UNIVERSITY OF NOTTINGHAM
WITH
FROM T

D1326704

Who's Who in America®

Biographical Titles Currently Published by Marquis Who's Who

Who's Who in America
Who's Who in America Junior & Senior High School Version
Who Was Who in America
  Historical Volume (1607–1896)
  Volume I (1897–1942)
  Volume II (1943–1950)
  Volume III (1951–1960)
  Volume IV (1961–1968)
  Volume V (1969–1973)
  Volume VI (1974–1976)
  Volume VII (1977–1981)
  Volume VIII (1982–1985)
  Volume IX (1985–1989)
  Volume X (1989–1993)
  Index Volume (1607–1993)
Who's Who in the World
Who's Who in the East
Who's Who in the Midwest
Who's Who in the South and Southwest
Who's Who in the West
Who's Who in American Education
Who's Who in American Law
Who's Who in American Nursing
Who's Who of American Women
Who's Who of Emerging Leaders in America
Who's Who in Finance and Industry
Who's Who in Medicine and Healthcare
Who's Who in Science and Engineering
Index to Marquis Who's Who Publications
The *Official* ABMS Directory of Board Certified Medical Specialists

Who'sWho in America®

Volume 3
Indexes

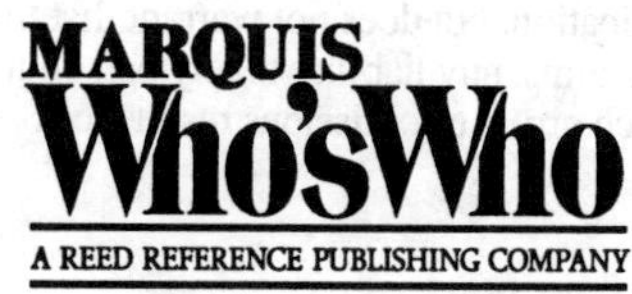

121 Chanlon Road
New Providence, NJ 07974 U.S.A.

Marquis Who's Who
Who'sWho in America®

Published by Marquis Who's Who, A Reed Reference Publishing Company.

Library of Congress Catalog Card Number 4-16934
International Standard Book Number 0-8379-0167-7 (set, Classic Edition)
0-8379-0170-7 (volume 3, Classic Edition)
0-8379-0171-5 (set, Deluxe Edition)
0-8379-0174-X (volume 3, Delxuxe Edition)

Manufactured in the United States of America

Table of Contents

Introduction

The *Who's Who in America* Geographic and Professional Indexes provide access to biographical information in the fiftieth edition through two avenues in alphabetical form—geography and profession. Each Biographee entry contains name and occupational description. A dagger symbol (†) indicates a new name first appearing in the fiftieth edition.

The Geographic Index lists names in the United States under state and city designations, as well as Biographees in American territories. Canadian listings include provinces and cities. Names in Mexico and other countries appear by city. Biographees whose addresses are not published in their sketches are found under Address Unpublished.

The Professional Index includes thirty-eight categories ranging alphabetically from Agriculture to Social Science. Within each area, the names appear under geographic subheadings. Names without published addresses appear at the end of each professional area listing under Address Unpublished. If the occupation does not fall within one of the specified areas, the name is listed under Unclassified.

Some Biographees have professions encompassing more than one area; each of these appears under the field best suited to the Biographee's occupation. Thus, while most bankers are listed under Finance: Banking Services, investment bankers are found in Finance: Investment Services. A Biographee with two or more diverse occupations is found under the area that best fits his or her professional profile.

The Retiree Index lists the names of those individuals whose biographical sketches last appeared in the forty-seventh, forty-eighth, or forty-ninth edition of *Who's Who in America*.

The Necrology lists Biographees of the forty-ninth edition whose deaths were reported to Marquis prior to the close of the compilation of this edition of *Who's Who in America*.

Alphabetical Practices

Names are arranged alphabetically according to the surnames, and under identical surnames according to the first given name. If both surname and first given name are identical, names are arranged alphabetically according to the second given name.

Surnames beginning with De, Des, Du, however capitalized or spaced, are recorded with the prefix preceding the surname and arranged alphabetically under the letter D.

Surnames beginning with Mac and Mc are arranged alphabetically under M.

Surnames beginning with Saint or St. appear after names that begin Sains, and are arranged according to the second part of the name, e.g. St. Clair before Saint Dennis.

Surnames beginning with Van, Von, or von are arranged alphabetically under the letter V.

Compound surnames are arranged according to the first member of the compound.

Many hyphenated Arabic names begin Al-, El-, or al-. These names are alphabetized according to each Biographee's designation of last name. Thus Al-Bahar, Neta may be listed either under Al- or under Bahar, depending on the preference of the listee.

Also, Arabic names have a variety of possible spellings when transposed to English. Spelling of these names is always based on the practice of the Biographee. Some Biographees use a Western form of word order, while others prefer the Arabic word sequence.

Similarly, Asian names may have no comma between family and given names, but some Biographees have chosen to add the comma. In each case, punctuation follows the preference of the Biographee.

Parentheses used in connection with a name indicate which part of the full name is usually deleted in common usage. Hence Chambers, E(lizabeth) Anne indicates that the usual form of the given name is E. Anne. In such a case, the parentheses are ignored in alphabetizing and the name would be arranged as Chambers, Elizabeth Anne. However, if the name is recorded Chambers, (Elizabeth) Anne, signifying that the entire name Elizabeth is not commonly used, the alphabetizing would be arranged as though the name were Chambers, Anne. If an entire middle or last name is enclosed in parentheses, that portion of the name is used in the alphabetical arrangement. Hence Chambers, Elizabeth (Anne) would be arranged as Chambers, Elizabeth Anne.

Where more than one spelling, word order, or name of an individual is frequently encountered, the sketch has been entered under the form preferred by the Biographee, with cross-references under alternate forms.

Geographic Index

†New name in *Who's Who in America*, Golden 50th Edition

UNITED STATES

ALABAMA

Abbeville
Rane, Michael Gregory *preservation company executive*

Albertville
Johnson, Clark Everette, Jr. *judge*

Alexander City
Adams, John C. *apparel company executive*
Gade, Marvin Francis *retired paper company executive*
Howell, H. Scott *apparel manufacturing company executive*
Shuler, Ellie Givan, Jr. *heritage center administrator*

Andalusia
Fuller, William Sidney *lawyer*
†Smith, J. E. Gene *electric power industry executive*

Anniston
Albritton, William Leonard *physician, microbiologist*
Andrews, Glenn *farmer, former congressman*
Ayers, Harry Brandt *editor, publisher, columnist*
Cain, William Vernon *academic administrator*
Harwell, Edwin Whitley *judge*
Klinefelter, James Louis *lawyer*

Arab
Hammond, Ralph Charles *real estate executive*

Athens
Jones, Joe Micheal *gifted education educator*
Ruth, Betty Muse *college administrator*

Auburn
Alderman, Charles Wayne *university dean*
Aldridge, Melvin Dayne *electrical engineering educator*
Amacher, Richard Earl *literature educator*
Andelson, Robert Vernon *social philosopher, educator*
Bailey, Wilford Sherrill *parisitology educator, science administrator, university president*
Ball, Donald Maury *agronomist, consultant*
Barker, Kenneth Neil *pharmacy administration educator*
Barker, Larry Lee *communications educator*
Barth, James Richard *finance educator*
Carr, Howard Earl *physicist, educator*
Cochran, John Euell, Jr. *aerospace engineer, educator, lawyer*
Crocker, Malcolm John *mechanical engineer, noise control engineer, educator*
Galbraith, Ruth Legg *retired university dean, home economist*
Irwin, John David *electrical engineering educator*
Jaeger, Richard Charles *electrical engineer, educator, science center director*
Klesius, Phillip Harry *microbiologist, researcher*
Lemke, Paul Arenz *botany educator*
Lewis, Walter David *historian*
Little, Ted David *lawyer*
Littleton, Taylor Dowe *humanities educator*
Millman, Richard George *architect, educator*
Molz, Fred John, III *hydrologist, educator*
Muse, William Van *university president*
Owens, John Murry *dean*
Perez, Joseph Dominique *physics educator*
Philpott, Harry Melvin *former university president*
Rainer, Rex Kelly *civil engineer, educator*
Reeve, Thomas Gilmour *physical education educator*
Rouse, Roy Dennis *retired university dean*
Samford, Thomas Drake, III *lawyer*
Schafer, Robert Louis *agricultural engineer, researcher*
Siginer, Dennis Aydeniz *mechanical engineering educator, researcher*
Skelton, Robert Beattie *language educator*
Teague, Sam Fuller *association executive, educator*
Turnquist, Paul Kenneth *agricultural engineer, educator*
Vaughan, John Thomas *veterinarian, educator, university dean*
Voitle, Robert Allen *college dean, physiologist*

Bessemer
Allison, Robert Arthur *retired professional stock car driver*
Bains, Lee Edmundson *lawyer, state official*

Birmingham
Acker, William Marsh, Jr. *federal judge*
Alexander, James Patrick *lawyer*
Allen, James Madison *family practice physician, lawyer, consultant*
Allen, Lee Norcross *historian, educator*
Allen, Maryon Pittman *former senator, journalist, lecturer, interior and clothing designer*
Alling, Charles Calvin, III *oral-maxillofacial surgeon, educator, writer*
Appleton, Joseph Hayne *civil engineer, educator*
Arrington, Richard, Jr. *mayor*
†Avent, Charles Kirk *medical educator*
Bailey, Thomas Edward *newspaper editor, book publisher*
Balch, Samuel Eason *lawyer*
Banton, Julian Watts *banker*
Barker, Samuel Booth *former university dean, physiology and biology educator*
Barker, Thomas Watson, Jr. *energy company executive*
Barrow, Richard Edward *architect*
†Bass, Richard O., Sr. *bishop*
Bauman, Robert Poe *physicist*
Benditt, Theodore Matthew *humanities educator*
Bennett, James Ronald *secretary of state*
Bennett, Joe Claude *university president*
Berte, Neal Richard *college president*
Blackburn, Sharon Lovelace *federal judge*
Blan, Ollie Lionel, Jr. *lawyer*
Boomershine, Donald Eugene *bureau executive, development official*
Booth, Rachel Zonelle *nursing educator*
Bowden, Travis J. *utilities executive*
Bowron, Richard Anderson *retired utilities executive*
Bradley, John M(iller), Jr. *forestry executive*
Brewer, Albert Preston *lawyer, former governor, law and government educator*
Bridgers, William Frank *physician, educator*
Brock, Harry Blackwell, Jr. *banker*
Brough, James A. *airport terminal executive*
Brown, Ephraim Taylor, Jr. *lawyer*
Brown, Jerry William *cell biology and anatomy educator*
Bruno, Anthony J. *consumer products executive*
Bruno, Joseph S. *meat products company executive*
Bruno, Ronald G. *food service executive*
Bueschen, Anton Joslyn *physician, educator*
Bugg, Charles Edward *biochemistry educator, scientist*
†Bulow, Jack Faye *library director*
†Burnham, James A. *museum director and consultant*
Cabaniss, William Jelks, Jr. *machining company executive, former state legislator*
†Callaway, Warren Eugene *hospital administrator*
Campbell, Elizabeth Todd *judge*
Caplan, Lester *optometrist, educator*
†Carlton, Michael *magazine editor*
Carruthers, Thomas Neely, Jr. *lawyer*
Carter, Frances Tunnell (Fran Carter) *fraternal organization administrator*
Carter, John Thomas *retired educational administrator, writer*
Casey, Ronald Bruce *journalist*
Caulfield, James Benjamin *pathologist, educator*
Chrencik, Frank *chemical company executive*
Clarke, Juanita M. Waiters *education educator*
Clemens, Peter John, III *manufacturing company financial executive*
Clemon, U. W. *federal judge*
Coleman, Brittin Turner *lawyer*
Collier, Felton Moreland *architect, planner, developer, detention, and recreation consultant, lecturer*
Comer, Donald, III *investment company executive*
Cooper, Jerome A. *lawyer*
Cooper, Max Dale *physician, medical educator, researcher*
Copeland, Hunter Armstrong *real estate executive*
Cornelius, Walter Felix *lawyer*
Corts, Thomas Edward *university president*
Crichton, Douglas Bentley *editor, writer*
Cullum, Mark Edward *editorial cartoonist*
Curtis, John J. *medical educator*
Dahl, Hilbert Douglas *mining company executive*
Daniel, Kenneth Rule *former iron and steel manufacturing company executive*
Davis, Julian Mason, Jr. *lawyer*
Denson, William Frank, III *lawyer*
Dentiste, Paul George *city and regional planning executive*
Devane, Denis James *health care company executive*
de Windt, Edward Mandell *manufacturing executive*
Diethelm, Arnold Gillespie *surgeon*
Dover, James Burrell *insurance executive*
Edmonds, William Fleming *retired engineering and construction company executive*
†Fallon, Harold Joseph *physician, pharmacology and biochemistry educator*
Farley, Joseph McConnell *lawyer*
†Faulkner, Charles Addison *health care administrator*
Fincher, John Albert *college official, consultant*
Finebaum, Paul Alan *sports columnist*
Finley, Sara Crews *medical geneticist, educator*
Finley, Wayne House *medical educator*
Floyd, John Alex, Jr. *editor, marketing executive, horticulturist*
Foft, John William *physician, educator*
Fowler, C. Thomas *power equipment manufacturing executive*
Franklin, H. Allen *electric company executive*
Fraser, Robert Gordon *diagnostic radiologist*
Friedel, Robert Oliver *physician*
Friedlander, Michael J. *neuroscientist, animal physiologist, medical educator*
†Friedman, Linda A. *lawyer*
Friend, Edward Malcolm, Jr. *lawyer*
Friend, Edward Malcolm, III *lawyer*
Fullmer, Harold Milton *dentist, educator*
Gaede, Anton Henry, Jr. *lawyer*
Gaffney, Michael Scully *diversified manufacturing company executive*
Gardner, Ronald Bruce *gas company executive*
Garrison, Paul F. *retail executive*
Geer, Jack Charles *retired pathology educator*
George, Frank Wade *small business owner, antiquarian book dealer*
Gerlach, Gary G. *botanical garden director, columnist*
Gewin, James W. *lawyer*
Gilbert, Rodney C. *engineering executive*
Gilbert, Roy W., Jr. *banker*
†Gilmore, Catherine Rye *ballet administrator*
†Glasscock, Gary M. *health care administrator*
Glaze, Robert Pinckney *retired university administrator*
Goldman, Jay *university dean, industrial engineer, educator*
Goodrich, Thomas Michael *engineering and construction executive*
Grant, Phyllis Hunt *hospital administrator*
Grayson, William Jackson, Jr. *manufacturing executive*
†Griffin, Eleanor *magazine editor*
Gross, Iris Lee *association executive*
Gross, Michael S. *secondary school principal*
Guin, Junius Foy, Jr. *federal judge*
Gunter, John Richmond *communications executive*
†Guthrie, Bill Myers *utility executive*
Hairston, W(illiam) George, III *nuclear power company executive*
†Hall, Dennis A. *hospital administrator*
Hames, Carl Martin *educational administrator, art dealer, consultant*
Hamilton, Virginia Van der Veer *historian, educator*
Hancock, James Hughes *federal judge*
Hanson, Victor Henry, II *newspaper publisher*
Harbert, Bill Lebold *construction corporation executive*
Harbert, Raymond J. *transportation executive*
Hardin, Edward Lester, Jr. *lawyer*
Harris, Aaron *management consultant*
Harris, Elmer Beseler *electric utility executive*
Heldman, Alan Wohl *lawyer*
Henderson, Louis Clifton, Jr. *management consultant*
Hendley, Dan Lunsford *retired university official*
Hendrick, Brice *academic administrator*
Herrera, Guillermo Antonio *pathologist*
Hess, Emil Carl *retail apparel company executive*
Hill, Samuel Richardson, Jr. *medical educator*
Hirschowitz, Basil Isaac *physician*
Holton, J(erry) Thomas *concrete company executive*
Horsley, Richard D. *banker*
Hubbard, Kenneth Earl *retail executive*
Hull, William Edward *provost, theology educator*
Hutchins, William Bruce, III *utility company executive*
Irons, George Vernon *history educator*
Jackson, Harold *journalist*
Jacobson, James Edmund *newspaper editor*
Johnsey, Walter F. *manufacturing executive*
Johnson, Emmett Raymond *hospital administrator*
Johnson, Joseph H., Jr. *lawyer*
Jones, Arthur McDonald, Sr. *consumer products company executive*
Jones, D. Paul, Jr. *banker, lawyer*
Jones, Warren Thomas *computer science educator*
†Kaimann, Frederick Daniel *music critic, reporter*
Kennedy, Joe David, Jr. (Joey Kennedy) *editor*
Kennedy, Theodore Clifford *engineering and construction company executive, consultant*
Kerr, Robert William *pipe fitting company executive*
Kirklin, John Webster *surgeon*
Kochakian, Charles Daniel *endocrinologist, educator*
Kuehn, Ronald L., Jr. *natural resources company executive*
Lacy, Alexander Shelton *lawyer*
Lammertsma, Koop *chemist, consultant*
Lee, James A. *health facility finance executive*
Lee, James Michael *religious education educator, publisher*
Left, Joan Marilyn *principal*
Lewis, James Eldon *health care executive*
Liu, Ray Ho *forensic science program director, educator*
Lloyd, Lewis Keith, Jr. *surgery and urology educator*
Loftin, Sister Mary Frances *health facility administrator*
Long, Thad Gladden *lawyer*
Longenecker, Herbert Eugene *biochemist, former university president*
†Lysinger, Rex Jackson *energy company executive*
Mackin, J. Stanley *banker*
Malone, Wallace D., Jr. *bank executive*
Manson-Hing, Lincoln Roy *dental educator*
Marks, Charles Caldwell *retired investment banker, retired industrial distribution company executive*
Massey, Richard Walter, Jr. *investment counselor*
Matthews, William Elliott, IV *gas company executive*
Mays, Joseph Barber, Jr. *lawyer*
Mc Callum, Charles Alexander *university official*
Mc Millan, George Duncan Hastie, Jr. *lawyer, former state official*
McWhorter, Hobart Amory, Jr. *lawyer*
Meezan, Elias *pharmacologist, educator*
Miller, Dennis Edward *corporate executive*
Miller, Edmond Trowbridge *civil engineer, educator, consultant*
Mills, William Hayes *lawyer*
Mitchell, Tamara O. *judge*
Molen, John Klauminzer *lawyer*
Monroe, Walter Harris, III *lawyer*
Montgomery, John Atterbury *research chemist, consultant*
Moor, Manly Eugene, Jr. *retired banker*
Moore, William Gower Innes *biochemist*
Morgan, Carolyn F. *lawyer*
Morgan, Hugh Jackson, Jr. *bank executive*
Morton, Marilyn Miller *genealogy and history educator, lecturer, researcher, travel executive, director*
Mowry, Robert Wilbur *pathologist, educator*
Nabers, Drayton, Jr. *insurance company executive*
Navia, Juan Marcelo *biologist, educator*
Neal, Phil Hudson, Jr. *manufacturing company executive*
Nelson, Dotson McGinnis, Jr. *clergyman*
Nelson, Edwin L. *federal judge*
Newfield, Mayer Ullman *lawyer*
Newton, Don Allen *association executive*
Nichol, Victor E., Jr. *banking executive*
Northen, Charles Swift, III *banker*
Nuckols, Frank Joseph *psychiatrist*
Nunn, Grady Harrison *political science educator emeritus*
Oakes, Walter Jerry *pediatric neurosurgeon*
Oglesby, Sabert, Jr. *retired research institute administrator*
Oliver, Samuel William, Jr. *lawyer*
Omura, George Adolf *medical oncologist*
Oparil, Suzanne *cardiologist, educator, researcher*
Pacifico, Albert Dominick *cardiovascular surgeon*
Parker, Israel Frank *national association consultant*
Parker, John Malcolm *management and financial consultant*
Peeples, William Dewey, Jr. *mathematics educator*
Peters, Henry Buckland *optometrist, educator*
Pewitt, James Dudley *academic administrator*
Peyser, Roxane D. *lawyer*
Pfister, Roswell Robert *ophthalmologist*
Phillips, James Linford *agricultural affairs journalist, editor*
Pittman, James Allen, Jr. *endocrinologist, dean emeritus, educator*
Pizitz, Richard Alan *retail and real estate group executive*
Pointer, Sam Clyde, Jr. *federal judge*
Polivnick, Paul *conductor, music director*
Pope, G. Phillip *insurance company executive*
Powell, William Arnold, Jr. *retired banker*
Powers, Edward Latell *accountant*
Propst, Robert Bruce *federal judge*
Putnam, Terry Michael *federal judge*
Quintana, Jose Booth *health care executive*
Redden, Lawrence Drew *lawyer*
Reeves, Garland Phillip *newspaper editor*
Renneker, Frederick Weyman, III *insurance executive*
Richards, J. Scott *rehabilitation medicine professional*
Richey, Ronald Kay *insurance company executive, lawyer*
Riegert, Robert Adolf *law educator, consultant*
Roberts, David Harrill *English language educator*
Robin, Theodore Tydings, Jr. *electric company executive, engineer*
Robinson, Edward Lee *retired physics educator, consultant*
†Roby, Jasper *bishop*
Rogers, Ernest Mabry *lawyer*
Rountree, Asa *lawyer*
Rouse, John Wilson, Jr. *research institute administrator*
Rozendale, David S. *engineering and construction firm executive*
Rubright, James Alfred *natural resources company executive*
Rushton, William James, III *insurance company executive*
Russell, Richard Olney, Jr. *cardiologist, educator*
Rynearson, W. John *association executive*
Salant, Nathan Nathaniel *athletic conference executive*
Savage, Kay Webb *lawyer, health center administrator, accountant*
Scarritt, Thomas Varnon *newspaper editor*
Schneyer, Charlotte Alper *physiologist, researcher, educator*
Seitz, Karl Raymond *editor*
Selfe, Edward Milton *lawyer*
Sellers, Fred Wilson *banker*
Shealy, David Lee *physicist, educator*
†Sheppard, Scott *magazine publisher*
Sibley, William Arthur *academic administrator, physics educator, consultant*
Skalka, Harold Walter *ophthalmologist, educator*
Sklenar, Herbert Anthony *industrial products manufacturing company executive*
†Slay, A. Michele *fundraiser*
Smith, Edward Samuel *federal judge*
Smith, John Joseph *lawyer*
Smith, Peter Garthwaite *energy consultant*
Spence, Paul Herbert *librarian*
Spotswood, Robert Keeling *lawyer*
Stabler, Lewis Vastine, Jr. *lawyer*
Stallworth, Anne Nall *writer, writing educator*
Starr, Bart (Bryan Bartlett Starr) *former professional football coach, former professional football player*
Stelling, Joan Donna *rehabilitation nurse*
Stelzenmuller, Cyril Vaughn *lawyer*
Stephens, James T. *publishing executive*
Stephens, Jerry Wayne *librarian, library director*
Stewart, George Ray *librarian*
Stone, Edmund Crispen, III *banker*
Sturgeon, Charles Edwin *management consultant*
Styslinger, Lee Joseph, Jr. *manufacturing company executive*
Sutowski, Thor Brian *choreographer*
Temple, William Norman *foundry executive*
Thompson, Wynelle Doggett *chemistry educator*
Tieszen, Ralph Leland, Sr. *internist*
Todd, James Averill, Jr. *steel company executive*
Truitt, John H. *insurance agency executive*
Tucker, Thomas James *investment manager*
Tyrrell, Thomas Neil *metal processing executive*
Upchurch, Samuel E., Jr. *lawyer*
Urry, Dan Wesley *research biophysicist, educator, science facility administrator*
Vinik, H(ymie) Ronald *anesthesiologist, physician*
Vinson, Laurence Duncan, Jr. *lawyer*
Vogelsang, John Martin *financial executive*
Wabler, Robert Charles, II *retail and distribution executive*
Walker, Evelyn *retired educational television executive*
Warnock, David Gene *nephrologist*
†Warren, William Michael, Jr. *utilities company executive*
Weatherly, Robert Stone, Jr. *banker*
Weeks, Arthur Andrew *lawyer, educator*
Weems, Frances Elizabeth *lawyer, county official*
†Weinsier, Roland Louis *nutrition educator and director*
Whitaker, Charles Larimore *lawyer*
Whitehead, Lewis E, Jr. *automotive consultant, management consultant*
Williams, N. Thomas *gas company executive*

Williams, Parham Henry, Jr. *lawyer*
Williams, Phillip Adger *insurance company executive*
Woodall, Norman Eugene *banker*
Woods, John Witherspoon *banker*
Wright, J. Raymond *manufacturing company executive*
Wrinkle, John Newton *lawyer*
Zeigler, Alan Karl *lawyer*

Brewton
Jones, Sherman J. *academic administrator, management educator*

Cherokee
†Oliver, Gerald Clifford *hospital administrator*

Clanton
Imgrund, William *oil company executive*
Williams, Paulette W. *state agency administrator*

Collinsville
Beasley, Mary Catherine *home economics educator, administrator, researcher*

Dadeville
Adair, Charles Robert, Jr. *lawyer*

Daphne
Gettig, Carl William *optometrist*
Jeffreys, Elystan Geoffrey *geological engineer, petroleum consultant and appraiser*

Dauphin Island
Porter, John Finley, Jr. *physicist, conservationist, retired educator*

Decatur
Caddell, John A. *lawyer*
Kuby, Patricia Ann Williams *early childhood educator*

Demopolis
Lloyd, Hugh Adams *lawyer*

Dothan
†Cross, Steven Jasper *dean, educator*
Garner, Alto Luther *retired education educator*
Harrison, Thomas E. *academic official*
Inscho, Jean Anderson *social worker*
Little, Charles Lawson *judge, lawyer*
Martin, Winn Farrar *banking executive*
Wright, Burton *sociologist*

Fairhope
Boyington, James Jerry *former state senator, insurance executive, restaurateur*

Florence
†Collins, Byron Griggs *hospital administrator*
Haltom, Elbert Bertram, Jr. *federal judge*
Howard, G. Daniel *dean*
Johnson, Johnny Ray *mathematics educator*
Mullins, Betty Johnson *realtor*
Peck, Richard Hyde *hospital administrator*
Potts, Robert Leslie *academic administrator*
Tease, James Edward *judge*
Wright, Mildred Anne (Milly Wright) *conservator, researcher*

Fort Rucker
Adams, Ronald Emerson *army officer*
†Petrosky, Daniel J. *army officer*

Gadsden
Hill, Anita Griffith *principal*
Hudgins, Don Franklin *city official*
Sledge, James Scott *federal judge*
Taylor, Fred M. *school system administrator*
†Weaver, Jerry *entrepreneur, holding company executive*
†Weaver, John B. *electronics executive, metal products executive*
†Williams, Walter Abner, Jr. *healthcare administrator, realtor*

Gulf Shores
Wallace, John Loys *aviation services executive*
Wingard, Raymond Randolph *transportation products executive*

Guntersville
Patterson, Harold Dean *superintendent of schools*
Sparkman, Brandon Buster *educator, writer, consultant*

Hartselle
Slate, Joe Hutson *psychologist, educator*

Harvest
Norman, Ralph Louis *physicist, consultant*

Helena
Smith, John Lee, Jr. *minister, former association administrator*

Homewood
Miller, John W. *management and financial consultant*

Hueytown
Gilbert, Melba Caldwell *special education and early childhood educator*

Huntsville
Allan, Barry David *research chemist, government official*
Anderson, Elmer Ebert *physicist, educator*
Billings, Nancy Carter *secondary education educator*
Boston, Edward Dale *hospital administrator*
Boykin, Betty Ruth Carroll *mortgage loan officer, bank executive*
Buckbee, Edward O'Dell *museum administrator*
Cleary, James Roy *lawyer*
Costes, Nicholas Constantine *aerospace technologist, government official*
Dannenberg, Konrad K. *aeronautical engineer*
Daussman, Grover Frederick *electrical engineer, consultant*
Decher, Rudolf *physicist*
de Loach, Anthony Cortelyou *solar physicist*
Dimmock, John Oliver *university research center director*
Douillard, Paul Arthur *engineering and financial executive, consultant*
Elliott, Sally Ann *special education educator*
Emerson, William Kary *engineering company executive*
Franz, Frank Andrew *academic administrator*
Garriott, Owen Kay *astronaut, scientist*
Graves, Benjamin Barnes *business administration educator*
Hettinger, Steve *mayor*
Holloway, Richard Allen *electronics company executive*
Huckaby, Gary Carlton *lawyer*
Hung, Ru J. *engineering educator, research scientist*
Johnson, Charles Leslie *aerospace physicist, consultant*
Joner, Bruno *aeronautical engineer*
Jones, Harvie Paul *architect*
King, Olin B. *electronics systems company executive*
Kowel, Stephen Thomas *electrical engineer, educator*
Leslie, Lottie Lyle *retired secondary education educator*
Loshuertos, Robert Herman *clergyman*
Lundquist, Charles Arthur *university official*
Mc Donough, George Francis, Jr. *aerospace engineer*
McKnight, William Baldwin *physics educator*
Mc Manus, Samuel Plyler *chemist, academic administrator*
McRary, John Walter, III *defense contract research and development company executive*
Meadlock, James W. *computer graphics company executive*
†Meadlock, Nancy B. *computer graphics company executive*
Mercieca, Charles *philosophy and political science educator*
Moore, Fletcher Brooks *engineering company executive*
Parnell, Thomas Alfred *physicist*
Perkins, James Francis *physicist*
Pittman, William Claude *electrical engineer*
Polites, Michael Edward *aerospace research engineer*
Potate, John Spencer, Sr. *engineering company executive, consultant*
Potter, Ernest Luther *lawyer*
Pruitt, Alice Fay *mathematician, engineer*
Ramsey, V. Bruce *electronics executive*
Reaves, Benjamin F. *academic administrator*
Rhett, Harry Moore, Jr. *investment executive*
Richter, William, Jr. *aerospace company executive*
Ritter, Alfred *aerospace consultant*
Roberts, Frances Cabaniss *history educator*
Russell, Lynn Darnell *engineering educator*
Sapp, A. Eugene, Jr. *electronics executive*
†Schonberg, William Peter *mechanical and civil engineering educator*
Schroer, Bernard Jon *industrial engineering educator*
Schwinghamer, Robert John *materials scientist*
†Simmons, Jennings (Jay) *aerospace engineer*
Smith, Philip Wayne *writer, communications company executive*
Smith, Robert Earl *space scientist*
Smith, Robert Sellers *lawyer*
Spencer, Guy J., Jr. *entrepreneur*
†Stevens, Edward Parker *military officer*
Stuhlinger, Ernst *physicist*
Sullivan, Michael Maurice *lawyer*
Taylor, James F., Jr. *computer graphics company executive*
Tietke, Wilhelm *gastroenterologist*
Traylor, Orba Forest *economist, lawyer, educator*
Vaughan, William Walton *atmospheric scientist*
Vinz, Frank Louis *electrical engineer*
Wessling, Francis Christopher *mechanical engineer, educator*
White, John Charles *historian*
Wilson, Allan Byron *graphics company executive*
Wright, John Collins *chemistry educator*
Zant, Robert Franklin *computer information educator*

Jacksonville
Boswell, Rupert Dean, Jr. *retired academic administrator, math educator*
Dunaway, Carolyn Bennett *sociology educator*
Dunaway, William Preston *retired administration educator*
McGee, Harold Johnston *university president*
Merrill, Martha *instructional media educator*
Quick, Edward Raymond *museum director*
Reid, William James *retired physicist, educator*

Jasper
Oliver, John Thomason, Jr. *commercial bank executive*
Rowland, David Jack *college chancellor*

Lanett
Fowler, Conrad Murphree *retired manufacturing company executive*

Leeds
Ritchey, James Salem *office furniture manufacturing company executive*

Lillian
Moyer, Kenneth Evan *psychologist, educator*
Shory, Naseeb Lein *dentist, retired state official*

Livingston
Green, Asa Norman *university president*

Madison
Brannan, Eulie Ross *education consultant*
Frakes, Lawrence Wright *retired career officer, businessman*
Hawk, Clark Wiliams *mechanical engineering educator*
Jellett, James Morgan *retired army officer, aerospace defense consultant*
Rosenberger, Franz Ernst *physics educator*
Stamps, Gladys A. *middle school educator*

Maplesville
Nichols, J. Hugh *economic development consultant*

Maxwell AFB
Kline, John Alvin *academic administrator*
Pendley, William Tyler *naval officer, international relations educator*
†Wendzel, Robert Leroy *political science educator*

Mc Calla
Gentry, Vicki Paulette *museum director*

Mentone
Herndon, Mark *musician*

Millry
Cowles, Milly *education educator*

Mobile
Anderson, Lewis Daniel *medical educator, orthopaedic surgeon*
Armbrecht, William Henry, III *lawyer*
Bahr, Alice Harrison *librarian*
†Baillio, O. Dallas, Jr. *library official*
Baker, Amanda Sirmon *university dean, nursing educator*
Beall, Samuel E., III *food service executive*
Bedsole, Ann Smith *state senator*
Bobo, James Robert *economics educator*
Boone, Louis Eugene *business and management educator, author*
Braswell, Louis Erskine *lawyer*
Brock, Paul Warrington *lawyer*
Brogdon, Byron Gilliam *physician, radiology educator*
Bryant, Thomas Earle, Jr. *lawyer*
†Busby, James Louie *electronics company executive*
Butler, Charles Randolph, Jr. *federal judge*
Byrd, Gwendolyn Pauline *school system superintendent*
Callahan, H. L. (Sonny Callahan) *congressman*
Clark, Jack *retired hospital company executive, accountant*
Conrad, Marcel Edward *hematologist, educator*
Copeland, Lewis *principal*
Cox, Emmett Ripley *federal judge*
Crow, James Sylvester *retired banker, railway executive*
Damico, James Anthony *library director*
DeBakey, Ernest George *physician, surgeon*
Delaney, Thomas Caldwell, Jr. *city official*
Delchamps, Randolph *grocery store executive*
Duvall, Charles Farmer *bishop*
Edwards, Jack *former congressman, lawyer*
Eichold, Samuel *medical educator, medical museum curator*
Fox, Sidney Walter *chemist, educator*
Gardner, William Albert, Jr. *pathologist, medical foundation executive*
Gottlieb, Sheldon Fred *biologist, educator*
Grady, Charles E. *marketing executive*
Hamid, Michael *electrical engineering educator, consultant*
Hand, William Brevard *federal judge*
Harris, Benjamin Harte, Jr. *lawyer*
Hearin, William Jefferson *newspaper publishing company executive*
Helmsing, Frederick George *lawyer*
Holberg, Ralph Gans, Jr. *lawyer*
Holland, Lyman Faith, Jr. *lawyer*
Holmes, Broox Garrett *lawyer*
Howard, Alex T., Jr. *federal judge*
Hunt, Pfilip Gardnyr *food service company executive*
Johnson, David Pittman *psychotheraphy consultant, social work educator*
Kahn, Gordon Barry *federal bankruptcy judge*
Kimbrough, William Adams, Jr. *lawyer*
Lager, Robert John *state agency administrator*
Lipscomb, Oscar Hugh *archbishop*
Littleton, Jesse Talbot, III *radiology educator*
Lyons, Champ, Jr. *lawyer*
Lyons, George Sage *lawyer, oil industry executive, former state legislator*
†Magnoli, Michael A. *academic official*
McCall, Daniel Thompson, Jr. *retired justice*
McCann, Clarence David, Jr. *special events coordinator, museum curator and director, artist*
McKnight, Charles Noel *lawyer*
Milling, Bert William, Jr. *federal judge*
Morelock, James Crutchfield *mathematician*
Moring, Rebecca Owen *university official*
†Parker, Donald Lester *technology company executive*
Parmley, Loren Francis, Jr. *medical educator*
Pitcock, James Kent *head and neck surgical oncologist*
Pittman, Virgil *federal judge*
Puhala, James Joseph *lawyer*
Rewak, William John *university president, clergyman*
Richelson, Paul William *curator*
†Schenk, Joseph B. *museum director*
Sessions, Jefferson Beauregard, III *lawyer*
Shepherd, Linda Pace *nurse, educator, administrator*
Smith, Jesse Graham, Jr. *dermatologist, educator*
Thomas, Daniel Holcombe *federal judge*
Thomson, H. Bailey *editor*
Thornton, J. Edward *lawyer*
Vacik, James Paul *university administrator*
Vitulli, William Francis *psychology educator*
Volkman, Beatrice Kramer *special education educator*
White, Lowell E., Jr. *medical educator*
Windom, Stephen Ralph *lawyer*
Winter, Arch Reese *architect*

Monroeville
Kniskern, Maynard *editor, writer*

Montevallo
McChesney, Robert Michael, Sr. *political science educator*

Montgomery
†Adair, Charles E. *medical products distribution company executive*
Albritton, William Harold, III *federal judge*
Almon, Reneau Pearson *state supreme court justice*
Amberg, Richard Hiller, Jr. *newspaper executive*
Baker, Clifford Cornell *state educational administrator*
Barnes, Robert E. *health care company executive*
Bass, Ray Dean *state highway director*
Bell, Katie Roberson *library educator*
Black, Robert Coleman *lawyer*
Blount, Winton Malcolm, Jr. *manufacturing company executive*
Blount, Winton Malcolm, III *investment executive*
Bobo, Thomas *school system administrator*
Bridges, Edwin Clifford *state official*
Brock, Eugene C. *landscape architect*
Brown, William Blake *newspaper editor*
Bullard, Mary Ellen *retired religious study center administrator*
†Butts, Terry L. *state supreme court justice*
Byars, Walter Ryland, Jr. *lawyer*
Caddell, John Allen *construction and engineering company executive*
Camp, Billy Joe *state official*
†Carnes, Edward E. *federal judge*
Cater, Douglass *former college president, former presidential assistant, writer, editor*
Clark, James S. *state legislator*
Cornett, Lloyd Harvey, Jr. *retired historian*
Dees, Morris Seligman, Jr. *lawyer*
De Ment, Ira *federal judge*
Dixon, Larry Dean *state legislator*
Dubina, Joel Fredrick *federal judge*
Evans, James Harold *state attorney general*
Findlay, R. B. *paper company executive*
Folsom, James, Jr. *investment company executive, consultant, former governor*
Franco, Ralph Abraham *lawyer*
Frazer, Nimrod Thompson *investment banker, financial services executive*
Gainous, Fred Jerome *state agency administrator*
Givhan, Edgar Gilmore *physician*
Godbold, John Cooper *federal judge*
Gorland, Ronald Kent *bank executive*
Graddick, Charles Allen *lawyer*
Gribben, Alan *English language educator, research consultant*
Hamner, Reginald Turner *lawyer*
†Harris, William Hamilton *academic administrator*
Hawthorne, Frank Howard *lawyer*
Hester, Douglas Benjamin *lawyer, federal official*
Hill, Thomas Bowen, III *lawyer*
Hobbs, Truman McGill *federal judge, lawyer*
Hoffman, Richard William *banker*
Holleman, John Albert *mortgage company executive*
Hornsby, Andrew Preston, Jr. *human services administrator*
Hornsby, (E.C.) Sonny *judge*
Houston, James Gorman, Jr. *state supreme court justice*
Ingram, Kenneth Frank *state supreme court justice*
†James, Forrest Hood, Jr. (Fob James) *governor*
Johnson, Andrew Emerson, III *educational administrator*
Johnson, Frank Minis, Jr. *federal judge*
†Klein, Richard Lee *wholesale pharmaceutical executive*
Kurth, Ronald James *university president, retired naval officer*
Langford, Charles Douglas *state legislator, lawyer*
Latham, Larry Lee *state administrator, psychologist*
Leslie, Henry Arthur *lawyer, retired banker*
Maddox, (Alva) Hugh *state supreme court justice, author*
McFadden, Frank Hampton *lawyer, business executive, former judge*
McPherson, Vanzetta Penn *federal judge*
Mendel, Perry *day care company executive*
Mitchell, Alfred Henry *state government official*
Morris, L. Daniel, Jr. *lawyer*
Myers, Ira Lee *physician*
Nachman, Merton Roland, Jr. *lawyer*
Norris, Robert Wheeler *lawyer, military officer*
Paddock, Austin Joseph *engineering executive*
Patterson, John Malcolm *judge*
Pickett, George Bibb, Jr. *retired military officer*
Robinson, Peter Clark *general management executive*
Rowan, John Robert *medical center director*
Saigo, Roy H. *chancellor*
Salay, Carolyn Jeanne *advertising agency executive*
Salmon, Joseph Thaddeus *lawyer*
Schloss, Samuel Leopold, Jr. *retired food service executive, consultant*
Schwarz, Joseph Edmund *artist*
Shorter, Walter Wyatt *forest products executive*
†Siegelman, Don Eugene *state official*
Sizemore, James Middleton, Jr. *state commissioner, lawyer*
Steele, Rodney Redfearn *federal judge*
Taylor, James Marion, II *automotive wholesale executive*
Teague, Barry Elvin *lawyer*
Teague, Larry Gene *editor*
Thompson, Myron H. *federal judge*
Torbert, Clement Clay, Jr. *state supreme court justice*
Varner, Robert Edward *federal judge*
Volz, Charles Harvie, Jr. *lawyer*
Walker, Claud Ladale, Sr. *state representative*
Wampold, Charles Henry, Jr. *lawyer*
Williams, James Orrin *university administrator, educator*
†Williams, Vicki *mortgage company executive*
†Williamson, William A., Jr. *medical products executive*
Wilson, John *protective services official*
Yow, John Stuart, Jr. *retired internist*

Mountain Brook
Haworth, Michael Elliott, Jr. *investor, former aerospace company executive*

Muscle Shoals
Roy, Amit H. *agricultural executive*
Smith, Harry Delano *educational administrator*

New Market
Lee, Thomas J. *aerospace scientist*

Normal
Caulfield, Henry John *physics educator*
Henson, David B. *academic administrator*
Okezie, B. Onuma *food scientist, nutritionist, educator*

Ohatchee
Ellis, Bernice Allred *personnel executive*

Opelika
Brown, Robert Glenn *plastic surgeon*
Jenkins, Richard Lee *manufacturing company executive*
Knecht, Charles Daniel *veterinarian*
Samford, Yetta Glenn, Jr. *lawyer*

Orange Beach
Adams, Daniel Fenton *legal educator*
Bennett, James Jefferson *higher education consultant*
Brennan, Lawrence Edward *electronics engineer*

Pelham
Turner, Malcolm Elijah *biomathematician, educator*
†Walker, William W, III *wholesale distribution executive*

Green Valley
Barich, Dewey Frederick *emeritus educational administrator*
Bates, Charles Carpenter *oceanographer*
Blickwede, Donald Johnson *retired steel company executive*
Brissman, Bernard Gustave *insurance company executive*
Crystall, Joseph N. *communications company executive*
Dmytryshyn, Basil *historian, educator*
Egger, Roscoe L., Jr. *consultant, former federal commissioner*
Ehrenfeld, John Henry *grocery company executive*
Lasch, Robert *former journalist*
McGibbon, William Alexander *rancher, photographer*
Miner, Earl Howard *retired trust banker*
Page, John Henry, Jr. *artist, educator*
Perry, Roger Lawrence *printing executive*
Peterson, Harold Albert *electrical engineer, educator*
Schirmer, Henry William *architect*
Smith, Raymond Lloyd *former university president, consultant*
Wasmuth, Carl Erwin *physician, lawyer*
White, Herbert Spencer *research library educator, university dean*

Lake Montezuma
Burkee, Irvin *artist*

Marana
Sederholm, Sarah Kathleen (Kathy Sederholm) *primary education educator*

Mesa
Allen, Merle Maeser, Jr. *lawyer*
Anderson, Herschel Vincent *librarian*
Bell, Daniel Carroll *realtor, ranch and land manager*
Boyd, Leona Potter *retired social worker*
DeRosa, Francis Dominic *chemical company executive*
†Evans, Don A. *healthcare company executive*
Fairbanks, Harold Vincent *metallurgical engineer, educator*
Garfield, Ernest *bank consultant*
Garwood, John Delvert *former college administrator*
Gaylor, Walter *writer, military historian*
Haggerty, Allen Charles *transportation company executive*
Johnson, Mary Elizabeth *elementary education educator*
Mead, Tray C. *museum administrator*
Murphy, Edward Francis *sales executive*
Roe, Carolyn *nursing educator*
Rummel, Robert Wiland *aeronautical engineer, author*
Shelley, James LaMar *lawyer*
Shill, Victor Lamar *architect*
Stott, Brian *software company executive*
Thompson, Ronald MacKinnon *family physician, artist, writer*
Unser, Bobby (Robert William Unser) *professional auto racer, television commentator*
†Whiteman, John O. *rental company executive*
†Wong, Willie *mayor, automotive executive*
Woods, Joe Eldon *general contractor*

Morenci
†Snider, Tim *mining executive*

New River
Bruder, William Paul *architect*

Nogales
†Castro, Raul Hector *lawyer, former ambassador, former governor*

Oracle
Rush, Andrew Wilson *artist*

Page
Hart, Marian Griffith *retired educator*

Paradise Valley
Alcantara, Theo *conductor*
Blumer, Harry Maynard *architect*
Carey, Ernestine Gilbreth (Mrs. Charles E. Carey) *writer, lecturer*
De Shazor, Ashley Dunn *business consultant*
Grimm, James R. (Ronald Grimm) *multi-industry executive*
Hann, J(ames) David *information systems company executive*
Heller, Jules *artist, writer*
Russell, Paul Edgar *electrical engineering educator*
Sapp, Donald Gene *minister*
Swanson, Robert Killen *management consultant*
Timmons, Evelyn Deering *pharmacist*

Payson
Rich, Frances Luther *sculptor*

Peoria
Bergmann, Fredrick Louis *English language educator, theater historian*
Bernstein, Eugene Merle *physicist, retired educator*
Degnan, Thomas Leonard *lawyer*
Jones, Lillie Agnes *retired educator*
Morrison, Manley Glenn *real estate investor, former army officer*
Palmer, Alice Eugenia *retired physician, educator*
Schindler, William Stanley *retired public relations executive*

Phoenix
Adams, Gail Hayes *interior designer*
Aguirre, Linda G. *state legislator*
Albrecht, Carol Lee *human resources consultant*
Allen, John Rybolt L. *chemist, biochemist*
Allen, Robert Eugene Barton *lawyer*
†Alsentzer, William James, Jr. *lawyer*
Alston, Lela *state senator*
Anderson, Edward Frederick *biology educator*
Armstrong, Nelson William, Jr. *gaming company executive*
Arriola, David Bruce *resort and hotel marketing executive*
Aschaffenburg, Walter Eugene *composer, music educator*
Babinec, Gehl P. *convenience store company executive*
Bachus, Benson Floyd *mechanical engineer, consultant*
Bacon, Roxana Collins *lawyer*
Bain, C. Randall *lawyer*
Baird, J. Ernest *lawyer, state representative*
Baker, William Dunlap *lawyer*
Bakker, Thomas Gordon *lawyer*
Ballantyne, Reginald Malcolm, III *healthcare executive*
†Baltes, Robert Thomas *electrical engineer*
Bansak, Stephen A., Jr. *investment banker, financial consultant*
Barkley, Charles Wade *professional basketball player*
Beauvais, Edward R. *airline executive*
Begam, Robert George *lawyer*
Beltrán, Anthony Natalicio *military non-commissioned officer, deacon*
Benson, Stephen R. *editorial cartoonist*
Bergamo, Ron *broadcasting company executive*
Bergin, Daniel Timothy *lawyer, banker*
Berkoff, David *Olympic athlete, swimmer*
†Bertholf, Neilson Allan, Jr. *aviation executive*
Bidwill, William V. *professional football executive*
Bimson, Carl Alfred *bank executive*
Binnie, Nancy Catherine *nurse, educator*
Bishop, C. Diane *state agency administrator, educator*
†Blake, George Alan, Jr. *non-profit association executive*
Blanchard, Charles Alan *lawyer, former state senator*
Bonny, Mary Cleinmark *nurse*
Bower, Willis Herman *retired psychiatrist, former medical administrator*
Bradley, Gilbert Francis *retired banker*
Breen, John *government official*
Brewer, Janice Kay *state legislator*
Broomfield, Robert Cameron *federal judge*
Brunacini, Alan Vincent *fire chief*
Bumpers, W. Carroll *finance corporation executive*
Burchard, John Kenneth *chemical engineer*
Burg, Jerome Stuart *financial planning consultant*
Burke, Timothy John *lawyer*
Burns, Brenda *state legislator*
Bylsma, Carol Ann *educational consultant, science consultant*
Cabot, Howard Ross *lawyer*
Cajero, Carmen *state legislator*
Calkins, Jerry Milan *anesthesiologist, educator, administrator, biomedical engineer*
Cameron, James Duke *lawyer, former state supreme court justice*
Canby, William Cameron, Jr. *federal judge*
Caputo, Salvatore *critic*
Carroll, Earl Hamblin *federal judge*
Carter, James Edward *judge*
Carter, Ronald Martin, Sr. *pharmaceutical company executive*
Chalmers, James A. *consulting company executive*
Charlton, John Kipp *pediatrician*
Cheifetz, Lorna Gale *psychologist*
Cheshire, William Polk *newspaper columnist*
Chisholm, Tom Shepherd *environmental engineer*
Chrisman, William Herring *property tax consultant*
Cohen, Jon Stephan *lawyer*
Cohen, Ronald Jay *lawyer*
Colangelo, Jerry John *professional basketball team executive*
Colburn, Donald D. *lawyer*
Conway, Michael J. *airline company executive*
Cooledge, Richard Calvin *lawyer*
Coppersmith, Sam *lawyer*
Copple, William Perry *federal judge*
Cordova, Alexander M. *city clerk*
Corson, Kimball Jay *lawyer*
†Covey, Donald David *school system administrator*
Cox, Robert Gene *management consultant*
Cozzi, Hugo Louis *psychiatrist*
Crews, James Cecil *hospital administrator*
†Crim, Jack C. *diversified industry executive*
Crockett, Clyll Webb *lawyer*
Curley, Sarah Sharer *federal bankruptcy judge*
Daniel, James Richard *accountant, computer company financial executive*
Daughton, Donald *lawyer*
Davies, David George *lawyer*
Davis, Kurt Reynolds *state government executive*
Dawson, John Joseph *lawyer*
†Day, Timothy Townley *food company executive*
DeBartolo, Jack, Jr. *architect*
DeBruhl, Richard R. *television reporter*
Deeny, Robert Joseph *lawyer*
deMatties, Nicholas Frank *artist, art educator*
DeMenna, Kevin Bolton *lobbyist*
De Michele, O. Mark *utility company executive*
Derasmo, Vito Joseph (Bill Derasmo) *marketing professional*
Derdenger, Patrick *lawyer*
DeSilva, Joseph J. *hospital administrator*
Dewalt, Judith K. *elementary school principal*
Dignac, Geny (Eugenia M. Bermudez) *sculptor*
†Dion, Philip Joseph *consumer products and services executive, real estate and construction company executive*
Donaldson, Wilburn Lester *property management corporation executive*
Donnelly, Charles Robert *retired college president*
Drain, Albert Sterling *business management consultant*
Dunipace, Ian Douglas *lawyer*
Durrant, Dan Martin *lawyer*
Early, Robert Joseph *magazine editor*
Eaton, Berrien Clark *retired lawyer, author*
Ebert, Richard J. *principal*
Edens, Gary Denton *broadcasting executive*
Edwards, Ralph M. *librarian*
Ekstrom, Walter F. *utility company executive*
Elien, Mona Marie *air transportation professional*
Ellison, Cyril Lee *publisher*
Elmore, James Walter *architect, retired university dean*
Emerson, Frederick George *transportation company executive*
Evans, Ronald Allen *lodging chain executive*
Everroad, John D. *lawyer*
†Fassler, Joseph K. *food service executive*
Faul, Gary Lyle *electrical engineering supervisor*
Feinstein, Allen Lewis *lawyer*
Feldman, Ira S. *accountant*
Feldman, Stanley George *state supreme court chief justice*
Fenzl, Terry Earle *lawyer*
Fine, Charles Leon *lawyer*
Fitzgerald, Joan *principal*
Fitzsimmons, (Lowell) Cotton *professional basketball executive, broadcaster, former coach*
†Fitzsimmons, Robert James *finance company executive*
†Flatt, Michael Oliver *manufacturing company executive*
†Foley, William Patrick, II *title insurance company executive*
Forsyth, Ben Ralph *academic administrator, medical educator*
Fournier, Donald Frederick *dentist*
Fox, Frances Juanice *retired librarian, educator, retired*
Frank, Anthony Melchior *federal official, former financial executive*
Frank, John Paul *lawyer, author*
Franke, William Augustus *corporate executive*
Freeman, Susan Maud *lawyer*
Freyermuth, Clifford L. *structural engineering consultant*
Friesen, Oris Dewayne *software engineer, historian*
Fulk, Roscoe Neal *retired accountant*
Gaines, Francis Pendleton, III *lawyer*
Galvan, Elias Gabriel *bishop*
Galvin, Elias *bishop*
Garrett, Dennis Andrew *police official*
Genrich, Mark L. *newspaper editor*
Gerard, Philip C. *lawyer*
Gibbs, William Harold *university administrator*
Giedt, Bruce Alan *paper company executive*
Gilbert, Donald R. *lawyer*
Gillis, William Freeman *telecommunications executive*
Gochnauer, Richard Wallis *consumer products company executive*
Goddard, Terry *lawyer*
Godwin, Mary Jo *editor, librarian consultant*
Goldman, Murray Abraham *semiconductor executive*
Goldstein, Stuart Wolf *lawyer*
Greenfield, Arthur Paul *lawyer*
Grier, James Edward *hotel company executive, lawyer*
Griffith, Ernest Ralph *physician, educator*
Griller, Gordon Moore *court administrator*
Grinell, Sheila *museum director*
Gunty, Christopher James *newspaper editor*
Gwozdz, Kim Elizabeth *interior designer*
Halliday, Keith *finance company executive*
Hallier, Gerard Edouard *hotel chain executive*
Halpern, Barry David *lawyer*
Hamilton, Ronald Ray *minister*
Hanley, Fred William *librarian, educator*
Hardy, Charles Leach *federal judge*
Harelson, Hugh *magazine publisher*
†Harrington, John Leonard, Jr. *hospital administrator*
Harris, Jean E. *lawyer*
Harrison, Mark I. *lawyer*
Harte, John Joseph Meakins *bishop*
Hawkins, Jasper Stillwell, Jr. *architect*
Hayden, William Robert *lawyer*
Haynes, James Earl, Jr. *association executive*
Heller, Mitchell Thomas *hotel company executive*
†Herbert, Victor *school system administrator*
Hicks, William Albert, III *lawyer*
Hill, Edward G. *food marketing executive*
Hoecker, Thomas Ralph *lawyer*
Hoffman, Robert B. *lawyer*
Holloway, Edgar Austin *retired diversified business executive*
Houseworth, Richard Court *banker*
Howard, William Matthew *lawyer, business executive, arbitrator, author*
Hoxie, Joel P. *lawyer*
Huck, Leonard William *retired banker*
Huffman, Edgar Joseph *oil company executive*
Hull, Jane Dee *state official, former state legislator*
Huntwork, James R. *lawyer*
†Iliff, Warren Jolidon *zoo administrator*
Inman, William Peter *lawyer*
Irwin, R. Neil *lawyer*
Jacobson, (Julian) Edward *lawyer*
James, Charles E., Jr. *lawyer*
Jirauch, Charles W. *lawyer*
Johnson, James Wayne *lawyer*
Johnson, Kevin Maurice *professional basketball player*
†Johnson, Peter Charles *neuropathologist*
Jones, Lucia Jean *physical education educator*
Jorgensen, Gordon David *engineering company executive*
Joyner, Seth *professional football player*
Kaufman, Roger Wayne *state judge*
Kennedy, Thomas J. *lawyer*
Khan, Ahmed Mohiuddin *finance, insurance executive*
Kimball, Bruce Arnold *soil scientist*
†Kitchell, Samuel Farrand *construction company executive*
Klausner, Jack Daniel *lawyer*
Kolbe, John William *newspaper columnist*
Kreutzberg, David W. *lawyer*
Kurn, Neal *lawyer*
Kurtz, Joan Helene *pediatrician*
Kyl, John Henry *former business executive*
Kyle, Richard Daniel *state legislator, fundraising consultant*
LaFave, Kenneth John *music critic, composer*
Lambert, Dennis Alvin *radio news director*
Land, George A. *philosopher, writer, educator, consultant*
†Landers, Teresa Price *librarian*
Lawrence, William Doran *physician*
Leach, John F. *newspaper editor, journalism educator*
Lee, Stephen E. *lawyer, educator*
Lemon, Leslie Gene *consumer products and services company executive, lawyer*
Leonard, George Edmund *finance company executive, consultant*
Lewis, Orme, Jr. *real estate company executive, land use adviser*
Lies, Richard Lorenz, Jr. *cosmetics executive*
Linxwiler, Louis Major, Jr. *retired finance company executive*
Lloyd, Llyn Allan *association executive*
Lorenzen, Robert Frederick *ophthalmologist*
Lowry, Edward Francis, Jr. *lawyer*
Maas, Terry Leo *investment banker*
Madden, Paul Robert *lawyer, director*
Mahoney, Richard *state official*
Majerle, Daniel Lewis *professional basketball player, olympic athlete*
Mallender, William Harry *lawyer*
Mallery, Richard K. *lawyer*
Mangum, John K. *lawyer*
Manion, Jerry Robert *hotel chain executive*
Manning, Daniel Ricardo *professional basketball player*
Manning, Michael C. *lawyer*
Mardian, Daniel *construction company director*
Marks, Merton Eleazer *lawyer*
Martin, Don P. *lawyer*
Martori, Joseph Peter *lawyer*
Mason, Anthony Halstead *lawyer, corporate executive*
May, Bruce Barnett *lawyer*
McClelland, Norman P. *food products executive*
Mc Clelland, W. Kent *food products executive*
Mc Clennen, Louis *lawyer, educator*
McDaniel, Joseph Chandler *lawyer*
McNamee, Stephen M. *federal judge*
McRae, Hamilton Eugene, III *lawyer*
Melczer, Joseph T., III *lawyer*
Melner, Sinclair Lewis *insurance company executive*
Merritt, Nancy-Jo *lawyer*
Meyer, Paul Joseph *lawyer*
Middleton, Lowell Glenn *bank executive*
Might, Thomas Owen *newspaper company executive*
Miller, Louis Rice *lawyer*
Miller, Michael Jon *survey engineer, local government manager*
Miller, Norman L. *lawyer*
Mitchell, George Hall *lawyer*
Moeller, James *state supreme court justice*
Moya, Patrick Robert *lawyer*
Moyer, Alan Dean *retired newspaper editor*
Muchmore, Charles J. *lawyer*
Muecke, Charles Andrew (Carl Muecke) *federal judge*
Mullen, Daniel Robert *finance company executive*
Murian, Richard Miller *book company executive*
Myers, Robert David *judge*
Nielson, Theo Gilbert *law enforcement official, university official*
Norberg, Jaron B. *public service company executive*
Norling, James A. *electronics company executive*
Novak, Edward Frank *lawyer*
Novak, Peter John *lawyer*
O'Brien, Thomas Joseph *bishop*
Olsen, Alfred Jon *lawyer*
Olsen, Gordon *retired lawyer*
Olson, Robert Howard *lawyer*
Oppedahl, John Fredrick *newspaper editor*
Parrett, Sherman O. *lawyer*
Patti, Andrew S. *consumer products company executive*
Paul, Elias *food company consultant*
Peck, Deana S. *lawyer*
Pena, Manuel, Jr. *state senator*
Phillips, Edwin Arthur *meteorologist*
†Pond, Kenneth W. *title company executive*
Porter, Amy R. *lawyer*
Preble, Lou-Ann M. *state legislator*
Pruitt, J. Doug *construction executive*
Puchi, Linda Carol *elementary school principal*
Pulaski, Charles Alexander, Jr. *lawyer*
Quinsler, William Thomson *retired investment advisor*
Radin, John William *agriculturalist, physiologist*
Rathwell, Peter John *lawyer*
Rau, David Edward *real estate company executive*
Reed, Wallace Allison *physician*
Reining, Beth LaVerne (Betty Reining) *public relations consultant, journalist*
Reins, Ralph Erich *automated service company executive*
Rethore, Bernard Gabriel *diversified company executive*
†Rimsza, Skip *mayor*
Rodgers, Anthony D. *hospital administrator*
†Rogers, A. Kay *construction company executive*
Romley, Richard M. *lawyer*
Rose, C. Kimball *judge*
Rosenblatt, Paul Gerhardt *federal judge*
Rowley, Beverley Davies *medical sociologist*
†Rubeli, Paul E. *gaming company executive*
Rudolph, Gilbert Lawrence *lawyer*
Ruffner, Jay Sturgis *lawyer*
Ryan, Buddy (James Ryan) *professional football coach*
Ryan, Patrick John *mining company executive*
Ryan, Thomas Grady *lawyer*
Ryan, Tula Fleshman *health service consultant and nursing facility administrator*
St. Clair, Thomas McBryar *mining and manufacturing company executive*
†Sargent, Henry Barry, Jr. *holding company executive*
Savage, Stephen Michael *lawyer*
Schatt, Paul *newspaper editor*
Schiffner, Charles Robert *architect*
Schiller, William Richard *surgeon*
†Schrader, William P. *organization executive, farmer*
Schroeder, Mary Murphy *federal judge*
Sedares, James L. *conductor*
Seiler, Steven Lawrence *health facility administrator*
Sellers, Joel Scott *sports medicine physician*
Shaw, Lillie Marie King *vocalist*
Sherk, Kenneth John *lawyer*
Shoen, Edward Joseph *transportation and insurance companies executive*
Simmons, Clyde *professional football player*
Snell, Richard *holding company executive*
Spencer, John Andrew *real estate development corporation executive*
Sperling, John Glen *education company executive*
Spitzer, Marc Lee *lawyer*
Stahl, Richard G. C. *journalist, editor*
Steckler, Phyllis Betty *publishing company executive*
Stern, Richard David *investment company executive*
Stine, George Harry *consulting engineer, author*
Storey, Norman C. *lawyer*
Strand, Roger Gordon *federal judge*
Sullivan, Martin Edward *museum director*
Susman, Alan Howard *lawyer*
Sutton, Samuel J. *lawyer, educator*
Symington, J. Fife, III *governor*
Tang, Thomas *federal judge*
Tatz, Paul H. *real estate executive*
Teets, John William *diversifed company executive*
Terry, Peter Anthony *lawyer*
Thomas, Harold William *avionics systems engineer, flight instructor*
Thompson, Charles Edward *electronics company executive*
Thor, Linda Maria *college president*
Traeger, Charles Henry, III *lawyer*
Trost, Eileen Bannon *lawyer*
Tubman, William Charles *lawyer*
Turner, Warren Austin *state legislator*
Turner, William Cochrane *international management consultant*
Udall, Calvin Hunt *lawyer*
Ulrich, Paul Graham *lawyer, author, publisher, editor*
†Uthoff, Michael *dancer, choreographer, artistic director*
Van Arsdale, Dick *professional basketball team executive*

Voorhees, John Henry military officer
Wales, Harold Webster lawyer
Walker, Richard K. lawyer
Wall, Donald Arthur lawyer
Ward, Yvette Hennig advertising executive
Watson, Harold George engineering executive, mechanical engineer
Weil, Louis Arthur, III newspaper publishing executive
Weinstein, Allan M. medical device company executive
†Wellinger, Charles H. health services company executive
†Welliver, Charles Harold hospital administrator
Westphal, Paul professional basketball coach
Whalen, Martin J. transportation executive, lawyer
Whisler, James Steven lawyer, mining and manufacturing executive
†White, Edward Allen electronics company executive
Wiley, Jay D. lawyer
Wilfried, Grau hotel executive officer
Williams, Bill academic administrator
Williams, Quinn Patrick lawyer
Wing, David Allan biochemistry educator
Winslow, Paul David architect
Winthrop, Lawrence Fredrick lawyer
Witherspoon, James Donald biology educator
Wolf, G. Van Velsor, Jr. lawyer
Woods, Bobby Joe transportation executive
Woods, Grant state attorney general
Woods, Joel Grant state attorney general
Woolf, Michael E. lawyer
Yarnell, Michael Allan lawyer
Yearley, Douglas Cain mining and manufacturing company executive
Zastrow, John Thurman judge
Zeilinger, Philip Thomas aeronautical engineer
Zerella, Joseph T. pediatric surgeon
Zine, Larry Joseph retail executive
†Zobell, Gregory Grant hospital administrator
Zoller, Richard Bernard investment counsel consultant
Zweifel, Terry L. aeronautical engineer, researcher

Portal
Zweifel, Richard George curator

Prescott
Anderson, Arthur George laboratory director, former computer company executive, consultant
Broadston, Donald Andrew real estate broker
Burke, Richard Kitchens lawyer, educator
Chesson, Eugene, Jr. civil engineering educator, consultant
Farrar, Elaine Willardson artist
Harris, Earl Edward business educator
Hasbrook, A. Howard aviation safety engineer, consultant
Kahne, Stephen James systems engineer, educator, academic administrator, engineering executive
Kleindienst, Richard Gordon lawyer
Longfellow, Layne Allen psychologist, educator
Markham, Richard Glover research executive
Mc Cormack, Fred Allen state social services administrator
Parkhurst, Charles Lloyd electronics company executive
Russo, Joseph Frank former college president
Stasack, Edward Armen artist

Queen Creek
Sossaman, James J. state legislator

Rio Rico
Le, Ton Da horticulturist, researcher

Rio Verde
Jordan, Richard Charles engineering executive

San Manuel
Hawk, Dawn Davah secondary education educator

Scottsdale
Aadland, Donald Ingvald engineering executive
Adams, Robert Granville marketing professional
Barbee, Joe Ed lawyer
Beesemyer, Fritz Timothy radio executive
Blackburn, Jack Bailey retired civil engineering educator
Burr, Edward Benjamin life insurance company executive, financial executive
Carney, Richard Edgar foundation executive
Chase, James Keller retired artist, museum director, educator
Christensen, Howard Alan consulting firm executive
Clement, Richard William plastic and reconstructive surgeon
Cole, George Thomas lawyer
Curtis, Philip C. artist
DeHaven, Kenneth Le Moyne retired physician
Doglione, Arthur George data processing executive
Donaldson, Scott English language educator, writer
Donnelly, Charles Francis management consultant
Douglas, John Clifton architect
Evans, Tommy Nicholas physician, educator
Fisher, John Richard engineering consultant, former naval officer
Foss, Joe association executive, speaker
Friedman, Shelly Arnold cosmetic surgeon
Furman, Robert Howard physician, educator
Gall, Donald Alan data processing executive
Garelick, Martin transportation executive
Golden, Libby artist
Goldwater, Barry Morris former senator
Gordon, Rena Joyce health services researcher, educator
Grenell, James Henry retired manufacturing company executive
Handy, Robert Maxwell patent lawyer
Hannah, Norman Britton former foreign service officer
Hansen, Donald W. insurance and financial services executive
Harrison, Harold Henry physician, scientist, educator
Haynie, Howard Edward lawyer
Hill, John deKoven architect
Hill, Louis Allen, Jr. former university dean, consultant
†Holliger, Fred Lee oil company executive
Howard, William Gates, Jr. electronics company executive
Howe, H(ugh) Philip banker
Huizingh, William former accounting educator
Jackson, Don Merrill lawyer
Jacobson, Frank Joel cultural organization adminisrator
Jenkins, William Walter psychologist, consultant
Kahn, Jeffrey Hay retired investment banker
Kitchel, Denison retired lawyer, writer
Kizziar, Janet Wright psychologist, author, lecturer
Kline, Arthur Jonathan electronics engineer
Kosick, Howard Allen accountant, finance executive
Krupp, Clarence William lawyer, personnel and hospital administrator
Kübler-Ross, Elisabeth physician
Lang, Margo Terzian artist
Leeser, David O. materials engineer, metallurgist
Linthicum, Gary Rex construction company executive
Lisa, Isabelle O'Neill mergers and acquisitions executive, law firm administrator
Malsack, James Thomas retired manufacturing company executive
Maturi, Raymond Rockne healthcare information services company executive
McGaw, Kenneth Roy wholesale distribution executive
McPherson, Donald J. metallurgist
Meyer, Madeline Anna librarian
Moeck, Walter F. conductor, music director
Newman, William Louis geologist
Osborn, Leslie Andrewartha psychiatrist
Panks, Gary Allen golf course architect
Pavlik, Nancy convention services executive
Peterson, Louis Robert retired consumer products company executive
Peyton, William Maupin treasurer, management educator
†Poll, Max Henry hospital administrator
Pomeroy, Kent Lytle physical medicine and rehabilitation physician
Prisbrey, Rex Prince insurance agent, underwriter, financial consultant
Pritzlaff, John Charles, Jr. former state senator
Rawles, Lewis Gene manufacturing executive
Rizzo, Mary Ann Frances international trade executive, former educator
Rudd, Eldon retired congressman
Ruhlman, Terrell Louis business executive
Rutes, Walter Alan architect
Sanderson, David R. physician
Scholder, Fritz artist
Shreffler, Genevieve author
Simon, Ernest Robert physician, business executive
Smith, Leonard Bingley musician
Smyth, Bernard John retired newspaper editor
Smyth, Joel Douglas newspaper executive
Soleri, Paolo architect, urban planner
Starr, Isidore law educator
Stuart, Derald Archie aerospace company consultant
Sullivan, George Edmund editorial and marketing company executive
Vairo, Robert John insurance company executive
Walsh, Edward Joseph toiletries and food company executive
Walsh, Mason retired newspaperman
Willoughby, Carroll Vernon retired motel chain executive
Wolfgang, Bonnie Arlene musician, bassoonist
Wright, James Corwin international management consultant

Sedona
Chicorel, Marietta Eva publisher
Converti, Vincenzo computer systems company executive
Eggert, Robert John, Sr. economist
Gregory, James actor
Hawkins, David Ramon psychiatrist, writer, researcher
Hoffmann, Joan Carol retired academic dean
Iverson, Wayne Dahl landscape architect, consultant
Johnson, Hoyt Charles publisher
Keane, Mark Edward public executive and educator
Preston, Edgar Harlan real estate broker
Sasmor, James Cecil publisher representative, educator
Shors, Clayton Marion cardiologist
Wolfe, Al marketing and advertising consultant

Sells
Fire Thunder, Sondra Nadine elementary educator

Show Low
Collins, Copp federal, corporate, institutional consultant

Sierra Vista
Dinges, Richard Allen entrepreneur
Lokensgard, Jon A. school system administrator
Meyer, William Trenholm defense company official, real estate executive
Morrison, Francis Martin real estate broker
Revak, JoAnn special education educator

Sonoita
Cook, William Howard architect
Scott, William Coryell medical executive

Sun City
Corcoran, Eileen Lynch special education educator emerita
Dapples, Edward Charles geologist, educator
Farwell, Albert Edmond retired government official, consultant
Jones, Alexander Elvin retired foundation executive
Lapsley, James Norvell, Jr. minister, pastoral theology educator
Morse, True Delbert business and agricultural consultant, former undersecretary of agriculture
Oppenheimer, Max, Jr. foreign language educator, consultant
Pallin, Irving M. anesthesiologist
Peterson, Leland Wilmer health facility administrator
Steffan, Wallace Allan entomologist, educator
Van Horssen, Arden Darrell retired manufacturing executive

Sun City West
Anderson, Ernest Washington manufacturing company executive
Becker, Wesley Clemence psychology educator emeritus
Black, Robert Frederick former oil company executive
Cohen, Abraham J. (Al Cohen) educational administrator
Curtin, Richard Daniel management consultant, retired air force officer, space pioneer
De Layo, Leonard Joseph former state education official
Edwards, F(loyd) Kenneth journalist, educator, management consultant, marketing executive
Madson, John Andrew architect
Mariella, Raymond P. chemistry educator, consultant
Mc Cune, John Francis, III retired architect
O'Brien, Gerald James utilities executive
Person, Robert John financial management consultant
Randall, Claire church executive
Schmitz, Charles Edison evangelist
Schrag, Adele Frisbie business education educator
Smith, Virginia Dodd (Mrs. Haven Smith) congresswoman
Stevens, George Richard business consultant, public policy commentator
Vrable, John Bernard retired oil corrosion engineer, consultant
Williams, William Harrison retired librarian
Woodruff, Neil Parker agricultural engineer

Sun Lakes
Houser, Harold Byron epidemiologist
Johnson, Marian Ilene education educator
Thompson, Loring Moore retired college administrator, writer

Surprise
Clark, Lloyd historian, educator

Tempe
Abell, James Logan architect
Abraham, Willard B. special education educator
Akers, Lex A. engineering educator
†Alexander, Thea Ann author, counseling psychologist
Alisky, Marvin Howard political science educator
Anand, Suresh Chandra physician
Aronson, Jerome Melville plant physiology educator
Arters, Linda Bromley public relations consultant, writer
Backus, Charles Edward engineering educator, researcher
Baker, Roland Jerald association executive
Balanis, Constantine Apostle electrical engineering educator
Begay, Jefferson Lee general contracting company executive
Bennett, ElDean mass communication educator, broadcaster
Berman, Neil Sheldon chemical engineering educator
Borovansky, Vladimir Theodore librarian
Brack, O. M., Jr. English language educator
Burgoyne, Edward Eynon chemistry educator
Buseck, Peter Robert geochemistry educator
Carpenter, Ray Warren materials scientist and engineer, educator
Christie, Clarence J. insurance brokerage executive
Clevenger, Jeffrey Griswold mining company executive
Coor, Lattie Finch university president
Cowley, John Maxwell physics educator
Dietz, Robert Sinclair retired geology educator
Duecy, Charles Michael retired lawyer
Evans, Lawrence Jack, Jr. lawyer
Farber, Bernard sociologist, educator
Farris, Martin Theodore economist, educator
Ferry, David Keane electrical engineering educator
Files, L(awrence) Burke financial consultant
Frischknecht, Lee Conrad retired broadcasting executive
Galician, Mary-Lou mass media educator
Gerking, Shelby Delos, Jr. zoologist, educator
Goodwin, Kemper retired architect
Gordon, Leonard sociology educator
Goronkin, Herbert physicist
†Greeley, Ronald geology educator
Grigsby, Jefferson Eugene, Jr. artist, educator
†Guilbeau, Eric J. biomedical engineer, electrical engineer, educator
Gwinner, Robert Fred, Jr. marketing educator
Hald, Alan P. computer company executive
Harris, Mark English educator, author
Herald, Cherry Lou research educator, research director
Hickson, Robin Julian mining company executive
Iverson, Peter James historian, educator
Juvet, Richard Spalding, Jr. chemistry educator
Karady, George Gyorgy electrical engineering educator, consultant
Kaufman, Irving retired engineering educator
Kelly, Rita Mae academic administrator, researcher
Klett, Mark C. photographer, educator
Krus, David James statistician
Lombardi, Eugene Patsy orchestra conductor, violinist, educator, recording artist
Lounsbury, John Frederick geographer, educator
MacKinnon, Stephen R. Asian studies administrator, educator
†Manz, Charles C. management educator
Marsh, Roberta Reynolds educator, consultant
Matheson, Alan Adams law educator
Mayer, James Walter materials science educator
McKeever, Jeffrey D. computer company executive
Mc Sheffrey, Gerald Rainey architect, educator, city planner
†Melnick, Rob research administrator
Metcalf, Virgil Alonzo economics educator
Metros, Mary Teresa librarian
Miller, Marc Douglas airline pilot
Miller, Warren Edward political scientist
Montero, Darrel Martin sociologist, social worker, educator
Nagrin, Daniel dancer, educator, choreographer, lecturer, writer
Ney, James Walter Edward Colby English language educator
Nigam, Bishan Perkash physics educator
Noce, Robert Henry neuropsychiatrist, educator
†O'Neil, Michael Joseph opinion survey executive, marketing consultant
Overman, Glenn Delbert college dean emeritus
Oxford, Sharon M. insurance company executive
Page, John Boyd physics educator
Pany, Kurt Joseph accounting educator, consultant
Patten, Duncan Theunissen ecologist educator
Pettit, George Robert chemistry educator, cancer researcher
Péwé, Troy Lewis geologist, educator
Poe, Jerry B. financial educator
Quadt, Raymond Adolph metallurgist, cement company executive
Raby, William Louis author
Richards, Gale Lee communications educator
Rios, Alberto Alvaro English educator
Ruiz, Vicki Lynn history educator
Sabine, Gordon Arthur educator, writer
Sackton, Frank Joseph university official, lecturer, retired army officer
Schroder, Dieter Karl electrical engineering educator
Scott, Judith Myers elementary education educator
Shaw, Milton Clayton mechanical engineering educator
Simon, Sheldon Weiss political science educator
Singhal, Avinash Chandra engineering administrator, educator
Skibitzke, Herbert Ernst, Jr. hydrologist
Smith, David John physicist, educator
Smith, Harvey Alvin mathematics educator, consultant
Starrfield, Sumner Grosby astrophysics educator, researcher
Tambs, Lewis Arthur diplomat, historian, educator
Thompson, Anna Blanche educator
Thums, Charles William designer, consultant
Tillery, Bill W. physics educator
Turk, Rudy Henry artist, retired museum director
Upson, Donald V. financial executive
Uttal, William R(eichenstein) psychology and engineering educator, research scientist
Vandenberg, Edwin James chemist, educator
Wales, Hugh Gregory marketing educator, business executive
Walker, Theodore Delbert landscape architect
Wang, Alan Ping-I mathematics educator
Weigend, Guido Gustav geographer, educator
Wesbury, Stuart Arnold, Jr. health administration and policy educator
Whitehurst, Harry Bernard chemistry educator
Wills, J. Robert academic administrator, drama educator, writer
Wilson, Lawrence Frank (Larry Wilson) professional football team executive
†Wood, Byard Dean mechanical engineering educator and researcher
Wyckoff, Susan astronomy researcher
Yau, Stephen Sik-sang computer science and engineering educator, computer scientist, researcher
Zeitlin, Marilyn Audrey museum director

Tolleson
Thompson, Bonnie Ransa secondary educator, chemistry educator

Tonopah
Brittingham, James Calvin nuclear engineer

Tubac
Miller, Frederick Robeson banker

Tucson
Abrams, Eric R. principal
Abrams, Herbert Kerman physician, educator
Acker, Robert Flint microbiologist
Alcorn, Stanley Marcus plant pathology educator
Alpert, Joseph Stephen physician, educator
Altman, Ellen librarian, educator
Anderson, Rachael Keller library administrator
Angel, James Roger Prior astronomer
Arnell, Walter James William mechanical engineering educator, consultant
Auslander, Steven Lawrence advertising executive, newspaper editor
Austin, John Norman classics educator
Banzhaf, Steven Michael utility company executive, lawyer
Barrett, Bruce Richard physics educator
Bartlett, David Carson state legislator
Bartocha, Bodo scientist, educator
Barton, Stanley Faulkner management consultant
Bates-Silva, Mary Louise land and cattle company executive
Battistelli, Joseph John electronics executive
Bayless, Charles Edward lawyer, utility executive
Beach, Lee Roy psychologist, educator
†Beckers, Jacques Maurice astrophysicist
Beigel, Allan psychiatry educator
Bermingham, Peter museum director
Bernhardt, Robert music director, conductor
Best, Gary Thorman real estate broker
Bilby, Richard Mansfield federal judge
Birkinbine, John, II philatelist
Block, Michael Kent economics and law educator, public policy association executive, former government official, consultant
Bohn, Hinrich Lorenz soil science educator
Bowers, William Sigmord entomology educator
Boyse, Edward Arthur research physician
Braswel, Kerry tax accountant, horsewoman
Breckenridge, Klindt Duncan architect
Briggs, Peter Stromme art historian, curator
Broadfoot, Albert Lyle physicist
Brodkey, Andrew Alan lawyer, copper company executive
Brosin, Henry Walter psychiatrist, educator
Brousseau, Georgia Cole school principal
Browning, William Docker federal judge
Bryant, Charles Austin, IV pediatrician, medical facility director
Burg, Walter A. airport terminal executive
Burrows, Benjamin physician, educator
Capp, Michael Paul physician, educator
Carleton, Willard Tracy finance educator
Carruthers, Peter Ambler physicist, educator
Cate, Rodney Michael academic administrator
Chafee, Judith Davidson architect
Champagne, John F., Jr. mining company executive
†Chapman, Clark Russell research astronomer
Chen, Chuan Fang mechanical engineering educator
Chidester, Otis Holden retired secondary education educator
Cisler, Theresa Ann osteopath
Clarke, James Weston political science educator, writer
Clay, James Ray mathematics educator
Clement, Nicholas I. principal
Conant, Howard Somers artist, educator
Cook, Gary Dennis music educator
Cortner, Hanna Joan science administrator, research scientist, educator
†Crawford, David L. astronomer
Cremer, Mabelle A. obstetrician, gynecologist
Dailey, Lynne secondary education educator
Dalen, James Eugene physician, educator
David, Ronald Sigmund psychiatrist
Davidson, Dalwyn Robert electric utility executive
Davidson, Lacinda Susan materials engineer, chemist
Davis, Daniel Edward museum director
Davis, James Luther retired utilities executive, lawyer
Davis, Stanley Nelson hydrologist, educator

Desai, Chandrakant S. civil engineering and engineering mechanics educator
Dessler, Alexander Jack space physics and astronomy educator, scientist
De Young, David Spencer astrophysicist
Dickinson, Donald Charles library science educator
Dickinson, Robert Earl atmospheric scientist, educator
Dinnerstein, Leonard historian, educator
Dinsmore, Philip Wade architect
Dobbs, Dan Byron lawyer
Dodd, Charles Gardner physical chemist
Dolph, Wilbert Emery lawyer
Drach, George Wisse urology educator
Dufner, Max retired German language educator
Eckdahl, Donald Edward manufacturing company executive
Eckhardt, August Gottlieb law educator
Elrod, Jerry David clergyman
Eshelman, Enos Grant, Jr. prosthodontist
Ewy, Gordon Allen cardiologist, educator
Falco, Charles Maurice physicist, educator
†Fang, Li-Zhi physicist, educator
Flint, Willis Wolfschmidt (Willi Wolfschmidt) artist
Forster, Leslie Stewart chemistry educator
Foster, Kennith Earl life sciences educator
Franklin, John Orland lawyer
Freeh, Edward James chemical engineer
†Freiser, Henry chemistry educator
Fritts, Harold Clark dendrochronology educator, researcher
Froman, Sandra Sue lawyer
Fuller, Wallace Hamilton research scientist, educator
Galloway, Kenneth Franklin electrical engineering educator
Ganapol, Barry Douglas nuclear engineering educator, consultant
Gantz, David Alfred lawyer, university official
Gerba, Charles Peter microbiologist, educator
†Gibson, Lay J. geography educator
Gieseler, Eugene C. lawyer
Gisi, John Joseph banker
Gissing, Bruce retired aerospace company executive
Golden, Judith Greene artist, educator
Gourley, Ronald Robert architect, educator
Grand, Marcia civic worker
Grand, Richard D. lawyer
Green, Jerrold David political science educator, academic administrator
Green, Robert Scott biotechnology company executive
Gross, Joseph Francis retired bio-engineering educator
Gruhl, James energy scientist, artist
Guice, John Thompson retired air force officer
Halonen, Marilyn Jean immunologist, pharmacologist, educator
Hampel, Alvin advertising executive
Hancocks, David Morgan museum director, architect
Harcleroad, Fred Farley education educator
Harrington, Roger Fuller electrical engineering educator, consultant
Hartmann, William Kenneth astronomy scientist
Hatfield, Charles Donald newspaper executive
Hawke, Robert Francis dentist
Haynes, Caleb Vance, Jr. geology and archaeology educator
Heins, Marilyn college dean, pediatrics educator, author
Heller, Frederick retired mining company executive
Henderson, Roger C. law educator, former dean
Hershberger, Robert Glen dean, architect
Heurlin, Bruce R. lawyer
Hildebrand, John G(rant) neurobiologist, educator
Hill, Henry Allen physicist, educator
Hoffmann, William Frederick astronomer
Houle, Joseph Adrien orthopaedic surgeon
Howard, Robert Franklin observatory administrator, astronomer
Hruby, Victor Joseph chemistry educator
Hubbard, William Bogel planetary sciences educator
Hull, Herbert Mitchell plant physiologist, researcher
Humphrey, John Julius university program director, historian, writer
Hunt, Bobby Ray electrical engineering educator, consultant
Hunten, Donald Mount planetary scientist, educator
Hurt, Charles D. college librarian
Hurt, Charlie Deuel, III library school director, educator
Hutchinson, Charles Smith, Jr. book publisher
Ingalls, Jeremy poet, educator
Ingram, Helen Moyer political science educator
Isenhower, Eleanor Anne Hexamer state government administrator
Jackson, Kenneth Arthur physicist, researcher
Jefferies, John Trevor astronomer, astrophysicist, observatory administrator
Jimmerson, J. Michael lawyer
Johnson, John Gray retired university chancellor
Jones, Frank Wyman management consultant, mechanical engineer
Jones, Roger Clyde retired electrical engineering educator
Jones, Warren David landscape architect, landscape architecture educator
Kaltenbach, C(arl) Colin dean, educator
Kaszniak, Alfred Wayne neuropsychologist
Kececioglu, Dimitri Basil reliability engineering educator
Kerwin, William James electrical engineering educator, consultant
Kessler, John Otto physicist, educator
Kiersch, George Alfred geological consultant, retired educator
Kimble, William Earl lawyer
King, Marcia management consultant
Kingsolver, Barbara Ellen writer
Kinney, Robert Bruce mechanical engineering educator
Kirk, Samuel Alexander psychologist, educator
Klotz, Arthur Paul physician, educator
Korn, Granino Arthur engineer
Krider, E. Philip atmospheric scientist, educator
Lacagnina, Michael Anthony judge
Laird, Wilbur David, Jr. librarian
Lamb, Ursula Schaefer history educator
Lamb, Willis Eugene, Jr. physicist, educator
Lane, Leonard J. hydrologist
Langendoen, Donald Terence linguistics educator
Law, John Harold biochemistry educator
Leavitt, Jerome Edward childhood educator
Lebowitz, Michael David epidemiologist
Lesher, Robert Overton lawyer
Levenson, Alan Ira psychiatrist, physician, educator
Levy, Eugene Howard planetary sciences educator, researcher
Lewis, Wilbur H. educational management consultant
Leydet, François Guillaume writer
Livermore, Joseph McMaster judge
Longan, George Baker, III real estate executive
Luningham, Robert Donald radio marketing consultant
†Marcialis, Robert Louis planetary astronomer
Marcus, Frank Isadore physician, educator
Marquez, Alfredo C. federal judge
Marshall, Robert Herman economics educator
Martin, Paul Edward retired insurance company executive
†Matthews, Mildred Shapley scientific editor, freelance writer
Maxon, Don Carlton construction company executive, mining company executive
Mc Connell, Robert Eastwood architect, educator
McCormick, Floyd Guy, Jr. agricultural educator, college administrator
†McCusker, J. Stephen zoo director
McCuskey, Robert Scott anatomy educator, researcher
Mc Donald, John Richard lawyer
McNulty, Michael Francis lawyer
Meeker, Robert Eldon retired manufacturing company executive
Meislin, Harvey Warren emergency healthcare physician, professional society administrator
Metcalfe, Darrel Seymour agronomist, educator
Meyer, Eric G. orchestra administrator
Miller, George mayor
Miller, Liz Rodriguez public library system director, librarian
Momaday, Navarre Scott English educator, author
Moreno, Manuel D. bishop
Morford, James Warren international health care executive
Morrow, James Franklin lawyer
Mullikin, Vernon Eugene aerospace executive
Myers, Douglas Scott advertising executive
Nadler, George L. orthodontist
Nagy, Bartholomew Stephen geochemist, educator
Nation, James Edward speech pathologist
Neal, James Madison, Jr. editor
Nelson, Edward Humphrey architect
Neuman, Shlomo P. hydrology educator
Neuts, Marcel Fernand statistician, educator
Nixon, Robert Obey, Sr. business educator
Nordby, Gene Milo engineering educator
Nugent, Charles Arter physician
O'Leary, Thomas Michael lawyer
Olson, Lute university athletic coach
Osborne, Thomas Cramer mineral industry consultant
Osterberg, Charles Lamar marine radioecologist, oceanographer
Pace, Thomas M. lawyer
Pacheco, Manuel Trinidad university president
Paley, Alfred Irving value engineering and consulting company executive, lecturer
Parmenter, Robert Haley physics educator
Pearson, Paul Brown nutritionist, educator
Peck, John Thomas newspaper editor
Peeler, Stuart Thorne petroleum industry executive and independent oil operator
Peete, Russell Fitch, Jr. aircraft appraiser
Pepper, Ian L. environmental microbiologist, research scientist, educator
Peters, Charles William research and development company manager
Peyghambarian, Nasser optical science educator
Pickrell, Timothy E. lawyer
†Pintozzi, Chestalene librarian
Porcello, Leonard Joseph engineering research and development executive
Powell, Richard C. physicist, educator, researcher
Prince, John Luther, III engineering educator
†Randolph, Alan Dean chemical engineering educator
Reid, Charles Phillip Patrick academic administrator, researcher, professor
Reinmuth, Oscar MacNaughton physician, educator
Renard, Kenneth George civil engineer
Re Velle, Jack B(oyer) statistician, consultant
Riggs, Frank Lewis foundation executive
Riggs, John B. architect
Rodeffer, Stephanie Lynn Holschlag archaeologist, government official
Roemer, Elizabeth astronomer, educator
Roll, John McCarthy federal judge
Roos, Nestor Robert consultant
Rose, Hugh management consultant
Ross, Glynn opera administrator
†Ross, Robert health agency administrator
Rountree, Janet Caryl astrophysicist
Russ, Joanna writer, English language educator
Saul, Kenneth Louis retired utility company executive
Schaefer, John Paul chemist, corporate executive
Schannep, John Dwight brokerage firm executive
Schorr, S. L. lawyer
Schottland, Charles Irwin retired legal educator
†Scotti, James Vernon astronomer
Seaman, Arlene Anna musician, educator
Sears, William Rees engineering educator
Seger, Martha Romayne financial economist
Seligman, Joel law educator
Shannon, Robert Rennie optical sciences center administrator, educator
Shropshire, Donald Gray hospital executive
Shubinski, Raymond planetarium director
Shultz, Silas Harold lawyer
Sibley, William Austin neurologist, educator
Silva, John Philip Costa newspaper editor
Smerdon, Ernest Thomas academic administrator
Smiley, Terah Leroy geosciences educator
Smith, David Wayne psychologist
Smith, Josef Riley internist
Smith, Vernon Lomax economist, researcher
Sonett, Charles Philip physicist
Soren, David archaeology educator, administrator
Speas, Robert Dixon aeronautical engineer, aviation company executive
†Stearns, Elliott Edmund, Jr. retired surgeon
Stini, William Arthur anthropologist, educator
Stoffle, Carla Joy dean university library
†Strausfeld, Nicholas neurobiology and entomology educator
Strittmatter, Peter Albert astronomer, educator
Strong, John William lawyer, educator
Sundt, Harry Wilson construction company executive
Sundt, Robert Stout construction company executive
Swalin, Richard Arthur scientist, company executive
Sypherd, Paul Starr microbiologist
Tang, Esther Don development consultant, retired social worker
†Thompson, Raymond Harris anthropologist, educator
Tifft, William Grant astronomer
Tirrell, John Albert religious organization executive, consultant
Tompkins, Jeannie Kay special education educator
Troup, Thomas James electronics company executive
Underwood, Jane Hainline Hammons anthropologist, educator
Van Kleek, Peter Eric college dean
Vicker, Ray writer
†Villa, Jacqueline I. newspaper editor
Volgy, Thomas John political science educator, organization official
Wahlke, John Charles political science educator
Wait, James Richard electrical engineering educator, scientist
Wallach, Leslie Rothaus architect
Weaver, Albert Bruce university administrator
Weber, Charles Walter nutrition educator
Weber, Samuel editor
Whiting, Allen Suess political science educator, writer, consultant
Wickham, John Adams, Jr. retired army officer
†Willert, Sister St. Joan health care corporation executive
Williams, Ben Franklin, Jr. mayor, lawyer
Willis, Clifford Leon geologist
Willoughby, Stephen Schuyler mathematics educator
Wilson, John Lewis university official
Winfree, Arthur Taylor biologist, educator
Wolfe, William Jerome librarian, English language educator
Wolfe, William Louis optics educator
Wolff, Sidney Carne astronomer, observatory administrator
Wood, Evelyn Nielsen reading dynamics business executive
†Woolfenden, James Manning nuclear medicine physician, educator
Wygnanski, Israel Jerzy aerospace engineering educator
Yassin, Robert Alan museum administrator, curator
Yocum, Harrison Gerald horticulturist, botanist, educator, researcher
Zeigler, Bernard Phillip electrical and computer engineering educator
Ziehler, Tony Joseph insurance agent
Zube, Ervin Herbert landscape architect, geographer, educator
†Zukoski, Charles F. surgeon, educator

Vail
Maierhauser, Joseph George entrepreneur
Reichlin, Seymour physician, educator

West Sedona
Lane, Margaret Anna Smith property manager developer

Whiteriver
†Lupe, Ronnie chairman of apache tribe

Window Rock
Zah, Peterson american indian tribal executive
Zion, James William lawyer

Youngtown
Gross, Al electrical engineer, consultant

Yuma
Hudson, John Irvin retired marine officer
Martin, James Franklin physician, lawyer
Norton, Dunbar Sutton economic developer
Young, Marilyn Rae school system adminstrative secretary, mayor

ARKANSAS

Arkadelphia
Dunn, Charles DeWitt academic administrator
Elrod, Ben Moody academic administrator
Grant, Daniel Ross retired university president
Martin, Marilyn Joan library director
Thomas, Herman L. school system administrator

Barling
Francis, Darryl Robert former banker

Batesville
Carius, Robert Wilhelm mathematics and science educator, retired naval officer
Griffith, John Vincent academic official
Harkey, John Norman state judge

Beebe
Owen, William Harold, Jr. academic administrator

Bella Vista
†Cooper, John Alfred, Jr. community development company executive
Johnson, A(lyn) William chemistry educator, researcher and consultant
†McMennamy, Roger Neal community development company executive
Medin, Myron James, Jr. city manager
Musacchia, X(avier) J(oseph) physiology and biophysics educator
Tucker, Willis Carleton retired academic administrator, retired journalism educator

Bentonville
Bruce, Robert Thomas retail executive
Carter, Paul R. retail executive
Coughlin, Thomas Martin wholesale goods company executive
Dietzman, Leslie retail executive
Fields, Bill discount department stores executive
Gildehaus, Roger Lee retail company executive
Glass, David D. department store company executive, professional baseball team executive
Gorman, David H. retail company executive
Hobbs, Lewis Ray merchandise executive
Martin, Bobby L. retail corporation executive
Schmidt, Mark Alan information systems executive
Shewmaker, Jack Clifford retired retail executive, rancher, consultant
Walton, S. Robson discount department store chain executive
White, Nicholas J. retail company executive

Blytheville
Fendler, Oscar lawyer

Camden
Brown, George J. academic administrator
Smith, Judy Seriale social services administrator, state legislator

Clarksville
Pennington, Donald Harris physician
Stephenson, C. Gene academic administrator

Conway
Bowman, Jim university dean
Brazil, William Clay lawyer
Daugherty, Billy Joe banker
Hamblin, Daniel Morgan economist
Holmes, Barbara Deveaux college president
Holt, Frank Ross retired aerospace engineer
Kearns, Terrance Brophy English language educator
Kline, Rodger S. marketing professional
Mc New, Bennie Banks economics and finance educator
Morgan, Charles Donald, Jr. manufacturing executive
Reddin, George religious organization administrator
Stiritz, Marette McCauley English language educator, consultant
†Summersett, James A., III health care executive, hospital administrator
Thompson, Winfred Lee university president, lawyer
Titlow, Larry Wayne physical education and kinesiology educator

Cotter
Naylor, George LeRoy lawyer, rail transportation executive

Dumas
Schexnayder, Charlotte Tillar state legislator

El Dorado
Anthony, Carol A. judge
Barnes, Harry F. federal judge
†Hogan, Robert Francis, Jr. cable company executive
Hopson, Brenda nursing administrator
Lee, Vernon Roy minister
McNutt, Jack Wray oil company executive
Murphy, Charles Haywood, Jr. petroleum company executive
Tommey, Charles Eldon surgeon
Vaughan, Odie Frank oil company executive
Watkins, Jerry West retired oil company executive, lawyer

Eureka Springs
Dragonwagon, Crescent writer
Epley, Lewis Everett, Jr. lawyer
Sackett, Ross DeForest publisher

Fayetteville
Ahlers, Glen-Peter, Sr. library director, educator, consultant
Andrews, John Frank civil and environmental engineering educator
Bassett, Woodson William, Jr. lawyer
Bell, Randall educational association administrator
Brown, Connell Jean retired animal science educator
Burggraf, Frank Bernard, Jr. landscape architect, educator
Clayton, Frances Elizabeth cytologist, scientist, educator
Cook, Doris Marie accountant, educator
Cramer, Gail Latimer economist
Davis, Wylie Herman lawyer, educator
Dulan, Harold Andrew former insurance company executive, educator
Evans, William Lee biologist
Faulkner, Claude Winston language professional
Ferritor, Daniel E. university official
Gaddy, James Leoma chemical engineer, educator
Gatewood, Willard Badgett, Jr. historian
Green, Thomas James archaeologist
Harrison, John Arthur library administrator
Hay, Robert Dean retired management educator
Jones, Douglas Clyde author
Jones, Euine Fay architect, educator
Jones, Fay architect
Kincaid, Hugh Reid lawyer
Knowles, Malcolm Shepherd education educator
LeFevre, Elbert Walter, Jr. civil engineering educator
Levine, Daniel Blank classical studies educator
Madison, Bernard L. academic dean, mathematics educator
Malone, David Roy university administrator, state senator
Mc Gimsey, Charles Robert, III anthropologist
Morris, Justin Roy food scientist, enologist, consultant
Musick, Gerald Joe entomology educator
Oxford, Charles William university dean, chemical engineer
Pearson, Charles Thomas, Jr. lawyer
Purvis, Hoyt Hughes political scientist, academic administrator, educator
Richardson, Nolan university athletic coach
Rosenberg, Leon Joseph marketing educator
Rutledge, Elliott Moye soil scientist, educator
Scharlau, Charles Edward, III natural gas company executive
Schmitt, Neil Martin biomedical engineer, electrical engineering educator
Schoppmeyer, Martin William education educator
Steele, Kenneth Franklin, Jr. hydrology educator, resource center director
Vorsanger, Fred S. university administrator
Waters, H. Franklin federal judge
West, Charles Patrick agronomist, educator
Williams, Doyle Z. university dean, educator
Williams, Miller poet, translator
Wilson, Charles Banks artist
Wolf, Duane Carl microbiologist

Flippin
Sanders, Steven Gill telecommunications executive

Forrest City
Brown, Patricia Ann child health nurse

Fort Smith
Banks, David Russell health care executive
Crow, Neil Edward radiologist
Dotson, Donald L. lawyer

Ellis, Mary Calline *nursing administrator*
Flanders, Donald Hargis *manufacturing company executive*
Flippin, Perry Welch *publishing executive*
Goins, Randall *grain company executive*
Gooden, Benny L. *school system administrator*
Hembree, Hugh Lawson, III *diversified holding company executive*
Hendren, Jimm Larry *federal judge*
Hendrickson, Boyde W. *health products executive*
Hoge, Marlin Boyd *surgeon*
Jesson, Bradley Dean *lawyer*
Kimbrough, Warren Oakley *judge*
Larson, Larry *librarian*
Marquard, William Albert *diversified manufacturing company executive*
Moseley, Jack Edwin *newspaper editor*
Pollan, Carolyn Joan *state legislator, job research administrator*
Pommerville, Robert W. *corporate lawyer*
Qualls, Robert L. *manufacturing executive, banker, former state official, educator*
Robinson, Opal Anne *secondary education educator*
Snider, James Rhodes *radiologist*
Stephens, Bobby Wayne *nursing home administrator*
Stites, Beverly R. *judge*
Udouj, Herman J. *diversified industries company executive*
†Wenderoth, Collier, Jr. *food products executive*
Yarbrough, Jerry A. *transportation company executive*
Young, Robert A., III *freight systems executive*

Garfield
Webb, Lance *bishop*

Glenwood
Klopfenstein, Philip Arthur *high school educator*

Greenwood
Walters, Bill *state senator, lawyer*

Hamburg
Murphy, N. B. (Nap Murphy) *state congressman, automobile dealer*

Harrison
Garrison, F. Sheridan *transportation executive*
Henley, J. Smith *federal judge*
Selby, Clark Linwood, Jr. *sales executive*

Helena
Roscopf, Charles Buford *lawyer*

Hiwasse
Sutherland, Gail Russell *retired industrial equipment manufacturing company executive*

Hot Springs National Park
Baer, Kenneth Peter *farmer cooperative executive*
Britt, Henry Middleton *retired judge*
Farley, Roy C. *rehabilitation researcher, educator*
Farris, Jefferson Davis *university administrator*
Phelps, Charlotte Mae *health educator*
Robinson, Donald Walter *university dean*
Tanenbaum, Bernard Jerome, Jr. *corporate executive*
Vaccaro, Charles G. *federal judge*
Wallace, William Hall *economic and financial consultant*

Hot Springs Village
Dellow, Reginald Leonard *advertising executive*
Schroeder, Donald Perry *retired food products company executive*

Huntsville
Carr, Gerald Paul *former astronaut, business executive, former marine officer*

Jefferson
Casciano, Daniel Anthony *biologist*
Hart, Ronald Wilson *radiobiologist, toxicologist, government research executive*
†Schwetz, Bernard Anthony *toxicologist*

Jonesboro
Elkins, Francis Clark *history educator, university official*
Peters, Mary Helen *library media specialist*
Smith, Eugene Wilson *retired university president and educator*

Little Rock
Ahlen, John William, III *state official, scientist, educator*
Anderson, Joel E., Jr. *university administrator*
Anderson, Philip Sidney *lawyer*
Andrews, Collins Adams, III *data processing company executive*
Arnold, Morris Sheppard *federal judge*
Arnold, Richard Sheppard *federal judge*
Bailin, David William *educational administrator*
Barron, Almen Leo *microbiologist*
Berube, Michael Edward *nursing administrator*
Bethea, William C. *financial administrator, lawyer*
Bisno, Alison Peck *investment banker*
Blandford, Sister Margaret Vincent *infirmary executive*
Blass, Noland, Jr. *retired architect*
Bobbitt, Max E. *telecommunications executive*
Bowen, William Harvey *banker, lawyer*
Bradbury, Curt *bank executive*
Brandon, Doug *state senator*
Brown, Dee Alexander *author*
Bryant, Winston *state attorney general*
Busfield, Roger Melvil, Jr. *retired trade association executive, educator*
Butler, Richard Colburn *banker, lawyer*
Campbell, George Emerson *lawyer*
Campbell, Gilbert Sadler *surgery educator, surgeon*
Cave, Mac Donald *anatomy educator*
Chilcote, Lugean Lester *architect*
Compton, Susan LaNell *retired librarian*
Corbin, Donald L. *judge*
Cromwell, Edwin Boykin *architect*
Cross, J. Bruce *lawyer*
Darr, James Earl, Jr. *lawyer*
Dillard, William, II *department store chain executive*
Dillard, William T. *department store chain executive*
Diner, Wilma Canada *radiologist, educator*
Doherty, James Edward, III *physician, educator*
Donovan, Herbert Alcorn, Jr. *bishop*
Doyle, Lee Lee *research scientist, educator*
Drummond, Winslow *lawyer*
DuBois, Alan Beekman *art museum administrator, curator*
Duffey, William Simon, Jr. *lawyer*
Dumeny, Marcel Jacque *lawyer*
Dyke, James Trester *building materials distributing company executive*
Eisele, Garnett Thomas *federal judge*
†Elliott, Burton *state education official*
Ferguson, John Lewis *state historian*
Ferris, Ernest Joseph *radiology educator*
Fisher, Jimmie Lou *state official*
Fogleman, John Albert *lawyer, retired judge*
Ford, Joe Thomas *telephone company executive, former state senator*
Forster, John Fredrick, Jr. *judge*
Foster, Lynn *law librarian, lawyer*
Fribourgh, James Henry *university administrator*
Fussell, Robert Foreman *federal judge*
Garcia-Rill, Edgar Enrique *neuroscientist*
Gardner, Kathleen D. *gas company executive, lawyer*
Givens, John Kenneth *manufacturing executive*
Glaze, Thomas A. *state supreme court justice*
Goss, Kay Gentry Collett *state official*
Goss, Kenneth George *physician, educator*
Gray, John Wylie *university dean, consultant*
Greenberg, Paul *newspaperman*
Guggenheim, Frederick Gibson *psychiatry educator*
Gulley, Wilbur Paul, Jr. *former savings and loan executive*
Gunter, Russell Allen *lawyer*
†Harrington, Russell Doyne, Jr. *hospital administrator*
Harris, Oren *retired federal judge*
Hatcher, Joe Branch *banker*
Hathaway, Charles E. *academic administrator*
Haught, William Dixon *lawyer*
†Hendren, James Knox *software development executive*
Hinshaw, Jerrold Eldon *state legislator*
Hinson, Jack Allsbrook *research toxicologist, educator*
†Hobbs, Ray David *editor*
Holt, Jack Wilson, Jr. *state supreme court chief justice*
Hough, Aubrey Johnston, Jr. *pathologist, physician, educator*
Howard, George, Jr. *federal judge*
Huckabee, Michael Dale *state official, minister*
Jansen, G. Thomas *dermatologist*
Jennings, Alston *lawyer*
Jones, Beverly Ward *state official*
Jones, Julia Hughes *state official*
Jones, Philip Lindsey *librarian*
King, Jack L. *electric power industry executive*
Ledbetter, Calvin Reville, Jr. (Cal Ledbetter) *political science educator, university dean, former legislator*
Levy, Eugene Pfeifer *architect*
Long, Walter Edward *international trade company executive, consultant*
Lucy, Dennis Durwood, Jr. *neurologist*
Lutgen, Robert R. *newspaper editor*
Maloney, Francis Patrick *physiatrist*
Martin, Rosemary Scarbrough *public library administrator*
Martin, William Auber *law association executive, lawyer, retired air force officer*
†Maulden, Jerry L. *utility company executive*
May, Ronald Alan *lawyer*
McAdams, Herbert Hall, II *banker*
McCarley, Robert Edward *real estate executive, real estate appraiser*
McConnell, John Wesley *real estate-resort developer, corporate executive*
McCuen, William James (Bill McCuen) *state official*
Mc Donald, Andrew J. *bishop*
McGowan, Michael Benedict *investment banker*
McMillan, Donald Edgar *pharmacologist*
McMullin, Carleton Eugene *automotive business executive*
Morris, Walter Scott *investment company executive*
Mulkey, Jack Clarendon *library director*
Murphey, Arthur Gage, Jr. *law educator*
Nelson, Edward Sheffield *lawyer, former utility company executive*
Newbern, William David *state supreme court justice*
Pagan, John Ruston *law educator*
Patten, Gerland Paul *lawyer*
Pierson, Richard Allen *hospital administrator*
Portis, Charles McColl *reporter, writer*
†Priest, Sharon Devlin *state official*
Purtle, John Ingram *lawyer, former state supreme court justice*
Reasoner, Stephen M. *federal judge*
Reeves, Rosser Scott, III *retired investment company executive*
Roberts, Jacqueline *state legislator, political consultant*
Roy, Elsijane Trimble *federal judge*
Scott, Mary Davies *federal judge*
Shults, Robert Lee *real estate executive, airline executive*
Shults, Robert Luther, Jr. *lawyer*
Simmons, Bill *newsman*
Smith, Charles Wilson, Jr. *university dean*
Smith, Sandra Lynn *lawyer*
Stead, William White *physician, educator, public health administrator*
Stephens, Jackson Thomas *investment executive*
Stephens, Warren A. *banking executive*
Suen, James Yee *otolaryngologist, educator*
Townsend, James Willis *computer scientist*
Truemper, John James, Jr. *retired architect*
Truex, Dorothy Adine *retired university administrator*
Tucker, Jim Guy, Jr. *governor*
Walker, L. T. *bishop*
Ward, Harry Pfeffer *physician, university chancellor*
Warner, Cecil Randolph, Jr. *lawyer*
Wassell, Irene Martin *food editor*
†Whillock, Carl Simpson *electric cooperative executive, former academic administrator*
Wilbourn, Gordon Gene *investment banker*
Wilcox, Jerry Cooper *architect*
Williams, C(harles) Fred *history professor*
Williams, Karmen Petersen *secondary school educator*
Williams, Norman F. *geologist, researcher*
Wilson, William R., Jr. *judge*
Witherspoon, Carolyn Brack *lawyer*
Wolfe, Jonathan James *pharmacy educator*
Wolfe, Townsend Durant, III *art museum director, curator*
Woodruff, John Douglas *non-profit association administrator, retired air force officer*
Woods, Henry *federal judge*
†Wright, Robert Ross, III *lawyer, educator*
Wright, Susan Webber *federal judge*

Lonoke
Ross, Philip Rowland *library director*

Lowell
Bergant, Paul R. *trucking company executive, lawyer*
Hunt, Johnnie B. *trucking company executive*
Palmer, Stephen *trucking company executive*
Thompson, James Kirk *transportation executive*

Mabelvale
Larch, Billie Bentley *nursing administrator*

Magnolia
Brinson, Harold Thomas *university president emeritus*
Davis, Elizabeth Hawk *English language educator*
Gamble, Steven G. *academic administrator*

Malvern
Hopkins, George *senator*

Monticello
Babin, Claude Hunter *history educator*
Ball, William Kenneth *lawyer*

Morrilton
Havener, Robert Dale *agricultural institute administrator*
Thompson, Robert Lee *agricultural economist, nonprofit executive*

Mountain Home
Anderson, Kenneth Norman *retired magazine editor, author*
Baker, Robert Leon *naval medical officer*
Saltzman, Benjamin Nathan *retired state health administrator, physician*
Seevers, Charles Junior *foundation executive, psychologist*

Newport
Boyce, Edward Wayne, Jr. *lawyer*
Thaxton, Marvin Dell *lawyer, farmer*

North Little Rock
Griffith, Jack William *medical librarian*
Harrison, Stephen Earle *manufacturing executive*
Hays, Patrick Henry *lawyer, mayor*
Holmes, James Frederick *minister*
Marshall, Terrell *lawyer*
Mc Elroy, Bobbie *furniture manufacturing executive*
Patty, Claibourne Watkins, Jr. *lawyer*
Vogler, Diane Clark *elementary school principal*

Osceola
Wilson, Ralph Edwin *lawyer, justice*

Pine Bluff
Adair, Toby Warren, Jr. *minister*
Bradford, Jay Turner *insurance executive, state legislator*
Burdick, David *library director*
Davis, Lawrence A. *academic administrator*
Engle, Carole Ruth *aquaculture economics educator*
Jones, John Harris *lawyer, banker*
Lea, George A., Jr. *retail food executive*
Long, Edward Arlo *business consultant, retired manufacturing company executive*
Ramsay, Louis Lafayette, Jr. *lawyer, banker*
Seawell, William Thomas *former airline executive*

Rogers
Hudson, James T. *food company executive*
Hudson, Michael T. *food company executive*
Scott, Harold Lee, Jr. *distribution executive*
Spainhower, James Ivan *retired college president*

Roland
Ebert, Richard Vincent *physician, educator*

Russellville
Chesnut, Franklin Gilmore *clergyman*
Hardin, Luther *state senator*
Inch, Morris Alton *theology educator*
Jones, James Rees *retired oil company executive*
†Morris, Lois Lawson *education educator*

Scranton
Uzman, Betty Geren *pathologist, retired educator*

Searcy
Beebe, Mike *state senator, lawyer*
Burks, David Basil *academic administrator, educator*
Miller, Ken Leroy *religious studies educator, consultant, writer*
Oldham, Bill W. *mathematics educator*
Organ, Dennis Michael *English educator*
Pryor, Joseph Ehrman *chemistry educator*

Sherwood
Wood, Marion Douglas *state legislator, lawyer*

Siloam Springs
†Butler, Lynch *food products executive*

Springdale
Cypert, Jimmy Dean *lawyer*
Hill, Peggy Sue *principal*
Johnston, Gerald McArthur *food company executive*
Pogue, William Reid *former astronaut, foundation executive, business and aerospace consultant*
Posey, Sandra Dalton *special education educator*
Rogers, Jerry *principal*
Rollins, Jimmy Don *school system administrator*
Sword, Russ Donald *hospital administrator*
Tollett, Leland Edward *food company executive*
Tyson, Donald John *food company executive*

State University
Fowler, Gilbert L. *dean, educator*
Jones, Charlott Ann *museum director, art educator*
Lindquist, Evan *artist, educator*
Mangieri, John Nicholas *university administrator*
Power, Mary Susan *political science educator*
Ruby, Ralph, Jr. *vocational business educator*
Whitis, Grace Ruth *nursing educator*

Stuttgart
Bell, Richard Eugene *grain and food company executive*
Hillman, Tommy *food products company executive*
Jessup, Stewart E. *agricultural products executive*

Texarkana
Henry, James Alvin *minister, benefits executive*
Stroud, John Fred, Jr. *state supreme court justice*

Walnut Ridge
Huckabay, Gary C. *academic administrator*

West Memphis
Fogleman, Julian Barton *lawyer*
Nance, Cecil Boone, Jr. *lawyer*

CALIFORNIA

Abingdon
Williams, Glen Morgan *federal judge*

Acton
†Butman, Harry Raymond *clergyman, author*

Agoura Hills
Chagall, David *journalist, author*
Chang, Chong Eun *chemical engineer*
deCiutiis, Alfred Charles Maria *medical oncologist, television producer*
Guarino, Salvatore Frank *hotel executive*
Maquipour, Iraj *consulting company executive*
Merchant, Roland Samuel, Sr. *hospital administrator, educator*
Naylor-Jackson, Jerry *entertainer, public relations consultant, producer*
†Scardina, Frank Joseph *real estate executive*
Schmidt, Frank Broaker *executive recruiter*
Teresi, Joseph *publishing executive*

Alameda
Bartalini, C. Richard *judge*
Billings, Thomas Neal *computer and publishing executive, management consultant*
Blatt, Beverly Faye *biologist, consultant*
Klehs, Henry John Wilhelm *civil engineer*
Stonehouse, James Adam *lawyer*
Taveggia, Thomas Charles *management educator*
Verrill, Kathleen Wills *special education educator*
Whorton, M. Donald *occupational and environmental health physician, epidemiologist*

Alamo
Bolles, Richard Nelson *author, clergyman*
Burchell, Mary Cecilia *surgeon*
Lee, Richard *martial arts educational executive*
Pritchett, Thomas Ronald *retired metal and chemical company executive*
Whalen, John Sydney *management consultant*

Albany
Boris, Ruthanna *dancer, choreographer, dance therapist, educator*
Chook, Edward Kongyen *academic administrator, disaster medicine educator*
†Sikora, Stephen Theodore *publisher*
†Weber, Barbara C. *research entomologist*

Albion
Martin, Bill *artist, art educator*

Alhambra
Anderson, Gordon MacKenzie *petroleum service contractors executive*
Anton, William R. *retired school system administrator, consultant*
Duke, Donald Norman *publisher*
Garber, C(harles) Stedman, Jr. *oil and mining industry executive*
Shannon, Edfred L., Jr. *gas and oil drilling company executive*
Siler, Walter Orlando, Jr. *retired business executive*
Szymanski, Joyce Ann *publicist*

Aliso Viejo
Sanford, Sarah J. *nurse, health care executive*

Alpine
Greenberg, Byron Stanley *newspaper and business executive, consultant*
Samuelson, Derrick William *lawyer*

Alta Loma
Cooper, George Robert *electrical engineer, educator*
Wu, Seng-Chai *financial planner, life insurance agency official*

Altadena
Burden, Jean (Prussing) *poet, writer, editor*
Gurnis, Michael Christopher *geological sciences educator*
Ikegawa, Shiro *artist*
Ziegler, Raymond Stewart *architect*

Anaheim
†Abramson, Norman *retail executive*
Balch, Glenn McClain, Jr. *academic administrator, minister, author*
Barnett, Holly Billings *public relations executive*
Bowman, Jeffrey R. *protective services official*
Brownhill, H. Bud *small business owner, canine behavior therapist*
Conlin, William Patrick *computer company executive*
†Daly, Tom *mayor*
Frontiere, Georgia *professional football team executive*
†Grennan, Cynthia *school superintendent*
Grose, Elinor Ruth *retired elementary education educator*
Hubbard, Charles Ronald *engineering executive*
Jackson, Bo (Vincent Edward Jackson) *professional baseball, former football player*
Jackson, David Robert *school system administrator*
Kallay, Michael Frank, II *medical devices company official*
Lachemann, Marcel *professional baseball manager*
Langston, Mark Edward *professional baseball player*
Lano, Charles Jack *management auditor*
Loeblich, Helen Nina Tappan *paleontologist, educator*

McGarry, Eugene L. *university official*
Nguyen, Tai Anh *minister*
Noorda, Raymond J. *computer software company executive*
Prince, Warren Victor *mechanical engineer*
Rivera, Armando Remonte *utilities engineer*
Rohrer, George John *lawyer*
Smith, Lee Arthur *professional baseball player*
Stark, Milton Dale *sports association executive*
†Steel, Alan Richard *financial executive*
Wrigley, William *corporation executive*

Angwin
Maxwell, D. Malcolm *college president*
†Maxwell, Malcolm *college president, minister*

Anza
Skelton, Red (Richard Skelton) *comedian, artist*

Apple Valley
Mays, George Walter, Jr. *educational technology educator, consultant*
Win, Khin Swe *anesthesiologist*

Aptos
Bohn, Ralph Carl *educational consultant, retired educator*
Dobey, James Kenneth *banker*
Heron, David Winston *librarian*
Hirsch, Bette G(ross) *college administrator, foreign language educator*
Mechlin, George Francis *electrical manufacturing company executive*
Mellenbruch, Giles (Johnny) Edward *orchestra leader, lyricist*
Woods, Gurdon Grant *sculptor*

Arcadia
Baillie, Charles Douglas *banker*
Broderick, Donald Leland *electronics engineer*
Eck, Dennis K. *supermarket chain executive*
Gamboa, George Charles *oral surgeon, educator*
Horner, Althea Jane *psychologist*
Mc Cormack, Francis Xavier *lawyer, former oil company executive*
Morse, Judy *science foundation administrator*
Nelson, Garrett R. *retail food company executive*
Seitz, Charles Lewis *computer scientist and engineer*
Sloane, Beverly LeBov *writer, consultant*
Stangeland, Roger Earl *retail chain store executive*

Arcata
Barratt, Raymond William *biologist, educator*
Bowker, Lee Harrington *academic administrator*
Emenhiser, JeDon Allen *political science educator, academic administrator*
Harvey, Carol Sammons *educator*
Hunt, Robert Weldon *mathematics educator, consultant*
Mc Crone, Alistair William *university president*
Wayne, Lowell Grant *air pollution scientist, consultant*

Aromas
Nutzle, Futzie (Bruce John Kleinsmith) *artist, author, cartoonist*

Arrowhead
Bauer, Ralph Leroy *business executive*

Artesia
Ferris, Pauline *principal*
Korsmeier, Gary *dairy products executive*
Moffett, Kenneth Lee *superintendent schools*
Taguchi, Aileen Takayo *special education educator*

Arvin
Pankey, Edgar Edward *rancher*

Atascadero
Eggertsen, Paul Fred *psychiatrist*
Ogier, Walter Thomas *retired physics educator*

Atherton
Bales, Royal Eugene *philosophy educator*
†Barker, Robert Jeffery *financial executive*
Chetkovich, Michael N. *accountant*
Fisher, Leon Harold *physicist, emeritus educator*
Goodman, Sam Richard *electronics company executive*
Heyns, Roger William *retired foundation executive and educator*
Hogan, Clarence Lester *retired electronics executive*
King, Jane Cudlip Coblentz *volunteer educator*
Lowry, Larry Lorn *management consulting company executive*
Mc Intyre, Henry Langenberg *former business executive, lawyer*
Starr, Chauncey *research institute executive*

Atwater
DeVoe, Kenneth Nickolas *food service executive, mayor*

Auburn
Hess, Patrick Henry *chemist*
Jeske, Howard Leigh *life insurance company executive, lawyer*

Avalon
Burns, Denise Ruth *artist*

Avila Beach
Kamm, Herbert *journalist*

Azusa
Felix, Richard E. *academic administrator*
Gray, Paul Wesley *university dean*
Kimnach, Myron William *botanist, horticulturist, consultant*

Bakersfield
Akers, Tom, Jr. *cotton broker, consultant*
Arciniega, Tomas Abel *university president*
Badgley, Theodore McBride *psychiatrist, neurologist*
Barro, Mary Helen *broadcast executive*
Boyd, William Harland *historian*
Clark, Michal Charles *social services director*
Corder, Michael Paul *physician, educator*
Decker, James Thomas *psychotherapist*
Dorer, Fred Harold *chemistry educator*
Duquette, Diane Rhea *library director*
Enriquez, Carola Rupert *museum director*
Frankel, Helen Bruce *county executive*
Friedman, Gloria A. *tennis coach*
Glynn, James A. *sociology educator, author*
Groefsema, Bruce *agricultural products executive*
Hart, Donald Milton *automotive and ranching executive, former mayor*
Hefner, John *principal*
Izenstark, Joseph Louis *radiologist, physician, educator*
Kegley, Jacquelyn Ann *philosophy educator*
Lundquist, Gene Alan *cotton company executive*
Martin, George Francis *lawyer*
McAlister, Michael Hillis *architect*
Murillo, Velda Jean *social worker, counselor*
Owen, Fred Wynne *lawyer*
Owens, Buck (Alvis Edgar, Jr.) *singer, musician, songwriter*
†Pratt, Brian *heavy manufacturing executive*
†Price, Robert O. *mayor*
Reep, Edward Arnold *artist*
Shell, Mary Katherine Jaynes Hosking (Mrs. Joseph C. Shell) (Mrs. Joseph C. Shell) *county official*

Balboa Island
Abramson, Albert *television historian, consultant*
Badham, Robert E. *former congressman*
Daughaday, William Hamilton *retired physician*

Baldwin Park
Gregory, George G. *lawyer*
Swartz, Stephen Arthur *banker, lawyer*

Barstow
Jones, Nathaniel *bishop*

Bayside
Bank, Ron *principal*
Cocks, George Gosson *retired chemical microscopy educator*
Pierce, Lester Laurin *retired pilot, aviation consultant*

Beale AFB
Carpenter, Adelbert Wall *air force officer*

Beaumont
†Lippert, Robert Lawrence *social services administrator*

Bellflower
Gillman, Greta Joanne *physician*
Martin, Melissa Carol *radiological physicist*

Belmont
†Carlson, Gary R. *publishing executive*
Glenn, Thomas Michael *science and technology executive*
Lake, David S. *publisher, lawyer*

Belvedere Tiburon
Behrman, Richard Elliot *pediatrician, neonatologist, university dean*
Caselli, Virgil P. *real estate executive*
Cook, Lyle Edwards *retired fund raising executive, consultant*
Cook, Robert Donald *financial service executive*
Crockett, Ethel Stacy *librarian*
Denton, Charles Mandaville *corporate consultant*
Elder, Rex Alfred *civil engineer*
Kramer, Lawrence Stephen *journalist*
Moffitt, Phillip William *magazine editor*
Power, Jules *television producer*

Berkeley
Aaker, David Allen *marketing educator*
Abel, Carlos Alberto *immunologist*
Abel, Ray *graphic artist*
Adelman, Irma Glicman *economics educator*
Alhadeff, David Albert *economics educator*
Allison, James Patrick *immunology educator, medical association administrator*
Alpen, Edward Lewis *biophysicist, educator*
Alpert, Norman Joseph *merchandising executive*
Alter, Robert B. *comparative literature educator and critic*
Alvarez, Walter *geology educator*
Ames, Bruce N(athan) *biochemist, molecular biologist*
Ames, Giovanna Ferro-Luzzi *biochemistry educator*
Anderson, John Richard *entomologist, educator*
Anderson, William Scovil *classics educator*
Angelakos, Diogenes James *electrical engineering educator*
Arbegast, David Elwood *landscape architect*
Arnon, Daniel I(srael) *biochemist, educator*
Arons, Jonathan *astrophysicist, educator*
Arveson, William Barnes *mathematics educator*
Attwood, David Thomas *physicist, educator*
Auerbach, Alan Jeffrey *economist*
Baas, Jacquelynn *art historian, museum administrator*
Bagdikian, Ben Haig *journalist, emeritus university educator*
†Baldwin, Bruce Gregg *botany educator, researcher*
Baletta, William *physics research administrator*
Barish, Jonas Alexander *English language educator*
Barker, Horace Albert *biochemist, microbiologist*
Barnes, Thomas G. *law educator*
Barnett, R(alph) Michael *theoretical physicist, educational agency administrator*
Barnett, Stephen R. *law educator*
Barrett, Reginald Haughton *wildlife management educator, biology educator*
Bartlett, Neil *chemist, educator*
†Bartlett, Paul A. *biochemist*
Barton, Babette B. *lawyer, educator*
†Basch, Reva *information services company executive*
Baumrind, Diana *research psychologist*
Bellah, Robert Neelly *sociologist, educator*
Bender, Richard *university dean, architect, educator*
Benedict, Burton *retired museum director, anthropology educator*
Berger, Stanley Allan *mechanical engineering educator*
Bergman, George Mark *mathematician, educator*
Bergman, Robert George *chemist, educator*
Berkner, Klaus Hans *laboratory administrator, physicist*
Berlekamp, Elwyn Ralph *former electronics company executive, mathematics educator*
Bern, Howard Alan *science educator, research biologist*
Berring, Robert Charles, Jr. *law educator, law librarian, former dean*
Berry, William Benjamin Newell *geologist, educator, former museum administrator*
Bickel, Peter John *statistician, educator*
Birdsall, Charles Kennedy *electrical engineer*
Blum, Manuel *computer science educator*
Blume, James Beryl *financial advisor*
Bogy, David B(eauregard) *mechanical engineering educator*
Bolt, Bruce Alan *seismologist, educator*
Bonnell, Victoria Eileen *sociologist*
Bourne, Samuel G. *mathematician, consultant, educator*
Bouwsma, William James *history educator*
Bowker, Albert Hosmer *retired university chancellor*
Bowyer, Stuart C(harles) *astrophysicist, educator*
Brandes, Stanley Howard *anthropology educator, writer*
Breslauer, George William *political science educator*
Brewer, Leo *physical chemist, educator*
Bronstein, Arthur J. *linguistics educator*
Browne, Walter Shawn *journalist, chess player*
Buckland, Michael Keeble *librarian, educator*
Bucklin, Louis Pierre *business educator, consultant*
Budinger, Thomas Francis *radiologist, educator*
Bukowinski, Mark Stefan Tadeusz *geophysics educator*
Burger, Edmund Ganes *architect*
Burger, Robert Eugene *author, chess expert*
Burnside, Mary Beth *biology educator, researcher*
Buxbaum, Richard M. *law educator, lawyer*
†Caetano, Raul *epidemiologist, educator*
Cahill, James Francis *art history educator*
Cain, Bruce Edward *political science educator, consultant*
Cairns, Elton James *chemical engineering educator*
Calame, Alexandre Emile *retired French literature educator*
Callenbach, Ernest *writer, editor*
Calloway, Doris Howes *nutrition educator*
Calvin, Melvin *chemist, educator*
Cardwell, Kenneth Harvey *architect, educator*
Carman, James Martin *business administration educator, consultant*
Carmichael, Ian Stuart Edward *geologist, educator*
Casida, John Edward *entomology educator*
Castro, Joseph Ronald *physician, oncology researcher, educator*
Catlin, James C. *conservationist, land use planner, electrical engineer*
Cerny, Joseph, III *chemistry educator, scientific laboratory administrator, university dean and official*
Chamberlain, Owen *nuclear physicist*
Chamberlin, Michael John *biochemistry educator*
Chandler, David *scientist, educator*
Chapman, G. Arnold *Romance languages educator*
Cheit, Earl Frank *economist, educator*
Chemsak, John Andrew *entomologist*
Chern, Shiing-Shen *mathematics educator*
Chew, Geoffrey Foucar *physicist*
Chopra, Anil Kumar *civil engineering educator*
Chorin, Alexandre Joel *mathematician, educator*
Chua, Leon O. *electrical engineering and computer science educator*
Clark, James Henry *publishing company executive*
Clark, John Desmond *anthropology educator*
Clark, Thomas Willard *poet*
Clarke, John *physics educator*
Clausen, John Adam *social psychologist*
Clemens, William Alvin *vertebrate paleontology educator*
Clifford, Geraldine Joncich (Mrs. William F. Clifford) *education educator*
Cohen, Marvin Lou *physics educator*
Cole, Robert H. *law educator*
Cole, Roger David *biochemist, educator*
Colson, Elizabeth Florence *anthropologist*
Concepción, David Alden *arbitrator, educator*
Coons, John E. *legal educator, lawyer*
Cooper, William Secord *information science educator*
Cooter, Robert *law educator*
Costa, Gustavo *Italian language educator*
Cozzarelli, Nicholas Robert *molecular biologist, educator*
Craib, Ralph Grant *reporter*
Crawford, James E. *law educator, lawyer*
Crews, Frederick Campbell *humanities educator, writer*
Cross, Kathryn Patricia *education educator*
Culler, David Ethan *computer science educator*
Curtis, Garniss Hearfield *geology educator*
Cutter, David Lee *pharmaceutical company executive*
Dahlsten, Donald Lee *enviromental biology and forest entomology educator*
Danton, Joseph Periam *librarian, educator*
Dauben, William Garfield *chemist, educator*
Davidson, Donald Herbert *philosophy educator*
Davis, Marc *astrophysics educator*
Debreu, Gerard *economics and mathematics educator*
De Goff, Victoria Joan *lawyer*
de Lumen, Benito O. *science educator*
Dempster, Lauramay Tinsley *botanist*
Denn, Morton Mace *chemical engineering educator*
DePaolo, Donald James *earth science educator*
de Pater, Imke *astronomy educator*
Desoer, Charles Auguste *electrical engineer*
Diamond, Marian Cleeves *anatomy educator*
Dornfeld, David Alan *engineering educator*
Drechsel, Edwin Jared *retired magazine editor*
Dresher, Paul Joseph *composer, music educator, performer*
Duesberg, Peter Heinz Hermann *molecular biology educator*
Dugger, Edwin Ellsworth *composer, educator*
Duhl, Leonard *psychiatrist, educator*
Dundes, Alan *writer, folklorist, educator*
Duster, Troy *sociology educator*
Dwyer, John P. *law educator*
Eckbo, Garrett *landscape architect, urban designer*
Eisenberg, Melvin A. *law educator*
Elberg, Sanford Samuel *university administrator*
Ely, Robert Pollock, Jr. *physics educator, researcher*
Enoch, Jay Martin *vision scientist, educator*
Evans, James William *metallurgical educator*
Falkner, Frank Tardrew *physician, educator*
Fateman, Richard J. *computer science educator, researcher*
Fatt, Irving *optometry and bioengineering educator*
Faulk, I. Carlton *religious organization executive*
Faulk, Sylvia *religious organization executive*
Feeley, Malcolm M. *law educator, political scientist*
Feldman, Jerome Arthur *computer scientist, educator*
Feller, David E. *arbitrator*
Ferrari, Domenico *computer science educator*
Finnie, Iain *mechanical engineer, educator*
Fleming, Scott *retired health services executive*
Fletcher, William A. *law educator*
Foster, George McClelland, Jr. *anthropologist*
Fowler, Thomas Kenneth *physicist*
Frankie, Gordon William *entomology educator*
Freedman, David Amiel *statistics educator, consultant*
Freedman, Sarah Warshauer *education educator*
Frisch, Joseph *mechanical engineer, educator, consultant*
Fuerstenau, Douglas Winston *mineral engineering educator*
Fuhs, G(eorg) Wolfgang *environmental research manager*
Furman, Deane Philip *parasitologist, emeritus educator*
Gaillard, Mary Katharine *physics educator*
Gall, Donald Arthur *minister*
Garrison, William Louis *civil engineering educator*
Genn, Nancy *artist*
Getz, Wayne Marcus *biomathematician, researcher, educator*
Gilbert, Neil Robin *social work educator, author, consultant*
Gilkerson, Tom Moffet *economist, company executive, education consultant*
Glaser, Donald Arthur *physicist*
Glenny, Lyman Albert *retired education educator*
†Godfrey, Charles Bruce *chemist, laboratory executive*
Goldhaber, Gerson *physicist, educator*
Goldsmith, Werner *mechanical engineering educator*
Gordley, James Russell *law educator*
Graburn, Nelson Hayes Henry *anthropologist, educator*
†Graham, James *astronomy educator*
Graham, Susan Lois *computer science educator, consultant*
Gray, Paul Russell *educator*
Greenblatt, Stephen J. *English language educator*
Greene, Albert Lawrence *hospital administrator*
Gregory, Joseph Tracy *paleontologist, educator*
Grossman, Elmer Roy *pediatrician*
Grossman, Joan Delaney *language and literature educator*
Grossman, Lawrence Morton *nuclear engineering educator*
Gruen, Erich Stephen *classics educator*
Guest, Barbara *author, poet*
Gurgin, Vonnie Ann *social scientist*
Hafey, Joseph Michael *health association executive*
†Hafter, Ervin R. *psychology educator*
Hahn, Erwin Louis *physicist, educator*
Hakansson, Nils Hemming *financial economics and accounting educator*
Halbach, Edward Christian, Jr. *legal educator*
Haley, George Patrick *lawyer*
Hammel, Eugene Alfred *anthropologist*
Hancock, Emily Stone *psychologist*
Hanff, Peter Edward *librarian, bibliographer*
Hardyck, Curtis Dale *psychology and education professor*
Harlan, Robert Dale *library and information studies educator, academic administrator*
Harris, Guy Hendrickson *chemical research engineer*
Harrison, Michael Alexander *computer scientist, educator, entrepreneur*
Harsanyi, John Charles *economics educator, researcher*
Hartman, Robert Leroy *artist, educator*
Hearst, John Eugene *chemistry educator*
Heathcock, Clayton Howell *chemistry educator, researcher*
Heilbron, John L. *historian*
Heiles, Carl Eugene *astronomer, educator*
Heineman, Heinz *chemist*
Heinemann, Heinz *chemist, researcher, consultant*
Helmholz, August Carl *physicist, educator emeritus*
Helson, Henry Berge *publisher, retired mathematics educator*
Henkin, Leon Albert *mathematician, educator*
Henry, Charles Patrick *political science educator*
Herr, Richard *history educator*
Hester, Randolph Thompson, Jr. *landscape architect, educator*
Hetland, John Robert *lawyer, educator*
Hirsch, Morris William *mathematics educator*
Hitch, Charles Johnston *economist, institution executive*
Hodges, David Albert *electrical engineering educator*
†Hoehn, Raymond Philip, Jr. *map librarian*
Hoffman, Darleane Christian *chemistry educator*
Holder, Harold D. *public health administrator, communications specialist, educator*
Holdren, John Paul *energy and resource educator, researcher, author, consultant*
Holmes, James Gordon *retired vascular surgeon, medical educator*
Holst, James E. *lawyer*
Holton, Richard Henry *business educator*
Howell, Francis Clark *anthropologist, educator*
Hsu, Chieh Su *applied mechanics engineering educator, researcher*
Hu, Chenming *electrical engineering educator*
Hunt, Frank Bouldin *architect, water color artist*
Hurley, Morris Elmer, Jr. *management consultant*
Hurst, Deborah *pediatric hematologist*
Hutcherson, Bobby *jazz vibraphonist*
Imbrie, Andrew Welsh *composer, educator*
Jackson, J(ohn) David *physicist, educator*
Jaffee, Dwight M. *economist, educator*
Jeanloz, Raymond *geophysicist, educator*
Jeffries, Carson Dunning *physicist, educator*
Jensen, Arthur Robert *psychology educator*
Jewell, Nicholas Patrick *statistics educator*
Jewell, William Sylvester *engineering educator*
Johanson, Donald Carl *physical anthropologist*
Johnson, Phillip E. *law educator*
Jolly, William Lee *chemistry educator*
Jordan, John Emory *language professional, educator*
Jordan, June M. *poet, English language educator*
Jorde, Thomas *law educator*
Kadish, Sanford Harold *law educator*
Kagan, Robert Michael *law educator*
Kahan, William M. *mathematics educator, consultant*
Kahn, Steven Michael *astrophysicist, educator*
Kallgren, Joyce Kislitzin *political science educator*
Kanafani, Adib *transportation think-tank administrator, civil engineering educator*
Kaplan, Donald Robert *biologist, educator*
Kaplansky, Irving *mathematician, educator, research institute director*
Karlinsky, Simon *language educator, author*
Karp, Richard Manning *computer sciences educator*
Kasten, Karl Albert *painter, printmaker*

Kastenberg, William Edward engineering and applied science educator
Kay, Herma Hill law educator
Kay, Paul de Young linguist
Keeler, Theodore Edwin economics educator
Kerman, Joseph Wilfred musicologist, critic
Kerr, Clark university president emeritus
Kerth, Leroy T. physics educator
†Kim, Sung-Hou chemistry educator, biophysical and biological chemist
King, Ivan Robert astronomy educator
King, Mary-Claire epidemiologist, educator, geneticist
Kingston, Maxine Hong author
Kirsch, Jack Frederick biochemistry educator
Kittel, Charles physicist, educator emeritus
Klinman, Judith Pollock biochemist, educator
Koshland, Daniel Edward, Jr. biochemist, educator
Koshland, Marian Elliott immunologist, educator
Kretchmer, Norman obstetrics, pediatrics and nutritional science educator
Kuh, Ernest Shiu-Jen electrical engineering educator
Kuttner, Stephan George law history educator
Lambert, Nadine Murphy psychologist, educator
Landau, Martin political science educator
Lane, Sylvia economist, educator
Lashof, Joyce C. public health educator
Lazarus, Richard Stanley psychology educator
Le Cam, Lucien Marie mathematics educator
Lee, Ronald Demos demographer, economist, educator
Lee, Yuan T(seh) chemistry educator
Leemans, Wim Pieter physicist
Lehmann, Erich Leo statistics educator
Leitmann, George mechanical engineering educator
Lennette, Edwin Herman virologist
Leopold, Luna Bergere geology educator
Lesser, Wendy literary magazine editor, writer, consultant
Lester, William Alexander, Jr. chemist, educator
Letiche, John Marion economist, educator
Lev, Baruch Itamar business administration educator, consultant
Lewis, Edwin Reynolds biomedical engineering educator
Licht, Paul zoologist, educator
Lichterman, Martin history educator
Lidicker, William Zander, Jr. zoologist, educator
Lieberman, David law educator
Light, Ken photojournalist, educator
Linn, Marcia Cyrog educator
Linn, Stuart Michael biochemist, educator
Lipps, Jere Henry paleontology educator
Lipson, Leslie Michael political science educator
Littlejohn, David journalism educator, writer
Litwack, Leon Frank historian, educator
Loher, Werner J. entomology educator
Long, Anthony Arthur classics educator
Lubin, Mary Luella nursing home administrator
Luker, Kristin sociology educator
Maisel, Sherman Joseph economist, educator
Malina, Roger F. astronomer
Mandelstam, Stanley physicist
Markowitz, Samuel Solomon chemistry educator
Maron, Melvin Earl philosopher, educator
Maslach, Christina psychology educator
Maslach, George James former university official
Mathies, Richard Alfred chemistry educator
†Matson, Pamela Anne environmental science educator
Maurer, Adah Electra psychologist
May, Adolf Darlington civil engineering educator
Mayali, Laurent legal history educator
McColl, John Graham plant and soil biology educator
Mc Cullough, Helen Craig Oriental languages educator
Mc Evilly, Thomas Vincent seismologist
McFadden, Daniel Little economics educator
McKee, Christopher Fulton astrophysics and astronomy educator
McKillop, William Lawie forest economics educator
McNulty, John Kent lawyer, educator
Mei, Kenneth K. electrical engineering and computer sciences educator
Meier, Richard Louis futurist, planner, behavioral scientist
Mel, Howard Charles biophysics educator
Meltzer, David author, musician
Merchant, Carolyn environmental history educator
Merrill, Richard James educational director
Messerschmitt, David Gavin engineering educator
Middlekauff, Robert Lawrence history educator, administrator
Miles, Raymond Edward former university dean, organizational behavior and industrial relations educator
Miller, William Hughes theoretical chemist, educator
Milosz, Czeslaw poet, author, educator
Minudri, Regina Ursula library director, consultant
Mishkin, Paul J. lawyer, educator
Miyasaki, George Joji artist
Monismith, Carl Leroy civil engineering educator
Montgomery, Roger dean
Moore, C. Bradley chemistry educator
Moran, Rachel lawyer, educator
Mote, Clayton Daniel, Jr. mechanical engineer, educator, administrator
Muir, William Ker, Jr. political science educator
Muller, Richard August physicist, author
Muller, Richard Stephen electrical engineer, educator
Muscatine, Charles English educator, author
Nagler, Michael Nicholas classics and comparative literature educator
Nandi, Satyabrata zoology educator
Nemeth, Charlan Jeanne psychology educator
Nero, Anthony Vincent, Jr. physicist, environmental scientist
Newman, Frank Cecil legal educator, retired state supreme court justice
Newman, John Scott chemical engineer, educator
Nonet, Philippe law educator
Odermatt, Robert Allen architect
Ogg, Wilson Reid poet, lyricist, curator, publisher, lawyer, retired judge, educator
Ohala, John Jerome linguistics educator
Oldham, William George electrical engineering and computer science educator
Ornduff, Robert botany educator
Osserman, Robert mathematician, educator
Ott, David Michael engineering company executive
Pagni, Patrick John mechanical and fire safety engineering science educator ,
Parsons, James Jerome geographer, educator
Pask, Joseph Adam ceramic engineering educator
Patterson, David Andrew computer scientist, educator, consultant
Paulling, John Randolph, Jr. naval architecture educator, consultant
Penzien, Joseph structural engineering educator
Penzl, Herbert German language and linguistics educator
Perez-Mendez, Victor physics educator
Perry, Dale Lynn chemist
Pigford, Thomas Harrington nuclear engineering educator
Pines, Alexander chemistry educator, researcher
Pitelka, Frank Alois zoologist, educator
Pitzer, Kenneth Sanborn chemist, educator
Polak, Elijah engineering educator, computer scientist
Policoff, Leonard David physician, educator
Popov, Egor Paul engineering educator
Post, Robert Charles law educator
Poulos-Woolley, Paige M. public relations executive
Prausnitz, John Michael chemical engineer, educator
Pritchard, Arthur Osborn retired business administrator
Purcell, Alexander Holmes entomologist, educator
Quigley, John Michael economist, educator
Ramamoorthy, Chittor V. computer science educator
Ranney, (Joseph) Austin political science educator
Rapoport, Sonya artist
Rasmussen, John Oscar chemist, scientist
Ratner, Marina mathematician, educator, researcher
Rauch, Irmengard linguist, educator
Rausser, Gordon C(lyde) agricultural and resource economics educator
Raymond, Kenneth Norman chemistry educator, research chemist
Reginato, Robert Joseph soil scientist
Reich, Michael economics educator
Reynolds, John Hamilton physicist, educator
Rice, Edward Earl former government official, author
Rice, Robert Arnot school administrator
Riesenfeld, Stefan Albrecht law educator, consultant
Ritchie, Robert Oliver materials science educator
Rohwer, William D., Jr. university dean
Roller, Robert Douglas, III psychiatrist
Rosberg, Carl Gustaf political science educator
Rosen, Kenneth T. economist
Rosenblatt, Gerd Matthew chemist
Rosenzweig, Mark Richard psychology educator
Rowe, John Howland anthropologist, educator
Rubinfeld, Daniel Lee law educator, consultant
Sadoulet, Bernard astrophysicist, educator
Sangiovanni-Vincentelli, Alberto Luigi electrical engineering and computer science educator, consultant
Sarich, Vincent M. anthropologist, educator
Sauer, Kenneth chemistry educator
Saykally, Richard James chemistry educator
Schachman, Howard Kapnek molecular biologist, educator
Scheiber, Harry N. law educator
†Schekman, Randy W. molecular biology administrator, biochemist
Schmalenberger, Jerry Lew pastor, seminary administrator
Schoenfeld, Alan Henry mathematics and education educator
†Schoenlein, Robert W. research scientist
Schommer, Trudy Marie pastoral minister, religion education
Schrock, Virgil Edwin mechanical and nuclear engineer
Schultz, Peter G. chemistry educator
Scordelis, Alexander Costicas civil engineering educator
Scott, Eugenie Carol science foundation director, anthropologist
Seaborg, Glenn Theodore chemistry educator
Sealey, B. Raphael classicist, educator
Searcy, Alan Winn chemist, educator
Seeba, Hinrich Claassen foreign language educator
Seitz, Walter Stanley cardiovascular research consultant
Selz, Peter Howard art historian, educator
Semoff, Deirdre Paula special education administrator, academic director
Sequin, Carlo H. computer science educator
Sessler, Andrew Marienhoff physicist
Shack, William Alfred anthropology educator, researcher, consultant
Shank, Charles Vernon science administrator, educator
Shannon, Thomas Frederic German language educator
Shapiro, Carl economics educator and consultant
Shapiro, Martin law educator
Shen, Yuen-Ron physics educator
Shu, Frank Hsia-San astronomy educator, researcher, author
Shugart, Howard Alan physicist, educator
†Silk, Joseph Ivor astronomy educator
Simpson, David William artist, educator
Siri, William E. physicist
Skolnick, Jerome H. law educator
Sloane, Thomas O. speech educator
Smith, Alan Jay computer science educator, consultant
Smith, Michael E. legal educator, lawyer
Smolensky, Eugene economics educator
Smoot, George Fitzgerald, III astrophysicist
Somorjai, Gabor Arpad chemist, educator
Spear, Robert Clinton environmental health educator, consultant
Speed, Terence Paul statistician, educator
Spinrad, Hyron astronomer
Srebnik, Herbert Harry retired anatomy educator
†Stacy, Angelica M. chemistry educator
Staubus, George Joseph accounting educator
Staw, Barry Martin business and psychology educator
Steiner, Herbert Max physics educator
Still, Gerald G. plant physiologist, research director
Stoller, Claude architect
Strauss, Herbert Leopold chemistry educator
Streitwieser, Andrew, Jr. chemistry educator
Stuhr, Walter M. seminary educator, clergyman
Superko, H. Robert research physician
Susskind, Charles engineering educator, author, publishing executive
Sutch, Richard Charles economics educator
Sweet, Justin law educator, lawyer
Syme, Sherman Leonard epidemiology educator
Symons, Timothy James McNeil physicist
Tannenbaum, Percy H. psychology educator
Tarter, Michael Ernest biostatistician, educator
Teece, David John economics and management educator
Teeguarden, Dennis Earl forest economist
Temko, Allan Bernard writer
Tempelis, Constantine Harry immunologist, educator
Thomas, Gareth metallurgy educator
Thomas, Paul Emery mathematics educator
Thompson, Anthony Wayne metallurgist, educator, consultant
Thornton, John Irvin forensic scientist, educator
†Thow, John H. music educator, composer
Tien, Chang-Lin chancellor
Tinoco, Ignacio, Jr. chemist, educator
Tobias, Charles William chemical engineer, educator
Townes, Charles Hard physics educator
Tracy, Robert (Edward) English educator, poetry translator
Trilling, George Henry physicist, educator
Tsina, Richard Vasil chemistry educator
Turin, George Lewis electrical engineering educator, university dean
Twiss, Robert Hamilton, Jr. environmental planning educator
Tyndall, David Gordon business educator
Valentine, James William paleobiology, educator, author
Van House, Nancy Anita library educator
Vaux, Henry James forest economist, educator
Vedros, Neylan Anthony microbiologist
Vetter, Jan legal educator
Vogel, David Jay business educator
Vollhardt, Kurt Peter Christian chemistry educator
Voulkos, Peter artist
Wake, David Burton biology educator, researcher
Wake, Marvalee Hendricks biology educator
Wakeman, Frederic Evans, Jr. historian
Waldron, Jeremy James law educator
†Walton, Ortiz Montaigne musician, sociologist
Waltz, Kenneth Neal political science educator
Wang, William Shi-Yuan linguistics educator
Washburn, Stan artist
Weidman, Anna Kathryn publishing company financial executive
Welch, Claude (Raymond) theology educator
†Welch, William John astronomer, educator
Westheimer, Gerald optometrist, educator
Whinnery, John Roy electrical engineering educator
White, Richard Manning electrical engineering educator
†White, Timothy Douglas biology educator
Wiegel, Robert Louis consulting engineering executive
Wilensky, Harold L. political science and industrial relations educator
Williamson, Oliver Eaton economics and law educator
†Witherspoon, Paul Adams, Jr. geological engineer, petroleum engineer
Wohletz, Leonard Ralph soil scientist, consultant
Wolf, Joseph Albert mathematician, educator
Wolfinger, Raymond Edwin political science educator
Wong, Eugene engineering educator
Wood, David Kennedy Cornell choreographer, educator
Wood, David L. entomologist, educator
†Xie, Ganquan mathematician, computational geophysical scientist, educator
Zaentz, Saul motion picture producer
Zimring, Franklin E. law educator
Zumino, Bruno physics educator, researcher
Zwerdling, Alex English educator
Zwoyer, Eugene Milton consulting engineering executive

Beverly Hills
Acheson, James costume designer
†Ackerman, Thomas cinematographer
Adams, Jane actress
Aguilera, Donna Conant psychologist, researcher
†Ahmad, Maher film production designer
Alexander, Jason (Jay Scott Greenspan) actor
Alice, Mary (Mary Alice Smith) actress
†Allen, Dede (Dorothea Carothers Allen) film editor
Allen, Howard Norman cardiologist, educator
Allen, Karen Jane actress
†Allen, Marit costume designer
†Anders, Allison film director, screenwriter
Anderson, Loni Kaye actress
Anderson, Richard Dean actor
Arnold, Tom actor, comedian, producer
†Arquette, Patricia actress
Arquette, Rosanna actress
August, Bille film director
†Avary, Roger Roberts film director, writer
Avildsen, John Guilbert film director
Aykroyd, Daniel Edward actor, writer
Bacon, Kevin actor
Bailey, John cinematographer
†Baird, Stuart film editor
Baker, Anita singer
Bakula, Scott actor
Baldwin, William actor
†Ballhaus, Michael director photography
Bancroft, Anne (Mrs. Mel Brooks) actress
†Banderas, Antonio actor
Bao, Katherine Sung pediatric cardiologist
Barbakow, Jeffery C. motion picture and television company executive
Barkin, Ellen actress
Barrie, Barbara Ann actress
Barrymore, Drew actress
Bartel, Paul film director
†Bartkowiak, Andrzej cinematographer
Basinger, Kim actress
Bass, Ronald screenwriter
Bates, Kathy actress
Bauer, Marty agent
Baxter, Meredith actress
Beals, Jennifer actress
Beatty, (Henry) Warren actor, producer, director
Beck, Marilyn Mohr columnist
Bedelia, Bonnie actress
Bellisario, Donald P. television director
Belushi, James actor
Benatar, Pat (Pat Andrzejewski) rock singer
Benedek, Barbara screenwriter
Bening, Annette actress
Benjamin, Richard actor, director
Benson, Robby actor, director, writer, producer
Berenger, Tom (Thomas Michael Moore) actor
Berg, Jeffrey Spencer talent agency executive
Bergman, Andrew motion picture director
Bergman, Nancy Palm real estate investment company executive
Bernhard, Harvey producer
Berry, Halle actress
Bishop, Joey (Joseph Abraham Gottlieb) comedian
Bisset, Jacqueline actress
Bloom, Jacob A. lawyer
†Bloom, John film editor
Boam, Jeffrey David screenwriter
Bolton, Michael singer, songwriter
Bracco, Lorraine actress
Brandauer, Klaus Maria actor
Brann, Alton Joseph oilfield services executive
Bridges, Beau (Lloyd Vernet Bridges, III) actor
Bridges, Jeff actor
Bridges, Lloyd actor
Brightman, Sarah singer, actress
†Brillstein, Bernie J. producer, talent manager
Brimley, Wilford actor
Broderick, Matthew actor
Brokaw, Norman Robert talent agency executive
Bronson, Charles (Charles Buchinsky) actor
Brooks, Mel producer, director, writer, actor
Brown, Hermione Kopp lawyer
Bugliosi, Vincent T. lawyer
†Bullock, Sandra actress
†Burgess, Don cinematographer
Burnett, Carol actress, comedienne, singer
Burstyn, Ellen (Edna Rae Gillooly) actress
Burton, Al producer, director, writer
Burton, Tim film director
†Burwell, Carter composer
Busey, Gary actor, musician
Busfield, Timothy actor
Buyse, Emile Jules film company executive
†Byrne, Gabriel actor
Caine, Michael actor
†Campion, Jane director, screenwriter
†Capshaw, Kate (Kathy Sue Nail) actress
Carpenter, John Howard screenwriter, director
Carrey, Jim actor
Carter, Nell actress, singer
Casey, Joseph T. corporate executive
Cates, Phoebe actress
Chamberlain, (George) Richard actor
Channing, Carol actress
Chaplin, Geraldine actress
†Chapman, Michael cinematographer, director
Cher, (Cherilyn Sarkisian) singer, actress
Chernin, Peter motion picture company executive
Chong, Thomas comedian, writer, director, musician
Chritton, George A. film producer
Cimino, Michael film director, writer
Clayburgh, Jill actress
†Clooney, George actor
Close, Glenn actress
†Coates, Anne V. film editor
Coen, Ethan film producer, writer
Coen, Joel film director, writer
Cohen, Larry film director, producer, screenwriter
Cole, Natalie Maria singer
Coleman, Dabney W. actor
Connery, Sean (Thomas Connery) actor
†Convertino, Michael composer
Coolidge, Martha film director
Corbin, Barry actor, writer
Corman, Eugene Harold motion picture producer
Cort, Robert W. film company executive
Corwin, Stanley Joel book publisher
Costa-Gavras, (Konstaninos Gavras) director, writer
Covitz, Carl D. state official, real estate and investment executive
†Cox, Courteney actress
Coyote, Peter (Peter Cohon) actor
Craven, Wes film director
Crenna, Richard actor
Crichton, (John) Michael author, film director
Cronenberg, David film director
Crowe, Cameron screenwriter
Crowe, Christopher director, screenwriter
Culkin, Macaulay actor
Cullum, John actor, singer
Culp, Robert actor, writer, director
†Cunliffe, Shay costume designer
Curry, Tim actor
Curtin, Jane Therese actress, writer
Curtin, Valerie screenwriter, actress
Curtis, Jamie Lee actress
Curtis, Tony (Bernard Schwartz) actor
Cusack, Joan actress
Cusack, John actor
Daly, Timothy actor
Daly, Tyne actress
D'Angelo, Beverly actress
Danson, Ted actor
†Darabont, Frank screenwriter, director
David, Clive events planning executive
David, Larry television scriptwriter
Davis, Geena (Virginia Davis) actress
Davis, Stuart savings and loan association executive
Davison, Bruce actor
Dawber, Pam actress
†Deakins, Roger cinematographer
Dearden, James director, screenwriter
†DeBont, Jan cinematographer, director
Dekom, Peter James lawyer
Delany, Dana actress
De Laurentiis, Dino motion picture producer
†Del Ruth, Thomas Anthony motion picture director of photography
De Niro, Robert actor
Dennehy, Brian actor
dePaolis, Potito Umberto food company executive
Depardieu, Gérard actor
Depp, Johnny actor
Dern, Bruce MacLeish actor
Dern, Laura actress
Devito, Danny Michael actor
†DiCaprio, Leonardo actor
†Dickerson, Ernest cinematographer, director
Dillon, Gregory Russell hotel executive
Doherty, Shannen actress
Dooley, Paul actor, writer
Douglas, Kirk (Issur Danielovitch Demsky) actor, motion picture producer
Douglas, Michael Kirk actor, film producer, director
Downey, Robert, Jr. actor
Dreyfuss, Richard Stephan actor
Duke, Patty (Anna Marie Duke) actress
Dunaway, (Dorothy) Faye actress
†Dunne, Griffin actor, producer
Duvall, Shelley actress
Eikenberry, Jill actress
Eisenshtat, Sidney Herbert architect
Elkins, Hillard producer
Elliott, Chris actor
†Elliott, Paul cinematographer
Elliott, Robert B. comedian
Elliott, Sam actor
Elwes, Cary actor
Epstein, Julius J. screenwriter, playwright, producer
Essex, Harry J. screenwriter, novelist
Estevez, Emilio actor, writer, director
Eszterhas, Joseph Anthony film scriptwriter
Evans, Linda actress
Evans, Louise psychologist, investor, philanthropist
Evans, Robert J. motion picture producer, actor
Evigan, Greg actor, musician

Factor, Max, III *lawyer, investment adviser*
Fahey, Jeff *actor*
Falk, Peter *actor*
†Faltermeyer, Harold *composer*
Farentino, James *actor*
Farwell, Lloyd S. *hotel executive*
Fein, William *ophthalmologist*
Feldshuh, Tovah S. *actress*
Fenn, Sherilyn *actress*
†Ferretti, Dante *production designer*
†Fiennes, Ralph Nathaniel *actor*
†Finfer, David *film editor*
Finney, Albert *actor, director*
Fitzgerald, Ella *singer*
Flaum, Marshall Allen *television producer, writer, director*
Fleischer, Richard O. *film director*
Fleming, Peggy Gale *professional ice skater*
Foch, Nina *actress, creative consultant, educator*
Fonda, Bridget *actress*
Fonda, Jane *actress*
Foonberg, Jay G. *lawyer, accountant*
Fox, Michael J. *actor*
Foxworth, Robert Heath *actor, director*
†Fraker, William A. *cinematographer, director*
Frank, Harriet, Jr. *screenwriter*
Frankenheimer, John Michael *film and stage director*
Franklin, Aretha *singer*
Frears, Stephen *film director*
Friedkin, William *film director*
†Fruchtman, Lisa *film editor*
Furth, George *actor, playwright*
Galbraith, James Ronald *hotel executive*
Gallagher, Peter *actor*
†Gardiner, Lizzy *costume designer*
Garr, Teri (Ann) *actress*
†Garwood, Norman *art director, production designer*
†Gassner, Dennis *production designer*
Gelbart, Larry *writer, producer*
Gere, Richard *actor*
Getchell, Robert *screenwriter*
Gilberg, Arnold L. *psychiatrist and psychoanalyst*
Gilbert, Melissa *actress*
Gillard, Stuart Thomas *film and television director, writer*
Giorgi, Elsie Agnes *physician*
Gleason, Joanna *actress*
Glenn, (Theodore) Scott *actor*
Gless, Sharon *actress*
Glover, Danny *actor*
Goldman, Bo *screenwriter, director*
Goldman, William *writer*
Goldsmith, Bram *banker*
†Goursaud, Anne Renee Mauricette Dominique *film editor*
Grant, Hugh *actor*
Graves, Peter *actor*
Gray, Spalding *actor, writer, performance artist*
†Green, Jack N. *cinematographer*
†Greenberg, Gerald B. *film editor*
Grey, Jennifer *actress*
Grey, Joel *actor*
Griffin, Merv Edward *former entertainer, television producer, entrepreneur*
Griffith, Andy (Andrew Samuel Griffith) *actor*
Grodin, Charles *actor, writer, director*
Grushow, Sandy *broadcast executive*
Guest, Christopher *actor, director, screenwriter*
Guttenberg, Steve *actor*
Hagman, Larry *actor*
†Hall, Roger *production designer*
Hallstrom, Lasse *director*
Hamel, Veronica *actress*
Hamilton, Linda *actress*
Hamlin, Harry Robinson *actor*
Hanks, Tom *actor*
†Hanley, Daniel *film editor*
Hannah, Daryl *actress*
Hanson, Curtis *director, writer*
Harmon, Mark *actor*
Harper, Valerie *actress*
Harrelson, Woody *actor*
Harris, Mel (Mary Ellen Harris) *actress*
Haskell, Peter Abraham *actor*
Hawke, Ethan *actor*
Hawn, Goldie *actress*
Headly, Glenne Aimée *actress*
Hefner, Hugh Marston *editor in chief*
Heller, Paul Michael *film company executive, producer*
Helmond, Katherine *actress*
Hemingway, Mariel *actress*
Henderson, Florence (Florence Henderson Bernstein) *actress, singer*
Henry, Buck *actor, writer*
Hepburn, Katharine Houghton *actress*
†Herring, Pembroke J. *film editor*
Herrmann, Edward Kirk *actor*
Hershey, Barbara (Barbara Herzstein) *actress*
Heston, Charlton (John Charlton Carter) *actor*
†Hill, David *broadcast executive*
†Hill, Michael J. *film editor*
Hill, Walter *film director, writer, producer*
Hilton, Barron *hotel executive*
Hilton, Eric Michael *hotel industry executive*
Hines, Gregory Oliver *actor, dancer*
Hinton, Leslie Frank *media executive*
†Hirsch, Paul Frederick *film editor*
Hoch, Orion Lindel *corporate executive*
†Hoenig, Dov *film editor*
Hopkins, Sir Anthony (Philip) *actor*
Hopper, Dennis *actor, writer, photographer, film director*
†Hornung, Richard *costume designer*
Howard, Ron *director, actor*
Hughes, John W. *film producer, screenwriter, film director*
Hulce, Tom *actor*
Hunt, Helen *actress*
Hunt, Linda *actress*
Hurd, Gale Anne *film producer*
Huston, Anjelica *actress*
†Hutshing, Joe *film editor*
Hutton, Timothy *actor*
†Isham, Mark *composer, jazz musician*
Jackson, Samuel L. *actor*
Jenner, Bruce *sportscaster, former Olympic athlete*
Jessup, W. Edgar, Jr. *lawyer*
Jillian, Ann (Ann Jura Nauseda) *actress, singer*
Johnson, Jimmy *sports commentator, former professional football coach*
†Johnson, Mark Mathis *film producer*
Jones, David Hugh *theater, film and television director*
†Jones, Robert C. *film editor*
Jordan, Glenn *theater director*
†Kahn, Michael *film editor*
Karpman, Harold Lew *cardiologist, educator, author*
Kasdan, Lawrence Edward *film director, screenwriter*
Kaufman, Philip *film director*
Keaton, Diane *actress*
Keaton, Michael *actor, comedian*
Keitel, Harvey *actor*
Kelly, Gene Curran *dancer, actor, director*
†Kemper, Victor J. *cinematographer*
Kilmer, Val *actor*
King, Alan *entertainer television, film producer*
King, Morgana *jazz vocalist*
Kinski, Nastassja (Nastassja Nakszynski) *actress*
Kirkwood, Gene *motion picture producer*
Klausen, Raymond *sculptor, television/theatre production designer*
Klein, Arnold William *dermatologist*
Kline, Kevin Delaney *actor*
Koepp, David *screenwriter*
Kravitz, Ellen King *musicologist, educator*
Kravitz, Lenny *singer, guitarist*
Kuhn, Michael *motion picture company executive*
Ladd, Diane *actress*
Landis, John David *film director, writer*
†Lane, Diane *actress*
Lane, Nathan (Joseph Lane) *actor*
Lange, Jessica *actress*
LaScala, Anthony Charles *financial company executive*
Laurie, Piper (Rosetta Jacobs) *actress*
Lawrence, Steve *entertainer*
Leachman, Cloris *actress*
Leary, Denis *comedian*
Lebo, William C., Jr. *hotel corporation executive, lawyer*
Lee, Peggy (Norma Delores Egstrom) *singer, actress*
Leibman, Ron *actor*
Leigh, Janet (Jeanette Helen Morrison) *actress*
Lemmon, Jack (John Uhler Lemmon, III) *actor*
Leonard, Robert Sean *actor*
Leonis, John Michael *aerospace executive*
†Levant, Brian *film director*
Levinson, Barry L. *film director*
Levy, David *broadcasting executive*
Levy, Eugene *actor, director, screenwriter*
†Levy, Peter *cinematographer*
Lewine, Robert F. *broadcasting company executive*
Lewis, Juliette *actress*
Linden, Hal *actor, singer*
Linkletter, Arthur Gordon *radio and television broadcaster*
Liotta, Ray *actor*
Lithgow, John Arthur *actor, director*
Little, Richard Caruthers (Rich Little) *comedian, impressionist, actor*
†Littleton, Carol *film editor*
Livingston, Myra Cohn *poet, writer, educator*
Lloyd, Emily (Emily Lloyd Pack) *actress*
Locklear, Heather *actress*
Loeffler, Richard Harlan *retail and technology company executive*
Loggia, Robert *actor*
Loggins, Kenny (Kenneth Clarke Loggins) *singer, songwriter*
†Lombardo, Tony *film editor*
Long, Shelley *actress*
Loughnane, Lee David *trumpeter*
Louis-Dreyfus, Julia *actress*
†Lovejoy, Ray *film editor*
Lovitz, Jon *actor, comedian*
Lowe, Rob *actor*
Lynch, David K. *film director, writer*
MacLachlan, Kyle *actor*
†MacMillan, Kenneth *cinematographer*
Macnee, (Daniel) Patrick *actor*
Madden, John *television sports commentator, former professional football coach*
Malkovich, John *actor*
Mandel, Babaloo *scriptwriter*
Manoff, Dinah Beth *actress*
Manulis, Martin *film producer*
Marin, Cheech (Richard Anthony Marin) *actor, writer, director*
Mark, John *film company executive*
†Marsh, Terence *production designer*
Marshall, (C.) Penny *actress, director*
Martin, Dean (Dino Crocetti) *actor, singer*
Martin, Steve *comedian, actor*
Mason, Marsha *actress, director, writer*
Masterson, Mary Stuart *actress*
Mastrantonio, Mary Elizabeth *actress*
Matlin, Marlee *actress*
†McAlpine, Andrew *production designer*
McDonnell, Mary *actress*
McGagh, William Gilbert *financial consultant*
McGavin, Darren *actor, director, producer*
Mc Kean, Michael *actor*
Mc Kenna, William Edward *entrepreneur*
McNaughton, John D. *director*
Mc Tiernan, John *film director*
†Mechanic, William M. *television and motion picture industry executive*
Menges, Chris *cinematographer, film director*
Menkes, John Hans *pediatric neurologist*
Menon, Vijaya Bhaskar *recording and entertainment company executive*
Metcalf, Laurie *actress*
Meyer, Nicholas *screenwriter, director*
Meyer, Ron *agent*
Meyers, Nancy Jane *screenwriter, producer*
Milius, John Frederick *film writer, director*
Miller, Dennis *comedian*
Modine, Matthew Avery *actor*
†Moffat, Donald *actor*
Moloney, Jay *agent*
Montalban, Ricardo *actor*
Moore, Demi (Demi Guynes) *actress*
Moore, Dudley Stuart John *actor, musician*
†Moore, J. Jamison *consulting firm executive, economist*
†Moore, Julianne *actress*
Moore, Michael *film director*
Moranis, Rick *actor*
†Moriarty, Cathy *actress*
†Mulgrew, Katherine Kiernan *actress*
Mulligan, Robert Patrick *film director, producer*
†Musky, Jane Michelle *film production designer*
Myers, Barton *architect*
†Myers, Ruth *costume designer*
Nabors, James Thurston *actor, singer*
†Nedd-Friendly, Priscilla Anne *motion picture film editor*
Neeson, Liam *actor*
Neill, Sam *actor*
Nelligan, Kate (Patricia Colleen Nelligan) *actress*
Nelson, Judd *actor*
Neuwirth, Bebe *dancer, actress*
Newton-John, Olivia *singer, actress*
Nichols, Mike *stage and film director*
Nicita, Rick *agent*
Nimoy, Leonard *actor, director*
†Nitzsche, Jack *composer*
Niven, Laurence Van Cott *author*
†Noble, (Terry) Thom *film editor*
†Noyce, Phillip *film director*
Nykvist, Sven Vilhem *cinematographer*
†O'Donnell, Chris *actor*
O'Donnell, Rosie *comedienne, actress*
O'Hara, Catherine *actress, comedienne*
Olin, Ken *actor*
Olin, Lena Maria Jonna *actress*
†Ondricek, Miroslav *cinematographer*
Orenstein, (Ian) Michael *philatelic dealer, columnist*
Ovitz, Michael S. *artists agency executive*
†Palminteri, Chazz *actor*
Pantoliano, Joe *actor*
Paquin, Anna *actress*
Parker, Alan William *film director, writer*
†Parker, Mary-Louise *actress*
†Parker, Sarah Jessica *actress*
†Paull, Lawrence G. *production designer*
†Paxton, Bill *actor, writer, director*
†Pedersen, Ken *recording industry executive*
Penderecki, Krzysztof *composer, conductor*
Penn, Sean *actor*
Perez, Rosie *actress, choreographer*
Perkins, Elizabeth Ann *actress*
Perlman, Rhea *actress*
Perry, Luke (Coy Luther Perry, III) *actor*
Pesci, Joe *actor*
†Pescucci, Gabriella *costume designer*
†Peterman, Donald *cinematographer*
Peters, Jon *film producer, film company executive*
Petersen, Wolfgang *film director*
Petrie, Daniel Mannix *film, theatre and television director*
Pfeiffer, Michelle *actress*
†Phillips, Erica Edell *costume designer*
Pierson, Frank Romer *screenwriter, director*
Pinchot, Bronson *actor*
Pitt, Brad *actor*
Pleskow, Eric Roy *motion picture company executive*
Plummer, Amanda *actress*
Plummer, (Arthur) Christopher (Orme) *actor*
Poitier, Sidney *actor, director*
Ponty, Jean-Luc *violinist, composer, producer*
Pop, Iggy (James Newell Osterberg) *composer, singer, musician*
†Pressman, Edward R. *motion picture producer*
Pressman, Michael *film director*
Ptak, John A. *talent agent*
†Pullman, Bill *actor*
†Quartararo, Phil *recording industry executive*
Quinn, Aidan *actor*
Raimi, Samuel M. *film director*
Ramer, Bruce M. *lawyer*
Ramis, Harold Allen *film director, screenwriter, actor*
Rapke, Jack *agent*
Ravetch, Irving *screenwriter*
Raymond, Gene *actor, producer, director*
Reed, Pamela *actress*
Reiner, Carl *actor, writer, director*
Reiner, Rob *actor, writer, director*
Reinhold, Judge (Edward Ernest Reinhold, Jr.) *actor*
Reiser, Paul *actor, comedian*
Reitman, Ivan *film director, producer*
Reynolds, Burt *actor, director*
Reynolds, Gene *television producer, director*
†Reynolds, William Henry *film editor*
Ribero, Michael Antonio *marketing executive*
Richardson, Patricia *actress*
Riegert, Peter *actor*
†Riess, Gordon Sanderson *management consultant*
†Rifkin, Arnold *film company executive*
†Robbins, Richard *composer*
Robbins, Tim (Timothy Francis Robbins) *actor*
Roberts, Eric *actor*
Roberts, Norman Leslie *lawyer*
Robinson, Phil Alden *director*
Roeg, Nicolas Jack *film director*
†Rolf, Tom *film editor*
Rolle, Esther *actress*
Rollins, Howard Ellsworth, Jr. *actor*
Romero, George A. *film director*
†Rosenzweig, Richard Stuart *publishing company executive*
Rosky, Burton Seymour *lawyer*
Ross, Herbert David *film director*
Ross, Stanley Ralph *writer, publisher, producer, software manufacturing executive*
†Roth, Eric *screenwriter*
Roth, Tim *actor*
†Rotunno, Giuseppe *cinematographer*
†Rousselot, Philippe *cinematographer*
†Rubeo, Bruno *production designer*
Rudnick, Paul *playwright, screenwriter*
Rudolph, Alan *film director*
Ruehl, Mercedes *actress*
Rush, Herman E. *television executive*
†Russell, Charles *film director, producer*
Russell, Ken (Henry Kenneth Alfred Russell) *film and theatre director*
Russell, Kurt Von Vogel *actor*
Ryan, Meg *actress*
Rydell, Mark *film director, producer, actor*
Ryder, Winona (Winona Laura Horowitz) *actress*
Sadwith, James Steven *screenwriter, director*
Sager, Carole Bayer *lyricist, singer*
†Sakamoto, Ryuichi *composer*
Sarandon, Susan Abigail *actress*
†Scharf, William *film editor*
Schiff, Gunther Hans *lawyer*
Schifrin, Lalo *composer*
Schine, Gerard David *entertainment company executive*
Schlatter, George H. *producer, director, writer*
Schrader, Paul Joseph *film writer, director*
Schulian, John (Nielsen Schulian) *screenwriter, author*
Schulman, Tom *screenwriter*
Schumacher, Joel *film writer, director*
Schwarzenegger, Arnold Alois *actor, author*
†Scott, Deborah L. *costume designer*
Seagal, Steven *actor*
Seinfeld, Jerry *comedian*
Selleck, Tom *actor*
Shanley, John Patrick *screenwriter*
Shapell, Nathan *financial and real estate executive*
Sharif, Omar (Michael Shalhoub) *actor*
Sheedy, Ally (Alexandra Elizabeth Sheedy) *actress*
Sheen, Charlie (Carlos Irwin Estevez) *actor*
Shepard, Sam (Samuel Shepard Rogers) *playwright, actor*
Sheridan, Jim *director, screenwriter*
Shoemaker, Bill (William Lee Shoemaker) *retired jockey, horse trainer*
Simmons, Jean *actress*
Simmons, Richard Milton Teagle *physical fitness specialist, television personality*
Singleton, Henry Earl *industrialist*
Singleton, John *director, screenwriter*
Sinise, Gary *actor, director*
Skerritt, Tom *actor*
Slater, Christian *actor*
†Smith, Roy Forge *art director, production designer*
Smith, Will *actor, rapper*
†Sonnenfeld, Barry *cinematographer, film director*
Sorvino, Paul *actor*
Spacek, Sissy (Mary Elizabeth Spacek) *actress*
Spader, James *actor*
Spence, Mary Anne *geneticist, medical association executive*
Spheeris, Penelope *film director*
Spielberg, Steven *motion picture director, producer*
Spikings, Barry Peter *film company executive*
Stack, Robert Langford *actor*
Stallone, Sylvester Enzio *actor, writer, director*
Stamos, John *actor*
Star, Darren *television writer, producer*
Steenburgen, Mary *actress*
Stefano, Joseph William *film and television producer, author*
Stein, Myron *internist, educator*
†Steinberg, David *comedian, author, actor*
Stern, Daniel *actor*
Stewart, Patrick *actor*
Stockwell, Dean *actor*
Stoltz, Eric *actor*
Stone, Sharon *actress*
Stowe, Madeleine *actress*
Strasberg, Susan *actress, writer, educator*
Strauss, Peter *actor*
Streep, Meryl (Mary Louise Streep) *actress*
Streisand, Barbra Joan *singer, actress, director*
Summerall, Pat (George Allan Summerall) *sportscaster*
†Suschitzky, Peter *cinematagrapher*
Sutherland, Donald *actor*
Tambor, Jeffrey *actor, theatre director, educator*
Terry, Clark *musician*
Thomas, Betty *actress*
Thomas, Marlo (Margaret Julia Thomas) *actress*
Thompson, Caroline Warner *film director, screenwriter*
Thompson, Emma *actress*
Thompson, Larry Angelo *producer, lawyer, personal manager*
Thompson, Tina Lewis Chryar *publisher*
†Thorin, Donald E. *cinematographer*
Thurman, Uma Karuna *actress*
†Tilly, Meg *actress*
Toffel, Alvin Eugene *corporate executive, business and governmental consultant*
Tomei, Marisa *actress*
Torme, Mel(vin) (Howard Torme) *musician, jazz vocalist*
Towers, Bernard Leonard *medical educator*
Towne, Robert *screenwriter*
†Travis, Nancy *actress*
Trumbull, Douglas *film director, writer, creator special effects*
Tucker, Michael *actor*
Turner, Janine *actress*
Turner, Kathleen *actress*
Turner, Tina (Anna Mae Bullock) *singer*
Turturro, John *actor*
Tyre, Norman Ronald *lawyer*
Tyson, Cicely *actress*
Ullman, Tracey *actress, singer*
Urich, Robert *actor*
Van Ark, Joan *actress*
Van Damme, Jean-Claude (Jean-Claude Van Varenberg) *actor*
Van Dyke, Dick *actor, comedian*
Van Sant, Gus, Jr. *director, screenwriter*
Victor, Robert Eugene *real estate corporation executive, lawyer*
†Virkler, Dennis M. *film editor*
Voight, Jon *actor*
von Sydow, Max (Carl Adolf von Sydow) *actor*
Wagner, Lindsay J. *actress*
Wagner, Robert *actor*
Walken, Christopher *actor*
†Walker, Lesley *film editor*
Walker, William Tidd, Jr. *investment banker*
Ward, David Schad *screenwriter, film director*
Warren, Lesley Ann *actress*
Washington, Denzel *actor*
Wayans, Damon *actor*
Wayans, Keenen Ivory *actor, producer*
Weaver, Fritz William *actor*
Weaver, Sigourney (Susan Alexandra Weaver) *actress*
Weir, Peter Lindsay *film director*
Welch, Raquel *actress*
Weller, Michael *playwright, screenwriter*
Weller, Peter *actor*
Weston, Paul *composer, arranger, conductor*
†Whalley-Kilmer, Joanne *actress*
Whitaker, Forest *actor*
White, Betty *actress, comedienne*
White, Jesse Marc *actor*
Williams, JoBeth *actress*
Williams, Treat (Richard Williams) *actor*
Willson, James Douglas *aerospace executive*
Wilson, Brian Douglas *recording artist, composer, record producer*
Wincer, Simon *film director*
Winkler, Henry Franklin *actor*
Winkler, Irwin *motion picture producer*
Winthrop, John *real estate executive, lawyer*
Wise, Robert *film producer, director*
Wood, Elijah *actor*
Woodard, Alfre *actress*
Woods, James Howard *actor*
†Wright, John *film editor*
†Wright, Robin *actress*
Yates, Peter *director, producer*
York, Michael (Michael York-Johnson) *actor*
Yorkin, Bud (Alan Yorkin) *producer, director*
†Young, Sean *actress*
Zanuck, Richard Darryl *motion picture company executive*
Zarem, Abe Mordecai *management consulting executive*
Zerbe, Anthony *actor*
Zevon, Warren *singer, songwriter*
Zimmerman, Don *film editor*
†Zwick, Edward M. *director, producer, scriptwriter*

Big Bear Lake

Dankanyin, Robert John *manufacturing executive*

Essman, Robert Norvel *small business owner, graphics designer*

Big Sur
Cross, Robert Louis *realtor, land use planner, writer*
Owings, Margaret Wentworth *conservationist, artist*

Bishop
Haber, Ralph Norman *psychology consultant, researcher, educator*
MacMillen, Richard Edward *biological sciences educator, researcher*

Blythe
Beumel, Wilford J. *college president*

Bodega
Hedrick, Wally Bill *artist*

Bodega Bay
Hand, Cadet Hammond, Jr. *marine biologist, educator*
Jeffery, William Richard *developmental biology educator*
King, Leland W. *architect*

Bolinas
Harris, Paul *sculptor*
Murch, Walter Scott *director, writer, film editor, sound designer*

Bonita
Curtis, Richard Earl *former naval officer, former company executive, business consultant*
Dresser, Jesse Dale *real estate investor*
Jacobsen, Adolf M.B. *university administrator, former naval officer*
Wood, Fergus James *geophysicist, consultant*

Boonville
Hanes, John Ward *sculptor, civil engineer consultant*

Borrego Springs
Scannell, William Edward *aerospace company executive, consultant, psychologist*
Shinn, Allen Mayhew *retired naval officer, business executive*

Brawley
Jaquith, George Oakes *ophthalmologist*

Brea
Dyer, Alice Mildred *psychotherapist*
Engleman, David S. *diversified financial services executive*
Hulsey, Neven C. *metal products executive*
Lowe, Randall Brian *lawyer*
Shell, Billy Joe *retired university president*
Tamura, Cary Kaoru *fundraiser*

Brisbane
Anargyros, Spero *sculptor*
Orban, Kurt *foreign trade company executive*

Buena Park
Arimoto, Masahiko *electronics company executive*
Elliott, Darrell Kenneth *minister, legal researcher*
Raup, Ronald B. *electronics executive*

Burbank
Aaronson, Robert Jay *aviation executive*
Allen, Tim *actor, comedian*
Arkoff, Samuel Z. *motion picture executive, producer*
Berman, Bruce *entertainment company executive*
Berry, Bill *popular musician*
Bollenbach, Stephen Frasier *entertainment executive*
Brankovich, Mark J. *restaurateur*
Brogliatti, Barbara Spencer *television and motion picture executive*
Bruckheimer, Jerry *producer*
Buck, Peter *musician, guitarist*
†Burke, Delta *actress*
Burke, Michele Christine *make-up artist*
Clark, Dick *performer, producer*
Clark, Susan (Nora Goulding) *actress*
Clements, Ronald Francis *animation director*
Costello, Elvis (Declan Patrick McManus) *musician, songwriter*
Costner, Kevin *actor*
Cunningham, Robert D. *lawyer*
Daly, Robert Anthony *film executive*
de Cordova, Frederick Timmins *television producer, director*
Disney, Roy Edward *broadcasting company executive*
Donner, Richard *film director, producer*
Droz, Henry *distribution company executive*
Eastwood, Clint *actor, director, former mayor*
Eisner, Michael Dammann *entertainment company executive*
Fagen, Donald *musician*
†Feldman, Edward S. *producer*
Ferry, Bryan *singer, songwriter*
Fisher, Lucy J. *motion picture company executive*
Flanagan, Tommy (Lee) *jazz pianist*
Fleetwood, Mick *musician*
†Frank, Richard H(arvey) *motion picture company executive*
†Frederickson, Harry Gray, Jr. *motion picture producer*
Godwin, Annabelle Palkes *retired early childhood education educator*
Gold, Jeffrey Alan *record company executive*
Gold, Stanley P. *chemical company executive, manufacturing company executive*
Griffith, Robert Douglas *broadcasting company executive*
Guy, Buddy *blues guitarist*
†Hagar, Sammy *musician, vocalist, composer*
†Hall, Deidre *actress*
Hartshorn, Terry O. *health facility administrator*
Hoberman, David *motion picture company executive*
Hope, Bob *actor, comedian*
Ingram, James *popular musician*
Isaak, Chris *popular musician, singer, songwriter, actor*
Karras, Alex *actor, former professional football player*
Katz, Marty *motion picture executive*
Katzenberg, Jeffrey *motion picture studio executive*
Keister, Jean Clare *lawyer*
Ketchum, Hal Michael *country music singer, songwriter*
Kidder, Margot *actress*
†LaLanne, Jack (François Henri LaLanne) *physical fitness specialist, entrepreneur*
Lanois, Daniel *record producer, musician, popular*
Lawrence, Vicki Schultz *singer, dancer, comedienne*
Leno, Jay (James Douglas Muir Leno) *comedian, writer*
†Littlefield, Warren *television executive*
Litvack, Sanford Martin *lawyer*
Marinace, Kenneth Anthony *financial advisor*
Mark, Laurence Maurice *film producer*
Marsalis, Branford *musician*
Mathis, Johnny *singer*
McCann, David DeWitt *motion picture company executive*
McQueen, Sherman John, Jr. *entertainment company executive*
Mc Vie, Christine Perfect *musician*
Mestres, Ricardo A., III *motion picture company executive*
Meyer, Barry Michael *motion picture executive*
Milchan, Arnon *film producer*
Miller, Clifford Albert *merchant banker, business consultant*
Moonves, Leslie *television company executive*
Nardino, Gary *television and motion picture producer*
Nicks, Stevie (Stephanie Nicks) *singer, songwriter*
Nolan, Peter Francis *lawyer, entertainment company executive*
O'Donnell, Scott Richard *aviation administrator*
Ohlmeyer, Donald Winfred, Jr. *film and television producer*
Peterson, Ralph *financial executive*
Pryor, Richard *actor, writer*
Raulinaitis, Pranas Algis *electronics executive*
Rich, Lee *entertainment industry executive*
Robinson, James G. *film production executive*
Roth, Joe *motion picture company executive*
Rundgren, Todd *musician, record producer*
Sago, Paul Edward *college administrator*
Seals, Dan Wayland *country music singer*
Semel, Terry *motion picture company executive*
Shao, Shiu *financial executive*
Shapiro, Joe *lawyer, entertainment company executive*
†Shuler-Donner, Lauren *film producer*
Silver, Joel *producer*
Simpson, Don *film producer*
Steiger, Rod *actor*
Stewart, Roderick David *singer*
Stipe, Michael *musician*
Tritt, Travis *country music singer, songwriter*
†Valdés, David Churchill *motion picture producer*
Volk, Robert Harkins *aviations company executive*
†Waronker, Leonard *record company executive*
Weintraub, Jerry *motion picture producer, executive*
Wolper, David Lloyd *motion picture and television executive*
Wonder, Stevie (Stevland Morris) *singer, musician, composer*

Burlingame
Bell, Herbert Aubrey Frederick *life insurance company executive*
Castetter, Sandra Lea *nursing executive*
Cotchett, Joseph Winters *lawyer, author*
Crawford, William Richard *psychologist*
Gradinger, Gilbert Paul *plastic surgeon*
Heath, Richard Raymond *investment executive*
Holmes, Richard Hugh Morris *investment management executive*
Hotz, Henry Palmer *physicist*
Loughead, Thomas A. *transportation executive*
Mc Dowell, Jack Sherman *political consultant*
Mendelson, Lee M. *film company executive, writer, producer, director*
Ocheltree, Richard Lawrence *lawyer, retired forest products company executive*
Souter, Robert Taylor *retired banker*
Truta, Marianne Patricia *oral and maxillofacial surgeon, educator, author*
Ward, William Reed *composer, educator*
Ziegler, R.W., Jr. *lawyer, consultant*
Zimmerman, Bryant Kable *lawyer*

Calabasas
Bartizal, Robert George *computer systems company executive, business consultant*
†Bastone, Peter Francis *hospital administrator*
Bleiweiss, Robert Morton *religious magazine editor, labor newspaper publisher*
Caren, Robert Poston *aerospace company executive*
Dworkoski, Robert John *headmaster*
Ghose, Rabindra Nath *technology research company executive*
Gressak, Anthony Raymond, Jr. *sales executive*
Kanaly, Steven Francis *actor*
Kitchen, Lawrence Oscar *aircraft and aerospace corporation executive*
Marafino, Vincent Norman *aerospace company executive*

California City
Friedl, Rick *former academic administrator, lawyer*

Calistoga
Spindler, George Dearborn *anthropologist, educator, author, editor*

Camarillo
†Cleary, Thomas Charles *technology company executive*
Denmark, Bernhardt *manufacturing executive*
DePatie, David Hudson *motion picture company executive*
Sime, Donald Rae *business administration educator*
Street, Dana Morris *orthopedic surgeon*

Cambria
Blundell, William Edward *journalist, consultant*
Crowther, H. David *aerospace company corporate communications executive*
DuFresne, Armand Frederick *management and engineering consultant*
Morse, Richard Jay *human resources and organizational development consultant, manufacturers' representative company executive*
Villeneuve, Donald Avila *biology educator*
Wallen, Vera S. *school superintendent*

Cameron Park
Buckles, Robert Edwin *chemistry educator*

Camp Pendleton
†Higginbotham, Geoffrey B. *military officer*

Campbell
Nicholson, Joseph Bruce *real estate developer*
Richards, Lisle Frederick *architect*
Ross, Hugh Courtney *electrical engineer*
Sack, Edgar Albert *electronics company executive*
Throndson, Edward Warner *residential association administrator*
†Walker, William R. *manufacturing executive, light*
Wu, William Lung-Shen (You-Ming Wu) *aerospace medical engineering design specialist, foreign intelligence analyst*

Campo
Charles, Blanche *retired elementary education educator*
Jermini, Ellen *academic spiritual administrator*

Canoga Park
Lederer, Marion Irvine *cultural administrator*
Norman, Arnold McCallum, Jr. *engineering specialist*
Taylor, Edna Jane *employment program counselor*

Capistrano Beach
Lewis, Jack (Cecil Paul Lewis) *publishing executive, editor*
Roemer, Edward Pier *neurologist*

Carlsbad
Anderson, Paul Irving *management executive*
Brown, Jack *magazine editor*
Callaway, Ely Reeves, Jr. *golf club manufacturer*
Crooke, Stanley Thomas *pharmaceutical company executive*
Gorsline, Samuel Gilbert, Jr. *school administrator*
Graham, Robert Klark *lens manufacturer*
Halberg, Charles John August, Jr. *mathematics educator*
Lange, Clifford E. *librarian*
Lynn, Fredric Michael *sportscaster, former professional baseball player*
McCracken, Steven Carl *lawyer*
Peasland, Bruce Randall *financial executive*
Rudolph, Charles Herman *computer software development executive*
Schumacher, John Christian *semiconductor materials and air pollution control equipment manufacturing company executive*
Smith, Warren James *optical scientist, consultant, lecturer*
Vincent, John Graham *administrator*
Wilson, Donald Grey *management consultant*

Carmel
Alsberg, Dietrich Anselm *electrical engineer*
Aurner, Robert Ray *author, corporate executive*
Barton, Gerald Gaylord *land development company executive*
Brahtz, John Frederick Peel *civil engineering educator*
Chung, Kyung Cho *Korean specialist, scholar, educator, author*
Creighton, John Wallis, Jr. *consultant, author, former management educator*
Eppler, Jerry Mack *management consultant*
Faul, George Johnson *former college president*
Felch, William Campbell *internist, editor*
Jordan, Edward George *business investor, former college president, former railroad executive*
Kennedy, John Edward *art dealer, appraiser, curator*
Koeppel, Gary Merle *publisher, art gallery owner*
Krugman, Stanley Lee *international management consultant*
Longman, Anne Strickland *educational consultant*
Merrill, William Dickey *architect*
Novak, Kim (Marilyn Novak) *actress*
Parker, Donald Henry *psychologist, author*
Pinkham, Frederick Oliver *foundation executive, consultant*
Robinson, John Minor *lawyer, retired business executive*
Skidmore, Howard Franklyn *public relations counsel*
Smith, Gordon Paul *management consulting company executive*
Steele, Charles Glen *retired accountant*
Stratton, Thomas Oliver *investment banker*
Weston, Theodore Brett *photographer*

Carmel Valley
Lorenzen, Coby *emeritus engineering educator*
Meckel, Peter Timothy *arts administrator, educator*

Carmichael
Areen, Gordon E. *finance company executive*
Bromberg, Walter *psychiatrist*
Givant, Philip Joachim *mathematics educator, real estate investment executive*
McHugh, James Joseph *retired associate dean*
Probasco, Calvin Henry Charles *clergyman, college administrator*
Sahs, Majorie Jane *art educator*
Wagner, Carruth John *physician*

Carpinteria
Ehrlich, Grant C(onklin) *business consultant*
Hansen, Robert William *artist, educator*
Lessler, Richard Sigmund *advertising executive*
Schmidhauser, John Richard *political science educator*
Wheeler, John Harvey *political scientist*

Carson
Brownell, John Arnold *retired university president*
Davidson, Mark *writer, educator*
Detweiler, Robert Chester *university president, historian*
Hirsch, Gilah Yelin *artist, writer*
Palmer, Beverly Blazey *psychologist, educator*
Suchenek, Marek Andrzej *computer science educator*

Castro Valley
Dance, Maurice Eugene *college administrator*
Denning, Eileen Bonar *management consultant*
Palmer, James Daniel *inspector*

Cathedral City
Jackman, Robert Alan *retail executive*

Cayucos
Hedlund, James Lane *retired psychologist, educator*

Cedar Ridge
Yeager, Charles Elwood (Chuck Yeager) *retired air force officer*

Central Valley
Emmerson, A. A. *sawmill executive*

Century City
Bishop, Stephen *singer, songwriter*
Blatt, Neil A. *cinema corporation executive*
Bogdanovich, Peter *film director, writer, producer, actor*
Thomas, Issac David Ellis *clergy member*

Cerritos
Robinson, Terence Vachel *secondary education educator*
Sarno, Maria Erlinda *lawyer, scientist*
†Webb, Lewis M. *retail executive*

Chatsworth
Adams, Charles Richard *manufacturing executive*
Alagem, Beny *electronics executive*
Arnold, Stanley Richard *lawyer*
Bartling, Judd Quenton *research corporation executive*
Dart, John Seward *religion news writer*
Klein, Jeffrey S. *lawyer, newspaper executive*
Montgomery, James Fischer *savings and loan association executive*
Palko, Michael James *finance company executive*
Rawitch, Robert Joe *newspaper editor*
†Southan, Arthur *insurance company executive*
Woodruff, Tom, Jr. *special effects designer*

Chico
Allen, Charles William *mechanical engineering educator*
Ediger, Robert Ike *botanist, educator*
Esteban, Manuel Antonio *university administrator, educator*
Farrer, Claire Anne Rafferty *anthropologist, folklorist, educator*
Greb, Gordon Barry *writer, educator*
†Hartman, Andrew Paul, Jr. *hospital association administrator*
Keithley, George *writer*
Kistner, David Harold *biology educator*
McIntyre, Valene Smith *anthropology educator*
Moore, Brooke Noel *philosophy educator*
Ruge, Neil Marshall *retired law educator*
Wolff, Howard Keith *computer science educator, consultant*

China Lake
Bennett, Jean Louise McPherson *physicist, research scientist*

Chino
Determan, John David *lawyer*
Johnston, Linda Joyce *educational company executive*
Outen, Dawn *secondary education educator*
Van Wagner, Ellen *lawyer, educator*

Chula Vista
Allen, David Russell *lawyer*
Allen, Henry Wesley *biomedical researcher*
Clement, Betty Waidlich *literacy educator, consultant*
Cohen, Elaine Helena *pediatrician, pediatric cardiologist*
Kerley, James J. *manufacturing executive*
Madsen, Richard Wellington *lawyer*
†Palumbo, Donald R. *metal products executive*
Schorr, Martin Mark *forensic psychologist, educator, writer*
Wolk, Martin *electronic engineer, physicist*

Citrus Heights
†Richards, Tom, III *real estate manager*

Claremont
Ackerman, Gerald Martin *art historian, consultant*
Albrecht, Paul Abraham *dean*
Alexander, John David, Jr. *college administrator*
Ansell, Edward Orin *lawyer*
Arndt, Sven William *economics educator*
†Arnn, Larry Paul *foundation executive, editor*
Atlas, Jay David *philosopher, consultant, linguist*
Barnes, Richard Gordon *English educator, poet*
Beardslee, William Armitage *religious organization administrator, educator*
Beckman, Tad Alan *philosophy educator*
Beilby, Alvin Lester *chemistry educator*
Bekavac, Nancy Yavor *academic administrator, lawyer*
Benjamin, Karl Stanley *artist, educator*
†Benjamin, Richard Keith *mycologist, botany educator*
Benson, George Charles Sumner *political science educator*
Bentley, Donald Lyon *mathematics and statistics educator*
Bjork, Gordon Carl *economist, educator*
Blizzard, Alan *artist*
Bond, Floyd Alden *economist, educator*
Bowman, Dean Orlando *economist, educator*
Burns, Richard Dean *history educator, publisher, author*
Casanova, Aldo John *sculptor*
Chambers, Robert Jefferson *educator, observatory administrator*
Coleman, Courtney Stafford *mathematician, educator*
Cooke, Kenneth Lloyd *mathematician, educator*
Davis, Nathaniel *humanities educator*
Douglass, Enid Hart *educational program director*
Dunbar, John Raine *retired English educator*
Dym, Clive Lionel *engineering educator*
Elderkin, Richard Howard *mathematician, educator*
Elsbree, Langdon *English language educator*
Erickson, Stephen A. *philosophy and humanities educator, programs director*
Fucaloro, Anthony Frank *academic dean*
Gold, Bela *educator, economist*
Goodrich, Norma Lorre (Mrs. John H. Howard) *French and comparative literature educator*
Grabiner, Sandy *mathematics educator*
Helliwell, Thomas McCaffree *physicist, educator*
Henriksen, Melvin *mathematician, educator*
Herschensohn, Bruce *film director, writer*
Hess, Dorothy Haldeman *college official*
Hick, John Harwood *theologian, philosopher, educator*

Hinshaw, Randall (Weston) economist, educator
Irish, Jerry Arthur academic administrator, religion educator
Kronenberg, Klaus J(ohannes) physicist
Kubota, Mitsuru chemistry educator
Kucheman, Clark Arthur religion educator
Lehman, James Alden economist, educator
Liggett, Thomas Jackson retired seminary president
Likens, James Dean economics educator
Lofgren, Charles Augustin legal and constitutional historian
Long, Franklin Asbury chemistry educator
Macaulay, Ronald Kerr Steven linguistics educator, former college dean
Maguire, John David university administrator, educator, writer
Massey, Marilyn Chapin academic administrator
McGaha, Michael Dennis Spanish educator
McKirahan, Richard Duncan, Jr. classics and philosophy educator
Mezey, Robert poet, educator
Miles, Jack (John Russiano) journalist, critic
Molinder, John Irving engineering educator, consultant
Monson, James Edward electrical engineer, educator
Moss, Myra Ellen (Myra Moss Rolle) philosophy educator
Mullikin, Harry Copeland mathematics educator
Neal, Fred Warner political scientist, educator
Neumann, Harry philosophy educator
Olson, Richard George historian, educator
Palmer, Hans Christian economics educator
†Parker, Pierson minister, religion educator
Pedersen, Richard Foote academic administrator
Phelps, Orme Wheelock economics educator emeritus
Phillips, John Richard engineering educator
Pinney, Thomas Clive English language educator
Platt, Joseph Beaven former college president
Post, Gaines, Jr. college educator, dean, administrator
Pronko, Leonard Cabell theater educator
Purves, William Kirkwood biologist, educator
Rankin, Robert retired educational foundation executive
Riggs, Henry Earle college president, engineering management educator
Rossum, Ralph Arthur political science educator
Roth, John King philosopher, educator
Sanders, James Alvin minister, biblical studies educator
Sellery, J'nan Morse English and American literature educator
Smith, Steven Albert philosophy educator
Sontag, Frederick Earl philosophy educator
Stanley, Peter William college president
Stark, Jack Lee college president
Tanenbaum, Basil Samuel engineering educator
Taylor, Roy Lewis botanist, educator
Wettack, F. Sheldon academic administrator
White, Alvin Murray mathematics educator, consultant
White, Kathleen Merritt geologist
Wykoff, Frank Champion economics educator
Young, Howard Thomas foreign language educator

Clayton
Wooten, Robert James executive

Cloverdale
Collins, John Wendler consumer products company executive

Clovis
Bronson, George A., Jr. school system administrator
Driscoll, Glen Robert former university president
Ensminger, Marion Eugene animal science educator, author

Coalinga
Harris, John Charles agriculturalist

Colton
Brown, Jack H. supermarket company executive
Halstead, Bruce Walter biotoxicologist

Columbia
†Maasberg, Bill Arthur publisher

Colusa
Carter, Jane Foster agriculture industry executive

Commerce
Conover, Robert Warren librarian

Compton
Allumbaugh, Byron grocery company executive
Bogdan, Carolyn Louetta financial specialist
Briskin, Bernard finance executive
Collins, Patrick W. grocery stores company executive
McNamara, E. Michael cosmetics executive
†Palmer, Curtis Howard diversified company executive, lawyer
Willmott, Peter Sherman retail executive

Concord
Allen, Toby resort executive
Anderberg, Roy Anthony journalist
†Cassidy, John Joseph hydraulic and hydrologic engineer
Clooney, Rosemary singer
Davis, Robert Leach retired government official, consultant
Headding, Lillian Susan (Sally Headding) writer, forensic clairvoyant
Jackson, Milton (Bags Jackson) jazz musician
Lee, Low Kee electronics engineer, consultant
Thall, Richard Vincent education program director
Williscroft, Beverly Ruth lawyer

Corona
Leo, Karen Ann library administrator
Ohmert, Richard Allan architect
Tillman, Joseph Nathaniel engineering executive

Corona Del Mar
Brandt, Rexford Elson artist
Britten, Roy John biophysicist
Brokaw, Charles Jacob educator, cellular biologist
Crump, Spencer publisher, business executive
Davis, Arthur David psychology educator, musician
Delap, Tony artist
Helphand, Ben J. actuary
Hill, Melvin James oil company executive
Hinderaker, Ivan political science educator
Richmond, Ronald LeRoy aerospace engineer
Tether, Anthony John aerospace executive
Wickman, Paul Everett public relations executive
Yeo, Ron architect

Coronado
Allen, Charles Richard retired financial executive
Axelson, Joseph Allen professional athletics executive, publisher
Brunton, Paul Edward retired diversified industry executive
Butcher, Bobby Gene retired military officer
Grant, Alan J. business executive
Hostler, Charles Warren international affairs consultant
Hudson, George Elbert retired research physicist
Merkin, William Leslie lawyer
Mock, David Clinton, Jr. internist
Trent-Ota, Jane Suzanne elementary school educator
Wagener, Hobart D. retired architect
Worthington, George Rhodes naval officer

Corte Madera
Epstein, William Louis dermatologist, educator

Costa Mesa
Anderson, Jon David lawyer
Argyros, George L. development company executive, former professional sports team owner
Billiter, William Overton, Jr. journalist
Crinella, Francis Michael neuropsychologist, science foundation director
Currie, Robert Emil lawyer
Damsky, Robert Philip communications executive
Daniels, James Walter lawyer
Davidson, Janet Toll lawyer
Elias, Rosalind mezzo-soprano
†Foell, Ronald R. builder
Frieden, Clifford E. lawyer
Gore, Thomas Gavin insurance and securities broker
Gritchen, Lyle Steven lawyer
Hamilton, James William lawyer
Hay, Howard Clinton lawyer
†Hecht, Duvall Y. publishing industry executive
Heylin, Michael magazine editor
Hugo, Nancy county official, alcohol and drug addiction professional
Jones, H(arold) Gilbert, Jr. lawyer
Labbe, Armand Joseph museum curator, anthropologist
Lattanzio, Stephen Paul astronomy educator
McIntyre, Joel Franklyn lawyer
Mittermeier, Janice commercial airport executive
Muller, Jerome Kenneth editor, photographer
Olson, Cal Oliver golf architect
†Panic, Milan pharmaceutical and health products company executive
Patterson, Dennis Joseph management consultant
Pearson, William James finance company executive
†Reppert, Joseph R. title company executive
Reveal, Ernest Ira, III lawyer
Riordan, George Nickerson investment banker
Savage, Sandra Hope Skeen mathematics educator, curriculum writer
Sognefest, Peter William manufacturing company executive
Speers, Roland Root, II lawyer
Thurston, Morris Ashcroft lawyer
Wall, James Edward petroleum, pharmaceutical executive
Williams, William Corey Old Testament educator, consultant

Covina
Fillius, Milton Franklin, Jr. food products company executive
Jackson, John Jay clergyman, denomination administrator
Phillips, Jill Meta novelist, critic, astrologer
Schneider, Calvin physician
Takei, Toshihisa otolaryngologist

Crestline
Merrill, Steven William research and development executive

Crockett
Somerset, Harold Richard sugar company executive

Cromberg
Kolb, Ken Lloyd writer

Culver City
Abdul, Paula (Julie) singer, dancer, choreographer
†Avnet, Jonathan Michael motion picture company executive, film director
Berland, James Fred software developer, computer management consultant
Bluth, Don animator, director, screenwriter
Boorman, John film director, producer, screenwriter
Brooks, James L. writer, director, producer
Canton, Mark motion picture company executive
Clodius, Albert Howard history educator
Eckel, James Robert, Jr. financial planner
Fetter, Trevor film executive
Gottlieb, Jerome television production company executive
Gregg, David Paul information storage media specialist
Guber, Peter producer
Kay, Kelly W. lawyer
Leve, Alan Donald electronic materials manufacturing company owner, executive
Levine, Alan J. entertainment company executive
Maltzman, Irving Myron psychology educator
Martin, Gary O. film company executive
†McNeill, Daniel Richard writer
Melnick, Daniel film producer
Moss, Eric Owen architect
Nathanson, Michael film company executive
†Netzel, Paul Arthur fund raising management executive, consultant
Proft, Pat screenwriter, film producer
Ray, Mary-Ann architect, educator
Real, Jack Garret helicopter company executive
Rose, Margarete Erika pathologist
Rosenfelt, Frank Edward motion picture company executive
Sagansky, Jeff broadcast executive
Sensiper, Samuel consulting electrical engineer
Stark, Ray motion picture producer
Tarantino, Quentin film director, screenwriter
Tinker, Grant A. broadcasting executive
†Tisch, Steven E. movie producer
Trebek, Alex television game show host
von Kalinowski, Julian Onesime lawyer
Weiss, Eric Robert lawyer
Williams, Kenneth Scott entertainment company executive
†Wilson, Nancy Linda church officer
†Ziskin, Laura film producer
Zucker, David director

Cupertino
Anderson, Charles Arthur former research institute administrator
Bossen, David August electronics company executive
Burg, John Parker signal processing executive
Cheeseman, Douglas Taylor, Jr. wildlife tour executive, photographer, educator
Compton, Dale Leonard retired space agency executive
†Eisenstat, Albert A. lawyer, corporate executive
Fenn, Raymond Wolcott, Jr. retired metallurgical engineer
Fletcher, Homer Lee librarian
Flynn, Ralph Melvin, Jr. sales executive, marketing consultant
Gingerich, John Charles manufacturing company executive
Graziano, Joseph A. computer company executive
Horn, Christian Friedrich venture capital company executive
Krambeck, Robert Harold communications and computer executive/researcher
Lindsay, Leslie packaging engineer
†Lundgren, David Albert product design engineer
Machamer, Sylvia Geraldine special education educator
Markkula, A. C., Jr. entrepreneur, computer company executive
Marshall, Robert Charles computer company executive
Mathias, Leslie Michael electronic manufacturing company executive
McAdams, Robert, Jr. electronics executive
Nelson, Richard Burton physicist, engineer, patent consultant
Norman, Donald Arthur cognitive scientist
Perkins, Thomas James venture capital company executive
Sarnoff, Jill Robin lawyer
Schmidt, Stephen C. computer company executive
Spindler, Michael H. computer company executive
†Starkweather, Gary Keith optical engineer, computer company executive
Tesler, Lawrence Gordon computer company executive
Togasaki, Shinobu corporate executive
Treybig, James G. computer company executive
Wiley, Richard Haven chemist, educator
Winslow, David Allen chaplain, naval officer
Zobel, Louise Purwin author, educator, lecturer, writing consultant

Cypress
Baugh, Coy Franklin corporate executive
Edmonds, Ivy Gordon writer
Hoops, Alan health care company executive
†Kiuchi, Takashi Tachi electronics company executive
Lowell, Wayne Brian financial officer
Naganuma, Kazue automotive executive
Olschwang, Alan Paul lawyer
Recchia, Richard D. automotive sales executive

Daly City
Hargrave, Sarah Quesenberry marketing, public relations company executive
Martin, Bernard Lee former college dean
Mullins, Anna Carrolle hospital administrator

Dana Point
Bruggeman, Lewis LeRoy radiologist
Frederickson, Arman Frederick minerals company executive
Jelinek, Robert advertising executive, writer
Kesselhaut, Arthur Melvyn financial consultant
Kleiner, Richard Arthur writer, editor
Krogius, Tristan Ernst Gunnar international marketing consultant, lawyer
Lacy, James Vincent government official
Robinson, Theodore Gould golf course architect

Danville
Amon, William Frederick, Jr. finance company executive
Arrol, John corporate executive
Behring, Kenneth E. professional sports team owner
Davis, James Ivey company president, laboratory associate
Frederickson, John Marcus insurance executive
Liggett, Lawrence Melvin vacuum equipment manufacturing company executive
Lowery, Lawrence Frank mathematic science and computer educator
Maninger, R(alph) Carroll engineering executive, consultant
Mattoon, Henry Amasa, Jr. advertising and marketing consultant, writer
McMillan, Terry L. writer, educator
Plummer, Marcie Stern real estate broker
Reed, John Theodore publisher, writer
Trezek, George James mechanical engineer

Davis
Addicott, Fredrick Taylor retired botany educator
Akesson, Norman Berndt agricultural engineer, emeritus educator
Alder, Henry Ludwig mathematics educator
Allard, Robert Wayne geneticist, educator
Andrews, Lawrence James chemistry educator, academic administrator
Ardans, Alexander Andrew veterinarian, laboratory director, educator
Axelrod, Daniel Isaac geology and botany educator
Ayer, John Demeritt law educator
Barbour, Michael G(eorge) botany educator, ecological consultant
Bartosic, Florian lawyer, artibrator, educator
Baskin, Ronald Joseph zoologist, physiologist, biophysicist educator, dean
Beadle, Charles Wilson retired mechanical engineering educator
Beagle, Peter Soyer writer
Biberstein, Ernst Ludwig veterinary medicine educator
Black, Arthur Leo biochemistry educator
Boulton, Lyndie McHenry professional society administrator
Bradbury, Edwin Morton biochemistry educator
Brandt, Harry mechanical engineering educator
Bruch, Carol Sophie lawyer, educator
Cahill, Thomas Andrew physicist, educator
Carlson, Don Marvin biochemist
Carman, Hoy Fred agricultural sciences educator
Carter, Harold O. agricultural economics educator
Chancellor, William Joseph agricultural engineering educator
Chang, Robert Shihman virology educator
Cheney, James Addison civil engineering educator
Cohen, Lawrence Edward sociology educator, criminologist
Colvin, Harry Walter, Jr. physiology educator
Conn, Eric Edward plant biochemist
Crane, Julian Coburn agriculturist,retired educator
Crowley, Daniel John anthropologist
Crummey, Robert Owen history educator, university dean
Day, Howard Wilman geology educator
DePaoli, Geri M. artist, art historian
Doi, Roy Hiroshi biochemist, educator
Dorf, Richard Carl electrical engineering and management educator
Dykstra, Daniel James lawyer, educator
Eldridge, Bruce Frederick entomology educator, researcher
Elmendorf, William Welcome anthropology educator
Enders, Allen Coffin anatomy educator
Epstein, Emanuel plant physiologist
Feeney, Floyd Fulton legal educator
Forbes, Jack D. ethnohistorian, educator, writer
Fowler, William Mayo, Jr. rehabilitation medicine physician
Freedland, Richard Allan retired biologist, educator
Fridley, Robert Bruce agricultural engineering educator
Gardner, Murray Briggs pathologist, educator
Gardner, William Allen electrical engineering educator
Gates, Bruce Clark chemical engineer, educator
Ghausi, Mohammed Shuaib electrical engineering educator, university dean
Giedt, Warren Harding mechanical engineer, educator
Gifford, Ernest Milton biologist, educator
Goldman, Marvin biophysicist, educator
Greenwood, M. R. C. college dean, biologist, nutrition educator
Grey, Robert Dean biology educator
Grossman, George Stefan library director, law eductor
Groth, Alexander Jacob political science educator
Gullón, Germán Spanish educator
Hakimi, S. Louis electrical and computer engineering educator
Halsted, Charles Hopkinson internist
†Hammock, Bruce Dupree research entomologist and toxicology educator
Harper, Lawrence Vernon human development educator
Hartmann, Hudson Thomas agriculturist, educator
Hawkes, Glenn Rogers psychology educator
Hayden, John Olin English literature educator, author
Hays, Peter L. English language and literature educator
Hedrick, Jerry Leo biochemistry and biophysics educator
Hendrickx, Andrew George anatomy educator
Hess, Charles Edward environmental horticulture educator
Higgins, Charles Graham geology educator
Hoffman, Michael Jerome humanities educator
Horwitz, Barbara Ann physiologist, educator, consultant
Hrdy, Sarah Blaffer anthropology educator
Hsieh, Dennis P. H. environmental toxicology educator
Hughes, John P. equine research adminstrator
Hullar, Theodore Lee environmental educator
Imwinkelried, Edward John law educator
Ives, John David (Jack Ives) geography and environmental sciences educator
Jackson, William Turrentine history educator
Jasper, Donald Edward clinical pathology educator
Jett, Stephen Clinton geography educator, researcher
Johnston, Warren Eugene agricultural economics educator, consultant
Jordan, Ellen Rausen law educator, consultant
Juenger, Friedrich Klaus lawyer, educator
Jungerman, John Albert physics educator
Kado, Clarence Isao molecular biologist
Keizer, Joel Edward chemistry educator, theoretical scientist
Kemper, John Dustin mechanical engineering educator
Kepner, Robert Allen agricultural engineering researcher, educator
Kimsey, Lynn Siri entomologist, educator
Kofranek, Anton Miles floriculturist, educator
Kunkee, Ralph Edward viticulture and enology educator
Laidlaw, Harry Hyde, Jr. entomology educator
Larock, Bruce Edward civil engineering educator
Lazarus, Gerald Sylvan physician
Learn, Elmer Warner agricultural economics educator, retired
Lipscomb, Paul Rogers orthopaedic surgeon, educator
Lofland, John Franklin sociologist, educator
Lofland, Lyn Hebert sociology educator
Major, Clarence Lee novelist, poet, educator
Martin, George Conner pomology educator
Mason, William A(lvin) psychologist, educator, researcher
McHenry, Henry Malcolm anthropologist, educator
McPherson, Sandra Jean poet, educator
Meyer, Margaret Eleanor microbiologist, educator
Moyle, Peter Briggs fisheries and biology educator
Mukherjee, Amiya K metallurgy and materials science educator
Murphy, Terence Martin biology educator
Musolf, Lloyd Daryl political science educator, institute administrator
Nash, Charles Presley chemistry educator
Overstreet, James Wilkins obstetrics and gynecology educator, administrator
Owings, Donald Henry psychology educator
Palmer, Philip Edward Stephen radiologist
Pappagianis, Demosthenes microbiology educator, physician
Pearcy, Robert Woodwell botany educator
Perschbacher, Rex Robert law educator
Plopper, Charles George anatomist, cell biologist
Pritchard, William Roy former university system administrator
Qualset, Calvin O. agronomy educator

Rappaport, Lawrence plant physiology and horticulture educator
Redenbach, Sandra Irene educational consultant
Rhode, Edward Albert veterinary medicine educator, veterinary cardiologist
Rick, Charles Madeira, Jr. geneticist, educator
Rocke, David Morton statistician, educator
Rost, Thomas Lowell plant biology educator
Rothstein, Morton historian, retired educator
Schenker, Marc Benet medical educator
Schneeman, Barbara Olds nutrition educator, dean
Schoener, Thomas William zoology educator, researcher
Schwabe, Calvin Walter veterinarian, medical historian, medical educator
Shapiro, Arthur Maurice biology educator
Sharrow, Marilyn Jane library administrator
Shelton, Robert Neal physics educator, researcher
Sillman, Arnold Joel physiologist, educator
Siverson, Randolph Martin political science educator
Skinner, G(eorge) William anthropologist, educator
Smiley, Robert Herschel university dean
Smith, Lloyd Muir chemist, educator
Smith, Michael Peter social science educator, researcher
Steffey, Eugene Paul veterinary medicine educator
Stewart, James Ian agricultural water scientist, cropping system developer, consultant
Stowell, Robert Eugene pathologist, retired educator
Stumpf, Paul Karl biochemistry educator emeritus
Sumner, Daniel Alan economist, educator
Swift, Richard G(ene) composer, educator
Tchobanoglous, George civil engineering educator
Theilen, Gordon Henry veterinary surgery educator
Tomlinson-Keasey, Carol Ann university administrator
Tupper, Charles John physician, educator
†Van Bruggen, Ariena Hendrika Cornelia plant pathologist
Vanderhoef, Larry Neil university administrator
Verosub, Kenneth Lee geology educator, researcher
Volman, David Herschel chemistry educator
Waddington, Raymond Bruce, Jr. English language educator
Wang, Shih-Ho electrical engineer, educator
Watt, Kenneth Edmund Ferguson zoology educator
Wegge, Leon Louis François economics educator
Williams, Hibbard Earl medical educator, physician
Williams, William Arnold agronomy educator
Williamson, Alan Bacher English literature educator, poet, writer
Willis, Frank Roy history educator
Wilson, Barry William biology educator
Wolk, Bruce Alan law educator
Woodress, James Leslie, Jr. English language educator
Wooten, Frederick (Oliver) applied science educator
Wydick, Richard Crews lawyer, educator
Yang, Linda Tsao financial consultant
Yang, Shang Fa biochemistry educator, plant physiologist
Youmans, Julian Ray neurosurgeon, educator

Del Mar
Comrie, Sandra Melton human resource executive
Cutrona, Louis John engineering executive
Faludi, Susan C. journalist, scholarly writer
Farquhar, Marilyn Gist cell biology and pathology educator
Jeub, Michael Leonard financial executive
Kaye, Peter Frederic newspaper editor
La Bonté, C(larence) Joseph weight management and lifestyle company executive
Reid, Joseph Lee physical oceanographer, educator
†Stevenson, Robert Everett oceanography consultant
Wilkinson, Eugene Parks nuclear engineer

Diablo
Pelandini, Thomas Francis mmarketing executive

Diamond Bar
Fisher, Louis Raymond insurance executive

Dillon Beach
Petersen, Roland artist, printmaker

Dinuba
Leps, Thomas MacMaster civil engineer, consultant

Downey
Baumann, Theodore Robert aerospace engineer, consultant, army officer
Brofman, Woody astronautical engineer, educator
Brooks, Lillian Hazel Ashton adult education educator
Demarchi, Ernest Nicholas aerospace company executive
Gong, Henry, Jr. physician, researcher
Hackney, Jack Dean physician
†Ingwerson, Donald W. educational administrator
Orden, Ted gasoline service stations executive
Perry, Jacquelin orthopedic surgeon
Redeker, Allan Grant physician, medical educator
Sapico, Francisco Lejano internist, educator
Schoettger, Theodore Leo city official
Schroeder, Robert J. veterinarian, association executive
Shapiro, Richard Stanley physician

Duarte
Chou, Chung-Kwang bio-engineer
Comings, David Edward physician, medical genetics scientist
Greenstein, Jesse Leonard astronomer, educator
Kovach, John Stephen oncologist, research center administrator
Levine, Rachmiel physician
Lundblad, Roger Lauren research director
Ohno, Susumu research scientist
Shapero, Sanford Marvin hospital executive, rabbi
Smith, Hallett Darius retired English literature educator
Smith, Steven Sidney molecular biologist

Dublin
Cope, Kenneth Wayne chain store executive
Del Santo, Lawrence A. retail merchandising company executive
Neff, James Dennis manufacturing company executive, consultant
Prince, Jimmie Dan retail food chain executive
†Webb, James William food products executive
†Whetten, John D. food products executive
Witt, Robert Louis materials manufacturing and sales company executive, lawyer

Edwards
Brand, Vance Devoe astronaut, government official
Deets, Dwain Aaron aeronautical research engineer
†Fugate, Robert Q. optical engineer

El Cajon
Burnett, Lowell Jay physicist, educator
Colling, Kenneth Frank hospital administrator
Fike, Edward Lake newspaper editor
Laffoon, Carthrae Merrette management consultant
McInerney, Joseph Aloysius hotel executive
Shoemaker, Joan mayor

El Centro
Flock, Robert Ashby retired entomologist
Gotti, Margaret Lynn library administrator
Lokey, Frank Marion, Jr. broadcast executive, consultant

El Cerrito
Conti, Isabella psychologist, consultant
Dillenberger, John theology educator emeritus, minister
Garbarino, Joseph William labor arbitrator, economics and business educator
Griffith, Ladd Ray retired chemical research director
Gwinn, William Dulaney physical chemist, educator, consultant
Komatsu, S. Richard architect
Kuo, Ping-chia historian, educator
Schomer, Howard retired clergyman, educator, social policy consultant

El Dorado Hills
Mansoor, John Jirius sports management executive

El Granada
Heere, Karen R. astrophysicist

El Macero
Raventos, Antolin radiology educator
Wheeler, Douglas Paul conservationist, government official, lawyer

El Monte
†Christ, Clifford Charles electronics executive

El Portal
Medley, Steven Paul association executive

El Segundo
Aldridge, Edward C., Jr. aerospace transportation executive
Amerman, John W. toy company executive
Autolitano, Astrid consumer products executive
Barad, Jill Elikann toy company executive
Brill, James Lathrop finance executive
Brown, Timothy Donell professional football player
Caslow, Richard Walker, Jr. manufacturing company executive
Clough, Charles Marvin electronics company executive
†Collazo, Jose Antonio computer company executive
Croft, Leonard Mathias toy company executive
Davis, Allen professional football team executive
Eskridge, James Arthur toy company executive
Gossett, Jeffrey Alan professional football player
Gupta, Madhu Sudan electrical engineering educator
Herrera, John professional football team executive
†Honeycutt, Van B. computer services company executive
Hostetler, Jeff W. professional football player
Ismail, Raghib (Rocket Ismail) professional football player
Jaeger, Jeff Todd professional football player
Kuelbs, John Thomas lawyer
Lantz, Norman Foster electrical engineer
†Leff, Robert S. computer company executive
Level, Leon Jules information services executive
†Lidow, Eric electrical parts manufacturing company executive
Mo, Roger Shih-Yah electronics engineering manager
Mosebar, Donald Howard professional football player
Neal, Jerry Eugene controller
Paulikas, George Algis physicist
Pickett, Michael D. computer hardware and software distributor
Radys, Raymond George laser scientist
Reames, Timothy Paul lawyer, toy company executive
Ricardi, Leon Joseph electrical engineer
Shell, Art professional football team coach
Tamrat, Befecadu aeronautical engineer
Tennant, Samuel McKibben aerospace systems company executive
Townsend, Greg professional football player
Wagman, David S. computer company executive
Wallace, Arthur agricultural educator
Wisniewski, Stephen Adam professional football player

Emeryville
Dezurick, Paul Anthony lawyer
Edginton, John Arthur lawyer
Hoover, Jessica Mary lawyer
Marcus, Frank biochemist
Masri, Merle Sid biochemist, consultant
†Penhoet, Edward biochemicals company executive
Weaver, Velather Edwards (Val Weaver) small business owner
Winger, Dennis Lawrence medical products company executive

Encinitas
Bloomberg, Warner, Jr. urban affairs educator emeritus
Dennish, George William, III cardiologist
Goldberg, Edward Davidow geochemist, educator
Hano, E. Gail mayor
Morrow, Charles Tabor aerospace consulting engineer
Peters, Leslie Ann television and radio producer
Satur, Nancy Marlene dermatologist

Encino
Acheson, Louis Kruzan, Jr. aerospace engineer and systems analyst
Bucks, Charles Alan airline industry consultant, former executive
Dor, Yoram health care executive
Dragutsky, Howard William estate planner
Eves, Jeffrey P. entertainment industry executive
Friedman, George Jerry aerospace company executive, engineer
Gasich, Welko Elton retired aerospace executive, management consultant
Hawthorne, Marion Frederick chemistry educator
Holman, Harland Eugene retired motion picture company executive
Hubbard, Frederick Dewayne trumpeter
Karlin, Myron D. motion picture executive
Kaufman, Albert I. lawyer
†Kerr, William Alexander glass company executive
†King, Peter DeWitt psychiatrist, educator, real estate developer
Knuth, Eldon Luverne engineering educator
Krueger, Kenneth John corporate executive, nutritionist, educator
Nicholson, Jack actor, director, producer
Nielsen, Leslie actor
Posnansky, Merrick history and archaeology educator
Roderick, Robert Lee aerospace executive
Singer, Gerald Michael lawyer, educator, author, arbitrator and mediator
Smith, Selma Moidel lawyer, composer
Stanton, Harry Dean actor
Webster, David Arthur life insurance company executive
Wood, Raymund Francis retired librarian
Zsigmond, Vilmos cinematographer, director

Escalon
Barton, Gerald Lee food company executive

Escondido
Allen, Donald Vail investment executive, author, concert pianist
Barrio, Raymond author, artist
Briggs, Edward Samuel naval officer
Damsbo, Ann Marie psychologist
Everton, Marta Ve ophthalmologist
Harper, Lilah Marie nursing service administrator
Moore, Marc Anthony university administrator, writer, retired military officer
Newman, Barry Ingalls retired banker, lawyer
O'Meara, David Collow retired banker
Ortiz, Angel Vicente church administrator
Packer, Russell Howard automotive company executive
†Pershing, Richard Wilson communications company executive, consultant
Sternberg, Harry artist
Stone, Ileane Gertrude gerontologist

Etna
Auxentios, (Bishop) clergyman
Chrysostomos, (González-Alexopoulos) bishop, clergyman, psychologist, educator

Eureka
†Kriger, Peter Wilson healthcare administrator

Fair Oaks
Agerbek, Sven mechanical engineer
Branch, Robert Lee retired educational administrator
Chernev, Melvin retired beverage company executive
Inglis, Andrew Franklin author, consultant
Luther, Florence Joan (Mrs. Charles W. Luther) lawyer
Smiley, Robert William industrial engineer

Fairfax
Gores, Joseph Nicholas novelist, scriptwriter
Novello, Don writer, comedian, actor

Fairfield
Martin, Clyde Verne psychiatrist
Moore, Marianna Gay law librarian, consultant

Fallbrook
Burge, Henry Charles architect
Freeman, Harry Lynwood accountant
Ragland, Jack Whitney artist

Felicity
Istel, Jacques Andre mayor

Fieldbrook
Schaaf, Miv writer, graphic designer, composer

Fish Camp
Schneider, Arthur Paul retired videotape and film editor, author

Folsom
Aldridge, Donald O'Neal military officer
Close, Gary E. pharmaceuticals executive
Ettlich, William F. electrical engineer
Whitmire, Melburn G. pharmaceutical distribution company executive

Fontana
Lardieri, Anthony J. school system administrator

Forestville
Benyo, Richard Stephen magazine editor, writer

Fort Ord
†Simpson, Kenneth Warren army officer

Fortuna
Fisher, Bruce David elementary educator
Fullerton, Gail Jackson university president emeritus

Foster City
Baselt, Randall Clint toxicologist
Dove, Millard retired transportation executive
Goldstein, Morris publishing company executive
Ham, Lee Edward civil engineer
Lonnquist, George Eric lawyer
MacNaughton, Angus Athole finance company executive
Malone, Michael Glen lawyer
Meredith, Allen Kent real estate developer
Paterson, Richard Denis financial executive
†Roberts, Lawrence Gilman telecommunications company executive
†Sewall, William Dana data processing manager
Thomlinson, Ralph demographer, educator
Turner, Ross James investment corporation executive

Fountain Valley
Gittleman, Morris metallurgist,consultant
Gumbiner, Robert health services executive
Jessup, R. Judd managed care executive
Olim, August Souza counselor
Price, Westcott Wilkin, III health care company executive
Smith, Marie Edmonds real estate agent, property manager

Frazier Park
Nelson, Harry journalist, medical writer

Fremont
Berry, Michael James scientist
Brown, David Richard school system administrator, minister
de Roque, Barbara Penberthy special education educator, consultant
Evenhuis, Henk J. research company executive
Gill, Stephen Paschall physicist, mathematician
†Harms, Ralph John financial executive
Lautzenheiser, Marvin Wendell computer software engineer
Ours, Marian Leah elementary education educator
Smith, Bernald Stephen retired airline pilot, aviation consultant
†Wood, Linda May librarian

Fresno
Andresen, Claudia principal
Beck, Dennis L. federal judge
Blum, Gerald Henry department store executive
Brahma, Chandra Sekhar civil engineering educator
Buzick, William Alonson, Jr. investor, lawyer, educator
Coe, William Charles psychology educator
Cohen, Moses Elias mathematician, educator
Coyle, Robert Everett federal judge
Crocker, Myron Donovan federal judge
Dackawich, S. John sociology educator
Dandoy, Maxima Antonio education educator emeritus
Darden, Edwin Speight, Sr. architect
Dauer, Donald Dean investment executive
Emrick, Terry Lamar financial business consultant
Falcone, Alfonso Benjamin physician
Flores, William Vincent Latin American studies educator
Gerster, Robert Gibson composer
Gorman, Michael Joseph library director, educator
Haak, Harold Howard university president
Holmes, Albert William, Jr. physician
Jamison, Oliver Morton retired lawyer
†Jimenez, Edward Rucobo editor
Kallenberg, John Kenneth librarian
Kauffman, George Bernard chemistry educator
Klassen, Peter James academic administrator, history educator
Kouymjian, Dickran art historian, Orientalist, educator
Krebs, John H. former congressman
Kuhlman, Josie-Lee social work administrator
Leigh, Hoyle psychiatrist, educator, writer
Levine, Philip poet, educator
Levy, Joseph William department stores executive
Mather, Allen Frederick lawyer
O'Brien, John Conway economist, educator, writer
†O'Connor, Kevin John psychologist
O'Donnell, Thomas Howard wheelchair manufacturing executive
Ogle, Mary Ellen nursing and surgical services executive
Ott, Michael Duane lawyer
Palmer, Samuel Copeland, III lawyer
Patnaude, William E. architect
Patterson, James mayor
†Petrucci, Vincent Emilio retired viticulture educator, consultant
Pings, Anthony Claude architect
Pinkerton, Richard LaDoyt management educator
Price, Edward Dean federal judge
Putman, Robert Dean golf course architect
Rank, Everett George government official
Rehart, Burton Schyler journalism educator, freelance writer
Saito, Paul Makoto landscape architect
Schofield, John-David Mercer bishop
†Setencich, Eli John columnist
Sexton, Richard school system administrator
Sobey, Edwin J. C. museum director, oceanographer, consultant
Steinbock, John T. bishop
Stude, Everett Wilson, Jr. rehabilitation counselor, educator
Tatarian, Hrach Roger journalist
Tellier, Richard Davis management educator
Wanger, Oliver Winston federal judge, educator
Welty, John Donald university president
†Wilson, Herman T., Jr. agricultural products supplier
Wilson, Warren Samuel clergyman, bishop

Fullerton
Atwell, Margaret Ann education educator
Axelson, Charles Frederic retired accounting educator
Ayala, John librarian, dean
Barchi, Barbara Ann education and training consultant
Begovich, Nicholas Anthony electrical engineer, consultant
Borst, Philip West academic administrator
Brattstrom, Bayard Holmes biology educator
Cole, Sherwood Orison psychologist
Coleman, Ronny Jack fire chief
Crosson, Albert J. food products executive
Curran, Darryl Joseph photographer, educator
Donoghue, Mildred Ransdorf education educator
Foster, Julian Francis Sherwood political science educator
Garrido, Augie university athletic coach
Goldstein, Edward David lawyer, former glass company executive
Gordon, Milton Andrew academic administrator
Hershey, Gerald Lee psychologist
Hollander, Gerhard Ludwig computer company executive
Hopping, Richard Lee college president
Hufnagel, Raymond Joseph, Jr. aerospace and commercial executive
Hugstad, Paul Steven college dean
Jones, Claris Eugene, Jr. botanist, educator
Kagiwada, Harriet Hatsune Natsuyama mathematician
Karson, Burton Lewis musician
Malakoff, James Leonard management information executive

May, William Hathaway instrument corporation executive, lawyer
McAuliffe, Clayton Doyle chemist
McGinnis, Joán Adell secondary school educator
Miller, Arnold electronics executive
Nowel, David John marketing professional
Patton, David Wayne health care executive
Rosso, Louis T. scientific instrument manufacturing company executive
†Sa, Julie mayor, restaurant chain owner
Shapiro, Mark Howard physicist, educator, academic dean, consultant
Smith, Ephraim Philip university dean, educator
Stollsteimer, John F. food company executive
Svinos, John Georgios software consulting firm executive
Taylor, James Walter marketing educator
Timm, Laurance Milo musician, educator
Walker, Mallory Elton tenor

Garden Grove
Ballesteros, Juventino Ray, Jr. minister
Banks, Ernest (Ernie Banks) moving company executive, retired professional baseball player
Bledsoe, Jane Kathryn art museum director, art historian
Ortlieb, Robert Eugene sculptor
Schuller, Robert Harold clergyman, author
Virgo, Muriel Agnes swimming school owner
Williams, J(ohn) Tilman insurance executive, real estate broker, city official

Gardena
Baker, Lillian L. author, historian, artist, lecturer
Crismond, Linda Fry association executive
†Kanner, Edwin Benjamin electrical manufacturing company executive
Kucij, Timothy Michael engineer, composer, organist, pianist, conductor, minister, theologian
†Mignanelli, Thomas D. automobile company executive
Winston, Morton Manuel equipment executive

Georgetown
Lengyel, Cornel Adam (Cornel Adam) author

Geyserville
Mc Clelland, John Peter winery executive

Gilroy
Barham, Warren Sandusky horticulturist
Blattman, H. Eugene foods corporation executive
Borton, George Robert airline captain
†Henry-John, Emmanuel Sylvester preacher, counselor

Glendale
Baker, Sheldon S. lawyer
Ball, James Herington lawyer
Beban, Gary Joseph real estate corporation officer
Burger, John Barclay systems architect, computer scientist
Colby, Barbara Diane interior designer, consultant
Courtney, Howard Perry clergyman
Cross, Richard John banker
Crull, Timm F. food company executive
Davidson, Suzanne Mouron lawyer
Day, John Francis city official, former savings and loan executive, former mayor
Dent, Ernest DuBose, Jr. pathologist
†Evans, Godfrey B. lawyer
Farmer, Crofton Bernard atmospheric physicist
Greenwood, Richard M. finance company executive, bank executive
Hadley, Paul Ervin international relations educator
Herzer, Richard Kimball franchising company executive
Hoffman, Donald M. lawyer
Howell, Jack Lynn financial executive
Kernen, Jules Alfred pathologist
Knoop, Vern Thomas civil engineer, consultant
Lathe, Robert Edward management and financial consultant
Lieber, Edward Joseph lawyer
Marr, Luther Reese communications executive, lawyer
Martin, John Hugh lawyer, retired
Misa, Kenneth Franklin management consultant
†Ravenhall, Colin chemicals executive
†Rosenberg, Robert M. food chain executive
Russell, Newton Requa state senator
Schult, Robert W. food products executive
Seegman, Irvin P. manufacturing company executive
Trafton, Stephen J. banking executive
Vilnrotter, Victor Alpár research engineer
Whalen, Lucille academic administrator

Glendora
Cahn, David Stephen cement company executive
Christofi, Andreas Charalambos finance educator
Lindly, Douglas Dean elementary school educator, administrator
Milhous, Robert E. advertising executive
Richey, Everett Eldon religion educator
Roland, Donald Edward advertising executive
Scheller, Sanford Gregory printing company executive
Schiele, Paul Ellsworth, Jr. educational business owner, writer
Yochem, Barbara June sales executive, lecturer

Goleta
Bartlett, James Lowell, III investment banker
†Frank, Harold Roy metal products executive
Thom, Richard David aerospace executive

Granada Hills
Aller, Wayne Kendall psychology educator, researcher, computer education company executive, property manager
Carradine, David actor, director
†Duffield, Thomas A. art director, production designer
Shoemaker, Harold Lloyd infosystem specialist

Granite Bay
Crossley, Frank Alphonso former metallurgical engineer

Grass Valley
Cartwright, Mary Lou laboratory scientist
Lawrence, Dean Grayson retired lawyer

Greenbrae
†Finkelstein, James Arthur management consultant
Levy, S. William dermatologist
Parnell, Francis William, Jr. physician

Gridley
Tanimoto, George agricultural executive, farmer

Gualala
Gaustad, Edwin Scott historian

Hacienda Heights
Love, Daniel Joseph consulting engineer
West, Linda Lea administrator

Half Moon Bay
Bonham, George Wolfgang magazine editor, writer, foundation executive
Fennell, Diane Marie marketing executive, process engineer
†Gross, Kenneth Paul management consultant
Hidy, George Martel chemical engineer, executive
Robertson, Abel L., Jr. pathologist

Hanford
Drosdick, John Girard oil company executive

Hawthorne
Ashkenas, Irving Louis aerospace executive
†McRuer, Duane Torrance aerospace engineering executive
Weiss, Max Tibor aerospace company executive

Hayward
Connors, Dennis Michael infosystems executive
Flora, Edward Benjamin research and development company executive, mechanical engineer
Hirschfeld, Sue Ellen geological sciences educator
Hwang, Kou Mau pharmaceutical executive
Mayers, Eugene David philosopher, educator
McCune, Ellis E. retired university system chief administrator, higher education consultant
Meyer, Ann Jane human development educator
Morgan, Joe Leonard investment company executive, former professional baseball player
Ramos, Melvin John artist, educator
Rees, Norma S. university president, educator
Resnikoff, George Joseph university dean, mathematics and statistics educator emeritus
Sabharwal, Ranjit Singh mathematician
Smith, J(ohn) Malcolm political science educator
Stern, Ralph David lawyer, county and municipal official
Tribus, Myron management consultant, engineer, educator
Warnke, Detlef Andreas geologist, educator
Whalen, Thomas Earl psychology educator

Healdsburg
Canfield, Grant Wellington, Jr. management consultant
Eade, George James retired air force officer, research executive, defense consultant
Erdman, Paul Emil author
Kamm, Thomas Allen lawyer, retired naval officer
Reed, Thomas Care business executive

Hemet
Berger, Lev Isaac physicist, educator
Bible, Frances Lillian mezzo-soprano, educator
Hall, John Thomas, Jr. patient care services administrator, consultant
Kopiloff, George psychiatrist
Shea, Robert Stanton retired academic administrator
Treece, Joseph Charles insurance broker

Hercules
Zhu, Mingde chemist

Hermosa Beach
Kokalj, James Edward retired aerospace administrator
McDowell, Edward R. H. chemical engineer

Hesperia
Butcher, Jack Robert manufacturing executive

Hillsborough
Blume, John August consulting civil engineer
Keller, John Francis retired wine company executive, mayor
†Kraft, Robert Arnold retired medical educator, physician
Willoughby, Rodney Erwin retired oil company executive

Hollister
Parker, Patrick Johnston entrepreneur, philantropist

Hollywood
Archuletta, Patti Stolkin performing arts association administrator
Bernstein, William film company executive
Bessman, Samuel Paul biochemist, pediatrician
Burkow, Judith Beth lawyer
Byrnes, James Bernard museum director emeritus
Carter, Bennett Lester (Benny Carter) musician, composer, conductor
Hovsepian, Vatche clergyman
Israel, David journalist, screenwriter, producer
Jordan, Stanley musician
Koch, Howard Winchel film and television producer
Lewis, Huey (Hugh Anthony Cregg, III) singer, composer, bandleader
Little Richard, (Richard Wayne Penniman) recording artist, pianist, songwriter, minister
Marshall, Conrad Joseph entrepreneur
Miller, Betty Jean feature film distribution company executive
Parks, Robert Myers appliance manufacturing company executive
Pollack, Sydney film director
Rudin, Scott film and theatre producer
Salomon, Mikael cinematographer, director
Schaefer, Carl George Lewis writer, public relations and advertising executive
Strock, Herbert Leonard motion picture producer, director, editor, writer
Wilder, Billy motion picture director, writer, producer

Hopland
Jones, Milton Bennion agronomist, educator

Huntington Beach
Anderson, Raymond Hartwell, Jr. metallurgical engineer
Falcon, Joseph A. mechanical engineering consultant
Frye, Judith Eleen Minor editor
Hildebrant, Andy McClellan retired electrical engineer
Martin, Wilfred Wesley Finny psychologist, property owner and manager
Shaffer, Richard James lawyer, former manufacturing company executive

Indian Wells
Carter, Paul Richard physician
Harris, Milton M. distributing company executive
Pace, Stanley Carter retired aeronautical engineer
Reed, A(lfred) Byron retired apparel and textile manufacturing company
Trotter, F(rederick) Thomas retired university president

Indio
Fischer, Craig Leland physician
Lloyd, Douglas George watercolor artist, educator

Inglewood
Alaniz, Miguel José Castañeda library director
Buss, Jerry Hatten real estate executive, sports team owner
Dymally, Mervyn Malcolm retired congressman, international business executive
Epstein, Marsha Ann public health administrator, physician
Gretzky, WayneDouglas professional hockey player
Guzy, Marguerita Linnes educator
Jefferson, Bernard S. academic administrator
Jobe, Frank Wilson orthopedic surgeon
Johnson, Earvin (Magic Johnson) professional sports team executive, former professional basketball coach
Kurri, Jari professional hockey player
Lewis, Roy Roosevelt physicist
†Long, Ophelia hospital administrator
Lynch, Linda Lou reading and language arts specialist/educator
McNall, Bruce professional sports executive, numismatist
Rothman, Claire Lynda entertainment executive
Sharman, William professional basketball team executive
Turner, Norris marketing professional
Vachon, Rogatien Rosaire (Rogie Vachon) professional hockey team executive
West, Jerry Alan professional basketball team executive
Worthy, James Ager former professional basketball player

Inverness
Welpott, Jack Warren photographer, educator

Irvine
Aigner, Dennis John economics educator, consultant
Allen, Joseph public relations executive
Alspach, Philip Halliday manufacturing company executive
Ang, Alfredo Hua-Sing civil engineering educator
Ayala, Francisco José geneticist, educator
Bander, Myron physics educator, university dean
Bartkus, Richard Anthony magazine publisher
Bastiaanse, Gerard C. lawyer
Beckman, Arnold Orville analytical instrument manufacturing company executive
Bennett, Albert Farrell biology educator
Bennett, Bruce Michael mathematics educator, musician
Bershad, Neil Jeremy electrical engineering educator
†Bonfield, Peter Leahy information technology executive
Bradley, Charles James, Jr. corporate human resources executive
Bradshaw, Ralph Alden biochemistry educator
Bron, Walter Ernest physics educator
†Bryant, Peter James biologist, educator
Burns, Donald Snow registered investment advisor, financial and business consultant
Burton, Michael Ladd anthropology educator
Butler, Merrill bank executive
Charles, M. Arthur endocrinologist, educator
Cheney, Darwin Leroy research foundation executive, medical educator
Cho, Zang Hee physics educator
Clark, Bruce Robert geology consultant
Clark, Karen Heath lawyer
Clark, Michael Phillip English educator
Cohen, Robert Stephen drama educator
Colino, Richard Ralph communications consultant
Combs, John Francis manufacturing company executive
Connolly, John Earle surgeon, educator
Cowart, Jim Cash business executive
Cunningham, Dennis Dean microbiology, molecular genetics educator
Cushman, Robert Fairchild political science educator, author, editor
Danziger, James Norris political science educator
Demetrescu, Mihai Constantin computer company executive, scientist
De Roes, Nanda Yvonne banker
Dorius, Kermit Parrish architect
Earhart, Donald Marion management consultant, health care company executive
Ericson, Jonathon Edward environmental science educator, researcher
Euster, Joanne Reed librarian
Fan, Hung Y. virology educator, consultant
Feldstein, Paul Joseph management educator
Felton, Jean Spencer physician
Fitch, Walter M(onroe) molecular biologist, educator
Fleischer, Everly Borah academic administrator
Freeman, Linton Clarke sociology educator
Friedenberg, Richard Myron radiology educator, physician
Friou, George Jacob immunologist, physician, educator
Garrison, Clayton university dean
Geis, Gilbert Lawrence sociology educator emeritus
George, Kattunilathu Oommen homoeopathic physician, educator
Gottschalk, Louis August neuropsychiatrist, psychoanalyst
Greenberger, Ellen psychologist, educator
Griffin, Gerald D. engineering company executive
Gupta, Sudhir immunologist, educator
Gutman, George Andre molecular biologist, educator
Guymon, Gary LeRoy civil engineering educator, consultant
Habermann, Norman restaurant group executive
Haggerty, Charles A. electronics executive
Halm, Dennis Ray academic administrator
†Henry, Walter L. cardiologist, educator
Herbert, Gavin Shearer health care products company executive
Hess, Cecil F. engineering executive
Hilker, Walter Robert, Jr. lawyer
Hine, Robert Van Norden, Jr. historian, educator
†Hoffman, Donald David cognitive and computer science educator
Holman, Diane Rosalie lawyer
Hoshi, Katsuo Kai international business executive
Jacobs, Donald Paul architect
Jamshidipour, Yousef bank executive, financial consultant, financial planner and advisor
Jeffers, Michael Bogue lawyer
Jones, Edward George anatomy and neurobiology professor, department chairman
Jones, Joie Pierce acoustician, educator, writer, scientist
Keating, James J. oil industry executive
Key, Mary Ritchie (Mrs. Audley E. Patton) linguist, author, educator
Kingman, Dong artist, educator
Kluger, Ruth German language educator, editor
Knight, Patricia Marie eye care company executive
Korb, Robert William former materials and processes engineer
Kossoff, Leslie Lynn quality improvement professional, educator
Kraemer, Kenneth Leo architect, urban planner, educator
†Krantz, Barry E. restaurant executive
Krieger, Murray English educator, author
Lambert, Robert Lowell scientific investigator
Lanyi, Janos Karoly biochemist, educator
Lave, Charles Arthur economics educator
Lehnert, Herbert Hermann foreign language educator
Lenhoff, Howard Maer biological sciences educator, academic administrator, activist
Lesonsky, Rieva editor in chief
Li, Peter Wai-Kwong mathematics educator
Lillyman, William John German language educator
Luce, R(obert) Duncan psychology educator
Maddy, Penelope Jo philosopher
Manara, James Anthony software executive, consultant
Margolis, Julius economist, educator
Marshall, Ellen Ruth lawyer
Martin, Jay Herbert psychoanalysis and English educator
McCann, Dean Merton lawyer, former pharmaceutical company executive
McCraw, Leslie G. engineering and construction company executive
Mc Culloch, Samuel Clyde history educator
Mc Gaugh, James Lafayette psychobiologist
McLaughlin, Calvin Sturgis biochemistry educator
McWilliams, Roger Dean physicist, educator
Menzel, Daniel Bruce toxicology educator
Miledi, Ricardo neurobiologist
Miller, Joseph Hillis comparative literature educator
Morrison, Gilbert Caffall psychiatrist
Mosier, Harry David, Jr. physician, educator
Moyer, Albert J. company executive, financial analyst
Muller, Edward Robert lawyer
Nalcioglu, Orhan physicist
Navajas, Gonzalo foreign language educator
Nelson, Robert E. public relations executive, political consultant
Nishida, Atsutoshi computer company executive
†Noda, Hiroshi automotive company executive
Nomura, Masayasu biological chemistry educator
Otth, Edward John, Jr. retired marine systems executive, retired naval officer
†Overman, Larry Eugene chemistry educator
Paul, Courtland Price landscape architect, planner
Penrod, James Wilford choreographer, dancer
Peterson, Arthur Jack finance company executive
Phalen, Robert F. community and environmental medicine educator, occupational health educator, research scientist
Power, Francis William newspaper publisher
†Quershey, Safi U. computer company executive
Qureshey, Safi U. electronics manufacturing company executive
†Radojevic, Danilo ballet dancer
Rady, Ernest S. thrift and loan association executive
Reines, Frederick physicist, educator
Rentzepis, Peter M. chemistry educator
Ristau, Kenneth Eugene, Jr. lawyer
Rollans, James O. service company executive
Rough, David S. marketing professional, consultant
Rowland, Frank Sherwood chemistry educator
Rubel, Arthur Joseph anthropologist, educator
Ruyter, Nancy Lee Chalfa dance educator
Rynn, Nathan physics educator, consultant
Santoro, Carmelo James electronics executive
Schonfeld, William Rost political science educator, researcher
Segal, D. Robert publishing and broadcast company executive
Shusterman, Neal Douglas author, screenwriter
Silverman, Paul Hyman parasitologist, former university official
Sirignano, William Alfonso aerospace and mechanical engineer, educator
Sklansky, Jack electrical and computer engineering educator, researcher
Small, Kenneth Alan economics educator
Sonoguchi, Kazuo automotive company executive
Sovie, Donald E. lawyer
Sperling, George cognitive scientist, educator
Stack, Geoffrey Lawrence real estate developer
Starr, Arnold neurologist, educator
Stolz, Neil N. financial services company executive
Stubberud, Allen Roger electrical engineering educator
Sutton, Dana Ferrin classics educator
†Swan, Richard Alan executive recruiter
Taagepera, Rein social science educator
Tennyson, Peter Joseph lawyer
Thomas, Joseph Allan lawyer
Tobis, Jerome Sanford physician
Treas, Judith Kay sociology educator
Trolinger, James Davis laser scientist
Tunney, Francis Richard, Jr. lawyer, corporate executive
van-den-Noort, Stanley physician, educator
†Van Vranken, David Lee chemist
Waggener, Susan Lee lawyer
Waitzkin, Howard Bruce physician, sociologist, educator

Wallis, Richard Fisher physicist, educator
Wan, Frederic Yui-Ming mathematician, educator
White, Douglas R. anthropology educator
White, Stephen Halley biophysicist, educator
Wiener, Jon history educator
Wilkening, Laurel Lynn university official, planetary scientist
Williams, James E. food products manufacturing company executive
Williams, S. Linn lawyer
Wintrode, Ralph Charles lawyer
Wolfsberg, Max chemist, educator
Woodruff, Truman O(wen) physicist, emeritus educator
†Yamano, Donald engineering executive
Young, Robert Anthony association director
Yuen, Thomas Chi Kwan business executive

Irwindale
DeKruif, Robert M. financial services company executive
Groom, John Miller food company executive
Hughes, Roger K. dairy and grocery store company executive
Rinehart, Charles R. savings and loan association executive

Jackson
Halvorson, William automotive executive

Keene
†Rodriguez, Arturo Salvador labor union official

Kensington
Connick, Robert Elwell chemistry educator
Loran, Erle artist
Malkiel, Yakov linguistics educator
Nathan, Leonard Edward writer, educator
Oppenheim, Antoni Kazimierz mechanical engineer
Stent, Gunther Siegmund molecular biologist, educator
Swanson, Guy Edwin social scientist, educator

Kentfield
Halprin, Anna Schuman (Mrs. Lawrence Halprin) dancer

La Canada Flintridge
Byrne, George Melvin physician
Clauser, Francis H. applied science educator
Costello, Francis William lawyer
Dales, Richard Clark history educator
Fry, Donald Owen broadcasting company executive
Lamson, Robert Woodrow retired school system administrator
Pickering, William Hayward physics educator, scientist
Read, William McClain retired oil company executive
Simmons, John Wesley oil company executive
Wallace, James Wendell lawyer

La Habra
Barnett, Albert E. physician
Burkle, Ronald W. food service executive
Chase, Cochrane advertising agency executive
Woyski, Margaret Skillman retired geology educator

La Honda
Waldhauer, Fred Donald health care executive

La Jolla
Alvariño De Leira, Angeles (Angeles Alvariño) biologist, oceanographer
Anderson, Richard William retired psychiatrist, educator
Anthony, Harry Antoniades city planner, architect, educator
Antin, David poet, critic
Antin, Eleanor artist
Arnold, James Richard chemist, educator
Arnold, Jean Ann health science facility administrator
†Asaro, Robert J. engineering educator
Asmus, John Fredrich physicist
Atkinson, Richard Chatham university chancellor, cognitive psychologist, educator
Attiyeh, Richard Eugene economics educator
Backus, George Edward theoretical geophysicist
Baesel, Stuart Oliver architect
Bardwick, Judith Marcia management consultant
Barnett, Tim P. meteorologist
Barrett-Connor, Elizabeth Louise epidemiologist, educator
Beebe, Mary Livingstone curator
Benson, Andrew Alm biochemistry educator
Bergan, John Jerome vascular surgeon
Bernstein, Eugene Felix vascular surgeon, medical educator
Beutler, Ernest physician, research scientist
Block, Melvin August surgeon, educator
Bloom, Floyd Elliott physician, research scientist
Boger, Dale L. chemistry educator
Borjas, George J(esus) economics educator
Bray, Nancy A. oceanographic administrator
Breitwieser, Charles John engineer, educator
Brueckner, Keith Allan theoretical physicist, educator
Buckingham, Michael John oceanography educator
Burbidge, E. Margaret astronomer, educator
Cain, William Stanley psychologist, educator
Carmichael, David Burton physician
Carson, John Congleton cardiologist, educator
Chang, William Shen Chie electrical engineering educator
Cheney, Carol endocrinologist
Chien, Shu physiology and bioengineering educator
Chodorow, Stanley Alan academic administrator
Christensen, Halvor Niels biochemist, educator
Conn, Robert William engineering science educator
†Continetti, Robert E. chemistry educator
Copley, David C. newspaper publishing company executive
Copley, Helen Kinney newspaper publisher
Cornelius, Wayne A., Jr. political scientist, educator
Cornette, William Magnus scientist, research director, company executive
Counts, Stanley Thomas aerospace consultant, retired naval officer, retired electronics company executive
Cox, Charles Shipley oceanography researcher, educator
Craig, Harmon geochemist, oceanographer
Cuevas, Jose Luis painter, illustrator
Dalessio, Donald John physician, neurologist, educator
Dashen, Roger Frederick physics educator, consultant
Davies, Hugh Marlais museum director
Dixon, Frank James medical scientist, educator
Doolittle, Russell Francis biochemist, educator
Dorsey, Dolores Florence corporate treasurer, business executive
Dreilinger, Charles Lewis (Chips Dreilinger) dean
Drell, William chemical company executive
Dulbecco, Renato biologist, educator
Dunn, David Joseph financial executive
Edelman, Gerald Maurice biochemist, educator
Edwards, Charles Cornell physician, research administrator
†Engvall, Eva biochemist
†Ewell, Charles Muse health care industry executive, consultant, educator
Farr, Richard Studley immunologist, educator, physician
Farson, Richard Evans psychologist
Feher, George physics and biophysics scientist, educator
Fisher, Frederick Hendrick oceanographer
Fishman, William Harold cancer research foundation executive, biochemist
Foley, L(ewis) Michael real estate executive
Fosburg, Richard Garrison cardiothoracic surgeon
Freedman, David Noel religion educator
Freedman, Michael Hartley mathematician, educator
Friedman, Paul Jay radiologist, chest radiologist, educator
Frieman, Edward Allan university administrator, educator
Fung, Yuan-Cheng Bertram bioengineering educator, author
†Garland, Cedric Frank epidemiologist, educator
Geckler, Richard Delph metal products company executive
Geiduschek, E(rnest) Peter biophysics and molecular biology educator
†Ghadiri, M. Reza chemistry educator
Gittes, Ruben Foster urological surgeon
Goldman, Stanford electrical engineer, scientist
Goodman, Murray chemistry educator
Gourevitch, Peter Alexis political science educator, dean
Granger, Clive William John economist, educator
Grier, Herbert Earl scientist, consultant
Grine, Donald Reaville geophysicist, research executive
Groves, Theodore Francis, Jr. economics educator
Guillemin, Roger C. L. physiologist
Haimo, Deborah Tepper mathematics educator
Halkin, Hubert mathematics educator, research mathematician
Harkins, Edwin L. music educator, performer
Harris, Philip Robert management and space psychologist
Harris, T George management and psychology editor
Haxo, Francis Theodore marine biologist
Helstrom, Carl Wilhelm electrical engineering educator
Hench, Philip Kahler physician
Hofmann, Alan Frederick biomedical educator, researcher
†Horres, Mary Milon medical librarian
Hoston, Germaine Annette political science educator
†Hudson, Richard Earl hospital administrator
Hunter, Tony (Anthony Rex Hunter) molecular biologist, educator
Imana, Jorge Garron artist
Intaglietta, Marcos bioengineering educator
Itano, Harvey Akio biochemistry educator
Jeffers, Donald E. retired insurance executive, consultant
Johnson, Allen Dress cardiologist
Jones, Charlie television sports announcer
Jones, Galen Everts microbiologist, educator
†Joyce, Gerald F. biochemist, educator
Kadonaga, James Takuro biochemist
Kaplan, Robert Malcolm health researcher, educator
Karten, Harvey Jules neurosciences educator
Keeling, Charles David oceanography educator
Keeney, Edmund Ludlow physician
Kerr, Donald MacLean, Jr. physicist
Kirchheimer, Arthur E(dward) lawyer, business executive
Klein, David foreign service officer
Klinman, Norman Ralph immunologist, medical educator
Knauss, John Atkinson federal agency administrator, oceanographer, educator, former university dean
Knox, Robert Arthur oceanographer, academic administrator
Lakier, Nancy S. health facility administrator
Lakoff, Sanford political scientist, educator
Lal, Devendra nuclear geophysics educator
Langacker, Ronald Wayne linguistics educator
Lauer, James Lothar physicist, educator
Lele, Padmakar Pratap physician, educator
Lerner, Richard Alan chemistry educator, scientist
Levy, Ralph engineering executive, consultant
Lewin, Ralph Arnold biologist
MacDonald, Gordon James Fraser geophysicist
MacDougall, John Douglas earth science educator
Maher, James R. laboratory administrator
Mandler, George psychologist
Mandler, Jean Matter psychologist, educator
Marti, Kurt chemistry educator
Martin, James John, Jr. retired consulting research firm executive, systems analyst
Masys, Daniel Richard medical school director
Mathews, Kenneth Pine physician, educator
McCammon, James Andrew chemistry educator
McDonald, Marianne classicist
Mc Elroy, William David biochemist, educator
McIlwain, Carl Edwin physicist
Milstein, Laurence Bennett electrical engineering educator, researcher
†Mirsky, Phyllis Simon librarian
Mogul, Leslie Anne marketing communications executive
Monaghan, Eileen artist
Monday, John Christian manufacturing company executive
Moore, F. Richard music educator
Morse, Jack Hatton utilities consultant
Mullis, Kary Banks biochemist
Munk, Walter Heinrich geophysics educator
†Myer, James Albert research science company executive
Nakamura, Robert Motoharu pathologist
Namias, Jerome meteorologist
Nelles, Maurice mechanical engineer, author
Newmark, Leonard Daniel linguistics educator
†Nicolaou, Kyriacos Costa chemistry educator
Nyhan, William Leo pediatrician, educator
Ogdon, Wilbur composer, music educator
Olafson, Frederick Arlan philosophy educator
O'Neil, Thomas Michael physicist, educator
†Orcutt, John Arthur geophysicist
Patton, Stuart biochemist, educator
Penhune, John Paul science company executive, electrical engineer
Penner, Stanford Solomon engineering educator
†Pierce, John Patrick epidemiology educator
Reissner, Eric (Max Erich Reissner) applied mechanics researcher
Reynolds, Roger Lee composer
Richey, Phil Horace former manufacturing executive, consultant
Ride, Sally Kristen physics educator, scientist, former astronaut
Robbins, John Michael, Jr. mortgage company executive
Rodin, Burton mathematics educator
Rosenblatt, Murray mathematics educator
Rosenbluth, Marshall Nicholas physicist, educator
Rotenberg, Manuel physics educator
Rudee, Mervyn Lea engineering educator, researcher
Ruiz, Ramon Eduardo history educator
Saier, Milton H, Jr. biology educator
Sandoval, Rik (Charles Sandoval) broadcasting executive
Schiller, Herbert Irving social scientist, author
Schmid-Schoenbein, Geert Wilfried biomedical engineer, educator
Sclater, John George geophysics educator
Shakespeare, Frank ambassador
Sham, Lu Jeu physics educator
Shannahan, William Paul lawyer
Sharpless, K. Barry chemist
Shor, George G., Jr. geophysicist, oceanographic administrator, engineer
Shuler, Kurt Egon chemist, educator
Siegan, Bernard Herbert lawyer, educator
Silverstone, Leon Martin pedodontist, cariologist, neuroscientist, educator, researcher
Simon, Ronald I. financial consultant
Skalak, Richard engineering mechanics educator, researcher
†Smith, Peter Hopkinson political scientist, consultant, author
Somerville, Richard Chapin James atmospheric scientist, educator
Spiess, Fred Noel oceanographer, educator
Spinweber, Cheryl Lynn research psychologist
Spiro, Melford Elliot anthropology educator
Spooner, Charles Edward university administrator, health educator
Starr, Ross Marc economist, educator
Steinberg, Daniel preventive medicine physician, educator
Stevens, Paul Irving manufacturing company executive
Stewart, John Lincoln university administrator
Streichler, Jerry human and technology resource development consultant
Suhl, Harry physics educator
Talke, Frank Eberhard education educator
Tan, Eng Meng immunologist, rheumatologist, biomedical scientist
Terras, Audrey Anne mathematics educator
Terry, Robert Davis neuropathologist, educator
Todd, Harry Williams aircraft propulsion system company executive
Van Lint, Victor Anton Jacobus physicist
Walker, Harold Osmonde newspaper and cable television executive
Wall, Frederick Theodore chemistry educator
Wallace, Robert George retired construction company executive, civil engineer
Watson, Kenneth Marshall physics educator
Weigle, William Oliver immunologist, educator
Wertheim, Robert Halley national security consultant
Wesling, Donald Truman English literature educator
West, John Burnard physiologist, educator
Whitaker, Eileen Monaghan artist
Wilkie, Donald Walter biologist, aquarium museum director
Wilkins, Floyd, Jr. retired lawyer, consultant
Williams, Forman Arthur engineering science educator, combustion theorist
Wolf, Jack Keil electrical engineer, educator
Wong, Chi-Huey chemistry educator
†Woodruff, David Scott biologist, educator
Wright, Andrew English literature educator
Wulbert, Daniel Eliot mathematician, educator
†Yang, Zhen research scientist
Yen, Samuel S(how)-C(hih) obstetrics and gynecology educator, reproductive endocrinologist
York, Herbert Frank physics educator, government official
ZoBell, Karl lawyer

La Mesa
Black, Eileen Mary elementary school educator
Burns, Kenneth Dean company executive, retired air force officer
Hansen, Grant Lewis retired aerospace and information systems executive
Schmidt, James Craig retired bank executive, bankruptcy examiner
Tarson, Herbert Harvey university administrator emeritus
Williams, Carlton Hinkle dentist

La Mirada
Brennan, Joan Stevenson federal judge
Henderson, Thelton Eugene federal judge
Legge, Charles Alexander federal judge
Lingenfelter, Sherwood Galen university provost, anthropology educator
Nash, Sylvia Dotseth religious organization executive, consultant
Walker, Vaughn R. federal judge
Zirpoli, Alfonso Joseph federal judge

La Puente
Perret, Joseph Aloysius banker, consultant
Reddy, Nagendranath K. biochemist, researcher
Reilly, John E. automotive executive
†Rieske, Gordon food products executive
Sheridan, Christopher Frederick human resources executive

La Quinta
Boysen, Harry obstetrician, gynecologist
Hartley, Celia Love nursing educator, nursing administrator

Houze, William Cunningham executive recruiter, management consultant

La Selva
Brown, Alan Charlton retired aeronautical engineer

La Verne
Morgan, Stephen Charles academic administrator

Lafayette
Alexander, Kenneth Lewis editorial cartoonist
Coffey, Susanne Norton communications company executive
Dethero, J. Hambright banker
Harlock, Michael J. architect
Hemphill, Norma Jo special event planning and tour company executive
Kahn, Robert Irving management consultant
Kapp, Eleanor Jeanne impressionistic artist, writer, researcher
Laird, Alan Douglas Kenneth mechanical engineering educator
Lewis, Sheldon Noah technology consultant
Moore, Calvin C. mathematics educator, administrator
Peirano, Lawrence Edward civil engineer
Sandberg, Robert Alexis former research organization administrator
Uilkema, Gayle Burns mayor, councilwoman, business educator

Laguna Beach
Adler, Jeffrey D. political consultant, public affairs consultant, crisis management expert
Arterburn, Stephen Forrest health care company executive
Banuelos, Betty Lou rehabilitation nurse
Bent, Alan Edward political science educator, administrator
Bezar, Gilbert Edward retired aerospace company executive, volunteer
Calderwood, James Lee former English literature educator, writer
Dale, Leon Andrew economist, educator
Fagin, Henry public administration consultant
Garfin, Louis actuary
Hanauer, Joe Franklin real estate executive
Smith, Leslie Roper hospital administrator
Taylor, Theodore Langhans author
Warner, Robert S. company director, former accountant
Wilson, James Newman retired laboratory executive
Wolf, Karl Everett aerospace and communications corporation executive
Youngquist, Andrew Lance construction executive

Laguna Hills
Batdorf, Samuel B(urbridge) physicist
Burrows, Gates Wilson retired architect
Faw, Duane Leslie retired military officer, law educator, lay worker, author
Herold, Ralph Elliott motion picture arts educator
Howard, Hildegarde (Mrs. Henry Anson Wylde) paleontologist
Hussey, William Bertrand retired foreign service officer
Iberall, Arthur Saul physicist, publisher
James, Sidney Lorraine television executive
Kaplan, Sidney Joseph sociologist, educator
Larson, Harry Thomas electronics engineer
Lederer, Jerome aerospace safety engineer, educator
Leydorf, Frederick Leroy lawyer
Lindquist, Raymond Irving clergyman
Linton, Frederick M. strategic planning consultant
Luhring, John William former bank executive
Mc Closkey, Paul N., Jr. lawyer, former congressman
Mc Guire, Joseph William business educator
Miller, Eldon Earl corporate business publications consultant, retired manufacturing company executive
Rabe, David William playwright
Rossiter, Bryant William chemistry consultant
Wheatley, Melvin Ernest, Jr. retired bishop

Laguna Niguel
Carr, Bernard Francis hospital administrator
Nelson, Alfred John retired pharmaceutical company executive
Pierce, Hilda (Hilda Herta Harmel) painter
York, James Orison real estate executive

Lagunitas
Holman, Arthur Stearns artist

Lake Elsinore
Corral, Jeanie Beleyn journalist, school board administrator
Wilson, Sonja Mary secondary education educator, consultant, poet

Lake Forest
Lindsell, Harold clergyman

Lakewood
Bogdan, James Thomas secondary education educator, electronics researcher and developer
Fenwick, James H(enry) editor

Lancaster
Crew, Aubrey Torquil aerospace inspector
Hodges, Vernon Wray mechanical engineer

Landers
Landers, Vernette Trosper writer, educator, association executive

Larkspur
Chilvers, Robert Merritt lawyer
Kirk, Gary Vincent investment advisor
Marker, Marc Linthacum lawyer, investment company executive
Roulac, Stephen E. real estate consultant
†Wilde, Paul K. computer company executive

Lemon Grove
Whitehead, Marvin Delbert plant pathologist

Lemoore
†Atwell, Clarence, Jr. Indian tribal leader

Livermore
Alder, Berni Julian *physicist*
Bennett, Alan Jerome *electronics executive, physicist*
Brown, Cathie *city official*
†Campbell, Edward Michael *research physicist, science administrator*
Carley, James French *chemical and plastics engineer*
†Dane, Paul Nelson *communication engineer, retired*
Dyer, Richard Hutchins *risk management executive*
†Glinsky, Michael Edwin *research physicist*
Hazen, Judi *elementary school educator*
Hulet, Ervin Kenneth *retired nuclear chemist*
Johnson, Roy Ragnar *electrical engineer*
Kidder, Ray Edward *physicist, consultant*
King, Ray John *electrical engineer*
Kirkwood, Robert Keith *applied physicist*
Leith, Cecil Eldon, Jr. *retired physicist*
Max, Claire Ellen *physicist*
Nuckolls, John Hopkins *physicist, researcher*
†Porter, James R. *computer company executive*
Schock, Robert Norman *geophysicist*
Sheem, Sang Keun *fiber optics engineering professional*
Shotts, Wayne J. *nuclear scientist, federal agency administrator*
Tarter, Curtis Bruce *physicist, science administrator*
Wong, Joe *physical chemist*
Wood, Donald Craig *marketing professional*

Livingston
Fox, Robert August *food company executive*

Lodi
Bennett, Michael William *museum and historical society director*

Loma Linda
Adey, William Ross *physician*
Bailey, Leonard Lee *surgeon*
Behrens, Berel Lyn *physician, academic administrator*
Bull, Brian Stanley *pathology educator, medical consultant, business executive*
Coggin, Charlotte Joan *cardiologist, educator*
Condon, Stanley Charles *gastroenterologist*
Hinshaw, David B., Sr. *hospital administrator*
Hinshaw, David B., Jr. *radiologist*
Johns, Varner Jay, Jr. *medical educator*
Klooster, Judson *academic administrator, dentistry educator*
Kuhn, Irvin Nelson *hematologist, oncologist*
Llaurado, Josep G. *nuclear medicine physician, scientist*
Longo, Lawrence Daniel *physiologist, gynecologist*
Mace, John Weldon *pediatrician*
Maurice, Don *personal care industry executive*
Moss, Susan Linda *nurse*
Peterson, John Eric *physician, educator*
Register, Ulma Doyle *nutrition educator*
Rendell-Baker, Leslie *anesthesiologist, educator*
Roberts, Walter Herbert Beatty *anatomist*
Slater, James Munro *radiation oncologist*
Slattery, Charles Wilbur *biochemistry educator*
Stilson, Walter Leslie *radiologist, educator*
Wilcox, Ronald Bruce *biochemistry educator, researcher*
Zolber, Kathleen Keen *nutrition educator*

Lompoc
Woodberry, Paul Francis *real estate executive*

Long Beach
Alibrandi, Joseph Francis *diversified industrial company executive*
Alkon, Ellen Skillen *physician*
Anand, Rajen S. *physiologist*
Anatol, Karl W. E. *provost*
Anderson, Gerald Verne *retired aerospace company executive*
Bauer, Roger Duane *chemistry educator, science consultant*
Beebe, Sandra E. *retired English language educator, artist, writer*
Beljan, John Richard *university administrator, medical educator*
Brent, Paul Leslie *mechanical engineering educator*
Brisco, Valerie *track and field athlete*
Chapman, Mayer *lawyer*
†Creel, Diane Claypoole *marketing professional*
Dean, Charles Thomas *industrial arts educator, academic administrator*
de Soto, Simon *mechanical engineer*
Dillon, Michael Earl *engineering executive, mechanical engineer, educator*
Domondon, Oscar *dentist*
Donald, Eric Paul *aeronautical engineer, inventor*
Dorrenbacher, Carl James *aerospace transportation executive*
Ferreira, Armando Thomas *sculptor, educator*
Fornia, Dorothy Louise *educator*
Giles, Jean Hall *retired corporate executive*
Giugni, Everett Thomas *school administrator*
Glenn, Constance White *art museum director, educator, consultant*
Hancock, John Walker, III *banker*
Harmon Brown, Valarie Jean *hospital laboratory director, information systems executive*
Hobgood, E(arl) Wade *college dean*
Hood, Robert H., Jr. *aircraft manufacturing company executive*
Hu, Chi Yu *physicist, educator*
Jeffery, James Nels *protective services official*
Jensen, James Leslie *chemistry educator, dean*
Kohn, Gerhard *psychologist, educator*
Kokaska, Charles James *educational psychologist*
Kumar, Rajendra *electrical engineering educator*
Kurnick, Nathaniel Bertrand *oncology educator, researcher*
Lathrop, Ann *librarian, educator*
Lathrop, Irvin Tunis *retired academic dean, educator*
Lauda, Donald Paul *university dean*
Lee, Isaiah Chong-Pie *social worker, educator*
†Levinson, David Maynard *music critic*
†Light, Richard Wayne *medical educator*
Lobdell, Robert Charles *retired newspaper executive*
Loganbill, G. Bruce *logopedic pathologist*
McDonough, Patrick Dennis *university executive*
McGuire, James Charles *aircraft company executive*
McMillan, James Thomas *aerospace company executive*
Mears, Gary H. *career military officer*
Mills, Don Harper *pathology and psychiatry educator*
Muchmore, Don Moncrief *museum, foundation, educational, financial fund raising and public opinion consulting firm administrator*
Mullins, Ruth Gladys *pediatrics nurse*
Munitz, Barry *chief university administrator, English literature educator, business consultant*
Myers, John Wescott *aviation executive*
†Nelson, Harold Bernhard *museum director*
†O'Neill, Beverly Lewis *mayor, former college president*
Owen, Christina L. *lawyer*
Patino, Douglas Xavier *foundation and university administrator*
Pokras, Sheila Frances *judge*
Polakoff, Keith Ian *historian, university administrator*
Rea, William *oil industry executive*
Ridder, Daniel Hickey *newspaper publisher*
Roth, Robert August *university administrator*
Ruszkiewicz, Carolyn Mae *newspaper editor*
Sato, Eunice Noda *former mayor, consultant*
Scepanski, Jordan Michael *librarian, administrator*
Schaufele, Roger Donald *aircraft company executive*
Schinnerer, Alan John *entrepreneur*
Seita, Yukifusa *electronics executive*
Snape, William John, Jr. *physician*
Stetler, Charles Edward *English language educator*
Sun, Chieh *electronics company executive*
Swatek, Frank Edward *microbiology educator*
Talmadge, Mary Christine *nursing educator*
Tang, Paul Chi Lung *philosophy educator*
Taylor, Reese Hale, Jr. *lawyer, former government administrator*
Thompson, William Ancker *intramural-recreational sports director, educator*
Todd, Malcolm Clifford *surgeon*
Vogel, William Charles *advertising executive*
Wheeler, Diana Jean Miller *secondary education educator*
Williams, Donald Clyde *lawyer*
Winget, Clifford *oil industry executive*
Wise, George Edward *lawyer*
Zappe, John Paul *city editor, educator*

Loomis
Hartmann, Frederick Howard *political science educator emeritus*

Los Alamitos
Ayling, Henry Faithful *writer, editor, consultant*
Booth, John Nicholls *minister, magician, writer, photographer*
†Egas, Sandy Steers *import/export and travel consultant*
Iceland, William Frederick *engineering consultant*
Myers, Edwin *think-tank executive*
Spiegel, Marilyn Harriet *real estate executive*
Weinberger, Frank *information systems advisor*

Los Altos
Allen, Michael Graham *management consultant*
Barker, William Alfred *physics educator*
Beer, Clara Louise Johnson *retired electronics executive*
Bell, Chester Gordon *computer engineering company executive*
Besser, Les *electrical engineer*
Carsten, Jack Craig *venture capitalist*
Critzer, William Ernest *association executive*
Drachler, Norman *retired education educator*
Fondahl, John Walker *civil engineering educator*
Fraknoi, Andrew *astronomy educator, astronomical society executive*
Fraser-Smith, Elizabeth Birdsey *biologist*
Frey, Christian Miller *research center executive*
Ginzton, Edward Leonard *retired engineering company executive*
Gray, Robert Donald *mayor*
Hall, Charles Frederick *space scientist, government administrator*
Hammond, Donald Leroy *computer company executive*
Hinckley, Gregory Keith *financial executive*
Johnson, Richard Damerau *aerospace scientist*
Jones, Robert Thomas *aerospace scientist*
Kazan, Benjamin *research engineer*
Miller, Ronald Grant *journalist*
Mullaley, Robert Charles *manufacturing company executive*
Oder, Frederic Carl Emil *retired aerospace company executive, consultant*
Peterson, Victor Lowell *aerospace engineer, management consultant*
†Robinson, Jacques Alan *electric manufacturing company executive*
Sharpe, Roland Leonard *retired engineering company executive, earthquake and structural engineering consultant*
Twersky, Victor *mathematical physicist, educator*
van Tamelen, Eugene Earle *chemist, educator*
Wickham, Kenneth Gregory *retired army officer, institute official*
Wilbur, Colburn Sloan *foundation administrator, chief executive officer*

Los Angeles
Aaron, Benjamin *law educator, arbitrator*
Abel, Richard L. *legal educator, lawyer*
†Abeles, Kim Victoria *artist*
Abernethy, Robert John *real estate developer*
Abrams, Norman *law educator, university administrator*
Adam, Ken *production designer*
Adamek, Charles Andrew *lawyer*
Adams, Bryan *vocalist, composer*
Adams, William Wesley, III *architect*
Adamson, Arthur Wilson *chemistry educator*
Adell, Hirsch *lawyer*
Adler, Douglas B. *lawyer*
Adler, Erwin Ellery *lawyer*
Afifi, Abdelmonem A. *biostatistics educator, academic dean*
†Ahlberg, Mac *cinematographer*
Aki, Keiiti *seismologist, educator*
Alarcon, Arthur Lawrence *federal judge*
Alexander, Herbert E. *political scientist*
Alkon, Paul Kent *English language educator*
Allen, Debbie *actress, dancer, director, choreographer*
Allen, Michael John Bridgman *English educator*
Allen, William Richard *retired economist*
Aller, Lawrence Hugh *astronomy educator, researcher*
Alley, Kirstie *actress*
Alleyne, Reginald H., Jr. *legal educator*
†Allison, Laird Burl *business educator*
†Alonzo, John A. *cinematographer, director*
Alpers, Edward Alter *history educator*
Altfeld, Sheldon Isaac *communications executive*
Alvarez, Rodolfo *sociology educator, consultant*
Amneus, D. A. *English language educator*
Amos, John *actor, producer, director*
Anastos, Rosemary Park *retired higher education educator*
Anawalt, Patricia Rieff *anthropologist*
Andersen, Henning *linguistics educator*
Andersen, Ronald Max *health services educator, researcher*
Anderson, Alison Grey *law educator*
Anderson, Austin Gilman *economics research company consultant*
Anderson, Daryl *actor*
Anderson, George Edward *financial services company executive*
Anderson, Jane A. *scriptwriter*
Anderson, Michael Joseph *film director*
Anderson, Richard Norman *actor, film producer*
Anderson, Robert *retired manufacturing company executive*
Anderson, W. French *genticist, biochemist, physician*
Angeloff, Dann V. *investment banking executive*
Anka, Paul *singer, composer*
Ansen, David B. *critic, writer*
Apfel, Gary *lawyer*
Appleby, Joyce Oldham *historian*
April, Rand Scott *lawyer*
Apt, Leonard *physician*
Arant, Eugene Wesley *lawyer*
Arbib, Michael Anthony *computer scientist, educator, neuroscientist, cybernetician*
Archer, Anne *actress*
Archerd, Army (Armand Archerd) *columnist, television commentator*
Argue, John Clifford *lawyer*
Armstrong, C. Michael *computer business executive*
Armstrong, Lloyd, Jr. *university official, physics educator*
Armstrong, Orville *judge*
Arnault, Ronald J. *petroleum company executive*
Arnold, Dennis B. *lawyer*
Arnold, Jeanne Eloise *anthropologist, educator*
Aroni, Samuel *architecture and urban planning educator*
Arora, Shirley Lease *Spanish language educator*
Ash, Roy Lawrence *business executive*
Ashforth, Alden *musician, educator*
Ashland, Calvin Kolle *federal judge*
Ashley, Sharon Anita *pediatric anesthesiologist*
Asimow, Michael R. *lawyer, educator*
Askanas-Engel, Valerie *neurologist, educator, researcher*
Askin, Richard Henry, Jr. *entertainment company executive*
Asner, Edward *actor*
†Asquith, Ronald H. *petroleum corporate executive*
Astin, Alexander William *education educator*
Astin, John Allen *actor, director, writer*
Avallone, Michael Angelo *author*
Avery, Robert Dean *lawyer*
Axon, Donald Carlton *architect*
Ayres, James Marx *mechanical engineer*
Babikian, George H. *petroleum products company executive*
Badie, Ronald Peter *banker*
Bahr, Ehrhard *Germanic languages and literature educator*
Bailey, Alan J. *film company executive*
Bain, Conrad Stafford *actor*
Baird, Lourdes G. *federal judge*
Baker, Kathy Whitton *actress*
Baker, Lawrence Colby, Jr. *insurance company executive*
Baker, Robert Frank *molecular biologist, educator*
Baker, William Garrett, Jr. *investment banker*
Bakshi, Ralph *film and television producer, director*
Banner, Bob *television producer, director*
Bao, Joseph Yue-Se *orthopaedist, microsurgeon, educator*
Barash, Anthony Harlan *lawyer*
†Barber, Gary *motion picture company executive*
Barbera, Joseph *motion picture and television producer, cartoonist*
Bardach, Sheldon Gilbert *lawyer*
Barker, Robert William *television personality*
Barker, Wiley Franklin *surgeon, educator*
Barrall, James D. C. *lawyer*
Barrio, Jorge Raul *medical educator*
Barry, Gene *actor*
†Barry, John *composer*
Barry, Julian *playwright, screenwriter*
Barry, Philip Semple *television and film producer*
Bart, Peter Benton *newspaper editor, film producer, novelist*
Barton, Alan Joel *lawyer*
Barza, Harold A. *lawyer*
Basil, Douglas Constantine *author, educator*
Bass, Barbara DeJong *film assistant director, free-lance writer*
Bass, Saul *graphic designer, filmmaker*
Bassett, Angela *actress*
Batres, Eduardo *computer model builder, animator*
Battaglia, Philip Maher *lawyer*
Bauman, John Andrew *law educator*
Baumann, Richard Gordon *lawyer*
Bauml, Franz Heinrich *German language educator*
†Baxter, Frank Edward *brokerage executive*
Bayless, Raymond *artist*
Baylor, Elgin Gay *professional basketball team executive*
Beach, Roger C. *oil company executive*
Beard, Ronald Stratton *lawyer*
†Beart, Robert W., Jr. *surgeon, educator*
Beck, John Christian *physician, educator*
Beckwith, Charles Emilio *English educator*
Bekey, George Albert *computer scientist, educator, engineer*
Bell, Lee Phillip *television personality, television producer*
Bell, Wayne Steven *lawyer*
Belleville, Philip Frederick *lawyer*
Belnap, David Foster *journalist*
†Belzer, Richard *comedian, TV show host, actor*
Bender, Charles William *lawyer*
Bendix, Helen Irene *lawyer*
Bennett, Charles Franklin, Jr. *biogeographer, educator*
Bennett, Harve (Harve Fischman) *television and film producer, writer*
Bennis, Warren Gameliel *business administration educator, author, consultant*
Benson, Sidney William *chemistry researcher*
Berg, Philip *religious denomination administrator*
Berger, Dan Lee *newspaper wine columnist*
†Berger, Peter E. *film editor*
Bergman, Alan *lyricist, writer*
Bergman, (Ernst) Ingmar *film director, writer*
Bergman, Marilyn Keith *lyricist, writer*
Bergman, Paul Bruce *law educator*
Berle, Milton (Milton Berlinger) *actor*
Berman, Arthur Malcolm *newspaper editor*
Bermingham, Richard P. *restaurant and food products company executive*
Bernacchi, Richard Lloyd *lawyer*
Bernhard, Herbert Ashley *lawyer*
Bernhard, Sandra *actress, comedienne, singer*
Bernheimer, Martin *music critic*
Bernstein, Arthur Harold *venture capital executive*
Bernstein, Elmer *composer, conductor*
Bernstein, Sol *cardiologist, educator*
Berry, Richard Douglas *architectural educator, urban planner and designer*
Bethune, Zina *actress, dancer, singer, choreographer*
Bhaumik, Mani Lal *physicist*
Bice, Scott Haas *lawyer, educator*
Biederman, Donald Ellis *lawyer*
Bierstedt, Peter Richard *lawyer, entertainment industry consultant*
Biles, John Alexander *pharmacology educator, chemistry educator*
Binder, David A. *lawyer, educator*
Bird, Peter *geology educator*
Birnbaum, Henrik *Slavic languages and literature educator*
Birren, James Emmett *university research center executive*
Bishop, Leah Margaret *lawyer*
Bishop, Sidney Willard *lawyer*
Black, Donna Ruth *lawyer*
Blackburn, Daniel M. *correspondent*
Blackman, Lee L. *lawyer*
Blackwelder, Ron Forest *engineering educator, consultant, researcher*
Blahd, William Henry *physician*
Blake, Michael *writer*
Blake, Robert (Michael Gubitosi) *actor*
Blakely, Edward James *economics educator*
Blankenship, Edward G. *architect*
Blitz, Stephen M. *lawyer*
Bloch, Paul *public relations executive*
Bloland, Paul Anson *psychology educator emeritus*
Bloom, Alan *lawyer*
Blumberg, Grace Ganz *law educator, lawyer*
Boak, Ruth Alice *physician, educator*
Bobbitt, Leroy *lawyer*
Bobrow, Michael Lawrence *architect*
Bochco, Steven *screenwriter, television producer*
Bodkin, Henry Grattan, Jr. *lawyer*
Boerlage, Frans Theodoor *opera director, music educator*
Bogaard, William Joseph *lawyer*
Bogen, Andrew E. *lawyer*
Bohle, Sue *public relations executive*
Boime, Albert Isaac *art history educator*
Bok, Dean *cell biologist, educator*
Bomes, Stephen D. *lawyer*
Bondareff, William *psychiatry educator*
Bonner, Robert Cleve *lawyer*
Boone, Pat (Charles Eugene Boone) *singer, actor*
Boonshaft, Hope Judith *public relations executive*
Borko, Harold *information scientist, psychologist, educator*
Borsch, Frederick Houk *bishop*
Borsting, Jack Raymond *business administration educator*
Bortman, David *lawyer*
Bosl, Phillip L. *lawyer*
Bosley, Tom *actor*
Bost, Thomas Glen *lawyer*
Bostwick, Barry *actor*
†Boswell, James Douglas *medical research executive*
Bothwell, Dorr *artist*
Bottger, William Carl, Jr. *lawyer*
Bower, Allan Maxwell *lawyer*
Bower, Paul George *lawyer*
†Bowers, John William *church official*
Bowlin, Michael Ray *oil company executive*
Boyarsky, Benjamin William *journalist*
Boyd, Harry Dalton *lawyer, former insurance company executive*
Boylan, John Patrick *record producer, songwriter*
Brach, Gérard *screenwriter*
Bradshaw, Carl John *investor, lawyer, consultant*
Bradshaw, Murray Charles *musicologist*
Braginsky, Stanislav Iosifovich *physicist, geophysicist, researcher*
Branca, John Gregory *lawyer, consultant*
Branch, Taylor *writer*
Brassell, Roselyn Strauss *lawyer*
Bratt, Bengt Erik *academic administrator, consulting engineer*
Braudy, Leo Beal *English language educator, author*
Braun, David A(dlai) *lawyer*
Braun, Zev *motion picture and television producer*
†Brecht, Albert Odell *library and information technology administrator*
Breidenbach, Francis Anthony *lawyer*
Breslow, Lester *physician, educator*
Bressan, Paul Louis *lawyer*
Brest, Martin *film director*
Breuer, Melvin Allen *electrical engineering educator*
Bricker, Seymour (Murray) *lawyer*
†Bricmont, Wendy Greene *motion picture film editor*
Bridges, B. Ried *lawyer*
Briley, John Richard *writer*
Brinsley, John Harrington *lawyer*
Broad, Eli *financial services executive*
Broadhurst, Norman Neil *manufacturing executive*
Broccoli, Albert Romolo *motion picture producer*
†Brochu, Don *film editor*
Brockett, Peter Charles *financial executive*
Broderick, Carlfred Bartholomew *sociology educator*
Broiles, Steven Anthony *lawyer*
Brolin, James (James Brunderlin) *actor*
Bromberg, Robert *aerospace company executive*
Brotman, David Joel *architectural firm executive*
Broussard, Thomas Rollins *lawyer*
†Brown, E. Lynn *minister*
Brown, Edmund Gerald (Pat Brown) *lawyer, former governor of California*
Brown, Louis Morris *lawyer, educator*
†Brubaker, William Rogers *sociology educator*
Buchman, Mark Edward *banker*
Buchwald, Nathaniel Avrom *neurophysiologist*
Buckley, Betty Lynn *actress*
Bucy, Richard Snowden *aerospace engineering and mathematics educator, consultant*
Bufford, Samuel Lawrence *federal judge*
Bulmer, Connie J. *film librarian*
Burch, Robert Dale *lawyer*
Burke, William M. *lawyer*
Burke, Yvonne Watson Brathwaite (Mrs. William A. Burke) *lawyer*
Burns, Dan W. *manufacturing company executive*
Burns, Marvin Gerald *lawyer*
Burns, Robert Ignatius *historian, educator, clergyman*

Burrows, James television and motion picture director, producer
Busby, Jheryl record company executive
Busse, Michael Clifford newspaper advertising executive
†Butler, Donald Earnest company executive
Butler, Jeffrey Sheridan publisher
†Butler, Octavia Estelle free-lance writer
Byers, Nina physics educator
Byrd, Christine Waterman Swent lawyer
Byrne, Jerome Camillus lawyer
Byrne, William Matthew, Jr. federal judge
Caan, James actor, director
†Cafaro, Albert recording industry executive
†Caldwell, Alethea Otti health care systems executive
Caldwell-Portenier, Patty Jean Grosskopf advocate, educator
Calhoun, Gordon James lawyer
Callender, William Lacey savings and loan executive, lawyer
†Cambern, Donn film editor
Campbell, Douglas Argyle securities broker
Campbell, Glen singer, entertainer
Campbell, Kenneth Eugene, Jr. vertebrate paleontologist
†Campbell, Malcolm film editor
Campion, Robert Thomas manufacturing company executive
Camron, Roxanne editor
Cannell, Stephen Joseph television writer, producer, director
Cannon, Louis Simeon journalist, author
Capron, Alexander Morgan lawyer, educator
Carabillo, Virginia Anne (Toni Carabillo) writer, editor, graphic designer
Cardone, Bonnie Jean photojournalist
Carlin, George Denis comedian
Carlson, Robert E. lawyer
Carlson, Terrance L. lawyer
Carpenter, David Roland life insurance executive
†Carpenter, Russell cinematographer
Carr, Allan film and stage producer, celebrity representative
Carr, Willard Zeller, Jr. lawyer
Carroll, Pat actress
Carson, Edward Mansfield banker
†Carter, Richard production designer
Caruso, David actor
Castaneda, Carlos anthropologist, author
Castro, Leonard Edward lawyer
Cates, Gilbert film, theater, television producer and director
Cathcart, David Arthur lawyer
Cato, Gloria Maxine secondary education educator, school program administrator
Catron, William G. lawyer
Catton, Ivan mechanical engineer
Cavanagh, John Edward lawyer
Cecchetti, Giovanni poet, Italian language educator, literary critic
Cecil, John Lamont retired bank executive, lawyer
†Chabin, James Boyd entertainment company executive
Chacko, George Kuttickal systems science educator, consultant
Chamberlain, Wilton Norman retired professional basketball player
†Champagne, Duane Willard sociology educator
Champlin, Charles Davenport television host, book critic, writer
Chandor, Stebbins Bryant pathologist
Chang, Henry Chung-Lien library administrator
Chapman, Orville Lamar chemist, educator
Charen, Mona syndicated columnist
Charisse, Cyd (Tula Ellice Finklea) actress, dancer
Charles, Glen television producer
Charles, Les television producer
Charles, Ray (Ray Charles Robinson) musician, singer, composer
Charwat, Andrew Franciszek engineering educator
Chase, Chevy (Cornelius Crane Chase) comedian, actor, author
Chassman, Leonard Fredric labor union administrator
Chavez, Victor Edwin judge
Cheng, Hsien Kei aeronautics educator
Cheng, Tsen-Chung electrical engineering educator
Chernesky, John Joseph, Jr. naval officer
Chernick, Richard lawyer
Cherry, James Donald physician
Chester, Marvin physics educator
Chetwynd, Lionel screenwriter, producer, director
†Chew, Richard film editor
Chiate, Kenneth Reed lawyer
Chilingarian, George Varos petroleum, environmental and civil engineering educator
Ching, Anthony lawyer
Chobotov, Vladimir Alexander aerospace engineer, educator
Chomsky, Marvin J. director
Christol, Carl Quimby lawyer, political science educator
Chu, Morgan lawyer
Chu, Wesley Wei-Chin computer science educator, consultant
Churchill, James Allen lawyer
Cicciarelli, James Carl immunology educator
Ciccone, Amy Navratil art librarian
Clark, Burton Robert sociologist, educator
†Clark, Marcia Rachel prosecutor
Clark, R. Bradbury lawyer
Clark, Richard lawyer
Clarke, Peter communications and health educator
Clay, Andrew (Dice) (Andrew Clay Silverstein) comedian
Clemente, Carmine Domenic anatomist, educator
Cline, David Bruce physicist, educator
Cobb, Jewel Plummer former college president, educator
Cochran, Johnnie L., Jr. lawyer
Cochran, Sachiko Tomie radiologist
Cocker, Joe popular musician
Coffey, C. Shelby, III newspaper editor
Cohan, John Robert lawyer
Cohen, Cynthia Marylyn lawyer
Cohen, Daniel Morris museum administrator, marine biology researcher
Cohen, Gary J. lawyer
Cohen, Leonard (Norman Cohen) poet, novelist, musician, songwriter
Cohen, S(tephen) Marshall philosophy educator
Cohen, William Alan marketing educator, author, consultant
†Colburn, Philip William automotive company executive
Cole, Curtis Allen lawyer
†Cole, Jay N. magazine publisher
Coleman, Charles Clyde physicist, educator
Coleman, Paul Jerome, Jr. physicist, educator
Coleman, Rexford Lee lawyer, educator
Coleman, Roger William institutional food distribution company executive
Collias, Elsie Cole zoologist
Collier, Charles Arthur, Jr. lawyer
Colton, Robert Craig lawyer
Conniff, Ray popular musician, conductor, composer, arranger
Cooder, Ry recording artist, guitarist
Cook, Lodwrick Monroe petroleum company executive
Coolbaugh, Carrie Weaver librarian
Coombs, John Wendell financial service executive
Coombs, Robert Holman sociologist, medical educator, author
Cooper, Edwin Lowell anatomy educator
Cooper, Leon Melvin lawyer
Coppola, Robert E. lawyer
Corea, Chick (Armando Corea) pianist, composer
Corman, Roger William motion picture producer, director
Cornwall, John Michael physics educator, consultant, researcher
Coroniti, Ferdinand Vincent physics educator, consultant
Corwin, Norman writer, director, producer
Cotliar, George J. newspaper editor
Cotter, George Edward former airline company executive
Coughlin, Sister Magdalen college chancellor
Counts, James Curtis management consultant
†Cox, Betsy costume designer
Cram, Donald James chemistry educator
Crandall, Edward David medical educator
†Cravens, Virginia Lee church official
Crippens, David Lee broadcast executive
Crispo, Lawrence Walter judge
†Crockett, Donald Harold composer, university educator
Crombie, Douglass Darnill aerospace communications engineer, former government official
Crosby, Peter Alan management consultant
Cross, Glenn Laban engineering executive, development planner
Cross, James Edwin lawyer
Crow, John Armstrong writer, educator
†Crow, Sheryl singer/songwriter, musician
Crystal, Billy comedian, actor
Cuadra, Carlos Albert information scientist, management executive
Cummings, Thomas Gerald management educator, consultant
Currie, Malcolm Roderick aerospace and automotive executive, scientist
Curtis, Daniel M. film director
Curtis, John E., Jr. lawyer
Curtiss, Thomas, Jr. lawyer, educator
D'Accone, Frank Anthony music educator
Dallek, Robert history educator
Dalton, Larry Raymond chemistry educator, researcher, consultant
Dangerfield, Rodney (Jack Roy Dangerfield) comedian, actor, author
Daniels, Jeff actor
Daniels, John Peter lawyer
Danoff, Dudley Seth surgeon, urologist
Dante, Joe film director
Danziger, Louis graphic designer, educator
Darby, G. Harrison lawyer
Darby, Michael Rucker economist, educator
†Darling, Juanita Marie correspondent
Davidson, Ezra C., Jr. physician, educator
Davidson, Gordon theatrical producer, director
Davidson, Herbert Alan Near Eastern languages and cultures educator
Davies, John G. federal judge
Davis, Andrew film director, screenwriter
Davis, Edmond Ray lawyer
†Davis, Gray state controller
Davis, Ossie actor, author
Davis, Ronald artist, printmaker
Davis, Sybil Alicia obstetrician gynecologist
Dawson, John Myrick plasma physics educator
Day, Anthony newspaper correspondent
Dearing, Vinton Adams retired English language educator
DeBard, Roger investment executive
De Brier, Donald Paul lawyer
de Castro, Hugo Daniel lawyer
DeChellis, Michael Anthony architectural illustrator, designer
Dee, Ruby (Ruby Dee Davis) actress, writer, director
†DeGovia, Jackson production designer
Dekmejian, Richard Hrair political science educator
De La Hoya, Oscar Olympic athlete, professional boxer
Del Olmo, Frank newspaper editor
DeLuce, Richard David lawyer
Delugach, Albert Lawrence journalist
De Meules, James Head lawyer
Demsetz, Harold economist, educator
Denlea, Leo Edward, Jr. insurance company executive
de Passe, Suzanne record company executive
Detels, Roger epidemiologist, physician, former university dean
Deukmejian, George lawyer, former governor
Dewey, Donald Odell university dean
Dhir, Vijay K. mechanical engineering educator
Diamond, Matthew Philip artistic director, choreographer, dancer
Diamond, Neil Leslie singer, composer
Diamond, Stanley Jay lawyer
Dickerson, Jaffe Dean lawyer
Didion, James J. real estate company executive
†Diederich, Francois Nico chemistry educator
Dignam, William Joseph obstetrician, gynecologist, educator
Dill, Donald consumer products company executive
Dillman, Bradford actor
Dillon, Paul Sanford artist
Dingwell, Everett W. food products company executive
Dismukes, Valena Grace Broussard physical education educator
Dixon, Andrew Derart retired academic administrator
Dockson, Robert Ray savings and loan executive
Dodds, Douglas Allen lawyer
Dolan, Mary Anne journalist, columnist
Dolan, Peter Brown lawyer
Dolinko, David Howard law educator
Doll, Lynne Marie public relations agency executive
Domantay, Norlito Valdez (Lito Domantay) communications executive
Domaradzki, Julian Andrzej physics educator
Domino, Fats (Antoine Domino) pianist, singer, songwriter
Donovan, John Arthur lawyer
†Dorleac, Jean-Pierre costume designer
Dorman, Albert A. consulting engineer executive, architect
Dorman, Thomas Patrick marketing professional, consultant
Doty, George Richard lawyer
Dougherty, Elmer Lloyd, Jr. chemical engineering educator, consultant
Dows, David Alan chemistry educator
Drake, Hudson Billings aerospace and electronics company executive
Drapkin, Steven G. lawyer
Dr. Dre, (Andre Young) rapper, record producer
Drew, Paul entrepreneur
Dreyfuss, John Alan journalist
Duffy, Patrick actor
Duke, William Edward public affairs executive
Dukeminier, Jesse law educator
Dummett, Clifton Orrin dentist, educator
Dundon, Brian R. motor company executive
Dunlavey, Dean Carl lawyer
†Dunn, Andrew cinematographer
Dunn, Arnold Samuel biochemistry educator
Dunn, Bruce Sidney materials science educator
Dunnahoo, Terry (Mrs. Thomas William Dunnahoo) editor, author
Dunton, James Kegebein investment management company executive
Duritz, Adam musician
Dworsky, Daniel Leonard architect
Dwyre, William Patrick journalist, public speaker
Dyck, Andrew Roy philologist
Eamer, Richard Keith health care company executive, lawyer
Earle, Timothy anthropology educator
Easterlin, Richard Ainley economist, educator
†Eastman, Donald church officer
†Edelman, Randy composer
Eden, Barbara Jean actress
Edgerton, Bradford Wheatly plastic surgeon
Edwards, Blake film director
Edwards, Howard Lee petroleum company executive
Edwards, Kenneth Neil chemist, consultant
Eger, Denise Leese rabbi
Eichler, Peter M. lawyer
†Eidelman, Cliff composer
Einstein, Clifford Jay advertising executive
Eisaman, Josiah Reamer, III advertising executive
Eisenberg, David Samuel molecular biologist, educator
Eiserling, Frederick Allen microbiologist, educator
Ela, Patrick Hobson museum director
†Ellickson, Bryan Carl economics educator
Ellingwood, Herbert E. government official, lawyer
Ellsworth, David G. lawyer
Ellsworth, Frank L. university administrator
†Elswit, Robert cinematographer
Emanuel, William Joseph lawyer
Emmeluth, Bruce Palmer investment banker, venture capitalist
Engler, George Nichols financial consultant, educator
English, Stephen Raymond lawyer
Ennis, Thomas Michael health foundation executive
Eno, Brian (Brian Peter George St. John De La Salle Eno) composer, musician, producer
Erburu, Robert F. media and information company executive
Erickson, Ralph Ernest lawyer
Esposito, Giancarlo actor
Estrich, Susan Rachel law educator
Estrin, Gerald computer scientist, engineering educator, academic administrator
Etra, Donald lawyer
†Ettenger, Robert Bruce physician, nephrologist
Eule, Julian Nathan law educator
Ewing, Edgar Louis artist, educator
Fahey, John Leslie immunologist
Fairbank, Robert Harold lawyer
Falk, EuGene L. publishing executive
Farman, Richard Donald gas company executive
Farmer, Robert Lindsay lawyer
Farrell, Joseph movie market analyst, producer, entertainment research company executive, writer, sculptor, designer
Farrell, Mike actor
Faulwell, Gerald Edward insurance company executive
Feidelson, Marc advertising executive
Feig, Stephen Arthur pediatrics educator, hematologist, oncologist
Feiman, Thomas E. accounting company executive
Fein, Ronald Lawrence lawyer
Fenimore, George Wiley management consultant
Fennelly, Jane Corey lawyer
Fenning, Lisa Hill federal judge
Fenster, Fred A. lawyer
Ferrell, Conchata Galen actress
Ferry, Richard Michael executive search firm executive
Feshbach, Seymour psychology educator
Field, Richard Clark lawyer
Field, Ted (Frederick Field) film and record industry executive
Fields, Bertram Harris lawyer
Fields, Henry Michael lawyer
Fifield, James G. recording industry executive
Finch, Caleb Ellicott neurobiologist, educator
Fine, Richard Isaac lawyer
†Finerman, Wendy film producer
†Fischer, Alfred George geology educator
Fish, Barbara psychiatrist, educator
Fishburne, Laurence, III actor
Fisher, Lawrence W. public relations company executive
Fisher, Raymond Corley lawyer
Fisher, Terry Louise television writer
Fitch, William C. professional basketball coach
Fitzgerald, Tikhon (Lee R. H. Fitzgerald) bishop
Fitzpatrick, William Joseph lawyer
Flanagan, Fionnula Manon actress, writer, producer
Flanigan, James J(oseph) journalist
Fleischmann, Ernest Martin music administrator
Floyd, Anne Marie Daze neonatology nurse, administrator
Fohrman, Burton H. lawyer
†Folk, Robert composer
Fonkalsrud, Eric Walter pediatric surgeon, educator
Foote, Christopher Spencer chemist, educator
Forbath, William E. law educator
Ford, Donald Hainline lawyer
Forester, Bernard I. recreational equipment company executive
Forgnone, Robert lawyer
Forness, Steven Robert educational psychologist
Forrest, Frederic actor
†Foster, David composer, record producer
Foster, Jodie (Alicia Christian Foster) actress
Foster, Mary Christine motion picture and television executive
†Fox, Saul Laurie physician, researcher
Frackman, Russell Jay lawyer
Fragner, Matthew Charles lawyer
Francis, Merrill Richard lawyer
†Franke, Christopher composer
Franklin, Bonnie Gail actress
†Franz, Dennis actor
Frazier, Joe retired professional boxer, performer
Fredman, Howard S lawyer
Freeman, Morgan actor
Freer, James Lewis accounting company executive
French, Susan F. law educator
Frey, Glenn songwriter, vocalist, guitarist
Fried, Burton David physicist, educator
Friedlander, Sheldon Kay chemical engineering educator
Friedman, Arthur Meeker magazine editor, professional motorcycle racer
Friedman, Robert Lee film company executive
Friedmann, Peretz Peter aerospace engineer, educator
Frimmer, Paul Norman lawyer
Frisch, Robert A. financial planning company executive
Fromholz, Haley James lawyer
Fromkin, Victoria Alexandra linguist, phonetician, educator
Fry, Michael Graham historian, educator
Fudge, Jack D. lawyer
†Fujimoto, Tak cinematographer
Fulco, Armand John biochemist
Fuller, Larry choreographer, director
Fuller, Samuel (Michael) scriptwriter, film director
Fybel, Richard D. lawyer
Gadbois, Richard A., Jr. federal judge
Gailys, John M. finance and operations executive
Gal, Kenneth Maurice advertising executive
Galanos, James fashion designer
Gale, Mary Ellen law educator
Gale, Robert Peter physician, scientist, researcher
Galef, Andrew Geoffrey investment and manufacturing company executive
Gallistel, Charles Ransom psychology educator
Galloway, Arnold John aerospace engineer
Gambino, Jerome James nuclear medicine educator
Ganas, Perry Spiros physicist
Garcia, Andy actor
†Garcia, Terry Donato lawyer
Garry, William James magazine editor
Garza, Oscar newspaper editor
Gaspari, Russell Arthur electrical engineer
Gates, Robert C. health system administrator
Gebb, Sheldon Alexander lawyer
Gebhart, Carl Grant security broker
Gelfand, Leonard H. insurance company executive
Gentile, Joseph F. lawyer, educator
†Gerber, Charles communications company executive
Gest, Howard David lawyer
Getto, Ernest John lawyer
Getty, Estelle actress
Geving, Steve William executive chef
Giacoletto, Joseph Richard electronics company executive
Gibbons, Leeza television talk show host, entertainment reporter
†Gibbs, Anthony film editor
Gibbs, Marla (Margaret Gibbs) actress
Gibson, Arthur Charles biologist, educator
Gibson, Mel actor
Gilbert, Judith Arlene lawyer
Giles, Anne Diener flutist
Gillcrist, Paul Thomas manufacturing executive, retired naval officer
Gilman, John Joseph research scientist
Gilman, Nelson Jay library director
†Gilmore, Mikal George critic, journalist, author
Gingrich, Harold insurance executive
Ginsburg, Seymour computer science educator
Girard, Robert David lawyer
Glad, Edward Newman lawyer
Glaser, Daniel sociologist
Glass, Herbert music critic, lecturer, editor
Glassner, Barry sociology educator, author
Glick, Earl A. lawyer
Glitz, Dohn George biochemistry educator
†Globus, Yoram motion picture company executive
Glover, John actor
Godbold, Wilford Darrington, Jr. enclosure manufacturing company executive, lawyer
Goette, Richard A. lawyer
Goff, Stanley Norman furniture retailing and manufacturing company executive
†Golan, Menahem motion picture company executive, film director
Gold, Arnold Henry judge
Gold, Bernard lawyer
Gold, Richard Horace radiologist
Goldberg, Gary David producer, writer
Goldberg Kent, Susan library director
Golden, Milton M. paint company executive
†Goldenthal, Elliot composer
Goldman, Allan Bailey lawyer
Goldman, Benjamin Edward lawyer
Goldman, Donald A. lawyer
Goldsmith, Jerry composer
†Goldstein, Harvey A. accountant
Goldstein, Mark A. zoo director
Goldstein, Robert David law educator
Goldwyn, Samuel John, Jr. motion picture producer
Göllner, Marie Louise musicologist, educator
Golomb, Solomon Wolf mathematician, electrical engineer, educator, university official
†Golub, Sidney Harris dean, educator
Gonick, Harvey Craig nephrologist, educator
Gooch, Lawrence Boyd accounting executive
Goodman, David Bryan musician, educator
Goodman, Max A. lawyer, educator
†Goodman, Miles composer
Gordon, Basil mathematics educator
Gordon, David Eliot lawyer
Gordon, Lawrence film producer
Gordon, Malcolm Stephen biology educator
Gordon, Milton G. real estate counselor, consultant
Gordy, Berry entrepreneur, record company executive, motion picture executive
Gorman, Cliff actor
Gorman, Joseph Gregory, Jr. lawyer
Gorney, Roderic psychiatry educator
Gorski, Roger Anthony neuroendocrinologist, educator

Gothold, Stuart E. *school system administrator, educator*
Gottfried, Ira Sidney *management consulting executive*
Gould, Charles Perry *lawyer*
Gould, David *lawyer*
Gould, Harold *actor*
†Goulding, Merrill Keith *engineer, consultant*
Grad, Laurie Burrows *food editor*
†Graham, Angelo *art director, production designer*
Gralnek, Donald D. *lawyer*
Grammer, Kelsey *actor*
Grant, Amy *singer, songwriter*
Grant, David *broadcasting executive*
Grant, David Browne *manufacturing executive*
Grantham, Richard Robert *real estate company executive*
Grausam, Jeffrey Leonard *lawyer*
Gray, Jan Charles *lawyer*
Gray, Linda *actress*
†Graysmark, John *production designer*
Grazer, Brian *film company executive*
Green, Guy Mervin Charles *film director*
Green, William Porter *lawyer*
Greenberg, Ira Arthur *psychologist*
Greenberger, Martin *computer and information scientist, educator*
Greene, Alvin *service company executive, management consultant*
Greene, Donald Johnson *retired English language educator, author*
Greenstadt, Melvin *investor, retired educator*
Gregg, Lucius Perry, Jr. *aerospace executive*
Gregory, Thomas Lang *restaurant chain executive*
Greiman, April *graphic designer*
Griffey, Linda Boyd *lawyer*
Grinnell, Alan Dale *neurobiologist, educator, researcher*
Grody, Mark Stephen *public relations executive*
Groh, Rupert James, Jr. *judge*
Groman, Arthur *lawyer*
Gross, Allen Jeffrey *lawyer*
Grosz, Philip J. *lawyer*
Groves, Martha *newspaper writer*
Grusin, Dave *film composer, record producer, pianist*
†Gruska, Jay *composer*
Gumpel, Glenn J. *association executive*
Gunn, Karen Sue *psychologist*
Gurash, John Thomas *insurance company executive*
Gurfein, Peter J. *lawyer*
Gutterridge, Larry G. *lawyer*
Haas, Edward Lee *business executive, consultant*
Habeishi, Fred Gabriel *engineering and construction services executive*
Hackford, Taylor *film director, producer*
Hackman, Gene *actor*
Hadda, Janet Ruth *Yiddish language educator, lay psychoanalyst*
Haden, Charles *jazz bassist, composer*
†Haegel, Nancy M. *materials, optics sciences educator*
Hahn, Elliott Julius *lawyer*
Hahn, Harlan Dean *political science educator, consultant*
Haight, James Theron *lawyer, corporate executive*
Haile, Lawrence Barclay *lawyer*
†Haimovitz, Jules *broadcasting company executive*
Haley, Jack, Jr. (John J. Haley) *director, producer, writer, executive*
Halgren, Jack *lawyer*
Halkett, Alan Neilson *lawyer*
Hall, Arsenio *television talk show host, comedian*
Hall, Carlyle Washington, Jr. *lawyer*
Hall, Clarence Albert, Jr. *geologist, educator*
Hall, Jeffrey Stuart *newspaper executive*
†Hallowell, Todd *art director, production designer*
†Halsey, Richard *film editor*
Halstead, Harry Moore *lawyer*
†Hambling, Gerald *film editor*
Hammer, (Stanley Kirk Burrell) *musician*
Hampton, Gordon Francis *lawyer*
Hancock, Herbert Jeffrey (Herbie Hancock) *composer, pianist, publisher*
Handelman, David Yale *film company executive, lawyer*
Handler, Carole Enid *lawyer, city planner*
Handler, Joel F. *law educator*
Handschumacher, Albert Gustave *retired corporate executive*
Handy, Lyman Lee *petroleum engineer, chemist, educator*
Handzlik, Jan Lawrence *lawyer*
Hanna, William Denby *motion picture and television producer, cartoonist*
Hanrahan, Thomas P. *lawyer*
Hansell, Dean *lawyer*
Hanson, John J. *lawyer*
Harbaugh, George Milton *hotel executive*
Harberger, Arnold Carl *economist, educator*
Harbert, Ted *broadcast executive*
Harbison, John Robert *management consultant*
Harlin, Renny (Renny Lauri Mauritz Harjola) *film director*
Harold, John Gordon *cardiologist, internist*
Harrick, Jim *university athletic coach*
Harris, Susan *television producer*
Harris, T. C. *water transportation executive*
Harris, Theodore Edward *mathematician, educator*
Hart, John Lewis (Johnny Hart) *cartoonist*
Hart, Mary *television talk show host*
†Harter, Robert Jackson, Jr. *lawyer, transportation holding company executive*
Hartigan, John Francis *lawyer*
Hartke, Stephen Paul *composer, educator*
Hartman, Lisa (Lisa Hartman Black) *actress, singer*
†Hartsough, Gayla Anne Kraetsch *management consultant*
Haskell, Charles Mortimer *medical oncologist, educator*
Hastings, Robert Pusey *lawyer*
Hathaway, Harry L. *lawyer*
Hatter, Terry Julius, Jr. *federal judge*
Hauk, A. Andrew *federal judge*
Havel, Richard W. *lawyer*
Hawley, Philip Metschan *retired retail executive, consultant*
Hayden, Tom *state legislator, author*
Hayes, Byron Jackson, Jr. *lawyer*
Hayes, Robert Mayo *university dean, library and information science educator*
Hayes, Vertis Clemon *painter, sculptor, educator*
Haythorn, J. Denny *law librarian*
Hayutin, David Lionel *lawyer*
Hayutin, Marc I. *lawyer*
Haywood, L. Julian *physician, educator*
Hazen, Steven Kelsey *lawyer*
Headlee, Rolland Dockeray *association executive*
Hearst, George Randolph, Jr. *publishing executive, diversified ranching and real estate executive*
†Heath, James R. *chemistry educator*
Heather, Fred Doenges *lawyer, educator*
Hecht, Harold Michael *retail executive*
Heer, David Macalpine *sociology educator*
†Heim, Alan *film editor*
Hein, Leonard William *accounting educator*
Heinisch, Robert Craig *sales and marketing executive, consultant*
Heinke, Rex S. *lawyer*
Hellwarth, Robert Willis *physicist, educator*
Helms, Harold Edwin *minister*
Hemion, Dwight Arlington *television producer, director*
Hemminger, Pamela Lynn *lawyer*
Hemmings, Peter William *orchestra and opera administrator*
Hendrick, Hal Wilmans *human factors educator*
Hennigan, James Michael *lawyer*
Hernandez, Antonia *lawyer*
Hertzberg, Paul Stuart *producer, publisher, writer*
Hesseman, Howard *actor*
Hessler, Curtis Alan *newspaper publishing company executive*
†Hester, John W. *film company executive*
Hettler, Paul *visual effects producer*
Heyert, Martin David *lawyer*
Heyler, Grover Ross *retired lawyer*
Hibner, Don Telfer, Jr. *lawyer*
Hieronymus, Edward Whittlesey *lawyer*
Higgins, John Joseph *corporate lawyer*
Highberger, William Foster *lawyer*
Hight, B. Boyd *lawyer*
Highwater, Jamake *author, lecturer*
Hill, Irving *judge*
Hiller, Arthur *motion picture director*
Hinerfeld, Robert Elliot *lawyer*
Hirsch, Barry L. *lawyer*
Hirsch, Werner Zvi *economist, educator*
Hoang, Duc Van *theoretical pathologist, educator*
Hoffenberg, Marvin *political science educator, consultant*
†Hoffman, Marvin *computer company executive*
Hoffman, Neil James *art school executive*
Hogan, Steven L. *lawyer*
Hogarth, Burne *cartoonist, illustrator*
Holbrook, Hal (Harold Rowe Holbrook, Jr.) *actor*
Holland, John Ray *minister*
Holliday, Thomas Edgar *lawyer*
Holman, Tomlinson *engineer, film educator*
Holmes, Gene L. *social services professional, child care specialist*
Holo, Selma Reuben *museum director, educator*
Holtzman, Robert Arthur *lawyer*
Hopkins, Carl Edward *public health educator*
Hopkins, Henry Tyler *art educator, university gallery director*
†Horner, James *composer*
Horowitz, Ben *medical center executive*
Horowitz, David Charles *consumer commentator, newspaper columnist*
Horwitz, David A. *medicine and microbiology educator*
Hospers, John *philosophy educator*
Houck, John Burton *retired lawyer*
Houk, Kendall Newcomb *chemistry educator*
House, John William *otologist*
Houston, Ivan James *insurance company executive*
Hovanessian, Shahen Alexander *electrical engineer, educator*
Hovannisian, Richard G. *Armenian and Near East history educator*
†Howard, James Newton *composer*
Howard, Sandy *motion picture producer*
Howe, John Thomas *film director, educator*
Howell, Kenneth Kennedy *lawyer*
†Hoy, Maysie *film editor*
†Hoy, William *film editor*
Hu, Sze-Tsen *mathematics educator*
Hubbard, John Randolph *university president emeritus, history educator, diplomat*
Hubbs, Donald Harvey *foundation president*
Huddleston, David William *actor, producer*
Hudson, Jeffrey Reid *lawyer*
Huebner, Harlan Pierce *lawyer*
Hufstedler, Seth Martin *lawyer*
Hufstedler, Shirley Mount (Mrs. Seth M. Hufstedler) *lawyer, former federal judge*
Hughes, Barnard *actor*
Hughes, Everett Clark *otolaryngology educator*
Hummel, Joseph William *hospital administrator*
Humphreys, Robert Lee *advertising agency executive*
Hundley, Norris Cecil, Jr. *history educator*
Hunter, Larry Dean *lawyer*
Hupp, Harry L. *federal judge*
Hurt, William *actor*
Hurt, William Holman *investment management company executive*
Hurwitz, Lawrence Neal *investment banking company executive*
Hutchins, Joan Morthland *manufacturing executive, farmer*
Hutton, Lauren (Mary Laurence Hutton) *actress, model*
Hyman, Milton Bernard *lawyer*
†Hyman, Richard Roven *composer, jazz musician*
Iamele, Richard Thomas *law librarian*
Iannaccone, Emil Anthony *advertising agency executive*
Ice Cube, (O'Shea Jackson) *rap singer, actor*
Ice-T, (Tracy Marrow) *rap singer, actor*
Ideman, James M. *federal judge*
Igo, George Jerome *physics educator*
Iman, (Iman Abdulmajid) *model*
Incaudo, Joseph August *engineering company executive*
Ingels, Marty *theatrical agent, television and motion picture production executive*
Intriligator, Michael David *economist, educator*
†Iovine, Jimmy *recording industry executive*
Irani, Ray R. *oil, gas and chemical company executive*
Ireland, Kathy *actress*
Irell, Lawrence E(lliott) *lawyer*
Irving, Jack Howard *technical consultant*
Irwin, Philip Donnan *lawyer*
Isinger, William R. *newspaper publishing executive*
Israel, Franklin David *architect*
†Ito, Lance Allan *judge*
Itoh, Tatsuo *engineering educator*
Jackson, Isaiah *conductor*
Jackson, Janet Damita *singer, dancer*
Jackson, Kingsbury Temple *educational contract consultant*
Jackson, Mary *actress*
Jackson, Michael (Joseph) *singer*
Jacob, Paul F., III *architectural firm executive*
Jacobs, Marilyn Susan *psychologist, author*
Jacobs, Marion Kramer *psychologist*
Jacobsen, Laren *programmer, analyst*
Jaffe, F. Filmore *judge*
Jaffe, Sigmund *educator, chemist*
James, Peter W. *lawyer*
Janofsky, Leonard S. *lawyer, association executive*
Jarmon, Lawrence *developmental communications educator*
†Jarre, Maurice Alexis *composer*
Jarrott, Charles *film and television director*
Jarvik, Lissy F. *psychiatrist*
Jarvik, Murray Elias *psychiatry, pharmacology educator*
Jenden, Donald James *pharmacologist, educator*
Jenkins, William *building materials and property development company executive*
Jensen, David Gram *university administrator*
Jeter, Michael *actor*
Joffe, Charles *motion picture producer, comedy management executive*
Johnson, Cage Saul *hematologist, educator*
Johnson, Earl, Jr. *judge, author*
Johnson, John H. *publisher, consumer products executive, chairman*
Johnson, Jonathan Edwin, II *lawyer*
Johnson, Martin Marion *lawyer*
Johnson, Patricia Gayle *public relations executive, writer*
Johnson, Scott *architect*
†Johnston, P. Michael *production designer, art director*
Johnston, Roy G. *consulting structural engineer*
Johnston, Ynez *artist*
Jones, Henry *actor*
Jones, James Earl *actor*
Jones, Quincy *producer, composer, arranger, conductor, trumpeter*
Jones, Tom *singer*
Jones, Walter Harrison *chemist*
Jordan, Judd L. *lawyer*
Jordan, Robert Leon *lawyer, educator*
Jorgensen, Paul Alfred *English language educator emeritus*
†Jung, Michael Ernest *chemistry educator*
Kadison, Stuart L. *lawyer*
Kagan, Benjamin M. *pediatrician*
Kagan, Jeremy Paul *director, filmmaker*
Kahn, Roger Charles *investment banker*
Kalaba, Robert Edwin *applied mathematician*
Kaliski, John *architectural firm executive*
Kambara, George Kiyoshi *retired ophthalmologist, educator*
†Kamen, Michael *composer, musician, conductor*
Kaminski, Janusz Zygmunt *photographer*
Kane, Carol *actress*
Kaneko, Mitsuru *production company executive, animation producer*
Kanemitsu, Matsumi *artist*
Kaplan, Isaac Raymond *chemistry educator, corporate executive*
Kaplan, Jonathan Stewart *film writer, director*
Kaplan, Robert B. *linguistics educator, consultant, researcher*
Kaplan, Samuel *pediatric cardiologist*
Karlin, Michael Jonathan Abraham *lawyer*
Karplus, Walter J. *engineering educator*
Karros, Eric Peter *professional baseball player*
Karst, Kenneth Leslie *legal educator*
Kashar, Lawrence Joseph *metallurgical engineer, consultant*
Kassar, Mario F. *film production company executive*
Katleman, Harris L. *television executive*
Katz, Jason Lawrence *lawyer, insurance executive*
Katz, Ronald Lewis *physician, educator*
†Kaula, William Mason *geophysicist, educator*
Kaus, Otto Michael *lawyer*
†Kaye, Barry *investment company executive*
†Kaye, Carole *museum director and curator*
Kaye, Jhani *radio station manager, director*
Keach, Stacy, Jr. *actor, director, producer, writer, musician, composer*
Kelleher, Robert *apparel executive*
Kelleher, Robert Joseph *federal judge*
Keller, William D. *federal judge*
Kellerman, Sally Claire *actress*
Kelley, Harold Harding *psychology educator*
Kelly, Arthur Paul *physician*
Kelly, Daniel Grady, Jr. *lawyer*
Kelly, Henry Ansgar *English language educator*
Kelly, Raymond Francis *commodity company executive*
Kelly, Roberto Conrado (Bobby Kelly) *professional baseball player*
†Kempster, Victor *art director, production designer*
Kendall, William Denis *medical electronic equipment company executive*
Kendig, Ellsworth Harold, Jr. *lawyer*
Kennedy, George *actor*
Kennedy, Kathleen *film producer*
Kennelly, Sister Karen Margaret *college administrator*
†Kent, Susan Goldberg *library director, consultant*
Kent, William *pilot, cameraman, special effects expert*
Kenyon, David V. *federal judge*
Ketchum, Robert Glenn *photographer, print maker*
Kidman, Nicole *actress*
Kienholz, Lyn Shearer *international arts projects coordinator*
Kikuchi, Ryoichi *physics educator*
Kilburn, Kaye Hatch *medical educator*
†Kimball, Jeffrey L. *director of photography*
Kindel, James Horace, Jr. *lawyer*
King, Joseph Paul *finance executive*
King, Robert Lucien *lawyer*
King, Sheldon Selig *medical center administrator, educator*
Kingsley, Walter Ingalls *television executive*
Kinney, James Howard *lawyer*
Kirkland, Sally *actress*
Kirschner, David *animation entertainment company executive*
Kirwan, Betty-Jane *lawyer*
Kirwan, Ralph DeWitt *lawyer*
Kivelson, Margaret Galland *physicist*
Klee, Kenneth Nathan *lawyer*
Klein, Benjamin *economics educator, consultant*
Klein, Joan Dempsey *judge*
Klein, William A. *lawyer, educator*
Kleinberg, Marvin H. *lawyer*
Kleingartner, Archie *business educator, academic administrator*
Kleinrock, Leonard *computer scientist*
Kleiser, (John) Randal *motion picture director*
Kline, Lee B. *architect*
Kline, Richard Stephen *public relations executive*
Klinger, Allen *computer science and engineering educator*
Klingman, Lynzee *film editor*
Klopf, Jeffrey A. *lawyer*
Klowden, Michael Louis *lawyer*
Knapp, Cleon Talboys *business executive*
Knight, Christopher Allen *art critic*
Knopoff, Leon *geophysics educator*
Knotts, Don *actor*
Kobin, William H. *television station executive*
Koch, Albin Cooper *lawyer*
Koch, Howard W., Jr. *film producer*
Koch, Richard *pediatrician, educator*
Koelzer, George Joseph *lawyer*
Koffler, Stephen Alexander *investment banker*
Kolin, Alexander *retired biophysics researcher*
Kolve, V. A. *English literature educator*
†Kopelson, Arnold *film producer*
Korenman, Stanley George *medical investigator, educator*
Korman, Harvey Herschel *actor*
Korn, Lester Bernard *business executive, diplomat*
Koshalek, Richard *museum director, consultant*
Kotcheff, William Theodore (Ted Kotcheff) *director*
Kramer, Stanley E. *motion picture producer, director*
Kresa, Kent *aerospace executive*
Krim, Mathilde *medical educator*
Kristoff, James *production company executive*
Kronenberg, John Robert *retired magistrate judge*
Krouse, Diane Murray *advertising company executive*
Krueger, Robert William *management consultant*
Kruger, Lawrence *neuroscientist*
Krupp, Edwin Charles *astronomer*
Kruse, Scott August *lawyer*
Kuechle, John Merrill *lawyer*
Kuehl, Hans Henry *electrical engineering educator*
Kulzick, Kenneth Edmund *lawyer, writer*
Kunc, Joseph Anthony *physics and engineering educator, consultant*
Kupchick, Alan Charles *advertising executive*
Kupietzky, Moshe J. *lawyer*
Kurtz, Swoosie *actress*
Kurtzman, Alan *cosmetics company executive*
Kuwayama, George *curator*
Laaly, Heshmat Ollah *research chemist, roofing consultant, author*
Laba, Marvin *management consultant*
Lachman, Morton *writer, theatrical director and producer*
Ladd, Alan Walbridge, Jr. *motion picture company executive*
Ladefoged, Peter Nielsen *phonetician*
La Force, James Clayburn, Jr. *economist, educator*
Lahti, Christine *actress*
Laird, David *humanities educator emeritus*
Lambro, Phillip *composer, conductor, pianist*
†Lamont, Peter *production designer, art director*
Landau, Martin *actor*
Lane, Joseph M. *orthopaedic surgeon, oncologist*
Lane, Marilyn Edith *treasurer, corporate executive*
Lane, Robert Gerhart *lawyer*
Langella, Frank *actor*
Langer, Glenn Arthur *cellular physiologist, educator*
Lansing, Sherry Lee *motion picture production executive*
Lappen, Chester I. *lawyer*
Lark, Raymond *artist, art scholar*
Larroquette, John Bernard *actor*
Lasarow, William Julius *federal judge retired*
Lasorda, Thomas Charles (Tommy Lasorda) *professional baseball team manager*
Lasswell, Marcia Lee *psychologist, educator*
Latham, Joseph Al, Jr. *lawyer*
Lauchengco, Jose Yujuico, Jr. *lawyer*
Launer, Dale Mark *screenwriter*
Laurance, Dale R. *oil company executive*
Laventhol, David Abram *newspaper editor*
Lavin, Linda *actress*
†Lavond, David G. *psychology educator*
Lawrence, Barry Howard *lawyer*
Lawrence, Sanford Hull *physician, immunochemist*
Lax, Kathleen Thompson *federal judge*
Laybourne, Everett Broadstone *lawyer*
Lazarus, Mell *cartoonist*
Lazzaro, Anthony Derek *university administrator*
Leach, Anthony Raymond *financial executive*
Leal, George D. *engineering company executive*
Lear, Norman Milton *producer, writer, director*
Leary, Timothy *psychologist, author*
†Lebenzon, Chris *film editor*
Lederman, Bruce Randolph *lawyer*
Lee, Amy Shiu *biochemist, educator*
Lee, Burns Wells *public relations executive*
Lee, Christopher Frank Carandini *actor, author*
Lee, R. Marilyn *employee relations executive*
Lee, Walter William, Jr. *film writer, consultant, publishing executive*
Leener, Jack Joseph *advertising executive*
Lehan, Richard D'Aubin *English language educator, writer*
Lehman, Robert Nathan *ophthalmologist, educator*
Leibow, Ronald Louis *lawyer*
†Leighton, Robert *film editor*
Leijonhufvud, Axel Stig Bengt *economics educator*
Lem, Richard Douglas *painter*
†Lenard, Michael Barry *merchant banker, lawyer*
Leo, Malcolm *producer, director, writer*
Leonard, Sheldon *television producer, director*
Leonetti, Matthew Frank *cinematographer*
†Lepine, Jean *cinematographer*
Lesser, Joan L. *lawyer*
Letts, J. Spencer *federal judge*
Letwin, Leon *legal educator*
Leung, Frankie Fook-Lun *lawyer*
Levine, Philip *classics educator*
Levine, Raphael David *chemistry educator*
Levine, Robert Arthur *economist, policy analyst*
Levine, Thomas Jeffrey Pello *lawyer*
Levy, Louis *chess master*
Levy, Norman *motion picture company executive*
Lew, Ronald S. W. *federal judge*
Lewin, David *management educator*
Lewin, Klaus J. *pathologist, educator*
Lewis, Charles Edwin *physician, educator*
Lewis, Craig Graham David *public relations executive*
Lewis, Samella Sanders *artist, educator*
Lewis, Shari *puppeteer, entertainer*
Lewitzky, Bella *choreographer*
Li, Gerald *architect, film producer*
Liberman, Robert Paul *psychiatry educator, researcher, writer*
Liebeler, Wesley J. *law educator, lawyer*
Lieber, David Leo *university president*
Lien, Eric Jung-chi *pharmacist, educator*
Light, John Robert *lawyer*

Limato, Edward Frank *talent agent*
Lin, Tung Hua *civil engineering educator*
†Linder, Stu *film editor*
Lindholm, Dwight Henry *lawyer*
†Lindley, John *cinematographer*
Lindsley, Donald Benjamin *physiological psychologist, educator*
Lindstedt-Siva, (Karen) June *marine biologist, oil company executive*
Link, George Hamilton *lawyer*
Linsk, Michael Stephen *real estate executive*
Lipsig, Ethan *lawyer*
Lipstone, Howard Harold *television executive*
Lishner, Laurence H. *lawyer*
Littlejohn, Bruce Every *film and television producer*
Littleton, Christine A. *law educator*
†Livingston, Alan Wendell *communications executive*
Lloyd, Christopher *actor*
†Lloyd, Walt *cinematographer*
Loeb, Ronald Marvin *lawyer*
Löfstedt, Bengt Torkel Magnus *classics educator*
Logan, Joseph Granville, Jr. *physicist*
Lond, Harley Weldon *editor, publisher*
Long, Gregory Alan *lawyer*
Longmire, William Polk, Jr. *physician, surgeon*
Looney, Gerald Lee *medical educator, administrator*
Lowenstein, Daniel Hays *lawyer, educator*
Lowenthal, Abraham Frederic *international relations educator*
Lublinski, Michael *lawyer*
Lucero, Gene A. *lawyer*
Ludlam, James Edward *lawyer*
†Lukasik, Stephen Joseph *information technology executive*
Lunt, Owen Raynal *biologist, educator*
Lurvey, Ira Harold *lawyer*
Lyman, John *psychology and engineering educator*
Lynch, Beverly Pfeifer *education and information studies educator*
Lynch, Patrick *lawyer*
Lyne, Adrian *director*
Lyons, James Elliott *lawyer*
†Macat, Julio *cinematographer*
Mac Dowell, Andie (Rose Anderson MacDowell) *actress*
MacGregor, Geddes *author, philosophy educator*
Mack, J. Curtis, II *civic organization administrator*
MacKenzie, John Douglas *engineering educator*
MacLaughlin, Francis Joseph *lawyer*
MacLeod, Robert Fredric *editor, publisher*
Mager, Artur *retired aerospace company executive, consultant*
Magner, Fredric Michael *financial services executive*
Magner, Martin *theatrical producer and director*
Mahony, Roger M. Cardinal *archbishop*
Maki, Kazumi *physicist, educator*
Malden, Karl (Malden Sekulovich) *actor*
Malecki, Edward Stanley, Jr. *political science educator*
Mall, William John, Jr. *aerospace executive, retired air force officer*
Malone, Nancy *actor, director, producer*
Maltin, Leonard *television commentator, writer*
Mancino, Douglas Michael *lawyer*
Mancuso, Frank G. *entertainment company executive*
Mandel, Joseph David *university official, lawyer*
Manilow, Barry *singer, composer, arranger*
Mann, Delbert *film, theater, television director and producer*
Mann, Nancy Louise (Nancy Louise Robbins) *entrepreneur*
Manning, Donald O. *protective services official*
Manning, Whipple Hall *savings and loan executive, real estate finance consultant*
Maquet, Jacques Jerome Pierre *anthropologist, writer*
March, Kathleen Patricia *federal judge*
Marciniak, Thaddeus J. *lawyer*
Margol, Irving *personnel consultant*
Margulies, Lee *newspaper editor*
Marion, Douglas Welch *magazine editor*
Markland, Francis Swaby, Jr. *biochemist, educator*
Marmor, Judd *psychiatrist, educator*
Maronde, Robert Francis *internist, clinical pharmacologist, educator*
Marrie, Thomas Phillip *bank executive*
Marsh, Dave Rodney *writer, publisher, editor*
†Marsh, Stephen F. *production designer*
Marshall, Arthur K. *lawyer, judge, arbitrator, educator, writer*
Marshall, Consuelo Bland *federal judge*
Marshall, E. G. *actor*
Marshall, Frank W. *film producer, director*
Martin, Albert Carey *architect*
†Martin, David R. *oil company executive*
Martin, Ernest H. *theatrical and motion picture executive*
†Martin, John A. *engineering company executive*
Martin, J(ohn) Edward *architectural engineer*
Martin, Ray *banker*
Martin, Vincent Francis, Jr. *real estate investment executive*
Martin, Walter Edwin *biology educator*
Martinez, Al *journalist, screenwriter*
Mason, Cheryl White *lawyer*
Mason, Marshall W. *theater director*
Masri, Sami F(aiz) *civil and mechanical engineering educator, consultant*
Matheson, Richard Burton *author, scriptwriter*
Matthau, Walter *actor*
Maxwell, Donald Stanley *publishing executive*
Maxworthy, Tony *mechanical and aerospace engineering educator*
†McAlpine, Donald *cinematographer*
McAuley, Skeet *artist*
McBurney, George William *lawyer*
Mc Callum, David *actor*
Mc Clanahan, Rue (Eddi-Rue Mc Clanahan) *actress*
†McClary, Susan *musicology educator, writer*
McDermott, Thomas John, Jr. *lawyer*
McDonald, Jeanne Gray (Mrs. John B. McDonald) *television producer*
Mc Donough, John Richard *lawyer*
McDonough, Patrick Joseph *lawyer*
Mc Dowall, Roddy *actor*
McGaughey, Emmett Connell *advertising agency executive*
McGee, Henry W., Jr. *legal educator, lawyer*
†McGoohan, Patrick Joseph *actor*
Mc Govern, William Montgomery, Jr. *law educator*
Mc Guire, Dorothy Hackett *actress*
McIntyre, Robert Malcolm *utility company executive*
McKee, Kathryn Dian Grant *banker*
McKnight, Frederick L. *lawyer*
Mc Kuen, Rod *poet, composer, author*
McLane, Frederick Berg *lawyer*
McLaren, Fred B. *supermarket chain executive*
McLarnan, Donald Edward *banker, corporation executive*
Mc Laughlin, Joseph Mailey *lawyer*
Mc Namar, Richard Timothy *merchant banker*
Mc Pherson, Rolf Kennedy *clergyman, church official*
McQueen, Justice Ellis (L. Q. Jones) *actor, director*
McSweeny, William Francis *petroleum company executive, author*
McWilliams, Peter *poet*
Medak, Peter *film director*
Meecham, William Corvell *engineering educator*
Melkonian, Harry G. *lawyer, rancher*
Mellinkoff, David *lawyer, educator*
Mellinkoff, Sherman Mussoff *medical educator*
Meloan, Taylor Wells *marketing educator*
Mendel, Jerry Marc *electrical engineering educator*
Menkel-Meadow, Carrie Joan *law educator*
Merkert, George *visual effects producer*
Merrifield, Donald Paul *university chancellor*
Merritt, Bruce Gordon *lawyer*
Metzger, Robert Streicher *lawyer*
Metzner, Richard Joel *psychiatrist, psychopharmacologist, educator*
Meuli, Judith K. *communications executive, real estate developer, small business owner*
Meyer, Michael Edwin *lawyer*
Michael, William Burton *psychologist, educator*
Michel, Donald Charles *editor*
Michelson, Lillian *motion picture researcher*
Middleton, James Arthur *oil and gas company executive*
Miech, Allen C. *financial services company executive*
Mihan, Richard *dermatologist*
Miles, Samuel Israel *psychiatrist*
Miley, Samuel A. *lawyer, electrical equipment company executive*
Millard, Neal Steven *lawyer*
Miller, Gavin *lawyer*
Miller, Jason *playwright*
†Miller, Michael Radgiff *film editor*
Miller, Milton Allen *lawyer*
Miller, Norman *psychology educator, researcher*
Miller, Norman Charles, Jr. *newspaper editor*
Miller, Timothy Alden *plastic and reconstructive surgeon*
Miller, Victoria Loren *designer, art director*
Milligan, Sister Mary *theology educator, religious consultant*
Mills, Donna *actress*
Mintz, Marshall Gary *lawyer*
†Mirisch, Lawrence Alan *motion picture agent*
Mischer, Donald Leo *television director and producer*
Mishell, Daniel R., Jr. *physician, educator*
Mitchell, Briane Nelson *lawyer*
Mitchell, Joni (Roberta Joan Anderson) *singer, songwriter*
Mitchell, Joseph Nathan *retired real estate executive*
†Mitchell, Theodore R. *dean, education educator*
Mitchell, Warren I. *utility company executive*
Mitchum, Robert Charles Durman (Charles Mitchum) *actor*
Mock, Theodore Jaye *accounting educator*
Mockary, Peter Ernest *clinical laboratory scientist, researcher*
Moe, Stanley Allen *architect, consultant*
Mohr, John Luther *biologist, environmental consultant*
Mommaerts, Wilfried Francis Henry Maria *physiologist, educator*
Monkewitz, Peter Alexis *mechanical and aerospace engineer, educator*
Montgomery, Richard Alan *sales executive*
Montoya Thompson, Velma *federal agency administrator*
Morava, Carol *lawyer*
Moreno, Rita *actress*
Morgan, Todd Michael *investment advisor*
Morgner, Aurelius *economist, educator*
Mori, Jun *lawyer*
Morphesis, James George *artist*
Morris, Garrett *actor, singer*
Morris, Herbert *lawyer, educator*
Morris, Larry Garner *transportation company executive*
Morris, Stephen James Michael *lawyer*
Morrison, Donald Graham *business educator, consultant*
Morrison, Robert Lewin *lawyer*
†Morriss, Frank *film editor*
Morrow, Winston Vaughan *financial executive*
†Morse, Susan E. *film editor*
Mortensen, Richard Edgar *engineering educator*
Moses, Gilbert *film and theatre director*
Mosich, Anelis Nick *accountant, author, educator, consultant*
Mosk, Richard Mitchell *lawyer*
Moskowitz, Joel Steven *lawyer*
Moss, Gary Curtis *lawyer*
Mossawir, Harve H., Jr. *lawyer*
Mossman, Thomas Mellish, Jr. *television manager*
Mosten, Forrest Steven *lawyer, educator*
Moxley, John Howard, III *physician*
Mueller, Carl Richard *theater arts educator, author*
Mueller, John C. *lawyer*
Muldaur, Diana Charlton *actress*
Mulder, Donald Gerrit *surgeon, educator*
Mullane, Donald A. *banker*
Muller, Peter *lawyer, entertainment company executive, retail company executive, consultant*
Mund, Geraldine *bankruptcy judge*
Muntz, Eric Phillip *aerospace engineering and radiology educator, consultant*
Munzer, Cynthia Brown *mezzo-soprano*
Munzer, Stephen R. *law educator*
Murphy, Eddie *comedian, actor*
Murphy, Gerald D. *agricultural products, grain company executive*
Murphy, Philip Edward *broadcast executive*
Murray, James Patrick *newspaper columnist*
Nadler, Gerald *engineering educator, management consultant*
Nahai, Hamid *lawyer*
Nakanishi, Don Toshiaki *Asian American studies educator, writer*
Nanus, Burton Benjamin *management educator, researcher*
Natzler, Otto *ceramic artist*
Neal, Joseph C., Jr. *church administrator*
Neely, Sally Schultz *lawyer*
Neiter, Gerald Irving *lawyer*
Nelson, Grant Steel *lawyer, educator*
Nelson, Howard Joseph *educator, geographer*
Nelson, J. Robert *lawyer*
Nelson, James Augustus, II *real estate executive, architect, banker*
Nelson, Mark Bruce *interior designer*
†Nemec, Joseph C., III *production designer*
Nesmith, Michael *film producer, video specialist*
Neufeld, Elizabeth Fondal *biochemist, educator*
Neufeld, Mace *film company executive*
Neumann, Alfred Kurt *public health physician, educator*
Neutra, Dion *architect*
Neville, Aaron *musician*
Neville, Art *musician*
Neville, Charles *musician*
Neville, Cyril *musician*
†Newborn, Ira *composer*
Newhart, Bob *entertainer*
Newhouse, Brian E. *lawyer*
Newman, David Wheeler *lawyer*
Newman, James Austin *financial journalist*
Newman, Richard *engineering executive*
†Newman, Thomas *composer*
Nibley, Robert Ricks *retired lawyer*
Nicholas, William Richard *lawyer*
Nicholaw, George *communications executive*
†Nichols, David *production designer*
†Niehaus, Lennie *composer, jazz saxophonist*
Niemeth, Charles Frederick *lawyer*
†Niemiec, Peter Jude *lawyer*
Niese, William A. *lawyer, newspaper publishing executive*
Nikolai, James A. *insurance executive*
Niles, John Gilbert *lawyer*
Nilles, John Mathias (Jack Nilles) *entrepreneur*
Nimni, Marcel Ephraim *biochemistry educator*
Nixon, John Harmon *economist*
Nobe, Ken *chemical engineering educator*
Noble, Ernest Pascal *physician, biochemist, educator*
Noble, James Wilkes *actor*
Noble, Richard Lloyd *lawyer*
Nocas, Andrew James *lawyer*
Noce, Walter William, Jr. *hospital administrator*
Nochimson, David *lawyer*
Nogales, Luis Guerrero *communications company executive*
Noguchi, Thomas Tsunetomi *author, forensic pathologist*
Norian, Roger W. *plastic manufacturing company executive*
Norris, Edwin L. *lawyer*
Norris, Floyd Hamilton *lawyer*
Norris, William Albert *federal judge*
Northrup, William Stephen, Jr. *television producer*
Nunis, Doyce Blackman, Jr. *historian, educator*
†Nyman, Michael Lawrence *composer*
Obrzut, Ted *lawyer*
Obst, Lynda Rosen *film company executive, producer, screenwriter*
O'Connell, Kevin *lawyer*
O'Day, Anita Belle Colton *entertainer, singer*
Oder, Kenneth William *lawyer*
O'Donnell, Pierce Henry *lawyer*
Ogle, Edward Proctor, Jr. *investment counseling executive*
Okeh, Samson Ewruje *psychiatric nurse*
Okrent, David *engineering educator*
Olah, George Andrew *chemist, educator*
Oldman, Gary *actor*
Olmos, Edward James *actor*
Olpin, Owen *lawyer*
Olsen, Frances Elisabeth *law educator, theorist*
Olsen, Roger Milton *lawyer*
Olson, Dale C. *public relations executive*
Olson, Gary *lawyer*
Olson, Ronald Leroy *lawyer*
O'Malley, Joseph James *lawyer*
O'Malley, Peter *professional baseball club executive*
Onak, Thomas Philip *chemistry educator*
O'Neal, Tatum *actress*
O'Neill, Russell Richard *engineering educator*
Orchard, Henry John *electrical engineer*
Ordin, Andrea Sheridan *lawyer*
O'Reilly, Richard Brooks *journalist*
Orme, Antony Ronald *geography educator*
Orr, Ronald Stewart *lawyer*
Orsatti, Alfred Kendall *organization executive*
†O'Steen, Sam *film editor, director*
Ostroff, Peter I. *lawyer*
Owen, Michael Lee *lawyer*
Owens, Stephen Thomas *lawyer*
Pace, Richard Randall *lawyer, educator*
Packard, Robert Charles *lawyer*
Pal, Pratapaditya *museum curator*
Palevsky, Max *industrialist*
Paparelli, Angelo A. *lawyer*
Papiano, Neil Leo *lawyer*
†Pappe, Stuart H. *film editor*
Paredes, Alfonso *psychiatrist*
Park, Chui Suh *pharmacist*
†Park, Ki Su *architectural firm executive*
Parker, John William *pathology educator, investigator*
Parker, Robert George *radiation oncology educator, academic administrator*
Parks, Michael Christopher *journalist*
Parmelee, Arthur Hawley, Jr. *pediatric medical educator*
Parsky, Gerald Lawrence *lawyer*
Patel, Chandra Kumar Naranbhai *communications company executive, educator, researcher*
†Patron, Susan Hall *librarian, writer*
Patterson, Charles Ernest *lawyer*
Patterson, Dawn Marie *dean, consultant, author, educator*
Paul, Lee Gilmour *lawyer*
Paulson, David L. *newspaper publishing executive*
Paulson, Donald Robert *chemistry educator*
Pearlstein, Leonard *advertising agency executive*
Peck, Austin H., Jr. *lawyer*
Pederson, Con *animator*
Peoples, David Webb *screenwriter*
Pepe, Stephen Phillip *lawyer*
Perenchio, Andrew Jerrold *film and television executive*
Pereyra-Suarez, Charles Albert *lawyer*
Perkins, William Clinton *company executive*
Perkins, William Hughes *speech pathologist, educator*
Perlmutter, Donna *music and dance critic*
Perloff, Joseph Kayle *cardiologist*
Perna, Frank, Jr. *manufacturing company executive*
†Peroni, Geraldine *film editor*
Perrine, Richard Leroy *environmental engineering educator*
†Perrine, Valerie *actress*
Perry, Joe *guitarist*
Perry, Ralph Barton, III *lawyer*
Perry, Robert Michael *consulting engineering company executive*
Perry, Troy D. *clergyman, church administrator*
Perry, William Joseph *food processing company executive*
†Petak, William John *systems management educator*
Peters, Aulana Louise *government agency commissioner, lawyer*
Peters, Richard T. *lawyer*
†Petersen, Robert E. *publisher*
Peterson, Linda S. *lawyer*
Petroni, Donald Victor *lawyer*
Pettit, Thomas Henry *ophthalmologist*
Petty, Tom *rock guitarist, band leader, composer*
Pfaelzer, Mariana R. *federal judge*
Phelps, Barton Chase *architect, educator*
Phillips, Julia Miller *film producer*
Phillips, Keith Wendall *minister*
Phinney, Jean Swift *psychology educator*
Piazza, Michael Joseph *professional baseball player*
Pieper, Darold D. *lawyer*
†Pierce-Roberts, Tony *cinematographer*
Pierskalla, William Peter *academic dean, management and engineering educator*
Pircher, Leo Joseph *lawyer*
Pitkin, Roy Macbeth *physician, educator*
Plate, Thomas Gordon *newspaper editor*
Platt, Mark E. *motion picture company executive*
Poindexter, William Mersereau *lawyer*
Polan, Morris *librarian*
Pollack, Daniel *concert pianist*
Pollock, John Phleger *lawyer*
Pope, Alexander H. *lawyer, former county official*
Port, Sidney Charles *mathematician, educator*
Portenier, Walter James *aerospace engineer*
Porter, Verna Louise *lawyer*
Post, Mike *composer*
Potts, Annie *actress*
Potts, Simon *record company executive*
Powell, James Lawrence *museum president*
Power, John Bruce *lawyer*
Prager, Susan Westerberg *dean, law educator*
Praw, Albert Z. *lawyer*
Preonas, George Elias *lawyer*
Presant, Sanford Calvin *lawyer*
Priestley, Jason *actor*
Principal, Victoria *actress*
Privett, Howard J. *lawyer*
†Proies, Michael Constantine *apparel company executive*
Puckett, Allen Emerson *aeronautical engineer*
Puhvel, Jaan *philologist, educator*
Purcell, Arthur Henry *environmental engineering educator, consultant*
Purcell, Lee *actress*
Puzo, Mario *author*
Quinn, Tom *communications executive*
Rabinovitz, Jason *film and television consultant*
Rabinovitz, Joel *lawyer, educator*
†Rabinowitz, Leonard *apparel executive*
Rachelefsky, Gary S. *medical educator*
Radloff, William Hamilton *editor, writer*
Rae, Matthew Sanderson, Jr. *lawyer*
Raeder, Myrna Sharon *lawyer, educator*
Rafeedie, Edward *federal judge*
Rafkin, Alan *television and film director*
Raitt, Bonnie Lynn *blues singer, guitarist*
Ramer, Lawrence Jerome *corporation executive*
Ramo, Simon *engineering executive*
Ramseyer, J. Mark *law educator*
Ramseyer, Loretta Lynne *lawyer*
Randolph, John *actor*
†Random, Ida *production designer*
Rangell, Leo *psychiatrist, psychoanalyst*
Rankaitis, Susan *artist*
Rapaport, Mark Samuel *lawyer*
Rappeport, Ira J. *lawyer*
Rath, Howard Grant, Jr. *lawyer*
Rathbun, John Wilbert *American studies educator*
Ratzenberger, John Deszo *actor, writer, director*
Rauch, Lawrence Lee *aerospace and electrical engineer, educator*
Raven, Bertram H(erbert) *psychology educator*
Ray, Gilbert T. *lawyer*
Ray, Kelley *production company technical director*
Rayfiel, David *screenwriter*
†Raymond, Arthur Emmons *aerospace engineer*
Rea, William J. *federal judge*
Reagan, Nancy Davis (Anne Francis Robbins) *volunteer, wife of former President of United States*
Reagan, Ronald Wilson *former President of United States*
Real, Manuel Lawrence *federal judge*
Reaney, Gilbert *musician, educator*
†Record, John F. *public relations executive*
Rector, Robert Wayman *mathematics and engineering educator, former association executive*
Redheffer, Raymond Moos *mathematician, educator*
†Reed, Donald Anthony *executive*
†Rees, Roger *actor, educator*
Reeves, Barbara Ann *lawyer*
Refuerzo, Ben J. *architectural educator, architectural firm executive*
Rehme, Robert G. *film company executive*
Reich, Kenneth Irvin *journalist*
Reiner, Ira *lawyer*
Reiss, Howard *chemistry educator*
Remy, Ray *chamber of commerce official*
†Renford, Edward J. *hospital administrator*
Rensch, Joseph Romaine *public utility holding company executive*
Rense, Paige *editor, publishing company executive*
†Reynolds, Norman *production designer, art director*
Rice, Donald Blessing *former secretary of air force, corporate executive*
Rice, Linda Johnson *publishing executive*
Rice, Susan F. *zoological park executive*
Rich, Alan *music critic, editor, author*
Rich, J(ay) Peter *lawyer*
Richards, Michael *actor, comedian*
Richardson, Douglas Fielding *lawyer*
Richardson, John Vinson, Jr. *library science educator*
Richardson, Rand Michael *public relations executive*
†Richardson, Robert *cinematographer*
Richman, Frederick Alexander *lawyer*
Richman, Peter Mark *actor, painter, writer*
Richter, W. D. *screenwriter, director, producer*
Rickles, Donald Jay *comedian, actor*
Rickman, Alan *actor*
†Riggs, Rita *costume designer*
Riley, Jack *actor, writer*
Riley, John Graham *economics educator*
Rimoin, David Lawrence *physician, geneticist*
Ring, Michael Wilson *lawyer*
Rinsch, Charles Emil *insurance company executive*
Riordan, Richard J. *mayor*
Ritchie, Michael Brunswick *film director and producer*
†Ritter, John(athan) (Southworth) *actor*

Ritvo, Edward Ross *psychiatrist*
†Riva, J. Michael *art director, production designer*
Rivers, Joan *entertainer*
†Roath, Kenneth B. *investment company executive*
Robards, Jason Nelson, Jr. *actor*
Robert, Patrick *playwright*
Roberts, Robert Winston *social work educator, dean*
Roberts, Sidney *biological chemist*
Roberts, Thomas G. *lawyer*
Roberts, Virgil Patrick *lawyer, business executive*
Robertson, Hugh Duff *lawyer*
Robertson, Robbie *musician, popular*
†Robinson, John Peter *film composer, keyboardist*
Robinson, Martha Stewart *retired legal educator*
Robinson, Smokey *singer, composer*
Rodgers, Aggie Guerard *costume designer*
Rodnick, Eliot Herman *psychologist, educator*
Roeder, Richard Kenneth *business owner, lawyer*
Roemer, Milton Irwin *physician, educator*
Rogan, Patrick Goode *lawyer*
†Rogers, James Wilson *church official*
Rogers, Kenneth Ray *entertainer, recording artist*
Rogger, Hans Jack *history educator*
†Rogoway, Lawrence Paul *civil engineer, consultant*
Rollins, Henry *musician, author, publisher*
Roney, John Harvey *lawyer*
Roos, Frederick Ried *film producer*
Rosecrance, Richard Newton *political scientist, educator*
†Rosen, Charles *production designer*
Rosen, Robert Charles *lawyer*
†Rosenman, Leonard *composer*
Rosenthal, Sol *lawyer*
Rosenthal, Stuart A. *retail executive*
Rosenzweig, David *newspaper editor*
Rosett, Arthur Irwin *lawyer, educator*
Rosner, T. *insurance executive*
Ross, Joseph Foster *physician, educator*
†Ross, Stan *accounting firm executive*
Ross, William H. *accountant*
Rosser, James Milton *university president*
Rosten, Irwin *writer, producer, director*
Rothenberg, Alan I. *professional sports association executive, lawyer*
Rothman, Frank *lawyer, motion picture company executive*
†Rotter, Stephen A. *film editor*
Rouse, Richard Hunter *historian, educator*
Roussey, Robert Stanley *accountant, educator*
Rubin, Bruce Joel *screenwriter, director, producer*
Rubin, Stanley Creamer *producer*
Rubinroit, Howard J. *lawyer*
†Rubinstein, Arthur B. *composer*
Rubinstein, Moshe Fajwel *engineering educator*
Rudolph, Jeffrey N. *museum director*
Ruskin, Joseph Richard *actor, director*
Ruth, Craig *business executive*
Rutledge, William P. *manufacturing company executive*
Ryan, Reade Haines, Jr. *lawyer*
Ryan, Stephen Joseph, Jr. *ophthalmology educator, university dean*
Saad, Mohammed Fathy *medical educator*
Safonov, Michael George *electrical engineering educator, consultant*
†Saget, Bob *actor, comedian*
Saltzman, Joseph *journalist, producer, educator*
Salvaty, Benjamin Benedict *lawyer*
Salzman, David Elliot *entertainment industry executive*
Samet, Jack I. *lawyer*
Sample, Steven Browning *university president*
Samuels, Donald L. *lawyer*
Sanders, Joseph Stanley *lawyer*
Sanders, Richard Kinard *actor*
Sanjian, Avedis Krikor *Armenian studies educator*
Sansweet, Stephen Jay *journalist, author*
Sarnat, Bernard George *plastic surgeon, educator, researcher*
Sarnoff, Thomas Warren *television executive*
†Sassoon, Vidal *hair stylist*
Savage, Edward Warren, Jr. *physician*
Savikas, Victor George *lawyer*
Sawyer, Charles Henry *anatomist, educator*
†Sawyer, Richard *art director, production designer*
Saxe, Deborah Crandall *lawyer*
Saxon, David Stephen *physics educator, university official*
Sayles, John Thomas *film director, writer, actor*
Saylor, Mark Julian *editor*
Schaefer, William David *English educator*
Scheibel, Arnold Bernard *psychiatrist, educator, researcher*
Scheifly, John Edward *retired lawyer*
Schell, Maximilian *actor, director*
Schepisi, Fred *director, screenwriter*
Schiff, Martin *physician, surgeon*
†Schifsky, Charles Mark *magazine editor*
Schlosberg, Richard T., III *newspaper publishing executive*
†Schmidt, Arthur *film editor*
Schmit, Lucien André, Jr. *structural engineer*
Schmutz, Arthur Walter *lawyer*
Schnabel, Rockwell Anthony *ambassador*
Schneider, Charles I. *newspaper executive*
Schneider, Edward Lewis *medicine educator, research administrator*
Schneider, Wolf *magazine editor, writer*
Scholtz, Robert Arno *electrical engineering educator*
†Schoonmaker Powell, Thelma *film editor*
Schopf, James William *paleobiologist*
Schroeder, Barbet G. *director*
Schroeder, Bill E. *lawyer*
Schumacher, Joseph Charles *chemical engineer*
Schurr, Carolyn *lawyer*
Schutz, John Adolph *historian, educator, former university dean*
Schwabe, Arthur David *physician, educator*
Schwartz, Gary T. *law educator*
Schwartz, Leon *foreign language educator*
Scott, A. Timothy *lawyer*
Scott, Allen John *educator*
Scott, Campbell *actor*
Scott, George Campbell *actor, director*
Scott, Kelly *newspaper editor*
Scott, Ridley *film director*
Scott, Robert Lane *chemist, educator*
Scott, Tony *film director*
Scully, Vincent Edward *sports broadcaster*
Seaver, Richard Carlton *oil field equipment company executive, lawyer*
†See, Carolyn *English educator, book critic*
Seebart, George E. *insurance executive*
Seeman, Melvin *sociologist, educator*
Segal, Morton *public relations executive*
Segil, Larraine Diane *materials company executive*
Seide, Paul *civil engineering educator*
Seidelman, Arthur Allan *director*
Seigel, Daniel A. *retail executive*
Selwood, Pierce Taylor *lawyer*
Seto, Joseph Tobey *virologist, educator*
Settles, F. Stan, Jr. *manufacturing executive, educator*
Seymour, Jane *actress*
†Seymour, Michael *production designer*
Shagan, Steve *screenwriter, novelist, film producer*
Shaiman, Marc *composer, arranger, orchestrator*
Shames, Henry Joseph *lawyer*
Shandling, Garry *comedian, scriptwriter, actor*
Shank, Russell *librarian, educator*
Shapiro, Isadore *materials scientist, consultant*
Shapiro, Marvin Seymour *lawyer*
Shapiro, Mel *playwright, director, drama educator*
Shapiro, Robert Leslie *lawyer*
Shapley, Lloyd Stowell *mathematics and economics educator*
Shatner, William *actor*
Shaw, David Lyle *journalist, author*
†Shearer, Derek N. *international studies educator, diplomat, administrator*
Sheehan, Lawrence James *lawyer*
Shelton, Turner Blair *diplomat*
Shepherd, Cybill *actress, singer*
Sheppard, Thomas Richard *lawyer*
Sherrell, John Bradford *lawyer*
Sherwood, Allen Joseph *lawyer*
Sherwood, Arthur Lawrence *lawyer*
Sherwood, Linda Kathleen *lawyer*
Shideler, Ross Patrick *foreign language and comparative literature educator, author, translator, poet*
Shire, David Lee *composer*
Shneidman, Edwin S. *psychologist, educator, thanatologist, suicidologist*
Shore, Herbert *writer, poet, educator*
Shorter, Wayne *musician*
Shortz, Richard Alan *lawyer*
Shultz, John David *lawyer*
Shutler, Mary Elizabeth *academic administrator*
Siart, William Eric Baxter *banker*
†Siegel, Michael Elliot *nuclear medicine physician, educator*
Siegel, Sheldon C. *physician*
Sigband, Norman Bruce *management communication educator*
Silbergeld, Arthur F. *lawyer*
Silverman, Bruce Gary *advertising executive*
Silverman, Leonard M. *university dean, electrical engineering educator*
Simpson, Allyson Bilich *lawyer*
Sinay, Hershel David *publisher*
Sinay, Joseph *retail executive*
Sinay, Ruth Doris *psychologist*
Sitrick, Michael Steven *communications executive*
Sklar, Richard Lawrence *political science educator*
Skotak, Robert F. *film production company executive*
Slater, Helen Rachel *actress*
Slaughter, John Brooks *university president*
Sloan, L. Lawrence *publishing executive*
Sloane, Robert Malcolm *hospital administrator*
Slonimsky, Nicolas *conductor, composer*
Smathers, James Burton *medical physicist, educator*
Smith, Byron Owen *lawyer*
Smith, Chester Leo *lawyer*
Smith, David King *publishing executive, newspaper*
Smith, Emil L. *biochemist, consultant*
†Smith, Howard *film editor*
Smith, Jack Clifford *journalist, author*
Smith, Jean Webb (Mrs. William French Smith) *civic worker*
†Smith, Joe *recording industry executive*
Smith, Joseph Benjamin *communications company executive*
Smith, Lane Jeffrey *automotive journalist, technical consultant*
Smith, Wallace A. *radio company executive*
Smith, William Ray *retired biophysicist, engineer*
Smits, Jimmy *actor*
Smothers, Tom *actor, singer*
Smulders, Anthony Peter *biology educator*
Snyder, Allegra Fuller *dance educator*
†Snyder, David L. *film production designer*
Snyder, David Markel *marketing executive*
Snyder, Sam A. *oil company executive, lawyer*
Sobelle, Richard E. *lawyer*
Solomon, David Harris *physician, educator*
Solomon, George Freeman *academic psychiatrist*
Soltman, Neil M. *lawyer*
Somers, Harold Milton *economist, educator*
Song, Moon Ki *biomedical research scientist*
Sonnenschein, Ralph Robert *physiologist*
Southern, Robert Allen *lawyer*
†Souza, Anthony P. *real estate developer, wholesale distribution services executive, finance company executive*
Span, Robert Steven *lawyer*
Spelling, Aaron *film and television producer, writer*
†Spencer, James H. *art director, production designer*
Spero, Stanley Leonard *broadcast executive*
Speyer, Jason Lee *engineer, educator*
†Spindler, Paul *public relations executive*
Spitzer, William George *university dean, physicist, educator, researcher*
Spofford, Robert Houston *advertising agency executive*
Spooner, Mark Jordan *lawyer*
Sprague, Norman Frederick, Jr. *surgeon, educator*
Spuehler, Donald Roy *retired lawyer, writer, mythologist*
Stamm, Alan *lawyer*
Stancill, James McNeill *finance educator, consultant*
Stanfill, Shelton G. *performing arts administrator*
†Stanton, Eric *wholesale distribution executive*
Stapleton, Jean (Jeanne Murray) *actress*
Starr, Steven Dawson *photographer*
Steckel, Richard J. *radiologist, academic administrator*
Steel, Dawn *motion picture producer*
Steel, Ronald Lewis *author, historian, educator*
†Steele, Victoria Lee *librarian*
Stegemeier, Richard Joseph *oil company executive*
Steinberg, Morris Albert *metallurgist*
Steinberg, Warren Linnington *principal*
†Steinkamp, Fredric *film editor*
†Steinkamp, William *film editor*
Stellwagen, Robert Harwood *biochemistry educator*
Stephens, Albert Lee, Jr. *federal judge*
Stephens, George Edward, Jr. *lawyer*
Sterling, Donald T. *professional basketball team executive*
Stern, Leonard Bernard *television and motion picture production company executive*
Stern, Marc Irwin *financial services executive*
Stern, Stephen Jeffrey *lawyer*
Stern, Walter Eugene *neurosurgeon, educator*
Stevens, Andrew *actor, producer, writer, director*
Stevens, Gerald D. *secondary education educator, consultant*
Stevens, Roy W. *distilled spirits executive*
Stevenson, Robert Murrell *music educator*
†Stewart, Marlene Jean *costume designer*
Stiehm, E. Richard *pediatrician, educator*
Stiers, David Ogden *actor, conductor*
Stinehart, William, Jr. *lawyer*
Stockwell, Robert Paul *linguist, educator*
Stoddard, Brandon *film and television company executive*
Stolberg, Sheryl Gay *journalist*
Stone, Lawrence Maurice *lawyer, educator*
Stone, Richard James *lawyer*
Stoterau, H. Peter *lawyer*
Straatsma, Bradley Ralph *ophthalmologist, educator*
†Strathairn, David *actor*
Stromberg, Ross Ernest *lawyer*
Sullivan, Peter M. *lawyer*
Sullivan, Stuart Francis *anesthesiologist, educator*
†Surace, Ronald J. *real estate executive*
†Sutherland, Michael Cruise *librarian*
Swayze, Patrick *actor, dancer*
Sweeney, Judith L. *newspaper publishing executive*
Szego, Clara Marian *cell biologist, educator*
Szwarc, Michael *polymer scientist*
Takasugi, Robert Mitsuhiro *federal judge*
Tally, Ted *screenwriter*
Talton, Chester Lovelle *bishop*
Tamkin, S. Jerome *business executive, consultant*
Tan, William Lew *lawyer*
Tanen, Ned Stone *motion picture company executive*
Tanzmann, Virginia Ward *architect*
Tardio, Thomas A. *public relations executive*
Tarr, Ralph William *lawyer, former federal government official*
Tartikoff, Brandon *broadcast executive*
Tashima, Atsushi Wallace *federal judge*
†Tashkin, Donald P. *physician*
Taylor, Leigh Herbert *college dean*
Taylor, Meshach *actor*
Tellem, Susan Mary *public relations executive*
Tennenbaum, Michael Ernest *investment banker*
Tennyson, G(eorg) B(ernhard) *English educator*
Terrell, Joseph Alcasar *interior designer*
Terry, Thomas Edward *investment company executive, lawyer*
Tesh, John *television talk show host*
Teutsch, Champion Kurt *psycho-geneticist*
Tevrizian, Dickran M., Jr. *federal judge*
Thoman, John Everett *architect, mediator*
Thomas, Christopher Robert *food products company executive*
Thomas, Jay *actor*
Thomas, Robert Joseph *columnist, author*
Thomas, Shirley *author, educator, business executive*
Thompson, Earl Albert *economics educator*
Thompson, Richard Frederick *psychologist, neuroscientist, educator*
Thompson, Shawna Margaret *lawyer*
†Thomson, Alex *cinematographer*
Thorne, Richard Mansergh *physicist*
Thrower, Norman Joseph William *geographer, educator*
Thune, Dale Gene *financial executive, appraiser*
†Tilly, Jennifer *actress*
Tinsley, Walton Eugene *lawyer*
Tischler, Gary Lowell *psychiatrist, educator*
Titus, Edward Depue *psychiatrist, administrator*
Tobia, Stephen Francis, Jr. *marketing professional, consultant*
Tobisman, Stuart Paul *lawyer*
†Toll, John *cinematographer*
Tomash, Erwin *retired computer equipment company executive*
Tompkins, Ronald K. *surgeon*
Topping, Norman Hawkins *former university chancellor*
Tornek, Terry E. *real estate executive*
Tortorici, Peter Frank *television executive*
Totten, George Oakley, III *political science educator*
Toulmin, Stephen Edelston *humanities educator*
Townley, Jon *production company creative director*
†Townsend, Jeffrey *production designer*
Townsend, Robert *film director*
Tranquada, Robert Ernest *medical educator, physician*
†Travis, Neil *film editor*
Treister, George Marvin *lawyer*
Trembly, Dennis Michael *musician*
Trimble, Phillip Richard *law educator*
Trimble, Stanley Wayne *hydrology and geography educator*
Triplett, Arlene Ann *travel company executive*
Troy, Joseph Freed *lawyer*
Trygstad, Lawrence Benson *lawyer*
Tuckson, Reed V. *university president*
Turchin, Carolyn *judge*
Turk, Herman *sociologist, educator, researcher*
Turner, Ralph Herbert *sociologist, educator*
Tuthill, Walter Warren *retail executive*
Tyler, Steven *singer*
Udwadia, Firdaus Erach *engineering educator, consultant*
Ufimtsev, Pyotr Yakovlevich *physicist, electrical engineer, educator*
Ukropina, James R. *lawyer*
Underwood, Vernon O., Jr. *grocery stores executive*
Unterman, Thomas E. *lawyer*
Urioste, Frank J. *film editor*
Utz, Sarah Winifred *nursing educator*
†Vacano, Jost *cinematographer*
Van Asperen, Morris Earl *banker*
van Dam, Heiman *psychoanalyst*
Van de Kamp, John Kalar *lawyer*
Vandeman, George Allen *lawyer*
Vanderet, Robert Charles *lawyer*
Van Der Meulen, Joseph Pierre *neurologist*
Van Dyke, David *broadcast executive*
Van Emburgh, Joanne *lawyer*
Van Horne, R. Richard *oil company executive*
Van Patten, Dick Vincent *actor*
†van Runkle, Theadora *costume designer*
Van Stekelenburg, Mark *food service executive*
Varat, Jonathan D. *law educator*
Vaughan, Joseph Robert *lawyer*
Vaughn, Robert (Francis Vaughn) *actor*
Vaughn, William Weaver *lawyer*
Vena, David Henry *lawyer*
Verdery, David Norwood *broadcast programming executive*
Vereen, Ben *actor, singer, dancer*
Verger, Morris David *architect, planner*
Verity, Maurice Anthony *pathologist, neuropathologist, educator, consultant*
Verrone, Patric Miller *lawyer, writer*
Villablanca, Jaime Rolando *medical scientist, educator*
†Villalobos, Reynaldo *cinematographers*
Vogel, Charles Stimmel *lawyer*
Volpert, Richard Sidney *lawyer*
Von Brandenstein, Patrizia *production designer*
Vradenburg, George, III *lawyer, corporate executive*
Vredevoe, Donna Lou *research immunologist, microbiologist, educator*
Wachs, Martin *urban planning educator*
Wagner, Christian Nikolaus Johann *materials engineering educator*
Wagner, D. William *lawyer*
Wagner, William Gerard *university dean, physicist, consultant, information scientist, investment manager*
Waits, Thomas Alan *composer, actor, singer*
Walcher, Alan Ernest *lawyer*
Walsh, John Harley *medical educator*
†Walsh, Thomas A. *production designer*
Ward, Fred *actor*
Ward, Leslie Allyson *journalist, editor*
Ward, Sela *actress*
†Warner, Mark Roy *film editor*
Warren, Mark Edward *shipping company executive, lawyer*
Wasserman, William Phillip *lawyer*
Waterman, Michael Spencer *mathematics educator, biology educator*
Waters, Laughlin Edward *federal judge*
Waterston, Samuel Atkinson *actor*
Watring, Watson Glenn *gynecologic oncologist, educator*
Watson, Sharon Gitin *psychologist, executive*
Watts, Quincy *track and field athlete*
Wayte, (Paul) Alan *lawyer*
Wazzan, Ahmed R(assem) Frank *engineering educator, dean*
Weaver, Don L. *lawyer*
Wedbush, Edward William *investment banker*
Wedgeworth, Ann *actress*
Wei, Jen Yu *physiologist, researcher, educator*
Weil, Jerry *animator*
Weiner, Leslie Philip *neurology educator, researcher*
Weinstein, Irwin Marshall *internist, hematologist*
Weinstock, Harold *lawyer*
Weiss, Martin Harvey *neurosurgeon, educator*
Weiss, Walter Stanley *lawyer*
Weitzman, Howard L. *lawyer*
Welch, Bo (Robert W. Welch, III) *production designer*
Welch, Lloyd Richard *electrical engineering educator, communications consultant*
†Welch, Robert W. *production designer, art director*
†Wellburn, Timothy *film editor*
Welles, Melinda Fassett *artist, educator*
Werner, Gloria S. *librarian*
Wessling, Robert Bruce *lawyer*
Westheimer, David Kaplan *novelist*
Weston, John Frederick *business educator, consultant*
Wexler, Robert *university administrator*
Wheat, Francis Millspaugh *retired lawyer*
Wheel, Lesley *design firm executive*
Whisman, Linda Anne *law librarian*
White, Leonard *motion picture company executive*
White, Robert Joel *lawyer*
Whitman, Kenneth Jay *advertising executive*
Whitmore, James Allen *actor*
Whitten, Charles Alexander, Jr. *physics educator*
Wiatt, James Anthony *theatrical agency executive*
Wickes, Mary *actress*
Wigmore, John Grant *lawyer*
Wilder, Gene *actor, director, writer*
Wilkerson, Kenneth L. *retail department stores executive*
Williams, David Welford *federal judge*
Williams, John Towner *composer, conductor*
Williams, Julie Ford *mutual fund specialist*
Williams, Paul Hamilton *composer, singer*
Williams, Phillip L. *newspaper publishing executive*
†Williams, Richard T. *hospital administrator*
Williams, Richard Thomas *lawyer*
Williams, Robert Martin *economist, consultant*
Williams, Robin *actor, comedian*
Williams, Theodore Earle *industrial distribution company executive*
Williams, Willie *protective services official*
Willison, Bruce Gray *banker*
Willner, Alan Eli *electrical engineer, educator*
Wills, John Elliot, Jr. *history educator, writer*
Willson, Alan Neil, Jr. *engineering educator, dean*
Wilson, Charles Zachary, Jr. *newspaper publisher*
Wilson, James Quinn *government, management educator*
Wilson, Miriam Geisendorfer *physician, educator*
Wilson, Stephen Victor *federal judge*
Wincor, Michael Z. *psychopharmacology educator, clinician, researcher*
Winfield, Paul Edward *actor*
Winger, Debra *actress*
Winkler, Howard Leslie *investment banker, stockbroker, business consultant*
Winterowd, Walter Ross *English educator*
Winters, Barbara Jo *musician*
Winters, Ralph E. *film editor*
Wiseley, Richard Eugene *securities corporation executive*
Wittrock, Merlin Carl *educational psychologist*
Wittry, David Beryle *physicist, educator*
Woelffer, Emerson Seville *artist*
Wolas, Herbert *lawyer*
Wolf, Alfred *rabbi*
Wolf, Lesley Sara *lawyer*
Wolfen, Werner F. *lawyer*
Wolinsky, Leo C. *newspaper editor*
Wong, Alfred Yiu-fai *physics educator*
Wood, Karen Sue *theatre manager, stage producer, consultant*
Wood, Nancy Elizabeth *psychologist, educator*
Wood, Willis Bowne, Jr. *utility holding company executive*
Woodruff, Fay *paleoceanographer, geological researcher*
Woods, Daniel James *lawyer*
Wooten, Cecil Aaron *religious organization administrator*
Wortham, Thomas Richard *English language educator*
Wright, Donald Franklin *newspaper executive*
Wright, Ernest Marshall *physiologist, consultant*
Wright, Kenneth Brooks *lawyer*
Wu, Li-Pei *banker*
Wu, Robert Chung Yung *space sciences educator*
Wurtele, Morton Gaither *meteorologist, educator*
Wyatt, James Luther *drapery hardware company executive*
Wyatt, Joseph Lucian, Jr. *lawyer, educator*

Wycoff, Robert E. *petroleum company executive*
Wyman, William George *musician*
Yablans, Frank *film company executive, motion picture producer*
Yagiela, John Allen *dental educator*
Yamamoto, Joe *psychiatrist, educator*
Yee, Stephen *airport executive*
Yeh, William Wen-Gong *civil engineering educator*
Yen, Teh Fu *civil engineering and environmental educator*
York, Gary Alan *lawyer*
Young, Bless Stritar *lawyer*
Young, Charles Edward *university chancellor*
Young, J. Anthony *entertainment company executive*
Young, Joseph Louis *artist*
Young, Loretta (Gretchen Young) *actress*
Yue, Alfred Shui-choh *metallurgical engineer, educator*
Zacchino, Narda *newspaper editor*
Zame, William R. *economist, educator, mathematician*
Zamir, Frances Roberta (Frances Roberta Weiss-Swede) *assistant principal*
Zarefsky, Ralph *lawyer*
†Zawacki, Bruce E. *surgeon, ethicist*
Zelon, Laurie Dee *lawyer*
Zemeckis, Robert L. *film director*
Ziering, Sigi *medical company executive*
Ziffren, Kenneth *lawyer*
Ziffren, Lester *lawyer*
†Zimmer, Hans *composer*
†Zimmerman, Herman F. *motion picture production designer*
Zohn, Martin Steven *lawyer*
Zolin, Frank Stanley *county administrator*
Zucker, Jerry *producer, director*

Los Gatos
Allan, Lionel Manning *lawyer, consultant*
Farley, Philip Judson *former government official*
Grubb, William Francis X. *consumer software executive, marketing executive*
Hartinger, Patricia Bernardine Curran *elementary school educator*
Henley, Jeffrey O. *restaurant executive*
Knudsen, William Claire *geophysicist*
Leverett, Miles Corrington *retired nuclear power consultant*
Lorincz, Albert Bela *physician, educator*
Meyers, Ann Elizabeth *sports broadcaster*
Naymark, Sherman *consulting nuclear engineer*
Olender, Beatrijs Tobi *psychologist, marriage and family therapist*
Simonson, Ted *principal*
Webster, John Chas *human resources management consultant*

Los Olivos
Buxton, Kenneth Arthur *educator, academic dean*
Cruft, Edgar Frank *mining company executive*

Los Osos
Brown, Mary Eleanor *physical therapist, educator*
Cloonan, Clifford B. *electrical engineer, educator*
Dorland, Frank Norton *art conservator*
Thomas, Robert Murray *educational psychology educator*

Lynwood
Jorgensen, Earle M. *metal products executive*

Magalia
Joffre, Stephen Paul *consulting chemist*

Malibu
Aiken, Lewis Roscoe, Jr. *psychologist, educator*
Baskin, Otis Wayne *business educator*
Chester, Arthur Noble *physicist*
Coben, William Allen *lawyer*
Davenport, David *university president, lawyer*
Ensign, Richard Papworth *transportation executive*
Felton, Norman Francis *motion picture producer*
Forward, Robert L(ull) *physicist, writer, consultant*
Gail, Maxwell Trowbridge, Jr. *actor, director, musician*
Klugman, Jack *actor*
Lilly, John Cunningham *medical scientist, author*
Louganis, Greg E. *former Olympic athlete, actor*
Margerum, J(ohn) David *chemist*
Morgenstern, Leon *surgeon*
Nolte, Nick *actor*
Palacio, June Rose Payne *professor of nutritional science*
Pepper, David M. *physicist, educator, author, inventor*
Phillips, Ronald Frank *legal educator, law school dean*
Reres, Mary Epiphany *health care and administration consultant*
Smith, George Foster *retired aerospace company executive*
†Tallal, Scott Victor *television research consultant*
Widmann, Glenn Roger *electrical engineer*
Wilson, John Francis *religion educator*
Yates, Jere Eugene *business educator, management consultant*
Young, Matt Norvel, Jr. *university chancellor emeritus*

Mammoth Lakes
Buchanan, Lee Ann *public relations executive*

Manhattan Beach
Anderson, Charles Michael *accountant*
Blanton, John Arthur *architect*
Bradburn, David Denison *engineer,retired air force officer*
Brooks, Edward Howard *college administrator*
Krienke, Carol Belle Manikowske (Mrs. Oliver Kenneth Krienke) *realtor*
Scott, Michael Dennis *lawyer*
Stern, Daniel Alan *business management consultant*
Weinstock, Herbert Frank *public relations executive*

Manteca
Tonn, Elverne Meryl *pediatric dentist, dental insurance consultant*

Marina
Myers, James David *municipal government official*

Marina Del Rey
Adams, Thomas Merritt *lawyer*
Collins, Russell Ambrose *advertising executive, creative director*
Doebler, Paul Dickerson *publishing management executive*
Gold, Carol Sapin *international management consultant, speaker*
Grobe, Charles Stephen *lawyer, accountant*
†Semler, Dean *cinematographer*
Smith, George Drury *publisher, editor, collagist, writer*
Smith, Steven Warren *public relations executive*
Tanaka, Ted Tokio *architect, educator*
Tennant, John Randall *management advisory company executive*
Waite, Ralph *actor*

Mariposa
Bruce, John Anthony *artist*
Rogers, Earl Leslie *artist, educator*
Shields, Allan Edwin *writer, photographer, retired educator*

Marshall
Evans, Robert James *architect*

Martinez
Bray, Absalom Francis, Jr. *lawyer*
Efron, Robert *neurology educator, research institute administrator*
Geokas, Michael C. *gastroenterologist*
Meyer, Jarold Alan *oil company research executive*
Thomas, Walter Dill, Jr. *forest pathologist, consultant*

Marysville
Hamilton, Richard Daniel *neurosurgeon*
Hardie, Robert C. *newspaper publishing executive*

Mc Kinleyville
Morris, Marjorie Hale *retail executive, appraiser, artist, writer*

Mendocino
Alexander, Joyce Mary *illustrator*

Menlo Park
Alexander, Theron *behavioral scientist, psychologist, writer*
†Altman, Drew E. *foundation executive*
Bader, William Reece *lawyer*
Baez, Joan Chandos *folk singer*
Bissell, Betty Dickson *retired stockbroker*
Bourne, Charles Percy *information scientist, educator*
Bremser, George, Jr. *electronics company executive*
Browne, Millard Child *former newspaper editor*
Bukry, John David *geologist*
†Cardon, Lon Ray *geneticist researcher*
†Chait, Arthur Lyle *management consultant*
Cook, Paul M. *technology company executive*
Craig, Gordon Alexander *historian, educator*
†Crall, Michael J. *insurance executive*
Crane, Hewitt David *science advisor*
Davis, William Emrys *religious organization official*
Duda, Richard Oswald *electrical engineering educator, researcher*
Edson, William Alden *electrical engineer*
Evans, Bob Overton *electronics executive*
Everett, Michael Thomas *lawyer*
Fassett, Hugh Gardner *investment counselor*
Fergason, James L. *optical company executive*
Ferris, Robert Albert *lawyer, venture capitalist*
Frisco, Louis Joseph *retired materials science company executive, electrical engineer*
Fuhrman, Frederick Alexander *physiology educator*
Funkhouser, Lawrence William *retired geologist*
Gardner, David Pierpont *foundation executive*
Gilburne, Miles R. *lawyer*
Glaser, Robert Joy *physician, foundation executive*
Graham, Howard Holmes *manufacturing executive*
Hiller, Stanley, Jr. *manufacturing company executive*
Hoagland, Laurance Redington, Jr. *investment executive*
Holzer, Thomas Lequear *geologist*
Honey, Richard Churchill *retired electrical engineer*
Jorgensen, Paul J. *research company executive*
Katz, Robert Lee *business executive*
Kohne, Richard Edward *retired engineering executive*
Kurtzig, Sandra L. *software company executive*
Lachenbruch, Arthur Herold *geophysicist*
Lane, Laurence William, Jr. *retired U.S. ambassador, publisher*
Leach, John Frank *transportation executive*
Leadabrand, Ray L. *engineering executive, defense industry consultant*
Lindh, Allan Goddard *seismologist*
Litfin, Richard Albert *retired news organization executive*
Lucas, Donald Leo *private investor*
MacGregor, James Thomas *toxicologist*
Marken, William Riley *magazine editor*
McCarthy, Roger Lee *mechanical engineer*
McCown, George E. *venture banking company executive*
McDonald, Warren George *accountant, former savings and loan executive*
†McMillen, Donald F. *chemist*
McMurtry, Burton John *venture capital investor, electrical engineer*
Morrell, James Wilson *consulting company executive*
Morrison, James Ian *research institute executive*
Nichols, William Ford, Jr. *foundation executive, business executive*
O'Brien, Raymond Francis *transportation executive*
Oronsky, Arnold Lewis *scientific research company executive, medical educator*
Pallotti, Marianne Marguerite *foundation administrator*
Parker, Donn Blanchard *information security consultant*
Phipps, Allen Mayhew *management consultant*
Pooley, James Henry Anderson *lawyer, author*
Postlewait, Harry Owen *chemical company executive*
Roberts, George R. *venture capital company executive*
†Saldich, Robert Joseph *electronics company executive*
Salmon, Vincent *acoustical consultant*
†Savage, James Crampton *geophysicist*
Scandling, William Fredric *retired food service company executive*
Shows, Winnie M. *public relations company executive, professional speaker*
Sidells, Arthur F. *architect*
Sommers, William Paul *management consultant*
Sparks, Robert Dean *medical administrator, physician*
Speidel, John Joseph *physician, foundation officer*
Storer, Morris Brewster *retired philosophy educator*
Surbeck, Leighton Homer *retired lawyer*
Sutherland, Robert Melvin *life sciences professional, educator*
Szentirmai, George *electrical engineer, corporate executive*
Taft, David Dakin *chemical executive*
Tietjen, James *research institute administrator*
Tokheim, Robert Edward *physicist*
Vickers, Roger Spencer *physicist, program director*
Vidale, John Emilio *geologist*
Wallace, Robert Earl *geologist*
Walsh, William Desmond *investor*
White, Phillip E. *technology company executive*
Wolaner, Robin Peggy *magazine publisher*

Mentone
Stockton, David Knapp *professional golfer*

Merced
Maytum, Harry Rodell *retired physician*
Olsen, David Magnor *science educator*

Mill Valley
Barbarich, Stanley Joseph *marketing executive*
Benezet, Louis Tomlinson *retired psychology educator, former college president*
Blatt, Morton Bernard *medical illustrator*
Crews, William Odell, Jr. *seminary administrator*
D'Amico, Michael *architect, urban planner*
Dillon, Richard Hugh *librarian, author*
Harner, Michael James *anthropologist, educator, author*
†Hurtado, Corydon Dicks *management consultant*
Ihle, John Livingston *artist, educator*
Leslie, Jacques Robert, Jr. *journalist*
Newman, Nancy Marilyn *ophthalmologist, educator, consultant, inventor, entrepreneur*
Padula, Fred David *filmmaker*
Pflueger, John Milton *architect*
Wallerstein, Robert Solomon *psychiatrist*
Winskill, Robert Wallace *manufacturing executive*

Millbrae
Li, David Wen-Chung *television company executive*

Milpitas
Berkley, Stephen Mark *computer peripherals manufacturing company executive*
Brown, David A. *computer hardware company executive*
Corrigan, Wilfred J. *data processing and computer company executive*
†Davis, Jeffrey L. *electronics company executive*
†Granchelli, Ralph S. *company executive*
Hodson, Roy Goode, Jr. *retired logistician*
Latimer, Linda Gay *small business owner*
Lee, Kenneth *physicist*
†Rostoker, Michael David *computer company executive, lawyer*
Wells, George Douglas *corporate executive*

Mission Hills
Cramer, Frank Brown *engineering executive, combustion engineer, systems consultant*
Krieg, Dorothy Linden *soprano, performing artist, educator*

Mission Viejo
Foulds, Donald Duane *aerospace executive*
Hough, J. Marie *vocational education educator*
Milunas, J. Robert *health care organization executive*
Pohl, John Henning *chemical engineer, consultant*
Ruben, Robert Joseph *lawyer*
Sabaroff, Rose Epstein *retired education educator*
Small, Richard F. *mechanical engineer, consultant*
†Smith, William K. *real estate developer*
Teitelbaum, Harry *English educator*

Modesto
Bairey, Marie *principal*
Bucknam, Mary Olivia Caswell *artist*
Crawford, Charles McNeil *winery science executive*
Ferreira, Judith Anne *librarian*
Ferrucci, Raymond Vincent *retired food company executive*
Gallo, Ernest *vintner*
Hedrick, Joseph Watson, Jr. *retired judge*
Kreissman, Starrett *librarian*
LaMont, Sanders Hickey *journalist*
†Lang, Richard Arthur *mayor, educator*
Mayhew, William A. *judge*
Mensinger, Peggy Boothe *retired mayor*
Owens, Jack Byron *lawyer*
Piccinini, Robert M. *grocery store chain executive*
Shastid, Jon Barton *wine company executive*
Smith, Glenda Irene *elementary school educator*
Snyder, Margaret Elizabeth *assemblywoman, paralegal*
Sprinkle, Charles Ray *wholesale grocery company executive*
†Webb, Erman A. *food products executive*
†Webb, Michael A. *food products executive*

Moffett Field
Baldwin, Betty Jo *computer specialist*
Cohen, Malcolm Martin *psychologist, researcher*
Dean, William Evans *aerospace agency executive*
Haines, Richard Foster *psychologist*
Kerr, Andrew W. *aerodynamics researcher*
Kittel, Peter *research scientist*
Lauber, John K. *research psychologist*
McCroskey, William James *aeronautical engineer*
†Morrison, David *science administrator*
†Munechika, Ken Kenji *research center administrator*
Park, Chul *aerospace engineer*
Ragent, Boris *physicist*
Scott, Donald Michael *educational association administrator, educator*
Seiff, Alvin *planetary scientist, atmosphere physics and aerodynamics consultant*
Statler, Irving Carl *aerospace engineer*
†Yelle, Roger V. *physical chemist*

Mojave
Rutan, Elbert L. (Burt Rutan) *aircraft designer*

Monrovia
Breen, Thomas Albert *financial services executive*
Jemelian, John Nazar *merchant, financial executive*
Mac Cready, Paul Beattie *aeronautical engineer*
Salaman, Maureen Kennedy *nutritionist*
Seiple, Robert Allen *Christian relief organization executive*

Montara
Gyemant, Robert Ernest *lawyer*

Montclair
Haage, Robert Mitchell *retired history educator, organization leader*

Monte Rio
Pemberton, John de Jarnette, Jr. *lawyer, educator*

Montebello
Dible, Rose Harpe McFee *special education educator*

Montecito
Atkins, Stuart (Pratt) *German language and literature educator*
Meghreblian, Robert Vartan *manufacturing executive, physicist*
Rose, Mark Allen *humanities educator*
Wheelon, Albert Dewell *physicist*

Monterey
Benjamin, David Joel, III *radio broadcasting executive*
Black, Robert Lincoln *pediatrician*
Bomberger, Russell Branson *lawyer, educator*
Bowman, Dorothy Louise *artist*
Bradford, Howard *graphic artist, painter*
Butler, Jon Terry *computer engineering educator, researcher*
Collins, Curtis Allan *oceanographer*
Cutino, Bert Paul *chef, restaurant owner*
Dedini, Eldon Lawrence *cartoonist*
Fenton, Lewis Lowry *lawyer*
Gaskell, Robert Eugene *mathematician, educator*
Haddad, Louis Nicholas *paralegal*
Hamming, Richard Wesley *computer scientist*
Hoivik, Thomas Harry *military educator, international consultant*
Kennedy-Minott, Rodney *international relations educator, former ambassador*
Ketcham, Henry King *cartoonist*
Leonardich, Agnes M. *school system administrator*
Lockhart, Brooks Javins *retired college dean*
Malone, James L. *lawyer, diplomat*
Marto, Paul James *mechanical engineering educator, researcher*
Miller, Susan Heilmann *publishing executive*
Mushkin, Leonard Barton *podiatrist*
Newberry, Conrad Floyde *aerospace engineering educator*
Newton, Robert Eugene *mechanical engineering educator*
Nowell, Elizabeth Cameron Clemons *author*
Packard, Julie *aquarium administrator*
Reneker, Maxine Hohman *librarian*
Ryan, Sylvester D. *bishop*
Sarpkaya, Turgut *mechanical engineering educator*
Schrady, David Alan *operations research educator*
Shull, Harrison *chemist, educator*
Spitler, Lee William *banker*
Stern, Gerald Daniel *lawyer*
Van Der Bijl, Willem *meteorology educator*
von Pagenhardt, Robert *policy sciences educator, diplomat*
Weaver, William Bruce *astronomer, research administrator*
Wright, Mary R. *state park superintendent*

Monterey Park
†Mastaler, Richard Michael *healthcare executive*
Tucker, Marcus Othello *judge*
Waiter, Serge-Albert *retired scientist, consultant*
Wilson, Linda *librarian*

Moorpark
Hall, Elton A. *philosophy educator*
†Kavli, Fred *manufacturing executive*

Moraga
Allen, Richard Garrett *health care and education consultant*
Anderson, Brother Mel *academic administrator*
Countryman, Vern *law educator*
†Frey, William Rayburn *healthcare educator, consultant*
Grassi, James Edward *recreational facility executive director*
Hollingsworth, Robert Edgar *nuclear consultant*
Sonenshein, Nathan *marine consulting company executive, retired naval officer*

Moreno Valley
Jaynes, Cherie Lou *early childhood education educator*

Morgan Hill
Freimark, Robert (Bob Freimark) *artist*
Hevia, Martha *principal, educational and counseling consultant*

Morro Bay
Lanser, Herbert Raymond *financial planner*

Moss Landing
†Johnston, Gail Liragis *laboratory director*
Lange, Lester Henry *mathematics educator*

Mount Shasta
Anderson, Lee Roger *landscape architect, solar, environmental, recreation and site planner*

Mountain View
Amdahl, Gene Myron *computer company executive*
Benham, James Mason *mutual fund executive*
Blachman, Nelson M(erle) *physicist*
Bowler, James S. *educational administrator*
Braun, Michael Alan *data processing executive*
Breitmeyer, Jo Anne *sales and marketing executive*
Clark, James H. *electronics executive*
Cusumano, James Anthony *chemical company executive, former recording artist*
Di Muccio, Mary Jo *retired librarian*
Elkus, Richard J., Jr. *electronics company executive*
†Fiester, Clark George *communications company executive*
†Gelpi, Armand Philippe *hemotologist/oncologist*
Johnson, Noel Lars *biomedical engineer*

Kobza, Dennis Jerome architect
Koo, George Ping Shan electronics executive
Lu, Wuan-Tsun microbiologist, immunologist
Marple, Stanley Lawrence, Jr. electrical engineer, signal processing researcher
Mc Nealy, Scott computer company executive
Michalko, James Paul library association administrator
Morris, Arlene Myers marketing professional
†North, Daniel Warner consulting analyst
Peters, Stanley Thomas materials engineer, consultant, educator
†Qureishi, A. Salam computer software and services company executive
†Raybould, Barry John computer software company executive
Rulifson, Johns Frederick computer company executive, computer scientist
Saifer, Mark Gary Pierce pharmaceutical executive
Slade, Bernard Newton electronics company executive
Tierney, Patrick John information services executive

Napa
Battisti, Paul Oreste county supervisor
Chiarella, Peter Ralph corporate executive
Ervin, Margaret Howie elementary educator, special education educator
Fawcett, F(rank) Conger lawyer
Folsom, Richard Gilman retired mechanical engineer and academic administrator, consultant
Francis, Marc Baruch pediatrician
Garnett, William photographer
Hill, Orion Alvah, Jr. retired banker
Kuntz, Charles Powers lawyer
LaRocque, Marilyn Ross Onderdonk public relations executive
Leavitt, Dana Gibson management consultant
Miller, John Laurence professional golfer
Muedeking, George Herbert editor
Smith, Robert Bruce former security consultant, retired army officer
Strock, David Randolph brokerage house executive
†Trice, Thomas Granville library director, history educator
†Zimmermann, John Paul plastic surgeon

National City
Potter, J(effrey) Stewart property manager

Newark
Ferber, Norman Alan retail executive
Joyce, Stephen Francis human resource executive
Moldaw, Stuart G. venture capitalist, retail clothing stores executive

Newbury Park
†Bullock, Gayle Nelson healthcare executive
Fredericks, Patricia Ann real estate executive
Guggenheim-Boucard, Alan Andre Albert Paul Edouard business executive, international consultant
Issari, M(ohammad) Ali film producer, educator, consultant

Newport Beach
Adams, William Gillette lawyer
Albright, Archie Earl, Jr. investment banker
Armstrong, Robert Arnold petroleum company executive
Baskin, Scott David lawyer
Bauer, Jay S. architect
Botwinick, Michael museum director
Brown, Giles Tyler history educator, lecturer
Bryant, Thos Lee magazine editor
Clark, Earnest Hubert, Jr. tool company executive
Cox, Christopher congressman
Curtis, Jesse William, Jr. retired federal judge
†Cvengros, William D. insurance company executive
Dean, Paul John magazine editor
Dougherty, Betsey Olenick architect
Dovring, Karin Elsa Ingeborg author, poet, playwright, communication analyst
Fletcher, Douglas Baden investment company executive
Frederick, Dolliver H. merchant banker
Gerken, Walter Bland insurance company executive
Giannini, Valerio Louis investment banker
Gross, William H. financial analyst, insurance company executive
Guilford, Andrew John lawyer
†Haskins, Larry Wayne health care administrator
Homan, Rich magazine editor
Indiek, Victor Henry finance corporation executive
Johnson, Thomas Webber, Jr. lawyer
Kahn, Douglas Gerard psychiatrist
Katayama, Arthur Shoji lawyer
Kaufman, Marcus Maurice retired judge, lawyer
†Kaye, Michael S. corporate executive
Kelly, James P. computer company executive
Kenney, William John, Jr. real estate development executive
†Kienitz, LaDonna Trapp librarian, city official
Klein, Maurice J. lawyer
Lipson, Melvin Alan technology and business management consultant
Lowe, Kathlene Winn lawyer
Lurie, Harold engineer, lawyer
†Lyon, William builder
†Maddock, Thomas Smothers engineering company executive, civil engineer
Mallory, Frank Linus lawyer
Marcoux, Carl Henry former insurance executive, writer, historian
Martens, Don Walter lawyer
Masotti, Louis Henry management educator, consultant
McAlister, Maurice L. savings and loan association executive
Millar, Richard William, Jr. lawyer
Morgridge, Howard Henry architect
Mortensen, Arvid LeGrande lawyer, insurance company executive
†Nadel, Steven J. marine instruments adjusting company executive
Panetti, Ramon Stanley investment company executive, consultant, lawyer
Phillips, Layn R. lawyer
Plat, Richard Vertin corporate finance executive
†Prince, Thomas E. bank executive
†Prough, Stephen W. savings and loan executive
Rehfeldt, David John savings and loan executive
Richardson, Walter John architect
†Roberts, Ralph S. restaurant chain executive
Rooklidge, William Charles lawyer
Rueb, Richard V., Sr. information systems management consultant
Schroeder, Charles Henry corporate treasurer
Simon, John Roger lawyer
Singer, Gary James lawyer
Solberg, Ronald Louis investment manager, international economist
Soliman, Anwar S. restaurant company executive
Spitz, Barbara Salomon artist
Stephens, Michael Dean hospital administrator
Strock, Arthur Van Zandt architect
Sutton, Thomas C. insurance company executive
Tanner, R. Marshall lawyer
†Teslow, Paul Andre retired health executive
Warren, William Robinson real estate broker
Wentworth, Theodore Sumner lawyer
Willard, Robert Edgar lawyer
Wimberly, George James architect
†Wirta, Ray real estate developer
Wood, George H. investment executive

Nipomo
Brantingham, Charles Ross podiatrist, ergonomics consultant

Norco
Parmer, Dan Gerald veterinarian

North Hollywood
†Badalamenti, Angelo composer
†Baker, Rick make-up artist
Boyle, Barbara Dorman motion picture company executive
Buffett, Jimmy singer, songwriter, author
Bull, David fine art conservator
†Clarke, Stanley Marvin musician, composer
†Colombier, Michel composer
†Flick, Stephen Hunter sound effects artist
Fox, Charles Ira composer, conductor
Frost, Mark director, producer, writer
†Gore, Michael composer
Grasso, Mary Ann theatre association administrator
Gregorius, Beverly June retired obstetrician-gynecologist
Hulse, Jerry journalist
Kapnick, Richard Allan international marketing and advertising consultant, educator, executive television producer, editor and publisher, broadcaster
Kreger, Melvin Joseph lawyer
†Laing, Robert production designer
†Lantieri, Michael special effects expert
Loper, James Leaders broadcasting executive
Maltz, Jerome Paul broadcasting executive
†McMartin, John actor
Milner, Howard M. real estate developer, international real estate financier
Mirisch, Marvin Elliot motion picture producer
†Neill, Ve make-up artist
†Omens, Sherwood cinematographer
Reynolds, Debbie (Mary Frances Reynolds) actress
Ribman, Ronald Burt playwright
Runquist, Lisa A. lawyer
†Safan, Craig Alan film composer
Schlosser, Anne Griffin librarian
Thomson, John Ansel Armstrong biochemist
Thurston, Alice Janet former college president
†Toussieng, Yolanda make-up artist

Northridge
Bassler, Robert Covey sculptor, educator
Bianchi, Donald Ernest academic administrator, biology educator
Boddington, Craig Thornton magazine editor
Bradshaw, Richard Rotherwood engineering executive
Butler, Karla psychologist
Chen, Joseph Tao historian, educator
Cleary, James W. retired university administrator
Curzon, Susan Carol library administrator
Davidson, Sheldon Jerome hematologist
Devol, Kenneth Stowe journalism educator
Ellner, Carolyn Lipton university dean, consultant
Harden, Marvin artist, educator
Jakobsen, Jakob Knudsen mechanical engineer
Kiddoo, Robert James engineering service company executive
Kuzma, George Martin bishop
Madison, Roberta Eleanor epidemiologist, educator, consultant
Molen, Gerald Robert film producer
Norris, Darell Forest retired insurance company executive
Oppenheimer, Steven Bernard biology educator
Segalman, Ralph sociology educator
Sparling, Mary Lee biology educator
Stark, Martin J. management consultant
Stout, Thomas Melville control system engineer
Tanis, Norman Earl retired university dean, library expert
Torgow, Eugene N. electrical engineer
Wilson, Blenda Jacqueline university chancellor

Norwalk
McCamly, Jerry Allen high school educator

Novato
Bozdech, Marek Jiri physician
Franklin, Robert Blair cardiologist
Hansmeyer, Herbert insurance company executive
Harding, Richard Swick engineering executive
Meyer, John F. insurance company executive
Obninsky, Victor Peter lawyer
Patterson, W. Morgan college president
Pfeiffer, Phyllis Kramer newspaper company executive
Simon, Lee Will astronomer
Womack, Thomas Houston manufacturing company executive

Oak Park
Caldwell, Stratton Franklin kinesiologist

Oakdale
Thomas, William LeRoy geography educator, cruise lecturer

Oakhurst
Bonham, Clifford Vernon social worker, educator

Oakland
Adelman, Rick professional basketball coach
Albers, William Marion retail food distribution executive
Alderson, Richard Lynn (Sandy) professional baseball team executive
Allen, Carole Geneva (Ward) college administrator
Allen, Jeffrey Michael lawyer
Ambrose, Tommy W. chemical engineer, executive
†Ausfahl, William Friend household products company executive
Bangham, Robert Arthur orthotist
†Bangs, Richard Johnston publishing executive
Barakat, Samir F. economic and strategic business consulting executive
Barlow, William Pusey, Jr. accountant
†Barricks, Michael Eli retinal surgeon
Beasley, Bruce Miller sculptor
Benham, Priscilla Carla religion educator, college president
Borum, William Donald engineer
Brocchini, Ronald Gene architect
Buckley, Mike Clifford lawyer, electronics company executive
Burnison, Boyd Edward lawyer
Burns, Catherine Elizabeth art dealer
†Burt, Christopher Clinton publisher
Caulfield, W. Harry health care industry executive, physician
Champlin, Malcolm McGregor retired municipal judge
Clancy, Thomas Gerald newspaper company executive
Cline, Wilson Ettason retired administrative law judge
Collen, Morris Frank physician
Cook, Lia art educator
Crane, Robert Meredith health care executive
Cray, Robert popular blues guitarist, singer, songwriter
Crompton, Arnold minister, educator
Cummins, John Stephen bishop
Cutter, Edward A(hern) consumer products company executive, lawyer
Davis, Frances M. lawyer, corporate executive
Davis, Roderick William retail executive
Deming, Willis Riley lawyer
Diaz, Sharon education administrator
Dibble, David Van Vlack educator of visually impaired, lawyer
Dickinson, Eleanor Creekmore artist, educator
Dolich, Andrew Bruce professional basketball team executive
Dommer, Donald Duane architect
Dunn, David Cameron entrepreneur, business executive
Eckersley, Dennis Lee professional baseball player
Farley, Thelma principal
†Farrell, Kenneth Royden economist
Fink, Diane Joanne physician
Finnane, Daniel F. professional basketball team executive
Fischer, Michael Ludwig environmental executive
Fogel, Paul David lawyer
Foley, Jack (John Wayne Harold Foley) poet, writer, editor
Friedman, Gary David epidemiologist, research facility administrator
Gantt, M. Dean retail food company executive
Gardner, Robert Alexander career counselor, career management consultant
Goldstine, Stephen Joseph college administrator
Gomes, Wayne Reginald academic administrator
Gomez, Martin library director
†Guidi, Ronn ballet company executive
Haas, Walter J. professional baseball team executive
Haiman, Franklyn Saul author, communications educator
Hardaway, Timothy Duane basketball player
Harris, Elihu Mason mayor
Haskell, Arthur Jacob retired steamship company executive
Heafey, Edwin Austin, Jr. lawyer
Helvey, Julius Louis, II finance company executive
Henderson, Rickey Henley professional baseball player
Heydman, Abby Maria academic dean
Hoopes, Lorenzo Neville former retailing executive
Isaac Nash, Eva Mae educator
Jacobus, Russell Lee retail store executive
Jensen, D. Lowell federal judge, lawyer, government official
Judd, James Thurston savings and loan executive
Jukes, Thomas Hughes biological chemist, educator
Kaplan, Alvin Irving lawyer, adjudicator, investigator
Kees, Beverly newspaper editor
Kennedy, Raoul Dion lawyer
King, Cary Judson, III chemical engineer, educator, university official
Kingman, Alton (Hayward), Jr. banker
Knight, Jeffrey William publishing and marketing executive
Kropschot, Richard H. physicist, science laboratory administrator
Lanier, Bob professional sports team executive, former basketball player
La Russa, Tony, Jr. (Anthony La Russa, Jr.) professional baseball manager
Laverne, Michel Marie-Jacques international relations consultant
Lawrence, David M. health facility administrator
Lee, Jong Hyuk accountant
Leon, Dennis sculptor
Lillie, John Mitchell transportation company executive
List, Raymond Edward engineering and construction executive, management consultant
Ludwig, LeRoy Frank retail store executive
Macmeeken, John Peebles foundation executive, educator
Marshall, George Dwire supermarket chain executive
Massey, Walter Eugene physicist, science foundation administrator
Matsumoto, George architect
†McCarthy, Michael Andrew banker, lawyer
McGwire, Mark David professional baseball player
McKinney, Judson Thad broadcast executive
Melchert, James Frederick artist
†Mesa, Richard school superintendent
Mikalow, Alfred Alexander, II deep sea diver, marine surveyor, marine diving consultant
Miller, Barry research administrator, psychologist
Miller, Kirk lawyer
Miller, Lyle G. bishop
Miller, Thomas Robbins lawyer, publisher
Mitrano, Joseph Charles school principal
Moon, Wayne health facility administrator
Mullin, Chris(topher) Paul professional basketball player
Newsome, Randall Jackson federal judge
Nicol, Robert Duncan architect
†O'Brien, George Donoghue, Jr. engineering consultant company executive
Okamura, Arthur artist, educator, writer
Patten, Bebe Harrison minister
Patton, Roger William lawyer, educator
Peltason, Jack Walter university president
Pierce, Ricky Charles professional basketball player
Pike, Douglas Eugene Indochina studies director
Poole, Monte LaRue sports columnist, consultant
†Potash, Jeremy Warner public relations executive
Potash, Stephen Jon international public relations practitioner
Power, Dennis Michael museum director
Quinby, William Albert lawyer
Rath, Alan T. sculptor
†Rosen, Corey M. professional association executive
Sandler, Herbert M. savings and loan association executive
Sandler, Marion Osher savings and loan association executive
Saperstein, Guy T. lawyer
Sargent, Arlene Hondl nursing educator
†Sass, Donald Jay anesthesiologist
Saunders, Ward Bishop, Jr. retired aluminum company executive
†Scalapino, Leslie poet
Schacht, Henry Mevis writer, consultant
Schwyn, Charles Edward accountant
Serenbetz, Robert manufacturing executive
Shinomiya, Yaeko librarian
Shoai, Elinor Josephine Kelly elementary school educator
Sierra, Ruben Angel Garcia professional baseball player
Silverberg, Robert author
Skaff, Andrew Joseph lawyer, public utilities, energy and transportation executive
Skinner, Clifford insurance company executive
Sullivan, G. Craig chemical executive
Sun, Cossette Tsung-hung Wu law library director
Talbert, Melvin George bishop
Tchaikovsky, Leslie J. judge
Totman, Patrick Steven lawyer, retail executive
Tracy, James Jared, Jr. law firm administrator
Vohs, James Arthur health care program executive
Weinmann, Robert Lewis neurologist
Whitsel, Richard Harry biologist, entomologist
Wick, William David lawyer
Winokur, Robert M. lawyer
Wolfe, Cameron Withgot, Sr. federal judge
Wood, James Michael lawyer
Wood, Larry (Mary Laird) journalist, author, university educator, public relations executive, environmental consultant

Oakville
Mondavi, Robert Gerald winery executive

Occidental
Rumsey, Victor Henry electrical engineering educator emeritus

Oceanside
Erickson, Frank William composer
Hertweck, E. Romayne psychology educator
Howard, Robert Staples newspaper publisher
Ladley, Karen J. nursing administrator, nurse
Lyon, Richard mayor, retired naval officer
Roberts, James McGregor retired professional association executive
Robinson, William Franklin retired legal consultant
Schuck, Carl Joseph lawyer

Oildale
Gallagher, Joseph Francis marketing executive

Ojai
Mankoff, Albert William cultural organization administrator, consultant
Weill, Samuel, Jr. automobile company executive
Wyman, Willard G. headmaster

Ontario
Ferguson, Michael Roger newspaper executive
Fry, Linda Sue hotel sales director, food products company executive
Johnson, Maurice Verner, Jr. agricultural research and development executive
Keel, Michael Clarence aerospace company executive
Luce, Susan Marie library director

Orange
Anzel, Sanford Harold orthopaedic surgeon
Armentrout, Steven Alexander oncologist
†Barr, Ronald Jeffrey dermatologist, pathologist
Berk, Jack Edward physician, educator
Braunstein, Phillip radiologist, educator
Crumley, Roger Lee surgeon, educator
Dana, Edward Runkle physician, educator
Dietrich, Rosalind radiology educator
DiSaia, Philip John gynecologist, obstetrician, radiology educator
Doti, James L. academic administrator
Fipps, Michael W. corporate executive
Fisk, Edward Ray retired civil engineer, author, educator
Furnas, David William plastic surgeon
Gerhard, Nancy Lucile Dege educator
Goble, Thomas Lee clergyman
Hamilton, Harry Lemuel, Jr. academic administrator
Levine, Howard Harris health facility executive
Lott, Ira Totz pediatric neurologist
†MacArthur, Carol Jeanne pediatric otolaryngology educator
Mc Farland, Norman Francis bishop
Morgan, Beverly Carver physician, educator
Quilligan, Edward James obstetrician/gynecologist, educator
Reed, David Andrew foundation executive
Rowen, Marshall radiologist
Sawdei, Milan A. lawyer
Schrodi, Tom instructional services director
Skilling, David van Diest manufacturing executive
Smith, Philip Walter savings and loan association executive, real estate consultant
†Sneed, Gail mortgage company executive
Stacho, Zoltan Aladar construction and engineering company executive
Starr, Richard William retired banker
Steffensen, Dwight A. medical products and data processing services executive
†Stickney, Douglas Henry biostatistician, consultant
Thompson, William Benbow, Jr. obstetrician/gynecologist, educator
Toeppe, William Joseph, Jr. retired aerospace engineer

Yu, Jen *medical educator*

Oregon House
Storm, Donald John *archaeologist, historian*

Orinda
Bowyer, Jane Baker *science educator*
Brookes, Valentine *retired lawyer*
Brown, Thomas Raymond *marketing company executive*
Conran, James Michael *state government official*
Cooper, Clare Dunlap *civic worker, writer*
Gilbert, Robert W. *secondary school principal*
Glasser, Charles Edward *academic administrator*
Hartsough, Walter Douglas *physicist*
Heftmann, Erich *biochemist*
McCormick, Loyd Weldon *lawyer*

Oroville
Ward, Chester Lawrence *physician, county health official, retired military officer*

Oxnard
Cathcart, Linda *art historian*
Dimitriadis, Andre C. *health care executive*
Frodsham, Olaf Milton *music educator*
Herlinger, Daniel Robert *hospital administrator*
Hill, Alice Lorraine *history, geneology, and social researcher, educator*
O'Connell, Hugh Mellen, Jr. *architect, retired*
Parriott, James Deforis *retired oil company executive, consultant*
Perrier, Barbara Sue *artist*

Pacific Grove
Adams, Margaret Bernice *retired museum official*
Brewer, Peter George *ocean geochemist*
Davis, Robert Edward *retired communication educator*
Epel, David *biologist, educator*
Fleischman, Paul *children's author*
Powers, Dennis Alpha *biology educator*
Roberts, William M. *publishing executive*
Verduin, Claire Leone *publishing company executive*

Pacific Palisades
Albert, Eddie (Edward Albert Heimberger) *actor*
Becker, Joseph *information scientist*
†Bode, Ralf D. *cinematographer*
†Boyd, Russell *cinematographer*
†Brown, Robert N. *film editor*
†Burum, Stephen H. *cinematographer*
†Butler, Wilmer C. *cinematographer*
Cale, Charles Griffin *lawyer*
Chesney, Lee Roy, Jr. *artist*
Claes, Daniel John *physician*
Clark, Bob H. *film director*
Crane, Richard Clement *paper manufacturing company executive*
Csendes, Ernest *chemist, corporate and financial executive*
†Cundey, Dean *cinematographer*
Diehl, Richard Kurth *retail business consultant*
Dignam, Robert Joseph *retired orthopaedic surgeon*
Fink, Robert Morgan *biological chemistry educator*
Flattery, Thomas Long *lawyer, legal administrator*
†Francis-Bruce, Richard *film editor*
Garwood, Victor Paul *retired speech communication educator*
†Goldblatt, Stephen *cinematographer*
†Gosnell, Raja *film editor*
Jones, Edgar Allan, Jr. *law educator, arbitrator, lawyer*
Klein, Joseph Mark *retired mining company executive*
Kovacs, Laszlo *cinematographer*
Kridel, James S. *banker*
Lewis, Frank Harlan *botanist, educator*
Longaker, Richard Pancoast *political science educator emeritus*
†MacDonald, Richard *production designer*
†Malley, William *production designer*
†Milsome, Douglas *cinematographer*
†Müller, Robby *cinematographer*
Mulryan, Henry Trist *mineral company executive, consultant*
Nash, Gary Baring *historian, educator*
†Norris, Patricia *costume designer*
†Norton, Rosanna *costume designer*
Purcell, Patrick B. *motion picture company executive*
Rode, James Dean *banker*
†Roizman, Owen *cinematographer*
†Rosenberg, Philip *production designer*
Rothenberg, Leslie Steven *lawyer, ethicist*
Salter, Robert Mundhenk, Jr. *physicist, consultant*
Schwartz, Murray Louis *lawyer, educator, academic administrator*
Sevilla, Stanley *lawyer*
†Spinotti, Dante *cinematographer*
†Washington, Dennis *production designer*
Zipper, Herbert *symphony conductor*

Palm Desert
Brown, James Briggs *retired business forms company executive*
Budge, Hamer Harold *mutual fund company executive*
Hartman, Ashley Powell *publishing executive, journalist, educator*
Humphrey, Charles Edward, Jr. *lawyer*
Hunt, Barnabas John *priest, religious order administrator*
Hunter, Patricia Rae *state legislator, nurse*
Krallinger, Joseph Charles *entrepreneur, business advisor, author*
McKissock, Paul Kendrick *plastic surgeon*
Sausman, Karen *zoological park administrator*
Sicuro, Natale Anthony *academic administrator*
Whelan, Francis C. *federal judge*
Wiedle, Gary Eugene *real estate management company executive*

Palm Springs
Aikens, Donald Thomas *educational administrator, consultant*
Arnold, Stanley Norman *manufacturing consultant*
Browning, Norma Lee (Mrs. Russell Joyner Ogg) *journalist*
Caesar, Sid *actor, comedian*
Cordier, Herbert *interior designer*
DeVore, Daun Aline *lawyer*
Fol, Monique Eliane *educator*
†Frauchiger, Fritz Arnold *museum director*
Frey, Albert *architect*
†Golden, Morton Jay *museum director*
Greenbaum, James Richard *liquor distributing company executive, real estate developer*
Hearst, Rosalie *philanthropist, foundation executive*
Jones, Milton Wakefield *publisher*
Jumonville, Felix Joseph, Jr. *physical education educator, realtor*
Krick, Irving Parkhurst *meteorologist*
Kroger, William Saul *obstetrician-gynecologist*
Maree, Wendy *painter, sculptor*
Weil, Max Harry *physician, medical educator, medical scientist*
Yantis, Richard William *investments executive*

Palmdale
Anderson, R(obert) Gregg *real estate company executive*
Grooms, Larry Willis *newspaper editor*
Harsha, Philip Thomas *aerospace engineer*
Rich, Ben Robert *aerospace executive, aero-thermodynamicist*
Storsteen, Linda Lee *librarian*
†Weiss, Richard R. *rocket propulsion technology executive*

Palo Alto
Adams, Marcia Howe *lawyer*
Adamson, Geoffrey David *reproductive endocrinologist, surgeon*
Agras, William Stewart *psychiatry educator*
Allen, Louis Alexander *management consultant*
Amylon, Michael David *physician, educator*
Attig, John Clare *history educator, consultant*
Bagshaw, Malcolm A. *radiation therapist, educator*
Baldwin, Gary Lee *electronics engineer, research laboratory administrator*
Ballam, Joseph *physicist, educator*
Balzhiser, Richard Earl *research and development company executive*
†Basso, Lawrence Vincent *physician*
Berger, Joseph *author, educator, counselor*
†Berry, Robert Emanuel *aerospace company executive*
Bhatt, Kiran *physician, educator*
Bienenstock, Arthur Irwin *physicist, educator*
Bird, Rose Elizabeth *former state chief justice, law educator*
Blau, Helen Margaret *molecular pharmacology educator*
Bohrnstedt, George William *educational researcher*
Borovoy, Roger Stuart *lawyer*
Bradley, Donald Edward *lawyer*
Briggs, Winslow Russell *plant biologist, educator*
Britton, M(elvin) C(reed), Jr. *physician, rheumatologist*
Brown, David Randolph *electrical engineer*
Brown, Robert McAfee *minister, religion educator*
Burke, Edmund Charles *retired aerospace company executive*
Buss, Claude Albert *history educator*
Carlson, Robert Wells *physician, educator*
†Case, Robbie *education educator, author*
Chase, Robert Arthur *surgeon, educator*
Childs, Wylie Jones *metallurgical engineer*
Climan, Richard Elliot *lawyer*
Cogan, John Francis *economist, researcher, educator*
Cohen, Elizabeth G. *education and sociology educator, researcher*
Cohen, Karl Paley *nuclear energy consultant*
Colin, Lawrence *aerospace scientist*
Cooper, Allen David *research scientist, educator*
Cutler, Leonard Samuel *physicist*
Dallin, Alexander *history and political science educator*
Dassoff, Christine Ellen *library administrator*
DeLustro, Frank Anthony *biomedical company executive, research immunologist*
Dement, William Charles *sleep researcher, medical educator*
Dornbusch, Sanford Maurice *sociology educator*
Duggan, Susan J. *educational administrator*
Early, James Michael *electronics research consultant*
Eggers, Alfred John, Jr. *research corporation executive*
Elliott, David Duncan, III *science research company executive*
Eng, Lawrence Fook *biochemistry educator, neurochemist*
Eulau, Heinz *political scientist, educator*
Farber, Eugene Mark *psoriasis research institute administrator*
Farquhar, John William *physician, educator*
†Feigenbaum, Edward Albert *computer science educator*
†Flory, Curt A. *research physicist*
Freiman, Paul E. *pharmaceutical company executive*
Fried, John H. *chemist*
Friedlander, Benjamin *electrical and computer engineering educator*
Fries, James Franklin *internal medicine educator*
Furbush, David Malcolm *lawyer*
Furthmayr, Heinz *pathologist, researcher*
Gerstel, Martin Stephen *pharmaceutical company executive*
Gibbons, James Franklin *university dean, electrical engineering educator*
†Giffard, Robin P. *computer engineer, industrial physicist*
Gilbert, Keith Duncan *electronics executive*
Goff, Harry Russell *retired manufacturing company executive*
†Goff, James Albert *medical center administrator*
Goldberg, Jacob *computer scientist, researcher*
Goldstein, Avram *pharmacology educator*
†Gribaldo, Albert C. *holding company executive*
Gubins, Samuel *museum administrator*
Guerard, Albert Joseph *retired modern literature educator, author*
Gunderson, Robert Vernon, Jr. *lawyer*
Halperin, Robert Milton *retired electrical machinery company executive*
Hammett, Benjamin Cowles *psychologist*
Haslam, Robert Thomas, III *lawyer*
Hays, Marguerite Thompson *physician*
Hecht, Lee Martin *software company executive*
Heinemann, Klaus W. *physical sciences research administrator*
Hewlett, William (Redington) *manufacturing company executive, electrical engineer*
Hinckley, Robert Craig *lawyer*
Hodge, Philip Gibson, Jr. *mechanical and aerospace engineering educator*
Holman, Halsted Reid *medical educator*
Holmes, John Richard *physicist, educator*
Hornak, Thomas *electronics company executive*
Horngren, Charles Thomas *accounting educator*
Itnyre, Jacqueline Harriet *programmer*
†Ivester, (Richard) Gavin *industrial designer*
Ivy, Benjamin Franklin, III *financial and real estate investment advisor*
Jamison, Rex Lindsay *medical educator*
Jamplis, Robert Warren *surgeon, medical foundation executive*
Johnson, Conor Deane *mechanical engineer*
Johnson, Noble Marshall *research scientist*
Johnston, Alan Cope *lawyer*
Jones, Robert Trent, Jr. *golf course architect*
Kaufman, Michael David *management executive*
Kennedy, W(ilbert) Keith, Jr. *electronics company executive, aerospace engineer*
Kino, Gordon Stanley *electrical engineering educator*
Kiremidjian, Anne Aghavny *civil engineering educator*
Knoles, George Harmon *history educator*
Knott, Donald Joseph *golf course architect*
Knudsen, Eric Ingvald *neuroscientist*
Krupp, Marcus Abraham *medical research director*
Lamport, Leslie B. *computer scientist*
Lane, William Kenneth *physician*
Lender, Adam *electrical engineer*
Lewis, John Wilson *political science educator*
Lindzey, Gardner *psychologist, educator*
Linn, Gary Dean *golf course architect*
Linna, Timo Juhani *immunologist, researcher, educator*
Loewenstein, Walter Bernard *nuclear power technologist*
Luenberger, David Gilbert *electrical engineer, educator*
†Marcus, George Mathew *real estate executive*
†Mario, Ernest *pharmaceutical company executive*
†Matthews, Zakee *psychiatrist, educator*
Mendelson, Alan Charles *lawyer*
Merrin, Seymour *computer marketing company executive*
Moffitt, Donald Eugene *transportation company executive*
†Moggridge, Bill G. *product designer, consultant*
Moll, John Lewis *electronics engineer*
Monroy, Gladys H. *lawyer*
Moretti, August Joseph *lawyer*
Morris, Randall Ellis *immunologist, university program director*
Morrison, David Fred *freight company executive*
Nordlund, Donald Craig *corporate lawyer*
Oliver, Bernard More *electrical engineer, technical consultant*
O'Rourke, J. Tracy *manufacturing company executive*
Packard, David *manufacturing company executive, electrical engineer*
Pake, George Edward *research executive, physicist*
Panofsky, Wolfgang Kurt Hermann *physicist, educator*
Partain, Larry Dean *solar research engineer*
Patterson, Robert Edward *lawyer*
Phair, Joseph Baschon *lawyer*
Platt, Lewis Emmett *electronics company executive*
†Powers, Richard P. *pharmaceutical executive*
†Proctor, Peter *pharmaceutical executive*
Quraishi, Marghoob A. *management consultant*
Reagan, Joseph Bernard *aerospace executive*
Remington, Jack Samuel *physician*
Rivette, Gerard Bertram *manufacturing company executive*
Roberts, Frank Emmett *financial executive*
Robinson, Thomas Nathaniel *pediatrician, educator, researcher*
Rosenzweig, Robert Myron *educational consultant*
Saltoun, Andre Meir *lawyer*
Sawyer, Wilbur Henderson *pharmacologist, educator*
Schrier, Stanley Leonard *physician, educator*
Scitovsky, Anne Aickelin *economist*
Scott, Edward William, Jr. *computer company executive*
Smelser, Neil Joseph *sociologist*
Sonsini, Larry W. *lawyer*
Spinrad, Robert Joseph *computer scientist*
Staprans, Armand *electronics executive*
†Street, Robert A. *research physicist*
Stringer, John *materials scientist*
Strober, Samuel *immunologist, educator*
Taylor, John Joseph *nuclear engineer*
Taylor, Robert William *research director*
†Thacker, Charles P. *computer engineer, engineering executive*
†Theeuwes, Felix *physical chemist*
Thompson, David Alfred *industrial engineer*
Ullman, Edwin Fisher *research chemist*
Urquhart, John *medical researcher, educator*
Van Atta, David Murray *lawyer*
Warne, William Elmo *irrigationist*
Watkins, Dean Allen *electronics executive, educator*
Wayman, Robert Paul *electronics company executive*
Weiser, Mark David *computer scientist, researcher*
Wheeler, Raymond Louis *lawyer*
Wiedmann, Tien-Wen Tao *medical scientist, educator*
Willrich, Mason *utility company executive, consultant*
†Wilson, James F. *pharmaceutical executive*
Yuan, Sidney Wei Kwun *cryogenic engineer, consultant*
Zuckerkandl, Emile *molecular evolutionary biologist, scientific institute executive*

Palo Cedro
Haggard, Merle Ronald *songwriter, recording artist*

Palos Verdes Estates
Christie, Hans Frederick *retired utility company subsidiaries executive, consultant*
†Davidson, Keith Thomas *industry association executive*
Mennis, Edmund Addi *investment management consultant*
Rechtin, Eberhardt *retired aerospace educator*
Yamaguchi, Tamotsu *bank executive*

Palos Verdes Peninsula
Dalton, James Edward *aerospace executive, retired air force officer*
Ebsen, Buddy (Christian Ebsen, Jr.) *actor, dancer*
Fischer, Robert Blanchard *university administrator, researcher*
Giles, Allen *pianist, composer, music educator*
Grant, Robert Ulysses *retired manufacturing company executive*
Haynes, Moses Alfred *physician*
Hurrell, Ann Patricia *assistant director, educator*
King, Nancy *communications educator*
Leone, William Charles *retired manufacturing executive*
Mirels, Harold *aerospace engineer*
Raue, Jorg Emil *electrical engineer*
Reynolds, Harry Lincoln *physicist*
Ryker, Charles Edwin *former aerospace company executive*
Savage, Terry Richard *information systems executive*
Slayden, James Bragdon *retired department store executive*
Spinks, John Lee *engineering executive*
Thomas, Claudewell Sidney *psychiatry educator*
Waaland, Irving Theodore *retired aerospace design executive*
Weiss, Herbert Klemm *aeronautical engineer*
Wilson, Theodore Henry *retired electronics company executive, aerospace engineer*
Yeomans, Russell Allen *lawyer, translator*

Panorama City
Bass, Harold Neal *pediatrician, medical geneticist*

Paradise
Fulton, Len *publisher*

Paramount
Cook, Karla Joan *elementary education educator*
Hall, Howard Harry *lawyer*
†McCune, William Minton *construction company executive*
†Strong, Warren Robert *construction company executive*

Parlier
Schaefer, Charles Herbert *physiologist, educator*

Pasadena
Abelson, John Norman *biology educator*
Adler, Fred Peter *electronics company executive*
Albee, Arden Leroy *geologist, educator*
Allen, Clarence Roderic *geologist, educator*
Allman, John Morgan *neurobiology educator*
Anderson, Don Lynn *geophysicist, educator*
Anson, Fred Colvig *chemistry educator*
Arnott, Robert Douglas *investment company executive*
Attardi, Giuseppe M. *biology educator*
†Atwood, Carol Ann *healthcare executive*
Babcock, Horace W. *astronomer*
†Bailey, James Edwin *chemical engineer*
Bakaly, Charles George, Jr. *lawyer, mediator*
Baldeschwieler, John Dickson *chemist, educator*
Bare, Bruce *life insurance company executive*
Barnes, Charles Andrew *physicist, educator*
†Barney, Kline Porter, Jr. *engineering company executive, consultant*
Baum, Dwight Crouse *investment banking executive*
Bean, Maurice Darrow *retired diplomat*
Beauchamp, Jesse Lee (Jack Beauchamp) *chemistry educator*
†Beaudet, Robert Arthur *chemistry educator*
Beer, Reinhard *atmospheric scientist*
Beichman, Charles Arnold *astrophysicist, academic director*
Bejczy, Antal Károly *research scientist, research facility administrator*
Bennett, Joel Herbert *construction company executive*
Bercaw, John Edward *chemistry educator, consultant*
Bergholz, Richard Cady *political writer*
†Bjorkman, Pamela *crystallographer*
Blandford, Roger David *astronomy educator*
Boehm, Felix Hans *physicist, educator*
Boochever, Robert *federal judge*
Boulos, Paul Fares *civil and environmental engineer*
Bourdeau, Paul Turgeon *insurance company executive*
Brady, John Francis *chemical engineering educator*
Breckinridge, James Bernard *research physicist*
Bridges, William Bruce *electrical engineer, researcher, educator*
Brooks, Norman Herrick *environmental and civil engineer, educator*
Buck, Anne Marie *library director, consultant*
Buckingham, Jerry L. *hospital administrator*
†Buratti, Bonnie J. *aerospace scientist*
Caillouette, James Clyde *physician*
Campbell, Judith Lynn *molecular biologist educator*
†Carlstrom, John E. *astronomy educator*
Carroll, William Jerome *civil engineer*
Chahine, Moustafa Toufic *atmospheric scientist*
Chamberlain, Willard Thomas *retired metals company executive*
Chan, Sunney Ignatius *chemist*
Chandy, Kanianthra Mani *computer sciences educator, consultant*
Cohen, Donald Sussman *mathematician, educator*
Cohen, Judith Gamora *astronomy educator*
Cohen, Marshall Harris *astronomer, educator*
Cole, Roberta Carley *nursing educator*
Coles, Donald Earl *aeronautics educator*
Culick, Fred Ellsworth Clow *physics and engineering educator*
†Dallas, Saterios (Sam) *aerospace engineer, researcher, consultant*
D'Angelo, Robert William *lawyer*
Davidson, Eric Harris *molecular and developmental biologist, educator*
Davidson, Norman Ralph *biochemistry educator*
Davis, Lance Edwin *economics educator*
Deihl, Richard Harry *savings and loan association executive*
Dervan, Peter Brendan *chemistry educator*
Diehl, Digby Robert *journalist*
Dimotakis, Paul Emmanuel *aeronautics and physics educator*
Dougherty, Dennis A. *chemistry educator*
Dowell, David Ray *library administrator*
Dressler, Alan Michael *astronomer*
Drutchas, Gerrick Gilbert *publishing executive*
†Duxbury, Thomas C. *planetary scientist*
Elliot, David Clephan *historian, educator*
Epstein, Samuel *geologist, educator*
Everhart, Thomas Eugene *university president, engineering educator*
Fay, Peter Ward *history educator*
Fernandez, Ferdinand Francis *federal judge*
Finnell, Michael Hartman *corporate executive*
Flagan, Richard Charles *chemical engineering educator*
Fowler, William Alfred *retired physics educator*
Franklin, Joel Nicholas *mathematician, educator*
Frautschi, Steven Clark *physicist, educator*
Freise, Earl Jerome *univeristy administrator, materials engineering educator*
†Friedman, Louis Dill *association executive, aerospace engineer*
†Fu, Lee-Lueng *oceanographer*
Gabel, Katherine *academic administrator*
Gavalas, George R. *chemical engineering educator*

Gilman, Richard Carleton museum executive, retired college president
Goddard, William Andrew, III chemist, applied physicist, educator
Goei, Bernard Thwan-Poo (Bert Goei) architectural and engineering firm executive
Goldreich, Peter Martin astrophysics and planetary physics educator
Goodstein, David Louis physics educator
Goodwin, Alfred Theodore federal judge
Gould, Roy Walter engineering educator
Graham, Lanier art and architecture historian, cultural planner
Gray, Harry Barkus chemistry educator
Grether, David Maclay economics educator
Grubbs, Robert Howard chemistry educator
Hale, Charles Russell lawyer
Hall, Cynthia Holcomb federal judge
Hall, William E. engineering and construction company executive
Harmsen, Tyrus George librarian
Harvey, Joseph Paul, Jr. orthopedist, educator
Hatheway, Alson Earle mechanical engineer
Heaton, Culver architect
Heindl, Clifford Joseph physicist
†Helin, Eleanor Kay astronomer, geologist
Helmberger, Donald Vincent geophysical educator, researcher
Hilbert, Robert S(aul) optical engineer
Hitlin, David George physicist, educator
Hopfield, John Joseph biophysicist, educator
Hornung, Hans Georg aeronautical engineering educator, science facility administrator
Housner, George William civil engineering educator, consultant
Howe, Graham Lloyd photographer, curator
Howes, Benjamin Durward, III mergers and acquisitions executive
Hudson, Donald Ellis civil engineering educator
Hunt, Gordon lawyer
Ingersoll, Andrew Perry planetary science educator
Iwan, Wilfred Dean engineering educator
Jacobs, Joseph Donovan engineering firm executive
Jacobs, Joseph John engineering company executive
Jastrow, Robert physicist
Jenkins, Royal Gregory manufacturing executive
Jennings, Paul Christian civil engineering educator, academic administrator
Johnson, Torrence Vaino astronomer
Johnson, William Lewis materials science educator
Kanamori, Hiroo geophysics educator
Kaplan, Gary executive recruiter
Kavanagh, Ralph William physics educator
Kevles, Daniel Jerome history educator, writer
†Knauss, Wolfgang Gustav engineering educator
Knowles, James Kenyon applied mechanics educator
Konishi, Masakazu neurobiologist
Koonin, Steven Elliot physicist, professor
Kousser, J(oseph) Morgan history educator
Kozinski, Alex federal judge
Lauter, James Donald stockbroker
Ledyard, John Odell economics educator, consultant
Leonard, Nelson Jordan chemistry educator
Lewis, Edward B. biology educator
Lewis, Nathan Saul chemistry educator
Liepmann, Hans Wolfgang physicist, educator
List, Ericson John environmental engineering science educator, engineering consultant
Loven, Andrew Witherspoon environmental engineering company executive
Luxemburg, Wilhelmus Anthonius Josephus mathematics educator
Lynch, Gerald John management consultant
MacLaren, Walter Rogers allergist, educator
Mandel, Oscar literature educator, writer
Marcus, Rudolph Arthur chemist, educator
Marlen, James S. chemical-plastics-building materials manufacturing company executive
Martin, Craig Lee engineering company executive
Mathies, Allen Wray, Jr. physician, hospital administrator
Mc Carthy, Frank Martin surgical sciences educator
Mc Duffie, Malcolm oil company executive
McEliece, Robert James electrical engineering educator, author, consultant
McGill, Thomas Conley physics educator
Mc Koy, Basil Vincent Charles theoretical chemist, educator
†McLaughlin, William Irving aerospace engineer
Mead, Carver Andress computer science educator
Messenger, Ron J. health facility administrator
Meye, Robert Paul retired seminary administrator, writer
Meyerowitz, Elliot Martin biologist, educator
Middlebrook, Robert David electronics educator
Miller, Charles Daly lumber company executive
Morari, Manfred chemical engineer, educator
Munger, Edwin Stanton political geography educator
Murray, Bruce C. planetary scientist, educator, administrator
Myers, R(alph) Chandler lawyer
Nackel, John George health care consulting director
Neal, Philip Mark diversified manufacturing executive
Nelson, Dorothy Wright (Mrs. James F. Nelson) federal judge
Neugebauer, Gerry astrophysicist, educator
Neugebauer, Marcia physicist, administrator
Newman, Joyce Kligerman sculptor
North, Wheeler James marine ecologist, educator
Nothmann, Gerhard Adolf retired engineering executive, research engineer
Oliver, Robert Warner economics educator
O'Neill, J. Norman, Jr. lawyer
Ott, George William, Jr. management consulting executive
Owen, Ray David biology educator
†Patterson, Clair Cameron nuclear chemist, biogeochemist, educator
Patterson, Paul H. biology educator, neuroscientist
Patton, Richard Weston mortgage company executive
Pianko, Theodore A. lawyer
Pieroni, Leonard J. engineering and construction company executive
Plott, Charles R. economics educator
Politzer, Hugh David physicist, educator
Presecan, Nicholas Lee civil, environmental engineer, consultant
Preskill, John Phillip physics educator
†Raichlen, Fredric civil engineering educator, consultant
Rapaport, David Alan corporate legal executive
Revel, Jean-Paul biology educator
Roberts, John D. chemist, educator
Rounds, Donald Edwin cell biologist
Rymer, Pamela Ann federal judge
Sabersky, Rolf Heinrich mechanical engineer
Saffman, Philip G. mathematician
Sandage, Allan Rex astronomer
Sano, Roy I. bishop
Sargent, Wallace Leslie William astronomer, educator
†Sauer, James Edward, Jr. hospital administrator
Schlinger, Warren Gleason retired chemical engineer
Schmidt, Maarten astronomy educator
Schwarz, John Henry theoretical physicist, educator
Scott, Ronald Fraser civil engineering educator, engineering consultant
Scudder, Thayer anthropologist, educator
Searle, Eleanor Millard history educator
Searle, Leonard astronomer, researcher
Seinfeld, John Hersh chemical engineering educator
†Sekanina, Zdenek astronomer
Sharp, Robert Phillip geology educator, researcher
Simon, Barry mathematician, physicist, educator
Simon, Marvin Kenneth electrical engineer, consultant
Slater, Richard James engineering company executive
Smith, Howard Russell manufacturing company executive
Smith, Richard Howard banker
†Spear, Anthony J. aerospace engineer
Spector, Phil record company executive
Springer, Edwin Kent mechanical engineer
†Stassi, Ronald V. electric power industry executive
Stehsel, Melvin Louis biology educator
Stevenson, David John planetary scientist
Stewart, Homer Joseph engineering educator
Stolper, Edward Manin geology educator
Stone, Edward Carroll physicist, educator
Stone, Willard John retired lawyer
Sudarsky, Jerry M. industrialist
Tanner, Dee Boshard lawyer
Terhune, Robert William optics scientist
Thomas, Joseph Fleshman architect
Todd, John mathematician, educator
Tollenaere, Lawrence Robert retired industrial products company executive
Tombrello, Thomas Anthony, Jr. physics educator, consultant
†Torres, Ralph Chon minister
Ulrich, Peter Henry banker
Van Amringe, John Howard retired oil industry executive, geologist
Vanoni, Vito August hydraulic engineer
Vaughn, John Vernon banker, industrialist
Vogt, Rochus Eugen physicist, educator
Wasserburg, Gerald Joseph geology and geophysics educator
†Waters, Daniel W. electrical power industry executive
Watkins, John Francis management consultant
Wayland, J(ames) Harold biomedical scientist, educator
Weisbin, Charles Richard nuclear engineer
Wernicke, Brian Philip geologist, educator
†Westphal, James Adolph planetary science educator
Whitham, Gerald Beresford mathematics educator
Wood, Nathaniel Fay editor, writer, public relations consultant
Wu, Theodore Yao-Tsu engineer
Wyllie, Peter John geologist, educator
Yamarone, Charles Anthony, Jr. aerospace engineer, consultant
Yariv, Amnon electrical engineering educator, scientist
Yeager, Caroline Hale radiologist, consultant
Yeh, Paul Pao electrical and electronics engineer, educator
†Yeomans, Donald Keith astronomer
Yohalem, Harry Morton lawyer
Zachariasen, Fredrik physics educator
Zammitt, Norman artist
Zewail, Ahmed Hassan chemistry and physics educator, editor, consultant

Paso Robles
Boxer, Jerome Harvey computer and management consultant, vintner, accountant
Brown, Benjamin Andrew journalist
Knecht, James Herbert lawyer

Pauma Valley
Dooley, George Elijah health facility administrator

Pebble Beach
Burkett, William Andrew banker
Cameron, JoAnna actress, director
Carns, Michael Patrick Chamberlain air force officer
Crossley, Randolph Allin retired corporate executive
Dennison, David Short, Jr. lawyer
Fergusson, Robert George retired army officer
Gianelli, William Reynolds foundation administrator, civil engineering consultant, former federal agency commissioner
Keene, Clifford Henry medical administrator
Mauz, Henry Herrward, Jr. retired naval officer
Maxeiner, Clarence William lawyer, construction company executive
Mortensen, Gordon Louis artist, printmaker
Sullivan, James Francis university administrator

Penn Valley
Throner, Guy Charles, Jr. engineering executive, scientist, engineer, inventor, consultant

Petaluma
Carr, Les psychologist, educator
Crawford, George Truett management systems company executive, consultant
Mc Chesney, Robert Pearson artist
O'Hare, Sandra Fernandez secondary education educator
Pronzini, Bill John (William Pronzini) author
Reichek, Jesse artist

Philo
Hill, Rolla B. pathologist

Piedmont
Cuttle, Tracy Donald physician, former naval officer
Daniels, Lydia M. health care administrator
Hoover, Robert Cleary retired bank executive
Hughes, James Paul physician
Montgomery, Theodore Ashton physician
Phillips, Betty Lou (Elizabeth Louise Phillips) author, interior designer
Putter, Irving French language educator
Smith, Charles Conard refractory company executive

Pinole
Gerbracht, Robert Thomas (Bob Gerbracht) painter, educator
Grogan, Stanley Joseph educational educator, consultant
Harvey, Elinor B. child psychiatrist

Pismo Beach
Saveker, David Richard naval and marine architectural engineering executive

Pittsburg
Chuderewicz, Leonard H. heavy industry executive

Placentia
Galvez, William artist
Gobar, Alfred Julian economic consultant, educator

Placerville
Craib, Kenneth Bryden resource development executive, physicist, economist
McIntosh, Paul Eugene county government official

Playa Del Rey
Copperman, William H value engineer, consultant
Weir, Alexander, Jr. utility consultant, inventor

Pleasant Hill
Gomez, Edward Casimiro physician, educator
Hassid, Sami architect, educator
Weiss, Lionel Edward geology educator

Pleasanton
Busboom, Larry D. food products company executive
Dunbar, Frank Rollin landscape architect
Fehlberg, Robert Erick architect
Giacolini, Earl L. agricultural products company executive
Goddard, John Wesley cable television company executive
†Gustafson, Lawrence Raymond lawyer
Hutchcraft, Arthur Stephens, Jr. aluminum and chemical company executive
†Marcy, Charles Frederick food products company executive
Miller, William Charles lawyer
Perry, James R. construction company executive
Petty, George Oliver lawyer
Shen, Mason Ming-Sun medical center administrator
Stager, Donald K. construction company executive
Tauscher, William Young pharmaceutical and cosmetic products executive
Weiss, Robert Stephen medical manufacturing and services company financial executive

Plymouth
Andreason, John Christian lawyer

Point Arena
Kohl, Herbert Ralph education educator

Point Mugu
Newman, William E. naval officer

Pollock Pines
Johnson, Stanford Leland marketing educator

Pomona
Aurilia, Antonio physicist, educator
Baker, Frederick John education educator
Bernau, Simon John mathematics educator
Burrill, Melinda Jane animal science educator
Collins, Catherine Clay finincial consultant
Coombs, Walter Paul retired lawyer, social science educator
Dev, Vasu chemistry educator
Eagleton, Robert Don physics educator
Eaves, Ronald Weldon university administrator
Fleck, Raymond Anthony, Jr. university administrator
Kauser, Fazal Bakhsh aerospace engineer, educator
Keating, Eugene Kneeland animal scientist, educator
Lyle, John Tillman landscape architecture educator
McCoy, Charles Wirth, Jr. superior court judge
Patten, Thomas Henry, Jr. management, human resources educator
†Pumerantz, Philip medical school president
Shieh, John Ting-chung economics educator
Suzuki, Bob H. university president
Thompson, Earlene civic volunteer

Port Hueneme
Chapla, P.A. civil engineering research administrator
Pathak, Sunit Rawly business owner, consultant, journalist

Porterville
†Wall, Fred Willard agricultural products supplier

Portola Valley
Berghold, Joseph Philip finance company executive
Cooper, John Joseph lawyer
Creevy, Donald Charles obstetrician-gynecologist
Garsh, Thomas Burton publisher
Graham, William James packaging company executive
Hanson, Raymond Lester retired lawyer
Hurd, Cuthbert C. computer company executive, mathematician
Kuo, Franklin F. computer scientist, electrical engineer
†Litton, Martin conservationist
Millard, Stephens Fillmore electronics company executive
Moses, Franklin Maxwell retired chemical marketing executive
Nycum, Susan Hubbell lawyer
Purl, O. Thomas retired electronics company executive
Ward, Robert Edward retired political science educator and university administrator

Poway
Brose, Cathy principal
Buncher, James Edward healthcare management executive
Remer, Vernon Ralph travel consultant
Shippey, Lyn reading center director

Ramona
Bennett, James Chester computer consultant, real estate developer
Cesinger, Joan author
Hoffman, Wayne Melvin retired airline official
Jordan, David Francis, Jr. retired judge
Vaughn, Robert Lockard aerospace and astronautics company executive

Rancho Cordova
Alenius, John Todd insurance executive
Ling, Robert Malcolm banker, publishing executive
Wilderotter, Maggie cable television executive

Rancho Cucamonga
Christopher, Gaylaird Wiley architect
Nelson, William O. pharmaceutical company executive
†Rankin, Jim real estate developer

Rancho Mirage
Buskirk, Richard Hobart marketing educator
Chambers, Milton Warren architect
Cone, Lawrence Arthur research medicine educator
Deiter, Newton Elliott clinical psychologist
Ford, Betty Bloomer (Elizabeth Ford) health facility executive, wife of former President of United States
Ford, Gerald Rudolph, Jr. former President of United States
Gardner, Donald LaVere development company executive
Kocen, Joel Evan financial planner
Kuhlmey, Walter Trowbridge lawyer
Rotman, Morris Bernard public relations consultant
Stenhouse, Everett Ray clergy administrator
Strickman, Arthur Edwin retired retail executive
†Wiskowski, Eugene health facility administrator

Rancho Palos Verdes
Lima, Luis Eduardo tenor
Marlett, De Otis Loring retired management consultant
McFadden, Thomas academic administrator

Rancho Santa Fe
Affeldt, John Ellsworth physician
Arms, Brewster Lee retired corporate lawyer, investor
Capen, Richard Goodwin, Jr. ambassador
Creutz, Edward Chester physicist, museum consultant
Gruenwald, George Henry new products development management consultant
Gunness, Robert Charles chemical engineer
Jordan, Charles Morrell retired automotive designer
Matthews, Leonard Sarver advertising executive, consultant
Schirra, Walter Marty, Jr. business consultant, former astronaut
Trout, Monroe Eugene hospital systems executive

Rancho Santa Margarita
Griffith Joyner, Florence DeLorez track and field athlete
Wong, Wallace medical supplies company executive, real estate investor

Redding
Becker, Stephen Arnold museum director
Buffum, Nancy Kay interior designer
Miller, Rodger Dale private investigator, intelligence analyst
Treadway, Douglas Morse academic administrator
Wilson, David Lee clinical psychologist

Redlands
Appleton, James Robert university president, educator
†Burgess, Larry Eugene library director, history educator
Ely, Northcutt lawyer
Skomal, Edward Nelson aerospace company executive, consultant
Skoog, William Arthur retired oncologist

Redondo Beach
Battles, Roxy Edith novelist, consultant, educator
Buchta, Edmund engineering executive
Burris, Harrison Robert computer and software developer
Chazen, Melvin Leonard chemical engineer
Cohen, Clarence Budd aerospace engineer
Heller, Anthony Ferdinand electronics engineer
Ilie, Paul foreign language educator
Kagiwada, Reynold Shigeru advanced technology manager
Marsee, Stuart (Earl) educational consultant, retired
McCann, Joseph John, Jr. lawyer
McWilliams, Margaret Ann home economics educator, author
Sackheim, Robert Lewis aerospace engineer, educator
Shellhorn, Ruth Patricia landscape architect

Redwood City
Bentley, John Martin lawyer
Bertram, Jack Renard information systems specialist
Bonino, Mark G. lawyer
Coddington, Clinton Hays lawyer
Eliassen, Rolf environmental engineer, emeritus educator
Elkus, Richard J. finance and industrial company executive
Ellison, Lawrence J. computer software company executive
Guinasso, Victor delivery service executive
Jenkins, Robert Lee management consultant
Jobs, Steven Paul computer corporation executive
Kalinske, Thomas J. video game and toy company executive
Logie, Dennis Wayne minister
Nacht, Sergio biochemist
Neville, Roy Gerald scientist, chemical management and environmental consultant
Russell, Charles T. bank executive
Seltzer, Ronald Anthony radiologist, educator
Silvestri, Philip Salvatore lawyer
Speziale, A. John organic chemist, consultant
Swinerton, William Arthur retired construction company executive
Tight, Dexter Corwin lawyer
Tyabji, Hatim Ahmedi computer systems company executive

Waller, Stephen *air transportation executive*
†Warmenhoven, Daniel John *communications equipment executive*
Wilhelm, Robert Oscar *lawyer, civil engineer, developer*
Wong, Nancy L. *dermatologist*

Redwood Shores
Abrahamson, James Alan *transportation executive, retired military officer*

Reedley
Dick, Henry Henry *minister*

Reseda
Anstad, Neil *director*
Hoover, Pearl Rollings *nurse*
Leahy, T. Liam *management consultant*

Richmond
Ayers, G. W. *church administrator*
Balakrishnan, Krishna (Balki Balakrishnan) *biotechnologist, corporate executive*
Beall, Frank Carroll *science director and educator*
Bertero, Vitelmo Victorio *civil engineer*
Colfack, Andrea Heckelman *elementary education educator*
Corbin, Rosemary Mac Gowan *mayor*
Doyle, William Thomas *retired newspaper editor*
Hedgpeth, Joe *molecular biologist, business executive*
Holmquist, Walter Richard *research chemist, molecular evolutionist, mathematics educator*
Moehle, Jack P. *civil engineer, engineering executive*
Rubanyi, Gabor Michael *medical research company executive*
Thomas, John Richard *chemist*
Ward, Carl Edward *research chemist*
Wessel, Henry *photographer*
Wilcox, W(ebster) Wayne *forest products pathologist, educator*
Zavarin, Eugene *forestry science educator*

Ridgecrest
Bennett, Harold Earl *physicist, optics researcher*
Pearson, John *mechanical engineer*
St. Amand, Pierre *geophysicist*

Riverside
Aderton, Jane Reynolds *lawyer*
Adrian, Charles Raymond *political science educator*
Balow, Irving Henry *retired education educator*
Barnes, Martin McRae *entomologist*
Bartnicki-Garcia, Salomon *microbiologist, educator*
Beni, Gerardo *electrical and computer engineering educator, robotics scientist*
Bergh, Berthold Orphie (Bob Bergh) *plant research scientist, human genetics educator*
Bhanu, Bir *computer information scientist, educator, director university program*
Bovell, Carlton Rowland *biology educator, microbiologist*
Bowers, Norene A. *nursing administrator, critical care nurse*
Brown, Albert Clarence *former mayor*
Carrillo, Gilberto *engineer*
Chang, Sylvia Tan *health facility administrator, educator*
Chute, Phillip Bruce *management consultant*
Clegg, Michael Tran *genetics educator, researcher*
†Coggins, Charles William *plant physiology educator*
Cohen, Kenneth Bruce *health agency director*
Crean, John C. *housing and recreational vehicles manufacturing company executive*
†Crebs, Raymond Lee *mortgage banking executive*
Elliott, Emory Bernard *English language educator, educational administrator*
Embleton, Tom William *horticultural science educator*
Erwin, Donald Carroll *plant pathology educator*
Eyman, Richard Kenneth *psychologist, educator*
Fagundo, Ana Maria *creative writing and Spanish literature educator*
Foreman, Thomas Elton *drama critic*
†Forney, Guy Sherman *electronics components manufacturing executive*
Geraty, Lawrence Thomas *academic administrator, archaeologist*
Gerdel, Miguel Antonio *manufacturing research engineer, researcher*
Green, Harry Western, II *geology/geophysics educator*
Green, Jonathan William *museum administrator and educator, artist, author*
Griffin, Keith Broadwell *economics educator*
Hackwood, Susan *electrical and computer engineering educator*
Hadfield, Tomi Senger *hospital administrator*
Hall, Anthony Elmitt *plant physiologist*
Ham, Gary Martin *psychologist*
Hanna, Ralph, III *English educator, author*
Hays, Howard H. (Tim Hays) *editor, publisher*
Hodgen, Maurice Denzil *financial development administrator, educator*
Inacker, Charles John *academic dean, business educator*
Jukkola, George Duane *obstetrician-gynecologist*
Kronenfeld, David Brian *anthropologist*
Kummer, Glenn F. *construction and automotive executive*
Lacy, Carolyn Jean *elementary education educator, secondary education educator*
Letey, John Joseph, Jr. *soil scientist, educator*
Maas, Sally Ann *newspaper editor, journalist*
Mc Laughlin, Leighton Bates, II *journalism educator, former newspaperman*
McQuern, Marcia Alice *newspaper publishing executive*
†Moore, John Alexander *biologist*
Norman, Anthony Westcott *biochemistry educator*
Opotowsky, Maurice Leon *newspaper editor*
Orbach, Raymond Lee *physicist, educator*
Page, Albert Lee *soil science educator, researcher*
Perkins, Van L. *university administrator, educator, conservationist*
Petrinovich, Lewis F. *psychology educator*
Pick, Arthur Joseph, Jr. *chamber of commerce executive*
Quinton, Paul Marquis *physiology educator*
Rabenstein, Dallas Leroy *chemistry educator*
Ratliff, Louis Jackson, Jr. *mathematics educator*
Ravitch, Norman *history educator*
Reuther, Walter *horticulture educator*
Reynolds, William Harold *music educator, choral conductor, music critic*
Ross, Delmer Gerrard *historian, educator*
Shapiro, Victor Lenard *mathematician*
Sherman, Irwin William *biological sciences educator, university official*
Shipley, Marilyn Elizabeth *school system administrator*
Snyder, Henry Leonard *history educator, bibliographer*
Sokolsky, Robert Lawrence *journalist, entertainment writer*
Spencer, William Franklin, Sr. *soil scientist, researcher*
Steckel, Barbara Jean *city financial officer*
Talbot, Prue *biology educator*
Trask, Grover C. *lawyer*
Turk, Austin Theodore *sociology educator*
Turner, Arthur Campbell *political science educator, author*
Van Gundy, Seymour Dean *nematologist, plant pathologist, educator*
Walter-Robinson, Carol Sue *investment executive*
Warren, David Hardy *psychology educator*
Weide, William Wolfe *housing and recreational vehicles manufacturer*
White, Robert Stephen *physics educator*
†White, Thomas Jeffrey *healthcare management educator*
Wild, Robert Lee *physics educator*
Wilkins, Charles L. *chemistry educator*
Wright, John MacNair, Jr. *retired army officer*
Yacoub, Ignatius I. *university dean*
Yeager, Jacques Stalder, Sr. *construction company executive*
Zentmyer, George Aubrey *plant pathology educator*

Rocklin
Ha, Chong Wan *state government executive*

Rohnert Park
Arminana, Ruben *university president, educator*
Babula, William *university dean*
Grivas, Theodore *retired historian, educator*
Johnston, Edward Elliott *insurance and management consultant*
Lord, Harold Wilbur *electrical engineer, electronics consultant*

Rolling Hills Estates
Bellis, Carroll Joseph *surgeon*
Rumbaugh, Charles Earl *lawyer, corporate executive*

Rosemead
Allen, Howard Pfeiffer *electric utility executive, lawyer*
Barry, David N., III *utility executive*
Bennett, Brian O'Leary *utilities executive*
Bryson, John E. *utilities company executive*
Bushey, Richard Kenneth *utility executive*
Hansen, Robert Dennis *educational administrator*
Noel, Michael Lee *utility executive*
†Pollay, Richard L. *title company executive*
Ray, Harold Byrd *utilities executive*

Roseville
Dupper, Frank Floyd *health care facility executive*
Hendricks, Ed Jerald *physician*
Leslie, (Robert) Tim *state legislator*
Robbins, Stephen J. M. *lawyer*
Simms, Thomas Haskell *chief of police*
Singer, Frank J. *insurance company executive, lawyer*

Ross
Fitzgerald, Richard Patrick *school administrator*
Godwin, Sara *writer*
Goulet, William Dawson *marketing professional*
Scott, John Walter *chemical engineer, research management executive*
Way, Walter Lee *anesthetist, pharmacologist, educator*

Rowland Heights
Perfetti, Robert Nickolas *career education coordinator, educator*

Rutherford
Eisele, Milton Douglas *viticulturist*
Staglin, Garen Kent *finance and computer service company executive*

Sacramento
Adelekan, Patricia Ann *school administrator*
Aldrich, Thomas Albert *consultant, former brewing executive*
Andrew, John Henry *lawyer, retail corporation executive*
Baccigaluppi, Roger John *agricultural company executive*
Baltake, Joe *film critic*
†Beckwith, Charles Allan *healthcare administrator, consultant*
Bell, Robert William *lawyer*
Benfield, John Richard *surgeon*
Bennett, Lawrence Allen *psychologist, criminal justice researcher*
Betts, Bert A. *former state treasurer, accountant*
Bezzone, Albert Paul *structural engineer*
Blackman, David Michael *lawyer*
Blackwell, Frederick Wayne *computer science educator*
Blum, Deborah *reporter*
Boatwright, Daniel E. *state legislator*
Bogren, Hugo Gunnar *radiology educator*
Bottel, Helen Alfea *columnist, writer*
Brookman, Anthony Raymond *lawyer*
Brown, Kathleen *state treasurer, lawyer*
Brown, Valerie *state legislator*
Brown, Willie Lewis, Jr. *state legislator, lawyer*
Bruce, Thomas Edward *thanatologist, psychology educator*
Cavigli, Henry James *petroleum engineer*
Chapman, Loring *psychologist, educator, neuroscientist*
Chapman, Michael William *orthopedist, educator*
†Cirona, James Michael *banker*
Cole, Glen David *minister*
Collings, Charles LeRoy *supermarket executive*
Collins, William Leroy *telecommunications engineer*
Connolly, Tom M. *state legislator, lawyer*
Cortese, Dominic L. *state legislator, farmer*
Cox, David W. *bank executive*
Cox, Whitson William *architect*
Crabbe, John Crozier *telecommunications consultant*
Crimmins, Philip Patrick *metallurgical engineer, lawyer*
Cunningham, Mary Elizabeth *physician*
Dahl, Loren Silvester *federal judge*
Dalkey, Fredric Dynan *artist*
Deitch, Arline Douglis *cell biologist*
Dorn, Robert Murray *physician, psychiatrist, educator, psychoanalyst*
Dreyfus, Pierre Marc *neurologist, educator*
Endicott, William F. *journalist*
Engel, Thomas P. *airport executive*
Evans, James Handel *university administrator, architect, educator*
Evrigenis, John Basil *obstetrician-gynecologist*
Farrell, Francine Annette *psychotherapist, educator*
Flournoy, Houston Irvine *public administration educator*
Forsyth, Raymond Arthur *civil engineer*
†Franz, Jennifer Danton *public opinion and marketing researcher*
Frey, Charles Frederick *surgeon, educator*
Friedman, Morton Lee *lawyer*
Gerth, Donald Rogers *university president*
Gibson, Edward Fergus *physicist, educator*
Glackin, William Charles *arts critic, editor*
Goodart, Nan L. *lawyer, educator*
Gottfredson, Don Martin *criminal justice educator*
Gray, Myles McClure *insurance company executive*
Gray, Walter P., III *museum director, consultant*
Greenfield, Carol Nathan *psychotherapist*
Grissom, Lee Alan *state official*
†Hallenbeck, Harry C. *architect*
†Hartman, Howard Levi *mining engineering educator, consultant*
Haugen, D. Peter *theatre critic*
Hay, John Thomas *trade association executive*
Hays, Patrick Gregory *health care executive*
Herman, Irving Leonard *business administration educator*
Hoagland, Dennis Roy *trust banker, financial consultant*
Holmes, Robert Eugene *state legislative consultant, journalist*
Hughes, Teresa P. *state legislator*
†Hunt, Dennis *public relations executive*
Karlton, Lawrence K. *federal judge*
Kerschner, Lee R(onald) *university president, political science educator*
Killian, Richard M. *library director*
Knight, William J. (Pete Knight) *state legislator, retired military officer*
Knudson, Thomas Jeffery *journalist*
Kolkey, Daniel Miles *lawyer*
Lagarias, John Samuel *engineering executive*
Lake, Carol Lee *anesthesiologist, educator*
†Lamb, Jerry A. *bishop*
LeBaron, Edward Wayne, Jr. *lawyer*
Levi, David F. *federal judge*
Lionakis, George *architect*
Loge, Frank Jean, II *hospital administrator*
Lukenbill, Gregg *sports promoter, real estate developer*
Lundstrom, Marjie *newspaper editor*
Lungren, Daniel Edward *state attorney general*
Lynch, Peter John *dermatologist*
MacBride, Thomas Jamison *federal judge*
Mack, Edward Gibson *retired business executive*
†Majesty, Melvin Sidney *psychologist, consultant*
McCarthy, Leo Tarcisius *state lieutenant governor*
McClatchy, James B. *editor, newspaper publisher*
McFarlane, William F. *wholesale nut company executive*
Meier, George Karl, III *pastor, lawyer*
Meindl, Robert James *English language educator*
Merwin, Edwin Preston *health care consultant, educator*
Mette, Joe *museum director*
Metzger, Bobbie Ann *public relations executive*
Moore, David Sumner *forensic document examiner*
Moulds, John F. *federal judge*
Muehleisen, Gene Sylvester *retired law enforcement officer, state official*
Mujumdar, Vilas Sitaram *structural engineer, management executive*
Nacht, Daniel Joseph *architect*
Napolitano, Grace F. *state legislator*
Nelson, Alan Curtis *government official, lawyer*
Newland, Chester Albert *public administration educator*
Nice, Carter *conductor, music director*
Nicholson, George *judge*
Nussenbaum, Siegfried Fred *chemistry educator*
O'Haire, Karen A. *lawyer*
Peck, Ellie Enriquez *retired state administrator*
Plant, Forrest Albert *lawyer*
Post, August Alan *economist, artist*
Potts, Erwin Rea *newspaper executive*
Presley, Robert Buel *state senator*
Quinn, Francis A. *bishop*
Ramirez, Raul Anthony *lawyer, former federal judge*
Redig, Dale Francis *dentist, association executive*
Richardson, Frank Kellogg *lawyer, former state justice*
Richman, David Paul *neurologist, researcher*
Riles, Wilson Camanza *educational consultant*
Ross, Terence William *architect*
Russell, Bill *former professional basketball team executive, former professional basketball player*
Russell, David E. *federal judge*
St. Jean, Garry *professional basketball coach*
Salamy, Farris Najeeb *lawyer*
Sawiris, Milad Youssef *statistician, educator*
Schaber, Gordon Duane *law educator, former judge*
Schmitz, Dennis Mathew *English language educator*
Schrag, Peter *editor, writer*
Schwabe, Peter Alexander, Jr. *judge*
Schwartz, Milton Lewis *federal judge*
Serna, Joe, Jr. *mayor*
Shaw, Eleanor Jane *newspaper editor*
Sherwood, Robert Petersen *retired sociology educator*
Shubb, William Barnet *federal judge*
Slater, Manning *broadcasting consultant*
Smith, Freda M. *minister*
Snow, Marina Sexton *reference librarian, playwright*
Stabenau, James Raymond *research psychiatrist, educator*
Stegenga, Preston Jay *international education consultant*
Strock, James Martin *state agency administrator, lawyer, conservationist*
Swatt, Stephen Benton *communications executive, consultant*
Takasugi, Nao *state official, business developer*
Thomas, Jim *professional basketball team executive*
Toman, Mary Ann *federal official*
Van Camp, Brian Ralph *lawyer*
†Venegas, Arturo, Jr. *chief police*
Wallace, Patricia Jean *artist, educator, writer*
Walsh, Denny Jay *reporter*
Walston, Roderick Eugene *state attorney general*
Walters, Daniel Raymond *political columnist*
Wasserman, Barry L(ee) *architect*
Whiteside, Carol Gordon *state official, former mayor*
Wightman, Thomas Valentine *rancher, researcher*
Wilkins, Philip Charles *judge*
Williams, Arthur Cozad *broadcasting executive*
Wilson, Pete *governor of California*
Wolfman, Earl Frank, Jr. *surgeon, educator*
Zeff, Ophelia Hope *lawyer*
Zumbrun, Ronald Arthur *lawyer*

Saint Helena
Amerine, Maynard Andrew *enologist, educator*
Hayes, James Edward *retired insurance executive*
Kamman, Alan Bertram *communications consulting company executive*

Salinas
Eifler, Carl Frederick *retired psychologist*
Francis, Alexandria Stephanie *psychologist*
†Kellogg, Donald Ray *surgeon, plastic surgeon*
Spinks, Paul *retired library director*
Stevens, Wilbur Hunt *accountant*
†Taylor, Steven Bruce *agriculture company executive*

San Andreas
Arkin, Michael Barry *lawyer, arbitrator*
Breed, Allen Forbes *correctional administrator*
Millsaps, Rita Rae *elementary school educator*

San Anselmo
Goodman, Carolyn *advertising executive*
Mudge, Lewis Seymour *theologian, educator, university dean*
Murphy, Barry Ames *lawyer*
Waetjen, Herman Charles *theologian, educator*

San Bernardino
Anderson, Barbara Louise *retired library director*
†Barnes, Gerald R. *bishop*
Bellis, David James *public administration educator*
Burgess, Mary Alice (Mary Alice Wickizer) *publisher*
Burgess, Michael *library science educator, publisher*
Evans, Anthony Howard *university president*
†Ewing, Robert Stirling *library administrator*
Fairley Raney, Rebecca *journalist*
Garson, Arnold Hugh *newspaper editor*
Heding, Thomas John *school system administrator*
Holtz, Tobenette *aerospace engineer*
Little, Thomas Warren *broadcast executive*
MacCauley, Hugh Bournonville *banker*
Nies, Boyd Arthur *hematologist, oncologist*
Robertson, Stewart *conductor*
Sagmeister, Edward Frank *small business owner, career officer, consultant*
Timmreck, Thomas C. *health sciences and health administration educator*
Turoci, Marsha May *county official*

San Bruno
†Agresti, Jack Joseph *construction company executive*
Arthur, Greer Martin *maritime container leasing firm executive*
Bradley, Charles William *podiatrist, educator*

San Carlos
Barnard, William Calvert *retired news service executive*
Bellack, Daniel Willard *advertising and public relations executive*
Curry, William Sims *procurement manager*
Gutow, Bernard Sidney *packaging manufacturing company executive*
Symons, Robert Spencer *electronics engineer*
True, Richard Brownell *scientist*

San Clemente
Fall, John Robert *management and computer consultant*
Fertik, Ira J. *medical laser company executive*
Khachigian, Kenneth Larry *lawyer*
Kim, Edward William *ophthalmic surgeon*
Singer, Kurt Deutsch *news commentator, author, publisher*
Stenzel, William A. *consulting services executive*
Walker, Joseph *retired research executive*
White, Stanley Archibald *research electrical engineer*

San Diego
†Aden, Gary Dee *healthcare company executive*
Adler, Louise DeCarl *bankruptcy judge*
Akeson, Wayne Henry *orthopedic surgeon, orthopedic educator*
Albritton, Robert Sanford *life insurance executive*
Albuquerque, Lita *artist*
Alpert, Deirdre Whittleton *state legislator*
Alpert, Michael Edward *lawyer*
Ames, Robert Forbes *lawyer*
Anderson, Paul Maurice *electrical engineering educator, researcher, consultant*
Anjard, Ronald Paul, Sr. *business and industry executive, consultant, educator, technologist, importer*
Arledge, Charles Stone *former aerospace executive, entrepreneur*
Bailey, David Nelson *pathologist, educator*
Bakko, Orville Edwin *retired health care executive, consultant*
Ballinger, Charles Edwin *educational association administrator*
Barckley, Robert Eugene *economics educator*
Bateman, Giles Hirst Litton *finance executive*
Bell, Gene *newspaper publishing executive*
Benes, Andrew Charles *professional baseball player*
Benirschke, Kurt *pathologist, educator*
Bennett, Ronald Thomas *photojournalist*
Berger, Bennett Maurice *sociology educator*
Beyster, John Robert *engineering company executive*
Bieler, Charles Linford *development director, zoo executive director emeritus*
Binkley, Nicholas Burns *banking executive*
Blakemore, Claude Coulehan *banker*
Bliesner, James Douglas *municipal/county official, consultant*
Blum, John Alan *urologist, educator*
Blumenfeld, Alfred Morton *industrial design consultant, educator*
Boarman, Patrick Madigan *economics and business administration educator, public official*
Boggs, Marcus Livingstone, Jr. *novelist, editor*
Bohrer, Robert Arnold *law educator*
Boller, John Hall, Jr. *minister*
Bolman, Pieter Simon Heinrich *publishing company executive, physicist*
Bowie, Peter Wentworth *lawyer, educator*

Boyd, Robert Giddings, Jr. mental health facility administrator
Bradley, Francis Xavier aluminum company executive
Bradley, John Edmund physician, emeritus educator
Bradley, Lawrence D., Jr. lawyer
Brandes, Raymond Stewart history educator
Branson, Harley Kenneth lawyer, finance executive
Brewster, Rudi Milton federal judge
Brezzo, Steven Louis museum director
Brimble, Alan business executive
†Brimner, Larry Dane author, editor, educational consultant
Brom, Robert H. bishop
Brooks, John White lawyer
Brown, Robert John accountant
†Bucker, Homer Park, Jr. acoustical engineer
Burge, David Russell concert pianist, composer, piano educator
Burgin, George Hans computer scientist, educator
Burke, John science technology company executive
Campbell, Ian David opera company director
†Cannon, Janell illustrator, writer
Carleson, Robert Bazil public policy consultant, corporation executive
Celentino, Anne Elizabeth lawyer
Chandler, Floyd Copeland fine arts educator
Charles, Carol Morgan education educator
Chen, Kao consulting electrical engineer
†Chory, Joanne plant biologist
Cobble, James Wikle chemistry educator
Cockell, William Arthur, Jr. naval officer
Conly, John Franklin engineering educator, researcher
Conner, Dennis manufacturing executive, yachtsman
Coox, Alvin David history educator
Copeland, Robert Glenn lawyer
Cornett, William Forrest, Jr. local government management consultant
Cota, John Francis utility executive
Crick, Francis Harry Compton research scientist, educator
Cross, C. Michael marine museum administrator
Crutchfield, Susan Ramsey neurophysiologist
Cunningham, Bruce Arthur biochemist
Cushman, Thomas Henry sports editor, columnist
Daley, Arthur Stuart retired humanities educator
Damoose, George Lynn lawyer
Darmstandler, Harry Max business executive, retired air force officer
Daub, Clarence Theodore, Jr. astronomer, educator
Day, Thomas Brennock university president
Delawie, Homer Torrence architect
DeMaria, Anthony Nicholas cardiologist, educator
Dendo, Albert Ulysses electronics executive
Devine, Brian Kiernan pet food and supplies company executive
†Diaz, David illustrator
DiMattio, Terry historic site administrator
Dolan, James Michael, Jr. zoological society executive
Donaldson, Milford Wayne architect, educator
†Douglas, Lee Wayland association executive
Downing, David Charles minister
Doyle, Thomas J. healthcare administrator, consultant, educator
Duddles, Charles Weller food company executive
Dziewanowska, Zofia Elizabeth neuropsychiatrist, pharmaceutical executive, physician
Early, Ames S. health facility administrator
Eckhart, Walter molecular biologist, educator
Ellsworth, Peter Kennedy health care executive
Enright, William Benner judge
Fagot, Joseph Burdell corporate executive
Feinberg, Lawrence Bernard university dean, psychologist
Feinberg, Leonard English language educator
Fernandez, Fernando Lawrence research company executive, aeronautical engineer
Fisher, Kathleen Mary biology educator
Flettner, Marianne opera administrator
Fontana, J. D. naval research administration
Freedman, Jonathan Borwick journalist, author, lecturer
Freeman, Dick professional baseball team executive
Freeman, Myrna Faye county schools official
Garrison, Betty Bernhardt mathematics educator
Garry, Frederick Wilton electrical manufacturing company executive
Gastil, Russell Gordon geologist, educator
Getis, Arthur geography educator
Gill, Gail Stoorza public relations executive
Gilliam, Earl Ben federal judge
Golding, Brage former university president
Golding, Susan mayor
Goltz, Robert William physician, educator
Gonzalez, Irma Elsa federal judge
Goodall, Jackson Wallace, Jr. restaurant company executive
Goode, John Martin manufacturing company executive
Gregor, Mary Jeanne educator
Griffin, Herschel Emmett epidemiology educator, administrator
Grosser, T.J. administrator, developer, fundraiser
Gu, Zu-Han research scientist
†Guerin, John P. air transportation company executive
Gwynn, Anthony Keith (Tony Gwynn) professional baseball player
Halasz, Nicholas Alexis surgeon
Hale, David Fredrick health care company executive
Hales, Alfred Washington mathematics educator, consultant
Hamburg, Marian Virginia health science educator
Haney, Raymond Lee gas and electric company executive
Hargrove, John James federal judge
Harmon, Harry William architect, former university administrator
Hart, Anne author
†Hartman, Harold W. academic admininstrator
Harwood, Ivan Richmond pediatric pulmonologist
Hawran, Paul William pharmaceutical executive
Hayes, Alice Bourke university official, biology educator
Hayes, Robert Emmet retired insurance company executive
Hays, Garry D. academic administrator
Helinski, Donald Raymond biologist, educator
Hemmingsen, Barbara Bruff microbiology educator
Henderson, Brian Edmond physician, educator
Henderson, John Drews architect
Heuschele, Werner Paul veterinary researcher
Hill, Frank Whitney, Jr. insurance company executive
Hofflund, Paul lawyer
Holl, Walter John architect, interior designer
Holman, J(ohn) Leonard retired manufacturing corporation executive
Hooper, Jere Mann consultant, retired hotel executive
Hope, Douglas Olerich newspaper editor
Hope, Frank Lewis, Jr. retired architect
Howell, Thomas Edwin manufacturing company executive
Huang, Chien Chang electrical engineer
Huff, Marilyn L. federal judge
Hughes, Author E. university president, association executive
Hughes, Gethin B. bishop
Huston, Kenneth Dale lawyer
†Huston, William Alvin engineering executive
Hutcheson, J(ames) Sterling lawyer
Igasaki, Masao, Jr. retired utilities company executive, controller
Ingle, John Ide dental educator
Isenberg, Jon Irwin gastroenterologist, educator
Ivans, William Stanley electronics company executive
†Jacobs, Irwin Mark communications executive
Jacoby, Irving physician
Jeste, Dilip Vishwanath psychiatrist, researcher
Johnson, Kenneth Owen retired audiologist
Jones, Welton H., Jr. critic
†Kaback, Michael medical educator
Kammer, William Nolan lawyer
Kaplan, George Willard urologist
Karin, Sidney research and development executive
Kaufman, Julian Mortimer broadcasting company executive, consultant
Kayler, Robert Samuel hospital administrator
Keep, Judith N. federal judge
†Keltner, Karen Lee conductor
Kendrick, Ronald H. banker
Kenneally, Dennis Michael government official
Kennedy, Peter Smithson personnel consultant
Kent, Theodore Charles psychologist
Keyser, Richard Lee hospital executive
Kidokoro, Yasuko physician
Klausmeier, Herbert John psychologist, educator
Klein, Herbert George newspaper editor
Koch, Charles Stephen hospital executive, economist
Koehler, John Edget electronics company executive
Kopp, Harriet Green communication specialist
Kripke, Kenneth Norman lawyer
Krulak, Victor Harold newspaper executive
†Krull, Kathleen juvenile fiction and nonfiction writer
†Kull, Lorenz A. scientific research company executive
Lane, Gloria Julian foundation administrator
†Lao, Lang Li nuclear fusion research physicist
Lathrop, Mitchell Lee lawyer
Lauer, Jeanette Carol history educator, author
LeBeau, Charles Paul lawyer
†Lee, Christopher Heinz destination management consultant
Lee, Jerry Carlton university administrator
Lee, Marianna editor
Lerach, William S. lawyer
Lewis, Alan James pharmaceutical executive, pharmacologist
Lewis, Gregory Williams scientist
Linn, Edward Allen writer
Linton, Roy Nathan graphic arts company executive
Litrownik, Alan Jay psychologist, educator
Livingston, Stanley C. architect
Lomeli, Marta elementary education educator
Long, Marie Katherine public relations consultant, researcher
†Lowenthal, Arline Mae marketing research executive
Lucchino, Lawrence lawyer, sports executive
Lynn, Mitchell Gordon retail company executive
Lyon, Waldo Kampmeier physicist
MacCracken, Peter James marketing executive, communications executive
Madhavan, Murugappa Chettiar economics educator, international consultant
Magnuson, Harold Joseph physician
†Maguire, Edward Francis hospital administrator
Maier, Paul Victor pharmaceutical executive
Malin, Michael Charles space scientist, former geology educator
Martin, Donald Ray chemist, educator, consultant
†Martinez, Albert computer peripherals company executive
Mattingly, Thomas K. astronaut
Maurer, Lawrence Michael acting school administrator, educator
Mayer, James Hock mediator, lawyer
McBrayer, Sandra L. educational director, homeless outreach educator
McCarroll, Mary Barbara social services administrator, retired
Mc Comic, Robert Barry real estate development company executive, lawyer
McGinnis, Robert E. lawyer
McGraw, Donald Jesse biologist, historian of science, writer
Mc Guigan, Frank Joseph psychologist, educator
McKee, Roger Curtis federal magistrate judge
Mc Kinnon, Clinton D. editor, former congressman
McManus, Richard Philip lawyer
Meyers, James William federal judge
Mickelson, Sig broadcasting executive, educator
Miles, Gordon Hugh restaurant company executive, lawyer
Mills, Lorna Henrietta banker
Mittermiller, James Joseph lawyer
Moe, Chesney Rudolph physics educator
Monahan, David Emory lawyer
Monson, Forrest Truman shop owner, clergyman
Moody, Rhea Phenon banking executive
Moossa, A. R. surgery educator
Morgan, Neil author, newspaper editor, lecturer, columnist
Morris, Grant Harold legal educator
Morris, Henry Madison, Jr. education educator
Morris, Richard Herbert physicist, educator
Morris, Sandra Joan lawyer
Moser, Kenneth Miles physician
Mullane, John Francis pharmaceutical company executive
Mulvaney, James Francis lawyer
Myers, Douglas George zoological society administrator
Nadler, Henry Louis pediatrician, geneticist, medical educator
Nassif, Thomas Anthony business executive, former ambassador
Nelson, Craig Alan management consultant
Netter, Irene M. secondary education educator
Neuman, Tom S. emergency medical physician, educator
Nichols, Charles Lee professional services executive
Nielsen, Leland C. federal judge
Noehren, Robert organist, organ builder
Noel, Craig performing arts company executive, producer
Normandy, George Mitchell, Jr. electrical engineer
Norrod, James Douglas computer subsystems company executive
Nugent, Robert J., Jr. fast food company executive
Ohkawa, Tihiro physicist
O'Malley, Edward physician, consultant
O'Malley, James Terence lawyer
Osby, Robert Edward protective services official
Owen, Sally Ann gifted and talented education educator
Owen-Towle, Carolyn Sheets clergywoman
Owsia, Nasrin Akbarnia pediatrician
Paderewski, Clarence Joseph architect
†Page, Thomas Alexander utility executive
Pecsok, Robert Louis chemist, educator
Perrill, Frederick Eugene information systems executive
Petersen, Martin Eugene museum curator
Peterson, Nad A. lawyer, corporate executive
Pettis, Ronald Eugene lawyer
Pfeffer, Rubin Harry publishing executive
Pfeiffer, John William publisher, management consultant
Phillips, Randall Clinger minister, university administrator
Pierson, Albert Chadwick business management educator
Pincus, Howard Jonah geologist, engineer, educator
Pincus, Robert Lawrence art critic, cultural historian
Pray, Ralph Marble, III lawyer
Price, Robert E. manufacturing company executive
Pugh, Richard Crawford lawyer
Quintana, Mack newspaper publishing executive
Ranney, Helen Margaret physician, educator
Ray, Gene Wells industrial executive
Rea, Amadeo Michael ethnobiologist, ornithologist
Reading, James Edward transportation executive
Reavey, William Anthony, III lawyer
Reinhard, Christopher John merchant banking company executive
Resnik, Robert medical educator
Rethmeier, Kenneth Wayne, Jr. publishing company executive
†Reyes, Greg electronics executive
Rhoades, John Skylstead, Sr. federal judge
Rice, Clare I. electronics company executive
Riedy, Mark Joseph finance educator
Ringer, Jerome public relations executive
Risser, Arthur Crane, Jr. zoo administrator
Ristine, Jeffrey Alan reporter
Robinson, David Brooks naval officer
Roeder, Stephen Bernhard Walter chemistry and physics educator
Ross, Vonia Pearl insurance agent, small business owner
Rotter, Paul Talbott retired insurance executive
Rowe, Peter A. newspaper columnist
Roy, Catherine Elizabeth physical therapist
Saidman, Lawrence Jay anesthesiologist
St. Clair, Hal Kay electrical engineer
St. George, William Ross lawyer, retired naval officer, consultant
Salamone, Gary P. (Pike Salamone) newspaper editor-in-chief, cartoonist
Salk, Jonas Edward physician, scientist
Sannwald, William Walter librarian
Sasaki, Tatsuo musician
Saunders, Russell Joseph utility company executive
Schade, Charlene Joanne adult and early childhood education educator
Schaechter, Moselio microbiology educator
Scher, Valerie Jean music critic
Schlotter, Wally chamber of commerce executive, television director
Schmidt, Patricia Fain nurse educator
Schmidt, Terry Lane health care executive
Schwartz, Alfred university dean
Schwartz, Edward J. federal judge
Seau, Junior (Jr. Tiana Seau) professional football player
Sesonske, Alexander nuclear and chemical engineer
Shaw, Richard Allan lawyer
Shearer, William Kennedy lawyer, publisher
Shelton, Dorothy Diehl Rees lawyer
Shevel, Wilbert Lee information systems executive
Shippey, Sandra Lee lawyer
Shneour, Elie Alexis biochemist
†Sidlin, Murry conductor
Silverberg, Lewis Henry management consultant
Simms, Maria Kay publishing and computer services executive
Slate, John Butler biomedical engineer
†Smull, Scott electronics executive
Snyder, David Richard lawyer
Sorrentino, Renate Maria illustrator
Spanos, Alexander Gus professional football team executive
Spanos, Dean A. business executive
†Stambaugh, Ronald physicist, researcher
Steen, Paul Joseph retired broadcasting executive
†Stein, Robert Benjamin biomedical researcher, physician
Stepner, Michael Jay architect
Sterrett, James Kelley, II lawyer
Stiska, John C. lawyer
Storer, Norman William sociology educator
Storms, Lowell Hanson psychologist
†Strait, Edward J. research physicist
Su, Shiaw-Der nuclear engineer
Sullivan, William Francis lawyer
Swoap, David Bruce children's relief administrator
†Taylor, Tony S. research scientist
Tennent, Valentine Leslie accountant
Tepedino, Francis Joseph business management company executive
Thomas, Charles Allen, Jr. molecular biologist, educator
Thomas, Jack E. utility company executive
Thompson, David Renwick federal judge
Thompson, Gordon, Jr. federal judge
Tillinghast, Charles Carpenter, III marketing company executive
Tricoles, Gus Peter electromagnetics engineer, physicist, consultant
Trybus, Raymond J. higher education executive, psychologist
Turrell, Eugene Snow psychiatrist
Vanderbilt, Kermit English language educator
Vause, Edwin Hamilton research foundation administrator
Verbeke, Frank Girard, Jr. mechanical engineer
Villani, Kevin Emil banker
Viterbi, Andrew James electrical engineering and computer science educator, business executive
Wagschal, Kathleen education educator
Walker, Donald Ezzell retired academic administrator
Wallace, Helen Margaret physician, educator
Wallace, J. Clifford federal judge
Wallace, Ted wholesale goods distribution executive
Ward-Steinman, David composer, music educator
Warner, John Hilliard, Jr. technical services, military and commercial systems and software company executive
Warren, Gerald Lee newspaper editor
Wasserman, Stephen Ira physician, educator
Weaver, Michael James lawyer
Weeks, John Robert geographer, sociology educator
Weisman, Irving social worker, educator
Werner, Tom television producer, professional baseball team executive
West, James Harold accounting company executive
Whitmore, Sharp lawyer
Wiesler, James Ballard retired banker
Wight, Nancy Elizabeth neonatologist
Willerding, Margaret Frances mathematician
Wilson, Richard Allan landscape architect
Winner, Karin newspaper editor
Wright, Jon Alan physicist
Yacovone, Ellen Elaine banker
Zedler, Joy Buswell ecological sciences educator
Ziegaus, Alan James public relations executive
Zisch, William E. technical services executive

San Dimas

Cameron, Judith Lynne secondary education educator, hypnotherapist
Flores, Frank Cortez health sciences administrator, public health educator
Johnson, Richard M. not-for-profit financial cooperative executive

San Fernando

Chiu, Dorothy pediatrician
Gosselin, Kenneth Stuart minister

San Francisco

Abbott, Barry A. lawyer
†Adams, John Coolidge composer, conductor
Adams, Lee Stephen lawyer, banker
Adams, Leon David author
Adams, Mark artist
Aird, Robert Burns neurologist, educator
Alderman, Margaret C. nursing administrator
†Alderson, Gerald Robert finance company executive
Alexander, Robert C. lawyer
Allan, Walter Robert lawyer
Allemann, Sabina ballet dancer
Allen, Jose R. lawyer
Amend, William John Conrad, Jr. physician, educator
Amidei, L. Neal public relations counselor
Ammiano, Tom school system administrator
Anderson, Carl West judge
Anderson, David E. zoological park administrator
Andrews, David Ralph lawyer
Angell, James Browne electrical engineering educator
Anschutz, Philip F. transportation executive
Anthony, of Sourozh (Anthony Emmanuel Gergiannakis) bishop
Apatoff, Michael John finance executive
Arabian, Armand state supreme court justice
Archer, Richard Joseph lawyer
Arieff, Allen Ives physician
Armstrong, Saundra Brown federal judge
Arnitz, Rick artist
Arnold, Kenneth James lawyer, publishing company executive
Ashby, Teri Helena lawyer
Asling, Clarence Willet anatomist, educator
Auerback, Alfred psychiatrist
August-deWilde, Katherine banker
Bachrach, Ira Nathaniel marketing executive
Backus, John computer scientist
Bagdonas, Kathy Joann lawyer
Baker, Cameron lawyer
Baker, Dusty (Johnnie B. Baker, Jr.) professional baseball team manager
Baker, Kenneth art critic, writer
Balin, Marty (Martyn Jerel Buchwald) musician
Bancroft, James Ramsey lawyer, business executive
Bantock, Nick writer, illustrator
Bara, Jean Marc advertising executive
Barbagelata, Robert Dominic lawyer
Bare, Joseph Edward, Jr. retired lawyer
Barondes, Samuel Herbert psychiatrist, educator
Barron, Patrick Kenneth bank executive
Bates, John Burnham lawyer
Bates, William, III lawyer
Batlin, Robert Alfred editor
Bauer, Michael newspaper editor
Baumhefner, Clarence Herman banker
Baxter, Marvin Ray state supreme court judge
Baxter, Ralph H., Jr. lawyer
Beall, Dennis Ray artist, educator
Bechtel, Riley Peart engineering company executive
Bechtel, Stephen Davison, Jr. engineering company executive
Bechtle, Robert Alan artist, educator
Beck, Edward William lawyer
Beck, Rodney Roy professional baseball player
Bedford, Daniel Ross lawyer
Bedford, Lyman D. lawyer
Bee, Robert Norman banker
Belli, Melvin Mouron lawyer, lecturer, writer
†Bellows, William public relations executive
Benet, Leslie Zachary pharmacokineticist
Benet, Thomas Carr journalist
Bennett, James Patrick lawyer
Bennett, William oboist
Bensinger, David August dentist, university dean
Benvenutti, Peter J. lawyer
†Berggruen, John Henry art gallery executive
Berman, Joanna dancer
Berns, Philip Allan lawyer
Bertain, G(eorge) Joseph, Jr. lawyer
Bertelsen, Thomas Elwood, Jr. investment banker
Bibel, Debra Jan microbiologist, immunologist
Biglieri, Edward George physician
Bishop, John Michael biomedical research scientist, educator
Blackburn, Elizabeth Helen molecular biologist
Blackstone, George Arthur retired lawyer
Bloch, Julia Chang bank executive, former government official
Blomstedt, Herbert Thorson conductor, symphony director
Boles, Roger otolaryngologist
Bolin, William Harvey banker
Bonapart, Alan David lawyer

Bonds, Barry Lamar *professional baseball player*
Bonetti, David *art critic*
Bonney, John Dennis *oil company executive*
Bookin, Daniel H. *lawyer*
Borne, Bonita H. *ballet dancer, assistant artistic director*
Borowsky, Philip *lawyer*
Boucher, Harold Irving *lawyer*
Bowers, Edgar *poet, educator*
Boyd, William Sprott *lawyer*
Boyer, Herbert Wayne *biochemist*
†Bradford, David S. *surgeon*
Brand, Donald A. *electrical engineer*
†Brandborg, Lloyd Leon *retired medical educator*
Brandel, Roland Eric *lawyer*
†Brandford, Napoleon *securities firm executive*
Brandin, Alf Elvin *retired mining and shipping company executive*
Brandin, Mark Semple *financial services executive*
Bray, Arthur Philip *management science corporation executive*
Bredt, David Scott *neuroscience and physiology educator*
Breeden, David *clarinetist*
Brick, Steven A. *lawyer*
Bridges, Robert Lysle *retired lawyer*
Briggs, Susan Shadinger *lawyer*
Brindley, Robert E. *food products executive*
Bromley, Dennis Karl *lawyer*
Brooks, William George *aeronautical engineer*
Broome, Burton Edward *insurance company executive*
Brosnahan, James Jerome *lawyer*
Broussard, Allen E. *lawyer, former state supreme court justice*
Brower, David Ross *conservationist*
Brown, Albert Jacob *lawyer*
Brown, Anthony P. *lawyer*
Brown, David Julian *lawyer*
Brown, Donald Wesley *lawyer*
Brown, H. Douglas *English educator*
Brown, Margaret deBeers *lawyer*
Brown, Robert L. *lawyer*
Browning, James Robert *federal judge*
Brubeck, David Warren *musician*
Bryan, Robert Russell *lawyer*
Buckner, John Knowles *pension administrator*
Budge, Hamilton Whithed *lawyer*
Bull, Henrik Helkand *architect*
Burgess, Leonard Randolph *business administration and economics educator, writer*
Burk, Gary Maurice *health care facility planner*
†Burkett, William Cleveland *management consultant*
Burlingame, Alma Lyman *chemist, educator*
Burns, Brian Patrick *lawyer, business executive*
†Burr, Michael *bassist*
Butenhoff, Susan *public relations executive*
Butz, Otto William *political science educator*
Caen, Herb *newspaper columnist, author*
Cain, Leo Francis *retired special education educator*
Callan, Terrence A. *lawyer*
Calvin, Allen David *psychologist, educator*
Campbell, Scott Robert *lawyer, former food company executive*
Caniparoli, Val William *choreographer, dancer*
Canty, James M. *lawyer*
Cape, Ronald Elliot *biotechnology company executive*
Carlson, John Earl *lawyer*
Carman, John Elwin *journalist*
Carmichael, Lynne A. *lawyer*
Carniglia, Stephen Davis *accountant, real estate consultant, lawyer*
Carroll, Jon *newspaper columnist*
Carter, George Kent *oil company executive*
Carter, John Douglas *lawyer*
Cartmell, Nathaniel Madison, III *lawyer*
Case, Daniel Hibbard, III *investment banker*
Casillas, Mark *lawyer*
Castilla, Antonio *ballet dancer*
Caulfield, Barbara Ann *lawyer*
Chao, Cedric C. *lawyer*
Chapin, Dwight Allan *columnist, writer*
Cheatham, Robert William *lawyer*
Cheng, Wan-Lee *mechanical engineer, industrial technology educator*
Cherny, Robert Wallace *history educator*
Chesnut, Carol Fitting *economist*
Chiaverini, John Edward *construction company executive*
Chickering, Allen Lawrence *research institute executive*
Chin, Sue Soone Marian (Suchin Chin) *conceptual artist, portraitist, photographer, community affairs activist*
Christensen, David William *mathematician, engineer*
Chu, Kuang-Han *structural engineer, educator*
Cirese, Robert Charles *economist, real estate investment counselor*
Cisneros, Evelyn *dancer*
Clark, Edgar Sanderford *insurance broker, consultant*
Clark, M(ary) Margaret *anthropology educator*
Clarke, Richard Alan *electric and gas utility company executive, lawyer*
†Cleaver, James Edward *radiologist, educator*
Clements, John Allen *physiologist*
Clever, Linda Hawes *physician*
†Close, Sandy *journalist*
Cluff, Lloyd Sterling *earthquake geologist*
Coblentz, William Kraemer *lawyer*
Coffin, Judy Sue *lawyer*
Colbert, Lester Lum, Jr. *technology products executive*
Cole, Richard Charles *lawyer*
Coleman, Thomas Young *lawyer*
Collar, Leo Linford *marine transportation company executive*
Collas, Juan Garduño, Jr. *lawyer*
Collins, Dennis Arthur *foundation executive*
Collins, Jeremy *dancer*
Colnett, Ronald Harry *advertising executive*
Colwell, Kent Leigh *real estate executive*
Conger, Harry Milton *mining company executive*
Connell, William D. *lawyer*
Coombe, George William, Jr. *banker, lawyer*
Coppola, Francis Ford *film director, producer, writer*
Corcoran, Maureen Elizabeth *lawyer*
Corrigan, Robert Anthony *university president*
Cortines, Ramon *school superintendent*
Counelis, James Steve *education educator*
Cowan, Stephen A. *lawyer*
Crain, William Edwin *oil company executive*
Cranston, Alan *former senator*
Cranston, Mary B. *lawyer*
Crawford, Roy Edgington, III *lawyer*
Crede, Robert Henry *physician, educator*
Cumming, George Anderson, Jr. *lawyer*
Cunningham, Arthur Francis *university dean, marketing educator*
Cunningham, Emmett Thomas, Jr. *physician, researcher*
Curley, John Peter *sports editor*
Currier, Frederick Plumer *market research company executive*
Curry, Francis John *physician*
†Curtis, David Lambert *rheumatologist, educator*
†Dachs, Alan Mark *investment company executive*
Daggett, Robert Sherman *lawyer*
Dail, Joseph Garner, Jr. *judge*
Daniels, Alfred Harvey *merchandising executive*
†Danko, Gary J. *chef*
Danoff, Eric Michael *lawyer*
Daugherty, Richard Bernard *lawyer*
Davies, Paul Lewis, Jr. *retired lawyer*
Davis, Roger Lewis *lawyer*
Davis, Roland Chenoweth *lawyer*
Dawes, Paul Harvey *lawyer*
Dawson, Chandler R. *ophthalmologist, educator*
Dean, Norman Emerson (Ned Dean) *coffee company executive*
Debas, Haile T. *gastrointestinal surgeon, physiologist, educator*
De Benedictis, Dario *arbitrator, mediator*
†De Coteau, Denis *music director, conductor*
†de Hostos, Eugenio Luis *cell biologist*
Del Campo, Martin Bernardelli *architect*
Dell, Robert Michael *lawyer*
Dellas, Robert Dennis *investment banker*
†DeLuca, Nicholas Anthony *broadcasting executive*
De Lutis, Donald Conse *investment manager, consultant*
Demarest, David Franklin, Jr. *banker, former government official*
Derr, Kenneth T. *oil company executive*
Dewey, Edward Allen *construction company executive*
Dewey, Phelps *publishing executive*
deWilde, David Michael *executive search consultant, financial services executive, lawyer*
Dewitt, John Belton *conservation executive*
Diamond, Philip Ernest *lawyer*
Dickey, Glenn Ernest, Jr. *sports columnist*
Dickinson, Wade *physicist, research and development company executive*
Diekmann, Gilmore Frederick, Jr. *lawyer*
Djerassi, Carl *chemist, educator, writer*
Djordjevich, Michael *insurance company executive*
Dodge, Peter Hampton *architect*
Dolby, Ray Milton *engineering company executive, electrical engineer*
Donnally, Patricia Broderick *newspaper fashion editor*
D'Ornellas, Robert W. *food products executive*
Dowlin, Kenneth Everett *librarian*
Doxsee, Lawrence Edward *corporate lawyer*
Dran, Robert Joseph *lawyer*
Draper, William Henry, III *business executive*
Drexler, Fred *insurance executive*
†Drexler, Millard S. *retail executive*
Dryden, Robert Eugene *lawyer*
Du Bain, Myron *foundation administrator*
Duff, James George *financial services executive*
Dugoni, Arthur A. *orthodontics educator, university dean*
Dullea, Charles W. *university chancellor emeritus, priest*
Dunn, Richard Joseph *investment counselor*
Dunne, Kevin Joseph *lawyer*
Dupree, Stanley M. *lawyer*
Duscha, Julius Carl *journalist*
Dyer, Noel John *lawyer*
Eastham, Thomas *foundation administrator*
Eastwood, Susan *medical scientific editor*
Eckersley, Norman Chadwick *banker*
Edgar, James Macmillan, Jr. *management consultant*
Edwards, John Hamilton *language professional*
Edwards, Robin Morse *lawyer*
Ehrlich, Thomas *law educator*
Eigner, Richard Martin *lawyer*
Eilenberg, Lawrence Ira *theater educator, artistic director*
Elderkin, E(dwin) Judge *retired lawyer*
Emmons, Donn *architect*
Enersen, Burnham *lawyer*
Enfield, D(onald) Michael *insurance executive*
Eng, Catherine *health care facility administrator, physician, medical educator*
Engel, G(eorge) Larry *lawyer*
Epstein, Charles Joseph *physician, medical geneticist, pediatrics and biochemistry educator*
Epstein, John Howard *dermatologist*
Epstein, Leon Joseph *psychiatrist*
Ericson, Bruce Alan *lawyer*
Erskine, John Morse *surgeon*
Eschmeyer, William Neil *marine scientist*
Esherick, Joseph *architect, educator*
Estes, Carroll Lynn *sociologist, educator*
†Faden, Alan Ira *neurology educator*
Fannon, John *paper company executive*
Farber, Seymour Morgan *physician, university administrator*
Farley, Leon Alex *executive search consultant*
Farrell, Edward Joseph *retired mathematics educator*
Featherstone, John Douglas Bernard *biochemistry educator*
Feld, Michael Sperry *advertising executive*
Ferlinghetti, Lawrence *poet*
Ferris, Russell James, II *freelance writer*
Festinger, Richard *music educator, composer*
Field, Carol Hart *writer, journalist, foreign correspondent*
Field, John Louis *architect*
Fielder, David R. *medical research administrator*
Filippi, Frank Joseph *lawyer*
Finberg, Laurence *pediatrician, educator, college dean*
Finigan, Vincent P., Jr. *lawyer*
Fink, Scott Alan *lawyer*
†Fischthal, Glenn Jay *symphony musician*
Fisher, Donald G. *casual apparel chain stores executive*
Fisher, Robert M. *foundation administrator, university administrator*
Fleishhacker, David *school administrator*
Flittie, Clifford Gilliland *retired petroleum company executive*
Folberg, Harold Jay *lawyer, mediator, educator, university dean*
Foster, David Scott *lawyer*
Foye, Laurance Vincent *physician, hospital administrator*
Frantz, John Corydon *librarian*
Fraser, Cosmo Lyle *medical educator, researcher*
Fredericks, Dale Edward *lawyer*
Freedman, Mervin Burton *psychologist, educator*
Freeman, Tom M. *lawyer*
Freund, Fredric S. *real estate broker, property manager*
Frick, Oscar Lionel *physician, educator*
Friedman, K. Bruce *lawyer*
Friedman, Meyer *physician*
Friese, Robert Charles *lawyer*
Fromm, Alfred *distributing company executive*
Fu, Karen King-Wah *radiation oncologist*
Fuller, James William *financial director*
Fuller, Maurice DeLano, Jr. *lawyer*
Furst, Arthur *toxicologist, educator*
Furth, Frederick Paul *lawyer*
Gaines, Ernest James *author*
Gaither, James C. *lawyer*
Ganong, William F(rancis) *physiologist, physician*
Garchik, Leah Lieberman *journalist*
Gardner, James Harkins *venture capitalist*
Garoutte, Bill Charles *neurophysiologist*
Garvey, Joanne Marie *lawyer*
Gates, Milo Sedgwick *construction company executive*
Gee, Juliet Leslie *lawyer*
†Gehb, Michael *public relations executive*
Geiger, Richard George *librarian*
†George, Donald Warner *newspaper editor, writer, lecturer*
†George, Vance *conductor*
German, William *newspaper editor*
Gertler, Alfred Martin *public relations executive*
Gerwick, Ben Clifford, Jr. *construction engineer, educator*
Getty, Gordon Peter *composer, philanthropist*
Gill, Margaret Gaskins *lawyer*
Gillmar, Stanley Frank *lawyer*
Ginn, Sam L. *telephone company executive*
Ginsberg, Allen *poet, photographer, musician*
Giovinco, Joseph *non-profit administrator, writer*
Glass, Laurel Ellen *gerontologist, developmental biologist, physician, retired educator*
Goldberg, Fred Sellmann *advertising executive*
Goldstein, Joyce Esersky *restaurant owner*
Golub, Howard Victor *lawyer*
Gomi, Yasumasa *bank executive*
Goode, Erica Tucker *internist*
Gooding, Charles Arthur *radiologist, physician, educator*
Gooding, Gretchen Ann Wagner *physician, educator*
Goodman, Joel Warren *microbiologist, research scientist*
Gordon, Robert Allen, Jr. *lawyer*
Gordon, Roger L. *savings and loan association executive*
Gortner, Susan Reichert *nursing educator*
Gottfried, Eugene Leslie *physician, educator*
Gowdy, Franklin Brockway *lawyer*
Graham, Robert Arlington *newspaper entertainment editor*
Grant, Isabella Horton *judge*
Gray, Frances M. *retired college president, lecturer*
Graysmith, Robert *political cartoonist, author*
Greber, Robert Martin *financial investments executive*
Greeley, Robert Emmett *financial analyst*
Green, Robert Leonard *hospital management company executive*
Greene, John Clifford *dentist, former university dean*
Greenspan, Deborah *oral medicine educator*
Greenspan, Francis S. *physician*
Gregory, Michael Strietmann *English language educator*
Gresham, Zane Oliver *lawyer*
Grier, William E. *petroleum company executive*
Grodsky, Gerold Morton *biochemistry educator*
Grubb, David H. *construction company president*
Grumbach, Melvin Malcolm *physician, educator*
Guggenhime, Richard Johnson *lawyer*
Guinn, Sam *telecommunications industry executive*
Gulbenkian, Paul *civil engineer, inventor*
Gumucio, Fernando Raul *foods and beverage company executive*
Gund, George, III *financier*
Gunn, Thom(son) (William) *poet*
Gunst, Robert Allen *consumer products executive*
Gunther, Herbert Chao *advertising agency executive*
Gutterman, Alan Spencer *lawyer*
Haas, Peter E., Sr. *retired manufacturing company executive*
Haas, Robert Douglas *apparel manufacturing company executive*
Haas, Walter A., Jr. *retired apparel company executive, professional baseball executive*
Haerle, Paul Raymond *judge*
Haire, James *theatrical producer*
Hale, Cecil *communications educator*
Halliday, John Meech *investment company executive*
Hambrecht, William R. *venture capitalist*
Hamilton, Phyllis Jean *judge*
Handler, Mark S. *retail executive*
Handlery, Paul Robert *hotel executive*
Hannawalt, Willis Dale *lawyer*
Hanschen, Peter Walter *lawyer*
Hardison, Donald Leigh *architect*
Hardy, David *lawyer, corporate executive*
Hargadon, Bernard Joseph, Jr. *consumer goods company executive*
Harlan, Neil Eugene *retired healthcare company executive*
Harrington, Rex *ballet dancer*
Harris, Richard Eugene Vassau *lawyer*
†Harrison, Blaine L. *engineering consulting company executive*
Harrison, E(rnest) Frank(lin) *management educator, consultant, author, former university president and chancellor*
Hartman, John E. *lawyer*
Harvey, James Ross *finance company executive*
†Harwood, Caroline Elizabeth *environmental organization administrator*
Hassard, Howard *lawyer*
Hasson, Kirke Michael *lawyer*
Hastings, Edward Walton *theater director*
Hatfield, Dale Charles *insurance company executive, banker*
Havel, Richard Joseph *physician, educator*
Haven, Thomas Edward *lawyer*
Hayes, Thomas Jay, III *management consultant, retired construction and engineering company executive, retired army officer*
Hazen, Paul Mandeville *banker*
Heilbron, David M(ichael) *lawyer*
Heilbron, Louis Henry *lawyer*
Hellman, F(rederick) Warren *investment advisor*
Helmich, Pamela Pence *architect*
Henderson, Horace Edward *public affairs consultant, military historian*
Heng, Donald James, Jr. *lawyer*
Henry, Margaret Elizabeth *physician, surgeon*
Henson, Ray David *legal educator, consultant*
Herbert, Chesley C. *psychiatrist*
Herringer, Frank Casper *diversified financial services company executive*
Hershman, Lynn Lester *artist*
Heyman, Melvin Bernard *pediatric gastroenterologist*
Heyneman, Donald *parasitology educator*
Hickerson, Glenn Lindsey *leasing company executive*
Hickman, Maxine Viola *social services administrator*
High, Thomas W. *utilities company executive*
Hill, Arthur Brian *auto insurance company executive*
†Hill, Greg *newspaper bureau chief*
Hills, Austin Edward *vineyard executive*
†Hindery, Leo Joseph, Jr. *media company executive*
Hinman, Frank, Jr. *urologist, educator*
Hinman, Harvey DeForest *lawyer*
Hoadley, Walter Evans *economist, financial executive, lay worker*
Hobbs, Carl Fredric *artist, filmmaker, author*
Hochschild, Adam *writer, commentator, journalist*
Hoffman, Arlene Faun *podiatric medicine educator, physiologist*
Hoffman, Julien Ivor Ellis *pediatric cardiologist, educator*
Hofmann, John Richard, Jr. *lawyer*
Holden, Frederick Douglass, Jr. *lawyer*
Holland, Tom *artist, educator*
†Holman, Thomas C. *lawyer*
Homer, Barry Wayne *lawyer*
Homsey, George W. *architectural firm executive*
Honig, Bill *state educational administrator*
Hooker, John Lee *blues singer, guitarist*
Hooper, Roger Fellowes *architect*
Hoppe, Arthur Watterson *columnist*
Horan, Joseph Patrick *interior designer*
Horne, Grant Nelson *corporate communications specialist*
Hotchkiss, Ralf David *engineer, educator*
Howard, Carl (Michael) *lawyer*
Howard, David E. *artist*
Howatt, Sister Helen Clare *human services director*
Howley, Peter Anthony *communications executive*
Hoyem, Andrew Lewison *publisher*
†Hsu, John Chao-Chun *retired pediatrician*
Hudner, Philip *lawyer, rancher*
Hull, Cordell William *business executive*
Humenesky, Gregory *personnel and labor relations executive*
Humphrey, Jayne Hulbert *real estate development and financial consultant*
Hunter, William Dennis *lawyer*
Hurlbert, Roger William *information service industry executive*
Hyde, Stuart Wallace *educator, author*
Iacono, James Michael *research center administrator*
Ikagawa, Tadaichi *banking executive*
Irwin, William Rankin *lawyer*
Jacobs, Edwin Max *oncologist, consultant*
Jacobs, John Howard *association executive*
†Jacobus, Arthur *dance company administrator*
Jaeger, Joseph C. *insurance company executive*
Jaffe, Robert Benton *obstetrician-gynecologist, reproductive endocrinologist*
James, David Lee *lawyer, international advisor, author*
James, George Barker, II *apparel industry executive*
Jarvis, Donald Bertram *judge*
Jenkins, Bruce *sportswriter*
†Jenkins, Margaret Ludmilla *choreographer, dancer*
Jewett, George Frederick, Jr. *forest products company executive*
Johnson, Herman Leonall *research nutritionist*
Johnson, Martin Wayne *lawyer*
Johnson, Reverdy *lawyer*
Johnstone, R. C., Jr. *engineering company executive*
Jones, Pirkle *photographer, educator*
Jordan, Frank M. *mayor*
Joseph, Allan Jay *lawyer*
Judd, Bruce Diven *architect*
Judson, Philip Livingston *lawyer*
Jundis, Orvy Lagasca *writer, consultant, educator*
Jung, David Joseph *law educator*
Kaapcke, Wallace Letcher *lawyer*
Kadushin, Karen D. *lawyer*
Kahn, Alice Joyce *columnist*
Kahn, Paul Markham *actuary*
Kallgren, Edward Eugene *lawyer*
Kalt, Howard Michael *public relations executive*
Kan, Yuet Wai *physician, investigator*
Kane, Mary Kay *law educator*
Kantner, Paul *musician*
†Karentz, Deneb *biology educator*
Kasanin, Mark Owen *lawyer*
Katz, Hilliard Joel *physician*
Katz, Ronald Stanley *lawyer*
Kaufman, Christopher Lee *lawyer*
Keesling, Francis Valentine, Jr. *management consultant*
Keller, Edward Lowell *electrical engineer, educator*
Keller, George Matthew *retired oil company executive*
Kemp, Alson Remington, Jr. *lawyer, legal educator*
Kennard, Joyce L. *judge*
Kenny, David Culber *lawyer*
Kern, John McDougall *lawyer*
Khosla, Ved Mitter *oral and maxillofacial surgeon, educator*
Kilgore, Eugene Sterling, Jr. *surgeon*
Kimport, David Lloyd *lawyer*
Kingsley, Leonard Edward *financial services executive*
Kirkham, Francis Robison *lawyer*
Kirkham, James Francis *lawyer*
Klafter, Cary Ira *lawyer*
Klammer, Joseph Francis *management consultant*
Kleeman, Michael Jeffrey *telecommunications and computer consultant*
†Klein, Jeremy Stephen *editor*
Klein, Marc S. *newspaper editor and publisher*
Kleinberg, David Lewis *education administrator*
Kline, John Anthony *state court justice*
Klinger, Marilyn Sydney *lawyer*
Klott, David Lee *lawyer*
Knebel, Jack Gillen *lawyer*
Kobayashi, Tom Toru *motion picture company executive*
Kobler, Raymond *concertmaster*
Koeppel, John A. *lawyer*
Koffel, Martin M. *engineering company executive*
†Kolb, Felix Oscar *physician*
Kolb, Theodore Alexander *lawyer*
†Kollman, Peter A. *chemistry educator*
Korins, Leopold *stock exchange executive*
Kozloff, Lloyd M. *university dean, educator, scientist*
Kozloff, Theodore J. *lawyer*
†Kramer, Steven G. *opthalmologist, educator*

Krause, Lawrence Allen financial adviser, financial planner
Krebs, Ernst Theodor, Jr. biochemist
Kreitzberg, Fred Charles construction management company executive
Krevans, Julius Richard university administrator, physician
Krevans, Rachel lawyer
Kriken, John Lund architect
Krippner, Stanley Curtis psychologist
Kuhl, Paul Beach lawyer
Kuhns, Craig Shaffer business educator
Kuzell, William Charles physician, instrument company executive
†LaBudde, Samuel Freeman biologist, environmental activist
Ladar, Jerrold Morton lawyer
LaFollette, Charles Sanborn business consultant
Lai, Him Mark writer
Lamberson, John Roger insurance company executive
Lambert, Frederick William lawyer, educator
Landahl, Herbert Daniel biophysicist, mathematical biologist, researcher, consultant
Lane, Fielding H. lawyer
Lane, John Rodger art museum director
Lara, Adair columnist, writer
†Larrouilh, Michel banker
Larson, John William lawyer
Lasky, Moses lawyer
Lathrope, Daniel John legal educator, administrator
Latzer, Richard Neal investment company executive
Laurie, Ronald Sheldon lawyer
Lautz, Lindsay Allan retained executive search consultant
LaVail, Jennifer Hart neurobiologist, educator, researcher
LeBlanc, Tina dancer
Lee, Brant Thomas lawyer, federal official
Lee, John Jin lawyer
Lee, Richard Diebold law educator
Legate, Stephen ballet dancer
Leonard, George Jay author
Levi, Julian Hirsch lawyer, educator
Levin, Alan Scott pathologist, allergist, immunologist
Levine, Norman Gene insurance company executive
Levit, Victor Bert lawyer, foreign representative, civic worker
Leviton, Alan Edward museum curator
Libbin, Anne Edna lawyer
Lim, Robert Cheong, Jr. surgeon, educator
Lin, Tung Yen civil engineer, educator
Lindh, Patricia Sullivan banker, former government official
Lindsay, George Edmund museum director
Lipkin, Jeffrey Alan lawyer
Lipton, Alvin E(lliot) lawyer
Little, Jan Nielsen lawyer
Littlefield, Edmund Wattis mining company executive
Livsey, Robert Callister lawyer
Lobdell, Frank artist
Lockhart, James Blakely public affairs executive
Lolli, Andrew Ralph industrial engineer, retired army officer
London, Barry Joseph lawyer
†Loscavio, Elizabeth dancer
Lo Schiavo, John Joseph university executive
Lotito, Michael Joseph lawyer
Lowry, Edwin R. petroleum company executive
Lucas, Malcolm Millar state supreme court chief justice
Luckow, Lynn D. W. publishing executive
Lufkin, Liz newspaper editor
Luft, Harold S. health economist
Luft, Rene Wilfred civil engineer
Luikart, John Ford investment banker
Lundquist, Weyman Ivan lawyer
Lynch, Eugene F. federal judge
Lynch, Timothy Jeremiah-Mahoney realty holding company executive, author, lawyer, theologian, law educator
Lyon, David William research executive
Macdonald, A. Ewan food products executive
MacDonald, Donald William architect
Mac Gowan, Mary Eugenia lawyer
MacGuinness, Rosemary Anne lawyer, real estate broker
Mach, David artist
MacLeamy, Patrick architectural firm executive
Maddux, Parker Ahrens lawyer
Madison, James Raymond lawyer
Maffre, Muriel ballet dancer
Magowan, Peter Alden professional baseball team executive, grocery chain executive
Maibach, Howard I. dermatologist
Majumdar, Sharmila research scientist, educator
Malin, Harold Martin, Jr. sexologist, educator
Malson, Rex Richard drug and health care corporation executive
Mandra, York T. geology educator
Maneatis, George A. retired utility company executive
Mann, Bruce Alan lawyer
Manson, Malcolm Hood educational administrator
Marchant, David J. lawyer
Marcus, Richard Leon lawyer
Marcus, Robert aluminum company executive
Margulis, Alexander Rafailo physician, educator
Marioni, Tom artist
Markun, Rachel lawyer, educator
Marshall, John Paul broadcast engineer
Marston, Michael urban economist, asset management executive
Martin, Fred artist, college administrator
Martin, Joseph, Jr. lawyer, former ambassador
Martin, Joseph Boyd neurologist, educator
Martin, Paul Egley investment banker
Martin, Stephen James lawyer
Martinson, Ida Marie nurse, physiologist, educator
Marvin, David Keith international relations educator
Mason, Dean Towle cardiologist
Mathes, Stephen John plastic and reconstructive surgeon, educator
Mathiason, Garry George lawyer
Mattes, Martin Anthony lawyer
Mayer, Patricia Jayne financial officer, management accountant
Mays, Willie Howard, Jr. (Say Hey Mays) former professional baseball player
McAniff, Edward John lawyer
†McAninch, Jack Weldon urological surgeon, educator
McCandless, Sandra Ravich lawyer
McClintock, Jessica fashion designer
McCorkle, Horace Jackson physician, educator
Mc Covey, Willie Lee former professional baseball player
McCrea, Peter oil company executive
McDowell, David E. pharmaceutical executive
McElhinny, Harold John lawyer
McEvoy, Nan Tucker publishing company executive
McGettigan, Charles Carroll, Jr. investment banker
McKee, William David lawyer
McKelvey, Judith Grant lawyer, educator, university dean
McKnight, Steven Lanier molecular biologist
Mc Laughlin, Herbert E. architect
Mc Laughlin, Jerome Michael lawyer, shipping company executive
McLeod, Robert Macfarlan lawyer, arbitrator
McLin, Stephen T. investment banker
Mc Mahan, John William real estate investment advisor
McNally, Thomas Charles, III lawyer
McNamara, John Stephen artist, educator
McNamara, Thomas Neal lawyer
McPhee, Sister Glenn Anne school system administrator
McQuaid, J. Dennis lawyer
†Mehta, Shailesh J. banker
Meleis, Afaf Ibrahim nurse sociologist, educator, clinician
Mellor, Michael Lawton lawyer
Mellor, Robert E. lawyer
Merrill, Charles Merton federal judge
Merrill, Harvie Martin manufacturing executive
Merritt, James Edward lawyer
Metzler, Roger James, Jr. lawyer
Meyer, Donald Robert banker, lawyer
Meyer, Thomas James editorial cartoonist
Mielke, Frederick William, Jr. retired utility company executive
Migden, Carole county official
Mihan, Ralph George lawyer
Miller, Burton Leibsle sales executive
Miller, James Lynn lawyer
Miller, Paul James coffee company executive
Miller, William Napier Cripps lawyer
†Milton, Catherine Higgs public service organization executive
Minnick, Malcolm David lawyer
Mitchell, Bruce Tyson lawyer
Mohan, D. Mike transportation company executive
Moll, Charles J., III lawyer
Molligan, Peter Nicholas lawyer
Monson, Arch, Jr. fire alarm manufacturing company executive
Montali, Dennis federal judge
†Moore, Richard public relations executive
Moris, Lamberto Giuliano architect
Morrin, Thomas Harvey engineering research company executive
Morris, Richard Ward nonprofit organization administrator, author
Morrissey, John Carroll lawyer
Mosk, Stanley state supreme court justice
Mostov, Keith Elliot cell biologist, educator
Mullenix, Travis H. food products company executive
Mumford, Christopher Greene corporate financial executive
Mundell, David Edward leasing company executive
Murray, G(lenn) Richard, Jr. lawyer
Murray, John Frederic physician, educator
Murrin, Thomas Edward insurance company executive
Musfelt, Duane Clark lawyer
Musser, Sandra G. lawyer
Mustacchi, Piero physician, educator
Myers, Howard Milton pharmacologist, educator
Nachman, Gerald Weil columnist, critic, author
Naegele, Carl Joseph university academic administrator, educator
Nafziger, Dean H. special education research executive
Needleman, Jacob philosophy educator, writer
Neerhout, John, Jr. petroleum company executive
Nelson, David Edward lawyer
Nemir, Donald Philip lawyer
Neri, Manuel sculptor
Nevins, Robert Charles insurance broker
Nichols, Robert E(dmund) editor, writer, journalist
Niehans, Daniel Jurg lawyer
Nodelman, Jared Robert investment advisor
Noonan, John T., Jr. federal judge, legal educator
Noonan, William Moss information systems executive, consultant
Nord, Paul Elliott accountant
O'Connor, G(eorge) Richard ophthalmologist
Odgers, Richard William lawyer
Offer, Stuart Jay lawyer
O'Flaherty, Terrence journalist
Oliveira, Nathan artist, educator
Olsen, Tillie author
Olson, Walter Gilbert lawyer
Oropallo, Deborah artist, educator
Orrick, William Horsley, Jr. federal judge
Osterhaus, William Eric television executive
Ostler, Scott newspaper sports columnist
Otto, George John investment banker
Otus, Simone public relations executive
Painter, Michael Robert landscape architect, urban designer
†Palmer, David dancer
Palmer, William Joseph accountant
Park, Roger Cook law educator
Parker, Harry S., III art museum administrator
Parry, Robert Troutt bank executive, economist
Pasahow, Lynn H(arold) lawyer
Pastreich, Peter orchestra executive director
Patel, Marilyn Hall federal judge
Pendleton, Alan R. conservation agency executive
Penman, Brian Edward radio personality
Penskar, Mark Howard lawyer
Peppercorn, John Edward chemical company executive
Perkins, Herbert Asa physician
Perlman, David science editor, journalist
Peterson, Harries-Clichy financial consultant
Peterson, Richard Hamlin utility executive, lawyer
Peterson, Rudolph A. banker
Peterson, Wayne Turner composer, pianist
Petrakis, Nicholas Louis physician, medical researcher, educator
Pfau, George Harold, Jr. stockbroker
†Pfister, Peter J. lawyer
Phillips, Theodore Locke radiation oncologist, educator
Pickett, Donn Philip lawyer
Piel, Carolyn Forman pediatrician, educator
Pincus, Joseph economist, educator
Placier, Philip R. lawyer
Platt, Peter Godfrey lawyer
Plishner, Michael Jon lawyer
Poole, Cecil F. federal judge
Popofsky, Melvin Laurence lawyer
Posin, Daniel Q. physics educator, television lecturer
†Posokhov, Iouri ballet dancer, educator
Pottruck, David Steven brokerage house executive
Powell, Sandra Theresa timber company executive
Preovolos, Penelope Athene lawyer
†Price, Jim engineering company executive, earth scientist
Price, Willis Joseph retired oil company executive
Pringle, Robert Bernard lawyer
Prunty, Bert Sherman, Jr. lawyer
Quiban, Estelita Cabrera controller
Quigley, Philip J. telecommunications industry executive
Quinn, John R. archbishop
Raciti, Cherie artist
Raeber, John Arthur architect, construction specifier consultant
Ragan, Charles Ransom lawyer
Ralston, Henry James, III neurobiologist, anatomist, educator
Ram, Tracy Schaefer ballet company manager
Ramsey, Robert Lee judge, lawyer
Ratner, David Louis legal educator
Ratzlaff, James W. investment company executive
Rautenberg, Robert Frank consulting statistician
Raven, Robert Dunbar lawyer
Read, Gregory Charles lawyer
Readmond, Ronald Warren investment banking firm executive
Ream, James Terrill architect, sculptor
Redo, David Lucien investment company executive
Reed, Robert Daniel publisher
Reese, John Robert lawyer
Reinsch, Harry Orville power company executive
Rembe, Toni lawyer
Renfrew, Charles Byron oil company executive, lawyer
Renne, Louise Hornbeck lawyer
†Renzi, Paul flutist
Rice, Denis Timlin lawyer
Rice, Dorothy Pechman (Mrs. John Donald Rice) medical economist
Rice, Jonathan C. educational television executive
Richards, John M. wood and paper products company executive
Richards, Norman Blanchard lawyer
Riney, Hal Patrick advertising executive
Rippel, Clarence W. academic administrator
Ripple, Helen Bernice nursing administrator
Risse, Guenter Bernhard physician, historian, educator
Roberts, Jerry newspaper editor
Robertson, Armand James, II lawyer
Robertson, David Govan lawyer
Robinson, Jerry H. lawyer
Rock, Arthur venture capitalist
Rockrise, George Thomas architect
Rockwell, Alvin John lawyer
Rockwell, Burton Lowe architect
Roe, Benson Bertheau surgeon, educator
Roemer, Elizabeth K. lawyer
Roethe, James Norton lawyer
†Rojas, Waldemar school superintendent
Rosch, John Thomas lawyer
Rosen, Moishe religious organization administrator
Rosen, Sanford Jay lawyer
Rosenberg, Claude Newman, Jr. investment adviser
Rosenberg, Richard Morris banker
Rosenberg, Sydney J. security company executive
Rosenheim, Daniel Edward journalist, newspaper editor
Rosenthal, James D. former ambassador, government and foundation executive
Rosinski, Edwin Francis health sciences educator
Ross, John J. petroleum products company executive
Ross, Sue entrepreneur, author, fundraising executive
Rosston, Edward William lawyer
Rowen, Harvey Allen investment company executive
Rowland, John Arthur lawyer
Rubenstein, Steven Paul newspaper columnist
Rubin, Michael lawyer
Rudolph, Abraham Morris physician, educator
Runnicles, Donald conductor
Rusco, Gene Earl radio broadcasting executive
Rusher, William Allen writer, commentator
Russell, Carol Ann personnel service company executive
†Rutter, William J. biochemist, educator
Ryan, Joan sportswriter
Ryan, Randel Edward, Jr. airline pilot
Ryland, David Ronald lawyer
Sachs, Marilyn Stickle author, lecturer, editor
Salomon, Darrell Joseph lawyer
Salzman, Richard William artist representative
Sanger, John Morton lawyer, urban planner
Santana, Carlos guitarist
Saras, James J. agricultural products, grain company executive
Sarsten, Gunnar Edward mechanical engineer, construction executive
†Sassoon, Janet ballerina, educator
Satin, Joseph language professional, university administrator
Saunders, Debra J. columnist
Saunders, Raymond Jennings artist, educator
Schiller, Francis neurologist, medical historian
Schlegel, John Peter university president
Schlesinger, Rudolf Berthold lawyer, educator
Schmid, Rudi (Rudolf Schmid) internist, educator, university official
Schmidt, Chauncey Everett banker
Schmidt, Robert Milton physician, scientist, educator
Scholten, Paul obstetrician-gynecologist, educator
Scholz, Garret Arthur financial executive
Schultz, Dean M. finance company executive
Schwartz, Louis Brown legal educator
Schwarz, Glenn Vernon editor
Schwarzer, William W federal judge
Sears, George Ames lawyer
Seebach, Lydia Marie physician
Seegal, John Franklin lawyer
Seelenfreund, Alan distribution company executive
Seip, Tom Decker securities executive
Selman, Roland Wooten, III lawyer
Sevier, Ernest Youle lawyer
Shackelford, Barton Warren retired utility executive
Shangraw, Clarence Frank museum official
Shansby, John Gary investment banker
Shapiro, Larry Jay pediatrician, scientist, educator
Sheinfeld, David composer
Shelton, Richard Fottrell investment executive
Shenk, George H. lawyer
Shiffer, James David utility executive
Shinefield, Henry Robert pediatrician
Shirpser, Clara former Democratic national committeewoman
Shor, Samuel Wendell Williston naval engineer
Shorenstein, Walter Herbert commercial real estate development company executive
Shulgasser, Barbara writer
Shumate, Charles Albert retired dermatologist
Sias, John B. multi-media company executive
Siegel, Louis Pendleton forest products executive
Silver, Steve producer, director, writer
Silverman, Alan accounting firm partner
†Silverman, Mervyn F. health science association administrator, consultant
Simini, Joseph Peter accountant, financial consultant, author, former educator
Simmons, Raymond Hedelius, Jr. lawyer
Simon, Cathy Jensen architect
Simone, Thomas B. distribution company executive
Singer, Allen Morris lawyer
Sinton, Peter newspaper editor, journalist
Skeen, John Kenneth sales executive
Skinner, Harry Bryant orthopaedic surgery educator
Skinner, Stanley Thayer utility company executive, lawyer
Small, Marshall Lee lawyer
Smegal, Thomas Frank, Jr. lawyer
†Smith, David A. real estate developer
Smith, David Elvin physician
Smith, Gordon Ray utilities executive
Smith, Gregory Allan lawyer
Smith, Kerry Clark lawyer
Smith, Lee Clark apparel company executive
†Smith, Theodore W. construction executive
Smuin, Michael choreographer, director, dancer
Sneed, Joseph Tyree, III federal judge
Snow, Tower Charles, Jr. lawyer
Sokolow, Maurice physician, educator
Sowder, Robert Robertson architect
Spander, Art sportswriter
Sparer, Malcolm Martin rabbi
Sparks, John Edward lawyer
Sparks, Thomas E., Jr. lawyer
†Spencer, William H. ophthalmologist
Spiegel, Hart Hunter retired lawyer
Sproul, John Allan retired public utility executive
†Stamper, Robert Lewis opthalmologist, educator
†Stanton, Michael architectural firm executive
Stanzler, Jordan lawyer
Staring, Graydon Shaw lawyer
Stauffer, Thomas Michael university president
Steer, Reginald David lawyer
Stein, Alan L. investment banker
Steinberg, Michael music critic, educator
Stephens, Shand Scott lawyer
Stetler, Russell Dearnley, Jr. private investigator
Stewart, Samuel B. banker, lawyer
Stone, Michael P. W. former federal official
Stotter, Lawrence Henry lawyer
Stowell, Christopher R. dancer
Stratton, Richard James lawyer
Stumbo, Richard William, Jr. mining company financial executive
Stupski, Lawrence J. investment company executive
Sturdivant, Frederick David consultant, business educator
Styles, Margretta Madden nursing educator
Sugarman, Myron George lawyer
Sugarman, Paul William lawyer
Sullivan, James N. fuel company executive
†Sullivan, John theater administrator
Sullivan, Robert Edward lawyer
Susskind, Teresa Gabriel publisher
Sutcliffe, Eric lawyer
Sutton, John Paul lawyer
Swing, William Edwin bishop
Szabo, Zoltan medical science educator, medical institute administrator
Sze, Helen Wang Yee lawyer
Taylor, Glenhall E. banker
Taylor, John Lockhart city official
Taylor, Robert P. lawyer
Taylor, William James (Zak Taylor) lawyer
†Tedeschi, Ernest Francis, Jr. naval officer
Terr, Lenore Cagen psychiatrist, writer
Thacher, Carter Pomeroy diversified manufacturing company executive
Thē, Hoang-Dinh middle school educator
Thelen, Max, Jr. foundation executive, lawyer
†Thiers, Harry Delbert biology educator, research mycologist
Thistlethwaite, David Richard architect
Thomas, William Geraint museum administrator
Thomas, William Scott lawyer
Thompson, Gary W. public relations executive
Thompson, Robert Charles lawyer
Thompson, Robert Randall (Robby Thompson) professional baseball player
Thompson, William Irwin humanities educator, author
Thor, Peter K. marketing executive
Thornton, D. Whitney, II lawyer
Tiano, Anthony Steven television producer, book publishing executive
Tierney, Kevin Hugh law educator
Tiffany, Joseph Raymond, II lawyer
Tingle, James O'Malley lawyer
Tobin, James Michael lawyer
Tomasson, Helgi dancer, choreographer, dance company executive
Toms, Michael Anthony broadcast journalist
Trautman, William Ellsworth lawyer
Traynor, J. Michael lawyer
Trowbridge, Thomas, Jr. mortgage banking company executive
Tulsky, Fredric Neal journalist
Turnbull, William, Jr. architect
Turner, Marshall Chittenden, Jr. venture capitalist
†Turnlund, Judith Rae nutrition scientist
Turpen, Louis A. airport terminal executive
Tusher, Thomas William apparel company executive
Ullman, Myron Edward, III retail executive
Underwood, Patricia Ruth clinical nursing educator, consultant
Uri, George Wolfsohn accountant
Valentine, William Edson architect
Van Dyck, Wendy dancer
Van Hoesen, Beth Marie artist, printmaker
Veaco, Kristina lawyer
Veitch, Stephen William investment counselor
Veith, Ilza retired psychiatric history educator
Venning, Robert Stanley lawyer
Volkmann, Daniel George, Jr. architect
Volpe, Peter Anthony surgeon
Vyas, Girish Narmadashankar virologist, immunohematologist
Waldo, Katita ballet dancer
Walker, Ralph Clifford lawyer
Wall, Brian Arthur sculptor

Wallace, Arthur, Jr. *college dean*
Wallerstein, Ralph Oliver *physician*
Walsh, Francis Richard *law educator*
Walsh, James Joseph *lawyer*
†Walsh, Robert Francis *oil company executive*
Wang, William Kai-Sheng *legal educator*
Ward, William T. *insurance company executive*
Warmer, Richard Craig *lawyer*
Warner, Harold Clay, Jr. *banker, investment management executive*
Watts, Malcolm S(tuart) M(cNeal) *physician, medical educator*
Way, E(dward) Leong *pharmacologist, toxicologist, educator*
Webb, J. A. *insurance company executive*
Weigel, Stanley Alexander *judge*
Weihrich, Heinz *management educator*
Weisberg, D. Kelly *law educator*
Welborn, Caryl Bartelman *lawyer*
Welch, Thomas Andrew *lawyer*
Wernick, Sandie Margot *advertising and public relations executive*
Werson, James Byrd *lawyer*
Wertheimer, Robert E. *paper company executive*
Westberg, Robert Myers *lawyer*
Westerdahl, John Brian *nutritionist, health educator*
Westerfield, Putney *management consulting executive*
Wetzel, Cherie Lalaine Rivers *biologist*
Whalen, Philip Glenn *poet, novelist*
†Wheater, Ashley *dancer*
Whelan, John William *lawyer, educator, consultant*
Whitaker, Clem, Jr. *advertising and public relations executive*
White, Mark N. *lawyer*
White, Rene *public relations executive*
Whitney, David Clay *business educator, consultant, writer*
Widman, Gary Lee *lawyer, former government official*
Wilbur, Brayton, Jr. *distribution company executive*
Wilcox, Collin M. *author*
Wilczek, John Franklin *history educator*
Wild, Nelson Hopkins *lawyer*
Wiley, Thomas Glen *retired investment company executive*
Wiley, William T. *artist*
Wilken, Claudia Ann *judge*
Williams, Matt (Matthew Derrick Williams) *professional baseball player*
Williams, Morgan Lloyd *retired investment banker*
Williford, Lawrence Harding *public relations company executive*
Willner, Jay R. *consulting company executive*
Willson, Prentiss, Jr. *lawyer*
Wilner, Paul Andrew *journalist*
Wilson, Charles B. *neurosurgeon, educator*
Wilson, Ian Robert *food company executive*
Wilson, John Oliver *economist, educator, banker*
Wilson, Kenneth Jay *writer*
Wilson, Matthew Frederick *newspaper editor*
Wingate, C. Keith *legal educator*
Winn, Steven Jay *critic*
Wintroub, Bruce Urich *dermatologist, educator, researcher*
Wolfe, Barbara Ahmajan *stock brokerage executive, administrator*
Wolfe, Cameron Withgot, Jr. *lawyer*
Wolff, Sheldon *radiobiologist, educator*
Wollen, W. Foster *lawyer*
Wood, Donald Frank *transportation educator, consultant*
Woodard, Clarence James *manufacturing company executive*
Woods, James Robert *lawyer*
Woolsey, David Arthur *leasing company executive*
Wright, Rosalie Muller *newspaper and magazine editor*
Wyle, Frederick S. *lawyer*
Yamakawa, David Kiyoshi, Jr. *lawyer*
†Yamamoto, Michael Toru *journalist*
Yamaoka, Seigen Haruo *bishop*
Yost, Nicholas Churchill *lawyer*
Young, Bryant Llewellyn *lawyer, business executive*
†Young, Lowell Sung-yi *medical administrator, educator*
Young, William Victor *banker*
Yu, Eleanor Ngan-Ling *advertising company executive*
Yuan, Shao Wen *aerospace engineer, educator*
Zaccaria, Adrian *utilities executive*
Zellerbach, William Joseph *retired paper company executive*
Zhukov, Yuri *ballet dancer*
Ziering, William Mark *lawyer*
Zimmerman, Bernard *lawyer*
Zippin, Calvin *epidemiologist*

San Jacinto

†Jones, Marshall Edward *retired environmental educator*

San Jose

Adams, William John, Jr. *mechanical engineer*
Almon, William Joseph *data processing company executive*
Anderson, Edward V. *lawyer*
Belluomini, Frank Stephen *accountant*
Bennett, Charles Turner *social welfare administrator*
Bentel, Dwight *emeritus journalism educator*
Blackwell, Jacqueline Pflughoeft *school district administrator*
Boldrey, Edwin Eastland *retinal surgeon, educator*
Brewer, Richard George *physicist*
Callan, Josi Irene *museum director*
†Campbell, Gordon A. *electronics executive*
Careaga, Rogelio Antonio *economics educator, consultant*
Caret, Robert Laurent *university president*
Carey, Peter Kevin *reporter*
Cedoline, Anthony John *psychologist*
Ceppos, Jerome Merle *newspaper editor*
Chen, Wen H. *engineering executive, educator*
Coburn, John Wyllie *physicist, researcher*
Collett, Jennie *principal*
Conner, Finis F. *electronics company executive*
†Crommie, Michael R. *research scientist*
Cruz, B. Robert *academic administrator*
Dalis, Irene *mezzo-soprano, opera company administrator, music educator*
Dean, Burton Victor *management educator*
Dougherty, John James *computer software company executive, consultant*
†Eigler, Donald Mark *physicist*
Elder, Robert Laurie *newspaper editor*
Estabrook, Reed *artist, educator*
Faggin, Federico *electronics executive*
Fiebiger, James Russell *manufacturing company executive*
Finnigan, Rogert Emmet *business owner*
Fish, James Henry *library director*
Forster, Julian *physicist, consultant*
Fowler, John Wellington *lawyer*
Franson, Paul Oscar, III *public relations executive*
Frauenfelder, Lewis *electronics executive*
Frymer, Murry *columnist, theater critic, critic-at-large*
Gonzales, Ron *county supervisor*
Granneman, Vernon Henry *lawyer*
Greenstein, Martin Richard *lawyer*
Gruber, John Balsbaugh *physics educator, university administrator*
Hall, Robert Emmett, Jr. *investment banker, realtor*
Halverson, George Clarence *business administration educator*
Hamilton, Judith Hall *computer company executive*
Hammer, Susan W. *mayor*
Harkins, Craig *management consultant*
Heiman, Frederic Paul *electronics company executive*
†Heneghan, John James *geotechnical engineer*
Higgins, James Bradley *dentist*
Hootnick, Laurence R. *electronics company executive*
Houle, Frances Anne *physical chemist*
Huang, Francis Fu-Tse *mechanical engineering educator*
Hucker, Robert Joseph *software engineer*
Ingle, Robert D. *newspaper editor, newspaper executive*
Ingram, William Austin *federal judge*
†Ito, Hiroshi *research chemist*
Jarrat, Henri Aaron *semiconductor company executive*
Johnson, Allen Halbert *surgeon*
Jordan, Thomas Vincent *advertising educator, consultant*
Kasley, Helen Mary *corporate secretary, legal counsel*
Kasson, James Matthews *electronics executive*
Kennedy, George Wendell *lawyer*
Kramer, Richard Jay *gastroenterologist*
Laskin, Barbara Virginia *legal association administrator*
Leavy, Paul Matthew *management consultant*
Lee, Sung W. *electronics executive*
Levy, Salomon *mechanical engineer*
Lippe, Philipp Maria *neurosurgeon, educator*
Lovell, Glenn Michael *film critic*
Loventhal, Milton *writer, playwright, lyricist*
†Lutz, Chris P. *research physicist*
†Markle, David A. *optical engineer*
McCarthy, Mary Ann Bartley *electrical engineer*
Mc Connell, John Douglas *retail corporation executive, owner*
McCoy, James M. *data processing, computer company executive*
McDowell, Jennifer *sociologist, composer, playwright, publisher*
Melendy, Howard Brett *historian, educator*
Migielicz, Geralyn *photojournalist*
Mitchell, David T. *electronic computing equipment company executive*
Mitchell, David Walker *lawyer*
Montgomery, Leslie David *biomedical engineer, cardiovascular physiologist*
Moody, Frederick Jerome *mechanical engineer, consultant thermal hydraulics*
Morgan, Marilyn *federal judge*
Morgan, William Robert *lawyer*
Morimoto, Carl Noboru *computer system engineer, crystallographer*
Neptune, John Addison *chemistry educator, consultant*
Nogawa, Kiyoshi *computer company executive*
Okerlund, Arlene Naylor *university official*
Okita, George T. *pharmacologist educator*
Ostrom, Philip Gardner *computer company executive*
†Parkin, Stuart S. P. *materials scientist*
Pausa, Clements Edward *electronics company executive*
Pellegrini, Robert J. *psychology educator*
†Praisner, Jan A. *electronics executive*
Rabolt, John Francis *optics scientist*
†Rao, Atambir Singh *nuclear engineer*
Rappaport, Stuart R. *lawyer*
†Rasdal, William D. *electronics executive*
Rha, Y. B. *electronics executive*
†Risinger, Paul N. *electronics executive*
Ritzheimer, Robert Alan *educational publishing executive*
†Rodgers, Thomas J. *electronics executive*
Rosendin, Raymond Joseph *electrical contracting company executive*
Rosenheim, Donald Edwin *electrical engineer*
Rothblatt, Donald Noah *urban and regional planner, educator*
Sanders, Adrian Lionel *education consultant*
Savage, Arthur L. *professional hockey team executive*
Scalise, George Martin *electronics company executive*
Schmidt, Cyril James *librarian*
Schofield, John Trevor *environmental management company executive*
Schroeder, William John *electronics executive*
Scifres, Donald R. *semiconductor laser, fiber optics and electronics company executive*
Sikora, James Robert *educational business administrator*
Slayen, Howard Theo *accounting company executive*
Smirni, Allan Desmond *lawyer*
Smith, David Eugene *business administration educator*
Smith, Joan Petersen *nursing administrator, educator*
†Smith, Rodney *electronics executive*
†Sola, Jure *electronics executive*
†Sollman, George Henry *telecommunications company executive*
Stacy, Richard A. *adminstrative law judge*
†Stafford, James F. *electronics executive*
†Steel, Gordon *electronics executive*
Steele, Shelby *writer, educator*
†Stein, Alfred J. *electronics executive, computer software company executive*
Sumrall, Harry *journalist*
Sweeny, Mary Ellen *public relations and advertising executive*
Tanaka, Richard Koichi, Jr. *architect, planner*
Trounstine, Philip J. *editor, journalist*
Valentine, Ralph Schuyler *chemical engineer, research director*
†Wang, Franny *electronics executive*
†Wang, Stanley *electronics executive*
Ware, James W. *federal judge*
Whyte, Ronald M. *federal judge*
Williams, John Lyle *lawyer*
Williams, Spencer M. *federal judge*
Winters, Harold Franklin *physicist*
†Yannoni, Costantino Sheldon *research chemist*
Yates, Kathleen Barrett *newspaper executive*
Yoshizumi, Donald Tetsuro *dentist*
Young, Katherine Curtin *manufacturing executive*
†Zaro, Brad A. *research company executive, biologist*
†Zenger, John Hancock *publishing company executive*

San Juan Capistrano

Braunstein, Herbert *pathologist, educator*
Curtis, John Joseph *lawyer*
Der Garabedian, Paul *energy and environmental company executive*
Fisher, Delbert Arthur *physician, educator*
Horn, Deborah Sue *organization administrator, writer, editor*
Purdy, Alan MacGregor *financial executive*
Robinson, Daniel Thomas *brokerage company executive*

San Leandro

†Bohne, David Rees *city government administrator*
Earle, Sylvia Alice *research biologist, oceanographer*
Leighton, Joseph *pathologist*
Nehls, Robert Louis, Jr. *school system administrator*
Odron, Edward Andrew *supermarket executive*
Pansky, Emil John *entrepreneur*
Stallings, Charles Henry *physicist*

San Lorenzo

Glenn, Jerome T. *secondary school principal*
Lantz, Charles Alan *chiropractor, researcher*
Morrison, Martin Earl *computer systems analyst*

San Luis Obispo

Bailey, Christina Anne *chemistry educator*
Bailey, Philip Sigmon, Jr. *university official, chemistry educator*
Baker, Warren J(oseph) *university president*
Blattner, Ernest Willi *mechanical engineering educator*
Brown, Howard C. *horticulture educator, consultant*
Buxbaum, James Monroe *business administration educator*
Daly, John Paul *lawyer*
Deasy, Cornelius Michael *architect*
Dickerson, Colleen Bernice Patton *artist, educator*
Ericson, Jon Meyer *academic administrator, rhetoric theory educator*
Fraser, Bruce Douglas, Jr. *architect, artist*
Grismore, Roger *physics educator, researcher*
Hasslein, George Johann *architectural educator*
Holder, Elaine Edith *psychologist, educator*
Jen, Joseph Jwu-Shan *food scientist, educator*
McCorkle, Robert Ellsworth *agribusiness educator*
Mc Donald, Henry Stanton *electrical engineer*
Perkins, Dale Warren *library director*
Riedlsperger, Max Ernst *history educator*
Rodman, Harry Eugene *architect, educator, acoustical and illumination consultant*
Smith, Joey Spauls *mental health nurse, biofeedback therapist, bodyworker, hypnotist*
Stream, Jay Wilson *financial consultant*
Wentz, Janet *principal*

San Marcos

Barnes, Howard G. *film company executive, film and video producer*
Ciurczak, Alexis *librarian*
Dhawan, Gulshan Kumar *chemical engineer*
Dixon, William Cornelius *lawyer*
Knight, Edward Howden *retired hospital administrator*
Lee, John Francis *retired international management consulting company executive, author*
Liggins, George Lawson *microbiologist-diagnostic company executive*
Lilly, Martin Stephen *university dean*
Melcher, Trini Urtuzuastegui *accounting educator*
Page, Leslie Andrew *disinfectant manufacturing company executive*
Radder, Bruce Milton *business owner*
Reed, H(orace) Curtis *insurance company executive, management consultant*
Sauer, David Andrew *writer, computer consultant*

San Marino

Baldwin, James William *lawyer*
Benzer, Seymour *neurosciences educator*
Footman, Gordon Elliott *educational administrator*
Galbraith, James Marshall *lawyer, business executive*
Hull, Suzanne White *retired cultural institution administrator, writer*
Karlstrom, Paul Johnson *art historian*
Man, Lawrence Kong *architect*
Medearis, Roger Norman *artist*
Meyer, William Danielson *retired department store executive*
Mortimer, Wendell Reed, Jr. *lawyer*
Ridge, Martin *historian, educator*
Robertson, Mary Louise *archivist, historian*
Rolle, Andrew F. *historian, educator, author*
Skotheim, Robert Allen *museum administrator*
Smith, Apollo Milton Olin *retired aerodynamics engineer*
Steadman, John Marcellus, III *English educator*
Thorpe, James *humanities scholar*
Wark, Robert Rodger *art curator*
Woodward, Daniel Holt *librarian, researcher*
Zall, Paul Maxwell *retired English language educator, consultant*
Zimmerman, William Robert *entrepreneur, engineering based manufacturing company executive*

San Mateo

Aadahl, Jorg *corporate executive*
Balles, John Joseph *banker, business consultant*
Bell, Frank Ouray, Jr. *lawyer*
Bohannon, David D. *community planner and developer*
Boyd, Robert Jamison *construction equipment company executive*
Briggs, Thorley D. *environmetal consultant*
Brubaker, John E. *bank executive*
†Burns, Harmon E. *investment company executive*
Everett, Lois Almen *executive director*
Felker, James M. *environmental engineering company executive*
Fenton, Noel John *venture capitalist*
Goble, Elise Joan H. *pediatric ophthalmologist*
Goldman, Bernard *leasing company executive*
Hawkins, William (Trip), III *software executive*
Helfert, Erich Anton *management consultant, author, educator*
Johnson, Charles Bartlett *mutual fund executive*
Jordan, Michelle Henrietta *public relations company executive*
Kane, Robert Francis *lawyer, former ambassador, consultant*
Kidera, George Jerome *physician*
Korn, Walter *writer*
Leeder, Stuart L. Sandy *real estate financial executive*
Poppel, Harvey Lee *management consultant*
Potts, David Malcolm *population specialist, administrator*
Poulos, Gary Peter *school system administrator*
†Probst, Lawrence F., III *computer company executive*
Riskas, Harry James *construction company executive*
Sanders, Charles Franklin *corporate executive*
Silver, William Robert *corporate finance executive*
Trabitz, Eugene Leonard *aerospace company executive*
Van Kirk, John Ellsworth *cardiologist*

San Pablo

Bristow, Lonnie Robert *physician*
†Woodruff, Kay Herrin *pathologist, educator*

San Pedro

Crutchfield, William Richard *artist, educator*
Ellis, George Edwin, Jr. *chemical engineer*
McCarty, Frederick Briggs *electrical engineer*
Price, Harrison Alan *business research company executive*
Simmons, William *physicist, aerospace research executive*

San Rafael

†Bartz, Carol *software company executive*
Brevig, Eric *special effects expert, executive*
Bruyn, Henry Bicker *physician*
Burtt, Ben *sound designer, director, editor*
Carson, Dave *special effects expert, executive*
†Ciampi, Mario Joseph *architect, planner*
Danse, Ilene Homnick Raisfeld *physician, educator, toxicologist*
Duston, Jennifer *performing arts association administrator*
Eekman, Thomas Adam *Slavic languages educator*
Elliott, Edward Procter *architect*
Farrar, Scott *special effects expert, executive*
Fink, Joseph Richardson *college president*
Friesecke, Raymond Francis *management consultant*
Goldman, Clint Paul *producer*
Gorman, Ned *film producer*
Gryson, Joseph Anthony *orthodontist*
†Hall, Allen *special effects expert*
Healy, Janet *graphics expert, producer*
Hinshaw, Horton Corwin *physician*
Kay, Douglas *graphics expert, executive*
Kennedy, James Waite *management consultant, author*
Kennedy, Thomas *executive producer*
Latno, Arthur Clement, Jr. *telephone company executive*
Lee, Robert *association executive, former theological educator, consultant, author*
Lesh, Philip Chapman *musician, composer*
Lucas, George W., Jr. *film director, producer, screenwriter*
Mann, Jeff *special effects expert, executive*
March, Ralph Burton *retired entomology educator*
†Murphy, George *special effects expert*
Napoles, Veronica Kleeman *graphic designer, consultant*
Nelson, James Carmer, Jr. *advertising executive, writer*
Nicholson, Bruce *graphics expert, executive*
Owens, Michael *camera graphics expert, executive*
Premo, Paul Mark *oil company executive*
Ralston, Ken *graphics expert*
Roffman, Howard *motion picture company executive*
Roth, Hadden Wing *lawyer*
Scanlan, John Joseph *retired bishop*
Sheldon, Gary *conductor, music director*
Shepard, James Edward *physician*
Squires, Scott William *special effects expert, executive*
Stout, Gregory Stansbury *lawyer*
Thompson, John William *international management consultant*
Thompson, Peter L. H. *golf course architect*
Tift, Mary Louise *artist*
Turner, William Weyand *author*
Wilson, Ian Holroyde *management consultant, futurist*

San Ramon

Kahane, Dennis Spencer *lawyer*
Lee, Robert *telecommunications executive*
Litman, Robert Barry *physician, author, television and radio commentator*
O'Connor, Paul Daniel *lawyer*
Weil, Jon David *psychologist, geneticist, administrator*

San Ysidro

Holderman, John Loran *financial broker*

Santa Ana

Abbruzzese, Carlo Enrico *physician, writer, educator*
†Adams, John M. *library director*
†Amoroso, Frank *retired communication system engineer, consultant*
Baik, Hyo Whi *automotive import company executive*
Barr, James Norman *federal judge*
Blaine, Dorothea Constance Ragetté *lawyer*
Buster, Edmond Bate *metal products company executive*
Capizzi, Michael Robert *lawyer*
Castruita, Rudy *school system administrator*
Cheverton, Richard E. *newspaper editor*
Dukes, David R. *computer company executive*
Fay-Schmidt, Patricia Ann *paralegal*
Ferguson, Warren John *federal judge*
Fitzgerald, Robert Lynn *small business owner*
Fouste, Donna H. *legal administrator*
Heckler, Gerard Vincent *lawyer*
Hernandez, Edward, Jr. *community college administrator*
Hickson, Ernest Charles *financial executive*
Holtz, Joseph Norman *marketing executive*
Idriss, Izzat M. *civil engineer, consultant*
Jacobsen, Eric Kasner *consulting engineer*
Jaffer, Rashida Amin *lawyer*

Katz, Tonnie newspaper editor
Kelly, James Patrick, Jr. retired engineering and construction executive
Kennedy, Donald Parker title insurance company executive
Lacy, Linwood A., Jr. computer company executive
Lydick, Lawrence Tupper federal judge
Maw, Sam H. restaurant chain executive
Mickelson, H(erald) Fred electric utility executive
Miller, Eric zoologist
Place, Geoffrey consumer goods manufacturing company executive
Potter, Charles Arthur, Jr. trust company executive
Pratt, Lawrence Arthur thoracic surgeon, foreign service officer
Richard, Robert John library director
Riddle, Lynne judge
Ryan, John Edward federal judge
St. Clair, Carl conductor, music director
Seoane, Emilio accountant
Shahin, Thomas John dry cleaning wholesale supply company executive
Shaw, David Allen magazine publisher
Stern, Sherry Ann journalist
Storer, Maryruth law librarian
Stotler, Alicemarie Huber federal judge
Vasquez, Gaddi county official
Ware, James Edwin retired international company executive
Washburn, Lawrence Robert manufacturing executive
Wilson, John James federal judge
Zabsky, John Mitchell engineering executive
Zaenglein, William George, Jr. lawyer

Santa Barbara

Ackerman, Marshall publishing company executive
Ahlers, B. Orwin marketing executive
Ahlers, Guenter physicist, educator
Aldisert, Ruggero John federal judge
Allaway, William Harris retired university official
Alldredge, Alice Louise biological oceanography educator
Amory, Thomas Carhart management consultant
Anderson, Darla Rae lawyer
Anderson, Donald Meredith bank executive
†Anderson, Stephen Thomas entertainment executive
Avalle-Arce, Juan Bautista language educator
Awramik, Stanley Michael geology educator
Badash, Lawrence science history educator
Baldwin, John David sociologist, educator
Bilhorn, William W. international mining company consultant
Bischel, Margaret DeMeritt physician, managed care consultant
Blasingame, Benjamin Paul electronics company executive
Blum, Gerald Saul psychologist, educator
Bock, Russell Samuel author
Boehm, Eric Hartzell information management executive
Boisse, Joseph Adonias library administrator
Bongiorno, James William electronics company executive
Boxer, Rubin software company owner, former research and development company executive
Boyan, Norman J. retired education educator
Brant, Henry composer
Brantingham, Barney journalist, writer
†Breunig, Robert G. natural history museum director
Brownlee, Wilson Elliot, Jr. history educator
Brun, Christian Magnus From university librarian
†Buratto, Steven K. chemistry educator, researcher
Byers, Horace Robert former meteorology educator
Caldwell, David Orville physics educator
†Cameron, Heather A. publishing executive
Campbell, Robert Charles clergyman, religious organization administrator
Campbell, William Steen writer, magazine publisher
Carleton, John Lowndes psychiatrist
†Carlson, Arthur W. lawyer
†Carlson, Jean M. physics educator
Chafe, Wallace LeSeur linguist, educator
Childress, James J. marine biologist, biological oceanographer
†Chmelka, Bradley Floyd chemical engineering educator
Christman, Arthur Castner, Jr. scientific advisor
Clinard, Marshall Barron sociologist, educator
Collins, Robert Oakley history educator
Comanor, William S. economist, educator
Conley, Philip James, Jr. retired air force officer
Corman, Cid (Sidney Corman) poet, editor
†Corman, Marvin Leonard surgeon
Crawford, Donald Wesley philosophy educator, university official
Crowell, John C(hambers) geology educator, researcher
Cunningham, Julia Woolfolk author
Dahl, John Anton education educator emeritus
Dauer, Francis Watanabe philosophy educator
Davidson, Eugene Arthur author
Del Chiaro, Mario Aldo art historian, archeologist, etruscologist, educator
Djordjevic, Dimitrije historian, educator
Dougan, Robert Ormes librarian
Doutt, Richard Leroy entomologist, lawyer, educator
Dudziak, Walter Francis physicist
Easton, Robert (Olney) author, environmentalist
Eck, Robert Edwin physicist
Edwardsen, Kenneth Robert administrator
Eguchi, Yasu artist
Eisberg, Robert Martin physics educator, computer software author and executive
Emmons, Robert John corporate executive
Enelow, Allen Jay psychiatrist, educator
Erasmus, Charles John anthropologist, educator
Fan, Ky mathematician, educator
Fingarette, Herbert philosopher, educator
Fisher, Steven Kay neurobiology eductor
Fleming, Brice Noel retired philosophy educator
Ford, Peter C. chemistry educator
Fredrickson, Glenn Harold chemical engineering and materials educator
Frizzell, William Kenneth architect
Gaines, Howard Clarke lawyer
Gallagher, James Wes journalist
Gebhard, David museum director, educator
Gibney, Frank Bray publisher, editor, writer, foundation executive
Gimbel, Norman lyricist, music publisher, television producer
Gossard, Arthur Charles physicist
Graham, Otis Livinston, Jr. history educator
Grayson, Robert Allen marketing executive, educator
Gunn, Giles Buckingham English educator, religion educator
Harris, James Dexter lawyer
Hay, Eloise Knapp English language educator
†Hedgepeth, John M(ills) aerospace engineer, mathematician, engineering executive
Heeger, Alan Jay physicist
†Helgerson, Richard English language educator
Hollister, Charles Warren history educator, author
Hsu, Immanuel Chung Yueh history educator
Hubbard, David Allan minister, educator, religious association administrator
Iselin, Donald Grote civil engineering and management consultant
Jackson, Beverley Joy Jacobson columnist, lecturer
Jacobson, Saul P. consumer products company executive
Jensen, Allen Reed lawyer
Jochim, Michael Allan archaeologist
Johnsen, Eugene Carlyle mathematician and educator
Juergensmeyer, Mark Karl sociology educator
Karpeles, David museum director
Keator, Carol Lynne library director
Kendler, Howard H(arvard) psychologist, educator
Kennett, James Peter geology and oceanography educator
Kohn, Walter educator, physicist
†Korenic, Lynette Marie librarian
Krieger, David Malcolm peace foundation executive, lawyer
Kruger, Kenneth Charles retired architect
Kryter, Karl David research scientist
Langer, James Stephen physicist, educator
Laub, Alan John engineering educator
Laverty, Roger Montgomery, III food products executive, lawyer
Lawrance, Charles Holway civil and sanitary engineer
Leal, Leslie Gary chemical engineering educator
Leckie, Frederick Alexander mechanical engineer, educator
Lick, Wilbert James mechanical engineering educator
Lockett, Barbara Ann librarian
Long, Charles Houston history of religion educator
Louis, Barbra Schantz dean
Lynch, Martin Andrew retail company executive
†Macdonald, Ken Craig geophysicist
Mac Intyre, Donald John college president
Marcus, Marvin mathematician, educator
Mathews, Barbara Edith gynecologist
Mayer, Richard Edwin psychology educator
McEwan, Willard Winfield, Jr. lawyer, judge
McGee, James Sears historian
Mehra, Rajnish finance educator
Meinel, Aden Baker optics scientist
Messick, Don actor
Minc, Henryk mathematics educator
Mitchell, Maurice B. publishing executive, educator
Mitra, Sanjit Kumar electrical and computer engineering educator
Moholy, Noel Francis clergyman
Moir, Alfred Kummer art history educator
Montgomery, Michael Davis advanced technology consultant, hotelier
†Morgan, Alfred V.
†Morse, Daniel E. biochemistry educator, science administrator
Narayanamurti, Venkatesh research administrator
Newman, Morris mathematician
Norris, Robert Matheson geologist
O'Dowd, Donald Davy retired university administrator
Ohyama, Heiichiro music educator, violist, conductor
Paradise, Phil(ip Herschel) artist
Peale, Stanton Jerrold physics educator
Peterson, Gregg Lee radio station executive
Philbrick, Ralph botanist
Potter, David Samuel former automotive company executive
†Prager, Elliot David surgeon, educator
Preston, Frederick Willard surgeon
Prindle, William Roscoe consultant, retired glass company executive
Pritchett, Charles Herman political science educator
Renehan, Robert Francis Xavier Greek and Latin educator
Riblet, Robin L. judge
Riemenschneider, Paul Arthur physician, radiologist
Robeck, Mildred Coen educator
Rockwell, Don Arthur psychiatrist
Rosenberg, Alex mathematician, educator
Russell, Charles Roberts chemical engineer
Russell, Jeffrey Burton historian, educator
Scalapino, Douglas James physics educator
Schneider, Edward Lee botanic garden administrator
Schultz, Arthur Warren communications company executive
Sears, Joanne Lewis retired educator, author
Shapiro, Perry economics educator
Sherman, Alan Robert psychologist, educator
Simons, Stephen mathematics educator, researcher
Sinsheimer, Robert Louis retired university chancellor and educator
Smith, Michael Townsend author, editor, stage director
Smith, Robert Nathaniel broadcasting executive, lawyer
†Sowle, David Hugh physicist
Sprecher, David A. university administrator, mathematician
†Stubbs, Christopher W. physics educator
Tapper, Joan Judith magazine editor
Taylor, Dermot Brownrigg pharmacology researcher
Terry, John Timothy insurance company executive
Tilton, David Lloyd savings and loan association executive
Tilton, George Robert geochemistry educator
Tobler, Waldo Rudolph geographer, cartographer
Tucker, Shirley Lois Cotter botany educator, researcher
Turner, Henry A. political science educator, author
Wade, Glen electrical engineer, educator
Wayland, L. C. Newton public health pediatrician
Wayland, Newton Hart conductor
Weaver, Sylvester Laflin, Jr. communications consultant
†Weinberg, William Henry chemical engineer, chemical physicist, educator
Wiemann, John Moritz communications educator, consultant
†Wilde, Gary Kezerian hospital administrator, business educator
Wilkins, Burleigh Taylor philosophy educator
Wilson, John Abraham Ross academic administrator
Wilson, Leslie biochemist, cell biologist, biology educator
Witherell, Michael S. physics educator
Wooldridge, Dean Everett engineering executive, scientist
Wright, Helene Segal editor
Wudl, Fred chemistry educator, consultant
Yang, Henry T. university chancellor, educator
Zelmanowitz, Julius Martin mathematics educator, university administrator
Zimmerman, Everett Lee English educator, academic administrator

Santa Clara

Abdaljabbar, Abdalhameed A. educational administrator
Alexander, George Jonathon legal educator, former dean
Alexanderson, Gerald Lee mathematician, educator, writer
Amelio, Gilbert Frank electronics company executive
Baird, Mellon Campbell, Jr. electronics industry executive
Barrett, Craig R. computer company executive
†Carey, D. John electronics executive
Carruthers, John Robert scientist
Chan, Shu-Park electrical engineering educator
Charles, Mary Louise newspaper columnist, photographer, editor
Cunningham, Andrea Lee public relations executive
DeLong, James J. lawyer
Delucchi, George Paul accountant
Dent, Richard Lamar professional football player
DuMaine, R. Pierre bishop
Endo, Makoto computer company executive
Facione, Peter Arthur dean, philosophy and education educator
†Fernbach, Stephen A. pediatrician
Glancy, Dorothy Jean lawyer, educator
Gordon, Mary McDougall history educator
Gozani, Tsahi nuclear physicist
Grove, Andrew S. electronics company executive
Halmos, Paul Richard mathematician, educator
Hanks, Merton Edward professional football player
Hoagland, Albert Smiley electrical engineer
†Hobart, James L. laser scientist
Hopkinson, Shirley Lois library and information science educator
House, David L. electronics components company executive
Jackson, Rickey professional football player
Krause, L. William manufacturing company executive
Kwock, Royal architect
Locatelli, Paul Leo university administrator
Lynch, Charles Allen investment executive, corporate director
Marken, Gideon Andrew, III advertising and public relations executive
Martin, Joseph Robert financial executive
McDonald, Tim professional football player
McVay, John Edward professional football club executive
Meier, Matthias S(ebastian) historian
Menkin, Christopher (Kit Menkin) leasing company executive
Moore, Gordon E. electronics company executive
Morgan, James C. electronics executive
Parden, Robert James engineering educator, management consultant
†Pribilla, Peter telecommunications industry executive
Rice, Jerry Lee professional football player
†Schapp, Rebecca Maria museum director
Seifert, George professional football coach
Siljak, Dragoslav D. engineering educator
Stockton, Anderson Berrian electronics company executive, consultant, genealogist
Vincent, David Ridgely management consulting executive
Yin, Gerald Zheyao technology and engineering executive
Young, Steven professional football player

Santa Clarita

Buck, Douglas Earl chemist
DeMieri, Joseph L. manufacturing company executive
Fritzke, Audrey Elmere artist
Lavine, Steven David college president
Lieberman, Paul aeronautical engineer, engineering research company executive
†Pederson, George Ludvig mayor, retired law enforcer
Powell, Mel composer
†Senter, Jack art director, production designer

Santa Cruz

Beevers, Harry biologist
Broadway, Nancy Ruth landscape design and construction company executive, consultant, model and actress
Brough, Bruce Alvin public relations and communications executive
Brown, George Stephen physicist
Bunnett, Joseph Frederick chemist, educator
Child, Frank Clayton economist, educator
Corrick, Ann Marjorie communications executive
Dasmann, Raymond Fredric ecologist
Dilbeck, Charles Stevens, Jr. real estate company executive
Dizikes, John American studies educator
Drake, Frank Donald astronomy educator
Dyson, Allan Judge librarian
Ellis, John Martin German literature educator
Faber, Sandra Moore astronomer, educator
Flatté, Stanley Martin physicist, educator
Fung, K. C. economics educator
Griggs, Gary Bruce earth sciences educator, oceanographer, geologist, consultant
Henderson, Ronald Wilbur psychology educator
Heusch, Clemens August physicist, educator
Hill, Terrell Leslie chemist, biophysicist
Huskey, Harry Douglas information and computer science educator
Kraft, Robert Paul astronomer, educator
Langdon, Glen George, Jr. electrical engineer
Langenheim, Jean Harmon biology educator
Laporte, Leo Frederic earth sciences educator
Lay, Thorne geosciences educator
Lease, Gary Lloyd religion educator, dean
Lieberman, Fredric ethnomusicologist, educator
Lynch, John Patrick classics educator, university official
Magid, Gail Avrum neurosurgery educator
Mc Henry, Dean Eugene academic administrator emeritus
Mumma, Gordon composer, educator, author
Musgrave, Richard Abel economics educator
Noller, Harry Francis, Jr. biochemist, educator
Oberdorfer, Jeff architect, firm executive
Osterbrock, Donald E(dward) astronomy educator
Pettigrew, Thomas Fraser social psychologist, educator
Pister, Karl Stark engineering educator
Prentiss, Charles Gary museum director
Rydell, Amnell Roy artist, landscape architect
Sands, Matthew Linzee physicist, educator
Shorenstein, Rosalind Greenberg physician
Silver, Mary Wilcox oceanography educator
Smith, M(ahlon) Brewster psychologist, educator
†Stevens, Stanley David local history researcher, retired librarian
Suckiel, Ellen Kappy philosophy educator
Summers, Carol artist
Tharp, Roland George psychology, education educator
†Welborn, Victoria Lee science librarian, educator
Williams, Quentin Christopher geophysicist, educator
Winston, George keyboardist, recording company executive
Wipke, W. Todd chemistry educator
Woosley, Stanford Earl astrophysicist

Santa Fe Springs

Butterworth, Edward Livingston retail company executive
Popejoy, William J. savings and loan association executive

Santa Margarita

Thomas, John Bowman educator, electrical engineer

Santa Maria

Arnell, Robert Edward technical writer
Dunn, Judith Louise secondary school educator
Musser, C. Walton physical scientist, consultant

Santa Monica

Abarbanel, Gail social service administrator, educator
Abrams, Irwin historian, educator, consultant
Ackerman, Helen Page librarian, educator
Alenikov, Vladimir motion picture director and writer
Allman, Gregg musician
Alpert, Herb musician, painter, recording artist, theatrical producer, philanthropist
Anderson, Robert Helms computer and management company executive
Augenstein, Bruno W. research scientist
Baer, Walter S. research executive
Barbakow, Jeffrey health facility administrator
Barren, Bruce Willard merchant banker
Bedrosian, Edward electrical engineer
Bedrosian, John C. health care executive
Black, Noel Anthony television and film director
Boltz, Gerald Edmund lawyer
Bonesteel, Michael John lawyer
Boyd, Malcolm minister, religious author
Brook, Robert Henry physician, educator, health services researcher
Brown, Scott McLean lawyer
Cameron, James film director, screenwriter, producer
Chartoff, Robert Irwin film producer
Chu, Deeing architect
Cohen, Leonard hospital management company executive
Cooper, Jackie actor, director, producer
Cowan, Andrew Glenn television writer
Crain, Cullen Malone electrical engineer
Daviau, Allen cinematographer
Demond, Joan marine biologist
De Palma, Brian Russell film director, writer
Dickson, Robert Lee lawyer
Edwards, Sarah Anne radio, cable television personality, clinical social worker
Eizenberg, Julie architect
Esber, Edward Michael, Jr. software company executive
Feitshans, Fred Rollin (Buzz Feitshans) film producer
Fleischman, Albert Sidney (Sid Fleischman) writer
†Flynt, Cynthia costume designer
Focht, Michael Harrison health care industry executive
Fogelberg, Daniel Grayling songwriter, singer
Foulkes, Llyn artist, educator
Garner, Donald K. lawyer
Gehry, Frank Owen architect
Graff, Todd screenwriter
†Greene, Michael C. art association administrator
Gritton, Eugene Charles nuclear engineer
Gupta, Rishab Kumar medical association administrator, educator, researcher
Hammond, R. Philip chemical engineer
†Heimbuch, Babette E. bank executive
†Hensler, Deborah Rosenfield public policy analyst, law educator
Holzman, D. Keith record company executive, producer, arts consultant
Intriligator, Devrie Shapiro physicist
Jacobson, Sidney editor
Janulaitis, M. Victor consulting company executive
Jarreau, Alwyn Lopez singer
Jenest, Jeffrey Mark video corporation executive
Jenkins, George stage designer, film art director
Jones, William Allen lawyer, entertainment company executive
Kahan, James Paul psychologist
Karlin, Robert automotive sales executive
Kauffman, Robert Craig artist, sculptor
Kayton, Myron engineering company executive
Koning, Hendrik architect
Leaf, Paul producer, director, writer
Liddicoat, Richard Thomas, Jr. association executive
†London, Andrew Barry film editor
Loo, Thomas S. lawyer
Lovelace, Jon B. investment management company executive
MacLaine, Shirley actress
†Maginnis, Molly costume designer
Mahal, Taj (Henry St. Clair Fredericks) composer, musician
Mann, Michael K. producer, director, writer
Marrs, Richard Preston gynecologist, obstetrician
Mayne, Thom architect
McGuire, Michael Francis plastic and reconstructive surgeon
Mc Intyre, James A. diversified financial services executive
Mc Kinney, Montgomery Nelson advertising executive
McMillan, M. Sean lawyer
Merideth, Frank E., Jr. lawyer

Michael, George (Gergios Kyriakou Panayiotou) *musician, singer, songwriter*
Miller, Leroy Benjamin *architect*
Morgan, Monroe *retired savings and loan executive*
Mortensen, William S. *banking executive*
Naidorf, Louis Murray *architect*
†Nettleship, Patricia Sharyn *investment group executive*
Nizze, Judith Anne *physician assistant*
Owens, Gary *broadcast personality, entrepreneur, author*
Pettit, John W. *hospital administrator*
Pisano, A. Robert *entertainment company executive, lawyer*
Powers, Marcus Eugene *lawyer*
Prewoznik, Jerome Frank *lawyer*
†Price, David *recreational facilities executive*
Price, Frank *motion picture and television company executive*
Rand, Robert Wheeler *neurosurgeon, educator*
Rich, Michael David *research corporation executive, lawyer*
Richards, David Kimball *investor*
Risman, Michael *lawyer, business executive, securities company executive*
†Roberts, Kevin *recreational facility executive*
Roney, Robert Kenneth *retired aerospace company executive*
Salveson, Melvin Erwin *business executive, educator*
Salzer, John Michael *technical and management consultant*
Schipper, Merle *art historian and critic, exhibition curator*
Schlei, Norbert Anthony *lawyer*
Schultz, Michael *stage and film director, film producer*
Sheller, John Willard *lawyer*
Sher, Allan L. *retired brokerage company executive*
Shubert, Gustave Harry *research executive, consultant, social scientist*
Singer, Frederick Raphael *medical researcher, educator*
Smith, James Patrick *economist*
Snedaker, Catherine Raupagh (Kit Snedaker) *editor*
Sperling, George Elmer, Jr. *lawyer*
Stern, Jan Peter *sculptor*
Stone, Oliver William *screenwriter, director*
Thompson, Dennis Peters *plastic surgeon*
Thomson, James Alan *research company executive*
Tunney, John Varick *lawyer, former senator*
Vajna, Andrew G. *film company executive*
Van Tilburg, Johannes *architectural firm executive*
Walker, Charles Montgomery *lawyer*
Walsh, John, Jr. *museum director*
Ware, Willis Howard *computer scientist*
Watrous, William Russell *trombonist, composer, conductor*
Watson, Doc (Arthel Lane Watson) *vocalist, guitarist, banjoist, recording artist*
Weatherup, Roy Garfield *lawyer*
Weber, Samuel Lloyd *tap dancer, choreographer*
Weil, Leonard *banker*
Weingarten, Victor I. *engineering educator*
Wexler, Haskell *film producer, cameraman*
Williams, Albert Paine *economist*
Williams, George Masayasu *religious organization administrator, editor*
Williams, Harold Marvin *foundation official*
Wolf, Charles, Jr. *economist, educator*
Wou, Leo S. *architect, planner*

Santa Rosa

Aman, Reinhold Albert *philologist, publisher*
Barr, Roger Terry *sculptor*
Brown, Corrick *musician, conductor*
Brunner, Howard William *professional land surveyor*
Cavanagh, John Charles *advertising agency executive*
Christiansen, Peggy *principal*
de Wys, Egbert Christiaan *geochemist*
Eilerman, Betty Jean *marriage and family counselor*
Fream, Ronald Warren *golf course architect*
Frowick, Robert Holmes *retired diplomat*
Lee, Young Woo *financial executive*
Mackay, Kenneth Donald *environmental services company executive*
Mc Donald, David William *chemist, educator*
O'Connor, Sister Ann Patricia *school system administrator*
Person, Evert Bertil *newspaper and radio executive*
Pipal, George Henry *journalist*
Rancourt, James Daniel *optical engineer*
Rider, Jane Louise *artist, educator*
Roland, Craig Williamson *architect*
Schudel, Hansjoerg *international business consultant*
Schulz, Charles Monroe *cartoonist*
Sibley, Charles Gald *biologist, educator*
Steinberger, Richard Lynn *lawyer, corporate executive*
Swofford, Robert Lee *newspaper editor, journalist*
Webb, Charles Richard *retired university president*
†Ziemann, G. Patrick *bishop*

Santa Ynez

Byrne, Joseph *retired oil company executive*
Ellion, M. Edmund *aerospace executive*
Stern, Marvin *management consultant*

Santee

Peters, Raymond Eugene *computer systems company executive*
Vanier, Kieran Francis *business forms printing company executive*

Saratoga

Cooper, George Emery *aerospace consultant*
Henderson, William Darryl *army officer, writer*
Lynch, Milton Terrence *retired advertising agency executive*
Park, Joseph Chul Hui *computer scientist*
Syvertson, Clarence Alfred *aerospace engineering consultant*
Wenzel, James Gottlieb *ocean engineering executive, consultant*

Sausalito

Berkman, William Roger *lawyer, army reserve officer*
Blunt, Peter Howe *capital company executive, lawyer*
Brand, Stewart *editor, writer*
Casals, Rosemary *professional tennis player*
Elliott, James Heyer *retired university art museum curator, fine arts consultant*
Glaser, Edwin Victor *rare book dealer*
Kuhlman, Walter Egel *artist, educator*
Lamoreaux, Phillip Addison *investment management company executive*
Leefe, James Morrison *architect*
Overton, John Blair *lawyer*
Slick, Grace Wing *singer*
Treat, John Elting *management consultant*
Trimmer, Harold Sharp, Jr. *lawyer, international telecommunications consultant*
Werner, William Arno *architect*

Scotts Valley

Bourret, Marjorie Ann *educational advocate, consultant*
Filler, Gary B. *computer company executive*
Shugart, Alan F. *electronic computing equipment company executive*

Seal Beach

Bacon, Paul Caldwell *training system company executive, aviation consultant, engineering test pilot*
Beall, Donald Ray *multi-industry high-technology company executive*
Black, Kent March *electronics company executive*
Burge, Willard, Jr. *software company executive*
Caesar, Vance Roy *newspaper executive*
Calise, William Joseph, Jr. *lawyer*
Hirsch, David L. *lawyer, corporate executive*
Iacobellis, Sam Frank *aerospace company executive*
Kee, Sharon Phillips *lawyer*
Merrick, George Boesch *aerospace company executive*
Mueth, Joseph Edward *lawyer*
†Robinson, Michael R. *aeronautical engineer*
Rossi, Mario Alexander *architect*
Thompson, Craig Snover *corporate communications executive*
Yarymovych, Michael Ihor *manufacturing company executive*

Seaside

Wilson, Robin Scott *university president, writer*

Sebastopol

†DeMartini, Rodney J. *executive director religious organization, priest*
Sabsay, David *library consultant*

Sepulveda

Costea, Nicolas Vincent *physician, researcher*

Sherman Oaks

Almeida, Laurindo *guitarist, composer*
Azpeitia, Lynne Marie *psychotherapist, educator, trainer, consultant*
Baumhoff, Walter Henry *headmaster*
†Beavan, Jenny *costume designer*
†Becker, Susan *costume designer*
Bower, Richard James *minister*
†Bright, John *costume designer*
†Bruckel, Jane C. *nonprofit organization executive*
†Bruno, Richard *costume designer*
Buckingham, Lindsey *musician*
Burton, Levar (Levardis Robert Martin Burton) *actor*
†Carter, Ruth E. *costume designer*
Cherones, Thomas Harry, Jr. *television producer, director*
Conrad, Robert (Conrad Robert Falk) *actor, singer, producer, director*
Cossette, Pierre *agent, producer*
†Dalton, Phyllis *costume designer*
Easton, Sheena *rock vocalist*
Ellison, Harlan Jay *author, screenwriter*
Farnsworth, Richard *actor, former stuntman*
†Fenton, George *composer*
†Finkelman, Wayne *costume designer*
Ghent, Peer *management consultant*
Gilmore, Art *television performer*
Green, Marjorie Biller *educational administrator*
†Greenberg, Adam *cinematographer*
†Gresham, Gloria *costume designer*
†Haigh, Nancy *set decorator*
Hamilton, Scott Scovell *professional figure skater, former Olympic athlete*
Hanlin, Russell L. *citrus products company executive*
†Heimann, Betsy Faith *costume designer*
Holst, Sanford *author, strategic consulting executive*
Hovland, Tim (The Hov) *volleyball player*
†Hurley, Jan *costume designer*
†Jamison-Tanchuck, Francine *costume designer*
†Johnston, Joanna *costume designer*
†Jones, Gary *costume designer*
†Jones, Trevor *composer*
Jourdan, Louis (Louis Gendre) *actor*
Kanter, Hal *television and film writer, producer, director*
Kennedy, Burt Raphael *film director*
†Komarov, Shelley *costume designer*
†Kurland, Jeffrey *costume designer*
Lamas, Lorenzo *actor, race car driver*
Laney, Michael L. *manufacturing executive*
Light, Robert M. *broadcasting association executive*
Lindgren, Timothy Joseph *supply company executive*
Majors, Lee *actor*
†McBride, Elizabeth *costume designer*
Miller, Margaret Haigh *librarian*
†Moorcroft, Judy *costume designer*
Morse, Robert Alan *actor*
Murray, Bill *actor, writer*
†Nadoolman, Deborah *costume designer*
Peplau, Hildegard Elizabeth *nursing educator*
†Pollack, Bernie *costume designer*
†Powell, Anthony *costume designer, set designer*
†Powell, Sandy *costume designer*
†Rand, Tom *costume designer*
†Ringwood, Bob *costume designer*
Rock, Angela *volleyball player*
Ross, Marion *actress*
Shapiro, Amy Rosemarie *film studio executive*
Silliphant, Stirling Dale *motion picture writer, producer, novelist*
Smith, Sinjin *volleyball player*
Steffes, Kent *volleyball player*
Stoklos, Randy (Stokey) *volleyball player*
Strauss, John *public relations executive*
Thomas, Julia Dessery *space designer*
Timmons, Steve (Red) *volleyball player*
†Tompkins, Joe I. *costume designer*
†Vance-Straker, Marilyn *costume designer*
†Weiss, Julie *costume designer*
Williams, Billy Dee *actor*
Winkler, Lee B. *business consultant*
Zemplenyi, Tibor Karol *cardiologist*

Shingle Springs

Crotti, Joseph Robert *aviation executive*

Sierra Madre

Brudvig, Glenn Lowell *library director*
Calleton, Theodore Edward *lawyer*
Dewey, Donald William *magazine editor and publisher, writer*
Nation, Earl F. *retired urologist, educator*
†O'Neil, William J. *aerospace engineer*
Whittingham, Charles Edward *thoroughbred race horse owner and trainer*

Signal Hill

Jarman, Donald Ray *public relations professional, minister, retired*

Simi Valley

Beck, Mat *special effects expert, photographer*
Bigelow, Michael *film director, visual effects expert*
Brown, Melbourne Thomas, Sr. *elementary education educator*
Deisenroth, Clinton Wilbur *electrical engineer*
Durst, Eric *television and commercial director*
Hoover, Richard *special effects expert, film director*
Killion, Jack Charles *newspaper columnist*
Mow, William *apparel executive*
Nesi, Vincent *apparel executive*
Shartle, Keith Robert *producer*
Stratton, Gregory Alexander *computer specialist, administrator, mayor*
Yeatman, Hoyt *special effects expert, executive*

Soda Bay

Fletcher, Leland Vernon *artist*

Solana Beach

Agnew, Harold Melvin *physicist*
Beare, Bruce Riley *trading company and sales executive*
Brody, Arthur *industrial executive*
Cvar, Duane Emil *marketing professional*
Ernst, Roger Charles *former government official, natural resources consultant, association executive*
Friedman, Maurice Stanley *religious educator*
Gildred, Theodore Edmonds *ambassador*
Hamilton, James Marvie *automotive company scientist*
Hecker, Bruce Albert *lawyer*
Kempf, Paul Stuart *optics company executive*

Solvang

Chandler, E(dwin) Russell *religious journalist, author*
Hegarty, William Kevin *medical center executive*
Morrow, Richard Towson *lawyer*
Shelesnyak, Moses Chaim *biodynamicist, physiologist*

Somerset

Collier, Clarence Robert *physician, educator*

Somis

Gius, Julius *retired newspaper editor*
Kehoe, Vincent Jeffré-Roux *photographer, author, cosmetic company executive*

Sonoma

Allen, Rex Whitaker *architect*
Beckmann, Jon Michael *publisher*
Kizer, Carolyn Ashley *poet, educator*
Lackey, Lawrence Bailis, Jr. *retired architect, urban designer*
Markey, William Alan *health care administrator*
Muchmore, Robert Boyer *engineering consultant executive*
Stadtman, Verne August *former foundation executive, editor*
Woodbridge, John Marshall *architect, urban planner*

Sonora

Price, Joe (Allen) *artist, former educator*
†Smith, Carlton Myles *military officer*
Walasek, Otto Frank *chemical engineer, biochemist, photographer*

South Lake Tahoe

†Nason, Rochelle *conservation organization administrator*
Null, Paul Bryan *minister*

South Pasadena

Askin, Walter Miller *artist, educator*
Girvigian, Raymond *architect*
Glad, Dain Sturgis *retired aerospace engineer, consultant*
Kopp, Eugene Howard *electrical engineer*
Saeta, Philip Max *judge*
Staehle, Robert L. *foundation executive*
White-Thomson, Ian Leonard *mining company executive*

South San Francisco

Alvarez, Robert Smyth *editor, publisher*
Crowley, Jerome Joseph, Jr. *manufacturing company executive*
Halligan, Thomas Walsh *construction company executive*
Henderson, Thomas James *construction company executive*
Levinson, Arthur David *molecular biologist*
Leylegian, Jack H., II *investment management company executive*
Masover, Gerald Kenneth *microbiologist*
Raab, G. Kirk *biotechnology company executive*
Swanson, Robert A. *genetic engineering company executive*
†Walsh, Gary L. *consumer products company executive*

Spring Valley

Gardner, Leonard Burton, II *industrial automation engineer*
Peterson, Donald Curtis *life care executive, consultant*
Runge, Paul Edward *baseball umpire, realtor*

Springs

Olofson, Roy Leonard *financial executive, accountant*

Stanford

Abramovitz, Moses *economist, educator*
Abrams, Herbert LeRoy *radiologist, educator*
Allen, Matthew Arnold *physicist*
Almond, Gabriel Abraham *political science educator*
Amemiya, Takeshi *economist, statistician*
Andersen, Hans Christian *chemistry educator*
Anderson, Annelise Graebner *economist*
Anderson, Martin Carl *economist*
Anderson, Theodore Wilbur *statistics educator*
Aoki, Masahiko *economics educator*
Arrow, Kenneth Joseph *economist, educator*
Atkin, J. Myron *science educator*
Ayres, Ian *law educator*
Aziz, Khalid *petroleum engineering educator*
Babcock, Barbara Allen *lawyer, educator*
Bai, Taeil Albert *research physicist*
†Bailey, Frank Ronald *technology educator, science administrator*
Baker, Bruce S. *molecular biologist*
Baker, Keith Michael *history educator*
Baldwin, Robert Lesh *biochemist, educator*
Bandura, Albert *psychologist*
Banks, Peter M. *aerospace science director*
Barkan, Philip *mechanical engineer*
Barnes, Grant Alan *book publisher*
Baron, David P. *business educator*
Baron, James Neal *organizational behavior and human resources educator, researcher*
Barton, John Hays *law educator*
Basch, Paul Frederick *international health educator, parasitologist*
†Bashaw, Matthew Charles *physicist*
Bauer, Eugene Andrew *dermatologist, educator*
Baugh, John *linguistics and anthropology educator, researcher*
Baxter, William Francis *lawyer, educator*
Baylor, Denis Aristide *neurobiology educator*
Beard, Rodney Rau *physician, educator*
Beasley, Malcolm Roy *physics educator*
Beaver, William Henry *accounting educator*
Beichman, Arnold *political scientist, educator, writer*
Bensch, Klaus George *pathology educator*
Berg, Paul *biochemist, educator*
Bershader, Daniel *aerophysics educator*
Bjorkman, Olle Erik *plant biologist, educator*
†Blaschke, Terrence F. *medicine and molecular pharmacology educator*
Bonner, William Andrew *chemistry educator*
Boskin, Michael Jay *economist, government official, university educator, consultant*
†Botstein, David *geneticist, educator*
Boudart, Michel *chemical engineer, chemist, educator*
†Boxer, Steven G. *physical chemistry educator*
Bracewell, Ronald Newbold *electrical engineering educator*
Bradshaw, Peter *engineering educator*
Brauman, John I. *chemist, educator*
Breitrose, Henry S. *communications educator*
Brest, Paul A. *law educator*
Bridges, Edwin Maxwell *education educator*
Brigham, William Everett *petroleum engineering educator*
Brown, Byron William, Jr. *biostatistician, educator*
Brown, Gordon E., Jr. *earth scientist, educator*
Brown, J. Martin *oncologist, educator*
Brumfiel, Gregory Wayne *mathematics educator*
Bryson, Arthur Earl, Jr. *retired engineering educator*
Bube, Richard Howard *materials scientist*
Bunzel, John Harvey *political science educator, researcher*
Calfee, Robert Chilton *psychologist, educational researcher*
Campbell, Allan McCulloch *bacteriology educator*
Campbell, Thomas J. *law educator*
Campbell, Wesley Glenn *economist, educator*
Cannon, Robert Hamilton, Jr. *aerospace engineering educator*
Carlsmith, James Merrill *psychologist, educator*
Carlson, Robert Codner *industrial engineering educator*
Carlsson, Gunnar Erik *mathematics educator*
Carnochan, Walter Bliss *retired English educator*
Carnoy, Martin *economics educator*
Carter, Dennis Robert *biomechanical engineer, educator*
Cavalli-Sforza, Luigi Luca *genetics educator*
Chaffee, Steven Henry *communication educator*
Chu, Steven *physics educator*
Cohen, Albert *musician, educator*
†Cohen, Harvey Joel *pediatric hematology and oncology educator*
Cohen, Stanley Norman *geneticist, educator*
Cohen, William *law educator*
Cole, Wendell Gordon *speech and drama educator*
Coleman, Robert Griffin *geology educator*
Collman, James Paddock *chemistry educator*
Conquest, (George) Robert (Acworth) *writer, historian, poet, critic, journalist*
Cover, Thomas M. *statistician, electrical engineer, educator*
Cox, Donald Clyde *electrical engineering educator*
Cutler, Cassius Chapin *physicist, educator*
†Dafoe, Donald Cameron *surgeon, educator*
Dantzig, George Bernard *applied mathematics educator*
†Date, Elaine Satomi *physician*
David, Paul Allan *economics educator*
Davis, Kingsley *sociologist, educator, researcher*
Davis, Mark M. *microbiologist, educator*
Davis, Robert T. *marketing educator*
Davis, Ronald Wayne *genetics researcher, biochemistry educator*
Deal, Bruce Elmer *physical chemist, educator*
DeBra, Daniel B. *mechanical engineering educator*
Degler, Carl Neumann *history educator*
Dekker, George Gilbert *literature educator, literary scholar, writer*
Derksen, Charlotte Ruth Meynink *librarian*
Dickson, Lance E. *law librarian, educator*
Dunlop, John Barrett *foreign language educator, research institution scholar*
Dutton, Robert Wilbur *electrical engineering educator*
Duus, Peter *history educator*
Eaton, John Kelly *mechanical engineering educator*
Efron, Bradley *mathematics educator*
†Egbert, Peter R. *ophthalmologist, educator*
†Ehrlich, Anne Howland *research associate*
Ehrlich, Paul Ralph *biology educator*
Eitner, Lorenz Edwin Alfred *art historian, educator*
Ely, John Hart *lawyer, university dean*
Enthoven, Alain Charles *economist, educator*
Ernst, Wallace Gary *geology educator*
Eshleman, Von Russel *electrical engineering educator*
Eustis, Robert Henry *mechanical engineer*
Falcon, Walter Phillip *economist*
Falkow, Stanley *microbiologist, educator*
Feferman, Solomon *mathematics and philosophy educator, researcher*
Fehrenbacher, Don Edward *retired history educator*

Fernald, Russell Dawson biologist, researcher
Ferziger, Joel Henry mechanical engineering educator, mathematician
Fetter, Alexander Lees theoretical physicist, educator
Flanagan, Robert Joseph economics educator
Flavell, John Hurley psychologist, educator
Flinn, Paul Anthony materials scientist
Follesdal, Dagfinn philosophy educator
Francke, Uta medical geneticist, genetics researcher, educator
Frank, Joseph Nathaniel comparative literature educator
Franklin, Gene Farthing electrical engineering educator, consultant
Franklin, Marc Adam law educator
Fredrickson, George Marsh history educator
Friedman, Lawrence M. law educator
Friedman, Milton economist, educator emeritus, author
Fuchs, Victor Robert economics educator
Gage, Nathaniel Lees psychologist, educator
Ganesan, Ann Katharine molecular biologist
Gardner, John William writer, educator
Geballe, Theodore Henry physics educator, communications technology consultant
Gelpi, Albert Joseph English educator, literary critic
George, Alexander Lawrence political scientist, educator
Gere, James Monroe civil engineering educator
Germane, Gayton Elwood business educator
Gibson, Count Dillon, Jr. physician, educator
Gilson, Ronald Jay law educator
Girard, René Noel author, educator
Giraud, Raymond Dorner retired language professional
†Glazer, Gary Mark radiology educator
Goldstein, Dora Benedict pharmacologist, educator
Goldstein, Paul lawyer, educator
Goodman, Joseph Wilfred electrical engineering educator
Graham, Stephan Alan earth sciences educator
Gray, Robert M(olten) electrical engineering educator
Green, Paul Barnett biology educator
Greenberg, Joseph H. anthropologist
Grey, Thomas C. lawyer, law educator
Gross, Richard Edmund education educator
Gunther, Gerald lawyer, educator
Hagstrom, Stig Bernt materials science and engineering educator
Hall, Robert Ernest economics educator
Hanawalt, Philip Courtland biology educator, researcher
Hanna, Stanley Sweet physicist, educator
Harbaugh, John Warvelle applied earth sciences educator
Harris, Donald J. economics educator
Harris, Edward D., Jr. physician
Harris, James Stewart, Jr. engineering educator, researcher
Harris, Stephen Ernest electrical engineering and applied physics educator
Harrison, Walter Ashley physicist, educator
Harvey, Van Austin religious studies educator
Heller, Horace Craig biologist, educator
Heller, Thomas C. law educator
Henriksen, Thomas Hollinger university official
Herring, William Conyers physicist, emeritus educator
Herrmann, George mechanical engineering educator
†Hesselink, Lambertus aeronautics, astronautics and electrical engineering educator
Hewett, Thomas Avery petroleum engineer, educator
Hickman, Bert George, Jr. economist, educator
Hilgard, Ernest Ropiequet psychologist
Hilton, Ronald international studies educator
†Hlatky, Mark Andrew cardiologist, health services researcher
Hoff, Nicholas John mechanical and aerospace engineer
Holloway, Charles Arthur public and private management educator
Holloway, David James political science educator
Howell, James Edwin economist, educator
Hubert, Helen Betty epidemiologist
Hughes, Thomas Joseph mechanical engineering educator, consultant
Inan, Umran Savas electrical engineering educator, researcher
Inkeles, Alex sociology educator
Jadvar, Hossein biomedical engineer, physician
Jaedicke, Robert K. university dean, accounting educator
Jardetzky, Oleg medical educator, scientist
Johnson, John J. historian, educator
Johnson, William Summer chemistry educator
Johnston, Bruce Foster economics educator
Johnstone, Iain Murray statistician, educator, consultant
Jones, Patricia Pearce biologist, educator
Kailath, Thomas electrical engineer, educator
Kaiser, Armin Dale biochemist, educator
Kane, Thomas Reif engineering educator
Karlin, Samuel mathematics educator, researcher
Kays, William Morrow university administrator, mechanical engineer
Keller, Joseph Bishop mathematician, educator
Keller, Michael Alan librarian, educator, musicologist
Kelman, Mark Gregory law educator
Kendig, Joan Johnston neurobiology educator
Kennedy, David Michael historian, educator
Kennedy, Donald environmental science educator, former academic administrator
Kirst, Michael Weile education educator, researcher
Kline, Stephen Jay mechanical engineer, educator
Knuth, Donald Ervin computer sciences educator
Korn, David educator, pathologist
Kornberg, Arthur biochemist
Kornberg, Roger David biochemist, structural biologist
Kovach, Robert Louis geophysics educator
Krauskopf, Konrad Bates geology educator
Krensky, Alan Michael pediatrician, educator
Kreps, David Marc economist, educator
Kruger, Charles Herman, Jr. mechanical engineering educator
Krumboltz, John Dwight psychologist, educator
Kurz, Mordecai economics educator
Lau, Lawrence Juen-Yee economics educator, consultant
Lawrence, Charles R. law educator
Lazear, Edward Paul economics and industrial relations educator, researcher
Leavitt, Harold Jack management educator
Leckie, James Oliver engineering educator
Lehman, (Israel) Robert biochemistry educator, consultant
Leifer, Larry John mechanical engineering design educator, health science facility administrator
Lepper, Mark Roger psychology educator
Levin, Henry Mordecai economist, educator
Levinthal, Elliott Charles physicist, educator
Levitt, Raymond Elliot civil engineering educator
†Levy, Ronald medical educator, researcher
L'Heureux, John Clarke English language educator
Lieberman, Gerald J. statistics educator
Lindenberger, Herbert Samuel writer, literature educator
Linvill, John Grimes engineering educator
Litt, Iris Figarsky pediatrics educator
Little, William Arthur physicist, educator
Loftis, John (Clyde), Jr. English language educator
Lohnes, Walter F. W. German language and literature educator
Long, Sharon Rugel molecular biologist, plant biology educator
Lopez, Gerald P. law educator
Lyman, Richard Wall foundation and university executive, historian
Lyons, Charles R. drama educator
Maccoby, Eleanor Emmons psychology educator
Macovski, Albert electrical engineering educator
Madix, Robert James chemical engineer, educator
Maffly, Roy Herrick medical educator
Maharidge, Dale Dimitro journalist, educator
Manley, John Frederick political scientist, educator
†Mann, J. Keith arbitrator, law educator
Mansour, Tag Eldin pharmacologist
March, James Gardner social scientist, educator
Mark, James B. D. surgeon
Marmor, Michael Franklin ophthalmologist, educator
Martin, Joanne business educator
Massy, William Francis education educator, academic administrator
Matisoff, Susan cultural research organization administrator
Mc Bride, Thomas Frederick lawyer, former university dean, government official
McCarthy, John computer scientist, educator
McCluskey, Edward Joseph engineering educator
McConnell, Harden Marsden biophysical chemistry researcher, chemistry educator
McDevitt, Hugh O'Neill immunology educator, physician
McDonald, John Gregory financial investment educator
McDougall, Iain Ross nuclear medicine educator
Mc Lure, Charles E., Jr. economist
Mc Namara, Joseph Donald researcher, retired police chief, novelist
Meier, Gerald M. economics educator
Melmon, Kenneth Lloyd physician, biologist, pharmacologist, consultant
Mendez-Longoria, Miguel Angel law educator
Merigan, Thomas Charles, Jr. physician, medical researcher, educator
Middlebrook, Diane Wood English language educator
Milgrom, Paul Robert economics educator
Miller, James Rumrill, III finance educator
Miller, William Frederick research company executive, educator, business consultant
Mommsen, Katharina German language and literature educator
Montgomery, David Bruce marketing educator
Mooney, Harold Alfred plant ecologist
Moore, Thomas Gale economist, educator
Moravcsik, Julius Matthew philosophy educator
Moses, Lincoln E. statistician, educator
†Mullins, James I. virologist, educator
Nelson, Lyle Morgan communications educator
Newman-Gordon, Pauline French language and literature educator
Niederhuber, John Edward surgical oncologist and molecular immunologist, university educator and administrator
Nilsson, Nils John computer science educator, researcher
Nivison, David Shepherd Chinese and philosophy educator
Nix, William Dale materials scientist, educator
Noddings, Nel education educator, writer
Noll, Roger Gordon economist, educator
North, Robert Carver political science educator
†Oberhelman, Harry Alvin, Jr. surgeon, educator
Olshen, Richard A. statistician, educator
Ornstein, Donald Samuel mathematician, educator
Orr, Franklin Mattes, Jr. petroleum engineering educator
Ortolano, Leonard civil engineering educator, water resources planner
Osheroff, Douglas Dean physicist, researcher
Ott, Wayne Robert environmental engineer
Paffenbarger, Ralph Seal, Jr. epidemiologist
Palm, Charles Gilman university official
Parkinson, Bradford W. aeronautical engineering educator
Paté-Cornell, Marie-Elisabeth Lucienne industrial engineering educator
Paul, Benjamin David anthropologist, educator
Paulson, Boyd Colton, Jr. civil engineering educator
Payne, Anita Hart reproductive endocrinologist, researcher
Pease, Roger Fabian Wedgwood electrical engineering educator
Pecora, Robert chemistry educator
Perloff, Marjorie Gabrielle English and comparative literature educator
Perry, John Richard philosophy educator
Petrosian, Vahé astrophysicist, educator
Pfeffer, Jeffrey business educator
Phillips, Denis Charles education and philosophy educator
Phillips, Ralph Saul mathematics educator
Pierce, John Robinson electrical engineer, educator
Plummer, James D. electrical engineering educator
†Polan, Mary Lake obstetrics and gynecology educator
Polinsky, A. Mitchell law and economics educator
Porterfield, James Temple Starke business administration educator
Pratt, Vaughan Ronald computer engineering educator
Quate, Calvin Forrest engineering educator
Rabin, Robert L. lawyer, educator
Raffin, Thomas A. physician
Raisian, John public policy institute executive, economist
Rees, John Robert physicist
†Reitz, Bruce Arnold cardiac surgeon, educator
Remson, Irwin retired hydrogeology educator
Reynolds, Clark Winton principal investigator, program director, educator
Reynolds, William Craig mechanical engineer, educator
Rhode, Deborah Lynn law educator
Ricardo-Campbell, Rita economist, educator
Richter, Burton physicist, educator
Risser, James Vaulx, Jr. journalist, educator
Roberts, Donald Frank, Jr. communications educator
Roberts, Donald John economics and business educator, consultant
Robinson, Paul Arnold historian, educator, author
Romer, Paul Michael economics educator
Rosaldo, Renato Ignacio, Jr. cultural anthropology educator
Rosenberg, Nathan economics educator
Rosenberg, Saul Allen oncologist, educator
Rosenhan, David L. psychologist, educator
Ross, Alexander Duncan art librarian
Ross, John physical chemist, educator
Rosse, James Nelson economics educator, educational administrator
Roster, Michael lawyer
Roth, Bernard mechanical engineering educator, researcher
Rott, Nicholas fluid mechanics educator
Rowen, Henry Stanislaus economics educator
Royden, Halsey Lawrence mathematics educator
Rubenstein, Edward physician, educator
Sa, Luiz Augusto Discher physicist
Saloner, Garth management educator
Sargent, Thomas John economics educator
Schatzberg, Alan Frederic psychiatrist, researcher
Schawlow, Arthur Leonard physicist, educator
†Schendel, Stephen Alfred plastic surgery educator, oral surgeon
Schimke, Robert Tod biochemist, educator
Schneider, Stephen Henry climatologist, environmental policy analyst, researcher
Scholes, Myron S. law and finance educator
†Schurman, David Jay orthopaedic surgeon, educator
Scott, Kenneth Eugene lawyer, educator
Scott, W(illiam) Richard sociology educator
Seligman, Thomas Knowles museum administrator
Serbein, Oscar Nicholas business educator, consultant
Shah, Haresh C. civil engineering educator
Shapiro, Lucille molecular biology educator
Shaw, Herbert John physics educator emeritus
Sheehan, James John historian, educator
Shepard, Roger Newland psychologist, educator
Shooter, Eric Manvers neurobiology educator, consultant
Shortliffe, Edward Hance internist, medical information science educator
†Shuer, Lawrence Mendel neurosurgery educator
Shultz, George Pratt former secretary of state, economics educator
Siegman, Anthony Edward electrical engineer, educator
Silverman, Frederic Noah physician
Simon, William H. legal educator
†Skeff, Kelley Michael health facility administrator
Sofaer, Abraham David lawyer, legal advisor, federal judge, legal educator
Solomon, Edward Ira chemistry educator and researcher
Solomon, Ezra economist, educator
Sorrentino, Gilbert English language educator, novelist, poet
Sowell, Thomas economist
Spence, A. Michael economics educator, academic administrator
†Spence, Michael finance educator, dean
Spicer, William Edward, III physicist, educator
Spitz, Lewis William historian, educator
Spreiter, John Robert engineering educator, space physics scientist
Springer, George Stephen mechanical engineering educator
Spudich, James A. biology educator
Staar, Richard Felix political scientist
†Stamey, Thomas Alexander physician, urology educator
Stansky, Peter David Lyman historian
†Stevenson, David A. materials science educator
Stinson, Edward Brad surgery educator
Stockdale, James Bond writer, research scholar, retired naval officer
Stone, William Edward association executive
Street, Robert Lynnwood civil and mechanical engineer
Strober, Myra Hoffenberg education educator, consultant
Stryer, Lubert biochemist, educator
Sturrock, Peter Andrew space science and astrophysics educator
Sweeney, James Lee engineering and economic systems educator
Switzer, Paul statistics educator
Taube, Henry chemistry educator
Taylor, John Brian economist, educator
Taylor, Richard Edward physicist, educator
Teicholz, Paul M. civil engineering educator, administrator
Teller, Edward physicist
Thompson, George Albert geophysics educator
Traugott, Elizabeth Closs linguistics educator and researcher
Triska, Jan Francis retired political science educator
Trost, Barry Martin chemist, educator
†Tsien, Richard Winyu biology educator
†Tune, Bruce M. pediatrics educator, renal toxicologist
Tyack, David B. education educator
†Tyler, G. Leonard electrical engineering educator
Ullman, Jeffrey David computer science educator
Van Derveer, Tara university athletic coach
Van Dyke, Milton Denman aeronautical engineering educator
Van Horne, James Carter economist, educator
Van Slyke, Lyman Page history educator
Vincenti, Walter Guido aeronautical engineer, emeritus educator
Wagoner, Robert Vernon astrophysicist, educator
Wald, Michael S. law educator
Walsh, William former football coach
Walt, Martin physicist, consulting educator
Warnke, Roger Allen pathology educator
Watt, Ian Pierre retired English literature educator
†Waymouth, Robert chemistry educator
Weber, David C(arter) librarian
†Wender, Paul Anthony chemistry educator
White, Robert Lee electrical engineer, educator
Widrow, Bernard electrical engineering educator
Williams, Howard Russell lawyer, educator
Winograd, Terry Allen computer science educator
Wojcicki, Stanley George physicist, educator
Wolfson, Mark Alan accounting and finance educator
Wooley, Bruce Allen electronics engineer, educator
Yanofsky, Charles biology educator
Zajonc, Robert B(oleslaw) psychology educator
Zare, Richard Neil chemistry educator
Zimbardo, Philip George psychologist, educator, writer
Zoback, Mark David geophysicist, educator

Stanton

Polk, Benjamin Kauffman retired architect, composer, educator

Stinson Beach

Metz, Mary Seawell university dean, retired college president

Stockton

Antoci, Mario savings and loan company executive
Atchley, Bill Lee university president
Barnum, Robert T. bank executive
Blewett, Robert Noall lawyer
Bookman, Philip newspaper editor
Clancy, Sister Madeline school system administrator
†Cuff, William, IV food company executive
Curtis, Orlie Lindsey, Jr. lawyer
DeRicco, Lawrence Albert college president emeritus
Haisley, Fay Beverley academic dean
Heyborne, Robert Linford electrical engineering educator
Hosie, William Carlton food products company executive
Jacobs, Marian advertising agency owner
Jantzen, J(ohn) Marc retired education educator
Klinger, Wayne Julius secondary education educator
†Kreikemeier, Kenneth G. pipe manufacturing company executive
Limbaugh, Ronald Hadley history educator, history center director
Matuszak, Alice Jean Boyer pharmacy educator
McNeal, Dale William, Jr. biological sciences educator
Meyer, Ursula library director
Montrose, Donald W. bishop
Oak, Claire Morisset artist, educator
Shao, Otis Hung-I corporate executive, educator
Simon, Karen Jordan retail executive
Sorby, Donald Lloyd university dean
Thompson, Thomas Sanford former college president
Whiteker, Roy Archie retired chemistry educator
Whittington, Robert Bruce retired publishing company executive
Won, Kyung-Soo symphony conductor, director

Studio City

Autry, Gene (Orvon Gene Autry) actor, entertainer, broadcasting executive, baseball team executive
Bergen, Polly actress
Bloodworth-Thomason, Linda television producer, writer
†Bumstead, Henry art director, production designer
Carsey, Marcia Lee Peterson television producer
Coolidge, Rita singer
English, Diane television producer, writer, communications executive
Fisher, Joel Marshall political scientist, legal recruiter
Frumkin, Simon political activist and columnist
†Galvin, Tim art director, production designer
Garver, Oliver Bailey, Jr. bishop
Gautier, Dick actor, writer
Goldthwait, Bob comedian, actor
Goodman, John actor
†Guerra, Robert art director, production designer
†Haber, David art director, production designer
Harrison, Gregory actor
†Hasselhoff, David actor
†Hole, Fred art director
†Hutman, Jon art director, production designer
Kenney, H(arry) Wesley, Jr. producer, director
†Kenney, William art director, production designer
†Kilvert, Lilly film production designer
Leider, Gerald J. motion picture and television company executive
†Mansbridge, John B. art director, production designer
†Mansbridge, Mark art director, production designer
†McClellan, Bennett Earl producer
†McDonald, Leslie art director, production designer
†McShirley, Marjorie Stone art director
Moore, Mary Tyler actress
Needham, Hal director, writer
Nieto del Rio, Juan Carlos marketing executive
Parish, James Robert author, cinema historian
Peerce, Larry film director
Pournelle, Jerry Eugene author
Roseanne actress, comedienne, producer, writer
†Sandell, William production designer
†Scarfiotti, Ferdinando production designer
†Scott, Elliot production designer
Shavelson, Melville writer, theatrical producer and director
†Smith, Peter Lansdown art director
†Sylbert, Paul production designer, art director
†Tavoularis, Dean motion picture production designer
†Taylor, Jack G., Jr. art director
†Thomas, Wynn P. art director, production designer
†Tomkins, Alan art director, production designer
von Zerneck, Frank Ernest television producer
Westmore, Michael George make-up artist
†Wissner, Gary Charles motion picture art director, production designer
†Woodruff, Donald B. art director, production designer
Yorty, Samuel lawyer, former mayor

Summerland

Calamar, Gloria artist
Hall, Lee Boaz publishing company consultant, author

Sun City

Newman, Glen Carroll superintendent of schools

Sun Valley

Kamins, Philip E. diversified manufacturing company executive

Sunnyvale

†Araki, Minoru S. aerospace engineer
Armistead, Robert Ashby, Jr. scientific research company executive
Bills, Robert Howard political party executive

DeMello, Austin Eastwood astrophysicist, concert artist, poet, writer
Evans, Barton, Jr. analytical instrument company executive
Fialer, Philip Anthony research scientist, electronics company executive
Guastaferro, Angelo aerospace company executive
Handschuh, G. Gregory lawyer
Hind, Harry William pharmaceutical company executive
†Holbrook, Anthony manufacturing company executive
Karp, Nathan political activist
Kim, Wan Hee electrical engineering educator, business executive
Leeson, David Brent electronics company executive
Lewis, John Clark, Jr. manufacturing company executive
Ludgus, Nancy Lucke lawyer
Ma, Fengchow Clarence agricultural engineering consultant
†Money, Arthur L. electronics executive
Omura, Jimmy Kazuhiro electrical engineer
Previte, Richard computer company executive
†Rankin, M. Douglas electronics executive
Rugge, Henry Ferdinand medical products executive
Sanders, Walter Jeremiah, III electronics company executive
Schubert, Ronald Hayward, Sr. retired aerospace engineer
Schumacher, Henry Jerold former career officer, business executive
†Simon, Ralph E. electronics executive
†Spilker, James J., Jr. electronics executive
Thissell, James Dennis physicist
†Thompson, Edward Francis corporate executive
Tramiel, Sam microcomputer and video game company executive
Trimble, Charles R. electronics executive
White, Eugene R. computer manufacturing company executive
Zebroski, Edwin Leopold nuclear engineer consultant
Zelencik, Stephen J. electronics company executive
Zemke, (E.) Joseph computer company executive

Sunset Beach
Faulkner, Adele Lloyd interior designer, color consultant

Susanville
†Bateson, Clarence Owen chiropractor
Blake, Larry Jay academic administrator

Sylmar
Hoggatt, Clela Allphin English language educator
Sholder, Jason Allen medical products company executive
Tully, Susan Balsley pediatrician, educator

Taft
Smith, Lee L. hotel executive

Tarzana
Abbott, Philip actor
Braun, Stanley insurance company executive
†Ferguson, Jay A. composer
Grill, Lawrence J. lawyer, accountant, management company executive
Hansen, Robert Clinton electrical engineering consultant
Lowy, Jay Stanton music industry executive
Macmillan, Robert Smith electronics engineer
†Michaelson, Richard Aaron health science facility administrator
†Newman, David composer
Shaw, Carole editor, publisher
Shaw-Cohen, Lori Eve magazine editor
†Small, Michael composer
Smith, Mark Lee architect
†Young, Christopher composer

Temecula
Minogue, Robert Brophy retired nuclear engineer

The Sea Ranch
Hayflick, Leonard microbiologist, cell biologist, gerontologist, educator, writer
Resch, Joseph Anthony neurologist

Thousand Oaks
Binder, Gordon M. health and medical products executive
Colburn, Keith W. electronics executive
DeLorenzo, David A. food products executive
Dorsey, Kimberly Lynne public relations executive
Dunaway, Robert Lee sales and marketing executive
Fitzgerald, Janet Marie cosmetic company executive, training consultant
Fore, Richard Lewis real estate development company executive
Gregory, Calvin insurance service executive
Hale, William Bryan, Jr. newspaper editor
Kehrer, Daniel M. publishing executive, author, journalist
Krumm, Charles Ferdinand electrical engineer
Luedtke, Luther S. academic administrator
Malmuth, Norman David program manager
McCune, David Franklin publisher
†Miller, Jim film editor
Rathmann, George Blatz genetic engineering company executive
Rooney, Mickey (Joe Yule, Jr.) actor
Sherman, Gerald financial estate planner, nuclear physicist
Sladek, Lyle Virgil mathematician, educator
Smyth, Glen Miller management consultant
Sparrow, Larry J. telecommunications executive
Van Mols, Brian publishing executive
Wang, I-Tung atmospheric scientist

Thousand Palms
Smith, Charles Thomas retired dentist, educator

Tiburon
Drury, Allen Stuart author
Heacox, Russel Louis mechanical engineer
Heller, H(einz) Robert financial executive
Robinson, Gordon Pringle forester

Toluca Lake
Belcher, Donald David manufacturing company executive
Whitesell, John Edwin motion picture company executive

Topanga
Redgrave, Lynn actress

Torrance
Adelsman, (Harriette) Jean newspaper editor
Alter, Gerald L. real estate executive
Amemiya, Koichi motor vehicle company executive
Ananth, Jambur psychiatrist, educator
Brasel, Jo Anne physician
Brodsky, Robert Fox aerospace engineer
Bruinsma, Theodore August retired business executive
Buckley, James W. librarian
Burnham, Daniel Patrick manufacturing company executive
Carey, Kathryn Ann advertising and public relations agency executive, consultant
Chandler, Richard Hill medical products company executive
Conrad, Paul Francis editorial cartoonist
Emmanouilides, George Christos physician, educator
Everts, Connor artist
Finer, William A. lawyer
Fledderjohn, Karl Ross manufacturing executive
Foley, Edward Joseph hospital administrator
Gurevitch, Arnold William dermatology educator
Harness, William Edward tenor
Itabashi, Hideo Henry neuropathologist, neurologist
Kaufman, Sanford Paul lawyer
Kay, Kenneth Jeffrey health care company executive
Krout, Boyd Merrill psychiatrist
Kulpa, John Edward management executive, former air force officer
Kurita, Masahiro computer company executive
Kwiker, Louis A. business executive
Leake, Donald Lewis oral and maxillofacial surgeon, oboist
Lin, Keh-Ming psychiatrist, researcher
Mann, Michael Martin electronics company executive
Mason, John Latimer engineering executive
McNamara, Brenda Norma secondary education educator
Miller, Milton Howard psychiatrist
Myhre, Byron Arnold pathologist, educator
Narasimhan, Padma Mandyam physician
Niwa, Norio computer company executive
O'Connor, William Charles automobile agency finance executive
†Perrish, Albert steel company executive
Petillon, Lee Ritchey lawyer
†Pitts, Robert Lynn automotive company executive
Prakash, Ravi physician, educator
Prell, Joel James medical group administrator
Riess, Susan Elizabeth lawyer
Rogers, Howard H. chemist
Rohrberg, Roderick George welding consultant
Sakai, Shinji finance company executive
Savitz, Maxine Lazarus aerospace company executive
Sheh, Robert Bardhyl environmental management company executive
Signorovitch, Dennis James communications executive
†Suzuki, Takuya telecommunications executive
Swerdloff, Ronald S. medical educator, researcher
Tanaka, Kouichi Robert physician, educator
†Togo, Yukiyasu automotive executive
Walti, Randal Fred management consultant
Westover, Samuel Lee insurance company executive
†Whitley, Ralph C. diversified financial services company executive
Woodhull, John Richard electronics company executive

Trabuco Canyon
Addy, Jo Alison Phears economist

Trinidad
Marshall, William Edward historical association executive

Tulare
Sickels, William Loyd secondary educator

Turlock
Ahlem, Lloyd Harold psychologist
Amrhein, John Kilian dean
Goedecke, David Stewart music educator, band educator, trumpet player
Williams, Delwyn Charles telephone company executive

Tustin
Bartlett, Arthur Eugene franchise executive
Clarke, Joyce Anne biochemist
†Crouch, Paul Franklin minister, church official
Hester, Norman Eric chemical company technical executive, chemist
Jay, David Jakubowicz management consultant
Kelley, Robert Paul, Jr. management consultation executive
Krumm, John McGill bishop
London, Ray William clinical and forensic psychologist

Twain Harte
Kinsinger, Robert Earl property company executive, educational consultant

Twentynine Palms
Clemente, Patrocinio Ablola psychology educator
Fultz, Philip Nathaniel management analyst

Universal City
Baker, Richard Eugene controller, corporate executive
Boulanger, Donald Richard financial services executive
Day, Doris (Doris von Kappelhoff) singer, actress
Horowitz, Zachary I. entertainment company executive
†Kahn, Sheldon F. film editor, producer
Katz, Perry Marc motion picture company executive
LaBelle, Patti singer
Lansbury, Angela Brigid actress
Lindheim, Richard David television company executive
Lovett, Lyle musician
Lynn, Loretta Webb (Mrs. Oliver Lynn, Jr.) singer
Masket, Edward Seymour television executive
Meat Loaf, (Marvin Lee Aday) popular musician, actor
Nelson, Craig T. actor
Paul, Charles S. motion picture and television company executive
Pollock, Thomas P. motion picture company executive
Sheinberg, Sidney Jay recreation and entertainment company executive
Teller, Alvin Norman music industry executive
Van Dyke, Jerry actor, comedian
Wasserman, Lew R. film, recording and publishing company executive
Yearwood, Trisha country music singer, songwriter

Upland
Hext, Kathleen Florence regulatory compliance consultant
Jones, Nancy Langdon financial planner, investment advisor
Lewis, Goldy Sarah real estate developer, corporation executive
Lewis, Ralph Milton real estate developer

Vacaville
Coulson, Kinsell Leroy meteorologist
Wisneski, Mary Jo Elizabeth reading specialist, educator

Valencia
Fiskin, Judith Anne artist educator
McGlasson, James Dean publishing executive

Valley Ford
Clowes, Garth Anthony electronics executive, consultant

Valley Village
Diller, Phyllis actress, author
†Stevenson, Michael Anson motion picture film editor

Van Nuys
Allen, Stephen Valentine Patrick William television comedian, author, pianist, songwriter
Altshiller, Arthur Leonard physics educator
Blinder, Martin S. business consultant, art dealer
Bodine, Ralph E. food products company executive
Brock, Richard Barrett hospital nursing administrator
Conway, Tim comedian
Cooper, Leroy Gordon, Jr. former astronaut, business consultant
Fraser, Julia Diane publishing executive
Frons, Brian Scott television executive
Gordon, Stuart film and theater producer, director, playwright
Halamandaris, Harry aerospace executive
Ivey, Judith actress
Jones, Dean Carroll actor
Kagan, Stephen Bruce (Sandy Kagan) travel agency executive
Mikesell, Richard Lyon lawyer, financial counselor
Mount, David Allen video specialist
Rosen, Alexander Carl psychologist, consultant
Simon, David Harold retired public relations executive
Sludikoff, Stanley Robert publisher, writer
†Sofro, Barney retail executive
Zucker, Alfred John English educator, academic administrator

Venice
Bengston, Billy Al artist
Berlant, Anthony artist
Bill, Tony actor, producer, director
Chiat, Jay advertising agency executive
Clow, Lee advertising agency executive
Ehrlich, Steven David architect
Eliot, Alexander author, mythologist
Eversley, Frederick John sculptor, engineer
†Ferry, April costume designer
Giaquinta, Gerald J. public relations executive
Gould, Elliott actor
Kuperman, Robert Ian advertising agency executive
O'Neill, Edward actor
Shapazian, Robert Michael publishing executive
Thomas, Bob public relations executive
Wolf, Robert Howard advertising executive, marketing consultant

Ventura
Adeniran, Dixie Darlene library administrator
Arita, George Shiro biology educator
Field, A. J. former oil drilling company executive, engineering consultant
Gaynor, Joseph technical and management consultant
Greig, William Taber, Jr. publishing company executive
Kirman, Charles Gary photojournalist
Matley, Benvenuto Gilbert (Ben Matley) computer engineer, educator, consultant
McElroy, Charlotte Ann principal
Wheeler, Harold Alden retired radio engineer

Victorville
Bascom, Earl Wesley artist, sculptor, writer
Caldwell, Patricia Frances management consultant, lecturer

Villa Park
Britton, Thomas Warren, Jr. management consultant

Visalia
Miller, Carl Duane transportation company executive
Riegel, Byron William ophthalmologist

Vista
Cavanaugh, Kenneth Clinton retired housing consultant
†Ferguson, Margaret Ann tax consultant
Johnson, Alan principal
Rader, Paul Alexander minister, administrator
Tiedeman, David Valentine education educator

Volcano
Prout, Ralph Eugene physician

Walnut
Ashford, Evelyn track and field athlete

Walnut Creek
Acosta, Julio Bernard obstetrician, gynecologist
Blackburn, Michael Philip lawyer
Caddy, Edmund Harrington Homer, Jr. architect
†Cadieux, Robert D. chemical company executive
Combs, William G. drug retailing company executive
Crandall, Ira Carlton consulting electrical engineer
Curtin, Daniel Joseph, Jr. lawyer
Farr, Lee Edward physician
Garlough, William Glenn marketing executive
Garrett, James Joseph lawyer, partner
Ginsburg, Gerald J. lawyer, business executive
Graham, Dee McDonald food company executive
Hallock, C. Wiles, Jr. athletic official
Hamilton, Allen Philip financial advisor
Hamlin, Kenneth Eldred, Jr. retired pharmaceutical company executive
Haswell, T. Clayton newspaper editor
Humphrey, William Albert mining company executive
Jackson, Dale Edward lawyer
Jones, Ebon Richard retail executive
Jones, Orlo Dow lawyer, drug store executive
Kieffer, William Franklinn chemistry educator
Lesher, Margaret Lisco newspaper publisher, songwriter
Long, Robert Merrill retail drug company executive
Madden, Palmer Brown lawyer
†Maslin, Harvey Lawrence staffing service company executive
McCauley, Bruce Gordon financial consultant
McGrath, Don John banker
Merritt, Robert Edward lawyer, educator
Morgan, Elmo Rich former university official
Nelson, Elmer Kingsholm, Jr. educator, writer, mediator, consultant
Newmark, Milton Maxwell lawyer
Pagter, Carl Richard lawyer
Plomgren, Ronald Arthur retail executive
Rhody, Ronald Edward banker, communications executive
Roach, John D. C. manufacturing company executive
Satz, Louis K. publishing executive
Seegers, Walter Henry hematology educator emeritus
Skaggs, Sanford Merle lawyer
Smith, Robert Houston archeologist, religious studies educator
†Stover, W. Robert lay worker, temporary services executive
†Wentzel, Dan R. title company executive
Wolcott, Oliver Dwight international trading company executive
Woodward, Richard Joseph, Jr. geotechnical engineer
Zander, Alvin Frederick social psychologist

Watsonville
Carpenter, Philip David laboratory administrator, environmental and organic chemist
Costanzo, Patrick M. constuction executive
Hernandez, Jo Farb museum and curatorial consultant
Roberts, Richard Heilbron construction company executive
Solari, R. C. heavy construction company executive

West Covina
Hamilton, Robert William lawyer
†Makowski, Peter Edgar hospital executive
McHale, Edward Robertson retired lawyer
†Pollak, Sam sports editor, columnist

West Hills
Freas, Frank Kelly illustrator
Straight, Beatrice Whitney actress

West Hollywood
Benson, George guitarist
Black, David writer, educator, producer
Black, Shane screenwriter
Bloom, Claire actress
Blumofe, Robert Fulton motion picture producer, association executive
Bogart, Paul film director
†Broughton, Bruce Harold composer
Brunell, Philip A. physician
Burns, George (Nathan Birnbaum) actor, comedian
Byrne, Edward Blake broadcasting company executive
Cage, Nicolas (Nicolas Coppola) actor
Conti, Bill film composer
†Copeland, Stewart composer, musician
Denver, John (Henry John Deutschendorf, Jr.) singer, songwriter
Deschanel, Caleb cinematographer, director
Dorsey, Helen Danner (Johna Blinn) writer, author, educator
Elfman, Danny composer
Erman, John film director
Etessami, Rambod endonontist
Fein, Irving Ashley television and motion picture executive
Fisher, Carrie Frances actress, writer
Geffen, David recording company executive, producer
†Gibbs, Richard composer
Grasshoff, Alex writer, producer, director
Helin, James Dennis advertising agency executive
Henley, Don singer, drummer, songwriter
Hockney, David artist
Holt, Dennis F. media buying company executive
Kingsley, Patricia public relations executive
Leblang, Steven Craig television executive
Leigh, Jennifer Jason (Jennifer Leigh Morrow) actress
Levine, Michael public relations executive, author
Lewis, Richard actor, comedian
Luckman, Charles architect
Males, William James film producer, make-up artist
Marsalis, Wynton musician
McKagan, Duff (Michael McKagan) bassist
Mull, Martin comedian, singer
Pasternak, Kathryn Ann filmmaker
†Portman, Rachel Mary Berkeley composer
Pozo, Santiago marketing executive
Reid, Antonio (L. A. Reid) musician, songwriter
†Revell, Graeme composer
Ronstadt, Linda Marie singer
Rose, W. Axl (William Bruce Bailey) singer
Sanello, Frank Anthony journalist, columnist
Shaye, Robert Kenneth cinema company executive
Sherman, Robert B(ernard) composer, lyricist, screenwriter
Slash, (Saul Hudson) guitarist
Taylor, James Vernon musician
Van Buren, Abigail (Pauline Friedman Phillips) columnist, author, writer, lecturer
Verhoeven, Paul film director
Wald, Donna Gene advertising executive
Walton, Brian lawyer, union negotiator
Wilson, Myron Robert, Jr. former psychiatrist

Young, Neil *musician, songwriter*

West Sacramento
†Teel, James E. *supermarket and drug store retail executive*
†Teel, Joyce *supermarket and drugstore retail executive*

Westlake Village
†Bevan, L. Darrell *telecommunication company executive, entrepreneur*
Caligiuri, Joseph Frank *retired engineering executive*
Doherty, Patrick Francis *communications executive, educator*
Easton, William Heyden *geology educator*
Fredericks, Ward Arthur *venture capitalist, food industry consultant*
Jessup, Warren T. *retired lawyer*
Murdock, David H. *diversified company executive*
Pang, Peter Chiusing *lawyer, business consultant*
Small, Richard David *research scientist*
Steadman, Lydia Duff *elementary school educator, symphony violinist*

Westminster
Allen, Merrill James *marine biologist*
Armstrong, Gene Lee *systems engineering consultant, retired aerospace company executive*
Ryan, James Edwin *industrial arts educator*

Westwood
Brydon, Harold Wesley *entomologist, writer*

Whittier
Arcadi, John Albert *urologist*
Arenowitz, Albert Harold *psychiatrist*
Ash, James Lee, Jr. *academic administrator*
†Briney, Allan King *radiologist*
Brown, Thomas Andrew *aircraft and weaponry manufacturing executive*
Connick, Charles Milo *retired religion educator, clergyman*
Davidson, Alan Charles *insurance executive*
Drake, E Maylon *academic administrator*
Lillevang, Omar Johansen *civil engineer*
Loughrin, Jay Richardson *mass communications educator, consultant*
Maxwell, Raymond Roger *accountant*
Solis, Hilda Lucia *educational administrator, state legislator*
Tunison, Elizabeth Lamb *education educator*

Wilmington
Hatch, Ronald Ray *engineer*
Smith, June Burlingame *English educator*

Winters
Low, Donald Gottlob *retired veterinary medicine educator*

Woodland
†Marler, Phillip Lynn *healthcare administrator*
Petre, Donna Marie *county judge*
Phan, Chuong Van *biotechnologist*
Stevens, M. Allen *geneticist, administrator*

Woodland Hills
Anaya, Richard Alfred, Jr. *accountant, investment banker*
Chernof, David *internist*
Conley, Robert Francis *aircraft and space industry executive*
Davidian, David *lighting and production designer*
DeWitt, Barbara Jane *journalist*
Firestone, Morton H. *business management executive*
Fisher, Gerald Saul *publisher, financial consultant, lawyer*
Fitzpatrick, Dennis Michael *information systems executive*
Freeman, Philip Conrad, Jr. *computer systems company executive*
Fricker, John Arthur *pediatrician, educator*
Goldberg, David Charles *electrical contracting executive*
Gray, Thomas Stephen *newspaper editor*
†Greaves, Roger F. *health maintenance organization executive*
Harris, Helen Josephine *foundation administrator*
†Hasan, Malik M. *health maintenance organization executive*
Hawkins, Willis Moore *aerospace and astronautical consultant*
Higginbotham, Lloyd William *mechanical engineer*
Horne, Lena *singer*
Janis, Conrad *actor, jazz musician, art dealer, film producer, director*
Labadie, George Sherman *retired art director*
Maeda, J. A. *data processing executive*
†Morishita, Akihiko *trading company executive*
Neill, William Alexander *magazine editor*
†Nicholas, Fayard Antonio *dancer, actor, entertainer*
Oltman, Henry George, Jr. *retired engineering executive*
O'Meara, Sara *foundation administrator*
Perlman, Itzhak *violinist*
Pregerson, Harry *federal judge*
Rapoport, Ronald Jon *journalist*
Robison, Frederick Mason *financial executive*
Schaeffer, Leonard David *health care executive*
Scheimer, Louis *film and television producer*
Sharma, Brahama Datta *chemistry educator*
Sigholtz, Sara O'Meara *non-profit organization executive*
Strote, Joel Richard *lawyer*
Swaim, Ruth Carolyn *educator*
Talbot, Matthew J. *oil company executive, rancher*
Taubitz, Fredricka *financial executive*
Taylor, Rowan Shaw *music educator, composer, conductor*
†Wasserman, Gerald B. *wholesale distribution executive*
†Weider, Joseph *wholesale distribution executive*
Weinberg, D. Mark *health insurance company executive*
Weiser, Paul David *manufacturing company executive*
Wester, Keith Albert *film and television recording engineer, television executive*
Zeitlin, Herbert Zakary *retired college president*

Woodside
Ashley, Holt *aerospace scientist, educator*
Blum, Richard Hosmer Adams *education educator, writer*
Kaisel, Stanley Francis *management consultant*
Poole, Gordon Leicester *lawyer*
Schneider, Steven Arnold *educational administrator, consultant*

Yorba Linda
Bailey, Don Matthew *aerospace and electronics company executive*
Eriksen, Otto Louis *retired manufacturing company executive*
Forth, Kevin Bernard *beverage distributing industry consultant*
Miller, Robert Lindsey *bishop*
†Naulty, Susan Louise *archivist*

Yountville
Goeglein, Richard John *hotel/casino chain executive*
Helzer, James Dennis *hospital executive*
Kay, Douglas Casey *leasing company executive*

Yreka
Beary, Shirley Lorraine *retired music educator*
McFadden, Leon Lambert *artist, inventor*

Yuba City
Falls, Edward Joseph *lawyer, insurance executive, educator*
Kemmerly, Jack Dale *retired state official, aviation consultant*

Yucaipa
Griesemer, Allan David *museum director*

COLORADO

Arvada
Elrick, Billy Lee *English language educator*
Holden, George Fredric *brewing company executive, policy specialist, consultant*
Ingalls, Gegory Kent *oral and maxillofacial sugeon*
Knight, William V. *geologist*

Aspen
Berkó, Ferenc *photographer*
Caudill, Samuel Jefferson *architect*
Eirman, Thomas Fredrick *music festival manager*
Ensign, Donald H. *landscape architect*
Harth, Robert James *music festival executive*
Jalili, Mahir *lawyer*
Levin, Barton John *aviation products and services company executive*
McDade, James Russell *management consultant*
Murray, Robert Bruce *theatre administrator*
O'Toole, James Joseph *business educator*
Soldner, Paul Edmund *artist, ceramist, educator*
Sullivan, Danny *professional race car driver*

Aurora
Barth, David Victor *computer systems designer, consultant*
Bauman, Earl William *accountant, government official*
Cowee, John Widmer *retired university chancellor*
Dye, Larry Wayne *political consultant*
Eames, Wilmer Ballou *dental educator*
Fedak, Barbara Kingry *technical center administrator*
Fish, Ruby Mae Bertram (Mrs. Frederick Goodrich Fish) *civic worker*
Hickman, Grace Marguerite *artist*
Huff, Paul Emlyn *insurance executive*
Hutchins, Charles Larry *educational association administrator, consultant*
Jarvis, Mary G. *principal*
Magalnick, Elliott Ben *retail medical supply company executive*
Matson, Merwyn Dean *educational consultant*
McPherson, Gary Lee *lawyer, state representative*
†Montgomery, John E. *federal medical association administrator*
Motz, Kenneth Lee *former farm organization official*
†Nicholas, Thomas Peter *library administrator, community television consultant, producer*
Schilling, Edwin Carlyle, III *lawyer*
Shearer, Carolyn Juanita *secondary education educator*

Basalt
Feliciano, José *entertainer*
Kazan, Lainie (Lainie Levine) *singer, actress*
Puente, Tito Anthony *orchestra leader, composer, arranger*
Severinsen, Doc (Carl H. Severinsen) *conductor, musician*
Sinatra, Frank (Francis Albert Sinatra) *singer, actor*
Williams, Joe *jazz and blues singer*

Bellvue
Bennett, Jim *retired university official*

Boulder
Albino, Judith E. N. *university president*
Albritton, Daniel L. *environmental scientist*
Alldredge, Leroy Romney *retired geophysicist*
Anderson, Robert K. *health care company executive*
Anderson, Ronald Delaine *education educator*
Andrews, James Rowland *electronics executive, consultant*
Anthes, Richard Allen *meteorologist*
Archambeau, Charles Bruce *physics educator, geophysics research scientist*
Armstrong, David Michael *biology educator*
Avery, Susan Kathryn *electrical engineering educator, researcher*
Bailey, Dana Kavanagh *radiophysicist, botanist*
†Baker, Daniel Neil *physicist*
Balog, James Dennis *photographer*
Bangs, F(rank) Kendrick *former business educator*
Barnes, Frank Stephenson *electrical engineer, educator*
Bartlett, David Farnham *physics educator*
Baughn, William Hubert *former business educator and academic administrator*
Beckmann, Petr *electrical engineer, educator*
Begelman, Mitchell C. *astrophysicist, educator*
Bintliff, Barbara Ann *law librarian, educator*
Birkenkamp, Dean Frederick *editor, publishing executive*
Birmingham, Bascom Wayne *retired government official*
†Born, George H. *aerospace engineer, educator*
Boss, Russel Wayne *business administration educator*
Boulding, Elise Marie *sociologist, educator*
Bourne, Lyle Eugene, Jr. *psychology educator*
Bowers, John Waite *communication educator*
Brakhage, James Stanley *filmmaker, educator*
Brault, James William *physicist*
Bright, William Oliver *linguistics educator*
Brutus, Dennis Vincent *African literature, poetry, creative writing educator*
Bryson, Gary Spath *cable television and telephone company executive*
Buchanan, Dodds Ireton *business educator, consultant*
Burns, Daniel Hobart *management consultant*
Byerly, Radford, Jr. *science policy official*
Calvert, Jack George *atmospheric chemist, educator*
Carlson, Devon McElvin *architect, educator*
†Carter, Laura Lee *academic librarian, psychologist*
Caruthers, Marvin Harry *biochemistry educator*
Cary, John Robert *physics educator*
Cathey, Wade Thomas *electrical engineering educator*
Cech, Thomas Robert *chemistry and biochemistry educator*
Chappell, Charles Franklin *meteorologist, consultant*
Chinnery, Michael Alistair *federal government official, geophysicist*
Choquette, Philip Wheeler *geologist, educator*
Clark, Melvin Eugene *chemical company executive*
Clifford, Steven Francis *science research director*
Codding, George Arthur, Jr. *political science educator*
Conti, Peter Selby *astronomy educator*
Corbridge, James Noel, Jr. *law educator*
Corotis, Ross Barry *civil engineering educator, academic administrator*
Cristol, Stanley Jerome *chemistry educator*
Crow, Edwin Louis *mathematical statistician, consultant*
Danilov, Victor Joseph *museum management program director, consultant, writer, educator*
Danna, Kathleen Janet *virologist, plant molecular biologist, educator*
Darling, Frank Clayton *former political science educator, educational institute administrator*
Daughenbaugh, Randall Jay *chemical company executive*
Davis, Donald Alan *author, news correspondent, lecturer*
De Fries, John Clarence *behavioral genetics educator, institute administrator*
Derr, Vernon Ellsworth *government research administrator*
Dilley, Barbara Jean *college administrator, choreographer, educator*
Dorn, Edward Merton *poet, educator*
Dryer, Murray *physicist*
Dubin, Mark William *educator, neuroscientist*
Duckworth, Guy *musician, educator*
Echohawk, John Ernest *lawyer*
Ekstrand, Bruce Rowland *university administrator, psychology educator*
Enarson, Harold L. *emeritus university president*
Fest, Thorrel Brooks *former speech educator, consultant*
Fiflis, Ted J. *lawyer, educator*
Fink, Robert Russell *music theorist, university dean*
Fleener, Terry Noel *marketing professional*
Fleming, Rex James *meteorologist*
Folsom, Franklin Brewster *author*
Fox, Joseph Leland *utilities executive*
†Frey, Julia Bloch *French language educator*
Fukae, Kensuke *infosystems specialist*
Fuller, Jackson Franklin *electrical engineering educator*
Gabridge, Michael Gregory *university administrator, science administrator*
Garstang, Roy Henry *astrophysicist, educator*
Geers, Thomas Lange *mechanical engineering educator*
Gerstle, Kurt Herman *retired civil engineering educator, consultant*
Gilman, Peter A. *national laboratory administrator, scientist*
Glover, Fred William *artificial intelligence and optimization research director, educator*
Goeldner, Charles Raymond *business educator*
Gossard, Earl Everett *physicist*
Gough, Bryan Ray *graphic designer*
Gralapp, Marcelee Gayl *librarian*
Greenberg, Edward Seymour *political science educator*
Greene, David Lee *physical anthropologist, educator*
Gupta, Kuldip Chand *electrical and computer engineering educator, researcher*
Hall, John Lewis *physicist, researcher*
Hanley, Howard James Mason *research scientist*
Hanna, William Johnson *electrical engineering educator*
†Hauser, Ray Louis *research engineer, entrepreneur*
Hawkins, David Cartwright *philosophy and history of science, educator*
Hay, William Winn *former museum director, natural history and geology educator*
Healy, Alice Fenvessy *psychology educator, researcher*
Helburn, Nicholas *geography educator*
Hermann, Allen Max *physics educator*
Hildner, Ernest Gotthold, III *solar physicist, science administrator*
Hill, Boyd H., Jr. *medieval history educator*
Hill, David Allan *electrical engineer*
†Hill, Norbert S., Jr. *executive director American Indian society*
Hoerig, Gerald Lee *chemical company executive*
Hofmann, David John *atmospheric science researcher, educator*
Hogg, David Clarence *physicist*
Holdsworth, Janet Nott *women's health nurse*
Holzer, Thomas E. *astronomer*
Horowitz, Isaac M. *control research consultant, writer*
†Jakosky, Bruce M. *planetary scientist*
Jerritts, Stephen G. *computer company executive*
Jessor, Richard *psychologist, educator*
Johnson, Edward Alden *dean of college*
Johnson, Maryanna Morse *business owner*
†Jonsen, Richard Wiliam *educational administrator*
Joselyn, Jo Ann *space scientist*
Kanda, Motohisa *electronics engineer*
Katz, Phyllis Alberts *developmental research psychologist*
Kauffman, Erle Galen *geologist, paleontologist*
Kaye, Evelyn Patricia (Evelyn Patricia Sarson) *author, publisher, travel expert*
Kellogg, William Welch *meteorologist*
Kelso, Alec John (Jack Kelso) *anthropologist, educator*
King, Edward Louis *retired chemistry educator*
Kintsch, Walter *psychology educator, director*
†Ko, Hon Yim *civil engineering educator, consultant*
Koch, Tad Harbison *chemistry educator, researcher*
†Lally, Vincent Edward *atmospheric scientist*
Lanham, Urless Norton *curator*
Lester, Robert Carlton *religious studies educator*
†Limerick, Patricia Nelson *history educator*
Lineberger, William Carl *chemistry educator*
Lodewyk, Eric *chemist, pharmaceutical executive*
Low, Boon Chye *physicist*
Mahanthappa, Kalyana Thipperudraiah *physicist, educator*
Main, Jackson Turner *history educator*
Malde, Harold Edwin *retired federal government geologist*
Maley, Samuel Wayne *electrical engineering educator*
Martin, Phillip Dwight *banking consulting company executive, mayor*
Mason, Leon Verne *financial planner*
Matthews, Eugene Edward *artist*
Matthews, Wanda Miller *artist*
McCabe, Richard Lee *real estate developer*
†McCray, Richard Alan *astrophysicist, educator*
Mc Intosh, J(ohn) Richard *biologist, educator*
McKenzie, James Milton *excavating company executive*
Meier, Mark F. *research scientist, glaciologist, educator*
Melicher, Ronald William *finance educator*
Metzger, H(owell) Peter *writer*
Middleton, Charles Ronald *educator, academic dean*
†Middleton, Paulette Bauer *atmospheric chemist*
Miller, Norman Richard *diversified manufacturing company executive*
Moses, Raphael Jacob *lawyer*
Mycielski, Jan *mathematician, educator*
Neinas, Charles Merrill *athletic association executive*
Norcross, David Warren *physicist, researcher*
Oesterle, Dale Arthur *law educator*
Pankove, Jacques Isaac *physicist*
Park, Roderic Bruce *university chancellor*
Peterson, Courtland Harry *law educator*
Phelps, Arthur Van Rensselaer *physicist, consultant*
Porzak, Glenn E. *lawyer*
Prescott, David Marshall *biology educator*
†Raudenbush, Michael H. *nuclear energy industry executive*
†Reitsema, Harold James *aerospace engineer*
Rich, Ben Arthur *lawyer, university official*
Rienner, Lynne Carol *publisher*
Robinson, Peter *paleontology educator, consultant*
Rodriguez, Juan Alfonso *technology corporation executive*
Rood, David S. *linguistics educator*
Sable, Barbara Kinsey *former music educator*
Sani, Robert LeRoy *chemical engineering educator*
Sarson, John Christopher *television producer, director, writer*
Schwarz, Josephine Lindeman *retired ballet company director, choreographer*
Serafin, Robert Joseph *science center administrator, electrical engineer*
Shanahan, Eugene Miles *flow measurement instrumentation company executive*
Sirotkin, Phillip Leonard *educational administrator*
Smith, Ernest Ketcham *electrical engineer*
Smythe, William Rodman *physicist, educator*
Snow, Theodore Peck *astrophysics educator*
Sodal, Ingvar Edmund *electrical engineer, scientist*
†Soll, Larry *pharmaceutical executive*
Speiser, Theodore Wesley *astrophysics, planetary and atmospheric sciences educator*
Staehelin, Lucas Andrew *cell biology educator*
Stanton, William John, Jr. *marketing educator, author*
Steuben, Norton Leslie *lawyer, educator*
Stull, Dean P. *chemical company executive*
Sullivan, Donald Barrett *physicist*
Symons, James Martin *theater and dance educator*
Tatarskii, Valerian Il'ich *physics researcher*
Taylor, Allan Ross *linguist, educator*
Thomas, Daniel Foley *telecommunications company executive*
†Thomas, Gary Edward *educator, researcher*
Timmerhaus, Klaus Dieter *chemical engineering educator*
Tippit, John Harlow *lawyer*
Tolbert, Bert Mills *biochemist, educator*
†Tolbert, Margaret A. *geochemistry educator*
Trenberth, Kevin Edward *atmospheric scientist*
Uberoi, Mahinder Singh *aerospace engineering educator*
Utlaut, William Frederick *electrical engineer*
†Van Vorous, Ted *manufacturing company executive*
Wahl, Floyd Michael *geologist*
Waldman, Anne Lesley *poet, performer, editor, publisher, educational administrator*
Walker, Deward Edgar, Jr. *anthropologist, educator*
Washington, Warren Morton *meteorologist*
Wheat, Joe Ben *anthropologist*
White, Gilbert F(owler) *geographer, educator*
Wieman, Carl E. *physics educator*
Williams, James Franklin, II *university dean, librarian*

Brighton
Vang, Timothy Teng *church executive*

Broomfield
Davis, Delmont Alvin, Jr. *manufacturing company executive*
Haas, John Allen *manufacturing company executive*
Rodriguez, Linda Takahashi *secondary education educator*

Brush
Cumberlin, Charles Edgar *auctioneer*

Canon City
Bendell, Donald Ray *writer, director, poet*
Mc Bride, John Alexander *retired chemical engineer*

Carbondale
Cowgill, Ursula Moser *biologist, educator, environmental consultant*

Castle Rock
Eppler, Jerome Cannon *private financial advisor*
Graf, Joseph Charles *retired foundation executive*
Thornbury, John Rousseau *radiologist, physician*

Cherry Hills Village
Meyer, Milton Edward, Jr. *lawyer, artist*

Cheyenne Mountain AFB
†Dekok, Roger G. air force officer
Horner, Charles Albert air force officer

Clark
Bartoe, Otto Edwin, Jr. aircraft company executive

Colorado Springs
Adams, Bernard Schroder retired college president
Allen, J. Lamar engineering company executive, educator
Allery, Kenneth Edward air force officer
Anderson, Lawrence Keith electrical engineer
Anderson, N. Christian, III newspaper publisher
Anderson, Paul Nathaniel oncologist, educator
Armstrong, Lance professional cyclist
Austin, Timothy Olympic athlete, boxer
Barrowman, Mike Olympic athlete, swimmer
Barry, William Patrick military officer
Barton, Gregory Mark Olympic athlete, kayak racer
Bates, Michael Olympic athlete, track and field
Biondi, Matt Olympic athlete, swimmer
Bishop, Leo Kenneth clergyman, educator
Blanchette, Jeanne Ellene Maxant artist, educator, performer
Bowen, Clotilde Dent retired army officer, psychiatrist
Breckner, William John, Jr. retired air force officer, corporate executive, consultant
Brooks, Glenn Ellis political science educator, educational administrator
Bubna, Paul F. church administrator
Budington, William Stone retired librarian
Buell, Bruce Temple lawyer
Burgess, Greg Olympic athlete, swimming
Burnley, Kenneth S. school system administrator
Byrd, Chris Olympic athlete, boxer
†Cameron, Paul Drummond research facility administrator
Christensen, Thomas Michael surface physicist
Cole, Julian Wayne (Perry Cole) computer educator, consultant, programmer, analyst
Conley, Mike track and field athlete
Conter, Thomas Michael publisher
Couger, James Daniel computer scientist, writer
Cramer, Owen Carver classics educator
Cray, Seymour R. computer designer
†Dassanowsky-Harris, Robert von writer, editor, educator
Davey, J. A. church administrator
Dees, Tony Olympic athlete, track and field
Dello Joio, Norman Olympic athlete, equestrian
Devers, Gail track and field athlete
Diebel, Nelson Olympic athlete, swimmer
Dimas, Trent Olympic athlete, gymnast
Doehrin, James Olympic athlete, track and field
Ehrhorn, Richard William electronics company executive
†Eisner, William lawyer
Eldredge, Todd figure skater
Engfer, Susan Marvel zoological park executive
Essick, Raymond Brooke, III amateur sports administrator
Faber, Michael Warren lawyer
Farr, Leonard Alfred hospital administrator
Feld, Werner Joachim political scientist, educator
†Flemke, Karl economic education association executive
Flynn, James T. lawyer
Forgan, David Waller retired air force officer
Foth, Bob Olympic athlete, riflery
Fowler, John Dale association executive
Fox, Douglas Allan religion educator
†Fox, James Joseph sports executive
Fujimura, Robert Kiyoshi executive director
Gillaspie, Richard C. banker
Goehring, Kenneth artist
Gray, Johnny Olympic athlete, track and field
Greene, Joe Olympic athlete, track and field
Groebli, Werner Fritz (Mr. Frick) professional ice skater, realtor
Guthrie, David Neal marketing executive
Hallenbeck, Kenneth Luster numismatist
Halling, Leonard William retired pathologist, laboratory administrator
†Hamilton, James Milton veterinarian
Hampton, Rex Herbert gold mining company executive, consultant
Hanifen, Richard Charles bishop
Hartwell, Erin Olympic athlete, cycling
Henrickson, Eiler Leonard geologist, educator
Hill, Roger Wendell sugar company executive
Hoffman, John Raleigh physicist
Hoge, Robert Wilson museum curator
Isaac, Robert Michael mayor, lawyer
Jacobi, Joe Olympic athlete, canoeist
Jager, Tom Olympic athlete, swimmer
Johnson, Dave Olympic athlete, track and field
Kelsey, Floyd Lamar, Jr. architect
Kendall, Phillip Alan lawyer
Kerrigan, Nancy professional figure skater, former Olympic athlete
Killian, George Ernest association executive
King, Peter Joseph, Jr. retired gas company executive
Kohlman, David Leslie engineering executive, consultant
LeMieux, Linda Dailey museum director
Lenzi, Mark Olympic athlete, springboard diver
Leuver, Robert Joseph former government official, association executive
Lewis, Steve Olympic athlete, track and field
Libby, Lauren Dean foundation president
†Loux, Gordon Dale organization executive
Macon, Jerry Lyn software company owner, software publisher
Mangham, R. H. church administrator
Margolis, Bernard Allen library administrator, antique book merchant and appraiser
Markert, Clement Lawrence biology educator
Marsh, Michael track and field athlete
May, Melvin Arthur computer software company executive
McIntyre, Elizabeth Geary Olympic athlete
Meagher, Thomas Francis Vincent research and development company executive
Metzler, Philip Lowry, Jr. air force officer
Midkiff, Donald Wayne program manager
Milton, Richard Henry retired diplomat
Mitchell, Dennis A. Olympic athlete, track and field
Mitchell, John Henderson retired army officer, management consultant
Mohrman, Kathryn academic administrator
Morales, Pablo Olympic athlete, swimmer
Morris, Jason Olympic athlete
Moses, Edwin former track and field athlete
Munro, Michael Donald entertainment and hospital consultant, professional voice talent
Murray, Ty (The Kid) professional rodeo cowboy
Nanfelt, P. N. church administrator
Nolan, Barry Hance publishing company executive
Noyes, Richard Hall bookseller
Olin, Kent Oliver banker
O'Rourke, Dennis lawyer
O'Shields, Richard Lee retired natural gas company executive
Payne, Billy (William A. Payne) real estate lawyer, sports association executive
Perkins, Floyd Jerry theology educator
Peterson, Amy Olympic athlete
Phibbs, Harry Albert interior designer, professional speaker, lecturer
Pierce, Jack Olympic athlete, track and field
†Rambo, David L. religious organization administrator
Robinson, Robert James retired manufacturing executive
Robinson, Ronald Alan oil company executive
Rochette, Edward Charles retired association executive
Rooney, Margaret Elaine nurse, educator
Rouse, Jeff Olympic athlete, swimmer
Rouss, Ruth lawyer
Sawyer, Thomas William air force officer
Schaeffer, Reiner Horst air force officer, retired librarian, foreign language professional
†Schauer, Ralph Floyd microelectronics company executive
Schwartz, Donald chemistry educator
Shafer, Dallas Eugene psychology gerontology educator, minister
Shaffer, Carolyn Lee (Cari Shaffer) staffing service executive
Shepard, Mikki Maureen Allison personal care company executive
Simmons, George Finlay mathematics educator
Simpkins, Charles Olympic athlete, track and field
Sinclair, William Donald church official, fundraising consultant, political activist
Stavig, Mark Luther English language educator
Stewart, Melvin Olympic athlete, swimmer
Stewart, Robert Lee retired army officer, astronaut
Strausbaugh, Scott David Olympic athlete, canoeist
Street, Picabo Olympic athlete
Stulce, Mike Olympic athlete, track and field
Tanous, Michael Allan consulting company executive
Thomas, Darrell Denman lawyer
Todd, Harold Wade retired air force officer, consultant
Turner, Cathy Olympic athlete
Vayhinger, John Monroe psychotherapist, minister
†Walker, LeRoy Olympic official
Waples, Eric Snowden headmaster
Warner, Michael D. museum director
Watts, Oliver Edward engineering consultancy company executive
Wells, Jeffrey M. state senator, lawyer, judge
West, Ralph Leland veterinarian
Wheeland, D. A. church administrator
Whitney, Jonathan Robert gas company executive
Wilcox, Rhoda Davis elementary education educator
Wilkins, Christopher Putnam conductor
Wood, Stephen minister
Worner, Lloyd Edson retired college president
Yaffe, James author
Yamaguchi, Kristi Tsuya ice skater
Young, Kevin track and field athlete
Zapel, Arthur L. book publishing executive
Ziemer, Rodger Edmund electrical engineering educator, consultant

Columbine Valley
Wittbrodt, Edwin Stanley consultant, former bank executive, former air force officer

Conifer
Powers, Edwin Malvin consulting engineer

Crawford
Mosher, Lawrence Forsyth journalist

Denver
Abo, Ronald Kent architect
Abram, Donald Eugene federal magistrate judge
Adkins, Jeanne M. state legislator
Adler, Charles Spencer psychiatrist
Aikawa, Jerry Kazuo physician, educator
Albrecht, Duane Taylor veterinarian
Alfers, Stephen Douglas lawyer
Allen, Deborah Colleen state legislator
Alsop, Marin conductor
Ames, A. Gary communications company executive
†Anderson, Donald H. gas industry executive
Anderson, John David architect
Antonoff, Gary L. real estate executive
Antonoff, Steven Ross educational consultant, author
Ashton, Rick James librarian
Atkins, Dale Morrell physician
Austin, H(arry) Gregory lawyer
Avrit, Richard Calvin defense consultant
Babcock, Lewis Thornton federal judge
Bain, Donald Knight lawyer
Ballhaus, William Francis, Jr. aerospace industry executive, research scientist
Bard, Richard H. financial service company executive
†Barger, Louise Baldwin religious organization administrator
Barkin, Roger Michael pediatrician, emergency physician, educator
Barnewall, Gordon Gouverneur news analyst, educator
Barry, Henry Ford chemical company executive
Bates, James Robert newspaper editor
Battaglia, Frederick Camillo physician
Bauder, Sister Marianna hospital administrator
Baylor, Don Edward professional baseball manager
Bearden, Thomas Howard news program producer, correspondent
Beckman, Sister Patricia school system administrator
Behrendt, John Charles research geophysicist
Belitz, Paul Edward lawyer
Benson, Robert Eugene lawyer
Benson, Thomas Quentin lawyer
Benton, Auburn Edgar lawyer
Beresford, Thomas Patrick psychiatry educator, alcoholism researcher
Berg, Karl A. architectural firm executive
Berger, John Milton state agency administrator
Berger, William Merriam Bart finance company executive
Berland, Karen Ina psychologist
Bermant, George Wilson lawyer
Berry, Charles Eugene (Chuck Berry) state legislator
Bickerstaff, Bernard Tyrone, Sr. (Bernie) professional basketball team executive
Bishop, Tilman Malcolm state senator, retired college administrator
Blager, Florence Berman voice pathology educator
Blair, Andrew Lane, Jr. lawyer, educator
Blatter, Frank Edward travel agency executive
†Bloor, John Holt gastroenterologist, educator
Blunk, Forrest Stewart lawyer
Bomberg, Thomas James dental educator
Boudreau, Robert Donald meteorology educator
Boulware, Richard Stark airport administrator
Bowman, Joseph Searles petroleum consultant
Bracken, Gary K. controller
Bradley, Jeff(rey) M. arts critic
Brainard, Edward Axdal academic administrator
Breck, Allen du Pont historian, educator
Brega, Charles Franklin lawyer
†Breitenbach, Eugene Allen oil company executive
Brimhall, Dennis C. hospital executive
Brom, Libor journalist, educator
Brown, Keith Lapham retired ambassador
†Browne, Spencer I. construction sales and financing executive
Brownlee, Judith Marilyn Wiccan minister, psychotherapist
Brownson, Jacques Calmon architect
Brumbaugh, Roland John federal judge
†Buckley, Vikki state official
Buechner, John C. academic administrator
Bunn, Paul A., Jr. oncologist, educator
Burford, Anne McGill lawyer
Burgess, Larry Lee aerospace executive
Burke, Kenneth John lawyer
Burrell, Calvin Archie minister
†Bury, Thomas L. construction executive
Butler, David lawyer
Butler, Owen Bradford securities advisor
Bye, James Edward lawyer
Cain, Douglas Mylchreest lawyer
Callender, Jonathan Ferris environmental consultant
Callihan, C. Michael lieutenant governor, former state senator
Campbell, Leonard Martin lawyer
Cann, William Hopson former mining company executive
Cantwell, William Patterson lawyer
Carr, James Francis lawyer
Carrigan, Jim Richard federal judge
Carver, Craig R. lawyer
Cassidy, Samuel H. lawyer, lieutenant governor, state legislator
Ceci, Jesse Arthur violinist
†Chandler, Thomas Franklin food products executive
Chapman, Karen Louise lawyer
Chappell, Willard Ray physics educator, environmental scientist
†Chase, H. Peter medical educator
Cheroutes, Michael Louis lawyer
Chidester, Alfred C. lawyer
Chinn, Peggy Lois nursing educator, editor
Chmelir, John David engineer, consultant
Clark, Drew secondary education educator, state legislator
Clark, Patricia Ann federal judge
Clarke, David Marshall academic administrator, priest
†Clayton, Mack Louis surgery professor, educator
Clinch, Nicholas Bayard, III business executive
Clough, Nadine Doerr school psychologist, psychotherapist
Cole, David Rodney mining executive
Collins, Martha Traudt lawyer
Collins, Susan Margaret archaeologist
Conger, John Janeway psychologist, educator
Conover, Frederic King lawyer
Conroy, Thomas Francis insurance company executive
Cook, Albert Thomas Thornton, Jr. financial advisor
Cooper, Paul Douglas lawyer
Coover-Clark, Carol architect
Cope, Thomas Field lawyer
Cordova, Donald E. lawyer
Cowley, Gerald Dean architect
Cox, William Vaughan lawyer
Craine, Thomas Knowlton academic administrator
Crawford, Richard A., Jr. corporate executive
Cubbison, Christopher Allen editor
†Curnow, Richard D. biologist, research ecologist
Curtis, George Bartlett lawyer
†Cutter, Gary Raymond biostatistician, epidemiologist
Daley, Richard Halbert foundation executive
Dallas, Sandra correspondent, writer
Dana, Richard E. oil industry executive
Danos, Robert McClure retired oil company executive
Darkey, Kermit Louis association executive, lawyer
Dauer, Edward Arnold law educator
Davis, Joseph Samuel retired department store executive, consultant
Davis, Marvin petroleum company executive, entrepreneur
Dean, James Benwell lawyer
Decker, David B. architect, educator
Deering, Fred Arthur insurance company executive
De Gette, Diana Louise lawyer, state legislator
Deitrich, Richard Adam pharmacology educator
DeLong, James Clifford air transportation executive
†Dempsey, Edward Charles thoracic surgeon
Dempsey, Howard Stanley lawyer, mining executive, investment banker
†Dennis, Evie school system administrator
DePew, Marie Kathryn retired secondary educator
Devine, Sharon Jean lawyer
DiGiorgio, Robert Michael dentist
Dobbs, Gregory Allan journalist
Doida, Stanley Y. dentist
Dolsen, David Horton mortician
Dominick, Peter Hoyt, Jr. architect
Doran, Maureen O'Keefe psychotherapist, psychiatric nursing consultant
Dougherty, Larry W. headmaster
Downey, Arthur Harold, Jr. lawyer
†Downing, Sybil S. state agency administrator
Drake, Sylvie (Jurras Drake) theater critic
Dubroff, Henry Allen journalist
Ducker, Bruce novelist, lawyer
Dunham, Stephen Sampson lawyer
†East, Donald Robert civil engineer
Eaton, Gareth Richard chemistry educator, university dean
Ebel, David M. federal judge
Edwards, Phyllis Mae accountant, graphologist
Eiberger, Carl Frederick trial lawyer
Eickhoff, Theodore Carl physician
Eklund, Carl Andrew lawyer
Engdahl, Todd Philip newspaper editor
Erickson, William Hurt state supreme court justice
Erisman, Frank lawyer
Espenoza, Cecelia M. law educator
Evans, Ginger Sunday civil engineer
Faatz, Jeanne Ryan state legislator
Fagin, David Kyle natural resource company executive
Fancher, George H., Jr. oil company executive, petroleum engineer
Farley, John Michael lawyer
Faxon, Thomas Baker lawyer
Featherstone, Bruce Alan lawyer
Feder, Harold Abram lawyer
Ferguson, Lloyd Elbert manufacturing engineer
Fernandez, Tomas Isidro accountant
Finesilver, Sherman Glenn federal judge
Firminger, Harlan Irwin pathologist, educator
Fischer, James Adrian clergyman
Fiske, Terry Noble lawyer
Flowers, William Harold, Jr. lawyer
Fognani, John Dennis lawyer
Foxley, Matthew C. art gallery administrator
Foxley, William Coleman cattleman
Frederickson, Charles Richard restaurant executive
Fredmann, Martin artistic director ballet, educator, choreographer
Freiheit, Clayton Fredric zoo director
Friedman, H. Harold cardiologist, internist
Fulginiti, Vincent university dean
Fulkerson, William Measey, Jr. college president
Fuller, Kenneth Roller architect
Galarraga, Andres Jose professional baseball player
Gallagher, Dennis Joseph state senator, educator
Gates, Charles Cassius rubber company executive
Gebhard, Bob professional baseball team executive
Gibson, Thomas Joseph diversified holding company executive
Giesen, John William advertising executive
Giffin, Glenn Orlando, II music critic, writer, newspaper editor
Gillis, Paul Leonard accountant
Gilman, Carol Elizabeth lawyer
Golitz, Loren Eugene dermatologist, pathologist, clinical administrator, educator
Graham, Linda Marie museum director, photographer
Grant, Patrick Alexander lawyer, former state legislator
Grant, William West, III banker
Green, Charles Walter newspaper editor
Green, Jersey Michael-Lee lawyer
Green, Larry Alton physician, educator
Green, Steven J. retail executive
Greenberg, David Ethan communications consultant
Greene, Leslie Speed lawyer
†Greenspahn, Barbara dean, law educator, librarian
Grissom, Garth Clyde lawyer
Groff, JoAnn organization administrator
Gutterman, Sheila Maydet lawyer
Haddon, Timothy John mining engineer
Halgren, Lee A. academic administrator
Hamblin, Kenneth Lorenzo radio talk show host, columnist
Hamilton, Warren Bell research geologist, educator
Hamilton, William T. English educator, former academic administrator
Hardy, Wayne Russell insurance broker
Harhai, Stephen John lawyer
Harris, Dale Ray lawyer
Harris, Ellen Gandy (Mrs. J. Ramsay Harris) civic worker
Harry, Robert Hayden lawyer
Hartley, James Edward lawyer
Hartman, Emily Lou botanist, educator, researcher
†Hatami, Marvin architect, educator, urban designer
Havekost, Daniel John architect
Hawley, Robert Cross lawyer
Hayes, Edward Lee religious organization administrator
Hendrix, Lynn Parker lawyer
Herz, Leonard financial consultant
Hesse, Stephen Max newspaper executive
Hetzel, Fredrick William biophysicist, educator
Hill, Diane Seldon corporate psychologist
†Hinkle, Betty Ruth educational administator
Hirschfeld, Arlene F. civic worker, homemaker
Hixon, Janet Kay Erickson education specialist
Hoagland, Donald Wright lawyer
Hobson, Harry Lee, Jr. lawyer
†Hock, Delwin D. utilities company executive
Hodges, Joseph Gilluly, Jr. lawyer
Hoffman, Daniel Steven lawyer, legal educator
Hogan, Curtis Jule union executive, industrial relations consultant
Holleman, Paul Douglas lawyer
Holme, Richard Phillips lawyer
Holmes, Fred Gillespie sugar company executive
Holte, Debra Leah investment executive, financial analyst
Hoover, George Schweke architect
Hopfenbeck, George Martin, Jr. lawyer
Hopkins, Donald J. lawyer
Horn, Gilbert minister
Hornbein, Victor architect
Horwitz, Kathryn Bloch molecular biologist
Howlett, John David urban planner, consultant
Hubbard, Kenneth Dean lawyer
Hunt, Donald F. newspaper publishing executive
Husband, John Michael lawyer
Imhoff, Walter Francis investment banker
Iona, Mario retired physics educator
Irvin, Robert D. lawyer
Iseman, Michael Dee medical educator
Jackson, Richard Brooke lawyer
Jacobs, Paul Alan lawyer
Jacobson, Eugene Donald educator, administrator, researcher
Jafek, Bruce William otolaryngologist, educator
Jensen, Peter L. accounting company executive
Johnston, Calvin George secondary education educator
Johnston, Gwinavere Adams public relations consultant
Jones, Richard Michael lawyer
Kauvar, Abraham J. gastroenterologist, medical administrator
Keats, Donald Howard composer, educator
Keely, George Clayton lawyer
Keller, Glen Elven, Jr. lawyer
Keppler, Peter lawyer
Kern, Fred, Jr. physician, educator
†Kikumoto, Charles David health insurance marketing executive
Kintzele, John Alfred lawyer
Kirgis, Frederic L. retired lawyer

Kirkpatrick, Charles Harvey *physician, immunology researcher*
Kirshbaum, Howard M. *judge*
Krane, Robert Alan *banker*
Krikos, George Alexander *pathologist, educator*
Krill, Arthur Melvin *engineering, architectural and planning company executive*
Laff, Seymour *health care executive*
LaRoche, Gloria Rosemarie *pilot*
Larsen, Gary Loy *physician, researcher*
Larson, Dayl Andrew *architect*
Law, John Manning *retired lawyer*
Lawless, Sarah Madison *theatrical executive*
†Lazarus, Steven S. *management consultant, marketing consultant*
Leather, Richard Brenk *mineral company executive*
Lee, Richard Kenneth *building products company executive*
Leiweke, Timothy *sales executive, marketing professional*
Leprino, James G. *food products executive*
Lesher, Donald Miles *lawyer*
Levy, Mark Ray *lawyer*
Lewis, Jerome A. *petroleum company executive, investment banker*
Lilly, John Russell *surgeon, educator*
Liu, Chaoqun *staff scientist*
Livingston, Johnston R. *manufacturing executive*
Lochmiller, Kurtis L. *real estate entrepreneur*
Lockwood, Barbara Jordan *nurse administrator*
Loeup, Kong *counselor*
Lohr, George E. *state supreme court justice*
†Longwell, John Dorney *petroleum engineer*
Low, John Wayland *lawyer*
Lubeck, Marvin Jay *ophthalmologist*
Lutz, John Shafroth *lawyer*
Lyle, Glenda Swanson *state legislator*
Macey, William Blackmore *oil company executive*
MacGregor, George Lescher, Jr. *freelance writer*
Magness, Bob John *telecommunications executive*
Makowski, Edgar Leonard *obstetrician and gynecologist*
Malone, Robert Joseph *bank executive*
†Mandarich, David D. *real estate corporation executive*
Mandelson, Richard S. *lawyer*
†Marcum, Walter Phillip *investment banker*
Markman, Howard J. *psychology educator*
Martin, James Russell *lawyer*
Martin, Richard Jay *medical educator*
Martin, William Truett *oral surgeon, state legislature*
Martz, Clyde Ollen *lawyer, educator*
Mason, Ronald Leonard *architect*
Matsch, Richard P. *federal judge*
Mauro, Richard Frank *lawyer, investment manager*
Maxfield, Thomas H. *lawyer*
May, Clifford Daniel *newspaper editor, journalist*
May, Francis Hart, Jr. *retired building materials manufacturing executive*
McAtee, Patricia Anne Rooney *medical educator*
Mc Candless, Bruce, II *engineer, former astronaut*
Mc Clenney, Byron Nelson *community college administrator*
McCoy, James Henry *oil company executive*
McGowan, Joseph Anthony, Jr. *news executive*
McGraw, Jack Wilson *government official*
McKibben, Ryan Timothy *newspaper executive*
Mc Kinney, Alexis *public relations consultant*
McWilliams, Robert Hugh *federal judge*
Mead, Beverly Mirium Anderson *writer, educator*
Mehring, Clinton Warren *engineering executive*
Meiklejohn, Alvin J., Jr. *state senator, lawyer, accountant*
Mendelsohn, Harold *sociologist, educator*
Merker, Steven Joseph *lawyer*
Messer, Donald Edward *theological school president*
Miller, Arlyn James *oil company executive*
Miller, Donald E. *rubber company executive*
Miller, Gale Timothy *lawyer*
Miller, Robert Nolen *lawyer*
Miller, Sarah Pearl *librarian*
Miller, Stanley Custer, Jr. *physicist, retired educator*
Misbrener, Joseph Michael *labor union official*
†Mizel, Larry A. *housing construction company executive*
Moore, Ernest Eugene, Jr. *surgeon, educator*
Moore, George Eugene *surgeon*
Moore, John Porfilio *federal judge*
†Moore, Ronald L. *bank executive*
Moorhead, John B. *lawyer*
Morgese, James N. *broadcast executive*
Morrison, Marcy *state legislator*
Movshovitz, Howard Paul *film critic, educator*
Moye, John Edward *lawyer*
Muldoon, Brian *lawyer*
Mullarkey, Mary J. *state supreme court justice*
Muller, Nicholas Guthrie *lawyer, business executive*
Mullineaux, Donal Ray *geologist*
Murane, William Edward *lawyer*
Murdy, Wayne William *mining company executive, financial officer*
Murret, Eugene John, Sr. *judicial administrator*
Musgraves, Robert E. *lawyer*
Musyl, Marc J. *lawyer*
Mutombo, DiKembe (Dikembe Mutombo Mpolondo Mukamba Jean Jacque Wamutombo) *professional basketball player*
Nakakuki, Masafumi *physician, psychiatry educator*
Nanda, Ved Prakash *law educator, university official*
Nash, Stella B. *government nutrition administrator*
Nelson, Bernard William *foundation executive, educator, physician*
Nelson, Nancy Eleanor *pediatrician, educator*
Nelson, Sarah Milledge *archaeology educator*
Neu, Carl Herbert, Jr. *management consultant*
Neumann, Herschel *physics educator*
Neville, Margaret Cobb *physiologist, educator*
Newton, James Quigg, Jr. *lawyer*
Nicholson, Will Faust, Jr. *bank holding company executive*
†Nields, Morgan Wesson *medical supply company executive*
Norman, John Barstow, Jr. *designer, educator*
North, Phillip J. *lawyer*
Norton, Gale A. *state attorney general*
Norton, Thomas Edmond *state senator, engineer*
Notari, Paul Celestin *communications executive*
Nottingham, Edward Willis, Jr. *federal judge*
†Novins, Douglas K. *psychiatrist, educator*
O'Keefe, Edward Franklin *lawyer*
Otten, Arthur Edward, Jr. *lawyer, corporate executive*
Otto, Jean Hammond *journalist*
Owen, James Churchill, Jr. *lawyer*
Owens, Marvin Franklin, Jr. *oil company executive*
Pakiser, Louis Charles, Jr. *geophysicist*
Palmer, David Gilbert *lawyer*
Palmreuter, Kenneth Richard Louis *principal*
Parker, Catherine Susanne *psychotherapist*
Peck, Neil *lawyer*
Perez, Jean-Yves *engineering company executive*
Petros, Raymond Louis, Jr. *lawyer*
Petty, Thomas Lee *physician, educator*
Pfenninger, Karl H. *cell biology and neuroscience educator*
Pfnister, Allan Orel *humanities educator*
Philip, Thomas Peter *mining executive*
†Phillips, Kay Randelle *association executive*
Phillips, Paul David, Jr. *lawyer*
Poirot, James Wesley *engineering company executive*
Pollard, William Sherman, Jr. *civil engineer, educator*
†Pomerantz, Marvin *thoracic surgeon*
†Post, Richard *real estate company executive*
Poulson, Robert Dean *lawyer*
Poynter, James Morrison *travel educator, travel company executive*
Pringle, Bruce D. *federal magistrate*
Pringle, Edward E. *legal educator, former state supreme court chief justice*
Prochnow, James R. *lawyer*
Prosser, John Martin *architect, educator, urban design consultant*
Puck, Theodore Thomas *geneticist, biophysicist, educator*
Purcell, Kenneth *psychology educator, university dean*
Purdy, Sherry Marie *lawyer*
Quail, Beverly J. *lawyer*
Quiat, Gerald M. *lawyer*
Rael, Henry Sylvester *health administrator*
Rainer, William Gerald *cardiac surgeon*
Ramon, David A. *consumer products company executive*
Ramsey, John Arthur *lawyer*
Randall, William Theodore *state official*
Rawls, Eugenia *actress*
Ray, Bruce David *lawyer*
Reisinger, George Lambert *management consultant*
Rendu, Jean-Michel Marie *mining executive*
Repine, John E. *internist, educator*
Reynolds, Collins James, III *association administrator*
Rich, Robert Stephen *lawyer*
†Riess, J. M. *gas and oil industry executive*
Ris, William Krakow *lawyer*
Ritchie, Daniel Lee *university administrator*
Roberts, Neil Fletcher *management consulting company executive*
Robinson, Carole Ann *insurance executive, retired*
Rockwell, Bruce McKee *retired banker, retired foundation executive*
Romer, Roy R. *governor*
Roslund, Carol L. *lawyer*
Rovira, Luis Dario *state supreme court justice*
Rubright, Royal Cushing *lawyer*
Ruge, Daniel August *retired neurosurgeon, educator*
Rule, Daniel Rhodes *opera company executive*
Ruppert, John Lawrence *lawyer*
Rutherford, Robert Barry *surgeon*
Sanders-Childears, Linda *banker*
Sandler, Thomas R. *accountant*
Sasso, Cassandra Gay *lawyer*
Savitz, David Barry *lawyer*
†Sawicki, Thomas *health care company executive*
Sayre, John Marshall *lawyer, former government official*
Schaffer, Robert Warren *state senator*
Schanfield, Moses Samuel *geneticist, educator*
Scherer, Ronald Callaway *voice scientist, educator*
Schertz, Morris *library director*
Schiff, Donald Wilfred *pediatrician, educator*
Schneck, Stuart Austin *neurologist, educator*
Schotters, Bernard William *communications company executive*
Schulzetenberg, John Martin *finance company executive, accountant*
Schwartz, Cherie Anne Karo *storyteller*
Seawell, Donald Ray *lawyer, publisher, arts center executive, producer*
Selbin, Joel *chemistry educator*
†Shaw, Ward Eric *information company executive*
Shea, Kevin Michael *lawyer*
Shearer, Cynthia Hodge *lawyer*
Sheeran, Michael John Leo *priest, educational administrator*
Shepherd, John Frederic *lawyer*
Shore, James H(enry) *psychiatrist*
Shulkin, Jerome Robert *insurance brokerage executive*
Silburn, Elaine Gwendolyn *banker*
Silverman, Arnold *physician*
Simons, Lynn Osborn *state education official*
Skaer, Laura Elizabeth *lawyer*
†Smith, Derrin Ray *information systems company executive*
Smith, Dwight Morrell *chemistry educator*
†Smith, Rita Sue *administrator*
Snyder, Stephen Edward *lawyer*
Sondheimer, Judith M. *pediatrician, educator*
†Sparkman, Cathryn *health facility administrator, lawyer*
Sparr, Daniel Beattie *federal judge*
Spencer, Frederick Gilman *newspaper editor in chief*
Spencer, Margaret Gilliam *lawyer*
Stafford, J. Francis *archbishop*
Steenhagen, Robert Lewis *landscape architect, consultant*
Stephens, Phillip *screenwriter, producer*
Stephens, William Thomas *forest products manufacturing company executive*
Stephenson, Arthur Emmet, Jr. *investment company executive, banker*
Stephenson, Toni Edwards *publisher, investment management executive*
Stockmar, Ted P. *lawyer*
Storey, Brit Allan *historian*
Strutton, Larry D. *newspaper executive*
Sudler, Barbara Welch *retired historical society administrator*
Sullivan, Claire Ferguson *marketing educator*
Sullivan, Mary Rose *English educator*
Sutton, Raymond L., Jr. *lawyer*
Sutton, Robert Edward *investment company executive*
Swenka, Arthur John *food products executive*
Swenson, Mary Ann *bishop*
Swift, William Charles *professional baseball player, olympic athlete*
Szefler, Stanley James *pediatrics and pharmacology educator*
Talmage, David Wilson *microbiology and medical educator, physician, former university administrator*
Tanner, Gloria Geraldine *state legislator*
Taylor, Edward Stewart *physician, educator*
Taylor-Little, Carol J(oyce) *legislator*
Teets, Peter B. *aerospace executive*
Terry, Ward Edgar, Jr. *lawyer*
Thomasch, Roger Paul *lawyer*
Thompson, Lohren Matthew *oil company executive*
Timothy, Robert Keller *telephone company executive*
Tipton, John J. *lawyer*
Todd, Donald Frederick *geologist*
Tomlinson, Warren Leon *lawyer*
Tormey, Douglass Cole *medical oncologist*
Tracey, Jay Walter, Jr. *retired lawyer*
Troy, Richard Hershey *lawyer*
Trueblood, Harry Albert, Jr. *oil company executive*
Udevitz, Norman *publishing executive*
Ulevich, Neal Hirsh *photojournalist*
Ulrich, Theodore Albert *lawyer*
Valot, Daniel L. *oil industry executive*
†Vela, David *lawyer*
Vigil, Charles S. *lawyer*
Wagner, Judith Buck *investment firm executive*
Walker, Timothy Blake *lawyer, educator*
Wallace, Victor L., II *lawyer*
†Waller, Frank S. *engineering company executive*
Washington, Reginald Louis *pediatric cardiologist*
Watson, William D. *lawyer*
†Weatherley-White, Roy Christopher Anthony *surgeon, consultant*
Webb, Wellington E. *mayor*
Weihaupt, John George *geosciences educator, scientist, university administrator*
Weil, Jack Baum *clothing manufacturing company executive*
†Weiman, Stephen L. *investment company executive*
Weinshienk, Zita Leeson *federal judge*
Weissenbuehler, Wayne *bishop*
Welch, Carol Mae *lawyer*
Weston, William Lee *dermatologist*
Wham, Dorothy Stonecipher *state legislator*
Wheeler, Malcolm Edward *lawyer, law educator*
Wiggs, Eugene Overbey *ophthalmologist, educator*
Williams, Michael Anthony *lawyer*
Williams, Wayne De Armond *lawyer*
Winterrond, William J. *bishop*
Wirkler, Norman Edward *architectural, engineering, construction management firm executive*
Wohlgenant, Richard Glen *lawyer*
Woodward, Lester Ray *lawyer*
Wunnicke, Brooke *lawyer*
Wynkoop, Donal Brooke *electric power company executive*
Yamamoto, Kaoru *psychology, education educator*
Yegge, Robert Bernard *lawyer, college dean emeritus, educator*
Zakhem, Sam Hanna *diplomat*
Zaranka, William F. *academic administrator, author*
Zeilig, Nancy Meeks *magazine editor*
Zimet, Carl Norman *psychologist, educator*
Zook, Kay Marie *nursing administrator*

Dillon
Follett, Robert John Richard *publisher*

Dolores
Kreyche, Gerald Francis *retired philosophy educator*

Durango
Ballantine, Morley Cowles (Mrs. Arthur Atwood Ballantine) *newspaper editor*
Burnham, Bryson Paine *retired lawyer*
Jones, Joel Mackey *college president*
Moore, John George, Jr. *medical educator*
Spencer, Donald Clayton *mathematician*
Steinhoff, Harold William *retired research institute executive*

Eagle
Sullivan, Selby William *lawyer, business executive*

Englewood
†Aguirre, Vukoslav Eneas *soils engineer*
Anderson, James Thomas *telecommunications executive*
†Arenberg, Irving Kaufman *ear surgeon, educator*
Arrington, Steve *oil company executive*
Atwater, Stephen Dennis *professional football player*
Barr, Kenneth John *retired mining company executive*
Beake, John *professional football team executive*
Beddow, David Pierce *broadcasting and cable executive*
Blair, Stewart D. *small business owner*
Busse, Lu Ann *audiologist*
Chesser, Al H. *union official*
Claussen, Bonnie Addison, II *aerospace company executive*
Craw, Nicholas Wesson *motor sports association executive*
Crowley, John Robert *real estate development company executive*
DeMuth, Laurence Wheeler, Jr. *lawyer, utility company executive*
DiSalle, Michael Danny *secondary education educator*
Eccles, Matthew Alan *golf course and landscape architect*
Edelman, Joel *medical center executive*
Elway, John Albert *professional football player*
English, Gerald Marion *otolaryngologist*
Fisher, Bob *real estate broker, franchisor*
Fisher, Donne Francis *telecommunications executive*
France, John Lyons *air force officer*
Gimbel, Alfred Adolf *employee benefits professional*
Hagan, Thomas Patrick *advertising executive*
†Hall, Kurt *movie theatre executive*
Harding, W. M. *cooperative financial institution executive*
Hart, Gary W. *former senator, lawyer*
Karsh, Philip Howard *advertising executive*
Loughrey, Kevin *lawyer*
Mahoney, Gerald Francis *manufacturing company executive*
Malone, John C. *telecommunications executive*
Manley, Richard Walter *insurance executive*
Massey, Leon R. *association executive*
Mc Adams, Ronald Earl *geologist*
McBeth, Ruben Jose, Jr. *retired criminal justice administrator*
McCormick, Richard David *telecommunications company executive*
Milford, Peggy R. *communications executive*
Neiser, Brent Allen *public affairs consultant*
O'Bryan, William Hall *insurance executive*
†Osterhoff, James Marvin *telecommunications company executive*
Parker, Gordon Rae *natural resource company executive*
Pearlman, David Samuel *allergist*
Perry, Michael Dean *professional football player*
†Reese, Monte Nelson *agricultural association executive*
Reilly, Laura J. *lawyer*
Rosser, Edwin Michael *mortgage company executive*
Rounds, Donald Michael *public relations executive*
Russ, Charles Paul, III *lawyer, corporate executive*
†Schirmer, Howard August, Jr. *civil engineer*
Schneider, Gene W. *cable television company executive, movie theater executive*
Sharpe, Shannon *professional football player*
Shields, Marlene Sue *elementary school educator*
Sims, Doug *bank executive*
Tanaka, Floyd Hideo *consulting firm executive*
†Timbers, Michael James *information technology executive*
Van Loucks, Mark Louis *venture capitalist, business advisor*
†Vierra, Fred A. *communications executive*
Ward, Milton Hawkins *mining company executive*
†Ware, Roger B. *insurance company executive*
Wilson, James Ernest *geological consultant, writer*
Wynar, Bohdan Stephen *librarian, author, editor*

Estes Park
Hillway, Tyrus *author, educator*
Moore, Omar Khayyam *experimental sociologist*
Thompson, James Bruce *national park administrator*
Webb, Richard C. *engineering company executive*

Evergreen
Baxter, Millie McLean *business owner, educator*
Benson, Robert Slater *restaurant executive*
Gerou, Phillip Howard *architect*
Haun, John Daniel *petroleum geologist, educator*
Jackson, William Richard *entrepreneur*
Jesser, Roger Franklyn *former brewing company engineering executive, consultant*
Link, Peter Karl *geologist*
Newkirk, John Burt *metallurgical engineer, administrator*
Phillips, Adran Abner (Abe Phillips) *geologist, oil and gas exploration consultant*

Fort Collins
Allgower, Eugene Leo *mathematics educator*
Altman, Jack *plant pathologist, educator*
Anderson, B(enard) Harold *educational administrator*
Bamburg, James Robert *biochemistry educator*
Bennett, Thomas LeRoy, Jr. *clinical neuropsychology educator*
Bernstein, Elliot Roy *chemistry educator*
†Berry, Kenneth J. *sociology educator*
Boyd, Landis Lee *agricultural engineer, educator*
Burns, Denver P. *forestry research administrator*
Cermak, Jack Edward *engineer, educator*
Chambers, Joan Louise *dean of libraries*
Christiansen, Norman Juhl *retired newspaper publisher*
Collins, Royal Eugene *physicist, engineering consultant, former educator*
Cummings, Sharon Sue *state extension service youth specialist*
Curthoys, Norman P. *biochemistry educator, consultant*
Eberhart, Steve A. *federal agency administrator, research geneticist*
Eitzen, David Stanley *sociologist, educator*
Elkind, Mortimer Murray *biophysicist, educator*
Fields, Robert Charles *retired printing company executive*
Fixman, Marshall *chemist, educator*
Follett, Ronald Francis *soil scientist*
Frasier, Gary W. *hydraulic engineer*
Frink, Eugene Hudson, Jr. *business and real estate consultant*
Garvey, Daniel Cyril *mechanical engineer*
Gilderhus, Mark Theodore *historian, educator*
Gillette, Edward LeRoy *radiation oncology educator*
†Gray, William Mason *meteorologist, atmospheric science educator*
Gubler, Duane J. *research scientist, administrator*
Hafford, Patricia Ann *electronic company executive*
Hanan, Joe John *horticulture educator*
Harper, Judson Morse *university administrator, consultant, educator*
Hecker, Richard Jacob *research geneticist*
Heermann, Dale Frank *agricultural engineer*
Irvine, Kevin Thomas *secondary education educator*
Jaros, Dean *university official*
Johnson, Robert Britten *geology educator*
Kaufman, Harold Richard *mechanical engineer and physics educator*
Keim, Wayne Franklin *retired agronomy educator, plant geneticist*
Kennedy, George Alexander *classicist, educator*
Ladanyi, Branka Maria *chemist, educator*
†Landsea, Christopher W. *meteorologist, educator*
†Laughlin, Charles William *agriculture educator, research administrator*
†Lauri, John Peter *hospital administrator*
Maga, Joseph Andrew *food science educator*
McHugh, Helen Frances *university dean, home economist*
Medearis, Kenneth Gordon *engineering research consultant, educator*
Meyers, Albert Irving *chemistry educator*
Mielke, Paul William, Jr. *statistician*
Mortvedt, John Jacob *soil scientist*
Mosier, Arvin Ray *chemist, researcher*
Niehaus, Merle H. *agricultural educator, international agriculture consultant*
Niswender, Gordon Dean *physiologist, educator*
Ogg, James Elvis *microbiologist, educator*
Patton, Carl Elliott *physics educator*
Peterson, Gary Andrew *agronomics researcher*
Richardson, Everett Vern *hydraulic engineer, educator, administrator*
†Roberts, Archibald E. *nonprofit corporation executive*
†Roberts, Archibald Edward *retired army officer, author*
Rock, Kenneth Willett *history educator*
Rogers, Garth Winfield *lawyer*
Rollin, Bernard Elliot *philosophy educator, consultant on animal ethics*
Rolston, Holmes, III *theologian, educator, philosopher*
Roos, Eric Eugene *plant physiologist*
†Runnells, Donald DeMar *geochemist, consultant*
Saferite, Linda Lee *library director*
Sandborn, Virgil Alvin *civil engineer, educator*
Schumm, Stanley Alfred *geologist, educator*

Seidel, George Elias, Jr. animal scientist, educator
Smith, Dwight Raymond ecology and wildlife educator, writer
Smith, Ralph Earl virologist
Sons, Raymond William journalist
Standing Bear, Zugguelgeres Galafach criminologist, forensic scientist, educator
Stendell, Rey ecological research director
Suinn, Richard Michael psychologist
Tweedie, Richard Lewis statistics educator, consultant
Voss, James Leo veterinarian
Walsh, Richard George agricultural economist
Wengert, Norman Irving political science educator
Wilber, Charles Grady forensic science educator, consultant
Woolhiser, David Arthur hydraulic engineer
Yates, Albert Carl university administrator, chemistry educator

Fort Morgan
Bond, Richard Randolph college administrator, legislator
Perdue, James Everett university vice chancellor emeritus

Fowler
Fox, Maxine Randall banker

Frisco
Bybee, Rodger Wayne science education administrator

Georgetown
Stern, Mort(imer) P(hillip) journalism and communications educator, academic administrator, consultant

Golden
Ansell, George Stephen metallurgical engineering educator, academic administrator
Babb, Alvin Charles beverage company executive
Baron, Robert Charles publishing executive
Baumgart, Norbert K. retired government official
Coors, Jeffrey H. technology manufacturing executive
Coors, William K. brewery executive
Danzberger, Alexander Harris chemical engineer, consultant
Deere, Cyril Thomas retired computer company executive
Eaton, Mark Rayner financial executive
Eckley, Wilton Earl, Jr. humanities educator
Grose, Thomas Lucius Trowbridge geologist, educator
Guettich, Bruce Michael sporting goods company executive
Hager, John Patrick metallurgy engineering educator
Harreld, James Bruce food company executive
Hopper, Sally state legislator
Hutchinson, Richard William geology educator, consultant
Johnson, Marvin Donald brewery executive
Johnstone, James George engineering educator
Kazmerski, Lawrence Lee scientist, research facility executive
Kennedy, George Hunt chemistry educator
Kotch, Alex chemistry educator
Krauss, George metallurgist
Lerud, Joanne Van Ornum library administrator
Lewis, Charles D. insurance executive, rancher
Lopez, Judith Carroll lawyer
Mathews, Anne Jones international consultant, library director
Morrison, Roger Barron geologist, executive
Mueller, William Martin former academic administrator, metallurgical engineering educator
Olson, Marian Katherine emergency management executive, consultant, publisher
Outerbridge, Cheryl lawyer
Pegis, Anton George English educator
Petrick, Alfred, Jr. mineral economics educator, consultant
Poettmann, Frederick Heinz retired petroleum engineering educator
Ponder, Herman geologist
Rodgers, Frederic Barker judge
Salamon, Miklos Dezso Gyorgy mining educator
†Shimanski, Charles Stuart organization executive
Sims, Paul Kibler geologist
Sneed, Joseph Donald philosophy educator, author
Stewart, Frank Maurice, Jr. federal agency administrator
Stokes, Robert Allan science research facility executive, physicist
Tilton, John Elvin mineral economics educator
Togerson, John Dennis computer software company executive
Toll, Jack Benjamin government official
Weimer, Robert Jay geology educator, energy consultant, civic leader
White, James Edward geophysicist
Wilson, James Robert lawyer
Woolsey, Robert Eugene Donald mineral economics, mathematics and business administration educator
Yarar, Baki metallurgical engineering educator

Grand Junction
Achen, Mark Kennedy city manager
Bacon, Phillip geographer, author, consultant
Bergen, Virginia Louise principal, language arts educator
Hammer, Jan Harold television station manager
Kribel, Robert Edward academic administrator, physicist
McDonald, Barbara Ann marketing educator
Moberly, Linden Emery educational adminstrator
†Morris, Rusty Lee administrative executive
Nelson, Paul William real estate broker
Olson, Sylvester Irwin government official
Pantenburg, Michel hospital administrator, health educator, holistic health coordinator
Rutz, Richard Frederick physicist, researcher
Sadler, Theodore R., Jr. thoracic and cardiovascular surgeon
Sewell, Beverly Jean financial executive
Young, Ralph Alden soil scientist, educator
Zumwalt, Roger Carl hospital administrator

Greeley
Caffarella, Edward Philip educational technology educator
Cook, Donald E. pediatrician
Duff, William Leroy, Jr. university dean emeritus, business educator
Hause, Jesse Gilbert retired college president
Houtchens, Barnard lawyer
Mapelli, Roland Lawrence food company executive
Monfort, Kenneth cattle production and meat processing executive
Morgensen, Jerry Lynn construction company executive
Mueller, Donald Dean food company executive
Riddoch, Gregory Lee professional baseball manager
Schulze, Robert Oscar university dean
Seager, Daniel Albert university librarian
†Thiesen, Gregory Alan accountant
Willis, Connie (Constance E. Willis) author
Worley, Lloyd Douglas English educator

Greenwood Village
†Haymons, Dan Lester, Jr. hospital administrator
Walker, Eljana M. du Vall civic worker

Keystone
Craig, Robert Wallace educational and policy center administrator

Lafayette
McNeill, William environmental scientist
Short, Ray Everett minister, sociology educator emeritus, author, lecturer

Lakewood
Battey, Charles W. gas industry executive
Beckman, L. David university chancellor
Craig, Lexie Ferrell career development specialist, career guidance counselor, educator
Elkins, Lincoln Feltch petroleum engineering consultant
Franta, Gregory Esser architect, energy consultant
Guyton, Samuel Percy retired lawyer
Hall, Larry D. energy company executive, lawyer
Horn, Steven Walter state agency official
Hosokawa, William K. newspaper columnist, author
Hurst, Leland Lyle natural gas company executive
Isely, Henry Philip association executive, integrative engineer, writer, educator
Knott, William Alan library director, library management and building consultant
Lu, Paul Haihsing mining engineer, geotechnical consultant
Mc Bride, Guy Thornton, Jr. college president emeritus
Milan, Marjorie Lucille early childhood educator
Myers, Harry J., Jr. publisher
Orullian, B. LaRae bank executive
Owen, Robert Roy manufacturing company executive
Shafer, J. M. utility administrator
†Spisak, John Francis environmental company executive
†Swan, Henry retired surgeon
Tucker, James Raymond elementary educator
Walton, Roger Alan public relations executive, mediator, writer
Wellisch, William Jeremiah social psychology educator
West, Marjorie Edith elementary education educator

Larkspur
Bierbaum, J. Armin petroleum company executive, consultant
Bierbaum, Janith Marie artist

Leadville
Gentile-Patti, Catherine Ann Olympic skier
McCabe, James R. school system administrator

Littleton
Bachman, David Christian orthopedic surgeon
Ballard, Jack Stokes educator
Barnard, Rollin Dwight retired financial executive
†Bass, Charles Morris financial and systems consultant
Cabell, Elizabeth Arlisse psychologist
Chapman, Richard LeRoy public policy researcher
Chavez, Cile school superintendent
Clift, William Orrin oil company executive, consultant
Fisher, Louis McLane, Jr. environmental engineering firm executive
Hadley, Marlin LeRoy direct sales financial consultant
Hansen, Bruce Whipple financial consultant
Kazemi, Hossein petroleum engineer
Kearney, Joseph Laurence athletic conference administrator
Kleinknecht, Kenneth Samuel retired aerospace company executive, former federal space agency official
Kullas, Albert John management and systems engineering consultant
Martinen, John A. travel company executive
Milliken, John Gordon research economist
Plusk, Ronald Frank manufacturing company executive
Smart, Marriott Wieckhoff research librarian consultant, information manager,
Snyder, William Harry financial advisor
Spelts, Richard John lawyer
Strang, Sandra Lee airline official
Thompson, Curtis Brooks manufacturing company executive
Thompson, Thomas Edward educator, administrator, researcher
Ulrich, John Ross Gerald aerospace engineer
Vail, Charles Daniel veterinarian, consultant

Livermore
Evans, Howard Ensign entomologist, educator

Longmont
†Adams, Robert Hickman photographer
Hahn, Yubong electro-optics company executive
Kaminsky, Glenn Francis deputy chief of police retired, business owner, teacher
Little, Charles Gordon geophysicist
Melendez, Joaquin orthopedic assistant
Stewart, William Gene broadcast executive

Louisville
Day, Robert Edgar retired artist, educator
Poppa, Ryal Robert manufacturing company executive
Qualley, Charles Albert fine arts educator

Loveland
Balsiger, David Wayne television-video director, researcher, producer
Churchill, Jerry M. environment company marketing executive

Mc Coy
Hastings, Merrill George, Jr. publisher, marketing consultant
Wolf, Charlotte Elizabeth sociologist

Middletown
Mac Lam, Helen editor, periodical

Montrose
Krumins, Girts lawyer, management consultant

Monument
Miele, Alfonse Ralph former government official

Parker
Jankura, Donald Eugene hotel executive, educator
Nelson, Marvin Ray retired life insurance company executive

Pueblo
Altman, Leo Sidney lawyer
Arveschoug, Steven Neil communications executive, state representative
Bates, Charles Emerson library administrator
Byrnes, Lawrence William dean
Carter, Jack Ralph broadcasting administrator, television personality
Casey, William Robert, Jr. ambassador, mining engineer
Farwell, Hermon Waldo, Jr. parliamentarian, educator, former speech communication educator
Horn, Thomas Carl retired banker
O'Callaghan, Robert Patrick lawyer
Occhiato, Michael Anthony city official
Penny, Laura Jean librarian
Post-Gorden, Joan Carolyn psychology educator
Rawlings, Robert Hoag newspaper publisher
Shirley, Robert Clark university president, strategic planning consultant, educator
Sisson, Ray L. dean
Tafoya, Arthur N. bishop

Pueblo West
Giffin, Walter Charles retired industrial engineer, educator, consultant

Rangely
Mullen, Robert Charles school system administrator

Ridgway
Decker, Peter Randolph rancher, former state official
Glenn, Gerald Marvin marketing, engineering and construction executive
Weaver, Dennis actor

Rifle
George, Russell Lloyd lawyer, legislator

Snowmass
Lovins, Amory Bloch physicist, energy consultant
Lovins, L. Hunter public policy institute executive

Snowmass Village
Diamond, Edward gynecologist, infertility specialist, clinician

Steamboat Springs
Langstaff, Gary Lee food service marketing executive

Sterling
Jackson, L. Duane agriculturist
Milander, Henry Martin community college president

Telluride
Madonia, Valerie dancer
Smith, Samuel David artist, educator

Thornton
Crowley, Judith Diane secondary educator

Trinidad
Potter, William Bartlett business executive
Rocha, Pedro, Jr. academic administrator

U S A F Academy
Coppock, Richard Miles nonprofit association administrator
†Cubero, Ruben A. dean, military officer
†Hopkins, James William career officer, educator
Hosmer, Bradley Clark retired military officer, educational consultant
Porter, David Bruce air force officer, behavioral scientist, educator

Univ Of Denver
Dance, Francis Esburn Xavier communication educator
†Rowe, Edward Thomas university administrator, educator

Univ Of No Colo
Lujan, Herman D. university president

University Of Colorado
Chamberlin, Henry Scott artist, educator
DePuy, Charles Herbert chemist, educator
Leone, Stephen Robert chemical physicist, educator
Miller, Gifford Hubbs geologist

Vail
Kelton, Arthur Marvin, Jr. real estate developer
Knight, Constance Bracken writer, realtor, interior decorator, corporate executive
Vosbeck, Robert Randall architect

Westminster
Dotson, Gerald Richard biology educator
Kober, Carl Leopold exploration company executive
Reed, John Howard school administrator
Silverberg, Stuart Owen obstetrician, gynecologist
Yocum, Charleen Elaine educational administrator, counselor

Wheat Ridge
Barrett, Michael Henry civil engineer
Hashimoto, Christine L. physician
LaMendola, Walter Franklin huamn services, information technology consultant
Meier, Thomas Joseph geologist, consultant, engineering firm executive
Scherich, Erwin Thomas civil engineer, consultant
Straits, Beverly Joan gynecologist

Winter Park
Johnson, William Potter newspaper publisher

CONNECTICUT

Andover
Domagala, Richard Edward mail marketing analyst

Ansonia
Carvalko, Joseph R., Jr. lawyer
Mendyk, Sandra L. English educator
Nichols, Russell James manufacturing company executive
Yale, Jeffrey Franklin podiatrist

Avon
Cain, Marcy communication executive
Goodson, Richard Carle, Jr. chemist, hazardous waste management consultant
Jarvis, Ronald Dean life insurance company executive
Johnson, Dean Adams landscape architect
Patricelli, Robert E. health care company executive
Rutland, George Patrick banker
Smith, Leonard Kelley former plastic and reconstructive surgeon, consultant
Wiechmann, Eric Watt lawyer

Berlin
Ellis, William Ben utility executive

Bethany
Forman, Charles William religious studies educator
Viens, Harry Henry, Jr. communications executive

Bethel
Ajay, Abe artist
Perrin, Charles R. light manufacturing executive

Bloomfield
Anderson, Buist Murfee lawyer
Desautelle, William Peter financial executive
Dooley, Thomas Howard insurance company executive
English, Lawrence P. insurance company executive
Hammer, Alfred Emil artist, educator
Handel, Morton Emanuel management consultation executive
Hilsenrath, Baruch M. principal
Houston, Howard Edwin retired government official
Kaman, Charles Huron diversified technologies corporation executive
Leonberger, Frederick John electrical engineer, photonics manager
Mackey, William Arthur Godfrey computer software company executive
Martin, Vernon Emil librarian
Messemer, Glenn Matthew lawyer
Reid, Hoch lawyer

Branford
Agassi, Andre Kirk tennis player
Blake, Peter Jost architect
Cohen, Myron Leslie mechanical engineer, business executive
Izenour, George Charles mechanical, electrical engineering educator
Krupp, James Arthur Gustave manufacturing materials executive, consultant
Leckerling, Jon Peter lawyer
Mancheski, Frederick John automotive company executive
Penner, Harry Harold Hamilton, Jr. pharmaceutical company executive, lawyer

Bridgeport
Allen, Richard Stanley (Dick Allen) English language educator, author
Brunale, Vito John aerospace engineer
Buckley, Eugene aircraft company executive
Carson, David Ellis Adams banker
DelGrego, Andrew August banker
Egan, Edward M. bishop
Eginton, Warren William federal judge
Garcia, Edna I. secondary education educator
Goettel, Gerard Louis federal judge
Goodspeed, Norwick Royall Givens banker
Helfrich, Bernard D. academic administrator
Henderson, Albert publishing company executive, dairy executive, consultant
Jacobsen, Daniel Tower banker
Johmann, Nancy librarian
†Kiam, Victor Kermit, II consumer products company executive
Margulies, Martin B. lawyer, educator
McGregor, Jack Edwin natural resource company executive
Nevas, Alan Harris federal judge
Norris, Louise religious organization executive
Semple, Cecil Snowdon retired manufacturing company executive
†Sheridan, Eileen librarian
Shiff, Alan Howard William federal judge
Thomas, Dudley Breckinridge newspaper pubisher
Tobin, Richard J. lawyer
†Trefry, Robert J. healthcare administrator
van der Kroef, Justus Maria political science educator
Wetzel, Edward Thomas investment company executive

Bristol
Abdul-Jabbar, Kareem (Lewis Ferdinand Alcindor) retired professional basketball player, sports commentator
Barnes, Carlyle Fuller manufacturing executive
Barnes, Wallace manufacturing executive
Besser, John Edward lawyer
Fenoglio, William Ronald manufacturing company executive
Krawiecki, Edward C., Jr. state legislator, lawyer
Melrose, Barry James sportscaster, former professional hockey team coach
Moffitt, George, Jr. foreign service officer

Simms, Phillip *sports commentator, former professional football player*
Wells, Arthur Stanton *manufacturing company executive*

Brookfield
Reynolds, Jean Edwards *publishing executive*
Rowe, Edward Lawrence, Jr. *graphic designer*
Schetky, Laurence McDonald *metallurgist, researcher*
Westermann, Horace Clifford *sculptor*
Whelan, Michael Raymond *artist, illustrator*

Brooklyn
Meigs, Joseph Carl, Jr. *retired English language educator*
Wendel, Richard Frederick *economist, educator, consultant*

Cheshire
Bozzuto, Michael Adam *wholesale grocery company executive*
Burton, Robert William *retired office products executive*
Fuller, Jack Glendon, Jr. *retired plastics engineer*
McKee, Margaret Jean *federal agency executive*
Rowland, Ralph Thomas *architect*
Wallace, Ralph *superintendent*

Chester
Cobb, Hubbard Hanford *magazine editor, writer*
Hays, David Arthur *theater producer, stage designer*

Colebrook
Mc Neill, William Hardy *retired history educator, writer*

Collinsville
Ford, Dexter *retired insurance company executive*

Cornwall Bridge
Galazka, Jacek Michal *publishing company executive*
Pfeiffer, Werner Bernhard *artist, educator*

Cos Cob
Donahue, Barbara Lynn Sean *television producer*
Hauptman, Michael *broadcasting company executive*
Kane, Margaret Brassler *sculptor*
Ketchum, Alton Harrington *retired advertising executive*
Pomerance, Ralph *retired architect*
Senter, William Joseph *publishing company executive*
Woodman, Harry Andrews *retired life insurance company executive, consultant*

Cromwell
Bushnell, Clarence William *retired hospital consultant*

Danbury
Baker, Leonard Morton *manufacturing company executive*
Barth, Elmer Ernest *wire and cable company executive*
Baruch, Eduard *management consultant*
Caparn, Rhys (Mrs. Herbert Johannes Steel) *sculptor*
Cassidy, Robert Joseph *consumer products company executive*
Dudley, Alfred Edward *home and auto products company executive*
Edelstein, David Simeon *historian, educator*
Geoghan, Joseph Edward *lawyer, chemical company executive*
Goldstein, Joel *management science educator, researcher*
Hawkes, Carol Ann *university dean*
Holzman, Robert Stuart *tax consultant*
Hull, Treat Clark *superior court trial referee*
†Joyce, William H. *chemist*
Kennedy, Robert Delmont *chemical company executive*
Leish, Kenneth William *publishing company executive*
Lichtenberger, Horst William *chemical company executive*
Lisimachio, Jean Louis *book publishing executive*
Malino, Jerome R. *rabbi*
McNabb, Frank William *consumer products company executive*
Nelson, Willie *musician, songwriter*
†Primm, Earl Russell, III *publishing executive*
Roach, James Richard *university president*
†Robilotti, Gerard Daniel *hospital administrator*
Rowland, Thomas William *lawyer, sugar company executive*
Rubin, Jacob Carl *mechanical research engineer*
Saghir, Adel Jamil *artist, painter, sculptor*
Skolan-Logue, Amanda Nicole *lawyer, consultant*
Soviero, Joseph C. *chemical company executive*
Stewart, Albert Clifton *college dean, marketing educator*
†Sweeney, Timm Raymond Paul *marketing research consultant*
Toland, John Willard *historian, writer*
Tolor, Alexander *psychologist, educator*
Toman, Stephen E. *educational publishing company executive*
†Weiner, Jonathan David *writer*

Darien
Allen, Joseph Henry *retired publishing company executive*
Bays, John Theophanis *consulting engineering executive*
Becker, Ralph Edward *broadcast executive, consultant*
Brooke, Avery Rogers *publisher, writer*
Brown, James Shelly *lawyer*
Buchanan, Robert Edgar *retired advertising agency executive*
Cowherd, Edwin Russell *management consultant*
Earle, Harry Woodward *printing company executive*
Forman, J(oseph) Charles *chemical engineer, consultant, writer*
Gammie, Anthony Petrie *pulp and paper manufacturing company executive*
Glenn, Roland Douglas *chemical engineer*
Grace, John Kenneth *communications executive*
Hart, Eric Mullins *finance company executive*
Hubner, Robert Wilmore *retired business machines company executive, consultant*
Kaynor, Sanford Bull *lawyer*
Kutz, Kenneth John *retired mining executive*
Lewis, A. Duff, Jr. *investment executive*
Mapel, William Marlen Raines *retired banking executive*
McCurdy, Richard Clark *engineering consultant*
Morse, Edmond Northrop *investment management executive*
Mundt, Barry Maynard *management consultant*
Nava, Eloy Luis *financial consultant*
O'Brien, Joseph Patrick, Jr. *apparel and textile company executive*
Owen, Robert Vaughan *financial company executive*
Saari, Leonard Mathew *paper company executive, lawyer*
Schell, James Munson *financial executive*
Smith, Elwin Earl *mining and oil company executive*
Spilman, Raymond *industrial designer*
Sprole, Frank Arnott *retired pharmaceutical company executive, lawyer*

Deep River
Healy, William Kent *environmental services executive*
Hieatt, Allen Kent *English language professional, educator*
Hieatt, Constance Bartlett *English language educator*

Derby
Brassil, Jean Ella *psychologist*

Durham
†Mack, Charles David *magazine educator*

East Glastonbury
Smith, David Clark *research scientist*

East Haddam
Borton, John Carter, Jr. (Terry Borton) *producer, theater*
Clarke, Logan, Jr. *management consultant*
Frost, Susan Beth *producer*

East Hartford
Ahlberg, John Harold *mathematician, educator*
Campbell, Jerry F. *insurance company executive*
Foyt, Arthur George *electronics research administrator*
Lundeberg, Roger Victor *inventor, scientist, writer*
Mordo, Jean Henri *financial executive*
Scholsky, Martin Joseph *priest*
Soppelsa, George Nicholas *artist*
Tanaka, Richard I. *computer products company executive*
Whiston, Richard Michael *lawyer*

East Haven
Conn, Harold O. *physician, educator*
Hegyi, Albert Paul *association executive, lawyer*

East Windsor
Folmsbee, Patricia Hurley *reading consultant*
Kaufmann, Sylvia Nadeau *office equipment sales company executive*

Easton
Meyer, Alice Virginia *state official*

Ellington
Setzer, Herbert John *chemical engineer*

Enfield
Berger, Robert Bertram *lawyer*
Hostetter, Amos Barr, Jr. *cable television executive*
Neher, Timothy Pyper *cable company executive*

Essex
Curtis, Alva Marsh *artist*
Grover, William Herbert *architect*
Harper, Robert Leslie *architect, educator*
Kenyon, Charles Moir *publishing company executive*
Keppel, John *writer, former diplomat*
McLaughlin, David J. *management consultant*
Russell, Thomas Wright, Jr. *retired manufacturing executive*
Simon, Mark *architect*

Fairfield
Allaby, Stanley Reynolds *clergyman*
Ambrosino, Ralph Thomas, Jr. *retired telecommunications executive*
Barone, Rose Marie Pace *writer, former educator*
Blau, Barry *advertising agency executive*
Brett, Arthur Cushman, Jr. *banker*
Bryan, Barbara Day *librarian*
Bunt, James Richard *electric company executive*
Caruso, Daniel F. *lawyer, judge, former state legislator*
Cernera, Anthony Joseph *academic administrator*
Cion, Richard M. *financial executive, lawyer*
Clark, Eleanor *author*
Cole, Richard John *marketing executive*
Cox, Richard Joseph *former broadcasting executive*
Currier, Jeffrey L. *manufacturing executive*
Dammerman, Dennis Dean *financial executive*
Dean, George Alden *advertising executive*
Eigel, Edwin George, Jr. *mathematics educator, retired university president*
Golub, Stephen Bruce *accountant, consultant, educator*
Heineman, Benjamin Walter, Jr. *lawyer*
Hergenhan, Joyce *public relations executive*
Hodgkinson, William James *marketing executive*
Jewitt, David Willard Pennock *retired banker*
Johnson, Alvin Roscoe *manufacturing executive*
Kantrowitz, Jonathan Daniel *educational software company executive, lawyer*
Kelley, Aloysius Paul *university president, priest*
Kenney, James Francis *lawyer*
Kijanka, Dorothy M. *library administrator*
Lachowicz, Franciszek *foreign language educator*
Limpitlaw, John Donald *retired publishing executive, clergyman*
Lumbard, Joseph Edward, Jr. *federal judge*
Mc Lean, Don *singer, instrumentalist, composer*
Newton, Lisa Haenlein *philosophy educator*
O'Connell, Robert John *insurance company executive*
Peirce, George Leighton *airport administrator*
Polin, Jane Louise *foundation official*
Sealy, Albert Henry *lawyer*
Shaffer, Dorothy Browne *retired mathematician, educator*
Smith, Clifford Vaughn, Jr. *academic administrator*
Spence, Barbara E. *publishing company executive*
Sutphen, Harold Amerman, Jr. *retired paper company executive*
Taylor, James Blackstone *aviation company executive*
Trager, Philip *photographer, lawyer*
Urquhart, John Alexander *management consultant*
Welch, John Francis, Jr. (Jack Welch) *electrical manufacturing company executive*
Wheeler, Henry Clark *manufacturing company executive*
Wolff, Steven Alexander *arts and entertainment consultant*

Falls Village
Cronin, Robert Lawrence *sculptor, painter*
Purcell, Dale *college administrator, consultant*
Toomey, Jeanne Elizabeth *animal activist*

Farmington
Bailey, Samuel, Jr. *investment advisor, lawyer*
†Besdine, Richard William *medical educator*
Bigler, Harold Edwin, Jr. *investment company executive*
Bronner, Felix *physiologist, biophysicist, educator, painter*
Cooperstein, Sherwin Jerome *medical educator*
Donaldson, James Oswell, III *neurology educator*
Escobar, Javier Ignacio *psychiatrist*
Frago, William S. *manufacturing executive*
Gossling, Harry Robert *orthopaedic surgeon, educator*
Halligan, Howard Ansel *investment management company executive*
Hartley, Harry J. *academic administrator*
Herbette, Leo Gerard *biophysics educator*
Hinz, Carl Frederick, Jr. *physician, educator*
Johnson, Robert E. *financial executive*
Katz, Arnold Martin *medical educator*
Kegeles, S. Stephen *behavioral science educator*
Löe, Harald *dentist, educator, researcher*
Maranzano, Miguel Franscisco *engineer*
Massey, Robert Unruh *physician, university dean*
Miser, Hugh Jordan *systems analyst, operations researcher, consultant*
Osborn, Mary Jane Merten *biochemist*
Paul, Christian Thomas *retired insurance company executive*
Powers, John Austin *alcoholic beverage company executive*
Raisz, Lawrence Gideon *medical educator, consultant*
Rothfield, Lawrence I. *microbiology educator*
Rothfield, Naomi Fox *physician*
Schenkman, John Boris *pharmacologist, educator*
Scott, David J. *beverage executive*
Sheeran, William James *engineering executive*
Spencer, Richard Paul *biochemist, educator, physician*
van Rooy, Jean-Pierre *international executive*
Walker, James Elliot Cabot *physician*

Georgetown
Roberts, Priscilla Warren *artist*

Glastonbury
Bruner, Robert B. *hospital consultant*
Googins, Sonya Forbes *state legislator, retired banker*
Hatch, D. Patricia P. *principal*
Roy, Kenneth Russell *school system administrator, educator*
Schroth, Peter W(illiam) *lawyer, management and law educator*

Glenbrook
Schofield, Herbert Spencer, III *insurance executive*

Goshen
Berleant, Arnold *philosopher*

Granby
Pestka, Stanley *secondary school principal*

Greens Farms
Deford, Frank *sportswriter, television and radio commentator, author*
McManus, John Francis, III *advertising executive*
St.Marie, Satenig *writer*

Greenwich
Allain, Emery Edgar *retired paper company executive*
†Amen, Robert Anthony *investor and corporate relations consultant*
Badman, John, III *real estate developer, architect, construction executive*
Baker, Charles Ernest *stockbroker*
Ball, John Fleming *advertising and film production executive*
Bam, Foster *lawyer*
Bantle, Louis Francis *tobacco company executive*
Barber, Charles Finch *retired metals company executive, financial services company executive*
†Barham, Robert Young, Jr. *communications company executive*
Barnum, William Milo *architect*
Bennett, Jack Franklin *oil company executive*
Bentley, Peter *lawyer*
Berkley, William Robert *insurance holding company executive*
Bogart, Robert B. *publishing company executive*
Cantor, Samuel C. *lawyer*
Cantwell, Robert *lawyer*
Carmichael, William Daniel *consultant, educator*
Chapman, Gilbert Whipple, Jr. *publishing company executive*
Chase, William Howard *public policy consultant, editor*
Chisholm, William Hardenbergh *management consultant*
Clements, Robert *insurance brokerage executive*
Collins, Richard Lawrence *magazine editor, publisher, author*
Combe, Ivan DeBlois *drug company executive*
Coudert, Victor Raphael, Jr. *marketing and sales executive*
Crowe, John Carl *aviation consultant, retired airline executive*
Damon, Edmund Holcombe *plastics company executive*
Davidson, Thomas Maxwell *international management company executive*
de Mar, Leoda Miller *fabric and wallcovering designer*
Dianis, Walter Joseph *retired banker*
Donahue, Donald Jordan *mining company executive*
Donley, James Walton *management consultant*
Dorme, Patrick John *electronic company executive*
Drake, Philip Meurer *lawyer*
duPont, Augustus Irénée *lawyer*
Egbert, Richard Cook *retired banker*
Ewald, William Bragg, Jr. *author, consultant*
Finn, Richard Galletly Francis *personal products executive*
Fisher, Everett *lawyer*
Foley, Thomas Coleman *investor*
Foraste, Roland *psychiatrist*
Forrow, Brian Derek *lawyer, corporation executive*
Fuller, Theodore *retired insurance executive*
Gabelli, Mario J. *diversified financial services company executive*
Gately, George (Gallagher Gately) *cartoonist*
Gierer, Vincent A., Jr. *tobacco and wine holding company executive*
Gillespie, Alexander Joseph, Jr. *lawyer*
Goldmann, Peter D. *editor*
Goodman, Lawrence Baron *retail executive*
Gorin, Robert Seymour *lawyer*
Grabe, William O. *investment company executive*
Graham, Diana *lawyer*
Grossman, Allen, III *educational administrator*
Hanson, Maurice Francis (Maury Hanson) *retired magazine publisher and editor*
Hasner, Rolf Kaare *management consultant*
Heath, Gloria Whitton *aerospace scientist, consultant*
Heer, Edwin LeRoy *insurance executive*
Hershaft, Elinor *space planner, interior designer*
Hicks, Paul B., Jr. *retired petroleum company executive*
Holten, John V. *food products executive*
Horton, Jared Churchill *retired corporation executive*
Howard, John Arnold *marketing educator*
Ix, Robert Edward *food company executive*
Jeffrey, Kim *food products executive*
Jones, Edwin Michael *lawyer, former insurance company executive*
Jordan, Jerry Neville *investment company executive*
Karraker, David Franklin *secondary educator, reading consultant*
Keegan, Richard John *advertising agency executive*
Keeshan, William Francis, Jr. *advertising executive*
Keogh, James *journalist*
Kestnbaum, Albert S. *advertising executive*
Kopenhaver, Patricia Ellsworth *podiatrist*
Kopp, W. Brewster *corporate director, advisor*
Kurtz, Melvin H. *lawyer, cosmetics company executive*
Larned, William Edmund, Jr. *international development and venture capital company executive*
Laudone, Anita Helene *lawyer*
Lawi, David Steven *energy, agriservice and thermoplastic resins industries executive*
Lawler, Richard Francis *lawyer*
Lederman, Ira Seth *insurance executive, lawyer*
Lewis, Audrey Gersh *financial marketing consultant*
Lewis, Perry Joshua *investment banker*
Long, James Alfred *financial services company executive*
Lowenstein, Peter David *lawyer*
Lozyniak, Andrew *manufacturing company executive*
Lurie, Ranan Raymond *political analyst, political cartoonist, artist, lecturer*
Lynch, William Redington *lawyer*
MacDonald, Gordon Chalmers *management consultant*
Mallardi, Joseph L. *manufacturing company executive*
Mann, Marvin L. *electronics executive*
Marchand, Nathan *electrical engineer, corporation president*
Maroni, Paul L. *finance executive*
Massey, James L. *investment banker*
McKee, Thomas J. *lawyer*
McLaughlin, Michael John *financial executive*
Mendenhall, John Ryan *retired lawyer, transportation executive*
Messud, Françis-Michel *manufacturing company executive*
Miles, Jesse Mc Lane *retired accounting company executive*
Mock, Robert Claude *architect*
Moller, William Richard, Jr. *banker*
Moonie, Clyde Wickliffe *financial consultant*
More, Douglas McLochlan *lawyer*
Neafsey, John Patrick *oil company executive*
Neal, Irene Collins *artist, educator*
Nelson, Don Harris *gas and oil industry executive*
†Nelson, Douglas W. *social service administrator*
Nevin, Crocker *investment banker*
†Nixon, James Alexander *cosmetic company executive*
†Oakley, Gary William *consulting company executive*
Ordway, John Danton *pension administrator, lawyer, accountant*
Paul, Roland Arthur *lawyer*
Paulson, Paul Joseph *advertising executive*
Perless, Robert L. *sculptor*
Pfeiffer, Jane Cahill *former broadcasting company executive, consultant*
Pivirotto, Richard Roy *former retail executive*
Pope, Ingrid Bloomquist *sculptor, lecturer, poet*
Pope, Marvin Hoyle *language educator, writer*
Pringle, Lewis Gordon *international trade and investment company executive*
†Ramanathan, Rama *foundation executive*
Randt, Clark Thorp *physician, educator*
Richards, Fred Tracy *finance company executive*
Rodenbach, Edward Francis *lawyer*
†Rooney, Francis Charles, Jr. *corporate executive*
Rose, Richard Loomis *lawyer*
Rossi, Ralph L. *tobacco company executive*
Rukeyser, Louis Richard *economic commentator*
Rutgers, Katharine Phillips (Mrs. Frederik Lodewijk Rutgers) *dancer*
Scheifele, Richard Paul *cosmetic and chemicals manufacturing company executive*
Schlafly, Hubert Joseph, Jr. *communications executive*
Schmidt, Herman J. *former oil company executive*
Schutz, Herbert Dietrich *publishing executive*
Scott, John Constante *marketing company executive*
Shaffer, David H. *publishing company executive*
Shepard, Thomas Rockwell, Jr. *publishing consultant*
Sheppard, Posy (Mrs. Jeremiah Milbank) *social worker*
Simonnard, Michel André *manufacturing executive*
Smith, Rodger Field *financial executive*
Springsteen, David Folger *financial consultant*
Squier, David Louis *manufacturing executive*

Srere, Benson M. *communications company executive, consultant*
Stern, Dennis M. *lawyer*
Taylor, Sir Cyril (Julian Hebden) *education association administrator, consultant*
Tiegs, Cheryl *model, designer*
Tournillon, Nicholas Brady *trade finance, international investments company executive*
Vance, Don Kelvin *baking industry consultant*
Wada, Sadami (Chris) *manufacturing executive*
Wallach, Philip C(harles) *financial, public relations consultant*
Wearly, William Levi *business executive*
Whitmore, George Merle, Jr. *management consulting company executive*
Willis, William Harold, Jr. *management consultant, executive search specialist*
Woelflein, Kevin Gerard *banker*
Wyman, Ralph Mark *corporate executive*
†Ziegler, Randall Keith *food service executive*

Groton
Auerbach, Michael Howard *chemical company research executive*
Cooper, Richard Arthur *oceanographer*
English, James Fairfield, Jr. *former college president*
Hinman, Richard Leslie *pharmaceutical company executive*
Pinson, Ellis Rex, Jr. *chemist, consultant*
Routien, John Broderick *mycologist*
Sheets, Herman Ernest *marine engineer*
Simpson, W. M. *career officer administrator*
Swindell, Archie Calhoun, Jr. *research biochemist, statistician*
Tassinari, Melissa Sherman *toxicologist*

Guilford
Baillie, Priscilla Woods *aquatic ecologist*
Boyle, Helen D. *entrepreneur*
Engelman, Donald Max *molecular biophysics and biochemistry educator*
Hayes, Michael Ernest *psychotherapist, educator*
Morgan, Leon Alford *retired utility executive*
Peters, William *author, producer, director*
Ragan, James Thomas *communications executive*
Warshaw, Joseph Bennett *pediatrician, educator*
Whitaker, Thomas Russell *English literature educator*

Hamden
Bennett, Harry Louis *college educator*
Cherry, Edward Earl *architect*
Clayman, Lillian Dudkiewicz *mayor*
Gay, Peter *history educator, author*
Gordon, Angus Neal, Jr. *retired electric company executive*
McClellan, Edwin *language educator*
Norberg-Caliendo, Lynda Joy *school system administrator*
Nuland, Sherwin *surgeon, author*
Parker, William Nelson *economics educator*
Peterson, George Emanuel, Jr. *lawyer, business executive*
Resnick, Idrian Navarre *foundation administrator*
Roche, (Eamonn) Kevin *architect*
Rosenthal, Franz *language educator*
Walker, Charles Allen *chemical engineer, educator*
Williams, Edward Gilman *retired banker*
Woodward, C. Vann *historian*

Hartford
Alfano, Charles Thomas, Sr. *lawyer*
Anthony, J(ulian) Danford, Jr. *lawyer*
Asmar, Mark Abdon *lawyer*
Baird, Zoë *insurance company executive, lawyer*
Baldwin, Howard J. *professional hockey team executive*
Benanav, Gary G. *insurance company counsel*
Berall, Frank Stewart *lawyer*
Berdon, Robert Irwin *state supreme court justice*
Bickford, Christopher Penny *association executive*
Bieluch, William Charles *judge*
†Blatti, Jo *historical institution administrator, historian*
Blumberg, Phillip Irvin *law educator*
Blumenthal, Richard *state attorney general*
Booth, Richard H. *insurance company executive*
Braithwaite, Ralph Rhey *executive search consultant*
Brauer, Rima Lois *psychiatrist*
Bronzino, Joseph Daniel *electrical engineer*
Buck, Gurdon Hall *lawyer, urban planner, real estate broker*
Buckingham, Harold Canute, Jr. *lawyer*
Budd, Edward Hey *insurance company executive*
†Burnham, Christopher Bancroft *state treasurer, investment banker*
Butterworth, Kenneth W. *manufacturing company executive*
Cain, George Harvey *lawyer, business executive*
Callahan, Robert J. *state supreme court justice*
Cantor, Donald Jerome *lawyer*
Carpenter, Michael Alan *securities firm executive*
†Carroon, Robert Girard *historian, clergyman*
Clarie, T. Emmet *federal judge*
Coburn, Richard Joseph *company executive, electrical engineer*
Cole, William Kaufman *lawyer*
Compton, Ronald E. *insurance and financial services executive*
Connelly, William Howard *retired foundation executive*
Conrad, Donald Glover *insurance executive*
Cooper, George Brinton *historian, educator*
Covello, Alfred Vincent *federal judge*
Crawford, Richard Bradway *biologist, biochemist, educator*
Cronin, Daniel Anthony *bishop*
Cullina, William Michael *lawyer*
Curran, Ward Schenk *economist, educator*
Daniell, Robert F. *diversified manufacturing company executive*
Decko, Kenneth Owen *association executive*
DePino, Chris Anthoney *state legislator*
D'Eramo, David *hospital administrator*
De Rocco, Andrew Gabriel *state commissioner, educator*
Donahue, John McFall *lawyer*
Donnelly, John *psychiatrist, educator*
Eagan, F(rancis) Owen *magistrate judge*
Elliot, Ralph Gregory *lawyer*
Endrst, James Bryan *television critic, columnist*
Englehart, Robert Wayne, Jr. *cartoonist*
Evans, William John *aerospace company executive*
Ewing, Robert *lawyer*
Fain, Joel Maurice *lawyer*
Faude, Wilson Hinsdale *museum director*
†Ferrandino, Vincent L. *stage agency administrator*
Fiondella, Robert William *insurance company executive*
Flaherty, Patrick John *state legislator, economist*
Fox, Bernard Michael *utilities company executive, electrical engineer*
Frahm, Donald Robert *insurance company executive*
Francis, Paul Wilbur, Jr. *association executive*
Freeman, David *chemical company executive*
Garfield, Gerald *lawyer*
†Gibbons, John Martin, Jr. *physician, educator*
Gill, Margaret S. *state legislator*
Gingold, George Norman *insurance company executive, lawyer*
Godfrey, Robert Douglas *lawyer*
Golden, Louis Joseph *former business news editor, newspaper executive*
Goodwin, Rodney Keith Grove *international bank and trade company executive*
Gorvett, Robert L. *accountant*
Green, Raymond Bert *lawyer*
Groark, Eunice *state official*
Guenter, Raymond Albert *lawyer, banker*
Gunderson, Gerald Axel *economics educator, administrator*
Gunther, George Lackman *state senator, natureopathic physician, retired*
Hamilton, James Carl *insurance company executive*
Hamilton, Thomas Stewart *physician, hospital administrator*
Harden, Jon Bixby *publishing executive*
Harris, James George, Jr. *social services administrator, consultant*
Harrison, Thomas Flatley *lawyer*
†Hedrick, Joan Doran *writer*
Heiman, Maxwell *state appellate court judge, lawyer*
Hermann, Robert Jay *manufacturing company engineering executive, consultant*
Hertel, Suzanne Marie *personnel administrator*
Hess, Marilyn Ann *state legislator*
Hess, Wheeler Herdman *insurance executive*
Hickey, Kevin Francis *insurance company executive*
†Himmelsbach, William Anthony, Jr. *healthcare executive*
Holmgren, Paul *professional hockey coach*
Holt, Timothy Arthur *insurance company executive*
Horgan, Denis Edward *journalist*
Irish, Leon Eugene *lawyer, educator, insurance company executive*
Ivey, Elizabeth S. *acoustician, physicist*
†Johnson, Dwight Alan *lawyer*
Jones, Richard F., III *obstetrician/gynecologist*
Jones, Thomas Chester *insurance company executive*
Joyce, Raymond M. H. *state legislator*
Kaimowitz, Jeffrey Hugh *librarian*
Kang, Juliana Haeng-Cha *anesthesiologist*
Kee Borges, Saundra Alice *city manager, lawyer*
Kelly, Peter Galbraith *lawyer*
Keyles, Sidney Alan *lawyer*
Killian, Robert Kenneth *former lieutenant governor*
King, Richard Hood *newspaper executive*
Knickerbocker, Robert Platt, Jr. *lawyer*
Knisel, Russell H. *banker*
Korzenik, Armand Alexander *lawyer*
Koupal, Raymond *newspaper publishing executive*
Kraus, Eileen S. *bank executive*
Kriebel, Robert H. *corporation executive*
Lamos, Mark *artistic director, administrator, actor*
Lane-Reticker, Edward *lawyer, educator*
Lautzenheiser, Barbara Jean *insurance executive*
Lewis, Lois A. *health services administrator*
Lipp, Robert I. *bank holding company executive*
Loomis, Worth (Alfred Worthington Loomis) *college president, manufacturer*
Lotstein, James I. *lawyer*
Lumsden, Lynne Ann *publishing company executive*
Lyman, Peggy *dancer, choreographer, educator*
Lyon, James Burroughs *lawyer*
Mahoney, Michael Robert Taylor *art historian, educator*
Maloney, James Henry *state senator, lawyer*
Marrs, Richard E. *insurance company executive*
Mattiello, Brian Edward *state legislator*
McKeon, George A. *lawyer*
McLane, James Woods *insurance executive*
Mc Lean, Jackie *jazz saxophonist, educator, composer, community activist*
McLoughlin, Philip Robert *insurance company executive*
Menses, Jan *artist, draftsman, etcher, lithographer, muralist*
Meotti, Michael Patrick *state legislator, lawyer*
Merriam, Dwight Haines *lawyer, land use planner*
Merrill, George Vanderneth *lawyer, investment executive*
Messmore, Thomas Ellison *insurance company executive*
Middlebrook, Stephen Beach *lawyer*
Miller, Jeffrey Clark *lawyer*
Milner, Thirman L. *state senator*
Morrison, Francis Henry *lawyer*
Morrissey, Robert John *communications executive*
Mueller, Marnie Wagstaff *insurance company executive, economist*
Murphy, Ann Burke *insurance company executive, computer engineer*
Murtha, John Stephen *lawyer*
Mushinsky, Mary M. *state legislator*
Newman, Jon O. *federal judge*
Nicholas, Robert B. *insurance executive*
Noel, Don Obert, Jr. *newspaper columnist*
Nolan, John Blanchard *lawyer*
O'Connor, Richard Dennis *lawyer*
O'Keefe, James William, Jr. *investment manager and banker*
O'Malley, Marjorie Glaubach *health care executive*
Opeka, John Frank *utility executive, electrical engineer*
Osborne, George Delano *performing arts company director*
Overstrom, Gunnar S., Jr. *banker*
Owen, H. Martyn *lawyer*
Pach, Peter Barnard *newspaper columnist and editor*
Palmer, Richard N. *judge*
Paul, William F. *manufacturing company executive*
Paydos, Charles J. *insurance company executive*
Peters, Ellen Ash *state supreme court chief justice*
Petry, Paul E. *insurance company executive*
Pinney, Sidney Dillingham, Jr. *lawyer*
Piotrowski, Richard Francis *state agency administrator, council chairman*
Polinsky, Janet Naboicheck *state official, former state legislator*
Quinn, Andrew Peter, Jr. *lawyer, insurance executive*
Randall, Gerald J. *insurance company executive*
†Rapoport, Miles S. *state official*
Reed, David Benson *bishop*
†Rell, M. Jodi *state official*
Renner, Gerald Anthony *journalist*
Richter, Donald Paul *lawyer*
Roberts, Henry Reginald *management consultant, former life insurance company executive*
Roberts, Melville Parker, Jr. *neurosurgeon, educator*
Roessner, Barbara *journalist*
Rolls, John Allison *electronics company executive*
Rome, Donald Lee *lawyer*
†Rosenberg, Steven H. *health facility administrator*
Ryan, David Thomas *lawyer*
Sargent, Joseph Denny *insurance company executive*
Schatz, S. Michael *lawyer*
Schatzki, George *law educator*
†Schneider, Craig William *biology educator, research botanist*
Schweitzer, N. Tina *photojournalist, television producer, director, writer, international consultant public relations, media relations, government relations*
Scott, Brian E. *insurance company executive*
Scully, John Carroll *life insurance marketing research company executive*
See, Edmund M. *lawyer*
Seidl, Jane Patricia *lawyer*
Shea, David Michael *state supreme court justice*
Shimelman, Susan Fromm *state administrator*
Siegel, Robert Gordon *lawyer*
Simmons, Robert Ruhl *state legislator, educator*
Smith, Donald Arthur *mechanical engineer, researcher*
†Solomon, Peter R. *physicist, physical chemist, engineering executive*
Space, Theodore Maxwell *lawyer*
Spear, H(enry) Dyke N(ewcome), Jr. *lawyer*
Speziale, John Albert *lawyer*
Springer, John Kelley *hospital administrator*
Stephen, Michael Anthony *insurance company executive*
†Sternberg, Betty J. *school system administrator*
Stoker, Warren Cady *university president*
Stone, Dennis J. *law librarian, educator*
Taylor, Allan Bert *lawyer*
Thomas, Calvert *lawyer*
Tingley, Floyd Warren *physician*
Trachsel, William Henry *corporate lawyer*
Trowbridge, Phillip Edmund *surgeon, educator*
Upson, Thomas Fisher *state legislator, lawyer*
Vohra, Ranbir *political scientist, educator*
Voigt, Richard *lawyer*
†Walters, Kirk W. *financial services holding company executive*
†Weintraub, Allen *diversified financial services executive*
Welch, John Paton *surgeon, educator*
Westervelt, James Joseph *insurance company executive*
White, David Oliver *museum executive*
Wilde, Wilson *insurance company executive*
Wilder, Michael Stephen *insurance company executive*
Wilkie, Everett Cleveland, Jr. *librarian*
†Williams, Sandra *insurance company executive*
†Winter, Miriam Therese (Gloria Frances Winter) *nun, religious education educator*
Wolman, Martin *lawyer*
Wright, Douglass Brownell *judge, lawyer*
Yoskowitz, Irving Benjamin *lawyer, manufacturing company executive*
Young, Leslie Towner *state legislator, stockbroker*
Zakarian, Albert *lawyer*
Zakarian, John J. *journalist*
Zikmund, Barbara Brown *minister, seminary president, church history educator*

Ivoryton
Bendig, William Charles *editor, artist, publisher*
LeCompte, Roger Burton *management consultant*
Osborne, John Walter *historian, educator, author*

Kensington
Colaiacovo, Christine Mary *secondary school educator*

Kent
Kilham, Walter H., Jr. *architect*

Lakeville
Barnes, Robert Goodwin *publishing consultant*
Bookman, George B. *public relations consultant*
Estabrook, Robert Harley *journalist*
Lovitt, George Harold *advertising executive*
Manassero, Henri J. P. *hotel executive*

Litchfield
Booth, John Thomas *investment banker*
Winter, Paul Theodore *musician*

Lyme
Bessie, Simon Michael *publisher*
Bloom, Barry Malcolm *medical consultant*
Friday, John Ernest, Jr. *retired securities company executive*
Greene, Joseph Nathaniel, Jr. *former foundation executive, former diplomat*

Madison
Anderson, Roy Ryden *former insurance executive, consultant*
Azarian, Martin Vartan *publishing company executive*
Carlson, Dale Bick *writer*
Egbert, Emerson Charles *publisher*
Golembeski, Jerome John *wire and cable company executive*
Haas, Frederick Peter *lawyer*
Houghton, Alan Nourse *association executive, educator, consultant*
Keim, Robert Phillip *retired advertising executive, consultant*
Kilbourne, Edwin Dennis *virologist, educator*
Peterkin, Albert Gordon *retired education educator*
Platt, Sherman Phelps, Jr. *publishing consultant*
Purcell, Bradford Moore *publishing company executive*
Snell, Richard Saxon *anatomist*

Manchester
Chung, Douglas Chu *pharmacist, consultant*
Galasso, Francis Salvatore *materials scientist*
†Reuter, James D. *aeronautical engineering manager*
Richard, Ann Bertha *nursing administrator*
Slaiby, Theodore George *aeronautical engineer, consultant*

Mansfield Center
Aldrich, Robert Adams *agricultural engineer*
Butler, Francelia McWilliams *retired English language educator, writer*
Liberman, Alvin Meyer *psychology educator*

Meriden
Bertolli, Eugene Emil *sculptor, goldsmith, designer, consultant*
†Friedheim, Michael *footwear and apparel company executive*
Gilbertson, Robert G. *computer company executive*
Luby, Thomas Stewart *lawyer*
†Stapleton, Richard D. *construction company executive*
Way, Carol Jane *non-profit organization administrator*
†Wetmore, Byron F. *construction company executive*

Middlebury
Binns, James W. *watch manufacturing company executive*
Coleman, Robert Elliott *secondary education educator*
Davis, Joanne Fatse *lawyer*
Fickenscher, Gerald H. *chemicals company executive*
Galie, Louis Michael *electronics company executive*
Mazaika, Robert J. *chemicals executive*
†Rowland, John G. *governor, former congressman*
Todt, Malcolm S. *company finance executive*

Middlefield
Thermenos, Nicholas *engineering company executive*

Middletown
Adams, David Bachrach *psychology educator*
Adams, John Robert *librarian*
Arnold, Herbert Anton *German language educator*
Bailey, Debra Sue *psychologist, neuropsychologist*
Balay, Robert Elmore *magazine editor, reference librarian*
Bennet, Douglas Joseph, Jr. *university president*
Beveridge, David Lewis *chemistry educator*
†Braxton, Anthony *musicologist*
Brewer, Timothy Francis, III *cardiologist*
Briggs, Morton Winfield *Romance language educator*
Buel, Richard Van Wyck, Jr. *history educator, writer, editor*
Comfort, William Wistar *mathematics educator*
Creighton, Joanne Vanish *academic administrator*
Crites, Stephen Decatur *religion educator*
Cumming, Robert Emil *editor*
Day, William Hudson *mechanical engineer, turbomachinery company executive*
D'Oench, Russell Grace, Jr. *publishing consultant*
Francisco, William H. *accounting educator*
Fry, Albert Joseph *chemistry educator*
Gerber, Murray A. *molding manufacturing company executive*
Gillmor, Charles Stewart *history and science educator, researcher*
Gourevitch, Victor *philosophy educator*
Haake, Paul *chemistry and biochemistry educator*
Hager, Anthony Wood *mathematics educator*
Harris, Dale Benner *psychology educator*
Horne, Gregory Stuart *geologist, educator*
Kerr, Clarence William *retired university administrator*
Lemert, Charles Clay *sociology educator*
Lensing, Leo A. *foreign language and humanities educator*
Linton, Fred Ernest Julius *mathematics educator*
Lovell, Michael C. *economics educator*
Manchester, William *writer*
Marteka, Vincent James, Jr. *magazine editor, writer*
Meyer, Priscilla Ann *Russian language and literature educator*
Miller, Richard Alan *economist, educator*
Pomper, Philip *history educator*
Reed, Joseph Wayne *American studies educator*
Reeve, Franklin D. *literature educator, writer*
Reid, James Dolan *mathematics educator, researcher*
Rose, Phyllis *English language professional, author*
Rosenbaum, Robert Abraham *mathematics educator*
Scheibe, Karl Edward *psychology educator*
Schwarcz, Vera *East Asian studies educator, history educator*
Sease, John W(illiam) *chemistry educator*
Seeley, J. *photography educator*
†Sergi, Theodore S. *educational administrator*
Shapiro, Norman Richard *Romance languages and literatures educator*
Slotkin, Richard Sidney *American studies educator, writer*
Steele, Robert Steven *psychology educator*
Stevens, Robert Edwin *bank executive, former insurance company executive*
Stowe, William Whitfield *English language educator*
Sumarsam *music educator*
Titus, David Anson *political science educator*
Turco, Alfred, Jr. *English language educator*
Upgren, Arthur Reinhold, Jr. *astronomer, educator, outdoor lighting consultant*
Wensinger, Arthur Stevens *German language and literature educator, author*
Winston, Krishna Ricarda *foreign language professional*

Milford
Berchem, Robert Lee, Sr. *lawyer*
†Blau, Stanley Marvin *information systems company executive*
Calabrese, Anthony *marine biologist*
Eadie, Cynthia *advertising executive*
†Kessman, Alan Stuart *telecommunications executive*
Madigan, Michael Scott *financial executive, treasurer*
Muth, Eric Peter *ophthalmic optician, consultant*
†Reichert, Bruce Robert *travel industry executive*
Taylor, Charles Henry *psychoanalyst, educator*
Wall, Robert Emmet *educational administrator, novelist*

Monroe
Turko, Alexander Anthony *biology educator*

Mystic
†Carr, J. Revell *museum executive, curator*
Connell, Hugh P. *aquarium executive*
Johnston, Waldo Cory Melrose *museum director*
Smith, Norman Clark *fund raising consultant*
Townsend, Thomas Perkins *former mining company executive*

Naugatuck
Flannery, Joseph Patrick *manufacturing company executive*

New Britain
Adams, John Francis, Jr. real estate executive
Ayers, Richard H. manufacturing company executive
Baskerville, Charles Alexander geologist, educator
Beal, Dallas Knight university president
†Davidson, Phillip Thomas retail company executive
Dethy, Ray Charles former university dean, management educator, consultant
Dimmick, Charles William geology educator
Donahugh, Robert Hayden library administrator
Frost, James Arthur former university president
Gallo, Donald Robert English educator
Hadlow, David Moore manufacturing executive
Jestin, Heimwarth B. retired university administrator
Judd, Richard Louis academic administrator
Kim, Ki Hoon economist, educator
Meskill, Thomas J. federal judge
Pearl, Helen Zalkan lawyer
Shumaker, John William university president
Sohn, Jeanne librarian
Tanner, Laurence Aram hospital administrator
Weddle, Stephen Shields manufacturing company executive

New Canaan
Bartlett, Dede Thompson company executive
Bergmann, Richard Ronald architect, photographer
Bosworth, Stephen Warren foundation executive
Burns, Ivan Alfred grocery products and industrial company executive
Caesar, Henry A., II sculptor
Congdon, Janet Zakryk counselor
Coughlin, Francis Raymond, Jr. surgeon, educator, lawyer
†Crawford, Kevin Francis mining company executive
Crossman, William Whittard retired wire cable and communications executive
Day, Castle Nason food company executive
de Selding, Edward Bertrand retired banker
Dillon, James McNulty retired banker
Foley, Patrick Martin computer manufacturing company executive
Gottlieb, Arnold dentist
Halan, John Paul human resources executive
Halverstadt, Robert Dale mechanical engineer, metals manufacturing company executive
Hanson, Joseph J. publishing executive
Harper, Anne Hopson environmental scientist, administrator
Hodgson, Richard electronics company executive
Jennings, William Christopher securities industry executive
Johnston, Douglas Frederick industrial holding company executive
Kovatch, Jak Gene artist
Marcus, Edward economist, educator
McClure, Grover Benjamin management consultant
McIvor, Donald Kenneth retired petroleum company executive, university administrator
Mc Mennamin, George Barry advertising agency executive
Means, David Hammond retired advertising executive
Mendez, Albert Orlando industrialist, financier
Mountcastle, Katharine Babcock foundation executive
O'Neill, Patrick Henry consulting mining engineer
Packard, Vance Oakley writer
Phypers, Dean Pinney retired computer company executive
Pike, William Edward business executive
Powell, Harold Fryburg food products executive
Powers, Thomas Moore author
Prescott, Peter Sherwin writer
Rendl-Marcus, Mildred artist, economist
Richards, Walter DuBois artist, illustrator
Richardson, Dana Roland video producer
Risom, Jens furniture designer, manufacturing executive
Rutledge, John William former watch company executive
Sachs, John Peter carbon company executive
Snyder, Nathan entrepreneur
Stack, J. William, Jr. management consultant
Thomas, Robert Dean publisher
Thompson, George Lee manufacturing company executive
Thomsen, Donald Laurence, Jr. institute executive, mathematician
Toumey, Hubert John (Hugh Toumey) textile company executive
Wallace, Kenneth Donald lawyer
Ward, Richard Vance, Jr. management executive
Wolfley, Alan corporate executive

New Fairfield
†Meyers, Abbey S. foundation administrator

New Hartford
Hall, Newman A. retired mechanical engineer

New Haven
Aaslestad, Halvor Gunerius university official
Abell, Millicent Demmin university library administrator
Abelson, Robert Paul psychologist, educator
Ackerman, Bruce Arnold lawyer, educator
Adair, Robert Kemp physicist, educator
Adelberg, Edward Allen genetics educator
Aghajanian, George Kevork medical educator
Alexandrov, Vladimir Eugene Russian literature educator
Altman, Sidney biology educator
Amar, Akhil Reed law educator
Ames, Louise Bates child psychologist
†Anderson, John Frederick science administrator, entomologist, researcher
Apfel, Robert Edmund mechanical engineering educator, applied physicist, research scientist
Apter, David Ernest political science educator
†Aronson, Peter Samuel medical scientist, physiology educator
†Askenase, Philip W. medicine and pathology educator
†Aylor, Donald Earl biophysicist, research meteorologist, plant pathology educator and reseacher
Bailey, William Harrison artist, educator
Baker, Robert Stevens organist, educator
Balkin, Jack M. law educator
Barash, Paul George anesthesiologist, educator
Barker, Richard Clark electrical engineering educator
Bartholomew, Alan Alfred librarian, educator
†Beardsley, G(eorge) Peter pediatric oncologist, biochemical pharmacologist
Beauchesne, Karen Sue nurse, administrator
Behan, Robert Francis bank executive
Behrman, Harold Richard endocrinologist, physiologist, educator
Bell, Wendell sociologist, educator, futurist
Bennett, Scott Boyce librarian
Bennett, William Ralph, Jr. physicist, educator
Berliner, Robert William physician, medical educator
Berner, Robert Arbuckle geochemist, educator
Bernstein, Ira Borah physics educator
Bers, Victor classics educator
Berson, Jerome Abraham chemistry educator
Blatt, Sidney Jules psychology educator, psychoanalyst
Bloom, Harold humanities educator
Blum, John Morton historian
Böowering, Gerhard H. Islamic studies educator
†Bormann, Frederick Herbert forest ecology educator
Borroff, Marie English language educator
Boulpaep, Emile Louis J. B. physiology educator, foundation administrator
Boyer, James Lorenzen physician, educator
Bracken, Paul political science educator
Brainard, Paul Henry musicologist, music educator
Brainard, William Crittenden economist, educator, university official
Braverman, Irwin Merton dermatologist, educator
Brewer, Charles H., Jr. bishop
Brewer, Garry Dwight social scientist, educator
Brewster, Carroll Worcester fund administrator
Brilmayer, R. Lea legal educator, lawyer
Bromley, David Allan physicist, educator
Brooks, Peter (Preston) French and comparative literature educator, writer
Brown, Arvin Bragin theater director
Brown, Ralph Sharp law educator
Brown, Thomas Huntington neuroscientist
Brownell, Kelly David psychologist, educator
Buck, Donald Tirrell finance educator
Bunney, Benjamin Stephenson psychiatrist
Burns, Ellen Bree federal judge
Burrow, Gerard Noel physician, educator
Burt, Robert Amsterdam lawyer, educator
Buss, Leo William biologist, educator
Butler, David J. newspaper editor
Byck, Robert Samuel psychiatrist, educator
Cabranes, José Alberto federal judge
Cahn, Walter B. art history educator
†Calabresi, Guido federal judge
†Calvi, Paul chemicals executive
Cappelli, Mary Antoinette principal
Carter, Stephen Lisle law educator
Casteras, Susan Paulette museum curator, educator
Chandler, William Knox physiologist
Chang, Richard Kounai physics educator
Child, Irvin Long psychologist, educator
Childs, Brevard Springs religious educator
Chupka, William Andrew chemical physicist, educator
Clark, Elias law educator
Clarke, Fred Webster, III architectural firm executive
Clizbe, John Anthony psychologist
Coe, Michael Douglas anthropologist, educator
Cohen, Donald Jay pediatrics, psychiatry and psychology educator, administrator
Cohen, Lawrence Baruch neurobiologist, educator
Cohen, Lawrence Sorel physician, educator
Cohen, Melvin Joseph neuroscientist
Cohen, Morris Leo law librarian, educator
†Cole, Laurence Anthony reproductive biology and cancer biology educator
Coleman, Joseph Emory biophysics and biochemistry educator
Coleman, Jules L. law educator
Collins, William F., Jr. neurosurgery educator
Comer, James Pierpont psychiatrist
Conklin, Harold Colyer anthropologist, educator
†Cooney, Leo Mathias, Jr. geriatrician, educator
Cooper, Jack Ross pharmacology educator, researcher
Cosham, Don architect
Cottrell, Mary-Patricia Tross banker
†Crossey, (John) Moore Davison librarian
Crothers, Donald Morris biochemist, educator
Crowder, Robert George psychology educator
Culler, Arthur Dwight English language educator
Cunningham, Walter Jack electrical engineering educator
Damaska, Mirjan Radovan law educator
Davey, Lycurgus Michael neurosurgeon
Davis, David Brion historian, educator
Davis, Deborah sociology educator
Davis, Michael medical educator
Dearington, Michael lawyer
Dechant, Virgil C. fraternal organization administrator
Deese, James LaMotte financial executive
Demos, John Putnam history educator, writer, consultant
De Rose, Sandra Michele psychotherapist, educator, supervisor, administrator
Deutsch, Jan Ginter law educator
Dittes, James Edward psychology of religion educator
Dolan, Thomas F., Jr. pediatrician, educator
Donaldson, Robert Macartney, Jr. physician
Donofrio, Richard Michael telecommunications company executive
Doob, Leonard William psychology educator, academic administrator
Dorsey, Peter Collins federal judge
DuBois, Arthur Brooks physiologist, educator
Duke, Steven Barry law educator
Dupré, Louis philosopher, educator
Edelson, Marshall psychiatry educator, psychoanalyst
†Edelson, Richard L. dermatology educator
Edelson, Zelda Sarah Toll editor
Eisenman, Alvin educator, graphic designer
†Elias, Jack Angel physician, educator
Ellickson, Robert Chester law educator
Elliott, Edwin Donald, Jr. law educator, federal administrator, environmental lawyer
Ember, Melvin Lawrence anthropologist, educator
Erikson, Kai sociologist, educator
Erlich, Victor Slavic languages educator
Evans, Alfred Spring physician, educator
Fassett, John D. retired utility executive, consultant
Feinstein, Alvan Richard physician
Feit, Walter mathematics educator
Fischer, Michael John computer science educator
Fiscus, Robert L. electric power industry executive
Fiss, Owen M. law educator
Franklin, Ralph William library director, literary scholar
French, Kenneth Ronald finance educator
French, Richard Frederic retired music educator
Fried, Charles A. accountant,financial executive
Friedlaender, Gary Elliott orthopedist, educator
Gallup, Donald Clifford bibliographer, educator
Galston, Arthur William biology educator
Garner, Wendell Richard psychology educator
Gastwirth, Donald Edward lawyer, literary agent
Geanakoplos, Deno John history educator
Genel, Myron pediatrician, educator
Gewirtz, Paul D. lawyer
†Gilbert, Creighton Eddy art historian
Gillis, C. Norman anesthesiology and pharmacology educator
Gilman, Richard drama educator, author
Glaser, Gilbert Herbert neuroscientist, physician, educator
Glier, Ingeborg Johanna German language and literature educator
Goldsmith, Mary Helen M. biology educator
Goldstein, Abraham S. lawyer, educator
Goldstein, Joseph law educator
Gordon, John Charles forestry educator
Gordon, Robert Boyd geophysics educator
Gordon, Robert W. law educator
†Gore, John Christopher medical physicist
Graetz, Michael J. law educator
†Gray, Bradford Hitch medical educator
Greene, Liliane French educator, editor
Greene, Thomas McLernon language professional, educator
Greenfield, James Robert lawyer
†Gross, Ian academic pediatrician, neonatologist
Grossi, Richard J. electric utility company executive
Guicharnaud, Jacques E. H. language educator
†Haddad, Gabriel G. physician, pediatrics educator
Haller, Gary Lee chemical engineering educator
Hallo, William Wolfgang Assyriologist
Handschumacher, Robert Edmund biochemistry educator
Hansmann, Henry Baethke law educator
Hanson, Anne Coffin art historian
Harries, Karsten philosophy educator, researcher
Harrison, Henry Starin real estate educator, appraiser, entrepreneur
Hartman, Geoffrey H. language professional, educator
Hartman, Willard Daniel marine biologist, educator
Hayslett, John Paul physician, medical educator, researcher
Heninger, George Robert psychiatry educator, researcher
Henrich, Victor Eugene physicist, educator
Herbert, Peter Noel physician, medical educator
Hersey, George Leonard art history educator
Herzenberg, Arvid physicist, educator
Hickey, Leo J(oseph) museum curator, educator
Hinds, Edward Allen physicist, educator
Hoffleit, Ellen Dorrit astronomer
Hoffman, Joseph Frederick physiology educator
Hohenberg, Pierre Claude research physicist
Holder, Angela Roddey lawyer, educator
Hole, Frank anthropology educator
†Holford, Theodore Richard biostatistician, educator
Hollander, John humanities educator, poet
Holmes, Frederic Lawrence science historian
Holquist, James Michael Russian and comparative literature educator
Horstmann, Dorothy Millicent physician, educator
Horváth, Csaba chemical engineering educator, researcher
†Howe, Roger Evans mathematician, educator
Hyman, Paula E(llen) history educator
Insler, Stanley philologist, educator
Jackson, Stanley Webber psychiatrist, medical historian
Jacobson, Nathan mathematics educator
Jacoby, Robert Ottinger comparative medicine educator
James, Paul Charles tire company executive
Jatlow, Peter I. pathologist, medical educator, researcher
Jekel, James Franklin physician, public health educator
Johnson, Eva Jo elementary education educator
Johnson, Lester Fredrick artist
Johnson, Robert Clyde theology educator
Johnstone, Quintin legal educator
Jorgensen, William L. chemistry educator
Kagan, Donald historian, educator
Kane, Patricia Ellen museum curator
Kashgarian, Michael pathologist, physician
Katz, Jay psychiatry and law educator
Kavanagh, Aidan Joseph priest, university educator
Kazemzadeh, Firuz history educator
Keck, Leander Earl theology educator
Kennedy, Paul Michael history educator
Kessen, William psychologist, educator
Kirchner, John Albert retired otolaryngology educator
Klein, Martin Jesse physicist, educator, science historian
Kleiner, Diana Elizabeth Edelman art history educator, administrator
†Kleinman, Charles Stephan physician, medical educator
Klevorick, Alvin K. law and economics educator
Koh, Harold Hongju law educator
Komp, Diane Marilyn pediatric oncologist, hematologist, writer
Konigsberg, William Henry molecular biophysics and biochemistry educator, administrator
Krauss, Judith Belliveau nursing educator
Krevit, Rita Recha alderwoman, retired business owner
Kronman, Anthony Townsend lawyer, educator
Kushlan, Samuel Daniel physician, educator, hospital administrator
Laderman, Ezra composer, educator, college dean
Lamar, Howard Roberts educational administrator, historian
Lang, Serge mathematics educator
Langbein, John Harriss lawyer, educator
LaPalombara, Joseph political science educator
Lasaga, Antonio C. geochemistry educator, researcher
Leeney, Robert Joseph newspaper editor
†Leffell, David Joel surgeon, dermatologist, educator, researcher
Lentz, Thomas Lawrence biomedical educator, dean, researcher
Levin, Richard Charles economist
Levine, Robert John physician, educator
Lewis, Melvin psychiatrist, pediatrician, psychoanalyst
Lipson, Leon law educator
Logue, Frank arbitrator, mediator, urban consultant, former mayor New Haven
Lord, George deForest English educator
Lorimer, Linda Koch college official
†Lorkovic, Tatjana librarian
Ma, Tso-Ping electrical engineering educator, researcher, consultant
MacAvoy, Paul Webster economics educator, university dean
Mac Dowell, Samuel Wallace physics educator
MacMullen, Ramsay retired history educator
Malherbe, Abraham Johannes, VI religion educator, writer
Malkin, Moses Montefiore employee benefits administration company executive
Marcus, Ruth Barcan philosopher, educator, writer, lecturer
Marks, Lawrence Edward psychologist
Marmor, Theodore Richard political science and public management educator
Marshall, Burke law educator
Martin, Samuel Elmo linguistics educator
Martz, Louis Lohr English literature educator
Mashaw, Jerry L. lawyer, educator
Massey, William S. mathematician, educator
Mayhew, David Raymond political educator
Mazzarella, Andrew James automotive products executive, accountant
Mazzotta, Giuseppe Francesco Italian language and literature educator
†McCarthy, Paul Louis pediatrics educator
McClatchy, J. D. editor, writer, educator
McDermott, Drew Vincent computer science educator
Mc Guire, William James social psychology educator
McMullin, Ruth Roney publishing company executive, management fellow
McMunn, Richard Earl editor, writer
Meeks, Wayne A. religious studies educator
†Mermann, Alan Cameron pediatrics educator, chaplain
†Merritt, John Augustus geriatrician, educator
Meyer, Patricia Ann veterinarian
†Miglio, Daniel Joseph telecommunications company executive
Miller, I. George physician, educator, researcher
Miller, Neal Elgar psychologist, emeritus educator
Miskimin, Harry Alvin history educator
Monteith, Walter Henry, Jr. utility company executive
Moore, Peter Bartlett biochemist, educator
Morgan, Robert P. music theorist, educator
Morriss, George W. banking executive
†Morrow, Jon Stanley pathology educator, medical scientist
Mostow, George Daniel mathematics educator
Mullen, Frank Albert university official, clergyman
Musto, David Franklin physician, historian, consultant
Myers, Jerome Keeley sociology educator
Naftolin, Frederick physician, reproductive biologist educator
Narendra, Kumpati Subrahmanya electrical engineer, educator
Natanson, Maurice Alexander philosopher, educator
Newick, Craig David architect
Newman, Harry Rudolph urologist, educator
Newman, Herbert S. architect, educator
Newman, Sasha Mary art historian, curator
Niederman, James Corson physician, educator
Nochlin, Linda art history educator
Nolan, Victoria Holmes theater director
Noon, Patrick museum curator
Novick, Alvin biology educator
Oemler, Augustus, Jr. astronomy educator
Oliver-Warren, Mary Elizabeth library science educator
Ostfeld, Adrian Michael physician
Ostrom, John H. vertebrate paleontologist, educator, museum curator
Outka, Gene Harold philosophy and Christian ethics educator
Palisca, Claude Victor musicologist, educator
Papageorge, Tod photographer, educator
Parker, Peter D.M. physicist, educator, researcher
Pease, David Gordon artist, educator
Peck, Merton Joseph educator, economist
Pelikan, Jaroslav Jan history educator
Pelli, Cesar architect
Peterson, Linda H. English language and literature educator
Phillips, Peter Charles Bonest economist, educator, researcher
Piatetski-Shapiro, Ilya mathematics educator
Piscottano, Ann Uscilla city official
Platner, Warren architect
Poirion, Daniel foreign language educator
Polayes, Irving Marvin plastic surgeon
Pollitt, Jerome Jordan art history educator
Porter, Charles Allan French language educator, educational administrator
Pospisil, Leopold Jaroslav anthropology educator
Priest, George L. law educator
†Prown, Jules David art historian educator
Pruett, Kyle Dean psychiatrist, writer, educator
Prusoff, William Herman biochemical pharmacologist, educator
Rakic, Pasko neuroscientist, educator
Ranis, Gustav economist, educator
Rawson, Claude Julien English educator
Rawson, Robert Orrin physiologist
Redmond, Donald Eugene, Jr. neuroscientist, educator
Reifsnyder, William Edward meteorologist
Reiser, Morton Francis psychiatrist, educator
Reisman, William M. lawyer, educator
Reiss, Albert John, Jr. sociology educator
†Reiss, Michael medical oncologist, researcher
Reynolds, Lloyd George economist, educator
Reynolds, Mary Trackett political scientist
†Richard, Alison Feltes anthropology educator
Richards, Frederic Middlebrook biochemist, educator
Rickart, Charles Earl mathematician, educator
Ritchie, J. Murdoch pharmacologist
Robbins, William Randolph minister
Robinson, (David) Duncan museum administrator, art historian
Robinson, Fred Colson English language educator
Rodgers, John geologist, educator
†Rodriguez, Cesar librarian
Romano, Roberta law educator
Rose-Ackerman, Susan law and political economy educator
Rosenblum, M. Edgar theater director
Roth, Harold architect
Rouse, Irving anthropologist, emeritus educator
Ruddle, Francis Hugh genetics educator
†Ruddle, Nancy Hartman microbiology educator
Rush, William John newspaper executive
Russett, Bruce Martin political science educator
Ryden, John Graham publishing executive

Saltzman, Barry *meteorologist, educator*
Sammons, Jeffrey Leonard *foreign language educator*
Sandweiss, Jack *physicist, educator*
Sanneh, Lamin *religion educator*
Sartorelli, Alan Clayton *pharmacology educator*
Sasaki, Clarence Takashi *surgeon, medical educator*
Scarf, Herbert Eli *economics educator*
Schenker, Alexander Marian *Slavic linguistics educator*
†Schepartz, Alanna *biochemist, educator*
Schmeer, Arline Catherine *cancer research development chemotherapy scientist*
†Schmuttenmaer, Charles A. *chemistry educator*
Schowalter, John Erwin *psychiatrist, educator*
Schultz, T. Paul *economics educator*
Schwartz, Ilsa Roslow *neuroscientist*
Schwartz, Peter Edward *physician, gynecologic oncology educator*
Scully, Vincent *art historian, retired educator, writer*
†Sears, Marvin *ophthalmologist, educator*
Seashore, Margretta Reed *physician*
Seligman, George Benham *mathematics educator*
Shubik, Martin *economics educator*
Shulman, Robert Gerson *biophysics educator*
†Siegel, Norman Joseph *pediatrician, educator*
Sigler, Paul Benjamin *molecular biology educator, protein crystallographer*
Silver, George Albert *physician, educator*
Simon, John Gerald *law educator*
Skinner, Helen Catherine Wild *biomineralogist*
Slayman, Carolyn Walch *geneticist, educator*
Slayman, Clifford Leroy, Jr. *biophysicist, educator*
Smith, David Martyn *forestry educator*
Smith, John Edwin *philosophy educator*
Smith, Rogers Mood *political scientist*
Smith, William Hulse *forestry and environmental studies educator*
Söll, Dieter *biochemistry educator*
Solnit, Albert Jay *commissioner, physician, educator*
Sparrow, Sara S. *psychology educator, psychologist*
Spence, Jonathan Dermot *historian, educator*
Spiro, Howard Marget *physician, educator*
Sreenivasan, Katepalli Raju *mechanical engineering educator*
Steitz, Joan Argetsinger *biochemistry educator*
Stenn, Kurt S. *dermatology and pathology educator*
Sternberg, Robert Jeffrey *psychology educator*
Stevens, Joseph Charles *psychology educator*
Stith, Kate *legal educator*
Stolberg, Irving J. *state legislator, consultant*
Stolwijk, Jan Adrianus Jozef *physiologist, biophysicist*
Stowe, Bruce Bernot *biology educator*
Stuehrenberg, Paul Frederick *librarian*
Summers, William Cofield *science educator*
Szczarba, Robert Henry *mathematics educator, mathematician*
Tamagawa, Tsuneo *mathematics educator*
†Tamborlane, William V., Jr. *physician, biomedical researcher, pediatrics educator*
Tanaka, Kay *genetics educator*
Taylor, Kenneth John W. *physician of diognostic imagery*
Theodore, Eustace D. *alumni association executive, management consultant*
Tilson, John Quillin *lawyer*
Tirro, Frank Pascale *music educator, author, composer*
Tobin, James *economics educator*
Totman, Conrad Davis *history educator*
Trinkaus, John Philip *cell and developmental biologist*
Tufte, Edward Rolf *statistics educator, publisher*
Turekian, Karl Karekin *geochemistry educator*
Turner, Caroline *theatre manager*
Underdown, David Edward *historian, educator*
Valesio, Paolo *Italian language and literature educator, writer*
Van Sinderen, Alfred White *former telephone company executive*
†Vogel, Susan Mullin *museum director*
Vroom, Victor Harold *management consultant, educator*
Waggoner, Paul Edward *agricultural scientist*
Wagner, Allan Ray *psychology educator, experimental psychologist*
Wagner, Günter Paul *biologist educator*
Wandycz, Piotr Stefan *history educator*
Wasserman, Harry Hershal *chemistry educator*
Waters, Donald Joseph *information services administrator*
Waxman, Stephen George *neurologist, researcher*
Weaver, Diana Jane *nursing administrator*
Wegener, Peter Paul *educator, author*
Weinstein, Stanley *Buddhist studies educator*
Weiss, Robert M. *urologist, educator*
Wentz, Howard Beck, Jr. *manufacturing company executive*
Wessel, Morris Arthur *pediatrician*
Westerfield, Holt Bradford *political scientist, educator*
Wheeler, Stanton *law and social science educator*
Wiberg, Kenneth Berle *chemist, educator*
Winks, Robin William *history educator*
Winter, Ralph Karl, Jr. *federal judge*
Wizner, Stephen *law educator*
Woerner, Peter Kurt *architect, builder*
†Wojewodski, Stan, Jr. *artistic director, dean*
Wolf, Werner Paul *physicist, educator*
Wright, Hastings Kemper *surgeon, educator*
Wyman, Robert J. *biology educator, neurophysiologist, neurogeneticist*
†Yandle, Stephen Thomas *law school dean*
Yeazell, Ruth Bernard *English educator*
Zaccagnino, Joseph Anthony *hospital administrator*
Zampano, Robert Carmine *federal judge*
Zaret, Barry Lewis *cardiologist, medical educator*
Zeller, Michael Edward *physicist*
†Zigler, Edward Frank *educator, psychologist*
Zinn, Robert James *astronomer*

New London
Bobruff, Jerome *physician*
Creviston, Richard L. *banker*
†Daragan, Patricia A. *librarian*
Doro, Marion Elizabeth *political scientist, educator*
Gaudiani, Claire Lynn *academic administrator*
Goodwin, Richard Hale *botany educator*
Knowles, Elizabeth Pringle *art museum director*
Lumadue, Donald Dean *hobby and crafts company executive*
MacCluggage, Reid *newspaper editor, publisher*
McGinley, Morgan *newspaper editor*
Mellberg, Leonard Evert *physicist*
Mulvey, Helen Frances *retired history educator*
Owsley, Norman Lee *electrical engineer, educator*
Pinhey, Frances Louise *physical education educator*
Rice, Argyll Pryor *Hispanic studies and Spanish language educator*
Rogers, Brian Deane *librarian*
Santaniello, Angelo Gary *state supreme court justice*
Wetmore, Thomas Trask, III *retired foundation administrator, retired coast guard officer*

New Milford
Edmondson, John Richard *lawyer, pharmaceutical manufacturing company executive*
Fabricand, Burton Paul *physicist, educator*
†Wedral, Elaine Regina *food chemist*

New Preston
Duffis, Allen Jacobus *polymer chemistry extrusion specialist*

Newington
Fleeson, William *psychiatry educator*
Sabatini, Vincent Fernando *lawyer*
Sumner, David George *association executive*
Vassar, William Gerald *gifted and talented education educator*

Newtown
Bockelman, Charles Kincaid *physics educator*
Cayne, Bernard Stanley *editor*
Verano, Anthony Frank *retired banker*

Niantic
Ashley, Eleanor Tidaback *retired elementary educator*
Bobruff, Carole Marks *radio show producer, personality*
Hunt, Francis Howard *retired navy laboratory official*

Noank
Bates, Gladys Edgerly *sculptor*

Norfolk
Lambros, Lambros John *lawyer, petroleum company executive*
Vagliano, Alexander Marino *banker*

North Branford
Gregan, Edmund Robert *landscape architect*
Logan, John Arthur, Jr. *retired foundation executive*
Mead, Lawrence Myers, Jr. *retired aerospace executive*

North Haven
Dahl, Robert Alan *political science educator*
Hoffmann, John J. *architect*
Mahl, George Franklin *psychoanalyst, psychologist, educator*
Seton, Fenmore Roger *manufacturing company executive, civic worker*
Walker, Fred Elmer *broadcasting executive*

North Stonington
Keane, John Patrick *retired secondary education educator*
Mollegen, Albert Theodore, Jr. *engineering company executive*
Nolf, David Manstan *financial executive*

Northford
James, Virginia Stowell *retired elementary education educator*
James, William Hall *former state official, educator*

Norwalk
Albanese, Licia *retired operatic soprano*
Balmuth, Marc I. *consumer products company executive*
Bell, Martin Jay *producer, writer*
Bennett, Carl *retired discount department store executive*
Bergere, C(lifford) Wendell, Jr. *lawyer*
Bermas, Stephen *lawyer*
†Booth, George Keefer *finanical service executive*
Bowman, Robert Gibson *publishing company executive*
Brandt, Richard Paul *communications and entertainment company executive*
Brod, Morton Shlevin *oral surgeon*
Brooks, Babert Vincent *publisher*
Brown, Beatrice *symphony conductor*
Bullard, Edward Payson, IV *non-profit executive*
Cammaker, Sheldon Ira *lawyer*
Caravatt, Paul Joseph, Jr. *communications company executive*
Caro, Warren *theatrical executive, lawyer*
Carswell, Bruce *communications executive*
†Cheifetz, David S. *small business owner*
Clarke, Don R. *consumer products company executive*
Crump, James G., Jr. *printing company executive*
†Digiovanna, Charles Vincent *chemical manufacturer*
Dresher, William Henry *research association executive*
Ettre, Leslie Stephen *chemist*
Floch, Martin Herbert *physician*
Foster, John McNeely *accounting standards executive*
Grace, Julianne Alice *manufacturing company executive*
Hart, James W., Jr. *manufacturing executive*
Hathaway, Carl Emil *investment management company executive*
Heeb, Louis F. *diversified corporation executive*
Hirsch, Leon Charles *medical company executive*
Howatson, Marianne *publisher*
Irving, Michael Henry *architect*
†Johnson, James Lawrence *telephone company executive*
Johnstone, Chauncey Olcott *pharmaceutical company executive*
Josefsen, Turi *medical supply company executive*
Kelley, Gaynor Nathaniel *instrumentation manufacturing company executive*
Korthoff, Herbert William *medical devices company executive*
Leonard, Stewart J. *dairy company executive*
Maarbjerg, Mary Penzold *office equipment company executive*
Maisano, Phillip Nicholas *investment company executive*
Manning, James Forrest *computer executive*
Marnane, Joseph Peter *maritime center executive*
McDonell, Horace George, Jr. *instrument company executive*
Mosso, David *accountant*
Needham, Charles William *neurosurgeon*
Nelson, David Leonard *process management systems company executive*
Neuman, Curtis William *computer systems company executive*
Partch, Kenneth Paul *editor, consultant*
Payne, Paul D. *finance company executive*
Peltz, Alan Howard *manufacturing company executive*
Perry, Charles Owen *sculptor*
Perschino, Arthur J. *secondary school principal*
Schmalzried, Marvin Eugene *financial consultant*
Smith, Wendell Murray *graphic arts control and equipment manufacturing executive*
Sturm, Donald L. *construction executive*
Tracey, Edward John *physician, surgeon*
Vanderbilt, Hugh Bedford, Sr. *mineral and chemical company executive*
†Vinciguerra, Salvatore Joseph *scientific instrument company executive*
Watson, H. Mitchell, Jr. *business machines company executive*
Wiggins, Charles *secondary education educator*
York, Theodore *electronics executive*

Norwich
Gualtieri, Joseph Peter *museum director*
Meseha, George Mansour *mechanical engineer*
Sharpe, Richard Samuel *architectural company executive*

Old Greenwich
Baritz, Loren *history educator*
Bonner, Charles William, III *community services executive, newspaper writer*
Fernous, Louis Ferdinand, Jr. *consumer products company executive*
Hittle, Richard Howard *corporate executive, international affairs consultant*
Islan, Gregory deFontaine *cable television executive*
Kenyon, Robert Edwin, Jr. *magazine journalist, magazine consultant, lecturer*
Maher, Stephen Albert *investment banker*
Mc Donough, Richard Doyle *retired paper company executive*
Mc Quinn, William P. *corporation executive*
Plancher, Robert Lawrence *manufacturing company executive*
Rukeyser, Robert James *manufacturing executive*
Scullion, Tsugiko Yamagami *non-profit organization executive*

Old Lyme
Anderson, Theodore Robert *physicist*
Bond, Niles Woodbridge *cultural institute executive, former foreign service officer*
Chandler, Elisabeth Gordon (Mrs. Laci De Gerenday) *sculptor, harpist*
Cook, Charles Davenport *pediatrician, educator*
de Gerenday, Laci Anthony *sculptor*
St. George, Judith Alexander *author*
Volland, Robert Stephen *financial executive*

Old Saybrook
Elrod, Harold Glenn *retired engineering science educator, consultant*
Hamilton, Donald Bengtsson *author*
Jensen, Oliver Ormerod *editor, writer*
Phillips, William Eugene *advertising agency executive*
Schneider, John Arnold *business investor*
Spencer, William Courtney *foundation executive, international business executive*

Orange
Bowerman, Richard Henry *utility company executive, lawyer*
Clark, John Phelps *lawyer, automotive executive*
Miller, Henry Forster *architect*
Ratcliffe, George Jackson, Jr. *business executive, lawyer*
Rowell, Harry Brown, Jr. *technology company executive*
Sinclair, Robert J. *automotive executive*

Plainville
Glassman, Gerald Seymour *metal finishing company executive*

Pomfret
Woodbridge, Henry Sewall *management consultant*

Preston
Makara, Carol Pattie *education educator, consultant*

Putnam
Desaulniers, Rene Gerard Lesieur *optometrist*

Redding
Benyei, Candace Reed *psychotherapist*
Foster, Edward John *engineering physicist*
Kipnis, Igor *harpsichordist, fortepianist, critic*
Mathews, Carmen Sylva *actress*
Russell, Allan David *lawyer*

Ridgefield
Bye, Arthur Edwin, Jr. *landscape architect*
Doran, Charles Edward *textile manufacturing executive*
Farina, Peter R. *biochemist*
Finneran, Thomas Aquinas *finance company executive*
Forbes, James Wendell *publishing consultant*
Julian, Alexander, II *menswear designer*
Kelley, Edward Allen *publisher*
Knortz, Herbert Charles *retired conglomerate company executive*
Levine, Paul Michael *paper industry executive, consultant*
Lodewick, Philip Hughes *equipment leasing company executive*
Malhotra, Surin M. *aerospace manufacturing executive*
Margolis, George *pathologist, medical educator*
Mattausch, Thomas Edward *public relations consultant, business owner*
McGovern, R(ichard) Gordon *food company executive*
Norman, Richard Arthur *educator*
Phelps, Judson Hewett *marketing sales executive*
Sadow, Harvey S. *health care company executive*
Tomanic, Joseph P(aul) *research scientist*
Wyton, Alec *composer, organist*

Riverside
Battat, Emile A. *management executive*
Coulson, Robert *retired association executive, lawyer*
Geismar, Richard Lee *communications executive*
Isaacson, Gerald Sidney *publishing company executive*
Juneja, Diljit Singh *retired management consultant*
Lovejoy, Allen Fraser *retired lawyer*
McCullough, Robert Willis *former textile executive*
McSpadden, Peter Ford *retired advertising agency executive*
Otto, Charles Edward *health care administrator*
Pearson, Robert Greenlees *writing services company executive*
Powers, Claudia McKenna *state government official*

Rocky Hill
Chuang, Frank Shiunn-Jea *engineering executive, consultant*
Geckle, Robert Alan *manufacturing company executive*
Hollis, Peter B. *retail executive*
Reese, Paul Wesley, Jr. *retail executive*

Rowayton
Moran, John Patrick, Jr. *publishing executive, marketing consultant*
Sills, David Lawrence *retired sociologist*

Roxbury
Anderson, Robert Woodruff *playwright, novelist, screenwriter*
Gurney, Albert Ramsdell *playwright, novelist, educator*
Miller, Arthur *playwright, author*

Salem
Diamond, Sigmund *editor, educator*

Salisbury
Bevan, Charles Albert, Jr. *minister*
Block, Zenas *management consultant, educator*
Blum, Robert Edward *business executive*

Sandy Hook
Karkut, Emil Joseph *manufacturing company executive*
Kellogg, Steven *author, illustrator*

Sharon
Gordon, Nicholas *broadcasting executive*
†Gottlieb, Richard Matthew *psychiatrist, consultant*
Murphy, Thomas Francis *federal judge*

Shelton
Bowron, John B. *transportation executive*
Crowe, Jeffrey C. *transportation executive*
Forbes, Richard E. *retired publishing company executive*
Harvey, Michael Lee *lawyer, transportation executive*
Lobsenz, Herbert Munter *data base company executive*
Mahoney, J. Daniel *federal judge*
McCurdy, Charles Gribbel *publishing company executive*
Shapiro, Glenn Alan *marketing executive, consultant*
Smith, Craig Richards *manufacturing executive*
Stauff, Michael Frederick *financial manager*
Wham, William Neil *publisher*
Zeller, Claude *physicist, researcher*

Sherman
Goodspeed, Barbara *artist*
Lee, Wallace Williams, Jr. *retired hotel executive*
Piel, William, Jr. *retired lawyer*
Valeriani, Richard Gerard *news broadcaster*

Simsbury
Hildebrandt, Frederick Dean, Jr. *management consultant*
Krisher, William K. *former insurance company executive*
Lance, Larry Kent *insurance company executive*
Long, Michael Thomas *lawyer, manufacturing company executive*
Nolan, Robert *management consulting company executive*
†Vander Putten, LeRoy Andrew *insurance company executive*

Somers
Blake, Stewart Prestley *retired ice cream company executive*
Hooper, Donald Robert *corporate chief executive officer*

South Windsor
Bapat, Vijaya *pediatrician, educator*
Gentile, George Michael *manufacturing company finance executive*
†Gerber, H. Joseph *manufacturing executive*
Gerber, Heinz Joseph *computer automation company executive*

Southbury
Atwood, Edward Charles *economist, educator*
Cassidy, James Joseph *public relations counsel*
Fabiani, Dante Carl *industrialist*
March, Xavier *systems analyst*
O'Neill, Arthur Julius *state legislator, lawyer*
Usher, Elizabeth Reuter (Mrs. William A. Scar) *retired librarian*
Wescott, Roger Williams *anthropologist*

Southport
Damson, Barrie Morton *oil and gas exploration company executive*
Greene, Herbert Bruce *lawyer, merchant banker*
Haas, Ward John *research and development executive*
Hill, David Lawrence *research corporation executive*
Kingsley, John McCall, Jr. *manufacturing company executive*
Miles, Leland Weber *university president*
Parker, David Scott *architect*
Perry, Vincent Aloysius *corporate executive*
Roache, Edward Francis *retired manufacturing company executive*
Ruger, William Batterman *firearms manufacturing company executive*
Walker, Charles Dodsley *conductor, organist*
Wheeler, Wilmot Fitch, Jr. *diversified manufacturing company executive*

Wilbur, E. Packer *investment company executive*

Stamford

Adams, Taggart D. *lawyer*
Allaire, Paul Arthur *office equipment company executive*
Alley, William Jack *holding company executive*
Anderson, Susan Stuebing *business equipment company executive*
Ashton, Harris John *business executive*
Ast, Steven Todd *executive search firm executive*
Axthelm, M. Bonnie *advertising executive*
Aylesworth, Thomas Gibbons *editor, author*
Ball, John A. *forest products company executive*
Barker, James Rex *water transportation executive*
Barlow, Clark W. *telephone company executive*
Barton, James Miller *lawyer*
Beiser, Gerald J. *paper products company executive*
Bell, W. James *manufacturing company executive*
Beyman, Jonathan Eric *information officer*
Bigelow, Eugene Thayer, Jr. *media company executive*
Bitter, Frank Gordon *manufacturing executive*
Block, Edward Martel *consultant, former telephone company executive*
Block, Ruth *retired insurance company executive*
Bowen, Patrick Harvey *lawyer, consultant*
Brakeley, George Archibald, Jr. *fundraising consultant*
†Breslawsky, Marc C. *manufacturing executive*
Britt, Glenn Alan *media company executive*
Britton, Robert Austin *manufacturing company executive*
Burchfield, William H. *forest products company executive*
Cahill, John C. *general industry company executive*
Calarco, Vincent Anthony *specialty chemicals company executive*
Carlin, Gabriel S. *corporate executive*
Carpenter, Edmund Mogford *manufacturing executive*
Carroll, Thomas Sylvester *business executive*
Cassetta, Sebastian Ernest *industry executive*
Castrignano, Robert Anthony *retired dean, retired broadcasting company executive*
Cavallon, Betty Gabler *interior designer*
Chiddix, James Alan *cable television engineering executive*
Coleman, Ernest Albert *plastics and materials consultant*
Collins, Joseph J. *television services company executive*
Condon, Joseph F. *engineering and services company executive*
Conover, Harvey *retired publisher*
Conti, Lee Ann *lawyer*
†Critelli, Michael J. *lawyer, manufacturing executive*
Davis, Ronald Vernon *beverage products executive*
Davison, Endicott Peabody *lawyer*
Dederick, Ronald Osburn *lawyer*
Dell, Warren Frank, II *management consultant*
Deneberg, Jeffrey N. *engineering executive*
Dolian, Robert Paul *lawyer*
Doolittle, James H. *cable television systems company executive*
Dorf, Robert L. *public relations executive, marketing and management consultant*
Duke, Robert Dominick *mining executive, lawyer*
Ekernas, Sven Anders *investment company executive*
Epstein, Simon Jules *psychiatrist*
Evans, Robert Sheldon *manufacturing executive*
Farrell, Joseph Christopher *mining executive, services executive*
Fein, Leah Gold *psychologist*
Ferguson, Ronald Eugene *reinsurance company executive*
Fernandez, Nino Joseph *manufacturing company executive*
Fillet, Mitchell Harris *financial services executive*
Filter, Eunice M. *business equipment manufacturing executive*
Forbes, Walter Alexander *consumer services company executive*
Fortune, Philip Robert *metal manufacturing company executive*
Fossel, Peter VanBrunt *magazine editor and publisher*
Frank, Charles Raphael, Jr. *financial executive*
Frey, Dale Franklin *financial investment company executive, manufacturing company executive*
†Friedman, Joel Stephen *manufacturing company executive*
Fuller, Mark Adin, Jr. *forest products company executive*
Garbacz, Gerald George *information services company executive*
Gardiner, Hobart Clive *petroleum company executive*
Gault, John Franklin *telecommunications industry executive*
Gefter, William Irvin *physician, educator*
Ginsky, Marvin H. *lawyer, corporate executive*
Gladstone, Herbert Jack *manufacturing company executive*
†Goldstein, Frederick Arya *marketing executive*
Griffin, Donald Wayne *diversified chemical company executive*
Gross, Ronald Martin *forest products executive*
Gudger, Robert H. *retired printing company executive*
Gupta, Dharam V. *chemical engineer*
Haber, Judith Ellen *nursing educator*
Hagner, Arthur Feodor *geologist, educator*
Hague, John William, Jr. *security company executive*
Harvey, George Burton *office equipment company executive*
Hawley, Frank Jordan, Jr. *venture capital executive*
Hedge, Arthur Joseph, Jr. *environmental executive*
Heist, Lewis Clark *forest products company executive*
Hicks, Wayland R. *electronic business equipment executive*
Higgins, Jay Francis *financial service executive*
Hollander, Milton Bernard *electronics corporate executive*
Hood, Edward Exum, Jr. *retired electrical manufacturing company executive*
Horrigan, D. Gregory *metal products executive*
Howard, Melvin *financial executive*
Hudson, Franklin Donald *diversified company executive*
Hudson, Harold Jordon, Jr. *retired insurance executive*
Hull, James Charles *industrial company executive*
Ingrum, Adrienne Gillette *book publisher*
Jacobson, Ishier *retired utility executive*
Jaffe, Elliot S. *women's clothing retail chain executive*
James, John Whitaker, Sr. *financial services executive*
Johnson, Martin Allen *publisher*
Johnstone, John William, Jr. *chemical company executive*
Karp, Steve *artistic director*
Kaufman, John E. *retired association executive*
Kavetas, Harry L. *finance leasing company executive*
Kellogg, Tommy Nason *reinsurance corporation executive*
Kinnear, James Wesley, III *retired petroleum company executive*
Kinsman, Robert Donald *art museum administrator, cartoonist*
Kloster, Burton John, Jr. *lawyer*
Knag, Paul Everett *lawyer*
Kobak, James Benedict *management consultant*
Kubisen, Steven Joseph, Jr. *chemical and plastics management consultant*
Lane, Hana Umlauf *editor*
Lee, Charles Robert *telecommunications company executive*
Lee, Charles Tomerlin *lawyer*
Lee, John J. *petroleum, fertilizer company executive*
†Leferman, Norman Bruce *marketing professional*
Lennard, Gerald *metal products executive*
Lockhart, Michael D. *electric company executive*
Loeffel, Bruce *software company executive, consultant*
Lowman, George Frederick *lawyer*
MacEwen, Edward Carter *communications executive*
Magidson, Michael D. *metals products executive*
Margolis, Emanuel *lawyer, educator*
Marlowe, Edward *research company executive*
Marsden, Charles Joseph *financial executive*
Martin, Patrick *business equipment company executive*
Maxwell, Anders John *corporate executive*
Mayhall, Dorothy Ann *museum director, curator of art, sculptor*
†McCabe, Sister Daniel Marie *nun, religious organization executive*
McCain, Arthur Williamson, Jr. *pension investment consultant*
McGeeney, John Stephen *lawyer*
McGrath, Richard Paul *lawyer*
Mc Kinley, John Key *retired oil company executive*
Mc Namara, Francis Joseph, Jr. *foundation executive, lawyer*
McNear, Barbara Baxter *financial communications executive, consultant*
Merritt, William Alfred, Jr. *lawyer, telecommunications company executive*
Miller, Wilbur Hobart *business diversification consultant*
Morgan, William J. *accounting company executive*
Morley, John C. *electronic equipment company executive*
Murphy, Robert Blair *management consulting company executive*
Nichols, Ralph Arthur *lawyer*
Nierenberg, Roger *symphony conductor*
Nightingale, William Joslyn *management consultant*
Norman, Geoffrey Robert *financial executive*
Nutter, Wallace Lee *paper manufacturing executive*
Oatway, Francis Carlyle *lumber products, paper company executive*
Obernauer, Marne *corporate executive*
Ogden, Dayton *executive search consultant*
O'Malley, Thomas D. *diversified company executive*
O'Neill, Robert Edward *business journal editor*
Owen, Nathan Richard *manufacturing company executive*
Ozanne, James Herbert *financial services executive*
Pacter, Paul Allan *accounting educator*
Pansini, Michael Samuel *energy company executive, consultant*
Paul, Thomas A. *book publisher*
Perle, Eugene Gabriel *lawyer*
Peterson, Carl Eric *banker, metals company executive*
Philipps, Edward William *banker, real estate appraiser*
Pollack, Gerald J. *financial executive*
†Porfeli, Joseph J. *computer and software development company, computer leasing company executive*
Porosoff, Harold *chemist, research and development director*
Prindiville, Robert Andrew *investment executive*
†Purcell, John R. *holding company executive*
Quest, James Howard *advertising executive*
Quinnell, Bruce Andrew *retail book chain executive*
†Rabey, T. W., Jr. *financial company executive*
†Raphael, Brett *artistic director, choreographer*
†Rasmussen, Gerald Elmer *museum director*
Reynolds, Robert Louis *financial services executive*
Rickard, Norman Edward *office equipment company executive*
Riggs, Douglas A. *lawyer*
Riggs, James Arthur *financial executive*
Rizzuto, Leandro Peter *corporate executive*
Rondepierre, Edmond Francois *insurance company executive*
Rosenberg, Charles Harvey *otorhinolaryngologist*
Ross, Stuart B. *corporate financial executive*
Rossman, Janet Kay *architectural interior designer*
Rowe, William John *newspaper publishing executive*
Rudman, Joan Eleanor *artist, educator*
Ryan, Raymond D. *retired steel company executive, insurance and marketing firm executive*
Salisbury, John Francis *distillery and chemical company executive, corporate lawyer*
Sarbin, Hershel Benjamin *management consultant, business publisher, lawyer*
Sayers, Richard James *newspaper editor*
Schectman, Herbert A. *lawyer, corporate executive*
†Schiff, Craig Mitchell *computer company executive*
Schilling, Albert Henry *former government agency administrator, corporate environmental consultant*
Schoonmaker, Samuel Vail, III *lawyer*
Scribner, Barbara Colvin *museum administrator*
Serrani, Thom *management consultant, former mayor*
Sharp, Edgar E. *diversified corporation executive*
Sigler, Andrew Clark *forest products company executive*
Silver, Charles Morton *communications company executive*
Silver, R. Philip *metal products executive*
Sisley, G. William *lawyer*
Skidd, Thomas Patrick, Jr. *lawyer*
Spindler, John Frederick *lawyer*
Stapleton, James Francis *lawyer*
Steinberg, Burt *retail executive*
Strone, Michael Jonathan *lawyer*
Strosahl, William Austin *artist, art director*
Sullivan, James Thomas *printing company executive*
Sveda, Michael *management and research consultant*
Teeters, Nancy Hays *economist*
Toy, Arthur Dock Fon *chemist*
Tregurtha, Paul Richard *marine transportation and construction materials company executive*
Trivisonno, Nicholas Louis *communications company executive, accountant*
Twardy, Stanley Albert, Jr. *lawyer*
Veronis, Peter *publisher*
Verrico, Ernest Joseph *banker*
Villarreal, Homero Atenógenes *human resources executive*
Vos, Frank *advertising and marketing executive*
Wall, Stephen James *senior executive consultant*
Wallfesh, Henry Maurice *business communications company executive, editor, writer*
Walsh, Thomas Joseph *neuro-ophthalmologist*
Weitzel, William Conrad, Jr. *lawyer*
Weyher, Harry Frederick, III *metals company executive*
White, Richard Booth *management consultant*
Wiggins, Rosalind Zeldina *lawyer*
Wilensky, Julius M. *publishing company executive*
Wilhelm, Gayle Brian *lawyer*
Williams, Ernest William, Jr. *economist, educator*
†Wise, Robert *computer services company executive*
†Worcester, Anne Person *sports association executive*
Yardis, Pamela Hintz *computer consulting company executive*
Yoder, Patricia Doherty *public relations executive*
Ziegler, William, III *diversified industry executive*
Zuckert, Donald Mack *marketing executive*

Stepney

Stokes, Charles Junius *economist, educator*

Stonington

†Bennett, Gary Paul *technical services company executive*
Dupont, Ralph Paul *lawyer, educator*
Van Rees, Cornelius S. *lawyer*

Storrs

Allen, George James *psychologist, educator*
Allen, John Logan *geographer*
Anderson, Stephen Alan *family psychology educator*
Bartram, Ralph Herbert *physicist*
Bobbitt, James McCue *chemist*
Charters, Ann *biographer, editor, educator*
Coons, Ronald Edward *historian, educator*
Dardick, Kenneth Regen *physician, educator*
De Maria, Anthony John *electrical engineer*
Devereux, Owen Francis *metallurgy educator*
Greene, John Colton *retired history educator*
†Gutteridge, Thomas G. *academic administrator, consultant and labor arbitrator*
Hinckley, Lynn Schellig *microbiologist*
†Katz, Leonard *psychology educator*
Long, Richard Paul *civil engineering educator, geotechnical engineering consultant*
Marcus, Philip Irving *virology educator, researcher*
†McGlamery, Thornton Patrick *map librarian*
Mc Innes, William Charles *priest, campus ministry director*
Nieforth, Karl Allen *university dean, educator*
†Pilar, Guillermo Roman *physiology and neurobiology educator*
Pitkin, Edward Thaddeus *aerospace engineer, consultant*
Rosen, William *English language educator*
Shaffer, Jerome Arthur *philosophy educator*
Spencer, Domina Eberle *mathematics educator*
Stwalley, William Calvin *physics and chemistry educator*
Walker, David Bradstreet *political science educator*
Wood, Wendy Deborah *filmmaker*

Storrs Mansfield

Abramson, Arthur Seymour *linguistics educator, researcher*
Anderson, Gregory Joseph *botanical sciences educator*
Azaroff, Leonid Vladimirovitch *physics educator*
Birdman, Jerome Moseley *drama educator, consultant*
Denenberg, Victor Hugo *psychology educator*
DiBenedetto, Anthony Thomas *engineering educator*
Glasser, Joseph *manufacturing and marketing executive*
Gray, Robert Hugh *college dean*
Guttay, Andrew John Robert *agronomy educator, researcher*
Howes, Trevor Denis *metallurgical engineering educator, researcher*
†Kerr, Kirklyn M. *veterinary pathologist, researcher*
Klemens, Paul Gustav *physicist, educator*
Koths, Jay Sanford *floriculture educator*
Ladd, Everett Carll *political science educator, author*
Laufer, Hans *developmental biologist, educator*
McFadden, Peter William *mechanical engineering educator*
Reed, Howard Alexander *historian, educator*
Schuster, Todd Mervyn *biophysics educator, biotechnology company executive*
Schwarz, J(ames) Conrad *psychology educator*
†Schwenk, Kurt *evolutionary biology educator*
Shaw, Montgomery Throop *chemical engineering educator*
Stevens, Norman Dennison *retired library director*
Zelanski, Paul John *art educator, author*

Stratford

Chase, J. Vincent *state legislator, shopping center executive*
Salzberg, Emmett Russell *new product developer*

Suffield

Black, Maureen McWeeny *special education educator*
Friedman, Dian Debra *elementary education educator*
Hanzalek, Astrid Teicher *public policy consultant*
Leavitt, Joel *consumer products company executive*
Leavitt, Julian J. *wholesale food company executive*

Tariffville

Johnson, Loering M. *design engineer, historian, consultant*

Thomaston

†Kirshner, Hal *cinematographer*

Thompson

Fisher, William Thomas *business administration educator*

Tolland

Wilde, Daniel Underwood *computer engineering educator*

Torrington

Wall, Robert Anthony, Jr. *lawyer*

Trumbull

Bravo, Anthony John *radiologist*
Doherty, Donna Kathryn *editor*
Ferm, David G. *magazine publisher*
FitzGerald, James W. (Jay) *magazine publisher*
Galvin, Terry *magazine editor*
Gladki, Hanna Zofia *civil engineer, hydraulic mixer specialist*
Mazza, David Lawrence *university athletic director, educator*
Norcel, Jacqueline Joyce Casale *educational administrator*
Schmitt, William Howard *cosmetics company executive*
Seitz, Nicholas Joseph *magazine editor*
Shaw, Ronald Gordon *manufacturing company executive*
Tarde, Gerard *magazine editor*
Watson, Donald Ralph *architect, universiity dean, author*

Uncasville

Meredith, William (Morris) *poet, English language educator*

Vernon Rockville

Herbst, Marie Antoinette *former state senator*
Marmer, Ellen Lucille *pediatrician*
†Sturgess, Geoffrey J. *aeronautical research engineer*
Wolff, Thomas John *insurance company executive, consultant, author*

Voluntown

Caddell, Foster *artist*

Wallingford

Augustyn, Walter Henry *physicist*
Cirasuolo, Joseph J. *school system administrator*
De George, Lawrence Joseph *diversified company executive*
Fritz, Mary G. *state legislator*
Hay, Leroy E. *school system administrator*
†Molinoff, Perry Brown *biology educator*
†Reiner, Bert Leo *consumer product engineering/manufacturing consultant*
Spero, Barry Melvin *medical center executive*

Warren

Abrams, Herbert E. *artist*
Gray, Cleve *artist*

Washington Depot

Chase, Alison Becker *modern dancer, choreographer, teacher*
Hardee, William Covington *banker, lawyer*
Leab, Daniel Josef *history educator*
Mandler, Susan Ruth *dance company administrator*
Pendleton, Moses Robert Andrew *dancer, choreographer*
Tracy, Michael Cameron *choreographer, performer*

Waterbury

Cohen, Andrew Stuart *architect, landscape architect*
Daly, T(homas) F(rancis) Gilroy *federal judge*
Dudrick, Stanley John *surgeon, scientist, educator*
Glass, Robert Davis *state legal administrator*
Hamilton, John Ross *financial consultant, educator*
Higgins, Dorothy Marie *academic dean*
Leever, Harold *chemical company executive*
Narkis, Robert Joseph *bank executive, lawyer*
Oliver, Eugene Alex *speech and language pathologist*
Olsen, T. Fred *timing instruments manufacturing company executive*
Pape, William James, II *newspaper publisher*
†Waite, Marguerite Frances *hospital administrator*
Zampiello, Richard Sidney *metals and trading company executive*
Zeitlin, Bruce Allen *superconducting material technology executive*

Waterford

Commire, Anne *playwright*
Hinkle, Muriel Ruth Nelson *naval warfare analysis company executive*
Kandetzki, Carl Arthur *engineer*
†Markowicz, John C. *engineering consulting company executive*
Sillin, Lelan Flor, Jr. *retired utility executive*
White, George Cooke *theater director, foundation executive*

West Cornwall

Klaw, Barbara Van Doren *author, editor*
Klaw, Spencer *writer, editor, educator*
Prentice, Tim *sculptor, architect*
Simont, Marc *artist*

West Granby

Conland, Stephen *publishing company executive*

West Hartford

Abbot, Quincy Sewall *retired insurance executive*
Chiarenza, Frank John *English language educator*
Clear, Albert F., Jr. *retired hardware manufacturing company executive*
Conard, Frederick Underwood, Jr. *lawyer*
†Cornell, Robert Witherspoon *engineering consultant*
Danker, Mervyn Kenneth *director of education*
Doran, James Martin *retired food products company executive*
Farren, J. Michael *former government official, lawyer*
Generas, George Paul, Jr. *accounting educator*
Glasson, Lloyd *sculptor, educator*
Glixon, David M(orris) *editor*
Glotzer, Mortimer M. *quality assurance consultant*
Hickcox, Curtiss Bronson *anesthesiologist*
Kramer, Karen Lee Van Brunt *business administration educator*
Lawson, Jonathan Nevin *academic administrator*
Libassi, Frank Peter *lawyer, dean*
Mason, George H. *business educator, consultant*
McCawley, Austin *psychiatrist, educator*
Miller, Elliott Cairns *retired bank executive, lawyer*
Mullane, Denis Francis *insurance executive*
Newell, Robert Lincoln *retired banker*

Raffay, Stephen Joseph *manufacturing company executive*
Reynolds, Philip Reeves *insurance company executive*
Streeter, Anne Paul *state senator*
Tonkin, Humphrey Richard *university president*
Uccello, Vincenza Agatha *artist, director, educator emerita*
Welna, Cecilia *mathematics educator*
Whitman, Robert *lawyer, educator*

West Haven
Callison, Charles Stuart *retired foreign service officer, development economist*
DeNardis, Lawrence J. *academic administrator*
Ellis, Lynn Webster *management educator, telecommunications consultant*
Gerritsen, Mary Ellen *vascular and cell biologist*
Lee, Ming Cho *set designer*
Turner, Frank Miller *historian, educator*

West Simsbury
Barney, Austin Cornelius Dunham, II *estate planner*
Brinkerhoff, Peter John *manufacturing company executive*
Morest, Donald Kent *neuroscientist*

Westbrook
Hall, Jane Anna *writer, model*

Weston
Bellin, Harvey Forrest *television producer, director*
Bleifeld, Stanley *sculptor*
Cadmus, Paul *artist, etcher*
Daniel, James *curator, business executive, writer, former editor,*
Diforio, Robert G. *literary agent*
Fredrik, Burry *theatrical producer, director*
Kilty, Jerome Timothy *playwright, stage director, actor*
Laikind, Donna *psychotherapist, consultant*
Liberatore, Nicholas Alfred *business consultant*
Lindsay, Charles Joseph *banker*
Murray, Thomas Joseph *advertising executive*
Offenhartz, Edward *aerospace executive*
Rand, Paul *graphic designer, educator*
Schnitzer, Robert C. *theater administrator*
Thompson, N(orman) David *insurance company executive*
Thorner, Peter *retail executive*

Westport
Aasen, Lawrence Obert *public relations executive*
Albani, Suzanne Beardsley *lawyer*
Allen, Robert Hugh *retired communications corporation executive*
Angle, Richard Warner, Jr. *not-for-profit and publishing executive*
Bishop, William Wade *advertising executive*
Breitbarth, S. Robert *manufacturing company executive*
Britt, David Van Buren *educational communications executive*
Bronson, Carole *publishing executive*
Brooks, Andrée Aelion *journalist, educator, author*
Brown, Mona *architect*
Cederbaum, Eugene E. *lawyer*
Chang, Robert Timothy *financial products company executive*
†Chernow, Ann Levy *artist, art educator*
†Chernow, Burt *artist, educator, writer*
Clausman, Gilbert Joseph *medical librarian*
Coleman, Joel Clifford *lawyer*
Davis, Joel *publisher*
Daw, Harold John *lawyer*
De Lay, Robert Francis *marketing executive, consultant*
Densen-Gerber, Judianne *psychiatrist, lawyer, educator*
Dickson, Sally I. *retired public relations executive*
Duncan, Joseph Wayman *business economist*
Dunton, James Raynor *publisher*
Enos, Randall *cartoonist, illustrator*
Ferris, Roger Patrick *architect*
†Fisher, Leonard Everett *artist, writer, educator*
Freedman, Judith Greenberg *state senator, importer*
Hagelstein, Robert Philip *publisher*
Hambleton, George Blow Elliott *management consultant*
Hanslip, Edward Robert *management consultant, marketing professional*
Harris, Cynthia Coolidge Mead *executive editor*
Hersey, Marilyn Elaine *performing company executive*
Hotchner, Aaron Edward *author*
Joseph, Michael Thomas *broadcast consultant*
Kalan, George Richard *venture capitalist*
Kelly, Paul Knox *investment banker*
Knopf, Alfred, Jr. *retired publisher*
Kramer, Sidney B. *publisher, lawyer, literary agent*
Krist, Peter Christopher *former petroleum company executive*
Lederer, Jack Lawrence *personnel director, human resources specialist*
Levinger, Beryl Beth *development specialist, organization administrator*
Martin, Ralph Guy *writer*
McCaig, Joseph J. *retail food chain executive*
McCormack, Donald Paul *newspaper consultant*
McCormack, Patricia Seger *independent press service editor, journalist*
McKane, David Bennett *business executive*
Meckler, Alan Marshall *publisher, author*
Murphy, Thomas John *publishing executive*
Nathan, Irwin *business systems company executive*
Nedom, H. Arthur *petroleum consultant*
Nolte, Richard Henry *political science researcher, consultant*
O'Keefe, John David *investment specialist*
O'Leary, James John *economist*
Poundstone, Sally *library director*
Radigan, Joseph Richard *human resources executive*
Ready, Robert James *financial company executive*
Rose, Reginald *television writer, producer*
Ross, John Michael *editor, magazine publisher*
Sabin, James Thomas *publisher*
Sacks, Herbert Simeon *psychiatrist, educator, consultant*
Sadler, David Gary *financial institution crisis management consultant*
Safran, Claire *writer, editor*
Sarn, James *physician, health association administrator*
Satinover, Jeffrey Burke *psychiatrist, health science facility administrator, lecturer, author*
Savage, Robert Heath *advertising executive*
Scheinman, Stanley Bruce *venture capital executive, lawyer*
Silk, George *photographer*
Singer, Henry A. *behavioral scientist, institute director*
Stashower, Michael David *retired manufacturing company executive*
†Stewart, Martha Kostyra *caterer, author, lecturer*
Tec, Leon *psychiatrist*
Tucker, Gardiner Luttrell *physicist, former paper company executive*
Walden, Amelia Elizabeth (Mrs. John William Harmon) *author*
Walton, Alan George *venture capitalist*
Weil, Ernst *oil industry executive*
Wexler, Herbert Ira *retail company executive*

Wethersfield
Edwards, Kenneth S. *principal*
Payne, Edward Carlton *archbishop*
Precourt, George Augustine *government official*
Tanguay, Norbert Arthur *municipal police training officer*

Whitneyville
Miller, Walter Richard, Jr. *banker*

Willimantic
Carter, David George, Sr. *university administrator*
Diehl, Lesley Ann *psychologist*
Loin, E. Linnea *social services administrator*
Peagler, Owen F. *colege administrator*
Philips, David Evan *English language educator*

Wilton
Billings, Edward Robert *accountant*
Black, Rita Ann *communications executive*
Brown, James Thompson, Jr. *computer information scientist*
Buchanan, William Hobart, Jr. *lawyer, publishing company executive*
Campbell, Robert Ayerst *accounting company executive*
Cassidy, George Thomas *international business development consultant*
Cook, Jay Michael *accounting company executive*
Cutler, Theodore John *cable company executive*
Farley, James Parker *retired advertising agency executive*
Finlayson, John L. *commodities company executive*
Finn, Daniel R., Jr. *investment company executive*
Forger, Robert Durkin *retired professional association administrator*
Fricke, Richard John *lawyer*
†Godfrey, Albert Blanton *research and management consulting company executive, writer, educator*
Green, John Orne *lawyer*
Heymann, Stephen T. *marketing management consultant*
Hoefling, Rudolf Joachim *power generating company executive*
Joseloff, Gordon Frederic *journalist, editor*
Juran, Joseph Moses *engineer*
Kangas, Edward A. *accounting firm executive*
Lamb, Frederic Davis *lawyer*
Martimucci, Richard Anthony *engineering company executive*
McCreight, John A. *management consultant*
Mc Dannald, Clyde Elliott, Jr. *management consultation company executive*
Morris, Michael J. *book publishing executive*
Nickel, Albert George *advertising agency executive*
Pemberton, Jeffery Kenneth *publisher*
Raikes, Charles FitzGerald *lawyer*
Ritter, Bruce *Commodities Company executive*
Stuart, Kenneth James *illustrator, art director*
Weissman, Robert Evan *information services company executive*

Windsor
Auten, Arthur Herbert *history educator*
Clarke, Cordelia Kay Knight Mazuy *marketing management executive*
Cowen, Bruce David *environmental service company executive*
Kamerschen, Robert Jerome *consumer products executive*
Mangold, John Frederic *manufacturing company executive, former naval officer*
Rocco, Vincent Anthony *consulting firm executive*
Scherer, A. Edward *nuclear engineering executive*
Stigler, David Mack *lawyer*

Windsor Locks
Coelho, Sandra Signorelli *secondary school educator*
Walker, K. Grahame *manufacturing company executive*

Wolcott
Gerace, Robert F. *secondary school principal*

Woodbridge
Alvine, Robert *industrialist, entrepreneur, international business leader*
Bondy, Philip Kramer *physician, educator*
Ecklund, Constance Cryer *French language educator*
Ostfeld, Alexander Marion *advertising agency executive*
Womer, Charles Berry *retired hospital executive, management consultant*

Woodbury
Farrell, Edgar Henry *building components manufacturing executive, lawyer*
Marsching, Ronald Lionel *lawyer, former precision instrument company executive*
Skinner, Brian John *geologist, educator*

Woodmont
Frazier, Howard Thomas *association executive*

Woodstock
Boote, Alfred Shepard *marketing researcher, educator*

DELAWARE

Dagsboro
Lally, Richard Francis *aviation security consultant, former association executive, former government official*

Dover
Bookhammer, Eugene Donald *state government official*
†Brady, M. Jane *state official*
Carey, V. George *farmer, state legislator*
Carper, Thomas Richard *governor*
Cohen, William John *urban and environmental planner, educator, photographer*
Delauder, William B. *academic administrator*
Ennis, Bruce Clifford *lawyer*
Forgione, Pascal D., Jr. *state superintendent*
Hedrick, JoAnn M. *legislative staff member*
Kern, John Rudolph *government administrator, historian*
Lahvis, Sylvia Leistyna *art historian, educator, curator*
†Lentini, James Salvatore *school librarian, fraternity executive*
Lowell, Howard Parsons *government records administrator*
Minner, Ruth Ann *state official*
Moran, Joseph Milbert *retired banker*
Ornauer, Richard Lewis *retired educational association administrator*
Sorenson, Liane Beth McDowell *university administrator, state legislator*
Vaughn, James T. *former state police officer, state senator*
Vawter, William Snyder *computer software consultant*
Wasfi, Sadiq Hassan *chemistry educator*
Wilson, Clealyn Bullock *elementary education educator*

Georgetown
Painter, John Cecil *library director*

Greenville
†Dombeck, Harold Arthur *engineering company executive*
†Levitt, George *retired chemist*
Reynolds, Nancy Bradford duPont (Mrs. William Glasgow Reynolds) *sculptor*
Schroeder, Herman Elbert *scientific consultant*

Hockessin
Bischoff, Joyce Arlene *information systems consultant, lecturer*
Bischoff, Kenneth Bruce *chemical engineer, educator*
Herzog, Kathryn Wedel *health care administrator, hospice consultant*
Sawin, Nancy Churchman *educator, artist, historian*
Sciance, Carroll Thomas *chemical engineer*

Lewes
Chapman, Janet Carter Goodrich (Mrs. John William Chapman) *economist, educator*
Fried, Jeffrey Michael *health care administrator*
Wilson, James L. *superintendent*

Middletown
Jackson, Donald Richard *marketing professional*

Milford
†Burris, John E. *food products executive*
Moses, Charles E. *superintendent*

Millsboro
Derrickson, Shirley Jean Baldwin *elementary school educator*
Jones, Lowell Robert *safety and industrial hygiene consultant*
Townsend, P(reston) Coleman *agricultural business executive*

New Castle
Almquist, Don *illustrator, artist*
Blackshear, L. T., Sr. *bishop*
Cansler, Leslie Ervin *retired newspaper editor*
†Freytag, Richard Arthur *finance executive*
Keillor, Sharon Ann *computer company executive*
Mac Ewen, George Dean *physician, medical institute executive*
Roddy, Edward Joseph *plastic pipe company executive*

Newark
Allen, Herbert Ellis *environmental chemistry educator*
Allmendinger, David Frederick, Jr. *history educator*
Barteau, Mark Alan *chemical engineering and chemistry educator*
Beris, Antony Nicolas *chemical engineer, educator*
Bilinsky, Yaroslav *political scientist*
Böer, Karl Wolfgang *physicist, educator*
Bohner, Charles Henry *English language educator*
Borgaonkar, Digamber Shankarrao *cytogeneticist, educator*
Brams, Marvin Robert *economist, mental health counselor, interfaith minister*
Burmeister, John Luther *chemistry educator*
Byrne, John Michael *energy and environmental policy educator, researcher*
Caffo, Betty Jane *nursing educator, medical/surgical nurse*
Campbell, Linzy Leon *microbiologist, educator*
Capek, Milic *retired philosophy educator*
Cawley, Charles M. *banker*
Cochran, John R. *bank executive*
Colton, David Lem *mathematician, educator*
Cooper, Stuart Leonard *chemical engineering educator, researcher, consultant*
†Curtis, James C. *cultural organization administrator/history educator*
Daniels, William Burton *physicist, educator*
Davies, Ronald Wynn *financial services executive*
Day, Robert Androus *English language educator, former library director, editor, publisher*
DiRenzo, Gordon James *sociologist, psychologist, educator*
Doberenz, Alexander R. *nutrition educator, chemist*
Dow, Lois Weyman *physician*
Elterich, Joachim Gustav *agricultural economics educator*
Enlow, Fred Clark *banker*
Evans, Dennis Hyde *chemist, educator*
Evenson, Paul Arthur *physics educator*
Graff, Harold *psychiatrist, psychoanalyst, hospital administrator*
Graham, David Tredway *medical educator, physician*
Graham, Frances Keesler (Mrs. David Tredway Graham) *psychologist, educator*
Gulick, Walter Lawrence *psychologist, former college president*
Halio, Jay Leon *language professional, educator*
Hammonds, Jay A. *educator, administrator*
Homer, William Innes *art history educator, art expert, author*
Hurst, Christina Marie *respiratory therapist*
Hutton, David Glenn *environmental scientist, consultant, chemical engineer*
Ih, Charles Chung Sen *electrical engineering educator, researcher*
Jones, Russel Cameron *civil engineering educator*
Jordan, Robert Reed *geologist, educator*
Kaufman, M(ichael) Scot *bank executive*
Keene, William Blair *state education official*
Kennedy, Christopher Robin *ceramist*
Klein, Michael Tully *chemical engineering educator, consultant*
Lemole, Gerald Michael *surgeon*
Mangone, Gerard J. *international and maritime law educator*
Mather, John Russell *climatologist, educator*
McCullough, Roy Lynn *chemical engineering educator*
McLaren, James Clark *French educator*
McNicholas, Kathleen Winifred *cardiac surgeon*
Mills, George Alexander *science administrator*
Mitchell, Peter Kenneth, Jr. *educational consultant, association administrator*
Moss, Joe Francis *sculptor, painter*
Mullen, Regina Marie *lawyer*
Murray, Richard Bennett *physics educator*
Neal, James Preston *state senator, project engineer*
Ness, Norman Frederick *astrophysicist, educator, administrator*
Nye, John Calvin *agricultural engineer, educator*
Raffel, Jeffrey Allen *urban affairs educator*
†Reid, Stephen Robert *power generation engineer, consultant*
Roselle, David Paul *university administrator, mathematician*
Rowe, Charles Alfred *artist, designer, educator*
Russell, Thomas William Fraser *chemical engineering educator*
Sandler, Stanley Irving *chemical engineering educator*
Scarpitti, Frank Roland *sociology educator*
Schiavelli, Melvyn David *university provost, chemistry educator, researcher*
Schultz, Jerold Marvin *materials scientist, educator*
Sheer, Barbara Lee *nursing educator*
Somers, George Fredrick *biology educator*
Stakgold, Ivar *mathematics educator*
Stark, Robert Martin *mathematician, civil engineer, educator*
Steiner, Roger Jacob *linguistics educator, author, researcher*
Szeri, Andras Z. *engineering educator*
Tannian, Francis Xavier *economist, educator*
Tolles, Bryant Franklin, Jr. *history and art history educator*
Urquhart, Andrew Willard *engineering and business executive*
Valbuena-Briones, Angel Julian *language educator, author*
Venezky, Richard Lawrence *English educator*
Webb, Richard Stephen *manufacturing executive*
Weslager, Clinton Alfred *historian, writer*
Wetlaufer, Donald Burton *biochemist, educator*
Wolters, Raymond *historian, educator*
Woo, S. B. (Shien-Biau Woo) *former lieutenant governor, physics educator*
Wright, Vernon Hugh Carroll *bank executive*
Wu, Jin *oceanographer, educator, engineer*

Newport
Kirkland, Joseph J. *research chemist*

Rockland
Levinson, John Milton *obstetrician-gynecologist*
Rubin, Alan A. *pharmaceutical and biotechnology consultant*

Smyrna
†Mays, William Fritz *health facility regional administrator, retired military career officer*

Wilmington
Adams, Wayne Verdun *pediatric psychologist, educator*
Aiken, Robert McCutchen *retired chemical company executive, management consultant*
Amick, Steven Hammond *lawyer, senator*
†Anderson, Paul S. *research chemist*
Arrington, Charles Hammond, Jr. *retired chemical company executive*
Bader, John Merwin *lawyer*
Balick, Helen Shaffer *federal judge*
†Baumann, Julian Henry, Jr. *lawyer*
Beardwood, Bruce Allan *chemical company executive*
Bell, Daniel Long, Jr. *lawyer, utilities executive*
Benson, Barbara Ellen *state agency administrator*
†Black, Robert C. *chemical company executive*
Bloch, Thomas Morton *tax company executive*
Bowler, Mary E. *lawyer*
Boyer, David Creighton *stockbroker*
Bredin, J(ohn) Bruce *retired real estate executive*
Bruni, Stephen Thomas *art museum director*
Campbell, Roger D. *utility company executive*
Carpenter, Edmund Nelson, II *lawyer, retired*
Carson, James Elijah *psychiatrist*
Cartwright, Albert Thomas *association executive*
Caspersen, Finn Michael Westby *diversified financial services company executive*
Cecala, Ted Thomas, Jr. *banker, accountant*
Ceci, Anthony Thomas *executive secretary*
Clark, Esther Frances *legal educator*
Connelly, Donald Preston *electric and gas utility company executive*
Connolly, Arthur Guild *lawyer, partner emeritus*
Corn, Jack W. *oil company executive*
Cornelison, Floyd Shovington, Jr. *retired psychiatrist, former educator*
Cosgrove, Howard Edward, Jr. *utility executive*
Crippen, Raymond C. *chemist, consultant*
Crittenden, Eugene Dwight, Jr. *chemical company executive*
Croom, John Henry, III *utility company executive*
Daly, John Dennis *utility company executive*
Danzeisen, John R. *chemical company executive*
Dayton, Richard Lee *architect*
DeBlieu, Ivan Knowlton *plastic pipe company executive, consultant*
Del Pesco, Susan Marie Carr *state judge*
delTufo, Theresa Lallana Izon *state official*
Desien, Mary Donna *principal*
DeVivo, Sal J. *newspaper executive*
Dewees, Donald Charles *securities company executive*

DiLiberto, Richard Anthony, Jr. *lawyer*
Doughty, Robert Allen *medical institute director*
Dunham, Archie W. *petroleum and chemical products company executive*
Du Pont, Pierre Samuel, IV *lawyer, former governor of Delaware*
Eichler, Thomas P. *state agency administrator*
Elliott, Richard Gibbons, Jr. *lawyer*
Elzea, Rowland Procter *art museum curator*
Emanuel, Abraham Gabriel *photo processing company executive, consultant*
†Engelmann, Glenn Matthew *lawyer*
Farnan, Joseph James, Jr. *federal judge*
Fenton, Wendell *lawyer*
Frank, George Andrew *lawyer*
Gadsby, Robin Edward *chemical company executive*
Galli, Paolo *chemical company executive*
Gebelein, Richard Stephen *judge, former state attorney general*
Gibson, Joseph Whitton, Jr. *retired chemical company executive*
Gilliam, James H., Jr. *lawyer*
Gilman, Marvin Stanley *real estate developer, educator*
Gossage, Thomas Layton *chemical company executive*
Graves, Thomas Ashley, Jr. *educational administrator*
Green, James Samuel *lawyer*
Grenz, Linda L. *Episcopal priest*
Gross, Lawrence Alan *lawyer*
Gunzenhauser, Stephen Charles *conductor*
Harley, Robison Dooling *physician, educator*
Harris, Robert Laird *minister, theology educator emeritus*
Hartzell, Charles R. *research administrator, biochemist, cell biologist*
Hendricks, Rayman Michael *chemical company executive*
Herdeg, John Andrew *lawyer*
†Howard, Richard James *biologist*
Huang, Hua-Feng *electrical engineer, researcher*
Ianni, Francis Alphonse *state official, former army officer*
Inselman, Laura Sue *pediatrician*
†Jacobson, Howard W. *research chemist*
Jaffe, Edward E(phraim) *retired research and development executive*
Johnson, Allen Leroy *hospital administrator*
Kane, Edward Rynex *retired chemical company executive, corporate director*
Karrh, Bruce Wakefield *industrial company executive*
Kassal, Robert James *polymer research scientist*
Kay, Jerome *psychiatrist, educator*
Kearns, James Francis *textile technology company executive*
Kimmel, Morton Richard *lawyer*
Kirkpatrick, Andrew Booth, Jr. *lawyer*
Kissa, Erik *retired chemist, consultant*
Kjellmark, Eric William, Jr. *management consultant, opera company director*
†Krol, John A. *diversified chemicals executive*
Kusheloff, David Leon *journalist*
Landon, Harry Raymond *utility company executive*
Lange, James Braxton *chemical company executive*
Latchum, James Levin *federal judge*
Linderman, Jeanne Herron *priest*
Longobardi, Joseph J. *federal judge*
Lukens, Paul Bourne *financial executive*
MacKenzie, George *controller, manufacturing executive*
Mackenzie, Malcolm Lewis *advertising executive*
Malloy, John Richard *lawyer, chemical company executive*
†Manzer, Leo E. *chemicals executive*
McKelvie, Roderick R. *federal judge*
Meitner, Pamela *lawyer, educator*
Mekler, Arlen B. *lawyer, chemist*
Miller, Hugh Edward *business executive*
Mollica, Joseph A. *pharmaceutical executive*
Molz, Robert Joseph *manufacturing company executive*
Moore, Carl Gordon *chemist, educator*
Morrione, Paolo *polypropylene company executive*
Morris, Kenneth Donald *lawyer*
Murphy, Arthur Thomas *systems engineer*
Nelson, Dewey Allen *neurologist, educator*
Nichols, David L. *retail executive*
Nottingham, Robinson Kendall *life insurance company executive*
Nwe, Khin May *physician, educator*
Oberly, Charles Monroe, III *state attorney general*
Ockun, Robert J. *manufacturing executive*
Olson, Leroy Calvin *retired educational administration educator*
Otey, Orlando *music executive, educator, pianist, theorist*
Pan, Henry Yue-Ming *clinical pharmacologist*
Parshall, George William *research chemist*
Partnoy, Ronald Allen *lawyer*
Peterson, Russell Wilbur *former association executive, former state governor*
Porter, Glenn *museum and library administrator*
Porter, John Francis, III *banker*
†Quill, Leonard Walter *banker*
Reeder, Charles Benton *economic consultant*
Renshaw, John Hubert *secondary education educator*
†Resnick, Paul R. *research chemist*
Rich, Michael Joseph *lawyer*
†Riegel, John Kent *corporate lawyer*
Robinson, Sue Lewis *federal judge*
Rogoski, Patricia Diana *financial executive*
†Rollins, John W., Jr. *transportation executive, environmental services administrator*
Rose, Selwyn H. *chemical company executive*
Roth, Jane Richards *federal judge*
Rothschild, Steven James *lawyer*
St. Clair, Jesse Walton, Jr. *retired savings and loan executive*
Salzstein, Richard Alan *biomedical engineer, researcher*
†Scherer, George W. *research chemist*
Schmutz, John F. *chemical company executive, corporate lawyer*
Schofield, Paul Michael *finance company executive*
Schwartz, Murray Merle *federal judge*
Seitz, Collins Jacques *federal judge*
Sganga, John B. *furniture holding company executive*
Shapiro, Irving Saul *lawyer*
Shipley, Samuel Lynn *advertising and public relations executive*
Simmons, Howard Ensign, Jr. *chemist, research administrator*
Skolas, John Argyle *lawyer*
Slook, George Francis *finance company executive*
Smith, June Ellen *secondary and special education educator*
Smook, Malcolm Andrew *chemist, chemical company executive*
Stapleton, Walter King *federal judge*
Steinberg, Marshall *toxicologist*
Stone, F. L. Peter *lawyer*
†Sullivan, Lawrence Matthew *lawyer*
Sutton, Richard Lauder *lawyer*
Tennis, Calvin Cabell *bishop*
Timmons, Earl L. *oil company executive*
†Tise, Mary Shackelford *public librarian*
Titus, H. Mark *librarian*
Tucker, Keith E. *pension fund executive, portfolio manager*
Turk, S. Maynard *lawyer*
Veasey, Eugene Norman *state supreme court justice, lawyer*
Walsh, Joseph Thomas *state supreme court justice*
Ward, Rodman, Jr. *lawyer*
Wasserman, Edel *scientist, executive*
†Wattman, Kenneth E. *chemical company executive*
†Weeks, Thomas Wesley *bishop*
Welch, Edward P. *lawyer*
Wheeler, M. Catherine *organization executive*
Wieland, Ferdinand *hotel executive, entrepreneur*
Wier, Richard Royal, Jr. *lawyer, inventor*
Wilhite, Colbert Roland *chemical and oil company executive*
†Willard, A. Keith *chemicals executive*
Williams, Richmond Dean *library appraiser, consultant*
Willis, Franklin Knight *lawyer, environmental services company executive*
Woods, Robert A. *chemical company executive*
Woodward, Anne Spivey *museum director*
Woolard, Edgar S., Jr. *chemical company executive*
Wyer, William Clarke *management consultant, development executive*

Winterthur

Buchter, Thomas *horticulturist, garden director*
Hummel, Charles Frederick *museum official*
Lanmon, Dwight Pierson *museum director*

DISTRICT OF COLUMBIA

Bolling AFB

Gardner, Jerry Dean *dentist, military officer*
†Hallion, Richard Paul *aerospace historian, museum consultant*
Jones, William Edward *air force officer*

Washington

Aaron, Henry Jacob *economics educator*
Aaronson, David Ernest *lawyer, educator*
†Abbott, Alden Francis *lawyer, government official, educator*
Abbott, Rebecca Phillips *museum director*
Abdalla, Abdalla Ahmed *agricultural educator*
Abel, Elie *reporter, broadcaster, educator*
Abeles, Charles Calvert *retired lawyer*
Abelson, Philip Hauge *physicist*
Abercrombie, Neil *congressman*
Ablard, Charles David *lawyer*
Able, Edward H. *association executive*
Abler, Ronald Francis *geography educator*
†Abraham, Spencer *senator*
Abrams, Elliott *writer, foreign affairs consultant and analyst*
Abrecht, Mary Ellen Benson *lawyer*
Abshire, David Manker *diplomat, research executive*
Acheson, David Campion *lawyer, author, policy analyst*
Achtenberg, Roberta *federal official*
Acker, Lawrence G. *lawyer*
Ackerman, Gary Leonard *congressman*
Ackerson, Nels J(ohn) *lawyer*
Adams, A. John Bertrand *public affairs consultant*
Adams, Andrew Joseph *army officer*
Adams, Arvil Van *economist, educator*
Adams, Gordon Merritt *federal agency administrator*
Adams, John Jillson *lawyer*
Adams, Linette M. *principal*
Adams, Lorraine *reporter*
Adams, Paul G. *bank executive*
Adams, Robert Edward *journalist*
Adams, Thomas Lynch, Jr. *lawyer*
Adamson, Richard Henry *pharmacologist*
Adamson, Terrence Burdett *lawyer*
Adler, Howard, Jr. *lawyer*
Adler, Howard Bruce *lawyer*
Adler, Robert Martin *lawyer*
Adoum, Mahamat Ali *minister of foreign relations*
Aein, Joseph Morris *electrical engineer*
Affronti, Lewis Francis, Sr. *microbiologist, educator*
Aggarwal, Satish Kumar *electrical engineer, government official*
†Aguirre-Sacasa, Francisco Xavier *international banker*
Ahmann, Mathew Hall *social action organization administrator, consultant*
Aikens, Joan Deacon *government official*
Aires, Randolf H. *retail company executive*
Aisenberg, Irwin Morton *lawyer*
Aiuto, Russell *science educators association executive*
Akaka, Daniel Kahikina *senator*
Alatis, James Efstathios *university dean emeritus*
Alberger, William Relph *lawyer, government official*
Alberts, Bruce Michael *foundation administrator, biochemist*
Albertson, Fred W(oodward) *retired lawyer, radio engineer*
Albertson, Terry L. *lawyer*
Albornoz, Francisco *government executive, urban planner, civil engineer*
Albright, Raymond Jacob *government official*
Alexander, Benjamin Harold *professional services firm executive, past government official*
Alexander, Bettina M. *lawyer*
Alexander, Clifford Joseph *lawyer*
Alexander, Clifford L., Jr. *management consultant, lawyer, former secretary of army*
†Alexander, Dawn Alicia *government official*
Alexander, Donald Crichton *lawyer*
Alexander, Jane *arts endowment administrator, actress, producer*
Alexander, Joseph Kunkle, Jr. *physicist*
Allard, Dean Conrad *historian, naval history center director*
Allard, Wayne A. *congressman, veterinarian*
Allbritton, Joe Lewis *diversified holding company executive*
Allen, Frederick Warner *federal agency executive*
†Allen, Henry Southworth *journalist*
†Allen, Joseph P. *aerospace company executive*
Allen, Richard Vincent *international business consultant, bank executive*
Allen, Toni K. *lawyer*
Allen, William Hayes *lawyer*
Allen, William Jere *minister*
†Allen, William L. *editor*
Allera, Edward John *lawyer*
Allison, Graham Tillett, Jr. *federal government official*
Allnutt, Robert Frederick *organization executive, lawyer*
Alpern, Robert Zellman *religious organization lobbyist/administrator*
Alperovitz, Gar *author*
Al-Saud, Prince Ibn Abdulaziz *government official*
Alter, Harvey *chemist, association executive*
Altman, Jeffrey Paul *lawyer*
Altman, Roger C. *former federal official*
Alton, Bruce Taylor *educational consultant*
Aluise, Timothy John *lawyer*
Ambach, Gordon Mac Kay *education association executive*
Ambrose, Myles Joseph *lawyer*
Ames, Frank Anthony *percussionist, film producer*
Amling, Frederick *economist, educator, investment manager*
Andersen, Robert Allen *government official*
†Anderson, Carl Albert *theology school dean, lawyer*
Anderson, David Lawrence *lawyer*
Anderson, David Turpeau *government official, judge*
Anderson, Dean William *educational administrator*
Anderson, Debra R. *state representative*
Anderson, Donald Morgan *entomologist*
Anderson, Frederick Randolph, Jr. *lawyer, law educator*
Anderson, John Bayard *lawyer, educator, former congressman*
Anderson, Marcus A. *career officer*
Andewelt, Roger B. *federal judge*
Andrews, Jessica Louise *performing arts company executive*
Andrews, John Frank *editor, author, educator*
Andrews, Laureen E. *foundation administrator*
Andrews, Mark Joseph *lawyer*
Andrews, Robert E. *congressman*
Andrews, William S. *lawyer*
Andrews, Wyatt *news correspondent*
Andringa, Calvin Bruce *investment banker*
Anfinson, Thomas Elmer *government financial administrator*
Angarola, Robert Thomas *lawyer*
Angier, Natalie Marie *science journalist*
Angula, Helmut Kangulohi *government executive*
Ansary, Cyrus A. *investment company executive, lawyer*
Anschuetz, Norbert Lee *retired diplomat, banker*
Anselmo, Philip Shepard *naval officer*
Anthony, David Vincent *lawyer*
Anthony, Sheila F. *federal official*
Anthony, Virginia Quinn Bausch *medical association executive*
Anton, Frank A. *publishing executive*
Apfel, Kenneth S. *federal government official*
†Aponte-Lebrón, Nilda I. *government executive, lawyer*
Apple, Martin Allen *scientific society executive*
Apple, Raymond Walter, Jr. *journalist*
Applebaum, Harvey Milton *lawyer*
Appleberry, James Bruce *higher education association executive*
Applegarth, Paul Vollmer *investment banking and finance executive*
Arbelbide, Cindy Lea *victim advocate, librarian, educator*
Archard, Douglas Bruce *foreign service officer*
Archer, Glenn LeRoy, Jr. *federal circuit judge*
Archer, William Reynolds, Jr. (Bill Reynolds) *congressman*
Areen, Judith Carol *law educator*
Arend, Anthony Clark *international relations educator*
Arent, Albert Ezra *lawyer*
†Argrett, Loretta Collins *assistant attorney general, educator*
†Arietti, Michael Ray *diplomat*
Arkilic, Galip Mehmet *mechanical engineer, educator*
Arling, Bryan Jeremy *internist*
Armaly, Mansour F(arid) *ophthalmologist, educator*
Armey, Richard Keith *congressman*
Armitage, Robert Allen *lawyer*
Armstrong, David Andrew *federal agency official, retired army officer*
Armstrong, Richard Burke *retired television director*
Arndt, Richard T. *writer, consultant*
Arnett, Peter *journalist*
Arnez, Nancy Levi *educational leadership educator*
Arnold, G. Dewey, Jr. *accountant*
Arnold, Gary Howard *film critic*
Arnold, William Edwin *foundation administrator*
Arnovitz, Benton Mayer *editor*
Arsht, Leslye Alene *public relations executive*
Aschheim, Joseph *economist, educator*
†Ashcroft, John David *senator*
Ashkenazi, Elliott Uriel *historian, lawyer*
†Ashton, Richard M. *federal lawyer*
Atherton, Alfred Leroy, Jr. *foundation executive, former foreign service officer*
Atherton, Charles Henry *federal commission administrator*
Atil, Esin *Islamic art historian, researcher*
Atiyeh, George Nicholas *library administrator, educator*
Atkin, James Blakesley *lawyer*
Atkinson, Francis Bolling (Frank Atkinson) *lawyer*
Attkisson, Sharyl T. *news correspondent, writer*
Atwell, Robert Herron *association executive*
Atwood, James R. *lawyer*
Atwood, John Brian *federal official, foundation administrator*
AuCoin, Les *lobbyist, former congressman*
Aucutt, Ronald David *lawyer*
Aug, Stephen M. *business journalist*
†Aukofer, Frank Alexander *journalist*
Auten, John Harold *government official*
Avery, George Allen *lawyer*
Avery, Gordon Bennett *medical educator, neonatologist*
Avil, Richard D., Jr. *lawyer*
Axelrod, Jonathan Gans *lawyer*
Ayer, Donald Belton *lawyer*
Ayres, Mary Ellen *government official*
Ayres, Richard Edward *lawyer*
Azcuenaga, Mary Laurie *government official*
Babbitt, Bruce Edward *U.S. secretary of the interior*
Babby, Ellen Reisman *education administrator*
†Baca, Polly *state senator*
Bachman, Kenneth Leroy, Jr. *lawyer*
Bachman, Leonard *physician, retired federal official*
Bachula, Gary R. *federal official*
Bachus, Spencer T., III *congressman, lawyer*
†Bacon, Kenneth H. *federal agency administrator, editor, journalist*
Bacon, Sylvia *judge*
Baena Soares, João Clemente *ambassador*
Baer, William J. *lawyer*
Baesler, Scotty *congressman*
Bagge, Carl Elmer *association executive, lawyer, consultant*
Bahr, Morton *trade union executive*
Bailey, Charles Waldo, II *journalist, author*
Bailey, John E. *federal agency administrator*
Bailey, Nancy Joyce *secondary education educator*
Bailey, Patricia Price *lawyer, government official*
Bainum, Peter Montgomery *aerospace engineer, consultant*
Bair, Sheila Colleen *commissioner*
Baird, Bruce Allen *lawyer*
Baker, David Harris *lawyer*
Baker, D(onald) James *government official, oceanographer*
Baker, Keith Leon *lawyer*
Baker, Melvin C. *advertising executive*
Baker, William P. (Bill Baker) *congressman*
†Baldacci, John Elias *congressman*
Baldwin, Deborah *editor*
Baldyga, Leonard J. *diplomat, international consultant, retired*
Ball, (Robert) Markham *lawyer*
Ball, Robert M. *social security, welfare and health policy specialist, writer, lecturer*
Ballantyne, Robert Jadwin *former foreign service officer, consultant*
Ballenger, Thomas Cass *congressman*
Ballentine, J. Gregory *economist*
Baltimore, Richard Lewis, III *foreign service officer*
Bancroft, Elizabeth Abercrombie *publisher, analytic chemist*
Bandow, Douglas Leighton *editor, columnist, policy consultant*
Bane, Mary Jo *federal agency administrator*
Banister, Judith *demographer, educator*
Banzhaf, John F., III *organization executive,lawyer*
Baquet, Charles R., III *federal agency administrator*
†Barach, Jeffrey Truxton *trade association executive*
Baran, Jan Witold *lawyer, educator*
Baranes, Shalom *architect*
Barbash, Fred *journalist, author*
Barbour, Haley *political organization administrator, lawyer*
Barcia, James A. *congressman*
Bardin, David J. *lawyer*
Barnes, Dennis Norman *lawyer*
Barnes, Donald Michael *lawyer*
Barnes, Frederic Wood, Jr. *journalist*
Barnes, Mark James *lawyer*
Barnes, Michael Darr *lawyer*
Barnes, Peter *lawyer*
Barnes, Samuel Henry *political scientist, educator*
Barnet, Richard Jackson *author, educator*
Barnett, Arthur Doak *political scientist, educator*
Barnett, John H. *judge*
Barnett, Robert Bruce *lawyer*
Barnett, Robert Warren *diplomat, author*
Barone, Michael D. *journalist*
Baroody, William Joseph, Jr. *research institute executive*
Barr, Michael Blanton *lawyer*
†Barr, Robert Laurence, Jr. *congressman, lawyer*
Barr, William Pelham *lawyer, former attorney general of United States*
Barram, David J. *federal official*
†Barreda, William E. *government executive*
Barrett, Andrew *federal agency administrator*
Barrett, Dennis P. *ambassador to Madagascar*
Barrett, Laurence Irwin *journalist*
Barrett, Richard David *director fundraising program, consultant*
Barrett, Thomas M. *congressman*
Barrett, William E. *congressman*
Barrett, William H. *lawyer*
Barringer, Philip E. *government official*
Barr-Kumar, Raj *architect*
Barron, Jerome Aure *law educator*
Barrow, Robert Earl *agricultural organization administrator*
†Barry, Marion Shepilov, Jr. *mayor*
Bartholomew, Reginald *diplomat*
Bartlett, Charles J. *think-tank executive*
Bartlett, Charles Leffingwell *foundation executive, former newspaperman*
†Bartlett, David Conant *journalist*
Bartlett, John Laurence *lawyer*
Bartlett, Michael John *lawyer*
Bartlett, Roscoe G. *congressman*
Bartnoff, Judith *judge*
Barton, Jean Marie *psychologist, educator*
Barton, William Russell *government official*
Baruch, Jordan Jay *management consultant*
Barusch, Ronald Charles *lawyer*
Baskir, Lawrence M. *lawyer*
†Bass, Charles F. *congressman*
Basseches, Harriet Itkin *psychoanalyst, clinical psychologist*
Basseches, Robert Treinis *lawyer*
Bassin, Jules *foreign service officer*
Bassman, Robert Stuart *lawyer*
Bateman, Herbert Harvell *congressman*
Bateman, Paul William *government official, business executive*
Bates, John Cecil, Jr. *lawyer*
Batjargal, Zambyn *Mongolian government official*
†Battle, Dolores *state official*
Battle, Lucius Durham *retired educational institution administrator, former diplomat*
†Baublitz, John Eberhart *chemical engineer*
Baucus, Max S. *senator*
Bauer, Gary Lee *government official*
Bauer, Robert Albert *public policy consultant*
Baum, Ingeborg Ruth *librarian*
Baumgarten, Jon A. *lawyer*
Baumgartner, Eileen Mary *government official*
†Baxter, Nevins Dennis *bank consultant*
†Bayer, Robert Edward *defense department official*
Bayh, Birch Evans, Jr. *lawyer, former senator*
Bayly, John Henry, Jr. *judge*
Baynard, Ernest Cornish, III *lawyer*
Beach, Milo C. *art museum director*
Beach, Walter Eggert *publishing organization executive*
Beale, Betty (Mrs. George K. Graeber) *columnist, writer*
Beale, Susan Yates *social worker*
Bear, Dinah *lawyer*

†Beard, Daniel P. federal government executive
Bearss, Edwin C(ole) historian
Beary, John Francis, III physician, pharmaceutical executive
Beatty, Richard Scrivener lawyer
Beauchamp, Tom L. philosophy educator
Beaumont, Enid Franklin public administration executive
Beazley, Hamilton Scott volunteer health organization executive
Becerra, Xavier congressman, lawyer
Becker, Brandon lawyer
Becker, Mary Louise political scientist
Becker, William Watters lawyer
Beckett, William Wade lawyer
Beckler, Richard William lawyer
†Beckner, Everet Hess diversified research and development laboratory executive
Beckwith, Edward Jay lawyer
Bedini, Silvio A. historian, author
Bednar, Richard John lawyer, law educator
Bednarek, Jana Maria biochemist
Beebe, Cora Prifold government official
Beecher, William Manuel government official
Beehler, Bruce McPherson research zoologist, ornithologist
Beerbower, Cynthia Gibson lawyer
Beghe, Renato federal judge
Begleiter, Ralph J. correspondent
†Behney, Clyde Joseph technology assessment manager
Beilenson, Anthony Charles congressman
Beisner, John Herbert lawyer
Beizer, Robert A. lawyer
Belford, Jane Golden lawyer
Bell, James Frederick lawyer
Bell, Olin Nile lawyer
Bell, Robert G. federal agency official
Bellanti, Joseph A. microbiologist, educator
Beller, Herbert N. lawyer
Bellinger, John B., Jr. federal official
Bello, Judith Hippler lawyer
Bellows, Michael Donald foreign service officer
Belman, A. Barry pediatric urologist
Belman, Murray Joel lawyer
Belmar, Warren lawyer
Belter, Leonard W. lawyer
Beltz, William Albert publisher
Bender, David Ray library association executive
Bendernagel, James F., Jr. lawyer
Benedick, Richard Elliot diplomat
Benezra, Neal curator
Benitez, Juan Antonio electronics company executive
Benjamin, Ben E. lawyer
Benjamin, Ernst professional association executive
Bennett, Alexander Elliot lawyer
Bennett, Betty T. English educator, university dean, writer
Bennett, David Michael naval officer
†Bennett, Marian Clae lawyer
Bennett, Marion Tinsley federal judge
Bennett, Robert F. senator
Bennett, Robert Stephen lawyer
Bennitt, Brent Martin naval officer
Bentley, James Daniel medical association executive
Bentley, James Luther journalist
†Bentsen, Ken, Jr. congressman
Ben-Veniste, Richard lawyer
Berenbaum, Michael G. museum director, theology educator
Berendzen, Richard astronomer, educator, author
Bereuter, Douglas Kent congressman
Berg, Norman Alf conservation consultant
Berg, Olena federal official
Berger, Samuel R. federal official
Berget, Grete Anni federal agency administrator
Bergmann, Barbara Rose economics educator
Bergmann, Fred Heinz genetic scientist, government official
Bergsten, C. Fred economist
Berl, Joseph M. lawyer
Berlack, Evan Raden lawyer
Berlin, Kenneth lawyer
Berlincourt, Marjorie Alkins government official
Berman, Howard Lawrence congressman
Berman, Marshall Fox lawyer
Berman, Paul J. lawyer
Berman, Sidney psychiatrist
Berner, Frederic George, Jr. lawyer
Bernhard, Berl lawyer
Bernstein, Caryl Salomon lawyer
Bernstein, Edwin S. federal judge
Bernstein, Harvey Michael research foundation executive, engineer
Bernstein, Mitchell Harris lawyer
Bernthal, Frederick Michael association executive
Berry, Mary Frances history and law educator
Berry, Max Nathan lawyer
Berryman, Richard Byron lawyer
Bertini, Judith Emerline government agency administrator
Berube, Raymond P. federal agency administrator
Berz, David R. lawyer
Besen, Stanley Martin economist
Best, Judah lawyer
†Best, William Jennings research scientist
Bevan, Robert Lewis lawyer
Bevill, Tom congressman, lawyer
†Beyer, John Carl economist, consultant
Bibby, Douglas Martin mortgage association executive
Bickart, David O. lawyer
Bickel, David Robert lawyer
Biddle, Livingston Ludlow, Jr. former government official, author
Biddle, Timothy Maurice lawyer
Biden, Joseph Robinette, Jr. senator
Bieber, Sander M. lawyer
Bier, Carol Manson museum curator
Bierbauer, Charles correspondent, news analyst
Bierman, James Norman lawyer
Bigelow, Donald Nevius educational administrator, historian, consultant
†Bilbray, Brain P. congressmant
†Biles, Brian Lewis government official
Bilirakis, Michael congressman, lawyer, business executive
Biller, Morris (Moe Biller) union executive
†Billingsley, Karen Anne federal agency administrator
Billington, James Hadley historian, librarian
Bingaman, Anne K. lawyer
Bingaman, Jeff senator
†Binnendijk, Johannes Albert institute administrator
Birnbaum, Norman author, humanities educator
Bishop, James Joseph dean
Bishop, Sanford Dixon, Jr. congressman
Bishop, Wayne Staton lawyer
Bishop, William Peter research scientist
Bissell, Richard Etter association administrator
Bittker, David religious organization administrator
Bittman, William Omar lawyer
Black, Charlie J. technical writer, educator, business consultant
Black, Stephen F. lawyer
Blackmun, Harry Andrew U.S. supreme court justice
Blackwelder, Brent Francis environmentalist
Blaine, Barbara S. lawyer
Blair, Bonnie former professional speedskater, former Olympic athlete
Blair, James Pease photographer, retired
Blair, William McCormick, Jr. lawyer
Blake, Jonathan Dewey lawyer
†Blanchette, Robert Wilfred business executive, lawyer
Blanck, Ronald Ray hospital administrator, internist, career officer
Blasier, Cole political scientist
Blaxall, Martha Ossoff economist
Blazek-White, Doris lawyer
Bleakley, Peter Kimberley lawyer
Bledsoe, Ralph Champion archivist
Bleicher, Samuel Abram lawyer
†Bleichner, Howard P. theological studies administrator
†Blickstein, Irving N. defense department executive
Blinder, Alan Stuart economist
Bliss, Donald Tiffany, Jr. lawyer
Blitzer, Charles educational administrator
†Bloch, Peter B. nuclear power commission administrator
Bloch, Richard Isaac labor arbitrator
Bloch, Susan Low law educator
Block, Herbert Lawrence (Herblock) editorial cartoonist
Bloom, David I. lawyer
Bloom, Thomas Richard accountant
Bloomfield, Arthur Irving economics educator
Bloomfield, Maxwell Herron, III historian, educator
Blum, Robert Allan psychiatrist
Blume, Jack Paul retired lawyer
Blumenfeld, Sue Deborah lawyer
Blumenthal, Ronnie lawyer
Blumenthal, Susan Jane physician
Blumenthal, William lawyer
Blute, Peter I. congressman
Bluth, B. J. (Elizabeth Jean Catherine Bluth) sociologist, aerospace educator
Boaz, David Douglas foundation executive
Bodde, William, Jr. foreign service officer
Bodner, John, Jr. lawyer
Boede, Marvin J. union official
Boehlert, Sherwood Louis congressman
Boehm, Richard Wood ambassador
Boehm, Steven Bruce lawyer
Boehner, John A. congressman
Boese, John T. lawyer
Bogard, Lawrence Joseph lawyer
Bogdan, Victor Michael mathematics educator, scientist
Boggs, George Trenholm lawyer
Bogosian, Richard Wayne diplomat
Boland, Christopher Thomas, II lawyer
Bold, Frances Ann librarian
Bolino, John Vincent federal agency administrator
Bolling, Landrum Rymer retired academic administrator, writer, consultant
Bolton, John Robert lawyer, former government official
Bond, Christopher Samuel (Kit Bond) senator, lawyer
Bond, Julian civil rights leader
Bond, Richard Norman political activist
Bonde, Count Peder Carlsson investment company executive
Bonilla, Henry congressman, broadcast executive
Bonior, David Edward congressman
Bonner, Walter Joseph lawyer
Bono, Gaspare Joseph lawyer
Bonosaro, Carol Alessandra professional association executive,former government official
Bonvillian, William Boone lawyer
Book, Edward R. consultant, retired association executive
Bookbinder, Hyman H(arry) public affairs counselor
Boorda, Jeremy Michael (Mike Boorda) naval officer
Boorstin, Daniel J. historian, lector, educator, author, editor
Boren, James Harlan business executive, association executive
Borg, Parker Webb ambassador
Borgiotti, Giorgio Vittorio research scientist, engineering consultant
Born, Brooksley Elizabeth lawyer
Borsari, George Robert, Jr. lawyer, broadcaster
Borski, Robert Anthony congressman
Borut, Donald J. association executive
Boskey, Bennett lawyer
Boucher, Frederick C. congressman, lawyer
†Bouchey, L. Francis diplomat
Boughton, James Murray economist
Bourne, Francis Stanley foundation administrator
Bourne, Peter Geoffrey physician, educator, author
Bowe, Richard Welbourn lawyer
Bowen, Margareta Maria interpretation and translation educator
†Bowes, William C. aerospace engineer
Bowie, Calvert S. architect
Bowles, Erskine White House staff member
Bowron, Edgar Peters art museum curator, administrator
Bowsher, Charles Arthur government official
Boxer, Barbara senator
Boyce, Peter Bradford astronomer, professional association executive
Boyd, Stephen Mather arbitrator, mediator, lawyer
Boyd, Susan Anne curator
Boyd, Thomas Marshall federal official, lawyer
†Boykin, Keith O. government official
Boyle, John Edward Whiteford cultural organization administrator
Boyle, Renée Kent cultural organization executive, translator, editor
Boyle, Terrence John lawyer
Braden, Efrem Mark lawyer
Bradford, William Allen, Jr. lawyer
Bradford, William Hollis, Jr. lawyer
Bradlee, Benjamin Crowninshield executive editor
Bradley, Bill senator
Bradley, Melvin LeRoy communications company executive
Brady, Nyle C. international consultant, science educator
Brady, Phillip Donley lawyer
Brady, Richard Alan lawyer
Brady, Sarah gun control activist
Braestrup, Peter editor
†Bragg, Lynn Munroe commissioner
Brahms, Thomas Walter engineering institute executive
Bramson, Leon social scientist, educator
Branigin, William Joseph journalist
Brannan, Beverly Wood curator of photography
Branson, David John lawyer
Branstool, Charles Eugene farmer, federal agency administrator
Braverman, Jordan columnist
Brazaitis, Thomas Joseph journalist
Breaux, John B. senator, former congressman
Bredemeier, Kenneth Herbert journalist
Breger, Marshall J. government official, legal educator
Brennan, William Joseph, Jr. former U.S. supreme court justice
Brenner, Janet Maybin Walker lawyer
Bresee, James Collins federal agency administrator
Bretzfelder, Deborah May museum exhibit designer, photographer
Brewster, Bill K. congressman
Brewster, Robert Charles diplomat, consultant
Brewster-Walker, Sandra JoAnn public relations executive, publishing executive, genealogist, historian, consultant
Breyer, Stephen Gerald U.S. supreme court justice
Briggs, Alan Leonard lawyer
Briggs, Harold Melvin corporate executive
Briggs, Steven Russell naval officer
Brinckman, Frederick Edward, Jr. retired research chemist, consultant
Brinkley, David McClure news commentator
†Brinkley, Joel Graham journalist
Briskman, Robert David engineering executive
Britt, Stanford R. architect
Britten, Gerald Hallbeck government official
Broadnax, Walter D. federal official
Brobeck, Stephen James consumer advocate
Broches, Aron international lawyer, arbitrator
Brock, Gerald Wayne telecommunications educator
Brockway, David Hunt lawyer
Broder, David Salzer reporter
Broderick, Anthony James federal government administrator
Brodie, M. J. (Jay Brodie) architect, city planner
Brody, Kenneth David investment banker
Broering, Naomi Cordero librarian
Bromwich, Michael Ray federal official
Bronstein, Alvin J. lawyer
Brooke, Edward William lawyer, former senator
Brooks, Daniel Townley lawyer
Broom, Richard Stuart lawyer
†Broomfield, Oree, Sr. bishop
Brotzman, Donald Glenn government official, lawyer
Broun, Elizabeth art historian, museum administrator
Browder, John Glen congressman, educator
Brown, Barbara Berish lawyer
Brown, Charles Freeman lawyer
Brown, Corrine congresswoman
Brown, Dale Susan government administrator, writer
Brown, David Nelson lawyer
Brown, David R. think-tank executive
Brown, David Springer retired public administration educator
Brown, Donald Arthur lawyer
†Brown, Donald Lee hospital administrator
Brown, Elizabeth Ann foreign service officer
Brown, George Edward, Jr. congressman
Brown, George Leslie legislative affairs and business development consultant, former manufacturing company executive, former lieutenant governor
Brown, Hank senator
Brown, Harold corporate director, former secretary of defense
Brown, Jesse federal official
Brown, John Carter art and education consultant, federal agency administrator
Brown, John Patrick newspaper executive, financial consultant
Brown, June Gibbs government official
Brown, Kent Newville ambassador
Brown, Lawrence Clifton, Jr. foundation administrator
Brown, Lee Patrick federal official, law enforcement educator
Brown, Lester Russell research institute executive
Brown, Michael Arthur lawyer
Brown, Omer Forrest, II lawyer
Brown, Oscar, Jr. writer, entertainer
Brown, Preston lawyer
Brown, Richard Laurence broadcast executive
Brown, Ronald Harmon U.S. secretary of commerce, political organization administrator, lawyer
Brown, Sherrod congressman, former state official
Brown, Thomas Philip, III lawyer
Brown, William Robert association executive, consultant
†Brownback, Sam congressman
Browne, Ray insurance broker
Browne, Richard Cullen lawyer
Browner, Carol federal official
†Browning, Stephen Carroll government official
Brownlee, Paula Pimlott association executive
Brownstein, Philip Nathan lawyer
Bruce, E(stel) Edward lawyer
Bruce, John Foster lawyer
Bruce, Robert Rockwell lawyer
Bruder, George Frederick lawyer
Bruggink, Eric G. federal judge
Brunner, Thomas William lawyer
Bruno, Harold Robinson, Jr. journalist
†Bruno, Michael Peter economist
Brunsvold, Brian Garrett lawyer, educator
†Bryan, A. Bradford, Jr. hotel corporation executive
Bryan, Richard H. senator
Bryant, Anne Lincoln association executive
Bryant, Arthur H. lawyer
†Bryant, Edward congressman
Bryant, John Wiley congressman
Bryant, Robert Edward architect
Bryant, William B. federal judge
Brynn, Edward Paul ambassador
†Bryson, William Curtis federal judge
Brzezinski, Zbigniew political science educator, author
†Buben, Jeffrey Alan restaurant owner, chef
Buc, Nancy Lillian lawyer
Bucholtz, Harold Ronald lawyer
Buchwald, Art columnist, writer
Buckalew, Judith Adele nurse, pharmaceutical industry executive
Buckley, Christopher Henry, Jr. lawyer
Buckley, James Lane federal judge
Buckley, Jeremiah Stephen lawyer
Bucklin, Donald Thomas lawyer
Buechner, Jack W(illiam) lawyer, government affairs consultant
Buente, David T. environmental lawyer
Buergenthal, Thomas lawyer, educator, international judge
Buffington, John Douglas ecologist, researcher
Buffon, Charles Edward lawyer
Buffum, Elizabeth V. federal agency administrator
†Buki, Dennis Gabor lawyer
Bullard, John Kilburn federal agency administrator
Bumpers, Dale L. senator, former governor
†Bunn, Jim congressman
Burack, Michael Leonard lawyer
Burch, John Thomas, Jr. lawyer
Burch, Michael Ira public relations executive, former government official
Burcroff, Richard Tomkinson, II economist
Buresh, C. John lawyer
†Burg, Robert Jules naval officer
Burgan, Mary Alice English language educator
Burk, Francis Lewis, Jr. lawyer, federal
Burka, Robert Alan lawyer
Burke, John priest
†Burleigh, A. Peter ambassador
Burnett, Arthur Louis, Sr. judge
†Burnett, Michael A. federal agency administrator
Burnham, David Bright writer
Burns, Conrad Ray senator
Burns, David Mitchell writer, musician, former diplomat
Burns, Joseph M. economist
Burns, Stephen Gilbert lawyer
†Burr, Richard M. congressman
Burris, James Frederick academic dean, educator
Burt, Jeffrey Amsterdam lawyer
Burt, John Alan federal agency administrator
Burton, Danny Lee congressman
Burzynski, Norman Stephen editor
Busby, David lawyer
Buscemi, Peter lawyer
Busey, George Brian lawyer
Bush, Robert Donald historical preservation organization executive
Butler, Michael Francis lawyer
Butterworth, Charles E. political science educator
Button, Kenneth Rodman international economist, consultant
Buyer, Steve E. congressman, lawyer
Byer, Robert Louis applied physics educator, university dean
Byrd, Joann Kathleen newswriter
Byrd, Robert Carlyle senator
Byrnes, Heidi academic administrator, German language educator
Byron, William James management educator, former university president
Bywater, William Harold labor union official
Cacciavillan, Agostino archbishop
Cain, Becky C. association executive
Calamaro, Raymond Stuart lawyer
Calderhead, William Dickson former foreign service officer
Caldwell, John L. corporate executive
Calhoun, John Alfred social services administrator
Calhoun, John Cozart financial services marketing executive
Calhoun, Michael Jeffery lawyer
Calhoun, Noah Robert oral maxillofacial surgeon, educator
Callaway, Clifford Wayne physician
Callender, Clive Orville surgeon
Calvani, Terry lawyer, former government official
Calvert, Ken congressman
Cambel, Ali Bulent engineering educator
Cameron, Don R. association director
Camp, Dave congressman
Camp, Donald A. diplomat
Campbell, Ben Nighthorse senator
Campbell, Donald Alfred government official
Campbell, Edmund Douglas lawyer
Campbell, James Sargent lawyer
Campbell, Nancy Edinger nuclear engineer
Campbell, Wallace Justin social welfare administrator, economist
Canady, Charles T. congressman, lawyer
Canapary, Herbert Carton insurance company executive
Candon, Mary Eva lawyer
Canes, Michael Edwin trade association administrator, economist
Canfield, Edward Francis lawyer, business executive
Cannon, Howard Walter former senator
Canter, Jerome Wolf surgeon, educator
Cantor, Muriel Goldsman sociologist, educator
Cantú, Norma V. federal official
†Caplan, Phillip M. government official
Caplin, Mortimer Maxwell lawyer, educator
Caputo, Lisa M. White House staff member
Carberry, Michael Glen public relations executive
†Card, Andrew H., Jr. government official
Cardin, Benjamin Louis congressman
Cardozo, Michael Hart lawyer
Carey, Hugh L. lawyer, former governor
†Carey, John Patrick, III lawyer
Carey, Ronald labor union leader
Carey, Sarah Collins lawyer
†Carhart, Homer W. science administrator, safety engineer
Carley, L. David investment consultant, former college administrator
Carlin, John William archivist, former governor
Carliner, Michael Simon economist, association executive
Carlisle, Linda Elizabeth lawyer
Carlisle, Margo Duer Black chief senatorial staff
Carlson, Richard Warner journalist, diplomat, federal agency administrator, broadcast executive
Carlson, William Dwight government agency administrator
Carlstrom, Robert E., Jr. government and public relations executive
Carlucci, Frank Charles, III former secretary of defense
Carman, Anne foundation executive
Carmody, John newspaper columnist
Carneal, George Upshur lawyer
Carnes, Bruce M. federal official
Carney, Nell Cardwell federal agency executive
Carney, Robert Thomas lawyer
Carome, Patrick Joseph lawyer
Carozza, Shirley Caviness government department administrator
Carpenter, Sheila Jane lawyer
Carpenter, Ted Galen political scientist
Carr, David Kenneth corporate executive
Carr, Lawrence Edward, Jr. lawyer
Carr, Ronald Gene lawyer
†Carr, Timothy Bernard librarian

Carrier, Joyce H. federal agency administrator
†Carrigan, Richard Alfred environmental scientist, chemist
Carroll, Raoul Lord lawyer, investment banker
Carrow, Milton Michael lawyer, educator
†Carson, Carol S. economist
Carson, Johnnie ambassador
Carter, Ashton Baldwin physicist, government agency executive
Carter, Barry Edward lawyer, educator, administrator
Carto, Willis Allison publishing executive
Caruana, Patrick Peter career officer
Case, Larry D. agricultural education specialist
Case, Stephen H. lawyer
Casellas, Gilbert F. lawyer, federal agency administrator
Casey, Bernard J. lawyer
Casey, Mary Ann diplomat
Cashen, Henry Christopher, II lawyer, former government official
Cashmore, Patsy Joy speechwriter, editor, author, consultant, educator
Casserly, Charley professional football team executive
Casserly, James Lund lawyer
Cassidy, Robert Charles, Jr. lawyer
Cassler, Robert Leslie lawyer
Casson, Joseph Edward lawyer
Casstevens, Kay L. federal official
Castle, Michael N. congressman, former governor of Delaware, lawyer
Catlett, D. Mark federal official
Catoe, Bette Lorrina physician, health educator
Cavanagh, John Henry political economist
Cavanaugh, Gordon lawyer
Cavnar, Samuel Melmon author, publisher, activist
Caws, Peter James philosopher, educator
Cenkner, William religion educator, academic administrator
Cerny, Louis Thomas civil engineer, association executive
†Ceroni, Andrew Joseph, Jr. air force officer
Chabot, Herbert L. federal judge
Chabot, Philip Louis, Jr. lawyer
†Chabot, Steven J. congressman
Chafee, John Hubbard senator
Challinor, David scientific institute administrator
Chalmers, Franklin Stevens, Jr. engineering consultant
†Chambliss, Saxby congressman
Chambliss, William Joseph educator, sociologist, author
Chameides, Steven B. lawyer
Chandler, John Wesley educational consultant
Chanin, Leah Farb law library administrator, lawyer, consultant, law educator
Chanin, Michael Henry lawyer
Chanin, Robert Howard lawyer
Chapman, James L. (Jim Chapman) congressman
†Chapman, Thomas William hospital executive
Charles, Kathleen J. federal agency official
Chavez, Linda government official
Cheatham, Linda Moye city manager
Checchi, Vincent Victor economist
Cheek, James Edward university president
Chen, Ho-Hong H. H. industrial engineering executive, educator
Chen, Yuki Y. Kuo industrial supplies company executive
Cheney, Dick (Richard Bruce Cheney) former secretary of defense, former congressman
Cheney, Lynne V. humanities educator, writer
Cheng, Tsung O. cardiologist, educator
Chennault, Anna Chen aviation executive, author, lecturer
†Chenoweth, Helen congresswoman
Cherian, Joy consulting company executive
Cheshes, Martin L. ambassador
†Chesser, Judy Lee federal agency administrator, lawyer
Chester, Alexander Campbell, III physician
Cheston, Sheila Carol lawyer
Chiazze, Leonard, Jr. biostatistician, epidemiologist, educator
Chierichella, John W. lawyer
Chilcote, Samuel Day, Jr. association executive
Childress, Fay Alice university administrator
Childs, Timothy Winston writer
Chilman, Catherine Earles Street social welfare educator, author
Chimerine, Lawrence economist
Chin, Cecilia Hui-Hsin librarian
Chopko, Mark E. lawyer
Choquette, William H. construction company executive
Chou, Wushow information scientist, federal agency official
Chrétien, Raymond A. J. ambassador
†Christensen, Jon congressman
Christensen, Karen Kay lawyer
Christensen, Sally Hayden government executive
Christian, Betty Jo lawyer
Christian, Ernest Silsbee, Jr. lawyer
†Christianson, Geryld B. Senate committee staff
Christina, Thomas Michael lawyer
Christopher, Warren U.S. secretary of state
Chronister, Gregory Michael newspaper editor
†Chrysler, Richard R. congressman
Chu, David S. C. economist
Chubb, Talbot Albert physicist
Church, Dale Walker lawyer
Chused, Richard Harris law educator
Chwalek, Adele Ruth library administrator
Cicconi, James William lawyer
Cikovsky, Nicolai, Jr. curator, art history educator
Cisneros, Henry G. U.S. secretary of housing and urban development
†Cisneros, Marc Anthony military officer
Clagett, Brice McAdoo lawyer, writer
Clapp, Charles E., II federal judge
Clark, Dick former senator, ambassador, foreign affairs specialist
Clark, Ian Douglas international agency official
Clark, Margaret Pruitt education and advocacy executive administrator
Clark, Robert William, III lawyer
Clark, Roger Arthur lawyer
Clark, Wendell Mark travelers organization executive
†Clark, William Patrick construction, engring & transportation co exec, lawyer, rancher
Clarke, Richard A. national security specialist
Clay, Don Richard environmental consulting firm executive
Clay, William Lacy congressman
Clayton, Eva M. congresswoman, former county commissioner
Clegg, Roger Burton lawyer
Clement, Bob congressman
Clemmer, Dan Orr librarian
Cleveland, Paul Matthews diplomat
Clevenger, Raymond C., III federal judge
Clifford, Clark McAdams lawyer
Clift, Eleanor magazine correspondent
Cline, Ray Steiner political scientist, historian
Cline, William Richard economist, educator
Clinger, William Floyd, Jr. congressman
Clinton, Bill (William Jefferson Clinton) President of the United States
Clinton, Hillary Rodham First Lady of United States, lawyer
Clodius, Robert LeRoy economist, educator
Close, David Palmer lawyer
Clubb, Bruce Edwin lawyer
Clurman, Michael newspaper publishing executive
Clyburn, James E. congressman
Coady, Philip James, Jr. naval officer
Coates, Joseph Francis futurist
Coats, Daniel Ray senator
Cobb, Calvin Hayes, Jr. lawyer
Cobb, Jane Overton legislative staff member
†Coburn, Tom A. congressman
Cocco, Marie Elizabeth journalist
Cochran, John Thomas professional association executive
Cocke, Erle, Jr. international business consultant
Cody, Thomas Gerald management consultant, writer
Coerper, Milo George lawyer
Coffey, Timothy physicist
Coffield, Shirley A. lawyer
Coffin, Laurence Edmondston, Jr. landscape architect, urban planner
Coffin, Tristram writer, editor
Cohen, Bonnie R. government official
Cohen, Charles I. lawyer
Cohen, Edward Barth lawyer
Cohen, Israel chain store executive
†Cohen, Jordan Jay medical association executive
Cohen, Lewis Isaac lawyer
Cohen, Mary Ann federal judge
Cohen, Richard Martin journalist
Cohen, Stephen Bruce law educator
Cohen, William Sebastian senator
Cohn, Herbert B. lawyer
Cohn, Ronald Dennis lawyer
Cohn, Sherman Louis lawyer, educator
Cohn, Victor Edward journalist
Coia, Arthur A. labor union executive
Colbert, Edward Tuck lawyer
†Colbert, Robert Ivan education association administrator
Colby, William Egan lawyer, international consultant
Cole, Charles Glaston lawyer
Cole, John Pope, Jr. lawyer
†Cole, Kenneth J. federal commissioner
Coleman, Bernell physiologist, educator
Coleman, Ronald D. (Ron Coleman) congressman
Coleman, Roy Melvin psychiatrist
Coleman, William Thaddeus, Jr. lawyer
†Colglazier, E. William science academy administrator, physicist
Coll, Stephen Wilson journalist
Collie, Homah, III trade association executive
Collins, Barbara-Rose congresswoman
Collins, Cardiss congresswoman
Collins, Daniel Francis lawyer
Collins, Herbert, Jr. retired elementary educator
Collins, Jeremiah C. lawyer
Collins, Michael A. (Mac Collins) congressman
Collins, Naomi F. higher education administrator
Colman, Richard Thomas lawyer
Colon, Gilbert federal official
Colson, Charles Wendell lay minister, writer
Colson, Earl M. lawyer
Colton, Deborah G. federal government official
Colton, Kent W. trade association executive
Colton, Sterling Don lawyer, business executive
Colvin, John O. federal judge
Combest, Larry Ed congressman
Compton, Ann Woodruff news correspondent
Conafay, Stephen Rogers trade association executive
†Conaway, John Bolyn national guard officer
Condit, Gary A. congressman
Congel, Frank Joseph federal agency administrator, physicist
Conklin, Kenneth Edward lawyer, industry executive
Conlon, Michael William lawyer
Connell, Alastair McCrae physician
Connell, Gerald A. lawyer
Conrad, Kent senator
Conroy, Sarah Booth columnist, novelist, speaker, editor
Constable, Elinor Greer federal official, diplomat
Constandy, John Peter lawyer
Conti, William J. lawyer
Converse, Robert E., Jr. lawyer
Conway, John Thomas government official, lawyer, engineer
†Conway, Stuart Nelson forestry project administrator
Conyers, John, Jr. congressman
Cook, Frances D. diplomat
Cook, Harry Clayton, Jr. lawyer
Cook, Michael Blanchard government executive
Cook, Richard Kelsey aerospace industry executive
Cook, Walter Anthony linguist, educator
Cooke, David Ohlmer government official
†Cooley, Wes Congressman
Cooney, John Fontana lawyer
Cooper, Alan Samuel lawyer
Cooper, Benita Ann federal agency administrator
Cooper, Jean Saralee judge
Cooper, Josephine Smith trade association and public relations executive
Cooper, Richard Melvin lawyer
Cooper, Susan Louise government agency executive
Cooper-Smith, Jeffrey Paul botanic garden administrator
Cope, James Dudley association executive
Cope, Jeannette Naylor human resources consultant
Cope, John R(obert) lawyer
†Coppelman, Peter David lawyer, government official
Corcoran, Thomas Joseph retired foreign service officer, former ambassador
Corden, Warner Max economics educator
Córdova, France Anne-Dominic astrophysics scientist, administrator
Coreth, Joseph Herman bank executive
†Corlett, Cleve Edward government administrator
Cornely, Paul Bertau physician, educator
Cornett, Richard Orin research educator, consultant
Cortese, Alfred William, Jr. lawyer, consultant
Cosgrove, John Patrick editor
Costello, Jerry F., Jr. congressman, former county official
Costigan, Constance Frances artist, educator
Cotruvo, Joseph Alfred federal agency administrator
Cotter, B. Paul, Jr. judge
Coughlin, Timothy Crathorne bank executive
Countryman, John Russell business executive, former ambassador
Coursen, Christopher Dennison lawyer
Courtney, William Harrison diplomat
Couvillion, David Irvin federal judge
Coverdell, Paul Douglas senator
Covington, Pamela Jean government official
Cowan, Edward journalist
Cowart, Jack museum executive
†Cowdry, Rex William physician, researcher
Cowen, Eugene Sherman broadcasting executive
Cowen, Wilson federal judge
Cox, Chapman Beecher lawyer, corporate executive
Cox, Kenneth Allen lawyer, communications consultant
Cox, Walter Thompson, III federal judge
Cox, Warren Jacob architect
†Coyle, Philip E. federal agency administrator, engineer
Coyne, James Kitchenman, III engineering executive
Coyne, William Joseph congressman
Craft, Robert Homan, Jr. lawyer
Cragin, Charles Langmaid lawyer
Craig, Gregory Bestor lawyer
Craig, John Tucker economist, consultant
Craig, Larry Edwin senator
Cramer, Robert E., Jr. (Bud Cramer) congressman
Crampton, Scott Paul lawyer
Crandall, David Hugh physicist
Crane, Edward Harrison, III institute executive
Crane, Philip Miller congressman
Crapo, Michael Dean congressman, lawyer
Crawford, Lester Mills, Jr. veterinarian
Crawford, Susan Jean federal judge, lawyer
Crawford, William Rex, Jr. former ambassador
Crawford-Mason, Clare Wootten television producer, journalist
Creekmore, Marion Virgil, Jr. diplomat
†Cremeans, Frank A. congressman
Cremona, Vincent Anthony federal agency administrator
Crenshaw, Albert Burford journalist
Crew, Spencer museum administrator
Crewdson, John Mark journalist, author
Crocker, Chester Arthur diplomat, scholar
Cromley, Allan Wray journalist
Cromley, Raymond Avolon syndicated columnist
Croser, Mary Doreen educational association executive
Crowder, Richard Thomas federal government official
Crowell, Eldon Hubbard lawyer
Crowley, Candy Alt news correspondent
Crowley, John Joseph, Jr. ambassador
†Cruden, John Charles lawyer
Crump, John lawyer
†Crunican, Grace federal agency administrator
Crutcher, John William federal agency commissioner
Crutchfield, Sam Shaw, Jr. association executive, lawyer
Cua, Antonio S. philosophy educator
Cude, Reginald Hodgin architect
Cullen, Thomas Francis, Jr. lawyer
Cummings, Frank lawyer
Cummings, Martin Marc medical educator, physician, scientific administrator
Cunningham, George Woody federal official, metallurgical engineer
Cunningham, Randy congressman
†Cunningham, William James labor lobbyist
Curfman, David Ralph neurological surgeon, musician
Curran, Donald Charles federal agency administrator, government librarian
Curry, George Edward journalist
Curtin, Kevin Gerard lawyer
Curtin, William Joseph lawyer
Curtis, Martha Louise parochial school social studies educator, administrator
Cusick, Ralph A., Jr. investment banking company executive
Custer, Benjamin Scott, Jr. lawyer
Cutler, Bernard Joseph editor-in-chief, writer
Cutler, Lloyd Norton lawyer, company director
Cutler, Walter Leon diplomat, foundation executive
Cylke, Frank Kurt librarian
Cymrot, Mark Alan lawyer
Cytowic, Richard Edmund neurologist
Czarra, Edgar F., Jr. lawyer
Czinkota, Ilona Vigh architect
Dabengwa, Dumiso foreign government official
Dach, Leslie Alan public relations executive
Daddario, Emilio Quincy lawyer
Daffron, MaryEllen librarian
Daileda, David Allen architect
Dalley, George Albert lawyer
Dalton, John Howard Secretary of the Navy, financial consultant
Dambach, Charles Frederick foundation administrator, management consultant
Dame, William Page, III bank executive, educational administrator
Dameron, William H., III ambassador
Damgard, John Michael trade association executive
Damus, Robert George lawyer
Danaher, James William federal government executive
Dancy, John Albert news correspondent
Dando, George William professional association executive
Danescu, George Ioan government official
Daniel, Aubrey Marshall, III lawyer
Daniel, Leon journalist, newspaper columnist, editor
D'Aniello, Daniel merchant banker
Daniels, Diana M. lawyer
Daniels, Michael Paul lawyer
Daniels, Stephen M. government official
Dankner, Donald K. lawyer
†D'Anna, Vincent P. federal commissioner
Danner, Patsy Ann (Mrs. C. M. Meyer) congresswoman
Dantone, Joseph John, Jr. naval officer
Danzig, Richard Jeffrey government official, lawyer
Danziger, Joan sculptor
Danziger, Martin Breitel lawyer
Dapice, Ronald R. government official
Darby, Joseph Branch, Jr. metallurgist, government official
Darman, Richard G. investor, former government official, former investment banker, former educator
Daschle, Thomas Andrew senator
Dash, Leon DeCosta, Jr. journalist
Dash, Samuel lawyer, educator
Dauster, William Gary lawyer, economist
Davidow, Joel lawyer
Davidson, Dan Eugene language educator, educational exchange administrator
†Davidson, Daniel I. lawyer
Davidson, Daniel Morton lawyer
Davidson, Eugene Abraham biochemist, university administrator
†Davidson, James Dale political economist, writer
Davidson, Michael lawyer
Davidson, Tom William lawyer
Davies, Tudor Thomas federal agency administrator
Davis, Carolyne Kahle health care consultant
Davis, David Oliver radiologist, educator
Davis, Donald Ray entomologist
Davis, Evelyn Y. editor, writer, publisher, investor
†Davis, Franklin Gary lawyer
Davis, Garry (S. Gareth Davis) publishing executive
Davis, Herbert Lowell utility company executive
†Davis, Hiram Logan librarian
Davis, James Richard military officer
Davis, Lance Alan research and development executive, metallurgical engineer
Davis, Lynn Etheridge political scientist, government official
Davis, Marilynn A. housing agency administrator
Davis, Ross Dane lawyer
Davis, Sid journalist
†Davis, Thomas M., III congressman
Davis, True corporate executive
Davis, Walter J., Jr. vice admiral
Davison, Calvin lawyer
Davison, Roderic Hollett historian, educator
Dawson, Howard Athalone, Jr. federal judge
Dawson, Mimi (Mimi Weyforth) public policy consultant, former government official
Dawson, Rhett electric power company executive, lawyer
Dawson, Robert Kent government relations expert
Day, J(ames) Edward lawyer, former postmaster general
Day, Mary artistic director, ballet company executive
Days, Drew S., III lawyer, law educator
Deal, Nathan J. congressman, lawyer
De Alwis, Susantha diplomat
Dealy, John Francis management consultant, lawyer, educator, arbitrator
Dean, Alan Loren government official
Dean, Edwin Robinson government official, economist
Dean, Leslie Alan foreign service officer
Dean, Paul Regis law educator
Deane, James Garner magazine editor, conservationist
Dearth, Jeffrey L. magazine publisher
†Deaver, Michael Keith public relations consultant
de Borchgrave, Arnaud editor, writer, lecturer
Deckelbaum, Nelson lawyer
†Deegan, Gene Austin marine corps officer
Deel, Frances Quinn retired librarian
Deer, Ada E. federal agency official, social worker, educator
Dees, C. Stanley lawyer
Deets, Horace association executive
DeFazio, Peter A. congressman
DeGeorge, Francis Donald federal official
DeGiovanni-Donnelly, Rosalie Frances biology researcher, educator
DeGrandi, Joseph Anthony lawyer
DeJarnette, Edmund ambassador
DeJong, Gerben hospital research executive
deKieffer, Donald Eulette lawyer
Deland, Michael Reeves energy executive
deLaski, Kathleen M. federal official
De La Torre-Leano, Jose Adolfo financial advisor, lawyer
DeLauro, Rosa L. congresswoman
DeLay, Thomas D. (Tom DeLay) congressman
de Leeuw, Frank economist
Deleon, Patrick Henry lawyer
de Leon, Sylvia A. lawyer
Dellums, Ronald V. congressman
†DeLong, James Bradford government official, economics educator
†DeLuca, Anthony J. director small and minority business program in United State Air Force
DeMars, Bruce naval administrator
Dembling, Paul Gerald lawyer, former government official
Demetrion, James Thomas art museum director
Dempsey, David B. lawyer
DeMuth, Christopher Clay lawyer, foundation executive
Denger, Michael L. lawyer
Denlinger, John Kenneth journalist
Denney, George Covert, Jr. organization administrator
Dennin, Joseph Francis lawyer, former government official
Denning, Dorothy Elizabeth Robling computer scientist
Dennis, Patricia Diaz communications Attorney
Denniston, John Baker lawyer
Denvir, James Peter, III lawyer
Denysyk, Bohdan marketing professional
De Pauw, Linda Grant history educator
†Derby, Adele government agency administrator
Derrick, Butler Carson, Jr. congressman
Derrick, John Martin, Jr. electric company executive
de Saint Phalle, Thibaut investment banker, educator, lawyer, financial consultant
DeSeve, G. Edward federal official
Detchon, Bryan Reid federal agency administrator
Determan, Sara-Ann lawyer
Deupi, Carlos architect
Deutch, John Mark federal official, chemist, academic administrator
Deutsch, Peter R. congressman, lawyer
Deutsch, Stanley anesthesiologist, educator
Devaney, Dennis Martin lawyer, legal educator
De Vault, Virgil Thomas physician
Dewhurst, Stephen B. government official, lawyer
DeWitt, Charles Barbour federal government official
Diaz-Balart, Lincoln congressman
DiBattiste, Carol A. assistant U.S. attorney, lawyer
DiBona, Charles Joseph association executive
DiCello, Francis P. lawyer
†Dickens, William Theodore economics educator
Dickey, George Edward federal government executive
Dickey, Jay W., Jr. congressman, lawyer
Dickinson, William Boyd, Jr. editorial consultant
Dicks, Norman De Valois congressman
Dickstein, Sidney lawyer
†Didion, Dale Albert social services administrator

Diercks, Walter Elmer lawyer
Dietrich, Paul George lawyer
diGenova, Joseph E. lawyer
Di Lella, Alexander Anthony biblical studies educator
Dillman, Grant journalist
Dillon, Robert Sherwood non-profit educational organization executive
Dillon, Wilton Sterling anthropologist, foundation administrator
DiMario, Michael Francis federal agency official, lawyer
Dinberg, Michael David industrial engineer, uniformed services officer
Dine, Thomas Alan government relations specialist
Dingell, John David, Jr. congressman
Dinneen, Gerald Paul electrical engineer, former government official
DiPerna, Frank Paul photographer, educator
Dirda, Michael book critic
Ditlow, Clarence M. think-tank executive
†Divone, Louis Vincent aerospace engineer, educator, author
Dixon, Jeane writer, lecturer, realtor, columnist
Dixon, Julian Carey congressman
Dixon, Phillip newspaper editor
Dizard, Wilson Paul, Jr. international affairs consultant, educator
Doan, Michael Frederick editor
Dobbins, James Francis, Jr. foreign service officer
Dobkin, James Allen lawyer, engineer, artist
Dobriansky, Paula Jon business and communications executive
Docter, Charles Alfred lawyer, former state legislator
Dodd, Christopher J. senator
Dodd, Thomas J. ambassador, educator
Doggett, Lloyd congressman, former state supreme court justice
Dolan, Edward Charles lawyer
Dolan, Michael William lawyer
Dole, Elizabeth Hanford charitable organization administrator, former secretary of labor, former secretary of transportation
Dole, Robert J. senator
†Dolibois, Robert Joseph trade association administrator
Domenici, Pete (Vichi Domenici) senator
Dommen, Arthur John agricultural economist
Donahue, John David federal official
Donahue, Thomas Reilly trade union official
Donaldson, Jeff Richardson visual artist, educator
Donaldson, Samuel Andrew journalist
Donegan, Charles Edward lawyer, educator
Donilon, Thomas E. federal official
Donley, Michael Bruce federal government executive, financial manager
Donley, Rosemary university official
Donohoe, Charles Richard general patent counsel
Donovan, George Joseph industry executive, consultant
Dooley, Calvin Millard congressman
Doolittle, Jesse William, Jr. lawyer
Doolittle, John Taylor congressman
Dorgan, Byron Leslie senator
Dorman, Craig Emery oceanographer, academic administrator
Dorn, James Andrew editor
Dorn, Jennifer Lynn charitable organization administrator
Dornan, Robert Kenneth congressman
Dorsen, David M(ilton) lawyer
Dougherty, Charlene legislative staff member
Dougherty, Jude Patrick dean
Douglas, Bruce Colman geophysicist
Douglas, Leslie investment banker
Dowd, John Maguire lawyer
Dowd, Thomas F. lawyer
Dowley, Joseph Kyran lawyer, member congressional staff
Downey, Arthur Thomas, III lawyer
Downey, Mortimer Leo, III transportation executive
Downie, Leonard, Jr. newspaper editor, author
Downs, Anthony urban economist, real estate consultant
Downs, Clark Evans lawyer
†Downs, Thomas Michael transportation facility administrator
Doyle, Francis Xavier religious organization administrator
Doyle, Gerard Francis lawyer
Doyle, Joyce Ann lawyer
†Doyle, Michael F. congressman
Drabkin, Murray lawyer
Dreier, David Timothy congressman
Drew, Elizabeth television commentator, journalist
Dreyer, David E. federal official
Drinan, Robert Frederick lawyer, former congressman, educator, clergyman
Droms, William George finance educator
Drouilhet, Paul Raymond, Jr. science laboratory director, electrical engineer
Dublin, Thomas David physician
DuBoff, Scott M. lawyer
DuCran, Claudette Deloris bank officer
†Dudley, Barbara environmental association administrator
Duemling, Robert Werner diplomat, museum director
Duffey, Joseph Daniel federal official
Dugan, Robert Perry, Jr. minister, religious organization administrator
Duggan, Ervin S. federal agency administrator
†Dujack, Stephen Raymond editor
Duke, Paul Robert lawyer
Dukert, Betty Cole television producer
†Dula, Brett M. military officer
Dulles, Eleanor Lansing diplomatic consultant, retired diplomat, educator
Dunbar, Charles Franklin diplomat
Duncan, Charles Tignor lawyer
Duncan, John Dean, Jr. lawyer
Duncan, John J., Jr. congressman
Dunn, H. Stewart, Jr. lawyer
Dunn, Jennifer Blackburn congresswoman
Dunn, Loretta Lynn lawyer
†Dunn, Michael V. federal agency administrator
Dunne, John Richard lawyer
Dunner, Donald Robert lawyer
Dunsmore, Barrie television news correspondent
Durbin, Richard Joseph congressman
Durfee, Harold Allen philosophy educator
Durham, Archer L. federal official, retired career officer
Durney, Michael Cavalier lawyer
†Durocher, Cort Louis aerospace engineer, association executive
Dutro, John Thomas, Jr. geologist, paleontologist
Duvall, Donald Knox lawyer
Dwyer, Jeffry R. lawyer
Dye, Alan Louis lawyer
Dye, Stuart S. lawyer
Dyk, Timothy Belcher lawyer, educator
Dyke, Charles William retired army officer
†Dyson, Lowell Keith historian
Dyvig, Peter P. ambassador
Dziewanowski, Kazimierz diplomat, journalist
Eads, George Curtis economics executive
Earle, Ralph, II lawyer
Earle, Richard Alan lawyer
Earll, Jerry Miller internist, educator
Earner, William Anthony, Jr. naval officer
Easley, William Webster, Jr. minister
East, Maurice Alden academic dean, political scientist
Easterling, Christine Davis educational administrator
Eastman, Ronald D. lawyer
Eastment, Thomas James lawyer
Easton, John Jay, Jr. lawyer
†Ebbitt, James Roger government official
Eckart, Dennis Edward lawyer, former congressman
Eckenhoff, Edward Alvin health care administrator
Eddy, David Corbett lawyer
Eddy, John Joseph diplomat
Edelman, Marian Wright (Mrs. Peter B. Edelman) lawyer
Edelman, Peter Benjamin lawyer
Edes, Nik Bruce lawyer
Edles, Gary J. lawyer
Edsall, Thomas Byrne reporter
Edson, Charles Louis lawyer, educator
Edwards, Bert Tvedt accountant
Edwards, Bob (Robert Alan Edwards) radio news anchor
Edwards, Chet congressman
Edwards, Gilbert Franklin sociologist, educator
Edwards, Harry T. chief federal judge
Edwards, Julia Spalding journalist
Edwards, Tony M. lawyer
Efron, Marc Fred lawyer
Efron, Samuel lawyer
Efros, Ellen Ann lawyer
†Eggenberger, Andrew Jon federal agency administrator
Ehlers, Vernon James congressman
Ehrenhaft, Peter David lawyer
Ehrlich, Clifford John hotel executive
Ehrlich, Everett Michael federal official, computer company executive
†Ehrlich, Robert L., Jr. congressman
Ein, Daniel allergist
Ein, Melvin Bennett government official
Einaudi, Luigi Roberto federal official, educator
Eisenberg, John Meyer physician, educator
Eisenberg, Jonathan Neil lawyer
Eisenberg, Meyer lawyer
Eisenberg, Milton lawyer
Eisenberg, Pablo Samuel non-profit organization executive
Eisenstat, David H. lawyer
Eisner, Howard engineering educator, engineering executive
Eisner, Neil Robert lawyer
†Elcano, Mary S. lawyer, federal agency administrator
Elfin, Mel magazine editor
Elgart, Mervyn L. dermatologist
Elias, Thomas Sam botanist, author
El Khadem, Hassan Saad chemistry educator, researcher
Eller, Jeff media affairs director, assistant to President
Ellicott, John LeMoyne lawyer
Elliott, Emerson John federal agency administrator, policy analyst
Elliott, Larry Paul cardiac radiologist, educator
Elliott, Lee Ann federal official
Elliott, Robert John lawyer
Elliott, Thomas Michael management services executive, educator, consultant
Elliott, Warren G. lawyer
Ellis, Courtenay lawyer
Ellis, Lee T., Jr. lawyer
Ellis, Brother Patrick (H. J. Ellis) academic administrator
Ellis, Rudolph Lawrence insurance company executive
Ellsworth, Robert Fred investment executive, former government official
Ellwood, David T. federal agency administrator
Elmer, Brian Christian lawyer
†Elms, Charles Patrick engineering company executive
Elrod, Eugene Richard lawyer
Elsasser, Glen Robert writer, editor
Elsey, George McKee association executive
Elwood, William Edward lawyer
Ely-Raphel, Nancy diplomat
Emerson, John Bonnell lawyer, partner
Emerson, William congressman
Emery, Nancy Beth lawyer
Emmett, Robert Addis, III lawyer
Emperado, Mercedes Lopez librarian
Endahl, Lowell Jerome retired electrical cooperative executive
Engberg, Eric Jon news correspondent
Engel, Eliot L. congressman
Engel, Ralph manufacturers association executive
Englert, Roy Theodore lawyer
English, Glenn association executive, former congressman
†English, Philip S. congressman
English, Richard Allyn sociologist, social work educator
Engman, Lewis August lawyer, trade association executive, former government official
Ennis, Bruce J. lawyer
Eno, Amos Stewart natural resource foundation adminstrator
†Ensign, John E. congressman
Ensign, William Lloyd architect
Epps, Charles H., Jr. medical educator, college dean
Epstein, David lawyer, arbitrator
Epstein, Gary Marvin lawyer
Epstein, Joseph editor, writer, educator
Epstein, Kalman Noel newspaper publishing company executive
Epstein, Lionel Charles lawyer
Epstein, Sidney editor
Epstien, Jay Alan lawyer
Erdreich, Ben Leader federal agency executive
†Erichsen, Peter Christian lawyer, government official
Ericsson, Sally Claire federal agency adminstrator
Ernst, Daniel Robinson law educator, legal historian
Erwin, Frank William personnel research and publishing executive
Escudero, Stanley ambassador
Eshoo, Anna Georges congresswoman
Eskridge, William Nichol, Jr. law educator
Espy, Mike (Alphonso Michael Espy) U.S. secretary of agriculture
†Esserman, Susan Gayle government official administrator
Esslinger, John Thomas lawyer
Esters, Donald J. audio and video company executive
Etters, Ronald Milton lawyer
Etzioni, Amitai Werner sociologist, educator
Evans, David C. lawyer
Evans, Lane congressman
†Evans, Michael Brock environmentalist
Evans, Rowland, Jr. newspaper columnist
†Evans, Thomas R. magazine publisher
Evelyn, Douglas Everett museum executive
Everett, R. Terry congressman, farmer, newspaper executive, bank executive
Everett, Ralph Bernard lawyer
Everett, Robinson Oscar federal judge, law educator
Ewing, Ky Pepper, Jr. lawyer
Ewing, Samuel Daniel, Jr. financial executive
Ewing, Thomas W. congressman, lawyer
Exon, J(ohn) James senator
Fahmy, Ibrahim Mounir hotel executive
Fahrenkopf, Frank Joseph, Jr. lawyer
Fairbanks, Richard Monroe, III lawyer, former ambassador at large
Fairchild, Samuel Wilson professional services company executive, former federal agency administrator
Faircloth, Duncan McLauchlin (Lauch Faircloth) senator, businessman, farmer
Falci, Kenneth Joseph food and nutrition scientist
Faleomavaega, Eni F. H. territorial diplomat
Falk, David B. lawyer, professional athletic representative
Falk, James Harvey, Sr. lawyer
Falter, Robert Gary correctional health care administrator
Falter, Vincent Eugene retired army officer, consultant
Fant, Lester G., III lawyer
Farabow, Ford Franklin, Jr. lawyer
Farer, Tom Joel legal educator, writer, consultant
Farley, John Joseph, III federal judge
Farley, John Michael steel industry executive
†Farmen, William Newton career officer
Farmer, Donald A(rthur), Jr. lawyer
Farmer, Thomas Laurence lawyer
Farr, Judith Banzer writer, literature educator
Farr, Sam Sharon congressman
Farrar, Donald Eugene capital markets advisor
Farrell, J. Michael lawyer
Farrell, Joseph Michael steamship company executive
Farrell, June Martinick public relations executive
Farrell, Suzanne ballerina
Fasman, Zachary Dean lawyer
†Fattah, Chaka congressman, former state legislator
Faust, Marcus G. lawyer
Faux, Jeff (Geoffrey Peter Faux) economist, writer
Favretto, Richard J. lawyer
Fawcett, John Thomas archivist
Fawell, Harris W. congressman
Fay, William Michael federal judge
Fazio, Vic congressman
Fedders, John Michael lawyer
Fedorochko, William, Jr. retired army officer, policy analyst
Feeney, Richard Joseph trade association executive, journalist
Feffer, Gerald Alan lawyer
Feighan, Edward Farrell lawyer, former congressman
Feinberg, Kenneth Roy lawyer, law educator
Feinberg, Richard E. federal official
Feingold, Russell Dana senator
Feingold, S. Norman psychologist
†Feinstein, Dianne senator
Feinstein, Martin opera director
Feld, Jonathan S. lawyer
Feld, Karen Irma columnist, journalist, public speaker
Feldhaus, Stephen Martin lawyer
Feldman, Adrienne Arsht lawyer, broadcasting company executive, banking executive
Feldman, Bruce Allen otolaryngologist
Feldman, Clarice Rochelle lawyer
Feldman, Mark B. lawyer
Feldman, Myer lawyer
Feldman, Roger David lawyer
Felker, Alex D. communications executive
Fell, James Carlton scientific and technical affairs executive, consultant
Feller, Lloyd Harris lawyer
Fellner, Baruch Abraham lawyer
Fels, Nicholas Wolff lawyer
Felton, Gordon H. retired publishing executive
Felts, William Robert, Jr. physician
†Feltus, William James legislative staff member
Fendrich, Roger Paul lawyer
Fenton, Kathryn Marie lawyer
Ferebee, John Spencer, Jr. corporate executive
Ferguson, Thomas Crooks lawyer
Ferguson, Thomas H. newspaper executive
Ferman, Irving lawyer, educator
Fern, Alan Maxwell art historian, museum director
Fernhall, Bo physical education educator
Ferrara, Peter Joseph federal official, lawyer, author, educator
Ferrara, Ralph C. lawyer
Ferren, John Maxwell federal judge
Ferris, Charles Daniel lawyer, former government official
Ferris, George Mallette, Jr. investment banker
Feuerstein, Donald Martin lawyer
Feulner, Edwin John, Jr. research foundation executive
Field, Andrea Bear lawyer
Fielding, Fred Fisher lawyer
Fields, Cleo congressman
Fields, Jack Milton, Jr. congressman
Fields, Stuart Howard employee relations specialist
Fields, Suzanne Bregman syndicated columnist
Fields, Wendy Lynn lawyer
Fielek, Etta state offical
Fifer Canby, Susan Melinda library administrator
Filerman, Gary Lewis health education executive
Filner, Bob congressman
Filstrup, E. Christian librarian, writer
†Finch, Johnny Charles government agency executive
Finerty, Martin Joseph, Jr. military officer, researcher
Fingerhut, Marilyn Ann federal agency administrator
Fink, Lois Marie art historian
Fink, Matthew Pollack trade association executive, lawyer
Finkel, Eugene Jay lawyer
Finkelstein, James David physician
Finkle, Jeffrey Alan professional association executive
Finn, Timothy John lawyer
Finney, Essex Eugene, Jr. agricultural research administrator
Fiorini, John E., III lawyer
Firestone, Charles Morton lawyer, educator
†Fischer, Dennis J. government official
Fischer, Stanley economist, educator
Fischetti, Michael Joseph accounting educator
Fishbaugh, Franklin James government intelligence officer, researcher, weapons specialist
Fishburne, Benjamin P., III lawyer
Fisher, Bart Steven lawyer, educator
Fisher, Benjamin Chatburn lawyer
Fisher, Farley chemist, federal agency administrator
Fisher, Joel Hilton lawyer
†Fisher, Joseph A. legislative official
Fisher, Miles Mark, IV education educator
Fisher, Robert Dale stockbroker, retired naval officer
†Fisher, Sam organization administrator, consultant
†Fisher, Stephen Todd naval officer
†Fisher, Timothy Mark non-profit administrator
Fiske, Richard Sewell geologist
Fitts, C. Austin investment banker, former federal agency administrator
†Fitzgerald, Joseph Edward, Jr. government official
FitzGerald, William Henry G. diplomat, corporation executive
Fitzhugh, David Michael lawyer
Fitz-Hugh, Glassell Slaughter, Jr. bank executive
Fitzmyer, Joseph Augustine theology educator, priest
Fitzpatrick, James Franklin lawyer
Fitzwater, (Max) Marlin former government official, press secretary, advertising executive
Flagg, Ronald Simon lawyer
Flake, Floyd Harold congressman
Flanagan, Francis Dennis retired corporate executive
†Flanagan, Michael Patrick congressman, lawyer
Flanigan, Alan H. ambassador
Flannery, Ellen Joanne lawyer
Flax, Alexander Henry aeronautical engineer, federal science agency administrator
Fleischaker, Marc L. lawyer
Fleischer, Michael chemist
Fleit, Martin lawyer
Fleming, Mack Gerald lawyer
Fleming, Robert Wright investment banker
Fletcher, Arthur A. federal official
†Fletcher, Carlton Henry artist
Fletcher, James Andrew information systems specialist
Flindt, Flemming ballet master
Flint, Myles Edward federal agency administrator, lawyer
Florance, Colden l'Hommedieu Ruggles architect
Flournoy, Nancy statistician, educator
Flowe, Carol Connor lawyer
†Flynn, Nancy Marie government executive
Foard, Douglas W. educational association administrator
Fogleman, Ronald Robert military officer
Fogt, Howard W., Jr. lawyer
†Fois, Andrew lawyer, educator
†Foley, Gary J. research chemical engineer, computer scientist, federal agency administrator
†Foley, Mark Adam congressman
Foote, Timothy Gilson editor
†Forbes, Michael P. congressman
†Force, Charles Thomas government executive
Ford, Charles A. federal official
Ford, Harold Eugene congressman
Ford, Robert Nelson government lawyer
Foreman, Anne N. lawyer
Foreman, Carol Lee Tucker corporate executive
Foreman, Dennis I. federal official, lawyer
Forester, John Gordon, Jr. lawyer
Forgey, Benjamin Franklin architecture and art critic
Forrest, Herbert Emerson lawyer
Forrest, Sidney clarinetist, music educator
Forster, Cecil R., Jr. lawyer
Fortune, Terence John lawyer
Fortuno, Victor M. lawyer
Fosler, R. Scott academic administrator, federal agency administrator
Fowler, Caleb L. insurance company executive, lawyer
†Fowler, Donald L. political organization leader, political science educator, retired US Army officer
Fowler, Earle Cabell physicist, administrator
†Fowler, Mary Emily federal agency administrator
†Fowler, Raymond Dalton professional association executive, psychologist
Fowler, Tillie Kidd congresswoman
†Fox, Charles Washington, III international broadcasting executive
†Fox, Harold Edward obstetrician/gynecologist, educator, researcher
†Fox, Jon D. congressman
Fox, Laurel R. community and population ecologist, researcher
Fox, Lynn Smith federal government official
Fox, Samuel Mickle, III physician, educator
Frame, Nancy Davis lawyer
Frampton, George Thomas, Jr. conservation organization executive
Francis, Samuel Todd columnist
Francke, Gloria Niemeyer pharmacist, editor, publisher
Francois, Francis Bernard association executive, lawyer
Frank, Barney congressman
Frank, Isaiah economist, educator
Frank, Richard Asher lawyer, health products executive
Frank, Richard Sanford magazine editor
Frank, Theodore David lawyer
Frank, Victor H., Jr. international financial consultant
†Frankel, Diane museum institute administrator
Frankel, Jeffrey Alexander economics educator, consultant
Frankel, Michael Henry accountant, lawyer
Frankle, Edward Alan lawyer
Franklin, Barbara Hackman former goverment official
Franklin, Charles E. career officer
Franklin, Hardy R. library director
Franks, Gary Alvin congressman, real estate professional
Franzen, Byron T. (John Franzen) media specialist
Frasure, Robert Conway diplomat
Frazier, Henry Bowen, III government official, lawyer

Frederick, Lafayette *botanist*
Freedberg, Sydney Joseph *retired museum curator, retired fine arts educator*
Freedman, Anthony Stephen *lawyer*
Freedman, Walter *lawyer*
Freeh, Louis J. *federal agency administrator*
Freeman, Chas. W., Jr. *government official, ambassador*
Freeman, Robert Turner, Jr. *insurance executive*
Freer, Robert Elliott, Jr. *lawyer*
Freije, Philip Charles *lawyer*
Freitag, Robert Frederick *government official*
†Frelinghuysen, Rodney P. *congressman*
†French, Catherine *association executive*
Freudenheim, Tom Lippmann *museum administrator*
Frey, Andrew Lewis *lawyer*
†Fricke, Heinz *conductor*
Fried, Edward R. *government official*
Friedlander, Charles *lawyer*
Friedlander, James Stuart *lawyer*
Friedlander, Michael E. *lawyer*
Friedman, Alvin *lawyer*
Friedman, Arthur Daniel *electrical engineering and computer science educator, investment management company executive*
Friedman, Daniel Mortimer *federal judge*
Friedman, Herbert *physicist*
Friedman, Miles *trade association executive, financial services company executive, university lecturer*
Friedman, Paul Lawrence *lawyer*
†Friedman, Paul Richard *government lawyer*
Friedman, Townsend B., Jr. *ambassador*
†Frisa, Daniel *congressman*
†Frist, William H. *senator, surgeon*
†Fritts, Edward O. *broadcast executive*
Fritz, Thomas Vincent *association and business executive, accountant*
Froehlich, Laurence Alan *lawyer*
Frohnmayer, John Edward *legal scholar, ethicist, writer*
Frost, Edmund Bowen *lawyer*
Frost, Ellen Louise *federal agency administrator*
Frost, Jonas Martin, III *congressman*
Frost, S. David *retired naval officer*
Fry, Louis Edwin, Jr. *architect*
Fry, Tom *federal official*
Fu, Shen C. Y. *curator, art historian*
Fuchs, Roland John *geography educator, university administrator*
Fugate, Wilbur Lindsay *lawyer*
Fuhrman, Robert Alexander *aerospace company executive*
Fukushima, Kiyohiko *economist*
Fulbright, Harriet Mayor *foundation administrator*
Fuller, Edwin Daniel *hotel executive*
†Fuller, Kathryn Scott *environmental association executive, lawyer*
Fuller, Lawrence Joseph *military officer, lawyer*
Fullerton, Lawrence Rae *lawyer*
Fulton, Richard Alsina *lawyer*
Funderburk, David B. *congressman, history educator, former ambassador*
Furash, Edward E. *management consultant*
Furgol, Edward Mackie *museum curator, historian*
Furgurson, Ernest Baker, Jr. (Pat Furgurson) *journalist*
†Furiga, Richard Daniel *government official*
Furse, Elizabeth *congresswoman, small business owner*
Futey, Bohdan A. *federal judge*
Futrell, Basil Lee *association executive*
Futrell, John William *institute executive, lawyer*
Futrell, Mary Alice Hatwood *education association administrator*
Gaff, Jerry Gene *academic administrator*
Gaffney, Susan *federal official*
Gaguine, Benito *lawyer*
Gaines, Ludwell Ebersole *investment executive*
Gale, Joseph H. *lawyer*
Galloway, William Jefferson *former foreign service officer*
Gallucci, Robert Louis *diplomat, federal government official*
Galston, William Arthur *political scientist, educator*
†Ganske, Greg *congressman*
Garavelli, John Stephen *biochemistry research scientist*
Gardner, Alvin Frederick *oral pathologist, government official*
†Gardner, Donald Ray *career officer*
Gardner, William Leonard *lawyer*
†Garfunkel, Sanford M. *medical administrator*
Garland, Merrick Brian *lawyer*
†Garner, Jay Montgomery *career officer*
Garrett, Theodore Louis *lawyer*
Garrish, Theodore John *lawyer*
Gart, Murray Joseph *journalist*
Garvey, Gerald Thomas *physicist, researcher*
Garvey, John Leo *lawyer, educator*
Gary, Marc *lawyer*
Gary, Nancy Elizabeth *nephrologist, academic administrator*
Gastwirth, Joseph Lewis *statistician, educator*
Gati, Toby T. *federal official*
Gauldin, Michael Glen *federal agency administrator*
Gaull, Gerald Edward *nutritionist, scientist, educator, food company executive*
Gaynor, Kevin Allen *lawyer*
Gearan, Mark D. *federal official*
Gehrig, Leo Joseph *surgeon*
Geisel, Harold Walter *diplomat*
Gejdenson, Sam *congressman*
Gekas, George William *congressman*
†Gelacak, Michael S. *legal administrator*
Geller, Kenneth Steven *lawyer*
Gellhorn, Ernest Albert Eugene *lawyer*
Gelman, Norman Ira *public policy consultant*
Geltman, Edward A. *lawyer*
†Genega, Stanley G. *career officer, federal agency administrator*
Geniesse, Robert John *lawyer*
George, Gerald William *author, administrator*
George, W. Peyton *lawyer*
Georgine, Robert Anthony *union executive*
Gephardt, Richard Andrew *congressman*
Gerber, Joel *federal judge*
Geren, Preston (Pete Geren) *congressman*
Gergen, David Richmond *federal official, magazine editor*
Gernand, Bradley Elton *archivist, manuscripts librarian*
†Gershman, Carl Samuel *foundation administrator*
Gerson, Stuart Michael *lawyer*
Gertig, June Munford *lawyer*
†Gessaman, Donald Eugene *government executive*
Gest, Kathryn Waters *press secretary*
Geyer, Georgie Anne *syndicated columnist, educator, author, biographer*
Giallorenzi, Thomas Gaetano *optical engineer*
Gibbons, John Howard (Jack Gibbons) *government official, physicist*
Gibbons, Samuel Melville (Sam Gibbons) *congressman*
Gibbs, Lawrence B. *lawyer*
Gibson, Paul Raymond *international trade and investment development executive*
Gibson, Reginald Walker *federal judge*
Gibson, Thomas Fenner, III *public affairs consultant, political cartoonist*
Gideon, Kenneth Wayne *lawyer*
Gifford, Prosser *library administrator*
Gilbert, Charles Richard Alsop *physician, medical educator*
Gilbert, Jackson B. *banker*
Gilchrest, Wayne Thomas *congressman, former high school educator*
Gildenhorn, Joseph Bernard *businessman, diplomat, lawyer*
Gilfoyle, Nathalie Floyd Preston *lawyer*
†Gilliam, Arleen Fain *labor union administrator, finance executive*
Gilliam, Dorothy Butler *columnist*
Gilliam, Sam *artist*
Gilliland, James Sevier *lawyer*
Gillingham, Robert Fenton *federal agency administrator, economist*
Gilliom, Judith Carr *government official*
Gillmor, Paul E. *congressman, lawyer*
Gilman, Benjamin Arthur *congressman*
Gilmour, Craddock Matthew, Jr. (Sandy Gilmour) *television news correspondent*
Gingrich, Newt (Newton Leroy Gingrich) *congressman*
Ginsburg, Charles David *lawyer*
Ginsburg, Douglas Howard *federal judge, educator*
Ginsburg, Gilbert J. *lawyer, law educator*
Ginsburg, Martin David *lawyer, educator*
Ginsburg, Ruth Bader *U.S. supreme court justice*
Girard, James Emery *chemistry educator*
Gitner, Geoffrey P. *lawyer*
Glancz, Ronald Robert *lawyer*
Glanzer, Seymour *lawyer*
Glaser, Vera Romans *journalist*
Glass, Andrew James *newspaper editor*
Glassman, James Kenneth *editor, writer, publishing executive*
Glauthier, T. James *federal official*
Gleason, Jean Wilbur *lawyer*
Glenn, John Herschel, Jr. *senator*
Glick, Leslie Alan *lawyer*
Glick, Warren W. *lawyer, banker*
Glickman, Daniel Robert *federal agency administrator*
Glogower, Michael Howard *housing program specialist, business and real estate consultant*
Glosser, Jeffrey Mark *lawyer*
Glynn, Thomas P. *federal agency administrator*
Gober, Hershel W. *government official*
Godsey, John Drew *minister, theology educator emeritus*
Goelzer, Daniel Lee *lawyer*
†Goforth, Wayne Reid *research administrator, biologist*
Goldberg, Avrum M. *lawyer*
Goldberg, Larry Joel *lawyer*
Goldberg, Seth A. *lawyer*
Goldberg, Stanley Joshua *federal judge*
Goldblatt, Steven Harris *law educator*
Golden, Cornelius Joseph, Jr. *lawyer*
†Golden, Myron *government official, diplomat*
Golden, Terence C. *realty corporation executive, former government official*
Goldfarb, Ronald Lawrence *lawyer*
Goldfield, Edwin David *statistician*
Goldhaber, Jacob Kopel *retired mathematician, educator*
Goldin, Daniel S. *government agency administrator*
Golding, Carolyn May *government administrator*
Goldman, Aaron *foundation executive, writer*
Goldman, Eugene I. *lawyer*
†Goldman, Lynn Rose *federal agency administrator*
Goldsmith, Willis Jay *lawyer*
Goldson, Alfred Lloyd *oncologist, educator*
Goldstein, Allan Leonard *biochemist, educator*
Goldstein, Frank Robert *lawyer*
Goldstein, Irving *communications company executive*
Goldstein, Michael B. *lawyer*
Goldstein, Murray *health organization official*
Goldstein, N. Linda *lawyer*
†Goldstein, Sheldon Robert *professional association administrator*
Golodner, Jack *labor association official*
†Gonzales, Richard Steven *broadcast journalist*
Gonzalez, Henry Barbosa *congressman*
Good, Mary Lowe (Mrs. Billy Jewel Good) *government official*
Goode, James Moore *historian*
Goode, Richard Benjamin *economist, educator*
Goodlatte, Robert William *congressman, lawyer*
Goodling, William F. *congressman*
Goodman, Margaret Gertrude *government administrator*
Goodpaster, Andrew Jackson *retired army officer*
Goodrich, George Herbert *judge*
Goodrich, Nathaniel Herman *lawyer, former government official*
†Goodwin, Larry Kenneth *federal government official*
Gordon, Barton Jennings (Bart Gordon) *congressman, lawyer*
Gordon, Harry Thomas *architectural firm executive*
Gordon, Nancy M. *congressional administrator*
Gordon, Shana *trade company executive*
Gore, Albert *Vice President of the United States*
Gore, Tipper (Mary Elizabeth Gore) *wife of vice president of the United States*
Gorelick, Jamie Shona *lawyer*
Gorham, William *organization executive*
Gorinson, Stanley M. *lawyer*
Gorman, Joyce J(ohanna) *lawyer*
Gorn, Janet Marie *government official*
Gorton, Slade *senator*
Goslin, David Alexander *research administrator, sociologist*
Gosnell, Jack Leslie *diplomat*
Gossage, John Ralph *photographer*
Gostin, Lawrence *lawyer*
Gottlieb, Anita F. *professional society executive*
Gottschalk, Thomas A. *lawyer*
Gould, William Benjamin, IV *federal official, lawyer, educator*
Grabow, John Charles *lawyer*
Gracey, James Steele *corporate director, retired coast guard officer, consultant*
†Gradison, Willis David, Jr. *congressman, investment broker*
Graefe, Frederick H. *lawyer*
Grafton, Robert Bruce *science foundation official*
Graham, D. Robert (Bob Graham) *senator, former governor*
Graham, Donald Edward *publisher*
Graham, Fred Patterson *journalist, lawyer*
Graham, Katharine *newspaper executive*
†Graham, Lindsey O. *congressman*
Graham, Thomas Richard *lawyer*
Gramm, William Philip (Phil Gramm) *senator, economist*
Grams, Rodney D. *congressman, construction executive, television producer and anchor*
Grandmaison, J. Joseph *political consultant*
Grant, Carl N. *communications executive*
Grant, David Alistair *lawyer*
Grant, Richard Evans *paleontologist, museum curator*
Grasselli, Margaret Morgan *curator*
Grassley, Charles Ernest *senator*
Graves, Ernest, Jr. *retired army officer, engineer*
Graves, Ruth Parker *educational executive*
Graves, William P. E. *editor*
Gray, Clayland Boyden *lawyer*
†Gray, Kenneth Darnell *career officer, judge*
Gray, Mary Wheat *statistician, lawyer*
Gray, Ralph *editor, writer*
Gray, Robert Keith *communications company executive*
Gray, Sheila Hafter *psychiatrist, psychoanalyst*
Grayson, Lawrence Peter *federal educational administrator*
Green, Darrell *professional football player*
Green, Donald Hugh *lawyer*
Green, Edward Crocker *health consulting firm executive*
Green, Gordon Woodrow, Jr. *economist, federal agency administrator*
Green, Joyce Hens *federal judge*
Green, June Lazenby *federal judge*
Green, Marshall *former ambassador, consultant*
Green, Monica *peace organization director*
Green, Richard Alan *lawyer*
Green, Richard James *federal agency administrator, aerospace engineer*
Green, Robert Lamar, Jr. *lawyer*
Green, Shirley Moore *public affairs and communications executive*
Green, Thomas Charles *lawyer*
Greenberg, Milton *political scientist, educator*
Greenberg, Robert E. *lawyer*
Greenberger, I. Michael *lawyer*
Greenburg, David Julius *professional association administrator, lawyer*
Greene, Harold H. *federal judge*
Greene, Ronald J. *lawyer*
Greene, Timothy Geddes *lawyer*
Greenebaum, Leonard Charles *lawyer*
Greenfield, Meg *journalist*
Greenspan, Alan *economist*
Greenspan, Michael Alan *lawyer*
Greenwald, Gerald Bernard *lawyer*
Greenwood, James Charles *congressman*
Greenwood, Janet Kae Daly *psychologist, educational administrator*
Greenwood, William Warren *journalist*
Grefé, Richard *graphic design executive*
Gregg, Judd *senator, former governor*
†Gregg, Richard Leo *federal commissioner*
Gregory, Bettina Louise *journalist*
†Gregory, Frederick D. *career officer, space agency administrator*
Greif, Joseph *lawyer*
Grenier, Edward Joseph, Jr. *lawyer*
Gribbin, David James, III *federal official*
Gribbon, Daniel McNamara *lawyer*
Grier, Phillip Michael *lawyer, association executive*
Griffenhagen, George Bernard *trade association executive*
†Griffin, Elaine B. *teacher*
Griffin, James Bennett *anthropologist, educator*
Griffin, Joseph Parker *lawyer, educator*
Griffin, Robert Thomas *automotive company executive*
Griffith, Patricia King *journalist*
Griffith, Ronald H. *military career officer*
Grimes, Larry Bruce *lawyer*
Grimmett, Richard Fieldon *government official*
Groner, Samuel Brian *lawyer*
Gros, Jeffrey *ecumenical theologian*
Gross, David Joseph *aquarium director*
Gross, Richard Alan *lawyer*
Grossi, Ralph Edward *agricultural conservation organization executive, farmer, rancher*
Grossman, Joanne Barbara *lawyer*
Grossman, John Henry, III *obstetrician, gynecologist, educator*
†Grossman, Marc *ambassador*
Grosvenor, Gilbert Melville *journalist, educator, business executive*
Grove, Brandon Hambright, Jr. *diplomat*
Gruenberg, Mark Jonathan *correspondent*
Grumbacher, Jacqueline W. *communications executive*
Guandolo, John *lawyer*
Gubser, Peter Anton *political scientist, writer, educator*
Guenther, Kenneth Allen *business association executive, economist*
Guggenheim, Charles E. *film, television producer, political media consultant*
Guimond, Richard Joseph *federal agency executive, environmental scientist*
†Gulbrandsen, Patricia Hughes *physician*
Gulland, Eugene D. *lawyer*
Gulya, Brigitta Rianna *federal government official*
Gumpert, Gunther *artist*
Gundersheimer, Werner Leonard *library director*
Gunderson, Steve Craig *congressman*
Gunther, Marc *television writer*
Gustini, Raymond J. *lawyer*
Gutierrez, Luis V. *congressman, elementary education educator*
Gutierrez-Santos, Luis Emiliano *economist*
Gutknecht, Gilbert William, Jr. *congressman, former state legislator, auctioneer*
Gutman, Harry Largman *lawyer*
Gutman, Roy William *reporter*
Gutter, Samuel I. *lawyer*
Guttman, Egon *law educator*
†Guzy, Carol *photojournalist*
Gwaltney, Corbin *editor, publishing executive*
Haas, Ellen *federal agency administrator*
Haass, Richard Nathan *federal agency administrator*
Hadar, Mary Ellen *newspaper editor*
Haft, Robert J. *law educator*
Hagenstad, M. Thomas *federal government administrator*
Hager, Robert *journalist*
Haggerty, James Joseph *writer*
Hahn, Gilbert, Jr. *lawyer*
Hahn, John Stephen *lawyer*
Haig, Alexander Meigs, Jr. *former secretary of state, former army officer, business executive*
†Haines, Milton L. (Lee Haines) *air force officer*
Haines, Ronald H. *bishop*
†Hair, Jay Dee *association executive*
†Halamandaris, Val J(ohn) *lawyer, association executive*
Hale, Marcia L. *federal official*
†Hale, Robert Fargo *government official*
Hales, Linda *newspaper editor*
Haley, George Williford Boyce *lawyer*
Haley, Roger Kendall *librarian*
Hall, Douglas K. *federal official*
Hall, Edwin King *lawyer*
Hall, Elliott Sawyer *lawyer*
Hall, Gerri Lynn *legislative staff member*
†Hall, James Evan *federal agency administrator, lawyer*
Hall, Keith R. *federal official*
Hall, Ralph Moody *congressman*
Hall, Tony P. *congressman*
Haller, Ralph A. *federal agency administrator*
Hallett, Carol Boyd *government official*
Hallgren, Richard Edwin *meteorologist*
Hallinan, Joseph Thomas *journalist, correspondent*
Halperin, Samuel *education and training policy analyst*
Halpern, James Bladen *lawyer*
Halpern, James S. *federal judge*
Halsey, Linda *newspaper editor*
Halstead, Dirck S. *photographer, journalist*
Halverson, Richard Christian *minister, chaplain*
Halvorson, Newman Thorbus, Jr. *lawyer*
Hamachek, Ross Frank *media company executive*
Hamarneh, Sami Khalaf *historian of medicine and science, author*
Hamblen, Lapsley Walker, Jr. *federal judge*
Hamilton, Lee Herbert *congressman*
Hamilton, Milton Holmes, Sr. *government executive, politic-military analyst*
Hammer, Carl *computer scientist, former computer company executive*
†Hammer, Charles F. *chemistry educator*
Hammond, Deanna Lindberg *linguist*
Hammond, Jerome Jerald *government program administrator, agricultural economist*
Hammond, Robert Alexander, III *lawyer*
†Hammonds, Timothy Merrill *scientific association executive, economist*
†Hampton, Delon *engineering consulting company executive*
†Hamre, John J. *legislative official*
Hancock, Mel *congressman*
†Hancock, Richard B. *performing company executive*
Hancock, William John *career officer*
Hand, John Oliver *museum curator*
Handelsman, M. Gene *association administrator*
Hanft, Ruth S. Samuels (Mrs. Herbert Hanft) *health care consultant, educator, economist*
Hanke, Byron Reidt *residential land planning and community associations consultant*
Hanley, Edward Thomas *union official*
Hanley, Frank *labor union official*
Hannaford, Peter Dor *public relations executive*
Hannigan, Vera Simmons *federal agency administrator*
Hansen, Frederic J. *state environmental agency director*
Hansen, Orval *lawyer, former congressman*
Hanson, Jean Elizabeth *lawyer*
Harbrant, Robert Francis *labor union executive*
Harden, Blaine Charles *journalist*
Hardesty, Charles Howard, Jr. *lawyer*
Hardiman, Joseph Raymond *securities industry executive*
Harding, Bertrand M., Jr. *lawyer*
Hardy, Robert Gerald *lawyer*
†Harkin, Ruth R. *federal agency administrator, lawyer*
Harkin, Thomas Richard *senator*
Harkins, Kenneth R. *federal judge*
Harkrader, Carleton Allen *lawyer*
Harlem, Susan Lynn *librarian*
Harman, Jane Frank *congresswoman, lawyer*
Harman, William Boys, Jr. *lawyer*
Harper, Conrad Kenneth *lawyer and government official*
Harper, Robert Allan *consulting psychologist*
Harpham, Virginia Ruth *violinist*
Harriman, Philip Darling *geneticist, science foundation executive*
Harrington, Anthony Stephen *lawyer*
Harris, David Ford *federal agency administrator*
Harris, Don Victor, Jr. *lawyer*
Harris, Jeffrey *lawyer*
Harris, Judith Linda *lawyer*
†Harris, Scott Blake *lawyer*
Harris, Stanley S. *federal judge*
Harris, Steven B. *lawyer*
Harris, Wesley L. *federal agency administrator*
Harrison, Donald *lawyer*
Harrison, Earl David *lawyer, real estate executive*
Harrison, Earl Grant, Jr. *educational administrator*
Harrison, Ellen Kroll *lawyer*
Harrison, Emmett Bruce, Jr. *public relations counselor*
Harrison, Jerry Calvin *army officer*
Harrison, Marion Edwyn *lawyer*
Harrison, Monika Edwards *business development executive*
Harrison, Patricia de Stacy *public relations consulting company executive*
Harrison, Rosalie Thornton (Mrs. Porter Harmon Harrison) *retired educator*
Harrop, William Caldwell *retired ambassador, foreign service officer*
†Hart, Christopher Alvin *lawyer*
Hart, John P. *federal official*
Hartman, Arthur A. *international business consultant*
Hartman, (Howard) Carl *newspaperman*
Hartman, George Eitel *architect*
†Hartmann, Heidi Irmgard Victoria *economist, political organization executive*
Hartwell, Stephen *investment company executive*
Harty, Sheila Therese *theologian, writer, editor*
Harvey, David Michael *lawyer*
Harvey, John Collins *physician, educator*
Harwit, Martin Otto *astrophysicist, educator, museum director*
Harwood, Richard Lee *journalist, newspaper editor*
Haseltine, John B. *think-tank executive*
Haskins, Caryl Parker *scientist, author*
Hass, Lawrence Joel *lawyer*

Hassett, Joseph Mark lawyer
Hastert, (J.) Dennis congressman
Hastings, Alcee Lamar congressman, former federal judge
†Hastings, Richard (Doc) congressmant
Hatfield, Mark O. senator
Hathaway, Fred William lawyer
Hathaway, William Dodd federal agency administrator
Haught, John Francis theology educator
†Haughton, Claiborne Douglass, Jr. government official
Hauser, Richard Alan lawyer
Havens, Charles W., III lawyer
Havlicek, Franklin J. communications executive
Hawk, Kathleen M. federal official
Hawke, John Daniel, Jr. lawyer
Hawkins, Edward Jackson lawyer
Hawkins, Wilbur federal official
†Hawksworth, K. J. engineering company executive
Hawley, Frederick William, III bank executive, former federal official
Hay, George Austin actor, producer, director, musician, artist
Hayes, David J. lawyer
Hayes, James Alison congressman
†Hayes, Nancy Keir government agency administrator
Hayes, Paula Freda governmental official
Hayes, Samuel Perkins social scientist, educator
Hayes, Webb Cook, III lawyer
Haynes, R. Michael lawyer
Haynes, William J(ames), II lawyer
Hays, Michael DeWayne lawyer
Haythe, Winston McDonald law educator, consultant, real estate investor
†Hayworth, John David, Jr. congressman, sportscaster, commentator, broadcaster
Hazelrigg, George Arthur, Jr. engineer
Hazen, Robert Miller research scientist, musician
Head, Anita Kessler law educator
Headden, Susan M. editor
Healey, John G. human services organization executive
Heanue, Anne Allen librarian
Heaphy, Eileen Michele diplomat
Hecht, Anthony Evan poet
Hecht, Marjorie Mazel editor
Heckman, Jerome Harold lawyer
Hedges, Harry George computer scientist, educator
Hedges, Kamla King library director
Hedrick, Floyd Dudley government official, author
Heelan, Patrick Aidan philosophy educator
Heffernan, James Vincent lawyer
Heffron, Howard A. lawyer
†Heflebower, Charles R. career officer
Hefley, Joel M. congressman
Heflin, Howell Thomas senator, lawyer, former state supreme court chief justice
Hefner, W. G. (Bill) congressman
Hefter, Laurence Roy lawyer
†Hehir, Thomas F. educational administrator
Heifetz, Alan William federal judge
Hein, Karen Kramer pediatrician, epidemiologist
Heindel, Ned Duane chemistry educator
†Heineman, Frederick K. (Fred Heineman) congressman
Heintz, John Edward lawyer
Heiss, Harry Glen archivist
†Helfer, Ricki Tigert federal agency administrator
Heller, Jack Isaac lawyer
Heller, John Roderick, III lawyer, business executive
Hellmuth, George William architect
Hellwig, Monika Konrad theology educator
Helms, Jesse senator
Helms, Richard McGarrah international consultant, former ambassador
Helms, Robert Brake economist, research director
Hemley, M. Rogue lawyer
Henderson, Donald Ainslie government science administrator
Henderson, Douglas Boyd lawyer
Henderson, Karen LeCraft federal judge
Henderson, Thomas Henry, Jr. lawyer, legal association executive
Henke, Michael John lawyer, educator
Henkin, Robert Irwin neurobiologist, internal medicine, nutrition and neurology educator, scientific products company executive, taste and smell disease physician
Hennemeyer, Robert Thomas diplomat
Hennessy, Ellen Anne lawyer, educator
Henry, Harold lawyer
Henry, Walter Lester, Jr. physician, educator
†Herberger, Albert J. federal agency administrator, retired naval officer
Herbers, Tod Arthur publisher
Herbert, James Charles education executive
Herbst, Robert LeRoy organization executive
Herbster, William Gibson university administrator, consultant
Herger, Wally W. congressman
Herlach, Mark Dayton lawyer
Herman, Alexis M. federal official
Herman, Andrea Maxine newspaper editor
Herman, George Edward radio and television correspondent
Herman, Mary Margaret pathologist
Hersh, Seymour M. journalist
Hershey, Robert Lewis mechanical engineer, management consultant
Hervey, Homer Vaughan federal agency administrator
Herzog, Richard Barnard lawyer
Herzstein, Robert Erwin lawyer
Hess, Stephen political scientist, author
Hess, Wilmot Norton science administrator
Heumann, Judith federal agency administrator
Hewitt, Frankie Lea theater producer
Hewitt, Paul Buck lawyer
Hey, Robert Pierpont editor association bulletin
Heyman, Ira Michael museum executive, law educator, former government official
Hibbert, Robert George lawyer, food company executive
Hickey, Edward Joseph, Jr. lawyer, diplomatic consultant
Hickey, James Aloysius Cardinal archbishop
Hickman, R(obert) Harrison political pollster, strategist
Hicks, Jocelyn Muriel laboratory medicine specialist
†Hicks, Robert Ruiz, Jr. army officer
Higginbotham, Edith Arleane radiologist, researcher
Higgins, James Henry, III marketing executive
Higgins, John Edward, Jr. lawyer
Higgins, William Robert college administrator
High, George Borman executive director, research organization
Hill, Bennett David history educator, Benedictine monk, priest
Hill, Elaine Brumfield elementary education educator
Hill, Jerry C. lawyer
Hill, Jimmie Dale government official
Hill, Stephen S. lawyer
†Hilleary, W. Van congressman
Hillgren, Sonja Dorothy journalist
Hilliard, Earl Frederick congressman, former state senator
†Hillman, Gracia association administrator
Hills, Carla Anderson lawyer, former federal official
Hills, John Merrill public policy research center executive, former educational administrator
Hills, Roderick M. lawyer, business executive, former government official
†Hilton, Steven Michael federal agency administrator
†Hilts, Philip James correspondent
Hinchey, Maurice D., Jr. congressman
Hinden, Stanley Jay newspaper editor
Hinds, Richard De Courcy lawyer
Hinson, David Russell airline company executive, federal agency administrator
Hinson, Hal film critic
Hirsch, Robert Bruce lawyer
Hirsch, Robert Louis energy and management consultant
Hirschhorn, Eric Leonard lawyer
Hitz, Frederick Porter federal agency administrator, lawyer
Hoagland, Jimmie Lee newspaper editor
Hoagland, Peter Jackson former congressman, lawyer
Hoar, Joseph P. military officer
Hobart, Lawrence Scott service organization administrator
Hobbs, Caswell O., III lawyer
†Hobbs, David L. foreign service officer
Hobbs, J. Timothy, Sr. lawyer
Hobbs, Vivian Lee lawyer
Hobelman, Carl Donald lawyer
Hobson, David Lee congressman, lawyer
Hobson, James Richmond lawyer
Hochberg, Jerome A. lawyer
Hodges, Robert H., Jr. federal judge
†Hodgson, Frederick Kimmel radio station executive
Hodgson, Morgan Day lawyer
Hodson, Kenneth Joe lawyer, criminal justice consultant, retired army officer
Hoehn, William Edwin federal goverment official
Hoekstra, Peter congressman, manufacturing executive
Hoewing, Raymond L. association executive
Hoffman, E. Leslie lawyer
Hoffman, Joel Elihu lawyer
Hoffman, Kenneth Myron mathematician, educator
Hoffmann, Robert Shaw museum administrator, educator
Hogan, John P. federal agency official
†Ho-Gonzalez, William lawyer
Hohlt, Deborah M. insurance company executive
Hoke, Martin Rossiter congressman
Holbrook, Douglas Cowen labor union administrator
Holdaway, Ronald M. federal judge
Holden, Glen A. ambassador
†Holden, Gwen A. professional society administrator
Holden, James Phillip lawyer
Holden, John Bernard former college president, educator
Holden, Raymond Thomas physician, educator
Holden, Tim congressman, protective official
Holder, Eric H. prosecutor
Holland, Christie Anna biochemist, virologist
Holland, James Ricks public relations executive, association executive
Holland, Robert Carl economist
Hollander, Richard Edward real estate executive
Holliman, John news broadcaster
Hollings, Ernest Frederick senator
Hollinshead, Ariel Cahill research oncologist
†Hollis, Walter W. government official
Hollister, Floyd Hill electrical engineer, engineering executive
Holloway, James Lemuel, III foundation executive, retired naval officer
Holloway, John Thomas physicist
Holmer, Alan Freeman lawyer
Holmes, Bradley Paul information technology management consultant
Holmes, Genta Hawkins diplomat
Holmes, Henry Allen government official
Holmstead, Jeffrey R. lawyer
Holt, Pamela Gail arts commission administrator
Holum, John D. government official
†Hoog, Thomas W. public relations executive
†Hooke, William Hines meteorologist
Hope, Judith Richards lawyer
Hope, William Duane zoologist, curator
†Hopewell, Luz Araoz trade association executive
Hopkinson, Shirley A. educator, consultant
Horahan, Edward Bernard, III lawyer
Horan, Harold Eugene university administrator, former diplomat
Hordell, Michael A. lawyer
Horlick, Gary Norman lawyer, legal educator
Horn, Charles M. lawyer
Horn, Donald Herbert lawyer
Horn, Marian Blank federal judge
Horn, (John) Stephen congressman, political science educator
Horne, Michael Stewart lawyer
†Horner, Constance J. federal agency administrator
Horowitz, Herbert Eugene educator, consultant, former ambassador
Horsky, Charles Antone lawyer
Horton, John Ernest motion picture industry consultant
Horyn, Cathy newspaper editor
Hosenball, S. Neil lawyer
†Hostettler, John N. congressman
Hotchkin, John Francis church official, priest
Houdek, Robert G. diplomat
Hough, Lawrence A. financial organization executive
Houghton, Amory, Jr. congressman
Houlihan, David Paul lawyer
House, W(illiam) Michael lawyer
Hove, Andrew Christian federal agency administrator
Hovey, Justus Allan, Jr. political scientist
Hoving, John Hannes Forester consulting firm executive
Howard, Glen Scott lawyer
Howard, Jack union executive
Howard, Jeffrey Hjalmar lawyer
Howard, Kenneth Calvin, Jr. lawyer
Howard, Kenneth Lee university official, consultant
Howard, Robert Elliott federal official
Howe, Fisher management consultant, former government official
Howerton, Helen Veronica federal agency administrator
Howes, Theodore Clark claims examiner
Howrey, Edward F. lawyer
Hoyer, Steny Hamilton congressman
Hoyt, David Richard federal agency official
Hoyt, John Arthur humane society executive
Hsu, Ming Chen federal agency administrator
Huband, Frank Louis educational association executive
Huberman, Benjamin defense consultant
†Huddleston, Vicki Jean diplomat
Hudec, Mary Suzanne nursing and patient services administrator
Hudgins, Michael Pharr internist
Hudson, Michael Craig political science educator
Hudson, Philip academic director
†Huerta, Michael Peter government official
Hufbauer, Gary Clyde economist, lawyer, educator
Hug, James Edward religious organization administrator
Hughes, Ann Hightower economist, government official
Hughes, Arthur H. ambassador to Yemen
Hughes, James Charles lawyer
Hughes, Marija Matich law librarian
Hughes, Thomas Lowe foundation executive
Hughes, William John congressman
Hulings, Joseph Simpson diplomat
Hume, Brit (Alexander Britton Hume) journalist
Hume, Paul Chandler music editor, music educator
Humphreys, Robert Russell lawyer
Hundt, Reed Eric federal official, lawyer
Hunkele, Lester Martin, III federal agency administrator
Hunnicutt, Charles Alvin lawyer
Hunt, Albert R. newspaper executive
Hunter, Ronald V. administrator
Huntress, Wesley Theodore, Jr. government official
Husemann, Robert William mechanical engineer
†Hussain, Syed Taseer anatomy educator, researcher
Huston, John Wilson air force officer, historian
Hutchinson, Tim congressman
Hutt, Peter Barton lawyer
Hyde, Henry John congressman
Hyland, William George international relations educator
Hylden, Thomas lawyer
Hyman, Lester Samuel lawyer
Hyun, Hong Choo ambassador
Iglesias, Enrique V. bank executive, former government minister
Ignatius, David newspaper editor
Iklé, Fred Charles former federal agency administrator, policy advisor, defense expert
Illig, James Michael humanitarian organization executive
Imam, M. Ashraf materials scientist, educator
Imig, David Gregg educational association executive
Ingersoll, John Joseph retired foreign service officer
Inglis, Robert D (Bob Inglis) congressman, lawyer
Ingoldsby, Thomas M. lawyer
Ingram, Richard Thomas association executive
†Ingrassia, Anthony Frank human resource specialist
Inhofe, James M. U.S. Senator
Innerst, Preston Eugene newspaper editor, journalist
Inouye, Daniel Ken senator
Ireland, Patricia association executive
Irey, Nelson Sumner pathologist
Irizarry, Estelle Diane foreign language educator, author, editor
Irvine, Reed John media critic, corporation executive
Irving, Clarence L., Jr. (Larry Irving) federal official
Irving, John Stiles, Jr. lawyer
Isaac, William Michael investment firm executive, former government official
Isaacs, Amy Fay political organization executive
Isbell, David Bradford lawyer, legal educator
Isenbergh, Max lawyer, musician, educator
Isom, Harriet Winsar ambassador
Israel, Barry John lawyer
Istook, Ernest James, Jr. (Jim Istook) congressman, lawyer
Itteilag, Anthony Louis government official
Ivers, Donald Louis federal judge
Iwry, J. Mark lawyer
Jackson, Karl Dion government official business executive, scholar
Jackson, Neal A. lawyer
†Jackson, Shirley Ann physicist
Jackson, Thomas Penfield federal judge
†Jackson-Lee, Sheila congresswoman
Jacobs, Andrew, Jr. congressman
Jacobs, Julian I. federal judge
Jacobsen, Hugh Newell architect
Jacobsen, Magdalena Gretchen mediator, federal agency executive
Jacobsen, William Ludwig, Jr. ambassador
Jacobson, David Edward lawyer
Jacobson, Michael Faraday consumer advocate, writer
Jagoda, Barry Lionel media adviser, communications consultant
James, Frederick Calhoun bishop
James, Julie Ann congressional staff member
Jamme, Albert Joseph archaeologist, educator
Janetatos, Jack Peter lawyer
Janis, Michael B. federal official
Jankowski, Gene F. broadcasting executive
Jankowsky, Joel lawyer
†Jansen, Bonnie federal agency administrator
Jansen, E. Harold bishop
†Jaramillo, Mari-Luci federal agency administrator
Jasinowski, Jerry Joseph economist, corporate executive
Jaskiewicz, Leonard Albert retired lawyer
Jaspersen, Frederick Zarr economist
Javits, Joshua Moses lawyer
Jaycox, Edward Van Kleeck bank executive
†Jeff, Gloria Jean federal government administrator
Jefferson, William L. (Jeff Jefferson) congressman
Jeffords, James Merrill senator
Jenkins, John Smith academic dean, lawyer
Jensen, Joseph (Norman) priest, educator
Jeremiah, David Elmer naval officer
Jesseramsing, Chitmansing ambassador
Jessup, Philip Caryl, Jr. lawyer, museum executive
Jeter, Howard F. ambassador
Jett, Dennis Coleman ambassador
Jetton, C. Loring, Jr. lawyer
Jewett, David Stuart federal agency administrator
†Jin, Leslie R. lawyer
Joe, Thomas think-tank
Joelson, Mark Rene lawyer
Johnson, Arlene Lytle government agency official
†Johnson, Broderick D. lawyer
Johnson, David Raymond lawyer
Johnson, Eddie Bernice congresswoman
Johnson, Haynes Bonner author, journalist
Johnson, James A. financial organization executive
Johnson, John A. communications company executive
†Johnson, John C. petroleum company executive
Johnson, John Griffith, Jr. lawyer
Johnson, Nancy Lee congresswoman
Johnson, Norma Holloway federal judge
Johnson, Oliver Thomas, Jr. lawyer
Johnson, Omotunde Evan George economist
Johnson, Philip McBride lawyer
Johnson, Ralph Raymond ambassador, federal agency administrator
Johnson, Richard Clark lawyer
Johnson, Richard Tenney lawyer
Johnson, Robert Henry political science educator
Johnson, Robert Louis cable television company executive
Johnson, Roger W. federal official, computer manufacturing company executive
Johnson, Samuel (Sam Johnson) congressman
Johnson, Stephen L. federal agency administrator
Johnson, Tim professional football player
Johnson, Timothy Peter congressman
Johnson, U. Alexis diplomat
Johnston, John Bennett, Jr. senator
†Johnston, Kenneth John astronomer
Johnston, Laurance Scott foundation director
Jones, Aidan Drexel lawyer
Jones, Alice Samuels elementary education educator, reading specialist
Jones, Boisfeuillet, Jr. lawyer, newspaper executive
Jones, Catherine Ann library administrator
Jones, Erika Ziebarth lawyer
Jones, Gerald Winfield lawyer
Jones, Howard St. Claire, Jr. electronics engineering executive
Jones, Leonade Diane newspaper publishing company executive
Jones, Lois Mailou (Mrs. Vergniaud Pierre-Noel) artist, educator
Jones, Philip Howard broadcast journalist
Jones, Richard Herbert lawyer, former government official
Jones, Stanley Boyd health policy analyst, priest
Jones, Theodore Lawrence lawyer
†Jones, Thomas Curtis army officer
†Jones, Walter B., Jr. congressman
Jones, William Bowdoin political scientist, retired diplomat, lawyer
Jones-Wilson, Faustine Clarisse education educator emeritus
Jordan, Emma Coleman law educator
Jordan, Irving King academic administrator
Jordan, John Patrick government agency executive, research scientist, educator
Jordan, Robert Elijah, III lawyer
Jordan, Vernon Eulion, Jr. lawyer, former association official
Joseph, Daniel Mordecai lawyer
Josephson, Diana Hayward aerospace executive
Jost, Peter Hafner lawyer
†Joulwan, George A. career military officer
Journey, Drexel Dahlke lawyer
Joyce, John T. labor union official
Juliana, James Nicholas ordnance company executive
Kabel, Robert James lawyer
Kafka, Gerald Andrew lawyer
Kahan, Jonathan Seth lawyer
Kahler, Elizabeth Sartor (Mrs. Ervin Newton Chapman) physician
†Kahler, Kathryn Schiller communications executive
Kahn, Edwin Leonard lawyer
Kahn, Michael stage director
Kahn, Walter Kurt engineering and applied science educator
Kaiser, Robert Greeley newspaper editor
Kakish, Bassam Eid ambassador
Kalbfeld, Brad Marshall television and radio executive, editor
Kalleres, Michael Peter career officer
Kalnay, Eugenia government official, meteorologist
Kamber, Victor Samuel political consultant
Kamm, Linda Heller lawyer
Kammerer, Kelly Christian lawyer
Kampelman, Max M. former ambassador, lawyer
Kane, Annette P. religious organization executive
Kane, Michael Barry education research executive
Kanjorski, Paul Edmund congressman, lawyer
Kant, Gloria Jean neuroscientist, researcher
Kanter, Arnold Lee policy analyst
Kantor, Michael (Mickey Kantor) federal trade representative
Kaplan, Gilbert B. lawyer
†Kaplan, Stephen H. federal agency administrator, lawyer
Kaplin, William Albert lawyer, educator, consultant
Kapp, Robert Harris lawyer
†Kappaz, Michael H. engineering company executive
Kappner, Augusta Souza government official
Kaptur, Marcia Carolyn congresswoman
Karalekas, Anne publishing executive
Karayn, James, Jr. broadcasting executive
Karelis, Charles Howard government official
Karklins, Vija L. librarian
Karle, Isabella L. chemist
Karle, Jerome physicist, researcher
Karmin, Monroe William senior editor
†Karp, Naomi Katherine United States government administrator
Kaseman, A. Carl, III lawyer
Kasich, John R. congressman
Kass, Benny Lee lawyer
Kassebaum, Donald Gene medical association administrator, physician, medical educator
Kassebaum, Nancy Landon senator
Kasten, Robert W., Jr. former senator
Kaswell, Maryann McCarthy lawyer
Katz, Jonathan Garber federal agency executive, lawyer
Katz, Sherman E. lawyer
Katz, Sol physician
Katzen, Sally lawyer
Kaufman, John Gilbert, Jr. materials engineer
Kaufman, Paul physician, former naval officer, association executive
Kaufman, Thomas Frederick lawyer, legal educator
Kaulkin, Donna Brookman editor, writer
Kautter, David John lawyer
Kauzlarich, Richard Dale U.S. ambassador, foreign service officer
Kavanaugh, Everett Edward, Jr. trade association executive
†Kawata, Paul Akio health association administrator
Kay, Kenneth Robert lawyer
Keane, William K. lawyer

Kearney, Stephen Michael *government official*
Keating, Robert B. *ambassador*
Keel, Alton Gold, Jr. *ambassador*
Keeley, Robert Vossler *academic administrator, retired ambassador*
Keener, Mary Lou *lawyer*
Keeney, E. Andrew *lawyer*
Keeney, John Christopher *lawyer*
Keeney, John Christopher, Jr. *lawyer*
†Keeney, Regina Markey *lawyer*
Keeny, Spurgeon Milton, Jr. *association executive*
Keevey, Richard Francis *government official, educator*
Kehoe, Patrick Emmett *law librarian, educator*
Keiner, R(obert) Bruce, Jr. *lawyer*
Keith, Kenton W. *ambassador to Qatar*
Kelley, Edward Watson, Jr. *federal agency administrator*
Kelley, Wayne Plumbley, Jr. *federal official*
Kellison, James Bruce *lawyer*
Kellogg, Frederic Rogers *lawyer*
Kelly, Charles J., Jr. *investment company executive*
Kelly, Eugene Walter, Jr. *counseling educator*
Kelly, Francis Joseph *strategic communications company executive*
Kelly, John Hubert *diplomat, business executive*
Kelly, Nancy Frieda Wolicki *lawyer*
†Kelly, Sue W. *congresswoman*
Kelly, William Charles, Jr. *lawyer*
Kelman, Steven Jay *government official*
Kemp, Geoffrey Thomas Howard *international affairs specialist*
Kemp, Jack French *association director, former U.S. secretary of housing and urban development, former congressman*
†Kemp, John D. *association administrator*
Kempley, Rita A. *film critic, editor*
Kempner, Jonathan L. *professional society administrator*
Kempster, Norman Roy *journalist*
Kempthorne, Dirk Arthur *senator*
Kendall, Peter Landis *television news executive*
Kendrick, John Whitefield *economist, educator, consultant*
†Kennedy, Allyson Ann *television producer*
Kennedy, Anthony McLeod *U.S. supreme court justice*
Kennedy, Edward Moore *senator*
Kennedy, Eugene Richard *microbiologist, university dean*
†Kennedy, James Keith *senate staff member*
Kennedy, Joseph Patrick, II *congressman*
Kennedy, Patrick F. *federal official*
†Kennedy, Patrick J. *congressman*
Kennedy, Richard Thomas *government official*
Kennedy, Robert Emmet, Jr. *history educator*
Kennedy, Roger George *park services executive*
Kennelly, Barbara B. *congresswoman*
Kenney, Robert James, Jr. *lawyer*
Kent, Alan Heywood *lawyer*
Kent, Jill Elspeth *academic administrator, lawyer, former government official*
Kent, Kenneth Mitchell *medical educator*
Kent, M. Elizabeth *lawyer*
Kenyon, Carleton Weller *librarian*
Kerber, Frank John *diplomat*
Kern, Harry Frederick *editor*
†Kern, Paul John *army officer*
Kerns, Wilmer Lee *social science researcher*
Kerrey, Bob (J. Robert Kerrey) *senator*
Kerry, John Forbes *senator*
Kerxton, Alan Smith *lawyer*
Kessler, Judd Lewis *lawyer*
Kesterman, Frank Raymond *investment banker*
Ketchum, James Roe *curator*
Keune, Russell Victor *architect, architectural association executive*
Keyes, Arthur Hawkins, Jr. *architect*
Keys, John R., Jr. *lawyer*
Keyworth, George Albert, II *physicist, consulting company executive*
Khadduri, Majid *international studies educator*
Kidd, Charles Vincent *former civil servant, educator*
Kier, Porter Martin *paleontologist*
Kies, Kenneth J. *lawyer*
Kieve, Loren *lawyer*
Kiko, Philip George *lawyer*
Kilborn, Peter Thurston *journalist*
Kilbourne, John Dwight *museum and library director*
Kildee, Dale Edward *congressman*
Kilgore, Edwin Carroll *retired government official, consultant*
Kilian, Michael David *journalist, columnist, writer*
Killgore, Andrew Ivy *former ambassador*
†Killion, Ruth Ann *statistical researcher*
Killory, Diane Silberstein *lawyer*
†Kilmartin, Thomas John, III *army officer*
Kim, Jay *congressman*
Kimball, Raymond Joel *lawyer*
†Kimbrough, Kenneth R. *commisioner public buildings service*
Kimmitt, Robert Michael *lawyer, banker, diplomat*
Kinard, Helen Marie Pawnee Madison *corporate executive*
Kind, Phyllis Dawn *immunologist*
King, Larry (Larry Zeiger) *broadcaster, radio personality*
†King, Marilou Meehan *lawyer, association executive*
King, Michelle Davis *lawyer*
King, Nina Davis *journalist*
King, Peter T. *congressman, lawyer*
King, Rufus *lawyer*
King, Thomas M. *theology educator, priest*
Kinghorn, Charles Morgan, Jr. *federal agency administrator*
Kingston, Jack *congressman*
Kinlow, Eugene *federal agency executive*
Kinsley, Michael E. *magazine editor*
Kiper, Ali Muhlis *mechanical engineering educator, consultant*
Kiplinger, Knight A. *journalist, publisher*
Kirby, Harmon E. *ambassador*
Kirby, Thomas Wesley *lawyer*
Kirk, Donald *journalist*
Kirkbride, Chalmer Gatlin *chemical engineer*
Kirkien-Rzeszotarski, Alicia Maria *academic administrator, researcher, educator*
Kirkland, Joseph Lane (Lane Kirkland) *labor union official*
†Kirkland, Lane *labor union administrator*
Kirkpatrick, Jeane Duane Jordan *political scientist, government official*
Kirtland, John C. *lawyer*
Kitchen, John Howard *economist*
Kittrell, Steven Dan *lawyer*
Kittrie, Nicholas N(orbert Nehemiah) *law educator, international consultant, author*
Kitzmiller, William Michael *government official*
Klain, Ronald Alan *lawyer*
Klass, Philip Julian *technical journalist, electrical engineer*
Klawiter, Donald Casimir *lawyer*
Klay, Andor C. *author, diplomat*
Kleczka, Gerald D. *congressman*
†Klein, Joel Irwin *lawyer*
†Klein, Leonard Robert *government official*
Klein, Michael Roger *lawyer, business executive*
Kleinknecht, Christian Frederick *Masonic official*
Klepner, Jerry D. *federal agency administrator*
Klepper, Martin *lawyer*
Kline, Jerry Robert *government official, ecologist*
Kline, Norman Douglas *federal judge*
Kling, William *economist, retired foreign service officer*
Klink, Ron *congressman, reporter, newscaster*
Klugh, James Richard *military officer*
Knapp, George M. *lawyer*
Knapp, Richard Maitland *association executive*
Knapp, Rosalind Ann *lawyer*
Knebel, John Albert *lawyer, former government official*
Knight, Athelia Wilhelmenia *journalist*
Knisely, Robert August *government official, lawyer*
Knoll, Jerry *former government official*
Knollenberg, Joseph (Joe Knollenberg) *congressman*
†Knopman, Debra S. *hydrologist, federal agency administrator*
Knotts, Joseph B. *lawyer*
Kobrine, Arthur *neurosurgeon*
Koch, George William *lawyer*
Koch, Kathleen Day *lawyer*
†Koenig, Harold Martin *U.S. Navy deputy surgeon general*
Koering, Marilyn Jean *anatomy educator, researcher*
Kohl, Herbert *senator, professional sports team owner*
Kohlhorst, Gail Lewis *librarian*
Kolasky, William Joseph, Jr. *lawyer*
Kolb, Charles Chester *humanities administrator*
Kolbe, James Thomas *congressman*
Kole, John William *writer*
Kolman, Mark Herbert *lawyer*
Komer, Robert William *government official, consultant*
Kondratas, Skirma Anna *policy analyst*
†Konetzni, Albert H., Jr. *naval officer*
Konschnik, David Michael *lawyer*
Koppel, Ted *broadcast journalist*
Kornblum, John Christian *foreign service officer*
Korner, Jules Gilmer, III *federal judge*
Kornheiser, Anthony I. *journalist*
Korologos, Tom Chris *government affairs consultant, former federal official*
Korth, Fred *lawyer*
Korth, Fritz-Alan *lawyer*
Korth, Penne Percy *ambassador*
Koskinen, John Andrew *federal government executive*
Kossak, Shelley *think-tank executive*
†Kostelnik, Michael Charles *military officer*
Kotler, Milton *marketing company executive*
†Kott, Robert Joseph *diplomat*
Kotz, Nathan Kallison (Nick Kotz) *news correspondent*
Kouts, Herbert John Cecil *physicist*
Kovach, Eugene George *government official, consultant*
Kovacs, William Lawrence *lawyer*
Koven, Joan Follin Hughes *marine biologist*
Kraemer, Jay Roy *lawyer*
†Kramek, Adm. Robert E. *U.S. coast guard officer*
†Kramer, Aaron J. *lawyer*
Kramer, Albert H. *lawyer*
Kramer, Kenneth Bentley *federal judge, former congressman*
Kramer, Kenneth Stephen *lawyer*
Kramer, Robert *dean*
Kramer, William David *lawyer*
Krasner, Wendy L. *lawyer*
Krasnostein, David M. *lawyer*
Krasnow, Erwin Gilbert *lawyer*
Kraus, Margery *management consultant*
Krebs, Martha *physicist, federal agency administrator*
Kreczko, Alan James *lawyer*
Kreidler, Charles W(illiam) *linguist, educator*
Kriesberg, Simeon M. *lawyer*
Kristol, Irving *social sciences educator, editor*
Kristol, William *public policy activist*
Kroener, William Frederick, III *lawyer*
Krogh, Peter Frederic *college dean, international affairs educator*
Krombein, Karl vonVorse *entomologist*
Kronstein, Werner J *lawyer*
Kropp, Arthur John *public interest organization executive*
Kruesi, Frank Eugene *federal agency administrator*
Krugman, Stanley Liebert *science administrator, geneticist*
Krulfeld, Ruth Marilyn *anthropologist, educator*
Krump, Gary Joseph *lawyer*
Kruse, Dennis K. *think-tank executive, career officer*
†Kruvant, William *federal agency administrator*
Kuchel, Roland Karl *ambassador*
Kuhn, Thomas R. *trade association executive*
Kullberg, John Francis *association executive*
†Kundanis, George *congressional aide*
Kunin, Madeleine May *federal agency administrator, former governor*
Kupperman, Helen Slotnick *lawyer*
Kupperman, Robert Harris *university official*
†Kurkjian, Stephen Anoosh *journalist*
Kurrelmeyer, Louis Hayner *lawyer*
†Kursch, Donald Bowman *foreign service officer*
Kurth, Walter Richard *association executive*
Kurtzke, John Francis, Sr. *neurologist, epidemiologist*
Kusnet, David *communications executive, speechwriter*
Kutscher, Ronald Earl *federal government executive*
Kyl, Jon *senator*
Lachance, Janice Rachel *federal agency administrator, lawyer*
Lachey, James Michael *professional football player*
Lackritz, Marc E. *securities trade association executive*
Laden, Ben Ellis *economist*
Laden, Susan *publishing consultant*
†Ladner, Joyce A. *academic administrator*
Laessig, Walter Bruce *publishing executive*
La Falce, John Joseph *congressman, lawyer*
†LaGamma, Robert Ronald *diplomat*
†LaHood, Ray *congressman*
Lahr, Jack Leroy *lawyer*
Laiou, Angeliki Evangelos *history educator*
Laird, Melvin Robert *former secretary of defense*
Lake, Anthony *federal official*
Lake, Joseph Edward *ambassador*
†Lakshmanan, T.R. *federal agency administrator, geography and environmental engineering educator, writer*
Lalley, Frank Edward *federal government official*
Lamb, Vincent P. *industrial executive*
Lambert, Jeremiah Daniel *lawyer*
Lambert, Steven Charles *lawyer*
Lamberth, Royce C. *federal judge*
Lambert Lincoln, Blanche M. *congresswoman*
Lamm, Carolyn Beth *lawyer*
Lampl, Peggy Ann *association administrator*
Lancaster, H(arold) Martin *congressman*
Landfair, Stanley W. *lawyer*
Lane, Bruce Stuart *lawyer*
Lane, John Dennis *lawyer*
Lane, Mark *lawyer, educator, author*
Lang, Ronald Anthony *trade association executive*
Langan, John Patrick *philosophy educator*
Langley, Chiara Maria Bini *society executive, research scientist*
Lanouette, William John *writer, public policy analyst*
Lanpher, E. Gibson *ambassador to Zimbabwe*
Lantos, Thomas Peter *congressman*
LaPidus, Jules Benjamin *association executive*
LaPlante, John Baptiste *naval officer*
Laporte, Gerald Joseph Sylvestre *lawyer*
Laqueur, Walter *history educator*
Lardner, George, Jr. *journalist*
†Largent, Steve *congressman, former professional football player*
LaRouche, Lyndon H., Jr. *economist*
Larroca, Raymond G. *lawyer*
Larry, David Heath *lawyer*
Larsen, Richard Gary *accounting firm executive*
Larson, Charles Fred *association executive*
Lash, Jonathan *environmental law executive*
Lash, Myles Perry *hospital administrator*
Lasko, Warren Anthony *mortgage banker, economist*
Lassman, Malcolm *lawyer*
Lastowka, James Anthony *former federal agency executive, lawyer*
†Latham, Tom *congressman*
Latham, Weldon Hurd *lawyer*
Latimer, Allie B. *lawyer, government official*
†LaTourette, Steven C. *congressman*
Lau, Cheryl A. *former state official*
Laughlin, Felix B. *lawyer*
Laughlin, Gregory H. (Greg Laughlin) *congressman*
Laughton, Katharine L. *career officer*
Lautenberg, Frank R. *senator*
LaVelle, Avis *federal administration official*
Lavine, Henry Wolfe *lawyer*
Law, David Hillis *physician*
Lawrence, Glenn Robert *federal administrative law judge*
†Lawrence, John Alan *legislative staff director*
†Laws, Elliott Pearson *federal agency administrator*
Lawson, D. Dale *public relations executive*
Lawson, Jennifer *broadcast executive*
Lawson, Richard Laverne *trade association executive, retired military officer*
Lawton, Thomas *art gallery director*
Layton, John C. *federal agency administrator*
Lazarus, Arthur, Jr. *lawyer*
Lazarus, Kenneth Anthony *lawyer*
Lazio, Rick A. *congressman, lawyer*
Leach, James Albert Smith *congressman*
Leaf, Howard Westley *retired air force officer, military official*
Leahy, Patrick Joseph *senator*
Leary, Thomas Barrett *lawyer*
Le Baron, Joseph Evan *diplomat*
Lebow, Irwin Leon *electronics engineering consultant*
LeBrecht, Thelma Jane Mossman *reporter*
Ledley, Robert Steven *biophysicist*
Lee, Chester Maurice *government official*
Lee, Philip Randolph *medical educator*
Lee, Ronald Barry *marketing company executive, retired military officer*
Leeds, Charles Alan *publishing executive*
†Leestma, Robert *federal agency administrator, educator*
Leetsar, Jaan *government official*
Lefever, Ernest W. *political philosopher, author, former institute president*
Lehmberg, Robert Henry *research physicist*
Lehner, George Alexander, Jr. *lawyer*
Lehr, Dennis James *lawyer*
Lehrer, James Charles *television journalist*
Lehrman, Margaret McBride *television news executive, producer*
†Leibach, Dale W. *public relations executive*
Leibold, Arthur William, Jr. *lawyer*
Leiden, Warren Robert *law association executive*
Leigh, Monroe *lawyer*
Leiter, Richard Allen *law educator, law librarian*
Le Mone, Archie *religious organization administrator*
Lenahan, Walter Clair *retired foreign service officer*
Lenhart, James Thomas *lawyer*
Lent, Norman Frederick, Jr. *former congressman*
LeoGrande, William Mark *political science educator, writer*
Leon, Donald Francis *university dean, medical educator*
Leon, Richard J. *lawyer, former government official*
Leonard, Michael *federal official*
Leonard, Will Ernest, Jr. *lawyer*
Lepkowski, Wil (Wilbert Charles Lepkowski) *journalist*
†Lese, William G(eorge), Jr. *government official*
Lesher, Richard Lee *association executive*
Leshy, John D. *lawyer, legal educator*
Leslie, John William *public relations and advertising executive*
Lessenco, Gilbert Barry *lawyer*
Lessin, Lawrence Stephen *hematologist, oncologist, educator*
Lessy, Roy Paul, Jr. *lawyer*
Lettow, Charles Frederick *lawyer*
Leubsdorf, Carl Philipp *newspaper executive*
Leva, Marx *lawyer*
Levalier, Dotian *harpist*
Leven, Ann Ruth *arts administrator*
Levey, Robert Frank *newspaper columnist*
Levin, Carl *senator*
Levin, Sander M. *congressman*
Levine, Henry David *lawyer*
Levine, Irving Raskin *news commentator, author, lecturer*
Levine, Joseph Manney *lawyer*
Levine, Theodore A. *lawyer*
Levinson, Daniel Ronald *lawyer*
Levitas, Elliott Harris *lawyer*
Levitt, Arthur, Jr. *securities and publishing executive, federal agency administrator*
Levy, David Corcos *museum director*
Levy, David Matthew *lawyer*
Levy, Mark Irving *lawyer*
Levy, Michael B. *federal official*
Lew, Ginger *lawyer*
Lewin, George Forest *former insurance company executive*
Lewin, Martin J. *lawyer*
Lewis, Ann Frank *social welfare association executive*
Lewis, Anne McCutcheon *architect*
Lewis, Charles Joseph *journalist*
Lewis, David John *lawyer*
†Lewis, Delano Eugene *broadcast executive*
Lewis, Douglas *art historian*
Lewis, E. Grey *lawyer*
Lewis, Emanuel Raymond *historian, librarian, psychologist*
Lewis, Forbes Downer *computer science educator, researcher*
†Lewis, Green Pryor, Jr. *community service administrator*
Lewis, Gregory Scott *lawyer*
Lewis, Jerry *congressman*
Lewis, John R. *congressman*
Lewis, Jordan David *management consultant, author, international speaker, educator*
†Lewis, Ron *congressman*
Lewis, W. Walker *cosmetics executive*
Lewis, William Henry, Jr. *lawyer*
Lewis, William Walker *management consultant*
Libin, Jerome B. *lawyer*
Lichtenstein, Elissa Charlene *legal association executive*
Liebenson, Herbert *economist, trade association executive*
Lieber, Robert J. *political science educator, writer*
†Lieberman, James *federal agency administrator*
Lieberman, Joseph I. *senator*
Lieberman, Myron *educational consulting firm executive*
Liebes, Raquel *import/export company executive, educator*
Liebman, Ronald Stanley *lawyer*
Liebowitz, Harold *aeronautical engineering educator, dean emeritus*
Liederman, David Samuel *child welfare administrator*
Lightfoot, James Ross *congressman*
Lighthizer, Robert E. *lawyer*
Lilienfield, Lawrence Spencer *physiology and biophysics educator*
Lilienthal, Alfred M(orton) *author, historian, editor*
Lillard, John Franklin, III *lawyer*
Lilley, James Roderick *foreign relations expert, former federal government official*
Lilley, William, III *communications business consultant*
Lilly, William Eldridge *government official*
†Limon, Lavinia *social services administrator*
Limpert, John Arthur *editor*
Lin, William Wen-Rong *economist*
Linder, John E *congressman, dentist*
Lindsey, Lawrence Benjamin *economist, federal official*
†Lindsey, Seth Mark *lawyer, federal agency administrator*
Linowes, Harry Michael *accountant*
Linowitz, Sol Myron *lawyer*
Lintz, Paul Rodgers *physicist, engineer, patent examiner*
Lion, Paul Michel, III *transportation engineer, executive*
Lipinski, William Oliver *congressman*
Lippman, Marc Estes *pharmacology educator*
Lipstein, Robert A. *lawyer*
Liska, George *political science educator, author*
Lister, Harry Joseph *financial company executive, consultant*
†Lister, Sara Elisabeth *lawyer*
Litan, Robert Eli *lawyer, economist*
Litke, Arthur Ludwig *business executive*
Litman, Harry Peter *lawyer, educator*
Litt, Nahum *federal judge*
Littig, Lawrence William *psychologist, educator*
Little, Elbert Luther, Jr. *botanist, dendrologist*
†Little, John Hadley *army officer*
Little, John William *plastic surgeon, educator*
Lively, Carol A. *association executive*
Livingston, Donald Ray *lawyer*
Livingston, Robert Gerald *university official, political scientist*
Livingston, Robert Linlithgow, Jr. (Bob Livingston, Jr.) *congressman*
†LoBiondo, Frank A. *congressman*
†Loeffke, Bernard *career officer*
Loeffler, Robert Hugh *lawyer*
Loevinger, Lee *lawyer*
†Lofgren, Zoe *congresswoman, former county government official*
Loftus, Stephen Francis *naval officer*
Logue-Kinder, Joan *government official*
Lohmiller, John M. (Chip Lohmiller) *professional football player*
†Loiello, John Peter *public affairs executive, consultant*
Loker, Elizabeth St. John *newspaper executive*
Lombard, Judith Marie *human resource policy specialist*
Long, Charles Thomas *lawyer*
Longanecker, David A. *federal official*
Longstreet, Victor Mendell *government official*
Loosbrock, Carol Marie *information management professional*
Lopatin, Alan G. *lawyer*
Lorber, Mortimer *physiology educator, researcher*
Lord, Jerome Edmund *federal education administrator, writer*
Lorenz, John George *librarian, consultant*
†Lorne, Simon Michael *lawyer*
Lorsung, Thomas Nicholas *editor-in-chief, director*
Lorton, Lewis *dentist, researcher, computer scientist*
Lott, Trent *senator*
Lourie, Alan David *federal judge*
Love, Margaret Colgate *lawyer*
Love, Michael Kenneth *lawyer*
Lovejoy, Thomas Eugene *tropical and conservation biologist, association executive*
Lovell, Malcolm Read, Jr. *public policy institute executive, educator, former government official, former trade association executive*
Low, Stephen *foundation executive, educator, former diplomat*
†Lowder, Rachael Della *company executive, consultant*
Lowe, Carol Hill *social services directo*r

Lowe, Florence Segal *retired public relations executive*
Lowe, Harry *museum director*
Lowe, Mary Frances *federal government official*
Lowenstein, James Gordon *former diplomat, international consultant*
Lowey, Nita M. *congresswoman*
Lowrie, Gerald M. *communications executive*
Loy, Frank Ernest *foundation executive*
Lozansky, Edward Dmitry *physicist, author, consultant*
Lubar, Jeffrey Stuart *journalist*
†Lucas, C. Payne *development organization executive*
Lucas, Frank D. *congressman*
Lucas, George Ramsdell, Jr. *philosophy educator*
Lucas, James Walter *federal government official*
Lucassen, Sigurd *labor union administrator*
Luce, Gregory M. *lawyer*
Ludwig, Eugene Allan *U.S. comptroller of the currency, lawyer*
Luffsey, Walter Stith *transportation executive*
†Lufrano, Michael Richard *federal government official*
Lugar, Richard Green *senator*
Luikart, Fordyce Whitney *management consultant*
Lund, Wendell Luther *lawyer*
Lurton, Horace VanDeventer *brokerage house executive*
Luskin, Robert David *lawyer*
Luth, William Clair *research manager*
†Luther, William P. *congressman*
Lutley, John H. *precious metals company executive*
Luttwak, Edward Nicolae *policy and business consultant, writer*
Lutz, Theodore Compton *newspaper publishing executive*
Lybecker, Martin Earl *lawyer*
Lydon, Thomas J. *federal judge*
Lyman, Princeton Nathan *ambassador*
Lynam, Terence Joseph *lawyer*
Lynch, Charles Theodore, Sr. *materials science engineering researcher, administrator, educator*
†Lynch, Robert N. *clergy member*
Lynch, Thomas C. *career military officer*
†Lynn, D. Joanne *physician, ethicist, health services researcher*
Lynn, James Thomas *investment banker, insurance company executive, government executive, lawyer*
Lynn, Larry *engineering executive*
†Lynn, William J., III *federal agency administrator*
Lyons, Dennis Gerald *lawyer*
Lyons, Ellis *lawyer*
Lyons, James Robert *federal official*
Maas, Joe (Melvin Joseph Maas) *federal agency administrator*
MacBeth, Angus *lawyer*
Macdonald, David Robert *lawyer*
MacDonald, John Thomas *educational administrator*
MacDonald, William Lloyd *architectural historian*
†MacHare, Peter Allen *law librarian*
Mack, Connie, III (Cornelius Mack) *senator*
Mack, Julia Cooper *judge*
Mack, Raymond Francis *newspaper executive*
Mack, Ronald J. *park superintendent*
Mackall, Laidler Bowie *lawyer*
†Mackie, Bert H. *postal service administrator*
Mackiewicz, Edward Robert *lawyer*
MacKinnon, George E. *federal judge*
MacLaury, Bruce King *research institution executive*
MacLean, Paul Donald *government institute medical research official*
MacLeod, William Cyrus *lawyer, economist*
Macomber, John D. *industrialist*
Macrory, Patrick Francis John *lawyer*
Madden, Joseph Michael *microbiologist*
Madden, Murdaugh Stuart *lawyer*
Madden, William J., Jr. *lawyer*
Maddock, Jerome Torrence *information services specialist*
Maddox, David M. *career military officer*
†Mader, David A. *federal agency executive*
Madigan, Kimberly A. *mediator, lawyer*
Madigan, Michael J. *lawyer*
Maechling, Charles, Jr. *lawyer, educator, writer*
Magaw, John W. *federal law enforcement official*
Magazine, Alan Harrison *association executive, consultant*
Magaziner, Ira *federal official*
Magielnicki, Robert L. *lawyer*
Magrath, C. Peter *educational association executive*
Maher, Patrick Joseph *utility company executive*
Maisel, Herbert *computer science educator*
Maisto, John F. *ambassador*
Maiwurm, James John *lawyer*
Majd, Massoud *radiology and nuclear medicine educator*
Majev, Howard Rudolph *lawyer*
Majors, Richard George *psychology educator*
Makris, Andreas *composer*
Malarkey, Martin Francis, Jr. *cable television executive*
Malashevich, Bruce Peter *economist*
Malcolm, Ellen Reighley *small business owner*
Maldon, Alphonso, Jr. *federal official, retired military officer*
Malek, Frederic Vincent *finance company executive*
Mallory, Charles King, III *lawyer*
Malmgren, Harald Bernard *economist*
Malone, Julia Louise *news reporter, White House correspondent*
Malott, Frank Stephen *foreign service officer*
Malott, John Raymond *foreign service officer*
Manatos, Andrew Emanuel *policy consultant, former government official*
Manatt, Charles T. *lawyer*
Manbeck, Harry Frederick, Jr. *lawyer*
Mandel, H(arold) George *pharmacologist*
Mandula, Jeffrey Ellis *physicist*
Mankin, Hart Tiller *federal judge*
Manley, Audrey Forbes *physician*
Manley, William Tanner *economist*
Manly, Marc Edward *lawyer*
Mann, Donegan *lawyer*
Mann, Marion *physician, educator*
Mann, Oscar *physician, internist, educator*
Mann, Thomas Edward *political scientist*
Manning, George Taylor *lawyer*
Mansfield, Edward Patrick, Jr. *advertising executive*
Mansfield, Michael Joseph *former ambassador, former senator*
Manson, Joseph Lloyd, III *lawyer*
Manthei, Richard Dale *lawyer, health care company executive*
Manton, Thomas Joseph *congressman*
Mantyla, Karen *sales executive*
Manzullo, Donald A *congressman, lawyer*
Maraniss, David *reporter*
Marans, J. Eugene *lawyer*
Marcum, Deanna Bowling *library administrator*
Marcuss, Stanley Joseph *lawyer*
Marfiak, Thomas Fletcher *career officer*
Margeton, Stephen George *law librarian*
Margolis, Daniel Herbert *lawyer*
Margolis, Eugene *lawyer, government official*
Margolis, James David *political consulting and advertising executive*
Margolis, Lawrence Stanley *federal judge*
Marinaccio, Charles Lindbergh *lawyer*
Mark, Alan Samuel *lawyer*
Markey, Edward John *congressman*
Markoski, Joseph Peter *lawyer*
Marks, Andrew H. *lawyer*
Marks, Herbert Edward *lawyer*
Marks, Leonard Harold *lawyer*
Marks, Richard Daniel *lawyer*
†Markus, Kent Richard *lawyer*
Marlowe, Howard David *lobbyist, public affairs company executive*
†Marquardt, Sandra Mary *activist, lobbyist, researcher*
Marquez, Joaquin Alfredo *lawyer*
Marquis, Christopher Holliday *newspaper correspondent*
Marrett, Michael McFarlene *chaplain*
Marriott, Alice Sheets (Mrs. John Willard Marriott) *restaurant chain executive*
Marriott, John Willard, Jr. *hotel and food service chain executive*
Marriott, Richard Edwin *hotel and contract services executive*
Marsh, Caryl Amsterdam *curator, psychologist*
Marsh, Quinton Neely *banker*
†Marshall, Andrew Walter *federal official*
Marshall, C. Travis *manufacturing executive, government relations specialist*
Martin, David Briton Hadden, Jr. *lawyer*
Martin, Guy *lawyer*
Martin, Jerry L. *federal agency administrator*
Martin, John Joseph *journalist*
Martin, Keith *lawyer*
Martin, Susan Katherine *librarian*
Martin, Thomas Stephen *lawyer*
†Martin, William Edwin *government official*
Martinez, Herminia S. *economist, banker*
Martinez, Matthew Gilbert *congressman*
†Martini, William J. *congressman*
Martyak, Joseph J. *lawyer*
Marumoto, William Hideo *management consultant*
Marvin, Douglas Raymond *lawyer*
Marzetti, Loretta A. *government agency executive, policy analyst*
Marzulla, Roger Joseph *lawyer*
†Mascara, Frank *congressman*
Masi, Dale A. *research company executive, social work educator*
Mason, Brian Harold *geologist, curator*
†Massey, William Lloyd *federal agency administrator, lawyer*
Masten, Charles C. *federal agency administrator*
Masters, Edward E. *association executive, former foreign service officer*
Matalin, Mary *political consultant*
†Mathews, Dan *animal rights activist*
Mathews, Jessica Tuchman *policy researcher, columnist*
Mathias, Charles McCurdy *lawyer, former senator*
Mathias, Edward Joseph *merchant banker*
Mathias, John Joseph *federal administrative law judge*
Mathis, William Walter *career officer*
Matsui, Robert Takeo *congressman*
Mattar, Philip *institute director, editor*
†Matthews, Dale Samuel *information scientist, media futurist*
†Mattingly, J. Virgil, Jr. *federal lawyer*
Maudlin, Robert V. *economics and government affairs consultant*
Maxa, Rudolph Joseph, Jr. *journalist*
Maxwell, David E. *academic administrator, educator*
Maxwell, David Ogden *government official, financial executive*
May, Edgar *former state legislator, nonprofit administrator*
May, Gregory Evers *lawyer*
May, Richard Edward *lawyer*
May, Stephen *writer, former government official*
May, Sterling Randolph *health association executive*
May, Timothy James *lawyer*
Mayer, Haldane Robert *federal judge*
Mayer, Walter Georg *physics educator*
Mayers, Daniel Kriegsman *lawyer*
Mayfield, Richard Heverin *lawyer*
Maynard, Nancy Gray *biological oceanographer*
Maynes, Charles William *editor, former government official*
Mayo, George Washington, Jr. *lawyer*
Mays, Janice Ann *lawyer*
Mazo, Mark Elliott *lawyer*
Mbila, Simon *government official, accountant*
Mbumba, Nangolo *government executive*
Mc Afee, William *government official*
McAllister, Patricia Anne *retail company executive*
McAllister, William Howard, III *newspaper reporter, columnist*
McArdle, Paul Francis *judge*
McAvoy, John Joseph *lawyer*
McBride, Jonathan Evans *executive search company executive*
McBride, Michael Flynn *lawyer*
McCabe, Edward Aeneas *lawyer, financial services corporation executive*
†McCaffrey, Barry Richard *army officer*
McCaffrey, Shellyn Gae *federal official*
McCahill, Barry Winslow *federal public affairs official*
McCain, John Sidney, III *senator*
McCallie, Marshall F. *ambassador*
McCammon, Helen Mary *government administrator*
McCargar, James Goodrich *diplomat, writer*
McCarten, William Weisel *financial executive*
McCarthy, Abigail Quigley *writer, columnist, educator*
Mc Carthy, Charles Joseph *lawyer, former government official*
McCarthy, Charles Richard *lawyer*
McCarthy, David Jerome, Jr. *legal educator*
McCarthy, John B. *veterinarian, veterinary association executive*
McCarthy, John Thomas *diplomat*
McCarthy, Karen P. *congresswoman, former state representative*
McCarthy, Wilbert Alan *mechanical engineer*
Mc Carty, Robert Lee *lawyer*
McClain, Charles William, Jr. (Bill McClain) *army officer*
McClain, William Thomas *lawyer*
McClintic, Howard Gresson *foundation executive*
McCloskey, J(ohn) Michael *association executive*
†McCloskey, Peter Francis *trade association executive*
McCobb, John Bradford, Jr. *lawyer*
McCollam, William, Jr. *utility company executive*
McCollum, Gary Wayne *federal agency administrator*
Mc Collum, Ira William, Jr. (Bill Mc Collum) *congressman*
McConnell, Addison Mitchell, Jr. (Mitch McConnell, Jr.) *senator, lawyer*
McConnell, Donald J. *ambassador*
McConnell, James Michael *federal official*
McCormack, Richard Thomas Fox *government official*
McCormick, Robert Junior *government official*
McCoy, Jerry Jack *lawyer*
†McCoy, John J. *engineering educator*
McCoy, Neal S. *lawyer*
McCoy, Patricia Ann *law educator, lawyer*
McCrery, James (Jim McCrery) *congressman*
Mc Curdy, Patrick Pierre *editor, consultant*
McCurry, Michael Demaree *government spokesman, press secretary*
McDade, Joseph Michael *congressman*
McDaniel, John Perry *health care company executive*
McDavid, J. Gary *lawyer*
McDavid, Janet Louise *lawyer*
Mc Dermott, Albert Leo *lawyer*
McDermott, Edward Aloysious *lawyer*
McDermott, James A. *congressman, psychiatrist*
McDermott, Robert Francis, Jr. *lawyer*
McDonald, Gail Clements *government official*
Mc Donald, John Warlick *diplomat, global strategist*
McDowell, Charles R. *columnist, news analyst, lecturer*
†McElroy, Edward J. *union officer*
McElroy, Frederick William *economics educator, consultant*
McElveen, Junius Carlisle, Jr. *lawyer*
McEntee, Gerald W. *labor union official*
Mc Fee, Thomas Stuart *government agency administrator*
McGarry, J. Michael, III *lawyer*
McGarry, John Warren *government official*
Mc Gaughan, Alexander Stanley *architect*
McGee, Robert Merrill *oil company executive*
McGeein, Mary Martha *health care organization executive*
Mc Giffert, David Eliot *lawyer, former government official*
McGinley, Ronald James *entomologist, researcher*
McGinnies, Elliott Morse *psychologist, educator*
Mc Ginnis, James Michael *physician*
McGinty, Michael Dennis *air force officer*
Mc Glothlin, James Harrison *lawyer*
McGlotten, Robert Miller *labor union official*
McGough, Duane Theodore *economist, government official*
McGovern, Michael Barbot *lawyer*
McGrath, Kathryn Bradley *lawyer*
†McGrath, Mary Helena *plastic surgeon, educator*
Mc Grory, Mary *columnist*
McGrory, Mary Kathleen *university official*
McGue, Christie *federal official*
McGuire, Patricia A. *lawyer, academic administrator*
McGuire, Roger Alan *foreign service officer*
McGuirl, Marlene Dana Callis *law librarian, educator*
McHenry, Donald F. *former diplomat, international affairs consultant, educator*
McHugh, James Lenahan, Jr. *lawyer*
McHugh, John Michael *congressman, former state senator*
McInnis, Scott Steve *congressman, lawyer*
†McIntosh, David M. *congressman*
Mc Kay, Emily Gantz *civil and human rights professional*
McKeon, Howard P. (Buck McKeon) *congressman, former mayor*
McKinless, Kathy Jean *accountant*
McKinley, Brunson *diplomat*
McKinney, Cynthia Ann *congresswoman*
McKinney, James Clayton *electronics executive, electrical engineer*
†McKune, Elizabeth D. *diplomat*
McLarty, Thomas F., III (Mack McLarty) *federal official*
McLaughlin, John Joseph *broadcast executive, television producer, political commentator, journalist*
McLaughlin, Maureen A. *federal agency administrator*
Mc Lean, George Francis *philosophy of religion educator, clergyman*
McLellan, Joseph Duncan *critic, journalist*
McLennan, Barbara Nancy *trade association executive, lawyer*
McLucas, William Robert *federal agency director*
McMahon, Joseph Einar *lawyer, consultant*
McMichael, Guy H., III *federal official*
McMillen, (Charles) Thomas *federal official*
McMiller, Anita Williams *army officer, transportation professional, educator*
Mc Namara, Robert Strange *former banking executive, cabinet member*
McNamara, Thomas Edmund *diplomat*
McNamee, Sister Catherine *educational association executive*
McNeill, John Henderson *government official, lawyer*
McNicol, David Leon *federal official*
McNulty, Michael Robert *congressman*
McNulty, Robert Holmes *civic association executive*
McPeak, Merrill Anthony *business executive, consultant, retired officer*
Mc Phee, Henry Roemer *lawyer*
Mc Pherson, Harry Cummings, Jr. *lawyer*
McQuinn, Michael Rand *lawyer*
McSteen, Martha Abernathy *organization executive*
Mead, Gilbert D(unbar) *geophysicist, lawyer*
Means, Marianne *political columnist*
Means, Thomas Cornell *lawyer*
Mears, Walter Robert *journalist*
Medalie, Richard James *lawyer*
Medero, Joanne Trimble *lawyer*
Mederos, Carolina Luisa *transportation policy consultant*
†Meehan, John J. *mortgage company executive*
Meehan, Martin Thomas *congressman, lawyer*
Meek, Carrie P. *congresswoman*
Megan, Thomas Ignatius *judge*
Meggers, Betty J(ane) *anthropologist*
Meijer, Paul Herman Ernst *educator, physicist*
Meikle, Philip G. *government agency executive*
Meissner, Doris *federal commissioner*
Melamed, Arthur Douglas *lawyer*
Melendez, Sara E. *academic administrator*
Melendy, David Russell *broadcast journalist*
Mellon, Paul *retired art gallery executive*
Mellor, John Williams *economist, policy consultant firm executive*
Melnick, Vijaya Lakshmi *biology educator, research center director*
Meloy, Sybil Piskur *lawyer*
Melton, Augustus Allen, Jr. *airport executive*
Meltzer, Steven Lee *lawyer*
Menard, Edith *English language educator, artist, poet, actress*
Mencher, Bruce Stephan *judge*
†Menendez, Adofo *engineering company executive*
Menendez, Robert *congressman, lawyer*
Menning, Edward Lee *veterinarian*
Menoher, Paul Edwin, Jr. *army officer*
Mercer, Lee William *lawyer, corporate executive, former government agency administrator*
Merchant, Carl William, II *retail executive*
Merino Castro, José Toribio *retired Chilean naval officer*
Merow, James F. *federal judge*
Merrell, Jesse Howard *writer*
Merrill, Philip *publisher*
Merry, Robert William *publishing executive*
Meserve, Richard Andrew *lawyer*
Messner, Howard Myron *professional association executive*
Meszar, Frank *publishing executive, former army officer*
†Metcalf, Jack *congressman, retired state senator*
Metz, Craig Huseman *legislative staff*
Metz, Douglas Wilber *association executive, lawyer*
Metzenbaum, Howard Morton *senator*
†Metzler, Cynthia A. *federal agency administrator, lawyer*
Meurlin, Keith W. *airport terminal executive*
Meyer, Alden Merrill *environmental association executive*
Meyer, Armin Henry *retired diplomat, author, educator*
Meyer, Dennis Irwin *lawyer*
Meyer, Lawrence George *lawyer*
Meyer, Lawrence Robert *journalist*
†Meyerhoff, James Lester *medical researcher*
Meyers, Jan *congresswoman*
Meyers, Tedson Jay *lawyer*
Meyers, Wayne Marvin *microbiologist*
Meyerson, Adam *magazine editor, foundation executive*
Meyung, Eugene J. *insurance company executive*
Mfume, Kweisi *congressman*
Michaelson, Martin *lawyer*
†Michel, David J. *metallurgist, crystallographer*
Michel, Paul Redmond *federal judge*
Mickey, Paul F(ogle), Jr. *lawyer*
Micozzi, Marc Stephen *museum director, physician, educator*
Mikel, Sarah Ann *librarian*
Miklaszewski, James Alan *television news correspondent*
Mikva, Abner Joseph *lawyer, retired federal judge*
Milam, William Bryant *diplomat, economist*
Miles, Ellen Gross *art historian, museum curator*
Millar, James Robert *economist, educator, university official*
Millenson, Debra Ann *lawyer*
Miller, Andrew Pickens *lawyer*
Miller, Charles A. *lawyer*
Miller, Christine Odell Cook *federal judge*
Miller, Dan *congressman*
Miller, George *congressman*
Miller, G(eorge) William *merchant banker, business executive*
Miller, H. Todd *lawyer*
Miller, Harry Charles, Jr. *physician, urologist, educator*
Miller, Herbert John, Jr. *lawyer*
Miller, Hope Ridings *author*
Miller, Iris Ann *landscape architect, urban designer, educator*
Miller, Jack Richard *federal judge*
Miller, James Clifford, III *economist*
Miller, Jeanne-Marie Anderson (Mrs. Nathan J. Miller) *English language educator, academic administrator*
Miller, John Francis *association executive, social scientist*
Miller, John T., Jr. *lawyer, educator*
Miller, Kenneth Gregory *air force officer*
Miller, Lawrence A. *lawyer*
Miller, Marshall Lee *lawyer*
Miller, Mary Hotchkiss *lay worker*
†Miller, Robert J. *financial executive*
Miller, Stephanie Lee *federal agency administrator*
Miller, Warren Lloyd *lawyer*
Miller, William Lawrence *government official*
Millhone, John Paul *federal laboratory administrator*
Millian, Kenneth Young *public policy consultant*
†Milliken, Christine Topping *legal association administrator, lawyer*
Millon, Henry Armand *fine arts educator, architectural historian*
Milstein, Elliott Steven *legal educator, academic administrator*
Minarik, Joseph John *economist, researcher*
Mineta, Norman Yoshio *congressman*
Minge, David *congressman, lawyer, law educator*
Mink, Patsy Takemoto *congresswoman*
Minnich, Nelson Hubert Joseph *historian, educator*
Mintz, Richard I. *federal official*
Mintz, Seymour Stanley *lawyer*
Mirabelli, Mario V. *lawyer*
Miranowski, John Alfred *agricultural economist*
Mitchell, Andrea *journalist*
†Mitchell, Edward Franklin *utility company executive*
Mitchell, Roy Shaw *lawyer*
Mitchell-Rankin, Zinora Mona *judge*
Mizroch, John F. *lawyer*
Mlay, Marian *government official*
Moakley, John Joseph *congressman*
Moates, G. Paul *lawyer*
Mobbs, Michael Hall *lawyer*
Mode, Paul J., Jr. *lawyer*
†Modiano, Albert Louis *gas, oil industry executive*
Moe, Richard Palmer *lawyer*
Moffett, Charles Simonton *museum director, curator, writer*
Mogel, William Allen *lawyer*
Mohler, Brian Jeffery *diplomat*
Moler, Elizabeth Anne *federal agency administrator, lawyer*
Molinari, Susan K. *congresswoman*
Mollohan, Alan B. *congressman, lawyer*

Monroe, Robert Rawson *engineering construction executive*
Montelongo, Michael *career officer*
Montgomery, George Cranwell *lawyer, former ambassador*
Montgomery, G(eorge) Franklin *electrical engineer, consultant*
Montgomery, Gillespie V. (Sonny Montgomery) *congressman*
Mooney, Marilyn *lawyer*
Moore, Arthur Cotton *architect*
Moore, Bob Stahly *communications executive*
†Moore, Elvi *performing company executive*
Moore, Jerry *religious organization administrator*
Moore, Julia Alice *non-profit executive*
Moore, Richard Anthony *diplomat, lawyer*
†Moore, Richard Thomas *federal agency administrator*
Moore, Robert Madison *food industry executive, lawyer*
†Moore, Walter Bruce *career officer*
Moorer, Thomas Hinman *retired naval officer*
Moorhead, Carlos J. *congressman*
Moos, Eugene *federal agency administrator*
Moose, George E. *government official*
Moose, Richard M. *federal official*
Moran, James Patrick, Jr. *congressman, stockbroker*
Moran, Ricardo Julio *economist*
Morehouse, David C. *military lawyer*
Morehouse, David Frank *geologist*
Morella, Constance Albanese *congresswoman*
Morgan, John Davis *government official*
Moring, John Frederick *lawyer*
Moritsugu, Kenneth Paul *physician, government official*
Morris, Daniel Kearns *journalist*
Morris, Stanley E. *federal official*
Morris, William *lawyer*
Morrison, David Lee *chemist, research institute executive*
Morrison, James William, Jr. *lobbyist and government relations consultant*
Morse, Richard McGee *historian*
Moscato, Anthony Charles *federal official*
Moseley-Braun, Carol *senator*
Mosemann, Lloyd Kenneth, II *government official*
Moser, Donald Bruce *magazine editor*
Mosettig, Michael David *television producer, writer*
†Moss, Madison Scott *editor*
†Mossel, Patricia Fleischer *opera executive*
Mossinghoff, Gerald Joseph *lawyer, association executive*
Mostoff, Allan Samuel *lawyer, consultant*
Moulton, David Aubin *library director*
Moynihan, Daniel Patrick *senator, educator*
Mtewa, Mekki *foundation administrator*
Muckenfuss, Cantwell Faulkner, III *lawyer*
Mueller, Robert Swan, III *lawyer, former federal official*
Mueller, Ronald Raymond *public relations executive*
Muir, J. Dapray *lawyer*
Mujica, Barbara Louise *foreign language educator, author*
Mulhern, John David *former academic dean, educator*
Muller, Scott William *lawyer*
Mulligan, Robert J. *retail store executive, accountant*
Mullin, Mark Hill *headmaster*
Munasinghe, Mohan *development economist*
Mundy, Carl Epting, Jr. *commandant of the marine corps*
Munnell, Alicia Haydock *economist*
Munsell, Elsie Louise *lawyer*
Munson, Richard Jay *congressional coalition policy analyst*
Muntzing, L(ewis) Manning *lawyer*
Murashige, Allen *defense analysis executive*
Murata, Ryohei *diplomat*
Murkowski, Frank Hughes *senator*
Murphy, Betty Jane Southard (Mrs. Cornelius F. Murphy) *lawyer*
Murphy, Caryle Marie *foreign correspondent*
Murphy, Frances Louise, II *newspaper publisher*
Murphy, Gerald *government official*
Murphy, James Paul *lawyer*
Murphy, John Condron, Jr. *lawyer*
Murphy, Kenneth Ray *non-governmental organization executive*
Murphy, Patrick Vincent *foundation executive*
Murphy, Reg *publishing executive*
Murphy, Robert Earl *scientist, government agency administrator*
Murphy, Stephen P. *lawyer*
Murphy, Terence Roche *lawyer*
†Murray, Alan Stewart *publishing executive*
Murray, Christopher Charles, III *architect*
Murray, James Joseph, III *association executive*
Murray, John Einar *lawyer, retired army officer, federal official*
Murray, Patty *senator*
Murray, Robert Fulton, Jr. *physician*
Murry, Harold David, Jr. *lawyer*
Murtha, John Patrick *congressman*
†Musselman, James Arthur *army officer*
Myers, Dee Dee (Margaret Jane Myers) *former press secretary*
Myers, John Holt *lawyer*
Myers, John Thomas *congressman*
Myers, Robert Manson *English educator, author*
Myers, Samuel Lloyd *education association executive*
†Myers, William Gerry, III *advocate, lawyer*
Myrick, Sue *congresswoman, former mayor*
Nace, Barry John *lawyer*
†Nach, James Peter *foreign service officer*
Nader, Ralph *consumer advocate, lawyer, author*
Nadler, Jerrold Lewis *congressman, lawyer*
Naifeh, Steven Woodward *writer*
Nakhleh, Emile A. *governmental sciences educator*
Napier, John Light *lawyer*
Nash, Bob J. (Bob Nash) *under-secretary agriculture rural and small development*
Nason, Charles Tuckey *financial services executive*
Natalie, Ronald Bruce *lawyer*
Natter, Robert, Jr. *federal official, military career officer*
Naughton, Paul Francis *financial executive*
Nauheim, Stephen Alan *lawyer*
Navarro, Bruce Charles *lawyer*
†Navas, William Antonio, Jr. *military officer, civil engineer*
Naylor, Brian *news correspondent*
Neal, Darwina Lee *government official*
Neal, Richard Edmund *congressman, former mayor*
Nebeker, Frank Quill *federal judge*
Nef, Evelyn Stefansson *psychotherapist, author, editor, specialist polar regions*
Nehmer, Stanley *economics consultant*
Neighmond, Patricia *reporter*
Neimark, Sheridan *lawyer*
Nelson, Alan Ray *internist, medical assocation executive*
Nelson, Charles J. *university administrator, international consultant, diplomat, consultant*
Nelson, David Brian *physicist*
Nelson, Gaylord Anton *former senator, association executive*
Nelson, John Howard (Jack Howard Nelson) *journalist*
Nelson, Lars-Erik *newspaperman*
Nelson, Richard Copeland *hotel executive*
Nelson, Robert Louis *lawyer*
Nemeroff, Michael Alan *lawyer*
Ness, Andrew David *lawyer*
†Nethercutt, George Rector, Jr. *congressman, lawyer*
Nethery, John Jay *government official*
†Neufeld, Michael John *curator, historian*
Neuman, Robert Henry *lawyer*
†Neumann, Mark W. *congressman*
Neviaser, Robert Jon *orthopedic surgeon, educator*
Nevins, Louis H. *lawyer*
Newhouse, Alan Russell *federal government executive*
†Newkirk, Ingrid *animal rights activist*
Newman, Barbara Pollock *journalist, television writer, producer.*
Newman, Don Melvin *federal agency administrator*
Newman, Frank Neil *federal official*
Newman, Monroe *retired economist, educator*
Newman, Pauline *federal judge*
Newman, William Bernard, Jr. *railroad executive*
Newquist, Don *federal agency administrator*
Newton, Virginia *archivist, historian, librarian*
†Ney, Robert W. *congressman*
Nicholas, Robert B. *lawyer*
Nichols, Henry Eliot *lawyer, savings and loan executive*
Nichols, Kenneth David *consulting engineer*
Nichols, Mary D. *federal agency administrator, lawyer*
Nicholson, Richard Selindh *educational association administrator*
Nickles, Donald (Don Nickles) *senator*
Niehoff, Karl Richard Besuden *financial executive*
Nies, Helen Wilson *federal judge*
Nightingale, Elena Ottolenghi *geneticist, physician, administrator*
Nikkel, Ronald Wilbert *social services administrator*
Nims, Arthur Lee, III *federal judge*
Nintemann, Terri *legislative staff member*
Nisbet, Robert A. *historian, sociologist*
Niskanen, William Arthur, Jr. *economist*
Nitze, Paul Henry *international studies educator*
Nitze, William Albert *lawyer, government official*
Noble, Ronald K. *government official, lawyer*
Nolan, Jean *federal agency official*
Nolan, John Edward, Jr. *lawyer*
†Noland, Marcus *economist, educator*
Norberg, Charles Robert *lawyer*
Norby, Ronald Brandon *nurse executive*
Norcross, David Frank Armstrong *lawyer*
Norcross, Marvin Augustus *veterinarian, government agency official*
Nordhaus, Robert Riggs *lawyer*
Nordquist, Myron Harry *lawyer*
Norland, Donald Richard *retired foreign service officer*
Norman, William Stanley *travel and tourism executive*
†Norris, Genie M. *political organization executive*
Northrop, Carl Wooden *lawyer*
Norton, Eleanor Holmes *congresswoman, lawyer, educator*
Norton, Floyd Ligon, IV *lawyer*
Norton, Gerald Patrick *lawyer*
Norton, James J. *union official*
†Norwood, Charles W., Jr. *congressman*
Noshpitz, Joseph Dove *child and adolescent psychiatrist*
Novak, Michael (John) *religion educator, author, editor*
Novak, Paul *hotel industry executive*
Novak, Robert David Sanders *newspaper columnist, television commentator*
Nover, Naomi *journalist, editor, author*
Novitch, Mark *physician, educator, retired pharmaceutical executive*
†Nowak, John Michael *air force officer*
Nunn, Samuel (Sam Nunn) *senator*
†Nussbaum, Karen *federal agency administrator*
Nussle, James Allen *congressman*
Nutter, Franklin Winston *lawyer*
Oakley, Diane *insurance executive, benefit consultant*
†Oakley, Phyllis Elliott *diplomat*
Oakley, Robert Louis *law librarian, educator*
Obee, Kent *foreign service officer*
†Obenschain, Stephen Philip *physicist*
Oberdorfer, Louis F. *federal judge*
O'Berry, Carl Gerald *air force officer, electrical engineer*
Oberstar, James L. *congressman*
Obey, David Ross *congressman*
O'Brien, Francis Anthony *lawyer*
O'Brien, Timothy Andrew *writer, journalist, lawyer*
O'Brien, William James, II *lawyer*
O'Brien, William Vincent *government educator*
O'Bryon, James Fredrick *defense executive*
†Ochmanek, David Alan *government official*
Ochs, Walter J. *civil engineer, drainage adviser*
O'Connell, Daniel Craig *psychology educator*
O'Connor, Charles Aloysius, III *lawyer*
O'Connor, Charles P. *lawyer*
†O'Connor, Jennifer *public administrator*
O'Connor, John Jay, III *lawyer*
O'Connor, Nancy Morrison *lawyer*
O'Connor, Sandra Day *U.S. supreme court justice*
O'Connor, Thomas Edward *petroleum geologist, world bank officer*
O'Connor, Tom *corporate executive, management consultant*
O'Day, Paul Thomas *trade association executive*
Odle, Robert Charles, Jr. *lawyer*
O'Doherty, Brian *playwright, filmmaker*
Odom, William Eldridge *army officer, educator*
†O'Donnell, Lawrence Francis, Jr. *legislative staff administrator, author*
O'Donnell, Terrence *lawyer*
O'Donovan, Leo Jeremiah *university president, theologian, priest*
Oehme, Wolfgang Walter *landscape architect*
Oertel, Goetz K. H. *physicist, professional association administrator*
Offutt, Gerald M. *lawyer*
†Ogden, David William *lawyer*
Ogilvie, Donald Gordon *bankers association executive*
Oh, John Kie-Chiang *political science educator, university official*
O'Hara, James Thomas *lawyer*
O'Hare, Patrick K. *lawyer*
O'Hern, Elizabeth Moot *microbiologist, writer*
Okay, John Louis *information scientist*
Olcott, John Whiting *aviation executive*
O'Leary, Hazel R. *U.S. secretary of energy, former power company executive, lawyer*
Olender, Jack Harvey *lawyer*
Oliver, Daniel *foundation fellow, lawyer*
Oliver, William Albert, Jr. *paleontologist*
Olmer, Lionel Herbert *lawyer*
Olmstead, Cecil Jay *lawyer*
Olsen, Kathie Lynn *neuroscientist, administrator*
Olson, Charles Eric *economist*
Olson, John Frederick *lawyer*
Olson, Theodore Bevry *lawyer, government official*
Olson, Walter Justus, Jr. *management consultant*
Olver, John Walter *congressman*
O'Neil, Joseph Francis *association executive*
O'Neill, Brian Dennis *lawyer*
O'Neill, John H., Jr. *lawyer*
O'Neill, Joseph Patrick *retail association executive*
O'Neill, William Patrick *lawyer*
Onek, Joseph Nathan *lawyer*
Ongman, John Will *lawyer*
Onto, John *think-tank executive*
Ooms, Van Doorn *economist*
Oppel, Richard Alfred *newspaper executive*
Oppenheimer, Franz Martin *lawyer*
Oppenheimer, Jerry L. *lawyer*
Oran, Elaine Surick *physicist*
†Ord, Robert L., III *military officer*
Ordway, Frederick Ira, III *educator, consultant, researcher, author*
Ornstein, Norman Jay *political scientist*
O'Rourke, C. Larry *lawyer*
Orr, J. Scott *newspaper correspondent*
†Orsini, Eric Andrew *army official*
Ortiz, Solomon P. *congressman*
†Ortner, Donald J. *biological anthropologist, educator*
Orton, William H. (Bill Orton) *congressman, lawyer*
Osnos, David Marvin *lawyer*
Ostar, Allan William *higher education consultant*
†Oster, Jeffrey Wayne *marine corps officer*
O'Sullivan, Lynda Troutman *lawyer*
Oswald, Robert Bernard *science administrator, nuclear engineer*
Oswald, Rudolph A. *economist*
O'Toole, Francis J. *lawyer*
O'Toole, Tara J. *federal official*
†Ottley, William Henry *professional association director, consultant*
Overbeck, Gene Edward *retired airline executive, lawyer*
Overman, Dean Lee *lawyer, investor, author*
Oweiss, Ibrahim Mohamed *economist, educator*
Owen, Henry *former ambassador, consultant*
Owen, Roberts Bishop *lawyer*
Owens, Major Robert Odell *congressman*
Oxley, Michael Garver *congressman*
Oxman, Stephen A. *federal official*
Oyler, Gregory Kenneth *lawyer*
Packard, George Randolph *journalist, educator*
Packard, Ronald *congressman*
Packwood, Bob *senator*
†Padgett, Nancy Weeks *law librarian, consultant, lawyer*
Page, Harry Robert *business administration educator*
Page, Joseph Anthony *law educator*
Page, Marcus William *federal official*
Page, Robert Wesley *engineering and construction company executive, federal official*
†Page, William Candler, Jr. *career officer*
Paige, Hilliard Wegner *corporate director, consultant*
Painter, William Hall *law educator*
Palast, Geri D. *federal agency administrator*
Pallone, Frank, Jr. *congressman*
Palmer, Alan Kenneth *lawyer*
Palmer, David Brent *lawyer*
Palmer, Ronald DeWayne Faisal *retired diplomat, educator, consultant*
Palmer, Steven O. *federal official*
Palmeter, N. David *lawyer*
Palumbo, Benjamin Lewis *public affairs consulting company executive*
Panetta, Leon Edward *federal official, former congressman*
Pang, Frederick F. Y. *federal official*
Panzer, Mary Caroline *museum curator*
Paoletta, Mark R. A. *federal lawyer*
Paper, Lewis J. *lawyer*
Papkin, Robert David *lawyer*
Parker, Edna G. *federal judge*
Parker, Gerald William *physician, medical center administrator, retired air force officer*
Parker, Michael (Mike Parker) *congressman*
Parker, Robert Allan Ridley *astronaut*
Parr, Carolyn Miller *federal court judge*
Parris, Robert *composer*
†Parris, Stanford E. *congressman*
Parrish, Alvin Edward *former university dean, medical educator*
Parrish, Edgar Lee *financial services executive*
Parrott, Robert Harold *pediatrician, educator*
Parshall, Gerald *journalist*
Partridge, William Russell *federal executive*
Pasmanick, Kenneth *bassoonist*
Pastor, Ed *congressman*
Patchan, Joseph *lawyer*
Pate, Michael Lynn *lawyer*
Patrick, Sue Ford *diplomat*
Patron, June Eileen *former government official*
Patten, Thomas Louis *lawyer*
Patton, Thomas Earl *lawyer*
Paul, Robert Dennis *lawyer*
Paul, William McCann *lawyer*
Paulsen, Thomas Dean *naval officer*
Paulson, Stanley Fay *association executive*
Paup, Michael Lee *lawyer*
Pawlson, Leonard Gregory *physician*
Paxon, L. William *congressman*
Paxson, Richard *newspaper editor*
Payne, Donald M. *congressman*
Payne, Kenneth Eugene *lawyer*
Payne, Lewis Franklin, Jr. (L.F. Payne) *congressman*
†Payne, Michael Lee *association management executive*
†Payzant, Thomas *government official*
Peapples, George Alan *automotive executive*
Pearlman, Ronald Alan *lawyer*
Pearse, Warren Harland *association executive, obstetrician and gynecologist*
Pearson, Jeremiah W., III *military career officer, federal agency official*
Pearson, Roger *organization executive*
Peavy, Robert A. *lawyer*
†Peck, Gary Lawrence *dermatologist, researcher*
Peck, Robert David *educational foundation administrator*
Peck, Robert Stephen *lawyer, educator*
Pedersen, Norman A. *lawyer*
Pedersen, Wesley Niels *public relations and public affairs executive*
Pedersen, William Francis, Jr. *lawyer*
Peele, Roger *hospital administrator*
Pehrson, Gordon Oscar, Jr. *lawyer*
Peirce, Neal R. *journalist*
Pelaez, Emmanuel N. *ambassador*
Pelavin, Diane Christine *small business owner, research analyst*
Pell, Claiborne *senator*
Pell, Ernest Eugene *broadcasting executive*
Pellegrino, Edmund Daniel *physician, educator, former university president*
Pelletreau, Robert Halsey *diplomat*
Pelosi, Nancy *congresswoman*
Peña, Federico Fabian *federal official*
Pendergast, William Ross *lawyer*
Pendleton, Mary Catherine *foreign service officer*
Penn, John Garrett *federal judge*
Penny, Timothy Joseph *congressman*
Perella, Susanne Brennan *librarian*
Perez, Lillian *non-profit association executive*
Perkins, Edward J. *diplomat*
Perkins, Jack Edwin *lawyer*
†Perkins, Lucian *photographer*
Perkins, Samuel Thomas *lawyer*
Perle, Richard Norman *government official*
Perlik, William R. *lawyer*
Perlin, Seymour *psychiatrist, educator*
Perlman, Matthew Saul *lawyer*
Perlmutter, Jack *artist, lithographer*
Perros, Theodore Peter *chemist, educator*
Perry, B(illy) Dwight *lawyer*
Perry, George Lewis *research economist, consultant*
Perry, Seymour Monroe *physician*
Perry, Spence William *lawyer*
Perry, William James *mathematical scientist, government official*
Persavich, Warren Dale *diversified manufacturing company executive*
Peter, Frances Marchbank *author, editor, research agency administrator, writer, strategic planner*
Peterman, John L. *economist*
Peters, Charles Given, Jr. *editor*
Peterson, Charles Hayes *trading company executive*
Peterson, Collin C. *congressman*
Peterson, Douglas Pete (Pete Peterson) *congressman*
Peterson, Esther *consumer advocate*
Peterson, Trudy Huskamp *national archivist*
Peterson, William Herbert *economist*
Petrash, Jeffrey Michael *lawyer*
Petri, Thomas Evert *congressman*
Pettengill, Harry Junior *federal agency administrator*
Pettit, John Whitney *lawyer*
Pettit, William Thomas *broadcasting journalist*
†Pettus, Mary Catherine *public relations executive*
Petty, John Robert *banker*
Pfeiffer, Leonard, IV *executive recruiter, consultant*
Pfeiffer, Margaret Kolodny *lawyer*
Pfeiffer, Steven Bernard *lawyer*
Pfnausch, Edward *religious association administrator*
Pfordresher, John Charles *English educator*
†Phelps, Timothy Miller *reporter*
Phemister, Thomas Alexander *lawyer*
Philbin, Edward James *federal agency commissioner, military officer, legal educator, engineer*
Philion, Norman Joseph, III *lawyer*
Philips, Malcolm H. *lawyer*
Phillips, Carter Glasgow *lawyer*
Phillips, Christopher Hallowell *diplomat*
Phillips, Cyrus Eastman, IV *lawyer*
Phillips, James D. *retired diplomat*
Phillips, Karen Borlaug *economist, association executive*
Phillips, Laughlin *museum president, former magazine editor*
Phillips, Richard L(overidge) *marine corps officer*
Phillips, Susan Meredith *financial economist, former university administrator*
Phlegar, Benjamin Focht *retired magazine editor*
Pickenpaugh, Thomas Edward *archaeologist*
Pickering, John Harold *lawyer*
Pickett, Owen B. *congressman*
Pickholtz, Raymond Lee *electrical engineering educator, consultant*
†Pierce, David R. *educational administrator*
Pierce, Margaret Hunter *government official*
Pietrowski, Robert Frank, Jr. *lawyer*
Pilecki, Paul Steven *lawyer*
Pinco, Robert G. *lawyer*
Pincus, Ann Terry *federal agency administrator*
Pincus, Walter Haskell *editor*
Pines, Burton Yale *broadcasting executive*
Pines, Wayne Lloyd *public relations counselor*
Pings, Cornelius John *educational association administrator*
Pinstrup-Andersen, Per *educational administrator*
†Pinzler, Isabelle Katz *lawyer*
Pipkin, James Harold, Jr. *lawyer*
Pirie, Robert Burns, Jr. *defense analyst*
Piroumian, Felix Ashot *Armenian government official*
Pitt, Harvey Lloyd *lawyer*
Pittman, Steuart Lansing *lawyer*
Pivik, Robert William *accounting executive*
Placke, James A(nthony) *foreign service officer, international affairs consultant*
Plager, S. Jay *federal judge*
Plaine, Daniel J. *lawyer*
Plaisted, Joan M. *diplomat*
Plante, William Madden *news correspondent*
†Plewes, Thomas Jeffrey *economic statistician, government executive*
Plotkin, Harry Morris *lawyer*
Plowman, R. Dean *federal agriculture agency administrator*
Podberesky, Samuel *lawyer*
Podgorny, Richard Joseph *biologist, science administrator*
Poe, Luke Harvey, Jr. *lawyer*
Pogue, Lloyd Welch *lawyer*
Pojeta, John, Jr. *geologist*
Polak, Jacques Jacobus *economist, foundation administrator*
Polan, Annette Lewis *artist*
Polebaum, Elliot Edward *lawyer*
Pombo, Richard *congressman, rancher, farmer*
Pomeroy, Earl R. *congressman, former state insurance commissioner*
Pomeroy, Harlan *lawyer*
Poneman, Daniel Bruce *federal official*
Pope, Michael Thor *chemist*

Poppeliers, John Charles architectural historian
Poppler, Doris Swords lawyer
Porter, Elisabeth Scott (Leezee Porter) political worker
Porter, John Edward congressman
Porter, Richard Howard lawyer
Portman, Rob congressman
Portnoy, Ian Karl lawyer
Poshard, Glenn W. congressman
Post, Boyd Wallace forester
Postol, Lawrence Philip lawyer
Poteete, Robert Arthur editor
Potter, Deborah Ann news correspondent, educator
Potter, John Francis surgical oncologist, educator
Potter, Trevor Alexander McClurg lawyer
Potts, Ramsay Douglas lawyer, aviator
Potts, Stephen Deaderick lawyer
Potvin, Raymond Herve sociology educator, author
Poulson, Richard Jasper Metcalfe lawyer
Povich, David lawyer
Povich, Shirley Lewis columnist, former sports editor
Powell, Anne Elizabeth editor
Powell, Joseph Lester (Jody Powell) public relations executive
Powell, Lewis Franklin, Jr. retired U.S. supreme court justice
†Power, John Jay labor union official
Power, Mark journalist, photographer, educator
Pozen, Walter lawyer
Prah, Pamela Marie journalist
Pratt, John Helm federal judge
Preeg, Ernest Henry strategic and international studies center executive
Preer, Jean Lyon university administrator, educator
Prell, Michael Jack economist
Press, Frank geophysicist, educator
Pressler, Larry senator
Preston, Colleen Ann lawyer
Preston, Lewis Thompson banker
Preston, Richard McKim lawyer
Prestowitz, Clyde Vincent economist, research administrator
Prettyman, Elijah Barrett, Jr. lawyer
Prewitt, Charles Thompson geochemist
Price, Griffith Baley, Jr. lawyer
Price, Joseph Hubbard lawyer
Price, Mark Michael building development consultant
†Price, Tom journalist
Prina, L(ouis) Edgar journalist
Principi, Anthony Joseph lawyer
†Pritchard, Paul Clement conservation association executive
Proctor, John P. lawyer
†Profitt, Glenn Arliss, II air force officer
Proto, Neil Thomas lawyer, educator
Pruden, James Wesley newspaper editor, columnist
Pruitt, Anne Loring university administrator, educator
Pryor, David Hampton senator
Pucie, Charles R., Jr. public affairs executive
Pugh, Keith E., Jr. lawyer
Pulliam, Howard Ronald federal agency administrator
Puryear, Martin artist
Pusey, William Anderson lawyer
Putzel, Michael journalist
Pyke, Thomas Nicholas, Jr. government science and engineering administrator
Pyle, Robert Noble public relations executive
Quainton, Anthony Cecil Eden diplomat
Quale, John Carter lawyer
Quarles, James Linwood, III lawyer
Queen, Evelyn E. Crawford judge, law educator
Queenan, John Thomas obstetrician, gynecologist, educator
Quello, James Henry government official
Quigley, Thomas J. lawyer
Quillen, James Henry (Jimmy Quillen) congressman
Quinn, Jack congressman, English language educator, sports coach
Quinn, Sally journalist
Quinn-Judge, Paul Malachy journalist
Quint, Arnold Harris lawyer
Quintiere, Gary G. lawyer
Raab, Harry Frederick, Jr. physicist
Raaflaub, Kurt A. classics educator
Rabb, Harriet Schaffer lawyer, educator
Rabel, Ed news correspondent
Rabin, Kenneth Hardy public relations executive
Rabin, Steve Arthur public affairs executive
Rabinowitz, Stanley Samuel rabbi
†Radanovich, George P. congressman
Rademaker, Stephen Geoffrey lawyer
Rader, Randall Ray federal judge
Rader, Robert Michael lawyer
Radin, Alex former association executive, consultant
Rafshoon, Gerald Monroe communications executive
Rahall, Nick Joe, II (Nick Rahall) congressman
Rahill, Margaret Fish retired museum curator
Rahn, Richard William economist, business executive
Raimo, Bernard, Jr. (Bernie) lawyer
Raines, Franklin Delano investment banker
Rainey, Jean Osgood public relations executive
Rales, Steven M. automotive parts company executive
Rall, David Platt pharmacologist, environmentalist
Ralls, Katherine zoologist
Ramberg, Walter Dodd architect
Ramey, Carl Robert lawyer
Ramsay, William Charles writer
Ramsey, Henry, Jr. university dean-official, lawyer, retired judge
Ramsey, William C. ambassador
Ramstad, Jim congressman, lawyer
Rand, Harry Zvi art historian, poet
Randall, Gene news correspondent, anchor
Randall, Robert L(ee) ecological economist
Randolph, Arthur Raymond federal judge, lawyer
Rangel, Charles Bernard congressman
Rankin, Haywood Forney diplomat
Rankin, Robert Arthur journalist
Rao, Desiraju Bhavanarayana meteorologist, oceanographer, educator
Raphael, Louise Arakelian mathematician, educator
Raphael-Howell, Frances Jayne clinical psychologist
Raphel, Robin federal official
Rasco, Carol Hampton federal official
Raskin, Marcus Goodman writer, educator
Raspberry, William James journalist
†Ratner, Ellen Faith radio talk show host, writer
Ratner, Rhoda Sue librarian
Rauh, Carl Stephen lawyer
Raul, Alan Charles lawyer
Raum, Arnold federal judge
Rausch, Howard information service executive
Ravenal, Earl Cedric international relations educator, author
Ravenhill, Philip Leonard curator, art historian
†Raviv, Sheila public relations executive
Rawson, David P. ambassador
Reade, Claire Elizabeth lawyer
Reade, Lewis Pollock diplomat, engineer
Reardon, Pearl Rance real estate executive, writer
Reason, Joseph Paul naval officer
Reaves, John Daniel lawyer, playwright, actor
Reaves, Wendy Wick museum curator
Reback, Joyce Ellen lawyer
Rechcigl, Miloslav, Jr. government official
Reck, Gregory Milton aerospace engineer
Reed, John Francis (Jack Reed) congressman, lawyer
Reed, John Hathaway former ambassador
Reed, Travis Dean public relations consultant
Reed, Vincent Emory federal education official
Reeder, Joe Robert federal official
†Rees, Raymond F. military officer
Reger, Lawrence Lee association executive
Regula, Ralph congressman, lawyer
Rehm, John Bartram lawyer
Rehnquist, William Hubbs U.S. supreme court chief justice
Reich, Alan Anderson association executive
Reich, Bernard political science educator
Reich, Otto Juan political analyst, business consultant
Reichardt, Glenn Richard lawyer
Reid, George Bernard, Jr. lawyer
Reid, Inez Smith lawyer, educator
Reid, Joseph Browning architect
Reid, Robert Newton lawyer, mortgage and financial consultant
Reidy, Gerald Patrick federal organization executive, arbitrator, mediator, fact-finder
Reilly, Gerard Denis judge
Reilly, William Kane former government official, educator, lawyer, conservationist
Rein, Bert Walter lawyer
Reingold, Nathan historian
Reining, Priscilla Copeland anthropologist
†Reinsch, William Alan government executive, educator
Reis, Victor H. mechanical engineer, government official
Relic, Peter academic administrator
Render, Arlene ambassador
Renninger, Mary Karen librarian
Reno, Janet U.S. attorney general
Retsinas, Nicolas P. federal official
Rettig, Richard Allen social sciences educator, policy analyst, administrator
Reynolds, Gary Kemp librarian
Reynolds, Joseph Hurley lawyer
Reynolds, Melvin J. (Mel Reynolds) congressman
Reynolds, Nicholas S. lawyer
Reynolds, Robert Joel economist, consultant
Rezneck, Daniel Albert lawyer
Rhodes, John Jacob lawyer, former congressman
Rice, Lois Dickson former computer company executive
Rice, Paul Jackson lawyer, educator
†Rich, Bruce Miller lawyer, environmental foundation executive
Rich, Giles Sutherland federal judge
†Richard, Mark M. government official, lawyer
Richard, Paul art critic
†Richards, Charles A. government official
Richards, Cory demographic think-tank executive
Richards, Suzanne V. lawyer
Richardson, Ann Bishop foundation executive, lawyer
Richardson, David Bacon writer, journalist
Richardson, Elliot Lee lawyer
Richardson, Margaret Milner federal agency administrator, lawyer
Richardson, William Blaine congressman
†Richburg, Keith Bernard journalist, foreign correspondent
Richey, Charles Robert federal judge
Richman, Phyllis Chasanow newspaper critic
Richmond, David Walker lawyer
Richmond, Marilyn Susan lawyer
Rickard, Lisa Ann lawyer
Riddell, Richard Anderson naval officer
Riddleberger, Hugh Compton, III headmaster
Ridgeway, James Fowler journalist
Ridgway, Rozanne LeJeanne government executive, former diplomat
Riecken, Henry William psychologist, research director
Rieke, Elizabeth Ann federal agency administrator
Rieser, Joseph A., Jr. lawyer
†Riggs, Frank congressman
Riley, Joseph Harry retired banker
†Riley, Michael Joseph government official
Riley, Richard Wilson U.S. secretary of education
Rill, James Franklin lawyer
Rimpel, Auguste Eugene, Jr. management and technical consulting executive
Rinzel, Daniel Francis lawyer
†RisCassi, Robert W. career military officer
Rishe, Melvin lawyer
Risher, John Robert, Jr. lawyer
Rissetto, Harry A. lawyer
Ritter, Donald Lawrence environmental policy institute administrator
Rittner, Edmund Sidney physicist
Rivas-Vazquez, Ana Victoria federal official
†Rivers, Lynn N. congresswoman
Rivers, Richard Robinson lawyer
Rivlin, Alice Mitchell economist
Roach, Arvid Edward, II lawyer
Robb, Charles Spittal senator, lawyer
Robb, James Willis Romance languages educator
Robbins, Robert B. lawyer
Robbins, Robert John biologist, computer scientist, educator
Roberts, Bert C., Jr. telecommunications company executive
Roberts, Charles Patrick congressman
Roberts, Corinne Boggs (Cokie Roberts) correspondent, news analyst
Roberts, Howard Richard food scientist, association administrator
Roberts, James Harold, III lawyer
Roberts, Jeanne Addison literature educator
Roberts, Markley economist, educator
Roberts, Paul Craig, III economics educator, author, consultant
†Roberts, Richard Y. federal agency administrator
Roberts, Walter Ronald political science educator, former government official
Robinson, Daniel Baruch banker
Robinson, Daniel N. psychology educator
Robinson, Davis Rowland lawyer
Robinson, Deborah A. judge
Robinson, Douglas George lawyer
Robinson, Laurie Overby lawyer
Robinson, Leonard Harrison, Jr. international government consultant, business executive
Robinson, Michael Hill zoological park director, biologist
Robinson, Randall think-tank executive
Robinson, Sharon Porter federal official
Robinson, Wilkes Coleman federal judge
Robison, Andrew Cliffe, Jr. museum curator
Rockefeller, Edwin Shaffer lawyer
Rockefeller, John Davison, IV (Jay Rockefeller) senator, former governor
Rockler, Walter James lawyer
Rockoff, S. David radiologist, physician, educator
Rocque, Vincent Joseph lawyer
Rodemeyer, Michael Leonard, Jr. lawyer
Rodgers, Paul lawyer, government official
Rodman, Peter Warren foreign policy specialist
Rodrigues, Eusebio L. humanities educator
Rodriguez, Rita Maria bank executive
Roemer, Timothy J. congressman
Roett, Riordan political science educator, consultant
Rogers, Harold Dallas (Hal Rogers) congressman
Rogers, James Albert lawyer
Rogers, Jerry L. federal agency administrator
†Rogers, Judith W. federal judge
Rogers, Paul Grant lawyer, former congressman
Rogers, Raymond Jesse federal railroad associate administrator
Rogers, Sharon J. university administrator
Rogers, Warren Joseph, Jr. journalist
Rogers, William Dill lawyer
Rogovin, Mitchell lawyer
†Rogowsky, Robert A. trade commission director
Rohner, Ralph John lawyer, educator, university dean
Rohr, David Baker federal agency commissioner
Rohrabacher, Dana congressman
Roiter, Eric D. lawyer
Rokke, Ervin Jerome air force officer, university president
Roley, Jerry bank executive
Roll, David Lee lawyer
Rollwagen, John A. federal official
Romanowski, Thomas Andrew physics educator
Romansky, Michael A. lawyer
Romeo, Peter John lawyer
Romero-Barceló, Carlos Antonio resident commissioner, former chairman New Progressive Party, former governor, lawyer, real estate agent
Rominger, Richard federal agency administrator
Rooney, William Richard magazine editor
Roosevelt, Edith Kermit journalist
Rope, William Frederick academic administrator
†Roque, Margarita government administrator
Roscher, Nina Matheny chemistry educator
Rose, Charles Grandison, III (Charlie Rose) congressman
Rose, Henry lawyer
Rose, James McKinley, Jr. lawyer, government official
Rose, Jonathan Chapman lawyer
Rose, Lloyd theatre critic
†Roseborough, Teresa Wynn lawyer
Rosebush, James Scott international management and public affairs consultant, former government official
Rosen, Gerald Robert editor
Rosenau, James Nathan political scientist, author
†Rosenberg, Mark Louis lawyer
Rosenberg, Norman Jack agricultural meteorologist, educator
Rosenberg, Ruth Helen Borsuk lawyer
Rosenberg, Sarah Zacher institute arts administration executive, humanities administration consultant
Rosenblatt, Jason Philip English language educator
Rosenblatt, Peter Ronald lawyer, former ambassador
Rosenbloom, H. David lawyer
Rosenbloom, Morris Victor author, publisher, public relations executive, government official
Rosendhal, Jeffrey David federal science agency administrator, astronomer
Rosenfeld, Stephen Samuel newspaper editor
Rosenquist, Glenn Carl pediatrician
Rosenstein, Peter Daniel association executive, medical educator
Rosensweig, Stanley Harold retail executive
Rosenthal, Aaron management consultant
Rosenthal, Alan Sayre government official
Rosenthal, Andrew newspaper editor
Rosenthal, Douglas Eurico lawyer, author
Rosenthal, Steven Siegmund lawyer
Ros-Lehtinen, Ileana congresswoman
Ross, Allan Michael physician, medical educator
Ross, Christopher Wade Stelyan diplomat
Ross, Douglas lawyer
Ross, Robinette Davis publisher
Ross, Stanford Gordon lawyer, former government official
Ross, Thomas Bernard federal government official
Ross, Wendy Clucas newspaper editor, journalist
Rossides, Eugene Telemachus lawyer, writer
Rossotti, Barbara Jill Margulies lawyer
Rostow, Eugene Victor lawyer, educator, economist
Rotberg, Eugene Harvey investment banker, lawyer
Roth, Alan J. lawyer, congressional aide
Roth, William V., Jr. senator
Rothenberg, Marc historian
Rother, John Charles association executive, lawyer
Rothkopf, David Jochanan federal official
Rothstein, Paul Frederick lawyer, educator
Rottman, Ellis public information officer
Roukema, Margaret Scafati congresswoman
†Roush, G. Jon organization administrator
Rousseau, Eva Rice principal
Rousselot, Peter Frese lawyer
Rouvelas, Emanuel Larry lawyer
Rovelstad, Mathilde Verner library science educator
Rowan, Carl Thomas columnist
Rowden, Marcus Aubrey lawyer, former government official
Rowe, Richard Holmes lawyer
Rowland, (James) Roy congressman
Rowlands, T. Dewi aerospace executive
Rowley, William Robert surgeon
Rowson, Richard Cavanagh publisher
Roybal-Allard, Lucille congresswoman
Royce, Edward R. (Ed Royce) congressman
Roycroft, Howard Francis lawyer
Rubin, Kenneth Allen lawyer
Rubin, Robert Edward U.S. secretary of the treasury
Rubin, Seymour Jeffrey lawyer, educator
†Rubinoff, Roberta Wolff government administrator
Ruby, Michael magazine executive
Ruckert, Edward M. lawyer
Rudder, Catherine Estelle political science association administrator
Ruddy, Frank S. lawyer, former ambassador
Rudman, Warren Bruce former senator, lawyer
Rudnick, Robert Alan lawyer
†Ruffer, Michael R. hotel company executive
Rugh, William Arthur diplomat
Ruhfus, Jürgen ambassador
†Ruiz, Vanessa lawyer
Rule, Charles Frederick (Rick Rule) lawyer
Rumford, Lewis, III real estate company executive
Runyon, Marvin Travis postmaster general
Rush, Bobby L. congressman
Russell, H. Diane museum curator, educator
Russell, Mark comedian
Russell, Michael James lawyer
Russell, Ted McKinnies electronics technician
†Russell, Theodore Emery diplomat
Russell, William Joseph association executive
Russert, Timothy John broadcast journalist, executive
Russin, Jonathan lawyer, consultant
Ruttenberg, Charles Byron lawyer
Ruttenberg, Stanley Harvey economist
Ruttinger, George David lawyer
Ruwe, Robert P. federal judge
Ruyak, Robert Francis lawyer
Ryan, Frederick Joseph, Jr. lawyer, public official
Ryan, Jerry William lawyer
Ryan, Joseph lawyer
Ryan, Mary A. diplomat
Ryerson, Paul Sommer lawyer
Ryn, Claes Gösta political science educator, author, research institute administrator
Sabo, Martin Olav congressman
Sabshin, Melvin psychiatrist, educator, medical association administrator
Sachar, Howard Morley history educator
Sacher, Steven Jay lawyer
Sachs, Stephen Howard lawyer
Sackler, Arthur Brian lawyer
Sacks, David Arnold lawyer
Sacksteder, Frederick Henry former foreign service officer
Safarian, Ashot Andraniki Armenian government official
Safire, William journalist, author
Sagalkin, Sanford lawyer
Sagawa, Shirley Sachi lawyer
Sagle, Robert Franklin lawyer
Sahanek, Tatana librarian, editor
†Sahli, Nancy Ann government agency administrator
St. John, Adrian, II retired army officer
Salamon, Linda Bradley university dean, English literature educator
Salant, Walter S. economist
Salem, George Richard lawyer
Salinger, Pierre Emil George journalist
Salmon, Matt congressman
Salmon, William Cooper mechanical engineer, engineering academy executive
Salop, Steven Charles economics educator
Saltzburg, Stephen Allan law educator, consultant
Salvado, August J. think-tank executive
Sam, Pierre Desforges ambassador
†Samet, Andrew government official
Samet, Kenneth Alan hospital administrator
Samman, George obstetrician, gynecologist
Sampas, Dorothy M. government official
Sampson, Daphne Rae library director
Sampson, Robert Neil association executive
Samuel, Howard David union official
Sandefur, James Tandy mathematics educator
Sanders, Bernard (Bernie Sanders) congressman
Sanderson, Fred Hugo economist
Sandler, Bernice Resnick women's rights specialist
Sandler, Sumner Gerald medical educator
Sanford, Bruce William lawyer
Sanford, Frederic Goodman career officer
†Sanford, Marshall (Mark Sanford) congressman
San Martin, Robert L. federal official
Santorum, Rick U.S. Senator
Santos, Leonard Ernest lawyer
Sapienza, John Thomas lawyer
Sarbanes, Paul Spyros senator
Sareeram, Ray Rupchand naval officer
†Sartore, Joel photojournalist
Sauntry, Susan Schaefer lawyer
Savage, Phillip Hezekiah federal agency administrator
Savage, Xyla Ruth government official
Savarese, Ralph J. lawyer
Sawhill, Isabel Van Devanter economist
Saworotnow, Parfeny Pavlovich mathematician, educator
Sawyer, Thomas C. congressman
†Saxon, Janet D. federal government official
Saxton, H. James congressman
†Saxton, James congressman
Sayre, Robert Marion ambassador
Sazima, Henry John oral and maxillofacial surgery educator
Scali, John Alfred journalist
Scalia, Antonin U.S. supreme court justice
Scanlon, Patrick Michael lawyer
Scanlon, Terrence Maurice research foundation administrator
†Scarborough, Joe congressman
Scarbrough, Frank Edward government official
Scassa, Eugene L. ambassador
Schachter, Barry economist
Schad, Theodore MacNeeve science research administrator, consultant
Schaefer, Dan L. congressman
Schall, Alvin Anthony judge
Schapiro, Mary federal agency administrator, lawyer
Scharff, Joseph Laurent lawyer
Schechter, Geraldine Poppa hematologist
†Scheibel, James Allen volunteer service executive
Scheibel, Kenneth Maynard journalist
Schenkel, Suzanne Chance natural resource specialist
Schenker, Carl Richard, Jr. lawyer
Scheppach, Raymond Carl, Jr. association executive, economist
Schiavo, A. Mary Fackler federal official, lawyer
Schiavone, Louise L. political correspondent, news analyst
Schick, Michael William public relations executive
Schiff, Margaret Scott newspaper publishing executive
Schiff, Stefan Otto zoologist, educator
Schiff, Steven Harvey congressman, lawyer
Schifter, Richard lawyer, government official
Schildhause, Sol lawyer
Schlagel, Richard H. philosophy educator
Schlesinger, B. Frank architect, educator
Schlesinger, James Rodney economist
Schley, Wayne A. postal rate commissioner
†Schlickeisen, Rodger O. non-profit environmental organization executive

Schlossberg, Stephen I. management consultant
Schmeltzer, Edward lawyer
Schmidt, Berlie Louis agricultural research administrator
Schmidt, John R. lawyer
Schmidt, Paul Wickham lawyer
Schmidt, Richard Marten, Jr. lawyer
Schneider, Keith Hilary news correspondent, journalist
Schneider, Mark Lewis government official
Schneider, Matthew Roger lawyer
Schoenbaum, Samuel English educator
Schoenberg, Mark George government agency administrator
Schoenberger, James Edwin federal agency administrator
Schorr, Lisbeth Bamberger child and family policy analyst, author, educator
Schosberg, Paul Alan trade association executive
Schotland, Roy Arnold lawyer, educator
Schotland, Sara Deutch lawyer
Schotta, Charles economist, government official
Schrag, Philip Gordon law educator
Schram, Martin Jay journalist
Schreiner, George E. nephrologist, educator, writer
Schriever, Bernard Adolph management consultant
Schroeder, Patricia Scott (Mrs. James White Schroeder) congresswoman
Schroeter, Richard B. federal official
Schropp, James Howard lawyer
Schubert, Richard Francis foundation administrator
Schuck, Victoria political science educator
†Schuker, Jill Anita federal official, consultant
Schultze, Charles Louis economist, educator
Schumer, Charles Ellis congressman
Schwaab, Richard Lewis lawyer, educator
Schwartz, Amy Elizabeth editorial writer, columnist
Schwartz, Daniel C. lawyer
Schwartz, Harry Kane lawyer
Schwartz, Marshall Zane pediatric surgeon
Schwartz, Richard Brenton English language educator, university dean, writer
Schwartz, Robert S. lawyer
Schwartz, Victor Elliot lawyer
Schwarz, Carl W. lawyer
Schweitzer, William H. lawyer
Sclafani, Frances Ann lawyer, federal agency executive
Scorca, Marc Azzolini arts administrator
Scott, Audrey Ebba federal agency administrator
Scott, Catherine Dorothy librarian, information consultant
Scott, Edward Philip lawyer
Scott, Irene Feagin federal judge
Scott, Joyce Alaine university official
Scott, Michael lawyer
Scott, Raymond Peter William chemistry research educator, writer
Scott, Robert Cortez congressman, lawyer
Scott, Thomas Jefferson, Jr. lawyer, electrical engineer
†Scouten, Rex W. curator
Scowcroft, Brent retired air force officer, government official
Scrimenti, Belinda Jayne lawyer
Sczudlo, Raymond Stanley lawyer
Seale, William Edward finance educator
Searing, Marjory Ellen government official, economist
Sears, John Patrick lawyer
Sears, Mary Helen lawyer
†Seastrand, Andrea H. congresswoman
Seelig, Steven Alfred government financial executive
†Seelman, Katherine Dolores institute administrator
Segal, Donald E. lawyer
Seidel, Milton Joseph government administrator
Seidman, Ellen Shapiro lawyer, government official
Seidman, L(ewis) William television commentator
Seidman, Ricki federal official
Seldman, Neil Norman cultural organization administrator
Selin, Ivan federal official
Sellin, Theodore foreign service officer, consultant
Seltzer, Bradley Marshall lawyer
Semas, Philip Wayne editor
Sender, Stanton P. lawyer
Sensenbrenner, Frank James, Jr. congressman, lawyer
Sentelle, David Bryan federal judge
Serafin, Barry D. television news correspondent
Sernoff, Louis R. lawyer
Serrano, Jose E. congressman
Sesno, Frank executive editor
Sethness, Charles Olin international financial official
Sever, Tom labor union administrator
Severino, Roberto foreign language educator, academic administration executive
Sewell, John Williamson research association executive
Seymour, Jon federal government official
†Shadegg, John B. congressman
Shafer, Jeffrey Richard federal official
Shafer, Raymond Philip lawyer, business executive
Shaffer, Jay Christopher lawyer
Shaheen, Michael Edmund, Jr. lawyer, government official
Shah-Jahan, M. M. economist
Shalala, Donna Edna federal official, political scientist, educator, university chancellor
Shales, Thomas William writer, journalist, television and film critic
Shalowitz, Erwin Emmanuel civil engineer
Shalwitz, Howard theater director, actor
Shank, Fred Ross federal agency administrator
Shanker, Albert labor union official
Shanks, Hershel editor, writer
Shanks, Robert Bruce lawyer
Shannon, Donald Hawkins retired newspaperman
Shapiro, David Israel lawyer
Shapiro, George Howard lawyer
Shapiro, Michael Henry government executive
Sharpe, Rochelle Phyllis journalist
Shattuck, John H. F. federal official
Shaw, Bernard television journalist
Shaw, E. Clay, Jr. (Clay Shaw) congressman
Shaw, Gaylord newspaper executive
Shaw, Russell Burnham association executive, author
Shaw, Sallye Brown women's health nurse
Shaw, William Frederick statistician
Shawhan, Samuel Frazier, Jr. telecommunications executive
Shays, Christopher congressman
Shea, Donald William career officer
Shearer, P. Scott government relations professional
Sheehan, Michael Terrence arts administrator, historian, consultant
Sheehan, Neil reporter, scholarly writer
Sheehy, Pat Murphy artistic director
Sheinbaum, Gilbert Harold international management consultant
Shelby, Richard Craig senator, former congressman
Shelley, Herbert Carl lawyer
Shelly, Christine Deborah foreign service officer
Shelton, Joanna Reed economist
†Shelton, Sally Angela political scientist, writer, educator, editor
Shenefield, John Hale lawyer
Shepherd, Karen congresswoman
Sher, Linda Rosenberg lawyer
Sherer, Samuel Ayers lawyer, urban planning consultant
Sherifis, Michael Eleftheriou ambassador
Sherman, Charles Edwin broadcasting executive, educator
Sherman, George M. manufacturing company executive
Sherman, Wendy Ruth federal agency administrator
Sherry, Robert Joseph lawyer
Sherwin, Michael Dennis government official
Sherzer, Harvey Gerald lawyer
Shestack, Alan museum administrator
Shields, Perry federal judge
Shih, J. Chung-wen Chinese language educator
†Shimberg, Steven Jay lawyer
Shine, Kenneth Irwin cardiologist, educator
Shiner, Josette Sheeran editor
Shinn, David Hamilton diplomat
Shinn, Linda Jane nurse, association executive
Shlaudeman, Harry Walter retired ambassador
Shniderman, Harry Louis lawyer
Shogan, Robert news correspondent
Shon, Frederick John nuclear engineer
Shook, Langley R. lawyer
Short, Elizabeth M. physician, educator, federal agency administrator
Short, Thomas Edward, Jr. educator
Shribman, David Marks editor
Shrier, Adam Louis investment firm executive
Shrinsky, Jason Lee lawyer
Shriver, Eunice Mary Kennedy (Mrs. Robert Sargent Shriver, Jr.) civic worker
Shriver, Robert Sargent, Jr. lawyer
†Shriver, Sargent organization executive, lawyer, ambassador
Shulman, Stephen Neal lawyer
Shuman, Michael Harrison lawyer, policy analyst
Shumate, John Page diplomat
Shurtleff, Leonard Grant ambassador
Shuster, Bud congressman
Siciliano, Rocco Carmine institute executive
Sidey, Hugh Swanson correspondent
Sidransky, Herschel pathologist
Siegel, Allen George lawyer
Siegel, Frederic Richard geology educator
Siegel, Jack S. federal official
Siegel, Lloyd Harvey architect, real estate developer, consultant
Siegel, Richard David lawyer, former government official
Siegel, Robert Charles broadcast journalist
Siemer, Deanne Clemence lawyer
Sierck, Alexander Wentworth lawyer
Sievers, Robert H. wholesale distributing company executive
Sieverts, Frank Arne government official
Siggins, Jack Arthur librarian
Sikes, Alfred C. communications executive
Silberg, Jay Eliot lawyer
Silberman, Rosalie Gaull federal official
Silby, Donald Wayne investment executive, entrepreneur
Sills, Hilary H. public relations executive
Silva, Omega Logan physician
Silver, Daniel B. lawyer
Silver, David financial executive, lawyer
Silver, Harry R. lawyer
†Silver, Jonathan Moses government official
Silverman, Alvin Michaels public relations consultant
Silverman, Ira Norton news producer
Simchak, Matthew Stephen lawyer
Simes, Dimitri Konstantin international affairs expert and educator
Simko, Jan English and foreign language literature educator
Simmons, Caroline Thompson civic worker
Simmons, Edwin Howard marine corps officer, historian
Simmons, Richard De Lacey mass media executive
†Simon, Gregory advisor to the Vice President
Simon, Jeanne Hurley federal commissioner
Simon, Justin Daniel lawyer
Simon, Karla Weber law educator
Simon, Kenneth Mark lawyer
Simon, Paul senator, educator, author
Simon, Rita James legal educator
Simon, Roger newspaper columnist, author
Simons, Barbara M. lawyer
Simons, Lawrence Brook lawyer
Simopoulos, Artemis Panageotis physician, educator
Simowitz, Lee H. lawyer
Simpson, Alan Kooi senator
Simpson, Carole Estelle broadcast journalist
Simpson, John W. lawyer
Simpson, Louis A. insurance company executive
Simpson, Michael Marcial science specialist, consultant
Sims, Joe lawyer
Sims, Robert Bell professional society administrator, public affairs official, newspaper publisher
Singer, Daniel Morris lawyer
Singer, Maxine Frank biochemist
Singer, Norman H. lawyer
Singer, Suzanne Fried editor
Singer, Thomas Kenyon international business consultant, farmer
Singleton, Harry Michael lawyer
Sinkford, Jeanne Craig dentist, educator
Sisco, Joseph John management consultant, corporation director, educator, government official
Sisisky, Norman congressman, soft drink bottler
Sivasubramanian, Kolinjavadi Nagarajan neonatologist, educator
Skadden, Donald Harvey professional society executive, accounting educator
Skaggs, David E. congressman
Skall, Gregg P. lawyer
Skeen, Joseph Richard congressman
Skelton, Isaac Newton, IV (Ike Skelton) congressman
Skene, G(eorge) Neil publisher, lawyer
Skinner, William Polk lawyer
Skog, Laurence Edgar botanist
Skol, Michael diplomat
†Skolfield, Melissa T. government official
Skolnik, Merrill I. electrical engineer
Slade, John Danton lobbyist, radio talk show host
Slagle, Larry B. human resources specialist
†Slate, Martin Ira pension benefit executive
Slater, Doris Ernestine Wilke business executive
Slater, Rodney E. federal administrator
Slatkin, Nora government official
Slattery, James Charles lawyer, real estate executive
Slaughter, Louise McIntosh congresswoman
Sloyan, Patrick Joseph journalist
Sly, Ridge Michael physician, educator
Small, Lawrence M. financial organization executive
Smedley, Lawrence Thomas organization executive
Smeeton, Thomas Rooney congressional staff director
Smiley, D. E. petroleum company executive
Smilow, Michael A. mortgage company exccutive
Smith, Alan W., Jr. management consultant
Smith, Anne Bowman academic administrator, editor
†Smith, Barbara Jeanne librarian
Smith, Brian William lawyer, former government official
Smith, Bruce David archaeologist
Smith, Bruce R. English language educator
Smith, Christopher Henry congressman
Smith, Dallas R. federal official
Smith, Daniel Clifford lawyer
Smith, Dean communications advisor, arbitrator
Smith, Elaine Diana foreign service officer
Smith, Geoffrey R.W. lawyer
Smith, George Patrick, II lawyer, educator
Smith, Jack Carl foreign trade consultant
Smith, Jack Prescott journalist
Smith, John Lewis, III lawyer
Smith, Lamar Seeligson congressman
Smith, Lee Elton surgery educator, retired military officer
Smith, Leighton Warren, Jr. naval officer
Smith, Loren Allan federal judge
Smith, Marshall Savidge government official, academic dean, educator
Smith, Nick congressman, farmer
Smith, Patricia Grace government official
Smith, Philip Meek science policy consultant, writer
Smith, Richard Melvyn government official
Smith, Robert Clinton senator
Smith, Roy Philip federal judge
Smith, Stephen Grant journalist
Smith, Stuart Seaborne writer, government official, union official
Smith, Terence Fitzgerald television news correspondent
Smith, William Dee naval officer
Smits, Helen Lida public adminstrator, physician, educator
Smoot, Oliver Reed, Jr. lawyer, trade association executive
Smuckler, Ralph Herbert university dean, political science educator
Smyth, Paul Burton lawyer
Smythe-Haith, Mabel Murphy consultant on African economic development, speaker, writer
Sneed, James H. lawyer
Snider, Jerome Guy lawyer
Snowden, Frank Martin, Jr. classics educator
Snowe, Olympia J. senator
Snyder, Allen Roger lawyer
Snyder, Daniel James military career officer
Sockwell, Oliver R., Jr. financial services company executive
Soderberg, David Lawrence chemist
Soderberg, Nancy federal agency administrator
Sohn, Louis Bruno lawyer, educator
Sokler, Bruce Douglas lawyer
Soldo, Beth Jean demography educator, researcher
Solomon, George M. newspaper editor
Solomon, Gerald Brooks Hunt congressman
Solomon, Henry university dean
Solomon, Richard Harvey political scientist
Solomon, Robert economist
Solomon, Sean Carl geophysicist, lab director
Solomons, Mark Elliott lawyer
Somerville, Walter Raleigh, Jr. government official
Sommer, Alphonse Adam, Jr. lawyer
Sommerfelt, Soren Christian foreign affairs, international trade consultant, former Norwegian diplomat, lawyer
Sonde, Theodore Irwin lawyer
Sonnenfeldt, Helmut former government official, educator, consultant, author
Sopher, Vicki Elaine museum director
Sorensen, John Noble mechanical and nuclear engineer
Sormani, Charles Robert insurance company executive, actuary
†Souder, Mark Edward congressman
Spaeder, Roger Campbell lawyer
†Spagnolo, Samuel Vincent medical educator
Spangler, Scott Michael private investor
Sparrowe, Rollin D. wildlife biologist
Spears, Gregory Luttrell journalist
Specter, Arlen senator
Spector, Eleanor Ruth government executive
Spence, Floyd Davidson congressman
Spence, Sandra association executive
Spencer, Samuel lawyer
Sperling, Godfrey, Jr. journalist
Spero, Joan Edelman federal agency administrator
Sphar, Raymond Leslie, Jr. physician, research administrator
Spingler, Frank Joseph lawyer
Spiro, Benjamin Paul economist, consultant
Splete, Allen Peterjohn association executive, educator
Spoon, Alan Gary communications and publishing executive
Sporkin, Stanley federal judge
Spratt, John McKee, Jr. congressman, lawyer
Spreiregen, Paul David architect, planner, author
†Springer, Fred Everett federal agency administrator
Springer, James van Roden lawyer
Springer, Michael Louis federal agency administrator
Sprott, John T. ambassador
Squier, Robert Dave political consultant, documentary filmmaker
Staats, Elmer Boyd foundation executive, former government official
†Stackpole, Laurie Eveleth library director
Stafford, Barbara Rose lawyer
Stahr, Elvis J(acob), Jr. lawyer, conservationist, educator
Stamberg, Susan Levitt radio broadcaster
Stanford, Dennis Joe archaeologist, museum curator
Stanley, Daniel Jean geological oceanographer, senior scientist
Stanley, Ronald Alwin environmental scientist, poet
Stanley, Timothy Wadsworth economist
Stanley, William Robert federal agency official
Stansbury, Philip Roger lawyer
Stanton, Robert historic site director
Stanwick, Tad systems engineering and business management executive
Stapleton, Jean think-tank executive
Stark, Fortney Hillman (Pete Stark) congressman
Stark, Nathan Julius association administrator, lawyer
†Stauber, Karl Neill federal executive
Stauffer, Ronald Eugene lawyer
Stavrou, Nikolaos Athanasios political science educator
Stayin, Randolph John lawyer
†Stayman, Allen Paul government executive
Steadman, Charles Walters lawyer, corporate executive, writer
Steadman, John Montague judge
Stearns, Clifford Bundy congressman, business executive
Stearns, James Gerry retired securities company executive
Steel, Adrian L., Jr. lawyer
Steele, Ana Mercedes government official
Steele, John Lawrence journalist
Steiger, Janet Dempsey government official
Steigman, Andrew L. academic dean
Stein, Herbert economist
Stein, Michael Henry lawyer
Steinbach, Sheldon Elliot lawyer
Steinberg, Jonathan Robert federal judge
Steinberg, Marcia Irene science foundation program director
Steinberg, Mark Robert lawyer
Steiner, Gilbert Yale political scientist
Steinhardt, Ralph Gustav, III law educator
Stemmler, Edward Joseph physician, retired association executive, retired academic dean
Stenholm, Charles W. congressman
Stephanopoulos, George Robert federal official
Stephens, James M. federal agency administrator
Stephens, Jay B. lawyer
Stephens, John Frank association executive, researcher
Stepp, Laura Sessions journalist
Steptoe, Mary Lou lawyer
Stern, Carl Leonard former news correspondent, federal official
Stern, Gerald Mann lawyer
Stern, Paula international trade advisor
Stern, Samuel Alan lawyer
Sterner, Michael Edmund international affairs consultant
†Sterrett, Samuel Black lawyer, former judge
Stevens, George, Jr. film and television producer, writer, director
Stevens, Herbert Francis lawyer, law educator
Stevens, John Paul U.S. supreme court justice
Stevens, Milton Lewis, Jr. trombonist
Stevens, Roger Lacey theatrical producer
Stevens, Theodore Fulton senator
Stevenson, A. Brockie artist
Stevenson, Eric Van Cortlandt mortgage banker, real estate executive, lawyer
Stevenson, John Reese lawyer
Stevenson, Russell B., Jr. lawyer
Stever, Horton Guyford aerospace scientist and engineer, educator, consultant
†Stewart, Dorothy K. educator, librarian
Stewart, George Cope, III (Scoop Stewart) lawyer
Stewart, John Daugherty publishing company executive
Stewart, John Irwin, Jr. lawyer
†Stewart, Julie nonprofit organization executive
Stewart, Ruth Ann public policy analyst, library administrator
Stillman, Elinor Hadley lawyer
†Stillman, Robert Donald government official
†Stiner, Carl Wade army officer
Stock, Stuart Chase lawyer
†Stockman, Stephen E. congressman
Stoer, Eric F. lawyer
Stokes, Arnold Paul mathematics educator
Stokes, Louis congressman
Stoll, Louise Frankel federal official
Stoll, Richard G(iles) lawyer
Stollman, Israel city planner
Stone, Donald Raymond lawyer
Stone, Elizabeth Wenger retired dean
Stone, Jeremy Judah association executive
Stone, Roger David environmentalist
Stone, Russell A. sociology educator
Stonehill, Robert Michael federal agency administrator
Stoner, Allan L. science foundation director
Stoner, John Richard federal government executive
Stookey, Laurence Hull clergyman, theology educator
Storing, Paul Edward foreign service officer
†Stout, Anthony Carder publisher
Strachan, David E. trade association executive
Stranahan, Robert Paul, Jr. lawyer
†Straub, Chester John, Jr. government official
†Strauss, David Vice Presidential Office official
Strauss, Elliott Bowman economic development consultant, retired naval officer
Strauss, Stanley Robert lawyer
Strickler, Frank Hunter lawyer
Stromberg, Clifford Douglas lawyer
Strong, Henry foundation executive
Stropp, Robert H., Jr. lawyer
Stuart, Raymond Wallace lawyer
Stuart, Sandra Kaplan federal official
Studds, Gerry Eastman congressman
Studeman, William Oliver naval officer
†Studley, Jamienne Shayne lawyer
Stump, Bob congressman
Stumpf, Mark Howard lawyer
Stuntz, Linda Gillespie government official, lawyer
Stupak, Bart T. congressman, lawyer
Sturtevant, William Curtis anthropologist
Sugarman, Jule M. children's services consultant, former public administrator
†Sugrue, Thomas Joseph lawyer
Sullivan, Brendan V., Jr. lawyer
Sullivan, Charles university dean, educator, author
Sullivan, Dennis F. transportation company executive, engineer
Sullivan, Eugene Raymond federal judge
Sullivan, Gordon R. career officer
Sullivan, John Fox publisher
Sullivan, Kathryn D. geologist, astronaut
Sullivan, Timothy lawyer
Sultan, Terrie Frances curator
Summerford, Ben Long retired artist, educator
Summers, Lawrence under secretary treasury department
Sundquist, James Lloyd political scientist
Sundquist, Maria Alexandra diplomat
Sunley, Emil McKee economist

Whiting, Richard Albert *lawyer*
Whitmore, Frank Clifford, Jr. *geologist*
Whyte, Martin King *sociology and Chinese studies educator*
†Wicker, Roger F. *congressman*
Widnall, Sheila Evans *federal official, air force officer, former aeronautical educator, former university official*
Widner, Ralph Randolph *civic executive*
Wiedemann, Kent M. *federal official*
Wiegley, Roger Douglas *lawyer*
Wiese, John Paul *federal judge*
Wilburn, Mary Nelson *lawyer, writer, educator*
Wilcher, LaJuana Sue *lawyer*
Wilcher, Shirley J. *lawyer*
Wilcox, Philip Connacher, Jr. *foreign service officer*
Wilensky, Gail Roggin *economist*
Wiley, Richard Emerson *lawyer*
Wilkinson, Christopher Foster *toxicologist, educator*
Wilkinson, John Burke *former government official, novelist, biographer*
Wilkinson, Ronald Sterne *science administrator, environmentalist, historian*
Will, George Frederick *editor, political columnist, news commentator*
Willard, Richard Kennon *lawyer*
Willenbrock, Frederick Karl *engineer, educator*
Willett, Edward Farrand, Jr. *lawyer*
Willging, Paul Raymond *trade association executive*
Williams, Abiodun *international relations educator*
Williams, Arthur E. *federal agency administrator*
Williams, B. John, Jr. *lawyer, former federal judge*
Williams, Eddie Nathan *research institution executive*
Williams, John Edward *lawyer*
Williams, Karen Hastie *lawyer*
†Williams, Lawrence Floyd *conservation organization official*
Williams, Margaret *federal official*
Williams, Maurice Jacoutot *development organization executive*
Williams, Neville *international development organization executive*
Williams, Pat *congressman*
Williams, Paul *federal agency administrator*
Williams, Richard Llewellyn *diplomat*
Williams, Ronald L. *pharmaceutical association executive*
Williams, Stephen Fain *federal judge*
Williams, Sylvia Hill *museum director*
Williams, T. Raymond *lawyer*
Williamson, Edwin Dargan *lawyer, former federal official*
Williamson, Richard Hall *association executive*
Williamson, Thomas Samuel, Jr. *lawyer*
Willis, Clayton *broadcaster, corporation executive, former government official, educator, arts consultant, photojournalist, lecturer*
†Willis, Mary Catherine *brigadier general*
Willmore, Robert Louis *lawyer*
Wilson, Carolyn Ross *school administrator*
Wilson, Charles (Charlie Wilson) *congressman*
Wilson, Ewen Maclellan *economist*
Wilson, Gary Dean *lawyer*
Wilson, Glen Parten *association administrator*
Wilson, Joseph Charles, IV *ambassador*
†Wilson, Norman Louis *psychiatrist, educator*
Wilson, R. Merinda D. *lawyer*
Wilson, Robert Spencer *magazine editor*
Wince-Smith, Deborah L. *federal agency administrator*
Wine, L. Mark *lawyer*
Winfield, Susan Rebecca *judge*
Winnefeld, James Alexander *defense analyst, former naval officer, author*
Winston, Judith Ann *lawyer*
Winter, Andrew J. *ambassador*
Winter, Douglas E. *lawyer, writer*
Winter, Harvey John *government official*
Winter, Roger Paul *government official*
Winter, Thomas Swanson *editor, newspaper executive*
Wintrol, John Patrick *lawyer*
Winzenried, Jesse David *retired petroleum executive*
Wirth, Timothy Endicott *federal official, former senator*
Wirtz, William Willard *lawyer*
Wise, Robert Ellsworth, Jr. (Bob Ellsworth) *congressman*
Wiseman, Alan M(itchell) *lawyer*
Wiseman, Laurence Donald *foundation executive*
Wisniewski, John William *mining engineer, bank engineering executive*
Wiss, Marcia A. *lawyer*
Witcover, Jules Joseph *newspaper columnist, author*
Witherspoon, Sharon *lawyer*
Withrow, Mary Ellen *treasurer of United States*
Witt, James Lee *federal agency administrator*
Wolanin, Barbara Ann Boese *art curator, art historian*
†Wolanin, Thomas Richard *federal government official*
Wolf, Frank R. *congressman, lawyer*
Wolfe, Janice E. *business development executive*
Wolfe, Leslie R. *think-tank executive*
Wolff, Alan William *lawyer*
Wolff, Elroy Harris *lawyer*
Wolfman, Brunetta Reid *education educator*
Wollenberg, J. Roger *lawyer*
Wolters, Curt Cornelis Frederik *foreign service officer*
Wood, John Martin *lawyer*
†Wood, Robert Winfield *science administrator, biophysicist*
Woodall, Samuel Roy, Jr. *trade association executive*
Woodruff, Judy Carline *broadcast journalist*
Woods, Harriett Ruth *academic administrator*
Woods, Millicent Wasell *federal official*
Woods, Walter Ralph *animal scientist, research administrator*
Woodward, Robert Forbes *retired government official, consultant*
Woodward, Robert Upshur *newspaper reporter, writer*
Woodward, Susan Ellen *economist, federal official*
Woolsey, Lynn *congresswoman*
Woolsey, R. James, Jr. *federal agency administrator*
Wooten, James Terrell *journalist*
Worden, Joan M. *public relations executive*
Work, Charles Robert *lawyer*
Work, Jane Magruder *professional society administrator*
Worsley, James Randolph, Jr. *lawyer*
Worthington, John Rice *communications company executive, lawyer*
Worthy, K(enneth) Martin *lawyer*
Worthy, Patricia Morris *municipal official, lawyer*
Wortley, George Cornelius *business consultant, investor*
Woteki, Catherine Ellen *nutritionist*
Wouk, Herman *writer*
Wraase, Dennis Richard *utilities company executive, accountant*
Wright, Lawrence A. *federal judge*
Wright, Thomas William Dunstan *architect*
Wruble, Bernhardt Karp *lawyer*
Wurtzel, Alan Leon *retail company executive*
Wyatt, Richard Jed *psychiatrist, educator*
Wyatt, Wilson Watkins, Jr. *finance association and public relations executive*
Wyden, Ronald Lee *congressman*
Wynn, Albert Russell *congressman*
†Wynn, William Harrison *union official*
Wyss, John Benedict *lawyer*
Yablon, Jeffery Lee *lawyer*
†Yager, Milan P. *government agency administrator*
†Yakeley, Jay B., III *naval officer*
Yancik, Joseph John *government official*
Yang, Tony Tien Sheng *engineering educator*
Yannucci, Thomas David *lawyer*
Yardley, Jonathan *journalist, columnist*
Yarowsky, Jonathan R. *lawyer*
Yates, Sidney Richard *congressman, lawyer*
Yatsevitch, Gratian Michael *retired army officer, diplomat, engineer*
†Yellen, Janet Louise *government official, economics educator*
Yerkes, David Norton *architect*
†Yim, Joan B. *federal agency administrator*
Yochelson, Ellis L(eon) *paleontologist*
Yochelson, John *political economist*
Yochim, Marie Hirst *retired association executive*
Yock, Robert John *federal judge*
Yoder, Hatten Schuyler, Jr. *petrologist*
Yoder, Ronnie A. *federal administrative law judge*
†Yoshikawa, Thomas T. *internist*
Yost, Paul Alexander, Jr. *foundation executive, retired coast guard officer*
Young, C. W. (Bill Young) *congressman*
Young, Donald Alan *physician*
Young, Donald E. *congressman*
Young, Kenneth Evans *educational consultant*
†Young, Loretta *government official*
Young, Patrick *editor*
Young, Peter Robert *librarian*
Young, William Fielding *lawyer*
Yulish, Charles Barry *public affairs executive*
Yurow, John Jesse *lawyer*
Yuspeh, Alan Ralph *lawyer*
Yzaguirre, Raul Humberto *civil rights administrator*
Zausner, L. Andrew *lawyer*
Zax, Leonard A. *lawyer*
Zeifang, Donald P. *lawyer*
Zelnick, Carl Robert *Congressional correspondent*
Zenowitz, Allan Ralph *government official*
Zevnik, Paul A. *lawyer*
Zielinski, Charles Anthony *lawyer*
Ziglar, James W. *former federal official, lawyer, investment banker*
Zimmer, Richard Alan *congressman, lawyer*
Zimmerman, Edwin Morton *lawyer*
Zimmerman, Hyman Joseph *internist, educator*
Zimmerman, John H. *communications company executive*
Zimmerman, Richard Gayford *journalist*
Zion, Roger H. *consulting firm executive, former congressman*
Zipp, Joel Frederick *lawyer*
†Zitnay, George Albert *foundation executive*
Zlatoper, Ronald Joseph *career officer*
Zoeller, Jack Carl *financial executive*
†Zonana, Victor F. *government agency official, writer, communications executive*
Zuck, Alfred Miller *association executive*
Zuckman, Harvey Lyle *legal educator*
Zweben, Murray *lawyer, consultant*
Zwick, Charles J. *think-tank executive*
Zwick, Kenneth Lowell *lawyer*

FLORIDA

Alachua
Gaines, Weaver Henderson *lawyer*
Gifford, George E. *immunology and medical microbiology educator*
Marston, Robert Quarles *university president*
Schneider, Richard T(heodore) *optics research executive, engineer*
Thornton, J. Ronald *university administrator*

Altamonte Springs
†Kirchman, Kenneth Paul *computer software services company executive*

Amelia Island
Harman, John Robert, Jr. *management consultant*

Anna Maria
Aubry, Eugene Edwards *architect*
Kaiser, Albert Farr *diversified corporation executive*

Apopka
Brandner, J. William *publishing company executive, insurance company executive*
Rufenacht, Roger Allen *accounting educator*
Shrum, Grant Arthur *non-profit organization executive*

Arcadia
Davis, Bruce Livingston, Jr. *retired accountant*
Schmidt, Harold Eugene *real estate company executive*
Turnbull, David John (Chief Piercing Eyes-Penn) *cultural association executive*

Atlantic Beach
Engelmann, Rudolph Herman *electronics consultant*
Herge, Henry Curtis, Sr. *education educator, dean emeritus*
Wheeler, William Crawford *agricultural engineer, educator*
Zechella, Alexander Philip *oil company executive, former naval officer*

Atlantis
Gough, Carolyn Harley *library director*
Minshall, Drexel David *retired manufacturing company executive*
Newmark, Emanuel *ophthalmologist*

Aventura
Kliger, Milton Richard *financial services executive*
Peshkin, Samuel David *lawyer*
†Susser, Allen *restaurateur, chef*

Avon Park
Cornelius, Catherine Petrey *college president*

Babson Park
Cloud, Linda Beal *retired secondary school educator*
Morrison, Kenneth Douglas *newspaper columnist*

Bal Harbour
Bernay, Betti *artist*
Field, Cyrus Adams *lawyer*
Gray, Phyllis Anne *librarian*
Hastings, Lawrence Vaeth *lawyer, physician, educator*
Horton, Jeanette *municipal government official*
Radford, Linda Robertson *psychologist*
Rosenbluth, Morton *periodontist, educator*

Bartow
McFarlin, Richard Francis *industrial chemist, researcher*

Bay Pines
†Johnson, David Porter *infectious diseases physician*
Keskiner, Ali *psychiatrist*
Robson, Martin Cecil *surgery educator, plastic surgeon*
†Stewart, Jonathan Taylor *psychiatrist, educator*
Weaver, Thomas Harold *health facility administrator*

Bayonet Point
Smith, Frank Edward *publisher, editor*

Belleair
Dexter, Helen Louise *dermatologist, consultant*

Belleair Beach
Fuentes, Martha Ayers *playwright*

Beverly Hills
Larsen, Erik *art history educator*

Boca Grande
Baldwin, William Howard *lawyer, retired foundation executive*
Brock, Mitchell *lawyer*
Dyche, David Bennett, Jr. *management consultant*
Frazetta, Frank *artist*
Nimitz, Chester William, Jr. *manufacturing company executive*
VanItallie, Theodore Bertus *physician*

Boca Raton
Africk, Jack *duty free company executive*
Albrecht, Arthur John *advertising agency executive*
Alvarado, Ricardo Raphael *retired corporate executive, lawyer*
Amen, Irving *artist*
Apelian, Clover B. *non-profit management consultant*
Arden, Eugene *retired university provost*
Arnold, Walter Martin *vocational education educator*
Arockiasamy, Madasamy *engineering educator*
Barton, William Blackburn *retired lawyer*
Baumgarten, Diana Virginia *geriatrics nurse*
Beber, Robert H. *lawyer, financial services executive*
Beck, Jan Scott *lawyer*
Bettmann, Otto Ludwig *picture archivist, graphic historian*
Blanton, Jeremy *dance company director*
Boer, F. Peter *chemical company executive*
Bolduc, J. P. *specialty chemicals and specialized health care company executive*
Bradley, George H. *furniture company executive*
Bressler, Steven L. *cognitive neuroscientist*
Broich, William John, Jr. *financial executive*
Burns, Gerald Phillip *education educator*
Butler, J. Murfree *chemical company executive*
Camilleri, Michael *lawyer, educator*
Cannon, Herbert Seth *investment banker*
Carraher, Charles Eugene, Jr. *chemistry educator, dean*
Catanese, Anthony James *academic administrator*
Chryssafopoulos, Nicholas *civil engineer*
Cohn, Jess Victor *psychiatrist*
Costello, Albert Joseph *diversified consumer products executive*
Deppe, Henry Adolph *insurance company executive*
Dorfman, Allen Bernard *international management consultant*
Dunhill, Robert W. *advertising direct mail executive*
Elliott, Robert M., Jr. *retail executive*
Epstein, Barry R. *public relations counselor*
Erdman, Joseph *lawyer*
Evert, Christine Marie (Chris Evert) *retired professional tennis player*
Fengler, John Peter *television producer, director, advertising executive*
Fetter, Richard Elwood *retired industrial company executive*
Feuerlein, Willy John Arthur *economist, educator*
Fey, Dorothy (Mrs. George Jay Fey) *former association executive*
Finegold, Ronald *computer service executive*
Finkl, Charles William, II *geologist, educator*
Frank, Stanley Donald *publishing company executive*
Garzarelli, Elaine Marie *brokerage house executive, economist*
Gold, Catherine Anne Dower *music history educator*
Goldstein, Bernard *transportation company executive*
Gordon, Marjorie *lyric coloratura soprano, opera producer*
Gralla, Eugene *natural gas company executive*
Hedrick, Frederic Cleveland, Jr. *lawyer*
Herst, Herman, Jr. *writer*
Hille, Stanley James *university dean*
Houraney, William George *company executive*
Ingwersen, Martin Lewis *shipyard executive*
Jaffe, Leonard Sigmund *financial executive*
Jessup, Joe Lee *business educator, management consultant*
Kelley, Eugene John *business educator*
Keyes, Daniel *author*
Klein, Robert *manufacturing company executive*
Kramer, Cecile E. *retired medical librarian*
Krause, Heinz Werner *computer and communications executive*
Lagin, Neil *property management executive*
Lampi, Juanita *principal*
Latané, Bibb *social psychologist*
Leahy, William F. *insurance company executive, lawyer*
†Lemasters, John N., III *management and marketing consultant*
Lin, Y. K. *engineer, educator*
Lipsey, John C. (Jack Lipsey) *insurance company executive*
Lucà-Moretti, Maurizio *scientist, nutrition researcher*
Lynn, Eugene Matthew *insurance company executive*
MacIntyre, A(lfonso) Everette *lawyer*
Mandor, Leonard Stewart *real estate company executive*
McLeod, John Wishart *architect*
Miller, Eugene *business educator, university official*
Miller, Kenneth Roy *management consultant*
Mills, Agnes Eunice Karlin *artist, printmaker, sculptor*
Mirkin, Abraham Jonathan *surgeon*
Monroe, William Lewis *human resources executive*
Murray, John Ralph *former college president*
Napsky, Martin Ben *insurance executive*
Nystrom, John Warren *geographer, educator*
Ortlip, Paul Daniel *artist*
Posner, Sidney *advertising executive*
Rasmussen, Lynn C. *fashion accessories company executive*
Reid, George Kell *biology educator, researcher, author*
Reinstein, Joel *lawyer*
Richardson, R(oss) Fred(erick) *insurance executive*
Rodman, R. Arlene *journalist*
Rosenthal, Myron Martin *retired electrical engineer, educator, author*
Rosner, M. Norton *business systems and financial services company executive*
Ross, Donald Edward *university administrator*
Rothbaum, Ira *advertising and marketing executive*
Rukeyser, M. S., Jr. *television consultant, writer*
Russo, Kathleen Marie *art educator*
Samuels, William Mason *physiology association executive*
Sarna, Nahum Mattathias *biblical studies educator*
Schaaf, Martha Eckert *author, library director, musician*
Selby, Roger Lowell *museum director*
Shane, Ronald *financial company executive*
Sigel, Marshall Elliot *financial consultant*
Stein, Irvin *orthopaedic surgeon, educator*
Tennies, Robert Hunter *headmaster*
Turano, Emanuel Nicolas *architect*
Turbeville, Gus *emeritus college president*
Turner, Lisa Phillips *human resources executive*
Wallis, John James (Jimmy Wallis) *entertainer, ventriloquist, video production executive*
Walsh, Robert Charles *chemical company executive*
Wiesenfeld, John Richard *chemistry educator*
Wolgin, David Lewis *psychology educator*

Bonifay
Quattlebaum, Walter Emmett, Jr. *telephone company executive*

Bonita Springs
Birky, John Edward *banker, consultant, financial advisor*
Cairns, Raymond Eldon, Jr. *consultant, retired chemical company executive*
Dacey, George Clement *retired laboratory administrator, consultant*
Johnson, Franklyn Arthur *academic administrator*
Miller, Richard Dwight *professional association executive*
Olander, Ray Gunnar *retired lawyer*
St. Mary, Edward Sylvester *direct mail marketing company executive*
Sargent, Charles Lee *recreation vehicle and pollution control systems manufacturing company executive*
Trudnak, Stephen Joseph *landscape architect*

Bowling Green
†Klein, Philip Howard *park ranger*

Boynton Beach
†Akridge, William David *hotel management company executive*
Allison, Dwight Leonard, Jr. *investor*
Babler, Wayne E. *retired telephone company executive, lawyer*
Balis, Moses Earl *biochemist, educator*
Bartholomew, Arthur Peck, Jr. *accountant*
Beisel, Daniel Cunningham *former newspaper publisher*
Bloede, Victor Gustav *retired advertising executive*
Brome, Robert Harrison *lawyer*
Bryant, Donald Loyd *insurance company executive*
Caras, Joseph Sheldon *life insurance company executive*
Crane, L(eo) Stanley *retired railroad executive*
Cross, Ralph Emerson *mechanical engineer*
Davant, James Waring *investment banker*
Falk, Bernard Henry *trade association executive*
Farace, Virginia Kapes *librarian*
Fields, Theodore *consulting medical radiation physicist*
Gilstein, Jacob Burrill *physicist*
Heckelmann, Charles Newman (Charles Lawton) *author, publishing consultant*
Jacobs, C. Bernard *banker*
Jensen, Reuben Rolland *former automotive company executive*
Johnson, Edward A. *manufacturing executive*
Koteen, Jack *management consultant, writer*
Kronman, Joseph Henry *orthodontist*
Miller, Emanuel *retired lawyer, banker*
Mirman, Irving R. *scientific adviser*
Peltzie, Kenneth Gerald *hospital administrator, educator*
Plossu, Bernard Pierre *photographer*
Saxbe, William Bart *lawyer, former government official*
Smith, Charles Henry, Jr. *industrial executive*
Snell, Thaddeus Stevens, III *lawyer, retired building materials manufacturing company executive*
†Spannuth, John R. *athletic association executive*
Stubbins, Hugh A(sher), Jr. *architect*
Turner, William Benjamin *electrical engineer*

Bradenton
†Aleppo, Joseph A. *foundation administrator*
Atkinson, Arlis D. *wall and ceiling contractor*
Balsley, Howard Lloyd *economist*
Beall, Robert Matthews, II *retail chain executive*
Blancett, Suzanne Smith *editor-in-chief*
Burton, Ralph Joseph *international development consultant*

Crouthamel, Thomas Grover, Sr. *editor*
Doenecke, Carol Anne *artist*
Feeley, John Paul *retired paper company executive*
Friedrich, Robert Edmund *retired electrical engineer, corporate consultant*
Godfrey, Paul *publisher*
Hare, John, IV *planetarium director*
Hodgell, Robert Overman *artist, art educator*
Jones, Horace Charles *former sales company executive*
Keane, Gustave Robert *architect, consultant*
†Klopp, Calvin Trexler *surgeon, educator*
Maynard, Donald Nelson *horticulturist, educator*
McFarland, Richard Macklin *retired journalist*
Phelan, John Densmore *insurance executive, consultant*
Price, Edgar Hilleary, Jr. *business consultant*
Ridings, Dorothy Sattes *communications executive, newspaper publisher*
Riha, William Edwin *beverage company executive*
Roeder, Myron A. *agricultural products company executive*
Sgroi, Mario *publishing executive*
†Tague, Karl Raymond *health care executive*
Thompson, Barbara Storck *state official*
Waters, Will Estel *horticulturist, researcher, educator*
Wendt, Lloyd *writer*
White, Dale Andrew *journalist*
Woodson-Howard, Marlene Erdley *former state legislator*

Bradenton Beach
Vega, Mario *family practice physician*

Brandon
Applegate, Minerva Irons *nursing educator, nurse*
Blomgren, David Kenneth *dean, pastor*
Lafferty, Beverly Lou Brookover *physician*
Mussenden, Gerald *psychologist*
Williamson, Robert Charles *marketing executive*

Brooksville
Anderson, Richard Edmund *city manager, management consultant*
Hetrick, Charles Brady *county official*
†Leftwich, Hal West *health facility administrator*
Slaatte, Howard Alexander *minister, philosophy educator*

Bushnell
Hagin, T. Richard *lawyer*

Cape Canaveral
†Block, David L. *solar engineering executive*
Clark, John F. *aerospace research and engineering educator*

Cape Coral
Brevoort, Richard William *public relations executive*
Lane, William C., Jr. *principal*
Mc Grath, William Restore *transportation planner, traffic engineer*
Peters, Donald Cameron *construction company executive*
Purdy, Alan Harris *biomedical engineer*
Seemann, Ernest Albright *lawyer*
West, John Merle *retired physicist, nuclear consultant*

Captiva
Fadiman, Clifton *writer, editor, radio and television entertainer*
Ronald, Peter *utility executive*

Casselberry
Medin, A. Louis *computer company executive*
Vincent, Thomas James *retired manufacturing company executive*

Cedar Key
Starnes, Earl Maxwell *urban and regional planner, architect*

Chattahoochee
Ivory, Peter B. C. B. *medical administrator*

Chuluota
Hatton, Thurman Timbrook, Jr. *retired horticulturist, consultant*

Clearwater
Alogna, John Joseph *advertising agency executive*
Beckwith, William Hunter *clergyman*
Berman, Elihu H. *lawyer*
Bertram, Frederic Amos *architect*
Birmingham, Richard Gregory *lawyer*
Bramante, Pietro Ottavio *physiology educator, retired pathology specialist*
Brown, Herbert Graham *entrepreneur*
Byrd, Mary Laager *life science researcher*
Carlson, Natalie Savage *author*
Caronis, George John *insurance executive*
Chamberlin, Terry McBride *sailing equipment company executive*
Churuti, Susan Hamilton *lawyer*
Darack, Arthur J. *editor*
De Lara, Mario, Jr. *psychologist, psychometrician, behavioral analyst*
Eshenbaugh, William Arthur *sales executive*
Free, E. LeBron *lawyer*
Fromhagen, Carl, Jr. *obstetrician and gynecologist*
Gibson, Barbara Arlene *nurse, writer*
Gilgar, Arthur Emery *bank executive*
Glindeman, Henry Peter, Jr. *real estate developer*
Graves, Robert Lee *hospital administration*
†Hallam, Arlita Warrick *library system administrator*
Hoornstra, Edward H. *retail company executive*
Horowitz, Harry I. *podiatrist*
Horton, Donna Alberg *technical writer*
Houtz, Duane Talbott *hospital administrator*
Howes, James Guerdon *airport director*
Jacobs, Marilyn Arlene Potoker *gifted education educator, consultant, author*
Jagger, Robert Edwin *lawyer*
Krosser, Howard S. *aerospace company executive*
Lansky, Zena *surgeon*
Leeds, Robert Lewis, Jr. *marketing and management educator*
Parks, Sallie Ann *county official, public relations executive, marketing professional*
Paxson, Lowell White *television station executive*
Pendleton, Sumner Alden *financial consultant*
Pinch, John G. *radio executive*
Raymund, Steven A. *computer company executive*
St. Clair, Jane Elizabeth *management executive*
Smith, Marion Pafford *avionics company executive*
Todd, Barbara Sheen *county commissioner*
Turley, Stewart *retail company executive*
Tutton, Betty Jane *humanities educator*
Werner, Elizabeth Helen *librarian, Spanish language educator*
Wheat, Myron William, Jr. *cardiothoracic surgeon*
Whedon, George Donald *medical administrator, researcher*
Yoho, Robert Wayne *company executive*
Youngberg, Robert Stanley *principal, consultant*

Clermont
Chandler, Robert Flint, Jr. *international agriculture consultant*
Dyson, Raymond Clegg *building contractor, construction consultant*

Clewiston
Boy, John Buckner *sugar company executive*

Cocoa
Linscott, Jacqueline C. *elementary school educator, consultant*

Cocoa Beach
Gunn, Kenneth David *explosives safety specialist, consultant*

Coconut Creek
Godofsky, Stanley *lawyer*

Coconut Grove
Cotton, John Pierce *principal*
Denaro, Gregory *lawyer*
McAmis, Edwin Earl *lawyer*

Coral Gables
Arcos, Cresencio S. *ambassador*
Baddour, Raymond Frederick *chemical engineer, educator, entrepreneur*
Bannard, Walter Darby *artist, art critic*
Blumberg, David *builder, developer*
Burini, Sonia Montes de Oca *apparel manufacturing and public relations executive*
Cegnar, Ronald William *food company executive*
Cobb, Charles E., Jr. *corporate executive, former ambassador*
Criss, Cecil M. *chemistry educator*
Davis, Mattie Belle Edwards *retired county judge*
Einspruch, Norman Gerald *physicist, educator*
Eisner, Peter Norman *reporter, correspondent*
Fung, Kee-Ying *engineer, educator, researcher*
Getman, Dennis Jon *lawyer*
Gutierrez, Jose Ramon *bank executive*
Hammes, Terry Marie *advertising, public relations and marketing executive*
Hertz, Arthur Herman *communications executive*
Higginbottom, Samuel Logan *retired aerospace company executive*
Howard, Bernard Eufinger *computer science and mathematics educator*
Jury, Eliahu Ibraham *electrical engineer, research educator*
Kirsner, Robert *language educator*
Kline, Jacob *biomedical engineering educator*
Kniskern, Joseph Warren *lawyer*
Latham, Jean Lee *writer*
Leblanc, Roger Maurice *chemistry educator*
Lemos, Ramon Marcelino *philosophy educator*
McCarthy, Patrick A. *English educator*
Minahan, John English *author*
Moss, Ambler Holmes, Jr. *academic administrator, lawyer, former ambassador*
Murfin, Ross C *university dean, English educator*
Nunez-Portuondo, Ricardo *investment company executive*
Perez, Josephine *psychiatrist, educator*
†Quillian, Warren Wilson, II *pediatrician, educator*
Ramsey, John Hansberry *executive search firm executive, investment banker*
Rodgers, Frank *librarian*
Rosenn, Keith Samuel *lawyer, educator*
Saffir, Herbert Seymour *structural engineer, consultant*
Shipley, Vergil Alan *political science educator*
Sumanth, David Jonnakoty *industrial engineer, educator*
Warburton, Ralph Joseph *architect, engineer, planner, educator*
Yarger, Sam Jacob *dean, educator*
Young, Tzay Y. *electrical and computer engineering educator*

Coral Springs
Averett-Short, Geneva Evelyn *college administrator*
†Burg, Ralph *art association executive*
Elmore, Walter A. *electrical engineer, consultant*
Luing, Gary Alan *financial management educator*
Sommerer, John *accountant*
Vandiver, Frances *principal*

Crescent City
García, Mary Elizabeth *Spanish and English as second languages educator*

Crystal River
Black, Charles Alvin *consulting engineering executive*

Cypress Gardens
Gobie, Henry Macaulay *philatelic researcher, retired postal executive*

Dade City
Burdick, Glenn Arthur *physicist, engineering educator*
McBath, Donald Linus *osteopathic physician*
Rine, Susan *principal*

Davie
Shula, Don Francis *professional football coach*

Daytona Beach
Alcott, Amy Strum *professional golfer*
Amick, William Walker *golf course architect*
Bronson, Oswald Perry *religious organization administrator, clergyman*
Collyer, Robert B. *association executive*
Connor, Edward Hollis, III *golf course architect*
Davidson, Herbert M. (Tippen), Jr. *newspaper publisher*
Davidson, Josephine F. *newspaper editor*
Earnhardt, (Ralph) Dale *professional race car driver*
Elliott, Carol Harris *nutrition counselor, dietitian*
Gardner, Joseph Lawrence *editor, writer*
Gauch, Eugene William, Jr. *former air force officer*
Geier, George *optical engineering consultant*
Haviland, Robert Paul *engineering executive, author*
Inkster, Juli *professional golfer*
King, Betsy *professional golfer*
Libby, Gary Russell *museum director*
Locke, Edwin Allen, Jr. *investment banker*
Mallon, Meg *professional golfer*
Marlin, Sterling *professional race car driver*
Mc Collister, John Charles *writer, clergyman, educator*
McCoy, Edward Fitzgerald *social services facility administrator*
Mechem, Charles Stanley, Jr. *former broadcasting executive, golf association executive*
Millar, Gordon Halstead *mechanical engineer, agricultural machinery manufacturing executive*
Mochrie, Dottie *professional golfer*
O'Reilly, Don *reporter, writer, photographer*
Osterholm, J(ohn) Roger *humanities educator*
Parker, Betty Morris *association administrator retired*
Petty, Kyle *professional stock car driver*
Reeves, Donna Andrews *golfer*
Sheehan, Patty *professional golfer*
Sliwa, Steven Mark *engineering executive, academic administrator*
Wehner, Henry Otto, III *pharmacist, consultant*
Whitworth, Kathrynne Ann *professional golfer*
Yarborough, William Caleb *former professional stock car race driver*

Deerfield Beach
Assaf, Ronald G. *electronics executive*
Bernstein, Stanley Robert *financial consultant, mortgage broker and banker*
Brown, Colin W(egand) *lawyer, diversified company executive*
Hochberger, Simon *communications educator*
Moran, James M. *automotive sales executive*
Moran, Patricia Genevieve *corporate executive*
Rung, Richard Allen *lawyer, retired air force officer, retired educator*
Van Arnem, Harold Louis *capital and technology equipment leasing company executive*

Deland
Brakeman, Louis Freeman *retired university administrator*
Coolidge, Edwin Channing *chemistry educator*
Dascher, Paul Edward *university dean, accounting educator*
Duncan, Pope Alexander *college administrator*
Fant, Clyde Edward, Jr. *religion educator*
Fortmueller, Heinz William Erich *quality assurance professional*
Gill, Donald George *education educator*
Horton, Thomas R. *business advisor*
Langston, Paul T. *music educator, university dean, composer*
Lee, Howard Douglas *university president*
MacMahon, Charles Hutchins, Jr. *architect*
McCormick, Lyle Bernard, Jr. *management consultant*
Morland, Richard Boyd *retired educator*
Sorensen, Jacki Faye *choreographer, aerobic dance company executive*
Tedros, Theodore Zaki *educator, real estate broker, appraiser*

Delray Beach
Barlow, Joel *retired lawyer*
Bryan, Robert Fessler *former investment analyst*
Cary, James Donald *journalist*
Charyk, Joseph Vincent *retired satellite telecommunications executive*
Coyle, William *educator*
Epley, Marion Jay *oil company executive*
Fuente, D. I. *office supply manufacturing executive*
Goldenberg, George *retired pharmaceutical company executive*
Groening, William Andrew, Jr. *lawyer, former chemical company executive*
Hegstrom, William Jean *mathematics educator*
Himmelright, Robert John, Jr. *rubber company executive*
Holmes, Walter Stephen, Jr. *retired financial executive*
Larry, R. Heath *lawyer*
Peoples, Thomas Edward *publisher, executive, writer*
Reef, Arthur *industry business consultant*
Rippeteau, Darrel Downing *architect*
Robinson, Richard Francis *writer, author*
Ross, Beatrice Brook *artist*
Saffer, Alfred *retired chemical company executive*
Shannon, Stephen Quinby, Jr. *broadcasting and human resources executive*
Shister, Joseph *labor arbitrator, law educator*
Sibigtroth, Joseph Clarence *insurance company executive*
Silver, Samuel Manuel *rabbi, author*
Smith, John Joseph, III *textile company executive, educator*
Stewart, Patricia Carry *foundation administrator*
Terry, Margaret Smoot *special education educator*
Zarwyn, Berthold *physical scientist*

Destin
Carlton, Paul Kendall *former air force officer, consultant*
Cunningham, James Everett *retired energy services company executive*
†Levin, Peter J. *hospital administrator, public health professor*

Dover
Pearson, Walter Donald *editor, columnist*

Dundee
Johnson, Gordon Selby *consulting electrical engineer*

Dunedin
Bradley, Robert Lee *surgeon*
Espy, Charles Clifford *English language educator, author, consultant, lecturer, administrator*
Geer, James Hamilton *retired broadcasting company executive*
Rosa, Raymond Ulric *retired banker*

Dunnellon
Dixon, W(illiam) Robert *retired educational psychology educator*

Eastpoint
Hoffer, Thomas William *communications educator*

Eglin AFB
Stewart, J. Daniel *air force development and test center administrator*

Englewood
Defliese, Philip Leroy *accountant, educator*
Marchand, Leslie Alexis *language educator, writer*
Schultz, Arthur Joseph, Jr. *retired trade association executive*
Simis, Theodore Luckey *investment banker, information technology executive*
Sisson, Robert F. *photographer, writer, lecturer, educator*
Suiter, John William *industrial engineer, consultant*

Fernandina Beach
Barlow, Anne Louise *pediatrician, medical research administrator*
Burns, Stephen Redding *golf course architect*
D'Agnese, Helen Jean *artist*
Hildebrand, Richard Allen *bishop*
Kurtz, Myers Richard *hospital administrator*
Rogers, Robert Burnett *naval officer*

Fisher Island
Trippe, Kenneth Alvin Battershill *shipping industry executive*

Flagler Beach
Nebil, Corinne Elizabeth *artist*

Fort Lauderdale
Adams, Alfred Hugh *college president*
Adams, Damon R. *city official*
Adams, Daniel Lee *lawyer*
Alberg, Mildred Freed *film and television producer, writer*
Aleff, Andrea Lee (Andy Aleff) *newspaper editor*
Andrews, John Harold *health care administrator*
Azrin, Nathan Harold *psychologist*
Bartelstone, Rona Sue *gerontologist*
Bayles, Samuel Heagan *advertising agency executive*
Becker, Edward A. *accounting educator, consultant*
Bimstein, Benjamin William *ice sculptor, caterer, chef*
Bleckner, Edward, Jr. *data communication products company executive*
Campbell, Donna Grayce *nursing administrator*
Caporella, Nick A. *diversified company executive*
Carney, Dennis Joseph *former steel company executive, consulting company executive*
Cicora, Kenneth Allan *public information officer*
Copelan, John Jefferson, Jr. *lawyer*
Cryer, Eugene Edward *newspaper editor*
Cumerford, William Richard *fund raising and public relations executive*
Cummings, Virginia J(eanne) *former real estate company executive*
Dawson, Muriel Amanda *legislator*
de Leon, Lidia Maria *magazine editor*
Dickinson, Richard *landscape architect*
Doane, Harold Everett *recording executive*
Dressler, Robert A. *lawyer*
Du Mont, Dolph Joseph *management consultant*
Durfey, Robert Walker *sea transportation consultant*
Eisner, Will *publishing company executive*
Feldman, Stephen *university president*
Ferris, Robert Edmund *lawyer*
Fine, Howard Alan *travel industry executive*
Fischler, Abraham Saul *university president*
Fitzpatrick, Mark *professional hockey player*
Fosback, Norman George *stock market econometrician, researcher*
Friedman, Sol *inventor, writer*
Gardner, Russell Menese *lawyer*
Gerbino, John *advertising executive*
Gilbert, Anne Wieland *journalist*
Gill, Richard Thomas *opera singer, economic analyst*
†Golnick, Howard Marshall *advertising executive*
†Golnick, Leon Shaffer *advertising and marketing executive*
Gonzalez, Jose Alejandro, Jr. *federal judge*
Greenberger, Sheldon Lee *newspaper advertising executive*
Grestner, Jonathan Neil *religious studies educator*
Gude, Nancy Carlson *systems consultant*
Gunzburger, Suzanne Nathan *county commissioner, social worker*
Hanbury, George Lafayette, II *city manager*
Hanson, Duane Elwood *sculptor*
Hargrove, John Russell *lawyer*
Hayes, Peter John *retail executive*
Hiaasen, Carl Andreas *lawyer*
Hirsch, Jeffrey Allan *lawyer*
Hirshson, William Roscoe *real estate consultant*
Holland, Beth *actress*
Holtzman, Gary Yale *recreational facility executive*
Honahan, H(enry) Robert *motion picture theatre executive*
Huizenga, Harry Wayne *entrepreneur, entertainment corporation executive, professional sports team executive*
Joseph, Paul R *law educator*
Jotcham, Thomas Denis *marketing communications consultant*
Keats, Harold Alan *corporate executive*
Keller, Larry Allan *reporter*
Kemper Littman, Marlyn *information scientist, educator*
King, Don *boxing promoter*
Klein, Bernard *publishing company executive*
Kobert, Norman Noah *asset management consultant*
Lataif, Lawrence P. *lawyer*
Lederman, Michael G. *consumer products company executive*
LeRoy, Joy *model*
Levi, Kurt *retired banker*
Lodwick, Gwilym Savage *radiologist, educator*
Lyons, Richard Chapman *former urologist*
Maher, Kim Leverton *museum administrator*
Marcus, Richard Alan *lawyer, distribution company executive*
Maucker, Earl Robert *newspaper editor, newspaper executive*
Morse, Edward J. *automotive executive*
Moss, Stephen B. *lawyer*
Murray, Bryan Clarence *professional sports team executive*

O'Bryan, William Monteith *lawyer*
Parkyn, John William *editor, writer*
Paulauskas, Edmund Walter *real estate broker*
†Peluso, David Anthony *clinical pharmacist, consultant*
Peterson, Colin Hampton *electronics company executive*
Pettijohn, Fred Phillips *retired newspaper executive, consultant*
Randi, James (Randall James Hamilton Zwinge) *magician, writer, educator*
Rasmussen, Geraldine Dorothy *composer, artist, musician, author*
Reigrod, Robert Hull *manufacturing executive*
†Richmond, Gail Levin *law educator*
†Roehrenbeck, Carol *law librarian, educator*
Roettger, Norman Charles, Jr. *federal judge*
Rosenstein, Samuel M. *federal judge*
Russo, Thomas Joseph *hospitality and consumer durables industry executive*
Sanders, Howard *investment company executive*
Schulte, Frederick James *newpaper editor*
Shaw, Bryan P. H. *retired investment company executive*
Shoemaker, William Edward *financial executive*
Singer, Donald Ivan *architect*
Skiddell, Elliot Lewis *rabbi*
Sklar, Alexander *electrical company executive*
Smith, James Edward *newspaper company executive*
Smith, Scott Clybourn *communications company executive*
Smolar, Edward Nelson *physician, consultant*
Snow, Lurana S. *judge*
Soeteber, Ellen *journalist, newspaper editor*
†Solomon, Barry Jason *healthcare administrator, consultant*
Sorensen, Allan Chresten *service company executive*
Stone, Edward Durell, Jr. *landscape architect*
Sutte, Donald T., Jr. *real estate executive*
Tenaglia, John Franc *broadcasting executive*
Thayer, Charles J. *investment banker*
Thomas, Everette Earl *federal judge*
Turner, Hugh Joseph, Jr. *lawyer*
Turner, Richard Stanley *health care financial executive*
Van Alstyne, Judith Sturges *English language educator*
Vanbiesbrouck, John *professional hockey player*
Vasquez, William Leroy *marketing professional, educator*
Wallace, Joan Scott *psychologist, social worker, international consultant*
Walton, Rodney Earl *lawyer*
†Waters, M. Jean *mortgage company executive*
†Waters, Richard W., Sr. *mortgage company executive*
Weinstein, Peter M. *lawyer, state senator*
White, Mary Lou *fundraiser, writer, educator*
Wynne, Brian James *former association executive, consultant*
Yaxley, Jack Thomas *secondary education educator*
Young, Lois Catherine Williams *university agency consultant*
Young, William Benjamin *special education educator*
Zikakis, John P. *educator, researcher, biochemist*
Zirkle, David H. *data processing company executive*
Zloch, William J. *federal judge*

Fort Myers
Adams, James Andrew *public school district official*
Aleo, Joseph John *pathology scientist, educator, academic research administrator*
Allen, Richard Chester *retired lawyer, educator*
Barbour, Hugh Revell *publisher*
Barbour, William Rinehart, Jr. *retired book publisher*
Brown, Earl Kent *historian, clergyman*
Censits, Richard John *electronic controls company executive*
Conger, Kyril B. *urologist*
Cyphert, Frederick Ralph *academic administrator*
Erickson, Roy Lydeen *lawyer*
Ferguson, James A. *surgeon*
Fromm, Winfield Eric *retired corporate executive, engineering consultant and investor*
Grove, William Johnson *physician, surgery educator*
Halgrim, Robert P. *museum director*
Harmer, Rose *marriage and family therapist, mental health counselor*
Hudson, Leonard Harlow *contractor*
Hughes, Judi E. *principal*
Idelson, Charles K. *bank executive*
Jones, Constance *principal*
Kelly, William E. *psychoanalyst*
Koehler, Robert Brien *priest*
Laboda, Gerald *oral and maxillofacial surgeon*
Mainous, Theresa Lei *nursing administrator*
Medvecky, Robert Stephen *lawyer*
Mergler, Harry Winston *engineering educator*
†Missimer, Thomas Michael *geologist*
Moeschl, Stanley Francis *electrical engineer, management consultant*
Morse, John Harleigh *lawyer*
Nathan, James Robert *hospital administrator*
Nottingham, James (Leroy Nottingham) *retired protective services official, professional society administrator*
O'Dell, William Francis *retired business executive, author*
Ölling, Edward Henry *aerospace engineer, consulting firm executive*
Peete, Calvin *professional golfer*
Powell, Richard Pitts *writer*
Rollason, Wendell Norton *social services administrator*
Ryan, William Joseph *communications company executive*
Schwartz, Carl Edward *artist, printmaker*
Scott, Kenneth Elsner *mechanical engineering educator*
Shafer, Robert Tinsley, Jr. *judge*
Simmons, Vaughan Pippen *medical consultant*
Solomon, Irvin D. *history educator, author*
Sypert, George Walter *neurosurgery educator, clinical neurosurgeon, research neurophysiologist*
Tyrer, John Lloyd *retired headmaster*
Wendeborn, Richard Donald *retired manufacturing company executive*
Zupko, Arthur George *consultant to drug industry, retired college administrator*

Fort Myers Beach
Arneson, Harold Elias Grant *manufacturing engineer, consultant*

Fort Pierce
Boucher, Mildred Eileen *state agency administrator*
Bynum, Henri Sue *education and French educator*
Calvert, David Victor *soil science educator*
Chapman, John Davol *communications brokerage executive*
Garment, Robert James *clergyman*

Fort Walton Beach
Brown, Gary Allen *defense analysis company executive*
Cooke, Fred Charles *real estate broker*
Gates, Philip Don *anesthesiologist*
Phillips, Loyal *newspaper executive*
†Sanders, Jimmy Devon *university official*

Gainesville
Abbaschian, Reza *materials science and engineering educator*
Abbott, Thomas Benjamin *speech educator*
Agrios, George Nicholas *plant pathology educator*
†Anderson, Timothy J. *chemical engineering educator*
Andrew, Edward Raymond *physicist*
Anghaie, Samim *nuclear engineer, educator*
Barber, Charles Edward *newspaper executive, journalist*
Barton, Allen Hoisington *sociologist*
Baughman, George Fechtig *foundation executive*
Bedell, George Chester *retired publisher, educator, priest*
Bednarek, Alexander Robert *mathematician, educator*
Behnke, Marylou *neonatologist, educator*
Bennett, Thomas Peter *museum director, educator, biologist*
Bernard, H. Russell *anthropology educator, scientific editor*
Besch, Emerson Louis *physiology educator, past academic administrator*
Bishop, Budd Harris *museum administrator*
Block, Seymour Stanton *chemical engineering educator, consultant, writer*
Bodine, Willis Ramsey, Jr. *music educator, organist*
Bodor, Nicholas Stephen *medicinal chemistry researcher, educator, consultant*
Boyes, Patrice Flinchbaugh *lawyer, environmental executive*
†Brown, Myra Suzanne *librarian*
Brown, William Samuel, Jr. *communication processes and disorders educator*
Bryan, Robert Armistead *university administrator, educator*
Burridge, Michael John *veterinarian, educator, academic administrator*
Canelas, Dale Brunelle *library director*
Cantliffe, Daniel James *horticulture educator*
Capaldi, Elizabeth Ann Deutsch *psychological sciences educator*
Capehart, Barney Lee *industrial and systems engineer*
Carr, Glenna Dodson *economics educator*
Challoner, David Reynolds *university official, physician*
Chang, Weilin Parrish *construction educator, administrator, researcher*
Chapin, Kenneth Lee *middle school educator*
Cheek, Jimmy Geary *university official, agricultural education and communications educator*
Childers, Donald Gene *electrical engineering educator, researcher*
Childers, Norman Franklin *horticulture educator*
Clark, Elmer J. *education educator*
Cluff, Leighton Eggertsen *physician*
Copeland, Edward Meadors, III *surgery educator*
Couch, Leon Worthington *electrical engineering educator*
Couch, Margaret Wheland *research chemist*
Cousins, Robert John *nutritional biochemist, educator*
Craven, Roy Curtis, Jr. *art educator emeritus, art gallery director*
Creel, Austin Bowman *religion educator*
Davidson, James Melvin *academic administrator, researcher, educator*
Davis, George Kelso *nutrition biochemist, educator*
Davis, Horance Gibbs, Jr. *retired educator, journalist*
Delfino, Joseph John *environmental engineering sciences educator*
Der-Houssikian, Haig *linguistics educator*
Detweiler, Steven Lawrence *physicist, educator*
Dewar, Michael James Steuart *chemistry educator*
Dewsbury, Donald Allen *historian of psychology, comparative psychologist*
Dickinson, Joshua Clifton, Jr. *museum director, educator*
Dierks, Richard Ernest *veterinarian, educational administrator*
Dilcher, David Leonard *paleobotany educator*
Dinculeanu, Nicolae *mathematician*
Drago, Russell Stephen *chemist, educator*
Drucker, Daniel Charles *engineer, educator*
Drury, Kenneth Clayton *biological scientist*
Eder, George Jackson *lawyer, economist*
†Edwardson, John Richard *agronomist*
Eichhorn, Heinrich Karl *astronomer, educator, consultant*
Elzinga, Donald Jack *industrial engineering researcher, educator*
Emch, Gerard Gustav *mathematics and physics educator*
Emch-Dériaz, Antoinette Suzanne *historian*
Feiss, Carl Lehman *retired urban planning educator*
Fossum, Jerry George *electrical engineering educator*
Gander, John Edward *biochemistry educator*
Gerberg, Eugene Jordan *entomologist*
Goggin, Margaret Knox *librarian, educator*
Goldhurst, William *retired humanities and English educator, writer*
Gravenstein, Joachim Stefan *anesthesiologist, educator*
Green, David Marvin *psychology educator, researcher, consultant*
Greer, Melvin *medical educator*
Grundy, Betty Lou Bottoms *anesthesiology and pharmaceutics educator*
Gutekunst, Richard Ralph *microbiology educator*
Haldeman, Joe William *novelist*
Hale, James Pierce *education educator*
†Hammer, Russell J. *corporate financial executive*
Hanrahan, Robert Joseph *chemist, educator*
Hanson, Harold Palmer *physicist, government official, editor, academic administrator*
Haring, Ellen Stone (Mrs. E. S. Haring) *philosophy educator*
Harrer, Gustave Adolphus *librarian, educator*
Harris, Marvin *anthropology educator*
†Harrison, Debia *chemistry educator*
Harrison, John Armstrong *historian, university dean*
Harrison, Willard W. *chemist, educator*
Hartigan, Karelisa Dorothy *classics educator*
Heflin, Martin Ganier *foreign service officer, international political economist*
Henson, (Betty) Ann *media specialist, educator*
Himes, James Albert *veterinary medicine educator emeritus*
Holland, Norman Norwood *English language educator*
Hollien, Harry Francis *speech and communications scientist, educator*
Holloway, Paul Howard *materials science educator*
Hoy, Marjorie Ann *entomology educator, researcher*
Isaacs, Gerald William *agricultural engineer, educator*
†Issacs, Gerald William *retired agricultural engineering educator, consultant*
Jacobs, Alan Martin *physicist, educator*
Jaeger, Boi Jon *health administrator educator*
†Johnson, Charles William *consulting firm executive*
Jones, Elizabeth Nordwall *county government official*
Jones, Richard Lamar *entomology educator*
Katritzky, Alan Roy *chemistry educator, consultant*
Keesling, James Edgar *mathematics educator*
Kenney, Thomas Frederick *broadcasting executive*
Kerslake, Kenneth Alvin *art educator, printmaker*
†Kiehne, Lynn Sheree *hospital administrator*
Klauder, John Rider *physics educator*
†Kucharek, Thomas A. *plant pathologist, educator*
Kurzweg, Ulrich Hermann *engineering science educator*
Kushner, David Zakeri *musicologist, educator*
†Law, Mark Edward *electrical engineer, educator*
Legler, Donald Wayne *university dean, dentist*
Lindholm, Fredrik Arthur *electrical engineering educator, researcher*
Liquori, Martin William, Jr. *athlete, business executive, television commentator*
Locascio, Salvadore Joseph *horticulturist*
Lombardi, John V. *university administrator, historian*
Lopez, Andy *university athletic coach*
Lowenstein, Ralph Lynn *university dean emeritus*
Malvern, Lawrence Earl *engineering educator, researcher*
†Maples, William Ross *anthropology educator, consultant*
Mautz, Robert Barbeau *lawyer, educator*
McKnew, Linda Alexander *health facility administrator*
Medina, Jose Enrique *dentist, educator*
Meredith, Julia Alice *nematologist, biologist, researcher*
Micha, David Allan *chemistry and physics educator*
Milanich, Jerald Thomas *archaeologist, museum curator*
Moberly, Robert Blakely *lawyer, educator*
Modell, Jerome Herbert *anesthesiologist, educator, dean*
Murray, Ernest Don *artist, educator*
Neims, Allen Howard *univeristy dean, medical scientist*
Neugroschel, Arnost *electrical engineering educator*
Nicoletti, Paul Lee *veterinarian, educator*
Oberlander, Herbert *insect physiologist, educator*
Ohanian, Mihran Jacob *engineering educator*
Ohrn, Nils Yngve *chemistry and physics educator*
Otis, Arthur Brooks *physiologist, educator*
†Park, Robert McIlwraith *science and engineering educator*
Peebles, Peyton Zimmerman, Jr. *electrical engineer, educator*
Penland, Arnold Clifford, Jr. *college dean, educator*
Pepine, Carl John *physician, educator*
Person, Willis Bagley *chemistry educator*
Pfaff, William Wallace *physician, educator*
Phillips, Winfred Marshall *dean, mechanical engineer*
Pierce, Robert Nash *writer*
†Popenoe, Hugh Llywelyn *soils educator*
Pop-Stojanovic, Zoran Rista *mathematics educator*
Price, Donald Ray *university official, agricultural engineer*
Probert, Walter *lawyer, educator*
Proctor, Samuel *history educator*
Purcifull, Dan Elwood *plant virologist, educator*
Putnam, Hugh Dyer *environmental scientist, educator, consultant*
Quarles, James Cliv *law educator*
Quesenberry, Kenneth Hays *agronomy educator*
Randall, Malcom *health care administrator*
Rhoton, Albert Loren, Jr. *neurological surgery educator*
Rosenbloom, Arlan Lee *physician, educator*
Rubin, Melvin Lynne *ophthalmologist, educator*
Schaub, James Hamilton *engineering educator*
Schiebler, Gerold Ludwig *physician, educator*
Schmeling, Gareth *classics educator*
Schmertmann, John Henry *civil engineer, educator, consultant*
Schmidt, Peter R. *anthropology educator*
Schmidt-Nielsen, Bodil Mimi (Mrs. Roger G. Chagnon) *physiologist*
Schueller, Wolfgang Augustus *architectural educator, writer*
Schwartz, Michael Averill *university dean, pharmaceutical scientist*
Severy, Lawrence James *psychologist, educator*
Shyy, Wei *aerospace, mechanical engineering researcher and educator*
Simmons, John Kaul *accounting educator*
Singer, Robert Norman *motor behavior educator*
Singley, John Edward, Jr. *environmental engineer, consultant*
Sisler, Harry Hall *chemist, educator*
Small, Parker Adams, Jr. *pediatrician, educator*
Smith, Alexander Goudy *physics and astronomy educator*
Smith, David C. *dean*
Smith, David Thornton *lawyer, educator*
Smith, Herrick Hayner *landscape architect, educator, consultant*
Smith, Jo Anne *writer, retired educator*
Smith, John James, Jr. *environmental engineering laboratory executive*
Sorensen, Andrew Aaron *provost*
Spurrier, Steve *university athletic coach, former professional football player*
Steadham, Charles Victor, Jr. *entertainment agent, producer*
Stehli, Francis Greenough *geologist, educator*
Stein, Jay M. *planning and design educator, consultant*
Stephan, Alexander F. *German language and literature educator*
Stern, William Louis *botanist, educator*
Stone, Williard Everard *accountant, educator*
Suzuki, Howard Kazuro *retired anatomist, educator*
Talbert, James Lewis *pediatric surgeon, educator*
†Taylor, Grace Elizabeth Woodall (Betty Taylor) *lawyer, educator, law library administrator*
Taylor, William Jape *physician*
Teitelbaum, Philip *psychologist*
Teixeira, Arthur Alves *food engineer, consultant*
Thompson, Neal Philip *food science and nutrition educator*
Thompson, Victor Alexander *political science educator*
†Toskes, Phillip Paul *physician, educator, clinical researcher*
Tou, Julius T. *electrical and computer engineering educator*
Uelsmann, Jerry Norman *photographer*
Valdés, Karen W. *art gallery director, educator*
Van Alstyne, W. Scott, Jr. *lawyer, educator*
Vasil, Indra Kumar *botanist*
Vaughn, Rufus Mahlon *psychiatrist*
Verink, Ellis Daniel, Jr. *metallurgical engineering educator, consultant*
Vierck, Charles John, Jr. *neuroscience educator, scientist*
Viessman, Warren, Jr. *academic dean, civil engineering educator, researcher*
von Mering, Otto Oswald *anthropology educator*
Walker, Robert Dixon, III *surgeon, urologist, educator*
Wass, Hannelore Lina *educational psychology educator emeritus*
Watson, Robert Joe *hospital administrator, retired career officer*
Wethington, John Abner, Jr. *retired nuclear engineering educator*
Weyrauch, Walter Otto *legal educator*
White, Jill Carolyn *lawyer*
White, John David *composer, theorist, cellist*
Wilcox, Charles Julian *geneticist, educator*
Williams, Hiram Draper *artist, educator*
Williams, Norris Hagan, Jr. *biologist, educator, curator*
Williams, Ralph Chester, Jr. *physician, educator*
Willocks, Robert Max *retired librarian*
Wing, Elizabeth Schwarz *museum curator, educator*
Woeste, John Theodore *academic administrator*
Wood, Frank Bradshaw *retired astronomy educator*
Wright, Jane Brooks *university foundation professional*
Wyatt-Brown, Bertram *historian, educator*
York, E. Travis, Jr. *academic administrator, former university chancellor, consultant*
Young, David Michael *biochemistry and molecular biology educator, physician*
Zabel, Edward *economist, educator*
Zerner, Michael Charles *chemistry and physics educator, consultant, researcher*

Goldenrod
Carmichael, William Jerome *publishing company executive*

Gonzalez
Plischke, Le Moyne Wilfred *research chemist*

Goulds
Taylor, Millicent Ruth *middle school educator*

Graceville
Kinchen, Thomas Alexander *college president*

Green Cove Springs
Lee, Ruth Davidson *tax collector*
Watson, Thomas Campbell *economic development consulting company executive*
Yelton, Eleanor O'Dell *reading specialist*

Groveland
Hamilton, Rhoda Lillian Rosen *educator, consultant*

Gulf Breeze
Lankton, Stephen Ryan *family therapist, management consultant*
Mayer, Foster Lee, Jr. *toxicologist*
Menzer, Robert Everett *toxicologist, educator*
Strength, Janis Grace *management executive, educator*

Gulf Stream
Stone, Franz Theodore *retired fabricated metal products manufacturing executive*

Haines City
Clement, Robert William *air force officer*

Hallandale
Contney, John Joseph *association executive*
Cornblatt, Max *automotive batteries manufacturing company executive*
Haspel, Arthur Carl *podiatrist, surgeon*
Kemp, Bernard *organizational development consultant*

Havana
Penson, Edward Martin *management consulting company executive*

Hawthorne
Fackler, Martin L(uther) *surgeon*
Ross, James Elmer *economist, administrator*

Hernando
Bell, Philip Wilkes *accounting and economics educator*

Hialeah
Economides, Christopher George *pathologist*
Edelcup, Norman Scott *management and financial consultant*
Heimbuch, Joseph William *marketing educator*
Kennedy, Thomas Patrick *financial executive*
Martinez, Julio J. *mayor*
Martinez, Raul L. *mayor, publisher*
Shaw, Steven John *retired marketing educator, academic administrator*
Stewart, Burch Byron *chemist, physicist*
†Strauss, Robert C. *manufacturing executive*
Wolter, Duane Roland *retail executive*

High Springs
Eaton, Wayne Carl *chiropractic physician*

Highland Beach
Collins, John Joseph *telecommunications executive*
Frager, Albert S. *retired retail food company executive*
Gaffey, Thomas Michael, Jr. *consumer products executive*
Schor, Stanley Sidney *mathematical sciences educator*
Stimson, Frederick Sparks *Hispanist, educator*
Summers, James Irvin *retired advertising executive*
Wegman, Harold Hugh *management consultant*

Hillsboro Bch
Gibbons, Joseph John *builders supply company financial executive*

Hobe Sound
Beddow, Thomas John *retired lawyer*
Casey, Edward Paul *manufacturing company executive*
Craig, David Jeoffrey *retired manufacturing company executive*
DeHority, Edward Havens, Jr. *retired accountant, lawyer*
Etherington, Edwin Deacon *lawyer, business executive, educator*
Fiske, Guy Wilbur *investment company executive*
Frank, Mary *sculptor, artist*
Graham, Bruce John *architect*
Havens, Oliver Hershman *lawyer, consultant*
Henley, Henry Howard, Jr. *retired manufacturing company executive*
Hotchkiss, Winchester Fitch *retired investment banker*
Markoe, Frank, Jr. *lawyer, business and hospital executive*
Matheson, William Lyon *lawyer, farmer*
McChristian, Joseph Alexander *international business executive*
Norman, Greg *professional golfer*
Simpson, Russell Gordon *lawyer, mayor, counselor to not-for-profit organiz*
Vanderbilt, Oliver Degray *financier*

Hollywood
Angstrom, Wayne Raymond *communications executive*
Bergman, Harry *urologist*
Blate, Michael *author, lecturer*
Blazzard, Norse Novar *lawyer*
Bujnicki, Sharon A. *health facility administrator*
Burton, John Jacob *real estate company executive, appraiser*
Cowan, Irving *real estate owner, developer*
Di Maggio, Joseph Paul *former professional baseball player*
Fell, Frederick Victor *publisher*
Giulianti, Mara Selena *mayor, civic worker*
Goldberg, Icchok Ignacy *retired special education educator*
Graves, Walter Albert *retired association executive, editor*
Harringer, Olaf Carl *architect, museum consultant*
King, Alma Jean *former health and physical education educator*
Korngold, Alvin Leonard *broadcasting company executive*
McQueen, Scott Robert *broadcasting company executive*
Nusim, Stanley Herbert *chemical engineer, consultant*
Sacco, Frank Vincent *hospital administrator*
Sadowski, Carol Johnson *fine artist, painter*
Sim, Robert Wilson *accountant*
Thomas, Thomas A. *lawyer*
Ward, James Theron *protective services official*
Weinberg, Harry Bernard *cardiologist*

Holmes Beach
Browning, Henry Prentice *banker*
Neustadt, Barbara Mae *artist, illustrator, etcher*

Homestead
Brammer, Barbara Allison *secondary school educator, consultant*
Crouse, John Oliver, II *journalist*
Reeder, Cecelia Painter *English educator*
Revuelta, René Sergio *marine scientist, educator*
†Risi, Louis J., Jr. *business executive*
Roberts, Larry Spurgeon *zoologist*

Homosassa
Acton, Norman *international organization executive*
Clement, Howard Wheeler *lawyer*

Indialantic
Bush, Norman *research and development executive*
Carroll, Charles Lemuel, Jr. *mathematician*
Lewis, Richard Stanley *author, former editor*

Indian Harbour Beach
Boan, Bobby Jack *chemist*
Denaburg, Charles Robert *metallurgical engineer, retired government official*
Traylor, Angelika *stained glass artist*

Indian Rocks Beach
Mortensen, James E. *management consultant*
Rocheleau, James Romig *academic administrator*
Sullivan, Paul William *communications specialist*

Interlachen
Hoffman, Edward Richard, III (Dick Hoffman) *retail and manufacturing executive*

Jacksonville
Adams, Henry *museum director*
Ade, James L. *lawyer*
Afflick, Clive Henry *minister, counselor*
Aftoora, Patricia Joan *transportation executive*
Ansbacher, Lewis *lawyer*
Austin, T. Edward (Ed Austin) *mayor*
†Baker, John Daniel, II *crushed stone company executive*
Barley, John McKim, II *architect*
Barrett, S. Barre *academic administrator, art educator*
Bartholomew, John Niles *church administrator*
Belin, Jacob Chapman *paper company executive*
Bennett, Charles Edward *former congressman, educator*
Birk, John R. *marketing/financial services executive*
Black, Susan Harrell *federal judge*
Blackburn, Robert McGrady *retired bishop*
Bodkin, Lawrence Edward *research development company executive, gemologist, inventor*
Bosworth, William Posey *physician, physical education educator*
Boyles, Carol Ann Patterson *career development educator*
Brady, James Joseph *university president*
Brann, William Paul *retired university official*
Bremer, Alfonso M. *neurosurgeon, neuro-oncologist*
Broward, Robert Charles *architect*
Brown, Lloyd Harcourt, Jr. *newspaper editor*
Bullock, Bruce Stanley *lawyer*
Carithers, Hugh Alfred *physician*
Carpenter, Alvin Rauso *transportation executive*
Cary, Cornelius Adams *executive search firm executive*
Cerveny, Frank Stanley *bishop*
Christian, Gary Irvin *lawyer*
Colby, Lestina Larsen *secondary education educator*
Commander, Charles Edward *lawyer, real estate consultant*
Criser, Marshall M. *lawyer*
†Cuny, John Dana *health care system executive*
Currie, Earl James *transportation company executive*
Davis, A. Dano *grocery store chain executive*
Davis, Jerry Ray *railroad company executive*
Dawes, Michael Francis *lawyer*
Drew, Horace Rainsford, Jr. *lawyer*
DuBow, Lawrence Jay *drug company executive*
Dundon, Margo Elaine *museum director*
Ehrlich, Raymond *lawyer*
El-Ansary, Adel Ibrahim *business educator*
Ernest, Albert Devery, Jr. *banker*
Farkas, Andrew *library director, educator, writer*
Farmer, Guy Otto, II *lawyer*
Fawbush, Andrew Jackson *lawyer*
Foster, Ronald H. *construction company executive*
Francis, James Delbert *oil company executive*
Frankland, G. Thomas *accountant, finance company executive*
Fredrickson, Arthur Allan *retired publishing company executive*
Freeman, Judson, Jr. *lawyer*
Fruit, Melvyn Herschel *lawyer, management consultant*
Gabel, George DeSaussure, Jr. *lawyer*
Getman, Willard Etheridge *lawyer*
Gibbons, G. Hunter *insurance executive*
Glocker, Theodore Wesley, Jr. *lawyer*
†Glover, Richard Bernard *association administrator*
Godfrey, John Munro *bank economist*
Goff, Charles Wesley, Jr. *management consultant*
Gregg, John Franklin *hospital administrator*
Groom, Dale *physician, educator*
Gunning, John Thaddeus *retired superintendent*
Hamilton, William Berry, Jr. *shipping company executive*
Hardrick, Charles M. *airport executive*
Harmon, Gary Lee *language professional, educator*
Hartmann, Frederick William *newspaper editor*
Haskell, Preston Hampton, III *construction company executive*
Hatch, Donald James (Jim Hatch) *business leadership and planning executive*
Herbert, Adam William, Jr. *university president*
Hill, James Clinkscales *federal judge*
Hodges, William Terrell *federal judge*
Howe, Jonathan Trumbull *naval officer*
Howell, John Floyd *insurance company executive*
Hrachovina, Frederick Vincent *osteopathic physician and surgeon*
Huebner, Jay Stanley *physicist, engineer, forensics consultant*
Jackson, Julian Ellis *food company executive*
Jeanes, Lincoln Douglas, Jr. *neurosurgeon*
Jenkins, Leerie Thurman, Jr. *architecture engineering planning firm executive*
Joyce, Edward Rowen *chemical engineer, educator*
Kelalis, Panayotis *pediatric urologist*
Kelly, Patrick Chastain *sales executive*
Kensey, Calvin D. *bishop*
Kent, Frederick Heber *lawyer*
Kinne, Frances Bartlett *chancellor emeritus*
Kirk, Robert Leonard *transportation company executive*
Klabosh, Charles Joseph *aerospace research and development executive*
Kress, Mary Elizabeth *newspaper editor*
Kufeldt, James *retail grocery store executive*
Lane, Edward Wood, Jr. *retired banker*
Lastinger, Allen Lane, Jr. *banker*
Lee, E. Denise *council woman*
Legler, Mitchell Wooten *lawyer*
Lestage, Daniel Barfield *retired naval officer, physician*
†Liebtag, Benford Gustav, III (Ben Liebtag) *engineer, consultant*
Lindner, Carl Henry, Jr. *financial holding company executive*
Loomis, Henry *former broadcasting company executive, former government official*
Lovett, Radford Dow *real estate and investment company executive*
Lyon, Sherman Orwig *rubber and chemical company executive*
Lyon, Wilford Charles, Jr. *insurance executive*
MacDonald, Carolyn Helms *gifted education educator*
Mann, Timothy *corporate executive*
Mason, William Cordell, III *hospital administrator*
Mass, M. F. *allergist, immunologist*
Massey, William Walter, Jr. *sales executive*
McCook, Richard Paul *grocery chain financial executive*
McCullough, Ray Daniel, Jr. *insurance company executive*
†McGehee, Frank Sutton *paper company executive*
McGehee, Thomas Rives *paper company executive*
McKellar, C. H. *grocery chain executive*
McWilliams, John Lawrence, III *lawyer*
Melton, Howell Webster, Sr. *federal judge*
Mikulas, Joseph Frank *graphic designer, educator, painter*
Monroe, Helen Leola *nurse, consultant, educator*
Monsky, John Bertrand *investment banking executive*
Moore, David Graham *sociologist, educator*
Moore, John Henry, II *federal judge*
†Morehead, Charles Richard *insurance company executive*
Morgan, William Newton *architect, educator*
Morris, William Shivers, III *newspaper executive*
Moseley, James Francis *lawyer*
Mueller, Edward Albert *transportation engineer executive*
Nelson, Julie D. *lawyer*
Nicolitz, Ernst *ophthalmologist, educator*
†Nicosia, Joseph A. *transportation company executive*
Oliver, Elizabeth Kimball *writer, historian*
O'Neal, Michael Scott, Sr. *lawyer*
Osborn, Marvin Griffing, Jr. *educational consultant*
†Osteen, H(oward) Kenneth, Jr. *real estate developer, hotel management executive*
Pappas, Ted Phillip *architect*
Parker, David Forster *real estate development consultant*
Pierson, David Lowell *orchestra manager*
Pillans, Charles Palmer, III *lawyer*
Prempree, Thongbliew *oncology radiologist*
Prom, Stephen George *lawyer*
Purcifull, Robert Otis *insurance company executive*
Rice, Charles Edward *banker*
Rinaman, James Curtis, Jr. *lawyer*
Rishel, Richard Clinton *banker*
Robbins, George William, III *chemical company executive*
Robinson, Christine Marie *mathematics educator*
Russell, David Emerson *mechanical engineer, consultant*
Sadler, Luther Fuller, Jr. *lawyer*
Schlageter, Robert William *museum administrator*
Schlesinger, Harvey Erwin *federal judge*
Schramm, Bernard Charles, Jr. *advertising agency executive*
Schultz, Frederick Henry *investor, former government official*
Sederbaum, William *marketing executive*
Sekely, George Frank *computer and communications executive*
Seroka, James Henry *social sciences educator, university administrator*
Shivler, James Fletcher, Jr. *retired civil engineer*
Singleton, Larry William *financial officer*
Slade, Thomas Bog, III *lawyer, investment banker*
Slaughter, Frank Gill *author, physician*
Smith, Ivan Huron *architect*
Snyder, John Joseph *bishop*
Stephenson, Samuel Edward, Jr. *physician*
Swenson, Courtland Sevander *retired musician*
Thornton, Winfred Lamotte *railroad executive*
Tierney, Patricia A. *school system administrator*
Tjoflat, Gerald Bard *federal judge*
Toker, Karen Harkavy *physician*
Tomlinson, William Holmes *management educator, retired army officer*
Travis, Forrest *investment firm executive*
Tsai, James Tarng *chemical and plastics company executive*
Vail, Patricia *lawyer*
Vincent, Norman Fuller *broadcasting executive*
Vines, Charles Jerry *minister*
Voss, Carl Hermann *clergyman, humanities educator, author*
Wallis, Donald Wills *lawyer*
Walters, John Sherwood *retired newspaperman*
Watford, John Hardin *bank executive*
Webster, David A. *lawyer*
Welch, Philip Burland *electronics and office products company executive*
Williams, Judith L. *library administrator*
Wilson, C. Nick *health educator, consultant, researcher, lecturer*
Winters, Robert Charles *architect*
Yamane, Stanley Joel *optometrist*

Jay
Peacock, Hugh Anthony *agricultural research director, educator*

Jensen Beach
Gamble, Raymond Wesley *marriage and family therapist, clergyman*
Kirjassoff, Gordon Louis *consulting civil engineer*
Sculfort, Maurice Charles *advertising agency executive*

Juno Beach
Migliaro, Marco William *electrical engineer*
Petillo, James Thomas *diversified utility company executive*

Jupiter
Anderson, Thomas Jefferson *publisher, rancher, public speaker, syndicated columnist*
Biebuyck, Daniel Prosper *retired anthropologist, educator*
Danforth, Arthur Edwards *finance executive*
Fazio, Tom *design firm executive, golf course designer*
Holbert, Theodore Frank *banker*
Komarek, Thomas Charles *retired government official*
Marker, Robert Sydney *management consultant*
Mc Call, Charles Barnard *health facility executive, educator*
McCall, Duke Kimbrough *clergyman*
Skully, Richard Patrick *airline consultant*
Taylor, Claude J. *sales executive, consultant*
Vanatta, Bob *athletic administrator*

Kennedy Space Center
Young, Richard Stuart *technical services executive*

Key Biscayne
Duffy, Earl Gavin *hotel executive*
Kraft, C. William, Jr. *federal judge*
Markell, Alan William *linguistic company executive*
Palmer, Roger Farley *pharmacology educator*

Key Largo
Brown, David *retired petrochemical corporation executive*
Chevins, Anthony Charles *advertising agency executive*
Daenzer, Bernard John *insurance company executive, legal consultant*
Daly, William Gerald *business executive*
Davidson, Thomas Noel *business executive*
Fundora, Thomas *artist, journalist, composer*
Mattson, James Stewart *lawyer, environmental scientist, educator*

Key West
Barnard, Scott *artist consultant*
Coudert, Ferdinand Wilmerding *lawyer*
Ellinghaus, William Maurice *communications executive*
Feeley, Henry Joseph, Jr. (Hank Feeley) *artist, former advertising agency executive*
Fizdale, Richard *advertising agency executive*
Henriquez, Armando Joseph *superintendent*
Lynch, William Thomas, Jr. *advertising agency executive*
Nolan, Robert D. *advertising company executive*
Oates, James G. *advertising executive*
Smith, John J. (Jack Smith) *advertising agency executive*
Trammell, Herbert Eugene *physicist, laboratory executive*

Lady Lake
Belok, Michael Victor *education educator*
Dore, Stephen Edward, Jr. *retired civil engineer*
Langevin, Thomas Harvey *higher education consultant*

Lake Alfred
Kender, Walter John *horticulturist, educator*
Nagy, Steven *biochemist*
Rouseff, Russell Lee *food chemistry educator, researcher*

Lake Buena Vista
Lomonosoff, James Marc *marketing executive*
Mc Mahon, Ed *television personality*
†Nunis, Richard Arlen *amusement parks executive*
Parke, Robert Leon *communications executive*

Lake City
Welborn, Elsie Elender Jenkins *nurse executive, nurse*
†Wheaton, T. Frederic, III *psychiatrist, retired naval officer*

Lake Mary
Franzen, Janice Marguerite Gosnell *magazine editor*
Strang, Stephen Edward *magazine editor, publisher*

Lake Park
McBride, Nancy Allyson *child resource center administrator*

Lake Placid
Layne, James Nathaniel *vertebrate biologist*

Lake Wales
Mumma, Albert G. *retired naval officer, retired manufacturing company executive, management consultant*

Lake Worth
Calder, Iain Wilson *publishing company executive*
Finch, Ronald M., Jr. *savings bank executive*
Kline, Gordon Mabey *chemist, editor*
Moore, Alderine Bernice Jennings (Mrs. James F. Moore) *association and organization administrator*
†Rabinowitz, Maynard *publishing executive*
Stevens, William John *management consultant, former association executive*

Lakeland
Campbell, James Arthur *professional baseball team executive*
Davis, Robert Aldine *college president*
Dufoe, William Stewart *lawyer*
Fadley, Ann Miller *English language and literature educator, writer*
Harritt, Norman L. *manufacturing company executive*
Hatten, William Seward *manufacturing company executive*
Hollis, Mark C. *supermarket company executive*
Hollis, Mark D. *federal official*
Hughes, Harold Hasbrouck, Jr. *bishop*
Jenkins, Charles H., Jr. *grocery company executive*
Jenkins, Howard M. *supermarket executive*
Kibler, David Burke, III *lawyer*
Kittleson, Henry Marshall *lawyer*
Koren, Edward Franz *lawyer*
Meads, Walter Frederick *executive recruitment consultant*
Miller, Robert Allen *hotel executive*
Peeler, Scott Loomis, Jr. *foreign language educator*
Perez, Louis Michael *newspaper editor*
Peterson, N. Curtis, Jr. *landscape architect, former state senator*
Reich, David Lee *library director*
Sheppard, Albert Parker, Jr. *mathematics educator*
Siedle, Robert Douglas *management consultant*
Smith, Levie David, Jr. *real estate appraiser, consultant*
Smith, Sherwood Draughon *retired hospital administrator*
Wade, Ben Frank *college administrator*

Lantana
†Rawls, L(oyd) Neal *communications executive*

Largo
Alpert, Barry Mark *insurance company and banking executive*
Boyle, John William *retail executive*
Brown, Warren Joseph *physician*
Craft Davis, Audrey Ellen *writer*
Criqui, William Edmund *lighting company financial executive*
Dolan, John E. *consultant, retired utility executive*
Fournier, Serge Raymond-Jean *orchestra conductor*
Gall, Keith D. *director*
Haile, James Francis *hospital administrator*
Hamlin, Robert Henry *public health educator, management consultant*
Hinesley, J. Howard *superintendent*
Keller, Gary William *printing manufacturing executive, accountant*
Loader, Jay Gordon *retired utility company executive*
Ray, Roger Buchanan *retired communications executive, lawyer*
Shapiro, Alan B. *secondary education educator*
†Slattery, James Lee *lawyer*
Williams, Harry George *minister*

Lecanto
Brogan, Howard Oakley *English language educator*

Leesburg
Entorf, Richard Carl *management consultant*
Houston, John Coates, Jr. *consultant*
Talley, William Giles, Jr. *container manufacturing company executive*

Lehigh Acres
Moore, John Newton *retired natural science educator*

Lighthouse Point
Farho, James Henry, Jr. *mechanical engineer, consultant*

Longboat Key
Cornelius, James Alfred *advertising executive*
Freeman, Richard Merrell *corporate director, lawyer*
Goldsmith, Jack Landman *former retail company executive*
Heitler, George *lawyer*
Maha, George Edward *research facility administrator, consultant*
Prizer, Charles John *chemical company executive*
Schoenberg, Lawrence Joseph *computer services company executive*

Longwood
†Bernabei, Raymond *management consultant*
Blumberg, Herbert Kurt *corporate executive*
Brooker, Robert Elton *corporate executive*
†Dunne, Nancy Anne *retired social services administrator*
Faller, Donald E. *marketing and operations executive*
Miller, William Jones *lawyer*
Reade, Richard Sill *manufacturing executive*
Smyth, Joseph Patrick *retired naval officer, physician*
Tomasulo, Virginia Merrills *retired lawyer*
Walters, Philip Raymond *foundation executive*
Yon, Eugene T. *process control company executive*

Lutz
Bedke, Ernest Alford *retired air force officer*
Garcia, Sandra Joanne Anderson *law and psychology educator*

Mac Dill AFB
†Downing, Wayne Allan *career officer*
LeMoyne, Irve Charles *career officer*
Passage, David *diplomat*
Schwendinger, Charles Joseph *public administration educator, researcher*
†Weinstein, Mark Steven *air force officer*

Madeira Beach
Beckerman, Milton Bernard *media broker*

Maitland
Blackburn, John Oliver *economist, consultant*
Braun, Charles Stuart *architect*
Crosby, Philip Bayard *company executive, author*
Davis, Paul Milton *television news administrator*
Fichthorn, Luke Eberly, III *investment banker*
†Galloway, Robert Thomas *aerospace engineer*
MacKenzie, Charles Sherrard *college president*
Nash, Ronald Herman *philosophy educator*
St. John, John *food company executive*
Vallee, Judith Delaney *environmentalist, fundraiser*
Whitlock, Luder Gradick, Jr. *seminary president*

Manalapan
Doherty, Thomas Joseph *financial services industry consultant*
Johnstone, Edmund Frank *advertising executive*

Marathon
Calvert, William Preston *radiologist*
Janicki, Robert Stephen *retired pharmaceutical company executive*
Kolker, Roger Russell *insurance executive*
Mc Cormick, Edward Allen *foreign language educator*
Wiecha, Joseph Augustine *linguist, educator*

Marco Island
Butler, Frederick George *retired drug company executive*
Fisher, Chester Lewis, Jr. *retired lawyer*
Guerrant, David Edward *retired food company executive*
Hurley, Patrick Mason *geology educator*
Jones, Edward Magruder *television producer and writer, correspondent*
Lavin, John Halley *editor, author*
Lesser, Joseph M. *retired business executive, retail store executive*
Pettersen, Kjell Will *stockbroker, consultant*
Poletti, Charles *lawyer*
Sundberg, R. Dorothy *physician, educator*
Thorson, Oswald Hagen *architect*
Wheeler, Warren G(age), Jr. *retired publishing executive*

Marianna
Flowers, Virginia Anne *academic administrator emerita*

Melbourne
Abbott, Robert Tucker *zoologist, author*
Babich, Michael Wayne *chemistry educator, educational administrator*
Baney, Richard Neil *physician, internist*
Barr, Constance R. *school system administrator*
Boyd, Joseph Aubrey *communications company executive*
Button, Kenneth John *physicist*
Cacciatore, S. Sammy, Jr. *lawyer*
Canfield, Constance Dale *accountant, nurse*
Cockriel, Russell George, Sr. *crime investigation official*
Edwards, David Northrop *retired university administrator*
Fay, Robert Woods *financial executive*
Gabriel, Roger Eugene *management consulting executive*
Hartley, John T., Jr. *electronic systems, semiconductor, communications and office equipment executive*
Helmstetter, Charles Edward *microbiologist*
Hogan, Henry Leon, III *business executive, retired air force officer*
Hollingsworth, Abner Thomas *university dean*
†Kehoe, Thomas A. *newspaper company executive*
Krieger, Robert Edward *publisher*
Lakshmikantham, Vangipuram *mathematics educator*
Lewis, Bernard Leroy *electronic scientist, consultant*
Means, Michael David *hospital administrator*
Michalski, Thomas Joseph *city planner, developer*
Nelson, Gordon Leigh *chemist, educator*
Noonan, Norine Elizabeth *academic administrator, researcher*
†Pruitt, J. Michael *real estate company executive*
†Pruitt, James H. *real estate company executive*
Roub, Bryan R(oger) *financial executive*
Scheuerer, Diane Thompson *home economics educator*
Sottile, James *financier*
Spezzano, Vincent Edward *newspaper publisher*
Stark, Bruce Gunsten *artist*
Storrs, Eleanor Emerett *research institute consultant*
Suojanen, Waino W. *management educator*
Swalm, Thomas Sterling *aerospace executive, retired military officer*
Van Arsdall, Robert Armes *engineer, retired air force officer*
Vilardebo, Angie Marie *management consultant, parochial school educator*
von Ohain, Hans Joachim P. *aerospace scientist*
Weaver, Lynn Edward *academic administrator, consultant, editor*
†Weldon, David Joseph, Jr. *congressman, physician*

Melrose
Burt, Alvin Victor, Jr. *journalist*
Harley, Ruth *artist, educator*
Meyer, Harvey Kessler, II *retired academic administrator*

Merritt Island
McClanahan, Leland *academic adminstrator*

Miami
Ajamil, Luis *civil engineer*
Alexenberg, Mel *artist, art educator*
Allen, Charles Norman *television, film and video producer*
Alonso, Antonio Enrique *lawyer*
Alschuler, Al *freelance writer, public relations counselor*
Altro, David A. *lawyer*
Anders, Walter Charles *human resources administrator*
Anderson, Douglas Richard *ophthalmologist, educator, scientist, researcher*
Anger, Paul *newspaper sports editor*
Anscher, Bernard *manufacturing executive, investor, management consultant*
Arango, Jorge Sanin *architect*
Arison, Micky *cruise line company executive*
Armstrong, James Louden, III *lawyer*
Aronovitz, Sidney M. *federal judge*
Astigarraga, Jose I(gnacio) *lawyer*
Atkins, C(arl) Clyde *federal judge*
Atlas, Randall I. *architect, criminologist*
Autrey, Frank Eugene *engineering company executive*
†Avino, Joaquin G. *county official*
Baena, Scott Louis *lawyer*
Balmaseda, Liz *columnist*
Barkett, Rosemary *federal judge*
Barnes, Donald Winfree *banker*
Barritt, Evelyn Ruth Berryman *nurse, educator, university dean*
Barry, Dave *columnist, author*
Basile, Michael *lawyer*
Bastian, James Harold *air transport company executive, lawyer*
Batten, James Knox *newspaper executive*
Bauer, Peter Alexander *clothing executive*
Beckley, Donald K. *fundraiser*
Bemis, Lawrence Perry *lawyer*
Berger, Arthur Seymour *author, lawyer, director cultural organization*
Berger, Joyce Muriel *foundation executive, author, editor*
Berkman, Harold William *marketing educator*
Berley, David Richard *lawyer*
Berman, Bruce Judson *lawyer*
†Bernstein, Stephen *healthcare executive*
Bezdek, Hugo Frank *scientific laboratory administrator*
Bishopric, Karl *investment banker, real estate executive, advertising executive*
Bitter, John *university dean emeritus, musician, businessman, diplomat*
Black, Creed Carter *newspaper executive*
Blackburn, James Ross, Jr. *business executive, retired airline pilot*
Blanco, Luciano-Nilo *physicist*
Bolooki, Hooshang *cardiac surgeon*
Bradley, Ronald Calvin *investment company executive*
Brady, Alexander Childs *dancer*
Braman, Norman *automotive executive, football club executive*
Breman, Joseph Eliot *school administrator, lawyer*
Brenner, Esther Hannah *elementary school educator*
Brinkman, Paul Del(bert) *foundation executive*
Brock, James Daniel *retired airline executive, consultant*
Brown, Morton Paul *lawyer*
Brown, Stephen Thomas *magistrate judge*
Brownell, Edwin Rowland *banker, civil engineer, land surveyor and mapper*
Bufman, Zev *stage producer, theater chain executive*
Bunge, Richard Paul *cell biologist, educator*
Burkett, Marjorie Theresa *nursing educator, gerontology nurse*
Burnett, Henry *lawyer*
Burns, Mitchel Anthony *transportation services company executive*
Capraro, Franz *investment management executive*
Carman, Gary Michael *lawyer*
Carr, Charles Lee Glenn, Jr. (Chuck Carr) *professional baseball player*
Casariego, Jorge Isaac *psychiatrist, psychoanalyst, educator*
Catanzaro, Tony *dancer*
Cesarano, Gregory Morgen *lawyer*
Cesarano, Michael Chapman *lawyer*
†Chaplin, Harvey *wine and liquor wholesale executive*
Chapman, Alvah Herman, Jr. *newspaper executive*
Chavin, Walter *biological science educator and researcher*
Cherry, Andrew Lawrence, Jr. *social work educator, researcher*
Clark, Ira C. *hospital association administrator, educator*
Clark, John Russell *ecologist*
Clark, Stephen P. *mayor*
Clarke, Mercer Kaye *lawyer*
Clifton, Douglas C. *newspaper editor*
Clot, Archlyn Ann *medical technologist*
Cohen, Alex *retired publisher*
Cohen, Eugene Erwin *university health institute administrator, accounting educator emeritus*
Cohen, Jacob *bishop*
Cohen, Sanford Irwin *physician, educator*
Cole, Robert Bates *lawyer*
Cole, Todd G. *management consultant transportation*
Colwin, Arthur Lentz *biologist, educator*
Comras, Rema *library director*
Conese, Eugene P., Jr. *aircraft maintenance executive*
Conese, Eugene Paul, Sr. *manufacturing company executive*
Connor, Terence Gregory *lawyer*
Conrad, Barry L. *hotel and restaurant executive*
Cooper, Thomas Astley *banking executive*
Cooper, William James *chemist*
Corcoran, Eugene Francis *chemist, educator*
Correll, Helen Butts *botanist, researcher*
Cosgrove, John Francis *state legislator, lawyer*
Coton, Carlos David *finance manager*
Courshon, Arthur Howard *banker, lawyer*
Courshon, Carol Biel *civic worker*
Cristol, A. Jay *federal judge*
Cubas, Jose M(anuel) *advertising agency executive*
Cullom, William Otis *trade association executive*
Dady, Robert Edward *lawyer*
Daughtry, DeWitt Cornell *surgeon, physician*
Davis, Edward Bertrand *federal judge*
†Davis, Richard Edmund *plastic surgeon*
Deaktor, Darryl Barnett *lawyer*
Dean, Stanley Rochelle *psychiatrist*
de la Guardia, Mario Francisco *electrical engineer*
Dellapa, Gary J. *airport terminal executive*
Denison, Floyd Gene *insurance executive*
Desautel, Helen Craig *health facility administrator*
Dickason, John Hamilton *foundation executive*
Dickey, Arden *newspaper publishing executive*
Dickinson, Robert H. *water transportation executive*
Dimond, Alan Theodore *lawyer*
Dolen, Christine Arnold *theater critic*
Dorion, Robert Charles *entrepreneur, investor*
Dottin, Erskine S. *education educator*
Downey, Ellen *transportation company executive*
Driscoll, Garrett Bates *telecommunications executive*
Dubocq, Tom *newspaper reporter*
Dunaway, Victor Allan *editor*
Dye, H. Michael *engineering executive*
Dyer, David William *federal judge*
Dyer, John Martin *lawyer, marketing educator*
Eaglstein, William Howard *dermatologist, educator*
Ehrlich, Morton *international finance executive*
England, Arthur Jay, Jr. *lawyer, former state justice*
Estefan, Gloria Maria *singer, songwriter*
Etling, Russell Hull *museum director, production company executive*
Evans, Peter Kenneth *advertising executive*
Fain, Richard David *cruise line executive*
Fascell, Dante B. *lawyer, congressman*
Fay, Peter Thorp *federal judge*
Feito, Jose *architect*
Ferguson, Wilkie D., Jr. *federal judge*
Ferrer, Esteban A. *lawyer*
Fichtner, Margaria *journalist*
Fine, Rana Arnold *chemical, physical oceanographer*
Fletcher, John Sheidley *lawyer*
Flynn, John T. *ophthalmology educator*
Fontaine, John C. *newspaper company executive, corporate lawyer*
Foote, Edward Thaddeus, II *university president, lawyer*
Frank, Walter Monroe, Jr. *media specialist*
Frei, Sister John Karen *university administrator*
Freitag, Dean Marco *lawyer*
Freshwater, Michael Felix *hand surgeon, educator*
Frigo, James Peter Paul *industrial hardware company executive*
Furia, Arthur Joseph *lawyer*
Garber, Barry L. *judge*
Garcia-Pedrosa, Jose Ramon *lawyer*
Garner, John Michael *investment company executive*
Gassen, Joseph Albert *lawyer, former judge*
Gelband, Henry *pediatric cardiologist*
Gerber, Seymour *publishing company executive*
Gibb, Maurice *vocalist, songwriter*
Gibbons, Barry J. *food service executive*
Giller, Norman Myer *banker, architect, author*
†Gimenez, Carlos Antonio *fire chief*
Ginsberg, Myron David *neurologist*
Gittess, Ronald Marvin *dentist*
Gittlin, Arthur Sam *industrialist, banker*
Glaskowsky, Elizabeth Pope *nutritionist, dietitian*
Godofsky, Lawrence *lawyer*
Gold, Alan Stephen *lawyer, educator, judge*
Goldenberg, I. Ira *academic administrator*
Golub, Alan *clothing company executive*
Gong, Edmond Joseph *lawyer*
Gonzales, Sylvia Alicia *academic administrator, communications executive*
Gonzalez-Pita, J. Alberto *lawyer*
Gordon, Jack David *senator, foundation executive*
Graboski, Thomas Walter *designer, artist*
Gragg, Karl Lawrence *lawyer*
Graham, Donald Lynn *federal judge*
Greene, Joe (Charles Edward Greene) *former professional football player, professional football coach*
Greer, Alan Graham *lawyer*
Halberg, F. David *principal*
Hall, Andrew Clifford *lawyer*
Hampton, John Lewis *newspaper editor*
Hampton, Mark Garrison *architect*
Hanlon, David Patrick *hotel and casino executive*
Hanna, Ronald Everette *art educator, consultant*
Harris, Douglas Clay *newspaper executive*
Harris, Steven Michael *lawyer*
Harvey, Bryan Stanley *professional baseball player*
Hayashi, Teru *zoologist, educator*
Hector, Louis Julius *lawyer*
†Heggen, Arthur William *insurance company executive*
Hendrickson, Harvey Sigbert *accounting educator*
Henson, John Denver *international management consulting firm executive*
Hern, Kenneth Truman *oil and gas industry executive*
Herron, James Michael *lawyer*
Hertz, David Bendel *management consultant, educator, lawyer*
Heuer, Robert Maynard, II *opera company executive*
Highsmith, Shelby *federal judge*
Higley, Bruce Wadsworth *orthodontist*
Hills, Lee *foundation administrator, newspaper executive, consultant*
Hoeveler, William M. *federal judge*
Hoffman, Larry J. *lawyer*
Holtz, Abel *bank executive*
Holtz, Daniel Martin *banker*
Houlihan, Gerald John *lawyer*
Howell, Ralph Rodney *pediatrician, educator*
Hoy, William Ivan *minister, religion educator*
Hoyt, Clark Freeland *journalist, newspaper editor*
Hudson, Robert Franklin, Jr. *lawyer*
Hurtgen, Peter Joseph *lawyer*
Huston, Edwin Allen *transportation company executive*
Huysman, Arlene Weiss *psychologist, educator*
Hyman, Milton *dental educator*
Johnson, Glendon E. *insurance company executive*
Johnson, Linnea R. *judge*
Jones y Diez Arguelles, Gastón Roberto *language educator*
Jude, James Roderick *cardiac surgeon*
Kanter, Joseph Hyman *banker, community developer*
Keeley, Brian E. *hospital administrator*
Kehoe, James W. *federal judge*
Kenin, David S. *lawyer*
Ketcham, Alfred Schutt *surgeon, educator*
King, James Lawrence *federal judge*
King, Shepard *lawyer*
Kline, Charles C. *lawyer*
Klock, Joseph Peter, Jr. *lawyer*
Knight, Charles Frasuer *architect*
Koch, William Henry *elementary education educator*
Korchin, Judith Miriam *lawyer*
Kozlowski, Ronald Stephan *librarian*
Kram, Michael Arnold *magazine publisher*
Kunce, Avon Estes *senior vocational rehabilitation counselor*
Kunstler, David B. *airline company executive*
Kutner, Maurice Jay *lawyer*
Lachemann, Rene George *professional sports manager*
Lampen, Richard Jay *lawyer, investment banker*
Landon, Robert Kirkwood *insurance company executive*
Landy, Burton Aaron *lawyer*
Lapidus, Morris *retired architect, interior designer*
Lasseter, Kenneth Carlyle *pharmacologist*
Lawrence, David, Jr. *newspaper editor, publisher*
Lazaga, Jose Ignacio *airline executive*
Le Duc, Albert Louis, Jr. *computer services director*
Leeder, Ellen Lismore *language and literature educator, literary critic*
Lehrman, Irving *rabbi*
Leite, Eduardo Cerqueira *lawyer*
Lemberg, Louis *cardiologist, educator*
Le Mehaute, Bernard Jean *marine physics educator*
Lewis, John Milton *cable television company executive*
Light, Alfred Robert *lawyer, political scientist*
Lindquist, Claude S. *electrical and computer engineering educator*
Long, Maxine Master *lawyer*
Louis, Paul Adolph *lawyer*
Maidique, Modesto Alex *academic administrator*
Man, Eugene Herbert *chemist, educator, business executive*
Mandine, Salvador G. *insurance executive*
Manov, Leslie Joan Boyle *radiologist, medical administrator*
Marano, Angeline Marie *hospital administrator*
Marcus, Stanley *federal judge*
Martínez, Luís Osvaldo *radiologist, educator*
Martinez, Walter Baldomero *architect*
Mathews, Byron Burnett, Jr. *lawyer*
†May, Peter William *business executive*
†McCabe, Robert Howard *educator, college president*
Mc Kenzie, John Maxwell *physician*
†Messing, Fred M. *health care executive*
Mettinger, Karl Lennart *neurologist*
†Meyer, Hank *public relations and publicity consultant*
Miller, Gene Edward *newspaper reporter and editor*
Mooers, Christopher Northrup Kennard *physical oceanographer, educator*
Moore, Kevin Michael *federal judge*
Moore, Michael T. *lawyer*
Moreno, Federico Antonio *federal judge*
Morgan, Andrew Wesley *artist, educator*
Morgan, Marabel *author*
Mozian, Gerard Paul *real estate company executive, business consultant*
Mudd, John Philip *lawyer*
Munn, Janet Teresa *lawyer*
Murphy, Stephen Edward *international media and finance consultant*
Myers, Joyce Anne *fast food chain company executive*
Myers, Kenneth M. *lawyer*
Myrberg, Arthur August, Jr. *marine biological sciences educator*
Nagel, Joachim Hans *biomedical engineer, educator*
Natoli, Joe *newspaper publishing executive*
Navarro, Antonio (Luis) *public relations executive*
Nesbitt, Lenore Carrero *federal judge*
Nicholson, William Mac *naval architect, marine engineer, consultant*
Nisonson, Ian *urologist*
†Noriega, Rudy Jorge *hospital administrator*
Nuernberg, William Richard *lawyer*
O'Bryon, Linda Elizabeth *television station executive*
O'Rourke, Jack *financial company administrator*
Osman, Edith Gabriella *lawyer*
Ostlund, H. Gote *atmospheric and marine scientist, educator*
Page, Larry Keith *neurosurgeon, educator*
Pancake, John *newspaper editor*
Papper, Emanuel Martin *anesthesiologist*
Parker, Alfred Browning *architect*
Parker, David Raymond *services industry executive*
Parker, Ree *real estate investor*
Parris, Nina Gumpert *curator, writer, researcher*
Pasano, Michael S. *lawyer*
Paul, Robert *lawyer*
Pearson, Daniel S. *lawyer*
Pearson, John Edward *lawyer*
†Peltz, Nelson *manufacturing company executive*
Pitts, Leonard Garvey, Jr. *columnist, writer*
Plater-Zyberk, Elizabeth Maria *architectural educator*
Plungis, Barbara Marie *health facility nursing administrator*
Politano, Victor Anthony *urology educator, physician*
Pomeranz, Felix *accounting educator*
Pope, John Edwin, III *newspaper sports editor*
Porter, Charles King *advertising executive*
Postel, Joachim Michael *cardiac surgeon*
Potter, James Douglas *pharmacology educator*
Powers, Joseph Edward *marine biologist*
Prineas, Ronald James *epidemiologist, educator*
Pyles, Carol DeLong *dean, consultant, educator*
Quencer, Robert Moore *neuroradiologist, researcher*
Quentel, Albert Drew *lawyer*
Raffel, Leroy B. *real estate development company executive*
Randolph, Jennings, Jr. (Jay Randolph) *sportscaster*

Ream, John K. banker
Rebozo, Charles Gregory banker
Reed, Alfred retired composer, conductor
Reed, George Francis architect
Reid, R(alph) Benjamine lawyer
Reisinger, Sandra Sue journalist, lawyer
Ripstein, Charles Benjamin surgeon
Robbie, Timothy John professional football team executive
Rockstein, Morris science writer, editor, consultant
Roemer, Elaine Sloane real estate broker
Rosenberg, Mark B. think-tank executive
Rosendahl, Bruce Ray dean, geophysicist, educator
Rosenthal, Stanley Lawrence meteorologist
Ross, David Lee lawyer
Rossie, Carlos Enrique computer school administrator
Rothchild, Howard Leslie advertising executive
Routh, Donald K(ent) psychology educator
†Rubin, Bruce S. public relations executive
Russell, Elbert Winslow neuropsychologist
Russell, James Webster, Jr. newspaper editor, columnist
Ryce, Donald Theodore lawyer
Sacher, Barton Stuart lawyer
Sackner, Marvin Arthur physician
Salazar-Carrillo, Jorge economics educator
Salvaneschi, Luigi real estate and development executive, business educator
Samole, Myron Michael lawyer
Sanchez, Robert Francis journalist
Sandoval, Arturo jazz musician
Santiago, Benito Rivera professional baseball player
Sapp, Neil Carleton international airline pilot, industrial consultant
Savage, James Francis editor
Scheinberg, Peritz neurologist
Scheinberg, Steven Eliot investment banker
Schiff, Eugene Roger medical educator, hepatologist
Schofield, Calvin Onderdonk, Jr. bishop
Schonbrun, Michael Keith health care executive
Schuetzenduebel, Wolfram Gerhard engineering executive
Schulman, Clifford A. lawyer
Schwartz, Kessel modern language educator
Seitz, Patricia Ann lawyer
Seline, Rex reporter
Shaklan, Allen Yale broadcast executive
Sharett, Alan Richard lawyer, environmental litigator, mediator and arbitrator, educator
Sheffield, Gary Antonian professional baseball player
Shepherd, Frank Andrew lawyer
Shevin, Robert Lewis lawyer
Shoemaker, Don (Donald Cleavenger Shoemaker) columnist
Shroder, Tom newspaper editor
Sieger, Charles Martin architect
Silber, Norman Jules lawyer
Silva, Felipe former tobacco company executive
Sims, James Larry hospital administrator, healthcare consultant
Sims, Keith professional football player
Smathers, Frank, Jr. banker, horticulturist
Smiley, Logan Henry journalist, public concern consultant
†Smirnoff, Bear recreational facility executive
Smith, Chesterfield Harvey lawyer
Smith, Samuel Stuart lawyer
†Sommerville, Mary Robinson library director
Sonnett, Neal Russell lawyer
Sonsky, Steve newspaper editor
Stanley, Sherry A. lawyer
Steinback, Robert Lamont newspaper columnist
Stephan, Egon, Sr. cinematographer, film equipment company executive
Stephens, Franklin Wilson transportation executive
Stickler, Daniel Lee health care management consultant
Stokes, Paul Mason lawyer
Stoller, Eric Chester stockbroker
Stover, James Howard real estate executive
Strait, Loraine Hall lawyer
Stratos, Kimarie Rose lawyer, sports agent
Strickland, Thomas Joseph artist
Strong, Charles Robert waste management administrator
Stuchins, Carol Mayberry nursing executive
Stuzin, Charles Bryan savings and loan association executive
Suarez, Roberto newspaper publishing executive
Suarez, Xavier Louis lawyer, former mayor
Sussex, James Neil psychiatrist, educator
Tarkoff, Michael Harris lawyer
Taylor, Ann Louise marketing executive
Taylor, Stephen Dewitt savings and loan association executive
Teicher, Morton Irving social worker, educator
Tejada, Francisco physician, educator
Telesca, Francis Eugene architect
Terilli, Samuel A., Jr. newspaper publishing executive
Tew, Jeffrey Allen lawyer
Thornton, Sandi Tokoa elementary education educator
Tifford, Arthur W. lawyer
Toro, Carlos Hans insurance/financial products marketing executive
Torres, Milton John industrial engineering educator
Treister, Kenneth architect, artist
Treyz, Joseph Henry librarian
Ungaro-Benages, Ursula Mancusi federal judge
Valdes-Dapena, Marie Agnes pediatric pathologist, educator
Valle, Laurence Francis lawyer
VanBrode, Derrick Brent, IV association executive
Van Wyck, George Richard insurance company executive
Verdeja, Sam newspaper publishing executive
Veziroglu, Turhan Nejat mechanical engineering educator, energy researcher
Wackenhut, George Russell security services executive
Wackenhut, Richard Russell security company executive
†Walsh, Bryan Oliver social services administrator, priest
Walters, David McLean lawyer
Webb, Richmond Jewel professional football player
Weber, Nancy Walker charitable trust administrator
Weeks, Marta Joan priest
Weigel, Rainer R. lawyer
Weiner, Morton David banker, insurance agent
Weinstein, Alan Edward lawyer
Weinstein, Andrew H. lawyer
Weiser, Ralph Raphael recovery company executive
Weiser, Sherwood Manuel hotel and corporation executive, lawyer
Weitzel, Peter Andre editor, newspaper
Weldon, Norman Ross manufacturing company executive
Wells, Daniel Ruth physics educator
Werth, Susan lawyer
Wessel, Jeffrey Hall bank executive
Whisenand, James Dudley lawyer
Wickstrom, Karl Youngert publishing company executive
Williams, James A. principal
Williamson, William Paul, Jr. journalist
Willis, Kevin Alvin professional basketball player
Wilson, Milner Bradley, III banker
Wolfenson, Azi U. electrical engineer
Wolper, Marshall insurance and financial consultant
Wragg, Joanna DiCarlo public relation executive, newspaper editor
Young, Freddie Gilliam educational administrator
Zanakis, Steve H. management/science/information systems educator
Zeiller, Warren former aquarium executive, consultant

Miami Beach
Abraham, William Michael physiologist
Balás, Irene Barbara artist
Chirovsky, Nicholas Ludomir economics educator, historian, author
Cunningham, Billy (William John Cunningham) professional basketball team executive, television sportscaster
Fort-Brescia, Bernardo architect
Gibb, Robin vocalist, songwriter
Gitlow, Abraham Leo retired university dean
Goldstein, Burton Jack psychiatrist
†Lawson, Eve Kennedy ballet mistress
Meyer, Sylvan Hugh editor, magazine executive, author
Schaffel, Lewis professional basketball team executive
Shapiro, Samuel Bernard management consultant
Spear, Laurinda Hope architect
Wax, William Edward photojournalist

Miami Lakes
Dominik, Jack Edward lawyer
Getz, Morton Ernest medical facility director, gastroenterologist

Miami Shores
Boyle, Judith Pullen clinical psychology, professor
O'Laughlin, Sister Jeanne university administrator

Micanopy
Cripe, Wyland Snyder veterinary medicine educator, consultant

Micco
Muller, Henry John real estate developer

Mount Dora
Adams, Carl Morgan, Jr. real estate appraiser, mortgage banker
Edgerton, Richard restaurant and hotel owner
Goodwin, Harry Eugene journalist, educator
Hensinger, Margaret Elizabeth horticultural and agricultural advertising and marketing executive
Hoag, Arthur Howard, Jr. retired architect
Myren, Richard Albert criminal justice consultant
Santini, John Amedeo educational consultant
Trussell, Charles Tait columnist

Mulberry
†Badcock, Wogan Stanhope, Jr. manufacturing company executive
Carrier, W(illiam) David, III geotechnical engineer

Murdock
Cross, George R. insurance consultant

Naples
Abbott, John Sheldon law school dean and chancellor emeritus
Alpert, Hollis writer
Ancker-Johnson, Betsy physicist, engineer, retired automotive company executive
Arthur, William Bolling retired editor
Baldwin, Ralph Belknap retired manufacturing company executive, astronomer
Barth-Wehrenalp, Gerhard chemical company executive
Beam, Robert Thompson retired lawyer
Benedict, Manson chemical engineer, educator
Berman, Robert S. marketing consultant
Biondo, Michael Thomas retired paper company executive
Buccello, Henry Louis advertising executive
Budd, David Glenn lawyer
Bush, John William business executive, federal official
Cantelon, John Edward academic administrator
Card, Orson Scott (Byron Walley) writer
Chartrand, Robert Lee information scientist
Ciano, James Francis computer systems analyst
Clapp, Roger Howland retired newspaper executive
Clark, Kenneth Edwin psychologist, former university dean
Craighead, Rodkey banker
Crehan, Joseph Edward lawyer
Crone, William Gerald hospital administrator
Daniels, Myra Janco (Mrs. Draper Daniels) advertising agency executive
Dion, Nancy Logan health care administrator, management consultant
Dodds, Robert James, Jr. retired lawyer
Dover, Clarence Joseph entrepreneur, public and employee relations executive, educator, consultant, communication director
Duff, Daniel Vincent former insurance company executive, former mayor
Dutton, Clarence Benjamin lawyer
Eldridge, David Carlton art appraiser
Elliott, Edward investment executive, financial planner
Emerson, John Williams, II lawyer
Evans, Elizabeth Ann West real estate agent
Farese, Lawrence Anthony lawyer
Fess, Philip Eugene accountant, educator
Frazer, John Howard tennis association executive, retired manufacturing company executive
Freedman, Stanley Marvin manufacturing company executive
Gahagan, Thomas Gail obstetrician, gynecologist
†Gardner, Frank museum director
Gilman, John Richard, Jr. organization behavior consultant
Gordon, Martin publisher, print dealer
Gresham, Robert Coleman transportation consultant
Griffin, Linda L. English language and speech educator
Gross, Paul pathologist, educator
Guarino, Roger Charles consulting company executive
Gushman, John Louis former corporation executive, lawyer
Hainsworth, Melody May information professional, researcher
Harvey, Curran Whitthorne, Jr. investment management executive
Hebald, Milton Elting sculptor
Hennessy, Brother Paul Kevin religion educator
Hobbs, Ranald Purcell publisher
Hochschwender, Herman Karl international consultant
Hooper, John Allen retired banker
Ivancevic, Walter Charles former gas distribution company executive
Johnson, Walter L. transportation company executive
Johnson, Zane Quentin retired petroleum company executive
Jones, Richard Wallace interior designer
Kapnick, Harvey Edward, Jr. retired corporate executive
Kay, Herbert retired natural resources company executive
Kennedy, Robert Emmet retired newspaperman
Kley, John Arthur banker
Leitner, Alfred mathematical physicist, educator, educational film producer
Levitt, LeRoy Paul psychiatrist, psychoanalyst
Lewis, Gordon Gilmer golf course architect
Mahoney, Sheila Irene middle school educator
Maloon, James Harold business executive, economist
Marshall, Charles communications company executive
Martinuzzi, Leo Sergio, Jr. banker
McCaffrey, Judith Elizabeth lawyer
Mc Combs, G. B. publishing company executive
Mc Queen, Robert Charles retired insurance executive
Montgomery, Ruth Shick author
Moore, Mechlin Dongan business consultant
Moorefield, James Lee retired insurance executive, lawyer
Myers, Charles Andrew retired economist
Oliver, Robert Bruce retired investment company executive
O'Neill, William Robert lawyer
Osias, Richard Allen international financier, investor, real estate investment executive, corporate investor
Parish, John Cook insurance executive
Passidomo, John Michael lawyer
Peck, Bernard Sidney lawyer
Perry, Jesse Laurence, Jr. investment manager, financier
Price, Thomas Benjamin former textile company executive
Putzell, Edwin Joseph, Jr. lawyer, mayor
Quigley, Jack Allen service company executive
Reed, John Franklin instrument manufacturing company executive
Richmond, Robert Linn management consultant
Roberts, William B. lawyer, business executive
Robinson, Nathaniel David physician
Rowe, Herbert Joseph retired trade association executive
Rowe, Jack Field retired electric utility executive
Scarlett, Harold O. retired retail executive, consultant
Schauer, Wilbert Edward, Jr. lawyer, manufacturing company executive
Sharpe, Robert Francis equipment manufacturing company executive
Smith, Willis Allen retired consultant, former food company executive
Snyder, Marion Gene lawyer, former congressman
Stevens, William Kenneth lawyer
Stewart, Harris Bates, Jr. oceanographer
Suziedelis, Vytautas A. engineering corporation executive
Tanner, Robert Hugh engineer, consultant
Terenzio, Peter Bernard hospital administrator
Van der Eb, Henry Gerard retired packaging company executive
Vickrey, Robert Remsen artist
von Arx, Dolph William food products executive
Waller, George Macgregor historian, educator
Weeks, Richard Ralph marketing educator
Westman, Carl Edward lawyer
White, Roy Bernard theater executive
Widman, Richard Gustave engineering and construction company executive
Williams, George Earnest engineer, retired business executive
Wodlinger, Mark Louis broadcast executive
Wyant, Corbin A. newspaper publisher

New Port Richey
Focht, Theodore Harold lawyer, educator
Oliveto, Frank Louis recreation consultant
Recchia, Susan Margaret artist, author
Rhodes, Eric Foster real estate and insurance executive, consultant
Sorensen, John Frederick retired minister

New Smyrna Beach
Hollis, Reginald archbishop
Makela, Benjamin R. editor, research director
Skove, Thomas Malcolm retired manufacturing company financial executive

Niceville
Burns, John Joseph consultant, retired aerospace executive, retired air force officer
†Hagwood, Henry Melvin, Jr. career officer
Litke, Donald Paul business executive, retired military officer
Phillips, Richard Wendell, Jr. air force officer

Nokomis
Cather, Donald Warren civil engineer
Halladay, Laurie Ann public relations consultant, former franchise executive
Meyerhoff, Jack Fulton financial executive
Peters, Farnsley Lewellyn retired association executive

North Fort Myers
Hoffman, Nelson Miles, Jr. retired academic administrator, consultant
Rogliano, Aldo Thomas publishing executive

North Miami
Cliff, Jimmy (James Chambers) vocalist, composer
Polley, Richard Donald microbiologist, polymer chemist

North Miami Beach
Averch, Harvey Allan economist, educator, academic administrator
Fishel, Peter Livingston accounting business executive
Terry, Morton academic administrator, physician

North Palm Beach
Bubrick, George Joseph corporate executive
Chane, George Warren management consultant
Connor, John Thomas retired bank and corporate executive, lawyer
†Crawford, Roberta association administrator
Doede, John Henry investment company executive
Edwards, William James broadcasting executive
Fauver, John William mayor, retired business executive
Gray, Harry Jack investment executive
Hayman, Richard Warren Joseph conductor
Hushing, William Collins retired corporate executive
Kenna, Edgar Douglas manufacturing company executive
Nicklaus, Jack William professional golfer
Oleksiw, Daniel Philip former foreign service officer, consultant
Rimmer, Jack retired chemical company executive
Staub, W. Arthur health care products executive
Yackira, Michael William power company executive

Ocala
Andrews, Richard L. bank executive
Booth, George Warren artist, advertising executive
Cabrera-Mendez, Fabio psychiatrist
Cini, Anthony Richard bookbinding craftsman
Corwin, William psychiatrist
Forgue, Stanley Vincent physics educator
Grissom, Robert Jesse, Sr. criminal justice educator
Johnson, Winston Conrad mathematics educator
Lewis, Richard Knox assitant city manager
Parker, Harry Lee retired military officer, counselor
Phillips, Margaret Crouse gifted and talented educator

Ocoee
Rose, Peter Edward former professional baseball player and manager

Odessa
Lister, Thomas Mosie composer, lyricist, publishing company executive, minister

Oldsmar
Brunner, George Matthew management consultant, former business executive
Burrows, William Claude aerospace executive, retired air force officer
Hirschman, Sherman Joseph lawyer, educator
Ligett, Waldo Buford chemist
Sloane, Thomas Charles lawyer
Thompson, Mack Eugene history educator

Ona
Pate, Findlay Moye agriculture educator, university center director
Rechcigl, Jack Edward soil and environmental sciences educator

Opa Locka
Clark, Gary C. football player
Dawson, Andre Nolan professional baseball player
Hopton, Janice elementary school principal
Kosar, Bernie, Jr. professional football player
Marino, Daniel Constantine, Jr. professional football player
Nelsen, Martin Claude management services professional
Pendleton, Terry Lee baseball player

Orange City
Gorman, Burton William retired education educator

Orange Park
Enney, James Crowe former air force officer, business executive
Kirkwood, Maurice Richard banker
Ratzlaff, Judith L. secondary school educator
Rice, Ronald James hospital administrator
Webb, Robert Lee chemical company executive

Orlando
Abbott, Edward Leroy finance executive
Allison, Anne Marie librarian
Andrews, Brad Francis zoological park administrator
Arnett, Warren Grant interior designer
Baker, Peter Mitchell laser scientist and executive, educator
Ball, G. Thomas lawyer
Ball, Joseph E. association executive
Bassett, Robert Cochem lawyer, publisher
Baumgardner, Theodore Rogers lawyer
Berry, Stephen Joseph reporter
†Bishop, Bill critic
Blackford, Robert Newton lawyer
Blair, Mardian John hospital management executive
Blue, Joseph Edward physicist
Bollen, Roger cartoonist
Brownlee, Thomas Marshall lighting manufacturing company executive
Buchanan, Walter Woolwine engineering educator, electrical engineer
Canan, Michael J. lawyer, author
Cardwell, David Earl lawyer
Cary, Freeman Hamilton physician
Connolly, Joseph Francis, II government consultant
Conti, Louis Thomas Moore lawyer
Conway, Anne Callaghan federal judge
Davis, William Albert theme park director
Deo, Narsingh computer science educator
Dorsey, Norbert M. bishop
Duane, William Francis lawyer
Dunn, William Bruna, III journalist
DuRose, Richard Arthur lawyer
Eagan, William Leon lawyer
Fawsett, Patricia Combs federal judge
Fulton, Richard T. lawyer
Gonong, Zoila Obmana medical, surgical nurse
Grady, Thomas J. bishop
Grant, Raymond Thomas arts administrator

Gray, Anthony Rollin *capital management company executive*
Guest, Larry Samuel *newspaper columnist*
Gustafson, Robert A. *air transportation and holding company executive*
Haile, L. John, Jr. *journalist, newspaper executive*
Hall, Richard C. Winton *psychiatrist*
Handley, Leon Hunter *lawyer*
Hansen, Richard Fred *architect*
Hanus, Thomas J. *air transportation services executive*
Harris, Martin Harvey *aerospace company executive*
Harvill-Dickson, Clara Gean *medical facility administrator*
Healy, Jane Elizabeth *newspaper editor*
Henry, William Oscar Eugene *lawyer*
Herrington, John Stewart *lawyer*
Hill, Brian *professional basketball team coach*
Hitt, John Charles *university president*
Hoepner, Theodore John *banker*
Horan, John Patrick *lawyer*
Hornick, Richard Bernard *physician*
Howe, John Wadsworth *bishop*
†Hughes, David Henry *manufacturing company executive*
Hyslop, Gary Lee *librarian*
Ioppolo, Frank Sebastian *lawyer*
Ispass, Alan Benjamin *utilities executive*
Ivey, James Burnett *political cartoonist*
Jones, Joseph Wayne *food and beverage company executive, entrepreneur*
Jontz, Jeffry Robert *lawyer*
†Kindlund, Newton C. *retail executive*
Kovaleski, Charles J. *title insurance company official, lawyer*
Laning, Richard Boyer *naval officer, writer, retired*
Leonhardt, Frederick Wayne *lawyer*
Linscott, Jerry R. *lawyer*
Llewellyn, Ralph Alvin *physics educator*
Maupin, Elizabeth Thatcher *theater critic*
McGee, William G. *air transportation company executive*
McNulty, Chester Howard *bank holding company executive*
Medin, Julia Adele *mathematics educator, researcher*
Miller, Charles Edward, Jr. *financial executive*
Mock, Frank Mackenzie *lawyer*
Moltzon, Richard Francis *manufacturing executive*
Morgan, Richard Thomas *publishing executive*
Morris, Max F. *lawyer*
Morrisey, Marena Grant *art museum administrator*
Norris, Franklin Gray *thoracic and cardiovascular surgeon*
O'Neal, Shaquille Rashaun *professional basketball player*
Pantuso, Vincent Joseph *food service consultant*
Pauley, Bruce Frederick *history educator*
Pearlman, Louis Jay *aviation and promotion company executive*
Pope, Theodore Campbell, Jr. *utilities executive, consultant*
Puerner, John *newspaper publishing executive*
Reed, John Alton *lawyer*
Reese, Charles Edgar *columnist*
Rice, Stephen Landon *engineering educator*
Roesner, Larry August *civil engineer*
Rolle, Christopher Davies *lawyer*
Rosenthal, Paul Edmond *lawyer*
Rush, Fletcher Grey, Jr. *lawyer*
Salmons, Joanna *health facility administrator*
Santiago, Carlos *minister*
Sathre, Leroy *mathematics educator, consultant*
Schott, James *educational administrator*
Sconiers, M. L. *bishop*
Sharp, George Kendall *federal judge*
Sharp, Joel H., Jr. *lawyer*
†Shaw, Brewster Hopkinson, Jr. *astronaut*
Silfvast, William T. *laser physics educator, consultant*
Simon, James Lowell *lawyer*
Skambis, Christopher Charles, Jr. *lawyer*
Smetheram, Herbert Edwin *business executive*
Smith, Paul Frederick *plant physiologist, consultant*
Soileau, Marion Joseph *engineering and physics educator*
Stephenson, Jan Lynn *professional golfer*
Strack, J. Gary *hospital administrator*
Strifler, Susan Victoria *nursing administrator*
†Sublette, William Edward *state representative*
Swedberg, Robert Mitchell *opera company director*
Tillotson, Frank Lee *naval officer*
Ting, Robert Yen-ying *physicist*
Todd, Troy W. *telecommunications company executive*
Urban, James Arthur *lawyer*
Ward, Sharon Polk *nursing administrator*
Werner, Thomas Lee *hospital administrator*
Wilkerson, John Lee *telecommunications executive*
Williamson, Thomas Arnold *publishing company executive*
Yesawich, Peter Charles *advertising executive*
Young, George Cressler *federal judge*

Ormond Beach
Barker, Robert Osborne (Bob Barker) *management and public relations consultant*
Coke, C(hauncey) Eugene *consulting company executive, scientist, educator, author*
Jacobson, Ira David *aerospace engineer, educator, researcher*
Nasser, Joseph Yousef *public safety adminstrator, consultant*
Riley, Daniel Edward *air force officer*
Wendelstedt, Harry Hunter, Jr. *umpire*
†Wild, Harry E. *engineering company executive*

Osprey
Allen, George Howard *publishing management consultant*
Coates, Clarence Leroy, Jr. *research engineer, educator*
Cort, Winifred Mitchell *microbiologist, biochemist*
Crispin, Mildred Swift (Mrs. Frederick Eaton Crispin) *civic worker, author*
Gross, James Dehnert *pathologist*
Kern, Jean Glotzbach *elementary education educator, gifted education educator*
Maddocks, Robert Allen *lawyer, manufacturing company executive*
Strongin, Theodore *journalist*
Ward, Jacqueline Ann Beas *nurse, healthcare administrator*
Woodall, William Leon *retired insurance executive*

Oviedo
Linhart, Letty Lemon *columnist*
Martin, Judson Phillips *retired education educator*

Whitworth, Hall Baker *forest products company executive*

Palm Bay
Galitello-Wolfe, Jane Maryann *artist, writer*
Jurgevich, Nancy J. *retail executive, educator*
Olejar, Paul Duncan *former information science administrator*
Regis, Nina *librarian, educator*

Palm Beach
Adduci, Vincent James *investment company executive*
Adler, Frederick Richard *lawyer, financier*
Alimanestianu, Calin *retired hotel consultant*
Alpert, Seymour *anesthesiologist, educator*
Artinian, Artine *French literature scholar, collector*
Asencio, Diego C. *state agency administrator, former federal commission administrator, consultant, business executive*
Bagby, Joseph Rigsby *financial investor*
†Bagby, Martha L. Green *real estate holding company, novelist, publisher*
Bane, Charles Arthur *lawyer*
Barness, Amnon Shemaya *financial service executive*
Beasley, James W., Jr. *lawyer*
Bishop, Warner Bader *finance company executive*
Black, Leonard Julius *retail store consultant*
Bonan, Seon Pierre *real estate developer*
Chittick, Elizabeth Lancaster *association executive, women's rights activist*
Chopin, L. Frank *lawyer*
Cole, Jonathan Edward *lawyer*
Cook, Edward Willingham *diversified industry executive*
Crawford, Sandra Kay *lawyer*
Curry, Bernard Francis *former banker, consultant*
Donnell, John Randolph *petroleum executive*
Druck, Kalman Breschel *public relations counselor*
Ferrin, Allan Wheeler *association executive*
Fitilis, Theodore Nicholas *portfolio manager*
Fogelson, David *retired lawyer*
Ford, Thomas Patrick *lawyer*
Gowdy, Curtis *sportscaster*
Graubard, Seymour *lawyer*
Gundlach, Heinz Ludwig *investment banker, lawyer*
Habicht, Frank Henry *industrial executive*
Hall, Kathryn Evangeline *writer, lecturer*
Halmos, Peter *investment company executive*
Isenberg, Abraham Charles *shoe manufacturing company executive*
Jackson, John Tillson *corporate executive*
Kaplan, Muriel Sheerr *sculptor*
Korn, David *investment company executive*
Levine, Laurence Brandt *investment banker*
†Mallardi, Vincent *organization executive*
Mandel, Carola Panerai (Mrs. Leon Mandel) *foundation trustee*
Pryor, Hubert *editor, writer*
Riefler, Donald Brown *financial consultant*
Rinker, Ruby Stewart *foundation administrator*
Robb, David Buzby, Jr. *financial services company executive, lawyer*
Roberts, Margaret Harold *editor, publisher*
Rudolph, Malcolm Rome *investment banker*
Rumbough, Stanley Maddox, Jr. *industrialist*
Smith, Lloyd Hilton *independent oil and gas producer*
Stoneman, Samuel Sidney *cinema company executive*
Tiecke, Richard William *pathologist, educator, association executive*
†Tremain, Alan *hotel executive*
Walsh, Cornelius Stephen *leasing company executive*
Wenzel, Joan Ellen *artist*
Winkler, Joseph Conrad *former recreational products manufacturing executive*
Wirtz, Willem Kindler *garden and lighting designer, public relations consultant*

Palm Beach Gardens
Awtrey, Jim L. *sports association executive*
Brackett, Sally Lee Martin *small business owner*
Calcevecchia, Mark *professional golfer*
Christian, Robert Henry *architect*
Daly, John *professional golfer*
Emiliani, Cesare *geology educator, author*
Harnett, Joseph Durham *oil company executive*
Herrick, John Dennis *financial consultant, former law firm executive, retired food products executive*
Howse, Robert Davis *business executive*
Lebed, Hartzel Zangwill *insurance company executive*
Mendelson, Richard Donald *former communications company executive*
Mergler, H. Kent *investment counselor*
Mize, Larry *professional golfer*
Player, Gary Jim *professional golfer*
Rodriguez, Chi Chi (Juan Rodriguez) *professional golfer*
Sabatini, Gabriela *tennis player*
Symons, J. Keith *bishop*

Palm City
Ammarell, John Samuel *retired college president, former security services executive*
Burton, John Routh *lawyer*
Henry, David Howe, II *former diplomat and international organization official*
Huntington, Earl Lloyd *lawyer, retired natural resources company executive*
Pepitone, Byron Vincent *former government official*
Senter, William Oscar *retired air force officer*
White, Eugene James *retired technology company executive*
Wirsig, Woodrow *magazine editor, trade organization executive, business executive*
Wishart, Ronald Sinclair *retired chemical company executive*

Palm Coast
Dickson, David Watson Daly *retired college president*
Franco, Annemarie Woletz *editor*
Godfrey, Eutha Marek *elementary school educator, consultant*

Palm Harbor
Curreri, John Robert *mechanical engineer, consultant*
Shaneyfelt, Patricia Tharin *elementary education educator*

Palmetto
Compton, Charles Daniel *chemistry educator*

Panama City
Childers, Perry Robert *psychology educator*
D'Arcy, Gerald Paul *engineering executive, consultant*
Dykes, James Edgar *advertising educator, consultant*
Green, Hubert *professional golfer*
Smith, Larry Glenn *retired state judge*
†Snapp, Manco *chemicals executive*

Panama City Beach
Miller, Robert William *personal property appraiser, writer*
Nelson, Edith Ellen *dietitian*

Patrick AFB
†Haggis, Arthur George, Jr. *retired career officer, educator, publisher*

Pembroke Pines
Armstrong, Ivy Claudette *nursing administrator*
Ladin, Eugene *communications company executive*

Penney Farms
Kimbrough, Ralph Bradley *educational administration educator emeritus*

Pensacola
Adams, Joseph Peter *retired lawyer, consultant*
Bowden, Jesse Earle *newspaper editor, author, cartoonist, journalism educator*
Bozeman, Frank Carmack *lawyer*
Bullock, Ellis Way, Jr. *architect*
Caton, Betty Ann *health science administrator*
Chang, Clifford W.J. *chemistry educator, researcher, consultant*
Cianciolo, Sister Rosemary *school system administrator*
Collier, Lacey Alexander *federal judge*
DeBardeleben, John Thomas, Jr. *retired insurance company executive*
Dillard, Robert Perkins *pediatrician, educator*
Dixon, James Andrew, Jr. *protective services official*
Frye, John William, III *retired senior circuit judge*
Furlong, George Morgan, Jr. *retired naval officer, museum foundation executive*
Geeker, Nicholas Peter *lawyer, judge*
Groner, Pat Neff *health care executive*
Hamilton, Robert Edward *oral and maxillofacial surgeon, naval officer*
Hass, Charles John William *criminal justice program coordinator*
Hutto, Earl *retired congressman*
Killian, Lewis Martin *sociology educator*
Lautier, Yves Laurent *physician*
Loesch, Harold C. *retired marine fisheries biologist, consultant*
Loesch, Mabel Lorraine *social worker*
Love, Robert William, Jr. *retired physician, government administrator*
Marx, Morris Leon *academic administrator*
Maygarden, Jerry Louis *health care foundation executive*
McCrary, Douglas L. *utility company executive*
McSwain, Richard Horace *materials engineer, consultant*
Moulton, Wilbur Wright, Jr. *lawyer*
Mountcastle, William Wallace, Jr. *philosophy and religion educator*
Novotny, Susan M. *judge*
Platz, Terrance Oscar *utilities company executive*
Rasmussen, Robert *museum director*
Ray, Donald Hensley *biologist*
Sargent, James O'Connor *freelance writer*
Shows, Clarence Oliver *dentist*
Smith, Jody Brant *philosophy and humanities educator*
†Smith, John M. *bishop*
†Tobin, Paul Edward, Jr. *naval officer*
Usry, Milton Franklin *accounting educator*
VanSlyke, Robert Emmett *health care executive*
Vinson, C. Roger *federal judge*
Watt, Stuart George *engineering contracting company executive*
Weisner, Maurice Franklin *former naval officer*
Woolf, Kenneth Howard *architect*
Yoder, Ronda Elaine *nursing educator*

Pineland
Doherty, Michel George *alcohol and drug treatment facility administrator*

Pinellas Park
Athanson, Mary Catheryne *elementary school principal*
Hall, Charles Allen *aerospace and energy company executive*
†Morris, Daniel *osteopath*
Perry, Paul Alverson *utility executive*
†Still, Craig Russell *publishing executive*

Placida
Grissom, Joseph Carol *retired leasing and investments business executive*
Schwarting, Arthur Ernest *university dean*

Plant City
Bruton, James DeWitt, Jr. *retired judge*
Holland, Gene Grigsby (Scottie Holland) *artist*
Patronelli, Raymond *church administrator*
Tully, Darrow *newspaper publisher*

Plantation
Baez, Manuel *health care executive*
Buck, Thomas Randolph *business executive*
Fershleiser, Steven Buckler *secondary education educator*

Plymouth
Voelker, Charles Robert *archbishop, academic dean*

Pompano Beach
Albert, Calvin *sculptor*
Ayres, John Cecil *retired public health executive*
Bliznakov, Emile George *biomedical research scientist*
Calatchi, Ralph Franklin *economist*
Crandell, K(enneth) James *management and strategic planning consultant, entrepreneur*
Elder, Robert Lee *professional golfer*
Freimark, Jeffrey Philip *retail supermarket executive*
Heir, Kal M. *financial executive*
Kester, Stewart Randolph *banker*

MacLaren, Neil Moorley, Jr. *musician, music educator*
Patterson, Alan Bruce *obstetrician, gynecologist*
Rifenburgh, Richard Philip *investment company executive*
Roen, Sheldon R. *publisher, psychologist*
Schwartz, Joseph *retired container company executive*
Slovin, Bruce *diversified holding company executive*
Szilassy, Sandor *retired lawyer, library director, educator*
Toppel, Harold H. *diversified company executive*
Wright, Joseph Robert, Jr. *corporate executive*
Zimmer, Paul Howard *housing and transportation manufacturing company executive*
Zinman, Jacques *former insurance agency executive*

Ponte Vedra Beach
Azinger, Paul *professional golfer*
Beman, Deane Randolph *association executive*
Chang, Michael *tennis player*
Cook, John *professional golfer*
Couples, Fred *professional golfer*
Edberg, Stefan *professional tennis player*
Elston, William Steger *food products company executive*
Faxon, Brad *professional golfer*
Fiorentino, Thomas Martin *transportation executive, lawyer*
Floyd, Raymond *professional golfer*
Forsman, Dan *professional golfer*
Green, Norman Kenneth *retired oil industry executive, former naval officer*
Hanigan, Marvin Frank *insurance executive*
Hartzell, Karl Drew *retired university dean, historian*
Janzen, Lee *professional golfer*
Kite, Thomas O., Jr. *professional golfer*
Klacsmann, John Anthony *retired chemical company executive*
Krusen, Henry Stanley *investment banker*
Kuhn, Bowie K. *lawyer, former professional baseball commissioner, consultant*
Love, Davis, III *professional golfer*
McMullan, William Patrick, Jr. *banker*
Milbrath, Robert Henry *retired petroleum executive*
Moore, Philip Walsh *appraisal company executive*
O'Brien, Raymond Vincent, Jr. *banker*
Pavin, Corey *professional golfer*
Phelan, Martin DuPont *retired film company executive*
Price, Nick *professional golfer*
ReMine, William Hervey, Jr. *surgeon*
Schultz, Andrew Schultz, Jr. *industrial engineering educator*
Spence, Richard Dee *paper products company executive, former railroad executive*
Stewart, Payne (William Payne Stewart) *professional golfer*
Thorndike, Richard King *former brokerage company executive*
Wadkins, Lanny *professional golfer*
Wilson, J. Tylee *business executive*
Zoeller, Fuzzy *professional golfer*

Port Charlotte
Flanders, Jefferson *publishing executive*
Munger, Elmer Lewis *civil engineer, educator*
Norris, Dolores June *elementary school educator*
Parvin, Philip E. *retired agricultural researcher and educator*
Ward-Presson, Kathryn M. *health facility administrator*

Port Manatee
Falls, William Wayne *aquaculturist*

Port Richey
Baiardi, John Charles *retired scientific laboratory director*
Radomski, Jack London *pharmacologist, consultant*

Port Saint Joe
Smith, Harry Lee *laboratory technician, chemist*

Port Saint Lucie
Clark, Harold Steve *architect*
Mottram-Doss, Renée *corporate executive*
Rhodes, Alfred William *former insurance company executive*
Sommers, Robert Thomas *editor, publisher, author*

Punta Gorda
Bulzacchelli, John G. *financial executive*
Harrington, John Vincent *retired communications company executive, engineer, educator*
Hepfer, John William, Jr. *consultant, retired air force officer*
Hill, Richard Earl *academic administrator*
Kavanaugh, Frank James *film producer, educator*
Wilson, Dwight Liston *former military officer, investment advisor*

Quincy
Lindquist, Mark Alvin *artist*
Teare, Iwan Dale *agronomy educator, research scientist*

River Ranch
Swett, Albert Hersey *retired lawyer, business executive, consultant*

Riviera Beach
Horowitz, Dennis *electronic components company executive*

Rockledge
Sutton, Betty Sheriff *elementary education educator*

Royal Palm Beach
Graham, Carl Francis *consultant, former chemical products company executive, chemist*

Ruskin
Nissen, Carl Andrew, Jr. *minister, retired procurement analyst*

Saint Augustine
Acito, Daniel Joseph *interior designer*
Adams, William Roger *historian*
Armstrong, John Alexander *political scientist, educator*
Baker, Norman Henderson *association executive*

Davis, Bertram George lawyer, association executive
Edwards, Page Lawrence, Jr. author, archivist, historical society administrator
Gilliland, Thomas consultant
Greenberg, Michael John biologist, research director
LeBeau, Hector Alton, Jr. management consultant, former confectionary company executive
Marsolais, Harold Raymond association executive
Matzke, Frank J. architect, consultant
Nolan, Joseph Thomas journalism educator, communications consultant
Proctor, William Lee college president
Russell, Josiah Cox historian, educator
Tadlock, R. Jerry manufacturing and logistics consultant
Theil, Henri economist, educator
Zellers, Carl Fredrick, Jr. railway executive

Saint Cloud
Everett, Woodrow Wilson electrical engineer, educator

Saint Leo
Mouch, Frank Messman college president, priest

Saint Petersburg
Allshouse, Merle Frederick higher education executive
Armacost, Peter Hayden college president
Barca, James Joseph fire department administrative services executive
Barnes, Andrew Earl newspaper editor
Battaglia, Anthony Sylvester lawyer
Belich, John Patrick, Sr. journalist
Benbow, Charles Clarence retired writer, critic
†Bercu, Barry B. pediatric endocrinologist
Blumenthal, Herman Bertram accountant
Brandimore, Stanley Albert lawyer, holding company executive
Bryant, John author, publisher
Byrd, Isaac Burlin fishery biologist, fisheries administrator
Carlson, Jeannie Ann writer
Carroll, Charles Michael music educator
Castle, Raymond Nielson chemist, educator
Clark, Carolyn Chambers nurse, author, educator
Collins, Carl Russell, Jr. architectural engineer
Cook, Marian Alice musician
Critchfield, Jack Barron utilities company executive
Dickson, Suzanne Elizabeth (Sue Dickson) educational administrator
DiFilippo, Fernando, Jr. lawyer
Donaldson, Merle Richard electrical engineering educator, consultant
Duval, Cynthia museum curator, adminstrator
Emerson, William Allen retired investment company executive
Escarraz, Enrique, III lawyer
Estenes, Joseph John, Jr. academic administrator
Favalora, John Clement bishop
Fischer, David J. mayor
Foley, Michael Francis newspaper executive
Freeman, Corinne financial services, former mayor
Galbraith, John William securities company executive
Giffin, Barbara Haines education coordinator
Godbold, Francis Stanley investment banker, real estate executive
Gonzalez, Hernan accountant, lawyer
†Good, Jeffrey journalist
Good, Robert Alan physician, educator
Greene, George E., III utility company executive
Grube, Karl Bertram judge
Haiman, Robert James newspaper editor, journalism educator
Hallock-Muller, Pamela oceanography educator, biogeologist, researcher
Hancock, John Allan utility company executive
Hansel, Paul George physicist, consultant
Hargrave, Victoria Elizabeth librarian
Harrington, Joan Kathryn counselor
Harris, Rogers S. bishop
Hines, Andrew Hampton, Jr. utilities executive
†Hinz, John English and American literature educator
Hull, Anne Victoria journalist
Jacob, Bruce Robert dean, academic administrator, law educator
†Jenkins, Robert Norman newswriter, editor
Jordan, William Reynier Van Evera, Sr. therapist, poet
Kazor, Walter Robert statistical process control and quality assurance consultant
†Keesler, Allen John, Jr. utilites executive
†Keller, Richard Donald accountant
Kuttler, Carl Martin, Jr. college president
Layton, William George computer company executive, management consultant, human resources executive
Leavell, William A. publisher, editor
Mann, Sam Henry, Jr. lawyer
Martin, Susan Taylor newspaper editor
Mc Connell, Robert Chalmers former city official
McIntyre, Deborah psychotherapist, author
Mc Lean, Thomas Edwin retired manufacturing company executive
McMurray, Joseph Patrick Brendan financial consultant
Meinke, Peter writer, retired educator
Meisels, Gerhard George academic administrator, chemist, educator
Mills, William Harold, Jr. construction company executive
Mosby, John Davenport, III investment banking executive
Neiser, Richard William utility executive
Nussbaum, Leo Lester retired college president, consultant
Ogletree, Thomas Vincent savings and loan association executive
O'Hearn, John Howard publishing company executive
Oleck, Howard Leoner legal educator, writer
Patterson, Eugene Corbett retired editor, publisher
Peterson, Arthur Laverne former college president
Pittman, Robert Turner retired newspaper editor
Putnam, J. Stephen financial executive
†Pyle, William Carmody human resource management educator, researcher
Rester, Alfred Carl, Jr. physicist
Roeder, Ross Eugene consulting company executive
Roney, Paul H(itch) federal judge
Root, Allen William pediatrician, educator
Rummel, Harold Edwin real estate developing executive
Runge, De Lyle Paul retired library director, consultant
Rydstrom, Carlton Lionel chemist, paint and coating consultant
Schell, Joan Bruning information specialist, business science librarian
Schuck, Marjorie Massey publisher, editor, consultant
Schultz, G. Robert lawyer
Scott, Lee Hansen retired holding company executive
Sembler, Mel company executive, former ambassador
Serrie, Hendrick anthropology and international business educator
Shank, Clare Brown Williams political leader
Sheen, Robert Tilton manufacturing company executive
Sherburne, Donald Wynne philosopher, educator
Shi, Feng Sheng mathematician
†Shuck, Robert F. financial executive
Sibley, Mark Anderson ophthalmologist
Silver, Lawrence Alan marketing executive
Snider, Eric Ross music critic
Söderberg, Bo Sigfrid marketing executive
Soechtig, Jacqueline Elizabeth telecommunications executive
Southworth, William Dixon retired education educator
Stevens, Edward Ira information systems educator
Stewart, Joseph Lester rubber company executive
Tash, Paul C. editor-in-chief
Walker, Brigitte Maria translator, linguistic consultant
†Wandler, Leslie Roy financial executive
Wedding, Charles Randolph architect
Westall, Sandra Thornton special education educator
Wisler, Willard Eugene health care management executive
Woodard, Joseph Lamar law librarian, law educator
Zahorian, Stephen Glen banker

Saint Petersburg Beach
Hurley, Frank Thomas, Jr. realtor

Sanford
Corp, William Thomas, Sr. purchasing executive
Osborne-Popp, Glenna Jean health services administrator
San Miguel, Sandra Bonilla social worker

Sanibel
Adair, Charles Valloyd retired physician
Ball, Armand Baer former association executive, consultant
Courtney, James Edmond real estate development
Crown, David Allan criminologist, educator
Herriott, Donald Richard optical physicist
Horecker, Bernard Leonard retired biochemistry educator
Kiernan, Edwin A., Jr. lawyer, corporation executive
Perkinson, Diana Agnes Zouzelka import company executive

Santa Rosa Beach
Wright, John Peale retired banker

Sarasota
Abbott, J. Carl architect, planner, inventor, educator
Adams, Richard Towsley university president, educational consultant
Altabe, Joan Augusta Berg artist, writer, art and architecture critic
Angelotti, Richard H. science administrator, banker
Arreola, John Bradley diversified financial service company executive, financial planner
Augsburger, Aaron Donald clergyman
Bailey, Robert Elliot financial executive
Balter, Frances Sunstein civic worker
Beck, George William retired industrial engineer
Beck, Robert Alfred hotel administration educator
Berkoff, Charles Edward pharmaceutical executive
Bewley, David Charles financial planner
Browdy, Alvin lawyer
Burket, Harriet (Mrs. Francis B. Taussig) editor
Byron, H. Thomas, Jr. veterinarian, educator
Chamberlain, John Angus sculptor
Christ-Janer, Arland Frederick college president
Christopher, William Garth lawyer
Connor, Robert T. former government official
Covert, Michael Henri healthcare facility administrator
Cox, Houston Abraham, Jr. futures markets consultant
Dearden, Robert James pharmacist
Dlesk, George retired pulp and paper industry executive
Downey, John Charles university dean, zoology educator
Eachus, Joseph J(ackson) computer scientist, consultant
Ebitz, David MacKinnon art historian, museum director
Eliscu, Frank sculptor
Estrin, Richard William newspaper editor
Fabrycy, Mark Zdzislaw retired economist
Feder, Allan Appel management executive, consultant
Felker, Ouida Jeanette Weissinger special education educator
Fendrick, Alan Burton retired advertising executive
Fowler, Charles William school administrator
Friedberg, Harold David cardiologist
Gerhardt, Paul Louis professional association executive
Gervais, Darwin banker, insurance executive
Gilbert, Perry Webster emeritus educator
Giordano, David Alfred internist, gastroenterologist
Gittelson, Bernard public relations consultant, author, lecturer
Glasser, Otto John former business executive, former air force officer
Gordon, Sanford Daniel economics educator
Graham, Otto Everett, Jr. retired athletic director
Gray, Hope Diffenderfer industrial relations specialist
Greene, Richard Efraim data processing executive
Greenfield, Robert Kauffman lawyer
Grubbs, Elven Judson retired newspaper publisher
Gurvitz, Milton Solomon psychologist
Hackl, Alphons J. publisher
Hagen, George Leon computer systems consultant
Hamberg, Daniel economist, educator
Hansen, Elisa Marie art historian
Harmon, (Loren) Foster art consultant
Hayes, Joseph author
Herbert, James Paul advertising executive
Highland, Marilyn M. principal
Hoffman, Oscar Allen retired forest products company executive
Hoover, Dwight Wesley history educator
Hrones, John Anthony mechanical engineering educator
Hull, J(ames) Richard retired lawyer, business executive
Irwin, Theodore writer
Ives, George Skinner arbitrator, former government official
Jacobs, Debra McQuaig banker
Jaeger, Leonard Henry former public utility executive
Jones, Tracey Kirk, Jr. minister, educator
Keitel, Hans George pediatrician
Kerker, Milton chemistry educator
Kimbrough, Robert Averyt lawyer
Kiplinger, Glenn Francis pharmacologist, medical-legal consultant
Lambert, John Phillip financial executive, consultant
Levitt, Irving Francis investment company executive
Lewis, Brian Kreglow computer consultant
Lindsay, David Breed, Jr. aircraft company executive, former editor and publisher
Long, Robert Radcliffe fluid mechanics educator
Loomis, Wesley Horace, III former publishing company executive
Loving, George Gilmer, Jr. retired air force officer
MacDonald, Robert Taylor newspaper executive
Mackey, Leonard Bruce lawyer, former diversified manufacturing corporation executive
Mahadevan, Kumar marine laboratory director, researcher
Marino, Eugene Louis publishing company executive
Mattran, Donald Albert management consultant, educator
McCollum, John Morris tenor
McFarlin, Diane H. newspaper editor
Meyer, B. Fred small business executive, home designer and builder, product designer
Miles, Arthur J. financial planner, consultant
Myerson, Albert Leon physical chemist
Neeley, Delmar George human resources executive
†Neff, Ray insurance company executive
Noether, Emiliana Pasca historian, educator
North, Marjorie Mary columnist
Page, George Keith banker
Pillot, Gene Merrill retired superintendent of schools
Powers, Dudley musician
Proffitt, Waldo, Jr. newspaper editor
Putterman, Florence Grace artist, printmaker
Radnay, Paul Andrew physician
Raimi, Burton Louis lawyer
Roberts, Merrill Joseph economist, educator
Ross, Gerald Fred engineering executive, researcher
Roth, James Frank manufacturing company executive, chemist
Sawyer, Helen Alton artist
Schersten, H. Donald management consultant, realtor, mortgage broker
Schwartz, Norman L. lawyer
Seibert, Russell Jacob botanist, research associate
Simon, Joseph Patrick food services executive
Sloan, Richard artist
Smith, Mark Hallard architect
Smith, Richard Emerson (Dick Smith) make-up artist
Solomon, Syd artist
Soran, Robert L. manufacturing executive
Swenson, Harold Francis crisis management consultant
Taplin, Winn Lowell historian, retired senior intelligence operations officer
Tatum, Joan Glennalyn John secondary school educator
Veinott, Cyril George electrical engineer, consultant
Vestal, Lucian LaRoe financier
Warner, Lee Howland cultural program director
Weeks, Albert Loren author, educator, journalist
Weeks, Walter LeRoy electrical engineering educator
Welch, John Dana urologist, performing arts association executive
White, Will Walter, III public relations consultant, writer
Wigton, Paul Norton steel company consultant, former executive
Winterhalter, Dolores August (Dee Winterhalter) art educator
Yordan, Carlos Manuel foreign service officer

Sebastian
Mauke, Otto Russell retired college president
Pieper, Patricia Rita artist, photographer

Sebring
Sherrick, Daniel Noah real estate broker

Seffner
Castellano, Sandra Lorrain curriculum director

Seminole
Nesbitt, Robert Edward Lee, Jr. physician, educator
Silver, Paul Robert marketing executive, consultant

Siesta
Held, Philip artist

South Bay
Fairbanks, J. Nelson sugar company executive

South Miami
Benbow, John Robert banker
Bruel, Iris Barbara psychologist
Fletcher, John Greenwood II lawyer, consultant

Spring Hill
Finney, Roy Pelham, Jr. urologist, surgeon, inventor
Rojas, Victor Hugo retired vocational education educator
Youngman, Henny comedian

Starke
Loper, George Wilson, Jr. physical education educator

Stuart
Ankrom, Charles Franklin golf course architect, consultant
Conklin, George Melville retired food company executive
DeRita, Thomas, Jr. automobile company executive
Derrickson, William Borden manufacturing executive
Haserick, John Roger retired dermatologist
Jefferson, Peter Augustus architect
Leibson, Irving industrial executive
Mc Kenna, Sidney F. technical company executive
McQuillan, William Hugh building company executive
Morena, John Joseph manufacturing engineer, executive
Murchake, John publishing executive
Pisani, Joseph Michael physician
Ragno, Nancy Nickell educational writer
Slade, Gerald Jack publishing company executive
Snider, Harlan Tanner former manufacturing company executive
Wasiele, Harry W., Jr. diversified electrical manufacturing company executive
Westlake, Robert Elmer, Sr. physician
Wood, Harleston Read retired manufacturing executive

Summerland Key
Muth, John Fraser economics educator

Sun City Center
Fleischman, Sol Joseph, Sr. retired television broadcasting executive
Hall, John Fry psychologist, educator
Jeffries, Robert Joseph retired engineering educator, business executive
McGrath, John Francis utility executive
Parsons, George Williams retired medical center administrator, cattle rancher
Sevold, Gordon James savings and loan executive
Weatherbee, Artemus Edwin former federal government official

Sunrise
Cronin, Mary Haag real estate referral agent
McBride, Wanda Lee psychiatric nurse

Surfside
Prystowsky, Harry physician, educator

Tallahassee
Adams, James Alfred natural science educator
Adams, Perry Ronald former college administrator
Anthony, William Philip management educator
Ashler, Philip Frederic international trade and development advisor
Aurell, John Karl lawyer
Avant, David Alonzo, Jr. realty company executive, photographer
Barnett, Martha Walters lawyer
Bartlett, Richard Adams American history educator, history consultant
Baum, Werner A. former academic administrator, meteorologist
Beach, Cecil Prentice librarian
Beck, Earl Ray historian, educator
†Boutwell, Wallace Kenneth, Jr. management consultant, health care executive
Bowden, Bobby university athletic coach
Boyd, Joseph Arthur, Jr. lawyer
Braswell, Robert Neil scientist, engineer, educator
Brennan, Mary M. state legislator
Brodsky, Lewis psychiatrist, educator
Brueckheimer, William Rogers social science educator
Burnette, Ada M. Puryear educational administrator
Burroway, Janet G. English language educator, novelist
Butterworth, Robert A. state attorney general
Bye, Raymond Erwin, Jr. academic administrator
Carson, Leonard Allen lawyer
Caspar, Donald Louis Dvorak biophysics and structural biology educator
Chen, Ching Jen mechanical engineering educator, research scientist
Chiles, Lawton Mainor governor, former senator
Choppin, Gregory Robert chemistry educator
Clark, Herbert Forrester state commissioner
Clarke, Allan J. oceanography educator, consultant
Clarkson, Julian Derieux lawyer
Colberg, Marshall Rudolph economist
Coleman, Hume Field lawyer
Collette, Charles T. (Chip Collette) lawyer
Coloney, Wayne Herndon civil engineer
Crow, Jack E. physics administrator
Dadisman, Joseph Carrol newspaper executive
D'Alemberte, Talbot (Sandy D'Alemberte) lawyer, educator
Davis, Bertram Hylton retired English educator
De Forest, Sherwood Searle agricultural engineer, agribusiness services executive
Dillingham, Marjorie Carter foreign language educator
Dorn, Charles Meeker art education educator
Durrence, James Larry state executive, history educator
Dye, Thomas Roy political science educator
Earhart, Eileen Magie retired home and family life educator
Ervin, Robert Marvin lawyer
Evans, Virden educator, academic administrator
Frechette, Ernest Albert foreign language educator emeritus
Friedmann, E(merich) Imre biologist, educator
Friedmann, Roseli Ocampo microbiologist, educator
Gil, Lazier university dean
Golden, Leon classicist, educator
Goodner, Dwight Benjamin mathematician, emeritus educator
Griffith, Elwin Jabez lawyer, university administrator
Grimes, Stephen Henry state supreme court chief justice
Gunter, William Dawson, Jr. (Bill Gunter) insurance company executive
Hafner, Lawrence Erhardt education educator
Hall, Houghton Alexander engineering professional
Harding, Major Best state supreme court justice
Harper, George Mills English language educator
Harris, Natholyn Dalton food science educator, researcher
Harrison, Thomas James electrical engineer, educator
Harsanyi, Janice soprano, educator
Hatchett, Joseph Woodrow federal judge
Heldman, Louis Marc newspaper editor
Herndon, Roy Clifford physicist
Holcombe, Randall Gregory economics educator
Holifield, Bishop Clarke lawyer
Housewright, Wiley Lee music educator
Humphries, Frederick S. university president
Hunt, John Edwin insurance company executive, consultant
†Hunter, Christopher mathematics educator
Johnsen, Russell Harold chemist, educator
Johnson, Benjamin F., VI real estate developer, consulting economist
Kaelin, Eugene Francis philosophy educator
Kemper, Kirby Wayne physics educator

Kenshalo, Daniel Ralph *psychologist, educator*
Kirk, Colleen Jean *conductor, educator*
Kogan, Gerald *state supreme court justice*
†Koontz, Christine Miller *research faculty*
Laird, William Everette, Jr. *economics educator, administrator*
Lannutti, Joseph Edward *physics educator*
Lick, Dale Wesley *academic administrator*
Lipner, Harry *physiologist, educator*
Macesich, George *econmomics professor*
MacKay, Kenneth Hood (Buddy MacKay) *state official, former congressman*
Maguire, Charlotte Edwards *retired physician*
Maier-Katkin, Daniel *criminology educator, administrator*
Makowski, Lee *science administrator, biology and chemistry educator*
Mandelkern, Leo *biophysics and chemistry educator*
Mann, Marcia L. *state agency administrator*
†Manning, Altha *education commissioner*
†Marshall, Alan George *chemistry and biochemistry educator*
Marshall, Stanley *former educator, business executive*
McBride, Donna Jannean *publisher*
McCrimmon, James McNab *language educator*
McDonald, Parker Lee *state supreme court justice*
Mc Knight, Paul James, Jr. *hospital corporate executive*
McTarnaghan, Roy E. *acadamic administrator*
Meredith, Michael *science educator, researcher*
Milligan, Robert F. *state agency administrator*
Moore, Duncan *healthcare executive*
Moore, John Hebron *history educator*
Morgan, Lucy W. *journalist*
Morgan, Robert Marion *educational research educator*
Morse, Joshua Marion, III *lawyer, educator*
Mortham, Sandra Barringer *state official*
Moulton, Grace Charbonnet *physics educator*
Mustian, Middleton Truett *hospital administrator*
Nam, Charles Benjamin *sociologist, demographer, educator*
Navon, Ionel Michael *mathematics educator*
Newell, Barbara Warne *economist, educator*
Nichols, Eugene Douglas *mathematics educator*
O'Brien, James Joseph *meteorology and oceanography educator*
Oldson, William Orville *history educator*
Overton, Benjamin Frederick *state supreme court justice*
Owen, William Cone *lawyer*
Palladino-Craig, Allys *museum director*
Paredes, James Anthony *anthropologist, educator*
†Parker, Herbert Gerald *state official*
Paul, Maurice M. *federal judge*
Pelham, Thomas Gerald *lawyer*
Penrod, Kenneth Earl *medical education consultant*
Peterson, Rodney Delos *mediator, forensic economist*
Pfeffer, Richard Lawrence *geophysics educator*
Reed, Charles Bass *university system chancellor*
Reid, Sue Titus *law educator*
†Rittberg, Eric Joseph *political consultant*
Robbins, Jane Borsch *library science educator, information science educator*
Roberts, B. K. *lawyer, former judge*
Robson, Donald *physics educator*
Rockwood, Ruth H. *former library science educator*
Rubenstein, Richard Lowell *theologian, educator*
Saunders, Ron *lawyer, former state legislator*
Schrieffer, John Robert *physics educator, science administrator*
Schroeder, Edwin Maher *law educator*
Serow, William John *economics educator*
Shaw, Leander Jerry, Jr. *state supreme court justice*
Sindler, Robert Brian *state legislator, veterinarian*
Smith, Eric Alan *meteorology educator*
Smith, James Cloudis *secretary of state, former state attorney general*
Stafford, William Henry, Jr. *federal judge*
Stino, Farid K.R. *biostatistician, educator, researcher, consultant*
Summers, Frank William *librarian*
Summers, Lorraine Dey Schaeffer *librarian*
Sundberg, Alan Carl *former state supreme court justice, lawyer*
Taylor, J(ames) Herbert *cell biology educator*
Trezza, Alphonse Fiore *librarian, educator*
Tuckman, Bruce Wayne *educational psychologist, educator, researcher*
Voran, James F. *principal*
Walborsky, Harry M. *chemistry educator, consultant*
Wilkins, (George) Barratt *librarian*
Williams, James Howard *sociologist, research agency executive*
Zachert, Martha Jane *retired librarian*
Zaiser, Kent Ames *lawyer*

Tamarac

Fish, Robert Jay *dental surgeon, lawyer, medico-legal consultant, diversified entrepreneur*
Krause, John L. *optometrist*

Tampa

Abell, Jan Mary *architect*
Acton, Emeline *lawyer*
Adams, Henry Lee, Jr. *federal judge*
Adkins, Edward Cleland *lawyer*
Afield, Walter Edward *psychiatrist, service executive*
Aitken, Thomas Dean *lawyer*
Alexander, William Olin *finance company executive*
†Anderson, Girard F. *utility company executive*
Anderson, Robert Henry *education educator*
Anton, John Peter *philosopher, educator*
Baker, Carleton Harold *physiology educator*
Barkin, Marvin E. *lawyer*
Barness, Lewis Abraham *physician*
Barton, Bernard Alan, Jr. *lawyer*
Battle, Jean Allen *writer, educator*
Baynes, Thomas Edward, Jr. *judge, lawyer, educator*
†Bean, George J. *airport executive*
Behnke, Roy Herbert *physician, educator*
Benjamin, Robert Spiers *foreign correspondent, writer, publicist*
Beytin, Kenneth Alan *lawyer*
Bice, Michael O. *health science association administrator*
Bierley, John Charles *lawyer*
Binford, Jesse Stone, Jr. *chemistry educator*
Bondi, Joseph Charles, Jr. *education educator, consultant*
Bowen, Thomas Edwin *cardiothoracic surgeon, retired army officer*
Branch, William Terrell *urologist, educator*
Brown, Troy Anderson, Jr. *electrical distributing company executive*
Bryant, Herbert McCoy, Jr. (Herbie DeLaney) *statistician*
Bucklew, Susan Cawthon *federal judge*
Bujones, Fernando Calleiro *ballet dancer*
Bukantz, Samuel Charles *physician, educator*
Burnette, Guy Ellington, Jr. *lawyer*
Bussone, David Eben *hospital administrator*
Butler, Paul Bascomb, Jr. *lawyer*
†Byrnes, Donald J. *consumer products company executive*
†Cameron, Susan *computer services company executive*
Campbell, David Ned *retired electric utility executive, business consultant*
Campbell, Richard Bruce *lawyer*
Carey, Larry Campbell *surgeon*
†Carideo, James Vincent *lawyer, telephone company executive*
Castagna, William John *federal judge*
Cavanagh, Denis *physician, educator*
Christopher, Wilford Scott *public relations consultant*
Corbitt, Doris Orene *real estate agent, dietitian*
Corcoran, C. Timothy, III *judge*
Crisp, Terry Arthur *professional hockey coach*
Crowe, Eugene Bertrand *retired investment counselor*
Culverhouse, Hugh Franklin *lawyer, professional sports team executive*
Cundiff, Paul Arthur *English language educator*
Cutler, Edward I. *lawyer*
Davis, Helen Gordon *former state senator*
Davis, Richard Earl *lawyer*
Davis, W. E. *clergyman, bishop*
Dawson, Richard Thomas *lawyer*
del Regato, Juan Angel *radio-therapeutist and oncologist, educator*
DeMontier, Paulette LaPointe *chemist*
Deutsch, Sid *bioengineer, educator*
DeVine, B. Mack *management consultant*
Doliner, Nathaniel Lee *lawyer*
Dunn, Henry Hampton *writer, former television commentator, former editor*
Ellwanger, Thomas John *lawyer*
Farrior, Joseph Brown *otologist*
Ferlita, Theresa Ann *clinical social worker*
Flom, Edward Leonard *retired steel company executive*
Floto, Ronald John *supermarket executive*
Frankowiak, James Raymond *public relations executive*
Franzen, Lavern Gerhard *bishop*
Freedman, Sandra Warshaw *mayor*
Frias, Jaime Luis *pediatrician, educator*
Friedlander, Edward Jay *journalism educator*
Gassler, Frank Henry *lawyer*
Germany, John Fredrick *lawyer*
Gilbert, Leonard Harold *lawyer*
Gilbert-Barness, Enid F. *pathologist, pathology and pediatrics educator*
Gillen, William Albert *lawyer*
Givens, Paul Edward *industrial engineer, educator*
Givens, Paul Ronald *former university chancellor*
Glasser, Stephen Paul *cardiologist*
Glickman, Ronnie Carl *state official, lawyer*
Gonzalez, Joe Manuel *lawyer*
Grady, Susanna Fenhagen *preparatory school administrator*
Grant, John Audley, Jr. *state senator, lawyer*
†Greco, Dick A. *mayor, hardware company executive*
Greenfield, George B. *radiologist*
Gregg, Charles Wayne *engineering executive*
Griffin, Christopher L. *lawyer*
†Guzzle, Timothy L. *energy corporation executive*
Hanford, Grail Stevenson *writer*
Hankenson, E(dward) Craig, Jr. *performing arts executive*
Harkness, Mary Lou *librarian*
Hartmann, William Herman *pathologist, educator*
Hayes, Don A. *data processing company executive*
Heck, James Baker *university official*
Hegarty, Thomas Joseph *academic administrator, educator*
Hemke, Donald Edward *lawyer*
Henning, Rudolf Ernst *electrical engineer, educator, consultant*
Hernandez, Gilberto Juan *accountant, auditor, management consultant*
Heuer, Martin *temporary services executive*
Hinsch, Gertrude Wilma *biology educator*
†Hoard, Jack Dale *hospital administrator*
Holder, Harold Douglas, Sr. *investor, industrialist*
Holmes, Dwight Ellis *architect*
Homan, Paul M. *financial consultant*
Howey, John Richard *architect*
†Hoyland, Fred *diversified products supply company executive*
Hoyt, Brooks Pettingill *lawyer*
Hyatt, Kenneth E(rnest) *building materials company executive*
Jacobson, Howard Newman *obstetrics/gynecology educator, researcher*
Jennewein, James Joseph *architect*
Johnson, Ewell Calvin *research and engineering executive*
†Johnson, James E. *airport executive*
Jones, John Arthur *lawyer*
Karl, Frederick Brennan *lawyer, former state justice*
Kase-Polisini, Judith Baker *educator*
Kaufman, Ronald Paul *physician, school official*
Kelly, Thomas Paine, Jr. *lawyer*
Kiernan, William Joseph, Jr. *lawyer, real estate investor*
Kimmel, Ellen Bishop *psychologist, educator*
Koehn, George Waldemar *bank executive*
Kovachevich, Elizabeth Anne *federal judge*
Kozlowski, Donna Maureen *hospital administrator*
Krentzman, Ben *federal judge*
Krzanowski, Joseph John, Jr. *pharmacology educator*
Leavengood, Victor Price *telephone company executive*
LeFevre, David E. *lawyer, professional sports team executive*
Levine, Jack Anton *lawyer*
Lim, Daniel Van *microbiology educator*
Ling, Jahja Wang-Chieh *conductor*
Litschgi, A. Byrne *lawyer*
Locker, Raymond Duncan *editor*
Lockey, Richard Funk *allergist, educator*
Loft, Kurt *newspaper editor, science writer, music critic*
Maass, R. Andrew *museum director*
MacDonald, Thomas Cook, Jr. *lawyer*
MacManus, Susan Ann *political science educator, researcher*
Martens, Ernesto *glass products company executive*
Martin, Gary Wayne *lawyer*
Martin, Robert Leslie *physician*
Matheny, Charles Woodburn, Jr. *retired army officer, retired civil engineer, former city official*
Matlock, Kenneth Jerome *building materials company executive*
McAdams, John P. *lawyer*
Mc Alister, Linda Lopez *educator, philosopher*
McCook, Kathleen de la Peña *university educator*
McDevitt, Sheila Marie *lawyer, energy company executive*
McIntosh, Henry Deane *cardiologist*
McMillan, Donald Ernest *internal medicine educator, state program director*
McNeel, Van Louis *chemical company executive*
Menendez, Manuel, Jr. *judge*
Merryday, Steven D. *federal judge*
Miller, Charles Leslie *civil engineer, planner, consultant*
Miller, Lesley James, Jr. *state representative*
Mirro, Richard Allen *bank executive*
Molnar, Lewis K. *health facility administrator*
Muroff, Lawrence Ross *nuclear medicine physician*
Nagera, Humberto *psychiatrist, psychoanalyst, educator, author*
Naimoli, Vincent Joseph *diversified operating and holding company executive*
Nakamura, Yoshio *professional sports team executive*
Neusner, Jacob *humanities and religious studies educator*
Nevins, Albert J. *publisher, editor, author*
Nimmons, Ralph Wilson, Jr. *federal judge*
Nord, Walter Robert *business administration educator, researcher, consultant*
Olson, Robert Eugene *physician, biochemist, educator*
O'Neill, Albert Clarence, Jr. *lawyer*
O'Sullivan, Brendan Patrick *lawyer*
Paskay, Alexander L. *federal judge, law educator*
Perry, James Frederic *philosophy educator, author*
Pfeiffer, Eric Armin *psychiatrist, gerontologist*
Pittman, Richard Frank, Jr. *newspaper publisher*
Platt, Jan Kaminis *former county official*
Plawecki, Judith Ann *nursing educator*
Poe, William Frederick *insurance agency executive, former mayor*
Pollara, Bernard *immunologist, pediatrician*
Porter, Nicolas Christopher *healthcare executive*
Preto-Rodas, Richard Anthony *foreign language educator*
†Rankin, Thompson L. *utilities executive, agricultural executive*
Read, Peter Kip *health care administrator*
Reading, Anthony John *physician*
Richardson, Edward James *federal government agency official*
Richardson, Sylvia Onesti *physician*
Ritterman, Stuart I. *speech pathologist, educator*
Roberson, Bruce H. *lawyer*
Roberts, Edwin Albert, Jr. *newspaper editor, journalist*
†Robinson, Charles E. *building materials executive*
†Rogal, Philip James *physician*
Rosenkranz, Stanley William *lawyer*
Rowlands, David Thomas *pathology educator*
Ruth, Daniel John *journalist*
Sada, Federico G. *glass manufacturing executive*
Saff, Edward Barry *mathematics educator*
†Salisbury, Charles A. (Lex) *zoo director, educator*
Sams, Robert Alan *lawyer*
Sanchez, Mary Anne *secondary school educator*
Schmidt, Paul Joseph *physician, educator*
Schnitzlein, Harold Norman *anatomy educator*
Schonwetter, Ronald Scott *physician, educator*
Schwenke, Roger Dean *lawyer*
Shively, John Adrian *pathologist*
Silver, Richard Abraham *hospital administrator*
Smith, Donn L. *university dean*
†Snyder, Richard G. *transportation services executive*
Soble, James Barry *lawyer*
Sodeman, William Anthony, Sr. *cardiologist*
Sparkman, Steven Leonard *lawyer*
Spellacy, William Nelson *obstetrician-gynecologist, educator*
Stafford, Josephine Howard *lawyer*
Stallings, (Charles) Norman *lawyer*
Starkey, William Edward *telephone company executive*
†Streeter, Richard Barry *academic official*
Studer, William Allen *county official*
Sullivan, Sister Marie Celeste *health care executive*
Tabor, Curtis Harold, Jr. *library director*
Taggart, James Knox *electric utility executive*
Taub, Theodore Calvin *lawyer*
Thomas, Carole Dolores *gerontologist*
Thomas, Wayne Lee *lawyer*
Tompkins, William David *corporate professional*
Villareal, Dewey R. *lawyer*
Wade, Thomas Edward *electrical engineering educator, university research administrator*
Wagner, Frederick William (Bill Wagner) *lawyer*
Walker, H(erbert) Leslie, Jr. *architect*
Watkins, Joan Marie *osteopath, occupational medicine physician*
Weiner, Irving Bernard *university administrator, psychologist, educator*
Whipple, Thomas A. *food marketing professional*
†Whiting, Paul L. *holding company executive*
Williams, Thomas Arthur *biomedical computing consultant, psychiatrist*
Wilson, Wallace *art educator, artist*
Wissman, Jack Paul *financial executive*
Wyche, Samuel David *professional football coach*
Zeno, Phyllis Wolfe *association executive, editor*
Zhou, Huanchun *chemist*

Tarpon Springs

Byrne, Richard Hill *counselor, educator*
Dempster, Richard Vreeland *environmental company executive*
Scala, Sinclaire Maximilian *aerospace engineer, retired*
Vajk, Hugo *manufacturing executive*

Tavernier

Mabbs, Edward Carl *management consultant*
Zim, Herbert Spencer *author, educator*

Temple Terrace

Rink, Wesley Winfred *banker*

Tequesta

Hart, Frederick Donald *retired utility association and manufacturing executive*
Holmes, Melvin Almont *insurance company executive*
Luster, George Orchard *professional society administrator*
Milton, Robert Mitchell *chemical company executive*
Peterson, James Robert *retired writing instrument manufacturing executive*
Ruoff, Andrew Christian, III *orthopedic surgeon, educator, consultant*
Seaman, William Bernard *physician, radiology educator*
Stanger, John William *finance company executive*
Turrell, Richard Horton, Sr. *retired banker*
Vollmer, James E. *consulting company executive*

Tierra Verde

Gaffney, Thomas Francis *investment company executive*
Kubiet, Leo Lawrence *newspaper advertising and marketing executive*
Schmitz, Dolores Jean *secondary education educator*

Titusville

Haise, Fred Wallace, Jr. *aerospace company executive, former astronaut*

Tyndall AFB

†Horn, Clinton Van *air force officer*

Valrico

Nelson, Norman Daniel *career officer*

Venice

Appel, Wallace Henry *retired industrial designer*
Bluhm, Barbara Jean *communications agency executive*
Concordia, Charles *consulting engineer*
Corrigan, William Thomas *retired broadcast news executive*
Dodderidge, Richard William *retired marketing executive*
Hardenburg, Robert Earle *horticulturist*
Hays, Herschel Martin *electrical engineer*
Jamrich, John Xavier *retired university administrator*
Kinney, Michael James *physician*
Leidheiser, Henry, Jr. *retired chemistry educator, consultant*
Miller, Allan John *lawyer*
Nevins, John J. *bishop*
Ogan, Russell Griffith *business executive, retired air force officer*
Palermo, Joseph *language educator*
Shaw, Bryce Robert *author*
Thomas, David Ansell *retired university dean*
Torrey, Richard Frank *utility executive*

Vero Beach

Allik, Michael *diversified industry executive*
Anderson, Rudolph J., Jr. *lawyer*
Berkovitch, Boris S. *retired trust company executive*
Bradford, Charles Lobdell *management consultant*
Brim, Orville Gilbert, Jr. *former foundation administrator, author*
Burton, Arthur Henry, Jr. *insurance company executive*
Cartwright, Alton Stuart *electrical manufacturing company executive*
Christy, Nicholas Pierson *physician*
Clawson, John Addison *financier, investor*
Conway, Earl Cranston *manufacturing company executive, educator*
Corr, Thomas L. *oil industry executive*
Dillard, Rodney Jefferson *real estate company executive*
Ebbitt, Kenneth Cooper *investor*
Feagles, Robert West *insurance company executive*
Fisher, Andrew *management consultant*
Furrer, John Rudolf *retired manufacturing business executive*
Glassmeyer, Edward *investment banker*
Grobman, Arnold Brams *retired biology educator and academic administrator*
Grobman, Hulda Gross (Mrs. Arnold B. Grobman) *horticulturist, retired public health educator*
Haywood, Oliver Garfield *engineer*
Hill, Henry Parker *accountant*
Kinard, Hargett Yingling *financial consultant*
Koontz, Alfred Joseph, Jr. *financial and operating management executive, consultant*
Lawrence, Merle *medical educator*
Leonsis, Theodore John *publishing company executive*
†Ludwig, William Frank *retired investment banker, lawyer*
MacTaggart, Barry *retired corporate executive*
Mc Afee, Jerry *retired oil company executive, chemical engineer*
Mc Namara, John J(oseph) *advertising executive, writer*
Michelson, Edward J. *journalist*
Nichols, Carl Wheeler *retired advertising agency executive*
Petersmeyer, C(harles) Wrede *retired broadcasting executive, venture capitalist*
Phillips, Ellis Laurimore, Jr. *legal educator, foundation executive*
Reed, Sherman Kennedy *chemical consultant*
Riley, Randy James *banker*
Ritterhoff, C(harles) William *retired steel company executive*
Schulman, Harold *obstetrician, gynecologist, perinatologist*
Sheehan, Charles Vincent *investment banker*
Slater, George Richard *retired banker*
Thompson, William David *investment banking executive*
Ward, William Binnington *agricultural communicator*
White, Thomas Patrick *county official, small business owner*
Wiegner, Edward Alex *multi-industry executive*

Viera

Ehrig, John Paul *architect*

Village Of Golf

Bates, Edward Brill *retired insurance company executive*

Wesley Chapel

Holloway, Marvin Lawrence *retired automobile club executive, rancher, vintager*

West Palm Beach

Aaron, M. Robert *electrical engineer*
Baker, Bernard Robert, II *lawyer*

Beall, Kenneth Sutter, Jr. *lawyer*
Bower, Ruth Lawther *retired mathematics educator*
Broadhead, James Lowell *business executive*
Brumback, Clarence Landen *physician*
Burck, Arthur Albert *lawyer, corporate merger expert*
Coar, Richard John *mechanical engineer, aerospace consultant*
Corts, Paul Richard *academic administrator*
†Coyle, Dennis Patrick *lawyer*
†Davis, Karen *sales executive*
Davis, Robert Edwin *manufacturing executive*
Diener, Bert *former food broker, artist*
Donovan, Ellen L. *museum director*
Elder, Stewart Taylor *dentist, retired naval officer*
Eppley, Roland Raymond, Jr. *retired financial services executive*
Eschbach, Jesse Ernest *federal judge*
Fairbanks, Richard Monroe *broadcasting company executive*
Flanagan, L. Martin *lawyer*
Freeland, James M. Jackson *lawyer, educator*
Freudenthal, Ralph Ira *toxicology consultant*
Giacco, Alexander Fortunatus *chemical industry executive*
Gillette, Frank C., Jr. *aeronautical engineer*
Giuffrida, Tom A. *publisher*
Hamilton, Neil Alfred *financial executive*
†Hawthorne, David Eugene *service hotel and resorts executive*
Hill, Thomas William, Jr. *lawyer, educator*
Hoewing, Mark Wesley *real estate association executive*
Hudson, Alice Peterson *chemistry consulting laboratory executive*
Jorandby, Richard Leroy *lawyer*
Kaslow, Florence W. *psychologist*
Katz, William David *psychologist, psychoanalytic psychotherapist, educator, mental health consultant*
Knott, James Robert *state judge, retired lawyer*
Knudsen, Raymond Barnett *clergyman, association executive, author*
Koff, Bernard Louis *engineering executive*
Lasnick, Julius *fabric company executive*
†Lavine, Alan *columnist, writer*
Lively, Edwin Lowe *sociology educator*
Livingstone, John Leslie *accountant, management consultant, business economist, educator*
Luckett, Paul Herbert, III *manufacturing executive*
Lynch, William Walker *savings and loan association executive*
MacDonald, Richard Annis *pathologist, physician, educator*
McGinnes, Paul R. *environmental chemist*
Miller, Richard Jackson *lawyer*
Montgomery, Robert Morel, Jr. *lawyer*
Moore, George Crawford Jackson *lawyer*
Mora, Abraham Martin *lawyer*
Nelson, Richard Henry *manufacturing company executive*
O'Brien, Robert Brownell, Jr. *investment banker, consultant, savings bank executive, yacht broker*
O'Brien, Thomas George, III *lawyer*
O'Flarity, James P. *lawyer*
O'Hara, Thomas Patrick *managing editor*
Olsak, Ivan Karel *civil engineer*
Orr-Cahall, Christina *art gallery director, art historian*
Paine, James Carriger *federal judge*
Passy, Charles *arts critic*
Patterson, Lydia Ross *industrial relations specialist, consulting company executive*
Petersen, David L. *lawyer*
Pledger, Thomas Rolon *holding company executive*
Pottash, A. Carter *psychiatrist, hospital executive*
Price, William James, IV *investment banker*
Rinker, Marshall Edison, Sr. *cement company executive*
Rivers, Marie Bie *broadcasting executive*
Roberts, Carol Antonia *county commissioner, real estate associate*
Roberts, Hyman Jacob *internist, researcher, author, historian, publisher*
Robinson, Raymond Edwin *musician, music educator, writer*
Ronan, William John *management consultant*
Royce, Raymond Watson *lawyer, rancher, citrus grower*
Ryskamp, Kenneth Lee *federal judge*
Sammond, John Stowell *lawyer*
Scheckner, Sy *former greeting card company executive*
Schuler, John Hamilton *holding company executive*
Sears, Edward Milner, Jr. *newspaper editor*
Sennett, Henry Herbert, Jr. *theatre arts educator*
Smith, David Shiverick *lawyer, former ambassador*
Snead, Samuel Jackson *former professional golfer*
Sokmensuer, Adil *physician, educator*
Still, Mary Jane (M. J. Still) *mathematics educator*
†Strickland, R. Michael *bank executive*
Sturrock, Thomas Tracy *botany educator, horticulturist*
Upledger, John Edwin *osteopath, physician*
Vanek, Cynthia Wilkinson *administrator*
Vecellio, Leo Arthur, Jr. *construction company executive*
Vitunac, Ann E. *judge*
Wagner, Arthur Ward, Jr. *lawyer*
Wilensky, Alvin *real estate investment trust executive*
Worsham, Ernest Lee *lawyer*
Wright, Donald Conway *editorial cartoonist*

Windermere
Alexander, Judd Harris *retired paper company executive*
Hylton, Hannelore Menke *retired manufacturing executive*

Winter Garden
Clifford, Margaret Louise *psychologist*

Winter Haven
Burns, Arthur Lee *architect*
Chase, Lucius Peter *lawyer, retired corporate executive*
Grierson, William *retired agricultural educator*
Lansdale, Daryl L. *retail executive*
Love, John Wesley, Jr. *English language and reading educator*
O'Connor, R. D. *health care executive*
Peck, Maryly VanLeer *college president, chemical engineer*
Turnquist, Donald Keith *orthodontist*

Winter Park
Armstrong, (Arthur) James *minister, religion educator, religious organization executive, consultant*
Balliett, Gene (Howard Eugene Balliett) *writer, lecturer*
Bornstein, Rita *academic administrator*
Britton, Erwin Adelbert *clergyman, college administrator*
Brooten, Kenneth Edward, Jr. *lawyer*
Dawson, Ray Fields *research scientist, educator, consultant, tropical agriculturist*
Edge, Findley Bartow *clergyman, religious education educator*
Fernandez, Joseph Anthony *educational administrator*
Flick, Carl *electrical engineer, consultant, free-lance author*
Fowler, Mark Stapleton *lawyer, corporation counsel*
Hawkins, Paula *federal official, former senator*
Hoche, Philip Anthony *life insurance company executive*
Holt, Georgina L. *ceramic artist*
Kiely, Dan Ray *lawyer, banking and real estate development executive*
Kost, Wayne L. *business executive*
Link, Raymond Arthur *construction company executive*
Mc Kean, Hugh Ferguson *college president, painter, writer*
Mc Kean, Keith Ferguson *former education educator*
McKean, Thomas Wayne *dentist, retired naval officer*
Mica, John L. *congressman*
Olsson, Nils William *former association executive*
Patterson, Robert Youngman, Jr. *retired lawyer, utility executive*
Perkins, James Patrick *advertising executive*
Plane, Donald Ray *management science educator*
Richards, Max De Voe *management educator, consultant, researcher, author*
Rogers, Donald Patrick *business administration educator*
Rogers, Rutherford David *librarian*
Ruggiero, Laurence Joseph *museum director*
Sedwick, (Benjamin) Frank *language educator*
Seymour, Thaddeus *English educator*
Spake, Ned Bernarr *energy company executive*
Weir, William C., III *lighting manufacturing company executive*

Winter Springs
Hagen, Kevin A. *performing company executive*

Zellwood
Wallcraft, Mary Jane Louise *religious organization executive, songwriter, author*

Zephyrhills
Jernstrom, Joan *secondary education educator*

GEORGIA

Adel
Darby, Marianne Talley *elementary school educator*

Ailey
Windsor, James Thomas, Jr. *printing company executive, newspaper publisher*

Albany
Greene, William Joshua, III *investment executive and consultant*
Marbury, Ritchey McGuire, III *engineering executive, surveyor*
Mayes, Helen *professional association administrator*
McManus, James William *chemist, researcher*
†Norwood, Geoffrey Alexander *hospital administrator*

Alpharetta
Balows, Albert *microbiologist, educator*
Barr, John Baldwin *chemist, reserach scientist*
Byrd, Bette Jean *artist, author*
Feuss, Linda Anne Upsall *lawyer*
Hung, William Mo-Wei *chemist*
Kingrea, Ann B. *principal*
Mills, Stephen Nathaniel *computer software company executive*
Zimmermann, John *financial consultant*

Americus
Capitan, William Harry *college president*
Counts, Wayne Boyd *chemistry educator*
Fuller, Millard Dean *charitable organization executive, lawyer*
Gray, Margaret Edna *nursing educator, dean*
Jernigan, Bob *utility company executive*
McGrady, Clyde A. *secondary school principal*
Stanford, Henry King *college president*

Andersonville
Boyles, Frederick Holdren *historian*

Athens
Agee, Warren Kendall *journalism educator*
Agosin, Moises Kankolsky *zoology educator*
Albersheim, Peter *biology educator*
Allinger, Norman Louis *chemistry educator*
Allsbrook, Ogden Olmstead, Jr. *economics educator*
Anderson, James L. *history educator, business developer*
Ansel, Howard Carl *pharmacist, educator*
Avise, John Charles *geneticist, educator*
Barry, John Reagan *psychology educator*
Beaird, James Ralph *legal educator*
Black, Clanton Candler, Jr. *biochemistry educator, researcher*
Bowen, John Metcalf *pharmacologist, toxicologist, educator*
Boyd, George Edward *physical chemist*
Boyd, Louis Jefferson *agricultural scientist, educator*
Bullock, Charles Spencer, III *political science educator, author, consultant*
Carlson, Ronald Lee *lawyer, educator*
Carter, Mary Eddie *government administrator*
Clute, Robert Eugene *political and social science educator*
Crowther, Ann Rollins *dean, political science educator*
Cutlip, Scott Munson *university dean*
Darvill, Alan G. *biochemist, botanist, educator*
Dickie, Margaret McKenzie *English language educator*
Dively, Frank Eugene *airport executive*
†Donoho, Clive W., Jr. *dean, research horticulturalist*
Dooley, Vincent Joseph *college athletics administrator*
Douglas, Dwight Oliver *university administrator*
Dunn, Delmer Delano *political science educator*
Ellington, Charles Ronald *lawyer, educator*
Eriksson, Karl-Erik Lennart *biochemist, educator*
Feldman, Edmund Burke *art critic*
Fincher, Cameron Lane *educator*
Fink, Conrad Charles *journalism educator, communications consultant*
Freer, Coburn *English language educator*
Fuller, Melvin Stuart *botany educator*
Garbin, Albeno Patrick *sociology educator*
Giles, Norman Henry *educator, geneticist*
Green, Frank C. *agricultural administrator*
Herbert, James Arthur *artist, filmmaker*
Hester, Albert Lee *journalism educator*
Hillenbrand, Martin Joseph *diplomat, educator*
Holcomb, Alice Willard Power *diversified investments executive*
Holder, Howard Randolph, Sr. *broadcasting company executive*
Horton, Gerald Talmadge *educator, public relations executive*
Hunt, Jacob Tate *special education educator emeritus*
Johnson, Michael Kenneth *chemistry educator*
Kamerschen, David Roy *economist, educator*
Kent, Robert B. *artist, educator*
King, Robert Bruce *chemistry educator, writer*
Knapp, Charles Boynton *economist, educator, academic administrator*
Kraszewski, Andrzej Wojciech *electrical engineer, researcher*
Kretzschmar, William Addison, Jr. *English language educator*
Landau, David Paul *physics educator*
Lane, Walter Ronald, Jr. *advertising executive, educator*
Levine, David Lawrence *social work educator*
†Lewis, A. Jefferson, III *botanical garden administrator*
Lindberg, Stanley William *English language educator, editor*
Mamatey, Victor Samuel *history educator*
Mc Feely, William Shield *historian, writer*
McGuire, John Murray *chemist, researcher*
Meeks, Carol Jean *educator*
Melton, Charles Estel *physicist, educator*
Miller, Herbert Elmer *accountant*
Miller, Ronald Baxter *English language educator, author*
Moore, Rayburn Sabatzky *American literature educator*
Morrison, Darrel Gene *landscape architecture educator*
Nelson, Stuart Owen *agricultural engineer, researcher, educator*
Neter, John *statistician*
Newsome, George Lane, Jr. *education educator*
Norred, William Preston, Jr. *pharmacologist, educator*
Nute, Donald E., Jr. *philosophy educator*
†Paul, William Dewitt, Jr. *artist, educator, photographer, museum director*
Pavlik, William Bruce *psychologist, educator*
Payne, William Jackson *microbiologist, educator*
Peacock, Lelon James *psychologist, educator*
Pelletier, S. William *chemistry educator*
Phillips, Walter Ray *lawyer, educator*
Plummer, Gayther L(ynn) *climatologist, ecologist, researcher*
Potter, William Gray, Jr. *library director*
Puckett, Elizabeth Ann *law librarian, law educator*
Rosenberg, Alexander *philosophy educator, author*
Schaefer, Henry Frederick, III *chemistry educator*
Smith, Howard Ross *economics educator, academic administrator, researcher, consultant*
Speering, Robin *computer specialist, educator*
Spurgeon, Edward Dutcher *law educator*
Staub, August William *drama educator, theatrical producer*
Steer, Alfred Gilbert, Jr. *foreign language educator*
Surrency, Erwin Campbell *librarian, educator*
Tesser, Abraham *social psychologist*
Tillman, Murray Howell *instructional technology educator*
Torrance, Ellis Paul *psychologist, educator*
Trim, Cynthia Mary *veterinarian, educator*
Tyler, David Earl *veterinary medical educator*
Van Eseltine, William Parker *microbiologist, educator*
Wall, Bennett Harrison *history educator*
Watson, William A. J. *law educator*
Wellman, Richard Vance *legal educator*
Wood, Betty A. *utilities executive*
Yamaguchi, Yukio *chemistry research scientist*
Yen, William Mao-Shung *physicist*
Younts, Sanford Eugene *university administrator*

Atlanta
Aaron, HenryL. (Hank Aaron) *professional baseball team executive*
Abdel-Khalik, Said Ibrahim *nuclear and mechanical engineering educator*
Abrams, Bernard William *construction manufacturing and property development executive*
Abrams, Edward Marvin *construction company executive*
Abrams, Harold Eugene *lawyer*
Ackerman, F. Duane *utility company executive*
Addison, Edward L. *retired utility holding company executive*
Akers, Sheldon Buckingham, Jr. *electrical and computer engineering educator*
Alexander, Cecil Abraham *college official, retired architect, consultant*
Alexander, Miles Jordan *lawyer*
Alexander, William Henry *judge*
Alford, Walter Helion *telecommunications executive, lawyer*
Alfred, Dewitt Clinton, Jr. *university dean, psychiatrist*
Allan, Frank Kellog *bishop*
Allen, Ivan, Jr. *office products company owner*
Allen, Ronald W. *airline company executive*
Allio, Robert John *management consultant, educator*
Ambrose, Samuel Sheridan, Jr. *urologist*
Ames, William Francis *mathematician, educator*
Amisano, Joseph *architect*
Anderson, Peter Joseph *lawyer*
Anderson, Ray C. *carpet company executive*
Andrews, Gary Blaylock *state judge, lawyer*
Arani, Ardy A. *professional sports marketing executive, lawyer*
†Arzewski, Cecylia *concertmaster*
†Ash, Thomas Gray *banker*
Ashe, Robert Lawrence, Jr. *lawyer*
†Atluri, Satya N(adham) *aerospace engineering educator*
Attridge, Richard Byron *lawyer*
Avery, Steven Thomas *professional baseball player*
Babcock, Peter Heartz *professional sports executive*
Bacon, Louis Albert *retired consulting civil engineer*
†Bahl, Roy Winford *economist, educator, consultant*
Bainbridge, Frederick Freeman, III *architect*
Bakay, Roy Arpad Earle *neurosurgeon, educator*
Baker, David S. *lawyer*
†Baker, Edward L. *physician, science facility executive*
Baker, Henry Grady, Jr. *utilities company executive*
Bakewell, Peter John *history educator*
Balke, Robert Roy *architect*
Banks, Bettie Sheppard *psychologist*
Baran, William Lee *food company executive*
Barker, William Daniel *hospital administrator*
Barkoff, Rupert Mitchell *lawyer*
Barksdale, Richard Dillon *civil engineer, educator*
Barnard, Susan Muller *zookeeper*
Barnes, Harry G., Jr. *human rights activist, retired ambassador*
Barnett, Crawford Fannin, Jr. *internist, educator, cardiologist*
Barnett, Elizabeth Hale *organizational consultant*
Barnett, Robert James *artistic director*
Barnwell, Thomas Pinkney, III *electrical engineering educator, business executive*
Barr, James Milton *business consultant*
†Barrow, Daniel Louis *neurosurgeon*
Bassett, Peter Q. *lawyer*
†Bates, Valentino Travis *engineering executive*
Batson, Richard Neal *lawyer*
Baxter, Arthur Pearce *financial services marketing company executive*
Baxter, Harry Stevens *lawyer*
Baxter, Robert Hampton, III *insurance executive*
Beard, Rick *cultural organization administrator*
Beattie, George *artist*
Beckham, Walter Hull, III *lawyer*
Bell, Gail McKnight *law educator*
Bell, Griffin B. *lawyer, former attorney general*
†Bell, Jack Atkins *percussionist, educator*
†Bell, Ronald Mack *university foundation administrator*
Benario, Herbert William *classics educator*
Benatar, Leo *packaging company executive*
Benham, Robert *state supreme court justice*
Bennett, Jay D. *lawyer*
Benson, Ronald Edward *state humanities program executive, clergyman, educator*
Benson, Thomas Hayden *utility company executive*
Benston, George James *accountant, economist*
Berry, Dennis *newspaper publishing executive*
Bevington, E(dmund) Milton *electrical machinery manufacturing company executive*
Biggers, William Joseph *retired manufacturing company executive*
Bihary, Joyce *federal judge*
Birch, Stanley Francis, Jr. *federal judge*
Bird, Wendell Raleigh *lawyer*
Bisher, James Furman *journalist, author*
Black, Kenneth, Jr. *insurance executive, educator, author*
Black, Kirby Samuel *biomedical engineer, immunologist, biologist, educator*
Blackburn, William Stanley *lawyer*
Blackstock, Jerry Byron *lawyer*
Blank, A(ndrew) Russell *lawyer*
Blank, Arthur M. *home and lumber retail chain executive*
Blauser, Jeffrey Michael *professional baseball player*
Bloodworth, A(lbert) W(illiam) Franklin *lawyer*
Blount, Ben B., Jr. *apparel executive*
Bobo, Genelle Tant (Nell Bobo) *office administrator*
Boeke, Eugene H., Jr. *construction executive*
Boisseau, Richard Robert *lawyer*
Boland, Thomas Edwin *banker*
Bolch, Carl Edward, Jr. *corporation executive, lawyer*
Boman, John Harris, Jr. *retired lawyer*
Bonds, John Wilfred, Jr. *lawyer*
Bondurant, Emmet Jopling, II *lawyer*
Boone, J. William *lawyer*
Booth, Gordon Dean, Jr. *lawyer*
Booth, Randolph Lee *broadcast executive*
Boren, Thomas Garner *utility executive*
Bourne, Henry Clark, Jr. *electrical engineering educator, former academic official*
Bowden, Henry Lumpkin, Jr. *lawyer*
Bowers, Michael Joseph *state attorney general*
Bowman, Juliette Joseph *interior decorator, gourmet food consultant*
Boyko, Gregory Andrew *insurance company executive*
Bradfield, Richard H. *architectural firm executive*
Bradley, William H. *lawyer*
Bragg, John Mackie *actuarial consultant*
Branch, Thomas Broughton, III *lawyer*
Brands, James Edwin *medical products executive*
Brandt, Harry *federal reserve bank executive*
Brannon, Lester Travis, Jr. *lawyer*
Bratton, James Henry, Jr. *lawyer*
Bridgewater, Herbert Jeremiah, Jr. *radio host*
Bright, David Forbes *academic administrator, classics and comparative literature educator*
Brighton, John Austin *mechanical engineer, educator*
Brill, Ronald Mitchel *retail executive*
Brinkley, Donald R. *oil industry executive*
Brooks, David William *farmer cooperative executive*
Brooks, Wilbur Clinton *lawyer*
Broome, Claire Veronica *epidemiologist, researcher*
Brown, Bennett Alexander *former banker*
Brown, John Robert *lawyer, priest, philanthropist*
Brown, Lorene B(yron) *library educator, educational administrator*
Brown-Olmstead, Amanda *public relations executive*
Buck, Lee Albert *retired insurance company executive, evangelist*
Burge, William Lee *retired business information executive*
†Burkart, Alan Ray *chemical company executive*
Burns, Carroll Dean *insurance company executive*
Burns, Thomas Samuel *history educator*
†Butts, Lester Wayne *principal*
Bynum, Richard Cary *publishing executive, author*
Byrd, Larry Donald *behavioral pharmacologist*
Byrne, Catherine *swimmer*
Cadenhead, Alfred Paul *lawyer*
Callahan, Harry Morey *photographer*

Callison, James W. former airline executive, lawyer
Cameron, Rondo economic history educator
Camp, Jack Tarpley, Jr. federal judge
Campbell, Bill mayor, broadcasting executive
Campbell, Colin McLeod journalist
Candler, John Slaughter, II retired lawyer
Cann, Sharon Lee librarian
Cannon, William Ragsdale bishop
Cantrell, Wesley Eugene, Sr. office equipment company executive
Caprio, Anthony S. university official
Carey, Gerald John, Jr. former air force officer, research institute director
Carlson, Robert Lee engineering educator
Carnes, Julie E. federal judge
†Carothers, Rick mortgage company executive
Carpenter, Charles Bernard medical educator
Carroll, James Michael retailing executive
Carter, Dan T. history educator
Carter, Jimmy (James Earl Carter, Jr.) former President of United States
Casey, Charles Francis diversified company executive
Chace, William Murdough university administrator
Chaiet, Alan Howard advertising agency executive
Chalmers, Alan Knight financial corporation executive
Chambers, Anne Cox newspaper executive
†Chandler, Robert Charles hospital administrator
Chapman, Hugh McMaster banker
†Chapman, Paul H. author
Charania, Barkat real estate consultant
Chasen, Sylvan Herbert computer applications consultant, investment advisor
Cheatham, Richard Reed lawyer
Chilivis, Nickolas Peter lawyer
Chilton, Horace Thomas pipeline company executive
Chisholm, Tommy lawyer, utility company executive
Chitwood, Harold Otis food company executive
Churchwell, Charles Darrett librarian
Circeo, Louis Joseph, Jr. research center director, civil engineer
Clark, Thomas Alonzo federal judge
Clark, William Franklin lawyer
Clarke, Clifford Montreville health foundation executive
Clarke, Thomas Hal lawyer
Cleland, Joseph Maxwell (Max Cleland) state official
Clements, James David psychiatry educator, physician
Clendenin, John L. telecommunications company executive
Clifton, David Samuel, Jr. research executive, economist
Clough, Gerald Wayne academic administrator
Coan, Gaylord O. agribusiness executive
Cohen, Ezra Harry lawyer
Cohen, George Leon lawyer
Cohen, N. Jerold lawyer
Cohn, Bob public relations executive
Cole, David Andrew management consultant executive
Cole, Johnnetta Betsch academic administrator
Cole, Thomas Winston, Jr. chancellor, college president, chemist
Coleman, Mattie Jones primary education educator
Collins, Marcus E., Sr. state agency administrator
Collins, Steven M. lawyer
Collura, Kathryn Jean communications executive, consultant
Connell-Tatum, Elizabeth Bishop physician
Connor, Charles William airline pilot
Cooper, Frederick Eansor lawyer
Cooper, Jerome Maurice architect
Cooper, Keith Harvey insurance consultant
Cooper, Thomas Luther retired printing company executive
Copeland, Alvin Charles fast food company executive
Copeland, Floyd Dean lawyer
Copeland, John Alexander, III physicist
Corr, James Vanis furniture manufacturing executive, investor, lawyer, accountant
Correll, Alston Dayton, Jr. forest products company executive
Cotton, James Perry, Jr. holding company executive
Cox, Albert Harrington, Jr. economist
Cox, Bobby (Robert Joe Cox) professional baseball manager
Coxe, Tench Charles lawyer
Cramer, Howard Ross geologist, environmental consultant
Creed, Thomas Wayne retired federal executive
Crews, William Edwin lawyer
Cross, Joyce Annette Oscar newscaster
Cupp, Robert Erhard golf course designer, land use planner
Cutshaw, Kenneth Andrew lawyer
Dahlberg, Alfred William electric company executive
Dahlke, Wayne Theodore civil engineer, corporate executive
Dalrymple, Gordon Bennett former engineering company executive
Dalton, John J. lawyer
Daly, Chuck (Charles Jerome Daly) sports commentator, former professional basketball coach
Davis, Eleanor Kay museum administrator
Davis, Frank Tradewell, Jr. lawyer
Davis, Lawrence William radiation oncologist
†DeConcini, Barbara association executive, religious studies educator
Dees, Julian Worth academic administrator
Dennison, Daniel Bassel chemist
Dennison, Stanley Scott retired lumber company executive, consultant
Denny, Richard Alden, Jr. lawyer
Dezell, James Elton, Jr. educational systems and computer company executive
Diedrich, Richard Joseph architect
Dillingham, William Byron literature educator, author
Dillon, John Robert, III communications executive
Dobson, Bridget McColl Hursley television executive and writer
Dodge, William Douglas risk management, insurance, benefits consultant
Dolive, Earl retired business executive
Dollar, Steve music critic
Donoghue, John Frances archbishop
Dorsey, J(onnie) Naomi vocational education educator, consultant
Dotson, Robert Charles news correspondent
Dougherty, John Ernest federal judge
Dowden, Thomas Clark telecommunication executive
Dowling, Roderick Anthony investment banker
Downs, Harry lawyer and retired corporate legal executive
Doyle, Michael Anthony lawyer
Drake, Miriam Anna librarian, educator
Drennen, Eileen Moira editor
Drucker, Melvin Bruce psychology educator
Dubberly, Ronald Alvah library director
DuBose, Charles Wilson lawyer
Dunahoo, Charles religious publisher, religious organization administrator
Durbetaki, Pandeli mechanical engineer, educator, researcher
Durrett, James Frazer, Jr. lawyer
Dykes, John Henry, Jr. finance executive
Dysart, Benjamin Clay, III environmental management consultant, conservationist, engineer
Eason, William Everette, Jr. lawyer
Easterly, David Eugene communications executive
Eber, Herbert Wolfgang psychologist
Ebneter, Stewart Dwight federal agency administrator
Eckert, Charles Alan chemical engineering educator
Eckert, Michael Joseph cable and broadcast television executive
Eden, Margie Cohen public relations executive
Edmondson, James Larry federal judge
Edwards, Howard Dawson business executive, physicist, academic administrator
Edwards, Louis Ward, Jr. diversified manufacturing company executive
Egan, Michael Joseph lawyer
Ehrlichman, John Daniel lawyer, company executive, author, former assistant to President of United States
Eisner, Rebecca Suzanne lawyer
Elam, Merrill L. architectural firm executive
Elliott, A(rthur) James lawyer
†Ellis, David Oliver merchant banker
Ellis, Elmo Israel broadcast executive, consultant, newspaper columnist
Elsas, Louis Jacob, II medical educator
El-Sayed, Mostafa Amr chemistry educator
Elsner, Carlene W. reproductive endocrinologist
Endicott, John Edgar international relations educator
Epstein, David Gustav lawyer
Erck, Theodore Augustus, Jr. lawyer
Etheridge, Jack Paul arbitrator, mediator, former judge
Evans, Edwin Curtis internist, educator, geriatrician
Evans, Orinda D. federal judge
Ezell, Reva Gross radio station manager, writer
†Falk, Henry pediatrician, research epidemiologist
Farley, Charles P. public relations executive
Farrington, Frank architect
Fash, William Leonard retired architecture educator, college dean
Feldman, Joel Martin magistrate judge
Felton, Jule Wimberly, Jr. lawyer
Finkelstein, David physicist, educator, consultant
Fitzgerald, David Patrick advertising agency executive
Fitzgerald, John Edmund civil engineering educator, dean
Fleming, Julian Denver, Jr. lawyer
Flemming, David Paul biologist
Fletcher, Norman S. state supreme court justice
Flinn, Patrick L. bank executive
Foley, James David computer science educator, consultant
Forbes, Theodore McCoy, Jr. lawyer, arbitrator, mediator
Ford, Basil H. packaging company executive
Foreman, Edward Rawson lawyer
Forrestal, Robert Patrick banker, lawyer
Forrester, J. Owen federal judge
Foster, Roger Sherman, Jr. surgeon, educator, health facility administrator
Fowler, Andrea teachers academy administrator
Fox, James Harold, Jr. superintendent of schools
Fox, Ronald Forrest physics educator
Fox-Genovese, Elizabeth Ann humanities educator
Francisco, Edgar Wiggin, III management information systems consultant
Frank, Ronald Edward marketing educator
Frank, William Pendleton sales and marketing executive
Franklin, Charles Scothern lawyer
Freeman, Richard Cameron federal judge
Frost, Norman Cooper retired telephone company executive
Frye, Billy Eugene university administrator, biologist
Fuqua, John Brooks retired consumer products and services company executive
Furr, Anthony Lloyd corporate executive
Gable, Carl Irwin business consultant, private investor, lawyer
Galambos, John Thomas medical educator, internist
Gallagher, Thomas C. diversified manufacturing executive
Gambrell, David Henry lawyer
Garland, LaRetta Matthews educational psychologist, nursing educator
Garner, Robert Edward Lee lawyer
†Garth, Thomas G. youth organization administrator
Gayer, Alan J. hospital administrator
Gayles, Joseph Nathan, Jr. medical educator, administrator
Gearon, John Michael professional basketball team executive
Geigerman, Clarice Furchgott writer, actress, consultant
†Gelardi, Robert Charles trade association executive, consultant
Genovese, Eugene Dominick historian, educator
Gianturco, Maurizio Antonio beverage company executive
Gifford, Anita Sheree lawyer
Gilchrist, Paul R. religious organization administrator
Gilmer, Harry Wesley publishing executive, educator
Girth, Marjorie Louisa lawyer, educator
†Gittens, Angela airport executive
Glassick, Charles Etzweiler cultural organization administrator
Glavine, Tom (Thomas Michael Glavine) professional baseball player
†Glover, John Trapnell real estate executive
Godard, James McFate retired educational consultant
Goizueta, Roberto Crispulo food and beverage company executive
Gokhale, Arun Mahadeo materials science and engineering educator
Goldman, Joel Stanley lawyer
Goldstein, Burton Benjamin, Jr. communications executive
Goldstein, Elliott lawyer
Goldstein, Jacob Herman retired physical chemist
Goodwin, George Evans public relations executive
Grace, Donald J. engineering researcher
Grant, Walter Matthews lawyer, diversified consumer products executive
Graves, Judson lawyer
Green, Holcombe Tucker, Jr. investment executive
†Green, William S. corporate executive, engineer
Greer, Bernard Lewis, Jr. lawyer
Gregory, Mel Hyatt, Jr. retired insurance company executive
Griffin, Clayton Houstoun retired power company engineer, lecturer
Grissom, Marquis Dean professional baseball player
Grove, Russell Sinclair, Jr. lawyer
Grumet, Priscilla Hecht fashion specialist, consultant, writer
Guberman, Sidney Thomas painter, writer
Guest, Rita Carson interior designer
Guinan, Mary Elizabeth physician, research scientist
Haas, George Aaron lawyer
Hackett, Stanley Hailey lawyer
†Haddad, Wassim Michael aerospace engineer, educator
Hahn, Thomas Marshall, Jr. forest products corporation executive
Hale, Jack K. mathematics educator, research center administrator
Hall, Jesse Seaborn banker
Hall, Robert Howell federal judge
Hall, Sarah E. magazine editor, educator
Hall, Wilbur Dallas, Jr. medical educator
Hansen, Jorgen Hartmann hotel corporation executive
Hanson, Victor Arthur surgeon
Harkey, Robert Shelton lawyer
Harlin, Robert Ray lawyer
Harmer, Lee DeLoache writer
Harmon, Nolan B. lawyer
Harney, Thomas C. lawyer
Harris, Henry Wood cable television executive
Harrison, John Raymond foundation executive, retired newspaper executive
Hartle, Robert Wyman retired foreign language and literature educator
Hasson, James Keith, Jr. lawyer
Hatch, Henry J. engineering executive
Hatcher, Charles Ross, Jr. cardiothoracic surgeon, medical center executive
Haverty, John Rhodes physician, former university dean
Haverty, Rawson retail furniture company executive
Hawkins, Robert Garvin management educator, consultant
Hawks, Barrett Kingsbury lawyer
Heil, Russell Howard air transportation company executive
Hemby, John Carlyle, Jr. utility company exeuctive
Henderson, Albert John federal judge
Hendrix, James Paisley, Jr. headmaster
Henry, John Dunklin hospital administrator
Henry, Ronald James Whyte university official
Henry, William Ray business administration educator
Herlong, D. C. agribusiness executive
Herold, David Mark management educator
Hiers, Mary A. museum director
Higgins, Richard J. microelectronics research administrator, educator
Hill, Harold Nelson, Jr. lawyer
Hill, Paul Drennen lawyer, banker
Hilliard, Robert Glenn insurance company executive, lawyer
Hinman, Alan Richard public health administrator, epidemiologist
Hodges, Dewey Harper aerospace engineer, educator
Hoenig, Gerald Jay lawyer, insurance company executive
Hoff, Gerhardt Michael lawyer, insurance company executive
Hogan, John Donald college dean, finance educator
Hollis, Charles Eugene, Jr. savings and loan association executive
Holmes, Malcolm Herbert telecommunications company executive
Holzel, David Benjamin newspaper editor
Honaman, J. Craig health facility administrator
Honan, James Terry construction company executive
Hoover, Ray Campbell, III architect
Hopkins, Donald Roswell public health physician
Hopkins, George Mathews Marks lawyer, business executive
Horsman, David A. Elliott writer, financial services executive, educator
Houpt, Corinne Anderson lawyer
Houpt, Jeffrey Lyle psychiatrist, educator
House, Donald Lee, Sr. software executive, private investor, management consultant
Howard, Harry Clay lawyer
Hubble, Don Wayne manufacturing company executive
Huber, Douglas Crawford pathologist
Huddleston, John Franklin obstetrics and gynecology educator
Hug, Carl Casmir, Jr. pharmacology and anesthesiology educator
Hughes, James Mitchell epidemiologist
Hughes, Rufus R., II architectural firm executive, architectural educator
Huie, William Stell lawyer
Hulbert, Daniel J. theater critic, entertainment writer
Humphrey, Charles Durham microbiologist, biomedical researcher
Hunter, Forrest Walker lawyer
Huntley, William Thomas, III insurance agent, consultant
Husband, J. D. bishop
Hutchins, Ralph Edwin, Jr. banker
†Hutton, Donald Henry hospital administrator
Ide, Roy William, III lawyer
Imlay, John Prescott, Jr. computer information science executive
Iodice, Joanna DiMeno (Jody Iodice) psychotherapist
Israili, Zafar Hasan scientist, clinical pharmacologist, educator
Ivester, Melvin Douglas beverage company executive
Izard, John lawyer
Jackson, Ernestine Hill elementary education educator
Janney, Donald Wayne lawyer
Jeffery, Geoffrey Marron medical parasitologist
Jeffries, McChesney Hill retired lawyer
Jenkins, Albert Felton, Jr. lawyer
Jeschke, Channing Renwick librarian
†Jobe, Warren Yancey electric utility company executive
Johnson, Barry Lee public health research administrator
Johnson, Ellis Lane mathematician
Johnson, Ronald Carl chemistry educator
Johnson, William B. hotel executive
Johnson, Wyatt Thomas, Jr. (Tom Johnson) cable news executive
Johnston, Lynn Henry insurance company executive
Jones, Christine Massey furniture company executive
†Jones, David R. gas company executive
Jones, Edward Marshall automotive parts distributing company executive
Jones, Frank Cater lawyer
Jones, George Henry university dean, research administrator, biology educator
Jones, Glower Whitehead lawyer
Jones, J. Kenley journalist
Jova, Henri Vatable architect
Joy, Edward Bennett electrical engineer, educator
Jurkiewicz, Maurice John surgeon, educator
Justice, David Christopher baseball player
Kahn, Bernd radiochemist, educator
Kaiser, Fred computer leasing company executive
Kalafut, George Wendell distribution company executive, retired naval officer
Kamm, Laurence Richard television producer, director
†Karahalis, George Gregory healthcare management consultant
Karp, Herbert Rubin neurologist, educator
Kasten, Stanley Harvey sports association executive
Kaufmann, James A. internist, educator
Keiller, James Bruce college dean, clergyman
Keith, Leroy, Jr. college president
Kelley, James Francis lawyer
Kelley, James P. delivery service executive
Kelly, James Patrick lawyer
Kelly, Michael Joseph academic administrator, consultant
Kelly, William Watkins educational association executive
Kennedy, Alfred Doby performing arts administrator
Kennedy, James C. publishing and media executive
Keough, Donald Raymond investment company executive
Kerr, Nancy Helen psychology educator
Killorin, Edward Wylly lawyer, tree farmer
King, Coretta Scott (Mrs. Martin Luther King, Jr.) educational association administrator, lecturer, writer, concert singer
King, Frederick Alexander neuroscientist, educator
Kinzer, William Luther lawyer
Klamon, Lawrence Paine lawyer
Klein, Luella Voogd obstetrics-gynecology educator
Klim, Michael Stephen legal publisher
Kloer, Philip Baldwin television critic
Kneisel, Edmund M. lawyer
Knobloch, Carl William, Jr. oil and gas services executive
Knowles, Marjorie Fine lawyer, educator, dean
Knox, James Lloyd bishop
Koplan, Jeffrey Powell physician
Korn, Steven W. broadcasting company executive, corporate lawyer
Kraft, Arthur academic dean
Kranzberg, Melvin history educator
Kravitch, Phyllis A. federal judge
Kuntz, Marion Lucile Leathers classicist, historian, educator
†Kuntz, Paul Grimley philosopher, educator
Kuse, James Russell chemical company executive
Lackland, Theodore Howard lawyer
La Farge, Timothy plant geneticist
Lamkin, William Pierce editor
Lamon, Harry Vincent, Jr. lawyer
Landon, James Henry lawyer
Lane, Louis musician, conductor
Langdale, Noah Noel, Jr. research educator, former university president
Lanier, John Hicks apparel company executive
Larche, James Clifford, II state agency administrator
Lawing, Jack L. lawyer, corporate executive
Lawson, A(bram) Venable retired librarian
†LeClercq, Jacques Jean retail grocery executive
Ledford, Hanna May state official
Lee, Kathryn Ellen corporate lawyer
Lee, R(aymond) William, Jr. apparel company executive
Lemen, Richard Alan epidemiologist, medical administrator
Lennon, A. Max food products company executive
Leonard, David Morse lawyer
Lester, Charles Turner, Jr. lawyer
Letton, Alva Hamblin surgeon, educator
Levi, Yoel orchestra conductor
Levy, David lawyer
Lewcock, Ronald Bentley architect, educator
Lewis, Larry Lynn college official, minister, denominational official
Liebmann, Seymour W. construction consultant
Lin, Ming-Chang physical chemistry educator, researcher
Linkous, William Joseph, Jr. lawyer
Lipman, Bernard internist, cardiologist
Lipshutz, Robert Jerome lawyer, former government official
Lobb, William Atkinson financial services executive
Lokey, Hamilton retired lawyer
Long, Leland Timothy geophysics educator, seismologist
Long, Maurice Wayne physicist, electrical engineer, radar consultant
Loory, Stuart Hugh journalist
Love, Edith Holmes theater producer
Lowe, Jonathan Wayne lawyer
Lower, Robert Cassel lawyer, educator
Lowery, Joseph E. clergyman
Lubin, Michael Frederick physician, educator
Lucchesi, John Charles genetics educator
†Luckovich, Mike cartoonist
Lunsford, Julius R(odgers), Jr. lawyer
Lurey, Alfred Saul lawyer
Lybarger, Jeffrey Allen epidemiology research administrator
Macey, Morris William lawyer
MacIntyre, R. Douglas information technology executive
Maddux, Greg (Gregory Alan Maddux) professional baseball player
Mafico, Temba Levi Jackson Old Testament and Semitic languages educator, clergy
Malaspina, Alex soft drink company executive
Malone, Perrillah Atkinson (Pat Malone) retired state official
Manley, Frank English language educator
Manners, George Emanuel business educator, emeritus dean
Marcus, Bernard retail executive
Margolis, Harold Stephen epidemiologist
Marr, David Franklin nurse, administrator
Marshall, John Donald, Jr. lawyer
Marshall, John Treutlen lawyer

Marshall, Thomas Oliver, Jr. *lawyer*
Martin, David Edward *health sciences educator*
Martin, James Francis *state legislator, lawyer*
Martin, Ron *newspaper editor in chief*
Martindale, Larry *hotel executive*
Marzilli, Luigi Gaetano *chemistry educator, consultant*
Massey, Charles Knox, Jr. *advertising agency executive*
Matula, Richard A(llan) *academic administrator*
†McBay, Henry Cecil *chemist, educator*
McBee, Mary Louise *state legislator, former academic administrator*
†McCall, Charles W. *computer company executive*
McClellan, James Harold *electrical engineering educator*
McCormick, Donald Bruce *biochemist, educator*
†McCoy, William O. *telecommunications executive*
McDonald, John C. *telecommunications company executive*
McDuffie, Frederic Clement *physician*
McEvoy, James F. *lawyer*
McGovern, John Francis *financial executive*
McGowan, John Edward, Jr. *microbiology educator*
McGriff, Fred (Frederick Stanley McGriff) *baseball player*
McGuinn, Michael Edward, III *retired army officer*
McGuire, Raymond L. *telecommunications company executive*
Mc Intosh, James Eugene, Jr. *interior designer*
McIntyre, John William *banker*
Mc Kenzie, Harold Cantrell, Jr. *retired manufacturing executive*
McLean, James Albert *artist, educator*
McMahon, Donald Aylward *investor, corporate director*
McMaster, Belle Miller *religious organization administrator*
McNeill, Thomas Ray *lawyer*
†McTier, Charles Harvey *foundation administrator*
Merdek, Andrew Austin *publishing/media executive, lawyer*
Merrigan, Eugene T. *financial company executive, marketing specialist*
Merritt, Lynn Garnard *trade association executive*
Miles, John Karl *marketing executive*
Millar, John Donald *occupational and environmental health consultant, educator*
†Miller, Frank L., Jr. *army officer*
Miller, James Hugh, Jr. *retired public utility executive*
Miller, Thomas Marshall *air transportation executive*
Miller, William Frederick *trust company executive*
Miller, Zell Bryan *governor*
Mobley, John Homer, II *lawyer*
Moderow, Joseph Robert *package distribution company executive*
Moeling, Walter Goos, IV *lawyer*
Molm, John Ralph *lawyer*
Montgomery, James Morton *public relations, marketing executive, association executive*
Moore, Henry Rogers *consulting engineer, retired railroad executive*
Moore, John W. *lawyer*
Moran, Thomas Francis *chemistry educator*
Moulthrop, Edward Allen *architect, artist*
Moye, Charles Allen, Jr. *federal judge*
Mull, Gale W. *lawyer*
Murphy, Gerald Patrick *urologist, educator*
Murphy, Margaret Hackett *federal bankruptcy judge*
Murphy, Michael Conlon *lawyer*
Murphy, Thomas Bailey *state legislator*
Muth, Richard Ferris *economics educator*
Nahmias, André Joseph *physician, educator, scientist*
Navalkar, Ramchandra Govindrao *microbiologist, immunologist*
Neaverth, Elmer Joseph, Jr. *dentist, endodontist, educator*
Neely, Edgar Adams, Jr. *lawyer*
Neisser, Ulric *psychology educator*
Nelson, Kent C. *delivery service executive*
Nelson, Robert Earl, Jr. *financial services company executive*
Nemeroff, Charles Barnet *neurobiology and psychiatry educator*
Nemhauser, George L. *industrial, systems engineer, operations research educator*
Nerem, Robert Michael *engineering educator, consultant*
Nethercut, Philip Edwin *honorary consul*
Newton, Richard Aaron *lawyer*
Nichols, Horace Elmo *state justice*
Nichols, William Curtis *psychologist, family therapist, consultant*
†Nickels, Robert Edward *plastic manufacturing company executive*
Norris, T. H. *retired oil industry executive*
†Oakley, Godfrey Porter, Jr. *health facility administrator, medical educator*
O'Brien, Mark Stephen *pediatric neurosurgeon*
O'Kelley, William Clark *federal judge*
Oliker, Vladimir *mathematician, educator*
Olson, Frank L. *electrical power industry executive*
Oppenlander, Robert *retired airline executive*
Ordover, Abraham Philip *lawyer*
O'Shea, Patricia A. *physician, educator*
Overstreet, Jim *public relations executive*
Owen, Robert Hubert *lawyer, real estate broker*
Owings, Francis Barre *surgeon*
Panlilio, Adelisa Lorna *public health physician*
†Pannone, Richard R. *treasurer*
Pantel, Stan Roy *newspaper publishing executive*
Paris, Demetrius Theodore *electrical engineering educator*
Parker, John Garrett *lawyer*
Parko, Edith Margaret *special education educator*
Parks, John Robert *lawyer*
†Parks, John Scott *pediatric endocrinologist*
Parks, R(obert) Keith *missionary, religious organization administrator*
Parsons, Leonard Jon *marketing educator, consultant*
Partain, Eugene Gartly *lawyer*
†Pate, Zack Taylor, Jr. *nuclear power company executive*
Patrick, Robert Winton, Jr. *lawyer*
Patterson, Anita Mattie *union administrator*
†Patterson, Solon P. *investment counselor*
Patterson, William Robert *lawyer*
Patti, Sister Josephine Marie *health science facility administrator*
Pattillo, Manning Mason, Jr. *academic administrator*
Patton, Carl Vernon *academic administrator, educator*
Patton, Matthew Henry *lawyer*
Payne, Maxwell Carr, Jr. *retired psychology educator*
Peacock, George Rowatt *retired life insurance company executive*
Peacock, Lamar Batts *retired physician*
Pence, Ira Wilson, Jr. *material handling research executive, engineer*
Perdue, Garland Day *surgeon, educator, hospital director*
Perkowitz, Sidney *physicist, educator, author*
Persons, J. Robert *lawyer*
Persons, Oscar N. *lawyer*
Phillips, Barry *lawyer*
Phillips, Herbert Alvin, Jr. *retired financial executive*
Piassick, Joel Bernard *lawyer*
Pierotti, Robert Amedeo *chemistry educator*
Pike, Larry Samuel *lawyer*
†Pinto, William A. *construction executive*
Poe, H. Sadler *lawyer*
Poehlein, Gary Wayne *chemical engineering educator*
Polstra, Larry John *lawyer*
Poole, John Jordan *lawyer*
Porter, Alan Leslie *industrial and systems engineering educator*
Porter, James Alexander *lawyer*
Portman, John C., Jr. *architect, developer*
Poythress, David Bryan *state commissioner, lawyer*
Pratt, John Sherman *lawyer*
Prince, Larry L. *automotive parts and supplies company executive*
Pucket, Susan *newspaper editor*
Pulgram, William Leopold *architect, space designer*
Purcell, Ann Rushing *state legislator, office manager medical business*
Raines, Mary Elizabeth *airline executive*
Ramsay, Ernest Canaday *lawyer*
Ramsey, Ira Clayton *pipeline company executive*
Raper, Charles Albert *retired management consultant*
†Reed, Bill *purchasing agent*
Reed, Glen Alfred *lawyer*
Reed, James Whitfield *physician, educator*
Reeder, Michael S. *consulting firm executive*
Reedy, Edward K. *system engineer administrator*
Reeves, Alexis Scott *journalist*
Regenstein, Lewis Graham *conservationist, author, lecturer, speech writer*
Reichardt, Delbert Dale *financial executive*
Reiman, Joey *advertising executive*
Reinhardt, Daniel Sargent *lawyer*
Reith, Carl Joseph *apparel industry executive*
†Rex, Christopher Davis *classical musician*
Richards, Robert Wadsworth *civil engineer, consultant*
†Richardson, Maurice M. *manufacturing executive*
Ridley, Clarence Haverty *lawyer*
Rierson, Robert Leak *broadcasting executive, television writer*
Ringel, Eleanor *film critic*
Robb, Felix Compton *association executive, consultant*
Roberts, Edward Graham *librarian*
Roberts, Thomasene Blount *entrepreneur*
Rock, John Aubrey *gynecologist and obstetrician, educator*
Rodrigue, George Pierre *electrical engineering educator, consultant*
Rogers, C. B. *lawyer*
Rogers, Werner *state superintendent schools*
Rojas, Carlos *Spanish literature educator*
Rollins, Gary Wayne *service company executive*
Rollins, R. Randall *diversified services company executive*
Roney, Shirley Fletcher *retail company executive*
Rosenberg, George A. *public relations company executive*
Rosenfeld, Arnold Solomon *newspaper editor*
†Rosenthal, Mark Elliott *hospital administrator*
Ross, E. Dennis *retail executive*
Rousseau, Ronald William *chemical engineering educator, researcher*
Russell, Harold Louis *lawyer*
†Russell, Herman Jerome *business executive*
Russell, Ralph Ernest *librarian, educator*
Ryan, J. Bruce *financial consulting company*
Saidman, Gary K. *lawyer*
Salter, Sally *reporter*
Sands, Don William *agricultural products company executive retired*
Satcher, David *public health service officer, federal official*
Satrum, Jerry R. *chemicals company executive*
Savell, Edward Lupo *lawyer*
Sawyer, Christopher Glenn *lawyer*
Saxena, Ashok *materials engineering educator, consultant*
Scalley, John J. *automotive parts company executive*
Schafer, Ronald William *electrical engineering educator*
Scharuda, Victoria *lawyer*
Schewe, Donald Bruce *archivist, library director*
Schimberg, Henry Aaron *soft drink company executive*
Schroder, Jack Spalding, Jr. *lawyer*
Schulte, Jeffrey Lewis *lawyer*
Schulze, Horst H. *hotel company executive*
Schumacher, Robert Alan *forest products company executive*
Schwartz, Dale Marvin *lawyer*
Schwartz, Herbert Marshall *business executive*
Schwartz, William A(llen) *broadcasting and cable executive*
Schwartz, William B., Jr. *ambassador*
Schweitzer, Conrad *timber company executive*
Scott, Charles R. *diversified company executive*
Scott, William Fred *cultural organization administrator*
Scovil, Roger Morris *engineering company executive*
Seabrook, Charles *reporter*
Sears, Curtis Thornton, Jr. *educational administrator*
†Seeger, Guenter Otto *chef*
Seffrin, John Reese *medical society executive*
Sessoms, Walter Woodrow *telecommunications executive*
Seto, William Roderick *public accounting company executive*
Sexson, Sandra Griffin Bishop *child psychiatrist, educator*
Shaw, Robert Lawson *symphony orchestra conductor*
Shepherd, James Harold, Jr. *hospital administrator, contruction executive*
Shepherd, Stephen Beers *construction executive*
Sherman, Roger Talbot *surgeon, educator*
Sherman, Ron *photographer*
Sherry, Henry Ivan *marketing consultant*
Sheth, Jagdish Nanchand *business administration educator*
Shirk, Richard D. *insurance company executive*
†Shivers, Jane *corporate communications executive, director*
Shoob, Marvin H. *federal judge*
Shutze, Virgil Cox *advertising executive*
Sibley, Celestine (Mrs. John C. Strong) *columnist, reporter*
Sibley, Horace Holden *lawyer*
Sibley, James Malcolm *retired lawyer*
Simms, Arthur Benjamin *management consultant, financier*
Sinanian, Loris R. *financial consultant, deacon*
Sink, John Davis *leadership consultant, scientist*
Sitter, John Edward *English literature educator*
Skillrud, Harold Clayton *minister*
Skinner, B. Franklin *retired telecommunications executive*
Skube, Michael *journalist, critic*
Slappey, Sterling Greene *writer, journalist, researcher*
Sloan, Stanley *management consultant*
Slotin, Ronald David *state legislator*
Smith, Alexander Wyly, Jr. *lawyer*
Smith, Glenn Stanley *electrical engineering educator*
Smith, James Louis, III *lawyer*
Smith, Janet Marie *professional sports team executive*
Smith, Jeffrey Michael *lawyer*
Smith, Joseph Newton, III *retired architect, educator*
Smith, Robert Boulware, III *vascular surgeon, educator*
Smith, Sidney Oslin, Jr. *lawyer*
Smith, Steven Delano *professional basketball player*
Smith, W. P., Jr. *food products executive*
Smith, Walton Napier *lawyer*
Smoltz, John Andrew *professional baseball player*
Snelling, George Arthur *banker*
Sonnenfeld, Jeffrey Alan *management educator*
Speer, G. William *lawyer*
Spiegel, John William *banker*
Spitznagel, John Keith *microbiologist, immunologist*
Spivey, Ted Ray *English educator*
Stacey, Weston Monroe, Jr. *nuclear engineer, educator*
Stanhope, William Henry *lawyer*
Stanton, Donald Sheldon *university administrator*
Steed, Robert Lee *lawyer, humor columnist*
Steinfals, Christian Werner *hotel executive*
Steinhaus, John Edward *physician, medical educator*
Stevens, James M. *food processing executive*
Stimpert, Michael Alan *agricultural products company executive*
†Stogner, James *airport executive*
Stokes, James Sewell *lawyer*
Stokes, Mack (Marion) Boyd *bishop*
Stormont, Richard Mansfield *hotel executive*
Strauss, Robert David *lawyer*
Streeb, Gordon Lee *diplomat, economist*
Strekowski, Lucjan *chemistry educator*
Strong-Tidman, Virginia Adele *marketing and advertising executive*
Stubbs, Thomas Hubert *company executive*
Su, Kendall Ling-Chiao *engineering educator*
Sullivan, Louis Wade *former secretary health and human services, physician*
Summerlin, Glenn Wood *advertising executive*
Surber, Eugene Lynn *architect*
Sutherland, Raymond Carter *clergyman, English educator emeritus*
Suttles, William Maurrelle *university administrator, clergyman*
Sutton, Berrien Daniel *beverage company executive*
Swan, James Robert Duncan *hotel executive*
Swann, Jerre Bailey *lawyer*
Swift, Frank Meador *lawyer*
Tanner, W(alter) Rhett *lawyer*
Tarkenton, Francis Asbury *computer comany executive, sports commentator, management consultant, former professional football player*
Tarver, Jackson Williams *newspaper executive*
Taylor, George Kimbrough, Jr. *lawyer*
Taylor, Virginia S. *lawyer*
Teepen, Thomas Henry *newspaper editor, journalist*
Teja, Amyn Sadrudin *chemical engineering educator, consultant*
Tennant, Thomas Michael *lawyer*
Thakker, Ashok *aerospace engineering company executive*
Tharpe, Frazier Eugene *journalist*
†Thomas, Kenneth Eastman *cardiothoracic surgeon*
Thomas, Mable *communications company executive, former state legislator*
Thomas, Patrick Herbert *information services company executive*
Thompson, James David *financial services company executive, lawyer*
†Thompson, James Wilber *symphony performer*
Thompson, Larry Dean *lawyer*
Thuesen, Gerald Jorgen *industrial engineer, educator*
Thumann, Albert *association executive, engineer*
Tidwell, George Ernest *federal judge*
Tierney, Michael Stewart *newspaper editor, journalist*
Tindall, George Taylor *neurosurgeon, educator*
Tipping, William Malcolm *social services administrator*
Tolar, Carroll T. *paper company executive, mechanical engineer*
Toler, James C. *electrical engineer*
Toner, Michael F. *journalist*
Tornabene, Thomas Guy *microbiologist, researcher, administrator*
Tracy, Thomas Kit *investment company executive*
Tschinkel, Sheila Lerner *banker, economist*
Tucker, Cynthia Anne *journalist*
Tucker, Robert Arnold *electrical engineer*
Tucker, Robert Dennard *health care products executive*
Tummala, Rao Ramamohana *engineering educator*
Turner, Ed Sims *broadcast executive, writer*
Turner, John Sidney, Jr. *otolaryngologist, educator*
Turner, Michael Griswold *advertising executive*
Turner, Ted (Robert Edward Turner) *television executive*
Tuttle, Elbert Parr *federal judge*
Tyler, Carl Walter, Jr. *physician, health research administrator*
Vaishnavi, Vijay Kumar *computer science educator, researcher*
Vanegas, Jorge Alberto *civil engineering educator*
VanLandingham, William Jennings *banker*
Varner, Chilton Davis *lawyer*
Ventulett, Thomas Walker, III *architect*
Verrill, F. Glenn *advertising executive*
Vickery, Trammell Eugene *lawyer*
Vigtel, Gudmund *museum director emeritus*
Voss, William Charles *retired oil company executive*
Walker, David Michael *compensation and benefits consultant, accountant*
Waller, John Louis *anesthesiology educator*
Walsh, W. Terence *lawyer*
Walter, John *newspaper editor*
†Walz, Jack *advertising executive*
Ward, Horace Taliaferro *federal judge*
Ward, Jackie M. *computer company executive*
Ward, Janet Lynn *magazine editor, sports wire reporter*
Ward, Richard Storer *child psychiatrist, educator emeritus*
Ware, Carl *bottling company executive*
Warner, Wayne Henry *elementary and secondary educator*
Warren, Edus Houston, Jr. *investment management executive*
Wartell, Roger Martin *biophysics educator*
†Watts, Robert *wholesale distribution executive*
Webb, Brainard Troutman, Jr. *lawyer, distribution company executive*
Webb, Roger Paul *electrical engineer, educator*
Weber, Donald W. *telephone company executive*
†Weiss, David *construction executive*
Weiss, Jay M(ichael) *psychologist, educator*
Wells, Donald Eugene *hospital administrator*
Wells, Everett Clayton, Jr. *economic development executive*
Weltner, Betsey *state art association administrator*
West, Richard Charles *construction company executive*
West, Ruth Tinsley *lawyer*
Westerhoff, John Henry, III *clergyman, theologian, educator*
White, Benjamin Taylor *lawyer*
White, Gayle Colquitt *religion writer, journalist*
White, John Austin, Jr. *engineering educator, dean, consultant*
White, Perry Merrill, Jr. *orthopedic surgeon*
White, Ronald Leon *financial management consultant*
Whitehead, John Jed *computer systems company executive*
Whitley, Joe Dally *lawyer*
Whitman, Homer William, Jr. *investment counseling company executive*
Whitt, Richard Ernest *reporter*
Whittington, Frederick Brown, Jr. *business administration educator*
Wiedeman, John Herman *civil engineer*
Wilkins, J. Ernest, Jr. *mathematician*
Williams, Charles Murray *computer information systems educator, consultant*
Williams, David Howard *lawyer*
Williams, Emily Allen *English language educator*
Williams, Ervin Eugene *religious organization administrator*
Williams, James Bryan *banker*
†Williams, John A. *real estate developer, property manger*
Williams, John Young *merchant banker*
Williams, Neil, Jr. *lawyer*
Williams, Ralph Watson, Jr. *retired securities company executive*
Williams, Thomas Franklin *architect*
†Williams, W. Clyde *religious organization administrator*
Wilson, Alexander Erwin, Jr. *lawyer, management consultant*
Wilson, James Hargrove, Jr. *lawyer*
†Wilson, Jimmy *computer service company executive*
Winer, Ward Otis *mechanical engineer, educator*
Winship, Wadleigh Chichester *holding company executive*
Winter, Wilburn Jackson, Jr. *financial executive*
Wolbrink, James Francis *real estate investor*
Wolensky, Michael K. *lawyer*
Womack, Mary Pauline *lawyer*
Woodard, John Roger *urologist*
Woodward, Richard Hollis, Jr. *utility company executive, lawyer*
Woody, Mary Florence *nursing educator, university administrator*
Wright, Peter Meldrim *lawyer*
Wu, James Chen-Yuan *aerospace engineering educator*
Wylly, Barbara Bentley *performing arts association administrator*
Wyvill, J. Craig *research engineer, program director*
Yates, Ella Gaines *library consultant*
Yeargin-Allsopp, Marshalyn *epidemiologist, pediatrician*
Yoganathan, Ajit Prithiviraj *biomedical engineer, educator*
Yother, Michele *publisher*
Young, Andrew *clergyman, civil rights leader, former mayor, former ambassador, former congressman*
Zaban, Erwin *diversified manufacturing company executive*
Zink, Charles Talbott *lawyer*
Zumpe, Doris *psychiatry researcher, educator*
Zunde, Pranas *information science educator, researcher*

Augusta

Barnard, Druie Douglas, Jr. *former congressman, former bank executive*
Bloodworth, William Andrew, Jr. *academic administrator*
Bowen, Dudley Hollingsworth, Jr. *federal judge*
Bray, Donald Claude *hospital administrator*
Cashin, Edward Joseph *history educator*
Chandler, Arthur Bleakley *pathologist, educator*
Colborn, Gene Louis *anatomy educator, researcher*
Cundey, Paul Edward, Jr. *cardiologist*
Davison, Frederick Corbet *foundation executive*
Feldman, Elaine Bossak *medical nutritionist, educator*
Gambrell, Richard Donald, Jr. *endocrinologist, educator*
Gillespie, Edward Malcolm *hospital administrator*
Given, Kenna Sidney *surgeon, educator*
Grier, Leamon Forest *social services administrator*
Hammer, Wade Burke *oral and maxillofacial surgeon, educator*
Lee, Lansing Burrows, Jr. *lawyer, corporate executive*
Luxenberg, Malcolm Neuwahl *ophthalmologist, educator*
Mahesh, Virendra Bhushan *endocrinologist*
Mansberger, Arlie Roland, Jr. *surgeon*
Martin, Willie Pauline *elementary school educator, illustrator*
Mayberry, Julius Eugene *realty company owner, investor*
Miller, Charles F. *insurance executive*
Oliver, John William Posegate *minister*
Parrish, Robert Alton *retired pediatric surgeon, educator*
Peloquin, Garry Wayne *retired hospital executive*

Pryor, Carol Graham *obstetrician-gynecologist*
Puchtler, Holde *histochemist, pathologist, educator*
Puryear, James Burton *college administrator*
Puryear, Joan Copeland *English language educator*
Rasmussen, Howard *medical educator, medical institute executive*
Richie, Sharon I. *army nursing officer*
Rosen, James Mahlon *artist, art historian, educator*
Rowland, Arthur Ray *librarian*
Ryan, James Walter *physician, medical researcher*
Solursh, Lionel Paul *psychiatrist*
Taylor, Janelle Diane Williams *writer*
Tedesco, Francis Joseph *health sciences university president*
Woodhurst, Robert Stanford, Jr. *architect*
Zachert, Virginia *psychologist, educator*

Austell
Friedrich, Stephen Miro *credit bureau company executive*

Bainbridge
Frieling, Thomas Jerome *library director*

Baxley
Reddy, Yenamala Ramachandra *metal processing executive*

Brunswick
Alaimo, Anthony A. *federal judge*
Brubaker, Robert Paul *food products executive*
Hammill, R. Joseph *health facility administrator*
Harper, Janet Sutherlin Lane *educational administrator, writer*
Iannicelli, Joseph *chemical company executive, consultant*
Rinkevich, Charles Francis *federal official*

Buford
Carswell, Virginia Colby *primary school educator, special education educator*
Ziegler, Delores *mezzo-soprano*

Canton
Hasty, William Grady, Jr. *lawyer*

Carrollton
Harrison, Earle *former county official*
Johnson, Harris Tucker *engineering educator, university administrator*
Morris, Robert Christian *education educator*
Richards, Roy, Jr. *wire and cable manufacturing company executive*
Sethna, Beheruz Nariman *college president, marketing/management educator*

Cartersville
Harris, Joe Frank *former governor*

Chatsworth
†Ralston, Merrell Edward *textiles executive*
†Williams, Edward *textile executive*

Clarkston
Downs, Jon Franklin *drama educator, director*
Negron, Jaime *college administrator*
Valenti, Rita *critical care nurse*

Clayton
†Knepp, Gerald Everett *hospital director*

Cleveland
Lewis, Richard, Sr. *securities broker, consultant*
Raznoff, Beverly Shultz *education educator*

Cochran
Ambardekar, Raj *library administrator*
Halaska, Thomas Edward *academic administrator, director, engineer*
Welch, Joe Ben *academic administrator*

Columbus
Amos, Daniel Paul *insurance executive*
Amos, Paul Shelby *insurance company executive*
Andrews, Gerald Bruce *textile executive*
Averill, Ellen Corbett *science educator, administrator*
Blanchard, James Hubert *finance company executive*
Brabson, Max LaFayette *health care executive*
Brinkley, Jack Thomas *lawyer, former congressman*
Brown, Frank Douglas *academic administrator*
Butler, Charles Thomas *museum director, curator*
†Butler, Stephen T. *manufacturing executive, light, wholesale distribution executive*
Cavezza, Carmen James *career officer*
Cloninger, Kriss, III *insurance company executive*
Collins, Wayne Winford *protective services official*
Diaz-Verson, Salvador, Jr. *investment advisor*
Elliott, James Robert *federal judge*
Harbison, Ed *state senator, broadcast journalist*
†Keaton, Charles Howard *health care administrator*
Lampton, Mason Houghland *construction company executive*
Laney, John Thomas, III *federal judge*
Lasseter, Earle Forrest *lawyer*
Leebern, Donald M. *distilled beverage executive*
†Martin, Frank Kieffer *mayor, lawyer*
McGlamry, Max Reginald *lawyer*
McIntosh, Joseph William *health administration consultant*
Oropeza, Mark *airport director*
Page, William Marion *lawyer*
Patrick, Carl Lloyd *theatre executive*
†Patrick, Michael Wynn *theatre executive*
Riggsby, Dutchie Sellers *education educator*
Riggsby, Ernest Duward *science educator*
Rothschild, Alan Friend *lawyer*
Salamanca, Merlina Espiritu *secondary education educator*
Slay, Ken *sales executive*
Watson, Billy *publishing executive, newspaper*
Zallen, Harold *corporate executive, scientist, former university official*

Conyers
†Florent, Gerald Philex *electronics executive, screen playwriter*
Mc Clung, Jim Hill *light manufacturing company executive*
Sheppard, Jacquelyn Smith *school system founder and administrator*
Smith, Michael Joseph *composer, pianist, lecturer*

Cordele
Wade, Benny Bernar *educational administrator*

Covington
Penland, John Thomas *import/export and development companies executive*
Silverman, Fred *television producer*
Womack, Samuel Edward *computer company executive*

Cumming
Pirkle, George Emory *television and film actor, director*

Dacula
Bascom, Perry Bagnall *retired marketing sales executive*

Dahlonega
Allen, Delmas James *anatomist, educator, university administrator*
Jones, William Benjamin, Jr. *electrical engineering educator*

Dallas
Calhoun, Patricia Hanson *secondary education educator*

Dalton
Clark, Winston Craig *neurosurgeon*
Kinnamon, Gregory Harold *lawyer*
Maffett, Joe Baxter *carpet manufacturing company executive*
†Norris, Kenneth L. *accountant*
Shaw, Julius C. *carpet manufacturing company executive*
Shaw, Robert E. *carpeting company executive*
Thomason, Frank W. *superintendent*

Decatur
Bain, James Arthur *pharmacologist, educator*
Baker, Stephen M. *school system administrator*
Carey, John Jesse *academic administrator, religion educator*
Cassity, (Allen) Turner *poet*
†Davis, John M. *educational association administrator*
Gay, Robert Derril *county official*
Gericke, Paul William *minister, educator*
Hill, Thomas Glenn, III *dermatologist*
Howard, Pierre *lieutenant governor, president senate*
Knight, Walker Leigh *editor, publisher, clergyman*
Loehle, Betty Barnes *artist, painter*
†Major, James Russell Richards *historian, educator*
Martinez-Maldonado, Manuel *medical service administrator, physician*
Mc Mahan, Robert Chandler *savings and loan association executive*
Middleton, James Boland *lawyer*
Myers, Clark Everett *retired business administration educator*
Myers, Orie Eugene, Jr. *university official*
Oakley, Mary Ann Bryant *lawyer*
Pepperdene, Margaret Williams *English educator*
Shaw, Jeanne Osborne *editor, poet*
Shulman, Arnold *judge, lawyer*
Strawn-Hamilton, Frank *jazz musician, folksinger, composer and arranger, educator*
Whitesides, Thomas Edward, Jr. *orthopaedic surgeon*
Wilkinson, Ben *chancellor, evangelist, ministry organizer, writer*
Winn, Albert Curry *clergyman*
Young, James Harvey *historian, educator*

Dillard
Wilkinson, Albert Mims, Jr. *lawyer*

Doraville
Wempner, Gerald Arthur *engineering educator*
Yancey, Eleanor Margaret Garrett *crisis intervention clinician*

Douglas
Palmer, Timothy Jackson *bank executive*

Dublin
Fatum, Delores Ruth *school counselor*
Greene, Jule Blounte *lawyer*
Watson, Mary Alice *academic administrator*

Duluth
Cardin, Charles Edward *lawyer*
Galfas, Timothy, II *franchising and turnaround administrator*
Holutiak-Hallick, Stephen Peter, Jr. *military officer*
Neuman, Ted R. *principal*
Taylor, Maria Centofanti *marketing professional*
Torian, Merville Russell, Sr. *construction company executive*

Dunwoody
Bartolo, Donna Marie *hospital administrator, nurse*

Elberton
Wheeler, Timothy Arneal *assistant superintendent*

Eton
†Weaver, Linda *textiles executive*

Evans
Beaudreau, David Eugene *dentist, educator*
Fournier, Joseph Andre Alphonse *nurse, social worker, psychotherapist*
Hartlage, Lawrence Clifton *neuropsychologist, educator*
Little, Robert Colby *physiologist, educator*

Fairburn
Montague, Mary Ellen *secondary school educator*

Fayetteville
Harris, Dorothy Clark *interior architect, designer, design instructor*

Folkston
Crumbley, Esther Helen Kendrick *realtor, retired educator*

Forsyth
Clarke, Harold Gravely *retired state supreme court chief justice*

Popper, Virginia Sowell *education educator*

Fort Benning
Grube, Dick DeWayne *museum director*
Ramsey, Russell Wilcox *national security affairs educator*
†White, Jerry Allen *career officer*

Fort Gordon
†Duffy, Walter James *psychiatrist*
†Spaulding, Vernon Charles, Jr. *military officer, gastroenterologist*
Xenakis, Stephen Nicholas *psychiatrist, army officer*

Fort McPherson
Champion, Charles Howell, Jr. *army officer*
Reimer, Dennis J. *career military officer*

Fort Oglethorpe
Stutz, Angela Lynn *health facility administrator*

Fort Valley
Marchman, Robert L., III *lawyer, pecan farmer*

Gainesville
Brasel, Michael Louis *library director*
Burd, John Stephen *academic administrator, music educator*
Hatfield, Joe Sweatt, Jr. *agricultural products company executive*
Hemmer, Jane Reynolds *state senator, real estate executive*
Kartzinel, Ronald *pharmaceutical company executive, neuroscientist*
Leet, Richard Hale *oil company executive*
Schuder, Raymond Francis *lawyer*
Wagner, Clarence *historian*

Georgetown
Connelly, Donald Webb *former military officer, business executive*

Greensboro
†Kuntz, Louis Edward *health science facility administrator*

Greenville
Johnson, Hardwick Smith, Jr. *school psychologist*

Griffin
Arkin, Gerald Franklin *agricultural research administrator, educator*
Champion, Ann Louverta *secondary school educator*
Doyle, Michael Patrick *food microbiologist, educator, researcher, administrator*
Duncan, Ronny Rush *agriculturist, researcher*
Gillaspie, Athey Graves, Jr. *pathologist, researcher*
†Newton, John T. *towel and baby products manufacturing company executive*
Shuman, Larry Myers *soil chemist*
Wilkinson, Robert Eugene *plant physiologist*

Grovetown
Baldwin, James Edwin *civil engineer, land development executive*

Hinesville
Gennrich, Robert Paul, II *radiologic technologist*

Jasper
Parrish, Carmelita *secondary school educator*

Jersey
Batchelor, Joseph Brooklyn, Jr. *electronics engineer, consultant*

Jesup
Childers, Anita Flowers *language arts educator*

Jonesboro
Fleming, Janelle Smith *gifted and talented education educator*
Pulliam, Brenda Jane *secondary school educator*
Sprayberry, Roslyn Raye *secondary school educator*

Juliette
Yancy, Cecil Henton, Jr. *editor*

Kennesaw
†Cissell, John *national park superintendent*
Gay, Albert Loyal, Jr. *mining company executive*
Rusche, Benard C. *engineering executive*

Kings Bay
Ellis, Winford Gerald *military career officer, federal agency administrator*

La Fayette
Hendrix, Bonnie Elizabeth Luellen *elementary school educator*

La Grange
Ault, Ethyl Lorita *academic administrator*
Copeland, Robert Bodine *internist, cardiologist*
Gordon, Robert Edward *university administrator*
Hudson, Charles Daugherty *insurance executive*
Murphy, Walter Young *college president, clergyman*
West, John Thomas *surgeon*

Lawrenceville
Fetner, Robert Henry *radiation biologist*
Henson, Gene Ethridge *retired legal administrator*
Wall, Clarence Vinson *congressman*

Lilburn
Bristow, Preston Abner, Jr. *civil engineer, environmental engineer*
Forsee, Joe Brown *library director*
Graham, Richard *container company executive*
Magill, Dodie Burns *early childhood education educator*
White, Jeffrey Lee *middle school educator*

Lithonia
Flanagan, James Lee *educational administrator*

Lookout Mountain
Hitching, Harry James *retired lawyer*

Macon
Ackerman, Robert Kilgo *college president, historian*
Alexander, David Lee *clergyman*
Anderson, Nancy *museum director*
Anderson, Robert Lanier, III *federal judge*
Bayliss, Sister Mary Rosina *principal*
†Bell, L. M. *bishop*
Bundy, John Franklin, Jr. *national monument superintendent*
Cockfield, Jamie Hartwell *history educator*
Crawford, Edwin Mack *health facilities executive*
Dantzler, Deryl Daugherty *dean, law educator*
Drinkard, Lawrence W. *health services executive*
Dunwody, Eugene Cox *architect*
Ennis, Edgar William, Jr. *lawyer*
Fickling, William Arthur, Jr. *health care manager*
Fitzpatrick, Duross *federal judge*
Gerson, Robert Walthall *judge, retired lawyer*
Godsey, R(aleigh) Kirby *university president*
Hails, Robert Emmet *aerospace consultant, business executive, former air force officer*
Hershner, Robert Franklin, Jr. *federal judge*
Hicks, C. J. *bishop*
Holliday, Peter Osborne, Jr. *dentist*
Innes, David Lyn *university official, educator*
Jones, John Ellis *real estate broker*
†King, Damon Dee *hospital executive*
Kinnel, Mary Lou *college recruitment executive*
Landry, Sara Griffin *social worker*
Laughlin, James Rodney *health care company executive*
Looney, Richard Carl *bishop*
Mac Crawford, Edwin *health facility administrator*
Marshall, Howard Lowen *music educator, musicologist*
†Mills, Cynthia Spraker *association administrator*
Mitchell, Carolyn Cochran *college official*
Murdoch, Bernard Constantine *psychology educator*
Oliver, Katherine C. *museum director*
Owens, Garland Chester *accounting educator*
Owens, Wilbur Dawson, Jr. *federal judge*
Rich, Arthur Lowndes *music educator*
Rutledge, Ivan Cate *retired legal educator, arbitrator*
Savage, Randall Ernest *journalist*
Schmidt, Charles J. *library administrator*
Sell, Edward Scott, Jr. *lawyer*
Snow, Cubbedge, Jr. *lawyer*
Steeples, Douglas Wayne *university dean, consultant, researcher*
Swartwout, Joseph Rodolph *obstetrics and gynecology educator, university administrator*
†Thomas, Richard D. *newspaper editor*
Volpe, Erminio Peter *biologist, educator*
Walton, DeWitt Talmage, Jr. *dentist*
†Weaver, William H. *newspaper editor*
Williamson, Christine Wilder *educational consultant, small business owner*

Madison
†Meixner, Richard *manufacturing executive, light*

Marietta
Aronoff, Craig Ellis *management educator, consultant*
Belcher, Julianna *lawyer*
Bemis, Royce Edwin *publishing executive*
Breese, John Allen *chemical industry executive*
Bridges, Alan Lynn *physicist, computer scientist, software engineer*
Burkey, J(acob) Brent *lawyer, company executive*
Cheshier, Stephen Robert *university president, electrical engineer*
Day, Afton J. *elementary school educator, administrator*
Derrick-White, Elizabeth *chaplain, international affairs consultant*
†Dewberry, James Terry *business executive*
Diercks, Chester William, Jr. *capital goods manufacturing company executive*
Dunwoody, Kenneth Reed *magazine editor*
Hammond, John William *lawyer*
Hayes, Robert Deming *electrical engineer, consultant*
Ingram, George Conley *lawyer*
Johnson, Herbert Frederick *sales executive, former university administrator, librarian*
Kiger, Ronald Lee *price analyst*
Lazenby, Gail R. *library director*
Norman, Peggy Rocker *retired secondary school educator*
North, John Adna, Jr. *accountant, real estate appraiser*
O'Haren, Thomas Joseph *financial services executive*
Overton, Bruce *personnel executive, consultant*
Petit, Parker Holmes *health care corporation executive*
Rainey, Kenneth Tyler *English language educator*
Ranu, Harcharan Singh *biomedical scientist, administrator, orthopaedic biomechanics educator*
Siegel, Betty Lentz *college president*
Smith, Baker Armstrong *management executive, lawyer*
Smith, George Thornewell *retired state supreme court justice*
Spann, George William *management consultant*
†Warren, James Walter, Jr. *pharmaceutical company executive*
†Welander, Bo *chemicals executive*
Wrege, Julia Bouchelle *tennis professional, physical education educator*

Metter
Doremus, Ogden *lawyer*

Midland
Hadden, Mayo Addison *chamber of commerce executive, military officer, educator*

Midway
Cobb, John Anthony *retired state veterinarian*

Milledgeville
Bouley, Eugene Edward, Jr. *sociology and criminal justice educator*
Engerrand, Doris Dieskow *business educator*
Evans, Frank Owen, Jr. *physician*
Kidd, E. Culver, Jr. *state senator, management professional*
Osborne, Paul Douglas *hospital administrator*

Monroe
Johnson, Robert Hoyt *minister*
Lynch, Lillian *retired secondary education educator*

Morrow
Samson, Linda Forrest *nursing educator and administrator*

Moultrie
Vereen, William Jerome *uniform manufacturing company executive*

Mount Berry
Mathis, Luster Doyle *college administrator, political scientist*
Mew, Thomas Joseph, III (Tommy Mew) *artist, educator*
Shatto, Gloria McDermith *college administrator, economist*

Newnan
Andrews, Rowena *public relations executive*
Morgan, Lewis Render *federal judge*

Norcross
Adams, Dee Briane *hydrologist, civil engineer*
Adams, Kenneth Francis *automobile executive*
†Balestrero, Gregory *association executive*
Born, Allen *mining executive*
Brown, Adrian Worley *manufacturing company executive*
†Campbell, Robert L. *holding company executive, computer software company executive*
Conway, Hobart McKinley, Jr. *geo-economist*
Crymes, Ronald Jack *draftsman, structural steel detailer*
Currey, Bradley, Jr. *paper company executive*
Darst, Bobby Charles *soil chemist, administrator*
Dibb, David Walter *research association administrator*
Drack, Paul E. *aluminum company executive*
Esher, Brian Richard *environmental company executive*
Harrison, Gordon Ray *engineering executive, consultant, research scientist*
Helander, Robert Charles *lawyer*
Johnson, Gary Ray *sales and marketing executive*
Kelly, William S. *automotive executive*
Kyle, John Emery *mission executive*
Milum-Wood, Joan *hospital administrator*
Nardelli-Olkowska, Krystyna Maria *ophthalmologist, educator*
Newman, James Michael *communications company executive*
Pippin, John Eldon *electronics engineer, electronics company executive*
Rouse, William Bradford *systems engineering executive, researcher, educator*
Sage, Gordon *metal products executive*
†Stanley, Robert L. *computer services executive*
†Strange, J. Leland *computer company executive*
Wagner, Harvey Alan *finance executive*
Wagner, Robert Earl *agronomist*

Oxford
Sitton, Claude Fox *newspaper editor*

Peachtree City
Eichelberger, Charles Bell *retired career officer*
Roobol, Norman Richard *chemistry educator, industrial painting consultant*
Thompson, Claude M. *finance officer, pharmacy consultant*
†Weingarten, Stephen C. *electronics executive*
Yeosock, John John *army officer*

Perry
Hinnant, Tony *superintendent*

Pine Mountain
Callaway, Howard Hollis *business executive*

Quitman
Baum, Joseph Herman *retired biomedical educator*

Rabun Gap
Dodd, Bruce C., Jr. *educational administrator*

Riverdale
Gibbs, Rose L. *interior designer*
King, Glynda B. *state legislator*
Lambert, Ethel Gibson Clark *secondary school educator*
Rhoden, Mary Norris *educational center director*
Waters, John W *minister, educator*

Rome
Hawley, Harold Patrick *educational consultant*
Janowski, Thaddeus Marian *architect*
Mosley, Mary Mac *retired librarian*
Murphy, Harold Loyd *federal judge*
Overbeck, James A. *library director, educator*
Papp, Leann Ilse Kline *respiratory therapy educator*
Perdue, Judy Clark *academic administrator*
Vining, Robert Luke, Jr. *federal judge*

Roswell
Burgess, John Frank *management consultant, former utility executive, former army officer*
DeVictor, D. J. *landscape architect*
Dickens, Gordon Lee, III *engineer, data processing company executive*
Forbes, John Ripley *museum executive, educator*
Graham, Charles Passmore *retired army officer*
Grosklaus, James G. *pulp and paper company executive*
Hill, Dennis James *trade show exhibition manager, consultant*
Jordan, DuPree, Jr. *management consultant, educator, journalist, publisher, business executive*
Peterson, Donald Robert *magazine editor, vintage automobile consultant*
Richkin, Barry Elliott *financial services executive*
†Thibaudeaux, Mary Frances *cultural organization administrator*

Saint Marys
Durr, Marguerite Denise *school system administrator*

Saint Simons Island
Douglas, William Ernest *retired government official*
Edwards, Brenda Faye *counselor*
King, Linda Orr *museum director*
Riedeburg, Theodore *management consultant*
†Tennent, Michael D. *park ranger administrator*
Tomberlin, William G. *principal*

Sandersville
Thiele, Paul Frederick *mining company executive*

Sapelo Island
Alberts, James Joseph *scientist, researcher*

Sautee Nacoochee
Miller, Wilbur Randolph *retired university educator and administrator*

Savannah
Albert, Theodore Merton *computer scientist*
Alley, James Pinckney, Jr. *computer art and graphic design educator*
†Aquadro, Jeana Lauren *graphic designer, educator*
Ball, Ardella Patricia *library science educator*
Beals, L(oren) Alan *association executive*
Bell, William Henry, Jr. *banker*
†Boland, John K. *bishop*
Breidenbach, Fred A. *aerospace company executive*
Burnett, Robert Adair *university administrator, history educator*
Cartledge, Raymond Eugene *retired paper company executive*
Cave, Kent R. *national park ranger*
Coffey, Thomas Francis, Jr. *editor*
Cooper, Robert H. *marketing executive*
Daubenspeck, Robert Donley *advertising agency executive*
Dickey, David Herschel *lawyer, accountant*
Eaves, George Newton *lecturer, consultant, research administrator*
Edenfield, Berry Avant *federal judge*
Forbes, Morton Gerald *lawyer*
Gillespie, Daniel Curtis, Sr. *retired non-profit company executive, consultant*
Glenn, Albert H. *aerospace company executive*
Graham, Patrick Samuel *air transportation executive*
Granger, Harvey, Jr. *manufacturing company executive*
Hale, Charlotte *author, publishing executive*
Horan, Leo Gallaspy *physician, educator*
Hsu, Ming-Yu *engineer, educator*
Innes, John Phythian, II *insurance company executive*
Ives, John Elway *hospital administrator*
Johnson, Victor L. *trucking executive*
Kenrich, John Lewis *lawyer*
Krahl, Enzo *retired surgeon*
Lessard, Raymond W. *bishop*
Lowe, William C. *business products and systems company executive*
McAlpin, Kirk Martin *lawyer*
Otter, John Martin, III *television advertising consultant, retired*
Painter, Paul Wain, Jr. *lawyer*
Rawson, William Robert *lawyer, retired manufacturing company executive*
Rousakis, John Paul *former mayor*
Schafer, Thomas Wilson *advertising agency executive*
Scott, Walter Coke *retired sugar company executive, lawyer*
Skipper, Henry T., Jr. *manufacturing company executive*
Sortor, Harold Edward *financial executive*
Spitz, Seymour James, Jr. *retired fragrance company executive*
Sprague, William Wallace, Jr. *food company executive*
Stillwell, Walter Brooks, III *lawyer*
Su, Helen Chien-fan *research chemist*
Taylor, James Marshall *food products executive*
†Terry, Elizabeth Bennett *chef, restaurant owner*
Theis, Francis William *business executive*
Thomas, Dwight Rembert *writer*
Tobey, Carl Wadsworth *retired publisher*
Wheeler, Ed Ray *mathematics educator*
†Wirth, Fremont Philip *neurosurgeon, educator*

Sea Island
Brown, Ann Catherine *investment company executive*
Brown, George Hay *investment counselor*
Carter, Don Earl *newspaper editor, publisher*
LaWare, John Patrick *retired banker, federal official*
Mattis, Louis Price *pharmaceutical and consumer products company executive*

Smyrna
Atkins, William A. (Bill) *state legislator*
†Chanoki, Fred *electronics component manufacturing company executive*
Head, John Francis, Jr. *distributing company executive*
Lenker, Max V. *consumer products company executive*
†Murata, Akira *manufacturing executive*
†Rineheart, Gary *mortgage company executive*
Wallace, Clifford Noble, III *public assembly facility management executive*
Welch, Jennifer Diane *lawyer*
Wilding, Diane *marketing, financial and information systems executive*

Snellville
Carlson, Roy Perry Merritt *retired banker*
†Maxwell, Clyde Edwin, Jr. *hospital administrator*

Sparta
†Holtz, Daniel Dwight *hospital administrator, retired air force officer*

Statesboro
Black, Charlene Rushton *university official, sociology educator*
Henry, Nicholas Llewellyn *college president, political science educator*
Murkison, Eugene Cox *business educator*
†Zellner, Benjamin Holmes *research astronomer*

Stockbridge
Davis, Raymond Gilbert *retired career officer, real estate developer*

Stone Mountain
Gotlieb, Jaquelin Smith *pediatrician*
Rogers, James Virgil, Jr. *retired radiologist and educator*
Speed, Billie Cheney (Mrs. Thomas S. Speed) *retired editor, journalist*
Wingate, Henry Taylor, Jr. *foundation administrator, fundraiser*

Suwanee
Doleman, Christopher John *professional football player*
Hebert, Bobby Joseph, Jr. *professional football player*
Jones, June *professional football coach*
Sanders, Ricky Wayne *professional football player*
Shelley, Elbert Vernell *professional football player*
Smith, Taylor *professional football team executive*

Thomaston
Hightower, Neil Hamilton *textile manufacturing company executive*

Thomasville
Buckner, James Lee *forester, biologist*
Crozer, Robert P. *food products company executive*
Flowers, Langdon Strong *foods company executive*
Flowers, William Howard, Jr. *food company executive*
Mc Mullian, Amos Ryals *food company executive*
Varnedoe, Heeth, III *food products company executive*
†Watt, William Vance *surgeon*
Wood, Charles Martin, III *food company executive*

Thomson
Smith, Robert L. *principal*

Tifton
Austin, Max Eugene *horticulture educator*
Butler, James Lee *agricultural engineer, researcher*
Douglas, Charles Francis *agronomist*
Miller, John David *retired agronomist*
Rogers, Charlie Ellic *entomologist*
Simpson, Juliette Rich *elementary educator*
Thomas, Adrian Wesley *laboratory director*

Toccoa
Maypole, John Floyd *real estate holding company executive*

Toccoa Falls
Alford, Paul Legare *college and religious foundation administrator*

Townsend
Collins, David Browning *religious institution administrator*

Tucker
Kilgore, Tom D. *electric power company executive*
O'Neil, Daniel Joseph *science research executive, university consultant*
Rogers, Richard Hilton *hotel company executive*
Smith, Leroy, Jr. *bank executive*
Valk, Henry Snowden *physicist, educator*

Valdosta
Bailey, Hugh Coleman *university president*
Beal, John M. *surgeon, medical educator*
Branan, John Maury *psychology educator, counselor*
Evans, Marie Annette Lister *school system administrator*
†Kinnan, Timothy Alan *air force officer*
McClain, Benjamin Richard *music educator, educational administrator*
Peace, Barbara Lou Jean *education educator*

Warm Springs
†Barnes, Charles Gerald *historic site administrator*

Warner Robins
Charkatz, Harry Marvin *psychiatrist*
DePriest, C(harles) David *engineer, retired air force officer*
Nugteren, Cornelius *air force officer*

Washington
McGill, Sam Peyton *state senator*

Watkinsville
Langdale, George Wilfred *research soil scientist*
Tate, Curtis E. *management educator*
Wedig, John Harrison *toxicologist, consultant*
Wright, Robert Joseph *lawyer*

West Point
Glover, Clifford Clarke *retired construction company executive*
Holland, John B. *textiles executive*
Jennings, Joseph Leslie, Jr. *textile executive*
Sauers, Clayton Henry *financial executive*
Terry, Richmond Bohler *textiles executive*

Winterville
Anderson, David Prewitt *university dean*
Shockley, W. Ray *travel trade association executive*

Woodbine
Christian, John H. *librarian*

Woodstock
Austin, John David *financial executive*

Young Harris
Richardson, Robert Janecek *library director*
Yow, Thomas Sidney, III *college administrator*

HAWAII

Aiea
Monk, Gregory Brittain *artist, business owner*

Camp H M Smith
†Christmas, George Ronald *career officer*
Macke, Richard Chester *naval officer*
Toney, Robert L. *naval officer*

Fort Shafter
Ivey, Claude Tarlton *military officer*

Haiku
Cost, James Peter *artist*

Haleiwa
Valentine, De Wain *artist*
Woolliams, Keith Richard *arboretum and botanical garden director*

Hanalei
Ching, Lawrence Lin Tai *retail executive*

Hilo
Dixon, Paul William *psychology educator*
Evans, Franklin Bachelder *marketing educator emeritus*
Gersting, Judith Lee *computer science educator, researcher*
Nagao, Mike Akira *horticulturist, county administrator*
Perrin, Kenneth Lynn *university chancellor*
Schnell, Russell Clifford *atmospheric scientist, researcher*
Taniguchi, Tokuso *surgeon*
Ushijima, John Takeji *state senator, lawyer*
Wang, James Chia-Fang *political science educator*
Werner, Marlin Spike *speech pathologist and audiologist*

Honaunau
†Shimoda, Jerry Yasutaka *national historic park administrator*

Honolulu
Abbott, Isabella Aiona *biology educator*
Ablon, R. Richard *service company executive*
Abramson, Norman *electronics executive*
Akinaka, Asa Masayoshi *lawyer*
Albano, Andres, Jr. *real estate developer, real estate broker*
Alm, Richard Sanford *education educator*
Amor, Simeon, Jr. *photographer, historian*
Andrasick, James Stephen *agribusiness company executive*
Antal, Michael Jerry, Jr. *mechanical engineering educator*
Aoude, Ibrahim Georges *ethnic studies educator*
Ashford, Clinton Rutledge *judge*
Ashton, Geoffrey Cyril *geneticist, educator*
Ayer, David Clay *architect*
Baker, Rosalyn *state legislator*
Barbieri, David Arthur *company executive*
Barr, Jon Michael *naval officer, federal official*
†Bates, George E. *oil industry executive*
Behnke, Richard Frederick *investment banking executive*
Beirne, Danielle Ululani *state legislator*
Bender, Byron Wilbur *linguistics educator*
Berg, Dennis Ray *air force officer*
Bess, Henry David *dean*
Betts, Barbara Stoke *artist, educator*
Bitterman, Morton Edward *psychologist, educator*
Bloede, Victor Carl *lawyer, academic executive*
†Bossert, Philip Joseph *information systems executive*
Botsai, Elmer Eugene *architect, educator, former university dean*
Brantley, Lee Reed *chemistry educator*
Brechin, Garry David *leasing company executive, real estate company executive*
Broder, Sherry Phyllis *lawyer*
Buyers, John William Amerman *agribusiness and specialty foods company executive*
Cachola, Romy Munoz *state representative*
Cades, Julius Russell *lawyer*
Cain, Raymond Frederick *landscape architect, planning company executive*
Callies, David Lee *lawyer, educator*
Case, James Hebard *lawyer*
†Cassiday, Paul Richard *estate administrator*
Cayetano, Benjamin Jerome *governor, former state senator and representative*
Chambers, Kenneth Carter *astronomer*
Chaplin, George *newspaper editor*
Char, Vernon Fook Leong *lawyer*
Chave, Keith Ernest *oceanographer, educator*
Chee, Percival Hon Yin *ophthalmologist*
Ching, Chauncey Tai Kin *agricultural economics educator*
Ching, Larry Fong Chow *construction company executive*
Cho, Lee-Jay *social scientist, demographer*
Choy, Herbert Young Cho *federal judge*
Chuck, Walter G(oonsun) *lawyer*
Chung, Kea Sung *television broadcasting executive*
Chun Oakland, Suzanne Nyuk Jun *state legislator*
Clark, Henry Benjamin, Jr. *retired food company executive, community service volunteer*
†Clarke, Robert F. *utilities company executive*
Copi, Irving Marmer *philosophy educator*
Cornuelle, Herbert Cumming *retired corporate executive*
Corsini, Raymond Joseph *psychologist*
Cotlar, Morton *organizational scientist, educator*
Couch, John Charles *diversified company executive*
Cowie, Lennox Lauchlan *astrophysicist*
Cox, Richard Horton *civil engineering executive*
Craven, John Piña *civil engineering and law educator, lawyer*
Cruthers, Evan Douglas *architect*
†Derieg, Thomas F. *airline executive*
Devenot, David Charles *human resource executive*
Devens, Paul *lawyer*
†DiLorenzo, Francis X. *bishop*
Dods, Walter Arthur, Jr. *bank executive*
D'Olier, H(enry) Mitchell *lawyer*
Dolly, John Patrick *university dean, educational psychologist*
Driskill, Thomas Malcolm, Jr. *military officer*
Duckworth, Walter Donald *museum executive, entomologist*
Dyen, Isidore *linguistic scientist, educator*
Edel, (Joseph) Leon *biographer, educator*
Ellis, George Richard *museum administrator*
Enoki, Donald Yukio *curriculum specialist*
Ezra, David A. *federal judge*
Fasi, Frank Francis *state senator*
Fernandes Salling, Lehua *lawyer, state senator*
†Fields, Harold Thomas, Jr. *career officer*
Fischer, Joel *social work educator*
Flanagan, John Michael *editor, publisher*
Fok, Agnes Kwan *cell biologist, educator*
Fong, Bernard W. D. *physician, educator*
Fong, Harold Michael *federal judge*
Fong, Hiram L. *former senator*
Fong, Peter C. K. *lawyer, judge*
Force, Roland Wynfield *anthropologist, museum executive*
†Fujioka, Roger Sadao *research microbiology educator*
Fullmer, Daniel Warren *psychologist, educator*
Gary, James Frederick *business and energy advising company executive*

Gay, E(mil) Laurence *lawyer*
Gelber, Don Jeffrey *lawyer*
George, Peter T. *orthodontist*
Gibb, Douglas Glenn *police chief*
Greenfield, David W. *academic dean, ichthyologist*
Greer, Howard Earl *former naval officer*
Hale, Nathan Robert *architect*
Hall, Donald Norman Blake *astronomer*
Halloran, Richard Colby *writer, former research executive, former news correspondent*
Hamada, Duane Takumi *architect*
Hanson, Dennis Michael *medical imaging executive*
†Harris, Jeremy *mayor*
Harrison, Jeremy Thomas *dean*
Hatfield, Elaine Catherine *psychology educator*
Hawke, Bernard Ray *planetary scientist*
Hays, Ronald Jackson *naval officer*
†Heenan, David A. *diversified products company executive*
Heller, Ronald Ian *lawyer*
Herbig, George Howard *astronomer, educator*
Hirono, Mazie Keiko *state official*
Ho, Donald Tai Loy *entertainer, singer*
Ho, Reginald Chi Shing *medical educator*
Ho, Stuart Tse Kong *investment company executive*
Hoag, John Arthur *retired bank executive*
Holland, Charles Malcolm, Jr. *retired health care executive, development corporation executive, retired banker*
Hong, Norman G. Y. *architect*
Hook, Ralph Clifford, Jr. *business educator*
Horner, Donald Gordon *banker*
Hubbard, Harold Mead *research executive*
Hughes, Robert Harrison *former agricultural products executive*
Ihrig, Judson La Moure *chemist*
Ikeda, Donna Rika *state senator*
Inaba, Lawrence Akio *educational director*
Iwase, Randall Yoshio *state senator*
Jackson, Miles Merrill *university dean*
Jellinek, Roger *editor*
Johanos, Donald *orchestra conductor*
Johnson, Lawrence M. *banker*
Jongeward, George Ronald *systems analyst*
Jordan, Amos Azariah, Jr. *foreign affairs educator, retired army officer*
Kaiser-Botsai, Sharon Kay *early chilhood educator*
Kamemoto, Fred Isamu *zoologist*
Kamemoto, Haruyuki *horticulture educator*
Kane, Bartholomew Aloysius *state librarian*
Kanehiro, Kenneth Kenji *insurance educator, risk analyst, consultant*
Katayama, Robert Nobuichi *lawyer*
Kay, Alan Cooke *federal judge*
Kay, Elizabeth Alison *zoology educator*
Keil, Klaus *geology educator, consultant*
Keir, Gerald Janes *newspaper editor*
Keith, Kent Marsteller *academic administrator, corporate executive, government official, lawyer*
Kelley, Richard Roy *hotel executive*
Kelly, James Andrew *policy reseach executive, former government official*
Kenda, Juanita Echeverria *artist, educator*
Khan, Mohammad Asad *geophysicist, educator, former energy minister and senator of Pakistan*
Kiessling, Ralph J. *health insurance company executive*
†Kim, Donald Chang Won *consulting engineering company executive*
King, Arthur R., Jr. *education educator, researcher*
King, Samuel Pailthorpe *federal judge*
Klein, Robert Gordon *judge*
Klobe, Tom *art gallery director*
Knowlton, Edgar Colby, Jr. *linguist, educator*
Kohloss, Frederick Henry *consulting engineer*
Koide, Frank Takayuki *electrical engineer*
Kolonel, Laurence Norman *epidemiologist, public health educator*
Krauss, Bob *newspaper columnist, author*
Krock, Hans-Jurgen *civil engineer*
Kugle, J. Alan *food company executive, lawyer*
Kuroda, Yasumasa *political science educator, researcher*
Lamoureux, Charles Harrington *botanist, arboretum administrator*
†Landovsky, John *artistic director*
Laney, Leroy Olan *economist, banker*
Langhans, Edward Allen *drama and theater educator*
Lau, Charles Kwok-Chiu *architect, architectural firm executive*
†Lau, H. Lorrin *physician, inventor*
Lee, Beverly Ing *educational administrator*
Levine, Aaron *city planner*
Lilly, Michael Alexander *lawyer*
Linman, James William *retired physician, educator*
Lum, Jean Loui Jin *nurse educator*
Luter, John *news correspondent, educator*
Mader, Charles Lavern *chemist*
†Magee, Donald Edward *national park service administrator*
†Mandel, Morton *molecular biologist*
Mark, Shelley Muin *economist, educator, government official*
Marks, Michael J. *lawyer, corporate executive*
†Marks, Robert Arthur *lawyer*
Marvit, Robert Charles *psychiatrist*
†Matelic, Candace Tangorra *museum studies educator, consultant, museum director*
Matsuda, Fujio *institute president*
Mattoch, Ian L. *lawyer*
McCready, William Floyd *venture capitalist, entrepreneur*
Mc Dermott, John Francis, Jr. *psychiatrist, physician*
McGinn, Susan Frances *musician*
Meagher, Michael *radiologist*
†Meech, Karen Jean *astronomer*
Meyer, Robert Allen *human resource management educator*
Miccio, Joseph V. *business educator, consultant*
Michael, Jerrold Mark *public health specialist, former university dean, educator*
Midkiff, Robert Richards *financial and trust company executive, consultant*
Miller, Richard Sherwin *legal educator*
Miyamoto, Owen *state agency administrator*
Moore, Willson Carr, Jr. *lawyer*
Morse, Richard *social scientist*
Murabayashi, Harris Nozomu *retired management analyst*
Nakagawa, Jean Harue *diversified corporation executive*
Nakashima, Mitsugi *state agency administrator*
Niles, Geddes Leroy *private investigator*
Nishimura, Pete Hideo *oral surgeon*
Nunn, G. Raymond *history educator*
Ogawa, Dennis Masaaki *American studies educator*
Ogburn, Hugh Bell *chemical engineer, consultant*
Okinaga, Lawrence Shoji *lawyer*
Olmsted, Ronald David *foundation executive, consultant*
Omori, Morio *lawyer*
O'Neill, Charles Kelly *marketing executive, former advertising agency executive*
Paige, Glenn Durland *political scientist, educator*
Pang, Herbert George *ophthalmologist*
Person, Donald Ames, Sr. *pediatrician, rheumatologist*
Peterson, Barbara Ann Bennett *history educator*
Pfeiffer, Robert John *transportation executive*
Pickens, Alexander Legrand *education educator*
†Pien, Francis D. *internist, microbiologist*
†Pollack, Richard W. *lawyer*
Porter, Michael Pell *lawyer*
Quinn, William Francis *lawyer*
Raleigh, Cecil Baring *geophysicist*
Rambo, A. Terry *anthropologist, research program director*
Ramler, Siegfried *school administrator*
Ramos, J. Mario *opera director, conductor*
Rapson, Richard L. *history educator*
Reed, Robert George, III *petroleum company executive*
Rehg, Kenneth Lee *linguistics educator*
Roberti, Mario Andrew *lawyer, former energy company executive*
Robertson, Gregg Westland *diversified company executive*
Robinson, Robert Blacque *association executive*
Russi, John Joseph *priest, educational administrator*
Rutherford, Robert L. *career military officer*
Sagawa, Yoneo *horticulturist, educator*
Saiki, Patricia (Mrs. Stanley Mitsuo Saiki) *former federal agency administrator, former congresswoman*
Salmon, Charles B., Jr. *diplomat*
†Sato, Richard Michio *consulting engineering company executive*
Schatz, Irwin Jacob *cardiologist*
Scheerer, Ernest William *dentist*
Scheuer, Paul Josef *chemistry educator*
Schnack, Gayle Hemingway Jepson (Mrs. Harold Clifford Schnack) *corporate executive*
Schubert, Glendon *political scientist, educator*
Sharma, Santosh Devraj *obstetrician and gynecologist, educator*
Sherman, Martin Nmi *entomologist*
Shibata, Shoji *pharmacology educator, researcher*
Siegel, Barbara Z(enz) *biology research scientist, educator*
Simonds, John Edward *newspaper editor*
Simpson, Andrea Lynn *energy communications executive*
Slain, George Cedric *finance executive*
Smith, Albert Charles *biologist, educator*
Smith, Barbara Barnard *music educator*
Smith, Christopher Case *newspaper editor*
†Smith, Thomas Kent *radiologist*
Smyser, Adam Albert *newspaper editor*
Solheim, Wilhelm Gerhard, II *anthropologist, educator*
Solidum, James *finance and insurance executive*
Sparks, Robert William *publishing executive*
Speicher, William Clayton *transportation executive*
Statler, Oliver Hadley *writer*
Stebbins, Dennis Robert *environmental management consultant*
Stephan, John Jason *historian, educator*
Stephenson, Herman Howard *banker*
Stevens, Robert David *librarian, educator*
Suh, Dae-Sook *political science educator*
Sutton, Charles Richard *architect, designer*
Swanson, Richard William *statistician*
Takumi, Roy Mitsuo *state representative*
†Tanabe, Barbara Jean *communications company executive*
Tanio, Tony *electrical engineer, hotel executive*
Tatibouet, André Stephan *condominium and resort management firm executive*
†Thompson, Henry Nainoa *hospital administrator*
Toole, Lee K. *telecommunications company executive*
Tuan, San Fu *theoretical physics, political science educator*
Turbin, Richard *lawyer*
Tuttle, Daniel Webster *retired political science educator*
Twigg-Smith, Thurston *newspaper publisher*
Ueberroth, John A. *air transportation executive*
Varley, Herbert Paul *Japanese language and cultural history educator*
†Wageman, Lynette Mena *librarian*
Wang, Jaw-Kai *agricultural engineering educator*
†Waterhouse, Blake E. *health facility administrator*
Weyand, Frederick Carlton *retired military officer*
Wiley, Bonnie Jean *journalism educator*
Williams, Carl Harwell *utilities executive*
Williamson, Harwood Danford *utility company executive*
Wolff, Herbert Eric *banker, former army officer*
Wong, Henry Li-Nan *bank executive, economist*
Wright, Chatt Grandison *academic administrator*
Wyrtki, Klaus *oceanography educator*
†Yamamoto, Harry Yoshimi *research institute director, educator*
Yamato, Kei C. *international business consultant*
Yee, Alfred Alphonse *structural engineer, consultant*
Yeh, Raymond Wei-Hwa *architect, educator*
Yount, David Eugene *physicist, educator*

Kahului
Piros, Cecille Patao *business owner*
Riecke, Hans Heinrich *architect*

Kailua
Bezanson, Ronald Scott, Jr. *clergyman, army chaplain*
Blue, Steven Joshua *nutritional physiologist*
Engelbardt, Robert Miles *telecommunications executive*
George, Mary Shannon *state senator*
Pence, Martin *federal judge*
Tam, William *secondary school principal*
Tokumaru, Roberta *principal*
†White, Terry Wayne *hospital administration executive*

Kailua Kona
Ashley, Darlene Joy *psychologist*
Clewett, Kenneth Vaughn *college official*
Feaver, Douglas David *university dean, classics educator*

Kamuela
Azzopardi, Marc Antoine *astrophysicist, scientist*

Kaneohe
Baker, Paul Thornell *anthropology educator*
Dever, Daniel *academic administrator*
Fisette, Scott Michael *golf course designer*
Hanson, Richard Edwin *civil engineer*
Ikeda, Moss Marcus Masanobu *retired state education official, lecturer, consultant*
Inamine, Sharon Ogawa *elementary school administrator*
Kamiyama, Linda *elementary school principal*
Lagoria, Georgianna Marie *curator, writer, editor, visual art consultant*
McGlaughlin, Thomas Howard *publisher, retired naval officer*
Smales, Fred Benson *corporate executive*
Winters-Maloney, Carol Emerson *nursing educator, academic administrator*

Kapaau
McFee, Richard *electrical engineer, physicist*

Kihei
Gaston, Joy Puu'olani *gifted and talented education educator*
Wilson, Brandon Laine *writer, advertising and public relations consultant, explorer*

Kula
Becker, Walter *guitarist, record producer*
Rohlfing, Frederick William *lawyer, judge*

Lahaina
Arnold, Joan Dean *publisher*
Nelson, Robert Bruce *lawyer*
Sato, Tadashi *artist*

Laie
Bradshaw, James R. *business educator*

Lihue
Cobb, Rowena Noelani Blake *real estate broker*

Makawao
Mascho, George Leroy *education educator emeritus*

Mililani
Gardner, Sheryl Paige *obstetrician/gynecologist*
Kiley, Thomas *rehabilitation counselor*

Oceanview
Gilliam, Jackson Earle *bishop*

Pearl City
Sue, Alan Kwai Keong *dentist*

Pearl Harbor
Fitzgerald, James Richard *naval officer*

Princeville
Kaye, Wilbur Irving *chemist, researcher, consultant*

Waialua
Krause-Diaz, Mary Jean *educational administrator*
Singlehurst, Dona Geisenheyner *horse farm owner*

Waianae
Kanno, Brian M. *volunteer worker*
Pinckney, Neal Theodore *psychologist, educator*

Waikoloa
Copman, Louis *radiologist*

Wailuku
Kinaka, William Tatsuo *lawyer*

Waipahu
Stevens, Adele Amy Kubota *physical education educator*

IDAHO

Aberdeen
Sparks, Walter Chappel *horticulturist, educator*

Blackfoot
†Peterson, Robert Marcellus *hospital and nursing home administrator*

Boise
Agee, William J. *transportation, engineering and construction company executive*
Aherns, Pamela Bengson *state legislator*
Andrus, Cecil Dale *academic administrator*
Bakes, Robert Eldon *retired state supreme court justice*
Barr, Robert Dale *university dean, educator*
Barrett, Lenore Hardy *state legislator, mining and investment consultant*
†Barton, Rayburn *educational administrator*
†Batt, Philip E. *governor*
Beaumont, Pamela Jo *marketing professional*
†Beebe, Stephen A. *agricultural products company executive*
Black, Max C. *insurance agent*
Black, Pete *state legislator, educator*
Blackbird, Mike *state senator, sales representative*
Board, Dwight Vernon *lawyer*
Bolles, Charles Avery *librarian*
Bowers, Daniel Kent *electric power industry executive*
Boyle, Larry Monroe *federal judge*
Brown, Tod David *bishop*
†Burnham, William A. *wildlife protection society administrator*
Callister, Marion Jones *federal judge*
Carley, John Blythe *retail grocery executive*
Cenarrusa, Pete T. *secretary of state*
Cleary, Edward William *retired diversified forest products company executive*
Cline, Glen Edwin *retired architect and planner*
Connolly, David I. *retail executive*
Crane, Charles Arthur *college president*
Daniels, Christopher Kent *pharmacologist, researcher*
Dorman, Rex Lee *forest products executive*
EchoHawk, Larry *state attorney general*
Evans, Jerry Lee *school system administrator*
Ferguson, E. Robert *construction and engineering company executive*
Ferrell, Yvonne Signe *state recreation commission administrator*
Fery, John Bruce *forest products company executive*
Garber, Jerold Allan *broadcasting executive*
Gloth, Alec Robert *retail grocery executive*
Glynn, William C. *natural gas company executive*
Griffin, Sylvia Gail *reading specialist*
Gurnsey, Kathleen Wallace *state legislator*
Hagan, Alfred Chris *federal judge*
Harad, George Jay *manufacturing company executive*
Hartung, Mary *state legislator*
Hawkins, James Victor *state official*
Hennessey, Alice Elizabeth *forest products company executive*
Hibbs, Robert Andrews *analytical chemistry educator*
Hollenbaugh, Kenneth M. *academic administrator, geology consultant*
Humpherys, A. Rich *state police administrator*
Hunsucker, (Carl) Wayne *architectural firm executive, educator*
Ilett, Frank, Jr. *trucking company executive*
Ingram, Cecil D. *accountant, state legislator*
Johnson, Byron Jerald *state supreme court judge*
Jones, D. Michael *banker*
Joyce, Claude Clinton *data processing executive*
Kayser, Donald Robert *financial executive*
Keane, Edmund J., Jr. *banker*
Kemp, J. Robert *beef industry consultant, food company executive*
Klein, Edith Miller *lawyer, former state senator*
Knight, Margot Haliday *oral historian*
Lance, Alan George *lawyer, legislator, attorney general*
Leroy, David Henry *lawyer, state and federal official*
Littman, Irving *forest products company executive*
Lodge, Edward James *federal judge*
Maloof, Giles Wilson *academic administrator, educator, author*
Manning, Darrell V. *national guard officer*
Marcus, Craig Brian *lawyer*
Maulin, Jack Doolin *construction company executive*
McClary, James Daly *retired contractor*
McDevitt, Charles Francis *state supreme court justice*
McKee, Joseph Fulton *engineering and construction executive*
McLaughlin, Marguerite P. *state senator, logging company executive*
Mc Quade, Henry Ford *state justice*
Mech, William Paul *mathematics educator, director honors program*
Michael, Gary G. *retail supermarket and drug chain executive*
Minnick, Walter Clifford *building materials company executive*
Mulick, Edward James *orthodontist*
Nafziger, Pattie Lois *state legislator*
Nelson, Thomas G. *federal judge*
Nguyen, King Xuan *language educator*
Norrie, K. Peter *manufacturing executive*
Nyborg, Lester Phil *physician*
Olson, Richard Dean *researcher, pharmacology educator*
O'Riordan, William Hugh *lawyer*
Otter, Clement Leroy *lieutenant governor*
Overgaard, Willard Michele *retired political scientist, jurisprudent*
†Parkinson, Joseph L. *electronics company executive, lawyer*
Parrish, Richard B. *manufacturing executive*
Peterson, Curtis Gerald *broadcast executive*
Pomeroy, Horace Burton, III *accountant, corporate executive*
Reuling, Michael Frederick *supermarket company, real estate executive*
Risch, James E. *lawyer*
Ruch, Charles P. *university official*
Rudd, Gerald Ray *retail food and drug company executive*
Ryals, Connie *state government department administrator*
Schwartz, Theodore B. *physician, educator*
Scudder, David Benjamin *economist, foundation administrator*
Shaver, Carl Hutchens *retail executive*
Shurtliff, Marvin Karl *lawyer*
Silak, Cathy R. *judge*
Simplot, John R. *agribusiness executive*
Slavich, Denis Michael *engineering and construction company executive*
Speer, William Thomas, Jr. *banker, investor, consultant, rancher*
Steinfort, James Richard *university program director*
Sullivan, James Kirk *forest products company executive*
Taylor, W.O. (Bill) *state legislator, business consultant*
Thornton, John S., IV *bishop*
†Tinstman, Robert A. *construction, real estate executive*
Trott, Stephen Spangler *federal judge, musician*
True, Leland Beyer *civil engineer, consultant*
VanHole, William Remi *lawyer*
Walk, Ronald Douglas *retail grocery chain executive*
Wells, Merle William *historian, state archivist*
Wilbur, Lyman Dwight *consulting engineering executive*
Wilson, Barbara Louise *communications executive*
Wilson, Jack Fredrick *retired federal government official*
Wood, Jeannine Kay *state official*
Woodard, Larry L. *Bible college official*
Young, Katherine Ann *education educator*

Bonners Ferry
McClintock, William Thomas *health care administrator*

Calder
Rechard, Ottis William *mathematics and computer science educator*

Caldwell
Attebery, Louie Wayne *English language educator, folklorist*
Gipson, Gordon *publishing company executive*
Hendren, Robert Lee, Jr. *academic administrator*
Kerrick, David Ellsworth *state senator, lawyer*
Lonergan, Wallace Gunn *economics educator, management consultant*

Coeur D Alene
Brown, Arthur *mining executive*
Green, Charlotte Kimball *educator*
Griffith, William Alexander *former mining company executive*
†Sabala, James Anthony *mining company executive*
Wheeler, Dennis Earl *mining company executive, lawyer*

Emmett
Farnham, Wallace Dean *historian*
Holverson, Harmon Elmer *family practice physician*

Hayden
Wogsland, James Willard *retired heavy machinery manufacturing executive*

Hayden Lake
Olson, Phillip David LeRoy *agriculturist, chemist*

Idaho Falls
Harris, Darryl Wayne *publishing executive*
Newman, Stanley Ray *oil refining company executive*
Reich, Charles William *nuclear physicist*
Riemke, Richard Allan *mechanical engineer*
Thorsen, Nancy Dain *real estate broker*
Williams, Phyllis Cutforth *retired realtor*

Island Park
Heinz, Don J. *agronomist*
Stratford, Ray Paul *electrical engineer, consultant*

Jerome
Bell, Maxine Toolson *state legislator, librarian*

Kamiah
Martin, Boyd Archer *political science educator emeritus*

Ketchum
Hogue, Terry Glynn *lawyer*
Kreitler, Richard Rogers *company executive*
†Ring, Terry William *company executive, environmentalist*

Kimberly
Carter, David LaVere *soil scientist, researcher, consultant*

Lewiston
Bjerke, Robert Keith *chemist*
Chinchinian, Harry *pathologist, educator*
Morgan, Glen D. *superintendent*
Peterson, Philip Everett *legal educator*
Ware, Marcus John *lawyer*

Mc Call
Evans, Darrell J. *art educator*

Moscow
Anderson, Clifton Einar *editor, writer*
Bartlett, Robert Watkins *academic dean, metallurgist*
Bobisud, Larry Eugene *mathematics educator*
Bray, R(obert) Bruce *music educator*
Butterfield, Samuel Hale *former government official and educator*
Crawford, Don Lee *microbiologist*
DeShazer, James Arthur *agricultural engineer, educator, administrator*
Force, Ronald Wayne *librarian*
Hendee, John Clare *college dean, natural resources educator*
Jackson, Melbourne Leslie *chemical engineering educator and administrator, consultant*
Jacobsen, Richard T. *mechanical engineering educator*
LeTourneau, Duane John *biochemist, educator*
MacFarland, Craig George *natural resource management professional*
Miller, Maynard Malcolm *geologist, educator, research foundation director, explorer, state legislator*
Peterson, Charles Loren *agricultural engineer, educator*
Renfrew, Malcolm MacKenzie *chemist, educator*
Roberts, Lorin Watson *botanist, educator*
Scott, J(ames) Michael *research biologist*
Seeger, Leinaala Robinson *law librarian, educator*
Shreeve, Jean'ne Marie *chemist, educator*
Woodall, David Monroe *research engineer*
Zinser, Elisabeth Ann *university president*

Nampa
Botimer, Allen Ray *retired surgeon, retirement center owner*
Rau, Shirley A. *secondary school educator*

Payette
Jones, Donna Marilyn *real estate broker, legislator*

Pocatello
Barnett, Mary Louise *elementary education educator*
Bowen, Richard Lee *academic administrator, political science educator*
†Collins, Clark L. *executive*
Hillyard, Ira William *pharmacologist, educator*
Hofman, Elaine D. *state legislator*
Jackson, Allen Keith *museum administrator*
McCune, Mary Joan Huxley *microbiology educator*
Nye, W. Marcus W. *lawyer*
Rowe, Ernest Ras *education educator, academic administrator*
Sagness, Richard Lee *education educator, former academic dean*
Seeley, Rod Ralph *physiology educator*
Stanek, Alan Edward *music educator, performer, music administrator*
Wilson, Albert Eugene *retired nuclear engineering educator*

Post Falls
Capener, Regner Alvin *minister, electronics engineer*
Chamberlain, Barbara Kaye *small business owner*

Rigby
Peterson, Erle Vidaillet *retired metallurgical engineer*

Rupert
Antone, Steve *state legislator, farmer*
Bellwood, Sherman Jean *arbitrator, consultant, retired judge*

Saint Maries
Carlson, George Arthur *artist*

Sandpoint
Glock, Charles Young *sociologist*
Murray, James Michael *librarian, law librarian, legal educator, lawyer*

Stanley
Kimpton, David Raymond *natural resource consultant, writer*

Sun Valley
Bryant, Woodrow Wesley *architect*

Twin Falls
Hartgen, Stephen Anthony *newspaper publisher*
Jones, Douglas Raymond *farming executive, state legislator*
†Katz, Edward Lyle *neurosurgeon*
McRoberts, Joyce *state legislator*

ILLINOIS

Abbott Park
Burnham, Duane Lee *pharmaceutical company executive*
Coughlan, Gary Patrick *pharmaceutical company executive*
†Hightower, Belinda Ann *pharmaceutical company official, researcher*
Hodgson, Thomas Richard *health care company executive*
Lussen, John Frederick *pharmaceutical laboratory executive*
McIntyre, John Duncan *health care executive*
Sasahara, Arthur Asao *cardiologist, educator, researcher*
Sazdanoff, Catherine Ann *lawyer*
Thompson, David Allen *health care company executive*

Addison
Brunken, Gerald Walter, Sr. *manufacturing company executive*
Turner, Eugene Andrew *manufacturing executive*

Alton
†Dickey, Keith Winfield *dentist, dental educator*
Heuertz, Sarah Jane *dentist*
Hoagland, Karl King, Jr. *lawyer*
Hodgson, Peter John *music educator*
†Kessler, William Eugene *health care executive*
King, Ordie Herbert, Jr. *oral pathologist*
Minsker, Robert Stanley *consultant, former industrial relations executive*
Schnabel, John Henry *music educator*
Struif, L. James *lawyer*

AMF Ohare
†Aron, Adam M. *air transportation executive*
Bateman, Sylvia Lilaine *lawyer*
Fisher, Patricia Sweeney *business executive, lawyer*
Guyette, James M. *airline executive*
Hartigan, James J. *retired airline executive*
Pope, John Charles *airline company executive*

Anna
†Livengood, Joanne Desler *healthcare administrator*
Wolfe, Martha *elementary education educator*

Antioch
Strang, Charles Daniel *marine engine manufacturing company executive*

Argonne
Arzoumanidis, Gregory G. *chemist*
Berger, Edmond Louis *theoretical physicist*
Berkowitz, Joseph *physicist, physical chemist, researcher*
Blander, Milton *chemist*
Braun, Joseph Carl *nuclear engineer, scientist*
Carpenter, John Marland *engineer, physicist*
Chang, Yoon Il *nuclear engineer*
Derrick, Malcolm *physicist*
†Dyrkacz, Gary R. *chemist*
Ferraro, John Ralph *chemist*
Fields, Paul Robert *research nuclear chemist, consultant*
Green, David William *chemist, educator*
Heine, James Arthur *utilities plant manager*
Herzenberg, Caroline Stuart Littlejohn *physicist*
Jorgensen, James Douglas *research physicist*
Krauss, Alan Robert *physicist*
Kumar, Romesh *chemical engineer*
Martin, Ronald Lavern *physicist*
Morss, Lester Robert *chemist*
Nolen, Jerry Aften, Jr. *physicist*
Perlow, Gilbert J(erome) *physicist, editor*
Peshkin, Murray *physicist*
Schiffer, John Paul *physicist*
Schriesheim, Alan *research administrator*
Steindler, Martin Joseph *chemist*
Zeidman, Benjamin *nuclear physicist*

Arlington Heights
Baumann, Daniel E. *newspaper executive*
Church, Herbert Stephen, Jr. *retired construction company executive*
Dickau, John C. *religious organization executive*
Hoops, Donald Lee *medical association administrator*
Jenny, Daniel P. *retired engineer*
Johnson, Clifford R. *retired retail executive, consultant*
†Kelson, Allen Howard *consultant, writer, dining critic*
Lampinen, John A. *newspaper editor*
Lewin, Seymour Zalman *chemistry educator, consultant*
Nerlinger, John William *association executive*
Paddock, Robert Young *publisher*
Paddock, Stuart R., Jr. *publishing executive*
Pochyly, Donald Frederick *physician, hospital administrator*
†Ray, C. Eugene *chemicals executive*
Ray, Douglas *newspaper editor*
Roderick, William Rodney *academic administrator*
Shetty, Mulki Radhakrishna *oncologist, consultant*
Smedley, Bernard Ronald (Bernie Smedley) *communications executive*
Staiano, Edward F. *electronics company executive*

terHorst, Cheryl Ann *journalist*
†Wilson, Debra *oil, gas industry executive*

Aurora
Alschuler, Sam *lawyer*
Ball, William James *pediatrician*
†Candlish, Malcolm *manufacturing executive*
Etheredge, Forest DeRoyce *former state senator, university administrator*
†Fisher, Thomas Lee *gas company executive*
Halloran, Kathleen L. *financial executive, accountant*
Lindner, Patricia Reid *state representative, lawyer*
Lowe, Ralph Edward *lawyer*
Tyler, Lloyd John *lawyer*
Zarle, Thomas Herbert *university president*

Bannockburn
Zorio, John William *financial services executive*

Barrington
Andler, Donald Andrew *marketing executive*
Bash, Philip Edwin *publishing executive*
Baxter, Reginald Robert *investment company executive*
Edwards, Wilbur Shields *communications company executive*
Farina, Nick Charles *investor relations consultant*
Flieder, John Joseph *insurance consultant, marketing professional*
Francis, Philip Hamilton *engineering executive, mechanical engineer*
Kartalia, Mitchell P. *electrical equipment manufacturing executive*
Kroha, Bradford King *electronics manufacturing corporation executive*
Ligare, Kathleen Meredith *strategy and marketing executive*
Marshall, Gordon Bruce *construction company executive*
Massé, Laurence Raymond *personnel search firm executive*
Mathis, Jack David *advertising executive*
Moses, Bruce Hadley *manufacturing company executive*
Perry, I. Chet *petroleum company executive*
Rechtsteiner, Steven Allen *import/export company executive*
Simmons, Damian *secondary education educator*
Smith, William Lewis *hotel executive*
Spak, Lorin Mitchell *office products industry executive*
Tomomatsu, Hideo *chemist*
Victor, Michael Gary *lawyer, physician*
Woltz, Kenneth Allen *consulting executive*
Wyatt, James Frank, Jr. *lawyer*

Bartlett
†Khan, Kalim Ullah *metallurgical engineer, consultant*

Batavia
Bardeen, William Allan *research physicist*
Chrisman, Bruce Lowell *physicist, administrator*
Jonckheere, Alan Mathew *physicist*
Lach, Joseph Theodore *physicist*
Nash, E(dward) Thomas *physicist*
Peoples, John, Jr. *physicist, researcher*
Schilling, Arlo Leonard *bank executive*
Tollestrup, Alvin Virgil *physicist*
Tweedy, Robert Hugh *retired equipment company executive*

Bedford Park
Batory, Ronald Louis *transportation executive*
Herbert, Victor James *association executive*
Wenstrup, H. Daniel *chemical executive*

Belleville
Bauman, John Duane *lawyer*
Berkley, Gary Lee *newspaper publisher*
Boyle, Richard Edward *lawyer*
Cagas, Cosme Ralota *pediatrician, endocrinologist*
Coghill, William Thomas, Jr. *lawyer*
Connors, Jimmy (James Scott Connors) *former professional tennis player*
Eichelberger, Geralyn Mary *nursing administrator, critical care nurse*
Ferguson, John Marshall *retired federal magistrate judge*
Fietsam, Robert Charles *accountant*
†Gregory, Wilton D. *bishop*
Heiligenstein, Christian E. *lawyer*
Hess, Frederick J. *lawyer*
Parham, James Robert *lawyer*
Stevens, C. Glenn *judge*

Bensenville
Lewis, Darrell L. *retail executive*
Matera, Richard Ernest *minister*

Benton
Foreman, James Louis *retired judge*
Gilbert, J. Phil *federal judge*

Bloomingdale
Pedicini, Louis James *manufacturing company executive*
†Wolande, Charles Sanford *corporate executive*

Bloomington
Beernink, Darrell Wayne *actuary, life insurance company executive*
Bower, Marvin D. *insurance company executive*
Bragg, Michael Ellis *lawyer*
Bray, Robert C. *literature educator*
Brown, Jared *theater director, educator, writer*
Callis, Bruce *insurance company executive*
Curry, Alan Chester *insurance company executive*
Edmondson, James William (Jay Edmondson) *insurance company executive*
Engelkes, Donald John *insurance company executive*
Friedman, Joan M. *educator*
Goebel, William Mathers *lawyer*
Gregor, Marlene Pierce *primary educator, elementary science consultant*
Johnson, Earle Bertrand *insurance executive*
Jones, Norman Thomas *agricultural products company executive*
Jordan, Leo John *lawyer*
Joslin, Roger Scott *insurance company executive*
Merwin, Davis Underwood *newspaper executive*
Miller, Duane Leon *insurance company executive*
Montgomery, William Adam *lawyer*

Myers, Minor, Jr. *college administrator, political science educator*
Poulson, Howard D. *agricultural products company executive*
Prescott, Richard Paul, Jr. *computer company consultant*
Rood, Don D *insurance executive*
Rust, Edward Barry, Jr. *insurance company executive, lawyer*
Shelley, Edward Herman, Jr. *retired insurance company executive*
Stevenson, Ernest Vail *retired farmer cooperative executive*
Stonier, Daryle L. *agricultural supplies company executive*
Sullivan, Laura Patricia *lawyer, insurance company executive*
Trosino, Vincent Joseph *insurance company executive*
Vayo, David Joseph *composer, music educator*
Vincent, Norman L. *insurance company executive*
Watkins, Lloyd Irion *university president*
Webb, O. Glenn *farm supplies company executive*
White, John, Jr. *insurance company executive, farm organization executive*
Wills, Edgar W. (Bill) *newspaper editor*
Wright, Charles Richard *insurance executive*

Blue Island
Kollmann, Hilda Hanna *banker*
Mueller, John D. *electric company executive*

Bolingbrook
Price, Theodora Hadzisteliou *individual and family therapist*

Broadview
Andrla, Valerie Etta *manufacturing company executive*
Hohage, Frederick William *automotive parts company executive*

Brookfield
Pawley, Ray Lynn *zoological park herpetology curator*
Rabb, George Bernard *zoologist*

Buffalo Grove
Clayton, Verna Lewis *state legislator*
Denov, Sam *musician*
Kaplan, Mitchell Philip *consulting engineer, marketing executive*
Siegel, Sid *composer, lyricist*
Smith, Justine Townsend *recreational association executive*

Burr Ridge
Danly, Donald Robert *retired manufacturing company executive*
Hatch, Edward William (Ted Hatch) *health care executive*
Sund, Jeffrey Owen *publishing company executive*

Cairo
Cobb, J. *bishop*

Calumet City
Edwards, James Clifford *finance company executive*
Self, Madison Allen *chemical company executive*

Carbondale
Ammon, Harry *history educator*
Bauner, Ruth Elizabeth *library administrator, reference librarian*
Best, Joel Gordon *sociology educator*
Bozzola, John Joseph *botany educator, researcher*
Brown, James Montgomery *retired English language and literature educator, academic administrator*
Buckley, John Joseph, Jr. *health care executive*
Burr, Brooks Milo *zoology educator*
Casey, John P. *special education educator*
Clemons, John Robert *lawyer*
Covington, Patricia Ann *university administrator*
Derge, David Richard *political science educator*
Dixon, Billy Gene *academic administrator*
Elkins, Donald Marcum *associate dean, agronomy educator*
Eynon, Thomas Grant *sociology educator*
Fladeland, Betty *historian, educator*
Gilbert, Glenn Gordon *linguistics educator*
Guyon, John Carl *university administrator*
Hahn, Lewis Edwin *philosopher, retired educator*
Handler, Jerome Sidney *anthropology educator*
Harper, Robert Alexander *geography educator*
Hart, James Warren *athletic director, restaurant owner, former professional football player*
Kionka, Edward James *lawyer*
†Koch, David Victor *librarian, administrator*
†Koch, Loretta Peterson *librarian, educator*
Lesar, Hiram Henry *lawyer, educator*
Matthews, Elizabeth Woodfin *law librarian, law educator*
Mead, John Stanley *university administrator*
Orthwein, William Coe *mechanical engineer*
Rubin, Harris B. *psychology educator*
Smith, James Gilbert *electrical engineer*
Snyder, Carolyn Ann *university dean, librarian*
Snyder, Charles Royce *sociologist, educator*
Somit, Albert *political educator*
Spees, Emil Ray *philosophy educator*
Takayama, Akira *economics educator*
Tao, Rongjia *physicist, educator*
Verduin, Jacob *botany educator*
Webb, Howard William, Jr. *humanities educator, university official*
Whitlock, John Joseph *museum director*
Wills, Walter Joe *agricultural marketing educator*
Woodbridge, Hensley Charles *retired foreign languages educator, librarian*
Wotiz, John Henry *chemist, educator*

Carlinville
Mc Conagha, Glenn Lowery *chancellor emeritus*
Schweizer, Melvin *food products executive*
Southwell, Leonard J. *dairy corporation executive*

Carmi
Edwards, Judith Elizabeth *advertising executive*

Carol Stream
Catone, Lucio *manufacturing executive*
Choice, Priscilla Kathryn Means (Penny Choice) *gifted education educator, international consultant*

Coffman, Roy Walter, III publishing company executive
Cook, Jeanette E. nursing administrator
Fricke, H. Walter minister
Myra, Harold Lawrence publisher
Pond, Byron O. manufacturing company executive
Schmerold, Wilfried Lothar dermatologist
Shorney, George Herbert publishing executive
Taylor, Kenneth Nathaniel publishing executive, author
†Waldrop, William Thomas executive
Yancey, Philip David editor, author

Carpentersville
Wilson, Delbert Ray publisher, author

Carrollton
Strickland, Hugh Alfred lawyer

Carthage
Glidden, John Redmond lawyer

Cary
Bowen, John Richard former chemical company executive

Centralia
Wargo, Tom professional golfer

Champaign
Arnould, Richard Julius economist, educator, consultant
Asaad, Kolleen Joyce special education educator
Bailey, Andrew Dewey, Jr. accounting educator
Baker, Jack Sherman architect, designer, educator
Batzli, George Oliver ecology educator
Bender, Paul Edward lawyer
Birdzell, Samuel Henry hospital administrator
Brems, Hans Julius economist, educator
Brighton, Gerald David accounting educator
Bryan, William Royal finance educator
Buschbach, Thomas Charles geologist, consultant
Cammack, Trank Emerson retired university dean
Cartwright, Keros hydrogeologist, researcher
Clark, Roger Gordon educational administrator
Cohen, Jozef psychophysicist, educator
Cribbet, John Edward legal educator, former university chancellor
Crummey, Donald Edward history educator
Davis, James Henry psychology educator
Due, John Fitzgerald economist, educator emeritus
Dulany, Elizabeth Gjelsness university press administrator
Eilbracht, Lee Paul retired association executive
Eriksen, Charles Walter psychologist, educator
Espeseth, Robert D. park and recreation planning educator
Feinberg, Walter philosophy educator
Foreman, John Richard newspaper editor
Frampton, George Thomas legal educator
Frankel, Marvin economist, educator
Fredrickson, L(awrence) Thomas composer
Friedberg, Maurice Russian literature educator
Froom, William Watkins banker
Garvey, John Charles violist, conductor, retired music educator
Getz, Lowell Lee zoology educator
Gross, David Lee geologist
Guttenberg, Albert Ziskind planning educator
Herzog, Beverly Leah hydrogeologist
Humphreys, Lloyd Girton research psychologist, educator
Jackson, Billy Morrow artist, retired art educator
Kanet, Roger Edward political science educator, university administrator
Kanfer, Frederick H. psychologist, educator
Keen, Maria Elizabeth retired educator
Khan, Latif Akbar mineral engineer
Kindt, John Warren, Sr. lawyer, educator, consultant
Knox, Charles Milton purchasing agent, consultant
Koenker, Diane P. history educator
Kotoske, Roger Allen artist, educator
Krause, Harry Dieter lawyer, educator
Kruger, William Arnold consulting civil engineer
Krummel, Donald William librarian, educator
Kuck, David Jerome computer system researcher, administrator
Levin, Geoffrey Arthur botanist
Loeb, Jane Rupley university administrator, educator
Love, Joseph L. history educator, cultural studies center administrator
Lyon, James Cyril chemical society executive
Maggs, Peter Blount lawyer, educator
Mamer, Stuart Mies lawyer
Mapother, Dillon Edward physicist, university official
McCulloh, Judith Marie editor
Meyer, August Christopher, Jr. broadcasting company executive, lawyer
Miller, Harold Arthur lawyer
Nagel, Stuart Samuel political science educator, lawyer
Neumann, Frederick Loomis accounting educator, academic administrator, consultant
Nowak, John E. law educator
†O'Connor, John T. civil engineering educator
O'Neill, John Joseph speech educator
Orr, Daniel educator, economist
Perry, Kenneth Wilbur accounting educator
Peterson, Roger Lyman insurance company executive
Philipp, Walter Viktor mathematician, educator
Phipps, John Tom lawyer
Puckett, Hoyle Brooks agricultural engineer, research scientist, consultant
Richards, Daniel Wells company executive
Ridlen, Samuel Franklin agriculture educator
Rotunda, Ronald Daniel law educator, consultant
†Scheetz, George Henry library director
Schoenfeld, Hanns-Martin Walter accounting educator
Schowalter, William Raymond college dean, educator
Semonin, Richard Gerard state official
Shupp, Franklin Richard economist
Simmons, Ralph Oliver physics educator
Slichter, Charles Pence physicist, educator
Smith, Ralph Alexander cultural and educational policy educator
Smith, Robert Lee agriculturalist
Spence, Clark Christian history educator
Spodek, Bernard curriculum educator
Sprenkle, Case Middleton economics educator
Sprugel, George, Jr. ecologist
Stapleton, Harvey James physics educator
Surles, Richard Hurlbut, Jr. law librarian
Sutton, Roger editor, writer, lecturer
†Taylor, James David health care executive
Vedder, Byron Charles newspaper executive
Wajenberg, Arnold Sherman retired librarian, educator
Wert, Lucille Mathena librarian, educator
Wolfram, Stephen physicist, computer company executive

Charleston
Buckellew, William Franklin retired education educator
Jorns, David Lee university president
Price, Dalias Adolph geography educator
Rives, Stanley Gene university president emeritus

Chester
Welge, Donald Edward food manufacturing executive

Chicago
Abbott, Jim (James Anthony Abbott) baseball player
Abbott, Kenneth Wayne law educator
Abcarian, Herand surgeon, educator
Abrahamson, Vicki Lafer lawyer
Abrams, Lee Norman lawyer
Abrams, Susan Elizabeth book editor, publisher
Acker, Frederick George lawyer
Acs, Joseph Steven transportation engineering consultant
Adair, Wendell Hinton, Jr. lawyer
Adams, Hall, Jr. (Cap Adams) advertising agency executive
Adams, John Richard psychiatrist, educator
Adams, Roy M. lawyer, writer
Adelman, Stanley Joseph lawyer
Adelman, Steven Herbert lawyer
Adkins, Arthur William Hope humanities educator
Adler, Mortimer Jerome philosopher, author
†Ady, Robert relocation consulting firm executive
Africano, Nicholas artist
Agarwal, Gyan Chand engineering educator
Agnew, David M. lawyer
Aitay, Victor concert violinist, music educator
Akerson, Daniel Francis telecommunications industry executive
Akos, Francis violinist
Aland, Robert H. lawyer
Albrecht, Ronald Frank anesthesiologist
Aldrich, Thomas Lawrence lawyer
Alesia, James H(enry) federal judge
Alexander, William Henry lawyer
Alexandroff, Mirron (Mike Alexandroff) academic administrator
Alexis, Geraldine M. lawyer
Aliber, Robert Z. economist, educator
Allan, Stanley Nance architect, consultant
Allard, Jean lawyer, urban planner
Allen, Belle management consulting firm executive, communications company executive
Allen, Richard Blose legal editor, lawyer
Allen, Ronald Jay law educator
Allen, Thomas Draper lawyer
Allgyer, Robert Earl accounting company executive
Almeida, Richard J. finance company executive
Almen, Lowell Gordon church official
Alschuler, Albert W. law educator
Altheimer, Alan J. lawyer
Altman, Louis lawyer, author, educator
Altmann, Jeanne zoologist, educator
Altmann, Stuart Allen biologist, educator
Amato, Isabella Antonia real estate executive
Amberg, Thomas Law public relations executive
Ambrose, Gerald A. lawyer
Amonte, Anthony Lewis professional hockey player
Amstadter, Laurence retired architect
Anagnost, Themis John lawyer
Andersen, Burton Robert physician, educator
†Andersen, Dana Kimball surgeon, educator
Andersen, Wayne R. federal judge
Anderson, David A. lawyer
Anderson, Donald W. lawyer
Anderson, Douglas Charles juvenile probation administrator
Anderson, J. Trent lawyer
Anderson, John Thomas lawyer
Anderson, Jon Stephen newswriter
Anderson, Kimball Richard lawyer
Anderson, Louise Eleanor biochemistry educator
Anderson, Paul Milton steel company executive
Anderson, Richard C. clothing company executive
Anderson, William Cornelius, III lawyer
Andreoli, Kathleen Gainor nurse, educator, administrator
†Andrews, Bernard W. retail company executive
Angelo, Percy L. lawyer
Angst, Gerald L. lawyer
Annable, James Edward economist
Anshaw, Carol writer
Anthony, Michael Francis lawyer
Anvaripour, M. A. lawyer
Apcel, Melissa Anne lawyer
Appel, Nina Schick law educator, dean
Applebaum, Edward Leon otolaryngologist, educator
Applegate, William Joseph broadcast executive
Appleton, Arthur Ivar retired electric products manufacturing company executive, horse breeder
Archambault, Bennett corporate executive
Arditti, Fred D. economist, educator
Arlow, Allan Joseph lawyer
Armstrong, Edwin Richard lawyer, publisher, editor
Arnason, Barry Gilbert Wyatt neurologist, educator
Arnsdorf, Morton Frank cardiologist, educator
Aronson, Howard Isaac linguist, educator
Aronson, Simon H. lawyer
Aronson, Virginia L. lawyer
Arroyo, Robert Edward lawyer
Artner, Alan Gustav art critic, journalist
Artwick, Frederic J. lawyer
Arzbaecher, Robert C(harles) research institute executive, electrical engineer, researcher
Ash, J. Marshall mathematician, educator
Ashwill, Terry M. advertising executive
Aspen, Marvin Edward federal judge
Athas, Gus James lawyer
Athens, Andrew A. steel company executive
Auerbach, Marshall Jay lawyer
Austin, Richard William lawyer
Austin, Robert B. lawyer
Auwarter, Franklin Paul lawyer
Avedisian, Armen George industrialist, financier
Axley, Frederick William lawyer
Babcock, Lyndon Ross, Jr. environmental engineer, educator
†Bacher, Robert Newell church official
Badel, Julie lawyer
Badger, Charles H. manufacturing company executive
Baer, John Richard Frederick lawyer
Baetz, W. Timothy lawyer
Baffes, Thomas Gus cardiac surgeon, lawyer
Bailar, Barbara Ann statistician, researcher
Bailey, Orville Taylor neuropathologist
Bailey, Robert, Jr. advertising executive
Bailey, Robert Short lawyer
Baird, Douglas Gordon law educator
Baird, Russell Miller lawyer
Baker, James Edward Sproul retired lawyer
Baker, Pamela lawyer
†Baker, Robert J. medical academic dean, surgeon
Bakwin, Edward Morris banker
Balasi, Mark Geoffrey architect
Baloun, John Charles wholesale grocery company executive
Balousek, John B. advertising executive
Balz, Douglas Charles journalist
Balzekas, Stanley, Jr. museum director
Ban, Stephen Dennis natural gas industry research institute executive
Banik, Douglas Heil advertising executive
Banks, Deirdre Margaret church organization administrator
Banoff, Sheldon Irwin lawyer
Banta, Merle Henry graphics equipment and service company executive
Baptist, Allwyn J. health care consultant
Barany, Kate biophysics educator
Barbour, Claude Marie minister
Bard, John Franklin consumer products executive
Barenberg, Sumner polymer physicist, business executive
Barker, Emmett Wilson, Jr. trade association executive
Barker, Walter Lee thoracic surgeon
Barker, William Thomas lawyer
Barliant, Ronald federal judge
Barnard, Morton John lawyer
Barnard, Robert N. lawyer
Barnard, Susan C. church administrator
Barnes, James Garland, Jr. lawyer
Barnett, Robert L. utilities executive
Barnette, Dennis Arthur management consultant
Barney, Carol Ross architect
Barr, John Robert lawyer
Barrett, Paulette Singer public relations executive
Barrett, Roger Watson lawyer
Barron, Howard Robert lawyer
Barrow, Charles Herbert investment banker
Barry, Norman J., Jr. lawyer
†Barry, Richard A. public relations executive
Bartholomay, William C. insurance brokerage company executive, professional baseball team executive
Bartlit, Fred Holcomb, Jr. lawyer, educator
Bartoletti, Bruno conductor
†Bartolotta, Paul Wenzel chef
Barton, Evan Mansfield physician
Bartter, Brit Jeffrey investment banker
Baruch, Hurd lawyer
Bashwiner, Steven Lacelle lawyer
Batlle, Daniel nephrologist
Bauer, William Joseph federal judge
Baugher, Peter V. lawyer
Baum, Bernard Helmut sociologist, educator
Baumgartner, William Hans, Jr. lawyer
Baumhart, Raymond Charles church administrator
Bayer, Gary Richard advertising executive
Beall, Ingrid Lillehei lawyer
Beattie, Janet Holtzman accounting firm executive
Beattie, Mary Jarvis public relations executive
†Beattie, Ted Arthur zoological gardens administrator
Beatty, William Kaye medical bibliography educator
Beaty, Harry Nelson internist, educator, university dean
Bechina, Melvin Jeremiah leasing company executive
Beck, Joan Wagner journalist
Beck, Philip S. lawyer
Beck, Robert N. nuclear medicine educator
Becker, Gary Stanley economist, educator
Becker, Mary E. law educator
†Becker, Michael A. physician, educator
Becker, Theodore Michaelson lawyer
Beckstrom, John H. lawyer, educator
Beeby, Thomas H. architect
Beecher, William John zoologist, museum director
Beem, Jack Darrel lawyer
Begando, Joseph Sheridan retired university chancellor, educator
Beggan, John Francis lawyer
Beigl, William physician, naturopath, hypnotist, acupuncturist, consultant
Beitler, J. Paul real estate developer
Belfour, Ed professional hockey player
Bell, Clark Wayne business editor, educator
†Bell, Kevin J. zoological park administrator
Bellas, Jean architect
Belluschi, Anthony C. architect
Belmore, F. Martin lawyer
Bender, Janet Pines artist
Bennett, Beverly newspaper editor
Bennett, Lerone, Jr. magazine editor, author
Bennett, M(ary) Elizabeth lawyer
Bennett, Russell Odbert lawyer
Bensinger, Peter Benjamin consulting firm executive
Bentley, Peter John Hilton lawyer
Berens, Mark Harry lawyer
Berg, Mildred M. church administrator
Bergel, Richard department store chain executive
Berger, Kay public relations executive
Berger, Robert Michael lawyer
Bergere, Carleton Mallory contractor
Berghoff, John C., Jr. lawyer
Bergonia, Raymond David venture capitalist
Bergstrom, Betty Howard consulting executive
Bergstrom, Robert William lawyer
Berkeley, Jill Brenda lawyer
Berkery, Michael John insurance company executive
Berland, Abel Edward lawyer, realtor
Berman, Arthur Leonard state senator
Berman, Bennett I. lawyer
Berman, Howard Allen rabbi
Bernadetta, Sister Maria special education educator
Bernard, Frank Charles lawyer
Bernardin, Joseph Louis Cardinal archbishop, university chancellor
Bernatowicz, Frank Allen management consultant, expert witness
Berner, Robert Lee, Jr. lawyer
Bernick, David M. lawyer
Berning, Larry D. lawyer
Bernstein, H. Bruce lawyer
Bernstein, Howard L. lawyer
Bernstein, Stuart lawyer
Berolzheimer, Karl lawyer
Berry, Alan M. lawyer
Berry, John Willard librarian, consultant
Berry, Leonidas Harris gastroenterologist, internist
Betke, James E. lawyer
Betts, Henry Brognard physician, health facility administrator, educator
Betz, Hans Dieter theology educator
Beugen, Joan Beth communications company executive
Bevington, David Martin English literature educator
†Bevington, Terry Paul professional baseball manager
Bezman, Victor H. lawyer
Bidwell, Charles Edward sociologist, educator
Biebel, Paul Philip, Jr. lawyer
Bielawski, Alan P. lawyer
Bierig, Jack R. lawyer
Biggles, Richard Robert marketing executive
Biggs, Robert Dale Near Eastern studies educator
Bilandic, Michael A. state supreme court chief justice, former mayor
Biljetina, Richard chemical engineering researcher
Bishop, Oliver Richard state official
Bitner, John Howard lawyer
Bixby, Frank Lyman lawyer
Bjorneberg, Paul Grant public relations executive
Blackman, Jana Cohen lawyer
Blair, Bowen investment banker
Blair, Edward McCormick investment banker
Blakemore, Thomas F. lawyer
Blanco, Jim L. lawyer
Blatt, Richard Lee lawyer
Bliwas, Ronald Lee advertising agency executive
†Bloch, Ralph Jay professional association executive
†Bloch, Spencer J. mathematician
Block, Neal Jay lawyer
Block, Philip Dee, III investment counselor
Bloom, Benjamin S. education educator
Bloom, Christopher Arthur lawyer
Blount, Michael Eugene lawyer
Bluhm, Neil Gary real estate company executive
Blum, Michael Stephen financial services executive
Blumberg, Avrom Aaron physical chemistry educator
Blutter, Joan Wernick interior designer
Boberg, Wayne D. lawyer
Bockelman, John Richard lawyer
Bodine, Laurence lawyer, editor, marketer
Boers, Terry John sportswriter, radio and television personality
Bogert, George Taylor lawyer
†Bogert, John Alden, II dental association executive
Boggess, Thomas Phillip, III graphic arts company executive
Boggs, Joseph Dodridge pediatric pathologist, educator
Bohmer, David Alan cable television executive
Bohne, Carl John, Jr. accountant
Boies, Wilber H. lawyer
Boley, John N. lawyer
Bolger, Anne Margaret hospital administrator
Bolnick, Howard Jeffrey insurance company executive
Bomchill, Fern Cheryl lawyer
Bonser, Sidney Henry diversified manufacturing company executive
Boodell, Thomas Joseph, Jr. lawyer
Bookshester, Dennis Steven retail company executive
Boonstra, Cornelis food products company executive
Booth, Wayne Clayson English literature and rhetoric educator, author
Borders, Thomas C. lawyer
Bornholdt, Laura Anna university administrator
Boshes, Louis D. physician, scientist, educator
Bosselman, Fred Paul law educator
Botica, Matthew J. lawyer
Bott, Harold Sheldon accountant, management consultant
Bottom, Dale Coyle association executive
Bouchard, Craig Thomas international banker
Bouma, Robert Edwin lawyer, diversified company executive
†Bourdon, Cathleen Jane executive director
Bowe, William John lawyer
Bowen, Stephen Stewart lawyer
Bowen, William Joseph management consultant
Bower, Bruce Lester lawyer
Bower, Glen Landis lawyer
Bowman, Barbara Taylor academic administrator
Bowman, George Arthur, Jr. federal judge
Bowman, James Edward physician, educator
Bowman, John architectural firm designer
Bowman, Leah fashion designer, consultant, photographer, educator
Bowytz, Robert B. lawyer
Boyce, David Edward transportation and regional science educator
Boyd, David J. lawyer
Boyd, Willard Lee museum administrator, educator, lawyer
Boyer, John William history educator, dean
Bradburn, Norman M. behavioral science educator
Braden, William Lou non-profit agency manager
Braidwood, Linda Schreiber archaeologist
Braidwood, Robert J. archaeologist, educator
Brake, Cecil Clifford diversified manufacturing executive
Bramnik, Robert Paul lawyer
Brashler, William author
†Brasitus, Thomas Albert gastroenterologist, educator
†Brasler, Wayne Michael journalism educator, writer
Breakstone, Donald S. lawyer
Brennan, Bernard Francis retail chain store executive
Brennan, Edward A. merchandising, insurance and real estate executive
Brennan, James Joseph lawyer
Brennan, Richard J. lawyer
Brennan, Richard Snyder bank executive, lawyer
Breslin, Michael Edward advertising agency executive, lawyer
Bresnahan, James Francis medical ethics educator
Brewer, John Isaac obstetrician, gynecologist
Breyer, Norman Nathan metallurgical engineering educator, consultant
Brice, James John retired accounting firm executive
Brice, Roger Thomas lawyer
Brickhouse, John B. (Jack Brickhouse) sports broadcaster
Bridewell, David Alexander lawyer
Bridgman, Thomas Francis lawyer
Brinkman, John Anthony historian, educator
Britton, Dennis A. newspaper editor, newspaper executive
Brizzolara, Charles Anthony lawyer
Brodsky, William J. futures options exchange executive

Brooker, Thomas Kimball oil company executive
Brooks, Gwendolyn writer, poet
Brooks, Robert Liss lawyer
Brookstone, Arnold F. paper packaging company executive
Brophy, Joan Edmonds lawyer
Brotman, Barbara Louise columnist, writer
Brown, Alan Crawford lawyer
Brown, Donald James, Jr. lawyer
Brown, Gregory K. lawyer
Brown, Richard Harris telecommunications industry executive
Brown, Richard Holbrook library administrator, historian
Brown, Rowine Hayes physician, former medical administrator
Browning, Don Spencer religion educator
Brubaker, Charles William architect
Brueschke, Erich Edward physician, researcher, educator
Brumback, Charles Tiedtke newspaper executive
Brummel, Mark Joseph magazine editor
Bruner, Stephen C. lawyer
Bruno, Kay Anderson public relations executive, speaker
†Brunson, Kathleen M. public relations executive
Bryan, John Henry food and consumer products company executive
Bryson, Cheryl Blackwell lawyer
Bua, Nicholas John retired federal judge
Buchholz, Edward J. lawyer
Buckle, Frederick Tarifero international holding company executive, political and business intelligence analyst
Buckley, Joseph Paul, III polygraph specialist
Bucklo, Elaine Edwards federal judge
Buckner, James Lowell dentist
Budenholzer, Roland Anthony mechanical engineering educator
Bueschel, David Alan management consultant
Bugielski, Robert Joseph state legislator
Bulger, Brian Wegg lawyer
Bunge, Jonathan Gunn lawyer
Burack, Elmer Howard management educator
†Buratto, Paddy Ann trade association executive
Burdelik, Thomas L. lawyer
Burditt, George Miller, Jr. lawyer
Burger, Mary Louise psychologist, educator
Burgett, George L. lawyer
Burhoe, Brian W. automotive service executive
Burhoe, Ralph Wendell religion and science educator
Burke, Thomas Joseph, Jr. lawyer
Burkey, Lee Melville lawyer
Burrell, Thomas J. marketing communication executive
Burt, Robert Norcross diversified manufacturing company executive
Burton, Raymond Charles, Jr. transportation company executive
Busey, Roxane C. lawyer
Buss, Daniel Frank environmental scientist
Butler, Richard Dean interior designer
Butler, Robert Allan psychologist, educator
†Butts, Edward A. lawyer
Byman, Robert Leslie lawyer
Bynoe, Peter Charles Bernard real estate developer, legal consultant
Caccamo, Nicholas James financial executive
Cahan, James N. lawyer
Calamaras, Louis Basil lawyer, association executive
Calderon, Alberto P. mathematician, educator
Caldwell, Ethel Louise Lynch academic administrator
Calenoff, Leonid radiologist
Callahan, Michael J. chemicals and manufacturing company executive
Callahan, Ronald E. petroleum company executive
Callaway, Karen A(lice) journalist
Campbell, Bruce Crichton hospital administrator
Campbell, Calvin Arthur, Jr. mining and plastics molding equipment manufacturing company executive
Campbell, Christian Larsen lawyer
Campbell, Edward Fay, Jr. religion educator
Campbell, Janie Lee patient services executive, researcher, abstractor
Campbell, Patricia K. public relations executive, writer, journalist
Campbell, Wendell Jerome architect
Camper, John Jacob writer, university administrator
Camras, Marvin electrical and computer engineering educator, inventor
Canning, John Anthony, Jr. venture capital company executive
Cannon, Bennie Marvin physical education educator
Caplis, Kevin J. lawyer
†Cappadoccia, Ronald food products executive
Cappo, Joseph C. publisher
†Carl, John L. petroleum industry executive
Carlin, Dennis J. lawyer
†Carlson, Rolland S. health facility adminstrator
Carlson, Stephen Curtis lawyer
Carlson, Walter Carl lawyer
Carlton, Dennis William economics educator
Carman, Charles Hallack legal business publisher, editor, lawyer
Carney, Jean Kathryn psychologist
Carnow, Bertram Warren occupational and environmental health consultant
Caro, William Allan physician
Carone, Frank medical educator, pathologist
Carpenter, Allan author, editor, publisher
Carpenter, David William lawyer
Carr, Anne Elizabeth theology educator
†Carr, Barbara Whitney foundation administrator
Carr, Robert Clifford petroleum company executive
Carren, Jeffrey P. lawyer
Carrier, Mark Anthony professional football player
Carroll, James J. lawyer
Carroll, John M. lawyer
Carroll, William Kenneth law educator, psychologist, theologian
Carton, Laurence Alfred lawyer
Casper, Regina Claire physician, researcher
Cassling, Donald Roger lawyer
Cavalier, Frank N. construction company executive, civil engineer
Center, Robert A. accounting firm executive
Chabraja, Nicholas D. lawyer
Chacko, Samuel association official
Chadwick, Joanne church administrator
Chaffetz, Hammond Edward lawyer
Chaitin, Anthony management services executive
Chakrabarty, Ananda Mohan microbiologist
Chaleff, Carl Thomas brokerage house executive
Chambers, Donald Arthur biochemistry and molecular medicine educator
Champagne, Ronald Oscar academic administrator, mathematics educator
Champion, Charles F. newspaper publishing executive
Chandler, Kent, Jr. lawyer
Chandrasekhar, Subrahmanyan astrophysicist, educator
Chanen, Franklin Allen lawyer
Chapman, Alger Baldwin finance executive, lawyer
Chapman, Delores elementary education educator
Chapman, Howard Stuart lawyer
Chapman, Stephen James columnist
Chappell, Sally art historian
Charles, Allan G. physician, educator
Charlesworth, Brian biologist, genetics and evolution educator
Charlier, Roger Henri oceanographer, geographer, educator
Chartier, Janellen Olsen airline service coordinator
Chatterton, Robert Treat, Jr. reproductive endocrinology educator
Cheely, Daniel Joseph lawyer
Chefitz, Joel Gerald lawyer
Chelios, Christos K professional hockey player
Chen, Wai-Kai electrical engineering and computer science educator, consultant
†Cherner, Paul Jordan lawyer
Cherney, James Alan lawyer
†Childers, J. Richard lawyer
Chiles, Stephen Michael lawyer
Chilstrom, Herbert Walfred bishop
Chippas, Denyse Leilani secondary mathematics educator, travel agent
Chlebowski, John Francis, Jr. financial executive
Chookaszian, Dennis Haig financial executive
Chorengel, Bernd international hotel corporation executive
Choyke, Phyllis May Ford (Mrs. Arthur Davis Choyke, Jr.) management executive, editor, poet
Christensen, George B. lawyer, retired
Christiansen, Richard Dean newspaper editor
†Christianson, Stanley David corporate executive
†Christopher, Robert Allan manufacturing company executive
Chung, Joseph Sang-hoon economics educator
Chung, Paul Myungha mechanical engineer, educator
Ciccarone, Richard Anthony financial executive
Ciccone, Richard newspaper editor
Cicero, Frank, Jr. lawyer
Ciotola, Nicholas Anthony financial executive
Citron, Diane lawyer
Claeys, Jerome Joseph, III real estate company executive
Clark, James Allen lawyer, educator
Clark, James E. lawyer
Clark, Jeanne (Barbara) police commander
Clark, John Whitcomb diagnostic radiologist
Clark, Terry Nichols sociology educator
Clarke, Philip Ream, Jr. investment banker
Clarke, Richard Stewart security company executive
Clay, John Ernest lawyer
Claypool, William, III hardware, garden equipment manufacturing company executive
†Claypoole, Robert Edwin distribution service company executive
Clayton, Robert Norman chemist, educator
Clemens, Richard Glenn lawyer
Cloonan, James Brian investment executive
Closen, Michael Lee law educator
Coar, David H. federal judge
Coase, Ronald Harry economics educator
Coe, Donald Kirk university official
Coe, Fredric L. physician, educator, researcher
Coffey, Raymond Richard newspaper editor, journalist
Cohan, George Sheldon advertising and public relations executive
Cohen, Christopher B. lawyer
Cohen, Edward Philip microbiology and immunology educator, physician
Cohen, Jerome psychology educator, electrophysiologist
Cohen, Melanie Rovner lawyer
Cohen, Melvin R. physician, educator
Cohen, Ted philosophy educator
Cohler, Bertram Joseph social sciences educator, clinical psychologist
Cohodes, Eli Aaron publisher
Cole, Franklin Alan investment company executive
Cole, Thomas Amor lawyer
Coleman, James Samuel sociologist, educator
Coleman, Roy Everett secondary education educator, computer programmer
Collen, Sheldon Orrin lawyer
Collens, Lewis Morton university president, legal educator
Colman, Jeffrey D. lawyer
Colter, Cyrus novelist, lawyer
Comiskey, Michael Peter lawyer
Conant, Howard Rosset steel company executive
Condon, Edward John, Jr. retail and financial services executive
Cone, Joseph Jay investment banking officer
Congalton, Susan Tichenor lawyer
Conibear, Shirley Ann occupational health consultant, physician
Conidi, Daniel Joseph private investigation agency executive
Conklin, Thomas William lawyer
Conlon, Suzanne B. federal judge
Conlon, William F. lawyer
Connelly, Vincent J. lawyer
Connolly, Eugene B., Jr. building materials company executive
†Connolly, Peter Dominic hotel executive, lawyer
Connors, Dorsey television and radio commentator, newspaper columnist
Connors, Mary Eileen psychologist
†Conrad, John R. utilities corporate executive
Consey, Kevin Edward museum administrator
Considine, Frank William container corporation executive
Constant, Anita Aurelia publisher
Conte, Richard Nicholas architect
Conviser, Richard James law educator, lawyer, publications company executive
Conway, James Joseph physician
Conway, Michael Maurice lawyer
†Conzen, Michael Peter geography educator
Cook, Richard Borreson architect
Cooke, Robert Phillip architect
Cooney, Robert John lawyer
Cooper, Charles Gilbert toiletries and cosmetics company executive
Coopersmith, Bernard Ira obstetrician/gynecologist, educator
Copeland, Edward Jerome lawyer
Copley, Stephen Michael materials science and engineering educator
Corboy, Philip Harnett lawyer
Corcoran, James Martin, Jr. lawyer, writer, lecturer
Corwin, Sherman Phillip lawyer
Costello, John William lawyer
Cotner, C(arol) Beth financial services company executive
Cotsonas, Nicholas John, Jr. physician, medical educator
Cotter, Daniel A. diversified company executive
Cotting, James Charles manufacturing company executive
Cotton, Eugene lawyer
Coughlan, Kenneth Lewis lawyer
Coughlin, Joseph E. lawyer
Coulson, John Selden retired marketing executive
Cousins, William, Jr. judge
Covalt, Robert Byron chemicals executive
Covey, Frank Michael, Jr. lawyer, educator
Covington, George Morse lawyer
Cox, Allan James management consultant
Cox, Charles C. economist
Crain, Gertrude Ramsay publishing company executive
Crain, Rance publishing company executive
Crane, Barbara Bachmann photographer, educator
Crane, Charlotte law educator
Crane, Mark lawyer
Craven, George W. lawyer
Crawford, Dewey Byers lawyer
Crawford, William Basil, Jr. journalist
Crawford, William F. corporate executive, consultant
Creamer, Robert Allan lawyer
Creighton, Neal foundation administrator, retired military officer
Cremin, Susan Elizabeth lawyer
Crihfield, Philip J. lawyer
Crisham, Thomas Michael lawyer
Crockett, George Ephriam secondary education educator
Croisant, Eugene R. banker
Cronin, James Watson physicist, educator
Cronin, Robert E. lawyer
Cropsey, Joseph political science educator
Cross, Dolores Evelyn university administrator, educator
Cross, Robert Clark journalist
Crossan, John Robert lawyer
†Crown, James Schine lawyer
Crown, Lester manufacturing company executive
Crumbaugh, David Gordon lawyer
Crusto, Mitchell Ferdinand lawyer, environmental management consultant
Csikszentmihalyi, Mihaly psychology educator
Cullen, Charles Thomas historian, librarian
Cummings, Maxine Gibson elementary school educator
Cummings, Walter J. federal judge
Cunningham, Robert James lawyer
†Cuny, Frederick C. disaster relief executive
Curatolo, Alphonse Frank architect
Curley, Robert E. lawyer
Currie, David Park lawyer, educator
Curwen, Randall William journalist, editor
Cusack, John Thomas lawyer
Cushman, Aaron D. public relations executive
Custer, Charles Francis lawyer
Cyr, Arthur association executive
D'Alexander, William Joseph publishing company executive
Daley, James P. lawyer
Daley, Richard Michael mayor
Daley, Rosie cook, writer
Daley, Susan Jean lawyer
Dam, Kenneth W. lawyer, law educator
D'Amato, Anthony law educator
Dammeyer, Rodney Foster distribution company executive
Dancewicz, John Edward investment banker
Darby, Edwin Wheeler retired newspaper financial columnist
Darnall, Robert J. steel company executive
Darr, Milton Freeman, Jr. banker
†Daum, Robert Steven pediatrics educator
Davidson, Stanley J. lawyer
Davies, Peter Francis pathology educator, medical educator
Davis, Andrew Bashaw publishing executive
Davis, J. Steve advertising agency executive
Davis, Michael W. lawyer
Davis, Muller lawyer
Davis, Ralph E. lawyer
Davis, Scott Jonathan lawyer
Davis, Sylvester, Jr. secondary education educator
Davison, Richard physician, educator
DeBat, Donald Joseph newspaper editor
Debus, Allen George history educator
DeCarlo, William S. lawyer
Dechene, James Charles lawyer
Decker, Richard Knore lawyer
De Costa, Edwin J. physician, surgeon
De Francesco, John Blaze, Jr. public relations company executive
deGrijs, Leo Charles banker
Degroot, Leslie Jacob medical educator
Dehmlow, Louis Henry Theodore wholesale and distribution company executive
de Hoyos, Debora M. lawyer
Deignan, Robert E. lawyer
Deitrick, William Edgar lawyer
del Greco, Francesco physician, educator
Delony, Patty Litton management consultant
Delp, Wilbur Charles, Jr. lawyer
Dembowski, Peter Florian foreign language educator
DeMoss, Jon W. insurance company executive, lawyer
Denvir, Robert F. lawyer
DePaul, Carol Stone lawyer
Depoy, Phil E. special studies think-tank executive
Derlacki, Eugene L(ubin) otolaryngologist, physician
Desch, Theodore Edward health insurance company executive, lawyer
D'Esposito, Julian C., Jr. lawyer
Despres, Leon Mathis lawyer, former city official
Detuno, Joseph Edward lawyer
DeWolfe, John Chauncey, Jr. lawyer
De Yoe, David P. lawyer
Diamond, Seymour physician
Diamond, Shari Seidman psychology educator, law researcher
Diefenbach, Viron Leroy dental, public health educator, university dean
Dilling, Kirkpatrick Wallwick lawyer
Dilworth, Robert Holden lawyer
Dimond, Robert Edward publisher
Dix, Rollin C(umming) mechanical engineering educator, consultant
Dixon, Stewart Strawn lawyer
Dobbs, Frank Wilbur chemistry educator
Dockterman, Michael lawyer
Dodds, Claudette La Vonn radio executive and consultant
Dolan, Thomas Christopher association executive
Dold, Robert Bruce journalist
Dondanville, John Wallace lawyer
Donenfeld, J. Douglas lawyer
Doniger, Wendy history of religions educator
Donlevy, John Dearden lawyer
Donnell, Harold Eugene, Jr. association executive
Donnelley, James Russell printing company executive
Donohoe, Jerome Francis lawyer
Donohue, John Joseph law educator
Donovan, Dianne Francys journalist
†Donovan, John Vincent consulting company executive
Donovan, Thomas B. lawyer
Donovan, Thomas Roy futures exchange executive
Doolittle, Sidney Newing retail executive
Dorf, Jerome clothing corporation executive
Dorman, Jeffrey Lawrence lawyer
Dorr, Williams Peter lawyer
Doty, Carl K. retired printing company executive
Douglas, Charles W. lawyer
Douglass, Andrew Ian lawyer, financial executive
Downing, Joan Forman editor
Downing, Robert Allan lawyer
Doyle, Daniel M. bank executive
Doyle, John Robert lawyer
Dreeben, Robert education educator
Drexler, Lloyd business executive
Drexler, Richard Allan manufacturing company executive
Driskell, Claude Evans dentist
Dropkin, Allen Hodes lawyer
Druick, Douglas Wesley museum administrator
Drymalski, Raymond Hibner lawyer, banker
Dubin, Arthur Detmers architect
Duecker, Robert Sheldon bishop
Duell, Daniel Paul artistic director, choreographer, lecturer
Duez, David Joseph lawyer
Duff, Brian Barnett federal judge
Duhl, Michael Foster lawyer
Dumbacher, John Philip evolutionary biologist
Duncan, John Patrick Cavanaugh lawyer
Duncan, Starkey Davis, Jr. behavioral sciences educator
Dunea, George nephrologist, educator
Dunford, Michael S. marketing professional
†Dunn, E(dward) Paul, Jr. treasurer
Dunphy, Thomas insurance company executive
Dupont, Todd F. mathematics and computer science educator
Durchslag, Stephen P. lawyer
Durso, John J. lawyer
Dykema, Henry L. manufacturing company financial executive
Dykla, K.H.S. Edward George social services administrator
Dykstra, Paul Hopkins lawyer
Dyrud, Jarl Edvard psychiatrist
Early, Bert Hylton lawyer, legal search consultant
Early, Patrick Joseph oil and gas company executive
Easterbrook, Frank Hoover federal judge
Eaton, John C. composer, educator
Eaton, Larry Ralph lawyer
Ebert, Paul Allen surgeon, educator
Ebert, Roger Joseph film critic
Echols, M(ary) Evelyn travel consultant
Eckel, John M. lawyer
Eddy, David Latimer banker
Edelman, Alvin lawyer
Edelman, Daniel Joseph public relations executive
Edelstein, Teri J. museum administrator, educator
Edwards, Charles Lloyd lawyer
Egan, Kevin James lawyer
Eggert, Russell Raymond lawyer
Egloff, Fred Robert manufacturers representative, writer, historian
Ehrman, Joseph S. lawyer
Eimer, Nathan Philip lawyer
Einhorn, Edward Martin (Eddie Einhorn) professional baseball team executive
Eisenberg, James food company executive
Eisenman, Trudy Fox dermatologist
†Eisenmann, Dale Richard dental educator
Eisner, Michael C. electric power industry executive
Ejiogu, Lem Onyeaduzim software engineer
Ekdahl, Jon Nels lawyer, corporate secretary
Elbaz, Sohair Wastawy library director, consultant
Elden, Gary Michael lawyer
Elleman, Barbara editor
Elliot, Willard Somers musician, composer
Ellwood, Scott lawyer
Elson, Alex lawyer, legal educator
Elson, John S. legal educator
Emerson, Carter Whitney lawyer
Ender, Jon T. investment management executive, banker
Engel, Joel Stanley telecommunications executive
Ephraim, Donald Morley lawyer
Eppen, Gary Dean business educator
Epstein, Laura social work educator, consultant
Epstein, Raymond engineering and architectural executive
Epstein, Richard A. law educator
Epstein, Sidney architect and engineer
Epstein, Wolfgang biochemist, educator
Erber, Thomas physics educator
Erdos, Ervin George pharmacology and biochemistry educator
Erens, Jay Allan lawyer
Ergas, Jean-Pierre Maurice packaging company executive
Ericson, Robert W. lawyer
Erlebacher, Albert history educator
Erlebacher, Arlene Cernik lawyer
†Ernest, J. Terry ocular physiologist, educator
Esmond, Truman H., Jr. health facility administrator
†Esposito, Rochelle Easton geneticist, educator
Esrick, Jerald Paul lawyer
Essex, Joseph Michael visual communication planner
Ettinger, Joseph Alan lawyer
Eubanks-Pope, Sharon G. real estate entrepreneur
Evans, Earl Alison, Jr. biochemist
Evans, Thelma Jean Mathis internist
Even, Francis Alphonse lawyer
Everett, Jonathan Jubal lawyer
Everson, Leonard Charles lawyer
Ewen, Malcolm Dawes stage manager
Ewers, R. Darrell food products company executive
Eyerman, Thomas Jude architect
Fahner, Tyrone C. lawyer, former state attorney general

Fahnestock, Jean Howe retired civil engineer
Fairchild, Thomas E. federal judge
Falls, Robert Arthur artistic director
Fano, Ugo physicist, educator
Fanta, Paul Edward chemist, educator
Farley, William F. corporation executive
Farrakhan, Louis religious leader
Farran, Carol J. nursing educator
Favors, Malachi jazz musician, bassist
Fayhee, Michael R. lawyer
Fazio, Peter Victor, Jr. lawyer
Feagley, Michael Rowe lawyer
Feder, Robert television and radio columnist
Fein, Roger Gary lawyer
Feinstein, Fred Ira lawyer
Feldman, Burton Gordon printing company executive
Feldman, Scott M. lawyer
Feldstein, Charles Robert fund raising consultant
Feldstein, Joel Robert public relations executive
Fellows, Jerry Kenneth lawyer
Felton, Cynthia principal
Fennessy, John James radiologist, educator
Fenton, Clifton Lucien investment banker
Ferencz, Robert Arnold lawyer
Ferguson, Bradford Lee lawyer
Ferguson, Donald John surgeon, educator
Ferrini, James Thomas lawyer
Fetridge, Bonnie-Jean Clark (Mrs. William Harrison Fetridge) civic volunteer
Fetridge, Clark Worthington publisher
Fickinger, Wayne Joseph advertising executive
Fiduccia, Paul C. lawyer
Fiechter, Charlotte E. church administrator
Field, Henry Frederick lawyer
Field, Marshall business executive
Field, Robert Edward lawyer
Fierer, Joshua Allan pathology educator
Fifield, William O. lawyer
Figge, Frederick Henry, Jr. retired publishing executive
Finch, David S. banker
Finch, Herman Manuel academic administrator
†Fine, Beth Anne genetic counselor, educator
Fink, John editor, newspaper
Finke, Robert Forge lawyer
Finley, Harold Marshall investment banker
Fiorella, Beverly Jean medical technologist, educator
Fiorentino, Leon Francis holding company executive
Fischel, Daniel R. law educator
Fischer, Fredric H. lawyer
Fisher, Herbert Hirsh lawyer
Fisher, Lester Emil zoo administrator
Fisher, Wendy Astley-Bell marketing executive
Fishman, Irving S. lawyer
Fishman, Ross Howard lawyer
Fisk, Carlton Ernest retired professional baseball player
Fitch, Frank Wesley pathologist, immunologist, educator, administrator
Fitch, Morgan Lewis, Jr. patent lawyer
Fitzgerald, Robert Maurice financial executive
Flagg, Michael James communications and graphics company executive
Flaherty, Emalee Gottbrath pediatrician
Flanagan, Joseph Patrick advertising executive
Flanagan, Kathy Marie circuit court judge
Flanagan, Thomas Patrick accountant
Flanagin, Neil lawyer
Flaum, Joel Martin federal judge
Fleischer, Cornell Hugh history educator
Fleming, Graham Richard chemistry educator
†Fleming, Richard H. finance executive
Fletcher, James L. lawyer
Flick, Warren Edmond retail executive
†Fligg, James Edward oil company executive
†Flynn, John J. museum curator
Flynn, Peter Anthony lawyer
Fogel, Henry orchestra administrator
Fogel, Robert William economist, educator, historian
Fogelson, Raymond David anthropology educator
Foldi, Andrew Harry singer, educator
Foley, Joseph Lawrence sales executive
Foote, Edward L. lawyer
Foote, William Chapin strategic planning and corporate development executive
Ford, L. H. bishop
Ford, Larry John computer company executive
Ford, Michael W. lawyer
Forrester, J(ohn) Paul lawyer
Fort, Jeffrey C. lawyer
Fortune, Michael Joseph religion educator
Foster, Hugh Warren transportation company executive
Foster, James Reuben investment company executive
Foudree, Bruce William lawyer
Fox, David Wayne banker
Fox, Jacob Logan lawyer
Fox, Paul T. lawyer
†Fozzard, Harry Allen physiologist, cardiologist
Franch, Richard Thomas lawyer
Francis, Clinton William legal educator
Francois, William Armand packaging company executive, lawyer
Franke, Richard James investment banker
Franklin, Richard Mark lawyer
Fraumann, Willard George lawyer
Frederiksen, Marilynn Elizabeth Conners physician
Freed, Karl Frederick chemistry educator
Freed, Mayer Goodman law educator
Freedman, Joyce Beth academic administrator
Freedman, Philip physician, educator
Freehling, Paul Edward lawyer
Freehling, Stanley Maxwell investment banker
Freehling, Willard Maxwell stockbroker
Freeman, Lee Allen, Jr. lawyer
Freeman, Leslie Gordon anthropologist, educator
Freeman, Louis S. lawyer
Freeman, Susan Tax anthropologist, educator
Freidheim, Cyrus F., Jr. management consultant
Fried, Josef chemist, educator
Fried, Walter hematologist, educator
Friedland, Joanne Benazzi lawyer
Friedland, Richard Stewart electronics company executive
Friedman, Lawrence Milton lawyer
Friedman, Roselyn L. lawyer
Friedrich, Paul anthropologist, linguist, poet
Frings, Manfred Servatius philosophy educator
Frisch, Henry Jonathan physics educator
Fritzsche, Hellmut physics educator
Frohman, Lawrence Asher endocrinology educator, scientist
Fromm, Erika (Mrs. Paul Fromm) clinical psychologist
Frommelt, Jeffrey James management consulting firm executive
Fross, Roger Raymond lawyer
Fruchter, Rosalie Klausner elementary school educator
Fuchs, Elaine V. molecular biologist, educator
Fujita, Tetsuya Theodore educator, meteorologist
Fukui, Yoshio biology educator
Fulgoni, Gian Marc market research company executive
Fullagar, William Watts lawyer
Fuller, D. Ward transportation equipment company executive
Fuller, Harry Laurance oil company executive
Fuller, Jack William writer, newspaper executive
Fuller, Perry Lucian lawyer
Fullmer, Paul public relations counselor
†Fulton, Paul food product executive
Fultz, Dave meteorology educator
Furcon, John Edward management and organizational consultant
Furda, Gregory H. lawyer
Furlane, Mark Elliott lawyer
Furman, James Merle foundation executive
Fuson, Douglas Finley lawyer
Gaggini, John Edmund lawyer
Gaines, Kenneth R. lawyer
Gaines, William Chester journalist
†Gale, Neil Jan finance company executive, consultant
Gallagher, John Pirie corporation executive
Gamwell, Franklin I. dean, educator
Gancer, Donald Charles lawyer
Gangemi, Columbus Rudolph, Jr. lawyer, educator
Gannon, Sister Ann Ida retired philosophy educator, former college administrator
Garber, Daniel Elliot philosophy educator
Garber, Samuel Baugh lawyer, retail company executive
Garbutt, Eugene James lawyer
Gardner, Bettiann hair care products executive
Gardner, Edward G. manufacturing company executive
Gardner, Howard Alan travel marketing executive, travel writer and editor
Gareis, Robert J. lawyer
Garnett, Marion Winston judge
Garrigan, Richard Thomas finance educator, consultant, editor
Garth, Bryant Geoffrey law educator, foundation executive
Gartner, Lawrence Mitchel pediatrician, medical college educator
Garvey, Michael J. lawyer
Garvey, Richard J. lawyer
Gates, Stephen Frye lawyer
Gaynor, James M., Jr. lawyer
Gearen, John J. lawyer
Gecht, Martin Louis physician, bank executive
Gehr, Mary illustrator, painter, printmaker
Geiman, J. Robert lawyer
Geis, Norman Winer lawyer
Genetski, Robert James economist
George, John Martin, Jr. lawyer
Geraghty, Thomas F. law educator
Geraldson, Raymond I. lawyer
Geraldson, Raymond I., Jr. lawyer
Gerber, Lawrence lawyer
Gerbie, Albert Bernard obstetrician, gynecologist, educator
Gerdes, Neil Wayne library director
Gerek, William Michael lawyer
Gerlits, Francis Joseph lawyer
Gerrish, Brian Albert theologian, educator
Gerson, Jerome Howard lawyer
Gerst, C(ornelius) Gary real estate executive
Gerstman, George Henry lawyer
Gerstner, Robert William structural engineering educator, consultant
Gertz, Elmer lawyer, author, educator
Getz, Bettina lawyer
†Getz, Godfrey Shalom dean, pathology educator
Getzels, Jacob Warren psychologist, educator
Getzendanner, Susan lawyer, former federal judge
Gewertz, Bruce Labe surgeon, educator
Giampietro, Wayne Bruce lawyer
Gibbons, William John lawyer
Gibson, McGuire archaeologist, educator
Gidwitz, Gerald cosmetics company executive
Gidwitz, Ronald J. personal care products company executive
Gies, Thomas Anthony publishing company executive
Giesen, Richard Allyn business executive
Gilbert, Howard N(orman) lawyer
Gilford, Steven Ross lawyer
Gill, Michael J. lawyer
Gill, William Haywood insurance broker
Gillette, Susan Downs advertising executive
Gilman, Sander Lawrence German language educator
Gilson, Jerome lawyer, writer
Gingiss, Benjamin Jack retired formal clothing stores executive
Ginley, Thomas J. banker
Ginsberg, Lewis Robbins lawyer
Ginsburg, Norton Sydney geography educator
Giovacchini, Peter Louis psychoanalyst
Gislason, Eric Arni chemistry educator
Given, Ronald B. lawyer
Gladden, James Walter, Jr. lawyer
Gladstone, Lee psychiatrist, addictionist
Glasner, LeRoy A. public relations executive
Glass, Ronald Lee real estate executive
Glasser, James J. leasing company executive
Gleeson, Paul Francis lawyer
Glieberman, Herbert Allen lawyer
Glovka, Richard Paul lawyer
Goeke, Joseph R. lawyer
Goepp, Robert August dental educator, oral pathologist
Goetz, John Bullock graphic designer
Golan, Stephen Leonard lawyer
Gold, Norman Myron lawyer
Goldberg, Arthur M. gaming and fitness company executive
†Goldberg, Bertrand architect
Goldberg, Sherman I. banking company executive
Goldberg, Stephanie Benson editor, magazine writer, lawyer
Goldberg, Stephen B. law educator
Goldblatt, Stanford Jay lawyer
Golden, Bruce Paul lawyer
Golden, William C. lawyer
Goldiamond, Israel experimental psychologist, educator
Goldman, Louis Budwig lawyer
†Goldmann, James A. healthcare consultant
Goldring, Norman Max advertising executive
Goldsborough, Robert Gerald publishing executive, author
Goldschmidt, Lynn Harvey lawyer
Goldsmith, John Anton linguist, educator
Goldsmith, Julian Royce geochemist, educator
Goldstein, Alfred George retail executive
Goldstein, Norman Ray alcoholic beverage company executive
Goldwasser, Eugene biochemist, educator
Golin, Alvin public relations company executive
Golomb, Harvey Morris oncologist, educator
Golomski, William Arthur consulting company executive
Gomer, Robert chemistry educator
Gonzalez, Ruben professional musician
Goodman, Elliott I(rvin) lawyer
Goodman, Gary Alan lawyer
Goodman, Stuart Lauren lawyer
Gordon, Ellen Rubin candy company executive
Gordon, Ezra architect, educator
Gordon, Jacques Nicholas real estate economist
†Gordon, Melvin Jay food company executive, diversified executive
Gordon, Phillip lawyer
Gordon, William A. lawyer
Gorter, James Polk investment banker
Goschi, Nicholas Peter lawyer
Goss, Howard S(imon) manufacturing executive
Goss, Richard Henry lawyer
Gossett, Philip musicologist
Gottlieb, Gidon Alain Guy law educator
Gottschall, Joan B. judge
Gould, Arthur Irwin lawyer
Gould, John Philip economist, educator
†Gould, Samuel Halpert pediatrics educator
Graber, Doris Appel political scientist, editor, author
Graber, Thomas M. orthodontist
Grabowski, Roger J. business, intangible assets, real estate appraiser
Grace, Mark Eugene professional baseball player
Gradowski, Stanley Joseph, Jr. publishing company executive
Grady, John F. federal judge
Grady, Mark F. law educator
Graettinger, John Sells physician, educator
Graham, David F. lawyer
Graham, Jarlath John publishing executive
Graham, Patricia Albjerg education educator, foundation executive
Graham, Robert L. lawyer
Gralen, Donald John lawyer
Granger, Bill columnist
Grant, Dennis newspaper publishing executive
Grant, Paul Bernard industrial relations educator
Grant, Robert McQueen humanities educator
Grant, Robert Nathan lawyer
Graupe, Daniel electrical and computer engineering educator, systems and biomedical engineer
Graves, Robert Lawrence mathematician, educator
Gray, Hanna Holborn history educator
Gray, James S. lawyer
Gray, Milton Hefter lawyer
†Gray, Paul L. art dealer
Gray, Richard art dealer, consultant, holding company executive
Grayck, Marcus Daniel lawyer
Grayhack, John Thomas urologist, educator
Green, William Robert architect
Greenbaum, Kenneth lawyer
Greenberg, Arthur A. diversified real estate and financial services executive, manufacturing company executive
Greenberg, Bernard entomologist, educator
Greenberger, Ernest lawyer
Greenblatt, Ray Harris lawyer
Greenblatt, Russell Edward lawyer, consultant
Greene, Robert Bernard, Jr. (Bob Greene) broadcast television correspondent, columnist, author
Greene-Mercier, Marie Zoe sculptor
Gregg, Jon Mann lawyer
Gregory, Byron L. lawyer
Grenesko, Donald C. publishing company executive
†Griffin, Andrew Joseph pediatrician
Griffin, Hugh C. lawyer
Griffin, Jean Latz newspaper reporter
Griffith, B(ezaleel) Herold physician, educator, plastic surgeon
Griffith, Donald Kendall lawyer
Grimes, Hugh Gavin physician
Grimm, Terry M. lawyer
Grimm, Victor E. lawyer
Griswold, Frank Tracy, III bishop
Gross, Dorothy-Ellen library director, dean
Gross, Theodore Lawrence university administrator, author
Grossi, Francis Xavier, Jr. lawyer, educator
Grossman, Robert Mayer lawyer
Grossweiner, Leonard Irwin physicist, educator
Grove, Helen Harriet historian, artist
Gruber, William Paul journalist
Grunsfeld, Ernest Alton, III architect
Gucker, Jane Gleason architect
Guenzel, Paul Walter corporate executive
Guillen, Oswaldo Jose Barrios (Ozzie Guillen) baseball player
Gunn, Robert Murray lawyer, farmer
Gupta, Krishna Chandra mechanical engineering educator
Guralnick, Sidney Aaron civil engineering educator
Guthman, Jack lawyer
Gutmann, David Leo psychology educator
Gwinn, Robert P. publishing executive
Haarlow, John B. lawyer
Haas, Howard Green bedding manufacturing company executive
Haas, Jonathan museum research organization executive
Haber, Meryl Harold physician, educator, author
Hablutzel, Margo Lynn lawyer
Hackl, Donald John architect
Haddad, James Brian lawyer, law educator
Haddix, Carol Ann Mighton journalist
Haderlein, Thomas M. lawyer
Haertel, Charles Wayne minister
Haffner, Charles Christian, III retired printing company executive
Hagan, Robert K. lawyer
Hague, Richard Norris architect
Hahn, Frederic Louis lawyer
Haines, Martha Mahan lawyer
Hales, Daniel B. lawyer
Haley, Clifton Edward car rental company executive
Haley, George Romance languages educator
Hall, Joan M. lawyer
Hall, Sophia Harriet judge
Hall, Tom T. songwriter, performer
Hall, William King manufacturing company executive
Hallagan, Robert E. management consultant
Halpern, Jack chemist, educator
Hamada, Robert S(eiji) economist, educator
Hambrick, Ernestine colon and rectal surgeon
Hamilton, Thomas Mackin, Jr. lawyer
Hamister, Donald Bruce electronics company executive
Hammesfahr, Robert Winter lawyer
Hamp, Eric Pratt linguist
Hanbury, Marshall E. lawyer
Hand, Elbert O. clothing manufacturing and retailing company executive
Hand, Roger physician, educator
Handler, Steven P. lawyer
Hannah, Wayne Robertson, Jr. lawyer
Hannan, C(hristie) Phillip health facility administrator
Hannay, William Mouat, III lawyer
Hansen, Carl R. management consultant
Hansen, Claire V. financial executive
Hanson, Floyd Bliss applied mathematician, computational scientist, mathematical biologist
Hanson, Richard A. lawyer
Hanson, Ronald William lawyer
Hanzlik, Paul F. lawyer
Hardgrove, James Alan lawyer
Harding, James Warren finance company executive
Hardy, David Jerry lawyer
Haring, Olga Munk medical educator, physician
Harmon, Robert Lon lawyer
Harper, Doyal Alexander, Jr. astronomer, educator
Harrington, Carol A. lawyer
Harrington, James Timothy lawyer
Harris, Chauncy Dennison geographer, educator
Harris, Donald Ray lawyer
Harris, Irving Brooks cosmetics executive
Harris, Jules Eli medical educator, physician, clinical scientist, administrator
†Harris, King William manufacturing company executive
Harris, Neil history educator
†Harrison, E. Hunter rail transportation executive
Harrold, Bernard lawyer
Hart, Cecil William Joseph otolaryngologist, head and neck surgeon
Hart, William Thomas federal judge
Hartigan, Neil F. lawyer, former state official
Hartnett, James Patrick engineering educator
Harvanek, Robert Francis philosophy educator, clergyman
Harvey, Katherine Abler civic worker
Harvey, Paul news commentator, author, columnist
Harvey, Ronald Gilbert research chemist
Haselkorn, Robert virology educator
Haselton, Forrest Ronald retail company executive
Hassan, M. Zia management educator
Hast, Malcolm Howard medical educator, scientist
Hasten, Michael V. lawyer
Haupt, Roger A. advertising executive
Havdala, Henri Salomon anesthesiologist, educator, consultant
Hawkinson, John former investment management company executive
Hay, Howard newspaper publishing executive
Hayden, Carla Diane librarian, educator
Hayes, David John Arthur, Jr. legal association executive
†Hayes, Patrick G. public health administrator
Hayes, Richard Johnson association executive, lawyer
Hayes, William Aloysius economics educator
Haymes, David Allen architect
Hayward, Thomas Zander, Jr. lawyer
Head, Patrick James lawyer
Headrick, Daniel Richard history and social sciences educator
Heagy, Thomas Charles banker
Heatwole, Mark M. lawyer
Heckman, James Joseph economist, econometrician, educator
Hefner, Christie Ann publishing executive and marketing executive
Hefner, Philip James theologian
Heidrick, Gardner Wilson management consultant
Heidrick, Robert Lindsay management consultant
Heilbrunn, Jeffrey trade association administrator
Heindl, Warren Anton law educator, retired
Heine, Spencer H. corporate lawyer, real estate executive
Heinecken, Robert Friedli art educator, artist
Heineman, Ben Walter corporation executive
Heineman, Natalie (Mrs. Ben W. Heineman) civic worker
Heinz, John Peter lawyer, educator
Heinz, William Denby lawyer
Heisler, Quentin George, Jr. lawyer
Heiss, Robin lawyer
Heitland, Ann Rae lawyer
Heller, Paul medical educator
Heller, Reinhold August art educator, consultant
Heller, Stanley J. lawyer, physician
Hellie, Richard Russian history educator, researcher
Hellman, Samuel radiologist, physician, educator
Helman, Robert Alan lawyer
Helmbold, Nancy Pearce classical languages educator
Helmholz, R(ichard) H(enry) law educator
Heltne, Paul Gregory museum executive
Hengstler, Gary Ardell publisher, editor, lawyer
Henikoff, Leo M., Jr. academic administrator, medical educator
Henning, Joel Frank lawyer, author, publisher, consultant
Henning, Mark G. lawyer
Henry, Charles Joseph options exchange board executive
Henry, Frederick Edward lawyer
Henry, Patricia Jean educational association administrator, consumer products company executive
Henry, Robert John lawyer
Hensel, Paul H. lawyer
Herbolsheimer, Henrietta physician, consultant
Herbst, Arthur Lee obstetrician-gynecologist
Herguth, Robert John columnist
Herman, Sidney N. lawyer
Hermann, Edward Robert occupational and environmental health consultant
Herpe, David A. lawyer
Herzel, Leo lawyer
Herzog, Fred F. legal educator
Hess, Peter A. lawyer
Hess, Sidney J., Jr. lawyer
Hesse, Carolyn Sue lawyer
Hester, Thomas Patrick lawyer
Heuer, Michael Alexander dentist, educator
Hewitt, Brian journalist
Hickey, John Thomas, Jr. lawyer
Hickman, Frederic W. lawyer
Hicks, Sherman Gregory bishop

Higgins, Jack *editorial cartoonist*
Higgins, Ruth Ellen *theatre producer*
Hilborn, Michael G. *lawyer, real estate development executive*
Hildebrand, Roger Henry *astrophysicist, physicist*
Hill, Arthur J. *real estate company executive*
Hiller, David Dean *lawyer*
Hilliard, David Craig *lawyer*
Hillis, Margaret *conductor, musician*
†Hillman, Lee Scott *financial executive*
Himes, Laurence Austin *professional baseball executive*
Himmelfarb, John David *artist*
Hinchliff, James Thomas *lawyer*
Hines, James Rodger *surgeon*
Hinkelman, Ruth Amidon *insurance company executive*
Hinojosa, Raul *physician, ear pathology researcher*
Hirshman, Harold Carl *lawyer*
Hirshman, Linda Redlick *law educator*
Hitch, James T., III *lawyer*
Hoban, George Savre *lawyer*
Hobbs, Marvin *engineering executive*
Hodes, Scott *lawyer*
Hoeft, Steven H. *lawyer*
Hoey, Rita Marie *public relations executive*
Hofer, Roy Ellis *lawyer*
Hoff, William Bruce, Jr. *lawyer*
Hoffman, Douglas W. *lawyer*
Hoffman, Richard Bruce *lawyer*
Hoffman, Valerie Jane *lawyer*
Hoffmann, Howard M. *lawyer*
Hogarth, Robin Miles *academic administrator, educator*
Holabird, John Augur, Jr. *retired architect*
Holderman, James F., Jr. *federal judge*
Holland, Eugene, Jr. *lumber company executive*
Holland, Jean *elementary education educator*
Hollies, Linda Hall *minister, educator, author, publisher*
Hollins, Mitchell Leslie *lawyer*
Hollis, Donald Roger *banker*
Holmberg, Ronald K. *insurance company executive*
Holmen, Neil E. *lawyer*
Holmes, Colgate Frederick *hotel executive*
Holmes, Stephen T. *political science and law educator*
Holt, Thomas Cleveland *history educator, consultant, writer, lecturer*
Holton, Lisa *newspaper editor, journalist*
Holtzman, Jerome *journalist, columnist, publisher*
Holzer, Edwin *advertising executive*
Homans, Peter *psychology and religious studies educator*
Honig, George Raymond *pediatrician*
†Hoover, Paul *poet*
Horne, John R. *farm equipment company executive*
Horwath, Leslie Kathleen *lawyer*
Horwich, Allan *lawyer*
Horwitz, Irwin Daniel *otolaryngologist, educator*
Hoskins, Richard Jerold *lawyer*
Hotz, V. Joseph *economics educator*
†Howard, Vance Francis *insurance company executive*
Howe, Jonathan Thomas *lawyer*
Howell, R(obert) Thomas, Jr. *lawyer, food company executive*
Hron, Michael G. *lawyer*
Hubbard, Antoinette Ziegler *telecommunications executive*
Huber, Richard Leslie *banker*
Hucker, Brian S. *lawyer*
Huckman, Michael Saul *neuroradiologist, educator*
Hudnut, William Herbert, III *civic federation executive, political scientist*
Huebsch, Robert P. *lawyer*
Huggins, Charles Brenton *surgical educator*
Huggins, Rollin Charles, Jr. *lawyer*
Hughes, John Russell *physician, educator*
Hughes, Joyce Anne *law educator*
Hummel, Gregory William *lawyer*
Hunt, Lawrence Halley, Jr. *lawyer*
Hunt, Roger Schermerhorn *hospital administrator*
Hunt, Steven J(ames) *media and advertising executive*
Hunter, James Alexander *surgeon, educator*
Hunter, J(ames) Paul *English language educator, literary critic, historian*
Huntley, Robert Stephen *newspaper editor*
Hurlbert, Robert P. *lawyer*
Hurley, William James, Jr. *English language educator*
Husar, John Paul *newspaper columnist, television panelist*
Hussey, Charles E., II *lawyer*
Husting, Peter Marden *advertising agency executive*
Huston, DeVerille Anne *lawyer*
Huston, John Leo *trade association executive*
Huston, John Lewis *chemistry educator*
Huston, Steven Craig *lawyer*
Hutchins, Harley *lawyer*
Hutchinson, Leland E. *lawyer*
Hutchison, Clyde Allen, Jr. *chemistry educator*
†Huttenlocher, Peter Richard *child neurologist*
Iakovos, (Iakovos Garmatis) *bishop*
Iltis, John Frederic *advertising and public relations company executive*
Inbau, Fred Edward *lawyer, educator, author*
Ingham, Norman William *Russian literature educator, genealogist*
Ingram, Randy Jan *television producer*
Inskeep, Kenneth W. *church administrator*
†Iqbal, Zafar Mohd *cancer researcher, biochemist, pharmacologist, toxicologist, consultant*
Isaacs, Roger David *public relations executive*
Isenbergh, Joseph *law educator*
Ishikawa, Kozo *securities executive*
Ivan, Thomas Nathaniel *professional hockey team executive*
Jachna, Joseph D. *photographer, educator*
Jackson, Jesse Louis *civic and political leader, clergyman*
Jackson, Philip Douglas *professional basketball coach*
Jacobson, David Cary *lawyer*
Jacobson, Harold LeLand *lawyer*
Jacobson, Marian Slutz *lawyer*
Jacobson, Richard Joseph *lawyer*
Jacoby, John Primm *lawyer*
Jacover, Jerold Alan *lawyer*
Jager, Melvin Francis *lawyer*
Jahn, Helmut *architect*
Jahns, Adam A. *banking executive*
Jahns, Jeffrey *lawyer*
Jakstas, Alfred John *museum conservator, consultant*
Jakubik, Jerome W. *lawyer*
Jambor, Robert Vernon *lawyer*

James, A. Lincoln, Sr. *minister, religious organization executive*
Janson, Patrick *singer, actor, conductor, educator*
Jarc, Frank Robert *printing company executive*
†Jasculca, Richard J. *public relations executive*
†Jast, Raymond Joseph *lawyer*
Jeffay, Henry *biochemistry educator*
Jefferson, Wayne *broadcast executive*
Jegen, Sister Carol Frances *religion educator*
†Jenkins, Neil Edmund *lawyer*
Jerome, Jerrold V. *insurance company executive*
Jerrick, Ronald M. *lawyer*
Jock, Paul F., II *lawyer*
Johnson, Argie K. *community school district superintendent*
Johnson, Beverly June *librarian, educator*
Johnson, C. Richard *lawyer*
†Johnson, Cathleen *public relations executive*
Johnson, Chauncey Paul *banker*
Johnson, Daniel Leroy *lawyer*
Johnson, David Gale *economist, educator*
Johnson, Elmer William *lawyer*
Johnson, Gary Thomas *lawyer*
Johnson, Glenn Thompson *judge*
Johnson, H. Arvid *lawyer*
Johnson, Howard Michael *professional baseball player*
Johnson, Janet Helen *Egyptology educator*
Johnson, Joan B. *cosmetics company executive*
Johnson, Lael Frederic *lawyer*
Johnson, Paul Joseph *manufacturing company executive*
Johnson, Richard Fred *lawyer*
Johnson, Robert Bruce *public relations executive*
Johnston, Alan Rogers *lawyer*
Johnston, Thomas Watts *lawyer*
†Joho, Jean Charles *chef, restaurateur*
Jonas, Harry S. *professional society administrator*
Jonasson, Olga *surgeon, educator*
Jones, Barbara Loretta *social services administrator*
†Jones, Dennis Paul *food and consumer goods company executive*
Jones, Emil, Jr. *state senator*
Jones, Peter d'Alroy *history educator, author*
Jones, Richard Cyrus *lawyer*
Jones, Thomas M. *lawyer*
Jordan, Michael Jeffery *professional basketball player, retired baseball player*
Jordan, Michelle Denise *lawyer*
Jordan, V. Craig *endocrine pharmacologist, educator*
Joseph, Robert Thomas *lawyer*
Josephson, Kenneth Bradley *artist, educator*
Joslin, Rodney Dean *lawyer*
Juhl, Loren Earl *lawyer*
Junewicz, James J. *lawyer*
Jurek, Kenneth J. *lawyer*
†Kabelin, Jerrald T. *diversified manufacturing company executive*
Kadanoff, Leo Philip *physicist*
Kahan, Samuel D. *economist*
Kahn, Harold *retail executive*
Kahn, Herta Hess (Mrs. Howard Kahn) *retired stockbroker*
Kahn, James Steven *museum director*
Kaiserlian, Penelope Jane *publishing company executive*
Kamin, Chester Thomas *lawyer*
Kamyszew, Christopher D. *museum curator, executive educator, art consultant*
Kanne, Michael Stephen *federal judge, educator*
Kanwit, Glen Harris *lawyer*
Kaplan, Harold L. *lawyer*
Kaplan, Jared *lawyer*
Kaplan, Morton A. *political science educator*
Kaplan, Sidney Mountbatten *lawyer*
Kaplan, Wayne S. *lawyer*
Karaba, Frank Andrew *lawyer*
Karanikas, Alexander *English language educator, author, actor*
Karge, Stewart W. *lawyer*
Kark, Robert M. *physician, educator*
Karl, Barry Dean *historian, educator*
Karlin, Bernard Richard *principal*
Karp, Robert *surgeon, educator*
Kasenter, Robert Albert *retail executive*
Kass, Leon Richard *life sciences educator*
Kastel, Howard L. *lawyer*
†Kateley, Richard *real estate consultant*
Katten, Melvin L. *lawyer*
Katz, Adrian Izhack *physician, educator*
Katz, Edwin I. *federal judge*
Katz, Harold Ambrose *lawyer, former state legislator*
Katz, Marilyn Faye *communications consultant, political strategist*
Katz, Robert Stephen *rheumatologist, educator*
Katz, Stuart Charles *lawyer, concert jazz musician*
Kaufman, Andrew Michael *lawyer*
Kaufman, Ira Jeffrey *investment banker*
Kazazis, Kostas *linguist, educator*
Kazik, John Stanley *newspaper executive*
Kearney, John Walter *sculptor, painter*
Keck, Robert Clifton *lawyer*
Keck, William *architect*
Keehn, Silas *retired bank executive*
Keenan, James George *classics educator*
†Keller, Eileen R. *chemical company executive accountant*
Kelley, Duane Matthew *lawyer*
Kelley, Michael John *newspaper editor*
Kelly, Arthur Lloyd *management and investment company executive*
Kelly, Charles Arthur *lawyer*
Kelly, Richard Smith *judge*
Kelly, Robert Donald *management consultant*
Kelman, Robert Andrew *lawyer*
Kempf, Donald G., Jr. *lawyer*
Kendrick, William Monroe *insurance company executive*
Kennedy, Eugene Cullen *psychology educator, writer*
Kennett, Robert L. *publisher*
Kenney, Frank Deming *lawyer*
Kenny, Edmund Joyce *lawyer*
Kent, Conrad S. *chemicals executive*
Kent, Geoffrey *pathology educator, physician*
Kerbis, Gertrude Lempp *architect*
Kessler, Stanton A. *lawyer*
Kestnbaum, Robert Dana *management consultant*
Khalidi, Rashid Ismail *history educator*
Kiel, William Frederick *architectural specifications consultant*
Kierscht, Charles M. *financial company executive*
Kiley, Roger J. *lawyer*
Kim, H. J. (Shaun Kim) *engineer*
King, Andre Richardson *architectural graphic designer*
King, Billie Jean Moffitt *former professional tennis player*

King, Clark Chapman, Jr. *lawyer*
King, David Edgar *librarian, editor*
King, Michael Howard *lawyer*
King, Sharon L. *lawyer*
Kins, Juris *lawyer*
Kinzie, Raymond Wyant *banker, lawyer*
Kipnis, Mark S. *lawyer*
Kipperman, Lawrence I. *lawyer*
Kirby, William Joseph *corporation executive*
Kirkland, John Leonard *lawyer*
Kirschner, Barbara Starrels *pediatric gastroenterologist*
Kirsner, Joseph Barnett *physician, educator*
Kisor, Henry Du Bois *newspaper editor, critic, columnist*
Kissel, Richard John *lawyer*
Kite, Steven B. *lawyer*
Kittle, Charles Frederick *surgeon*
Klapperich, Frank Lawrence, Jr. *investment banker*
Klarich, Nina Marie *economic development executive*
Klaviter, Helen Lothrop *magazine editor*
†Kleckner, Robert A. *accounting firm executive*
Klegerman, Neal Alan *lawyer*
Klein, Michael Sherman *manufacturing executive*
Klement, Vera *artist*
Klenk, James Andrew *lawyer*
Kloc, Emily Alvina *elementary principal*
Klutz, C. H. *church administrator*
Knapp, Donald Roy *musician, educator*
†Knappenberger, Paul Henry, Jr. *science museum director*
Knight, Christopher Nichols *lawyer*
Knoblauch, Mark George *librarian*
Knox, James Edwin *lawyer*
Knox, Lance Lethbridge *venture capital executive*
Knuti, Robert A. *lawyer*
Kobs, James Fred *advertising agency executive*
Kocoras, Charles Petros *federal judge*
Koehler, Irmgard Kilb *dermatologist, educator*
Koenig, Bonnie *non-profit organization administrator*
Koester, Robert Gregg *record company executive*
Koga, Mary *artist, photographer, social worker*
Kohn, Shalom L. *lawyer*
Kohn, William Irwin *lawyer*
Kohrman, Arthur Fisher *pediatric educator*
Kolb, Gwin Jackson *language professional, educator*
Kolek, Robert Edward *lawyer*
Koltin, Allan David *accountant*
Komie, Stephen Mark *lawyer*
Koncel, James E. *electrical engineer*
Kopec, Joseph Arthur *public relations executive*
Kopel, David *psychologist, educator*
Koran, Janet M. *lawyer*
Kornel, Ludwig *medical educator, physician, scientist*
Kortright, Richard T. *lawyer*
Koten, John A. *retired communications executive*
Kotulak, Ronald *newspaper science writer*
Kouvel, James Spyros *physicist, educator*
Koven, Howard Richard *lawyer*
Kowitt, Arthur Jay *lawyer*
Kozitka, Richard Eugene *consumer products company executive*
Kraft, Sumner Charles *physician, educator*
Krainik, Ardis *opera company executive*
Kraus, Herbert Myron *public relations executive*
Kravitt, Jason Harris Paperno *lawyer*
Krawetz, Arthur Altshuler *chemist, science administrator*
Kriss, Robert J. *lawyer*
Kroch, Carl Adolph *retail executive*
Kroll, Barry Lewis *lawyer*
Krueger, Bonnie Lee *editor, writer*
Krueger, Herbert William *lawyer*
Krug, Judith Fingeret *association administrator*
Krupka, Robert George *lawyer*
Krupnik, Vee M. *financial company executive*
Kruskal, William Henry *statistician, educator*
Kubida, Judith Ann *museum administrator*
Kucera, Daniel Jerome *lawyer*
Kuchta, Thomas Walter *accountant, tax consultant*
Kudish, David J. *financial executive*
†Kudo, Irma Setsuko *not-for-profit executive director*
Kullberg, Duane Reuben *accounting firm executive*
Kunkle, Sandra Lee *brokerage house executive, sales executive*
Kunkle, William Joseph, Jr. *lawyer*
Kupcinet, Irv *columnist*
Kupperman, Melvin *civil engineer, construction and development company executive*
Kurland, Philip B. *lawyer, educator*
Kurtich, John William *architect, film-maker, educator*
Kuta, Jeffrey Theodore *lawyer*
Kyle, Robert Campbell, II *publishing executive*
Lach, Alma Elizabeth *food and cooking writer, consultant*
Ladd, Jeffrey Raymond *lawyer*
Lafontant-Mankarious, Jewel (Mrs. Naguib S. Mankarious) *diplomat, lawyer*
Laidlaw, Andrew R. *lawyer*
Laitin, David Dennis *political science educator*
Lamb, Gordon Howard *academic administrator*
Landan, Henry Sinclair *lawyer*
Landau, Richard L. *physician, educator*
Landers, Ann (Mrs. Esther P. Lederer) *columnist*
Landes, William M. *law educator*
Landow-Esser, Janine Marise *lawyer*
Landsberg, Lewis *endocrinologist, medical researcher*
Landsman, Stephen A. *lawyer*
Lane, Kenneth Edwin *retired advertising agency executive*
Lane, Robert G. *lawyer*
Lane, Ronald Alan *lawyer*
Laner, Richard Warren *lawyer*
Lang, Richard A. *lawyer*
Langbaum, Gary Alan *financial executive*
Langhenry, John Godfred, Jr. *lawyer*
Langsley, Donald Gene *psychiatrist, medical board executive*
Lannert, Robert Cornelius *manufacturing company executive*
Lanzl, Lawrence Herman *medical physicist*
Lapidus, Allan E. *lawyer*
LaPointe-Peterson, Kittie Vadis *choreographer, ballet school director, educator*
Lappin, Richard C. *corporate executive*
Larsen, Paul Emanuel *religious organization administrator*
Larson, Allan Louis *political scientist, educator, lay church worker*
Larson, Harry Robert *investment banking executive*
LaRue, Paul Hubert *lawyer*
LaRue, Paul Hubert, Jr. *lawyer*
LaSage, John David *public relations firm executive*
Lasky, Laurence D. *lawyer*

Lassar, Scott R. *lawyer*
Lassers, Willard J. *judge*
Latimer, Kenneth Alan *lawyer*
Lauer, Robert Lee *consumer products executive*
Laumann, Edward Otto *sociology educator*
LaVelle, Arthur *anatomy educator*
Lawler, James Ronald *French language educator*
Lazar, Ludmila *concert pianist, educator*
Lazarus, George Milton *newspaper columnist*
Leahigh, Alan Kent *public relations executive*
Lebedow, Aaron Louis *consulting company executive*
Lecker, Abraham *former banker*
Leckey, Andrew A. *financial columnist*
Lederman, Leon Max *physicist, educator*
LeDuc, John Andre *lawyer*
†Lee, Raphael Carl *plastic surgeon*
Lee, William Marshall *lawyer*
LeFevre, Perry Deyo *minister, theology educator*
Leff, Alan Richard *medical educator*
Lefkow, Joan Humphrey *judge*
Legge Kemp, Diane *architect, landscape architect*
Lehman, George Morgan *food sales executive*
Lehner, Mark *archaeologist, educator*
Lehrman, Nat *magazine editor*
†Leiden, Jeffrey Marc *molecular biologist, cardiologist*
Leigh, Sherren *communications executive, editor, publisher*
Leighton, George Neves *retired federal judge*
Leinenweber, Harry D. *federal judge*
Leiseca, Sergio A. Jr. *lawyer*
Leisten, Arthur Gaynor *lawyer*
Lemein, Gregg D. *lawyer*
Lennes, Gregory *manufacturing and financing company executive*
Lerner, Nathan Bernard *artist*
Lesly, Philip *public relations counsel*
†Lester, June *library, information management educator*
Lester, Robin Dale *private school educator, author, former headmaster*
Lev, Allen P. *lawyer*
Levenfeld, Milton Arthur *lawyer*
†Leventhal, Bennett Lee *psychiatry and pediatrics educator, administrator*
Levi, Edward Hirsch *former attorney general, university president emeritus*
Levi, John G. *lawyer*
Levin, Charles Edward *lawyer*
Levin, Jack S. *lawyer*
Levin, Michael David *lawyer*
Levine, Donald Nathan *sociologist, educator*
Levine, Laurence Harvey *lawyer*
Levi-Setti, Riccardo *physicist, director*
Levit, Louis William *lawyer*
Levitan, Valerie Fassler *fraternal organization executive*
Levy, Arnold S(tuart) *real estate company executive*
Levy, Donald Harris *chemistry educator*
Levy, Richard Herbert *lawyer*
Lewis, Charles A. *investment company executive*
Lewis, Harriet Gerbert *plumbing fixtures manufacturing company executive*
Lewis, John D. *financial services company executive*
Lewis, Julius *lawyer*
Lewis, Philip *educational and technical consultant*
Lewis, Phillip Harold *museum curator*
Lewis, Ramsey Emanuel, Jr. *pianist, composer*
Lewis, Sylvia Gail *journalist*
Lewy, Ralph I. *hotel executive*
Liao, Shutsung *biochemist*
Lichter, Edward Arthur *physician, educator*
Liddy, Edward M. *manufacturing company executive*
Lieb, Michael *English educator, humanities educator*
Lieberman, Myron *lawyer*
Light, John Caldwell *chemistry educator*
Light, Kenneth Benjamin *manufacturing company executive*
Lin, Chin-Chu *physician, educator, researcher*
Lin, James Chih-I *biomedical and electrical engineer, educator*
Lincoln, Sandy *investment management executive*
Lind, Jon Robert *lawyer*
Lindberg, George W. *federal judge*
Linde, Ronald Keith *corporate executive, private investor*
Linden, Henry Robert *chemical engineering research executive*
Linklater, William Joseph *lawyer*
Lipinski, Ann Marie *newspaper editor*
Lippe, Melvin Karl *lawyer*
Lipton, Lois Jean *lawyer*
Lipton, Richard M. *lawyer*
List, David Patton *lawyer*
Listrom, Linda L. *lawyer*
Litweiler, John Berkey *writer, editor*
Litwin, Burton Howard *lawyer*
Liu, Ben-chieh *economist*
Livingston, Homer J., Jr. *stock exchange executive*
Livingston, Theodore A., Jr. *lawyer*
Lloyd, William F. *lawyer*
Locher, Richard Earl *editorial cartoonist*
Lockwood, Frank James *manufacturing company executive*
Lockwood, Gary Lee *lawyer*
Loesch, Katharine Taylor (Mrs. John George Loesch) *communication and theatre educator*
Logemann, Jerilyn Ann *speech pathologist, educator*
Lohan, Dirk *architect*
Lohman, Gordon R. *manufacturing executive*
Long, Earline Davis *elementary education educator*
Longman, Gary Lee *accountant*
Longworth, Richard Cole *journalist*
Looman, James R. *lawyer*
Lopata, Helena Znaniecka *sociologist, researcher, educator*
Lorand, Laszlo *biochemist, educator*
Lorch, Kenneth F. *lawyer*
Lorenz, Hugo Albert *insurance executive*
Lorenz, Katherine Mary *banker*
Lorenz, Richard Theodore, Jr. *lawyer*
Lorie, James Hirsch *business administration educator*
Lorincz, Allan Levente *physician, educator*
Lotocky, Innocent Hilarius *bishop*
Lott, David Stuart *lawyer*
Loucks, Ralph Bruce, Jr. *investment company executive*
Love, Clinton Kenneth *finance company executive*
†Lowenstine, James R. *metal products manufacturing company executive*
Lowrie, William G. *oil company executive*
Lowry, James Hamilton *management consultant*
Lubawski, James Lawrence *health care administrator*
Lubet, Steven *law educator*
Lubin, Donald G. *lawyer*
Lucas, Jo Desha *law educator, editor*
Lucas, John Kenneth *lawyer*

Lumpkin, John Robert *public health physician, state official*
Lundberg, George David, II *medical editor, pathologist*
Lundergan, Barbara Keough *lawyer*
Lundy, Joseph R. *lawyer*
Lurie, Paul Michael *lawyer*
Luscombe, George A. II *lawyer*
Lutter, Paul Allen *lawyer*
Lutz, Karl Evan *lawyer*
Lykos, Peter George *educator, scientist*
Lyman, Arthur Joseph *financial executive*
Lynch, John Peter *lawyer*
Lynn, Laurence Edwin, Jr. *university administrator, educator*
Lyon, Jeffrey *journalist, author*
Lyons, Jeffrey *film critic*
Lythcott, Marcia A. *newspaper editor*
†Ma, Tai-Loi *library curator, Chinese studies specialist*
MacCarthy, Terence Francis *lawyer*
MacDougal, Gary Edward *corporate director, foundation trustee*
Macey, Jonathan R. *law educator*
MacLane, Saunders *mathematician, educator*
Macneil, Ian Roderick *lawyer, educator*
Macsai, John *architect*
Madansky, Albert *statistics educator*
Madigan, John William *publishing executive*
Maggio, Michael John *artistic director*
Maher, David Willard *lawyer*
Maher, Francesca Marciniak *lawyer*
Mahowald, Anthony Peter *geneticist, cell biologist, educator*
Makinen, Marvin William *biophysicist, educator*
Malato, Stephen H. *lawyer*
Malik, Raymond Howard *economist, scientist, corporate executive, multi-lingual, inventor, educator*
Malkin, Cary Jay *lawyer*
Malkin, Judd D. *diversified corporation executive*
Mallory, Robert Mark *controller, finance executive*
Malone, James Laurence, III *lawyer*
Malott, Robert Harvey *manufacturing company executive*
Malovance, Gregory J. *lawyer*
Malstrom, Robert A. *lawyer*
Maltz, J. Herbert *physician, hospital director*
Mancoff, Neal Alan *lawyer*
Mandell, Floyd A. *lawyer*
Manelli, Donald Dean *screenwriter, film producer*
Mangler, Robert James *lawyer*
Mann, H. George *lawyer*
Manning, Frederick James *insurance company executive*
Manny, Carter Hugh, Jr. *architect, foundation administrator*
†Manos, John *editor-in-chief*
Maram, Barry S. *lawyer*
Marcus, Joseph *child psychiatrist*
Marcus, Stephen A. *lawyer*
Marcuse, Manfred Joachim *paper products executive*
Margoliash, Emanuel *biochemist, educator*
Margolis, Jeremy *lawyer*
Marineau, Philip Albert *food company executive*
Mariotti, Jay Anthony *journalist*
Marks, Dennis A. *lawyer*
Marks, Jerome *lawyer*
Markus, Robert Michael *journalist*
Marovich, George M. *federal judge*
Marovitz, Abraham Lincoln *judge*
Marovitz, James Lee *lawyer*
Marovitz, William A. *state senator, lawyer*
Marsh, Jeanne Cay *social welfare educator, researcher*
Marshall, Cody *bishop*
Marshall, Donald Glenn *English language and literature educator*
Marshall, Eric C. *lawyer*
Marshall, John David *lawyer*
Marshall, Prentice H., Jr. *lawyer*
Marshall, Prentice Henry *federal judge*
Marston-Scott, Mary Vesta *nurse, educator*
Martin, Arthur Mead *lawyer*
Martin, Barbara Jean *elementary school principal*
Martin, R. Eden *lawyer*
Marty, Martin Emil *religion educator, editor*
Marwedel, Warren John *lawyer*
Marx, David, Jr. *lawyer*
Mason, Bruce *advertising agency executive*
†Mason, Earl Leonard *steel company executive*
Mason, Henry Lowell, III *lawyer*
Massolo, Arthur James *banker*
Matasar, Ann B. *former dean, business and political science educator*
Mateles, Richard Isaac *biotechnologist*
Matis, Nina B. *lawyer*
Matthei, Edward Hodge *architect*
Mattos Neto, Sebastiao De Souza *lawyer*
Mattson, Stephen Joseph *lawyer*
Maxson, M. Finley *lawyer*
May, J. Peter *mathematics educator*
Mayer, Frank D., Jr. *lawyer*
Mayer, Raymond Richard *business administration educator*
Mayers, Barbara W. *lawyer*
Mayo, J. Haskell, Jr. *bishop*
Mazenko, Gene Francis *physics educator*
†McAuliffe, Richard L. *church official*
McBreen, Maura Ann *lawyer*
McCaleb, Malcolm, Jr. *lawyer*
McCarron, John Francis *columnist*
Mc Carter, John Wilbur, Jr. *corporation executive*
McCarthy, Paul *lawyer*
McCarville, Mark John *food company executive*
McCaskey, Edward W. *professional football team executive*
Mc Caskey, Raymond F. *insurance company executive*
McCausland, Thomas James, Jr. *brokerage house executive*
Mc Clure, James J., Jr. *lawyer, former municipal executive*
McCombs, Hugh R., Jr. *lawyer*
McConahey, Stephen George *securities company executive*
McConnell, E. Hoy, II *advertising executive*
Mc Connell, Michael W. *law educator*
McCormack, Robert Cornelius *investment banker*
McCormick, Steven D. *lawyer*
McCracken, Thomas James, Jr. *lawyer*
McCrone, Walter Cox *research institute executive*
McCue, Howard McDowell, III *lawyer, educator*
McCue, Judith W. *lawyer*
McCullagh, Grant Gibson *architect*
McCullough, Michael William, Jr. *minister, educator, researcher, writer, missionary, gospel singer, consultant*
McCullough, Richard Lawrence *advertising agency executive*
McCurry, Margaret Irene *architect, educator*
McDaniel, Charles-Gene *journalism educator, writer*
McDermott, John H(enry) *lawyer*
McDermott, Robert B. *lawyer*
McDonald, Thomas Alexander *lawyer*
McDonough, John Michael *lawyer*
McDougal, Alfred Leroy *publisher*
Mc Dougall, Dugald Stewart *retired lawyer*
McDowell, William S. *lawyer*
McFarland, Claudette *real estate executive*
McGarr, Frank James *retired federal judge, dispute resolution consultant*
McGinn, Bernard John *religious educator*
McGivern, Arthur J. *corporate lawyer, food products company executive*
McGrath, William Joseph *lawyer*
McGuigan, John V. *lawyer*
Mc Guirt, Wayne Robert *publishing company executive*
McIntyre, Kathryn Joan *publisher, editorial director*
Mc Kay, Neil *banker*
McKee, Keith Earl *manufacturing technology executive*
Mc Kenna, Thomas Joseph *advertising executive*
McKenzie, Robert E. *lawyer*
McKinley, Vicky Lynn *biology educator*
†McKinney, William T. *psychiatrist, educator*
McLaughlin, John Michael, Jr. *engineer, engineering company executive*
McLaughlin, T. Mark *lawyer*
McLean, Robert David *lawyer*
McMahon, Thomas Michael *lawyer*
McMenamin, John Robert *lawyer*
McMillan, C. Steven *manufacturing company executive*
McNeely, Stephen Allen *outdoor advertising company executive*
McNeill, G. David *psychologist, educator*
McNeill, Robert Patrick *investment counselor*
McNeill, Thomas B. *lawyer*
McQueen, Thomas K. *lawyer*
McVisk, William Kilburn *lawyer*
McWhirter, Bruce J. *lawyer*
McWilliams, Dennis Michael *lawyer*
Measelle, Richard L. *accountant*
Mecklenburg, Gary Alan *hospital executive*
Medved, Michael *film critic, author*
Medvin, Harvey Norman *financial executive, treasurer*
Meers, Henry W. *investment banker*
Mehlman, Mark Franklin *lawyer*
Melamed, Leo *investment company executive*
Melbinger, Michael S. *lawyer*
Meleney, John Alexander *lawyer*
Melton, David Reuben *lawyer*
Meltzer, Bernard David *legal educator*
Menchin, Robert Stanley *marketing executive*
Menson, Richard L. *lawyer*
†Menzer, John Bruce *financial executive*
Mercer, David Robinson *association executive*
†Meritt, Dennis Andrew *zoo administrator*
Merrill, Thomas Wendell *lawyer, law educator*
Metz, Charles Edgar *radiology educator*
Meyer, Charles Appleton *former retailing executive*
Meyer, Donald Gordon *college dean, educator*
Meyer, Edward Paul *advertising executive*
Meyer, J. Theodore *lawyer*
Meyer, Michael Louis *lawyer*
Meyer, Paul Reims, Jr. *orthopedic surgeon*
Meyer, Peter *physicist, educator*
Meyer, Raymond Joseph *former college basketball coach*
Meyers, Dorothy *adult education educator, writer*
Michalak, Edward Francis *lawyer*
Michelson, Irving *aerospace engineer*
Migala, Lucyna Jozefa *broadcast journalist, arts administrator, radio station executive*
Migdal, Sheldon Paul *lawyer*
Mikesell, Marvin Wray *geography educator*
Miletich, Ivo *library and information scientist, bibliographer, educator, linguist, literature research specialist*
Millard, Richard Steven *lawyer*
Miller, Bernard Joseph, Jr. *advertising executive*
Miller, Charles S. *clergy member, church administrator*
Miller, Frederick Staten *music educator, academic administrator*
Miller, Geoffrey Parsons *law educator*
Miller, Irving Franklin *chemical engineering educator, academic administrator*
Miller, James Edwin, Jr. *English language educator*
Miller, Jay Alan *civil rights association executive*
Miller, Mark *newspaper editor*
Miller, Maurice James *lawyer*
Miller, Merton Howard *finance educator*
Miller, Michael I. *lawyer*
Miller, Patrick William *research administrator, educator*
Miller, Paul J. *lawyer*
†Miller, Sheldon Irvin *psychiatrist, educator*
Miller, Stephen Ralph *lawyer*
Miller, Theodore Norman *lawyer*
Miller, William H. *public relations executive*
Millichap, Joseph Gordon *neurologist, educator*
Millner, Robert B. *lawyer*
Mills, Martha Alice *lawyer*
Milnikel, Robert Saxon *lawyer*
Milstein, Albert *lawyer*
Mindes, Gayle Dean *education educator*
Miner, Thomas Hawley *international entrepreneur*
Minichello, Dennis *lawyer*
Minkowycz, W. J. *mechanical engineering educator*
Minnick, Malcolm L., Jr. *clergy member, church administrator*
Minogue, John P. *academic administrator, priest, educator*
Minow, Josephine Baskin *civic worker*
Minow, Newton Norman *lawyer*
Mintz, Harry *artist, educator*
Mirkin, Bernard Leo *clinical pharmacologist, pediatrician*
Mirza, David Brown *economist, educator*
Mitchell, Daniel Ray *lawyer*
Mitchell, Douglas Farrell *trust company executive, lawyer*
Mitchell, Lee Mark *communications executive, investment fund manager, lawyer*
Mitchell, W. J. T. *English language, literature and visual arts educator, editor*
Mlsna, Timothy Martin *lawyer*
Moawad, Atef *obstetrician-gynecologist, educator*
Moelmann, Lawrence R. *lawyer*
Moffatt, Joyce Anne *performing arts executive*
Moller-Gunderson, Mark Robert *minister, administrator*
Moller-Gunderson, Mary Ann *clergy member, church administrator*
Molloy, James B. *corrugated packaging executive*
Moltz, Marshall Jerome *lawyer*
Mone, Peter John *lawyer*
Montgomery, Charles Barry *lawyer*
Montgomery, Charles Howard *retired bank executive*
Moor, Roy Edward *finance educator*
Moore, John Ronald *manufacturing executive*
Moore, Paul Brian *geophysical sciences educator*
Moran, James Byron *federal judge*
Moran, John Thomas, Jr. *lawyer*
Morency, Paula J. *lawyer*
Morgan, Howard Campbell *banker*
Morisato, Susan Cay *actuary*
Morris, Norval *criminologist, educator*
Morris, Ralph William *chronopharmacologist*
Morrison, John Horton *lawyer*
Morrison, Michael P. *lawyer*
Morrison, Portia Owen *lawyer*
Morrissey, Francis Daniel *lawyer*
Morrow, John Ellsworth *lawyer*
Morrow, Richard Martin *retired oil company executive*
Morsch, Thomas Harvey *lawyer*
Mortensen, Audrey R. *church administrator*
Mosena, David R. *aviation commissioner*
Moses, Irving Byron *architect*
Moskow, Michael H. *federal official*
Mosley, Elaine Christian Savage *principal, chief education officer, consultant*
†Moss, Gerald S. *dean, medical educator*
Mourek, Joseph Edward *musician*
Moutoussamy, John Warren *architect*
Mrozek, Donald L. *lawyer*
Muchin, Allan B. *lawyer*
Mueller, Gregory M. *museum curator, botanist, researcher*
Muench, John E. *lawyer*
Mukoyama, James Hidefumi, Jr. *securities executive*
Mullan, John Francis (Sean Mullan) *neurosurgeon, educator*
Mullen, J. Thomas *lawyer*
Muller, Dietrich Alfred Helmut *physicist, educator*
Muller, Ralph W. *hospital administrator*
Mullin, Leo Francis *banker*
Mulvihill, Terence Joseph *investment banking executive*
Mumford, Manly Whitman *lawyer*
Mundlak, Yair *agriculture and economics educator*
Munitz, Gerald F. *lawyer*
Munizzi, Pam *state senator*
Munson, James Calfee *lawyer*
Murata, Tadao *engineering and computer science educator*
Murdock, Charles William *lawyer, educator*
Murphy, Barth T. *insurance company executive*
Murphy, Ellis *association management executive*
Murphy, Michael Emmett *food company executive*
†Murphy, Newton Jerome *steel company executive, holding company executive*
Murray, Daniel Richard *lawyer*
Murray, Gregory S. *lawyer*
Murray, James Cunningham, Jr. *lawyer*
Murray, Michael J. *bank executive*
Murtaugh, Christopher David *lawyer*
Murtaugh, Michael K. *lawyer*
Murtaugh, Rodger W. *oil company executive*
Musa, Mahmoud Nimir *psychiatry educator*
Myers, Jim *church administrator*
Myers, Lonn William *lawyer*
Myers, Randall Kirk (Randy Myers) *professional baseball player*
†Nachman, Frederick *public relations executive*
Nachman, James L. *lawyer*
Nachman, Norman Harry *lawyer*
Nadherny, Ferdinand *executive recruiting company executive*
Nadler, Mark B. *executive editor*
Nagel, Sidney Robert *physics educator*
Nahrwold, David Lange *surgeon, educator*
Najita, Tetsuo *history educator*
Nakajima, Yasuko *medical educator*
Nambu, Yoichiro *physics educator*
Narahashi, Toshio *pharmacology educator*
Nash, Donald Gene *commodities specialist*
Nash, Robert Coutts *lawyer*
Nason, Robert E. *accountant*
Nault, William Henry *publishing executive*
Neal, John Eric *banking executive*
Neal, Stephen C. *lawyer*
Neal, Steven George *journalist*
Nebel, Kai Allen *lawyer*
Nechin, Herbert Benjamin *lawyer*
†Needham, George Michael *library association executive*
Neis, James M. *lawyer*
Nelsen, Timothy Alan *lawyer*
Nelson, H(arry) Donald *communications executive*
Nelson, Kenneth Edward *consulting engineer*
Nelson, Richard David *lawyer*
Nelson, Thomas R. *lawyer*
Nemerovski, Steven H. *lawyer*
Nesburg, Alan D. *lawyer*
Neubauer, Charles Frederick *investigative reporter*
Neugarten, Bernice Levin *social scientist*
Neuhausen, Benjamin Simon *auditor, accountant*
Newell, Frank William *ophthalmologist, educator*
Newey, Paul Davis *lawyer*
Newlin, Charles Fremont *lawyer*
Newman, Ralph Geoffrey *literary scholar historian*
Newman, Terry E. *lawyer*
Newsome, Mary de Sévigné *psychoanalyst*
Nicastro, Neil David *business executive, lawyer*
Nichol, Norman J. *manufacturing executive*
Nicholas, Arthur Soterios *manufacturing company executive*
Nicholas, Ralph Wallace *anthropologist, educator*
Nicholls, David G. *editor*
Nickel, Melvin Edwin *metallurgical engineer*
Nicklin, Emily *lawyer*
Nicolaides, Mary *lawyer*
Nims, John Frederick *writer, educator*
Nisenholtz, Martin Abram *telecommunications executive, educator*
Nissen, William John *lawyer*
Nitikman, Franklin W. *lawyer*
Nixon, Harvey *lawyer*
Noha, Edward J. *insurance company executive*
Nolan, Carole Rita *broadcasting executive*
Nord, Henry J. *transportation executive*
Nord, Robert Eamor *lawyer*
Nordberg, John Albert *federal judge*
Nordland, Gerald *art museum administrator, historian, consultant*
Nordstrand, Raymond William *broadcasting company executive*
Norgle, Charles Ronald, Sr. *federal judge*
Norris, James Rufus, Jr. *chemist, educator, consultant*
Norton, Peter Bowes *publishing company executive*
Norum, David P. *retail company executive*
Notebaert, Richard C. *telecommunications industry executive*
Notz, John Kranz, Jr. *lawyer*
Novick, David *civil engineer, educator*
Novick, Peter *historian, educator*
Nowacki, James Nelson *lawyer*
Nussbaum, Bernard J. *lawyer*
Nussbaum, Martha Craven *philosophy and classics educator*
Nutt, Jim *artist*
Nye, Sandra Gayle *lawyer, psychiatric social worker, consultant*
Nyhus, Lloyd Milton *surgeon, educator*
O'Brien, James Phillip *lawyer*
O'Brien, Patrick William *lawyer*
O'Connell, Harold Patrick, Jr. *banker*
O'Connor, Daniel J. *lawyer*
O'Connor, James John *utility company executive*
O'Connor, John Killeen *lawyer*
O'Dell, James E. *newspaper publishing executive*
Odorizzi, Michele L. *lawyer*
Oehme, Reinhard *physicist, educator*
Oesterle, Eric Adam *lawyer*
Offer, Daniel *psychiatrist*
O'Flaherty, Paul Benedict *lawyer*
O'Hagan, James Joseph *lawyer*
O'Hara, Paul M. *clothing manufacturing company executive*
O'Hare, John Mitchell *lawyer*
O'Hare, Linda Parsons *management consultant*
Oka, Takeshi *physicist, chemist, astronomer, educator*
O'Leary, Daniel Vincent, Jr. *lawyer*
O'Leary, Frank J. *lawyer*
Olian, Robert Martin *lawyer*
Olins, Robert Abbot *communications research executive*
Oliver, Harry Maynard, Jr. *retired brokerage house executive*
Olsen, Edward John *geologist, educator*
Olsen, Rex Norman *trade association executive*
O'Malley, John Daniel *legal educator, banker*
Onasch, Donald Carl *business executive*
Orbon, Margaret J. *lawyer*
O'Reilly, Charles Terrance *university dean*
Organ, Joseph B. *lawyer*
Orozco, Raymond E. *protective services official*
Orr, Richard Tuttle *journalist*
Ortmann, Jeffrey *theater producer, director*
Oryshkevich, Roman Sviatoslav *physician, physiatrist, dentist, educator*
O'Shea, Lynne Edeen *advertising executive, educator*
Osiyoye, Adekunle *obstetrician/gynecologist, educator*
O'Sullivan, Gerald Joseph *association executive*
Oswald, William H. *lawyer*
Ouzounian, Armenuhi *dentist*
Overgaard, Mitchell Jersild *lawyer*
Overton, George Washington *lawyer*
Overton, Jane Vincent Harper *biology educator*
Oxtoby, David William *chemistry educator*
Ozog, Edward J. *lawyer*
Pachman, Daniel J. *physician, educator*
Page, Clarence E. *newspaper columnist*
Page, Ernest *medical educator*
Page, Janice Ellen *retail executive*
†Page, John Arthur *professional association executive, educator*
Pallasch, B. Michael *lawyer*
Pallmeyer, Rebecca Ruth *federal judge*
Palm, Gary Howard *lawyer, educator*
Palmer, John Bernard, III *lawyer*
Palmer, Patrick Edward *radio astronomer, educator*
Palmer, Robert Erwin *association executive*
Palmer, Robert Towne *lawyer*
Palmore, Roderick Alan *lawyer*
Panich, Danuta Bembenista *lawyer*
Panko, Jessie Symington *dean*
Pape, Arthur Edward *lawyer*
Pappageorge, George C. *architect*
Pappas, George Demetrios *anatomy and cell biology educator, scientist*
Parisi, Joseph (Anthony) *magazine editor, writer-consultant, educator*
Park, Chung Il *librarian*
Parrish, Overton Burgin, Jr. *pharmaceutical corporation executive*
Parsons, John Russell *retail company executive*
Parsons, Keith I. *lawyer*
Partridge, Mark Van Buren *lawyer*
Parzen, Stanley Julius *lawyer*
Pascal, Roger *lawyer*
Pascale, Daniel Richard *judge*
Paschke, Edward F. *artist, illustrator*
Patel, Homi Burjor *apparel company executive*
Pattishall, Beverly Wyckliffe *lawyer*
Patton, Stephen Ray *lawyer*
Paul, Arthur *artist, graphic designer, illustrator, art and design consultant*
Paul, Ronald Neale *management consultant*
Pavalon, Eugene Irving *lawyer*
Pavik, Malvin A. *department stores executive*
Pearl, Melvin E. *lawyer, film producer*
Peck, Donald Vincent *musician*
Peerman, Dean Gordon *magazine editor*
Peirson, Walter Russell *oil company executive*
Pell, Wilbur Frank, Jr. *federal judge*
Pelton, Russell Meredith, Jr. *lawyer*
Peltzman, Sam *economics educator*
Peres, Judith May *journalist*
Perkins, James L. *lawyer*
Perlberg, Jules Martin *lawyer*
Perlman, Judy Platt *lawyer*
Perlman, Robert L. *pediatrics, pharmacology, and physiology educator*
Perlstadt, Sidney Morris *lawyer*
Perry, Michael John *law educator*
Pestureau, Pierre Gilbert *literature educator, literary critic, editor*
Petacque, Arthur M. *journalist*
Peters, Gordon Benes *musician*
Petersen, Donald Sondergaard *lawyer*
Petersen, William Otto *lawyer*
Peterson, Gerald C. *lawyer*
Peterson, Marybeth A. *church administrator*
Peterson, Mildred Othmer (Mrs. Howard R. Peterson) *lecturer, writer, librarian, civic leader*
Petrakis, Peter *lawyer*
Pezzella, Jerry James, Jr. *investment and real estate corporation executive*
Phelan, Richard John *county administrator, lawyer*
Phelps, Paul Michael *lawyer*
Philipps, Louis Edward *data systems manufacturing company executive*

Phillips, Donald Wright *investment company executive*
Phillips, Frederick Falley *architect*
Piccirilli, Robert James, Jr. *small business owner*
Pick, Ruth *research scientist, physician, educator*
Piderit, John J. *university educator*
†Piecewicz, Walter Michael *lawyer*
Piekarski, Victor J. *lawyer*
Pierce, Daniel Marshall *lawyer, mayor*
Pierson, Don *sports columnist*
Pigott, Richard J. *food company executive*
Pikler, Charles *musician*
Pilkington, Alan Ralph *advertising executive*
Pincus, Theodore Henry *public relations executive*
Pippen, Scottie *professional basketball player*
†Pitser, Tom G. *manufacturing executive, heavy*
Pitt, George *lawyer*
Pitts, Robert Eugene, Jr. *marketing educator, consultant*
Pizer, Howard Charles *professional baseball team executive, lawyer*
Plank, Betsy Ann (Mrs. Sherman V. Rosenfield) *public relations counsel*
Platz, George Arthur, III *lawyer*
Platzman, George William *geophysicist, educator*
Pless, Vera *mathematics and computer science educator*
Plotkin, Manuel D. *management consultant, educator, former corporate executive and government official*
Plotnick, Harvey Barry *publishing executive*
Plotnik, Arthur *publishing executive*
Plunkett, Paul Edward *federal judge*
Podesta, Robert Angelo *investment banker*
Poe, Douglas Allan *lawyer*
Polaski, Anne Spencer *lawyer*
†Pollay, Richard L. *real estate title insurance company executive*
Polley, Edward Herman *anatomist, educator*
Pollick, G. David *college president, philosopher*
Pollock, Alexander John *banker*
Pollock, Earl Edward *lawyer*
Pollock, George Howard *psychiatrist, psychoanalyst*
Pollock, Sheldon Ivan *language professional, educator*
Polsby, Daniel D. *law educator*
Pomerantz, Rhoda Silverstein *geriatrician, internist, health center executive*
Pope, Daniel James *lawyer*
Pope, Jerome W. *lawyer*
Pope, Kerig Rodgers *magazine executive*
Pope, Richard M. *rheumatologist*
†Pope, Steven Francois *association executive*
Posner, Richard Allen *federal judge*
Postlewaite, Philip Frederick *law educator*
Powell, Allen Royal *bishop*
†Powers, James *engineering company executive*
Powles, Peter B. *lawyer*
Poznanski, Andrew Karol *pediatric radiologist*
Pratt, Robert Windsor *lawyer*
Prekop, Martin D. *art educator, artist*
Preschlack, John Edward *management consultant*
Presser, Stephen Bruce *lawyer, educator*
Prior, Gary L. *lawyer*
Pritikin, David T. *lawyer*
Pritikin, James B. *lawyer, employee benefits consultant*
Pritzker, Nicholas J. *diversified services corporation executive*
Pritzker, Robert Alan *manufacturing company executive*
Pritzker, Thomas Jay *lawyer, business executive*
Prochnow, Douglas Lee *lawyer*
Prochnow, Herbert Victor *former government official, banker, author*
Prochnow, Herbert Victor, Jr. *lawyer*
Proctor, Barbara Gardner *advertising agency executive*
Proctor, Edward George *lawyer*
Proops, Jay D. *agricultural products executive*
Prosperi, David Philip *public relations executive*
Provus, Barbara Lee *executive search consultant*
Pugh, Roderick Wellington *psychologist, educator*
Pugliese, Robert J. *lawyer*
Pumper, Robert William *microbiologist*
Quaal, Ward Louis *broadcast executive*
Quade, Victoria Catherine *editor, writer*
Quebe, Jerry Lee *architect*
†Queeney, Jack *public relations executive*
Quinlan, William Joseph, Jr. *lawyer*
†Rabin, Paul *insurance company executive*
Rachwalski, Frank Joseph, Jr. *financial executive*
†Raczkiewicz, Maciej A. *engineering company executive*
Radell, Nicholas John *management consultant*
Rafelson, Max Emanuel, Jr. *biochemist, medical school administrator*
Ragir, John Arthur *theatrical company executive*
Rahe, Maribeth Sembach *bank executive*
Raines, Timothy *professional baseball player*
Rajan, Fred E. N. *clergy member, church administrator*
Ralph, William J. *lawyer*
Ramberg, Christina *artist, educator*
Ramsey-Goldman, Rosalind *physician*
Ran, Shulamit *composer*
Rank, John Thomas *lawyer*
Rankin, James Winton *lawyer*
†Ranney, David C. *urban economics educator*
Ranney, George A., Jr. *lawyer*
Raphaelson, Joel *retired advertising agency executive*
Rapoport, David E. *lawyer*
Rasin, Rudolph Stephen *corporate executive*
Rasor, Robert D. *lawyer*
Ratner, Gerald *lawyer*
Ratny, Ruth Lucille *publishing company executive, writer*
Rattner, William Edward *lawyer*
Rauch, George Washington *lawyer*
Raup, David Malcolm *paleontology educator*
Raven, Corinne *principal*
Raymond, Spencer Henry *lawyer*
Rearick, J. Arden *lawyer*
Redish, Martin Harris *legal educator*
Reed, Charles Allen *anthropologist*
Reed, Cordell *utility company executive*
Reed, Janet Lynn *lawyer*
Reed, John Shedd *former railway executive*
Reed, Keith Allen *lawyer*
Reedy, Jerry Edward *editor, writer*
Reeves, Michael Stanley *public utility executive*
Refo, Patricia Lee *lawyer*
Regensteiner, Else Friedsam (Mrs. Bertold Regensteiner) *textile designer, educator*
Reggio, Vito Anthony *management consultant*
Reice, Charles Thomas *department store, food service and lodging executive*
Reich, Allan J. *lawyer*
Reicin, Ronald Ian *lawyer*
†Reid, Daniel James *public relations executive*
Reiffel, Leonard *physicist, scientific consultant*
Reilly, Robert Frederick *valuation consultant*
Reingold, Haim *mathematics educator*
Reinke, John Henry *clergyman, educational administrator*
Reinsdorf, Jerry Michael *professional sports teams executive, real estate executive, lawyer, accountant*
Reiss, Dale Anne *accounting executive*
Reiter, Michael A. *lawyer*
Reitman, Jerry Irving *advertising agency executive*
Relias, John Alexis *lawyer*
Renshaw, Charles Clark, Jr. *retired publishing executive*
Reschke, Michael W. *real estate executive*
Resnick, Donald Ira *lawyer*
Reuben, Don Harold *lawyer*
Reum, James Michael *lawyer*
Reynolds, Frank Everett *religious studies educator*
Reynolds, Thomas A., Jr. *lawyer*
Reynolds, Thomas A., III *lawyer*
Rhind, James Thomas *lawyer*
Rhoads, Paul Kelly *lawyer*
Rhodes, Charles Harker, Jr. *lawyer*
Rhone, Douglas Pierce *pathologist, educator*
Rible, Morton *manufacturing executive, lawyer*
Rice, William Edward *newspaper columnist*
Rich, S. Judith *public relations executive*
Richardson, Jerome Johnson *food service company executive*
Richardson, John Thomas *university chancellor, clergyman*
Richardson, William F. *lawyer*
Richman, Harold Alan *social welfare policy educator*
Richman, John Marshall *lawyer, business executive*
Richman, William Sheldon *furniture company executive*
Richmond, William Patrick *lawyer*
Riddell, Matthew Donald Rutherford *consulting environmental engineer*
Rieger, Mitchell Sheridan *lawyer*
Rielly, John Edward *association executive*
Riggleman, James David *professional baseball team manager*
Rikoski, Richard Anthony *engineering executive, electrical engineer*
Rissman, Burton Richard *lawyer*
Ritchie, Albert *lawyer*
Ritchie, William Paul *lawyer*
Rizzo, Ronald Stephen *lawyer*
Robbins, Henry Zane *public relations and marketing executive*
Roberts, Harry Vivian *statistics educator*
Roberts, Jo Ann Wooden *school system administrator*
Roberts, Theodore Harris *banker*
Robertson, Sara Stewart *portfolio manager*
†Robinson, June Kerswell *dermatologist, educator*
Robinson, Martin F. *lawyer*
Robinson, Theodore Curtis, Jr. *lawyer*
Rocek, Jan *chemist, educator*
Roche, James McMillan *lawyer*
Rodgers, James Foster *association executive, economist*
Rodgers, Johnathan *broadcast executive*
Rodriguez, Matt L. *protective services professional*
Roebuck, John Clifford *lawyer*
Roenick, Jeremy *professional hockey player*
Roeper, Richard *columnist*
†Roger, John W. *parks and recreation director*
Rogers, Desiree Glapion *state official*
Rogers, Eddy J. *lawyer*
Rogers, John Washington, Jr. *investment management company executive*
Rohlin, Diane Elizabeth *financial public relations executive*
Roin, Howard James *lawyer*
Roizman, Bernard *virologist, educator*
Rollhaus, Philip Edward, Jr. *diversified manufacturing company executive*
Rooney, Matthew A. *lawyer*
Ropski, Gary Melchior *lawyer*
Roque, Roberto Dizon *city official*
Rose, Merrill *public relations counselor*
Rosemarin, Carey Stephen *lawyer*
Rosen, George *economist, educator*
Rosen, Sherwin *economist, educator*
Rosen, Steven Terry *oncologist, hematologist*
Rosenbaum, Michael A. *investor relations consultant*
Rosenberg, Gary Aron *construction executive, lawyer*
Rosenberg, Richard M. *lawyer*
Rosenberg, Robert Brinkmann *research organization executive*
Rosenbloom, Lewis Stanley *lawyer*
Rosenbloom, Steve *sportswriter*
Rosenblum, Michael F. *lawyer*
Rosenblum, Victor Gregory *political science and law educator*
Rosenfield, Robert Lee *pediatric endocrinologist, educator*
Rosenheim, Edward Weil *English educator*
Rosenheim, Margaret Keeney *social welfare policy educator*
Rosenthal, Albert Jay *advertising agency executive*
Rosenthal, Earl Edgar *art history educator*
Rosenthal, Ira Maurice *pediatrician, educator*
Rosner, Jonathan Lincoln *physicist, educator*
Rosner, Robert *astrophysicist*
Ross, Edward W. *diversified corporation executive*
Ross, Jeffrey Kenneth *lawyer*
Rostenkowski, Dan *congressman*
Roston, David C. *lawyer*
Roth, Sanford Irwin *pathologist, educator*
Rothman-Denes, Lucia Beatriz *biology educator*
Rothschild, George William *judge, lawyer*
Rothstein, Ruth M. *hospital adminstrator*
Rotman, Carlotta J. H. *physician*
†Rotunno, Joseph Rocco *construction company executive*
Rovner, Ilana Kara Diamond *federal judge*
Rowder, William Louis *lawyer*
Rowen, Robert G. *savings and loan executive*
Rowley, Janet Davison *physician*
Roy, David Tod *Chinese literature educator*
Royer, Kathleen Rose *pilot*
Royko, Mike *newspaper columnist*
Rubenstein, Arthur Harold *physician, educator*
Rubin, Bonnie Miller *journalist*
Rubin, E(rwin) Leonard *lawyer*
Rubin, Robert J. *lawyer*
Rubinowitz, Leonard S. *lawyer, educator*
Ruder, David Sturtevant *lawyer, educator, government official*
Rudnick, Paul David *lawyer*
Rudolph, Lloyd Irving *political science educator*
Rudolph, Susanne Hoeber *political and social science educator*
Rudstein, David Stewart *law educator*
Rudy, Lester Howard *psychiatrist*
Rumsfeld, Donald Henry *former government official, corporate executive*
Rundio, Louis Michael, Jr. *lawyer*
Runkle, Martin Davey *library director*
Rupert, Donald William *lawyer*
Rusch, William Graham *religious organization administrator*
Russell, James H. *lawyer*
Russell, Lillian *medical, surgical nurse*
Russell, Paul Frederick *lawyer*
†Russo, William *composer, educator*
Rutigliano, Louis J. *telecommunications industry executive*
Rutkoff, Alan Stuart *lawyer*
†Ryan, James E. *attorney general*
Ryan, Leo Vincent *business educator*
Ryan, Patrick G. *insurance company executive*
Ryan, Robert Collins *lawyer*
Ryan, Thomas F. *lawyer*
Rychlak, Joseph Frank *psychology educator, theoretician*
Rycroft, Donald Cahill *insurance executive*
Ryder, David R. *lawyer*
Rydholm, Ralph Williams *advertising agency executive*
Rymer, William Zev *research scientist, administrator*
Rynkiewicz, Stephen Michael *journalist*
Sabl, John J. *lawyer*
Sachs, Lloyd Robert *entertainment critic, writer*
Sachs, Robert Green *physicist, educator, laboratory administrator*
†Safar, Michael *information scientist*
Sager, William F. *retired chemistry educator*
Salenger, Lucy Lee *producer, consultant*
Saller, Richard Paul *classics educator*
Salpeter, Alan N. *lawyer*
†Sandberg, Harold Raymond *civil engineer*
Sanders, David P. *lawyer*
Sanders, Jacquelyn Seevak *psychologist, educator*
Sanders, Richard Henry *lawyer*
†Sandlow, Leslie J. *physician, educator*
Sandner, John Francis *commodity futures broker, lawyer*
Sandquist, Elroy Charles, Jr. *lawyer*
Sangerman, Harry M. *lawyer*
Santangelo, Mario Vincent *dental association executive, educator*
Sarchi, Bernard *healthcare administrator*
Sauer, Kenneth H. *bishop*
Saul, Peter *artist*
Saunders, George Lawton, Jr. *lawyer*
Saunders, Terry Rose *lawyer*
†Sautter, Dianne Lee *children's museum director*
Savard, Denis Joseph *professional hockey player*
Savner, David A. *lawyer*
Sawdey, Richard Marshall *lawyer*
Sawinski, Vincent John *chemistry educator*
Sawyier, Calvin P. *lawyer*
Sawyier, David R. *lawyer*
Scalish, Frank Anthony *labor union administrator*
Scanlan, Thomas Cleary *publishing executive, editor*
Scarse, Olivia Marie *cardiologist, consultant*
Schafer, Michael Frederick *orthopedic surgeon*
Schauer, Louis Frank *lawyer*
Schechter, Allen E(dward) *retired publishing company executive*
Scheinkman, José Alexandre *economics educator*
Scherer, Ross Paul *retired sociology educator*
Schieser, Hans Alois *education educator*
Schiffman, David M. *lawyer*
Schild, Joyce Anna *otolaryngologist, surgeon*
Schiller, Donald Charles *lawyer*
Schiller, Eric M. *lawyer*
Schillinger, Edwin Joseph *physics educator*
Schilsky, Richard Lewis *oncologist, researcher*
Schimberg, A(rmand) Bruce *retired lawyer*
Schindel, Donald Marvin *lawyer*
Schink, James Harvey *lawyer*
Schippers, David Philip *lawyer*
Schirn, Janet Sugerman *interior designer*
Schlickman, J. Andrew *lawyer*
Schlitter, Stanley Allen *lawyer*
Schloss, Nathan *economist*
Schlossman, John Isaac *architect*
Schmiege, Robert *railroad executive*
Schneider, Dan W. *lawyer, consultant*
Schneider, Robert Jerome *lawyer*
†Schoeller, Dale Alan *nutrition research educator*
†Schoenberg, Harry W. *urologic surgeon*
Scholle, Roger Hal *dentist*
Schommer, Carol Marie *principal*
Schoonhoven, Ray James *retired lawyer*
Schorer, Joseph U. *lawyer*
Schornack, John James *accountant*
Schoumacher, Bruce Herbert *lawyer*
Schramm, David Norman *astrophysicist, educator*
Schreck, Robert A., Jr. *lawyer*
Schriver, John T., III *lawyer*
Schroeder, Charles Edgar *banker, investment management executive*
Schroeder, Douglas Fredrick *architect*
Schroeder, W(illiam) Widick *religion educator*
Schubert, William Henry *curriculum studies educator*
Schuerman, John Richard *social work educator*
Schuette, Michael *lawyer*
Schug, Kenneth Robert *chemistry educator*
Schulfer, Roche Edward *theater executive director*
Schulhofer, Stephen Joseph *law educator*
Schulman, Sidney *neurologist, educator*
Schulte, David Michael *investment banker*
Schulte, Stephen Charles *lawyer*
Schultz, Heidi Flynn *publisher*
Schultz, Kurt Lee *lawyer*
Schultz, Theodore William *retired educator, economist*
Schulz, Keith Donald *corporate lawyer*
†Schulze, Theodora Economou *music director, educator, investment firm executive*
Schumer, William *surgeon, educator*
Schupp, Ronald Irving *clergyman, civil rights leader*
Schuyler, Daniel Merrick *lawyer, educator*
†Schwartz, Alan Gifford *sport company executive*
Schwartz, Charles Phineas, Jr. *replacement auto parts company executive, lawyer*
Schwartz, Donald Lee *lawyer*
Schwartz, John Norman *health care executive*
Schweikert, Norman Carl *musician*
Scogland, William Lee *lawyer*
Scott, Alice H. *librarian*
Scott, John Brooks *research institute executive*
Scott, Louis Edward *advertising agency executive*
Scott, Theodore R. *lawyer*
Scullion, Annette Murphy *lawyer, educator*
Scully, Joseph C. *bank executive*
Seaman, Irving, Jr. *public relations consultant*
Seamons, Quinton Frank *lawyer*
Sedelmaier, John Josef *film director, cinematographer*
Seely, Robert Fleming *lawyer*
Seewald, Elsbeth M. *law firm executive, fraternal organization administrator*
Seidenfeld, Glenn Kenneth *lawyer*
Seidner, Frederic Jay *public relations executive*
Seitz, Tim *church administrator*
Seki, Hoken S. *lawyer*
Selander, Larry *lawyer*
Seligman, Richard Michael *lawyer*
Sen, Ashish Kumar *urban planner, educator*
Seng, Ann Frances *civic organization executive*
Sengstacke, John Herman Henry *publishing company executive*
Senturia, Yvonne Dreyfus *pediatrician, epidemiologist*
Sereno, Paul C. *paleontologist, educator*
Serritella, James Anthony *lawyer*
Serritella, William David *lawyer*
Serwer, Alan Michael *lawyer*
Sexton, Carol Burke *financial institution executive*
Sfikas, Peter Michael *lawyer, educator*
Shadur, Milton I. *judge*
Shadur, Robert H. *lawyer*
Shafer, Eric Christopher *minister*
†Shah, Manu Hirachand *civil and structural engineer*
Shambaugh, George Elmer, III *internist*
Shanahan, Edmond Michael *savings and loan executive*
Shanas, Ethel *sociology educator*
Shank, William O. *lawyer*
Shanks, Gerald Robert *insurance company executive*
Shannon, Peter Michael, Jr. *lawyer*
Shapey, Ralph *composer, conductor, educator*
Shapiro, Harold David *lawyer, educator*
Shapiro, Stanley *materials scientist*
Shapiro, Stephen Michael *lawyer*
Shapo, Helene S. *law educator*
Shapo, Marshall Schambelan *lawyer, educator*
†Shedlock, James *library director, consultant*
Sheldon, Harvey M. *lawyer*
Shepherd, Daniel Marston *executive recruiter*
Shepherd, Stewart Robert *lawyer*
Shepro, Richard W. *lawyer*
Sherck, Timothy C. *lawyer*
Shere, Dennis *publishing executive*
Sherwin, Byron Lee *religion educator, college official*
Shields, Thomas Charles *lawyer*
Shields, Thomas William *surgeon, educator*
Shindler, Donald A. *lawyer*
Shirley, Virginia Lee *advertising executive*
Shuman, Nicholas Roman *journalist, educator*
Shute, David *retail executive, lawyer*
Sibbald, John Ristow *management consultant*
Sido, Kevin Richard *lawyer*
Siegel, Arthur *corporate executive*
Siegel, Howard Jerome *lawyer*
Siegler, Mark *internist, educator*
Sigal, Michael Stephen *lawyer*
Sigmon, Joyce Elizabeth *association executive*
Silberman, Alan Harvey *lawyer*
Silets, Harvey Marvin *lawyer*
Simmons, Adele Smith *foundation president, former educator*
Simon, Bernece Kern *social work educator*
Simon, John Bern *lawyer*
Simon, John P. *lawyer*
Simon, Mordecai *religious association administrator, clergyman*
Simon, Ralph *rabbi*
Simon, Seymour *lawyer, former state supreme court justice*
Simons, Helen *school psychologist, psychotherapist*
Simonson, Margaret *newspaper publishing executive*
Simpson, John Alexander *physicist*
Singer, Emel *staffing industry executive*
Singh, Manmohan *orthopedic surgeon, educator*
Siske, Roger Charles *lawyer*
Siskel, Gene (Eugene Kal Siskel) *film critic*
Sive, Rebecca Anne *public affairs company executive*
Skilling, Raymond Inwood *lawyer*
Skinner, Samuel Knox *utilities executive, lawyer*
Sklarsky, Charles B. *lawyer*
†Skom, Joseph Harry *medical educator*
Skrebneski, Victor *photographer*
Slansky, Jerry William *investment company executive*
Slavitt, Earl Benton *lawyer*
Slocomb, Paul D. *lawyer*
Smart, Allen Rich, II *lawyer*
Smedinghoff, Thomas J. *lawyer*
Smith, Adrian Devaun *architect*
Smith, Arthur B(everly), Jr. *lawyer*
Smith, David Waldo Edward *pathology educator, physician*
Smith, Freddye L(ee) *financial planner*
Smith, Gordon Howell *lawyer*
Smith, John Gelston *lawyer*
Smith, Kenneth Bryant *seminary administrator*
Smith, Lawrence R. *lawyer*
Smith, Mary Anne *lawyer*
Smith, Michele *lawyer*
Smith, Raymond Thomas *anthropology educator*
Smith, Robert Drake *railroad executive*
†Smith, Sam P. *columnist, author*
Smith, Spencer Bailey *engineering and business educator*
Smith, Stan Vladimir *economist, financial service company executive*
Smith, Tefft W. *lawyer*
Smithburg, William Dean *food manufacturing company executive*
Sneed, Michael (Michele) *columnist*
Snider, Lawrence K. *lawyer*
Snyder, Jean Maclean *lawyer*
†Snyder, William E. *lawyer*
†Sobel, Arnold I. *mining executive*
Sochen, June *history educator*
Socolofsky, Jon Edward *banker*
Solomon, Jack Avrum *lawyer, automotive distributor, art dealer*
Solomonson, Charles D. *corporate executive*
Solotorovsky, Julian *lawyer*
Solovy, Jerold Sherwin *lawyer*
Solti, Sir Georg *conductor*
Sonderby, Peter R. *lawyer*
Sonderby, Susan Pierson *federal bankruptcy judge*
Sopranos, Orpheus Javaras *manufacturing company executive*
Sorensen, Leif Boge *physician, educator*
Sorensen, W. Robert *clergy member, church administrator*
Soto, Ramona *training specialist*
Sparberg, Marshall Stuart *gastroenterologist, educator*

Spector, David M. *lawyer*
Spector, Harold Norman *physics educator*
Speigel, I. Joshua *neurosurgery educator*
Spellmire, George W. *lawyer*
Spencer, Lewis Douglas *lawyer*
Spencer, Rozelle Jeffery *moving and storage company executive*
Sperling, Robert Y. *lawyer*
Spindler, George S. *lawyer, oil industry executive*
Spiotto, James Ernest *lawyer*
Spivey, Bruce E. *integrated delivery systems management executive*
Springer, David Edward *lawyer*
Sproger, Charles Edmund *lawyer*
Sprowl, Charles Riggs *lawyer*
Squires, John Henry *federal bankruptcy judge*
Stack, John Wallace *lawyer*
Stack, Stephen S. *manufacturing company executive*
Stahl, Charles Eugene *lawyer*
Stahl, David M. *lawyer*
Staley, Augustus Eugene, III *advertising executive*
Standberry, Herman Lee *school system administrator, consultant*
Stanley, James Richard *lawyer*
Stanley, Justin Armstrong *lawyer*
Staples, James G. *lawyer*
Starkman, Gary Lee *lawyer*
Starr, Rick *broadcasting executive*
Stassen, John Henry *lawyer*
Stead, James Joseph, Jr. *securities company executive*
Stearns, Neele Edward, Jr. *diversified holding company executive*
Steck, Theodore Lyle *biochemistry and molecular biology educator, physician*
Stegemoeller, Harvey A. *clergy member, church administrator*
Stein, A. C. *clergy member, church administrator*
Stein, Carey M. *lawyer*
Stein, Paula Jean Anne Barton *hotel real estate consultant*
Stein, Richard Allen *real estate developer*
Steinberg, Morton M. *lawyer*
Steiner, Barbara S. *lawyer*
Steiner, Donald Frederick *biochemist, physician, educator*
Steinfeld, Manfred *furniture manufacturing executive*
Steingraber, Frederick George *management consultant*
Stelmack, Gloria Joy *elementary education educator*
Stelzel, Walter Tell, Jr. *accountant, financial company executive*
Stephan, Edmund Anton *lawyer*
Steptoe, Philip P., III *lawyer*
Stern, Carl William, Jr. *management consultant*
Stern, Richard Gustave *author, educator*
Stern, Robert Louis *lawyer*
Sternberg, Paul *retired ophthalmologist*
Sternstein, Allan J. *lawyer*
Stevenson, Adlai Ewing, III *lawyer, former senator*
†Stewart, S. Jay *chemical company executive*
Stickler, K. Bruce *lawyer*
Stigler, Stephen Mack *statistician, educator*
Stillman, Nina Gidden *lawyer*
Stinson, James R. *lawyer*
Stirling, James Paulman *investment banker*
Stock, Leon Milo *chemist, educator*
Stocking, George Ward, Jr. *anthropology educator*
Stoll, John Robert *lawyer, educator*
Stone, Alan *container company executive*
Stone, Daniel Hunter *metallurgical engineer, researcher*
Stone, Geoffrey Richard *law educator, lawyer*
Stone, Howard Lawrence *lawyer*
Stone, James Howard *management consultant*
Stone, Randolph Noel *law educator*
Stone, Roger Warren *container company executive*
Stone, Steven Michael *sports announcer, former baseball player*
Storb, Ursula Beate *molecular genetics and cell biology educator*
Storer, John W. *lawyer, consultant*
Stotter, David W. *marketing executive*
Stover, Leon (Eugene) *anthropology educator, writer, critic*
Stowell, Joseph, III *academic administrator*
Strasburger, Joseph Julius *retired lawyer*
Strauch, Gerald Otto *surgeon*
Straus, Helen Lorna Puttkammer *biologist, educator*
Streff, William Albert, Jr. *lawyer*
Strenski, James B. *communications executive*
Strobel, Pamela B. *lawyer*
Strobel, Russ M. *lawyer*
Strubel, Richard Perry *manufacturing company executive*
Struggles, John Edward *management consultant*
Stuart, Robert *container manufacturing executive*
Studwell, Thomas W. *lawyer*
Stukel, James Joseph *university official, mechanical engineering educator*
Sulkin, Howard Allen *college president*
Sullivan, Bernard James *accountant*
Sullivan, Cornelius J. *lawyer*
Sullivan, Marcia Waite *lawyer*
Sullivan, Peggy (Anne) *librarian*
Sullivan, Thomas Patrick *lawyer*
Sumner, William Marvin *anthropology and archaeology educator*
Sunstein, Cass R. *law educator*
Sussman, Arthur M. *law educator*
Sutherland, Joe Allen *lawyer*
Sutter, William Paul *lawyer*
Swan, Richard Gordon *mathematics educator*
Swaney, Thomas Edward *lawyer*
Swanson, Bernet Steven *consulting engineer, former educator*
Swanson, Don Richard *university dean*
Swanson, Patricia K. *university official*
Swartz, William John *transportation resources company executive/retired*
Sweeney, James Raymond *lawyer*
Sweeney, Michael J. *lawyer*
Sweet, Charles Wheeler *executive recruiter*
Swerdlow, Martin Abraham *physician, pathologist*
Swett, Daniel Robert *lawyer*
Swibel, Steven Warren *lawyer*
Swift, Dolores Monica Marcinkevich *public relations executive*
Swift, Edward Foster, III *investment banker*
Swiger, Elinor Porter *lawyer*
Szala, Scott J. *lawyer*
Szczepanski, Slawomir Zbigniew Steven *lawyer*
Tabin, Julius *patent lawyer, physicist*
Talbot, Earl Armour *lawyer*
Talbot, Pamela *public relations executive*
Tallant, David, Jr. *lawyer*
Tannenberg, Dieter E. A. *manufacturing company executive*
Tanner, Helen Hornbeck *historian*
Tardy, Medney Eugene, Jr. *otolaryngologist*
Tarun, Robert Walter *lawyer*
Tassani, Sally Marie *communications executive, marketing consultant*
Taswell, Howard Filmore *pathologist, blood bank specialist, educator*
Tatooles, Constantine John *cardiovascular and thoracic surgeon*
Taub, Richard Paul *social sciences educator*
Taylor, George Allen *advertising agency executive*
Taylor, John Wilkinson *education educator*
Taylor, Roger Lee *lawyer*
Teichner, Lester *management consulting executive*
Telling, Edward Riggs *former retail, insurance, real estate and financial services executive*
Terkel, Studs (Louis Terkel) *author, interviewer*
Terp, Dana George *architect*
Terry, Richard Edward *public utility holding company executive*
Thaden, Edward Carl *history educator*
Thatcher, Kristine Marie *actress, writer*
Theobald, Edward Robert *lawyer*
Theobald, Thomas Charles *banker*
Thies, Richard Brian *lawyer*
Thomas, Dale E. *lawyer*
Thomas, Frank Edward *professional baseball player*
Thomas, Frederick Bradley *lawyer*
Thomas, John Thieme *management consultant*
Thomas, Lawrason Dale *oil company executive*
Thomas, Leroy *newspaper executive editor*
Thomas, Richard Lee *banker*
Thomas, Stephen Paul *lawyer*
Thompson, James Robert, Jr. *lawyer, former governor*
Thomsen, Mark William *religious organization administrator*
Thomson, George Ronald *lawyer, educator*
Thorne-Thomsen, Thomas *lawyer*
Thornton, Theodore Kean *investment advisor*
Tibble, Douglas Clair *lawyer*
Tienda, Marta *demographer, educator*
Tigerman, Stanley *architect, educator*
Tijunelis, Donatas *engineering executive*
Tillett, Samuel Raymond *lawyer*
Tippins, Bedell A. *lawyer*
Tobin, Calvin Jay *architect*
Tobin, Thomas F. *lawyer*
Todd, James S. *surgeon, educator, medical association administrator*
Todd, James Stiles *surgeon, professional executive association*
Todd Copley, Judith Ann *materials and metallurgical engineering educator*
†Toft, Richard P(aul) *title insurance executive*
Toles, Edward Bernard *retired judge*
Toll, Daniel Roger *corporate executive, civic leader*
Tompsett, William C. *lawyer*
Tone, Jeffrey R. *lawyer*
†Tone, Michael P. *lawyer*
Tone, Philip Willis *lawyer, former federal judge*
Toohey, James Kevin *lawyer*
Topinka, Judy Baar *state official*
Topol, Clive M. *lawyer*
Torbert, Preston M. *lawyer*
Torgersen, Torwald Harold *architect, designer*
Torshen, Jerome Harold *lawyer*
Totlis, Gust John *title insurance company executive*
Towne, L. Stanton *lawyer*
Tozer, Forrest Leigh *lawyer*
Tracy, David *theology educator*
Trapp, James McCreery *lawyer*
Trauscht, Donald C. *security services executive*
†Travis, David B. *curator*
Travis, Dempsey Jerome *real estate executive, mortgage banker*
†Trczinski, Robert A. *public relations executive*
Treece, John W. *lawyer*
Trexler, Edgar Ray *minister, editor*
Trienens, Howard Joseph *lawyer*
Tritter, Richard Paul *strategic consulting executive*
Trukenbrod, William Sellery *banker*
Truran, James Wellington, Jr. *astrophysicist*
Truskowski, John Budd *lawyer*
Tsoris, Stephen A. *lawyer*
Tsou, Tang *political science educator, researcher*
Tucker, Watson Billopp *lawyer*
Tulsky, Alex Sol *physician*
Turkevich, Anthony Leonid *chemist, educator*
Turner, Jack Henry *can manufacturing company executive*
Turner, Lynne Alison (Mrs. Paul H. Singer) *harpist*
Turner, Michael Stanley *physics educator*
Turow, Scott F. *lawyer, author*
Tyler, Thomas Shephard *lawyer*
Tyler, W(illiam) Ed *printing company executive*
Tymm, William E. *lawyer*
Tyner, Howard A. *newspaper editor, journalist*
Ulbricht, Robert E. *savings and loan executive, lawyer*
Ultmann, John Ernest *physician, educator*
Umsted, Louis Franklin *manufacturing executive*
Uvena, Frank John *retired printing company executive, lawyer*
Valdes, Miguel A. *lawyer*
Valerio, Joseph M. *architectural firm executive, educator*
VanderBeke, Patricia K. *architect*
Vander Wilt, Carl Eugene *banker*
Vanecko, Robert Michael *surgeon, educator*
Van Valen, Leigh Maiorana *biologist, educator*
Varro, Barbara Joan *editor*
Varsbergs, Vilis *minister, former religious organization administrator*
Veit, Fritz *librarian*
Ventura, Robin Mark *professional baseball player*
Verschoor, Curtis Carl *business educator, consultant*
†Viall, J(ohn) Thomas *non-profit organization executive, fundraiser*
Vie, Richard Carl *insurance company executive*
Vieregg, Robert Todd *lawyer*
Vilim, Nancy Catherine *advertising agency executive*
Vinci, John Nicholas *architect, educator*
Vittum, Daniel Weeks, Jr. *lawyer*
Vogler, James R. *lawyer*
von Rhein, John Richard *music critic, editor*
Voortman, John J. *lawyer*
Vrablik, Edward Robert *import/export company executive*
Vrechek, George Gerald *architectural firm executive*
Vree, Roger Allen *lawyer*
Wackerle, Frederick William *management consultant*
Wadden, Richard Albert *environmental science educator, consultant, researcher*
Wade, Edwin Lee *writer, lawyer*
†Wade, Michael John *ecology and evolution educator, researcher*
Wagner, Joseph M. *church administrator*
Wahlen, Edwin Alfred *lawyer*
Waintroob, Andrea Ruth *lawyer*
Waite, Dennis Vernon *investor relations consultant*
Waite, Ellen Jane *vice president*
Waite, Norman, Jr. *lawyer*
Walberg, Herbert John *psychologist, educator, consultant*
Waldstein, Sheldon Saul *physician, educator*
Walker, John Patrick *theater director, actor*
Walker, Ronald Edward *psychologist, educator*
Wall, James McKendree *minister, editor*
Wall, Robert F. *lawyer*
Wallace, Julia Diane *newspaper editor*
Walsh, Joseph A., Jr. *lawyer*
Walter, Douglas Hanson *lawyer*
Walter, Priscilla Anne *lawyer*
Walton, Stanley Anthony, III *lawyer*
Waltz, Jon Richard *lawyer, educator, author*
Wander, Herbert Stanton *lawyer*
Wang, Albert James *violinist, educator*
Wang, Gung H. *management consultant*
Wanke, Ronald Lee *lawyer*
Ward, Daniel Patrick *lawyer*
Ward, James Frank *pension fund administrator*
Wardell, Jay Howard *association executive*
Wardropper, Ian Bruce *museum curator, educator*
Warnecke, Michael O. *lawyer*
Warnecke, Richard Basley *sociologist, educational administrator*
†Warshauer, Myron C. *land use planner*
Wasan, Darsh Tilakchand *university official, chemical engineer educator*
Wasik, John Francis *editor, writer, publisher*
Wasiolek, Edward *literary critic, language and literature educator*
Watkins, Cheryl Denise *special education educator*
Watson, Lee Ann *lawyer*
Watson, Robert R. *lawyer*
Waxler, Beverly Jean *anesthesiologist, physician*
Weaver, Donna Rae *company executive*
Weaver, William Townsend *laywer*
Webb, Dan K. *lawyer*
Weber, Arthur *magazine executive*
Weber, Daniel E. *marketing professional*
Weber, Donald B. *advertising and marketing executive*
Weber, Frederic *lawyer*
Weber, Hanno *architect*
Weber, Merrill Evan *lawyer, business executive*
Webster, Albert Knickerbocker *consultant in performing arts*
Webster, James Randolph, Jr. *physician*
Weclew, Victor T. *dentist*
Weese, Benjamin Horace *architect*
†Weichselbaum, Ralph R. *oncologist chairman*
Weil, John David *envelope company executive*
Weil, Roman Lee *accounting educator*
Weimer, Jean Elaine *nursing educator*
Weinberg, David B. *lawyer*
Weinberg, Harvey A. *apparel company executive*
Weinberg, Lila Shaffer *writer, editor*
Weinberg, Meyer *humanities educator*
Weinberger, Seth Jay *lawyer*
†Weingart, Jeanne *public relations executive*
Weinkopf, Friedrich J. *lawyer*
Weinsheimer, William Cyrus *lawyer*
Weintraub, Joseph Barton *publishing executive*
Weintraub, Karl Joachim *history educator*
†Weir, Bryce K. A. *neurosurgeon, neurology educator*
†Weiss, Stanley C. *electrical and electronics products wholesale distribution executive*
Weissman, Michael Lewis *lawyer*
Weitzman, Robert Harold *investment company executive*
Wellington, Robert Hall *manufacturing company executive*
Wells, Joel Freeman *editor, author*
West, Byron Kenneth *banker*
Westbrooks, Alphonso *public relations executive*
Wexler, Raymond P. *lawyer*
Wexler, Richard Lewis *lawyer*
Whalen, Wayne W. *lawyer*
White, Barry A. *lawyer*
White, Craig Mitchell *lawyer*
White, H. Blair *lawyer*
White, John Abiathar *pilot, consultant*
White, Linda Diane *lawyer*
White, R. Quincy *lawyer*
White, William J. *lawyer*
Whitehead, James S. *lawyer*
Whiteley, Sandra Marie *librarian, editor*
†Whitington, Peter Frank *pediatrics educator, pediatric hepatologist*
†Whitley, Douglas L. *telecommunications industry executive*
Wied, George Ludwig *physician*
Wier, Patricia Ann *publishing executive, consultant*
Wiggins, Charles Henry, Jr. *lawyer*
Wilcox, Mark Dean *lawyer*
Wilczek, Robert Joseph *lawyer*
Wildermuth, Gordon Lee *architect*
Wildman, Max Edward *lawyer*
Wilhelm, David C. *political organization administrator*
Wilkerson, Isabel *journalist*
†Wilks, Charles E. *chemicals executive*
Will, Hubert Louis *federal judge*
Williams, Ann Claire *federal judge*
Williams, Billy Leo *professional baseball coach*
Williams, Carl Chanson *oil company executive*
Williams, Douglas H. *lawyer*
Williams, Edward Joseph *banker*
Williams, George Howard *lawyer, association executive*
Williams, H. Randolph *lawyer*
Williams, John Cobb *lawyer*
Williams, Mark H. *advertising agency executive*
Williams, Richard Lucas, III *electronics company executive, lawyer*
Williams, Thurmon *retail company executive*
Williams-Ashman, Howard Guy *biochemistry educator*
Williamson, Joel V. *lawyer*
Williamson, Richard Salisbury *lawyer*
Willoughby, William Franklin, II *physician, researcher*
Wilmouth, Robert K. *commodities executive*
Wilson, Bruce G. *lawyer*
Wilson, Gahan *cartoonist, author*
Wilson, Harry L. *lawyer*
Wilson, Karen Lee *museum curator*
Wilson, Richard Harold *government official*
Wilson, Roger Goodwin *lawyer*
Wilson, Ruby Lee *nurse, director*
Wilson, William Julius *sociologist, educator*
Winfrey, Oprah *television talk show host, actress, producer*
Wing, John Adams *financial services executive*
Winger, Howard Woodrow *library educator*
Winnie, Alon Palm *anesthesiologist, educator*
Winninghoff, Albert C. M. *advertising company executive*
Winston, Roland *physicist, educator*
Wirsching, Charles Philipp, Jr. *brokerage house executive, investor*
Wirszup, Izaak *mathematician, educator*
Wirtz, Arthur Michael, Jr. *professional hockey team executive*
Wirtz, William Wadsworth *real estate and sports executive*
Wise, William Jerrard *lawyer*
Wiser, James Louis *political science educator*
Wishner, Maynard Ira *finance company executive, lawyer*
Witcoff, Sheldon William *lawyer*
Witwer, Samuel Weiler, Sr. *lawyer*
†Wiwchar, Michael *bishop*
Wojcik, Lawrence A. *lawyer*
Wolf, Charles Benno *lawyer*
Wolf, Neal Lloyd *lawyer*
Wolf, Stephen M. *airline executive*
Wolfe, David Louis *lawyer*
Wolfe, Sheila A. *journalist*
Wolfson, Larry M. *lawyer*
Wolpert, Edward Alan *psychiatrist*
Wood, Arthur MacDougall *retired retail executive*
Wood, James Clarence *lawyer*
Wood, James Nowell *museum director and executive*
Woodruff, Teresa K. *cell biologist*
Woods, Robert Archer *investment counsel*
Wool, Ira Goodwin *biochemist, molecular biologist, educator*
Wootton, Robert Ray *lawyer*
Wright, Benjamin Drake *psychology, statistics, education educator*
Wright, Judith Margaret *law librarian, educator*
Wright, Patricia Donovan *communications executive*
Wycliff, Noel Don *journalist, newspaper editor*
Wynn, Thomas Joseph *county judge, educator*
Yacktman, Donald Arthur *financial executive, investment counselor*
Yale, Seymour Hershel *dental radiologist, educator, university dean, gerontologist*
Yamakawa, Allan Hitoshi *university administrator*
Yarkony, Gary Michael *physician, researcher*
Yee, Edmond *church administrator*
York, Donald Gilbert *astronomy educator, researcher*
Young, Ronald Faris *commodity trader*
Youngman, Owen Ralph *newspaper editor*
Yu, Anthony C. *religion and literature educator*
Yuenger, James Laury *journalist*
Zabel, Sheldon Alter *lawyer, educator*
Zagel, James Block *federal judge*
Zajicek, Jeronym *music educator*
Zaki, Abdelmoneim Emam *dental educator*
Zaremski, Miles Jay *lawyer*
Zarnowitz, Victor *economist, educator*
Zaslow, Jeffrey Lloyd *syndicated columnist*
Zatuchni, Gerald Irving *physician, educator*
Zavis, Michael William *lawyer*
Zeffren, Eugene *toiletries company executive*
Zekman, Pamela Lois (Mrs. Fredric Soll) *reporter*
Zell, Samuel *transportation leasing company executive*
†Zelmanov, Efim Isaakovich *mathematician educator*
Zemans, Frances Kahn *legal association executive*
Zemm, Sandra Phyllis *lawyer*
Zenner, Sheldon Toby *lawyer*
Zimmer, Robert J. *mathematician*
Zimmerman, Martin E. *financial executive*
Zlatoff-Mirsky, Everett Igor *violinist*
Zmuda, Sharon Louise *construction executive*
Zolno, Mark S. *lawyer*
Zonis, Marvin *political scientist, educator*
Zoon, William K. *packaging company executive*
Zorn, Eric J. *newspaper columnist*
Zucaro, Aldo Charles *insurance company executive*
Zukowsky, John Robert *curator*
Zulkey, Edward John *lawyer, author*

Chicago Heights

Cifelli, John Louis *lawyer*
Hurd, Byron Thomas *newspaper executive*

Clarendon Hills

Moritz, Donald Brooks *mechanical engineer, consultant*

Crete

Langer, Steven *human resources management consultant and industrial psychologist*

Crystal Lake

Althoff, J(ames) L. *construction company executive*
Anderson, Lyle Arthur *manufacturing company executive*
Chamberlain, Charles James *railroad labor union executive*
Keller, William Francis *publishing consultant*
Knox, Susan Marie *paralegal*
Linklater, Isabelle Stanislawa Yarosh-Galazka (Lee Linklater) *secondary education educator*
Smyth, Joseph Vincent *manufacturing company executive*

Danville

Baker, Harold Albert *federal judge*
Burnside, William Charles *investment company executive*
Kettling, Virginia *administrator*
Pittelkow, Richard T. *grain company executive*
Prabhudesai, Mukund M. *pathology educator, laboratory director, researcher, administrator*

Darien

Sieracki, Aloysius Alfred *religious organization administrator*

De Kalb

Ashmann, Jon *art professor, designer*
Aung-Thwin, Michael Arthur *history educator*
Bach, Jan Morris *composer, educator*
Bickner, Bruce Pierce *agriculture executive*
Buckner, Kathleen E. *nursing educator, maternal-child health nurse*
Even, Robert Lawrence *art educator*
Hagelman, Charles William, Jr. *language professional, educator*
Hanna, Nessim *marketing educator*
Kevill, Dennis Neil *chemistry educator*
Kies, Cosette Nell *library science educator, consultant*
Kimball, Clyde William *physicist, educator*

Kleppner, Paul social studies think-tank administrator
La Tourette, John Ernest academic administrator
Monat, William Robert university official
Rossing, Thomas D. physics educator
Shur, George Michael lawyer
Skeels, Jack William economics educator, consultant
Sons, Linda Ruth mathematics educator
Troyer, Alvah Forrest seed corn company executive, plant breeder
Vance Siebrasse, Kathy Ann newspaper publishing executive
Wenner, Lettie McSpadden political science educator
Wit, Daniel international consultant
Witmer, John Harper, Jr. lawyer
Young, Arthur Price librarian, educator
Zar, Jerrold H(oward) biology educator, statistician

Decatur
Andreas, Michael Dwayne agricultural business executive
Blake, William Henry credit and public relations consultant
Braun, William Joseph underwriter
Cain, Richard Duane small business owner
Decker, Charles Richard business educator
Dunn, John Francis lawyer, state representative
Graf, Karl Rockwell nuclear engineer
Haab, Larry David utility company executive
Harris, Donald Wayne research scientist
Kelley, Wendell J. retired utilities executive
Koucky, John Richard metallurgical engineer, manufacturing executive
Kraft, Burnell D. agricultural products company executive
McCray, Curtis Lee university president
Mohan, J. Patrick lawyer
Moorman, John A. librarian
Morgan, E. A. church administrator
Perry, Anthony John retired hospital executive
Randall, James R. manufacturing company executive
Requarth, William Henry surgeon
Staley, Henry Mueller manufacturing company executive
Stetzner, Leah Manning lawyer, utilities executive
Strong, John David insurance company executive
Wells, Charles William utility executive
Womeldorff, Porter John utilities executive

Deerfield
Abbey, G(eorge) Marshall lawyer, former health care company executive, general counsel
Ames, Craig L. lawyer
Batts, Warren Leighton diversified industry executive
Boyd, Joseph Don financial services executive
Brunner, Vernon Anthony marketing executive
Chapman, Douglas Kenneth office equipment executive
Charlson, David Harvey executive search company professional
Chieger, Kathryn Jean oil company executive
†Chromizky, William Rudolph accountant
†Clement, Philip A. electronics executive
Cruikshank, John W., III life insurance underwriter
Eramo, John Jeffrey marketing executive
†Flynn, Robert Emmett food products company executive
Foght, James Loren banker
Gaples, Harry Seraphim computer service company executive
Gash, Lauren Beth lawyer, state legislator
†Goings, Everett Vernon cosmetics executive
Graham, William B. pharmaceutical company executive
Halaska, Robert H. health care executive
Hannafan, Kay H. Pierce lawyer
Heiman, Marvin Stewart financial services company executive
Hersher, Richard Donald management consultant
Howell, George Bedell equity investing and managing executive
Hunter, Charles David retail company executive
Jorndt, Louis Daniel retail drug store chain executive
Kinzelberg, Harvey leasing company executive
Krause, Jerry (Jerome Richard Krause) professional basketball team executive
Kushner, Jeffrey L. manufacturing company executive
Larrimore, Randall Walter manufacturing company executive
Loucks, Vernon R., Jr. healthcare products and services company executive
Meyer, Kenneth Marven academic administrator
O'Donnell, Lawrence James architect
Oettinger, Julian Alan lawyer, pharmacy company executive
Pigozzi, Raymond Anthony architect
†Polich, James W. environmental services consultant
†Ringler, James M. cookware company executive
Rucci, Anthony Joseph health care products and services executive
Scheiber, Stephen Carl psychiatrist
Simon, David Sidney consumer goods manufacturing executive
†Slavin, Craig Steven management and franchising consultant
Smith, Marschall Imboden lawyer
Staubitz, Arthur Frederick lawyer, healthcare products company executive
Thorne, Oakleigh Blakeman publishing company executive
Van Sickle, Paul Brunton financial executive
Vollen, Robert Jay lawyer
Walgreen, Charles Rudolph, III retail store executive
White, Tony L. health and medical products executive
†Wieseneck, Robert L. credit manager
Williams, Robert Jene lawyer, rail car company executive
Zywicki, Robert Albert electrical distribution company executive

Des Moines
Kelley, Bruce Gunn insurance company executive, lawyer

Des Plaines
Babb, Michael Paul engineering magazine editor
†Bardagy, Robert A. computer leasing company executive
†Beck, Lowell Richard lawyer, association executive
Brodl, Raymond Frank lawyer, former lumber company executive
Carroll, Barry Joseph manufacturing and real estate executive
Clapper, Marie Anne magazine publisher
Coburn, James LeRoy educational administrator
Demouth, Robin Madison lawyer, corporate executive
Dlouhy, Phillip Edward engineering, construction executive
Farley, James Newton manufacturing executive, engineer
†Frank, James Alan marketing professional
Frank, James S. automotive executive
Geisler, Rosemary P. computer dealer, marketing executive
Grahn, Barbara Ascher publisher
Henrikson, Lois Elizabeth photojournalist
Hlavacek, Roy George publishing executive, magazine editor
Jacobs, William Russell, II lawyer
Kelly, Timothy Michael magazine publisher
Klemens, Thomas Lloyd editor
Koffman, Morley trucking executive
Krupa, John Henry English language educator
Kubalanza, Ronald J. bank executive
Lakier, Thelma child development specialist, librarian
Lamey, William Lawrence, Jr. manufacturing company executive
Lee, Bernard Shing-Shu research company executive
Lee, Margaret Burke college administrator
Le Menager, Lois M. incentive merchandise and travel company executive
Li, Norman N. chemicals executive
Malchow, Dennis food products executive
Meinert, John Raymond clothing manufacturing and retailing executive, investment banker
Munden, Robin Ghezzi lawyer
Neel, Judy Murphy association executive
†Nelson, Thomas Carl association executive
Newman, Wade Davis trade association executive
†Pontikes, William N. computer rental and leasing company executive
Saporta, Jack psychologist, educator
Schmidt, Robert L. export company executive
Shoults, Harold E. social services administrator
Sisson, George Allen, Sr. physician, educator
Soble, David S. steel company executive
†Spungin, Joel D. wholesale office supplies and equipment executive
Tenhoeve, Thomas academic administrator
Tory, John A. newspaper publishing executive
†Winfield, Michael D. engineering company executive
Yarnell, Jeffrey Alan regional credit executive

Dixon
Belcher-Redebaugh-Levi, Caroline Louise nursing home administrator, nurse
Shaw, Thomas Douglas newspaper executive

Dolton
†Bennett, Joe bishop

Downers Grove
Appelman, Evan Hugh retired chemist
Armstrong, Richard A. diversified service company executive
Boese, Robert Alan forensic chemist
†Cantu, Carlos holding company executive
Colbert, Marvin Jay retired internist, educator
†Dietz, Charles Kenneth chemical engineer
Divis, Deborah B. lawyer
Erickson, Robert Daniel management services company executive
Fruin, Robert Cornelius physician, hospital administrator
Gioioso, Joseph Vincent psychologist
Kinsinger, Jack Burl chemist, educator
Kirkegaard, R. Lawrence architectural acoustician
†Lewis, Robert J. secondary education educator
Pollard, Charles William diversified services company executive
Pollock, John Glennon facilities management services company executive
Ryan, John Michael landscape architect

Dundee
Burger, George Vanderkarr wildlife ecologist, researcher

Dunlap
Bailey, John Maxwell retired mechanical engineer, consultant

DuQuoin
Smith, Lucius Skinner, III educational foundation administrator

Dwight
Oughton, James Henry, Jr. corporate executive, farmer

East Moline
Puffer, Richard Judson retired college chancellor
Silliman, Richard George retired lawyer, retired farm machinery company executive

East Peoria
Grisham, George Robert mathematics educator
Walker, Philip Chamberlain, II health care executive

East Saint Louis
Beatty, William Louis federal judge
Cohn, Gerald Bernard federal judge
Dunham, Katherine choreographer, dancer, anthropologist
Lindsley, James Bruce sales and marketing executive
Reilly, Michael K. mining executive
Stiehl, William D. federal judge

Edwardsville
Carlson, Jon Gordon lawyer
†Fortado, Robert Joseph librarian, educator
Going, William Thornbury English educator
Haley, Johnetta Randolph musician, educator, university administrator
Lazerson, Earl Edwin university president emeritus
Malone, Robert Roy artist, art educator
Ottwein, Merrill William George real estate company executive, veterinarian
Virgo, John Michael economist, researcher, educator

Elburn
Etter, David Pearson poet, editor
Hansen, H. Jack management consultant

Elgin
Brinckman, Donald Wesley industrial company executive
Burian, Robert J human resources executive
Butera, Paul retail grocery company executive
Deeter, Joan G. church administrator
Didier, James William college executive, administrator, consultant
Ericson, Burton E. diversified corporation executive
Furst, Warren Arthur retired holding company executive
Gwillim, Russell Adams manufacturing company executive
Hoeft, Elizabeth Bayless speech and language pathologist
Juister, Barbara Joyce mathematics educator
Kelly, Matthew Edward association executive
Kirkland, Alfred Younges, Sr. federal judge
†Miller, Donald Eugene minister, educator
Minnich, Dale E. religious administrator
Myers, Anne M. church administrator
Nelson, John Thilgen hospital administrator, physician
Nolen, Wilfred E. church administrator
Ratthahao, Sisouphanh minister
Saliba, Jacob manufacturing executive
Seigle, Harry Jay building supply company executive
Steiner, Duane religious administrator
Timmons, Glenn F. church administrator
Weber, Harm Allen college chancellor, former college president
Zack, Daniel Gerard library director
Ziegler, Earl Keller minister

Elk Grove Village
Best, Willis D. retired international union official
†Braznell, Gerald K. printing company executive
†Dzurinko, Joseph J. corporate executive, controller
Edwardson, John Albert airline executive
Flaherty, John Joseph quality assurance company executive
Halloran, James Joseph editor
Nadig, Gerald George manufacturing executive
Sertich, Tony artistic director
Sutton, Norma J. lawyer, educator

Elmhurst
†Baker, Robert I. business executive
Balcerzak, Marion John mechanical engineer
Blain, Charlotte Marie physician, educator
Burton, Darrell Irvin engineering executive
Cureton, Bryant Lewis college president, educator, political scientist
†Duchossois, Richard Louis manufacturing executive, racetrack executive
Ephland, John Russell magazine editor
Fornatto, Elio Joseph otolaryngologist, educator
Garvin, Thomas Michael food products company executive
Gerber, C. Allen food products executive
Grisim, J. Terrence safety consulting company executive
Hildreth, R(oland) James foundation executive, economist
Townsend, Merton LeRoy metal products executive
Wyman, Thomas H. food products executive

Elmwood Park
Spina, Anthony Ferdinand lawyer

Erie
Latham, LaVonne Marlys physical education educator

Eureka
Hearne, George Archer academic administrator

Evanston
Aagaard, James Stuart computer system developer
Abnee, A. Victor trade association executive
Achenbach, Jan Drewes engineer and scientist
Alexander, Ellen Jo lawyer, arbitrator, mediator
Alexis, Marcus economics educator
Allred, Albert Louis chemistry educator
Balachandran, Bala Venkataraman accounting systems educator
Bankoff, Seymour George chemical engineer, educator
Bareiss, Erwin Hans computer scientist, mathematician, nuclear engineer, educator
Bashook, Philip G. medical association executive, educator
Basolo, Fred chemistry educator
Bazant, Zdenek Pavel structural engineering educator, scientist, consultant
†Bedzyk, Michael J. ctystallographer, materials scientist
Bellow, Alexandra mathematician, educator
Belytschko, Ted Bohdan civil, mechanical engineering educator
Bernstein, Susan Powell development and fundraising consultant
Bishop, David Fulton library administrator
Borcover, Alfred Seymour journalist
†Bordwell, Frederick George chemistry educator
Boye, Roger Carl academic administrator, journalism educator, writer
Braeutigam, Ronald Ray economics educator
Branch, William B. school system administrator
Brazelton, William Thomas chemical engineering educator
†Breslin, Paul English language educator
Brown, Laurie Mark physicist, educator
Buchbinder-Green, Barbara Joyce art and architectural historian
Butt, John Baecher chemical engineering educator
Carr, Stephen Howard materials engineer, educator
Cassell, Frank Hyde business educator
Cates, Jo Ann librarian, management consultant
Catlett, George Roudebush accountant
Chang, R. P. H. materials science educator
Cheng, Herbert Su-Yuen mechanical engineering educator
Christian, Richard Carlton university dean, former advertising agency executive
Chung, Yip-Wah engineering educator
Cohen, Jerome Bernard materials science educator
Cole, Douglas English literature educator
Collins, Rives Berryman theater educator, artisitc director
Colton, Frank Benjamin retired chemist
Condit, Carl Wilbur history educator
Conger, William Frame artist, educator
Corey, Gordon Richard financial advisor, former utilities executive
Crawford, James Weldon psychiatrist, educator, administrator
Crawford, Susan library director, educator
Crotty, William political science educator
Dallos, Peter John neurobiologist, educator
Daniel, Isaac Mordochai mechanical engineering educator
Daskin, Mark Stephen civil engineering educator
Davis, Stephen Howard applied mathematics educator
De Coster, Cyrus Cole Spanish language and literature educator
Devinatz, Allen mathematics educator
Dockery, J. Lee medical school administrator
Domowitz, Ian economics educator
Dowen, David Earl investment banking executive
Duncan, Robert Bannerman strategy and organizations educator
Dwass, Meyer mathematician, educator
Eagly, Alice Hendrickson social psychology educator
Eberley, Helen-Kay opera singer, classical record company executive, poet
Ehmann, Kornel F. mechanical engineering educator
Eichenbaum, Martin Stewart economist, educator, consultant
Eisner, Robert economics educator
Ellis, Donald Edwin physicist, educator
Enroth-Cugell, Christina Alma Elisabeth neurophysiologist, educator
Epstein, Max electrical engineering educator
Fine, Arthur I. philosopher
Fine, Morris Eugene materials engineer, educator
Fisher, Neal Floyd minister
Fisher, Stephen David mathematics educator, university official
†Fourer, Robert H. industrial engineering educator, consultant
Fox, Edward Inman education administrator and Spanish educator
Freeman, Arthur J. physics educator
Frey, Donald Nelson industrial engineer, educator, manufacturing company executive
Friedman, Hans Adolf architect
Fryburger, Vernon Ray, Jr. advertising and marketing educator
Galati, Frank Joseph stage and opera director, educator, screen writer, actor
Galvin, Kathleen Malone communications educator
Gasper, George, Jr. mathematics educator
Gibbons, William Reginald, Jr. poet, novelist, editor
Giordano, August Thomas (Gus Giordano) choreographer, dancer
Goldman, Jerry political science educator, researcher
Goldstick, Thomas Karl biomedical engineering educator
Gordon, Julie Peyton foundation administrator
Gordon, Robert James economics educator
Gormley, R(obert) James retired lawyer
†Greenberg, Douglas Stuart history educator
Haberman, Shelby Joel statistician, educator
Haddad, Abraham Herzl electrical engineering educator, researcher
Halperin, William Paul physicist, educator
Harlow, Robert Dean packaging company executive
Herron, Orley R. college president
Heyck, Bill historian
Hill, Winfred Farrington psychology educator
Hoffman, Brian M. chemist, educator
Howard, Kenneth Irwin psychology educator
Huff, Stanley Eugene dermatologist
Hughes, Edward Francis Xavier physician, educator
Hurter, Arthur Patrick economist, educator
Ibers, James Arthur chemist, educator
Ihlanfeldt, William university administrator, consultant
Ingersoll, Robert Stephen former diplomat, federal agency administrator
Ionescu Tulcea, Cassius research mathematician, educator
Irons, William George anthropology educator
Jacob, Herbert political science educator
Jacobs, Donald P. banking and finance educator
Jacobs, Norman Joseph publishing company executive
Janda, Kenneth Frank political science educator
Janeway, Michael Charles journalism educator, school dean
†Jelinek, Richard Carl hospital management consultant company executive, educator
Jencks, Christopher Sandys sociology educator
Jerome, Joseph Walter mathematics educator
Johnson, David Lynn materials scientist, educator
Jones, Robert Russell magazine editor
Kaatz, Ronald B. advertising educator, consultant
Kalai, Ehud decision sciences educator, researcher in economics and decision sciences
Karlins, M(artin) William composer, educator
Keer, Leon Morris engineering educator
Kern, Charles William university official, chemistry educator
Kerr, Thomas Jefferson, IV academic official
Ketterson, John Boyd physics educator
Khandekar, Janardan Dinkar oncologist, educator
King, Robert Charles biologist, educator
Kistler, Alan Lee engineering educator
Kliphardt, Raymond A. engineering educator
Klotz, Irving Myron chemist, educator
Kotler, Philip marketing educator, consultant, educator
Kovitz, Arthur A. mechanical engineering educator
Kreml, Franklin Martin educational administrator, association executive
Krizek, Raymond John civil engineering educator, consultant
Krulee, Gilbert Koreb computer scientist, educator
Kuenster, John Joseph magazine editor
Kujala, Walfrid Eugene musician, educator
Kung, Harold Hing-chuen educational association administrator
Lambert, Joseph Buckley chemistry educator
Larson, Roy journalist, publisher
Lavengood, Lawrence Gene management educator, historian
Lavine, John M. journalism educator, newspaper publisher
Leslie, Joshua Allensworth mathematics educator
Letsinger, Robert Lewis chemistry educator
Lewis, Dan Albert education educator
Lippincott, James Andrew biochemistry and biological sciences educator
Liu, Wing Kam mechanical and civil engineering educator
Mack, Raymond Wright university provost
Magee, Robert Paul accounting and information systems educator
Mah, Richard Sze Hao chemical engineering educator

Manheim, Marvin Lee *business management educator, consultant*
Marhic, Michel Edmond *engineering educator, entrepreneur, consultant*
Marks, Tobin Jay *chemistry educator*
Matkowsky, Bernard Judah *applied mathematician, educator*
McCoy, Marilyn *university official*
Mc Nerney, Walter James *health policy educator, consultant*
Meshii, Masahiro *materials science educator*
Miller, Thomas Williams *former university dean*
Mills, Edwin Smith *economics educator*
Mineka, Susan *psychology educator*
Mintzer, David *physics educator*
Mitchell, Kendall *writer, literary critic*
Moses, Leon Nathan *economist, educator*
Moskos, Charles C. *sociology educator*
Mura, Toshio *civil engineering educator*
Murphy, Gordon John *engineering educator*
Myerson, Roger Bruce *game theorist, economist, educator*
†Neaman, Mark A. *health facility administrator*
Neaman, Mark Robert *hospital administrator*
Neuschel, Robert Percy *educator, former management consultant*
Novales, Ronald Richards *zoologist, educator*
Oakes, Robert James *physics educator*
Olmstead, William Edward *mathematics educator*
Olson, Gregory Bruce *materials science and engineering educator, academic director*
Ottino, Julio Mario *chemical engineering educator, scientist*
Otwell, Ralph Maurice *retired newspaper editor*
Pabst, Edmund G. *retired insurance company executive, lawyer*
Page, Benjamin Ingrim *political science educator, researcher*
Panzar, John C. *economist, educator, consultant*
Parker, James Floyd *minister, pension fund executive*
Paynter, John Philip *conductor*
Peck, Abraham *editor, writer, educator, magazine consultant*
Perkin, Harold James *social historian*
Pines, Herman *chemistry educator, consultant*
†Pinto, Lawrence Henry *neurobiologist, educator*
Plaut, Eric Alfred *psychiatrist, educator*
Plonus, Martin Algirdas *electrical engineering educator*
Poeppelmeier, Kenneth Reinhard *chemistry educator*
Polzin, John Theodore *lawyer*
Pople, John Anthony *chemistry educator*
Porter, Robert Hugh *economics educator*
Prince, Thomas Richard *accountant, educator*
†Quigley, Robert Lawrence *cardiothoracic surgeon, educator*
Rath, Gustave J(oseph) *industrial engineering educator, psychologist*
Ratner, Mark Alan *chemistry educator*
Reimer, Bennett *music educator, writer*
Reiter, Stanley *economist, educator*
Revelle, William Roger *psychology educator*
Revsine, Lawrence *accounting educator, consultant*
Robinson, R. Clark *mathematician, educator*
Rolfe, Michael N. *management consulting firm executive*
Rosenbaum, James Edward *psychologist, educator*
Rubenstein, Albert Harold *industrial engineering and management sciences educator*
Rudnicki, John Walter *engineering educator*
Saari, Donald Gene *mathematician*
Sachtler, Wolfgang Max Hugo *chemistry educator*
Salzman, Arthur George *architect*
Samter, Max *physician, educator*
Samuels, Ernest *author, educator*
Sandor, Ellen Ruth *artist*
Schank, Roger Carl *computer science and psychology educator*
Schnaiberg, Allan *sociology educator*
Schultz, Don Edward *academic administrator*
Schwartz, Neena Betty *endocrinologist, educator*
Schwarzlose, Richard Allen *journalism educator*
Scott, Walter Dill *management educator*
Seidman, David N(athaniel) *materials science and engineering educator*
Shah, Surendra Poonamchand *engineering educator, researcher*
Sheridan, James Edward *history educator*
Shriver, Duward Felix *chemistry educator, researcher, consultant*
Silverman, Richard Bruce *chemist, biochemist, educator*
Slaughter-Defoe, Diana Tresa *education educator*
Sobel, Alan *electrical engineer, physicist*
Spears, Kenneth George *chemistry educator*
Sprang, Milton LeRoy *obstetrician, gynecologist, educator*
Stern, Louis William *marketing educator, consultant*
Taam, Ronald Everett *physics and astronomy educator*
Taflove, Allen *electrical engineer, educator, researcher, consultant*
†Takahashi, Joseph S. *neuroscientist*
Tamhane, Ajit C. *statistician, engineer, educator*
Tankin, Richard Samuel *fluid dynamics engineer, educator*
Taronji, Jaime, Jr. *lawyer*
Thompson, Tyler *minister, philosophy educator*
Thrash, Patricia Ann *association executive*
Tornabene, Russell C. *communications executive*
Traisman, Howard Sevin *pediatrician*
Ulmer, Melville Paul *physics and astronomy educator*
Van Demark, Ruth Elaine *lawyer*
Vandenbroucke, Russell James *theatre director*
Vanderstappen, Harrie Albert *Far Eastern art educator*
Van Duyne, Richard Palmer *analytical chemistry and chemical physics educator*
Vanneman, Edgar, Jr. *lawyer*
Van Ness, James Edward *electrical engineering educator*
Ver Steeg, Clarence Lester *historian, educator*
Wagner, Durrett *former publisher, picture service executive*
Walker, Harold Blake *minister*
Walker, John Andrew *mechanical engineer, educator*
Weber, Arnold R. *university chancellor*
Weertman, Julia Randall *materials science and engineering educator*
Weil, Irwin *Slavic languages and literature educator*
Well, Irwin *language educator*
Werckmeister, Otto Karl *art historian and educator*
Wessels, Bruce W. *materials scientist, educator*
Weston, Michael C. *lawyer*
White, Willmon Lee *magazine editor*
Wick, John William *education educator, author*
Wilber, Laura Ann *audiologist*
Wilks, Ivor Gordon Hughes *historian, educator*
Wills, Garry *journalist, educator*
Worthy, James Carson *educator*
Wright, Donald Eugene *retired librarian*
Wright, John *classics educator*
Wu, Tai Te *biological sciences and engineering educator*
Yoder, Frederick Floyd *fraternity executive*
Zarefsky, David Harris *academic administrator, communication studies educator*
Zelinsky, Daniel *mathematics educator*
Ziomek, Jonathan S. *journalist, educator*
Zolomij, Robert William *landscape architect, consultant*

Evergreen Park

Ephraim, Max, Jr. *mechanical engineer*
Lucas, Shirley Agnes Hoyt *management executive*
Smith, Lawrence J. *bishop*

Fairview Heights

Barkofske, Francis Lee *lawyer, coal company executive*
Cunningham, Joseph Francis, Jr. *retired state supreme court justice*
Hughes, John W. *mining executive*
†Smith, John R. *agricultural products executive*
Sullivan, Joseph Patrick *agricultural product company executive*
Vyas, Chand Bhaourbhai *coal company executive*

Flossmoor

Ferreira, Daniel Alves *Spanish language educator*
Garrison, Ray Harlan *lawyer*
Lis, Edward Francis *pediatrician, consultant*
Ripling, Edward Joseph *metallurgical engineer, researcher*
Tiernan, James Scott, Jr. *association executive*
Vogt, John Henry *corporate executive*
Wagner, Alvin Louis, Jr. *real estate appraiser, consultant*
Walker, George W. *bishop*

Forest Park

Johnson, Calvin Keith *research executive, chemist*
Orland, Frank *oral microbiologist, educator*

Fort Sheridan

†Lenhardt, Alfonso Emanual *army officer*

Fox River Grove

Abboud, Alfred Robert *banker, consultant, investor*

Frankfort

Dennis, Peter Ray *environmental corporate executive*
Pearson, Gerald P. *hospital administrator*
Ruggles, Barbara Ann *elementary education educator*

Franklin Park

Dean, Howard M., Jr. *food company executive*
†Roche, Burke Bernard *manufacturing company executive*
Simpson, Michael *metals service center executive*
Watts, Ernest Francis *manufacturing company executive*
†Wilson, Steve *metal products executive*

Freeport

Ferguson, Daniel C. *diversified company executive*
Matschullat, Dale Lewis *lawyer*

Galena

Hermann, Paul David *retired association executive*

Galesburg

Hane, Mikiso *history educator*
Haywood, Bruce *retired college president*
Kirk, Sherwood *librarian*
Kowalski, Richard Sheldon *hospital administrator*
Tourlentes, Thomas Theodore *psychiatrist*

Galva

Massie, Michael Earl *lawyer*

Garden Prairie

Channick, Herbert S. *lawyer, arbitrator, retired real estate and broadcasting corporation executive*

Gays

Finley, Gary Roger *financial company executive*

Geneseo

Cherry, Robert Earl Patrick *retired food company executive*

Geneva

Barney, Charles Richard *transportation company executive*
Conterato, Bruno Paul *architect*
Goulet, Charles Ryan *retired insurance company executive*
Pershing, Robert George *retired telecommunications company executive*
†Stamps, David M. *publishing executive*
†Whitfield, Richard *publishing executive*
Young, Jack Allison *financial executive*

Genoa

Cromley, Jon Lowell *lawyer*

Gilman

Ireland, Herbert Orin *engineering educator*

Glen Ellyn

Conti, Paul Louis *management consulting company executive*
Crumbaugh, Lee Forrest *publisher, consultant*
Dieter, Raymond Andrew, Jr. *physician, surgeon*
Egan, Richard Leo *medical association administrator, medical educator*
Frateschi, Lawrence Jan *economist, statistician, educator*
Kirkpatrick, Clayton *former newspaper executive*
Larson, Ward Jerome *lawyer, retired banker*
Lischer, Ludwig Frederick *consultant, former utility company executive*
Logan, Henry Vincent *transportation executive*
McAninch, Harold D. *college president*
Patten, Ronald James *university dean*
Sigalos, George Peter *corporate executive*
Temple, Donald *allergist, dermatologist*
Wilhoit, Carol Lynn *physician*

Glencoe

Baer, Joseph Winslow *retired lawyer, mediator, arbitrator*
Bendix, William Emanuel *business director, consultant*
Fenninger, Leonard Davis *medical educator, consultant*
Gordon, Bernard *management and communications consultant*
Grabow, Beverly *learning disability therapist*
Nebenzahl, Kenneth *rare book and map dealer, author*
Niefeld, Jaye Sutter *advertising executive*
Rubin, David Robert *corporate executive*
Silver, Ralph David *distilling company director*
Stewart, Charles Leslie *lawyer*
Webb, James Okrum, Jr. *insurance company executive*

Glenview

Adler, Robert *electronics engineer*
Ampel, Leon Louis *anesthesiologist*
Berkman, Michael G. *lawyer, chemical consultant*
Bible, Geoffrey Cyril *tobacco company executive*
Blattner, Simon James, III *manufacturing executive*
Bradtke, Philip Joseph *architect*
Corley, Jenny Lynd Wertheim *educator*
Cozad, James William *retired oil company executive*
Dawson, Suzanne Stockus *lawyer*
†Durrett, Joseph Park *food company executive*
Franklin, Lynne *business communications consultant, writer*
Groh, Thomas Joseph *real estate executive*
Hafner, Arthur Wayne *author, information scientist, medical librarian*
Harris, Ronald David *chemical engineer*
†Hillebrand, Jeffrey Henry *hospital executive*
Hudnut, Stewart Skinner *manufacturing company executive, lawyer*
Kramer, Ferdinand *mortgage banker*
Lacy, Herman Edgar *management consultant*
Levine, Edwin Burton *retired classics educator*
Mabley, Jack *newspaper columnist, communications consultant*
McCarthy, Gerald Michael *electronics executive*
Mc Cormick, James Charles *leasing and financial services company executive*
McGrew, Jean B. *superintendent*
Miller, Edward Boone *lawyer*
Nichols, John Doane *diversified manufacturing corporation executive*
Panarese, William C. *civil engineer*
Pearlman, Jerry Kent *electronics company executive*
Powers, John Glenn, Jr. *manufacturing company executive*
Ptak, Frank S. *manufacturing executive*
Rorig, Kurt Joachim *chemist, research director*
Russell, Henry George *structural engineer*
Sherman, Elaine C. *gourmet foods company executive, educator*
Smith, Harold B. *manufacturing executive*
Stern, Gerald Joseph *advertising executive*
Taylor, D(arl) Coder *architect, engineer*
Traudt, Mary B. *elementary education educator*
Van Zelst, Theodore William *civil engineer, natural resource exploration company executive*
White, John Francis *retired corporate executive*
†Wilcoxson, Roy Dell *plant pathology educator and researcher*
Winett, Samuel Joseph *manufacturing company executive*
Young, Richard Alan *publishing company executive*

Godfrey

Harner, Linda Jeane *allied health educator*
McDaniels, John Louis *mathematics educator*

Goreville

Fosse, E(rwin) Ray *insurance company executive*

Granite City

†Raczkiewicz, Paul Edward *hospital administrator*

Great Lakes

Andrews, Carolyn Fraser *psychologist*
Gaston, Mack Charles *naval officer*

Greenville

Stephens, William Richard *college president emeritus*

Gurnee

†Funk, Carla Jean *medical librarian*
Meyer, Joyce *special education educator*

Hartford

Christian, Nelson Frederick *chemical engineer*

Harvey

Jensen, Harold Leroy *physician*
Krengel, Theodore H. *diversified metal manufacturing company executive*
Liem, Khian Kioe *medical entomologist*
Shotts, David Allison *manufacturing executive*

Hawthorn Woods

Schmitz, Shirley Gertrude *marketing and sales executive*

Hennepin

Bumgarner, James McNabb *judge*

Hickory Hills

Johnson, (Mary) Anita *physician, medical service administrator*

Highland

Baumer, Martha Ann *minister*
Rikli, Donald Carl *lawyer*

Highland Park

Asher, Frederick *former mail order company executive*
Bluefarb, Samuel Mitchell *physician*
Boruszak, James Martin *insurance company executive*
Dolin, Albert Harry *lawyer*
Friend, Peter Michael *hospital executive*
Gordon, Edward *music association executive*
Grimmer, Margot *dancer, choreographer, director*
Haight, Edward Allen *lawyer*
Harris, Thomas L. *public relations executive*
Herbert, Edward Franklin *public relations executive*
Hirsch, Jay G. *psychiatrist, educator*
†Hulseman, Robert L. *manufacturing company executive*
Johnson, Curtis Lee *publisher, editor, writer*
Karol, Nathaniel H. *lawyer, consultant*
Maas, Duane Harris *distilling company executive*
Markman, Raymond Jerome *marketing executive*
Mehta, Zarin *music association administrator*
Mordini, Marilyn Heuer *physical education educator*
Moschin, Susan Kamin *school board executive*
Pokorny, Virginia Anne *elementary education educator*
Rudo, Milton *retired manufacturing company executive, consultant*
Rutenberg-Rosenberg, Sharon Leslie *journalist*
Singer, Norman Sol *food products executive, inventor*
Smith, Malcolm Norman *manufacturing company executive*
Uhlmann, Frederick Godfrey *commodity and securities broker*
Weinberg, Michael, Jr. *commodities broker*

Highwood

Brown, Lawrence Haas *banker*

Hines

Daane, Kathryn D. *nursing administrator*
Green, Joseph Barnet *neurologist, educator*
Mason, George Robert *surgeon, educator*
Trimble, John Leonard *sensor psychophysicist, biomedical engineer*
Zvetina, James Raymond *pulmonary physician*

Hinsdale

Anderson, Harry Frederick, Jr. *architect*
†Bauer, C. William *contractor*
Berry, Virgil Jennings, Jr. *management consultant*
Birnholz, Jason Cordell *radiologist, consultant, educator*
Bloom, Stephen Joel *distribution company executive*
Burrows, Donald Albert *artist, painter, college dean*
Butler, Margaret Kampschaefer *retired computer scientist*
Cannon, Patrick Francis *public relations executive*
Cohen, Burton David *franchising executive, lawyer*
Dederick, Robert Gogan *economist*
Dyer, Goudyloch Erwin *state legislator*
Flynn, Donald Francis *waste management executive*
Gauthier, Clarence Joseph *retired utility executive*
Gustafson, F. Edward *food company executive*
Hodnik, David F. *retail company executive*
†Johnson, Lowell W. *management consultant*
Kalus, Richard A. *university program director*
Kaminsky, Manfred Stephan *physicist*
Kinney, Kenneth Parrish *banker, retired*
Lee, Patricia Hureston *lawyer*
Lowenstine, Maurice Richard, Jr. *retired steel executive*
Lynch, Charles J. *secondary school principal*
Mikos, David Edward *architect*
Mulhern, Joseph Patrick *lawyer*
Ochiltree, Ned A., Jr. *retired metals manufacturing executive*
Paloyan, Edward *physician, educator, reseacher*
†Passaneau, Robert J. *computer company executive*
Rinder, George Greer *retired retail company executive*
Shea, John J. *catalog and retail company executive*
Sheehan, Dennis William *lawyer, business executive*
Taylor, T(homas) Roger *educational consultant, educator*
Urbik, Jerome Anthony *financial consultant*
Wheeler, Paul James *real estate executive*
Whitney, William Elliot, Jr. *advertising agency executive*
†Wisniewski, Henry George *wholesale distribution executive*
Withers, Alton Merrill *retail store executive*

Hodgkins

Winn, Elwood F. *consumer product company executive*

Hoffman Estates

Baffico, Paul Anthony *retail executive*
†Biggins, James J. *fundraiser*
Costello, John H., III *business and marketing executive*
Dennis, Steven Pellowe *retail executive*
Laubenstein, Vernon Alfred *state agency administrator*
Martinez, Arthur C. *retail company executive*
Pagonis, William Gus *retired army officer*
Pasen, Robert Martin *psychologist*
Rooney, John Edward, Jr. *communications company executive*
Saunders, Eric Don *retail company executive*
Weston, Roger Lance *banker*

Homer

Gilhaus, Barbara Jean *home economics secondary educator*

Homewood

Brunst-May, Lois *accounting & association management firm executive*
Dietch, Henry Xerxes *judge*
Gray, Melvin *construction services company executive*
Grunwald, Arnold Paul *communications executive, engineer*
MacMaster, Daniel Miller *retired museum official*
Manson, Bruce Malcolm *construction company executive*
McClellan, Larry Allen *minister, writer*
Parker, Eugene Newman *retired physicist, educator*
†Reed, Michael A. *agricultural products supplier*
Schumacher, Gebhard Friederich Bernhard *obstetrician-gynecologist*

Hudson

Mills, Lois Jean *legislative aide, former education educator*

Huntley

Glickman, Louis *industrial sewing equipment executive*
Suzuki, Mikio *machine manufacturing executive*

Indianhead Park
Frisque, Alvin Joseph *retired chemical company executive*

Ingleside
Propst, Catherine Lamb *biotechnology company executive*

Inverness
Hetzel, William Gelal *executive search consultant*

Island Lake
Benson, John Earl *construction executive*

Itasca
Bingham, Bruce Bryan *real estate developer*
Fowler, Jack W. *printing company executive*
†Garratt, Reginald George *electronics executive*
Grue, Howard Wood *former insurance company executive*
†Nytko, Edward C. *printing company executive*
Rowsey, Michael *printing company executive*
Sheridan, James Leslie *real estate developer*

Jacksonville
Findley, Paul *former congressman, author, educator*
Gallas, Martin Hans *librarian*
Hack, Carole Mae *media generalist*
Olinger, Glenn Slocum *entrepreneur, consultant, investor*
Pfau, Richard Anthony *college president*

Joliet
Barber, Andrew Bollons *bank executive*
Benfer, David William *hospital administrator*
Caamano, Kathleen Ann Folz *gifted education professional*
Dunn, Thomas Aquinas *lawyer, state legislator*
Imesch, Joseph Leopold *bishop*
†Johnson, Mary Ann *computer training/vocational school owner*
Johnston, James Robert *library director*
Kaffer, Roger Louis *bishop*
Marion, Marjorie Anne *English educator*
McCullough, Henry G(lenn) L(uther) *nuclear engineer*
O'Connell, James Joseph *port official*
Pietak, Raymond Adam *academic administrator*
Ring, Alvin Manuel *pathologist*
Sova, Rita Wolz *community health nurse, educator*

Kankakee
Berkenkamp, Fred Julius *management consultant*
Bowling, John C. *academic administrator*
†Feth, Joseph S. *healthcare administrator*
Sayes, James Ottis *religion educator, minister*
Schroeder, David Harold *health care facility executive*
†Van Fossan, Kathryn Ruth *library director*

Kenilworth
Corrigan, John Edward, Jr. *banker, lawyer*
Frederick, Earl James *healthcare consultant*
Guelich, Robert Vernon *retired management consultant*
Hodson, Thomas William *health care company executive*
McKittrick, William Wood *lawyer*
Weiner, Joel David *retired food products executive*

Kildeer
Harrod, Scott *consulting manufacturing executive*

Knoxville
Johnson, Robert Oliver, Jr. *school system administrator*

La Grange
Carroll, Thomas John *advertising executive*
Kerr, Alexander Duncan, Jr. *lawyer*
Norby, William Charles *financial consultant*

Lafox
Seils, William George *lawyer*

Lake Bluff
Albrecht, Edward Daniel *metals manufacturing company executive*
Anderson, Roger E. *bank executive*
Felknor, Bruce Lester *editorial consultant*
Fromm, Henry Gordon *retired manufacturing and marketing executive*
Gage, Calvin William *retired marketing executive*
Grant, John Robert *management consultant*
Kelly, Daniel John *physician*
Ott, James Forgan *finance company executive*
Schreiber, George Richard *association executive, writer*
Stetson, John Charles *corporate executive*
Wacker, Frederick Glade, Jr. *manufacturing company executive*

Lake Forest
Anderluh, John Russell *business forms and information management company executive*
Bernthal, Harold George *health care company executive*
Bransfield, Joan *principal*
Brown, Cameron *insurance company consultant*
Carter, Donald Patton *advertising executive*
Coutts, John Wallace *chemist, educator*
Deters, James Raymond *retired manufacturing and services company executive*
Ditka, Michael Keller *restaurateur, former professional football coach*
Eckert, Ralph John *insurance company executive*
Emerson, William Harry *lawyer, oil company executive*
Ford, Donald James *retired insurance company executive, consultant, lawyer*
Frederick, Virginia Fiester *state legislator*
Fuhs-Smith, Wendy L. *foundation executive*
Hammar, Lester Everett *health care manufacturing company executive*
Hanlon, James Allison *confectionery company executive*
Hillman, Stanley Eric Gordon *former corporate executive*
Hotchkiss, Eugene, III *college president emeritus*
Jones, Dante Delaneo *professional football player*
Kenly, Granger Farwell *marketing consultant, college official*
Kreischer, Gary C. *secondary school educator*
Krouse, Ann Wolk *publishing executive*
Lambert, John Boyd *chemical engineer, consultant*
Levy, Nelson Louis *physician, scientist, corporate executive*
McCaskey, Michael B. *professional football team executive*
†McClure, Michael Clyde *corporate executive*
Miller, Arthur Hawks, Jr. *librarian, consultant*
Mohr, Roger John *advertising agency executive*
Murad, Ferid *physician*
O'Loughlin, John Kirby *retired insurance executive*
O'Mara, Thomas Patrick *manufacturing company executive*
Peterson, Donald Matthew *insurance company executive*
Rand, Kathy Sue *public relations executive*
Reichert, Jack Frank *manufacturing company executive*
Reichert, Norman Vernon *financial services consultant*
†Salaam, Rashaan *professional football player*
Salter, Edwin Carroll *physician*
Schulze, Franz, Jr. *art critic, educator*
Sikorovsky, Eugene Frank *retired lawyer*
Singletary, Michael *retired professional football player*
Stirling, Ellen Adair *retail executive*
Swanton, Virginia Lee *author, publisher, bookseller*
Van Gorkom, Jerome William *financial executive*
Vuckovich, Dragomir Michael *neurologist, educator*
Walter, Robert Irving *chemistry educator, chemist*
Wannstedt, David Raymond *professional football team coach*
Weston, Arthur Walter *chemist, scientific and business executive*
Wilbur, Richard Sloan *physician, foundation executive*
Woolford, Donnell *professional football player*
Yaconetti, Dianne Mary *business executive*

Lake Zurich
Schultz, Carl Herbert *real estate management and development company executive*

Lansing
†Colander, Patricia Marie *newspaper publisher*
†Gamble, Harry M. *newspaper editor*
†Kutzko, Nicholas, Jr. *marketing professional*

Lawrenceville
†Sudhaus, William S. *petroleum company executive*
Wright, John D. R. *oil industry executive*

Lemont
Chen, Shoei-Sheng *mechanical engineer*
Herriford, Robert Levi, Sr. *army officer*
Katz, Joseph Jacob *chemist, educator*
Tomkins, Frank Sargent *physicist*
Williams, Jack Marvin *chemist*

Lerna
†Vance, Thomas Carter *historic site director*

Libertyville
Burrows, Brian William *research and development manufacturing executive*
Goodman, Evan Besey *dentist*
Kremkau, Paul *principal*
Krolopp, Rudolph William *industrial designer, consultant*
Kummer, Daniel William *insurance executive*
Mraz, Alana L. *elementary school principal*
Ranney, George Alfred *lawyer, former steel company executive*
Ransom, Margaret Palmquist *public relations executive*
Thompson, David Jerome *chemical company executive, biochemist, nutritionist*

Lincoln
Wilson, Robert Allen *religion educator*

Lincolnshire
Berkey, Timothy Bruce *principal*
DuFour, Richard P. *school system administrator*
Freund, Charles Gibson *retired holding company executive*
Guist, Fredric Michael *minerals, chemicals and waste services corporation executive*
Hughes, William Franklin, Jr. *ophthalmologist, emeritus educator*
Iosue, Carmine A. *marketing executive*
Kotynek, George Roy *mechanical engineer, educator, marketing executive*
O'Connell, Edward Joseph, III *financial executive, accountant*
Reilly, John Paul *manufacturing company executive*
Speer, David Blakeney *industrial executive*
Tucker, Arlie G. *manufacturing executive*

Lincolnwood
Astrin, Marvin H. *broadcasting company executive*
Pattis, S. William *publisher*

Lisle
Aprati, Robert L. *lawyer, car rental company executive*
Becker, Richard Charles *college president*
†Bingham, Carleton Dille *science administrator, chemist*
Birck, Michael John *manufacturing company executive, electrical engineer*
†Donnelly, Gerard Thomas *arboretum director*
†Guglielmi, Peter Anthony *data and voice communications executive*
Hecht, Louis Alan *lawyer*
Krehbiel, Frederick August, II *electronics company executive*
Krehbiel, John H., Jr. *electronics company executive*
Long, Charles Franklin *corporate communications executive*
Melsa, James Louis *electrical engineer*
Psaltis, John Costas *manufacturing company executive*
Reum, W. Robert *manufacturing executive*
Sandrok, Richard William *lawyer*
Schwemm, John Butler *printing company executive, lawyer*
Tyson, Kirk W. M. *management consultant*
Wouch, Gerald *materials scientist*

Litchfield
Jackson, David A. *retired newspaper editor*

Lombard
Ahlstrom, Ronald Gustin *artist*
Branum, William Howell *engineering company executive*
Johnson, Dennis Lester *marketing consultant*
†Riordan, John Francis *oil and gas corporate executive*
†Robinson, Richard Clark *engineering company executive*
Velardo, Joseph Thomas *molecular biology and endocrinology educator*
Yeager, David P. *management consultant*
Yeager, Phillip Charles *transportation company executive*

Long Grove
Ausman, Robert K. *surgeon, research executive*
Connor, James Richard *foundation administrator*
Fitzpatrick, John Henry *insurance company executive*
Gallichio, Kathleen Anne *lawyer, insurance and financial services company executive*
Hayes, Percy B. *retired insurance company training executive*
Liuzzi, Robert C. *chemical company executive*
Maatman, Gerald Leonard *insurance company executive*
Mathis, David B. *financial services and insurance company executive*
Obert, Paul Richard *manufacturing company executive, lawyer*
Standbridge, Peter Thomas *insurance company executive*
Tarjan, Robert Wegg *information services executive*
Timbers, Stephen Bryan *financial services company executive*
Wilson, Stephen Ray *fertilizer manufacturing company executive*

Loves Park
Canova, John Richard *educational administrator*

Lynwood
Dyer-Dawson, Diane Faye *educational administrator*

Macomb
Anderson, Richard Vernon *ecology educator, researcher*
Brown, Spencer Hunter *historian*
Dexter, Donald Harvey *surgeon*
Goehner, Donna Marie *university dean*
Hopper, Stephen Rodger *hospital administrator*
Malpass, Leslie Frederick *retired university president*
Spencer, Donald Spurgeon *historian, academic administrator*
Vos, Morris *foreign languages educator, language services consultant*
†Walzer, Norman Charles *economics educator*
Witthuhn, Burton Orrin *university official*

Madison
Pope, Sarah Ann *elementary education educator*

Marengo
Franks, Herbert Hoover *lawyer*
Mrkvicka, Edward Francis, Jr. *financial writer, publisher, consultant*

Marion
Lincoln, Lucian Abraham *coal company executive*
Livengood, Richard Vaughn *healthcare executive*

Matteson
Yager, Vincent Cook *banker*

Mattoon
Horsley, Jack Everett *lawyer, author*
Phipps, John Randolph *retired army officer*
Sherline, Harold Albert *adult education professional*

Maywood
Blumenthal, Harold Jay *microbiologist, educator*
†Canavan, William J. *food products executive*
Canning, John Rafton *urologist*
Celesia, Gastone Guglielmo *neurologist, neurophysiologist, researcher*
Cera, Lee Marie *veterinarian*
†Cohen, Elliot Gene *hospital administrator*
Ellington, Mildred L. *librarian*
Freeark, Robert James *surgeon, educator*
Gamelli, Richard Louis *surgeon, educator*
Greenlee, Herbert Breckenridge *surgeon, educator*
Hanin, Israel *pharmacologist, educator*
†Radke, Jan Rodger *pulmonologist, hospital program administrator*
Slogoff, Stephen *anesthesiologist, educator*
Welty, William John *transportation executive, accountant*
†Winship, Daniel Holcomb *medicine educator, university dean*

Mc Henry
Duel, Ward Calvin *health care consultant*

Melrose Park
Bernick, Howard Barry *manufacturing company executive*
Cernugel, William John *hair care products company financial executive*
Di Matteo, Dominick, Jr. *supermarket chain executive*
Gass, Raymond William *lawyer, consumer products company executive*
Lavin, Bernice E. *cosmetics executive*
Lavin, Leonard H. *personal care products company executive*
Umans, Alvin Robert *manufacturing company executive*

Mendota
Du Bois, Clarence Hazel, Jr. *clergy member*
Hume, Horace Delbert *manufacturing company executive*

Metamora
Crow, Mary Jo Ann *elementary education educator*

Mokena
Janssen, Sister Norma *hospital administrator*
Sangmeister, George Edward *congressman, lawyer*

Moline
Arnell, Richard Anthony *radiologist*
Becherer, Hans Walter *agricultural equipment manufacturing executive*
Cottrell, Frank Stewart *lawyer, manufacturing executive*
England, Joseph Walker *heavy equipment manufacturing company executive*
Hallene, Alan Montgomery *retired elevator and escalator company executive*
Hanson, Robert Arthur *retired agricultural equipment executive*
Harrington, Roy Edwards *agricultural engineer, author*
†Irish, James Richard *national trade association executive*
Larson, Sandra Mae *nursing educator*
Leroy, Pierre Elie *manufacturing executive*
Morrison, Deborah Jean *lawyer*
Stowe, David Henry, Jr. *agricultural and industrial equipment company executive*

Monmouth
Johnson, John Prescott *philosophy educator*

Mooseheart
Ross, Donald Hugh *fraternal organization executive*

Morrison
French, Raymond Douglas *insurance agent, realtor,*

Morton Grove
Farber, Isadore E. *psychologist, educator*
McKenna, Andrew James *paper distribution and printing company executive, baseball club executive*

Mount Prospect
Alexy, R. James *manufacturing company executive*
Basar, Ronald John *research engineer, engineering executive*
Cucco, Ulisse P. *obstetrician, gynecologist*
Feingold, Diana *middle school educator, conservationist*
Jacobsen, Charlene Marie *music educator, band director*
†Lo, Robert *process engineering company executive, computer support company executive*
†Ottenfeld, Marshall *marketing research company executive*
†Randhava, Serge *electronics executive*
Rogers, Richard F. *construction company executive, architect, engineer*
Scott, Norman Laurence *engineering consultant*
Stamper, James M. *retired English language educator*
Wilks, Alan Delbert *chemical research and technology executive, researcher*

Mount Vernon
Withers, W. Russell, Jr. *broadcast executive*

Mundelein
Burns, Kenneth Jones, Jr. *lawyer, consultant*
Kennedy, George Danner *chemical company executive*
†MacLean, Barry L. *plastic and metal products company executive*
Mills, James Stephen *medical supply company executive*
Terris, William *publishing executive*

Murphysboro
Brewer, Donald Louis *school superintendent*
Jacobs, Robert *education educator emeritus*
Miller, Donald Morton *physiology educator*

Naperville
Clark, Worley H., Jr. *specialty chemical company executive*
Cline, Richard Gordon *business executive*
Cowlishaw, Mary Lou *state legislator*
Crawford, Raymond Maxwell, Jr. *nuclear engineer*
Dranias, Dean Anthony *financial and sports marketing executive*
Fields, Ellis Kirby *research chemist*
Fleisher, Robert E. R. *trucking executive*
Frank, Dieter *technical consultant, retired chemical company executive*
Fritz, Roger Jay *management consultant*
Grimley, Jeffrey Michael *dentist*
†Hannon, Steven Kevin *hospital administrator*
Hauptmann, Randal Mark *molecular biologist*
Hensley, Albert Lloyd, Jr. *research chemist, technical consultant*
Karayannis, Nicholas Marios *chemist*
Katai, Andrew Andras *chemical company executive*
L'Allier, James Joseph *educational multimedia company executive, instructional designer*
Landwehr, Arthur John *minister*
†Lannon, John Joseph *energy holding company executive*
†Marion, Daniel J(oseph) *hospital executive*
Mooney, Edward Joseph, Jr. *chemical company executive*
Olliver, Denis G. *transportation company executive*
Olson, Donald W. *transportation executive*
Oxenreiter, Maurice Frank *chemical engineer*
†Patel, Ramanlal L. *engineering executive*
†Pearson, Roger Lee *library administrator*
Reuss, Robert Pershing *telecommunications executive, consultant*
Rovner, Jack Alan *lawyer*
Sadowski, Anthony James *chemical company executive, physical chemist*
Schaack, Philip Anthony *retired beverage company executive*
Schultz, Theodore Edward *retail executive*
Schwab, Paul Josiah *psychiatrist educator*
Scullen, Thomas G. *superintendent*
Shaw, Michael Allan *lawyer, mail order company executive*
Spiotta, Raymond Herman *consulting editor*
Thomas, Joseph Erumappettical *psychologist*
Triggiani, Leonard Vincent *corporate executive*
Ulrich, Werner *patent lawyer*
†Vora, Manu Kishandas *chemical engineer, quality consultant*
†Wake, William S. *wholesale distribution executive*
†Wellek, Richard Lee *business executive*
Wilde, Harold Richard *college president*
Wolfram, Thomas *physicist*

Niles
Chertack, Melvin M. *internist*
Herb, Marvin J. *food products executive*
Powell, David *manufacturing company executive*
Schreiber, Jeffrey Lee *computer sales executive*
†Walker, A. Harris *lawyer, manufacturing executive*

Normal
Bolen, Charles Warren *university dean*
Brown, Francis Robert *mathematics educator*
Jelks, Edward Baker *archaeologist, educator*
Jones, Graham Alfred *mathematics educator*
Matsler, Franklin Giles *higher education educator*
Mc Knight, William Warren, Jr. *publisher*
Ohinouye, Tsuneo *automobile manufacturing executive*
Peterson, Fred McCrae *librarian*
Shields, John Charles *American studies and African American studies and literature educator*
Strand, David Axel *university executive*
Towner, Naomi Whiting *fiber artist, educator*
Wallace, Thomas Patrick *university administrator*
Williams, Michael Roy *marketing research, management educator*
Young, Robert Donald *physicist, educator*

North Chicago
Beer, Alan Earl *physician, medical educator*
Clark, Paul Newton *pharmaceutical company executive*
Ehrenpreis, Seymour *pharmacology educator*
Freese, Uwe Ernest *physician, educator*
Gall, Eric Papineau *physician educator*
Hawkins, Richard Albert *medical educator, administrator*
Kim, Yoon Berm *immunologist, educator*
Kringel, John G. *health products company executive*
Loga, Sanda *physicist, educator*
Morris, Charles Elliot *neurologist*
Nair, Velayudhan *pharmacologist, medical educator*
Rogers, Eugene Jack *medical educator*
Rudy, David Robert *physician, educator*
Schneider, Arthur Sanford *physician, educator*
Sierles, Frederick Stephen *psychiatrist, educator*
Sladek, Celia Davis *neuroscientist, educator*
Taylor, Michael Alan *psychiatrist*

Northbrook
Afterman, Allan B. *accountant, educator, researcher*
Boyce, Donald Nelson *diversified industry executive*
†Burgman, J. A. *manufacturing executive, light*
Clarey, John Robert *executive search consultant*
Cohen, Seymour *lawyer*
†Courtheoux, Richard James *management consultant*
Cunningham, R. John *financial consultant*
Day, Emerson *physician*
Degen, Bernard John, II *association executive*
Demaree, David Harry *utilities executive*
Fortune, Patrick John *packaging company executive*
Freedman, Walter G. *corporate services executive*
Gardner, Marshall Allen *merchant banker*
Hedberg, Richard J. *chemicals company executive*
Hirsch, Lawrence Leonard *physician, retired educator*
Hoffman, Charles Steven *fertilizer company executive*
Ingle, M(orton) Blakeman *corporate executive*
Jacobs, Richard Alan *management consultant*
Kasperson, Richard Willet *retired pharmaceutical company executive*
Kubek, Ralph A. *management consultant, accountant*
†Lane, William Noble, III *financial executive*
Lapin, Harvey I. *lawyer*
Lenon, Richard Allen *chemical corporation executive*
Lever, Alvin *health science association administrator*
Lower, Louis Gordon, II *insurance company executive*
Magad, Samuel *orchestra concertmaster, conductor*
Marshall, Irl Houston, Jr. *residential and commercial cleaning company executive*
McFadden, Joseph Patrick *insurance company executive*
Mc Laren, John Alexander *retired physician*
†Newman, Lawrence William *financial executive*
Nordman, Richard Dennis *chemical company executive*
Pesmen, Sandra (Mrs. Harold William Pesmen) *editor*
Piccolo, C. A. Lance *healthcare company executive*
Pinsof, Nathan *retired advertising executive*
Riskind, Kenneth Jay *metals company executive*
Rodriguez-Erdmann, Franz *physician*
Rudnick, Ellen Ava *health care executive*
Russell, William Steven *finance executive*
Salomon, Richard Adley *business executive, lawyer*
Saunders, Kenneth D. *insurance company executive, consultant, arbitrator*
Sayatovic, Wayne Peter *manufacturing company executive*
Scanlon, Edward F. *surgeon, educator*
Searle, William Louis *investment company executive*
Segal, Gordon I. *retail executive*
†Simon, Steve *public relations executive*
Slattery, James Joseph (Joe Slattery) *actor*
Snader, Jack Ross *publishing company executive*
Terra, Daniel James *chemical company executive*
Tolan, James Francis *corporate and financial communications executive, marketing consultant, financial analyst*
Tucker, Frederick Thomas *electronics company executive*
Turner, Billie B. *chemical company executive*
Turner, Lee *travel company executive*
Wajer, Ronald Edward *management consultant*
Weinstein, Ira Phillip *advertising executive*
Ziemann, Edward Frances *food service company executive, sales and marketing professional*

Northfield
Bruns, Nicolaus, Jr. *retired agricultural chemicals company executive, lawyer*
Carlin, Donald Walter *retired food products executive, consultant*
Cartwright, Howard E(ugene) *retired association executive*
Cutler, Robert Porter *psychiatrist, psychoanalyst*
Edelson, Ira J. *venture banker*
Fodrea, Carolyn Wrobel *educational researcher, publisher*
Fraenkel, Stephen Joseph *engineering and research executive*
Giffin, Mary Elizabeth *psychiatrist, educator*
Glass, Henry Peter *industrial designer, interior architect, educator*
Hotze, Charles Wayne *publisher, printer*
Hough, Richard T. *chemical company executive*
Lawrie, Henry DeVos, Jr. *lawyer*
Leslie, John Hampton *manufacturing executive*
Louis, John (Jeffry), Jr. *former ambassador*
Mayer, Richard Philip *food executive*
Morrison, Robert Scheck *food processing company executive*
O'Brien, Maurice James *business executive*
Otis, James, Jr. *architect*
Porter, Helen Viney (Mrs. Lewis M. Porter, Jr.) *lawyer*
Sernett, Richard Patrick *lawyer*
Shabica, Charles Wright *earth science educator*
Smart, Jackson Wyman, Jr. *business executive*
Smeds, Edward William *food company executive*
Stepan, Frank Quinn *chemical company executive*
Stern, Grace Mary *former state legislator*
Tenuta, Jean Louise *sports reporter, medical technologist*

Northlake
Di Matteo, James S. *food products executive*
Jasper, Paul Tucker *food company executive*

O'Fallon
Jenner, William Alexander *meteorologist, educator*

Oak Brook
†Akin, Lewis E. *mechanical engineer*
Baker, Robert J(ohn) *hospital administrator*
Barnes, Karen Kay *lawyer*
Bergerson, J. Steven *lawyer*
Buntrock, Dean Lewis *waste management company executive*
†Burzynski, William *chemicals executive, manufacturing executive, heavy*
Caldarazzo, Richard Joseph *lawyer*
Cantalupo, James Richard *restaurant company executive*
†Challenger, James Edgar, Jr. *computer software executive*
Cosenza, G. Joseph *real estate executive*
Degerstrom, James Marvin *engineering manager*
DeLorey, John Alfred *printing company executive*
Duerinck, Louis T. *retired railroad executive, attorney*
Flynn, Patrick J. *food products company executive*
Getz, Herbert A. *lawyer*
Gibson, James Thomas, Jr. *lawyer, consultant, antique dealer*
Goodwin, Daniel L. *real estate company executive*
Greenberg, Jack M. *food products executive*
Holsinger, Wayne Townsend *apparel manufacturing executive*
Honeywell, Larry Gene *publishing company executive, travel company executive*
Iorgulescu, Jorge *international chemicals executive, chemical engineer*
Johnson, Grant Lester *lawyer, retired manufacturing company executive*
Jones, John Earl *construction company executive*
Kelly, Donald Philip *entrepreneur*
Kramer, Janice Kay *real estate marketing executive*
Maher, David L. *drug store company executive*
Peterson, Roger Eric *hardware wholesale company executive*
Quinlan, Michael Robert *fast food franchise company executive*
Rensi, Edward Henry *restaurant chain executive*
Riley, Georgianne Marie *lawyer*
Risk, Richard R. *health facility administrator*
Root, Lynal A. *fast food company executive*
Schrage, Paul Daniel *fast food executive*
Schueppert, George Louis *financial executive*
Stauffer, Delmar J. *professional association executive*
Stonich, Timothy Whitman *financial executive*
Wardell, Kevin Stuart *hospital administrator*

Oak Brook Mall
Christian, Joseph Ralph *physician*
†Laskowski, Richard E. *retail hardware company executive*
O'Leary, Dennis Sophian *medical organization executive*
†Peterson, Allen Kenneth *healthcare administrator*

Oak Forest
Hull, Charles William *special education educator*

Oak Lawn
†Gordon, Edward Earl *training company executive, educator*
Massura, Eileen Kathleen *family therapist*
Rathi, Manohar Lal *pediatrician, neonatologist*

Oak Park
Adelman, William John *university labor and industrial relations educator*
Bell, Robert Alan *architect*
Bowman, James Henry *writer*
Brackett, Edward Boone, III *orthopedic surgeon*
Cary, William Sterling *retired church executive*
Clark, John Peter, III *engineering consultant*
Davis, Christine Eurich *elementary education educator*
Devereux, Timothy Edward *advertising agency executive*
Douglas, Kenneth Jay *food products executive*
Edwards, Linda H. *public health professional*
Knight, Robert Milton *journalist, educator*
Kotlowitz, Alex *writer, journalist*
Lyles, Jean Elizabeth Caffey *journalist*
Notaro, Michael R. *data processing and computer service executive*
Schultz, Bryan Christopher *dermatologist, educator*
Thompson, Charles Edwin *import consultant and manufacturer*
Tomek, Laura Lindemann *marketing executive*
Valinsky, Mark Steven *podiatrist*
Varchmin, Thomas Edward *environmental health administrator*
Worley, Marvin George, Jr. *architect*

Oglesby
Zeller, Francis Joseph *academic administrator*

Okawville
Schmale, Allen Lee *financial services company executive*

Olney
Edwards, Ian Keith *obstetrician, gynecologist*

Olympia Fields
Haley, David Alan *preferred provider organization executive*
Purdy, Charles Robert *corporate executive*
Sprinkel, Beryl Wayne *economist, consultant*

Oregon
Abbott, David Henry *manufacturing company executive*

Orland Park
Dyott, Richard Burnaby *research engineering executive*
English, Floyd Leroy *telecommunications company executive*
Gittelman, Marc Jeffrey *manufacturing and financial executive*
Leonard, Robert Dougherty *communications company executive*
Schultz, Barbara Marie *insurance company executive*

Oswego
Stephens, Steve Arnold *real estate broker*

Palatine
Butler, John Musgrave *business financial consultant*
Claassen, W(alter) Marshall *employment company executive*
Fitzgerald, Gerald Francis *retired banker*
Fitzgerald, Peter Gosselin *state senator, lawyer*
Flavin, Patrick Brian *investment company executive, securities analyst*
Hull, Elizabeth Anne *English language educator*
Kasten, Richard John *accountant*
Kern, Byron Mehl *retired chemical company executive*
Lee, Tien Shuey *chemical firm executive*
Makowski, M. Paul *electronics research executive*
Medin, Lowell Ansgard *security company executive*
Nagatoshi, Konrad R. *anthropology educator, information systems specialist*
Novak, Robert Louis *civil engineer, pavement management consultant*
Perez, Gerard Vincent *art publishing company executive*
Pohl, Frederik *writer*
†Roggeveen, Richard *operation services executive, executive recruiter*
Smith-Pierce, Patricia A. *speech professional*

Palos Heights
Higgins, Francis Edward *history educator*
Nederhood, Joel H. *church organization executive, minister*

Palos Hills
Crawley, Vernon Obadiah *academic adminstrator*

Palos Park
Crewe, Albert Victor *physicist, business executive, former research administrator*
Lawler, Susan George *elementary education educator*
Nelson, Lawrence Evan *business consultant*

Park Forest
Billig, Etel Jewel *theater director, actress*
Goodrich, John Bernard *lawyer, consultant*
McDonald, Stanford Laurel *clinical psychologist*
Putnam, Robert E. *writer, editor*
Steinmetz, Jon David *mental health facility administrator, psychologist*

Park Ridge
Adkins, Howard Eugene *aluminum company executive*
Boe, Gerard Patrick *health science association administrator*
Bridges, Jack Edgar *electronics engineer*
Carr, Gilbert Randle *retired railroad executive*
Casten, Carol Elizabeth *nursing administrator*
Curtis, Philip James *lawyer*
Ellis, Robert Griswold *engineering executive*
Howlett, Phyllis Lou *athletics conference administrator*
Kleckner, Dean Ralph *trade association executive*
Kukla, Robert John *association executive*
Margolies, Raymond *management consulting company executive*
McCarthy, Michael Shawn *health care company executive, lawyer*
Peterson, Richard Elton *publisher*
Raffel, Louis B. *association executive*
Rosenheim, Howard Harris *management consultant*
Ryan, Judith Andre *health care executive, hospital administrator, nurse*
Schultz, Richard Carlton *plastic surgeon*
Tongue, William Walter *economics and business consultant, educator emeritus*
Ummel, Stephen L. *health facility administrator*
Weber, Philip Joseph *retired manufacturing company executive*
Weinberg, Milton, Jr. *cardiovascular-thoracic surgeon*

Pekin
Bell, John Richard *dentist*
Clevenger, Robert Vincent *lawyer*
†Frison, Rick *agricultural company executive*
Heiple, James Dee *state supreme court justice*
Herbstreith, Yvonne Mae *primary education educator*
Scheffler, Robert W. *insurance company executive*

Peoria
Allen, Lyle Wallace *lawyer*
Ballowe, James *English educator, author*
Brazil, John Russell *academic administrator*
Chamberlain, Joseph Miles *astronomer, educator*
Christison, William Henry, III *lawyer*
Cunningham, Raymond Leo *research chemist*
Dabney, Seth Mason, III *lawyer*
Dancey, Charles Lohman *newspaper executive*
Doyle, Richard Lee *architect, engineer*
Eissfeldt, Theodore L. *lawyer*
Fites, Donald Vester *tractor company executive*
Francis, John Elbert *university dean*
Gould, David Scott *equipment manufacturing company executive*
Grundbacher, Frederick John *geneticist, educator*
Guerindon, Pierre Claude *construction equipment company executive*
Herring, Susan Kay *library director*
Kenyon, Leslie Harrison *architect*
King, Jerry Wayne *research chemist*
Lindgren, William Dale *librarian*
MacBurney, Edward Harding *bishop*
Maloof, James A(loysius) *mayor, real estate company executive*
McCollum, Jean Hubble *medical assistant*
McConnell, John Thomas *newspaper executive, publisher*
McDade, Joe Billy *federal judge*
Meriden, Terry *physician*
Michael, Jonathan Edward *insurance company executive*
Mihm, Michael Martin *federal judge*
Mikulecky, Thomas J. *city manager*
Morgan, Robert Dale *federal judge*
Murphy, Sharon Margaret *university official, educator*
Myers, John Joseph *bishop*
Nielsen, Harald Christian *retired chemist*
Osborn, Terry Wayne *biochemist, executive*
Parsons, Donald James *retired bishop*
Peak, William Roy *newspaper editor*
Poupard, James J. *controller*
Price Boday, Mary Kathryn *choreographer, small business owner, educator*
Rainson, Ronald Lee *engineering executive, consultant*
Rothfus, John Arden *chemist*
Ryan, Michael Beecher *lawyer, former government official*
Slane, Henry Pindell *broadcasting executive*
Slone, R. Wayne *utility company executive*
Smith, Clyde R. *counselor educator*
Stephens, Gerald D. *insurance company executive*
Strodel, Robert Carl *lawyer*
Sullivan, Paul J. *legal administrator*
Thompson, William Scott *lawyer*
Viets, Robert O. *utilities executive*
Watson, Ellen I. *academic administrator*

Peru
Benning, Joseph Raymond *principal*
Carus, André Wolfgang *educational publishing firm executive*
Carus, Milton Blouke *chemical company executive, publisher*

Plainfield
Aldinger, Thomas Lee *construction executive*
Chakrabarti, Subrata Kumar *marine research engineer*
Chase, Maria Elaine Garoufalis *publishing company executive*
Schinderle, Robert Frank *hospital administrator*

Poplar Grove
Hullah, Ann Marie *elementary education educator*

Princeton
Johnson, Watts Carey *lawyer*
Schultz, Robert Vernon *entrepreneur*

Princeville
Erickson, Marianna Cuany *family physician*

Prophetstown
Thompson, George Howard *livestock transportation company executive*

Prospect Heights
Clark, Donald Cameron *financial services company executive*
Clark, Donald Robert *retired insurance company executive*
Hindo, Walid Afram *radiology educator, researcher*

Quincy
Dorsey, Jeffrey Alan *broadcaster*
Liebig, Richard Arthur *retired manufacturing company executive*
†Niemann, Richard Henry *grocery executive*
Points, Roy Wilson *municipal official*
Shade, Thomas L. *agricultural products executive*
Toal, James Francis *academic administrator*
Tyer, Travis Earl *librarian*

River Forest
Columbus, Chris Joseph *film director, screenwriter*
Hamper, Robert Joseph *marketing executive*
Koenig, Michael Edward Davison *information science educator*
Krentz, Eugene Leo *university president, educator, minister*
Li, Tze-chung *lawyer, educator*
Lund, Sister Candida *college chancellor*
Marco, Guy Anthony *library educator*
McCusker, Mary Lauretta *library science educator*
Murray, Sister Jean Carolyn *college president*
Rimbach, Evangeline Lois *music educator*
Sloan, Jeanette Pasin *artist*
Wanamaker, Robert Joseph *advertising company executive*
White, Philip Butler *artist*

River Grove
Hillert, Gloria Bonnin *anatomist, educator*
Litzsinger, Paul Richard *publishing company executive*

Riverdale
Hoekwater, James Warren *treasurer*
Saulsbury, Ruth Eva *retired special education educator*

Riverside
Fleck, Gordon Pierce *accounting firm executive*
Howlett, Carolyn Svrluga *art educator*
Perkins, William H., Jr. *finance company executive*
Potokar, Richard Albert *architect*

Riverwoods
Bartlett, Robert William *lawyer, publishing executive*
Douglas, Bruce Lee *oral and maxillofacial surgeon, educator, health consultant, gerontology consultant*
Hynes, Mary Ann *publishing executive, lawyer*
Kirby, Emily Baruch *psychologist, writer*
Leatham, John Tonkin *business executive*

Rochelle
†Ray, Gary J. *food products executive*

Rock Falls
Bippus, David Paul *manufacturing company executive*

Rock Island
Bergendoff, Conrad John Immanuel *clergyman*
Brauch, Merry Ruth Moore *gifted education consultant*
Cheney, Thomas Ward *insurance company executive*
Forlini, Frank John, Jr. *cardiologist*
†Hickerson, William Joseph, Jr. *geology researcher, educator*
Horstmann, James Douglas *college official*
Lardner, Henry Petersen (Peter Lardner) *insurance company executive*
Mulich, Steve Francis *safety engineer*
Sundelius, Harold W. *geology educator*
Telleen, John Martin *retired judge*
Tredway, Thomas *college president*
Wallace, Franklin Sherwood *lawyer*
Whitmore, Charles Horace *utility executive, lawyer, management consultant*

Rockford
Anderson, LaVerne Eric *lawyer*
Barrick, William Henry *lawyer*
Bradley, Charles MacArthur *architect*
Chitwood, Julius Richard *librarian*
†Delavan, John *freight transportation company executive*
DeLuca, August Frank, Jr. *financial executive*
Donovan, Paul *aerospace executive*
†Doran, Thomas George *bishop*
Eliason, Jon Tate *electrical engineer*
†Gaylord, Edson I. *manufacturing company executive*
Hasley, Ronald K. *bishop*
Heerens, Robert Edward *physician*
†Hess, George J. *electrical engineer, consultant*
Hill, Scott Alan *architect, farmer*
Horst, Bruce Everett *manufacturing company executive*
Howard, John Addison *former college president, institute executive*
Larsen, Steven *orchestra conductor*
Lynn, Janet (Janet Lynn Nowicki Salomon) *professional figure skater*
Marelli, Sister M. Anthony *secondary school principal*
Maysent, Harold Wayne *hospital administrator*
Meuleman, Robert Joseph *banker*
Muck, George Arthur *food products executive*
O'Donnell, William David *construction firm executive*
O'Hare, Don R. *corporate executive*
Olson, Stanley William *physician, educator, medical school dean*
Pritikin, Roland I. *opthalmologic surgeon, writer, lecturer*
Reinhard, Philip G. *federal judge*
Reno, Roger *lawyer*
†Rosenfeld, Joel Charles *librarian*
Roszkowski, Stanley Julian *federal judge*
Schilling, Richard M. *lawyer, corporate executive*
Steele, Carl Lavern *academic administrator*
Van Vleet, William Benjamin *lawyer, life insurance company executive*
†Vincenti-Brown, Crispin Rufus William *engineering executive*
Walhout, Justine Simon *chemistry educator*
Ward, Sylvan Donald *music conductor, educator*
Weissbard, David Raymond *minister*
Whitsell, Doris Benner *retired educator*
†Wilson, Fred C. *manufacturing company executive*

Rolling Meadows
Brennan, Charles Martin, III *construction company executive*
†Cain, R. Wayne *rental leasing company executive*
Cushing, Robert Charles *beverage company executive*
†Ferguson, C. David *electronics company executive*
Grogan, Kenneth Augustine *publishing company executive*
Mynatt, John Rupert, Jr. *soft drink bottling executive*
Sturmon, Patricia Montgomery *public relations executive*

Romeoville
Lifka, Mary Lauranne *history educator*

Roscoe
Dorsey-Wong, Kathleen M. *critical care nurse, administrator*

Rosemont
Baldwin, Gerald Erwin *airline pilot*
Burkhardt, Edward Arnold *transportation company executive*
Good, William Allen *professional society executive*
Isenberg, Howard Lee *manufacturing company executive*
Stanton, James Adkins *technology equipment leasing company executive, consultant*
Trznadel, Frank Dwight, Jr. *leasing company executive*
Walsh, Martin R. *computer company executive*

Round Lake
Johnston, William David *health care company executive*
Kingdon, Henry Shannon *physician, biochemist, educator, executive*

Saint Charles
Alfini, James Joseph *dean, lawyer, educator*
McCartney, Charles Price *retired obstetrician-gynecologist*
Mc Kay, Thomas, Jr. *lawyer*
Stone, John McWilliams, Jr. *electronics executive*
Urhausen, James Nicholas *real estate developer, construction executive*
Zito, James Anthony *retired railroad company executive*

Savanna
Foulk, David Wingerd *military civilian executive*

Savoy
Bosworth, Douglas LeRoy *farm implement company executive*

Scales Mound
Lieberman, Archie *photographer, writer*

Schaumburg
Bauchiero, James *transportation executive*
Bolinder, William Howard *insurance company executive*
Boston, Leona *organization executive*
Brenner, Arnold S. *electronics company executive*
Chitwood, Lera Catherine *information professional, manufacturing company manager*
Collins, James Francis *lawyer*
Edmunds, Jane Clara *communications consultant*
Galvin, Christopher B. *electronics company executive*
Galvin, Robert W. *electronics executive*
Geiger, Joseph Francis *financial planner*
Harmon, Nancy Jean *elementary school educator*
Heaton, Syd N. *computer company executive*
Hickey, John Thomas *electronics company executive*
Hill, Raymond Joseph *packaging company executive*
Kadish, Steven A. *retail executive*
Katzir, Levy *electronics company executive*
Keene, Floyd Stanley *lawyer*
Keil, M. David *international association executive*
Krebs, Robert Duncan *transportation company executive*
Langsdorf, Alexander, Jr. *physicist*
Meltzer, Brian *lawyer*
Miller, Vernon Dallace *minister*
†Mitchell, John Francis *electronics company executive*
Morgan, David Ernest *computer and communications research executive*
†Nauert, Robert F. *insurance company executive*
Nettleton, David *religious administrator*
†O'Connor, John E(dward), Jr. *association executive*
Oldberg, Carl Malcolm *public relations executive*
Payton, Walter (Sweetness) *professional race car driver, former professional football player*
Poth, Edward Cornelius *construction company executive*
Rashkow, Ronald *home improvement company executive*
Roach, William Russell *training and education executive*
Schulmeyer, Gerhard *manufacturing executive*
Schwab, Susan Carol *electronics company executive*
Stephens, Norval Blair, Jr. *marketing consultant*
Tompson, Marian Leonard *association executive*
Tooker, Gary Lamarr *electronics company executive*
Wagner, Betty Valiree *medical organization executive*
Walker, Robert Giles, Jr. *architect*
Weise, Richard Henry *lawyer, corporate executive*
Weisz, William Julius *electronics company executive*
Wine-Banks, Jill Susan *lawyer*
Wojcik, Kathleen Louise *state representative*
Wyslotsky, Ihor *engineering company executive*

Schiller Park
Ring, Alice Ruth Bishop *physician*

Scott A F B
†Hemingway, Thomas L. *career officer*

Shelbyville
Gloede, Richard *management consulting executive*
Hullinger, Golden E. *manufacturing company executive*

Skokie
Alexander, John Charles *pharmaceutical company executive, physician*
Altschul, Alfred Samuel *airline executive*
Bakalar, John Stephen *printing and publishing company executive*
Bellows, Randall Trueblood *ophthalmologist, educator*
†Bielinski, Donald Edward *financial executive*
Bogomolny, Robert Lee *lawyer*
Boxer, Robert William *allergist*
†Buckardt, Everett L. *marketing executive*
†Buonanno, Vincent J. *metal products executive*
†Caldwell, Wiley North *retired distribution company executive*
Childers, John Henry *talent company executive, personality representative*
Corley, William Gene *engineering research executive*
†DeSchutter, Richard U. *pharmaceutical company executive*
Dishman, Leonard I. *accountant*
Filler, Robert *chemistry educator*
Fluno, Jere David *business executive*
Gleason, John Patrick, Jr. *trade association executive*
Goldberg, Arthur Lewis *manufacturing company executive*
Goldberg, Vicki Comm *employment services executive*
Goldmann, Morton Aaron *cardiologist*
Grainger, David William *distribution company executive*
Hedien, Wayne Evans *retired insurance company executive*
Herting, Robert Leslie *pharmaceutical executive*
Hognestad, Eivind *retired civil engineer*
Johansson, Nils A. *manufacturing executive*
Kranz, Norman *advertising executive*
Krucks, William *electronics manufacturing executive*
Mayes, Frank Gorr *food company executive*
McNally, Andrew, III *printer, publisher*
McNally, Andrew, IV *publishing executive*
Olwin, John Hurst *surgeon*
Pappano, Robert Daniel *financial company executive*
Rubow, W. Steven *food company executive*
Sayers, Gale *computer company executive, retired professional football player*
Siegal, Burton Lee *product designer, consultant, inventor*
Siegal, Rita Goran *engineering company executive*
Steele, Kurt D. *publishing company executive*
Van Wagner, Bruce *telecommunications equipment distribution company executive*
†Weinberg, David *chemicals executive*
White, William James *information management and services company executive;*
Wildermuth, Roger Gregory *publishing company executive*
†Zakin, Jonathan Newell *computer industry executive*

South Elgin
Burdett, George Craig *plastics industry executive*

South Holland
Mulder, Dennis Marlin *religious organization executive*

Schaap, Marcia *special education educator*

Springfield
Blackman, Jeanne A. *lobbyist*
Budinger, Charles Jude *state agency insurance analyst*
Burris, Roland Wallace *state attorney general*
Byers, Gary William *religious organization administrator*
Cadigan, Patrick Joseph *lawyer*
Clarke, John Patrick *newspaper publisher*
Currie, Barbara Flynn *state legislator*
†Davis, George Cullom, Jr. *history educator*
Dodd, Robert Bruce *physician, educator*
Edgar, Jim *governor*
Ferguson, Mark Harmon *banker, lawyer*
Fischoff, Ephraim *humanities educator, sociologist, social worker*
Frank, Stuart *cardiologist*
Gallina, Charles Onofrio *nuclear scientist*
†Gottfried, Theodore Alexander *lawyer*
Greenwalt, Clifford Lloyd *utility executive*
Hahn, Ralph Crane *structural engineer, consultant*
Hallmark, Donald Parker *museum director*
Hanson, Walter Edmund *consulting civil engineer*
Heintz, Jack *publishing company executive*
Holland, John Madison *family practice physician*
Hudson, Claude Earl *banker*
Hughes, Ann *state legislator*
Humphrey, Howard C. *insurance company executive*
Jackson, Robert William *utility company executive*
Kaitschuk, John Paul *bishop*
†Kustra, Robert W. (Bob Kustra) *lieutenant governor, political scientist, educator*
Laabs, Allison C. *hospital administrator*
Layzell, Thomas D. *academic administrator*
Lessen, Larry Lee *federal judge*
Lohman, Walter Rearick *banker*
Lynn, Naomi B. *university chancellor*
Lyons, J. Rolland *civil engineer*
Madigan, Michael Joseph *state legislator*
Mc Millan, R(obert) Bruce *museum executive, anthropologist*
Mervis, Louis *school system administrator*
Miller, Benjamin K. *state supreme court justice*
Mills, Richard Henry *federal judge*
Mogerman, Susan *state agency administrator*
Moore, Andrea S. *state legislator*
Moy, Richard Henry *academic dean, educator*
Munyer, Edward A. *zoologist, museum adminstrator*
Myers, Phillip Ward *otolaryngologist*
Nanavati, Grace Luttrell *dancer, choreographer, instructor*
Netsch, Dawn Clark *state official, law educator*
Oxtoby, Robert Boynton *lawyer*
Petterchak, Janice A. *library director*
Philip, James (Pate Philip) *state senator*
Phillips, John Robert *college dean, educator*
Poorman, Robert Lewis *education educator, consultant, academic administrator*
Rabinovich, Sergio *physician, educator*
†Rockey, Paul Henry *physician, medical educator, university official*
Ronen, Carol *state legislator*
Rowe, Max L. *lawyer, corporate executive, management consultant, judge*
Ryan, Daniel Leo *bishop*
Satterthwaite, Helen Foster *state legislator*
Severns, Penny L. *state legislator*
Shim, Sang Koo *state mental health official*
Shotwell, Malcolm Green *minister*
Sondag, Michael Robert *association executive*
Stroh, Raymond Eugene *personnel executive*
Tarr, Paul Cresson, III *insurance company executive*
Temple, Wayne Calhoun *historian*
Thomas, Payne Edward Lloyd *publisher*
†Thompson, Donald Edward *engineering company executive*
Thompson, Joyce Elizabeth *arts management educator*
Travis, Lawrence Allan *accountant*
Trstensky, Sister Jomary *hospital administrator*
Van Meter, Abram DeBois *lawyer, retired banker*
Wehrle, Leroy Snyder *economist, educator*
Welch, Patrick Daniel *state senator*
Whitney, John Freeman, Jr. *political science educator*
Wood, Harlington, Jr. *federal judge*
Worthing, Carol Marie *minister*
Zollar, Nikki Michelle *state agency administrator*
Zook, Elvin Glenn *plastic surgeon, educator*

Sterling
Albrecht, Beverly Jean *special education educator*
Gurnitz, Robert Ned *steel industry company executive*
Knight, Herbert Borwell *manufacturing company executive*
von Bergen Wessels, Pennie Lea *state legislator*

Streator
Harrison, Frank Joseph *lawyer*

Summit Argo
Abramowicz, Alfred L. *bishop*
Urban, Patricia A. *former elementary school educator*

Sumner
Trent, Wendell Campbell *business owner*

Sycamore
Grace, John Eugene *business forms company executive*
Johnson, Yvonne Amalia *elementary education educator, science consultant*

Taylorville
Ford, Ellen Hodson *composer*

Tinley Park
Denys, Edward Paul *education educator*
Johnson, Herman *secondary education educator*

Tonica
Ryan, Howard Chris *retired state supreme court justice*

University Park
Lingamneni, Jaganmohan Rao *criminology educator*
Strukoff, Rudolf Stephen *music educator*
Wentz, Walter John *health administration educator*

Urbana
Addy, Alva Leroy *mechanical engineer*
Albrecht, Felix Robert *mathematics educator*
Aldridge, Alfred Owen *English language educator*
Alkire, Richard Collin *chemical engineering educator*
Andersen, Kenneth Eldon *speech communication educator*
Antonsen, Elmer Harold *Germanic languages and literature educator*
Arnstein, Walter Leonard *historian, educator*
Axford, Roy Arthur *nuclear engineering educator*
Baer, Werner *economist, educator*
Baker, David Hiram *biochemist, biochemistry educator*
Balbach, Stanley Byron *lawyer*
Banwart, Wayne Lee *agronomy, environmental science educator*
Basar, Tamer *electrical engineering educator*
Bateman, John Jay *classics educator*
Bateman, Paul Trevier *mathematician, educator*
Bates, James Leonard *historian*
Baym, Nina *English educator*
Bayne, James Wilmer *mechanical engineering educator*
Beak, Peter Andrew *chemistry educator*
Beavers, Alvin Herman *soil science educator*
Beck, Paul Adams *metallurgist, educator*
Becker, Donald Eugene *animal science educator*
Bedford, Norton Moore *accounting educator*
Bell, Gerald Wayne *physical education educator*
Bentley, Orville George *retired agricultural educator, dean emeritus*
Bergeron, Clifton George *ceramic engineer, educator*
Birnbaum, Howard Kent *materials science educator*
Blahut, Richard Edward *electrical and computer engineering educator*
Blair, Lachlan Ferguson *urban planner, educator*
Bloomfield, Daniel Kermit *college dean, physician*
Boardman, Eunice *music educator*
Brichford, Maynard Jay *archivist*
Broudy, Harry Samuel *retired philosophy educator*
Brown, Theodore Lawrence *chemistry educator*
Brün, Herbert *composer*
Bruner, Edward M. *anthropology educator*
Bryant, Marvin Pierce *bacteriologist, microbiologist, educator*
Buck, William Boyd *toxicology educator*
Buetow, Dennis Edward *physiology educator*
Burdge, Rabel James *sociology educator*
Burger, Ambrose William *agronomy educator*
†Burger, Robert Harold *librarian*
Burkholder, Donald Lyman *mathematician, educator*
†Carbonneau, Beth Ellen *association administrator*
Carmen, Ira Harris *political scientist, educator*
Carroll, Robert Wayne *mathematics educator*
Chao, Bei Tse *mechanical engineering educator*
Chato, John Clark *mechanical engineering educator*
Cheng, Chin-Chuan *linguistics educator*
Cheryan, Munir *agricultural studies educator, biochemical engineering educator*
Choldin, Marianna Tax *librarian, educator*
Chow, Poo *wood technologist, scientist*
Clausing, Arthur M. *mechanical engineering educator*
Cohen, Stephen Philip *political science and history educator*
Cole, Michael Allen *microbiologist, educator*
Coleman, Paul Dare *electrical engineering educator*
Conry, Thomas Francis *mechanical engineering educator, consultant*
Courson, Roger Lee *agricultural educator*
Crang, Richard Francis Earl *plant and cell biologist, research center administrator*
Crofts, Antony Richard *biophysics educator*
Cunningham, Clark Edward *anthropology educator*
Curtin, David Yarrow *chemist, educator*
Cusano, Cristino *mechanical engineer, educator*
†Davis, Elisabeth Bachman *librarian, library administration educator*
Dawn, Clarence Ernest *history educator*
Debrunner, Peter George *physics educator*
Dickinson, David Budd, Jr. *horticulture educator*
Dobrovolny, Jerry Stanley *engineering educator*
Doob, Joseph Leo *mathematician, educator*
Dovring, Folke *land economics educator, consultant*
Drickamer, Harry George *retired chemistry educator*
Due, Jean Margaret *agricultural economist, educator*
Dunn, Floyd *biophysicist, bioengineer, educator*
Dziuk, Philip John *animal scientist educator*
Economy, James *polymer researcher, consultant*
Edelsbrunner, Herbert *computer scientist, mathematician*
Eden, James Gary *electrical engineering and physics educator, researcher*
Ehrlich, Gert *science educator, researcher*
Elyn, Mark *opera singer, educator*
†Endress, Anton G. *horticulturist, educator*
Engelbrecht, Richard Stevens *environmental engineering educator*
†Everly, Jack Crittenden *agriculturist, educator*
Faulkner, Larry Ray *chemistry educator, academic officer*
Fitz-Gerald, Roger Miller *lawyer*
Forbes, Richard Mather *biochemistry educator*
Ford, Richard Earl *plant virologist, educator, academic administrator*
Fossum, Robert Merle *mathematician, educator*
Frazzetta, Thomas H. *evolutionary biologist, functional morphologist, educator*
Friedman, Stanley *insect physiologist, educator*
Gabriel, Michael *psychology educator*
Gaddy, Oscar Lee *electrical engineering educator*
Gaeng, Paul Ami *foreign language educator*
Garfield, Evelyn Picon *Spanish educator*
Garrigus, Upson Stanley *animal science and international agriculture educator*
Giertz, J. Fred *economics educator*
Giles, Eugene *anthropology educator*
†Glaser, Janet H. *science administrator, biochemistry educator*
†Glawe, Dean A. *mycology educator*
Goering, Carroll E. *agricultural engineering educator*
Goldberg, Samuel Irving *mathematics educator*
Goldwasser, Edwin Leo *physicist*
Goodman, William I. *urban planner, educator*
Gorecki, Jan *sociologist, educator*
Gove, Samuel Kimball *political science educator*
Govindjee *biophysics and biology educator*
Gray, John Walker *mathematician, educator*
Greene, Laura Helen *physicist*
Greenough, William Tallant *psychobiologist, educator*
Greenwold, Warren Eldon *retired physician, medical educator*
†Gruebele, Martin *chemistry educator*
Gutowsky, Herbert Sander *chemistry educator*
Haile, H. G. *German language and literature educator*

Hajj, Ibrahim Nasri *electrical and computer engineering educator*
Haken, Wolfgang *mathematics educator*
Hall, William Joel *civil engineer, educator*
Hannon, Bruce Michael *engineer, educator*
Hanratty, Thomas Joseph *chemical engineer, educator*
Harlan, Jack Rodney *geneticist, emeritus educator*
Harper, James Eugene *plant physiologist*
Hay, Richard Le Roy *geology educator*
Heichel, Gary Harold *agronomy educator*
Helle, Steven James *educator, lawyer*
Hendrick, George *English language educator*
Henson, C. Ward *mathematician, educator*
Herrin, Moreland *civil engineering educator, consultant*
Hess, Karl *electrical and computer engineering educator*
Hill, Lowell Dean *agricultural marketing educator*
Hixon, James Edward *physiology educator*
Hobgood, Burnet M. *theater educator*
Hoeft, Robert Gene *agriculture educator*
Hoffmeister, Donald Frederick *zoology educator*
Holonyak, Nick, Jr. *electrical engineering educator*
Holt, Donald A. *university administrator, agronomist, consultant, researcher*
Horwitz, Alan Fredrick *cell and molecular biology educator*
Huang, Thomas Shi-Tao *electrical engineering educator, researcher*
Hunt, Donnell Ray *agricultural engineering educator*
Hurt, James Riggins *English language educator*
Hymowitz, Theodore *plant geneticist, educator*
Iben, Icko, Jr. *astrophysicist, educator*
Ikenberry, Stanley Oliver *university president*
Isaacson, Richard Evan *microbiologist*
Jackson, Edwin Atlee *physicist, educator*
Jacobson, Howard *classics educator*
Jenkins, William Kenneth *electrical engineering educator*
Jerrard, Richard Patterson *mathematics educator*
Jockusch, Carl Groos, Jr. *mathematics educator*
Jonas, Jiri *chemistry educator*
Jones, Benjamin Angus, Jr. *retired agricultural engineering educator, administrator*
Kachru, Braj Behari *linguist*
Kachru, Yamuna *linguist*
Kang, Sung-Mo (Steve Kang) *electrical engineering educator*
Kesler, Clyde Ervin *engineering educator*
Kim, Chin-Woo *linguist, educator*
Kirkpatrick, R(obert) James *geology educator*
Klein, Miles Vincent *physics educator*
Knake, Ellery Louis *weed science educator*
Knight, Frank Bardsley *mathematics educator*
Kolodziej, Edward Albert *political scientist, educator*
Konisky, Jordan *microbiology educator*
Kumar, Panganamala Ramana *electrical and computer engineering educator*
Langenheim, Ralph Louis, Jr. *geology educator*
Lauterbur, Paul C(hristian) *chemistry educator*
Lawrie, Duncan H. *computer science educator, consultant*
Lazarus, David *physicist, educator*
Leuthold, Raymond Martin *agricultural economics educator*
Lieberman, Laurence *poet, educator*
Liebman, Judith Rae Stenzel *operations research educator*
Linowes, David Francis *political economist, educator, corporate executive*
Littlewood, Thomas Benjamin *journalism educator*
Lo, Kwok-Yung *astronomer*
Lodge, James Robert *dairy science educator*
Mainous, Bruce Hale *foreign language educator*
Makri, Nancy *chemistry educator*
Manning, Sylvia *English studies educator*
Marcovich, Miroslav *classics educator*
Maxwell, William Hall Christie *civil engineering educator*
May, Walter Grant *chemical engineer*
Mayer, Enrique José *anthropology educator*
Mayer, Robert Wallace *emeritus finance educator*
Mayes, Paul Eugene *engineering educator, technical consultant*
Mazumder, Jyotirmoy *mechanical and industrial engineering educator*
Mc Clellan, William Monson *library administrator*
McColley, Robert McNair *history educator*
Mc Conkie, George Wilson *education educator*
Mc Glamery, Marshal Dean *agronomy, weed science educator*
Melby, John B. *composer, educator*
Merkelo, Henri *electronics and computer scientist*
Meyer, Richard Charles *microbiologist*
Mihalas, Dimitri Manuel *astronomer, educator*
Miley, George Hunter *nuclear engineering educator*
Miller, Robert Earl *engineer, educator*
†Morkoç, Hadis *electrical engineer, educator*
Nanney, David Ledbetter *genetics educator*
†Nardulli, Peter F. *political science educator*
Nelson, Ralph Alfred *physician*
Nettl, Bruno *anthropology and musicology educator*
Newman, John Kevin *classics educator*
†O'Brien, Nancy Patricia *librarian, educator*
Ogren, William Lewis *physiologist, educator*
O'Morchoe, Charles Christopher Creagh *administrator, anatomical sciences educator*
O'Morchoe, Patricia Jean *pathologist, educator*
Ormsbee, Allen Ives *aeronautical and astronautical engineering educator, researcher, consultant*
Pai, Anantha Mangalore *electrical engineering educator, consultant*
Parker, Alan John *veterinary neurologist, educator, researcher*
Perkins, William Randolph *electrical engineer, educator*
Peterson, Theodore Bernard *retired journalism educator*
Pethick, Christopher John *physicist*
†Pirkle, William H. *chemistry educator*
Poss, Jeffery Scott *architect, educator*
Prosser, C. Ladd *physiology educator, researcher*
Prussing, Laurel Lunt *state official, economist*
Queller, Donald Edward *historian, educator*
Rao, Nannapaneni Narayana *electrical engineer*
Rebeiz, Constantin Anis *plant physiology educator*
Replinger, John Gordon *architect*
Resek, Robert William *university administrator*
Ricketts, Gary Eugene *animal scientist*
Riley, Robert Bartlett *landscape architect*
Rotzoll, Kim Brewer *advertising and communications educator*
Rowland, Theodore Justin *physicist, educator*
Salamon, Myron Ben *physicist, educator*
Sameh, Ahmed Hamdy *computer science educator*
Sandage, Charles Harold *advertising educator*
†Sargent, Malcolm Lee *research biochemist, research geneticist, botany educator and researcher*
Satterthwaite, Cameron B. *physics educator*
Scanlan, Richard Thomas *classics educator*
Schacht, Richard Lawrence *philosopher, educator*
Schmidt, Stephen Christopher *agricultural economist, educator*
Schweizer, Kenneth Steven *physics educator*
Seigler, David Stanley *botanist, chemist, educator*
Seitz, Wesley Donald *agricultural economics educator*
†Shaffer, Louis Richard *engineering research administrator, civil engineering educator*
Shtohryn, Dmytro Michael *librarian, educator*
Shuman, R(obert) Baird *academic program director, writer, english educator, educational consultant*
Shurtleff, Malcolm C. *plant pathologist, consultant, educator, extension specialist*
Siedler, Arthur James *nutrition and food science educator*
Siess, Chester Paul *civil engineering educator*
Simon, Jack Aaron *geologist, former state official*
†Sinclair, James Burton *plant pathology educator, consultant*
Small, Erwin *veterinarian, educator*
Snyder, Lewis Emil *astrophysicist*
Socie, Darrell Frederick *mechanical engineering educator*
Solberg, Winton Udell *history educator*
Sonka, Steven T. *agricultural economics educator, consultant*
Soo, Shao Lee *mechanical engineer, educator*
Spence, Mary Lee *historian*
Spitze, Robert George Frederick *agricultural economics educator*
Splittstoesser, Walter Emil *plant physiologist*
Stallmeyer, James Edward *engineer, educator*
Stillinger, Jack Clifford *English educator*
Stout, Glenn Emanuel *water resources center administrator*
†Suslick, Kenneth Sanders *chemistry educator*
Suzuki, Michio *mathematics educator*
Swenson, George Warner, Jr. *electronics engineer, radio astronomer, educator*
Switzer, Robert Lee *biochemistry educator*
Talbot, Emile Joseph *French language educator*
Tang, Wilson Hon-chung *engineering educator*
Thompson, Margaret M. *physical education educator*
Tondeur, Philippe Maurice *mathematician, educator*
Trick, Timothy Noel *electrical and computer engineering educator, researcher*
Trigger, Kenneth James *manufacturing engineering educator*
Visek, Willard James *nutritionist, animal scientist, physician, educator*
Voss, Edward William, Jr. *immunologist, educator*
Wagner, William Charles *veterinarian*
Waldbauer, Gilbert Peter *entomologist, educator*
Warfield, William Caesar *singer, actor, educator*
Watson, Paula D. *library administrator*
Wattenberg, Albert *physicist, educator*
Watts, Emily Stipes *English educator*
Wedgeworth, Robert *university librarian, dean, former association executive*
Weir, Morton Webster *retired university chancellor and educator*
Wert, Charles Allen *metallurgical and mining engineering educator*
Westwater, James William *chemical engineering educator*
White, W(illiam) Arthur *geologist*
Whitt, Gregory Sidney *molecular phylogenetics, evolution educator*
Williams, Martha Ethelyn *information science educator*
Wirt, Frederick Marshall *political scientist*
Wisniewski, Thomas Joseph *music educator*
Wolfe, Ralph Stoner *microbiology educator*
Wolynes, Peter Guy *chemistry researcher, educator*
Yoerger, Roger Raymond *agricultural engineer, educator*
Yu, George Tzuchiao *political science educator*

Venice
Purdes, Alice Marie *secondary education educator*

Vernon Hills
Donovan, Nancy S. *financial services executive*
Ferkenhoff, Robert J. *retail executive*
Powers, Anthony Richard, Jr. *educational sales professional*
Skidmore, Paul Harold *insurance broker*
Wilson, J. Steven *lumber company executive*

Villa Park
Becker, Robert Jerome *allergist, health care consultant*
Binder, John *minister, religious organization executive*
Brown, C(harles) Foster, III *construction services and building products executive*
Devlin, Barbara Jo *school district administrator*
Effa, Herman *clergy member, religious organization administrator*
Evans, Austin James *hospital administrator*
Fenech, Joseph C. *lawyer*
†Kay, Robert Lee *hospital administrator*
Kohlstedt, James August *lawyer*
Leston, Patrick John *lawyer*
†Loewer, Jackie *church official*
McDonnell, Dennis J. *securities industry executive*
†Norman, Ronald *church officer*
Rogers, Peter Norman *food company executive*
Russell, Richard *religious organization admnstrator*
Taylor, Ronald Lee *school administrator*
Williams, David Arthur *marketing professional*

Washington
McKinney-Keller, Margaret Frances *retired special education educator*

Wauconda
Bolchazy, Ladislaus Joseph *publishing company executive*

Waukegan
Beeler, Thomas Joseph *lawyer, manufacturing company executive*
Bleck, Virginia Eleanore *illustrator*
Chapman, James Claude *marine equipment manufacturing executive*
Cherry, Peter Ballard *electrical products corporation executive*
Cherry, Walter Lorain *electronics executive, engineer*
Hall, Albert Leander *lawyer*
Marks, Martha Alford *author*
†Martin, Darnell *medical care products corporation executive*
†Stover, William Ruffner *insurance company executive, retired*

Westchester
Clarke, Richard Lewis *health science association administrator*
†Ingalls, Harold W. *vice president, CFO, environmental services company*
Masterson, John Patrick *retired English language educator*
†Schulte, Margaret Florence *personnel firm executive*
Walsh, Thomas James *state senator*
†Weinstein, Alan *health care management executive*

Western Springs
Carroll, Jeanne *public relations executive*
Hanson, Heidi Elizabeth *lawyer*
Mudd, Anne Chestney *small business owner, mathematics educator, real estate agent*
Tiefenthal, Marguerite Aurand *school social worker*
Zamora, Marjorie Dixon *retired political science educator*

Wheaton
†Algeo, John Thomas *retired educator, association executive*
Beers, V(ictor) Gilbert *publishing executive*
Bellock, Patricia Rigney *county government official*
Bogdonoff, Maurice Lambert *physician*
Botti, Aldo E. *lawyer*
Burnham, Robert Danner *electronics executive, scientist*
Butt, Edward Thomas, Jr. *lawyer*
Corum, William Thomas, III *computer information systems executive*
Estep, John Hayes *religious denomination executive, clergyman*
Fawell, Beverly Jean *state legislator*
Flynn, James Rourke *retired insurance company executive*
Haenszel, William Manning *epidemiologist, educator*
Holman, James Lewis *financial and management consultant*
Jack, Nancy Rayford *supplemental resource company executive, consultant*
Jett, Charles Cranston *management consultant*
Kelly, Robert Thomas *publisher*
Loebig, Wilfred F. *health care executive*
Maibenco, Helen Craig *anatomist, educator*
Mellott, Robert Vernon *advertising executive*
Pint, Sister Rose Mary *nun, religious order administrator, health care executive*
Provenzale, Maryellen Kirby *judge, educator*
Reszka, Alfons *computer systems architect*
Roberts, Keith Edward, Sr. *lawyer*
Roskam, Peter James *state legislator, lawyer*
Spedale, Vincent John *manufacturing executive*
Stone, Irene Mildred *county commissioner*
Sweeney, Mark Owen *publisher*
Sweetser, Ruth Emilie Ziemann *university administrator*
Taylor, Mark Douglas *publishing executive*
Thompson, Bert Allen *retired librarian*
Ward, Patricia Ann *dean*

Wheeling
†Burrows, George J. *wholesale distribution executive*
Carmichael, Leonard Lawrence *manufacturing executive, accountant*
Hammer, Donald Price *librarian*
Koch, Peter F. *management consultant*
Long, Sarah Ann *librarian*
Mc Clarren, Robert Royce *librarian*
Saranow, Mitchell Harris *investment banker, financial consultant*
†Wesley, Norman H. *metal products executive*

Wilmette
Albright, Townsend Shaul *investment banker, government benefits consultant*
Barnett, Ralph Lipsey *engineering educator*
Barth, David Keck *industrial distribution industry consultant*
Beane, Marjorie Noterman *academic administrator*
Biedron, Theodore John *newspaper executive*
Brink, Marion Francis *association executive*
Bro, Kenneth Arthur *plastic manufacturing company executive*
Chen, Shau-Tsyh *architect*
Espenshade, Edward Bowman, Jr. *geographer, educator*
Fries, Robert Francis *historian, educator*
Gary, James Francis *mental health counselor, educational counselor*
Hansen, Andrew Marius *retired library association executive*
Kurtzman, Allan Roger *advertising executive*
Mc Nitt, Willard Charles *business executive*
Merrier, Helen *actress, director*
Muhlenbruch, Carl W. *civil engineer*
Nash, Jay Robert, III *author, playwright, publisher*
Nelson, James F. *judge, religious organization administrator*
Randolph, Lillian Larson *medical association executive*
Smutny, Joan Franklin *academic director, educator*
Stipp, John Edgar *financial consultant, lawyer*
Williams, Emory *former retail company executive, banker*

Wilmington
Anderson, Mary Jane *public library director*

Winfield
Calvin, Patricia Lynn *hospital administrator*

Winnetka
Abell, David Robert *lawyer*
Andersen, Kenneth Benjamin *retired association executive*
Bartlett, William McGillivray *hospital and scientific products company executive*
Bogart, Homer Gordon *marketing executive*
Carrow, Leon Albert *physician*
Crowe, Robert William *lawyer, mediator*
Davis, Britton Anthony *lawyer*
dePeyster, Frederic Augustus *surgeon*
Earle, David Prince, Jr. *physician, educator*
Folds, Charles Weston *merchandising consultant*
Gavin, James John, Jr. *diversified company executive*
Greeley, Joseph May *retired advertising executive*
Hartman, Robert S. *retired paper company executive*
Hudnut, Robert Kilborne *clergyman, author*
Jones, Philip Newton *physician, medical educator*
Kahn, Paul Frederick *executive search company executive*
Kapnick, Richard Bradshaw *lawyer*
Keller, John Paul *industrial company executive*
Lindsay, Dianna Marie *educational administrator*
Mancuso, James Vincent *automobile columnist*
Mathers, Thomas Nesbit *financial consultant*
Mc Millen, Thomas Roberts *lawyer, arbitrator, mediator, retired judge*
Menke, Allen Carl *industrial corporation executive*
Owens, Luvie Moore *association executive*
Pattison, Abbott Lawrence *sculptor*
Piper, Robert Johnston *architect, urban planner*
Plowden, David *photographer*
Puth, John Wells *consulting company executive*
Sharboneau, Lorna Rosina *artist, educator, writer*
Sick, William Norman, Jr. *investment company executive*
Weber, John Bertram *architect*
Weldon, Theodore Tefft, Jr. *retail company executive*

Wood Dale
Kearns, Janet Catherine *corporate secretary*
Thompson, John Henry *consulting executive*

Woodridge
Allen, Charles Joseph, II *advertising agency executive*

Woodstock
Gitlin, H. Joseph *lawyer*
Hale, Hamilton Orin *retired lawyer*
Kuhajek, Eugene James *chemical research executive*

INDIANA

Anderson
Conrad, Harold August *retired religious pension board executive*
Dale, Doris *religious organization executive*
Dye, Dwight Latimer *minister*
Edwards, James L. *university president*
Foggs, Edward L. *church administrator*
Gay, David Earl, Sr. *experimental chemist*
Grubbs, J. Perry *church administrator*
Hayes, Sherill D. *religious organization administrator*
King, Charles Ross *physician*
Nicholson, Robert Arthur *college president*
Olson, Carol Lea *lithographer, educator, photographer*
Patton, Norman S. *church adminstrator*
Rist, Robert G. *religious publishing executive*

Angola
Elliott, Carl Hartley *former university president*

Attica
Harrison, Joseph William *state senator*

Auburn
Kempf, Jane Elmira *marketing executive*
Mountz, Louise Carson Smith *retired librarian*
Record, Lincoln Fredrick *speech communications educator, communications consultant*

Batesville
Hillenbrand, Daniel A. *manufacturing company executive*
Hillenbrand, W. August *manufacturing company executive*
Rosebrough, Walter M., Jr. *manufacturing executive*
Smith, Lonnie Max *diversified industries executive*

Beech Grove
Clapper, George Raymond *accountant, computer consultant*

Berne
Lehman, Doyle *superintendent*

Beverly Shores
Ruzic, Neil Pierce *author, publisher, scientist*

Bloomington
Adams, William Richard *archaeologist, lecturer, curator*
Allison, Tomilea *mayor*
Aman, Alfred Charles, Jr. *law educator*
Anderson, Judith Helena *English language educator*
Arnove, Robert Frederick *education educator*
Bain, Wilfred Conwell *former university dean, music educator, opera theater director*
Bair, Edward Jay *chemistry educator*
Barnes, A. James *academic dean*
Barnstone, Willis (Robert Barnstone) *language literature educator, poet, scholar*
Battenhouse, Roy Wesley *English educator*
Bauman, Richard *anthropologist, educator*
Baxter, Maurice Glen *historian, educator*
Beckwith, Christopher Irving *social sciences educator, writer, composer*
Belth, Joseph Morton *retired business educator*
Bent, Robert Demo *physicist, educator*
Bishop, Michael D. *emergency physician*
†Black, William Richard *transportation geography educator*
Boerner, Peter *language and literature educator*
Bonham, Russell Aubrey *chemistry educator*
Bonser, Charles Franklin *public administration educator*
Brand, Myles *academic administrator*
Bregel, Yuri *history educator*
Brown, Keith *musician, educator*
Buelow, George John *musicologist, educator*
Bundy, Wayne M. *retired geologist, consultant*
Burton, Philip Ward *advertising executive, educator*
Byrnes, Robert Francis *history educator*
Cagle, William Rea *librarian*
Caldwell, Lynton Keith *social scientist, educator*
Calinescu, Adriana Gabriela *museum curator, art historian*
Campaigne, Ernest Edward *chemistry educator*
Chisholm, Malcolm Harold *chemistry educator*
Clevenger, Sarah *botanist, computer consultant*
Cohen, William Benjamin *historian, educator*
Cole, Bruce Milan *art historian*
Conrad, Geoffrey Wentworth *archaeologist, educator*
Counsilman, James Edward *physical education educator*
†Crowe, James W. *university administrator, educator*
Davidson, Ernest Roy *chemist, educator*

Davis, Charles Hargis information scientist, educator
DeHayes, Daniel Wesley management executive, educator
DeVoe, Robert Donald visual physiologist
Diamant, Alfred political science educator
Dieterle, Donald Lyle accountant, educator
Dinsmoor, James Arthur psychology educator
Dodd, James Robert geologist, educator
Dunn, Jon Michael philosophy educator
Edgerton, William B. foreign language educator
Edmondson, Frank Kelley astronomer
Eisenberg, Paul David philosophy educator
Ferrell, Robert Hugh historian, educator
Foster, Kathleen Adair art historian, museum curator
Gealt, Adelheid Maria museum director
Gest, Howard microbiologist, educator
Goodman, Charles David physicist, educator
Gordon, Paul John business management educator
Gough, Pauline Bjerke magazine editor
Grieco, Paul Anthony chemistry educator
Gros Louis, Kenneth Richard Russell university chancellor
†Gubar, Susan (David) English educator, writer
Guth, Sherman Leon (S. Lee Guth) psychologist, educator
Hagen, Charles William, Jr. botany educator
Hamburger, Michael Wile geology educator
Hammel, Harold Theodore physiology and biophysics educator, researcher
Hanson, Karen philosopher, educator
Harder, John E. electrical engineer
Haitin, Donald Edward geologist, educator
Hegeman, George Downing microbiology educator
Heidt, Robert Harold law educator, consultant
Heise, George Armstrong psychologist, educator
Heiser, Charles Bixler, Jr. botany educator
Hites, Ronald Atlee environmental science educator, chemist
Hodge, Carleton Taylor linguist, educator
Hofstadter, Douglas Richard cognitive, computer scientist, educator
Hopkins, Jack Walker former university administrator, environmental educator
Ingersoll, Gary Michael educational psychologist
Jacobi, Peter Paul journalism educator, author
Johnson, Hollis Ralph astronomy educator
Johnson, Owen Verne program director
Johnson, Sidney Malcolm foreign language educator
Juergens, George Ivar history educator
Kibbey, Hal Stephen science writer
Klotman, Robert Howard music educator
Knight, Bob college basketball coach
Kohr, Roland Ellsworth hospital administrator
Komunyakaa, Yusef (James Willie Brown, Jr.) poet
Lebano, Edoardo Antonio foreign language educator
Lee, Don Yoon publisher, academic researcher and writer
Leftwich, Richard Henry economist, educator
Long, John D. retired insurance educator
Lowe, Marvin artist
Macfarlane, Malcolm Harris physics educator
Mac Watters, Virginia Elizabeth singer, music educator, actress
Markman, Ronald artist, educator
Martins, Heitor Miranda foreign language educator
Mc Clung, Leland Swint microbiologist, educator
McDowell, John Holmes folklore educator, institute director
Mehlinger, Howard Dean education educator
Mitchell, Bert Breon literary translator
Mobley, Tony Allen university dean, recreation educator
Moore, Ward Wilfred medical educator
Murray, Haydn Herbert geology educator
Nolan, Val, Jr. biologist, lawyer
Nordloh, David Joseph English language educator
Novotny, Milos Vlastislav chemistry educator
O'Hearn, Robert Raymond stage designer
Oinas, Felix Johannes foreign language educator
O'Meara, Patrick O. political science educator
Orrego-Salas, Juan Antonio composer, retired music educator
Ostrom, Elinor political science educator, researcher
Ostrom, Vincent A(lfred) political science educator
Otteson, Schuyler Franklin former university dean, educator
Pagels, Jürgen Heinrich balletmaster, dance educator, dancer, choreographer, author
Parmenter, Charles Stedman chemistry educator
Patrick, John Joseph social sciences educator
Patterson, James Milton marketing specialist, educator
Peters, Dennis Gail chemist
Phillips, Harvey musician, music educator, arts consultant
Pletcher, David Mitchell history educator
Pollock, Robert Elwood nuclear physicist
Pozzatti, Rudy Otto artist
Preer, John Randolph, Jr. biology educator
Prosser, Franklin Pierce computer scientist
Purdom, Paul Walton, Jr. computer scientist
Puri, Madan Lal mathematics educator
Putnam, Frank William biochemistry and immunology educator
Randolph, James C. professor
Rebec, George Vincent neuroscience researcher, educator, administrator
Remak, Henry H.H. foreign language educator
Rink, Lawrence Donald cardiologist
Rosenberg, Samuel Nathan French and Italian language educator
†Roush, William R. chemistry educator
Rousseau, Eugene Ellsworth musician, music educator, consultant
Rudolph, Lavere Christian library director
Ruesink, Albert William biologist, plant sciences educator
Ryan, John William retired university president
Salmon, Russell Owen, II Latin American studies educator, administrator
Samuelsen, Roy bass-baritone
Scannell, Dale Paul dean, university educator
Schaich, William L. physics educator
Schmidt, Nancy J. anthropologist, educator
Schroeder, Henry J. health science organization administrator
Schuessler, Karl Frederick sociologist, educator
Schurz, Scott Clark journalist, publisher
Sebeok, Thomas Albert linguistics educator
Sebok, Gyorgy pianist, educator
Simmons, Merle Edwin foreign language educator
Sinor, Denis Orientalist, educator
Smith, Carl Bernard education educator
Smith, Frederick Robert, Jr. social studies educator
†Smith, J. Steven electric power industry executive
Sperling, Elliot Harris history educator
Spulber, Nicolas economics educator emeritus
Stolnitz, George Joseph economist, educator, demographer
Stryker, Sheldon sociologist, educator
Sullivan, Michael Francis, III executive
Svetlova, Marina ballerina, choreographer, educator
Swanson, Robert Mclean retired business educator
Thelin, John Robert academic administrator, education educator, historian
Vincent, Jeff Robert labor studies educator
Vitaliano, Charles J(oseph) geologist, educator
von Furstenberg, George Michael economics educator, researcher
Warren, Donald university dean, education educator
Weaver, David Hugh journalism educator, communications researcher
Webb, Charles Haizlip, Jr. university dean
Weinberg, Eugene David microbiologist, educator
Wells, Herman B. university chancellor
Wentworth, Jack Roberts business educator, consultant
Westfall, Richard Samuel historian
Williams, Camilla soprano, voice educator
Williams, Edgar Gene university administrator
Wilson, George Macklin history educator, cultural studies center administrator
Wittlich, Gary Eugene music theory educator
†Wolin, Jeffrey Alan artist
†Yeager, Janice Skinner library director
Young, Frank Nelson, Jr. biology educator, entomologist

Bluffton
Brockmann, William Frank medical facility administrator
Lawson, William Hogan, III electrical motor manufacturing executive

Boggstown
Gray, Carlos Gibson restaurateur, seedsman, entertainer

Brownsburg
Gregory, Susan B. lawyer

Burns Harbor
Brown, Gene W. steel company executive

Butler
Ford, Lee Ellen (Leola Ford) scientist, educator, retired lawyer

Carmel
Chittenden, Michael Dennis hospital administrator
Dick, Rollin Merle insurance company executive
Eden, Barbara Janiece commercial and residential interior designer
Ferrero, Louis Peter computer services company executive
Gongaware, Donald Francis insurance company executive
Hartman, Robert D. superintendent
Herr, Earl Binkley, Jr. pharmaceutical company executive
Hilbert, Stephen C. insurance company executive
Kolda, Thomas Joseph non-profit organization executive
†Magliery, Frank Thomas hospital administrator
Mc Laughlin, Harry Roll architect
Monical, Robert Duane consulting structural engineer
Pickens, Robert Bruce accountant
Quayle, J(ames) Danforth former vice president of United States, investment company executive
Read, Frank Thompson law educator
Roche, James Richard pediatric dentist, university dean
Russell, Richard L. van line executive
Shoup, Charles Samuel, Jr. chemicals and materials executive
Smith, John Burnside transportation company executive
Smith, Michael L. transportation company executive
†Stauder, Alfred Max wire products company executive

Charlestown
Schmidt, Jakob Edward medical and medicolegal lexicographer, physician, author, inventor

Chesterfield
Fry, Meredith Warren civil engineer, consultant

Chesterton
Martino, Robert Salvatore orthopedic surgeon
Petrakis, Harry Mark author

Clinton
Cloyd, George Thomas dentist

Columbus
Abts, Henry William banker
Baker, James Kendrick auto parts manufacturing company executive
Berman, Lewis Paul financial executive
Boll, Charles Raymond engine company executive
†Claypool, Edward Lavern engine company executive
Draeger, Wayne Harold manufacturing company executive
Durham, James Michael, Sr. marketing executive
Evans, Loren Kenneth manufacturing company executive
Garton, Robert Dean state senator
Hackett, John Thomas economist
Hamilton, Peter Bannerman lawyer, manufacturing company executive
Hartley, James Michaelis aerospace systems, printing and hardwood products manufacturing executive
Henderson, James Alan engine company executive
Higgins, Harold Bailey executive search company executive
Jolly, Bruce Dwight manufacturing company executive
Kamo, Roy engineering company executive
Kubo, Isoroku mechanical engineer
Miller, Joseph Irwin automotive manufacturing company executive
Nash, John Arthur bank executive
Orben, Robert Allen engine company executive
Sales, A. R. financial executive
Schacht, Henry Brewer diesel engine manufacturing company executive
Stoner, R(ichard) B(urkett) manufacturing company executive, member of Democratic national committee

Connersville
Kuntz, William Henry lawyer, mediator

Crawfordsville
Barnes, James John history educator
Fisher, A. James theater educator, director, actor
Ford, Andrew Thomas academic administrator
Michal, Philip Quentin veterinarian, mayor
†Simmons, Emory G. mycologist

Crown Point
Haines, Robert Earl retired industrial construction executive

Culver
Holaday, Allan Gibson English educator
Manuel, Ralph Nixon private school executive

Dale
Hayes, Mary Joanne special education educator

Danville
†Dawes, Dennis William hospital executive

Dyer
Teuscher, George William dental educator

East Chicago
Crum, James Francis waste recycling company executive
Papachronis, Darlene R. hospital administrator
Platis, James G. secondary education educator
Vis, Mary A. Murga elementary education educator

Elkhart
Bender, Ross Thomas minister
Bowers, Richard Stewart, Jr. lawyer
Bryant, Donald Loudon pharmaceutical company executive
Corson, Keith Daniel business executive
Corson, Thomas Harold manufacturing company executive
Decio, Arthur Julius manufacturing company executive
Free, Helen M. chemist, consultant
Gassere, Eugene Arthur lawyer, business executive
Groom, Gary Lee recreational vehicle manufacturing executive
Harman, John Royden lawyer
Hill, Thomas Stewart electronics executive, consultant, engineer
Holtz, Glenn Edward bank instrument manufacturing executive
Kerich, James Patrick manufacturing company executive
Kloska, Ronald Frank manufacturing company executive
Kovach, John Michael museum director, historian
Lapp, James Merrill clergyman, marriage and family therapist
†Meyer, Albert James educational administrator
Mischke, Frederick Charles manufacturing company executive
O'Hagan, William D. metal products executive
Oltz, Richard John publishing executive, minister
Preheim, John S. secondary education educator
Rand, Phillip Gordon chemist
†Renbarger, Larry D. prefabricated housing manufacturing executive
†Snyder, James R. wholesale distribution executive, textiles executive
Speas, Charles Stuart personnel director
Tatum, Rita communications executive
Treckelo, Richard M. lawyer
†Van Es, Richard John, Jr. electronics executive
Vite, Frank Anthony realtor

Elwood
†Baer, James Edward hospital administrator
Vance, Joan Emily Jackson (Mrs. Norval E. Vance) elementary school educator

Evansville
Able, Warren Walter natural resource company executive, physician
Anderson, Milton Henry psychiatrist
Barber, Charles Turner political science educator
Brill, Alan Richard entrepreneur
Brooks, Gene Edward federal judge
Capshaw, Tommie Dean federal judge
Clouse, John Daniel lawyer
Dailey, Donald Earl industrial design consultant
Denner, Melvin Walter life sciences educator
Egan, Raymond C. pharmaceutical comapny executive
Fagan, Thomas Perry transportation executive
Faw, Melvin Lee retired physician
Gaither, John Francis accountant, consultant
Gerhart, Philip Mark mechanical engineering educator
Gettelfinger, Gerald Andrew bishop
†Graham, Dellas business executive
Graves, Wallace Billingsley retired university executive
Guthrie, Catherine S. Nicholson (Catherine S. Nicholson-Guthrie) research scientist
Hargrave, Robert Webb banker
Hartsaw, William O. mechanical engineering educator
Howard, Edward Allen library administrator, consultant
Jackson, Bill D. newspaper editor
Kiechlin, Robert Jerome retired coal company executive, financial consultant
Kitch, Frederick David advertising executive
Koch, Robert Louis, II manufacturing company executive, mechanical engineer
†Mathews, W. Garret columnist
†Mitchell, Daniel Wertz banking executive
Muehlbauer, James Herman manufacturing executive
Penkava, Robert Ray radiologist, educator
Prybil, Lawrence Dewey health system executive
Reherman, Ronald Gilbert gas and electric company executive
Riechmann, Fred B. retired newspaper publisher
Ryder, Thomas Michael newspaper editor
Savia, Alfred conductor
Schoffstall, Phil school superintendent
Shaffer, Michael L. transportation company executive
Shaw, Margery Wayne Schlamp geneticist, physician, lawyer
Streetman, John William, III museum official
Tuley, Thomas Wayne newspaper executive
Vandeveer, Michael D. city official
Vinson, James Spangler university president
White, Linda Elaine nursing administrator
Young Lively, Sandra Lee nurse

Fishers
Gatto, Louis Constantine retired college president
Jontz, Polly college official, musuem director

Fort Branch
Bertram, Michael Wayne secondary education educator

Fort Wayne
Abbott, Jacquelyn Meng lawyer
Andorfer, Donald Joseph academic administrator, educator
Anker, Robert Alvin insurance company executive
Atzeff, Efrodita fraternal organization administrator
Baker, Carl Leroy lawyer
Beals, Duane church administrator
Beineke, Lowell Wayne mathematics educator
Bender, Linda Arlene bank officer
Brown, Ronald Wayne fire chief
Bunkowske, Eugene Walter religious studies educator
Burns, Thagrus Asher manufacturing company executive, former life insurance company executive
Carpenter, Charles religious organization administrator
Clarke, Kenneth Stevens insurance company executive
Cole, Kenneth Duane architect
Connavino, Nicholas Anthony food company executive
Cox, David Jackson biochemistry educator
Curtis, Douglas Homer small business owner
D'Arcy, John Michael bishop
Dax, Janice M. nursing administrator
Donesa, Antonio Braganza neurosurgeon
Dorman, Barry waste management executive
Dunsire, P(eter) Kenneth insurance company executive
Edris, Charles Lawrence insurance company executive
Fairchild, David Lawrence philosophy educator
Flynn, Pauline T. speech pathologist, educator
Gerberding, Miles Carston lawyer
Goeglein, Gloria J. state legislator
Graf, Robert Arlan financial services executive
Guerin, Christopher David arts administrator
Helmke, (Walter) Paul, Jr. mayor, lawyer
Henschen, Bob religious foundation executive
Hirschy, Gordon Harold real estate agent
Hoffer, Alma Jeanne nursing educator
Hunter, Jack Duval lawyer
Jackson, Paul Howard librarian, educator
Kam, Jeanette Virginia school system administrator
Keefer, J(ames) Michael lawyer
Kerr, Frederick Hohmann hospital administrator, college president
Klugman, Stephan Craig newspaper editor
Krull, Jeffrey Robert library director
Labernik, Mary Sue nurse
Latz, G. Irving, II manufacturing company executive
Lee, Shuishih Sage pathologist
Lee, William Charles federal judge
Lewark, Carol Ann special education educator
Liechty, Eric church administrator
Lockwood, Robert Philip publishing executive
Loutsenhizer, Marvin Jerry manufacturing executive
Lupke, Duane Eugene insurance company executive
Lyons, Jerry Lee mechanical engineer
Mahmoud, Aly Ahmed electrical engineering educator
†Maier, Walter Arthur church official
Mann, David William minister
Mansfield, Maynard Joseph computer science educator, academic dean
Marine, Clyde Lockwood agricultural business consultant
†McAllister, Gene Robert electronics company executive, electrical engineer
McClelland, Michael wholesale distribution executive
McFarlane, Neil church administrator
Menge, Richard Cramer electric utility executive
Mills, Rodney Daniel engineering company executive
Moran, John religious organization administrator
Morehart, Donald Hadley food products executive
Niewyk, Anthony lawyer
Overmyer, John Eugene manufacturing company executive
Pease, Ella Louise elementary education educator
Peebles, Carter David lawyer
Pellegrene, Thomas James, Jr. editor, researcher
Pope, Mark Andrew lawyer
Quinby, Charles Edward, Jr. manufacturing company executive
Quinn, C. Jack mechanical engineering educator, consultant
†Reitz, William supermarket company executive
Richardson, Joseph Hill physician, medical educator
Ridderheim, David Sigfrid hospital administrator
Riemen, David Clarence chief of police
Rifkin, Leonard metals company executive
Robertson, Richard Stuart insurance holding company executive
Rolland, Ian McKenzie insurance executive
Sack, James McDonald, Jr. radio and television producer, marketing executive
Sandeson, William Seymour cartoonist
Scheetz, Sister Mary JoEllen English language educator
Schmiel, David Gerhard clergyman, religious education administrator
Shaffer, Paul E. banker
Shoaff, Thomas Mitchell lawyer
Speicher, Opal church administrator
Steinbronn, Richard Eugene lawyer
Stevenson, Kenneth Lee chemist, educator
Stucky, Ken clergy member, religious publication editor, church organization administrator
Szuhaj, Bernard Francis food research director
Vachon, Marilyn Ann retired insurance company executive
von Gunten, David church administrator
†Waterfield, Richard Dallas bank executive, mortgage company executive
Weatherford, George Edward civil engineer
Weiler, Joseph Ashby newspaper editor
West, Thomas Meade insurance company executive
Williams, Walter Jackson, Jr. electrical engineer, consultant
†Wolf, Don Allen hardware wholesale executive

Fowler
Brouillette, Donald G. *grain company executive*

Frankfort
Borland, Kathryn Kilby *author*

Franklin
Jacobs, Harvey Collins *newspaper editor, writer*

Gary
Barnes, Thomas Vernon *mayor, lawyer*
Bosley, John Scott *editor*
Gaughan, Norbert F. *bishop*
Knight, Harriette *secondary educator*
Meyerson, Seymour *retired chemist*
Moran, Robert Francis, Jr. *library director*
Richards, Hilda *university administrator*
Roberts, Samuel Alden *secondary education educator*
Smith, Vernon G. *education educator, state representative*
Sutton, William Wallace, Jr. *editor, newspaper executive*

Goshen
Gunden, Elizabeth Ann *nursing administrator*
Lehman, Karl Franklyn *accountant*
†Liegl, Peter J. *company executive*
Morris, Robert Julian, Jr. *art gallery owner*
Schrock, Harold Arthur *manufacturing company executive*
Stoltzfus, Victor Ezra *academic administrator*

Granger
Brissey, Ruben Marion *retired container company executive*
Chmiel, Chester T. *adhesive chemist, consultant*

Greencastle
Anderson, John Robert *retired mathematics educator*
Bonifield, William C. *economist, educator*
Bottoms, Robert Garvin *academic administrator*
DiLillo, Leonard Michael *Spanish educator, researcher, academic administrator*
†Dittmer, John Avery *history educator*
Gass, Clinton Burke *mathematics educator*
Houck, Carolyn Marie Kumpf *special education educator*
Phillips, Clifton J. *history educator*
Weiss, Robert Orr *speech educator*

Greenfield
Bettler, Janet Louise Bell *foreign language educator*

Greensburg
Ricke, David Louis *agricultural and environmental consultant*
Small, Ralph Milton *publisher, clergyman*

Greentown
Healy, Stephen C. *seconadry school principal*

Greenwood
Means, George Robert *organization executive*

Hammond
Adik, Stephen Peter *energy company executive*
Albright, John Rupp *physics educator*
Ammeraal, Robert Neal *biochemist*
Ash, Frederick Melvin *manufacturing company executive*
Bahls, Gene Charles *agricultural products company executive*
Delph, Donna Jean (Maroc) *education educator, consultant, university administrator*
Diamond, Eugene Christopher *lawyer, hospital administrator*
Eichhorn, Frederick Foltz, Jr. *lawyer*
Gerard, Peggy S. *critical care nurse, researcher*
Goodman, Samuel J. *lawyer*
Lozano, Rudolpho *federal judge*
Marshall, Philomena Ann *health care administration*
†Meyers, Arthur Solomon *library director*
Moore, Carolyn Lannin *video specialist*
Neale, Gary Lee *utilities executive*
Neff, Gregory Pall *manufacturing engineering educator, consultant*
Pierson, Edward Samuel *engineering educator, consultant*
Rodovich, Andrew Paul *lawyer, federal magistrate*
Schroer, Edmund Armin *utility company executive*
Steen, Lowell Harrison *physician*
Watson, Steven Ellis *school district administrator*
Yackel, James William *mathematician, academic administrator*
Yovich, Daniel John *educator*

Highland
Gregory, Marian Frances *educator, counselor*
Purcell, James Francis *consultant, former utility executive*

Hobart
Rajsic, Robert *secondary education educator*

Hope
Golden, Eloise Elizabeth *community health nurse*

Huntington
Doermann, Paul Edmund *retired surgeon*
Kaehr, Robert Eugene *librarian, educator*
Kopp, Clarence Adam, Jr. *clergyman*
†Seilhamer, Ray A. *bishop*

Indianapolis
Albright, Terrill D. *lawyer*
Alexander, Gary Lee *architect*
Allan, Marc David *music critic*
Allen, David James *lawyer*
Allen, Stephen D(ean) *pathologist, microbiologist*
Allerheiligen, Sandra Renee *pharmacokineticist*
Alsop, Thomas Walter *secondary education educator*
Andretti, John *professional race car driver*
Antich, Rose Ann *state legislator*
Applegate, Malcolm W. *newspaper executive*
Aprison, Morris Herman *biochemist, neurobiologist, educator*
Aschleman, James Allan *lawyer*
Austin, Spencer Peter *minister*
Avery, Dennis Teel *agricultural analyst*
Badger, David Harry *lawyer*
Baetzhold, Howard George *English language educator*
Bannister, Geoffrey *university president, geographer*
Barcus, Mary Evelyn *primary school educator*
Barcus, Robert Gene *educational association administrator*
Barker, Sarah Evans *federal judge*
Barman, Charles Roy *science educator*
Bash, James Francis *insurance company executive*
Bates, Gerald Earl *bishop*
Bayh, Evan *governor*
Bayt, Robert Louis *federal bankruptcy judge*
Becker, Vaneta G. *state representative*
Beckwith, Lewis Daniel *lawyer*
Beeler, Virgil L. *lawyer*
Behar, Lucien E. *church administrator*
Bennett, Bruce W. *construction company executive, civil engineer*
Bennett, Claire Richardson *landscape architect*
Bepko, Gerald Lewis *academic administrator, law educator, lecturer, consultant, lawyer*
Besch, Henry Roland, Jr. *pharmacologist, educator*
Bessey, William Higgins *physicist, educator*
Betley, Leonard John *lawyer*
Bindley, William Edward *pharmaceutical executive*
Birky, Nathan Dale *publishing company executive*
Blackwell, Henry Barlow, II *lawyer*
Block, Amanda Roth *artist*
Boldt, Michael Herbert *lawyer*
†Bolin, Daniel Paul *music educator*
Bonney, M. Doane *religious organization director*
Born, Emily Marie *editor, association executive*
Born, Samuel Roydon, II *lawyer*
Bower, Sandra Irwin *communications executive*
†Bowes, Edward (Bud) *superintendent of schools*
Brady, Mary Sue *pediatric dietitian, educator*
Brandt, Ira Kive *pediatrician, medical geneticist*
Brannon, Ronald Roy *minister*
Brannon-Peppas, Lisa *chemical engineer, researcher*
Brashear, Diane Lee *marital and sex therapist*
Bray, Donald Lawrence *religious organization executive, minister*
Brickley, Richard Agar *retired surgeon*
Brinkerhoff, Tom J. *financial services executive*
Brown, Edwin Wilson, Jr. *physician, educator*
Brown, Lawrence Harvey (Larry Brown) *basketball coach*
Browne, William Albert, Jr. *architectural firm executive*
Broxmeyer, Hal Edward *medical educator*
Bruess, Charles Edward *lawyer*
Budak, Mary Kay *state legislator*
Buechlein, Daniel Mark *bishop*
Bundy, David Dale *librarian, educator*
Buttrey, Donald Wayne *lawyer*
Campbell, Judith Lowe *child psychiatrist*
Capehart, Homer Earl, Jr. *lawyer*
Caperton, Albert Franklin *newspaper editor*
Carey, Edward Marshel, Jr. *accounting company executive*
Carney, Joseph Buckingham *lawyer*
Carpenter, Susan Karen *lawyer*
Carr, William H(enry) A. *public relations executive, author*
Carter, Pamela Lynn *state attorney general*
Casebeer, Edwin Frank, Jr. *English language educator*
Cassel, Herbert William *religion educator*
Castle, Howard Blaine *religious organization administrator*
Chapman, Linda Brown *school system administrator*
Chernish, Stanley Michael *physician*
Choplin, John M., II *lawyer*
Christenson, Le Roy Howard *insurance company officer*
Christian, Joe Clark *medical genetics researcher, educator*
Ciotti, Eugene Barney *paper packaging company executive*
Clark, Charles M., Jr. *research institution administrator*
Cliff, Johnnie Marie *mathematics and chemistry educator*
Cofield, Howard John *lawyer*
Cohen, Gabriel Murrel *editor, publisher*
Cohen, Marlene Lois *pharmacologist*
Cones, Van Buren *electronics engineer, consultant*
Conley, James Daniel *retired foundation executive*
Corley, William Edward *hospital administrator*
Cramer, Betty F. *life insurance company executive*
Cross, Leland Briggs, Jr. *lawyer*
Crow, Paul Abernathy, Jr. *clergyman, religious council executive, educator*
†Dailey, Donald Harry *adult education educator, volunteer*
Daly, Walter Joseph *physician, educator*
Das, Eula *hospital administrator*
DeBruler, Roger O. *state supreme court justice*
Deer, Richard Elliott *lawyer*
†DeHaan, Christel *vacation exchange and travel company executive*
DeLaney, Edward O'Donnell *lawyer*
†DeMars, Dan Richard *construction executive*
†De Rosa, Guy Paul *orthopedic surgery educator*
Dickinson, Richard Donald Nye *clergyman, educator, theological seminary administrator*
Dietz, William Ronald *financial services executive*
Dillin, S. Hugh *federal judge*
Dortch, Carl Raymond *former association executive*
Dougherty, Douglas Wayne *retail executive*
Duncan-Ladd, Georgia Jones *elementary education educator*
Durbin, Robert Cain *hotel executive*
Dutton, Stephen James *lawyer*
Eigen, Howard *pediatrician, educator*
Einhorn, Lawrence Henry *medical educator*
Ellerbrook, Niel Cochran *gas company executive*
Ellis, Carollyn *religious organization administrator*
Ellis, Raymond W. *religious organization executive, consultant*
Emerson, Andrew Craig *lawyer, insurance executive*
Emtman, Steven Charles *professional football player*
Endsley, J(ohn) Patrick *federal magistrate judge*
Engle, Barbara Louise *state legislator*
Engledow, Jack Lee *college administrator, consultant, researcher*
Evans, Daniel Fraley *college administrator, banker, retail executive*
Evans, Daniel Fraley, Jr. *lawyer*
Ewick, Charles Ray *librarian*
Farris, Bain Joseph *health care executive*
Faulk, Ward Page *immunologist*
Feigenbaum, Harvey *cardiologist, educator*
Felicetti, Daniel A. *academic administrator, educator*
Fisch, Charles *physician*
Fischler, Barbara Brand *librarian*
Fisher, Gene Lawrence *financial executive*
Fisher, James R. *lawyer*
FitzGibbon, Daniel Harvey *lawyer*
Fleming, Marcella *journalist*
Fortune, William Lemcke *journalist*
Foster, David Mark *bishop*
Foulkes, John R. *minister*
French, Philip Franks *agricultural cooperative corporate executive*
Frenzel, Otto N., III *banker*
Fritz, Cecil Morgan *investment company executive*
Fruehwald, Kristin G. *lawyer*
Fuller, Samuel Ashby *lawyer, mining company executive*
Funk, David Albert *law educator*
Furlow, Mack Vernon, Jr. *financial executive, treasurer*
Fuson, Wayne Edward *sports editor*
Gable, Robert William, Jr. *aerospace engineer*
Gabovitch, Edward Robert *internist*
Galbraith, Bruce W. *educational administrator*
Gantz, Richard Alan *museum administrator*
Garmel, Marion Bess Simon *journalist*
Gehring, Perry James *toxicologist, chemical company executive*
Geisler, Hans Emanuel *gynecologic oncologist*
Ghetti, Bernardino Francesco *neuropathologist, neurobiology researcher*
Gibson, David Mark *biochemist, educator*
Gibson, James Edwin *toxicologist*
†Gilbert, Shirl Edward *school system administrator*
Gilman, Alan B. *restaurant company executive*
Gilmore, H. William *college dean, dentistry educator*
†Gilroy, Sue Anne *state official*
Givan, Richard Martin *state supreme court justice, retired*
Givens, David W. *banker*
Glazner, Raymond Charles *technical services manager*
Gnat, Raymond Earl *librarian*
Godich, John Paul *federal magistrate judge*
†Golder, Morris Ellis *minister*
Goldsmith, Stephen *mayor*
Goodwin, William Maxwell *financial executive*
Gould, Karen J. *elementary school principal*
Grant, Claudia Ewing *minister*
Gray, Mary Jo Zimmer *medical/surgical nurse*
Grayson, John Allan *lawyer*
Green, James Murney *software products executive*
Green, Morris *physician, educator*
Greist, Mary Coffey *dermatologist*
Griffiths, David Neil *utility executive*
Grosfeld, Jay Lazar *pediatric surgeon, educator*
Grossman, Elizabeth Korn *nursing administrator, retired college dean*
Grube, Elizabeth *investment company executive*
Haines, Lee Mark, Jr. *religious denomination administrator*
Hall, Newell J. *chain drug store company executive*
Hamburger, Richard James *physician, educator*
Handel, David Jonathan *health care administrator*
Harden, Mary Louise *human resources management specialist*
Hardin, Boniface *academic administrator*
Harp, Pamela Jo *special education consultant*
Harris, Robert Allison *biochemistry educator*
Haslam, Robert B. *religious publication editor*
†Hayes, John Robert *health care executive, psychiatrist*
Haynes, Thomas Joseph *marketing executive*
Heard, William Robert *retired insurance company executive*
Hegel, Carolyn Marie *farmer, farm bureau executive*
Heger, Martin L. *bank executive*
Helmkamp, John G. *accounting educator, consultant*
Helveston, Eugene McGillis *pediatric ophthalmologist, educator*
Henderson, Eugene Leroy *lawyer*
Henderson, Linda Kay *state legislator*
Herman, Barbara F. *psychologist*
†Hicks, Allen Morley *hospital administrator*
Higgins, William Robert, III *journalist*
Highfield, Robert Edward *lawyer*
Hillman, Charlene Hamilton *public relations executive*
Hingtgen, Joseph Nicholas *psychologist, neuroscientist, educator*
Ho, Thomas Inn Min *computer scientist, educator*
Hodes, Marion Edward *genetics educator, physician*
Hodowal, John Raymond *lawyer, holding company executive, utility company executive*
Hogsett, Joseph H. *state official*
Hubbard, Jesse Donald *pathology educator*
Huber, Richard C. *insurance company executive*
Huffman-Hine, Ruth Carson *adult education administrator, educator*
Hunt, Robert Chester *construction company executive*
Husman, Catherine Bigot *insurance company executive, actuary*
Husted, Ralph Waldo *former utility executive*
Huston, Michael Joe *lawyer*
Ilangyi, Bya'ene Akulu *bishop*
Ilchman, Warren Frederick *university administrator, political science educator*
Irsay, James Steven *professional football team executive*
Irvine, George *professional basketball coach*
Irwin, Glenn Ward, Jr. *medical educator, physician, university official*
Irwin, H. William *lawyer*
Israelov, Rhoda *financial planner, writer, entrepreneur*
Jackson, Valerie Pascuzzi *radiologist, educator*
Janis, F. Timothy *technology company executive*
Jegen, Lawrence A., III *law educator*
Jewett, John Rhodes *real estate executive*
Johnson, David Allen *singer, songwriter, investor*
Johnson, James P. *religious organization executive*
Johnstone, Joyce Visintine *education educator*
Johnstone, Robert Philip *lawyer*
Jones, Katharine Jean *research physicist*
Jones, Robert C. *symphony orchestra administrator*
Joyner, John Erwin *medical educator, neurological surgeon*
Justice, Brady Richmond, Jr. *medical services executive*
Kacek, Don J. *management consultant, business owner*
Kahlenbeck, Howard, Jr. *lawyer*
Kappes, Philip Spangler *lawyer*
Kashani, Hamid Reza *lawyer, computer consultant*
Kaufman, Barton Lowell *financial services company executive*
Kaufman, Karl Lincoln *consultant, former state agency administrator*
Kemper, James Dee *lawyer*
Kempski, Ralph Aloisius *bishop*
Kerr, M. D. *highway and street contracting company executive*
Kerr, William Andrew *lawyer, educator*
Khalil, Michael O. *actuary*
Kilgore, Gary M. *church administrator*
King, J. B. *pharmaceutical company executive, lawyer*
Kirk, Carol *state official, lawyer*
Kitchen, John Milton *lawyer*
Klaper, Martin Jay *lawyer*
Kleiman, David Harold *lawyer*
†Klug, Michael Gregory *physician*
†Klusas, Roman J. *chemical company executive*
Knebel, Donald Earl *lawyer*
Knoebel, Suzanne Buckner *cardiologist, medical educator*
Koppel, Gary Allen *chemist, immunologist*
Krasean, Thomas Karl *historian*
Kreegar, Phillip Keith *educational administrator*
Kreuscher, Wayne Charles *lawyer*
Krueger, Alan Douglas *communications company executive*
Krueger, Betty Jane *telecommunications company executive*
Lanford, Luke Dean *electronics company executive*
Lantz, George Benjamin, Jr. *business executive, college executive, consultant*
Lee, Stephen W. *lawyer*
Lefstein, Norman *lawyer, educator*
Lemberger, Louis *pharmacologist, physician*
Lent, James A. *analytical equipment company executive*
Lewis, Dale Kenton *retired lawyer*
Lindemann, Donald Lee *utility executive*
Lindseth, Richard Emil *orthopedic surgeon*
Liu, Pingyu *physicist, educator*
Lobley, Alan Haigh *lawyer*
†Lofton, Thomas Milton *lawyer*
Long, Clarence William *accountant*
Long, Timothy Scott *chemist, consultant*
Long, William Allan *retired forest products company executive*
Loveday, William John *hospital administrator*
Lugar, Thomas R. *manufacturing executive*
Lyst, John Henry *newspaper editor*
Lytle, L(arry) Ben *insurance company executive, lawyer*
MacVittie, Paula Rae *advertising executive*
Maine, Michael Roland *lawyer*
Mallon, David Joseph, Jr. *lawyer*
Manders, Karl Lee *neurosurgeon*
Manworren, Donald B. *church administrator*
Marchibroda, Ted (Theodore Joseph Marchibroda) *professional football coach*
Marsh, Don Ermal *supermarket executive*
Massey, James D. *bank holding company executive*
McBride, Angela Barron *nursing educator*
Mc Carthy, Harold Charles *retired insurance company executive*
McDermott, James Alexander *lawyer*
†McDonell, Katherine Mandusic *association executive*
Mc Farland, H. Richard *food company executive*
McGowan, Hugh Barry *insurance agency executive*
McIntyre, Rita Ann *nursing consultant*
McKinney, E. Kirk, Jr. *retired insurance company executive*
McKinney, Larry J. *federal judge*
Merrill, William H., Jr. *lawyer, corporate professional*
Merritt, Doris Honig *pediatrics educator*
Miller, David W. *lawyer*
Miller, Patricia Louise *state legislator, nurse*
Miller, Reginald Wayne *professional basketball player*
Mirsky, Arthur *geologist, educator*
Miyamoto, Richard Takashi *otolaryngologist*
Morris, James Thomas *utilities executive*
Mullen, Thomas Edgar *real estate consultant*
Mutz, Oscar Ulysses *manufacturing and distribution executive*
Myers, Woodrow Augustus, Jr. *physician, corporate medical director*
Neal, Richard Edward *finance company executive*
Nolan, Alan Tucker *retired lawyer*
†Noone, Stephen J. *association executive*
Norins, Arthur Leonard *physician, educator*
Norman, LaLander Stadig *insurance company executive*
Nugent, Johnny *tractor company executive, state senator*
Nugent, Thomas D. *food products executive*
Nyhart, Eldon Howard *employee benefits consultant, lawyer*
†Nzeyimana, Noah *bishop*
O'Bannon, Frank Lewis *state official, lawyer*
Ochs, Sidney *neurophysiology educator*
Orcutt, Daniel C. *airport terminal executive*
Paine, Andrew J., Jr. *banker*
Palmer, Lester Davis *minister*
Pattyn, Remi Ceasar *management consultant*
Paul, Stephen Howard *lawyer*
Pearlstein, Robert M. *physics educator*
Perelman, Melvin *pharmaceutical company executive*
Peters, Garry Lowell *wholesale grocery executive*
Petersen, James L. *lawyer*
Peterson, John Dwight *investment company executive*
Pettinga, Cornelius Wesley *pharmaceutical company executive*
Phillippi, Wendell Crane *editor*
Plater, William Marmaduke *English language educator, academic administrator*
Pless, John Edward *forensic pathologist, educator*
Polston, Mark Franklin *minister*
Ponder, Lester McConnico *lawyer, educator*
†Poray, John Lawrence *professional association executive*
Powlen, David Michael *lawyer*
Pratt, Arthur D. *printing company executive*
†Prible, Larry R. *insurance company executive*
Prosser, Kathy *state official*
Pulliam, Eugene Smith *newspaper publisher*
Pulliam, Russell Bleecker *editor, elder*
Quayle, Marilyn Tucker *lawyer, wife of former vice president of U.S.*
†Race, John Stephen *electronics manufacturing and technology executive*
Ralph, Roger Paul *arbitrator*
†Reed, Suellen Kinder *state education administrator*
Reeve, Ronald Cropper, Jr. *manufacturing executive*
Reich, Jack Egan *insurance company executive*
Reid, William Hill *mathematics educator*
Renda, Randolph Bruce *university dean*
Reynolds, Alan Anthony *economist, writer, consultant*
Reynolds, Robert Hugh *lawyer*
Richmond, James Ellis *restaurant company executive*
Richter, Judith Anne *pharmacology educator*
†Rieck, Theodore J. *city official*

Riegsecker, Marvin Dean pharmacist, state senator
Riemenschneider, Dan LaVerne religious organization administrator
Rinck, Elizabeth Appel editor
Risk, John Fred banker, investment banker
Roberts, William Everett lawyer
Robinson, Larry Robert insurance company executive
Rogers, Robert Ernest medical educator
Ross, Edward cardiologist
Ross, Steven Carter entertainment executive
Roth, Lawrence Max pathologist, educator
Ruben, Gary A. marketing and communications consultant
†Rump, Erwin Elmer state agency administrator
Russell, Frank Eli newspaper publishing executive
Rusthoven, Peter James lawyer
Ryder, Henry C(lay) lawyer
Salentine, Thomas James pharmaceutical company executive
Sayre, Larry D. religious organization executive
Scaletta, Phillip Ralph, III lawyer
Scanlon, Thomas Michael lawyer
Schellen, Nando opera director
Schlegel, Fred Eugene lawyer
Schmidt, William C. chemical company executive
Scholer, Sue Wyant state legislator
Schwindt, Robert F. diagnostic medical products executive
Scism, Daniel Reed lawyer
Segar, Geoffrey retired lawyer
Seitz, Melvin Christian, Jr. distributing company executive
Semler, Jerry D. insurance company executive
Seneff, Smiley Howard business owner
SerVaas, Beurt Richard corporate executive
†Shaffer, Alfred Garfield Terry service organization executive
Shepard, Randall Terry judge
†Sherman, Stuart physician
Shideler, Shirley Ann Williams lawyer
Shipp, Travis education educator, author
Shula, Robert Joseph lawyer
Silver, David Mayer former university official
Simon, Herbert professional basketball team executive
Simpson, Vi state senator
Sindlinger, Verne E. bishop
Slaymaker, Gene Arthur public relations executive
Small, Joyce Graham psychiatrist, educator
†Smith, Donald Eugene healthcare facility management administrator owner
†Smith, Eric wholesale distribution executive
Smith, Kathy Ann educator, state senator
Smith, Keith protective services official
Smith, Stephen Kendall lawyer
Snyder, Jack Ralph lawyer
Soper, Quentin Francis chemist
†Spanogle, Robert William marketing and advertising company executive, association administrator
Speth, Gerald Lennus education and business educator
Staff, Charles Bancroft, Jr. music and theater critic
Standish, Samuel Miles oral pathologist, college dean
Stark, Rohn Taylor professional football player
Stayton, Thomas George lawyer
Steger, Evan Evans, III lawyer
Stein, Richard Paul lawyer
Step, Eugene Lee retired pharmaceutical company executive
†Stephenson, Kathryn Burg performing company executive
Stern, Raymond principal
Stockard, Robert Thomas secondary school administrator
Stoelting, Robert K. anesthesiologist, medical association executive
Stone, Donald Crawford public administrator, educator
Stout, William Jewell department store executive
Strauss, Jerome Manfred lawyer, banker
Sullivan, Frank, Jr. judge
Sutherland, Donald Gray lawyer
Suzuki, Hidetaro violinist
Swaim, David Dee diversified company financial executive
Sweezy, John William political party official
Swhier, Claudia Versfelt lawyer
Tabler, Bryan G. lawyer
Tabler, Norman Gardner, Jr. lawyer
†Taurel, Sidney pharmaceutical executive
Thomas, Beth Eileen Wood (Mrs. Raymond O. Thomas) editor
Tinder, John Daniel federal judge
Tinkle, Carolyn J. state legislative staff member
Tobias, Randall L. pharmaceutical company executive
Todd, Zane Grey utility executive
Tomlinson, Joseph Ernest manufacturing company executive
Ton, L. Eugene church official
Townsend, Earl Cunningham, Jr. lawyer, writer
Trigg, Donald Clark lawyer, insurance company executive
Updegraff Spleth, Ann L. church executive, pastor
†Usher, Phyllis Land state official
Vandivier, Richard White federal judge
Van Valin, John Ernest publisher
Vereen, Robert Charles retired trade association executive
Vobach, William H. state senator
Walker, Frank Dilling market research executive
Walker, Thomas Cole telephone company executive
Wallace, F. Blake aerospace executive, mechanical engineer
Waller, Aaron Bret, III museum director
Walls, John William association executive
Walsh, Donnie sports club executive
Walsh, John Charles metallurgical company executive
Wampler, Lloyd Charles retired lawyer
Watanabe, August Masaru physician, scientist, medical educator, corporate executive
Watkins, Harold Robert minister
Weber, George oncology and pharmacology researcher, educator
Webster, Daniel Robert lawyer
Weinberger, Myron Hilmar medical educator
Wellman, Henry Nelson nuclear medicine specialist
Welsh, Robert K. religious organization executive
Werner, Charles George cartoonist
Whale, Arthur Richard lawyer
Wheeler, Daniel Scott publishing executive, editor
Whelan, John Martin insurance executive
White, Arthur Clinton physician
White, James Patrick law educator
Wilson, Charles Edward lawyer
Wilson, Earle Lawrence church administrator
†Wilson, Fred M., II ophthalmologist, educator
Wilson, Harry Cochrane clergyman
Wishard, Gordon Davis lawyer
Wolsiffer, Patricia Rae insurance company executive
Wong, David T. biochemist
Wood, Richard Donald pharmaceutical company executive
Wood, William Jerome lawyer
Woodard, Harold Raymond lawyer
Wooden, Reba Faye Boyd guidance counselor
Woodring, DeWayne Stanley religion association executive
Woods, Marcus Eugene electric utility company executive, lawyer
Woody, John Frederick secondary education educator
Woollen, Evans architectural firm executive
Worrell, David Charles lawyer
Wright, David Burton retired newspaper publishing company executive
Yan, Sau-Chi Betty biochemist
Young, Philip Howard library director
Young, Richard religious organization executive
Yovits, Marshall Clinton computer and information science educator, university dean
Zapapas, James Richard pharmaceutical company executive
Zipes, Douglas Peter cardiologist, researcher
Zoeller, David Louis lawyer

Jasper
Birk, Jim business and home furnishings company executive
Fleck, Albert Henry, Jr. insurance agency executive
Habig, Douglas Arnold manufacturing company executive
Habig, Thomas Louis manufacturing executive
Kohler, Jeffrey Martin office furniture manufacturing executive
Oser, Roman Bernard manufacturing company executive
Thyen, Herbert Edward furniture company executive
Thyen, John T. furniture company executive
Thyen, Ronald Joseph furniture company executive

Jeffersonville
Bobzien, H.J., Jr. transportation company executive
Hoehn, Elmer Louis lawyer, state and federal agency administrator, educator, consultant
Pettyjohn, Shirley Ellis lawyer, real estate executive
Reisert, Charles Edward, Jr. real estate executive

Kokomo
Hall, Milton L. bishop
Hill, Emita Brady academic administrator
Schraut, Kenneth Charles mathematician, educator

La Porte
Grott, Geraldine librarian
Hancock, John D. film director
Heiden, Susan Jane elementary education educator
Hiler, John Patrick former government official, former congressman, business executive
Morris, Leigh Edward hospital executive officer

Lafayette
Andrews, Frederick Newcomb emeritus university administrator
Bement, Arden Lee, Jr. engineering educator
Brewster, James Henry retired chemistry educator
Christensen, Nikolas Ivan geophysicist, educator
Claflin, Robert Malden veterinary educator, university dean
Coburn, Patricia Ellen oncological nurse
de Branges de Bourcia, Louis mathematics educator
Emery, Alden Hayes, Jr. chemical engineer, educator
Etzel, James Edward environmental engineering educator
Feuer, Henry chemist, educator
Fox, Robert William mechanical engineering educator
Gartenhaus, Solomon physicist
Gautschi, Walter mathematics educator
Geddes, LaNelle Evelyn nursing educator, physiologist
Geddes, Leslie Alexander bioengineer, physiologist, educator
Gordon, Irene Marlow radiology educator
Gustafson, Winthrop Adolph aeronautical and astronautical engineering educator
Higi, William L. bishop
Hobbs, James Allen insurance executive
Howarth, David H. retired bank executive
Judd, William Robert engineering geologist, educator
Loeffler, Frank Joseph physicist, educator
Maickel, Roger Philip pharmacologist, educator
Mc Laughlin, John Francis civil engineer, educator
Melhorn, Wilton Newton geosciences educator
Meyer, Brud Richard pharmaceutical company executive
Naumann, Hans Richard Ernst manufacturing executive
†Nicholson, Ralph Lester botanist, educator
Ott, Karl Otto nuclear engineering educator, consultant
Porile, Norbert Thomas chemistry educator
Posey, Edwin Dalfield librarian
Price, David Robert construction company executive
Rubin, Jean Estelle mathematics educator
Sato, Hiroshi materials science educator
Sperandio, Glen Joseph pharmacy educator
Stob, Martin physiology educator
Truce, William Everett chemist, educator
VanHandel, Ralph Anthony librarian
Veenker, Claude Harold health education educator
Whitsel, Robert Malcolm insurance company executive

Lakeville
Mangus, Richard W. farmer

Lanesville
Cleveland, Peggy Rose Richey cytotechnologist

Lawrenceburg
Dautel, Charles Shreve retired mining company executive

Leo
Worman, Richard W. insurance company executive, state senator

Liberty Mills
Gross, Rachel Ann human services coordinator

Linden
Lefebvre, Gren Gordon school superintendent

Lowell
Boller, Carole Ann visual artist
Myers, Charlotte secondary educator

Madison
Gunter, Frank Elliott artist

Marion
Barnes, James Byron university president
Fisher, Pierre James, Jr. physician
McIntyre, Robert Walter church official

Martinsville
Kendall, Robert Stanton newspaper editor, journalist

Michigan City
Brockway, Lee J. architect
Higgins, William Henry Clay, III retired telecommunications consultant
Musgrave, Charles Edward music director, correctional facility official
Ruby, Burton Bennett men's apparel manufacturer

Middlebury
Guequierre, John Phillip manufacturing company executive
†Wells, Walter E. prefabricated housing manufacturing executive

Mishawaka
Goebel, Richard Alan veterinarian
Hagiwara, Kokichi steel company executive
Kapson, Jordan automotive executive
Ponko, William Reuben architect
Scott, Darrel Joseph healthcare executive
Troyer, LeRoy Seth architect

Monroeville
Geldien, Judith Ruth Motter elementary educator

Monrovia
Bennett, James Edward retired plastic surgeon, educator

Monticello
Hardin, Lowell Stewart retired economics educator
Wolf, Katie Louise state legislator

Montpelier
Neff, Kenneth D. realtor, mayor

Morgantown
Boyce, Gerald G. artist, educator

Mount Vernon
Bach, Steve Crawford lawyer

Muncie
Anderson, Stefan Stolen bank executive
Barber, Earl Eugene consulting firm executive
Bell, Stephen Scott (Steve Bell) journalist, educator
Bennon, Saul electrical engineer, transformer consultant
Carmin, Robert Leighton retired geography educator
†Clark, Nicholas L. museum director, ethnic consultant
Connally, Sandra Jane Oppy art educator
Eddy, Darlene Mathis poet, educator
Emerson, Duane E. corporate executive
Fisher, John Wesley manufacturing company executive
Harris, Joseph McAllister chemist
†Hayashi, Tetsumaro English educator, author, editor
Hendrix, Jon Richard biology educator
Henzlik, Raymond Eugene zoophysiologist, educator
Joyaux, Alain Georges art museum director
Kumbula, Tendayi Sengerwe journalism educator
Marsh, Helen Unger retired educational administrator
Mertens, Thomas Robert biology educator
Owsley, Alvin manufacturing executive, lawyer
Radcliff, William Franklin lawyer
†Rippy, Frances Marguerite Mayhew English educator
Robold, Alice Ilene mathematician, educator
Sappenfield, Charles Madison architect, educator
Sargent, Thomas Andrew political science educator, university program director
Schlesinger, Albert Reuben diversified products company executive, controller
Schuessler, Annemarie pianist, educator
Shondell, Donald Stuart physical education educator
Sissel, George Allen lawyer, manufacturing executive
Sursa, Charles David banker
Swartz, B(enjamin) K(insell), Jr. archaeologist, educator
Wheeler, David Laurie university dean

Munster
Corsiglia, Robert Joseph electrical construction company executive
Fort, Gene secondary educator
Luerssen, Frank Wonson retired steel company executive
Sherman, Mona Diane school system administrator

Nappanee
Borger, Michael Hinton Ivers osteopathic physician, educator

Nashville
McDermott, Renée R(assler) lawyer

New Albany
Baker, Claude Douglas biology educator, researcher
Braden, Samuel Edward economics educator
Crooks, Edwin William former academic administrator
Rand, Leon university administrator

New Castle
Dudley, Harry Bruce oil company executive
Walburn, John Clifford mental health services professional

New Haven
Chapman, Reid Gillis former broadcasting company executive

New Palestine
Saunders, Toni Lynne construction company executive

Newburgh
Tierney, Gordon Paul real estate broker, genealogist

Noblesville
Almquist, Donald John retired electronics company executive
Wechter, Larry Scot retail food executive
Wilson, Norman Glenn church administrator, writer

North Manchester
Harshbarger, Richard B. economics educator

Notre Dame
Adams, Howard Glen education association administrator
Aldous, Joan sociology educator
Arnold, Peri Ethan political scientist
Bartell, Ernest economist, educator
Bella, Salvatore Joseph management educator
†Blenkinsopp, Joseph biblical studies educator
Bruns, Gerald L. English literature educator
Burrell, David Bakewell philosophy educator
Cason, Neal Martin physics educator
Castellino, Francis Joseph university dean
Craig, George Brownlee, Jr. entomologist
Craypo, Charles labor economics educator
Crosson, Frederick James former university dean, humanities educator
Cunningham, Lawrence Springer theology educator
Delaney, Cornelius Francis philosophy educator
De Santis, Vincent Paul historian, educator
Despres, Leo Arthur sociology and anthropology educator, academic administrator
Dougherty, James Patrick English language educator
Dowty, Alan Kent political scientist, educator
Fehlner, Thomas Patrick chemistry educator
Feigl, Dorothy Marie chemistry educator, university official
Fuchs, Morton S. biology educator
Gabriel, Astrik Ladislas medieval studies educator, scholar
Goerner, Edward Alfred political science educator
Goulet, Denis André political science educator, writer, development ethicist
Gray, William Guerin civil engineering educator
Grazin, Igor Nikolai law educator, former state official
Gunn, Alan law educator
Gurulé, Jimmy legal educator
Gutting, Gary Michael philosophy educator
Hallinan, Maureen Theresa sociologist
Hatch, Nathan Orr university administrator
Hayes, Stephen Matthew librarian
Helquist, Paul M. chemistry educator, researcher
Hesburgh, Theodore Martin clergyman, former university president
Holtz, Louis Leo college football coach
Howard, George Stephen psychology educator
Jemielity, Thomas John English educator
Jensen, Richard Jorg biology educator
Jerger, Edward William mechanical engineer, university dean
Kennedy, John Joseph political science educator
Kmiec, Douglas William government official, law educator
Kogge, Peter Michael computer scientist, educator
Kohn, James Paul engineering educator
Langford, James Rouleau university press administrator
Lanzinger, Klaus language educator
Lauck, Anthony Joseph artist, retired art educator, priest
Leege, David Calhoun political scientist, educator
Loescher, Gilburt Damian international relations educator
Loux, Michael Joseph philosophy educator
Malloy, Edward Aloysius priest, university administrator, educator
Manier, August Edward philosophy of biology educator
Marshalek, Eugene Richard physics educator
Matthias, John Edward English literature educator
McBrien, Richard Peter theology educator
McCormick, Richard Arthur priest, religion educator, writer
McInerny, Ralph Matthew philosophy educator, author
Mc Mullin, Ernan Vincent philosophy educator
Merz, James Logan electrical engineering and materials educator, researcher
Michel, Anthony Nikolaus electrical engineering educator, researcher
Miller, Robert Carl library director
Mirowski, Philip Edward economics educator
Nugent, Walter Terry King historian
O'Meara, Onorato Timothy academic administrator, mathematician
O'Meara, Thomas Franklin priest, educator
O'Rourke, William Andrew English language educator, author
Plantinga, Alvin philosophy educator, author
Pollak, Barth mathematics educator
Pollard, Morris microbiologist, educator
†Porter, Dean Allen art museum director, art historian, educator
Quinn, Philip Lawrence philosophy educator
Reilly, Frank Kelly business educator
Rice, (Ethel) Ann publishing executive, editor
Robinson, John Hayes law educator
Rosenberg, Charles Michael art historian, educator
†Ross, Alberta Barkley chemist
Sain, Michael Kent electrical engineering educator
Sayre, Kenneth Malcolm philosophy educator
Scheidt, W. Robert chemistry educator, researcher
Schmitz, Roger Anthony chemical engineering educator, academic administrator
Schuler, Robert Hugo chemist, educator
Scully, Timothy Richard priest, academic administrator
Shaffer, Thomas Lindsay law educator
Shannon, William Norman, III marketing and international business educator, food service executive
Sommese, Andrew John mathematics educator
Stoll, Wilhelm mathematics educator
Swartz, Thomas R. economist, educator
Sweeney, Thomas Leonard chemical engineering educator, researcher

Szewczyk, Albin Anthony *engineering educator*
Tavis, Lee A. *business educator*
Thomas, John Kerry *chemistry educator*
Trozzolo, Anthony Marion *chemistry educator*
Valenzuela, Julio Samuel *sociologist, educator*
Varma, Arvind *chemical engineering educator, researcher*
Vecchio, Robert Peter *business management educator*
Wadsworth, Michael A. *ambassador, director of athletics, former professional football player*
Walicki, Andrzej Stanislaw *history educator*
Walshe, Aubrey Peter *political science educator*
Weigert, Andrew Joseph *sociology educator*
White, James Floyd *theology educator*
Wong, Warren James *mathematics educator*
Yoder, John Howard *theology educator*

Ogden Dunes
Mulvaney, Mary Jean *physical education educator*

Orleans
Keys, Steven Franklin *chemical engineer*

Pendleton
Kischuk, Richard Karl *insurance company executive*
Phenis, Nancy Sue *educational administrator*

Peru
Bronson, Kenneth Caldean *newspaper company executive*
Stackhouse, John Wesley *publishing executive*

Plainfield
Hay, John Franklin *church administrator*
Menscer, Darrell V. *utility company executive*
†Noland, Jon David *utilities executive, lawyer*

Portage
Gasser, Wilbert (Warner), Jr. *retired banker*

Princeton
Fair, Robert James *lawyer*
Mullins, Richard Austin *chemical engineer*

Reelsville
Powell, Audrey Lee *nursing administrator, critical care nurse*

Rensselaer
Shannon, Albert Joseph *educator*

Richmond
Farber, Evan Ira *librarian*
Kirk, Thomas Garrett, Jr. *librarian*
Maurer, Johan Fredrik *religious denomination administrator*
Muzzillo, Rachel Evelyn Sheeley *reporter*
Passmore, Jan William *investment company executive*
Robinson, Dixie Faye *school system administrator*
†Smuck, Harold Vernon *retired minister, religious organization administrator*
Talbot, Ardith Ann *editor*
Wood, Richard J. *college president*

Saint Mary Of The Woods
Doherty, Sister Barbara (Ann Doherty) *academic administrator*

Saint Meinrad
Daly, Simeon Philip John *librarian*

Santa Claus
Platthy, Jeno *cultural association executive*

Seymour
Bollinger, Don Mills *grocery company executive*
Terkhorn, Henry K. *food company executive*

Shelby
†Kurzeja, Richard Eugene *association executive*

South Bend
Altman, Arnold David *business executive*
Armour, James Author *military vehicle manufacturing company executive*
Bancroft, Bruce Richard *lawyer*
Black, Virginia Morrow *writer*
Burkhart, Charles Barclay *outdoor advertising executive*
Carey, John Leo *lawyer*
Charles, Isabel *university administrator*
Clarke, Thomas Crawford *lawyer*
Cohen, Ronald S. *accountant*
Costello, Donald Paul *English educator*
Ecker, Carol Adele *veterinarian*
Ford, George Burt *lawyer*
Grant, Robert Allen *federal judge*
Gray, Francis Campbell *bishop*
Gray, Frank C. *bishop*
Harriman, Gerald Eugene *retired business administrator, economics educator*
Horsbrugh, Patrick *architect, educator*
Kalamaros, Edward Nicholas *lawyer*
Korbuly, Laszlo John *architect*
Lake, Brian James *lawyer*
MacLeod, John *college basketball coach*
Manion, Daniel Anthony *federal judge*
McGill, Warren Everett *lawyer, consultant*
McKernan, Leo Joseph *manufacturing company executive*
Meyer, John Bernard *public relations executive*
Miller, Robert L., Jr. *federal judge*
Mills, Nancy Anne *elementary education educator*
Mullins, James Lee *library director*
Murphy, Christopher Joseph, III *financial executive*
†Naus, James H. *accountant*
Niemeyer, Gerhart *political science educator*
Pfeil, Richard John *electric company executive*
Raclin, Ernestine Morris *banker*
Reinke, William John *lawyer*
Ripple, Kenneth Francis *federal judge*
Rodibaugh, Robert Kurtz *federal judge*
Schurz, Franklin Dunn, Jr. *media executive*
Seall, Stephen Albert *lawyer*
Sharp, Allen *chief federal judge*
Sumrall, Lester Frank *missionary, evangelist*
Szarwark, Ernest John *lawyer*
Vandenberg, Sister Patricia Clasina *health system executive*
van Inwagen, Peter Jan *philosophy educator*
Vogel, Nelson J., Jr. *lawyer*
†Wensits, James Emrich *newspaper editor*
Yeh, Tsung *orchestral conductor*

Speedway
†Knoy, Ernest Crone *management consultant*
Unser, Alfred, Jr. *professional race car driver*

Terre Haute
Baker, Ronald Lee *English educator*
Bopp, James, Jr. *lawyer*
Campbell, Judith May *physical education educator*
Carmony, Marvin Dale *linguist, educator*
De Marr, Mary Jean *English language educator*
Frantz, Welby Marion *transportation executive*
Gilman, David Alan *education educator, editor*
Grimley, Liam Kelly *special education educator*
Guthrie, Frank Albert *chemistry educator*
Hulbert, Samuel Foster *college president*
Hunt, Effie Neva *former college dean, former English educator*
Jerry, Robert Howard *education educator*
Johnson, Jack Thomas *political science educator*
Kicklighter, Clois Earl *academic administrator*
Kunkler, Arnold William *surgeon*
Lamis, Leroy *artist, retired educator*
Landini, Richard George *university president, emeritus English educator*
Leach, Ronald George *university dean, librarian*
Little, Robert David *library science educator*
Martin, Betty Carolyn *library director*
Mausel, Paul Warner *geography educator*
Meany, John Joseph *newspaper publisher*
Moore, John W. *academic administrator*
Moore, John William *university administrator*
Pease, Edward Allan *lawyer, former state legislator, university official*
Perry, Eston Lee *real estate and equipment leasing company executive*
Puckett, Robert Hugh *political scientist, educator*
†Ralston, Patrick Robert *state government official*
Smith, Charles Oliver *engineer*
Smith, Donald Eugene *banker*
Van Til, William *education educator, writer*
Wheelock, Larry Arthur *engineer, consultant*

Unionville
Franklin, Frederick Russell *retired legal association executive*

Upland
Kesler, Jay Lewis *university president*
Shulze, Frederick Bennett *music educator*

Valparaiso
Carr, Wiley Nelson *hospital administrator*
Cook, Addison Gilbert *chemistry educator*
Ehren, Charles Alexander, Jr. *lawyer, educator*
Harre, Alan Frederick *university president*
Hillila, Bernhard Hugo Paul *education educator*
Miller, John Albert *university administrator, marketing consultant*
Mundinger, Donald Charles *college president retired*
Persyn, Mary Geraldine *law librarian, law educator*
Peters, Howard Nevin *foreign language educator*
Schlender, William Elmer *management sciences educator*
Schnabel, Robert Victor *retired academic administrator*
Taylor, Kenard Lyle, Jr. *senior manager training*

Veedersburg
Marshall, Carolyn Ann M. *church official, consultant*

Vincennes
Rose, Robert Carlisle *banker*

Wabash
Curless, Larry Dean *tax consultant, farm manager*
Flott, Leslie William *quality control professional*
Scales, Richard Lewis *manufacturer's representative*

Walton
Chu, Johnson Chin Sheng *physician*

Warsaw
Dalton, William Matthews *retired foundry executive*
†McCaffrey, R. Michael *orthopedic company executive*

West Lafayette
Abhyankar, Shreeram S. *mathematics and industrial engineering educator*
Adelman, Steven Allen *theoretical physical chemist, chemistry educator*
Albright, Jack Lawrence *animal science and veterinary educator*
Albright, Lyle Frederick *chemical engineering educator*
Allen, Durward Leon *biologist, educator*
Altman, Joseph *biological sciences educator*
Altschaeffl, Adolph George *civil engineering educator*
Amstutz, Harold Emerson *veterinarian, educator*
Amy, Jonathan Weekes *scientist, educator*
Anderson, James George *sociologist, educator*
Andres, Ronald Paul *chemical engineer, educator*
Axtell, John David *genetics educator, researcher*
Baird, William McKenzie *chemical carcinogenesis researcher, biochemistry educator*
Barany, James Walter *industrial engineering educator*
Barber, Stanley Arthur *agronomy educator*
Barnes, Virgil Everett, II *physics educator*
Baumgardt, Billy Ray *university official, agriculturist*
Beering, Steven Claus *university president, medical educator*
Belcastro, Patrick Frank *pharmaceutical scientist*
BeMiller, James Noble *biochemist, educator*
Bogdanoff, John Lee *aeronautical engineering educator*
Borowitz, Joseph Leo *pharmacologist*
†Bracker, Charles E. *plant pathology educator and researcher*
Bray, Ralph *physics educator*
Broden, Thomas Francis, III *French educator*
Brown, Donald Ray *psychologist, university administrator*
Brown, Herbert Charles *chemistry educator*
Butler, Larry Gene *biochemistry educator, researcher*
Byrn, Stephen R. *medical educator*
Christian, John Edward *health science educator*
Cicirelli, Victor George *psychologist*
Cohen, Raymond *mechanical engineer, educator*
Conte, Samuel Daniel *computer scientist, educator*
Contreni, John Joseph, Jr. *humanities educator*
Cooper, James Albert, Jr. *electrical engineering educator*
Cramer, William Anthony *biochemistry and biophysics researcher, educator*
Curtis, Kenneth Stewart *land surveyor*
Dayananda, Mysore Ananthamurthy *materials engineering educator*
Delleur, Jacques William *civil engineering educator*
Diamond, Sidney *chemist, educator*
Dilley, Richard A. *biochemist, plant physiologist, educator*
Dolch, William Lee *retired engineering materials educator*
Drake, John Warren *aviation consultant*
Drnevich, Vincent Paul *civil engineering educator*
Eckert, Roger E(arl) *chemical engineering educator*
Farris, Paul Leonard *agricultural economist*
Farris, Thomas N. *engineering educator, researcher*
Feinberg, Richard Alan *consumer science educator, consultant*
Feldhusen, John Frederick *educational psychology educator*
Ferris, Virginia Rogers *nematologist, educator*
Fischbach, Ephraim *physicist*
Ford, Frederick Ross *university official*
Franzmeier, Donald Paul *agronomy educator, soil scientist*
Frick, Gene Armin *university administrator*
Friedlaender, Fritz Josef *electrical engineering educator*
Fukunaga, Keinosuke *engineering educator*
Gappa, Judith M. *university administrator*
Garfinkel, Alan *Spanish language and education educator*
Gentry, Don Kenneth *academic dean*
Gottfried, Leon Albert *English language educator*
Grace, Richard Edward *engineering educator*
Grant, Edward Robert *chemistry educator*
Greenkorn, Robert Albert *chemical engineering educator*
Grimley, Robert Thomas *chemistry educator*
Gruen, Gerald Elmer *psychologist, educator*
Gupta, Shanti Swarup *statistician, educator*
Haas, Felix *former mathematics educator, university administrator*
Haelterman, Edward Omer *veterinary microbiologist, educator*
Hanks, Alan R. *chemistry educator*
Haring, Marilyn Joan *academic dean*
Harmon, Bud Gene *animal sciences educator, consultant*
Harr, Milton Edward *civil engineering professor, engineering consultant*
Hem, Stanley Lawrence *pharmacy educator, researcher*
Herrick, Robert James *electrical engineering technology educator, electronics engineer*
Hillberry, Ben(ny) M(ax) *mechanical engineering educator*
Hinkle, Charles Nelson *retired agricultural engineering educator*
Ho, Cho-Yen *scientific research director*
Hoover, William Leichtler *forestry and natural resources educator, financial consultant*
Horwich, George *economist, educator*
Hunt, Michael O'Leary *wood science and engineering educator*
Ichiyama, Dennis Yoshihide *design educator, consultant*
Incropera, Frank Paul *mechanical engineering educator*
Janick, Jules *horticultural scientist, educator*
Johannsen, Chris Jakob *agronomist, educator, administrator*
Johnson, Robert Willard *management educator*
Kampen, Emerson *chemical company executive*
Kashyap, Rangasami Lakshmi Narayan *electrical engineering educator*
Kessler, Wayne Vincent *health sciences educator, researcher, consultant*
Kim, Yeong Ell *physics educator, researcher, consultant*
King, Donald C. *psychologist, educator*
Kirksey, Avanelle *nutrition educator*
Knevel, Adelbert Michael *pharmacy educator*
Knudsen, Dean DeWayne *sociology educator*
Knudson, Douglas Marvin *forestry educator*
Landgrebe, David Allen *electrical engineer*
Laskowski, Michael, Jr. *chemist, educator*
Leap, Darrell Ivan *hydrogeologist*
Leimkuhler, Ferdinand Francis *industrial engineering educator*
Leitch, Vincent Barry *literary studies educator*
Le Master, Dennis Clyde *forest economics and policy educator*
Lewellen, Wilbur Garrett *management educator, consultant*
Liley, Peter Edward *mechanical engineering educator*
Lin, Pen-Min *electrical engineer, educator*
Lipschutz, Michael Elazar *chemistry educator, consultant, researcher*
Low, Philip Funk *soil chemistry educator, consultant, researcher*
Lynch, Robert Emmett *mathematics educator*
Mannering, Jerry Vincent *agronomist, educator*
Margerum, Dale William *chemistry educator*
Markee, Katherine Madigan *librarian, educator*
Marshall, Francis Joseph *aerospace engineer*
Mc Bride, William Leon *philosopher, educator*
McDonald, Robert Bond *chemical company executive*
McFee, William Warren *soil scientist*
McGee, Reece Jerome *sociology educator, researcher*
Mc Gillem, Clare Duane *electrical engineering educator*
McMillin, David Robert *chemistry educator*
Mengel, David Bruce *agronomy and soil science educator*
Michael, Harold Louis *civil engineering educator*
Michaud, Howard Henry *conservation educator*
Mobley, Emily Ruth *library dean, educator*
Molnar, Donald Joseph *landscape architecture educator*
Monke, Edwin John *agricultural engineering educator*
Morrison, Harry *chemistry educator, university dean*
Moskowitz, Herbert *management educator*
Moyars-Johnson, Mary Annis *university administrator*
Mullen, James Gentry *physics educator*
Nelson, John Howard *food company research executive*
Nelson, Philip Edwin *food scientist, educator*
Neudeck, Gerold Walter *electrical engineering educator*
Newby, Timothy James *education educator, researcher*
†Nixon, Judith May *librarian*
O'Connor, Ruth Susan *physician, educator*
Ohm, Herbert Willis *agronomy educator*
Ong, Chee-Mun *engineering educator*
Ortman, Eldon E. *entomologist, educator*
Overhauser, Albert Warner *physicist*
†Pardue, Harry L. *chemist, educator*
Peck, Garnet Edward *pharmacist, educator*
Peppas, Nikolaos Athanassiou *chemical engineering educator, consultant*
Perrucci, Robert *sociologist, educator*
Pratt, Dan Edwin *chemistry educator*
Pritsker, A. Alan B. *engineering executive, educator*
†Ramdas, Anant Krishna *physicist, optics scientist*
Reichard, Hugo Manley *English literature educator*
Rice, John Rischard *computer scientist, researcher, educator*
Richey, Clarence Bentley *agricultural engineering educator*
Ringel, Robert Lewis *university administrator*
Robinson, Farrel Richard *pathologist, toxicologist*
Rossmann, Michael George *biochemist, educator*
Rothenberg, Gunther Erich *history educator*
Rutledge, Charles Ozwin *pharmacologist, educator*
Salvendy, Gavriel *industrial engineer*
Schendel, Dan Eldon *management consultant, business educator*
Schönemann, Peter Hans *psychology educator*
Schrader, Lee Frederick *agricultural economist*
Schreiber, Marvin Mandel *agronomist, educator*
Schuhmann, Reinhardt, Jr. *metallurgical engineering educator, consultant*
Schwartz, Richard John *electrical engineering educator, researcher*
Shaw, Stanley Miner *nuclear pharmacy scientist*
Shell, Kevin Duane *human services researcher, psychologist*
Sherman, Louis Allen *biologist, researcher*
Shertzer, Bruce Eldon *education educator*
Shoup, Ronald Edward *chemicals executive*
Skelton, Robert Eugene *aeronautics and astronautics educator*
Solberg, James Joseph *industrial engineering educator*
Sozen, Mete Avni *civil engineering educator*
Stevenson, Warren Howard *mechanical engineering educator*
Stone, Beverley *former university dean, former dean of students*
Stump, John Edward *veterinary anatomy educator, ethologist*
Swensen, Clifford Henrik, Jr. *psychologist, educator*
Taber, Margaret Ruth *electrical engineering technology educator, electrical engineer*
Tacker, Willis Arnold, Jr. *academic administrator, medical educator, researcher*
Taylor, Raymond Ellory *mechanical engineering researcher*
Theen, Rolf Heinz-Wilhelm *political science educator*
Thomas, Marlin Uluess *industrial engineering educator*
†Tucker, John Mark *librarian, educator*
Tyner, Wallace Edward *economics educator*
Vest, Robert Wilson *ceramic engineering educator*
Viskanta, Raymond *mechanical engineering educator*
Wankat, Phillip Charles *chemical engineering educator*
Weidenaar, Dennis Jay *college dean*
Weinstein, Michael Alan *political science educator*
White, Joe Lloyd *soil scientist, educator*
Williams, Theodore Joseph *engineering educator*
Wilson, Franklin Leondus, III *political science educator*
Woodman, Harold David *historian*
Wright, Alfred George James *band symphony orchestra conductor, educator*
Wright, Gordon Pribyl *management, operations research educator*
Wright, Jeff Regan *civil engineering educator*

Westfield
Nolan, Paul T. *telephone company executive*

Westville
Alspaugh, Dale William *university administrator, aeronautics and astronautics educator*

Winona Lake
Ashman, Charles H. *retired minister*
Davis, John James *religion educator*
Julien, Thomas Theodore *religious denomination administrator*
Lewis, Edward Alan *religious organization adminstrator*

Zionsville
Hansen, Arthur Gene *former academic administrator, consultant*
Meyer, William Michael *mortgage banking executive*

IOWA

Adel
Garst, Elizabeth *bank executive*

Akron
Johnson, Marlys Dianne *utility company executive*

Amana
Setzer, Kirk *religious leader*

Ames
Ahmann, John Stanley *psychology educator*
Ahrens, Franklin Alfred *veterinary pharmacology educator*
Anderson, Lloyd Lee *animal science educator*
Anderson, Robert Morris, Jr. *electrical engineer*
Angelici, Robert J. *chemistry educator*
Barnes, Richard George *physicist, educator*
Basart, John Philip *electrical engineering and radio astronomy researcher, educator*
Baumann, Edward Robert *sanitary engineering educator*
Benbow, Camilla Persson *psychology educator, researcher*
Beran, George Wesley *veterinary microbiology educator*
Berger, P(hilip) Jeffrey *animal science educator, quantitative geneticist*
Black, Charles Allen *soil scientist, educator*

Bowen, George Hamilton, Jr. *astrophysicist, educator*
Boylan, David Ray *retired chemical engineer, educator*
Bremner, John McColl *agronomy and biochemistry educator*
Brown, Frederick Gramm *psychology educator*
Brown, Robert Grover *engineering educator*
Bruner, Charlotte Hughes *French language educator*
Buchele, Wesley Fisher *agricultural engineering educator, consultant*
Burnet, George, Jr. *engineering educator*
Burris, Joseph Stephen *agronomy educator*
Cantrell, Ronald Paul *agronomy educator, plant breeder*
Christensen, George Curtis *university official*
Cleasby, John LeRoy *civil engineer, educator*
Clem, John Richard *physicist, educator*
Colvin, Thomas Stuart *agricultural engineer, farmer*
Corbett, John Dudley *chemistry educator*
Crabtree, Beverly June *college dean*
Curry, Norval Herbert *retired agricultural engineer*
David, Herbert Aron *statistics educator*
Dobson, John McCullough *historian*
Eaton, Nancy Ruth Linton *librarian, dean*
Ebbers, Larry Harold *education educator*
Edwards, David Charles *psychology educator*
Ekberg, Carl Edwin, Jr. *civil engineering educator*
Finnemore, Douglas Kirby *physics educator*
Flora, Cornelia Butler *sociologist, educator*
Fox, Karl August *economist, eco-behavioral scientist*
Freeman, Albert E. *agricultural science educator*
Fritz, James Sherwood *chemist, educator*
Fuller, Wayne Arthur *statistics educator*
Gaertner, Richard Francis *manufacturing research center executive*
Gartner, Michael Gay *editor, television executive*
Gerlach, Gary Gene *newspaper publisher*
Ghoshal, Nani Gopal *veterinary anatomist, educator*
Greve, John Henry *veterinary parasitologist, educator*
Gschneidner, Karl Albert, Jr. *metallurgist, educator, editor, consultant*
Hadwiger, Don Frank *retired political science educator, researcher*
Hallauer, Arnel Roy *geneticist*
Hansen, Robert Suttle *chemist, educator*
Harl, Neil Eugene *economist, lawyer, educator*
Hatfield, Jerry Lee *plant physiologist, biometeorologist*
Herrnstadt, Richard Lawrence *American literature educator*
Horowitz, Jack *biochemistry educator*
Houk, Robert Samuel *chemistry educator*
Inger, George Roe *aerospace engineering educator*
Isely, Duane *biology and botany educator*
Iversen, James Delano *aerospace engineering educator, consultant*
Jacobson, Norman L. *retired agricultural educator, researcher*
Jacobson, Robert Andrew *chemistry educator*
Jischke, Martin C. *academic administrator*
Johnson, Howard Paul *agricultural engineering educator*
Johnson, Lawrence Alan *cereal technologist, educator, researcher, administrator*
Johnson, Stanley R. *economist, educator*
Jones, Edwin Channing, Jr. *electrical engineering educator*
Kainlauri, Eino Olavi *architect*
Kalton, Robert Rankin *crop scientist*
Karlen, Douglas Lawrence *soil scientist*
Keeney, Dennis Raymond *soil science educator*
Kelly, William Harold *physicist, physics educator*
Kempthorne, Oscar *retired statistics educator*
Kirkham, Don *soil physicist, educator*
Klonglan, Gerald Edward *sociology educator*
Larsen, William Lawrence *materials science and engineering educator*
Larson, Maurice Allen *chemical engineer, educator*
Lynch, David William *physicist, educator*
Manatt, Richard *education educator*
Maze, Thomas H. *engineering educator*
Mengeling, William Lloyd *veterinarian, virologist, researcher*
†Meyers, William Henry *economics educator*
Mischke, Charles Russell *mechanical engineering educator*
Moon, Harley William *veterinarian*
†Moore, Kenneth James *agronomy educator*
Mullen, Russell Edward *agricultural studies educator*
O'Berry, Phillip Aaron *veterinarian*
Okiishi, Theodore Hisao *mechanical engineering educator*
†Osweiler, Gary Douglas *veterinary medicine educator, toxicologist*
Palermo, Gregory Sebastian *architect*
Papadakis, Emmanuel Philippos *physicist, university research director, consultant*
Pearson, Phillip Theodore *veterinary clinical sciences and biomedical engineering educator*
Porter, Max L. *engineering educator*
Redmond, James Ronald *zoology educator, researcher*
Rice, Ronald Max *superintendent*
Riley, William Franklin *mechanical engineering educator*
Rosenberg, Ralph *former state senator, lawyer, consultant, educator*
Ross, Richard Francis *veterinarian, microbiologist, educator*
Ruedenberg, Klaus *theoretical chemist, educator*
Russell, Glen Allan *chemist, educator*
Sanders, Wallace Wolfred, Jr. *civil engineer*
Seaton, Vaughn Allen *veterinary pathology educator*
Smiley, Jane Graves *author, educator*
Smith, John Francis *materials science educator*
†Snow, Joel Alan *research director*
Starleaf, Dennis Roy *economics educator*
Svec, Harry John *chemist, educator*
Tannehill, John C. *aerospace engineer, educator*
Thompson, Joan Kathryn *university official*
Thompson, Louis Milton *agronomy educator, scientist*
Topel, David Glen *college dean, animal science educator*
Voss, Regis Dale *agronomist, educator*
Wallin, Jack Robb *research plant pathology educator*
Wass, Wallace Milton *veterinarian, clinical science educator*
Wilder, David Randolph *materials engineer, consultant*
Wilhelm, Harley A(lmey) *chemist, educator, mechanical engineer, retired*
Willham, Richard Lewis *animal science educator*
Wilson, Lennox Norwood *aeronautical engineering educator*
Wilt, Alan Freese *history educator*
Yeung, Edward Szeshing *chemist*
Young, Donald Fredrick *engineering educator*
Young, Jerry Wesley *animal nutrition educator*

Ankeny
Hartog, John, II *theology educator, librarian*

Bettendorf
Edgerton, Winfield Dow *gynecologist*
Evans, David Lynn *management consultant, executive*
Shenk, John Christian, Jr. *retired savings bank executive*

Burlington
Brocket, Judith Ann *mathematics educator*
Grinde, Douglas *banker*
Hirsch, David Alan *lawyer*
Hoth, Steven Sergey *lawyer*
Longanecker, Edwin Snyder, Jr. *special education services educator*

Camanche
Rittmer, Elaine Heneke *library media specialist*

Cambridge
Frederick, Lloyd Randall *soil microbiologist*

Cedar Falls
Austin, Calvin Murray *geography educator*
Carlson, Jerry Alan *editor*
Hanson, Roger James *physics educator*
Maier, Donna Jane-Ellen *history educator*
Oster, Merrill James *entrepreneur, publisher, author, lecturer*
Thompson, Thomas Henry *philosophy educator*
Wilson, Robley Conant, Jr. *English educator, editor, author*

Cedar Rapids
Albright, Justin W. *lawyer*
Armitage, Thomas Edward *library director*
Barta, James Omer *priest, psychology educator, church administrator*
†Blankenship, David Lynn *insurance company executive*
Boettcher, Norbe Birosel *chemist*
Bowers, M. Joan *nursing administrator*
Brown, John Edward *college president*
†Brown, Larry G. *corporate lawyer*
†Carlson, LeRoy Theodore, Jr. *telecommunications industry executive*
Chapman, Kathleen Halloran *state legislator, lawyer*
Damrow, Richard G. *advertising executive*
Dunmire, Ronald Warren *manufacturing company executive*
Faches, William George *lawyer*
Falconio, Patrick E. *insurance company executive*
Feld, Thomas Robert *college president*
Fick, E(arl) Dean *insurance executive*
Hansen, David Rasmussen *federal judge*
Healey, Edward Hopkins *architect*
Hinzman, Gerald Richard *chief of police*
Hladky, Joseph F., III *publishing executive*
Huber, Rita Norma *civic worker*
Kasparek, Ann Janine *health facility administrator*
Kucharski, Robert Joseph *power industry financial executive*
Ledford, Sandra *principal*
Lisio, Donald John *historian, educator*
Mc Manus, Edward Joseph *federal judge*
Melloy, Michael J. *federal judge*
Nazette, Richard Follett *lawyer*
Nielsen, Joyce *former state legislator*
Norris, Albert Stanley *psychiatrist, educator*
Novetzke, Sally Johnson *former ambassador*
Plagman, Ralph *principal*
Quarton, William Barlow *broadcasting company executive*
Riley, Tom Joseph *lawyer*
Root, Larry Donald *utilities executive*
Roth, Sister M. Augustine *nun, educator*
Schrimper, Vernon L. *manufacturing, marketing executive*
†Smith, Herald Alvin, Jr. *transportation executive*
†Smith, John M. *trucking executive*
Stadlen, Diane Elizabeth *marketing professional*
Stone, Herbert Marshall *architect*
Wallace, Samuel Taylor *hospital administrator*
Wax, Nadine Virginia *retired banker*
Wilson, Robert Foster *lawyer*

Center Point
Neenan, Thomas Francis *association executive, consultant*

Chariton
Pearson, Ronald Dale *retail food stores corporation executive*
Pickens, Earl *consumer products company executive*
Vredenburg, Dwight Charles *retired supermarket chain executive*

Charles City
Mc Cartney, Ralph Farnham *lawyer*

Clinton
Weil, Myron *retired banker*

Coon Rapids
Shirbroun, Richard Elmer *veterinarian, cattleman*

Council Bluffs
Nelson, H. H. Red *insurance company executive*
Peterson, Richard William *lawyer, magistrate judge*

Dallas Center
McDonald, John Cecil *lawyer*

Davenport
Bhatti, Iftikhar Hamid *chiropractic educator*
†Bradley, William Steven *art museum director*
Bright, Stanley J. *utilities executive*
Burgess, Janet Helen *interior designer*
Copes, Marvin Lee *college dean*
Gottlieb, Richard Douglas *media executive*
Jecklin, Lois Underwood *art corporation executive, consultant*
Juckem, Wilfred Philip *manufacturing company executive*
Kanzaki, George Akaki *industrial engineer, educator*
Le Grand, Clay *former state justice*
†Lense, Marcia *television anchor, producer, reporter*
Luzkow, Jack Lawrence *history educator, writer, consultant*
Moeller, Donald Joseph *academic administrator, educator*
O'Keefe, Gerald Francis *bishop, retired*
Potter, Corinne Jean *librarian*
Rogalski, Edward J. *university administrator*
Rohlf, Paul Leon *urologist*
Runge, Kay Kretschmar *library director*
Schermer, Lloyd G. *publishing and broadcasting company executive*
Schmidt, W. Robert *school system administrator*
Shaw, Donald Hardy *lawyer*
Tinsman, Margaret Neir *state senator*
Wenz, Richard L. *school system and church administrator*

Davis City
Boswell, Leonard L. *state senator*

Decorah
Belay, Stephen Joseph *lawyer*
Erdman, Lowell Paul *civil engineer, land surveyor*
Farwell, Elwin D. *minister, educational consultant*

Des Moines
Baxter, Elaine *state government official*
Beatty, Linda L. *state legislator*
Begleiter, Martin David *law educator, consultant*
Belin, David William *lawyer*
†Bowlin, Patrick L. *church officer*
Boyle, Bruce James *publisher*
Branstad, Terry Edward *governor, lawyer*
Bremer, Celeste F. *judge*
Bucksbaum, Martin *real estate developer*
Bucksbaum, Matthew *real estate development company president*
Burnett, Robert A. *publisher*
†Butkiewicz, Ronald M. *insurance company executive*
Campbell, Bonnie Jean *former state attorney general*
Canfield, Earle Lloyd *university dean, mathematics educator*
†Charron, Joseph L. *bishop*
Christiansen, Russell *utility company executive*
Clark, Beverly Ann *lawyer*
Clark, Robert Loy *social services administrator*
Claypool, David L. *lawyer*
†Cochran, Susan Mills *librarian*
Conlin, Roxanne Barton *lawyer*
Corning, Joy Cole *state official*
Daggett, Horace Clinton *state legislator*
Dahl, Harry Waldemar *lawyer*
de Gravelles, William Decatur, Jr. *physician*
Drake, Richard Francis *state senator*
Duncan, Hearst Randolph *lawyer*
Durrenberger, William John *retired army general, educator, investor*
Edwards, Charles C., Jr. *newspaper publisher*
Edwards, John Duncan *law educator, librarian*
Ehrle, Roy W. *insurance company executive*
Ellis, Mary Louise Helgeson *insurance company executive*
Elmets, Harry Barnard *osteopath, dermatologist*
†Epp, Telfer L. *church official*
Epting, C. Christopher *bishop*
Estes, Elaine Rose Graham *librarian*
†Evans, John Erik *insurance company executive*
Fagg, George Gardner *federal judge*
Ferrari, Michael Richard, Jr. *university administrator*
Fisher, Thomas George *lawyer*
Fitzgerald, Michael Lee *state official*
Fitzpatrick, Sister Jude *academic administrator*
Flansburg, James Sherman *editor, columnist*
Foster, James Franklin *professional sports management executive*
Fox, Marcia Helen *nursing administrator, medical-surgical nurse*
Frohock, Joan (Joan Walton) *industrial supply company executive*
Garman, Teresa Agnes *state legislator*
Giunta, Joseph *conductor, music director*
Glomset, Daniel Anders *physician*
Goldsmith, Janet Jane *pediatric nurse practitioner*
Grefe, Rolland Eugene *lawyer*
Grubbs, Steven Eric *state representative*
Grundberg, Betty *state legislator, property manager*
Hansell, Edgar Frank *lawyer*
Harper, Patricia M. *state legislator*
Harris, Charles Elmer *lawyer*
Harris, K. David *state supreme court justice*
Hennesy, Craig *insurance company executive*
Hill, Luther Lyons, Jr. *lawyer*
†Hoak, James McClain, Jr. *communications corporation executive, lawyer*
Hockenberg, Harlan David *lawyer*
Hubbell, James Windsor, Jr. *retired insurance company executive*
Hurd, G. David *insurance company executive*
Hutchison, Theodore Murtagh *insurance company executive*
Jensen, Dick Leroy *lawyer*
Jordan, Charles Wesley *bishop*
Jordan, David Loran *editor*
Josten, Robert E. *lawyer*
Kalainov, Sam Charles *insurance company executive*
†Kaplan, Jerry *magazine publisher*
Kelley, Robb Beardsley *insurance company executive*
Kerr, William T. *publishing and broadcasting executive*
Kramer, Mary Elizabeth *health services executive, state legislator*
Kruidenier, David *newspaper executive*
Langdon, Herschel Garrett *lawyer*
Larson, Jerry L. *state supreme court justice*
Lawless, James L. *editor, columnist*
Leighton, Paul Joe *lawyer*
LemMon, Jean Marie *editor-in-chief*
Lepley, William *state education official*
Lewis, Calvin Fred *architect, educator*
Little, Christopher Mark *publishing company executive, lawyer*
Longstaff, Ronald E. *federal judge*
Lund, Doris Hibbs *dietitian*
Lundby, Mary A. *state legislator*
Lynch, James Alexander *architect*
Lyon, James Robert *utilities executive*
MacDonald, Kenneth *journalist, former editor*
Marker, David George *university president*
Martin, Christina Marie *public relations executive*
McGiverin, Arthur A. *state supreme court justice*
†McKitrick, James Thomas *retail executive*
Meredith, Edwin Thomas, III *media executive*
Merriman, John Allen *lawyer, insurance executive*
Mertz, Dolores Mary *farmer, legislator*
Miller, Kenneth Edward *sociologist, educator*
†Miller, Thomas J. *state attorney general*
Mitchell, Orlan E. *clergyman, former college president*
Moulder, William H. *chief of police*
Murphy, Patrick Joseph *state representative*
Myers, Mary Kathleen *publishing executive*
Neis, Arthur Veral *healthcare and development company executive*
Newsome, Jon P. *insurance company executive*
Nyemaster, Ray *lawyer*
Odell, Mary Jane *former state official*
Peddicord, Roland Dale *lawyer*
Peterson, David Charles *photojournalist*
Powell, Sharon Lee *social welfare organization administrator*
†Powell, Watson (Scot) W., III *insurance company executive*
†Powell, Watson W., Jr. *insurance executive*
Power, Joseph Edward *lawyer*
Proctor, William Zinsmaster *lawyer*
Puotinen, Arthur Edwin *college president, clergyman*
Ramsey, David Selmer *hospital executive*
Ray, Robert D. *health insurance company executive*
Reece, Maynard Fred *artist, author*
Rehm, Jack Daniel *publishing executive*
†Reitinger, Thomas Anthony *hospital administrator*
Richards, Riley Harry *insurance company executive*
Rittmer, Sheldon *farmer, senator*
†Roberts, Howard L. *wholesale distribution executive*
†Roberts, Ted *manufacturing executive*
Rogers, Rodney Albert *biologist, educator*
Rohm, Charles Edward *insurance company executive*
Rosen, Matthew Stephen *botanist, consultant*
†Ruan, John *transportation executive*
Schneider, William George *former life insurance company executive*
Schroeder, Jack Walter *insurance executive, lawyer*
Shoff, Patricia Ann *lawyer*
Simbro, William Charles *journalist*
Slade, Llewellyn Eugene *lawyer, engineer*
Smith, Diana Marie *business educator*
Smith, Mary Louise *politics and public affairs consultant*
†Smith, Ray E. *church officer*
†Smith, Sharman Bridges *state librarian*
Snell, Bruce M., Jr. *state supreme court justice*
Snyder, Carolyn Swick (Carrie Snyder) *special education educator, vocational program administrator*
Speas, Raymond Aaron *retired insurance company executive*
Stauffer, William Albert *insurance company executive*
Stoffer, Terry James *advertising executive*
Stuart, William Corwin *federal judge*
Sullivan, Patricia Clare *hospital administrator*
Szymoniak, Elaine Eisfelder *state senator*
Thoman, Mark Edward *pediatrician*
Urban, Thomas Nelson *agricultural products company executive*
Vande Krol, Jerry Lee *architect*
Van Zante, Shirley M(ae) *magazine editor*
Vietor, Harold Duane *federal judge*
Vorbrich, Lynn Karl *lawyer, utility executive*
Wegenke, Gary L. *school systems administrator*
Wells, Samuel Joseph *insurance company executive*
Wine, Donald Arthur *lawyer*
Winick, Alfred Zell *data services corporation executive*
Witke, David Rodney *newspaper editor*
Wolle, Charles Robert *federal judge*
†Yepsen, David Arlon *reporter*
Young, Dennis Eugene *financial services executive*

Dubuque
Agria, John Joseph *college official*
Bertsch, Frank Henry *furniture manufacturing company executive*
Brown, William Clifford *publishing company executive*
Crahan, Jack Bertsch *manufacturing company executive*
Drummond, Richard Henry *religion educator*
Dunn, M. Catherine *college administrator, educator*
Ernst, Daniel Pearson *lawyer*
†Hammer, David Lindley *lawyer, author*
Hanus, Jerome *archbishop*
Hemmer, Paul Edward *musician, broadcasting executive*
Herzberger, Eugene E. *retired neurosurgeon*
Kolz, Beverly Anne *publishing executive*
McDonald, Robert Delos *manufacturing company executive*
Peterson, Walter Fritiof *academic administrator*
Pike, George Harold, Jr. *religious organization executive, clergyman*
Toale, Thomas Edward *school system administrator, priest*
Tully, Thomas Alois *building materials executive, consultant, educator*
Wahlert, Robert Henry *food company executive*

Dysart
Wieck, Paul Hans *fraternal organization executive*

Fairfield
Hawthorne, Timothy Robert *direct response advertising and communications company executive*
Schaefer, Jimmie Wayne, Jr. *agricultural company executive*

Forest City
Beebe, Raymond Mark *lawyer*
Hanson, John Kendrick *recreational vehicle manufacturing company executive*
Vammen, James Oliver *human services administrator*

Fort Dodge
Pratt, Diane Adele *elementary education educator*

Glenwood
Campbell, William Edward *state hospital school administrator*

Grinnell
Adelberg, Arnold Melvin *mathematics educator, researcher*
Cervene, Richard T. *art educator*
Christiansen, Kenneth Allen *biologist, educator*
Erickson, Luther Eugene *chemist, educator*
Ferguson, Pamela Anderson *mathematics educator, educational administrator*
Fitzgerald, Michael J. *secondary school principal*

Herman, Eugene Alexander *mathematics educator*
Kaiser, Daniel Hugh *historian, educator*
Kintner, Philip L. *history educator*
Kissane, James Donald *English literature educator*
Leggett, Glenn *former English language educator, academic administrator*
McKee, Christopher Fulton *librarian, naval historian, educator*
Michaels, Jennifer Tonks *foreign language educator*
Walker, Waldo Sylvester *academic administrator*
Wall, Joseph Frazier *historian, educator*

Independence
Handy, Charles Brooks *accountant, educator*

Indianola
Jennings, Stephen Grant *academic administrator*
Larsen, Robert LeRoy *artistic director*

Iowa City
Abboud, Francois Mitry *physician, educator*
Addis, Laird Clark, Jr. *philosopher, educator, musician*
Afifi, Adel Kassim *physician*
Albrecht, William Price *economist, educator, government official*
Andreasen, Nancy Coover *psychiatrist, educator*
Andrews, Clarence Adelbert *historian, educator, writer, publisher*
Arora, Jasbir Singh *engineering educator*
Aydelotte, Myrtle Kitchell *nursing administrator, educator, consultant*
Baird, Robert Dahlen *religious educator*
Baker, Richard Graves *geology educator, palynologist*
Balukas, Jean *professional pocket billiard player*
Banker, Gilbert Stephen *industrial and physical pharmacy educator, administrator*
Bar, Robert S. *endocrinologist*
Barkan, Joel David *political science educator*
Baron, Jeffrey *pharmacologist, educator*
Bayne, David Cowan *priest, lawyer, law educator*
Bedell, George Noble *physician, educator*
†Bell, Marvin Hartley *poet, English language educator*
Bentz, Dale Monroe *librarian*
Bergman, Ronald Arly *anatomist, educator*
Bishara, Samir Edward *orthodontist*
Bonfield, Arthur Earl *lawyer, educator*
Bonfiglio, Michael *surgeon, educator*
Brennan, Robert Lawrence *psychometrician*
Bruch, Delores Ruth *education educator, musician*
†Buckwalter, Joseph Addison *orthopaedic surgeon, educator*
Burns, C(harles) Patrick *hematologist-oncologist*
Burton, Donald Joseph *chemistry educator*
Butchvarov, Panayot Krustev *philosophy educator*
Cain, Patricia A. *law educator*
Carmichael, Gregory Richard *chemical engineering educator*
Chen, Lea D. *engineering educator, researcher*
Clifton, James Albert *physician*
Coffman, William Eugene *educational psychologist*
Collins, Daniel W. *accountant, educator*
Colloton, John William *university health care executive*
Cooper, Reginald Rudyard *orthopedic surgeon, educator*
Cruden, Robert William *botany educator*
Damasio, Antonio R. *physician, neurologist*
Daniels, Lacy *microbiology educator*
Deligiorgis, Stavros G. *literature educator*
Dickeson, Robert Celmer *retired university president, corporation president, political science educator*
DiPardo, Anne *English language and education educator*
†Domsic, Dennis Michael *dean, university medical department official*
Donelson, John Everett *biochemistry educator, molecular biologist*
Downer, Robert Nelson *lawyer*
Duck, Steve Weatherill *communications educator*
Dudziak, Mary Louise *law educator, lecturer*
Eckhardt, Richard Dale *physician, educator*
Eckstein, John William *physician, educator*
Ehrenhaft, Johann Leo *surgeon*
Eyman, Earl Duane *electrical science educator, consultant*
Feldt, Leonard Samuel *university educator and administrator*
Fellows, Robert Ellis *medical educator, medical scientist*
Ferguson, Richard L. *educational administrator*
Filer, Lloyd Jackson, Jr. *pediatric educator, clinical investigator*
Fitz, Annette Elaine *physician, educator*
Forell, George Wolfgang *religion educator*
Forsythe, Robert Elliott *economics educator*
Franken, Edmund Anthony, Jr. *radiologist, educator*
Fry, Hayden *university athletic coach*
Fuller, John Williams *economics educator*
Galask, Rudolph Peter *obstetrician-gynecologist*
†Galbraith, William Bruce *physician, educator*
Gantz, Bruce Jay *otolaryngologist, educator*
Gelfand, Lawrence Emerson *historian, educator*
Gerber, John Christian *English language educator*
Gergis, Samir Danial *anesthesiologist, educator*
Gittler, Josephine *law educator*
Goff, Harold Milton *chemistry educator*
Goldstein, Jonathan Amos *ancient history and classics educator*
Gompper, David *music educator*
Goodridge, Alan Gardner *research biochemist, educator*
†Graham, Jorie *author*
Green, Michael David *law educator*
Green, William *archaeologist*
Gurnett, Donald Alfred *physics educator*
Hammond, Harold Logan *pathology educator, oral pathologist*
Hanley, Sarah *history educator*
Hardt, Hanno Richard Eduard *communications educator*
Hardy, James Chester *speech pathologist, educator*
Haug, Edward Joseph, Jr. *mechanical engineering educator, simulation research engineer*
Hausler, William John, Jr. *microbiologist, educator, public health laboratory administrator*
Hawley, Ellis Wayne *historian, educator*
Helm, June *anthropologist, educator*
Hering, Robert Gustave *mechanical engineer, educator, university administrator*
Hines, N. William *law educator, administrator*
Hoffmann, Louis Gerhard *immunologist, educator, sex therapist*
Hogg, Robert Vincent, Jr. *mathematical statistician, educator*
Holstein, Jay Allen *Judaic studies educator*
Hornsby, Roger Allen *classics educator*
Jacobs, Richard Matthew *dentist, orthodontics educator*
January, Lewis Edward *physician, educator*
Johnson, Eugene Walter *mathematician*
†Jones, Thom Douglas *writer*
Justice, Donald Rodney *poet, educator*
Kelch, Robert Paul *pediatric endocrinologist*
Keller, Eliot Aaron *broadcasting executive*
Kelley, Robert E. *English language educator*
Kerber, Linda Kaufman *historian, educator*
Kessel, Richard Glen *zoology educator*
Kim, Chong Lim *political science educator*
Kirchner, Peter Thomas *physician nuclear medicine, educator, consultant*
Kleinfeld, Erwin *mathematician, educator*
Knutson, John Franklin *psychology educator, clinical psychologist*
Koch, Donald LeRoy *geologist, state agency administrator*
Korpel, Adrian *electrical and computer engineering educator, consultant*
Kottick, Edward Leon *music educator, harpsichord maker*
Krause, Walter *retired economics educator, consultant*
Kurtz, Sheldon Francis *lawyer, educator*
Kusiak, Andrew *manufacturing engineer, educator*
Lance, George Milward *mechanical engineering educator*
Levey, Samuel *health care administration educator*
†Linhardt, Robert John *medicinal chemistry educator*
Loewenberg, Gerhard *political science educator*
Long, John Paul *pharmacologist, educator*
Longren, Karl Erik *electrical and computer engineering educator*
Lopes, Lola Lynn *psychologist, educator*
MacVey, Alan Mokler *program director*
Madsen, Donald Howard *engineering educator, consultant*
Marshall, Jeffrey Scott *mechanical engineer, educator*
Mason, Edward Eaton *surgeon*
Mather, Betty Bang *musician, educator*
Mather, Roger Frederick *music educator, freelance technical writer*
Mc Leran, James Herbert *university dean, oral surgeon*
Milkman, Roger Dawson *genetics educator, molecular evolution researcher*
Montgomery, Rex *biochemist, educator*
Morriss, Frank Howard, Jr. *pediatrics educator*
Nathan, Peter E. *psychologist, educator*
Nelson, Herbert Leroy *psychiatrist*
Neumann, Roy Covert *architect*
Obermann, C. Esco *psychologist, rehabilitation consultant*
Olin, William Harold *orthodontist, educator*
Osborne, James William *radiation biologist*
Patel, Virendra Chaturbhai *mechanical engineering educator*
Percas de Ponseti, Helena *foreign language and literature educator*
Persons, Stow Spaulding *historian, educator*
Pietrzyk, Donald John *chemistry educator*
Plapp, Bryce Vernon *biochemistry educator*
Ponseti, Ignacio Vives *orthopaedic surgery educator*
Potra, Florian Alexander *mathematics educator*
Prokopoff, Stephen Stephen *art museum director, educator*
Raeburn, John Hay *English language educator*
Richerson, Hal Bates *physician, internist, allergist, immunologist, educator*
Riesz, Peter Charles *marketing educator, consultant*
Ringen, Catherine Oleson *linguistics educator*
Robertson, Timothy Joel *statistician, educator*
Ross, Russell Marion *political science educator*
Saks, Michael Jay *law educator*
Sayre, Robert Freeman *English language educator*
Schmidt, Julius *sculptor*
Schoenbaum, David Leon *historian*
Schultz, Louis William *judge*
Schulz, Rudolph Walter *university dean*
Shannon, Lyle William *sociology educator*
Siebert, Calvin D. *economist, educator*
Sinicropi, Stephen Anthony *radio station executive*
Skorton, David Jan *university official, physician, educator*
Small, Arnold McCollum *psychologist, educator*
Solbrig, Ingeborg Hildegard *German literature educator, author*
Stay, Barbara *zoologist, educator*
Steele, Oliver *English educator*
Stensvaag, John-Mark *legal educator, lawyer*
Stern, Gerald Daniel *poet*
Strauss, John Steinert *dermatologist, educator*
Tephly, Thomas Robert *pharmacologist, toxicologist, educator*
Thompson, Herbert Stanley *neuro-ophthalmologist*
Titze, Ingo Roland *physics educator*
Tomkovicz, James Joseph *law educator*
Trank, Douglas Monty *rhetoric and speech communications educator*
Van Allen, James Alfred *physicist, educator*
Van Gilder, John Corley *neurosurgeon, educator*
Vaughan, Emmett John *academic dean, insurance educator*
Vernon, David Harvey *lawyer, educator*
Wachal, Robert Stanley *linguistics educator, consultant*
Wasserman, Edward Arnold *psychology educator*
Weinberger, Miles M. *physician, pediatric educator*
Weingeist, Thomas Alan *ophthalmology educator*
Werger, Paul Myron *bishop*
Weston, Burns Humphrey *law educator*
Widiss, Alan I. *lawyer, educator*
Wiley, Robert Allen *pharmaceutical educator*
Williams, Richard Dwayne *physician, educator*
Winokur, George *psychiatrist, educator*
Wunder, Charles C(ooper) *physiology and biophysics educator, gravitational biologist*
Wurster, Dale Erwin *pharmacy educator, university dean*
Ziegler, Ekhard Erich *pediatrics educator*
Zimmer, Paul Jerome *publisher, editor, poet*

Janesville
Ehmen, James Edward *elementary educator*

Johnston
Churchill, Steven Wayne *fund-raising consultant*
Duvick, Donald Nelson *plant breeder*
Steele, Betty Louise *retired banker*

Keokuk
Atterberg, Douglas Keith *financial planner*

Knoxville
Joslyn, Wallace Danforth *psychologist*

Lamoni
Higdon, Barbara J. *college president*

Larchwood
Onet, Virginia C(onstantinescu) *research scientist, educator, writer*
Zangger, Russell George *organization executive, flying school executive*

Le Mars
†Wells, Fay R. *food products executive*
†Wells, Fred D. *food products executive*

Madrid
Handy, Richard Lincoln *civil engineer, educator*

Marion
Starr, David Evan *corporate executive*

Marshalltown
Brennecke, Allen Eugene *lawyer*

Mason City
†Alexandres, Richard Bernard *manufacturing company executive*
†Collison, Jim *business executive*
MacNider, Jack *retired cement company executive*
Rosenberg, Dale Norman *psychology educator*
Schumacher, Larry P. *health facility administrator*
Wallace, Ralph Howes *retired engineering company executive*

Mc Callsburg
Lounsberry, Robert Horace *former state government administrator*

Mount Pleasant
Haselmayer, Louis August *college president emeritus*

Mount Vernon
Ruppel, Howard James, Jr. *sociologist*

Muscatine
Carver, Martin Gregory *tire manufacturing company executive*
Coulter, Charles Roy *lawyer*
Dahl, Arthur Ernest *former manufacturing executive, consultant*
Dvorchak, Thomas Edward *financial executive*
Fosholt, Sanford Kenneth *consulting engineer*
Howe, Stanley Merrill *manufacturing company executive*
Johnson, Donald Lee *agricultural materials processing company executive*
Kautz, John T. *agricultural business executive*
Kautz, Richard Carl *chemical and feed company executive*
†Kent, James H. *food products company executive*
Koll, Richard Leroy *retired chemical company executive*
McMains, Melvin L(ee) *controller*
Schoeffel, Jon Michael *lawyer*
Stanley, Richard Holt *consulting engineer*
Thomopulos, Gregs G. *consulting engineering company executive*

Nevada
Countryman, Dayton Wendell *lawyer*

Newton
Bennett, Edward James *lawyer*
Hadley, Leonard Anson *appliance manufacturing corporation executive*
†Haines, Richard Joseph *appliance manufacturing executive*
Schiller, Jerry A. *retired manufacturing company executive*

Oakdale
Spriestersbach, Duane Caryl *university administrator, speech pathology educator*

Oelwein
McFarlane, Beth Lucetta Troester *former mayor*

Orange City
Scorza, Sylvio Joseph *religion educator*

Osceola
Reynoldson, Walter Ward *state supreme court chief justice*

Oskaloosa
Porter, David Lindsey *history and political science educator, author*

Ottumwa
Roseberry, Donald G. *chief administrator*

Pella
†Andringa, Mary Vermeer *manufacturing executive*
Bevis, James Wayne *manufacturing company executive*
Farver, Mary Joan *building products company executive*

Plainfield
Lynes, James William, Sr. *communications company executive*

Red Oak
Anderson, Ronald G. *newspaper publisher*

Schaller
Currie, James Morton *bank executive*

Shenandoah
Rose, Jennifer Joan *lawyer*

Sioux Center
Hulst, John B. *academic administrator*

Sioux City
†Biorn, David Olaf *hospital administrator*
Deck, Paul Wayne, Jr. *federal judge*
Delk, Ira Edwin *utilities and diversified company executive*
Engle, Richard Carlyle *utilities executive*
Hagen, R. E. *bank executive*
Hansen, Doris Anne *accountant*
Harward, Gary John *utility company executive*
Juon, Lester Allen *utility executive*
Madsen, George Frank *lawyer*
Marks, Bernard Bailin *lawyer*
Nymann, P. L. *lawyer*
O'Brien, Donald Eugene *federal judge*
Rants, Carolyn Jean *college official*
Rocklin, Isadore J. *manufacturing executive, consultant, engineer*
Rooney, Gail Schields *college administrator*
Silverberg, David S. *financial consultant*
Soens, Lawrence D. *bishop*
Spellman, George Geneser, Sr. *internist*
Tommeraasen, Miles *college president*
Walker, Jimmie Kent *mechanical engineer*
Wharton, Beverly Ann *utility company executive*
Wick, Sister Margaret *college administrator*

Spencer
Pearson, Gerald Leon *food company executive*

Spirit Lake
Brett, George Wendell *retired geologist, philatelist*
Hedberg, Paul Clifford *broadcasting executive*

Springville
Nyquist, John Davis *retired radio manufacturing company executive*

Steamboat Rock
Taylor, Ray *state senator*

Storm Lake
Briscoe, Keith G. *college president*
Miller, Curtis Herman *bishop*
Shafer, Everett Earl *business administration educator*

Urbandale
Alumbaugh, JoAnn McCalla *magazine editor*

Walnut
Everhart, Robert Phillip (Bobby Williams) *entertainer, songwriter, recording artist*

Waterloo
Broshar, Robert Clare *architect*
Kimm, Robert George *animal science educator*
Kober, Arletta Refshauge (Mrs. Kay L. Kober) *educational administrator*
†Lindberg, Duane R. *minister*
Mast, Frederick William *construction company executive*
Taylor, Lyle Dewey *economic development company executive*

Waverly
Vogel, Robert Lee *college administrator, clergyman*

West Branch
Mather, Mildred Eunice *retired archivist*
Sulg, Madis *corporation executive*
†Walch, Timothy George *library administrator*

West Des Moines
Alberts, Marion Edward *physician*
Barnett, Duane Alan *school system administrator*
Brooks, Roger Kay *insurance company executive*
Bump, Wilbur Neil *retired lawyer*
Davis, James Casey *lawyer*
Davis, Ronald Arthur *life insurance brokerage executive*
Dooley, Donald John *publishing executive*
Marshall, Russell Frank *research company executive*
Neiman, John Hammond *lawyer*
†Plunk, Robert Malcome *insurance company executive*
Pomerantz, Marvin Alvin *container corporation executive*
Richard, Harold Irvin *agricultural business executive*
Sather, Everett Norman *accountant*
Schroder, Andrea Ruth Lundeen *realtor*
Starr, V. Hale *communications executive*
Trebilcock, William Everett *food products executive*
Westerbeck, Kenneth Edward *retired insurance company executive*
Zimmerman, Jo Ann *health services and educational consultant, former lieutenant governor*

West Union
Vettrus, Richard James *minister*

Windsor Heights
Ansorge, Iona Marie *retired real estate agent, musician, high school and college instructor*
Demorest, Allan Frederick *psychologist, consultant*

KANSAS

Atchison
Cray, Cloud Lanor, Jr. *grain products company executive*

Auburn
Good, Martha Gail *educational administrator*

Baldwin City
Keeling, Joe Keith *academic administrator, provost*
Lambert, Daniel Michael *academic administrator*

Beloit
Conroy, Thomas Hyde *lawyer*

Bonner Springs
Elliott-Watson, Doris Jean *psychiatric, mental health and gerontological nursing educator*

Burr Oak
O'Brien, Kimberly K. *secondary education educator*

Chanute
Mitchell, Donald E. *rehabilitation counselor, transition counselor*

Clay Center
Braden, James Dale *former state legislator*

Coffeyville
Garner, Jim David *state legislator, lawyer*
Seaton, Richard Melvin *newspaper and broadcasting executive*

Colby
Finley, Philip Bruce *retired state adjutant general*
Frahm, Sheila *lieutenant governor, former state legislator*

Concordia
Buechel, William Benjamin *lawyer*
Casado, Antonio Francisco *retired real estate executive*

Derby
†Guntly, Gregory G. *health facility administrator*

Dighton
Stanley, Ellen May *historian, consultant*

Dodge City
Chaffin, Gary Roger *business executive*
Clifton-Smith, Rhonda Darleen *art center director*
Schlarman, Stanley Gerard *bishop*

Downs
La Barge, William Joseph *tutor, researcher*

El Dorado
Edwards, James Lynn *college dean*

Emporia
Christiansen, David K. *hospital administrator*
Glennen, Robert Eugene, Jr. *university president*
†Hale, Martha Larsen *librarian*
Hashmi, Sajjad Ahmad *business educator, university dean*
O'Reilly, Hugh Joseph *restaurant executive*

Enterprise
Wickman, John Edward *librarian, historian*

Fairway
Marquardt, Christel Elisabeth *lawyer*

Fort Leavenworth
†Allie, Stephen J. *museum curator*
Miller, John Edward *army officer*
Oliver, Thornal Goodloe *health care executive*

Fort Riley
†Bright, Patricia Spurrier *executive director*
†Gorsline, Stephen Paul *medical technician*
†House, Randolph Watkins *military officer*

Fort Scott
Emery, Frank Eugene *publishing executive*

Goddard
Kastens, Beverly Ann *special and elementary education educator*

Goodland
Sharp, Glenn (Skip Sharp) *vocational education administrator*

Great Bend
Jones, Edward *physician, pathologist*

Haven
Schlickau, George Hans *cattle breeder, professional association executive*

Hays
Budke, Charles Henry *secondary education educator*
Coyne, Patrick Ivan *physiological ecologist*
Hammond, Edward H. *university president*
Lee, Carla Ann Bouska *nursing educator*

Hesston
Yost, Lyle Edgar *farm equipment manufacturing company executive*

Hiawatha
Pennel, Marie Lucille Hunziger *elementary education educator*

Hugoton
Nordling, Bernard Erick *lawyer*

Hutchinson
Baumer, Beverly Belle *journalist*
Buzbee, Richard Edgar *newspaper editor*
Dick, Harold L. *manufacturing executive*
Dillon, David Brian *retail grocery executive*
Hayes, John Francis *lawyer*
Kerr, David Mills *state legislator*
O'Neal, Michael Ralph *state legislator, lawyer*
Schmidt, Gene Earl *hospital administrator*
†Smith, Steve *retail executive*

Independence
Swearingen, Harold Lyndon *oil company executive*

Industrial Airport
Mendelson, Lewis Aaron *manufacturing company executive*

Iola
Talkington, Robert Van *state senator*

Junction City
Werts, Merrill Harmon *management consultant*

Kansas City
Anderson, Harrison Clarke *pathology educator, biomedical researcher*
Arakawa, Kasumi *physician, educator*
Baska, James Louis *wholesale grocery company executive*
Behbehani, Abbas M. *clinical virologist, educator*
Cade, Walter *church administrator*
Campbell, Joseph Leonard *trade association executive*
†Cargin, Thomas C. *controller*
Carolan, Douglas *wholesale company executive*
Cho, Cheng Tsung *pediatrician, educator*
Coles, Anna Louise Bailey *university official, nurse*
DeFabis, Mike *food products company executive*
†Doull, John *toxicologist, pharmacologist*
Dunn, Marvin Irvin *physician*
Ebner, Kurt Ewald *biochemistry educator*
Forst, Marion Francis *bishop*
Godfrey, Robert Gordon *physician*
Godwin, Harold Norman *pharmacist, educator*
Goldberg, Ivan D. *microbiologist, educator*
Goodwin, Donald William *psychiatrist, educator*
Grantham, Jared James *nephrologist, educator*
Greenberger, Norton Jerald *physician*
Greenwald, Gilbert Saul *physiologist*
Hassanein, Khatab M. *biostatistics educator, consultant*
Hollander, Daniel *gastroenterologist, medical educator*
Hollenbeck, Marynell *municipal government official*
Hudson, Robert Paul *medical educator*
Jerome, Norge Winifred *nutritionist, anthropologist*
Jones, Charles W. *labor union executive*
Jones, Sherman Jarvis *state senator*
Keleher, James P. *bishop*
Krantz, Kermit Edward *physician, educator*
†Loosen, Sister Sister Ann Marita *nun, health care executive*
Lungstrum, John W. *federal judge*
Maher, Sylvia Arlene *nurse administrator*
Mathews, Paul Joseph *allied health educator*
Mathewson, Hugh Spalding *anesthesiologist, educator*
Merritt, Carol Ruth *middle school educator*
Mohn, Melvin Paul *anatomist, educator*
Moore, Wayne V. *pediatrician, educator, endocrinologist*
Morrison, David Campbell *immunology educator*
O'Connor, Earl Eugene *federal judge*
Olofson, Tom William *private investor, business executive*
Phillips, Gary Lynn *wholesale grocery distribution company executive*
Potter, Glenn Edward *hospital administrator*
Powell, Nancy Egan *elementary education educator*
†Reed, V. Keith *pension fund administrator*
Robinson, David Weaver *surgeon, educator*
Samson, Frederick Eugene, Jr. *neuroscientist, educator*
Schloerb, Paul Richard *surgeon, educator*
Simpson, Laura Kay *lawyer*
Stoskopf, William Howard *retired music educator*
Strecker, Ignatius J. *archbishop*
Van Bebber, George Thomas *federal judge*
Vratil, Kathryn Hoefer *federal judge*
Walaszek, Edward Joseph *pharmacology educator*
Waxman, David *physician, university consultant*
Whelan, Richard J. *director special education and pediatrics programs, academic administrator*
Ziegler, Dewey Kiper *neurologist*

Kingman
Burket, George Edward, Jr. *family physician*

Lake Quivira
Hall, R. Vance *psychology researcher, educator, administrator, consultant, business executive*

Lawrence
Alexander, John Thorndike *historian, educator*
Ammar, Raymond George *physicist, educator*
Andrews, William Leake *English educator*
Angino, Ernest Edward *geology educator*
Armitage, Kenneth Barclay *biology educator, ecologist*
Augelli, John Pat *geography educator, author, consultant, rancher*
Baumgartel, Howard J., Jr. *psychology educator, academic administrator*
Beedles, William LeRoy *finance educator, financial consultant*
Benjamin, Bezaleel Solomon *architecture and architectural engineering educator*
Borchardt, Ronald Terrance *biochemistry and pharmaceutical chemistry educator, consultant*
Bovee, Eugene Cleveland *protozoologist, emeritus educator*
Bowman, Laird Price *retired foundation administrator*
Brawley, Robert Julius *artist, art educator*
Bulgren, William Gerald *computer science educator, researcher*
Burroughs, William Seward *writer*
Byers, George William *retired entomology educator*
Carlson, Robert Gideon *chemistry educator*
Casad, Robert Clair *legal educator*
Cherniss, Michael David *English educator*
Crowe, William Joseph *dean of libraries, educator*
Darwin, David *civil engineering educator, researcher, consultant*
Debicki, Andrew Peter *foreign language educator*
De George, Richard Thomas *philosophy educator*
Dreschhoff, Gisela Auguste Marie *physicist, educator*
Duerksen, George Louis *music educator, music therapist*
Eblen, George Thomas (Tom Eblen) *journalist*
Eldredge, Charles Child, III *art history educator*
†El-Hodiri, Mohamed A. *economics educator*
Enos, Paul *geologist, educator*
Farokhi, Saeed *aerospace engineering educator, consultant*
Forman, George Whiteman *mechanical design consultant*
Frederickson, Horace George *former college president, public administration educator*
Genova, Anthony Charles *philosophy educator*
Gerhard, Lee Clarence *geologist, educator*
Ginn, John Charles *journalism educator, former newspaper publisher*
Grabow, Stephen Harris *architecture educator*
Green, Don Wesley *chemical and petroleum engineering educator*
Gunn, James E. *English educator*
Harmony, Marlin Dale *chemistry educator, researcher*
Haufler, Christopher Hardin *botany educator*
Heller, Francis H(oward) *law and political science educator emeritus*
Himmelberg, Charles John, III *mathematics educator, researcher*
Holtzman, Julian Charles *electrical engineer*
Johnston, Richard Fourness *biologist*
Kleinberg, Jacob *chemist, educator*
Koepp, Donna Pauline Petersen *librarian*
Laird, Roy Dean *political science educator*
Landgrebe, John Allan *chemistry educator*
Lane, Meredith Anne *botany educator, museum director*
Leonard, Roy Junior *civil engineering educator*
Levine, Stuart George *editor, English literature educator, author*
Li, Chu-Tsing *art history educator*
†Lichtwardt, Robert William *mycologist*
Locke, Carl Edwin, Jr. *academic administrator, engineering educator*
Lucas, William Max, Jr. *structural engineer, university dean*
Lundsgaarde, Henry Peder *anthropology educator, researcher*
Mackenzie, Kenneth Donald *management consultant, educator*
Martin, Edwin J(ohn) *psychologist*
Mc Coy, Donald Richard *historian*
Mc Kinney, Ross Erwin *civil engineering educator*
Michener, Charles Duncan *entomologist, biologist, educator*
Miller, Don Robert *surgeon*
Mitscher, Lester Allen *chemist, educator*
Moore, Richard Kerr *electrical engineering educator*
†Morgan, Scott Ellingwood *publisher, lawyer*
Muirhead, Vincent Uriel *aerospace engineer*
Norris, Andrea Spaulding *art museum director*
†Ohlen, Robert Bruce *hospital executive*
Orel, Harold *literary critic, educator*
Papanek, Victor *designer, educator, writer*
Paretsky, David *microbiology educator*
Phillips, Oliver C. *classics educator*
Pickett, Calder Marcus *retired journalism educator*
Pinet, Frank Samuel *former university dean*
Pozdro, John Walter *music educator, composer*
Quinn, Dennis B. *English language and literature educator*
Robinson, Walter Stitt, Jr. *historian*
Rolfe, Stanley Theodore *civil engineer, educator*
Roskam, Jan *aerospace engineer*
Ross, Jack Lewis *psychiatrist*
Rowland, James Richard *electrical engineering educator*
Saul, Norman Eugene *history educator*
Schiefelbusch, Richard L. *research administrator*
Schoeck, Richard Joseph *English and humanities scholar*
Schroeder, Stephen Robert *psychology researcher*
Seaver, James Everett *historian, educator*
Seibold, Ronald Lee *sociologist, writer*
Sheridan, Richard Bert *economics educator*
Simons, Dolph Collins, Jr. *newspaper publisher*
Smith, Glee Sidney, Jr. *lawyer*
Smith, Howard Wesley *engineering educator*
Smith, Robert Lee *retired civil engineering educator*
Spires, Robert Cecil *foreign language educator*
Stella, Valentino John *pharmaceutical chemistry educator*
Stokstad, Marilyn Jane *art history educator, curator*
Tacha, Deanell Reece *federal judge*
Tsubaki, Andrew Takahisa *theater director, educator*
Turnbull, Ann Patterson *special education educator, consultant*
Tuttle, William McCullough, Jr. *history educator*
Vincent, Jon Stephen *foreign language educator*
Williams, Roy *university athletic coach*
Willner, Ann Ruth *political scientist, educator*
Wilson, Paul Edwin *lawyer, educator*
Winter, Winton Allen, Jr. *lawyer, state senator*
Woelfel, James Warren *philosophy educator*
Woodward, Frederick Miller *publisher*
Worth, George John *English literature educator*
Young, J(ohn) Michael *philosophy educator*
Zeller, Edward Jacob *physics, astronomy and geology educator, consultant*
Zerwekh, Robert Paul *engineering administrator, engineering management educator, researcher, consultant, artist*

Leavenworth
Glatt, Sister Marie Damian *healthcare corporation executive*
Haag, Donald Richard *director facilities and services*
McGilley, Sister Mary Janet *nun, educator, writer, academic administrator*
Mengel, Charles Edmund *physician, medical educator*
Stanley, Arthur Jehu, Jr. *federal judge*

Leawood
Ballard, John William, Jr. *banker*
Snyder, Willard Breidenthal *lawyer*

Lebanon
Colwell, John Edwin *retired aerospace scientist*

Lecompton
Conard, John Joseph *financial official*

Lenexa
Ascher, James John *pharmaceutical executive*
Parkinson, Mark Vincent *state legislator, lawyer*
Rayburn, George Marvin *business executive, investment executive*
Stephan, Robert Taft *state attorney general*

Liberal
Holmes, Carl Dean *landowner, state legislator*

Lyons
Hodgson, Arthur Clay *lawyer*

Manhattan
Appl, Fredric Carl *retired mechanical engineering educator*
Babcock, Michael Ward *economics educator*
Barkley, Theodore Mitchell *biology educator*
Chang, Amos Ih-Tiao *retired educator*
Coffman, James Richard *academic administrator, veterinarian*
Cogley, Allen C. *mechanical engineering educator, administrator*
Davis, Kenneth Sidney *writer*
Durkee, William Robert *retired physician*
Ealy, Robert Phillip *horticulture and landscape architecture educator*
Erickson, Howard Hugh *veterinarian*
Erickson, Larry Eugene *chemical engineering educator*
Fateley, William Gene *scientist, educator, inventor, administrator*
Fenton, Donald Lee *mechanical engineering educator, consultant*
Flaherty, Roberta D. *university official*
Foerster, Bernd *architecture educator*
Hagen, Lawrence Jacob *agricultural engineer*
Higham, Robin *historian, editor, publisher*
Hoyt, Kenneth Boyd *educational psychology educator*
Janke, Rhonda Rae *agronomist, educator*
Johnson, Marc Anton *agricultural economics educator*
Johnson, Terry Charles *biologist, researcher*
Johnson, William Howard *agricultural engineer, educator*
Kaufman, Donald Wayne *research ecologist*
Kirkham, M. B. *plant physiologist, educator*
Kirmser, Philip George *engineering educator*
Kremer, Eugene R. *architecture educator*
Kruh, Robert F. *university administrator*
Lee, E(ugene) Stanley *industrial engineer, mathematician, educator*
Lee, William Franklin, III *association administrator*
Lorenz, Michael Duane *veterinary medicine educator*
Marsh, Harry Dean *journalism educator*
McCulloh, John Marshall *historian*
McKee, Richard Miles *animal studies educator*
Murray, John Patrick *psychologist, educator, researcher*
Nafziger, Estel Wayne *economics educator*
†Oblander, Charles P. *university official*
Oehme, Frederick Wolfgang *medical researcher and educator*
Parish, Thomas Scanlan *human development educator*
Phares, E. Jerry *psychology educator*
†Posler, Gerry Lynn *agronomist, educator*
Sears, Rollin George *wheat geneticist, small grains researcher*
Seaton, Edward Lee *newspaper editor and publisher*
Setser, Carole Sue *food science educator*
Setser, Donald Wayne *chemistry educator*
Simons, Gale Gene *nuclear engineering educator, university administrator*
Spears, Marian Caddy *dietetics and institutional management educator*
Stolzer, Leo William *bank executive*
Thomas, Lloyd Brewster *economics educator*
Twiss, Page Charles *geology educator*
Vetter, James Louis *food research association administrator*
Vorhies, Mahlon Wesley *veterinary pathologist, educator*

Marion
Meyer, Bill *newspaper publisher, editor*

Mc Pherson
Hull, Robert Glenn *retired financial administrator*
Mason, Stephen Olin *academic administrator*
Nichols, Richard Dale *former congressman, banker*
Shriver, Garner Edward *lawyer, former congressman*
Steffes, Don Clarence *state senator*
Williams, Larry Emmett *oil company executive*

Merriam
Miller, Stanford *reinsurance executive, arbitrator, lawyer*

Mission
Novak, Alfred *retired biology educator*
Thomas, Christopher Yancey, III *surgeon, educator*

Neosho Falls
Bader, Robert Smith *biology, zoology educator and researcher*

Newton
Preheim, Vern Quincy *religious organization administrator, minister*

North Newton
Fast, Darrell W. *minister*

Oakley
Squibb, Sandra Hildyard *special education educator*

Olathe
Booth, Jody Shelton *executive director*
Burke, Paul E., Jr. *state senator, investment banker*
Chipman, Marion Walter *judge*
Hackler, Ruth Ann *state legislator*
O'Connor, Kay *state legislator*
Snowbarger, Vincent Keith *lawyer, state representative*
†Summe, Gregory Louis *management consultant*

Ottawa
Howe, William Hugh *artist*

Overland Park
Baker, Charles H. *engineering company executive*
Balloun, Joseph Eugene *lawyer*
†Browning, Roy Wilson, III *mortgage banking executive*
Burger, Henry G. *anthropologist, vocabulary scientist, publisher*
Burton, Delmar Lee *insurance company executive*
Cummings, Penelope Dirrig *special education educator*
†Dempsey, Cedric W. *sports association administrator*
Dore, James Francis *financial services executive*
Gaar, Norman Edward *lawyer, former state senator*
Green, John Lafayette, Jr. *education executive*
Krauss, Carl F. *lawyer*
Linn, James Herbert *retired banker*
Mealman, Glenn *corporate marketing executive*
Murphy, Stephen P. *corporate lawyer*
Neal, Louise Kathleen *life insurance company executive, accountant*
Oldham, Dale Ralph *life insurance company executive, actuary*
Powell, George Everett, Jr. *motor freight company executive*
Powell, George Everett, III *trucking company executive*
Ruse, Steven Douglas *lawyer*
Sampson, William Roth *lawyer*
Shipman, David Norval *healthcare consultant*
Short, Joel Bradley *lawyer, consultant, software publisher*
Stanton, Roger D. *lawyer*

Van Dyke, Thomas Wesley *lawyer*
Walter, Alan Stuart *crop insurance industry association executive*
Waxse, David John *lawyer*
Webb, William Duncan *lawyer, investment executive*

Parsons
Lomas, Lyle Wayne *agricultural research administrator, educator*
†Tignor, George *principal*

Pittsburg
Behlar, Patricia Ann *political science educator*
Nettels, George Edward, Jr. *mining executive*
Sullivan, Frank Victor *academic dean, industrial arts educator*
Wilson, Donald Wallin *university president, educator*

Prairie Village
Franking, Holly Mae *software publisher*
Lytle, Robert Frank *lawyer*
Souders, James P. *professional association executive*
Stock, Gregg Francis *retired association executive*

Pratt
Loomis, Howard Krey *banker*

Saint Marys
Latham, Dudley Eugene, III (Del Latham) *printing and paper converting executive*

Salina
Ashby, John Forsythe *bishop*
Cosco, John Anthony *health care executive, educator*
Crawford, Lewis Cleaver *engineering executive*
Fitzsimons, George K. *bishop*
Piper, Jon Kingsbury *ecologist, researcher*
Ryan, Stephen Collister *funeral director*
Stanton, Marshall P. *academic administrator, clergyman*
Tompkins, John Andrew *school system administrator*

Shawnee Mission
Arneson, George Stephen *manufacturing company executive, management consultant*
Barton, C. Robert *insurance company executive*
Bell, Deloris Wiley *physician*
Bennett, Robert Frederick *lawyer, former governor*
Biggs, J. O. *lawyer, general industry company executive*
Bogina, August, Jr. *state senator*
Bond, Richard Lee *lawyer, state senator*
Boyd, John Kent *advertising executive*
†Boyle, James Wilbur *hospital administrator*
Boysen, Melicent Pearl *finance company executive*
Burdick, Robert William *transportation company executive*
Burm, Forrest Henry *transportation executive*
Byers, Walter *athletic association executive*
Cahal, Mac Fullerton *lawyer, publisher*
Callahan, Harry Leslie *civil engineer*
†Campbell, Mark S. *food products executive*
Clay, George Harry *lawyer*
Clifford, James Michael *clinical research administrator*
Connelly, John Matthew *lawyer, insurance company executive*
Deaver, Darwin Holloway *former utility executive*
Dineen, Robert Joseph *diversified manufacturing company executive*
Dockhorn, Robert John *physician*
Dougherty, Robert Anthony *manufacturing company executive*
Dozois, Gardner *editor, writer*
Fairchild, Robert Charles *pediatrician*
Findlay, Theodore Bernard *management consultant*
Gamet, Donald Max *appliance company executive*
Goetz, Kenneth Lee *cardiovascular physiologist*
Haggard, Forrest Deloss *minister*
Hechler, Robert Lee *financial services company executive*
Herring, Raymond Mark *marketing and planning executive*
Hershman, Mark Steven *lighting designer*
Holliday, John Moffitt *insurance company executive*
Holter, Don Wendell *retired bishop*
Howard, Theodore Walter *mutual fund corporation executive*
Kaplan, Marjorie Ann Pashkow *school district administrator*
Kemp, John Bernard *retired state secretary of transportation*
Langworthy, Audrey Hansen *state legislator*
McEachen, Richard Edward *banker, lawyer*
Mindlin, Richard Barnett *market research executive*
Mischler, Paul *grain company executive*
Mitlyng, Errol Paul *financial executive*
Myhre, Roger L. *agricultural products executive*
Nauer, Paula Lou *physician*
Nulton, William Clements *lawyer*
Olsen, Stanley Severn *minister*
Pierson, John Theodore, Jr. *manufacturer*
Price, James Gordon *physician*
Putman, Dale Cornelius *management consultant, lawyer*
†Reichert, Patricia *mortgage company executive*
Robinson, Thomas Bullene *retired civil engineer*
Rubin, Charles Elliott *lawyer, sports agent*
Sader, Carol Hope *former state legislator*
Schweitzer, Jon Anton *broadcasting executive*
†Smith, Howard E. *manufacturing executive, light*
†Smith, Michael L. *transportation executive*
Smith, Robert Hugh *engineering construction company executive*
Steinkamp, Robert Theodore *lawyer*
Stevens, James Hervey, Jr. *financial advisor*
Strubbe, Thomas R. *diagnostic testing industry executive*
Sunderland, Robert *cement company executive*
†Walsh, Robert *publishing executive*
Watanabe, Hirosuko *grain merchandising company executive*
Watson, Thomas Sturges *professional golfer*
Wenner, Herbert Allan *pediatrician*
Whitaker, Kathleen K. *gifted education facilitator*
Widder, Willard Graves *retired banker*

Silver Lake
Rueck, Jon Michael *manufacturing executive*

South Hutchinson
Myers, Theodore Ash *financial executive*

Stilwell
Keith, Dale Martin *utilities management consultant*

Topeka
Abbott, Bob *state supreme court justice*
Abrahams, John Hambleton *life insurance company executive*
Allegrucci, Donald Lee *state supreme court justice*
Ayres, Ted Dean *lawyer, academic counsel*
Benlon, Lisa L. *state legislator*
Blackburn, Harold Lee, Jr. *state agency administrator*
†Brown, William Ernest *utility executive*
Carpenter, William Randolph, Jr. *judge*
†Chase, Howard Marion *hospital administrator*
Chronister, Rochelle Beach *state legislator*
Clarke, Gary Kendrick *zoologist*
Cohen, Sheldon Hersh *chemistry educator*
Comstock, Glen David *civil engineer*
Conroy, Robert Warren *psychiatrist*
Crow, Sam Alfred *federal judge*
Davis, Robert Edward *judge*
Dicus, John Carmack *savings and loan association executive*
Douglas, Joe J., Jr. *fire chief*
Droegmueller, Lee *state education official*
Eisenbarth, Gary *insurance company executive*
Elrod, Linda Diane Henry *lawyer, educator*
Fink, H. Bernerd *corporate professional*
Fink, Ruth Garvey *diversified company executive*
Francisco, James L. *lieutenant governor*
Franklin, Benjamin Barnum *dinner club executive*
†Freden, Sharon Elsie Christman *state education agency administrator*
Fricke, Howard R. *insurance company executive*
Gabbard, Glen Owens *psychiatrist, psychoanalyst*
Gannon, Richard Galen *state senator, rancher, farmer*
Graves, William Preston *governor*
Harper, Patricia Nelsen *psychiatrist*
Hayes, John Edward, Jr. *electric power industry executive*
Heitz, Mark V. *insurance company executive*
Hilpert, Dale W. *retail shoe company executive*
Holmes, Richard Winn *state supreme court justice*
Johnson, Arnold William *mortgage company executive*
Karr, Gerald Lee *agricultural economist, state senator*
Karst, Gary Gene *architect*
Kuether, John Frederick *law educator*
Kuether, Ronald Clarence *utility company executive*
Laster, Ralph William, Jr. *insurance company executive, accountant*
Lockett, Tyler Charles *state supreme court justice*
Lynch, Eloise *state legislator*
Mara, John Lawrence *veterinarian, consultant*
Marshall, Herbert A. *lawyer*
Marvin, James Conway *librarian, consultant*
Mays, M. Douglas *state legislator, financial consultant*
McCandless, Barbara J. *auditor*
McClure, Janice Lee *state legislator, farmer, graphic designer*
McFarland, Kay Eleanor *state supreme court justice*
Menninger, Roy Wright *medical foundation executive, psychiatrist*
Menninger, William Walter *psychiatrist*
Metzler, Dwight Fox *civil engineer, retired state official*
Miller, Robert Haskins *retired state chief justice*
Miller, Thomas L. *insurance company executive*
Mutti, Albert Frederick *minister*
Oleen, Lana *state legislator*
Peavler, Nancy Jean *editor*
Petty, Marge *state senator*
†Platis, Tom Gust *lawyer, oil company executive*
Powers, Harris Pat *broadcasting executive*
Powers, Ramon Sidney *historical society administrator, historian*
Praeger, Sandy *state legislator*
Pusateri, James Anthony *federal bankruptcy judge*
Randall, Elizabeth Ellen *personnel manager*
Rogers, Richard Dean *federal judge*
Rosenberg, John K. *lawyer*
Saffels, Dale Emerson *federal judge*
Salisbury, Alicia Laing *state legislator*
Samuelson, Ellen Banman *state legislator*
Samuelson, Marvin Lee *veterinarian*
Schneider, Raymond Clinton *architect, educator*
Sebelius, Kathleen Gilligan *state legislator*
Sheffel, Irving Eugene *psychiatric institution executive*
Shuler, Howard L. *superintendent*
Simpson, William Stewart *retired psychiatrist, sex therapist*
Six, Fred N. *state supreme court justice*
Skoog, Ralph Edward *lawyer*
Smalley, William Edward *bishop*
Spohn, Herbert Emil *psychologist*
Spring, Raymond Lewis *legal educator*
Standifer, Sabrina *state legislator*
Stauffer, John H. *newspaper and broadcast executive*
Stauffer, Stanley Howard *newspaper and broadcasting executive*
†Stovall, Carla Jo *state official, lawyer*
Swogger, Glenn, Jr. *psychiatrist*
Thompson, Hugh Lee *university president*
Thompson, Sally Engstrom *state official*
Tillotson, Carolyn *state legislator*
Varner, Charleen LaVerne McClanahan (Mrs. Robert B. Varner) *nutritionist, educator, administrator, dietitian*
Vidricksen, Ben Eugene *food service executive, state legislator*
Wagle, Susan *state legislator, small business owner*
Wagnon, Joan *former state legislator, association executive*
Wagnon, William Odell, Jr. *history educator*
Ware, Lucile Mahieu *child psychiatrist, educator, researcher*
Welshimer, Gwen R. *state legislator, real estate broker, appraiser, tax consultant*

Ulysses
Palmer, Barbara Jean *special education administrator*

University Of Kansas
Ashe, James S. *entomologist, educator*
Ballard, Barbara W. *state legislator*
†Craig, Susan Virginia *librarian*
Hemenway, Robert E. *university administrator, language educator*
Humphrey, Philip Strong *university museum director*
Kraft, David Christian *civil engineering educator*
Kuznesof, Elizabeth Anne *history educator*
†Neeley, Kathleen Louise *librarian*

†Turnbull, H. Rutherford, III *law educator, lawyer*

Vassar
Visser, John Evert *university president emeritus, historian*

Wellington
Ferguson, William McDonald *retired lawyer, rancher, author, banker, former state official*

Westwood
Buckner, William Claiborne *real estate broker*
Devlin, James Richard *lawyer*
Esrey, William Todd *telecommunications company executive*
Schultz, Richard Dale *national athletic organizations executive*

Wichita
Andrew, Kenneth L. *research physicist, physics educator*
†Banks, Michael A. *hospital administrator*
Barents, Brian Edward *marketing executive*
Bell, Baillis F. *airport terminal executive*
Bell, Charles Robert, Jr. *judge*
Biltz, Jim *hospital administrator*
Brown, Wesley Ernest *federal judge*
Bunten, William Daniel *banker*
Cadman, Wilson Kennedy *retired utility company executive*
Cheesman, John Michael *aeronautics company executive, civic leader*
Chen, Zuohuang *conductor*
Claassen, Sherida Dill *newspaper executive*
Clark, Susan Matthews *psychologist*
Curfman, Lawrence Everett *lawyer*
Curtright, Robert Eugene *newspaper critic and columnist*
Davis, Robert Louis *lawyer*
Denger, Elsie Sue *nursing administrator*
Docking, Thomas Robert *lawyer, former state lieutenant governor*
Durst, Martha Lynn *insurance agent*
Dyck, George *psychiatry educator*
Eastburn, Jeannette Rose *religious publishing executive*
Eby, Martin Keller, Jr. *construction company executive*
Egan, Sister M. Sylvia *hospital administrator*
Egbert, Robert Iman *electrical engineering educator, academic administrator*
Ellington, Howard Wesley *architect*
Gates, Walter Edward *rental company executive, business owner*
Gerber, Eugene J. *bishop*
Getz, Robert Lee *newspaper columnist*
Gosman, Albert Louis *mechanical engineering educator*
Guthrie, Richard Alan *physician*
Hanna, William W. *chemical company executive*
Hatteberg, Larry Merle *photojournalist*
Hicks, M. Elizabeth *pharmacist*
Jabara, Francis Dwight *merchant banker, educator, entrepreneur*
Johnson, Kenneth O. *petroleum company executive*
Jones, Lawrence Marion *food distribution company executive*
Karp, Harvey Lawrence *metal products manufacturing company executive*
Kelly, Patrick F. *federal judge*
Knight, Robert G. *mayor, investment banker*
Knudsen, Darrell G. *diversified financial services company executive*
Koch, Charles de Ganahl *oil industry executive*
Lahti, Richard *quality improvement administrator*
Lair, Robert Louis *catering company executive*
Lusk, William Edward *real estate, oil company executive*
Manning, Robert Thomas *physician, educator*
Mc Kee, George Moffitt, Jr. *civil engineer, consultant*
Meyer, Russel William, Jr. *aircraft company executive*
North, Doris Griffin *physician, educator*
†Oxley, Dwight K(ahala) *pathologist*
Peterman, Bruce Edgar *aircraft company executive*
Pohlman, Randolph Allen *business administration educator, dean*
Pottorff, Jo Ann *state legislator*
Rademacher, Richard Joseph *librarian*
Rainey, William Joel *lawyer*
Reals, William Joseph *pathologist, academic administrator, educator*
Redman, Peter *finance company executive*
Reed, Darwin Cramer *health care consultant*
Reinemund, Steven S. *restaurant chain executive*
†Rhodes, Darryl W. *bank executive*
†Roberts, Alice *reservations service executive*
Sowers, Wesley Hoyt *lawyer, management consultant*
Theis, Frank Gordon *federal judge*
Thompson, M(orris) Lee *lawyer*
Thomsen, Marcia Rozen *marketing executive*
Varner, Sterling Verl *retired oil company executive*
†Watson, Dean *agricultural products*
Wentz, William Henry, Jr. *aerospace engineer, educator*
Wilhelm, William Jean *civil engineering educator*
Williams, Ronald Paul *lawyer*
Zehr, Clyde James *church administrator*
Zytkow, Jan Mikolaj *computer science educator*

Winfield
Crowley, Marilyn *critical care nurse, educator*
Miller, Franklin Rush *retired internist, educator*
Willoughby, John Wallace *former college dean, provost*

KENTUCKY

Ashland
Boyd, James Robert *oil company executive*
Brothers, John Alfred *oil company executive*
Carter, David Edward *communications executive*
Chellgren, Paul Wilbur *petroleum company executive*
Compton, Robert H. *lawyer*
Dansby, John Walter *oil company executive*
Feazell, Thomas Lee *lawyer, oil company executive*
Hall, John Richard *oil company executive*
Hartl, William Parker *oil company executive*
Justice, Franklin Pierce, Jr. *oil company executive*
Lacy, James Daniel *oil company executive*
Luellen, Charles J. *retired oil company executive*
Mc Cowan, Robert Taylor *oil company executive*
Spears, Richard W. *oil company executive*
Weaver, Carlton Davis *retired oil company executive*
Wilhoit, Henry Rupert, Jr. *federal judge*
Yancey, Robert Earl, Jr. *oil company executive*
Zachem, Harry M. *oil company executive*

Barbourville
Phillips, Jack Carter *educational administrator*

Bardstown
Carter, Carmen M. *elementary education educator, consultant*

Benton
Lewis, Richard Hayes *lawyer, former state legislator*

Berea
Hager, Paul Calvin *college administrator, educator*
Lamb, Irene Hendricks *medical researcher*

Bowling Green
Campbell, Joe Bill *lawyer*
Cangemi, Joseph Peter *psychologist, consultant, educator*
Constans, Henry Philip, Jr. *philosopher, educator*
Cravens, Raymond Lewis *political science educator*
†Daniel, Patricia Lynne *educator, consultant*
Dewhurst, William Harvey *psychiatrist*
Haynes, Robert Vaughn *university administrator, historian*
Holland, John Ben *clothing manufacturing company executive*
Kalab, Kathleen Alice *sociology educator*
Meredith, Thomas C. *academic administrator*
Minton, John Dean *historian, educator*
Murrell, Estelle C. *elementary school educator*
Russell, Joyce M. *lawyer, apparel executive*
Slocum, Donald Warren *chemist*
Tapp, John Cecil *physician, educator, futures trader*

Burkesville
Smith, Paul Traylor *mayor, former business executive, former army officer*

Corbin
Barton-Collings, Nelda Ann *political activist, newspaper, bank and nursing home executive*

Covington
Bensman, Charles J. *academic administrator*
Clabes, Judith Grisham *newspaper editor*
Gross, Joseph Wallace *hospital administrator*
Harper, Kenneth Franklin *state legislator, retired, real estate broker*
Head, Joseph Henry, Jr. *lawyer*
Kerr, Thomas Robert *lawyer*
Mc Ginness, William George, III *manufacturing company executive*
Oppmann, Andrew James *newspaper editor*
Trimble, Vance Henry *retired newspaper editor*

Crestwood
Upchurch, Paul *principal*

Danville
Adams, Michael F. *academic administrator, political communications specialist*
Breeze, William Hancock *college administrator*
Campbell, Stanley Richard *library services director*
Lively, Pierce *federal judge*
Newhall, David Sowle *history educator*
Rowland, Robert E. *secondary school principal*
Spragens, Thomas Arthur *educational consultant*

Elizabethtown
Modderman, Melvin Earl *health administrator*

Erlanger
Hughes, William Anthony *bishop*

Fairdale
Steffen, Pamela Bray *secondary school educator*

Florence
Walker, H. Lawson *lawyer*

Fort Knox
†Funk, Paul Edward *army officer*

Fort Thomas
†Goetz, Robert Clifford *army officer*
Gooch, Deborah Ann Grimme *medical/surgical nurse, administrator*
†Hoyle, John Douglas *hospital administrator*
Pendery, Edward Stuart *deputy county judge*

Frankfort
Babbage, Robert A. *state official*
Brown, Viola Davis *state agency administrator*
Carroll, Julian Morton *lawyer, former governor*
Gale, Steven Hershel *humanities educator*
Geddes, LaDonna McMurray *speech educator*
Gorman, Chris *state attorney general*
Jones, Brereton C. *governor*
Klotter, James C. *state historical organization administrator, consultant*
Leibson, Charles M. *state supreme court justice*
McDonald, Alice Coig *state education official*
Miller, Mary Helen *public administrator*
Mills, Frances Jones *state official*
Nelson, James Albert *librarian, state official*
Northup, Anne Meagher *state legislator*
Palmore, John Stanley, Jr. *lawyer*
Patton, Paul E. *state official*
Reese, Lowell D. *editor, publisher*
†Reidy, Edward, Jr. *state official*
Stephens, Robert F. *state supreme court chief justice*
†Trapp, Leslie Combs *state legislator*
Wallace, Peggy Marie *state commissioner*
Wintersheimer, Donald Carl *state supreme court justice*
Wolfe, John Thomas, Jr. *university president*

Franklin
Clark, James Benton *railroad industry consultant, former executive*
Herndon, Wallace Eugene, Jr. *human resources manager*

Georgetown
Warren, Alex McLean, Jr. *automotive executive*

Gilbertsville
Mathues, Thomas Oliver *retired automobile company executive*

Glasgow
†Baker, Walter A. *lawyer, state senator*

Goshen
Mc Clinton, Donald G. *diversified holding company executive*
Strode, William Hall, III *photojournalist, publisher*

Harrods Creek
Chandler, James Williams *retired securities company executive*

Harrodsburg
Lunger, Irvin Eugene *university president emeritus, clergyman*

Hebron
Holscher, Robert F. *county official*

Highland Heights
Bell, Sheila Trice *lawyer*
Boothe, Leon Estel *university president*
Carr, George Francis, Jr. *lawyer*
Jones, William Rex *lawyer, educator*
Redding, Rogers Walker *physics educator*
Seaver, Robert Leslie *law educator*
Wallace, Harold Lew *historian, educator*

Hopkinsville
Dixon, John Morris, Jr. *lawyer*
Freer, John Herschel *psychiatrist*
Riley, Thomas Leslie *retired college president*
Watson, Roger Elton *human resources administrator*

Independence
Boster, Judy Landen *primary school educator*

Lexington
Allison, James Claybrooke, II *broadcasting executive*
Anderson, Richard L(oree) *mathematician, educator*
Avant, Robert Frank *physician, educator*
Barnhart, Charles Elmer *animal sciences educator*
Baumann, Robert Jay *child neurology educator*
Beshear, Steven L. *lawyer*
Bhattacharya-Chatterjee, Malaya *cancer research scientist*
Birchfield, Martha *librarian*
Blanton, Jack Christopher *academic administrator*
Bosomworth, Peter Palliser *university medical administrator*
Boyer, Lillian Buckley *artist, educator*
Breathitt, Edward Thompson, Jr. *lawyer, railroad executive*
Brown, William Randall *geology educator*
Bryant, Joseph Allen, Jr. *English language educator*
Butler, Frank Anthony *hospital administrator*
†Calico, Forrest W. *health facility adminstrator*
Calvert, C(lyde) Emmett *state agency adminstrator, retired*
Caroland, William Bourne *structural engineer*
Cheniae, George Maurice *plant biochemist*
Chesser, Roger Moreton *broadcasting executive*
Clawson, David Kay *orthopedic surgeon*
Cochran, Lewis W. *physicist, university official*
Coffman, Edward McKenzie *history educator*
Cole, Henry Philip *educational psychologist*
Cremers, Clifford John *mechanical engineering educator*
Davenport, Guy Mattison, Jr. *author, retired educator*
David, Miriam Lang *physician*
Davis, Vincent *political science educator*
Deitchle, Gerald Wayne *restaurant company executive*
DeLong, Lance Eric *physics educator, researcher*
DeLuca, Patrick Phillip *pharmaceutical scientist, educator, administrator*
Diana, John Nicholas *physiologist*
Diedrich, Donald Frank *pharmacology educator*
Dittert, Lewis William *pharmacy educator*
Eberle, Todd Bailey *lawyer, educator*
Ehmann, William Donald *chemistry educator*
Eller, Ronald D *historian, educator*
†Ely, George Melvin, Jr. *civil engineer*
Ettensohn, Frank Robert *geologist, educator*
Flynn, Peter Francis *superintendent of schools*
†Foree, Edward Golden *environmental engineer, consultant*
Forester, Karl S. *federal judge*
Fowler, Harriet Whittemore *art museum director*
Fox, Virginia Gaines *public broadcasting executive*
Friedell, Gilbert Hugo *pathologist, hospital administrator, educator, cancer center director*
Frye, Wilbur Wayne *soil science educator, researcher, administrator*
Gable, Robert Elledy *real estate investment company executive*
Gilliam, M(elvin) Randolph *urologist, educator*
Girone, Vito Anthony *architect, city planner, educator emeritus, artist*
Glenn, James Francis *urologist, educator*
Goldman, Alvin Lee *lawyer, educator*
Grabau, Larry J. *crop physiologist, educator*
Griffen, Ward O., Jr. *surgeon, educator, medical board executive*
Grimes, Dale Mills *electrical engineering educator*
Gunn, Wendell Lavelle *insurance company executive*
Hagan, Wallace Woodrow *geologist*
Hagen, Michael Dale *medical educator, family practice researcher*
Hamburg, Joseph *physician, educator*
Hanson, Mark Tod *engineering mechanics educator*
Heitzman, Robert Edward *retired materials handling equipment manufacturing company executive*
Henderson, Hubert Platt *fine arts association executive*
Hochstrasser, Donald Lee *cultural anthropologist, community health and public administration educator*
Holsinger, James Wilson, Jr. *physician*
Host, W. James *public relations and advertising executive*
Hultman, Charles William *economics educator*
Kasperbauer, Michael John *plant physiology educator, researcher*
Keeling, Larry Dale *journalist*
Kelly, Timothy Michael *newspaper editor*
Kern, Bernard Donald *retired educator, physicist*
†King, James Orell *public administrator*
Kissling, Fred Ralph, Jr. *insurance agency executive*
Knapp, Vaughn Robert *coal company executive*
Krone, Julie *jockey*
Kuc, Joseph A. *educator, consultant*
Landon, John William *minister, social worker, educator*
Lee, Joe *federal judge*
Lewis, Robert Kay, Jr. *fundraising executive*
Lewis, Thomas Proctor *legal educator*
†Little, Charles Oran *agriculture director, animal scientist*
Liu, Keh-Fei Frank *physicist, educator*
Lodder, Robert Andrew *chemistry and pharmaceutics educator*
Logan, Joyce Polley *education educator*
Madden, Edward Harry *philosopher, educator*
Markesbery, William R. *neurology and pathology educator, physician*
Mason, Ellsworth Goodwin *librarian*
McCann, William H., Sr. *lawyer*
Mercer, Leonard Preston, II *biochemistry educator*
Miller, Harry B(enjamin) *lawyer*
Miller, Pamela Gundersen *mayor*
Mink, John Robert *dental educator*
Mitchell, George Ernest, Jr. *animal scientist, educator*
Mostert, Paul Stallings *mathematician, educator*
Nasar, Syed Abu *electrical engineering educator*
†Nathan, Richard Arnold *research and development company executive*
Newton, John Thomas *utility company executive*
Noonan, Jacqueline Anne *pediatrics educator*
Nyere, Robert Alan *banker*
Oberst, Paul *law educator*
Owens, Lewis E. *newspaper executive*
Parks, Harold Francis *anatomist, educator*
Pass, Bobby Clifton *entomology educator*
Perdue, Theda *history educator, author*
Philpott, James Alvin, Jr. *lawyer*
Pirone, Thomas Pascal *plant pathology educator*
Pitino, Richard *college basketball coach*
Reed, Michael Robert *agricultural economist*
Robinson, Thomas Christopher *academic administrator, educator*
Rodriguez, Juan Guadalupe *entomologist*
Rogers, Lon B(rown) *lawyer*
Romanowitz, Byron Foster *architect, engineer*
Sands, Donald Edgar *chemistry educator*
Schaeffer, Edwin Frank, Jr. *lawyer*
Schneider, George William *horticulturist, educator, researcher*
Scruggs, John Dudley *landscape architect*
Sexton, Robert Fenimore *educational organization executive*
Shepherd, Robert James *plant pathology researcher, educator*
Shipley, David Elliott *university dean, lawyer*
Shuler, Scott *civil engineer*
Sineath, Timothy Wayne *library educator, university dean*
Singletary, Otis Arnold, Jr. *university president emeritus*
Steele, Earl Larsen *electrical engineering educator*
†Steensland, Ronald Paul *librarian*
Stober, William John, II *economics educator*
Straus, Robert *behavioral sciences educator*
Tauchert, Theodore Richmond *mechanical engineer, educator*
Tietz, Norbert Wolfgang *clinical chemistry educator, administrator*
Timoney, Peter Joseph *veterinarian, virologist, educator, consultant*
Traynor, Harry Sheehy *engineering consultant*
Turner, Larry William *agricultural engineer, educator*
Ulmer, Shirley Sidney *political science educator, researcher, consultant*
Varellas, Sandra Motte *judge*
Vittetoe, Marie Clare *retired medical technology educator*
Vore, Mary Edith *pharmacology educator, researcher*
Wagner, Alan Burton *entrepreneur*
Walker, John Neal *agricultural engineering educator*
Wallace, Donald Querk *architect, civil engineer*
Ward, Richard C. *lawyer*
Warth, Robert Douglas *history educator*
Wethington, Charles T., Jr. *academic administrator*
Whitley, Michael R. *utilities executive*
Williams, James Kendrick *bishop*
Willis, Paul Allen *librarian*
Worell, Judith P. *psychologist, educator*
Young, Paul Ray *medical board executive, physician*
Zack, George J. *conductor, music director*

London
Coffman, Jennifer B. *federal judge*
Early, Jack Jones *college administrator*
Siler, Eugene Edward, Jr. *federal judge*
†Spencer, Thomas W. *mining executive, energy executive*

Louisville
Aberson, Leslie Donald *lawyer*
Adams, Christine Beate Lieber *psychiatrist, educator*
Adams, Robert Waugh *state agency administrator, economics educator*
†Allen, Charles Ethelbert, III *lawyer*
Allen, Charles Mengel *federal judge*
Allen, Phillip E. *insurance company executive*
Andrews, Billy Franklin *pediatrician, educator*
Andrews, James Edgar *church official, minister*
Ardery, Joseph Lord *lawyer*
Ardery, Philip Pendleton *lawyer*
Aronoff, George Rodger *medicine and pharmacology educator*
Ayotte, Robert C. *metal products executive*
Bailey, Irving Widmer, II *insurance holding company executive*
Baron, Martin Raymond *psychology educator*
Baxter, James William, III *insurance and investment executive*
Becker, Gail Roselyn *museum director*
Belanger, William Joseph *chemist, polymer applications consultant*
Benfield, Ann Kolb *lawyer*
Berman, Edward Henry *education educator*
Bingham, George Barry, Jr. *publishing and broadcasting executive*
Boggs, Danny Julian *federal judge*
Bow, Stephen Tyler, Jr. *insurance company executive*
†Boyd, Morton *banker*
Brennan, William Bernard, Jr. *small business owner*
Brockwell, Charles Wilbur, Jr. *history educator*
Brown, Owsley, II *diversified consumer products company executive*
Brown, William Lee Lyons, Jr. *consumer products company executive*
Bryant, Oscar Sims, Jr. *investment advisor*
Bujake, John Edward, Jr. *beverage company executive*
Bullard, Claude Earl *newspaper, commercial printing and radio and television executive*
Burse, Raymond Malcolm *lawyer*
Callen, Jeffrey Phillip *dermatologist, educator*
Carden, Joy Cabbage *educational consultant*
Carpenter, Marj Collier *religious organization news director*
Chancey, Malcolm B., Jr. *bank executive*
Clark, John Hallett, III *consulting engineering executive*
Clements, Kerry *religious organization administrator*
Coffin, John *religious organization administrator*
Coggins, Homer Dale *retired hospital administrator*
Cohn, David V(alor) *biochemistry educator*
Conner, Stewart Edmund *lawyer*
Cornelius, Wayne Anderson *engineering technology educator, consultant*
†Corradino, Joseph Carmen *civil engineer*
Cowan, Frederic Joseph *lawyer*
Cranor, John *food service executive*
†Crawford, Byron Garrison *newswriter, journalist*
Crum, Denny (Denzel Edwin Crum) *collegiate basketball coach*
Crutcher, Michael Bayard *lawyer*
Cybulski, Joanne Karen *nutritionist, diabetes educator*
Dabney, Watson Barr *investment banker*
Dale, Judy Ries *religious organization administrator*
Danzl, Daniel Frank *emergency physician*
Daulton, David Coleman *actuary*
Davenport, Gwen (Mrs. John Davenport) *author*
Davidson, Gordon Byron *lawyer*
Davidson, Michael Walker *energy company executive*
Davis, Finis E. *printing company executive*
Davis, Harry Scott, Jr. *banker*
Deering, Ronald Franklin *librarian, minister*
DeVries, William Castle *surgeon, educator*
Dorr, Ralze Wheeler *librarian*
Drury, Ralph Leon *newspaper executive*
Dudley, George Ellsworth *lawyer*
Early, Glen Alan *biology educator*
Ehrlich, Virginia Lee *nursing administrator*
Eighmey, Douglas Joseph, Jr. *hospital administrator*
Ekstrom, William Ferdinand *college administrator*
Ellison, William Louie, Jr. *newspaper editor, journalist*
Ethridge, Larry Clayton *lawyer*
Ferguson, Duncan Sheldon *education administrator*
Ferguson, Jo McCown *lawyer*
Fitch, Howard Mercer *lawyer, labor arbitrator, travelogue exhibitor and producer*
Ford, Gordon Buell, Jr. *English language and linguistics educator, author, retired hospital industry financial management executive*
Frazier, Owsley B. *beverage company executive*
Fuller, Thomas Ralph *retired manufacturing company executive*
Garcia, Rafael Jorge *chemical engineer*
Garcia-Varela, Jesus *language educator, literature educator*
Garfinkel, Herbert *university official*
Garretson, Henry David *neurosurgeon*
Glore-Seward, Linda Jo *primary school educator*
†Goff, Jim *religious organization administrator*
Granady, Juanita H. *religious organization administrator*
†Guillaume, Raymond Kendrick *banker*
Gummere, Walter Cooper *educator, consultant*
Hale, Roger W. *utilities company executive*
Hanley, Thomas Richard *engineering educator*
Hawpe, David Vaughn *newspaper editor, journalist*
Haynes, Douglas Martin *physician, educator*
Hazen, Elizabeth Frances *retired special education educator*
Heiden, Charles Kenneth *former army officer, metals company executive*
Helm, Joseph Burge *lawyer*
Hendricks, William Lawrence *theology educator*
Heyburn, John Gilpin, II *federal judge*
Higgins, Walter M., III *electric power industry executive*
Hockenberger, Susan Jane *nurse educator*
Hower, Frank Beard, Jr. *retired banker*
Hoye, Robert Earl *higher education educator, health care consultant*
Huang, Kee Chang *pharmacology educator, physician*
Hunter, William Jay, Jr. *lawyer*
Jenkins, C(arle) Frederick *religious organization executive, minister, lawyer*
Johnson, Alan Arthur *physicist, educator*
Jones, David Allen *health facility executive*
Keeney, Arthur Hail *physician, educator*
Kelley, Noble Henry *former psychologist, educator*
Kelly, Thomas Cajetan *archbishop*
Kinsey, William Charles *building materials company executive*
Kirkpatrick, Clifton *minister, church administrator*
Kleinert, Harold Earl *plastic surgery educator*
Klotter, John Charles *retired legal educator*
Kmetz, Donald R. *academic administrator*
Kohnhorst, Earl Eugene *tobacco company executive*
Krainer, Edward Frank *engineering executive*
Lansing, Allan Meredith *cardiovascular surgeon, educator*
Lay, Norvie Lee *legal educator*
Lomicka, William Henry *investor*
Lonergan, Jeanette Nancy *nurse*
Luber, Thomas J(ulian) *lawyer*
Lundy, Mary Ann Weese *religious organization administrator*
Luvisi, Lee *concert pianist*
MacKinnon, Cyrus Leland *retired newspaper executive*
Maddox, Robert Lytton *lawyer*
Martin, Boyce Ficklen, Jr. *federal judge*
Marvin, Oscar McDowell *retired hospital administrator*
Mateus, Lois *manufacturing executive*
Mather, Elizabeth Vivian *health care executive*
Mather, Roland Donald *judge*
McCall, John Richard *lawyer*
McCormick, Steven Thomas *insurance company executive*
McDowell, James W., Jr. *milk products company executive*
McLellan, Harold Linden *health care company executive*
Melnykovych, Andrew O. *journalist*
Meuter, Maria Coolman *lawyer*
Miller, John Ulman *minister, author*
Miller, Robert Henry *English educator*
Minchin, Michael M., Jr. *food industry consultant*
Morrin, Peter Patrick *museum director*
Mountz, Wade *retired health service management executive*
Mueller, James E. *agricultural products executive*
Neely, J. Randall *public relations executive*
Neustadt, David Harold *physician*
†Niblock, William Robert *manufacturing executive*
Nystrand, Raphael Owens *university dean, educator*
Osborn, John Simcoe, Jr. *lawyer*
Parkins, Frederick Milton *dental educator, university dean*
Peden, Katherine Graham *industrial consultant*
Peebles, Robert Alvin *horse breed registry executive*
Phelps, Joseph William *banker*
Pickle, James C. *hospital administrator*
Polk, Hiram Carey, Jr. *surgeon, educator*
Pollard, Carl F. *health insurance company executive*
Porter, Henry Homes, Jr. *investor*
Potvin, Suzanne Hilda *chief nurse*
P'Pool, Gerald W. *manufacturing executive*
Prough, Russell Allen *biochemistry educator*
Quinn, Joseph Michael *coatings industry executive*
Ratterman, David Burger *lawyer*
Ready, William Andrew *mergers/acquisitions and management consultant*
Rice, Jerry W. *insurance company executive*
Roberts, J. Wendell *federal judge*
†Robinson, Mark Alexander, III *heavy construction, mining equipment executive*
Rollo, F. David *hospital management company executive, radiology educator*
Rompf, Clifford G., Jr. *distillery executive*
Rosky, Theodore Samuel *insurance company executive*
Royer, Robert Lewis *retired utility company executive*
Runyon, Keith Leslie *lawyer, newspaper editor*
St. Clair, Robert Neal *English language and linguistics educator*
Sandefur, Thomas Edwin, Jr. *tobacco company executive*
Schaefer, J. Scott *religious organization administrator*
†Scheu, Lynn McLaughlin *scientific publication editor*
Schmidt, Stephen Robert *lawyer*
Schwab, John Joseph *psychiatrist, educator*
Scott, Ralph Mason *physician, radiaiton oncology educator*
Shaver, Jesse Milton, Jr. *manufacturing company executive*
Shaw, Robert T. *life insurance holding company executive*
Shoemaker, Gradus Lawrence *chemist, educator*
Silverthorn, Robert Sterner, Jr. *lawyer*
Simpson, Charles R., III *federal judge*
Skees, William Leonard, Jr. *lawyer*
Slater, Marilee Hebert *theatre administrator, producer, director, consultant*
Smillie, Thomson John *opera producer*
Smith, Hal W. *restaurant management company executive*
†Smith, R. Gene *health facility administrator*
Smith, Wayne Thomas *healthcare company executive*
Speed, John Sackett *insurance company executive*
†Sprague, William *insurance company executive, farmer*
Strachan, Gladys *executive director*
Straus, R(obert) James *lawyer*
Street, William May *beverage company executive*
Swain, Donald Christie *university president, history educator*
Swann, Rande Nortof *public relations executive*
Talbott, Ben Johnson, Jr. *lawyer*
Tallichet, Leon Edgar *retired publishing executive, financial administrator*
†Tanguay, Peter Eugene *child and adolescent psychiatry educator*
Taylor, Kenneth Grant *chemistry educator*
Taylor, Robert Lewis *academic administrator*
Teller, David Norton *neurochemist*
Thorp, James Harrison, III *aquatic ecologist*
Tinsley, Tuck, III *book publishing executive*
Towles, Donald Blackburn *retired newspaper publishing executive*
Tsai, Tsu-Min *surgeon*
Tucker, Ray Moss *agricultural products cooperative executive*
Turner, Gene *religious organization administrator*
Tyrrell, Gerald Gettys *banker*
Uhde, George Irvin *physician*
Vandewater, David *hospital administrator*
VanMeter, Vandelia L. *library director*
Volz, Marlin Milton *legal educator*
Waddell, William Joseph *pharmacologist, toxicologist*
†Wagner, Henry Carrh, III *health care executive*
Ward, Jasper Dudley, III *architect*
Ward, Thomas Leon *engineering educator*
Weisskopf, Bernard *pediatrician, child behavior, development and genetics specialist, educator*
Wenz, Rodney E. *public relations executive*
Wiedman, Wayne Rentchler *retired association executive*
†Williams, Steven A. *hospital administrator*
Wingenbach, Gregory Charles *minister, religious-ecumenical agency director*
†Winters, Donald *finance company executive*
Woolsey, Frederick William *retired journalist, music critic*
Wyatt, Wilson Watkins *lawyer*
Zimmerman, Gideon K. *minister*
Zimmerman, Thom Jay *ophthalmologist, educator*
Zingman, Edgar Alan *lawyer*

Madisonville
Monhollon, Leland *lawyer*
Sneed, Joanne Lawson *elementary school educator, author*
Veazey, Doris Anne *field office administrator*

Marrowbone
Clark, Betty Pace *banking executive*

Mayfield
Harris, Isaac Henson *university dean*

Midway
Clay, Robert N. *thoroughbred breeder*
Minister, Kristina *speech communication educator*

Morehead
Besant, Larry Xon *librarian, administrator, consultant*

Murray
Hunt, Charles Brownlow, Jr. *university dean, musician*
Hunt, Mark Alan *museum director*
Pogue, Forrest Carlisle *retired historian*

Nazareth
Dundon, Mark Walden *hospital administrator*

Newport
Hopgood, James F. *anthropologist*
Siverd, Robert Joseph *lawyer*

Owensboro
Best, Robert Wayne *gas transmission company executive, lawyer*
Cocklin, Kim Roland *lawyer*
Eaton, Clara Barbour *librarian*
Hood, Mary Bryan *museum director, painter*
Hulse, George Althouse *steel company executive*
McRaith, John Jeremiah *bishop*
Neal, Wilmer Lewis *clinical neurophysiologist*
Poling, Wesley Henry *college president*
Vickery, Robert Bruce *oil industry executive, consultant*
Wright, Patrick E. *grain company executive*

Paducah
Brown, Laverne Kindred *health facility administrator, nurse*
Johnstone, Edward Huggins *federal judge*
Walden, Robert Thomas *physicist educator, consultant*
Westberry, Billy Murry *lawyer*

Pewee Valley
Gill, George Norman *newspaper publishing company executive*

Pikeville
Hood, Joseph M. *federal judge*

Pineville
Whittaker, Bill Douglas *minister*

Pleasureville
O'Nan, Martha *foreign language educator*

Port Royal
Berry, Wendell *farmer, author*

Prospect
Dunbar, Wallace Huntington *manufacturing company executive*

Richmond
Branson, Branley Allan *biology educator*
Burkhart, Robert Edward *English language educator*
Funderburk, H(enry) Hanly, Jr. *college president*
Kirkpatrick, Dorothy Louise *education educator, program coordinator*
Martin, Robert Richard *emeritus college president, former senator*
Shearon, Forrest Bedford *humanities educator*
Witt, Robert Wayne *English educator*

Russell
Crimmins, Sean T(homas) *oil company executive*
Gates, Deborah Wolin *petroleum company executive, lawyer*

Russellville
Harper, Shirley Fay *nutritionist, educator, consultant*

Saint Catherine
Collins, Martha Layne *college president, former governor*

Salvisa
†Lancaster, Clay *architecture/design educator, writer*

Scottsville
Turner, Cal, Sr. (H. Calister Turner) *discount stores executive*
Wilcher, Larry Keith *lawyer*

Somerset
Jasper, Patrick Lee *pediatrician, medical association executive*

Trappist
Hart, Patrick Joseph *editor*

Union
Cook, Janice Eleanor Nolan *elementary school educator*

Versailles
Freehling, William Wilhartz *historian, educator*

West Liberty
Blevins, Walter, Jr. *dentist, state legislator*

Wilmore
Faupel, David William *minister, theological librarian*
Kinlaw, Dennis Franklin *clergyman, society executive*
†Kuhn, Anne Naomi Wicker (Mrs. Harold B. Kuhn) *foreign language educator*
McKenna, David Loren *seminary president, clergyman*

LOUISIANA

Alexandria
Bolton, Robert Harvey *banker*
Brady, James Joseph *lawyer*
Brocato, Joseph Myron *architect*
Gist, Howard Battle, Jr. *lawyer*
Hargrove, Robert Jefferson, Jr. *bishop*
†Jacobs, Sam G. *bishop*
Keller, Christoph, Jr. *bishop*
Little, F. A., Jr. *federal judge*
Mayeux, Ronald N. *school system administrator*
Smith, Joe Dorsey, Jr. *newspaper executive*
Sneed, Ellouise Bruce *nursing educator*
Ward-Steinman, Irving *lawyer*

Arnaudville
LaGrange, Claire Mae *special education educator*

Baker
Moody, Lamon Lamar, Jr. *retired civil engineer*
Roberson, Patt Foster *mass communications educator*

Baton Rouge
Acar, Yalcin Bekir *civil engineer, soil remediation technology executive, educator*
Aghazadeh, Fereydoun *industrial engineer, educator*
Arceneaux, William *historian, educator, association official*
Arman, Ara *civil engineering educator*
Arveson, Raymond G. *state superintendent*
Bayard, Alton Ernest, III *lawyer*
†Beckman, Joseph Alfred *research and development administrator*
Beckner, Donald Lee *lawyer*
Bedeian, Arthur George *business educator*
Berg, Irwin August *psychology educator*
Besch, Everett Dickman *veterinarian, university dean emeritus*
Blackman, John Calhoun, IV *lawyer*
Booth, George Geoffrey *finance educator*
Boyce, Bert Roy *university dean, library and information science educator*
Bray, George August *physician, scientist, educator*
Brickman, Kenneth Alan *state lottery executive*
Brockway, William Robert *architect*
Brown, Dale Duward *basketball coach*
Brown, James H., Jr. *state official, lawyer*
Brun, Judith *principal*
Bybee, Jay Scott *lawyer, educator*
Byrd, Warren Edgar, II *lawyer*
Caffey, H(orace) Rouse *academic administrator, consultant*
†Chandler, Brue Stanhope, III *hospital administrator*
Chen, Peter Pin-Shan *electrical engineering and computer science educator, data processing executive*
Cherry, William Ashley *surgeon, state health officer*
Cole, Luther Francis *former state supreme court associate justice*
Coleman, James Malcolm *marine geology educator*
Constant, William David *chemical engineer, educator*
Constantinides, Dinos Demetrios (Constantine Constantinides) *music educator, composer, conductor*
Cooper, William James, Jr. *history educator*
Copping, Allen Anthony *university president*
Cox, Hollis Utah *veterinarian*
Davis, William Eugene *university administrator*
Desbrandes, Robert *petroleum engineering educator, consultant*
Desmond, John Jacob *architect*
Duffy, John *history educator*
Edgeworth, Robert Joseph *classical languages educator*
Edwards, Edwin Washington *governor*
Flournoy, Melissa *state legislator*
Geiselman, Paula Jeanne *psychologist*
Gernon, Clarke Joseph, Sr. *mechanical and forensic engineering consultant*
Gibbs, Arnold James *lawyer*
†Gikas, Carol Sommerfeldt *museum director*
Giles, William Elmer *journalism educator, former newspaper editor*
Gilmore, Clarence Percy *writer, magazine editor*
Goldstein, Jerome Arthur *mathematics educator*
Gopu, Vijaya K.A. *engineer, consultant*
Graves, Robert Glen *transportation company executivw*
Greer, Robert Stephenson *insurance company executive*
Griffin, G. Lee *banker*
†Groat, Charles George *geologist, science administrator*
Guedry, Leo J. *agricultural economics educator*
Hancock, Paul Byron *headmaster*
Hansel, William *biology educator*
Hardy, John Edward *English language educator, author*
Harrison, Betty Carolyn Cook *vocational educator, administrator*
Hatfield, Jack Daniel *newspaper editor*
Hawkland, William Dennis *law educator*
Haynes, Leonard L., Jr. *philosophy educator, clergyman*
Hazel, Joseph Ernest *geology educator, stratigrapher*
Hill, Ralph Kelly *physician*
Hoover, Jimmie Hartman *librarian, educator*
Hoyt, Robert Emmet *business and industry association executive*
Hughes, Alfred Clifton *bishop*
Hunter, Kim Antoinette *state official*
Ieyoub, Richard Phillip *state attorney general*
Jaques, Thomas Francis *librarian*
Jenkins, Louis (Woody) *television executive, state legislator*
Kendrick, Brian Edward *financial executive*
Krotoski, Wojciech Antoni *research physician, educator*
Lambremont, Edward Nelson, Jr. *nuclear science educator*
Lamonica, P(aul) Raymond *lawyer, academic administrator, educator*
Landolt, Arlo Udell *astronomer, educator*
Larkin, John Montague *microbiology educator, researcher*
Lee, Betty Redding *architect*
Leonard, Paul Haralson *retired lawyer*
Le Vine, Jerome Edward *retired ophthalmologist, educator*
Liuzzo, Joseph Anthony *food science educator*
Lucas, Fred Vance *pathology educator, university administrator*
Madden, David *author*
Manship, Douglas *broadcast and newspaper executive*
Marshak, Alan Howard *electrical engineer, educator*
Martin, Freddie Anthony *agronomist, educator*
Mathews, Sharon Walker *artistic director, secondary school educator*
Mayfield, William Stephen *law educator*
Mc Cameron, Fritz Allen *university administrator*
Mc Clendon, William Hutchinson, III *lawyer*
Mc Glynn, Sean Patrick *physical chemist, educator*
McKeithen, Walter Fox *secretary of state*
McLaughlin, Edward *chemical engineering educator, dean*
McLindon, Gerald Joseph *planning and environmental design consultant, university dean emeritus*
Merliss, William Sidney *retired architect, engineer*
Middleton, Frank Walters, Jr. *lawyer*
Moody, Gene Byron *engineering executive, small business owner*
Moyse, Hermann, Jr. *banker*
Noland, Christina A. *magistrate judge*
Norem, Richard Frederick, Sr. *musician, music educator*
O'Connell, Robert Francis *physics educator*
Oden, William Bryant *bishop, educator*
Olney, James *English language educator*
Parish, Richard Lee *engineer, consultant*
Parker, John Victor *federal judge*
Patrick, William Hardy, Jr. *wetland biogeochemist, educator, laboratory director*
Patterson, Charles Darold *librarian, educator*
Philabaum, Leslie Ervin *publisher*
Pike, Ralph Webster *chemical engineer, educator, university official*
Polozola, Frank Joseph *federal judge*
Pope, David E. *geologist, micropaleontologist*
†Powell, Larry R. *chemicals executive*
Prestage, James Jordan *university chancellor*
†Prinzo, Felix J. *chemicals executive*
Pryor, William Austin *chemistry educator*
Pugh, George Willard *legal educator*
Rabideau, Peter Wayne *university dean, chemistry educator*
Rayburn, B. B. *state senator, farmer*
†Redman, Dale E. *diversified financial services company executive, title company executive*
Reich, Robert Sigmund *retired landscape architect*
Remsen, James Vanderbeek, Jr. *biologist, museum curator*
Riopelle, Arthur Jean *psychologist*
Robertson, George Leven *retired association executive*
Sawyer, Thomas Harry *health care facility administrator*
Schulz, Michael Anthony, Jr. *construction company executive, real estate developer*
Schwegmann, Melinda *state official*
Schwing, Charles E. *architect*
Shaw, Richard Francis *fisheries administrator, oceanography educator*
Smith, David Jeddie *American literature educator*
Smyth, David John *economist*
Soderbergh, Peter Andrew *education educator*
Stanford, Donald Elwin *English educator, editor, poet, critic*
Stopher, Peter Robert *civil and transportation engineering educator, consultant*
Swaggart, Jimmy Lee *evangelist, gospel singer*
Timmons, Edwin O'Neal *psychologist*
Tipton, Kenneth Warren *agricultural administrator, researcher*
Traynham, James Gibson *chemist, educator*
Tumay, Mehmet Taner *geotechnical consultant, educator, research administrator*
Turner, Bert S. *construction executive*
Urban, Gilbert William *banker*
Van Lopik, Jack Richard *geologist, educator*
Walker, Florence Ann *preschool educator, insurance underwriter*
Watson, J(ames) Hugh *banker*
West, Philip William *chemistry educator*
West, Robert Cooper *geography educator*
Wheeler, Otis Bullard *academic administrator, educator emeritus*
Williams, Hulen Brown *former university dean*
Williamson, William Floyd, Jr. *architect*
Willis, Guye Henry, Jr. *soil chemist*
Witcher, Robert Campbell *bishop*
Woodin, Martin Dwight *retired university system president*
Yarbrough, Martha Cornelia *music educator*
Yiannopoulos, Athanassios Nicholas *law educator*
Zwirn, Robert *architect, architecture educator*

Belle Chasse
Yandle, Sylvester Elwood, II *sales executive, inventor*

Benton
Dunnihoo, Dale Russell *physician, medical educator*

Bossier City
Johnson, Ruby LaVerne *retail executive*

Boyce
Chilton, St. John Poindexter *retired plant pathology educator, farm owner*

Calhoun
Robbins, Marion Le Ron *agricultural research executive*

Carencro
Clark, George Bryan *geophysicist*

Chalmette
Wheeler, Genevieve Stutes *library administrator, educator*

Chauvin
Sammarco, Paul William *ecologist*

Covington
Bankston, Terry *school system administrator*
Blossman, Alfred Rhody, Jr. *banker*
Files, Mark Willard *business and financial consultant*
Krauss, Steven James *clothing executive*
Roberts, James Allen *urologist*
Stroup, Sheila Tierney *columnist*
†Wilcox, Richard *grain company executive*

Deridder
Lytle, Ellen Juanita Wilson *special education educator*

Deville
McCann, Norma Reed *health facility administrator*

Eunice
Rogers, Donald Onis *language educator*

Franklin
Broussard, Bernard B. *social activist, publisher, writer*
Fairchild, Phyllis Elaine *counselor*

Geismar
Coombs, Douglas A. L. *chemical company executive*

Grambling
Fields, Hall Ratcliff *finance educator*
Robinson, Eddie Gay *college football coach*
Smith, Betty Edmiston *university dean, nurse*
Wilkerson, Pinkie Carolyn *state legislator, lawyer*

Gretna
Calhoun, Milburn *publishing executive, rare book dealer, physician*
Lupin, Ellis Ralph *physician, lawyer, coroner*

Hammond
Hejtmancik, Milton Rudolph *medical educator*
Jackson, Joy Juanita *history educator*
Kemp, John Randolph *journalist, author, academic administrator*
Matheny, Tom Harrell *lawyer*
Parker, Clea Edward *university president*
Smith, Grant Warren, II *university administrator, physical sciences educator*
Thorburn, James Alexander *humanities educator*

Harahan
Bowler, Shirley *state legislator*

Harvey
Chee, Shirley *real estate broker*
Romagosa, Elmo Lawrence *clergyman, retired editor*

Houma
Boudreaux, Warren Louis *retired bishop*
†Jarrell, Charles Michael *bishop*
Lemoine, Pamela Allyson *assistant principal*
Paisant, Sister Immaculata *school system administrator*
Saia, Louis P., III *transportation executive*

Independence
Vaccaro, Nick Anthony *principal*

Kenner
Cook, Willie Chunn *elementary school educator*
Scherich, Edward Baptiste *retired diversified company executive*
Siebel, Mathias Paul *mechanical engineer*
Treuting, Edna Gannon *retired nursing administrator*
Zito, Michael Steven *protective services official*

Lacombe
Hendricks, Donald Duane *librarian*

Lafayette
Andrew, Catherine Vige *elementary school educator*
Benoit, Robert Patrick *protective services official*
Bertrand, Harry C. *health facility administrator*
†Branch, Sonya Meyer *library director*
Burnam, Paul Wayne *accountant, educator*
Carstens, Jane Ellen *retired library science educator*
Castellini, Patricia Bennett *business management educator*
Cook, David Sherman *lawyer*
Davidson, James Joseph, III *lawyer*
Davis, William Eugene *federal judge*
Doherty, Rebecca Feeney *federal judge*
Domingue, Emery *consulting engineering company executive*
Duhe, John Malcolm, Jr. *federal judge*
Dur, Philip Francis *political scientist, educator, retired foreign service officer*
Haik, Richard T., Sr. *federal judge*
Heatherly, Henry Edward *mathematics educator*
Kline, Roger V. *health science facility adminstrator*
Lenox, Charles N(ewton), Jr. *newspaper editor*
Leon, Benjamin Joseph *electrical engineering educator, consultant*
Methvin, Mildred E. *judge*
Mickel, Joseph Thomas *lawyer*
Nolan, Paul Thomas *retired English and humanities educator*
O'Donnell, Edward Joseph *bishop, former editor*
Perkins, David Layne, Sr. *architect*
Poe, (Lydia) Virginia *reading educator*
Putnam, Richard Johnson *federal judge*
Redding, Evelyn A. *dean, nursing educator*
Shaw, John Malach *federal judge*
†Sides, Larry Eugene *advertising executive*
Stuart, Walter Bynum, III *banker*
Tynes, Pamela Anne *federal judge*

Lake Charles
Beam, James C. (Jim Beam) *editor, newspaper*
Butler, Robert Olen *writer, educator*
Cain, Sister Gloria *school system administrator*
Cox, James Joseph *lawyer*
Douglas, Wanda Sue Lenard *middle school educator*
Drez, David Jacob, Jr. *orthopaedic surgeon, educator*
Everett, John Prentis, Jr. *lawyer*
Hathaway, Leah *artistic director*
Hebert, Robert D. *academic administrator*
Hebert, Robert D. *academic administrator*
Heiserman, Russell Lee *electronics educator*
Hunter, Edwin Ford, Jr. *federal judge*
Lawton, William Burton *bank executive*
Leder, Sandra Juanita *elementary school educator*
McHale, Robert Michael *lawyer*
McLeod, William Lasater, Jr. *judge, former state legislator*
Mount, Willie Landry *mayor*
Shaddock, William Edward, Jr. *lawyer*
Speyrer, Jude *bishop*
Trimble, James T., Jr. *federal judge*

Leesville
Boren, Lynda Sue *educator*
Russell, Gerald Edward *social worker, retired army officer*

Mandeville
Christian, John Catlett, Jr. *lawyer*
Deano, Edward Joseph, Jr. *lawyer, state legislator*
Rohrbough, Elsa Claire Hartman *artist*

Mansfield
Smelley, Joyce Marie *special education supervisor*

Marksville
Riddle, Charles Addison, III *state legislator, lawyer*

Marrero
Hebert, Clifford Joseph *data processing executive*

Metairie
Ammon, James E. *retail executive*
Andersen, Morten *football player*
Benson, Jerome *automotive sales executive*
Benson, Tom *professional football executive*

Bower, Philip Jeffrey *cardiologist, administrator*
Brisolara, Ashton *substance abuse and employee assistance programs consultant*
Buetow, Paul Elmer *principal*
Caplan, Merry Wassom *non-profit educational corporation executive*
Carter, Rebecca Davilene *general surgeon, surgical oncology educator*
†Cheveallier, J. Clint *religious organization executive*
Colbert, Charles Ralph *architect*
Costello, Joseph Mark, III *broadcasting and motion picture executive*
Denegre, George *lawyer*
†Derbes, Max Joseph, Jr. *real estate appraiser*
Falco, Maria Josephine *political scientist, academic administrator*
Flake, Leone Elizabeth *special education educator*
Gauthier, Wendell Haynes *lawyer*
†Gereighty, Andrea Saunders *polling company executive, poet*
Goss, Donald Davis *consultant, author, lecturer*
†Grimm, John Lloyd *business executive, marketing professional*
†Hartman, James Austin *retired geologist*
Heim, Charles William, Jr. *fund raising executive*
†Holland, Jeffrey Stuart *hospital executive*
Johnson, Beth Michael *principal*
Johnson, Vaughan *professional football player*
McShan, Clyde Griffin, II *financial executive*
Mora, James Ernest *professional football coach, professional sports team executive*
Murphy, Alvin Leo *educational administrator*
Myers, Iona Raymer *real estate and property manager*
†Perlis, Sharon A. *lawyer*
Roaf, William Layton *professional football player*
Spruiell, Vann *psychoanalyst*
Turnbull, Renaldo *professional football player*
Walsh, Maurice David, Jr. *former librarian, business executive*

Minden
Doerge, Everett Gail *retired school system adminstrator, state rep*

Monroe
Cage, Bobby Nyle *university dean*
Curry, Robert Lee, III *lawyer*
Marsala, Theresa Clark *nurse, adminstrator*
†Reppond, Jim D. *communications executive*
Rose, Charles David *consulting company executive*
Sartor, Daniel Ryan, Jr. *lawyer*
Stewart, Joe R. *law enforcement official*
Wall, Jerry Leon *management educator, university administrator*

Napoleonville
Gunnell, William N. *school system administrator*

Natchitoches
Alost, Robert Allen *university executive*
Christensen, Raymond Lyle *electrical engineer, educator*
Egan, Shirley Anne *retired nursing educator*

New Iberia
Cavalier, David J. *school system administrator*
Henton, Willis Ryan *bishop*

New Orleans
Abad, Rosario Dalida *elementary educator*
Acomb, Robert Bailey, Jr. *lawyer, educator*
Agrawal, Krishna Chandra *pharmacology educator*
Allen, F(rank) C(linton), Jr. *manufacturing executive, lawyer*
Allen, Gary Curtiss *geology educator*
Alsobrook, Henry Bernis, Jr. *lawyer*
Ambrose, Stephen Edward *history educator, author*
Amoss, W. James, Jr. *shipping company executive*
Amoss, Walter James, III *editor*
Andrews, Bethlehem Kottes *research chemist*
Andrus, Gerald Louis *utilities holding company consultant*
Arnof, Ian *banker*
Ates, J. Robert *lawyer*
Azaceta, Luis Cruz *artist*
Bachmann, Richard Arthur *oil company executive*
Ball, Millie (Mildred Porteons Ball) *editor, journalist*
Barham, Mack Elwin *lawyer, educator*
Barnett, Walter Michael *lawyer*
Baron, John Herschel *music educator, musicologist*
Barry, Francis Julian, Jr. *lawyer*
Beard, Elizabeth Letitia *physiologist, educator*
Beason, Amos Theodore *banker*
Beckerman, Robert Cy *pediatrician, educator*
Beer, Peter Hill *federal judge*
Benerito, Ruth Rogan (Mrs. Frank H. Benerito) *chemist*
Benjamin, Edward Bernard, Jr. *lawyer*
Bennett, Joan Wennstrom *biology educator*
Berenson, Gerald Sanders *physician*
Berger, Walter Jasper, Jr. *financial executive*
Berlin, Charles I. *audiologist, scientist*
Bernstein, Joseph *lawyer*
†Bertoniere, Noelie Rita *research chemist*
Bertrand, William Ellis *public health educator, international health center administrator*
Besthoff, Sydney J., III *drug store company executive*
Bieck, Robert Barton, Jr. *lawyer*
Birtel, Frank Thomas *mathematician, philosopher, educator*
Blitch, James Buchanan *architect*
Blitch, Ronald Buchanan *architect*
Boudreaux, Kenneth Justin *finance and economics educator, consultant*
Boyle, Edward J., Sr. *federal judge*
Brannan, William *urologist, educator*
Bricker, Harvey Miller *anthropology educator*
Bricker, Victoria Reifler *anthropology educator*
Brown, James Barrow *bishop*
Brown, Wood, III *lawyer*
Buccino, Salvatore George *physics educator*
Buckley, Samuel Olliphant, III *lawyer*
Bullard, Edgar John, III *museum director*
Burns, Mary W. *school system administrator*
Calogero, Pascal Frank, Jr. *state supreme court chief justice*
Campbell, Margaret M. *social work educator*
Carr, Patrick E. *judge*
Carter, James Clarence *university administrator*
Casellas, Joachim *art gallery executive*
Cassibry, Fred James *lawyer, retired federal court judge*
†Cazayoux, Charles *airport executive*
Cheatwood, Roy Clifton *lawyer*
Christman, John Francis *science administrator, former university administrator*
Claverie, Philip deVilliers *lawyer*
Clayton, Paul David *savings and loan executive*
Clement, Edith Brown *federal judge*
Cody, Wilmer St. Clair *educational administrator*
Cohen, Joseph *English literature educator, writer, business owner*
Cohn, Isidore, Jr. *surgeon, educator*
Coleman, James Julian, Jr. *lawyer, industrialist, real estate executive*
Combe, David Alfred *law librarian, educator*
Combe, John Clifford, Jr. *lawyer*
Connolly, Edward S. *neurological surgeon*
Cook, Samuel DuBois *university president, political scientist*
Cook, Victor Joseph, Jr. *marketing educator, consultant*
Copelin, Sherman Nathaniel, Jr. *state legislator, enterpreneur, business executive*
Corey, Orlin Russell *publisher, editor*
Correro, Anthony James, III *lawyer*
Corrigan, James John, Jr. *pediatrician*
Cosenza, Arthur George *opera director*
†Cospolich, James Donald *electrical engineering executive, consultant*
Couch, Harvey Crowley, III *law educator*
Couhig, Robert Emmet *lawyer*
Crisp, John N. *engineering educator*
Cummings, Anthony Michael *music historian, educator, academic administrator*
†Curry, Dale B. *journalist*
D'Ambrosia, Robert Dominick *orthopaedic educator*
Daniels, Robert Sanford *psychiatrist, medical school dean*
Deasy, William John *construction, marine dredging, engineering and mining company executive*
Defenbaugh, Richard Eugene *marine ecologist*
Dennery, Moise Waldhorn *lawyer, educator*
Dennis, James Leon *state supreme court justice*
Dickinson, Catherine Schatz *microbiologist*
Dittmann, Albert Stephen, Jr. *lawyer*
Dixon, Irma Muse *state commissioner, former state legislator, social worker*
Dodds, Richard Crofton *theater critic*
Domer, Floyd Ray *pharmacologist, educator*
Domingue, Gerald James *medical scientist, microbiology, immunology and urology educator, researcher, clinical bacteriologist*
Duffy, John Charles *psychiatrist, physician*
Duncan, Margaret Caroline *physician*
Duplantier, Adrian Guy *federal judge*
Easson, William McAlpine *psychiatrist*
†Edisen, Clayton Byron *physician*
Edmonson, Munro Sterling *anthropologist, educator*
Epstein, Arthur William *physician, educator*
Ewin, Dabney Minor *surgeon*
Fagaly, William Arthur *curator*
Fantaci, James Michael *lawyer*
Feldman, Martin L. C. *federal judge*
Ferguson, Charles Austin *retired newspaper editor*
Filson, Ronald Coulter *architect, educator, college dean*
Fine, David Jeffrey *hospital executive, educator, consultant, lecturer*
Fingerman, Milton *biologist, educator*
Fisher, James William *medical educator, pharmacologist*
Fishman, Louis Yarrut *lawyer*
Force, Robert *law educator*
Forman, L. Ronald *park and zoological garden administrator*
Fountain, Peter Dewey, Jr. (Pete Fountain) *clarinetist*
Franco, Philip Anthony *lawyer*
Frantz, Phares Albert *architect*
Freeman, Montine McDaniel *museum trustee*
Freudenberger, Herman *retired economics educator*
Friedlander, Miles Herbert *ophthalmologist*
Friedman, Joel William *law educator*
Frohlich, Edward David *physician*
Garcia, Patricia A. *lawyer*
García Oller, José Luis *neurosurgeon*
Gathright, John Byron, Jr. *colon and rectal surgeon, educator*
Gelfand, M. David *lawyer, educator*
Gelpi, C. James (Jim Gelpi) *lawyer*
Gerber, Michael Albert *pathologist, researcher*
Glasgow, Vaughn Leslie *museum curator and administrator*
Goins, Richard Anthony *lawyer, educator*
Gonzales, Brother Alexis (Joseph M. Gonzales) *theater and communications educator*
Gordon, Joseph Elwell *university official, educator*
Gottlieb, A(braham) Arthur *medical educator, biotechnology corporate executive*
Grau, Shirley Ann (Mrs. James Kern Feibleman) *writer*
Greenleaf, Richard Edward *Latin American history educator*
Hall, Luther Egbert, Jr. *retired lawyer*
Hamlin, James Turner, III *university dean, physician*
Hansel, Stephen Arthur *holding company executive*
†Harness, Francis William *naval officer*
Harper, Robert John, Jr. *chemist, researcher*
Harris, Aurand *playwright*
Hassenboehler, Donalyn *principal*
Healy, George William, III *lawyer*
Heebe, Frederick Jacob Regan *federal judge*
Hewitt, Robert Lee *surgeon, educator*
Hilbert, Peter Louis, Jr. *lawyer*
Hinton, James Forrest, Jr. *lawyer*
†Holmes, Morris L., Jr. *school superintendent*
Howard, Ernest E., III *lawyer, natural resource company executive*
Howson, Robert E. *construction company executive*
Huot, Rachel Irene *cell biologist*
Hyman, Albert Lewis *cardiologist*
Ivens, Mary Sue *microbiologist, mycologist*
Jackson, Jerry Donald *utility company executive, lawyer*
Jacobsen, Thomas Warren *archaeologist, educator*
Jaffe, Bernard Michael *surgeon*
Jefferson, Patrick O'Neal *university program director, administrative assistant*
Jenkins, Howard J. *church education administrator*
Jimirro, James P. *broadcasting and telecommunications executive*
Johnsen, Erik Frithjof *transportation executive*
Johnson, Lee Harnie *dean, educator*
Jones, John Anderson, Jr. *school system administrator*
Jung, Rodney C. *internist, academic administrator*
†Kaufman, Herbert Edward *ophthalmologist, educator*
Keller, Thomas Clements *lawyer*
Kelly, Eamon Michael *university president*
Kemp, James Bradley, Jr. *lawyer*
Kilanowski, Michael Charles, Jr. *oil, natural gas, minerals exploration company executive, lawyer*
Kline, David Gellinger *neurosurgery educator*
Klingman, John Philip *architect, educator*
Krementz, Edward Thomas *surgeon*
†Kukla, Jon (Keith) *historian, museum director*
Laborde, Alden James *oil company executive*
Laborde, John Peter *retired international energy company executive*
Lambert, Olaf Cecil *hotel executive*
Lang, Erich Karl *physician, radiologist*
Lannes, William Joseph, III *electrical engineer*
Latiolais, René Louis *natural resources company executive, chemical engineer*
Latorre, Robert George *naval architecture and engineering educator*
LaValle, Irving Howard *decision analysis educator*
Lavelle, Paul Michael *lawyer*
Lee, Griff Calicutt *civil engineer*
Leger, Walter John, Jr. *lawyer*
Leinbach, Philip Eaton *librarian*
Le Jeune, Francis Ernest, Jr. *otolaryngologist*
Lemann, Thomas Berthelot *lawyer*
Levell, Edward, Jr. *city official*
Levert, John Bertels, Jr. *investment executive*
Levy, Sam *consumer products company executive*
Lewis, Floyd Wallace *former electric utility executive*
Lewy, John Edwin *pediatric nephrologist*
†Lief, Thomas Parrish *sociologist, educator*
Lind, Thomas Otto *barge transportation company executive*
Litwin, Martin Stanley *surgeon*
Livaudais, Marcel, Jr. *federal judge*
†Livingston, James Evertte *marine corps officer*
Locke, William *endocrinologist*
†Lopez, Manuel *immunology and allergy educator*
Lovejoy, Barbara Campbell *sculptor, architectural designer*
Lovett, William Anthony *law and economics educator*
Low, Frank Norman *anatomist, educator*
Lowe, Robert Charles *lawyer*
Luza, Radomir Vaclav *historian, educator*
Lykes, Joseph T., III *shipping company executive*
Mackin, Cooper Richerson *university chancellor*
Marcus, Bernard *lawyer*
Marcus, Walter F., Jr. *state supreme court justice*
Marks, Charles Dennery *insurance salesman*
†Martin, David Hubert *physician, educator*
Martinez, Andrew Tredway *lawyer*
Mason, Henry Lloyd *political science educator*
†Massare, John Steve *medical association administrator, educator*
McCormick, Eugene F., Jr. *transportation company executive*
McDougal, Luther Love, III *law educator*
McFarland, James W. *academic administrator*
McMahon, Maeve *principal*
McMillan, Lee Richards, II *lawyer*
McNamara, A. J. *federal judge*
Mealey, George Allan *mining executive*
Mentz, Henry Alvan, Jr. *federal judge*
Mickal, Abe *retired physician*
†Miller, Robert Harold *otolaryngologist, educator*
Milling, R(oswell) King *bank executive, lawyer*
Mintz, Albert *lawyer*
Mitchell, Lansing Leroy *federal judge*
Moely, Barbara E. *psychology educator*
Moffett, James Robert *oil and gas company executive*
Mogabgab, William Joseph *epidemiologist, educator*
Molony, Michael Janssens, Jr. *lawyer*
Monachino, Francis Leonard *music educator*
Monroe, James Walter *organization executive*
Morial, Marc Haydel *mayor*
Morrell, Arthur Anthony *lawyer, state legislator*
Murrish, Charles Howard *oil and gas exploration company executive, geologist*
Navar, Luis Gabriel *physiology educator, researcher*
Nehrbass, Seth Martin *lawyer*
Nelson, James Smith *pathologist, educator*
†Nelson, Waldemar Stanley *civil engineer, consultant*
Nice, Charles Monroe, Jr. *physician, educator*
Nichols, Ronald Lee *surgeon, educator*
Novakov, George John, Jr. *gifted and talented education educator*
Nuzum, Robert Weston *lawyer*
Ochsner, John Lockwood *thoracic-cardiovascular surgeon*
Olson, Richard David *psychology educator*
O'Meallie, Kitty *artist*
O'Neal, Edgar Carl *psychology educator*
Orihel, Thomas Charles *parasitology educator, research scientist*
Ortique, Revius Oliver, Jr. *city official*
Pankey, George Atkinson *physician, educator*
Paolini, Gilbert *literature and science educator*
Paradise, Louis Vincent *psychology educator, university provost*
Perdew, John Paul *physics educator, condensed matter and density functional theorist*
Peyroux, Robert Albert *accounting company executive*
Pfister, Richard Charles *physician, radiology educator*
Phelps, Ashton, Jr. *newspaper publisher*
Pittman, Jacquelyn *mental health nurse, nursing educator*
Pizer, Donald *author, educator*
Plaeger, Frederick Joseph, II *lawyer*
Plavsic, Branko Milenko *radiology educator*
Poesch, Jessie Jean *art historian*
Poitevent, Edward Butts, II *lawyer*
Pope, John M. *journalist*
Purtell, Lawrence Robert *lawyer*
Purvis, George Frank, Jr. *life insurance company executive*
Puyau, Francis Albert *physician, radiology educator*
Quirk, Peter Richard *engineering company executive*
Rayson, Jack Henry *dentist, educator, retired*
†Re, Richard N. *endocrinologist*
Reck, Andrew Joseph *philosophy educator*
Redmon, Harry Smith, Jr. *lawyer*
Reisin, Efrain *nephrologist, researcher, educator*
Remley, Theodore Phant, Jr. *counselor, educator and lawyer*
Richardson, Donald Edward *neurosurgery educator*
†Riddick, Frank Adams, Jr. *physician, health care facility administrator*
Riedlinger, Brian A. *principal*
Riess, George Febiger *lawyer, educator*
Rigby, Perry Gardner *medical center administrator, educator, former university dean, physician*
Roberts, Elliott C., Sr. *hospital administrator*
Roberts, John Kenneth, Jr. *life insurance company executive*
Roberts, Louise Nisbet *philosopher*
Robins, Robert Sidwar *political science educator, administrator*
Roesler, Robert Harry *city official*
Rosen, Charles, II *lawyer*
Rosen, William Warren *lawyer*
Rosensteel, George T. *physics educator, nuclear physicist*
Roskoski, Robert, Jr. *biochemist, educator, author*
Rossowska, Magdalena Joanna *physiology educator, research scientist*
Salvaggio, John Edmond *physician, educator*
Sarpy, Leon *lawyer*
Schally, Andrew Victor *endocrine oncologist, researcher*
Schneider, George T. *obstetrician-gynecologist*
Schulte, Francis B. *archbishop*
Schwartz, Charles, Jr. *federal judge*
†Schwartz, Daniel K. *chemistry educator*
Schwegmann, John F. *consumer products company executive*
Sear, Morey Leonard *federal judge, educator*
Sellin, Eric *linguist, poet, educator*
Sharma, Bhu Dev *mathematics educator, researcher*
Shinn, Clinton Wesley *lawyer*
Sibley, David Emile *oil company executive*
†Simms, Ellenese Brooks *civic leader, retired school system administrator*
Simon, H(uey) Paul *lawyer*
Sims, John William *lawyer*
Sinor, Howard Earl, Jr. *lawyer*
Smith, John Webster *retired naval officer, company executive*
Snyder, Charles Aubrey *lawyer*
†Stanback, Lawrence *conservationist*
Stapp, Dan Ernest *retired lawyer, utility executive*
Steg, J(ames) L(ouis) *artist*
Steinmetz, Deborah Susan *interior designer*
Steinmetz, Robert Charles *architect*
Stephens, Richard Bernard *natural resource company executive*
Stevenson, Bobbie Lee *education director*
Straumanis, John Janis, Jr. *psychiatry educator*
Sumrell, Gene *research chemist*
Surprenant, Mark Christopher *lawyer*
Sweeney, Joseph Modeste *lawyer, educator*
Tarver, Michael Keith *lawyer*
Taylor, Kenneth Byron, Jr. *librarian, minister, religion educator*
Tewell, Joseph Robert, Jr. *electrical engineer*
†Thomas, Robert Allen *environmental policy administrator, educator*
Thompson, Annie Laura *foreign language educator*
Thornell, Jack Randolph *photographer*
Toussaint, Allen Richard *recording studio executive, composer, pianist*
Trapolin, Frank Winter *retired insurance executive*
Trostorff, Alexander Peter *lawyer*
Usdin, Gene Leonard *physician, psychiatrist*
Vance, Robert Patrick *lawyer*
Vanselow, Neal Arthur *university administrator, physician*
†Verges, Ernest E. *architectural firm executive*
Villavaso, Stephen Donald *urban planner, lawyer*
Waechter, Arthur Joseph, Jr. *lawyer*
Waggonner, Joseph David, III *architect*
Wakefield, Benton McMillin, Jr. *banker*
Walk, Frank Humphrey *consulting engineer*
Walsh, John Joseph *medical school administrator, physician*
Waring, William Winburn *pediatric pulmonologist, educator*
Washington, Robert Orlanda *educator, former university administrator*
Watson, Jack Crozier *state supreme court justice*
Webb, Watts Rankin *surgeon*
Weigel, John J. *lawyer*
Weill, Hans *physician, educator*
Weiss, Kenneth Andrew *lawyer, law educator*
Weiss, Thomas Edward *physician*
Welch, Robert Ballinger *investment planner*
Welden, Arthur Luna *biology educator*
Welsh, Ronald Arthur *physician, educator*
White, Charles Albert, Jr. *medical educator, obstetrician-gynecologist*
Wilford, Walton Terry *economics educator*
†Wilkinson, Joel *oil company executive*
†Willems, Constance Charles *lawyer*
Williamson, Ernest Lavone *petroleum company executive*
Wilson, C. Daniel, Jr. *library director*
Wilson, Peggy Henican *city official*
Wisdom, John Minor *federal judge*
Womack, Edgar Allen, Jr. *technology executive*
Woodward, Madison Truman, Jr. *lawyer*
Woodward, Ralph Lee, Jr. *historian, educator*
Wright, Thomas Joe *electric utility executive*
Yates, Robert Doyle *anatomy educator*
Young, Lucy Cleaver *physician*
Zimny, Marilyn Lucile *anatomist, educator*

New Roads
Haag, William George *anthropologist, educator*

Pineville
Boswell, Bill Reeser *religious organization executive*
Howell, Thomas *history educator*
Martin, W. Terry *librarian*
Matthews, Betty Parker *special education educator*
Swearingen, David Clarke *general practice physician, musician*
Tapley, Philip Allen *English language and literature educator*

Ruston
Barron, Randall Franklin *mechanical engineer, educator, consultant*
Freasier, Aileen W. *special education educator*
Halliburton, Lloyd *Romance philology educator*
Maxfield, John Edward *retired university dean*
Painter, Jack Timberlake *civil engineer*
Posey, Clyde Lee *business administration and accounting educator*
Reneau, Daniel D. *university administrator*
Sale, Tom S., III *financial economist, educator*
Taylor, Foster Jay *retired university president*
Warrington, Robert O'Neil, Jr. *mechanical engineering educator and administrator, researcher*
Wicker, William Walter *librarian*

Saint Bernard
Gilbert, Norman Sutcliffe *research physician*
Lee, Melvin Joseph *minister*

Saint Gabriel
Das, Dilip Kumar *chemical engineer*

Scott
Stockton, Robert Standeford *writer, real estate development, construction, sales and management consultant*

Shreveport
Achee, Roland Joseph *lawyer*
Beaird, Charles T. *publishing executive*
Boyd, Clarence Elmo *retired surgeon*
Bradley, Ronald James *neuroscientist*
Breffeilh, Louis Andrew *ophthalmologist, educator*
Bremer, Richard H. *electric power company executive*
Carmody, Arthur Roderick, Jr. *lawyer*
Crissinger, Karen Denise *pediatric gastroenterologist, physiologist*
Darling, John Rothburn, Jr. *university administrator, educator*
Demopulos, Chris *engineering company executive*
Dilworth, Edwin Earle *obstetrician, gynecologist*
Elberson, Edwin Wallace *architect*
Fort, Arthur Tomlinson, III *physician*
Friend, William Benedict *bishop*
Ganley, James Powell *ophthalmologist, educator*
Gentry, Hubert, Jr. *lawyer*
George, Ronald Baylis *physician*
†Gilmore, Marshall *bishop*
Greene, Dallas Whorton, Jr. *fire chief*
Grigsby, Chester Poole, Jr. *oil and investments company executive*
Haas, Lester Carl *architect*
Hall, John Whitling *geography educator*
Jamison, Richard Melvin *virologist, educator*
Jones, Ernest Edward *minister, religious organization administrator*
Kelley, Marie Nichols *hospital administrator*
Lazarus, Allan Matthew *retired newspaper editor*
McDonald, John Clifton *surgeon*
Misra, Raghunath Prasad *physician, educator*
Nelson, Sydney B. *lawyer, state senator*
Payne, Roy Steven *judge*
Pederson, William David *political scientist, educator*
Pelton, James Rodger *librarian*
Politz, Henry Anthony *federal judge*
Preston, Loyce Elaine *retired social work educator*
Pugh, Robert Gahagan *lawyer*
Ramey, Cecil Edward, Jr. *lawyer*
Reddy, Pratap Chandupatla *cardiologist, educator, researcher*
†Schneider, Thomas Richard *hospital administrator*
Schober, Charles Coleman, III *psychiatrist, psychoanalyst*
Schwab, Kenneth Lynn *college president*
Shannon, George Ward, Jr. *museum director, anthropologist, archaeologist*
Shelby, James Stanford *cardiovascular surgeon*
†Smith, Clair S., Jr. *oil industry executive*
†Smith, Clair Scott, III *petroleum company executive*
Stagg, Tom *federal judge*
†Stewart, Carl E. *judge*
Thurmon, Theodore Francis *medical educator*
Tiner, Stanley Ray *business communications executive, former editor*
Tullis, John Ledbetter *retired wholesale distributing company executive*
Walter, Donald Ellsworth *federal judge*
Webb, Donald Arthur *minister*
Wiener, Jacques Loeb, Jr. *federal judge*
Winham, George Keeth *mental health nurse*
†Wion, J. Mike *oil industry executive*
Witt, Elizabeth Nowlin (Beth Witt) *special education educator*
Woodman, Walter James *lawyer*

Slaughter
Gremillion, Curtis Lionel, Jr. *psychologist, hospital administrator, musician*

Slidell
Faust, Marilyn B. *elementary school principal*
Hall, Ogden Henderson *allied health educator*

Springhill
Schoenrock, James V. *religious organization administrator*

Tallulah
Ragland, Alwine Mulhearn *judge*

Thibodaux
Delozier, Maynard Wayne *marketing educator*
Fairchild, Joseph Virgil, Jr. *accounting educator*
Nunn, Thomas Calvin *school supervisor, retired army officer*
Swetman, Glenn Robert *English language educator, poet*
Worthington, Janet Evans *academic director, English language educator*

West Monroe
Johnson, Thomas H. *manufacturing company executive*
Rentfro, Larry Dean *hospital administrator*

Winnsboro
Wilson, Rose Eaton *elementary education educator*

Zachary
Hull, Donnie Faye *special education director, educator*

MAINE

Alfred
Jordan, Anne Harrison *lawyer*

Alna
Herz, Michael Joseph *marine environmental scientist*

Andover
Ellis, George Hathaway *retired banker and utility company executive*

Auburn
Clifford, Robert William *judge*
Phillips, Charles Franklin *economic consultant*

Augusta
Barth, Alvin Ludwig *state legislator*
Billings, Richard Whitten *association executive*
Brawn, Linda Curtis *state legislator*
Bustin, Beverly Miner *state legislator*
†Butland, Jeffrey H. *president of senate, customer service representative*
Carpenter, Michael E. *state attorney general*
Cheng, Hsueh Ching *physician*
Cohen, Richard Stockman *lawyer*
Diamond, G. William *secretary of state*
Gervais, Paul Nelson *foundation administrator, psychologist, public relations executive*
Kany, Judy C(asperson) *health policy analyst, former state senator*
Kilkelly, Marjorie Lee *state legislator*
Martin, John L. *state legislator*
†Martin, Leo G. *educational administrator*
Moody, Stanley Alton *entrepreneur, financial consultant*
Nickerson, John Mitchell *political science educator*
Phillips, Joseph Robert *museum director*
Richard, Debrah Jane *environmental planner*
Roberts, Donald Albert *advertising, public relations, marketing and media consultant*
Saxl, Jane Wilhelm *state legislator*
Scribner, Rodney Latham *state official*
Sewell, Dwight A. *state government official*
Sotir, Thomas Alfred *healthcare executive, retired shipbuilder*
Winn, Julie *state representative*

Bailey Island
Carter, William Caswell *computer systems scientist*

Bangor
Albrecht, Ronald Lewis *financial services executive*
Brody, Morton Aaron *federal judge*
Bullock, William Clapp, Jr. *banker*
†Libbey, Robert David *television producer*
Mills, David Harlow *psychologist, association executive*
Rea, Ann W. *librarian*
Roderick, Richard Michael *petroleum distribution and real estate company financial executive*
Turner, Marta Dawn *youth program specialist*
Warren, Richard Jordan *newspaper publisher*
Warren, Richard Kearney *newspaper publisher*
Watkins, Julia M. *university dean*

Bar Harbor
Davisson, Muriel Trask *geneticist*
Dworak, Marcia Lynn *library director, library building consultant*
Green, Earl Leroy *retired biomedical research administrator, geneticist*
Hoppe, Peter Christian *biologist, geneticist*
†Mooser, Stephen *author*
Paigen, Kenneth *geneticist, educator*
Swazey, Judith Pound *institute president, sociomedical science educator*

Bath
Ipcar, Dahlov *illustrator, painter, author*
O'Keefe, Patrick *transportation executive*
Webb, Todd (Charles Clayton Webb) *photographer, writer*
Weiss, David Raymond *lawyer*

Belfast
Porter, Bernard Harden *consulting physicist, author, publisher*
Worth, Mary Page *mayor*

Biddeford
Ford, Charles Willard *university administrator, educator*
Reynolds, Thomas Hedley *university president*

Blue Hill
Lowry, James David *author, consultant*

Blue Hill Falls
Stookey, Noel Paul *folksinger, composer*

Boothbay Harbor
Cavanaugh, Tom Richard *artist, antiques dealer, retired art educator*
Eames, John Heagan *etcher*
Grossman, Morton S. *artist*
Lenthall, Franklyn *theatre historian*

Bridgton
Thompson, Larry A. *principal*

Bristol
Schmidt, Thomas Carson *international development banker*

Brooklin
Schmidt, Klaus Dieter *management consultant, university administrator, marketing and management educator*
Yglesias, Helen Bassine *author, educator*

Brownfield
Kloskowski, Vincent John, Jr. *educational consultant, writer*

Brunswick
Chandler, John, Jr. *retired educational consultant*
Dixon, Thomas Francis *aviation company executive*
Edwards, Robert Hazard *college president*
Fuchs, Alfred Herman *psychologist, college dean, educator*
Geoghegan, William Davidson *religion educator, minister*
Greason, Arthur LeRoy, Jr. *university administrator*
Hodge, James Lee *German language educator*
Huntington, Charles Ellsworth *biologist, educator*
Morgan, Richard Ernest *political scientist, educator*
Pfeiffer, Sophia Douglass *state legislator, lawyer*
Porter, Richard Sterling *retired metal processing company executive, lawyer*
Schwartz, Elliott Shelling *composer, author, music educator*
Tucker, Allen Brown, Jr. *computer science educator*
Watson, Katharine Johnson *art museum director, art historian*

Bryant Pond
Conary, David Arlan *investment company executive*

Camden
Anderson, George Harding *broadcasting company executive*
Lavenson, James H. *hotel industry executive*
Lavenson, Susan Barker *hotel corporate executive, consultant*
Shuman, Samuel Irving *lawyer, law educator*
Spock, Benjamin McLane *physician, educator*
Thomas, (Charles) Davis *editor*
Weidman, Hazel Hitson *anthropologist, educator*

Canaan
Walker, Willard Brewer *anthropology educator, linguist*
Zikorus, Albert Michael *golf course architect*

Cape Elizabeth
Emerson, Paul Carlton *retired publishing executive*
Simonds, Stephen Paige *former state legislator*

Caribou
McElwain, Franklin Roy *educational administrator*

Castine
Booth, Philip *poet, educator*
Davis, Peter Frank *filmmaker, author*
Hall, David *sound archivist, writer*
Wiswall, Frank Lawrence, Jr. *lawyer, educator*

Center Lovell
Adams, Herbert Ryan *management consultant, retired clergyman, educator, publishing executive*

Cumb Foreside
Dill, William Rankin *college president*
Harper, Ralph Champlin *retired banker*

Cushing
Magee, A. Alan *artist*

Damariscotta
Blake, Bud (Julian Watson) *cartoonist*
Haas, Warren James *librarian, consultant*
Hauschka, Theodore Spaeth *biologist, researcher, educator*
Johnson, Arthur Menzies *retired college president, historian, educator*
Robinson, Walter George *arts management and funding consultant*

East Blue Hill
Taylor, Samuel Albert *playwright*

East Boothbay
Eldred, Kenneth McKechnie *acoustical consultant*
Smith, Merlin Gale *engineering executive, researcher*

Ellsworth
Dudman, Richard Beebe *communications company executive, journalist*
Eustice, Russell Clifford *consulting company executive*
Goodyear, Austin *electronics and retail company executive*
Wiggins, James Russell *newspaper editor*

Fairfield
Gwadosky, Dan A. *state legislator*

Falmouth
Mansfield, Kenneth Eugene *retail executive*
Sadik, Marvin Sherwood *art consultant, former museum director*

Farmington
Kalikow, Theodora June *university president*

Freeport
Clark, Nancy Randall *former state legislator*
Gorman, Leon A. *mail order company executive*
Lea, Lola Stendig *lawyer*
Poole, Norman A. *retail executive*

Friendship
MacIlvaine, Chalmers Acheson *retired financial executive, former association executive*
Owen, Wadsworth *oceanographer, consultant*
†Walker, Douglass Willey *retired pediatrician-medical center administrator*

Gardiner
Nowell, Glenna Greely *librarian, consultant*

Gorham
Bearce, Jeana Dale *artist, educator*

Gouldsboro
Wexler, Ginia Davis *singer, association executive*

Hallowell
Treat, Sharon Anglin *state legislator*

Hampden
Brown, Robert Horatio *retired orthopedic surgeon*

Hartland
Larochelle, Richard Clement *tanning company executive*

Hebron
Farwell, Margaret Wheeler *elementary education educator*

Jefferson
Fiore, Joseph Albert *artist*

Kennebunk
Alling, Charles Booth, Jr. *management consultant*
Betts, Edward *artist*
Dyer, Robert Darlington *elementary education educator*
Escalet, Frank Diaz *art gallery owner, artist, educator*
McConnell, David M. *secondary school principal*

Kittery Point
Howells, William White *anthropology educator*

Leeds
Lynn, Robert Wood *theologian, educator, dean*

Lewiston
Baxter, William MacNeil *priest*
†Cassidy, James Edward *hospital executive*
Chute, Robert Maurice *retired biologist, educator, poet*
Gauvreau, Norman Paul *lawyer*
Harward, Donald *academic official*
Murray, Michael Peter *educator, economist*
Stauffer, Charles Henry *retired chemistry educator*

Lincoln
Kneeland, Douglas Eugene *retired newspaper editor*

Lincolnville
Nichols, David Arthur *mediator, retired state justice*
Williams, Robert Luther *city planning consultant*

Little Deer Isle
Mc Closkey, Robert *artist*

Machias
Hudson, Miles *special education educator*

Madawaska
†St. Jean, Andre *paper executive*
Vollmann, John Jacob, Jr. *cosmetic packaging executive*

Milbridge
Enslin, Theodore Vernon *poet*

Monhegan Island
Hudson, Jacqueline *artist*

Monmouth
Carlson, Marsha George *performing company executive*

New Harbor
Brown, Donald Vaughn *technical educator, engineering consultant*
Fradley, Frederick Macdonell *architect*
Lyford, Cabot *sculptor*

New Vineyard
West, Arthur James, II *biologist*

North Fryeburg
Bolomey, Roger Henry *sculptor*

North Yarmouth
Fecteau, Rosemary Louise *educational consultant*

Oakland
Albanese, J. Duke *school system administrator*
Koons, Donaldson *geologist, educator*
Poulin, Thomas Edward *marine engineer, state legislator, retail business owner*

Old Orchard Beach
Bartner, Jay B. *school system administrator*
Holmes, Reed M. *clergyman, former religious organization administrator*

Orient
Chenevert, Edward Valmore, Jr. *retired librarian, real estate broker*

Orono
Albright, Elaine McClay *dean*
Borns, Harold William, Jr. *geologist, educator*
Campana, Richard John *retired plant pathology educator, writer, consultant*
Clapham, William Montgomery *plant physiologist*
Coupe, John Donald *university official, economics educator*
Csavinszky, Peter John *physicist, educator*
Devino, William Stanley *economist, educator*
Goldstone, Sanford *psychology educator*
Hartgen, Vincent Andrew *museum director, educator, artist*
Hatlen, Burton Norval *English educator*
Hutchinson, Frederick Edward *university president*
Ives, Edward Dawson *folklore educator*
Knight, Fred Barrows *forester, entomologist, educator*
†Kornfield, Irv *zoology educator*
Norton, Stephen Allen *geological sciences educator*
Rauch, Charles Frederick, Jr. *academic official*
Rivard, William Charles *mechanical engineering educator*
Tarr, Charles Edwin *physicist, educator*
Weber, Jean MacPhail *museum director*
Wiersma, G. Bruce *dean, forest resources educator*
Wilson, Dorothy Clarke *author*

Oxford
Bensen, Pamela Parke *emergency medicine physician, educator*

Pejepscot
Chonko, Lorraine Nancy *state legislator*

Phippsburg
Mc Lanathan, Richard (Barton Kennedy) *author, consultant*
Schuman, Howard *sociologist, educator*

Port Clyde
Thon, William *artist*

Portland
Allen, Charles William *lawyer*
Bonney, Weston Leonard *bank executive*
Bradford, Carl O. *judge*
†Burns, Robert E. *bank executive*
Carter, Gene *federal judge*
Cecil, Alex Thomson *travel executive*
Chalfant, Edward Cole *bishop*
Chisholm, Colin Alexander Joseph, III *media professional*
Coffin, Frank Morey *federal judge*
Coughlan, Patrick Campbell *lawyer*
Crispin, Robert William *investment company executive*
DiMatteo, John R. *health facility administrator*
Durgin, Frank Albert, Jr. *economics educator*

Freilinger, James Edward *insurance and investments company executive*
Gerry, Joseph John *bishop*
Gilmore, Roger *academic administrator*
Glassman, Caroline Duby *state supreme court justice*
Goodman, James A. *federal judge*
Graffam, Ward Irving *lawyer*
Grosset, Alexander Donald, Jr. *banker*
Harte, Christopher McCutcheon *former newspaper executive, investment manager*
Haynes, Peter Lancaster *utility holding company executive*
Hirshon, Robert Edward *lawyer*
Hornby, David Brock *federal judge*
Kendrick, Peter Murray *communications executive, investor*
Lancaster, Ralph Ivan, Jr. *lawyer*
Loper, Merle William *law educator*
McDowell, Donald L. *hospital administrator*
McKusick, Vincent Lee *former state supreme judicial court chief justice, lawyer*
Mooers, Daniel William *lawyer*
Murray, Peter Loos *lawyer, educator*
Neavoll, George Franklin *newspaper editor*
Nixon, Philip Andrews *diversified company executive*
Nosanow, Barbara Shissler *museum director*
O'Leary, Edward Cornelius *bishop*
Orr, James F., III *insurance company executive*
Parks, George Richard *librarian*
Philbrick, Donald Lockey *lawyer*
Politis, Timothy Jude *insurance company executive*
Potter, Lillian Florence *business executive secretary*
Powell, Larson Merrill *investment advisory service executive*
Raisbeck, Gordon *systems engineer*
Roberts, David Glendenning *state supreme court justice*
Ryan, William J. *bank executive*
Santomenna, Robert Charles *lawyer*
Saufley, William Edward *banker, lawyer*
Schwanauer, Francis *philosopher, educator*
Shaffer, James Burgess *communications executive*
Shimada, Toshiyuki *orchestra conductor, music director*
Simmonds, Rae Nichols *musician, educator*
Skolnik, Barnet David *lawyer*
Smith, William Charles *lawyer*
Stier, Robert H., Jr. *lawyer*
Ureneck, Louis Adam *newspaper editor, newspaper executive*
Wathen, Daniel Everett *state supreme court chief justice*
Wroth, L(awrence) Kinvin *lawyer, educator*
Zarr, Melvyn *lawyer, educator*
Zieff, Ralph Morrison *psychologist*

Presque Isle
Donnelly, James Owen *state legislator, bank executive*
Gallagher, John *church administrator*

Prospect Harbor
Shipman, Charles William *chemical engineer*

Readfield
Metzler, Glenn Elam *minister*

Rockland
Collins, Samuel W., Jr. *judge*
Crosman, Christopher Byron *art museum administrator*
McGuigan, Charles James *rehabilitation therapist*
Taylor, Roger Conant *writer*

Rockport
Fernald, Harold Allen *publishing executive*
Jackson, David Pingree *publishing executive*
Swenson, Orvar *surgeon*

Saint Francis
Ellwood, Stephen Charles, IV *education educator*

Sanford
Zandman, Felix *electronics executive*

Scarborough
Brackett, Norman E. *retail company executive*
Farrington, Hugh G. *wholesale food and retail drug company executive*
Moody, James L., Jr. *retail food distribution company executive*

Sebago Lake
Murray, Wallace Shordon *publisher, educator*

Sedgwick
Mc Millan, Brockway *former communications executive*
Schroth, Thomas Nolan *editor*

South Berwick
Carroll, Gladys Hasty *author*

South Harpswell
Barnes, George William *architecture and engineering company executive*

South Portland
Connell, Lawrence *lawyer*
Dalbeck, Richard Bruce *insurance executive*
Katz, Steven Edward *psychiatrist, state health official*

Southwest Harbor
Delehanty, Edward John *investment company executive*

Springvale
Eastman, Harland Horace *former foreign service officer*

Spruce Head
Bird, John Adams *educational consultant*

Standish
Hart, Loring Edward *academic administrator*

Surry
Kilgore, John Edward, Jr. *former petroleum company executive*
Pickett, Betty Horenstein *psychologist*
Sopkin, George *cellist, music educator*

Whitcomb, Benjamin Bradford, Jr. *neurosurgeon*

Thorndike
Treleaven, Phillips Albert *retired publishing company executive*

Topsham
Tierney, James Edward *attorney general*

Union
Buchan, Ronald Forbes *preventive medicine physician*

Vinalhaven
Indiana, Robert *artist*

Waterville
Bassett, Charles Walker *English language educator*
Bennett, Miriam Frances *biologist, educator*
Cotter, William Reckling *college president*
Ezhaya, Joseph Bernard *brokerage house executive*
Gemery, Henry Albert *economics educator*
Hudson, Yeager *philosophy educator, minister*
Muehlner, Suanne Wilson *library director*
Zukowski, Walter Henry *administrative science educator*

Wells
Carleton, Joseph George, Jr. *lawyer, state legislator*
Grimes, William Alvan *retired state supreme court chief justice*
Neilson, Elizabeth Anastasia *health sciences educator, association executive, author, editor*

Windham
Henry, Harriet Putnam *judge*

Winthrop
Skeete, F. Herbert *bishop*

Wiscasset
Leslie, Seaver *artist*

Yarmouth
Hertz, Willard Joel *foundations and nonprofit organizations consultant*

York
†Peterson, Karen Ida *marketing research company executive*

York Beach
Davison, Nancy Reynolds *artist*
Dutton, Robert Edward, Jr. *medical educator*

York Harbor
Curtis, Edward Joseph, Jr. *gas industry executive, management consultant*

MARYLAND

Aberdeen
Bonsack, Rose Mary Hatem *state legislator, physician*

Aberdeen Proving Ground
Coburn, John G. *career officer*
Frasier, John T. *research administrator*
Hackley, Brennie Elias, Jr. *chemist*
Paules, Palmer L. *engineering director*
Steger, Ralph James *chemist*

Adamstown
Ohlke, Clarence Carl *public affairs consultant*

Adelphi
DeMonte, Vito J. *physical sciences research administrator*
Langenberg, Donald Newton *academic administrator, physicist*
Lyons, John W(inship) *government agency administrator, chemist*

Annapolis
Aery, Shaila Rosalie *state educational administrator*
Allen, John Loyd *technical engineering consultant*
Anderson, William Carl *association executive, environmental engineer, consultant*
†Athey, Tyras S. *state official*
Baldwin, John Ashby, Jr. *retired naval officer*
Barber, James Alden *military officer*
Boergers, Mary H. *senator*
Bontoyan, Warren Roberts *chemist, state laboratories administrator*
Brady, Frank Benton *retired technical society executive*
Brann, Eva Toni Helene *dean*
Brock, William Emerson *former secretary of labor*
Brunk, William Edward *astronomer*
Cabral, Judith Ann *telecommunications executive*
Cade, John A. *state senator*
Casey, Edward Dennis *newspaper editor*
Chambers, Ronald D. *book publishing executive*
Cheevers, James William *museum curator*
Clotworthy, John Harris *oceanographic consultant*
Colussy, Dan Alfred *aviation executive*
Coogle, Joseph Moore, Jr. *management consultant*
Coulter, James Bennett *state official*
Dembrow, Dana Lee *lawyer*
DiAiso, Robert Joseph *civil engineer*
Elder, Samuel Adams *physics educator*
Eldridge, John Cole *judge*
Ellis, George Fitzallen, Jr. *energy services company executive*
Evans, William Davidson, Jr. *lawyer*
Forehand, Jennie Meador *state legislator*
†Gallis, John Nicholas *naval officer, healthcare executive*
†Glendening, Parris Nelson *governor, political science educator*
Goldstein, Louis Lazarus *state official*
Granger, Robert Alan *aerospace engineer*
Groves, George L., Jr. *air freight service company executive*
†Hagan, Kenneth James *historian, museum director*
Henderson, William Boyd *engineering consulting company executive*
Hixson, Sheila Ellis *state legislator*
Ho, Louis Ting *mechanical engineer*
Hollinger, Paula Colodny *state senator*
Holmberg, Lawrence Oscar, Jr. *documentary film producer, photographer, writer*
Holmes, David Charles *broadcasting company executive*
†Holtgrewe, Henry Logan *urologist*
Howell, Barbara Fennema *research chemist*
Hutchinson, Leslie E *state legislator, fiscal programs manager, consultant*
Hyde, Lawrence Henry, Jr. *industrial company executive*
Jackson, Elmer Martin, Jr. *newspaper executive*
Jansson, John Phillip *architect, consultant*
Johnson, Bruce *engineering educator*
Johnson, David Simonds *meteorologist*
Jones, Sylvanus Benson *adjudicator, consultant*
Kapland, Mitchell Arthur *engineering firm executive*
Kelley, Delores Goodwin *state legislator*
Klima, Martha Scanlan *state legislator*
Koscianski, Leonard Joseph *artist*
Lapides, Julian Lee *state senator, lawyer*
Larson, Charles Robert *naval officer*
Lee, T. Girard *architect*
Levitan, Laurence *lawyer, former state senator*
Long, Robert Lyman John *naval officer*
Lustbader, Philip Lawrence *lawyer*
Madden, Martin Gerard *state legislator, insurance agent*
Maloney, Timothy Francis *state legislator, lawyer*
†Massie, Samuel Proctor, Jr. *chemistry educator*
Maurer, Lucille Darvin *state treasurer*
McAfee, Lawrance Wiley *finance executive*
McDonough, Joseph Corbett *former army officer, aviation consultant*
Meima, Ralph Chester, Jr. *corporate execuitve, former foreign service officer*
Menes, Pauline H. *state legislator*
Mitchell, R. Clayton, Jr. *state legislator*
Moellering, John Henry *aviation maintenance company executive*
Montague, Brian John *consulting company executive*
Montague, Kenneth Charles *congressman*
Morgan, John Stephen *state representative, materials science researcher*
Muller, Richard W. (Wilhelm Gustav Muller) *retired textile importer*
Murphy, Robert C(harles) *judge*
Ness, Frederic William *former academic administrator, educator, consultant*
Nuesse, Celestine Joseph *retired university official*
Papenfuse, Edward Carl, Jr. *archivist, state official*
Papet, Louis M. *federal official, civil engineer*
Perry, Marsha Gratz *legislator, professional skating coach*
†Pierce, James Lee *engineering and information systems company executive*
Roesser, Jean Wolberg *state legislator*
Rowell, Charles Frederick *chemistry educator*
Ruben, Ida Gass *state senator*
†Russell, William T. *government executive, nuclear engineer*
Schleicher, Nora Elizabeth *banker, treasurer, accountant*
Shea, Walter James *labor union executive*
Sheppard, John Wilbur *computer research scientist*
Steinberg, Melvin Allen *lieutenant governor, lawyer*
Taussig, Joseph Knefler, Jr. *retired government official, lawyer*
†Townsend, Kathleen Kennedy *state official*
Waugh, Robert James *aerospace company executive*
Weitzel, Harry John, Jr. *banker*
Werking, Richard Hume *librarian, historian, academic administrator*
Wilkes, Joseph Allen *architect*
Winegrad, Gerald William *lawyer, state senator, educator*

Arnold
Barrett, John Anthony *printing company financial executive*
Green, John Cawley *lawyer*
Smith, Clifford Lee *clergyman*

Ashton
Leibowitz, Jack Richard *physicist, educator*

Baldwin
Bressler, Philip Jack *food products executive, consultant*

Baltimore
Abato, F. Rozann *federal government administrator, nurse*
Abeloff, Martin David *medical administrator, educator, researcher*
Abrams, Rosalie Silber *state agency administrator*
Achinstein, Peter Jacob *philosopher, educator*
Adams, Harold Lynn *architect*
Adkins, Edward James *lawyer*
†Adkinson, N. Franklin, Jr. *clinical immunologist*
Ahearn, John Stephen *research physicist*
Albinak, Marvin Joseph *chemistry educator*
Allen, Ronald John *astrophysics educator, researcher*
Alliker, Stanford Arnold *hospital administrator*
Ambler, Bruce Melville *finance company executive*
†Amprey, Walter G. *school system administrator*
Anderson, Gary Dean *architect, planner, educator*
Anderson, Gerard Fenton *economist, university program administrator*
Anderson, John William *protective services official*
Anderson, Wilda Christine *French literature educator*
Andres, Reubin *gerontologist*
Angelos, Peter G. *lawyer*
Apgar, Mahlon, IV *real estate management counselor*
†Applebaum, Gary E. *medical director, executive*
Archibald, James Kenway *lawyer*
Astrachan, James Barry *lawyer*
†August, Joseph Thomas *pharmacology educator*
Ayers, Richard Winston *architect*
Ayres, Jeffrey Peabody *lawyer*
Bachur, Nicholas Robert, Sr. *research physician*
Bacigalupo, Charles Anthony *brokerage company executive*
Backas, James Jacob *foundation administrator*
Badder, Susan Stevenson *art historian, educator*
Baines, Harold Douglass *professional baseball player*
Bair, Robert Rippel *lawyer*
Baker, R. Robinson *surgeon*
Baker, Susan P. *public health educator*
Baker, Timothy Danforth *physician, educator*
Baldwin, Henry Furlong *banker*
Baldwin, John Chandler *lawyer*
Baldwin, John Wesley *history educator*
†Ballantyne, Harry Clay *actuary*
Barber, John Merrell *banker*
Barker, Stephen Francis *philosophy educator*
Barnhouse, Robert Bolon *lawyer*
Bart, Polly Turner *commercial real estate developer*
Barth, John Simmons *writer, educator*
Bartlett, James Wilson, III *lawyer*
Bastedo, Ralph W(alter) *museum administrator, educator*
Battle, Mark Garvey *social services executive*
Bayless, Theodore M(orris) *gastroenterologist, educator, researcher*
Beall, George *lawyer*
Beasley, Robert Scott *financial executive*
Beckenstein, Myron *journalist*
Beemon, Karen Louise *biology educator*
Beer, Michael *biophysicist, educator*
Behm, Mark Edward *university administrator, consultant*
Benton, George Stock *meteorologist, educator*
Bereston, Eugene Sydney *dermatologist*
Berg, Jeremy M. *chemistry educator*
†Berger, Stuart David *school superintendent*
Berlin, Fred Saul *psychiatrist*
Berman, Barnett *internist, educator*
Berman, Barry David *lawyer*
Bernhardt, Herbert Nelson *lawyer, educator*
Bigelow, George E. *psychology and pharmacology scientist*
Black, Walter Evan, Jr. *federal judge*
Blake, Catherine C. *judge*
Blake, Norman Perkins, Jr. *finance company executive*
Blanton, Edward Lee, Jr. *lawyer*
Block, James A. *hospital administrator, pediatrician*
Blumenfeld, Barry Jay *physics educator*
Boardman, John Michael *mathematician, educator*
Boone, Harold Thomas *retired lawyer*
Bor, Jonathan Steven *journalist*
Borden, Ernest Carleton *physician, educator*
†Boughman, Joann Ashley *dean*
Bowen, Kit Hansel, Jr. *chemistry educator*
Bowen, Lowell Reed *lawyer*
Bradley, Thomas Andrew *insurance company executive*
Brady, Joseph Vincent *behavioral biologist, educator*
Bramble, Frank P. *bank executive*
Brand, Ludwig *biology educator, biophysicist*
Bready, James Hall *reporter*
Breitenecker, Rudiger *pathologist*
Brewster, Gerry Leiper *lawyer*
Bridges, Leon *architect*
Brieger, Gert Henry *medical historian, educator*
Bright, Margaret *sociologist*
Brinkley, James Wellons *investment company executive*
Brock, Mary Anne *research biologist, consultant*
Brody, Eugene B. *psychiatrist, educator*
Brotman, Phyllis Block *advertising and public relations executive*
Brown, Donald David *biology educator*
Brown, Florence S. *librarian, administrator*
Brown, John Walter *vocational education supervisor*
†Brown, Robert Alan *physicist*
Brumbaugh, John Maynard *lawyer, educator*
Brunson, Dorothy Edwards *broadcasting executive*
Brush, Lucien Munson, Jr. *hydrologist, educator*
Brusilow, Saul *pediatrics educator*
Burch, Francis Boucher, Jr. *lawyer*
Byrnes, Robert Michael *diversified manufacturing company executive*
Byrnes, William Gerard *investment banker*
Cacossa, Anthony Alexander *Romance languages educator*
Cahill, William Walsh, Jr. *lawyer*
Cain, Rosa Marie *nurse, educator*
†Cameron, John Lemuel *general surgeon*
Campazzi, Earl James *physician*
Carbine, James Edmond *lawyer*
Cardin, Meyer M. *retired judge*
Carey, Anthony Morris *lawyer*
Carey, Jana Howard *lawyer*
Carlin, Paul Victor *legal association executive*
Carlton, Sara Boehlke *rehabilitation services administrator*
Carney, Bradford George Yost *lawyer, educator*
Carroll, John Sawyer *newspaper editor*
Cashman, Edmund Joseph, Jr. *investment banker*
Castro-Klaren, Sara *Latin American literature educator*
Catania, A(nthony) Charles *psychology educator*
Chapanis, Alphonse *human factors engineer, ergonomist*
Chaplin, Peggy Fannon *lawyer*
Charache, Samuel *hematologist*
Chartrand, Mark Ray *astronomer, telecommunications consultant*
Chater, Shirley Sears *federal commissioner*
Chavis, Benjamin Franklin, Jr. *civil rights advocate, minister*
Chiarello, Donald Frederick *lawyer*
Chien, Chia-Ling *physics educator*
Chien, Chih-Yung *physics educator, researcher*
Childs, Barton *physician, educator*
Chisolm, James Julian, Jr. *pediatrics educator*
Chiu, Hungdah *lawyer, legal educator*
Chylinski-Polubinski, Roger *academic administrator*
Civiletti, Benjamin R. *lawyer, former U.S. attorney general*
Clapp, Roger Alvin *lawyer*
Clark, Gilbert Michael *association executive, lawyer*
Clark, Raymond Skinner *retired transportation and distribution company executive*
Clements, Mary Lou *epidemiologist, educator*
Coe, Ward Baldwin, Jr. *retired lawyer*
Cohen, Warren I. *history educator*
Cole, Charles W., Jr. *bank holding company executive*
Colhoun, Howard Post *financial executive*
Collins, George Joseph *investment counselor*
†Colombani, Paul Michael *general pediatric and transplant surgeon*
Cone, Richard Allen *biophysics educator*
Conley, Carroll Lockard *physician, emeritus educator*
Connaughton, James Patrick *psychiatrist*
Cook, Bryson Leitch *lawyer*
Cooper, Jerrold Stephen *historian, educator*
Cooper, Joseph *political scientist, educator*
Corn, Morton *environmental engineer, educator*
Cornblath, Marvin *pediatrician, educator*
Couper, William *banker*
Creagh, David Michael *public radio executive*
Crenshaw, Marion Carlyle, Jr. *obstetrician, educator*
Crenson, Matthew Allen *political science educator*
Crooke, Edward A. *utility company executive*
Cropper, M. Elizabeth *art history educator*
Crowe, Thomas Leonard *lawyer*
Cruz, Bobby *professional boxer*
Cullen, James Patrick *international trading company executive*

Cummings, Charles William physician, educator
Cunningham, M(urray) Hunt, Jr. aerospace company executive, mechanical engineer, author
†Cunningham, Terence Thomas, III hospital administrator
Curley, John Francis, Jr. securities company executive
Curran, J. Joseph, Jr. state attorney general
Curran, Robert Bruce lawyer
Dagdigian, Paul Joseph chemistry educator
Dailey, George R., Jr. insurance company executive
Dale, James Michael advertising executive, writer
Dall'Acqua, Charles Robert marketing executive
Daly, Warren B., Jr. lawyer
Dannenberg, Arthur Milton, Jr. experimental pathologist, immunologist, educator
Davis, Ada Romaine nursing educator
Davison, Warren Malcolm lawyer
Degenford, James Edward electrical engineer, educator
Delpit, Lisa D. education educator, researcher, consultant
Dempsey, Charles Gates art historian, educator
Deoul, Neal electronics company executive
Derby, Ernest Stephen federal judge
Desoto, Clinton Burgel psychologist, educator
Dicello, John Francis, Jr. physicist, educator
Dickman, James Gary marketing professional
Dietze, Gottfried political science educator
Digges, Dudley Perkins retired editor
Dilloff, Neil Joel lawyer
DiPentima, Renato Anthony government agency official
Ditz, Toby Lee history educator
Dodge, Calvert Renaul education and training executive, author, educator
Dodge, Douglas Walker banker
Domokos, Gabor research physicist
Donkervoet, Richard Cornelius architect
Donohue, Marc David chemical engineering educator
Doory, Robert Leonard, Jr. lawyer
Dorsey, John Russell art critic, journalist
Dorst, John Phillips physician, radiology and pediatrics educator
Dunne, Richard Edwin, III lawyer
Eanes, Joseph Cabel, Jr. surety company executive
Ebinger, Mary Ritzman pastoral counselor
Edidin, Michael Aaron biologist
Eichhorn, Gunther Louis chemist
Eisenberg, Howard Michael neurosurgeon
Eisner, Henry Wolfgang advertising executive
†Eleff, Scott Marshall anesthesiology educator, brain damage researcher
Elias, Amy Pumpian public relations executive
Ellin, Marvin lawyer
Ellingwood, Bruce Russell structural engineering researcher
Engel, Bernard Theodore psychologist, educator
Engel, Paul Bernard lawyer
Englund, Paul Theodore biochemist, educator
Entwisle, Doris Roberts sociology educator
Epstein, Daniel Mark poet, dramatist
†Evers-Williams, Myrlie cultural organization administrator
†Eyler, James R. lawyer
Fambrough, Douglas McIntosh, Jr. biology educator, researcher
†Fantry, George Thomas gastroenterologist
Fedoroff, Nina Vsevolod research scientist, consultant
Feldman, Gordon physics educator
†Feldman, Paul Donald physics educator, research astronomer
Felsenthal, Gerald physiatrist, educator
Fenselau, Catherine Clarke chemistry educator
Fenton, Charles E. lawyer
Fergenson, Arthur Friend lawyer
Ferrara, Steven educational administrator, researcher, consultant
Files, Jon M. utilities executive
Finch, Walter Goss Gilchrist lawyer, engineer, accountant, retired army officer
Finnerty, Joseph Gregory, Jr. lawyer
Fishbein, Estelle Ackerman lawyer
Fisher, George Wescott geology educator
Fisher, Jack Carrington environmental engineering educator
Fisher, Jay McKean museum curator
Fisher, Morton Poe, Jr. lawyer
Fishman, Bernard Philip museum director
Fishman, Jacob Robert psychiatrist, educator, corporate executive, investor
Fitzgerald, Thomas Rollins university administrator
Flathman, Richard Earl political science educator
Fleishman, Avrom Hirsch English educator
Ford, John Gilmore interior designer
Foreman, Ellen S. manufacturing executive
Forster, Robert history educator
Fowler, Bruce Andrew toxicologist, marine biologist
Frank, Jerome David psychiatrist, educator
Frank, Robert Allen real estate securities investment analyst
Franyo, Richard Louis investment banker
Freeman, John Mark pediatric neurologist
Fried, Herbert Daniel advertising executive
Friedman, Louis Frank lawyer
Fuentealba, Victor William professional society administrator
†Fulton, Thomas theoretical physicist, educator
Gall, Joseph Grafton biologist, researcher, educator
Garbis, Marvin Joseph federal judge
Gardner, R. H. (Rufus Hallette Gardner, III) retired drama and film critic
Gately, Mark Donohue lawyer
Gauvey, Susan K. lawyer
Gaver, Barbara Anne child and adolescent psychotherapist
Gibbons, Thomas Michael communications executive
Giddens, Don Peyton engineering educator, researcher
†Gidwitz, John David symphony orchestra executive
Gillece, James Patrick, Jr. lawyer
Ginsberg, Benjamin political science educator
Glasgow, Jesse Edward newspaper editor
Glassgold, Israel Leon construction company executive, engineer, consultant
Glynn, Edward college administrator
Godenne, Ghislaine Dudley physician, psychoanalyst
Goedicke, Hans archeology educator
Goellner, Jack Gordon publishing executive
Goldberg, Alan Marvin toxicologist, educator
Goldberg, Jonathan English literature educator
Goldberg, Morton Falk ophthalmologist, educator
Goldman, Brian Arthur lawyer, accountant
Goldscheider, Sidney lawyer
Goldstein, Franklin lawyer
Goldstein, Gary W. rehabilitation research administrator
Gordis, Leon physician
Graham, George Gordon physician
Graham, Jerry Fisher bank executive, accountant
Graham, John Stuart, III lawyer
Grasmick, Nancy S. superintendent of schools
Graves, Pirkko Maija-Leena clinical psychologist, psychoanalyst
Gray, Carol Joyce nurse, educator
Gray, Dahli accounting educator and administrator
Gray, Frank Truan lawyer
Green, Benjamin Louis wholesale food distribution executive
Green, Bernard food products executive
Green, Bert Franklin, Jr. psychologist
Green, Robert Edward, Jr. physicist, educator
Greene, Jack Phillip historian, educator
Greenough, William Bates, III medical educator
Greenspan, Arnold Michael computer company executive
Grieb, Elizabeth lawyer
Griffin, Diane Edmund research physician, virologist, educator
Griffith, Lawrence Stacey Cameron cardiologist
Griswold, Benjamin Howell, IV investment banker
Grossman, Allen Richard poet, educator
Grossman, Lawrence biochemist, educator
Guest, James Alfred public service official
†Guggino, William Biagio medical administrator, physiology educator
Habermann, Helen Margaret plant physiologist, educator
Hafets, Richard Jay lawyer
Haig, Frank Rawle physics educator, clergyman
Haines, Thomas W. W. lawyer
Hale, Danny Lyman bank executive
Hall, Merrill Souel, III head master
Hall, Richard Leland food processing company consultant
†Hall, Wiley A. columnist, journalist
†Handelsman, Jacob Charles surgeon
Hanks, James Judge, Jr. lawyer
Hanle, Paul Arthur museum administrator
Hansen, Barbara Caleen physiology educator, scientist
Hansen, Jeanne Bodine retired counselor
Hargrove, John R. federal judge
Harmening, Denise M. academic administrator, educator
Harp, Solomon, III airport executive
†Harris, Milton Michael management consultant
Harrison, Michael opera company executive
Hart, Robert Gordon federal agency administrator
Hartigan, Grace artist
Hartman, Charles Henry association executive, educator
Hartman, Philip Emil biology educator
Harvey, Abner McGehee physician, educator
Harvey, Alexander, II federal judge
Harvey, Robert Dixon Hopkins banker
Hayes, Charles Lawton insurance company executive, holding company executive
†Hayes, Dennis C. lawyer
Haysbert, Raymond Victor food company executive
Hebb, Donald Bruce, Jr. investment banker
Hecht, Alan Dannenberg insurance executive
Heckman, Timothy Martin astronomy and physics educator
Helrich, Martin anesthesiologist, educator
†Henderson, Duncan airport administrator
Henderson, Lenneal Joseph, Jr. political science educator
†Henderson, Robin pediatrics educator, pediatric nutritionist
Henry, Richard Conn astrophysicist, educator
Heptinstall, Robert Hodgson physician
Higham, John history educator
Hilgenberg, Eve Brantly Handy government official
Hillers, Delbert Roy Near East language educator
Hillman, Robert Sandor lawyer
Himelfarb, Richard Jay securities firm executive
Hirsch, Richard Arthur mechanical engineer
Hirsh, Allan T., III book publisher
Hirsh, Allan Thurman, Jr. publishing executive
Hirsh, Theodore William lawyer
Hochberg, Bayard Zabdial lawyer
Honemann, Daniel Henry lawyer
Hooper, William Edwin advertising agency executive
Hopkins, Samuel retired investment banker
Houck, John Roland clergyman
Howard, J. Woodford, Jr. political science educator
Huang, Pien Chien biochemistry educator, scientist
Huang, Ru Chih Chow molecular biology educator
Hubbard, Herbert Hendrix lawyer
Hug, Richard Ernest environmental company executive
Huggins, William Herbert electrical engineering educator
Hughes, Harry Roe lawyer
Hulse, Stewart Harding, Jr. educator, experimental psychologist
Hungerford, David Samuel orthopaedic surgeon, educator
Hussels Maumenee, Irene E. ophthalmology educator
Hutchins, Grover MacGregor pathologist, educator
Hyman, Harris, IV investment banker
Igusa, Jun-Ichi mathematician, educator
Ihrie, Robert oil, gas and real estate company executive
Immelt, Stephen J. lawyer
Inglehart, Lorretta Jeannette physicist
Irwin, John Thomas humanities educator
Ivey, Jean Eichelberger composer
Jacobs, Richard James banker, educator
Jacox, Ada Kathryn nurse, educator
Jelinek, Frederick electrical engineer, educator
Jenkins, Benjamin Larry insurance company executive
Jensen, Arthur Seigfried consulting engineering physicist
Jernigan, Kenneth association executive
Johns, Carol Johnson physician, educator
Johns, Michael Marieb Edward otolaryngologist, university dean
Johns, Richard James physician
Johnson, Kenneth Peter neurologist, medical researcher
Johnson, Michael Paul history educator
Johnston, George W. lawyer
Johnston, William Ralph museum curator
Jones, John Martin, Jr. lawyer
Jones, Raymond Moylan strategy and public policy educator
Joseph, Richard Isaac electrical engineering and computer science educator
Judd, Brian Raymond physicist, educator
Judson, Horace Freeland history of science, writer, educator
Junghans, Paula Marie lawyer
Kagan, Richard Lauren history educator
Kaplan, Alexander Efimovich physics educator, engineering educator
Karni, Edi economics educator
Kastor, John Alfred cardiologist, educator
Katz, Joseph Louis chemical engineer, educator
Katz, Richard Stephen political science educator
Kaufman, Frank Albert federal judge
Keller, George Charles higher education consultant, editor
Keller, Robert community organization adminstrator
Kelly, Thomas Jesse, Jr. molecular biologist
Kent, Edgar Robert, Jr. investment banker
Kessler, Herbert Leon art historian, educator
Khan, Mohammed Ali economics educator
Kidd, Langford pediatrician, cardiologist, educator
Killebrew, Robert Sterling, Jr. investment manager
Kim, Chung Wook physics educator, researcher
King, Ora Sterling education educator
Kingsbury, David T. microbiologist, science administrator
Kinnard, William James, Jr. pharmacy educator
Kirk, Robert L. rail transportation executive
Klarman, Herbert Elias economist, educator
Kleiner, Arnold Joel television executive
Klitzke, Theodore Elmer former college dean, arts consultant
Knapp, David Allan pharmaceutical educator, researcher
Knight, Franklin W. history educator
Knoedler, Elmer L. retired chemical engineer
Kohn, Melvin L. sociologist
Kosaraju, S. Rao computer science educator, researcher
Koski, Walter S. chemistry educator, scientist
Kowal, Charles Thomas astronomer
Kowal, Robert Paul hospital administrator
Kowarski, Allen Avinoam endocrinologist, educator
Kramer, Morton biostatistician, epidemiologist
Krolik, Julian Henry astrophysicist, educator
Kruger, Jerome materials science educator, consultant
Kues, Irvin William health care financial executive
Kumin, Libby Barbara speech language pathologist, educator
Kurth, Lieselotte foreign language educator
Kwiterovich, Peter Oscar, Jr. medical science educator, researcher, physician
Lafferty, Joyce G. Zvonar retired educator
†Lakatta, Edward Gerard biomedical researcher
Lamp, Frederick John museum curator
Lane, Malcolm Daniel biological chemistry educator
Larrabee, Martin Glover biophysics educator
Lavin, Charles Blaise, Jr. realtor, association executive
Lawrence, Robert Swan physician, educator, academic administrator
Lazarus, Fred, IV college president
Lebowitz, Harvey M. lawyer
Lee, Yung-Keun physicist, educator
Legg, Benson Everett federal judge
Legum, Jeffrey Alfred automobile company executive
Lehman, Arnold Lester museum official, art historian
Lemer, Andrew Charles engineer, economist
Leonard, John Wirth English educator, retailer
Levin, Betsy lawyer, educator, university dean
Levin, Edward Jesse lawyer
Levine, Richard E. lawyer
Lewis, Alexander Ingersoll, III lawyer
Liberto, Joseph Salvatore banker
Lichtenstein, Lawrence Mark allergy, immunology educator, physician
Lidtke, Doris Keefe computer science educator
Lidtke, Vernon LeRoy history educator
Liebmann, George William lawyer
Lin, Shin biophysics educator
Littlefield, John Walley physiology educator, geneticist, cell biologist, pediatrician
Loewy, Steven A. lawyer
†Loftus, Donald Gregory hospital administrator
Lohr, Walter George, Jr. lawyer
Long, Donlin Martin surgeon, educator
Love, Warner Edwards biophysics educator
Lucas, Barbara B. electrical equipment manufacturing executive
Luck, Georg Hans Bhawani classics educator
Lyle, Charles Thomas association executive
Maccini, Louis John economic educator
Machen, Arthur Webster, Jr. lawyer
Macleod, Donald clergyman, educator
Madansky, Leon particle physicist, educator
Magida, Arthur Jay newspaper editor, writer
Magnuson, Nancy librarian
Maletz, Herbert Naaman federal judge
Mallette, Phyllis Cooper Spencer medical/surgical nurse
Marimow, William Kalmon journalist
Marriot, Salima Siler state legislator, social work educator
Marsh, Bruce David geologist, educator
Martin, Emily anthropologist, educator
Martin, George Reilly federal agency administrator
Maslen, Stephen Harold research engineer, consultant
Mason, Raymond Adams brokerage company executive
Massof, Robert William neuroscientist, educator
Maurer, Marc Morgan federation administrator, lawyer
McCarter, P(ete) Kyle, Jr. Near Eastern studies educator
McCarthy, Carol M. health care association executive, lawyer
McCarty, Harry Downman tool manufacturing company executive
McCarty, Richard Earl biochemist, biochemistry educator
McClung, A(lexander) Keith, Jr. lawyer
Mc Cord, Kenneth Armstrong consulting engineer
McDowell, Elizabeth Mary pathology educator
McGowan, George Vincent public utility executive
McGuire, Charles Carroll, Jr. banking executive
McGuirk, Ronald Charles banker
Mc Hugh, Paul R. psychiatrist, neurologist, educator
Mc Kenney, Walter Gibbs, Jr. lawyer, publishing company executive
McKhann, Guy Mead physician, educator
McKinney, Richard Ishmael philosophy educator
McManus, Walter Leonard investment executive
McPartland, James Michael university official
McPherson, Donald Paxton, III lawyer
McWilliams, John Michael lawyer
Medani, Charles Richard pediatric nephrology educator
Meehan, David Howard insurance company executive
Melvin, Norman Cecil lawyer
Merritt, Betty L. medical/surgical and mental health nurse
Meyer, Jean-Pierre Gustave mathematician, educator
Migeon, Claude Jean pediatrics educator
Miller, Decatur Howard lawyer
Miller, Edward Doring, Jr. anesthesiologist
Milnor, William Robert physician
Mintz, Sidney Wilfred anthropologist
Mocko, George Paul minister
Mogol, Alan Jay lawyer
†Mohraz, Judy Jolley college president
Money, John William psychologist
Monroe, Russell Ronald psychiatrist, educator
Montgomery, Paula Kay school editor, publishing executive
Moos, H. Warren physicist, astronomer, educator, administrator
Moreland, Ernest Ferman dean
Morrel, William Griffin, Jr. banker
Morris, Edwin Thaddeus construction consultant
Moser, Hugo Wolfgang physician
Moser, M(artin) Peter lawyer
Moszkowski, Lena Iggers secondary school educator
†Motz, Diana Gribbon judge
Motz, John Frederick federal judge
Moudrianakis, Evangelos N. cell biology and biochemistry educator, biomedical researcher
†Mulholland, John Henry physician, educator
Mulligan, Joseph Francis physics educator
Munster, Andrew Michael surgeon, educator
Murnaghan, Francis Dominic, Jr. federal judge
Murphy, Philip Francis bishop
Murray, Joseph William banker
Mussina, Michael Cole professional baseball player
Nägele, Rainer German and comparative literary educator
Nathans, Daniel biologist
Nathanson, Constance A. health science organization administrator, sociology educator
†Nevin, Joseph Francis computer systems engineer
Newhall, Charles Watson, III venture capitalist
Newman, William C. bishop
Nichols, Stephen George Romance languages educator
Nickerson, William Milnor federal judge
Nickon, Alex chemist, educator
Niemeyer, Paul Victor federal judge
Nilson, George Albert lawyer
Norman, Colin Arthur astrophysics educator
Norman, Philip Sidney physician
Northrop, Edward Skottowe federal judge
Nuckolls, Robert Theodore cemetery executive
Ober, Douglas Gary investment company executive
O'Connell, Kevin Michael lawyer
O'Hare, Thomas J(ames), Jr. federal commissioner
Ohly, D. Christopher lawyer
O'Keefe, Kevin public relations executive
Orman, Leonard Arnold lawyer
Oski, Frank Aram physician, educator
Ott, John Harlow museum administrator
Owen, Stephen Lee lawyer
Owens, Albert Henry, Jr. oncologist, educator
Pappas, George Frank lawyer
Park, Mary Woodfill information consultant
Passano, E. Magruder, Jr. publishing executive
Passano, Edward Magruder printing company executive
Paternotte, William Leslie brokerage house executive
Patz, Arnall physician
Patz, Edward Frank lawyer
Paulson, Ronald Howard English and humanities educator
Peabody, Robert Lee political science educator, researcher
Peck, James Stevenson banker
Peirce, Carol Marshall English educator
Permutt, Solbert physiologist, physician
Pettijohn, Francis John geology educator
Pevsner, Aihud physicist, educator
Phillips, Owen Martin oceanographer, geophysicist, educator
†Pierce, Ruth A. federal agency administrator
†Pinkard, Walter Devier, Jr. real estate executive
Piotrow, Phyllis Tilson public health educator, international development specialist
Pittman, Carolyn artist
Plant, Albin MacDonough lawyer
Platt, William Rady pathology educator
Plummer, Risque Wilson lawyer
Pocock, John Greville Agard historian, educator
Poindexter, Christian Herndon utility company executive
Pokempner, Joseph Kres lawyer
Pollak, Mark lawyer
Pollard, Shirley employment training director, consultant
Pollard, Thomas Dean biologist, educator
Popel, Aleksander S. engineering educator
Portes, Alejandro sociologist, educator
Posner, Gary Herbert chemist, educator
Prendergast, Robert A. pathologist educator
Preston, Mark I. investment company executive
Price, Leigh banker
Price, Thomas Ransone neurologist, educator
Prince, Charles O., III lawyer
Prince, Jerry Ladd engineering educator
Privalov, Peter L. biology and biophysics educator
Proctor, Donald Frederick otolaryngology educator, physician
Proctor, Kenneth Donald lawyer
Provorny, Frederick Alan lawyer
†Provost, Thomas Taylor dermatology educator, researcher
Putzel, Constance Kellner lawyer
Quinn, Michael Desmond diversified financial services executive
Rabb, Bernard Paul book publisher, consultant
Rafferty, William Bernard lawyer
Randall, Lilian Maria Charlotte museum curator
Rank, Larry Gene executive director
Ranum, Orest Allen historian, educator
Ray, Robert Franklin banker
Rayson, Glendon Ennes internist, preventive medicine specialist, writer
Redden, Roger Duffey lawyer
Redman, Barbara Klug nursing educator
Reeder, Ellen Dryden museum curator
Reeder, Oliver Howard paint products manufacturing executive
Reese, Errol Lynn university administrator, dentist
†Regan, Philip Raymond professional baseball coach
†Reich, Daniel H. physics educator
Rennels, Marshall Leigh neuroanatomist, biomedical scientist, educator
Reno, Russell Ronald, Jr. lawyer

ReVelle, Charles S. *environmental engineer, geophysicist, systems analysis and economics educator*
Reynolds, William Leroy *lawyer, educator*
Ricard, John H. *bishop, educator*
Richardson, Brenda *musuem administrator*
Richardson, Loretta M. *college dean, medical/surgical nurse*
Richardson, William Chase *university administrator*
Richlin, W. Gar *investment banking executive, lawyer*
Riepe, James Sellers *investment company executive*
Ripken, Calvin Edwin, Jr. (Cal Ripken) *professional baseball player*
Robinson, Dean Wentworth *chemist, educator*
Robinson, Frank *professional baseball team executive, former coach, former player*
Rodowsky, Lawrence Francis *judge*
Rodricks, Daniel John *columnist, television commentator*
†Rose, Sister Cecilia *healthcare management administrator*
Rose, Hugh *retired economics educator*
Rose, Noel Richard *immunologist, microbiologist, educator*
Roseman, Saul *biochemist, educator*
Rosenberg, Henry A., Jr. *petroleum executive*
Rosenstein, Beryl Joel *physician*
Rosenthal, William J. *lawyer*
Ross, Dorothy *history educator*
Ross, Richard Starr *medical school dean emeritus, physician, cardiologist*
Roth, George Stanley *research biochemist, physiologist*
Rothschild, Amalie Rosenfeld *artist*
Rousuck, J. Wynn *theater critic*
Rugh, Wilson John, II *electrical engineering educator*
Russell-Wood, Anthony John R. *history educator*
†Rutledge, Brian Aaron *zoo director*
Ryan, Judith W. *geriatrics nurse, adult nurse practitioner, educator, researcher*
Sack, Sylvan Hanan *lawyer*
Sagett, Jan Jeffrey *lawyer, former government official*
†St. John, David Marshall *poet, English educator*
Salamon, Lester Milton *political science educator*
Sandler, Paul Mark *lawyer*
†Sanfilippo, Alfred Paul *pathologist, educator*
Schaefer, Robert Wayne *banker*
Scheeler, Charles *construction company executive*
Schimpff, Stephen Callender *internist, oncologist*
Schleif, Robert F. *biology educator*
Schmoke, Kurt L. *mayor*
Schneewind, Jerome Borges *philosophy educator*
Schoenrich, Edyth Hull *academic administrator, physician*
Scott, Frederick Isadore, Jr. *editor, business executive*
Scriggins, Larry Palmer *lawyer*
Seaman, Tony *university athletic coach*
Semans, Truman Thomas *investment company executive*
Sfekas, Stephen James *lawyer*
Shaeffer, Charles Wayne *investment counselor*
Shamoo, Adil Elias *biochemist, biophysicist, educator*
Shapiro, Harry Dean *lawyer*
Shapiro, Sam *health care analyst, biostatistician*
Sharfstein, Steven Samuel *health care executive, medical director*
Sharpe, Donald Edward *lawyer*
Sharpe, William Norman, Jr. *mechanical engineer, educator*
Shattuck, Mayo Adams, III *investment banking executive*
Shiffman, Bernard *mathematician, educator*
Shokurov, Vyacheslav Vladimirovich *mathematics educator*
Short, Alexander Campbell *lawyer*
Silbergeld, Ellen Kovner *environmental epidemiologist and toxicologist*
Silverstein, Arthur Matthew *ophthalmic immunologist, educator, historian*
Silverstone, Harris J. *chemistry educator*
Simon, David *principal*
†Simpson, Thomas William *physician*
Slatkin, Murray *paint sundry distribution executive*
Slepian, Paul *mathematician, educator*
Smalkin, Frederic N. *federal judge*
Smith, Elmer W. *federal government administrator*
Smith, Gardner Watkins *physician*
Smith, Hamilton Othanel *molecular biologist, educator*
Smith, Hoke LaFollette *university president*
Smith, James F. *oil industry executive*
Smith, Julian Payne *gynecological oncologist, educator*
Smouse, H(ervey) Russell *lawyer*
Snead, James Arrington *architect*
Snyder, Solomon Halbert *psychiatrist, pharmacologist*
Snyder, William Russell *oil company executive*
Somerville, Romaine Stec *arts administrator*
Sommer, Alfred *public health professional, ophthalmologist, epidemiologist*
Sorkin, Alan Lowell *economist, educator*
Spicer, Joaneath A. *museum curator*
Stalfort, John Arthur *lawyer*
Stanley, Jay *sociologist, educator*
Stanley, Julian Cecil, Jr. *psychology educator*
Stanley, Steven Mitchell *paleobiologist, educator*
Starfield, Barbara Helen *physician, educator*
Stein, Bernard Alvin *business consultant*
Steiner, Robert Frank *biochemist*
Steinwachs, Donald Michael *public health educator*
Sternberger, Ludwig Amadeus *neurologist, educator*
Sterne, Joseph Robert Livingston *newspaper editor*
Stevens, Elisabeth Goss (Mrs. Robert Schleussner, Jr.) *writer, journalist*
Stewart, C(ornelius) Van Leuven *lawyer*
Stewart, Doris Mae *biology educator*
Stobo, John David *physician, educator*
Stolley, Paul David *medical educator, researcher*
Stone, Norman R., Jr. *state legislator*
†Storrs, Alexander David *astronomer*
Strickland, George Thomas, Jr. *physician, researcher, educator*
Strickland, Marshall Hayward *bishop*
Strull, Gene *technology consultant, retired electrical manufacturing company executive*
Suskind, Sigmund Richard *microbiology educator*
Swani, Parvesh *transportation company executive*
Sweeting, Linda Marie *chemist*
Sykes, Melvin Julius *lawyer*
Tabatznik, Bernard *physician, educator*
Talalay, Paul *pharmacologist, physician*
Talbot, Donald Roy *consulting services executive*
Taylor, Carl Ernest *physician, educator*
Taylor, Meldrick *professional boxer, Olympic athlete*
Tepper, Michael Howard *publishing company executive*
Terborg-Penn, Rosalyn Marian *historian, educator*
Teret, Stephen Paul *health law educator*
Thalheimer, Louis B. *diversified corporation executive*
Thomas, Gary Lynn *financial executive*
Thompson, Lawrence Hyde *federal agency official*
†Townsend, Craig Arthur *chemistry educator*
Trimble, William Cattell, Jr. *lawyer*
Trostel, Michael Frederick *architect*
Trouillot, Michel-Rolph *anthropology educator, educational administrator*
Trpis, Milan *vector biologist, scientist, educator*
Truesdell, Clifford Ambrose, III *author, editor*
Ts'o, Paul On-Pong *biophysical chemist, educator*
†Turnock, James McClymonds *healthcare executive*
Tyler, Anne (Mrs. Taghi M. Modarressi) *author*
Tyler, George Thomas *lawyer*
Tyler, John W. *historic site administrator*
†Van Metre, Thomas Earle *physician, allergist*
Vasile, Gennaro James *health care executive*
Verdery, Katherine Maureen *anthropologist, educator*
Vikan, Gary Kent *art museum administrator*
Vogelstein, Bert *oncology educator*
Wagner, Henry Nicholas, Jr. *physician*
Walker, Irving Edward *lawyer*
Walker, Mack *historian, educator*
Wallach, Edward Eliot *physician, educator*
Walser, Mackenzie *physician, educator*
†Walsh, Patrick Craig *urologist*
Wasserman, Richard Leo *lawyer*
Webb, Myrtle Bailey *elementary school reading teacher*
Weidman, Gregory Rowlett *curator, historic interiors consultant*
†Weiss, James Lloyd *cardiology educator*
Welch, Robert Bond *ophthalmologist, educator*
Westerhout, Gart *retired astronomer*
Wheeler, John Ernest, Jr. *oil company executive*
Whelton, Paul K. *medical educator, researcher*
White, Emil Henry *chemistry educator*
White, Pamela Janice *lawyer*
Wierman, John Charles *mathematician, educator*
Wilgis, Herbert E., Jr. *corporate executive*
Williams, Harold Anthony *retired newspaper editor*
†Williams, Richard F. *banker*
†Williams, Robert Eugene *astronomer*
Wilmot, Louise C. *charitable organization executive*
Wilson, Donald Edward *physician, educator*
Wilson, W. Stephen *mathematics educator*
Wilzack, Adele *state health official*
Winn, James Julius, Jr. *lawyer*
Wintriss, Lynn *lawyer*
Wolf, Fred, III *lawyer*
Wolman, M. Gordon *geography educator*
Wood, Howard Graham *banker*
†Woods, Alan Churchill, Jr. *retired surgery educator*
Woodward, Robert A. *radio broadcasting executive*
Woodward, Theodore Englar *medical educator, internist*
Yannuzzi, William A(nthony) *conductor*
Yarmolinsky, Adam *lawyer, educator, university administrator*
Young, Barbara *psychiatrist, psychoanalyst, psychiatry educator, photographer*
Young, Joseph H. *federal judge*
Zaiman, Joel Hirsh *rabbi*
Zassenhaus, Hiltgunt Margret *physician*
Ziff, Larzer *English language educator*
Ziger, Steven Gary *architect*
Zinman, David Joel *conductor*
Zizic, Thomas Michael *physician, educator*

Bel Air

Crocker, Michael Pue *lawyer*
Eichelberger, Robert John *retired government research and development administrator, consultant*
†Klett, Shirley Louise *columnist, writer, critic, researcher*
Miller, Max Dunham, Jr. *lawyer*
Powers, Doris Hurt *engineering company executive*

Beltsville

Adams, Jean Ruth *entomologist*
Andre, Pamela Q. J. *library director*
Appell, Louise Sophia *consulting company executive*
Carroll, Stephen John, Jr. *business educator*
†Chapela, Ignacio H. *biologist, researcher*
Diener, Theodor Otto *plant pathologist*
Duke, James Alan *botanist, author, consultant*
Faust, Robert McNeer *science research administrator*
Guttman, Helene Nathan *research science executive*
Hoberg, Eric Paul *parasitologist*
Kasprick, Lyle Clinton *medical products company executive*
Kearney, Philip Charles *biochemist*
Levin, Gilbert Victor *health information, bioengineering and environmental control company executive*
Lincicome, David Richard *biomedical and animal scientist*
Marten, Gordon Cornelius *research agronomist, educator, federal agency administrator*
Murphy, Charles Franklin *agriculturist*
†Palm, Mary Egdahl *mycologist*
Quirk, Frank Joseph *management consulting company executive*
†Sexton, Thomas John *science administrator, research physiologist*
Shands, Henry Lee *plant geneticist, administrator*
†Swales, Thomas G. *electronics executive*
Tallent, William Hugh *chemist, research administrator*
Terrill, Clair Elman *animal scientist, geneticist, consultant*
Tso, Tien Chioh *federal agency official, plant physiologist*
van Schilfgaarde, Jan *agricultural engineer, government agricultural service administrator*

Berlin

Crawford, Norman Crane, Jr. *academic administrator, consultant*
Horner, William Harry *biochemist*
Howarth, Thomas *tax consultant*
Passwater, Barbara Gayhart *real estate broker*
Passwater, Richard Albert *biochemist, writer*

Bethesda

Abbrecht, Peter Herman *medical educator*
Abrams, Samuel K. *lawyer*
†Ahmed, S. Basheer *research company executive, educator*
Alexander, Duane Frederick *pediatrician, research administrator*
Alper, Jerome Milton *lawyer*
Altobello, Daniel Joseph *service executive*
Anestos, Harry Peter *lawyer*
Asbell, Fred Thomas *telecommunications company executive*
Atlas, David *meteorologist, research scientist*
Atwell, Constance Woodruff *health services executive, researcher*
Auerbach, Seymour *architect*
Augustine, Norman Ralph *industrial executive*
Axelrod, Julius *pharmacologist, biochemist*
Bailey, William Wesley *insurance company executive*
Baird, Charles Fitz *minings and metals company executive*
Banik, Sambhu Nath *psychologist*
Barber, Arthur Whiting *communications company executive*
Barquín, Ramón Carlos *consulting company executive*
Barter, Robert Henry *physician, retired educator*
Bauersfeld, Carl Frederick *lawyer*
Beall, Robert Joseph *foundation executive*
Becker, Edwin Demuth *chemist, laboratory director*
Bennett, Lawrence Herman *physicist*
Benson, Elizabeth Polk *Pre-Columbian art specialist*
Berendes, Heinz Werner *medical epidemiologist, pediatrician*
Berger, Robert Lewis *biophysicist, researcher*
Bernardini, Isa *biochemist*
Berns, Walter Fred *political scientist, educator*
Bick, Katherine Livingstone *scientist, international liaison consultant*
Blush, Steven Michael *nuclear scientist, safety consultant*
Bosnak, Robert John *mechanical engineer, federal agency administrator*
Bowles, Walter Donald *economist, educator*
Brady, Roscoe Owen *neurogeneticist, educator*
Breggin, Peter Roger *psychiatrist, author*
Bregman, Jacob Israel *environmental consulting company executive*
Brickfield, Cyril Francis *lawyer, association executive*
Briggs, Shirley Ann *organization executive*
Brinley, F(loyd) J(ohn), Jr. *health science institution executive, physician*
Brodine, Charles Edward *physician*
†Brossi, Arnold R. *research chemist*
Brouha, Paul *association executive, fishery-wildlife biologist*
Brown, Ann *federal agency administrator*
Brown, Dudley Earl, Jr. *psychiatrist, educator, health executive, former federal agency administrator, former naval officer*
Brown, Earle Palmer *advertising agency executive*
Brown, Jeremy Earle *advertising executive*
†Brownstein, Michael Jay *pharmacologist, neuroscientist*
Bryan, Billie Marie (Mrs. James A. Mackey) *biologist*
Bryant, Bertha Estelle *retired nurse*
Buccino, Alphonse *university dean*
Bucherre, Veronique *environmental company executive*
†Burdeshaw, William Brooksbank *engineering executive*
Burton, Benjamin Theodore *government official*
Burton, Charles Henning *lawyer*
Butler, Sydney J. *zoological and aquarium association administrator*
Callmer, James Peter *architect*
Calvert, Gordon Lee *retired legal association executive*
Campbell, Arthur Andrews *government official*
Cantoni, Giulio Leonardo *biochemist, government official*
Cass, Millard *lawyer, arbitrator*
Cassman, Marvin *biochemist*
Castelli, Alexander Gerard *accountant*
Cath, Stanley Howard *psychiatrist, psychoanalyst*
Catravas, George Nicholas *biologist*
†Chappell, Raymond Edward *real estate company executive*
Chase, Thomas Newell *neurologist, researcher, educator*
Cheever, Allen Williams *pathologist*
Chen, Philip S., Jr. *government official*
Clark, Blake *author, business executive*
Clark, William Doran *former government official*
†Cleary, Timothy Finbar *professional society administrator*
Clema, Joe Kotouc *computer scientist*
Cohen, Allan Yale *social science research administrator*
Cohen, Max Harry *surgeon*
Cohen, Robert Abraham *retired physician*
Cohen, Sheldon Gilbert *physician, historian*
Collins, Francis S. *medical research scientist*
Comings, William Daniel, Jr. *mortgage banker, housing development executive*
Conrad, Edward Ezra *physicist, nuclear engineer, scientific corporation executive*
Cooney, David Martin *organization administrator, retired naval officer*
Cooper, Merri-Ann *psychologist*
Cooper, Roger Merlin *information technology executive, federal government official, educator*
Cooper, William Ewing, Jr. *retired army officer*
Corbett, Jack Elliott *mutual fund officer, clergyman, author*
Corn, Milton *academic dean, physician*
Cornish, Edward Seymour *magazine editor*
Cottony, Herman Vladimir *electronic engineer, consultant*
Cowie, Catherine Christine *epidemiologist*
†Crockett, Bruce Larmour *communications company executive*
Crout, J(ohn) Richard *physician, pharmaceutical researcher*
Cummings, Nancy Boucot *nephrologist*
Daly, John W. *chemistry research administrator*
Daniel, Charles Dwelle, Jr. *consultant, retired army officer*
Dawid, Igor Bert *biologist*
Dawson, John Frederick *architect*
Day, Robert Dwain, Jr. *foundation executive, lawyer*
Decker, John Laws *physician*
Delappe, Irving Pierce *scientist, government official*
de Vries, Margaret Garritsen *economist*
Dietrich, Robert Anthony *pathologist, medical administrator, consultant*
Di Paolo, Joseph Amedeo *geneticist*
Dogoloff, Lee Israel *clinical social worker, psychotherapist, consultant*
Dresing, Robert K. *health care executive*
Drucker, William Richard *surgeon*
Dubner, Ronald *neurobiologist*
Duma, Richard Joseph *microbiologist, physician, pathologist, researcher, educator*
Duncan, Francis *historian, government official*
Dunning, Herbert Neal *government official, physical chemist*
Dyer, Ann *headmistress*
Dyer, Frederick Charles *writer, consultant*
Dykstra, Vergil Homer *retired academic administrator*
Eden, Murray *electrical engineer, emeritus educator*
Egan, John Frederick *electronics executive*
Ehrenstein, Gerald *biophysicist*
Elin, Ronald John *pathologist*
Elman, Philip *lawyer*
Epps, Roselyn Elizabeth Payne *pediatrician, educator*
Ernst, Roger *consultant, university educator*
Estrin, Melvyn J. *computer products company executive*
Eule, Norman L. *lawyer*
Evans, Charles Hawes, Jr. *immunologist, medical researcher*
Fales, Henry Marshall *chemist*
Farmer, Richard Gilbert *physician, foundation administrator, medical advisor*
Fauci, Anthony Stephen *health facility administrator, physician*
Feller, William Frank *surgery educator*
Ferris, Frederick Joseph *gerontologist, social worker*
†Fleisher, Thomas Arthur *physician*
†Ford, John Bassett *broadcasting executive*
Fowler, Emil Eugene *nuclear technology consultant*
Frank, Martin *physiology educator, health scientist, association executive*
Fraser, James Cavender *research center executive*
†Fratantoni, Joseph Charles *medical researcher, hematologist, medical association administrator*
Fraumeni, Joseph F., Jr. *scientific researcher, medical educator, physician, military officer*
Free, Ann Cottrell *writer*
Freedman, Joseph *sanitary and public health engineering consultant*
Freedman, Laurence Stuart *statistician*
Fri, Robert Wheeler *non-profit research executive*
Frommer, Peter Leslie *physician, medical institute administrator*
Gaarder, Marie *speech pathologist*
Gallagher, Hubert R. *governmental consultant*
Gallin, John I. *physician/scientist/medical research administrator*
Gallin, John Isaac *health science association administrator*
Gallo, Robert Charles *research scientist*
Garges, Susan *microbiologist*
Gartland, William Joseph, Jr. *research institute administrator*
Gates, Theodore Ross *economic consultant*
Gelboin, Harry Victor *biochemistry educator, researcher*
†Geller, Ronald Gene *health administrator*
Gershon, Elliot Sheldon *psychiatrist*
Gerwin, Brenda Isen *research biochemist*
Gibson, Sam Thompson *internist, educator*
Gilbert, Daniel Lee *physiologist*
Ginsburg, Ann *biochemist, researcher*
Gleazer, Edmund John, Jr. *retired education educator*
Gluckstein, Fritz Paul *veterinarian, biomedical information specialist*
Gohagan, John Kenneth *medical institute administrator, educator*
Gold, Philip William *neurobiologist*
Goldberg, Herman Raphael *government agency official, educator*
Goldstein, Robert Arnold *physician*
†Gorden, Phillip *federal agency administrator*
Grau, John Michael *trade association executive*
Green, Jerome George *federal government official*
Greenwald, Peter *physician, government medical research director*
Gruber, Jack *medical virologist, biomedical research administrator*
Gude, Gilbert *former state and federal legislator, nurseryman, writer*
Gutheim, Robert Julius *government official*
Hall, John Allen *international nuclear consultant*
Hall, William Darlington *lawyer*
Hallett, Mark *physician, neurologist, health research institute administrator*
Halstead, Scott Barker *foundation administrator*
Hancock, Charles Cavanaugh, Jr. *scientific association administrator*
Hanley, (Charles) Robert, Jr. *computer systems executive, real estate developer*
Harding, Fann *health scientist, administrator*
Harlan, William Robert, Jr. *physician, educator, researcher*
Harney, Kenneth Robert *editor, columnist*
Hartmann, Robert Trowbridge *author, consultant*
Haseltine, Florence Pat *research administrator, obstetrician, gynecologist*
Hauck, Frederick Hamilton *retired naval officer, astronaut, business executive*
Hausman, Steven Jack *health science administrator*
Helke, Cinda Jane *pharmacology and neuroscience educator, researcher*
Helm, Lewis Marshall *public affairs executive*
Hempstone, Smith, Jr. *diplomat, journalist*
Henze, Paul Bernard *author, former government official*
Herman, Edith Carol *journalist*
Herman, Stephen Allen *lawyer*
Hersh, Stephen Peter *psychiatrist, educator*
Higgins, Robert Louis *trade association executive*
Highfill, Philip Henry, Jr. *retired language educator*
Hill, Hugh Kenneth *retired diplomat, former ambassador*
Hoak, John Charles *physician, educator*
Hodgdon, Harry Edward *association executive, wildlife biologist*
Hoenack, August Frederick *architect*
Holmes, Randall Kent *microbiology educator, physician, university administrator*
Holt, Helen Keil *physicist*
Hoover, Roland Armitage *publisher, printer*
Horakova, Zdenka Zahutova *retired toxicologist, pharmacologist*
Hoth, Daniel Floyd *infectious diseases administrator*
†Howard, Frances Estella Humphrey *government official*
Hughes, Carl Wilson *physician*
Hurd, Suzanne Sheldon *federal agency health science director*
Hutcheson, Janet Reid *radiologist*
Hutton, John Evans, Jr. *surgery educator, retired military officer*

Hyson, Charles David economist, consultant
Iglehart, John K. journalist
Ingraham, Edward Clarke, Jr. foreign service officer
Jackson, Michael John physiologist, association executive
Jayson, Lester Samuel lawyer, educator
Johnson, Joyce Marie psychiatrist, epidemiologist
Jonas, Gary Fred health care center executive
Jones, John Courts wildlife biologist
Jones-Smith, Jacqueline federal commission administrator, lawyer
Jordan, Elke molecular biologist, government medical research institute executive
Joy, Robert John Thomas medical history educator
†Kalt, Marvin Robert health organization administrator, cell biologist
Kamenske, Bernard Harold journalist, communications specialist
Kamerow, Martin Laurence accountant
Kampf-Singman, Cindy Alise public relations executive
Kapikian, Albert Zaven physician, epidemiologist
Kaufman, Seymour biochemist
Keiser, Harry Robert physician
Keith, Jerry M. molecular biologist
Kelly, William Clark science administrator
Kety, Seymour S(olomon) physiologist, neuroscientist
King, Charles McDonald, Jr. association foundation executive
Kingsley, Thomas Drowne economist
Kirschstein, Ruth Lillian physician
Kleine, Herman economist
Knachel, Philip Atherton librarian
Kohlmeier, Louis Martin, Jr. newspaper reporter
Koltnow, Peter Gregory engineering consultant
Kopin, Irwin Jerome physician, pharmacologist
Korn, Edward David biochemist
Krause, Richard Michael medical scientist, government official, educator
Kriegsman, William Edwin consulting firm executive
Kruger, Gustav Otto, Jr. oral surgeon, educator
Kupfer, Carl ophthalmologist, science administrator
Kynoch, James Brent environmental engineering executive
Laingen, Lowell Bruce diplomat
Larrabee, Donald Richard publishing company executive
Larson, Clarence Edward association executive
Lauret, Curtis Bernard, Jr. international marketing professional
Law, Lloyd William geneticist
Lee, Edward Brooke, Jr. real estate executive, fund raiser
Lee, Young Jack federal agency administrator
Lenfant, Claude Jean-Marie physician
Leonard, James Joseph physician, educator
Leonard, Sugar Ray (Ray Charles Leonard) retired professional boxer
Leventhal, Carl M. neurologist, government official
Levin, Carl public and government relations consultant
Levine, Arthur Samuel physician, scientist
Lewis, David association executive
Lewis, David Eldridge airport development executive
Lewis, James Histed retired foreign service officer
Lindberg, Donald Allan Bror library administrator, pathologist, educator
Liotta, Lance Allen pathologist
†Lockshin, Michael Dan rheumatologist
Lugt, Hans Josef physicist
Lystad, Mary Hanemann (Mrs. Robert Lystad) sociologist, author, consultant
Lystad, Robert Arthur Lunde retired university dean, educator
Macnamara, Thomas Edward physician, educator
Malone, Winfred Francis health scientist
Malouff, Frank Joseph health care association executive
†Mann, Gary T. engineering company executive
Mansfield, Carl Major radiation oncology educator
†Martino, Robert Louis computational scientist and engineer, researcher
Massa, Paul Peter publisher
Mastny-Fox, Catherine Louise administrator, consultant
McAfee, John Gilmour nuclear medicine physician
McClure, Brooks management consultant
McCurdy, Harry Ward otolaryngologist
Mc Gurn, Barrett communications executive, writer
Mc Kenna, James Aloysius broadcasting executive, former lawyer
McKeon, Kathryn Lothschuetz nursing administrator
McManus, Edward Hubbard government official
McNamara, Francis John writer
†Mead, Loren Benjamin writer, consultant
Meier, Louis Leonard, Jr. lawyer
Meltzer, Jack consultant, retired college dean
Meredith, Ellis Edson association and business executive
Metzger, Henry federal research institution administrator
†Millard, Kenneth E. communications company executive
Miller, Bennett physicist, former government official
Miller, Louis Howard biologist, researcher
Mishkin, Mortimer neuropsychologist
Morgan, William Bruce naval architect
Morton, Herbert Charles editor, economist
Moshman, Jack statistical consultant
Moss, Bernard virologist, researcher
†Mujica, Mauro E. architect
Murayama, Makio biochemist
Nash, Howard Allen biochemist, researcher
Navarro, Joseph Anthony statistician, consultant
Naylor, Phyllis Reynolds author
Neill, Denis Michael government relations consulting executive
Nelligan, William David professional association executive
Nelson, Karin Becker child neurologist
Nessen, Ronald Harold public affairs executive
Neumann, Robert Gerhard ambassador, consultant
Neva, Franklin Allen physician, educator
Newsom, David Dunlop foreign service officer, educator
Nirenberg, Marshall Warren biochemist
North, William Haven foreign service officer
Norwood, Bernard economist
Notkins, Abner Louis physician, researcher
Nyirjesy, Istvan obstetrician, gynecologist
Obrams, Gunta Iris research administrator
O'Brien, Lawrence Francis, III lawyer
O'Callaghan, Jerry Alexander government official
O'Connell, Quinn lawyer
Oddis, Joseph Anthony association executive
O'Donnell, James Francis health science administrator
Okunieff, Paul radiation oncologist, physician
Olmsted, Jerauld Lockwood telephone company executive
Ommaya, Ayub Khan neurosurgeon
Onufrock, Richard Shade pharmacist, researcher
Ory, Marcia Gail social science researcher
O'Shaughnessy, Gary William military officer
Otte, Ruth L. cable television executive
Owen, Thomas Barron retired naval officer, space company executive
Packard, Barbara Baugh science institute administrator, physician, physiologist
Pankopf, Arthur, Jr. lawyer
Parkman, Paul Douglas federal agency administrator
Parry, Hugh Jones (James Cross) social scientist, educator, author
Pastan, Ira Harry biomedical science researcher
Paul, William Erwin immunologist, researcher
Peck, Edward Lionel retired foreign service officer, corporate executive
Peterson, Shirley D. federal agency administrator
Petralia, Ronald Sebastian entomologist, neurobiologist, educator
Phillips, Kevin Price columnist, author
Pickerell, James Howard photojournalist
Pitofsky, Robert lawyer, educator, university administrator
Podolsky, Richard James biophysicist
Pogue, Mary Ellen E. (Mrs. L. Welch Pogue) youth and community worker
Pollard, Harvey B. physician, neuroscientist
Pompa, James Robert computer industry executive
Pospisil, George Curtis biomedical research administrator
Post, Robert M. psychiatrist
Potter, Michael genetics researcher, medical researcher
Pras, Robert Thomas hotel executive
Pratt, Dana Joseph publishing consultant
Pritchard, Wilbur Louis telecommunications engineering executive
Pritchard Schoch, Teresa Noreen lawyer, law librarian, executive
Purcell, Robert Harry virologist
Quinnan, Gerald Vincent, Jr. medical educator
Quraishi, Mohammed Sayeed health scientist, administrator
†Rabson, Alan Saul physician, educator
Rall, Joseph Edward physician
Rapoport, Judith psychiatrist
Raullerson, Calvin Henry political scientist, consultant
Reese, Thomas Sargent neurobiology educator and researcher
Reeves, Richard Allen government aerospace program executive, lawyer
Reichard, John Francis educational consultant
†Reid, Clarice Delores physician
Reighard, Homer Leroy physician
Resnik, Harvey Lewis Paul psychiatrist
Richards, Merlon Foss retired diversified technical services company executive
Richardson, John retired international relations executive
Riley, Matilda White (Mrs. John W. Riley, Jr.) sociology educator
Robbins, Keith Cranston research scientist
Roberts, Chalmers McGeagh reporter
Roberts, Doris Emma epidemiologist, consultant
Robinson, David Mason physiologist
Rosen, Saul Woolf research scientist, health facility administrator
Rosenberg, Steven Aaron surgeon, medical researcher
Ross, William Warfield lawyer
Roth, Harold Philmore physician
Rowell, Edward Morgan retired foreign service officer, lecturer
Rubin, William editor
Ruppe, Loret Miller former ambassador
Safer, John artist, lecturer
Saffiotti, Umberto pathologist
Salisbury, Franklin Cary foundation executive, lawyer
Salisbury, Tamara Paula foundation executive
Salmoiraghi, Gian Carlo physiologist, educator
Sams, James Farid real estate development company executive
Sanford, Katherine Koontz cancer researcher
Sarnoff, Lili-Charlotte Dreyfus (Lolo Sarnoff) artist, business executive
Saunders, Charles Baskerville, Jr. retired association executive
Sausville, Edward Anthony medical oncologist
Saville, Thorndike, Jr. coastal engineer, consultant
Sayre, E(noch) Phillip political scientist, state official
Schambra, Philip Ellis federal agency administrator, radiobiologist
Schinski, Vernon David navy officer
Schlom, Jeffrey Bert research scientist
Schmeltzer, David lawyer
Schneider, John Hoke health science administrator
Schoch, Claude Martin computer scientist, publishing company executive
Schurman, Joseph Rathborne lawyer
Schwartz, Charles Frederick economist, consultant
Sevik, Maurice engineer
Shapiro, Irving S. medical think-tank executive
Shellow, Robert management service company executive, consultant
Sheridan, Philip Henry pediatrician, neurologist
Shipler, David Karr journalist, correspondent, author
Shulman, Lawrence Edward biomedical research administrator, rheumatologist
Simonds, Peggy Muñoz writer, lecturer, retired literature educator
Sinclair, Warren Keith radiation biophysicist, organization executive, consultant
Sindelar, William Francis surgeon, researcher
Small, William Edwin, Jr. association executive
Smith, Ruth Lillian Schluchter librarian
Snow, James Byron, Jr. physician, research administrator
Sokoloff, Louis physiologist, neurochemist
Sontag, James Mitchell cancer researcher
†Southard, Bill public relations executive
Southwick, Paul retired public relations executive
Spangler, Miller Brant science and technology analyst, planner, consultant
Spector, Melbourne Louis management consultant
Spivak, Alvin A. retired public relations executive
Sponsler, George Curtis, III research administrator, lawyer
Sprott, Richard Lawrence government official, researcher
Spurling, Everett Gordon, Jr. architect, construction specifications consultant
Stadtman, Earl Reece biochemist
Stadtman, Thressa Campbell biochemist
Stewart, Harold Leroy physician, educator
Stolz, Walter Sargent health scientist administrator
Striner, Herbert Edward economics educator
Sturtz, Donald Lee physician, naval officer
Sulkin, Sidney editor, writer
†Tabor, Edward physician, researcher
Tabor, Herbert biochemist
Talbot, Bernard government medical research facility official, physician
Taylor, Jimmie Wilkes naval officer
Tellep, Daniel Michael aerospace executive, mechanical engineer
Thorgeirsson, Snorri Sveinn physician, pharmacologist
Thursz, Daniel retired service organization executive, consultant
Tilley, Carolyn Bittner technical information specialist
†Timbers, William Homer, Jr. nuclear fuel company executive
Toomey, Thomas Murray lawyer
Trumbull, Richard psychologist
†Trus, Benes Louis chemist
Tsuneishi, Warren Michio librarian
Vaitukaitis, Judith Louise medical research administrator
†Van Dyke, Joseph Gary Owen computer consulting executive
Varmus, Harold Eliot government health institutes administrator
Vasta, Bruno Morreale information scientist, chemist
Vaughan, Martha biochemist
Vest, George Southall diplomat
Vickers, James Hudson veterinarian, research pathologist
von Kann, Clifton Ferdinand aviation and space executive, software executive
Vosburgh, Frederick George writer, editor
Waldmann, Thomas Alexander medical research scientist, physician
Walker, Lannon foreign service officer
Walker, Mallory real estate executive
Walleigh, Robert Shuler consultant
Walter, Robert think-tank executive, career officer
Walter, William Arnold, Jr. physician
Walters, Judith Richmond neuropharmacologist
Webster, Henry deForest neuroscientist
Wehr, Thomas A. psychiatrist, researcher
Weinberger, Alan David corporate executive
Weiss, George Herbert mathematician, consultant
Wertheimer, Franc retired corporate executive
Whaley, Storm Hammond retired government official, consultant
White, Beverly J. cytogeneticist
Wilbourn, Edgar Sherman, III construction company executive, consultant
Willner, Dorothy anthropologist, educator
Winkler, James B. health care consultant
Wishart, Leonard Plumer, III army officer
Witkop, Bernhard chemist
Wolffe, Alan Paul molecular embryologist, molecular biologist
Wolfsheimer, Ronald Milton financial services executive
Wong, Ma-Li psychiatrist
Woolley, George Walter biologist, geneticist, educator
Work, Henry Harcus physician, educator
Wright, Helen Patton association executive
Wright, James Roscoe chemist
Wurtz, Robert Henry physiologist, scientist
Yaffe, Sumner Jason pediatrician, research center administrator, educator
Yamada, Kenneth Manao cell biologist
Young, A. Thomas defense, aerospace, energy and information systems company executive
Zimble, James Allen naval officer, physician

Bowie
Forrester, Donald Dean principal
Green, Leo Edward lawyer, state legislator
Purcell, Steven Richard international management consultant, engineer, economist
Sterling, Richard Leroy English and foreign language educator
Stone, Edward Harris, II landscape architect
Sullivan, Francis Edward research administrator
Towle, Laird Charles book publisher

Bozman
Peterson, H. William chemical executive, consultant

Braddock Heights
Wirths, Theodore William public policy consultant

Brentwood
†Fiedler, Maureen Ellen nun
Kaskey, Raymond John sculptor

Brookeville
Johns, Warren LeRoi lawyer
Wilson, Vincent Joseph, Jr. writer, historian, publisher

Brooklandville
Darcy, George Robert public relations executive
Miller, Paul George computer company executive

Burkittsville
Aughenbaugh, Deborah Ann mayor, retired educator

Burtonsville
Peck, Carol Faulkner poet, writer, publisher, educator
Yang, Jackson aerospace engineering company executive

Cabin John
Dragoumis, Paul electric utility company executive
Gallagher, Hugh Gregory government affairs author, consultant
Sewell, Winifred pharmaceutical librarian
Shropshire, Walter, Jr. biophysicist emeritus, pastor

Calverton
Parker, Stephen L. architectural firm executive

Catonsville
Cadman, Theodore Wesley chemical engineering educator
Loerke, William Carl art history educator
Stowe, David Henry arbitrator
Vanderlinde, Raymond Edward clinical chemist
†Wilt, Lawrence J.M. librarian
Wynn, John Charles clergyman, retired religion educator

Centreville
Amos, James Lysle photographer
Wharton, Kay Karole special education educator

Chester
Dabich, Eli, Jr. insurance company executive
Pelczar, Michael Joseph, Jr. microbiologist, educator

Chestertown
Clarke, Garry Evans composer, educator, musician, administrator
Gordon, James Braund management consultant
Newlin, Peter Caverly architect
Sener, Joseph Ward, Jr. securities company executive
Trout, Charles Hathaway historian, educator
Williams, Henry Thomas retired banker, real estate agent

Cheverly
Lockyer, Charles Warren, Jr. corporate executive

Chevy Chase
Adler, James Barron publisher
Anderson, Owen Raymond scientific and educational organization executive
Asher, Lila Oliver artist
Bacon, Donald Conrad author, editor
Bissinger, Frederick Lewis retired manufacturing executive, consultant
Blair, William Draper, Jr. conservationist
Broumas, John George retired banker, retired theatre owner
Bush, Frederick Morris federal official
Calfee, William Howard sculptor, painter
Casey, Thomas J. lawyer
Chase, Nicholas Joseph lawyer, educator
Chaseman, Joel media executive
Choppin, Purnell Whittington research administrator, virology researcher, educator
Coleman, Joseph Michael truck lease consultant
Corrigan, Robert Foster business consultant, retired diplomat
Cowan, William Maxwell neurobiologist
Crain, Darrell Clayton, Jr. physician
Crawford, Meredith Pullen research psychologist
Cross, Christopher T. association executive
Delano, Victor retired naval officer
Durant, Frederick Clark, III aerospace history and space art consultant
Dyer, Robert Francis, Jr. internist, educator
Edelson, Burton Irving electrical engineering educator
Ellis, Sydney pharmacological scientist, former pharmacology educator
Emery, Robert Firestone economist, educator
Ferguson, James Joseph, Jr. researcher, educator
Freeman, Harry Louis investment executive
Freeman, Raymond Lee landscape architect, planning consultant
Geber, Anthony economist, retired foreign service officer
Gellermann, Marian DeBelle lawyer
Ginzburg, Yankel artist
Goodwin, Ralph Roger historian, editor
Greenberg, Robert Milton retired psychiatrist
Harr, Karl Gottlieb, Jr. lawyer
Harter, Donald Harry research administrator, medical educator
Hudson, Anthony Webster retired federal agency administrator
Hudson, Ralph P. physicist
Ikenberry, Henry Cephas, Jr. lawyer
Kainen, Jacob artist, former museum curator
Ketcham, Orman Weston lawyer, former judge
Key, Kerim Kami historian, educator
Lukens, Alan Wood retired ambassador and foreign service officer
Mayers, Jean aeronautical engineering educator
Mc Closkey, Robert James former diplomat
Michaelis, Michael management and technical consultant
Miller, Ralph Eli consulting economist
Mulligan, James Kenneth government official
Oler, Wesley Marion, III physician, educator
Oudens, Gerald Francis architect, architectural firm executive
Pancoast, Edwin C. retired foreign service officer, writer, researcher
Prince, Julius S. (Bud) retired foreign service reserve officer
Promisel, Nathan E. materials scientist, metallurgical engineer
Quinn, Eugene Frederick government official, clergyman
Riley, John Winchell, Jr. consulting sociologist
Ritchie, Royal Daniel economic development executive
Rockwell, Theodore nuclear engineer
Romansky, Monroe James physician, educator
Rose, John Charles physician, educator
Sauer, Richard John association executive
Saul, B. Francis, II bank executive
Scammon, Richard Montgomery political scientist
Schlegel, John Frederick management consultant, speaker, trainer
Stetler, C. Joseph lawyer
Strauss, Jon Calvert medical research administrator
Teitel, Simon economist
Vance, Sheldon Baird lawyer, former diplomat
Vanderryn, Jack philanthropic foundation administrator
Walk, Richard David retired psychology educator
Wallerstein, Leibert Benet economist
†Weber, Shirley Bowers retired management analyst, networking communicator
Weisman, John author
Welch, Arnold DeMerritt pharmacologist, biochemist
Williams, Charles Laval, Jr. physician, international organization official
Zurkowski, Paul George information company executive

Churchton
†Morrison, Joel Lynn cartographer, geographer

Claiborne
Moorhead, Paul Sidney geneticist

Clarksburg
Arnold, Jay engineering executive
Bargellini, Pier Luigi electrical engineer
Hyde, Geoffrey satellite communications research executive
Mahle, Christoph Erhard electrical engineer
Townsend, John William, Jr. physicist, retired federal aerospace agency executive

Clarksville
Brancato, Emanuel Leonard electrical engineering consultant

Clinton
Cruz, Wilhelmina Mangahas nephrologist, educator
Garner, William Darrell health services executive, management consultant
Johns, Jayne Howell elementary education educator, administrator, achievement specialist
Sizemore, Carolyn Lee nuclear medicine technologist
Ward, Sue Elleanore Fryer social worker, state agency administrator

Cobb Island
Vanderslice, Joseph Thomas chemist

Cockeysville
Futcher, Palmer Howard physician, educator
Jacobsen, Josephine author
Marsik, Frederic John microbiologist

Cockeysville Hunt Valley
Brown, Adrienne Jean microbiology diagnostic testing company official
Edgett, William Maloy lawyer, labor arbitrator
Kunisch, Robert Dietrich business services company executive
Peirce, Brooke English language educator
Simms, Charles Averill environmental management company executive
Whitehurst, William Wilfred, Jr. management consultant

College Park
†Ahearn, Michael Francis astronomer, educator
Aloimonos, Yiannis John computer sciences educator
Anderson, John David, Jr. aerospace engineer
Antman, Stuart Sheldon mathematician, educator
Barbe, David Franklin electrical engineer, educator
Benesch, William Milton molecular physicist, atmospheric researcher, educator
Berman, Louise Marguerite education educator
Birnbaum, Robert higher education educator
Blankenship, Gilmer Leroy electrical engineering educator, engineering company executive
Blewett, John Paul retired physicist
Brill, Dieter Rudolf physicist
Brodsky, Marc Herbert physicist, research and publishing executive
Brown, Peter Gilbert philosopher, educator
Burke, Frank Gerard archivist
Castellan, Gilbert William chemistry educator
Clark, Eugenie zoologist, educator
Cleghorn, Reese journalist, educator
Colwell, Rita Rossi microbiologist, molecular biologist
Coughlin, Peter Joseph economics educator, researcher
Cunniff, Patrick Francis mechanical engineer
Dally, James William mechanical engineering educator, consultant
Davidson, Roger H(arry) political scientist, educator
DeMonte, Claudia Ann artist, educator
DeSilva, Alan W. physics educator, researcher
Destler, I. M(ac) political scientist, foreign policy writer
Dieter, George Elwood, Jr. university official
Dietrich, Martha Jane (Martha Jane Shultz) genealogist
Dorsey, John Wesley, Jr. university administrator, economist
Efrat, Isaac mathematician, financial analyst
Ehrensberger, Ray university chancellor
Ehrlich, Gertrude retired mathematics educator
Embody, Daniel Robert biometrician
Ephremides, Anthony electrical engineering educator
Fallon, Daniel university administrator
Fanning, Delvin Seymour soil science educator
†Fawcett, Sharon Kay Atchison archivist
Finkelstein, Barbara education educator
Fisher, Michael Ellis mathematical physicist, chemist
Fuegi, John comparative literature educator, author, filmmaker
†Gantt, Elisabeth botany educator and researcher
Gaylin, Ned L. psychology educator
Gentry, James Walter chemical engineer, educator
Gessow, Alfred aerospace engineer, educator
Gluckstern, Robert Leonard physics educator
Gordon, Lawrence Allan accounting educator
Gouin, Francis Romeo physiologist
Granatstein, Victor Lawrence electrical engineer, educator
Greenberg, Jerrold Selig health education educator
Greenberg, Oscar Wallace physicist, educator
Greer, Thomas Vernon business consultant and educator
Griem, Hans Rudolf physicist, educator
Griffin, James Joseph physics educator
Grim, Samuel Oram chemistry educator
Grunig, James Elmer communications educator, researcher, public relations consultant
Gupta, Ashwani Kumar mechanical engineering educator
Gurr, Ted Robert political science educator, author
Hardy, Robert Charles human development educator
Harlan, Louis Rudolph history educator, writer
Heath, James Lee food science educator, researcher
†Hendler, James Alexander computer science educator, consultant
Hey, Nancy Henson educational administrator
Hiebert, Ray Eldon journalism educator, author, consultant
Hill, Clara Edith psychology educator
Holder, Sallie Lou training and meeting management consultant
Holton, William Milne English language and literature educator
Irwin, George Rankin physicist, mechanical engineering educator
Jaquith, Richard Herbert chemistry educator, retired university official
Just, Richard Eugene agricultural and resource economics educator consultant
Keller, Samuel William aerospace administrator
Kerr, Frank John astronomer, educator
Kirwan, William English, II mathematics educator, university official
Kolodny, Richard finance educator
Kotz, Samuel statistician, educator, translator
Kundu, Mukul Ranjan physics and astronomy educator
Lamone, Rudolph Philip business educator
Lapinski, Tadeusz Andrew artist, educator
Levine, William Silver electrical engineering educator
Lewis, Roger Kutnow architect, educator, author
Lightfoot, David William linguistics educator
Locke, Edwin Allen, III psychologist, educator
Lubkin, Gloria Becker physicist
Lyon, Andrew Bennet economics educator
Marcus, Steven Irl electrical engineering educator
Massey, Thomas Benjamin educator
Mayer, William Emilio dean
Mc Donald, Frank Bethune physicist
Michels, Eugene physical therapist
Mikulski, Piotr Witold mathematics educator
Miller, Alan Stanley ecology center administrator, law educator
Miller, Raymond Edward computer science educator
Miller, Raymond Jarvis agronomy educator
Minker, Jack computer scientist, educator
Misner, Charles William physics educator
Moss, Lawrence Kenneth composer, educator
Nerlove, Marc Leon economics educator
Newcomb, Robert Wayne electrical engineer
†Norman, Howard A. writer
Olson, Keith Waldemar history educator
Olson, Mancur Lloyd economics educator
Oster, Rose Marie Gunhild foreign language professional, educator
Pai, Shih I. aeronautical engineer
Pasch, Alan philosophy educator
Patterson, Glenn Wayne botany educator
Peterson, David Frederick government agency executive
Piper, Don Courtney political science educator
Polakoff, Murray Emanuel university dean, economics and finance educator
Popper, Arthur N. zoology educator
Prentice, Ann Ethelynd academic adminstrator
Presser, Harriet Betty sociology educator
†Presser, Stanley survey researcher, educator
Quebedeaux, Bruno horticulture educator
Quester, George Herman political science educator
Rabin, Herbert physics educator, university official
Rosenfeld, Azriel computer science educator, consultant
Russell, John David English literature educator
Sagoff, Mark philosopher, educator, academic administrator
Schelling, Thomas Crombie economist, educator
Schneider, Benjamin psychology educator
Seefeldt, Carol education educator
Sigall, Harold Fred psychology educator
Silverman, Joseph chemistry educator, scientist
Simon, Julian Lincoln economics educator
†Sims, Henry P. management educator
Singh, Amarjit engineering executive, scientist, management consultant
Smith, Betty Faye textile chemist
Smith, Theodore Goodwin chemical engineering educator
Snow, George Abraham physicist
Stark, Francis C., Jr. horticulturist, educator
Stewart, Gilbert Wright computer science educator
Stover, Carl Frederick foundation executive
Stumpff, Robert Thomas academic administrator
Taylor, Leonard Stuart engineering educator, consultant
Toll, John Sampson university administrator, physics educator
Ulmer, Melville Jack economist, educator
Vandersall, John Henry dairy science educator
Wasserman, Paul library and information science educator
†Weart, Spencer Richard historian
Webb, Richard Alan physicist
Weeks, John David chemistry and physical science educator
Weil, Raymond Richard soil scientist
†White, Marilyn Domas information science educator
Whittemore, Edward Reed, II poet, retired educator
Williams, Aubrey Willis anthropology educator
Winik, Jay B. writer, political scientist, consultant
Yaney, George history educator
Zen, E-an research geologist
Zimmerman, Mary Ann university purchasing agent

Colton Point
Humphries, Michael Elwood museum director

Columbia
Alexander, Bruce Donald real estate executive
Askew, Laurin Barker, Jr. architect
Bailey, John Martin retired transportation planner, educator
Baker, Russell Tremaine, Jr. lawyer
Barrow, Lionel Ceon, Jr. communications and marketing consultant
Bitonti, James Anthony business machinery company executive
Blackwell, Camellia Ann art educator
Bretz, Thurman Wilbur corporate professional
Bruley, Duane Frederick academic administrator, consultant, engineer
Butcher, (Charles) Philip English language educator, author
Byington, S. John medical products executive, lawyer
Carr, Charles Jelleff pharmacologist, educator, toxicology consultant
Clark, Billy Pat physicist
Cook, Stephen Bernard homebuilding company executive
Deering, Anthony Wayne Marion real estate developer
Deutsch, Robert William physicist
DeVito, Mathias Joseph real estate executive
Fisher, Dale John chemist, instrumentation and medical diagnostic device investigator
Harrison, Elza Stanley medical association executive
Hartman, Lee Ann Walraff educator
Hegedus, L. Louis chemical engineer, research and development executive
Hilderbrandt, Donald Franklin, II urban designer, landscape architect, artist
Hotchkies, Barry financial executive
Hyman, Lawrence Robert psychiatrist
Keeton, Morris Teuton research institute director
Khare, Mohan chemist
Kime, J. William career officer, engineer
Lapides, Jeffrey Rolf corporate executive
Letaw, Harry, Jr. technology corporation executive
Lijinsky, William biochemist
McCauley, Richard Gray real estate developer, lawyer
McCuan, William Patrick real estate company executive
†McIndoe, Darrell Bruce, Sr. communications executive
Millspaugh, Martin Laurence real estate developer, urban development consultant
Morgan, Walter Edward management consultant
†Northrop, Thomas Webster health care facility administrator
Peck, Charles Edward retired construction and mortgage executive
†Potts, Thomas H. trust company executive
Slater, John Blackwell landscape architect
Steele, Richard J. management consultant
Ulman, Louis Jay lawyer
van Remoortere, Francois Petrus chemical company research and development executive
Whiting, Albert Nathaniel former university chancellor
†Willoughby, Anthony R. satellite support services executive
Wolter, John Amadeus librarian, government official
†Wright, Abraham English language educator, college lecturer

Crofton
Clark, Marcia Hileman special education educator
Eastman, John Robert educator
Kelley, Albert Benjamin consulting company executive
Reich, Merrill Drury intelligence consultant, writer
Watson, Robert Tanner physical scientist

Crownsville
Lawrence, William Porter former naval officer, academic administrator
Wright, Harry Forrest, Jr. retired banker

Cumberland
Fiedler, Lee N. automotive products executive

Darnestown
Knox, Bernard MacGregor Walker retired classics educator

Davidsonville
Mahaffey, Redge Allan movie producer, director, writer

Denton
Doster, Rose Eleanor Wilhelm artist
Thornton, Robert Alan, Jr. state legislator, lawyer

Dundalk
Arnick, John Stephen lawyer, legislator

Dunkirk
Ewing, Richard Tucker diplomat, educator, publisher

Easton
Belmont, August investment banker
Burns, Michael Joseph operations and sales-marketing executive
Engle, Mary Allen English physician
Engle, Ralph Landis, Jr. internist, educator
Jacobs, Michael Joseph lawyer
Lockwood, Willard Atkinson publisher
Maffitt, James Strawbridge lawyer
Peterson, James Kenneth manufacturing company executive
Quinn, William Wilson army officer, manufacturing executive
Read, William Lawrence business executive, former naval officer
Woods, William Ellis lawyer, pharmacist, association executive

Edgewater
†Gross, M(eredith) Grant oceanographer, science administrator
Holm, Jeanne Marjorie author, consultant, government official, former air force officer
†Malley, Kenneth Cornelius military officer

Eldersburg
Bastress, Robert Lewis principal

Elkridge
Calton, Gary Jim chemical company executive, medical educator

Elkton
Harrington, Benjamin Franklin, III business consultant
Scherf, Christopher N. association executive
Smith, James Morton museum administrator, historian

Ellicott City
Faulstich, Albert Joseph banking consultant
Gleaves, Leon Rogers marketing and sales executive
Hickey, Michael E. school system administrator
Hoffberger, Jerold Charles corporation executive
†Longuemare, R. Noel, Jr. federal official
Neil, Fred Applestein public relations executive
Phelps, Catherine elementary school principal
Robison, Susan Miller psychologist, educator, consultant
Tillman, Elizabeth Carlotta nurse, educator
†Wehland, Granville Warren Pearson lawyer, consultant
Weingarten, Murray manufacturing executive

Faulkner
Freeze, James Donald administrator, clergyman

Forestville
Povey, Thomas George office systems company executive

Fort George G Meade
McConnell, John Michael federal agency administrator

Fort Washington
Alexander, Gary R. lawyer, state legislator
Cameron, Rita Giovannetti writer, publisher
Coffey, Matthew B. association executive
Fielding, Elizabeth M(ay) public relations executive, editor, writer
McKenzie, Ruth Bates Harris diversity human relations consultant, writer
Stiver, William Earl retired government administrator

Frederick
Anderson, William Bert import company executive
Beran, Denis Carl publisher
Brown, Frederick James education educator
Bryan, John Leland retired engineering educator
Cragg, Gordon Mitchell government chemist
Farmer, Noel T., Jr. school system administrator
Floerchinger, Thomas Allen computer company executive
Garver, Robert Vernon research physicist
Hoff, Charles Worthington, III banker
Hogan, Ilona Modly lawyer
Housewright, Riley Dee microbiologist, former society executive
Kappe, David Syme environmental chemist
Lewis, Robert Alan biologist, physiologist, environmental scientist, researcher, educator, administrator, author
†Nathanson, Kim computer support executive
†Nathanson, Rick computer company sales and support services executive
Pyne, Frederick Wallace genealogist, clergyman, retired civil engineer, retired mathematics educator
Rice, Jerry Mercer medical research center administrator
Smith, Sharron Williams chemistry educator
Vande Woude, George Franklin molecular biologist, cancer researcher
Wohlgemuth, John Harold solid state physicist

Frostburg
Gira, Catherine Russell university president
Root, Edward Lakin university dean, educator
Tam, Francis Man Kei physics educator

Ft Washington
Miller, John Richard interior designer

Gaithersburg
†Amato, Ivan Abel science writer
Ambler, Ernest government official
Arrowsmith, Peter D. engineering executive
Attix, Frank Herbert medical physics educator, researcher
Berger, Harold physicist
Bochicchio, Jill Arden photographer
Boddiger, George Cyrus insurance corporate executive, consultant
Brown, Dorothea Williams technology consulting company executive
†Bruggeman, John Robert publishing executive
Buckley, Gerard Duke science facility administrator
Cahn, John Werner metallurgist, educator
Casella, Russell Carl physicist
Caswell, Randall Smith physicist
†Celotta, Robert James physicist
Clark, Alan Fred physicist
Cook, Vincent N. information processing and business machinery company executive
Cookson, Alan Howard electrical engineer, researcher
Costrell, Louis physicist
Crisp, Elizabeth Amanda physician
Danos, Michael physicist
Dean, Stephen Odell physicist
Deprit, Andre Albert mathematician, consultant
Deutsch, Judith Sloan journalist, newspaper editor
Ewing, Frank Marion lumber company executive, industrial land developer
†Eyman, L. Dean environmental company executive
Fleming-Durdin, Jennie elementary school educator
Flickinger, Harry Harner organization and business executive, management consultant
French, Judson Cull government official
Fuhrman, Ralph Edward civil and environmental engineer
Gebbie, Katharine Blodgett astrophysicist
Hall, Arthur Raymond, Jr. minister
Harman, George Gibson physicist, consultant
Hegyeli, Ruth Ingeborg Elisabeth Johnsson pathologist, government official
Hertz, Harry Steven government official
Hougen, Jon Torger physical chemist, researcher
Hsu, Stephen M. materials scientist, chemical engineer
Hubbell, John Howard radiation physicist
Isbister, James David pharmaceutical business executive
Jefferson, David computer scientist
Kammer, Raymond Gerard, Jr. government official
Karch, Karen Brooke principal
Kessler, Karl Gunther physicist
Klein, Sami Weiner librarian
Kushner, Lawrence Maurice physical chemist
Kuyatt, Chris E(rnie) (Earl) physicist, administrator
Lee, John Chonghoon, Sr. financial executive, international laywer
Levelt Sengers, Johanna Maria Henrica research physicist
Levine, Robert Sidney chemical engineer
Marozsan, John Robert publishing company executive
†Martin, Roger John computer scientist
†Marx, Paul Benno author, social service administrator, missionary
Mathias, Joseph Simon metallurgical engineer, consultant
McShefferty, John research company executive
Mills, Kevin Lee government executive
Nayyar, Mohinder Lal mechanical engineer
Nemecek, Albert Duncan, Jr. retail company executive, investment banker, management consultant
Oettinger, Frank Frederic electronics executive, researcher
Penniman, W. David information scientist, management consultant
†Pierce, Daniel Thornton physicist
Prabhakar, Arati federal administration research director, electrical engineer
Pugh, Edison Neville metallurgist
Rabinow, Jacob electrical engineer, consultant
Reader, Joseph physicist
Rollow, Thomas A. federal official
Rosenblatt, Joan Raup mathematical statistician
Ross, Sherman psychologist, educator
Rupert, (Lynn) Hoover minister
Ruth, James Perry financial planning executive
Schaefer, William G. lawyer
Schrenk, W(illi) Juergen chemicals executive

Schwartz, Lyle H. *materials scientist, government official*
Schwartzberg, Allan Zelig *psychiatrist, educator*
Semerjian, Hratch Gregory *research and development executive*
Smith, Leslie E. *physical chemist*
Snell, Jack Eastlake *federal agency administrator*
†Stein, Stephen Ellery *research chemist, software engineer*
Taylor, Barry Norman *physicist*
Watkins, Michael Dean *town planner*
Weber, Alfons *physicist*
Whallon, Evan Arthur, Jr. *orchestra conductor*
Wicklein, John Frederick *journalist, educator*
Wiese, Wolfgang Lothar *physicist*
Witzgall, Christoph Johann *mathematician*
Wohl, Ronald H. *management consultant, readability expert*
Wright, Richard Newport, III *civil engineer, government official*

Galena
Haenlein, George Friedrich Wilhelm *dairy scientist, educator*

Garrett Park
Baldwin, Calvin Benham, Jr. *retired medical research administrator*
Friedman, Edward David *lawyer, arbitrator*
Kornberg, Warren Stanley *science journalist*
McDowell, Eugene Charles *systems analyst*
Melville, Robert Seaman *chemist*
Silbergeld, Sam *psychiatrist*

Germantown
Christian, John Kenton *organization executive, publisher, writer, marketing consultant*
†Davis, Karen Elizabeth *social concern administrator*
Golding, Leonard Sheldon *telecommunications executive, scientist*
Price, William James *organization executive*
Shaw, Jack Allen *communications company executive*

Glen Arm
Jackson, Theodore Marshall *retired oil company executive*
Mc Cord, Marshal *civil engineer*

Glen Echo
Simpson, Robert Edward *economist, consultant*

Glenelg
Williams, Donald John *research physicist*

Grantsville
Ruddell, Gary Ronald *publisher*

Grasonville
Andrews, Archie Moulton *government official*
Prout, George Russell, Jr. *medical educator, urologist*

Greenbelt
Boarman, Gerald L. *principal*
Chasanow, Deborah K. *federal judge*
Cooper, Robert Shanklin *engineering executive, former government official*
Day, John H. *physicist*
Ekstrand, Richard Edward *lawyer, educator*
†Emerson, Jeff Douglas *healthcare executive*
Fichtel, Carl Edwin *physicist*
Gehrels, Neil *astrophysicist*
Hauser, Michael George *astrophysicist*
Holt, Stephen S. *astrophysicist*
Jascourt, Hugh D. *lawyer, arbitrator, mediator*
Kenkel, James Edward *judge*
†Krulisch, Lee *science facility administrator*
Langel, Robert Allan, III *geophysicist*
Lubetzky, Carole Diane *elementary education educator, math-science specialist*
Mannes, Paul *federal judge*
Maran, Stephen Paul *astronomer*
Mather, John Cromwell *astrophysicist*
Messitte, Peter Jo *judge*
Mumma, Michael Jon *physicist*
O'Mara, Arthur James *civil engineer*
†Ormes, Jonathan Fairfield *astrophysicist, science administrator, researcher*
O'Sullivan, Judith Roberta *state administrator, author*
Ramaty, Reuven Robert *physicist, researcher*
†Reid, Hubert M. *computer software company executive, electronics executive*
Rothenberg, Joseph Howard *federal agency administrator*
Simpson, Joanne Malkus *meteorologist*
Smith, David Edmund *geophysicist*
Stief, Louis John *chemist*
†Weinman, James A. *meteorologist*

Hagerstown
Coles, Robert Nelson, Sr. *religious organization administrator*
Fisher, Charles Worley *editor*
Harrison, Lois Smith *hospital executive, educator*
Palmisano, Sister Maria Goretti *principal*
Poole, D. Bruce *lawyer*
Tuckwell, Barry Emmanuel *musician, music educator*
Warner, Harry Backer, Jr. *retired journalist, freelance writer*
Wolford, Patricia Weber *management company executive*

Hampstead
Staub, Martha Lou *elementary education educator*

Hancock
Popenoe, John *horticultural consultant, retired botanical garden administrator*

Hanover
Hay, Lewis *food marketing executive*
Miller, James L. *food products executive*

Havre De Grace
Wetter, Edward *broadcasting executive*

Hollywood
Hertz, Roy *physician, educator, researcher*

Hunt Valley
Kinstlinger, Jack *engineer executive, consultant*
McKay, Jack Alexander *electronics engineer, physicist*
Mulligan, Martin Frederick *clothing executive, professional tennis player*
Parker, Lewis E. S. *orthopedic company executive, commercial vineyard operator*
Yow, Raymond Murray *insurance company executive, retired physician*

Huntingtown
Merrion, Arthur Benjamin *mathematics educator, tree farmer*
Mitchell, Robert Greene *industrial manufacturing executive, consultant*

Hyattsville
Choi, Jai Won *mathematical statistician, researcher*
Herrmann, Douglas J. *psychology educator, researcher*
Houle, Philip P. *lawyer*
Lovick, Norman *accountant*
Manos, Pete Lazaros *supermarket executive*
McLin, William Merriman *foundation administrator*
Moylan, John L. *secondary school principal*
Rodgers, Mary Columbro *university chancellor, English educator, author*

Indian Head
Wamsley, Barbara Simborski *federal agency administrator*

Jessup
†Smelkinson, Robert N. *wholesale distribution executive*

Kensington
†Booz, Elisabeth Benson *geographer*
Braden, Joan Kay *mental health counselor*
Clarke, Frederic B., III *risk analysis consultant*
Daisley, William Prescott *lawyer*
DeConcini, John Cyrus *retired labor organization executive*
Jackson, Mary Jane McHale Flickinger *principal*
Jackson, William David *research executive*
Marienthal, George *telecommunications company executive*
Rather, Lucia Porcher Johnson *library administrator*
Revoile, Charles Patrick *lawyer*
Rogers, Kenneth Norman *retired foreign service officer, lawyer, international political and commercial consultant*
Root, William Alden *export control consultant*
Schmerling, Erwin Robert *volunteer, retired government official*
Suraci, Charles Xavier, Jr. *retired federal agency administrator, aerospace education consultant*

Kingsville
Pullen, Keats A., Jr. *electronics engineer*

La Plata
Galvin, Noreen Ann *nurse, educator*

Landover
Bachand, Stephen E. *manufacturing company executive*
Colyer, Sheryl Lynn *psychologist*
Drahmann, Brother Theodore *academic administrator*
Freeman, Ernest Robert *engineering executive*
Hechinger, John W., Jr. *home improvement company executive*
Hechinger, John Walter *hardware chain executive*
Huggins, David *custom software development executive*
Lynam, Jim *professional basketball coach*
McClelland, W. Clark *retail company financial executive*
Nash, John N. *professional basketball team executive*
O'Malley, Susan *professional basketball team executive*
Patrick, Richard M. *professional hockey team executive*
Poile, David Robert *professional hockey team executive*
Pollin, Abe *professional basketball team executive, builder*
Sachs, Jerry *professional basketball team executive*
Schoenfeld, Jim *professional hockey coach*
Unseld, Westley Sissel *professional sports team executive, former professional basketball coach, former professional basketball player*

Lanham Seabrook
Blanchard, David Lawrence *aerospace executive, real estate developer*
Bowen, Robert Stevenson *diversified company executive*
Connors, Maureen Stotler *publishing executive*
Fellers, Raymond *publisher*
Fischel, David *astrophysicist, remote sensing specialist*
Henry, Gisèle Byrd *publishing executive, book designer*
Herman, Kenneth *food marketing executive*
Horowitz, David Joel *author*
Jones, Robert Lee, Jr. *veterans service organization executive*
Lucido, Chester Charles, Jr. *marketing company executive*
McCarthy, Kevin John *lawyer*
Nagan, Peter Seymour *publisher*
Youman, Lillian Hobson Lincoln *building services contractor*

Largo
Isom, Virginia Annette Veazey *nursing educator*

Laurel
Abbagnaro, Louis Anthony *corporate executive*
Apel, John Ralph *physicist*
Avery, William Hinckley *physicist, chemist*
Billig, Frederick Stucky *mechanical engineer*
Corrothers, Helen Gladys *criminal justice official*
Dallman, Paul Jerald *engineer, writer*
Eaton, Alvin Ralph *aeronautical and systems engineer, research and development administrator*
Ellis, David H. *biologist, research behaviorist*
Fristrom, Robert Maurice *chemist*
Gieszl, Louis Roger *mathematician*
Gottsman, Earl Eugene *academic administrator*
Halushynsky, George Dobroslav *systems engineer*

Kossiakoff, Alexander *chemist*
Krimigis, Stamatios Mike *physicist, researcher, space science/engineering manager, consultant*
Linevsky, Milton Joshua *physical chemist*
O'Connor, Harold J. *wildlife research administrator*
Perrone, Nicholas *mechanical engineer, business executive*
Robbins, Chandler S(eymour) *research biologist*
Sharpless, Joseph Benjamin *former county official*
Sherwood, Aaron Wiley *aerodynamics educator*
†Springer, Jeffrey R. *bank officer*
Wales, Sister Patrice *school system administrator*
†Ward, James D. *bank executive building material executive*
Westhaver, Lawrence Albert *electronics engineer, consultant*

Lavale
Heckert, Paul Charles *sociologist, educator*

Leonardtown
Briscoe, John Hanson *judge, lawyer, former state legislator*

Libertytown
Lindblad, Richard Arthur *health services administrator, drug abuse epidemiologist*

Linthicum Heights
Skillman, William Alfred *consulting engineering executive*

Lusby
Eshelman, Ralph Ellsworth *historian, consultant*
Howell, James Theodore *medical consultant, internist*
Radcliffe, Redonia Wheeler (Donnie Radcliffe) *journalist, author*
Simpich, William Morris *public affairs consultant*
Sprague, Edward Auchincloss *retired association executive, economist*

Lutherville
Barton, Meta Packard *property management executive, financial planner*
Corcoran, Loma M. *hospital administrator*
Morgan, James Gilmor *insurance executive*
Sagerholm, James Alvin *retired naval officer*
Sanders, Roger Cobban *radiologist*
Tebay, James Elwood *retired foundation executive*

Lutherville Timonium
Bond, Calhoun *lawyer, retired*
Bundick, William Ross *dermatologist*
Cappiello, Frank Anthony, Jr. *investment advisor*
Cedrone, Louis Robert, Jr. *critic*
Chapman, Robert Breckenridge, III *management consulting company executive*
Hambleton, Thomas Edward *theatrical producer*
Kerr, Patrick Corbitt *real estate appraiser, consultant*
Park, Lee Crandall *psychiatrist*
Shriver, Pamela Howard *professional tennis player*
†Thompson, Wayne Paul *healthcare executive*

Mardela Springs
Harcum, Louise Mary Davis *retired elementary education educator*

Marriottsville
Fitzgerald, John L. *hospital administrator*

Mechanicsville
Henderson, Madeline Mary (Berry) (Berry Henderson) *chemist, researcher, consultant*

Mitchellville
Bever, Christopher Theodore *psychiatrist*
Blough, Roy *retired economist*
Kendall, Katherine Anne *social worker*
Manvel, Allen Dailey *fiscal economist*
Phelps, Flora L(ouise) Lewis *editor, anthropologist, photographer*

Monkton
Mountcastle, Vernon Benjamin *neurophysiologist*
Ryker, Norman J., Jr. *retired manufacturing company executive*

Monrovia
Atanasoff, John Vincent *physicist*
†Cooney, William Joseph, Jr. *communications company executive*

Mount Airy
Collins, Henry James, III *insurance company executive*

Myersville
Blake, John Ballard *retired historian*

North Potomac
Bavier, Robert Newton, III *architect*
Passantino, Richard J. *architect*
Solomon, Joel Martin *retired professional society administrator*

Oakland
Farrar, Richard Bartlett, Jr. *secondary education educator*

Olney
Aylward, Thomas James, Jr. *communication arts and theatre educator*
Delmar, Eugene Anthony *architect*
Graham, William Howard *theatre producer, consultant*
Pines, Nancy Freitag *psychotherapist*

Owings
Oring, Stuart August *visual information specialist, writer/photographer*

Owings Mills
Disharoon, Leslie Benjamin *retired insurance executive*
†Elkins, Robert N. *association executive*
Gloth, Fred M., Jr. *insurance company executive*
†Hindman, W. James *service agency administrator*
Holdridge, Barbara *book publisher*
Kershaw, Robert Alan *corporate treasurer*

†Parviainen, Asko *engineering company executive, consultant*
Walsh, Semmes Guest *retired insurance company executive*
Wieczynski, Frank Robert *insurance brokerage executive*

Oxford
Mc Kee, Kinnaird Rowe *retired naval officer*
Radcliffe, George Grove *retired life insurance company executive*
Stanley, Edmund Allport, Jr. *foundation administrator, philanthropist*
Waetjen, Walter Bernhard *university president emeritus*

Oxon Hill
Boerrigter, Glenn Charles *educational administrator*

Parkton
Fitzgerald, Edwin Roger *physicist, educator*

Parkville
Munson, Paul Lewis *pharmacologist*

Pasadena
Kreps, Robert Wilson *research chemist*
Young, Russell Dawson *physics consultant*

Perry Point
Peszke, Michael Alfred *psychiatrist, educator*

Phoenix
†Byrd, Harvey Clifford, III *information management company executive*

Pocomoke City
Kerbin, Diane Leithiser *history educator*

Port Republic
Miller, Ewing Harry *architect*

Potomac
Affeldt, David Allan *lawyer, legal consultant*
Antoniou, Lucy D. *internist, nephrologist*
Bollum, Frederick James *biotechnology executive*
Bradley, Mark Edmund *physician, consultant*
Brewer, Nathan Ronald *veterinarian, consultant*
Broderick, John Caruthers *retired librarian, educator*
Conner, Troy Blaine, Jr. *lawyer, writer*
Cotton, William Robert *dentist*
Elisburg, Donald Earl *lawyer*
Engelmann, Rudolf Jacob *meteorologist*
Epstein, Edward S. *meteorologist*
Evanega, George Ronald *medical company executive*
Evans, Christine Burnett *health care executive*
Fink, Daniel Julien *management consultant*
Fox, Arthur Joseph, Jr. *editor*
Frey, James McKnight *government official*
Haddy, Francis John *physician, educator*
Heller, Peggy Osna *poetry therapist, psychotherapist*
Jones, Sidney Lewis *economist, government official*
Jung, Richard K. *headmaster*
Karson, Emile *international business executive*
Kessler, Ronald Borek *journalist*
Lemley, Barbara Wink *business educator*
Mc Bryde, F. Webster *geographer, ecologist, consultant*
Munroe, Pat *retired newsman*
Nichol, Henry Ferris *former government official, environment consultant*
Noonan, Patrick Francis *conservation executive*
†Owen, Jack Walden *retired hospital association administrator*
†Pastan, Linda Olenik *poet*
Peter, Phillips Smith *lawyer*
Peters, Frank Albert *retired chemical engineer*
Proffitt, John Richard *investment banking executive*
Reichart, Stuart Richard *lawyer*
Reynolds, Frank Miller *retired government administrator*
Rhode, Alfred Shimon *business consultant, educator*
Rotberg, Iris Comens *social scientist*
Schonholtz, Joan Sondra Hirsch *banker, civic worker*
Shapiro, Richard Gerald *retired department store executive, consultant*
Shepard, William Seth *government official, diplomat*
Stupak, Ronald Joseph *dean, management educator, researcher*
Terragno, Paul James *information industry executive*
Whang, Yun Chow *space science educator*

Preston
Suggs, Leo H. *transportation executive*

Princess Anne
Hytche, William Percy *university president*

Queenstown
Bancroft, Paul, III *investment company executive, venture capitalist*
Beall, Robert Milton *restaurant executive*
Mc Laughlin, David Thomas *academic administrator, business executive*

Riva
Powers, Margaret A. *nursing administrator*

Riverdale
Ahl, Alwynelle Self *zoology, ecology and veterinary medical executive*
Hedgepeth, Leroy J. *park director*
Kanal, Laveen N. *computer science educator, data processing company executive*
Love, Richard Harvey *lawyer*
O'Reilly, Thomas Patrick *state senator, lawyer*

Riverside
Guetzkow, Daniel Steere *technology company entrepreneur*

Rockville
Aamodt, Roger Louis *federal agency administrator*
†Abron, Lilia A. *chemical engineer*
Akhter, Mohammad Nasir *physician, government public health administrator*
Anderson, Walter Dixon *trade association management consultant*
Arnstein, Sherry Phyllis *health care executive*
Barkley, Brian Evan *lawyer, political consultant*
Beattie, Donald A. *energy scientist, consultant*

Bell, William Coleman *agricultural engineer, consultant*
Birns, Mark Theodore *physician*
Brandhorst, Wesley Theodore *information manager*
Bruck, Stephen Desiderius *biochemist*
Brumback, Gary Bruce *industrial and organizational psychologist*
Bryant, Edward Clark *statistician*
Buchanan, John Donald *health physicist, radiochemist*
†Burns, Kevin J. *computer software services executive*
†Campbell, Barry G. *engineering company executive*
†Canter, Mark A. *insurance company executive*
Carey, John Edward *information services executive*
†Chang, Kung-Li (Charlie) *engineering consulting firm executive*
Chapin, James Chris *lawyer*
†Chavez, Nelba *federal agency administrator*
Chiogioji, Melvin Hiroaki *government official*
Christie, R(obert) Brent *entrepreneur, real estate and hotel executive*
Cowart, Elgin Courtland, Jr. *naval medical officer*
Cramer, Mercade Adonis, Jr. *computer company executive*
Day, LeRoy Edward *aerospace scientist, consultant*
Dockser, William Barnet *real estate management and mortgages executive*
Doub, William Offutt *lawyer*
Drzewiecki, Tadeusz Maria *corporate executive, defense consultant*
Dubey, Satya Deva *biomedical and statistical scientist, researcher, executive*
Dunn, Bonnie Brill *chemist*
DuPont, Robert Louis *psychiatrist, physician*
Elliott, Benjamin Paul *architect*
Fenton, Wayne S. *psychiatrist*
Finlayson, John Sylvester *biochemist*
Fischer, Irene Kaminka *retired research geodesist, mathematician*
Fischetti, Michael *public administration educator, arbitrator*
Foa, Joseph Victor *aeronautical engineer, educator*
Forbes, Allan Louis *physician, foods and nutrition consultant*
†Forest, Harvey *electronics executive*
Fouchard, Joseph James *retired government agency administrator*
†Freiman, StephenWeil *ceramic engineering researcher*
Fthenakis, Emanuel John *diversified aerospace company executive*
†Gabelnick, Henry Lewis *medical research director*
Geier, Mark Robin *obstetrical genetics and infertility physician*
†Goldenberg, Melvyn Joel *company executive*
†Gordis, Enoch *science administrator, internist*
Gordon, Joan Irma *lawyer*
Gordon, Michael Robert *lawyer*
Gougé, Susan Cornelia Jones *microbiologist*
Grady, Lee Timothy *pharmaceutical chemist*
Graff, Stuart Leslie *accounting executive*
Griffen, Agnes Marthe *library administrator*
Griffith, Jerry Dice *energy consultant*
Haffner, Marlene Elisabeth *internist, health care administrator*
Halperin, Jerome Arthur *pharmacopeial convention executive*
Hanna, Michael George, Jr. *immunologist, institute administrator*
†Hardegree, Mary Carolyn *medical association administrator, pediatrician, immunologist*
Harvey, Donald Phillips *retired naval officer*
Haudenschild, Christian Charles *pathologist, educator*
Hawkins, James Alexander, II *mental health fund executive*
Henderson, Edward Shelton *oncologist*
Hewlett, Richard Greening *historian*
Hoffman, C. Michael *federal agency administrator*
†Holston, Sharon Smith *government official*
Hoobler, James Ferguson *federal executive*
Horowitz, Harold *architect*
Howard, Lee Milton *international health consultant*
Hoyer, Leon William *physician, educator*
†Hubbard, William Keith *government executive*
Huber, John Michael *director non-profit organization*
Hunt, Joseph A. *statistical survey research executive*
Jamieson, Graham A. *biochemist, organization official*
Jochum, George T. *management company executive*
Johnson, Elaine McDowell *federal government administrator*
Johnson, Emery Allen *physician*
Kadish, Richard L. *lawyer*
Kalton, Graham *survey statistician, research scientist*
Karnow, Stanley *journalist, writer*
Kawazoe, Robin Inada *federal official*
Kelsey, Frances Oldham (Mrs. Fremont Ellis Kelsey) *government official*
Kessler, David A. *health services commissioner*
Kindt, Thomas James *chemist*
Kline, Raymond Adam *professional organization executive*
Knox, C. Neal *political and governmental affairs consultant, writer*
Koslow, Stephen Hugh *science administrator, pharmacologist*
Krahnke, Betty Ann *county official*
Krear, Gail Richardson *elementary education educator, consultant*
Landon, John Campbell *medical research company executive*
Lee, James Jieh *environmental educator, computer specialist*
Leslie, John Walter *development consultant*
Ley, Herbert Leonard, Jr. *retired epidemiologist*
Liard, Jean-Francois *cardiovascular physiologist, researcher, educator*
Lim, David Jong-Jai *otolaryngology educator, researcher*
Liu, Darrell Teh Yung *biochemist, researcher*
Lloyd, Douglas Seward *physician, public health administrator*
Lutwak, Leo *physician, educator*
Matthews, Daniel George *editorial consultant*
McCormick, Kathleen Ann Krym *geriatrics nurse, computer information specialist, federal agency administrator*
McDonald, Capers Walter *biomedical engineer, corporate executive*
McMahon, Edward Peter *systems engineer, consultant*
†Meade, Kenneth Albert *minister*
Menkello, Frederick Vincent *computer scientist*
Mertz, Walter *retired government research executive*
Meyer, F. Weller *bank executive*
Milan, Thomas Lawrence *accountant*
Miller, Kenneth Michael *electronics executive*
†Millstein, Richard Allen *federal agency administrator*
Milner, Max *food and nutrition consultant*
†Minor, Marilyn T. *engineering company executive*
Missar, Charles Donald *librarian*
Molitor, Graham Thomas Tate *lawyer*
†Motayed, Asok K. *engineering company executive*
Murray, Peter *metallurgist, manufacturing company executive*
Naft, Barry Niel *waste management administrator, chemical engineer*
Nash, Jonathon Michael *program manager, mechanical engineer*
Naunton, Ralph Frederick *surgeon, educator*
Nelson, Joseph Conrad *lawyer, business executive, educator*
Nguyen, Truyen Thanh *computer and communications company executive*
Niewiaroski, Trudi Osmers (Gertrude Niewiaroski) *social studies educator*
†Nightingale, Stuart Lester *physician, public health officer*
Nora, Audrey Hart *physician*
Nora, James Jackson *physician, author, educator*
Nystrom, Harold Charles *lawyer, labor consultant*
Pagan Martinez, Juan *administrative corps officer*
Parler, William Carlos *lawyer*
Petzold, Carol Stoker *state legislator*
Poljak, Roberto J(uan) *research director, biotechnology educator*
Pollack, Louis *telecommunications company executive*
Pollard, George Marvin *economist*
Porter, John Robert, Jr. *space technology company executive, geochemist*
Rafajko, Robert Richard *medical research company executive*
†Ramsey, James P. *marine engineering consultant, computer services company consultant*
Ramsey, William Edward *retired naval officer, space systems executive*
Regeimbal, Neil Robert, Sr. *retired journalist*
Rheinstein, Peter Howard *government official, physician, lawyer*
†Robinson, William Andrew *health service executive, physician*
Rosenberg, Judith Lynne *middle school educator*
Rosenstein, Marvin *public health administrator*
†Rosenthal, Richard Scott *information management company executive*
Sacchet, Edward M. *foreign service officer*
Sanks, Charles Randolph, Jr. *minister, psychotherapist*
†Scearce, P. Jennings, Jr. *engineering executive*
Schindler, Albert Isadore *physicist, educator*
Schweickart, Russell Louis *communications executive, astronaut*
Seltser, Raymond *epidemiologist, educator*
Shadoan, George Woodson *lawyer*
Shaw, Robert William, Jr. *management consultant, venture capitalist*
Shelton, Wayne Vernon *professional services and systems integration company executive*
Shepherd, Alan J. *construction executive, management consultant*
†Smith, Vivian Louise *substance abuse prevention professional, social worker*
Snyder, Marvin *neuropsychologist*
Sontag, Peter Michael *travel management company executive*
Sparks, David Stanley *university administrator*
Stansfield, Charles W. *educational administrator*
Stern, Joyce Reuben *lawyer*
†Stoiber, Carlton Ray *government agency official*
Sumaya, Ciro Valent *pediatrician, educator*
Szabo, Daniel *government official*
†Taylor, Michael R. *federal agency administrator, lawyer*
Teske, Richard Henry *veterinarian*
Titus, Roger Warren *lawyer*
Tripp, Frederick Gerald *investment advisor*
Trost, Carlisle Albert Herman *retired naval officer*
Ulbrecht, Jaromir Josef *chemical engineer*
†Vollmer, Richard Henry *federal agency administrator*
†Waugaman, Richard Merle *psychiatrist*
Weinberger, Leon Walter *sanitary engineer*
Whitney, Robert A., Jr. *veterinarian, government public health executive*
Wonnacott, (Gordon) Paul *economics educator*
Zoon, Kathryn Egloff *biochemist*

Royal Oak
Israel, Lesley Lowe *political consultant*

Saint Leonard
Andrews, John Stewart *management consultant*
Sanders, James Grady *biogeochemist*

Saint Michaels
Jones, Raymond Edward, Jr. *brewing executive*
Marshall, Robert Gerald *language educator*
Rever, George Wright *psychiatrist, health facility administrator*

Salisbury
Becker, Thomas McKean *architect*
Houlihan, Hilda Imelio *physician*
Kleiman, Gary Howard *broadcast, advertising and cellular communications consultant*
Moultrie, Fred *geneticist*
Perdue, Franklin P. *poultry products company executive*
Perdue, James *food products executive*
Poisker, Karen Coons *nursing administrator*

Sandy Spring
Cope, Harold Cary *former university president, higher education association executive*
Gibian, Thomas George *chemical company executive*
Kanarowski, Stanley Martin *chemist, chemical engineer, government official*

Savage
Filby, Percy William *library consultant*

Seabrook
Brugger, George Albert *lawyer*
Durrani, Sajjad Haidar *space communications engineer*
Laurenson, Robert Mark *mechanical engineer*

Severna Park
Darden, Alverta Eleanor *elementary educator*
Davis, John Adams, Jr. *electrical engineer, roboticist, corporate research executive*
Greulich, Richard Curtice *anatomist, gerontologist*
Moore, John Leo, Jr. *journalist, writer, editor*
Retterer, Bernard Lee *electronic engineering consultant*
Schick, Edgar Brehob *German literature educator*

Silver Spring
Ahmad, Mirza Muzaffar *economic advisor*
Attaway, David Henry *federal research administrator, oceanographer*
Avram, Henriette Davidson *librarian, government official*
Bainum, Stewart *health care and lodging company executive*
Ball, Anne H. *writer, editor, public relations consultant*
†Baptiste, Harold W. *religious organization administrator*
Barber, Ben Bernard Andrew *journalist*
Barkin, Robert Allan *graphic designer, newspaper executive, consultant*
Beach, Bert Beverly *clergyman*
Berger, Allan Sidney *psychiatrist*
Blake, Lamont Vincent *electronics consultant*
Blankenheimer, Bernard *economics consultant*
†Borkovec, Vera Z. *Russian studies educator*
Briscoe, Melbourne G. *oceanographer, administrator*
Brog, David *consultant, former air force officer*
Brooks, Bruce Delos *writer*
†Brown, Carolyn Thompson *librarian*
Butler, Broadus Nathaniel *retired university administrator*
Cain, David Lee *corporate executive*
Calinger, Ronald Steve *historian*
Carnell, Paul Herbert *federal education official*
Coates, Robert Jay *retired electronic scientist*
Cole, Wayne Stanley *historian, educator*
Craig, Paul Max, Jr. *lawyer*
Dale, Charles *trade association executive*
Day, Daniel Edgar *government information officer*
DeMartini, Richard Michael *financial services company executive*
Dimino, Joseph T. *archbishop*
Doerr, Edd *religious liberty organization administrator*
Doherty, William Thomas, Jr. *historian, retired educator*
Douglass, Carl Dean *biochemistry consultant, former government official*
Eades, James Beverly, Jr. *aeronautical engineer*
Eiserer, Leonard Albert Carl *publishing executive*
Fanelli, Joseph James *retired public affairs executive, consultant*
†Fiorito, Ralph Bruno *research physicist, consultant*
Flieger, Howard Wentworth *editor*
Fockler, Herbert Hill *foundation executive*
Folkenberg, Robert S. *religious organization administrator*
Foresti, Roy, Jr. *chemical engineer*
Friday, Elbert Walter, Jr. *federal agency administrator, meteorologist*
Gaunaurd, Guillermo C. *physicist, engineer, researcher*
Geiger, Anne Ellis *secondary educator*
Gilbert, Arthur Charles Francis *psychologist*
Gilbert, Donald Floyd *church administrator*
Glenn, Robert Edward *industrial hygienist, trade association executive, former government research administrator*
Goott, Daniel *government official, consultant*
Grubbs, Donald Shaw, Jr. *actuary*
Hackett, John Francis *archivist*
†Hall, J. Michael *federal agency administrator, meteorologist*
Hamill, James Paul *hospital administrator*
Hannan, Myles *lawyer, banker*
Hanson, Angus Alexander *geneticist*
Hayman, Harry *association executive, electrical engineer*
Haynes, Leonard L., III *government official, consultant, educator*
†Hazard, Robert Culver, Jr. *hotel executive*
Hegstad, Roland Rex *magazine editor*
Hermach, Francis Lewis *consulting engineer*
Hermanson Ogilvie, Judith *foundation executive*
Hersey, David Floyd *information resources management consultant, government official;*
Holloway, William Jimmerson *retired educator*
Howze, Karen Aileen *newspaper editor, lawyer, multi-cultural communications consultant*
Hsueh, Chun-tu *political science educator, foundation executive*
Humphries, Weldon R. *real estate/hotel executive*
Jacobs, George *telecommunications engineering consulting company executive*
Jaskot, John Joseph *insurance company executive*
†Johnson, Charles Christopher, Jr. *consulting environmental engineer*
Kendrick, James Earl *business consultant*
Kohler, Max Adam *consulting hydrologist, weather service administrator*
Kotler, Martin *management consultant*
Kronstadt, Arnold Mayo *community and architectural planner*
Leedy, Daniel Loney *ecologist*
Lynch, Sonia *data processing consultant*
Manduley, Jose Carlos *government official*
†Michelson, Stephan *economist*
Milligan, Glenn Ellis *psychologist*
Mitchell, Milton *lawyer*
Mooney, James Hugh *newspaper editor*
Morrison, Roy Dennis, II *philosophy, religion and science educator emeritus*
Mundel, Marvin Everett *industrial engineer*
Munson, John Christian *acoustician*
Myers, Evelyn Stephenson *editor, writer*
Odland, Gerald Clark *association executive*
Orkand, Donald Saul *management consultant*
Ostenso, Ned Allen *oceanographer, government official*
Pearman, Reginald James *educational administrator*
Peiperl, Adam *kinetic and video sculptor*
Pellerzi, Leo Maurice *lawyer*
Perlmutter, Jerome Herbert *communications specialist*
Phillips, Craig *aquarium administrator*
Popkin, Roy Sandor *emergency management consultant, writer, researcher*
Porter, Dwight Johnson *former electric company executive, foreign affairs consultant*
Raphael, Coleman *business school dean*
Rasi, Humberto Mario *educational administrator, editor, minister*
Rayburn, Carole (Mary Aida) Ann *psychologist, researcher, writer*
Rueger, Lauren John *retired physicist*
†Rule, Donald *research physicist*
Sampugnaro, Trudy M. *principal*
Scheer, Milton David *physical chemist*
Schick, Irvin Henry *educator*
Schneider, William Charles *aerospace consultant*
Scipio, L(ouis) Albert, II *aerospace science engineering educator, architect, military historian*
†Sellers, Barney *professional society administrator*
Senseman, Ronald Sylvester *architect*
Shames, Irving Herman *engineering educator*
Shih-Carducci, Joan Chia-mo *cooking educator, biochemist, medical technologist*
Shira, Robert Bruce *university administrator, oral surgery educator*
Simon, Donald John *financial planner, insurance and investment broker*
Straub, Sylvia Ann *association executive*
Sweetland, Loraine Fern *librarian, educator*
Telesetsky, Walter *government official*
Thompson, George Ralph *church denomination administrator*
Ventre, Francis Thomas *environmental design and policy educator*
von Hake, Margaret Joan *librarian*
Waldrop, Francis Neil *physician*
Ware, Thomas Earle *building consultant*
†Watts, Ralph S. *social services administrator*
Whalen, John Philip *retired educational administrator*
Whitten, Leslie Hunter, Jr. *author, newspaper reporter*
Wilson, William Stanley *oceanographer*
Winston, Michael Russell *foundation executive, historian*
Wood, Robert Elkington, II *financial services company executive*
Yasher, Michael *accountant*
Yeakel, Joseph Hughes *clergyman*
†Young, Jay Alfred *chemical safety and health consultant, writer, editor*
Young, Kenneth Laurence *union official*

Solomons
Samuels, Sheldon Wilfred *philosophy educator, writer*

Sparks
Barr, Irwin Robert *retired aeronautical engineer*
Felton, John Walter *spice company executive*
Harrison, James Joshua, Jr. *food products executive*
McCormick, Charles Perry, Jr. *food products company executive*
Single, Richard Wayne, Sr. *lawyer*
Suarez-Murias, Marguerite C. *retired language and literature educator*

Sparks Glencoe
†Swackhamer, Gene L. *bank executive*

Stevenson
Hendler, Nelson Howard *physician, medical clinic director*
Jacobs, Bradford McElderry *newspaper editor*
Schnering, Philip Blessed *investment banker*

Stevensville
Deen, Thomas Blackburn *transportation research executive*
Kepley, Thomas Alvin *management consultant*

Sykesville
Buck, John Bonner *retired biologist*
Enoff, Louis D. *international consultant*

Takoma Park
Carpenter, Mary Chapin *singer, songwriter*
†Tucker, Kathleen M. *lawyer*

Temple Hills
Day, Mary Jane Thomas *cartographer*
Whidden, Stanley John *physiologist, physician*
Wilcox, Richard Hoag *information scientist*

Towson
Baker, Jean Harvey *history educator*
Chappell, Annette M. *university dean*
DiCamillo, Gary Thomas *manufacturing executive*
Hildebrand, Joan Martin *education educator*
Howell, Harley Thomas *lawyer*
Irwin, Sister Marie Cecilia *hospital administrator*
Johnston, Edward Allan *lawyer*
Lerch, Richard Heaphy *lawyer*
Levasseur, William Ryan *lawyer*
Mark, Michael Laurence *music educator*
Mc Indoe, Darrell Winfred *nuclear medicine physician, former air force officer*
Muuss, Rolf Eduard *psychologist, educator*
Peacock, James Daniel *lawyer*
Spodak, Michael Kenneth *forensic psychiatrist*
Udvarhelyi, George Bela *neurosurgery educator emeritus, cultural affairs administrator*

Trappe
Anderson, Andrew Herbert *retired army officer*

Union Bridge
Laughlin, Henry Prather *physician, psychiatrist, educator, author, editor*

Upper Marlboro
Aluisi, James Vincent *protective services official, security specialist*
†Anderson, Neil R. *oceanographer*
Bowles, Liza K. *construction executive*
Chasanow, Howard Stuart *judge, lecturer*
Elwood, Patricia *educator, political consultant*
Kourpias, George J. *international union administrator*
MacFadyen, David Jerry *building research executive*
Smith, Ralph Lee *author, musician*
Street, Patricia Lynn *secondary education educator*
Underdue, Marilyn Rosetta *special education educator*

Westminster
Bryson, Brady Oliver *lawyer*
Chambers, Robert Hunter, III *college president, American studies educator*
Cueman, Edmund Robert *county planner*
Dulany, William Bevard *lawyer*

Wheaton
Whiddon, Jerry B. *artistic director, actor, educator*

White Hall
Radigan, Frank Xavier *pharmaceutical company executive*

Williamsport
Chesnut, Nondis Lorine *English language educator, writer, consultant*

Woodbine
Brush, Peter Norman *federal agency administrator, lawyer*

Woodstock
Ballweber, Hettie Lou *archaeologist*
Fitzgerald, John *health facility executive*
Price, John Roy, Jr. *financial executive*

Wye Mills
Schnaitman, William Kenneth *finance company executive*

MASSACHUSETTS

Acton
Barrett, James *computer software company executive*
Golden, John Joseph, Jr. *manufacturing company executive*
Kittross, John Michael *retired communications educator*
Lee, Shih-Ying *mechanical engineering educator*
Leighton, Charles Milton *specialty consumer products company executive*
Peterson, Bob *environmental company executive, consultant*
†Russo, Peter Robert, Jr. *data instrument company executive*
Tod, G. Robert *consumer marketing executive*
†Ziminski, Richard William *engineering executive*

Agawam
Charest, Gabrielle Marya *educational administrator*

Allston
Becton, Henry Prentiss, Jr. *broadcasting company executive*
Bley, Carla Borg *jazz composer*
Metheny, Patrick Bruce *musician*
Mills, Daniel Quinn *business educator, consultant, author*
Sanders, Pharoah *saxophonist, composer*
Silk, Alvin John *business educator*

Amesbury
Dowd, Frances Connelly *librarian*
Labaree, Benjamin Woods *history educator*

Amherst
Abbott, Douglas Eugene *engineering educator*
Adrion, William Richards *academic administrator, computer and information sciences educator, author*
Alfange, Dean, Jr. *political science educator*
Anderson, Ronald Trent *art educator*
Archer, Ronald Dean *chemist, educator*
Arkes, Hadley P. *political science and jurisprudence educator*
Averill, James Reed *psychology educator*
Bagg, Robert Ely *English educator, poet*
Baker, Lynne Rudder *philosophy educator*
Beals, Ralph Everett *economist, educator*
Belt, Edward Scudder *sedimentologist, educator*
†Benitez-Rojo, Antonio *Romance languages educator*
Benson, Lucy Peters Wilson *political and diplomatic consultant*
Bentley, Richard Norcross *regional planner, educator*
Berger, Bernard Ben *environmental and civil engineer, former educator and public health officer*
Berger, Seymour Maurice *social psychologist*
Bestor, Charles Lemon *composer, educator*
Bezucha, Robert Joseph *history educator*
Bischoff, David Canby *university dean*
Bozone, Billie Rae *librarian, consultant*
Brandon, Liane *filmmaker, educator*
Bridegam, Willis Edward, Jr. *librarian*
Bromery, Randolph Wilson *geologist, educator*
Buell, Victor Paul *marketing educator, author, editor*
Byron, Frederick William, Jr. *physicist, educator, university vice chancellor*
Carpino, Louis A. *chemist, educator*
Chappell, Vere Claiborne *philosophy educator*
Coppinger, Raymond Parke *biologist, educator*
Cornish, Geoffrey St. John *golf course architect*
Creed, Robert Payson, Sr. *literature educator*
Demerath, Nicholas Jay, III *sociology educator*
Donohue, Therese Brady *artistic director, choreographer, designer*
Ehrlich, Paul *chemist, educator*
Fink, Richard David *chemist, educator*
Fleischman, Paul R. *psychiatrist, writer*
Fox, Thomas Walton *veterinary science educator*
Franks, Lewis E. *electrical and computer engineering educator, researcher*
Gerety, Tom *college administrator, educator*
Gibson, Walker *retired English language educator, poet, writer*
Godfrey, Paul Joseph *science foundation director*
Goldman, Sheldon *political science educator*
Goldstein, Joseph Irwin *materials scientist, educator*
Gordon, Joel Ethan *physics educator*
Grose, Robert Freeman *psychology educator*
Haensel, Vladimir *chemical engineering educator*
Harrison, Edward Robert *physicist, educator*
Hendricks, James Powell *artist*
Hernon, Joseph Martin, Jr. *history educator*
Hewlett, Horace Wilson *former educational administrator, association executive*
Hillel, Daniel *soil physics and hydrology educator, researcher, consultant*
Holmes, Francis William *plant pathologist*
Holmes, Helen Bequaert *researcher*
Inglis, David Rittenhouse *physicist*
Jenkins, Paul Randall *poet, editor*
Kantor, Simon William *chemistry educator*
Kinney, Arthur Frederick *literary history educator, author, editor*
Klare, Michael Thomas *social science educator, program director*
Langland, Joseph Thomas *author, emeritus educator*
Larson, Joseph Stanley *environmentalist, educator, researcher*
Laurence, Robert Lionel *chemical engineering educator*
Lenz, Robert William *polymer chemistry educator*
Liebling, Jerome *photographer, educator*
MacKnight, William John *chemist, educator*
Marcum, James Benton *college dean*
Mc Donagh, Edward Charles *sociologist, university administrator*
Mc Garrah, Robert Eynon *business administration educator*
McIntosh, Robert Edward, Jr. *electrical engineering educator, consultant, electronics executive*
McNeal, Ann P. *Woodhull physiology professor*
Menon, Premachandran Rama *electrical engineering educator*
Motherway, Joseph Edward *mechanical engineer, educator*
Nash, William Arthur *civil engineer, educator*
Nicholson, Walter *economist, educator*
Oates, Stephen Baery *history educator*
O'Brien, Richard Desmond *university administrator, neurobiologist*
Palser, Barbara F. *botany researcher, retired educator*
Parkhurst, Charles *retired museum director, art historian*
Partee, Barbara Hall *linguist, educator*
Peterson, Gerald Alvin *physicist*
Porter, Dennis Dudley *foreign language educator*
Porter, Roger Stephen *chemistry educator*
Prince, Gregory Smith, Jr. *academic administrator*
Quin, Louis DuBose *chemist, educator*
Ragle, John Linn *chemistry educator*
Rodovich, Arlene Guyotte *administrator, small business owner*
Rohde, Richard A. *plant pathologist educator*
Rosbottom, Ronald Carlisle *academic administrator, French culture and literature educator*
Rossi, Alice S. *sociology educator, author*
Rupp, William John *architect*
Sandweiss, Martha A. *museum director, author, American studies educator*
Sarat, Austin D. *jurisprudence and political science educator*
Schaubert, Daniel Harold *electrical engineering educator*
Scott, David Knight *physicist, university administrator*
Singleton, Philip Arthur *corporate executive*
Slakey, Linda Louise *biochemistry educator*
Stein, Otto Ludwig *botany educator*
Stein, Richard Stephen *chemistry educator*
Strickland, Bonnie Ruth *psychologist, educator*
†Strom, Stephen Eric *astronomer*
Swift, Calvin Thomas *electrical and computer engineering educator*
Tager, Jack *historian, educator*
Talbot, Richard Joseph *library administrator*
Tate, James Vincent *poet, English educator*
Taubman, Jane Andelman *Russian literature educator*
Taubman, William Chase *political science educator*
Tenenbaum, Jeffrey Mark *academic librarian*
Tippo, Oswald *botanist, educator, university administrator*
Torras, Joseph Hill *pulp and paper company executive*
Wideman, John Edgar *English literature educator, novelist*
Wilcox, Bruce Gordon *publisher*
Wills, David Wood *minister, educator*
Wolff, Robert Paul *philosophy educator*
Woodbury, Richard Benjamin *anthropologist, educator*
Wyman, David Sword *historian, educator*

Andover
Anderson, Amelia E. *nursing administrator, geriatrics nurse*
Butler, Fred Jay, Jr. *manufacturing company executive*
†Caledonia, George E. *research company executive*
Chase, Barbara Landis *headmistress*
Cook, Christopher Capen *artist, educator*
Fan, Rulin *organic chemist, researcher*
Fitzgerald, Michael Anthony *insurance company executive*
Jakes, William Chester *electrical engineer*
Lloyd, Robert Andrew *art educator*
Mac Neish, Richard Stockton *archaeologist, educator*
Maguire, Robert Edward *retired public utility executive*
Sullivan, John Vincent *life insurance company executive*
Wise, Kelly *private school educator, photographer, critic*

Arlington
Fulmer, Vincent Anthony *retired college president*
Gumpertz, Werner Herbert *structural engineering company executive*
O'Connell, Paul Edmund *publisher*
Spengler, Kenneth C. *meteorologist, professional society administrator*
Whitehead, George William *retired mathematician*

Ashfield
Nye, Edwin Packard *mechanical engineering educator*
Pepyne, Edward Walter *lawyer, former educator*

Ashland
Borgeson, Earl Charles *law librarian, educator*
Gohlke, Frank William *photographer*

Attleboro
DeWerth, Gordon Henry *corporate finance executive*
Glenn, James *sales executive*
Griffin, Edwin H., Jr. (Hank Griffin) *chemist*
Hammerle, Fredric Joseph *metal processing executive*
†King, Melvin James *internist*

Auburn
Baker, David Arthur *small business owner, manufacturer*

Babson Park
Genovese, Francis Charles (Frank Genovese) *economist, consultant, editor*
Glavin, William Francis *academic administrator*

Bedford
Alarcon, Rogelio Alfonso *physician, researcher*
Aronstein, Laurence W. *middle school principal*
Brady, Upton Birnie *editor*
†Carpenter, Chadwick H., Jr. *computer software company executive*
Carr, Paul Henry *physicist*
Cronson, Harry Marvin *electronics engineer*
Dill, Melville Reese, Jr. *industrial engineering consultant*
Dulchinos, Peter *lawyer*
†Elkinton, Joseph Russell *medical educator*
Fante, Ronald Louis *engineering scientist*
Gilmartin, John A. *medical products company executive*
Goodman, William Beehler *editor, literary agent*
Griffin, Donald R(edfield) *zoology educator*
Hicks, Walter Joseph *electrical engineer, consultant*
Horowitz, Barry Martin *systems research and engineering company executive*
Jelalian, Albert V. *electrical engineer*
Kennedy, X. J. (Joseph Kennedy) *writer*
Kouyoumjian, Charles H. *diversified financial services company executive*
Kovaly, John Joseph *consulting engineering executive, educator*
Landry, John Bernard, III *data processing executive*
Nunes, Geoffrey *lawyer, corporate executive*
Ren, Chung-Li *engineer*
Sizer, Irwin Whiting *biochemistry educator*
Taylor, C(harles) Richard *biological sciences educator*
Volicer, Ladislav *physician, educator*
†Wilson, Raymond P. *communications systems marketing professional*
Winter, David Louis *systems engineer, human factors scientist, retired*
Zraket, Charles Anthony *systems research and engineering company executive*

Belmont
Allison, Elisabeth Kovacs *information company executive*
Bergson, Abram *economist, educator*
Bird, Edward Dennis *physician*
Buckley, Jerome Hamilton *English language educator*
Cavarnos, Constantine Peter *writer, philosopher*
Cohen, Bruce Michael *psychiatrist, educator, scientist*
†Coyle, Joseph Thomas *psychiatrist*
de Marneffe, Francis *psychiatrist, hospital administrator*
Frey, John Ward *landscape architect*
Gui, James Edmund *architect*
Haralampu, George Stelios *electric power engineer, former engineering executive electric utility company*
Haselkorn, David *teacher recruiting executive*
Keil, Alfred Adolf Heinrich *marine engineering educator*
Klein, Martin Samuel *management consulting executive*
Levendusky, Philip George *clinical psychologist, administrator*
Levine, Sarah Loewenberg *developmental psychologist, school director*
Luick, Robert Burns *lawyer*
Merrill, Edward Wilson *chemical engineering educator*
Nixon, Ralph Angus *psychiatrist, educator, research neuroscientist*
Onesti, Silvio Joseph *psychiatrist*
Pope, Harrison Graham, Jr. *psychiatrist, educator*
Rowe, Richard R. *on-line information and management services company executive*
Seifert, William Walther *electrical engineering educator*
Sifneos, Peter Emanuel *psychiatrist*

Beverly
Barger, Richard Wilson *hotel executive*
Bemberis, Ivars *marketing professional*
Roberts, Richard John *molecular biologist*
†St. Laurent, David Francis *insurance company executive*

Billerica
Brebbia, Carlos Alberto *educator, engineering consultant*
Gray, Charles Agustus *chemical company research executive*
Kolb, Charles Eugene *research corporation executive*
Leblois, Axel *computer company executive*
Mackenzie, Ward D. *computer company executive*
McCaffrey, Robert Henry, Jr. *retired manufacturing company executive*
Pike, Albert Louis, Jr. *educational administrator, consultant*
†Rennie, John Coyne *aerospace company executive*
Schmidt, James Robert *facilities engineer*

Bolton
Kadak, Andrew C. *engineering company executive*

Boston
Ablow, Joseph *artist, educator*
Aborn, Foster Litchfield *insurance company executive*
Abraham, Nicholas Albert *lawyer, real estate developer*
Abrams, Ruth Ida *state supreme court justice*
Achatz, John *lawyer*
Acton, Lloyd Phelps, Jr. *architect*
Adams, Douglass Franklin *radiologist, educator*
Adams, John Randolph *neurologist, educator*
Adams, Phoebe-Lou *journalist*
Adelstein, S(tanley) James *physician, educator*
Adler, David Avram *psychiatrist*
Aikman, William Francis *venture capitalist*
Aisenberg, Alan C. *physician, educator, researcher*
Akin, Steven Paul *financial company executive*
Alden, Vernon Roger *corporate director, trustee*
Aldrich, Bailey *federal judge*
Alexander, James Garth *architect*
Alexander, Joyce London *judge*
Allard, David Henry *judge*
Allen, Nancy Schuster *librarian*
Alpert, Joel Jacobs *medical educator, pediatrician*
Ames, Damaris *publishing executive*
Ames, James Barr *lawyer*
Amirault, Richard B. *career officer*
Amy-Moreno de Toro, Angel Alberto *social sciences educator, writer, oral historian*
Anderson, Arthur Irvin *lawyer*
Andre, Rae *writer, organizational behavior educator*
Andrews, Kenneth Richmond *business administration educator*
Angelo, E. Joanne *child, adolescent and adult psychiatrist*
Angelou, Maya *author*
Annas, George J. *health law educator*
Anselme, Jean-Pierre Louis Marie *chemist*
Ansin, Betsey Iris *psychotherapist, clinical social worker*
Antoniades, Harry Nicholas *educator, research biochemist*
Appelbaum, Diana Karter *author*
Aresty, Jeffrey M. *lawyer*
Argyris, Chris *organizational behavior educator*
Arias, Irwin Monroe *physician, educator*
Arky, Ronald Alfred *medical educator*
Armand, Patrick *dancer*
Armstrong, Rodney *librarian*
Arnold, John David *management counselor, consultant*
Aronow, Saul *physicist*
Astrue, Michael James *lawyer*
Atherton, William *insurance company executive*
Auerbach, Arnold (Red Auerbach) *professional basketball team executive*
Auerbach, Joseph *lawyer, educator*
Austen, K(arl) Frank *physician*
Austen, W(illiam) Gerald *surgeon, educator*
Avery, Mary Ellen *pediatrician, educator*
Avison, David *photographer*
Bae, Frank S. H. *law educator, law librarian*
Baer, Michael Alan *political scientist, educator*
Bailey, Richard Briggs *investment company executive*
Bailey, Stephen *newspaper reporter*
Baker, Charles Duane *business administration educator, former management executive*
Bangs, Will Johnston *lawyer*
Banks, Henry H. *academic dean, physician*
Barger, A(braham) Clifford *physiology educator*
Bargmann, Joel David *architect*
Barlow, Charles Franklin *physician, educator*
Barlow, John Sutton *neurophysiologist, electroencephalographer*
Barry, Patricia Pound *physician, educator*
Batchelder, Samuel Lawrence, Jr. *corporate lawyer*
Bates, Jeffrey C. *lawyer*
Bauer, Elaine Louise *ballet dancer*
Beal, Ilene *bank executive*
Beal, Robert Lawrence *real estate executive*
Beard, Charles Julian *lawyer*
Beard, John Edwards *lawyer*
Beatty, Jack J. *magazine editor*
Beck, William Samson *physician, educator, biochemist*
Becker, Fred Ronald *lawyer*
Beinhocker, Gilbert David *investment banker*
Belin, Gaspard d'Andelot *lawyer*
Bellefontaine, Edgar John *law librarian, lawyer*
Benjamin, William Chase *lawyer*
Bennett, George Frederick *investment manager*
Benning, John Alan *financial services executive*
Berenberg, William *physician, educator*
Berenson, Paul Stewart *advertising executive*
Berg, Norman Asplund *management educator*
Berg, Warren Stanley *retired banker*
Bergen, Kenneth William *lawyer*
Berger, Francine Ellis *radio station executive, communications executive*
Berkey, Dennis D. *mathematics educator*
Berlew, Frank Kingston *lawyer*
Berman, Kenneth R. *lawyer*
Bernfield, Merton Ronald *pediatrician, scientist, educator*
Bernhard, Alexander Alfred *lawyer*
Bernhard, William Francis *thoracic and cardiovascular surgeon*
Berry, Janis Marie *lawyer*
Berson, Eliot Lawrence *ophthalmologist, medical educator*
Bertman, Richard Jay *architect*
Bertonazzi, Louis Peter *state senator*
Berube, Margery Stanwood *publishing executive*
Bettenhausen, Elizabeth Ann *theology educator*
Biederman, Joseph *psychiatrist*
Bines, Harvey Ernest *lawyer, educator, writer*
Bird, Larry Joe *retired professional basketball player*
Bissell, George S. *insurance company executive*
Blampied, Peter J. *banker*
Blau, Monte *radiology educator*
Blendon, Robert Jay *health policy educator*
Bloch, Kurt Julius *physician*
Blout, Elkan Rogers *biological chemistry educator, university dean*
Bodman, Samuel Wright, III *specialty chemicals and materials company executive*
Bohnen, Michael J. *lawyer*
Bok, John Fairfield *lawyer*
Bondoc, Conrado Cervania *surgeon, educator*
Borenstein, Milton Conrad *lawyer, manufacturing company executive*
Bornheimer, Allen Millard *lawyer*
Borod, Ronald Sam *lawyer*
Boudin, Michael *federal judge*
Bourne, Katherine Day *journalist, educator*
Bourque, Michael H. *interior designer*
Bourque, Ray *professional hockey player*
Bower, Joseph Lyon *business administration educator*
Bowler, Marianne Bianca *judge*
Bownes, Hugh Henry *federal judge*
Boyan, William L., Jr. *insurance company executive*
Boyden, W(alter) Lincoln *lawyer*
Brain, Joseph David *biomedical scientist*
Brandt, Allan M. *medical history educator*
Braunwald, Eugene *physician, educator*
Braver, Barbara Leix *religious organization communications administrator*
Brazelton, Thomas Berry *pediatrician, educator*
Brecher, Kenneth *astrophysicist*
Breitman, Leo R. *banker*
Brenner, Barry Morton *physician*
Brenton, Marianne Webber *state legislator, technical librarian*
Britton, Richard Lindsay *advertising executive*
Brody, Richard Eric *lawyer*
Broitman, Selwyn Arthur *microbiologist, educator*
Bromsen, Maury Austin *historian, bibliographer, antiquarian bookseller*
†Brooke, Marvin McClatchey *rehabilitative medicine physician, educator*
Brountas, Paul Peter *lawyer*
Brovarski, Edward Joseph *curator, Egyptologist*
Brown, David A.B. *strategy consultant*
Brown, Judith Olans *lawyer, educator*
Brown, Matthew *lawyer*
Brown, Michael *information technology executive*
Brown, Michael Robert *lawyer*

Brown, Stephen Lee insurance company executive
Brown, William L. banker
Browne, Kingsbury lawyer
Brownell, Gordon Lee physicist, educator
Bruns, William John, Jr. business administration educator
Buccella, William Victor lawyer
Buchanan, Robert McLeod lawyer
Buchin, Stanley Ira management consultant, educator
Buckley, Joseph W. insurance company executive
Buckley, Mortimer Joseph physician
Burack, Sylvia Kamerman editor, publisher
Burakoff, Steven James immunologist, educator
Burgess, John Allen lawyer
Burgess, R. William, Jr. investment banking executive
Burke, John Francis surgeon, educator, researcher
Burleigh, Lewis Albert lawyer
Burley, Dexter Lishon gerontologist, consultant
Burnes, Kennett Farrar chemical company executive
Burns, James John information systems executive
Burns, Padraic physician, psychiatrist, psychoanalyst, educator
Burns, Richard Michael public utility company executive
Burns, Thomas David lawyer
Burr, Francis Hardon lawyer
Bustin, Edouard Jean political scientist, educator
†Buxbaum, Robert C. internist
Cabot, Charles Codman, Jr. lawyer
Cabot, Louis Wellington chemical manufacturing company executive
Cabot, Thomas Dudley chemical company executive
Calderwood, Stanford Matson investment management executive
Caldwell, Gail book critic
†Callahan, James T. engineering company executive
Callow, Allan Dana surgeon
Campbell, Levin Hicks federal judge
Campbell, Richard P. lawyer
Caner, George Colket, Jr. lawyer
Canseco, Jose professional baseball player
Cantella, Vincent Michele stockbroker
Cantor, Charles Robert biochemistry educator
Caplan, Louis Robert neurology educator
Cardona, Rodolfo Spanish language and literature educator
Cariseo, David Joseph financial services executive
Carr, Jay Phillip critic
Carr, Michael Leon professional sports team executive, former professional basketball player
Carroll, James author
Carroll, Matthew Shaun reporter
Carter, Lewis Aaron, Jr. public relations executive
†Carton, Lonnie Caming educational psychologist
Cashel, Thomas William lawyer, educator
Casner, Truman Snell lawyer
Caso, Gasper librarian, lawyer
Cassidy, Carl Eugene physician
Cassilly, Richard tenor, voice educator
†Castaneda, Aldo R. pediatric cardiac surgeon
Cederholm, Theresa Miriam Dickason museum director
Cellucci, Argeo Paul state official
Cervieri, John Anthony, Jr. real estate company officer
†Chandler, David Luscombe science writer
Chapin, Melville lawyer
Cheever, Daniel Sargent international affairs educator, editor
Chen, Ching-chih information science educator, consultant
Chen, Lincoln Chin-ho medical educator
Chilvers, Derek insurance company executive
Chinlund, Christine newspaper editor
Chobanian, Aram Van medical school dean, cardiologist
Christensen, Carl Roland business administration educator
Christensen, Charles Harold college publishing company executive
Christenson, Charles John business educator
Clancy, John M. architectural firm executive
Clapp, Eugene Howard, II financial executive
Clarke, Terence Michael public relations and advertising executive
Clemens, William Roger professional baseball player
Cleveland, Richard Joseph surgeon
Cleven, Carol Chapman state legislator
†Coffin, John Miller molecular biologist, educator
Coffman, Jay Denton physician, educator
Cogan, John Francis, Jr. lawyer
Cogan, Robert David composer, school official
†Coggins, Cecil Hammond physician, educator
Cohen, Alan Seymour internist
Cohen, Jonathan Brewer molecular neurobiologist, biochemist
Cohen, Rachelle Sharon journalist
Cohen, Robert Sonné physicist, philosopher, educator
Cohn, Andrew Howard lawyer
Cole, Carolyn Jo brokerage company executive
Coleman, C. Norman radiologist, oncologist, researcher, educator
Coleman, John Joseph telephone company executive
Collings, Robert Biddlecombe federal judge
Collins, John Joseph, Jr. cardiac and thoracic surgeon
Collins, Monica Ann journalist
Colloredo-Mansfeld, Ferdinand real estate company executive
Comegys, Walker Brockton lawyer
Cone, Carol Lynn public relations executive
Connell, William Francis diversified company executive
Conners, John Brendan insurance company executive
Connolly, Michael Joseph state official
Connolly, Paul K., Jr. lawyer
Connolly, Thomas Edward state court judge
Connors, Donald Louis lawyer, land use planner
Connors, John Michael, Jr. advertising agency executive
Conroy, Pat (Donald Patrick Conroy) writer
Cook, David editor
Coolidge, Francis Lowell lawyer
Copeland, Anne Pitcairn psychologist
Corcoran, Paul John physician
Cornwall, Deborah Joyce consulting firm executive, management consultant
Costellese, Linda E. Grace banker
Cotran, Ramzi S. pathologist, educator
†Cotton, Deborah Jean physician
†Coughlin, Margaret Ann marketing communications executive
Countryman, Gary Lee insurance company executive
Cousy, Bob Joseph sports commentator
Cox, Howard Ellis, Jr. venture capitalist
Crandall, Rhona personnel manager
Crane, Andrew B. state official
Cravalho, Ernest George biomedical engineering educator
Craver, James Bernard lawyer
Crocker, Allen Carrol pediatrician
Crofwell, James B. stock exchange executive
Cronin, Bonnie Kathryn Lamb legislative staff executive
Cronin, Philip Mark lawyer
Crook, Robert Wayne mutual funds executive
Crozier, William Marshall, Jr. bank holding company executive
Curley, Arthur library director
Curran, Emily Katherine museum director
Curry, John Anthony, Jr. university administrator
Curry, John Michael investment banker
Curtin, John Joseph, Jr. lawyer
Curtin, Phyllis music educator, former dean, operatic singer
Curtis, Christopher Michael magazine editor
Cutler, Arnold Robert lawyer
†Cyker, Marvin Myer dental equipment company executive
Dacey, Kathleen Ryan judge
D'Agostino, Ralph Benedict mathematician, statistician, educator, consultant
D'Alessandro, David Francis financial services company executive
†Daley, James A. hotel executive
Daley, Paul Patrick lawyer
Dana, Jerilyn ballet company administrator
Danziger, Jeff political cartoonist, writer
Darehshori, Nader Farhang publishing sales executive
Davies, Don education educator
Davis, David William transportation consultant
Davis, George Wilmot electric utility executive
Davis, Harold Truscott retired lawyer
Davis, Michael Richard architect
Davis, William Arthur writer, editor
Davison, Peter Fitzgerald retired science administrator, consultant
Davison, Peter Hubert editor, poet
Dawson, James Ambrose printing industry executive
Dean, Robert Charles architect
de Burlo, Comegys Russell, Jr. investment advisor, educator
De Cherney, Alan Hersh obstetrics and gynecology educator
Dederer, William Bowne music educator, dean
Deissler, Mary A. foundation executive
Delaney, John White lawyer
Delbanco, Thomas Lewis medical educator, researcher
Delinsky, Stephen R. lawyer
De Luca, Carlo John biomedical engineer
Denniston, Brackett Badger, III lawyer
Dentler, Robert Arnold sociologist, educator
de Rham, Casimir, Jr. lawyer
DeSanctis, Roman William cardiologist
Desforges, Jane Fay medical educator, physician
†Desnoyers, Megan Floyd archivist, educator
Deutsch, Stephen B. lawyer
Di Domenica, Robert Anthony musician, composer
Diener, Betty Jane university administrator
DiFranza, Virginia principal
Dignan, Thomas Gregory, Jr. lawyer
Dillin, John Woodward, Jr. newspaper correspondent
Dillon, James Joseph lawyer
Dineen, John K. lawyer
DiStasio, James Shannon accountant
Dixon, Andrew Lee, Jr. cable television company executive, lawyer
†Dluhy, Robert George physician
Doebler, James Carl naval officer, engineering executive
Donahue, Douglas Aidan, Jr. business executive
Donovan, Carol Ann state legislator
Donovan, Helen W. newspaper editor
Dooley, Arch Richard business administration educator
Doorley, Thomas Lawrence, III management consulting firm executive
Doris, Francis D. state senator
Dreben, Raya Spiegel judge
Driver, William Raymond, Jr. banker
Drohan, Thomas H. investment management executive
†Druhot, Theodore J(oseph) hospital adminintrator
Duffy, Kenneth J. insurance company executive
Dumaine, F. C. diversified corporation executive
Durand, Robert Alan state senator
Dusseault, C. Dean lawyer
Dvorak, Harold F. pathologist, educator, scientist
Eastman, Thomas George investment management executive
Eckstein, Marlene R. vascular radiologist
Eder, Richard Gray newspaper critic
Egdahl, Richard Harrison surgeon, medical educator, health science administrator
Ehrlich, M. Gordon lawyer
Eichorn, John Frederick Gerard, Jr. utility executive
Eisenberg, Leon psychiatrist, educator
Eisner, Sister Janet Margaret college president
El-Baz, Farouk program director, educator
Eldridge, Larry (William Lawrence Eldridge) journalist
Elfers, William retired investment company director
Elfner, Albert Henry, III mutual fund management company executive
Elkus, Howard Felix architect
Elliott, Byron Kauffman lawyer, business executive
Ellis, David Wertz museum director
Ellis, Franklin Henry, Jr. surgeon, educator
End, William Thomas business executive
Epstein, Franklin Harold physician, educator
Erickson, Kenneth W. lawyer
Eskandarian, Edward advertising agency executive
Essex, Myron Elmer microbiology educator
Estabrooks, Gordon Charles secondary education educator
Estin, Hans Howard investment executive
Evans, Donald John lawyer
Fairbanks, Jonathan Leo museum curator
Falb, Peter Lawrence mathematician, educator, investment company executive
Faller, Douglas V. cancer research scientist, physician
Fanning, Katherine Woodruff editor, journalism educator
Farrah, Elias George lawyer
Fausch, David Arthur public relations executive
Fay, Michael Leo lawyer
Fazzone, David A. lawyer
Feder, Donald Albert syndicated columnist
†Federman, Daniel David medical educator, educational administrator, endocrinologist
Feeney, Mark newspaper editor
Feldman, Robert George neurologist, medical educator
Feldman, Roger David lawyer
Felsen, Leopold B. engineer, educator
Felter, John Kenneth lawyer
Ferris, Benjamin Greeley, Jr. retired physician, environmental researcher, educator
Fesus, George John banker
Field, James Bernard internist, educator
Fieleke, Norman Siegfried economist
Fine, Samuel biomedical engineering educator, consultant
Fineberg, Harvey Vernon physician, educator
Finegold, Maurice Nathan architect
Fink, Joanna Elizabeth art dealer
Finnegan, Neal Francis banker
†Fischbach, Gerald D. neurobiology educator
Fischer, Eric Robert lawyer, educator
Fischer, Thomas Covell law educator, consultant, writer, lawyer
Fish, David Earl insurance company executive
Fisher, Champe Andrews lawyer
Fitzgibbons, James M. diversified company executive
Fitzpatrick, Thomas Bernard dermatologist, educator
Flansburgh, Earl Robert architect
Fletcher, Robert Hillman medical educator
Fletcher, Suzanne Wright physician, educator
Flint, Anthony Evans journalist
Floor, Richard Earl lawyer
Folkman, Moses Judah surgeon
Fonvielle, William Harold management consultant
Forbes, Peter architect
Foss, Clive Frank Wilson history educator
Fox, Bernard Hayman cancer epidemiologist, educator
Fox, Francis Haney lawyer
Frankenheim, Samuel lawyer
Frankl, Spencer Nelson dentist, university dean
Fraser, Robert Burchmore lawyer
Freed, Rita Evelyn curator, Egyptologist, educator
Freedberg, A. Stone physician
Freehling, Daniel Joseph law educator, law library director
Frei, Emil, III physician, medical researcher, educator
Freiman, David Galland pathologist, educator
Freishtat, Harvey W. lawyer
Fremont-Smith, Marion R. lawyer
†Friedmann, Robert Frederick advertising executive
Frigoletto, Fredric David, Jr. physician
Fruitt, Paul N. manufacturing executive
Furman, John Rockwell wholesale lumber company executive
Gabel, Creighton anthropologist, educator
†Gaintner, J(ohn) Richard health facility executive, medical educator
Galaburda, Albert Mark neurologist, researcher, educator
Galvani, Paul B. lawyer
†Galvin, William Francis secretary of state, lawyer
Gamson, Zelda sociologist, researcher
Gamst, Frederick Charles anthropology educator
Gang, Stephen R. motion picture executive, consultant
Garcia, Adolfo Ramon lawyer
Gardner, Dorsey Robertson finance company executive
Gaudreau, Russell A., Jr. lawyer
Gault, Robert Mellor lawyer
Gavitt, David R. (Dave Gavitt) professional sports team executive
Gellis, Sydney Saul physician
Gendron, George magazine editor
Gens, Peter David lawyer
Gergely, John biochemistry educator
Gerstmayr, John Wolfgang lawyer
Gesmer, Henry lawyer
Gibbons, Ronald John microbiologist, educator
Gibran, Kahlil sculptor
Gibson, Barry Joseph magazine editor
†Giesser, Richard A. transportation executive, financial and management consultant
Gifford, Charles Kilvert banker
Gifford, Nelson Sage financial company executive
Gilmore, Daniel J., III lawyer
Gimbrone, Michael Anthony, Jr. research scientist, pathologist, educator
Giso, Frank, III lawyer
Glass, Milton Louis retired manufacturing company executive
Glassman, Herbert Haskel architect
Glazer, Donald Wayne business executive, lawyer, educator
Glazer, Michael H. lawyer
Gleason, Jean Berko psychology educator
†Glickman, Robert Morris physician, educator
Glimcher, Melvin Jacob orthopedic surgeon
Glosband, Daniel Martin lawyer
Goldberg, Avram Jacob consulting and investing company executive, arbitrator
Goldberg, Irving Hyman molecular pharmacology and biochemistry educator
Goldman, David consumer products company executive
Goldsmith, Harry Sawyer surgeon, educator
Golomb, Claire psychology educator
Goodglass, Harold psychologist, neurology educator
Goodman, Abbie Rebecca state agency executive
Goodman, Bruce Gerald lawyer
Goodman, Louis Allan lawyer
Goodman, Sherri Wasserman lawyer
Goody, Joan architect
Gordon, Philip H. jewelry industry executive
Gordon, Ralph Dearing bank executive
Gorham, William Hartshorne lawyer
Gottlieb, Leonard Solomon pathology educator
Gould, James Spencer financial consultant
Gould, John Joseph communications executive
Goyal, Raj Kumar medical educator
Graham, Gary Lee architect, facilitator
Graham, John David public health educator
Greco, Michael S. lawyer
Greeley, Walter Franklin management and acquisition corporation executive, lawyer
Green, Gareth Montraville physician, educator, scientist
Green, Howard cellular physiologist, educator, administrator
Green, Jerry Richard economist, educator
Greenblatt, David J. pharmacologist, educator
Greene, Leonard J. newspaper columnist
Greene, Robert Allan former university administrator
Greenwald, Sheila Ellen writer, illustrator
Greer, Gordon Bruce lawyer
†Gresham, David Melvin designer, small business owner
Grillo, Hermes Conrad surgeon
Griswold, Frank Matthew, Jr. investment executive
Grossfeld, Stan newspaper photography executive, author
Grossman, Frances Kaplan psychologist
Gulley, Joan Long banker
Guthary, Barry Curtis lawyer
Haas, Kenneth Gregg orchestra executive
Haber, Edgar physician, educator
Haber, Robert J. mutual fund manager
Haddad, Ernest Mudarri lawyer
Hagler, Jon Lewis investment executive
Hailey, Arthur writer
Haley, Joseph William lawyer
†Hall, Donald holding company executive
Hall, Henry Lyon, Jr. lawyer
Hall, John Emmett orthopedic surgeon, educator
Hall, Lyle Gillis manufacturing company executive
Hamill, John P. bank executive
Hamilton, John Dayton, Jr. lawyer
Hammock, John Calvin international economic developer, consultant
Hammond, Norman David Curle archaeology educator, researcher
Hampton, Henry Eugene film and television producer
Hand, John lawyer
Handford, Martin John illustrator, author
Harkins, Lida E. state legislator, educator
Harold, Paul Dennis state senator
Harrington, Edward F. federal judge
Harrington, John Leo baseball company executive
Harrington, John Michael, Jr. lawyer
Harrington, Joseph John environmental engineering educator
Harrington, William David utility executive
Harris, Barbara C(lementine) bishop
Harris, Burton Henry surgeon
Harris, William Hamilton orthopedic surgeon
Harrison, Carter Henry banker
†Harrison-Jones, Lois school system administrator
Harshbarger, Scott state attorney general
Hartmann, Edward George historian, educator
Harvey, Les composer, producer
Harvey, William Burnett retired law educator
Hassan, William Ephriam, Jr. lawyer
Haussermann, Oscar William, Jr. lawyer
Hawke, Robert Douglas state legislator
Hawkey, G. Michael lawyer
Hawley, Anne museum director
Hay, Elizabeth Dexter embryology researcher, educator
Haydock, Robert, Jr. lawyer
Hayes, Andrew Wallace, II consumer products company executive
Hayes, Robert Francis lawyer
Hayes, Robert Herrick technology management educator
Hayes, Samuel Linton, III business educator
Hayward, Charles E. publishing company executive
Hedley-Whyte, Elizabeth Tessa neuropathologist
Heigham, James Crichton lawyer
Hein, John William dentist, educator
Heineman, Robert M. architectural firm executive
Hennekens, Charles Henry physician, epidemiologist
Henry, DeWitt Pawling, II creative writing educator, writer, arts administrator
Henry, Joseph Louis university dean
Heros, Roberto Cosme neurosurgeon
Hiatt, Howard H. physician, educator
Higgins, George Vincent journalist, lawyer, author, educator
Hill, George Jackson, III advertising agency executive
Hill, Richard Devereux retired banker
Hillman, Carol Barbara communications executive
Hillman, William Chernick federal bankruptcy judge
Hills, Patricia Gorton Schulze curator
Hines, Marion Ernest electronic engineering consultant
Hingson, Ralph W. medical educator
Hintikka, Jaakko philosopher, educator
Hirtle, Richard C. insurance company executive
Hjerpe, Edward Alfred, III finance and banking executive
Hobbs, Matthew Hallock investment banker
Hobson, John Allan psychiatrist, researcher, educator
Hoffman, Christian Matthew lawyer
Hoffman, David Alan lawyer
Holder, Timothy Scott fundraising and management consultant
Holey, Ronald Loren retired construction company executive
†Holick, Michael Francis nutritionist
Holland, Hubert Brian lawyer
Holloway, Bruce Keener former air force officer
†Holman, B. Leonard radiology educator, researcher
Hooker, Michael Kenneth college president
Hoort, Steven Thomas lawyer
Hornig, Donald Frederick scientist
Horowitz, Morris A. economist
Hotchkiss, Andra Ruth lawyer
Houston, Douglas White advertising company executive, creative director
Howe, Jas. Murray lawyer
Howlett, D(onald) Roger art gallery executive, art historian
†Howley, Peter Maxwell pathology educator
Hoyt, Herbert Austin Aikins television producer
Hubel, David Hunter physiologist, educator
†Humphrey, John William management and sales training executive, human resources consultant
Hurd, J. Nicholas executive recruiting consultant, former banker
Hutchinson, Bernard Thomas ophthalmologist
Hutter, Adolph Matthew, Jr. cardiologist, educator
Iafrate, Al Anthony professional hockey player
Isaacs, Helen Coolidge Adams (Mrs. Kenneth L. Isaacs) artist
Isham, Carolynn Clough advertising executive
Jackson, Cleotha human resource director
Jandl, James Harriman physician, educator
Jaroch, Timothy D. lawyer
†Jellinek, Michael Steven psychiatrist, pediatrician
Jensen, Michael Cole economics educator
Jochum, Veronica pianist
Johannsen, Peter George lawyer
Johnson, Dennis professional basketball player
Johnson, Edward Crosby, III financial company executive
Johnston, Richard Alan lawyer
Jones, Jeffrey Foster lawyer
Jones, Rodney G. poet, English educator
Jones, Sheldon Atwell lawyer
Jordan, Alexander Joseph, Jr. lawyer

Judson, Arnold Sidney management consultant
Julian, Sheryl newspaper writer
Kahn, Carl Ronald research laboratory administrator
Kamer, Joel Victor insurance company executive, actuary
Kames, Kenneth F. manufacturing company executive
Kane, Louis Isaac merchant
Kanin, Dennis Roy lawyer
Kanter, Rosabeth Moss management educator, consultant, writer
Kapiotas, John hotel company executive
Kaplan, Lawrence Edward lawyer
†Kaplan, Marshall Myles gastroenterologist, researcher, educator
†Karelitz, Richard Alan financial executive, lawyer
Karelitz, Robert N(elson) lawyer
†Karger, Barry L. chemistry educator
Karnovsky, Manfred L. biochemistry educator
Karnovsky, Morris John pathologist, biologist
Katz, Larry writer
Katz, Peter lawyer
†Katzmann, Gary Stephen lawyer
Kauffman, Godfrey newspaper publishing executive
Kazemi, Homayoun physician, medical educator
Kearns, Ellen Cecelia lawyer
Keating, Michael Burns lawyer
Keeton, Robert Ernest federal judge
Kehoe, William Francis lawyer
Keller, Stanley lawyer
†Kelley, Kevin H. insurance company executive
Kelly, Edmund F. insurance company executive
Kelly, Thomas J. lawyer
Kennedy, Eugene Patrick biochemist, educator
Kennedy, Kevin Curtis professional baseball team manager
Kenney, Raymond Joseph, Jr. lawyer
Kerry, Cameron F. lawyer
Kieff, Elliott Dan medical educator
Kim, Ducksoo radiologist and educator
Kimball, George Edward, III sports columnist
Kimura, Robert Shigetsugu otologic researcher
†Kindl, Patrice writer
King, Kernan Francis insurance company executive, lawyer
King, Nick newspaper editor
King, Robert David insurance company executive
King, William Bruce lawyer
Kingman, William Lockwood financial consultant
Kirchick, William Dean lawyer
Kirk, Paul Grattan, Jr. lawyer, former political organization official
Kirkpatrick, Edward Thomson college administrator, mechanical engineer
†Kirschner, Marc Wallace biochemist, cell biologist
Kitz, Richard John anesthesiologist, educator
Klarfeld, Jonathan Michael journalism educator
Kleiner, Fred Scott art history and archaeology educator, editor
Klem, Christopher A. lawyer
Klempner, Mark Steven Joel physician, research scientist, educator
Klotz, Charles Rodger shipping company executive
Knight, Norman broadcast executive
Knox, Richard Albert journalist
Koetter, Fred architectural firm executive, educator, dean
Koffel, William Barry lawyer
Kolodner, Richard David biochemist, educator
Kopelman, Leonard lawyer
Korb, Kenneth Allan lawyer
Korff, Yitzchok Aharon rabbi
Kotter, John Paul organizational behavior educator, management consultant
Kowal, Ruth Elizabeth library administrator
Krakow, Barbara Levy art gallery executive
Krane, Stephen Martin physician, educator
Kubzansky, Philip Eugene environmental and organizational psychologist
Kunkel, Louis Martens research scientist, educator
Kurzweil, Edith sociology educator, editor
Kwasnick, Paul Jack retail executive
La Fontaine, Raymond M. insurance company executive
Laine, Richard R. banking executive
Lamere, Robert Kent lawyer
Lampert, James B. lawyer
Lane, Harold Edwin retired management educator, consultant
Lane, Newton Alexander lawyer
Langer, Lawrence Lee English educator, writer
Langer, Robert Martin retired chemical engineering company executive, consultant
Langermann, John W. R. institutional equity salesperson
Lanner, Michael research administrator, consultant
Lapatin, Philip Stuart lawyer
Largey, Kathleen Kiernan lawyer, marketing director
Larkin, Michael John newspaper editor, journalist
LaRosa, Robert A. trade association executive
Lasagna, Louis Cesare medical educator
Lasker, Morris E. federal judge
Last, Michael P. lawyer
Latham, James David lawyer
Lawrence, Merloyd Ludington editor
Lawrence, Paul Roger retired organizational behavior educator
Leaf, Alexander physician, educator
Lee, David Stoddart investment counselor
Lee, Donald Young (Don Lee) publishing executive, editor, writer
Lee, Jonathan Owen financial services company executive, lawyer
Lee, Robin S. surgeon, researcher
Leeman, Susan Epstein neuroscientist, educator
Lees, Sidney research facility administrator, bioengineering educator
Leibensperger, Edward Paul lawyer
Leibler, Kenneth Robert financial service executive
Leonard, Laurence Barberie, Jr. investment company executive
Leone, Peter R. lawyer
Le Quesne, Philip William chemistry educator, researcher
Lesser, Laurence music conservatory president, cellist, educator
Lettieri, Richard Joseph lawyer
Levine, Ruth Rothenberg biomedical science educator
Levine, Sol sociologist
Levinsky, Norman George physician, educator
Lewis, Anthony newspaper columnist
Ley, Andrew James lawyer
Liacos, Paul Julian state supreme judicial court chief justice
Liang, Matthew H. medical director
Libby, Peter cardiologist, medical researcher
†Licata, Arthur Frank lawyer
Lichtenberg, Margaret Klee publishing company executive
Lichtin, Norman Nahum chemistry educator
Lipton, Stuart Arthur neuroscientist
Little, Arthur Dehon investment banker
Little, John Bertram physician, radiobiology educator, researcher
Liukkonen, Karen Elaine financial company executive
Livingston, David Morse biomedical scientist, physician, internist
†Lockhart, Keith Alan conductor
Lockwood, Rhodes Greene retired lawyer
Lodge, George C(abot) business administration educator
Loeser, Hans Ferdinand lawyer
Logue, Edward Joseph development company executive
Lonkart, Georgia Faith banker
Looney, William Francis, Jr. lawyer
Loring, Arthur lawyer, financial services company executive
Loring, Caleb, Jr. investment company executive
Lorsch, Jay William business educator
†Loscalzo, Joseph biochemist, cardiologist
Love, David accountant
Lovell, Francis Joseph, III investment company executive
Lovett, Miller Currier management educator, clergyman
Lowry, Bates art historian, museum director
Lowry, Lois (Hammersberg) author
Luongo, C. Paul public relations executive
Lykins, Marshall Herbert insurance company executive
Lyman, Henry retired publisher, marine fisheries consultant
Lynch, Francis Charles lawyer
Lynch, Peter S. retired portfolio manager
Lynch, Sandra Lea lawyer
Lyons, David Barry philosophy and law educator
Lyons, Paul Vincent lawyer
MacCombie, Bruce Franklin composer, college administrator
Macdonald, Alan G. trade association administrator
Macdonald, Mary Elizabeth nursing administrator, educator
MacDougall, Peter lawyer
Macera, Salvatore industrial executive
Macomber, John D. construction executive
Madara, James L. epitheliologist, pathologist, educator
Maher, Peter Sutton banker
Malamy, Michael Howard molecular biology and microbiology educator
Malenka, Bertram Julian physicist, educator
Malone, Joseph D. state treasurer
Mandell, Samuel W. W. corporate lawyer
Manfredi, David Peter architect
Mankin, Henry Jay physician, educator
Mannick, John Anthony surgeon
Manning, Robert Joseph editor
Manning, Thomas Allen publishing company executive
Manning, William Frederick wire service photographer
Mansfield, Christopher Charles insurance company legal executive
Marcellino, James J. lawyer
Markham, Jesse William economist
Marks, Bruce artistic director, choreographer
Marshall, Martin Vivan business administration educator, business consultant
Martin, Dale vocational rehabilitation executive
Martin, Stanley A. lawyer
†Maso, Michael Harvey managing director
Mason, Herbert Warren, Jr. religion and history educator, author
Mason, Nancy Tolman state agency director
Matthews, Roger Hardin lawyer
May, James Warren, Jr. plastic surgeon, medical association executive
Mazzone, A. David federal judge
McArdle, John publishing company executive
Mc Arthur, Janet Ward endocrinologist, educator
Mc Carthy, Denis Michael investment executive
Mc Carthy, Joseph Michael historian
Mc Carthy, Patrick Edward institute president
McChesney, S. Elaine lawyer
McClean, Graham J. commercial printing company executive
McCluskey, Jean Louise civil and consulting engineer
McCluskey, Robert Timmons physician
McCormick, Marie Clare pediatrician, educator
McCraw, Thomas Kincaid business history educator, editor, author
Mc Dermott, William Vincent, Jr. physician, educator
Mc Donough, William corporate lawyer
McDougal, William Scott urology educator
McFarlan, Franklin Warren business administration educator
McGovern, A. Lane lawyer
McHugh, Edward Francis, Jr. lawyer
McKinnell, Noel Michael architect, educator
Mc Kinnon, Alan Leo banker
McLennan, Bernice Claire human resources professional
Mc Neice, John Ambrose, Jr. investment company executive
McNeil, Barbara Joyce radiologist
McPhee, Jonathan music director, conductor
Medearis, Donald Norman, Jr. physician, educator
Meister, Doris Powers investment management executive
Meister, Mark Jay museum director, professional society administrator
Melconian, Linda Jean state senator, lawyer
Mellins, Harry Zachary radiologist, educator
Menino, Thomas M. mayor
Menoyo, Eric Felix lawyer
Menyuk, Paula developmental psycholinguistics educator
Menzies, Ian Stuart newspaper editor
Mercer, Douglas lawyer
Merton, Robert C. economist, educator
Meserve, Robert William lawyer
Meserve, William George lawyer
Messerle, Judith Rose medical librarian, public relations director
Messing, Arnold Philip lawyer
Metcalf, Arthur George Bradford electronics company executive
Metzer, Patricia Ann lawyer
†Metzger, Mark Kavanaugh public relations company executive
Michael, Michael L. lawyer, brokerage house executive
†Michel, Thomas Mark internal medicine educator
Mihaly, Eugene Bramer consultant, corporate executive, writer, educator
Mikels, Richard Eliot lawyer
Miliora, Maria Teresa chemist, psychotherapist, psychoanalyst, educator
Millar, Sally Gray nurse
Miller, Alan Gershon lawyer
Miller, Alan Robert lawyer
Miller, J. Philip television producer, director, educator
Miller, John A., Jr. public relations executive
Miller, John B. lawyer
Miller, Keith Wyatt pharmacology educator
Miller, Naomi art historian
Milley, Jane Elizabeth academic administrator
Mills, Andrew Geoffrey financial executive
Mitchell, W. Randle, Jr. textile company executive
Modugno, Maria publishing executive
Moellering, Robert Charles, Jr. internist, educator
Monaco, Anthony Peter surgery educator, medical institute administrator
Moncreiff, Robert P. lawyer
Monrad, Ernest Ejner trust company executive
Montgomery, William Wayne surgeon
Mooney, Michael Edward lawyer
Moore, Francis Daniels retired surgeon, educator, consultant, editor
Moore, Richard Lawrence structural engineer, consultant
Moran, James J., Jr. lawyer
Morby, Jacqueline venture capitalist
Morgan, Frank Brown Webb, Jr. journalist, consultant
Morgan, James Philip pharmacologist, cardiologist, educator
Morgentaler, Abraham urologist, researcher
Moriarty, George Marshall lawyer
Moriarty, John opera administrator, artistic director
Morris, Gerald Douglas newspaper editor
Morrison, Gordon Mackay, Jr. investment company executive
†Morrissey, Peter A. public relations executive
Morse, Garlan, Jr. real estate investment counseling officer
Morton, Edward James insurance company executive
Morton, William Gilbert, Jr. stock exchange executive
Moseby, LeBaron Clarence, Jr. mathematics and computer science educator
Moseley, Frederick Strong, III investment banker
Moss, Guy B. lawyer
Motley, Thomas, Jr. lawyer
Muldoon, Robert Joseph, Jr. lawyer
Mullaney, Joseph E. lawyer
Mulligan, Gerald Thomas banker
Mulvoy, Thomas F., Jr. newspaper editor, journalist
Munro, Meredith Vance lawyer
Munsat, Theodore L. neurologist, researcher
Murphy, Dennis Michael state legislator
Murphy, Evelyn Frances healthcare administrator, former lieutenant governor
Murray, Robert J. consumer products company executive
Mygatt, Susan Hall lawyer
Myrick, Ronald Ernest lawyer, educator
Nadas, Alexander Sandor pediatric cardiologist
Naeser, Margaret Ann linguist, medical researcher
Naimi, Shapur cardiologist, educator
Nashe, Carol association executive, public relations consultant
Nathan, David Gordon physician, educator
Neely, Cameron Michael professional hockey player
Neely, Thomas Emerson lawyer
Nelson, David S. federal judge
Nesmith, Richard Duey clergyman, theology educator
Nesson, H. Richard medical administrator, physician
Neville, Robert Cummings philosophy and religion educator
Newberg, Joseph H. lawyer
†Newbrander, William Carl health economist, management consultant
Newhouse, Joseph Paul economics educator
Newman, Richard Alan publisher, editor and consultant
Nichols, David Harry gynecologic surgeon, obstetrics and gynecology educator, author
Nichols, William Deming lawyer
Nixon, Ralph Edward financial executive
Norris, Melvin lawyer
Norton, Augustus Richard political science educator
Notopoulos, Alexander Anastasios, Jr. lawyer
Nutt, Robert L. lawyer
Nutt, William James investment, management and mutual funds company executive
Nylander, Jane Louise museum director
Oates, Adam R. professional hockey player
Oates, William Armstrong, Jr. investment company executive
O'Block, Robert Paul management consultant
†O'Brien, Paul Charles telephone company executive
O'Connell, Kevin George priest, fundraiser, former college president
O'Dell, Edward Thomas, Jr. lawyer
O'Donnell, Thomas Lawrence Patrick lawyer
O'Hern, Jane Susan psychologist, educator
Ojemann, Robert Gerdes neurosurgeon
O'Leary, Joseph Evans lawyer
O'Neil, William Francis academic administrator
O'Neill, Philip Daniel, Jr. lawyer, educator
O'Neill, Timothy P. lawyer
Orenstein, Theodore Paul lawyer
Orr, Bobby (Robert Gordon Orr) former hockey player
Osteen, Carolyn McCue lawyer
†Ostheimer, Gerard William anesthesiology educator
Packer, Rekha Desai lawyer
Page, Patricia M. health science association administrator
Paladino, Albert Edward venture capitalist
Palmer, David Scott political scientist, educator
Pardee, Arthur Beck biochemist, educator
Pardus, Donald Gene utility executive
Park, James Theodore microbiologist, educator
Park, William H(erron) financial executive
Park, William Wynnewood law educator
Parker, Christopher William lawyer
Parks, Paul corporate executive
†Parrish, John Albert dermatologist, research administrator
Partan, Daniel Gordon lawyer, educator
Patterson, John de la Roche, Jr. lawyer
Patterson, Robert Logan librarian, country and western dance promoter
Paul, Oglesby physician
†Paulin, Sven Josef Karl radiologist, educator
Pechilis, William John lawyer
Peckham, John Munroe, III investment executive, author
Penney, Sherry Hood university chancellor, educator
Peppercorn, Mark Allen gastroenterologist, educator
Perera, Lawrence Thacher lawyer
Perkins, James Wood lawyer
Perkins, John Allen lawyer
Perkins, Malcolm Donald lawyer
Perkins, Samuel lawyer
Perocchi, Paul Patrick lawyer
Peterson, Roger Tory ornithologist, artist
Phillips, Daniel Anthony trust company executive
Phillips, Derwyn Fraser manufacturing company executive
Phillips, William English language educator, editor, author
Pierce, Allan Dale engineering educator, researcher
Pierce, Daniel investment company executive
Pierce, Joel Farwell lawyer
Pierce, Martin E., Jr. fire commissioner
†Pile, Walter Mitchell, Jr. advertising agency executive
Pineda, Marianna sculptor, educator
Pines, Lois G. state legislator
Pinsky, Robert Neal poet, educator
Piret, Marguerite Alice investment banker
Ploszaj, Stephen Charles lawyer
Pochi, Peter Ernest physician
Pomeroy, Robert Corttis lawyer
Popeo, R. Robert lawyer
Poser, Charles Marcel neurology educator
†Potts, John Thomas, Jr. physician, educator
Poussaint, Alvin Francis psychiatrist, educator
Powers, Charles William environmental ethicist
Pratt, Albert financial consultant, trustee
Pratt, John Winsor statistics educator
Prescott, John Hernage aquarium executive
Preston, Malcolm artist, art critic
Prior, Ronald L. animal scientist, nutritionist
Provost, David Emile financial services executive
Psathas, George sociologist, educator
Purcell, Patrick Joseph newspaper publisher
†Purvis, George Porter, III health services company executive, consultant
Pynchon, Thomas Ruggles, Jr. author
Quelle, Frederick William, Jr. physicist
Quickel, Kenneth Elwood, Jr. physician, medical center executive
Rabadjija, Neven lawyer
Rabkin, Mitchell Thornton physician, hospital administrator, educator
Radloff, Robert Albert real estate executive
Raemer, Harold Roy electrical engineering educator
Raish, David Langdon lawyer
Raskin, Paul D. resource management and environmental research administrator
Rawn, William Leete, III architect
Ray, William F. banker
Reck, Joel M(arvin) lawyer
Regan, Peter John banker
Reid, Lynne McArthur pathologist
Reiling, Henry Bernard business educator
Reinherz, Helen Zarsky social services educator
Reinschmidt, Kenneth Frank engineering and construction executive
Relman, Arnold Seymour physician, educator, editor
Reppert, Steven Marion pediatrician, educator
Resnik, Peter L. lawyer
†Reznicek, Bernard William power company executive
Rhinesmith, Stephen Headley international management consultant
Rice, William Phipps investment counselor
Richie, Jerome Paul surgeon, educator
Richter, James Michael physician, clinical investigator
Rieper, Alan George brokerage company executive
Riley, Robert Edward financial services company executive
Riley, Stephen Thomas historian, librarian
Ritt, Roger Merrill lawyer
Rittner, Carl Frederick educational administrator
Rizzo, William Ober lawyer
Roach, Sister Ann Dominic school system administrator
Roache, Francis Michael law enforcement official
Robinson, Sumner Martin college administrator
Robinson, Walter newspaper editor
†Robinson, William R. health facility adminstrator
†Rockoff, Mark Alan anesthesiologist
Rodman, Oliver newspaper publishing executive
Roehrig, C(harles) Burns internist, health policy consultant, editor
Roffey, Robert C., Jr. insurance company executive
Rogeness, Mary Speer state legislator
†Rogers, Malcolm Austin museum curator, art historian
Rohda, Rodney Raymond insurance company executive
Romney, W. Mitt investment company executive
Ronayne, Michael Richard, Jr. academic dean
Rose, Alan Douglas lawyer
†Rose, John M., Jr. advertising executive
Rosen, Fred Saul pediatrics educator
Rosen, Stanley Howard humanities educator
Rosenberg, James William marketing executive
Rosenberg, Manuel retail company executive
Rosenblatt, Michael medical researcher, educator
Rosensteel, John William insurance company executive
Rossell, Christine Hamilton political science educator
Rossman, Stuart T. lawyer
Rostow, Charles Nicholas lawyer, educator
Rotenberg, Sheldon violinist
†Rothman, Martha L. architectural firm executive
Row, Peter L. musician, educator
†Ruby, Leonard Kenneth hand surgeon, orthopaedic surgeon, educator
Rush, David medical investigator, epidemiologist
Rushing, Byron Douglas state legislator
Russell, Paul Snowden surgeon, educator
Rutstein, Stanley Harold apparel retailing company executive
Ryan, Kenneth John physician, educator
Ryder, Kenneth Gilmore university chancellor
Sager, Ruth geneticist
St. Clair, James Draper lawyer
Saleh, Bahaa E. A. electrical engineering educator
Sales, Robert Julian newspaper editor
Salzberg, Betty Joan computer science educator
Samp, Edward Joseph, Jr. lawyer
†Sanborn, George Freeman, Jr. genealogist
Sanders, Irwin Taylor sociology educator
Sandson, John I. physician, educator, retired university dean

Saparoff, Peter M. lawyer
Saper, Clifford Baird neurobiology and neurology educator
†Sapers, Carl Martin lawyer
Sargeant, Ernest James lawyer
Sargent, David Jasper university executive, lawyer
Saris, Patti B. federal judge
Saunders, Donald Leslie hotel executive, commercial real estate company executive
Saunders, Roger Alfred hotel group executive
Savrann, Richard Allen lawyer
Saxe, Edward A. lawyer
Say, Allen children's writer, illustrator
Scanlon, Dorothy Therese history educator
Schlossman, Stuart Franklin physician, educator, researcher
Schmelzer, Henry Louis Phillip lawyer, financial company executive
Schnitzer, Iris Taymore financial management executive
†Schnitzer, Jan Eugeniusz medical educator, scientist
†Schorr, Marvin G. technology company executive
Schrader, William Cutler banker
Schram, Ronald Byard lawyer
Schuknecht, Harold Frederick physician, educator
Schwartz, Bernard physician
Schwartz, Jules Jacob management educator
Schwartz, Lloyd music critic, poet
Scipione, Richard Stephen insurance company executive, lawyer
Scott, A. Hugh lawyer
Scott, Arnold Duane lawyer
Scrimshaw, Nevin Stewart physician, nutrition and health educator
Scuderi, Louis Anthony climatology educator
Sears, John Winthrop lawyer
Seddon, Johanna Margaret ophthalmologist, epidemiologist
Segal, Robert Mandal lawyer
Selkoe, Dennis Jesse neurologist, researcher, educator
Shader, Richard Irwin psychiatrist, educator
Shafto, Robert Austin insurance company executive
Shapiro, Eli business consultant, educator, economist
Shapiro, Jerome Herbert radiologist, educator
Shapiro, Sandra lawyer
Shattuck, Roger Whitney author, educator
Shaw, Henry D. insurance company executive
Shaw, James Headon nutritionist, educator
Shemin, Barry L. insurance company executive
Shepard, Henry Bradbury, Jr. lawyer
Shepley, Hugh architect
Sherman, Elliot Mark lawyer
Shields, Lawrence Thornton orthopedic surgeon, educator
Shklar, Gerald oral pathologist, periodontist, educator
Short, Marion Priscilla neurologist
Shucart, William Arthur neurosurgeon
Silber, John Robert university president
Silberman, Robert A. S. lawyer
†Silen, William physician, surgery educator
Silvey, Anita Lynne editor
Simmons, Sylvia Jeanne Quarles (Mrs. Herbert G. Simmons, Jr.) university administrator, educator, senior manager
Simons, Steven J(ay) lawyer
Sinai, Allen Leo economist, educator
Sinden, Harry professional hockey team executive
Sinex, Francis Marott biochemist, educator
Singer, Thomas Eric industrial company executive
Sirkin, Joel H. lawyer
Skelly, Thomas Francis manufacturing company executive
Skinner, Walter Jay federal judge
Skinner, Wickham business administration educator
Skwar, Donald R. newspaper editor
Slechta, Robert Frank biologist, educator
†Sledge, Clement Blount orthopedic surgeon, educator
Slinger, Michael Jeffery law library director
Sloane, Carl Stuart business educator, management consultant
Slosberg, Mike advertising executive
Smith, Edwin Eric lawyer
Smith, Keith A. artist
†Smith, Louise Zandberg English studies educator, writer
Smith, Philip Jones lawyer
Smith, Thomas Woodward cardiologist, educator
Smyth, Peter Hayes radio executive
Snyder, Richard Joseph lawyer
Sobin, Julian Melvin international consultant
Soden, Richard Allan lawyer
Solet, Maxwell David lawyer
Solomon, Arthur Kaskel biophysics educator
†Solomon, David investment banker
Sommerfeld, Nicholas Ulrich lawyer
Sonnabend, Roger Philip hotel company executive
Sonnenschein, Adam lawyer
Southard, William G. lawyer
Spackman, David Glendinning lawyer
Spilhaus, Karl Henry textiles executive, lawyer
Stanley, H(arry) Eugene physicist, educator
Stare, Fredrick John nutritionist, biochemist, physician
Stearns, Richard Gaylore judge
Steele, Glenn Daniel, Jr. surgical oncologist
Steere, Allen Caruthers, Jr. physician, educator
Steig, William author, artist
Stein, Marshall David lawyer
Steinhauer, Gillian lawyer
Stepanian, Ira banker
Stevens, Marilyn Ruth editor
Stevenson, Howard Higginbotham business educator
Stevenson, Philip Davis lawyer
Stobaugh, Robert Blair business educator, business executive
Stokes, James Christopher lawyer
Stollerman, Gene Howard physician, educator
Stone, Arthur Harold mathematics educator
Stone, David Barnes investment advisor
Stone, James J. photographer
Stone, John Ware management consultant
†Storer, Thomas Perry lawyer
Storey, James Moorfield lawyer
Storin, Matthew Victor newspaper editor
Strauss, Phyllis R. biology educator
Streeter, Henry Schofield lawyer
Strom, Terry Barton immunologist
Strothman, Wendy Jo book publisher
Stull, Donald LeRoy architect
Sugarman, Paul Ronald lawyer, educator, academic administrator
Sullivan, James Leo organization executive
Sullivan, John Louis, Jr. retired search company executive
Summerville, David pediatrician, chemist
Swaim, Charles Hall lawyer
Swartz, Morton Norman medical educator
†Swift, Humphrey Hathaway manufacturing executive
Swift, Jane Maria state senator
Swope, Jeffrey Peyton lawyer
Szep, Paul Michael editorial cartoonist
Tappé, Albert Anthony architect
Taqqu, Murad Salman mathematics educator
Tarlov, Alvin Richard former philanthropic foundation administrator, physician, educator, researcher
Tauber, Alfred Imre hematologist, immunologist, philosopher of science
Taubman, Martin Arnold immunologist
Tauro, Joseph Louis federal judge
Taveras, Juan Manuel physician, educator
Taylor, Benjamin B. newspaper publishing executive
Taylor, Hal Winslow lawyer
Taylor, Julius Willard director student health services, physician
Taylor, Stephen Emlyn publishing executive
Taylor, Thomas William lawyer
Teixeira, Joseph advertising executive
Teller, Richard E. lawyer
Temkin, Robert Harvey accountant
Tempel, Jean C. bank executive
Tempel, Jean Curtin venture capitalist
Terrill, Ross Gladwin author, educator
Terry, Jannie Lee elementary education educator
Thibedeau, Richard Herbert environmental planner, administrator
Thorn, George Widmer physician, educator
Thorndike, John Lowell investment executive
†Thrall, James Hunter radiology educator
Tierney, Robert Thomas civil engineer
†Tocco, Stephen airport administrator
Todd, J. Owen judge
†Tompkins, Ronald Gary surgeon, educator, biomedical investigator
Toran, Daniel James insurance executive
Torto, Raymond Gerald economist
†Tosteson, Daniel Charles physiologist, medical school dean
Totenberg, Roman violinist, music educator
Towles, Stokley Porter commercial and investment banking executive
Trier, Jerry Steven gastroenterologist, educator
Trimmier, Roscoe, Jr. lawyer
Tsongas, Paul Efthemios lawyer, former senator
Tuchmann, Robert lawyer
Tucker, Louis Leonard historical society administrator
Tucker, Richard Lee financial executive
Turek, Sonia Fay journalist
Turillo, Michael Joseph, Jr. management consultant
Turlish, Molly Buffum academic administrator
Tyrrell, Joseph Patrick public utility executive
Utiger, Robert David medical editor
Uyterhoeven, Hugo Emil Robert business educator and consultant
Vaccarelli, Marie C. lawyer
Vaillant, George Eman psychiatrist
Van, Peter lawyer
Vance, Verne Widney, Jr. lawyer
†Vanderweil, Raimund Gerhard, Jr. consulting firm executive, mechanical engineer
Van Domelen, John Francis academic administrator
van Gestel, Allan lawyer
Vatter, Paul August business administration educator, dean
Vaughan, Herbert Wiley lawyer
Vaughn, Maurice Samuel (Mo Vaughn) professional baseball player
Vermeule, Cornelius Clarkson, III museum curator
Vermilye, Peter Hoagland banker
Verrot, Pascal conductor, educator
Vershbow, Arthur Emmanuel mechanical engineer
Villee, Claude Alvin, Jr. biochemistry educator
Vineburgh, James Hollander banking executive
Vinik, Jeffrey investment portfolio manager
Volk, Jan professional sports team executive
Volpe, Joseph John pediatric neurologist, educator
Waddick, Sheryl F. Baiky lawyer
Wainberg, Alan footwear company executive
Wakefield, Dan author, screenwriter
Walcott, Derek Alton poet, playwright
Walker, Gordon T. lawyer
Wallace, David Dunsmore architect
Wallraff, Barbara Jean magazine editor, writer
Walrath, Patricia A. state legislator
†Walsh, Christopher Thomas biochemist, department chairman
Walton, Bill (William Theodore Walton, III) sportscaster, former professional basketball player
Walton, Richard Eugene business educator
†Wang, Timothy C. gastroenterologist
Warga, Jack mathematician, educator
†Warren, Rosanna poet
Warshaw, Andrew Louis surgeon, researcher
Washburn, H. Bradford, Jr. museum administrator, cartographer, photographer
Watts, Charles Henry, II university administrator
†Weadock, Daniel Peter corporate executive
Weaver, Paul David lawyer
Webb, Alexander, III investment company executive
Webster, Edward William medical physicist
Wechsler, Henry research psychologist
Weiner, Stephen Mark lawyer
Weinstein, David Carl lawyer
Weinstein, Milton Charles health policy educator
Weiss, Earle Burton physician
Weiss, Rainer physics educator
Weitzel, John Patterson lawyer
Weitzman, Arthur Joshua English educator
Welch, Claude Emerson surgeon
Weld, William Floyd governor, lawyer
Weltman, David Lee lawyer
Wentworth, Michael Justin curator
Wermuth, Paul Charles retired English educator
Westcott, John McMahon, Jr. lawyer
Westling, Jon university administrator
Wheatland, Richard, II fiduciary services executive, museum executive
Wheelwright, Steven C. religious organization administrator, business educator
Whitburn, Gerald state agency administrator
White, Barry Bennett lawyer
Whitlock, John L. lawyer
Whitters, James Payton, III lawyer, university administrator
Whitworth, William A. magazine editor
Wieckowski, Zdislaw Wladyslaw lawyer
Wiesel, Elie writer, educator
Wiesner, David illustrator, children's writer
Wilkes, Brent Ames management consultant
Wilkins, (Jacques) Dominique professional basketball player
Wilkins, Herbert Putnam judge
Willens, Alan Rush management consultant
Williams, Charles Marvin commercial banking educator
†Williams, Gordon Harold medical educator, researcher
Williams, John Taylor lawyer
Williams, Rhys minister
Williams, Robert D. cable television advertiser
Williams, Robert Dana lawyer
Willock, Marcelle Monica medical educator
Wilson, Robert Gould management consultant
Winkelman, James Warren hospital administrator, pathology educator
Winter, Donald Francis lawyer
Wirth, Peter lawyer
Wiseman, James Richard classicist, archaeologist, educator
Wodlinger, Eric W. lawyer
Wolf, David lawyer
†Wolf, Gary Herbert architect
Wolf, Mark Lawrence federal judge
Wood, Henry Austin architect
†Wood, Lawrence Crane medical association administrator, educator
Woodburn, Ralph Robert, Jr. lawyer
Woodlock, Douglas Preston federal judge
Woolsey, John Munro, Jr. lawyer
Worthen, John A. insurance executive
Worthley, Harold Field minister, educator
Wortzel, Lawrence Herbert marketing educator
Wu, Tung curator, art historian, art educator, artist
Wyman, Stanley Moore radiologist
Yamamoto, Tamotsu art educator, artist, architectural illustrator
Yastrzemski, Carl Michael former baseball player, public relations executive
Yemma, John newspaper editor
Young, David William accounting educator
Young, Laura dance educator, choreographer
Young, Raymond Henry lawyer
Young, William Glover federal judge
Zack, Arnold Marshall lawyer, mediator, arbitrator
Zahn, Carl Frederick museum publications director, designer, photographer
Zaleznik, Abraham psychoanalyst, management specialist, educator
Zannieri, Nina museum director
Zarins, Bertram orthopaedic surgeon
Zeien, Alfred M. consumer products company executive
Zelen, Marvin statistics educator
Zellman, Ande editor
Zervas, Nicholas Themistocles neurosurgeon
Zimmerman, George Ogurek physicist, educator
Zinner, Michael Jeffrey surgeon, educator
Zobel, Hiller Bellin judge
Zobel, Rya Weickert federal judge
Zupcofska, Peter F. lawyer

Boxboro
Gary, Benjamin Walter, Jr. landscape architect
Murphy, Paul James high technology company executive
Nitta, Kenjiro Computer company executive

Boxford
Siegert, Barbara (Marie) health care administrator

Boylston
Brazelton, Roy Dale real estate executive

Braintree
Berman, Stanley retail executive
Conlon, Eugene artist, administrator
Davis, Robert Jocelyn engineering executive
Fish, Edward Anthony, Jr. construction company executive
Flowers, Robert L. retail executive
Foster, Arthur Rowe mechanical engineering educator
Gittleman, Sol university official, humanities educator
Grossman, Everett Philip retail executive
Guertin, Robert Powell physics educator, university dean
Harris, Jeffrey Sherman direct marketing company executive
Kent, Richard Edmund lawyer
Latham, Allen, Jr. manufacturing company consultant
†O'Donnell, Michael Paul restaurant executive
†O'Toole, Lawrence William lawyer, educational finance professional
Paven, Nathan Samuel lawyer
Piraino, Thomas writer, retired electrical engineer
†Remondi, John F. student aid administrator
†Tobin, Robert G. supermarket chain executive

Brewster
Coburn, John Bowen retired bishop
Hay, John writer
Hemsing, Albert E. public affairs adviser
Lindquist, Susan Pratzner museum executive

Bridgewater
Anderson, Marcia Kay physical education educator
Bardo, John William university administrator
Cost, Richard Willard educator
†Heffernan, Peter John state official
Neubauer, Richard A. library science educator, consultant
Rondileau, Adrian college president
Tinsley, Adrian college president

Brighton
Bernstein, Emil Steven financial executive
Herron, Carolivia novelist, English educator
Law, Bernard Francis Cardinal archbishop
Walker, Ruth Ann journalist

Brockton
Buote, Rosemarie Boschen special education educator
Carlson, Desiree Anice pathologist
Clark, Carleton Earl tax consultant
Droukas, Ann Hantis management executive
Hart, Daniel Anthony bishop

Brookfield
Kring, Walter Donald minister

Brookline
Ames, Adelbert, III neurophysiologist, educator
Barron, Ros artist
Blake, Ran jazz pianist, composer
Blom, Gaston Eugene psychiatrist
Brooks, Joae Graham psychiatrist, educator
Burnstein, Daniel lawyer
Cromwell, Adelaide M. sociology educator
Feinberg, Robert I(ra) lawyer
Frankel, Ernst Gabriel shipping and aviation business executive, educator
Gray, Seymour medical educator, author
Gyger, Terrell Lee minister
Jakab, Irene psychiatrist
Kadin, Marshall Edward hematopathologist, educator
Katz, Israel engineering educator, retired
Kibrick, Anne nursing educator, university dean
Krasner, Louis concert violinist
Lynton, Ernest Albert physicist, educator, former university official
Mc Cormick, Thomas Julian art history educator
Mesch, Barry academic administrator
Nadelson, Carol Cooperman psychiatrist, educator
Papademetriou, George Constantine priest, director, educator
Perry, Frederick Sayward, Jr. corporate executive
Shaw, Samuel Ervine, II retired insurance company executive, consultant
Swan, Barbara artist
Tournas, Methodios (Methodios of Boston) bishop, academic administrator
Tuchman, Maurice Simon library director
Tyler, H. Richard physician
Vallee, Bert Lester biochemist, physician, educator
Walter, Helen Joy executive director, teacher
Wax, Bernard research and development consultant, lecturer
Wilson, John artist

Burlington
Bright, Willard Mead manufacturing company executive
Clerkin, Eugene Patrick physician
Connors, Richard J. principal
Crow, Howard Morrison, Jr. electronics company executive
Fager, Charles Anthony physician, neurosurgeon
Freeman, Donald Chester, Jr. health care company executive
Hall, John Reginald, II retired army officer, electronics company executive
†Labovitz, George Harold business executive, educator
Lynch, John Joseph electronics company executive
Moschella, Samuel L. dermatology educator
Mosher, Giles Edmund, Jr. banker
Prosperi, Robert manufacturing company executive
†Reno, John F. communications equipment company executive
Reno, John Findley corporate executive
Schoetz, David John, Jr. colon and rectal surgeon
Seckel, Brooke Rutledge plastic surgeon
Veidenheimer, Malcolm Charles surgeon
Wise, Robert Edward radiologist

Buzzards Bay
Mitchell, Peter McQuilkin educational administrator
Roper, Burns Worthington retired opinion research company executive

Byfield
Bragdon, Peter Wilkinson headmaster
Kozol, Jonathan writer

Cambridge
Abernathy, Frederick H. mechanical engineering educator
Abt, Clark C. social scientist, executive, engineer, publisher, educator
Ackerman, James Sloss fine arts educator
Akylas, Triantaphyllos R. mechanical engineering educator
Alberty, Robert Arnold chemistry educator
Alcalay, Albert S. artist, educator
Alevizos, Susan Bamberger lawyer, santouri player, author
Alevizos, Theodore G. lawyer, singer, author
Alexiou, Margaret Beatrice Greek studies educator
Alford, William P. lawyer, educator
Alfred, William author, educator
Allen, Lew, Jr. laboratory executive, former air force officer
Allen, Samuel Miller metallurgical engineer
Allen, Thomas John management educator
Alonso, William population studies educator, demographer
Alt, James Edward political science educator
Anderson, Donald Gordon Marcus mathematics educator
†Anderson, James Gilbert chemistry educator
Anderson, Stanford Owen architect, architectural historian, educator
Anderson, William Henry psychobiologist, educator
Anderson-Imbert, Enrique retired Hispanic literature educator, author
Andrews, William Dorey lawyer, educator
Annis, Martin technology company executive
Antoniadis, Dimitri Alexander electrical engineering educator
Appiah, Kwame Anthony philosophy educator
Appley, Mortimer Herbert psychologist, university president emeritus
Areeda, Phillip lawyer, educator
Argon, Ali Suphi mechanical engineering educator
Aronson, Michael Andrew editor
†Ashoori, Raymond physics educator
Ashton, Peter Shaw tropical forest science educator
Athans, Michael electrical engineering educator, consultant
†Athey, Susan economist educator
Babson, David Leveau retired investment counsel
Badian, Ernst history educator
Bailyn, Bernard historian, educator
Bailyn, Lotte psychology and management educator
Baker, James Gilbert optics scientist
Baltimore, David microbiologist, educator
Banfield, Edward Christie political science educator
Bapst, Sarah artist, educator
Barger, James Edwin physicist
Barnet, Sylvan English literature educator
Baron, Judson Richard aerospace educator
Baron, Sheldon research and development company executive
Barro, Robert Joseph economics educator, consultant
Bartee, Thomas Creson computer scientist, educator
Bartholet, Elizabeth law educator
Bartus, Raymond Thomas neuroscientist, pharmaceutical executive, writer

Bate, Walter Jackson *English literature educator*
Bator, Francis Michel *economist, educator*
Battin, Richard Horace *astronautical engineer*
Baum, Michael Scott *lawyer, consultant*
Bazzaz, Fakhri A. *plant biology educator, administrator*
Bebchuk, Luclan Arye *law educator*
Becker, Ulrich J. *physics educator, particle physics researcher*
Bedrosian, Edward Robert *investment management company executive*
Beér, János Miklós *engineering educator*
Bekefi, George *physics educator*
Bell, Daniel *sociologist*
Bellow, Gary *lawyer, educator*
Ben-Akiva, Moshe Emanuel *civil engineering educator*
†Benedek, George Bernard *physicist, educator*
Beranek, Leo Leroy *scientific foundation executive, acoustical design consultant*
Berg, Howard C. *biology educator*
Berger, Harvey James *pharmaceutical company executive, physician, educator*
Berger, Suzanne *political science educator*
Berliner, Joseph Scholom *economics educator*
Bernays, Anne Fleischman *writer, educator*
Berndt, Ernst Rudolf *economist, educator*
Bernstein, Joseph N. *mathematician, researcher, educator*
Berwick, Robert Cregar *computer science educator*
Biemann, Klaus *chemistry educator*
Billings, Marland Pratt *geologist, educator*
Birgeneau, Robert Joseph *physicist, educator*
Bishop, Robert Lyle *economist, educator*
Bizzi, Emilio *neurophysiologist, educator*
Blackmer, Donald Laurence Morton *political scientist*
Bloch, Konrad Emil *biochemist*
Block, Ned *philosophy educator*
Bloembergen, Nicolaas *physicist, educator*
Bloomfield, Lincoln Palmer *political scientist*
Bloomfield, Richard J. *international relations executive*
†Bloxham, Jeremy *geologist*
Bluestone, Hugh Lawrence *architect*
Bogorad, Lawrence *biologist*
Bok, Derek *law educator, former university president*
Bol, Peter Kees *Chinese history educator*
Bolster, Arthur Stanley, Jr. *history educator*
Bond, William Henry *librarian, educator*
Boolos, George Stephen *philosophy educator*
Booth, I(srael) MacAllister *photography products company executive*
Boss, Kenneth Jay *biology educator, museum curator*
Bott, Raoul *mathematician, educator*
Bottiglia, William Filbert *humanities educator*
Bowen, H. Kent *engineering educator, consultant*
Bowes, Frederick, III *publishing executive*
Boyle, Edward Allen *oceanography educator*
Bradt, Hale Van Dorn *physicist, x-ray astronomer, educator*
Braida, Louis Benjamin Daniel *electrical engineering educator*
Branscomb, Lewis McAdory *physicist*
Branton, Daniel *biology educator*
Bras, Rafael Luis *engineering educator*
Brenner, Howard *chemical engineering educator*
Brinton, Joyce Marie *university adminsitrator*
Brody, Alan *playwright*
†Brooks, Harvey *physics educator*
Brown, Edgar Cary *retired economics educator*
Brown, Gene Monte *biochemist, educator*
Brown, Robert Arthur *chemical engineering educator*
Brown, Roger William *psychologist, educator*
Bruce, James Donald *academic administrator*
Bruck, Ferdinand Frederick *architect*
Bruck, Phoebe Ann Mason *landscape architect*
Brusch, John Lynch *physician*
Brustein, Robert Sanford *English language educator, theatre director, author*
Buchanan, John Robert *physician, educator*
Buchi, George Hermann *chemistry educator*
†Buchwald, Jed Zachary *science history educator*
Buckler, Sheldon A. *energy company executive*
Budiansky, Bernard *engineering educator*
Buell, Lawrence Ingalls *English language educator*
†Buffa, Sebastian Joseph *art history educator, consultant*
Bullock, Francis Jeremiah *pharmaceutical research executive*
Burchfiel, Burrell Clark *geology educator*
Burke, Bernard Flood *physicist, educator*
Burlage, Dorothy Dawson *clinical psychologist*
Burnham, Charles Wilson *mineralogy educator*
Burns, Carol J. *architect, educator*
Butler, James Newton *chemist, educator*
†Buttenwieser, Paul Arthur *writer, psychiatrist*
Cameron, Alastair Graham Walter *astrophysicist, educator*
Campbell, John Young *economics educator*
Campbell, Robert *architect, writer*
Canizares, Claude Roger *astrophysicist, educator*
Caramazza, Alfonso *psychology educator*
Carliner, Geoffrey Owen *economist, director*
Carmichael, Alexander Douglas *engineering educator*
Carpenter, Kenneth E. *librarian, bibliographer*
Carrier, George Francis *applied mathematics educator*
Castaldi, David Lawrence *health care company executive*
Cavanagh, Richard Edward *university dean*
Cavell, Stanley *philosophy educator, writer*
Chall, Jeanne Sternlicht *psychologist, educator*
Champion, (Charles) Hale *political science educator, former public official*
Chang, Kwang-Chih *anthropologist, educator*
Chapin, Richard *arbitrator, consultant*
Charren, Peggy *consumer activist*
Chayes, Abram *law educator, lawyer*
Chen, Sow-Hsin *nuclear engineering educator, researcher*
Chernoff, Herman *statistics educator*
Chisholm, Sallie Watson *biological oceanography educator, researcher*
Chomsky, Avram Noam *linguistics and philosophy educator*
Chubb, Stephen Darrow *medical corporation executive*
Chvany, Catherine Vakar *foreign language educator*
Ciappenelli, Donald John *chemist, electronics company executive*
Clark, George Whipple *physics educator*
Clark, Joel Phillip *engineering educator, consultant*
†Clark, Peter P. *optical engineer*
Clark, Robert Charles *lawyer, educator, dean*
Clark, William Cummin *academic director, educator*
Clausen, Wendell Vernon *classics educator*
Clendenning, Bonnie Ryon *college administrator*
Cobb, Carolus Melville *science company executive, chemical researcher*
Cohen, Morris *engineering educator*
Cohen, Robert Edward *chemical engineering educator, consultant*
Cohn, Marjorie Benedict *curator, art historian, educator*
Colby, Anne *psychologist*
Cole, Heather Ellen *librarian*
Coleman, Sidney Richard *physicist, educator*
Coles, Robert *child psychiatrist, educator, author*
Collins, Allan Meakin *cognitive scientist, psychologist, educator*
†Collins, John William, III *librarian*
Colton, Clark Kenneth *chemical engineering educator*
†Conrades, George Henry *information systems company executive*
Conway, Jill Kathryn Ker *former college president*
Cook, Robert Edward *plant ecology researcher, educator*
Cooper, Richard Newell *economist, educator*
†Coppi, Bruno *physicist, educator*
Corbato, Fernando Jose *electrical engineer and computer science educator*
Corey, Elias James *chemistry educator*
Coser, Lewis Alfred *sociology educator*
Counselman, Charles Claude, III *electrical engineering educator*
Covert, Eugene Edzards *aerophysics educator*
Cox, Archibald *lawyer, educator*
Craig, Albert Morton *Asian studies educator*
Crandall, Stephen Harry *engineering educator*
Crawley, Edward Francis *aerospace engineering educator*
Cross, Frank Moore, Jr. *foreign language educator*
Cumings, Edwin Harlan *biology educator*
Cuno, James *art museum director*
Daley, Royston Tuttle *architect*
Dalgarno, Alexander *astronomy educator*
†Danheiser, Rick Lane *biochemistry educator*
Daniels, Ronald George *theater director*
Davidson, Charles Sprecher *physician*
Davie, Joseph Myrten *physician, pathology and immunology educator, science administrator*
Davis, Edgar Glenn *science and health policy executive*
De Gennaro, Richard *library director*
Demain, Arnold Lester *microbiologist, educator*
de Neufville, Richard Lawrence *engineering educator*
Dennis, Jack Bonnell *computer consultant*
Dershowitz, Alan Morton *lawyer, educator*
Dertouzos, Michael Leonidas *computer scientist, electrical engineer, educator*
Desai, Anita *writer*
de Varon, Lorna Cooke *choral conductor*
Dewey, Clarence Forbes, Jr. *engineering educator*
Diaconis, Persi W. *mathematical statistician, educator*
Diamond, Peter Arthur *economics educator*
Dickson, William Robert *academic administrator*
Doering, William von Eggers *organic chemist, educator*
Domar, Evsey David *economics educator*
Dominguez, Jorge Ignacio *government educator*
Donahue, Charles, Jr. *law educator, author*
Donald, Aida DiPace *publishing executive*
Donnelly, Thomas William *physicist*
Donoghue, Daniel Gerard *English language educator*
Dorfman, Robert *economics educator*
Dornbusch, Rudiger *economics educator*
†Doty, Paul Mead *biochemist, educator, arms control specialist*
Dowling, John Elliott *biology educator*
Downey, Richard Ralph *lawyer, consultant*
Drake, Elisabeth Mertz *chemical engineer*
Dreben, Burton Spencer *philosopher,educator*
Dresselhaus, Mildred Spiewak *physics and engineering educator*
Dubowsky, Steven *mechanical engineering educator*
Dudley, Richard Mansfield *mathematician, educator*
Duecker, Heyman Clarke *chemical executive, researcher*
Duffy, Robert Aloysius *aeronautical engineer*
Dugundji, John *aeronautical engineer*
Dunlop, John Thomas *economics educator, former secretary of labor*
Dunn, Charles William *Celtic languages and literature educator, author*
Dupree, Anderson Hunter *historian, educator*
Durant, Graham John *medicinal chemist, drug researcher*
†Durlach, Nathaniel I. *acoustical engineering educator*
Dyck, Arthur James *ethicist, educator*
Dyck, Martin *literary theorist, mathematics historian*
Eagar, Thomas Waddy *metallurgist, educator*
Eagleson, Peter Sturges *hydrologist, educator*
Eckaus, Richard Samuel *economist, educator*
Edgerly, William Skelton *banker*
Edley, Christopher F., Jr. *law educator*
Edsall, John Tileston *biological chemistry educator*
Ehrenreich, Henry *physicist, educator*
Einsweiler, Robert Charles *research director*
Eisen, Herman Nathaniel *immunology educator, medical researcher*
Eisenberg, Carola *psychiatry educator*
Elias, Peter *electrical engineering educator*
Elliot, James Ludlow *astronomer, educator*
Emanuel, Kerry Andrew *earth sciences educator*
Emerson, Anne Devereux *university administrator*
Emmons, Howard Wilson *engineer, educator, consultant, researcher*
Engell, James Theodore *English educator*
Epstein, David Mayer *composer, conductor*
Epstein, Henry David *electronics company executive*
Erdely, Stephen Lajos *music educator*
Erikson, Raymond Leo *biology educator*
Estes, William Kaye *psychologist, educator*
Eurich, Nell P. *educational consultant*
Evans, David A(lbert) *chemistry educator*
Evans, Robley Dunglison *physicist*
Fagans, Karl Preston *real estate facilities administration executive*
Fallon, Richard H., Jr. *law educator*
Fanger, Donald Lee *Slavic language and literature educator*
Fano, Robert Mario *electrical engineering educator*
Fay, James Alan *mechanical engineering educator*
Feininger, Theodore Lux *artist*
Feld, Michael Stephen *physics educator*
Feldman, Gary Jay *physicist, educator*
Feldstein, Martin Stuart *economist, educator*
Fernandez-Cifuentes, Luis I. *foreign language educator, researcher*
Feshbach, Herman *physicist, educator*
Field, George Brooks *theoretical astrophysicist*
Field, Martha Amanda *law educator, lawyer*
Field, Robert Warren *chemistry educator*
Fink, Gerald Ralph *geneticist, biochemist*
Fiorenza, Francis P. *religion educator*
Fischer, Kurt Walter *education educator*
Fisher, Franklin Marvin *economist*
Fisher, Philip J. *English language and literature educator*
Fisher, Roger Dummer *lawyer, educator, negotiation expert*
FitzGerald, Maura *public relations executive*
†Flannery, Susan Marie *library administrator*
Fleischer, Dorothy Ann *administrative assistant*
Fleming, Donald Harnish *historian, educator*
Fleming, Ronald Lee *urban designer, administrator, preservation planner, environmental educator*
Flemings, Merton Corson *engineering educator, materials scientist*
Fletcher, Norman Collings *architect*
Flier, Michael Stephen *Slavic languages educator*
†Flowers, Woodie Claude *mechanical engineering educator and researcher, engineering director*
Foner, Simon *research physicist*
Ford, Franklin Lewis *history educator, historian*
Ford, Patrick Kildea *Celtic studies educator*
Forman, Richard T. T. *ecology educator*
Forrester, Jay Wright *management specialist, educator*
Fortmann, Thomas Edward *research and development company executive*
Fox, John Bayley, Jr. *university dean*
Fox, Maurice Sanford *molecular biologist, educator*
French, Anthony Philip *physicist, educator*
Freund, Robert Michael *management science educator*
Frey, Frederick August *geochemistry researcher, educator*
Fried, Charles *lawyer, educator*
Friedman, Benjamin Morton *economics educator*
Friedman, Jerome Isaac *physics educator, researcher*
Friend, Cynthia M. *chemist, educator*
Frisch, Rose Epstein *population sciences researcher*
Frosch, Robert Alan *retired automobile manufacturing executive, physicist*
Frug, Gerald E. *law educator*
Frye, Richard Nelson *historian, educator*
Fujimoto, James G. *electrical engineering educator*
†Furman, Thomas D., Jr. *engineering company executive*
Gage, (Leonard) Patrick *research company executive*
Gakenheimer, Ralph Albert *urban planning educator, consultant*
Galbraith, John Kenneth *retired economist*
Gallager, Robert Gray *electrical engineering educator*
Ganley, Oswald Harold *university official*
Gardner, Howard Earl *psychologist, author*
Garland, Carl Wesley *chemist, educator*
Gaskell, Ivan George Alexander De Wend *art museum curator*
Gates, Henry Louis, Jr. *English language educator*
Gatos, Harry Constantine *engineering educator*
†Geller, Margaret Joan *astrophysicist, educator*
Georgi, Howard *physics educator*
Gerrish, Hollis G. *confectionery company executive*
Gienapp, William Eugene *history educator*
Gilbert, Walter *molecular biologist, educator*
Gilligan, Carol F. *psychologist, writer*
Gingerich, Owen Jay *astronomer, educator*
Glaser, Peter Edward *mechanical engineer, consultant*
Glauber, Roy Jay *theoretical physics educator*
Glauner, Alfred William *lawyer, engineering company executive*
Glazer, Nathan *sociologist, educator*
Gleason, Andrew Mattei *mathematician, educator*
Glendon, Mary Ann *law educator*
Golay, Michael Warren *nuclear engineering educator*
Goldberg, Ray Allan *agribusiness educator*
Goldblith, Samuel Abraham *food science educator*
Goldfarb, Warren (David) *philosophy educator*
Goldin, Claudia Dale *economics educator*
Goldman, Laura Nan *physician*
Goldman, Ralph Frederick *research physiologist, educator*
Goldstone, Jeffrey *physicist*
Golovchenko, Jene Andrew *physics and applied physics educator*
Gomes, Peter John *clergyman, educator*
Gonson, S. Donald *lawyer*
†Goode, William Josiah *sociology educator*
Gordon, Roy Gerald *chemistry educator*
Gould, Stephen Jay *paleontologist, educator*
Graham, Loren Raymond *historian, educator*
Graham, William Albert *religion educator*
Graubard, Stephen Richards *history educator, editor*
Gray, Paul Edward *academic official*
Green, Richard John *architect*
†Greenberg, Arthur Wayne *financial executive*
Greene, Frederick D., II *chemistry educator*
Greeno, J(ohn) Ladd *consulting company executive*
Greenspan, Harvey Philip *applied mathematician, educator*
Gregory, Bruce Nicholas *astrophysicist, educator*
Greitzer, Edward Marc *aeronautical engineering educator, consultant*
Greytak, Thomas John *physics educator*
Griffin, Robert G. *chemistry administrator*
Griffith, Peter *mechanical engineering educator, researcher*
Griliches, Zvi *educator, economist*
Grindlay, Jonathan Ellis *astrophysics educator*
Grosz, Barbara Jean *computer science educator*
†Grotzinger, John P. *surgeon*
Grove, Timothy Lynn *geology educator*
†Guerra, John Michael *optical engineer*
Guth, Alan Harvey *physicist, educator*
Guthke, Karl Siegfried *foreign language educator*
Gyftopoulos, Elias Panayiotis *mechanical and nuclear engineering educator*
Hall, Peter Andrew *social scientist, educator, writer*
Halle, Morris *linguist, educator*
Halperin, Bertrand Israel *physics educator*
Hamilton, Malcolm Cowan *librarian, editor, indexer, personnel educator*
Hamner, W. Easley *architect*
Hanan, Patrick Dewes *foreign language professional, educator*
Handlin, Oscar *historian, educator*
Hansen, Kent Forrest *nuclear engineering educator*
Hansman, Robert John, Jr. *aeronautics and astronautics educator*
Hanson, Paul David *religion educator*
Harbison, John *composer*
Harkness, John Cheesman *architect*
Harleman, Donald Robert Fergusson *environmental engineering educator*
Harling, Otto Karl *nuclear engineering educator, researcher*
Harris, Charles Ward *landscape architect and educator, land development consultant, editor*
Hart, Donald Purple *bishop*
Hart, Oliver D'Arcy *economics educator*
Hartl, Daniel Lee *genetics educator*
Hass, Michael Shepherdson *architect*
Hastings, John Woodland *biologist, educator*
Haus, Hermann Anton *electrical engineering educator*
Hauser, John Richard *marketing and management science educator*
Hausman, Jerry Allen *economics educator, consultant*
Hausmann, Leonard J. *academic administrator, educator*
Havens, Leston Laycock *psychiatrist, educator*
Hax, Arnoldo Cubillos *management educator, industrial engineer*
Heaney, Seamus Justin *poet, educator*
†Heifetz, Ronald Abadian *psychiatrist, educator*
Heimert, Alan Edward *humanities educator*
Helgason, Sigurdur *mathematician, educator*
Heney, Joseph Edward *environmental engineer*
Henrichs, Albert Maximinus *classicist, educator*
Henry, Allan Francis *nuclear engineering educator, consultant, researcher*
Herrnstein, Richard Julius *psychology educator*
Herschbach, Dudley Robert *chemistry educator*
Herwitz, David Richard *law educator*
Heymann, Philip B. *law educator, academic director*
Heywood, John Benjamin *mechanical engineering educator*
Ho, Yu-Chi *electrical engineering educator*
Hoag, David Garratt *aerospace engineer*
Hobbs, Linn Walker *materials science educator*
Hoffman, Paul Felix *geologist, educator*
Hoffmann, Stanley *political science, French educator*
Holbik, Karel *economics educator*
Holm, Richard Hadley *chemist, educator*
Holmes, Michael Denison *trust company executive*
Holton, Gerald *physicist, science historian*
Holzman, Philip Seidman *psychologist, educator*
Homburger, Freddy *physician, scientist, artist*
Horowitz, Paul *physicist, educator*
Horrell, Jeffrey Lanier *library administrator*
Horvitz, Howard Robert *biology educator, researcher*
Horwitz, Morton J. *law educator*
Horwitz, Paul *physicist*
Houtchens, Robert Austin, Jr. *biochemist*
Houthakker, Hendrik S(amuel) *economics educator, consultant*
Howard, Jack Benny *chemical engineer, educator, researcher*
Hsiao, William C. *economist, actuary, educator*
Huang, Kerson *physics educator*
Hubbard, Ruth *biology educator*
Huchra, John Peter *astronomer, educator*
Huehnergard, John *semitic philology educator*
Huntington, Samuel Phillips *political science educator*
Hynes, Richard Olding *biology educator*
Ippen, Erich Peter *electrical engineering educator*
Iriye, Akira *historian, educator*
Jackiw, Roman *physicist, educator*
Jackson, Francis Joseph *research and development company executive*
Jacob, Daniel James *atmospheric chemist*
†Jacobsen, Eric N. *chemistry educator*
Jacobson, Ralph Henry *laboratory executive, former air force officer*
Jacoby, Henry Donnan *economist, educator*
Jaffe, Robert Loren *theoretical physicist, educator*
Javan, Ali *educator, physicist*
Jenkins, Glen Paul *economics educator*
Jensen, Klavs Fleming *chemical engineering educator*
John, Richard Rodda *transportation executive*
Johnson, Carol Roxane *landscape architect*
Johnson, Howard Wesley *former university president, business executive*
Johnson, Willard Raymond *political science educator, consultant*
†Jones, Cherry *actress*
Jones, Christopher Prestige *classicist, historian, educator, consultant*
Jones, Robert Emmet *French language educator*
Jordan, Thomas Hillman *geophysicist, educator*
Jorgenson, Dale Weldeau *economist, educator*
Joskow, Paul Lewis *economist, educator*
Joss, Paul Christopher *astrophysicist, educator*
Kac, Victor G. *mathematician, educator*
Kagan, Jerome *psychologist, educator*
Kalb, Marvin *public policy and government educator*
Kalelkar, Ashok Satish *consulting company executive*
Kamentsky, Louis Aaron *biophysicist*
Kamm, Roger Dale *biomedical engineer, educator*
Kaplan, Benjamin *judge*
Kaplan, Justin *author*
Kaplow, Louis *law educator*
Karplus, Martin *chemistry educator*
†Kassakian, John Gabriel *research electrical engineer, engineering director*
Kassman, Herbert Seymour *lawyer, management consultant*
Katayama, Toshihiro *artist, educator*
Katz, Milton *legal educator, public official*
Kaufman, Andrew Lee *law educator*
Kaufman, Gordon Dester *theology educator*
Kaysen, Carl *economics educator*
Kazhdan, David *mathematician, educator*
Kazimi, Mujid Suliman *nuclear engineer, educator*
Keenan, Edward Louis *history educator*
Kelley, Albert Joseph *management educator, executive consultant*
Kelman, Herbert Chanoch *psychology educator*
Kendall, Henry Way *physicist*
Kennedy, David W. *law educator*
Kennedy, Randall L. *law educator*
Kennedy, Robert Spayde *electrical engineering educator*
Kennedy, Stephen Dandridge *economist, researcher*
Kerman, Arthur Kent *physicist, educator*
Kerpelman, Larry Cyril *consulting firm executive*
Kerrebrock, Jack Leo *aeronautics and astronautics engineering educator*
Keyfitz, Nathan *educator, sociologist, demographer*
Keyser, Samuel Jay *linguistics educator, university official*
Khorana, Har Gobind *chemist, educator*
Khoury, Philip S. *social sciences educator, historian*
Kiang, Nelson Yuan-sheng *medical educator*
Kilson, Martin Luther, Jr. *government educator*
Kim, Peter Sungbai *biochemistry educator*
King, John Gordon *physicist, educator*

King, Jonathan Alan *molecular biology educator*
King, Ronold Wyeth Percival *physics educator*
Kirby, Kate Page *physicist*
Kirshner, Robert P. *astrophysicist, educator*
Kishi, Yoshito *chemist, educator*
Kistiakowsky, Vera *physics researcher, educator*
Kleiman, Steven Lawrence *mathematics educator*
Klemperer, William *chemistry educator*
Klibanov, Alexander Maxim *chemistry educator*
Kliem, Peter Otto *imaging company executive*
Knoll, Andrew Herbert *biology educator*
Knowles, Jeremy Randall *chemist, educator*
Kobus, Richard Lawrence *architectural company executive*
Koerner, Joseph Leo *art history educator*
Koester, Helmut Heinrich *theologian, educator*
Kong, Jin Au *electrical engineering educator*
Kosslyn, Stephen M. *psychologist educator*
Kostant, Bertram *mathematician, educator*
Kovach, Bill *educational foundation administrator*
Kraakman, Reinier H. *law educator*
Krieger, Alex *architecture and design educator*
Krueger, Winslow Bruce, Jr. *retail executive*
Kruger, Kenneth *architect*
Krugman, Paul Robin *economics educator*
Kugel, James Lewis *Hebrew literature educator*
Kung, H. T. *computer science and engineering educator, consultant*
Kyhl, Robert Louis *electrical engineering educator*
Ladd, Charles Cushing, III *civil engineering educator*
Ladjevardi, Habib *historian*
†Laibinis, Paul Edward *chemical engineering educator*
LaMantia, Charles Robert *management consulting company executive*
Lamberg-Karlovsky, Clifford Charles *anthropologist, archaeologist*
Lamport, Felicia (Mrs. Benjamin Kaplan) *writer*
†Lander, Eric S. *biologist, educator*
Langer, Ellen Jane *psychologist, educator, writer*
Langer, Robert Samuel *chemical, biomedical engineering educator*
Langstaff, John Meredith *musician*
Latanision, Ronald Michael *materials science and engineering educator, consultant*
Layzer, David *astrophysicist, educator*
Lee, Leo Ou-fan *Far Eastern languages educator*
Lee, Patrick A. *physics educator*
Lee, Thomas Henry *electrical engineer, educator*
Leehey, Patrick *mechanical and ocean engineering educator*
Leibowitz, Ann Galperin *lawyer*
†LeMessurier, William James *structural engineer*
Leonard, Herman Beukema (Dutch Leonard) *public finance and management educator*
Lerman, Leonard Solomon *science educator, scientist*
Lessard, Donald Roy *management educator*
Levi, Herbert Walter *biologist, educator*
Levins, Richard *science educator*
Levinson, Harry *psychologist, educator*
Levy, Stephen Raymond *diversified high technology company executive*
Lewin, Walter H. G. *physics educator*
Lieberson, Stanley *sociologist, educator*
Liem, Karel Frederik *biologist, educator*
Light, Richard Jay *statistician, education educator*
Lightman, Alan Paige *physicist, writer*
Lindzen, Richard Siegmund *meteorologist, educator*
Lippard, Stephen James *chemist, educator*
Lipscomb, William Nunn, Jr. *retired physical chemistry educator*
Lipsky, Michael *political science educator*
Litster, James David *physics educator, dean*
Little, John Dutton Conant *management scientist, educator*
Littlefield, Paul Damon *management consultant*
Livingston, James Duane *physicist, educator*
Lloyd, Boardman *investment executive*
Lodish, Harvey Franklin *biologist, educator*
Lomon, Earle Leonard *physicist, educator, consultant*
Longwell, John Ploeger *chemical engineering educator*
Lorenz, Edward Norton *meteorologist, educator*
Loss, Louis *lawyer, retired educator*
Low, Francis Eugene *physics educator*
Luchetti, Robert James *architect, industrial designer*
Lucker, Jay K. *library administrator, consultant*
Lunt, Horace Gray *linguist, educator*
Lynch, Harry James *biologist*
Lynch, Nancy Ann *computer scientist, educator*
Lyon, Richard Harold *educator, physicist*
Maass, Arthur *political science and environmental studies educator*
Mack, Robert Whiting *lawyer*
Mackey, George Whitelaw *mathematician, educator*
MacMaster, Robert Ellsworth *historian, educator*
Madsen, Peter Eric *architecture and real estate development firms executive*
Magee, John Francis *research company executive*
Magnanti, Thomas L. *management and engineering educator*
Maher, Brendan Arnold *psychology educator, editor*
Mahoney, Thomas Henry Donald *historian, educator, government official*
Maier, Charles Steven *history educator*
Maier, Pauline *history educator*
Makhoul, John Ibrahim *electrical engineer, researcher*
Malkus, Willem Van Rensselaer *mathematics educator*
Malmstad, John Earl *Slavic languages and literatures, educator*
Maniatis, Thomas Peter *molecular biology educator*
Mann, Robert Wellesley *biomedical engineer, educator*
Mansfield, John H. *lawyer, educator*
Manzi, Jim *computer software company executive*
Marini, Robert Charles *environmental engineering executive*
Markey, Winston Roscoe *aeronautical engineering educator*
Marks, David Hunter *civil engineering educator*
Marolda, Anthony Joseph *management consulting company executive*
Marsden, Brian Geoffrey *astronomer*
Marshall, Margaret Hilary *lawyer*
Martin, Harry Stratton, III *law librarian*
Martin, Paul Cecil *physicist, educator*
Martino, Donald James *composer, educator*
Marvin, Ursula Bailey *geologist*
Marx, Leo *retired American cultural history educator*
Masamune, Satoru *chemistry educator, consultant*
May, Ernest Richard *historian, educator*
Mayr, Ernst *emeritus zoology educator, author*
Mazlish, Bruce *historian, educator*
Mazur, Eric *physicist, educator*
Mazur, Michael *artist*
McArthur, John Hector *university dean, business educator*
McCarthy, James Joseph *oceanography educator*
McCormick, Michael *history educator*
McCue, Gerald Mallon *architect, educator*
McElroy, Michael *physicist, researcher*
McGarry, Frederick Jerome *civil engineering educator*
McKenna, Margaret Anne *college president*
Mc Kie, Todd Stoddard *artist*
McMahon, Thomas Arthur *biology and applied mechanics educator*
McNemar, Donald William *consultant*
McNutt, Marcia Kemper *geophysicist*
Medoff, James Lawrence *economics educator*
Meltzer, Daniel J. *law educator*
Mendelsohn, Everett Irwin *science educator*
Meselson, Matthew Stanley *biochemist, educator*
Meyer, John Edward *nuclear engineering educator*
Meyer, John Robert *economist, educator*
Michelman, Frank I. *lawyer, educator*
Milgram, Jerome H. *marine and ocean engineer, educator*
Miller, Arthur Raphael *legal educator*
Miller, Rene Harcourt *aerospace engineer, educator*
Minow, Martha L. *law educator*
Minsky, Marvin Lee *mathematician, educator*
Mitchell, Ralph *microbiologist*
Mitten, David Gordon *classical archaeologist*
Mitter, Sanjoy K. *electrical engineering educator*
Mnookin, Robert Harris *lawyer, educator*
Modigliani, Lazzaro G. *chemicals executive*
Molina, Mario Jose *physical chemist, educator*
Moneo, José Rafael *architecture educator*
Mongan, Agnes *museum curator, art historian, educator*
Moniz, Ernest Jeffrey *physics educator*
Montgomery, John Dickey *political science educator*
Moore, Mark Harrison *criminal justice, public policy educator*
Moore, Sally Falk *anthropology educator*
Moran, James Michael, Jr. *astronomer*
†Moran, W. Dennis *engineering consulting executive*
Morgenthaler, Frederic Richard *physics educator*
†Morris, Errol M. *filmmaker*
Moses, Joel *computer scientist, educator*
Mosteller, Frederick *mathematical statistician, educator*
Mowry, Robert Dean *art museum curator, educator*
Mueller, Robert Kirk *management consulting company executive*
Mumford, David Bryant *mathematics educator*
Murman, Earll M. *aeronautics and astronautics educator*
†Nadol, Joseph B., Jr. *otolaryngologist, educator*
Nakayama, Ken *psychology educator*
Narayan, Ramesh *astronomy educator*
†Neale, Timothy Arthur *hospital administrator*
Negele, John William *physics educator, consultant*
Nelson, David Robert *physics educator*
Nelson, Keith Adam *chemistry educator*
Nesson, Charles R. *lawyer, educator*
Neustadt, Richard Elliott *political scientist, educator*
Newell, Reginald Edward *physics educator*
Newman, John Nicholas *naval architect educator*
†Nichols, Albert L. *economics consultant*
Nordell, Hans Roderick *journalist, retired editor*
Norkus, Michael *management consultant*
Notkin, Leonard Sheldon *architect*
Nozick, Robert *philosophy educator, author*
Nykrog, Per *French literature educator*
Oettinger, Anthony Gervin *mathematician, educator*
Ogilvie, T(homas) Francis *engineer, educator*
Oldman, Oliver *law educator*
O'Neil, Wayne *linguist, educator*
O'Neil, William Francis *financial executive*
Oommen, George *architect, painter*
Oppenheim, Alan Victor *electrical engineering educator*
Oppenheim, Irwin *chemical physicist, educator*
Orchard, Robert John *theater producer, educator*
Orlen, Joel *association executive*
Orlin, James Berger *mathematician, management scientist, educator*
Orme-Johnson, William Henry, III *chemist, educator*
Owen, Stephen *Chinese literature educator*
Owen, Walter Shepherd *materials science and engineering educator*
Oye, Kenneth A. *political scientist, educator*
Ozment, Steven *historian, educator*
Papaliolios, Costas Demetrios *physics educator*
Papert, Seymour Aubrey *mathematician, educator, writer*
Paradis, James Gardiner *historian*
Pardue, Mary Lou *biology educator*
Parker, Harry Lambert *university rowing coach*
Parker, Richard Davies *lawyer, educator*
Parker, Sam *finance company executive*
Parsons, Charles Dacre *philosophy educator*
Parthum, Charles Albert *civil engineer*
Patterson, Orlando *sociologist*
Paul, William *physicist, educator*
Payne, Harry Morse, Jr. *architect*
Peattie, Lisa Redfield *urban anthropology educator*
Pelloux, Regis Marc Noel *materials engineering educator*
Penfield, Paul Livingstone, Jr. *electrical engineering educator*
Penman, Sheldon *biology educator*
Perkins, David *English language educator*
Perkins, Dwight Heald *economics educator*
Pershan, Peter Silas *physicist, educator*
Petersen, Ulrich *geology educator*
†Peterson, Carl Richard *mechanical engineering educator, consultant*
Pettengill, Gordon H(emenway) *physicist, educator*
†Pettinella, Nicholas Anthony *financial executive*
†Pfaltzgraff, Robert Louis, Jr. *political scientist, educator*
Pfister, Donald Henry *biology educator*
Pian, Rulan Chao *musicologist, scholar*
Pian, Theodore Hsueh-Huang *engineering educator, consultant*
Piene, Otto *artist, educator*
Pierce, Naomi Ellen *biology educator, researcher*
Pilbeam, David Roger *paleoanthropology educator*
Pinkham, Daniel *composer*
Piore, Michael Joseph *educator*
Pipes, Richard *historian, educator*
Poggio, Tomaso Armando *physicist, educator, computer scientist, researcher*
Polenske, Karen Rosel *economics educator*
Pollock, Wilson F. *architectural firm executive*
Porter, Roger Blaine *government official, educator*
Porter, William Lyman *architect, educator*
Poterba, James Michael *economist, educator*
Potter, Ralph Benajah, Jr. *theology and social ethics educator*
Pounds, William Frank *management educator*
Powers, Michael Kevin *architectural and engineering executive*
Press, William Henry *astrophysicist, computer scientist*
Preston, John Thomas *engineering executive*
Preyer, Robert Otto *English literature educator*
Price, Don K. *political science educator*
Pritchard, David Edward *physics educator*
Probstein, Ronald Filmore *mechanical engineering educator*
Ptashne, Mark Steven *biochemistry educator*
Purcell, Edward Mills *physics educator*
Pye, Lucian Wilmot *political science educator*
Quine, Willard Van Orman *philosophy educator*
Rabinowicz, Ernest *mechanical engineer, tribologist, educator*
Ragone, David Vincent *former university president*
Rakoff, Todd D. *law educator*
Ramsey, Norman F. *physicist, educator*
Rands, Bernard *composer, educator*
Rasmussen, Norman Carl *nuclear engineer*
Rathbone, Perry Townsend *art museum director*
Rathjens, George William *political scientist, educator*
Raymond, John Charles *physicist*
Rebek, Julius, Jr. *chemistry educator, consultant*
Rediker, Robert Harmon *physicist*
Redwine, Robert Page *physicist, educator*
Reid, Robert Clark *chemical engineering educator*
Reimann, William Page *artist, educator*
Rein, Martin *educator, social worker*
Rey, Margret Elizabeth *writer*
Rice, James Robert *engineering scientist, geophysicist*
Rich, Alexander *molecular biologist, educator*
Riesman, David *lawyer, social scientist*
†Ris, Howard C., Jr. *nonprofit public policy organization administrator*
Robbins, Phillips Wesley *biology educator*
Roberts, Edward Baer *technology management educator*
Roberts, Nancy *computer educator*
Robinson, Allan Richard *oceanography educator*
†Robinson, David G. *management consultant*
Robinson, Marguerite Stern *anthropologist, educator, consultant*
Roche, John Jefferson *lawyer*
Rockart, John Fralick *information systems reseacher*
Roedder, Edwin Woods *geologist*
Rogers, Peter Philips *environmental engineering educator, city planner*
Rohsenow, Warren Max *retired mechanical engineer, educator*
Roos, Daniel *civil engineering educator*
Rose, Robert Michael *materials science and engineering educator*
Rosenberg, David *law educator*
Rosenblith, Walter Alter *scientist, educator*
Rosenbloom, Richard Selig *business administration educator*
Rosenfeld, Walter David, Jr. *architect, writer*
Rosenfield, John Max *art educator*
Rosenkrantz, Barbara Gutmann *retired history educator*
Rosenthal, Robert *psychology educator*
Rosovsky, Henry *economist, educator*
Rota, Gian-Carlo *mathematician, educator*
Rotemberg, Julio Jacobo *economist, educator, consultant*
Rowe, Mary P. *university official, educator*
Rowe, Peter Grimmond *architecture educator, researcher*
Rubin, Donald Bruce *statistician, educator, research company executive*
Rubin, Jeffrey Zachary *psychologist, educator*
Rubin, Jerome Sanford *publishing company executive, lawyer*
Rubin, Lawrence Gilbert *physicist, laboratory manager*
Rudenstine, Neil Leon *academic administrator, educator*
Ruina, Jack Philip *electrical engineer, educator*
Russell, George Allen *composer, musicologist*
Russell, Kenneth Calvin *metallurgical engineer, educator*
Ryan, Allan Andrew, Jr. *lawyer, author, lecturer*
Ryan, Judith Lyndal *German language and literature educator*
Sadoway, Donald Robert *materials science educator*
Safran, Edward Myron *financial service company executive*
Saltzer, Jerome Howard *computer science educator*
Samuelson, Paul Anthony *economics educator*
Sander, Frank Ernest Arnold *law educator*
Sanders, John Lyell, Jr. *educator, researcher*
Sapolsky, Harvey Morton *political scientist, educator*
Sargentich, Lewis D. *legal educator*
Satterfield, Charles Nelson *chemical engineer, educator*
Schauer, Frederick Franklin *legal educator*
Scheffler, Israel *philosopher, educator*
Schein, Edgar Henry *management educator*
Scherer, Frederic Michael *economics educator*
Schild, Rudolph Ernst *astronomer, educator*
Schimmel, Paul Reinhard *biochemist, biophysicist, educator*
Schmalensee, Richard Lee *economist, former government official, educator*
Schmid, Wilfried *mathematician*
Schreiber, William Francis *electrical engineering educator*
Schuessler Fiorenza, Elisabeth *theology educator*
Schultes, Richard Evans *ethnobotanist, museum executive, educator, conservationist*
Scott, Hal S. *law educator*
Scott Morton, Michael Stewart *business management educator*
Seamans, Robert Channing, Jr. *astronautical engineering educator*
Seamans, Warren Arthur *museum director*
Segal, Charles Paul *classics educator, author*
Segal, Irving Ezra *mathematics educator*
Sekler, Eduard Franz *architect, educator*
Sen, Amartya Kumar *economist*
Septimus, Bernard Mark *religion educator*
Sevcenko, Ihor *history and literature educator*
Seyferth, Dietmar *chemist, educator*
Shapiro, David Louis *lawyer, educator*
Shapiro, Irwin Ira *physicist, educator*
Shapiro, Jeremy Frank *management educator*
Sharp, Phillip Allen *academic administrator, biologist, educator*
Shavell, Steven *law educator*
†Shea, Joseph F. *aeronautical engineering educator*
Sheridan, Thomas Brown *mechanical engineering and applied psychology educator, researcher, consultant*
†Shieber, Stuart Merrill *natural sciences educator*
Shinagel, Michael *English literature educator*
Shore, Miles Frederick *psychiatrist, educator*
Shultz, Leila McReynolds *botanist, educator*
Siebert, William McConway *electrical engineering educator*
Siegel, Abraham J. *economics educator, academic administrator*
Siever, Raymond *geology educator*
Signer, Ethan Royal *biology educator*
Silbey, Robert James *chemistry educator, researcher*
Silvera, Isaac Franklin *physics educator*
Simon, Eckehard (Peter) *foreign language educator*
Sims, Ezra *composer*
Singer, Irving *philosopher*
Singer, Isadore Manuel *mathematician, educator*
Sinskey, Anthony John *microbiology educator*
Sisler, William Philip *publishing executive*
Skolnikoff, Eugene B. *political science educator*
Slater, Jonathan E. *director*
Slive, Seymour *museum director, fine arts educator*
Smith, Kenneth Alan *chemical engineer, educator*
Smith, Merritt Roe *history educator*
Smith, Ronald Lee *academic administrator, public policy educator*
Snider, Eliot I. *lumber company executive*
Solbrig, Otto Thomas *population biologist, educator*
Sollors, Werner *English language, literature and American studies educator*
Solow, Robert Merton *economist, educator*
Sonin, Ain A. *mechanical engineering educator, consultant*
Spaepen, Frans August *applied physics researcher, educator*
Spunt, Shepard Armin *real estate executive, management and financial consultant*
Squire, James Robert *retired publisher, consultant*
Staelin, David Hudson *electrical engineering educator, consultant*
Stager, Lawrence E. *archaeologist, educator*
Stanley, Richard P. *mathematics educator*
Steiner, Henry Jacob *law and human rights educator*
Steiner, Lisa A(melia) *immunologist, educator*
Steinfeld, Jeffrey Irwin *chemistry educator, consultant, author*
†Steller, Hermann *neurobiologist, educator*
Stephanopoulos, Gregory *chemical engineering educator, consultant, researcher*
Stevens, Kenneth Noble *electrical engineering educator*
Stoddard, Roger Eliot *librarian*
Stoker, Thomas M. *economics educator*
Stone, Alan A. *law educator, psychiatry educator*
Stone, Andrew Grover *lawyer*
Strandberg, Malcom Woodrow Pershing *physicist*
Strang, William Gilbert *mathematician, educator*
Strauch, Karl *physicist, educator*
Striedter, Jurij *foreign language educator*
Striker, Gisela *philosophy educator*
Stroock, Daniel Wyler *mathematician, educator*
Stubbe, JoAnne *chemistry educator*
Suh, Nam Pyo *mechanical engineering educator*
Sullivan, Jeremiah David *physicist, educator*
Sulloway, Frank Jones *historian*
Susskind, Lawrence Elliott *urban and environmental planner, educator, mediator*
Swets, John Arthur *psychologist, scientist*
Szabo, Albert *architect, educator*
Ta, Tai Van *lawyer, researcher*
Tambiah, Stanley Jeyarajah *anthropologist*
Tanaka, Toyoichi *science educator*
Tannenbaum, Steven Robert *toxicologist, chemist*
Tarrant, R(ichard) J(ohn) *classicist, educator*
†Tassell, Jon Van *optical engineer*
Taubes, Clifford H. *mathematician, educator*
Tayler, Irene *English educator*
Teeter, Karl van Duyn *retired linguistic scientist, educator*
Tema-Lyn, Laurie *management consultant*
Temin, Peter *economics educator*
Termeer, Henricus Adrianus *biotechnology company executive*
Thaddeus, Patrick *physicist, educator*
Thernstrom, Stephan Albert *historian, educator*
Thiemann, Ronald Frank *dean, religion educator*
Thomas, Edwin L. *materials engineering educator*
Thomas, Harold Allen, Jr. *civil engineer, educator*
Thomas, Owen Clark *clergyman, educator*
Thompson, Dennis Frank *political science and ethics educator, consultant*
Thompson, James Burleigh, Jr. *geologist, educator*
Thorburn, David *literature educator*
Thurow, Lester Carl *economics educator*
Timmer, Charles Peter *agricultural economist*
Ting, Samuel Chao Chung *physicist, educator*
Tinkham, Michael *physicist, educator*
Tobin, James Robert *biotechnology company executive*
Todreas, Neil Emmanuel *nuclear engineering educator*
Tonegawa, Susumu *biology educator*
†Toomre, Alar *applied mathematician, theoretical astronomer*
Torriani-Gorini, Annamaria *microbiologist*
Trainor, Bernard Edmund *journalist, educator, retired marine corps officer*
Triantafyllou, Michael Stefanos *ocean engineering educator*
Tribe, Laurence Henry *lawyer, educator*
Trilling, Leon *aeronautical engineering educator*
†Tromp, Jeroen *earth scientist*
Troxel, Donald Eugene *electrical engineering educator*
Tsipis, Kosta Michael *science educator*
Tsoi, Edward Tze Ming *architect, interior designer, urban planner*
Tuller, Harry Louis *materials science and engineering educator*
Turkle, Sherry *sociologist, psychologist, educator*
Turnbull, David *physical chemist, educator*
Ulam, Adam B. *history and political science educator*
Ulrich, Laurel Thatcher *historian, educator*
Ungar, Eric Edward *mechanical engineer*
†Urban, Glen L. *management educator*
Urbanowski, Frank *publishing company executive*
Vagts, Detlev Frederick *lawyer, educator*
Valiant, Leslie Gabriel *computer scientist*
van der Merwe, Nikolaas Johannes *archaeologist*
Vander Velde, Wallace Earl *aeronautical and astronautical educator*
Vanger, Milton Isadore *history educator*
Vendler, Helen Hennessy *literature educator, poetry critic*
†Vér, István László *acoustical consultant*

Verba, Sidney *political scientist, educator*
†Verdine, Gregory Lawrence *chemist, educator*
Vermeule, Emily Townsend (Mrs. Cornelius C. Vermeule, III) *classicist, educator*
Vernon, Raymond *economist, educator*
Vessot, Robert Frederick Charles *physicist*
Vest, Charles Marstiller *university president*
Vigier, François Claude Denis *city planning educator*
Villars, Felix Marc Hermann *physicist, educator*
Vincent, James Louis *biotechnology company executive*
Vivian, Johnson Edward *retired chemical engineering educator*
Vogel, Ezra F. *sociology educator*
Vogt, Evon Zartman, Jr. *anthropologist*
von Mehren, Arthur Taylor *lawyer, educator*
Vorenberg, James *lawyer, educator, university dean*
Voss, John *retired association executive*
Wacker, Warren Ernest Clyde *physician, educator*
Wald, George *biochemist, educator*
Walker, Graham Charles *biology educator*
Wang, James Chuo *biochemistry and molecular biology educator*
Wang, Jian-Sheng *materials scientist*
Ward, John Milton *music educator*
Ward, Robertson, Jr. *architect*
Wardell, William Michael *drug development executive*
Warren, Alvin Clifford, Jr. *lawyer*
Waugh, John Stewart *chemist, educator*
Weber, Larry *public relations executive*
Wechsler, Alfred Elliot *engineering executive, consultant, chemical engineer*
Weiler, Paul Cronin *law educator*
Weinberg, Robert Allan *biochemist, educator*
Weiner, Charles *historian, educator*
Weiner, Myron *political science educator*
Weinreb, Lloyd Lobell *law educator*
Weiss, Stanley Irwin *engineering executive, aeronautical engineer*
Weiss, Thomas Fischer *electrical engineering educator, biophysicist*
Wendorf, Richard Harold *library director, educator*
Wenger, Luke Huber *educational association executive, editor*
West, Cornel *philosopher, writer*
Westervelt, Robert Moore *physics educator*
Westfall, David *lawyer, educator*
Westheimer, Frank Henry *chemist, educator*
Wexler, Kenneth Norman *psychology educator*
Whipple, Fred Lawrence *astronomer*
White, David Calvin *electrical engineer, energy educator, consultant*
Whitesides, George McClelland *chemistry educator*
Whitlock, Charles Preston *former university dean*
Whitman, Robert Van Duyne *civil engineer, educator*
Whitney, Charles Allen *astronomer, writer*
Wilcox, Maud *editor*
Wiley, Don Craig *biochemistry and biophysics educator*
Willard, Louis Charles *librarian*
Williams, George Huntston *church historian, educator*
Williams, James Henry, Jr. *mechanical engineer, educator, consultant*
Williams, Preston Noah *theology educator*
Willie, Charles Vert *sociology educator*
Wilson, David Gordon *mechanical engineering educator*
Wilson, Edward Osborne *biologist, educator*
Wilson, Gerald Loomis *electrical engineer, college dean*
Wilson, Linda Smith *university administrator*
Wilson, Mary Elizabeth *physician*
Wilson, Robert Woodrow *radio astronomer*
Winner, Thomas G. *foreign literature educator*
†Wisdom, Jack Leach *physicist, educator*
Wiseman, Frederick *filmmaker*
Wogan, Gerald Norman *toxicology educator*
Wolff, Christoph Johannes *music historian, educator*
Wolff, Cynthia Griffin *humanities educator, author*
Wolfman, Bernard *lawyer, educator*
Wood, John Armstead *planetary scientist, geological sciences educator*
Wrangham, Richard Walter *anthropology educator*
Wu, Tai Tsun *physicist, educator*
Wuensch, Bernhardt John *ceramic engineering educator*
Wunderlich, Renner *film producer, cinematographer*
Wunsch, Carl Isaac *oceanographer, educator*
Wurtman, Judith Joy *research scientist*
Wurtman, Richard Jay *physician, educator*
Yamamoto, Richard Kumeo *physics educator*
Yannas, Ioannis Vassilios *polymer science and engineering educator*
Yau, Shing-Tung *mathematics educator*
Yergin, Daniel Howard *writer, consultant*
Zahn, Markus *electrical engineering educator*
†Zeckhauser, Richard Jay *economist, educator*
Zeidenstein, George *population educator*
Zerner, Henri Thomas *art historian*
Zinberg, Dorothy Shore *science policy educator*
Ziolkowski, Jan M. *English educator*
†Zur Loye, Hans-Conrad *research chemist*

Canton
Bihldorff, John Pearson *hospital director*
Brouillard, John Charles *retail company executive*
†Ferrera, Alfred William *food distribution company executive*
Ferrera, Arthur Rocco *food distribution company executive*
Ferrera, Kenneth Grant *food distribution company executive*
Friend, William Kagay *lawyer*
Galligan, Thomas Joseph, III *retail footwear company executive*
Hirsh, Jane *pharmaceutical executive*
Holt, Donald Edward, Jr. *retail executive*
Lewis, Henry Rafalsky *manufacturing company executive*
Lyman, Charles Peirson *comparative physiologist*
Miller, Carl Eugene *marketing executive*
O'Donnell, Eugene J. *department stores executive*
Pitts, Virginia M. *human resources executive*
†Socol, Jerry M. *retail executive*
Tockman, Ronald Chester *accountant*

Carlisle
Fohl, Timothy *consulting and investment company executive*

Centerville
Anderson, Gerald Edwin *utilities executive*
Kiernan, Owen Burns *educational consultant*

Scherer, Harold Nicholas, Jr. *electric utility company executive, engineer*

Charlestown
Armstrong, Nancy L. *soprano, voice coach*
Bonventre, Joseph Vincent *physician, scientist, medical educator*
Isselbacher, Kurt Julius *physician, educator*
Lamont-Havers, Ronald William *physician, research administrator*
Moskowitz, Michael Arthur *neuroscientist, neurologist*
Talmage, John H. *food company executive*
Waldfogel, Morton Sumner *prefabricated housing/plywood company executive*

Chatham
Anderson, Barbara Graham *philanthropic resources development consultant*
Leighten, Edward Henry *publisher, consultant*
Miles, Robert Henry *management educator, university dean, consultant*
Pacun, Norman *lawyer*

Chelmsford
Fulks, Robert Grady *engineering computer executive*
Grossman, Debra A. *lawyer, real estate manager, radio talk show host*
†Howard, Terry Thomas *obstetrician/gynecologist*
Shepp, Allan *chemist and physicist*

Chelsea
Dunn, Norman Samuel *plastics and textiles company executive*
†Kaneb, Gary *oil industry executive*

Chestnut Hill
Altbach, Philip *higher education director, educator*
Barth, John Robert *English educator, priest*
Baum, Jules Leonard *ophthalmologist, educator*
Belsley, David Alan *economics educator, consultant*
Blanchette, Oliva *philosophy educator*
Bresky, H. Harry *diversified manufacturing company executive*
Bursley, Kathleen A. *lawyer*
Casper, Leonard Ralph *American literature educator*
Collins, Arthur Worth (Bud), Jr. *sports commentator*
Courtiss, Eugene Howard *plastic surgeon, educator*
Daly, Robert Joseph *theology educator*
Daniel-Dreyfus, Susan B. Russe *civic worker*
Duhamel, Pierre Albert *English language professional*
Fouraker, Lawrence Edward *social and business organizations director, former business administration educator*
†Fourkas, John T. *chemistry educator*
†Geller, Eric P. *lawyer, cinema company executive*
Glynn, Arthur Lawrence *business administration and accounting educator*
Goldweitz, Saul *publishing company executive*
Hawkins, Joellen Margaret Beck *nursing educator*
Hunt-Clerici, Carol Elizabeth *academic personnel assistant*
Kane, Edward James *economics educator*
Knapp, Robert Charles *retired obstetrics and gynecology educator*
Kosasky, Harold Jack *gynecologist*
Levy, James Peter *publishing company executive*
Lowell, Juliet *author*
Mahoney, John L. *English literature educator*
McAleer, John Joseph *English literature educator*
Meissner, William Walter *psychiatrist, clergyman*
Monan, James Donald *college president*
†Reichman, Joel H. *retail executive*
Rodrigues, Joseph E. *grain company executive*
Smith, Richard Alan *publishing and speciality retailing executive*
Stanbury, John Bruton *physician, educator*
Tarr, Robert Joseph, Jr. *publishing executive, retail executive*
Thier, Samuel Osiah *physician, educator*
Valette, Rebecca Marianne *Romance languages educator*

Chicopee
Anderson, Nancy Elaine *home economics educator*
Fishman, Gail Barbara *special education educator*

Chilmark
Geyer, Harold Carl *artist, writer*
Low, Joseph *artist*

Cohasset
Campbell, John Coert *political scientist, author*
Lyne, Austin Francis *sporting goods business executive*
Rabstejnek, George John *management consultant*
Sewall, Tingey Haig *banker*

Concord
Berger, Raoul *lawyer, educator, violinist*
Bloom, Edwin John, Jr. *human resources consultant*
Cavazos, Lauro Fred *former U.S. secretary of education, former university president, educator*
Cutting, Heyward *designer, planner*
Daltas, Arthur John *management consultant*
Drew, Philip Garfield *consultant engineering company executive*
Edmonds, Walter Dumaux *author*
Hogan, Daniel Bolten *management consultant*
†Howe, Harold, II *former foundation executive, educator*
Ihara, Michio *sculptor*
Link, David M. *medical products consultant*
Lombardo, Gaetano (Guy) *venture capitalist*
Meistas, Mary Therese *endocrinologist, diabetes researcher*
Moore, Robert Lowell, Jr. (Robin Moore) *author*
Palay, Sanford Louis *retired scientist, educator*
Rathore, Naeem Gul *United Nations official, retired*
Schiller, Pieter Jon *venture capital executive*
Smith, Peter Walker *finance executive*
Valley, George Edward, Jr. *physicist, educator*
Villers, Philippe *mechanical engineer*
White, James Barr *lawyer, real estate investor, consultant*
Woll, Harry J. *electrical engineer*

Conway
Mallary, Robert *sculptor*

Cotuit
Miller, Robert Charles *retired physicist*

Cummington
Wilbur, Richard Purdy *writer, educator*

Danvers
†Gaut, Norman Eugene *electronics firm executive*
Langford, Dean Ted *electronics executive*
Manganello, James Angelo *psychologist*
†Rubinstein, Sidney Jacob *orthopaedic technologist*
Traicoff, George *college president*
Waite, Charles Morrison *food company executive*

Dartmouth
Kahalas, Harvey *business educator*

Dedham
Culver, Edward Holland *marketing executive*
Firth, Everett Joseph *timpanist*
Lake, Ann Winslow *lawyer*
Magner, Jerome Allen *entertainment company executive*
†Maloof, Richard C. *engineering executive*
Redstone, Sumner Murray *entertainment company executive*
Russo, Peter Francis *financial executive, accountant*
Spoolstra, Linda Carol *minister, educator, religious organization administrator*
Weiss, Bruce Jordan *academic administrator*

Deerfield
Friary, Donald Richard *museum administrator*

Dennis
Weilbacher, William Manning *advertising and marketing consultant*

Dighton
Chu, David Yuk *chemical engineer*

Dorchester
Brelis, Matthew Dean Burns *journalist*
Bruzelius, Nils Johan Axel *journalist*
Daly, Charles Ulick *foundation executive, investor*
Garrison, Althea *goverment official*
Goodman, Ellen Holtz *journalist*
Greenway, Hugh Davids Scott *journalist*
Hatfield, Julie Stockwell *journalist, newspaper editor*
Huff, William Braid *publication company executive*
Kaufman, Jonathan Reed *journalist*
Larkin, Alfred Sinnott, Jr. *newspaper editor*
Lee, June Warren *dentist*
Leland, Timothy *newspaper executive*
Lewis, Elma I. *cultural organization artistic director*
Steller, Arthur Wayne *educational administrator*
Taylor, William Osgood *newspaper executive*

Dover
Aldrich, Frank Nathan *bank executive*
Bonis, Laszlo Joseph *business executive, scientist*
Borel, Richard Wilson *communications executive, consultant*
Buyse, Marylou *pediatrician, clinical geneticist, medical administrator*
Chattoraj, Sati Charan *biochemistry educator, researcher*
Crittenden, Gazaway Lamar *retired banker*
Fulchino, Paul Edward *management consultant*
Roberts, Francis Donald *manufacturing company executive*
Ryburn, Samuel McChesney *marketing executive*
Smith, William Henry Preston *writer, editor, former corporate executive*
Stockwell, Ernest Farnham, Jr. *banker*

Duxbury
Albritton, William Hoyle *training and consulting executive, lecturer, writer*
Mc Carthy, D. Justin *college president*
Thrasher, Dianne Elizabeth *mathematics educator, computer consultant*
Vose, Robert Churchill, Jr. *former art gallery executive*
Wangler, William Clarence *retired insurance company executive*

East Bridgewater
Jenkins, David B. *supermarket chain executive*

East Falmouth
George, M(erton) Baron T(isdale) *aerospace researcher, aviation artist*

East Longmeadow
Cushman, Elizabeth *English educator*

East Orleans
Hallowell, Burton Crosby *economist, educator*
MacMillan, Douglas Clark *naval architect*
McDermott, Thomas Curtis *health care and consumer products company executive*
Nenneman, Richard Arthur *retired publishing executive*
Rath, George Edward *bishop*

East Sandwich
Cober, Alan Edwin *artist, illustrator, printmaker, educator*

East Wareham
Dormitzer, Henry, II *retired manufacturing company executive*

East Weymouth
Hedlund, Robert L. *state senator, automobile executive*

Eastham
McLaughlin, Richard Warren *retired insurance company executive*

Easthampton
Grubbs, Dennis H. *secondary school principal*
Perkins, Homer Guy *manufacturing company executive*

Edgartown
Piper, George Earle *retailing design and financial consulting company executive*
Treat, Lawrence *author*
Walsh, Philip Cornelius *mining consultant*

Essex
McMillen, Louis Albert *architect*

Everett
Jenkins, Alexander, III *financial business executive*

Fall River
Correia, Robert *state legislator*
Ingles, James H. *learning resources academic director*
O'Malley, Sean *bishop*
Sullivan, Ruth Anne *librarian*

Falmouth
Bonn, Theodore Hertz *computer scientist, consultant*
Brewer, William Dodd *former ambassador, political science educator emeritus*
Gilmour, Edward Ellis *psychiatrist*
Goody, Richard Mead *geophysicist*
Hollister, Charles Davis *oceanographer*
Litschgi, Richard John *computer manufacturing company executive*
Mitchell, Charles Archie *financial planning consultant, engineer*

Fitchburg
Anderson, Charles Lee Royal *academic administrator*
Bogdasarian, John Robert *otolaryngologist*
Bourque, Anita Mary *school principal*
†Cronin, Francis Joseph, Jr. *hospital administrator*
†Fredette, Raymond David *healthcare executive*
Mara, Vincent Joseph *college president*
Timms, Peter Rowland *art museum administrator*
Wiegersma, Nan *economics educator*

Foxboro
Armstrong, Bruce Charles *professional football player*
Bowditch, Hoel Lawrence *design engineer inventor, consultant*
Bush, Raymond T. *accountant, corporate professional*
Ghosh, Asish *control engineer*
Morris, Gerald Francis *manufacturing company executive*
Parcells, Bill (Duane Charles Parcells) *professional football coach*
Pierce, Francis Casimir *civil engineer*
Pitt, Earle William *manufacturing company executive*
Sullivan, William Hallisey, Jr. *professional football team executive*

Framingham
Atsumi, Ikuko *management school administrator, educator*
Ballou, Kenneth Walter *retired transportation executive, university dean*
Bogard, Carole Christine *lyric soprano*
Bose, Amar Gopal *electrical engineering educator*
†Campbell, Kirk *information systems executives*
†Castelli, William Peter *cardiovascular epidemiologist, educator*
Feldberg, Sumner Lee *retail company executive*
Gaffin, Gerald Eliot *lawyer*
Gray, John Bullard *manufacturing company executive*
Hoffer, Edward Peter *physician*
Kuklinski, Joan Lindsey *librarian*
Lipton, Leah *art historian, educator, museum curator*
†McGovern, Patrick J. *communications executive*
Meltzer, Jay H. *lawyer, retail company executive*
Merser, Francis Gerard *manufacturing company executive, consultant*
Oleskiewicz, Francis Stanley *retired insurance executive*
Perini, David B. *construction company executive*
Perini, Joseph R. *corporate executive*
Sposato, Charles *secondary education educator*
Stuart, Anne Elizabeth *journalist, freelance writer, educator*
Vermette, Raymond Edward *clinical laboratories administrator*
Waters, James Logan *analytical instrument manufacturing executive*
Wilson, John Benedict *office supplies company executive*
Wishner, Steven R. *retail executive*

Framington
Scherr, Allan Lee *computer scientist, executive*

Franklin
Bonin, Paul Joseph *real estate and banking executive*
Hoffman, S. Joseph *advertising agency executive*

Gardner
McCarthy, Albert Henry *human resources executive*
Wagenknecht, Edward *author*

Gloucester
Baird, Gordon Prentiss *publisher*
Curtis, Roger William *artist, educator*
Duca, Alfred Milton *artist*
Erkkila, Barbara Howell Louise *writer, photographer*
Hancock, Walker Kirtland *sculptor*
Hausman, William Ray *fund raising and management consultant*
Lauenstein, Milton Charles *management consultant*
Socolow, Arthur Abraham *geologist*
Warhover, Stephen Hunt *food company executive*

Grafton
Haggerty, John Edward *research center administrator, former army officer*

Granville
†Brown, Stephen Pat *artist*

Great Barrington
Gilmour, Robert Arthur *foundation executive, educator*
Rodgers, Bernard F., Jr. *academic administrator, dean*
Schenck, Benjamin Robinson *insurance consultant*
Stonier, Tom *educator, author*

Greenfield
Curtiss, Carol Perry *nursing consultant*
Lee, Marilyn (Irma) Modarelli *law librarian*
Robinson, John Alan *logic and computer science educator*

Groton
†Rhoads, Richard H. *printing company executive*
Smith, Alan Harvey *former editor*

Halifax
Fanning, Margaret Beverly *psychotherapist*

Hanover
Fantozzi, Peggy Ryone *environmental planner*
Hart, Richard Nevel, Jr. *financial exective, consultant*
Lonborg, James Reynold *dentist, former professional baseball player*

Hanscom AFB
†Eckhardt, Donald Henry *geophysicist*
Mailloux, Robert Joseph *physicist*

Hanson
Norris, John Anthony *health sciences executive, lawyer, educator*

Harvard
†Becker, Ray Everett *data processing executive*
†Larson, Roland Elmer *health care executive*
Sutherland, Malcolm Read, Jr. *clergyman, educator*

Harwich
Bush, Richard James *engineering executive, lay church worker*
Randolph, Robert Lee *economist, educator*
Rigg, Charles Andrew *pediatrician*
Thorndike, Joseph Jacobs, Jr. *editor*

Harwich Port
Mc Cormick, Richard Patrick *history educator*
Staszesky, Francis Myron *electric company consultant*

Hatfield
Yolen, Jane *author*

Haverhill
Dimitry, John Randolph *college president*
Ehrig, Ulrich *physician*
Haritos, Dolores Jean *nursing educator*
Mignanelli, James Robert *manufacturing executive*
Niccolini, Drew George *gastroenterologist*

Hingham
Dassori, Frederic Davis, Jr. *lawyer*
Ford, Joseph *retired superior court judge*
Hinkley, Clark J. *retail executive*
†Kutsch, Michael R. *oil company financial executive, finance company executive*
Lane, Frederick Stanley *lawyer*
Replogle, David Robert *publishing company executive*
Zetcher, Arnold B. *apparel executive*

Holbrook
†Crandlemere, Robert Wayne *engineering executive*

Holden
Botty, Kenneth John *editor, newspaper executive*

Holliston
Scibelli, Arthur Peter, Jr. *lawyer*

Holyoke
Dwight, William, Jr. *former newspaper executive, restaurateur*
†Parent, Mark *engring company executive, computer support company executive*
Radner, Sidney Hollis *retired rug company executive*

Hopkinton
Desmarais, Maurice *trade association administrator*
Leamon, Tom B. *industrial engineer, educator*
Nickerson, Richard Gorham *research company executive*
Novich, Bruce Eric *materials engineer*
Preston, William Hubbard *consultant to specialty businesses*
Ruettgers, Michael Cadet *electronics executive*

Housatonic
Levy, Sy *advertising and direct marketing executive*

Hull
Anderson, Timothy Christopher *consulting company executive*
Burgess, David Lowry *artist*
Chase, David Marion *applied physicist, mathematical modeler*

Hyannis
Chiotellis, Philip Nicos *cardiologist*
Himstead, Scott *newspaper publisher*
White, Timothy Oliver *newspaper editor*

Hyannis Port
Ludtke, James Buren *business and finance educator*

Hyde Park
Riley, Lawrence Joseph *bishop*

Ipswich
Berggren, Dick *editor*
Bryant, Edward Curtis *educational association executive*
Getchell, Charles Willard, Jr. *lawyer, publisher*

Jamaica Plain
Cushing, Steven *software educator, researcher, consultant*
Pierce, Chester Middlebrook *psychiatrist, educator*
Shapiro, Ascher Herman *mechanical engineer, educator, consultant*
Snider, Gordon Lloyd *physician*

Kingston
Rispettoso, George Alphonse *vocational educator, diesel technology consultant*
Squarcia, Paul Andrew *school superintendent*
Stair, Gobin *publishing executive, painter, graphic designer*
Walters, Alan Stanley *distribution company executive*

Lawrence
†Dionne, Joseph Robert *public library director, fundraising consultant*
Mosca, Anthony John *substance abuse professional*
Ochiltree, Stuart A. *cosmetics company executive*

Lee
Smith, Elske Van Panhuys *retired university administrator*

Leeds
Baskin, Leonard *sculptor, graphic artist*

Lenox
Curtis, William Edgar *conductor, composer*
Krofta, Milos *engineer*
LiMarzi, Joseph *artist*
Novak, William Arnold *author, lecturer*
Pierson, John Herman Groesbeck *economist, writer*
Ripps, Rodney *artist*
Slavin, Simon *social administration educator*

Leominster
Cormier, Robert Edmund *writer*

Leverett
Barkin, Solomon *economist*

Lexington
Aldrich, Ralph Edward *physicist*
Alloway, Robert Malcombe *computer consulting executive*
Bailey, Fred Coolidge *retired engineering consulting company executive*
Bainbridge, Kenneth Tompkins *physicist, educator*
Bartlett, Paul Doughty *chemist, educator*
Barton, David Knox *engineering executive, radar engineer*
Bell, Carolyn Shaw *economist, educator*
Bernardi, John Lawrence, Jr. *economic historian, educator, consultant*
Berstein, Irving Aaron *biotechnology and medical technology executive*
Bishop, Robert Calvin *pharmaceutical company executive*
Bleck, Max Emil *aircraft company executive*
Brick, Donald Bernard *consulting company executive*
Brookner, Eli *electrical engineer*
Buchanan, John Machlin *biochemistry educator*
Bursma, Albert, Jr. *publishing company executive*
Cathou, Renata Egone *chemist, consultant*
Chaskelson, Marsha Ina *neuropsychologist*
Ciampa, Dan *management consultant*
Colburn, Kenneth Hersey *investment banker*
Cooper, William Eugene *consultant engineer*
Deitcher, Herbert *financial executive*
Della Penna, Joan Frances *secondary educator*
Duboff, Robert Samuel *marketing professional*
Eaton, Allen Ober *lawyer*
Eberle, William Denman *international management consultant*
Fallon, John Golden *banker*
Fillios, Louis Charles *retired science educator*
Fray, Lionel Louis *management consultant*
Freed, Charles *engineering consultant, researcher*
Freitag, Wolfgang Martin *librarian, educator*
Garing, John Seymour *retired physicist, research executive*
Gibbs, Martin *biologist, educator*
Gilbert, David *computer company executive*
Harkness, Sarah Pillsbury *architect*
Hoffmann, Christoph Ludwig *lawyer*
Holzman, Franklyn Dunn *economics educator*
Hoopes, Walter Ronald *chemical company executive*
Jensen, Mona Dickson *chemist, researcher*
Kanter, Irving *mathematical physicist*
Kindleberger, Charles P., II *economist, educator*
Kingston, Robert Hildreth *engineering educator*
Kirkpatrick, Francis H(ubbard), Jr. *biophysicist, consultant*
Korte, Loren A. *publishing company executive*
Lawton, Eugene Alfred *banking executive*
Litchfield, Ruth France *reading, literacy specialist*
Mack, Jane Louise *early childhood educator, administrator*
McWhorter, Alan Louis *electronics researcher, engineering educator*
Melngailis, Ivars *solid state research executive*
Mollo-Christensen, Erik Leonard *oceanographer*
†Moren, Nicholas Charles *investment and holding company executive*
Morrow, Walter Edwin, Jr. *electrical engineer, university laboratory administrator*
Nash, Leonard Kollender *chemistry educator*
O'Donnell, Robert Michael *electrical engineering executive*
Osepchuk, John Moses *engineering physicist, consultant*
Papanek, Gustav Fritz *economist, educator*
Phalon, Philip Anthony *marketing executive*
Phillips, Thomas L. *corporate executive*
Picard, Dennis J. *electronics company executive*
Pierce, Walter S. *architect*
Risch, Martin Donald *marketing-management consulting company executive*
Ross, Douglas Taylor *retired software company executive*
Samour, Carlos Miguel *chemist*
Schloemann, Ernst Fritz (Rudolf August) *physicist, engineer*
Schultz, Samuel Jacob *clergyman, educator*
Seaman, Robert LeRoy *technology company executive*
Shull, Clifford G. *physicist, educator*
Smith, Edgar Eugene *biochemist, university administrator*
Smith, Robert Louis *construction company executive*
Stern, Ernest *science research executive, electrical engineer*
Wallace, John Edwin *retired meteorologist, consultant*
Wathne, Carl Norman *hospital administrator*
Williamson, Richard Cardinal *physicist*
Wyss, David Alen *financial service executive*

Lincoln
Adams, Thomas Boylston *journalist*
Barrett, Beatrice Helene *psychologist*
Brown, Linda Weaver *academic administrator*
Cannon, Bradford *surgeon*
Donald, David Herbert *author, history educator*
Eschenroeder, Alan Quade *environmental scientist*
Fernald, George Herbert, Jr. *retired photographic company executive*
Godine, David Richard *publishing company executive*
Green, David Henry *manufacturing company executive*
Holberton, Philip Vaughan *biotechnology company executive*
Kalba, Kas *international communications consultant*
LeGates, John Crews Boulton *information scientist*
Master-Karnik, Paul Joseph *art museum director*
Merrill, Vincent Nichols *landscape architect*
Schwann, William Joseph *publisher, musician, discographer*
Schwartz, Edward Arthur *lawyer, foundation executive*
Sprague, John Louis *management consultant*

Littleton
Fuller, Samuel Henry, III *computer engineer*
Mikes, Thomas Louis *optical design engineer*

Longmeadow
Cobbs, Russell L(ewis) *English language educator*
Ferris, Theodore Vincent *chemical engineer, consulting technologist*
Hopfe, Harold Herbert *chemical engineer*
Keady, George Cregan, Jr. *judge*
Leary, Carol Ann *academic administrator*
Lo Bello, Joseph David *banking executive*
Locklin, Wilbert Edwin *management consultant*
Louargand, Marc Andrew *real estate executive, financial consultant*
Skelton, Don Richard *consulting actuary, retired insurance company executive*
Stewart, Alexander Doig *bishop*
Wright, Jeanette Tornow *college president*

Lowell
Baker, Adolph *physicist*
Carr, George Leroy *physicist, educator*
Coleman, Robert Marshall *biology educator*
Greenwald, John Edward *newspaper and magazine executive*
Hoffman, Paul Roger *aerospace executive*
Hosking, Douglas Gordon *printing company executive*
Kumnick, Albert Joseph *engineering executive*
Natsios, Nicholas Andrew *retired foreign service officer*
Osenton, Thomas George *publisher*
Rayfield, Allan Laverne *electronics company executive*
Reinisch, Bodo Walter *electrical engineering educator*
Ruskai, Mary Beth *mathematics researcher, educator*
Salamone, Joseph Charles *polymer chemistry educator*
Sheldon, Eric *physics educator*
Shirvani, Hamid *philosophy educator, university dean, critic*
Sullivan, Anne Dorothy Hevner *artist*
Tripathy, Sukant Kishore *chemistry educator*
Tucci, Joseph M. *computer software and services executive*
Vanderslice, Thomas Aquinas *electronics executive*

Ludlow
Cox, Geraldine Vang *engineering executive*

Lynn
Kercher, David Max *mechanical engineer*
Lukowski, Stanley J. *banker*
Stark, Dennis Edwin *banker*

Lynnfield
Gianino, John Joseph *former insurance executive*

Manchester
Bundy, Harvey Hollister *retired bank executive*
Cabot, John G. L. *chemical manufacturing company executive*
Lothrop, Kristin Curtis *sculptor*

Mansfield
Forney, G(eorge) David, Jr. *electronics company executive*
Khan, Gordon Simeon *financial executive*
Meelia, Richard J. *healthcare products executive*
Rosa, Edward A. *principal*
Roskothen, Michael S. *health care supply company executive*

Marblehead
Dolan, John Ralph *retired corporation executive*
Ehrich, Fredric F. *aeronautical engineer*
Kemelman, Harry *author*
Pruyn, William J. *energy industry executive*
Rogow, Bruce Joel *information technology consultant*
Sanders, Frederick *meteorologist*
Zawinul, Josef *bandleader, composer, keyboardist, synthesist*

Marion
†Walsh, William Egan, Jr. *electronics executive*

Marlborough
Axline, Robert Paul *electronics executive*
Bennett, C. Leonard *consulting engineer*
Bethel, Tamara Ann *psychiatric nurse, consultant*
Birstein, Seymour Joseph *aerospace company executive*
†Koutros, Stephen Anthony *business executive, computer consultant*
Lohr, Harold Russell *bishop*
Palihnich, Nicholas Joseph, Jr. *retail chain executive*
Stiffler, Jack Justin *electrical engineer*

Marshfield
Mc Carthy, Thomas Patrick *magazine publisher*

Marshfield Hills
Stacey, Kathleen Mary *advertising and public relations executive*

Marstons Mills
Martin, Vincent George *management consultant*
Vila, Robert Joseph *television host, designer, real estate developer*
Wheeler, Richard Warren *banker*

Maynard
Palmer, Robert B. *computer company executive*
Siekman, Thomas Clement *lawyer*
Smith, John F. *computer company executive*

Medford
Anderson, Thomas Jefferson, Jr. *composer, educator*
Astill, Kenneth Norman *mechanical engineering educator*
Balabanian, Norman *electrical engineering educator*
Bedau, Hugo Adam *philosophy educator*
Berman, David *lawyer, poet*
†Brooke, John L. *history educator*
Brown, Althea T. *secondary education educator*
Burke, Edward Newell *radiologist*
Burnim, Kalman Aaron *theatre educator emeritus*
Cartwright, Helen Morris *philosophy educator, writer*
Caviness, Madeline Harrison *art history educator, researcher*
Cavitch, David *English language educator*
Conklin, John Evan *sociology educator*
Cormack, Allan MacLeod *physicist, educator*
Daniels, Norman *philosopher, educator*
DeBold, Joseph Francis *psychology educator*
Dennett, Daniel Clement *philosopher, author, educator*
DiBiaggio, John A. *university administrator*
Elkind, David *psychology educator*
Fyler, John Morgan *English language educator*
Galvin, John Rogers *educator, retired army officer*
Garrelick, Joel Marc *acoustical scientist, consultant*
Greif, Robert *mechanical engineering educator*
Gunther, Leon *physicist*
Howell, Alvin Harold *engineer*
Junger, Miguel Chapero *acoustics researcher*
Kanarek, Robin Beth *psychology educator, nutrition educator, researcher*
Klema, Ernest Donald *nuclear physicist, educator*
Laurent, Pierre-Henri *history educator*
Luria, Zella Hurwitz *psychology educator*
Mancke, Richard Bell *university dean, economics educator*
Manno, Vincent Paul *mechanical engineer*
Marcopoulos, George John *history educator*
Mc Carthy, Kathryn A. *physicist*
Miczek, Klaus Alexander *psychology educator*
Milburn, Richard Henry *physics educator*
Mumford, George Saltonstall, Jr. *former university dean, astronomy educator*
Nelson, Frederick Carl *mechanical engineering educator*
Nitecki, Zbigniew Henry *mathematician, educator*
Noonan, Joseph Patrick *engineering educator*
†O'Connell, Brian *community organizer, public administrator, writer, educator*
Reynolds, William Francis *mathematics educator*
Romero, Christiane *German language educator*
Salacuse, Jeswald William *lawyer, educator*
Schneps, Jack *physics educator*
Senelick, Laurence Philip *theatre educator, director, writer*
Simches, Seymour Oliver *language educator*
Sloane, Marshall M. *banker*
†Smith, Hale *data processing services executive*
Sung, Nak-Ho *science educator*
Sussman, Martin Victor *chemical engineering educator, inventor, consultant*
Swap, Walter Charles *academic dean, psychology educator*
Uhlir, Arthur, Jr. *electrical engineer, university administrator*
Urry, Grant Wayne *chemistry educator*
Wechsler, Judith Glatzer *art historian, filmmaker, educator*

Medway
Yonda, Alfred William *mathematician*

Melrose
Fremont-Smith, Thayer *judge*
Gibbons, Patrice Ellen *critical care nurse*

Methuen
†Pollack, Herbert William *electronics executive*

Middleboro
Beeby, Kenneth Jack *lawyer, food products executive*
Collison, Curtis Lee, Jr. *processed food and beverage company executive*
Llewellyn, John Schofield, Jr. *food company executive*

Middleton
Stover, Matthew Joseph *communications company executive*

Milford
Carson, Charles Henry *electronics engineer*
Gliksberg, Alexander David *engineering executive*
Graziano, Chancey Lee *business executive*

Millbury
Noonan, Stephen Joseph *accounting firm executive*
Pan, Coda H. T. *mechanical engineering educator, consultant, researcher*

Milton
Berzon, Faye Clark *retired nursing educator*
Dunn, Martin Joseph *dentist*
Giuliano, Frank J., Jr. *school system administrator*
Ingold, Catherine White *academic administrator*
Kennedy, Thomas Leo *investment management company executive*
Place, David Elliott *lawyer*

Monson
Krach, Mitchell Peter *retired financial services executive*

Montague
Coughlin, Jack *printmaker, sculptor, art educator*

Nantucket
Holch, Eric Sanford *artist*
Jesser, Benn Wainwright *chemical engineering and construction company executive*
Lethbridge, Francis Donald *architect*
Lobl, Herbert Max *lawyer*
Mercer, Richard Joseph *retired advertising executive, freelance writer*
Murray, Caroline Fish *psychologist*
Rorem, Ned *composer, author*

Natick
Babson, Arthur Clifford *financial executive*

Bensel, Carolyn Kirkbride *psychologist*
Cukor, Peter *chemical research and development executive, educator, consultant*
Current, Richard Nelson *historian, educator*
Deutsch, Marshall E(manuel) *medical products company executive, inventor*
Donovan, R. Michael *management consultant*
Geller, Esther (Bailey Geller) *artist*
Gomberg, Sydelle *dancer educator*
Milius, Richard A. *organic chemist*
Narayan, K(rishnamurthi) Ananth *biochemist*
Neumeyer, John Leopold *research company administrator, chemistry educator*
Perrin, Stephanie B. *headmistress*
Planitzer, Russell E. *computer company executive*
Savage, James Cathey, III *lawyer, military officer, educator*
Strauss, Harlee Sue *environmental consultant*
Strayton, Robert Gerard *public communications executive*
Wang, Chia Ping *physicist, educator*

Needham
Burrell, Sidney Alexander *history educator*
Cantor, Pamela Corliss *psychologist*
Carey, Robert Williams *retired insurance company executive*
Chattoraj, Aparna *gynecologist, educator*
Cogswell, John Heyland *retired telecommunications executive, financial consultant*
Cohen, Lewis Cobrain *security products firm executive*
Cowens, David William (Dave Cowens) *insurance executive, retired professional basketball player, basketball school executive*
Hopson, James Warren *newspaper publisher*
Hunter, Elizabeth Ives-Valsam *consultant*
Kung, Patrick Chung-Shu *biotechnology executive*
Lebowitz, Marshall *publishing company executive*
Pucel, Robert Albin *electronics research engineer*
Sabosik, Patricia Elizabeth *publisher, editor*
Tarsky, Eugene Stanley *accountant, management and systems consultant*
Toner, Walter Joseph, Jr. *transportation engineer, financial consultant*
Walworth, Arthur *author*
Weller, Thomas Huckle *physician, emeritus educator*

New Bedford
Benoit, Richard Armand *police chief, lawyer*
Chang, Robin *engineering executive*
Hodgson, James Stanley *antiquarian bookseller*
McCarter, Robert *banking executive*
Merolla, Michele Edward *chiropractor*
Robbins, Orren Bourne *newspaper publisher*
Shapiro, Gilbert Lawrence *orthopedist*
Tierney, Rosemary *mayor*
Young, Janie Chester *museum consultant*

New Salem
Lenherr, Frederick Keith *neurophysiologist, computer scientist*

Newburyport
Howard, John Tasker *city planner*
†Strem, Michael Edward *chemicals executive*

Newton
Barclay, Stanton Dewitt *engineering executive, consultant*
Baron, Charles Hillel *lawyer, educator*
Bernard, Michael Mark *city planning consultant, lawyer*
Bewick, John Arters *consulting firm executive*
Blacher, Richard Stanley *psychiatrist*
Caldwell, Sarah *opera producer, conductor, stage director and administrator*
†Capon, Edwin Gould *church organization administrator, clergyman*
Chlamtac, Imrich *computer company executive, educator*
Coleman, Gerald Christopher *management consultant*
Coquillette, Daniel Robert *lawyer, educator*
Deats, Paul Kindred, Jr. *religion educator, clergyman*
Dunlap, William Crawford *physicist*
Forsberg, Roy Walter *publishing company executive*
Frieden, Bernard Joel *urban studies educator*
Gerrity, J(ames) Frank, II *building materials company executive*
Gill, Benjamin Franklin *physician*
†Glick-Weil, Kathy *library director*
Guidotti, Guido *biochemist, educator*
Hauser, Harry Raymond *lawyer*
†Heck, William Henry *hotel executive*
Heins, Ethel L. *children's literature consultant, critic*
Henderson, Kenneth Atwood *investment counseling executive*
Heyn, Arno Harry Albert *retired chemistry educator*
Horbaczewski, Henry Zygmunt *lawyer, publishing executive*
Kaplan, Steven F. *business management executive*
Katz, Sanford Noah *lawyer, educator*
Kosowsky, David I. *retired biotechnical company executive*
Krakoff, Robert Leonard *publishing executive*
†Landers, Renée Marie *law educator, government lawyer*
Manners, Robert Alan *anthropologist*
†Marram, Edward P. *engineering company executive*
Mason, Charles Ellis, III *magazine editor*
Myerson, Paul Graves *psychiatrist, educator*
Oles, Paul Stevenson (Steve Oles) *architect, perspectivist, educator*
Porter, Jack Nusan *writer, sociologist*
Rakay, William R. *publishing company executive*
Rodman, Sumner *insurance executive*
Rogoff, Jerome Howard *psychiatrist, psychoanalyst, forensic expert*
Saffran, Kalman *engineering consulting company executive, entrepreneur*
Sbordon, William G. *publisher*
Simon, Harold *radiologist*
Stein, Seymour *electronic scientist*
Stundza, Thomas John *journalist*
Tannenwald, Leslie Keiter *educational administrator*
Thompson, Stephen Arthur *publishing executive*
Weisskopf, Victor Frederick *physicist*
White, Burton Leonard *educational psychologist, author*
Young, James Morningstar *physician, naval officer*
Zander, Benjamin *conductor, educator*

Newton Center
Ault, Hugh Joseph *legal educator*
Mark, Melvin *consulting mechanical engineer, educator*
Mautner, Henry George *chemist*
Sandman, Peter M. *communications risk consultant*
Schuller, Gunther Alexander *composer*
Walker, Bradford C. *architect*

Newtonville
Polonsky, Arthur *artist, educator*

Norfolk
Beard, Carol Elaine *art educator*

North Adams
Thurston, Donald Allen *broadcasting executive*

North Amherst
Andersen, Richard Arnold *writer, consultant*
Lester, Julius B. *author*

North Andover
Buchanan, Ellery Rives *sales executive*
Goldstein, Charles Henry *architect, consultant*
Olney, Peter Butler, Jr. *retired management consulting firm executive*
Rivard, Paul Edmund *museum director*
Scully, Stephen J. *plastic surgeon*

North Attleboro
†Friend, Dale Gilbert *retired medical educator*

North Billerica
Fink, David A. *rail transportation executive*
Sodini, Peter J. *food service executive*

North Brookfield
Neal, Avon *artist, author*
Parker, Ann (Ann Parker Neal) *photographer, graphic artist*

North Chatham
Hiscock, Richard Carson *marine safety investigator*
McCarthy, Joseph Harold *consultant, former retail food company executive*
Rowlands, Marvin Lloyd, Jr. *publishing and communications consultant*

North Dartmouth
Andersen, Laird Bryce *retired university administrator*
Cressy, Peter Hollon *naval officer, academic administrator*
Dace, Tish *drama educator*
Law, Frederick Masom *engineering educator, structural engineering firm executive*
Noel, Barbara Hughes McMurtry *music educator*
Tuttle, Clifford Horace, Jr. *electronics manufacturing company executive*
Waxler, Robert Phillip *university educator, consultant*
Yoken, Mel B. *French language educator, author*

North Dighton
Cserr, Robert *psychiatrist, physician, hospital administrator*

North Eastham
Simmel, Marianne Lenore *graphic designer*

North Easton
†Holland, David Vernon *minister*

North Egremont
Le Comte, Edward Semple *author, educator*

North Falmouth
Bass, Norman Herbert *physician, scientist, university and hospital administrator, health care executive*
Morse, Robert Warren *research administrator*

North Grafton
Loew, Franklin Martin *medical and biological scientist*
Nelson, John Martin *corporate executive*
Ross, James Neil, Jr. *veterinary educator*
Schwartz, Anthony *veterinary surgeon, educator*

North Quincy
Allinson, A. Edward *banking executive*
Porter, John Stephen *television executive*

North Reading
Dolan, Edward Corcoran *real estate developer and investor*
†Ford, Gilbert (Gib Ford) *sporting goods company executive*
Green, Jack Allen *lawyer*
O'Neil, John P(atrick) *athletic footwear company executive*

Northampton
Burk, Carl John *biological sciences educator*
Crosby, Faye Jacqueline *psychology educator, author*
Dashef, Stephen Sewell *psychiatrist*
Derr, Thomas Sieger *religion educator*
Donfried, Karl Paul *minister, theology educator*
Dunn, Mary Maples *college president*
Elkins, Stanley Maurice *historian, educator*
Ellis, Frank Hale *English literature professional*
Fleck, George Morrison *chemistry educator*
Flesher, Hubert Louis *religion educator*
Heartt, Charlotte Beebe *university official*
Hoyt, Nelly Schargo (Mrs. N. Deming Hoyt) *history educator*
Lehmann, Phyllis Williams *archaeologist, educator*
Little, Lester Knox *historian, educator*
MacLachlan, Patricia *author*
Munson, Richard Howard *horticulturist*
Naegele, Philipp Otto *violinist, violist, music educator*
Olivo, Margaret Ellen Anderson (Margaret Ellen Anderson) *physiologist, educator*
Piccinino, Rocco Michael *librarian*
Pickrel, Paul *English educator*
Robinson, Donald Leonard *social scientist, educator*
Rose, Peter Isaac *sociologist, writer*
Rupp, Sheron Adeline *photographer, educator*
Smith, Malcolm Barry Estes *philosophy educator, lawyer*
Vaget, Hans Rudolf *language professional, educator*
Vesely, Alexander *civil engineer*
Volkmann, Frances Cooper *psychologist, educator*
von Klemperer, Klemens *historian, educator*

Northborough
Fulmer, Hugh Scott *physician, educator*
Jeas, William C. *electronics and aerospace engineering executive*

Norton
Dahl, Curtis *English literature educator*
†Marshall, Dale Rogers *college president, political scientist, educator*
Norris, Curtis Bird *writer, journalist*
Olson, Roberta Jeanne Marie *art historian, author, educator*
Taylor, Robert Sundling *English educator, art critic*

Norwell
Brett, Jan Churchill *illustrator, author*
Mullare, T(homas) Kenwood, Jr. *lawyer*
Rolnik, Zachary Jacob *senior editor, publisher*
†Samra, Hisham *pharmaceutical executive*
Wentworth, Murray Jackson *artist, educator*

Norwood
Berliner, Allen Irwin *dermatologist*
Florian, Agustin Max *thoracic and cardiovascular surgeon*
Freni, Anthony *church administrator*
Imbault, James Joseph *engineering executive*
Pence, Robert Dudley *biomedical research administrator, hospital administrator*
Rasmussen, David George *lawyer*
Sheingold, Daniel H. *electrical engineer*
†Stata, Raymond *data processing and computer company executive*

Orange
Bate, Judith Ellen *artist*
Preece, Warren Eversleigh *editor*

Orleans
Dessauer, John Phillip *publisher, financial management company executive*
Hughes, Libby *author*
Lawton, Nancy *artist*
Russell, David L(awson) *psychology educator*

Osterville
Old, Bruce Scott *chemical and metallurgical engineer*

Palmer
Dupuis, Robert Simeon *sales executive*

Peabody
Goldberg, Harold Seymour *electrical engineer, academic administrator*
†Peters, Leo Francis *environmental engineer*
Wood, Richard Robinson *real estate executive*

Pittsfield
Cornelio, Albert Carmen *insurance executive*
Feigenbaum, Armand Vallin *systems engineer, systems equipment executive*
Gregware, James Murray *financial planner*
Poland, Susan Lee *lawyer*
Shammas, Nazih Kheirallah *environmental engineering educator, consultant*

Plymouth
Atkinson, Christine Gagner *chemist, environmental engineer, consultant*
Barreira, Brian Ernest *lawyer*
†Ehrlich, Richard L. *museum executive*
Forman, Peter *sheriff, former state legislator*
Gregory, Dick *comedian, civil rights activist*
Joseph, Rodney Randy *artist, arts society executive*

Provincetown
Brock, Alice May *restaurateur, author*
Doty, Mark *poet*
Oliver, Mary *poet*

Quincy
Bierman, George William *technical consulting executive, food technologist*
†Gorfinkle, Constance Sue *journalist*
Hagar, William Gardner, III *photobiology educator*
Hayes, Bernardine Frances *computer systems analyst*
Hill, Kent Richmond *college president*
Levin, Robert Joseph *retail grocery chain store executive*
Lippincott, Joseph P. *photojournalist, educator*
Mancini, Rocco Anthony *civil engineer*
McGlinchey, Joseph Dennis *retail corporation executive*
Miller, George David *retired air force officer, marketing consultant*
Pitts, James Atwater *financial executive*
Shuster, Herbert Victor *corporate executive, consultant*
Watson, Warren Edward *retired library administrator*
Young, Richard William *corporate director*

Randolph
Morrissey, Edmond Joseph *classical philologist*
Rosenberg, Robert Michael *restaurant franchise company executive*
Ross, Edward Joseph *architect*

Reading
Burbank, Nelson Stone *investment banker*
McKinley, William Thomas *composer, performer, educator*
Stone, Warren R. *book publishing executive*

Revere
Taubert, Frederick Wayne *oil company executive*

Richmond
Curtiss, Trumbull Cary *banker*
Sexton, William Cottrell *journalist*

Rockland
Campbell, David Stetson *civil engineer, engineering executive*

Rockport
Bakrow, William John *college president emeritus*
Bissell, Phil (Charles P. Bissell) *cartoonist*
Cotter, Joseph Francis *bank officer*
Deedy, John Gerard, Jr. *writer*
Delakas, Daniel Liudviko *retired foreign language educator*
Morrell, Wayne Beam, Jr. *artist*
Nicholas, Thomas Andrew *artist*
Strisik, Paul *artist*
Walen, Harry Leonard *historian, lecturer, author*
Wiberg, Lars-Erik *human resources consultant*

Roxbury
Berman, Marlene Oscar *neuropsychologist, educator*
Caldini, Maria Pia *physician*
Franzblau, Carl *biochemist, consultant, researcher*
Jacobs, Annette *health facilities administrator*
MacNichol, Edward Ford, Jr. *biophysicist, educator*
Peters, Alan *anatomy educator*
Short, Janet Marie *principal*
Simons, Elizabeth R(eiman) *biochemist, educator*

Salem
Ettinger, Mort *marketing educator*
Fetchko, Peter J. *museum administrator*
Finamore, Daniel Robert *museum curator*
Galaris, John Daniel *director of athletics*
Griffin, Thomas McLean *retired lawyer*
Harrington, Nancy D. *college president*
Hope, Lawrence Latimer *physicist*
La Moy, William Thomas *library director, editor*
Moran, Philip David *lawyer*
O'Brien, Robert Kenneth *insurance company executive*
Piro, Anthony John *radiologist*
†Rich, Howard *retail executive*

Sandwich
Terrill, Robert Carl *hospital administrator*

Saugus
Austill, Allen *dean emeritus*

Sharon
Olum, Paul *mathematician, former university president*
Segersten, Robert Hagy *lawyer, investment banker*

Sheffield
Haworth, Donald Robert *educator, retired association executive*
Unsworth, Richard Preston *minister, school administrator*
Velmans, Loet Abraham *retired public relations executive*

Sherborn
Kennedy, Chester Ralph, Jr. *former state official, art director*
Pickhardt, Carl Emile, Jr. *artist*

Shirley
Field, Hermann Haviland *architect, educator*

Shrewsbury
Pederson, Thoru Judd *biologist, research institute director*
Piggford, Roland Rayburn *library and information services consultant*
Zamecnik, Paul Charles *oncologist, medical research scientist*

Somerville
Bailey, James Martin *minister, ecumenical executive, public relations consultant*
Bakanowsky, Louis Joseph *visual arts educator, architect, artist*
Korobkin, Barry Jay *architect*
Safdie, Moshe *architect*
Verderber, Joseph Anthony *capital equipment company executive*
Wheeler, Katherine Frazier (Kate Wheeler) *writer*
Wong, Po Kee *research company executive, educator*

South Dartmouth
Lenci, Gordon Kent *headmaster*
Stern, T. Noel *political scientist, educator*
Ward, Richard Joseph *university official, educator, author*

South Deerfield
Bete, Channing Lindquist, Jr. *publishing company executive*
Fritz, Nancy *elementary education educator*

South Easton
Clarke, Cornelius Wilder *superintendent, minister*

South Hadley
Berek, Peter *English educator*
Brodsky, Joseph (Alexandrovich) *poet, educator*
Brownlow, Frank Walsh *English language educator*
Campbell, Mary Kathryn *chemistry educator*
Ciruti, Joan Estelle *Spanish language and literature educator*
Farnham, Anthony Edward *English language educator*
Hall, Lee *artist, educator*
Harrison, Anna Jane *chemist, educator*
Herbert, Robert Louis *art history educator*
Johnson, Richard August *English language educator*
Kennan, Elizabeth Topham *college president*
Kraske, Karl Vincent *paper company executive*
Mazzocco, Angelo *language educator*
Quinn, Betty Nye *former classics educator*
Robin, Richard Shale *philosophy educator*
†Salter, Mary Jo *poet*
Townsend, Jane Kaltenbach *zoologist, educator*
Viereck, Peter *poet, historian, educator*

South Hamilton
Kalland, Lloyd Austin *minister*
Patton, George Smith *military officer*

South Harwich
Micciche, Salvatore Joseph *journalist, lawyer*

South Lancaster
Chopra, Deepak *writer*

South Orleans
Hickok, Richard Sanford *accountant*

South Wellfleet
Macauley, Robie Mayhew *retired editor*

South Yarmouth
Arthur, George Roland *accountant, engineer, mathematician*
Benoit, Leroy James *language educator*
McIlveen, Edward E. *electrical engineer, association executive*

Southborough
Dews, P(eter) B(ooth) *medical scientist, educator*

Southbridge
Ghiglione, Loren Frank *newspaper editor*
Mangion, Richard Michael *health care executive*

Southwick
MacEwan, Barbara Ann *middle school educator*

Springfield
Bixby, Allan Barton *insurance company executive*
Bode, Susan Mary *nursing administrator*
Brennen, Patrick Wayne *library director*
Canavan, John James, Jr. *employment services executive*
Clark, William James *insurance company executive*
Daly, Michael Joseph *hospital administrator*
Dastgeer, Ghulam Mohammad *surgeon*
Dooley, Richard Gordon *insurance company executive*
Dunn, Donald Jack *law librarian, law educator, lawyer*
Esposito, Joseph John *publishing company executive*
Finnegan, Thomas Joseph, Jr. *insurance executive, lawyer*
Frankel, Kenneth Mark *thoracic surgeon*
Freedman, Frank Harlan *federal judge*
Gallup, John Gardiner *retired paper company executive*
Garvey, Richard Conrad *journalist*
Gordon, Ronni Anne *journalist*
Haggerty, Thomas Francis *newspaper editor*
Johnson, Robert Allison *life insurance company executive*
Keough, Francis Paul *librarian*
Koeninger, Edward Calvin *chemical engineer*
Lees, Brian Paul *state senator*
Liptzin, Benjamin *psychiatrist*
Long, Brian Joseph *newspaper publishing executive*
Markel, Robert Thomas *mayor*
Marshall, John Aloysius *bishop*
McGee, William Tobin *intensivist*
Miller, Beverly White *college president*
Miller, J(ohn) Wesley, III *lawyer, writer*
Milstein, Richard Sherman *lawyer*
Mish, Frederick Crittenden *editor*
Morse, John M. *book publishing executive*
Muhlberger, Richard Charles *former museum administrator, writer*
Naughton, John M. *insurance company executive*
†Navab, Farhad *medical educator*
Negroni, Peter Joseph *school system administrator*
Norton, Peter J. *publishing executive*
Oldershaw, Louis Frederick *lawyer*
Ponsor, Michael A. *federal judge*
Porter, Burton Frederick *philosophy educator, author*
Riddle, James Douglass *college administrator*
Stack, May Elizabeth *library director*
Stanley, Thomas Edward *publishing company executive*
Sturges, Hollister, III *museum director*
Utley, F. Knowlton *library director, educator*
Wheeler, Thomas Beardsley *insurance company executive*
†Whitt, David Virgel *insurance company executive*
Winder, Alvin Eliot *public health educator, clinical psychologist*
Woods, David Fitzwilliam *insurance, estate and financial planner*

Stockbridge
Gibson, William *author*
Rich, Philip Dewey *publishing executive*
Shapiro, Edward Robert *psychiatrist, educator, psychoanalyst*
Storch, Arthur *theater director*

Stoneham
Igou, Raymond Alvin, Jr. *orthopedic surgeon*
Mc Donald, Andrew Jewett *securities firm executive*

Stoughton
Amirault, Carol Jean *nurse*
Cammarata, Bernard *retail company executive*
Douglas, John Breed, III *lawyer*
Duerden, John H. *sports apparel company executive*
Duncan, Paul R. *athletic footwear company executive*
Fireman, Paul B. *footwear and apparel company executive*

Stow
Olsen, Kenneth Harry *manufacturing company executive*
Shrader, William Whitney *radar consulting scientist*

Sturbridge
Flynn, Richard Jerome *manufacturing company executive*
McMahon, Maribeth Lovette *physicist*

Sudbury
Aronson, David *artist, retired art educator*
Blackey, Edwin Arthur, Jr. *geologist*
Bradstreet, Bernard Francis *computer company executive*
Fowler, Charles Albert *electronics engineer*
Freund, Mitchell David *cable television executive, producer, director*
Henderson, Ernest, III *health care executive*
Hillery, Mary Jane Larato *columnist, producer, television host, reserve army officer*
Kaplan, Aline Michele *advertising executive*
Meltzer, Donald Richard *treasurer*
Nyman, Georgianna Beatrice *painter*
Read, Philip Lloyd *computer design and manufacturing executive*

Swampscott
Fountain, Eugenia Ferris *library director*
Mulcahy, John J. *bishop*
Truog, Dean-Daniel Wesley *educator, consultant*

Swansea
Holmes, Hank Eugene *broadcast journalist*

Taunton
Donly, Michael J. *headmaster*
Iannoni, F. Joseph, Jr. *finance executive, hospital executive*
Lopes, Maria Fernandina *commissioner*
Wall, Erving Henry, Jr. *sales agency executive, state senator*
Weeks, Sinclair, Jr. *silverware manufacturing company executive*

Tewksbury
DeMoulas, Telemachus A. *retail grocery company executive*
Miamis, James D. *retail grocery chain executive*

Topsfield
Peirce, John Wentworth *architect*
Webster, Larry Russell *artist*

Truro
Falk, Lee Harrison *performing arts executive, cartoonist*
Woolley, Catherine (Jane Thayer) *writer*

Vineyard Haven
Billingham, Rupert Everett *zoologist, educator*
Hough, George Anthony, III *journalism educator*
Jacobs, Gretchen Huntley *psychiatrist*
Porter, James H. *chemical engineering executive*

Wakefield
Bartl, Frederick J. *marketing professional*
†Carr, Greg C. *electronics executive*
Hunt, Samuel Pancoast, III *lawyer, corporate executive*
Kelley, John Dennis *librarian*
†Paltiel, A. Robert *engineering consulting company executive*
Roberts, Louis Wright *transportation executive*

Walpole
Dexter, Lewis *physician*
Warthin, Thomas Angell *physician, educator*

Waltham
Abeles, Robert Heinz *biochemistry educator*
Adamian, Gregory Harry *academic administrator*
Altman, Stuart Harold *economist*
Arena, Albert A. *museum director*
Belz, Carl Irvin *museum director*
Berger, Arthur Victor *music educator, composer, critic*
Bernstein, Stanley Joseph *manufacturing executive*
Black, Eugene Charlton *historian, educator*
Bohlen, Nina *artist*
Boykan, Martin *composer, music educator*
Brown, Edgar Henry, Jr. *mathematician, educator*
Brown, Seyom *international relations educator, government consultant*
Bumpus, Frederick Joseph *insurance executive*
Carter, Anne Pitts *economist, educator*
Cohen, Saul G. *chemist, educator*
Curnan, Susan Patricia Anne *human development and social policy educator, executive director, consultant*
Decker, C(harles) David *research and development executive*
De Rosier, David John *biophysicist, educator*
Deser, Stanley *educator, physicist*
Ellenbogen, George *poet, educator*
†Ellenbogen, S. David *electronics company executive*
Engelberg, Edward *comparative literature educator*
Epstein, Irving Robert *chemistry educator*
Evans, Robert, Jr. *economics educator*
Farrington, Thomas Alex *business executive*
Fasman, Gerald David *biochemistry educator*
Feldman, Mark Russel *architect, policy consultant*
Floyd, John Taylor *electronics executive*
Foxman, Bruce Mayer *chemist, educator*
Fuchs, Lawrence Howard *government official, educator*
†Galinat, Walton C. *research scientist*
Ganong, William Francis, III *speech sciences research executive*
Gerety, Robert John *microbiologist, pharmaceutical company executive, pediatrician, vaccinologist*
Hahn, Bessie King *library administrator, lecturer*
Harth, Erica *French language and comparative literature educator*
Hatsopoulos, George Nicholas *mechanical engineer, thermodynamicist, educator*
Hatsopoulos, John Nicholas *high-technology company executive*
Hayes, Sherman Lee *library director*
Hennessey, Robert John *pharmaceutical company executive*
Hindus, Milton *writer, literature educator*
Howard, Robert Clark *energy company executive*
Huxley, Hugh Esmor *molecular biologist, educator*
Jackendoff, Ray Saul *linguistics educator*
Jeanloz, Roger William *biochemist, educator*
Jencks, William Platt *biochemist, educator*
Jewett, John Persinger *electronics executive, lawyer*
Johnson, William Alexander *clergyman, philosophy educator*
Kasputys, Joseph Edward *data processing executive, economist*
Kern, Fred Robert, Jr. *engineer*
Kunkel, Barbara *psychologist, consultant, educator*
Kustin, Kenneth *chemist*
Lackner, James Robert *aerospace medicine educator*
Leach, Robert Ellis *physician, educator*
Lees, Marjorie Berman *biochemist, neuroscientist*
Levitan, Irwin Barry *neuroscience educator, academic administrator*
†Lowe, Justus Frederick, Jr. *software company executive*
Marshall, Robert Lewis *musicologist, educator*
McCulloch, Rachel *economics researcher, educator*
McManmon, Thomas Arthur, Jr. *oil industry executive*
Mitchell, Janet Brew *health services researcher*
Monia, Joan *management consultant*
Morant, Ricardo Bernardino *psychology educator*
Nelson, Arthur Hunt *real estate management development company executive*
Nisonoff, Alfred *biochemist, educator*
Nogelo, Anthony Miles *health care company executive*
Pantazelos, Peter George *financial executive*
†Patkin, Judith Kent *human rights agency executive*
Petri, Peter Alexander *economist, educator, director*
Petsko, Gregory Anthony *chemistry and biochemistry educator*
Poduska, John William, Sr. *computer company executive*
Reilly, Philip Raymond *medical research administrator*
Reinharz, Jehuda *university president, history educator*
Reisman, Bernard *theology educator*
Riley, Henry Charles *banker*
Rosenblum, Myron *chemist, educator*
Ross, George William *social scientist, educator*
†Rufeh, Firooz *energy research firm administrator*
Sakhuja, Ravinder Kumar *electronics executive*
Schiff, Jerome Arnold *biologist, educator*
Schweber, Silvan Samuel *physics and history educator*
Sekuler, Robert William *psychology educator, scientist*
†Shapero, Harold (Samuel) *composer, pianist, educator*
Slifka, Alfred A. *oil corporation executive*
Stambaugh, Armstrong A., Jr. *restaurant and hotel executive*
Staves, Susan *English educator*
Storer, Donald Edgar *corporate executive*
Titcomb, Caldwell *music and theatre historian*
Touster, Saul *legal educator*
Wallace, John *investment company executive*
†Wallack, Stanley S. *healthcare administrator*
†Walske, Steven C. *computer software company executive*
Wasserstein, Bernard Mano Julius *historian*
Weaver, William Charles *manufacturing executive*
Weckstein, Richard Selig *economics consultant*
Weinert, Henry M. *biomedical company executive*
†Wilczek, Joseph *health facilities administrator*
Wyner, Yehudi *composer, pianist, conductor, educator*
Young, Dwight Wayne *ancient civilization educator*
Zohn, Harry *author, educator*

Ware
Shirtcliff, Christine Fay *healthcare facility executive*

Watertown
†Appell, Michael Monroe *foundation executive*
Crissman, James Hudson *architect*
Dawson, Stuart Owen *landscape architect, urban designer*
El-Bisi, Hamed Mohamed *scientist*
Goodheart, Eugene *English language educator*
Katz, William Emanuel *chemical engineer*
Lampkin, M. Martha *architect, city planner*
Loney, Linda Christine *pediatrician*
†Montagu, Jean Ivan *electro-optic company executive*
Pellegrom, Daniel Earl *international health and development executive*
Rivers, Wilga Marie *foreign language educator*
Semonian, Robert Alexander *energy and lighting consultant*
True, Edward Keene *architectural engineer*
Ward, Alan L. *architectural landscape designer*
Wright, Edward S. *materials technology administrator*

Wayland
Blair, John *consulting scientist*
Bullard, Robert Oliver, Jr. *lawyer*
Clark, Melville, Jr. *physicist, electrical engineer, consultant*
Ebert, Robert Higgins *physician, educator, foundation consultant*
Freed, Murray Monroe *physician, medical educator*
Hagenstein, Perry Reginald *economist*
Huygens, Remmert William *architect*
Weil, Thomas Alexander *electronics engineer*
Williams, James P., Jr. (Jay Williams) *broadcasting executive*
Wolf, Irving *clinical psychologist*

Wellesley
Aldrich, Richard Orth *lawyer*
Allen, Michael W *management consultant*
Anathan, James Mone, III *retail executive*
Anthony, Edward Lovell, II *retired investments executive*
Auerbach, Jerold S. *university educator*
Beckedorff, David Lawrence *investment manager, computer scientist*
Carlson, Christopher Tapley *lawyer*
Coyne, Mary Downey *biologist, endocrinologist, educator*
Doku, Hristo Chris *dental educator*
Eilts, Hermann Frederick *international relations educator, former diplomat*
Farnham, Sherman Brett *retired electrical engineer*
Freeman, Judi H. *museum curator, art historian*
Gailius, Gilbert Keistutis *manufacturing company executive*
Gerson, Samuel J. *apparel executive*
Giddon, Donald B(ernard) *psychologist, educator*
Gladstone, Richard Bennett *retired publishing company executive*
Hildebrand, Francis Begnaud *mathematics educator*
†Hornig, Lilli Schwenk *educational administrator, researcher*
Jacobs, Ruth Harriet *poet, playwright, sociologist, gerontologist*
Jacoff, Rachel *Italian language and literature educator*
Kobayashi, Yutaka *biochemist, consultant*
Kucharski, John Michael *scientific instruments manufacturing company executive*
Lefkowitz, Mary Rosenthal *Greek literature educator*
Levin, Burton *diplomat*
Ma, Jing-Heng Sheng *East Asian languages educator*
Marcus, William Michael *rubber and vinyl products manufacturing company executive*
Miller, Linda B. *political scientist*
Mistacco, Vicki E. *foreign language educator*
Montague, Joel Gedney *public health consultant*
Murray, Joseph Edward *plastic surgeon*
Myers, Arthur B. *journalist, author*
Nagler, Leon Gregory *management consultant*
O'Gorman, James Francis *art educator, writer*
Papageorgiou, John Constantine *management science educator*
Parker, William H., III *federal official*
Piper, Adrian Margaret Smith *philosopher, artist, educator*
Putnam, Ruth Anna *philosopher, educator*
Rayen, James Wilson *art educator, artist*
Reiss, Martin Harold *engineering executive*
Ritt, Paul Edward *communications and electronics company executive*
†Roche, Daniel F. *retail executive*
Rubinovitz, Samuel *diversified manufacturing company executive*
Ruiz-de-Conde, Justina *retired foreign language educator*
Shea, Robert McConnell *lawyer*
Shuchat, Alan Howard *mathematician, educator*
Siskind, Paul M. *retired executive*
Valente, Louis Patrick (Dan Valente) *technical corporation executive*
†Walsh, Diana Chapman *academic administrator, social and behavioral sciences educator*

Wellesley Hills
Coco, Samuel Barbin *venture consultant*

Wellfleet
Dugger, Ronnie E. *writer, publisher*
Piercy, Marge *poet, novelist, essayist*

West Barnstable
Bowman, George Leo *artist*
†Breisky, William John *editor*
Corsa, Helen Storm *language professional*

West Boylston
McKenna, William Stuart *sales and marketing executive*

West Bridgewater
†Roberts, David *wholesale distribution executive*
Wyner, Justin L. *laminating company executive*

West Brookfield
Higgins, Brian Alton *art gallery executive*

West Chatham
McHale, Thomas Anthony *sales and marketing consultant*

West Chelmsford
†Michaud, Norman Paul *association administrator, logistics consultant*

West Falmouth
Scranton, William Maxwell *manufacturing company executive, consultant*
Vaccaro, Ralph Francis *marine biologist*

West Newbury
Coit, Margaret Louise *writer*
Dooley, Ann Elizabeth *freelance writers cooperative executive, editor*

West Newton
Elya, John Adel *bishop*

West Roxbury
Hedley-Whyte, John *anesthesiologist, educator*
Wiegner, Allen Walter *biomedical engineering educator, researcher*

West Springfield
Butterfield, Jack Arlington *hockey league executive*
Engebretson, Douglas Kenneth *architect*

West Tisbury
Smith, Henry Clay *retired psychology educator*

Westborough
Bok, Joan Toland *utility executive*
†Dickson, John H. *utilities executive*
Frank, Jacob *lawyer*
Gionfriddo, Maurice Paul *research and development manager, aeronautical engineer*
Greenman, Frederic Edward *utility executive*
Houston, Alfred Dearborn *energy company executive*
Jackson, Frederick Herbert *educational administrator*
Nichols, Guy Warren *institute executive, former utilities executive*
Rowe, John William *utility executive*
Skates, Ronald Louis *computer manufacturing executive*
†Solvell, Stefan *pharmaceutical executive*
Strauss, Judith Feigin *physician*
Young, Douglas Ryan *technology company executive*
Young, Roger Austin *natural gas distribution company executive*

Westfield
Applbaum, Ronald Lee *academic administrator*
Ashley, Cynthia Elizabeth *psychotherapist, human service administrator*
Buckmore, Alvah Clarence, Jr. *computer scientist, ballistician*
Hahn, Celia Ferner *state legislator, broadcaster*
†Reed, John E. *manufacturing executive*
†Reed, Stewart B. *manufacturing executive*
Tower, Horace Linwood, III *consumer products company executive*

Westford
Dennison, Byron Lee *electrical engineering educator, consultant*
†Hanna, Steven Rogers *meteorologist*
Salah, Joseph Elias *research scientist, educator*
Stansberry, James Wesley *air force officer*

Westminster
Moran, M. Marcus, Jr. *retail executive*

Weston
Anthony, Michael Thomas *consulting engineering firm executive*
Aquilino, Daniel *banker*
Bales, Robert Freed *social psychologist, educator*
Brooks, John Robinson *surgeon, educator*
Chu, Jeffrey Chuan *business executive, consultant*
Clayton, Richard Reese *holding company executive*
El-Hage, Nabil Nazih *financial company executive*
Fine, Bernard J. *retired psychologist, consultant*
Haas, Jacqueline Crawford *lawyer*
Higgins, Sister Therese *English educator, former college president*
Ives, J. Atwood *financial executive*
Kendall, Julius *consulting engineer*
Kraft, Gerald *economist*

Mc Elwee, John Gerard *retired life insurance company executive*
Oelgeschlager, Guenther Karl *publisher*
Paresky, David S. *travel company executive*
Resden, Ronald Everette *medical devices product development engineer*
Rockwell, George Barcus *financial consultant*
Rogers, Howard Gardner *consultant, photographic company research director emeritus*
Saad, Theodore Shafick *retired microwave company executive*
Sack, Burton Marshall *restaurant company executive*
Sanzone, Donna S. *editor-in-chief*
Sturgis, Robert Shaw *architect*
Sullivan, Barbara Boyle *management consultant*
Thomas, Roger Meriwether *lawyer*
Wacker, John Lee *landscape architect*
Whitehouse, David Rempfer *physicist*
Wind, Herbert Warren *writer*

Westport
Howard, James Merriam, Jr. *education writer*
Somerson, Rosanne *artist*

Westport Point
Fanning, William Henry, Jr. *computer scientist*

Westwood
Bernfeld, Peter Harry William *biochemist*
Borgman, George Allan *journalist*
Donahue, Charles Lee, Jr. *health network executive*
Funkhouser, Elmer Newton, Jr. *retired academic official*
Gillette, Hyde *investment banker*
Philbrick, Margaret Elder *artist*
Plaut, James Sachs *foundation executive*
†Polimeno, Lawrence A. *computer softwear company executive*
Thomas, Abdelnour Simon *software company executive*

Weymouth
Connor, Jerome Joseph *civil engineering educator*
Parsons, Edwin Spencer *clergyman, educator*

Wilbraham
Anderson, Eric William *retired food service company executive*
Gale, William Henry *artist*
O'Shaughnessy, Joseph A. *restaurant company executive*
Wise, Warren Roberts *lawyer*

Williamsburg
Healy, Robert Danforth *manufacturing executive*
Snow, Elizabeth Jean *poet, inventor, farmer, small business owner*

Williamstown
Art, Henry Warren *biology educator*
Bahlman, Dudley Ward Rhodes *history educator*
Bell, Michael Davitt *history and literature educator*
Bell-Villada, Gene H. *literature educator, writer*
Bleezarde, Thomas Warren *magazine editor*
Bolton, Roger Edwin *economist, educator*
†Burns, James MacGregor *political scientist, historian*
Conforti, Michael Peter *museum director, art historian*
Conklin, Susan Joan *psychotherapist*
Cramer, Phebe *psychologist*
Crampton, Stuart Jessup Bigelow *physicist, educator*
Crider, Andrew Blake *psychologist*
Dalzell, Robert Fenton, Jr. *historian*
Dew, Charles Burgess *historian, educator*
Dickerson, Dennis Clark *history educator*
Dunn, Susan *literature and history educator*
Edgerton, Samuel Youngs, Jr. *art historian, educator*
Erickson, Peter Brown *librarian, scholar, writer*
Eusden, John Dykstra *theology educator, minister*
Filipczak, Zirka Zaremba *art historian, educator*
Fox, William Templeton *geologist, educator*
Fuqua, Charles John *classics educator*
Gibson, Sarah Ann Scott *art librarian*
Goethals, George R., II *psychology educator*
Graver, Lawrence Stanley *English language professional*
Graver, Suzanne Levy *English language educator*
Hamilton, George Heard *curator*
Hastings, Philip Kay *psychology educator*
Hill, Victor Ernst, IV *mathematics educator, musician*
Hyde, John Michael *history educator*
Johnson, Eugene Joseph, III *art historian, educator*
Lee, Arthur Virgil, III *biotechnology company executive*
†Lovett, Charles M. *genetics educator*
Markgraf, J(ohn) Hodge *chemist, educator*
McGill, Robert Ernest, III *retired manufacturing company executive*
McGill, Thomas Emerson *psychology educator*
Morgan, Frank *mathematician*
Norton, Glyn Peter *French literature educator*
Oakley, Francis Christopher *history educator, former college president*
Park, David Allen *physicist, educator*
Pasachoff, Jay Myron *astronomer, educator*
Payne, Harry Charles *historian, educator*
Petersen, Norman Richard, Jr. *religious studies educator*
Pistorius, George *language educator*
Raab, Lawrence Edward *English educator*
Rudolph, Frederick *history educator*
Shainman, Irwin *music educator, musician*
Sheahan, John Bernard *economist, educator*
Solomon, Paul Robert *neuropsychologist, educator*
Stamelman, Richard Howard *French and humanities educator*
Waite, Robert George Leeson *history educator*
Welch, Neal William *retired electric company executive*
Wikander, Lawrence Einar *librarian*
Wilkins, Earle Wayne, Jr. *surgery educator emeritus*
Winston, Gordon Chester *economic educator, former academic administrator*
Wobus, Reinhard Arthur *geologist, educator*

Wilmington
†Altschuler, Samuel *electronics company executive*
Bartlett, John Bruen *financial executive*
Buckley, Robert Paul *aerospace company executive*
DiFilippo, Anthony Francis *service company executive*
Faccini, Ernest Carlo *mechanical engineer*
Foster, Henry Louis *veterinarian, laboratory executive*
†McCard, Harold Kenneth *aerospace company executive*
†Rand, Albert *computer systems company executive*
Reeves, Barry Lucas *aerophysics research engineer*
Rice, Frederick Colton *environmental management consultant*
Tuchman, Avraham *physicist, researcher*

Winchester
Bigelow, Robert P. *arbitrator, writer*
Blackham, Ann Rosemary (Mrs. J. W. Blackham) *realtor*
Brennan, Francis Patrick *banker*
Casey, Norine Therese *school principal*
Cecich, Donald Edward *business executive*
Cowgill, F(rank) Brooks *retired insurance company executive*
Ewing, David Walkley *magazine editor*
Hansen, Robert Joseph *civil engineer*
Hirschfeld, Ronald Colman *retired consulting engineering executive*
Hottel, Hoyt Clarke *consulting chemical engineer*
Neuman, Robert Sterling *art educator, artist*
Ockerbloom, Richard C. *newspaper executive*
Shannon, Claude Elwood *mathematician, educator*
Smith, Robert Moors *anesthesiologist*
Taggart, Ganson Powers *management consultant*

Winthrop
Costantino, Frank Mathew *architectural illustrator*
Moses, Ronald Elliot *retired toiletries products executive*

Woburn
Breazeale, Kelly Wade *health care association executive, consultant*
Donadio, Robert Nicholas *mechanical engineer*
Eddison, Elizabeth Bole *entrepreneur, information specialist*
Flummerfelt, J. Kent *electronics executive*
Gelb, Arthur *science association executive, electrical and systems engineer*
†Ginwala, Kymus *engineering executive*
Klein, Michael James *broadcast executive, engineer*
Mehra, Raman Kumar *data processing executive, automation and control engineering researcher*
†Reid, Martin J. *electronics executive*
St. Onge, Vincent A. *electronics executive*
Tomaszewski, James M. *electronics executive*

Woods Hole
Ballard, Robert Duane *marine scientist*
Burris, John Edward *biologist*
Butman, Bradford *oceanographer*
Cohen, Seymour Stanley *biochemist, educator*
Copeland, Donald Eugene *research marine biologist*
Ebert, James David *research biologist, educator*
Emery, Kenneth Orris *marine geologist*
Fofonoff, Nicholas Paul *oceanographer, educator*
Grice, George Daniel *marine biologist, science administrator*
Hart, Stanley Robert *geochemist, educator*
Inoué, Shinya *microscopy and cell biology scientist, educator*
Rafferty, Nancy Schwarz *anatomy educator*
Steele, John Hyslop *marine scientist, oceanographic institute administrator*
Von Herzen, Richard Pierre *research scientist, consultant*
Woodwell, George Masters *ecologist, educator, author, lecturer*

Worcester
Apelian, Diran *materials scientist, provost*
Appelbaum, Paul Stuart *psychiatrist, educator*
Bagshaw, Joseph Charles *molecular biologist, educator*
Barnhill, Georgia Brady *print curator*
Baughman, Susan S. *library director*
Bell, Peter Mayo *geophysicist*
Berth, Donald Frank *university official, consultant*
Biederman, Ronald R. *mechanical engineer, educator*
Billias, George Athan *history educator*
Bonkovsky, Herbert Lloyd *gastroenterologist, educator*
Bourgeois, Anne Mary *nursing administrator*
Brill, A. Bertrand *nuclear medicine educator*
Brooks, John Edward *college president emeritus*
Brown, John Lott *retired university president, educator*
Cabot, Harold *banker*
Candib, Murray A. *business executive, retail management consultant*
Carlson, Suzanne Olive *architect*
Charney, Evan *pediatrician, educator*
Clarke, Edward Nielsen *engineering science educator*
Clements, Kevin Anthony *dean, electrical engineering educator, consultant*
Cowan, Fairman Chaffee *lawyer*
DeFalco, Frank Damian *civil engineering educator*
Densmore, William Phillips *management consultant*
Dewey, Henry Bowen *retired lawyer*
Dorman, Harry Gaylord, III *hospital administrator*
Drachman, David Alexander *neurologist*
Dufault, Wilfrid Joseph *religious organization administrator*
Dunlap, Ellen S. *library administrator*
Dunlop, George Rodgers *surgeon*
Fries, Donald Eugene *lawyer, insurance executive*
Fuller, Gilbert Amos *manufacturing company executive*
Gorton, Nathaniel M. *federal judge, lawyer*
Greenberg, Nathan *accountant*
Grogan, William Robert *university dean*
Hagan, Joseph Henry *college president*
Hanshaw, James Barry *physician, educator*
Hanson, Susan Easton *geography educator*
Harkavy, Donna *curator*
Hohenemser, Christoph *physics educator, researcher*
Hunt, John David *retired banker*
Hunter, Richard Edward *physician*
Isaksen, Robert L. *bishop*
Jareckie, Stephen Barlow *museum curator*
Johnson, Penelope B. *librarian*
Kaplan, Melvin Hyman *immunology, rheumatology, medical educator*
Kelly, John Francis *lawyer*
King, Anthony Gabriel *museum administrator*
Klein, Michael William *physics educator*
Laster, Leonard *physician, consultant, author*
Levine, Peter Hughes *physician, health facility administrator*
Ludlum, David Blodgett *pharmacologist, educator*
Lutz, Francis Charles *university dean, civil engineering educator*
Magiera, Frank Edward *journalist, critic*
Malone, Joseph James *mathematics educator, researcher*
Mancini, Valerie *health facility administrator*
†Mattar, Edward Paul, III *academic administrator*
McCorison, Marcus Allen *librarian, cultural organization administrator*
McManus, Charles E. *school system administrator*
McQuarrie, Bruce Cale *mathematics educator*
Menon, Mani *urological surgeon, educator*
O'Brien, John F. *insurance company executive*
Olson, Robert Leonard *retired insurance company executive*
Onorato, Nicholas Louis *program director, economist*
Pavlik, James William *chemistry educator*
†Plummer, Edward Bruce *college librarian*
Queenan, James F., Jr. *judge*
Quinlan, John Michael *insurance company executive*
Reilly, Daniel Patrick *bishop*
Sharp, Joann M. *county official*
Sioui, Richard Henry *chemical engineer*
Smith, Edward Herbert *radiologist, educator*
Soule, Charles Everett *insurance executive*
Spencer, Harry Irving, Jr. *retired banker*
Tonkonogy, Joseph Moses *physician, neuropsychiatrist, researcher*
Torraco, Stephen Francis *priest, theologian, educator*
Townes, Philip Leonard *pediatrician, educator*
Traina, Richard Paul *university president*
Ullrich, Robert Albert *business management educator*
Vaughan, Alden True *history educator*
Von Laue, Theodore Herman *historian, educator*
Wapner, Seymour *psychologist, educator, administrator*
Weiss, Alvin Harvey *chemical engineering educator, catalysis researcher and consultant*
Welu, James A. *art museum director*
Wheeler, Hewitt Brownell *surgeon, educator*
Wilbur, Leslie Clifford *mechanical engineering educator*
Wilkinson, Harold Arthur *neurosurgeon*
Zeugner, John Finn *history educator, writer*
Zurier, Robert Burton *medical educator, clinical investigator*
Zwiep, Donald Nelson *mechanical engineering educator, administrator*

Worthington
Hastings, Wilmot Reed *lawyer*

Wrentham
Brown, Millie Louise *mental health nurse*
Teplow, Theodore Herzl *valve company executive*

Yarmouth Port
Brundage, Gloria Swegman *public relations executive*
Gorey, Edward St. John *author, artist*
Hall, James Frederick *retired college president*
Stauffer, Robert Allen *former research company executive*
Stott, Thomas Edward, Jr. *engineering executive*
Teague, Edward B., III *insurance and investment broker*

MICHIGAN

Ada
Beutner, Roger Earl *manufacturing executive*
DeVos, Richard Marvin *network marketing company executive*
DeVos, Richard Marvin, Jr. (Dick DeVos) *direct sales company executive*
Grochoski, Gregory Thomas *marketing company research executive*
Mitchell, Kim Sarahjane *lawyer*
Van Andel, Jay *home and personal products company executive*

Addison
Knight, V. C. *manufacturing executive*

Adrian
Caine, Stanley Paul *college administrator*
Dombrowski, Mark Anthony *librarian*
Hinkley Thompson, Carol Joyce *fund raising consultant, motivational speaker*
Weathers, Milledge Wright *retired economics educator*

Albion
Vulgamore, Melvin L. *college president*

Allendale
Lubbers, Arend Donselaar *university president*
Murray, Diane Elizabeth *librarian*
Niemeyer, Glenn Alan *academic administrator, history educator*

Alma
Sanders, Jack Ford *physician*
Stone, Alan Jay *college administrator*
Swanson, Robert Draper *college president*

Ann Arbor
Abrams, Gerald David *physician, educator*
Adamson, Thomas Charles, Jr. *aerospace engineering educator, consultant*
Agno, John G. *management consultant*
Agranoff, Bernard William *biochemist, educator*
Akcasu, Ahmet Ziyaeddin *nuclear engineer, educator*
Akerlof, Carl William *physics educator*
Aldridge, John Watson *English language educator, author*
Aleinikoff, T. Alexander *law educator*
Allen, Layman Edward *law educator, research scientist*
Allen, Sally Lyman *biologist*
Aller, Margo Friedel *astronomer*
Alpern, Mathew *physiological optics educator*
Amann, Peter Henry *historian, educator*
Anderson, Austin Gothard *university administrator, lawyer*
Anderson, Barbara A. *sociologist, educator*
Anderson, William R. *botanist, educator, curator, director*
Ansbacher, Rudi *physician*
Apperson, Jean *psychologist*
Arlinghaus, Sandra Judith Lach *mathematical geographer, educator*
Arthos, John *English language educator*
Ash, Major McKinley, Jr. *dentist, educator*
Ashe, Arthur James, III *chemistry educator*
Assanis, Dennis N. (Dionissios Assanis) *mechanical engineering educator*
Atreya, Sushil Kumar *astronomy educator, astrophysicist, researcher*
Avery, James Knuckey *dental educator*
Bailey, David Roy Shackleton *classics educator*
Bailey, Reeve Maclaren *museum curator*
Bailey, Richard Weld *English educator*
Baker, Sheridan *English educator, author*
Banks, Peter Morgan *electrical engineering educator*
Barbarin, Oscar Anthony *psychologist*
Bartell, Lawrence Sims *chemist, educator*
Bartle, Robert Gardner *mathematics educator*
Bassett, Leslie Raymond *composer, educator*
Beaubien, Anne Kathleen *librarian*
Beaver, Frank Eugene *communication educator, film critic and historian*
Becher, William Don *electrical engineering educator, engineering consultant*
Becker, Marvin Burton *historian*
Beckley, Robert Mark *architect, educator*
Bedard, Patrick Joseph *editor, writer, consultant*
Beeton, Alfred Merle *laboratory director, limnologist, educator*
Belcher, Louis David *marketing and operations executive, former mayor*
Benford, Harry Bell *naval architect*
Bernstein, Isadore Abraham *biochemistry educator, researcher*
Beutler, Frederick Joseph *information scientist*
Bhattacharya, Pallab Kumar *electrical engineering educator, researcher*
Bidlack, Russell Eugene *librarian, educator, former dean*
Bilello, John Charles *materials science and engineering educator*
Bitondo, Domenic *engineering executive*
Blinder, Seymour Michael *chemistry educator*
Blotner, Joseph Leo *English language educator*
Blouin, Francis Xavier, Jr. *history educator*
Bolcom, William Elden *musician, composer, educator, pianist*
Bole, Giles G. *physician, researcher, medical educator*
Bornstein, George Jay *literary educator*
Bornstein, Morris *economist, educator*
Boylan, Paul Charles *music educator, academic administrator*
Brandt, Richard Booker *former philosophy educator*
Britton, Clarold Lawrence *lawyer, consultant*
Brown, Deming Bronson *Slavic languages and literature educator*
Brown, Donald Robert *psychology educator*
Brown, Morton B. *biostatistics educator*
Bryant, Barbara Everitt *academic researcher, market research consultant, former federal agency administrator*
Buchanan, Robert Alexander *pharmaceutical company executive, physician*
Burbank, Jane Richardson *Russian and European studies educator*
Burdi, Alphonse Rocco *anatomist*
Buyse, Leone Karena *orchestral musician, educator*
Cain, Albert Clifford *psychology educator*
Cain, Charles Alan *electrical engineering educator, researcher*
Calahan, Donald Albert *electrical engineering educator*
†Cameron, Oliver Gene *psychiatrist, educator psychobiology reseacher*
Cannell, Charles Frederick *psychologist, educator*
Cantrall, Irving J(ames) *entomologist, educator*
Carlen, Sister Claudia *librarian*
Carnahan, Robert Dean *business development executive*
Cart, Pauline Harmon *minister, educator*
Casey, Kenneth Lyman *neurologist*
Cassara, Frank *artist, printmaker*
Castor, C. William, Jr. *physician, educator*
Chambers, David Laurance, III *legal educator*
Chambers, Leigh Ross *French language educator*
Christensen, A(lbert) Kent *anatomy educator*
Christiansen, Richard Louis *orthodontics educator, research director, former dean*
Christman, James Edward *landscape architect*
Chupp, Timothy E. *physicist, educator, nuclear scientist, academic administrator*
Clark, John Alden *mechanical engineering educator*
Clark, Noreen Morrison *behavioral science educator, researcher*
Clark, Thomas Bertram, Sr. *real estate broker*
Clarke, Roy *physicist, educator*
Cohen, Malcolm Stuart *economist, research institute director*
Cole, David Edward *university administrator*
Cole, Juan R.I. *history educator*
Converse, Philip Ernest *social science educator*
Conway, Lynn Ann *computer scientist, educator*
Cooper, Edward Hayes *lawyer, educator*
Coran, Arnold Gerald *pediatric surgeon, educator*
Cornelius, Kenneth Cremer, Jr. *finance executive*
Counsell, Raymond Ernest *pharmacology educator*
Courant, Paul Noah *economist, educator*
Cowen, Roy Chadwell, Jr. *German language educator*
Craig, Holly Kathlyn *director communicative disorders clinic*
Craig, Robert George *dental science educator*
Crane, Horace Richard *educator, physicist*
Crawford, Charles Merle *business administration educator*
†Cresswell, Ronald Morton *pharmaceutical and biotechnology company executive*
Csere, Csaba *magazine editor*
Curley, Edwin Munson *philosophy educator*
Curtis, George Clifton *psychiatry educator, clinical research investigator*
Danly, Robert Lyons *Japanese studies educator, author, translator*
D'Arms, John Haughton *classics educator, university dean*
Darwall, Stephen Leicester *educator*
†Daub, Peggy Ellen *library administrator*
Davenport, Horace Willard *physiologist*
Davis, Wayne Kay *university dean, educator*
Dawson, William Ryan *zoology educator*
Day, Colin Leslie *publisher*
Decker, Raymond Frank *scientist, technology transfer executive*
Dekker, Eugene Earl *biochemistry educator*
De La Iglesia, Felix Alberto *pathologist, toxicologist*
Delonis, Robert Joseph *bank executive*
DeVine, Edmond Francis *lawyer*
DeWeese, Marion Spencer *educator, surgeon*
Diana, Joseph A. *retired foundation executive*

Dirks, Nicholas B. cultural research organization administrator/history educator
†Dixon, Jack E. biological chemistry educator, consultant
Domino, Edward Felix pharmacologist, educator
Donabedian, Avedis physician
Donahue, Thomas Michael physics educator
Dougherty, Richard Martin library and information science educator
Douvan, Elizabeth social psychologist, educator
Dow, William Gould electrical engineer, educator
Drach, John Charles researcher, dental basic science educator
Dubin, Howard Victor dermatologist
Duderstadt, James Johnson university president
Duke, Richard De La Barre urban planner, educator
Dunlap, Connie librarian
†Dunnick, N. Reed physician, radiologist, educator
Duquette, Donald Norman law educator
Duren, Peter Larkin mathematician, educator
Easter, Stephen Sherman, Jr. biology educator
Eberbach, Steven John consumer electronics company executive
Eby, Cecil DeGrotte English language educator, writer
Eisenberg, Marvin Julius art history educator
Eisenberg, Rebecca S. law educator
Eisendrath, Charles Rice journalism educator, manufacturer, farmer, consultant
Eisenstein, Elizabeth Lewisohn historian, educator
Ellmann, William Marshall lawyer, mediator, arbitrator, researcher
Ellsworth, Phoebe Clemencia psychology educator
England, Anthony Wayne electrical engineering and computer science educator, astronaut, geophysicist
Enns, Mark Kynaston electrical engineer
Eron, Leonard David psychology educator
Evans, Francis Cope ecologist
Fader, Daniel Nelson English language educator
Faeth, Gerard Michael aerospace engineering educator, researcher
Fajans, Stefan Stanislaus internist, retired educator
Farrand, William Richard geology educator
Faulkner, John Arthur physiologist, educator
†Fekety, Robert physician, educator
Feuerwerker, Albert history educator
Fifield, Russell Hunt political science educator
Filisko, Frank Edward physicist, educator
Finch, Debra Ann registered nurse
Finney, Ross Lee composer
Fitzsimmons, Joseph John publishing executive
Fleming, Suzanne Marie university official, chemistry educator
Fogler, Hugh Scott chemical engineer, educator, consultant
Foley, Daniel Ronald business and personnel executive
Forsyth, Ilene Haering art historian
Forsyth, John D. hospital administrator
Foster, Alan Herbert financial consultant
Fox, Merritt B. law educator
Fraser, Russell Alfred author, educator
Freedman, Ronald sociology educator
Freeth, Douglas Duncan banker
Friedman, Richard D. law educator
Frier, Bruce W. law educator
†Frueh, Bartley Richard surgeon
Fry, Richard E. architectural firm executive
Fusfeld, Daniel Roland economist
Gans, Carl zoologist, educator
Gehring, Frederick William mathematician, educator
Gelehrter, Thomas David medical and genetics educator, physician
Gibala, Ronald metallurgical engineering educator
Gikas, Paul William medical educator
Gilbert, Elmer Grant aerospace engineering educator, control theorist
Gilbert, Robert Edward lawyer
Gillespie, Thomas David mechanical engineer, researcher
Gilman, Sid neurologist
Gingerich, Philip Derstine paleontologist, evolutionary biologist, educator
Ginsburg, David human genetics educator, researcher
Goad, Linda May research scientist
Goldstein, Irwin Joseph medical research executive
Goldstein, Steven Alan medical and engineering educator
Gomberg, Edith S. Lisansky psychologist, educator
Gomberg, Henry Jacob nuclear engineer
Gomez, Luis Oscar Asian and religious studies educator
Grassmuck, George Ludwig political science educator
Gray, Robert Howard toxicology educator, researcher
Gray, Whitmore law educator, lawyer
Greden, John Francis psychiatrist, educator
Green, Thomas Andrew lawyer, law and history educator
Greene, Douglas A. internist, educator
†Greenfield, Lazar John surgeon, educator
Griffin, Carleton Hadlock accountant, educator
Griffith, John Randall health services administrator, educator
Grisham, Rita Miller automotive executive
Guardo, Carol J. association executive
Guthrie, Harvey Henry, Jr. clergyman
Guy, Ralph B., Jr. federal judge
Hackett, Roger Fleming history educator
Haddad, George Ilyas engineering educator, research scientist
Haddock, Fred T. astronomer, educator
Haddox, Mark electronic engineer
Hagen, John William psychology educator
†Halter, Jeffrey B. internal medicine educator, geriatrician
Hansen, Will civil engineer, educator, consultant
Hanson, Robert Duane civil engineering educator
Hawkins, Joseph Elmer, Jr. retired acoustic physiologist, educator
Hawthorne, Victor Morrison epidemiologist, educator
Hayes, John Patrick electrical engineering and computer science educator, consultant
Heidelberger, Kathleen Patricia physician
Henderson, John Woodworth ophthalmologist, educator
Hennessey, William John museum director
Herzog, Bertram computer scientist, educator
Hess, Bartlett Leonard clergyman
Hessler, David William information management educator, information systems consultant
Hill, Bruce Marvin statistician, scientist, educator
Hiss, Roland Graham physician, medical educator
Hochster, Melvin mathematician, educator
Hoff, Julian Theodore physician, educator
Holbrook, Robert Sumner economist, educator
Horowitz, Samuel Boris biomedical researcher, educational consultant
House, James Stephen social psychologist, educator
Howell, Joel DuBose physician, educator
Howrey, Eugene Philip economics educator, consultant
Huelke, Donald Fred anatomy and cell biology educator, research scientist
Huetteman, Raymond Theodore, Jr. lawyer
Huntington, Curtis Edward actuary
Israel, Jerold Harvey law educator
Jackson, James Sidney psychology educator
Jackson, John Howard lawyer, educator
Jacobson, Harold Karan political science educator, researcher
Jelinek, Fran school system administrator
Johnson, Harold R. social work and gerontology educator, academic administrator
Johnston, Lloyd Douglas social scientist
Joiner, Charles Wycliffe judge
Jones, Beverly Ann critical care and pediatrics nurse
Jones, Lawrence William educator, physicist
Jones, Phillip Sanford mathematics educator emeritus
Joscelyn, Kent Buckley lawyer, research scientist
†Julius, Stevo physician, educator, physiologist
Kahn, Douglas Allen legal educator
Kalisch, Beatrice Jean nursing educator, consultant
Kamisar, Yale lawyer, educator
Kamrowski, Gerome artist
Kauffman, Charles William aerospace engineer
Kaufman, Peter Bishop biological sciences educator
Kauper, Thomas Eugene lawyer, educator
Kelly, Raymond Case anthropology educator
Kennedy, David Boyd foundation executive, lawyer
Kennedy, Frank Robert lawyer
Kerr, William nuclear engineering educator
Kesler, Stephen Edward economic geology educator
Ketefian, Shaké nursing educator
Kim, E. Han finance and business administration educator
Kimbrough, William Walter, III psychiatrist
Kingdon, John Wells political science educator
Kirkendall, John Neal judge
Kirkpatrick, Dorothy Ann early childhood education educator
Kish, Leslie research statistician, educator
Kister, James Milton mathematician, educator
Kleinsmith, Lewis Joel cell biologist, educator
Kmenta, Jan economics educator
Knoll, Glenn Frederick nuclear engineering educator
Knott, John Ray, Jr. language professional, educator
Koenen, Ludwig classical studies educator
Konigsberg, Ira film and literature educator, writer
Kostyo, Jack Lawrence physiology educator
Kozma, Adam electrical engineer
Kramer, Charles Henry psychiatrist
Krause, Charles Joseph otolaryngologist
Krier, James Edward law educator, author
Krimm, Samuel physicist, educator
Krisch, Alan David physics educator
Kuhl, David Edmund physician, nuclear medicine educator
La Du, Bert Nichols, Jr. pharmacology educator, physician
Lapides, Jack urologist, medical educator
La Plata, George federal judge
Leith, Emmett Norman electrical engineer, educator
Lempert, Richard Owen lawyer, educator
Leonard, Joanne photographer, educator
Lewis, Donald John mathematics educator
Lewis, Robert Enzer lexicographer, educator
Lichter, Paul Richard ophthalmology educator
Lillya, Clifford Peter musician, educator
Liu, Vi-Cheng aerospace engineering educator
Livingstone, Frank Brown anthropologist, educator
Longone, Daniel Thomas chemistry educator
Lopatin, Dennis Edward immunologist, educator
Losada, Marcial Francisco research scientist, psychologist
Lowe, John Burton molecular biology educator, pathologist
MacKinnon, Catharine A. lawyer, law educator, legal scholar, writer
Macnee, Alan Breck electrical engineer, educator
Manis, Melvin psychologist, educator
Marans, Robert Warren architect, planner, educator
Margolis, Philip Marcus psychiatrist, educator
†Marietta, Michael biochemistry and medicinal chemistry educator
Martel, William radiologist, educator
†Martin, Bruce James newspaper editor
Martin, Claude Raymond, Jr. marketing consultant, educator
Martin, William Russell nuclear engineering educator
Massey, Vincent biochemist, educator
Matthews, Rowena Green biological chemistry educator
McCarus, Ernest Nasseph language educator
McClamroch, N. Harris aerospace engineering educator, consultant, researcher
Mc Cracken, Paul Winston economist, business educator
McDougal, Stuart Yeatman comparative literature educator, author
Mc Gibbon, William landscape architect
McKeachie, Wilbert James psychologist, educator
Mersereau, John, Jr. Slavic languages and literatures educator
Merte, Herman, Jr. educator, mechanical engineer
Metcalf, Robert Clarence architect, educator
Meyer, John Frederick engineering and computer science educator, researcher, consultant
Midgley, A(lvin) Rees, Jr. reproductive endocrinology educator, researcher
Miller, William Ian legal educator
Miskel, Cecil G. academic dean
Mitchell, Edward John economist, retired educator
Mitzelfeld, Jim newspaper reporter
Monaghan, Thomas Stephen restaurant chain executive
†Monto, Arnold S. epidemiology educator
Moore, Thomas E. biology educator, museum director
Morakinyo, Akinbola Oluwole mechanical, energy engineer
Morgan, James Newton research economist, educator
Morgan, Raleigh, Jr. linguistics educator
Morley, George William gynecologist
Morris, Phyllis Sutton philosophy educator
Moss, Cruse Watson automobile company executive
Munro, Donald Jacques philosopher, educator
Murphey, Rhoads history educator
Nagy, Andrew Francis engineering educator
Neal, Homer Alfred physics educator, researcher, university administrator
Neidhardt, Frederick Carl microbiologist
Nelson, Virginia Simson pediatrician, educator
Newman, Sarah Winans neuroanatomist, educator
Nisbett, Richard Eugene psychology educator
Nordman, Christer Eric chemistry educator
Nugent, Theodore Anthony musician
Oakley, Deborah Jane researcher, educator
O'Brien, William Joseph educator, consultant
Oliver, William John pediatrician, educator
†Olson, Gary Monroe psychology educator
Organski, Abramo Fimo Kenneth political scientist, educator
Orringer, Mark B. thoracic surgeon
Osborn, June Elaine pediatrician, microbiologist, educator
Packard, P. Kim diversified products company executive
Paige, Jeffery Mayland sociologist, educator
Parkinson, William Charles physicist, educator
Parsons, Jeffrey Robinson anthropologist, educator
Paul, Ara Garo university dean
Paulsen, Serenus Glen architect, educator
Paulson, William Ross foreign language educator, researcher
Payton, Sallyanne law educator
Pedley, John Griffiths archaeologist, educator
Pehlke, Robert Donald materials and metallurgical engineering educator
Pender, Nola J. community health nursing educator, researcher
Pepe, Steven Douglas federal judge
Petrick, Ernest Nicholas mechanical engineer
Pierce, Roy political science educator
Pierce, William James law educator
Pierpont, Wilbur K. retired acounting educator
Pitt, Bertram cardiologist, consultant
Ploger, Robert Riis retired military officer, engineer
Pollack, Henry Nathan geophysics educator
Pollock, Stephen Michael industrial engineering educator, consultant
Porter, John Wilson education executive
Powell, Linda Rae educational healthcare consultant
Pulgram, Ernst linguist, philologist, Romance and classical linguistics educator, writer
Radock, Michael foundation executive
Rea, David K. geology and oceanography educator
Reed, John Wesley lawyer, educator
Richardson, Rudy James toxicology and neurosciences educator
Riggs, Donald Eugene librarian, university dean
Ringler, Daniel Howard lab animal medicine educator
Roach, Thomas Adair lawyer
Robbins, Jerry Hal educational administration educator
Robertson, Richard Earl physical chemist, educator
Rockwell, Richard Cook association executive
Roe, Byron Paul physics educator
Romani, John Henry health administration educator
Root, William Lucas electrical engineering educator
Rosenthal, Amnon pediatric cardiologist
Rosseels, Gustave Alois music educator
Ruff, Larry geology educator
Rumman, Wadi (Saliba Rumman) civil engineer
Rupp, Ralph Russell audiologist, educator, author
Ryan, William Frank management consultant
Rycus, Mitchell Julian urban planning educator, urban security and energy planning consultant
St. Antoine, Theodore Joseph legal educator
†Samson, Perry J. environmental scientist, educator
Sandalow, Terrance law educator
Saussele, Charles William marking systems company executive
Savageau, Michael Antonio microbiology and immunology educator
Schacht, Jochen Heinrich biochemistry educator
Scharp-Radovic, Carol Ann choreographer, classical ballet educator, artistic director
Schenck, John Frederic physician
Schneider, Carl Edward law educator
Schottenfeld, David epidemiologist, educator
Schriber, Thomas Jude computer and information systems educator, researcher
†Schteingart, David Eduardo internist
Schultz, Albert Barry engineering educator
Schwank, Johannes Walter chemical engineering educator
Scott, Norman Ross electrical engineering educator
†Semion, A. Kay editor
Senior, Thomas Bryan A. electrical engineering educator, researcher, consultant
†Shapiro, Matthew David economist
Shappirio, David Gordon biologist, educator
Shayman, James Alan nephrologist, educator
Sheldon, Ingrid Kristina mayor
Silverman, Albert Jack psychiatrist, educator
Simpson, A. W. B. law educator
Singer, Eleanor sociologist, editor
Singer, Joel David political science educator
Slavens, Thomas Paul information and library studies educator
Smith, David John, Jr. plastic surgeon
Smith, J(ames) E(verett) Keith psychologist, educator
Snyder, Jeanne Anne interior designer, educator
Solomon, David Eugene engineering company executive
Southwick, Arthur Frederick legal educator
Sparling, Peter David dancer, dance educator
Stafford, Frank Peter, Jr. economics educator, consultant
Stark, Joan Scism education educator
Starr, Chester G. history educator
Steel, Duncan Gregory physics educator
Stein, Eric retired law educator
Steiner, Erich Ernst botany educator
Steiner, Peter Otto economics educator, dean
Steinhoff, William Richard English literature educator
Steiss, Alan Walter research administrator, educator
Stevenson, Harold William psychology educator
†Stoermer, Eugene Filmore biologist, educator
Stolper, Wolfgang Friedrich retired economist, educator
Stolz, Benjamin Armond foreign language educator
Stowe, Leland journalist, writer
Strang, Ruth Hancock pediatric educator, pediatric cardiologist, priest
Striffler, David Frank dental public health educator
Stross, Jeoffrey Knight physician, educator
Sullivan, Donald John health care corporation executive
Super, Robert Henry English educator
Surovell, Edward David real estate company executive
Tai, Chen-To electrical engineering educator
Tamres, Milton chemistry educator
Tandon, Rajiv psychiatrist, educator
Taren, James Arthur neurosurgeon, educator
Taylor, William Brooks, II retired dermatologist
Terpstra, Vern marketing educator
Thompson, Norman Winslow surgeon, educator
Tice, Carol Hoff educator, consultant
Townsend, LeRoy B. chemistry educator, university administrator, researcher
Trautmann, Thomas Roger history and anthropology educator
†Tremper, Kevin K. anesthesiologist, educator
Turcotte, Jeremiah George physician, surgery educator
Ulaby, Fawwaz Tayssir electrical engineering and computer science educator, research center administrator
Upatnieks, Juris optical engineer, researcher, educator
Van der Voo, Rob geophysicist
Van Houweling, Douglas Edward university administrator, educator
Varian, Hal Ronald economics educator
Veltman, Martinus J. physics educator
Vesecky, John F. science educator, electrical engineering educator, researcher
†Vinh, Nguyen Xuan aerospace engineer, educator
Vining, (George) Joseph law educator
†Voorhees, John James dermatologist
Waggoner, Lawrence William law educator
Waggoner, Raymond Walter neuropsychiatrist
Wagman, Frederick Herbert librarian, educator, deceased
Wagner, Warren Herbert, Jr. botanist, educator
Wahl, Richard Leo radiology educator, nuclear medicine cancer researcher
Wall, Carroll Edward librarian, publisher
Waller, Patricia Fossum transportation executive, researcher, psychologist
†Wan, Weiying library curator
†Wang, Henry Y. chemical engineering educator
Ward, Peter Allan pathologist, educator
Ware, Richard Anderson foundation executive
Warner, Kenneth E. public health educator, consultant
Warner, Robert Mark archivist, historian, university dean
Warshaw, Martin Richard marketing educator
Watkins, Paul B. academic research center administrator, medical educator
Watson, Andrew Samuel psychiatry and law educator
†Weber, Roy Edwin savings and loan association executive
Weber, Walter Jacob, Jr. engineering educator
Weber, Wendell William pharmacologist
Weg, John Gerard physician
Wegman, Myron Ezra physician, educator
Weinreich, Gabriel physicist, minister, educator
Weisbuch, Robert Alan English educator
Westen, Peter law educator
Whitaker, Gilbert Riley, Jr. academic administrator, business economist
†White, B. Joseph university dean
White, James Boyd law educator
White, James Justesen legal educator
White, Michelle Jo economics educator
Whitman, Christina Brooks law educator
Whitman, Marina Von Neumann economist
Wicha, Max S. oncologist, educator
Wight, James K. civil engineer, research scientist, educator
Williams, John Andrew physiology educator, consultant
Williams, John Troy librarian, educator
Williams, William James electrical engineering educator
Willmarth, William Walter aerospace engineering educator
Wilson, Richard Christian engineering firm executive
Wineman, Alan Stuart mechanical engineering and applied mechanics educator
Wolpoff, Milford Howell paleoanthropologist, educator, author
Woodcock, Leonard humanities educator, former ambassador
Wylie, Evan Benjamin civil engineering educator, consultant, researcher
Yang, Ralph Tzu-bow chemical engineer
Yates, Brock Wendel editor, journal
Yeh, Chai electrical engineer, educator
Yeh, Gregory Soh-Yu physicist, educator
Yih, Chia-Shun fluid mechanics educator
Yocum, Charles Fredrick biology educator
Young, Edwin Harold chemical and metallurgical engineering educator
Zarafonetis, Chris John Dimiter physician, emeritus educator
†Zhang, Youxue geology educator
†Zhou, Xiaoyuan paleobiologist, researcher
Zimmerman, William political science educator
Zucker, Robert A(lpert) psychologist

Auburn Hills

Dumars, Joe, III professional basketball player
Farrar, Stephen Prescott company executive
Gerson, Ralph Joseph corporate executive
Grava, Alfred H. automotive and business equipment manufacturing company executive
Kerr, John E. automotive executive
Neumann, Charles Henry mathematics educator
Robertson, Alvin Cyrrale professional basketball player
Schuler, V. Edmund light manufacturing executive
Wagner, Bruce Stanley marketing communications executive

Battle Creek

Adkins-Overton, Betty Jean foundation administrator
Bruce, Thomas Allen physician, philanthropic administrator
Clark, Richard McCourt lawyer, food company executive
Cline, Charles William poet, pianist, rhetoric and literature educator
Costley, Gary Edward food company executive
Davis, Laura Arlene foundation administrator
DeVries, Robert Allen foundation administrator
Elliott, Charles W. food products company executive
Fritz, William Warren accountant, foundation executive
Grace, Helen Kennedy foundation administrator
Hutson, Don D. insurance company executive
Knowlton, Thomas A. food products executive
Langbo, Arnold Gordon food company executive
Mawby, Russell George foundation executive
McKay, Eugene Henry, Jr. food company executive
Nichols, Robert Lee food company executive
Pattullo, Andrew former foundation executive

Starrett, Pamela Elizabeth symphony executive director, violinist, conductor
Stewart, Joseph Melvin food products executive
Thar, Ferdinand August (Bud Thar) trade company executive

Bay City
Churchill, James Paul federal judge
Cleland, Robert Hardy federal judge
McDermott, Larry Arnold newspaper publisher, newspaper editor
Van Dyke, Clifford Craig retired banker
Zuraw, Kathleen Ann special education and physical education educator

Belding
Mason, Donald Roger protective services official, city official

Benton Harbor
Frey, Robert Imbrie lawyer
Goldin, Sol marketing consultant
Hopp, Daniel Frederick manufacturing company executive, lawyer
LeBlanc, James E. financial services company executive
Putnam, Charles Duane manufacturing company executive
Rasmussen, Alice Call nursing educator
Samartini, James Rogers appliance company executive
Whitwam, David Ray appliance manufacturing company executive

Berrien Springs
Ali, Muhammad (Cassius Marcellus Clay) retired professional boxer
Andreasen, Niels-Erik Albinus religious educator
Lesher, William Richard retired university president
Waller, John Oscar English language educator

Beulah
Auch, Walter Edward securities company executive
Edwards, Wallace Winfield retired automotive company executive

Beverly Hills
Landuyt, Bernard Francis economist, educator

Big Rapids
Barnes, Isabel Janet microbiology educator, college dean
Mathison, Ian William chemistry educator, academic dean
Popovich, Helen Houser university administrator
Santer, Richard Arthur geography educator
Thapa, Khagendra survey engineering educator
Weinlander, Max Martin retired psychologist

Bingham Farms
Berline, James H. advertising executive, public relations agency executive
Garpow, James Edward financial executive
Martin, J(oseph) Patrick lawyer, arbitrator, educator
†McKeen, Alexander C. engineering consulting company owner
Williams, Edson Poe retired automotive company executive

Birmingham
Birkerts, Gunnar architect
Bromberg, Stephen Aaron lawyer
Bublys, Algimantas Vladas architect
Buesser, Anthony Carpenter lawyer
Chodorkoff, Bernard psychoanalyst, psychiatrist
Donald, Larry Watson sports journalist
Elsman, James Leonard, Jr. lawyer
Gold, Edward David lawyer
Hirschhorn, Austin lawyer
Kosak, Anthony James transportation company executive
McCuen, John Joachim financial company executive
McIntyre, Bruce Herbert publishing company executive
Ortman, George Earl artist
†Robinette, Gary E. lumber executive, wholesale distribution executive, retail executive
Schaefer, John Frederick lawyer
VanDeusen, Bruce Dudley company executive
Van Dine, Harold Forster, Jr. architect
Wittlinger, Timothy David lawyer
Ziegelman, Robert Lee architect

Bloomfield Hills
Adams, Charles Francis advertising and real estate executive
Adams, Thomas Brooks advertising consultant
Allen, Maurice Bartelle, Jr. architect
Andrews, Frank Lewis lawyer
Avant, Grady, Jr. lawyer, financial executive
Baker, Robert Edward lawyer, retired financial corporation executive
Ball, Patricia Ann physician
Bates, Baron Kent automobile company executive
Behring, Daniel William educational administrator
Benton, Robert Austin, Jr. investment banker, broker
Benton, William Pettigrew advertising agency executive
Bianco, Joseph Paul, Jr. foundation and art museum executive
Bissell, John Howard marketing executive
Bonner, Thomas Neville history and higher education educator
Brown, Jack Wyman architect
Brown, Lynette Ralya journalist, publicist
Bruegel, David Robert lawyer
Burgess, Robert K. construction company executive
Caldwell, Will M. former automobile company executive
Cannon, John Kemper lawyer
Caplan, John David retired automotive company executive, research director
Carr, Robin advertising executive
Casey, John Patrick (Jack Casey) public relations executive, political analyst
Chason, Jacob (Leon Chason) neuropathologist
Clippert, Charles Frederick lawyer
Colladay, Robert S. trust company executive, consultant
Cooper, John Arnold financial analyst
Cumbey, Constance Elizabeth lawyer, author, lecturer
Dawson, Stephen Everette lawyer
Doyle, Jill J. elementary school principal
Forrester, Alan McKay capital company executive
Frey, Stuart Macklin automobile manufacturing company executive
Fulton, Patsy Jo educational administrator, writer
Googasian, George Ara lawyer
Haidostian, Alice Berberian concert pianist, civic volunteer and fundraiser
Harlan, John Marshall construction company executive
Hertz, Richard Cornell rabbi
Hillman, Donald M. middle school principal
Houston, E. James, Jr. bank officer
Hsu, John J. psychiatrist
James, William Ramsay cable television executive
Johnson, John K. advertising executive
Kasischke, Louis Walter lawyer
Klingler, Eugene Herman consulting engineer, educator
Knudsen, Semon Emil manufacturing company executive
Kollins, Michael Jerome automotive engineer, historian, writer
Leonard, Elmore John novelist, screenwriter
Leonard, Michael A. automotive executive
LoPrete, James Hugh lawyer
Marko, Harold Meyron diversified industry executive
Marks, Craig management educator, consultant, engineer
Maxwell, Jack Erwin manufacturing company executive
McCoy, Katherine Braden designer, educator
McCoy, Michael Dale designer, educator
Mc Donald, Patrick Allen lawyer, arbitrator, educator
McNeil, Joseph Malcolm advertising executive
Meyer, George Herbert lawyer
Mills, Peter Richard advertising executive
Nolte, Henry R., Jr. lawyer, former automobile company executive
Norris, John Hart lawyer
Pappas, Edward Harvey lawyer
Pero, Joseph John retired insurance company executive
Pingel, John Spencer advertising executive
Plaut, Jonathan Victor rabbi
Poth, Stefan Michael retired sales financing company executive
Preston, David Michael lawyer
Rader, Ralph Terrance lawyer
Rom, (Melvin) Martin securities executive
Rosenfeld, Joel ophthalmologist, lawyer
Rusin, Edward A. bank executive
Sillman, Herbert Phillip accounting firm executive
Smith, Richard Allen retired manufacturing company executive
Snyder, George Edward lawyer
Stivender, Donald Lewis mechanical engineering consultant
Thurber, John Alexander lawyer
Tunstall, Sharon Sue advertising executive
Vlasic, Robert Joseph food company executive
Ward, Richard C. advertising executive
Weil, John William technology management consultant
Williams, Walter Joseph lawyer
Winograd, Bernard financial adviser

Brighton
Jensen, Baiba principal

Buchanan
French, Robert Warren economics educator emeritus, writer, consultant

Cadillac
†Gravelle, Peter W. durable goods manufacturing company executive
†Kempton, George Roger manufacturing company executive

Canton
†Spitler, Kenneth F. wholesale distribution executive

Carsonville
Kummerow, Arnold A. superintendent of schools

Cass City
Althaver, Lambert Ewing manufacturing company executive
†Walpole, Robert heavy manufacturing executive

Clarkston
Erkfritz, Donald Spencer mechanical engineer

Clinton Township
†Brown, Ronald Delano endocrinologist

Coldwater
Jones, Ora McConner foundation administrator
Spittle, James Pratt arts administrator

Coloma
Tallman, Clifford Wayne school system administrator, consultant

Copemish
Wells, Herschel James physician, former hospital administrator

Cross Village
Stowe, Robert Allen catalytic and chemical technology consultant

Croswell
Anderson, Sandy Fay healthcare executive, nurse

Dearborn
Benton, Philip Eglin, Jr. retired automobile company executive
Bixby, Harold Glenn manufacturing company executive
Bobb, Richard Allen credit company executive
Brennan, Leo Joseph, Jr. foundation executive
Brown, James Ward mathematician, educator, author
Brucker, Eric academic administrator
Cairns, James Robert mechanical engineering educator
Caldwell, John Thomas, Jr. communications executive
†Cape, James Odies E. fashion designer
Christy, Perry Thomas lawyer, air transport company executive
Coady, Reginald Patrick library director
Coburn, Ronald Murray ophthalmic surgeon, researcher
Currier, Gene Mark lawyer
Czarnecki, Richard Edward business educator
†Devine, John M. automotive company executive
Fair, Jean Everhard education educator
Fitzgerald, Gerald Dennis hospital administrator
Ford, William Clay automotive company executive
†Ghafari, Yousif Butrus chemical engineer
Gilmour, Allan Dana automotive company executive
Hagenlocker, Edward E. automobile company executive
Hirsch, Lore psychiatrist
†Hoffman, David W. research scientist
Jelinek, John Joseph public relations executive
Joseph, Ramon Rafael physician, educator
Kasle, Roger H. steel company executive
Kienbaum, Karen Smith lawyer
Klein, Bernard W. academic administrator
Little, Robert Eugene mechanical engineering educator, materials behavior researcher, consultant
Lundy, J(oseph) Edward retired automobile company executive
Manning, Mervyn H. automobile manufacturing company executive
†Manoogian, John A. manufacturing engineer
Marquis, Rollin Park retired librarian
Martin, John William, Jr. lawyer, automotive industry executive
Mc Cammon, David Noel automobile company executive
McTague, John Paul automobile manufacturing company executive, chemist
Meitzler, Allen Henry electrical engineering educator, automotive scientist
Morshead, Richard Williams philosophy of education educator
Odom, William E. automobile finance company executive
Otto, Klaus physicist, physical chemist
Pestillo, Peter John lawyer, automotive executive
Poling, Harold Arthur retired automobile company executive
Powers, William Francis automobile manufacturing company executive
Ross, Louis Robert automotive company executive
Sagan, John former automobile company executive
Schneider, Michael Joseph biologist
Simon, Evelyn lawyer
Skramstad, Harold Kenneth museum administrator, consultant
Smith, Stanton Kinnie, Jr. utility executive
Tai, Julia Chow chemistry educator
Taub, Robert Allan lawyer
†Telnack, John J. automobile designer
Trotman, Alexander J. automobile manufacturing company executive
†Werling, Donn Paul environmental educator
Whipple, Kenneth automotive company executive

Detroit
Abramson, Hanley Norman pharmacy educator
Abt, Jeffrey art and art history educator
Adams, William Johnston financial and tax consultant
Albom, Mitch David sports columnist
Amerman, John Ellis lawyer
Amsden, Ted Thomas lawyer
†Anderson, John Albert physician
†Anderson, Moses B. bishop
Anderson, Sparky (George Lee Anderson) professional baseball team manager
Anstett, Pat newspaper editor
Archer, Dennis Wayne mayor
Ashenfelter, David Louis editor, former newspaper reporter
Audia, Christina librarian
Baba, Marietta Lynn business anthropologist
Babcock, Charles Witten, Jr. lawyer
Bahr, Mark A. construction company executive
Bainbridge, Leesa newspaper editor
Banas, Christine Leslie lawyer
Barden, Don H. communications executive
Barr, Martin health care and higher education adminstrator
Barringer, Leland David lawyer
Bassett, Tina communications executive
Battista, Robert James lawyer
Beaufait, Frederick W(illiam) civil engineering educator
Beltaire, Beverly Ann public relations executive
Bennett, Margaret Ethel Booker psychotherapist
Bergeron, Jeffrey David accountant
Betanzos, Louis banker
Bieber, Owen F. labor union official
Blain, Alexander, III surgeon, educator
Bohm, Henry Victor physicist
Borman, Paul retail chain company executive
Bradford, Christina newspaper editor
Brady, Edmund Matthew, Jr. lawyer
Brammer, Forest Evert electrical engineering educator
Brand, George Edward, Jr. lawyer
Braun, Richard Lane, II lawyer
Braun, Robert C. airport executive
Bray, Thomas Joseph journalist, editor
Brodhead, William McNulty lawyer, former congressman
†Broughton, Paul Laurence hospital administrator
Brown, Eli Matthew anesthesiologist
Brown, Ray Kent biochemist, physician, educator
Brown, Stratton Shartel lawyer
Brown, William Paul investment executive
Brustad, Orin Daniel lawyer
Bryfonski, Dedria Anne publishing company executive
Bullard, George newspaper editor
Burstein, Richard Joel lawyer
Burzynski, Susan Marie newspaper editor
Buselmeier, Bernard Joseph insurance company executive
Bushnell, George Edward, Jr. lawyer
Calarco, N. Joseph theater educator
Callaway, David Henry, Jr. investment banker
Campbell, David James hospital administrator
Candler, James Nall, Jr. lawyer
Cantoni, Louis Joseph psychologist, poet, sculptor
Cantor, George Nathan journalist
Cerny, Joseph Charles urologist, educator
Chapin, Roy Dikeman, Jr. automobile company executive
Charfoos, Lawrence Selig lawyer
Charla, Leonard Francis lawyer
Choate, Robert Alden lawyer
Clarke, Edwin Richards, III financial executive
Coffey, Paul professional hockey player
Cohan, Leon Sumner lawyer, retired electric company executive
Cohen, Sanford Ned pediatrics educator, academic administrator
Colby, Joy Hakanson art critic
Coleman, David Manley chemistry educator
Collier, James Warren lawyer
Connor, Laurence Davis lawyer
†Cordes, James F. gas transmission company executive
Cortada, Rafael Leon university president
Cothorn, John Arthur lawyer
Cox, Clifford Ernest deputy superintendent, chief information officer
Cox, John William architect, educator
†Crutcher, Gabriel bishop
Cunningham, Alexander Alan retired automotive company executive
Curtis, Jean Trawick library director
Czarnecki, Walter P. truck rental company executive
Darlow, Julia Donovan lawyer
Darr, Alan Phipps curator, historian
Dart, Judith C(andelor) Lalka lawyer
Dauch, Richard E. automobile manufacturing company executive
Davis, Eric Keith former professional baseball player
DeRamus, Betty Jean columnist
Devellano, James Charles professional hockey manager
DeVine, (Joseph) Lawrence drama critic
Diamond, Michael P. obstetrician-gynecologist, educator
Di Chiera, David performing arts impresario
Dickerson, Brian editor, periodical
Diebolt, Judy newspaper editor
Dobranski, Bernard law educator
Dortch, Heyward utility company executive
Draper, James Wilson lawyer
Driker, Eugene lawyer
DuBois, Melodee Ann performing company executive
Dudley, Arthur, II lawyer
Dudley, John Henry, Jr. lawyer
Duggan, Patrick James federal judge
Dunham, Frank L. accounting company executive
Dunn, William Bradley lawyer
Dykema, John Russel retired lawyer
Dziuba, Henry Frank dental school administrator
†Dzwonkowski, Ronald Edward newspaper editor
Earley, Anthony Francis, Jr. utilities company executive, lawyer
Easlick, David Kenneth telephone company executive
Eaton, Robert James automotive company executive
Ebbing, Darrell Delmar chemist, educator
Edmunds, Nancy Garlock federal judge
Eggertsen, John Hale lawyer
Ellison, James Morton secondary education educator
Elsila, David August editor
Ernst, Calvin Bradley vascular surgeon, surgery educator
†Eustis, Mark Arthur hospital administrator
†Evans, Mark Ira obstetrician, geneticist
†Ewing, Stephen E. natural gas company executive
Falls, Joseph Francis sportswriter, editor
Fay, Sister Maureen A. university president
Feikens, John federal judge
Ferguson, James Peter distilling company executive
Fielder, Cecil Grant professional baseball player
Fisher, Charles Thomas, III banker
Fisher, Max Martin diversified company executive
Fitzgerald, Robert Hannon, Jr. orthopedic surgeon
Flint, Robert H. printing ink company executive
Frade, Peter Daniel chemist
Fradkin, David Milton physicist, educator
Francis, Edward D. architect
Franco, Anthony M. public relations executive
Friedman, Bernard Alvin federal judge
Fromm, David surgeon
Fryman, David Travis professional baseball player
Gadola, Paul V. federal judge
Garberding, Larry Gilbert utilities companies executive
Garcia, Julio Hernan pathology educator
Garzia, Samuel Angelo lawyer
Gelder, John William lawyer
Gerstel, Judith Ross film critic
Gerwert, Philip Edward automotive executive
Getz, Ernest John lawyer
Giles, Robert Hartmann newspaper editor
Gilmore, Horace Weldon federal judge
Giocondi, Gino J. automotive company executive
Givhan, Robin Deneen journalist
Glancy, Alfred Robinson, III public utility company executive
Go, Robert A. management consultant
Goodman, Allen Charles economics educator
Gormley, Dennis James manufacturing and distribution company executive
Gould, Wesley Larson political science educator
Graves, Ray Reynolds federal judge
Grow, Richard Dennis lawyer
Guinn, John Rockne music critic
Gumbleton, Thomas J. bishop
Gupta, Suraj Narayan physicist, educator
Gushee, Richard Bordley lawyer
Hackett, Barbara (Kloka) federal judge
Halperin, Jerome Yale accountant, consultant
Hampton, Verne Churchill, II lawyer
Hanson, David Bigelow construction company executive, engineer
Hardon, John Anthony priest, research educator
Harling, Carlos Gene savings and loan executive
Hatie, George Daniel lawyer
Hay, Frederick Dale automotive supply company executive
Heaphy, John Merrill lawyer
Hearns, Thomas professional boxer
Henry, William Lockwood sales and marketing executive
Heppner, Gloria Hill science administrator
Herstein, Carl William lawyer
Hill, Draper editorial cartoonist
Holmes, Peter Douglas lawyer
Holness, Gordon Victor Rix engineering executive, mechanical engineer
Hough, Leslie Seldon educational administrator
Housley, Charles Edward hospital system executive
Howbert, Edgar Charles lawyer
Hutton, Carole Leigh newspaper editor
Iacobell, Frank Peter hospital administrator
Ilitch, Marian professional hockey team executive
Ilitch, Michael professional hockey team executive
Istock, Verne George banker
Jarrell, John W. automobile company executive
Jarvi, Neeme conductor
Jeffries, Charles Dean microbiology educator, scientist

Jeffs, Thomas Hamilton, II banker
Johnson, Carl Randolph chemist, educator
Johnson, Robert Bertram hospital administrator
Kachadoorian, Zubel artist, educator
Kalman, Andrew manufacturing company executive
Kantrowitz, Adrian surgeon, educator
Kaplan, Bernice Antoville anthropologist, educator
Kaufman, Richard C. judge
Keith, Damon Jerome federal judge
Kelleher, Timothy John publishing company executive
Kennedy, Cornelia Groefsema federal judge
Kessler, Philip Joel lawyer
Kessler, William Henry architect
Keydel, Frederick Reid lawyer
Kienbaum, Thomas Gerd lawyer
King, John Lane lawyer
Kinnaird, Charles Roemler lawyer
Kirschner, Stanley chemist
Kiska, Timothy Olin newspaper columnist
Kline, Kenneth Alan mechanical engineering educator
Klont, Barbara Anne librarian
Kowalczyk, Richard Leon English language educator, technical writing consultant
Krauss, Charles A(nthony), Jr. finance company executive
Krawetz, Stephen Andrew molecular biology and genetics educator
Krull, Edward Alexander dermatologist
Kuehn, George E. lawyer, beverage company executive
Kummler, Ralph H. chemical engineering educator
Kushma, David William journalist
Laitner, Bill reporter
Lamborn, LeRoy Leslie legal educator
Lane, James McConkey investment executive
Lannon, Linnea newspaper editor
Lasker, Gabriel Ward anthropologist, educator
Laughlin, Nancy newspaper editor
Lawrence, John Kidder lawyer
Ledwidge, Patrick Joseph lawyer
†Lee, André Lafayette hospital administrator
Lee, James Edward, Jr. educational administrator
Leininger, Madeleine Monica nurse, anthropologist, administrator, consultant, editor
Lenga, J. Thomas lawyer
Lerner, Stephen Alexander microbiologist, physician, educator
Lesch, Michael cardiologist
Levin, Charles Leonard state supreme court justice
Levy, Edward Charles, Jr. manufacturing company executive
†Leyh, George Francis association executive
Lindow, Donald August insurance company executive
†Liu, Gang-Yu chemist, educator
Livingood, Clarence S. dermatologist
Lobbia, John E. utility company executive
Lockman, Stuart M. lawyer
Lombard, Arthur J. law educator
Longhofer, Ronald Stephen lawyer
Lucow, Milton lawyer
Lupulescu, Aurel Peter medical educator, researcher, physician
Lusher, Jeanne Marie pediatric hematologist, educator
Lutz, Robert Anthony automotive company executive
Mack, Robert Emmet hospital administrator
†Macoska, Jill Anne urology and cancer biology educator, researcher
Madgett, Naomi Long poet, editor, educator
Maibach, Ben C., III construction company executive
Maida, Adam Joseph archbishop
Majzoub, Mona Kathryne lawyer
Mallett, Conrad LeRoy, Jr. state supreme court justice
Mamat, Frank Trustick lawyer
Mandel, Leon, III author
Margerum, Roger Williams, Jr. architect
Martin, Fred retired municipal official
Martin, John Gustin investment banker
Marx, Thomas George economist
Massie, Noel David lawyer
Massura, Edward Anthony accountant
Mathes, Caryn G. broadcast executive
†Mathieson, J. Douglas engineering association executive
Maurer, David L. lawyer
Maycock, Joseph Farwell, Jr. lawyer
McCracken, Caron Francis data processing consultant
McCrackin, William K. gas company executive
Mc Gehee, H(arry) Coleman, Jr. bishop
McGriff, Deborah school system administrator
McGruder, Robert newspaper publishing executive
McHugh, Richard Walker lawyer
McIntyre, Ronald Llewellyn electric utility executive
McKim, Samuel John, III lawyer
McKinnon, Isaiah police chief
Mc Millan, James manufacturing executive
McNair, Russell Arthur, Jr. lawyer
McNamara, Edward Howard county official, former mayor
McWilliams, Michael G. writer, television critic
Meilgaard, Morten Christian food products executive, international consultant
Meisel, Jerome electrical engineer
Mengden, Joseph Michael investment banker
Meriwether, Heath J. newspaper editor
Mika, Joseph John library director, consultant
Mikon, Arnold architect
Miller, Dorothy Anne Smith cytogenetics educator
Miller, Eugene Albert banker
Miller, George DeWitt, Jr. lawyer
Miller, Orlando Jack physician, educator
†Mirer, Franklin Emanuel industrial hygienist
Mitseff, Carl lawyer
Moldenhauer, Judith A. graphic design educator
†Moore, James Terrence, II industrial distribution company executive
Morgan, Virginia magistrate judge
Moss, Leslie Otha court administrator
Murphy, Thomas Aquinas former automobile manufacturing company executive
Musone, Fred James manufacturing and logistic executive
Negrepontis, Michael (Timothy) bishop
Nordmann, Gary Arnold corporate executive
Novak, Raymond Francis research institute director, pharmacology educator
O'Gorman, Kathleen newspaper editor
O'Hair, John D. lawyer, prosecutor
Oliver, John Preston chemistry educator, academic administrator
Olmstead, Laurence Daniel journalist
O'Meara, John Corbett federal judge
Orton, Colin George medical physicist
Ownby, Dennis Randall pediatrician, allergist, educator, researcher
Parker, George Edward, III lawyer
Parry, Dale D. newspaper editor
Patton, George Thomas, Jr. credit agency executive
Paul, Richard Wright lawyer
Pearce, Harry Jonathan lawyer
Peck, William Henry museum curator, art historian, archaeologist, author, lecturer
Penske, Roger S. manufacturing and transportation executive
Pepper, Jonathon Lester newspaper columnist
Peters, William P. oncologist, science administrator, educator
Phillips, Elliott Hunter lawyer
Phillis, John Whitfield physiologist, educator
Ponitz, John Allan lawyer
Porter, Arthur T. oncologist, educator
Pouncy, Marva Nell elementary education educator
†Powsner, Edward Raphael physician
Prasad, Ananda Shiva medical educator
Raden, Louis tape and label corporation executive
†Ragains, Charles C. public relations executive
Rajlich, Vaclav Thomas computer science educator, researcher, consultant
Rakolta, John construction company executive
Reuss, Lloyd Edwin Armin automobile manufacturing company executive
Richardson, Joan reporter
Richie, Leroy C. lawyer, automotive executive
Riley, Dorothy Comstock state supreme court justice
Rines, John Randolph automotive company executive
Rintelmann, William Fred audiology educator
Roberts, Peter Allen physical education educator
Roberts, Seymour M. (Skip Roberts) advertising agency executive
Robinson, James Kenneth lawyer
Roche, Douglas David lawyer, bar examiner
Roehling, Carl David architect
Ronca, Luciano Bruno geologist, educator
Rosen, Gerald Ellis federal judge
Ross, Mary O. religious organization administrator
Rossen, Jordan lawyer
Ross-Flanigan, Nancy reporter
Rossman, Richard Alan lawyer
Rozof, Phyllis Claire lawyer
Ruffner, Frederick G., Jr. book publisher
Russell, Robert Gilmore lawyer
Ruwart, David Peter lawyer
Ryan, Earl M. public affairs analyst
Ryan, James Leo federal judge
Sachs, Samuel, II museum director
St. John, Anthony Paul automotive executive
Santo, Ronald Joseph lawyer
Saurbier, Scott Alan lawyer
Sax, Stanley Paul manufacturing company executive
Saxton, William Marvin lawyer
Saylor, Larry James lawyer
†Schaengold, Phillip S. hospital adiministrator
Scherer, Karla foundation executive, venture capitalist
Schiffer, Daniel L. gas company executive
Schindler, Marvin Samuel foreign language educator
Schmidt, Robert mechanics and civil engineering educator
Schreiber, Bertram Manuel mathematics educator
Schultz, Dennis Bernard lawyer
Schuster, Elaine civil rights professional, state official
Schwartz, Alan E. lawyer
Schwartz, Jerome Merrill lawyer
Schweitzer, Peter advertising agency executive
Scott, John Edward Smith lawyer
Semanik, Anthony James university program administrator
Semple, Lloyd Ashby lawyer
Sengupta, Dipak Lal electrical engineering and physics educator, researcher
Shaevsky, Mark lawyer
Shannon, Margaret Anne lawyer
Shaw, Nancy Rivard museum curator, art historian, educator
Shay, John E., Jr. college president
Sheffield, Horace Lindsey, Jr. union official
Shine, Neal James newspaper editor
Simpkin, Lawrence James utilities executive
Small, Melvin history educator
Smith, F. Alan automobile manufacturing company executive
Smith, John Francis, Jr. automobile company executive
Smith, William Huston communication company executive
Smyntek, John Eugene, Jr. newspaper editor
Snead, David L. superintendent
†Sokol, Robert James obstetrician, gynecologist, educator
Sott, Herbert lawyer
Sparrow, Herbert George, III lawyer
Spencer, Milton Harry economics and finance educator
Spina, Anthony photojournalist
Spyers-Duran, Peter librarian, educator
Stark, Susan R. film critic
Stein, Paul David cardiologist
Stella, Frank Dante food service and dining equipment executive
Stewart, Melbourne George, Jr. physicist, educator
Stone, Robert B. automotive company executive
Stroh, Peter Wetherill brewery executive
Stroud, Joe Hinton newspaper editor
Stynes, Stanley Kenneth retired chemical engineer, educator
Sullivan, Joseph B. retired judge
Surdam, Robert McClellan retired banker
†Sutton, Lynn Sorensen librarian
Sylvain, Rick newspaper editor
Szary, Richard M. manufacturing company executive
Szilagyi, D(esiderius) Emerick surgeon, researcher, educator
Talbert, Bob newspaper columnist
Taylor, Anna Diggs federal judge
Teagan, John Gerard newspaper executive
Thelen, Bruce Cyril lawyer
Thomas, Edward St. Clair hospital administrator
Thomas, Robert Leighton physicist, researcher
Thorpe, Norman Ralph lawyer, automobile company executive, retired air force officer
Thurber, Peter Palms lawyer
Toll, Sheldon Samuel lawyer
Tunac, Josefino Ballesteros biotechnology administrator
Turnley, David Carl photojournalist
Uicker, James Leo mechanical engineer
Uicker, Joseph Bernard engineering company executive
Ursache, Victorin (His Eminence The Most Reverend Archbishop Victorin) archbishop
Vaitkevicius, Vainutis Kazys foundation administrator, medical educator
van der Marck, Jan art historian
Vaughan, Clifford James automotive manufacturing company executive
Vega, Frank J. newspaper publishing executive
Vincent, Charles Eagar, Jr. sports columnist
Vititoe, William Paul natural gas company executive
Volz, William Harry legal educator, administrator
Wagner, Harvey Arthur nuclear engineer
Waldmeir, Peter Nielsen journalist
Waldmeir, Peter William lawyer
Walt, Alexander Jeffrey surgeon, educator
Walton, Jonathan Taylor banker
Warden, Gail Lee health care executive
Warren, William Gerald lawyer
Watson, Susan newspaper columnist
Weiss, Mark Lawrence anthropology educator
Weiss, Robert Benjamin lawyer
Werba, Gabriel public relations consultant
Wesselmann, Glenn Allen hospital executive
White, Joseph B. reporter
Whitehouse, Fred Waite endocrinologist, researcher
Wiedyk, Gerald M. union welfare fund administrator
Wiener, Joseph pathologist
†Wilkes, James E. telecommunications industry executive
Williams, J. Bryan lawyer
Williamson, Marilyn Lammert English educator, university adminstrator
Winsten, I. W. lawyer, law educator
Wise, John Augustus lawyer
Wittrup, Richard Derald health care executive
Wood, R. Stewart bishop
Woods, George Edward federal judge
Worden, William Michael city agency administrator, preservation consultant
Wynne, James Earl lawyer
Young, Donald E. computer manufacturing company executive
Young, Gordon Ellsworth composer, organist
Young, Shirley automotive industry executive, strategic marketing consultant
Youngren, Ralph Park architect
Yzerman, Steve professional hockey player
Zatkoff, Lawrence P. federal judge
Ziegler, John Augustus, Jr. lawyer
Zuckerman, Richard Engle lawyer, educator

Dowagiac

Mulder, Patricia Marie educator

Dundee

Byland, Peter construction materials company executive
Moir, Robert Jesse manufacturing company executive, lawyer
Yhouse, Paul Alan manufacturing executive

East Lansing

Abeles, Norman psychologist, educator
Abolins, Maris Arvids physics researcher and educator
Abramson, Paul Robert political scientist, educator
Allen, Bruce Templeton economics educator
Andersland, Orlando Baldwin civil engineering educator
Anderson, David Daniel retired humanities educator, writer, editor
Anderson, James Henry university dean
Appel, John J. history educator
Asmussen, Jes, Jr. electrical engineer
Austin, Sam M. physics educator
Axinn, George Harold rural sociology educator
Bandes, Susan Jane museum director, educator
Beckmeyer, Henry Ernest anesthesiologist, medical educator
Benenson, Walter nuclear physics educator
Bergen, Werner Gerhard animal science educator, nutritionist
Bettinghaus, Erwin Paul university dean
Bickart, Theodore Albert electrical and computer engineering educator, university dean
Bonham, Vence Lee, Jr. lawyer, educator
Brody, Theodore Meyer pharmacologist, educator
Brophy, Jere Edward education educator, researcher
Brown, Boyd Alex physicist, educator
Bukovac, Martin John horticulturist, educator
Butcher, James Walter biologist
Byerrum, Richard Uglow college dean
Chapin, Richard Earl librarian
Chen, Kun-Mu electrical engineering educator
Cherney, Elaine Ethel education educator
Courtney, Gladys (Atkins) nursing educator, former dean
Cross, Aureal Theophilus geology and botany educator
Cutts, Charles Eugene civil engineering educator
De Benko, Eugene librarian, consultant
Dennis, Frank George, Jr. horticulture educator
Dewhurst, Charles Kurt museum director, curator, folklorist, English educator
Dilley, David Ross plant physiologist, researcher
D'Itri, Frank Michael environmental research chemist
Dye, James Louis chemistry educator
Eadie, John William history educator
Eulenberg, John Bryson artificial languages educator, administrator
Falk, Julia S. linguist, educator
Fischer, Lawrence Joseph toxicologist, educator
Fisher, Alan Washburn historian, educator
Fisher, Ronald C. economics educator
Fluck, Michele M(arguerite) biology educator
Foss, John Frank mechanical engineering educator
Frame, James Sutherland retired mathematics educator
Fromm, Paul Oliver physiology educator
Gast, Robert Gale agriculture educator, experiment station administrator
Gelbke, Claus-Konrad nuclear physics educator
Gerhardt, Philipp microbiologist, educator
Goodman, Erik David engineering educator
Gottschalk, Alexander radiologist, diagnostic radiology educator
Greenberg, Bradley Sander communications educator
Greer, Thomas Hoag historian, educator
Grimes, Margaret Whitehurst medievalist, educator
Hackel, Emanuel science educator
Hackett, Wesley Phelps, Jr. lawyer
Hamlin, Roger Eugene urban planning educator, economic and financial analyst
Harrison, Michael Jay physicist, educator
Hildebrand, Verna Lee human ecology educator
Hocking, John Gilbert mathematics educator
Hollander, Stanley Charles marketing educator
Honhart, Frederick Lewis, III academic director
Hoppensteadt, Frank Charles mathematician, university dean
Hull, Jerome, Jr. horticultural extension specialist
Huzar, Eleanor Goltz history educator
Ilgen, Daniel Richard psychology educator
Johnson, J. David communication educator
Johnson, John Irwin, Jr. neuroscientist
Johnson, Theodore Oliver, Jr. musician, educator
Jones, Kensinger advertising executive
†Kamrin, Michael Arnold toxicology educator
Kaplan, Thomas Abraham physics educator
Kay, Bernard Melvin osteopathic pediatrician, educational administrator
Kende, Hans Janos plant physiology educator
Kevern, Niles Russell aquatic ecologist, educator
Kirk, Edgar Lee musician, educator
Klomparens, Karen Lee optics scientist, educator
Krecke, Charles Francis radiologist, educator
Kreinin, Mordechai Eliahu economics educator
Kronegger, Maria Elisabeth French and comparative literature educator
Kurz, Mary Elizabeth lawyer
†Lacy, Melvyn Leroy plant pathology educator and reseacher
Lang, Marvel urban affairs educator
Larrowe, Charles Patrick economist, educator
Lashbrooke, Elvin Carroll, Jr. legal educator, consultant
Leepa, Allen artist, educator
Lerner, Richard M. special education director
Lloyd, John Raymond mechanical engineering educator
Lockwood, John LeBaron plant pathologist
Lowe, Kenneth Stephen magazine editor
Lucas, Robert Elmer soil scientist
Luecke, Richard William biochemist
Lund, Lois A. food science and human nutrition educator
Mackey, Maurice Cecil university president, economist, lawyer
Macrakis, Kristie Irene history of science educator
Manderscheid, Lester Vincent agricultural economics educator
Manning, Peter Kirby sociology educator
Mansour, George P. Spanish language and literature educator
Martin, Michael J. university administrator, consultant
McConnell, David Graham research biochemist, educator
McMeekin, Dorothy botany, plant pathology educator
Merva, George Ellis agricultural engineer, educator, researcher
Miller, Gerald Raymond communications educator
Miracle, Gordon Eldon advertising educator
Montgomery, Donald Joseph physicist, educator
Moore, Kenneth Edwin pharmacology educator
Moran, Daniel Austin mathematician
Mukherjee, Kalinath materials science and engineering educator, researcher
Munger, Benson Scott association executive
Murray, Raymond Harold physician
Nelson, Ronald Harvey animal science educator, researcher
Netzloff, Michael Lawrence pediatric educator, endocrinologist
Ohlrogge, John B. botany and plant pathology educator
Olson, Judy Mae geography, cartography educator
Paananen, Victor Niles English educator
Papsidero, Joseph Anthony social scientist, educator
Patterson, Maria Jevitz microbiology-pediatric infectious disease educator
Paul, Eldor Alvin agriculture, ecology educator
Peterson, Penelope Loraine education educator
Phillips, Richard Edward mathematics educator
Platt, Franklin Dewitt history educator
Poland, Robert Paul business educator, consultant
Pollack, Gerald Leslie physicist, educator
Pollack, Norman history educator
Potchen, E. James radiology educator
Preiss, Jack biochemistry educator
Press, Charles retired political science educator
Ralph, David Clinton communications educator
Rasche, Robert Harold economics educator
†Reed, Thomas H. livestock exchange executive
Reinhart, Mary Ann medical board executive
Ricks, Donald Jay agricultural economist
Ries, Stanley K. plant physiologist, university educator
Ristow, George Edward neurologist, educator
Robbins, Lawrence Harry anthropologist
Root-Bernstein, Robert Scott biologist, educator
Rovner, David Richard endocrinology educator
Rudman, Herbert Charles education educator
Saul, William Edward academic administrator, civil engineering educator
Schlesinger, Joseph Abraham political scientist
Shaw, Robert Eugene minister, administrator
Silverman, Henry Jacob history educator
Smith, Victor Earle economist, educator
Snell, John Raymond civil engineer
Snoddy, James Ernest education educator
Sommers, Lawrence Melvin geographer, educator
Soutas-Little, Robert William mechanical engineer, educator
Sparks, Harvey Vise, Jr. physiologist
Spence, Robert Dean physics educator
Stapleton, James Hall statistician, educator
Strassmann, W. Paul economics educator
Suits, Daniel Burbidge economist
Summitt, (William) Robert chemist, educator
Tasker, John Baker veterinary medical educator, college dean
Tesar, Milo Benjamin agricultural researcher and educator
Tiedje, James Michael microbiology educator, ecologist
Tien, H. Ti biophysics and physiology educator, scientist
Tolbert, Nathan Edward biochemistry educator, plant science researcher
Useem, John Hearld sociologist, anthropologist
Useem, Ruth Hill sociology educator
van der Smissen, M. E. Betty educator
Velicer, Leland Frank veterinarian, microbiologist, virologist, educator
VerBurg, Kenneth political scientist, educator, writer
von Bernuth, Robert Dean agricultural engineering educator, consultant
Von Tersch, Lawrence Wayne electrical engineering educator, university dean
Wakoski, Diane poet
Walker, Bruce Edward anatomy educator
Whallon, William literature educator

Williams, Donald Herbert *psychiatric education administrator*
Wilson, R. Dale *marketing educator, consultant*
Winder, Clarence Leland *psychologist, educator*
Witter, Richard Lawrence *veterinarian, educator*
Wojcik, Anthony Stephen *computer science educator*
Wolterink, Lester Floyd *biophysicist, educator*
†Wood, Douglas L. *medical educator*
Wronski, Stanley Paul *education educator*
Yussouff, Mohammed *physicist, educator*

Elk Rapids
Briggs, Robert Peter *banker*

Farmington
Baker, Edward Martin *engineering and industrial psychologist*
†Booth, Eric D. *bank executive*
Britt, Gerald F. *food products company executive*
Burns, Sister Elizabeth Mary *hospital administrator*
Elder, Jean Katherine *education administrator*
†Haydon, Glen Edgar *healthcare administrator*
Headlee, Richard Harold *insurance company executive*
Lakritz, Isaac *fundraising organization executive*
Lomason, Harry Austin, II *automotive company executive*
Mylod, Robert Joseph *banker*
†Neyer, Jerome Charles *consulting civil engineer*
†Richards, Robert W. *mortgage company executive*
Salabounis, Manuel *computer information scientist, mathematician*
Schwartz, Michael Robinson *health administrator*
Shoop, Deborah *lawyer*
Stark, Werner E. *food broker*
Wine, Sherwin Theodore *rabbi*

Farmington Hills
Abrams, Roberta Busky *hospital administrator, nurse*
Birnkrant, Sherwin Maurice *lawyer*
Ethridge, James Merritt *editor, former publishing company executive, writer*
Fox, Dean Frederick *coporate executive*
Haliw, Andrew Jerome, III *lawyer, engineer*
Heid, Sister Mary Corita *hospital administrator*
Heiss, Richard Walter *banker, consultant*
Landry, Thomas Henry *construction executive*
†Papai, Beverly Daffern *library director*
Pelham, Judith *hospital administrator*
Prady, Norman *advertising executive, writer, marketing consultant*

Ferndale
Braude, Edwin Simon *manufacturing company executive*
Dunn, Elwood *minister*
Lenz, Randolph W. *manufacturing company executive*

Flint
Campbell, Phyllis *nursing administrator*
Diemecke, Enrique Arturo *conductor*
Duckett, Bernadine Johnal *elementary principal*
Duncan, Clydell *police chief, educator*
Edson, Ray Zachariah *middle school educator*
Farrehi, Cyrus *cardiologist, educator*
Germann, Steven James *museum director*
Gratch, Serge *mechanical engineering educator*
Hackworth, Donald E. *automotive manufacturing company executive*
Hamady, Jack Ameen *retail food company executive*
Heymoss, Jennifer Marie *librarian*
Himes, George Elliott *pathologist*
†Incarnati, Philip Anthony *hospital administrator*
Jayabalan, Vemblaserry *nuclear medicine physician, radiologist*
Kugler, Lawrence Dean *mathematics educator*
Lehman, Richard Leroy *lawyer*
Lorenz, John Douglas *college official*
Lovejoy, William Joseph *automotive company executive*
Mahey, John Andrew *museum director*
Nelms, Charlie *academic administrator*
Newblatt, Stewart Albert *federal judge*
†Pelavin, Michael Allen *lawyer*
Piper, Mark Harry *retired banker*
Rappleye, Richard Kent *financial executive, consultant, educator*
†Reetz, Gary *medical facility administrator*
Tauscher, John Walter *retired pediatrician, emeritus educator*
Tomblinson, James Edmond *architect*
White, William Samuel *foundation executive*
Wong, Victor Kenneth *physics educator, academic administrator*

Flushing
Schriner, Jon Leslie *sports medicine physician*

Frankfort
Acker, Nathaniel Hull *retired educational administrator*
Foster, Robert Carmichael *banker*

Franklin
Adler, Philip *osteopathic physician*
†Navarre, Robert Ward *manufacturing company executive*
Rassel, Richard Edward *lawyer*
Sessamen, Donald William *communications company executive*
Zylanoff, Phillipa Louise *anesthesiologist*

Fremont
Clark, Stephen R. *children's food and clothing company executive*
Johnston, Robert Lloyd, Jr. *food products executive*

Gaylord
Cooney, Patrick Ronald *bishop*
Magsig, Judith Anne *early childhood educator*

Glenn
Rizzolo, Louis B. M. *artist, educator*

Grand Blanc
Corbin, Gary George *state legislator*
Tomlinson, James Lawrence *mechanical engineer*

Grand Haven
Anderson, Cynthia Finkbeiner Sjoberg *speech and language pathologist*

Grand Ledge
Farnsworth, Judith Marie *elementary education educator*

Grand Rapids
Anderson, Roger Gordon *minister*
Andrews, Alice French *neonatologist educator*
Arthur, Charthel Estner *artistic director*
Auwers, Stanley John *motor carrier executive*
Babcock, Wendell Keith *religion educator*
Baker, Hollis MacLure *furniture manufacturing company executive*
Baker, Richard Lee *book publishing company executive*
Barnes, Thomas John *lawyer*
Bartek, Gordon Luke *radiologist*
Beeke, Joel Robert *minister, theology educator, writer*
Bell, Robert Holmes *federal judge*
Blovits, Larry John *retired art educator*
Bolinder, Scott W. *publishing company executive*
Bolt, Eunice Mildred DeVries *artist*
Borgdorff, Peter *church administrator*
†Bowers, Paul Duane, Jr. *architecture, engineering and planning firm executive*
Boyden, Joel Michael *lawyer*
Bradshaw, Conrad Allan *lawyer*
Brady, James S. *lawyer*
Bransdorfer, Stephen Christie *lawyer*
Brenneman, Hugh Warren, Jr. *federal magistrate judge*
Brent, Helen Teressa *mental health nurse*
Brink, William P. *clergyman*
Buick, James Gordon *corporate executive*
Calkins, Richard W. *college president*
Canepa, John Charles *banking executive*
†Chester, Timothy J. *museum director*
Comet, Catherine *conductor*
Curtin, Timothy John *lawyer*
Daniels, Joseph *neuropsychiatrist*
Deems, Nyal David *lawyer, mayor*
DeHaan, John *religious organization administrator*
Deihl, Charles L. *college president*
Delnick, Martha Joyce *elementary education educator*
DeVries, Robert K. *religious book publisher*
DeWitt, Jon Francis *lawyer*
Dickerson, Allen Bruce *interior designer, consultant*
Diekema, Anthony J. *college president*
Emery, Marcia Rose *parapsychologist, psychologist, consultant*
Engel, Albert Joseph *federal judge*
Frankforter, Weldon DeLoss *retired museum administrator*
Fry, David Stow *lawyer*
Fulton, James A. *financial executive*
Gantos, LeRoy Douglas *retail clothing executive*
Garcia, Joseph Everett *public library director*
Gibson, Benjamin F. *chief federal judge*
Gregg, James D. *federal judge*
Gross, Michael *school system administrator*
Gundry, Stanley N. *publishing company executive*
Hardy, Michael C. *performing arts administrator*
Heiden, Thomas John *lawyer*
Hillman, Douglas Woodruff *federal judge*
Hoekema, David Andrew *philosophy educator, academic administrator*
Hofman, Leonard John *minister*
Holton, Earl D. *retail company executive*
Howard, Laurence Edward *federal judge*
Jackson, Beth Ann *nursing administrator*
Jacobsen, Arnold *archivist*
†Kaczmarczyk, Jeffrey Allen *journalist, classical music critic*
Kara, Paul Mark *lawyer*
†Koop, Donald J. *food products distribution executive*
†Lewis, John Robert *zoo administrator*
Lloyd, Michael Stuart *newspaper editor*
Logie, John Hoult *mayor, lawyer*
†Marchido, William F. *finance executive, accountant*
Maxfield, Michael Gerald *forest products and restaurant company executive*
Mc Callum, Charles Edward *lawyer*
McGarry, John Everett *lawyer*
Mears, Patrick Edward *lawyer*
Meijer, Douglas *retail company executive*
Meijer, Frederik *retail company executive*
Meijer, Hendrik *retail company executive*
Meijer, Mark *retail executive*
Miglore, Joseph James *furniture manufacturing executive*
Miles, Wendell A. *federal judge*
Monsma, Marvin Eugene *library director*
Morin, William Raymond *bookstore chain executive*
Mulder, Gary *religious publisher*
Myers, Jerry K. *medal products executive*
†Nadel, Mark Alan *hospital executive*
Perez, Peter Manuel *woodworking products company executive*
Pestle, John William *lawyer*
Pew, Robert Cunningham, II *office equipment manufacturing company executive*
Quinn, Patrick Michael *wholesale food executive*
Quist, Gordon Jay *federal judge*
†Raz, Robert Eugene *librarian*
Rougier-Chapman, Alwyn Spencer Douglas *furniture manufacturing company executive*
Rozeboom, John A. *religious organization administrator*
Ryskamp, Bruce E. *publishing executive*
Sadler, Robert Livingston *banker*
†Schwanda, Tom *religious studies educator*
Smith, Peter Wilson *symphony orchestra administrator*
Sobol, Judith Ellen *museum director, art historian*
Stevenson, Jo Ann C. *federal bankruptcy judge*
Stevenson, William Alexander *architect*
Sytsma, Fredric Alan *lawyer*
Titley, Larry J. *lawyer*
VanderLaan, Robert D. *lawyer*
Vander Meer, Harry *church administrator*
Vander Weele, Ray *religious organization administrator*
VanHarn, Gordon Lee *college administrator and provost*
Van't Hof, William Keith *lawyer*
Van Tol, William *religious organization administrator*
Viehl, Marjorie Alice *nursing educator*
Vinton, Samuel R., Jr. *religious organizatoin administrator*
Vrancken, Robert Danloy *facilities management educator*
†Wagner, David James *banker*
Wege, Peter M. *office furniture manufacturing company executive*
Wold, Robert Lee *architect, engineer*

Grass Lake
Popp, Nathaniel *bishop*

Greenbush
Paulson, James Marvin *engineering educator*

Grosse Ile
Frisch, Kurt Charles *educator, administrator*
Smith, Veronica Latta *real estate corporation officer*

Grosse Pointe
Allen, Lee Harrison *wholesale company executive, industrial consultant*
Beierwaltes, William Henry *physician, educator*
Beltz, Charles Robert *engineering executive*
Blevins, William Edward *management consultant*
Brucker, Wilber Marion *lawyer*
Canfield, Francis Xavier *priest, English language educator*
Christian, Edward Kieren *radio and television station executive*
Couzens, Frank, Jr. *banker*
Darke, Richard Francis *lawyer*
Droll, Marian Clarke *energy company public affairs executive*
Gilbert, Ronald Rhea *organization executive, lawyer*
Gilbride, William Donald *lawyer*
Gofrank, Frank Louis *retired machine tool company executive*
Mc Bride, Robert Dana *steel company executive*
McWhirter, Glenna Suzanne (Nickie McWhirter) *newspaper columnist*
Mecke, Theodore Hart McCalla, Jr. *management consultant*
Mogk, John Edward *legal educator, association executive*
Nicholson, George Albert, Jr. *financial analyst*
Peters, Thomas Robert *English educator, writer*
Pytell, Robert Henry *lawyer, former judge*
Richardson, Dean Eugene *retired banker*
Robie, Joan *elementary school principal*
Sphire, Raymond Daniel *anesthesiologist*
Thurber, Cleveland, Jr. *trust banker*
Thurber, Donald MacDonald Dickinson *public relations counsel*
Trebilcott, James Joseph *former utility executive*
Valk, Robert Earl *corporate executive*
Whittaker, Jeanne Evans *former newspaper columnist*
Wilkinson, Warren Scripps *manufacturing company executive*
Wilson, Henry Arthur, Jr. *management consultant*

Grosse Pointe Farms
Axe, John Randolph *lawyer, financial executive*
Cartmill, George Edwin, Jr. *retired hospital administrator*
Obolensky, Marilyn Wall (Mrs. Serge Obolensky) *metals company executive*

Gwinn
Lasich, Vivian Esther Layne *secondary education educator*

Hancock
Dresch, Stephen Paul *economist, state legislator*

Harbert
Morrissette, Bruce Archer *Romance languages educator*

Harbor Springs
Graham, Robert C. *management consultant*
Judge, John Emmet *manufacturing company marketing executive*

Harper Woods
DeGiusti, Dominic Lawrence *medical science educator, academic administrator*

Harrison Township
Suchecki, Lucy Anne *elementary education educator*

Harsens Island
Slade, Roy *artist, college president, museum director*

Haslett
Andrew, Gwen *university dean emerita, retired*
Hotaling, Robert Bachman *community planner, educator*

Hastings
Adrounie, V. Harry *dean, environmental scientist, educator*

Hickory Corners
Bristol, Norman *lawyer, arbitrator, former food company executive*
Brown, Norman A. *consultant*
Hubbard, William Neill, Jr. *pharmaceutical company executive*
Lauff, George Howard *biologist*

Highland
Doyle, James H. *school system administrator*

Hillsdale
Castel, Albert Edward *history educator*
Roche, George Charles, III *college administrator*
Trowbridge, Ronald Lee *college admininstrator*

Holland
Cook, James Ivan *clergyman, religion educator*
Haworth, Gerrard Wendell *office systems manufacturing company executive*
Haworth, Richard G. *office furniture manufacturer*
Hountras, Peter Timothy *psychologist, educator*
Ingham, Mark Gordon *physicist, educator*
Jacobson, John Howard, Jr. *college president*
Johanneson, Gerald Benedict *office products company executive*
Quimby, Robert Sherman *retired humanities educator*
Van Wylen, Gordon John *former college president*

Houghton
Heckel, Richard Wayne *metallurgical engineering educator*
Huang, Eugene Yuching *civil engineer, educator*
Krenitsky, Michael V. *librarian*
Lumsdaine, Edward *mechanical engineering educator, university dean*
Pelc, Karol I. *engineering management educator, researcher*
Smith, Darrell Wayne *metallurgical engineering educator, consultant*
Tompkins, Curtis Johnston *university president*

Huntington Woods
Gutmann, Joseph *art history educator*
Logan, Linda Mary *art education educator*

Inkster
Ruehle, Dianne Marie *elementary education educator*

Ishpeming
Andriacchi, Dominic Francis *lawyer*
Cope, Robert Gary *management educator, author, consultant*

Jackson
Feldmann, Judith G. *language professional, educator*
Fowler, John Russell *retail executive*
Genyk, Ruth Bel *psychotherapist*
Henderson, John William *chemistry educator*
†Hockenbrocht, David William *manufacturing and oil company executive*
Howell, Stephen Haviland *utility executive*
Kelly, Robert Vincent, Jr. *metal company executive*
Lincoln, Raynard C., Jr. *utility company executive*
Marcoux, William Joseph *lawyer*
McCormick, William Thomas, Jr. *electric and gas company executive*
Patrick, Ueal Eugene *oil company executive*
Rosenfeld, Mark Kenneth *retail store executive*
†Smith, John J. *manufacturing company executive*
Vischer, Harold Harry *manufacturing company executive*
Weaver, Franklin Thomas *newspaper executive*
†Wilkinson, Howard R. *association administrator*

Kalamazoo
Aladjem, Silvio *obstetrician, gynecologist, educator*
†Amdursky, Saul Jack *library director*
Barrett, Nancy Smith *university administrator*
Breisach, Ernst A. *historian, educator*
Bridenstine, James Aloysius *museum director*
Brown, Eric Vandyke, Jr. *lawyer*
Bryan, Lawrence Dow *college administrator*
Calloway, Jean Mitchener *mathematician, educator*
Carver, Norman Francis, Jr. *architect, photographer*
Chodos, Dale David Jerome *physician, consumer advocate*
Clarke, Allen Bruce *mathematics educator, retired academic administrator*
Connable, Alfred Barnes *retired business executive*
Cyrus, Kenneth M. *pharmaceutical company executive, lawyer*
†Dybek, Stuart *English educator, writer*
Dykstra, David Allen *corporate executive*
Edmondson, Keith Henry *chemical company executive*
Enslen, Richard Alan *federal judge*
Fitch, W. Chester *industrial engineer*
Fredericks, Sharon Kay *nurses aide*
Freed, Karl Francis *professional planner*
Gilmore, James Stanley, Jr. *broadcast executive*
Gladstone, William Sheldon, Jr. *radiologist*
Gordon, Jaimy *English educator*
Greenfield, John Charles *bio-organic chemist*
Gregory, Ross *history educator, author*
Grotzinger, Laurel Ann *university librarian*
Haenicke, Diether Hans *university president*
Hite, Judson Cary *retired pharmaceutical company executive*
Holland, Harold Herbert *banker*
Hooker, Richard Alfred *lawyer*
Hustoles, Thomas Paul *lawyer*
Inselberg, Rachel *education educator, researcher*
Johnson, Tom Milroy *academic dean, medical educator, physician*
Klein, Richard Dean *banker*
Lawrence, William Joseph, Jr. *retired corporate executive*
Lee, Edward L. *bishop*
†Lennon, Elizabeth M. *retired educator*
Light, Christopher Upjohn *writer, computer musician*
Light, Timothy *linguistics, religious and Asian studies educator, academic administrator*
Lowrie, Jean Elizabeth *librarian, educator*
†Ludwig, Patric E. *health care group executive*
Maier, Paul Luther *history educator, author, chaplain*
Markin, David Robert *motor company executive*
Marshall, Vincent de Paul *industrial microbiologist, researcher*
McCarty, Theodore Frederick *banker*
McDonald, Kenneth William *principal*
Moritz, Edward *historian, educator*
Norris, Richard Patrick *museum director, history educator*
O'Boyle, Robert L. *landscape architect*
Parfet, Donald Reid *pharmaceutical executive*
Ritter, Charles Edward *lawyer*
Rowland, Doyle Alfred *federal judge*
Ruoff, Cynthia Osowiec *foreign language educator*
Salisbury, Robert Cameron *financial executive*
Smith, Daniel R. *bank holding company executive*
†Smith, Ley S. *pharmaceutical company executive*
Smith, Robert James *immunopharmacologist*
†Stack, R. Timothy *health facility administrator*
†Stasik, Randy *health facility administrator*
Stufflebeam, Daniel LeRoy *education educator*
Taborn, Jeannette Ann *real estate investor*
Tessler, Allan R. *trucking company executive*
Thomas, Philip Stanley *economics educator*
Vescovi, Selvi *pharmaceutical company executive*
Waring, Walter Weyler *English language educator*
Welborn, John Alva *former state senator, small business owner*
†Zabriskie, John L. *healthcare and agricultural products manufacturing company executive*
Zupko, Ramon *composer, music professor*

Kincheloe
Light, Kenneth Freeman *college administrator*

Lake Angelus
Kresge, Bruce Anderson *retired physician*

Lake Leelanau
Shannahan, John Henry Kelly *energy consultant*

Lake Orion
†Brendel, Albert E. small business owner, mechanical engineer

Lansing
Anderton, James Franklin, IV holdings company executive
Anthony, Vernice Davis public health officer
Arends, Herman Joseph insurance company executive
Baker, Frederick Milton, Jr. lawyer
Ballbach, Philip Thornton political consultant
Barns, Justine state legislator
Beardmore, Dorothy state education administrator
Binsfeld, Connie Berube lieutenant governor
Boyle, Patricia Jean judge
Braunstein, Diane Karen state agency administrator
Brennan, Thomas Emmett law school president
Brickley, James H. judge
Bullard, Willis Clare, Jr. state legislator
Cavanagh, Michael Francis state supreme court chief justice
Crandall, Nancy Lee geriatrics service professional, nurse
Cropsey, Alan Lee state legislator, lawyer
DeHaven, Clark Edwin business educator
Demlow, Daniel J. lawyer
Dobronski, Agnes Marie state legislator
Dolan, Jan Clark state legislator
Emmons, Joanne state senator
Fink, Joseph Allen lawyer
Fitzgerald, John Warner legal educator
Foster, Joe C., Jr. lawyer
Freedman, Eric journalist
Geake, Raymond Robert state senator
Hammerstrom, Beverly Swoish state representative
Harrison, Michael Gregory judge
Harvey, Joanne H. genealogist
†Hawks, Gary D. state education official
Hoffman, Philip Edward state legislator
Holle, Reginald Henry bishop
Kaza, Greg John state representative, economist
Kelley, Frank Joseph state attorney general
Kilpatrick, Carolyn Cheeks state legislator, educator
Kindinger, Paul Eugene state director of agriculture
Kluge, Len H. director, actor, theater educator
Lindemer, Lawrence Boyd lawyer, former utility executive, former state justice
McKeague, David William district judge
McLellan, Richard Douglas lawyer
†McRee, Edward Barxdale hospital administrator
Miller, Candice S. state official
†Neumann, Forrest Karl hospital administrator
Perry, Maxine Lewis state official
Pitoniak, Gregory Edward state representative
Povish, Kenneth Joseph bishop
Rooney, John Philip law educator
Saltzman, Robert Paul insurance company executive
†Schiller, Robert E. state official
Schroer, Mary state legislator
Schwarz, John J.H. state senator, surgeon
Smith, Virgil Clark state legislator
Stockmeyer, Norman Otto, Jr. law educator, consultant
Suhrheinrich, Richard Fred federal judge
Valade, Alan Michael lawyer
Vaughn, Jackie, III state legislator
Wiegenstein, John Gerald physician
Wilkinson, William Sherwood lawyer
Wotiska, Sister Dorita school system administrator

Leland
Small, Hamish chemist

Livonia
Brandon, David A. marketing and publishing executive
Campbell, Barbara Ann editor
†Davis, Lawrence Edward church official
Hanket, Mark John lawyer
Holtzman, Roberta Lee French and Spanish language educator
Marinelli, Joseph John educational administrator
McCuen, John Francis, Jr. lawyer
Needham, Kathleen Ann gerontology educator, consultant
Sobel, Howard Bernard osteopath
Utley, John Eddy automotive supplies executive
Van de Vyver, Sister Mary Francilene academic administrator

Mackinac Island
†Mc Cabe, John Charles, III writer

Madison Heights
Chapman, Gilbert Bryant physicist
Jeffe, Sidney David automotive engineer
Kafarski, Mitchell I. chemical processing company executive
†Keisoglou, Abraham Nikolaos engineering company executive
O'Hara, Thomas Edwin association executive
Pricer, Wayne Francis counseling administrator
†Tersigni, Anthony health science facility administrator

Mancelona
Whelan, Joseph L(eo) neurologist

Maple City
Morris, Donald Arthur Adams college president

Marine City
Cronenworth, Charles Douglas manufacturing company executive

Marquette
Burt, John Harris bishop
Camerius, James Walter marketing educator, corporate researcher
†Garland, James H. bishop
Geiger, David Scott mathematician, researcher
Heldreth, Leonard Guy university administrator
Hill, Betty Jean academic administator
Ray, Thomas Kreider bishop
Skogman, Dale R. bishop
Vandament, William Eugene academic administrator, educator

Metamora
Blass, Gerhard Alois physics educator

Midland
Barker, Nancy Lepard university official
Boulanger, Rodney Edmund energy company executive
Byers, Rosemarie library director
Carson, Gordon Bloom engineering executive
Chao, Marshall chemist
Cuthbert, Robert Lowell product specialist
Dorman, Linneaus Cuthbert retired chemist
Downey, Joseph L. chemical company executive
Falla, Enrique Crabb chemical company executive
Gant, George Arlington Lee chemist
Hampton, Leroy retired chemical company executive
Hanes, James Henry consulting business executive, lawyer
Hazleton, Richard A. chemicals executive
†Heinlein, Gregory John chemical company executive
Hyde, Geraldine Veola secondary education educator, retired
Jenkins, James Robert lawyer, corporate executive
Ludington, John Samuel manufacturing company executive
Maneri, Remo R. management consultant
Mansfield, Marc Lewis chemist, research scientist
Meister, Bernard John chemical engineer
Oreffice, Paul Fausto retired chemical company executive
Popoff, Frank Peter chemical company executive
Powell, Rebecca Ann secondary education educator
†Roels, Philip insurance company executive
†Schrenk, Walter John research chemical engineer
Speier, John Leo, Jr. chemist
†Stavropoulos, William S. chemical executive
Stull, Daniel Richard research thermochemist, educator, consultant
Tabor, Theodore Emmett chemical company research manager
Weyenberg, Donald Richard chemist

Monroe
Foster, Ronald G. automotive parts company executive
Heselton, Patricia Ann clinical psychologist
Keck, Merel Fogg bank executive
Knabusch, Charles Thair manufacturing company executive
Lipford, Rocque Edward lawyer, corporate executive
Mlocek, Sister Frances Angeline financial executive
Siciliano, Elizabeth Marie secondary education educator
White, Gary L. trucking executive

Mount Clemens
Fraser, Blanche E. school system administrator
Kolakowski, Diana Jean county commissioner

Mount Pleasant
Dietrich, Richard Vincent geologist, educator
Grabinski, C. Joanne gerontologist, educator
Lippert, Robert J. administrator and culinary arts educator, consultant
Lovinger, Sophie Lehner child psychologist
McBryde, James Edward state legislator
Meltzer, Bernard N(athan) sociologist, educator
Orlik, Peter Blythe media educator, author, musician
Plachta, Leonard E. academic administrator
Zimmerman, Helene Loretta business educator

Muskegon
Austin, William Lamont educational consultant, former superintendent of schools
†Bliss, David C. retail executive
Hadiaris, Marie Ellen special education educator
Johnson, Dale A. manufacturing company executive
Mason, Robert Joseph automotive parts company executive
Roy, Paul Emile, Jr. county official
Van Leuven, Robert Joseph lawyer
Werner, R(ichard) Budd business executive

Negaunee
Friggens, Thomas George state official, historian

New Buffalo
Laird, Evalyn Walsh lawyer

Newaygo
Grodus, Edward T. secondary school principal

Northville
Lockett, Harold James physician, psychiatrist
Opre, Thomas Edward magazine editor, film company executive, corporate travel company executive

Novi
Andrus, Leonard Carl marketing executive
Chow, Chi-Ming retired mathematics educator
Kinsey, Charles John industrial auctioneer, consultant, cattle breeder, farmer
Kirkpatrick, Elwood milk products company and association executive
†Kowalski, Thomas P. environmental consulting executive
Singh, Jaswant environmental company executive

Oak Park
McManus, Martin Joseph lawyer, priest
Novick, Marvin investment company executive, former automotive supplier executive, accountant

Okemos
Giacoletto, Lawrence Joseph electronics engineering educator, researcher, consultant
Hickey, Howard Wesley retired education educator
Huddleston, Eugene Lee retired American studies educator
Killingsworth, Charles Clinton economist
Oberg, Roger Winston management educator
Ochberg, Frank Martin psychiatrist, health science facility administrator, author
Solo, Robert Alexander economist, educator

Olivet
Bassis, Michael Steven academic administrator

Onondaga
Byrum, Dianne state legislator

Orchard Lake
Haven, Thomas Kenneth financial consultant

Owosso
Hoddy, George Warren electric company executive, electrical engineer

Paw Paw
Warner, James John small business owner

Pinckney
Hernandez, Ramon Robert clergyman

Pleasant Ridge
Krabbenhoft, Kenneth Lester radiologist, educator

Plymouth
Bates, J(ohn) Bertram retired chemical company executive
Grannan, William Stephen safety engineer, consultant
Maresca, Daniel G. retail executive
McClendon, Edwin James health science educator
Merrill, Kenneth Coleman retired automobile company executive
Mondry, Ira electronic appliance company executive
Moore, Joan Elizabeth human resources executive, lawyer
Morgan, Donald Crane lawyer
Scott, George Ernest publisher, writer
†Trim, Donald Roy consulting engineer
Vlcek, Donald Joseph, Jr. food distribution company executive

Pontiac
Berlow, Robert Alan lawyer
Blades, Horatio Benedict (Bennie Blades) professional football player
Brown, Lomas, Jr. professional football player
Carter, Anthony football player
Decker, Peter William academic administrator
Fontes, Wayne professional football team head coach
Grant, Barry M(arvin) judge
Gray, Mel professional football player
Huntoon, Donna R. commissioner
Mahone, Barbara Jean automotive company executive
McClellan, Thomas James educator
Robinson, Jack Albert retail drug stores executive
Sanders, Barry football player
Schmidt, Chuck professional football team executive
Seeley, Fred Cooley retail executive
Smith, Roger Bonham automotive manufacturing executive
Spielman, Chris professional football player
Swilling, Pat professional football player
Wilcox, Joann Rose Court hospital administrator

Port Huron
Coury, John, Jr. surgeon
DeMascio, Robert Edward federal judge
Hoover, Herbert Arnold chemical manufacturing company executive
Kirby, Ward Nelson gas company executive
McDaniels, Peggy Ellen special education educator
Rowark, Maureen fine arts photographer
Thomson, Robert James natural gas distribution company executive
Wu, Harry Pao-Tung librarian

Portland
Adams, Bill principal
Rich, Joseph John accountant

Redford
Flint, H. Howard, II printing company executive
Koci, Ludvik Frank automotive manufacturing company executive

Richmond
Huvaere, Richard Floyd auto dealer

Riverdale
Kirby, Kent Bruce artist, educator

Rochester
Callewaert, Denis Marc biochemistry educator
Daniels, David Wilder conductor, music educator
†Hage, Christine Lind library administrator
Horwitz, Ronald M. business administration educator
Hovanesian, Joseph Der mechanical engineering educator
Packard, Sandra Podolin association administrator
Polis, Michael Philip academic administrator, electrical engineering educator
Thomas, S. Bernard history educator
Unakar, Nalin Jayantilal biological sciences educator

Rochester Hills
Cook, Leonard Clarence manufacturing company executive
Ferguson, Harley Robert service company executive
Matthews, George Tennyson history educator
†Pfister, Karl Anton industrial company executive
Stryker, James William automotive executive, former military officer

Rockford
Gleason, Thomas Daues shoe company executive

Romulus
Archer, Hugh Morris consulting engineer, manufacturing professional
Gulda, Edward James automotive executive

Royal Oak
Bernstein, Jay pathologist, researcher, educator
Dworkin, Howard Jerry nuclear physician, educator
Fredericks, Marshall Maynard sculptor
Karavite, Carlene Marie psychologist, real estate property manager
Klosinski, Deanna Dupree medical laboratory sciences educator
LaBan, Myron Miles physician, administrator
Matzick, Kenneth John hospital administrator
Myers, Kenneth Ellis hospital administrator
Proctor, Conrad Arnold physician
Stephens, Martha Foster advertising executive
Walker, Richard Harold pathologist, educator

Saginaw
Chaffee, Paul Charles newspaper editor
Cline, Thomas William real estate leasing company executive, management consultant
Doud, Kenneth Eugene, Jr. accountant
Evans, Harold Edward banker
Kern, Franklin Lorenz auditor
Kinney, Yvonne Marie primary grades educator
†Manning, John Warren, III retired surgeon, medical educator
Najar, Leo Michael conductor, arranger, educator
Puravs, John Andris journalist
Thatcher, Rex Howard newspaper publisher
Untener, Kenneth E. bishop
Williams, Herbert J. bishop
Wilson, J. Parrish religious organization administrator

Saint Clair Shores
Gordon, Steven Stanley automotive parts company executive
Rownd, Robert Harvey biochemistry and molecular biology educator
Seppala, Katherine Seaman (Mrs. Leslie W. Seppala) retail company executive
Shehan, Wayne Charles lawyer
Walker, Frank Banghart pathologist
†Woodford, Arthur MacKinnon library director, historian

Saint Joseph
Butt, Jimmy Lee retired association executive
Castenson, Roger R. agricultural engineer, association executive
Maley, Wayne Allen engineering consultant
Michelotti, Carl Anthony electronics company executive

Saline
Cornell, Richard Garth biostatistics educator
Frank, Richard Calhoun architect

Sault Sainte Marie
Johnson, Gary Robert political scientist, editor

South Haven
Nequist, John Leonard retired food company executive

Southfield
Barnett, Marilyn advertising agency executive
†Barrett, John Eugene, Jr. health care administrator
†Beuerlein, Sister Juliana hospital administrator
Borden, John Anthony manufacturing company executive
Brown, June journalist
Cantwell, Dennis Michael finance company executive
Caponigro, Jeffrey Ralph public relations counselor
Chambers, Charles MacKay university president
Cohen, Norton Jacob lawyer
Considine, John Joseph advertising executive
Darin, Frank Victor John management consultant
Dawson, Dennis Ray lawyer, manufacturing company executive
Doctoroff, Martin Myles judge
Dorfman, Henry S. meat products company executive
Dorfman, Joel Marvin meat products company executive
Ellis, Robert William engineering educator
Fleming, Mac Arthur labor union administrator
Hammel, Ernest Martin medical educator, academic administrator
Hotelling, Harold law and economics educator
†Ibrahim, Ibrahim N. bishop
Jacobs, John Patrick lawyer
Jeffrey, Walter Leslie corporation executive
Johnson, Richard Alan advertising executive
Kalter, Alan advertising agency executive
Kevorkian, Jack pathologist
Koch, Albert Acheson management consultant
Link, Robert Allen lawyer, financial company executive
Maibach, Ben C., Jr. service executive
Makupson, Amyre Porter television station executive
Mathog, Robert Henry otolaryngologist, educator
Matthes, Gerald Stephen advertising agency executive
Mikelberg, Arnold meat packing company executive
Moran, Frank Sullivan accounting executive
Morganroth, Fred lawyer
Morganroth, Mayer lawyer
Nadel, Roger radio executive
Neman, Thomas Edward advertising and marketing executive
†O'Donovan, Thomas Raphael professional association administrator
Ohtake, Yoshito metal products executive
Olsen, Douglas H. superintendent
Papazian, Dennis Richard history educator, political commentator
Redstone, Daniel Aaron architect
Redstone, Louis Gordon architect
Rosenzweig, Norman psychiatry educator
Rossiter, Robert E. diversified corporation executive
Rowe, Arthur Edgar manufacturing company executive
Satovsky, Abraham lawyer
Smith, Nancy Hohendorf sales and marketing executive
Stern, Guy German language educator, writer
Tauber, Joel David manufacturing company executive
Thimotheose, Kadakampallil George psychologist
Welch, Martin E., III manufacturing company executive
†Wiggins, Timothy J. metal products executive
†Wisne, Anthony E. metal products executive
†Wisne, Lawrence A. metal products executive

Southgate
Brodhun, Andrew R. banker
Torok, Margaret Louise insurance company executive

Spring Arbor
Dillman, Charles Norman religion educator
Thompson, Stanley B. church administrator

Stanwood
Cawthorne, Kenneth Clifford financial planner

Sterling Heights
Duchane, Stephen Michael city manager
†Frank, Michael Sanford dermatologist
Ice, Orva Lee, Jr. history educator

Stevensville
†Vegter, William Charles *wholesale supply executive*

Sturgis
Mackay, Edward *engineer*

Suttons Bay
Skinner, Thomas *broadcasting and film executive*
Whitney, William Chowning *retired banker, financial consultant*

Taylor
Billig, Erwin H. *manufacturing company executive*
Bright, Gerald *lawyer, manufacturing company executive*
Leekley, John Robert *lawyer*
Lyon, Wayne Barton *manufacturing company executive*
Manoogian, Alex *manufacturing company executive*
Manoogian, Richard Alexander *manufacturing company executive*
Rosowski, Robert Bernard *manufacturing company executive*
Ullrich, John Frederick *diversified manufacturing company executive*

Tecumseh
Herrick, Kenneth Gilbert *manufacturing company executive*
Herrick, Todd W. *manufacturing company executive*
Hood, Douglas Crary *retired electronics educator*
Taylor, Robert Lee *financial services and sales executive, information systems account executive, educator*

Temperance
†Kinney, Mark B. *educator*

Thompsonville
Perry, Margaret *librarian, writer*

Traverse City
†Abeel, Samantha Lynn *juvenile fiction author*
†Bay, John Cantrell *retired hospital administrator*
Brown, Paul Bradley *architect*
Chang, Ching-I Eugene *insurance executive*
Howe, Gordon *former professional hockey player, sports association executive*
LeJeune, Dennis Edward *investment counsel*
Rosser, Richard Franklin *education consultant*
Taylor, Donald Arthur *marketing educator*
Warrington, Willard Glade *former university official*
Wolfe, Richard Ratcliffe *lawyer*
Zimmerman, Paul Albert *retired college president, minister*

Troy
Adderley, Terence E. *corporate executive*
Alterman, Irwin Michael *lawyer*
Anderson, Iain Mair *automobile manufacturing company executive*
Antonini, Joseph E. *discount department store executive*
Avedisian, Edward *artist*
Baker, Ernest Waldo, Jr. *advertising executive*
Behnke, Bruce Ivan *manufacturing company executive*
Buschmann, Siegfried *manufacturing executive*
Cantor, Bernard Jack *patent lawyer*
Carlson, David Martin *retail executive*
†Chinni, Charles Ross *retail executive*
Corace, Joseph Russell *automotive parts company executive*
Crane, Louis Arthur *retired labor arbitrator*
Drakos, Irene Sasso *chemist*
Fellingham, David Andrew *mortgage banker*
Fritz, Jock Thane *radio executive*
Gardon, John Leslie *paint company research executive*
Handleman, David *audio products company executive*
Hartwig, Eugene Lawrence *lawyer*
†Haven, Carl Ole *hospital administrator*
Hunia, Edward Mark *foundation executive*
†Jablonski, Dale Z. *public relations and publishing executive*
Kelly, William R. *employment agency executive*
†Klingmann, Horst *automotive company executive*
Kruse, John Alphonse *lawyer*
LaDuke, Nancie *lawyer, corporate executive*
Leach, Ralph F. *banker*
Marshall, John Elbert, III *foundation executive*
McDonald, Alonzo Lowry, Jr. *manufacturing executive*
Meyers, Christine Laine *publishing and media executive, consultant*
†Milidrag, George D. *engineering company executive*
Montross, Albert Edward *electronics company executive*
Moore, Oliver Semon, III *publishing executive, consultant*
Ovshinsky, Stanford Robert *physicist, inventor, energy and information company executive*
†Perkins, Donald S. *department store chain executive*
Powell, Robert Barrows *architectural firm executive*
Powers, James *record and tape company executive*
Reickert, Erick Arthur *automotive executive*
Ricketts, Thomas Roland *bank executive*
Sandy, William Haskell *training and communications systems executive*
Schafer, Sharon Marie *anesthesiologist*
Sharf, Stephan *automotive company executive*
Simons, Leonard Norman Rashall *advertising executive*
Sloan, Hugh Walter, Jr. *automotive industry executive*
Smith, Glen B. *consumer products company executive*
†Stanalјczo, Gregg *computer services executive*
Stine, Jeanne M. *mayor, educator*
Strome, Stephen *distribution company executive*
Taylor, Alfred Hendricks, Jr. *former foundation executive*
Thomas, Joseph R. *retail chain stores executive*
Thompson, Robert Eugene *employment agency executive*
Wetstein, Gary M. *accountant, company executive*
Williams, David Perry *manufacturing company executive*

Union Lake
Boulos, Nadia Ebid *medical/surgical nurse*

Union Pier
Howland, Bette *writer*

University Center
Carlyon, Don J. *college president*
Gilbertson, Eric Raymond *academic administrator, lawyer*
Lange, Crystal Marie *nursing educator*
Miller, Roberta Balstad *science administrator*

Utica
Williams, Robert Joseph, Sr. *automotive executive*

Warren
Agley, Randolph J. *pharmaceutical company executive*
Bell, Bradley J. *household appliance manufacturing company executive*
Bonkowski, Ronald Lawrence *mayor*
Brayer, Robert Marvin *program manager, engineer*
Campbell, David Douglas *automotive company executive*
†Dedeurwaerder, Jose Joseph *automotive executive*
Dow, Peter Anthony *advertising agency executive*
Foxworth, John Edwin, Jr. *automotive executive, philatelist*
Gallopoulos, Nicholas Efstratios *chemical engineer*
Gilbert, Suzanne Harris *advertising executive*
Ginsberg, Myron *computer scientist*
Gothard, Donald Lee *auto company executive*
Haas, Ronald Henry *automotive company executive, mechanical engineer*
Herbst, Jan Francis *physicist, researcher*
Hopp, Anthony James *advertising agency executive*
Horton, William David, Jr. *army officer*
Jacovides, Linos Jacovou *electrical engineering research manager*
†Kirby, Patrick G. *engineering executive*
Lau, Ian Van *safety research engineer, biomechanics expert*
Lett, Philip Wood, Jr. *defense consultant*
Lorenzo, Albert L. *academic administrator*
Morelli, William Annibale, Sr. *aerospace manufacturing company executive*
Nagy, Louis Leonard *engineering executive, researcher*
†Plummer, Raymond J. *furniture manufacturing executive*
Schirmer, Robert Hamilton *advertising executive*
Schultz, Louis Michael *advertising agency executive*
Schwartz, Shirley E. *chemist*
Smith, George Wolfram *physicist, educator*
Smith, John Robert *physicist*
Tausch, William Joseph *advertising agency executive*
Valerio, Michael Anthony *financial executive*
Viano, David Charles *automotive safety research scientist*

Waterford
Hampton, Phillip Michael *consulting engineering company executive*

West Bloomfield
Childress, Carl T. *principal*
Colton, Victor Robert *real estate developer, investor*
†Di Pietro, Frank Anthony *manufacturing engineer*
Green, Shirley Laak *nursing administrator*
Ho, Leo Chi Chien *education administrator*
Meyers, Gerald Carl *management consultant, author, educator, lecturer, former automobile company executive*
Peterson, Esther *secondary school principal*
Sarwer-Foner, Gerald Jacob *physician, educator*
Sawyer, Howard Jerome *physician*

Whitehall
Youngquist, Alvin Menvid, Jr. *publisher, editor*

Williamsburg
Goodell, Warren Franklin *retired university administrator*

Williamston
Landis, Elwood Winton *retired newspaper editor*

Wixom
Boynton, Irvin Parker *educational administrator*

Ypsilanti
Barnes, James Milton *physics and astronomy educator*
Beck, Mary Clare *librarian*
Boone, Morell Douglas *academic administrator, information and instructional technology educator*
Caswell, Herbert Hall, Jr. *retired biology educator*
Corriveau, Arlene Josephine *educational specialist*
Duncan, Charles Howard *business education educator*
Evans, Gary Lee *communications educator and consultant*
Gledhill, Roger Clayton *statistician, engineer, mathematician, educator*
Goldenberg, Ronald Edwin *university dean*
Gwaltney, Thomas Marion *education educator, researcher*
Holland, Joy *health care facility executive*
McNutt, Kristen Wallwork *consumer affairs executive*
Norton, Jody (John Douglas Norton) *English language educator*
Olmsted, Patricia Palmer *education educator, researcher*
Perkins, Bradford *history educator*
Randolph, Linda Jane *mathematics educator*
Ritter, Frank Nicholas *otolaryngologist, educator*
Shelton, William Everett *university president*
Sullivan, Thomas Patrick *college president*
Ullman, Nelly Szabo *statistician, educator*
Weinstein, Jay A. *social science educator, researcher*
Williams, Regina Marion *nursing educator*
Wilson, Lorraine M. *medical, surgical nurse, nursing educator*

Zeeland
Campbell, J. Kermit *office products company executive*
De Pree, Max O. *furniture manufacturing company executive*
Ruch, Richard Hurley *manufacturing company executive*

MINNESOTA

Alexandria
Hultstrand, Donald Maynard *bishop*
Templin, Kenneth Elwood *paper company executive*

Annandale
Johnson, Jon E. *magazine editor and publisher*

Anoka
Sekhon, Kathleen *state legislator*

Apple Valley
†Seal, Ulysses S. *animal scientist*

Arden Hills
Lindmark, Ronald Dorance *retired federal agency administrator*
Ousley, James E. *systems integrator*

Austin
Hodapp, Don Joseph *food company executive*
Holman, Ralph Theodore *biochemistry and nutrition educator*
Knowlton, Richard L. *food and meat processing company executive*
Schmid, Harald Heinrich Otto *biochemistry educator, academic director*

Avon
†Blattner, William Henry *construction company executive*

Babbitt
†de Marcken, Baudouin François *foreign service officer*

Bayport
Hulings, A. D. *manufacturing company execuitve*
Johnson, Alan *retired window/patio door manufacturer*
Meissner, Harold C. *window manufacturing company executive*

Bemidji
Bridston, Paul Joseph *insurance company executive, consultant*
Kief, Paul Allan *lawyer*
Martel, Petra Jean Hegstad *elementary school educator*
Paul, Sherman *retired English language educator*

Bloomington
Allen, Mary Louise Hook *physical education educator*
Cuthill, Robert T. *church administrator*
Dahlberg, Burton Francis *real estate corporation executive*
Huttner, Marian Alice *library administrator*
Jodsaas, Larry Elvin *computer components company executive*
Krueger, Eugene Rex *academic program director*
Kuntz, Lila Elaine *secondary business education educator*
Lakin, James Dennis *allergist, immunologist*
McDill, Thomas Allison *minister*
McGrath, Dennis Britton *public relations executive*
Meyer, Scott D. *public relations firm executive*
Mona, David L. *public relations executive*
Smith, Henry Charles, III *symphony orchestra conductor*
Thomas, Margaret Jean *clergywoman, religious research consultant*
Thorndyke, Lloyd Milton *computer company executive*

Brooklyn Park
Peterson, Donn Neal *forensic engineer*
Spencer, LaVyrle *writer*

Burnsville
Gardner, Dennis (Den Gardner) *public relations executive*
Knutson, David Lee *lawyer, state senator*
†Weksel, William *electronics executive*

Chanhassen
Severson, Roger Allan *bank executive*
Thorson, John Martin, Jr. *electrical engineer, consultant*

Chisago City
Bergstrand, Wilton Everet *minister*

Circle Pines
McClellan, John R. *school system administrator*

Cloud
Holthaus, Thomas Anthony *hospital administrator*

Cokato
Thomas, Paul S. *principal*

Collegeville
Haile, Getatchew *archivist, educator*
Henry, Patrick G. *religious research administrator*
Reinhart, Dietrich Thomas *university president, history educator*

Cottage Grove
Glazebrook, Rita Susan *nursing educator*

Crookston
Balke, Victor H. *bishop*

Dassel
Kay, Craig *principal*

Detroit Lakes
Eginton, Charles Theodore *surgeon, educator*

Dresbach
Saline, Lindon Edgar *industrial company executive*

Duluth
Aadland, Thomas Vernon *minister*
Aufderheide, Arthur Carl *pathologist*
Balmer, James Walter *lawyer*
Billig, Thomas Clifford *publishing and marketing executive*
Bowman, Roger Manwaring *real estate executive*
Chee, Cheng-Khee *artist*
Coffman, Phillip Hudson *music educator, arts administrator*
Eisenberg, Richard Martin *pharmacology educator*
Fischer, Roger Adrian *history educator*
Franks, Ronald Dwyer *university dean, psychiatrist, educator*
Gallinger, Lois Mae *medical technologist*
Heaney, Gerald William *federal judge*
Heller, Lois Jane *physiologist, educator, researcher*
Ianni, Lawrence Albert *university administrator, English language educator*
Jankofsky, Klaus Peter *medieval studies educator*
Johnson, Arthur Gilbert *microbiology educator*
Latto, Lewis M., Jr. *broadcasting company executive*
Lease, Martin Harry, Jr. *retired political science educator*
Pearce, Donald Joslin *retired librarian*
Rapp, George Robert, Jr. (Rip) *geology and archeology educator*
Salmela, David Daniel *architect*
Sandbulte, Arend John *utility executive*
Schroeder, Fred Erich Harald *humanities educator*
Schwietz, Roger L. *bishop*
Whiteman, Richard Frank *architect*
Wood, Douglas *author, composer, musician*

Eagan
Opperman, Dwight Darwin *publishing company executive*
Scott, Andrew *corporate executive*

Eden Prairie
Berra, John Michael *measurement and control instrumentation company executive*
Cooper, Adrian *football player*
Emison, James W. *petroleum company executive*
Green, Dennis *professional football coach*
Hanson, Dale S. *banker*
Headrick, Roger Lewis *professional sports executive*
Heath, Vernon H. *manufacturing company executive*
Higgins, Robert Arthur *electrical engineer, educator, consultant*
Hinton, Christopher Jerrod *professional football player*
Knotek, Robert Frank *management consultant, educator*
Lau, Michele Denise *advertising consultant, sales trainer, television personality*
†Levy, David Franklin *sales and marketing executive*
McCoy, Gerald Leo *superintendent of schools*
McDaniel, Randall Cornell *professional football player*
Moon, Harold Warren, Jr. *professional football player*
Morrissey, John Edward *wholesale grocery company executive*
†Roth, Thomas *marketing executive*
Rusch, Thomas William *manufacturing executive*
Schaeffer, Brenda Mae *psychologist*
†Schulze, Richard M. *consumer products executive*
Skoglund, John C. *former professional football team executive*
†Steel, John M. *electronics executive*
Thomas, Henry Lee, Jr. *professional football player*
†Thorstad, Dale J. *manufacturing company executive*

Edina
Brown, Charles Eugene *retired electronics company executive*
Burdick, Lou Brum *public relations executive*
Emmerich, Karol Denise *former retail company executive, consultant*
Enger, Kathleen May *preschool administrator*
†Esbensen, Barbara Juster *author*
Prince, Robb Lincoln *manufacturing company executive*
Putnam, Frederick Warren, Jr. *bishop*
Saltzman, William *painter, sculptor, designer*
Schwarzrock, Shirley Pratt *author, lecturer, educator*

Elysian
Nickerson, James Findley *education consultant*

Excelsior
Bilka, Paul Joseph *physician*
Deikel, Theodore *marketing company executive*
French, Lyle Albert *surgeon*
Rich, Willis Frank, Jr. *banker*

Faribault
Saufferer, William Charles *health center executive*
Turnbull, Charles Vincent *real estate broker*

Farmington
†Johnson, Eldon Wayne *electric utility manager*

Fergus Falls
Egge, Joel *clergy member, academic administrator*
Emmen, Dennis R. *electric utility executive*
†MacFarlane, John Charles *utility company executive*
Olson, Iarle *clergy member, Church administrator*
Overgaard, Robert Milton *religious organization administrator*
Rinden, David Lee *editor*
Westby, Armin *clergy member, church administrator*

Forest Lake
Marchese, Ronald Thomas *ancient history and archaeology educator*

Fridley
Rajamannan, Ambrose Harry *agriculture products supplier*
Vernier, Robert Lawrence *physician, educator*

Golden Valley
†Cepure, Uldis *church official*
Van Hauer, Robert *former health care company executive*

Grand Rapids
King, Sheryl Jayne *secondary education educator, counselor*
Radecki, Anthony Eugene *paper company executive*

Hermantown
Leland, Paula Susan *educational administrator, educator*

Hopkins
Beeler, Donald Daryl *retail executive*
Burke, Steven Francis *organization executive*
†Haley, Thomas William *corporate executive*
Haugen, Gerald Alan *financial consultant*
Hunter, Donald Forrest *lawyer*
Passi, Beth *school administrator*
†Peterson, D. Bruce *data processing computer services company executive*
Rappaport, Gary Burton *defense equipment and computer company executive*
Tempero, Kenneth Floyd *pharmaceutical company executive, physician, clinical pharmacologist*

Hutchinson
Graf, Laurance James *communications executive*

International Falls
Clary, Ben *park superintendent*

Inver Grove
Webster, Elroy *diversified supplies and machinery executive*

Ivanhoe
Hoversten, Ellsworth Gary *insurance executive, producer*

Lake Elmo
Shervheim, Lloyd Oliver *insurance company executive, lawyer*

Lakeville
Krueger, Richard Arnold *state legislator*
Phinney, William Charles *retired geologist*

Little Falls
Zirbes, Mary Kenneth *social justice ministry coordinator*

Long Lake
Lurton, H. William *retired retail executive*

Lutsen
Napadensky, Hyla Sarane *engineering consultant*

Madison
Husby, Donald Evans *engineering company executive*

Mankato
Gage, Fred Kelton *lawyer*
Hottinger, John Creighton *state legislator, lawyer*
Hustoles, Paul John *theater educator*
Larson, Michael Len *newspaper editor*
Orvick, George Myron *church denomination executive, minister*
Rush, Richard R. *university administrator*
Zeller, Michael James *psychologist, educator*

Maple Grove
Lamon, Beverly Ann *school system administrator*

Maple Plain
Larson, Mark Allan *financial executive*

Mapleton
John, Hugo Herman *natural resources educator*

Marcell
Aldrich, Richard John *agronomist, educator*

Marshall
Libby, Ronald Theodore *political science educator, consultant, researcher*
Schwan, Alfred *food products executive*

Mendota Heights
Dennis, Clarence *surgeon, educator*
Frechette, Peter Loren *dental products executive*

Minneapolis
Abrams, Richard Brill *lawyer*
Ackerman, Eugene *biophysics educator*
Ackman, Lauress V. *lawyer*
Adams, John Stephen *geography educator*
Adams, Thomas Lewis *lawyer*
Adamson, Oscar Charles, II *lawyer*
Aguilera, Richard Warren (Rick Aguilera) *professional baseball player*
Albertson, Vernon Duane *electrical engineering educator*
Albright, Susan *newspaper editor*
Alcott, James Arthur *communications executive*
Alton, Ann Leslie *judge, lawyer, educator*
Amdahl, Byrdelle John *business consulting executive*
Amdahl, Douglas Kenneth *retired state supreme court justice*
Anderson, Albert Esten *publisher*
Anderson, Charles S. *college president, clergyman*
Anderson, Chester Grant *English educator*
Anderson, Clyde Bailey *musician, educator*
Anderson, Eric Scott *lawyer*
Anderson, John Edward *mechanical engineering educator*
Anderson, Laurence Alexis *lawyer*
Anderson, Lowell Carlton *insurance company executive*
Anderson, Robert Marshall *bishop*
Anderson, Thomas Willman *lawyer*
Andreas, David Lowell *banker*
Appel, William Frank *pharmacist*
Aris, Rutherford *applied mathematician, educator*
Arndt, Roger Edward Anthony *hydraulic engineer, educator*
Arthur, Lindsay Grier *retired judge, editor, author*
Asp, William George *librarian*
Asplin, Edward William *retired packaging company executive*
Atwater, Horace Brewster, Jr. *food company executive*
Baillie, James Leonard *lawyer*
Baker, John Stevenson (Michael Dyregrov) *writer*
Baker, Michael Harry *chemical engineer*
Bakken, Earl Elmer *electrical engineer, bioengineering company executive*
Bales, Kent Roslyn *English language educator*
Balfour, Henry Hallowell, Jr. *medical educator, researcher, physician, writer*
†Barany, George *chemistry educator, researcher, consultant*
Barnard, Allen Donald *lawyer*
Barnhill, Howard Eugene *insurance company executive*
Bartels, Juergen E. *hotel company executive*
Bartkowski, William Patrick *public relations executive*
Bartle, Emery W(arness) *lawyer*
Baum, David Roy *research psychologist*
Beardsley, John Ray *public relations firm executive*
Bearmon, Lee *lawyer*
Bell, Jerry *professional sports team executive*
Belton, Sharon Sayles *mayor*
Benson, Donald Erick *holding company executive*
Bentz, Frederick Jacob *architect*
Berens, William Joseph *lawyer*
Berg, Stanton Oneal *firearms and ballistics consultant*
Berg, Thomas Kenneth *lawyer*
Bergerson, Stephen Richard *lawyer*
Berry, David J. *financial services company executive*
Berryman, Robert Glen *accounting educator, consultant*
Berscheid, Ellen S. *psychology educator, author, researcher*
Beukema, John Frederick *lawyer*
Bileydi, Sumer *advertising agency executive*
Bisping, Bruce Henry *photojournalist*
Blackburn, Henry Webster, Jr. *physician*
Blair, Craig John *utilities executive*
Blanton, W. C. *lawyer*
†Blau, Robert Alan *marketing executive*
Bleck, Michael John *lawyer*
Blomquist, Robert Oscar *insurance company executive*
Blood, Edward Linford *consumer products company executive*
Bloom, Roger Fredric *lawyer*
Bly, Robert *poet*
Boelter, Philip Floyd *lawyer*
Bolan, Richard Stuart *urban planner, educator, researcher*
Bonsignore, Michael Robert *electronics company executive*
Borger, John Philip *lawyer*
Boubelik, Henry Fredrick, Jr. *car rental company executive*
Bouchard, Thomas Joseph, Jr. *psychology educator, researcher*
Bowie, Norman Ernest *university official, educator*
Brand, Steve Aaron *lawyer*
Brasket, Curt Justin *systems analyst, chess player*
Breimayer, Joseph Frederick *patent lawyer*
Bress, Michael E. *lawyer*
Brings, Lawrence Martin *publisher*
Brink, David Ryrie *lawyer*
Brosnahan, Roger Paul *lawyer*
Brown, David M. *physician, educator, dean*
Brown, Laurence David *retired bishop*
Browne, Donald Roger *speech communication educator*
Browne, Michael Dennis *poet, educator*
Brummer, Donald E. *food company executive*
Bruner, Philip Lane *lawyer*
Buchwald, Henry *surgeon, educator, researcher*
Buckley, John William *financial company executive*
Buoen, Roger *newspaper editor*
Buratti, Dennis P. *lawyer*
Burk, Robert S. *lawyer*
Burke, Martin Nicholas *lawyer*
Burns, Neal Murray *advertising agency executive*
Burns, Robert A. *lawyer*
Burton, Charles Victor *physician, surgeon, inventor*
Busa, Stephen K. *artistic director*
Busdicker, Gordon G. *lawyer*
Cadogan, William J. *telecommunications company executive*
Campbell, James Robert *banker*
Campbell, Karlyn Kohrs *speech and communication educator*
Cardozo, Richard Nunez *marketing, entrepreneurship and business educator*
Caretta, Raul Alberto *chemical engineering educator*
Carlson, Curtis LeRoy *corporate executive*
Carlson, Don D. *lawyer*
†Carlson, Gerald K. *metal products executive*
Carlson, Norman A. *government official*
Carlson, Thomas David *lawyer*
Carlton, Steven Norman *retired professional baseball player*
Carmody, John *architectural educator*
Carpenter, Norman Roblee *lawyer*
Carr, Charles William *biochemist, emeritus educator*
Carr, Robert Wilson, Jr. *chemistry educator*
Carter, Roy Ernest, Jr. *journalist, educator*
Cavert, Henry Mead *physician, retired educator*
Cedar, Paul Arnold *church executive, minister*
Champlin, Steven Kirk *lawyer*
Chavers, Blanche Marie *pediatrician, educator, reseacher*
Chen, William Shao-Chang *retired army officer*
Chipman, John Somerset *economist, educator*
Chisholm, Tague Clement *pediatric surgeon, educator*
Chou, Shelley Nien-chun *neurosurgeon, university official, educator*
Christiansen, Jay David *lawyer*
Ciresi, Michael Vincent *lawyer*
Clemence, Roger Davidson *landscape architect, educator*
Cleveland, (James) Harlan *political scientist, public affairs executive*
Clinton, Joseph Edward *emergency physician*
Cohen, Arnold A. *electrical engineer*
Comstock, Rebecca Ann *lawyer*
Conley, Tom Clark *literature educator*
Conn, Gordon Brainard, Jr. *lawyer*
Cook, Jay F. *lawyer*
Cooper, William Allen *banking executive*
Cope, Lewis *journalist*
Corcoran, Mary Elizabeth *educational psychology educator emeritus*
Cowles, John, III *newspaper publishing executive*
Cox, David Carson *media company executive*
Craig, James Lynn *physician, consumer products company executive*
Crawford, Bryce Low, Jr. *chemist, educator*
Crosby, Jacqueline Garton *newspaper editor, journalist*
Crosby, Thomas Manville, Jr. *lawyer*
Cummings, Larry Lee *psychologist, educator*
Cutler, Kenneth Lance *lawyer*
Dabill, Phillip Alvin *wholesale foods executive*
Dahl, Christopher T. *broadcasting executive*
Dahler, John Spillers *chemist, educator*
Davies, R. Scott *lawyer*
Davis, Howard Ted *chemical engineering educator*
Davis, Julia McBroom *college dean, speech pathology and audiology educator*
Dawis, René V. *psychology educator, research consultant*
Degenhardt, Robert Allan *architectural and engineering firm executive*
Degnan, Joseph *magazine editor*
Deming, Frederick Lewis *banker*
DeNero, Henry T. *department store chain executive*
Desbois, Barbra Berlovitz *artistic director, actor*
DiGangi, Frank Edward *academic administrator*
Diracles, John Michael, Jr. *financial executive*
Doroschak, John Z. *dentist*
Dorsey, Peter *lawyer*
Doty, David Singleton *federal judge*
Dove, William Edwin *banker*
Drawz, John Englund *lawyer*
Dreher, Nancy C. *federal judge*
Dugmore, Edward *artist*
Dunlap, William DeWayne, Jr. *advertising agency executive*
Dworkin, Martin *microbiologist, educator*
Eames, Earl Ward, Jr. *management educator, development specialist*
Eastwood, J. Marquis *lawyer*
Eck, George Gregory *lawyer*
Eckert, Ernst R. G. *mechanical engineering educator*
†Eisenreich, Steven John *chemistry educator, environmental scientist*
Elzay, Richard Paul *dental school administrator*
Endorf, Verlane L. *lawyer*
Engebrecht, Julie *newspaper sports editor*
Erickson, Gerald Meyer *classical studies educator*
Erickson, W(alter) Bruce *business and economics educator, entrepreneur*
Etchelecu, Albert Dominic *energy company executive*
Etzwiler, Donnell Dencil *pediatrician*
Eyberg, Donald Theodore, Jr. *architect*
Fairhurst, Charles *civil and mining engineering educator*
Falker, John Richard *investor relations counsel*
Farah, Caesar Elie *Middle Eastern and Islamic studies educator*
Farber, Daniel Alan *law educator*
Feld, Barry Charles *law educator*
Ferner, David Charles *non-profit management and development consultant*
Ferrera, Robert James *superintendent of schools*
Fetler, Paul *composer*
Findorff, Robert Lewis *retired air filtration equipment company executive*
Finzen, Bruce Arthur *lawyer*
Firchow, Evelyn Scherabon *German educator, author*
Firchow, Peter Edgerly *language professional, educator, author*
Firestone, Jon *advertising executive*
Fisch, Robert Otto *medical educator*
Fischer, Robert William *financial executive*
Fisher, Michael Bruce *lawyer*
Fisher, Orville Earl, Jr. *lawyer, venture capital consultant*
†FitzGerald, Richard Joseph, Jr. *lawyer, educator*
Flanagan, Barbara *journalist*
Flannery, George Perry *lawyer*
†Flaten, Alfred N. *food and consumer products executive*
Fleezanis, Jorja Kay *violinist, educator*
Fleischer, Daniel *minister, religious organization administrator*
Fletcher, Edward Abraham *engineering educator*
Flittie, John Howard *insurance company executive*
Flom, Gerald Trossen *lawyer*
Fox, Howard Tall, Jr. *professional baseball team executive*
Frame, J. Leonard *engineering company executive, retail company executive*
Franklin, Robert Brewer *journalist*
Frase, Richard Stockwell *law educator*
Fraser, Arvonne Skelton *former United Nations ambassador*
Frecon, Alain *lawyer*
French, John Dwyer *lawyer*
Friedman, Avner *mathematician, educator*
Fronek, David N. *lawyer*
Fulton, Robert Lester *sociology educator*
Gage, Edwin C., III (Skip Gage) *travel, marketing services executive*
Gagnon, Craig William *lawyer*
Gainor, Thomas Edward *banker*
Galambos, Theodore Victor *civil engineer, educator*
Gallagher, Gerald Raphael *venture capitalist*
Galloway, Robert Lee *manufacturing executive*
Gandrud, Robert P. *insurance company executive*
Gannon, Mary Carol *nutritional biochemist*
Gardner, William Earl *university dean*
Garmezy, Norman *psychology educator*
Garner, Shirley Nelson *English language educator*
Garon, Philip Stephen *lawyer*
Garton, Thomas William *lawyer*
Gasiorowicz, Stephen George *physics educator*
Gault, N. L., Jr. *physician, educator*
†Gavin, Sara *public relations executive*
Gearty, Edward Joseph *lawyer*
Gedgaudas, Eugene *radiologist, educator*
Gehrz, Robert Douglas *astrophysicist, educator, researcher*
Geistfeld, Ronald Elwood *dental educator*
George, Melvin Douglas *university official*
George, William Wallace *manufacturing company executive*
Gerberich, William Warren *engineering educator*
Gerlach, Luther Paul *anthropologist*
Geweke, John Frederick *economics educator*
Gherty, John E. *food products and agricultural products company executive*
Gifford, Daniel Joseph *lawyer, educator, antitrust consultant*
Gill, Richard Lawrence *lawyer*
Gilpin, Larry Vincent *retail executive*
Goldberg, Luella Gross *business executive*
Goldfus, Donald Wayne *glass company executive*
Goldman, Allen Marshall *physics educator*
Goldstein, Mark David *advertising agency executive*
Goldstein, Richard Jay *mechanical engineer, educator*
Good, David Franklin *economic historian, educator*
Goodman, Elizabeth Ann *lawyer*
Gopinath, Anand *electrical engineer, research scientist*
Gordon, John Bennett *lawyer*
Gorham, Eville *science educator*
Gorlin, Robert James *medical educator*
Gottier, Richard Chalmers *computer company executive*
Gottschalk, Stephen Elmer *lawyer*
Graham, William Franklin (Billy Graham) *evangelist*
Grant, David James William *pharmacy educator*
Gray, Virginia Hickman *political science educator*
Grayson, Edward Davis *lawyer, manufacturing company executive*
Greener, Ralph Bertram *lawyer*
Grieman, John Joseph *communications executive*
Griffin, Edward Michael *language professional, educator*
Griffith, G. Larry *lawyer*
Grim, Eugene Donald *physiology educator*
Groves, Franklin Nelson *construction company executive*
Grundhofer, John F. *banker*
Gudeman, Stephen Frederick *anthropology educator*
Gudorf, Kenneth Francis *business executive*
Guillaume, Marnix Leo Karl *insurance company executive*
Gullickson, Glenn, Jr. *physician, educator*
Gumucio, Marcelo Andres *electronics executive*
Gustafson, Richard Charles *rental and leasing company executive*
Haase, Ashley Thomson *microbiology educator, scientist*
Hagglund, Clarance Edward *lawyer, publishing company owner*
Halbreich, Kathy *museum director*
Hale, Roger Loucks *manufacturing company executive*
Halley, James Woods, Jr. *physicist*
Hallman, Gary L. *photographer, educator*
†Hamel, William John *church administrator, minister*
Hamermesh, Morton *physicist, educator*
Hansen, Jo-Ida Charlotte *psychology educator, researcher*
Hanson, A. Stuart *medical foundation executive, physician*
Hardman, James Charles *lawyer, motor carrier executive*
Hargens, William Garman *architect*
Harper, Donald Victor *transportation and logistics educator*
Harris, Jean Louise *physician*
Harris, John Edward *lawyer*
Hasselquist, Maynard Burton *retired lawyer*
Haugen, Rolf Eugene *leasing company executive*
Hayward, Edward Joseph *lawyer*
Heiberg, Robert Alan *lawyer*
Heider, David Arthur *hardware wholesale company executive*
Hempel, William J. *lawyer*
Hemphill, Stuart R. *lawyer*
Hendrixson, Peter S. *lawyer*
Henson, Robert Frank *lawyer*
†Herrick, Gregory Evans *technology corporation executive*
Hertogs, Mary Helen *educational administrator*
Hetland, James Lyman, Jr. *banker, lawyer, educator*
Hibbs, John Stanley *lawyer*
Hibbs, William R. *lawyer*
Hilary, Sandra Marie *councilwoman*
Hinderaker, John Hadley *lawyer*
Hippee, William H., Jr. *lawyer*
Hitch, Horace *lawyer*
Hobbie, Russell Klyver *physicist*
Hobbins, Robert Leo *lawyer*
Hodder, William Alan *fabricated metal products company executive*
†Hoelscher, Douglas Richard *engineering company executive, educator*
Hoffmann, Thomas Russell *business management educator*
Hogenkamp, Henricus Petrus Cornelis *biochemistry researcher, biochemistry educator*
Holgaard, Conrad J. *company executive*
Holt, Robert Theodore *political scientist, dean, educator*
Holter, Arlen Rolf *cardiothoracic surgeon*
Hooke, Roger LeBaron *geomorphology and glaciology educator*
Horns, Howard Lowell *physician, educator*
Horsch, Lawrence Leonard *venture capitalist, corporate revitalization executive*
†Howe, Craig Walter Sandell *medical organization executive, internist*
Howland, Joan Sidney *law librarian, law educator*
Hoyer, Harvey Conrad *retired college president, clergyman*
Hubers, David Ray *financial services company executive*
Hudec, Robert Emil *lawyer, educator*
Hull, Bill *clergy member, church administrator*
Hull, William Henry *publishing company executive*
Humphreys, Roberta Marie *astronomer, educator*
Hurwicz, Leonid *economist, educator*
Huston, Beatrice Louise *banker*
†Hyslop, David Johnson *arts administrator*
Infante, Ettore Ferrari *mathematician, educator, university administrator*
Isbin, Herbert Stanford *chemical engineering educator*
Ison, Christopher John *investigative reporter*
Jackson, J. David *lawyer*
Jacob, Bernard Michel *architect*
†Jacobs, Irwin Lawrence *diversified corporate executive*
Jarboe, Mark Alan *lawyer*
†Jeffries, Mary L. *public relations executive*
†Jensen, Robert P. *investment banking executive*
Jensen, Roland Jens *utility company executive*
Johnson, Cheryl *newspaper columnist*
Johnson, Clark Eugene, Jr. *electronics and computer company executive, magnetics physicist*
Johnson, David Wolcott *psychologist, educator*
†Johnson, Donald Clay *librarian, curator*
Johnson, Eugene Laurence *lawyer*
†Johnson, Gary Leroy *publisher*
Johnson, Gary M. *lawyer*
Johnson, John Warren *association executive*
Johnson, Larry Walter *lawyer*
Johnson, Lloyd Peter *banker*
Johnson, Paul Owen *lawyer*
Johnson, Sankey Anton *manufacturing company executive*
Johnson, Scott William *lawyer, manufacturing company executive*
Johnson, Vernon A. *retired labor saving equipment company executive*
Johnson, Walter Kline *civil engineer*
Jones, Bradley Mitchell *lawyer*
Jones, Norman M. *finance executive*
Jones, Thomas Walter *astrophysics educator, researcher*
Jones, Will (William Arnold) *writer, former newspaper columnist*
Joseph, Burton M. *grain merchant*
Joseph, Daniel Donald *aeronautical engineer, educator*
Joseph, Geri Mack (Geraldine Joseph) *former ambassador, educator*

Joseph, Marilyn Susan gynecologist
Kain, Richard Yerkes electrical engineer, researcher, educator
Kallok, Michael John physiologist, research administrator
Kampf, William Ira lawyer
Kane, Robert Lewis public health educator
Kapanke, John church administator
Kaplan, Manuel E. physician, educator
Kaplan, Sheldon lawyer
Karan, Bradlee lawyer, educator
Karigan, James Andrew lawyer
Keane, William Francis nephrology educator, research foundation executive
Kelly, A. David lawyer
Kelly, Tom (Jay Thomas Kelly) major league baseball club manager
Kelts, Kerry R. geology educator
Kennedy, B(yrl) J(ames) medicine and oncology educator
Keppel, William James lawyer
Keyes, Jeffrey J. lawyer
Kidwell, David Stephen academic administrator
Kilbourn, William Douglas, Jr. law educator
Kilzer, Louis Charles journalist
Kinderwater, Joseph C. (Jack Kinderwater) publishing company executive
King, Lyndel Irene Saunders art museum director
King, Richard Harding financial consultant, retired food processing company executive
King, Robert Cotton association consultant
Kinney, Earl Robert mutual funds company executive
Kirby, John D. lawyer
Kirshbaum, Jane Kaplan lawyer
Kitchak, Peter Ramon lawyer
Klaas, Paul Barry lawyer
Kling, Richard William financial services executive
Klobuchar, James John columnist
Knoke, David Harmon sociology educator
Knopman, David S. neurologist
Koeppen, Bart law educator, consultant
Kohlstedt, Sally Gregory history educator
Kolehmainen, Jan Waldroy association executive
Koneck, John M. lawyer
Konopka, Gisela Peiper (Mrs. Erhardt Paul Konopka) social worker, author, lecturer, educator
Korotkin, Fred writer, philatelist
†Koschinska, Gregory Don accountant
Koutsky, Dean Roger advertising executive
Kovacevich, Richard M. banker
Kralewski, John Edward health service administration educator
Kramer, Joel Roy journalist, newspaper executive
Kramp, Richard William biotechnology executive
Kraut, Gerald Anthony investment banker
Krislov, Samuel political science educator
Krohnke, Duane W. lawyer
Kruse, Paul Walters, Jr. physicist, consultant
Kudrle, Robert Thomas economist, educator
Kuhi, Leonard Vello astronomer, university administrator
Kvalseth, Tarald Oddvar mechanical engineer, educator
Laettner, Christian Donald professional basketball player
Laing, Karel Ann magazine publishing executive
Lambert, Robert Frank electrical engineer, educator
Landry, Paul Leonard lawyer
Langer, Leonard O., Jr. radiologist, educator
Lareau, Richard George lawyer
Larkin, Eugene David artist, educator
Larson, Dale Irving lawyer
Larson, Earl Richard federal judge
Layton, Edwin Thomas, Jr. science and technology history educator, writer
Lazar, Raymond Michael lawyer, educator
Lebedoff, David M. lawyer, author
Lebedoff, Jonathan Galanter federal judge
Lebedoff, Randy Miller lawyer
Lee, E. Bruce electrical engineering educator
Lee, Joe R. food products company executive
†Lee, Robert Lloyd pastor, religious association executive
Lehmberg, Stanford Eugene historian, educator
LeMond, Gregory James former professional bicycle racer
Leon, Arthur Sol research cardiologist, exercise physiologist
Leppert, Richard David humanities educator
Lerner, Harry Jonas publishing company executive
†Lettmann, John William cereal manufacturing company executive
Levine, John David lawyer
Levitt, Seymour Herbert physician, radiology educator
Levy, Robert Joseph lawyer, educator
Lindau, James H. grain exchange executive
Lindell, Edward Albert former college president, religious organization administrator
Lindgren, D(erbin) Kenneth, Jr. lawyer
Liszt, Howard Paul advertising executive
Liu, Benjamin Young-hwai engineering educator
Loh, Horace H. pharmacology educator
Loud, Warren Simms mathematician
Lubben, David J. lawyer
Luepker, Russell Vincent epidemiology educator
Luiso, Anthony international food company executive
Lumry, Rufus Worth, II chemist, educator
Luthringshauser, Daniel Rene manufacturing company executive
Macke, Kenneth A. retail executive
MacLaughlin, Harry Hunter federal judge
MacMillan, Whitney food products and import/export company executive
Magnuson, Roger James lawyer
Mahaffey, Gary John architect
Mahoney, Jerry C. D. lawyer
Malfeld, Diane D. lawyer
Mammel, Russell Norman retired food distribution company executive
Manning, Patrick James veterinarian, experimental pathologist, educator
Manning, William Henry lawyer
Manthey, Thomas Richard lawyer
Markopoulos, Andrew John retail executive
Marks, Florence Carlin Elliott nursing informaticist
Markus, Lawrence retired mathematics educator
Marshak, Marvin Lloyd physicist, educator
Marshall, Sherrie newspaper editor
Martenson, Edward Allen theater manager
Martin, Kathleen Minder lawyer
†Martin, Le Roy accounting firm executive
Martin, Phillip Hammond lawyer
Martin, Roger Bond landscape architect, educator
Matson, Wesley Jennings educational administrator
Matthews, James Shadley lawyer
Maurer, Evan Maclyn art museum director
Mazze, Roger Steven medical educator, researcher
McBurney, Thomas Ross food company executive
McClintock, George Dunlap lawyer
McDonald, William Andrew classics educator
McEnroe, Paul reporter
McErlane, Joseph James insurance company executive
McGlynn, Michael James bakery company executive
McGuire, Timothy James newspaper editor, lawyer
McHale, Kevin Edward former professional basketball player
McKenna, Robert J. car rental company executive
†McMurry, Peter Howard mechanical engineer, educator
McQuarrie, Donald Gray surgeon, educator
Meador, Ron newspaper editor, writer
Meehl, Paul Everett psychologist, educator
Mellum, Gale Robert lawyer
Melrose, Kendrick Bascom manufacturing company executive
Meshbesher, Ronald I. lawyer
Meyer, Maurice Wesley physiologist, dentist, neurologist
Michael, Alfred Frederick, Jr. physician, medical educator
Miller, Donald Muxlow accountant, administrator
Miller, John William, Jr. bassoonist
Miller, Willard, Jr. mathematician, educator
Miller, William Alvin clergyman, author
Minish, Robert Arthur lawyer
Mitau, Lee R. lawyer
Mitchell, James Austin insurance company executive
Moe, Thomas O. lawyer
†Mohr, L. Thomas newspaper executive
Monson, Dianne Lynn literacy educator
Montgomery, Henry Irving financial planner
Mooty, John William lawyer
Moraczewski, Robert Leo publisher
Morath, Julianne Mollie nursing administrator
Morgan, Arthur Edward technology company executive
Morgan, Carol Miró marketing executive
Morris, C. Robert law educator
Morris, David Hugh manufacturing and marketing executive
Morrison, Clinton banker
Morrison, Fred LaMont law educator
†Morrison, John Lewis former food company executive, investor
Mortenson, M. A., Jr. construction executive
Moscowitz, Albert Joseph chemist, educator
Murphy, Diana E. federal judge
Murphy, Joseph Edward, Jr. broadcast executive
Myers, Malcolm Haynie artist, art educator
Nagel, Paul Chester historian, writer, lecturer
Najarian, John Sarkis surgeon, educator
Nathan, Marshall Ira electrical engineering educator
Nelson, Glen David medical products executive, physician
Nelson, Richard Arthur lawyer
Nelson, Steven Craig lawyer
Nestor, Susan E. health services executive
Neumann, L. N. grain company executive
Newman, Margaret Ann nursing educator
Nicholson, Bruce J. insurance company executive
Nilles, John Michael lawyer
Nitsche, Johannes Carl Christian mathematics educator
Noonan, Thomas Schaub history educator, Russian studies educator
Norberg, Arthur Lawrence, Jr. historian, physicist educator
Norton, Elizabeth Wychgel lawyer
Nyrop, Donald William airline executive
Ogata, Katsuhiko engineering educator
O'Keefe, Daniel P. lawyer
O'Keefe, Thomas Michael foundation executive
Oliver, Edward Carl state senator, retired investment executive
Olson, Clifford Larry management consultant, entrepreneur
Olson, Ronald Dale grain company executive
Olson, Theodore Alexander former environmental biology educator
O'Neill, Brian Boru lawyer
Oppenheimer, Jack Hans internist, scientist, educator
Oriani, Richard Anthony metallurgical engineering educator
†Pajor, Robert E. paint and plastics company executive
Palmer, Brian Eugene lawyer
Palmer, Deborah Jean lawyer
Palms, Roger Curtis religious magazine editor, clergyman
Paparella, Michael M. otolaryngologist
Parker, Leonard Sam architect, educator
Parkinson, Roger P. publishing company executive
Patterson, Joan Marie maternal/child health educator, psychologist
Payne, Elizabeth Eleanore surgeon, otolaryngologist
Payne, William Bruce lawyer
Pazandak, Carol Hendrickson liberal arts educator
Pedoe, Daniel mathematician, writer, artist
Perlman, Lawrence technology company executive
Persson, Erland Karl electrical engineer
Pfender, Emil mechanical engineering educator
Pfleider, James Kenneth motivation company executive
Phibbs, Clifford Matthew surgeon, educator
Philipson, Willard Dale curriculum and instructional educator
Pile, Robert Bennett advertising executive, writer, consultant
†Pilgrim, Richard D. engineering company executive
Pillsbury, George Sturgis investment adviser
Piper, Addison Lewis securities executive
Pitt, Helen K. nurse, hospital administrator
Pluimer, Edward J. lawyer
Poehling, Robert Edward plumbing supply company executive
Pohlad, Carl R. professional baseball team executive, bottling company executive
Porter, Philip Wayland geography educator
Porter, William L. electrical engineer
Portoghese, Philip Salvatore medicinal chemist, educator
Potuznik, Charles Laddy lawyer
Pour-El, Marian Boykan mathematician, educator
Prager, Stephen chemistry educator
Pratte, Robert John lawyer
Prem, Konald Arthur physician, educator
Preuss, Roger E(mil) artist
Price, Joseph Michael lawyer
Puckett, Kirby professional baseball player
Quie, Paul Gerhardt physician, educator
Rachie, Cyrus lawyer
Radmer, Michael John lawyer, educator
Rahman, Yueh-Erh biologist
Rahn, Alvin Albert former banker
Rand, Peter Anders architect
Rand, Sidney Anders retired college administrator
Ranheim, David A. lawyer
Rapson, Ralph architect, educator
Rath, R. John historian, educator
Ratner, Harvey professional basketball team owner
Rauenhorst, Gerald design and construction company executive
Read, John Conyers management consultant
Rebane, John T. lawyer
Reichgott Junge, Ember D. state legislator, lawyer
Reilly, George lawyer
Rein, Stanley Michael lawyer
Reinhart, Robert Rountree, Jr. lawyer
Reiss, Ira Leonard sociology educator, writer
Reister, Raymond Alex lawyer
Renier, James J. diversified electronic equipment manufacturing company executive
Retzler, Kurt Egon diversified management company executive, hospitality, travel and marketing company executive
Reuter, James William lawyer
Reynolds, David G(eorge) physiologist, educator
Robins, Michael Harry theater executive producing director
Rockenstein, Walter Harrison, II lawyer
Rockwell, Winthrop Adams lawyer
Roe, John H. manufacturing company executive
Rogers, David apparel executive
Rogers, William Cecil political science educator
Rohr, Daniel C. banker
Rose, Thomas Albert artist, art educator
Rosen, Judah Ben computer scientist
Rosenbaum, James Michael federal judge
Ross, Donald, Jr. English language educator, university administrator
Ross, Percy Nathan business executive, newspaper columnist
Rubens, Sidney Michel physicist, technical advisor
Rudelius, William marketing educator
Ruvelson, Alan Kenneth investment company executive
Sabath, Leon David internist, educator
Saeks, Allen Irving lawyer
Safley, James Robert lawyer
†St Germain, George retail executive
Salyer, Stephen Lee broadcast executive
Sampson, John Eugene food company executive
Sanger, Stephen W. consumer products company executive
Sanner, Royce Norman lawyer
Satorius, John Arthur lawyer
Saunders, R. Reed financial services company executive
Savelkoul, Donald Charles lawyer
Sawchuk, Ronald John pharmaceutical scientist, educator
Scallen, Stephen Burns law educator
Scallen, Thomas Kaine broadcasting executive
Scheerer, Paul J. lawyer
†Schmidt, Lanny D. chemical engineering educator and researcher, physical chemist
Schnell, Robert Lee, Jr. lawyer
Schnobrich, Roger William lawyer
Schoettle, Ferdinand P. lawyer, educator
Schofield, William psychologist, educator
Schreiner, John Christian economics consultant, software publisher
Schuh, G(eorge) Edward university dean, agricultural economist
Schultz, Louis Edwin management consultant
Schulze, Arthur Robert, Jr. food company executive
Schwartzbauer, Robert Alan lawyer
Scott, Robert Lee speech educator
Scoville, James Griffin economics educator
Scriven, L. E(dward) chemical engineering educator, scientist
Seaman, William Casper retired news photographer
Serrin, James Burton mathematics educator
†Severinson, Kenneth J. athletic and electronic equipment manufacturing executive
Shapiro, Burton Leonard experimental pathologist, geneticist, educator
Shapiro, Fred Louis physician, educator
Shaughnessy, Thomas William librarian, consultant
Sheehy, Lee Edward lawyer
Sherry, Suzanna law educator
Shiels, Barbara L. lawyer
Shipp, Roger Lee finance company executive
Shively, William Phillips political scientist, educator
Shnider, Bruce Jay lawyer
Shulman, Yechiel engineering educator
†Siepmann, Joern Ilja chemistry educator
Silverman, Robert Joseph lawyer
Skrowaczewski, Stanislaw conductor, composer
Slagle, James Robert computer science educator
Slorp, John S. academic administrator
Slovut, Gordon reporter
Smetanka, Mary Jane reporter
Smith, Eldred Reid library educator
†Smith, Norman E. metal products executive
Snyder, Richard Allen manufacturing executive, accountant, treasurer
Somrock, John Douglas electronic marketing and manufacturing executive
Sonkowsky, Robert Paul classicist, educator, actor
Sorbo, Allen Jon actuary, consultant
Sowada, Alphonse Augustus bishop
Sparrow, Ephraim Maurice mechanical engineering scientist, educator
Speer, David James public relations executive
Spencer, David James lawyer
Spinner, Robert Keith hospital administrator
Spoor, William Howard food company executive
Sprenger, Gordon M. hospital administrator
Spring, John Benham car rental company executive
Staba, Emil John pharmacognosy and medicinal chemistry educator
Steilen, James R. lawyer
Stein, Bob professional basketball team executive
Stenwick, Michael William internist, geriatric medicine consultant
Sterling, Raymond Leslie civil engineering educator, researcher, consultant
Stern, Leo G. lawyer
Stodder, John Wesley jewelry company executive
Strickler, Jeff newspaper movie critic
Stroup, Stanley Stephenson lawyer, educator
Struyk, Robert John lawyer
†Stuart, John Malcolm public defender
Stubbs, Jan Didra travel industry executive
Stuebner, James Cloyd real estate developer, contractor
Sullivan, Austin P(adraic), Jr. diversified food company executive
Sullivan, Michael Patrick food service executive
Susanka, Sarah Hills architect
Sveinson, Pamela J. human resources executive
Swaiman, Kenneth Fred pediatric neurologist, educator
Swanson, Lloyd Oscar former savings and loan association executive
Swartz, Donald Everett television executive
Swatsky, Ben church administrator
Symchych, Janice M. lawyer
Tagatz, George Elmo obstetrician, gynecologist, educator
†Tanner, Travis travel company executive
Teachout, Noreen Ruth writer
†Theisen, Edwin Mathew utility company executive
Thompson, Leonard Allen insurance sales and marketing specialist, consultant
Thompson, Theodore Robert pediatric educator
Thompson, William Moreau radiologist, educator
Thornton, John T. corporate financial executive
†Tibbetts, Pamela Lee health facility administrator
Tinkham, Thomas W. lawyer
†Tirrell, Matthew chemical engineering/materials science educator
Todd, John Joseph lawyer
Torres, Gerald law educator
Toscano, James Vincent medical institute administration
Toupin, Harold Ovid chemical company executive
Tracy, James Donald historian
Tree, David L. advertising agency executive
Trestman, Frank D. distribution company executive
Trucano, Michael lawyer
Truhlar, Donald Gene chemist, educator
Tufte, Obert Norman retired research executive
Turner, John Gosney insurance company executive
Tygesson, Gary Lincoln lawyer
Ueland, Sigurd, Jr. lawyer
†Ulrich, Robert J. retail discount chain stores executive
Vander Molen, Thomas Dale lawyer
Van Dyke, William Grant manufacturing company executive
Van Housen, Thomas Corwin, III architect, designer, builder
Vaughan, Peter Hugh theater critic
Vecoli, Rudolph John history educator
Viera, James Joseph financial executive
Wade, Lewis V. mineral research director
Wahoske, Michael James lawyer
Wainwright, Charles Anthony advertising company executive
Waldera, Wayne Eugene crisis management specialist
Walker, Elva Mae Dawson health consultant
Waller, Joel N. consumer products executive
Wallin, Winston Roger manufacturing company executive
Walsh, Paul S. food products executive
Walter, Frank Sherman retired health care corporation executive
Walters, Glen Robert banker
Walters, Jay B. banker
Wang, L. Edwin church official
Ward, David Allen sociology educator
Ward, Wallace Dixon medical educator
Ware, D. Clifton singer, educator
Warner, William Hamer applied mathematician
Warwick, Warren J. pediatrics educator
†Watkins, James David food products executive
Watson, Catherine Elaine journalist
Watson, Dennis Wallace microbiology educator, scientist
Webb, Martha Jeanne film producer
†Weber, Don finance company executive
Webster, Melville Jay, III bank executive
†Wegmiller, Donald Charles health care corporation executive
Weinberg, Richard Alan psychologist
Weir, Edward Kenneth cardiologist
Weisberg, Leonard R. research and engineering executive, retired
Weiss, Gerhard Hans German language educator
Weiss, James Michael financial analyst, portfolio manager
Weissbrodt, David Samuel law educator
Welch, David C. advertising agency executive
Weyler, Walter Eugen manufacturing company executive
White, James George pediatrician, hematologist, pathologist, educator
White, Robert James newspaper editor, columnist
Whitehill, Clifford Lane lawyer
Whitlock, William Abel lawyer
Wickesberg, Albert Klumb retired management educator
Wiener, Daniel Norman psychologist
†Wilbur, David E., Jr. chemicals executive
Wild, John Julian physician, director medical research institute
Wille, Karin L. lawyer
Willes, Mark Hinckley food industry executive
Willis, Raymond Edson strategic management and organization educator
Wilson, Leonard Gilchrist history of medicine educator
Windhorst, John William, Jr. lawyer
Wine, Mark Philip lawyer
Winter, Robert Bruce orthopaedic surgeon, educator
Wolfenson, Marv professional basketball team executive
Wolff, Larry F. dental educator, researcher
Wood, Joseph George neurobiologist, educator
Woods, Robert Edward lawyer
Wright, Frank Gardner newspaper editor
Wright, Herbert E(dgar), Jr. geologist
Wright, Michael William wholesale food company executive
Wurtele, Christopher Angus paint and coatings company executive
Wyman, James Thomas petroleum company executive
†Yonas, Albert psychology educator
Youngblood, Richard Neil columnist
Younger, Judith Tess lawyer, educator
Yourzak, Robert Joseph management consultant, engineer, educator
Ysseldyke, James Edward psychology educator, research center administrator
Yuen, David Alexander geophysics and computational physics educator
Zalk, Robert H. lawyer
Ziebarth, E. William news analyst, educator
†Ziegenhagen, David M. healthcare company executive

Minnetonka

Ehlert, John Ambrose publisher
Eugster, Jack Wilson retail executive

Gillies, Donald Richard advertising agency and marketing consultant
Henningsen, Peter, Jr. diversified industry executive
Johnson, Kay Durbahn real estate manager, consultant
List, Charles Edward management and organization development consultant
Maxwell, Robert Oliver insurance company executive
Mc Guire, William W. health maintenance organization executive
Palmer, John Marshall lawyer
Randall, Dean Bowman retired electronics manufacturing company executive
Robbins, Orem Olford insurance company executive
Rogers, James Devitt judge
Sorensen, Stuart L. actuary
Vanstrom, Marilyn June retired elementary education educator

Minnetonka Mills
Hoard, Heidi Marie lawyer

Moorhead
Anderson, Jerry Maynard speech educator
Coomber, James Elwood English language educator
Dille, Roland Paul college president
Gee, Robert LeRoy agriculturist, dairy farmer
Heuer, Gerald Arthur mathematician, educator
Noblitt, Harding Coolidge political scientist, educator
Nyquist, Robert sugar company executive
Revzen, Joel conductor
Rimmereid, Arthur V. bishop
Sinner, George Albert former state governor, farmer, corporate executive
Sun, Li-Teh economics educator
Trainor, John Felix retired economics educator
Treumann, William Borgen university dean

Morris
Johnson, David Chester university chancellor, sociology educator
Kahng, Sun Myong economics educator
Kemble, Ernest Dell psychology educator
Ordway, Ellen biology educator, entomology researcher

New Brighton
†Sharma, Raghu Nandan engineering executive
Shier, Gloria Bulan mathematics educator

New Ulm
Lucker, Raymond Alphonse bishop

Nisswa
Marmas, James Gust retired businees educator, retired college dean

Northfield
Appleyard, David Frank mathematics and computer science educator
Berwald, Helen Dorothy education educator
Bonner, Robert Elliott dean
Buchwald, Caryl Edward geology educator, environmental consultant, educational consultant
Burton, Alice Jean biology educator
Casper, Barry Michael physics educator
Clark, Clifford Edward, Jr. history educator
Clark, William Hartley political science educator
Crouter, Richard Earl religion educator
Dittmann, Reidar art educator
†Edwards, Mark U., Jr. college president, history educator, author
Flaten, Robert Arnold ambassador, retired
Foss, Harlan Funston religious education educator, academic administrator
Haworth, Dale Keith art history educator, gallery director
Hong, Howard Vincent library administrator, philosophy educator, editor, translator
Hvistendahl, Joyce Kilmer journalism and communications educator
Iseminger, Gary H. philosophy educator
Lamson, George Herbert economics educator
†Lewis, Stephen Richmond, Jr. economist, academic administrator
Lloyd, Timothy L. art educator
Mason, Perry Carter philosophy educator
McDonnell, James English educator
McKinsey, Elizabeth college dean
Metz, T(heodore) John librarian, consultant
Morral, Frank Rolf English educator, psychologist
Noer, Richard J. physics educator, researcher
†Paas, John Roger German language educator
Ramette, Richard Wales chemistry educator
Schuster, Seymour mathematician, educator
Sipfle, David Arthur philosophy educator
Sostek, Edward Leon theater educator, director
Soth, Lauren art history educator
Soule, George Alan literature educator
Sovik, Edward Anders architect, consultant
†Steen, Lynn Arthur mathematician, educator
Will, Robert Erwin economics educator
Yandell, Cathy Marleen foreign language educator
Zelliot, Eleanor Mae history educator

Osseo
Haun, James William chemical engineer, retired food company executive, consultant
Hersch, Russell LeRoy secondary education educator
Ramsey, Mark school system administrator
†Spencer, Dale A. medical products executive

Ottertail
†Hanson, Al financial newsletter editor and publisher

Owatonna
Buxton, Charles Ingraham, II insurance company executive
Nelson, Kirk N. insurance company executive

Park Rapids
McNulty-Majors, Susan Rose special education administrator
Tonn, Robert James entomologist

Pipestone
Scott, William Paul lawyer

Plymouth
Fowler, James D., Jr. manufacturing company financial executive
Friswold, Fred Ravndahl manufacturing executive
Froemming, Herbert Dean retail executive
Kahler, Herbert Frederick diversified business executive

Red Wing
Seymour, Arthur Hallock retired newspaper editor

Redlake
Ceterski, Dorothy nutritionist

Richfield
†Thompson, Steve Allan writer

Robbinsdale
Anderson, Scott Robbins hospital administrator

Rochester
Anderson, James Gerard hospital administrator
Bartholomew, Lloyd Gibson physician
Beahrs, Oliver Howard surgeon
†Beckett, Victoria Ling physician
Berge, Kenneth George retired internist, educator
Bisel, Harry Ferree oncologist
Brimijoin, William Stephen pharmacology educator, neuroscience researcher
Bulbulian, Arthur H. biomedical scientist, medical graphics and facial prosthetics specialist
Butt, Hugh Roland gastroenterologist, educator
Carlson, Roger Allan manufacturing company executive, accountant
Corbin, Kendall Brooks physician, scientist
Danielson, Gordon Kenneth, Jr. cardiovascular surgeon, educator
DeRemee, Richard Arthur physician, educator, researcher
†Dickson, Edgar Rolland gastroenterologist
Douglass, Bruce E. physician
Du Shane, James William physician, educator
Engel, Andrew George neurologist
Feldt, Robert Hewitt pediatric cardiologist, educator
Gastineau, Clifford Felix retired physician
Gervais, Sister Generose hospital consultant
Gilchrist, Gerald Seymour pediatric hematologist, oncologist, educator
Gomez, Manuel Rodriguez physician
Gracey, Douglas Robert physician, physiologist, educator
Hattery, Robert R. radiologist, educator
Hudson, Winthrop Still minister, history educator
Huffine, Coy Lee retired chemical engineer, consultant
Husband, Richard Lorin, Sr. consulting company executive
Kao, Pai Chih clinical chemist
Kempers, Roger Dyke obstetrics and gynecology educator
Key, Jack Dayton librarian
Keys, Thomas Edward medical library consultant
Krom, Ruud Arne Finco surgeon
Kurland, Leonard Terry epidemiologist educator
Kyle, Robert Arthur medical educator, oncologist
Lantz, William Charles lawyer
Larson, April U. bishop
Leachman, Roger Mack librarian
Leonard, David Arthur hospital executive emeritus
Lofgren, Karl Adolph surgeon
Lucas, Alexander Ralph child psychiatrist, educator
Malkasian, George Durand, Jr. physician, educator
Martin, Gordon Mather physician, educator, administrator
Martin, Maurice John psychiatrist
Mc Conahey, William McConnell, Jr. physician, educator
Mc Goon, Dwight Charles retired surgeon, educator
Michenfelder, John Donahue anesthesiology educator
Milner, Harold William hotel executive
Morlock, Carl Grismore physician, medical educator
Mulder, Donald William physician, educator
Muller, Sigfrid Augustine dermatologist, educator
Neel, Harry Bryan, III surgeon, scientist, educator
Nichols, Donald Richardson medical educator
Nycklemoe, Glenn Winston bishop
Olsen, Arthur Martin physician, educator
†Opitz, Joachim Ludwig physiatrist
Payne, W(illiam) Spencer retired surgeon
Perry, Harold Otto dermatologist
Phillips, Sidney Frederick gastroenterologist
Pittelkow, Mark Robert dermatology educator, researcher
Polley, Howard Freeman physician
Pratt, Joseph Hyde, Jr. surgeon
Reitemeier, Richard Joseph physician
Riggs, Byron Lawrence, Jr. physician, educator
Rosenow, Edward Carl, III medical educator
Seeger, Ronald L. lawyer
Shepherd, John Thompson physiologist
†Shulman, Carole Karen professional society administrator
Siekert, Robert George neurologist
Spencer, Edson White computer systems company executive
Stillwell, G(eorge) Keith physician
Symmonds, Richard Earl gynecologist
Szurszewski, Joseph Henry physiologist
Waller, Robert Rex ophthalmologist, educator, foundation executive
Whisnant, Jack Page neurologist
Wicks, John R. lawyer
Wojcik, Martin Henry foundation development official
Wood, Earl Howard physiologist, educator
Woods, John Elmer plastic surgeon

Rosemount
Bohan, Wanda M. secondary school educator
Walter, Kenneth Luverne agricultural facility director

Roseville
Berry, James Frederick biochemistry educator
†Be Vier, William A. religious studies educator

Saginaw
Stauber, Marilyn Jean educator, consultant

Saint Cloud
Berling, John George academic dean
Bess, Robert O. academic administrator
Gruys, Robert Irving physician, surgeon
Henry, Edward LeRoy former foundation executive, consultant, college president, public official
Hofsommer, Donovan Lowell educator, consultant
Kallhoff, Sister Catherine school system administrator
Lindula, Pamela O'Hara lawyer
Pribble, Edward David Lalor labor and employment arbitrator, lawyer
†Thrune, Elaine M. biotechnician
Wertz, John Alan secondary school educator

Saint Joseph
O'Connell, Sister Colman college president, nun
Rowland, Howard Ray mass communications educator

Saint Louis Park
Dooley, David J. elementary school principal
Gerike, Ann Elizabeth psychologist
Knighton, David Reed vascular surgeon, educator
Rothenberg, Elliot Calvin lawyer, writer
Svendsbye, Lloyd August college president, clergyman, educator

Saint Paul
Alsop, Donald Douglas federal judge
Andersen, Anthony L. chemical company executive
Andersen, Elmer Lee manufacturing and publishing executive, former governor of Minnesota
†Anderson, John Freeman marketing executive
Anderson, Tim airport terminal executive
Appelhof, Ruth Stevens museum director, curator, art historian
Archabal, Nina M(archetti) historical society director
Asch, Marc consultant
Ashton, Sister Mary Madonna healthcare administrator
Assink, Brent E. performing arts executive
†Aune, R. Benjamin healthcare alliance administrator
Baker, Donald Gardner retired soil science educator
Baker, Thomas F. agricultural grain company executive
Barnwell, Franklin Hershel zoology educator
Baukol, Ronald Oliver manufacturing company executive
Benson, Joanne lieutenant governor
Berglin, Linda state senator
Bertram, Jeff Nickolas farmer, state legislator
Best, Eugene Crawford, Jr. musician
Betz, Charles W. manufacturing company executive
Betzold, Donald Richard state senator
Bingham, Christopher statistics educator
Bjorklund, Frederick savings and loan association executive
Bloomfield, Coleman insurance company executive
Bloomfield, Victor Alfred biochemistry educator
Boehnen, David Leo grocery company executive, lawyer
Bothun, Donald Dean controller
Boudreau, James Lawton insurance company executive
Bremer, Victor John broadcasting executive
Brink, John William financial corporation executive
Brooks, Conley, Jr. investment management executive
Brown, Kay state legislator
Brushaber, George Karl academic president, minister
Buckheit, James E. primary and secondary education administrator
Burchell, Howard Bertram retired physician, educator
Burnside, Orvin Charles agronomy educator, researcher
Bushnell, William Rodgers agricultural research scientist
Caldwell, Elwood Fleming food science educator, researcher, editor
Carlson, Arne Helge governor
Carlson, Lyndon Richard state legislator, educator
Carlson, Marjorie J. retired church administrator
Carruthers, Philip Charles lawyer
Checchi, Alfred A. airline company executive
Cheng, H(wei) H(sien) soil scientist, agriculture and environmental scie
Chiang, Huai Chang entomologist, educator
Clapp, C(harles) Edward research chemist, soil biochemistry educator
Clark, Karen state legislator
Clark, Ronald Dean newspaper editor
Clary, Bradley Grayson lawyer, educator
Close, Elizabeth Scheu architect
Close, Winston Arthur retired architect
†Coleman, Norm mayor
Collins, Theodore Joseph lawyer, educator
Corn, Joseph Edward, Jr. arts management consultant
Coyne, M(ary) Jeanne state supreme court justice
Crippin, Byron Miles, Jr. lawyer, religious organization professional, consultant
Crookston, Robert Kent agronomy educator
Culp, Bethany Kelly lawyer
Cummings, Roger David powder coatings consultant, sales executive
Czarnecki, Caroline MaryAnne veterinary anatomy educator
Czarniecki, Myron James, III art museum director, cultural planner
Dahl, Reynold Paul agricultural economics educator
Dalton, Howard Edward accounting executive
Daly, Joseph Leo law educator
Davis, Margaret Bryan paleoecology researcher, educator
Desimone, Livio Diego diversified manufacturing company executive
Diesch, Stanley La Verne veterinarian, educator
Dietz, Charlton Henry lawyer
Dille, Stephen Everett farmer, state legislator, veterinarian
Doctor, Kenneth Jay editor
Doermann, Humphrey foundation administrator
Dunlop, Robert Hugh veterinary medicine educator
Dyrstad, Joanell M. former lieutenant governor
Ebert, Robert Alvin retired lawyer, retired airline executive
Edwards, Jesse Efrem physician, educator
Ehramjian, Vartkes Hagop manufacturing company financial executive
Ek, Alan Ryan forestry educator
Elrod, Bernett Richard (Sam Elrod) newspaper editor
Enfield, Franklin D. geneticist
Engle, Donald Edward retired railway executive, lawyer
Estenson, Noel K. gas, oil industry executive
Faricy, Richard Thomas architect
Farnum, Sylvia Arlyce physical chemist
Feinberg, David Erwin publishing company executive
Fesler, David Richard foundation director
†Fetrow, John Patrick veterinary medicine educator
Fingerson, Leroy Malvin engineering executive, mechanical engineer
Finnegan, John Robert, Sr. retired newspaper executive
Flynn, Harry Joseph bishop
Fogg, James W. printing company executive
Fogg, Richard Lloyd food products company executive
Frame, Clarence George retired oil and gas refining company executive
†Francis, D. Max healthcare management executive
Frederickson, Dennis Russel state legislator, farmer
Friel, Bernard Preston lawyer
Fryxell, David Allen publishing executive, newspaper editor
Fuchs, James A. biochemistry educator
Fuller, Benjamin Franklin physician, educator
Galvin, Michael John, Jr. lawyer
Gardebring, Sandra S. judge
†Garland, Robert Field health facility executive
Garretson, Donald Everett retired manufacturing company executive
Gavin, Robert Michael, Jr. college president
Gehrz, Robert Gustave retired railroad executive
Geis, Jerome Arthur lawyer, legal educator
Goff, Lila Johnson historical society administrator
Goodman, Lawrence Eugene structural analyst, educator
Goodrich, Leon Raymond lawyer
Graham, Charles John university educator, former university president
Green, Philip Bevington publishing company executive
Grieve, Pierson MacDonald specialty chemicals and services company executive
Growe, Joan Anderson state official
Halverson, Richard Paul investment management company executive
Hammond, Frank Joseph lawyer
Hansen, Robyn L. lawyer
Hanson, Allen Dennis grain marketing and processing cooperative executive
Hanson, Paula E. state legislator
Haukoos, Melvin Robert state representative
Haverty, Harold V. forms and check printing company executive
Haynsworth, Harry Jay, IV lawyer, educator
†Heasley, Philip financial services company executive
Heidenreich, Douglas Robert lawyer
Herman, William Sparkes zoology educator
Hill, James Stanley computer consulting company executive
Holbert, Sue Elisabeth archivist, writer, consultant
Holmen, Reynold Emanuel chemist
Hopper, David Henry religion educator
Hubbard, Stanley Stub broadcast executive
Huber, Sister Alberta college president
Huber, Allan J. diversified manufacturing company executive
†Hudson, Gail Brown television news producer
Hughes, Jerome Michael state senator, educator
Humphrey, Hubert Horatio, III state attorney general
†Jacob, Rosamond Tryon librarian
Janavaras, Basil John business consultant, business educator
Jensen, James Robert dentist, educator
Jessup, Paul Frederick financial economist, educator
Johnson, Kenneth Harvey veterinary pathologist
Johnson, Margaret Ann library administrator
Johnson, Paul Oren lawyer
Jones, C. Paul lawyer, educator
Jones, Thomas Neal manufacturing executive, mechanical engineer
Kane, Lucile Marie archivist, historian
Kane, Patricia Lanegran language professional, educator
Kane, Stanley Phillip insurance company executive
Kane, Thomas Patrick lawyer
Kaner, Harvey Sheldon lawyer, executive
Keffer, Charles Joseph academic administrator
Keillor, Garrison Edward writer, radio host, storyteller
Keith, Alexander MacDonald state supreme court chief justice
Kelso, Becky state legislator
Kenyon, Jane Jennifer poet, writer
Kerr, Sylvia Joann educator
Kirwin, Kenneth F. law educator
Kiscaden, Sheila M. state legislator
Kishel, Gregory Francis federal judge
Kling, William Hugh broadcasting executive
Kommedahl, Thor plant pathology educator
Kuhrmeyer, Carl Albert manufacturing company executive
Kyle, Richard House federal judge
†Lawton, Lois health facility administrator
Lay, Donald Pomeroy federal judge
Leatherdale, Douglas West insurance company executive
Lehr, Lewis Wylie diversified manufacturing company executive
Lein, Malcolm Emil architect
Leonard, Kurt John plant pathologist, university program director
Leppik, Margaret White state legislator
Levi, Arlo Dane lawyer
Lillehei, Clarence Walton surgeon
Ling, Joseph Tso-Ti manufacturing company executive, environmental engineer
Loken, James Burton federal judge
Long, Dee state legislator
Lourey, Becky J. state legislator
Lund, Bert Oscar, Jr. publisher
Lundy, Walker newspaper editor
Luther, Darlene state legislator
Lynch, Teresa Ann state legislator
MacDonald, Roderick library director
Maclin, Alan Hall lawyer
MacTaggart, Terrence Joseph academic administrator
Magee, Paul Terry geneticist and molecular biologist, college dean
Magnuson, Norris Alden librarian, history educator
Magnuson, Paul Arthur federal judge
Marty, John state senator, writer
Mason, John Milton (Jack Mason) judge
Mather, Richard Burroughs retired Chinese language and literature educator
McCollum, Betty state legislator
McCoy, Mary Ann state official
McGrath, Michael Alan state government officer
McGuire, Mary Jo state legislator
McKinnell, Robert Gilmore zoology, genetics and cell biology educator
McLaughlin, David Jordan botanist

McMillan, Mary Bigelow *retired minister, volunteer*
McNeely, John J. *lawyer*
Merrill, Arthur Lewis *retired theology educator*
Mitchell, Pamela Ann *airline pilot*
Mitsch, Ronald Allen *chemical company executive*
Molnau, Carol *state legislator*
Mondale, Theodore Adams *state senator*
Morrow, Patrice Ann *biology educator*
Mrkonich, Dorothy Evanson *nursing educator*
Murphy, Mary C. *state legislator*
Murphy, Steven Leslie *state senator, utilities company official*
Murray, Peter Bryant *English language educator*
Nash, Nicholas David *retailing executive*
Neary, Pamela *state legislator*
Nicholson, Morris Emmons, Jr. *metallurgist, educator*
Noel, Franklin Linwood *federal magistrate judge*
Nugent, Daniel Eugene *business executive*
Olson, Katy *state legislator, farmer*
Olson, Sigmund Lars *corporate finance executive*
Oppenheimer, James Richard *lawyer*
Orfield, Myron Willard, Jr. *state legislator, educator*
Osman, Stephen Eugene *historic site administrator*
Osnes, Larry G. *academic administrator*
Ostby, Ronald *dairy and food products company executive*
Ostman, Eleanor A. *food writer*
Page, Alan Cedric *judge*
Palmer, Roger Raymond *accounting educator*
Pampusch, Anita Marie *academic administrator*
Pappas, Sandra Lee *state senator*
Paulus, Stephen Harrison *composer*
†Perry, James Alfred *natural resources and policy management educator, researcher, consultant*
†Perryman, Margaret E. *hospital executive*
Peterson, James Lincoln *museum executive*
Peterson, Robert Austin *manufacturing company executive retired*
Peterson, Willis Lester *economics educator*
Phillips, Ronald Lewis *plant geneticist, educator*
Piper, Pat Kathryn *state senator*
Podolak, Douglas John *marketing consultant*
Popovich, Peter Stephen *lawyer, former state supreme court chief justice*
Powell, Linda *state education official*
Preus, David Walter *bishop, minister*
†Pustovar, Thomas M. *manufacturing executive, heavy*
Rafferty, Craig Elliot *architect, educator*
Rastogi, Anil Kumar *medical device manufacturer executive*
Renner, Robert George *federal judge*
Ridder, Bernard Herman, Jr. *newspaper publisher*
Roach, John Robert *archbishop*
Robertson, Jerry Earl *retired mining and manufacturing company executive*
Robertson, Martha Rappaport *state senator, consultant*
Rogosheske, Walter Frederick *lawyer, former state justice*
Rosengren, William R. *lawyer, corporation executive*
Rossmann, Jack Eugene *psychology educator*
Rothmeier, Steven George *merchant banker, investment manager*
Rowe, Clarence John *psychiatrist*
Ruttan, Vernon Wesley *agricultural economist*
Ryan, Lehan Jerome *lawyer*
Schafer, John Francis *plant pathologist*
Schuman, Allan L. *chemical company executive*
Seagren, Alice *state legislator*
Seymour, McNeil Vernam *lawyer*
Shannon, Michael Edward *specialty chemical company executive*
Simonett, John E. *state supreme court justice*
Sippel, William Leroy *lawyer*
Solberg, Loren Albin *state legislator, secondary education educator*
Spear, Allan Henry *state senator, historian, educator*
Stadelmann, Eduard Joseph *plant physiologist, educator*
Stewart, James Brewer *historian, author, college administrator*
Sullivan, Alfred Dewitt *university administrator*
Sullivan, William E. *public relations executive*
Tate, Jeffrey L. *biology institute administrator*
Tecco, Romuald Gilbert Louis Joseph *violinist, concertmaster*
Tester, John Robert *biologist, educator*
Thomas, Brenda C. *county official*
Thompson, Mary Eileen *chemistry educator*
Thwaits, James Arthur *manufacturing executive*
Titus, Jack L. *pathologist, educator*
Todd, Henry Reynolds, Jr. *director state tourism office*
Tomljanovich, Esther M. *judge*
Tompkins, Eileen *state legislator*
Tordoff, Harrison Bruce *retired zoologist, educator*
Trubeck, William Lewis *air transportation company executive*
Tuominen, F(rancis) William *research and engineering company executive*
Ursu, John Joseph *lawyer*
Vaughn, John Rolland *auditor*
Vellenga, Kathleen Osborne *former state legislator*
Wagenius, Jean *state representative*
Wagner, Mary Margaret *library and information science educator*
Walker, Charles Thomas *physicist, educator*
Walton, Matt Savage *geologist, educator*
†Wanek, Stephen J. *electronics executive*
Washburn, Donald Arthur *business executive*
Weiner, Carl Dorian *historian*
Wendt, Hans W. *life scientist*
Whelpley, Dennis Porter *lawyer*
†White, Duane E. *mortgage company executive*
Williams, Chester Arthur, Jr. *insurance educator*
Wollner, Thomas Edward *manufacturing company executive*
Zander, Janet Adele *psychiatrist*
Zeyen, Richard John *plant pathology educator*
Zylstra, Stanley James *farmer, food company executive*

Saint Peter
Haeuser, Michael John *library administrator*
Mc Rostie, Clair Neil *economics educator*
Nelsen, William Cameron *foundation president, former college president*
Ostrom, Don *state legislator, political science educator*

Scandia
Borchert, John Robert *geography educator*

Slayton
Anderson, Merlyn Dean *lawyer*

South Saint Paul
Kampmeier, Donald George *livestock association executive*
Pugh, Thomas Wilfred *lawyer*

Spicer
Wescoe, W(illiam) Clarke *physician*

Spring Grove
Hellyer, Clement David *writer*
Roverud, Eleanor *pathologist, neuropathologist*

Spring Park
Nelson, Craig Wayne *academy administrator*

Stillwater
Anderson, Burnell *principal*
Asch, Susan McClellan *pediatrician*
Carter, Orwin L. *chemical executive*
O'Brien, Daniel William *lawyer, corporation executive*
Sowman, Harold Gene *ceramic engineer, researcher*

Victoria
Courtney, Eugene Whitmal *computer company executive*

Virginia
Knabe, George William, Jr. *pathologist, educator*

Waseca
Frederick, Edward Charles *university official*

Waubun
Christensen, Marvin Nelson *venture capitalist*

Wayzata
Alton, Howard Robert, Jr. *lawyer, real estate and food company executive*
Bergerson, David Raymond *lawyer*
Blodgett, Frank Caleb *retired food company executive*
Detlefsen, Guy-Robert *management consultant*
Fish, James Stuart *college dean, advertising consultant*
Hoffman, Gene D. *food company executive, consultant*
Mithun, Raymond O. *advertising agency executive, banker, real estate and insurance executive*
Reutiman, Robert William, Jr. *lawyer*
Shannon, James Patrick *foundation consultant, retired food company executive*
Swanson, Donald Frederick *retired food company executive*

West Saint Paul
Markwardt, Kenneth Marvin *former chemical company executive*

White Bear Lake
Gabrick, Robert William *secondary education educator*
Gutchë, Gene *composer*
Williams, Julie Belle *psychiatric social worker*

Winona
DeThomasis, Brother Louis *college president*
Krueger, Darrell William *academic administrator*
Preska, Margaret Louise Robinson *education educator, institute executive*
Towers, James Mc *education educator*
Vlazny, John George *bishop*

Woodbury
Benforado, David M. *environmental engineer*
Clancy, Robert J. *insurances company executive*

MISSISSIPPI

Aberdeen
Davidson, Glen Harris *federal judge*
Davis, Jerry Arnold *judge*
Senter, Lyonel Thomas, Jr. *federal judge*

Ackerman
Coleman, Frances McLean *secondary school educator*

Amory
Bryan, Hob *lawyer, state senator*

Bay Saint Louis
Sidders, Patrick Michael *financial executive*

Belzoni
Halbrook, Rita Robertshaw *artist, sculptor*

Biloxi
Bramlette, David C., III *federal judge*
Cozzi, Sister Joanne *school system administrator*
Gex, Walter Joseph, III *federal judge*
Hagood, Annabel Dunham *speech communication educator, communication consultant*
Hash, John Frank *broadcasting executive*
Howze, Joseph Lawson Edward *bishop*
Roper, John Marlin *federal magistrate judge*
Weeks, Roland, Jr. *newspaper publisher*
Young, Walter Richard *controller*

Brandon
Buckley, Frank Wilson *newspaper executive*
Nelson, Norman Crooks *surgeon, academic administrator, educator*
Samsel, Maebell Scroggins (Midge Samsel) *paralegal*

Brookhaven
†Perkins, Thomas Hayes, III *furniture company executive*

Carriere
Wilson, Raymond Clark *former hospital executive*

Carrollton
McConnell, David Stuart *insurance agent, retired federal executive*

Clarksdale
Curtis, Chester Harris *lawyer, retired bank executive*
Williams, Kenneth Ogden *farmer*

Cleveland
Alexander, William Brooks *lawyer, former state senator*
Cash, William McKinley *history educator*
Howorth, Lucy Somerville *lawyer*
Macon, Myra Faye *library director*
Thornton, Larry Lee *psychotherapist, author, educator*
Wyatt, Forest Kent *university president*

Clinton
Bigelow, Martha Mitchell *retired historian*
Eichelberger, Lisa Wright *academic administrator, nursing educator*
Hensley, John Clark *religious organization administrator, minister*
Montgomery, Keith Norris, Sr. *insurance executive, state legislator*
Nobles, Lewis *college president*

Columbia
Simmons, Miriam Quinn *state legislator*

Columbus
Atkinson, Gloria L. *archivist*
†Duke, Lance Brittain *hospital administrator*
Fant, Joseph Lewis, III *retired army officer, educator*
Hudnall, Jarrett, Jr. *management and marketing educator*
Ivy, Robert Adams, Jr. *architect, writer*
Kaye, Samuel Harvey *architect, educator*
Rent, Clyda Stokes *university president*
Stringer, Mary Evelyn *art historian, educator*

Crenshaw
Cooke, Gloria Grayson *trust fund director*

Diamondhead
Jaumot, Frank Edward, Jr. *automobile parts manufacturing company executive*

Fayette
La Salle, Arthur Edward *historic foundation executive*

Greenville
†Carter, Peggy Wolfe *artist*

Greenwood
†Eastland, Woods Eugene *agricultural products executive*

Gulfport
Allen, Harry Roger *lawyer*
Brignac, Wanda Anne *nursing educator*
Daffron, Martha *retired education educator*
Freret, René Joseph *minister*
Guice, Daniel Dicks, Jr. *state legislator*
Harral, John Menteith *lawyer*
Hewes, William Gardner, III *insurance executive, real estate agent, legislator*
Hinkle, Walter C., Jr. *banker*
Pickering, Shelbie Jean *mortgage loan executive*
Russell, Dan M., Jr. *federal judge*
Schloegel, George Anthony *banker*
Seal, Leo William, Jr. *banker*
Thatcher, George Robert *banker*
Walker, Harry Grey *retired state supreme court justice*
Yeager, Andrea Wheaton *editor*

Hattiesburg
Burrus, John N(ewell) *sociology educator*
Gonzales, John Edmond *history educator*
Gordon, Granville Hollis *church official*
Graves, Sid Foster, Jr. *library and museum director*
Lucas, Aubrey Keith *university president*
Miller, James Edward *computer scientist, educator*
Noonkester, James Ralph *retired college president*
Pickering, Charles W. *federal judge*
Rawlings, Paul C. *retired government official*
Riley, Thomas Jackson *lawyer*
Saucier Lundy, Karen *college dean, educator*
Sims, James Hylbert *English educator, former university administrator*
Traylor, Joan Sadler *interior design educator*
Wood, Vivian Poates *mezzo soprano, voice educator*
Woodall, Lowery A. *hospital administrator*

Hazlehurst
Lowenkamp, William Charles, Jr. *medical device engineer, researcher, consultant*

Holly Springs
Beckley, David Lenard *academic administrator*

Houlka
Washington, Gerald *manufacturing executive*

Indianola
Crouse, Ted *grocery company executive*
Matthews, David *clergyman*
Powell, Anice Carpenter *librarian*

Inverness
Pratt, William Hunter *insurance agent, small business owner*

Itta Bena
Henderson, Robbye Robinson *library director*
Ware, William Levi *physical education educator, researcher*

Jackson
Achord, James Lee *gastroenterologist, educator*
Allin, John Maury *bishop*
Anderson, Reuben V. *state supreme court justice*
Ball, Carroll Raybourne *anatomist, medical educator, researcher*
Baltz, Richard Jay *health care company executive*
Barbour, William H., Jr. *federal judge*
Barksdale, Rhesa Hawkins *federal judge*
Barnett, Robert Glenn *lawyer*
Batson, Blair Everett *pediatrician, educator*
Bender, Kaye W. *nursing administrator*
Biggs, Thomas Jones *architect*
Bloom, Sherman *pathologist, educator*
Bourdeaux, Norma Sanders *state legislator*
Breese, Frank Chandler, III *newsprint company executive, lawyer*
Briggs, Eddie J. *state official*
Brooks, Thomas Joseph, Jr. *preventive medicine educator*
Burnham, Tom *state school system administrator*
Burns, Robert, Jr. *architect, freelance writer, artist*
Burwell, Dudley Sale *retired investment executive and food executive*
Butler, George Harrison *lawyer*
Campbell, James Boyd *office supply company executive*
Capers, Charlotte *retired state archives and history administrator*
†Cavanaugh, William, III *electric utility company executive*
Christ, Mary Ann *academic administrator, nursing educator*
†Chustz, J. Steve *lawyer*
Clark, Charles *lawyer*
Clark, David Wright *lawyer*
Cruse, Julius Major, Jr. *pathologist*
Cullen, William *school system administrator*
Currier, Robert David *neurologist*
Dallas, Thomas Abraham *retired utility company executive*
Das, Suman Kumar *plastic surgeon, researcher*
†Day, Frank R. *bank executive*
Dean, Jack Pearce *retired insurance company executive*
Ditto, (John) Kane *mayor*
Dodson, William H. *school system administrator*
Downing, Margaret Mary *newspaper editor*
Draper, Edgar *psychiatrist*
Dubbert, Patricia Marie *psychologist*
Fordice, Daniel Kirkwood, Jr. (Kirk Fordice) *governor, construction company executive, engineer*
Forks, Thomas Paul *osteopathic physician*
Freeland, Alan Edward *orthopedic surgery educator, physician*
Fulmer, (Mary) Jeannine *broadcasting executive*
Fuselier, Louis Alfred *lawyer*
Galloway, Patricia Kay *systems analyst, ethnohistorian*
†Graham, Charlotte Ann *religion writer, consultant*
Gray, Duncan Montgomery, Jr. *retired bishop*
Green, Tomie Turner *lawyer, state legislator*
Gunn, Frank Michael *direct marketing professional*
Guyton, Arthur Clifton *physician, educator*
Halaris, Angelos *psychiatrist, educator*
Hall, Dick *state legislator*
Harmon, George Marion *college president*
Harrison, Robert Vernon McElroy *architect*
Hawkins, Armis Eugene *state supreme court chief justice*
Henderson, W. Guy *editor, minister*
Hiatt, Jane Crater *arts agency administrator*
Holman, William Henry, Jr. *retail executive*
Hosemann, C. Delbert, Jr. *lawyer*
Houck, William Russell *bishop*
Houston, Gerry Ann *oncologist*
Hutchison, William Forrest *parasitologist, educator*
Irby, Stuart Charles, Jr. *construction company executive*
Jolly, E. Grady *federal judge*
Knapp, Richard S. *planetarium director*
Lampton, Leslie B., Sr. *oil industry executive*
Langford, James Jerry *lawyer*
Lee, Tom Stewart *federal judge*
Lewis, Robert Edwin, Jr. *pathology immunology educator, researcher*
Lilly, Thomas Gerald *lawyer*
Lutken, Donald C. *utility company executive*
Malloy, James Matthew *managed care executive, health care consultant*
McCarty, William Bonner, Jr. *retail grocery executive*
McKnight, William Edwin *minister*
McMillan, Howard Lamar, Jr. *banker*
Miller, Hainon Alfred *lawyer, investor*
Miller, Larry D. *broadcasting executive*
Moize, Jerry Dee *lawyer*
Molpus, Dick *state official*
Moore, Mike *state attorney general*
Parks, James Franklin, Jr. *librarian*
Pearce, Colman Cormac *conductor, pianist, composer*
Pearce, David Harry *biomedical engineer*
Penick, George Dial, Jr. *foundation executive*
Phillips, George L. *prosecutor*
Pittman, Edwin Lloyd *state supreme court justice*
Prather, Lenore Loving *state supreme court presiding justice*
Price, Alfred Lee *lawyer, mining company executive*
Ray, H. M. *lawyer*
Rayborn, William Lee *state senator*
Reid-Petty, Jane *artistic director, actor, playwright*
Robinson, E. B., Jr. *bank executive*
Saunders, Doris Evans *editor, educator, business executive*
Seltzer, Ada May *librarian, medical library director*
Sewell, Charles Haslett *banker*
Stampley, Norris Lochlen *former electric utility executive*
Stovall, Jerry (Coleman Stovall) *insurance company executive*
Stubbs, James Carlton *retired hospital administrator*
Sugg, Robert Perkins *former state supreme court justice*
Sullivan, Michael David *state supreme court justice*
Thrash, Edsel E. *educational administrator*
Timmer, Wayne F. *architectural firm executive*
Tullos, John Baxter *banker*
Vance, Ralph Brooks *oncologist and educator*
†Vanderleest, Dirk *airport executive*
Watts, John McCleave *financial services executive*
Welty, Eudora *author*
†Wilder, Margaret T. *bank holding company executive*
Williams, James Kelley *diversified resources company executive*
Williams, William Lane *university administrator, anatomist*
Wingate, Henry Travillion *federal judge*
Winter, William Forrest *former governor, lawyer*
Wise, Sherwood Willing *lawyer*
Woodfield, Clyde Vernon *senator*
Woodrell, Frederick Dale *health care executive*
Wright, Maria Gloria *nursing administrator*

Kosciusko
Kearley, F. Furman *minister, religious educator, magazine editor*

Laurel
Masters, Beda Doris *elementary educator*

Learned
Barrett, Richard *lawyer*

Long Beach
Horton, Jerry Smith *minister*

Lorman
†Williams, Richard, Jr. *animal scientist*

Madison
Harpole, Jerry Lee *agri-business executive*
Hays, Donald Osborne *retired government official*
Robinson, John David *retired army officer*

Mc Comb
Bancroft, Joseph C. *metal products company executive*

Meridian
Balliet, James Lee *manufacturing company executive*
Blackwell, Cecil *science association executive*
Church, George Millord *real estate executive*
Drawdy, Larry A. *school system administrator*
Lindstrom, Donald Fredrick, Jr. *priest*
Marshall, John Steven *artist, educator, museum administrator*
†Peavey, Hartley Davis *electronics company executive*
†Peavey, Melia McRae *electronics company executive*
Phillips, Patricia Jeanne *retired school administrator, consultant*

Mississippi State
Bishop, Calvin Thomas *landscape architect, educator*
Cliett, Charles Buren *aeronautical engineer, educator, academic administrator*
Clynch, Edward John *political science educator, researcher*
Crowell, Lorenzo Mayo *historian, educator*
Donaghy, Henry James *English literature educator, academic administrator*
Dorough, H. Wyman *toxicologist, educator, consultant*
Hawkins, Merrill Morris *college administrator*
Howell, Everette Irl *physicist, educator*
Jacob, Paul Bernard, Jr. *electrical engineering educator*
Khatena, Joe *psychology educator*
Lee, John Edward, Jr. *university administrator*
Lowery, Charles Douglas *history educator, academic administrator*
Mabry, Donald Joseph *university administrator, history educator*
Man, Cameron Robert James *landscape architect*
Martin, Edward Curtis, Jr. *landscape architect, educator*
McGilberry, Joe Herman *food service executive*
McRae, John Malcolm *college dean, architect*
Minyard, James Patrick, Jr. *chemist, educator*
Nash, Henry Warren *marketing educator*
Parrish, William Earl *history educator*
Parsons, George William *city planner, educator*
Powe, Ralph Elward *university administrator*
†Reddy, Kambham Raja *plant physiology educator*
Shillingsburg, Peter LeRoy *English language educator*
Taylor, Clayborne Dudley *engineering educator*
Thompson, Joe Floyd *aerospace engineer, research director*
Thompson, Warren S. *forestry educator, university dean*
†White, Charles H. *food science and technology educator*
Wiltrout, Ann Elizabeth *foreign language educator*
Zacharias, Donald Wayne *university president*

Monticello
Allen, Frank Carroll *retired banker*

Morton
†Rogers, John M. *food Products executive*

Natchez
Parker, Mary Evelyn *former state treasurer*

Nettleton
Sides, Kermit Franklin *furniture company executive*

Ocean Springs
McNulty, Matthew Francis, Jr. *health sciences and health services administrator, educator, university administrator, consultant, horse and cattle breeder*
Morrison, Mable Johnson *business technology educator*

Oxford
Biggers, Neal Brooks, Jr. *federal judge*
Dunbar, Wylene Wisby *lawyer, writer*
Foster, George Rainey *soil erosion research scientist*
Meyer, L. Donald *agricultural engineer, researcher, educator*
Moorhead, Sylvester Andrew *education educator retired*

Pascagoula
Carlson, John Henry *lawyer*
Corben, Herbert Charles *physicist, educator*
McIlwain, Thomas David *fishery administrator, marine biologist, educator*
St. Pe, Gerald J. *manufacturing company executive*

Pass Christian
Clark, John Walter, Jr. *shipping company executive*
McCardell, James Elton *retired naval officer*

Perkinston
Parker, Ora Dean Simmons *elementary school educator*

Picayune
Pardue, Larry G. *botanical garden administrator, educator*

Poplarville
Edwards, Ned Carmack, Jr. *agronomist, university program director*

Ridgeland
Dye, Bradford Johnson, Jr. *former lieutenant governor, lawyer, partner*
Morgan, Madel Jacobs *retired archives and library administrator*
Morrison, Francis Secrest *physician*

Rose Hill
Young, Thomas Daniel *retired humanities educator, author*

Ruleville
Crook, Robert Lacey *lawyer*

Scott
†Malkin, Roger D. *agricultural products executive*
†Robinson, Frederic M. *agricultural products company executive*

Southaven
Utroska, William Robert *veterinarian*

Starkville
Carley, Charles Team, Jr. *mechanical engineer*
Emerich, Donald Warren *retired chemistry educator*
Ford, Robert MacDonald, III *architect, educator*
Loftin, Marion Theo *sociologist, educator*
Martin, Theodore Krinn *former university administrator (deceased)*
Palmertree, Ruth Godron *counselor*
Priest, Melville Stanton *retired consulting hydraulic engineer*
Wolverton, Robert Earl *classics educator*
Yancey, Jimmie Isaac *marketing professional*

Stennis Space Center
Baker, Robert Andrew *environmental research scientist*
Blair, Ruth Reba *government official*
Gaffney, Paul Golden, II *military officer*
Mc Call, Jerry Chalmers *government official*
Royestess, Roy *aerospace science administrator*

Stoneville
Hardee, D. D. *laboratory director, research program leader*
Ranney, Carleton David *plant pathology researcher, administrator*

Summit
Jones, Lawrence David *insurance and medical consultant*

Tupelo
†Bland, Alvin E. *manufacturing executive*
Bush, Fred Marshall, Jr. *lawyer*
†Hicks, John David *hospital administrator*
Johnson, Ruth Allen *elementary school educator*
Patterson, Aubrey Burns, Jr. *banker*
Radojcsics, Anne Parsons *librarian*
Smith, John Willis *banker*

University
Cooker, Philip George *psychology educator*
Cottle, Rex L. *college dean*
Ferris, William Reynolds *folklore educator*
Hannah, Barry *educator, writer*
Horton, Thomas Edward, Jr. *mechanical engineering educator*
Jordan, Winthrop Donaldson *historian, educator*
Keiser, Edmund Davis, Jr. *biologist, educator*
Kiger, Joseph Charles *history educator*
Kushlan, James A. *biology educator*
†Landon, Michael de Laval *historian, educator*
Leary, William James *educational administrator*
Meador, John Milward, Jr. *university dean*
Paterson, Alan Leonard Tuke *mathematics educator*
Sam, Joseph *retired university dean*
Smith, Allie Maitland *university dean*
Walton, Gerald Wayne *English educator, university officiala*

Vicksburg
Albritton, Gayle Edward *structural engineer*
Briuer, Elke Moersch *editor*
Herrmann, Frank Adolph, Jr. *hydraulics laboratory director, researcher*
†Howard, Bruce Kenneth *army officer, environmental engineer*
Mather, Bryant *research administrator*

West Point
Vicks, JoAnn *biology educator*

Whitfield
Morton, James Irwin *hospital administrator*

Yazoo City
Arnold, David Walker *chemical company executive, engineer*
Brown, Marion Lipscomb, Jr. *publisher, retired chemical company executive*
Hawkins, William F. *chemical company executive*

MISSOURI

Arrow Rock
Bollinger, Michael *artistic director*

Ballwin
Cornell, William Daniel *mechanical engineer*
Kern, Gary L. *golf course architect*
Tyler, William Howard, Jr. *advertising executive, educator*

Blue Springs
Foudree, Charles M. *financial executive*
Hatley, Patricia Ruth *school system administrator*
Nelson, Freda Nell Hein *librarian*
Olsson, Björn Eskil *railroad supply company executive*
Reed, Tony Norman *aviation company executive*
†Yahn-Kramer, Bettie Lynn *forester, horticulturist*

Bolivar
Jackson, James Larry *recreation educator*

Boonville
Cline, Dorothy May Stammerjohn (Mrs. Edward Wilburn Cline) *vocational school educator*

Branson
Tillis, Mel(vin) *musician, songwriter*
†Todd, Cecil William *ministry director*
Williams, Andy *entertainer*

Bridgeton
Brauer, Stephen Franklin *manufacturing company executive*
Joyner Kersee, Jacqueline *track and field athlete*
McSweeney, Michael Terrence *manufacturing executive*

California
Wood, Mary Marie *secondary education educator*

Cameron
Griffin, Bob Franklin *state legislator, lawyer*

Cape Girardeau
Blackwelder, Richard E(liot) *entomologist, zoology educator, archivist*
Dahiya, Jai Narain *physics educator, researcher*
Southard-Ritter, Marcia *nursing administrator*
Stroup, Kala Mays *university president*

Carthage
Cornell, Harry M., Jr. *furnishings company executive*
Glauber, Michael A. *manufacturing company executive*
Jefferies, Robert Aaron, Jr. *furniture company executive, lawyer*
Wright, Felix E. *manufacturing company executive*

Cassville
Melton, Emory Leon *state legislator, lawyer, publisher*

Centralia
Harmon, Robert Wayne *electrical engineering executive*
Lomo, Leif *electrical manufacturing company executive*

Chesterfield
Armstrong, Theodore Morelock *corporate utilities executive*
Bowling, William Glasgow *English educator*
Bradshaw, Stanley J. *financial holding company executive*
Carpenter, Will Dockery *chemical company executive*
†Gervais, Russell F. *plastics company executive*
Henry, Roy Monroe *financial planner*
Huffer, Dan L. *public relations executive*
Humphreys, James Burnham *hospital administrator*
Hunter, Harlen Charles *orthopedic surgeon*
Jacobsen, James Conrad *apparel manufacturing executive*
King, William Terry *manufacturing company executive*
Klarich, David John *lawyer, state senator*
Levin, Marvin Edgar *physician*
Liggett, Hiram Shaw, Jr. *retired diversified industry financial executive*
Malvern, Donald *retired aircraft manufacturing company executive*
McCarthy, Paul Fenton *aerospace executive, former naval officer*
Palazzi, Joseph L(azarro) *manufacturing executive*
Payne, Meredith Jorstad *physician*
Pollihan, Thomas Henry *lawyer*
†Ritzie, Robert F. *metal products executive*
Thomas, Violeta de los Angeles *real estate broker*
Toombs, Eugene Martin, III *manufacturing executive*
Turley, Clarence M., Jr. *finance company executive*
Unterreiner, C. Martin *financial advisor*
Upbin, Hal Jay *consumer products executive*
Welshans, Merle Talmadge *management consultant*
Willis, Frank Edward *retired air force officer*
Yardley, John Finley *aerospace engineer*

Clayton
Bartlett, Joe Michael *school system administrator*
Belz, Mark *lawyer*
Buechler, Bradley Bruce *plastic processing company executive, accountant*
Christner, Theodore Carroll *architect*
Kohm, Barbara *principal*
Turner, Terry Madison *architect*
†Vecchiotti, Robert Anthony *management and organizational consultant*
Zimmerman, Harold Seymour *elementary school educator*

Clinton
Deskins, Gary *school system administrator*

Columbia
Adams, Algalee Pool *college dean, art educator*
Alexander, Martha Sue *librarian*
Alexander, Thomas Benjamin *history educator*
Allen, William Cecil *physician, educator*
Almony, Robert Allen, Jr. *librarian, businessman*
Anderson, Donald Kennedy, Jr. *English educator*
Archer, Stephen Murphy *theater educator*
Atwater, James David *journalist, educator*
Basu, Asit Prakas *statistician*
Bauman, John E., Jr. *chemistry educator*
Beem, John Kelly *mathematician, educator*
Biddle, Bruce Jesse *social psychologist, educator*
Bien, Joseph Julius *philosophy educator*
Blaine, Edward H. *health science association administrator*
Blevins, Dale Glenn *agronomy educator*
Blount, Don H. *physiology educator*
Breimyer, Harold Frederick *agricultural economist*
Brown, Olen Ray *medical microbiology research educator*
Bryant, Lester R. *surgeon, educator*
Bunn, Ronald Freeze *political science educator, lawyer*
Burchett, Betty Martela *science education educator*
Burdick, Allan Bernard *geneticist*
Calabrese, Diane Marie *entomologist, writer*
Carroll, Carmal Edward *librarian, educator, clergyman*
Coe, Edward Harold, Jr. *geneticist, agronomist, educator*
Colwill, Jack Marshall *physician, educator*
Cunningham, Milamari Antoinella *anesthesiologist*
Darrah, Larry Lynn *plant breeder*
Davis, James O(thello) *physician, educator*
Day, Cecil LeRoy *agricultural engineering educator*
Decker, Wayne Leroy *meteorologist, educator*
Denney, Arthur Hugh *consultant*
Dolliver, Robert Henry *psychology educator*
Duncan, Donald Pendleton *retired forestry educator*
Dyrenfurth, Michael John *vocational technical and industrial arts educator, consultant*
Eggers, George William Nordholtz, Jr. *anesthesiologist, educator*
El-Gizawy, Ahmed Sherif *mechanical and aerospace engineering educator, manufacturing engineer, consultant*
Ethington, Raymond Lindsay *geology educator, researcher*
Finkelstein, Richard Alan *microbiologist*
Fisch, William Bales *lawyer*
Frew, Bud L. *agricultural products company executive*
Frisby, James Curtis *agricultural engineering educator*
Fulweiler, Howard Wells *language professional*
Gehrke, Charles William *biochemistry educator*
Geiger, Louis George *historian*
Geiger, Mark Watson *management educator*
Goodrich, James William *historian, association executive*
Gysbers, Norman Charles *education educator*
Hatley, Richard V(on) *education educator*
Heldman, Dennis Ray *engineering educator*
Hensley, Elizabeth Catherine *nutritionist, educator*
Hillman, Richard Ephraim *pediatrician, educator*
Holden, Sandra S(ue) *insurance executive*
†Howden, Norman, III *library science educator, consultant*
Ignoffo, Carlo Michael *insect pathologist-virologist*
Johns, Williams Davis, Jr. *geologist, educator*
Jones, William McKendrey *language professional, educator*
Kashani, Javad Hassan-Nejad *physician*
Kausler, Donald Harvey *psychology educator*
Keith, Everett Earnest *educator, education administrator*
Kiesler, Charles Adolphus *psychologist, academic administrator*
Lago, Mary McClelland *English language educator, author*
Lambeth, Victor Neal *horticulturist, researcher*
Larson, Sidney *art educator, artist, writer, painting conservator*
Lenox, Mary Frances *academic dean*
Long, Edwin Tutt *surgeon*
LoPiccolo, Joseph *psychologist, educator, author*
Martin, Mark Edward *molecular biologist, biochemist*
Mayer, Dennis Thomas *biochemist, educator*
McCollum, Clifford Glenn *college dean emeritus*
Mc Ginnes, Edgar Allen, Jr. *forestry educator*
Miller, Paul Ausborn *adult education educator*
Mitchell, Roger Lowry *agronomy educator*
Monroe, Haskell M., Jr. *university educator*
Morehouse, Lawrence Glen *veterinarian, educational administrator*
Mullen, Edward John, Jr. *Spanish language educator*
Nikolai, Loren Alfred *accounting educator, author*
Novacky, Anton Jan *plant pathologist, educator*
Overby, Osmund Rudolf *art historian, educator*
Palo, Nicholas Edwin *professional society administrator*
Parrigin, Elizabeth Ellington *lawyer*
Perkoff, Gerald Thomas *physician, educator*
Perry, Michael Clinton *physician, medical educator, academic administrator*
Plummer, Patricia Lynne Moore *chemistry and physics educator*
Poehlmann, Carl John *agronomist, researcher*
Pringle, Oran Allan *mechanical and aerospace engineering educator*
Puckett, C. Lin *plastic surgeon, educator*
Pugh, Robert Kenneth *textbook distributing company executive*
Rabjohn, Norman *chemistry educator emeritus*
Ratti, Ronald Andrew *economics educator*
Reid, Loren Dudley *speech educator*
Rothwell, Robert Clark *agricultural products executive*
Rowlett, Ralph Morgan *archaeologist, educator*
Russell, George Albert *university president*
†Sanders, Keith Page *journalism educator*
†Schoettger, Richard A. *physiologist, marine biology researcher, science administrator*
Schrader, Keith William *mathematician*
Silver, Donald *surgeon, educator*
Silvoso, Joseph Anton *accounting educator*
†Smith, Bruce L. *secondary education educator*
Sphar, Gail Ellen *insurance company executive*
Springsteel, Frederick Neil *computer science educator*
Stephenson, Hugh Edward, Jr. *retired physician, educator*
Strickland, Arvarh Eunice *history educator*
Taft, William Howard *journalism educator*
†Thomas, Thomas Stanton *health system executive*
Thompson, Warren A. *mental health services educator, director*
Timberlake, Charles Edward *history educator*
Twaddle, Andrew Christian *sociology educator*
Unklesbay, Athel Glyde *geologist, educator*
Viswanath, Dabir Srikantiah *chemical engineer*
Wagner, Joseph Edward *veterinarian, educator*
Wagner, William Burdette *business educator*
Walkenbach, Ronald Joseph *foundation executive, pharmacology educator*
Weiss, James Moses Aaron *psychiatrist, educator*
Welliver, Warren Dee *lawyer, retired state supreme court justice*
Westbrook, James Edwin *lawyer, educator*
Wheeler, Otis V., Jr. *public school principal*
Williams, Frederick *statistics educator*
Witten, David Melvin *radiology educator*
Yanders, Armon Frederick *biological sciences educator, research administrator*
Yarwood, Dean Lesley *political science educator*
Yasuda, Hirotsugu Koge *chemical engineering professor*
Zemmer, Joseph Lawrence, Jr. *mathematics educator*

Crestwood
Reitter, Charles Andrew *personal financial planner*

Cuba
Work, Bruce Van Syoc *business consultant*

Des Peres
Smith, Barbara Martin *art educator*

Eagle Rock
Rowan, Gerald Burdette *insurance company executive, lawyer*

Earth City
Anderhalter, Oliver Frank *educational organization executive*

Eminence
Staples, Danny Lew *state senator*

Eureka
Coles, Richard W(arren) *biology educator, research administrator*
†Lindsey, Susan Lyndaker *zoologist*

Fenton
Greenblatt, Maurice Theodore *transportation executive*
Korn, Irene Elizabeth *elementary education educator, consultant*
Maritz, William E. *communications company executive*
Richardson, Thomas Hampton *design consulting engineer*
Stadler, Gerald P. *transportation executive*
Stolar, Henry Samuel *corporate lawyer*

Florissant
Bartlett, Robert James *principal*
Betts, Warren R. *retired health facility administrator*
†Cochran, Robert Emmett *sales executive*
Kelly, James Joseph *printing company executive*
Martin, Edward Brian *electrical engineer*
Pomeroy, Robert Lee *food distribution executive*
Reese, Alferd George *retired army civilian logistics specialist*
Tanphaichitr, Kongsak *rheumatologist, allergist, immunologist, internist*

Fort Leonard Wood
†Broyles, Thomas Edwin *career officer, healthcare facility executive*

Fortuna
Ramer, James LeRoy *civil engineer*

Fulton
Barnett, Jahnae Harper *academic administrator*
Davidson, Robert Laurenson Dashiell *college president emeritus, philatelist*
Gish, Edward Rutledge *surgeon*
Remley, Audrey Wright *educational administrator, psychologist*

Gallatin
Wilsted, Joy *elementary education educator, reading specialist, parenting consultant*

Grandview
Brown, Bob Oliver *retired manufacturing company executive*
Dietrich, William Gale *lawyer, real estate developer, consultant*
Justesen, Don Robert *psychologist*

Hale
Danner, Steve *senator*

Hallsville
McFate, Kenneth Leverne *association administrator*

Hamilton
Esry, Cordelia Cochran *community health nurse*

Hannibal
Dothager, Julie Ann *librarian*
Sweets, Henry Hayes, III *museum director*

Hattiesburg
Saucier, Gene Duane *state legislator, import/export company executive*

Hazelwood
†Dalton, Dick Newton *communications executive*
McClintock, Eugene Jerome *minister*
Mohrmann, Robert E. *wholesale distribution executive*
Purvines, Verne Ewald, Jr. *lawyer*
Rose, Joseph Hugh *clergyman*
Seitz, Harold A. *supermarket executive*
Urshan, Nathaniel Andrew *minister, church administrator*
†Wetterau, Theodore C. *diversified food wholesaler*

Hermann
†Renn, Erin McCawley *museum administrator*

Highlandville
Pruter, Karl Hugo *bishop*

Hillsboro
Adkins, Gregory D. *academic administrator*

Hollister
Thominet, Maurice J. *architect*

Independence
Booth, Paul Wayne *minister*
Ferguson, John Wayne, Sr. *librarian*
Hansen, Francis Eugene *minister*
Henley, Robert Lee *school system administrator*
Kaufman, Lawrence Clark *city official*
Lammers, Joseph Edwin *hospital executive*
†Lindgren, A. Bruce *church administrator*
Mitchell, Earl Wesley *clergyman*
Potts, Barbara Joyce *historical society executive*
Sheehy, Howard Sherman, Jr. *minister*
Smith, Wallace Bunnell *physician, church official*
†Spencer, Geoffrey F. *church administrator*
Strang, Marian Boundy *librarian*
†Swails, Norman E. *church officer*
Tyree, Alan Dean *clergyman*
Vigen, Kathryn L. Voss *nursing administrator, educator*
Walsh, Rodger John *lawyer*

Ironton
Douma, Harry Hein *social service agency administrator*

Jefferson City
Backer, Gracia Yancey *state legislator*
Bartlett, Alex *lawyer*
Bartman, Robert E. *state education official*
Benton, W. Duane *judge*
Blunt, Roy D. *state official*
Bray, Joan *state legislator*
Carnahan, Mel *governor, lawyer*
Clay, William Lacy, Jr. *state legislator*
Cook, Sam B. *banker*
Covington, Ann K. *judge, lawyer*
Deutsch, James Bernard *lawyer*
Dey, Charlotte Jane *community health nurse*
Donnelly, Robert True *retired state supreme court justice*
Gaw, Robert Steven *lawyer, state representative*
Goode, Wayne *state senator, corporate executive*
Griesheimer, John Elmer *state representative*
Hale, David Clovis *former state representative*
Hearn, Rosemary *English language educator*
Holden, Bob *state official*
Holstein, John Charles *state supreme court justice*
Karll, Jo Ann *state agency administrator, lawyer*
Kauffman, Sandra Daley *state legislator*
Kelley, Pat *minister, state legislator*
Kelly, Margaret Blake *auditor, state official*
Limbaugh, Stephen Nathaniel, Jr. *judge*
Lumpe, Sheila *state legislator*
Maxwell, Joe *state representative, lawyer*
Mays, Carol Jean *state legislator*
Mc Auliffe, Michael F. *bishop*
McClain, Charles James *state educational administrator*
McClelland, Emma L. *state legislator*
Morgan, Annette N. *state legislator*
Moriarty, Judith Kay Spry *state official*
Nixon, Jeremiah W. (Jay Nixon) *state attorney general*
Park, Carole Roper *state legislator*
Parr, Lloyd Byron *state official*
Peeno, Larry Noyle *state agency administrator, consultant*
Price, William Ray, Jr. *state supreme court judge*
Rayburn, Wendell Gilbert *college president*
Reidinger, Russell Frederick, Jr. *fish and wildlife scientist*
Robertson, Edward D., Jr. *state supreme court chief justice*
Scott, Gary Kuper *academic administrator*
Steinmetz, Kaye H. *state legislator*
Tettlebaum, Harvey M. *lawyer*
Thomas, Elwood Lauren *state supreme court justice*
Treppler, Irene Esther *state senator*
Waters, Stephen Russell *state agency administrator*
Wiggins, Harry *state senator, lawyer*
Wilson, Roger B. *lieutenant governor, school administrator*
Winn, Kenneth Hugh *archivist, historian*

Joplin
Burke, Charles Don *church administrator, minister*
Fancher, Robert Burney *electric utility executive, entrepreneur*
Gee, James David *minister*
Harris, Robert A. *music educator*
Hughes, Fred George *retired newspaper publisher*
Lamb, Robert Lewis *electric utility executive*
Malzahn, Ray Andrew *chemistry educator, university dean*
†Minor, Ronald Ray *minister*
Pulliam, Frederick Cameron *educational administrator*
Singleton, Marvin Ayers *otolaryngologist, senator*
Williams, Rex Enoch *international union representative*
Wilson, Aaron Martin *religious studies educator, college executive*

Kahoka
Huffman, Robert Merle *insurance company executive*

Kansas City
Abdou, Nabih I. *physician, educator*
Acheson, Allen Morrow *retired engineering executive*
Adam, Paul James *engineering company executive, mechanical engineer*
Allen, Marcus *professional football player*
Alt, John *football player*
Anderson, Christopher James *lawyer*
Anderson, David *church administrator*
Anderson, David Charles *media specialist*
Anderson, James Keith *retired magazine editor*
Andrews, Kathleen W. *book publishing executive*
Appier, (Robert) Kevin *professional baseball player*
Aslin, M. M. *banker*
Ayres, John Samuel *retired chemical engineer*
Baker, John Russell *utilities executive*
Baker, Robert Thomas *interior designer*
Barnes, Donald Gayle *management consultant*
Bartlett, D. Brook *federal judge*
Bartlett, Paul Dana, Jr. *agribusiness executive*
Bates, William Hubert *lawyer*
Batiuk, Thomas Martin *cartoonist*
Becker, Thomas Bain *lawyer*
Beckett, Theodore Charles *lawyer*
Beihl, Frederick *lawyer*
Benner, Richard Edward, Jr. *management and marketing consultant, investor*
Berard, Dennis *church administrator*
Berardi, John Francis *food products and chemical manufacturing executive*
Berg, W. Robert *agricultural products company executive*
Berkley, Eugene Bertram (Bert Berkley) *envelope company executive*
Berkowitz, Lawrence M. *lawyer*
Berrey, Robert Wilson, III *lawyer, judge*
Bixby, Walter E. *insurance company executive*
Black, John Sheldon *lawyer*
Blackwell, Menefee Davis *lawyer*
Blim, Richard Don *pediatrician*
Bloch, Henry Wollman *tax preparation company executive*
Boland, Raymond James *bishop*
Bolender, Todd *choreographer*
Bombeck, Erma Louise (Mrs. William Bombeck) *author, columnist*
†Boone, Robert Raymond *professional baseball coach*
Bowers, Curtis Ray, Jr. *chaplain*
Bowman, Pasco Middleton, II *federal judge*
Boyd, John Addison, Jr. *civil engineer*
Bradbury, Daniel Joseph *library administrator*
Bradshaw, Jean Paul, II *lawyer*
Bradshaw, William David *insurance company executive*
Brannon, Wilbur *church administrator*
Bransby, Eric James *muralist, educator*
Braude, Michael *commodity exchange executive*
Brenner, Daniel Leon *lawyer*
Brett, George Howard *baseball executive, former professional baseball player*
Brisbane, Arthur Seward *newspaper editor*
Brouillette, Gary Joseph *lawyer*
Brown, John O. *banker*
Brown, Peter W. *lawyer*
Bruening, Richard P(atrick) *lawyer*
Buchanan, John Clark *bishop*
Bugher, Robert Dean *association executive*
Burg, George Roscoe *journalist*
Burk, Norman *oral surgeon*
Busby, Marjorie Jean (Marjean Busby) *journalist*
Butler, Martin *church administrator*
Bywaters, David R. *management consultant*
Cahill, Patricia Deal *radio station executive*
Callo, Joseph Francis *corporate communications consultant, writer*
Canfield, Robert Cleo *lawyer*
Cantrell, (Thomas) Scott *newspaper music critic*
Cappon, Alexander Patterson *English language educator*
Carr, Jack Richard *candy company executive*
Chastain, Larry Kent *insurance company executive*
Ching, Wai Yim *physics educator, researcher*
Chisholm, Donald Herbert *lawyer*
Clarke, Milton Charles *lawyer*
Clarkson, William Edwin *construction company executive*
Cleberg, Harry C. *food products company executive*
Cloud, Randall R. *church administrator*
†Cohen, Martin D. *ballet company administrator*
Cohen, Roger L. *real estate executive*
Collins, Mark *professional football player*
Conrad, William Merrill *architect*
Conway, Thomas James *lawyer*
Cook, Bart R. *dancer*
Cook, Mary Rozella *psychophysiologist*
Cooper, Corinne *law educator*
Costin, James D. *performing arts company executive*
Couch, Daniel Michael *healthcare executive*
Courson, Marna B. P. *public relations executive*
Cowley, Samuel Parkinson *utility company executive, lawyer*
Crawford, Howard Allen *lawyer*
Crider, Stephen Wayne *banker, lawyer*
Cross, William Dennis *lawyer*
Davis, F(rancis) Keith *civil engineer*
Davis, James Robert *cartoonist*
Davis, John Charles *lawyer*
Davis, Richard Francis *city government official*
Deacy, Thomas Edward, Jr. *lawyer*
Dees, Stephen Phillip *petroleum, farm and food products company executive, lawyer*
Dillingham, John Allen *marketing professional*
Dimond, Edmunds Grey *medical educator*
Diuguid, Lewis Walter *editor, metrocolumnist*
Dodd, Monroe *newspaper editor*
†Doughty, Clark Ronald *healthcare executive, government official*
Doyle, Wendell E. *retired educator*
Driscoll, Robert Louis *lawyer*
Dumovich, Loretta *real estate and transportation company executive*
Durig, James Robert *college dean*
Durwood, Edward D. *motion picture corporation executive*
†Durwood, Stanley H. *entertainment industry executive*
Eddy, William Bahret *psychology educator, university dean*
Edgar, John M. *lawyer*
Edwards, George W., Jr. *railway company executive*
Edwards, Horace Burton *former state official, former oil pipeline company executive, management consultant*
Egan, Charles Joseph, Jr. *greeting card company executive, lawyer*
Eldridge, Truman Kermit, Jr. *lawyer*
Ellfeldt, Howard James *orthopedic surgeon*
Estep, Michael R. *church administrator*
Eubanks, Eugene Emerson *education educator, consultant*
Evans, Gary *food products executive*
Field, Lyman *lawyer*
Fields, Curtis Grey *public utility executive*
Flora, Jairus Dale, Jr. *statistician*
Foster, Mark Stephen *lawyer*
Fox, Thomas Charles *editor, publisher, writer*
Frank, Eugene Maxwell *bishop*
Frederick, Joseph Francis, Jr. *hotel executive*
Freilich, Robert H. *lawyer, educator*
French, Linda Jean *lawyer*
Freund, Ronald S. *management consultant, marketing company executive*
Fries, James Lawrence *trade association executive*
Frigon, Henry Frederick *diversified company executive*
Frost, Earle Wesley *lawyer, retired judge*
Fullerton, Fred *church administrator*
Gaitan, Fernando J., Jr. *federal judge*
Gardner, Brian E. *lawyer*
†Genovese, Peter J. *banker*
Getty, Carol Pavilack *government official*
Gibson, Floyd Robert *federal judge*
Gibson, John Robert *federal judge*
Gier, Audra May Calhoon *environmental chemist*
Giffin, Reggie Craig *lawyer*
†Gilbert, John R. *advertising and public relations agency executive*
Gile, Herbert R., Jr. *airport terminal executive*
Gorman, Gerald Warner *lawyer*
Graham, James Robert, III *physician, medical society administrator*
Gray, Helen Theresa Gott *religion editor*
Grider, Joseph Kenneth *theology educator, writer*
Grosskreutz, Joseph Charles *physicist, engineering researcher, educator*
Grossman, Jerome Barnett *retired service firm executive*
Grunt, Jerome Alvin *pediatric endocrinologist*
Gunter, Moody *church administrator*
Gusewelle, Charles Wesley *journalist*
Hagans, Robert Frank *industrial clothing cleaning company executive*
Hagsten, Ib *animal scientist, educator*
Hall, Donald Joyce *greeting card company executive*
Hall, Miriam *church administrator*
Hartley, Richard Glendale *association executive*
Hartzler, Geoffrey Oliver *cardiologist*
Harvey, Thomas D. *headmaster*
Hasting, Glen Richard, II *health care executive, educator*
Hazlett, James Arthur *insurance administrator*
Hebenstreit, James Bryant *agricultural products executive, bank and venture capital executive*
Hendrickson, Marshall David *banker*
Hendrix, Ray *church administrator*
Henson, Paul Harry *telecommunications corporate executive*
Hicks, Lawrence Wayne *manufacturing company executive*
Hockaday, Irvine O., Jr. *greeting card company executive*
Hoenig, Thomas M. *bank executive*
Hoffer, Sharon Marie *educator*
Hoffman, Alfred John *retired mutual fund executive*
Hoffman, John Raymond *lawyer*
Hoffmann, Donald *architectural historian*
Holder, Thomas Martin *physician*
Horsely, Willie Woodruff *educational administrator*
Hoskins, William Keller *lawyer, pharmaceutical company executive*
Hubbell, Ernest *lawyer*
Hunerberg, David W. *accounting firm executive*
Hunt, Lamar *professional football team executive*
Hunter, Elmo Bolton *federal judge*
Hunzicker, Warren John *research consultant, physician, cardiologist*
Huston, Kent Allen *rheumatologist*
Ingram, Robert Palmer *magazine publisher*
Isler, Mamie *secondary school principal*
Jenkins, Orville Wesley *retired religious administrator*
Jennings, A. Drue *utility company executive*
Johnson, Jerald D. *religious organization administrator*
Johnson, Mark Eugene *lawyer*
Julian, Lanny *printing company executive*
Karmeier, Delbert Fred *consulting engineer*
Kemper, David Woods, II *banker*
Kemper, James Madison, Jr. *banker*
Kemper, Rufus Crosby, Jr. *banker*
Kilroy, John Muir *lawyer*
Kilroy, William Terrence *lawyer*
King, Richard Allen *lawyer*
Kingsley, James Gordon *health care executive*
Kipp, Robert Almy *greeting card company executive*
Kittoe, Larry *grain company executive*
Knadle, Richard D. *grain product company executive*
†Knight, John Allan *clergyman, philosophy and religion educator*
Koger, Frank Williams *federal judge*
Kramer, Lawrence John *college president*
Kroenert, Robert Morgan *lawyer*
Kronschnabel, Robert James *manufacturing company executive*
Kunz, Larry P. *lumber and building materials company executive*
La Budde, Kenneth James *librarian*
Langworthy, Robert Burton *lawyer*
Larson, Gary *cartoonist*
Latshaw, John *entrepreneur*
Lee, Margaret Norma *artist*
†Leikam, Dale Francis *agronomist*
Levi, Peter Steven *chamber of commerce executive, lawyer*
Lindsey, David Hosford *lawyer*
†Lindstrom, Charles Clifford *hospital administrator*
Lombardi, Cornelius Ennis, Jr. *lawyer*
Lott, Ronnie (Ronald Mandel Lott) *professional football player*
Loudon, Donald Hoover *lawyer*
Lubin, Bernard *psychologist, educator*
Lyons, Frederick William, Jr. *pharmaceutical company executive*
Lysaught, Patrick *lawyer*
†MacNair, Rachel Mary *editor*
Malacarne, C. John *insurance company executive, lawyer*
Manka, Ronald Eugene *lawyer*
†Marks, Walter *school system administrator*
†Martin, Deanna Coleman *university director*
Martin, Donna Lee *publishing company executive*
Martin-Bowen, (Carole) Lindsey *freelance writer*
Martinez-Carrion, Marino *biochemist, educator*
Martucci, William Christopher *lawyer*
Matheny, Edward Taylor, Jr. *lawyer*
Maughmer, John Townsend *federal judge*
Mc Coy, Frederick John *retired plastic surgeon*
McDowell, Robert *farmer*
McGarry, Robert George *safety engineer*
Mc Gee, Joseph John, Jr. *former insurance company executive*
McGuff, Joe *newspaper editor*
Mc Kelvey, John Clifford *research institute executive*
McKenna, George LaVerne *art museum curator*
McLarney, Charles Patrick *lawyer*
McManus, James William *lawyer*
Mc Meel, John Paul *newspaper syndicate and publishing executive*
McSweeney, William Lincoln, Jr. *publishing executive*
Mebust, Winston Keith *surgeon, educator*
Merriman, Joe Jack *insurance company executive*
Mick, Howard Harold *lawyer*
Milton, Chad Earl *lawyer*
Moffatt, David John *anatomy educator*
Molz, Otis *oil industry executive*
Mongan, James John *physician*
Montgomery, Jeffrey Thomas *professional baseball player*
Moore, David Lowell *dentist*
Moore, Dorsey Jerome *dentistry educator, maxillofacial prosthetist*
Mordy, James Calvin *lawyer*
Moseley, Furman C. *timber company executive*
Murdock, Stuart Laird *banker, investment adviser*
Myers, Wendy Suzanne *editor*
Newsom, James T. *lawyer*
Noback, Richardson Kilbourne *medical educator*
†Nofsinger, William Morris *engineering executive*
Northrip, Robert Earl *lawyer*
O'Hearne, John Joseph *psychiatrist*
Oliphant, Patrick *editorial cartoonist*
Olson, Kay Melchisedech *magazine editor*
†Owens, Donald D. *church officer*
Palmer, Cruise *newspaper editor*
Palmer, Dennis Dale *lawyer*
Parizek, Eldon Joseph *geologist, college dean*
Patterson, Russell *conductor, opera executive*
†Patty, R. Bruce *architect*
Pedram, Marilyn Beth *reference librarian*
Pelofsky, Joel *lawyer*
Pendleton, Barbara Jean *retired banker*
Perkins, Sister Victoria Marie *school system administrator*
Perrin, John Paul *medical school president*
Peterson, Carl *professional football team executive*
Petosa, Jason Joseph *publisher*
Piepho, Robert Walter *pharmacy educator, researcher*
Piette, Edward James *television executive*

Pistilli, Philip *hotel executive*
Popham, Arthur Cobb, Jr. *lawyer*
Popper, Robert *law educator, former dean*
Pratt, Donald Henry *manufacturing company executive*
Presson, Ellis Wynn *health services executive*
Price, Charles H., II *former ambassador*
†Prince, William J. *church officer*
Quirk, Barbara Long *medical center executive, nurse*
Reaves, Charles William *insurance company executive, writer, educator, investment advisor*
Reiter, Robert Edward *banker*
Rice, H. Wayne *food products executive*
Robb, Gary Charles *lawyer*
Robertson, Leon H. *management consultant, educator*
Robinson, John Hamilton *civil engineer*
Robinson, Spencer T. (Herk Robinson) *professional baseball team executive*
Rost, William Joseph *chemist*
Rowland, Landon Hill *diversified holding company executive*
Sachs, Howard F(rederic) *federal judge*
Samuel, Robert Thompson *optometrist*
Sauer, Gordon Chenoweth *physician, educator*
Savage, Thomas Joseph *college president, governance and planning consultant, educator, priest*
Sayler, J. W., Jr. *insurance company executive*
Schoolman, Arnold *neurological surgeon*
Schottenheimer, Martin Edward *professional football coach*
Scott, Deborah Emont *curator*
Scott, James White *newspaper editor*
See, Karen Mason *federal judge*
Seligson, Theodore H. *architect, interior designer, art consultant*
Semegen, Patrick William *lawyer*
Session, William Terrell *lawyer*
Setzler, Edward Allan *lawyer*
Sexton, Donald Lee *business administration educator*
Shaw, John W. *lawyer*
Sheldon, Ted Preston *library director*
Shutz, Byron Christopher *real estate executive*
Skahan, Paul L(aurence) *bank executive, lawyer*
Skiles, Paul *church administrator*
Smee, John *church administrator*
Smith, Neil *professional football player*
Smithson, Lowell Lee *lawyer*
Solberg, Elizabeth Transou *public relations executive*
Solomon, John Davis *aviation executive*
Spalty, Edward Robert *lawyer*
Spencer, Richard Henry *lawyer*
Stanley, David *retail company executive*
Steadman, Jack W. *professional football team executive*
Steele, Kathleen Frances *federal official*
Stevens, Joseph Edward, Jr. *federal judge*
Stewart, Albert Elisha *safety engineer, industrial hygienist*
Stites, C. Thomas *journalist, publisher*
Stone, Jack *religious organization administrator*
Stowers, James Evans, Jr. *investment company executive*
Strandjord, Mary Jeannine *telecommunications executive*
Sullivan, Bill *church administrator*
Sullivan, Charles A. *food products executive*
Svadlenak, Jean Hayden *museum administrator, consultant*
Tammeus, William David *journalist, columnist*
Taylor, Jeff *reporter*
Temple, Joseph George, Jr. *pharmaceutical company executive*
Thornton, Thomas Noel *publishing executive*
Toll, Perry Mark *lawyer*
Townsend, Harold Guyon, Jr. *publishing company executive*
Tripp, David Richard *lawyer*
Ucko, David Alan *museum director*
Ulrich, Robert Gene *judge*
Van Ackeren, Maurice Edward *college administrator*
Vandever, William Dirk *lawyer*
Varner, Barton Douglas *lawyer*
Vaughan, Kirk William *banker*
Vering, John Albert *lawyer*
Viani, James L. *lawyer*
Vogel, Arthur Anton *clergyman*
Ward, Louis Larrick *candy company executive*
Watterson, Bill *cartoonist*
†Weathers, K. Russell *hospital foundation executive, mayor*
†Wells, J. Lyle, Jr. *bank executive*
Wheeler, Charles Bertan *pathologist*
Whipple, Dean *federal judge*
†Wiener, Mark Seth *health facility administrator*
Wiggins, Kip Acker *lawyer*
Wilson, Eugene Rolland *foundation executive*
Wilson, Marc Fraser *art museum administrator and curator*
Wilson, Tom *cartoonist, greeting card company executive*
Woods, Richard Dale *lawyer*
†Wourms, Mark Kenneth *zoological park director*
Wright, Scott Olin *federal judge*
Wrobley, Ralph Gene *lawyer*
Wyrsch, James Robert *lawyer, educator, author*
Zeller, Marilynn Kay *librarian*

Kirksville
Festa, Roger Reginald *chemist, educator*

Kirkwood
Gibbons, Michael Randolph *lawyer*
Holsen, James Noble, Jr. *retired chemical engineer*

Laddonia
Scheffler, Lewis Francis *pastor, educator, research scientist*

Lake Lotawana
Heineman, Paul Lowe *consulting civil engineer*
Zobrist, Benedict Karl *library director, historian*

Lake Saint Louis
Czarnik, Marvin Ray *retired aerospace engineer*
German, John George *transportation consultant*
Royal, William Henry *real estate developer, architect*

Lamar
†Riegel, T. E. *manfacturing executive, light*

Lambert Airport
Griggs, Leonard LeRoy, Jr. *federal agency administrator*

Lebanon
Hutson, Don *lawyer*

Lees Summit
Hall, Glenn Allen *lawyer, state representative*
Hurley, Marjorie Bryan *marketing consultant*
Korschot, Benjamin Calvin *investment executive*
Puglisi, Philip James *electrical engineer*
Timmons, Joseph Dean *insurance company executive*
Waite, Daniel Elmer *retired oral surgeon*

Liberty
Ferrell, James Edwin *energy company executive*
Harriman, Richard Lee *performing arts administrator, educator*
Sizemore, William Christian *college president*
Tanner, Jimmie Eugene *college dean*

Liguori
O'Connor, Francine Marie *magazine editor*

Manchester
Warner, Vinnie *principal*

Mansfield
Wallace, Dorothy Alene *special education administrator*

Marshall
Gruber, Loren Charles *English language educator, writer*
Tweito, Eleanor Marie *social services administrator, educator*
Wymore, Luann Courtney *elementary education educator*

Maryland Heights
Baker, Newell Alden *oil company executive*
Beumer, Richard Eugene *engineer, architect, construction firm executive*
Dokoudovsky, Nina Ludmila *dance educator*
Schwartz, Henry Gerard, Jr. *consulting engineering company executive*
Smith, Brice Reynolds, Jr. *engineering company executive*
Sobol, Lawrence Raymond *lawyer*
Uselton, James Clayton *engineering executive*

Maryville
Hubbard, Dean Leon *university president*
Jonagan, Glenn E. *principal*
Strating, Sharon L. *elementary school educator*

Mexico
Hummer, Paul F., II *manufacturing company executive*
Stover, Harry M. *corporate executive*

Moberly
Blackmar, Charles Blakey *state supreme court justice*
Pelfrey, Lloyd Marvin *college president*

Neosho
Hargis, Billy James *minister*

Nevada
Ewing, Lynn Moore, Jr. *lawyer*
Hizer, Marlene Brown *library director*
Hornback, Joseph Hope *mathematics educator*
Morton, John, III *banker*

Normandy
Meyer, Ruth Ann *physical education and dance educator*

North Kansas City
Hagan, John Charles, III *ophthalmologist*

Parkville
Breckon, Donald John *academic administrator*

Point Lookout
Klinefelter, Sarah Stephens *division dean, radio station manager*

Poplar Bluff
Alexander, C. Alex *physician*
Black, Ronnie Delane *religious organization administrator, mayor*
Carr, Charles Louis *religious organization administrator*
Duncan, Leland Ray *mission administrator*

Richmond Heights
Chandler, James Barton *international education consultant*

Rolla
Adawi, Ibrahim Hasan *physics educator*
Alexander, Ralph William, Jr. *physics educator*
†Allison, Sandy *genealogist, appraiser, political consultant*
Armstrong, Daniel Wayne *chemist, educator*
Babcock, Daniel Lawrence *chemical engineer, educator*
Barr, David John *civil, geological engineering educator*
Crosbie, Alfred Linden *mechanical engineering educator*
Datz, Israel Mortimer *information systems specialist*
Day, Delbert Edwin *ceramic engineering educator*
Grimm, Louis John *mathematician, educator*
Hagni, Richard Davis *geology and geophysics educator*
Ingram, William Thomas, III *mathematics educator*
Irion, Arthur Lloyd *psychologist, educator*
James, William Joseph *chemistry educator*
Johnson, James Winston *chemical engineering educator*
Mc Farland, Robert Harold *physicist, educator*
Munger, Paul R. *civil engineering educator*
O'Keefe, Thomas Joseph *metallurgical engineer*
Omurtag, Yildirim (Bill) *engineering educator*
Rao, Vittal Srirangam *electrical engineering educator*
Saperstein, Lee Waldo *mining engineering educator*
Sarchet, Bernard Reginald *retired chemical engineering educator*
Sauer, Harry John, Jr. *mechanical engineering educator, university administrator*
†Scott, James J. *retired mining engineer*
†Summers, David Archibald *research mining engineer, engineering educator and director*
Tsoulfanidis, Nicholas *nuclear engineering educator*
Warner, Don Lee *dean emeritus*
Zobrist, George Winston *computer scientist, educator*

Saint Ann
†Drury, Charles Louis, Jr. *hotel executive*

Saint Charles
Barnett, Howard Albert *English language educator*
Castro, Jan Garden *author, arts consultant, educator*
Dauphinais, George Arthur *import company executive*
Dieterich, Russell Burks *obstetrician/gynecologist*
Gross, Charles Robert *personnel executive, legislator, appraiser*
Porterfield, Patricia Rough *education educator*
Radke, Rodney Owen *agricultural research executive*

Saint Joseph
Chilcote, Gary M. *museum director, reporter*
Head, J. Michael *transportation executive*
Johnson, Marvin Melrose *industrial engineer, consultant*
Kelly, Glenda Marie *former mayor*
Kranitz, Theodore Mitchell *lawyer*
Lockwood, George J. *newspaper editor*
Miller, Lloyd Daniel *real estate agent*
†Murphy, Janet Gorman *college president*
Sprong, Gerald Rudolph *banker*

Saint Louis
Abelov, Stephen Lawrence *uniform clothing company executive*
Abrahamson, Barry *chemical company executive*
Ackerman, Joseph J. H. *chemistry educator*
Ackers, Gary Keith *biophysical chemistry educator, researcher*
Adams, Albert Willie, Jr. *lubrication company executive*
Adorjan, J(ulius) Joe *electric company executive*
Agrawal, Harish Chandra *neurobiologist, researcher, educator*
Akerson, Alan W. *public relations company executive*
Allen, Garland Edward *biology educator, science historian*
Allen, Renee *principal*
Alpers, David Hershel *physician, educator*
Anderson, Charles Bernard *surgeon, educator*
†Anderson, William K. *public relations executive*
Andes, G. Thomas *banker*
Appleton, R. O., Jr. *lawyer*
Arnold, John Fox *lawyer*
†Arrington, Barbara *public health educator*
Arvidson, Raymond Ernst *planetary geology educator*
Asa, Cheryl Suzanne *biologist*
Attanasio, John Baptist *law educator*
Atwood, Hollye Stolz *lawyer*
Avis, Robert Grier *investment company executive, civil engineer*
Aylward, Ronald Lee *lawyer*
Babb, Ralph Wheeler, Jr. *banker*
Babington, Charles Martin, III *lawyer*
Bachmann, John William *securities firm executive*
Backer, Matthias, Jr. *obstetrician-gynecologist*
Bader, Kenneth Leroy *association executive*
Badgley, William S. *multi-bank holding company executive*
Baernstein, Albert, II *mathematician*
Bagley, Mary Carol *literature educator, writer, broadcaster*
Baile, Clifton A. *biologist, researcher*
Baker, Barry *broadcast executive*
Baker, Shirley Kistler *university library administrator*
Baldwin, Edwin Steedman *lawyer*
Ball, William Ernest *computer science educator*
Ballinger, Walter Francis *surgeon, educator*
Baloff, Nicholas *business educator, consultant*
Barken, Bernard Allen *lawyer*
Barksdale, Clarence Caulfield *banker*
Barmann, Lawrence Francis *history educator*
Barnes, Harper Henderson *movie critic*
Barnes, Zane Edison *communications company executive*
Barnett, William Arnold *economics educator*
Barney, Steven Matthew *human resources executive*
Barrie, John Paul *lawyer, educator*
†Barry, A. L. *church official*
Barta, James Joseph *federal judge*
Barth, Karl Luther *retired seminary president*
Bartlett, Walter E. *communications company executive*
Bascom, C. Perry *lawyer*
Bateman, Sharon Louise *public relations executive*
Battram, Richard L. *retail executive*
Baue, Arthur Edward *surgeon, educator, administrator*
Bauman, George Duncan *former newspaper publisher*
Bealke, Linn Hemingway *bank executive*
Bean, Bourne *lawyer*
Beare, Gene Kerwin *electric company executive*
Beck, Lois Grant *anthropologist, educator*
Becker, David Mandel *legal educator, author, consultant*
Becker, Rex Louis *architect*
Beckman, Tamela Jean (T.J. Wright) *disc jockey, entertainer*
Benberry, Cuesta Ray *historian*
Bender, Carl Martin *physics educator, consultant*
Benson, Robert John *computer science educator, administrator*
Bentele, Raymond F. *retired minerals corporate executive*
Beracha, Barry Harris *brewery executive*
Berg, Leonard *neurologist, educator, researcher*
Berger, John Torrey, Jr. *lawyer*
Bernstein, Donald Chester *brokerage company executive, lawyer*
Bernstein, Merton Clay *lawyer, educator, arbitrator*
Berthoff, Rowland Tappan *historian, educator*
Biondi, Lawrence *university administrator, priest*
Bloemer, Rosemary Celeste *bookkeeper*
Bloomberg, Terry *early childhood education administrator*
†Blowers, Richard M. *professional society administrator*
Bock, Edward John *retired chemical manufacturing company executive*
Bohle, Bruce William *editor*
Bohne, Jeanette Kathryn *mathematics and science educator*
Boldt, H. James *church administrator*
Boothby, William Munger *mathematics educator*
Bosley, Freeman Robertson, Jr. *mayor*
Bottini, Thomas H. *lawyer*
Bourke, Vernon Joseph *philosophy educator*
Bowen, James Ronald *banker*
Bowen, Stephen Francis, Jr. *ophthalmic surgeon*
Boyd, Robert Cotton *English educator*
Bracken, Robert W. *food products executive*
†Brandt, Donald Edward *utilities company executive*
Brasunas, Anton de Sales *metallurgical engineering educator*
Breece, Robert William, Jr. *lawyer*
Breihan, Erwin Robert *civil engineer, consultant*
Brickey, Kathleen Fitzgerald *law educator*
Brickson, Richard Alan *lawyer*
Bridgewater, Bernard Adolphus, Jr. *footwear company executive*
Briggs, William Benajah *aeronautical engineer*
Brock, Louis Clark *business executive, former professional baseball player*
Brodeur, Armand Edward *pediatric radiologist*
Brodsky, Philip Hyman *chemical executive, research director*
Brody, Lawrence *lawyer, educator*
Broeg, Bob (Robert William Broeg) *writer*
Broers, J. Terry *medical products manufacturing company executive*
Browde, Anatole *electronics company executive, consultant*
Browman, David L(udvig) *archaeologist*
†Brown, Frederick Lee *health care executive*
Brown, Jay Wright *food manufacturing company executive*
Brown, Melvin F. *executive*
Brownlee, Robert Hammel *lawyer*
Bryan, Henry C(lark), Jr. *lawyer*
Bryant, Ruth Alyne *banker*
Buck, Jack *sportscaster*
Burgess, James Harland *physics educator, researcher*
Burke, James Donald *museum administrator*
Burke, Mary Leyhe *school administrator*
Burkett, Randy James *lighting designer*
Burks, Verner Irwin *architect*
Burnet, Roger Hasted *construction company executive*
Burnett, Roger H. *construction executive*
Busch, August Adolphus, III *brewery executive*
Butler, James Lawrence *financial planner*
Byrnes, Christopher Ian *academic dean, researcher*
Cahill, Clyde S. *federal judge*
†Cahill, John Conway *air transportation company executive*
Cain, James Nelson *arts school administrator*
Cairns, Donald Fredrick *engineering educator, management consultant*
Callis, Clayton Fowler *research chemist*
Capellupo, John P. *air transportation executive*
†Carberry, John J. Cardinal *former archbishop*
Carey, Patricia Elaine Stedman *hospital administrator*
†Carlson, Arthur Eugene *accounting educator*
Carmody, Gerard Timothy *lawyer*
Caron, Ronald Jacques *professional sports team executive*
Carp, Richard Lawrence (Larry Carp) *lawyer*
Carr, Gary Thomas *lawyer*
†Carr, Julian Lanier, Jr. *healthcare and educational services industries executive*
Cejka, Susan Ann *executive search company executive*
Chaplin, Hugh, Jr. *physician, educator*
Chivetta, Anthony Joseph *architect*
Christopher, Glenn A. *publishing company executive*
Clear, John Michael *lawyer*
Cleary, Thomas John *aluminum products company executive*
Clement, Richard Francis *retired investment company executive*
†Clifton, Regina Marie *health association executive*
Cloninger, Claude Robert *psychiatric researcher, educator, genetic epdemiologist*
Cobb, Donna Deanne Hill *physical therapist*
Coco, Charles Edward *food products company executive*
Coerver, Elizabeth Ann *data base consultant*
Cole, Barbara Ruth *pediatrician, nephrologist*
Cole, William Porter *librarian*
Colten, Harvey Radin *pediatrician, educator*
Conaway, Mary Ann *professional counselor, educator*
Conerly, Richard Pugh *retired corporation executive*
Conran, Joseph Palmer *lawyer*
†Cook, Patricia Florence *nursing administrator*
Cooper, David Booth, Jr. *financial executive*
Cooper, Scott Kendrick *professional baseball player*
Cori, Carl Tom *chemicals executive*
Cornelius, William Edward *utilities company executive*
Cornfeld, Dave Louis *lawyer*
Costigan, Edward John *investment banker*
Cotton, W(illiam) Philip, Jr. *architect*
Cox, Jerome Rockhold, Jr. *electrical engineer*
Cox, Robert M., Jr. *electrical products manufacturing company executive*
†Craib, Donald Forsyth, Jr. *insurance company executive*
Craig, Andrew Billings, III *bank holding company executive*
Crampton, William DeVer *tax lawyer*
Crandell, Dwight Samuel *museum director*
†Crawford, Walter Clyde, Jr. *ornithologist*
Crebs, P(aul) Terence *lawyer*
Crutsinger, Robert Keane *diversified food wholesale company executive*
Cryer, Philip Eugene *medical educator, scientist, endocrinologist*
†Cummings, James M. *urology educator*
Cunningham, Charles Baker, III *manufacturing company executive*
†Curley, John E., Jr. *religious health association director*
Curran, Michael Walter *scientist*
Curtiss, Roy, III *biology educator*
Dames, Joan Foster (Mrs. Urban L. Dames) *magazine editor, columnist*
Danforth, John Claggett *senator, lawyer, clergyman*
Danforth, William Henry *academic administrator, physician*
†Davis, Irvin *broadcasting company executive*
Davis, Steven L. *lawyer*
†Davis, Stuart Alan *real estate company executive*
Davis, W. L., III *electrical products company executive*
Deal, Joseph Maurice *university dean, art educator, photographer*
Delaney, Robert Vernon *logistics and transportation executive*

Denneen, John Paul *lawyer*
DesRosiers, Roger I. *artist, educator*
Devantier, Paul W. *communications executive, broadcaster*
Dewald, Paul Adolph *psychiatrist*
Dierdorf, Daniel Lee (Dan Dierdorf) *football analyst, sports commentator, former professional football player*
Dill, Charles Anthony *manufacturing and computer company executive*
Dill, John Francis *publishing company executive*
Dill, Virginia S. *accountant*
Dodge, Philip Rogers *physician, educator*
Domjan, Laszlo Karoly *newspaper executive*
Dommermuth, William P. *marketing consultant, educator*
Donohue, Carroll John *lawyer*
Dorsey, Gray Lankford *law educator emeritus*
Dorwart, Donald Bruce *lawyer*
Dougherty, Charles Joseph *retired utility executive*
Dowd, Edward L., Jr. *prosecutor*
Dreifke, Gerald Edmond *electrical engineering educator*
Dressel, Roy Robert *insurance company executive*
Drews, Robert Carrel *physician*
Du Bois, Philip Hunter *psychologist, educator*
†Dudukovic, Milorad P. *chemical engineering educator, consultant*
Duesenberg, Richard William *lawyer*
Duhme, H(erman) Richard, Jr. *sculptor, educator*
Dunivent, John Thomas *artist, educator*
Earle, James A. *educational administrator*
†Early, Gerald *writer*
Eckhoff, Sister Mary Ann *academic administrator*
Edison, Bernard Alan *retired retail apparel company executive*
Ehrlich, Ava *television executive producer*
Elkin, Stanley Lawrence *author, literature educator*
Elkins, Ken Joe *broadcasting executive*
Elliott, Howard, Jr. *gas distribution company executive*
†Elliott, Susan Spoehrer *data processing executive*
Ellis, Dorsey Daniel, Jr. *dean*
Elsesser, James R. *food products company executive*
Engelhardt, Thomas Alexander *editorial cartoonist*
Epner, Steven Arthur *computer consultant*
Erwin, James Walter *lawyer*
Essman, Alyn V. *photographic studios company executive*
Etzkorn, K. Peter *sociologist, educator, author*
Evens, Ronald Gene *radiologist, medical center administrator*
Ewan, Joseph (Andorfer) *botanist, biohistorian, research bibliographer*
Falk, William James *lawyer*
Farrell, David Coakley *department store executive*
Farrell, John Timothy *hospital administrator*
Farrell, Neal Joseph *banker*
Farris, Charles Lowell *city official*
Fascia, Remo Mario *aviation consultant, airplane manufacturing company executive*
Faught, Harold Franklin *electrical equipment manufacturing company executive*
Feir, Dorothy Jean *entomologist, physiologist, educator*
Ferguson, Gary Warren *public relations executive*
Ferrendelli, James Anthony *neurologist, educator*
Filippine, Edward Louis *federal judge*
Fillenwarth, Albert F. *advertising agency financial executive*
Finan, John Joseph *hospital administrator*
Finkel, Donald *poet*
Finnigan, Joseph Townsend *public relations executive*
Fischer, Harry William *radiologist, educator*
Fitch, Coy Dean *physician, educator*
Fleming, Richard Carl Dunne *city planner, business executive*
Fletcher, James Warren *physician*
Flye, M. Wayne *surgeon, immunologist, educator*
Fogarty, William Martin, Jr. *physician*
Folk, Roger Maurice *laboratory director*
Forrestal, Patrick George *sales promotion agency executive*
Fournie, Raymond Richard *lawyer*
†Fox, Sam *business executive*
Frager, Norman *stockbroker*
Frawley, Thomas Francis *physician*
Frederick, William Sherrad *manufacturing and retailing company executive*
Fredrickson, John Murray *otolaryngologist*
Freeland, A. Jerome *publishing executive*
Frieden, Carl *biochemist, educator*
Friedlander, Michael Wulf *physicist, educator*
Friedman, William Hersh *otolaryngologist, educator*
Fryer, Edwin Samuel *lawyer*
†Gaertner, Donell J. *library director*
†Gain, Jeffrey W. *agricultural organization executive*
Garr, Louis Joseph, Jr. *lawyer, retail company executive*
Gass, William H. *author, educator*
Gauen, Patrick Emil *newspaper correspondent*
Gelman, Warren Jay *metals trading company executive*
Gerard, Jules Bernard *law educator*
Gerdine, Leigh *retired academic administrator*
Gershenson, Harry *lawyer*
Gibbons, Patrick Chandler *physicist, educator*
Gibson, Robert *broadcaster, former baseball player*
Gilbert, Allan Arthur *manufacturing executive*
†Gilcrest, James P. *mortgage banker*
Gilligan, Sandra Kaye *private school director*
Gladding, Nicholas C. *lawyer*
Godiner, Donald Leonard *lawyer*
Godsey, C. Wayne *broadcasting executive*
Goebel, John J. *lawyer*
Goldberg, Anne Carol *physician, educator*
Goldberg, Norman Albert *music publisher, writer*
Goldstein, Michael Gerald *lawyer*
Goldstein, Samuel R. *oil company executive*
Goldstein, Steven *lawyer*
Gomes, Edward Clayton, Jr. *construction company executive*
Goodman, Harold S. *lawyer*
Gould, Phillip L. *civil engineering educator, consultant*
Graff, George Stephen *aerospace company executive*
Graham, Colin *stage director*
Graham, John Dalby *public relations executive*
Gray, Charles Elmer *lawyer, rancher, investor*
Gray, Walter Franklin *retired banker*
Green, Dennis Joseph *lawyer*
Green, Maurice *molecular biologist, virologist, educator*
Greenbaum, Stuart I. *economist, educator*
Griffin, W(illiam) L(ester) Hadley *shoe company executive*
Groennert, Charles Willis *electric company executive*
Gross, Michael Lawrence *chemistry educator*
Guenther, Charles John *librarian, writer*
Guerri, William Grant *lawyer*
Gunn, George F., Jr. *federal judge*
Gupta, Surendra Kumar *chemical firm executive*
Guze, Samuel Barry *psychiatrist, educator, university official*
Haake, Arthur C. *church administrator*
Haberstroh, Richard David *insurance agent*
Hamburger, Viktor *retired biology educator*
Hamilton, Jean Constance *federal judge*
Handel, Peter H. *physics educator*
Hansen, Charles *lawyer*
Harmon, Robert Lee *corporate executive*
Harris, Whitney Robson *lawyer*
Hasl, Rudolph Carl *university dean, law educator, lawyer*
Hastings, Bryce *architect*
Hayes, Samuel Banks, III *banking company executive*
Hays, Ruth *lawyer*
Hecker, George Sprake *lawyer*
Heininger, S(amuel) Allen *retired chemical company executive*
Heinrich, Ross Raymond *geophysicist, educator*
Hellmuth, George Francis *architect*
Hellmuth, Theodore Henning *lawyer*
Hempstead, Gerard Francis *lawyer*
Henle, Robert John *former university president*
Herbert, Kevin Barry John *classics educator*
Hermann, Robert Ringen *conglomerate company executive*
Hershey, Falls Bacon *surgeon, educator*
Hewitt, Thomas Edward *financial executive*
Hexter, Jack H. *historian, educator*
Higgins, Edward Aloysius *newspaper editor*
Hilgert, Raymond Lewis *management and industrial relations educator, consultant, arbitrator*
Hillard, Robert Ellsworth *public relations consultant*
Hillis, Mark B. *lawyer*
†Hirsch, Ira Jean *otolaryngologist, educator*
Hirsch, Raymond Robert *chemical company executive, lawyer*
Hirsh, Ira Jean *psychology educator, researcher*
Hoblitzelle, George Knapp *former state legislator*
Hoessle, Charles Herman *zoo director*
Hofstatter, Leopold *psychiatrist, researcher*
Hohenberg, Charles Morris *physics educator*
Holmes, Nancy Elizabeth *pediatrician*
Holt, Glen Edward *library administrator*
†Holt, Leslie Edmonds *librarian*
Holten, James Joseph *meat processing company executive*
Holtzer, Alfred Melvin *chemistry educator*
†Horner, Robert David *mortgage banking executive*
Horstmeyer, John A. *manufacturing company executive*
Horwitt, Max Kenneth *biochemist, educator*
Howard, Walter Burke *chemical engineer*
Hsu, Chung Yi *neurologist*
Hull, Brett A. *professional hockey player*
Hungate, William Leonard *retired federal judge, former congressman*
Hunter, Earle Leslie, III *professional association executive*
†Hunter, Michael Thomas *natural gas pipeline company executive*
Hunter, Thom Hugh *seminary administrator*
Husar, Rudolf Bertalan *mechanical engineering educator*
Ihde, Daniel Carlyle *health science executive*
Immel, Vincent Clare *retired law educator*
Inkley, John James, Jr. *lawyer*
Irwin, Hale S. *professional golfer*
Israel, Martin Henry *astrophysicist, educator, academic administrator*
Isselhard, Donald Edward *dentist*
Ittner, H. Curtis *architect*
Jackson, Carol E. *federal judge*
Jackson, Rebecca R. *lawyer*
Jacobsen, Thomas H(erbert) *banker*
James, William W. *banker*
Jaudes, William E. *lawyer*
Jenkins, James Allister *mathematician, educator*
Jenks, Downing Bland *railroad executive*
Jensen, Gary Richard *mathematics educator*
Jobe, Muriel Ida *medical technologist*
Johnsen, Richard Alan *manufacturing executive*
Johnson, E. Perry *lawyer*
Johnson, Kennett Conrad *advertising agency executive*
Joist, Johann Heinrich *hematologist, medical researcher, educator*
Jones, Robert E. *company executive*
Jones, Ronald Woodbridge *human resources specialist, small business owner*
Jones, Wilbur Boardman, Jr. *trust company executive*
Jones, William Catron *legal educator*
Kagan, Sioma *economics educator*
Kanne, Marvin George *newspaper publishing executive*
Kaplan, Henry Jerrold *ophthalmologist, educator*
Kauffman, William Ray *lawyer*
Keller, Juan Dane *lawyer*
Keltner, Raymond Marion, Jr. *surgeon, educator*
Kerrick, Gray *corporate communications executive*
Kerwin, Richard G. *grain company executive*
Kessler, Nathan *technology consultant*
Ketner, Joseph Dale *museum director, art historian*
Khoury, George Gilbert *printing company executive, baseball association executive*
†Kilkenny, John E. *geologist*
Killenberg, George Andrew *newspaper consultant, former newspaper editor*
Kimmey, James Richard, Jr. *medical educator, consultant*
King, Morris Kenton *medical school dean*
King, Robert Henry *minister, church denomination executive, former educator*
Kinsella, Ralph Aloysius, Jr. *physician*
Kipnis, David Morris *physician, educator*
Kirberg, Leonard Carl *engineering executive*
Klahr, Saulo *physician, educator*
Kling, Merle *political scientist, university official*
Kling, S(tephen) Lee *banker*
Klobasa, John Anthony *lawyer*
Kniffen, Jan Rogers *finance executive*
Knight, Charles Field *electrical equipment manufacturing company executive*
Kodner, Ira J. *surgeon, educator*
Koff, Robert Hess *program director*
Kolker, Allan Erwin *ophthalmologist*
Korando, Donna Kay *journalist*
Kornblet, Donald Ross *communications company executive*
Kornfeld, Rosalind Hauk *research biochemist*
Kouchoukos, Nicholas Thomas *surgeon*
†Kowalskey, Zygmont John, Jr. *aerospace executive*
Krekorian, Elizabeth Anne *nursing college administrator*
Krenzke, Richard L. *church administrator, clergy member, social worker*
Krukowski, Lucian *philosophy educator, artist*
Kuhlmann, Fred L. *brewery consultant, lawyer, baseball executive*
Kultermann, Udo *architectural and art historian*
Kummer, Fred S. *construction company executive*
Kurz, Joseph Louis *chemistry educator*
Lacy, Norris Joiner *French language and literature educator*
Lacy, Paul Eston *pathologist*
Lagunoff, David *physician, educator*
Lambright, Stephen Kirk *brewing company executive*
Lamoreux, Frederick Holmes *financial executive*
Landau, William Milton *neurologist*
Lander, David Allan *lawyer*
Lanese, Herbert J. *air and aerospace transportation manufacturing executive*
Laskowski, Leonard Francis, Jr. *microbiologist*
Lause, Michael Francis *lawyer*
Lazorko, Anthony, Jr. *art director*
Lebowitz, Albert *lawyer, author*
Leer, Steven F. *mining executive*
Lents, Don Glaude *lawyer*
Leonard, Eugene Albert *banker*
Leven, Charles Louis *economics educator*
Levin, Ronald Mark *law educator*
Le Vine, Victor Theodore *political science educator*
Liberman, Lee Marvin *utility executive*
Lickhalter, Merlin Eugene *architect*
Liddy, Richard A. *insurance company executive*
Lieberman, Edward Jay *lawyer*
Limbaugh, Stephen Nathaniel *federal judge*
Lipeles, Maxine Ina *lawyer*
Lipkin, David *chemist*
Lipman, David *multimedia company executive*
Loeb, Jerome Thomas *retail executive*
Loeb, Virgil, Jr. *oncologist, hematologist*
Loewenstein, Joseph F. *English literature educator*
Logan, Joseph Prescott *lawyer*
Long, Helen Halter *author, retired educator*
Loomstein, Arthur *real estate company executive*
Lorenzini, Paul G. *manufacturing executive*
Lovelace, Eldridge Hirst *retired landscape architect, city planner*
Lovin, Keith Harold *university administrator, philosophy educator*
Loynd, Richard Birkett *consumer products company executive*
Lucking, Peter Stephen *marketing consultant, industrial engineering consultant*
Lucy, Robert Meredith *lawyer*
Luedde, Charles Edwin Howell *lawyer, corporation executive*
Luepke, Henry Francis, Jr. *lawyer*
Luther, George Aubrey *orthopedic surgeon*
MacCarthy, John Peters *banker*
Macias, Edward S. *chemistry educator, university official*
Maguire, John Patrick *investment company executive*
Mahsman, David Lawrence *religious publications editor*
Majerus, Philip Warren *physician*
Mall, Ida *church administrator*
Mandelker, Daniel Robert *law educator*
Mandelstamm, Jerome Robert *lawyer*
Manske, Paul Robert *orthopedic hand surgeon, educator*
Marcus, Larry David *broadcasting executive*
Marsh, James C., Jr. *secondary school principal*
Marsh, Miles L. *holding company executive*
Marshall, Garland Ross *biochemist, biophysicist, medical educator*
Massey, Raymond Lee *lawyer*
Masters, William Howell *physician, educator*
Mattern, Keith Edward *lawyer*
Mattison, Richard *psychiatry educator*
Mattson, William Royce, Jr. *health care consulting company executive*
†Mazzotta, Bruno Robert *hospital administrator, former military officer*
McCarter, Charles Chase *lawyer*
Mc Carthy, Francis F. *construction executive*
McCorkle, Michael *construction company executive*
McCracken, Ellis W., Jr. *lawyer, corporation executive*
Mc Daniel, James Edwin *lawyer*
McDonnell, John Finney *aerospace and aircraft manufacturing company executive*
McDonnell, Sanford Noyes *aircraft company executive*
McFarland, Mary A. *elementary/secondary school educator/administrator*
McGinnis, W. Patrick *diversified company executive*
McGinty, John *marketing consultant*
McGrath, Edward A. *electrical equipment company executive*
McKelvey, James Morgan *chemical engineering educator*
McKenna, William John *textile products executive*
McKinney, John Benjamin *steel company executive*
McKinnis, Michael B. *lawyer*
McKissack, Patricia Carwell *children's book author*
McMillian, Theodore *federal judge*
Meisel, George Vincent *lawyer*
Meissner, Edwin Benjamin, Jr. *real estate broker*
†Melnuk, Paul D. *diversified financial services company executive*
†Mennicke, August Theodore *church officer*
Merbaum, Michael *psychology educator, clinical psychologist*
Merrell, James Lee *religious editor, clergyman*
Merrill, Charles Eugene *lawyer*
Mertz, Stuart Moulton *landscape architect*
Metcalfe, Walter Lee, Jr. *lawyer*
Meyer, John *church administrator*
Meyer, William F. *church administrator*
Michaelides, Constantine Evangelos *architect, educator*
Middelkamp, John Neal *pediatrician, educator*
Miller, Frank William *legal educator*
Miller, Gary J. *political economist*
Miller, James Gegan *research scientist, physics educator*
Miller, Theresa Ann *management consultant*
Mills, Linda S. *public relations executive*
Mink, Eric P. *newspaper columnist*
Minnich, Virginia *retired medical researcher, educator*
Mohan, John J. *lawyer*
Monroe, Thomas Edward *industrial corporation executive*
Moore, McPherson Dorsett *lawyer*
Morgan, Lawrence Allison *headmaster, educational administrator*
Morgan, Robert Peter *engineering educator*
Morice, James L. *public relations executive*
Morley, Harry Thomas, Jr. *real estate executive*
Morrow, Ralph Ernest *historian, educator*
Mueller, Charles William *electric utility executive*
Mueller, David Brian *accountant, chief financial officer*
†Mulcahy, J. Patrick *food company executive*
Muller, Lyle Dean *religious organization administrator*
Muller, Marcel W(ettstein) *electrical engineering educator*
Mulligan, Michael Dennis *lawyer*
Mulligan, Robert William *university official, clergyman*
Munk, Peter *oil industry executive*
Murphy, George Earl *psychiatrist, educator*
Murray, Robert Wallace *chemistry educator*
Myers, Raymond Irvin *optometrist, researcher*
Myerson, Robert J. *radiologist, educator*
Myler, Russell Clinton *social services association administrator*
Nathanson, Wayne Richard *aerospace company executive*
Nelson, Michael Underhill *aerospace company executive, association executive*
Nemanick, Richard Charles *business executive*
Neufeind, Wilhelm *economics educator, university administrator*
Neville, James Morton *food company executive, lawyer*
Newman, Andrew Edison *retail executive*
Newman, Charles A. *lawyer*
Newman, Eric Pfeiffer *retail chain store executive*
Newman, Joan Meskiel *lawyer*
Newton, George Addison *investment banker, lawyer*
†Nichols, Colin Graham *bioscience educator*
Noel, Edwin Lawrence *lawyer*
Norberg, Richard Edwin *physicist, educator*
Norman, Charles Henry *broadcasting executive*
North, Douglass Cecil *economist, educator*
Novelly, Paul A. *petrochemical and refining company executive*
Nussbaum, A(dolf) Edward *mathematician, educator*
Obata, Gyo *architect*
O'Brien, Albert James *management consultant*
O'Brien, Thomas Francis *manufacturing company executive*
O'Connell, Dennis E. *lawyer*
Oetter, Bruce Christian *lawyer*
O'Keefe, Michael Daniel *lawyer*
Olson, Clarence Elmer, Jr. *newspaper editor*
Olson, Robert Grant *lawyer*
O'Malley, Kevin Francis *lawyer, writer, educator*
O'Neill, Eugene Milton *mergers and acquisitions consultant*
O'Neill, John Robert *airline executive*
O'Neill, Sheila *principal*
Ong, Walter Jackson *priest, English educator, author*
Orton, George Frederick *aerospace engineer*
O'Shoney, Glenn *church administrator*
Osterloh, Everett William *county official*
O'Toole, Terrence J. *lawyer*
Owens, William Don *anesthesiology educator*
Owyoung, Steven David *curator*
Ozawa, Martha Naoko *social work educator*
Palans, Lloyd Alex *lawyer*
Paris, Paul Croce *mechanics educator, engineering consultant, researcher*
Patton, Thomas F. *college administrator, pharmaceutical chemist*
Peck, William Arno *physician*
Peiser, Robert Alan *financial executive*
Pellett, Thomas Rowand *retired food company executive*
Penniman, Nicholas Griffith, IV *newspaper publisher*
Peper, Christian Baird *lawyer*
Perez, Carlos A. *radiation oncologist, educator*
Perry, Catherine D. *judge*
Peters, David Allen *mechanical engineering educator, consultant*
Peters, Frank Lewis, Jr. *retired arts editor*
†Peterson, T. Roger *engineering company executive*
Petrie, Roy H. *obstetrician, gynecologist, educator*
Pfautch, Roy *minister, public affairs consultant*
Pfefferkorn, Michael Gene, Sr. *secondary education educator, writer*
Pfefferkorn, Sandra J. *secondary education educator*
Pflueger, M(elba) Lee *academic administrator*
†Phillips, Oliver *botany educator*
Pickens, Buford Lindsay *architectural educator, historian*
Pickle, Robert Douglas *lawyer, diversified industry executive*
Pittman, David Joshua *sociologist, educator, researcher, consultant*
Pollack, Joe *newspaper critic and columnist, free-lance writer*
Pollack, Seymour Victor *computer science educator*
†Pope, Robert Eugene *fraternal organization administrator*
Poscover, Maury B. *lawyer*
†Prather, Thomas Levi, Jr. *army officer*
Prensky, Arthur Lawrence *pediatric neurologist, educator*
Price, Joseph Levering *neuroscientist, educator*
Prickett, Gordon Odin *mining, mineral and energy engineer*
†Privott, W. J. *agricultural products company executive*
Pulitzer, Emily S Rauh (Mrs. Joseph Pulitzer, Jr.) *art consultant*
Pulitzer, Michael Edgar *publishing executive*
Pylipow, Stanley Ross *retired manufacturing company executive*
Quenon, Robert Hagerty *mining consultant, retired holding company executive*
Quinn, Jack J. *professional hockey team executive*
Ractliffe, Robert Edward George *management executive*
†Ramey, Peter M. *holding company executive*
Ramming, Michael Alexander *school system administrator*
Randolph, Joe Wayne *machine manufacturing executive*
†Rasmussen, David Tab *physical anthropology educator*
Rataj, Edward William *lawyer*
Raven, Peter Hamilton *botanical garden director, botany educator*
†Reding, Nicholas Lee *chemical company executive*
Reinert, Paul Clare *university chancellor emeritus*
Reinhard, James Richard *judge*
Reynolds, James E. *lawyer*
Rich, Harry E. *footwear and specialty retailing financial executive*
†Richey, Donald L. *retail executive*
Richmond, Richard Thomas *journalist*

Riddle, Veryl Lee lawyer
†Rigali, Justin F. archbishop
†Riley, Joe real estate executive
Ritter, Robert Forcier lawyer
Ritterskamp, Douglas Dolvin lawyer
†Robert, Bruce G. manufacturing executive, light
Roberts, Hugh Evan business investment services company executive
Robins, Lee Nelken medical educator
Rocklage, Sister Mary Roch health system executive
Rockwell, Hays Hamilton bishop
Rodin, Ervin Yechiel László mathematician
†Rosenberg, Kim David banker
Rosenthal, Harold Leslie biochemistry educator
Rosenzweig, Saul psychologist, educator, administrator
†Rosin, Walter L. religious organization administrator
Ross, Donald Kenneth consulting engineering executive
Ross, Monte electrical engineer
Rubenstein, Jerome Max lawyer
Ruland, Richard Eugene English and American literature educator, critic, literary historian
Ryall, Jo-Ellyn M. psychiatrist
†Ryan, Barbara Ann church official
Ryckman, DeVere Wellington consulting environmental engineer
Sachs, Alan Arthur lawyer, corporate executive
Sale, Llewellyn, III lawyer
Sale, William Merritt classicist, comparatist, educator
Saligman, Harvey consumer products and services company executive
Salisbury, Robert Holt political science educator
Samples, Ronald Eugene coal company executive
Sanders, Fred Joseph aerospace company executive
Sanders, Steven Paul lawyer
Sant, John Talbot lawyer
Santiago, Julio Victor medical educator, researcher and administrator
Saperstein, Marc Eli religious history educator, rabbi
Sathe, Sharad Somnath chemical company executive
Sauer, Robert C. religious organization administrator
Schierholz, William Francis, Jr. real estate developer
Schlafly, Phyllis Stewart author
Schmidt, Robert Charles, Jr. finance company executive
†Schneiderman, Herbert Barry hospital administrator
Schnuck, Craig grocery stores company executive
Schoemehl, Vincent Charles, Jr. mayor
Schoendienst, Albert Fred (Red Schoendienst) professional baseball coach, former baseball player
Schoeneberg, Joyce Eileen secondary school biology educator
Schoenhard, William Charles, Jr. health care executive
Schonfeld, Gustav medical educator, researcher
Schumacher, Frederick Carl former insurance company executive
Schwartz, Alan Leigh pediatrician, educator
Schwartz, Henry Gerard surgeon, educator
Schwarz, Egon humanities and German language educator, author, literary critic
Scott, Hugh, III diesel engine distributor
Searls, Eileen Haughey lawyer, librarian, educator
Self, Larry Douglas architectural firm executive
Selfridge, George Dever dentist, retired naval officer
Sestric, Anthony James lawyer
Sexton, Owen James vertebrate ecology educator, conservationist
Shanahan, Michael Francis manufacturing executive, hockey team executive
Shands, Courtney, Jr. lawyer
Shank, Robert Ely physician, preventive medicine educator emeritus
†Shapiro, Robert B. manufacturing executive
Shaw, Charles Alexander judge
Shaw, James church administrator
Shaw, John Arthur lawyer
Shea, Daniel Bartholomew, Jr. English language educator, actor
Shelton, O. L. state legislator
Shipton, Harold William biomedical engineering educator, researcher
Shrauner, Barbara Wayne Abraham electrical engineering educator
Siemer, Paul Jennings public relations executive
Sigurdson, Erik D. oil industry executive
†Sikorski, James Alan research chemist
Siteman, Alvin Jerome banker
Slatkin, Leonard Edward conductor, music director, pianist
Slatopolsky, Eduardo nephrologist, educator
Slavin, Raymond Granam allergist, immunologist
†Smith, Gene R. engineering company executive
Smith, Jeffrey E. historian, educator
†Smith, Morton Edward ophthalmology educator, dean
Smith, Ozzie (Osborne Earl Smith) professional baseball player
†Smith, Wayman Flynn, III brewery executive, lawyer
Smurfit, Michael William Joseph manufacturing company executive
Sneider, Martin Karl retail company executive
Snyder, Peter Larsen public relations executive
Sonnino, Carlo Benvenuto electrical manufacturing company executive
Sparks, Robert Edward chemical engineering educator
Spector, Gershon Jerry physician, educator, researcher
Spector, Stanley foreign language educator
†Spehr, Steven real estate company executive
Stahl, Philip Damien physiology and cell biology educator
Staley, Robert W. mechanical engineer, electric company executive
Stauder, William Vincent geophysics educator
Stearley, Robert Jay retired packaging company executive
Stefoff, James Edward retired clothing company executive
†Stevens, Warren Douglas botanist
Stewart, John Harger music educator
Stiritz, William P. food company executive
†Stodghill, Ronald school system administrator
Stoecker, David Thomas banker
Stohr, Donald J. federal judge
Stokes, Patrick T. brewery company executive
Stonecipher, Harry Curtis manufacturing company executive
†Stoneman, William, III physician, educator
Storandt, Martha psychologist
Stork, Donald Arthur advertising executive
Stretch, John Joseph social work educator, management and evaluation consultant
Strunk, Robert Charles physician
Suba, Antonio Ronquillo surgeon
Suelflow, August Robert historical institute consultant, educator
Suggs, James C. publishing executive
Suhre, Walter Anthony, Jr. retired lawyer and brewery executive
Suter, Albert Edward manufacturing company executive
Sutera, Salvatore Philip mechanical engineering educator
Sutter, Richard Anthony physician
Szabo, Barna Aladar mechanical engineering educator, mining engineer
Takano, Masaharu physical chemist
Tamke, George William electronics and electrical equipment executive
Taylor, Jack C. automobile company executive
Teasdale, Kenneth Fulbright lawyer
Teasdale, Thomas Hennings architect
Teitelbaum, Steven Lazarus pathology educator
Templeton, Alan Robert biology educator
Ternberg, Jessie Lamoin pediatric surgeon
Thalden, Barry R. architect
Thayer, Gerald Campbell beer company executive
Thomas, Lewis Jones, Jr. anesthesiology educator, biomedical researcher
Thomas, Rhonda Churchill lawyer
Thompson, James Clark utilities executive
†Thompson, Robert W. surgeon
Throdahl, Monte Corden former chemical company executive
Tober, Lester Victor shoe company executive
Touhill, Blanche Marie university chancellor, history-education educator
Tremayne, Bertram William, Jr. lawyer
Trova, Ernest Tino artist, sculptor
Truitt, William Harvey private school educator
Trusheim, H. Edwin insurance executive
Tulloch, George Sherlock, Jr. electrical equipment distribution company executive, lawyer
Turley, Michael Roy lawyer
Turner, Harold Edward education educator
Ulett, George Andrew psychiatrist
Ullian, Joseph Silbert philosophy educator
Van Bokkelen, William Requa health facility administrator
Van Cleve, William Moore lawyer
Vandover, Samuel Taylor lawyer
Varner, Joseph Elmer biology educator, researcher
†Vonk, Hans conductor
Wack, Thomas E. lawyer
Waggle, Doyle Hans food company executive, scientist/researcher
Walentik, Corinne Anne pediatrician
Walker, Dale Rush banker
Walker, Earl E. manufacturing executive
Walker, George Herbert, III investment banking company executive, lawyer
Walker, Robert Mowbray physicist, educator
Walsh, John E., Jr. business educator, consultant
Walsh, Thomas Charles lawyer
Walz, Bruce James radiation oncologist
Wandling, Marilyn Elizabeth Branson artist, art educator
Ward, R. J. bishop
Waters, Richard retired publishing company executive
Watkins, Hortense Catherine middle school educator
Watson, Richard Allan philosophy educator, writer
Weaver, William Clair, Jr. (Mike Weaver) human resources development executive
Weber, Gloria Richie minister, retired state representative
Weber, Morton M. microbial biochemist, educator
Weeks, Paul Martin plastic surgeon, educator
Weidenbaum, Murray Lew economics educator
Weil, Paul P. lawyer
Weiss, Charles Andrew lawyer
Weiss, Robert Francis former academic administrator, religious organization administrator, consultant
Wellman, Carl Pierce philosophy educator
Wells, Ben Harris retired beverage company executive
Wells, Samuel Alonzo, Jr. surgeon, educator
Wente, Patricia Ann radio executive
Wenzel, Fred William apparel manufacturing executive
West, Robert C. engineering company executive
†Wetzel, Sister Damian health care administrator
Wheeler, Burton M. literature educator, higher education consultant, college dean
Whyte, Michael Peter medicine and pediatrics educator, research director
Wickline, Samuel Alan cardiologist, educator
Wiley, Gregory Robert publisher
Wilke, LeRoy church administrator
Will, Clifford Martin physicist, educator
Williams, Frank James, Jr. department store chain executive, lawyer
Williamson, Donald Ray retired career Army officer
Willman, John Norman management consultant
Willman, Vallee Louis physician, surgery educator
Wilson, Betty May finance company executive
Wilson, Edward Nathan mathematician, educator
Wilson, Harry Burgoyne retired public relations company executive
Wilson, Margaret Bush lawyer, civil rights leader
Winer, Warren James insurance executive
Winter, David Ferdinand electrical engineering educator, consultant
Winter, William Earl mayor, retired beverage company executive
Wissner, Seth Ernst gynecologist, educator
Withers, W. Wayne lawyer
Witherspoon, William investment economist
Wolfe, Charles Morgan electrical engineering educator
Wolff, Frank Pierce, Jr. lawyer
Wolzenski, Ben H. insurance company executive
Woo, William Franklin newspaper editor
Wood, Frederick S. manufacturing company executive
Woodruff, Bruce Emery lawyer
Worseck, Raymond Adams economist
Wrighton, Mark Stephen chemistry educator
Wu, Nelson Ikon art history educator, author, artist
Young, Marvin Oscar lawyer
Young, Paul Andrew anatomist
Zavaglia, Greg J. management consultant
Zuker, Michael biomathematician
Zurheide, Charles Henry consulting electrical engineer

Saint Peters
Krey, Mary Ann Reynolds beer wholesaler executive

Sedalia
Noland, Gary Lloyd vocation educational administrator

Sibley
Morrow, Elizabeth business owner, sculptress, museum association administrator, educator

Sparta
Madore, Joyce Louise gerontology nurse

Springfield
Abraham, Yohannan management educator
Ames, Jimmy Ray education educator
Berger, Jerry Allen museum director
Boehm, Robert Kenneth telecommunications consultant
†Booze, Joyce Wells publishing executive
Carlson, Thomas Joseph lawyer, mayor, real estate developer
Champion, Norma Jean communications educator, state legislator
Clark, Russell Gentry federal judge
Collinson, William R. federal judge
Cox, Lester Lee broadcasting executive
Criswell, Charles Harrison analytical chemist, environmental and forensic consultant, executive
Cunningham, Robert Cyril clergyman, editor
Dailey, Parker Stokes minister
Dearmore, Thomas Lee retired journalist
Delaney, Jean Marie art educator
Denton, D. Keith management educator
Edwards, Charles M. hospital administrator
Flower, Joseph Reynolds administrative executive
Glazier, Robert Carl publishing executive
Groves, Sharon Sue elementary education educator
Gruhn, Robert Stephen parole officer
Hackett, Earl Randolph neurologist
Hagerty, Paul James school superintendent
Hanman, Gary Edwin dairy company executive
Hansen, John Paul metallurgical engineer
H'Doubler, Francis Todd, Jr. surgeon
Himstedt, Ronald Eugene union official
Hulston, John Kenton lawyer
Jacobi, Fredrick Thomas newspaper publisher
Jura, James J. electric utility executive
King, (Jack) Weldon photographer
Leibrecht, John Joseph bishop
Linnemeyer-Busch, Annie library director
Liu, Yuan Hsiung drafting and design educator
Lowther, Gerald Halbert lawyer
McCartney, N.L. investment banker
†McDonald, William Henry lawyer
Moore, John Edwin, Jr. college president
Nuccitelli, Saul Arnold civil engineer, consultant
Orms, Howard Raymond dramatics educator
Ostergren, Gregory Victor insurance company executive
Ownby, Jerry Steve landscape architect, educator
Shealy, Clyde Norman neurosurgeon
Spicer, Holt Vandercook speech and theater educator
Starnes, James Wright lawyer
Stone, Allan David economics educator
Stovall, Richard L. academic administrator
Strickler, Ivan K. dairy farmer
Swift, James William health care executive
Sylvester, Ronald Charles newspaper writer
Thompson, Clifton C. chemistry educator, university administrator
Trask, Thomas Edward religious organization administrator
Triplett, Loren O. religious organization administrator
Van Cleave, William Robert international relations educator
Westphal, Leonard Wyrick health care executive, consultant

Stockton
Jackson, Betty L. Deason real estate developer

University City
Flanagan, Joan Wheat (Maggie Flanagan) educational therapist
Shen, Jerome Tseng Yung pediatrician

Valley Park
Benedict, Gary Clarence psychotherapist

Viburnum
West, Roberta Bertha writer

Warrensburg
Elliott, Eddie Mayes college president
Harmon, Lynn Adrian banker
Limback, E(dna) Rebecca vocational education educator
Smith, Dolores Maxine Plunk dancer, educator

Warrenton
Dapron, Elmer Joseph, Jr. communications executive

Webster Groves
Kramer, Gerhardt Theodore architect
Osver, Arthur artist
Schenkenberg, Mary Martin principal

Wentzville
Berry, Chuck (Charles Edward Anderson Berry) singer, composer

MONTANA

Anaconda
McCarthy, Bea state legislator

Antelope
Olson, Betty-Jean elementary education educator

Arlee
Gregory, Russell Arthur education and training consultant

Big Timber
Yuzeitis, James Richard information specialist

Bigfork
Blumberg, Nathan(iel) Bernard journalist, educator, writer and publisher
Keller, Barbara Lynn special education educator
Shennum, Robert Herman retired telephone company executive

Billings
Barnea, Uri N. music director, conductor, composer, violinist
Battin, James Franklin judge, former congressman
Carpenter, Bruce H. academic administrator
Cochran, William Michael librarian
DeRosier, Arthur Henry, Jr. college president
Fagg, Russell judge, lawyer
Haughey, James McCrea lawyer, artist
Heiny, Robert Wayne special education educator
†Hylton, Robert Ralph anesthesiologist
Jones, James Leonard lawyer
Jones, Ronald Vance broadcast executive
Larsen, Richard Lee former city manager, business, municipal and labor relations consultant, arbitrator
Marcovitz, Leonard Edward retail executive
McCracken, Joe C. school system administrator
Moss, Lynda Bourque museum director
Murphy, Gregory Gerard lawyer
Pihlaja, Maxine Muriel Mead orchestra executive
Reed, Kenneth G. petroleum company executive
Russell, Angela Veta state legislator, social worker
Sample, Joseph Scanlon foundation executive
Shanstrom, Jack D. federal judge
Sites, James Philip lawyer, consul
Small, Lawrence Farnsworth history educator
Surwill, Benedict Joseph, Jr. college dean, educator
Thompson, James William lawyer
Towe, Thomas Edward lawyer
Williams, Judy Carol teacher
Williamson, Jerry Dean radio station executive

Bozeman
Berg, Lloyd chemical engineering educator
Characklis, William Gregory university research center director, engineering educator
Cundy, Vic Arnold mechanical engineer, educator
Davis, Nicholas Homans Clark finance company executive
DeHaas, John Neff, Jr. retired architecture educator
Goering, Kenneth Justin college administrator
Gray, Philip Howard psychologist, educator
Harris, Christopher Kirk lawyer
†Horner, John Robert paleontologist, researcher
Hovin, Arne William agronomist, educator
†Lavin, Matthew T. horticultural educator
Malone, Michael Peter academic administrator, historian
Mattson, George Arthur architect
Mertz, Edwin Theodore biochemist, emeritus educator
Onsager, Jerome Andrew research entomologist
Pagenkopf, Andrea LeSuer university official
Pittendrigh, Colin Stephenson retired biologist, educator
Ratliff, Gerald Lee dean, speech and theatre educator
Refsland, Gary Arlan retired sociology educator
Sanks, Robert Leland environmental engineer, emeritus educator
Spencer, Robert C. political science educator
Stanislao, Joseph consulting engineer, educator
Stroup, Richard Lyndell economics educator, writer
Todd, Kenneth S., Jr. parasitologist, educator

Browning
Scriver, Robert Macfie sculptor

Butte
Beuerman, Donald Roy chemistry educator
Burke, John James utility executive
†De Voe, Irving Woodrow microbiologist, educator
Gannon, Robert P. utility company executive
Mc Elwain, Joseph Arthur retired power company executive
Peterson, John Leonard lawyer, judge
Poore, James Albert, III lawyer
Sherick, John Matthew (Jack Sherick) technical services company executive
Studebaker, Irving Glen engineering educator, researcher
Volborth, Alexis geochemistry and geological engineering educator

Cascade
Mesaros, Kenneth Lee rancher, state senator

Corvallis
Koch, Peter wood scientist

Crow Agency
Ditmanson, Dennis L. national monument administrator

Darby
Brandborg, Stewart Monroe conservationist, government official

Dayton
Catalfomo, Philip university dean

Deer Lodge
Baehr, Robert E. electrical contractor

Dillon
Ross, Deborah Lynn (Debbie Ross) reporter, photographer

Dutton
DeBruycker, Jane Crystal state legislator

Forsyth
Smith, Jeffry Alan health administrator, physician, consultant

Gallatin Gateway
Monaco, Paul academic administrator, educator, artist, writer

Great Falls
Christiaens, Chris (Bernard Francis Christiaens) financial analyst, state senator
Davidson, David Scott architect
Day, James Lawrence psychiatrist
Doherty, Steve lawyer, state legislator
Downer, William John, Jr. retired hospital administrator, consultant
Hatfield, Paul Gerhart federal judge, lawyer
Hoiland, Andrew Calvin architect

Kochman, Carl Jessee *media executive, consultant, educator*
Manning, John Willard *lawyer*
Milone, Anthony M. *bishop*
Overfelt, Clarence Lahugh *lawyer*
Ryan, William Matthew *lineman, state legislator*
Sletten, John Robert *construction company executive*
Stevens, George Alexander *realtor*
Walker, Leland Jasper *civil engineer*
Weissman, Jerrold *metal products executive*
†Wilson, Kirk George *medical service executive*

Hamilton
Garon, Claude Francis *laboratory administrator, researcher*
Munoz, John Joaquin *research microbiologist*
Rudbach, Jon Anthony *biotechnical company executive*

Harrison
Jackson, Peter Vorious, III *retired association executive*

Havre
Leeds, Debra Ann *primary school educator*
Windel, Robert Eugene *school system administrator*

Helena
Barnhart, Beverly Homyak *management consultant*
Bartlett, Sue *state legislator*
Blair, Gary Charles *military officer*
Brooke, Vivian M. *state legislator*
Brown, Jan Whitney *small business owner*
†Brunett, Alexander J. *bishop*
†Cain, Alan F. *insurance company executive*
Cocchiarella, Vicki Marshall *state legislator*
†Cooney, Mike *state official*
Fitzpatrick, Lois Ann *library administrator*
Gray, Karla Marie *state supreme court justice*
Hanson, Marian W. *state legislator*
Harrison, John Conway *state supreme court justice*
Hunt, William E., Sr. *state supreme court justice*
Jacobson, Judith Helen *state senator*
Johnson, David Sellie *civil engineer*
Jones, Charles Irving *bishop*
Kasten, Betty Lou *state legislator*
†Keenan, Nancy A. *state agency administrator*
Lovell, Charles C. *federal judge*
Malcolm, Andrew Hogarth *journalist, writer*
Marks, Robert L. (Bob Marks) *treasurer ex-officio, rancher*
Marquardt, Kathleen Patricia *association executive*
Mazurek, Joseph P. *state attorney general*
McDonough, Russell Charles *retired state supreme court justice*
†Meadows, Judith Adams *law librarian, educator*
†Morrison, John Haddow, Jr. *engineering company executive*
Opitz, John Marius *clinical geneticist, pediatrician*
Racicot, Marc F. *governor*
Rehberg, Dennis R. *state official*
Swanson, Emily *state legislator*
Trieweiler, Terry Nicholas *state supreme court justice*
Turnage, Jean A. *state supreme court chief justice*
Vaughn, Eleanor *state legislator*
Weber, Fred J. *state supreme court justice*

Hot Springs
Erickson, James Gardner *retired artist, cartoonist*

Kalispell
James, Marion Ray *magazine founder, editor*
Ormiston, Patricia Jane *elementary education educator*
Ruder, Melvin Harvey *retired newspaper editor*

Livingston
Feldstein, Albert B. *retired editor, artist, writer*
Harrison, James Thomas (Jim Harrison) *author*
†LeBlond, Richard Foard *internist, educator*

Mc Leod
Hjortsberg, William Reinhold *author*
McGuane, Thomas Francis, III *author, screenwriter*

Miles City
Heitschmidt, Rodney Keith *rangeland ecologist*

Missoula
Banaugh, Robert Peter *computer science educator*
Brown, Robert Munro *museum director*
Dennison, George Marshel *academic administrator*
Erickson, Leif B. *federal judge*
Fawcett, Don Wayne *anatomist*
Fisher, William Henry *education educator*
Haddon, Sam Ellis *lawyer*
Jakobson, Mark John *physics educator*
Jenni, Donald Alison *zoology educator*
Kemmis, Daniel Orra *mayor, author*
Kindrick, Robert LeRoy *academic administrator, dean, English educator*
Knowles, William Leroy (Bill Knowles) *television news producer, journalism educator*
Kraft, Dennis *school system administrator*
Lopach, James Joseph *political science educator*
Murray, Raymond Carl *forensic geologist, educator*
Nakamura, Mitsuru James *microbiologist, educator*
Osterheld, R(obert) Keith *chemistry educator*
Peterson, James Algert *geologist, educator*
Power, Thomas Michael *economist, educator*
Rippon, Thomas Michael *art educator, artist*
Sogard, Jeffrey W. *lawyer*
Stevenson, Marolane *counselor*
Strobel, David Allen *psychology educator*
Turman, George *former lieutenant governor*
Watkins, John Goodrich *psychologist, educator*
Winston, Bente *academic administrator*
Wollersheim, Janet Puccinelli *psychology educator*
Wright, Barbara Evelyn *microbiologist*

Polson
Flamm, Barry Russell *ecologist*
Stanford, Jack Arthur *biological station administrator*

Red Lodge
Kauffman, Marvin Earl *geoscience consultant*

Troy
Sherman, Signe Lidfeldt *securities analyst, former research chemist*

Twin Bridges
Ruppel, Edward Thompson *geologist*

Victor
Stewart, JoAnne *secondary school educator*

West Glacier
Lusk, Harlan Gilbert *national park superintendent*
Mihalic, David Anthony *national park administrator*

Whitefish
Daggett, Charles Edward *construction company executive*
Miller, Ronald Alfred *family physician*

Wibaux
Bruski-Maus, Betty Jean *state legislator*

Wolf Point
Listerud, Mark Boyd *retired surgeon*

NEBRASKA

Alliance
Haefele, Edwin Theodore *political theorist, consultant*

Auburn
Winegardner, Rose Mary *special education educator*

Bellevue
Hinz, Calvin L. *architectural firm executive*
Muller, John Bartlett *university president*
Raynor, Dennis L. *architect, firm executive*

Boys Town
†Lynch, Thomas Joseph *museum manager*
Peter, Val Joseph *social service administrator, educator, priest*

Chadron
Hanson, Charles Easton, Jr. *museum director, consultant*

Clay Center
Hahn, George LeRoy *agricultural engineer, biometeorologist*
Laster, Danny Bruce *animal scientist*

Columbus
Whitehead, John C. *state judge*

Crete
Brakke, Myron Kendall *retired research chemist and educator*

Dakota City
Andriessen, Roel *management consulting company executive*
Broyhill, Roy Franklin *manufacturing executive*
Grigsby, Lonnie Oscar *food company executive*
Haines, Perry Vansant *cattle company executive*
Leman, Eugene D. *meat industry executive*
Peterson, Robert L. *meat processing executive*
Tinstman, Dale Clinton *investment company executive*

Fremont
Dunklau, Rupert Louis *personal investments consultant*

Gering
Harvey, Karon Lee *secondary education educator*
Weihing, John Lawson *plant pathologist, state senator*

Gibbon
Wiley, Ronald LeRoy *financial executive*

Grand Island
Dobesh, Ernest Leonard *farmer, mayor*
Etheridge, Margaret Dwyer *medical center director*
MacDonald, Joseph Faber *bishop*
Mc Namara, Lawrence J. *bishop*
Ryan, Thomas A. *school system administrator*
Zichek, Shannon Elaine *secondary school educator*

Gretna
Riley, Kevin M. *principal*

Hartington
Meyer, Betty Jean *physical education educator*

Hastings
Larsen, Glen L. *school system administrator*
McEwen, Larry Burdette *retired English and theater arts educator, author*

Herman
Korshoj, Franklin Delano *retail lumberyard owner*

Holdrege
Hendrickson, Bruce Carl *life insurance company executive*

Humboldt
Rumbaugh, Melvin Dale *geneticist, agronomist*

Kearney
De Los Angeles, Reynaldo Adrillana *psychiatrist, consultant*
Wice, Paul Clinton *news director, educator*
Young, Ann Elizabeth O'Quinn *historian, educator*

Lincoln
Acklie, Duane William *transportation company executive*
Adams, Charles Henry *retired animal scientist, educator*
Angle, John Charles *retired life insurance company executive*
Arth, Lawrence Joseph *insurance executive*
Babchuk, Nicholas *sociology educator, researcher*
Bahar, Ezekiel *electrical engineering educator*
Bailey, Dudley *English educator*
Beam, Clarence Arlen *federal judge*
Beermann, Allen J. *state official*
Blad, Blaine L. *agricultural meteorology educator, consultant*
Bleich, Michael Robert *nursing administrator and consultant*
Boslaugh, Leslie *judge*
Bradley, Richard Edwin *retired university president*
Broman, Keith Leroy *finance educator, financial planner*
†Bruskewitz, Fabian W. *bishop*
Caporale, D. Nick *state supreme court justice*
Cederberg, John Edwin *accountant*
Childs, Gayle B(ernard) *retired education educator*
Crompton, Louis William *English literature educator*
Curtis, Carl Thomas *former senator*
Day, Richard Putnam *marketing and employee benefits consultant*
Diamond, Judy *museum administrator*
Digman, Lester Aloysius *management educator*
†Dixon, Wheeler Winston *film and video studies educator, writer*
Dyer, William Earl, Jr. *retired newspaper editor*
Eckhardt, Craig Jon *chemistry educator*
Edison, Allen Ray *electrical engineer, educator*
Edwards, Donald Mervin *biological systems engineering educator, university dean*
Elias, Samy E. G. *engineering executive*
Fahrnbruch, Dale E. *state supreme court justice*
Fisher, Calvin David *food manufacturing company executive*
Francis, Charles Andrew *agronomy educator, consultant*
Fuenning, Samuel Isaiah *sports medicine research director*
Gardner, Charles Olda *plant geneticist and breeder, design consultant, analyst*
Genoways, Hugh Howard *biologist*
Gibbs, Dale L. *architect, educator*
Grew, Priscilla Croswell *university official, geology educator*
Hamilton, David Wendell *medical services executive*
Hanway, Donald Grant *retired agronomist, educator*
Hastings, William Charles *retired state supreme court chief justice*
Hendrickson, Kent Herman *dean, librarian*
Heng, Stanley Mark *military officer*
Hermance, Lyle Herbert *college official*
Hewitt, James Watt *lawyer*
Hillegass, Clifton Keith *publisher*
Hirai, Denitsu *surgeon*
Hodges, Clarence Eugene *charitable organization executive, former government official*
Janzow, Walter Theophilus *retired college administrator*
Johnson, Margaret Kathleen *business educator*
Johnson, Raymond Allen Constan *state auditor of public accounts, accountant*
Johnson, Virgil Allen *retired agronomist*
Jolliff, Carl R. *clinical biochemist, immunologist, laboratory administrator*
Jones, Alice Jane *soil scientist, educator, federal agency administrator*
Jones, Lee Bennett *chemist, educator*
Kivett, Marvin Franklin *anthropologist*
Kopf, Richard G. *federal judge*
Koszewski, Bohdan Julius *internist, medical educator*
Landis, David Morrison *state legislator*
Lanphier, David J. *judge*
Laursen, Paul Herbert *retired university educator*
Leinieks, Valdis *classicist, educator*
Liggett, Twila Marie Christensen *public television company executive, academic administrator*
Louis, Kenneth Clair *insurance company executive*
Luedtke, Roland Alfred *lawyer*
Lutjeharms, Joseph Earl *commissioner*
MacPhee, Craig Robert *economist, educator*
†Margolis, Stuart W. *computer science and engineering educator*
Marsh, Frank (Irving) *former state official*
Massengale, Martin Andrew *agronomist, university president*
McClurg, James Edward *research laboratory executive*
Minahan, John C., Jr. *federal judge*
†Moore, Scott *state official*
Morris, M(ary) Rosalind *cytogeneticist, educator*
Morrow, Andrew Nesbit *interior designer, business owner*
Moul, Maxine Burnett *state official*
Moyer, Robert Theodore *newspaper editor*
Nelson, Darrell Wayne *university administrator, scientist*
Nelson, Don Jerome *electrical engineering and computer science educator*
Nelson, E. Benjamin *governor*
Neubert, George W. *museum director, sculptor*
Nolte, Walter Eduard *retired retirement home executive, foundation counsel, former banker*
Oldfather, Charles Eugene *lawyer*
O'Leary, Marion Hugh *chemistry educator*
Osborne, Tom *college football coach*
Ottoson, Howard Warren *agricultural economist, former university administrator*
Pedersen, Dwite A. *state senator, alcohol/drug abuse counselor*
Peterson, Wallace Carroll, Sr. *economics educator*
Piester, David L(ee) *magistrate judge*
Pirsch, Carol McBride *state senator, community relations manager*
Powers, David Richard *educational administrator*
Preister, Donald George *greeting card manufacturer, state senator*
Rawley, Ann Keyser *small business owner, picture framer*
Rawley, James Albert *history educator*
Raz, Hilda *editor-in-chief periodical, educator*
Robak, Kim M. *state official*
Robson, John Merritt *library and media administrator*
Rogers, Vance Donald *former university president*
Rosenow, John Edward *foundation executive*
Sander, Donald Henry *soil scientist, researcher*
Sawyer, Robert McLaran *history educator*
†Schepers, James Stuart *soil scientist*
Schimek, DiAnna Ruth Rebman *state legislator*
Schmidt, John Wesley *agronomy educator*
Schmitz, John Albert *veterinary pathologist*
†Schultz, Kathleen Anne *executive director*
Schwendiman, Gary *business administration educator*
Sellmyer, David Julian *physicist, educator*
Sheffield, Leslie Floyd *retired agricultural educator*
†Smith, Donald Eugene *financial analyst*
Smith, Lewis Dennis *academic administrator*
Sonderegger, Theo Brown *psychology educator*
Spellman, J. R. *book publishing executive*
Splinter, William Eldon *agricultural engineering educator*
Stange, James Henry *architect*
Stenberg, Donald B. *state attorney general*
Steward, Weldon Cecil *architecture educator, architect, consultant*
Stover, John Ford *railroad historian, educator*
Stuart, James *banker, broadcaster*
Swartz, Jack *association executive*
Swartzendruber, Dale *soil physicist, educator*
Swihart, Fred Jacob *lawyer*
Tavlin, Michael John *telecommunications company executive*
Taylor, Stephen Lloyd *food toxicology educator*
Thorson, Thomas Bertel *zoologist, educator*
Treves, Samuel Blain *geologist, educator, administrator*
Tyner, Neal Edward *retired insurance company executive*
Ullman, Frank Gordon *electrical engineering educator*
Urbom, Warren Keith *federal judge*
Vicary, Duane S. *chamber of commerce executive*
Wagner, Rod *library director*
Wesely, Donald Raymond *state senator*
White, C. Thomas *state supreme court justice*
White, John Wesley, Jr. *university president*
Wiegand, Sylvia Margaret *mathematician, educator*
Wiersbe, Warren Wendell *clergyman, author, lecturer*
Will, Eric John *state senator*
Woollam, John Arthur *electrical engineering educator*
Young, Dale Lee *banker*

Madison
Mortensen-Say, Marlys (Mrs. John Theodore Say) *school system administrator*

Malcolm
Hudkins, Carol L. *state legislator*

Norfolk
Froehlich, Virgil *food products company executive*
Kubik, James Donald *educator*
Stites, Ray Dean *minister, college president*
Wehrer, Charles Siecke *business educator*
Wilson, Robert *food products executive*
Wozniak, Richard Michael, Sr. *city and regional planner*

North Bend
Johnson, Lowell C. *commissioner*

Offutt A F B
†Butler, George L. *career military officer*
Curtin, Gary Lee *air force officer*
Tindal, Ralph Lawrence *career officer*

Omaha
Abboud, Christopher William *state senator*
Albert, Michael L. *food broker*
Ames, George Ronald *insurance marketing executive*
Andersen, Harold Wayne *contributing editor, newspaper executive, director*
Andrews, Richard Vincent *physiologist, educator*
Ansorge, Luella M. *retired association administrator*
Aschenbrener, Carol Ann *pathologist, educator*
Badeer, Henry Sarkis *physiology educator*
Banville, Guy Rene *academic dean*
Barmettler, Joseph John *lawyer*
Barrett, Frank Joseph *insurance company executive*
Bauer, Otto Frank *university official, communication educator*
Beal, Graham William John *museum director*
Bechtel, James M. *retired civil servant*
Bell, C(lyde) R(oberts) (Bob Bell) *association executive*
Ben-Yaacov, Gideon *computer system designer*
Bergquist, Gordon Neil *English educator*
Bookout, John G. *insurance company executive*
Bowen, Gary Roger *architect*
Brody, Alfred Walter *pulmonologist*
Buffett, Warren Edward *entrepreneur*
Cambridge, William G. *federal judge*
Casey, Murray Joseph *physician*
Christensen, Curtis Lee *lawyer*
Cohen, Paul G(erson) *management consultant*
Conley, Eugene Allen *retired insurance company executive*
Council, Brenda Joyce *lawyer*
Cox, Robert Sayre, Jr. *pathologist, researcher, educator*
Coy, William Raymond *civil engineer*
Crummer, Murray Thomas, Jr. *insurance company executive*
Cunningham, Glenn Clarence *government official*
Cunningham, William Francis, Jr. *English language educator, university administrator*
Curtiss, Elden F. *bishop*
Davidson, Richard K. *railroad company executive*
Davis, Chip *record producer, arranger*
Davis, John Byron *surgeon*
Dickerson, Lon Richard *library administrator*
Dolan, James Vincent *lawyer*
†Donaldson, William L. *newspaper publishing company executive*
Dougherty, Charles John *philosophy and medical ethics educator*
Dubes, George Richard *geneticist*
Eggers, James Wesley *executive search consultant*
Erickson, James Paul *financial service company executive*
Faust, Harlan R. *architect*
Ferer, Harvey Dean *metals company executive*
Fitzgerald, William Allingham *savings and loan association executive*
Fjell, Mick *principal*
Fletcher, Philip B. *food products company executive*
Flickinger, Thomas Leslie *hospital alliance executive*
Forbes, Franklin Sim *lawyer, educator*
Fowler, Stephen Eugene *retired military officer/human resource specialist*
†Fraser, John Martin *hospital administrator*
Frazier, Chet June *advertising agency executive*
Frederickson, Keith Alvin *advertising agency executive*
Fusaro, Ramon Michael *dermatologist, researcher*
Gambal, David *biochemistry educator*
Gano, Clifton Wayne, Jr. *risk management executive*
Gardner, Paul Jay *anatomist, educator*
Garofolo, Ronald Joseph *drafting and architecture education educator*
†Geary, Richard *construction company executive*
†Giltner, F. P. *bank executive*
Goaley, Donald Joseph *insurance company executive, accountant*
Gordon, John Leo *anesthesiologist*
Graham, Wayne *insurance company executive*

Grant, John Thomas retired state supreme court justice
Greer, Randall Dewey investment company executive
Grewcock, William L. mining company executive
†Gupta, Vinod business lists company executive
Hachten, Richard Arthur, II hospital administrator
Hamann, Deryl Frederick lawyer, bank executive
Haney, J. Terrence insurance consultant
Hangen, Bruce Boyer conductor, music director
Harned, Roger Kent radiology educator
Harr, Lawrence Francis lawyer
Harter, David John radiation oncologist
Haselwood, Eldon LaVerne education educator
Heaney, Robert Proulx physician, educator
Hodgson, Paul Edmund surgeon
Horning, Ross Charles, Jr. historian, educator
Howe, G(ary) Woodson newspaper editor, newspaper executive
Hruska, Roman Lee lawyer, retired senator
Hultquist, Paul Fredrick electrical engineer, educator
Imray, Thomas John radiologist, educator
Jaudzemis, Kathleen A. judge
Jay, Burton Dean insurance actuary
Jensen, Sam lawyer
Jugel, Richard Dennis corporate executive, management consultant
Kaiman, Jerome J. supermarket executive
Key, Stephen Lewis food company exective
Klassen, Lynell W. rheumatologist, transplant immunologist
Knobbe, Urban food products executive
Korbitz, Bernard Carl oncologist, hematologist, educator, consultant
Krogstad, Jack Lynn accounting educator
Krotz, James Edward bishop
Larson, Roberta M. children's theater director
Lauritzen, John Ronnow banker
Lemon, Henry Martyn physician, educator
Lindsay, James Wiley agricultural company executive
Lochiano, Rocco natural gas company executive
†Lozier, Allan G. manufacturing company executive
Lynch, Benjamin Leo oral surgeon educator
Maginn, John Leo insurance company executive
†Maher, L. James, III molecular biologist
Matthies, Frederick John architectural engineer
Maurer, Harold Maurice pediatrician
McDaniels, B. T. bishop
McEniry, Robert Francis education educator
Miller, Morris Folsom banker
Moeller, A. Diane health facility administrator
Mohiuddin, Syed Maqdoom cardiologist, educator
Monaghan, Thomas Justin prosecutor
Monasee, Charles Arthur healthcare foundation executive
†Moriarty, Jeanne Marie medical center administrator
Morrison, Michael Gordon university president, clergyman, history educator
Mulcahey, Sister Patricia school system administrator
Munger, Charles T. diversified company executive
Myers, Herman E., Jr. life insurance company executive
Nethers, Elena Soto lawyer
Newton, John Milton acadmeic administrator, psychology educator
O'Brien, Richard L(ee) academic administrator, physician, cell biologist
O'Donohue, Walter John, Jr. medical educator
Omer, Robert Wendell hospital administrator
†Parks, J. Michael telecommunications executive
Pearson, Paul Hammond physician
Peck, Ernest James, Jr. academic administrator
Peck, Richard Cleon judge
Phares, Lynn Levisay public relations communications executive
Polsky, Donald Perry architect
Power, Kenneth D. utilities company executive
Ramm, Richard W. retail executive
†Regan, Timothy James grain company executive
†Richard, Oliver Gonzard, III (Rick Richard) lawyer, business executive
Rikkers, Layton F. surgeon
†Rikkers, Layton Frederick surgeon
Rock, Harold L. lawyer
Rogan, Eleanor Groeniger cancer researcher, educator
Roskens, Ronald William association administrator
Ruddon, Raymond Walter, Jr. pharmacology educator
Rupp, Mark Edmund medical educator
Sanders, W(illiam) Eugene, Jr. physician, educator
Sawtell, Stephen M. private investor, lawyer
Schlessinger, Bernard S. retired university dean
Schmidman, Jo Ann artistic director
†Schuerman, Norbert Joel school superintendent
Schwartz, C. Edward hospital administrator
Scott, Robert Michael data processing executive
Scott, Walter, Jr. construction company executive
Severa, Gordon L. utility executive
Shanahan, Thomas M. judge
Sheehan, John Francis cytopathologist, educator
Simmons, Lee Guyton, Jr. zoological park director
Skoog, Donald Paul retired physician, educator
Skutt, Thomas James insurance company executive
Sokolof, Phil industrialist, consumer advocate
Soshnik, Joseph investment banking consultant
Strom, Lyle Elmer federal judge
Tollman, Thomas Andrew librarian
†Townley, Robert Gordon medical educator
Truhlsen, Stanley Marshall physician, educator
Tucker, Michael elementary school principal
Tunnicliff, David George civil engineer
Velde, John Ernest, Jr. business executive
Waggener, Ronald Edgar radiologist
Watt, Dean Day retired biochemistry educator
Weber, Delbert Dean university administrator
Weekly, John William insurance company executive
Werner, Clarence L. transportation executive
Wright, Norman Harold lawyer
Wunsch, James Stevenson political science educator
Zepf, Thomas Herman physics educator, researcher

Papillion
Dvorak, Allen Dale radiologist

Plainview
Mauch, Jeannine Ann elementary education educator

Scottsbluff
Fisher, J. R. marketing executive
Scovil, Larry Emery minister
Weichenthal, Burton A. educational administrator, beef specialist

Seward
Vrana, Verlon Kenneth professional society administrator, conservationist

Valley
Chapman, John Arthur agricultural engineering executive
Lerew, Everett Duane special education administrator

Wayne
Mash, Donald J. college president

West Point
Paschang, John Linus retired bishop

Wood River
Bish, Milan David former ambassador, consultant

Wymore
Meyer, Melvin A. lumber and hardware executive, freelance designer

NEVADA

Battle Mountain
Hensley, E. Leon school system administrator

Boulder City
Ferraro, Arthur Kevin broadcasting executive
Wyman, Richard Vaughn engineering educator, exploration company executive

Carson City
Ayres, Janice Ruth social service executive
Crawford, John Edward geologist, scientist
Del Papa, Frankie Sue state attorney general
Gunderson, Elmer Millard state supreme court justice, law educator
†Hammargren, Lonnie lieutenant governor
†Heller, Dean state official
†Jackson, James Jeffrey lawyer
Larson, Gerald Lee auditor
Lowden, Suzanne state legislator
McLain, John Lowell resource specialist, consultant
Miller, Robert Joseph governor, lawyer
Noland, Robert LeRoy retired manufacturing company executive
O'Connell, Mary Ann state senator, business owner
Paslov, Eugene T. state education official
Rocha, Guy Louis archivist, historian
Rose, Robert E(dgar) state supreme court justice
Santor, Ken state treasurer
Seale, Robert L. state treasurer
Springer, Charles Edward state supreme court justice
†Sullivan, Carley Hayden political party executive
Tiffany, Sandra L. state legislator
Titus, Alice Cestandina (Dina Titus) state legislator
Van Wagoner, Robert Louis lawyer
Wagner, Sue Ellen former state official
Young, C. Clifton judge

Dyer
Howard, Sherwin Ward college president

East Ely
Alderman, Minnis Amelia psychologist, educator, small business owner

Fallon
Plants, Walter Dale elementary education educator, minister

Gardnerville
Harlander, Leslie Albert naval architectural consultant
Manoukian, Noel Edwin lawyer, former state supreme court chief justice

Glenbrook
Buscaglia, (Felice) Leo(nardo) special education educator, author
Jabara, Michael Dean investment banker

Hawthorne
Graham, Lois Charlotte retired educator
Sortland, Trudith Ann educator, speech and language therapist

Henderson
Benson, James DeWayne university administrator
Creech, Wilbur Lyman air force officer
Durante, Salvatore (Rusty Durante) broadcast executive
Freyd, William Pattinson fund raising executive, consultant
McKinney, Sally Vitkus realty company executive, business owner
Turner, Florence Frances ceramist

Incline Village
Cordingley, Mary Jeanette Bowles (Mrs. William Andrew Cordingley) social worker, psychologist, artist, writer
Dale, Martin Albert investment banking executive
Diederich, J(ohn) William financial consultant
Eastin, Keith E. lawyer
Henderson, Paul Bargas, Jr. economic development consultant
Hiatt, Robert Worth former university president
Johnson, James Arnold business consultant, venture capitalist
Jones, Robert Alonzo economist
McCartney, Patrick Kevin newspaper reporter
McCormac, Billy Murray physicist, research institution executive, former army officer
Merdinger, Charles John civil engineer, naval officer, academic adminstrator
Strack, Harold Arthur retired electronics company executive, retired air force officer, planner, analyst, author, musician
Wahl, Howard Wayne retired construction company executive, engineer

Incline Vlg
White, Richard Hugh dean student affairs

Jean
Schaeffer, Glenn William casino corporate financial executive

Las Vegas
Ackerman, H. Don automotive dealership executive
Adams, Charles Lynford English language educator
Ann-Margret, (Ann-Margret Olsson) actress, performer
†Aquilina, Nick C. government agency administrator
Aranow, Peter Jones service company executive
Arce, Phillip William hotel and casino executive
Atkins, Cholly (Charles Atkinson) choreographer, consultant
†Baker, Chuck journalist, author
Bandt, Paul Douglas physician
Barger, James Daniel physician
Barnes, Wesley Edward energy and environmental executive
Barth, Delbert Sylvester environmental studies educator
Basile, Richard Emanuel retired management consultant, educator
†Batson, Darrell Lynn librarian, consultant
†Bausher, Leslie J. home building company executive
Bennett, William Gordon casino executive
Bilbray, James Hubert former congressman, lawyer, consultant
Boehm, Robert Foty mechanical engineer, educator, researcher
Brandsness, David R. hospital administrator
Brebbia, John Henry lawyer
Bretthauer, Erich Walter chemist
Broadbent, Robert N. government official, pharmacist
Brown, Brice Norman surgeon, educator
Brown, Lori Lipman secondary school educator
†Canarelli, Lawrence D. real estate developer
Capelle, Madelene Carole opera singer, educator, music therapist
Caro, Mike gaming authority
†Cling, Carol Susan movie critic, writer
†Cram, Brian Manning school system administrator
Cwerenz-Maxime, Virginia Margaret secondary education educator
Di Palma, Joseph Alphonse brokerage house executive, lawyer
Eastwood, DeLyle chemist
Fehr, Gregory Paris marketing and distribution company executive
Foley, Roger D. federal judge
Fortier, Quincy Ernest obstetrician, gynecologist
Galane, Morton Robert lawyer
George, Lloyd D. federal judge
Goodall, Leonard Edwin public administration educator
Goodwin, Nancy Lee corporate executive
Goulet, Robert Gerard singer, actor
Gowdy, Miriam Betts nutritionist
Haas, Robert John aerospace engineer
Hamilton, Richard Lee surgeon
Hardbeck, George William economics educator
Hardie, George Graham casino executive
Harpster, Robert Eugene engineering geologist
Harter, Carol Clancey university president, English language educator
Healy, Mary (Mrs. Peter Lind Hayes) singer, actress
Herte, Mary Charlotte plastic surgeon
Herzlich, Harold J. chemical engineer
Hess, John Warren scientific institute administrator, educator
Hilbrecht, Norman Ty lawyer
Hill, Michael John newspaper editor
Holmes, David Leo recreation and leisure educator
Horner, Lee foundation executive, speaker, consultant, computer specialist
Hosier, Gerald Douglas lawyer
Hunsberger, Charles Wesley library consultant
Iorio, John Emil retired education educator
Johns, Albert Cameron political scientist
Johnston, Robert Jake federal magistrate judge
Jones, Jan Laverty mayor
Jones, Robert Clive judge
Kaiser, Glen David construction company executive
Kenny, Erin Leigh advertising executive, state legislator
Kerkorian, Kirk motion picture company executive, consultant
Knight, Gladys (Maria) singer
Kornstein, Don Robert investment banker
Landau, Ellis gaming company executive
Laub, William Murray retired utility executive
Law, Flora Elizabeth (Libby Law) retired community health and pediatrics nurse
Lazerson, Jack pediatrician, educator
Lenzie, Charles Albert utility company executive
Levich, Robert Alan geologist
Levin, Bruce Alan lawyer, real estate developer
Levy, Franklin I. mail order food service company executive
Lewis, Jerry (Joseph Levitch) comedian
Lovell, Carl Erwin, Jr. lawyer
Lurie, Ron mayor
Mack, Jerome D. banker
Mahan, James Cameron lawyer
Martin, Thomas E. motel chain executive
McDonald, Malcolm Gideon education educator
Mc Kenzie, Jeremy Alec food service and baking company executive
Messenger, George Clement engineering executive, consultant
Michel, Mary Ann Kedzuf nursing educator
Miel, George Joseph computer scientist
Ogren, Carroll Woodrow retired hospital administrator
Popeil, Ron consumer products company executive
Pridham, Thomas Grenville research microbiologist
Pro, Philip Martin federal judge
†Randall, William bank executive
Rawson, Raymond D. dentist
Reichartz, W. Dan hotel executive
Riddell, Richard Harry retired lawyer
Riegle, Linda B. federal judge
†Ritchie, James E. hotel executive
Rogers, David Hughes finance executive
Rogich, Sig advertising executive
Root, Alan Charles diversified manufacturing company executive
Rossin, Herbert Yale television broadcaster
Sandvick, Frederick gaming company executive, lawyer, accountant
Sawyer, Grant lawyer
Sestini, Virgil Andrew secondary education educator
Sharits, Dean Paul motion picture company executive
Shepard, Kathryn Irene public relations executive
Shettles, Landrum Brewer obstetrician-gynecologist
Shields, Brooke Christa Camille actress, model
Smith, Fred Wesley communications company executive
Smith, Stephanie Marie lawyer
Stevens, Arthur Wilber, Jr. English literature educator, writer, editor
Thomas, Peter M. real estate developer
Thomas-Orr, Betty Jo retired public relations specialist
Trimble, Thomas James utility company executive, lawyer
Troidl, Richard John banker
Turner, Clyde T. service executive
Vanatta, Chester B. business executive, educator
Wada, Harry Nobuyoshi training company executive
Walsh, Daniel Francis bishop
Wiemer, Robert Ernest film and television producer, writer, director
Wiener, Valerie communications company owner
Wilson, Warner Rushing psychology educator
Wynn, Kenneth Richard design and furnishings company executive
Wynn, Stephen A. hotel, entertainment facility executive
Zehm, Stanley James education educator

Logandale
Smiley, Robert William, Jr. investment banker

Lovelock
Kiley, James P. retired school system administrator

Nellis AFB
Trippy, Donald R. illustrator

North Las Vegas
Marchand, Russell David, II fire chief
Regan, John Bernard (Jack Regan) community relations executive, assemblyman
†Whiteman, Steven science administrator
Williams, Mary Irene college administrator

Pahrump
Hersman, Marion Frank professional administrator, lawyer

Reno
Bandurraga, Peter Louis museum director, historian
Barnet, Robert Joseph cardiologist
Bijou, Sidney William psychology educator
Binns, James Edward banker
Bohmont, Dale Wendell agricultural consultant
Broili, Robert Howard lawyer
Brunetti, Melvin T. federal judge
Cain, Edmund Joseph education educator, emeritus dean
Carr, Thomas Jefferson, Jr. gaming executive
Clarke, Janice Cessna principal
Crowley, Joseph Neil academic administrator
Cummings, Nicholas Andrew psychologist
Dalrymple, Margaret Fisher university press editor, writer
Daugherty, Robert Melvin, Jr. university dean, medical educator
Day, Kevin Thomas banker, community services director
Delaney, William Francis, Jr. reinsurance broker
Derby, Jill Talbot anthropologist, educator, consultant
Dulgar, Pam realtor
Fox, Carl Alan research institute executive
Gibbons, Dawn managwment consultant
Gifford, Gerald Frederic education educator
Guild, Clark Joseph, Jr. lawyer
Guinn, Janet Martin psychologist, consultant
Hagen, David W. judge
Harder, Kelsie T. artist, educator
Haynes, Gary Anthony archaeologist
Helm, Donald Cairney hydrogeologist, educator
Hendricksen, Holmes G. hotel executive
Hibbs, Loyal Robert lawyer
Hill, Earl McColl lawyer
Horton, Gary Bruce transportation company executive
Horton, Robert Carlton geologist
Hug, Procter Ralph, Jr. federal judge
Humphrey, Neil Darwin university president, retired
Hynek, Frederick James architect
Johnson, Arthur William, Jr. planetarium executive
Jordan, Joseph Rembert airline pilot
Keepers, William L. utility company executive
Krenkel, Peter Ashton engineer, educator
Larwood, Laurie psychologist
Leipper, Dale Frederick physical oceanographer, educator
Leland, Joy Hanson anthropologist, alcohol research specialist
Locke, William Louis pharmacist
Loveless, Edward Eugene education educator, musician
Martz, John Roger lawyer
Mathewson, Charles Norman manufacturing company executive
May, Jerry Russell psychologist
McKibben, Howard D. federal judge
Middlebrooks, Eddie Joe environmental engineer
Mildon, Marie Roberta association executive
Miller, Newton Edd, Jr. communications educator
Neidert, Kalo Edward accountant, educator
Newberg, Dorothy Beck (Mrs. William C. Newberg) portrait artist
Pagliarini, James broadcast executive
Perry, Jean Louise dean
Pierson, William Roy chemist
Pinson, Larry Lee pharmacist
Pough, Frederick Harvey mineralogist
Price, Jonathan G. geologist
Raggio, William John state senator
Reed, Edward Cornelius, Jr. federal judge
Richards, Paul A. lawyer
Ritter, Dale Franklin geologist, research association administrator
Savoy, Douglas Eugene bishop, religion educator, explorer, writer
Sladek, Ronald John physics educator
Small, Elisabeth Chan psychiatrist, educator
Smith, Aaron research director, clinical psychologist
Straling, Phillip Francis bishop
Taranik, James Vladimir geologist, educator
Thompson, James Harold judge
Weems, Robert Cicero economist, educator
†Weideking, W. automotive holding company
Weinberg, Leonard Burton political scientist
Wells, Richard H. gaming research executive
Wiggins, Charles Edward federal judge

Smith
Weaver, William Merritt, Jr. investment banker

Sparks
Allen, Judith Martha nursing administrator, career officer
Bentley, Kenton Earl aerospace scientist, researcher
Chapman, Samuel Greeley political science educator, criminologist
Kleppe, John Arthur electrical engineering educator, business executive

Yerington
Dini, Joseph Edward, Jr. state legislator

Zephyr Cove
Proctor, Robert Swope retired petroleum company executive

NEW HAMPSHIRE

Alstead
Fiske, Edward Bogardus editor, journalist, educational consultant
Hanson, George Fulford geologist
Lyon, Bryce Dale historian, educator

Amherst
Collins, Paul D. principal
Lalley, Richard A. school system administrator
†Morley, Richard E. manufacturing engineer

Bedford
Collins, Diana Josephine psychologist
Cronin, Timothy Cornelius, III computer manufacturing executive
Effenberger, John Albert research chemist
Hall, Pamela S. environmental consulting firm executive

Berlin
Doherty, Katherine Mann librarian, writer

Canterbury
†Chamberlin, Robert West medical educator

Center Sandwich
Booty, John Everitt historiographer
Folch-Pi, Willa Babcock Romance language educator
Shoup, Carl Sumner retired economist
Simmons, Alan Jay electrical engineer, consultant

Chester
Preston, Faith college president

Concord
Arnold, Thomas Ivan, Jr. legislator
Bagley, Amy L. state legislator
Barbadoro, Paul J. federal judge
Barry, William H., Jr. federal judge
Bartlett, William Stuart, Jr. state legislator, realtor
Batchelder, William F. state supreme court justice
†Bofinger, Paul O. conservationist
Brock, David Allen state supreme court chief justice
Brunelle, Robert L. retired state education director
Cann, William Francis judge
Chambers, Mary Peyton state legislator
Cote, David Edward state legislator
Crosier, John David association administrator
Currie, Glenn Kenneth financial consultant
Day, Russell Clover federal agency administrator
Delahunty, Joseph Lawrence state senator, business investor
Devine, Shane federal judge
Dunn, Miriam D. legislative research firm executive
Dupuis, Sylvio Louis optometrist, educator, administrator
Foss, Patricia Howland state legislator, insurance agency manager
†Frisbee, John Lee historical society director
Gardner, William Michael state official
Hager, Elizabeth Sears state legislator
Hayes, Robert Cunningham financial executive
Horton, Sherman D., Jr. state supreme court justice
Hosmer, Bradley Edwin corporate executive
Hurst, Sharleene Page state legislator
Johnson, William R. state supreme court justice
Kalipolites, June E. Turner rehabilitation professional
Lederer, Richard Henry writer, educator, columnist
Levins, John Raymond investment advisor, management consultant, educator
Loughlin, Martin Francis federal judge
Marston, Charles state education official
McAuliffe, Steven James federal judge
McRae, Karen K. state legislator
Merrill, Stephen governor
Mevers, Frank Clement state archivist, historian
Newland, Matthew John state legislator
O'Rourke, Joanne A. state legislator
Packard, Bonnie Bennett state legislator
Pearson, Gertrude Booth state legislator
Pignatelli, Debora Becker state legislator
Podles, Eleanor Pauline state senator
Preston, Robert Francis state legislator
Randlett, Gloria clerk of the New Hampshire Senate
Rath, Thomas David lawyer, former state attorney general
Roberts, George Bernard, Jr. business and government affairs consultant, former state legislator
Rogers, David H. banker
Rogers, Katherine Diane political consultant, state legislator
Shaw, Randall Francis state legislator
Stahl, Norman H. federal judge
Swope, John Franklin retired insurance executive
Teschner, Douglass Paul state legislator
Thayer, W(alter) Stephen, III state supreme court justice
Theuner, Douglas Edwin bishop
†White, Jeffrey George healthcare consultant, educator
Wiggin, Kendall French state librarian
Zusy, Catherine curator

Conway
Solomon, Richard Lester retired psychology educator

Cornish
Atkinson, James Blakely writer, editor

Derry
Aranda, Mary Kathryn state legislator
Katsakiores, George Nicholas state legislator, retired restauranteur

Dover
Burr, Peter Haskell publisher, political consultant
Catalfo, Alfred, Jr. (Alfio Catalfo) lawyer
Merritt, Deborah Foote state legislator, counselor
Parks, Joe Benjamin state legislator
Pelletier, Arthur Joseph state legislator, industrial arts and computer programming educator
Pelletier, Marsha Lynn state legislator, secondary school educator
Trites, Donald George human service foundation executive

Dublin
Biklen, Paul retired advertising executive
Hale, Judson Drake, Sr. editor
Wolfe, Albert Blakeslee lawyer

Durham
Aber, John David global ecosystem research adminstrator
Appel, Kenneth I. mathematician, educator
Beckett, John Angus management educator, consultant
Farrell, William Joseph university chancellor
Flynn, Paul Bartholomew marketing executive
Ford, Daniel (Francis) writer
Hapgood, Robert Derry English educator
Harter, Robert Duane soil scientist, educator
Lawson, John H. university official
Nitzschke, Dale Frederick university president
Palmer, Stuart Hunter academic dean, sociology educator
Perry, Bradford Kent academic administrator
Pistole, Thomas Gordon microbiology educator, researcher
Powers, John H. school system administrator
†Puffer, Winthrop Freeman, Jr. behavioral science company executive, clergyman
Ritvo, Roger Alan university dean, health management-policy educator
Romoser, George Kenneth political science educator
Rosen, Sam economics educator emeritus
Rouman, John Christ classics educator
Tischler, Herbert geologist, educator
Voll, John Obert history educator
Wheeler, Katherine Wells state legislator

Etna
Ferm, Vergil Harkness anatomist, embryologist

Exeter
Beck, Albert manufacturing company executive
Boggess, Jerry Reid protective services official
Brownell, David Paul business executive
Dailey, Daniel Owen artist, educator, designer
Erickson, Raymond Leroy dean, psychologist
Jackson, Patrick John public relations counsel
Kozlowski, L. Dennis manufacturing company executive
McLaughlin, Anne Elizabeth secondary education educator
O'Donnell, Kendra Stearns principal
†Power, Richard D. manufacturing executive
†Saltonstall, Cecilia Drinker musician
Slabon, Roland Michael writer
Thomas, Jacquelyn May librarian
†Weeder, Dana Nixon surgeon

Francestown
White, Ruth O'Brien (Mrs. Wallace B. White) civic worker

Franconia
Merwin, John David lawyer, former governor

Franklin
Asplund, Bronwyn Lorraine state legislator
Wiehl, John Jack foundry executive

Freedom
Bickford, Gail Holmgren publishing executive
Kucera, Henry linguistics educator

Fremont
Richardson, Artemas P(artridge) landscape architect

Gilmanton
Osler, Howard Lloyd controller

Goffstown
Gillmore, Robert syndicated columnist, author, editor, publisher
Glines, Jon Malcolm secondary education educator

Grantham
Boothroyd, Herbert J. insurance company executive
Feldman, Roger Bruce government official
Hansen, Herbert W. management consultant
Knights, Edwin Munroe pathologist
MacNeill, Arthur Edson physician, science consultant
Wells, Edward Phillips radiologist

Greenfield
†Wheelock, Major William, Jr. college administrator

Groveton
Kegeles, Gerson chemistry educator

Hampton
†Best, Jacob Hilmer (Jerry), Jr. hotel chain executive
Canas, Jon hotel executive
Coviello, Robert Frank retail executive
D'Amato, Anthony Salvatore food products company executive
Montrone, Paul Michael scientific instruments company executive
Morton, Donald John librarian
Vogel, Phillip T. manufacturing executive
†Weber, Kenneth J. hotel executive

Hampton Falls
Buckingham, Richard L(eroy) computer company executive

Hancock
Brown, David Warfield retired academic administrator
Carney, David Mitchel political party official

Hanover
Almy, Thomas Pattison physician, educator
Anthony, Robert Newton management educator emeritus
Arndt, Walter Werner Slavic scholar, linguist, writer, translator
Baumgartner, James Earl mathematics educator
Bien, Peter Adolph English language educator, author
Birnie, Richard Williams graduate studies dean
Blaydon, Colin Campbell university professor
Bogart, Kenneth Paul mathematics educator, consultant
Boghosian, Varujan Yegan sculptor
Bollinger, Lee Carroll law educator
Bower, Richard Stuart economist, educator
Braun, Charles Louis chemistry educator, researcher
Brooks, H. Allen architectural educator, author, lecturer
Browning, James Alexander engineering company executive,inventor
Cahill, George Francis, Jr. physician, educator
Campbell, Colin Dearborn economist, educator
Chamberlain, Charles Page earth science educator
Chapman, Carleton Burke physician
Clement, Meredith Owen economist, educator
Crory, Elizabeth L. state legislator
Crowell, Richard Henry mathematician, educator
Daniell, Jere Rogers, II history educator, consultant, public lecturer
Dean, Robert Charles, Jr. mechanical engineer, entrepreneur, innovator
Demko, George Joseph geographer
Deshpandé, Rohit marketing educator
Dodge, Charles Malcolm composer, music educator
Doenges, Norman Arthur classics educator
Doney, Willis Frederick philosophy educator
Doyle, William Thomas physicist, educator
Duncan, Bruce foreign language educator
Eberhart, Richard poet
Ermenc, Joseph John mechanical engineering educator
Flaccus, Edward retired biology educator
†Fogelin, Robert John philosophy educator
Freedman, James Oliver university president, lawyer
Garthwaite, Gene Ralph historian, educator
Gert, Bernard philosopher, educator
Green, Mary Jean Matthews foreign language educator
Green, Ronald Michael ethics and religious studies educator
Guest, Robert Henry state legislator, management educator
Gustman, Alan Leslie economics educator
Harbury, Henry Alexander biochemist, educator
Hart, Katherine Wainwright curator
Heffernan, James Anthony Walsh English language and literature educator
Hennessey, John William, Jr. academic administrator
Hill, Errol Gaston drama educator, director, author
Huppe, Alex public relations executive
Hutchinson, Charles Edgar engineering educator, dean emeritus
Jacobus, John M., Jr. educator, author, photographer
Kantrowitz, Arthur physicist, educator
Kleck, Robert Eldon psychology educator
Knetter, Michael Mark economics educator
Koop, Charles Everett surgeon, government official
Kritzman, Lawrence David humanities educator
Kurtz, Thomas Eugene mathematics educator
Lahr, Charles Dwight mathematics educator, college dean
Lamperti, John Williams mathematician, educator
Lathem, Edward Connery librarian, editor, educator
Lawrence, Louis James, Jr. automotive company executive
Logue, Dennis Emhardt financial economics educator, consultant
Long, Carl Ferdinand engineering educator
Loseff, Lev Lifschutz Russian educator
Lubin, Martin cell physiologist educator
Lyons, Gene Martin political scientist, educator
Malmstrom, Vincent Herschel geography educator
Mansell, Darrel Lee, Jr. English educator
Marvin, Eugene L. civil engineer
Masters, Roger Davis government educator
McCollum, Robert Wayne physician, educator
Mc Farland, Thomas L. book publishing executive
†Meadows, Donella environmentalist
Montgomery, David Campbell physicist, educator
Montgomery, William J. finance company executive
Moss, Ben Frank, III art educator, painter
Otto, Margaret Amelia librarian
Oxenhandler, Neal language educator, writer
Paganucci, Paul Donnelly banker, lawyer, former college official
Parton, James historian
Penner, Hans Henry historian
Perrin, Noel environmental studies educator
Queneau, Paul Etienne metallurgical engineer, educator
Rawnsley, Howard Melody physician, educator
†Richards, Daniel Thomas library director
Rieser, Leonard Moos college administrator, physics educator
Riggs, Lorrin Andrews psychologist, educator
Roos, Thomas Bloom biological scientist, educator
Russell, Robert Hilton Romance languages and literature educator
Rutter, Jeremy Bentham archaeologist, educator
Sabinson, Mara Beth theatre educator, director, actress
Scher, Steven Paul literature educator
Scherr, Barry Paul foreign language educator
Sheldon, Richard Robert Russian language and literature educator
Shewmaker, Kenneth Earl history educator
Slesnick, William Ellis mathematician, educator
Snell, James Laurie mathematician, educator
Spiegel, Evelyn Sclufer biology educator, researcher
Spiegel, Melvin retired biology educator
Spitzer, Leo historian, educator
Staples, O. Sherwin orthopaedic surgeon
Starzinger, Vincent Evans political science educator
Stearns, Stephen Russell civil engineer, forensic engineer, educator
Stockmayer, Walter H(ugo) chemistry educator
Sturge, Michael Dudley physicist
Wallace, Andrew Grover physician
Wallis, Graham Blair engineer, educator
Webster, Frederick Elmer, Jr. marketing educator, consultant
Wegner, Gary Alan astronomer
Weiss, Ira Francis retired banker
Wetterhahn, Karen Elizabeth chemistry educator
White, Cleveland Stuart, Jr. architect
Wolff, Christian composer, music and classics educator
Wood, Charles Tuttle history educator
Wright, James Edward dean, history educator
Wykes, David English educator
Young, Oran Reed political scientist, educator

Henniker
Arnesen, Deborah Arnie educator
Braiterman, Thea Gilda economics educator, state legislator
Cowan, Stuart DuBois publisher, consultant, writer
Cummiskey, J. Kenneth former college president
O'Connell, William Raymond, Jr. college president

Hill
Thierry, John Adams heavy machinery manufacturing company executive, lawyer

Hillsboro
†Gefvert, Jane V. association executive
Gibson, Raymond Eugene clergyman
Marsh, Richard J. strategic management consultant
Walmsley, Arthur Edward bishop

Hinsdale
Smith, Edwin O. real estate executive, state legislator

Holderness
Cutler, Laurence Stephan architect, urban designer, advertising executive, educator

Hollis
Lerner, Arnold Stanley radio station executive
Merritt, Thomas Butler lawyer
Wright, George Walter aeronautical engineer, state legislator

Hooksett
Bagan, Merwyn neurological surgeon

Hudson
Blanchard, Glenn Robert principal

Jackson
Johnson, Ned (Edward Christopher Johnson) publishing company executive
Synnott, William Raymond retired management consultant

Jaffrey
Alderman, Bissell architect
Schott, John (Robert) international consultant, educator
Schulte, Henry Frank journalism educator
Von Eckardt, Wolf design critic, educator
Walling, Cheves Thomson chemistry educator

Keene
Baldwin, Peter Arthur psychologist, educator, minister
Bell, Ernest Lorne, III lawyer
Burkart, Walter Mark manufacturing company executive
Colby, Kenneth Poole insurance company executive
Fachada, Ederito Paul podiatrist
Hickey, Delina Rose education educator
†Koontz, James L. manufacturing executive
Lyon, Ronald Edward management consultant, computer consultant
Plaut, Nathan Michael retired lawyer
Yarosewick, Stanley J. academic administrator, physicist

Kingston
Curtis, Staton Russell university dean
Johnston, Robert Everett information management administrator

Laconia
Carbon, Susan Berkson lawyer, consultant
Caverly, Gardner A. foundation executive
Heald, Bruce Day English and music educator, historian

Lancaster
Drapeau, Phillip David banking executive
Pratt, Leighton Calvin state legislator

Lebanon
Clendenning, William Edmund dermatologist
Cornwell, Gibbons Gray, III physician, medical educator
Emery, Virginia Olga Beattie psychologist, researcher
Galton, Valerie Anne endocrinology educator
†Glass, D. David anesthesiologist
Jillette, Arthur George, Jr. school system administrator
Kelley, Maurice Leslie, Jr. gastroenterologist, educator
Mc Cann, Frances Veronica physiologist, educator
Morain, William Douglas surgeon, educator
Munck, Allan Ulf physiologist, educator
Myers, Warren Powers Laird physician, educator
Rolett, Ellis Lawrence medical educator, cardiologist
Rous, Stephen Norman urologist, educator
†Silberfarb, Peter Michael psychiatrist, educator
Smith, Barry David obstetrician-gynecologist, educator
Sox, Harold Carleton, Jr. physician, educator
Varnum, James William hospital administrator
Wallace, Harold James, Jr. physician

Londonderry
Dean, Richard T. pharmaceutical company executive
Nelson, Lloyd Steadman statistics consultant

Loudon
Heath, Roger Charles state senator, writer
Moore, Bea religious organization executive

Lyme
Darion, Joe librettist, lyricist

Dwight, Donald Rathbun *newspaper publisher, corporate communications executive*
McIntyre, Oswald Ross *physician*

Lyndeborough
Morison, John Hopkins *casting manufacturing company executive*

Madbury
Bruce, Robert Vance *historian, educator*

Manchester
†Angoff, Gerald Harvey *cardiologist*
Arnold, Barbara Eileen *state legislator*
Backus, Ann Swift Newell *educator, consultant*
Blake, Jeannette Belisle *psychotherapist*
Brensinger, Barry L. *architectural firm executive*
Bryan, Roland Henry *dentist*
Cameron, David Pierre Guyot, Jr. *utility company executive, lawyer*
Comeau, Reginald Alfred *academic administrator, consultant*
Constance, Joseph William, Jr. *library director*
Coolidge, Daniel Scott *lawyer*
DeFelice, Jonathan Peter *college president, priest*
DesRochers, Gerard Camille *surgeon*
Dobbins, James Joseph *artist*
Emery, Paul Emile *psychiatrist*
Gustafson, Richard Alrick *college president*
Kissmeyer-Nielsen, Perla M.S. *psychiatrist*
Loeb, Nackey Scripps *publisher*
Mc Lane, John Roy, Jr. *lawyer*
McQuaid, Joseph Woodbury *newspaper executive*
Middleton, Jack Baer *lawyer*
Millimet, Joseph Allen *retired lawyer*
Mires, Dennis Burnard *architect*
Monson, John Rudolph *lawyer*
Nixon, David Lee *lawyer*
†O'Brien, L. Douglas *banking executive*
O'Neil, Leo E. *bishop*
Perkins, Charles, III *newspaper editor*
Ryan, Philip Browne *investment banker*
Thurber, Cleveland, Jr. *trust banker*
Zachos, Kimon Stephen *lawyer*

Marlborough
†Walton, Russell Sparey *foundation administrator*

Meredith
Williams, Christopher Peele *architect*

Merrimack
Hower, Philip Leland *semiconductor device engineer*
Kotelly, George Vincent *editor, writer*
Malley, James Henry Michael *industrial engineer*

Nashua
Bickford, Andrew Thomas *newspaper publisher*
Carter, John Avery *architect*
Clough, Charles Elmer *consumer products company executive*
Gregg, Hugh *former cabinet manufacturing company executive, former governor New Hampshire*
Hanson, Arnold Philip *retired lawyer*
Hargreaves, David William *communications company executive*
Hemming, Walter William *business financial consultant*
Hippauf, Georgette Laurin *company executive*
Lee, Paul King-lung *electronics engineer, researcher*
Light, James Forest *English educator*
†Magnano, Salvatore Paul *financial executive, treasurer*
Moskowitz, Ronald *electronics executive*
Nelson, Mary S. *former state legislator*
Pressly, Barbara *state legislator*
Rudolph, John W. *architectural firm executive*
Stein, Robert *consumer products company executive*
Taeuber, Conrad *demography educator, former government statistician*
Webber, Howard Rodney *computer company executive*
Weinstein, Jeffrey Allen *consumer products company executive, lawyer*
Woodruff, Thomas Ellis *electronics consulting executive*

New Castle
Friese, George Ralph *retail executive*
Silva, Joseph Donald *English language educator*
Stevenson, Robert Edwin *microbiologist, culture collection executive*

New London
Cleveland, James Colgate *lawyer, former congressman*
Foote, Robert Stephens *physician*
Nye, Thomas Russell *retired drafting, reproduction and surveying company executive*
Pearson, Roy Messer, Jr. *clergyman*
Phillips, Roscoe Wendell, Jr. *architect*
Sheerr, Deirdre McCrystal *architectural firm executive*
Wheaton, Perry Lee *management consultant*

Newmarket
Getchell, Sylvia Fitts *librarian*

Newport
Stamatakis, Carol Marie *state legislator, lawyer*

North Hampton
Goldberger, Stephen A. *retail stores executive*
White, Ralph Paul *automotive executive, consultant*

North Salem
†Stone, Robert Eldred *small business owner, museum director*

Oxford
Richardson, John Carroll *lawyer, tax legislative consultant*

Pelham
Holmes, Richard Dale *secondary educator, historical consultant*

Peterborough
Calvin, Jerry Gene *industrial executive*

Plaistow
Senter, Merilyn P(atricia) *state legislator, retired freelance reporter*

Plymouth
Swift, Robert Frederic *music educator*

Portsmouth
Bulmer, Edward E. *oil industry executive*
Doleac, Charles Bartholomew *lawyer*
Hopkins, Jeannette Ethel *book publisher, editor*
Hynes, Carolyn Elizabeth *consumer products company executive*
Lyman, William W., Jr. *retired architect*
Morin, Carlton Paul *private investments executive*
O'Toole, Dennis Allen *museum director*
Powers, Henry Martin, Jr. *oil company executive*
Silverman, George Alan *broadcasting executive*
Smith, Stanton Thomas *insurance company executive*
Thornhill, Arthur Horace, Jr. *retired book publisher*
Tillinghast, John Avery *utilities executive*
Tober, Stephen Lloyd *lawyer*
Volk, Kenneth Hohne *lawyer*

Raymond
Warburton, (Nathaniel) Calvin, Jr. *state legislator, retired clergyman*

Rochester
Bickford, Drucilla *state legislator*
Dupont, Edward Charles, Jr. *petroleum distribution company executive, state senator*
†Dworkin, Gary Steven *insurance company executive*
Hambrick, Patricia *state legislator*

Rumney
King, Wayne Douglas *state senator*

Salem
†Chasse, François *consulting company executive*
Cooper, Warren Stanley *manufacturing executive*
King, Thomas L. *diversified manufacturing company executive*
Simmons, Marvin Gene *geophysics educator*
Sununu, John H. *former chief of staff President of U.S., former governor*

Sanbornton
Andrews, Henry Nathaniel, Jr. *botanist, scientist, educator*
Meader, Ralph Gibson *medical administrator*

Sandown
Densen, Paul Maximillian *former health administrator, educator*

Silver Lake
Pallone, Adrian Joseph *research scientist*

Strafford
Simic, Charles *English language educator, poet*

Stratham
Bjorkman, Gordon Stuart, Jr. *structural engineer, consultant*

Sunapee
Cary, Charles Oswald *aviation executive*
Chait, Lawrence G. *marketing consultant*
MacKinnon, Malcolm D(avid) *retired insurance company executive*
Rauh, John David *manufacturing company executive*

Walpole
Burns, Kenneth Lauren *filmmaker, historian*
Gooding, Judson *writer*
Szmit, Frederick Andrew *paper manufacturing company executive*

Warner
Hunt, Everett Clair *engineering educator, researcher, consultant*

Washington
Halverson, Wendell Quelprud *former educational association executive, clergyman, educator*

Waterville Valley
Grimes, Howard Ray *management consultant*

West Lebanon
Chalmers, Thomas Clark *physician, educational and research administrator*
MacAdam, Walter Kavanagh *consulting engineering executive*

West Peterborough
Dyer, Merton S. *pharmacist, state legislator*

Winchester
MacKay, Neil Duncan *plastic company executive*

Wolfeboro
Meredith, David Robert *investor*
Murphy, Gordon Laurence *insurance company executive*
Murray, Roger Franklin *economist, educator*
Steadman, David Rosslyn Ayton *business executive, corporate director*

NEW JERSEY

Absecon
Steinruck, Charles Francis, Jr. *management consultant, lawyer*

Allendale
Birdsall, Blair *consulting engineering executive*
Castor, William Stuart, Jr. *chemist, consultant, laboratory executive, educator*
Hollands, John Henry *electronics consultant*

Allenhurst
Hinson, Robert William *advertising executive, consultant*

Allenwood
Shortess, Edwin Steevin *marketing consultant*

Alpine
Yuelys, Alexander *former cosmetics company executive*

Andover
Gioseffi, Daniela *poet, author, educator*
Klein, Joseph Michelman *musical director*

Annandale
Cohen, Morrel Herman *physicist, biologist, educator*
Drakeman, Donald Lee *corporate executive, lawyer*
†Drakeman, Lisa N. *biotechnology company executive*
Gorbaty, Martin Leo *chemist, researcher*
Lohse, David John *physicist*
†Milner, Scott T. *chemical engineer*
Rosensweig, Ronald Ellis *research scientist*
Sinfelt, John Henry *chemist*

Asbury
Konrad, Adolf Ferdinand *artist*

Atlantic City
Blaziek, William Louis *casino and hotel executive*
†Gluck, Henry *resort complex executive*
Harris, Paul Smith *human resources professional*
Knight, Edward R. *judge, law educator, psychologist*
Maland, Tim *hospitality company executive*
Stuart, Eve Lynne *elementary education educator*
Tucci, Mark A. *state agency administrator*
†Wagner, Roger Philip *hotel executive*

Atlantic Highlands
Crowley, Cynthia Johnson *secondary school educator*
Fink, Dolores Hesse *special education educator*
Kevenides, Herve Arnaud *economic and real estate consultant*
Royce, Paul Chadwick *medical administrator*

Avalon
Yochum, Philip Theodore *retired motel and cafeteria chain executive*

Avon By The Sea
Bruno, Grace Angelia *accountant, educator*

Barnegat
Hawk, Frank Carkhuff, Sr. *industrial engineer*
Schmoll, Harry F., Jr. *lawyer, educator*

Barnegat Light
Gibbs, Frederick Winfield *lawyer, communications company executive*

Barrington
Florio, Maryanne J. *state health research scientist*

Basking Ridge
Allen, Robert Eugene *communications and computer company executive*
Bodman, Richard Stockwell *telecommunications executive*
Collis, Sidney Robert *retired telephone company executive*
Condon, Verner Holmes, Jr. *retired utility executive*
Echikson, Richard *retail consultant*
Ferguson, Forest D. *marketing executive*
Heckendorf, Glenn *sales and marketing executive*
†Laurie, Marilyn *communications and computer company executive*
Miller, Richard Wesley *telecommunications company executive*
Munch, Douglas Francis *pharmaceutical and health industry consultant*
Willcoxon, Sam Randolph *communications executive*

Bay Head
Benning, Joseph Francis, Jr. *portfolio manager, financial analyst*

Bayonne
Gorman, William David *artist, graphic artist*
Pelosi, Marco Antonio *obstetrician/gynecologist*

Beach Haven
Brunt, Harry Herman, Jr. *psychiatrist*

Beachwood
Newman, Justina Anne *nursery school administrator, consultant*

Bedminster
Bovey, Frank Alden *research chemist*
Darr, John Keith *finance executive*
David, Edward Emil, Jr. *electrical engineer, business executive*

Belle Mead
Evans, Frederick John *psychologist*
Hansen, Ralph Holm *chemist*
Murphy, Barry John *publishing executive*
Singley, Mark Eldridge *agricultural engineering educator*

Belleville
Pincus, George *university dean, engineering educator*

Bellmawr
Hughes, James Sinclair *electronic engineer, executive*
Wilke, Constance Regina *elementary education educator*

Bergenfield
Pei, Ming L. *civil engineering educator*

Berkeley Heights
†Collard, Ross Theo *management consultant*
Geusic, Joseph Edward *retired physicist*
Gottheimer, George Malcolm, Jr. *insurance executive, educator*
Marx, William B., Jr. *telecommunications industry executive*
Rabiner, Lawrence Richard *electrical engineer*
Thomsen, Thomas Richard *communications company executive*

Bernardsville
Abeles, James David *manufacturing company executive*
Coheleach, Guy Joseph *artist*
Cooperman, Saul *foundation administrator*
DiDomenico, Mauro, Jr. *communication executive*
Dixon, Richard Wayne *retired communications company executive*
Spofford, Sally Hyslop *artist*

Blairstown
Bean, Bennett *artist*

Bloomfield
Becker, Robert Clarence *clergyman*
Hutcheon, Forbes Clifford Robert *engineer*
Martel, Eugene Harvey *engineering company executive*
Solomon, Stephen Michael *chemical engineer, company executive*
Stella, John Anthony *investment company executive*
Vincent, Tony *cable television/radio executive and personality*

Bloomingdale
Baeder, Donald Lee *petroleum and chemical company executive, financial consultant*

Bogota
Condon, Francis Edward *former foundation administrator*

Boonton
Ahmad, Mehmood Riaz *cardiologist*

Bordentown
Brown, Hershel M. *newspaper publisher*
Walther, John Henry *banker*

Bound Brook
Chandler, Marguerite Nella *real estate corporation executive*
Furst, E(rrol) Kenneth *transportation executive, accountant*
Gould, Donald Everett *retired chemical company executive*
Karol, Frederick John *industrial chemist*

Branchville
Hallowell, Walter Henry *insurance company executive*

Brick
Gluck, Lucille Gindoff *educator*

Bridgewater
Albert, Robert Bertrand *chemical executive*
Albrethsen, Adrian Edysel *metallurgist, consultant*
Allen, Randy Lee *corporate executive*
Bernson, Marcella Shelley *psychiatrist*
Conroy, Robert John *lawyer*
Freeman, Henry McCall *newspaper publisher*
Glesmann, Sylvia-Maria *artist*
Harrigan, Laura G. *newspaper editor*
Healey, Lynne Kover *editor, broadcaster, writer, educator*
Hillegass, Christine Ann *psychologist*
Iovine, Carmine P. *chemicals executive*
Kennedy, James Andrew *chemical company executive*
Lewis, Donald Emerson *banker*
McFarland, Richard M. *executive recruiting consultant*
Patton, Diana Lee Wilkoc *artist*
Pickett, Doyle Clay *employment and training counselor, consultant*
Skidmore, James Albert, Jr. *management, computer technology and engineering services company executive*
Weingast, Marvin *laboratory director*

Brielle
Palisi, Anthony Thomas *psychologist, educator*

Brigantine
†Schoelkopf, Robert Carl *non-profit organization administrator*

Butler
Klaas, Nicholas Paul *management and technical consultant*
Ward, Robert Allen, Jr. *advertising executive*

Caldwell
Chatlos, William Edward *management consultant*
Stanton, George Basil, Jr. *engineering executive, chemical engineer, consultant*

Califon
Hannigan, Frank *sportswriter, television writer and commentator, golf course design consultant*
Rosen, Carol Mendes *artist*

Camden
†Abbott, Ann Augustine *social worker, educator*
Ances, I. G(eorge) *obstetrician/gynecologist, educator*
Beck, David Paul *biochemist*
Brotman, Stanley Seymour *federal judge*
Coleman, John Michael *lawyer, food products executive*
Cottrol, Robert James *lawyer, history educator*
Denton, Arnold Eugene *retired food company executive*
Edgerton, Brenda Evans *soup company executive, treasurer*
Fairbanks, Russell Norman *law educator, university dean*
Ford, Joseph Raymond *manufacturing company executive*
Gerry, John Francis *federal judge*
Gordon, Walter Kelly *provost, English language educator*
†Halpern, Kevin Gregg *hospital administrator*
Holman, Joseph S. *automotive sales executive*
Irenas, Joseph Eron *federal judge*
Johnson, David Willis *food products executive*
Kirk, James Robert *research development and quality assurance executive*
Mancini, Nicholas Angelo *psychologist*
McHugh, James T. *bishop*

Morrison, Ashton Byrom *pathologist, medical school official*
Peacock, Patricia Anne *academic program director*
Polin, Claire *musician*
Pomorski, Stanislaw *lawyer, educator*
Rapaport, Robert M. *financial executive*
Rodriguez, Joseph H. *federal judge*
Showalter, English, Jr. *French language educator*
Sigler, Jay Adrian *political scientist, educator*
Simandle, Jerome B. *federal judge*
Weise, Frank Earl, III *food products company executive*
Wellington, Judith Lynn *cultural organization administrator*
Wizmur, Judith H. *federal judge*
Wood, Martha Oakwell *obstetrics-gynecology nurse practitioner*

Cape May
Cadge, William Fleming *gallery owner, photographer*
Janosik, Edward Gabriel *retired political science educator*
Lassner, Franz George *historian, educator*
Wilson, H(arold) Fred(erick) *chemist, research scientist*

Cape May Court House
Cohen, Daniel Edward *writer*
Cohen, Susan Lois *author*
Kurtz, James Eugene *freelance writer, minister*
Poel, Robert Walter *career officer, physician*

Carlstadt
Daniels, Robert Alan *marketing executive*

Carteret
Corliss, Robert *sporting goods company executive*
Didieo, James *sporting goods stores executive*
Timinski, Robert *sporting goods store executive*

Cedar Grove
Brownstein, Alan P. *health foundation executive, consultant*
Nash, Annamarie *secondary education educator*
Spagnardi, Ronald Lee *publishing executive*
Thiel, Thelma King *foundation executive*

Cedar Knolls
Lingnau, Lutz *pharmaceutical executive*

Chatham
Barnes, William Oliver, Jr. *lawyer*
Bast, Ray Roger *retired utility company executive*
Feeney, John Robert *banker*
Glatt, Mitchell Steven *corporate executive*
Gonzalez, Efren William *science information services administrator*
Kaulakis, Arnold Francis *management consultant*
Lenz, Henry Paul *management consultant*
Manning, Frederick William *retired retail executive*
Rockwood, Thomas Julian *management services executive, information technolgy consultant*
Sayles, Thomas Dyke, Jr. *banker*
Woods, Reginald Foster *management consulting executive*

Cherry Hill
Beebe, Leo Clair *industrial equipment executive, former educator*
Belin, Henry A., Jr. *bishop*
Biddle, Daniel R. *reporter*
Boyer, Peter Jay *lawyer*
Callaway, Ben Anderson *journalist*
Cazes, Jack *chemist, marketing consultant, editor*
Dunfee, Thomas Wylie *law educator*
Getz, Solomon *defense consulting executive, aerospace engineer*
†Gibson, Thomas Richard *automobile import company executive*
Gillespie, Colleen Patricia *lawyer*
Hayasi, Nisiki *physicist, business executive, inventor*
Higurashi, Takeshi *automotive executive*
Iglewicz, Raja *state agency administrator, researcher, industrial hygienist*
Israelsky, Roberta Schwartz *speech pathologist, audiologist*
Lamm, Harvey H. *foreign car and parts importer*
Laskin, Lee B. *judge, laywer, former state senator*
Luchak, Frank Alexander *lawyer*
Margolis, Gerald Joseph *psychiatrist, educator*
McGuire, Mavis Louise *professional society administrator*
Muller, George T. *automotive executive*
Myers, Daniel William, II *lawyer*
Newell, Eric James *financial planner, tax consultant, former insurance executive*
Olearchyk, Andrew S. *cardiothoracic surgeon, educator*
Rabil, Mitchell Joseph *lawyer*
Radey, Frank Herbert, Jr. *architect*
Riesenbach, Marvin S. *automotive corporation executive*
Rose, Joel Alan *legal consultant*
Rudman, Solomon Kal *magazine publisher*
Sax, Robert Edward *food service equipment company executive*
Schad, James L. *bishop*
Schelm, Roger Leonard *information systems specialist*
Simmerman, Gary F. *bank executive*
†Singh, Krishna Pal *mechanical engineer*
Weinstein, Steven David *lawyer*
Werbitt, Warren *gastroenterologist, educator*
†Wolff, Ferida *author*

Chester
Gurian, Mal *telecommunications executive*
Maddalena, Lucille Ann *management executive*

Cinnaminson
Johnson, Victor Lawrence *banker*
Lippincott, Sarah Lee *astronomer, graphologist*

Clark
Augeri, Joseph *personal care industry executive*
Kinley, David *physical therapist, acupuncturist*
Levy, Jean *cosmetics company executive*
†Stepanski, Anthony Francis, Jr. *computer company executive*

Cliffside Park
Jaspen, Nathan *educational statistics educator*
Pushkarev, Boris S. *research foundation director, writer*

Clifton
Adelsberg, Harvey *hospital administrator*
Feinstein, Miles Roger *lawyer*
Magnus, Frederick Samuel *investment banker*
Petrucelli, Frank *school system administrator*
Roberts, Robert Charles *secondary education educator*
Rodimer, Frank Joseph *bishop*
Sheehan, Deborah Ann *radio station and theater executive*
Silber, Judy G. *dermatologist*
Srinivasachari, Samavedam *chemical engineer*
Swystun-Rives, Bohdana Alexandra *dentist*

Clinton
Acerra, Michele (Mike Acerra) *engineering and construction company executive*
Atwater, N. William *engineering and construction executive*
Boyland, Joseph Francis *corporate controller*
DeGhetto, Kenneth Anselm *engineering and construction company executive*
Deones, Jack E. *corporate executive*
†Hansen, Arthur Magne *engineering and manufacturing executive*
Kennedy, Harold Edward *lawyer*
Moser, Elizabeth Marie *lawyer*
Newman, Stephen Alexander *chemical engineer, thermodynamicist*
†Swift, Richard J. *engineering company executive*
Winkin, Justin Philip *engineering executive*
Wolsky, Murray *corporation executive*

Collingswood
Mohrfeld, Richard Gentel *heating oil distributing company executive*

Colonia
Wiesenfeld, Bess Gazevitz *business executive, real estate developer*

Colts Neck
French, Charles Ferris, Jr. *banker*
Rode, Leif *real estate personal computer consultant*

Columbus
Sikora, Jane Ann *secondary education educator, reference librarian*

Convent Station
Weber, Joseph H. *communications company executive*
Wright, Robert Burroughs *financial consultant*

Cranbury
Boulanger, Robert N. *insurance company executive*
Cuthbert, Robert Allen *pet products company executive*
Daoust, Donald Roger *pharmaceutical and toiletries company executive, microbiologist*
Fiore, Anthony N. *marketing company executive, strategic planning consultant*
Koras, William *concessions, restaurants and publishing company executive*
Lee-Smith, Hughie *artist, educator*
Raymond, Maurice A. *corporate director research*
Rector, Milton Gage *social work educator, former association executive*
Reichek, Morton Arthur *retired magazine editor, writer*
Wang, Chih Chun *material scientist, business executive*
Yoseloff, Julien David *publishing company executive*
Yoseloff, Thomas *publisher*

Cranford
Bardwil, Joseph Anthony *investments consultant*
Bodian, Nat G. *publishing, marketing consultant, author, lecturer, lexicographer*
Cleaver, William Pennington *retired sugar refining company executive, consultant*
Eisenberg, R. Neal *restoration company executive*
Schink, Frank Edward *electrical engineer*
Sommerlad, Robert Edward *environmental research engineer*
Thomson, Robert Hennessey *manufacturing executive*

Cresskill
Bogner, Stephen D. *marketing professional*
Gardner, Richard Alan *psychiatrist, writer*
Smyth, Craig Hugh *fine arts educator*

Dayton
†Hess, Alan Marshall *toy company executive*

Deal
Becker, Richard Stanley *music publisher*

Demarest
Ahr, Ernest Stephan *business archive executive*

Denville
Breed, Ria *anthropologist*
Coes, Kent Day *artist*
Fisher, Sharon Mary *musician*
Minter, Jerry Burnett *electronic component company executive, engineer*

Dover
Mc Donald, John Joseph *electronics executive*

East Brunswick
Candelmo, Lee France *special education educator*
Chang, Stephen S. *food scientist, educator, researcher, inventor*
Daniel, Eleanor Sauer *economist, real estate executive*
Fisher, Lucille *principal*
Georgantas, Aristides William *banking executive*
Haupin, Elizabeth Carol *retired secondary school educator*
Johnson, Edward Elemuel *psychologist, educator*
Kabela, Frank, Jr. *broadcast executive*
Karmazin, Sharon Elyse *library director*
King, Charles M. *principal*
Lund, Daryl Bert *college dean*
McDonough, Patrick Joseph, Jr. *lawyer*
Mooney, William Piatt *actor*
Nemser, Robert Solomon *visual communications consultant, art director, designer, educator*
Rosenberg, Norman *surgeon*
Thompson, Robert McBroom *publishing executive*
Wagman, Gerald Howard *retired biochemist*

East Hanover
Anderson, Gary William *physician*
Finkel, Marion Judith *physician*
Hassan, Frederich *pharmaceutical executive*
Leveille, Gilbert Antonio *food products executive*
Morris, Patricia Smith *media specialist, author, educator*
Nemecek, Georgina Marie *molecular pharmacologist*
Rejeange, Jacques F. *pharmaceutical executive*
†Rothwell, Timothy Gordon *pharmaceutical company executive*
Towey, Robert *pharmaceutical company executive*

East Orange
Bowe, Riddick Lamont *professional boxer*
Brown, Paulette *lawyer*
Brundage, Gertrude Barnes *pediatrician*
Gibson, Althea *retired professional tennis player, golfer, state official*
Green, David *insurance company executive*
Holyfield, Evander *boxer*
Howe, James Everett *investment company executive*
Medley, Alex Roy *executive minister*
Moorer, Michael *professional boxer*
†Weck, Thomas Lincoln *consulting company executive*
Wolff, Derish Michael *economist, company executive*

East Rutherford
Aufzien, Alan L. *professional sports team executive*
Beard, Alfred (Butch) *former basketball player, former commentator*
Coleman, Derrick D. *professional basketball player*
Gerstein, David Brown *hardware manufacturing company executive, professional basketball team executive*
Kempner, Michael W. *public relations executive*
Lamoriello, Louis Anthony *professional hockey team executive*
Lemaire, Jacques *professional hockey coach*
†Lemieux, Claude *professional hockey player*
Mann, Bernard (Bernie Mann) *professional basketball team executive*
Mara, John K. *professional sports team executive*
Mara, Wellington T. *professional football team executive*
McMullen, John J. *professional hockey team executive*
Mc Nab, Maxwell Douglas *professional sports executive*
Reed, Willis *professional basketball team executive, former head coach*
Reeves, Daniel Edward *professional football coach*
Taylor, Lawrence *sports commentator, former professional football player*
Wadler, Arnold L. *lawyer*
Walker, Herschel *professional football player*
Young, George Bernard, Jr. *professional football team executive*

East Windsor
Phelan, Richard Paul *trust company executive*

Eatontown
Dalton, John Joseph *healthcare consultant*

Edison
Applebaum, Charles *lawyer*
Behr, Marion Ray *artist, author*
Behr, Omri M. *lawyer*
†Berg, Carol Scherer *financial executive*
†Bonini, Victor *accountant*
Burke, James *wholesale executive*
Cangemi, Michael Paul *accountant, financial executive*
Carretta, Richard Louis *beverage company executive*
Cavanaugh, James Henry *corporate executive, former government official*
Comstock, Robert Ray *journalism educator, newspaper editor*
Corman, Randy *lawyer*
Danzis, Rose Marie *emeritus college president*
Ensor, Richard Joseph *athletic conference commissioner, lawyer*
Francis, Peter T. *gas and oil industry executive*
†Hare, Richard Bergin *market research company executive*
Huber, Michael W. *petroleum company executive*
Huber, Peter C. *diversified chemicals manufacturing company executive*
Hunter, Michael *publishing executive*
Kott, Joseph Hilton *lawyer, bank executive*
Lo Surdo, Antonio *physical chemist, educator*
Lubetkin, Charles Schiller *retail executive*
Maeroff, Gene I. *educational association administrator, journalist*
Marash, Stanley Albert *consulting company executive*
Parker, Barbara Z. *bank executive*
†Peraino, Roy T. *banker*
Romano, Dominick V. *food products executive*
Schenk, George *oil industry executive*
Scheuring, Garry Joseph *banker*
Shulman, Hyman *food service executive*
Silberstein, Alan Mark *banker*
Sullivan, Cornelius Francis, Jr. *banking executive*
Warsh, Jeffrey Alan *state legislator, lawyer*

Egg Harbor City
Dittenhafer, Brian Douglas *banker, economist*
Hamilton, Thomas Herman *savings and loan association executive*
Melick, George Fleury *mechanical engineer, educator*

Elizabeth
Beglin, Edward W., Jr. *judge*
Buonanni, Brian Francis *health care facility administrator, consultant*
Clare, Thomas J. *consumer products company executive*
Gellert, George Geza *food importing company executive*
Infusino, Thomas P. *food distribution company executive*
Keenan, Joseph James, Jr. *library director*
Klein, Peter Martin *lawyer, transportation company executive*
Leonett, Anthony Arthur *banker*
Power, Frank Raymond *transportation company executive*
Stender, Linda de Milt *county official*

Elmer
Slavoff, Harriet Emonds *learning disabilities teacher, consultant*

Elmwood Park
Blume, Paula Jollin *special education educator*
Hazama, Hajime *electronics executive*
Wygod, Martin J. *pharmaceuticals executive*

Emerson
Rooney, John Edward *state legislator, electrical company executive*

Englewood
Anuszkiewicz, Richard Joseph *artist*
Beer, Jeanette Mary Scott *foreign language educator*
Bullough, John Frank *organist, music educator*
Casarella, Edmond *sculptor, printmaker*
Chiorazzi, Mary Lorraine *psychiatrist*
Deresiewicz, Herbert *mechanical engineering educator*
Essey, Basil *bishop*
Friedman, Emanuel *publishing company executive*
Gambee, Eleanor Brown *writer, lecturer, civic worker*
Hertzberg, Arthur *rabbi, educator*
Hess, Blaine R. *manufacturing company executive*
Jones, Stephen Powell *school administrator*
Kane, Daniel A. *hospital administrator*
Khouri, Antoun *church administrator*
Lapidus, Arnold *mathematician*
Mc Mullan, Dorothy *nurse educator*
Miles, Virginia (Mrs. Fred C. Miles) *marketing consultant*
Neis, Arnold Hayward *pharmaceutical company executive*
Orlando, George (Joseph) *union executive*
Saliba, Philip E. *archbishop*
Schmidt, Ronald Hans *architect*
†Vane, Dena *magazine editor-in-chief*
Zwilich, Ellen Taaffe *composer*

Englewood Cliffs
Abdela, Angelo Solomon *manufacturing company executive*
†Baumgarten, Herbert Joseph *chemical company executive, lawyer*
Brandreth, John Breckenridge, II *chemical importer*
Brissie, Eugene Field, Jr. *publisher*
Byrne, John N. *food company executive*
Cantwell, John Walsh *advertising executive*
Dojny, Richard Francis *publishing company executive*
†Farrell, Patricia Ann *psychologist, educator*
Feliciotti, Enio *food company executive*
Green, Alvin *lawyer, corporate executive*
Guiher, James Morford, Jr. *publisher*
Haltiwanger, Robert Sidney, Jr. *book publishing executive*
Hurst, Kenneth Thurston *publisher*
Meendsen, Fred Charles *food company executive*
†Saible, Stephanie *magazine editor*
Schlatter, Konrad *corporate executive*
Scott, John William *food processing executive*
†Shimoyama, Hideo *construction company executive*
Shoemate, Charles Richard *food company executive*
Shrem, Charles Joseph *metals corporation executive*
Storms, Clifford Beekman *lawyer*
†Weiderholz, Conrad *magazine publisher*

Englishtown
Rudins, Leonids (Lee Rudins) *retired chemical company executive, financial executive*

Fair Haven
Gagnebin, Albert Paul *retired mining executive*
Labrecque, Theodore Joseph *lawyer*

Fair Lawn
†Brandt, Ronald Elliot *chemical company executive*
Hayden, Neil Steven *communications company executive*
†Matsumoto, Atsushi *electronics executive*
Motin, Revell Judith *data processing executive*
†Ozawa, Ted *electronics executive*
Panella, Elizabeth M. *secondary school principal*
Parker, Adrienne Natalie *art educator, art historian, lecturer*

Fairfield
Boccone, Andrew Albert *chemical company executive*
Dean, John L. *sales and marketing executive, educator*
Finn, James Francis *consulting engineering executive*
Giambalvo, Vincent *manufacturing company executive*
Mehta, Narinder Kumar *marketing executive*
Meilan, Celia *food products executive*
Oolie, Sam *investment company executive*
Prince, Daniel Lloyd *molecular biologist, virologist, validation scientist, industrial microbiologist, computer network administrator, consultant*
Stein, Robert Alan *electronics company executive*

Fairview
Anton, Harvey *textile company executive*

Far Hills
Barnum, William Douglas *communications company executive*
Ellsworth, Duncan Steuart, Jr. *retired utility company executive*
Fay, David B. *sports association executive*
Holt, Jonathan Turner *public relations executive*
McCall, David Warren *chemist, administrator, materials consultant*
Ross, Stephen Bruce *public affairs consultant*

Farmingdale
Schluter, Peter Mueller *electronics company executive*
Smith, Sibley Judson, Jr. *historic site administrator*

Flemington
Accettola, Albert Bernard *orthopedic surgeon, educator*
†Gilbert, Jack Alan *company executive*
Katcher, Avrum L. *pediatrician*
Kettler, Carl Frederick *airline executive*
Lance, Leonard *assemblyman*
McGregor, Walter *medical products company designer, inventor, consultant, educator*

Roth, Lee Britton *lawyer*

Florham Park
Aden, Laura *performing arts association administrator*
Bossen, Wendell John *insurance company executive*
Bottelli, Richard *architect*
Clayton, William L. *investment banking executive*
Eidt, Clarence Martin, Jr. *research and development executive*
Erickson, Charles Edward *insurance company executive*
Fischer, Pamela Shadel *public relations executive*
Griffo, James Vincent, Jr. *retired biology educator*
Hardin, William Downer *lawyer*
Jameson, J(ames) Larry *cable company executive*
Kluge, J. Hans *company executive*
Laulicht, Murray Jack *lawyer*
Lieberman, Lester Zane *engineering company executive*
Lovell, Robert Marlow, Jr. *investment company executive*
Marshall, Philips Williamson *insurance agency executive*
McDonagh, Thomas Joseph *physician*
Monks, Donald Richard *banker*
Mott, Vincent Valmon *publisher, author*
Naimark, George Modell *marketing and management consultant*
Perham, Roy Gates, III *industrial psychologist*
†Smith, Randy P. *metal products executive*
Smith, Robert William *former insurance company executive, lawyer*
†Sperber, Martin *pharmaceutical company executive, pharmacist*
Stanton, Patrick Michael *lawyer*
Whitley, Arthur Francis *retired international consulting company executive, engineer, lawyer*

Fords
†Blond, Stuart Richard *newsletter editor*
Brown, James *singer, broadcasting executive*
Chryss, George *chemical company executive, consultant*
Kaufman, Alex *chemicals executive*
Lynch, Charles Andrew *chemical company executive*

Fort Hancock
Klein, George D. *geologist, executive*

Fort Lee
Abut, Charles C. *lawyer*
Barr, Edward Evan *chemical company executive*
†Berdy, Jack M. *software and consultation company executive*
Fischel, Daniel Norman *publishing consultant*
Gauci, Charles Leon *health care company executive*
Gharib, Susie *television newscaster*
Goldberg, Harry Finck *lawyer, business consultant*
Houston, Whitney *vocalist, recording artist*
Huppuch, Winfield Adelbert, III *secondary education educator, publishing executive*
Insana, Ronald Gerard *newscaster*
Jacobs, Marisa Frances *lawyer*
Kim, Gil *minister*
Kiriakopoulos, George Constantine *dentist*
Lippman, William Jennings *investment company executive*
Lynaugh, Joseph T. *health care executive*
Manniello, John Baptiste Louis *research scientist*
Ramsey, Douglas Kenneth *television anchor, journalist*
Roglieri, John Louis *health facility administrator*
Schiessler, Robert Walter *retired chemical and oil company executive*
Seitel, Fraser Paul *public relations executive*
†Sigona, Ralph John *international business consulant*
†Smith, Jeffrey E. *pharmaceutical executive*
Sugarman, Alan William *educational administrator*
Vignolo, Biagio Nickolas, Jr. *chemical company executive*
Weitzer, Bernard *telecommunications executive*
Williams, Edwin William *publisher*

Fort Monmouth
Ignoffo, Matthew Frederick *English language educator, writer, counselor*
Kalwinsky, Charles Knowlton *government official*
Lymberis, Costas Triantafillos *environmental engineer*
McCarthy, Timothy Michael *career non-commissioned officer*
Perlman, Barry Stuart *electrical engineer, researcher*
Schwering, Felix Karl *electronics engineer, researcher*
Thornton, Clarence Gould *electronics engineering executive*

Franklin Lakes
Andrews, Willard Douglas *retired medical products manufacturer, consultant*
Berger, Murry P. *food company executive*
†Castellini, Clateo *medical products manufacturing executive*
Friedman, Martin Burton *chemical company executive*
Galiardo, John William *lawyer*
Ginsberg, Barry Howard *physician, researcher*
Hegelmann, Julius *retired pharmacy educator*
Hetzel, Donald Stanford *chemist*
Howe, Wesley Jackson *medical supplies company executive*

Freehold
Fisher, Clarkson Sherman, Jr. *judge*
Foster, Eric H., Jr. *retail executive*
Handlin, Amy Harwood *marketing educator*
Laden, Karl *toiletries company executive*
Shapiro, Michael *supermarket corporate officer*

Frenchtown
Scaglione, Aldo Domenico *language educator*

Garfield
Kodaka, Kunio *plastics company executive*

Gladstone
Detwiler, Peter Mead *investment banker*

Glassboro
Gephardt, Donald Louis *college official*
James, Herman Delano *college administrator*
Marcus, Laurence Richard *state official*
Stone, Don Charles *computer science educator*

Glen Ridge
Agnew, Peter Tomlin *employee benefit consultant*
Bracken, Eddie (Edward Vincent) *actor, director, writer, singer, artist*
Clemente, Celestino *physician, surgeon*
Szamek, Pierre Ervin *research anthropologist*

Glen Rock
Blackin, Jack Milton *banker*
Fine, Seymour Howard *marketing educator, lecturer, author, consultant*
†Riggs, Gina Ginsberg *educational association administrator*
Shell, Glenn Harmen *bank executive*

Green Village
Castenschiold, René *engineering company executive, author, consultant*

Hackensack
Ahearn, James *newspaper columnist*
Araki, K. *electronics company executive*
Baker, Andrew Hartill *clinical laboratory executive*
Benfield, Richard Ernest *journalist*
Blomquist, David Wels *journalist*
Borg, Malcolm Austin *communications company executive*
Delaney, Patrick James *investment company executive*
Fahy, John J. *lawyer*
†Feldberg, Robert Moses *theater critic*
Ferguson, John Patrick *medical center executive*
Fiore, Antoinette *nursing administrator*
Gross, Peter Alan *epidemiologist, researcher*
Judge, Jean Frances *management consultant*
Kestin, Howard H. *judge*
Mack, Patricia Johnson *newspaper editor*
Margulies, James Howard *editorial cartoonist*
Massler, Howard Arnold *lawyer, corporate executive*
Mavrovic, Ivo *chemical engineer*
Mehta, Jay *financial executive*
Michel, Robert Charles *retired engineering company executive*
Pennington, William Mark *sportswriter*
Pollinger, William Joshua *lawyer*
Schuber, William Patrick *lawyer*
Spackman, Thomas James *radiologist*
Waixel, Vivian *journalist*
Walsh, Joseph Michael *magazine distribution executive*
†Yagoda, Harry Nathan *system engineering executive*

Hackettstown
Mulligan, Elinor Patterson *lawyer*

Haddon Heights
Gwiazda, Stanley John *university dean*
O'Toole, Marie Theresa *rehabilitation nursing educator*

Haddonfield
Adler, John Herbert *lawyer, state legislator*
Bauer, Raymond Gale *sales professional*
Capelli, John Placido *nephrologist*
†Carter, Joan Pauline *medical services company executive*
Cheney, Daniel Lavern *retired magazine publisher*
Iavicoli, Mario Anthony *lawyer*
LaBarge, Richard Allen *financial analyst, educator*
Shaub, Harold Arthur *food products executive*
Siskin, Edward Joseph *engineering and construction company executive*

Hainesport
Sylk, Leonard Allen *housing company executive, real estate developer*

Hamburg
Buist, Richardson *corporate executive, retired banker*

Hammonton
Levitt, Gerald Steven *natural gas company executive*

Hanover
Salans, Lester Barry *physician, scientist, educator*

Harrington Park
McGlynn, Richard Bruce *lawyer*
†McKelvey, Don Richard *finance company executive*

Harrison
Winnerman, Robert Henry *home building company executive*

Harvey Cedars
Elliott, Joseph Gordon, Jr. *retired newspaper executive*

Haworth
Stokvis, Jack Raphael *urban planner and developer, government agency administrator*

Hawthorne
Cole, Leonard Aaron *political scientist, dentist*

Hazlet
Miller, Duane King *health and beauty care company executive*
Morrison, James Frederick *flavor and fragrance company administrator*

Hewitt
Selwyn, Donald *engineering administrator, researcher, inventor, educator*

Highland Lakes
Ansorge, Helen J. *retired elementary school educator*
†Kiraly, Bèla Kàlmàn *retired history educator, Hungarian army officer*

Highland Park
Broggi, Barbara Ann *elementary education educator, staff developer*
Brudner, Harvey Jerome *physicist*
Coughlin, Caroline Mary *library consultant, educator*
Feigenbaum, Abraham Samuel *nutritional biochemist*
Green, James Weston *educator, physiologist*
Pane, Remigio Ugo *Romance languages educator*

Hightstown
Arnold, Matthew Charles *real estate corporation officer*
Brodman, Estelle *librarian, retired educator*
†Bronner, William Roche *lawyer*
DeSesa, Michael Anthony *chemical company executive*
Howard, Barbara Sue Mesner *artist*
Kilborne, William Skinner *retired business consultant*

Ho Ho Kus
Tobin, John Everard *retired lawyer*

Hoboken
Abel, Robert Berger *science administrator*
Boesch, Francis Theodore *electrical engineer, educator*
Bonsal, Richard Irving *textile marketing executive*
Buckman, Thomas Richard *foundation executive, educator*
Fajans, Jack *physics educator*
Gans, Manfred *chemical engineer*
Gerstein, Richard *medical research executive*
Griskey, Richard George *chemical engineering educator*
Johnson, James Myron *psychologist, educator*
Jurkat, Martin Peter *management educator*
Kunhardt, Erich Enrique *physicist, educator*
Raveché, Harold Joseph *university administrator, physical chemist*
Regazzi, John James, III *publishing executive*
Savitsky, Daniel *engineer, educator*
Schmidt, George *physicist*
Seessel, Adam H. *writer, journalist*
Sisto, Fernando *mechanical engineering educator*
Swern, Frederic Lee *engineering educator*
Widdicombe, Richard Palmer *librarian*

Holmdel
Abate, John E. *electrical and electronic engineer, communications consultant*
Ayub, Yacub *financial consultant*
Bjorkholm, John Ernst *physicist*
Boyd, Gary Delane *electro-optical engineer, researcher*
Burrus, Charles Andrew, Jr. *research physicist*
Haskell, Barry Geoffry *communications company research administrator*
Heirman, Donald Nestor *telecommunications engineering company manager*
Johannes, Virgil Ivancich *electrical engineer*
Jukes, Terence Douglas *marketing professional*
Kaminow, Ivan Paul *physicist*
Kogelnik, Herwig Werner *electronics company executive*
Li, Tingye *electrical engineer*
Mac Rae, Alfred Urquhart *physicist, electrical engineer*
Meadors, Howard Clarence, Jr. *electrical engineer*
Miller, David Andrew Barclay *physicist*
Mollenauer, Linn Frederick *physicist*
Netravali, Arun N. *communications executive*
Opie, William Robert *retired metallurgical engineer*
Ross, Ian Munro *electrical engineer*
Shah, Jagdeep *physicist, researcher*
Tien, Ping King *electronics engineer*
Wyndrum, Ralph W., Jr. *communications company executive*

Hopatcong
Harsanyi, Andrew *bishop*
Reese, Harry Edwin, Jr. *electronics executive*

Hopewell
Halpern, Daniel *poet, editor, educator*

Howell
Borowick, Bernadine Ann *supervisor of instruction*

Imlaystown
Richardson, Donald Campbell *land planner, landscape architect*

Irvington
McConnell, Lorelei Catherine *library director*

Iselin
Clarke, David H. *industrial products executive*
Dornbusch, Arthur A., II *lawyer*
Garfinkel, Harmon Mark *specialty chemicals company executive*
Guyett, Robert Losee *specialty chemicals and metals executive*
Hecht, William David *accountant*
LaTorre, L. Donald *chemical company executive*
Mackinnon, Robert *medical products executive*
Raos, John G. *manufacturing executive*
Smith, Orin Robert *chemical company executive*
Tice, George A(ndrew) *photographer*
Vitt, David Aaron *medical manufacturing company executive*
White, Sir (Vincent) Gordon Lindsay *textile company executive*

Jackson
Hagberg, Carl Thomas *financial executive*

Jamesburg
Chase, Aurin Moody, Jr. *biology educator*
Denton, John Joseph *retired pharmaceutical company executive*
Maxwell, Bryce *engineer,educator*
Miller, Theodore Robert *surgeon, educator*

Jersey City
Alfano, Michael Charles *pharmaceutical company executive*
Basso, Kathleen Alyssa *lawyer*
Bavasi, Peter Joseph *professional baseball team executive*
Block, Leonard Nathan *drug company executive*
Chatterjee, Amit *structural engineer*
Collins, Doris L. *nursing educator, psychiatric-mental health nurse*
D'Amico, Thomas F. *economist, educator*
Dreman, David Nasaniel *investment counselor, security analyst*
Dubin, Michael *financial services executive*
†Field, James Samuel *stevedore company executive*
Fortune, Robert Russell *financial consultant*
Foster, Delores Jackson *elementary school principal*
Fox, Thomas George *academic adminstrator, healthscience educator*
Gurevich, Grigory *visual artist, educator*
Hernon, Richard Francis *engineer*
Holmes, Aline MacDonnell *nursing administrator*
Howard, Stanley Louis *investment banker*
Ingrassia, Paul Joseph *publishing executive*
Katz, Colleen *editor in chief*
LiBrizzi, Rose Marie Meola *library administrator, counselor*
Luthi, Wilfried T. *manufacturing executive*
Manischewitz, Bernard *food products company executive*
Means, Fred Ernest *dean*
Melnick, Gilbert Stanley *radiologist, educator*
Metsch, Jonathan Martin *health facility executive*
Meyer, Howard Robert *lawyer*
Mortensen, Eugene Phillips *hospital administrator*
Nash, Lee J. *banker*
Niemiec, Edward Walter *professional association executive*
Patterson, Grace Limerick *library director*
Poiani, Eileen Louise *mathematics educator, college administrator, higher education planner*
Reynolds, Scott Walton *academic administrator*
Sanders, Franklin D. *insurance company executive*
Serra-Badue, Daniel Francisco *artist, educator*
Shildneck, Barbara Jean *accounting magazine editor*
Smith, James Frederick *securities executive*
Tognino, John Nicholas *financial services executive*
Tugwell, John *bank executive*
Tymon, Leo F., Jr. *banker*
Wagner, Douglas Walker Ellyson *journal editor*
†Welfeld, Joseph Alan *healthcare consultant*
Zuckerberg, David Alan *pharmaceutical company executive*

Kearny
†Goodman, Leonard *personal products company executive*

Keasbey
†Hari, Kenneth Stephen *painter*

Kendall Park
Goldberg, Bertram J. *social agency admininistrator*
Hershenov, Bernard Zion *electronics research and development company executive*

Kenilworth
Conklin, Donald Ransford *pharmaceutical company executive*
Darrow, William Richard *pharmaceutical company executive*
Ganguly, Ashit Kumar *organic chemist*
Hoffman, John Fletcher *lawyer*

Keyport
Graupe-Pillard, Grace *artist, educator*
Warren, Craig Bishop *flavor and fragrance company executive, researcher*

Kinnelon
Davis, Dorinne Sue Taylor Lovas *audiologist*
Haller, Charles Edward *engineering consultant*
Preston, Andrew Joseph *pharmacist, drug company executive*
Richardson, Irene M. *health facility administrator*
Schafer, John Stephen *foundation administrator*

Lake Hiawatha
Schonfeld, Rudolf Leopold *secondary school educator*

Lake Hopatcong
Dowling, Robert Murray *oil company executive*

Lakehurst
Millar, John Francis *industrial products company executive*

Lakewood
Bowers, John Zimmerman *physician, educator*
Levovitz, Pesach Zechariah *rabbi*
Nolan, Harold Joseph, Jr. *marketing educator*
Shawl, S. Nicole *counseling psychologist*
Sloyan, Sister Stephanie *mathematics educator*
Williams, Barbara Anne *college president*

Laurel Springs
Cleveland, Susan Elizabeth *library administrator, researcher*

Lawrenceville
Coleman, Wade Hampton, III *management consultant, mechanical engineer, former banker*
†Farrar, Donald Keith *financial executive*
Iversen, David Stewart *librarian*
Kihn, Harry *electronics engineer, manufacturing company executive*
Moser, Robert Lawrence *pathologist, health facility administrator*
Stehle, Edward Raymond *secondary education educator, school system administrator*
Terracciano, Anthony Patrick *banker*
Tharney, Leonard John *education educator, consultant*

Lebanon
Goulazian, Peter Robert *retired broadcasting executive*
Kone, Russell Joseph *advertising agency executive, film producer*
Lager, Henry S. *transporation executive*
Pollazzi, Roger G. *transportation executive*

Leonia
Hollinshead, May Block *anatomist, educator*

Liberty Corner
Apruzzese, Vincent John *lawyer*
Gall, Martin *project chemist, research and development manager*
Rajani, Prem Rajaram *transportation company financial executive*
Stoll, Roger G. *health insurance company executive*

Lincroft
Keenan, Robert Anthony *financial services company executive, educator, consultant*
Morehouse, Dorothy Van Winkle *museum director*

Pollock, William John *secondary school administrator*
Sullivan, Brother Jeremiah Stephen *former college president*

Linden
Covino, Charles Peter *metal products company executive*
Foege, Rose Ann Scudiero *human resources professional*
Hansen, Christian Andreas, Jr. *chemical company executive*
Hart, Paul *dean, poet, educator*
Malec, Ruth Ellen *special services director*
Tamarelli, Alan Wayne *chemical company executive*

Lindenwold
Tucker-Keto, Claudia A. *academic administrator*

Linwood
McCormick, Robert Matthew, III *newspaper executive*
Voigt, John Jacob *telecommunication executives, international investment banker*

Litte Falls
Glasser, Lynn Schreiber *publisher*

Little Falls
Armellino, Michael Ralph *retired asset management executive*
Dohr, Donald R. *metallurgical engineer, researcher*
Glasser, Stephen Andrew *publishing executive, lawyer*
Nash, James John *superintendent*
Stiles, John Callender *physicist*

Little Ferry
Barbarow, Thomas Steven *public school system administrator*

Little Silver
Finch, Rogers Burton *association management consultant*
Fleischer, Paul E. *electrical engineer*
Labbett, John Edgar *pet food products executive*

Livingston
Barlotta, Flora Maria *hematologist*
Caballes, Romeo Lopez *pathologist, bone tumor researcher*
Daman, Ernest Ludwig *mechanical engineer*
Del Mauro, Ronald *hospital administrator*
Heilmeier, George Harry *electrical engineer, researcher*
†Ho, Robert P. *plastics company executive*
†Jacobs, Richard Moss *consulting engineer*
Keswani, Satty Gill *reproductive endocrinologist*
Krieger, Abbott Joel *neurosurgeon*
Kuzmak, Lubomyr Ihor *surgeon*
Mandelbaum, Howard Arnold *marketing/ management consultant*
†Pai, David H(sien)-C(hung) *research engineer*
Pantages, Louis James *lawyer*
†Wang, Walter *chemicals executive*
†Wang, Y. C. *chemicals executive*
Zappulla, Lawrence Joseph *bank executive*

Lodi
Karetzky, Stephen *library director, educator, researcher*
Meno, John Peter *chorepiscopus*
Samuel, Athanasius Yeshue *archbishop*

Long Branch
Arvanitis, Cyril Steven *surgeon, educator*
Barnett, Lester Alfred *surgeon*
Caron, Patrick Edward *protective services official*
†Dadlez, Christopher M. *hospital administrator*
Evangelista, Paula Lee *public policy and communications director*
†Fox, Howard Alan *physician, medical educator*
Lagowski, Barbara Jean *writer, book editor*
Makhija, Mohan *nuclear medicine physician*
Nahavandi, Amir Nezameddin *retired engineering firm executive*
†Sacco, Robert Anthony *financial executive*

Long Valley
Levich, Cecilia Cortes *psychiatrist*

Lyndhurst
Albosta, Richard Francis *engineering and construction company executive*
Lasky, David *lawyer, corporate executive*
Mosher, Howard Ira *automotive executive*
†Rim, B. C. *wholesale distribution executive, retail executive*
Sieger, Charles *librarian*

Lyons
Kidd, A. Paul *hospital administrator, government official*

Madison
Byrd, Stephen Fred *human resource consultant*
Calligan, William Dennis *retired life insurance company executive*
Campbell, William Cecil *biologist*
†Collins, David Edmond *pharmaceutical company executive, lawyer*
Comey, J. Martin *pharmaceutical company executive*
D'Andrade, Hugh A(lfred) *pharmaceutical company executive, lawyer*
deStevens, George *chemist, educator*
Ellenbogen, Leon *nutritionist, pharmaceutical company executive*
Fogarty, John Thomas *lawyer*
Gibson, William Ford *author*
Gnichtel, William Van Orden *lawyer*
†Goodman, Michael B(arry) *communications educator*
Irons, Neil L. *bishop*
Johnson, William Joseph *stockbroker*
Kean, Thomas H. *academic administrator, former governor*
Knox, John, Jr. *philosopher, educator*
Kogan, Richard Jay *pharmaceutical company executive*
Leak, Margaret Elizabeth *insurance company executive*
Luciano, Robert Peter *pharmaceutical company executive*
McCulloch, James Callahan *manufacturing company executive*
Mc Mullen, Edwin Wallace, Jr. *English language educator*
Monte, Bonnie J. *performing company executive*
O'Brien, Mary Devon *communications executive, consultant*
Siegel, George Henry *international business development consultant*
Stafford, John Rogers *pharmaceutical and household products company executive*
†Stotts, Michael W. *theatrical producer*
Yrigoyen, Charles, Jr. *church denomination executive*

Mahwah
Borowitz, Grace Burchman *chemistry educator, researcher*
Bram, Leon Leonard *publishing company executive*
Bryan, Thomas Lynn *lawyer, educator*
Eiger, Richard William *publisher*
Hansen, Rosanna Lee *publishing executive*
Hirooka, Sueyuki *electronics company executive*
Hollerith, Richard, Jr. *industrial designer, consultant*
Lynch, Kevin A. *book publishing executive*
Padovano, Anthony Thomas *theologian, educator*
Schecter, M. *book publishing executive*
Scott, Robert Allyn *college administrator*
Weinberg, Sydney Stahl *historian*

Manahawkin
†Docheff, Ivan *lawyer*

Manalapan
Harrison-Johnson, Yvonne Elois *pharmacologist*
Stone, Fred Michael *lawyer*

Mantoloking
Morris, Robert *lawyer, writer*

Maplewood
Hammond, Caleb Dean, Jr. *cartographer, publisher*
Hammond, Caleb Dean, III *publishing executive*
Lev, Alexander Shulim *mechanical engineer*
MacWhorter, Robert Bruce *retired lawyer*
†Safian, Gail Robyn *public relations executive*
Weston, Randy (Randolph Edward Weston) *pianist, composer*

Margate City
Kennedy, Berenice Connor (Mrs. Jefferson Kennedy, Jr.) *magazine executive, writer, consultant*
Weiss, Mordechai *principal*

Marlboro
Leveson, Irving Frederick *economist*
Schwartz, Perry Lester *information systems engineer, consultant*

Marlton
Byerly, LeRoy James *psychiatrist, educator*
Forbes, Gordon Maxwell *sports journalist, commentator*

Matawan
Kesselman, Bruce Alan *marketing executive, consultant, composer, writer*

Maywood
Fitzpatrick, Judith *immunochemist*

McGuire AFB
†Armstrong, Malcolm Buron *career officer*
†Gray, George A., III *retired military officer*

Medford
Dunn, Roy J. *landscape architect*
Hogan, Thomas Harlan *publisher*
Katzell, Raymond A. *psychologist, educator*
Kesty, Robert Edward *chemical manufacturing company executive*
Klugman, Peter Jay *psychologist, consultant*
Konstantinos, K. Kiki *school system administrator*
Sanders, Phyllis Aden *retired radio and television broadcaster*
Vereb, Michael Joseph *pharmaceutical and cosmetic executive*
Wallis, Robert Ray *psychologist, entrepreneur*

Mendham
Desjardins, Raoul *medical association administrator, financial consultant*
Fenner, Peter David *communications executive, management consultant*
Kaprelian, Edward K. *mechanical engineer, physicist*
Kirby, Allan Price, Jr. *investment company executive*
Posunko, Barbara *elementary education educator*
Posunko, Linda Mary *elementary education educator*

Mercerville
†Kraus, Ted Richard *real estate consultant*

Metuchen
Horrocks, Norman *publisher*
Hughes, Edward T. *bishop*
Vercammen, Kenneth Albert *lawyer*

Middletown
Levi, Ilan Mosche *computer and communications company executive*
O'Neill, Eugene Francis *communications engineer*
Roesner, Peter Lowell *manufacturing company executive*

Midland Park
Koster, John Peter, Jr. *journalist, author*

Milford
Carter, Clarence Holbrook *artist*

Millburn
Cohen, Geoffrey Merrill *theater executive*
†Duberstein, Joel Lawrence *physician*
Gitner, Deanne *writer*
Ogden, Maureen Black *state legislator*
Raff, Gilbert *publishing company executive*

Millington
Donaldson, John Cecil, Jr. *consumer products company executive*
Thompson, Larry Flack *semicondurctor equipment company executive*

Milltown
Bradley, Edward William *sports foundation executive*

Millville
†Johnson, James Robert *county agricultural official, educator*

Monmouth Beach
Herbert, LeRoy James *retired accounting firm executive*

Monmouth Junction
Neff, Peter John *chemicals, mining and metal processing executive*

Montclair
Alexander, Fernande Gardner *writer, photographer*
Beerman, Miriam *artist, educator*
Behrle, Franklin Charles *retired pediatrician and educator*
Bolden, Theodore Edward *dentist, educator*
Boyd, Hugh Alan *architect*
Brown, Geraldine Reed *lawyer, consulting executive*
Brownrigg, Walter Grant *cartoonist, corporate executive*
Campbell, Stewart Fred *foundation executive*
Conant, Herbert D. *construction executive*
Draper, Daniel Clay *lawyer*
Dubrow, Marsha Ann *high technology company executive, composer*
Fleming, Thomas Crawley *physician, medical director, former editor*
Gogick, Kathleen Christine *magazine editor, publisher*
†Griffith, Nanci *singer, songwriter*
Hardin, John Alexander *retired broadcasting consultant*
Jacoby, Tamar *journalist, author*
Jones, Rees Lee *golf course architect*
Mc Carthy, Daniel Christopher, Jr. *manufacturing company executive*
Mills, James Thoburn *association executive*
Mochary, Mary Veronica *lawyer*
Morris, John Lunden *international transportation executive*
Pierson, Robert David *banker*
Richart, John Douglas *investment banker*
Sabin, William Albert *editor*
Schlesinger, Stephen Lyons *nurseryman*
Stevens, John Galen *mathematics and computer science educator*
Strobert, Barbara *principal*
Tobia, Ronald Lawrence *lawyer*
Tonges, Mary Crabtree *nurse executive*
Walker, George Theophilus, Jr. *composer, pianist, music educator*
Ward, Roger Coursen *lawyer*

Montvale
Bassermann, Michael N. *automotive executive*
Beattie, James Raymond *lawyer*
Borman, Earle Kirkpatrick, Jr. *chemical company executive*
Bowman, Patricia Imig *microbiologist*
Brecht, Warren Frederick *business executive*
†Burnett, Ed *direct marketing executive*
†Chambers, Patrick Joseph, Jr. *utility company executive*
Corrado, Fred *food company executive*
Gallagher, Michael Robert *consumer products company executive*
Kanter, Carl Irwin *lawyer*
Kennedy, John Raymond *pulp and paper company executive*
Kennedy, Quentin J., Sr. *lawyer, paper company executive*
Larkin, Michael Joseph *retail food executive*
Moritz, James R. *financial executive*
O'Gorman, Peter Joseph *retail company executive*
Pfister, James Joseph *publishing company executive*
†Quinot, Jean Michel *chemicals executive*
Rowe, James W. *food chain executive*
Sbarbaro, Robert Arthur *banker*
Scopes, Gary Martin *professional association executive*
Sifton, David Whittier *magazine editor*
Steinberg, Charles Allan *electronics manufacturing company executive*
Ulrich, Robert Gardner *retail food chain executive, lawyer*
Wood, James *supermarket executive*

Montville
Klapper, Byron D. *financial company executive*
Teubner, Ferdinand Cary, Jr. *retired publishing company executive*

Moonachie
Colburn, Janet *data processing administrator*
Robinson, Hugh R. *retired marketing executive*

Moorestown
Andrews, Ronald Allen *laboratory director, physicist, researcher*
Bennington, William Jay *public relations executive*
Fischer, Frank Ernest *utility executive*
Hassinger, Herman A. *architect*
Schwerin, Horace S. *marketing research executive*
Springer, Douglas Hyde *retired food company executive, lawyer*

Morris Plains
de Vink, Lodewijk J. R. *consumer pharmaceutical products company executive*
Fielding, Stuart *psychopharmacologist*
Goodes, Melvin Russell *manufacturing company executive*
Krull, Kevin Charles *publishing company executive, lawyer*
Kumar, Surinder *food company executive*
Picozzi, Anthony *dentistry educator, educational administrator*
Williams, Joseph Dalton *pharmaceutical company executive*

Morristown
Ahl, David Howard *writer, editor*
Arnow, Leslie Earle *scientist*
Aspero, Benedict Vincent *lawyer*
Azzato, Louis Enrico *manufacturing company executive*
†Baldassari, Dennis *utilities executive*
Baldwin, Robert Hayes Burns *business executive*
Barpal, Isaac Ruben *technology and operations executive*
Bauhs, David J. *manufacturing executive*
Belzer, Alan *diversified manufacturing company executive*
Bergstein, Stanley Francis *horse racing executive*
Berkley, Peter Lee *lawyer*
Berndt, John Edward *telecommunications company executive*
Bickerton, John Thorburn *retired pharmaceutical executive*
Booth, Albert Edward, II *real estate executive*
Bossidy, Lawrence Arthur *industrial manufacturing executive*
Bromberg, Myron James *lawyer*
Callahan, Edward William *chemical engineer, manufacturing company executive*
Cameron, Nicholas Allen *diversified corporation executive*
Campion, Thomas Francis *lawyer*
Clemen, John Douglas *lawyer*
Clifford, Robert L. *state supreme court justice*
Colby, Lewis James, Jr. *manufacturing company executive*
†Cortellessa, Dominick Ralph *information systems executive*
Cregan, Frank Robert *financial executive, consultant*
DeLury, Bernard E. *vice president labor relations*
Fredericks, Robert Joseph *language company executive*
Graham, Paul E(ugene) *lawyer*
Granet, Roger B. *psychiatrist, educator*
Herman, Robert Lewis *cork company executive*
Herzberg, Peter Jay *lawyer*
Hesselink, Ann Patrice *financial executive, lawyer*
Hittinger, William Charles *electronics company executive*
Hyland, William Francis *lawyer*
Kandravy, John *lawyer*
Katzenbach, Nicholas deBelleville *lawyer*
Kearns, William Michael, Jr. *investment banker*
Kirby, Fred Morgan, II *corporation executive*
Klindt, Steven *art museum director*
Kreindler, Peter Michael *lawyer*
Krumholz, Dennis Jonathan *lawyer*
Kurtz, Bruce Edward *chemical engineer, research and development executive*
Lavey, Stewart Evan *lawyer*
Lindner, Joseph, Jr. *physician, medical administrator*
Lunin, Joseph *lawyer*
Martin, Alvin Charles *lawyer*
Maskaleris, Stephen Nicholas *lawyer*
McCarthy, G. Daniel *lawyer*
Mc Elroy, William Theodore *lawyer*
Miller, Hasbrouck Bailey *financial and travel services company executive*
Munson, William Leslie *insurance company executive*
Nadaskay, Raymond *architect*
Newhouse, Robert J., Jr. *insurance executive*
Nittoly, Paul Gerard *lawyer*
O'Connor, Francis X. *financial executive*
O'Grady, Dennis Joseph *lawyer*
Oishi, Satoshi *architectural and engineering executive*
†Oths, Richard Philip *hospital administrator, insurance firm executive*
Pantel, Glenn Steven *lawyer*
Parr, Grant Van Siclen *surgeon*
Personick, Stewart David *electrical engineer*
Pollock, Stewart Glasson *state supreme court justice*
Powell, David Greatorex *public affairs executive*
Reed, Rex Raymond *retired telephone company executive*
Reid, Charles Adams, III *lawyer*
Rose, Robert Gordon *lawyer*
Rosenthal, Meyer L(ouis) *lawyer*
Samet, Andrew Benjamin *lawyer*
Scott, Susan *lawyer*
†Shanahan, William Stephen *consumer products company executive*
Sharkey, Vincent Joseph *lawyer*
Shumate, Paul William, Jr. *communications executive*
Simon, William Edward *investment banker, former secretary of treasury*
Szuch, Clyde Andrew *lawyer*
Teiger, David *management consultant*
Tierney, Raymond Moran, Jr. *lawyer*
Tokar, Edward Thomas *manufacturing company executive*
†Urban, John S. *engineering company executive*
Van Uitert, LeGrand Gerard *chemist*
Wajnert, Thomas C. *leasing company executive*
Warlick, Robert Patterson *investment management company executive*
Whitmer, Frederick Lee *lawyer*

Mount Arlington
Cohen, Irving David *science administrator*

Mount Holly
Tiedeken, Kathleen Helen *health facilities administrator*

Mount Laurel
†Barba, Evans Michael *civil engineer*
Buchan, Alan Bradley *land planner, consultant, civil engineer*
Calzolano, John Joseph *engineering and construction company executive*
Grey, Richard E. *toy company executive*
Hart, Larry Edward *communications company executive*
Instone, John Clifford *manufacturing company executive*
Klein, Anne Sceia *public relations executive*
Laubach, Roger Alvin *accountant*
Taylor, Henry Roth *marketing executive*
†Vidas, Vincent George *engineering executive*

Mount Olive
Cornish, Jeannette Carter *lawyer*
Stein, J. Dieter *chemical company executive*

Mount Tabor
Lender, Herman Joseph *reinsurance company executive*

Mountain Lakes
Case, Manning Eugene, Jr. *corporate executive*
Cook, Charles Francis *insurance executive*
Mattes, Hans George *communications system design scientist, researcher*
Turnheim, Palmer *banker*
Williams, Edward David *consulting executive*
Wolff, Ivan Lawrence *venture capitalist*

Mountainside
Abrams, Joseph computer company executive
Cardoni, Horace Robert retired lawyer
DiPietro, Ralph Anthony marketing and management consultant, educator
Horner, Shirley Jaye writer, columnist
Lipton, Bronna Jane marketing communications executive
Lissenden, Carolkay pediatrician

Mullica Hill
Demola, James, Sr. church administrator

Murray Hill
Atal, Bishnu Saroop speech research executive
Baker, William Oliver research chemist, educator
†Batlogg, Bertram physicist
Bonnes, Charles Andrew lawyer
Brinkman, William Frank physicist, research executive
Capasso, Federico physicist, research administrator
Cho, Alfred Yi electrical engineer
Cohen, Melvin Irwin telephone company executive
Coppersmith, Susan Nan physicist
Dyer, Alexander Patrick industrial gas manufacturing company executive
Field, Michael Stanley information services company executive
Glass, Alastair Malcolm physicist, research director
Graham, Ronald Lewis mathematician
Helfand, Eugene chemist
†Hutchinson, Albert L. research physicist
Johnson, David Wilfred, Jr. ceramic scientist, researcher
†Kurkjian, Charles R(obert) ceramic engineer, researcher
Mayo, John Sullivan telecommunications company executive
Morgan, Samuel P(ope) physicist, applied mathematician
Murthy, Srinivasa K. engineering corporation executive
Musa, John Davis computer and infosystems executive, software reliability engineering researcher and expert
Pinczuk, Aron physicist
Radner, Roy economist, educator, researcher
Rayner, Robert Martin financial executive
†Sirtori, Carlo research physicist
†Sivco, Deborah L. research physicist
Sloane, Neil James Alexander mathematician, researcher
Stillinger, Frank Henry chemist, educator
†Taylor, Volney marketing company executive
†Tully, John Charles research chemical physicist
†van Dover, Robert Bruce physicist
Wagner, Edward Kurt publishing company executive
Wernick, Jack Harry chemist
White, Alice Elizabeth physicist, researcher

Neptune
Aguiar, Adam Martin chemist, educator
Axelrod, Herbert Richard ichthyologist, publishing executive
Clurfeld, Andrea editor, food critic
†Falvo, Peter S., Jr. lawyer
Harrigan, John Thomas, Jr. physician, obstetrician-gynecologist
Lass, E(rnest) Donald communications company executive
Lloyd, John Koons hospital administrator
Ollwerther, William Raymond newspaper editor
Plangere, Jules L., III newpaper company executive
†Spencer, James Jeffrey executive director
Suozzo, Frank Vincent insurance company executive

Neshanic Station
Muckenhoupt, Benjamin retired mathematics educator
Weicksel, Charlene Marie principal

Netcong
Sekula, Edward Joseph, Jr. financial executive

New Brunswick
Aisner, Joseph oncologist, physician
Alexander, Robert Jackson economist, educator
Amarel, Saul computer scientist, educator
Anderson, James Doig library and information science educator
Ballou, Janice Marie research director
Becker, Ronald Leonard archivist
Bern, Ronald Lawrence consulting company executive
Boehm, Werner William social work educator
Boocock, Sarane Spence sociologist
†Bowden, Henry Warner religion educator
Budd, Richard Wade communications scientist, educator, lecturer, consultant, university dean
Burke, James Edward consumer products company executive
Campbell, Robert E. retired health care products company executive
Carman, John Herbert elementary education educator
Cate, Phillip Dennis art museum director
Chelius, James Robert economics educator
Daubechies, Ingrid mathematics educator
Day, Peter Rodney geneticist, educator
Dill, Ellis Harold university dean
Dinerman, Miriam social work educator
Eager, George Sidney, Jr. electrical engineer, business executive
Edelman, Hendrik library and information science educator
Ehrenfeld, David William biology educator, author
†Eisinger, Robert Peter nephrologist, educator
Elinson, Jack sociology educator
Ettinger, Lawrence Jay pediatric hematologist-oncologist, educator
†Ferris, Harris Nichols ballet company director, dancer, educator
Flaherty, Charles Foster, Jr. psychology educator, researcher
Funk, Cyril Reed, Jr. agronomist, educator
Gardner, Lloyd Calvin, Jr. history educator
Garner, Charles William educational administration educator, consultant
†Gelfand, Israel Moseevich mathematician
Gillette, William historian, educator
Glass, David Carter psychology educator
Glasser, Paul Harold sociologist, educator, university administrator, social worker
Gocke, David Joseph immunology educator, physician, medical scientist
Goffen, Rona art educator
Goodyear, John Lake artist, educator
Grassle, John Frederick oceanographer, marine sciences educator
Greco, Ralph Steven surgeon, researcher, medical educator
Grob, Gerald N. historian, educator
Gupta, Ayodhya Prasad entomologist, immunologist, cell biologist
Gussin, Robert Zalmon health care company executive
Hartman, Mary S. historian
Hayakawa, Kan-Ichi food science educator
Ho, Chi-Tang food chemistry educator
Holzberg, Harvey Alan hospital administrator
Horowitz, Irving Louis publisher, educator
†House, Renee S. theological librarian, minister
Hurst, Gregory Squire artistic director, director, producer
Jacob, Charles Elmer political scientist, educator
Johnson, Clark Hughes financial executive
Katz, Carlos electrical engineer
Kelley, Donald Reed historian
Kovach, Barbara Ellen management and psychology educator
Kruskal, Martin David mathematical physicist, educator
Kulikowski, Casimir Alexander computer science educator, research program director
Lachance, Paul Albert food science educator, clergyman
Laraya-Cuasay, Lourdes Redublo pediatric pulmonologist, educator
Larsen, Ralph S(tanley) health care company executive
Lebowitz, Joel Louis mathematical physicist, educator
Lee, Barbara Anne lawyer, educator
Leggett, John Carl sociology educator
Lettvin, Theodore concert pianist
Levine, George Lewis English language educator, literature critic
Lewis, David Levering history educator
Liao, Mei-June biopharmaceutical company executive
Lynch, John A. lawyer, state senator
Mandel, Ruth B. political science educator, educational association administrator, researcher
Maramorosch, Karl virologist, educator
Markey, Andrew Joseph health care products company executive
Matuska, John E. hospital administrator
Mc Laren, Malcolm Grant, IV ceramic engineering educator
Mechanic, David social sciences educator
Midlarsky, Manus Issachar political scientist, educator
Morrison, Karl Frederick history educator
Nawy, Edward George civil engineer, educator
Nelson, Douglas Lee insurance company executive
Nelson, Jack Lee education educator
O'Neill, William Lawrence history educator
†Ostriker, Alicia Suskin poet
Peterson, Donald Robert psychologist, educator, university administrator
Plano, Richard James physicist, educator
Poirier, Richard English educator, literary critic
Psuty, Norbert Phillip marine sciences educator
Reed, James Wesley social historian, educator
†Reeling, Patricia Glueck library educator, educational consultant
Reock, Ernest C., Jr. retired government services educator and academic director
Roberts, Albert Roy social work educator
Rosen, Robert Thomas analytical and food chemist
Rosenberg, Seymour psychologist, educator
Roth, Herbert, Jr. corporate executive
Ruben, Brent David communication educator
Russell, Louise Bennett economist, educator
Scanlon, Jane Cronin mathematics educator
Scully, John Thomas obstetrician, gynecologist, educator
Seibold, James Richard physician, researcher
Snyderman, Reuven Kenneth plastic surgeon, educator
Solberg, Myron food scientist, educator
Stewart, Joseph Turner, Jr. retired pharmaceutical company executive
Stimpson, Catharine Roslyn English language educator, writer
Strauss, Ulrich Paul educator, chemist
Strawderman, William E. statistics educator
Stuart, Robert Crampton economics educator
Szarka, Laslo Joseph pharmaceutical company executive
Taft, Earl Jay mathematics educator
Tanner, Daniel curriculum theory educator
Tedrow, John Charles Fremont soils educator
Temmer, Georges Maxime physicist
Tiger, Lionel social scientist, anthropology consultant
Toby, Jackson sociologist, educator
Turock, Betty Jane library and information science educator, educational association administrator
Vieth, Wolf Randolph chemical engineering educator
Walters, Arthur Scott neurologist, educator, clinical research scientist
Wasson, Richard Howard English language educator
†Webre, Septime ballet company artistic director, choreographer
Wheeler, Kenneth William historian, educator
Wilkinson, Louise Cherry psychology educator, dean
Wilson, Donald Malcolm publishing executive
Wolfe, Robert Richard bioresource engineer, educator
†Woodward, John Taylor, III lawyer
Yttrehus, Rolv Berger composer, educator

New Monmouth
Donnelly, Gerard Kevin retail executive

New Providence
Barnes, Sandra Henley publishing company executive
Bishop, David John physicist
Chatterji, Debajyoti manufacturing company executive
Cooper, Carol Diane publishing company executive
Fishburn, Peter Clingerman research mathematician, economist
Flink, Richard Allen lawyer, manufacturing company executive
Gaylord, Norman Grant chemical and polymer consultant
Lanzerotti, Louis John physicist
Laudise, Robert Alfred research chemist
Longfield, William Herman health care company executive
Maloney, George Thomas health industry executive
Mitchell, James Winfield science administrator
Murray, Cherry Ann physicist, researcher
Shepp, Lawrence Alan mathematician, educator
Stormer, Horst Ludwig physicist
Sundberg, Carl-Erik Wilhelm telecommunications executive, researcher
Symanski, Robert Anthony treasurer
Walker, Stanley P. publishing executive
Wertheim, Gunther Klaus physicist
Wyner, Aaron Daniel mathematician

New Vernon
Dugan, John Leslie, Jr. foundation executive
Huck, John Lloyd pharmaceutical company executive
Le Buhn, Robert investment executive
Margetts, W. Thomas automobile parts company executive, lawyer

Newark
Abrams, Roger I. academic dean, labor arbitrator
Ackerman, Harold A. federal judge
Alito, Samuel Anthony, Jr. federal judge
Allen, David newspaper editor
Arabie, Phipps marketing educator, researcher
Aregood, Richard Lloyd editor
Askin, Frank law educator
Auth, Susan Handler curator, educator
Baker, Herman vitaminologist
Bar-Ness, Yeheskel electrical engineer, educator
Barry, Maryanne Trump federal judge
Bartner, Martin newspaper executive
Bassler, William G. federal judge
Beck, Robert Arthur insurance company executive
Ben-Menachem, Yoram radiologist
Bergen, Stanley Silvers, Jr. university president, physician
Beyer-Mears, Annette physiologist
Bigley, William Joseph, Jr. control engineer
Bischoff, William Ludwig curator
Bishop, Gordon Bruce journalist
Bissell, John W. federal judge
Blount, Alice McDaniel museum curator
Bonaventura, Vincent E. transportation executive
Bornstein, Lester Milton medical center executive
Bossert, Carol Jo museum administrator
Braun, Robert newspaper editor
Cahn, Jeffrey Barton lawyer
Caldwell, Wesley Stuart, III lawyer, lobbyist
Canfield, William Newton editorial cartoonist
†Capra, Ralph transportation executive
Carroll, John Douglas mathematical and statistical psychologist
Chagnon, Joseph V. school system administrator
Cheng, Mei-Fang psychobiology educator, neuroethology researcher
Chesler, Stanley Richard federal judge
Chinard, Francis Pierre physiologist, physician
Christakos, Sylvia biochemist, educator, researcher
Christodoulou, Aris Peter pharmaceutical executive, investment banker
Cinotti, Alfonse Anthony ophthalmologist, educator
Clark, Dewey P. insurance company executive
Cocchia, Neal newspaper editor
Codey, Lawrence R. electric power company executive
Colli, Bart Joseph lawyer
Contractor, Farok business and management educator
Cook, Stuart Donald physician, educator
Covington-Winrow, Carolyn school administrator
Crane, Samuel association executive
Crew, Louie (Li Min Hua) language professional, educator
Crimmins, Thomas Michael, Jr. utilities company executive
Day, Edward Francis, Jr. lawyer
Debevoise, Dickinson Richards federal judge
De Lisa, Joel Alan rehabilitation physician
Del Tufo, Robert J. lawyer, former state prosecutor
Dickson, Jim playwright, stage director, arts consultant
D'Uva, Robert Carmen insurance and real estate broker
Dwane, James E. insurance company executive
Eittreim, Richard MacNutt lawyer
English, Nicholas Conover lawyer
English, Woodruff Jones lawyer
Eslami, Hossein Hojatol surgeon, educator
Estrin, Herman Albert English language educator
Evans, Hugh E. pediatrician
Everett, Richard G. newspaper editor
Feldman, Susan Carol neurobiologist, anatomy educator
Fenster, Saul K. university president
Ferland, E. James electric utility executive
Fink, Aaron Herman box manufacturing company executive
Flaherty, John Edmund lawyer
Foushee, Geraldine George municipal county government official, detective
Friedland, Bernard engineer, educator
Futter, Victor lawyer
Gambardella, Rosemary federal judge
Gardner, Bernard surgeon, educator
Garth, Leonard I. federal judge
Genzer, Stephen Bruce lawyer, educator
Gerathy, E. Carroll former insurance executive, real estate developer
Gilbert, Stephen Alan lawyer
Gillett, Jonathan Newell publishing executive
Goldenberg, David Milton experimental pathologist, oncologist
Gossett, George Boyd human service executive
Greenbaum, Jeffrey J. lawyer
Greendorfer, Terese Grosman fashion editor
Greenfield, Sanford Raymond architect
Griffinger, Michael R. lawyer
Guenzel, Frank Bernhard chemical engineer
Hadas, Rachel poet, educator
Hanesian, Deran chemical engineer, chemistry and environmental science educator, consultant
Hannon, John Robert investment company executive
Haring, Eugene Miller lawyer
Harrison, Charles newspaper editor
Harrison, Roslyn Siman lawyer
Henderson, Dorland John retired electrical engineer
Hermann, Steven Istvan textile executive
Hill, George James surgeon, educator
Hiltz, Starr Roxanne sociologist, educator, computer scientist, writer, lecturer, consultant
Hobson, Robert Wayne, II surgeon
Hollander, Toby Edward education educator
Holzer, Marc public administrator educator
Horii, Howard Nobuo architect, educator
Howe, Carroll Victor construction equipment company executive
Hrycak, Peter mechanical engineer, educator
Hsieh, Jui Sheng mechanical engineer, educator
Hsu, Cheng-Tzu Thomas civil engineering educator
†Hull, Joan Carol historical society executive, consultant
Hutcheon, Duncan Elliot physician, educator
Iffy, Leslie medical educator
Jakubowski, Hieronim biochemistry educator
James, Sharpe mayor
Jones, Etta singer
Kaltenbacher, Philip D(avid) industrialist, former public official
Kanzler, George journalist, critic
Karp, Donald Mathew lawyer, banker
Keith, Garnett Lee, Jr. insurance company investment executive
Klein, Willie newspaper editor
Knapp, Edward D. banker
Knee, Stephen H. lawyer
Koeppe, Alfred C. telecommunications company executive
Kosof, Anna Clara radio station executive
Kott, David Russell lawyer
Lanzoni, Vincent medical school dean
Latini, Anthony A. insurance company financial executive
Lawatsch, Frank Emil, Jr. lawyer
Layman, William Arthur psychiatrist, educator
Lechner, Alfred James, Jr. federal judge
Ledeen, Robert Wagner neurochemist, educator
Lederman, Peter (Bernd) environmental services executive, consultant, educator
Leevy, Carroll Moton medical educator, hepatology researcher
Lenehan, Art newspaper editor
Levin, Simon lawyer
Lieberman, Leonard retired supermarket executive
Lifland, John C. federal judge
Light, Dorothy Kaplan insurance executive, lawyer
Link, William P. insurance company executive
Lory, Marc H. hospital administrator
Mahler, Harry Bez architect, planner
Marano, Rocco John telephone company executive
Martinez, Arturo newspaper editor
Maske, Monica newspaper editor
Materna, Thomas Walter ophthalmologist
Mc Carrick, Theodore Edgar archbishop
McGuire, William B(enedict) lawyer
McKelvey, Jack M. bishop
McKinney, John Adams, Jr. lawyer
Mitchell, James Lowry lawyer, former government official
Morgenstern, Dan Michael jazz historian, educator, editor
Moskowitz, Sam (Sam Martin) author, editor, publisher
Murnick, Daniel Ely physicist, educator
Murray, Constance Ann college dean
Murray, John Peter insurance company executive
Muscato, Andrew lawyer
Newhouse, Donald E. newspaper publishing executive
Newhouse, Mark William publishing executive
O'Leary, Paul Gerard investment executive
†Ostroff, Allen J. insurance company executive
Paul, James Caverly Newlin law educator, former university dean
Pfeffer, Edward Israel educational administrator
Pfeffer, Robert chemical engineer, academic administrator, educator
Pignataro, Louis James engineering educator
Politan, Nicholas H. federal judge
Quinn, John Joseph bank executive
Ralson, Lesley Lloyd insurance company executive
Reichman, Lee Brodersohn physician
Reilly, William Thomas lawyer
Reynolds, Valrae museum curator
Riepl, Francis Joseph utilities executive
Robertson, William Withers lawyer
Rosenberg, Jerry Martin business administration educator
Roth, Allan Robert lawyer, educator
†Ryan, Arthur Frederick insurance company executive
Samojlik, Eugeniusz administrator, medical educator
Sarokin, H. Lee federal judge
Schweizer, Karl Wolfgang historian, writer
Silipigni, Alfredo opera conductor
Silverman, A(lan) Jared state agency administrator, lawyer
Simmons, Peter urban planning educator
Spillers, William Russell civil engineering educator
Spong, John Shelby bishop
Starks, Florence Elizabeth special education educator
†Stavitsky, Jeffrey wholesale distribution executive
Stein, Donald Gerald psychology educator
Stults, Laurence Allen airline pilot
Tallal, Paula cognitive neuroscientist
Thomas, Gary L. academic administrator
Tischman, Michael Bernard lawyer
Tremayne, William Howard insurance company executive
Tuohey, William F. federal judge
Vevier, Charles historian, educator, consultant, university administrator
Von Glahn, Keith G. lawyer
Wachenfeld, William Thomas lawyer, foundation executive
Weis, Judith Shulman biology educator
Weiss, Gerson physician, educator
†Willse, James Patrick newspaper editor
Winfield, Novalyn L. federal bankruptcy judge
Winters, Robert Cushing insurance company executive
Wolin, Alfred M. federal judge
Wolper, Allan L. journalist, educator
Wyer, James Ingersoll lawyer
Yamner, Morris lawyer
Yu, Yi-Yuan mechanical engineering educator
Zinbarg, Edward Donald insurance company executive

Newfield
McKee, Mary Elizabeth producer

Newton
Carstens, Harold Henry publisher
†Jones, Matthew T. editorial director

North Bergen
Andriani, Marino N. electronics company executive
Chazen, Jerome A. apparel company executive
Kelly, Thomas James finance executive
Lanier, Thomas chemical and export company executive
Miller, Samuel Martin apparel company finance executive
Nobile, John Frank food flavor company executive

Scarne, John game company executive

North Branch
Gartlan, Philip M. secondary school director

North Brunswick
Awan, Ahmad Noor civil engineer
Barcus, Gilbert Martin medical products executive, business educator
Mills, George Marshall insurance and financial consultant
Phillips, Daniel Miller lawyer

North Caldwell
Stevens, William Dollard consulting mechanical engineer

North Haledon
Brown, James Joseph manufacturing company executive

Northvale
Aronson, Jason publisher
Goodman, Stanley Leonard advertising executive
Kurzweil, Arthur publisher, writer, educator
Peer, George Joseph metals company executive

Nutley
Burns, John Joseph pharmacology educator
Conrad, Herbert J. pharmaceutical executive
Drews, Jürgen pharmaceutical researcher
English, Robert Joseph electronic corporation executive
Kuntzman, Ronald pharmacology research executive
Lerner, Irwin pharmaceutical company executive
Mallard, Stephen Anthony retired utility company executive
Mostillo, Ralph medical association executive
Seyffarth, Linda Jean Wilcox corporate executive, controller
Udenfriend, Sidney biochemist
Weissbach, Herbert biochemist

Oakhurst
Konvitz, Milton Ridbaz legal educator
Seltzer, Ronald retail company executive
Wilentz, Robert Nathan state supreme court justice

Oakland
Bacaloglu, Radu chemical engineer
†Berrie, Russell sales executive, business owner
Bloom, Arnold Sanford lawyer
†Cooke, A. Curts business executive
Peterson, John Douglas museum administrator

Ocean
Abrams, Robert Allen lawyer
Schell, James Edward, II computer company executive, consultant
Winograd, Audrey Lesser advertising executive

Ocean City
Brown, Frederick Harold insurance company executive
Speitel, Gerald Eugene consulting environmental engineer

Ocean Gate
Campbell, Edward Wallace nutritionist

Old Bridge
Engel, John Jacob communications executive
†Fields, Edward management consultant
†Meisel, Philip L. chemical company executive
†Meisel, Robert P. financial company executive
Mount, Karl A. manufacturing executive
Swett, Stephen Frederick, Jr. principal

Old Tappan
Dubnick, Bernard retired pharmaceutical company administrator
Ferriter, Warren Joseph information systems executive

Oldwick
Blewitt, George Augustine physician, pharmaceutical company executive
Hitchcock, Ethan Allen lawyer
Purcell, Richard Fick lawyer, food companies advisor and counsel
Snyder, Arthur publishing company executive

Oradell
Clark, Laura magazine editor, writer
Dinsmore, Gordon Griffith management consultant
Regazzi, John Henry retired corporate executive
Roe, Kenneth Keith power and industrial engineering/construction company executive

Orange
Chlopak, Donna Gayle marketing and management consultant

Palmyra
Overholt, Miles Harvard, III management consultant, family therapist

Paramus
Adams, Eda Ann Fischer nursing educator
†Ascher, David Mark lawyer
Baczko, Joseph R. consumer products executive
Bagli, Vincent Joseph plastic surgeon
Balter, Leslie Marvin business communications educator
Birchby, Kenneth Lee banker
DiGeronimo, Suzanne Kay architect
Fader, Shirley Sloan writer
Gingras, Paul Joseph real estate management company executive
Goldstein, Michael retail executive
†Gunther, Timothy zoo director
Kenney, Martin Edward, Jr. publishing company executive
Lazarus, Charles retail toy company executive
†Liva, Edward Louis eye surgeon
Machlin, Lawrence J. nutritionist, biochemist, educator
Maclin, Ernest biomedical diagnostics company executive
Nakasone, Robert C. retail toy and game company executive
Plucinsky, Constance Marie school counselor, supervisor
Ross, William financial planner
Salizzoni, Frank Louis financial executive
†Samuels, Reuben engineering consultant
Stone, Lawrence retail executive
Wilcha, John Samuel food products company executive
Yegen, Christian Conrad, Jr. lawyer, business executive

Park Ridge
De Pol, John artist
Kaplan, Daniel I. leasing company executive
Kennedy, Brian James marketing executive
Koch, Craig R. automobile rental and leasing company executive
Noyes, Robert Edwin publisher, writer
Olson, Frank Albert car rental company executive
†Tschirhart, Paul M. corporate lawyer
Wells, Peter Raymond architect

Parlin
Chernow, Jay Howard music industry executive

Parsippany
Agostini, Rosemarie Coniglio human services administrator
Askins, Wallace Boyd manufacturing company executive
Bean, Bruce Winfield investment banker, lawyer
†Belmonte, Steven Joseph hotel chain executive
Bernthal, Frederick W. chemical company executive
Bridwell, Robert Kennedy lawyer
Brualdi, Ulysses J., Jr. electrical company executive
Clark, Philip Raymond nuclear utility executive, engineer
Cochran, Larry B. amusement park executive
Dudrow, Peter Warren human resources executive, consultant
Dvorkin, Donald electronic design and marketing company executive
Fleisher, Seymour manufacturing company executive
Florio, Jim lawyer, former governor
Geyer, Thomas Powick newspaper publisher
Graham, John Gourlay utility company executive
Graham, Stuart Edward construction company executive
Greeniaus, H. John food products company executive
Harber, Joseph F. food marketing executive
Haselmann, John Philip marketing executive
Hopp, Manfred Ernst chemical company executive
Hoyt, Monty communications executive
Jenkins, Katherine Erskine advertising executive
Jolles, Ira Hervey lawyer
Kallmann, Stanley Walter lawyer
Karpf, Ilene Phyllis lawyer
Kirkman, James A. food products executive
Kleinberg, Lawrence H. food industry executive
Lane, Stephen L. electronic equipment company executive
Leva, James Robert electric utility company executive
Manfredi, John Frederick food products executive
Morrell, Michael Preston utility executive
Muratore, Robert Peter advertising executive
Nalewako, Mary Anne corporate secretary
Olsen, Robert John savings and loan association executive
Parrish, Barry Jay marketing executive
Rowland, Jan Brownstein marketing statistician
†Simon, Richard A. insurance company executive
Singleterry, Gary Lee investment banker
Visocki, Nancy Gayle infosystems design consultant
Waggoner, Leland Tate insurance company executive
†Wiedenmayer, Christopher M. writing instrument manufacturer, distributor
Winters, Robert W. medical educator, pediatrician

Passaic
Haddad, Jamil Raouf physician
Levine, David M. newspaper editor
Lindholm, Clifford Falstrom, II engineering executive, mayor
†Pogorelec, Steven Martin fraternal organization administrator
Scudder, Richard B. newspaper executive
†Starr, Michael Seth critic

Paterson
Danziger, Glenn Norman chemical sales company executive
Deffaa, Chip jazz critic
†Duffy, Joseph Frederick hospital administrator
Pulhamus, Marlene Louise elementary school educator
Reiss, Sidney H. judge, lawyer

Peapack
Tyler, Richard Dale, Jr. air conditioning manufacturing company executive
Weiss, Allan Joseph transport company executive, lawyer

Pennington
Calvo, Roque John association executive
Halasi-Kun, George Joseph hydrologist, educator
Harris, Frederick George publishing company executive
Wallace, John Duncan banker
Widmer, Kemble geologist

Pennsauken
Alday, Paul Stackhouse, Jr. mechanical engineer
Connor, Wilda government health agency administrator
O'Brien, James Jerome construction management consultant

Pequannock
MacMurren, Harold Henry, Jr. psychologist, lawyer

Perrineville
Hoffman, Maryhelen H. Paulick communications company executive

Perth Amboy
DeFiore, Leonard F. academic administrator
Gemmell, Joseph Paul banker

Phillipsburg
Cooper, Paul mechanical engineer, research director
Paige, Richard Bruce financial information executive
Rosenthal, Marvin Bernard pediatrician, educator
Stull, Frank Walter educator

Pilesgrove
Koehler, George Applegate broadcasting company executive

Piscataway
Alderfer, Clayton Paul organizational psychologist, educator, author, administrator
Bretschneider, Ann Margery histotechnologist
Burke, Jacqueline Yvonne telecommunications executive
†Burzin, Klaus chemicals executive
Cagan, Robert H. manufacturing company research executive, biochemist
Chien, Yie W. pharmaceutics educator
Classon, Rolf Allan pharmaceutical company executive
Colaizzi, John Louis college dean
Conney, Allan Howard pharmacologist
Denhardt, David Tilton molecular and cell biology educator
†Devlin, Thomas Joseph physicist
Edelman, Norman H. medical educator
Flanagan, James Loton electrical engineer, educator
Fogiel, Max publishing executive
Freeman, Herbert computer engineering educator
Glickman, Norman Jay economist, urban policy analyst
Goldstein, Bernard David physician, educator
Goodwin, Douglas Ira steel distribution company executive
Gotsch, Audrey Rose environmental health sciences educator, researcher
Hidalgo, Alberto F. chemical engineering executive
Julesz, Bela experimental psychologist, educator, electrical engineer
Kampouris, Emmanuel Andrew corporate executive
Kear, Bernard Henry materials scientist
Lazarus, Arnold Allan psychologist, educator
Lindenfeld, Peter physics educator
Lioy, Paul James environmental health scientist
Liu, Alice Yee-Chang biology educator
McCrady, Barbara Sachs psychologist, educator
Messing, Joachim Wilhelm molecular biology educator
Moliteus, Magnus pharmaceutical and biotechnology company executive
Murphree, Henry Bernard Scott psychiatry educator, consultant
Ortiz, Raphael Montañez performance artist, educator
Passmore, Howard Clinton, Jr. geneticist, biological sciences educator
Pollack, Irwin William psychiatrist, educator
Pond, Thomas Alexander physics educator
Pramer, David microbiologist, educator, research administrator
Rhoads, George Grant medical epidemiologist
Robbins, Allen Bishop physics educator
Rudczynski, Andrew B. academic administrator, medical researcher
Salkind, Alvin J. electrochemical engineer, educator
Sannuti, Peddapullaiah electrical engineering educator
Schlesinger, Robert Walter microbiologist, microbiology educator emeritus
Schwebel, Milton psychologist, educator
Shanefield, Daniel Jay ceramics engineering educator
Shatkin, Aaron Jeffrey biochemistry educator
Shea, Stephen Michael physician, educator
Smith, Robert G. lawyer, assemblyman, educator
Snitzer, Elias physicist
Spence, Donald Pond psychologist, psychoanalyst
Welkowitz, Walter biomedical engineer, educator
Williams, James Richard human factors engineering psychologist
Witkin, Evelyn Maisel geneticist
Yacowitz, Harold biochemist, nutritionist
Young, James Earl ceramics educator, educational administrator

Pittstown
Jacob, Harry Myles mining executive

Plainfield
†Eisenstat, Theodore Ellis colon and rectal surgeon, educator
Granstrom, Marvin Leroy civil and sanitary engineering educator
Kopicki, John R. hospital administrator
Turnbull, Kenneth W. bank executive
Yood, Harold Stanley internist

Plainsboro
†Glenn, Terry Kimball investment management executive, lawyer
Hewitt, N. J. investment company executive
Jones, Allen N. insurance company executive
Lindsay, Nathan James aerospace company executive, retired career officer
Schreyer, William Allen retired investment firm executive
Talkington, William Ale publishing company executive
Urciuoli, J. Arthur investment executive
Yun, Samuel minister, educator

Pleasantville
Briant, Maryjane newspaper editor
Freeman, Lillie Brooks communications company administrator
Huggard, Ernest Douglas utility company executive

Point Pleasant
Albano, Pasquale Charles management educator, management and organization development consultant
Feeks, J. Michael bank executive
Perdunn, Richard Francis management consultant

Point Pleasant Beach
Motley, John Paul psychiatrist, consultant

Pomona
Bukowski, Elaine Louise physical therapist
†Dunn, Stephen poet
Farris, Vera King college president
Gasbarro, Norman John, Jr. educational administrator
Sung, Edward physician

Port Murray
Kunzler, John Eugene physicist

Pottersville
Goodenough, Marion P. nursing administrator
Lynch, James Henry, Jr. lawyer

Princeton
Aandahl, Fredrick historian, editor
Aarsleff, Hans linguistics educator
Ackourey, Peter Paul lawyer
Adler, Stephen Louis physicist
Allen, Diogenes clergyman, philosophy educator
Almgren, Frederick Justin, Jr. mathematician
Anderson, Ellis Bernard retired lawyer, pharmaceutical company executive
Appelbaum, Michael Arthur finance company executive
Armstrong, James Franklin religion educator
Armstrong, Richard Stoll minister, ministry and evangelism educator
Ashenfelter, Orley Clark economics educator
Autera, Michael Edward health care products company executive
Axtmann, Robert Clark nuclear and chemical engineering educator
Ayers, William McLean electrochemical engineering company executive
Bahcall, John Norris astrophysicist
Baker, Richard Wheeler, Jr. real estate executive
†Balch, Stephen Howard association administrator
Banse, Robert Lee lawyer
Barker, Richard Gordon corporate research and development executive
Barlow, Walter Greenwood public opinion analyst, management consultant
Bartolini, Robert Alfred electrical engineer, researcher
Baumol, William Jack economist, educator
Beeners, Wilbert John speech professional, minister
Begel, Thomas M. manufacturing company executive
Beidler, Marsha Wolf lawyer
Benacerraf, Paul Joseph Salomon philosophy educator
Bergman, Richard Isaac engineering executive, consultant
Bernanke, Ben Shalom economist, educator
Berry, Charles Horace economist, educator
Bhatt, Ravindra N. physicist, educator
Bien, Frederic Vincent mathematics educator
Bienen, Henry Samuel political science educator
Billington, David Perkins civil engineering educator
Bogan, Elizabeth Chapin economist, educator
Bogdonoff, Seymour Moses aeronautical engineer
Bonini, William Emory geophysics educator
Borel, Armand mathematics educator
Bowersock, Glen Warren historian
Boyer, Ernest LeRoy foundation executive
Bracco, Frediano Vittorio mechanical engineering educator
Bradford, David Frantz economist
Brennan, William Joseph, III lawyer
Broach, James Riley molecular biology educator
Brombert, Victor Henri literature educator, author
Browder, William mathematician, educator
Brown, Leon Carl history educator
†Bryan, Kirk, Jr. research meteorologist, research oceanographer
Bunn, William Bernice, III physician, lawyer, epidemiologist
Bunnell, Peter Curtis photography and art educator, museum curator
Burgess, Robert Kyle lawyer
Buttenheim, Edgar Marion publishing executive
Caffarelli, Luis Angel mathematician, educator
Cakmak, Ahmet Sefik civil engineering educator
Canright, Sarah Anne artist, educator
Carlson, Charlotte Booth book illustrator
Carnes, James Edward electronics executive
Carver, David Harold physician, educator
Cassidy, Brendan Francis art educator and director
Chamberlin, John Stephen investor, former cosmetics company executive
Champlin, Edward James classics educator
Chandler, George Alfred manufacturing executive
Chandler, James John surgeon
Chang, Clarence Dayton chemist
Chow, Gregory Chi-Chong economist, educator
Cinlar, Erhan engineering educator
Coale, Ansley Johnson economics educator
Coffey, Joseph Irving international affairs educator
Coffin, David Robbins art historian, educator
Cole, Nancy Stooksberry educational research executive
Colquhoun, Alan H. architectural educator
Conn, Hadley Lewis, Jr. physician, educator
Connor, Geoffrey Michael lawyer
Cook, Michael Allan social sciences educator
Cooke, Theodore Frederic, Jr. chemist
Cooper, Joel psychology educator
Cooper, John Madison philosophy educator
†Cooper, Michael R. opinion research corporation executive
Corngold, Stanley Alan German and comparative literature educator, writer
Cox, Edward Charles biology educator
Crerar, David Alexander geochemistry educator, consultant
Crespi, Irving public opinion and market research consultant
Cryer, Dennis Robert pharmaceutical company executive, researcher
Cuoco, Daniel Anthony lawyer
Curschmann, Michael Johann Hendrik German language and literature educator
Curtiss, Howard Crosby, Jr. mechanical engineer, educator
Cushmore, Carole Lee publisher
Danson, Lawrence Neil English language educator
Darley, John McConnon psychologist
Darnton, Robert Choate history educator
Davidson, Ronald Crosby physicist, educator
Davies, Horton Marlais clergyman, religion educator
Davies, Robert Abel, III consumer products company executive
Davis, Natalie Zemon history educator
Davis, Richard K. management consultant executive
Deaton, Angus Stewart economist, educator
de Grazia, Sebastian political philosopher, author
Deligné, Pierre R. mathematician
Denlinger, Edgar Jacob electronics engineering research executive
†Devine, Hugh James, Jr. marketing executive, consultant
de Vries, Jacobus E. investment banker
Diamond, Malcolm Luria retired religion educator, therapist

Dickinson, Bradley William *electrical engineering educator*
Dilworth, Joseph Richardson *investment banker*
Dobkin, David Paul *computer science educator*
Doherty, Leonard Edward *financial publishing company executive*
Doig, Jameson Wallace *political science educator*
Douglass, Jane Dempsey *theology educator*
Dovey, Brian Hugh *health care products company executive, venture capitalist*
Draper, Theodore *author*
Durbin, Enoch Job *aeronautical engineering educator*
Dyson, Freeman John *physicist*
†Ebright, George Watson *health care company executive*
Ehrenberg, Edward *executive, investor*
Ekstrom, Ruth Burt *psychologist*
Emmerich, Walter *psychologist*
Ermolaev, Herman Sergei *Slavic languages educator*
Estey, Audree Phipps *artistic director*
Farley, Edward Raymond, Jr. *mining and manufacturing company executive*
Fefferman, Charles Louis *mathematics educator*
Fenichel, Richard Lee *biochemist*
Ferguson, Stephen *librarian*
Fernandes, Prabhavathi Bhat *molecular biologist*
File, Joseph *research physics engineer*
Fill, Dennis C. *pharmaceutical company executive*
Finch, Jeremiah Stanton *English language educator*
Fisch, Nathaniel Joseph *physicist*
Fitch, Val Logsdon *physics educator*
Fleming, John Vincent *humanities educator*
Flint, Sarah Jane *molecular biologist, educator*
Florey, Klaus Georg *chemist, pharmaceutical consultant*
Forcione, Alban Keith *language educator*
Ford, Jeremiah, III *architect*
†Forest, Carey *research physicist*
Fornaess, John Erik *mathematics educator*
Fouss, James H. *marketing executive*
Fox, Mary Ann Williams *librarian*
Fresco, Jacques Robert *biochemist, educator*
Funk, Peter V. K. *writer, scholarly, lexical semanticist*
Gale, Paula Jane *chemist*
Ganoe, Charles Stratford *banker*
Gear, Charles William *computer scientist*
Geertz, Clifford James *anthropology educator*
Geertz, Hildred Storey *anthropology educator*
George, Thomas *artist*
Gibson, James John *electronics engineer, consultant*
Gillespie, Richard Joseph *advertising agency executive*
Gillespie, Thomas William *theological seminary administrator, religion educator*
Gillham, John Kinsey *chemical engineering educator*
Gilpin, Robert George, Jr. *political science educator*
Gips, Walter Fuld, Jr. *manufacturing company executive*
Girgus, Joan Stern *psychologist, university administrator*
Glassman, Irvin *mechanical and aeronautical engineering educator, consultant*
Glucksberg, Sam *psychology educator*
Goheen, Robert Francis *classicist, educator, former ambassador*
Goldfeld, Stephen Michael *economics educator, university official*
Goldman, Clifford Alan *financial advisor*
Goldman, Michael Paul *language professional, educator, writer*
Goldsholle, Gerry H(arvey) *insurance executive, lawyer*
Gordenker, Leon *political sciences educator*
Gordon, Ernest *clergyman*
Gott, J. Richard, III *astrophysicist*
Gould, James L. *biology educator*
Grabar, Oleg *art educator*
Graessley, William Walter *chemical engineering educator*
†Grafton, Anthony Thomas *history educator*
Gramlich, James Vandle *chemical products company executive*
Grant, Peter Raymond *biologist, researcher, educator*
Grasselli, Robert Karl *physical chemist, research scientist*
Graves, Michael *architect, educator*
Green, Joseph *chemist*
Greenberg, Herbert M(arvin) *psychologist, corporate executive*
Greenberg, Joel S. *management consultant, engineer*
Greene, Andrew Richard *foundation executive*
Greenstein, Fred Irwin *political science educator*
Griffiths, Phillip A. *mathematician, academic administrator*
Gross, Charles Gordon *psychology educator, neuroscientist*
Groves, John Taylor, III *chemist, educator*
Gunn, James Edward *astrophysicist*
Gunning, Robert Clifford *mathematician, educator*
Habicht, Christian Herbert *history educator*
Haggerty, John Richard *banker*
Haldane, Frederick Duncan Michael *physics educator*
Halpern, Manfred *political science educator*
Happer, William, Jr. *physicist, educator*
Hardy, Daniel Wayne *theological center director, theologian, educator*
Harford, James Joseph *retired aerospace association executive*
Harman, Gilbert Helms *philosophy educator*
Harris, Robert *lawyer, investment company executive*
Harvey, Norman Ronald *finance company executive*
Hathaway, David Roger *physician, medical educator, scientist*
Hawryluk, Richard Janusz *physicist*
Hawver, Dennis Arthur *psychological consultant*
Hayes, Edwin Junius, Jr. *business executive*
Hearn, Ruby Puryear *foundation executive*
Hendrickson, Robert Frederick *pharmaceutical company executive*
Henkel, William *financial services executive*
Henneman, John Bell, Jr. *library bibliographer*
Hill, James Scott *lawyer*
Hillier, James *communications executive, researcher*
Hillier, J(ames) Robert *architect*
Hirschman, Albert Otto *political economist, educator*
Hoebel, Bartley Gore *psychology educator*
Hollander, Robert B., Jr. *Romance languages educator*
Holst, Willem *oil company executive*
Holt, Philetus Havens, III *architect*
Holzinger, James Jay *bank executive*
Horn, Elizabeth Gates *museum curator*
Horn, Henry Stainken *biology educator*
Howarth, William (Louis) *education educator, writer*
Hulse, Russell Alan *physicist*
Hunter, John Stuart *statistician, consultant*
Hynes, Samuel *English language educator, author*
Inderbitzin, Paul Herold *reinsurance company executive*
Issawi, Charles Philip *economist, educator*
Itzkowitz, Norman *history educator*
†Jackson, Roy *chemical engineering educator*
†Jacobs, William Paul *botanist, educator*
Jacobson, Herbert Leonard *electronics company executive*
Jahn, Robert George *university dean, engineering educator*
Jansen, Marius Berthus *historian, educator*
Jeffery, Peter Grant *musicologist, fine arts educator*
Jeffrey, Richard Carl *philosophy educator*
Jellinek, Paul S. *foundation executive, health economist*
Jenkins, Edward Beynon *research astronomer*
Jobe, Edward B. *insurance company executive*
Johnson, Ernest Frederick *chemical engineer, educator*
Johnson, Walter Curtis *electrical engineering educator*
Johnston, Robert Chapman *lawyer*
Johnston, Robert Fowler *venture capitalist*
Jones, Maitland, Jr. *chemistry educator*
Jordan, William Chester *history educator*
Joyce, Carol Bertani *social studies educator*
Joyce, William Leonard *librarian*
Judge, Marty M. *lawyer*
Judson, Sheldon *geology educator*
Karol, Reuben Hirsh *civil engineer, sculptor*
Kateb, George Anthony *political science educator*
Kaufman, Nancy J. *health foundation executive*
Kaufmann, Thomas DaCosta *art history educator*
Kauzmann, Walter Joseph *chemistry educator*
Keaney, John Joseph *classics educator*
Keeley, Edmund LeRoy *English, creative writing and modern Greek studies educator, author*
Kehrt, Allan W. *architectural firm executive*
Kemmerer, Peter Ream *financial executive*
Kenen, Peter Bain *economist, educator*
Kennan, George Frost *historian, educator, former ambassador,*
Kenyon, Regan Clair *research foundation executive*
†Kessel, Charles *plasma engineer, research physicist*
Khachadurian, Avedis *physician*
Knoepflmacher, Ulrich Camillus *literature educator*
Kobayashi, Hisashi *computer scientist, communication theorist, educator*
Kohn, Joseph John *mathematician, educator*
Kuenne, Robert Eugene *economics educator*
Kuh, Charlotte Virginia *economist*
Kull, F. Thomas, Jr. *newspaper publishing executive*
†Kulsrud, Russell Marion *physicist*
Kung, Sun-Yuan *electrical engineering educator*
Labalme, Patricia Hochschild *educational administrator*
Lange, Victor *language educator, author*
Langlands, Robert Phelan *mathematician*
Law, Chung King *aerospace engineering educator, researcher*
Lawrence, Barbara *information manager*
Lechner, Bernard Joseph *consulting electrical engineer*
Lemonick, Aaron *physicist, educator*
Lerner, Ralph *architect, university dean*
Lester, Richard Allen *economist, educator*
Levin, Simon Asher *mathematician, ecologist, educator*
Levine, Arnold Jay *molecular biology educator, researcher*
Levy, Kenneth *music educator*
Lewis, Bernard *Near Eastern studies educator*
Lewis, David Kellogg *philosopher, educator*
Libchaber, Albert Joseph *physics educator*
Liben, Michael Paul *magazine publisher*
Lieb, Elliott Hershel *physicist, mathematician, educator*
Lieberman, David Ira *mathematician, administrator*
Lippincott, Walter Heulings, Jr. *publishing executive*
Litz, Arthur Walton, Jr. *English language educator*
Liu, Bede *electrical engineering educator*
Lopresti, Philip Vincent *electrical engineer, researcher, consultant*
†Los, Marinus *agrochemical researcher*
Ludwig, Richard Milton *English literature educator, librarian*
Mahlman, Jerry David *research meteorologist*
Mahoney, Michael Sean *history educator*
Majda, Andrew J. *mathematician, educator*
Malkiel, Burton Gordon *economics educator*
Malkiel, Nancy Weiss *college dean, history educator*
Manabe, Syukuro *climatologist*
Manning, Winton Howard *psychologist, educational administrator*
Marks, John Henry *Near Eastern studies educator*
Mather, John Norman *mathematics educator*
Mayer, Arno Joseph *history educator*
Mc Clure, Donald Stuart *physical chemist, educator*
Mc Cullough, John Price *retired oil company executive*
Mc Pherson, James Munro *history educator*
†Meade, Dale Michael *laboratory director*
Merrill, Leland Gilbert, Jr. *retired environmental science educator*
Metzger, Bruce Manning *clergyman, educator*
Miles, Richard Bryant *mechanical and aerospace engineering educator*
Miller, George Armitage *psychologist, educator*
Miller, Patrick Dwight, Jr. *religion educator, minister*
Mills, Bradford *merchant banker*
Mills, Michael James *architect*
Mills, Robert Gail *retired physicist*
Miner, Earl Roy *English educator*
Minton, Dwight Church *manufacturing company executive*
Miyakoda, Kikuro *meteorologist, lecturer*
Montagu, Ashley *anthropologist, social biologist*
Montgomery, Ronald Eugene *chemist, research and development director*
Moote, A. Lloyd *history educator*
Morel, François Marie Michel *environmental geology educator*
Morrill, William Ashley *research executive*
Morris, Mac Glenn *advertising bureau executive*
Morrison, Toni (Chloe Anthony Morrison) *novelist*
Moynahan, Julian Lane *English language educator, author*
Mueller, Peter Sterling *psychiatrist, educator*
Nadler, Georgia Jane *nursing administrator*
Napoliello, Michael John *psychiatrist*
†Nash, John C. *research mathematician*
Navrotsky, Alexandra *geophysics educator*
Nehamas, Alexander *philosophy educator*
Nucciarone, A. Patrick *lawyer*
Oates, Joyce Carol *author*
Ober, Josiah *history educator*
O'Connor, Neal William *former advertising agency executive*
O'Donnell, Laurence Gerard *newspaper editor*
Ondetti, Miguel Angel *chemist, consultant*
Oort, Abraham Hans *meteorologist, researcher, educator*
Orleans, Jeffrey Howard *lawyer*
Orszag, Steven Alan *applied mathematician, educator*
Ostriker, Jeremiah Paul *astrophysicist, educator*
Paczynski, Bohdan *astrophysicist, educator*
†Page, Lyman Alexander, Jr. *physicist*
Painter, Nell Irvin *historian, educator*
Palsho, Dorothea Coccoli *information services executive*
Paneyko, Stephen Hobbs *banker*
Paret, Peter *historian*
Paris, Peter Junior *religion educator, minister*
Patel, Mukund Ranchhodlal *electrical engineer, researcher*
Peebles, Phillip James E. *physicist, educator*
Penick, Joe Edward *petroleum consultant*
Perhach, James Lawrence *pharmaceutical company executive*
Peterson, Willard James *Chinese history educator*
Phinney, Robert Alden *geophysics educator*
Poor, Harold Vincent *electrical engineering educator*
Popper, Robert David *computer and management consultant*
Prud'homme, Robert Krafft *chemical engineering educator*
Putnam, Peter Brock *author, lecturer*
Quandt, Richard Emeric *economics educator*
Rabb, Theodore K. *historian, educator*
Rabitz, Herschel Albert *chemistry educator*
Rampersad, Arnold *writer, literature educator*
Rebenfeld, Ludwig *chemist*
Reinhardt, Uwe Ernst *economist, educator*
Reynolds, George Thomas *physics educator, researcher, consultant*
Reynolds, Richard Clyde *physician, foundation administrator*
Rhett, Haskell Emery Smith *foundation executive, educator*
Rich, Jude T. *management consulting firm executive*
Rigolot, François *French literature educator, literary critic*
Roberts, Peter A. *banker*
Robertson, Nat Clifton *chemist*
Rodgers, Daniel Tracy *history educator*
Rodwell, John Dennis *biochemist*
Rogoff, Kenneth S. *economics educator*
Rosen, Arye *microwave, optoelectronics and medicine researcher*
Rosen, Harvey Sheldon *economics educator*
Rosen, Norman Edward *lawyer*
Rosenbaum, Allen *art museum administrator*
Rosenberg, Leon Emanuel *medical educator, geneticist, university dean*
Rosenthal, Howard Lewis *political science educator*
Roth, William Matson *former corporate executive*
Rothschild, Michael *economics educator*
Royce, Barrie Saunders Hart *physicist*
Rozman, Gilbert Friedell *sociologist, educator*
Rutherford, Paul Harding *physicist*
Savage, Naomi *photographer*
Saville, Dudley Albert *chemical engineering educator*
Schafer, Carl Walter *investment executive*
Schoen, Alvin E., Jr. *environmental engineer*
Schofield, Robert E(dwin) *history educator, academic administrator*
Schorske, Carl Emil *historian, educator*
Schroeder, Alfred Christian *electronics research engineer*
Schroeder, Steven Alfred *medical educator, researcher, foundation executive*
Schwartz, Stuart Carl *electrical engineering educator*
Scoles, Giacinto *chemistry educator*
Seawright, James L., Jr. *sculptor, educator*
Seizinger, Bernd Robert *molecular geneticist, physician, researcher*
Semrod, T. Joseph *banker*
Sethi, Shyam Sunder *management consultant*
Shapiro, Harold Tafler *university president, economist*
Shear, Theodore Leslie, Jr. *archaeologist, educator*
Shenk, Thomas Eugene *molecular biology educator*
Shimizu, Yoshiaki *art historian, educator*
Shinozuka, Masanobu *civil engineer, educator*
Shoemaker, Frank Crawford *physicist, educator*
Showalter, Elaine *humanities educator*
Sigmund, Paul Eugene *political science educator*
Silhavy, Thomas Joseph *molecular biology educator*
Simmons, Jean Elizabeth Margaret (Mrs. Glen R. Simmons) *chemistry educator*
Singer, Burton Herbert *statistics educator*
Smagorinsky, Joseph *meteorologist*
Smith, Arthur John Stewart *physicist, educator*
Smith, Margaret Phyllis *editor, consultant*
Smith, Michael A. *aerospace engineer, engineering executive*
Soames, Scott *philosophy educator*
Socolow, Robert Harry *engineering educator, scientist*
†Spergel, David Nathaniel *astrophysicist*
Spies, Claudio *composer, educator*
Spiro, Thomas George *chemistry educator*
Starr, Paul Elliot *sociologist, writer, editor, educator*
Steinberg, Malcolm Saul *biologist, educator*
Steiner, Robert Lisle *language consultant*
Stengel, Robert Frank *mechanical and aerospace engineering educator*
Stern, Gail Frieda *historical association director*
Sterzer, Fred *research physicist*
Stix, Thomas Howard *physicist, educator*
Stokes, Donald Elkinton *political science educator*
Stone, Lawrence *historian*
Sullivan, John Mark *manufacturing company executive*
†Suppe, John *geology educator*
†Sussman, Steven David *management consulting executive*
Sussna, Robert Earl *architect*
Tabell, Anthony *financial analyst*
Tarbox, Dick *communications engineering executive*
Tarjan, Robert Endre *computer scientist, educator*
Taylor, Edward Curtis *chemistry educator*
Taylor, Joseph Hooton, Jr. *radio astronomer, physicist*
Tierney, Bill *university athletic coach*
Tignor, Robert Lee *historian, educator*
Tilghman, Shirley Marie *biology educator*
Timpane, Philip Michael *educator, foundation official*
Torquato, Salvatore *materials science engineer, researcher*
Townsend, Charles Edward *Slavic languages educator*
†Tregoe, Benjamin Bainbridge *management consultant, researcher*
Treiman, Sam Bard *physics educator*
†Treu, Jesse Isaiah *venture capitalist*
Turner, Edwin Lewis *astronomy educator, researcher*
†Udovitch, Abraham Labe *historian, educator*
Uitti, Karl David *language educator*
Ullman, Richard Henry *political science educator*
Umscheid, Ludwig Joseph *computer specialist*
Vahaviolos, Sotirios John *electrical engineer, scientist, corporate executive*
Van Houten, Franklyn Bosworth *geologist, educator*
Vanmarcke, Erik Hector *civil engineering educator*
†Verlinde, Herman L. *physics educator*
Villafranca, Joseph J. *biochemistry educator*
Von Hippel, Frank Niels *public and international affairs educator*
Wallace, Walter L. *sociologist, educator*
Walzer, Michael Laban *political science educator*
Wei, James *chemical engineering educator, academic dean*
Weigmann, Hans-Dietrich H. *chemist*
†Weil, Andre *mathematics educator and researcher*
Weimer, Paul K(essler) *electrical engineer*
Weinmann, Roberto *molecular biologist, educator*
Weinstein, Stephen Brant *communications executive, researcher, writer*
Weiss, Renée Karol *editor, writer, musician*
Weiss, Robert Jerome *psychiatrist, educator*
Weiss, Theodore Russell *poet, editor*
Wentz, Sidney Frederick *insurance company executive, foundation executive*
West, Charles Converse *theologian, educator*
Westergaard, Peter Talbot *composer, music educator*
Westoff, Charles Francis *demographer, educator*
Wheeler, John Archibald *physicist, educator*
White, Lynn Townsend, III *political science educator*
White, Morton Gabriel *philosopher, author*
Wightman, Arthur Strong *physicist, educator*
Wilczek, Frank Anthony *physics educator*
Wilentz, Robert Sean *history educator, author*
Wiles, Andrew J. *mathematician, educator*
Wilkinson, David Todd *physics educator*
Williams, Bertha Elizabeth Griffin *elementary education educator*
Williams, Brown F *television media services company executive*
Willig, Robert Daniel *economics educator*
Willingham, Warren Willcox *psychologist, testing service executive*
Wilmerding, John *art history educator, museum curator*
Wilson, Margaret Dauler *philosophy educator*
Wise, John James *oil company executive*
Witten, Edward *mathematical physicist*
Wolfson, Susan Jean *English literature educator*
Wong, Ching-Ping *chemist*
Wood, Eric Franklin *earth and environmental sciences educator*
Wood, Joshua Warren, III *lawyer, foundation executive*
Woolf, Harry *historian, educator*
Wright, Thomas H., Jr. *lawyer*
Wuthnow, Robert *sociology educator*
Yu, Ying Shih *history educator, researcher*
Zeitlin, Froma I. *classics educator*
Zierler, Neal *mathematician*
Ziolkowski, Theodore Joseph *comparative literature educator*
Zissman, Lorin *marketing research, consulting company executive*

Princeton Junction

Haddad, James Henry *chemical engineering consultant*
Norback, Craig Thomas *writer*

Rahway

†Ashkenazi, Ely Ezra *electronics company executive*
Byles, Daniel William *lawyer*
Cohen, Abraham Ezekiel *retired health care company executive*
Horan, John J. *pharmaceutical company executive*
Kaczorowski, Gregory John *biochemist, researcher, science administrator*
Linemeyer, David Lee *molecular biologist*
McDonald, Mary M. *lawyer*
†Rasmusson, Gary Henry *medicinal chemist*
Reynolds, Glenn Franklin *medicinal research scientist*
†Scolnick, Edward Mark *science administrator*
Shapiro, Bennett Michaels *biochemist, educator*

Ramsey

DeLio, Richard Michael *management consultant*
Eklund, Donald Arthur *trade association executive*
Founds, Henry William *pharmaceutical executive, microbiologist*
Kusumoto, Sadahei *light manufacturing executive*
Markowitz, Arthur Walter *food brokerage executive*
Oliver, Joseph J. *consumer products company executive*
Underwood, Steven Clark *publishing executive*

Randolph

Raber, Marvin *consultant, retired utility company executive*

Raritan

Alatzas, George *delivery service company executive*
†Goldstein, Jack *health science executive, microbiologist*

Red Bank

Auerbach, Philip Gary *lawyer*
Chynoweth, Alan Gerald *retired telecommunications executive, consultant*
Dale, Madeline Houston McWhinney *banker*
Harbison, James Prescott *research physicist*
Hertz, Daniel Leroy, Jr. *entrepreneur*
Hollywood, John Matthew *electronics consultant*
Hovnanian, Kevork S. *real estate developer*
Koch, Udo *oil industry executive*
Liao, Paul Foo-Hung *communications research company executive, physicist*
Lucky, Robert Wendell *electrical engineer*
McCann, John Francis *financial services company executive*
McWhinney, Madeline H. (Mrs. John Denny Dale) *economist*
Meredith, George (Marlor) *association executive, writer*

Reinhart, Peter Sargent *corporate executive, lawyer*
Rogers, Lee Jasper *lawyer*
Schimpf, John Joseph *real estate developer*
Schneider, Sol *electronic engineer, consultant, researcher*
Sorsby, James Larry *home building company executive*
Trofino, Joan Alhanati *health care facility administrator*
Weiant, William Morrow *investment banking executive*

Ridgefield
Goldman, Arnold Ira *biophysicist, statistical analyst*

Ridgefield Park
Case, Gerard Ramon *drafting technician*
Kim, Ok-Nyun *manufacturing executive*
Ranone, John Louis *school board executive*

Ridgewood
Abplanalp, Glen Harold *civil engineer*
Anderson, Thomas Kemp, Jr. *editor*
Azzara, Michael William *hospital administration executive*
Clements, Lynne Fleming *family therapist, programmer*
Economaki, Chris Constantine (Christopher Economaki) *publisher, editor*
Fokine, Irine *ballet educator*
Geraghty, Margaret Karl *financial consultant, portfolio manager*
Harris, Micalyn Shafer *lawyer*
Healey, Frank Henry *retired research executive*
Kiernan, Richard Francis *publisher*
Knies, Paul Henry *former life insurance company executive*
Lucca, John James *retired dental educator*
McBride, William Bernard *treasurer*
Molnar, Thomas *philosophy of religion educator, author*

Ringoes
Price, Liza *entrepreneur*

River Edge
Gass, Manus M. *accountant, business executive*
Hochhauser, Richard Michael *marketing professional*
†Lennon, Michael T. *public relations executive*
Sommer, Robert George *public relations executive*

River Vale
Moderacki, Edmund Anthony *music educator, conductor*

Riverside
Gouda, Moustafa Abdel-Hamid *geotechnical engineer consultant*

Robbinsville
Goldstein, Norman Robert *safety engineer*
Moustafa, Fikry Sayed *accountant*

Rochelle Park
Laskey, Richard Anthony *medical device company executive*
Mack, Earle Irving *real estate company executive*
Schapiro, Jerome Bentley *chemical company executive*

Rockaway
Allen, Dorothea *secondary education educator*
Laine, Cleo (Clementina Dinah Dankworth) *singer*
Ruch, William Vaughn *writer, educator, consultant*

Rockleigh
Heslin, Cathleen Jane *artist, designer, entrepreneur*
Heslin, John Thomas *entrepreneur, historic preservationist*
†Plaskett, Thomas G. *transportation company executive*

Roosevelt
Landau, Jacob *artist*

Roseland
Berkowitz, Bernard Solomon *lawyer*
Casale, Robert J. *communications executive*
Costanzo, Hilda Alba *retired banker*
D'Avella, Bernard Johnson, Jr. *lawyer*
Drasco, Dennis J. *lawyer*
Eakeley, Douglas Scott *lawyer*
Fleischman, Joseph Jacob *lawyer*
Greenberg, Stephen Michael *lawyer, businesss executive*
Kemph, Carleton Richard *lawyer*
Kohl, Benedict M. *lawyer*
Korf, Gene Robert *lawyer*
†Kranson, Gerald Irwin *employee benefits consultant, lawyer*
Lafer, Fred Seymour *data processing company executive*
Lowenstein, Alan Victor *lawyer*
MacKay, John Robert, II *lawyer*
Malafronte, Donald *health executive*
McElwee, Andrew Allison *finance executive, lawyer*
Shoulson, Bruce Dove *lawyer*
Slutsky, Kenneth Joel *lawyer*
Steinhart, Ashley *lawyer*
Stern, Herbert Jay *lawyer*
Sturtz, Ronald M. *lawyer*
Taub, Henry *retired computer services company executive*
Turner, William J. *data processing company executive*
Weinbach, Arthur Frederic *computing services company executive*
Wells, Theodore V., Jr. *lawyer*
Weston, Josh S. *data processing company executive*
Wovsaniker, Alan *lawyer*

Roselle Park
Wilchins, Sidney A. *gynecologist*
Zahumeny, Janet Mae *secondary education educator*

Rumson
Brennan, William Joseph *manufacturing company executive*
Brenner, Theodore Engelbert *retired trade association executive*
†Bryan, Richard D.S. *conservationist*
Christianson, Lloyd Fenton *management consultant*
Cocker, Barbara Joan *marine artist, interior designer*
Creamer, William Henry, III *insurance company executive*
Freeman, David Forgan *foundation executive*
Macdonald, Donald Arthur *publishing executive*
Robinson, William Wheeler *editor*
Rosen, Bernard H. *chemical engineer*
Swartz, Renee Becker *civic volunteer*

Rutherford
Barzanti, Sergio *educator*
Gerety, Peter Leo *archbishop*
Law, Janet Mary *music educator*
Liptak, Irene Frances *retired business executive*
Petrie, Ferdinand Ralph *illustrator, artist*

Saddle Brook
Anderson, David J. *metals company executive*
†Barbieri, Rocco A. *manufacturing company executive*
†Byrne, John J. *chemicals executive*

Saddle River
Amman, Robert J. *telecommunications financial services company executive*
Buckler, Beatrice *editor*
Caulo, Ralph Daniel *publishing executive*
Dowden, Carroll Vincent *publishing company executive*
Leavitt, Horace Madison, Jr. *communications company executive, former naval officer*
Lehmann, Doris Elizabeth *elementary education educator*
McClelland, William Craig *paper company executive*
Warrington, Clayton Linwood, Jr. *advertising executive*

Salem
Foster, Paul *playwright*
Petrin, Helen Fite *lawyer, consultant*
Seabrook, John Martin *retired food products executive, chemical engineer*

Scotch Plains
Abramson, Clarence Allen *pharmaceutical company executive, lawyer*
Avery, James Stephen *oil company executive*
Barnard, Kurt *retail marketing forecaster, publisher*
Bishop, Robert Milton *former stock exchange official*
Cleminshaw, Frank Foster *electronic company executive*
Edwards, Thomas Robert, Jr. *language professional, investment company executive*
Johnson, Valerie Anne *elementary education educator*
Klock, John Henry *lawyer*
Ungar, Manya Shayon *volunteer, education consultant*

Sea Bright
Plummer, Dirk Arnold *electrical engineer*

Secaucus
Bender, Bruce F. *book publishing executive*
Bidermann, Maurice *textiles executive*
Bolt, J. Andrew *textiles executive*
Brown, Ira Bernard *data processing executive*
Donovan, Raymond James *U.S. secretary of labor*
Endyke, Mary Beth *lawyer*
Fisher, Herbert *retail executive*
Gerstein, Hilda Kirschbaum *clothing company executive*
†Gomes, Celeste Regina *writer, editor*
Heller, Fred *illumination manufacturing company executive*
†Imura, Akiya *industrial and consumer electronics company executive*
Kilburn, Edwin Allen *lawyer*
Kraft, Richard A. *electronics executive*
Lazarus, Arlie Gary *retail corporate executive*
Marcus, Alan C. *public relations consultant*
Newton, V. Miller *medical psychotherapist, neuropsychologist, writer*
Pinsker, Penny Collias (Pangeota Pinsker) *television producer*
Rakov, Barbara Streem *marketing executive*
Rockland, Barry Clifford *retail financial executive*
Schenck, Frederick A. *business executive*
Thomas, Ian Leslie Maurice *publisher*
Unanue, Joseph *food products executive*
Zorn, Eric Stuart *retail department store chain executive*

Short Hills
Aviado, Domingo M. *pharmacologist, toxicologist*
Bartels, Stanley Leonard *investment banker*
Broder, Patricia Janis *art historian, writer*
Brous, Philip *retail consultant*
Good, Allen Hovey *acquisitions broker, real estate broker*
Good, Joan Duffey *artist*
Greenberg, Carl *lawyer*
Harwood, Jerry *market research executive*
Hazlehurst, Robert Purviance, Jr. *lawyer*
Jackson, William Ward *chemical company executive*
Kaye, Jerome R. *retired engineering and construction company executive*
Klemme, Carl William *banker*
Mebane, William Black *controller, financial consultant*
Meredith, George Davis *advertising executive, publisher*
Middleton, Timothy George *writer*
Moore, Robert Condit *civil engineer*
Parks, Robert Henry *consulting economist, educator*
Pilchik, Ely Emanuel *rabbi, writer*
Schaefer, Charles James, III *advertising agency executive, consultant*
Schaffer, Edmund John *management consultant, retired engineering executive*
Siegfried, David Charles *lawyer*
Soderlind, Sterling Eugene *newspaper industry consultant*
Stefanile, Lawrence Vincent *management counsulting company executive*
Wharton, Lennard *engineering company executive*
Winter, Ruth Grosman (Mrs. Arthur Winter) *journalist*
Yorks, Richard Alan *investment banker*

Shrewsbury
Duff, Thomas M. *textiles executive*
Hopkins, Charles Peter, II *lawyer*
Jones, Charles Hill, Jr. *banker*
Reich, Bernard *telecommunications engineer*

Skillman
Brill, Yvonne Claeys *engineer, consultant*
Kral, Frank *biophysical chemist*
Messner, Richard Stephen *school system administrator*
Wang, Jonas Chia-Tsung *pharmaceutical executive*

Somerdale
Morgan, Mary Anne *secondary education educator*

Somerset
Aronson, Dana Lynne *program/public relations executive*
Aronson, Louis Vincent, II *manufacturing executive*
Brophy, Joseph Thomas *insurance company executive*
DeVaris, Jeannette Mary *psychologist*
Goldberg, Arthur M. *food products executive, lawyer*
†Gunji, Hiromi *manufacturing executive*
†King, David T. *communications company financial executive*
Kozlowski, Thomas Joseph, Jr. *lawyer, trust company executive*
Kroll, William John, Jr. *manufacturing company executive*
†Marinari, Donald J. *advertising executive*
Neff, Richard B. *consumer products company executive*
Nemeth, Patricia A. *school nurse*
Noonan, William Francis *public relations company executive*
Plenty, Royal Homer *writer*

Somerville
Beck, Eckardt C. *engineering executive*
Benz, Harry R. *business executive*
Cirello, John *environmental management and engineering company executive*
Cohen, Walter Stanley *accountant, financial consultant*
Deieso, Donald Allan *environmental goods and services executive*
Dormann, Juergen *chemical company executive*
Drew, Ernest Harold *chemical company executive*
Glenn, Arthur L. *engineering company executive*
Grant, Robert James *animal nutritional research manager*
Hildebrandt, Bradford Walter *consulting company executive*
Hutcheon, Peter David *lawyer*
Hyde, Mary Morley Crapo (Viscountess Eccles) *author*
Johnson, Nicholas *writer, lawyer, lecturer*
Shive, Richard Byron *architect*

South Hackensack
Ragals, William Charles, Jr. *lawyer, business executive*

South Orange
De Varis, Panayotis Eric *architect*
Fleming, Edward J. *priest, educator*
Goldman, Harvey S. *therapist, rabbi*
Green, Donald Webb *economist*
Harahan, Robert E. *rector*
Houle, Joseph E. *mathematics educator*
Reilly, George Love Anthony *history educator*
Sontag, Frederick H. *public affairs and research consultant*

South Plainfield
Becker, Erich Peter *metals company executive*
Borah, Kripanath *pharmacist*
Goode, Bobby Claude *secondary education educator*
Kopley, Catherine S. *investment company executive*
Saltz, Ralph *corporate lawyer*

Southampton
Knortz, Walter Robert *accountant, former insurance company executive*

Sparta
Buist, Jean Mackerley *veterinarian*
Granieri, Michael Nicholas *electronics executive, educator*
Harrison, Alice Kathleen *retired elementary educator*
Saxe, Thelma Richards *secondary education educator, consultant*
Spence, Robert Leroy *publishing executive*

Spring Lake
Ernst, John Louis *management consultant*
McEntee, Robert Edward *management consultant*

Springfield
Adams, James Mills *chemicals executive*
†Coleman, James H., Jr. *state supreme court justice*
Enslow, Ridley Madison, Jr. *book publisher*
Merachnik, Donald *superintendent of schools*
Panish, Morton B. *physical chemist, consultant*
Shilling, A. Gary *economic consultant, investment advisor*
†Stoller, Mitchell R. *non-profit organization administrator*

Stillwater
Finkelstein, Louis *retired art educator*

Stockholm
dePaolo, Ronald Francis *editor, publisher*

Stockton
Griffin, Bryant Wade *retired judge*
Kent, George Cantine, Jr. *zoology educator*
Mahon, Robert *photographer*
Schoenherr, John (Carl) *artist, illustrator*
Tunley, Roul *author*

Stratford
Mendels, Joseph *psychiatrist, educator*

Summit
Batzer, R. Kirk *accountant*
†Beyer, Charlotte Bishop *investment management marketing executive, consultant*
Bostwick, Randell A. *retired retail food company executive*
†Earle, Jean Buist *hospital administrator*
Fuess, Billings Sibley, Jr. *advertising executive*
Fukui, Hatsuaki *electrical engineer, art historian*
Geiger, Richard Lawrence *entrepreneur*
Gonnella, Nina Celeste *biophysical chemist*
Kenyon, Edward Tipton *lawyer*
Mathis, James Forrest *retired petroleum company executive*
May, Ernest Max *charitable organization official*
Moore, Milo Anderson *banker*
Mueller, Paul Henry *retired banker*
Mulreany, Robert Henry *retired lawyer*
Natkin, Alvin Martin *environmental company executive*
Nessen, Ward Henry *former typography company executive, lawyer*
Pace, Leonard *retired management consultant*
Parsons, Judson Aspinwall, Jr. *lawyer*
Phillips, James Charles *physicist, educator*
Pincus, Jillian Ruth *physician*
Pollak, Henry Otto *retired utility research executive, educator*
Rossey, Paul William *school superintendent, university president*
Rousseau, Irene Victoria *artist, sculptor*
Scudder, Edward Wallace, Jr. *newspaper and broadcasting executive*
Sheldon, William Charles *marketing professional*
Slepian, David *mathematician, communications engineer*
Sniffen, Michael Joseph *hospital administrator*
Vogel, Julius *consulting actuary, former insurance company executive*
Wissbrun, Kurt Falke *chemist, consultant*

Surf City
Aurner, Robert Ray, II *oil company, auto diagnostic, restaurant franchise and company development executive*

Swedesboro
Lovell, Theodore *electrical engineer, consultant*

Teaneck
Borg, Sidney Fred *mechanical engineer, educator*
†Brophy, John Martin *information management services executive*
Browne, Robert Span *economist*
Brudner, Helen Gross *social sciences educator*
Cassimatis, Peter John *economics educator*
Churg, Jacob *pathologist*
Ehrlich, Ira Robert *mechanical engineering consultant*
Fairfield, Betty Elaine Smith *psychologist*
Fanshel, David *social worker*
Fatemi, Faramarz Saifpour *history and political science educator, consultant*
Feinberg, Robert S. *plastics manufacturing company executive, marketing consultant*
Forson, Norman Ray *controller*
Gordon, Jonathan David *psychologist*
Gordon, Lois Goldfein *English language educator*
Gordon, Maxwell *pharmaceutical company executive*
Gund, Sharon Smallwood *information services company executive*
Herman, Kenneth *psychologist*
Jugenheimer, Donald Wayne *advertising and communications educator, university administrator*
Kramer, Bernard *physicist, educator*
Lehrer, Joel Fredric *otolaryngologist*
Margolis, Sidney O. *textile and apparel company executive*
Mertz, Francis James *academic administrator*
Ngai, Shih Hsun *physician*
Palitz, Clarence Yale, Jr. *commercial finance executive*
Pischl, Adolph John *school administrator*
Rudy, Willis *historian*
Walsh, Peter Joseph *physics educator*
Williams, John A. *English language educator, author*
Zwass, Vladimir *computer scientist, educator*

Tenafly
Badr, Gamal Moursi *Arab laws consultant*
Cosgriff, Stuart Worcester *internist, consultant*
Gerst, Elizabeth Carlsen (Mrs. Paul H. Gerst) *university dean, researcher, educator*
Gibbons, Robert Philip *management consultant*
Heghinian, Elizabeth Alban Trumbower *artist, educator*
Katzman, Merle Hershel *orthopaedic surgeon*
Koons, Irvin Louis *design and marketing executive, graphic artist, consultant*
Kronenwett, Frederick Rudolph *microbiologist*
Lang, Hans Joachim *engineering company executive*
Levy, Norman Jay *investment banker, financial consultant*
Lilley, Theodore Robert *financial executive*
Stowe, David Metz *clergyman*
Vinocur, M. Richard *publisher*

Teterboro
†Engle, Phillip *airport executive*
Gambino, S(alvatore) Raymond *medical laboratory executive, educator*

Three Bridges
Lawrence, Gerald Graham *management consultant*

Tinton Falls
Furman, Samuel Elliott *dentist*
Orlando, Carl *medical research and development executive*
Priesand, Sally Jane *rabbi*
Van Winkle, William *financial planner*

Titusville
Marden, Kenneth Allen *advertising executive*
†May, J. Joel *health care management consultant*
†Swissler, Robert *educational consultant*

Toms River
Fanuele, Michael Anthony *electronics engineer, research engineer*
Gottesman, Roy Tully *chemical company executive*
Gross, Leroy *sugar company executive*
Kanarkowski, Edward Joseph *data processing company executive*
Pilla, Mark Domenick *hospital administrator*
Unger, Howard Albert *artist, photographer, educator*
Whitman, Russell Wilson *lawyer*

Totowa
Badke, Ronald E. *retail shoe company executive*
Jelliffe, Charles Gordon *banker*
Solomon, Edward David *chain store executive*

Trenton
Agocs, Stephen F. *instrument and electronic equipment manufacturing company executive*
Bakelaar, Donna *state assembly staff member*
Bigham, William J. *lawyer*
Brandinger, Jay Jerome *electronics executive, state official*
Brown, Garrett Edward, Jr. *federal judge*
Butorac, Frank George *administrative librarian*
Chavooshian, Marge *artist, educator*
Clymer, Brian William *state official*
Courtney, Esau *bishop*
Cowen, Robert E. *federal judge*
Crom, William Hampton *engineer*
Cushman, David Wayne *research biochemist*
Dalton, Daniel J. *secretary of state*
DiFrancesco, Donald T. *state senator*
Domm, Alice *lawyer*
Eickhoff, Harold Walter *college president, humanities educator*
Farina, David *church administrator*
Fisher, Clarkson Sherman *federal judge*
George, Emery Edward *foreign language and studies educator*
Giddings, S. Arthur *chemical engineer*
Gindin, William Howard *federal judge*
Greenberg, Morton Ira *federal judge*
Haberle, Joan Baker *state official*
Handler, Alan B. *state supreme court justice*
Jester, Roberts Charles, Jr. *engineering services company executive*
Kelly, Thomas Joseph, III *photojournalist*
Kirk, Dolores Ann *government administrative assistant*
Losty, Barbara Paul *college official*
Megna, Jerome Francis *academic administrator, educator*
Meyer, Robert *bank executive*
O'Hern, Daniel Joseph *state supreme court justice*
Parell, Mary Little *federal judge, former banking commissioner*
Peacock, Douglas W. *manufacturing executive*
Pettit, Vincent King *bishop*
Pollock, John Crothers, III *opinion research executive, educator*
†Poritz, Deborah T. *state attorney general*
Pruitt, George Albert *college president*
Prusinowski, Julie Ellen *artistic director*
Reiss, John C. *bishop*
Robinson, Susan Mittleman *data processing executive*
Russell, Joyce Anne Rogers *librarian*
Schirber, Annamarie Riddering *speech and language pathologist, educator*
†Sloshberg, Leah Phyfer *museum director*
Stein, Sandra Lou *educational psychologist, educator*
Sterns, Joel Henry *lawyer*
Stewart, Barbara Elizabeth *free-lance magazine editor, artist*
Stockman, Gerald Richard *lawyer*
Summerfield, Martin *physicist*
Thompson, Anne Elise *federal judge*
Trainor, Lillian (Midge Trainor) *elections official*
Tucker, Robert Keith *environmental scientist, research administrator*
Weinberg, Martin Herbert *psychiatrist*
Weissman, Daniel *journalist*
Whitman, Christine Todd *governor*
Wolfe, Deborah Cannon Partridge *government education consultant*
Wolfson, Freda L. *judge*

Tuckerton
Egan, Roger Edward *publishing executive*

Union
Bassano, C. Louis *state senator, fuel oil company executive*
Doren, Henry Julius Thaddeus *artist, painter*
Franks, Robert D. (Bob Franks) *congressman*
Hennings, Dorothy Grant (Mrs. George Hennings) *educational educator*
Kaplan, Doris Weiler *social worker*
Lapidus, Norman Israel *food broker*
Pasvolsky, Richard Lloyd *parks, recreation, and environment educator*
Schiffman, Robert S. *environmental test equipment manufacturing executive*
Zois, Constantine Nicholas Athanasios *meteorology educator*

Union City
†Arias, David *bishop*
Bozoyan, Sylvia *elementary school educator*
Conklin, Anna Immaculata Zotti *mathematics and language arts educator*
Stier, Edwin H. *lawyer*

Upper Montclair
Aronson, David *chemical and mechanical engineer*
Coffin, Charlsa Lee *Montessori educator, writer, artist*
Cordasco, Francesco *sociologist, educator, author*
Kidde, John Lyon *investment manager*
Kowalski, Stephen Wesley *chemistry educator*
Reid, Irvin D. *academic official*

Upper Saddle River
Butterfield, Bruce Scott *publishing company executive*
Wallace, William, III *engineering executive*

Ventnor City
Bolton, Kenneth Albert *management consultant*
Panico, Elaine Hartman *nurse*
Robbins, Hulda Dornblatt *artist, printmaker*
Zuckerman, Stuart *psychiatrist, educator*

Vernon
Gillman, Richard *hotel, casino company executive*

Verona
Ayaso, Manuel *artist*
Brightman, Robert Lloyd *importer, textile company executive, consultant*
Greenwald, Robert *public relations executive*
Meyer, Helen (Mrs. Abraham J. Meyer) *retired editorial consultant*

Vineland
Hunt, Howard F(rancis) *psychologist, educator*
†Pranckun, John *manufacturing executive*
†Redwine, Richard H. *manufacturing executive, light*

Voorhees
Barone, Donald Anthony *neurologist, educator*
Hutchinson, Susan Elaine *hospital administrator*
Johnstone, George W. *utility company executive*
LaFrankie, James V. *water utility holding company executive*
Lewis, Marilyn Ware *water company executive*
Myslowka, Myron William (Ron Myslowka) *labor union executive*
Swiecicki, Martin *neurosurgeon*

Waldwick
Surdoval, Donald James *accounting and management consulting company executive*

Wall
Colford, Francis Xavier *gas industry executive*
†Downes, Laurence M. *treasurer*

Warren
Blass, Walter Paul *consultant, management educator*
Chubb, Percy, III *insurance company executive*
Cohen, Bertram David *psychologist, educator*
Hartman, David Gardiner *actuary*
Jackson, John Wyant *medical products executive*
Knox, William T., IV *lawyer*
Maull, George Marriner *music director, conductor*
Norton, Donn H. *insurance company executive*
O'Hare, Dean Raymond *insurance company executive*
Parker, Henry Griffith, III *insurance executive*
Salem, Eli *chemical engineer*
Sartor, Anthony Joseph *environmental engineer*
Smith, Dudley Renwick *insurance company executive*
Smith, Richard D. *insurance holding company executive*
Wright, Richard G. *optical and health care company executive*

Washington
De Sanctis, Vincent *college president*

Watchung
Knudson, Harry Edward, Jr. *retired electrical manufacturing company executive*
Nadeau, Earl Raymond *electronics executive*
Schaefer, Jacob Wernli *military systems consultant*

Wayne
†Atlee, Frank V. *chemical company executive*
Benedict, Theresa Marie *mathematics educator*
Benjamin, James Anthony *electrical engineer, educator*
Blauvelt, John Clifford *diversified consumer products company executive*
Boekenheide, Russell William *forest products company executive*
Bridges, Beryl Clarke *marketing executive*
Buckstein, Mark Aaron *lawyer, educator*
Cheng, David Hong *mechanical engineering educator*
Coslow, Richard David *electronics company executive*
Crane, Thomas R., Jr. *oil industry executive*
Donald, Robert Graham *retail food chain personnel executive*
Drossman, Jay Lewis *aerospace executive*
Droste, Donald Casper *corporate lawyer, diversified manufacturing company executive*
Eckardt, Carl R. *chemical and building materials executive*
Garcia C., Elisa Dolores *lawyer*
†Gollance, Robert Barnett *ophthalmologist*
Haswell, Carleton Radley *banker*
Haxton, David *computer graphics educator, computer animator, photographer*
Heyman, Samuel J. *chemicals and building materials manufacturing company executive*
Hirsch, Gary D. *supermarket executive*
Howes, William Browning *forest products company executive*
Jeffrey, Robert George, Jr. *industrial company executive*
Kagan, Irving *specialty chemicals and building materials executive*
Katz, Leandro *artist, filmmaker*
Louttit, William A. *supermarket chain executive*
Mallik, Arjun *biomedical chemist*
Nicastro, Francis Efisio *defense electronics and retailing executive*
O'Connor, John Morris, III *philosophy educator*
Sergey, John Michael, Jr. *manufacturing company executive*
†Southway, Peter *bank holding company executive*
Speert, Arnold *college president, chemistry educator*
Trice, William Henry *paper company executive*
Wendowski, Kathleen Cecelia *hospital administrator*
White, Doris Gnauck *science educator, biochemical and biophysics researcher*
Wolynic, Edward Thomas *specialty chemicals technology executive*

Weehawken
Hayden, Joseph A., Jr. *lawyer*
Hess, Dennis John *investment banker*

West Bridgewater
Hulse, Robert Douglas *high technology executive*

West Caldwell
Chun, Edward Hong Yun *psychiatrist*
Jacobs, Howard *distribution executive*
Page, Frederick West *business consultant*
Sostilio, Robert Francis *office equipment marketing executive*
†Terranova, Paul *former corporate executive*

West Long Branch
Rouse, Robert Sumner *former college official*
Stafford, Rebecca *college president, sociologist*

West Milford
Stelpstra, William John *minister*

West New York
Aquino, Felix John *college administrator*
Gruenberg, Elliot Lewis *electronics company executive*
Kelly, Lucie Stirm Young *nursing educator*
Rolston, Robert John *accountant, consultant*

West Orange
Berman, Mona S. *actress, playwright, theatrical director and producer*
Brodkin, Roger Harrison *dermatologist, educator*
Ghali, Anwar Youssef *psychiatrist, educator*
†Housman, Harry J. *pharmaceutical company executive*
Kushen, Allan Stanford *lawyer, retired*
Mandelbaum, Barry Richard *lawyer*
Rayfield, Gordon Elliott *playwright, political risk consultant*
Richmond, Harold Nicholas *lawyer*
Sosnow, Lawrence Ira *health care company executive*
Wu, Nan Faion *pediatrician*

West Paterson
†Fry, Darryl Diamond *chemical company executive*
Kaufman, Allan M. *actuary, consultant*
Ruibal, Charles Adrian *chemical company executive*
Vandervoort, Peter *lawyer*

West Trenton
Roshon, George Kenneth *manufacturing company executive*

Westfield
Alayeto, George I. *food products company executive*
Bartok, William *environmental technologies consultant*
Boutillier, Robert John *accountant*
Connell, Grover *food company executive*
Connell, Ted *food products company executive*
Connell, Terry *agricultural products company executive*
Connolly, Ronald Cavanagh *financial services executive*
Cushman, Helen Merle Baker *retired management consultant*
Feret, Adam Edward, Jr. *dentist*
Lloyd, Eugene Walter *construction company executive*
McDevitt, Brian Peter *educational consultant*
McLean, Vincent Ronald *former manufacturing company financial executive*
Miller, Gabriel Lorimer *physicist, researcher*
Priest, William Wallace, Jr. *investment counselor*
Simon, Martin Stanley *commodity marketing company executive, economist*
†Torcivia, Benedict J., Sr. *construction company executive*
†Torcivia, Benedict Joseph, Jr. *construction company executive*

Westmont
Danner, Charles L. *elementary education educator*

Westville
Doughty, A. Glenn *minister*

Westwood
Andolsek, Charles Merrick *land development consultant*
Bennett, Thomas E. *machinery company executive*
Black, Theodore Halsey *retired manufacturing company executive*
Cullen, Ruth Enck *reading specialist, elementary education educator*
Folley, Clyde H. *diversified manufacturing executive*
Gerlinger, Karl *automotive executive*
McBride, Thomas Francis *machinery company executive*
Mulligan, William G(oeckel) *machinery manufacturing company executive*
Nachtigal, Patricia *equipment manufacturing company executive, general counsel*
†Perrella, James Elbert *manufacturing company executive*
Schutz, Donald Frank *geochemist, corporate executive*

Wharton
Loughlin, William Joseph *priest, religious organization administrator*
Rodzianko, Paul *energy company executive*

Whippany
Colmenares, Narses Jose *electrical engineer*
Curwin, Ronald *home equipment stores executive*
Golden, John F. *packaging company executive*
Golden, Michael Frank *packaging sales company executive*
Michaelis, Paul Charles *engineering physicist executive*
Mimnaugh, John M. *advertising executive*
Spina, Dennis J. *gas industry executive*

Whitehouse Station
Atieh, Michael Gerard *accountant*
Darien, Steven Martin *pharmaceutical executive*
Douglas, Robert Gordon, Jr. *physician*
Gilmartin, Raymond V. *health care products company executive*
Lewent, Judy C. *pharmaceutical executive*
†Spiegel, Francis Herman, Jr. *pharmaceutical company executive*

Whiting
Williams, Roger Wright *public health educator*

Willingboro
Bertolino, Angela Maria *educational association administrator*
Schnapf, Abraham *aerospace engineer, consultant*

Wood Ridge
Castagnetta, Grace Sharp *pianist, piano educator*

Woodbridge
Amato, Vincent Vito *business executive*
Becker, Frederic Kenneth *lawyer*
Brauth, Marvin Jeffrey *lawyer*
Brown, Morris *lawyer*
Buchsbaum, Peter A. *lawyer*
Cirafesi, Robert J. *lawyer*
Cuti, Anthony J. *consumer products company executive*
D'Amico, Andrew John *oil company executive*
Futterman, Jack *retail executive*
Greenbaum, Robert S. *lawyer*
Hoberman, Stuart A. *lawyer*
Jaffe, Sheldon Eugene *lawyer*
Molloy, Brian Joseph *lawyer*
Murray, Arthur G. *food products executive*

Woodbury
Wallace, Jesse Wyatt *pharmaceutical company executive*
White, John Lindsey *lawyer*
Zane, Raymond J. *lawyer, state senator*

Woodcliff Lake
†Robson, Brian *electronics executive*

Wyckoff
Abdelrahman, Talaat Ahmad Mohammad *financial executive*
Anstatt, Peter Jan *marketing services executive*
Bauer, Theodore James *physician*
Bucko, John Joseph *investment corporation executive*
Lavery, Daniel P. *marketing management consultant*
Miller, Walter Neal *insurance company consultant*
Stahl, Alice Slater *psychiatrist*

NEW MEXICO

Alameda
Hooker, Van Dorn *architect, artist*

Alamogordo
Hawkins, James Lowell, Jr. *bank executive*
Stapp, John Paul *surgeon, former air force officer*

Albuquerque
Ackerman, John Tryon *gas company executive*
Adams, Clinton *artist, historian*
Anaya, Rudolfo *educator, writer*
Anderson, Darrell Edward *psychologist, educator*
Anspach, Judith Ford *law librarian, law educator*
Antreasian, Garo Zareh *artist, lithographer, art educator*
Armstrong, Glenn Garnett *artist, retired postal executive*
Austin, Edward Marvin *mechanical engineer, researcher, consultant*
Bahm, Archie John *philosophy educator*
Ballard, David Eugene *anesthesiologist*
Barbo, Dorothy Marie *obstetrician-gynecologist, educator*
Bardacke, Paul Gregory *lawyer, former attorney general*
Barrow, Thomas Francis *artist, educator*
Barry, Steve *sculptor, educator*
Basso, Keith Hamilton *cultural anthropologist, linguist, educator*
Beckel, Charles Leroy *physics educator*
Beeler, Gary *materials science administrator*
Bell, Stoughton *computer scientist, mathematician, educator*
Bennett, Marianne *lawyer, health care company executive*
Binkley, J. S. *physical sciences research administrator*
Black, Craig Call *retired museum administrator*
Bleiweis, Paul Benjamin *environmental services executive*
Bolie, Victor Wayne *electrical and computer engineering educator*
Buss, William Charles *research pharmacology educator*
Campbell, C(harles) Robert *architect*
Caplan, Edwin Harvey *university dean, accounting educator*
Cargo, David Francis *lawyer*
Carraro, Joseph John *senator, small business owner, consultant*
Carrick, David Stanley *electrical engineer*
Caruso, Mark John *lawyer*
Chavez, Martin Joseph *mayor, attorney*
Clark, Alan Barthwell *city administrator*
Clark, James A. *banker*
Cofer, Charles Norval *psychologist, educator*
Cole, Terri Lynn *organization administrator*
Condie, Carol Joy *anthropologist, research facility administrator*
Conway, John E. *federal judge*
Corliss, John Ozro *zoology educator*
Crawford, Dale Lee *architect*
Danziger, Jerry *broadcasting executive*
Deaton, William Weldon, Jr. *federal judge*
†De Santis, Nunzio Pasquale *nuclear pharmacy executive*
Dixon, George Lane, Jr. *orthopaedic surgeon*
†Dodson-Barnhart, Jan Mary *library development specialist, writer*
Dorato, Peter *electrical and computer engineering educator*
Drummond, Harold Dean *education educator*
Easley, Mack *retired state supreme court chief justice*
Eaton, George Wesley, Jr. *petroleum engineer, oil company executive*
Edwards, William Sterling, III *cardiovascular surgeon*
Eglinton, William Matthew *utility company executive*
Evans, Bill (James William Evans) *dancer, choreographer, educator, arts administrator*
Evans, Max Allen *writer, artist*
Findley, James Smith *biology and zoology educator, museum director*
Ford, Wallace Roy *clergyman, religious organization executive*
Friberg, George Joseph *electronics company executive*
Friederich, Jan *retail grocery executive*
Fuller, Anne Elizabeth Havens *English educator, consultant*
Garcia, F. Chris *academic administrator, political science educator, public opinion researcher*
Garland, James Wilson, Jr. *retired physics educator*
Geary, David Leslie *communications executive, educator, consultant*
George, Roy Kenneth *minister*
Goldston, Barbara M. Harral *editor*
Gordon, Larry Jean *public health administrator and educator*
Gorham, Frank DeVore, Jr. *petroleum company executive*
Graham, Robert Albert *research physicist*
Griffin, W. C. *bishop*
Guthrie, Patricia Sue *newspaper reporter, free-lance writer*
Hadas, Elizabeth Chamberlayne *publisher*
Haddad, Edward Raouf *civil engineer, consultant*
Hahn, Betty *artist, photographer, educator*
Hale, Bruce Donald *marketing professional*
Hall, Jerome William *research engineering educator*
Haltom, B(illy) Reid *lawyer*

Hancock, Don Ray *researcher*
Hanna, Robert Cecil *lawyer, lecturer, hotelier*
Hansen, Curtis LeRoy *federal judge*
Harris, Fred R. *political science educator, former senator*
Harrison, Charles Wagner, Jr. *applied physicist*
Hart, Frederick Michael *law educator*
Heady, Ferrel *retired political science educator*
†Henderson, Rogene Faulkner *toxicologist, researcher*
Howard, William Jack *mechanical engineer, retired*
Hsi, David Ching Heng *plant pathologist and geneticist, educator*
Hutton, Paul Andrew *history educator, writer*
Johnson, Robert Hersel *journalist*
Johnson, William Hugh, Jr. *hospital administrator*
Jones, Donald L. *lawyer*
Karni, Shlomo *electrical engineering educator*
Kelley, Robert Otis *medical science educator*
Kellshaw, Terence *bishop*
Kelshaw, Terence *bishop*
King, James Claude *physicist*
King, James Nedwed *construction company executive, lawyer*
Knospe, William Herbert *medical educator*
Korman, Nathaniel Irving *research and development company executive*
Kramarsic, Roman Joseph *engineering consultant*
Kutvirt, Duda Chytilova (Ruzena) *scientific translator*
Lang, Thompson Hughes *publishing company executive*
Lattman, Laurence Harold *retired academic administrator*
Levin, Thomas Augustus *health care corporation executive*
Liberman, Ira L. *real estate broker*
Loftfield, Robert Berner *biochemistry educator*
Looney, Ralph Edwin *newspaper editor, author, photographer*
Loubet, Jeffrey W. *lawyer*
Lujan, Manuel, Jr. *former U.S. secretary of the interior, former congressman*
MacCurdy, Raymond Ralph, Jr. *modern language educator*
Malina, Robert S. *investment company executive*
†Matthew, Kathryn Kahrs *museum director*
Mauderly, Joe Lloyd *pulmonologist*
May, Gerald William *university administrator, educator, civil engineering consultant*
McCabe, Robert R. *architect, city planner*
McCarty, W(illard) Duane *obstetrician-gynecologist, physician executive*
McFeeley, Mark B. *federal judge*
McKiernan, John William *mechanical engineer*
Mc Million, John Macon *retired newspaper publisher*
Mechem, Edwin Leard *judge*
Meiering, Mark C. *lawyer*
Minahan, Daniel Francis *manufacturing company executive, lawyer*
Mitovich, John *association executive*
Molzen, Dayton Frank *consulting engineering executive*
†Moore, James Collins *museum director*
Moore, John Ashton *zoo director*
†Mora, Federico *neurosurgeon*
Murphy, Walter Francis *political science educator, author*
†Nagatani, Patrick Allan Ryoichi *artist, art educator*
Napolitano, Leonard Michael *anatomist, university administrator*
Narath, Albert *laboratory administrator*
Nash, Gerald David *historian*
Neidhart, James Allen *physician, educator*
Newsom, Melvin Max *retired research company executive*
Norman, Ralph David *consulting psychologist, former university administrator*
Omer, George Elbert, Jr. *orthopaedic surgeon, hand surgeon, educator*
Osbourn, Gordon Cecil *materials scientist*
Ottensmeyer, David Joseph *neurosurgeon, health care executive*
Papike, James Joseph *geology educator, science institute director*
Parker, James Aubrey *federal judge*
Pearl, George Clayton *architect*
Peck, Ralph Brazelton *civil engineering educator, consultant*
Peck, Richard Earl *academic administrator, playwright, novelist*
Phillips, Ronald Edward *artist, sales executive*
Ramo, Roberta Cooper *lawyer*
Rezac, Stephan Robert *trade association executive*
Riley, Ann J. *state legislator, technology specialist*
Riordan, William F. *lawyer*
Roberts, Dennis William *association executive*
Robinson, Charles Paul *nuclear physicist, diplomat, business executive*
Roehl, Jerrald J(oseph) *lawyer*
Roehl, Joseph E. *lawyer*
Rosenberg, Arthur James *research science company executive*
Rotherham, Larry Charles *insurance executive*
Rust, John Laurence *manufacturing company executive*
Rutherford, Thomas Truxtun, II *state senator, lawyer*
Sabatini, William Quinn *architect*
Saland, Linda Carol *anatomy educator*
Sanchez, Robert Fortune *archbishop*
Sanchez, Victoria Wagner *science educator*
Schmitt, Harrison Hagan *former senator, geologist, astronaut, consultant*
Schoen, Stevan Jay *lawyer*
Schwerin, Karl Henry *anthropology educator, researcher*
Scully, Marlan Orvil *physics educator*
Serna, David C. *lawyer*
Shedd, Ben Alvin *film producer, director, production company executive*
Sheehan, Michael Jarboe *archbishop*
Sickels, Robert Judd *political science educator*
†Simpson, Steven Quentin *physician, researcher*
Sisk, Daniel Arthur *lawyer*
Slade, Lynn H. *lawyer*
Smith, Elvin T. *communications executive*
Snell, Patricia Poldervaart *librarian, consultant*
†Sobolewski, John Stephen *computer information scientist, director computer services, consultant*
Solomon, Arthur Charles *pharmacist*
Sparks, Morgan *physicist*
Stahl, Jack Leland *real estate company executive*
Stamm, Robert Jenne *building contractor, construction company executive*
Stephenson, Barbera Wertz *lawyer*
Strati, Tony J. *accountant*
Stulberg, Neal Howard *conductor, pianist*
Sturm, Fred Gillette *philosopher, educator*
Tatum, Ronald Winston *physician, endocrinologist*
Thompson, Rufus E. *lawyer*
Thorson, Connie Capers *library educator*
Tope, Dwight Harold *retired management consultant*
Travelstead, Chester Coleman *former educational administrator*
Uhlenhuth, Eberhard Henry *psychiatrist, educator*
Unser, Al *professional auto racer*
†Van Devender, J. Pace *physical scientist*
Vook, Frederick Ludwig *physicist*
Walch, Peter Sanborn *museum director, publisher*
Ward, Charles Richard *extension and research entomologist, educator*
Wellborn, Charles Ivey *lawyer*
Westwood, Albert Ronald Clifton *engineer*
Whiddon, Carol Price *writer, editor, consultant*
Wildin, Maurice Wilbert *mechanical engineering educator*
Winslow, Walter William *psychiatrist*
Witkin, Joel-Peter *photographer*
Wolf, Cynthia Tribelhorn *librarian, library educator*
Wollman, Nathaniel *economist, educator*
Worrell, Audrey Martiny *geriatric psychiatrist*
Worrell, Richard Vernon *orthopedic surgeon, educator*
Young, Joan Crawford *advertising executive*
Youngdahl, James Edward *lawyer*
Zink, Lee B. *academic administrator, economist, educator*
†Zumwalt, Ross Eugene *forensic pathologist, educator*

Angel Fire
Dillon, Robert Morton *retired association executive, architectural consultant*

Artesia
Sarwar, Barbara Duce *school system administrator*

Belen
Chicago, Judy *artist*
Gutjahr, Allan Leo *mathematics educator, researcher*
Toliver, Lee *mechanical engineer*

Carlsbad
Cooper, Richard *zoological park administrator*
Markle, George Bushar, IV *surgeon*
Ricer, N. Dean *park superintendent*
Watts, Marvin Lee *minerals company executive, chemist, educator*

Cedar Crest
Sheppard, Jack W. *retired air force officer*

Chama
Moser, Robert Harlan *physician, educator, writer*

Church Rock
Linford, Laurance Dee *cultural organization administrator*

Clovis
Rehorn, Lois Marie Smith *nursing administrator*

Corrales
Adams, James Frederick *psychologist, educational administrator*
†Cobb, John Candler *medical educator*
Eaton, Pauline *artist*
Eisenstadt, Pauline Doreen Bauman *investment company executive*
Hamilton, Jerald *musician*
Martin, Harold Clark *humanities educator*
Page, Jake (James K. Page, Jr.) *writer, editor*
Tice, Clifford Ray *state legislator, oil company executive*

Crownpoint
Tolino, Arlene Becenti *elementary education educator*

Cuba
Lopez, Joe A. *school system administrator*

Farmington
Garretson, Owen Loren *engineer*
Little, Sylvia Ford *oil industry executive*
Plummer, Steven Tsosie *bishop*
Risley, Larry L. *air transportation executive*
Swetnam, Monte Newton *petroleum exploration executive*

Gallup
Crouch, Altha Marie *health educator, consultant*
Maikowski, Thomas Robert *priest, educational director*

Glenwood
Tackman, Arthur Lester *newspaper publisher, management consultant*

Glorieta
Mc Coy, Robert Baker *publisher*

Grants
Lowney, Bruce Stark *artist*

Hobbs
Garey, Donald Lee *pipeline and oil company executive*
Reagan, Gary Don *state legislator, lawyer*

Kirtland AFB
†Anderson, Christine Marlene *software engineer*
Baum, Carl Edward *electromagnetic theorist*
Harrison, George Brooks *career officer*
†Miller, Leonard Doy *army officer*

Lamy
Holt, Nancy Louise *artist*

Las Cruces
Bloom, John Porter *historian, editor, administrator, archivist*
Borman, Frank *former astronaut, laser patent company executive*
Bratton, Howard Calvin *federal judge*
Coburn, Horace Hunter *retired physics educator*
Cochrun, John Wesley *insurance agent*
Dickinson, James Gordon *editor*
Easterling, Kathy *elementary school principal*
Elliott, Richard L. *school administrator*
Ford, Clarence Quentin *mechanical engineer, educator*
Gale, Thomas Martin *university dean*
Harary, Frank *mathematician, computer scientist, educator*
Jacobs, Kent Frederick *dermatologist*
Kemp, John Daniel *biochemist, educator*
Ketchum, Rhonda J. *hospital administrator*
Kilmer, Neal Harold *physical scientist*
Lease, Richard Jay *police science educator, former police officer*
Lutz, William Lan *lawyer*
Matthews, Larryl Kent *mechanical engineering educator*
Medoff, Mark Howard *playwright, screenwriter, novelist*
Morgan, John Derald *electrical engineer*
†Myers, R. David *library director, dean*
Papen, Frank O'Brien *banker, former state senator*
Peterson, Robin Tucker *marketing educator*
Porter, William Emme *state legislator, small business owner*
Ramirez, Ricardo *bishop*
Reeves, Billy Dean *obstetrics/gynecology educator emeritus*
Reinfelds, Juris *computer science educator*
Roscoe, Stanley Nelson *psychologist, aeronautical engineer*
Sandenaw, Thomas Arthur, Jr. *lawyer*
Schemnitz, Sanford David *wildlife biology educator*
Southward, Glen Morris *statistician, educator*
Thode, Edward Frederick *chemical engineer, educator*
Way, Jacob Edson, III *museum director*
Weigle, Robert Edward *mechanical engineer, research director*

Las Tablas
Laos, Jeffery Baffert *health services specialist*

Las Vegas
Flores, Benny E. *judge*
Riley, Carroll Lavern *anthropology educator*

Los Alamos
Allred, John Caldwell *physicist*
Andrews, Andrew Edward *nuclear engineer*
Bame, Samuel Jarvis, Jr. *research scientist*
†Becker, Stephen A. *physicist, designer*
Bell, George Irving *biophysics researcher*
†Bishop, Alan Reginald *research scientist*
Bradbury, Norris Edwin *physicist*
Campbell, Mary Margaret Stinecipher *research chemist, educator*
Colgate, Stirling Auchincloss *physicist*
Engel, Emily Flachmeier *school administrator*
Engelhardt, Albert George *physicist*
Flynn, Edward Robert *physicist*
Friar, James Lewis *physicist*
†Gancarz, Alexander John *science administrator, research chemist*
Gibson, Benjamin Franklin *physicist*
Ginocchio, Joseph Natale *theoretical physicist*
Goldstone, Philip David *physicist*
Gregg, Charles Thornton *research company executive*
Grilly, Edward Rogers *physicist*
Hecker, Siegfried Stephen *metallurgist*
Jackson, James F. *nuclear engineer*
Jarmie, Nelson *physicist*
Johnson, Mikkel Borlaug *physicist*
Judd, O'Dean P. *physicist*
Keene, Douglas Ralph *diplomat*
Keepin, George Robert, Jr. *physicist*
Kelly, Robert Emmett *physicist, educator*
Kubas, Gregory Joseph *research chemist*
Linford, Rulon Kesler *physicist, engineer*
Matlack, George Miller *radiochemist*
†McComas, David John *science administrator, space physicist*
McNally, James Henry *physicist, defense consultant*
Mendius, Patricia Dodd Winter *editor, educator, writer*
Metropolis, Nicholas Constantine *mathematical physicist*
Mitchell, Terence Edward *materials scientist*
Nix, James Rayford *nuclear physicist, consultant*
Nunz, Gregory Joseph *program manager, aerospace engineer, educator*
Pack, Russell T *theoretical chemist*
Penneman, Robert Allen *retired chemist*
Pynn, Roger *physicist*
Rosen, Louis *physicist*
Selden, Robert Wentworth *physicist, science advisor*
†Shaner, John Wesley *physicist*
Sharp, Jane Ellyn *operations executive*
Smith, Fredrica Emrich *rheumatologist, internist*
Smith, James Lawrence *research physicist*
Stoddard, Stephen Davidson *ceramic engineer, former state senator*
Strottman, Daniel David *physicist*
Terrell, (Nelson) James *physicist*
Thompson, Lois Jean Heidke Ore *industrial psychologist*
Wade, Rodger Grant *financial systems analyst*
Wahl, Arthur Charles *retired chemistry educator*
Wallace, Jeannette Owens *state legislator*
Whetten, John Theodore *geologist*
†WoldeGabriel, Giday *research geologist*
Zurek, Wojciech Hubert *physicist*
Zweig, George *physicist, neurobiologist*

Los Lunas
Mateju, Joseph Frank *hospital administrator*

Mesilla
Willey, Darrell S. *education educator*

Mesilla Park
Shutt, Frances Barton *special education educator*
Tombaugh, Clyde William *astronomer, educator*

Montezuma
Geier, Philip Otto, III *college president*

New Mexico State Capitol
Lambert, Martha Lowery *state legislator*
Morgan, Lynda M. *state legislator*
Nava, Cynthia D. *state legislator*
Stefanics, Elizabeth T. (Liz Stefanics) *state legislator*

Pecos
Price, Thomas Munro *computer consultant*

Placitas
Dunmire, William Werden *author, photographer*
Forrest, Suzanne Sims *research historian*
Pirkl, James Joseph *industrial designer, educator*
Smith, Richard Bowen *retired national park superintendent*

Portales
Agogino, George Allen *anthropologist, educator*
Matheny, Robert Lavesco *history educator, former university president*
Paschke, Donald Vernon *music educator*
Williamson, Jack (John Stewart Williamson) *writer*

Ranchos De Taos
Marx, Nicki D. *sculptor, painter*

Raton
Robinson, Janie Monette *education educator*

Roswell
Anderson, Donald Bernard *oil company executive*
Anderson, Robert Orville *oil and gas company executive*
Baldock, Bobby Ray *federal judge*
Casey, Barbara A. Perea *state representative, educator*
Ebie, William D. *museum director*
Jennings, Emmit M. *surgeon*
Knowles, Richard Thomas *state legislator, retired army officer*
Lewis, George Raymond *clinical social worker*
†Nasi, John Roderick *manufacturing executive*
Olson, Richard Earl *lawyer, state legislator*
Pretti, Bradford Joseph *lay worker, insurance company executive*

Ruidoso
Coe, Elizabeth Ann *elementary education educator*

Ruidoso Downs
Knapp, Thomas Edwin *sculptor, painter*

Sandia Park
Greenwell, Ronald Everett *communications executive*

Santa Fe
Abeyta, Santiago Audoro (Jim Abeyta) *human services administrator*
Agresto, John *college president*
Alexander, John Bradfield *weaponry manager, retired army officer*
Ancona, George Ephrain *photographer, film producer, author*
Arthur, William Brian *economist, educator*
Baca, Edward Dionicio *national guard officer*
Baca, Joseph Francis *state supreme court chief justice*
Ballard, Louis Wayne *composer*
Baustian, Robert Frederick *conductor*
Bejnar, Thaddeus Putnam *lawyer, law librarian*
Bergé, Carol *author*
Bond, Thomas Alden *university president*
†Bradley, Walter D. *lieutenant governor, real estate broker*
Brockway, Merrill LaMonte *television producer and director*
Burton, John Paul (Jack Burton) *lawyer*
Calloway, Larry *columnist*
Campos, Santiago E. *federal judge*
Candelaria, Judith (Watt) *nursing administrator*
Cannon, Helen Leighton *retired geologist, government official*
Cerny, Charlene Ann *museum director*
Chatfield, Cheryl Ann *nonprofit organization executive, educator*
Citrin, Phillip Marshall *retired lawyer*
Clift, William Brooks, III *photographer*
Connell, Evan Shelby, Jr. *author*
Conron, John Phelan *architect*
Cowan, George Arthur *chemist, bank executive, director*
Crosby, John O'Hea *conductor, opera manager*
Cuming, George Scott *retired lawyer, retired gas company official*
Curran, Neil Willis *state police chief*
Davis, Shelby M. C. *investment executive, consultant*
Dennison, Charles Stuart *institutional executive*
Dirks, Lee Edward *newspaper executive*
Dodds, Robert James, III *lawyer*
Drabanski, Emily Ann *editor*
Dreisbach, John Gustave *investment banker*
Duval, Michael Raoul *investment banker*
Erdman, Barbara *visual artist*
Espinosa, Judith M. *state agency administrator*
Ettinger, Richard Prentice *publishing company executive*
Fisher, Robert Alan *laser physicist*
Forsdale, (Chalmers) Louis *education and communication educator*
Franchini, Gene Edward *state supreme court justice*
Frenkel, Jacob Karl *physician, consultant, researcher*
Gaddes, Richard *performing arts administrator*
Gell-Mann, Murray *theoretical physicist, educator*
Giovanielli, Damon Vincent *physicist, consulting company executive*
Gonzales, Stephanie *state official*
Grover, Phyllis Bradman *artist, consultant*
Hall, Edward Twitchell *anthropologist, educator, author*
†Handell, Albert George *artist*
Hatch, John Davis *design consultant, art historian*
Hawkanson, David Robert *theater managing director*
Humphries, William R. *state land commissioner*
Jaramillo, Arthur Lewis *lawyer*
†Johnson, Gary Earl *governor*
Johnson, William Stewart *cultural arts administrator*
Kasbeer, Stephen Frederick *university official*
Kelly, Paul Joseph, Jr. *federal judge*
Knapp, Edward Alan *scientist, government administrator*
Koessel, Donald Ray *retired banker*
Leon, Bruno *architect, educator*
Livesay, Thomas Andrew *museum administrator, lecturer*
Longley, Bernique *artist, painter, sculptor*
Loriaux, Maurice Lucien *artist, ecclesiologist*
Mann, Herbie *flutist*
Mauldin, William H. (Bill Mauldin) *cartoonist*
Mc Kinney, Robert Moody *newspaper editor and publisher*

McLaughlin, Ted John *speech educator*
Moellenbeck, Albert John, Jr. *engineering executive*
Morgan, Alan D. *state education official*
Noble, Merrill Emmett *retired psychology educator, psychologist*
Nuckolls, Leonard Arnold *retired hospital administrator*
Nurock, Robert Jay *investment analysis company executive*
Pearson, Margit Linnea *real estate company executive*
Phipps, Claude Raymond *research scientist*
Phister, Montgomery, Jr. *computer engineering consultant, writer*
Pickrell, Thomas Richard *retired oil company executive*
Pollock, Marvin Erwin *lawyer*
†Quintana, Sammy J. *lawyer*
Ransom, Richard Edward *state supreme court justice*
Ratliff, Floyd *biophysics educator, scientist*
Samora, Joseph E., Jr. *lawyer*
Scheinbaum, David *photography educator*
Schwartz, George R. *physician*
Schwarz, Michael *lawyer*
Seth, Oliver *federal judge*
Shubart, Dorothy Louise Tepfer *artist, educator*
†Spencer, Steven Sears *medical consultant*
Stephenson, Donnan *lawyer, former state supreme court justice*
Stevens, Ron A. *lawyer, public interest organization administrator*
Stieber, Tamar *writer*
Tarn, Nathaniel *poet, translator, educator*
Udall, Thomas *state attorney general*
Upton, Arthur Canfield *experimental pathologist, educator*
Vazquez, Martha Alicia *judge*
Watkins, Stephen Edward *accountant*
White, David Hywel *physics educator*
Whiteford, Andrew Hunter *anthropologist*
Williams, Stephen *anthropologist, educator*
Yalman, Ann *judge*

Seneca
Monroe, Kendyl Kurth *lawyer*

Silver City
Bettison, Cynthia Ann *museum director, archaeologist*
Foy, Thomas Paul *lawyer, state legislator, banker*
Paez, Carolyn Jean *secondary education educator*
Snedeker, John Haggner *university president*

Socorro
Kottlowski, Frank Edward *geologist*
†Lyons, William Claypool *engineering educator and consultant*
Petschek, Albert George *physics educator*

Sunspot
Altrock, Richard Charles *astrophysicist*
Leibacher, John William *astronomer*

Taos
Bacon, Wallace Alger *speech communications educator, author*
Bell, Larry Stuart *artist*
Crespin, Leslie Ann *artist*
Dickey, Robert Preston *author, educator, poet*
Ellis, Robert Malcolm *artist, foundation administrator*
Murphey, Michael Martin *country western singer, songwriter*
Witt, David L. *curator, writer*
Young, Jon Nathan *archeologist*

Tesuque
Poedtke, Carl Henry George, Jr. *management consultant*

Tijeras
Vizcaino, Henry P. *mining engineer, consultant*

Univ Of New Mexico
Ellis, Willis Hill *lawyer, educator*
Goodin, Julia C. *medical investigator, state official, educator*
Hull, McAllister Hobart, Jr. *retired university administrator*
Sarto, Gloria Elizabeth *obstetrician/gynecologist, educator*
Thorson, James Llewellyn *English language educator*

Wagon Mound
Abeyta, Jose Reynato *retired pharmacist, state legislator, cattle rancher*

White Sands Missle Range
Arthur, Paul Keith *electronic engineer*

NEW YORK

Afton
Schwartz, Aubrey Earl *artist*

Albany
Aceto, Vincent John *librarian, educator*
Arseneau, James Charles *physician*
Ashe, Bernard Flemming *lawyer*
Beach, John Arthur *lawyer*
Beebe, Richard Townsend *physician*
Begg, Robert Thomas *law library adminstrator, law librarian, lawyer*
Beharriell, Frederick John *German and comparative literature educator*
Bellacosa, Joseph W. *judge*
Bellizzi, John J. *law enforcement association administrator, educator, pharmacist*
Biggs, Donald Anthony *psychologist, educator*
†Block, Eric *chemist*
Blount, Stanley Freeman *marketing educator*
Bosart, Lance Frank *meteorology educator*
Bowen, Mary Lu *ecumenical developer*
Bradford, Peter Amory *state official*
Bradley, Wesley Holmes *physician*
Brantlinger, Frank Herbert *insurance company executive*
Brown, Albert Joseph, Jr. *banker*
Brown, Judith Anne *law librarian*
†Brown, Lester *social work educator*
Burke, Joseph C. *university administrator*
Calhoun, Nancy *state legislator*
Carovano, John Martin *not-for-profit adminstrator, conservationist*
Carpenter, Howard Grant, Jr. *lawyer, savings and loan association executive*
Case, Forrest N., Jr. *lawyer*
Catalano, Jane Donna *lawyer*
Cholakis, Constantine George *federal judge*
Chorbajian, Herbert G. *bank executive*
Connelly, Elizabeth Ann *state legislator*
Cotter, William Donald *state commissioner, former newspaper editor*
Coughlin, Thomas A., III *state official*
Creegan, Robert Francis *philosophy educator*
Csiza, Charles Karoly *veterinarian, microbiologist*
Davis, Paul Joseph *endocrinologist*
DeFelice, Eugene Anthony *physician, medical educator, consultant, magician*
Demerjian, Kenneth Leo *atmospheric science educator, research center director*
DeNuzzo, Rinaldo Vincent *pharmacy educator*
Donovan, Robert Alan *English educator*
Dougherty, James *orthopedic surgeon, educator*
Doyle, Joseph Theobald *physician, educator*
Eckstein, Jerome *philosopher, educator*
Engel, David Anthony *lawyer*
Falk, Dean *anthropology educator*
Farley, Hugh Thomas *state senator, law educator*
Ferguson, Henry *international management consultant*
Fitzgerald, Frank Thomas *sociology educator*
Frisch, Harry Lloyd *chemist, educator*
Frost, Robert Edwin *chemistry educator*
Furlong, Patrick Louis *health science association administrator*
Galiber, Joseph Lionel *state senator*
Galvin, Thomas John *information science policy educator, librarian, information scientist*
Gay, Charles *church administrator*
Gellhorn, Alfred *physician, educator*
Giblin, Mary Ellen *mental health professional*
Gottfried, Richard Norman *state legislator*
Grove, William Boyd *bishop*
Gruber, Scott Alan *medical educator*
Hagoort, Thomas Henry *lawyer*
Halsey, Richard Sweeney *information scientist, educator*
Han, Jaok *cardiologist, researcher, educator*
Happ, Harvey Heinz *electrical engineer, educator*
Harenberg, Paul E. *state legislator*
Haydock, Michael Damean *commissioner*
Herman, Robert S. *former state official, economist, educator*
Hill, Earlene Hooper *state legislator*
Hitchcock, Karen Ruth *biology educator, university dean, academic administrator*
Hof, Liselotte Bertha *biochemist*
Hoffmeister, Jana Marie *cardiologist*
Holland, Joseph Robert *state senator*
Holstein, William Kurt *business administration educator*
Holt-Harris, John Evan, Jr. *lawyer*
Hubbard, Howard James *bishop*
Hughs, Richard Earl *business school dean*
†Kadamus, James A. *educational administrator*
Katz, William Armstrong *library science educator*
Kaye, Gordon Israel *pathologist, anatomist, educator*
Kaye, Judith Smith *judge*
Kekes, John *philosopher, educator*
Kennedy, William Joseph *novelist, educator*
Kiepper, James Julius *education educator*
Kim, Jai Soo *physics educator*
Kinney, Thomas J. *adult education educator*
Kuivila, Henry Gabriel *chemist, educator, consultant*
Lack, James J. *state senator, lawyer*
Langlitz, Harold N. *pension fund administrator*
Leichter, Franz S. *state senator*
Lenardon, Robert Joseph *classics educator*
Levine, Louis David *museum director, archaeologist*
Ley, Ronald *psychologist, educator*
Lumpkin, Lee Roy *dermatologist, educator*
Lundine, Stanley Nelson *state government official, former congressman, lawyer*
Luster, Martin Arnold *state legislator*
Lynch, Daniel *newspaper editor, writer*
Macario, Alberto Juan Lorenzo *physician*
MacFarland, Robert Frederick *bank executive*
Marchi, John Joseph *state senator, lawyer*
Margolis, Natalie *nursing administrator, educator*
McCarthy, Mary Lynn *social work educator*
†McCaughey, Elizabeth P. (Betsy McCaughey) *state official*
†Meader, John Daniel *state agency administrator, judge*
Mihm, Martin Charles, Jr. *pathologist, educator*
Miles, Christine Marie *museum director*
Miller, Melvin Howard *state legislator*
Miner, Roger Jeffrey *federal judge*
Moelleken, Wolfgang Wilfried *Germanic languages and literature educator*
Morga Bellizzi, Celeste *editor*
Morgan, George Jefferson *interior designer*
Mullin, Lenore Marie Restifo *computer scientist, researcher*
Murphy, Thomas Joseph *strategic communications consultant*
Murray, David *journalist, author*
†Murray, Francis J., Jr. *energy executive*
Nathan, Richard P(erle) *political scientist, educator*
O'Connell, George Edward *state official*
O'Neil, Chloe Ann *state legislator*
Ortloff, George Christian, Sr. (Chris Ortloff) *journalist, state legislator*
†Pataki, George E. *governor*
Paulson, Peter John *librarian, publishing company executive*
Picotte, Michael Bernard *real estate developer*
Pohlsander, Hans Achim *classics educator*
†Prieto, Claudio R. *academic administrator, lawyer*
Purves, Alan Carroll *English language educator, education educator*
Quellmalz, Henry *printing company executive*
Reese, William Lewis *philosophy educator*
Reichert, Leo Edmund, Jr. *biochemist, endocrinologist*
Reid, William James *social work educator*
Reynolds, Joseph P. *publishing executive, educational consultant*
Riley, Victor J., Jr. *financial services company executive*
Robbins, Cornelius (Van Vorse) *education administration educator*
†Roberts, Hugh D. *real estate company executive*
†Roberts, Katherine Christina *real estate executive*
Roberts, Warren Errol *history educator*
Robinson, John Bowers, Jr. *bank holding company executive*
Rosenfeld, Harry Morris *editor*
Rosenkrantz, Daniel J. *computer science educator*
Roth, Laura Maurer *physics educator, researcher*
Sacklow, Stewart Irwin *advertising executive*
Salkin, Patricia E. *law educator*
Santiago, Nellie *state legislator*
†Schmidt, John Thomas *neurobiologist*
Schneider, Allan Stanford *biochemistry and pharmacology educator, biomedical research scientist*
Shaffer, Gail S. *state government official*
Shea, Maurice P., III *bank executive*
Shubert, Joseph Francis *librarian*
Siegel, David Donald *law educator*
Simons, Richard Duncan *judge*
Singer, Cecile Doris *state legislator*
Skelos, Dean G. *senator*
Smith, Ada L. *state legislator*
Smith, Ralph Wesley, Jr. *federal judge*
Smith, Rex William *journalist*
Sobol, Thomas *state education commissioner*
Solomon, Martin M. *state senator*
Sprow, Howard Thomas *lawyer, educator*
Stachowski, William T. *state senator*
Standish, John Spencer *textile manufacturing company executive*
Stewart, Margaret McBride *biology educator, researcher*
Swartz, Donald Percy *physician*
Tedeschi, James Theodore, Jr. *psychologist educator*
Teevan, Richard Collier *psychology educator*
Thompson, Frank Joseph *political science educator*
Thornberry, Terence Patrick *criminologist, educator*
Thornton, Maurice *university administrator*
Tieman, Suzannah Bliss *neurobiologist*
Titone, Vito Joseph *judge*
Vaccaro, Louis Charles *college president*
Vachon, Russell Bertrand *transportation executive*
†Valentino, F. William *energy executive*
Vitaliano, Eric Nicholas *state legislator, lawyer*
Volker, Dale Martin *state senator, lawyer*
Wallender, Michael Todd *lawyer*
†Walton, Arthur L. *state education official*
Ward, Frank Jay *banker*
Wierzbicki, Ronald Gerard *auditor*
Wright, Theodore Paul, Jr. *political science educator*
Zacek, Joseph Frederick *history educator, international studies consultant, East European affairs specialist*
Zimmerman, Joseph Francis *political scientist, educator*

Alfred
Billeci, Andre George *art educator, sculptor*
Coll, Edward Girard, Jr. *university president*
Frechette, Van Derck *ceramic engineer*
Higby, (Donald) Wayne *artist, educator*
Keith, Timothy Zook *psychology educator*
McCauley, James Weymann *ceramics engineer, educator*
Ott, Walter Richard *academic administrator*
Potter, Barrett George *historian, educator*
Rand, Joella Mae *nursing educator*
Rossington, David Ralph *physical chemistry educator*
Spriggs, Richard Moore *ceramic engineer, research center administrator*

Alfred Station
Love, Robert Lyman *educational consulting company executive*

Amagansett
Opper, John *painter, retired educator*

Amenia
Gilbert, Linda Johanna *special education administrator*

Amherst
Alfiero, Salvatore Harry *manufacturing company executive*
Arrison, Clement R. *manufacturing company executive*
Brown, Stephen Ira *mathematics educator*
Clark, Donald Malin *association executive*
Cohen, Herman Nathan *private investigator*
Coover, James Burrell *music educator*
Cramer, Stanley Howard *psychology educator, author*
Eberlein, Patricia James *mathematician, computer scientist, educator*
Fujita, Peter Kozo *tire manufacturing executive*
Gracia, Jorge Jesus Emiliano *philosopher, educator*
Graf, Paul Edward *electronics company executive*
Jen, Frank Chifeng *finance and management educator*
Kurtz, Paul *publisher, philosopher, educator*
Mills, Theodore Mason *sociologist, educator*
Reinhorn, Andrei M. *civil engineering educator, consultant*
Roby, Edgar Maclin *electronic equipment manufacturing company executive*
Rossberg, Robert Howard *psychology educator, former university dean*

Amityville
Brennan, Patrick Thomas *meteorology company executive*
†Gordon, Saul Wolfe *technology educator*
Linehan, Patrick Francis, Jr. *financial planner*

Annandale On Hudson
Achebe, Chinua *humanist, humanities educator*
Ashbery, John Lawrence *language educator, poet, playwright*
†Botstein, Leon *college president, historian, conductor, music critic*
Frank, Elizabeth *English literature educator, author*
Kelly, Robert *poet, educator*
Kiviat, Erik *ecologist, administrator, educator*
Manea, Norman *writer, educator*
Sullivan, Jim *artist*

Apalachin
Linder, Fannie Ruth *psychotherapist, concert soprano*

Ardsley
Barth, Richard *pharmaceutical executive*
Barton, Joan Chi-Hung Lo *sales executive*
Benjamin, Jeff *lawyer*
Gayle, Joseph Central, Jr. *computer information professional*
Habermeier, Jeurgen *chemical company executive*
Mohl, Allan S. *social worker*
O'Brien, Charles O. *chemical company executive*
†Pires, Mary Ann *public relations consultant*
Ricklin, Arthur H. *hospital administrator*
Sanders, Robert Martin *commodity trader*
Sullivan, Joseph Thomas *chemical executive, chemical engineer*

Armonk
Bailey, William O. *retired insurance company executive*
Behr, Richard Henry *architect, educator*
Bergson, Henry Paul *association executive*
Berlin, Caren Ann *marketing professional*
Bolduc, Ernest Joseph *management consultant*
Bolton, John Roger *public relations executive*
Eastman, Dean Eric *science research executive*
Elliott, David H. *insurance company executive*
Elson, Charles *stage designer, educator*
Evangelista, Donato A. *lawyer, computer and infosystems manufacturing company executive*
Forese, James John *business machine company executive*
Gerstner, Louis Vincent, Jr. *diversified company executive*
Godfrey, Robert R. *financial services executive*
Grove, David Lawrence *economist*
Levy, Kenneth James *advertising executive*
Lynett, Lawrence Wilson *electronics company executive*
†Mc Groddy, James Cleary *computer company executive*
Mellors, Robert Charles *physician scientist*
Quinn, James W. *lawyer*
†Rizzo, Paul J. *information processing company executive*
Sayers, Ken W(illiam) *writer and public relations executive*
Sharpe, Myron Emanuel *publisher, editor, writer*
Turner, Mary Lee *data processing executive*
†Weber, Michael *editor*
Weill, Richard L. *lawyer*
York, Jerome B. *computer company executive*

Astoria
Fox, R. Steven *psychotherapist, theologian*
Koszarski, Richard *film historian, writer*
McCormick, Douglas Walter *cable, broadcast executive*
†See Fong Chan *retired linguist, composer*

Athens
Lew, Roger Alan *manufacturing company executive*

Auburn
Eldred, Thomas Gilbert *secondary education educator, historian*
Sayles, Edward Thomas *theatrical producer*

Aurora
Shilepsky, Arnold Charles *mathematics educator, computer consultant*
Slocum, George Sigman *energy company executive*

Averill Park
Haines, Walter Wells *retired economics educator*

Babylon
Collis, Charles *aircraft company executive*
Haley, Priscilla Jane *artist, printmaker*
Hennelly, Edmund Paul *lawyer, oil company executive*
Keane, Daniel J. *banker*
Lopez, Joseph Jack *oil company executive, consultant*
Meirowitz, Claire Cecile *public relations executive*

Baldwin Place
Kurian, George Thomas *publisher*

Ballston Lake
Fiedler, Harold Joseph *electrical engineer, consultant*
Lambert, Lloyd Tupper *writer, civic volunteer*
Proskin, Arnold W. *state assemblyman, lawyer*

Ballston Spa
Barba, Harry *author, educator, publisher*

Bangall
†Cetrone, Gene Leonard *author, producer, screenwriter*

Barrytown
Higgins, Dick (Richard Carter Higgins) *writer, publisher, composer, artist*

Batavia
Maher, John Francis *personnel executive*
Steiner, Stuart *college president*

Bath
Sandt, John Joseph *psychiatrist, educator*

Bay Shore
Merolla, Carmine Ralph *banker*
Pinsker, Walter *allergist, immunologist*

Bayport
Courant, Ernest David *physicist*
Poli, Kenneth Joseph *editor*

Bayside
D'Amato, Domenico Donald *lawyer*
Goldstein, Milton *art educator, printmaker, painter*
Zinn, William *violinist, composer, business executive*

Beacon
Flagello, Ezio Domenico *basso*
Garell, Paul Charles *family physician*
Pollart, Dale F(lavian) *petroleum company research executive*

Bearsville
Wickiser, Ralph Lewanda *painter, educator, author*

Bedford
Atkins, Ronald Raymond *lawyer*
Benedek, Armand *landscape architect*
Bonsal, Dudley Baldwin *federal judge*
Bowman, James Kinsey *publishing company executive, rare book specialist*

Clifford, Lawrence M. investment company executive
Damora, Robert Matthew architect
Jalkut, Richard Alan telecommunications executive
Philip, Peter Van Ness former trust company executive
Ruppel, George Robert accountant
Weinman, Robert Alexander sculptor

Bedford Corners
Singer, Craig broker, consultant, investor

Bedford Hills
Diebold, John management consultant
Fissell, William Henry investment advisor
Ludlum, Robert author
Marshall, William Emmett biotechnology company executive, biochemistry researcher
Nichols, C. Walter, III retired trust company executive
Previn, Andre composer, conductor
Waller, Wilhelmine Kirby (Mrs. Thomas Mercer Waller) civic worker, organization official

Bellmore
Crouch, Howard Earle health service organization executive
Schlossberg, Fred Paul elementary education educator

Bellport
Barton, Mark Quayle physicist
Hughes, Elinor Lambert drama and film critic

Berlin
Stephens, Donald Joseph retired architect

Bethpage
Anderson, John Robert manufacturing executive
Freese, Robert Gerard financial executive
Melnik, Robert Edward aeronautical engineer
Rockensies, John William mechanical engineer

Binghamton
Anderson, Warren Mattice lawyer
†Atkin, William Walter insurance company executive
Babb, Harold psychology educator
Balla, Wesley G. museum curator, historian
Banks, Arthur Sparrow political scientist, educator
Bearsch, Lee Palmer architect, city planner
Best, Robert Mulvane insurance company executive
Block, Haskell Mayer humanities educator
Brehm, Sharon Stephens psychology educator, university administrator
Carrigg, James A. utility company executive
Coates, Donald Robert geology educator, scientist
Cornacchio, Joseph Vincent engineering educator, computer researcher, consultant
Dalke, Robert Lynn insurance company executive
Defleur, Lois B. university president, sociology educator
Dunn, Melvin Bernard insurance company executive
Eisch, John Joseph chemist, educator
Farley, Daniel W. lawyer, utility company executive
Feisel, Lyle Dean university dean, electrical engineering educator
Feldsine, Frances Teresa nursing administrator
Gaddis Rose, Marilyn comparative literature educator, translator
Gerhart, Eugene Clifton lawyer
Hilton, Peter John mathematician, educator
Hinman, George Lyon lawyer
Ippolito, Angelo artist, educator
Isaacson, Robert Lee psychology educator, researcher
Jennings, Frank Louis engineering company executive, engineer
Kessler, Milton English language educator, poet
Klir, George Jiri systems science educator
Komar, Paul utility company executive
Levis, Donald James psychologist, educator
Libous, Thomas William state senator
Lowen, Walter mechanical engineering educator
Mazrui, Ali Al'Amin political science educator, researcher
McAvoy, Thomas James federal judge
Michael, Sandra Dale reproductive endocrinology educator, researcher
Pearson, Paul Holding insurance company executive
Pomeroy, John Eric electronics company executive
Salem-Murdock, Muneera anthropologist
Schwartz, Richard Frederick electrical engineering educator
Shillestad, John Gardner financial services company executive
Sklar, Kathryn Kish historian, educator
Stein, George Henry historian, educator, administrator
Su, Stephen Y. H. computer science and engineering educator, consultant

Bloomingdale
†Ketchledge, Edwin H. conservationist

Bloomington
Ruffing, Anne Elizabeth artist

Bohemia
Kern, Harry developmental engineer
Manley, Gertrude Ella librarian, media specialist

Brasher Falls
Patterson, Florence Ghoram real estate broker

Brewster
Barnhart, Robert Knox writer, editor
†Shepard, Jean Heck publishing company consultant

Briarcliff Manor
Bhargava, Rameshwar Nath physicist
Bingham, J. Peter electronics research executive
Bornmann, Carl M(alcolm) lawyer
Callahan, Daniel John institute director
Carey, James Henry banker
Dolmatch, Theodore Bieley management consultant
Gaylin, Willard physician, educator
Glassman, Jerome Martin clinical pharmacologist, educator
Haddad, Jerrier Abdo engineering management consultant
Leiser, Burton Myron philosophy and law educator
Luck, Edward Carmichael association executive
†McLeish, David James Dow employee benefits consulting executive, actuary
Pruitt, Peter Taliaferro insurance company executive
Radandt, Friedhelm K. college president
†Reynolds, Michael Joseph consulting company executive
Weintraub, Michael Ira neurologist
Zimmar, George Peter publishing executive, psychology educator

Briarwood
Danna, Jo J. publisher, author, anthropologist

Bridgehampton
Edwards, John W. school superintendent
Jackson, Lee artist
Needham, James Joseph consultant
Phillips, Warren Henry publisher

Brockport
Bretton, Henry L. political scientist, educator
Harter, Michael Thomas college dean, health sciences consultant
Leslie, William Bruce history educator
Marcus, Robert D. historian, educator
Stack, George Joseph philosophy educator
Studer, Ginny college dean
Van de Wetering, John E(dward) college president

Bronx
Adams, Alice sculptor
Aiken, William accountant
Ansbro, John Joseph philosophy educator
Balka, Sigmund Ronell lawyer
Bamberger, Phylis Skloot judge
Barton, Lewis food manufacturing company executive
Bhalodkar, Narendra Chandrakant cardiologist
†Biasiny-Rivera, Charles cultural organization administrator
Blaufox, Morton Donald physician, educator
Bloom, Barry R. microbiologist, immunologist, educator
Boggs, Wade Anthony professional baseball player
Bowers, Francis Robert literature educator
Brescia, Michael Joseph nephrologist, educator
Bruenn, Howard Gerald physician
Bryant, Roy, Sr. bishop
Burde, Ronald Marshall neuro-ophthalmologist
Buschke, Herman neurologist
Caffin, Louise Anne library media educator
Carrick, Bruce Robert publishing company executive
Cimino, James Ernest physician
Cohen, Herbert Jesse physician, educator
Conway, William Gaylord zoologist, zoo director, conservationist
Cornfield, Melvin lawyer, university institute director
DeMartino, Anthony Gabriel cardiologist, internist
Dulles, Avery priest, theologian
Duncalf, Deryck anesthesiologist
Edelmann, Chester Monroe, Jr. pediatrician, medical school dean
Eder, Howard Abram physician
Eliasoph, Joan radiologist, educator
Elkin, Milton radiologist, physician, educator
Fernandez, Ricardo R. university administrator
Fernandez, Tony (Octavio Antonio Castro Fernandez) baseball player
Fishman, Joshua Aaron sociolinguist, educator
Foreman, Spencer pulmonary specialist, hospital executive
Forero, Enrique botanical garden research director
Frater, Robert William Mayo surgeon, educator
Freeman, Leonard Murray radiologist, nuclear medicine physician, educator
Friedman, Joel Matthew oral and maxillofacial surgeon, educator
Fulop, Milford physician
Gandhi, Bhanumati Bhagwandas anesthesiologist
Garance, Dominick (D. G. Garan) lawyer, author
Gerst, Paul Howard physician
Gliedman, Marvin L. surgeon, educator
Gootzeit, Jack Michael rehabilitation institute executive
Greenberg, Blu author
Gross, Ludwik physician
Hait, Gershon pediatric cardiologist
Hallett, Charles Arthur, Jr. English and humanities educator
Hankin, Leonard J. merchant
Heath, Cedric Alexander nurse, health services administrator
Heilbrun, James economist, educator
Hennessy, Thomas Christopher clergyman, educator, retired university dean
Himmelberg, Robert Franklin historian, educator
Hirano, Asao neuropathologist
Hovnanian, H. Philip biomedical engineer
Howell, Alfred Hunt former banker
Humphry, James, III librarian
Hurwitz, Ted Harold sports conference administrator
Iazetti, Anthony M. school system administrator
Jacobson, Harold Gordon radiologist, educator
Jaffé, Ernst Richard medical educator and administrator
Jennings, Ralph Merwin broadcasting executive
Kahn, Thomas medical educator
Karasu, T(oksoz) Byram psychiatry educator
Karmen, Arthur physician, science administrator, educator
Karp, Abraham Joseph historian, rabbi, educator
Kassoy, Hortense (Honey Kassoy) artist
Key, Jimmy (James Edward Key) professional baseball player
Kitzie, John, Jr. retail electronic products executive
Koranyi, Adam mathematics educator
Koss, Leopold G. pathologist, educator, physician
Kucic, Joseph management consultant, industrial engineer
Lattis, Richard Lynn zoo director
Lawn, John C. professional baseball team executive, former federal government official
Lieber, Charles Saul physician, educator
Lilly, Frank oncogenetic biomedical researcher
Linden, Barnard Jay electrical engineer
Macklin, Ruth bioethics educator
Maddox, Utricia Antoinette English educator, communications educator
Martinez-Tabone, Raquel school psychologist supervisor
Marx, Gertie Florentine anesthesiologist
Mattingly, Donald Arthur professional baseball player
McCabe, James Patrick library director
McDowell, Jack Burns professional baseball player
†McShane, Joseph M. priest, dean, theology educator
Michelsen, W(olfgang) Jost neurosurgeon, educator
Mittler, Diana (Diana Mittler-Battipaglia) music educator and administrator, pianist
Moritz, Charles Fredric book editor
Mulholland, Terence John (Terry Mulholland) professional baseball player
Muschel, Louis Henry immunologist, educator
Nagler, Arnold Leon pathologist, scientist, educator
Nathanson, Melvyn Bernard university provost, mathematician
Nathenson, Stanley Gail immunology educator
Orkin, Louis Richard physician, educator
Ottenberg, James Simon hospital executive
Parker, Everett Carlton clergyman
Pearl, Mary Corliss wildlife conservationist
Pitchumoni, Capecomorin Sankar gastroenterologist, educator
Potkin, Harvey food company executive
Purpura, Dominick P. neuroscientist, university dean
Rapin, Isabelle physician
Revelle, Donald Gene manufacturing and health care company executive, consultant
Reynolds, Benedict Michael surgeon
Richman, Arthur Sherman sports association executive
Rizzuto, Philip Francis (Scooter) sports broadcaster, former professional baseball player
Roberts, Burton Bennett administrative judge
†Robinson, John Gwilym conservationist
Romney, Seymour Leonard physician, educator
Rose, Israel Harold mathematics educator
Rosenstock, Morton librarian
Rothstein, Anne Louise education educator, college official
Ruben, Robert Joel physician, educator
Scanlan, Thomas Joseph college president, educator
Schaller, George Beals zoologist
Scharff, Matthew Daniel immunologist, cell biologist, educator
Scharrer, Berta Vogel anatomy and neuroscience educator
Schaumburg, Herbert Howard neurology educator
Schwam, Marvin Albert graphic design company executive
Seltzer, William statistician, social researcher, former international organization director
Shafritz, David Andrew physician, research scientist
Shamos, Morris Herbert physicist educator
Sherman, Judith Dorothy producer, recording company owner, recording engineer
Shinnar, Shlomo child neurologist, educator
Showalter, Buck (William Nathaniel Showalter, III) major league baseball team manager
Smith, Sharon Patricia university dean
Spitzer, Adrian pediatrician, medical educator
Sprecher, Baron Baron William pianist, composer, conductor, diplomat
Stanley, Pamela Mary cell biologist
Stein, Ruth Elizabeth Klein physician
Steinbrenner, George Michael, III professional baseball team executive, shipbuilding company executive
Stuhr, David Paul business educator, consultant
Surks, Martin I. medical educator, endocrinologist
Sussman, David William lawyer
Tong, Hing mathematician, educator
Tregde, Lorraine C. hospital administrator
Tusiani, Joseph foreign language educator, author
Ultan, Lloyd historian
Waelsch, Salome Gluecksohn geneticist, educator
Waltz, Joseph McKendree neurosurgeon, educator
Weins, Leo Matthew publishing company executive
Wiernik, Peter Harris oncologist, educator
Williams, Marshall Henry, Jr. physician, educator
Wolf, Robert Thomas lawyer
Yalow, Rosalyn Sussman medical physicist
Zalaznick, Sheldon editor, journalist
Zeichner, Oscar historian, educator

Bronxville
Armstrong, John Kremer lawyer, artist
Arndt, Kenneth Eugene banker
Barkhuus, Arne physician
Barnhart, Clarence Lewis lexicographer, editor
Biscardi, Chester composer, educator
Blank, Richard Mark advertising licensing and product development executive
Conant, Miriam Bernheim political scientist, educator
Cook, Charles David international lawyer, arbitrator, consultant
Dvorak, Roger Gran health facility executive
Farber, Viola Anna dancer, choreographer, educator
Forester, Erica Simms decorative arts historian, consultant, educator
Franklin, Margery Bodansky psychology educator, researcher
Graham, Nancy O. nurse, administrator
Hutchison, Dorris Jeannette retired microbiologist, educator
Ilchman, Alice Stone college president, former government official
Kaplan, Barbara college dean
Kirk, Grayson Louis retired political science educator, retired universtiy president, trustee
Knapp, George Griff Prather insurance consultant, arbitrator
Krupat, Arnold English educator, writer
Levitt, Miriam pediatrician
L'Huillier, Peter (Peter) archbishop
Lombardo, Philip Joseph broadcasting company executive
Lukash, Barbara Lynne dermatologist
Martin, R. Keith business and information systems educator, consultant
Mau, Dwayne Holger minister
Noble, James Kendrick, Jr. media industry consultant
Penisten, Gary Dean entrepreneur
Peters, Sarah Whitaker art historian, writer, lecturer
Prakapas, Eugene Joseph art gallery director
Randall, Francis Ballard historian, educator, writer
Root, Stuart Dowling lawyer, former banker and government official
Schönberg, Bessie dance educator
Shuker, Gregory Brown publishing and production company executive
Wilson, John Donald banker, economist

Brooklyn
Abrahamsen, Samuel retired Judaic studies educator
Adams, George Harold hospital and health executive
Adasko, Mary speech pathologist
Agard, Emma Estornel psychotherapist
Ahrens, Thomas H. production company executive
Alfano, Edward Charles, Jr. elementary education educator
Alfonso, Antonio Escolar surgeon
Al-Hafeez, Humza minister, editor
Allen, Percy, II hospital administrator
Alley, Frederick Don hospital executive
Altura, Burton Myron physiologist, educator
Amon, Carol Bagley federal judge
Anderson, Lennart artist
Artschwager, Richard Ernst artist
Ashley, Leonard Raymond Nelligan English language educator
Azrack, Joan M. judge
Bachman, George mathematics educator
†Baltakis, Paul Antanas bishop
Barabash, Claire special education administrator, psychologist
Bartels, John Ries federal judge
Barth, Robert Henry nephrologist
Battle, Turner Charles, III art educator, educational association administrator
Bergeron, R. Thomas radiologist, educator
Bertoni, Henry Louis electrical engineering educator
Bianco, Anthony Joseph, III newswriter
Birenbaum, William M. former university president
Biro, Laszlo dermatologist
Blackman, Robert Irwin real estate developer and investor, lawyer, accountant
Blasi, Alberto Romance languages educator, writer
Bode, Walter Albert editor
Bowers, Patricia Eleanor Fritz economist
Bramwell, Henry federal judge
†Broas, Donald Sanford hospital executive
Brownstone, Paul Lotan retired speech communications and drama educator
Buck, Robert Treat, Jr. museum director, educator
Bugliarello, George university president
Carlile, Janet Louise artist, educator
Carlson, Ralph Lawrence book publisher
Carruthers, Walter Edward Royden (Roy Carruthers) graphic designer, artist
Carswell, Lois Malakoff botanical gardens executive, consultant
Carter, Betty (Lillie Mae Jones) jazz singer, songwriter
Castleman, Louis Samuel metallurgist, educator
Castro, Nikki Marie dancer
Catell, Robert Barry gas utility executive
Charton, Marvin chemist, educator
Chernow, Ron writer, columnist
Clark, Peggy theatrical lighting designer
Clune, John Richard library administrator
Comer, John F. superintendent
Contino, Rosalie Helene English educator, costume designer
Cornell, Thomas Browne artist, educator
Corry, Emmett Brother librarian, educator, researcher, archivist
Costantino, Giuseppe psychologist, researcher, administrator, educator
Cracco, Roger Quinlan medical educator, neurologist
Crum, Albert Byrd psychiatrist, consultant
Daily, Thomas V. bishop
Dearie, Raymond Joseph federal judge
DeBock, Florent Alphonse controller
DeCarava, Roy R. photographer, educator
Dellomo, Frank A. banker
Delson, Elizabeth artist
Delson, Sidney Leon architect
Dinnerstein, Harvey artist
Dinnerstein, Simon Abraham artist, educator
Duberstein, Conrad B. federal judge
Edelstein, Brenda school administrator
Edemeka, Udo Edemeka surgeon
Eirich, Frederick Roland chemist, educator
†Erber, William Franklin gastroenterologist
Eschen, Albert Herman optometrist
Everdell, William Romeyn humanities educator
Faison, Seth Shepard retired insurance broker
†Falcocchio, John Carlo civil engineer
Faunce, Sarah Cushing museum curator
Federici, William Vito newspaper reporter
Ferber, Linda S. museum curator
Flam, Jack Donald art historian, educator
Fodstad, Harald neurosurgeon
Ford, Vandelette mental health educator
Forest, Charlene Lynn cell biologist, educator
Franco, Victor theoretical physics educator
Friedman, Eli Arnold nephrologist
Friedman, Gerald Manfred geologist, educator
Friedman, Howard Samuel cardiologist, educator
Friedman, Paul chemistry educator
Friis, Erik Johan editor, publisher
Frisch, Ivan Thomas computer and communications company executive
Gabriel, Mordecai Lionel biologist, educator
Garcia, Marc Anthony diplomat
Geller, Sheldon consumer products company executive
Gintautas, Jonas physician, scientist, administrator
Giordano, Anthony Bruno electrical engineering educator, retired college dean
Glasser, Israel Leo federal judge
Glickman, Franklin Sheldon dermatologist, educator
Goodman, Alvin S. engineering educator, consultant
Gootman, Phyllis Myrna educator
Gordon, Conrad J. financial executive
Gotta, Alexander Walter anesthesiologist, educator
Grado, Angelo John artist
Graham, Arnold Harold lawyer, educator
Grayson, D. W. bishop
Gresser, Carol A. school system administrator
Gross, Stephen Mark pharmacist, academic dean
†Gustin, Mark Douglas hospital administrator
Hamm, Charles John banker
Handlin, James Patrick headmaster
Harris, James Arthur, Sr. economics educator, consultant
Harvey, Edmund Huxley, Jr. (Tad Harvey) editor
Heidtmann, Susan Ann nursing administrator
Helly, Walter Sigmund engineering educator
Herman, Susan N. legal educator
Hochstadt, Harry mathematician, educator
Hohenrath, William Edward retired banker
Holden, David Morgan medical educator
Hood, Ernest Alva, Sr. pharmaceutical company executive
Hoogenboom, Ari Arthur historian, educator
Hopkins, Karen art administrator
Imperato, Pascal James physician, health administrator, author, editor, medical educator
Ireys, Alice Recknagel landscape architect
Jacobson, Leslie Sari biologist, educator
Jarman, Joseph jazz musician
Jenkins, Leroy violinist, composer
Jindrak, Karel Francis pathologist, researcher, educator
Jofen, Jean foreign language educator
Johnson, Sterling, Jr. federal judge
Jones, Blanche nursing administrator, orthopaedic and gerontology consultant

Jones, Susan Emily *fashion educator, administrator, educator*
Kamholz, Stephan L. *physician*
Kaplan, Frada M. *principal, special education educator*
Karamouz, Mohammad *engineering educator*
Kehl, Shelley Sanders *lawyer, academic administrator*
Kempner, Joseph *aerospace engineering educator*
Kimmich, Christoph Martin *academic administrator, educator*
King, Margaret Leah *history educator*
Kippel, Gary M. *psychologist*
Kjeldaas, Terje, Jr. *physics educator emeritus*
Klainberg, Marilyn Blau *community health educator*
Korman, Edward R. *federal judge*
Kotik, Charlotta *curator, museum administrator*
Kravath, Richard Elliot *pediatrician, educator*
Kuskin, Karla *writer, illustrator*
†La Corte, John J. *philososhy educator, historical society executive*
Langer, Arthur Mark *mineralogist*
Lebouitz, Martin Frederick *financial services industry executive, consultant*
Lederman, Stephanie Brody *artist*
Lee, Spike (Shelton Jackson Lee) *filmmaker*
Lee, Stanley *physician, educator*
Leeman, Cavin Philip *psychiatrist, educator*
Leiman, Sid Zalman *Judaic studies educator*
Levere, Richard David *physician, academic administrator, educator*
†Lewin, Ted Bert *writer, illustrator*
Lewis, Felice Flanery *lawyer, educator*
Leyh, Richard Edmund, Sr. *retired investment executive*
Lichtenstein, Harvey *performing arts executive*
†Light, Harold L. *health care facility executive*
Lindo, J. Trevor *psychiatrist, consultant*
Lobron, Barbara L. *writer, editor, photographer*
Maddalena, Frank Joseph *health care executive*
†Madigan, Richard Allen *museum director*
Malach, Monte *physician*
Marcus, Harold *physician, health facility administrator*
Margolin, Harold *metallurgical educator*
Marsala-Cervasio, Kathleen Ann *medical/surgical nurse*
Masterson, Charles Francis *retired social scientist*
Matthews, Craig Gerard *gas company executive*
Mendelson, Sol *physical science educator, consultant*
Milhorat, Thomas Herrick *neurosurgeon*
Milman, Doris Hope *pediatrics educator, psychiatrist*
Minkoff, Jack *economics educator*
Mohaideen, A. Hassan *surgeon, healthcare consultant*
Montgomery, Velmanette *state legislator*
Moore, Arthur James *editor*
Morawetz, Herbert *chemistry educator*
Mundy, Mark James *hospital administrator*
Murillo-Rohde, Ildaura Maria *marriage and family therapist, consultant, educator, dean*
Murphy, Edward Patrick, Jr. *gas utility company executive*
Namba, Tatsuji *physician, medical researcher*
†Nelson, Karl Emil *hospital administrator, healthcare consultant*
Nickerson, Eugene H. *federal judge*
Norstrand, Iris Fletcher *psychiatrist, neurologist, educator*
Nurhussein, Mohammed Alamin *internist, geriatrician, educator*
O'Connor, Sister George Aquin (Margaret M. O'Connor) *college president, sociology educator*
Olson, Robert Goodwin *philosophy educator*
Onken, George Marcellus *lawyer*
Oussani, James John *stapling company executive*
Pagala, Murali Krishna *physiologist*
Pan, Huo-Hsi *mechanical engineer, educator*
Pearlstein, Seymour *artist*
Pennisten, John William *computer scientist, linguist, actuary*
Peter, Helmut W. *gas company executive*
Pfaffman, William Scott *sculptor*
Phillips, Gretchen *clinical social worker*
Plotz, Charles Mindell *physician*
Pollack, Bruce *banker, real estate consultant*
Poser, Norman Stanley *law educator*
†Primm, Beny Jene *addiction treatment foundation administrator*
Provine, John C. *lawyer*
†Puccio, John *hospital administrator*
Purdy, James *writer*
Raggi, Reena *federal judge*
Raskind, Leo Joseph *law educator*
Ravitz, Leonard J., Jr. *physician, scientist, consultant*
Reich, Nathaniel Edwin *physician, poet, author, artist, educator*
Reinisch, June Machover *psychologist, educator*
Reissman, Maurice L. *bank executive*
Reynolds, Nancy Remick *editor, writer*
Rice, John Thomas *architecture educator*
Rocco, Ron *artist*
Roess, Roger Peter *engineering educator*
Ross, Allyne R. *federal judge*
Ryan, Leonard Eames *administrative law judge*
Safir, Howard *fire commissioner*
Sands, Edith Sylvia Abeloff (Mrs. Abraham M. Sands) *finance educator, author*
Sanduja, Mohan L. *chemist, researcher, executive*
Sanford, David Boyer *writer, editor*
Schaefer, Marilyn Louise *artist, writer, educator*
Schiffman, Gerald *microbiologist, educator*
Schmidt, Fred (Orval Frederick Schmidt) *editor*
Scholtz, Elizabeth *botanical garden administrator*
Schussler, Theodore *lawyer, physician, educator*
Shalita, Alan Remi *dermatologist*
Sharify, Nasser *librarian, educator, author*
Shaw, Doris *creative marketing consultant*
Shaw, Leonard Glazer *electrical engineering educator, consultant*
Shechter, Ben-Zion *artist, illustrator*
Shechter, Laura Judith *artist*
Sher, Norman *psychiatrist, child psychiatrist*
Shooman, Martin Lawrence *electrical engineer, computer scientist, educator*
†Shubert, Gabrielle S. *museum executive director*
Shulman, Max L. *corporate executive*
Sifton, Charles Proctor *federal judge*
Silver, Horace Ward Martin Tavares *composer, pianist*
Slade, Rejane De Oliveira *Portuguese language educator*
Sonenberg, Jack *artist*
Spector, Robert Donald *language professional, educator*
Spivack, Frieda Kugler *psychologist, administrator, educator, academician*
Sternlight, Peter Donn *economist, retired banker*
Stevenson, Gale *librarian*
Stracher, Alfred *biochemistry educator*
Sullivan, Colleen Anne *physician, educator*
Sullivan, Donald *college president*
Sullivan, Joseph M. *bishop*
Sultzer, Barnet Martin *microbiology and immunology researcher, educator*
Swenson, Karen *poet, journalist*
Swirsky, Judith Perlman *arts administrator, consultant*
Szenberg, Michael *economics educator, editor, consultant*
Tamir, Theodor *electrophysics researcher, educator*
Tesoro, Giuliana Cavaglieri *chemistry research educator, consultant*
Trager, David G. *judge, lawyer, educator*
Vogl, Otto *polymer science and engineering educator*
†von Rydingsvard, Ursula Karoliszyn *sculptor*
Walsh, George William *publishing company executive, editor*
Wasserman, Arnold Saul *academic dean, industrial design executive*
Weill, Georges Gustave *mathematics educator*
Weiner, Irwin M. *medical educator, college dean, researcher*
Weinstein, Jack Bertrand *federal judge*
Weston, I. Donald *architect*
†Williams, Carl E., Sr. *bishop*
Williams, Emma Louise *elementary education educator*
Williams, William Magavern *headmaster*
Wise, Leslie *surgeon, educator*
Wolf, Edward Lincoln *physics educator*
Wolfe, Ethyle Renee (Mrs. Coleman Hamilton Benedict) *college administrator*
Wolintz, Arthur Harry *physician, neuro-ophthalmologist*
Wollman, Leo *physician*
Woolley, Margaret Anne (Margot Woolley) *architect*
Zelin, Jerome *retail executive*
†Zivari, Bashir *architect, industrial designer*

Brookville
Huber, Don Lawrence *publisher*
Woodsworth, Anne *university dean, librarian*

Buchanan
Somerstein, Aurc ·a Abrera *educator*

Buffalo
Abate, Ralph Francis *structural engineer*
Abrahams, Athol Denis *geography researcher, educator*
Ackerman, Philip Charles *utility executive, lawyer*
Allen, Barbara Jo *health facility administrator*
Allen, William Sheridan *history educator*
Ambrus, Clara Maria *physician*
Ambrus, Julian L. *physician, medical educator*
Ament, Richard *anesthesiologist, educator*
Anbar, Michael *biophysics educator*
Anderson, Wayne Arthur *electrical engineering educator*
Arcara, Richard Joseph *federal judge*
Ashgriz, Nasser *mechanical and aerospace engineer, educator*
Aurbach, Herbert Alexander *sociology educator*
Bakay, Louis *neurosurgeon*
†Ballow, Mark *physician, educator*
†Bannon, Anthony L. *museum director*
Barcelona, Charles B. *wholesale food company executive*
Bardos, Thomas Joseph *chemist, educator*
Barney, Thomas McNamee *lawyer*
Basu, Rajat Subhra *physicist, researcher*
Batty, J. Michael *geographer, educator*
Bayles, Jennifer Lucene *museum education curator*
Bean, Edwin Temple, Jr. *lawyer*
Behling, Charles Frederick *psychology educator*
Benenson, David Maurice *engineering educator*
Berlin, Lorna Chumley *artist*
Berner, Robert Frank *statistics educator*
Birch, David William *college official*
Bishop, Beverly Petterson *physiologist*
Blaine, Charles Gillespie *lawyer*
Blane, Howard Thomas *research institute administrator*
Bobinski, George Sylvan *librarian, educator*
Borst, Lyle Benjamin *physicist, educator*
Brady-Borland, Karen *reporter*
Brandt, Barbara Berryman *cultural organization administrator*
Brody, Harold *neuroanatomist, gerontologist*
Brooks, John Samuel Joseph *pathologist, researcher*
Bross, Irwin Dudley Jackson *biostatistician*
Brown, John M. *gas company executive*
Bruckenstein, Stanley *chemistry educator*
Brutvan, Cheryl Ann *curator, art history educator*
Calkins, Evan *physician, educator*
†Campbell, David N. *data processing executive*
Carmichael, Donald Scott *lawyer, business executive*
Chapman, Frederick John *manufacturing executive*
Chrisman, Diane J. *librarian*
Christopher, James Roy *executive director*
Chu, Tsann Ming *immunochemist, educator*
Chutkow, Jerry Grant *neurologist, educator*
Ciancio, Sebastian Gene *periodontist, educator*
Clark, Randall Livingston *manufacturing company executive*
Cleave, James H. *bank executive*
Cloudsley, Donald Hugh *library administrator*
Coburn, Lewis Alan *mathematics educator*
Coles, Robert Traynham *architect*
Collins, J. Michael *public broadcasting executive*
Coppens, Philip *chemist*
Cordes, Alexander Charles *lawyer*
Crandall, Robert Mason *pharmaceutical executive*
Creaven, Patrick Joseph *physician, research oncologist*
Creeley, Robert White *author, English educator*
Curran, Robert *columnist*
Curtin, John T. *federal judge*
Day, Donald Sheldon *lawyer*
Draper, Verden Rolland *accountant*
Drew, Fraser Bragg Robert *English language educator*
Drinnan, Alan John *oral pathologist*
†Drury, Colin Gordon *engineering consultant, educator*
Duax, William Leo *biological researcher*
Duke, Emanuel *lawyer*
Eagan, John Gayle *business educator*
Elfvin, John Thomas *federal judge*
†Esmonde, Donn Patrick *newspaper columnist*
Fay, Albert Hill *building materials executive*
Federman, Raymond *novelist, English and comparative literature educator*
Feldman, Irving *poet*
Fiedler, Leslie Aaron *English educator, actor, author*
Flint, Mark Addison *financial executive*
Floyd, David Kenneth *lawyer, judge*
Foley, Timothy Francis *food company executive*
Foschio, Leslie George *lawyer*
Frake, Charles Oliver *anthropology educator*
Freschi, Bruno Basilio *architect, educator*
Friedlander, John Eastburn *health facility administrator*
Fuhr, Grant *professional hockey player*
Fung, Ho-Leung *pharmacy educator, researcher, consultant*
Fuzak, Victor Thaddeus *lawyer*
Gardner, Arnold Burton *lawyer*
Garvey, James Anthony *lawyer*
Gemmett, Robert James *university dean, English language educator*
Genco, Robert Joseph *scientist, immunologist, periodontist, educator*
Gerstman, Sharon Stern *lawyer*
Glanville, Robert Edward *lawyer*
Glasauer, Franz Ernst *neurosurgeon*
Glickman, Marlene *social organization administrator*
Goldberg, Neil A. *lawyer*
Goldhaber, Gerald Martin *communication educator, author, consultant*
Gona, M. Jayakumari *nuclear medicine physician*
Goodell, Joseph Edward *manufacturing executive*
Gort, Michael *economics educator*
Graham, (Lloyd) Saxon *epidemiology educator*
Grasser, George Robert *lawyer*
Gray, F(rederick) William, III *lawyer*
Greiner, William Robert *university administrator, educator, lawyer*
Gresham, Glen Edward *physician*
Gruen, David Henry *financial executive, consultant*
Halbreich, Uriel Morav *psychiatrist, educator*
Hall, David Edward *lawyer*
†Hall, Linda M. *biochemical pharmacology educator, consultant*
†Hall, Miles W. *electronics company executive*
Halpern, Ralph Lawrence *lawyer*
Halpert, Leonard Walter *retired editor*
Hare, Daphne Kean *medical association director, educator*
Hare, Peter Hewitt *philosophy educator*
Hauptman, Herbert Aaron *mathematician, educator, researcher*
Hawerchuk, Dale *professional hockey player*
He, Guang Sheng *research scientist*
†Head, Christopher Alan *lawyer*
Head, Edward Dennis *bishop*
Headrick, Thomas Edward *lawyer, educator*
Heilman, Pamela Davis *lawyer*
†Hein, August Henry *transportation company executive*
Helm, Frederick *dermatology educator*
Hetzner, Donald Raymund *social studies educator*
Horoszewicz, Juliusz Stanislaw *oncologist, cancer researcher, laboratory administrator*
Hull, Elaine Mangelsdorf *psychology educator*
†Huntington, Richard (John) *art critic*
Iggers, Georg Gerson *history educator*
Ireland, Barbara Hennig *newspaper editor*
Irwin, Robert James Armstrong *investment company executive*
Jacobs, Jeremy M. *diversified holding company executive, hockey team owner*
Jain, Piyare Lal *physics educator*
Jasen, Matthew Joseph *state justice*
Jerge, Marie Charlotte *minister*
Johnstone, D. Bruce *university administrator*
Joslin, Norman Earl *judge*
Kaeser, Clifford Richard *lawyer, food service industry executive*
Katz, Jack *audiology educator*
Katz, Leonard Allen *medical director, educator*
Kelley, Sister Helen *hospital executive*
Kellner, Douglas Ernest *financial executive*
†Kennedy, Bernard Joseph *utility executive*
Kenzie, Ross Bruce *retired banker*
Kieffer, James Marshall *lawyer*
Kinzly, Robert Edward *engineering company executive*
Kiser, Kenneth M(aynard) *chemical engineering educator*
Knox, Northrup Rand *banker*
Kostyniak, Paul John *toxicology educator*
Kris, Edward Joseph *chemist*
Kurlan, Marvin Zeft *surgeon*
Lafontaine, Pat *professional hockey player*
Lamb, Charles F. *minister*
Lammert, Richard Alan *corporate lawyer*
Landi, Dale Michael *industrial engineer, academic administrator*
Langway, Chester Charles, Jr. *geological sciences educator*
Larson, Wilfred Joseph *chemical company executive*
Laurenzo, Vincent Dennis *industrial management company executive*
Layton, Rodney Eugene *controller, newspaper executive*
Lee, George C. *civil engineer, university administrator*
Lee, Richard Vaille *physician, educator*
Leland, Harold Robert *research and development corporation executive, electronics engineer*
Levine, George Richard *English language educator*
Levine, Murray *psychology educator*
Levy, Kenneth Jay *psychology educator, academic administrator*
Liew, Fah Pow *mechanical engineer*
Light, Murray Benjamin *newspaper editor*
Lippes, Gerald Sanford *lawyer, business executive*
Littlewood, Douglas Burden *business brokerage executive*
Loew, Ralph William *clergyman, columnist*
Lucey, Thomas William *banker*
MacLeod, Gordon Albert *lawyer*
Manes, Stephen Gabriel *concert pianist, educator*
Marinelli, Lynn M. *county official*
Markwart, Paul Martin *architect*
†Masiello, Anthony M. (Tony Masiello) *mayor*
McGuire, Beryl Edward *retired federal judge*
McHale, Magda Cordell *academic administrator, trend analyst*
Meehan, Gerry *professional hockey team executive*
Menasco, William Wyatt *mathematics educator*
Meredith, Dale Dean *civil engineering educator*
Metzger, Ernest Hugh *aerospace engineer, scientist*
Middleton, Elliott, Jr. *physician*
Mihich, Enrico *medical researcher*
Milgrom, Felix *immunologist, educator*
Millane, Lynn *town official*
Milligan, John Drane *historian, educator*
Mindell, Eugene Robert *surgeon, educator*
Miner, John Burnham *industrial relations educator, writer*
Minter, Edgar Frederick *industrial executive*
Mirand, Edwin Albert *medical scientist*
Moriarty, Robert Brian *lawyer*
Muckler, John *professional hockey coach, professional team executive*
Nanula, Savino P. *supermarket and convenience store company executive*
Naughton, John Patrick *cardiologist, medical school administrator*
Newman, Stephen Michael *lawyer*
Okun, Janice *food editor*
†Orlowski, Ronald Joseph *wood preserving company executive*
Ortolani, Minot Henry *zoo director*
Ottenbacher, Kenneth John *dean, educator*
Panaro, Victor Anthony *radiologist*
†Paul, Philip Franklin, Jr. *management consultant*
Payne, Frances Anne *literature educator, researcher*
Pearson, Paul David *lawyer, mediator*
Pegels, C. Carl *management science and systems educator*
Peradotto, John Joseph *classics educator, editor*
Petrocco, William Patrick *retail executive*
Pett, John Lyman *banker*
Phillips, Stanley F *restaurant company executive*
Piccillo, Joseph *artist*
Piech, Margaret Ann *mathematics educator*
Pierce, Frederick Smythe *envelope company executive*
Piver, M. Steven *gynecologic oncologist*
Priore, Roger L. *biostatistics educator, consultant*
Pruitt, Dean Garner *psychologist, educator*
Rachlin, Lauren David *lawyer*
Rappolt, William Carl *banker*
Regan, Peter Francis, III *physician, psychiatry educator*
Reif, Louis Raymond *lawyer, utilities executive*
Reismann, Herbert *engineer, educator*
Reitan, Paul Hartman *geologist, educator*
Rekate, Albert C. *physician*
Rice, Victor Albert *global industrial company executive*
Rich, Robert E., Sr. *frozen foods company executive*
Rich, Robert E., Jr. *food products company executive*
Richards, David Gleyre *German language educator*
Richardson, F. C. *academic administrator*
Richmond, Allen Martin *speech pathologist, educator*
Riepe, Dale Maurice *philosopher, writer, illustrator, educator, Asian art dealer*
Robinson, David Clinton *reporter*
Rochwarger, Leonard *former ambassador*
Rogovin, Milton *photographer, retired optometrist*
Rooney, Paul Monroe *former library administrator*
Rosenthal, Donald B. *political scientist, educator*
Ruch, Paul Edward *banker*
Ruckenstein, Eli *chemical engineering educator*
Rumer, Ralph Raymond, Jr. *civil engineer, educator*
Sahlem, James Robert *law librarian*
Salisbury, Eugene W. *lawyer, justice*
Saperston, Howard Truman, Sr. *lawyer*
Sarjeant, Walter James *electrical and computer engineering educator*
Saveth, Edward Norman *history educator*
Schatz, Lillian Lee *playwright, molecular biologist, educator*
Schentag, Jerome John *pharmacy educator*
Schroeder, Harold Kenneth, Jr. *lawyer*
Schultz, Douglas George *art museum director*
Schutte, Alden Frederick *advertising executive*
Seidl, Fredrick William *dean, social work educator*
Seller, Robert Herman *cardiologist, family physician*
Serafin, James Adam *organization executive, management consultant*
Shanahan, Robert B. *banker*
Shanahan, Thomas J. *lawyer*
Shapiro, Stuart Charles *computer scientist, educator*
Sharma, Sushil Chandra *hospital administrator*
Sharpe, Daniel Roger *lawyer*
Shaw, David Tai-Ko *electrical and computer engineering educator, university administrator*
Shedd, Donald Pomroy *surgeon*
Sherwood, Arthur Morley *lawyer*
Siedlecki, Peter Anthony *English educator*
Siener, William Harold *museum director, historian, consultant*
Skretny, William Marion *federal judge*
Small, S(aul) Mouchly *psychiatrist, educator*
Smith, Barbara *camping administrator*
Solo, Alan Jere *medicinal chemistry educator, consultant*
Spaulding, Robert Mark *lawyer*
Spencer, Foster Lewis *newspaper editor*
Stainrook, Harry Richard *banker*
Starks, Fred William *chemical company executive*
Steegmann, Albert Theodore, Jr. *anthropology educator*
Stein, William Warner *anthropology educator*
†Stevens, Raymond Donald, Jr. *chemical company executive*
Stoll, Howard Lester, Jr. *dermatologist*
†Stone, Robert A. *airport administrator*
Stull, G. Alan *university dean, health professions educator*
Tedlock, Dennis *anthropology and literature educator*
Thompson, Michael F. *food service executive*
Toles, Thomas Gregory *editorial cartoonist*
Tomasi, Thomas B. *cell biologist, administrator*
Treanor, Charles Edward *physicist*
Triggle, David John *university dean, consultant*
Trotter, Herman Eager, Jr. (Herman Trotter) *music critic*
Tufariello, Joseph James *chemistry educator*
Urban, Henry Zeller *newspaperman*
†Vacco, Dennis C. *lawyer*
Valdes, Maximiano *conductor*
Vardon, James Lewes *bank executive*
Vogel, Michael N. *journalist, writer, historian*
Voorhess, Mary Louise *pediatric endocrinologist*
Wang, Jui Hsin *biochemistry educator*
Weber, Thomas William *chemical engineering educator*
Weller, Sol William *chemical engineering educator*
Wickser, John Philip *lawyer*
Wiesen, Richard A. *academic administrator, educator*
Williams, Reginald Victor, III *marketing communications company executive*
Wilmers, Robert George *banker*
Wirth, Sandra Lee *real estate company owner*
Wisbaum, Wayne David *lawyer*
Wolck, Wolfgang Hans-Joachim *linguist, educator*
Wright, John Robert *pathologist*
Zaleski, Marek Bohdan *immunologist*

Zarembka, Paul *economics educator*
†Zimmerman, Nancy Picciano *library science educator*

Burdett
Stillman, Joyce L. *artist, educator, consultant*

Buskirk
Johanson, Patricia Maureen *artist, architect, park designer*

Cambridge
Guma, Greg William *producer, writer, administrator*
Sullivan, Patricia W. (Terry Sullivan) *real estate trainer*

Campbell Hall
Greenly, Colin *artist*
Ottaway, James Haller, Jr. *newspaper publisher*
Stone, Peter George *lawyer, publishing company executive*

Canaan
Bell, James Milton *psychiatrist*
Pennell, William Brooke *lawyer*
Rothenberg, Albert *psychiatrist, educator*
Walker, William Bond *retired librarian*

Canandaigua
†Sands, Marvin *wine company executive*
†Sands, Richard E. *food products executive*

Canton
Fleming, Barbara Joan *university administrator*
Goldberg, Rita Maria *foreign language educator*
O'Connor, Daniel William *retired religious studies and classical languages educator*
Peterson, Patti McGill *college president*
Pollard, Fred Don *finance company executive*
Romey, William Dowden *geologist, educator*

Carle Place
Kahn, Leonard Richard *communications and electronics company executive*
Linchitz, Richard Michael *pain medicine specialist, psychiatrist, physician*

Carmel
Carruth, David Barrow *landscape architect*
†Gosline, Peter Lawrence *hospital administrator*
Huckabee, Carol Brooks *psychologist*
Laporte, Cloyd, Jr. *retired manufacturing executive, lawyer*
†Leach, William Riley *writer, historian*
Shen, Chia Theng *former steamship company executive, religious institute official*

Castle Point
Greene, Jerry George *physician*

Castleton On Hudson
Lanford, Oscar Erasmus, Jr. *retired university vice chancellor*

Catskill
Kingsley, John Piersall *lawyer*

Cedarhurst
Cohen, David B. *optical company executive*
Cohen, Harris L. *diagnostic radiologist, consultant*
Cohen, Philip Herman *accountant*

Centereach
McAllister, Dee Theresa *elementary education educator*

Centerport
Caputi, William James, Jr. *engineering consultant*
Fischel, Edward Elliot *physician*
Mallett, Helene Gettler *elementary education educator*

Central Islip
Finnin, Mary Josephine *nurse, consultant*
McGowan, Harold *real estate developer, investor, scientist, author, philanthropist*

Chappaqua
Boal, Lyndall Elizabeth *social worker*
Brockway, George Pond *economist*
Cronin, Raymond Valentine *financial executive*
de Janosi, Peter Engel *research manager*
Fischer, David C. *lawyer*
George, Jean Craighead *author, illustrator*
Gstalder, Herbert William *publisher*
Kingsley, Emily Perl *writer*
Laun, Louis Frederick *government official*
Lundberg, Ferdinand Edgar *author*
Maloney, John Frederick *retired marketing and opinion research specialist*
O'Neill, Robert Charles *consultant, inventor*
Pomerene, James Herbert *retired computer engineer*
Whittingham, Charles Arthur *library administrator, publisher*

Chestnut Ridge
Bickel, Henry Joseph *electronics company executive*
Day, Stacey Biswas *physician, educator*

Chittenango
Cassell, William Walter *retired accounting operations consultant*
Schultz, Ruth Anne *home economics educator, parenting educator, consultant*

Chucktowaga
Howland, Murray Shipley, Jr. *gastroenterologist*

Circleville
Hazan, Marcella Maddalena *author, educator, consultant*

Clarence
Greatbatch, Wilson *biomedical engineer*
Hubler, Julius *artist*
Mehaffy, Thomas N. *retired tire company executive*

Clifton Park
Farley, John Joseph *library science educator emeritus*
Favreau, Donald Francis *corporate executive*
Panek, Jan *electrical power engineer, consultant*
Scher, Robert Sander *instrument design company executive*
Schmitt, Roland Walter *retired academic administrator*

Climax
Adler, Lee *artist, educator, marketing executive*

Clinton
Anthony, Donald Charles *librarian, educator*
Blackwood, Russell Thorn, III *philosophy educator*
Couper, Richard Watrous *foundation executive, educator*
Fuller, Ruthann *principal*
Ring, James Walter *physics educator*
Rupprecht, Carol Schreier *comparative literature educator, dream researcher*
Wagner, Frederick Reese *language professional*
Wertimer, Sidney *economics educator*

Cobleskill
Ingels, Jack Edward *horticulture educator*

Cohoes
Kennedy, Kathleen Ann *nursing administrator*

Cold Spring
Brill, Ralph David *architect, real estate developer, venture capitalist*

Cold Spring Harbor
Freeman, Ira Henry *author, journalist*
Hargraves, Gordon Sellers *banker*
Huffman, Carol Koster *middle school educator*
Nightingale, Geoffrey J. *communications company executive, consultant*
Roberts, Francis Joy *secondary education educator, journalist*
Watson, James Dewey *molecular biologist, educator*
Wigler, Michael H. *molecular biologist*

College Point
Hegarty, Michael John *financial officer*

Colton
Bulger, Dennis Bernard *military officer, engineer*

Commack
Nelson, Marvin Bernard *financial executive*

Conesus
Dadrian, Vahakn Norair *sociology educator*

Cooperstown
†Bordley, James, IV *surgeon*
Carew, Rodney Cline *batting coach, former professional baseball player*
Evans, Abigail Winifred *theatrical executive*
†Franck, Walter Alfred *rheumatologist, medical administrator, educator*
Harman, Willard Nelson *malacologist, educator*
Hermann, William Henry *retired hospital administrator, consultant*
†Jackson, Felicity Anne *performing arts organization administrator*
Jenkins, Ferguson Arthur, Jr. (Fergie Jenkins) *former baseball player*
MacLeish, Archibald Bruce *museum director*
Pearson, Thomas Arthur *epidemiologist, educator*
Reynolds, Jack Mason *manufacturing company executive*

Copake Falls
Chalk, Howard Wolfe *marketing company executive*

Corning
Ahrens, Kent *museum director, art historian*
†Beall, George Halsey *ceramic engineer*
Behm, Forrest Edwin *glass manufacturing company executive*
Booth, C(hesley) Peter Washburn *manufacturing company executive*
Buechner, Thomas Scharman *artist, retired glass manufacturing company executive, museum director*
Campbell, Van C. *manufacturing company executive*
Duke, David Allen *glass company executive*
Dulude, Richard *glass manufacturing company executive*
Ecklin, Robert Luther *glass company executive*
Flynn, James Leonard *manufacturing executive*
Hauselt, Denise Ann *lawyer*
Houghton, James Richardson *glass manufacturing company executive*
Josbeno, Larry Joseph *physics educator*
Keck, Donald Bruce *physicist*
Luther, David Byron *glass company executive*
Maurer, Robert Distler *retired industrial physicist*
Meiling, Gerald Stewart *materials scientist*
Peck, Arthur John, Jr. *diversified manufacturing executive*
Riesbeck, James Edward *glass company executive*
Spillman, Jane Shadel *curator, researcher, writer*
Stuart, Ben R. *manufacturing company executive*
Ughetta, William Casper *lawyer, manufacturing company executive*
†Whitehouse, David Bryn *museum director*

Cornwall
Gentile, Melanie Marie *record producer, marketing and public relations consultant, writer*

Cornwall On Hudson
Abrams, Vivien *artist*
Grant, Joanne Catherine *auctioneer*
Weiss, Egon Arthur *retired library administrator*

Corona
Cole, Donald H. *middle school educator*
Jackson, Andrew Preston *library director*

Cortland
Anderson, Donna Kay *musicologist, educator*
†Gration, Selby Upton *library director*
Kaminsky, Alice Richkin *English language educator*
Miller, John David *manufacturing company executive*
Zipp, Arden Peter *chemistry educator*

Cranberry Lake
Glavin, James Edward *landscape architect*

Craryville
Figols, Priscilla Gordon de *soprano*
Payson, Ronald Sears *biology educator*

Cross River
Smith, Lawrence Beall *artist*

Croton On Hudson
Adelson, Alexander M. *physicist*
Coleman, Earl Maxwell *publishing company executive*
Henderson, Harry Brinton, Jr. *author, editor*
Hoffman, Paul Shafer *lawyer*
Kahn, Roger *author*
Miranda, Robert Nicholas *publishing company executive*
Nelson, Charles Arthur *publisher, consultant*
Plotch, Walter *management consultant, fund raising counselor*
Rubinfien, Leo H. *photographer, filmmaker*
Shatzkin, Leonard *publishing consultant*
Straka, Laszlo Richard *publishing consultant*
Turner, David Reuben *publisher, author*
†Wandel, Thaddeus *ophthalmologist*

Cutchogue
Dank, Leonard Dewey *medical illustrator, audio-visual consultant*
O'Connell, Francis Joseph *lawyer, arbitrator*

De Witt
Ball, Baxter Fenton, Jr. *secondary school administrator*

Deer Park
Taub, Jesse J. *electrical engineering researcher*

Delhi
MacDonald, Robert Bruce *county official*

Delmar
Birdsey, Anna Campas *civil engineer, architect*
Button, Rena Pritsker *public relations company executive*
Mangouni, Norman *publisher*
Nitecki, Joseph Zbigniew *librarian*
Odenkirchen, Carl Josef *Romance languages and literatures educator*
Quackenbush, Roger E. *secondary education educator*

Denver
Brockway, Amie *artistic director*

Dexter
Hayes, Eugene P. *airport administrator*

Dix Hills
Fisher, Fenimore *business development consultant*
Murphy, Edward J. *school system administrator*

Dobbs Ferry
Clarke, Pamela Jones *headmaster*
Clarke, Richard M. *chemicals executive*
Cohen, Philip Francis *publishing company executive*
Fritz, Jean Guttery *writer*
Grunebaum, Ernest Michael *investment banker*
Holtz, Sidney *publishing company executive*
Juettner, Diana D'Amico *lawyer, educator*
Kapp, Richard P. *conductor, arts administrator*
Kraetzer, Mary C. *sociologist, educator, consultant*
Maiocchi, Christine *lawyer*
Moore, Sandra M. *director of admissions*
Newman, Edwin Stanley *lawyer, publishing company executive*
Panitz, Esther Leah *English language educator*
Perelle, Ira B. *psychologist, educator*
Simon, Lothar *publishing company executive*
Sutton, Francis Xavier *social scientist, consultant*
Triplett, Kelly B. *chemist*
Whiting, John Randolph *publisher, writer, editor*
Wilcauskas, Eugene *chemicals executive*

Douglaston
Costa, Ernest Fiorenzo *graphic designer*
Helfat, Lucile *social services professional*

Dundee
Pfendt, Henry George *retired information systems executive, management consultant*

Dunkirk
Smith, Claire Laremont *language educator*

East Amherst
Bauer, Paul David *retired food service executive*
Soong, Tsu-Teh *engineering science educator*

East Aurora
Bingham, William *toy manufacturing executive*
Brott, Irving Deerin, Jr. *lawyer, judge*
Hawk, George Wayne *retired electronics company executive*
Hayes, Bonaventure Francis *priest*
Spahn, Mary Attea *retired educator*
Woodard, Carol Jane *educational consultant*

East Berne
Grenander, M. E. *English language educator, critic*

East Garden City
Baker, J. A., II *monetary architect, financial engineer*

East Hampton
Dalzell, Fred Briggs *financial consultant*
Damaz, Paul F. *architect*
De Bruhl, Marshall *writer, editor, publishing consultant*
Dello Joio, Norman *composer*
Garrett, Charles Geoffrey Blythe *physicist*
Ignatow, David *poet*
Jacobs, Helen Hull *former tennis player, writer*
Lassaw, Ibram *sculptor, painter*
Munson, Lawrence Shipley *management consultant*
Paxton, Tom *songwriter, entertainer, author*
Praetorius, William Albert, Sr. *artist, former advertising and real estate executive*
Richenburg, Robert Bartlett *artist, retired art educator*
Stein, Ronald Jay *artist, airline transport pilot*

East Islip
Fleishman, Philip Robert *internist*
Somerville, Daphine Holmes *elementary educator*

East Meadow
Adler, Ira Jay *lawyer*
Albert, Gerald *clinical psychologist*
Beyer, Norma Warren *secondary education educator*
†Fuchs, Jerome Herbert *management consultant*

East Northport
Hayo, George Edward *management consultant*
Reed, Robert Monroe *publishing executive*

East Rochester
†Gundlach, Robert William *physicist*
Murray, James Doyle *accountant*
Rauscher, Tomlinson Gene *electronics company executive, management consultant*

East Setauket
Briggs, Philip Terry *biologist*
Englebright, Steven Cale *assemblyman*
Layton, Billy Jim *composer*
Thom, Joseph M. *librarian*

East Syracuse
Duffy, Nancy Keogh *television broadcast professional*
Landsberg, Dennis Robert *engineering executive, consultant*

Eatons Neck
Altner, Peter Christian *orthopedic surgeon, medical educator*

Edmeston
Price, James Melford *physician*
†Robinson, D. Theodore *insurance company executive*
†Robinson, Van Ness D. *insurance company executive*

Elizabethtown
Davis, George Donald *land use policy consultant*
Lawrence, Richard Wesley, Jr. *foundation administrator*

Ellenville
Baer, Albert Max *metal products executive*
Straus, R. Peter *communications company executive, broadcasting executive*

Elmhurst
Lester, Lance Gary *education educator, researcher*
Wachsteter, George *illustrator*

Elmira
Burke, Rita Hoffmann *educational administrator*
Farley, H. Fred *nursing educator*
Hall, Geraldine Cristofaro *biology educator*
Kintz, Ronald Joseph *hospital financial executive, treasurer*
Meier, Thomas Keith *college president, English educator*
Orsillo, James Edward *computer systems engineer, company executive*

Elmont
Cusack, Thomas Joseph *banker*
Stephens, Woodford Cefis (Woody Stephens) *horse trainer, breeder*

Elmsford
Bostin, Marvin Jay *hospital and health services consultant*
Bouw, Pieter *airline company executive*
Caswell, Hollis Leland *computer company executive, electrical engineer*
Shaviv, Eddie *marketing and sales executive*
Sklarew, Robert Jay *biomedical research educator, consultant*

Endicott
Murray, Charles Coursen *footwear manufacturing and retail company executive*

Endwell
Wagner, Peter Ewing *physics and electrical engineering educator*

Erieville
Snodgrass, W. D. *writer, educator*

Esopus
Tetlow, Edwin *author*

Fairport
Haylett, Margaret Wendy *television director, engineer*
Oldshue, James Y. *chemical engineering consultant*
Van Bortel, Howard Martin *automarketing consultant*

Far Rockaway
Kelly, George Anthony *clergyman, author, educator*

Farmingdale
Blum, Melvin *chemical company executive, researcher*
Bolle, Donald Martin *engineering educator*
Bongiorno, Joseph John, Jr. *electrical engineering educator*
Cipriani, Frank Anthony *college president*
Dordelman, William Forsyth *food company executive*
Engelhardt, Dean Lee *biotechnology company executive*
Goodstein, Edward Marc *communications executive*
Guggenheimer, Heinrich Walter *mathematician, educator*
†Hinkaty, Charles John *drug company executive*
Horowitz, Sidney *manufacturing executive*
Klosner, Jerome Martin *mechanical engineer, educator*
Kostanoski, John Ivan *criminal justice educator*

Lamberg, Stanley Lawrence medical technologist, educator
LaTourrette, James Thomas retired electrical engineering and computer science educator
Marcuvitz, Nathan electrophysics educator
Marshall, Clifford Wallace mathematics educator
Nolan, Peter John physics educator
Smith, Joseph Seton electronics company executive, consultant
Steckler, Larry publisher, editor

Fayetteville
Cantwell, John Dalzell, Jr. management consultant
Dosanjh, Darshan S(ingh) aeronautical engineer, educator
Evans, Nolly Seymour lawyer
Pachter, Irwin Jacob pharmaceutical consultant
Pulos, Arthur Jon industrial design executive
Sager, Roderick Cooper retired life insurance company executive
Sears, Bradford George landscape architect
Wallace, Spencer Miller, Jr. hotel executive

Feura Bush
Byrne, Donn Erwin psychologist, educator

Floral Park
Chatoff, Michael Alan legal editor
Corbett, William John government and public relations consultant, lawyer
Goldstein, George A. school system administrator
Heyderman, Mark Baron sales and marketing company executive
Moskowitz, Stanley Alan financial executive
Scricca, Diane Bernadette principal
Weinrib, Sidney retired optometric and optical products and services executive

Florida
Bronstein, David G. food products executive
Koppele, Gary S. food service executive
Madera, Cornelius J. J., Jr. supermarket chain executive, lawyer, mayor
Mench, John William retail store executive, electrical engineer
Rosenberg, A. Richard supermarket company executive
Rosenberg, William supermarket company executive

Flushing
Allen, Ralph Gilmore dramatist, producer, drama educator
Birnstiel, Charles consulting engineer
Bonilla, Bobby (Roberto Martin Antonio Bonilla) professional baseball player
Boylan, Elizabeth Shippee biology educator, academic administrator
Bruder, Harold Jacob artist, educator
Brush, George W. college president
Carlson, Cynthia Joanne artist, educator
Cashen, J. Frank professional baseball team executive
Cathcart, Robert Stephen mass media consultant
Chabora, Peter Christian academic administrator, researcher, educator
Commoner, Barry biologist, educator
Cooke, Constance Blandy librarian
†Cooper, Marianne (Abonyi Cooper) librarian, educator
Curzio, Francis Xavier finance company executive
Diehl, Stephen Anthony banker
Doubleday, Nelson professional baseball team executive
Dubocq, Carole Ann nursing administrator
Dubov, Spencer Floyd podiatrist, educator
Ellis, John Taylor pathologist, educator
Farkas, Edward Barrister airport program/project manager, engineer
Fichtel, Rudolph Robert retired association executive
Finks, Robert Melvin paleontologist, educator
Friedman, Alan Jacob museum director
Gafney, Harry D. chemistry educator
Goldman, Norman Lewis chemistry educator
Goldsmith, Howard writer, consultant
Grace, Richard Anthony construction company executive
Green, Dallas (George Dallas Green) professional baseball team manager
Grossman, Julius conductor
Hacker, Andrew political science educator
Hatcher, Robert Douglas physicist, educator
Henshel, Harry Bulova watch manufacturer
Hirshson, Stanley Philip history educator
Hoffman, Merle Holly political activist, social psychologist, author
Johnson, Thomas Stephen banker
Kaplan, Stephen parapsychologist
Kiner, Ralph McPherran sports commentator, former baseball player
Kornhauser, Stanley Henry medical administrator, educator, consultant
Laderman, Gabriel artist
Lamont, Rosette Clementine Romance languages educator, theatre journalist, translator
Lee, Paul Ching-Lai banker, real estate developer
Madden, Joseph Daniel trade association executive
Mendelson, Elliott mathematician, educator
Michael, Carola designer, weaver
Moriarty, Michael actor
Nelson, Ralph Lowell economics educator
Nicotra, Joseph Charles artist
Parmet, Herbert Samuel historian, educator
Patai, Raphael former anthropology educator
Psomiades, Harry John political science educator
Rabassa, Gregory Romance languages educator, translator
Rafanelli, Kenneth Robert physics educator
Saberhagen, Bret William professional baseball player
Sanborn, Anna Lucille pension and insurance consultant
Schnall, Edith Lea (Mrs. Herbert Schnall) microbiologist, educator
Sessoms, Allen Lee academic administrator, former diplomat, physicist
Shen, Ronger artist, Qigong educator
Smaldone, Edward Michael composer
†Smith, Charles William social sciences educator, sociologist
Speidel, David Harold geology educator
Stahl, Frank Ludwig civil engineer
Sutherland, Alan Roy association executive
Tytell, John humanities educator, writer
Valero, René Arnold clergyman
Vasilachi, Gheorghe Vasile priest, vicar
Wilpon, Fred real estate developer, baseball team executive
Wolz, Henry George philosophy educator

Fly Creek
Dusenbery, Walter Condit sculptor

Forest Hills
Crystal, Boris artist
Gayner, Esther K. artist
LeFrak, Richard Stone real estate developer
Lipkin, Seymour pianist, conductor, educator
Miller, Donald Ross management consultant
Phelan, Arthur Joseph financial executive
Pinto, Rosalind retired educator, civic volunteer
Polakoff, Abe baritone
Prager, Alice Heinecke music company executive
Rogers, Philip Virgilius, Jr. headmaster
Silver, Sheila Jane composer, music educator
Stinson, Richard James editor
Tewi, Thea sculptor

Fort Covington
Dunwich, Gerina magazine editor, author, astrologer, witch

Franklin Square
Doyle, Will Lee writer, editor
Indiviglia, Salvatore Joseph artist, retired naval officer

Fredonia
Barnard, Walther M. geosciences educator
Benton, Allen Haydon biology educator
Dowd, Morgan Daniel political science educator
Jordan, Robert concert pianist, educator
MacPhee, Donald Albert academic administrator
Mac Vittie, Robert William retired college administrator
Sonnenfeld, Marion linguist, educator

Freeport
Pullman, Maynard Edward biochemist
Terris, Albert metal sculptor

Fresh Meadows
Ganz, Samuel human resource and management professional

Friendship
Kingdon, Mary Oneida Grace elementary education educator

Fulton
Long, Robert Emmet author

Garden City
Accordino, Frank Joseph architect, car rental company executive
Bovino, Charles Anthony rental car company executive, lawyer
Conlon, Thomas James marketing executive
Cook, George Valentine lawyer
Corsi, Philip Donald lawyer
†Covich, Frank J. business transfer consultant
Crom, James Oliver professional training company executive
De Mille, Nelson Richard writer
Desch, Carl William banker, consultant
Diamandopoulos, Peter philosopher, educator
Doucette, Mary-Alyce computer company executive
Feingold, Ronald Sherwin physical education educator
Fishberg, Gerard lawyer
Fleisig, Ross aeronautical engineer, engineering manager
Fristedt, Hans manufacturing company executive
Glass, Arthur L. mining company executive
Gordon, Barry Joel investment advisor
Gordon, Jay F(isher) lawyer
Guttenplan, Harold Esau food company executive
Harr, Alma Elizabeth Tagliabue nursing educator
Harwood, Stanley retired judge, lawyer
Jenkins, Kenneth Vincent literature educator, writer
Kane, Jeffrey academic dean
Korshak, Yvonne art historian
Krieger, Benjamin William paper company executive
Larocca, James Lawrence lawyer
Larsson, Hans Lennart match company executive
Lioz, Lawrence Stephen lawyer, accountant
†Lipka, David H. food company executive
Lovely, Thomas Dixon banker
Makapela, Alven history educator
Marlin, Jenesta banker
McNicholas, David Paul automobile rental company executive
Minicucci, Richard Francis lawyer, former hospital administrator
Nicklin, George Leslie, Jr. psychoanalyst, educator, physician
Ohrenstein, Roman Abraham economics educator, economist, rabbi
Okulski, John Allen principal
Olcott, William Alfred magazine editor
Roche, John Edward human resources management consultant, educator
Shirk, Evelyn Urban retired philosophy educator
Shneidman, J. Lee historian, educator
Tucker, William Philip lawyer, writer
Vigilante, Joseph Louis social worker, social policy educator
Vittoria, Joseph V. car rental company executive
Webb, Igor Michael university administrator
Westermann, David lawyer, educator, electronics industry executive
Williams, Irving Laurence physics educator
Zirkel, Gene computer science educator and mathematics

Gardiner
Mabee, Carleton historian, educator

Garrison
Chasins, Edward A. communications company executive
Egan, Daniel Francis priest
Pierpont, Robert fund raising executive, consultant

Geneseo
Battersby, Harold Ronald anthropologist, archaeologist, linguist
Edgar, William John philosophy educator
Fausold, Martin Luther history educator
Forest, Herman Silva biology educator
Hickman, John Hampton, III entrepreneurial investment banker, industrialist, educator
Moore, Gary Alan economist
Small, William Andrew mathematics educator

Geneva
Berta, Joseph Michel music educator, musician
Caponegro, Mary English language educator
Hersh, Richard H. academic administrator
Roelofs, Wendell Lee biochemistry educator, consultant
Roenke, Henry Merrill, Jr. curator
Siebert, Karl Joseph food science educator, consultant
Wilcox, Wayne F. plant pathologist, educator, researcher

Germantown
Rollins, (Theodore) Sonny composer, musician

Gilbertsville
Roos, Casper actor

Glen Cove
Burnham, Harold Arthur pharmaceutical company executive, physician
Casem, Conrado Sibayan civil, structural engineer
Conti, James Joseph chemical engineer, educator
Dehn, Joseph William, Jr. chemist
Deming, Donald Livingston lawyer
Greenberg, Allan advertising and marketing research consultant
Krasnoff, Abraham business executive
Maxwell, J. Douglas, Jr. chemical service company executive
Mills, Charles Gardner lawyer

Glen Head
Boyrer, Elaine M. principal
Cohen, Lawrence N. health care management consultant
Feinberg, Irwin L. retired manufacturing company executive
†Sutherland, Denise Jackson ballerina
Sutherland, Donald James investment company executive

Glen Oaks
Ryan, Therese Eileen nursing administrator

Glendale
Hess, Karsten trading company executive
Maltese, Serphin Ralph state senator, lawyer
†Peetz-Larsen, Hans trading company executive

Glenham
Douglas, Fred Robert cost engineering consultant

Glenmont
Block, Murray Harold educational consultant
Kolb, Lawrence Coleman psychiatrist
Robillard, Donald J. elementary school principal

Glens Falls
Allard, Edward F. engineering company executive
Bartlett, Richard James lawyer, former university dean
Bitner, William Lawrence, III retired banker, educator
†Carota, Richard J. paper company executive
Malkki, Olli paper company executive
McMillen, Robert Stewart lawyer

Glenville
Anderson, Roy Everett electrical engineering consultant

Goldens Bridge
Ambrose, Daniel Michael publishing executive

Goshen
Goodreds, John Stanton newspaper publisher
Hall, Wanda Jean mental health professional, consultant
Ward, William Francis, Jr. real estate investment banker

Grand Island
Rader, Charles George chemical company executive
White, Ralph David retired editor and writer

Great Neck
Arlow, Jacob A. psychiatrist, educator
Brand, Oscar folksinger, author, educator
Busner, Philip H. lawyer, arbitrator, judge
Donenfeld, Kenneth Jay management consultant
Elkowitz, Lloyd Kent dental anesthesiologist, dentist, pharmacist
Fialkov, Herman investment banker
Fiel, Maxine Lucille journalist, behavioral analyst, lecturer
Friedland, Louis N. retired communications executive
Gellman, Yale H. lawyer
Gillett, Charles travel executive
Glushien, Morris P. lawyer, arbitrator
Goldberg, Melvin Arthur communications executive
Green, Dan publishing company executive
Hamovitch, William economist, educator, university official
Hampton, Benjamin Bertram brokerage house executive
Harris, Rosalie psychotherapist, clinical counselor, Spanish language professional and multi-linguist, English as second language educator
Hurwitz, Johanna (Frank) author, librarian
Joskow, Jules economic research company executive
Katz, Edward Morris banker
Kraft, Leo Abraham composer
Lampel, Ronald B. human resources executive
Lees, Benjamin composer
Levy, Joel N. financial executive
Machiz, Leon electronic equipment manufacturing executive
Mc Quade, Walter author
Panes, Jack Samuel publishing company executive
Pohl, Gunther Erich retired library administrator
Pollack, Paul Robert airline service company executive
Roth, Harvey Paul publisher
Rubin, Irving editor
Samanowitz, Ronald Arthur lawyer
Satinskas, Henry Anthony airline services company executive
Seidler, Doris artist
Shaffer, Bernard William mechanical and aerospace engineering educator
Simon, Arthur pharmacologist, research laboratory executive
Turofsky, Charles Sheldon landscape architect
Unger, Robert Martin lawyer, author, professional speaker, singer
Velie, Lester journalist
Wachsman, Harvey Frederick lawyer, neurosurgeon
Wank, Gerald Sidney periodontist
Zirinsky, Daniel real estate investor and photographer

Greece
Ryan-Johnson, Deborah principal

Greene
Raymond, George Gamble, Jr. material handling equipment company executive
Sternberg, Paul J. lawyer

Greenfield Center
Conant, Robert Scott harpsichordist, music educator
Fonseca, John dos Reis writer, former law educator
Templin, John Leon, Jr. healthcare consulting executive

Greenlawn
Bachman, Henry Lee electrical engineer, engineering executive
Engle, Merle L. manufacturing executive
†Newman, Edward M. engineering executive
Stevens, John Richard architectural historian

Greenport
Breeze, Roger Gerrard federal agency administrator

Greenvale
Araoz, Daniel Leon psychologist, educator
Cook, Edward Joseph college president
Gillespie, John Thomas university administrator
Halper, Emanuel B(arry) real estate lawyer, developer, consultant, author
Leipzig, Arthur photographer, educator emeritus
Pall, David B. manufacturing company executive, chemist
†Shields, Joan E. chemistry educator
Steinberg, David Joel academic administrator, historian, educator

Greenwich
Leone, Louis J. marketing and communications executive

Greenwood
Rollins, June Elizabeth elementary education educator

Guilderland
Gordon, Leonard Victor psychologist, educator emeritus
Persico, Joseph Edward author

Hamburg
Killeen, Henry Walter lawyer

Hamilton
Appley, Lawrence A. business executive
Aveni, Anthony Francis astronomy and anthropology educator, researcher
Bergen, Daniel Patrick librarian, retired educator
Berlind, Bruce Peter poet, educator
Blackton, Charles S(tuart) history educator
†Blackton, John Stuart diplomat
Busch, Briton Cooper historian
Busch, Frederick Matthew writer, literature educator
Cappeto, Michael Arnold educator
Carter, John Ross philosophy and religion educator
Cochran, John Charles chemistry educator
DeBoer, George Edward education educator
Dovidio, John Francis psychology educator
Edmonston, William Edward, Jr. publisher
Farnsworth, Frank Albert economics educator
Garland, Robert Sandford John classical studies educator
†Grabois, Neil Robert college president
Hathaway, Robert Lawton Romance languages educator
Hoffmann, Dierk Otto German language educator
Holbrow, Charles Howard physicist, educator
Johnston, (William) Michael political science educator, university administrator
Jones, Frank William language educator
Jones, Howard Langworthy educational administrator, consultant
Kessler, Dietrich biology educator
Kraynak, Robert political science educator
Lantz, David Carson mathematics educator
Levy, Jacques educator, theater director, lyricist, writer
Linsley, Robert Martin retired geology educator
Little, Daniel Eastman philosophy educator, associate dean
Loveless, James King art educator
Nakhimovsky, Alice Stone foreign language educator
Nevison, Christopher Harry computer science educator
Noyes, Judith Gibson library director
Pownall, Malcolm Wilmor mathematics educator
Staley, Lynn English educator
Tucker, Thomas William mathematics professor
Van Schaack, Eric art historian, educator

Hampton Bays
Yavitz, Boris business educator and dean emeritus

Hancock
DeLuca, Ronald consultant, former advertising agency executive

Harrison
Fuchs, Hanno communications consultant
Herrick, Doris Eileen Schlesinger sports association administrator
Krantz, Melissa Marianne public relations company executive
McCaffrey, Neil publishing executive
Mc Coy, William Daniel manufacturing executive
Serenbetz, Warren Lewis financial management company executive

Wadsworth, Frank Whittemore *foundation executive, literature educator*

Hartsdale
Carroll, Albert *corporate executive*
Gillingham, Stephen Thomas *financial planner*
Katz, John *investment banker, business consultant, lawyer*

Hastings On Hudson
Clark, Kenneth Bancroft *psychologist, educator*
Shillinglaw, Gordon *accounting educator, consultant, writer*
Weil, Edward David *chemist*
Weinstein, Edward Michael *architect, consultant*
Wolfe, Stanley *composer, educator*

Hauppauge
Arams, Frank Robert *electronics company executive*
Carpenter, Angie M. *small business owner, editor*
†Costa, Pat Vincent *automation sciences executive*
Hausman, Howard *electronics executive*
Hershberg, David E. *communications corporation executive*
Hurley, Denis R. *federal judge*
Katz, Burton *electronics distribution company executive*
Miller, Kenneth Allen *electrical engineer*
Miller, Ronald M. *manufacturing executive*
Oschmann, Joan Edythe *gifted and elementary education educator*
Reich, William Michael *advertising executive*
Reis, Don *publishing executive*
Shalam, John Joseph *car stereo and cellular telephone company executive*
Stemple, Joel Gilbert *computer company executive*
Vignola, William J. *communications executive*
Wexler, Leonard D. *federal judge*

Hawthorne
†Batstone, Joanna L. *computer scientist*
Hooley, Robert Childs *banker*
McConnell, John Edward *electrical engineer, company executive*
Press, Jeffery Bruce *chemist*
Sandbank, Henry *photographer, film director*
Swift, Michael Ronald *physician, scientist, educator*

Hempstead
Adams, Robert Hugo *business news publisher, English teacher*
Agata, Burton C. *lawyer, educator*
Altimari, Frank X. *federal judge*
Andrews, Charles Rolland *library administrator*
Berliner, Herman Albert *university provost and dean, economics educator*
Block, Jules Richard *psychologist, educator, university official*
Chapman, Ronald Thomas *musician, educator*
Esiason, Boomer (Norman Julius Esiason) *professional football player*
Freedman, Monroe Henry *lawyer, educator*
Freese, Melanie Louise *librarian, professor*
Goldstein, Stanley Philip *engineering educator*
Gutman, Steve *professional football team executive*
Haynes, Ulric St. Clair, Jr. *university dean*
Hextall, Ron *professional hockey player*
Hijuelos, Oscar *novelist*
Kotite, Rich *professional football coach*
Laano, Archie Bienvenido Maaño *cardiologist*
Lewis, Mo *professional football player*
Lowery, Dominic Gerald (Nick) *professional football player*
Mahon, Malachy Thomas *lawyer, educator*
Maier, Henry B. *environmental engineer*
Masheck, Joseph Daniel *art critic, educator*
Montana, Patrick Joseph *management educator*
Pell, Arthur Robert *human resources development consultant, author*
Regan, John J. *law educator*
Roble, Carole Marcia *accountant*
Shuart, James Martin *university president*
Sparberg, Esther B. *chemist, educator*
Steinberg, Dick *professional football team executive*
Turgeon, Edgar Lynn *economics educator*
Wattel, Harold Louis *economics educator*

Henrietta
Carmel, Simon J(acob) *anthropologist*
Snyder, Donald Edward *corporate executive*

Herkimer
Mitchell, Donald J. *former congressman*

Hewlett
Dalrymple, Richard William *banker*
Kislik, Louis A. *marketing company executive*
Large, James Mifflin, Jr. *banker*
Wolff, Eleanor Blunk *actress*

Hicksville
Calabrese, Alphonse Francis Xavier *psychotherapist*
Kneitel, Thomas Stephen *writer, consultant, editor*
O'Flaherty, Lucy Louise *secondary education educator*
Salsberg, Arthur Philip *publishing company executive*
Tinghitella, Stephen *publishing company executive*
Walsh, Charles Richard *banker*

Highland
Rosenberger, David A. *research scientist, cooperative extension specialist*

Hillsdale
Richards, Joseph Edward *artist*

Hilton
Scutt, Ed *English language educator*

Holbrook
Lissman, Barry Alan *veterinarian*

Holland
Blair, Robert Noel *artist*

Hollis
Vai, Steve *guitarist*

Homer
Gustafson, John Alfred *biology educator*
†Twentyman, Lee *foreign service officer, economist*

Hoosick Falls
Dodge, Cleveland Earl, Jr. *manufacturing executive*
Hatfield, David Underhill *artist*

Hopewell Junction
†Mohammad, Shaikh Noor *electronics engineer, educator*
Walden, Stanley Eugene *composer, clarinetist*

Horseheads
Cusimano, Adeline Mary *educational administrator*
Huffman, Patricia Joan *accounting coordinator*
Mortimer, Garth Eugene *mathematics educator*

Houghton
Chamberlain, Daniel Robert *college president*
Luckey, Robert Reuel Raphael *retired academic administrator*

Howard Beach
Berliner, Patricia Mary *psychologist*
Krein, Catherine Cecilia *public relations professional*

Hudson Falls
Bronk, William *writer, retail businessman*

Hunter
Jaeckel, Christopher Carol *memorablia company executive, antiquarian*

Huntington
Augello, William Joseph *lawyer*
Bendiner, Robert *writer, editor*
Christiansen, Donald David *engineer, editor, publishing consultant*
Connor, Joseph Robert *editor*
Coraor, John Edward *museum director*
D'Addario, Alice Marie *school administrator*
Glickstein, Howard Alan *law educator*
Hayden, Ralph Frederick *accountant, financial consultant*
Holahan, Richard Vincent *former magazine and book publisher*
Jackson, Richard Montgomery *former airline executive*
Jordan, Daniel Patrick, Jr. *law librarian*
Munson, Nancy Kay *lawyer*
Myers, Robert Jay *retired aerospace company executive*
Noll, Anna Cecilia *curator*
Papoulis, Athanasios *electrical engineering educator*
Pratt, George Cheney *law educator, retired federal judge*
Schulz, William Frederick *human rights association executive*
Twardowicz, Stanley Jan *artist, photographer*
Vale, Margo Rose *physician*

Huntington Station
Agosta, Vito *mechanical/aerospace engineering educator*
Braun, Ludwig *educational technology consultant*
Lanzano, Ralph Eugene *civil engineer*
Liguori, Frank Nickolas *temporary personnel company executive*
Pierce, Charles R. *electric company consultant*
Schell, Jonathan Edward *writer*
Schoenfeld, Michael P. *lawyer*

Hyde Park
Dayson, Diane Harris *superintendent, park ranger*
Newton, Verne Wester *library director*

Interlaken
Bleiler, Everett Franklin *writer, publishing company executive*

Irvington
Angelakis, Manos G(eorge) *filmmaker, communications executive*
Devons, Samuel *educator, physicist*
Evans, Bruce Max *foundation executive*
Holden, Donald *author, artist*
Lugenbeel, Edward Elmer *publisher*
Massie, Robert Kinloch *author*
Steinberg, James Ian *marketing executive*
Turk, Stanley Martin *advertising agency executive*
Wolf, Eric Robert *anthropologist, educator*

Island
Kaslick, Ralph Sidney *dentist, educator*

Islandia
Wang, Charles B. *computer software company executive*

Islip
Muuss, John *public safety and emergency management executive*

Islip Terrace
Hartley-Leonard, Darryl *hotel company executive*

Ithaca
Abrams, Meyer Howard *English language educator*
Adler, Kraig (Kerr) *biology educator*
Alexander, Gregory Stewart *law educator*
Alexander, Martin *microbiology educator, researcher*
Ammons, Archie Randolph *poet, English educator*
Anderson, Benedict Richard O'Gorman *political science educator*
Arntzen, Charles Joel *bioscience educator*
Ascher, Robert *anthropologist, archaeologist, educator, filmmaker*
Ashcroft, Neil William *physics educator, researcher*
Bail, Joe Paul *agricultural educator emeritus*
Barcelo, John James, III *law educator*
Barker, Robert *biochemistry educator*
Barney, John Charles *lawyer*
Bassett, William Akers *geologist, educator*
Bates, David Martin *botanist, educator*
Batterman, Boris William *physicist, educator, academic director*
Bauer, Simon Harvey *chemistry educator*
Bauman, Dale Elton *nutritional biochemistry educator*
Ben Daniel, David Jacob *entrepreneurship educator, consultant*
†Beneria, Lourdes *sociologist, educator*
Berger, Toby *electrical engineer*
Bergstrom, Gary Carlton *physiologist*
Berkelman, Karl *physics educator*
Bethe, Hans Albrecht *physicist, educator*
Blackler, Antonie William Charles *biologist*
Blau, Francine Dee *economics educator*
Booker, John Franklin *mechanical engineer, educator*
Bourne, Russell *publisher, author*
Bramble, James Henry *mathematician, educator*
Brazell, Karen Woodard *Japanese literature educator*
Briggs, Vernon Mason, Jr. *economics educator*
Bronfenbrenner, Urie *psychologist*
Brown, Theodore Morey *art history educator*
Brunk, Max Edwin *marketing educator emeritus*
Burns, Joseph Arthur *planetary science educator*
Call, David Lincoln *agricultural economics educator, administrator*
Caputi, Anthony *comparative literature educator*
Carlin, Herbert J. *electrical engineering educator, researcher*
Carpenter, Barry Keith *chemistry educator, researcher*
Caughey, David Alan *engineering educator, researcher*
†Clardy, Jon Christel *chemistry educator, consultant*
Clark, David Delano *physicist, educator*
Clermont, Kevin Michael *law educator*
Coffman, William Ronnie *plant breeding educator*
Colby-Hall, Alice Mary *Romance studies educator*
Conway, Richard Walter *computer scientist, educator*
Cooke, William Donald *university administrator, chemistry educator*
Corson, Dale Raymond *retired university president, physicist*
Cotton, Dorothy Foreman *former director student activities, consultant*
Craft, Harold Dumont, Jr. *university official, radio astronomer*
Craighead, Harold G. *physics educator*
Cramton, Roger Conant *lawyer, legal educator*
Crepet, William Louis *botanist, educator*
Culler, Jonathan Dwight *English language educator*
Dalman, Gisli Conrad *electrical engineering educator*
Darlington, Richard Benjamin *psychology educator*
Davies, Peter John *plant physiology educator, researcher*
De Boer, Pieter Cornelis Tobias *mechanical and aerospace engineering educator*
Dick, Richard Irwin *environmental engineer, educator*
Dietert, Rodney Reynolds *immunology/toxicology educator*
Dobson, Alan *veterinary physiology educator*
Dodd, Jack Gordon, Jr. *physicist, educator*
Dworsky, Leonard B. *civil and environmental engineer, educator*
Dyckman, Thomas Richard *accounting educator*
Earle, Clifford John, Jr. *mathematician*
Earle, Elizabeth Deutsch *biology educator*
Easley, David *economics educator*
Eastman, Lester Fuess *electrical engineer, educator*
Eddy, Donald Davis *English language educator*
Eisenberg, Theodore *law educator*
Eisner, Thomas *biologist, educator*
Elledge, Scott Bowen *language professional, educator*
Elliot, John *accountant, educator*
Farley, Jennie Tiffany Towle *industrial and labor relations educator*
Fay, Robert Clinton *chemist, educator*
Fick, Gary Warren *agronomy educator, forage crops researcher*
Finch, C. Herbert *archivist, library administrator, historian*
Fine, Terrence Leon *electrical engineering and statistics educator*
Firebaugh, Francille Maloch *university official*
Fireside, Harvey Francis *political scientist, educator*
Fitchen, Douglas Beach *physicist, educator*
Fleischmann, Hans Hermann Paul *physics educator*
Foote, Robert Hutchinson *animal physiology educator*
Forker, Olan Dean *agricultural economics educator*
Fox, Francis Henry *veterinarian*
Fréchet, Jean Marie Joseph *chemistry educator*
Freed, Jack Herschel *chemist, educator*
Fuchs, Wolfgang Heinrich *mathematics educator*
Geller, A. Neal *business educator, financial consultant*
George, Albert Richard *aerospace and mechanical engineering educator*
†Germain, Claire Madeleine *law librarian, educator*
Gibian, George *Russian and comparative literature educator*
Gibson, Quentin Howieson *biochemist*
Gierasch, Peter Jay *astronomy educator*
Gilbert, Robert Owen *veterinary educator, researcher*
Gillespie, James Howard *veterinary microbiologist, educator*
Gillett, James Warren *toxicologist*
Giovanelli, Riccardo *astronomer*
Glock, Marvin David *retired psychology educator*
Gold, Daniel *religious studies educator*
Gold, Thomas *astronomer, educator*
Goldsmith, Paul Felix *physics and astronomy educator*
Goldsmith, William Woodbridge *city and regional planning educator*
Gottfried, Kurt *physicist, educator*
Green, Nancy Elizabeth *curator, writer*
Greisen, Kenneth Ingvard *physicist, emeritus educator*
Gries, David Joseph *computer science researcher, educator*
Grippi, Salvatore William *artist*
Groos, Arthur Bernhard, Jr. *German literature educator*
Grunes, David Leon *research soil scientist, educator, editor*
Gubbins, Keith Edmund *chemical engineering educator*
Guckenheimer, John *mathematician*
†Haas, Jere Douglas *nutritional sciences educator, researcher*
Habicht, Jean-Pierre *public health researcher, educator, consultant*
Hairston, Nelson George, Jr. *ecologist, educator*
Halpern, Bruce Peter *physiologist, consultant*
Hammond, Jane Laura *retired law librarian, lawyer*
Hardy, Ralph W. F. *biochemist, biotechnology executive*
Hardy, Ralph Wilbur Frederick *science administrator, biochemist, molecular biologist*
Hart, Edward Walter *physicist*
Hartmanis, Juris *computer scientist, educator*
Hay, George Alan *law and economics educator*
Haynes, Martha Patricia *astronomer*
Heath, David Clay *mathematics educator, consultant*
Henderson, James A., Jr. *law educator*
Hess, George Paul *biochemist, educator*
Hillman, Robert Andrew *law educator, university dean*
Hockett, Charles Francis *anthropology educator*
Hoffmann, Roald *chemist, educator*
Hohendahl, Peter Uwe *German language and literature educator*
Holcomb, Donald Frank *physicist, academic administrator*
Hopcroft, John Edward *dean, computer science educator*
†Howell, Bonnie Howard *hospital administrator*
Hsu, John Tseng Hsin *music educator, cellist, gambist, barytonist, conductor*
Husa, Karel Jaroslav *composer, conductor, educator*
Isard, Walter *economics educator*
Isen, Alice M. *experimental social psychologist, behavioral science educator*
Jagendorf, Andre Tridon *plant physiologist*
Jarrow, Robert Alan *finance and economics educator, consultant*
Kahin, George McTurnan *political science and history educator*
Kahn, Alfred Edward *economist, educator, government official*
Kallfelz, Francis A. *veterinary medicine educator*
Kammen, Michael *historian, educator*
Katz, Steven Theodore *religion studies educator*
Kendler, Bernhard *editor*
Kennedy, Kenneth Adrian Raine *biological anthropologist, forensic anthropologist*
Kennedy, Wilbert Keith, Sr. *agronomy educator, retired university official*
Kent, Robert Brydon *law educator*
Kingsbury, John Merriam *botanist, educator*
Kirsch, A(nthony) Thomas *anthropology and Asian studies educator, researcher*
†Korf, Richard Paul *mycology educator*
Kramer, Edward John *materials science and engineering educator*
Kramer, John Paul *entomologist, educator*
Kramnick, Isaac *government educator*
Kronik, John William *Romance studies educator*
Kubiak, John Michael *academic administrator*
Kubota, Joe *soil scientist*
LaCapra, Dominick Charles *historian*
LaFeber, Walter Frederick *history educator, author*
Lambert, William Wilson *psychology educator*
†Law, Gordon Theodore, Jr. *library director*
Ledford, Richard Allison *food science educator, food microbiologist*
Lee, David Morris *physics educator*
Leibovich, Sidney *engineering educator*
Lengemann, Frederick William *physiology educator, scientist*
Lesser, William Henri *marketing educator*
Liboff, Richard Lawrence *physicist, educator*
Little, George Daniel *clergyman*
Longin, Thomas Charles *academic administrator*
Loucks, Daniel Peter *environmental systems engineer*
Lowi, Theodore J(ay) *political science educator*
Lumley, John Leask *physicist, educator*
Lurie, Alison *author*
Lust, Barbara C. *psychology and linguistics educator*
Lynn, Walter Royal *civil engineering educator, university administrator*
Lyons, Thomas Patrick *economics educator*
Maas, James Beryl *psychology educator, lecturer, filmmaker*
Martin, Peter William *lawyer, educator*
Maxwell, William Laughlin *industrial engineering educator*
McConkey, James Rodney *English educator, writer*
McDaniel, Boyce Dawkins *physicist, educator*
Mc Guire, William *civil engineer, educator*
McIsaac, Paul Rowley *electrical engineer, educator*
McLafferty, Fred Warren *chemist, educator*
McMurry, John Edward *chemistry educator*
Meinwald, Jerrold *chemist, educator*
Mermin, N. David *physicist, educator, essayist*
Merten, Alan Gilbert *university dean*
Meyburg, Arnim Hans *transportation engineer, educator, consultant*
Mikus, Eleanore Ann *artist*
Miller, J(ames) Gormly *retired librarian, educator*
Moore, Charles Hewes, Jr. *industrial and engineered products executive*
Moore, Norman Slawson *physician*
Morrison, George Harold *chemist, educator*
Mortlock, Robert Paul *microbiologist, educator*
Mueller, Betty Jeanne *social work educator*
Murra, John Victor *anthropologist, educator*
Nesheim, Malden C. *university administrator*
†Niklas, Karl J. *plant biology educator*
Norton, Mary Beth *history educator, author*
Novak, Joseph Donald *science educator, knowlege studies specialist*
Oblak, John Byron *academic administrator*
Oglesby, Ray Thurmond *aquatic science educator*
Oliver, Jack Ertle *geophysicist*
Orear, Jay *physics educator, researcher*
O'Rourke, Thomas Denis *civil engineer, educator*
Osgood, Russell King *law educator*
Palmer, Larry Isaac *lawyer, educator*
Park, Roy Hampton, Jr. *advertising media executive*
Parks, Thomas W. *electrical engineering educator, consultant*
Parsons, Kermit Carlyle *urban planning educator, former university dean*
Payne, Lawrence Edward *mathematics educator*
Phelan, Richard Magruder *mechanical engineer*
Phemister, Robert David *college dean*
Pimentel, David *entomologist, educator*
Plaisted, Robert Leroy *plant breeder, educator*
Pohl, Robert Otto *physics educator*
Polenberg, Richard *history educator*
Poleskie, Stephen Francis *artist, educator*
Pope, Stephen Bailey *engineering educator*
Poppensiek, George Charles *veterinary scientist, educator*
Porte, Joel Miles *English educator*
Porter, Michael R. *manufacturing executive*
Radzinowicz, Mary Ann *language educator*
Rawlings, Hunter Ripley, III *university administrator*
Rehkugler, Gerald Edwin *agricultural engineering educator, consultant*
Relihan, Walter J., Jr. *lawyer*
Rhodin, Thor Nathaniel *educational administrator*
Richardson, Robert Coleman *physics educator, researcher*
Roberts, E. F. *lawyer, educator*
Robinson, Franklin Westcott *museum director, art historian*
Rodríguez, Ferdinand *chemical engineer, educator*
Rossi, Faust F. *lawyer, educator*
Rossiter, Margaret Walsh *history of science educator*
Ruoff, Arthur Louis *physicist, educator*
Sagan, Carl Edward *astronomer, educator, author*

Salpeter, Edwin Ernest physical sciences educator
Salton, Gerard computer science educator
Saltzman, Sidney city and regional planning educator
Scammell, Michael foreign language educator, translator, writer
Scheraga, Harold Abraham physical chemistry educator
Scheuer, Katherine Dunn editor
Schlafer, Donald Hughes veterinary pathologist
Schwab, Stewart Jon law educator
Schwartz, Donald Franklin communication educator
Scott, Fredric Winthrop veterinarian
Scott, Norman Roy academic administrator, agricultural engineering educator
Seeley, Harry Wilbur, Jr. microbiology educator
Seibert, Mary Lee college official
Shell, Karl economics educator
Shiffrin, Steven H. law educator
Shoemaker, Sydney S. philosophy educator
Shore, Richard Arnold mathematics educator
Shuler, Michael Louis biochemical engineering educator, consultant
Sievers, Albert John, III physics educator
Silbey, Joel Henry history educator
Silcox, John physicist, educator
Sims, William Riley, Jr. design and facility management educator, consultant
Simson, Gary Joseph law educator
Skipper, James Everett librarian
Slate, Floyd Owen chemist, materials scientist, civil engineer, educator, researcher
Smith, Julian Cleveland, Jr. chemical engineering educator
Smith, Robert John anthropology educator
Smith, Robert Samuel banker, former agricultural finance educator
Squier, Jack Leslie sculptor, educator
Stamp, Neal Roger lawyer
Staples, Richard Cromwell microbiologist, researcher
Streett, William Bernard university dean, engineering educator
Strout, Sewall Cushing, Jr. humanities educator
Stycos, Joseph Mayone demographer, educator
Sudan, Ravindra Nath electrical engineer, physicist, educator
Summers, Robert Samuel lawyer, author, educator
Terzian, Yervant astronomy and astrophysics educator
Thaler, Richard H. economics educator
Thomas, J. Earl physicist
Thorbecke, Erik economics educator
Thorp, James Shelby electrical engineering educator
Tigner, Maurice physicist, educator
Tomek, William Goodrich agricultural economist
Torng, Hwa C. engineering educator, researcher
Trautmann, Charles Home museum director, civil engineer
Trotter, Leslie Earl operations research educator, consultant
Turcotte, Donald Lawson geophysical sciences educator
Tynes, Theodore Archibald educational administrator
Van Campen, Darrell Robert chemist
Vandenberg, John Donald entomologist
Vanek, Jaroslav economist, educator
Van Houtte, Raymond A. financial executive
Walcott, Charles neurobiology and behvior educator
Wang, Kuo-King manufacturing engineer, educator
Wasserman, Robert Harold biology educator
Webb, Watt Wetmore physicist, educator
Weinstein, Leonard Harlan institute program director
Welch, Ross Maynard plant physiologist, researcher, educator
Whalen, James Joseph college president
Whitaker, Susanne Kanis veterinary medical librarian
White, Richard Norman civil and environmental engineering educator
Whyte, William Foote industrial relations educator, author
Widom, Benjamin chemistry educator
Williams, David Vandergrift organizational psychologist
Williams, Leslie Pearce history educator
Williams, Robin Murphy, Jr. sociology educator
Wilson, Robert Rathbun retired physicist
Windmuller, John Philip industrial relations educator, consultant
Wolf, Edward Dean electrical engineering educator
Wootton, John Francis physiology educator
Wu, Ray Jui biochemistry educator
Zall, Robert Rouben food scientist, educator
Zilversmit, Donald Berthold nutritional biochemist, educator

Jackson Heights
Grebey, Clarence Raymond, Jr. airline executive
Schiavina, Laura Margaret artist
Sklar, Morty E. publisher, editor

Jamaica
Angione, Howard Francis lawyer, editor
Barry, J. Kevin librarian
Bartilucci, Andrew Joseph university administrator
Beard, Joseph James law educator
†Benson, James Allen library science educator, academic administrator
Berman, Richard Miles lawyer
Cade, Walter, III artist, musician, singer, actor
Clemmons, Ithiel bishop
Cline, Janice Claire education educator
Conway, Alvin James hospital administrator
Crivelli, Joseph Louis security specialist
Desser, Maxwell Milton artist, art director, filmstrip producer
Dragone, Allan R. manufacturing company executive
Etzel, Joseph Vincent pharmacy educator
Fay, Thomas A. philosopher, educator
Geffner, Donna Sue speech pathologist, audiologist
Greenberg, Jacob biochemist, educator, consultant
Hammer, Deborah Marie librarian
Harmond, Richard Peter historian, educator
Harrington, Donald James university president
Kay, Mary Ellen nurse
†Kelly, Robert airport executive
Lengyel, István chemist, educator
†Lin, Shu-Fang Hsia librarian
Mc Kinnon, Clinton Dan aerospace transportation executive
Melton, Marie Frances university dean
Paolucci, Anne Attura playwright, poet, English and comparative literature educator
†Prendergast, Thomas F. railroad executive
Re, Edward Domenic law educator, retired federal judge
Reams, Bernard Dinsmore, Jr. lawyer, educator
Rosner, Fred physician, educator
Rowe, Richard Lloyd aviation executive, management consultant
Sciame, Joseph university administrator
Strong, Gary Eugene librarian
Trepel, Mindy J. county official, lawyer
Tschinkel, Andrew Joseph, Jr. law librarian
Vasilopoulos, Athanasios V. engineering educator
Wetherington, Roger Vincent journalism educator, newspaper copy editor

Jamestown
Anderson, R. Quintus diversified company executive
Bargar, Robert Sellstrom investor
Benke, Paul Arthur college president
Goldman, Simon broadcasting executive
Idzik, Martin Francis lawyer
†Nauleau, Heidi A. holding company executive, metal products executive
Okwumabua, Benjamin Nkem corporate executive

Jamesville
DeCrow, Karen lawyer, author, lecturer
Mazer, Norma Fox writer
Morton, William Gilbert banker

Jeffersonville
Craft, Douglas Durwood artist
Harms, Elizabeth Louise artist
Wooddell, Philo Glenn fine arts educator, radio broadcaster and producer

Jericho
Astuto, Philip Louis retired Spanish educator
Axinn, Donald Everett real estate investor, developer
Berger, Charles Martin food company executive
Blau, Harvey Ronald lawyer
Fitteron, John Joseph petroleum products company executive
†Harris, Elaine K. medical consultant
Khan, Arfa radiologist, educator
†Liebowitz, Leo oil company executive
Mandery, Mathew M. principal
Martin, David S. educator, administrator
Rosen, Robert Arnold management company executive, real estate investor
Shinners, Stanley Marvin electrical engineer
Spivack, Henry Archer life insurance company executive

Johnson City
Aswad, Betsy (Betsy Becker) writer
Sargent, Pamela writer

Johnstown
Zinnecker, Robert Wallace telecommunications company executive

Katonah
Baker, John Milnes architect
Bashkow, Theodore Robert electrical engineering consultant, former educator
Fry, John magazine editor
Giobbi, Edward Giacchino artist
Krefting, Robert J(ohn) publishing company executive
Levine, Pamela Gail business owner
Raymond, Jack journalist, public relations executive, foundation executive
Simpson, William Kelly curator, Egyptologist, educator
Toney, Anthony artist
White, Harold Tredway, III management consultant

Keene
†Twichell, Chase poet

Kenmore
Schimminger, Robin state legislator
Vienne, Dorothy Titus school principal

Kew Gardens
Schnakenberg, Donald G. financial administrator
Silver, Jonathan lawyer

Kinderhook
Benamati, Dennis Charles law librarian, editor, consultant
Lankhof, Frederik Jan publishing executive

Kings Park
Calviello, Joseph Anthony research electrophysicist, consultant
Greene, Robert William media consultant
LoPresti, Marilyn Angela school system administrator
Smith, Norma Jane elementary education educator

Kings Point
Billy, George John library director
Bloom, Murray Teigh author
Matteson, Thomas T. academic administrator
Mazek, Warren F(elix) academic administrator, economics educator

Kingston
Agerwala, Tilak Krishna Mahesh computer company executive
Lanitis, Tony Andrew market researcher
Tsirpanlis, Constantine N. theology, classics and history educator

Lagrangeville
LaMont, Barbara Gibson librarian

Lake Placid
†Caguiat, Carlos Jose health care administrator, episcopal priest
Sato, Gordon Hisashi retired biologist, researcher

Lake Success
Fujii, Kenji medical equipment executive
Lee, Brian Edward lawyer

Lancaster
Neumaier, Gerhard John environment consulting company executive
Van Nortwick, Thomas H. radio broadcast executive
Weinberg, Norman Louis electrochemist

Larchmont
Aburdene, Odeh Felix banker
Bellak, Leopold psychiatrist, psychoanalyst, psychologist
Berridge, George Bradford retired lawyer
Bloom, Lee Hurley lawyer, public affairs consultant, retired household products manufacturing executive
Emery, Jonathan Willard lawyer
Engel, Ralph Manuel lawyer
Fletcher, Denise Koen strategic and financial consultant
Gallaher, Carolyn Combs secondary education educator
Gillman, Arthur Emanuel psychiatrist
Greenwald, Carol Schiro professional services marketing research executive
Hinerfeld, Ruth J. civic organization executive
Holleb, Arthur Irving surgeon
Josevie, Arnold Jean Phillipe physicist, scientific consultant
Kaufmann, Henry Mark mortgage banker
Kerr, Jean writer
Kerr, Walter F. retired drama critic, author
Levi, James Harry real estate executive, investment banker
Pelton, Russell Gilbert lawyer
Plumez, Jean Paul advertising agency executive, consultant
Rosenberg, Paul physicist, consultant
Schwatka, Mark Andrew advertising agency executive
Seton, Charles B. lawyer
Silverstone, David advertising executive
Sonneborn, Henry, III former chemical company executive, business consultant
Swire, Edith Wypler music educator, musician, violist, violinist
Tobey, Alton Stanley artist
Wielgus, Charles Joseph information services company executive

Laurel Hollow
Tantleff, Irwin food products executive

Lawrence
Sklarin, Burton S. endocrinologist
Wurzburger, Walter Samuel rabbi, philosophy educator

Levittown
Rubin, Arnold Jesse aeronautical engineer

Lewiston
Dexter, Theodore Henry chemist
Kennedy, G. Alfred federal agency administrator
Newlin, Lyman Wilbur bookseller, consultant

Lido Beach
Billauer, Barbara Pfeffer lawyer, educator

Lily Dale
Merrill, Joseph Hartwell religious association executive
Wittich, Brenda June religious organization executive, minister

Lima
Reynolds, Lewis Dayton administrator
Spencer, Ivan Carlton clergyman

Lindenhurst
Boltz, Mary Ann aerospace materials company executive, travel agency executive
Farrell-Logan, Vivian actress
Gentile, Patricia M. elementary education educator
Hamilton, Daniel Stephen clergyman

Little Falls
Barlow, Phyllis L. nurse manager, coordinator
Feeney, Mary Katherine O'Shea retired public health nurse

Liverpool
†Greenway, William Charles electronics executive, design engineer
†Kark, Pieter Robert Adriaan neurologist
Kogut, John Anthony retail executive, pharmacist
Morabito, Bruno Paul machinery manufacturing executive
O'Leary, Daniel J. retail trade executive
Sharp, Walter Len secondary educator
Winahradsky, Michael Francis drug company executive
Wolfson, Warren David lawyer, specialty retail store executive

Lockport
Carr, Edward Albert, Jr. medical educator, physician
Cull, John Joseph novelist, playwright
Hoyme, Chad Earl packaging company executive
Penney, Charles Rand lawyer, civic worker
Shah, Ramesh Keshavlal automotive company executive

Lockwood
Keating, Keith Anthony English language educator

Locust Valley
Benson, Robert Elliott investment banker, consultant
Bentel, Frederick Richard architect, educator
Bentel, Maria-Luise Ramona Azzarone (Mrs. Frederick R. Bentel) architect, educator
Davison, Daniel Pomeroy retired banking executive
Devendorf, Barbara Lancaster (Bonnie Lancaster Devendorf) real estate broker
Lippold, Richard sculptor
McGee, Dorothy Horton writer, historian
Schaffner, Charles Etzel consulting engineering executive
Schor, Joseph Martin pharmaceutical executive, biochemist
Sunderland, Ray, Jr. retired insurance company executive
Webel, Richard Karl landscape architect
Zulch, Joan Carolyn retired medical publishing company executive, consultant

Long Beach
Bernstein, Lester editorial consultant
Robbins, Jeffrey Howard media consultant, research writer, educator
†Sherman, Zachary civil and aerospace engineer, consultant
Siegel, Herbert Bernard certified professional management consultant
Thompson, Dorothy Barnard elementary school educator

Long Eddy
Hoiby, Lee composer, concert pianist

Long Island City
Brustein, Lawrence financial executive
Carson, Kent (Lovett Carson) paper company executive
Cushing, Robert Hunter lawyer, real estate investment executive
Di Suvero, Mark sculptor
Donneson, Seena Sand artist
Fife, Bernard automobile products manufacturing company executive
Gussow, Roy sculptor, educator
Jablowsky, Albert Isaac civil engineer
Lang, William Charles retail executive
Modell, Michael Steven lawyer, business executive
Mojica, Aurora association executive
Sadao, Shoji architect
Schlosser, Herbert S. broadcasting company executive
Ulrich, Werner Richard union education administrator
Villinski, Paul Stephen artist
†Weitz, Bruce retail executive

Loudonville
McConville, William academic administrator

Lowville
Becker, Robert Otto orthopedic surgery educator

Madison
Blount, Robert Grier pharmaceutical company executive

Mahopac
Gould, Sandra M. elementary school principal
Richards, Edgar Lester psychologist, educator
†Silbert, Alvin Jay secondary physics educator
Silbert, Linda Bress educational counselor, therapist

Mahopac Falls
Karimi, Reza artist

Malverne
Engoren, Sampson Seymour interior designer
Freund, Richard L. communications company executive, consultant, lawyer
Knight, John Francis insurance company executive
Ryan, Suzanne Irene nursing educator

Mamaroneck
Allensworth, Dorothy Alice education foundation administrator
Halpern, Abraham Leon psychiatrist
Holz, Harold A. chemical and plastics manufacturing company executive
Mazzola, Claude Joseph physicist, small business owner
Mines, Herbert Thomas executive recruiter
Mizrahi, Abraham Mordechay cosmetics and health care company executive, retired physician
Pugh, Grace Huntley artist

Manhasset
Anderson, Arthur N. retired utility company executive
Arnold, Charles Burle, Jr. psychiatric resident, epidemiologist, writer
Barrett, James P. lawyer
Carucci, Samuel Anthony lawyer
Corva, Angelo Francis architect
Croce, Anne Lally nurse, commissioner
Enquist, Irving Fridtjof surgeon
†Fendt, John W. minister, religious organization administrator
Fenton, Arnold N. obstetrician, gynecologist, educator
Frankum, James Edward airlines company executive
Gallagher, John S. T. (Jack Gallagher) hospital administrator
Grossi, Olindo architect, educator
Hayes, Arthur Michael lawyer
†Hinds, Glester Samuel financier, advertising executive, tax consultant
Keen, Constantine retired manufacturing company executive
Kreis, Willi physician
Lindow, John Wesley banker, corporate executive
Orenstein-Bellia, Jessica publishing company manager
Rostky, George Harold editor
Scherr, Lawrence physician, educator
Schiller, Arthur A. architect, educator
Spitz, Charles Thomas, Jr. clergyman
Wallace, Richard editor, writer
Wallace, Richard K. editor, journalist
Warren, Kenneth S. medical educator, physician
Wettereau, Richard Bradway editor, writer

Marcellus
Lafferty, Richard Thomas architect

Marcy
Fay, Rowan Hamilton minister

Maryknoll
Gormley, Robert John book publisher

Maspeth
Wykurz, Ireneusz Wojciech stage director, actor

Massapequa
Aiello-Contessa, Angela Marie physician
Hughes, Spencer Edward, Jr. financial executive, consultant
Vaccaro, Nicholas Carmine English language and media educator

Massapequa Park
Plotkin, Martin retired electrical engineer
Zizzo, Alicia concert pianist

Massena
Pellegrino, James Martin *dentist*

Mattituck
Paulsen, Joanna *publishing executive*

Mechanicville
Mahoney, Michael Nicholas *newspaper owner*

Melville
Bass, Elizabeth Ruth *editor*
Brandt, Robert Frederic, III *newspaper editor, journalist*
Colen, B. D. *journalist*
Cooke, Robert William *science journalist*
†Donovan, Brian *reporter, journalist*
Dooley, James C. *newspaper editor*
Green, Carol H. *lawyer, educator, journalist*
Hall, Charlotte Hauch *publishing executive*
Hildebrand, John Frederick *newspaper columnist*
Isenberg, Steven Lawrence *newspaper executive*
Jagoda, Donald Robert *sales promotion agency executive*
†Jansen, Raymond A., Jr. *newspaper publishing executive*
†Jurick, Robert Herbert *marketing executive*
Kahn, David *editor, author*
Kaufman, Stephen P. *electronics company executive*
Kett, Herbert Joseph *retail executive*
†Kissinger, Walter Bernhard *automotive test and service equipment manufacturing executive*
Klatell, Robert Edward *lawyer, electronics company executive*
Klurfeld, James Michael *journalist*
Krueger, Gerald Peter *psychologist*
Krusos, Denis Angelo *communications company executive*
Large, G. Gordon M. *data processing company executive*
Lengel, David Lee *electronics manufacturing executive*
Lynn, James Dougal *newspaper editor, journalist*
Maller, Robert Russell *certified management consultant, banker*
Marchesano, John Edward *electro-optical engineer*
Marro, Anthony James *newspaper editor*
McMillan, Robert Ralph *lawyer*
Miller, Robert C. *telecommunications industry executive*
Moran, Paul James *journalist, columnist*
Nassberg, Edward *chemicals executive*
Olson, Gary Robert *banker*
Patrick, Allan *drug store and variety store executive*
Payne, Leslie *newspaper editor, columnist, journalist, author*
Ray, Gordon Thompson *communications executive*
Redder, Thomas H. *newspaper publishing executive*
Robins, Marjorie Kaplan *newspaper editor*
Roel, Ron *newspaper editor*
†Saul, Stephanie *journalist*
Sommer, Jeff *journalist*
Toedtman, James Smith *newspaper editor, journalist*
Viklund, William Edwin *banker*
Woldt, Harold Frederick, Jr. *newspaper publishing executive*

Merrick
Beckman, Judith Kalb *financial counselor and planner, educator, writer*
Cariola, Robert Joseph *artist*
Cherry, Harold *insurance company executive*
Copperman, Stuart Morton *pediatrician*
Doyle, James Aloysius *retired association executive*
O'Brien, Kenneth Robert *life insurance company executive*
Paul, Martin Ambrose *physical chemist*

Mexico
Sade, Donald Stone *anthropology educator*

Middle Island
†Andrews, Gaylen *advertising executive*
†Linick, Andrew S. *marketing executive*
Mastrion, Guy *secondary school principal*

Middle Village
Farb, Edith Himel *chemist*
Kolatch, Alfred Jacob *publisher*
Meyers, Edward *photographer, writer, publisher*

Middleport
Schwan, Judith Alecia *photographic researcher*

Middletown
Bedell, Barbara Lee *newspaperwoman*
Blumenthal, Fritz *printmaker, painter*
Sprick, Dennis Michael *critic, copy editor*
Waddill, Graham Walker *retail executive*

Mill Neck
Grieve, William Roy *educational administrator, researcher, consultant*

Millbrook
Johnston, Robert Cossin *consulting engineer executive*
Likens, Gene Elden *ecologist*

Mineola
Bartlett, Clifford Adams, Jr. *lawyer*
Cirker, Hayward *publisher*
Delaney, Martin Joseph *hospital administrator*
English, John F. *lawyer*
Hankin, Errol Patrick *hospital administrator*
Hendler, Samuel I. *lawyer*
Klein, Arnold Spencer *lawyer*
McGonigle, James Gregory *training consultant*
Meyer, Bernard Stern *lawyer, former judge*
Mogil, Bernard Marc *judge*
Murphy, George Austin *judge*
Newman, Malcolm *civil engineering consultant*
Paterson, Basil Alexander *lawyer*
Rains, Harry Hano *lawyer, arbitrator, mediator*
Rozzi, Santa Caputo *county official*
Rushmore, Stephen *hotel consulting and appraisal specialist*
Salten, David George *university administrator, educator*
Schaffer, David Irving *lawyer*
Shperling, Irena *internist*
Smolev, Terence Elliot *lawyer, educator*
Twist, Paul Francis, Jr. *neonatologist*
Wurzel, Leonard *retired candy manufacturing company executive*
Yeh, James Kuen-Jann *nutritionist*

Monroe
Werzberger, Alan *pediatrician*

Monsey
Schore, Robert *social worker, educator*

Montauk
Duryea, Perry Belmont, Jr. *former state legislator, business executive*
First, Wesley *publishing company executive*
Garvey, Richard Anthony *lawyer*
Lavenas, Suzanne *writer, editor, consultant*

Monticello
Cooke, Lawrence Henry *lawyer, former state chief judge*
Lauterstein, Joseph *cardiologist*

Moriches
Casciano, Paul *principal*

Morrisville
Rouse, Robert Moorefield *mathematician, educator*

Mount Kisco
Couture, Ronald David *art administrator, design consultant*
Eckhoff, Carl D. *manufacturing executive*
Goodhue, Mary Brier *lawyer, former state senator*
Icahn, Carl C. *arbitrator, options specialist, corporation executive*
Keesee, Thomas Woodfin, Jr. *financial consultant*
Laster, Richard *biotechnology executive*
Pastorelle, Peter John *film company executive, radiological services and waste management company executive*
Schwarz, Wolfgang *psychologist*
Senkier, Robert Joseph *foundation administrator, educator*
Weiss, Caryl Shander *interior designer, educator*
Wilson, Robert R. H. *airline company executive*
Wood, James *broker*

Mount Vernon
Camerano, Franklin *medical center administrator*
Leonard, John Harry *advertising executive*
Mc Neill, Charles James *publishing executive*
Richardson, W. Franklyn *religious organization administrator*
Rossini, Joseph *contracting and development corporate executive*
†Wasserspring, Fredric R. *securities trader*

Munnsville
Carruth, Hayden *poet*

Nanuet
Burden, Ordway Partridge *investment banker*
Gold, Arline *educational administrator*
Savitz, Martin Harold *neurosurgeon*
Vamvaketis, Carole *nursing educator*

Naples
Beal, Myron Clarence *osteopathic physician*

Nedrow
†Lyons, Oren *Native American chieftain, conservationist*

New City
Elberg, Darryl Gerald *publisher, educator*
Esser, Aristide Henri *psychiatrist*
Feld, Joseph *construction executive*
Gromack, Alexander Joseph *state legislator*
Rosenbaum, Joseph Irving *lawyer, educator*
Wasserman, Walter Leonard *magnetics company executive*

New Hartford
Jones, Hugh Richard *lawyer*
Maurer, Gernant Elmer *metallurgical executive, consultant*
Muzyka, Donald Richard *specialty metals executive, metallurgist*

New Hyde Park
Anderson, Ronald Howard *consumer packaged goods company marketing executive*
Baldwin, Thomas James *restaurant chain financial executive, accountant, educator*
Biddle, David *neurologist*
Chafitz, Alan Herbert *financial services company executive*
Chardavoyne, David Edwin *utility executive*
Cooper, Milton *real estate investment trust executive*
Daley, John Terence *priest*
Fink, Martin Neil *hospital administrator*
Frankel, Arnold J. *chemical company executive*
Isenberg, Henry David *microbiology educator*
Jacob, Gary Steven *real estate developer*
Koplewicz, Harold Samuel *child and adolescent psychiatrist*
Mulvihill, James Edward *periodontist, university administrator, educator, health care executive*
Offner, Eric Delmonte *lawyer*
Pappas, Christine Ann *nursing administrator*
Reddan, Harold Jerome *sociologist, educator*
†Redman, Monte N. *bank executive*
Richards, Bernard *investment company executive*
Seltzer, Vicki Lynn *obstetrician-gynecologist*
Shenker, Ira Ronald *pediatrician*
†Smoot, E. Philip *chemicals executive*
Stevens, Gary *professional jockey*
Wingate, David Aaron *manufacturing company executive*
Wolf, Julius *medical educator*

New Kingston
Maffei, Dorothy Jean *theatre manager*

New Paltz
Chandler, Alice *university president, educator*
Fleisher, Harold *computer scientist*
Hathaway, Richard Dean *language professional, educator*
Nyquist, Thomas Eugene *consulting business executive, mayor*
Richbart, Carolyn Mae *mathematics educator*
Ryan, Marleigh Grayer *Japanese language educator*
Schneemann, Carolee *painter, performing artist, filmmaker, writer*
Schnell, George Adam *geographer, educator*

New Rochelle
Beardsley, Robert Eugene *microbiologist, educator*
Behren, Robert Alan *lawyer, accountant*
Berlage, Gai Ingham *sociologist, educator*
Blotner, Norman David *lawyer, real estate broker, corporate executive*
Branch, William Blackwell *playwright, producer*
Brodie, Norman *retired financial actuary*
Burns, Joseph William *lawyer*
Dobrin, Bernard Robert *financial executive*
Frenkel, Michael *lawyer*
Gallagher, John Francis *academic administrator, education educator*
Golub, James Robert *internist, allergist*
Golub, Sharon Bramson *psychologist, educator*
Gunning, Francis Patrick *lawyer, insurance association executive*
Hayes, Arthur Hull, Jr. *physician, clinical pharmacology educator, medical school dean, business executive, consultant*
Jacobs, Doran *travel marketing executive*
Kelly, Sister Dorothy Ann *college president*
Klein, Arthur Luce *theatrical company executive*
Lulla, Jack David *polymer engineer*
Malach, Herbert John *lawyer*
†Mamangakis, John Paul *health facility administrator*
Merrill, Robert *baritone*
Murphy, Austin de la Salle *economist, educator, banker*
Nienburg, George Frank *photographer*
Petrucelli, R(occo) Joseph, II *nephrologist*
Rovinsky, Joseph Judah *obstetrician, gynecologist*
Saperstein, David Allan *novelist, screenwriter, film director*
Saunders, Rubie Agnes *former magazine editor, author*
Schaffer, Monroe S. *grocery company executive*
Slotnick, Mortimer H. *artist*
Sweeny, Stephen Jude *academic administrator*
Tassone, Gelsomina (Gessie Tassone) *metal processing executive*
Vernon, Lillian *mail order company executive*
Wolotsky, Hyman *retired college dean*

New Windsor
†Lawrence, Albert James *association executive*

New York
Aaron, Lynn *dancer*
†Abatemarco, Fred *editor in chief*
Abberley, John J. *lawyer*
Abbey, Scott Gerson *computer information scientist*
Abboud, Joseph M. *fashion designer*
Abel, Reuben *humanities educator*
Abeles, Sigmund M. *artist, printmaker*
Abelson, Alan *columnist*
Abercrombie, Stanley *magazine editor*
Abernathy, James Logan *public relations executive*
Abish, Cecile *artist*
Ablon, Ralph E. *manufacturing company executive*
Abraham, F(ahrid) Murray *actor, educator*
Abrahams, William Miller *editor, author*
Abrahamsen, David *psychiatrist, psychoanalyst, author*
Abram, Prudence Beatty *federal judge*
Abramovitz, Max *architect*
Abrams, Alan M. *lawyer*
Abrams, Bertram Alan *lawyer*
Abrams, Floyd *lawyer*
Abrams, Marc R. *lawyer*
Abrams, Muhal Richard *pianist, composer*
Abrams, Robert *former state attorney general*
Abramson, Sara Jane *radiologist, educator*
Abularach, Rodolfo Marco Antonio *artist*
Abu-Lughod, Janet Lippman *sociologist, educator*
Acampora, Anthony Salvator *electrical engineer, educator*
Acampora, Ralph Joseph *brokerage firm executive*
Acconci, Vito (Hannibal) *conceptual artist*
Achenbaum, Alvin Allen *marketing and management consultant*
Achtert, Walter Scott *publisher*
Ackman, Milton Roy *lawyer*
Acrivos, Andreas *chemical engineering educator*
Adams, Alice *writer*
Adams, Dennis Paul *artist*
Adams, Douglas Noel *writer*
Adams, Edward Thomas (Eddie Adams) *photographer*
Adams, Joey *comedian, author*
Adams, John Hamilton *lawyer*
Adamson, John William *hematologist*
Addison, Herbert John *publishing executive*
Adler, Freda Schaffer (Mrs. G. O. W. Mueller) *criminologist, educator*
Adler, Joel A. *lawyer*
Adler, Richard *composer, lyricist*
Adolfo, (Adolfo F. Sardiña) *fashion designer*
Adri, (Adrienne Steckling) *fashion designer*
Adrian, Barbara (Mrs. Franklin C. Tramutola) *artist*
Agate, Robert M. *diversified manufacturing company executive*
Agha, Mahmoud Fikry *architectural firm executive*
Agisim, Philip *advertising and marketing company executive*
Agosta, William Carleton *chemist, educator*
Agostinelli, Robert Francesco *investment banker*
Ahmad, Jameel *civil engineer, researcher, educator*
Ahrens, Edward Hamblin, Jr. *physician*
Aibel, Howard J. *lawyer*
Aidinoff, M(erton) Bernard *lawyer*
Aiello, Danny *actor*
Aiello, Stephen *public relations executive*
Ailes, Roger Eugene *television producer, consultant*
Ainslie, Michael Lewis *art-related holding company executive*
Aisenbrey, Stuart Keith *trust company official*
Akabas, Sheila Helene *social work educator*
Akalaitis, JoAnne *theater director, writer, actress*
Akins, Ellen *writer*
Akiyoshi, Toshiko *jazz composer, pianist*
Aksen, Gerald *lawyer, educator*
Aksin, Mustafa *diplomat*
Aktar, A.S. (Art Aktar) *civil engineer, consultant*
Alazraki, Jaime *Romance languages educator*
Albee, Edward Franklin *author, playwright*
Albenda, David *lawyer*
Albers, Charles Edgar *investment manager, insurance executive*
Albert, Marv *sportscaster, program director*
Albert, Neale Malcolm *lawyer*
Albert, Rory Judd *lawyer*
Albright, Harry Wesley, Jr. *banking executive, former government official, lawyer*
Albright, Madeleine Korbel *diplomat, political scientist*
Albright, Warren Edward *advertising executive*
Alcott, Mark Howard *lawyer*
Aldea, Patricia *architect*
Alden, Steven Michael *lawyer*
Alderson, Philip Otis *radiologist, educator*
Aldredge, Theoni Vachliotis *costume designer*
Alessandroni, Venan Joseph *lawyer*
Alexander, Barbara Toll *investment banker*
Alexander, Harold *bioengineer, educator*
Alexander, Norman E. *diversified manufacturing company executive*
Alexander, Roy *public relations executive, editor, author*
Alexander, Shana *journalist, author, lecturer*
Alexopoulos, Helene *ballet dancer*
†Alfaro, Victor *fashion designer*
Alford, Robert Ross *sociologist*
Ali, Mehdi *financial services company executive*
Alicea-Baez, Johnny *religious organization administrator*
Alland, Alexander, Jr. *anthropology educator*
Allard, Linda Marie *fashion designer*
Allardice, Bruce *art association executive*
Allardice, Robert B., III *financial services company executive*
Allen, Alice Catherine Towsley *public relations professional, writer, consultant*
Allen, Betty (Mrs. Ritten Edward Lee, III) *mezzo-soprano*
Allen, Herbert *investment banker*
Allen, Jay Presson *writer, producer*
Allen, Leon Arthur, Jr. *lawyer*
Allen, Nancy *musician, educator*
Allen, Ralph Dean *telecommunications corporate executive*
Allen, Roberta L. *fiction and nonfiction writer, conceptual artist*
Allen, William Frederick, Jr. *mechanical engineer*
Allison, David Bradley *psychologist*
Allison, Herbert Monroe, Jr. *investment firm executive*
Allmendinger, Paul Florin *retired engineering association executive*
Allner, Walter Heinz *designer, painter, art director*
Alloggiamento, Nancy Thomas *advertising agency executive, consultant, business owner*
Alonzo, Martin Vincent *mining and aluminum company executive, investor, financial consultant*
Alper, Merlin Lionel *financial executive*
Alpern, Andrew *lawyer, architect*
Alpern, David Mark *magazine editor, broadcast journalist and producer*
Alpert, Gordon Myles *lawyer*
Alpert, Warren *oil company executive, philanthropist*
Alprin, William Samuel *women's accessory company executive*
Alten, Jerry *art director*
Alter, David *lawyer*
Alter, Eleanor Breitel *lawyer*
Alter, Jonathan Hammerman *journalist*
Altfest, Lewis Jay *financial and investment advisor*
Altman, Lawrence Kimball *physician, journalist*
Altman, Robert B. *film director, writer, producer*
Altman, Roy Peter *pediatric surgeon*
Altschul, Arthur Goodhart *investment banker*
Alvarez-Recio, Emilio De La Torre *personal care products company executive*
Alvary, Lorenzo *bass*
Alworth, Sandra Ann *municipal bond salesperson, brokerage house executive*
Amara, Lucine *opera and concert singer*
Amberg, Stanley Louis *lawyer*
Amdur, Martin Bennett *lawyer*
Amdur, Neil Lester *sports editor, writer*
Ames, George Joseph *investment banker*
Ames, Richard Pollard *physician, author, educator*
Amhowitz, Harris J. *lawyer, educator*
Ammirati, Ralph *advertising agency executive*
Amory, Cleveland *writer*
Amos, Tori *singer, musician*
Amram, David Werner *composer, conductor, musician*
Amster, Linda Evelyn *newspaper executive, consultant*
Amsterdam, Anthony Guy *law educator*
Anchlia, Than Mal *wholesale distribution executive*
Ancona, Barry *publishing and marketing consultant*
Andersen, K(ent) Tucker *investment executive*
Andersen, Kurt Byars *magazine editor, critic, writer*
Anderson, Arthur Allan *management consultant*
Anderson, Bradley Jay *cartoonist*
Anderson, David Poole *sportswriter*
Anderson, Eugene Robert *lawyer*
Anderson, Gavin *public relations consultant*
Anderson, George W. *metal industry executive, retired*
Anderson, Jack Northman *newspaper columnist*
†Anderson, Kevin James *writer*
Anderson, Laurie *performance artist*
Anderson, O(rvil) Roger *biology educator, marine biology and protozoology, researcher*
Anderson, Poul William *author*
Anderson, Quentin *English language educator, critic*
Anderson, Ron *advertising executive*
Anderson, Sydney *biologist, museum curator*
Anderson, Theodore Wellington *portfolio strategist*
Anderson, Walter Herman *magazine editor*
Andolsen, Alan Anthony *management consultant*
Andre, Carl *sculptor*
Andrews, E. Lee *paper company executive*
Andrews, Frederick Franck *newspaper editor*
Andrews, Gordon Clark *lawyer*
Andrus, Roger Douglas *lawyer*
Andruskevich, Thomas A(nthony) *corporate executive*
Anfield, Frank A. *advertising executive*
Angell, Roger *writer, magazine editor*
Angell, Wayne D. *economist, banker*
Angland, Joseph *lawyer*
Ankerson, Robert William *management consultant*
Anneken, William B. *apparel company executive*
Annese, Domenico *landscape architect*
Anshen, Melvin *business educator*
Anspach, Ernst *economist, lawyer*
Anthoine, Robert *lawyer, educator*
Anthony, Piers *science fiction writer*
Anthony, William Graham *artist*
Antilla, Susan *journalist*
Antonacci, Lori (Loretta Marie Antonacci) *marketing executive, consultant*
Antonakos, Stephen *sculptor*
Antonell, Walter John *publishing executive*

Antonuccio, Joseph Albert hospitality industry executive
Antrobus, John Simmons psychologist, educator
Antupit, Samuel Nathaniel art director
Apostolakis, James John shipping company executive
Appel, Alfred lawyer
Appel, Karel artist, illustrator
Appel, Michael R(obert) corporation treasurer
Appelbaum, Alan lawyer
Apple, Max Isaac English educator
Applebaum, Stuart S. public relations executive
Appleton, Myra magazine editor, writer
Aquilino, Thomas Joseph, Jr. federal judge, law educator
Araskog, Rand Vincent diversified telecommunications multinational company executive
Arcara, James Amadeus broadcasting company executive
Arcaro, Eddie (George Edward) sports broadcasting journalist, former jockey, horse trainer
Archer, James G. lawyer
Archer, Kenneth Davidson lawyer, insurance executive
Archibald, Reginald Mac Gregor physician, chemist, educator
Archimedes, Verdun Joseph art consultant, mental health nurse
Arcilesi, Vincent Jasper artist
Ardrey, Rushton Leigh, Jr. banker
Arenson, Gregory K. lawyer
Arenson, Karen Wattel journalist
Arenstein, Robert David lawyer
Arias, Jimmy professional tennis player
Arkin, Alan Wolf actor
Arledge, Roone television executive
Arlow, Arnold Jack advertising agency executive
Arman, Armand Pierre sculptor
Armani, Giorgio fashion designer
Armitage, Karole dancer, choreographer
Armstrong, James Sinclair retired lawyer, foundation director
Armstrong, Michael Francis lawyer
Arnhold, Henry H. investment banker
Arning, John Fredrick lawyer
Arnold, Eddy singer
Arnold, Kenneth Lloyd publisher, playwright
Arnold, Martin journalist
†Arnold, Skip performance artist
Arnold, Thomas Elijah, Jr. (Tim Arnold) advertising executive, blues guitar player
Arnot, Bob physician, medical correspondent
Aron, Alan Milford pediatric neurology educator
Aronoff, Michael Stephen psychiatrist
Arons, Michael Eugene physicist, academic administrator
Aronson, Arnold H. retail company executive
Aronson, Donald Eric professional services firms consultant
Aronson, Edgar David venture capitalist
Aronson, Esther Leah association administrator, psychotherapist
Aronstam, Neil Lee media marketing firm executive
Arouh, Jeffrey Alan lawyer
Arpino, Gerald Peter performing company executive
Arquit, Kevin James lawyer
Arsene, Vladimir architect
Arther, Richard Oberlin polygraphist, educator
Arvystas, Michael Geciauskas orthodontist, educator
Asahina, Robert James editor, publishing company executive
Asakawa, Takako dancer, dance teacher
Asanuma, Hiroshi physician, educator
Asch, Arthur Louis apparel company executive
Ascher, Michael transportation executive
Ashdown, Marie Matranga (Mrs. Cecil Spanton Ashdown, Jr.) writer, lecturer
Asher, Aaron editor, publisher
Ashinoff, Reid L. lawyer
Ashjian, Mesrob archbishop
Ashkinazy, Larry Robert dentist
†Ashley, Diane S. advertising executive
Ashley, Elizabeth actress
Ashley, Merrill ballerina
Ashrafi, Dariush apparel company executive
Ashton, Dore author, educator
Ashton, Jean Willoughby library director
Ashton, Robert W. lawyer, foundation administrator
Assael, Henry marketing educator
Athanassiades, Ted insurance company executive
Atkins, Peter Allan lawyer
Atkins, Robert Emmett, Jr. lawyer
Atkinson, Holly Gail physician, journalist, author, lecturer
Atkinson, Paul C. newspaper publishing executive
Atlas, James Robert magazine editor, writer
Atwater, Verne Stafford finance educator
†Atwood, Colleen costume designer
Auchincloss, Kenneth magazine editor
Auchincloss, Louis Stanton writer
†Aucoin, Kevyn J. make-up artist
Auel, Jean Marie author
Auerbach, William lawyer
Aufses, Arthur H(arold), Jr. surgeon, medical educator
Augeri, Joseph Leonard packaging engineer
Auld, Larry Elwood foundation executive
†Aulisi, Joseph Garibaldi costume designer
Auriemmo, Frank Joseph, Jr. financial holding company executive
Austad, Vigdis computer software company executive
Auster, Paul writer
Austerlitz, Robert Paul linguistics educator
Austin, Danforth Whitley newspaper executive
Austin, Gabriel Christopher publisher
Austrian, Neil R. football league executive
Avedon, Richard photographer
Avi, (Avi Wortis) author
Avrett, John Glenn advertising executive
Ax, Emanuel pianist
Axel, Richard pathology and biochemistry educator
Axelrod, Charles Paul lawyer
Axelrod, Norman N(athan) technology application and technical planning consultant
Axinn, Stephen Mark lawyer
Aycock, Alice artist
Ayers, Emory Daniel management consultant
†Azenberg, Emanuel theatrical producer
Babcock, Michael Joseph retail company executive
Babson, Irving K. publishing company executive
Babyface, (Kenny Edmunds) popular musician
Bacall, Lauren actress
Bach, Arthur James investment banker
Bache, Theodore Stephen recording company executive
Bachelder, Joseph Elmer, III lawyer
Bacher, Judith St. George executive search consultant
Backer, William Montague retired advertising agency executive
Backman, Gerald Stephen lawyer
Bacot, John Carter banker
Baden, Michael M. pathologist, educator
Badertscher, David Glen law librarian, consultant
Baer, Harold, Jr. judge
Baer, Norbert Sebastian art conservation educator, chemist
Baer, Rudolf Lewis dermatologist, educator
Baer, Thomas James lawyer
Baeza, Mario Leon lawyer
Bagger, Richard Hartvig lawyer
Bagnall, Roger Shaler history educator
Bagnoli, Vincent James, Jr. construction company executive, engineer
Bahash, Robert J. publishing executive
Bahr, Lauren S. publishing company executive
Bahrenburg, D. Claeys publishing executive
Bailey, Glenn Waldemar manufacturing company executive
Bailey, Janet Dee publishing company executive
Bains, Harrison MacKellar, Jr. financial executive
Bains, Leslie Elizabeth banker
Bainton, J(ohn) Joseph lawyer
Baird, Dugald Euan telecommunications industry executive
Baity, John Cooley lawyer
Baitz, Jon Robin playwright
Bakal, Carl writer, public relations counsel, photojournalist
Baker, David Remember lawyer
Baker, Edwin Herbert lawyer
Baker, Elizabeth Calhoun magazine editor
Baker, Elmer Elias, Jr. speech pathology and communication educator
Baker, James Barnes architect
Baker, James Estes foreign service officer
Baker, Norman Hodgson, Jr. astronomy educator
Baker, Paul Raymond history educator
Baker, Russell Wayne columnist, author
Baker, Stephen advertising executive, author
Baker, Stuart David lawyer
Baker, Wilder DuPuy advertising executive
Baker, William Franklin public broadcasting company executive
Baker, William George publishing company financial executive
Baker-Riker, Margery television executive
Balakian, Anna foreign language educator, scholar, critic, writer
Balbin, Julius foreign language educator, poet, translator
Baldasaro, P. Michael tax consultant
Baldassano, Corinne Leslie radio executive
Baldwin, David Allen political science educator
Baldwin, David Shepard physician
†Balick, Kenneth D. securities and investment bank executive
Balkind, Aubrey advertising executive
Ball, George L. securities company executive
Ball, John H(anstein) lawyer
Ball, John Paul publishing company executive
Ballard, Charles Alan investment banker
†Ballard, Claude Mark, Jr. real estate investment executive
Balliett, Whitney writer, critic
Bamberger, Gabrielle public relations executive
Bamberger, Michael Albert lawyer
Bancroft, Alexander Clerihew lawyer
Bancroft, Margaret Armstrong lawyer
Bandier, Martin music publisher
Bandy, Mary Lea museum official
Banerjee, (Bimal) artist, educator
Banker, Stephen M. lawyer
Banks, Russell chemical company executive
Bankston, Archie Moore, Jr. lawyer
Banner, Stephen Edward company executive, lawyer
Baquero, José Maria architect, artist
Baragwanath, Albert Kingsmill curator
Baraka, Amiri (Everett LeRoi Jones) author
Barandes, Robert lawyer
Baranik, Rudolf artist
Baranski, Joan Sullivan publisher
Barasch, Clarence Sylvan lawyer
Barasch, Mal Livingston lawyer
Barbash, Joseph lawyer, arbitrator
Barbee, Victor ballet dancer
Barber, Russell Brooks Butler television producer
Bardach, Joan Lucile clinical psychologist
Bardin, Clyde Wayne biomedical researcher and developer of contraceptives
Barist, Jeffrey A. lawyer
Barker, Barbara Ann ophthalmologist
Barker, Charles conductor
Barker, Edwin Bogue musician
Barkhorn, Henry Charles, III investment banker
Barksdale, Phillip Dunlap, Jr. banker
Barletta, Joseph Francis newspaper executive, lawyer
Barnes, B. Jack manufacturing executive
Barnes, Clive Alexander drama and dance critic
Barnes, Duncan magazine editor, writer
Barnes, Edward Larrabee architect
Barnes, Jack Whittier political party official
Barnes, Jhane Elizabeth fashion design company executive, designer
Barnet, Will artist, educator
Barnett, Bernard accountant
Barnett, Henry Lewis medical educator, pediatrician
Barnett, Jonathan architect, city planner
Barnett, Richard Blair lawyer
Barnett, Vivian Endicott curator
Barolini, Teodolinda foreign language educator
Baron, Carolyn editor, author, publishing executive
Baron, Maureen Walsh editor, writer
Baron, Melvin Leon civil engineer, consultant
Baron, Mitchell Neal lawyer
Baron, Theodore public relations executive
Barondess, Jeremiah Abraham physician
Barondess, Linda Hiddemen professional society executive
Barr, Michael Charles securities analyst, investment banker
Barr, Thomas D. lawyer
Barratt, Michael Scott architect
Barrett, Bill sculptor
Barrett, Herbert artists management executive
Barrett, Richard James investment banker
Barrett, William L. D. lawyer
Barron, Francis Patrick lawyer
Barron, James Turman journalist
Barron, Susan clinical psychologist
Barry, David Earl lawyer
Barry, Desmond Thomas, Jr. lawyer
Barry, Edward William publisher
Barry, Lynda cartoonist, playwright, author
Barry, Thomas Corcoran investment counsellor
Barry, William Garrett, III publishing company executive
Barsalona, Frank Samuel theatrical agent
Barsamian, Khajag Sarkis primate
Bartel, Ann Pelcovits economist
Barth, Mark Harold lawyer
Bartle, Annette Gruber (Mrs. Thomas R. Bartle) artist, writer, photographer
Bartlett, C(raig) Scott, Jr. banker
Bartlett, Dwight Kellogg, III insurance company executive
Bartlett, Jennifer Losch artist
Bartlett, John fashion designer
Bartlett, Joseph Warren lawyer
†Bartlett, Thomas Foster international management consultant
Bartley, Robert LeRoy newspaper editor
Baruch, Ralph M. communications executive
Baryshnikov, Mikhail ballet dancer
Barzilay, Isaac Eisenstein historian
Barzun, Jacques author, literary consultant
Basden, Cameron ballet mistress, dancer
Basile, Thomas J. accountant
Baskin, Stuart Jay lawyer
Bason, George R., Jr. lawyer
Bass, Hyman mathematician, educator
Bass, Joel Leonard artist
Bass, Max S. natural resources and chemical production company executive
Bassen, Ned Henry lawyer
Bates, Don public relations and marketing executive
Bates, Michael Lawrence curator
Batscha, Robert Michael museum executive
Battle, Kathleen Deanna soprano
Baudendistel, Daniel dancer
Bauer, Douglas F. lawyer
Bauer, Frances Brand research mathematician
Bauer, Marion Dane writer
Bauer, Ralph Glenn lawyer, maritime arbitrator
Baum, Eleanor electrical engineering educator, academic administrator
Baum, Willow Ann public relations executive
Bauman, Martin Harold executive search firm executive
Baumann, Gary Joseph accountant
Baumann, Karl H. health and medical products executive
Baumgardner, John Ellwood, Jr. lawyer
Baumgarten, Paul Anthony lawyer
Baumgarten, Sidney lawyer
Baumrin, Bernard Stefan Herbert lawyer, educator
Bausch, James John foundation executive
Baxter, Adrienne Marshall art editor
Baylis, Robert Montague investment banker
Bazell, Robert Joseph science correspondent
Bazerman, Steven Howard lawyer
Beal, Jack artist
Beale, Christopher William investment banker
Bear, Donald law firm executive director
Bear, Larry Alan lawyer, educator
Beard, Anson McCook, Jr. investment banker
Beard, Eugene P. advertising agency executive
Beardsley, Charles William engineering publisher, editor, writer
Beardsley, Theodore S(terling), Jr. association executive
Bearn, Alexander Gordon physician scientist, former pharmaceutical company executive
Beattie, Ann author
Beattie, Edward James surgeon, educator
†Beattie, Richard Irwin lawyer
Beatty, John Lee scenic designer
Beatty, Talley choreographer
Beaumont, Richard Austin management consultant
Beck, Adrian Robert surgeon, educator
Beck, James (Henry) art historian, author
Beck, Martha Ann art curator, director
Beck, Rosemarie artist, educator
Becker, Don Crandall newspaper executive
Becker, Isidore A. business executive
Becker, Ivan advertising executive
Becker, Michael Lewis advertising executive
Becker, Robert A. advertising executive
Becker, Stanley R. advertising executive
Beckham, Edgar Frederick foundation administrator
Beckhard, Herbert architect
Beckwith, Rodney Fisk management consulting firm executive
Becofsky, Arthur Luke arts administrator, writer
Bederson, Benjamin physicist, educator
Bedford, Brian actor
Bednar, Rudy Gerard television producer, director
Beene, Geoffrey fashion designer
Beeney, Garrard Russ lawyer
Beerbower, John Edwin lawyer
Beers, Charlotte Lenore advertising agency executive
Beeson, Jack Hamilton composer, educator, writer
Begell, William publisher
Begley, Louis lawyer, writer
Behrendt, John Thomas lawyer
Behrens, Hildegard soprano
Beim, David Odell investment banker, educator
Beim, Norman playwright, actor, director
Beinecke, Candace Krugman lawyer
Beinecke, Frederick William investment company executive
Beinecke, William Sperry corporate executive
Belden, David Leigh professional association executive, engineering educator
Belford, Richard David lawyer
Bel Geddes, Joan writer
Belkin, Boris David violinist
Belknap, Norton petroleum company consultant
Belknap, Robert Lamont Slavic language educator
Belkov, Meredith Ann landmark administrator
Bell, David Arthur advertising agency executive
Bell, Derrick Albert legal educator, author, lecturer
Bell, James Halsey lawyer
Bell, Jonathan Robert lawyer
Bell, Martin Allen investment company executive
Bell, Thomas Devereaux, Jr. public affairs company executive
Bellamy, Carol international organization executive
Bellanger, Serge René banker
Bellas, Albert Constantine investment banker, advisor
Belle, John Leighton architect, planner
Belle, Regina popular musician
Bellin, Howard Theodore plastic surgeon
Bellin, Milton Rockwell artist
Belliveau, Gerard Joseph, Jr. librarian
Bellows, Howard Arthur, Jr. marketing research executive
Bellson, Louis Paul drummer
Bellwin, Janna H. J. lawyer
Belnick, Mark Alan lawyer
Belson, Jerome investment company executive, real estate developer
Bemis, Mary Ferguson magazine editor
Benchley, Peter Bradford author
Bendelius, Arthur George engineering firm executive
Bender, Thomas history and humanities educator, writer
Bendixen, Henrik Holt physician, educator, dean
Benedetto, M. William investment banker
Benedict, James Nelson lawyer
Benedikt, Michael poet, educator, author, editor, free-lance consultant
Ben-Eli, Michael Uri management consultant
Benenson, Edward Hartley realty company executive
Benenson, Mark Keith lawyer
Benglis, Lynda artist, sculptor
Ben-Haim, Zigi artist
Ben-Hur, Ehud research scientist
Benichou, Pascal dancer
Benjamin, George David retired insurance company executive, risk consultant
Benjamin, Harvey E. lawyer, sports executive
Benkard, James W. B. lawyer
Benn, T(heodore) Alexander (Alec Benn) writer
Bennack, Frank Anthony, Jr. publishing company executive
Benner, Mary Wright marketing professional
Bennett, Edward A. broadcast company executive
Bennett, Georgette communications and planning consultant
Bennett, Reynold lawyer
Bennett, Saul public relations agency executive
Bennett, Tony (Anthony Dominick Benedetto) entertainer
Benshoof, Janet L. lawyer, association executive
Bent, Ian David musicologist
Bentley, Eric author, playwright, comparative literature educator
Benton, Nicholas theater producer
Benton, Robert film director, screenwriter
Benway, Joseph Calise advertising agency financial executive
Bercovitch, Hanna Margareta editor
Berend, Robert William lawyer
†Berendt, John Lawrence writer, editor
Berens, Rodney Bristol investment banker
Berenson, Robert Leonard advertising agency executive
Berenstain, Janice author, illustrator
Berenstain, Stanley author, illustrator
Berezin, Tanya artistic director, actress
Berg, David author, artist
Berg, Jonathan Albert investment company executive
Berg, Wayne architect, educator
Bergan, Philip James lawyer
Bergen, D. Thomas business executive
Bergen, G. S. Peter lawyer
Bergen, John Donald communications, public affairs executive
Berger, Arnold Robert advertising executive
Berger, Curtis Jay law educator
Berger, Frank Milan biomedical researcher, scientist, former pharmaceutical company executive
Berger, George lawyer
Berger, Oscar artist
Berger, Pearl library director
Berger, Stephen financial services company executive
Berger, Vivian Olivia lawyer, educator
Bergeret, Albert Hamilton artistic director, conductor, singer, theatrical technician
Bergin, John Francis advertising agency executive
Bergonzi, Carlo tenor, voice educator
Bergstein, Daniel Gerard lawyer
Berk, Alan S. law firm executive
Berk, Paul David physician, scientist, educator
Berkman, Lillian foundation executive, corporation executive, art collector
Berkow, Ira Harvey author, journalist
Berkwitt, George Joseph editor
Berle, Peter Adolf Augustus lawyer, association executive
Berlin, Andrew Mark advertising agency executive
Berlin, Emily lawyer
Berlin, Howard Richard investment advisory company executive
Berlin, Jordan Stuart investment company executive
Berlind, Robert Elliot artist
Berlind, Roger Stuart stage and film producer
Berliner, Barbara librarian, consultant
Berliner, Ruth Shirley real estate company executive
Berliner, William Michael business educator
Berman, Ariane R. artist
Berman, Joshua Mordecai lawyer, manufacturing company executive
Berman, Julius lawyer
Berman, Lazar pianist
Berman, Martin M. television producer
Berman, Mira advertising agency executive
Berman, Philip Averill journalist, consultant
Berman, Simeon Moses mathematician, educator
Bermann, George Alan law educator, lawyer
Bernard, David George management consultant
Bernard, Kenneth (Otis Bernard) poet, author, playwright
Bernard, Lewis W. foundation executive
Bernard, Richard Phillip lawyer
Bernard, Viola Wertheim psychiatrist
Bernard, Walter art director
Bernardi, Mario conductor
Bernbach, John Lincoln advertising agency executive
Berne, Bruce J. chemistry educator
†Berner, Andrew Jay library director, writer
Berns, Kenneth Ira physician
Bernstein, Alan Arthur oil company executive
Bernstein, Anne Elayne psychoanalyst
Bernstein, Bernard lawyer, corporate executive
Bernstein, Carl author, journalist
Bernstein, Daniel Lewis lawyer
Bernstein, Elliot Louis television executive
Bernstein, Richard Allen publishing company executive
Bernstein, Robert Louis publishing company executive
Bernstein, Thomas Paul political science educator
Bernstein, Zalman C. research and money management executive
Berresford, Susan Vail philanthropic foundation executive
Berrien, James Stuart magazine publisher
Berry, Charles Gordon lawyer
Berry, Edna Janet lawyer, chemist
†Berry, John Nichols, III publishing executive, editor
Berry, Joseph John brokerage house executive
Berry, Joyce Charlotte university press editor
Berry, Nancy Michaels nonprofit development executive
Berry, Walter baritone
Berthot, Jake artist

Bertino, Joseph Rocco physician, educator
Bertles, John Francis physician, educator
Berton, Lee writer
Bertuccioli, Bruno petrochemical company executive
Beshar, Christine lawyer
Bessey, Edward Cushing health care company executive
Best, Geoffry D. C. lawyer
Betcher, Albert Maxwell anesthesiologist
Betley, John Robert accountant
Bettman, Gary Bruce lawyer
Betts, Dicky (Richard Forrest Betts) guitarist, songwriter, vocalist
Betts, Richard Kevin political science educator
Beuchert, Edward William lawyer
Beuth, Philip Roy television executive
Bewkes, Eugene Garrett, Jr. investment company executive, consultant
Bewkes, Jeff television broadcasting company executive
Bezahler, Donald Jay lawyer
Bezanson, Thomas Edward lawyer
Bezikos, Lynne A. lawyer
Bhavsar, Natvar Prahladji artist
Bialer, Seweryn political science educator, author, consultant
Bialkin, Kenneth Jules lawyer
Bialo, Kenneth Marc lawyer
†Bibliowicz, Jessica M. financial analyst
Bickers, David Rinsey physician, educator
Bickford, Jewelle Wooten investment banker
Bicks, David Peter lawyer
Biddle, Flora Miller art museum administrator
Biderman, Mark Charles investment banker
Bidwell, James Truman, Jr. lawyer
Biebelberg, David Mark marketing professional
Biederman, Barron Zachary (Barry Biederman) advertising agency executive
Bienenstock, Martin J. lawyer
Bierman, Steven M. lawyer
Biewen, Robert L. publishing executive
Bigger, John Thomas, Jr. physician, educator
Biggs, Barton Michael investment company executive
Biggs, Jeremy Hunt trust company executive
Biggs, John Herron insurance company executive
†Bigham, James John agribusiness company executive
Bijur, Arthur William advertising executive
Bikel, Theodore actor, singer
Biller, Hugh Frederick medical educator
Billian, Cathey R. sculptor, educator
Binger, Wilson Valentine civil engineer
Binkert, Alvin John hospital administrator
Binkowski, Edward Stephan research analysis director, lawyer, educator
Biondi, Frank J., Jr. broadcast executive
Bird, Mary Lynne Miller association executive
Birenbaum, Jonathan lawyer
Birkelund, John Peter investment banking executive
Birkenhead, Thomas Bruce theatrical producer and manager, educator
Birman, Joan S. mathematician, educator
Birmingham, Stephen writer
Birnbaum, Edward Lester lawyer
Birnbaum, Henry librarian
Birnbaum, Irwin Morton lawyer
Birnbaum, Robert Jack lawyer
Birnbaum, Sheila L. lawyer, educator
Birnhak, Sandra Jean film company executive
†Bischoff, Theresa medical center administrator
Bishop, André artistic director, producer
Bishop, Susan Katharine executive search company executive
†Bisson, Terry Ballantine author, editor
Bite-Dickson, Guna newspaper editor
Bizar, Irving lawyer
Black, Barbara Aronstein legal history educator
†Black, Daniel James chemical company executive
Black, Hillel Moses publisher
Black, James Isaac, III lawyer
Black, Jerry Bernard lawyer
Black, Neil Spencer magazine publishing executive
Black, Rosemary newspaper editor
Black, Shawn Morgado, . dancer
Blackiston, Henry Curtis, III lawyer
Blackman, Kenneth Robert lawyer
Blackwell, John Wesley securities industry executive, consultant
Blackwell, Richard Manning lawyer
Blades, Carol Brady public relations executive
Blades, Ruben singer, songwriter, composer
Blaine, Nell artist, printmaker
Blair, William Granger retired newspaperman
Blake, Richard Charles lawyer
Blakeslee, Edward Eaton lawyer, insurance executive
Blalock, Sherrill investment advisor
Blanc, Roger David lawyer
Bland, Frederick Aves architect
Bland, Peter George bank executive
Blaney, John advertising executive
Blank, Blanche Davis political science educator
Blank, Marion Sue psychologist
Blasi, Vincent A. lawyer, educator
Blass, Bill (William Ralph Blass) apparel and home furnishings designer
Blattmachr, Jonathan George lawyer
Blatty, William Peter writer
Blechman, R. O. artist, filmmaker
Bleiberg, Robert Marvin retired financial editor
Blind, William Charles lawyer
Blinder, Richard Lewis architect
Blinken, Robert James manufacturing and communications company executive
Blitzer, Andrew otolaryngologist, educator
Bliven, Bruce, Jr. writer
Bliven, Naomi book reviewer
Bliwise, Lester Martin lawyer
Blobel, Günter cell biologist, educator
†Bloch, Peter editor
Block, Dennis Jeffery lawyer
†Block, Francesca Lia writer
Block, John Douglas auction house executive
Block, Lawrence author
Block, Paul J. cosmetic company executive
†Blondeau, Jacques Patrick Adrien reinsurance company executive
Bloom, David E. university educator
Bloom, Robert Avrum lawyer
Bloomer, Harold Franklin, Jr. lawyer
Bloomfield, Peter statistics educator
Bloomgarden, Kathy Finn public relations executive
Blos, Joan W. author, critic, lecturer
Blum, Howard Louria, Jr. investment banking executive
Blumberg, Gerald lawyer
Blume, Judy Sussman author
Blume, Lawrence Dayton lawyer
Blumenthal, W(erner) Michael manufacturing company executive, former secretary of treasury, investment banker
Blumkin, Linda Ruth lawyer
Blumstein, Allan lawyer
Blumstein, Reneé J. research and statistical consultant
Blyth, Myrna Greenstein publishing executive, editor, author
Blythe, William LeGette, II editor, writer
Boal, Peter Cadbury dancer
Boardman, Seymour artist
Boast, Molly Shryer lawyer
Bocca, Julio dancer
Bochner, Mel artist
Bock, Joseph Reto industrial relations executive
Bock, Walter Joseph zoology educator
Bockstein, Herbert lawyer
Boehm, David Alfred publisher, producer
Boelzner, Gordon orchestral conductor
Boes, Lawrence William lawyer
Bogdonoff, Morton David physician, educator
Boggs, Gil principal ballet dancer
Bohan, Thomas E. advertising company executive
Bohn, John Augustus, Jr. banker, lawyer
Boice, Craig Kendall management consultant
Bolebruch, John J. investment banking company executive
Boley, Bruno Adrian engineering educator
Boley Bolaffio, Rita artist
Bollman, Mark Brooks, Jr. communications executive
Bolt, Thomas writer, artist
Bolter, Eugene P. investment counselor
Bona, Frederick Emil public relations executive
Bonazzi, Elaine Claire mezzo-soprano
Bond, George Clement anthropologist, educator
Bond, J. Max, Jr. architect, educational administrator
Bond, Jonathan Halbert advertising executive
Bond, Victoria Ellen conductor, composer
Bonfante, Larissa classics educator
Bonino, Fernanda art dealer
Bon Jovi, Jon rock singer, composer
†Bonmati, Reynald G. investment banking executive
Bonniwell, Katherine magazine executive
Bono, (Paul Hewson) singer, songwriter
Bonomi, John Gurnee lawyer
Boodey, Cecil Webster, Jr. political science educator
Bookhardt, Fred Barringer, Jr. architect
Booth, Edgar Hirsch lawyer
Booth, Margaret A(nn) communications company executive
Booth, Mitchell B. lawyer
Boothby, Willard Sands, III bank executive
Boothe, Power visual artist, educator, filmmaker, set designer
Borchard, William Marshall lawyer
Borda, Deborah symphony orchestra executive
Borden, Elizabeth B. publishing executive
Borders, William Alexander journalist
Bordiga, Benno automotive parts manufacturing company executive
Borelli, Francis J(oseph) (Frank Borelli) insurance brokerage and consulting firm financial executive
Borenstein, Abe Isaac securities industry executive
Borer, Jeffrey Stephen cardiologist
Borge, Victor entertainer, comedian, pianist
Borisoff, Richard Stuart lawyer
Bornet, Stephen Folwell public relations and marketing communications executive
Borofsky, Jonathan artist
Borowitz, Sidney retired physics educator
Borsody, Robert Peter lawyer
Bosco, Philip Michael actor
Boshkov, Stefan Hristov mining engineer, educator
Boshkov, Stefan Robert lawyer
†Boskey, Adele Ludin biochemistry educator, researcher
Bosniak, Morton Arthur physician, educator
Bostock, Roy Jackson advertising agency executive
†Boston, Gretha mezzo-soprano, actress
Botero, Fernando artist
Bothmer, Dietrich Felix von museum curator, archaeologist
Bottner, Irving Joseph cosmetic company executive
Boucher, Henry Joseph (Bud Boucher) management consultant
Boulanger, Jacques Pierre investment banker
Bouloukos, Don P. broadcast company executive
Boultinghouse, Marion Craig Bettinger editor
Boundas, Louise Gooch editor
Bourdon, David art critic, writer
Bourgeois, Louise sculptor
Bourjaily, Vance novelist
†Bourke, Thomas Anthony librarian, writer
†Bourne, Mel production designer, art director
Boutros-Ghali, Boutros United Nations official
Bove, John Louis chemistry and environmental engineering educator, researcher
Bovin, Denis Alan finance company executive
Bowden, Sally Ann choreographer, teacher, dancer
Bowden, William P., Jr. lawyer, banker
Bowen, Jean music librarian, consultant
Bowen, John Sheets advertising agency executive
Bowen, William Gordon economist, educator, foundation administrator
Bowie, Jonathan Munford lawyer
Bowling, James Chandler food products company consultant
Bowman, Robert A. hotel company executive
Boxer, Leonard lawyer
Boyarski, Joel I. financial executive
Boyce, Joseph Nelson journalist
Boyd, Michael Alan investment banking company executive, lawyer
Bozorth, Squire Newland lawyer
Brack, Reginald Kufeld, Jr. publisher
Bradbury, Ray Douglas author
Brademas, John retired university president, former congressman
Bradford, Barbara Taylor writer, journalist, novelist
Bradford, John Carroll retired magazine executive
Bradford, Richard Roark writer
Bradford, Robert Ernest motion picture producer
Bradley, E. Michael lawyer
Bradley, Edward R. news correspondent
Bradley, Lisa M. artist
Bradner, William Murray, Jr. lawyer
Bradstock, John advertising executive
Brady, Adelaide Burks public relations agency executive, giftware catalog executive
Brady, James Winston writer, television commentator
Braham, Randolph Lewis political science educator
Brams, Steven John political scientist, educator, game theorist
Brancato, Carolyn Kay economist, consultant
Brand, Leonard physician, educator
Brandt, Grace Borgenicht art dealer
Brandt, Warren artist
Branson, Richard airline executive, entrepreneur, adventurer
Brant, Sandra J. magazine publisher
†Bratton, William J. police commissioner
Braude, Robert Michael medical library administrator
†Braudy, Susan Orr writer
Braun, Craig Allen producer
Braun, Jeffrey Louis lawyer
Braun, Lilian Jackson writer
Braverman, Robert Jay international consultant, public policy educator
Bravmann, Ludwig investment banker
Bravo, Rose Marie retail executive
Braxton, Toni popular musician
Brazinsky, Irving chemical engineering educator
Brecher, John newspaper editor
Brechner, Stanley artistic director
Brecker, Manfred retail company executive
†Breger, William N. architect, educator
Breglio, John F. lawyer
Bregman, Martin film producer
Breindel, Eric Marc editor, columnist, educator
Breines, Simon architect
Breinin, Goodwin M. physician
Brendel, Alfred concert pianist
Brennan, Daniel L. accounting, consulting firm executive
Brennan, Donald P. aircraft parts manufacturing executive
Brennan, Donald P. investment company executive
Brennan, Henry Higginson architect
Brennan, Timothy William entertainment company executive
†Brenner, Beth Fuchs publishing executive
Brenner, Egon university official, education consultant
Brenner, Erma author
Brenner, Frank lawyer, venture capitalist
Brenner, Gita Kedar Voivodas small business owner, research and editing consultant
Brenner, Howard Martin banker
Brenner, Paul R. lawyer
Bresani, Federico Fernando business executive
Bresler, Martin I. lawyer
Breslin, Jimmy columnist, author
Breslow, Jan Leslie scientist, educator, physician
Breslow, Ronald Charles chemist, educator
Bressler, Bernard lawyer
Breuer, Lee playwright, theatrical director, producer, actor
Brewer, John Charles journalist
Brewer, Karen librarian
Brewster, Robert Gene concert singer, educator
Brezenoff, Stanley bi-state agency administrator
Bricken, Barry Irwin fashion designer
Brickman, Marshall screenwriter, director
Brief, Henry association executive
Brier, Pamela Sara health facility administrator
Briess, Roger Charles brewing and food industry executive
Briggs, Jean Audrey publishing company executive
Briggs, Philip insurance company executive
Briggs, Taylor Rastrick lawyer
Brigstocke, David Hugh Charles investment banker
Brill, Steven magazine editor
Brilliant, Richard art history educator
Brilliant, Robert Lee advertising agency executive
Brimelow, Peter journalist
Bring, Murray H. lawyer
Brinker, Robert J. investment company executive, radio talk show host
Brinkley, Christie model
Bristah, Pamela Jean librarian
Britell, Peter Stuart lawyer
Brittenham, Raymond Lee investment company executive
Broadwater, Douglas Dwight lawyer
Broches, Paul Elias architect
Brocksmith, James G., Jr. accounting, management consulting firm executive
Broder, Douglas Fisher lawyer
Brodkey, Harold Roy writer
Brodsky, Edward lawyer
Brodsky, Samuel lawyer
Brody, Alan Jeffrey investment company executive
Brody, Alexander advertising executive
Brody, Eugene David investment company executive
Brody, Jacqueline editor
Brody, Jane Ellen journalist
†Brody, Martin food service company executive
Brody, Saul Nathaniel English literature educator
Brofman, Lance Mark portfolio manager, mutual fund executive
Brokaw, Thomas John television broadcast executive, correspondent
Brome, Thomas Reed lawyer
Bronfman, Edgar M., Jr. food products executive
Bronfman, Edgar Miles beverage company executive
Bronkema, Frederick Hollander minister, church official
Bronkesh, Annette Cylia public relations executive
Bronstein, Richard J. lawyer
Brook, David William psychiatrist
Brooke, Paul Alan finance company executive
Brooks, Diana D. auction house executive
Brooks, Geraldine reporter, correspondent
Brooks, Jerome Bernard English and Afro-American literature educator
Brooks, Lorimer Page patent lawyer
Brooks, Russell Edwin lawyer
Brooks, Timothy H. media executive
Brooks, Tyrone dancer
Brooksbank, Randolph Wood broadcasting executive
Brophy, Francis L. chemical company executive
Bross, Steward Richard, Jr. lawyer
Brothers, Joyce Diane television personality, psychologist
Broude, Richard Frederick lawyer, educator
Broughton, Phillip Charles lawyer
Browar, Lisa M. librarian
Browdy, Joseph Eugene lawyer
Brown, Arthur Edward physician
Brown, Carroll diplomat, association executive
Brown, Charles Dodgson lawyer
Brown, Daniel Herbert lawyer, manufacturing company executive
Brown, David motion picture producer, writer
Brown, Edward Glenn chef, restaurateur
†Brown, Eric Lucasen art gallery director, art dealer
Brown, Francis Cabell, Jr. lawyer
Brown, Fred Elmore investment executive
Brown, Helen Gurley editor, writer
Brown, Hobson, Jr. executive search firm consultant and executive
Brown, Jason Walter neurologist, educator, researcher
Brown, Jeffrey Wisner publishing company executive
Brown, Jonathan art historian, fine arts educator
Brown, Les (Lester Louis) journalist
Brown, Meredith M. lawyer
Brown, Milton Wolf art historian, educator
Brown, Paul M. lawyer
Brown, Peter Megargee lawyer, writer, lecturer
Brown, Ralph Sawyer, Jr. lawyer, business executive
Brown, Raymond Edward educator, priest
Brown, Robert Delford artist
Brown, Robert William baseball league executive, physician
Brown, Ronald stockbroker
Brown, Seymour William engineering executive, consultant
Brown, Terrence Charles art association executive, researcher, lecturer
Brown, Thomas J. real estate syndication company executive
Brown, Tina magazine editor
Brown, Trisha dancer
Browne, Arthur newspaper editor
Browne, Jeffrey Francis lawyer
Browne, Malcolm Wilde journalist
Browning, Edmond Lee bishop
Browning, John pianist
Brownwood, David Owen lawyer
Brozman, Tina L. federal judge
Bruce, Duncan Archibald financier
Bruckmann, Donald John investment banker
Bruckmann, Mark F. lawyer
Brumback-Henry, Sarah Elizabeth industrial psychologist, management and corporate consultant
Brumm, James Earl trading company executive
Brundage, Susan art dealer, gallery director
Brundige, Robert W., Jr. lawyer
Brunie, Charles Henry investment manager
Brusca, Robert Andrew economist
Brush, Charles Francis anthropologist
Brush, Craig Balcombe French language and computer educator
Bruzs, Boris Olgerd management consultant
Bryan, Barry Richard lawyer
Bryant, Gay magazine editor, writer
Brydon, Donald James media consultant, former news service executive
Brzustowicz, Stanislaw Henry clinical dentistry educator
Bschorr, Paul Joseph lawyer
Buatta, Mario interior designer
Buchwald, Elias public relations executive
Buchwald, Naomi Reice federal magistrate judge
Buck, James E. financial exchange executive
Buck, Louise Zierdt psychologist
Buckles, Robert Howard investment company executive
†Buckley, Kevin magazine editor
Buckley, Priscilla Langford magazine editor
Buckley, Virginia Laura editor
Buckley, William Frank, Jr. magazine editor, writer
†Buford, Bill editor, writer
Buhagiar, Marion editor, author
Bujold, Lois McMaster science fiction writer
Bullen, Richard Hatch former corporate executive
Bulliet, Richard Williams history educator, novelist
Bullock, H. Ridgely management and investment executive, lawyer
Bullock, Hugh investment banker
Bumbry, Grace soprano
Bundschuh, George August William insurance company executive
Bundy, Mary Lothrop social worker
Bundy, McGeorge former government official, history educator
Bungey, Michael advertising executive
Bunts, Frank Emory artist
Burak, H(oward) Paul lawyer
Burback, Steven Brent military administrator
Burenga, Kenneth L. publishing executive
Burg, Mitchell Marc advertising executive
†Burge, Christopher auction house executive
Burgee, John Henry architect
Burger, Chester retired management consultant
Burgheim, Richard Allan magazine editor
Burgweger, Francis Joseph Dewes, Jr. lawyer
Burke, Chris actor
Burke, Daniel Barnett retired communications corporation executive
Burke, James Joseph, Jr. investment banker
Burke, Mary Griggs (Mrs. Jackson Burke) art collector
Burke, Thomas Edmund lawyer
Burkhardt, Ronald Robert advertising executive
Burland, Brian Berkeley novelist, poet, artist, scenarist, playwright
Burlingame, Lloyd Lamson design instructor
Burns, Arnold Irwin lawyer
Burns, John F. reporter
Burns, John Joseph, Jr. manufacturing executive
Burns, Robin cosmetics company executive
Burns, Ronald S. advertising company executive
Burns, Ward textile company executive
Burnshaw, Stanley writer
Burrell, Kenneth Earl guitarist, composer
Burrill, Kathleen R. F. (Kathleen R. F. Griffin-Burrill) Turkologist, educator
Burrows, Michael Donald lawyer
Burrows, Selig Saul industrialist
Bursky, Herman Aaron lawyer
Burson, Harold public relations executive
Burton, John Campbell university dean, educator, consultant
Burton, Robert Gene printing and publishing executive
†Busch, Andrew textile executive
†Bush, Harry Leonard, Jr. surgery educator
Bush, Kate (Catherine Bush) singer, songwriter
Bushey, Alan Scott insurance holding company executive
Bushman, Richard L. history educator, writer, consultant
Bushnell, John Alden diplomat, economist
Butcher, Willard Carlisle banker
Butler, Jonathan Putnam architect
Butler, Robert Neil gerontologist, psychiatrist, writer, educator
Butler, Samuel Coles lawyer
Butler, Vincent Paul, Jr. physician, educator
Butler, William Joseph lawyer
Butowsky, David Martin lawyer
†Butrom, Carl broadcasting executive
Buttenwieser, Lawrence Benjamin lawyer
Butterfield, R. Keith financial company executive
Buttner, Jean Bernhard publishing company executive

Button, Richard Totten *television and stage producer, former figure skating champion*
Buttrick, Harold *architect*
Buxton, Jorge Norman *ophthalmologist*
Byer, Diana *performing arts company executive*
Byington, Homer Morrison, III *financial consultant*
Bylinsky, Gene Michael *magazine editor*
Byrne, Gerard Anthony *publishing company executive, marketing consultant*
Bystryn, Jean-Claude *dermatologist, educator*
†Cabot, Jane Fenderson *public relations executive*
Cadwell, Franchellie Margaret *advertising agency executive, writer*
Cafiero, Eugene Anthony *manufacturing company executive*
Caggiano, Joseph *advertising executive*
Caggiano, Michael Vincent *financial services company executive*
Cahan, William George *surgeon, educator*
Cahn, Joshua Binion *lawyer*
Cahn, Steven M. *philosopher, educator*
Cajigal, Joseph A. *financial services executive*
Cajori, Charles Florian *artist, educator*
Calabrese, Rosalie Sue *arts management consultant, writer*
Calame, Kathryn Lee *microbiologist, educator*
Calder, Kenneth Thomas *psychiatrist, psychoanalyst, educator*
Caldwell, Earl *newspaper columnist*
Caldwell, Paulette M. *law educator*
Caldwell, Philip *financial services company executive, retired automobile manufacturing company executive*
Caldwell, Susan Hanes *art dealer*
Caldwell, Zoe *actress, director*
Caliban, Richard Allen *artistic director*
Calise, Ronald Jan *investment banking executive*
Calisher, Hortense (Mrs. Curtis Harnack) *writer*
Call, Neil Judson *corporate executive*
Callahan, Joseph Patrick *lawyer*
Callahan, Robert F., Jr. *radio network executive*
Callen, John Holmes, Jr. *executive search consultant*
Callum, Myles *magazine editor, writer*
Calvey, Brian J. *lawyer*
Calvillo, Ricardo C. *communications executive*
Cameron, Eleanor *author*
†Campbell, Alan *actor*
Campbell, Colin (Soupy Campbell) *professional hockey coach*
Campbell, Colin Goetze *foundation president*
Campbell, Douglass *banker*
Campbell, George, Jr. *physicist, administrator*
Campbell, Mary Schmidt *dean art school*
Campbell, Naomi *model*
Campbell, Robert Chambers *critic, playwright*
Campbell, Ronald Neil *magazine designer*
Campbell, Scott G. *lawyer*
Campbell, Timothy Reid *financial services company executive*
Campbell, William I. *cigarette company executive*
Campbell, Woodrow Wilson, Jr. *lawyer*
Campi, John G. *newspaper publishing executive*
Campo, Benjamin Paul *lawyer*
Campos, Fernando *editor-in-chief*
†Canada, Geoffrey *social welfare administrator*
Canavan, Bernard *retired pharmaceuticals executive, physician*
Canby, Vincent *film critic*
Cancro, Robert *psychiatrist*
Candia, Oscar A. *ophthalmologist, physiology educator*
Cane, Myles Adrian *lawyer, not-for-profit organization executive*
Canin, Ethan *writer*
Cannaliato, Vincent, Jr. *investment banker, mathematician*
Cannell, John Redferne *lawyer*
Cannella, John Matthew *federal judge*
Cannon, James Anthony *advertising executive*
Cannon, John Haile *retail executive*
†Canonero, Milena *costume designer*
Canoni, John David *lawyer*
Canter, Stanley D. *retired marketing consulting company executive*
Cantilli, Edmund Joseph *safety engineering educator, writer*
Cantor, Alexandra *professional society administrator*
Cantor, Bernard Gerald *financial executive*
Cantor, Melvyn Leon *lawyer*
Cantor, Norman Frank *history educator, writer*
Cantor, Richard Ira *physician, corporate health executive*
Cantrell, Lana *actress, singer*
Cantwell, Mary *journalist*
Caouette, John Bernard *insurance company executive*
Capa, Cornell *photographer, director photography museum*
Capalbo, Carmen Charles *director, producer*
Caples, Richard James *dance company executive, lawyer*
Capone, Robert *retail store executive*
†Capouya, Emile *writer*
Cappello, Juan C. *business executive*
Cappon, Andre Alfred *management consultant*
Capriati, Jennifer Maria *professional tennis player*
Caputo, David Armand *university president, political scientist educator*
Caputo, Philip Joseph *author, journalist, screenwriter*
Caraley, Demetrios *political scientist, educator, author*
Caras, Roger Andrew *author, motion picture company executive, television correspondent, radio commentator*
Carb, Stephen Ames *lawyer*
Carberry, Charles Michael *lawyer*
Cardew, William Joseph *bank executive*
Cardinali, Albert John *lawyer*
Cardozo, Benjamin Mordecai *lawyer*
Cardozo, Michael A. *lawyer*
Carelli, Gabor Paul *opera singer*
Carey, Edward John *utility executive*
Carey, J. Edwin *lawyer*
Carey, James William *university dean, educator, researcher*
Carey, Thomas Hilton *advertising agency executive*
Carey, William Polk *investment banker*
Cariou, Len Joseph *actor, director*
Carling, Francis *lawyer*
Carlson, David Bret *lawyer, consultant*
Carlson, Loren Dale *finance executive*
Carlson, Marian Bille *geneticist, researcher, educator*
Carlson, Marvin Albert *theater educator*
Carlson, P(atricia) M(cElroy) *writer*
Carlson, Theodore Joshua *lawyer, retired utility company executive*
Carman, Gregory Wright *federal judge*
Carnase, Thomas Paul *graphic designer, typographic consultant*
Carnella, Frank Thomas *information executive*
Caro, Robert Allan *author*
Caroff, Phyllis M. *social work educator*
Carpenter, Patricia *music educator*
Carr, Arthur Charles *psychologist, educator*
Carr, Gladys Justin *publishing company executive*
Carr, Ronald Edward *ophthalmologist, educator*
Carra, Andrew Joseph *advertising executive*
Carreras, José *tenor*
Carret, Philip Lord *corporate executive*
Carroll, J. Speed *lawyer*
Carroll, Joseph J(ohn) *lawyer*
Carroll, Kent *book publishing executive*
Carroll, Thomas Joseph *investment services company executive*
†Carter, Betsy L. *magazine editor*
Carter, Carolyn Houchin *advertising agency executive*
Carter, Cary Warren *investment banking executive*
Carter, Edward Graydon *editor*
Carter, James Hal, Jr. *lawyer*
Carter, Kevin *photographer*
Carter, Marshall Nichols *banker*
Carter, Sylvia *journalist*
Carthaus, James Arthur *financial service company executive*
Cartland, Barbara *author*
†Carton, Ellen *association executive*
Caruso, Victor Guy *investment banker*
Carver, Brent *actor*
Casals-Ariet, Jordi *physician*
Case, Eugene Lawrence *advertising agency executive*
Case, Hadley *oil company executive*
Casebere, James Edward *artist*
Cash, Rosanne *country singer, songwriter*
Cashin, Richard Marshall *international aid official*
Caso, Ronald George *lawyer, accountant*
Casper, Jack H. *advertising executive*
Cassell, Eric Jonathan *physician*
Cassell, Kay Ann *librarian*
Cassella, William Nathan, Jr. *organization executive*
†Cassidy, John Joseph *journalist*
Castel, Nico *tenor, educator*
Castel, P. Kevin *lawyer*
Castelli, Leo *art dealer*
Castellino, Ronald Augustus Dietrich *radiologist*
Castle, John Krob *merchant banker*
Castleman, (Esther) Riva *museum curator*
Castronovo, David *English language educator*
Catley-Carlson, Margaret *association executive*
Cato, John David *religious organization administrator*
Catsimatidis, John Andreas *retail chain executive, airline executive*
Catuzzi, J. P., Jr. *lawyer*
Cauthen, Steve *former jockey, sportscaster*
Cavaglieri, Giorgio *architect*
Cavior, Warren Joseph *communications executive*
Caws, Mary Ann *French language and comparative literature educator, critic*
Cayne, James E. *investment banker*
Cazeaux, Isabelle Anne Marie *retired musicology educator*
Cecil, Robert Salisbury *telecommunications company executive*
Cedarbaum, Miriam Goldman *federal judge*
Ceresney, Ian *lawyer*
Cesarani, Sal *fashion designer*
Chahinian, Aram Philippe *oncologist*
†Chaitkin, David *composer*
Chajet, Clive *communications consultant*
Chalif, Seymour H. *lawyer*
Chalsty, John Steele *investment banker*
Chamberlin, Ward Bryan, Jr. *public broadcasting executive*
Chammah, Walid A. *investment banker*
Chamson, Sandra Potkorony *psychologist*
†Chan, Eric Ping-Pang *industrial designer*
Chan, Lo-Yi Cheung Yuen *architect*
Chan, W. Y. *pharmacologist, educator*
Chancellor, John William *former news correspondent*
Chandler, Kenneth A. *newspaper editor*
Chandler, Robert Leslie *public relations executive*
Chaney, Verne Edward, Jr. *surgeon, foundation executive, educator*
†Chaney, William R. *former cosmetics executive*
Channing, Alan Harold *hospital administrator*
Channing, Stockard (Susan Stockard) *actress*
Chapin, Hugh A. *lawyer*
Chapin, Schuyler Garrison *cultural affairs executive, university dean*
†Chapin, Theodore Steinway *entertainment company executive*
Chapman, Peter Herbert *investment company executive*
Chapman, Wes *dancer*
Chapnick, David B. *lawyer*
Chappell, John Charles *lawyer*
Chargaff, Erwin *biochemistry educator emeritus, writer*
Charlesworth, Sarah E. *photographer, conceptual artist*
Charnin, Martin *theatrical director, lyricist, producer*
Charrier, Michael Edward *investment banker*
Charron, Paul Richard *apparel company executive*
Chase, Merrill Wallace *immunologist, educator*
Chase, Sylvia B. *journalist*
Chaves, Jose Maria *diplomat, foundation administrator, lawyer, educator*
†Chaya, Masazumi *dancer*
†Chazanoff, Jay David *investment company executive*
Chazen, Hartley James *lawyer*
Checker, Chubby (Ernest Evans) *musician*
Checketts, David Wayne *professional basketball team executive*
Chefitz, Harold Neal *investment banker*
Cheh, Huk Yuk *engineering educator, electrochemist*
Chell, Beverly C. *lawyer*
Chen, Chi (Chen Chi) *artist*
†Chen, Philip Minkang *investment banker, corporate executive, lawyer, engineer*
Chenault, Kenneth Irvine *financial services company executive*
Cheney, Richard Eugene *public relations executive*
Cheng, Chuen Yan *biochemist, educator*
Chenok, Philip Barry *accountant, association executive*
Chermayeff, Ivan *graphic designer*
Chernin, Fredric David *advertising agency executive*
Chernoff, Allan *correspondent*
Chernow, David A. *former distillery executive, consultant*
Cherovsky, Erwin Louis *lawyer, writer*
Cherry, Rona Beatrice *magazine editor, writer*
Chesnutt, Jane *publishing executive*
Chester, Giraud *television executive*
Chester, John Geoffrey *lawyer*
Cheung, Ambrose Lin-Yau *microbiologist, researcher*
Chevalier, Samuel Fletcher *banker*
Chevigny, Paul Graves *lawyer, educator*
Chevray, Rene *physics educator*
Chiarchiaro, Frank John *lawyer*
Chichilnisky, Graciela *economics educator, mathematician, consultant*
Child, Julia McWilliams (Mrs. Paul Child) *cooking expert, television personality, author*
Childs, John Farnsworth *investment banker*
Chiles, Nick *newspaper reporter*
Chilstrom, Robert Meade *lawyer*
Chimsky, Mark Evan *editorial executive*
Chin, Sylvia Fung *lawyer*
Chinnis, Pamela P. *religion organization administrator*
Chirelstein, Marvin A. *law educator*
Chiu, David Tak Wai *surgeon*
Choi, Ye-Chin *microbial geneticist*
Cholak, Paul Michael *financial services personnel executive*
Chook, Paul Howard *publishing executive*
Chorazy, Sandra Marie *advertising agency executive*
Chow, Yuan Shih *mathematician, educator*
Christaldi, Brian *lawyer*
Christensen, Dieter *ethnomusicologist*
Christensen, Henry, III *lawyer*
Christensen, Thomas Gordon Steffen *law educator*
Christesen, Russell J. *construction company executive*
†Christian, Charles Leigh *physician, educator*
Christian, Darrell L. *journalist*
Christo, (Christo Vladimirov Javacheff) *artist*
Christopher, Maurine Brooks *foundation administrator, writer, editor*
†Christopher, Nicholas *poet, novelist*
Christy, Arthur Hill *lawyer*
Chromow, Sheri P. *lawyer*
Chryst, Gary *ballet dancer*
Chu, C. K. *applied mathematician, educator*
†Chu, David *apparel executive*
Chu, Richard Shao-hung *investment banker*
Chu, Roderick Gong-Wah *management consultant*
Chua, Nam-Hai *plant molecular biologist, educator*
†Chudnovsky, David Volfovich *mathematician, computer designer*
Chudnovsky, Gregory Volfovich *mathematician, educator*
Chung, Chia Mou (Charles) *oriental art business owner*
Chung, Connie (Constance Yu-hwa Chung) *broadcast journalist*
Church, Frank Forrester *minister, author, columnist*
†Church, George John *journalist*
Churchill, Mary Carey *public relations executive*
Chwast, Seymour *graphic artist*
Ciccone, Peter M. *telephone company executive*
Ciechanover, Joseph *banker, lawyer*
†Ciociola, Melvin J. *advertising agency executive*
†Cisneros, Sandra *poet, short story writer, essayist*
Citron, Richard Ira *management consultant*
Clabby, William Robert *editor*
Claire, Thomas Andrew *business executive, writer*
Clamar, Aphrodite J. *psychologist*
Clancy, Thomas L., Jr. *novelist*
Clapman, Peter Carlyle *insurance company executive, lawyer*
Clapton, Eric *musician*
Clarens, John Gaston *investment executive*
Clark, Cameron *lawyer*
Clark, Carolyn Cochran *lawyer*
Clark, Howard Longstreth, Jr. *finance company executive*
Clark, J. Thomas *advertising agency executive*
Clark, Jonathan Montgomery *lawyer*
Clark, Joseph Gilbert *opera company executive*
Clark, Matt *science writer*
Clark, Merrell Edward, Jr. *lawyer*
Clark, Ramsey *lawyer*
Clark, Robert Henry, Jr. *holding company executive*
Clark, Thomas Carlyle *banker*
Clark, William Stratton *physician*
Clarke, Frank William *advertising agency executive*
Clarke, John Clem *artist*
Clarke, Kenneth Kingsley *electrical equipment company executive*
Claro, Jaime *metal trading company executive*
Clary, Richard Wayland *lawyer*
Claster, Jill Nadell *university administrator, history educator*
Clauson, James Wilson *accountant*
Clayton, Joe Don *lawyer*
Clayton, Jon Kerry *holding company executive*
Clayton, Jonathan Alan *banker*
Cleary, Beverly Atlee (Mrs. Clarence T. Cleary) *author*
Clemente, Constantine Louis *lawyer, health care company executive*
Cliff, Walter Conway *lawyer*
Clifford, Stewart Burnett *banker*
Close, Chuck (Charles Thomas Close) *artist*
Close, Michael John *lawyer*
Cloward, Richard Andrew *social work educator*
Clurman, Richard Michael *journalist*
Cobb, Henry Nichols *architect*
Cochrane, James Louis *economist*
Coffee, John Collins, Jr. *legal educator*
†Coffin, Dwight Clay *grain company executive*
Coffin, John Devereux *import-export company executive*
Cogan, James Richard *lawyer*
Cogan, Marshall S. *entrepreneur*
Cohen, Abby Joseph *securities analyst*
Cohen, Alan Norman *business executive*
Cohen, Arnold *apparel executive*
Cohen, Arthur Morris *artist*
†Cohen, Audrey C. *college president*
Cohen, Burton Jerome *financial service executive*
†Cohen, Claire Gorham *investors service company executive*
Cohen, Cora *artist*
Cohen, David Harris *neurobiology educator, university official*
Cohen, Edmund Stephen *lawyer*
Cohen, Edward *civil engineer*
Cohen, Edward Herschel *lawyer*
Cohen, Eli Edward *sociology educator*
Cohen, Ezechiel Godert David *physicist, educator*
Cohen, Fred Howard *investment banker*
Cohen, Henry Rodgin *lawyer*
Cohen, Irving Elias *real estate executive*
Cohen, Irving I. *finance company executive*
Cohen, Jerome Alan *lawyer, educator*
Cohen, Joel Ephraim *scientist, educator*
Cohen, Joel J. *lawyer, investment banker*
Cohen, Jonathan Little *investment banker*
Cohen, Lawrence Alan *real estate executive*
Cohen, Mildred Thaler *art gallery director*
†Cohen, Naomi Wiener *historian, educator*
Cohen, Noel Lee *otolaryngologist, educator*
Cohen, Richard Gerard *lawyer*
Cohen, Samuel Israel *clergyman, organization executive*
Cohen, Saul Bernard *former college president, geographer*
Cohen, Selma *reference librarian, researcher*
Cohen, Selma Jeanne *dance historian*
Cohen, Stephen Frand *political scientist, historian, educator, author, broadcaster*
Cohl, Claudia Hope *editor*
Cohn, Bertram Josiah *investment banker*
Cohn, David Herc *retired foreign service officer*
Cohn, Harvey *mathematician*
Cohn, Sam *motion picture and theatrical agent*
Cohn, Theodore *management consultant*
Coigney, Martha Wadsworth *theater executive*
Colasuonno, Louis Christopher *newspaper editor*
Colby, Marvelle Seitman *business management educator, administrator*
Colby, Robert Alan *retired library science educator*
Cole, Elma Phillipson (Mrs. John Strickler Cole) *social welfare executive*
Cole, Jonathan Richard *sociologist, academic administrator*
Cole, Lewis George *lawyer*
Cole, Max *artist*
Cole, Sylvan, Jr. *art dealer*
Cole, Vinson *tenor*
Coleman, Cy *pianist, composer, producer*
Coleman, George Edward *tenor, alto and soprano saxophonist*
Coleman, Leonard S., Jr. *sports association executive*
Coleman, Lester Laudy *otolaryngologist*
Coleman, Martin Stone *office furniture company executive*
Coleman, Morton *oncologist, hematologist, educator*
Coleman, Ornette *jazz musician*
Coler, Myron A(braham) *chemical engineer, educator*
†Coles, Bruce C. *engineering company executive*
Coles, Michael H. *investment banker*
Colker, Edward *artist, educator*
Coll, John Peter, Jr. *lawyer*
Collamore, Thomas Jones *corporate executive*
Collins, Daniel G. *law educator*
†Collins, J. Barclay, II *oil company executive, lawyer*
Collins, Judy Marjorie *singer, songwriter*
Collins, Wayne Dale *lawyer*
Collins, William T. *lawyer*
Collinson, Dale Stanley *lawyer*
Collyer, Michael *lawyer*
Colombo, Frank V. *securities company executive*
Colombo, Furio *writer, journalist*
Colonel, Sheri Lynn *advertising agency executive*
Comden, Betty *writer, dramatist, lyricist, performer*
Comey, Dale Raymond *insurance company executive*
Comfort, William Twyman, Jr. *banker*
Comfrey, Kathleen Marie *lawyer*
Comissiona, Sergiu *conductor*
Comitas, Lambros *anthropologist*
Como, Perry *singer*
Compagnon, Antoine Marcel *French language educator*
Conarroe, Joel Osborne *foundation administrator, educator, editor*
Conboy, Kenneth *lawyer, former federal judge*
Concannon, Richard James *lawyer*
Cone, James Hal *theologian, educator, author*
Conforti, Joanne *advertising executive*
Conklin, Thomas J. *insurance company executive*
Conlon, James Joseph *conductor*
Connelly, Albert R. *lawyer*
Connick, Harry, Jr. *jazz musician, actor, singer*
Connolly, John Joseph *health care company executive*
Connolly, William Gerard *newspaper editor*
Connor, John Thomas, Jr. *lawyer*
Connor, Joseph E. *accountant*
Conover, Robert Fremont *artist, educator*
Conrad, Winthrop Brown, Jr. *lawyer*
Conroy, Dennis Joseph *management consultant*
Consagra, Sophie Chandler *academy administrator*
Constance, Thomas Ernest *lawyer*
Constantine, Gus *physical education educator, coach*
Constantine, Jan Friedman *lawyer*
Conston, Henry Siegismund *lawyer*
Conway, David Antony *communications executive, marketing professional*
Conway, Kevin *actor, director*
Conyard, Shirley Jean *college dean*
Cook, Blanche Wiesen *history educator, journalist*
Cook, James *magazine editor*
Cook, Michael Lewis *lawyer*
Cook, Robert Stansfield, Jr. *lawyer*
Cook, Robin *author*
Cooke, Alfred Alistair *correspondent, broadcaster*
Cooke, Gordon Richard *retail executive*
Cooke, Mary A. *hospice director*
Cooney, Joan Ganz *broadcasting executive*
Cooney, John Patrick, Jr. *lawyer*
†Cooney, Lenore *public relations executive*
Cooper, Alice (Vincent Furnier) *popular musician*
Cooper, Andrew *public relations executive*
Cooper, Arthur Gerald *cable television executive*
Cooper, Arthur Martin *magazine editor*
Cooper, Deborah Ellen *lawyer*
Cooper, Irving Ben *federal judge*
Cooper, James H. *book publishing company executive, lawyer*
Cooper, Mario *artist, educator*
Cooper, Michael Anthony *lawyer*
Cooper, Norman Streich *pathologist, medical educator*
Cooper, Paulette Marcia *writer*
Cooper, R. John, III *advertising agency executive, lawyer*
Cooper, Roger Frank *publishing company executive*
Cooper, Stephen Herbert *lawyer*
Coplan, Norman Allan *lawyer*
Coppel, Alfred *author*
Corbin, Herbert Leonard *public relations executive*
Corbin, Sol Neil *lawyer*
Corcoran, David *newspaper editor*
Corcoran, James P. *lawyer*
Corcoran, Robert Lee, Jr. *banker*
Cordero, Angel T., Jr. *former jockey, horse trainer*
Core, Mary Carolyn W. Parsons *radiologic technologist*
Corigliano, John Paul *composer*
Corley, Leslie M. *investment banker*
Corliss, Richard Nelson *critic, magazine editor*
Corman, Avery *author*
Corn, Bennett Julian *commodity exchange executive*
Cornell, George W. *journalist*
Cornez, Gerald H. *association executive*
Cornstein, David B. *finance executive*

Corporon, John Robert broadcasting executive
Corr, Gary Alan finance company executive
Corrigan, E. Gerald investment banker
Corry, Carl dancer
Corry, John Adams lawyer
Corsaro, Frank Andrew theater, musical and opera director
Corso, (Nunzio) Gregory poet
Cortor, Eldzier artist, printmaker
Cory, Charles Robinson investment banker
Corzine, Jon Stevens investment banker
Cose, Ellis journalist, author
Cossotto, Fiorenza mezzo-soprano
Costa, Max health facility administrator, pharmacology educator, environmental medicine educator
Costello, Gerald Michael editor
Costello, John Robert linguistics educator
Costello, Richard Neumann advertising agency executive
Costikyan, Edward N(azar) lawyer
Coté, Anne Alexis hospital nursing administrator
Cotter, James Michael lawyer
Coulter, Catherine writer
Coupland, Douglas C. writer
Couric, Katherine broadcast journalist
Court, Kathryn Diana editor
Cowan, Martin B. lawyer
Cowan, Wallace Edgar lawyer
Cowen, Edward S. lawyer
Cowen, Robert Nathan lawyer
Cowin, Stephen Corteen biomedical engineering educator, consultant
Cowles, Charles art dealer
Cowles, Frederick Oliver lawyer
Cox, Archibald, Jr. investment banker
Cox, Darlene Louise health care executive, nurse
Cox, James Oliver, III public relations company executive
Cox, Marshall lawyer
Cox, Winston H. television executive
†Coyne, Nancy Carol advertising executive
Craft, Randal Robert, Jr. lawyer
Craig, Charles Samuel marketing educator
Craig, George publishing executive
Crain, Irving Jay psychiatrist, educator
Cramer, Edward Morton lawyer, music company executive
Cramer, Marjorie plastic surgeon
Crames, Michael J. lawyer
Crane, Benjamin Field lawyer
Crane, Stephen Andrew insurance company executive
Crary, Miner Dunham, Jr. lawyer
Crawford, Bruce Edgar advertising executive
Crawford, Cindy model
Crawford, Harold Bernard publisher
Crawley, John Boevey publisher
†Creech, Sharon children's author
Creedon, John J. insurance company executive
Creel, Thomas Leonard lawyer
Crevier, Roger L. banker
Crews, Harry Eugene author
Crier, Catherine television news correspondent
Crile, Susan artist
Crimmins, Robert John insurance company executive

NEw York

Crisci, Mathew G. marketing executive

New York

Crisona, James Joseph lawyer
†Crispino, Mike sportscaster
Crist, Judith film and drama critic
Critchlow, Charles Howard lawyer
Crivello, Anthony actor
Croce, Arlene Louise critic
Cromwell, Oliver Dean investment banker
Cronholm, Lois S. biology educator
Cronkite, Walter radio and television news correspondent
Crosby, Gordon Eugene, Jr. insurance company executive
Crosby, John Griffith investment banker
Crosland, Philip Crawford advertising company executive
Cross, George Alan Martin biochemistry educator, researcher
Cross, Peter A. lawyer
Cross, Theodore Lamont publisher, author
Cross, William Redmond, Jr. corporate director, foundation executive
†Crouch, Stanley writer, jazz musician
Crow, Elizabeth Smith publishing company executive
Crowdus, Gary Alan film company executive
Crowley, Mark investment company executive
Croy, Sandra Lee bank officer
†Cruz, Celia vocalist
Cryer, Gretchen playwright, lyricist, actress
Crystal, James William insurance company executive
Crystal, Lester Martin television producer
Cubitto, Robert J. lawyer
Culhane, John William journalist, author, film historian
Culhane, Shamus producer, author
Cullen, Patrick Colborn English educator
Culligan, John William retired corporate executive
Cullman, Edgar M., Jr. tobacco products company executive
Cullman, Edgar Meyer diversified consumer products company executive
Culp, Michael securities company executive, research director
Cumming, Ian M. holding company executive
Cummings, Josephine Anna writer
Cummins, Herman Zachary physicist
Cuneo, Donald Lane lawyer, educator
Cunha, Mark Geoffrey lawyer
Cunningham, Bill photographer
Cunningham, Jeffrey Milton publishing executive
Cunningham, Merce dancer
Cunningham, Noel B. lawyer, educator
Cunningham, Patrick Joseph advertising agency executive
Cuomo, Mario Matthew lawyer, former governor
Cuozzo, Steven David newspaper editor
Curley, Walter Joseph Patrick diplomat, investment banker
Curran, William James, III lawyer
Currie, Bruce artist
Curry, Ann correspondent, anchor
Curry, Jack magazine editor
Curry, Jane Louise writer
Curtin, Brian Joseph ophthalmologist
Curtis, Frank R. lawyer
Curtis, Paul James American mime
Curtis, Sheldon lawyer
Curtis, Susan Grace lawyer
Cushing, Harry Cooke, IV investment banker
Cutie, James A. newspaper publishing executive
Cutler, Kenneth Burnett lawyer, investment company executive
Cutler, Laurel advertising agency executive
Cutler, Rhoda psychologist
Cutler, Richard J. metal products executive
Czerwinski, Edward Joseph foreign language educator
Dabah, Haim apparel executive
Dabah, Isaac apparel company executive
Dacey, Eileen M. lawyer
Dailey, Benjamin Peter chemistry educator
Daily, John Charles software company executive
Daitz, Ronald Frederick lawyer
Dajani, Virginia arts administrator
Dakin, Christine Whitney dancer, educator
Daldry, Stephen theatrical director
Dale, Harvey Philip law educator
Dale, Jim actor
Daley, James E. accounting firm executive
Dallas, William Moffit, Jr. lawyer
Dallmann, Daniel F. artist, educator
Dalrymple, Jean Van Kirk theatrical producer, publicist, author
Dalton, Dennis Gilmore political science educator
Daly, Charles Patrick publishing company executive
Daly, George Garman college dean, educator
Daly, Joe Ann Godown publishing company executive
Daly, John Neal investment company executive
Daly, Margaret V. magazine editor
Daly, Michael newspaper columnist
d'Amboise, Jacques Joseph dancer, choreographer
Damrosch, Lori Fisler law educator
Dana, F(rank) Mitchell theatrical lighting designer
Danaher, Frank Erwin transportation technologist
Dane, Maxwell former advertising executive
†Danese, Renato art gallery director
D'Angelo, Joseph Francis publishing company executive
Dangler, Richard Reiss corporate service companies executive, entrepreneur
Daniel, David Ronald management consultant
Daniel, Gerard Lucian physician, pharmaceutical company executive
Daniel, Richard Nicholas fabricated metals manufacturing company executive
Daniels, Faith newscaster
Daniels, Joanne D. publisher
Danilek, Donald J. lawyer
Danilova, Alexandra ballet dancer, choreographer
Danitz, Marilynn Patricia choreographer
Danne, Richard Franklin graphic designer
Dannhauser, Stephen J. lawyer
Danto, Arthur Coleman author, philosophy educator
Danzig, Aaron Leon lawyer
Danzig, Frederick Paul newspaper editor
Danzig, Jerome Alan (Jerry) management consultant
Danzig, Sarah Palfrey retired advertising agency executive, writer
Danziger, Bruce Edward structural engineer
Danziger, Paula author
Daphnis, Nassos artist
DaPuzzo, Peter James investment banker, trader, financial consultant
Darling, Robert Edward designer, stage director
Darlington, Henry, Jr. investment broker
†Darnton, John Townsend journalist
Darrell, Norris, Jr. lawyer
Darrow, Jill E(llen) lawyer
Darrow, Katherine Prager lawyer, publishing executive
Darst, David Martin investment banking company executive, writer, educator
Darvarova, Elmira violinist, concertmaster
Dattner, Richard architect, educator
Dauben, Joseph Warren history educator
D'Auria, Anthony J. lawyer
David, Hal lyricist
David, Miles association and marketing executive
David, Theoharis Lambros architect, educator
Davidovich, Bella pianist
Davidovich, Jaime video artist, researcher
Davidson, Donald William advertising executive
Davidson, George Allan lawyer
Davidson, Joy Elaine mezzo-soprano
Davidson, Mark Edward lawyer
Davidson, Nancy Brachman artist, educator
Davidson, Robert Bruce lawyer
†Davidson, Wayne A. pharmaceutical and consumer products company executive
David-Weill, Michel Alexandre investment banker
Davies, Dennis Russell conductor, music director, pianist
Davies, Jane B(adger) (Mrs. Lyn Davies) architectural historian
Davies, Martha Hill dance educator
Davis, Andrew Frank conductor
†Davis, Anthony composer, pianist, educator
Davis, Clive Jay record company executive
Davis, Douglas Matthew artist, educator, author
Davis, Edward Shippen lawyer
Davis, Evan Anderson lawyer
Davis, Frederick Townsend lawyer
Davis, George Linn banker
Davis, Jerry Albert architect
Davis, Karen Padgett fund executive
Davis, Kathryn Wasserman foundation executive, writer, lecturer
Davis, Kenneth Leon psychiatrist, pharmacologist, medical educator
Davis, Leonard violist
Davis, Lorraine Jensen writer, editor
Davis, Martin S. investment company executive
Davis, Orlin Ray publisher, consultant
Davis, Peggy Cooper law educator
Davis, Richard Bruce investment banker
Davis, Richard Joel lawyer, former government official
Davis, Richard Ralph lawyer
Davis, Samuel hospital administrator, educator, consultant
Davis, Steven Howard lawyer
Davis, Susan Lynn public relations executive
Davis, Wendell, Jr. lawyer
Davoe, David publishing executive
Dawn, Deborah dancer
Dawson, Thomas Cleland, II financial executive
Day, John W. international corporation executive
Dayan, Rodney S. lawyer
Deak, Istvan historian, educator
Dean, Sidney Walter, Jr. business and marketing executive
Deane, James Richard lawyer
Deare, Jennifer Laurie marketing professional
de Bary, William Theodore Asian studies educator
De Blasio, Michael Peter electronics company executive
Debo, Vincent Joseph lawyer
DeBow, Jay Howard Camden public relations company executive
DeBow, Thomas Joseph, Jr. advertising executive
Debs, Richard A. investment banker, government official
DeBusschere, David Albert brokerage executive, retired professional basketball player and team executive
Decaminada, Joseph Pio insurance company executive, educator
DeCarlo, Donald Thomas lawyer, insurance company executive
de Champlain, Vera Chopak artist, painter
†Decker, Dennis Dale industrial designer
de Cou, Emil conductor
Decter, Midge writer
De Deo, Joseph E. advertising executive
Dedman, Bill journalist
de Duve, Christian René chemist, biologist, educator
Deem, George artist
Deems, Richard Emmet magazine publisher
De Ferrari, Gabriella curator, writer
Deffenbaugh, Ralston H., Jr. immigration agency executive, lawyer
De Gaster, Zachary engineering company executive
DeGroff, Ralph Lynn, Jr. retired investment banker
de Hartog, Jan writer
Deitz, Paula magazine editor
De Jaegher, Jean F. textile and apparel company executive
De Johnette, Jack musician
†De Keyzer, Carl-Georges photographer
Dekker, Marcel publishing company executive
de Kooning, Willem artist
de la Falaise, Lucie model
de la Gueronniere, Raphael securities firm executive
Delaney, Robert Vincent former gas company executive, economic development consultant
Delano, Lester Almy, Jr. advertising executive
de la Renta, Oscar fashion designer
DeLay, Dorothy (Mrs. Edward Newhouse) violinist, educator
Delikat, Michael lawyer
DeLillo, Don author
Dell, Ralph Bishop pediatrician, researcher
Della Femina, Jerry advertising agency executive
Delman, Stephen Bennett lawyer
Delson, Robert lawyer
Delz, William Ronald petroleum company executive
DeMarco, Robert Thomas investment company executive
Demarest, Daniel Anthony retired lawyer
Demaria, Walter sculptor
Demaris, Ovid (Ovid Desmarais) author
deMause, Lloyd psychohistorian
de Menil, Lois Pattison philanthropist
DeMichele, Robert Michael management corporation executive
Demme, Jonathan director, producer, writer
de Montebello, Philippe Lannes museum administrator
Dempsey, Edward A. securities company executive
Dempsey, Louis F(rancis), III banker
Dempster, (Frank) Curt artistic director, producer
De Natale, Andrew Peter lawyer
Denes, Agnes C. environmental artist
Denham, Robert Edwin lawyer, investment company executive
Denhof, Miki graphic designer
Denker, Henry playwright, author, director
Dennis, Donna Frances sculptor, art educator
Dennis, Everette Eugene, Jr. foundation executive, journalism educator, media critic, author
Dennis, Robert (Arthur) composer, educator
Dennis, Walter Decoster suffragan bishop
Denoon, David Baugh Holden economist, educator, consultant
Dent, V. Edward former advertising and communications company executive
DeNunzio, Ralph Dwight investment banker
dePaola, Thomas Anthony illustrator, children's author
de Planque, E. Gail physicist
Derchin, Michael Wayne research director, investment banker, financial analyst
Derman, Cyrus mathematical statistician
DeRoma, Leonard James securities firm executive
Derow, Peter Alfred publishing company executive
Desai, Padma economist, educator, political scientist
Desai, Vishakha N. gallery director, society administrator
de Saint Phalle, Pierre Claude lawyer
De Santo, Samuel J. architectural firm executive, educator
De Sear, Edward Marshall lawyer
Desnick, Robert John human geneticist
Despommier, Dickson Donald microbiology educator, parasitologist, researcher
des Rioux, Deena Victoria Coty artist, graphics designer
Dessi, Adrian Frank marketing, communications executive
Destino, Ralph, Jr. retail executive
Deupree, Marvin Mattox accountant, business consultant
Deuss, Jean librarian
Deutsch, Martin Bernard Joseph editor, publisher
deVeer, Robert Kipp, Jr. investment banker
Deveraux, Jude (Jude Gilliam White) writer
Devers, Peter Dix lawyer
De Vido, Alfredo Eduardo architect
Devine, W. John retail executive
DeVita, Vincent Theodore, Jr. oncologist
DeVito, Francis Joseph advertising agency executive
de Vries, Rimmer economist
Dewey, Robert Manson, Jr. investment company executive
Dewing, Merlin Eugene diversified financial services company executive
de Zagon, Baroness Monique S. lawyer
Dhrymes, Phoebus James economist, educator
Diamant, Anita literary agent
Diamant, Aviva F. lawyer
Diament, Paul electrical engineering educator, consultant
Diamond, David Howard lawyer
Diamond, David Jeremy performing arts company administrator, consultant
Diamond, Edwin journalism educator, editor, columnist
Diamond, Freda designer, home furnishings consultant, lecturer
Diamond, Harris corporate communications executive, lawyer
Diamond, Irene foundation administrator
Diamond, Judy Kay publishing executive
Diamond, Robert Stephen publishing company executive
Diamondstone, Lawrence paper company executive
Diamonstein-Spielvogel, Barbaralee writer, television interviewer/ producer
DiBenedetto, Joseph A. lawyer
diBuono, Anthony Joseph lawyer, business executive
DiCarlo, Dominick L. federal judge
Dichter, Misha concert pianist
Dicker, Marvin lawyer
Dicterow, Glenn Eugene violinist
Didion, Joan author
DiDonna, Richard A. lawyer, diversified company executive
Diemente, Damon L. chemistry educator
Di Franco, Loretta Elizabeth lyric coloratura soprano
Diggins, Peter Sheehan ballet company administrator
Dilenschneider, Robert Louis public relations company executive
Dillard, Annie author
Dillingham, Robert Bulger publishing executive
Dillon, Clarence Douglas retired investment company executive
Dillon, Matt actor
DiMaggio, Frank Louis civil engineering educator
Dimen, Muriel Vera psychoanalyst
Di Meo, Dominick artist, sculptor, painter
Di Mitri, Piero fashion designer
Dimling, John Arthur marketing executive
Dimon, James financial services executive
Dinaburg, Mary Ellen art education and curatorial consultant
Dine, Jim artist
Dintenfass, Terry art dealer
Dionne, Joseph Lewis publishing company executive
Di Paola, Robert Arnold mathematics and computer science educator
Di Paolo, Nicholas P. corporate executive, real estate investor
Dirks, Dennis John financial services executive
Di Salvo, Nicholas Armand dental educator, orthodontist
Diskant, Gregory L. lawyer
Disney, Anthea editor
Dispeker, Thea artists' representative
Diver, William linguistics educator
Dixon, Paul Edward chemical company executive, lawyer
D'Lower, Del manufacturing executive
Dobbs, John Barnes artist, educator
†Dobbs, Lou television executive, managing editor
Dobell, Byron Maxwell magazine consultant
Dobrof, Rose Wiesman geriatric services professional
Doctorow, Edgar Lawrence novelist, English educator
Dodd, Lois artist, art professor
Dodson, Daryl Theodore ballet administrator, arts consultant
Doerr, Harriet writer
Doherty, Thomas publisher
Dohrenwend, Bruce Philip psychiatric epidemiologist, social psychologist, educator
Dolan, James Francis lawyer
Dolan, Raymond Bernard insurance executive
Dole, Vincent Paul medical research executive, educator
Dolgen, Jonathan L. motion picture company executive
Dolger, Jonathan editor, literary agent
Dolgin, Martin cardiologist
Doman, Nicholas R. lawyer
Domingo, Placido tenor
Dominianni, Emilio Anthony (Mike Dominianni) lawyer, accountant
Donahue, Phil television personality
Donald, Norman Henderson, III lawyer
Donald, Roger Thomas publishing executive
Donaldson, Stephen Reeder author
Donaldson, William Henry financial executive
Donati, Enrico artist
Doner, Frederick Nathan advertising and communications executive
Donohue, William Anthony religious organization administrator
Dooner, John Joseph, Jr. advertising executive
Dooskin, Herbert P. manufacturing company executive
Doppelt, Earl H. communications corporation executive
Dormann, Henry O. magazine publisher
Dormire, Corwin Brooke lawyer
†Dorn, Sue Bricker hospital and medical school administrator
Dornemann, Michael book publishing executive
Dorris, Michael Anthony anthropologist, writer
Dorsen, Harriette K. lawyer
Dorsen, Norman lawyer, educator
Douglas, Paul Wolff retired mining executive
Douglas, Philip Le Breton lawyer
Douglass, Robert Royal banker, lawyer
Dowell, Anthony James ballet dancer
Dowling, Edward Thomas economics educator
Downes, Edward Olin Davenport musicologist, critic, radio broadcaster
Downey, John Alexander physician, educator
†Downing, Arthur librarian
Downs, Hugh Malcolm radio and television broadcaster
Doyle, Eugenie Fleri pediatric cardiologist, educator
Doyle, Joseph Anthony lawyer
Doyle, L. F. Boker trust company executive
Doyle, Paul Francis lawyer
Doyle, William Stowell venture capitalist
Doza, Lawrence O. food company executive, accountant
Draper, James David art museum curator
Draper, William Franklin artist, portrait and landscape painter
Drapkin, Arnold Howard consulting picture editor, journalist, program director
Drasner, Fred newspaper publishing executive
Drawbaugh, Kevin Alan journalist
Drebsky, Dennis Jay lawyer
Dreier, Douglas H. construction executive
Dreizen, Alison M. lawyer
Dressner, Howard Roy foundation executive, lawyer
Drewry, Elizabeth newspaper publishing executive
Drexler, Joanne Lee art appraiser
Dreyfus, Alfred Stanley rabbi
Dreyfuss, Rochelle Cooper law educator
Dritz, Michael A. securities company executive
Driver, Tom Faw theology educator, writer, justice/ peace advocate
Drobis, David R. public relations company executive
Druck, Mark David director, producer, writer
Druckenmiller, Robert T. public relations executive

Drucker, Mort commercial artist
Druckman, Jacob Raphael composer
Druker, Henry Leo investment banker
Druker, Isaac E. lawyer
Drusin, Lewis Martin physician, educator
Duberman, Martin historian
Dubin, James Michael lawyer
Dubin, Morton Donald management consultant, film producer
Dubin, Seth Harris lawyer
DuBois, Jonathan Delafield lawyer
Dubroff, Charles Mark lawyer
Duchin, Peter Oelrichs musician
Dudack, Gail Marie brokerage house executive
Duddy, Joan Frances performing arts administrator, dancer
Dueves, Henry C. computer company executive
Duff, John Ewing sculptor
Duff, Patricia foundation administrator
Duffy, David L. public relations executive
Duffy, Edmund Charles lawyer
Duffy, James Henry writer, former lawyer
Duffy, Kevin Thomas federal judge
Duffy, Nicole dancer
Duffy, W. Leslie lawyer
Dufour, Val (Albert Valery Dufour) actor
Dugan, Edward Francis bank executive
DuGan, Gordon F. investment banker
Dugan, Michael J. former air force officer, health agency executive
Duggan, Dennis Michael newspaper editor
Duggan, Rosemary H. vocational administrator
Dukakis, Olympia actress
Duke, Angier Biddle retired diplomat
Duke, Anthony Drexel sociologist, educator, philanthropist
Duke, Robin Chandler Tippett retired public relations executive
Dulaine, Pierre ballroom dancer
Duncan, Richard magazine editor
Dundas, Philip Blair, Jr. lawyer
Dune, Steve Charles lawyer
Dunham, Christine dancer
Dunham, Corydon Busnell lawyer, broadcasting executive
Dunham, Donald Carl diplomat
Dunham, Wolcott Balestier, Jr. lawyer
Dunleavy, Rosemary ballet dancer
Dunn, James Joseph magazine publisher
Dunn, James Robert geologist
Dunn, Martin newspaper editor-in-chief
Dunn, M(orris) Douglas lawyer
Dunn, Susan singer
Dunne, Dominick writer
Dunne, John Gregory author
Dunne, Thomas Leo editor, author, publisher
Dunst, Laurence David advertising executive
Dupuy, Frank Russell, Jr. magazine publisher
†Durang, Christopher actor, playwright
Dusenberry, Philip Bernard advertising executive
Dutter, Andrew Allen editor
du Vair, Pierre Henri Serge Marie banker
Dwek, Cyril S. banker
Dworetzky, Murray physician, educator
Dworin, Steve advertising executive
Dworkin, David Lee retail executive
Dworkin, Ronald Myles legal educator
†Dwyer, Jim reporter, columnist
Dykhouse, David Wayne lawyer
Dylan, Bob (Robert Allen Zimmerman) singer, composer
Dyson, Robert R. investment company executive
Dystel, Jane Dee literary agent
Dyyon, Frazier (LeRoy Frazier) artist
Dzodin, Harvey Cary communications executive
Earle, Victor Montagne, III lawyer
Easum, Donald Boyd consultant, educator, former institute executive, diplomat
Ebbitt, Kenneth Cooper, Jr. investment company executive
Ebersol, Dick television broadcasting executive
Eberstein, Arthur biomedical engineering educator, researcher
Ebin, Robert Felix lawyer
Eckert, Allan W. author
Eckhaus, Jay Elliot business executive, lawyer
Eckman, Fern Marja journalist
Eckstut, Michael Kauder management consultant
Edelbaum, Philip R. lawyer
Edelman, Harold architect
Edelman, Herbert Stephen lawyer
Edelman, Isidore Samuel biochemist and medical educator
Edelman, Judith Hochberg architect
Edelman, Paul Sterling lawyer
Edelman, Richard Winston public relations executive
Edelson, Gilbert Seymour lawyer
Edelstein, David Northon federal judge
Edelstein, Haskell banker, tax lawyer
Edgar, Harold Simmons Hull legal educator
Edinger, Lewis Joachim political science educator
Edlow, Kenneth Lewis securities brokerage official
Edmiston, Mark Morton publishing company executive
Edmonds, Robert Scott lawyer
Edmunds, Robert Thomas retired surgeon
Edson, Andrew Stephen public relations executive
Edwards, Christine Annette lawyer
Edwards, Franklin R. economist, educator, consultant
Edwards, Harold Mortimer mathematics educator
Edwards, James D. accounting company executive
Edwards, James Malone lawyer
Edwards, Robert Randle law educator
Effel, Laura lawyer
Eger, Joseph conductor, music director
Eggers, Ernest Russell management consultant
Egielski, Richard illustrator
Ego-Aguirre, Ernesto surgeon
Ehinger, Albert Louis, Jr. securities trader
Ehlers, Kathryn Hawes (Mrs. James D. Gabler) physician
Ehlers, Walter George retired insurance executive
Ehrenbard, Robert lawyer
Ehrenkranz, Joel S. lawyer
Eidson, Thomas E. writer, public relations firm executive
Eig, Norman investment company executive
Einarson, Baldvin Oliver lawyer
Einbender, Alvin H. securities dealer
Einhorn, Eric John advertising executive
Einhorn, Harold lawyer
Einiger, Carol Blum foundation executive
Einiger, Roger W. brokerage house executive
Eisen, Mark fashion designer
Eisenberg, Alan association executive
Eisenberg, Sonja Miriam artist
Eisenberg, Steven securities analyst
Eisenman, Peter David architect, educator
Eisenstadt, G. Michael diplomat, author, lecturer, research scholar
Eisenstadt, Samuel investment company executive
Eisenstaedt, Alfred photojournalist
Eisenthal, Kenneth B. physical chemistry educator
Eisert, Edward Gaver lawyer
Eisler, Colin Tobias art historian, curator
†Eisner, Jack P. writer
Eisner, Richard Alan accountant
Ekern, George Patrick lawyer
Ekman, Richard foundation executive, educator
Elam, Leslie Albert association executive
Elder, Eldon stage designer, theatre consultant
Elderfield, John art historian, museum curator
El-Erian, Tahani library administrator
Elia, Claudio manufacturing executive
Elicker, Gordon Leonard lawyer
Eliopoulos, Nicholas construction company executive
Eliot, Lucy Carter artist
Elkes, Terrence Allen communications executive
Elkin, Jeffrey H. lawyer
Ellenbogen, Rudolph Solomon library curator
Ellerbee, Linda broadcast journalist
Ellig, Bruce Robert personnel executive
Elliman, Donald magazine company executive
Ellington, Mercer Kennedy trumpeter, conductor, composer
Elliott, A. Wright banker
Elliott, John, Jr. advertising agency executive
Elliott, Osborn journalist, educator, former university dean
Elliott, Tim C. advertising agency executive
Elliott-Smith, Paul Henry marketing and economics consultant
Ellis, Albert clinical psychologist, educator, author
Ellis, Bret Easton author
Ellis, Carolyn Terry lawyer
Ellis, Charles Richard publishing executive
Ellis, Kent radiologist, consultant
Ellison, Solon Arthur microbiology and dentistry educator
†Ellroy, James writer
Ellsworth, Arthur Whitney publishing consultant
Elman, Naomi Geist artist, producer
Elrod, James Lake, Jr. investment banker
Elsen, Sheldon Howard lawyer
Elster, Samuel Kase college dean, medical educator, physician
Embree, Ainslie Thomas history educator
Emerson, Alice Frey political scientist, educator emerita
Emerson, Ken newspaper editor
Emick, Jarrod actor
Emil, Arthur D. lawyer
Emmerich, Andre art gallery executive, author
Emmerman, Michael N financial analyst
Emmert, Richard Eugene professional association executive
Emmons, Delia McQuade investment industry executive
Enberg, Dick sportscaster
Enders, Anthony Talcott banker
Enders, Elizabeth McGuire artist
Engelhardt, Sara Lawrence organization executive
†Engen, D(onald) Travis diversified telecommunications company executive
Englander, Roger Leslie television producer, director
Engler, Robert political science educator, author
English, John Winfield foundation administrator
†Engstrom, Erik publishing company executive
Entremont, Philippe conductor, pianist
Ephron, Nora writer
Epling, Richard Louis lawyer
Eppley, Stephen Clyde investment banker
Eppner, Gerald Allen lawyer
Epstein, Barbara editor
Epstein, Cynthia Fuchs sociology educator, writer
Epstein, Harriet Pike public relations executive
Epstein, Jason publishing company executive
Epstein, Jeremy G. lawyer
Epstein, Matthew performing company director
Epstein, Melvin lawyer
Epstein, Michael Alan lawyer
Erbsen, Claude Ernest journalist
Ercklentz, Alexander Tonio insurance company executive
Ercklentz, Enno Wilhelm, Jr. lawyer
Erdrich, (Karen) Louise fiction writer, poet
Ergas, Enrique orthopedic surgeon
Erhardt, Edward Richard advertising company executive
Erlanger, Bernard Ferdinand biochemist, educator
Erlanger, Steven Jay journalist
Erosh, William Daniel financial services company executive
Ertegun, Ahmet Munir record company executive
Erwitt, Elliott Romano photographer, cinematographer
Eschenbach, Christoph conductor, pianist
Esman, Aaron H. physician, psychiatrist
Esman, Rosa Mencher art gallery executive
Esposito, Michael Patrick, Jr. banker
Esposito, Richard Joseph journalist, executive
Espy, Willard Richardson author
Esquivel, Laura writer
Essandoh, Hilda Brathwaite kindergarten educator
Estabrook, Alison breast surgeon, surgical oncologist, educator
Esterow, Milton magazine editor, publisher
Estes, Richard artist
†Estreicher, Samuel lawyer, educator
Eswein, Bruce James, II human resources executive
Etra, Aaron lawyer
Eustice, James Samuel lawyer, educator
Evangelista, Linda model
Evans, Alfred Lee, Jr. advertising executive
Evans, Edward Parker former publishing company executive
Evans, Harold M. publishing executive, writer
†Evans, James Bremond (Jim Evans) major league baseball umpire
Evans, James Hurlburt retired transportation and natural resources executive
Evans, Jerry Norman television director
Evans, John artist
Evans, Martin Frederic lawyer
Evans, Mary Johnston transportation company director
Evans, Thomas Chives Newton communications executive
Evans, Thomas William lawyer
Evans, Van Michael advertising agency executive, consultant
Eveillard, Jean-Marie financial company executive
Everaert, P. J. electronics executive
Everett, James William, Jr. lawyer
Everette, Cheryl newspaper editor
Everhart, Angie model
Everly, Jack conductor
Evnin, Anthony Basil venture capital investor
Ewers, Patricia O'Donnell university administrator
Ewing, Maria Louise soprano
Ewing, Patrick Aloysius professional basketball player
Fabbri, Brian John economist, investment strategist
Faber, Neil advertising executive
Faber, Peter Lewis lawyer
Fabian, George Stephen advertising agency executive
Fabian, Larry Louis non-profit institution executive
Fabio, (Fabio Lanzoni) model
Fabricant, Neil lawyer, educator
Fader, Ellen Strahs communications company executive
Fagen, Leslie Gordon lawyer
Fahey, Peter M(atthew) investment banker
Fahn, Stanley neurologist, educator
Fair, William Robert physician
Fairbanks, Douglas Elton, Jr. actor, producer, writer, corporation director
Fairchild, John Burr publisher
Fales, Haliburton, II lawyer
Falk, Edgar Alan public relations consulting executive, author
Falk, Harvey L. apparel company executive
Fallaci, Oriana writer, journalist
Falletta, Jo Ann musician
Falvey, Patrick Joseph lawyer
Farah, Roger retail company executive
Faran, Ellen Webster publishing executive
Farber, Jackie editor
Farber, John J. chemical company executive
Farber, Saul Joseph physician, educator
Farberman, Harold conductor, composer
†Farella, Steven advertising executive
Fargis, Paul McKenna publishing consultant, book developer, editor
Farinelli, Jean L. public relations firm executive
Farkas, Robin Lewis retail company executive
Farley, Carole soprano
Farley, James Bernard retired financial services company executive
Farley, Peggy Ann finance company executive
Farley, Robert Donald lawyer, business executive
Farley, Terrence Michael banker
Farney, Dennis journalist
Farnham, George Railton lawyer
Farnsworth, E(dward) Allan lawyer, educator
Farnsworth, Philip Richeson lawyer, broadcasting and publishing executive
Farrell, Eileen soprano
Fass, Peter Michael lawyer, educator
Fass, Sim medical products executive
Fast, Howard Melvin author
Fast, Julius author, editor
†Fasullo, Eugene Jack state official
Fates, Joseph Gilbert television producer
Faulkner, Frank M. artist
Faulkner, Walter Thomas lawyer
Faurer, Louis photographer
Feder, Arthur A. lawyer
Feder, Saul E. lawyer
Federico, Gene graphic designer
Feders, Sid journalist, television producer
Fehr, Donald M. baseball union executive
Feigelson, Philip biochemist, educator
Feigen, Richard L. art dealer
Feigin, Barbara Sommer advertising executive
Feiler, Jo Alison artist
Fein, Bernard investments executive
Feinberg, Mortimer Robert psychologist, educator
Feinberg, Robert Edward advertising agency executive, writer
Feinberg, Samuel retired newspaper columnist
Feinberg, Wilfred federal judge
Feininger, Andreas Bernhard Lyonel photographer
Feist, Gene theater director
Feist, Leonard association executive
Feit, Glenn M. lawyer
Felcher, Peter L. lawyer
Feld, Eliot dancer, choreographer
Feldberg, Chester Ben banker, lawyer
Feldberg, Meyer university dean
Feldberg, Michael Svetkey lawyer
Feldman, Franklin lawyer, printmaker
Feldman, Jerome Ira lawyer, patent development executive
Feldman, Justin Newton lawyer
†Feldman, Robert C. public relations executive
Feldman, Ronald art gallery director
Feldman, Ronald Arthur social work educator, researcher
Feldman, Samuel Mitchell neuroscientist, educator
Feldmann, Shirley Clark psychology educator
Feldtmose, John Nielsen management consulting executive
Felfe, Peter Franz lawyer
Fellner, Michael Josef dermatologist
Felsher, Celia Ann lawyer
Feniger, Jerome Roland, Jr. broadcasting executive
†Fennell, John magazine publisher
†Fenster, Albert M. lawyer
Fensterstock, Blair Courtney lawyer
Fensterstock, Lee securities firm executive
Fenton, Thomas Trail journalist
Ferber, Samuel publishing executive
Feretic, Eileen Susan editor
Ferguson, Frances Hand volunteer, civic worker
Ferguson, Milton Carr, Jr. lawyer
Ferguson, Robert A. law educator
Ferguson, Robert Harry Munro lawyer
Ferguson, William Charles telecommunications executive
Fernandez, Jose Walfredo lawyer
Fernández-Velazquez, Juan Ramon university chancellor
†Fernando, Lakshman G. accountant
Ferra, Max stage director
Ferrante, Joan Marguerite English and comparative literature educator
Ferrara, Arthur Vincent insurance company executive
Ferrara, Peter Biagio, Jr. radio broadcast executive
Ferrari, Alberto Mario health care company executive
Ferrell, John Frederick advertising executive
Ferrer, Marie Irene physician
Ferri, Alessandra Maria ballet dancer
Ferries, John Charles advertising executive
Ferris, Barton Purdy, Jr. investment banker
†Ferris, Robert public relations executive
Ferris, Robert Dominick public relations executive
Fertig, Howard publisher, editor
Fetscher, Paul George William brokerage house executive
Fetter, Theodore Henry entertainment consultant
Feuer, Cy motion picture and theatrical producer, director
Fewell, Christine Huff psychoanalyst, alchohol counselor
Fidanza, Giovanni securities broker, dealer, executive
Fiedler, Lawrence Elliot real estate investment company executive
Field, Crystal artistic director, actor
Fields, Douglas Philip building supply and home furnishings wholesale company executive
Fields, Harry industry executive
Fier, Elihu lawyer
Fierstein, Harvey Forbes playwright, actor
Filer, Elizabeth Ann psychotherapist
Filler, Ronald Howard lawyer
Finberg, Alan Robert retired newspaper executive, lawyer
Finberg, Barbara Denning foundation executive
Finch, Edward Ridley lawyer, former diplomat, author, lecturer
Findlay, Michael Alistair auction house executive, poet
Findlay, Ronald Edsel economist
Fine, Donald Irving editor, publisher
Fine, Michael Joseph publishing and communications company executive
Fineman, Martha Albertson law educator
Finger, Seymour Maxwell political science educator, former ambassador
Fink, Donald Glen engineering executive, editor
Fink, Robert Steven lawyer, writer, educator
Fink, Stuart Simon business management educator
Finkelstein, Bernard lawyer
Finkelstein, Edward Sydney department store executive
Finlay, Thomas Hiram biochemist, researcher
Finn, David public relations company executive, artist
Finn, Joan Lockwood public relations executive, writer, educator
Finn, Peter public relations executive
Finnerud, Kenneth Percival marketing executive
Finocchiaro, Alfonso G. bank executive
Fiorato, Hugo conductor
Fiore, Mary magazine editor
Fiorillo, John A(nthony) health care executive
Fires, Earlie Stancel jockey
First, Harry legal educator
Fischer, Carl photographer, graphic designer
Fischer, Lindsay Koehler dancer
Fischman, Bernard D. lawyer
Fish, Hamilton public interest executive
Fishbein, Peter Melvin lawyer
Fishel, Stanley Irvyng advertising executive
Fisher, Ann Bailen lawyer
Fisher, Arthur magazine editor
Fisher, Bennett Lawson investment executive
Fisher, Gary Alan publishing executive
Fisher, Harold Leonard lawyer, banker
Fisher, Herbert Franklin lawyer
Fisher, Jules Edward producer, lighting designer, theatre consultant
Fisher, Richard B. investment banker
Fisher, Rick lighting designer
Fisher, Robert Allen advertising executive
Fisher, Robert I. lawyer
Fishman, Fred Norman lawyer
Fishman, James H. magazine executive
Fishman, Jay Steven financial services executive
Fishman, Mitchell Steven lawyer
Fiske, Robert Bishop, Jr. lawyer
Fitch, James Marston architectural preservationist, architectural historian, critic
Fitch, Lyle Craig economist, administrator
Fitzgerald, James E. newspaper publishing executive
Fitzpatrick, Nancy S. advertising executive
Fitzsimmons, Sophie Sonia interior designer
Fiumefreddo, Charles A. investment management company executive
Flack, Roberta singer
Flagg, Jeanne Bodin editor
Flaherty, Tina Santi corporate communications executive
Flaherty, William E. chemicals and metals company executive
Flanagan, Bernard newspaper publishing executive
Flanagan, Dennis journalist
Flanagan, Thomas James Bonner writer, fiction, non-fiction
Flanigan, Peter Magnus investment banker
Flannery, Anne Catherine lawyer
Flatley, Guy writer, magazine editor
Flatt, Ernest Orville choreographer, director
Flaum, Sander Allen advertising and marketing executive
Fleder, Robert Charles lawyer
Fleischer, Arthur, Jr. lawyer
Fleischer, Joseph Linden architect
Fleischman, Edward Hirsh lawyer
Fleischman, Lawrence Arthur art dealer, publisher, consultant
Fleishman, Wendy Ruth lawyer
†Fleiss, David Jonathan orthopedist
Fleming, Alice Carew Mulcahey (Mrs. Thomas J. Fleming) author
Fleming, Charles Stephen ambassador
Fleming, Peter Emmet, Jr. lawyer
†Fleming, Renée L. opera singer
Fleming, Thomas James writer
Fletcher, Anthony L. lawyer
Fletcher, Colin author
Fletcher, George P. law educator
Fletcher, Harry George, III curator
Fletcher, Raymond Russwald, Jr. lawyer
Flexner, James Thomas author
Flint, George Squire lawyer
Flom, Joseph Harold lawyer
†Florio, Lori Zelikow magazine publisher
Florio, Steven T. magazine executive
Flowers, William Ellwood lawyer
Fluhr, Howard consulting firm executive
Flumenbaum, Martin lawyer
Flynn, George William chemistry educator, researcher
Flynn, James T. banker
Flynn, Richard Michael utilities executive
Fodor, Eugene Nicholas concert violinist
Fodor, Susanna Serena lawyer
†Foerst, John George, Jr. fundraising executive
Fogarty, John Thomas business executive, former association executive
Fogel, Irving Martin consulting engineering company executive
Fogg, Blaine Viles lawyer
Fogge, Len advertising executive
Foley, Duncan Karl economist, educator
Foley, Joseph Bernard retired business publishing executive

Foley, Kathleen M. neurologist, educator, researcher
Fondiller, David Stewart journalist
Foner, Eric historian, educator
Fontaine, Edward Paul mining company executive
Fontana, Thomas Michael producer, scriptwriter
Fontana, Vincent Robert lawyer
Foote, Horton playwright, scriptwriter
Forbes, Christopher (Kip Forbes) publisher
†Forbes, Colin Ames graphic design consultant
Forbes, Malcolm Stevenson, Jr. publishing executive
Forbes, Timothy Carter publisher
Ford, Eileen Otte (Mrs. Gerard W. Ford) modeling agency executive
Ford, John Charles communications executive
Ford, Silas M. personal care, household products company executive
Foreman, Laura dancer, choreographer, conceptual artist, writer, educator
Foreman, Richard theater director, playwright
Foresman, Bruce Chalfin treasurer
Forlano, Anthony retired investment company executive
Forman, Leonard P. media company executive
Fornes, Maria Irene playwright, director
Forst, Donald newspaper editor
Forst, Judith Doris mezzo-soprano
Forstadt, Joseph Lawrence lawyer
Forster, Arnold lawyer, author
Forte, Wesley Elbert insurance company executive, lawyer
Fortenbaugh, Samuel Byrod, III lawyer
Fortner, Joseph Gerald surgeon, educator
Foster, David Lee lawyer
Foster, James Henry advertising and public relations executive
Foulke, William Green, Jr. banker
Fowler, Henry Hamill investment banker
Fowler, Robert Ramsay Canadian deputy defence minister
Fox, Arthur Charles physician, educator
Fox, Daniel Michael foundation administrator, author
Fox, Donald Thomas lawyer
Fox, Jack Jay chemist, educator
†Fox, Mitchell magazine publisher
Fox, Paula (Mrs. Martin Greenberg) author
Fox, Robert Frederick, Jr. architect
Fox, Stephen Cress television correspondent, writer
Fox, Sylvan journalist
†Foxman, Abraham H. advocacy organization administrator
Foxworth, Jo advertising agency executive
Frackman, Richard Benoit investment banker
Fraenkel, George Kessler chemistry educator
Fraidin, Stephen lawyer
Fraiman, Genevieve Lam lawyer
France, Joseph David securities analyst
Francis, Dick (Richard Stanley Francis) novelist
Francis, Richard Herman transportation executive
Franck, Thomas Martin law educator
Franco, Jean Spanish language educator
†Frangione, Blas physician
Frangopoulos, Zissimos A. banker
Frank, David Abraham finance executive
Frank, Frederick investment banker
Frank, James Aaron magazine editor, author
Frank, Lloyd lawyer, chemical company executive
Frank, Robert Allen advertising executive
Frank, William Fielding computer systems design executive, consultant
Frankel, Alice Kross physician, director
Frankel, Benjamin Harrison lawyer
Frankel, Gene theater director, author, producer, educator
Frankel, Martin Richard statistician, educator, consultant
Frankel, Marvin E. lawyer
Frankel, Max journalist
†Franken, Martin public relations company executive
Frankenthaler, Helen artist
Frankl, Kenneth Richard lawyer
Franklin, Blake Timothy lawyer
Franklin, Edward Ward international investment consultant, lawyer, actor
Franklin, Julian Harold political science educator
Franklin, Phyllis professional association administrator
Franks, Lucinda Laura journalist
Frantz, Andrew Gibson physician, educator
Frantz, Jack Thomas advertising executive
Frantzen, Henry Arthur investment company executive
Franz, Donald Eugene, Jr. merchant banker, security analyst
Franzen, Ulrich J. architect
Frassetto, Floriana Domina performer, choreographer, costume designer
Fratti, Mario playwright, educator
Frawley, Sean Paul publishing executive
Frazier, Walter, Jr. (Clyde Frazier) radio announcer, television analyst, retired professional basketball player
†Fréchette, Louise Canadian diplomat
Fredericks, Wesley Charles, Jr. lawyer
Freeburg, Richard Gorman financial derivatives company executive
Freed, James Ingo architect
Freed, Stanley Arthur museum curator
Freedberg, David Adrian art educator, historian
Freedberg, Irwin Mark dermatologist
Freedgood, Anne Goodman editor
Freedman, Albert Z. publishing company executive
Freedman, Alfred Mordecai psychiatrist, educator
Freedman, Allen Royal business executive, lawyer
Freedman, Audrey Willock economist
Freedman, Eugene M. accounting firm executive
Freedman, Gerald M. lawyer
Freedman, Helen Edelstein justice
Freedman, Theodore Levy lawyer
Freeman, Clifford Lee advertising agency executive
Freeman, Elaine Lavalle sculptor
Freeman, Mark artist
Freeman, Michael J. consumer products company executive
Freiberg, Lowell Carl financial executive
Freid, Jacob association executive, educator
Freilicher, Morton lawyer
Freizer, Louis A. radio news producer
French, Harold Stanley food company executive
French, John, III lawyer
French, Marilyn author, critic
Freudenberger, Herbert Justin psychoanalyst
†Freudenheim, Milton B. journalist
Freudenstein, Ferdinand mechanical engineering educator
Freund, Fred A. lawyer
Freund, Gerald foundation administrator
Freund, James Coleman lawyer
Freund, William Curt economist
Fribourg, Michel international agribusiness executive
Fricke, Janie (Jane Marie Fricke) singer
Fried, Albert, Jr. investment banker
Fried, Burton Theodore lawyer
Fried, Donald David lawyer
Fried, Walter Jay lawyer
Friedan, Betty Naomi author, feminist leader
Friedberg, Barry Sewell investment banker
Friedberg, Marvin Paul landscape architect
Friedberg, Richard M. physicist, educator
Friedenberg, Daniel Meyer financial investor
Friedewald, William Thomas physician
Friedheim, Eric Arthur publisher, editor
Friedhoff, Arnold J. psychiatrist, medical scientist
Friedlander, Ralph thoracic and vascular surgeon
Friedman, Alan Herbert ophthalmologist
Friedman, Alan Roy lawyer
Friedman, Alvin Edward investment executive
Friedman, Bart lawyer
Friedman, B(ernard) H(arper) writer
Friedman, Emanuel A. medical educator
Friedman, Frances public relations executive
Friedman, Howard Martin financial executive
Friedman, Howard W. retired real estate company executive
Friedman, Ira Hugh surgeon
Friedman, J. Roger publisher
Friedman, John Maxwell, Jr. lawyer
Friedman, Joshua M. journalist, educator
Friedman, Leon law educator, lawyer
Friedman, Mickey (Michaele T. Friedman) novelist
Friedman, Robert editor
Friedman, Robert Laurence lawyer
Friedman, Robert N. retail executive
Friedman, Samuel Selig lawyer
Friedman, Stephen James lawyer
Friedman, Victor Stanley lawyer
Friedman, Wilbur Harvey lawyer
Friend, Jonathan Joseph opera administrator
Friendly, Fred W. journalist, educator
Friesner, Richard A. chemistry educator
Frimerman, Leslie financial services company executive
Frisch, Harry David lawyer, consultant
Frischling, Carl lawyer
Frisell-Schröder, Sonja Bettie opera producer, stage director
Frith, Margaret publishing company executive
Fritz, Joanie M. theater director, actor
†Fritz, Mark reporter, journalist
Fritzlen, Thomas L., Jr. investment banker and broker
Froewiss, Kenneth Clark corporate finance executive
†Fromme, Irwin industrial raw materials marketing company executive
Frommer, Henry financial executive
Frost, Diana lawyer
Frost, Robert financial consulting firm executive
Frost, William Lee lawyer
Frumkin, Allan art dealer
Frye, Clayton Wesley, Jr. financial executive
Fryer, Judith Dorothy lawyer
Fryer, Robert Sherwood theatrical producer
Fuchs, Anna-Riitta medical educator, scientist
Fuchs, Joseph Louis magazine publisher
Fuchs, Michael Joseph television executive
Fuersich, Janet Theresa compensation consultant, corporate executive
Fugate, Judith ballet dancer
Fugate-Wilcox, Terry artist
Fuhrer, Arthur K. lawyer
Fujitani, Yoshitaka heavy manufacturing executive
Fujiwara, Nobuo trading company executive
Fuks, Zvi Y. medical educator
Fuld, James Jeffrey lawyer
Fuld, Stanley H. lawyer
Fulghum, Robert L. author, lecturer
Fullem, Lawrence Robert lawyer
Fuller, Charles Henry, Jr. playwright
Furlaud, Richard Mortimer pharmaceutical company executive
Furlong, Charles Richard broadcasting executive
Furman, Anthony Michael public relations executive
Furman, Roy L. investment banker
Furmanski, Philip cancer research scientist
Furnas, Joseph Chamberlain writer
Fursland, Richard Curtis public relations executive
Furuhata, Taketo (Mike Furuhata) trading company executive
Fuster, Valentin cardiologist, educator
Futia, Leo Richard former insurance company executive
Futter, Ellen Victoria museum administrator
Fuzesi, Stephen, Jr. lawyer, communications executive
Gabay, Donald David lawyer
Gabrilove, Jacques Lester physician
Gaddis, William writer
Gaertner, Christopher Wolfgang electronics company executive
Gagosian, Larry art dealer
Gaines, Boyd actor
Gaines, James Russell magazine editor, author
Gaines, Jay S. executive recruiter
Gainsburg, Roy Ellis publishing executive
Galant, Herbert Lewis lawyer
Galanter, Eugene psychologist, educator
Galanter, Marc psychiatrist, educator
Galassi, Jonathan White book publishing company executive
Galassi, Peter museum curator
Galbraith, Evan Griffith investment banker
Gale, John banker
Galin, Miles A. ophthalmologist, educator
Gallagher, Edward Peter arts association administrator
Gallagher, Patrick Ximenes mathematics educator, researcher
Gallagher, Terence Joseph lawyer
Gallagher, Thomas Joseph banker
Gallantz, George Gerald lawyer
Galleno, Anthony Massimo bank executive
Gallo, Gregory sports editor
Gallo, William Victor cartoonist
Galotti, Donna publishing executive
Galotti, Ronald A. magazine publisher
Galston, Clarence Elkus lawyer
Galway, James flutist
Gambee, Robert Rankin investment banker
Gambro, Michael S. lawyer
Gambuti, Gary hospital administrator
Gammell, Stephen illustrator
Gammill, Lee Morgan, Jr. insurance company executive
Gamper, Albert R., Jr. insurance executive
Gamson, Annabelle dancer
Gandolf, Raymond L. media correspondent
Gannon, Jerome Aylward construction and contracting management executive
Gans, Herbert J. sociologist, educator
Gans, Walter Gideon lawyer
Gant, Donald Ross investment banker
†Gantcher, Nathan financial services company executive
Ganz, Howard L. lawyer
Ganzi, Victor Frederick lawyer
Garagiola, Joe sports broadcaster
Garba, Edward Aloysius financial executive
Garber, Harry Douglas life insurance executive
Garber, Robert Edward lawyer, insurance company executive
Gardiner, E. Nicholas P. executive search executive
Gardino, Vincent Anthony broadcast executive
Gardner, James Richard pharmaceutical company executive
Gardner, Ralph David advertising executive
Gardner, Richard Newton diplomat, lawyer, educator
Garfinkel, Barry Herbert lawyer
Gargano, Amil advertising agency executive
Garland, Sylvia Dillof lawyer
Garner, Albert Headden investment banker
Garnett, Stanley Iredale, II lawyer, utility company executive
Garratt, Graham publishing executive
Garrett, Robert financial advisory executive
Garrison, John Raymond organization executive
Garrow, David Jeffries historian, author
Gartner, Alan P. university official, author
Gartner, Murray lawyer
Garver, Robert S. banker
Garvin, Andrew Paul information company executive, author, consultant
Gassel, Philip Michael lawyer
Gatch, Milton McCormick, Jr. library administrator, clergyman, educator
Gates, Jodie dancer
Gatje, Robert Frederick architect
Gatti, Frank R. publishing executive
Gattie, Erma Charlotte opera singer
Gatto, John Taylor educational consultant, writer
Gaudieri, Millicent Hall association executive
Gaughan, Eugene Francis accountant
Gavrity, John Decker insurance company executive
Gazouleas, Panagiotis J. journalist
Gazzara, Ben actor
Gebbie, Kristine Moore health science educator, health official
Gechtoff, Sonia artist
Geduld, Emanuel Edward equity trading company executive
Geduldig, Alfred corporate communications consultant
Geer, John Farr religious organization administrator
Gehringer, Richard George publishing executive
Geier, Philip Henry, Jr. advertising executive
Geiger, H. Jack medical educator
Geis, Bernard book publisher
Geiser, Elizabeth Able publishing company executive
Geismar, Thomas H. graphic designer
Geissbuhler, Stephan graphic designer
Gelb, Arthur newspaper editor
Gelb, Bruce S. city commissioner
Gelb, Harold Seymour investor
Gelb, Joseph W. lawyer
Gelb, Judith Anne lawyer
Gelb, Leslie Howard organization president, lecturer
Gelb, Richard Lee pharmaceutical corporation executive
Gelber, Herbert Donald diplomat
Gelber, Jack playwright, director
Geldzahler, Janet Thiele lawyer
Gelfand, Neal oil company executive
Gelfman, Robert William lawyer
†Geller, Jeffrey Lawrence financier
Geller, Robert James advertising agency executive
Gellert, Michael Erwin investment banker
Gellhorn, Walter law and political science educator, author
Gellman, Isaiah environmental consultant
Geltzer, Sheila Simon public relations executive
Genin, Roland energy executive
Genkins, Gabriel physician
Genova, Joseph Steven lawyer
Geoghegan, Patricia lawyer
George, Beauford James, Jr. lawyer, educator
George, David Alan investment banker
George, Gladys hospital administrator
Georges, Paul Gordon artist
Georgescu, Peter Andrew advertising executive
Georgopoulos, Maria architect
Geraghty, Kenneth George financial services company executive
Gerard, Emanuel investment banking executive
Gerard, Fred N. lawyer
Gerard, Whitney Ian lawyer
Gerber, Robert Evan lawyer
Gerber, Roger Alan lawyer, business executive
Gerdts, William Henry art history educator
Gergiev, Valery artistic director, conductor
Gerhardt, Lillian Noreen magazine editor
Germano, William Paul publisher
Gerra, Ralph A., Jr. lawyer
Gerry, Elbridge Thomas, Jr. banker
Gershengorn, Marvin Carl physician, scientist, educator
†Gershon, Michael David anatomist, educator
Gershon, Nina federal judge
Gershuny, Donald Nevin lawyer
Gerson, Irwin Conrad advertising executive
Gersony, Welton Mark physician, pediatric cardiologist, educator
Gersten, Bernard theatrical producer
Gertler, Menard M. physician, educator
Gertner, Joseph Michael physician, educator
Gessner, Charles Herman apparel company executive
Gewirtz, Elliot lawyer
Gewirtz, Gerry editor
†Giakas, Wallace Martin investment banker
Giannetti, Thomas Leonard lawyer
Giannini, Cynthia dancer
Giaquinto, Philip M. banker
Gibb, Barry vocalist, songwriter
Gibbs, Joe Jackson former professional football coach, broadcaster, professional sports team executive
†Gibbs, L(ippman) Martin lawyer
Gibbs, Richard Leslie public relations executive
Giblin, James Cross author, editor
Gibson, Charles DeWolf broadcast journalist
Gibson, Ralph H(olmes) photographer
Gibson, William B. advertising, marketing executive
Gibson, William Francis investment banking executive
Gibson, William Shepard insurance executive
Giddins, Gary Mitchell music critic, columnist
Gifford, Frank Newton sportscaster, commentator, former professional football player
Gifford, Kathie Lee television personality, singer
Gifford, William C. lawyer
Gilbert, Bradley professional tennis player, Olympic athlete, professional tennis coach
Gilbert, Edes Powell headmistress
Gilbert, Phil Edward, Jr. lawyer
Gilbert, Pia S. musical educator, composer
Gilbert, Thomas Strong investment banker, venture capitalist
Gilinsky, Stanley Ellis department store executive
Gill, Ardian C. actuary
Gill, Brendan writer
Gill, E. Ann lawyer
Gill, Vince country musician, singer
Gillers, Stephen law educator
Gillespie, George Joseph, III lawyer
Gillham, Robert bank executive
Gilliatt, Neal advertising executive, consultant
Gilman, Charles Alan lawyer
Gilman, Richard H. newspaper publishing executive
Gilmont, Ernest Rich chemist
†Gilmore, Louise Jacobson labor union adiminstrator
Gilmore, Robert Gordon insurance company executive
Gilpatric, Roswell Leavitt lawyer
Giniger, Kenneth Seeman publisher
Ginsberg, David Lawrence architect
Ginsberg, Ernest lawyer, banker
Ginsberg, Frank Charles advertising executive
Ginsberg, Harold Samuel virologist, educator
Ginsberg, Hersh Meier rabbi, religious organization executive
Ginsberg-Fellner, Fredda pediatric endocrinologist, researcher
Ginsburg, Ellin Louis public relations executive
†Ginsburg, Faye D. anthropology educator, ethnologist
Ginsburg, Sigmund G. museum administrator
Ginter, Valerian Alexius urban historian
Ginzberg, Eli economist, emeritus educator, government consultant, author
Ginzburg, Ralph editor, writer
Giraldi, Robert Nicholas film director
Girden, Eugene Lawrence lawyer
Giroux, Robert editor, book publisher, author
Gitner, Gerald L. aviation and investment banking executive
Gitter, Max lawyer
Gitterman, Alex social work educator
Giuliani, Rudolph W. mayor, former lawyer
Giusti, Gino Paul natural resources company executive
Gladstone, William Louis accountant
Glasberg, Paula Drillman advertising executive
Glasco, Joseph Milton artist
Glaser, Milton interior designer
Glass, Daniel S. record company executive
Glass, Philip composer, musician
Glasser, Ira Saul civil liberties organization executive
Glassgold, Alfred Emanuel physicist, educator
Glassman, Alexander Howard psychiatrist, researcher
Glassman, Steven J. lawyer
Glazer, Esther violinist
Gleason, Edward L. manufacturing executive
†Gleason, John Francis paint and chemical coatings company executive
Gleason, John James theatrical lighting designer
Glekel, Jeffrey Ives lawyer
Glick, Allan H. business executive
Glickstein, Steven lawyer
Glidden, Allan Hartwell insurance company executive
†Glimcher, Arnold B. art gallery executive
Glisenti, Paolo chemical, oil company executive
Glissant, Edouard Mathieu French language educator, writer
Glos, Margaret Beach management company executive, real estate developer
†Glover, Ron K. business information services company executive
Gluck, Carol history educator
Glynn, Gary Allen pension fund executive
Gnehm, Edward W., Jr. ambassador
Gochberg, Thomas real estate investor, financial executive
Goddess, Lynn Barbara commercial real estate broker
Godman, Gabriel Charles pathology educator
Godson, Godfrey Nigel molecular geneticist, educator
Goelet, Robert G. corporate executive
Goertz, Augustus Frederick, III artist
Goetz, Cecelia Helen lawyer, retired judge
Goetz, Maurice Harold lawyer
Goff, Stephen Payne molecular biologist, educator
Goings, Ralph artist
Gold, Albert artist
Gold, Jay D. broadcasting company executive
Gold, Jeffrey Mark investment banker, financial adviser
Gold, Leonard Singer librarian, translator
Gold, Mari S. public relations executive
Gold, Martin Elliot lawyer, educator
Gold, Simeon lawyer
Gold, Stuart Walter lawyer
Gold, Sylviane entertainment editor, writer, critic
Goldberg, Arthur Abba merchant banker, financial advisor
Goldberg, Bernard R. news correspondent
Goldberg, David lawyer, law educator
Goldberg, David Alan investment banker, lawyer
Goldberg, Edward L. financial services executive
Goldberg, Leslie Daniel advertising executive
Goldberg, Melvin A. non-profit organization executive
Goldberg, Michael artist
Goldberg, Richard W. federal judge
Goldberg, Samuel holding company executive
Goldberg, Sidney editor
Goldberg, Steven M. architect
Goldberg, Victor Paul law educator
Goldberger, Paul Jesse architecture critic, writer, educator, editor
Goldblatt, David Ira lawyer
Golde, David William physician, educator
Golden, Arthur F. lawyer
Golden, Robert Charles brokerage executive
Golden, Soma newspaper editor
Golden, Stephen publishing executive, forest products company executive
Golden, William Robert, Jr. lawyer
Golden, William Theodore corporate trustee, director

Goldenberg, Charles Lawrence real estate company executive
Goldfarb, Donald industrial engineering educator
Goldfeld, Dorian mathematics educator
Goldfield, Alfred Sherman lawyer
Goldin, Alan Gary advertising executive
Goldin, Leon artist, educator
Goldman, Charles Norton lawyer, corporation executive
Goldman, Donald Howard lawyer
Goldman, Francisco writer
Goldman, George David psychologist, psychoanalyst
Goldman, James playwright, screenwriter, novelist
†Goldman, James M. financial executive
Goldman, Lawrence Saul lawyer
Goldman, Leo psychologist, educator
Goldman, Marvin Gerald lawyer
Goldman, Robert Irving financial services company executive
Goldmark, Peter Carl, Jr. foundation executive
Goldschmid, Harvey Jerome law educator
Goldschmidt, Robert Alphonse financial executive
Goldsmith, Barbara author, social historian, journalist
Goldsmith, Clifford Henry former tobacco company executive
Goldsmith, Donald Alan lawyer
Goldsmith, Gary L. advertising executive
Goldsmith, Lee Selig lawyer, physician
Goldsmith, Merwin actor, theater director
Goldsmith, Robert Lewis youth association magazine executive
Goldsmith, Stanley Joseph nuclear medicine physician, educator
Goldstein, Alvin lawyer
Goldstein, Bernard Herbert lawyer
Goldstein, Charles Arthur lawyer
Goldstein, Fred accountant
Goldstein, Gary S. executive recruiter
Goldstein, Howard Warren lawyer
Goldstein, Jack transportation executive
Goldstein, Jonathan lawyer
†Goldstein, Lisa Joy writer
Goldstein, Marc microsurgeon, urology educator, academic administrator
Goldstein, Marcia Landweber lawyer
Goldstein, Menek neurochemistry educator
Goldstein, Norm editor, writer
Goldstein, Richard A. consumer products company executive
Goldstone, Steven F. lawyer
Gollin, Albert Edwin media research executive, sociologist
Gollin, Stuart Allen accountant
Gollob, Herman Cohen publishing company executive, editor
Golomb, Frederick Martin surgeon, educator
Golson, George Barry editor
Golub, Harvey financial services company executive
Golub, Leon Albert artist
Gomory, Ralph Edward mathematician, manufacturing company executive, foundation executive
Gonzalez, Eugene Robert investment banker
Gooch, Anthony Cushing lawyer
Goodacre, Jill model
Goodale, James Campbell lawyer
Goodale, Toni Krissel development consultant
Goodchild, Robert Marshall trust company executive
Goode, Richard Stephen pianist, educator
Goodfriend, Herbert Jay lawyer
Goodhartz, Gerald law librarian
Gooding, Richard newspaper editor
Goodkind, Louis William lawyer
Goodman, Gary A. lawyer
Goodman, George Jerome Waldo (Adam Smith) author, television journalist, editor
Goodman, Jordan Elliot journalist
†Goodman, Roy Matz senator, business executive
Goodman, Stuart Franklyn brokerage house executive
Goodman, Thomas Andrew public relations executive
Goodridge, Allan D. lawyer
Goodstein, Les newspaper publishing executive
Goodstone, Edward Harold retired insurance company executive
Goodwillie, Eugene William, Jr. lawyer
Goodwin, Bernard lawyer, executive, educator
†Goodwin, Doris Helen Kearns history educator, writer
Goodwin, Todd banker
Gordimer, Nadine author
Gordon, Albert Hamilton investment banker
Gordon, David playwright, director, choreographer
Gordon, David Jamieson tenor
Gordon, Diana Russell political science educator
Gordon, Elizabeth Jane publisher
Gordon, Jeffrey Neil law educator
Gordon, Mary Catherine author
Gordon, Michael Mackin lawyer
Gordon, Nicole Ann lawyer
Gordon, Roy Harris engineering design firm executive
Goren, Arnold Louis educator, former university official
Gorham, David L. newspaper executive
Gorlin, Richard physician, educator
Gormley, Nancy H. lawyer, electric power industry executive
Goss, Mary E. Weber sociology educator
Gossage, Wayne library director, management consultant, executive recruiter
Gossett, Oscar Milton advertising executive
Gossett, Robert Francis, Jr. merchant banker
Gotlieb, Irwin I. broadcast executive
Gottesman, Callman lawyer
Gottesman, David Sanford investment executive
Gottlieb, Jane Ellen librarian
Gottlieb, Jerrold Howard advertising executive
Gottlieb, Morton Edgar theatrical and film producer
Gottlieb, Paul publishing company executive
Gottlieb, Robert Adams publisher
Gottschall, Edward Maurice graphic arts company executive
Gouilloud, Michel oil industry servicing and equipment company executive
†Gould, Eleanor Lois (Eleanor Gould Packard) editor, grammarian
Gould, Harry Edward, Jr. industrialist
Gould, Jay Martin economist, consultant
Gould, Milton Samuel lawyer, business executive
Goulden, Joseph Chesley author
Goulianos, Konstantin physics educator
Gourdine, Simon Peter professional basketball executive
Graber, Edward Alex obstetrician, gynecologist, educator
Grace, E. engineering executive
Grace, Jason Roy advertising agency executive
Grad, Frank Paul lawyer
Graf, Peter Gustav accountant, lawyer
Graff, George Leonard lawyer
Graff, Randy actress
Graffin, Guillaume ballet dancer
Grafstein, Bernice physiology and neuroscience educator, researcher
Graham, Alma Eleanor magazine editor, writer, educational consultant
Graham, Jesse Japhet, II lawyer
Gralla, Lawrence publishing company executive
Gralla, Milton publisher
Gralnick, Jeff broadcasting company executive
Gramatte, Joan Helen graphic designer, art director
Granger, David investment banker
Grano, Joseph J., Jr. securities industry executive
Grant, Alfred David orthopaedic surgeon, educator
Grant, Cynthia D. writer
Grant, Dale B. consulting company executive
Grant, James Deneale health care company executive
Grant, Leonard Tydings educational association president
Grant, Merrill Theodore producer
Grant, Stephen Allen lawyer
Grant, Virginia Annette newspaper editor, journalist
Grant, William Robert investment banker
Grappelli, Stephane jazz violinist
Grashof, August Edward lawyer
Grasso, Richard A. stock exchange executive
Graves, Adam professional hockey player
Graves, Earl Gilbert publisher
Graves, Fred Hill librarian
Graves, Nancy Stevenson artist
Gray, Arthur, Jr. investment counselor
Gray, Barry Sherman radio commentator
Gray, C(harles) Jackson retail executive
Gray, Diane dancer, choreographer
Gray, George mural painter
Graziano, Joseph Harold scientist, educator
Greaney, Patrick Joseph electronics executive
Grebow, Edward television executive, banker
Greco, Jose choreographer
Green, Adolph playwright, lyricist
Green, Al soul and gospel singer
Green, Ashbel publishing executive, book editor
Green, David Edward librarian, priest, translator
Green, David O. accounting educator, educational administrator
Green, George Joseph publishing executive
Green, Gerald author
Green, Jack Peter pharmacology educator, medical scientist
Green, Jay M. diversified manufacturing and development company executive
Green, Maurice Richard neuropsychiatrist
Green, Robert S. lawyer
Greenawalt, Peggy Freed Tomarkin advertising executive
Greenawalt, Robert Kent lawyer
Greenawalt, William Sloan lawyer
Greenbaum, Maurice Coleman lawyer
Greenberg, Alan Courtney (Ace Greenberg) stockbroker
Greenberg, Daniel Herbert lawyer
Greenberg, Freddi Jane editor-in-chief, magazine
Greenberg, Ira George lawyer
Greenberg, Jack lawyer
Greenberg, Jerome advertising executive
Greenberg, Joshua F. lawyer, educator
Greenberg, Maurice Raymond insurance company executive
Greenberg, Robert A. financial consultant
Greenberg, Ronald David law educator
Greenberger, Daniel Mordecai physics researcher and educator
Greenberger, Howard Leroy lawyer, educator
Greene, A(lvin) C(arl) author
Greene, Bernard Harold lawyer
Greene, Carl William utility company executive
Greene, David Elsworth advertising agency executive, accountant
Greene, Howard Paul communications executive
Greene, Lloyd Asher pathology educator
Greene, Shecky entertainer
Greenfield, Gordon Kraus software company executive
Greenfield, Jay lawyer
Greenfield, (Henry) Jeff news analyst
Greenfield, Seymour Stephen mechanical engineer
Greengard, Paul neuroscientist
Greenhill, Robert Foster investment banker
†Greenhouse, Barry David historic and archeological consulting firm executive
Greenland, Leo advertising executive
Greenman, Jane Friedlieb lawyer
Greenstein, Abraham Jacob mortgage company executive, accountant
Greenwald, James L. broadcasting and communications executive
Greenwald, Martin publishing company executive
†Greenwood, Jane costume designer, educator
Greer, Allen Curtis, II lawyer
Greer, James Alexander, II lawyer
Gregg, Donald Phinney federal agency administrator, lecturer
Gregorio, Luis Justino Lopes transportation executive
Greig, Robert Thomson lawyer
Greilsheimer, James Gans lawyer
Grein, Richard Frank bishop, pastoral theology educator
Grele, Ronald John historian
Grenquist, Peter Carl publishing executive
Gresov, Boris (Vladimir) economist
Grey, Linda book publisher
Griefen, John Adams artist, educator
Griesa, Thomas Poole federal judge
Griffin, Judith Ann strategic planning and operating executive
Griffith, Alan Richard banker
Griffith, Katherine Scott communications executive
Griffiths, Daniel Edward dean emeritus
Griffiths, Sylvia Preston physician
Grigsby, Henry Jefferson, Jr. editor
Grillo, Joann Danielle mezzo-soprano
Grimaldi, Nicholas Lawrence social services administrator
Grimes, Martha author
Grimm, Donald E. petroleum company executive
Grimsley, Will Henry author
Grindea, Daniel international economist
Grisanti, Eugene Philip flavors and fragrances company executive
Grisham, John writer
†Grishman, Ronnie Joyce magazine editor
Grisi, Jeanmarie Conte finance executive
Grizzard, George actor
Groban, Robert Sidney, Jr. lawyer
Groberg, James Jay information sciences company executive
†Gromada, Thaddeus V. historian, administrator
Gropp, Louis Oliver editor in chief
Gropper, Allan Louis lawyer
Grose, Molly Pickering performing company executive
Grose, William Rush publishing executive
Groseclose, Everett Harrison editor
Gross, Abraham rabbi, educator
Gross, Ernest Arnold lawyer
Gross, Jonathan Light computer scientist, mathematician, educator
Gross, Lawrence Robert manufacturing executive
Gross, Robert Alfred engineering and physics educator
Gross, Steven Ross lawyer
Grossman, Barbara Susanne publisher
Grossman, Dan Steven lawyer
Grossman, Jack advertising agency executive
Grossman, Jacob S. structural engineer
Grossman, Janice publisher
Grossman, Nancy artist
Grossman, Ronald financial executive, lawyer
Grossman, Sanford lawyer
Grove, Barry theater executive
Groves, Ray John accountant
Gruber, Alan Richard insurance company executive
Grubin, Sharon E. federal judge
Grubman, Allen J. lawyer
Gruenberger, Peter lawyer
Grumbach, Doris novelist, editor, critic, educator, bookseller
Grumbach, George Jacques, Jr. lawyer
Grunberger, Dezider biochemist, researcher
Grune, George Vincent publishing company executive
Grunes, Robert Lewis engineering consulting firm executive
Grunewald, Raymond Bernhard lawyer
Grunfeld, Ernst metals company executive
Gruson, Michael lawyer
Gruss, Martin David private investor
Gruver, William Rolfe investment banker
Guare, John playwright
Guccione, Robert Charles Joseph Edward Sabatini publisher
Guenther, Jack Donald banker
Guenther, Paul Bernard securities company executive
Guest, Judith Ann author
Guettel, Henry Arthur retired arts executive
Gugel, Craig Thomas advertising and new media executive
Guggenheimer, Elinor civic leader, writer
Guida, Peter Matthew surgeon, educator
Guillen, Michael Arthur mathematical physicist, educator, writer, television journalist
†Guillermoprieto, Alma journalist, non-fiction writer
Guimaraes, George Gomes advertising agency executive
Guise, David Earl architect, educator
Guldimann, Till M. banker
Gumbel, Bryant Charles broadcaster
Gumbinner, Paul S. advertising and executive recruitment agency executive
†Gunn, John Reginald medical institution executive, consultant
†Gunther, Jack Disbrow, Jr. lawyer
Gunther, Jane Perry (Mrs. John Gunther) editor, writer
Gurin, Meg dancer
Gusberg, Saul Bernard physician, educator
†Guterson, David writer
Guth, Paul C. lawyer
Guth, William Donald business educator
Guthrie, Randolph Hobson, Jr. plastic surgeon
Gutman, Jeremiah Sheldon lawyer
Gutman, Robert William retired fine arts educator
Guttentag, Lucas lawyer
Gutterman, Gerald S. diversified manufacturing company executive
Guttman, Zoltan Lou exchange executive
Gwathmey, Charles architect
Gwertzman, Bernard newspaper editor
Gwilt, John Ruff pharmaceutical company executive
Gyulassy, Miklos physics educator
Haacke, Hans Christoph Carl artist, educator
Haas, Frederick Carl paper and chemical company executive
Habecker, Eugene Brubaker religious association executive
Haber, Ira Joel artist, art educator
Haber, Pierre Claude psychologist
Hackett, Bruce Clayton investment banking company executive
Hackett, Buddy actor
Hackett, Kevin R. lawyer
Hacklin, Allan artist, art educator
Haddad, Heskel Marshall ophthalmologist
Haddock, Robert Lynn information services entrepreneur, writer
Hadley, Jerry opera singer
Hadley, Leila Eliott-Burton (Mrs. Henry Luce, III) author
Haerer, Carol artist
Haessle, Jean-Marie Georges artist
Haffner, Alden Norman university official
Haffner, Alfred Loveland, Jr. intellectual property lawyer
Haft, Marilyn Geisler lawyer
Hagen, Uta Thyra actress
Hagendorn, William lawyer
Hager, Charles Read lawyer
Hager, Larry Stanley book editor, publishing executive
Haggerty, Robert Henry lawyer
Haggerty, Robert Johns physician, educator
Hahn, Fred retired political science and history educator
Haidt, Harold lawyer
Haig, Robert Leighton lawyer
Haiken, Leatrice Brown periodical editor
Haims, Bruce David lawyer
†Haire, Jack magazine publisher
Haire, John Russell corporate executive, lawyer
Haje, Peter Robert lawyer
Hajim, Edmund A. financial services executive
Halberg, G. Peter ophthalmologist
Halberstam, David journalist, author
Halberstam, Malvina legal educator, lawyer
Hall, Daryl musician
Hall, Gus (Arvo Kusta Halberg) political party official
Hall, John Herbert lawyer
Hall, Nancy Christensen publishing company executive, author, editor
Hall, Susan author, film producer
Hallam, Beverly (Beverly Linney) artist
Halliday, Joseph William lawyer
Hallingby, Paul, Jr. investment banker
Halloran, Leo Augustine retired financial executive
Halper, Harlan Richard executive search consultant
Halper, Thomas political science educator
Halperin, Richard E. lawyer, holding company executive
Halpern, Alvin Michael physicist, educator
Halpern, Charles Robert foundation executive, educator, lawyer
Halpern, Nathan Loren communications company executive
Halpin, Anna Marie architect
Halsband, Frances architect
Hamblen, L. Jane lawyer
Hambrick, George Walter, Jr. dermatologist, educator
Hamburg, Beatrix Ann medical educator, researcher
Hamburg, Charles Bruce lawyer
Hamburg, David A. psychiatrist, foundation executive
Hamburger, Philip (Paul) writer
Hamel, Rodolphe lawyer, pharmaceutical company executive
Hamilton, Bill advertising executive
Hamilton, Patricia Rose artist's agent
Hamm, David Bernard lawyer
Hammer, Emanuel Frederick clinical psychologist, psychoanalyst
Hammerling, Robert Charles lawyer
Hammerman, Stephen Lawrence lawyer, financial services company executive
Hammett, William M. H. foundation executive
Hammond, Lou Rena Charlotte public relations executive
Hammond, Steven Alan lawyer
Hampton, Philip McCune banker
Han, Yingshi medical educator and medical researcher
Hanafusa, Hidesaburo virologist
Hancock, Gerre Edward musician
Handberg, Irene Deak educational executive
Handelsman, Lawrence Marc lawyer
Handler, Arthur M. lawyer
Handler, Milton lawyer
Hanemann, John H. commodity exchange executive
Hansen, James E. physicist, meteorologist, federal agency administrator
Hansen, Richard Arthur insurance company executive, psychologist
Hansmann, Ralph Emil investment executive
Happel, John chemical engineer, researcher
Harbison, James Wesley, Jr. lawyer
Harder, Lewis Bradley ore bodies development company executive
Hardison, Ruth Inge sculptor
Hardwick, Elizabeth author
Hardy, Gordon Alfred music educator, music school president
Hardy, Hugh architect
Hardy, Thomas Austin sculptor
†Hardy, Thomas George chemical agricultural products and fertilizer company executive
Harfst, Jeffrey Loren accountant
Hariri, Gisue architect, educator
Harkarvy, Benjamin artistic director
Harkna, Eric advertising executive
Harkrader, Milton Keene, Jr. corporate executive
Harlan, Leonard Morton merchant banker
Harleston, Bernard Warren college president
Harley, Colin Emile lawyer
Harley, Naomi Hallden radiation specialist, environmental medicine educator
Harlow, George Eugene mineralogist, curator
Harmon, James Allen investment banker
Harmon, Lily artist, author
Harnedy, Edmund Richard insurance executive
Harnett, Thomas Aquinas lawyer
Harnick, Sheldon Mayer lyricist
Harper, Charles Michel food company executive
Harper, Emery Walter lawyer
Harper, Gerard Edward lawyer
Harrell, Lynn Morris cellist
Harrington, John Patrick English language educator, college dean
Harris, Allen lawyer, educator
Harris, Ann S. editor
Harris, Arlene lawyer
Harris, Charles Frederick book publishing executive
Harris, Colin Cyril mineral engineer, educator
Harris, Cyril Manton physicist, engineering and architecture educator, consulting acoustical engineer
Harris, David Alan not-for-profit organization executive
Harris, David Henry retired life insurance company executive
Harris, Ed(ward Allen) actor
Harris, Ellen W. lawyer
Harris, Henry William physician
Harris, Joel B(ruce) lawyer
Harris, Julie (Ann) actress
Harris, Richard Max corporate executive
†Harris, Rosemary Ann actress
Harris, Thomas author
Harris, William Vernon history educator
Harrison, Gerald publisher
Harrison, John Alexander financial executive
Harrison, S. David lawyer
Harrod, B(illy) J(oe) professional association executive
Harrow, Nancy (Mrs. Jan Krukowski) jazz singer, songwriter, editor
Harry, Deborah Ann singer
Hart, Gurnee Fellows investment counselor
Hart, Kenneth Nelson lawyer
Hart, Kitty Carlisle arts administrator
Hart, Robert M. lawyer
Harter, Hugh Anthony foreign language educator
Hartford, Huntington financier, art patron
Hartford, William H. magazine editor, writer, lecturer
Harth, Sidney musician, educator
Hartley, Duncan fundraising executive
Hartman, Stephen Jennings, Jr. banker
Hartman-Goldsmith, Joan art historian
Hartmann, Sven Richard physicist, educator
Hartzell, Andrew Cornelius, Jr. lawyer
Harvey, Cynthia ballet dancer
Harvey, Donald Joseph history educator
Hasen, Burton Stanley artist
Hashim, George A. immunologist, biomedical researcher, educator
Haskell, Barbara curator
Haskell, John Henry Farrell, Jr. investment banking company executive

Hassler, Howard E. retail stores executive
Hasso, Signe Eleonora Cecilia actress
Hastings, Baird conductor, music educator, writer
Hastings, Deborah bass guitarist
Hastings, Donald Francis actor, writer
Hatfield, Robert Sherman former packaging company executive
Hatheway, John Harris advertising agency executive
Haubert, Alaine ballet dancer
Hauck, Marguerite Hall broadcasting executive
†Hauck, Mary Elizabeth portfolio manager
Hauptman, William playwright
Hauser, Fred P. insurance company executive
Hauser, Gustave M. cable and electronic communications company executive
Hauser, Rita Eleanore Abrams lawyer
Hawes, Douglas Wesson lawyer
Hawke, Roger Jewett lawyer
Hawkey, Penelope J. advertising agency executive
Hawkins, Ashton museum executive, lawyer
Hawkins, Katherine Ann hematologist, educator
Hawley, John Stratton religious studies educator
Hayden, Raymond Paul lawyer
Hayes, Gerald Joseph lawyer
Hayes, Isaac rhythm and blues singer, composer
†Hayes, John advertising agency executive
Hayne, Thomas Arthur banker
Haynes, Jean Reed lawyer
Haynes, Todd film writer, producer, director
Hayon, Jack publishing executive
Haywood, H(erbert) Carl(ton) psychologist, educator
Hazen, William Harris finance executive
Hazlitt, Donald Robert artist
Hazzard, Shirley author
Heal, Geoffrey Martin economics educator
†Heald, Anthony actor
Healy, Harold Harris, Jr. lawyer
Healy, Nicholas Joseph lawyer, educator
Heard, Edwin Anthony banker
Hearle, Douglas Geoffrey public relations consultant
†Hearn, George actor
Hearn, George Henry lawyer, steamship corporate executive
Hearst, Randolph Apperson publishing executive
Heber, Ruth R. psychologist, consultant
Hebert, Bliss Edmund opera director
Hechinger, Fred Michael newspaper editor, columnist, foundation executive
†Heck, Warren W. insurance company executive
Heckart, Robert Lee lawyer
Heckscher, August journalist, author, foundation executive
Heckscher, Morrison Harris museum curator, architectural historian
Hedley, David Van Houten investment banker
Hedlund, Ronald baritone
Hedstrom, Mitchell Warren banker
Heekin, James Robson, III advertising executive
Heese, William John music publishing company executive
Heffner, Richard Douglas historian, educator, communications consultant, television producer
Heilbroner, Robert Louis economist, author
†Heiler, Lynn publishing executive
Heiloms, May (Mrs. Samuel Heiloms) artist
Heimann, John Gaines investment banker
Heimarck, Gregory James psychoanalyst, child psychiatrist
Heimbold, Charles Andreas, Jr. pharmaceutical company executive
Heine, Edward Joseph, Jr. lawyer
Heineman, Andrew David lawyer
†Heinrich, Amy Vladeck library director
Heinzerling, Larry Edward communications executive
Heisel, Ralph Arthur architect
Heisler, Stanley Dean lawyer
Heitner, Kenneth Howard lawyer
Hejduk, John Quentin dean, architect
Held, Al artist, educator
Held, Virginia philosophy educator
Helferich, Gerard Marion book editor
Helfgott, Samson lawyer
Heliker, John artist
Helioff, Anne Graile painter
Hellawell, Robert law educator
Hellenbrand, Samuel Henry lawyer, diversified industry executive
Heller, Arthur advertising agency executive
Heller, Edwin lawyer
Heller, Joseph writer
Heller, Robert Martin lawyer
Hellerstein, Alvin Kenneth lawyer
Hellerstein, Jerome Robert lawyer
Hellmold, Ralph O. investment banker
Helmreich, William Benno sociology educator, consultant
†Helmsley, Harry B. real estate company executive
Heloise columnist, lecturer, broadcaster, author
Helpern, David Moses shoe corporation executive
Helwig, George James securities trader, dealer
Heming, Charles E. lawyer
Hemmerdinger, H. Dale real estate executive
Hemming, Roy G. writer, magazine editor, broadcaster
Henderson, Donald Bernard, Jr. lawyer
Henderson, Joe jazz tenor saxophonist
Henderson, Skitch (Lyle Russell Cedric) pianist, conductor
Hendricks, Edward David association executive
Hendrickson, Robert Augustus lawyer
†Hendrickson, Wayne A(rthur) biochemist, educator
Hendry, Andrew Delaney lawyer, consumer products company executive
Henkin, Louis lawyer, law educator
Henley, Arthur author, editor, television consultant
Henley, Beth playwright, actress
Henley, Deborah newspaper editor
Hennes, Robert Taft former management consultant, investment executive
†Hennessy, John Francis, III engineering executive, mechanical engineer
Hennessy, John M. brokerage house executive
Hennig, Frederick E. retail company executive
Henning, Alyson Balfour advertising executive
Henninger, Daniel Paul editor
Henry, Elizabeth Powers lawyer
Henry, Marguerite author
Henry, Sally McDonald lawyer
Hensler, Guenter Manfred record company executive
Hentoff, Margot columnist
Hentoff, Nathan Irving writer
Herbert, Bob newspaper columnist
Herbits, Stephen Edward alcoholic beverage company executive
†Herbst, Edward Ian brokerage firm executive
Herbst, Martin publishing company executive
†Herder, Gwendolin Elisabeth Maria publishing executive
Herkness, Lindsay Coates, III securities broker
Herman, Jerry composer, lyricist
Herman, Kenneth Beaumont lawyer
Hernstadt, Judith Filenbaum city planner, real estate executive, broadcasting executive
†Hero, Byron A. investment banker, lawyer
Herold, Karl Guenter lawyer
Heron, Nye Brian artistic director
Herr, Kenneth Julian retired charitable foundation executive
Herregat, Guy-Georges Jacques banker
Herrera, Carolina fashion designer
Herrera, Paloma dancer
Herrera, Paul Fredrick accountant
Herrmann, Lacy Bunnell investment company executive, financial entrepreneur, venture capitalist
Hersch, Dennis Steven lawyer
Hershfield, Allan Frankel academic administrator
Herstand, Theodore theatre artist, educator
Hertz, Leon publishing executive
Hertz, Rudolf Heinrich banker
Hertzberg, Daniel journalist
Hertzberg, Hendrik magazine editor, writer
Herz, Andrew Lee lawyer
Heslin, James J. association executive
Hess, Leon oil company executive
†Hesse, Karen (Sue) writer, educator
Hesselbein, Frances Richards foundation executive, consultant
Hester, James McNaughton foundation administrator
Hetfield, James singer
Hetherington, John Warner lawyer
Heuer, Kenneth John publishing company executive
Hewes, Henry drama critic
Hewitt, Carl Herbert lawyer
Hewitt, Dennis Edwin financial executive
Hewitt, Don S. television news producer
Hewitt, Vivian Ann Davidson (Mrs. John Hamilton Hewitt, Jr.) librarian
Heyde, Martha Bennett (Mrs. Ernest R. Heyde) psychologist
Heydebrand, Wolf Von sociology educator
Heyer, Paul Otto college president, architect
Heyman, George Harrison, Jr. securities company executive
Heyman, William Herbert securities firm executive
Heyn, Ernest V. author, editor
Heyward, Andrew John television producer
Heyworth, James O. communications company executive
Hiatt, John musician, country, popular
Hibel, Bernard financial consultant, former apparel company executive
Hickey, Catherine Josephine school system administrator
Hickman, J. Kenneth accounting company executive
Hiden, Robert Battaile, Jr. lawyer
Higginbotham, A. Leon, Jr. lawyer, educator
Higgins, Harrison Scott investment company executive
Higginson, James Jackson lawyer
Higgs, John H. lawyer
Highleyman, Samuel Locke, III lawyer
Hilfiger, Tommy fashion designer
Hilgartner, Margaret Wehr pediatric hematologist, educator
Hill, Alfred lawyer, educator
Hill, Clinton artist
Hill, Elizabeth Starr writer
Hill, George Roy film director
Hill, J(ames) Tomilson investment banker
Hill, Robert Arthur ballet dancer
Hilliard, Landon banker
Hillman, Howard Budrow author, editor, publisher, consultant
Hillman, Patrick advertising agency executive
Hills, Frederic Wheeler editor, publishing company executive
Hilton, Alice Mary cybernetics and computing systems consultant, author, mathematician, art historian
Hilton, Andrew Carson management consultant, former manufacturing company executive
†Hinckley, David Malcolm journalist, editor, critic
Hinds, Thomas Sheldon publisher, organization executive
Hinerfeld, Norman Martin manufacturing company executive
Hines, Anna Grossnickle author, illustrator
Hinrichs, Horst manufactoring executive
Hinton, S(usan) E(loise) author
Hinz, Dorothy Elizabeth writer, editor, international corporate communications and public affairs specialist
Hinz, Theodore Vincent architect
Hios, Theodore painter, graphic artist
Hirata, H. grain company executive
Hirota, Yutaro metal products executive
Hirsch, Barry lawyer
Hirsch, George Aaron publisher
Hirsch, Jerome Seth lawyer
Hirsch, Judd actor
Hirsch, Jules physician, scientist
Hirsch, Roseann Conte publisher
Hirschfeld, Albert artist
Hirschfeld, Michael lawyer
Hirschfield, Robert S. political science educator
Hirschhorn, Kurt pediatrics educator
Hirschhorn, Rochelle genetics educator
Hirschman, Shalom Zarach physician
Hirshfield, Stuart lawyer
Hirshon, Sheldon Ira lawyer
Hirshowitz, Melvin Stephen lawyer
Hiss, Tony writer
Hlinka, Nichol dancer
Hoagland, Edward author
Hobbs, Franklin Warren, IV investment banker
Hoberman, Charles Steven mechanical engineer, inventor
Hoch, Frank William banker
Hochberg, Irving audiologist, educator
Hochberg, Julian psychologist
Hochman, Charles Bruce lawyer
Hochstadt, Joy biomedical research scientist, scientific and research director
Hockenberry, John television journalist
Hodapp, Siegfried petroleum industry executive
†Hodes, Bernard S. advertising agency executive
Hodes, Robert Bernard lawyer
Hoeflin, Ronald Kent philosopher, test designer, newsletter publisher
Hoeft, Julius Albert publishing company executive
Hofer, Myron A(rms) psychiatrist, researcher
Hoff, Jonathan M(orind) lawyer
Hoff, Syd(ney) cartoonist, author
Hoffenberg, Harvey advertising executive
Hoffert, Martin Irving applied science educator
Hoffman, Alice writer
Hoffman, Dustin Lee actor
Hoffman, John Ernest, Jr. retired lawyer
Hoffman, Martin Leon psychology educator
Hoffman, Mathew lawyer
Hoffman, Michael Eugene editor, publisher, museum curator
Hoffman, William M(oses) playwright, editor
Hoffmann, Malcolm Arthur lawyer
Hoffner, Marilyn university administrator
Hogan, Charles Carlton psychiatrist
Hogan, William E. law educator, lawyer
Hoge, Warren M. newspaper and magazine editor
Hohn, Harry George insurance company executive, lawyer
Holabird, Katherine children's book author
Holder, Geoffrey Lamont dancer, actor, choreographer, director
Holderness, Algernon Sidney, Jr. lawyer
Holderness, G(eorge) Malcolm lawyer
Holl, Steven Myron architect
Holland, Bradford Wayne artist
Holland, Michael Francis investment company executive
Hollander, David lawyer
Hollander, Edwin Paul psychologist, educator
Hollander, Lorin pianist
Hollander, Stacy Candice Foster museum curator
Hollenbeck, Ralph Anthony retired editor, book reviewer
Holliday, Jennifer Yvette singer, actress
Holliday, Polly Dean actress
Hollinshead, Byron Sharpe, Jr. publishing company executive
Holloway, David baritone
Holloway, Ralph Leslie anthropology educator
Holman, Bud George lawyer
Holman, Margaret Mezoff fundraising consultant
Holmes, Miriam H. publisher
Holmgren, Laton Earle clergyman
Holroyd, Michael author
Holt, Donald Dale magazine editor
Holt, Peter Rolf physician, educator
Holtzman, Alexander lawyer, consultant
Holtzman, Ellen A. foundation executive
Holtzmann, Howard Marshall lawyer, judge
Holtzschue, Karl Bressem lawyer, author, educator
Holub, Martin architect
Holzer, Hans author
Holzer, Jenny artist
Holzman, Malcolm architect
Hommes, Frits Aukustinus biology educator
Honan, William Holmes journalist, writer
Honig, Barry Hirsh biophysics educator
Hood, Donald Charles university administrator, psychology educator
Hooper, Ian (John Derek Glass) marketing communications executive
†Hoover, James Bentley private investor
Hoover, James Lloyd law librarian, educator
Hope, Michael S. entertainment and communications company executive
Hopkins, Harold Anthony, Jr. bishop
†Hopkins, Speed Elliott art director
Hopkins, Thomas Arscott lawyer
Hopper, Walter Everett lawyer
Hopple, Richard Van Tromp, Jr. advertising agency executive
Hormats, Robert David economist, investment banker
Horn, Charles G. textile executive
Horn, Shirley vocalist, pianist
Hornby, Geoffrey oil industry executive
Horne, Marilyn mezzo-soprano
Horner, Larry Dean retired accounting firm executive, brokerage firm executive
Hornick, Robert Newton lawyer
Horovitz, Israel Arthur playwright
Horowitz, David H. communications industry executive, lawyer, consultant
Horowitz, Frances Degen academic administrator, psychology educator
Horowitz, Gedale Bob investment banker
Horowitz, Lewis Jay stock exchange executive
Horowitz, Raymond J. lawyer
Hoser, Albert electronics executive
Hoskins, William John obstetrician and gynecologist, educator
Hosokawa, David advertising executive
Host, Stig oil company executive
Hotz, Robert Henry investment banking executive
Houghton, Charles Norris stage director, author, educator
Hould-Ward, Ann theatrical costume designer
House, Karen Elliott company executive, former editor, reporter
Hovde, Carl Frederick language professional, educator
Hovdesven, Arne lawyer
Hover, John Calvin, II banker
Hoving, Thomas museum and cultural affairs consultant, author
Howard, Clifton Merton, Jr. psychiatrist
Howard, David ballet school administrator
Howard, Elizabeth corporate communications and marketing executive
Howard, M(oses) William, Jr. minister, seminary president
Howard, Nathan Southard investment banker, lawyer
Howat, John Keith museum executive
Howe, Florence English educator, writer, publisher
Howe, Richard Rives lawyer
Howe, Tina playwright
Howell, Wesley Grant, Jr. lawyer
Howes, Alfred S. business and insurance consultant
Hoxie, Ralph Gordon educational administrator, author
Hoxter, Allegra Branson radio news and freelance writer
Hoxter, Curtis Joseph international economic adviser, public relations and affairs counselor
Hoynes, Louis LeNoir, Jr. lawyer
Hoyt, Charles King architect, editor
Hoyt, Henry Hamilton, Jr. pharmaceutical and toiletry company executive
Hoyt, Seth publisher
Hruska, Alan J. lawyer
Hsu, Charles Jui-cheng manufacturing company executive, advertising agent
Hu, Joseph Chi-Ping mortgage securities analyst
Huang, Alice Shih-hou microbiology and molecular genetics educator
Hubbe, Nikolaj dancer
†Hubbell, Robert C. public relations executive
Hubler, Bruce Albert management executive
Hudlin, Warrington writer, producer, director
Hudson, Dawn Emily advertising executive
Hudspeth, Stephen Mason lawyer
Huettner, Richard Alfred lawyer
Huffstodt, Karen opera singer, recitalist
Hufham, Barbara Frances publishing executive, lawyer
Hughes, Allen music critic
Hughes, Kevin Peter lawyer
Hughes, Robert Studley Forrest art critic
Hugo, Norman Eliot plastic surgeon, medical educator
Huhs, John I. lawyer
Hulbert, Richard Woodward lawyer
Hull, Cathy artist, illustrator
Hull, Philip Glasgow lawyer
Hultberg, John artist
Hultquist, Timothy Allen investment banker
Humperdinck, Engelbert (Arnold George Dorsey) singer
Humphreys, Richard advertising executive
Hundt, Paul Robert diversified industry executive, lawyer
Hunnewell, Francis O. bank executive
Hunt, Franklin Griggs lawyer
Hunt, Richard sculptor
Hunte, Beryl Eleanor mathematics educator, consultant
Hunter, Evan (Ed Mc Bain) author
Hunter, Rachel model
Hunter-Gault, Charlayne journalist
Hunter-Stiebel, Penelope art historian, art dealer
Huntington, Lawrence Smith investment banker
Hupp, Robert Martin artistic director, educator
Hupper, John Roscoe lawyer
Hurewitz, J(acob) C(oleman) retired international relations educator, author, consultant
Hurford, John Boyce investment counselor
Hurley, Cheryl Joyce book publishing executive
Hurley, Geoffrey Kevin lawyer
Hurlock, James Bickford lawyer
Hurst, Robert Jay securities company executive
Hurvitz, Arthur Isaac pathologist, researcher
Hurwitz, Sol business policy organization executive
Hutchens, John Kennedy journalist, editor
Hutchings, Peter Lounsbery insurance company executive
Hutner, Seymour Herbert microbiologist, protozoologist
Hutter, Rudolf Gustav Emil physics educator
Hutton, Ernest Watson, Jr. urban designer, city planner
Huxtable, Ada Louise architecture critic
Huyssen, Andreas German literature educator
Hwang, David Henry playwright, screenwriter
Hyams, Joseph writer
Hyde, David Rowley lawyer
Hyman, Alan Barry lawyer
Hyman, Bruce Malcolm ophthalmologist
Hyman, Jerome Elliot lawyer
Hyman, Morton Peter shipping company executive
Hyman, Seymour capital and product development company executive
Hymes, Norma internist
Hytner, Nicholas theatrical director
Iakovos, (Demetrios A. Coucouzis) archbishop
Ianni, Francis Anthony James anthropologist, psychoanalyst, educator
Iannuzzi, John Nicholas lawyer, author, educator
Ibarguen, Alberto newspaper executive
Idleman, Lee Hillis investment company executive
Idzik, Daniel Ronald lawyer
Iger, Robert A. broadcast executive
Imparato, Anthony Michael vascular surgeon, medical educator, researcher
†Imperato-McGinley, Julianne L. endocrinologist, educator
Incandela, Gerald Jean-Marie artist
Indursky, Arthur lawyer
Inez, Colette poet
Ingraham, David Wood broadcast executive
Ingraham, John Wright banker
Ingram, Samuel William, Jr. lawyer
Ink, Dwight A. government agency administrator
Innaurato, Albert Francis playwright
Innis, Roy Emile Alfredo organization executive
Inoue, Minoru manufacturing executive
Insel, Michael S. lawyer
Iovenko, Michael lawyer
Ireland, Patrick artist
Irvin, Patricia Louise lawyer
Irvin, Tinsley Hoyt insurance broker
Isaacson, Allen Ira lawyer
Isaacson, Melvin Stuart library director
Isaacson, Walter Seff editor
Isay, Jane Franzblau publisher
Isay, Richard Alexander psychiatrist
Iselin, John Jay university president
Isley, Alexander Max graphic designer, lecturer
Isogai, Masaharu women's apparel executive
Isquith, Fred Taylor lawyer
Israel, Margie Olanoff psychotherapist
Issler, Harry lawyer
Ittleson, H(enry) Anthony bicycle vacation company executive
Ivanick, Carol W. Trencher lawyer
Ivanov, Lyuben Dimitrov naval architecture researcher, educator
Ives, Colta Feller museum curator, educator
Ivory, James Francis film director
Jablons, Jane Ellen lawyer
Jacey, Charles Frederick, Jr. accounting company executive, consultant
Jackel, Lawrence publishing company executive
Jacker, Corinne Litvin playwright
Jackson, Anne (Anne Jackson Wallach) actress
Jackson, David Parker radio news anchor
Jackson, Joe musician, singer, composer, songwriter
†Jackson, Kate Morgan children's book editor
Jackson, Keith MacKenzie television commentator, writer, producer
Jackson, Kenneth Terry historian, educator
Jackson, Reginald Martinez former professional baseball player
Jackson, Richard George advertising agency executive
Jackson, Thomas Gene lawyer
Jackson, Ward artist
Jackson, William Eldred lawyer
Jacob, Edwin J. lawyer
Jacob, John Edward social service agency executive
Jacob, Marvin Eugene lawyer
Jacobs, Arnold Stephen lawyer
Jacobs, Bernard B. theater executive
Jacobs, Dennis G. federal judge
Jacobs, James B. law educator
Jacobs, Jane Brand lawyer
Jacobs, Jim actor, playwright, composer, lyricist

Jacobs, Marc *fashion designer*
Jacobs, Mark Neil *financial services corporation executive, lawyer*
Jacobs, Robert Alan *lawyer*
Jacobsen, Theodore H. (Ted H. Jacobsen) *labor union official, educator*
Jacobson, Gary Steven *lawyer*
Jacobson, Gaynor I. *retired association executive*
Jacobson, Jerold Dennis *lawyer*
Jacobson, Willard James *science educator*
Jacoby, A. James *securities brokerage firm executive*
Jacoby, Jacob *consumer psychology educator*
Jacoby, Robert Harold *management consulting executive*
Jacquet, Hervé Michel *mathematics educator*
Jacquette, Yvonne Helene *artist*
Jaffe, Alan Steven *lawyer*
Jaffe, Andrew Mark *editor, publisher*
Jaffe, Caroline Ruth *association communications executive*
Jaffe, Rona *author*
Jaffe, Susan *ballerina*
Jaffe, Suzanne Denbo *investment banker, entrepreneur*
Jaffee, Sandra Schuyler *financial executive*
Jaffin, Charles Leonard *lawyer*
Jagger, Mick (Michael Philip Jagger) *singer, musician*
Jagiello, Georgiana M. *geneticist, educator*
Jakes, John *author*
James, Frank Munger *brokerage house executive*
James, Hamilton Evans *investment banking firm executive*
James, Robert Leo *advertising agency executive*
Jameson, Richard *magazine editor, film critic*
Jamieson, Edward Leo *magazine editor*
Jamieson, Robert John *television journalist*
Jamin, Gerald Alan *petroleum company executive*
†Jamison, Jayne *magazine publisher*
Jamison, Judith *dancer*
Jampolis, Neil Peter *designer*
Jander, Klaus Heinrich *lawyer*
Janeway, Elizabeth Hall *author*
Janiak, Anthony Richard, Jr. *investment banker*
Janklow, Linda LeRoy *civic worker, volunteer*
Janney, Stuart Symington, III *investment company executive*
Janowitz, Henry David *physician, researcher, medical educator*
Janssen, Peter Anton *magazine editor and publisher*
Jánszky, Andrew Béla *lawyer*
Jaramillo, Virginia *artist*
Jarecki, Henry George *physician, financial executive*
Jaroff, Leon Morton *magazine editor*
Jarriel, Thomas Edwin *correspondent*
Jarvis, Gale Rall *retail executive*
Jassy, Everett Lewis *lawyer*
Jaudon, Valerie *artist*
Javits, Eric Moses *lawyer*
Jedlicka, Judith Ann *organization executive*
Jefferies, Jack P. *lawyer*
Jefferson, Denise *dance school director*
†Jefferson, Margo L. *theater critic*
Jelinek, Josef Emil *dermatologist*
Jellinek, George *broadcast executive, writer, music educator*
Jenkins, Newell *conductor*
Jenkins, Paul *artist*
Jenkins, Robert Nesbit *real estate executive*
Jennings, Frank Gerard *editor*
Jennings, Peter Charles *television anchorman*
Jenrette, Richard Hampton *investment and insurance company executive*
Jensen, Michael Charles *journalist, lecturer, author*
Jepson, Hans Godfrey *investment company executive*
Jerome, Fred Louis *science organization executive*
Jervis, Robert *political science educator*
Jessup, John Baker *lawyer*
Jeydel, Richard K. *lawyer*
Jeynes, Mary Kay *college dean*
Jhabvala, Ruth Prawer *author*
Jinnett, Robert Jefferson *lawyer*
Joel, Billy (William Martin Joel) *musician*
Joffe, Robert David *lawyer*
Johansen, David (Buster Poindexter) *popular musician, actor*
Johns, Jasper *artist*
†Johns, William Potter *non-profit organization administrator*
Johnsen, Niels Winchester *ocean shipping company executive*
Johnson, Angela *children's book author*
Johnson, Betsey Lee *fashion designer*
Johnson, Charles Richard *writer, teacher*
Johnson, Clarke Courtney *finance educator*
Johnson, Denis *poet, writer*
Johnson, Freda S. *public finance consultant*
Johnson, Harold Earl *personnel executive*
Johnson, Horton Anton *pathologist*
Johnson, J. Chester *financial executive, poet*
Johnson, James Gann, Jr. *lawyer*
Johnson, James M. *orchestra executive*
Johnson, John William, Jr. *executive recruiter*
Johnson, Kate *dancer*
Johnson, Philip Cortelyou *architect*
Johnson, Virginia Alma Fairfax *ballerina*
†Johnson, Warren Douglas *infectious diseases physician, researcher*
†Johnston, Catherine V. *magazine publisher*
Johnston, Harry Melville, III *lawyer*
Johnston, Michael J. *brokerage house executive*
†Johnston, Philip *association executive*
Jonas, Gilbert *public relations and fund raising executive*
Jonas, Joan *artist*
Jonas, Ruth Haber *psychologist*
Jonas, Saran *neurologist, educator*
Jones, Abbott C. *investment banking executive*
Jones, Alex S. *reporter*
Jones, Anne *librarian*
Jones, Barclay Gibbs, III *investment banker*
Jones, Bill T. *dancer, choreographer*
Jones, Caroline Robinson *advertising executive*
Jones, Colin Howard *publishing company executive*
Jones, David Milton *economist, educator*
Jones, David Rhodes *newspaper editor*
Jones, Diana Wynne *writer*
Jones, Edward Powis *artist*
Jones, Elaine R. *civil rights advocate*
Jones, Gwenyth Ellen *director information systems*
Jones, Landon Y., Jr. *magazine editor*
Jones, Laurie Lynn *magazine editor*
Jones, Lucian Cox *lawyer*
†Jones, Malcolm Wheeler *writer, editor*
†Jones, Paul Tudor, II *investment executive*
Jones, Rickie Lee *singer, songwriter*
Jones, Robert Quince *securities company executive*
Jones, Ronald David *lawyer*
Jones, Thomas Wade *financial services executive*
Jones, William Kenneth *law educator*
Jones, William Randall *publisher*
Jong, Erica Mann *writer, poet*
Jordan, John W., II *holding company executive*
Jordan, Susan *newspaper editor*
Jordan, Thomas Richard *public relations executive*
Jordon, Deborah Elizabeth *lawyer*
Joseph, Frederick Harold *investment banker*
Joseph, Gregory Paul *lawyer*
Joseph, L. Anthony, Jr. *lawyer*
Joseph, Leonard *lawyer*
Joseph, Michael Sarkies *accountant*
Josephs, Ray *public relations and advertising executive, writer, international relations consultant*
Josephson, Marvin *talent and literary agency executive*
Josephson, William Howard *lawyer*
†Joyce, William Edward *writer, illustrator*
Juceam, Robert E. *lawyer*
Judson, Jeannette Alexander *artist*
Jung, Doris *dramatic soprano*
Jurka, Edith Mila *psychiatrist, researcher*
Kabat, Elvin Abraham *immunochemist, biochemist, educator*
Kaden, Ellen Oran *lawyer, broadcasting corporation executive*
Kaden, Lewis B. *law educator*
Kadet, Samuel *lawyer*
Kael, Pauline *film critic, author*
Kafin, Robert Joseph *lawyer*
Kagan, Julia Lee *magazine editor*
Kaggen, Lois Sheila *non-profit organization executive*
Kahan, Marlene *professional association executive*
Kahana, Aron *bank executive*
Kahen, Harold I. *lawyer*
Kahler, Steve Carl *publishing executive*
Kahn, Alfred Joseph *social worker and planner, educator*
Kahn, Anthony F. *lawyer*
Kahn, Joseph Gabriel *newspaperman*
Kahn, Norman *pharmacology and dentistry educator*
Kahn, Richard Dreyfus *lawyer*
Kahn, Robert Theodore *photojournalist*
Kahn, Walter *steel company executive*
Kahn, Wolf *artist*
Kailas, Leo George *lawyer*
Kaish, Luise Clayborn *sculptor*
Kaish, Morton *artist, educator*
†Kaku, Michio *theoretical nuclear physicist*
Kalech, Marc *newspaper editor*
Kalikow, Peter Stephen *real estate developer, former newspaper owner, publisher*
Kalish, Arthur *lawyer*
Kalish, Myron *lawyer*
Kallir, Jane Katherine *art gallery director, author*
Kalmanoff, Martin *composer*
Kalmus, Allan Henry *public relations executive*
Kals, Stephen A. *lawyer*
Kalsner, Stanley *pharmacologist, physiologist, educator*
Kamali, Norma *fashion designer*
Kamen, Harry Paul *life insurance company executive, lawyer*
Kamerman, Sheila Brody *educator, social worker*
Kamiel, Jerald *apparel executive*
Kamihara, Takashi *electronics firm executive*
Kamin, Sherwin *lawyer*
Kaminer, Peter H. *lawyer*
Kaminsky, Arthur Charles *lawyer*
Kaminsky, Howard *publisher*
Kamlot, Robert *performing arts executive*
Kamsky, Leonard *economist, retired manufacturing executive, financial advisor*
Kan, Diana Artemis Mann Shu *artist*
Kanade, I. *manufacturing executive*
Kandel, William Lloyd *lawyer, educator, author*
Kander, John Harold *composer*
Kane, Daniel Hipwell *lawyer*
Kane, Herman William *research company executive, political scientist*
Kane, Jay Brassler *banker*
Kanick, Virginia *radiologist*
Kann, Peter Robert *journalist, business reporting and services company executive*
Kanovitz, Howard *artist*
Kanter, Norman A. *publishing executive*
Kanuk, Leslie Lazar *management consultant, educator*
Kaplan, Carl Eliot *lawyer*
Kaplan, Harold Irwin *psychiatrist, psychoanalyst, educator*
†Kaplan, Helene Lois *lawyer*
Kaplan, Joseph Solte *lawyer*
Kaplan, Larry *public relations executive*
Kaplan, Leo Sylvan *social scientist, former college administrator*
Kaplan, Lewis A. *lawyer*
Kaplan, Lloyd Arthur *public relations executive*
Kaplan, Madeline *legal administrator*
Kaplan, Mark Norman *lawyer*
Kaplan, Peter James *lawyer*
Kaplan, Philip Thomas *lawyer*
Kaplan, Richard James *producer, director, writer, educator, consultant*
Kaplan, Robert Arthur *association executive*
Kappas, Attallah *physician, medical scientist*
Karalekas, George Steven *advertising agency executive, political consultant*
Karan, Donna (Donna Faske) *fashion designer*
Karasz, Peter *lawyer*
Karatz, William Warren *lawyer*
Karchin, Louis Samuel *composer*
Karmel, Roberta Segal *lawyer, educator*
Karotkin, Stephen K. *lawyer*
Karp, Marshall Warren *creative director, writer*
Karp, Martin Everett *management consultant*
Karp, Richard M. *advertising agency executive*
Karpel, Craig S. *journalist, editor*
Karpen, Marian Joan *financial executive*
Karr, Norman *association executive*
Karsen, Sonja Petra *retired Spanish educator*
Karter, Jerome *reinsurance company executive*
Kartiganer, Joseph *lawyer*
†Kasaks, Sally Frame *apparel executive*
Kasinec, Edward Joseph *library administrator*
Kaskell, Peter Howard *association executive, lawyer*
Kasowitz, Marc Elliot *lawyer*
Kassebaum, John Philip *lawyer*
Kassel, Virginia Weltmer *television producer, writer*
Katalinich, Peggy *magazine editor*
Katsh, Abraham Isaac *university president emeritus, educator*
Katsh, Salem Michael *lawyer*
Katz, Abraham *retired foreign service officer*
Katz, Alex *artist*
Katz, Daniel Roger *conservation executive*
Katz, Gregory *lawyer*
Katz, Hilda *artist*
Katz, Howard Carl *coffee company executive*
Katz, Jerome Charles *lawyer*
Katz, Jose *cardiologist, theoretical physicist, educator*
Katz, Marcia *public relations company executive*
Katz, Norman *manufacturing company executive*
Katz, Phyllis Pollak *magazine publisher and editor*
Katz, Ronald S. *lawyer*
Katz, Stanley Nider *law history educator, association executive*
Katz, Susan R. *publisher*
†Katz, Thomas J. *chemistry educator*
Katz, William Loren *author*
Katzman, Herbert Henry *artist*
Kauffmann, Stanley Jules *author*
Kaufman, Arthur Stephen *lawyer*
Kaufman, Bel *author, educator*
Kaufman, Frank Joseph *lawyer*
Kaufman, Martin N. *metal processing company executive*
Kaufman, Robert Max *lawyer*
Kaufman, Victor A. *film company executive*
Kaufmann, Jack *lawyer*
Kaufmann, Mark Steiner *banker*
Kautz, James Charles *investment banker*
Kavaler, Thomas J. *lawyer*
Kavee, Robert Charles *insurance company executive*
Kavesh, Robert A. *economist, educator*
Kavner, Robert M. *communications company executive*
Kavoukjian, Michael Edward *lawyer*
Kay, Allen Steven *advertising executive*
Kaye, Stephen Rackow *lawyer*
Kaye, Walter *financial executive*
Kaynor, William Akin *lawyer*
Kaz, Nathaniel *sculptor*
Kazanjian, John Harold *lawyer*
Kazanjian, Shant *religious organization administrator*
Kazemi, Farhad *political science educator*
Kazin, Alfred *writer*
Kealy, William James *investment executive*
Kean, Hamilton Fish *lawyer*
Keane, Bil *cartoonist*
Keany, Sutton *lawyer*
Kearney, Michael John *banker*
Kearse, Amalya Lyle *federal judge*
Keating, Cornelius Francis *record company executive*
Keating, Robert Edward *public relations executive*
Keegan, Gerard C. *bank executive*
Keenan, John Fontaine *federal judge*
Keenan, Michael Edgar *advertising executive*
Keene, Christopher *conductor, author, librettist, musician*
Keeshan, Bob *television producer, actor*
Keeshan, Michael *advertising agency executive*
Keeton, Kathy Merle *publisher*
Keevil, Philip Clement *investment banker*
Kehr, David *film critic*
Kehret, Peg *writer*
Keilin, Eugene Jacob *investment banker, lawyer*
Keill, Stuart Langdon *psychiatrist*
Keith, John Pirie *urban planner*
†Kekst, Gershon *public relations consultant*
Kellen, Stephen Max *investment banker*
Keller, Bill *journalist*
Keller, Kenneth Harrison *engineering educator, science policy analyst*
Keller, Richard Charles *banker*
Kellerman, Jonathan Seth *pediatric psychologist, writer*
Kelley, Sheila Seymour *public relations executive, crisis consultant*
Kellman, Barnet Kramer *film, stage and television director*
Kellner, Irwin L. *economist*
Kellogg, Cal Stewart, II *conductor, composer*
Kellogg, David *publisher*
Kellogg, Herbert Humphrey *metallurgist, educator*
Kellogg, Peter R. *securities dealer*
Kelly, David Austin *food and chemical products executive*
Kelly, James *artist*
Kelly, Robert J. *accounting firm executive*
Kelm, Linda *opera singer*
Kelman, Charles D. *ophthalmologist, educator*
Kelmenson, Leo-Arthur *advertising executive*
Kelne, Nathan *editorial and public relations consultant*
Kempa, Gerald *manufacturing company executive*
Kemper, Randolph E. *fashion designer*
Kennedy, Ian Glen *art appraiser*
Kennedy, John Joseph *lawyer, educator*
Kennedy, Michael John *lawyer*
Kennedy, Moorhead *foundation administrator*
Kennedy, Thomas H. *lawyer*
Kenney, Jerome P. *finance company executive*
Kenney, John Joseph *lawyer*
Kenney, Matthew *chef*
Kenny, Roger Michael *executive search consultant*
Kent, Barbara *real estate investor*
Kent, Julie Ann *ballet dancer, actress, model*
Kent, Linda Gail *dancer*
Keogh, Kevin *lawyer*
Kepets, Hugh Michael *artist*
Keppler, Herbert *publishing company executive*
Kern, George Calvin, Jr. *lawyer*
Kern, Jerome H. *lawyer*
Kern, Martin H(arold) *supermarket chain executive*
†Kernis, Aaron Jay *composer*
Kernochan, John Marshall *lawyer, educator*
Kerrison, Ray *newspaper columnist*
Kerschner, Edward *brokerage house executive*
Kessel, Mark *lawyer*
Kesselman, Mark Jonathan *political science educator, writer*
Kessler, Jeffrey L. *lawyer*
Kessler, Ralph Kenneth *lawyer, manufacturing company executive*
Kesting, Theodore *magazine editor*
Kevlin, Mary Louise *lawyer*
Kezsbom, Allen *lawyer*
Khan, Chaka (Yvette Marie Stevens) *singer*
Khanzadian, Vahan *tenor*
Khayatt, Shaker Albert *investment banker*
Kheel, Theodore Woodrow *lawyer, labor arbitrator and mediator*
Khuri, Nicola Najib *physicist, educator*
Kidd, John Edward *lawyer, corporate executive*
Kidd, Michael (Milton Greenwald) *choreographer, director*
Kidder, (John) Tracy *writer*
Kiechel, Walter, III *magazine editor*
Kieren, Thomas Henry *management consultant*
Kifner, John William *journalist, newspaper correspondent*
Kilburn, H(enry) T(homas), Jr. *investment banker*
Kill, Lawrence *lawyer*
Killefer, Tom *banker*
Killeffer, Louis MacMillan *advertising executive*
Kim, Willa *costume designer*
Kimball, Richard Arthur, Jr. *lawyer*
Kinberg, Judy *television producer, director*
King, B. B. (Riley B. King) *singer, guitarist*
King, Carole *songwriter, singer*
King, Douglas Lohr *insurance executive, lawyer*
King, Henry Lawrence *lawyer*
King, Lawrence Philip *lawyer, educator*
King, Marvin *research executive*
King, Thomas Creighton *thoracic surgeon, educator*
King, Woodie, Jr. *producer, actor, director*
Kingsberg, Harold Joseph *investment management company executive*
Kingsland, James Arthur *architect*
Kingsley, April *art critic, curator, historian, art educator*
Kinnell, Galway *poet, translator*
Kinney, Stephen Hoyt, Jr. *lawyer*
Kinser, Richard Edward *management consultant*
Kinsolving, Augustus Blagden *lawyer*
Kinsolving, Charles McIlvaine, Jr. *marketing executive*
Kinstler, Everett Raymond *artist*
Kinzler, Thomas Benjamin *lawyer*
Kirby, John Joseph, Jr. *lawyer*
Kirk, Alexis Vemian *designer*
Kirk, Donald James *consultant, accounting educator*
Kirk, Susanne Smith *editor*
Kirkland, Gelsey *dancer*
†Kirsch, Arthur William *investment banker*
†Kirsch, Donald *financial consultant, author*
Kirschbaum, Myron *lawyer*
Kirschner, Marc Steven *lawyer*
Kirshbaum, Laurence J. *book publishing executive*
Kirshenbaum, Richard Warren *creative director*
Kirstein, Lincoln *ballet promoter*
Kish, Joseph Laurence, Jr. *management consultant*
Kismaric, Carole Lee *editor, writer, book packaging company executive*
Kisner, Jacob *poet, editor*
Kissel, Howard William *drama critic*
Kissiloff, William *industrial designer*
Kistler, Darci Anna *ballet dancer*
Kitt, Eartha Mae *actress, singer*
Kittell, Donald D. *investment firm executive*
Kivette, Ruth Montgomery *English language educator*
Klaperman, Joel Simcha *lawyer*
Klass, Morton *anthropology educator, consultant*
Klatell, Jack *dentist*
Klatsky, Bruce J. *apparel company executive*
Klausmann, Walter Joseph *financial executive*
Kleeberg, John Martin *museum curator*
†Klein, Anton J. *school superintendent*
Klein, Calvin Richard *fashion designer*
Klein, Donald Franklin *scientist, psychiatrist, educator*
Klein, Elaine *magazine publishing executive*
†Klein, Harvey *physician, educagtor*
Klein, Herbert Sanford *historian*
Klein, John E. *agricultural products company executive*
Klein, Morton *industrial engineer, educator*
Klein, Paul E. *insurance company executive, lawyer*
Klein, Robert *comedian, actor*
Klein, Robert Majer *retired bank executive*
Klein, T(heodore) E(ibon) D(onald) *writer*
Klein, William, II *lawyer*
Kleinbard, Edward D. *lawyer*
Kleinberg, Norman Charles *lawyer*
Kleinberg, Robert Irwin *lawyer*
Klemm, Richard Henry *investment company executive*
Kligfield, Paul David *physician, medicine educator*
Kliment, Robert Michael *architect*
Kliment, Stephen Alexander *architect, editor*
Kline, Eugene Monroe *lawyer*
Klingenstein, Frederick Adler *investment banking executive*
†Klinghoffer, David *journalist*
Klingsberg, David *lawyer*
Klink, Fredric J. *lawyer*
Klipper, Mitchell S. *book publishing executive*
Kloos, Edward John Michael, Jr. *minister*
Klopf, Gordon John *college dean, educational consultant*
Klotz, Florence *costume designer*
Kluberdanz, Wallace *publishing executive*
Kmiotek, Jacqueline J. *lawyer*
Knapp, Charles Lincoln *law educator*
Knapp, Whitman *federal judge*
Knell, Gary Evan *media executive, lawyer*
Kneller, John William *French language educator*
Kner, Andrew Peter *art director*
Kness, Richard Maynard *tenor*
Knickerbocker, Daniel Candee, Jr. *legal educator*
Knight, Howard Atwood *investment banking executive, consultant*
Knight, Robert Huntington *lawyer, bank executive*
Knight, Townsend Jones *lawyer*
Knisley, Patrick Allen *advertising company executive*
Knobler, Alfred Everett *ceramic engineer, manufacturing company executive, publisher*
Knobler, Peter Stephen *magazine editor, writer*
Knowles, Edward F(rank) *architect*
Knowles, Richard James Robert *medical physicist, educator, consultant*
Knox, George L(evi), III *consumer products company executive*
Knudsen, Rudolph Edgar, Jr. *insurance company executive*
Knutson, David Harry *lawyer, banker*
Kobak, James Benedict, Jr. *lawyer, educator*
Kobayashi, Hisao *financial company executive*
Kober, Jane *lawyer*
Kobler, John *writer*
Kobrin, Lawrence Alan *lawyer*
Koch, Edward I. *former mayor, lawyer*
Koch, Kenneth *poet, playwright*
Koegel, William Fisher *lawyer*
Koeltl, John George *judge*
Koenig, Marvin *heavy manufacturing executive*
Koenigsberg, I. Fred *lawyer*
Koeppel, Noel Immanuel *financial planner, securities and real estate broker*
Kogstad, Rolf Egil *sales company executive*
†Kohlberg, Jerome, Jr. *lawyer, business executive*
Kohlenberg, Stanley *marketing executive*
Kohn, A. Eugene *architect*
Kohn, Stephen Jerome *accounting company executive*
Kohut, John Walter *corporate executive*
Kok, Hans Gebhard *consulting engineer*

Koke, Richard Joseph author, exhibit designer, museum curator
Kolatch, Myron magazine editor
Kolb, Daniel Francis lawyer
Kolbe, Karl William, Jr. lawyer
Kolbert, Kathryn lawyer, educator
Kole, Adrian G. banker
Kolesar, Peter John business and engineering educator
Kolmer, John H., Jr. banker
Kolodny, Edwin Hillel neurologist, geneticist, medical administrator
Kolpakova, Irina dancer, educator, coach
†Komansky, David H. financial services executive
Komar, Arthur B. physicist, educator
Komaroff, Stanley lawyer
Komarovsky, Mirra (Mrs. Marcus A. Heyman) sociology educator
Komisar, Arnold otolaryngologist, educator
Kondas, Nicholas Frank shipping company executive
Kondylis, Costas Andrew architect
Kong, Deyong research center administrator
Konner, Joan Weiner university administrator, educator, broadcasting executive, television producer
Kono, Toshihiko cellist
Koob, Charles Edward lawyer
Koons, Linda Gleitsman publishing executive
Koontz, Dean Ray writer
Koontz, Richard Harvey financial printing company executive
Kopech, Robert Irving banker
Kopelman, Richard Eric management educator
Kopit, Arthur playwright
Koplik, Michael R. durable goods company executive
Koplik, Perry H. durable goods company executive
Koplovitz, Kay communication network executive
Kopp, Wendy teaching program administrator
Koppelman, Chaim artist
Koppelman, Charles record company executive
Koppelman, Dorothy Myers artist, consultant
Koppenaal, Richard John psychology educator
Koral, Alan M. lawyer
Koren, Edward Benjamin cartoonist, educator
Korman, Jess J. advertising executive
Korman, Lewis J. film company executive, consultant, lawyer
Korn, Harold Leon law educator
Kornberg, Alan William lawyer
Kornblit, Sandra Cohen lawyer
Korner, Anthony David publisher
Kornhauser, Henry advertising executive
Kornhauser, Lewis law educator
Kornreich, Edward Scott lawyer
Kornreich, Morton Alan insurance brokerage company executive
Korotkin, Michael Paul lawyer
Kors, Michael (Karl Anderson, Jr.) fashion designer
Kortepeter, Carl Max history educator, columnist
Koshar, Louis David civil engineer
†Koslow, Sally editor-in-chief
Kosner, Edward A(lan) magazine editor and publisher
Kosovich, Dushan Radovan psychiatrist
Kostelanetz, Boris lawyer
Kostelanetz, Richard writer, artist
Koster, Elaine Landis publishing executive
Kotcher, Raymond Lowell public relations executive
Kotecha, Mahesh Kanjibhai financial guarantee insurance company executive
Kotlowitz, Robert writer,editor
Kotzwinkle, William author
Kourides, Peter Theologos lawyer
Kovacs, Elizabeth Ann professional society administrator
Kovak, Ellen B. public relations firm executive
Kovalcik, Kenneth John accountant
Kozlova, Valentina ballerina
Kozodoy, Neal magazine editor
Kra, Pauline Skornicki French language educator
Kraemer, Lillian Elizabeth lawyer
Kraft, Marcijane lawyer
Kram, Shirley Wohl federal judge
†Kramberg, Ross arts administrator
Kramer, Alan Sharfsin lawyer
Kramer, Fred Russell molecular biologist
Kramer, George P. lawyer
Kramer, Jane writer
Kramer, Jonathan Donald composer
†Kramer, Kenneth Merin lawyer
Kramer, Linda Konheim curator, art historian
Kramer, Marc B. forensic audiologist
Kramer, Morris Joseph lawyer
Kramer, Philip retired petroleum refining executive
Kranwinkle, Conrad Douglas lawyer
Krasna, Alvin Isaac biochemist, educator
Krasner, Daniel Walter lawyer
Krasno, Richard Michael educational organization executive, educator
Kraus, Douglas M. lawyer
Kraus, Norma Jean industrial relations executive
Kraushar, Jonathan Pollack communications and media consultant
Krauss, Herbert Harris psychologist
Kravis, Henry R. venture financier
Krawitz, Herman Everett television producer
Kreh, Kent Q. magazine publishing executive
Kreisberg, Neil Ivan advertising executive
Kreitman, Benjamin Zvi rabbi, Judaic studies educator
Kreitzman, Ralph J. lawyer
Krementz, Jill photographer, author
Krenek, Debby newspaper editor
Krens, Thomas museum director
Krensky, Harold retired retail store executive, investor
Krents, Milton Ellis broadcast executive
Kressel, Henry venture capitalist
Kreston, Martin Howard advertising, marketing, public relations, and publishing executive
Kretschmer, Keith Hughes stockbroker
Kretschmer, Paul Robert investment banker
Kreutzer, Franklin David lawyer
Krickstein, Aaron professional tennis player
Krieger, Sanford lawyer
Krimendahl, Herbert Frederick, II investment banker
Kriney, Marilyn Walker publishing executive
Krinsky, Carol Herselle art history educator
Krinsky, Robert Daniel consulting firm executive
Krinsly, Stuart Zalmy lawyer, manufacturing company executive
Krisher, Patterson Howard management consultant
Kristeller, Paul Oskar former philosophy educator
Kroeber, Karl English language educator
Kroeger, Lin J. management consultant
Kroft, Steve news correspondent, editor
Kroll, Alexander S. advertising agency executive
Kroll, Arnold Howard investment banker
Kroll, Arthur Herbert lawyer, law educator
Krominga, Lynn cosmetic and health care company executive, lawyer
Krone, Gerald Sidney theatrical and television producer
Krone, Helmut consultant, former advertising executive
Krosnick, Joel cellist
Krouse, George Raymond, Jr. lawyer
Krown, Susan Ellen physician, researcher
Kruech, Paul C. bank executive
Krueger, Harvey Mark investment banker, lawyer
Krugman, Saul physician, educator, researcher
Krulik, Barbara S. director, curator
Krulwich, Terry Ann biochemistry researcher
Krupman, William Allan lawyer
Krupp, Frederic D. lawyer, environmental agency executive
Krupska, Danya (Mrs. Ted Thurston) theater director, choreographer
Krushenick, Nicholas artist
Krzyzanowski, Eve broadcasting executive
Kubek, Anthony Christopher (Tony Kubek) sports announcer
Kubin, Michael Ernest advertising and marketing executive
Kufeld, William Manuel lawyer
Kuh, Joyce Dattel education administrator
Kuh, Richard Henry lawyer
Kuhn, Denis Glen architectural firm executive
Kuklin, Anthony Bennett lawyer
Kullberg, Gary Walter advertising agency executive
Kumble, Steven Jay lawyer
Kumin, Maxine Winokur poet, author
Kummel, Eugene H. advertising agency executive
Kunitz, Stanley Jasspon poet, editor, educator
Kunstler, William Moses lawyer, educator, lecturer, author
Kuntz, Lee Allan lawyer
Kuo, John Tsungfen geophysicist, educator, researcher
Kupfer, Sherman physician, educator, researcher
Kupferman, Theodore R. state justice
Kuralt, Charles Bishop writer, former television news correspondent
Kuriansky, Judy television and radio talk show host, reporter, psychologist, writer, lecturer
Kurnit, Paul David advertising executive
Kurnit, Shepard advertising agency executive
Kurnow, Ernest statistician, educator
†Kuropat, Rosemary Louise marketing executive
Kurtis, William Horton (Bill Kurtis) broadcast journalist
Kurtyka, Ruthanne lawyer
Kurtz, Jerome lawyer, educator
Kury, Bernard Edward lawyer
Kurz, Mitchell Howard marketing communications executive
Kurzweil, Harvey lawyer
Kushner, Robert Ellis artist
Kushner, Tony playwright
Kvint, Vladimir Lev finance educator, mining engineer
Kwa, Raymond Pain-Boon cardiologist
LaBarre, Dennis W. lawyer
Labrecque, Thomas G. banker
Labunski, Stephen Bronislaw association executive
Lacey, Frederick Bernard lawyer, former federal judge
Lachenbruch, David editor, writer
†Lachman, Edward cinematographer
Lachman, Lawrence business consultant, former department store executive
Lachman, Marguerite Leanne real estate investment advisor
Lacovara, Philip Allen lawyer
Lacy, Robinson Burrell lawyer
Lacy, Steve jazz musician
Ladau, Robert Francis architect, planner
Lader, Lawrence writer
Ladjevardi, Hamid fund manager
Lafferty, Charles Douglas Joseph advertising agency executive
LaForce, William Leonard, Jr. photojournalist
La Fosse, Robert ballet dancer, choreographer
Lai, W(ei) Michael mechanical engineer, educator
Laird, Robert Winslow journalist
Lakah, Jacqueline Rabbat political scientist, educator
Lala, Dominick J. manufacturing company executive
Lalli, Cele Goldsmith editor
Lalli, Frank magazine editor
Lamb, George Richard foundation executive
Lambert, Eleanor (Mrs. Seymour Berkson) public relations executive, fashion authority, journalist
Lambert, Paul Christopher lawyer, former ambassador
Lamel, Linda Helen insurance company executive, college president, lawyer
Lamia, Thomas Roger lawyer
Lamirande, Arthur Gordon editor, organist
Lamm, Donald Stephen publishing company executive
Lamont, Corliss philosopher, educator, author
Lamont, Lansing journalist, public affairs executive, author
Lamont, Lee art management executive
Lancaster, Kelvin John economics educator
Lanchner, Bertrand Martin lawyer, advertising executive
Land, David Potts lawyer
Landa, Howard Martin lawyer, business executive
Landau, Peter Edward editor
Landau, Ralph chemical engineer
Landau, Sidney I. publishing executive, lexicographer
Landau, Walter Loeber lawyer
†Landegger, Carl Clement machinery and pulp manufacturing executive
Landes, Robert Nathan lawyer
Landesman, Heidi set designer
Landrigan, Philip John epidemiologist
†Landy, Joanne Veit foreign policy analyst
Lane, Alvin S. lawyer
Lane, Arthur Alan lawyer
Lane, Frederick Carpenter investment banker
Lane, Jeffrey Bruce financial services company executive
Lane, Kenneth Jay jewelry designer
Lane, Leonard Charles manufacturing company executive
Lane, Lois N. artist
Lane, Nancy editor
Lane, William W. electronics executive
Lang, Daniel S. artist
Lang, Eugene M. technology development company executive
Lang, George restaurateur
Lang, John Francis lawyer
lang, k. d. (Katherine Dawn Lang) country music singer, composer
Lang, Pearl dancer, choreographer
Lang, Robert Todd lawyer
Lang, Stephen R. lawyer
Lang, Theresa investment banker
Lange, Marvin Robert lawyer
Lange, Phil C. retired education educator
Langer, Andrew J. advertising agency executive
Langer, Horst financial corporate executive
Langham, Michael theatrical director
Langton, Cleve Swanson advertising executive
Lannamann, Richard Stuart executive recruiting consultant
La Noue, Terence David artist, educator
Lans, Asher Bob lawyer
Lansbury, Edgar George theatrical producer
Lansner, Kermit Irvin editor, consultant
Lantay, George Charles (Wagner) psychologist, psychotherapist, consultant
Lanyon, Ellen (Mrs. Roland Ginzel) artist, educator
Lanza, Frank C. electronics executive
La Penta, Robert Vincent electronics company executive
Lapham, Lewis Henry editor, author, television host
LaPier, Theodore lawyer
Lapierre, Dominique writer, historian, philanthropist
Lapine, James Elliot playwright, director
Lappin, Joan E. financial executive
Laragh, John Henry physician, scientist, educator
Lareau, Marybeth Bass marketing professional
Laren, Kuno investment banker
Larkin, Leo Paul, Jr. lawyer
†Larmore, Jennifer mezzo-soprano
La Rossa, James M(ichael) lawyer
Larsen, Anne editor
Larsen, Robert Dhu lawyer
La Rue, (Adrian) Jan (Pieters) musicologist, educator, author
Lascher, Alan Alfred lawyer
Lash, Stephen Sycle auction company executive
†Laskawy, Philip A. accounting and management consulting firm executive
Lasker, Jonathan Lewis artist
Lasker, Joseph L. artist, illustrator
Lassen, Robert Maurie graphic artist, photographer, editor
Lasser, Joseph Robert investment company executive
Lassiter, Phillip B. insurance company executive
Lattes, Raffaele physician, educator
Lattimer, John Kingsley physician, educator
Lattin, Albert Floyd banker
Lauder, Estée cosmetics company executive
†Lauder, Evelyn cosmetics executive
Lauder, Leonard Alan cosmetic and fragrance company executive
Lauer, Eliot lawyer
Lauersen, Niels Helth physician, educator
Laufer, Beatrice composer
Laufer, Donald L. lawyer
Laufman, Harold surgeon
Laughlin, James publishing company executive, writer, lecturer
Laughlin, John Seth physicist, educator
Laughren, Terry marketing executive
Lauren, Ralph fashion designer
Laurence, Jeffrey Conrad immunologist
Laurus, (Laurus Skurla) archbishop
Lavey, Kenneth Henry advertising agency executive, designer
Lavin, Thomas J. A. investment banker
Lavine, Lawrence Neal investment banker
Lavinsky, Larry Monroe lawyer, consultant
Lavitt, Mel S. investment banking professional
Law, Sylvia A. law educator
Lawrence, Bryan Hunt investment banking executive
Lawrence, Henry Sherwood physician, educator
Lawrence, James Bland advertising executive
Lawrence, Ruddick Carpenter public relations executive
Lawry, Sylvia (Mrs. Stanley Englander) association executive
Laws, Robert E. diversified company executive
Lawson-Johnston, Peter Orman foundation executive
Lax, Melvin theoretical physicist
Lax, Peter David mathematics educator
Laybourne, Geraldine broadcasting executive
Layton, Donald Harvey banker
Layton, Robert lawyer
Lazarus, Rochelle Braff advertising executive
Leach, Michael Glen publisher
Leach, Robin producer, writer, television host
Leaf, Robert Jay dental insurance consultant
Leaf, Roger Warren business consultant
†Leahey, Lynn editor-in-chief
Leahy, Michael Joseph newspaper editor
Lear, Evelyn soprano
Lear, Robert William holding company executive
Leavitt, Charles Loyal English language educator, administrator
Leavitt, David Adam writer
Leavitt, Michael P(aul) performing arts manager and concert producer
Lebec, Alain investment banker
Lebensfeld, Harry manufacturing company executive
Leber, Lester advertising agency executive
Leber, Steven Edward film producer, corporate executive
LeBlond, Richard Knight, II banker
LeBow, Bennett S. communications executive
Lebow, Mark Denis lawyer
Lechay, James artist, emeritus art educator
LeClerc, Paul library director
†LeCompte, Elizabeth theater director
Lederberg, Joshua geneticist, educator
Lederer, Edith Madelon journalist
Lederer, Peter David lawyer
Lederman, Lawrence lawyer, writer, educator
Ledger, William Joe physician, educator
LeDoux, Harold Anthony cartoonist, painter
Lee, Barbara A. federal magistrate judge
Lee, Catherine sculptor, painter
Lee, Chin O. physiologist, educator
Lee, Clement William Khan association administrator
Lee, Dai-Keong composer
Lee, David James lawyer
Lee, J. Daniel, Jr. insurance company executive
Lee, Jerome G. lawyer
Lee, Martin Yongho (Kyung-Joo Lee) mechanical engineer
Lee, Paul L. lawyer
Lee, Robert Sanford psychologist
†Lee, Sally A. editor-in-chief
Lee, Sarah Tomerlin design executive
Lee, Sidney Phillip chemical engineer, state senator
Lee, Stan (Stanley Martin Lieber) cartoon publisher, writer
Lee, Tsung-Dao physicist, educator
Lee, Wonyong physicist, educator
Leebron, David Wayne law educator
Leeds, Douglas Brecker advertising agency executive, theatre producer
Leet, Mildred Robbins corporate executive, consultant
Leetch, Brian Joseph hockey player
Le Fevre, William Mathias, Jr. brokerage company executive
Lefferts, Gillet, Jr. architect
Lefkovits, Albert Meyer dermatologist
Lefkowitz, Howard N. lawyer
Lefkowitz, Lawrence lawyer
LeFrak, Francine theatre and film producer
†Legrand, Michel Jean composer
Lehman, Edward William sociology educator, researcher
Lehman, Mark E. lawyer
Lehman, Orin retired state official
Lehmann, Frederick Gliessmann university administrator
Lehmann-Haupt, Christopher Charles Herbert book reviewer
Lehr, Janet art dealer, publisher, author
Lehrer, Leonard artist, educator
Lehrer, Sander lawyer
Leiber, Gerson August artist
Leiber, Judith Maria designer, manufacturer
Leibovitz, Annie photographer
Leibowitz, Herbert Akiba English language educator, author
Leichtling, Michael Alfred lawyer
Leigh, Stephen industrial designer
Leighton, Lawrence Ward investment banker
Leisure, George Stanley, Jr. lawyer
Leisure, Peter Keeton federal judge
Leiter, Elliot urologist
Leland, Richard G. lawyer
Leland, Sara ballet dancer
Lelchuk, Alan author, educator
Lelyveld, Joseph Salem newspaper editor, correspondent
Le Mener, Georges Philippe hotel executive
Lemesh, Nicholas Thomas designer, filmmaker
Lencek, Rado L. Slavic languages educator
Leness, George Crawford lawyer
L'Engle, Madeleine (Mrs. Hugh Franklin) author
Lengyel, Peter Emery banker
Lennox, Annie rock musician
Leo, Jacqueline M. publishing company executive
Leonard, Edward F. chemical engineer, educator
Leonard, Edwin Deane lawyer
Leontief, Wassily economist, educator
Lepore, Michael Joseph gastroenterologist, educator
Leppard, Raymond John conductor, harpsichordist
Lepri, Daniel B. light manufacturing executive
†Lerer, Kenneth public relations executive
Leritz, Lawrence choreographer, dancer, actor
Lerner, Martin museum curator
Lerner, Ralph E. lawyer
Lerner, Sandy Richard art educator, art restorer, appraiser, painter, sculptor, lithographer
Lescaze, Lee Adrien editor
Lesch, Michael Oscar lawyer
Leser, Bernard H. publishing executive
Leslie, John Webster, Jr. communications company executive
Leslie, Seymour Marvin communications executive
Lesser, Edward Arnold banker
Lesser, Lawrence J. advertising agency executive
Letterman, David television personality, comedian, writer
Letzig, Betty Jean association executive
Leubert, Alfred Otto Paul international business consultant
Leute, William Russell, III bank executive
Leval, Pierre Nelson federal judge
Leve, Samuel scenic designer
Levenstein, Alan Peter advertising executive
Leventhal, Kathy Neisloss magazine publisher
Levertov, Denise poet
†Levesque, Roger Raymond trading company executive
Levi, Isaac philosophy educator
Levie, Joseph Henry lawyer
Levin, Alan M. television journalist
Levin, Ezra Gurion lawyer
Levin, Gerald Manuel media and entertainment company executive
Levin, Ira author, playwright
Levin, Jerry Wayne cosmetics executive
Levin, Martin P. publishing executive, lawyer
Levin, Neil D. bank executive
Levine, Arthur Elliott academic administrator, educator
Levine, Carl Morton motion picture exhibition, real estate executive
Levine, Charles Michael publishing company executive, consultant
Levine, David artist
†Levine, Douglas Gary music industry executive
Levine, Edward Leslie lawyer
Levine, Ellen R. magazine editor
Levine, Gerald Richard investment banker, finanical advisor, estate planning and philanthropy specialist
Levine, Israel E. writer
Levine, James conductor, pianist, artistic director
Levine, Laurence William lawyer
Levine, Lawrence Steven lawyer
Levine, Mark Leonard lawyer
Levine, Martin Robert executive search and recruiting company executive
Levine, Naomi Bronheim university administrator
Levine, Richard James publishing executive
Levine, Robert Jay lawyer
Levine, Ronald Jay lawyer
Levine, Suzanne Braun magazine editor
†Levins, Ilyssa public relations executive
Levinson, Rascha psychotherapist
Levinson, Robert Alan textile company executive
Levinson, Warren Mitchell broadcast journalist
Levison, Harold George lawyer
Levitan, Dan investment banker
Levitan, David M(aurice) lawyer, educator
Levitan, James A. lawyer
Levitas, Mitchel Ramsey editor
Levitt, Mitchell Alan management consultant
Levitz, Paul Elliot publishing executive
Levoy, Myron author
Levy, Alain M. record company executive
Levy, Alan Joseph editor, journalist, writer
Levy, Benjamin artist
Levy, Joseph lawyer
Levy, Leon investment company executive

Levy, Mark Allan *lawyer*
Levy, Marvin David *composer*
†Levy, Reynold *communication company executive*
Levy, Stanley Herbert *lawyer*
Levy, Walter James *oil consultant*
Levy, Walter Kahn *management consultant executive*
Lewins, Steven *security analyst, investment advisor, corporate executive*
Lewinton, Christopher *business executive*
Lewis, Allan *conductor, ballet company music director*
Lewis, Edwin A. *communications company executive*
Lewis, George Ralph *consumer goods company executive*
Lewis, Grant Stephen *lawyer*
Lewis, Hylan Garnet *sociologist, educator*
Lewis, James Berton *law educator*
Lewis, Jerry Lee *country-rock singer, musician*
Lewis, John Leeman, Jr. *obstetrician, gynecologist*
†Lewis, Loida Nicolas *food products holding company executive*
Lewis, Robert Charles *lawyer*
Lewis, Russell T. *newspaper publishing executive*
Lewis, Sherman Richard, Jr. *investment banker*
†Lewis, Sylvia Davidson *association executive*
Lewis, William Scheer *electrical engineer*
LeWitt, Sol *artist*
Lewyn, Thomas Mark *lawyer*
Libby, John Kelway *financial services company executive*
Liberman, Alexander *artist, editor*
Libin, Paul *theatre executive, producer*
Licari, Joseph *real estate company executive*
Lichtblau, John H. *economist*
Lichtenstein, Seymour *clothing manufacturing company executive*
Liddell, Donald Macy, Jr. *retired investment counsellor*
Lieberman, Charles *economist*
Lieberman, Gail Forman *finance executive*
Lieberman, Seymour *biochemistry educator emeritus*
Liebermann, Lowell *composer, pianist, conductor*
Liebman, Lance Malcolm *dean, lawyer*
Liebman, Theodore *architect*
Lifland, William Thomas *lawyer*
Liftin, John Matthew *lawyer*
Lifton, Robert Jay *psychiatrist, author*
Lifton, Robert Kenneth *diversified companies executive*
Liggio, Carl Donald *lawyer*
Lightfoot, Gordon Meredith *singer, songwriter*
Lilien, Mark Ira *publishing, retailing and systems executive*
Lilley, Albert Frederick *lawyer*
Lillie, James Woodruff, Jr. *lawyer*
Liman, Arthur Lawrence *lawyer*
Limbaugh, Rush Hudson *radio and talk show host*
Lin, Joseph Pen-Tze *neuroradiologist, clinical administrator, educator*
Lin, Wuu-Long *economist*
Lincoln, Abbey (Anna Marie Woolridge, Gaby Lee, Aminata Moseka) *jazz singer, actress*
Lincoln, Edmond Lynch *investment banker*
Lindblom, Marjorie Press *lawyer*
Lindenbaum, Sandford Richard *lawyer*
Linder, Bertram Norman *foundation administrator, horse-breeder, actor*
†Lindheim, James Bruce *public relations executive*
Lindley, David Morrison *lawyer*
Lindsay, George Nelson *lawyer*
Lindsay, George Peter *lawyer*
Lindsay, Robert Van Cleef *trust company executive*
Lindskog, David Richard *lawyer*
Lingeman, Richard Roberts *editor, writer*
Linney, Romulus *author, educator*
Linsenmeyer, John Michael *lawyer*
Linz, Werner Mark *publishing executive*
Lionni, Leonard *author, artist*
Lipkin, Martin *physician, scientist*
Lipsey, Robert Edward *economist, educator*
Lipton, Charles *public relations executive*
†Lipton, Charles Jules *lawyer*
Lipton, Joan Elaine *advertising executive*
Lipton, Martin *lawyer*
Lipton, Robert Steven *lawyer*
Lipton, William James *accountant, lawyer*
Lish, Gordon *author, educator, editor*
†Lisle, Janet Taylor *writer*
Lissack, Michael Robert *investment banker*
Litman, Helena D. *lawyer*
†Litrell, Barbara *publishing executive*
Littledale, Freya Lota Brown *writer, editor*
Littlefield, Martin (Martin Kleinwald) *book publishing executive*
Liu, Brian Cheong-Seng *urology and oncology educator, researcher*
Livengood, Victoria Ann *opera singer*
Livingston, Jay Harold *composer, lyricist*
†Livingston, Sharon Hollander *advertising executive*
Livnat, Joshua *accounting educator, consultant*
LL Cool J, (James Todd Smith) *rap singer, actor*
Lloyd-Jones, Donald J. *transportation executive*
Localio, S. Arthur *retired surgeon, educator*
Lochner, Philip Raymond, Jr. *lawyer*
Lockett, Pierre *dancer*
Lockhart, James Bicknell, III *investment banker*
Lockwood, Molly Ann *communications company executive*
Loeb, Frances Lehman *civic leader*
Loeb, John Langeloth *banker, broker*
Loeb, John Langeloth, Jr. *investment counselor*
Loeb, Marshall Robert *journalist, magazine editor*
Loeb, Peter Kenneth *money manager*
Loeb, Steven Michael *lawyer*
†Loeks, James *theater chain executive*
Loengard, John Borg *photographer; editor*
Loengard, Richard Otto, Jr. *lawyer*
LoFrisco, Anthony F. *lawyer*
Logan, Francis Dummer *lawyer*
Logan, J. Murray *investment manager*
Logan, Kenneth Richard *lawyer*
Logan, Vicki *advertising executive*
Logsdon, Richard Henry *retired librarian and educator*
Lohf, Kenneth A. *librarian, writer*
Lohse, Austin Webb *banker*
†Lois, George *advertising agency executive*
Lokken, Lawrence *law educator*
London, Herbert Ira *humanities educator*
London, Martin *lawyer*
Londoner, David Jay *investment banker, analyst*
Loney, Glenn Meredith *drama educator*
†Long, David L. *magazine publisher*
Long, Elizabeth Valk *magazine publisher*
Long, Melvin Durward *university president*
Long, Robert Douglas *financial service executive*
Long, Thomas Michael *investment banker*
†Longchampt, Michel *steel executive*
Longley, Marjorie Watters *newspaper executive*
Longman, Richard Winston *mechanical engineering educator*
Longstreth, Bevis *lawyer*
†Lookstein, Haskel *rabbi*
Loomis, Carol J. *journalist*
Loomis, Philip Clark *investment executive*
Loomis, Robert Duane *publishing company executive, author*
Lopez, Lourdes *ballerina*
†Lopez, Ramon *recording industry executive*
Lorch, Ernest Henry *lawyer*
Lorch, Maristella De Panizza (Mrs. Inama von Brunnenwald) *Romance languages educator, writer, lecturer*
Lord, M. G. *writer*
Lord, Marvin *apparel company executive*
Lore, Martin Maxwell *lawyer*
Lorentzen, Carl Warren *chemical company executive*
Lorenz, Lee Sharp *cartoonist*
Loring, John Robbins *artist*
Lortel, Lucille *theatrical producer*
LoSchiavo, Linda Bosco *library director*
Losee, Thomas Penny, Jr. *publisher*
Losh, Clifford William *lawyer*
Loss, Margaret Ruth *lawyer*
Loss, Stuart Harold *financial executive*
Lotas, Judith Patton *advertising executive*
†Lottman, Evan *film editor*
Lotwin, Stanford Gerald *lawyer*
Loudon, Dorothy *actress*
Louis, Murray *dancer, choreographer, dance teacher*
Louis-Cotton d'Englesqueville, Francois Pierre *automobile company executive*
Love, Kenneth Del *design company director, consultant*
Love, Richard Emerson *equipment manufacturing company executive*
Loveless, Patty (Patty Ramey) *country music singer*
Loving, Alvin Demar, Jr. *artist, educator*
Low, Anthony *English language educator*
Low, Barbara Wharton *biochemist, biophysicist*
Low, Dana Evarts *consulting engineer*
Low, Richard H. *broadcasting executive, producer*
Lowe, Frank Budge *business executive*
Lowe, Mary Johnson *federal judge*
Lowen, Gerard Gunther *mechanical engineering educator*
Lowenfeld, Andreas Frank *legal educator, arbitrator*
Lowenfels, Fred M. *lawyer*
Lowenfels, Lewis David *lawyer*
Lowenstein, Louis *legal educator*
Lowenthal, Constance *art historian*
Lowenthal, Jacob *finance executive*
Lowry, Glenn David *art gallery director*
Lowry, William Ketchin, Jr. *insurance company executive*
Lowy, George Theodore *lawyer*
Lubetski, Edith Esther *librarian*
Lubic, Ruth Watson *association executive, nurse-midwife*
Lubkin, Virginia Leila *ophthalmologist*
Lubovitch, Lar *dancer, choreographer*
Lucas, Craig *playwright, screenwriter*
Lucas, Henry Cameron, Jr. *information systems educator, writer, consultant*
Lucas, James E(vans) *operatic director*
Lucchesi, Bruno *sculptor*
Lucci, Susan *actress*
Luce, Charles Franklin *former utilities executive, lawyer*
Luce, Henry, III *foundation executive*
Lucht, John Charles *management consultant, executive recruiter, writer*
Lucido, Louis Charles *finance company executive*
Luck, David Jonathan Lewis *biologist, educator*
Luckman, Sharon Gersten *arts administrator*
Luders, Adam *ballet dancer*
Ludgin, Chester Hall *baritone, actor*
Ludovici, Anthony *security investment executive*
Luening, Otto *composer, conductor, flutist, educator*
Luers, William Henry *art museum administrator*
Luftglass, Murray Arnold *manufacturing company executive*
Luke, John A., Jr. *paper, packaging and chemical company executive*
Luke, John Anderson *paper company executive*
Lumet, Sidney *film director*
Lund, Peter Anthony *broadcast executive*
Lunden, Joan *television personality*
Lunding, Christopher Hanna *lawyer*
Lundquist, James Harold *lawyer*
Lundquist, John Milton *librarian, author, lecturer, travel writer*
Lundy, Daniel Francis *communications company executive*
Luo, Gangming *mechanical engineer*
Lupert, Leslie Allan *lawyer*
Lupica, Michael Thomas *sports columnist*
Lupkin, Stanley Neil *lawyer*
Lupo, Frank Michael *architect*
LuPone, Patti *actress*
Lupton, Ellen *curator, graphic designer*
Luria, Mary Mercer *lawyer*
Lurie, Alvin David *lawyer*
Lusky, Louis *legal educator*
Lustenberger, Louis Charles, Jr. *lawyer*
Lustgarten, Ira Howard *lawyer*
Lutringer, Richard Emil *lawyer*
Luttinger, Joaquin Mazdak *retired physics educator, researcher*
Lynch, Frank Joseph *insurance company executive*
Lynch, Gerald Weldon *college president, psychologist*
Lynch, Gerard E. *law educator*
Lynch, Hollis Ralph *history educator*
Lynch, James C. *newspaper editor*
Lynch, John T. *management consultant*
†Lynch, Ronald P. *financial manager*
Lynch, William Dennis, Jr. *broadcast journalist*
Lyne, Susan *magazine editor*
Lyne, Susan Markham *magazine editor, publication director*
Lynn, Evadna Saywell *investment analyst*
Lynn, Theodore Stanley *lawyer*
Lynton, Harold Stephen *lawyer*
Lyon, Carl Francis, Jr. *lawyer*
Lyons, Laurence *securities executive*
Ma, Yo Yo *cellist*
Maas, Peter *writer*
Maas, Werner Karl *microbiology educator*
Macan, William Alexander, IV *lawyer*
MacArthur, John Roderick C. G. (Rick MacArthur) *magazine publisher, journalist*
MacCallum, Robert Kenneth *lawyer*
Macchiarola, Frank Joseph *political science, business and law educator*
MacCrate, Robert *lawyer*
Macdonald, Clifford Palmer *editor, writer*
Macdonald, Robert Rigg, Jr. *museum director*
MacEwan, Nigel Savage *merchant banker*
MacGrath, C. Richard *retired business executive*
MacHale, Joseph P. *financial executive*
Machida, Naoshi *airline company executive*
Machlin, Eugene Solomon *metallurgy educator, consultant*
Machlin, Milton Robert *magazine editor, writer*
Macioce, Frank Michael, Jr. *lawyer, financial services company executive*
MacIver, Loren *artist*
†Mack, Consuelo Cotter *news anchor and editor*
Mack, Daniel Richard *furniture designer*
Mack, Dennis Wayne *lawyer*
Mack, Joseph P. *advertising agency executive*
MacKay, Malcolm *executive search consultant*
MacKenzie, John Pettibone *journalist*
Mackerodt, Fred *public relations specialist*
†Mackey, Patricia Elaine *librarian*
Mackie, Robert Gordon *costume and fashion designer*
MacKinnon, John Alexander *lawyer*
MacKinnon, Roger Alan *psychiatrist*
Mackler, Tina *artist*
Mac Namara, Donal Eoin Joseph *criminologist*
MacNeil, Robert Breckenridge Ware *broadcast journalist*
Macpherson, Elle *model*
MacRae, Cameron Farquhar, III *lawyer*
Macri, Theodore William *book publisher*
Macro, Lucia Ann *editor*
Macurdy, John Edward *basso*
Madden, Donald Paul *lawyer*
Madden, John Kevin *publishing executive*
Madden, Michael Daniel *finance company executive*
†Madden, Thomas J., III *management consultant*
Madoff, Bernard Lawrence *investment dealer*
Madonna, (Madonna Louise Veronica Ciccone) *singer, actress*
Madonna, Jon C. *accounting firm executive*
Madsen, Loren Wakefield *sculptor*
Madsen, Stephen Stewart *lawyer*
Maffei, Gregory B. *investment banker*
Magdol, Michael Orin *bank executive*
Mager, Ezra Pascal *automobile dealership group executive*
Maggin, Bruce *communications executive*
Maguire, Robert Alan *Slavic languages and literatures educator*
†Maher, Bill *talk show host, comedian, producer*
Mahon, Arthur J. *lawyer*
Mahon, John Joseph *federal agency adminstrator*
Mahoney, John *actor*
Mahoney, Margaret Ellerbe *foundation executive*
Maidman, Richard Harvey Mortimer *lawyer*
Mailer, Norman *author*
Makin, Edward *food products executive*
Makrianes, James Konstantin, Jr. *management consultant*
Malabre, Alfred Leopold, Jr. *journalist, author*
Malamed, Seymour H. *motion picture company executive*
Malamud, Phyllis Carole *journalist, magazine editor*
Maldonado-Bear, Rita Marinita *economist, educator*
Malefakis, Edward E. *history educator*
Maleska, Martin Edmund *publishing executive*
Malgieri, Nick *chef, author, educator*
Malin, Irving *English educator, literary critic*
Malin, Robert Abernethy *investment management executive*
Malina, Judith *actress, director, producer, writer*
Malina, Michael *lawyer*
Malino, John Gray *real estate executive*
Malis, Leonard Irving *neurosurgeon*
Malitz, Sidney *psychiatrist, educator, researcher*
†Malkin, Barry *film editor, consultant*
Malkin, Peter Laurence *lawyer*
Malkin, Stanley Lee *neurologist*
Mallardi, Michael Patrick *broadcasting company executive*
Malle, Louis *film director*
Mallory, Kenneth W. *religious organization administrator*
Malloy, William Michael *book editor, reviewer, writer*
Mallozzi, Cos M. *public relations executive*
Malm, James Royal *surgeon*
Malman, Laurie L. *law educator*
Malone, Joseph Lawrence *linguistics educator*
Maloney, Michael Patrick *lawyer, corporate executive*
Maloney, William Gerard *retired investment company executive*
Malozemoff, Plato *mining executive*
Maltby, Richard Eldridge, Jr. *theater director, lyricist*
Mamlok, Ursula *composer, educator*
Mamorsky, Jeffrey Dean *lawyer*
Mandel, Irwin Daniel *dentist*
Mandelstam, Charles Lawrence *lawyer*
†Mandl, Alex J(ohann) *telecommunications company executive*
Maneker, Morton M. *lawyer*
Maney, Michael Mason *lawyer*
Mangan, Mona *association executive, lawyer*
Manger, William Muir *internist*
Manges, James Horace *investment banker*
Mangino, Robert *insurance company executive*
Mango, Wilfred Gilbert, Jr. *construction company executive*
Mangold, Glenn E. *securities industry executive*
Mangold, Robert Peter *artist*
Mankin, Robert Stephen *financial executive*
Mann, James Brooks *lawyer*
Mann, Theodore *theatrical producer and artistic director*
Manning, Burt *advertising executive*
Manning, Jack *photographer, columnist, author*
Manning, Jerome Alan *lawyer*
Manning, William Joseph *lawyer*
Manoff, Richard Kalman *advertising executive, nutrition policy consultant*
Mansi, Joseph Anneillo *public relations company executive*
Manski, Wladyslaw Julian *microbiology educator, medical scientist*
Mantegna, Joe Anthony *actor, playwright*
Mantell, Lester J. *financial business executive*
Mantell, Suzanne *editor*
Mantle, Raymond Allan *lawyer*
Manton, Edwin Alfred Grenville *insurance company executive*
†Manuel, Bernard M. *investment banker*
Mapes, Glynn Dempsey *newspaper editor*
Mapes, Pierson *broadcasting company executive*
†Maple, John E. *protective services official*
Maraldo, Pamela Jean *nursing association executive, lecturer, consultant*
Maraynes, Allan Lawrence *filmmaker, television producer*
Marceau, Yvonne *ballroom dancer*
Marchi, Lorraine June *association executive*
Marchioni, Allen *publishing company executive*
Marcosson, Thomas I. *service company executive*
Marcus, Barry Philip *lawyer*
Marcus, Beth E. *religious organization administrator*
Marcus, Eric Peter *lawyer*
Marcus, Eric Robert *psychiatrist*
Marcus, Hyman *business executive*
Marcus, James Stewart *investment banker*
Marcus, Norman *lawyer*
Marcus, Steven *dean, English educator*
Marcusa, Fred Haye *lawyer*
Marcuse, Adrian Gregory *college administrator*
Marden, John Newcomb *lawyer*
Mardenborough, Leslie A. *newspaper publishing company executive*
Marder, John G. *real estate investor, marketing consultant, corporate director*
Marder, Michael Zachary *dentist, researcher, educator*
Marella, Philip Daniel *broadcasting company executive*
Margaritis, John Paul *public relations executive*
Margolin, Arthur Stanley *distillery company executive*
Margolis, David I(srael) *corporate executive*
Margolis, Karl L. *retail company executive*
Margolis, Louis Irving *financial executive*
Margolis, Milton Joseph *marketing executive*
Margulis, Les *advertising executive*
Marion, John Louis *fine arts auctioneer and appraiser*
Marisol, (Marisol Escobar) *sculptor*
Mark, Jonathan I. *lawyer*
Mark, Reuben *consumer products company executive*
Marke, Julius Jay *law librarian, educator*
Markle, Cheri Virginia Cummins *nurse*
Markowitz, Harry M. *finance and economics educator*
Marks, Barbara Hanzel *publishing executive*
Marks, Edward B. *international social service administrator*
Marks, Edwin S. *investment company executive*
Marks, Paul Alan *oncologist, cell biologist, educator*
Marks, Theodore Lee *lawyer*
Marlas, James Constantine *holding company executive*
Marlette, Douglas Nigel *editorial cartoonist, comic strip creator*
Marlin, Richard *lawyer*
Marron, Donald Baird *investment banker*
Marsh, Jean Lyndsey Torren *actress, writer*
Marsh, William Laurence *retired research pathology executive*
Marshall, Alton Garwood *real estate counselor*
Marshall, Daniel Stuart *advertising executive*
Marshall, Geoffrey *university administrator*
Marshall, John *association administrator*
Marshall, John Patrick *lawyer*
Marshall, Sheila Hermes *lawyer*
†Marshall, Susan *artistic director*
Marshall, Thomas Carlisle *applied physics educator*
Marston, Robert Andrew *public relations executive*
Martin, Agnes *artist*
Martin, Andrea Louise *actress, comedienne, writer*
Martin, Ann Matthews *writer, juvenile*
†Martin, Betsy *magazine publishing executive*
Martin, Elliot Edwards *theatrical producer*
Martin, George J., Jr. *lawyer*
Martin, James Smith *insurance executive*
Martin, John S., Jr. *federal judge*
Martin, Joseph Paul *human rights administrator*
Martin, Judith Sylvia *journalist, author*
Martin, Malcolm Elliot *lawyer*
Martin, Mary-Anne *art gallery owner*
Martin, Richard Harrison *curator, art historian*
Martin, Richard L. *insurance executive*
†Martinez, Julio J. *chemical company executive*
Martinez, Roman, IV *financial executive*
Martins, Nilas *dancer*
Martins, Peter *ballet master, choreographer, dancer*
Martone, Patricia Ann *lawyer*
Marx, Owen Cox *lawyer*
Marzulli, John Anthony, Jr. *lawyer*
Masey, Jack *exhibition designer*
Mashberg, Gregg M. *lawyer*
Masin, Michael Terry *lawyer*
Masinter, Edgar Martin *lawyer*
Maskin, Arvin *lawyer*
Maslin, Janet *film critic*
Maslow, Melanie Jane *physician*
Maslow, Will *lawyer, association executive*
Mason, Bobbie Ann *novelist, short story writer*
Mason, Jackie *comedian, actor*
Massey, Stephen Charles *auctioneer*
Masters, Jon Joseph *lawyer*
Masterson, James Francis *psychiatrist*
Mastromonaco-Adler, Ellen G. *publishing company executive*
Masur, Kurt *conductor*
Matalon, Vivian *theatrical director*
Mathers, William Harris *lawyer*
Mathes, Sorrell Mark *investment banker*
Mathews, Jack Wayne *journalist, film critic*
Mathews, Linda McVeigh *newspaper editor*
Matlock, Jack Foust, Jr. *diplomat*
Matsakis, Steven C. *bank executive, retail executive*
Matteson, William Bleecker *lawyer*
Matthews, Edward E. *insurance company executive*
Matthews, Edwin Spencer, Jr. *lawyer*
Matthews, Gilbert Elliott *investment banker*
Matthews, Norman Stuart *department store executive*
Matthews, Peter F. *electrical contracting company executive*
Matthews, Westina L. *finance and banking executive*
Matthews, William Procter *English educator*
Mattone, Vincent J. *investment banker*
Mattson, Francis Oscar *retired librarian and rare books curator*
Mattson, Marlin Roy Albin *health facility administrator, psychiatry educator*
Mattson, Walter Edward *retired publishing company executive*
Matz, Robert *physician, educator*
Maubert, Jacques Claude *headmaster*
Maughan, Deryck C. *investment banker*
Maulsby, Allen Farish *lawyer*
Maupin, Armistead Jones, Jr. *writer*
Maurer, Gilbert Charles *media company executive*
Maurer, Jeffrey Stuart *finance executive*

Mauzerall, David Charles biophysics educator, research scientist
Max, Herbert B. lawyer
Max, Peter artist
Maxey, Thomas F. advertising agency executive
Maxfield, Guy Budd lawyer, educator
Maxwell, Carla Lena dancer, choreographer, educator
Maxwell, Hamish diversified consumer products company executive
Maxwell, William writer
May, Elaine actress, theatre and film director
May, Gita French language and literature educator
May, William Frederick manufacturing executive
Mayden, Barbara Mendel lawyer
Mayer, Carl Joseph lawyer, town official
Mayer, Margery Weil publishing executive
Mayer, Theodore V.H. lawyer
Mayerson, Philip classics educator
Mayerson, Sandra Elaine lawyer
Mayfield, Curtis Lee musician
Mayle, Peter writer
Maynard, John Rogers English educator
Maynard, Parrish ballet dancer
Mayo, Joan Bradley microbiologist, epidemiologist
Mazur, Jay J. trade union official
Mazza, Thomas Carmen lawyer
Mazzia, Valentino Don Bosco physician, educator, lawyer
Mazzilli, Paul John investment banker
Mazzo, Kay ballet dancer, educator
Mazzola, Anthony Thomas editor, art consultant, designer
Mazzola, John William former performing arts center executive, consultant
†McAniff, Nora P. publishing executive
McAward, Patrick Joseph, Jr. architectural and engineering company executive
McBaine, John Neylan lawyer
McBride, David Alan business information services executive
McBride, Rodney Lester investment counselor
McBryde, Thomas Henry lawyer
McCabe, Edward Arthur communications company executive
McCaffrey, Carlyn Sundberg lawyer
McCaffrey, William Thomas financial services company executive
McCall, David Bruce advertising executive
McCall, Marsh cardiologist
McCandless, Carolyn Keller entertainment, media company executive
McCandless, Stephen Porter financial executive
Mc Cann, John Joseph lawyer
McCann, Raymond J. utility company executive
†McCarrick, Edward R. magazine publisher
Mc Carter, Thomas N., III investment counseling company executive
McCarthy, Bernard William lawyer
McCarthy, Bryant accounting firm executive
McCarthy, Cormac (Charles McCarthy, Jr.) writer
McCarthy, Denis artist, educator
McCarthy, James sociology researcher, educator
McCarthy, Joseph Gerald plastic surgeon, educator
McCarthy, Michael Anthony architecture executive
†McCarthy, Patrick magazine publishing executive
McCarty, Maclyn medical scientist
McCarty, Michiel Cleve investment banker
McCarver, James Timothy sportscaster
McCleary, Benjamin Ward investment banker
McClellan, Anne Starr environmentalist
McClelland, Timothy Reid baseball umpire
McClimon, Timothy John lawyer
McClung, Richard Goehring lawyer
Mc Clure, Michael Thomas poet, playwright, educator
McConnell, Charles Warren marketing management executive
McCormack, John Joseph, Jr. insurance executive
McCormack, Thomas Joseph publishing company executive
McCormick, Donald E. librarian, archivist
McCormick, Hugh Thomas lawyer
McCormick, James Michael management consultant
Mc Cormick, Kenneth Dale retired editor
McCoy, Ann artist
McCoy, Millington F. management recruitment company executive
McCracken, A. Michael accounting firm executive
Mc Cracken, Daniel Delbert computer science educator, author
†McCredie, James Robert fine arts educator
†McCree, Donald Hanna, Jr. banker
Mc Crie, Robert Delbert editor, publisher, educator
Mc Crory, Wallace Willard pediatrician, educator
McCullough, David author
Mc Cullough, Donald Frederick textile manufacturing executive
McCully, Emily Arnold illustrator, writer
McDarrah, Fred William photographer, editor, writer, photography reviewer
McDavid, William Henry lawyer
McDermott, Richard T. lawyer, educator
McDonald, Audra Ann actress
Mcdonald, Gregory Christopher author
McDonald, James L. accounting firm executive
McDonald, Willis, IV lawyer
McDonell, Robert Terry magazine editor, novelist
Mc Donnell, Edward Francis distillery executive
McDonough, William J. banker
McDormand, Frances actress
McDowell, Jay Hortenstine lawyer
McDowell, Robert Neil accounting company executive
Mc Elrath, Richard Elsworth insurance company executive
McEnroe, John Patrick lawyer
McEnroe, John Patrick, Jr. professional tennis player
McEnroe, Patrick professional tennis player
†McEwen, James publishing executive
McFadden, David Revere museum director and curator
Mc Fadden, G. Bruce hospital administrator
Mc Fadden, James Patrick publisher
McFadden, Mary Josephine fashion industry executive
Mc Fadden, Robert Dennis reporter
†McFeely, William Drake publishing company executive
McFerrin, Bobby singer, musician, composer and conductor
McGanney, Thomas lawyer
McGarry, John Patrick, Jr. advertising agency executive
McGeady, Sister Mary Rose religious organization administrator, psychologist
†McGill, Jay magazine publisher
Mc Gillicuddy, John Francis retired banker
Mc Ginnis, Arthur Joseph publisher
McGinnis, Arthur Joseph, Jr. public relations executive
McGinnis, John Oldham lawyer, educator
Mc Ginniss, Joe writer
McGirr, David William John investment banker
Mc Goldrick, John Gardiner lawyer
McGonigal, Richard M. lawyer
McGovern, John Hugh urologist, educator
McGovern, Thomas Aquinas utility executive
Mc Gowin, William Edward artist
McGrath, Eugene R. utility company executive
†McGrath, Judith broadcast executive
McGrath, Thomas J. lawyer, writer, film producer
McGraw, Harold Whittlesey, Jr. publisher
McGraw, Robert Pierce publishing executive
Mc Gruder, Stephen Jones portfolio manager
Mc Guire, Alfred James former basketball coach, sports equipment company executive, basketball commentator
McGunigle, Brian Edward lawyer
McHenry, Barnabas lawyer
Mc Inerney, Denis lawyer
McInerney, Jay author
McInnis, Helen Louise publishing company executive
McIntyre, Douglas Alexander magazine publisher
†McIntyre, Thomas recording industry executive
†McKay, Craig film editor
Mc Kay, Jim television sports commentator
McKean, Henry P. mathematics institute administrator
McKelvey, Andrew J. advertising executive
McKenna, Lawrence M. federal judge
Mc Kenna, Malcolm Carnegie vertebrate paleontologist, curator, educator
McKenzie, Kevin Patrick ballet dancer
McKenzie, Mary Beth artist
Mc Keown, William Taylor magazine editor, author
McKerrow, Amanda ballet dancer
McKesson, John Alexander, III international relations educator
McKessy, Stephen W. accounting firm executive
McKillop, Daniel James insurance company real estate executive
McKinley, (Jennifer Carolyn) Robin writer
McKinnon, Floyd Wingfield textile executive
Mc Kitrick, Eric Louis historian, educator
McKnew, Robert David banker
McLaughlin, Joseph lawyer
McLaughlin, Joseph Michael federal judge, law educator
McLaughlin, Joseph Thomas lawyer
McLaughlin, Mary Rittling magazine editor
McLaughlin, Michael John insurance company executive
McLean, Edward Peter executive search consultant
McLearn, Michael Baylis lawyer
Mc Lendon, Heath Brian securities investment company executive
McMahon, Colleen lawyer
McManus, Jason Donald editor
McMeen, Albert Ralph, III writer, lecturer
McMeen, Elmer Ellsworth, III lawyer, guitarist
McMenamin, Joan Stitt headmistress
McMenamy, Kristen model
McMullan, William Patrick, III investment banker
Mc Murtry, James Gilmer, III neurosurgeon
McMurtry, Larry Jeff author
McNally, John Joseph lawyer
McNally, Terrence playwright
Mc Namara, J(ohn) Donald lawyer, business executive
McNamara, John Jeffrey advertising executive
McNamee, Daniel Vincent, III management consultant
McNamee, Louise advertising agency executive
McNeary, Joseph Allen apparel executive
McNeill, Alfred Thomas, Jr. construction executive
Mc Nicol, Donald Edward lawyer
Mc Pherson, Paul Francis publishing and investment banking executive
†McQuade, Charles Brian data processing executive
Mc Queeney, Henry Martin, Sr. publisher
McQuillen, Harry A. publishing company executive
†McQuown, Judith Hershkowitz author, financial advisor
†McWilliam, Joanne Elizabeth religion educator
Meachin, David James Percy investment banker, import-export executive
†Mead, Wayland McCon lawyer
Meaders, Paul Le Sourd lawyer
Meadow, Lynne (Carolyn Meadow) theatrical producer and director
Meagher, Mark Joseph publishing company executive
Medenica, Gordon corporate planner
Medford-Rosow, Traci lawyer
Medina, Standish Forde, Jr. lawyer
Medwick, Craig Steven lawyer
Mee, Charles L., Jr. playwright, historian, editor
Meehan, John Joseph brokerage house executive
Meek, Phillip Joseph communications executive
Mehta, A. Sonny publishing company executive
Mehta, Ved (Parkash) writer, literature and history educator
Meier, August historian, educator
Meier, Paul statistician, mathematics educator
Meier, Richard Alan architect
Meigher, S. Christopher, III communications and media investor
Meikle, Thomas Harry, Jr. foundation administrator, neuroscientist, educator
Meisel, Louis Koenig art dealer, art historian, writer
Meisel, Martin English and comparative literature educator
Meisel, Perry English educator
Meisel, Steven advertising photographer
Meiselas, Susan Clay photographer
Meislich, Herbert chemistry educator emeritus
Melamid, Alexander economics educator, consultant
Mellencamp, John (John Cougar) singer, songwriter
Mellins, Robert B. pediatrician, educator
Melone, Joseph James insurance company executive
Meltzer, Milton author
Melvin, Russell Johnston magazine publishing consultant
†Menaker, Ronald Herbert banking executive
Mencher, Melvin journalist, retired educator
Mendell, Oliver M. banking executive
Mendelsohn, John oncologist, hematologist, educator
Mendelsohn, Walter lawyer
Mendelson, Edward James English literature educator
Mendelson, Haim artist, educator, art gallery director
Menges, Carl Braun investment banker
Menk, Carl William executive search company executive
Menken, Alan composer
Menninger, Edward Joseph public relations executive
Menschel, Richard Lee investment banker
Menschel, Robert Benjamin investment banker
Menuez, D. Barry religious organization administrator
Menuhin, Yehudi violinist
Meranus, Arthur Richard advertising agency executive
Mercer, Robert B. automobile corporation executive
Merchant, Ismail Noormohamed film producer
Mercorella, Anthony J. lawyer, former state supreme court justice
Meron, Theodor law educator, researcher
Merow, John Edward lawyer
Merrifield, Robert Bruce biochemist, educator
Merrill, Newton Phelps Stokes financial executive
Merriss, Philip Ramsay, Jr. banker
Mertens, Joan R. museum curator, art historian
Merton, Robert K. sociologist, educator
Merwin, William Stanley poet
Merz, Carl Allen financial services company executive
Mesches, Arnold artist
Mescon, Richard Alan lawyer
Mesnikoff, Alvin Murray psychiatry educator
Messer, Thomas Maria museum director
Messier, Mark Douglas professional hockey player
Messineo, Karen newspaper publishing executive
Messing, Mark P. advertising executive
Messinger, Ruth W. borough president
Messinger, Scott James advertising executive
Messner, Thomas G. advertising executive, copywriter
Mester, Jorge conductor
Mestres, Ricardo Angelo, Jr. lawyer
Mesznik, Joel R. investment banker
Metcalf, Karen foundation executive
Metcalf, William Edwards museum curator
Metz, Emmanuel Michael investment company executive, lawyer
Metz, Robert Roy publisher, editor
Meyaart, Paul Jan distilling company executive
Meyer, Edward Henry advertising agency executive
Meyer, Edward N. lawyer
Meyer, Fred Josef advertising executive
Meyer, Jackie Merri publishing executive
Meyer, Karl Ernest journalist
Meyer, Pearl executive compensation consultant
Meyer, Pucci newspaper editor
Meyer, Richard E. insurance agent
Meyer, Sandra W(asserstein) bank executive, management consultant
Meyer, Susan E. publisher
Meyer-Bahlburg, Heino F. L. psychologist
Meyerhoff, Erich librarian, administrator
Meyers, Dale (Mrs. Mario Cooper) artist
Meyers, John Allen magazine publisher
Meyerson, Morton communications executive
Miano, Louis Stephen advertising executive
Michaels, Alan Richard sports commentator
Michaels, James Walker magazine editor
Michaels, Lorne television writer, producer
Michaelson, Arthur M. lawyer
Michals, Duane photographer
Michel, Clifford Lloyd lawyer, investment executive
Michel, Harriet R. association executive
Michel, Henry Ludwig civil engineer
Michels, Robert psychiatrist
Michelsen, Christopher Bruce Hermann surgeon
Michelson, Gertrude Geraldine retired retail company executive
Michenfelder, Joseph Francis public relations executive
Middendorf, John Harlan English literature educator
Middleton, David physicist, applied mathematician, educator
Midler, Bette singer, entertainer, actress
Midori, (Midori Goto) classical violinist
Miele, Joel Arthur, Sr. civil engineer
Mikita, Joseph Karl broadcasting executive
Milbank, Jeremiah foundation executive
Mildvan, Donna infectious diseases physician
Miles, Michael Arnold consumer products executive
Milgrim, Roger Michael lawyer
Millard, John Alden lawyer
Millard, Wenda Harris magazine publisher
Miller, B. Jack investment company executive
†Miller, Caroline editor-in-chief
Miller, Charles Hampton lawyer
Miller, David lawyer, advertising executive
Miller, Donald Keith venture capitalist, asset management executive
Miller, Donald LeSessne publishing executive
Miller, Edward Daniel banker
Miller, Ernest Charles management consultant
Miller, Gerri magazine editor, writer
Miller, Harry Brill scenic designer, director, acting instructor, lyricist, interior designer
Miller, Harvey R. lawyer, bankruptcy reorganization specialist
Miller, Harvey S. Shipley foundation trustee
Miller, Israel rabbi, university administrator
Miller, Joel E. accountant, finance company executive
Miller, Laurence Glenn art gallery owner and director
Miller, Lawrence Edward lawyer
Miller, Lee Anne artist, educator
Miller, Lenore labor union official
Miller, Morgan Lincoln textile manufacturing company executive
Miller, Neil S. financial officer, advertising executive
Miller, Nicole Jacqueline fashion designer
Miller, Paul health care products company executive
Miller, Paul Lukens investment banker
Miller, Philip Boyd retail executive
Miller, Philip Efrem librarian
Miller, Raymond F. banker
Miller, Richard B. publishing executive
Miller, Richard Jerome bank executive
Miller, Richard Kidwell artist, actor, educator
Miller, Richard McDermott sculptor
Miller, Richard Steven lawyer
Miller, Robert advertising executive
Miller, Robert L. publishing company executive
Miller, Roberta Davis editor
†Miller, Robin Davis professional society administrator
Miller, Sam Scott lawyer
Millett, Katherine Murray (Kate Millett) political activist, sculptor, artist, writer
Milliken, Roger textile company executive
Millman, Robert Barnet psychiatry and public health educator
Millo, Aprile Elizabeth opera singer
Millstein, Ira M. lawyer, lecturer
Milnes, Sherrill Eustace baritone
Milosh, Eugene John international trade association executive
Minard, Everett Lawrence, III journalist, magazine editor
Minard, Frank Pell Lawrence investment manager
Mincer, Jacob economics educator
Minick, Michael publishing executive
Minicucci, Robert A. management consultant
Minikes, Michael investment banker
Minkel, Herbert Philip, Jr. lawyer
Minkowitz, Martin lawyer, former state government official
Minnelli, Liza singer, actress
Minor, Raleigh Colston management consultant
Mintz, Donald Edward psychologist, educator
Mintz, Norman Nelson investment banker, educator
Mintz, Shlomo conductor, violist, violinist
Mintz, Walter investment company executive
Mirabella, Grace magazine publishing executive
†Mirante, Arthur J., II real estate company executive
Mirsky, Sonya Wohl librarian, curator
Mishkin, Edwin B. lawyer
Mishkin, Jeffrey Alan lawyer
Miss, Mary artist
Missan, Richard Sherman lawyer
Mitchell, Arthur dancer, choreographer, educator
Mitchell, John Dietrich theatre arts institute executive
Mitchell, Joseph (Quincy) writer
Mitchell, Richard Boyle advertising executive
Mitgang, Herbert author, journalist
Mittelstadt, Charles Anthony advertising executive
Miyake, Issey fashion designer
Miyaoka, K. grain company executive
Mizrahi, Isaac fashion designer
Mizuno, Masaru retail executive
Moak-Mazur, Connie J. investment consultant, marketing professional
Mobius, Michael chemicals executive
Model, Iris cosmetics executive
Model, Peter molecular biologist
Modlin, Howard S. lawyer
Moeller, Achim Ferdinand Gerd art dealer, consultant, publisher
Moerdler, Charles Gerard lawyer
Mohler, Mary Gail magazine editor
Mohr, Jay Preston neurologist
Moise, Edwin Evariste mathematician, educator
Mok, Ngaiming mathematics educator
Molho, Emanuel publisher
Molholt, Pat university official
†Molino, Patricia Mary communications executive
Moloney, Thomas Joseph lawyer
Moloney, Thomas Walter consulting firm executive
Moltz, James Edward brokerage company executive
Molz, Redmond Kathleen public administration educator
Monaco, Michael P. finance company executive
Monaghan, Henry P. lawyer, educator
Mondlin, Marvin retail executive, antiquarian book dealer
Monge, Jay Parry lawyer
Monk, Debra actress
Monk, Meredith Jane artistic director, composer, choreographer, film maker, director
Monroe, Vernon Earl, Jr. (The Pearl Monroe) former professional basketball player
Montemayor, Jesus Samson physician
Montgomery, Robert Humphrey, Jr. lawyer
Montgomery, Walter George communications executive, consultant
Montorio, John Angelo magazine editor
Moody, John Stephen real estate executive
Mooney, Richard E. editorial writer
Moore, Andrew Given Tobias, II investment banker, educator
Moore, Brian writer
Moore, Donald Francis lawyer
Moore, Geoffrey Hoyt economist
Moore, Jane Ross librarian
Moore, John Dennis publisher
Moore, John Joseph lawyer
Moore, Kathleen dancer
Moore, Malcolm Andrew Stephen cancer researcher
†Moore, Mary advertising agency executive
Moore, Paul, Jr. bishop
Moore, Susanna writer
Moore, Thomas Ronald lawyer
Moorhead, Thomas Burch lawyer, pharmaceutical company executive
Morahan, Matthew Joseph investment banker
Moran, Charles A. securities executive
Moran, John A. investment company executive
Moran, Juliette M. management consultant
Moran, Martin Joseph fundraising company executive
Morath, Inge photographer
Morawetz, Cathleen Synge mathematician
Moreira, Marcio Martins advertising executive
Morgado, Robert music company executive
Morgan, Frank Edward, II lawyer
Morgan, (George) Frederick poet, editor
Morgan, Jacqui illustrator, painter, educator
Morgan, Robin Evonne poet, author, journalist, activist, editor
Morgan, Thomas Bruce public affairs executive, author, editor
Morgen, Lynn public relations executive
Morgenthau, Robert Morris lawyer
Mori, Hanae fashion designer
†Morin, William J. management consultant
†Morley, Michael pubic relations executive
Morley, Michael B. public relations executive
Morosani, John Warrington brokerage house executive
Morris, Clayton Leslie priest
Morris, Douglas Peter recording company executive
Morris, Eugene Jerome lawyer
Morris, James Peppler bass
†Morris, John composer, conductor, arranger
Morris, John E. lawyer
Morris, Kenneth Baker mergers, acquisition and real estate executive
Morris, Mark Ronald advertising agency executive
Morris, Mark William choreographer
Morris, Michael Howard public relations executive
Morris, Robert artist
Morris, Robert C. historian, archivist, educator
Morris, Robert Lee gallery administrator, jewelry designer
Morris, Stephen Burritt marketing information executive
Morris, Thomas Quinlan hospital administrator, physician
Morris, William Charles investor
Morris, Wright novelist, critic
Morrisett, Lloyd N. foundation executive

Morrison, Michael Ian Donald insurance company executive
Morrissey, Dolores Josephine insurance executive
Morrissey, Thomas Jerome investment banker
Morrow, E. Frederic financial consultant, retired banker
Morrow, Lance writer
Mortimer, Henry Tilford, Jr. financial assurance executive
Mortimer, Peter Michael lawyer
†Morton, Brian writer, editor, educator
Morton, Frederic author
Mosbacher, Martin Bruce public relations executive
Moseley, Carlos DuPre former music executive, musician
Moskin, John Robert editor, writer
Moskin, Morton lawyer
Moskowitz, Arnold X. strategist, economist, educator
†Mosley, Walter writer
Moss, Charles advertising agency executive
Moss, Kate model
Moss, Melvin Lionel anatomist
Moss, Mitchell Lawrence urban planning educator
Moss, William John lawyer
Mossbrucker, Tom dancer
Mosse, Peter John Charles financial services executive
†Moss-Salentijn, Letty (Aleida Moss-Salentijn) anatomist
Most, Jack Lawrence lawyer, consultant
Most, Nathan securities exchange executive
Motley, Constance Baker (Mrs. Joel Wilson Motley) federal judge, former city official
Mottola, Gary F. lawyer
Mouchly-Weiss, Harriet business executive
Mountcastle, Kenneth Franklin, Jr. stockbroker
Mow, Van C. engineering educator, researcher
Moyers, Bill D. journalist
Moynahan, John Daniel, Jr. insurance executive
Moyne, John Abel computer scientist, linguist, educator
Mroz, John Edwin political scientist
Mukasey, Michael B. federal judge
Mulder, Edwin George minister, church official
Mullen, Peter P. lawyer
Muller, Charlotte Feldman economist, educator
Muller, Frank B. advertising executive
Muller, Henry James journalist, magazine editor
Muller, Jennifer choreographer, dancer
Muller, Priscilla Elkow curator
Muller, Robert Joseph, Jr. manufacturing company executive
Mulligan, Gerald Joseph (Gerry Mulligan) composer, arranger, musician, songwriter
Mulligan, Hugh Augustine journalist
Mulvihill, Roger Denis lawyer
Mulvoy, Mark journalist
†Mundell, Robert Alexander economics educator
Mundheim, Robert Harry law educator
Mundy, John Hine history educator
Munera, Gerard Emmanuel manufacturing company executive
Munhall, Edgar curator, art history educator
Munro, Alice author
Munro, J. Richard publishing company executive
Munroe, George Barber former metals company executive
Muradian, Vazgen composer, viola d'amore player
Murase, Jiro lawyer
Muratore, Peter Frederick securities executive
Murchie, Edward Michael accountant
Murdock, Robert Mead art consultant, curator
Muro, Roy Alfred independent media service corporation executive
Murphy, Ann Pleshette magazine editor-in-chief
Murphy, Arthur William lawyer, educator
Murphy, Catherine painter
Murphy, Charles Joseph investment banker
Murphy, Daniel Hayes, II lawyer
Murphy, Donna actress
Murphy, Eugene Francis consultant, retired government official
†Murphy, George William insurance executive
†Murphy, Helen recording industry executive
Murphy, James E. public relations and marketing executive
Murphy, Jill public relations executive
Murphy, John Arthur tobacco, food and brewing company executive
Murphy, John Cullen illustrator
Murphy, Joseph Samson political science educator
Murphy, Richard William retired foreign service officer, Middle East specialist, consultant
Murphy, Rosemary actress
Murphy, Russell Stephen theater company executive
Murphy, Thomas S. media company executive
Murray, Elizabeth artist
†Murray, Henry Wilke physician, educator
Murray, Paul Brady lawyer, banker
Murray, Richard Maximilian insurance executive
†Murray, Robert William diversified company executive
Murray, Thomas Francis real estate executive
Murray, William food products executive
Muse, Martha Twitchell foundation executive
Musgrave, R. Kenton federal judge
Musser, Tharon theatrical lighting designer, theatre consultant
Muth, John Francis newspaper editor, columnist
Myerberg, Marcia investment banker
Myers, Gerald E. humanities educator
Myers, Wayne Alan psychiatrist, educator
Myers, William S. magazine publishing executive
Myerson, Toby Salter lawyer
Nabatoff, Robert Allan vascular surgeon, educator
Nabi, Stanley Andrew investment executive
†Nachman, Ralph Louis physician, educator
†Nachtwey, James Alan photojournalist
Nadel, Elliott investment firm executive
Nadich, Judah rabbi
Nadiri, M. Ishaq economics educator, researcher, lecturer, consultant
†Nadler, Allan Lawrence institute director
Naftalis, Gary Philip lawyer, educator
Nagamiya, Shoji physicist, educator
Nagle, Arthur Joseph investment banker
Nagler, Stewart Gordon insurance company executive
Nagourney, Herbert publishing company executive
Nagy, Stephen Felsobuki investment company executive
Nahas, Gabriel Georges pharmacologist, educator
Naiburg, Irving B., Jr. publisher
Najarian, Haigazoun church administrator
Nakamura, James I. economics educator
Nakanishi, Koji chemistry educator, research institute administrator
Namath, Joseph William entertainer, former professional football player
Nance, Allan Taylor lawyer
Narasimhan, Subha law educator
Nash, Edward L. advertising agency executive
Nash, Graham William singer, composer
†Nash, Jack investment banker
Nash, June Caprice anthropology professor
Nash, Paul LeNoir lawyer
Nassau, Michael Jay lawyer
Nathan, Andrew James political science educator
Nathan, Carl Francis medical educator
Nathan, Frederic Solis lawyer
Nathan, Paul S. editor, writer
Natori, Josie Cruz apparel executive
Nauert, Roger Charles health care executive
Navasky, Victor Saul magazine editor
Navratil, Gerald Anton physicist, educator
†Nay, Howard Riley surgeon, educator
Nayden, Denis J. diversified financial services company executive
Nazareth, Annette LaPorte lawyer
Nazem, Fereydoun F. venture capitalist, financier
Neal, James Weatherly investment banker
Neal, Leora Louise Haskett social services administrator
Neal, Philip dancer
†Neary, Robert D. accounting firm executive
Necarsulmer, Henry investment banker
Nederlander, James Morton theater executive
Nederlander, Robert E. entertainment and television executive, lawyer
Neeck, Bernard J. insurance company executive
Needham, George Austin investment banker
Needham, Richard Lee magazine editor
Neff, Craig periodical editor
Neff, Thomas Joseph executive search firm executive
Neff, Walter Perry financial consultant
Neft, David Samuel marketing professional
Neidell, Martin H. lawyer
Neilly, Andrew Hutchinson, Jr. publisher
Neiman, LeRoy artist
Nelkin, Dorothy sociology and science policy educator, researcher
Nelson, Bruce Sherman advertising agency executive
Nelson, Donald Arvid (Nellie Nelson) professional basketball coach
Nelson, Gareth Jon zoologist, curator, educator
Nelson, Lindsey sportscaster
Nelson, Merlin Edward international business consultant, company director
Nelson, Richard John playwright
Nelson, Richard R. law educator
Nelson, William Edward lawyer, educator
Nemser, Earl Harold lawyer
Nesbit, Robert Grover management consultant
Netzer, Dick economics educator
Neu, Harold Conrad physician, educator
Neubauer, Peter Bela psychoanalyst
Neuberger, Roy R. investment counselor
Neuborne, Burt law educator
Neufeld, Victor television executive
Neuhaus, Max artist, composer
Neuhaus, Sydney Ann public relations executive
Neumark, Gertrude Fanny materials science educator
Neuthaler, Paul David publisher
Neuwirth, Alan James lawyer
Neuwirth, Robert Samuel obstetrician, gynecologist
Neveloff, Jay A. lawyer
Nevling, J. Kelley, Jr. lawyer
New, Maria Iandolo physician, educator
Newbauer, John Arthur editor
Newbold, John Lowe banker
Newborn, Jud cultural anthropologist, writer
Newcomb, Danforth lawyer
Newcomb, Jonathan publishing executive
Newcombe, George Michael lawyer
Newell, Norman Dennis paleontologist, geologist, museum curator, educator
Newfield, Jack columnist
Newhouse, Nancy Riley newspaper editor
Newhouse, Samuel I., Jr. publishing executive
Newman, Arnold photographer
Newman, Bruce Murray antiques dealer
Newman, Edwin David textile company executive
Newman, Elias artist
Newman, Fredric Samuel lawyer, business executive
Newman, Geraldine Anne advertising executive
Newman, Howard Neal law educator, lawyer
Newman, Jane advertising agency executive
Newman, Lawrence lawyer
Newman, Lawrence Walker lawyer
Newman, Norman lawyer
Newman, Rachel magazine editor
Newman, Robert Gabriel physician
Newman, Scott David lawyer
Newman, William real estate executive
Newton, Blake Tyler, III lawyer
Ney, Edward N. ambassador, advertising and public relations company executive
Nibley, Andrew Mathews editorial executive
Nicholls, Richard H. lawyer
Nichols, Carol D. real estate professional, association executive
Nichols, Kyra ballerina
Nicholson, William Thomas advertising executive
Nicola, James B. stage director, composer, playwright
†Nicola, James C. theater director
Nidetch, Jean health service executive
Nied, Thomas H. publishing company executive
Nielsen, Nancy publishing executive
Nieman, John Francis advertising executive
Niemiec, David Wallace investment company executive
Niesen, James Louis theater director
Niles, Nicholas Hemelright publisher
Nimetz, Matthew lawyer
Nimkin, Bernard William retired lawyer
Nirenberg, Louis mathematician, educator
Nixon, Joan Lowery writer
Noback, Charles Robert anatomist, educator
Noia, Alan James utility company executive
Nolan, Terrance Joseph, Jr. lawyer
Nolan, William Joseph, III banker
Nolte, Judith Ann magazine editor
Nonna, John Michael lawyer
Noonan, Susan Abert public relations counselor
Norcia, Stephen William advertising executive
Nord, Peter Robert advertising executive
†Norell, Mark Allen paleontology educator
Norfolk, William Ray lawyer
Norgren, William Andrew religious denomination administrator
Norman, Jessye soprano
Norman, Marsha playwright
Norman, Stephen Peckham financial services company executive
†Norrgard, Kristin Ann magazine publisher
†Norris, Floyd Hamilton financial journalist
Norton, Paul Allen insurance executive
Norvell, Patsy artist
Norville, Deborah news correspondent
Norz, Charles Henry oil company executive
Notarbartolo, Albert artist
Novacek, Michael John curator, museum administrator
Novak, Barbara art history educator
Novak, Eugene Francis advertising executive
Novello, Antonia Coello United Nations official, former U.S. surgeon general
Novick, Nelson Lee dermatologist, internist, writer
Novick, Robert physicist, educator
Novitz, Charles Richard television executive
Novogrod, Nancy Ellen editor
Nowick, Arthur Stanley metallurgy, materials science educator
Nugent, Nelle theater, film and television producer
Nusbacher, Gloria W. lawyer
Nussbaum, Mark Stephen securities trader
†Nussbaumer, Gerhard Karl metals company executive
Nuzum, John M., Jr. banker
Nyren, Neil Sebastian publisher, editor
Oakes, John Bertram writer, editor
Ober, Eric W. broadcasting executive
Oberman, Michael Stewart lawyer
Obernauer, Marne, Jr. investment company executive
Obolensky, Ivan investment banker, foundation consultant, writer, publisher
O'Brian, Jack journalist
O'Brien, Conan writer, performer, talk show host
O'Brien, Donal Clare, Jr. lawyer
O'Brien, Geoffrey Paul editor
O'Brien, John M. newspaper publishing company executive
O'Brien, Kevin J. lawyer
O'Brien, Orin Ynez musician, educator
O'Brien, Richard Francis advertising agency executive
O'Brien, Thomas Ignatius lawyer
O'Brien, Timothy James lawyer
O'Brien, William K. accounting firm executive
†Ochs, Carol Rebecca philosophy and religion educator, writer
Ochs, Michael editor, librarian, music educator
O'Connell, Carmela Digristina appraisal executive, consultant
O'Connell, Daniel S. private investments and management buyouts
O'Connell, Frank Joseph apparel company executive
O'Connor, Carroll actor, writer, producer
O'Connor, John Joseph Cardinal archbishop, former naval officer
O'Connor, Robert James publishing executive
O'Connor, Sinead singer, songwriter
O'Dea, Dennis Michael lawyer
Odell, Stuart Irwin lawyer
Odenweller, Robert Paul philatelist, association executive, airline pilot
O'Donnell, John Logan lawyer
O'Donnell, Richard Walter lawyer, accountant, brokerage company executive
Oettgen, Herbert Friedrich physician
Offensend, David Glenn investment executive
Offit, Morris Wolf investment management executive
Offit, Sidney writer, educator
Ogden, Alfred lawyer
O'Grady, John Joseph, III lawyer
O'Grady, William M. manufacturing executive
Ohannessian, Griselda Jackson publishing executive
O'Hara, Alfred Peck lawyer
†O'Hara, Robert Sydney, Jr. lawyer
O'Hare, Jean Ann lawyer
O'Hare, Joseph Aloysius university president, priest
O'Healy, Quill insurance company executive
Ohira, Kazuto theatre company executive, writer
Ohlson, Douglas Dean artist
O'Horgan, Thomas Foster composer, director
Ohrenstein, Manfred state senator, lawyer
Ohtsu, Masakazu electronics executive
†Okada, Takuya food service and retail executive
O'Keefe, Vincent Thomas clergyman, educational administrator
Okun, Herbert Stuart ambassador, international executive
Olafsson, Olafur J. publishing company executive
Old, Lloyd John cancer biologist
Oldenburg, Claes Thure artist
Oldenburg, Richard Erik auction house executive
†Oldham, Joe editor
Oldham, John Michael physician, psychiatrist, educator
Oldham, Todd fashion designer
Olds, John Theodore banker
†Olds, Sharon poet
Olian, JoAnne Constance curator, art historian
Olick, Arthur Seymour lawyer
Olick, Philip Stewart lawyer
Oliensis, Sheldon lawyer
Oliveira, Elmar violinist
Oliver, Alexander R. management consultant
Oliver, Stephanie Stokes magazine editor
Oliver, Steven Wiles banker
Olmstead, Clarence Walter, Jr. lawyer
Olsen, David Alexander insurance executive
Olshan, Kenneth S. advertising agency executive
Olsinski, Peter Kevin international outplacement executive
Olson, Thomas Francis, II communications company executive
Olson, Wanda Jean lawyer
Olsson, Carl Alfred urologist
O'Malley, Shaun F. accounting firm executive
O'Neal, Hank entertainment producer, business owner
O'Neil, James Peter financial printing company executive
O'Neil, John Joseph lawyer
O'Neill, Daniel Joseph lawyer
O'Neill, Francis Xavier, III marketing executive
O'Neill, George Dorr business executive
O'Neill, Harry William survey research company executive
O'Neill, June Ellenoff economist
†O'Neill, Thomas J. engineering company executive
O'Neill Bidwell, Katharine Thomas fine arts association executive, performing arts executive
Opel, John R. business machines company executive
Opotowsky, Stuart Berger holding company executive
Oppenheim, Ellen W. media director, advertising executive
Oppenheimer, Martin J. lawyer
Oppenheimer, Michael physicist
†Oppenheimer, Paul Eugene English comparative literature educator, poet, author
Oram, John L. chemical company executive
Orben, Jack Richard investment company executive
Orce, Kenneth W. lawyer
†O'Reilly, Vincent M. accounting firm executive
Oreskes, Irwin biochemistry educator
Oresman, Donald entertainment and publishing company executive, corporate lawyer
Orkin, Leonard lawyer
Orlowsky, Martin L. retail company executive
Ornitz, Richard Martin lawyer, business executive
O'Rorke, James Francis, Jr. lawyer
O'Rourke, P. J. (Patrick Jake O'Rourke) writer, humorist
Orr, Terrence S. dancer
Orrmont, Arthur writer, editor
Osborn, Donald Robert lawyer
Osborn, Frederick Henry, III fundraiser, investment advisor
†Osborne, Mary Pope writer
Osborne, Richard de Jongh mining and metals company executive
Osborne, Stanley de Jongh investment banker
Osgood, Charles news broadcaster, journalist
Osgood, Richard M., Jr. applied physics and electrical engineering educator, research administrator
Osgood, Robert Mansfield lawyer
Osnos, Gilbert Charles management consultant
Osnos, Peter Lionel Winston publishing executive
Ostberg, Henry Dean corporate executive
Ostergard, Paul Michael bank executive
Osterhout, Dan Roderick insurance executive
Ostling, Paul James lawyer
Ostling, Richard Neil journalist, author, broadcaster
Ostrager, Barry Robert lawyer
Ostrander, Thomas William investment banker
Ostrow, Joseph W. advertising executive
Ostrow, Samuel David public relations executive
Ostrum, Dean Gardner actor, writer, calligrapher
O'Sullivan, Eugene Henry retired advertising executive
O'Sullivan, Thomas J. lawyer
O'Toole, John E. advertising executive
Ott, Gilbert Russell, Jr. lawyer
Ott, Jurg geneticist, educator
Overlock, Willard Joseph, Jr. investment banker
Owen, Michael ballet dancer
Owen, Richard federal judge
Owen, Sylvia interior design executive
Owen, Thomas Llewellyn, Sr. investment executive
Owett, Adam Thomas advertising creative director, writer
Owsley, David Thomas art consultant, appraiser, lecturer, author
Oxman, David Craig lawyer
Oz, Frank (Frank Richard Oznowicz) puppeteer, film director
Ozawa, Seiji conductor, music director
Ozero, Brian John chemical engineer
Ozick, Cynthia author
Paalz, Anthony L. beverage company executive
Paaswell, Robert Emil civil engineer, educator
Pace, Eric Dwight journalist
Pace, Norma economist, consulting firm executive
Pace, Stephen Shell artist, educator
Pacella, Bernard Leonardo psychiatrist
Pacino, Al (Alfredo James Pacino) actor
Pack, Leonard Brecher lawyer
Padberg, Manfred Wilhelm mathematics educator
Paddock, Anthony Conaway financial consultant
Padilla, James Earl lawyer
Pados, Frank John, Jr. trust company executive
†Page, Jonathan Roy investment analyst
Pagnozzi, Amy columnist
Pais, Abraham physicist, educator
Paisner, Bruce Lawrence lawyer, television and film executive
Pakula, Alan J. producer, director
Paladino, Daniel R. lawyer, beverage corporation executive
Palermo, Nicholas J. banker
†Palermo, Steve sportscaster, color analyst, former umpire
Palitz, Bernard G. finance company executive
Palladino, Vincent Neil lawyer
Palmer, Edward Lewis banker
Palmer, Robert Baylis librarian
Palmer, Robert J(oseph) advertising executive, winery owner
Palmieri, Victor Henry lawyer, business executive
Paluszek, John L. public relations firm executive
Pampel, Joseph Philip Stevenson investment executive
Pandolfi, Francis P. publishing executive
Paneth, Donald J. editor, writer
Panitch, Michael B. brokerage house executive
Panken, Peter Michael lawyer
Papa, Vincent T. insurance company executive
Papalia, Diane Ellen human development educator
Papernik, Joel Ira lawyer
Pappas, Alceste Thetis consulting company executive, educator
Pardee, Scott Edward securities dealer
Pardes, Herbert psychiatrist, educator
Pardo, Dominick George (Don Pardo) broadcasting announcer
Parent, Louise Marie lawyer
Parfit, Gavin J. international management executive
Parish, J. Michael lawyer, writer
Parker, Charles A. insurance company executive
Parker, Douglas Martin lawyer
Parker, James retired curator
†Parker, Joan public relations executive
Parker, Kellis E., Sr. legal educator, lawyer, musician
Parker, Lynda Michele psychiatrist
Parker, Maceo jazz musician, alto saxophone
Parker, Maynard Michael journalist, magazine executive
Parker, Mel editor
Parker, Nancy Winslow artist, writer
Parker, Olivia photographer
Parker, Robert Andrew artist
Parker, Susan Brooks rehabilitation administrator
Parkin, Gerard Francis Ralph chemistry educator, researcher
Parkinson, Georgina ballet mistress
Parkinson, Thomas Ignatius, Jr. lawyer
Parks, Gordon Roger Alexander Buchanan film director, author, photographer, composer
Parmelee, Harold J. construction company executive
Parr, Ferdinand Van Siclen, Jr. lawyer
Parrish, Thomas Kirkpatrick, III marketing consultant
Parseghian, Gene talent agent

Parsons, Andrew John management consultant
Parsons, David artistic director, choreographer
Parsons, Estelle actress
Parsons, Richard Dean banker, lawyer
Parver, Jane W. lawyer
Pasanella, Giovanni architect, architectural educator
Pasanella, Marco furniture designer
Pascal, David artist
Pasquarelli, Joseph J. real estate, engineering and construction executive
Passage, Stephen Scott energy company executive
Passow, Aaron Harry education educator
†Paster, Howard G. public relations/public affairs company executive
Paterson, Katherine Womeldorf writer
Paton, Leland B. investment banker
Patrick, Hugh Talbot economist, educator
Patrick, Thomas H. brokerage house executive
Patrikis, Ernest T. lawyer
Patten, John W. magazine publisher
Patterson, Ellmore Clark banker
Patterson, James Brendan, Jr. advertising agency executive
Patterson, Jerry Eugene author
Patterson, Robert Porter, Jr. federal judge
Patterson, Russel Hugo, Jr. neurosurgeon, educator
Patton, Joanna advertising executive
Patton, Joëlle Delbourgo publishing executive
Paugh, Thomas Francis magazine editor, writer, photographer
†Paul, Andrew Mitchell venture capitalist
Paul, Douglas Allan insurance executive
Paul, Eve W. lawyer
Paul, James William lawyer
Paul, Robert Carey lawyer
Paul, Robert David management consultant
Pauley, Jane television journalist
Paulsen, Diana religious organization administrator
Paumgarten, Nicholas Biddle investment banker
Pavarotti, Luciano lyric tenor
Paxton, Robert Owen historian, educator
Payson, Martin David entertainment company executive, lawyer
†Peacock, Molly poet
Pearlstine, Norman editor
Pearsall, Otis Pratt lawyer
Pearson, Clarence Edward management consultant
Pearson, Henry Charles artist
Peasback, David R. recruiting company executive
Pease, Denise Louise state bank regulator
Peaslee, James M. lawyer
Pechukas, Philip chemistry educator
Peck, Fred Neil economist, educator
Peck, M(organ) Scott psychiatrist, writer
Peck, Richard Wayne novelist
Pecker, David J. magazine publishing company executive, financial executive
Peckolick, Alan graphic designer
†Pedraza, Pedro academic director
Peebler, Charles David, Jr. advertising executive
Peerce, Stuart Bernard lawyer
Peet, Charles D., Jr. lawyer
Peet, Creighton Houck brokerage firm executive
Pegram, John Braxton lawyer
Pei, Ieoh Ming architect
Pekarik, Andrew Joseph museum administrator
Pelé, (Edson Arantes do Nascimento) professional soccer player
Pellegrini, Anna Maria soprano
Peloso, John Francis Xavier lawyer
Pelster, William C. lawyer
Pelz, Robert Leon lawyer
Penicnak, A. John manufacturing company executive
Penn, Arthur Hiller film and theatre producer
Penn, Stanley William journalist
Penney, Alexandra magazine editor-in-chief, writer
Pennoyer, Paul Geddes, Jr. lawyer
Pennoyer, Robert M. lawyer
Peper, George Frederick editor
Pepper, Allan Michael lawyer
Pepper, Beverly artist, sculptor
Peppers, Jerry P. lawyer
Peppet, Russell Frederick accountant
Perahia, Murray pianist
Percus, Jerome Kenneth physicist, educator
Perell, Edward Andrew lawyer
Perelman, Ronald Owen diversified holding company executive
Peress, Gilles photographer
Peress, Maurice symphony conductor, musicologist
Peretz, Eileen interior designer
Peritz, Abraham Daniel business executive
Perkiel, Mitchel H. lawyer
Perkins, Lawrence Bradford, Jr. architect
Perkins, Leeman Lloyd music educator, musicologist
Perkins, Roswell Burchard lawyer
Perless, Ellen advertising executive
Perlis, Donald M. artist
†Perlman, Willa M. publishing executive
Perlmuth, William Alan lawyer
Perlmutter, Alvin Howard television and film producer
Perlmutter, Diane F. communications executive
Perlmutter, Louis investment banker, lawyer
Perrotta, Fioravante Gerald lawyer
Perry, David priest
Perry, Douglas opera singer
Perry, Frank motion picture executive, director, producer, writer
Perschetz, Martin L. lawyer
Persell, Caroline Hodges sociologist, educator, author, researcher, consultant
Pershan, Richard Henry lawyer
†Pesce, Gaetano architectural, interior, industrial and graphic designer
Pesner, Carole Manishin art gallery owner
†Petchesky, Rosalind Pollack political science and women's studies educator
Peters, Alton Emil lawyer
Peters, Arthur King international trade executive, author, consultant
Peters, Bernadette (Bernadette Lazzara) actress
†Peters, Robert Wayne organization executive, lawyer
Peters, Roberta soprano
Peters, Ronald George investment banker
Petersen, Raymond Joseph publishing company executive
Peterson, Charles Gordon retired lawyer
Peterson, Kirk Charles ballet dancer
Peterson, Kristina publishing company executive
Peterson, Nadeen advertising agency executive
Peterson, Peter G. banker
Petrie, Donald Joseph banker
†Petrocelli, Anthony Joseph management executive, consultant
Pettibone, Peter John lawyer
Pettus, Barbara Wyper bank executive
Petz, Edwin V. real estate executive, lawyer
Petzal, David Elias editor, writer
†Peugeot, Patrick insurance executive
Peyronnin, Joseph Felix, III network news executive
Pfeffer, David H. lawyer
Pflaum, Susanna Whitney college dean
†Pfrang, Edward Oscar association executive
†Phelan, Kathleen McGrath public relations executive
Phelps, Edmund Strother economics educator
Philbin, Regis television personality
Phillips, Anthony Francis lawyer
Phillips, Anthony Mark auction house executive
Phillips, Barnet, IV lawyer
Phillips, Charles Gorham lawyer
Phillips, Elizabeth Joan marketing executive
Phillips, Ethel C. (Mrs. Lloyd J. Phillips) writer
Phillips, Gerald Baer internal medicine educator, scientist
Phillips, Graham Holmes advertising executive
Phillips, Howard William investment banker
Phillips, John David management consultant
Phillips, Joyce Martha human resources executive
Phillips, Lawrence S. apparel company executive
Phillips, Pamela Kim lawyer
Phillips, Russell Alexander, Jr. foundation executive
Philp, Richard Nilson writer, editor
Pickholz, Jerome Walter advertising agency executive
Pickholz, Marvin G. lawyer
Picower, Warren Michael magazine editor
Pidot, Whitney Dean lawyer
Piel, Gerard editor, publisher
Piemonte, Robert Victor association executive
Pierce, Charles Eliot, Jr. library director, educator
Pierce, Lawrence Warren federal judge
Pierce, Morton Allen lawyer
Pierce, Richard James, Jr. legal educator, consultant
Pierpoint, Powell lawyer
Pierson, Richard Norris, Jr. medical educator
Pietersen, William Gerard pharmaceutical company executive
Pietrini, Andrew Gabriel automotive aftermarket executive
Pietruski, John Michael, Jr. biotechnology company executive, pharmaceuticals executive
Pietrzak, Alfred Robert lawyer
Pike, Laurence Bruce retired lawyer
Pilcz, Maleta psychotherapist
Pilgrim, Dianne Hauserman art museum director
Piliguian, Tro advertising executive
Pimsler, Alvin J. artist
Pincay, Laffit, Jr. jockey
Pincus, Lionel Irwin venture banker
Piore, Emanuel Ruben physicist
Piper, Thomas Laurence, III investment banker
Pirani, Conrad Levi pathologist, educator
Pirie, Robert S. investment banker, lawyer
Pirner, David musician, songwriter
Pirsig, Robert Maynard author
Pisano, Ronald George art consultant
Pi-Sunyer, F. Xavier medical educator, medical investigator
Pittaway, David Bruce investment banker, lawyer
Pitti, Donald Robert financial service company executive
Pittman, Robert Warren entertainment executive
Pitts, Thomas E. lawyer
Piven, Frances Fox political scientist, educator
Placzek, Adolf Kurt librarian
Plain, Belva writer
Plant, David William lawyer
Platnick, Norman I. curator, arachnologist
Platt, Charles Adams architect, planner
Platt, Nicholas Asian affairs specialist, ambassador
Plavoukos, Spencer advertising executive
Plimpton, George Ames writer, editor, television host
†Plotnicki, Steven Joel record company executive
Plottel, Jeanine Parisier foreign language educator
†Plum, Fred neurologist
Plunkett, Maryann actress
Pluzynski, Edward Dale advertising executive
Podd, Ann newspaper editor
Podhoretz, Norman magazine editor, writer
Podos-Untermeyer, Salle lawyer
Pogo, Beatriz Teresa Garcia-Tunon cell biologist, virologist, educator
Pogrebin, Letty Cottin writer, lecturer
†Polacco, Patricia children's author, illustrator
Polak, Vivian Louise lawyer
Polak, Werner L. lawyer
Polisi, Joseph W(illiam) college administrator
Poll, Robert Eugene, Jr. bank executive
Pollack, Milton federal judge
Pollack, Robert Elliot biological sciences educator, writer, scientist
Pollack, Stanley P. lawyer
Pollack, Stephen J. stockbroker
Pollak, Martin Marshall lawyer, patent development company executive
Pollak, Richard writer, editor
Pollak, Tim advertising agency executive
Pollak, William L. newspaper publishing executive
Pollicino, Joseph Anthony investment company executive
†Pollitt, Katha writer, poet, educator
Pollock-O'Brien, Louise Mary public relations executive
Polshek, James Stewart architect
Pomerance, Norman publishing company executive
Pomerantz, Charlotte writer
Pomerantz, John J. manufacturing executive
Pomerantz, Laura apparel company executive
Pomeroy, Lee Harris architect
Pompadur, I. Martin communications executive
Pool, Mary Jane design consultant, author, lecturer
Poons, Larry artist
Poor, Anne artist
Poor, Peter Varnum producer, director
Poppe, Fred Christoph advertising agency executive
Poppel, Seth Raphael corporate executive
Poppen, Alvin J. religious organization administrator
Porizkova, Paulina model, actress
Porretta, Emanuele Peter banker
†Portas, Jose oil industry executive
Porter, Karl Hampton orchestra musical director, conductor
Porter, Liliana Alicia artist, printmaker
Porter, Stephen Winthrop stage director
Portnoy, Sara S. lawyer
Posamentier, Alfred Steven mathematics educator, university administrator
Posen, Susan Orzack lawyer
Posner, Donald art historian
Posner, Edward Mark brokerage company executive
†Posner, Gerald author, lawyer
Posner, Jerome Beebe neurologist, educator
Posner, Roy Edward finance executive
Post, Emily (Elizabeth Lindley Post) author
Poster, June performing company executive
Potoker, Edward Martin English language educator, author
Potter, Cary Nicholas banker
†Potter, Delcour S. finance company executive
Potter, Guy Dill radiologist, educator
Potter, Hamilton Fish, Jr. lawyer, consultant, author
Potter, William James investment banker
Pounder, Richard A. advertising executive
Poussaint, Renee Francine journalist
Povell, Roy Albert lawyer
Povich, (Maurice) Maury Richard broadcast journalist, talk show host, television producer
Powell, James Henry lawyer
Powell, Mike olympic athlete, track and field
Powell, Richard Gordon retired lawyer
Powers, Edward Alton minister, educator
Powers, Richard F., III finance company executive
Pratt, Michael Theodore book publishing company executive, marketing, sales and publishing specialist
Pratt, Richardson, Jr. retired college president
Preble, Laurence George lawyer
Preiskel, Barbara Scott lawyer, association executive
Prem, F. Herbert, Jr. lawyer
Prendergast, John Patrick accounting company executive
Prentice, Eugene Miles, III lawyer
Presby, J. Thomas financial advisor
Preska, Loretta A. federal judge
Prestbo, John Andrew newspaper editor, journalist, author
Preston, Frances W. performing rights organization executive
Preston, James E. cosmetics company executive
Prewitt, Kenneth political science educator, foundation executive
Price, Hugh B. foundation executive, lawyer
Price, Leontyne concert and opera singer, soprano
Price, Reynolds novelist, poet, playwright, essayist, educator
Price, Robert lawyer, media executive, investment banker
Priest, Aaron Mendell publishing executive
Primis, Lance Roy newspaper executive
Primps, William Guthrie lawyer
Prince, Carl E. historian, educator
Prince, Harold theatrical producer
Prince, Kenneth Stephen lawyer
Princz, Judith publishing executive
Prizzi, Jack Anthony investment banking executive
Profusek, Robert Alan lawyer
Prosky, Robert Joseph actor
Protas, Ron dance company executive
Proudfoot, Wayne Lee religion educator
Proulx, Edna Annie writer
Prouty, Norman R. investment banker
Pryce, Jonathan actor
Pryor, Alan Mark banker
Puleo, Frank Charles lawyer
Pulitzer, Roslyn K. social worker, psychotherapist
Pulling, Thomas Leffingwell investment advisor
Purcell, James Lawrence lawyer
Puris, Martin Ford advertising agency executive
Purse, Charles Roe real estate company executive
†Puschel, Philip P. textiles executive
Putney, John Alden, Jr. insurance company executive
Pye, Gordon Bruce economist
Pye, Lenwood David materials science educator, researcher, consultant
Pyle, Robert Milner, Jr. financial services company executive
Pyne, Eben Wright banker
†Quackenbush, Margery Clouser psychoanalyst, administrator
Quackenbush, Robert Mead artist, author, psychoanalyst
Quain, Mitchell I. investment executive
Quaintance, Robert Forsyth, Jr. lawyer
Quale, Andrew Christopher, Jr. lawyer
Quaytman, Harvey painter
Queler, Eve conductor
Quennell, Nicholas landscape architect, educator
Questel, Mae actress
†Quick, Leslie Charles, III brokerage house executive
Quick, Thomas Clarkson brokerage house executive
Quigley, Austin Edmund literature and language educator
Quigley, Martin Schofield publishing company executive, educator
Quilico, Louis baritone
Quinlan, Guy Christian lawyer
Quinn, Anthony Rudolph Oaxaca actor, writer, artist
Quinn, Jane Bryant journalist, writer
Quinn, Yvonne Susan lawyer
Quinson, Bruno Andre publishing executive
Quint, Ira retail executive
Quintero, Jose theatrical director
Quintero, Ronald Gary management consultant
Quirk, John James investment company executive
Quisgard, Liz Whitney artist, sculptor
Quraishi, Nisar Ali internist
Raab, Selwyn journalist
Raab, Sheldon lawyer
†Raasch, Ernest Martin company executive
Rabb, Bruce lawyer
Rabb, Maxwell M. lawyer, former ambassador
Rabetafika, Joseph Albert Blaise UN representative
Rabin, Jack lawyer
Rabiner, Susan editor
Rabinowitch, David George sculptor
Rabinowitz, Jack Grant radiologist, educator
Rabinowitz, Mayer Elya librarian, educator
Rachleff, Owen Spencer (Owen Spencer Rackleff) actor, author
Rachow, Louis A(ugust) librarian
Raffael, Joseph artist
Rafferty, Brian Joseph investor relations consultant
†Rafii, Shahin medicine educator
Ragan, David publishing company executive
Ragusa, Olga Maria Italian language educator
Rahm, David Alan lawyer
Rahm, Susan Berkman lawyer
Rainer, John David psychiatrist
Raines, Howell Hiram newspaper editor, journalist
Raines, Joan Binder literary agent
Rainess, Alan Edward psychiatrist
Rainier, Robert Paul publisher
Rainis, Eugene Charles brokerage house executive
Rainone, Salvatore Raffaello vocalist
Raisler, Kenneth Mark lawyer
†Rajski, Peggy film director, film producer
Rakoff, Jed Saul lawyer, author
Ralli, Constantine Pandia lawyer
Ramat, Charles S. apparel executive
Ramey, Samuel Edward bass soloist
Ramirez, Maria Fiorini economist, investment advisor
†Ramirez, Tina artistic director
Ramsay, Gustavus Remak actor
Ramsey, Peter Christie bank executive
Ramsier, Paul composer, psychotherapist
†Ranadive, Prakash Kamlakant government official, diplomat
Rand, Calvin Gordon arts and education producer and consultant
Rand, Harry Israel lawyer
Rand, Lawrence Anthony investor and financial relations executive
Rand, William lawyer, former state justice
Randall, Tony (Leonard Rosenberg) actor
Randazzo, Anthony dancer
Randolph, David conductor
Rankin, Clyde Evan, III lawyer
Rao, Sethuramiah Lakshminarayana United Nations official
Rapaczynski, Andrzej law educator
Raphael, Sally Jessy talk-show host
Rapoport, Bernard Robert lawyer
Rappaport, Charles Owen lawyer
Rappaport, Steven N. financial information services executive
Rashad, Ahmad (Bobby Moore) sports broadcaster, former professional football player
Rasmus, John A. magazine executive
Rather, Dan broadcast journalist
Rattazzi, Serena art museum and association administrator
Rattner, Steven Lawrence investment banker
Rauch, Arthur Irving management consultant
Rauch, Rudolph Stewart, III periodical editor, arts education executive
Rauschenberg, Robert artist
Ravitch, Beverly lawyer
Ravitch, Diane Silvers historian, educator, author, government official
Ravitz, Robert Allan advertising agency executive
Rawl, Arthur Julian retail executive, accountant, consultant, author
Rawson, Eleanor S. publishing company executive
Raylesberg, Alan Ira lawyer
Raynolds, John F., III executive search consultant
Raynor, Richard Benjamin neurosurgeon, educator
Read, David Haxton Carswell clergyman
Rebay, Luciano Italian literature educator, literary critic
Recanati, Raphael shipping and banking executive
Rechy, John Francisco author
†Redden, Nigel A. performing company executive
Reddy, Krishna Narayana artist, educator
Redlich, Norman lawyer, educator
Redo, S(averio) Frank surgeon
Reed, Ishmael Scott (Emmett Coleman) writer
Reed, James Donald journalist, author
Reed, John Shepard banker
Reed, John W. religious organization administrator
Reed, Joseph Verner, Jr. diplomat
Reed, Rex author, critic
†Reemtsma, Keith surgeon, educator
Reese, Ann N. financial executive
Reeve, Christopher actor
†Reeves, Daniel McDonough video artist
†Reeves, Richard writer, historian
Reff, Theodore art historian
Regan, Judith Theresa publishing executive
†Regan, Muriel small business owner
Regan, Sylvia playwright
Reges, Marianna Alice marketing executive
Reibstein, Richard Jay lawyer
Reich, Larry Sam lawyer
Reich, Seymour David lawyer, former fraternal organization executive
Reich, Steve composer
Reich, Yaron Z. lawyer
Reichel, Walter Emil advertising executive
Reichl, Ruth Molly restaurant critic
Reid, John Phillip law educator
Reid, Sarah Layfield lawyer
Reid-Crisp, Wendy publishing executive
Reidenberg, Marcus Milton physician, educator
Reidy, Carolyn Kroll publisher
Reig, June Wilson writer, director, producer
Reilly, Edward Arthur lawyer
†Reilly, Edward J. public relations executive
Reilly, Edward T., Jr. publisher
Reilly, William Francis publishing company executive
Reiman, Donald Henry English language educator
Rein, Catherine Amelia financial services executive, lawyer
Reinhard, Keith Leon advertising executive
Reinhold, Richard Lawrence lawyer
Reininghaus, Ruth artist
Reinstein, Paul Michael lawyer
Reinthaler, Richard Walter lawyer
Reis, Arthur Robert, Jr. men's furnishings manufacturer
Reis, Donald Jeffery neurologist, neurobiologist, educator
Reis, Judson Patterson investment banker
Reis, Muriel Henle lawyer, broadcast executive, commentator
Reisberg, Barry geropsychiatrist, neuropsychopharmacologist
Reisner, Milton psychiatrist, psychoanalyst
Reiss, Alvin writer
Reiss, Jeffrey Charles television executive
Reiss, Steven Alan lawyer, law educator
Reiss, Timothy James comparative literature educator, writer
†Relkin, Allen commodities executive
Relson, Morris patent lawyer
Rembar, Charles (Isaiah) lawyer, writer
Remington, Deborah Williams artist
Remnick, David J. journalist
Rendino, Anthony trust company executive
Reneberg, Richard (Richey Reneberg) professional tennis player
Renick, Kyle artistic director
Renvall, Johan ballet dancer
Repko, William Clarke banker
Resika, Paul artist
Resnick, Marcia Aylene photographic artist, educator
Resnick, Milton artist
Resnik, Frank Edward tobacco company executive
Resnik, Regina operatic singer
Resor, Stanley Rogers lawyer
Restani, Jane A. federal judge
Reuben, Alvin Bernard entertainment executive
Reuter, Carol Joan insurance company executive

Reuther, David Louis *children's book publisher, writer*
Reutter, Eberhard Edmund, Jr. *education and law educator*
Reverdin, Bernard J. *lawyer*
Revesz, Richard Luis *law educator*
Reyes, Andre *ballet dancer*
Reynolds, Brett W. *managing director, playwright*
Reynolds, Clayton S. *lawyer*
Reynolds, Donald Martin *art historian, foundation administrator, educator*
†Reynolds, James *management consultant*
Reynolds, Warren Jay *retired publisher*
Reynolds, W(ynetka) Ann *university system administrator, educator*
Reznikov, Hanon *theater director, actor*
Rhoads, Geraldine Emeline *editor*
Rhodes, Dennis Earl *public relations executive*
Rhodes, John Bower *management consultant*
Rhodes, Milton *arts association administrator*
Rhodes, Richard Lee *writer*
Rhodes, Samuel *violist*
†Rhodes, William Reginald *banker*
Rhodes, Yorke E(dward) *chemist*
†Rhone, Sylvia *recording industry executive*
Ribicoff, Abraham A. *lawyer, former senator*
Ricci, Kenneth *architect*
Ricciardi, Lawrence R. *food products company executive, lawyer*
Ricciarelli, Katia *soprano*
Rice, Anne *author*
Rice, Charles Duncan *university official*
Rice, Donald Sands *lawyer*
Rice, Eugene Franklin, Jr. *history educator*
Rice, James A. *investment company executive*
Rice, Joseph Lee, III *lawyer*
Rice, T. Walker *actor, theatre adminstrator*
Rich, Adrienne *writer*
Rich, Frank Hart *critic*
Rich, Kenneth Malcolm *executive search and management consultant*
Rich, R(obert) Bruce *lawyer*
Richard, Ellen *theater executive*
Richards, David A. J. *lawyer, educator*
Richards, David Alan *lawyer*
Richards, Keith *musician*
Richards, Lloyd George *theatrical director, university administrator*
Richards, Reuben Francis *natural resource company executive*
Richardson, David John *ballet dancer, educator*
Richardson, Midge Turk *magazine editor*
Richardson, Miranda *actress*
Richman, Howard *surgeon*
Richman, Martin Franklin *lawyer*
Richmond, Eero *music librarian, composer*
Richter, Georg *book publishing executive*
Richter, Michael Thomas *professional hockey player*
Ricker, John Boykin, Jr. *insurance counselor*
Ridder, Eric *newspaper publisher*
Riddle, Sturgis Lee *minister*
Rideout, Philip Munroe *publishing company executive*
†Rieff, David Sontag *editor, writer, critic*
Riffaterre, Michael *foreign language educator, writer*
Rifkin, Harold *physician, educator*
Rifkind, Arleen B. *physician, researcher*
Rifkind, Robert S(inger) *lawyer*
Rifkind, Simon Hirsch *lawyer*
Rigby, Paul Crispin *artist, cartoonist*
Riggio, Leonard *book publishing executive*
Riggio, Stephen *book store chain executive*
Riggs, Andy J., Jr. *newspaper publishing executive*
Riggs, Michael David *magazine editor, writer*
Riker, Walter F., Jr. *pharmacologist, physician*
Riklis, Meshulam *manufacturing and retail executive*
Riley, Ivers Whitman *stock exchange executive*
Riley, Patrick James *former professional basketball coach*
Riley, William *corporate executive, writer*
Rimerman, Ira Stephen *banker*
Rinaldini, Luis Emilio *investment banker*
Rindlaub, John Wade *advertising agency executive*
Rinehart, Jonathan *public relations executive*
Rines, S. Melvin *investment banker*
Ring, Renee E. *lawyer*
Ringel, Dean *lawyer*
Ringer, James Milton *lawyer*
Ringgold, Faith *artist, writer*
Ringler, Lenore *educational psychologist*
Rinsland, Roland DeLano *university official*
Riordan, James Quentin *retired company executive*
Riss, Eric *psychologist*
Ritch, Herald LaVern *finance company executive*
Ritch, Kathleen *diversified company executive*
Ritter, Robert Joseph *lawyer*
Rivera, Chita (Conchita del Rivero) *actress, singer, dancer*
Rivera, Geraldo *television personality, journalist*
Rivlin, Benjamin *political science educator*
†Rizk, Mohammed M. *import/export executive*
Rizzo, Francis *arts administrator, writer, stage director*
Roach, John Hendee, Jr. *bank executive, investment banker*
Roach, Maxwell Lemuel *musician*
Roath, Robert S. *food products executive*
Robbins, Edith Schultz *microscopy educator*
Robbins, Harold *author*
Robbins, Jerome *choreographer, director*
Robbins, John Clapp *management consultant*
Robbins, Kenneth L. *advertising agency executive*
†Robert, Stephen *investment firm executive*
†Roberti, William Vincent *retail executive*
Roberts, Donald Munier *banker, trust company executive*
†Roberts, Eugene Leslie, Jr. *newspaper executive, editor*
Roberts, Francis Stone *advertising executive*
Roberts, John J. *accounting firm executive*
Roberts, John Joseph *insurance company executive*
Roberts, Kathleen Anne *judge*
Roberts, Sidney I. *lawyer*
Roberts, Tony (David Anthony Roberts) *actor*
Robertson, Edwin David *lawyer*
Robertson, Jaquelin Taylor *architect, educator*
Robertson, Leslie Earl *structural engineer*
Robertson, Michael Brian *advertising executive*
Robertson, Nan *journalist, correspondent*
Robinowitz, Stuart *lawyer*
Robinson, Barbara Paul *lawyer*
Robinson, David Zav *foundation administrator*
Robinson, Enders Anthony *geophysics educator, writer*
Robinson, Irwin Jay *lawyer*
Robinson, James Dixon, III *corporate executive*
Robinson, James LeRoy *architect, educator, developer*
Robinson, L. Donald *advertising executive*
Robinson, Lee Harris *lawyer*
Robinson, Maurice Richard, Jr. *publishing executive*
Robinson, Nan Senior *not-for-profit organization consultant*
Robinson, Richard *publishing company executive*
Robinson, Robert Armstrong *pension fund executive*
Robison, Paula Judith *flutist*
Robock, Stefan Hyman *economics educator emeritus*
Roby, Joe Lindell *investment banker*
Roche, John J. *banking company executive, corporate lawyer*
Roche, Kevin Joseph *finance executive*
Rochell, Carlton Charles *librarian*
Rochlis, James Joseph *manufacturing company executive*
Rockefeller, David *banker*
Rocklen, Kathy Hellenbrand *lawyer, banker*
Rockwell, John Sargent *arts administrator, music critic, writer*
Rodgers, John Joseph, III *school administrator*
Rodman, Leroy Eli *lawyer*
Rodriguez, Beatriz *ballerina*
Rodriguez, Geno (Eugene Rodriguez) *artist, arts administrator*
Rodriguez, Vincent Angel *lawyer*
Roe, Mark J. *law educator*
Roeder, Robert Gayle *biochemist, educator*
Roehm, Carolyne Jane *fashion designer*
Roehm, MacDonell, Jr. *investment firm executive*
Roellig, Leonard Oscar *physics educator*
†Roen, Philip Ruben *urologist, surgeon, medical educator*
Roerick, William (George) (William Roehrick) *actor, author*
Roessler, Ronald James *lawyer*
Roethenmund, Otto Emil *financial and banking executive*
Rogalin, Roger Richard *publishing executive*
Rogers, Arthur Merriam, Jr. *banker*
Rogers, Edmund Pendleton, III *lawyer*
Rogers, Elizabeth Barlow *municipal park administrator*
Rogers, Eugene Charles *investment firm executive*
Rogers, Kenneth R. *advertising executive*
Rogers, Theodore Courtney *investment company executive*
Rogin, Gilbert Leslie *editor, author*
Rohatyn, Felix George *investment company executive*
Rolfe, Robin Ann *trade association executive, lawyer*
Rolfe, Ronald Stuart *lawyer*
Rollin, Betty *author, television journalist*
Rollins, Jack *motion picture producer*
Rollins, Sherrie Sandy *television executive*
Rolontz, Robert *recording company executive*
Roman, Kenneth, Jr. *corporate communications executive*
Roman, Stanford Augustus, Jr. *medical educator, dean*
Romans, John Niebrugge *lawyer*
Romney, Richard Bruce *lawyer*
Roney, Wallace *musician*
Ronson, Raoul R. *publishing executive*
Rooney, Andrew Aitken *writer, columnist*
Rooney, Michael Francis *publisher*
Rooney, Paul C., Jr. *lawyer*
Rooney, Terence *public relations executive*
Roosevelt, Theodore, IV *investment banker*
Root, Nina J. *librarian*
Root, William Pitt *poet, educator*
Rosand, David *art history educator*
Rosdeitcher, Sidney Samuel *lawyer*
Rose, Charles *television journalist*
†Rose, Daniel *real estate company executive, consultant*
Rose, Elihu *real estate executive*
Rose, Herman *artist*
Rose, Jerome Gerald *lawyer*
Rose, Leatrice *artist, educator*
Rose, Milton Curtiss *lawyer*
Rose, Robert Neal *brokerage house executive*
†Rose, Victoria Lasdon *magazine publisher*
Rose, Zeldon E. *public relations consultant*
Rosen, Benjamin Maurice *venture capitalist, computer company executive*
Rosen, David Michael *university administrator, public affairs consultant*
†Rosen, David Paul *book editor*
Rosen, J(oshua) Philip *lawyer*
Rosen, Marcella *advertising executive*
Rosen, Nathaniel Kent *cellist*
Rosen, Richard Lewis *lawyer, real estate developer*
Rosenbaum, Joan Hannah *museum director*
Rosenbaum, Steven Ira *public relations and publishing executive, photographer*
Rosenberg, Alan Stewart *lawyer*
Rosenberg, Burton M. *apparel company executive*
Rosenberg, Jerome I. *lawyer*
Rosenberg, John David *English educator, literary critic*
Rosenberg, Judith Meta *brokerage executive*
Rosenberg, Marianne *lawyer*
Rosenberg, Maurice *lawyer, educator*
Rosenberg, Michael Joseph *financial executive*
Rosenberg, Robert Charles *housing corporation executive*
Rosenberg, Stephen *lawyer*
Rosenberger, Carol *concert pianist*
Rosenberger, Ernst Hey *judge*
Rosenblatt, Arthur Isaac *architect, former museum director*
Rosenblatt, Lester *naval architect*
Rosenbloom, Daniel *investment banker, lawyer*
Rosenblum, Constance *newspaper editor*
Rosenblum, Robert *art historian, educator*
Rosenbluth, Lucille Maxine *health research facility administrator*
Rosenfeld, Arthur H. *lawyer, publisher*
Rosenfeld, Herb *educational consultant*
Rosenfeld, Ronald Marvin *advertising executive*
Rosenfeld, Steven B. *lawyer*
Rosenfield, Allan *physician*
Rosenfield, Jay Gary *publisher*
Rosenhouse, Irwin J. *artist, designer*
Rosensaft, Menachem Zwi *lawyer, author, community activist*
Rosenshine, Allen Gilbert *advertising agency executive*
Rosenthal, Albert Joseph *university dean, law educator, lawyer*
Rosenthal, Charles Michael *financial executive*
Rosenthal, Imre *financial company executive*
Rosenthal, Jacob (Jack Rosenthal) *newspaper editor*
Rosenthal, Lucy Gabrielle *writer, editor, educator*
Rosenthal, Macha Louis *author, educator*
Rosenthal, Milton Frederick *minerals and chemical company executive*
Rosenthal, Nan *curator, author*
Rosenthal, Peter *public relations executive*
Rosenthal, Tony (Bernard) *sculptor*
Rosenwald, E. John, Jr. *brokerage house executive, investment banker*
Rosenwald, William *investment executive, philanthropist*
Roskind, E. Robert *real estate company executive*
Rosner, Lydia S. *sociology educator, author*
Rosoff, Jeannie I. *association administrator*
Rosow, Stuart L. *lawyer*
Ross, Brian Elliott *news correspondent*
Ross, Charles *artist*
Ross, Coleman DeVane *accountant, insurance company consultant*
Ross, David A. *art museum director*
Ross, Diana *singer, actress, entertainer, fashion designer*
Ross, Donald Edward *engineering company executive*
Ross, Donald Keith *retired insurance company executive*
Ross, Jeffrey Allan *political scientist, educator*
Ross, Michael Aaron *lawyer*
Ross, Norman Alan *publisher*
Ross, Rhoda *artist*
Rossant, James Stephane *architect, artist*
Rossellini, Isabella *actress, model*
Rosset, Barnet Lee, Jr. *publisher*
Rosset, Lisa Krug *editor*
Rossi, Dominick F., Jr. *advertising agency executive*
Rossner, Judith *novelist*
Rostagno, Derrick *professional tennis player*
Rosten, Leo Calvin (Leonard Q. Ross) *author, political scientist*
Rostropovich, Mstislav Leopoldovich *musician*
†Rotan, Walter *sculptor*
Rotenstreich, Jon W. *insurance company executive*
Roth, Ann *costume designer*
Roth, Henry *writer*
Roth, Judith Shulman *lawyer*
Roth, Michael I. *lawyer, financial executive*
Roth, Paul Norman *lawyer*
Roth, Philip *writer*
Roth, Richard, Jr. *architect*
Roth, Sol *rabbi*
Rothberg, Gerald *editor, publisher*
Rothenberg, Jerome *author*
Rothenberg, Peter Jay *lawyer*
Rothenberg, Robert Edward *physician, surgeon, author*
Rothenberg, Robert Philip *public relations counselor*
Rothenberg, Susan *artist*
Rothholz, Peter Lutz *public relations executive*
Rothman, Bernard *lawyer*
Rothman, David J. *history and medical educator*
Rothman, Henry Isaac *lawyer*
Rothman, Howard Joel *lawyer*
Rothman, James Edward *cell biologist, educator*
Rothschild, Diane *advertising agency executive*
Rothschild, Joseph *political science educator*
Rothstein, Fred H. *clothing executive*
Rothstein, Gerald Alan *investment company executive*
Rothstein, Richard *public relations executive*
Rotter, Steve *advertising executive*
Roubos, Gary Lynn *diversified manufacturing company executive*
Roughsedge, Carolyn Dunn *advertising agency executive*
Rover, Edward Frank *lawyer*
Rovine, Arthur William *lawyer*
Rowe, John Wallis *academic administrator, hospital administrator*
†Rowen, Daniel *architect*
Rowen, Ruth Halle *musicologist, educator*
Rowland, Esther E(delman) *college dean*
Rowland, Herbert Leslie *public relations executive*
Rowland, Lewis Phillip *neurologist, medical editor, educator*
Roy, Melinda *dancer*
Rozel, Samuel Joseph *lawyer*
Rozelle, Pete (Alvin Ray Rozelle) *former commissioner athletic league*
Rozen, Jerome George, Jr. *research entomologist, museum curator and research administrator*
Ruben, Lawrence *real estate developer, building company executive, lawyer*
Ruben, William Samuel *marketing consultant*
Rubenfeld, Stanley Irwin *lawyer*
Rubenstein, Howard Joseph *public relations executive*
Rubenstein, Joshua Seth *lawyer*
Rubenstein, Stanley Ellis *public relations consultant*
Rubin, Albert L. *physician, educator*
Rubin, Edwin Manning *advertising executive*
Rubin, Gustav *orthopedic surgeon, consultant, researcher*
Rubin, Harry Meyer *entertainment industry executive*
Rubin, Herbert *lawyer*
Rubin, Jane Lockhart Gregory *lawyer*
Rubin, Joel Edward *consulting company executive*
Rubin, Mel *advertising executive*
Rubin, Norman Julius *columnist*
Rubin, Richard Allan *lawyer*
Rubin, Robert Samuel *investment banker*
Rubin, Stephen Edward *editor, journalist*
Rubin, Stephen Wayne *lawyer*
Rubin, Theodore Isaac *psychiatrist*
Rubino, Victor Joseph *law institute executive*
Rubinstein, Aaron *lawyer*
Rubinstein, Frederic Armand *lawyer*
Rubinstein, Laurence Henry *university administrator, fund raiser*
Ruckert, Ann Johns *musician, singer*
Rudd, Nicholas *marketing communications company executive*
Rudel, Julius *conductor*
Ruder, William *public relations executive*
Ruding, Herman Onno *banker, former Dutch government official*
†Rudman, Mark *poet, educator*
Rudoff, Sheldon *lawyer, former religious organization executive*
Ruebhausen, Oscar Melick *lawyer*
Ruegger, Philip Theophil, III *lawyer*
Ruello, Samuel Angus *management consultant*
Ruffle, John Frederick *banker*
Ruggiero, Thomas William *lawyer*
Rupp, George Erik *university president*
Ruscha, Edward *artist*
Rushnell, Squire Derrick *television executive*
Rusmisel, Stephen R. *lawyer*
Russell, Charles F. *newspaper publishing executive*
Russell, Charlotte Sananes *biochemistry educator, researcher*
Russell, John St. Clair, Jr. *lawyer*
Russo, Anthony Joseph *public relations professional*
Russo, Gregory Thomas *lawyer*
Russo, Thomas Anthony *lawyer*
Rust, Frances O'Connell *education educator*
Ruth, Carol A. *public relations executive*
Ruthchild, Geraldine Quietlake *training and development consultant, writer, poet*
Rutkin, Seymour *architect*
Rutman, Mark Charles *public relations executive*
Ruvane, John Austin *pharmaceutical industry consultant*
Ryan, J. Richard *lawyer*
Ryan, Michael Clifford *lawyer*
Ryan, Michael Lee *lawyer*
Ryan, Regina Claire (Mrs. Paul Deutschman) *editor, book packager, literary agent*
Ryan, Thomas Timothy, Jr. *banker, lawyer, government official*
Ryden, Katherine *publishing executive, human resources executive*
Ryder, Thomas O. *magazine publishing executive*
Ryle, Joseph Donald *public relations executive*
Ryman, Robert Tracy *artist*
Rysanek, Leonie *soprano*
Ryskamp, Charles Andrew *museum executive, educator*
Saal, Hubert Daniel *journalist*
Sabel, Bradley Kent *lawyer*
Sabinson, Harvey Barnett *cultural organiztion administrator*
Sacerdote, Peter M. *investment banker*
Sachar, David Bernard *gastroenterologist, medical educator*
Sachdev, Ved Parkash *neurosurgeon*
Sachs, David *lawyer*
Sachs, Susan F. *publishing executive*
Sack, Robert David *lawyer*
Sackeim, Harold *psychologist, educator*
Sacks, David G. *retired distilling company executive, lawyer*
Sacks, Ira Stephen *lawyer*
Sacks, Oliver Wolf *neurologist, writer*
Sacks, Temi J. *public relations executive*
Saddler, Donald Edward *choreographer, dancer*
Sadegh, Ali M. *mechanical engineering educator, researcher, consultant*
Sadock, Benjamin James *psychiatrist, educator*
†Sadove, Stephen Irving *consumer products company executive*
Safer, Jay Gerald *lawyer*
Safer, Morley *journalist*
†Saff, Donald Jay *artist, educator*
Safiol, George E. *electronics company executive*
Sagami, Kim *dancer*
Sager, Clifford J(ulius) *psychiatrist, educator*
Sager, Lawrence Gene *law educator*
Sahid, Joseph Robert *lawyer*
Said, Edward W. *English language and literature educator*
Saiman, Martin S. *lawyer*
Sainer, Arthur *writer, theater educator*
St. Clair, Michael *art dealer*
Sainty, Guy Stair *art dealer*
Sakita, Bunji *physicist, educator*
Saks, Arnold *graphic designer*
Saladino, John F. *architect, interior decorator, furniture designer*
Salberg, Melvin *lawyer*
Sale, (John) Kirkpatrick *writer*
Salembier, Valerie Birnbaum *publishing executive*
†Salerno-Sonnenberg, Nadja *violinist*
Salgado, Lissette *dancer*
Salinger, Jerome David *author*
Salisbury, Nancy *convent director*
Salle, David *artist*
Salmans, Charles Gardiner *banker*
Salomon, Richard *investor*
Salomon, Robert S., Jr. *portfolio manager*
Salonga, Lea *actress, singer*
†Salter, Kevin Thornton *lawyer*
Salvadori, Mario *mathematical engineer*
Salzman, Eric *artistic director*
Salzman, Robert Jay *accountant*
Samers, Bernard Norman *fund raising organization executive*
Samuels, Leslie B. *federal agency administrator, lawyer*
Samuels, Nathaniel *business executive, government administrator*
Sand, Leonard B. *federal judge*
Sandalls, William Thomas, Jr. *financial services company executive*
Sanders, Fredric M. *lawyer*
Sanders, Lawrence *author*
†Sanders, Lewis A. *investment research and management executive*
Sanders, Richard Louis *assistant managing editor*
Sandler, Jenny *dancer*
Sandler, Lucy Freeman *art history educator*
Sandler, Richard Jay *lawyer*
Sandler, Robert Michael *insurance company executive, actuary*
Sandler, Ross *law educator*
Sanford, Charles Steadman, Jr. *banker*
†Sanger, Alexander Campbell *family planning executive*
Sanger, Gail *lawyer*
†Sanhueza, Hernan *demographer, physician*
Santulli, Thomas Vincent *surgeon*
Sapinsky, Joseph Charles *magazine executive, photographer*
Sarachik, Myriam Paula *physics educator*
Sarazen, Richard Allen *media company executive*
Sard, George *public relations company executive*
Sardanis, Andrew S. *investment company executive*
Sargent, James Cunningham *lawyer*
Sarnelle, Joseph R. *electronic publishing specialist, magazine and newspaper editor*
Sarnoff, Albert *communications executive*
Sarnoff, William *publishing company executive*
†Sarris, Shirley Cornelia *publishing company executive*
Sartori, Giovanni *political scientist*
Sarver, Eugene *finance educator*
Sasaki, Mikio *import/export company exeutive*
Satine, Barry Roy *lawyer*
†Satz, Michael Ellis *insurance executive*
Sauerhaft, Stan *public relations executive, consultant*
Saul, John Woodruff, III *writer*
Saunders, Arlene *opera singer*
Saunders, Dero Ames *writer, editor*
Saunders, Paul Christopher *lawyer*
Savas, Emanuel S. *public management educator*
Savelli, Angelo *artist*
Savich, René *broadway theater executive, producer*
Savrin, Louis *lawyer*
Sawyer, (L.) Diane *television journalist*
Sawyer, Forrest *newscaster*

Sawyer, William Dale physician, educator, university dean, foundation administrator
Saxe, Leonard social psychologist, educator
Saxena, Brij B. biochemist, endocrinologist, educator
Saylor, Steven Warren writer prose, fiction
Scala, Gale G. lawyer
Scanlon, Peter Redmond accountant
Scanlon, Rosemary economist
Scarborough, Charles Bishop, III broadcast journalist, writer
Scardino, Michael Christopher advertising executive
Scaturro, Philip David investment banker
Scavullo, Francesco photographer
Scelsa, Joseph Vincent sociologist
Schaap, Richard Jay journalist
Schacht, Ronald Stuart lawyer
Schachter, Oscar lawyer, educator, arbitrator
Schachter, Stanley psychology educator
Schade, Malcolm Robert lawyer
†Schaffer, Kenneth B. communications executive, satellite engineer, inventor, consultant
Schaffer, Seth Andrew lawyer
†Schaffner, Bertram Henry psychiatrist
Schaffran, Charles Brad investment company executive
Schallert, Edwin Glenn lawyer
Schama, Simon historian, educator, author
Schanberg, Sydney Hillel newspaper editor, columnist
Schapiro, Donald lawyer
Schapiro, Miriam artist
Schapiro, Morris A. investment banker
Schaub, Sherwood Anhder, Jr. management consultant
Schechner, Richard theater director, author, educator
Schechter, Daniel Philip lawyer
Scheeder, Louis theater producer, director, educator
Scheinberg, Labe Charles physician, educator
Scheindlin, Raymond Paul Hebrew literature educator, translator
Scheler, Brad Eric lawyer
Schenk, Deborah Huffman law educator
Scher, Irving lawyer
Scher, Stanley Jules lawyer
Schiavi, Raul Constante psychiatrist, educator, researcher
Schick, Elliot business executive
Schick, Harry Leon investment company executive
Schickele, Peter composer
Schieffer, Bob broadcast journalist
Schiff, David Tevele investment banker
Schiffer, Claudia model
†Schiffman, Stephan management consultant, writer
Schiffrin, Andre publisher
Schilling, Warner Roller political scientist, educator
Schindler, Alexander Moshe rabbi, organization executive
Schirmeister, Charles F. lawyer
Schisgal, Murray Joseph playwright
Schizer, Zevie Baruch lawyer
Schlaifer, Charles advertising executive
Schlein, Carol Leslie lawyer
Schlein, Dov C. banker
Schlesinger, Arthur (Meier), Jr. writer, educator
Schlesinger, David Harvey medical educator, researcher
Schlesinger, Edward Bruce neurological surgeon
Schlesinger, Sanford Joel lawyer
Schless, Phyllis Ross investment banker
Schlessinger, Joseph pharmacology educator
†Schley, William Shain otorhinolaryngologist
Schmemann, Serge journalist
Schmertz, Eric Joseph lawyer, educator
Schmertz, Herbert public relations and advertising executive
Schmertz, Mildred Floyd editor, writer
Schmetterer, Robert Allen advertising executive
Schmidt, Richard Frederick business executive
Schmidt, Stanley Albert editor, writer
Schmitter, Charles Harry electronics manufacturing company executive, lawyer
Schmitz, Robert Allen publishing executive, investor
Schmolka, Leo Louis law educator
Schnabel, Julian artist
Schnackenberg, Gjertrud Cecelia poet
Schnall, Flora lawyer
Schneck, Jerome M. psychiatrist, medical historian, educator
Schneider, Bernard industrial machinery executive
Schneider, Donald Frederic banker
Schneider, Howard lawyer
Schneider, JoAnne artist
Schneider, Martin Aaron photojournalist, ecologist, engineer, writer, artist, television director, public intervenor, educator, university instructor, lecturer
Schneider, Norman M. food manufacturing company executive
Schneider, Willys Hope lawyer
Schneiderman, David Abbott publisher, journalist
Schneiderman, Irwin lawyer
Schneier, Harvey Allen physician, pharmaceutical researcher
Schnell, Joseph dancer
Schonberg, Harold Charles music critic, columnist
Schoonover, Jean Way public relations consultant
Schor, Laura Strumingher historian, academic administrator
Schorer, Suki ballet teacher
Schorsch, Ismar clergyman, Jewish history educator
Schotter, Andrew Roye economics educator, consultant
Schrag, Karl artist
Schragis, Steven M. publisher, lawyer
Schramm, Texas E. football league executive
Schreiber, Paul Solomon lawyer
Schreyer, Leslie John lawyer
Schriever, Fred Martin energy, environmental and information technology executive
Schroder, Raymond A. petroleum company executive
Schroeder, Aaron Harold songwriter
Schroeder, Edmund R. lawyer
Schrutt, Norman broadcast company executive
Schubart, Mark Allen arts and education executive
Schuchert, Joseph light manufacturing executive
Schueller, Thomas George lawyer
Schulberg, Budd author
Schulhof, Michael Peter entertainment, electronics company executive
Schulman, Grace poet, English language educator
†Schulman, Mark Allen market research company executive
Schulman, Paul Martin advertising executive
Schulte, Stephen John lawyer, educator
†Schumacher, Hans Heinrich steel company executive
Schumacher, Robert Denison banker
Schupak, Leslie Allen public relations company executive
Schur, Jeffrey advertising executive
Schuster, Karen Sutton administrator
Schuur, Robert George lawyer
Schwab, Frank, Jr. management consultant
Schwab, George David social science educator
Schwab, Terrance Walter lawyer
Schwarcz, Steven Lance lawyer
†Schwartz, Alan Victor advertising executive
Schwartz, Allen G. federal judge
†Schwartz, Amy Margaret children's book author, illustrator
Schwartz, Anna Jacobson economic historian
Schwartz, Arthur Robert food writer, critic, consultant
Schwartz, Bernard L. electronics company executive
Schwartz, Daniel Bennett artist
Schwartz, Eugene M. art collector, patron
Schwartz, Felice N. social activist, educator
Schwartz, Herbert Frederick lawyer
Schwartz, Irving Leon physician, scientist, educator
Schwartz, Jack Theodore retired publisher
Schwartz, Marvin lawyer
Schwartz, Melvin physics educator, laboratory administrator
Schwartz, Mischa electrical engineering educator
Schwartz, R. Malcolm management consultant
Schwartz, Renee Gerstler lawyer
Schwartz, Robert George retired insurance company executive
Schwartz, Roselind Shirley Grant podiatrist
Schwartz, Stephen Lawrence composer, lyricist
Schwartz, William lawyer, educator
Schwartzman, David economist, educator
Schwarz, Gerard conductor, musician
Schwarz, H. Marshall trust company executive
Schwarz, Melvin A. lawyer
Schwarz, Ralph Jacques engineering educator
Schwarz, Richard Howard obstetrician/gynecologist, educator
Schwarzkopf, H. Norman retired army officer, engineer
Schwed, Peter author, retired editor and publisher
Schweitzer, Melvin L. commissioner, lawyer
Schwerin, Warren Lyons real estate developer
Schwind, Michael Angelo law educator
Sciarratta, Patrick Louis director, educator, artistic director
Scieszka, Jon children's author
Scofield, John jazz guitarist
Scopaz, John Matthew banker
Scorsese, Martin film director, writer
†Scott, Dale Allan major league umpire
Scott, Helen S. law educator
†Scott, Michael Lester artist, educator
Scott, Mimi Koblenz actress, psychotherapist
Scott, Willard Herman radio and television performer
Scott, William Clement, III entertainment industry executive
Scotto, Renata soprano
Scowcroft, John Arthur portfolio manager
Scribner, Charles, III publisher, art historian, lecturer
Scroggins, Richard Muir real estate executive
Scully, Sean Paul artist
Scurry, Richardson Gano, Jr. real estate company financial executive
Scutt, Der architect
Seadler, Stephen Edward business and computer consultant, social scientist
Seaman, Alfred Barrett journalist
Seaman, Alfred Jarvis retired advertising agency executive
Seaman, Barbara (Ann Rosner) author
Seaman, Robert Lee lawyer
Searle, Ronald artist
Seaver, Tom (George Thomas Seaver) former professional baseball player
†Secrist, Richard A. industrial company executive
Secunda, Arthur (Holland Secunda) artist
Secunda, Don Elliott lawyer, realtor
Secunda, Eugene marketing communications executive, educator
Sedaka, Neil singer, songwriter
Sederbaum, Arthur David lawyer
Sedlin, Elias David physician, orthopedic researcher, educator
Seegal, Herbert Leonard department store executive
Seeger, Pete folk singer, songwriter
Seely, Robert Daniel physician, medical educator
Seessel, Thomas Vining nonprofit organization executive
Seff, Leslie S. securities trader
Segal, George actor
Segal, George sculptor
Segal, Joel Michael advertising executive
Segal, Jonathan Bruce editor
Segal, Lore writer
Segal, Martin Eli retired actuarial and consulting company executive
Segal, Sheldon Jerome biologist, educator, foundation administrator
Segal, Stephen Martin advertising executive
Segalas, Hercules Anthony investment banker
Segall, Harold Abraham lawyer
Segesváry, Victor Győző retired diplomat
Seidelman, Susan film director
Seiden, Henry (Hank Seiden) advertising executive
†Seidenberg, Ivan G. telecommunications company executive
Seidler, Lynn L. foundation executive
Seidler, Norman Howard lawyer
Seidman, Herta Lande international trade and information company executive
Seidman, Samuel Nathan investment banker, economist
Seifert, Thomas Lloyd lawyer
Seigel, Jerrold Edward historian, writer
Seigel, Stuart Evan lawyer
Seippel, Thomas J. insurance executive
Seitz, Frederick university president emeritus
Selby, Cecily Cannan dean, educator, scientist
Selig, Karl-Ludwig language and literature educator
Seliger, Charles artist
Seliger, Mark Alan photographer
Seligman, Daniel editor
Seligson, Carl H. investment banker
Selkowitz, Arthur advertising agency executive
Sellers, Peter Hoadley mathematician
†Sellers, Wallace Osborne financial services company executive
Sells, Harold E. retail company executive
Seltzer, Leo filmmaker, educator, lecturer
Seltzer, Richard C. lawyer
Selver, Paul Darryl lawyer
Semaya, Francine L. lawyer
Semmel, Bernard historian, educator
Sendak, Maurice Bernard writer, illustrator
Sendax, Victor Irven dentist, educator, dental implant researcher
Sendrovic, Israel bank executive
Senior, Enrique Francisco investment banker
Sennett, Richard sociologist, writer
†Senter, Alan Zachary communications company executive
Senzel, Martin Lee lawyer
Sepahpur, Hayedeh C(hristine) investment executive
Seraphine, Danny Peter drummer
Serbaroli, Francis J. lawyer, educator, writer
Serkin, Peter pianist
Serota, James Ian lawyer
Serota, Susan Perlstadt lawyer
Serra, Richard sculptor
†Servedio, Dominick Michael engineering executive
Serwatka, Walter Dennis publishing executive
Seth, Vikram writer
Setrakian, Berge lawyer
Settipani, Frank G. news correspondent
Settle, Mary Lee author
Severs, Charles A., III lawyer
Seward, George Chester lawyer
Sexton, John Edward lawyer, educator
Sexton, Richard lawyer, diversified manufacturing company executive
Seymore, James W., Jr. magazine editor
Shachar, Avishai lawyer
Shadwell, Wendy Joan curator, writer
Shaffer, David psychiatrist
Shaffer, Paul musician, bandleader
Shaffer, Peter Levin playwright
Shaffer, Russell K. advertising agency executive
†Shain, Harold magazine publisher
Shaine, Theodore Harris advertising agency executive
Shainess, Natalie psychiatrist, educator
Shair, David Ira human resources executive
Shane, Rita opera singer
Shange, Ntozake (Paulette Williams) playwright, poet
Shanks, David publishing executive
Shanks, Eugene B., Jr. banker
Shanley, Ellen costume curator
Shanley, William C., III sugar company executive
Shanman, James Alan lawyer
Shapiro, Babe artist
Shapiro, Ellen Marie graphic design company executive, writer
Shapiro, George M. lawyer
Shapiro, Harvey poet
Shapiro, Howard Alan lawyer
Shapiro, Ivan lawyer
Shapiro, Jerome Gerson lawyer
Shapiro, Joel Elias artist
Shapiro, Judith R. anthropology educator, academic administrator
Shapiro, Marvin Lincoln communications company executive
Shapiro, Murray structural engineer
Shapiro, Myra Stein poet
Shapiro, Robert Frank investment banking company executive
Shapiro, Theodore psychiatrist, educator
Shapley, Robert Martin neurophysiology and perception educator
Shapoff, Stephen H. financial executive
Sharbel, Jean M. editor
Sharp, Daniel Asher foundation executive, corporate consultant
Sharpe, Jean Elizabeth lawyer
Shattuck, Scott Harlan performing company executive
Shaviro, Daniel Nathan law educator
Shaw, Alan Roger financial executive, educator
Shaw, (Francis) Harold performing arts administrator
Shaw, (George) Kendall artist, educator
Shaw, L. Edward, Jr. lawyer
Shaw, William diversified telecommunications company executive
Shawn, Wallace playwright, actor
Shaykin, Leonard P. investor
Shays, Rona Joyce lawyer
Shea, Dion Warren Joseph association executive
Shea, Edward Emmett lawyer, educator, author
Shea, James William lawyer
Sheehan, Robert W. lawyer
Sheehan, Susan writer
Sheehy, Eugene Paul retired librarian, author
Sheets, Michael Jay consumer products company executive
Sheinkman, Jack union official, lawyer
Shelanski, Michael L. cell biologist, educator
Shelby, Jerome lawyer
Sheldon, Eleanor Harriet Bernert sociologist
Sheldon, Sidney author
Shelley, Carole Augusta actress
Shellman, Eddie J. ballet dancer, teacher, choreographer
Shelp, Ronald Kent non-profit business and trade association executive, author, lecturer, consultant
Shen, Theodore Ping investment banker
Shenker, Joseph college administrator
Shenton, James Patrick history educator
Shepard, Elaine Elizabeth writer, lecturer
Shepard, Robert M. lawyer, investment banker, engineer
Shepard, Stephen Benjamin journalist, magazine editor
†Shepard, Thomas Rockwell, III magazine executive
Sheppard, William Stevens investment banker
Sherak, Thomas Mitchell motion picture company executive
Sherman, Arlene television producer
Sherman, Cindy artist
Sherman, Eugene Jay marketing executive, economist
Sherman, Jeffrey Barry retail executive
Sherman, Norman Mark advertising agency executive
Sherman, Randolph S. lawyer
Sherman, Saul Lawrence lawyer, government official
†Sherman, Saul S. manufacturing company executive
Sherr, Lynn Beth TV news correspondent
Sherrill, H. Virgil securities company executive, manufacturing company executive
Sherrod, Lonnie Ray foundation administrator, researcher, psychologist
Sherry, George Leon political science educator
Sherva, Dennis G. investment company executive
Shestack, Melvin Bernard editor, author, filmmaker, television producer
Shevack, Brett David advertising agency executive
Shields, James Joseph, Jr. educator, educational administrator, author
Shientag, Florence Perlow lawyer
Shier, Shelley M. production company executive
Shikler, Aaron artist
Shimer, Zachary lawyer
Shineman, Edward William, Jr. retired pharmaceutical executive
Shinn, George Latimer investment banker, consultant, educator
Shinn, Richard Randolph former insurance executive, former stock exchange executive
Shinnar, Reuel chemical engineering educator, industrial consultant
Shipley, L. Parks, Jr. banker
Shipley, Walter Vincent banker
Shnayerson, Robert Beahan editor
Shore, Stephen photographer
Short, Robert Waltrip (Bobby Short) entertainer, author
Shorter, James Russell, Jr. lawyer
Shortz, Will puzzle editor
Shoss, Cynthia Renée lawyer
Shostakovich, Maxim Dmitriyevich symphonic conductor
Shpilberg, David management consultant, artificial intelligence researcher
Shriver, Donald Woods, Jr. theology educator
Shriver, Maria Owings news correspondent
Shuff, Lily artist, wood engraver
Shulevitz, Uri author, illustrator
Shull, Richard Bruce actor
Shuman, Stanley S. investment banker
Shupack, Paul Martin law educator
Shur, Walter retired insurance company executive
Shwartz, Robert N. lawyer
Shyer, John D. lawyer
†Sibley, Alden Kingsland former organization executive, retired army officer
Sidamon-Eristoff, Anne Phipps museum official
Sidamon-Eristoff, Constantine lawyer
Sidney, Sylvia (Sophia Kossow) actress
Sidran, Miriam retired physics educator, researcher
Siebert, Muriel brokerage house executive, former state banking official
Siegal, Allan Marshall newspaper editor
Siegel, Jeffrey Norton lawyer
Siegel, Joel Steven television news correspondent
Siegel, Marc Monroe television and film producer, writer, director
Siegel, Martin Jay lawyer, investment advisor
Siegel, Marvin newspaper editor
Siegel, Morton Kallos religious organization administrator, educational administrator
Siegel, Stanley lawyer, educator
Siegler, Thomas Edmund investment banking executive
†Siegman, Henry association executive
Siekevitz, Philip biology educator
Siemer, Fred Harold securities analyst
Sienkiewicz, John Casimir insurance company executive
Siffert, Robert Spencer orthopedic surgeon
Sifton, Elisabeth book publisher
Siguler, George William financial services executive
Silber, William L. finance educator
Silberberg, Richard Howard lawyer
Silberman, Charles Eliot magazine editor, author
Silberman, H. Lee public relations executive
Silberman, James Henry editor, publisher
Silberman, John Alan lawyer
Silberman, Linda Joy lawyer, educator
Silfen, David M. investment banker
Silkenat, James Robert lawyer
Silleck, Harry Garrison lawyer
Sills, Beverly (Mrs. Peter B. Greenough) opera company director, coloratura soprano
Silver, Joan Micklin film director, screenwriter
Silver, Morris economist, educator
Silver, Paul architect
Silver, Philip Warnock Spanish language educator
Silver, Richard Tobias physician, educator
Silver, Ron actor, director
Silver, Sheldon lawyer, state legislator
Silverberg, Michael Joel lawyer
Silverman, Al editor
Silverman, Arthur Charles lawyer
Silverman, Burton Philip artist
Silverman, Henry Richard diversified business executive, lawyer
Silverman, Herbert R. corporate financial executive
Silverman, Jeffrey Stuart manufacturing executive
Silverman, Kenneth Eugene English educator, writer
Silverman, Marylin A. advertising agency executive
Silverman, Moses lawyer
Silverman, Samuel Joshua lawyer
Silverman, Stephen Meredith journalist, screenwriter, producer
†Silverman, Sydel Finfer anthropologist
Silvers, Eileen S. lawyer
Silvers, Robert Benjamin editor
Silvers, Sally choreographer, performing company executive
Silverstein, Howard Alan investment banker
Silverstein, Samuel Charles cellular biology and physiology educator, researcher
Silverstein, Shelby (Shel Silverstein) author, cartoonist, composer, folksinger
Sim, Craig Stephen investment banker
Simmons, Charles author
Simmons, Dan science fiction writer
Simmons, Gene musician
Simmons, Hardwick investment banker
Simmons, J. Gerald management consultant
Simmons, John Derek investment banker
Simmons, Russell recording industry executive
Simmons, Samuel Lee corporate executive
Simon, Caroline K(lein) lawyer
Simon, Eric Jacob neurochemist, educator
Simon, Jacqueline Albert political scientist, writer
Simon, Joanna singer
Simon, John Ivan film and drama critic
Simon, Neil playwright, television writer
Simon, Norma Plavnick psychologist
Simon, Ronald Charles curator
Simone, Joseph R. lawyer
Simons, Albert, III lawyer
Simons, Kent Cobb mutual fund executive
Simonson, Lee Stuart broadcast company executive
Simpson, Linda Ann lawyer
Simpson, Mary Michael priest, psychotherapist
Simpson, William Arthur insurance company executive
Sinclair, Daisy advertising executive, casting director
Singer, Arthur Louis, Jr. foundation executive
Singer-Magdoff, Laura Joan Silver (Mrs. Samuel Magdoff) psychotherapist
Singerman, Martin newspaper publishing executive
Singh, Jyoti Shankar political organization director
Singleton, Donald Edward journalist
Sinsheimer, Warren Jack lawyer
Siphron, Joseph Rider lawyer
†Siris, Ethel Silverman endocrinologist
Sirowitz, Leonard advertising agency executive

Sis, Peter *illustrator, children's book author, artist, filmmaker*
Sischy, Ingrid Barbara *magazine editor, art critic*
Sisk, Robert Joseph *lawyer*
Siskind, Arthur *lawyer, director*
Siskind, Donald Henry *lawyer*
Sisman, Elaine Rochelle *musicology educator*
Sitarz, Anneliese Lotte *pediatrics educator, physician*
Sitrick, James Baker *lawyer*
Sive, David *lawyer*
Skigen, Patricia Sue *lawyer*
Skillin, Edward Simeon *magazine publisher*
†Skinner, David Bernt *surgeon, educator*
Skinner, Peter Graeme *publishing executive, lawyer*
Skirnick, Robert Andrew *lawyer*
Sklaren, Cary Stewart *lawyer*
Skomorowsky, Peter P. *accounting company executive*
Skupinski, Bogdan Kazimierz *artist*
Skwiersky, Paul *accountant*
Sky, Alison *artist, designer*
Slade, Bernard *playwright*
Slain, John Joseph *legal educator*
Slate, William Kenneth, II *international dispute resolution association executive*
Slater, Jill Sherry *lawyer*
Slater, Joseph Elliott *educational institute administrator*
Slavin, Arlene *artist*
Slavin, Neal *photographer*
†Sleator, Tycho *physics educator*
Sleed, Joel *newspaper editor*
Sleigh, Sylvia *artist, educator*
†Sloan, Allan Herbert *journalist*
Sloan, Stephen Stehly *investment banker*
Slomanson, Lloyd Howard *architect, musician*
Slonaker, Norman Dale *lawyer*
Slone, Adolph *liquor manufacturing executive*
Slusser, William Peter *investment banker*
Slutsky, Lorie Ann *foundation executive*
Small, Elaine Luchak *banker*
Small, George LeRoy *geographer, educator*
Small, Jeffrey *lawyer, law educator*
Small, Jonathan Andrew *lawyer*
Smalley, David Vincent *lawyer*
Smart, L(ouis) Edwin, Jr. *lawyer, business executive*
Smethurst, E(dward) William, Jr. *brokerage house executive*
Smit, Hans *law educator, academic administrator, lawyer*
Smith, Alexander John Court *insurance executive*
Smith, Anna Deavere *actress, playwright*
Smith, Anna Nicole *model*
Smith, Bradley Youle *lawyer*
Smith, Brian J. *diversified chemical executive*
Smith, Clarence O'Farrell *publishing company executive*
Smith, Corlies Morgan *publishing executive*
Smith, Datus Clifford, Jr. *former foundation executive, publisher*
Smith, Derek Armand *publishing company executive*
Smith, Edward Paul, Jr. *lawyer*
Smith, G. E. Kidder *architect, author*
Smith, George S., Jr. *communications financial executive*
Smith, Gordon H. *civil engineer*
Smith, Guy Lincoln, IV *strategic communications company executive*
†Smith, Harold Charles *private pension fund executive*
Smith, Hilary Cranwell Bowen *investment banker*
Smith, J. Kellum, Jr. *foundation executive, lawyer*
Smith, James Oscar (Jimmy Smith) *jazz organist*
Smith, Jim *advertising executive*
Smith, John Matthew *insurance company executive*
Smith, Joseph Phelan *film company executive*
Smith, Kathleen Tener *bank executive*
†Smith, Lane *illustrator, author*
Smith, Leon Polk *artist*
Smith, Liz (Mary Elizabeth Smith) *newspaper columnist, broadcast journalist*
Smith, Lowell *dancer*
Smith, Malcolm Bernard *investment company executive*
Smith, Malcolm Sommerville *bass*
Smith, Murray Livingstone *advertising executive*
Smith, Norman Obed *physical chemist, educator*
Smith, Paul J. *museum adminstrator*
Smith, Paul Thomas *financial services company executive*
Smith, Peter Bennett *banker*
†Smith, Peter Douglas *dean*
Smith, Phillips Guy *banker*
Smith, Pierce Reiland *stock brokerage, investment banking executive*
Smith, R. Evan *lawyer*
Smith, R. Jeffery *grain company executive*
Smith, Richard Mills *editor in chief, magazine executive*
Smith, Robert Everett *lawyer*
Smith, Robert Kimmel *author*
Smith, Shirley *artist*
Smith, Steven James *insurance company executive*
Smith, Stuart A. *lawyer*
Smith, Vincent DaCosta *artist*
Smith, Vincent Milton *lawyer*
Smith, William Jay *author*
Smith, Winthrop Hiram, Jr. *financial services executive*
Smith-Miller, Henry Houck *architect*
Smithson, Luther Harris *diversified electronics research company executive*
Smolinski, Edward Albert *holding company executive, lawyer, accountant, deacon*
Smotrich, David Isadore *architect*
Snibbe, Richard W. *architect*
Snitow, Charles *lawyer*
Snyder, Richard Elliott *publishing company executive*
Sobel, Shepard Michael *artistic director*
Softness, John *public relations executive*
Sohmer, Bernard *mathematics educator, administrator*
Soika, Helmut Emil *retirement plan administrator*
†Sokol, Marc Jeffrey *arts administrator*
Solar, Richard Leon *banker*
Soldatos, Paul W. *holding company executive*
Solender, Sanford *social worker*
Solender, Stephen David *philanthropic organization executive*
Solheim, James Edward *church executive, journalist*
Solinger, David Morris *lawyer*
Soiman, Joseph *artist*
Solomon, Howard *pharmaceutical company executive*
Solomon, Joseph *lawyer*
Solomon, Maynard Elliott *music historian, former recording company executive*
Solomon, Zachary Leon *apparel manufacturing company executive*
Solomons, Gus, Jr. (Gustave Martinez) *choreographer, dancer, writer*
Solov, Zachary *choreographer, ballet artist*
Somasundaran, Ponisseril *surface and colloid engineering, applied science educator*
Somers, John Arthur *insurance company executive*
Somerville, Robert Eugene *historian*
Somerville, Theodore Elkin *lawyer*
Somnolet, Michel Pierre *cosmetics company financial executive*
Sompolski, Timothy Andrew *benefits compensation executive*
Sonenberg, Martin *biochemistry educator, physician*
Songster, John Hugh *legal administrator*
Sonneman, Eve *artist*
Sonnenberg, Ben *playwright, poet, editor*
Sontag, Susan *writer*
Sookram, Atma Ram *transportation engineer*
Soreff, Stephen Mayer *artist*
Sorel, Claudette Marguerite *pianist*
†Soren, Howard *textiles executive*
Soren, Tabitha L. *television newscaster, writer*
Sorensen, Burton Erhard *investment banker*
Sorensen, Gillian Martin *United Nations official*
Sorensen, Theodore Chaikin *lawyer, former special counsel to President of U.S.*
Sorkin, Laurence Truman *lawyer*
Soros, George *fund management executive*
Sorrel, William Edwin *psychiatrist, educator, psychoanalyst*
Sorrentino, Ralph Joseph *controller*
Sorter, George Hans *accounting and law educator, consultant*
Soter, George Nicholas *advertising executive*
Soto, Jock *dancer*
Sotomayor, Sonia *federal judge*
Souham, Gérard *communications executive*
Soule, Gardner Bosworth *writer*
Soutar, Charles Frederick *utilities executive*
Southall, Ivan Francis *author*
Sovern, Michael Ira *law educator*
Soyer, David *cellist, music educator*
Soyster, Margaret Blair *lawyer*
Spacey, Kevin *actor*
Spaeh, Winfried Heinrich *banker*
Spangler, Arnold Eugene *investment banker*
Sparano, Vincent Thomas *editor*
Spatt, Robert Edward *lawyer*
Spear, Harvey M. *lawyer*
Speciale, Richard *bank executive*
†Speck, William T. *health facility administrator*
Spector, Abraham *ophthalmic biochemist, educator, laboratory administrator*
Spelker, Arnold William *banker*
Spence, James Robert, Jr. *television sports executive*
Spencer, Henry Benning *insurance industry investment advisor*
Spencer, Scott *novelist*
Sperakis, Nicholas George *artist*
Sperling, Allan George *lawyer*
Sperry, Sandra Phillips *nursing administrator*
Speth, James Gustave *United Nations executive, lawyer*
Spiegel, Arthur Henry, III *managing director, president*
Spiegel, Edward A. *astrophysicist, fluid dynamicist, educator*
Spiegel, Herbert *psychiatrist, educator*
Spiegelman, Art *author, cartoonist*
Spielvogel, Carl *international marketing executive*
Spielvogel, Sidney Meyer *investment banker*
Spilerman, Seymour *sociologist, educator*
Spinella, Stephen *actor*
Spinks, Michael *retired professional boxer*
Spira, Patricia G. *performing arts association executive*
Spivack, Gordon Bernard *lawyer, lecturer*
†Spivak, Joan Carol *medical public relations specialist*
Spizzirri, Richard Dominic *lawyer*
Spooner, Forrest Allen *insurance company executive*
Sprague, Peter Julian *semiconductor company executive, lecturer*
Spring, Michael *editor, writer*
Springer, John Shipman *public relations executive*
Springsteen, Bruce *singer, songwriter, guitarist*
Sprinson, David Benjamin *biochemistry educator*
Sprizzo, John Emilio *federal judge*
Sproat, Christopher Townsend *artist*
Spruch, Larry *physicist, educator*
Squire, Walter Charles *lawyer*
Stack, Edward William *business management and foundation executive*
Stade, George Gustav *humanities educator*
Staheli, Donald L. *grain company executive*
Stahl, Alan Michael *curator*
Stahl, Lesley R. *journalist*
Staley, Delbert C. *telecommunications executive*
Stamas, Stephen *investment executive*
Stamos, Theodoros *artist*
Standen, Michael *metal products company executive*
Stanger, Abraham M. *lawyer*
Stanger, Ila *writer, editor*
Staniar, Burton B. *entertainment company executive*
Stanley, Bob *artist*
Stanton, Alexander *public relations executive*
Stanton, Edward M. *public relations company executive*
Stanton, Frank *communications executive*
Stanton, Ronald P. *export company executive*
Stapp, Olivia Brewer *opera singer*
Stark, Richard Boies *surgeon, artist*
Starn, Douglas *artist, photographer*
Starn, Mike P. *artist, photographer*
Starr, Martin Kenneth *management educator*
Stasior, William F. *engineering company executive*
Stauffer, Michael Kirk *communications executive, consultant*
Stawasz, Cherie *public relations executive*
Steedman, Doria Lynne Silberberg *advertising agency executive*
Steel, Danielle Fernande *author*
Steele, Harry Gerard *diversified company executive*
Steere, William Campbell, Jr. *pharmaceutical company executive*
Stefanelli, Joseph James (Joe Stefanelli) *artist*
Steffen, Christopher J. *bank executive*
Steffens, John Laundon *brokerage house executive*
Steiger, Heidi Schwarzbauer *investment executive*
Steiger, Paul Ernest *newspaper editor, journalist*
Stein, Bennett Mueller *neurosurgeon*
Stein, Bernard *stockbroker*
Stein, Carl *architect*
Stein, David Fred *investment executive*
Stein, Gilbert *professional hockey executive*
Stein, Howard *mutual fund executive*
Stein, Howard S. *banker*
Stein, Joseph *playwright*
Stein, Martin Donald *architect*
Stein, Marvin *psychiatrist, educator*
Stein, Robert William *actuary, accountant*
Stein, Stephen William *lawyer*
Steinberg, Arthur Jay *lawyer*
Steinberg, Howard Eli *lawyer, holding company executive*
Steinberg, Joseph Saul *investment company executive*
Steinberg, Leo *art historian, educator*
Steinberg, Michael *department store executive*
Steinberg, Robert M. *holding company executive*
Steinberg, Saul *artist*
Steinberg, Saul Phillip *holding company executive*
Steinberg, Stephen Arthur *information systems executive*
Steinem, Gloria *writer, editor, lecturer*
Steiner, Jeffrey Josef *industrial manufacturing company executive*
Steiner, Lee Nathan *lawyer*
Steinfeld, Thomas Albert *publisher*
Steinfels, Margaret O'Brien *editor*
†Steinfels, Peter Francis *newspaper correspondent, writer*
Steinmetz, Richard Bird, Jr. *holding company executive, lawyer*
†Steinmetz, Sol *publishing company editor*
Steir, Pat Iris *artist*
Stella, Frank Philip *artist*
Stemmer, Wayne J. *real estate and financial services company executive*
Stenzel, Kurt Hodgson *physician, nephrologist, educator*
Stepan, Alfred C. *political science educator, author*
Stephens, Gary Ralph *American literature and journalism educator*
Stephens, Lester John, Jr. *banker*
Stephens, Olin James, II *naval architect, yacht designer*
Stephenson, Alan Clements *lawyer*
†Stepler, Richard Lewis *magazine editor*
Stergios, Peter Doe *lawyer*
Sterling, David M. *graphic designer*
Sterling, Robert Lee, Jr. *investment company executive*
Stern, David Joel *basketball association executive*
Stern, Fritz Richard *historian, educator*
Stern, Howard Allan *radio disc jockey, television show host*
Stern, Isaac *violinist*
Stern, James Andrew *investment banker*
Stern, Joseph A. *lawyer*
Stern, Leonard Norman *pet supply manufacturing company executive*
Stern, Leslie Warren *management consultant*
Stern, Lewis Arthur *lawyer*
Stern, Madeleine Bettina *rare books dealer, author*
Stern, Marvin *psychiatrist, educator*
Stern, Robert Arthur Morton *architect, educator*
Stern, Robert D. *publishing executive*
Stern, Roslyne Paige *magazine publisher*
Stern, Stanley B. *investment banker*
†Stern, Walter Phillips *investment executive*
Sternberg, Seymour *insurance company executive*
Sternglass, Lila M. *advertising agency executive*
Sternman, Joel W. *lawyer*
Sterrett, Jane Evelyne *illustrator, artist*
Steuer, Richard Marc *lawyer*
Stevens, Art *public relations executive*
Stevens, Martin *English educator*
Stevens, Shane *novelist*
Stevenson, Justin Jason, III *lawyer*
†Stevenson, Nikolai *medical association executive*
Stevenson, William Henri *author*
Stever, Donald Winfred *lawyer*
Steves, Gale C. *editor*
Stewart, Charles Evan *lawyer*
Stewart, Duncan James *lawyer*
Stewart, James B. *journalist*
Stewart, James M. *merchant banker*
Stewart, James Montgomery *banker*
Stewart, Jeff *advertising agency executive*
Stewart, Kirk T. *public relations executive*
Stewart, Mary Florence Elinor *author*
Stewart, Richard Burleson *lawyer, educator*
Steyer, Roy Henry *retired lawyer*
Stiebel, Gerald Gustave *art dealer*
Stiefler, Jeffrey E. *financial services executive*
†Stiles, Ned Berry *lawyer*
Stiles, Thomas Beveridge, II *investment banking executive*
Still, William Clark, Jr. *chemistry educator*
Stills, Stephen *musician, vocalist, composer*
Stilwell, Richard Dale *baritone*
Stimmel, Barry *cardiologist, internist, educator, university dean*
Stocker, Jule E(lias) *lawyer*
Stockman, David Allen *former federal official, congressman, financier*
Stoddard, George Earl *investment company financial executive*
Stoddard, Laurence Ralph, Jr. *advertising executive*
Stoll, Neal Richard *lawyer*
Stolper, Pinchas Aryeh *religious organization executive, rabbi*
Stoltzman, Richard Leslie *clarinetist*
Stone, Allan Barry *art gallery director*
Stone, Bonnie Carol *healthcare executive*
Stone, David Kendall *financial executive*
Stone, David Philip *lawyer*
Stone, Lewis Bart *lawyer*
Stone, Merrill Brent *lawyer*
Stone, Peter *playwright, scenarist*
Stone, Richard B. *law educator*
Stone, Robert Anthony *author*
Stookey, John Hoyt *chemical company executive*
Storette, Ronald Frank *lawyer*
Stork, Gilbert (Josse) *chemistry educator, investigator*
Storke, William Frederick Joseph *film producer*
Storr, Robert *curator painting and sculpture, artist, writer*
Stossel, John *news analyst*
Stovall, Robert H(enry) *money management company executive*
Stowers, Carlton Eugene *writer*
Stram, Hank Louis *former professional football coach, television and radio commentator*
Strand, Curt Robert *hotel executive*
Strand, Mark *poet*
Strasfogel, Ian *stage director*
Stratas, Teresa (Anastasia Strataki) *opera singer, soprano*
Straton, John Charles, Jr. *investment banker*
Stratton, Walter Love *lawyer*
Straub, Chester John *lawyer*
Strauber, Donald I. *lawyer*
Straus, Alan Gordon *lawyer*
Straus, Donald Blun *retired company executive*
Straus, Irving Lehman *public relations executive*
Straus, Kenneth Hollister *former retail store executive*
Straus, Melville *investment company executive*
Straus, Oscar S., II *foundation executive*
Straus, Roger W., Jr. *publishing company executive*
Straus, Roger W, III *book publishing executive, photographer*
Strauss, Audrey *lawyer*
Strauss, Edward Robert *carpet company executive*
Strauss, Peter L(ester) *law educator*
Strear, Joseph D. *public relations executive*
Strelzer, Martin *religious organization administrator*
Stretton, Ross *ballet dancer*
Strevey, Tracy Elmer, Jr. *army officer, surgeon*
Strickon, Harvey Alan *lawyer*
Stringer, Howard *television executive*
Stroke, Hinko Henry *physicist, educator*
Strom, Milton Gary *lawyer*
Strong, Robert S. *banker*
Strong, William L., III *investment executive*
Stroock, Mark Edwin, II *public relations company executive*
Strossen, Nadine *law educator, human rights activist*
Strum, Brian J. *real estate executive*
Strum, Jay Gerson *lawyer*
Strupp, David John *lawyer*
Struve, Guy Miller *lawyer*
Stuart, Carole *publishing executive*
Stuart, John McHugh, Jr. *public relations consultant, retired foreign service officer*
Stuart, Lyle *publishing company executive*
Sturges, John Siebrand *management consultant*
Sturtevant, Peter Mann, Jr. *television news executive*
†Stutzmann, Nathalie *classical vocalist*
Stux, Ivan Ernest *financial executive*
Subak-Sharpe, Genell Jackson *editor, writer*
Subak-Sharpe, Gerald Emil *electrical engineer, educator*
Sugarman, George *artist*
Sugarman, Irwin J. *lawyer*
Sugarman, Robert Gary *lawyer*
Sugihara, Kenzi *publishing executive*
Sugimoto, Yoshihisa *import/export company executive*
Suhr, J. Nicholas *lawyer*
Sui, Anna *fashion designer*
Sulcer, Frederick Durham *advertising executive*
Sulger, Francis Xavier *lawyer*
Sulimirski, Witold Stanislaw *investment company executive*
Sullivan, Anne Elizabeth *publishing executive*
Sullivan, Eugene John Joseph *manufacturing company executive*
Sullivan, Joseph Peter *insurance broker*
Sullivan, Thomas John *communications company executive*
Sullivan, Walter Seager *editor, author*
Sultan, Donald Keith *artist, printmaker*
Sulzberger, Arthur Ochs *newspaper executive*
Sulzberger, Arthur Ochs, Jr. *newspaper publisher*
Summers, Andy (Andrew James Somers) *popular musician*
Surrey, Milt *artist*
Suskind, Dennis A. *investment banker*
Susser, Mervyn Wilfred *epidemiologist, educator*
Sussman, Alexander Ralph *lawyer*
Sussman, Gerald *publishing company executive*
Sussman, Leonard Richard *foundation executive*
Sutresna, Nana S. *ambassador*
Sutter, Laurence Brener *lawyer*
Sutton, Kelso Furbush *publishing executive*
Sutton, Pat Lipsky *artist, educator*
Sutton-Straus, Joan M. *journalist*
Suzuki, Ryosuke *securities firm executive*
Svenson, Charles Oscar *investment banker*
Swados, Elizabeth A. *composer, director, writer*
Swain, Robert *artist*
Swan, William *actor*
Swanke, Albert Homer *architect*
Swann, Brian *writer, humanities educator*
Swanson, David Heath *agricultural company executive*
Swanzey, Robert Joseph *data processing executive*
Sweeney, Sister Margaret Mary *hospital administrator, nun*
Sweeney, Thomas Joseph, Jr. *lawyer*
Sweet, Robert Workman *federal judge*
Sweezy, Paul Marlor *editor, publisher*
†Swenson, Emily Barron *broadcast executive*
Swenson, Eric Pierson *publishing company executive*
Swid, Stephen Claar *business executive*
Swift, Isabel Davidson *editorial director*
Swift, John Francis *health care advertising company executive*
Swing, John Temple *lawyer, association executive*
†Sylbert, Richard *production designer, art director*
Symmers, William Garth *international maritime lawyer*
Syron, Richard Francis *financial services executive, economist*
Szer, Wlodzimierz *biochemist, educator*
Tabak, Ronald Jerome *lawyer*
Taber, Carol A. *magazine publisher*
Taddei, Giuseppe *baritone*
Tafel, Edgar *architect*
Tagliabue, Paul John *national football league commissioner*
Tagliaferri, Lee Gene *investment banker*
Tagliaferro, John Anthony *broadcasting company executive*
Tagliarino, Scott Alan *public relations executive*
Taguchi, Tadao *electronics company executive*
Talbot, Phillips *Asian affairs specialist*
Talese, Gay *writer*
Talese, Nan Ahearn *publishing company executive*
Tallackson, Jeffrey Stephen *lawyer*
Talley, Truman Macdonald *publisher*
Tallmer, Margot Sallop *psychologist, psychoanalyst, gerontologist*
Talmi, Yoav *conductor, composer*
Tanenbaum, Gerald Stephen *lawyer*
Taney, J. Charles *advertising agency executive*
Tanler, Ronald F. *retail executive*
Tannenbaum, Bernice Salpeter *religious organization executive*
Tanner, Harold *investment banker*
Tanselle, George Thomas *English language educator, foundation executive*
Tapella, Gary Louis *manufacturing company executive*
Tapley, Donald Fraser *university official, physician, educator*
Taran, Leonardo *classicist, educator*
Tarantino, Dominic A. *accounting firm executive*
Tarbox, Katharine Riggs *investor relations executive*

†Targoff, Michael Bart defense corporation executive, lawyer
Tarnopol, Michael L. bank executive
Tarter, Fred Barry advertising executive
Taschetti, Vincent S. advertising executive
Tash, Martin Elias publishing company executive
Tauber, Ronald Steven investment banker
†Taubes, Gary scientific writer
Taubin, Robin Livingston lawyer
Tavel, Mark Kivey money management company executive, economist
Tavon, Mary E. public relations, marketing and communications executive
Tayler, Edward William English language educator
Taylor, Clyde Calvin, Jr. literary agent
Taylor, Elizabeth Rosemond actress
Taylor, Humphrey John Fausitt information services executive
Taylor, John Chestnut, III lawyer
Taylor, Lance Jerome economics educator
Taylor, Nicole Renée model
†Taylor, Patricia theater company managing director
Taylor, Paul choreographer
Taylor, Paul B. dancer
Taylor, Regina actress
Taylor, Richard Trelore retired lawyer
Taylor, Richard William investment banker, securities broker
Taylor, Sherril Wightman broadcasting company executive
Taylor, Telford lawyer, educator
Tcherkassky, Marianna Alexsavena ballerina
Teclaff, Ludwik Andrzej law educator, consultant, author, lawyer
Tehan, John Bashir lawyer
Teich, Malvin Carl electrical engineering educator
Teiman, Richard B. lawyer
Te Kanawa, Kiri opera and concert singer
Telang, Nitin T. cancer biologist, educator
Tellefsen, Gerald management consultant
Telles, Martin Jack marketing executive
Temple, Wick journalist
Tendler, David international trade company executive
Tengi, Frank R. lawyer, insurance company executive
Tenney, Dudley Bradstreet lawyer
Tepper, Lynn Marsha gerontology educator
Teran, Timothy Eric Alba marketing professional
Terborgh, Bert dancer
Terenzio, Joseph Vincent hospital administrator
†Terkuhle, Abby graphic designer
Terrace, Herbert S(ydney) psychologist, educator
Terrell, J. Anthony lawyer
Terry, F. Davis, Jr. investment company executive
Terry, Frederick Arthur, Jr. lawyer
Terry, James Joseph, Jr. lawyer
Terry, Megan playwright, performer , photographer
†Tertzakian, Hovhannes bishop
Tesich, Steve author
Testa, Michael Harold lawyer
Tetley, Glen choreographer
Tetzeli, Frederick Edward banker
Thackeray, Jonathan E. lawyer
Thalacker, Arbie Robert lawyer
Tharp, Twyla dancer, choreographer
Themelis, Nickolas John metallurgical and chemical engineering educator
Thesing, James J. arts organization executive
†Thiebaud, Wayne artist
Thoman, Mark lawyer
Thomas, Brooks publishing company executive
Thomas, David Hurst archaeologist
Thomas, Debi (Debra J. Thomas) ice skater
Thomas, Gladys Roberts foundation executive
Thomas, John Cox, Jr. publisher
Thomas, Richard actor
Thomas, Robert Morton, Jr. lawyer
Thomas, Roger Warren lawyer
Thompson, David Duvall physician
Thompson, Hunter Stockton author, political analyst, journalist
Thompson, Martin Christian news service executive
Thompson, Robert L., Jr. lawyer
Thompson, William Cannon, Jr. advertising agency executive
Thomson, William Barry retail company executive
Thorne, Francis composer
Thorne, John Watson, III advertising and marketing executive
Thornton, John Vincent lawyer, educator
Thoyer, Judith Reinhardt lawyer
Thrall, Donald Stuart artist
†Thrower, Ellen academic administrator
Thurman, Ralph Holloway health care company executive
†Tian, Gang mathematics educator
Tierney, Paul E., Jr. investment company executive
Tietjen, John Henry biology and oceanography educator, consultant
Tigay, Alan Merrill editor
Tilberis, Elizabeth editor-in-chief
Tillinghast, David Rollhaus lawyer
Tillis, Pam country singer, songwriter
Tilly, Louise Audino history and sociology educator
Tilson, Dorothy Ruth word processing executive
Tilson, M(artin) David surgeon, scientist
Tilson Thomas, Michael symphony conductor
Tilton, James Floyd theatrical designer, art director
Timothy, Raymond Joseph television executive
Tinker, Thomas Eaton headmaster
Tipton, Jennifer lighting designer
Tirakis, Judith Angelina financial company executive
†Tisch, Andrew Herbert corporate executive
†Tisch, James S. diversified holding company executive
†Tisch, Jonathan Mark hotel company executive
Tisch, Laurence Alan broadcast corporation executive
Tisch, Preston Robert finance executive
Tishman, John L. realty and construction company executive
Tishman, Robert V. real estate and construction company executive
†Tison, Joseph Southwood food products company executive
Tison-Braun, Micheline Lucie French language educator
Tizzio, Thomas Ralph brokerage executive
Tobach, Ethel retired curator
Tober, Barbara D. (Mrs. Donald Gibbs Tober) editor
Tobias, Julius sculptor
Tobin, Peter J. financial executive
Tocklin, Adrian Martha insurance company executive, lawyer
Todd, David Fenton Michie architect
Todd, Patricia Anne publishing executive
Todd, Ronald Gary lawyer
Toepfer, Susan Jill editor
Toepke, Utz Peter lawyer
Toff, Nancy Ellen book editor
†Toffler, Heidi author, futurist
Tollerson, Ernest newspaper editor
Tomkins, Calvin writer
Tomlinson, James Francis retired news agency executive
Tondel, Lawrence Chapman lawyer
Tooker, George artist
Toote, Gloria E. A. developer, lawyer, columnist
Topol, Robert Martin financial services executive, securities trader
Torell, John Raymond, III banker
†Torman, Howard Alan cardiologist, medical correspondent
Torre, Douglas Paul dermatologist
Torrence, (John) Richard fundraising executive, special events producer
Torrenzano, Richard public affairs executive
Torres, Edwin state judge, writer
Tortorella, Albert James public relations executive, consultant
Tortoriello, Robert Laurence lawyer
Towbin, A(braham) Robert investment banker
Townsend, Charles H. publishing executive
Townsend, M. Wilbur manufacturing company executive
Townshend, Peter musician, composer, singer
Tozer, W. James, Jr. investment company executive
Tracey, Margaret dancer
Trachtenberg, Matthew J. bank holding company executive
Tracy, Janet Ruth legal educator, librarian
Trager, Alan Martin financial services company executive
Trager, William biology educator
Train, John investment counselor, writer, government official
Traina, Albert Salvatore publishing executive
Tramontine, John O. lawyer
Traub, J(oseph) F(rederick) computer scientist, educator
Traub, Richard Kenneth lawyer
Traum, Jerome S. lawyer
Treadway, James Curran investment company executive, lawyer, former government official
Treadway, Stephen Joseph investment banking and brokerage executive
Treaster, Joseph B. (Bland) journalist
Tree, Michael violinist, violist, educator
Treitler, Leo musicologist, educator
Treuhold, Charles Richard investment banker
Trigere, Pauline fashion designer
Trillin, Calvin Marshall writer, columnist
Tripodi, Louis Anthony advertising agency executive
Troeger, Curtis Ralph advertising executive
Trost, J. Ronald lawyer
Troubetzkoy, Alexis Serge foundation administrator, educator
†Trowbridge, Edward Kenneth insurance executive
Trubin, John lawyer
Trueman, Walter retired advertising agency executive
Truesdell, Wesley Edwin public relations and investor relations consultant
Truitt, Richard Hunt public relations agency executive
Trygg, Steve Lennart advertising executive
Tryhane, Gerald newspaper publishing executive
Tscherny, George graphic designer
Tse, Stephen Yung Nien insurance executive
Tsividis, Yannis P. electrical engineering educator
Tsoucalas, Nicholas federal judge
Tuck, Edward Hallam lawyer
Tucker, Alan David publisher
Tucker, Marcia museum director, curator
Tucker, Paul Thomas information systems executive
Tudryn, Joyce Marie professional society administrator
Tufts, David Albert, Jr. securities company executive
Tulchin, David Bruce lawyer
Tully, Daniel Patrick financial services executive
Tumminello, Stephen Charles consumer electronics manufacturing executive
Tune, Tommy (Thomas James Tune) musical theater director, dancer, choreographer, actor
Tung, Ko-Yung lawyer
Turino, Gerard Michael physician, medical scientist, educator
†Turk, Patricia Avedon dance company executive
Turkel, Stanley hotel consultant, management executive
Turlington, Christy model
Turnbaugh, Douglas Blair arts administration executive, author
Turner, Almon Richard art historian, educator
Turner, E. Deane lawyer
Turner, Hester Hill management consultant
Turner, Roderick L. retired consumer packaged products manufacturing company executive
Turner, Stuart paper company executive
Turo, Joann K. psychoanalyst, psychotherapist, consultant
Turrentine, Stanley William musician
Turro, Nicholas John chemistry educator
Tushman, Michael business educator
Tuttleton, James Wesley English educator
Tutun, Edward H. retired retail executive
Twell, Nicholas J. financial analyst
Twiname, John Dean minister, health care executive
†Twombly, Cy artist
Tyler, David Alan auction house executive
Tyler, Harold Russell, Jr. lawyer, former government official
Tyler, Richard fashion designer
Typermass, Arthur G. insurance company executive
Tyson, Harry James investment banker
†Tyson, Mike G. professional boxer
Tzimas, Nicholas Achilles orthopedic surgeon, educator
Ubell, Robert Neil editor, publisher, consultant, literary agent
Uchitelle, Louis journalist
Udell, Richard lawyer
Ufford, Charles Wilbur, Jr. lawyer
Uhry, Alfred Fox playwright
Ulanov, Barry author, educator
Ullmark, Hans advertising agency executive
Ulrich, Lars drummer
Ulrich, Max Marsh executive search consultant
Underberg, Mark Alan lawyer
Underhill, Jacob Berry, III retired insurance company executive
Underweiser, Irwin Philip mining company executive, lawyer
Underwood, Joanna DeHaven environmental research and education organizations president
Underwood, Paul brokerage house executive
Ungaro, Susan Kelliher magazine editor
Unger, Irwin historian, educator
Unger, Peter Kenneth philosophy educator
Unger, Ronald Lawrence lawyer
Unger, Stephen Herbert electrical engineer, computer scientist
Upbin, Shari theatrical producer, director, agent, educator
Updike, Helen Hill economist, investment manager, financial planner
Uppman, Theodor concert and opera singer, voice educator
Upright, Diane Warner auction house executive
Upshaw, Dawn soprano
Upson, Stuart Barnard advertising agency executive
Urdang, Alexandra book publishing executive
Urkowitz, Michael banker
Urowsky, Richard J. lawyer
Urquia, Rafael, II lawyer
Urstadt, Charles Jordan real estate executive
Uviller, H. Richard law educator
Vaadia, Boaz sculptor
Vai, Marjorie Theresa language educator, university administrator, author
Vaicaitis, Rimas civil engineering and engineering mechanics educator
Vale, Norman advertising executive
Valenstein, Suzanne Gebhart art historian
Valenti, Carl M. newspaper publisher
Valles, Jean-Paul finance company executive
Valletta, Amber model
Van Brunt, Albert Daniel advertising agency executive
Van Campen, Stephen Bernard executive recruiter, consultant
Vance, Andrew Peter lawyer
Vance, Cyrus Roberts lawyer, former government official
van den Akker, Koos fashion designer
Van Dine, Vance investment banker
Van Doren, Glenn Henry professional association executive, management consultant
†Van Dyk, Stephen Henry librarian
Van Eysinga, Frans W. publisher
Van Gundy, Gregory Frank lawyer
Van Halen, Eddie guitarist, rock musician
van Hengel, Maarten banker
Van Nostrand, Morris Abbott, Jr. publisher
Van Sant, Peter Richard news correspondent
van Vogt, Alfred Elton author
Varet, Michael A. lawyer
Vargas, Eduardo advertising executive
Varnedoe, John Kirk Train museum curator
Varney, Carleton Bates, Jr. interior designer, columnist, educator, author
Vass, Joan fashion designer
Vaughan, Edwin Darracott, Jr. urologist, surgeon
†Vaughan, Linda publishing executive
Vaughan, Samuel Snell editor, author
†Vaughan, Susan Carole psychiatrist, psychoanalyst
Vecchione, Joseph John newspaper editor
Vecsey, George Spencer sports columnist
Vedder, Eddie singer
Vega, Marylois Purdy journalist
Vega, Matias Alfonso lawyer
Velasquez, Jorge Luis, Jr. jockey
Vendela model
Ventres, Romeo John manufacturing company executive
Venza, Jac broadcast executive, cultural and arts program administrator
Verbridge, Gerald religious organization administrator
Verdi, David Joseph broadcast news executive
Verdol, Joseph Arthur chemist
Verdon, Gwen (Gwyneth Evelyn) actress, dancer, choreographer
Vermeer, Maureen Dorothy sales executive
Versace, Gianni fashion designer
Versfelt, David Scott lawyer
†Veru, Theodore advertising agency executive
Vestal, Jeanne Marie Goodspeed book publishing company executive
Vialardi, Enzo Joseph publishing company executive
Vick, James Albert publishing executive, consultant
Vickrey, William Spencer economist, emeritus educator
Victor, A. Paul lawyer
†Viemeister, Tucker L. industrial designer
Viener, John D. lawyer
Viermetz, Kurt F. banker
†Viertel, Jack theatrical producer, writer
Vig, Vernon Edward lawyer
Vignelli, Massimo architecture and design executive
†Vignola, Leonard Robert foundation executive
Vignone, Ronald John advertising agency executive
Vilcek, Jan Tomas medical educator
Violenus, Agnes A. school system administrator
Vitale, Alberto Aldo publishing company executive
Vitale, Dick color commentator, sports writer
Vitkowsky, Vincent Joseph lawyer
Vitt, Sam Bradshaw communications media services executive
Vittadini, Adrienne fashion designer
Vittorini, Carlo publishing company executive
Vitz, Paul Clayton psychologist, educator
Viviano, Sam Joseph illustrator
Vizard, Frank Joseph journalist
Voell, Richard Allen real estate services company executive
Vogel, Eugene L. lawyer
Vogel, Stephen Eugene systems analyst
Vogelman, Joseph Herbert scientific engineering company executive
Volckhausen, William Alexander lawyer, banker
Volk, Norman Hans financial executive
Volk, Stephen Richard lawyer
Volney, Taylor financial executive
Volpe, Joseph opera company administrator
Volpe, Thomas J. advertising executive
Vona, Carmine banker
von der Heyden, Karl Ingolf Mueller manufacturing company executive
Von Fraunhofer-Kosinski, Katherina bank executive
von Furstenberg, Betsy actress, writer
Von Furstenberg, Diane Simone Michelle fashion designer
von Knorring, Henrik Johan publisher
†von Mehren, Jane editor
von Mehren, Robert Brandt lawyer
Vonnegut, Kurt, Jr. writer
Von Ringelheim, Paul Helmut sculptor
Von Stade, Frederica mezzo-soprano
Voorsanger, Bartholomew architect
Vora, Ashok financial economist
Vuilleumier, Francois curator
Wachner, Linda Joy apparel marketing and manufacturing executive
Wachsman, Phyllis Geri advertising executive
Wachtel, Harry H. lawyer, chain store executive
Wachtel, Norman Jay lawyer
Waddell, Harry Lee editor, publisher
Waddell, John Comer electronics distribution company executive
Wade, George Joseph lawyer
Wade, James O'Shea publisher
Wade, Nicholas Michael Landon journalist
Wadsworth, Charles William pianist
Wadsworth, Christopher headmaster
Wadsworth, Dyer Seymour lawyer
Wadsworth, Robert David advertising agency executive
Wager, Walter Herman author, communications director
Wagner, Alan Cyril television and film producer
Wagner, Christina Breuer media company executive
Wagner, Robin Samuel Anton stage and set designer
Wailand, George lawyer
Wainwright, Carroll Livingston, Jr. lawyer
Waks, Jay Warren lawyer
Waksman, Byron Halsted neuroimmunologist, experimental pathologist, educator, medical association administrator
Waksman, Ted Stewart lawyer
Wald, Bernard Joseph lawyer
Wald, Sylvia artist
Waldbaum, Maxim Howard lawyer
Waldman, Diane museum deputy director
Wales, Gwynne Huntington lawyer
Walke, David Michael public relations executive
Walker, Alice Malsenior author
Walker, Charles R., III lawyer
Walker, Douglas Craig publishing company executive
Walker, Joan H. public relations executive
Walker, John Lockwood lawyer
Walker, John Mercer, Jr. federal judge
Walker, Kenneth Henry architect
Walker, Mark A. lawyer
Walker, Mort cartoonist
Walker, Sally Barbara retired glass company executive
Walker, Sandra mezzo-soprano
Walkley, Barbara Ann public relations executive
Walkowitz, Daniel J. historian, filmmaker, educator
†Wallace, Ken magazine publisher
Wallace, Mike television interviewer and reporter
†Wallace, Paul F. real estate company officer
Wallace, Robert Fergus banker
Wallace, Thomas C(hristopher) editor, literary agent
Wallace, Thomas J. magazine editor-in-chief
Wallace, Thomas Robert public relations executive
Wallace, Walter C. lawyer, government official
Wallach, Allan Henry former senior critic
Wallach, Eric Jean lawyer
Wallach, Ira writer
Wallach, John Paul foundation administrator, author
Wallach, Stanley medical educator, consultant, administrator
Wallance, Gregory J. lawyer
Waller, Robert James writer
Walpin, Gerald lawyer
Walsh, Kevin A. lawyer
Walsh, Thomas Gerard actuary
Walter, Ingo economics educator
Walters, Barbara television journalist
Walters, Milton James investment banker
Walters, Raymond, Jr. newspaper editor, author
†Walther, Robert R. physician, educator
Walton, Anthony John (Tony Walton) theater and film designer, book illustrator
Walton, Eileen Rowan lawyer
Walzer, Judith Borodovko university administrator, educator
Walzog, Nancy Lee film and television executive
Wanek, William Charles public relations executive
Wang, Arthur Woods publisher
Wang, Charles Pei social service administrator
Wang, Julie Caroline public relations executive
Wang, Vera fashion designer
†Wankel, Robert E. financial executive
Wanner, Eric foundation executive, researcher, writer, editor
Ward, Geoffrey Champion author, editor
†Ward, Robert property manager
Ward, Robert Joseph federal judge
Warden, Jack actor
Warden, John L. lawyer
Wardwell, Allen art historian
Wareham, Raymond Noble investment banker
Waren, Stanley A. university administrator, theatre and arts center administrator, director
Warfield, Gerald Alexander composer, writer
Warhaftig, Solomon L. lawyer
Warner, Douglas Alexander, III banker
Warner, Edward Waide, Jr. lawyer
Warner, John Edward advertising executive
†Warner, Miner Hill investment banker
Warner, Peter David publishing executive
Warner, Rawleigh, Jr. oil company executive
Warren, Irwin Howard lawyer
Warren, William Bradford lawyer
Warren, William Clements lawyer, educator
Warsawer, Harold Newton real estate appraiser and consultant
Warshauer, Irene Conrad lawyer
Warshaw, Leon J(oseph) physician
Warsoff, Stanley L. lawyer
Warwick, Dionne singer
Warwick, John Petersen advertising executive
Washburn, David Thacher lawyer
Wasser, Henry retired English educator
Wasserman, Albert writer, director
Wasserman, Bert W. communications and publishing company executive
Wasserman, Charles banker
Wasserman, Dale playwright
Wasserman, Louis Robert physician, educator
Wasserman, Steve publisher
Wasserstein, Bruce investment banker
Watanabe, Kyoichi A(loysius) chemist, researcher, pharmacology educator
Waters, Sylvia dance company artistic director
Waters, William Francis financial services executive
†Wathne, Stefan, Jr. consulting company executive
Watkins, Charles Booker, Jr. mechanical engineering educator
Watkins, Stanley academic director
Watson, Albert MacKenzie photographer
Watson, Anthony L. health facility executive
Watson, James Lopez federal judge
Watson, John King, Jr. lawyer
Watson, John Lawrence, III trade association executive

Watson, Solomon Brown, IV *lawyer, business executive*
Watt, Douglas (Benjamin Watt) *writer, critic*
Wattles, Joshua *motion picture studio executive*
Wattleton, (Alyce) Faye *association executive*
Wattman, Malcolm Peter *lawyer*
Watts, André *concert pianist*
Watts, David Eide *lawyer*
Watts, Harold Wesley *economist, educator*
Watts, Henry Miller, Jr. *stockbroker*
Waugh, Theodore Rogers *orthopedic surgeon*
Wax, Edward L. *advertising executive*
Waxenberg, Alan M. *publisher*
Way, Kenneth L. *seat company executive*
Waylett, Thomas Robert *management consultant executive*
Weare, Ashley *banker*
Weathersby, George Byron *investment management executive*
Weatherstone, Dennis *trust company executive*
Weaver, Martin Edward *historic conservation educator, administrator*
Webb, Veronica *fashion model, journalist*
Weber, Robert Maxwell *cartoonist*
Webster, John Kimball *investment executive*
Wechsler, Herbert *retired legal educator*
Wechsler, Raymond Henry *management company executive*
Wecker, William A. *preventive medicine physician, neuropsychiatrist*
Weeks, Brigitte *publishing executive*
Weeks, David Frank *foundation administrator*
Wegman, William George *artist*
Weida, Lewis Dixon *marketing analyst, consultant*
Weidlinger, Paul *civil engineer*
Weidman, Jerome *author*
Weil, Frank A. *investment banker, lawyer*
Weil, Gilbert Harry *lawyer*
Weil, Leon Jerome *diplomat*
Weil, Peter Henry *lawyer*
Weil-Garris Brandt, Kathleen *art historian*
Weill, Gus, Jr. *communications consultant*
Weill, Sanford I. *banker*
Weinbach, Lawrence Allen *accounting executive*
Weinberg, H. Barbara *art historian, educator, curator paintings and sculpture*
Weinberg, Herschel Mayer *lawyer*
Weinberg, Jeffrey J. *lawyer*
Weinberg, John Livingston *investment banker*
Weinberger, Caspar Willard *publishing executive, former secretary of defense*
Weinberger, Harold Paul *lawyer*
Weiner, Annette Barbara *university dean, anthropology educator*
Weiner, Earl David *lawyer*
Weiner, Max *educational psychology educator*
Weiner, Richard *public relations executive*
Weiner, Ronald Gary *accounting executive*
Weiner, Stephen Arthur *lawyer*
Weiner, Walter Herman *banker, lawyer*
Weingrow, Howard L. *financial executive, investor*
Weinschel, Alan Jay *lawyer*
Weinstein, Harvey *film company executive*
Weinstein, Herbert *chemical engineer, educator*
Weinstein, I. Bernard *physician*
Weinstein, Mark Michael *lawyer*
Weinstein, Martin *aerospace manufacturing executive, materials scientist*
Weinstein, Robert *film company executive*
Weinstein, Ruth Joseph *lawyer*
Weinstein, Sidney *university program director*
Weinstock, Leonard *lawyer*
Weintraub, Daniel Ralph *social welfare administrator*
Weintz, Walter Louis *book publishing company executive*
Weir, Peter Frank *lawyer*
Weisberg, Jonathan Mark *public relations executive*
†Weisbrod, Carl Barry *lawyer, public official*
Weisenburger, Randall *company executive*
Weisfeldt, Myron Lee *physician, educator*
Weisgall, Hugo David *composer, conductor*
Weiss, Brian *lawyer*
Weiss, Charles Stanard *investment banker*
Weiss, David *religion educator*
Weiss, Donald L(ogan) *retired sports association executive*
Weiss, George C. *lawyer*
Weiss, Lewis Stephen *pharmaceutical executive*
Weiss, Mark *public relations executive*
Weiss, Melvyn I. *lawyer*
Weiss, Myrna Grace *business consultant*
Weiss, Ronald Whitman *real estate executive, lawyer*
Weiss, Stephen Henry *investment firm executive*
Weissman, Gail Kuhn *nursing administrator*
†Weissman, Morris *printing compnany company*
Weissman, Norman *public relations executive*
Weissman, Paul Marshall *investment company executive*
Weissmann, Gerald *medical educator, researcher, writer, editor*
Weiswasser, Stephen Anthony *lawyer, broadcast executive*
Weithas, William Vincent *advertising agency executive*
Weitz, John *fashion designer, writer*
Weitzner, Harold *mathematics educator*
†Weksler, Marc Edward *physician, educator*
Weld, Jonathan Minot *lawyer*
Welikson, Jeffrey Alan *lawyer*
Welles, James Bell, Jr. *lawyer*
Wellington, Harry Hillel *lawyer, educator*
Wellington, Sheila Wacks *foundation administrator, psychiatry educator*
Wells, Linda Ann *editor-in-chief*
Wells, Melissa Foelsch *foreign service officer*
Wells, Victor Hugh, Jr. *advertising agency executive*
Welsh, Donald Emory *publisher*
Weltchek, Paul Richard *lawyer*
Wemple, William *lawyer*
Wendel, Thomas Michael *financial services company executive*
Wender, Ira Tensard *lawyer*
Wender, Phyllis Bellows *literary agent*
Wenders, Wim *film director*
Wenglowski, Gary Martin *economist*
Wenner, Jann Simon *editor, publisher*
Werner, Robert L. *lawyer*
†Werthamer, N. Richard *physicist*
Wertkin, Gerard Charles *museum director, lawyer*
Wertsman, Vladimir Filip *librarian, information specialist, author*
Weschler, Anita *sculptor, painter*
Weschler, Lawrence Michael *writer, journalist*
Wesely, Edwin Joseph *lawyer*
Wesley, John Mercer *artist*
Wessinger, W. David *management consultant*
Wessler, Sheenah Hankin *psychotherapist, consultant*
West, Bernard *investor*
West, Paul Noden *author*
West, Stephen Kingsbury *lawyer*
Westerman, Sylvia Hewitt *journalist, university official*
Westheimer, Ruth Siegel (Karola Ruth Siegel Westheimer) *psychologist, television personality*
Westin, Alan Furman *political science educator*
Westin, David Lawrence *lawyer*
Westlake, Donald Edwin *author*
Weston, M. Moran, II *educator, real estate developer, banker, clergyman*
Wetzler, James Warren *economist*
Wetzler, Monte Edwin *lawyer*
†Wexler, Nancy Sabin *clinical neuropsychology educator*
Wexler, Peter John *producer, director, set designer*
Weyher, Harry Frederick *lawyer*
Wham, George Sims *publishing executive*
Wharton, Clifton Reginald, Jr. *former university president, former government official, former insurance executive*
†Wharton, Danny Carroll *zoo biologist*
Wheeler, Wesley Dreer *marine engineer, naval architect, consultant*
Whelan, Elizabeth Ann Murphy *epidemiologist*
Whelan, Stephen Thomas *lawyer*
Whelan, Wendy *ballet dancer*
Whisnand, Roy Van Arsdel *investment management executive*
Whitcraft, Edward C. R. *investment banker*
White, Edmund Valentine *author*
White, Harrison Colyar *sociology educator*
White, Harry Edward, Jr. *lawyer*
White, John Simon *opera director*
White, Kate *editor-in-chief*
White, Kerr Lachlan *physician, foundation director*
White, Lawrence J. *economics educator*
White, Norval Crawford *architect*
White, Richard David *managing director*
White, Thomas Edward *lawyer*
White, Timothy Thomas Anthony *writer, editor, broadcaster*
White, William Dekova (Bill White) *baseball league executive*
Whitehead, E. Douglas *urology educator*
Whitehead, John Cunningham *investment executive*
Whitehead, Robert *theatrical producer*
Whiteman, Douglas E. *publisher*
Whiteman, H(orace) Clifton *banker*
Whiting, Richard Brooke *retired investment banker*
Whitman, Bruce Nairn *flight safety executive*
Whitmer, Kevin *newspaper sports editor*
Whitmore, John Rogers *banker*
Whitney, Edward Bonner *investment banker*
Whitney, Ruth Reinke *magazine editor*
Whittemore, Laurence Frederick *private banker*
Whitworth, John Harvey, Jr. *lawyer*
Whoriskey, Robert Donald *lawyer*
Wickes, R(ichard) Paul *lawyer*
Widlund, Olof Bertil *computer science educator*
Widmann, Nancy C. *broadcast executive*
Widney, Marilyn Edith (Marilyn Perry) *international finance and real estate executive, television producer*
Wiegers, George Anthony *investment banker*
Wiener, Hesh (Harold Frederic Wiener) *publisher, editor, consultant*
Wiener, Malcolm Hewitt *investment management company executive*
Wiener, Marvin S. *rabbi, editor, executive*
Wiener, Robert Alvin *accountant*
Wiener, Solomon *writer, consultant, former city official*
Wiesel, Torsten Nils *neurobiologist, educator*
Wiest, Dianne *actress*
Wigmore, Barrie Atherton *investment banker*
Wilby, William Langfitt *international portfolio manager, economist*
Wilcox, John Caven *lawyer, corporate consultant*
Wildes, Leon *lawyer, educator*
Wiley, Deborah E. *publishing executive*
Wilford, John Noble, Jr. *news correspondent*
Wilhite, Clayton Edward *advertising executive*
Wilkinson, Donald Michael, Jr. *lawyer*
Wilkinson, John Hart *lawyer*
Williams, Anthony *lawyer*
Williams, Dave Harrell *investment executive*
Williams, David Benton *advertising agency executive*
Williams, Donald Maxey *dancer, singer, actor*
Williams, Garth Montgomery *illustrator*
Williams, Lowell Craig *lawyer, employee relations executive*
Williams, Lucinda *country musician*
Williams, Milton Lawrence *judge, educator*
Williams, Omer S. J. *lawyer*
†Williams, Robert L. *pharmaceutical executive*
Williams, Stanley *ballet dancer and teacher*
Williams, Thomas Allison *lawyer*
Williams, Tod Culpan *architect*
Williams, Tony *jazz drummer*
Williams, Vanessa *recording artist, actress*
Williams, Vaughn Charles *lawyer*
Williams, William Thomas *artist, educator*
Williamson, Douglas Franklin, Jr. *lawyer*
†Willis, Beverly Ann *architect*
Willis, Everett Irving *lawyer*
Willis, Gordon *cinematographer*
Willis, John Alvin *editor*
Willis, Thornton Wilson *painter*
Willis, William Ervin *lawyer*
Willkie, Wendell Lewis, II *lawyer*
Wilson, August *playwright*
Wilson, Edgar Byron *business executive*
Wilson, F(rancis) Paul *novelist*
Wilson, Fredric Woodbridge *musicologist, library curator*
Wilson, John Hill Tucker *investment banker*
Wilson, Paul Holliday, Jr. *lawyer*
Wilson, Robert M. *theatrical artist*
Winawer, Sidney Jerome *physician, clinical investigator, educator*
Wincenc, Carol *concertizing flutist, educator*
Windels, Paul, Jr. *lawyer*
Windhager, Erich Ernst *physiologist, educator*
Windsor, Laurence Charles, Jr. *publishing executive*
Windsor, Patricia (Katonah Summertree) *author, educator, lecturer*
Winfrey, Carey Wells *journalist, magazine editor*
Wing, John Russell *lawyer*
Winger, Ralph O. *lawyer*
Winick, Charles *sociologist, educator*
Winick, Myron *educator, physician*
Winikoff, Beverly *physician*
Winkel, Fred Michael *marketing professional*
Winokur, Herbert Simon, Jr. *transportation company executive*
Winship, Frederick Moery *journalist*
Winsor, Jackie *artist*
Winsor, Kathleen *writer*
Winston, Judith Ellen *marine biologist, curator*
Winterer, Philip Steele *lawyer*
Wintour, Anna *editor*
Wirz, Pascal Francois *trust company executive*
Wise, David *author, journalist*
Wise, Robert F., Jr. *lawyer*
Wisehart, Arthur McKee *lawyer*
Wishnick, Marcia Margolis *pediatrician, geneticist, educator*
Wit, Harold Maurice *investment banker, lawyer, investor*
Witkin, Georgia Hope *clinical psychologist*
Witkin, Mildred Hope Fisher *psychotherapist, educator*
Wittreich, Joseph Anthony, Jr. *English language educator, author*
Wittstein, Edwin Frank *stage and film production designer*
Wixom, William David *art historian, museum administrator, educator*
Woetzel, Damian Abdo *ballet dancer, educator*
Wogan, Robert *broadcasting company executive*
Woglom, Eric Cooke *lawyer*
Wohl, Ronald Gene *lawyer*
Wohlgelernter, Beth *organization executive*
Wohlstetter, Charles *telephone company executive*
Woit, Erik Peter *corporate executive, lawyer*
Woitach, Richard *conductor, pianist*
Wojnilower, Albert Martin *economist*
Wolcott, Samuel H., III *investment banker*
Wolf, Gary Wickert *lawyer*
Wolf, James Anthony *insurance company executive*
Wolf, Naomi *writer*
Wolf, Peter Michael *investment and land planning consultant, educator, author*
Wolfe, George C. *theater director, producer, playwright*
Wolfe, James Ronald *lawyer*
Wolfe, Thomas Kennerly, Jr. *writer, journalist*
Wolfensohn, James David *bank executive*
Wolff, Jesse David *lawyer*
Wolff, Kurt Jakob *lawyer*
Wolff, Sanford Irving *lawyer*
Wolff, Virginia Euwer *writer, secondary education educator*
Wolff, William F., III *investment banker*
†Wolff, William I. *surgeon, educator*
Wolfson, Harold *corporate executive*
Wolfson, Michael George *lawyer*
Wolins, Joseph *artist*
Wolinsky, David *metal processing company executive*
Wolitzer, Steven Barry *investment banker*
Wolkoff, Eugene Arnold *lawyer*
Wolman, William *economist, journalist, broadcaster*
Wolowitz, Steven *lawyer*
†Wolsky, Albert *costume designer*
Wolson, Craig Alan *lawyer*
Wong, Kwan Shut *art appraiser, artist*
Woo, Frances Mei Soo *lawyer*
Wood, Christopher L. J. *real estate consulting firm executive*
Wood, Kimba M. *federal judge*
Wood, Paul F. *national health agency executive*
Wood, Ronald *musician*
Woodbury, Marion A. *insurance company executive*
Woodbury, Thomas Bowring, II *lawyer, public utility executive*
Wooden, Ruth A. *public service advertising executive*
Woodman, Timothy *artist*
Woodman, William E. *theater, opera and television director*
Woodrum, Robert Lee *executive search consultant*
Woods, Laurie *lawyer*
Woods, Rodney Ian *banker*
Woodside, William Stewart *service company executive, museum official*
Woodward, M. Cabell, Jr. *financial executive*
Worenklein, Jacob Joshua *lawyer*
Worley, Robert William, Jr. *lawyer*
Worman, Howard Jay *physician, educator*
Worth, Irene *actress*
Wortman, Richard S. *historian, educator*
Wray, Cecil, Jr. *lawyer*
Wray, Gilda Gates *foundation administrator*
Wright, Franklin Leatherbury, Jr. *lawyer, banker*
Wright, Gwendolyn *art center director, writer, educator*
Wright, Hugh Elliott, Jr. *association executive, writer*
Wright, Irving Sherwood *physician, retired educator*
Wright, Jane Cooke *physician, educator, consultant*
Wright, Jeanne Elizabeth Jason *advertising executive*
Wright, Jeffrey *actor*
Wright, Laurali R. (Bunny Wright) *writer*
Wright, P(aul) Bruce *lawyer*
Wright, Richard John *business executive*
Wright, Robert C. *broadcasting executive*
Wright, Robert F. *petroleum products company executive*
Wriston, Walter Bigelow *retired banker*
Wrong, Dennis Hume *sociologist, educator*
†Wu, Chien Shiung *physicist*
WuDunn, Sheryl *journalist, correspondent*
Wulf, Melvin Lawrence *lawyer*
Wunderman, Jan Darcourt *artist*
Wunderman, Lester *advertising agency executive*
Wuorinen, Charles P. *composer*
Wurmfeld, Sanford *artist, educator*
Wyatt, Mary Jean (M.J. Wyatt) *public relations executive*
Wyckoff, Edward Lisk, Jr. *lawyer*
Wynder, Ernst Ludwig *science foundation director, epidemiologist*
Wynette, Tammy *singer*
Wyse, Lois *advertising executive, author*
Wyser-Pratte, John Michael *lawyer*
Yablon, Leonard Harold *publishing company executive*
Yahr, Melvin David *physician*
Yalen, Gary N. *insurance company executive*
Yancey, Richard Charles *investment banker*
Yang, Edward S. *electrical engineering educator*
Yankelovich, Daniel *social researcher, public opinion analyst*
Yanowitch, Michael H. *lawyer*
Yao, David Da-Wei *engineering science educator*
Yassky, Lester *lawyer, banker*
Yegulalp, Tuncel M. *mining engineer, educator*
Yelle, Richard Wilfred *artist, product designer*
Yellin, Thomas Gilmer *broadcast executive*
Yellin, Victor Fell *composer, music educator*
Yeo, Edwin Harley, III *bank executive*
Yerman, Fredric Warren *lawyer*
Yerushalmi, Yosef Hayim *historian, educator*
Yeston, Maury *composer, lyricist, educator*
Yetman, Leith Eleanor *administrator, educator*
†Yohe, James Lyle *art gallery director, art dealer*
Yonkman, Fredrick Albers *lawyer, management consultant*
Yorburg, Betty (Mrs. Leon Yorburg) *sociology educator*
Yorinks, Arthur *children's author*
York, Richard Travis *art dealer*
Young, Alice *lawyer*
Young, Ed (Tse-chun) *illustrator, children's author*
Young, Genevieve Leman *publishing executive, editor*
Young, Harrison Hurst, III *banker*
Young, John Edward *lawyer*
Young, Michael Warren *geneticist, educator*
Young, Morris *electrical engineering consultant*
Young, Nancy *lawyer*
Young, Robert Francis *publisher*
Young, William F. *legal educator*
Youngerman, Jack *artist, sculptor*
Youngwood, Alfred Donald *lawyer*
Yuncker, Barbara *science writer*
Yunich, David Lawrence *consumer goods consultant*
Yunich, Peter B. *publishing executive*
Yurchenco, Henrietta Weiss *ethnomusicologist, writer*
†Yurt, Roger William *surgeon, educator*
Zabel, William David *lawyer*
Zabriskie, Virginia M. *art dealer*
Zacharius, Walter *publishing company executive*
Zackheim, Adrian Walter *editor*
Zahn, Paula *newscaster*
Zahn, Timothy *writer*
Zahnd, Richard Hugo *professional sports team executive, lawyer*
Zaitzeff, Roger Michael *lawyer*
Zakanitch, Robert Rahway *artist*
Zakim, David *biochemist*
Zakkay, Victor *aeronautical engineering educator, scientist*
Zaks, Jerry *theatrical director, actor*
Zampaglione, Arturo *newspaper publishing executive*
Zand, Dale Ezra *business management educator*
Zara, Louis *author, editor*
Zarb, Frank Gustave *insurance brokerage executive*
Zawistowski, Stephen Louis *psychologist, educator*
Zeckendorf, William, Jr. *real estate developer*
Zedrosser, Joseph John *lawyer*
Zehring, Karen *information executive*
Zeikel, Arthur *investment company executive*
Zeisler, Richard Spiro *investor*
Zeldin, Richard Packer *publisher*
Zelnick, Strauss *entertainment company executive*
Zerin, Steven David *lawyer*
Zeuschner, Erwin Arnold *investment advisory company executive*
Zevon, Susan Jane *editor*
Zhu, Ai-Lan *opera singer*
Ziegler, Michael Lewis *lawyer*
Ziegler, Richard Ferdinand *lawyer*
Ziegler, William Alexander *lawyer*
Zifchak, William C. *lawyer*
Ziff, William Bernard, Jr. *publishing executive*
Zimand, Harvey Folks *lawyer*
Zimmerman, Diane Leenheer *law educator, lawyer*
Zimmerman, George Abraham *lawyer*
Zimmerman, William Edwin *newspaper editor and publisher*
Zimmett, Mark Paul *lawyer*
Zindel, Paul *author*
Zinder, Norton David *genetics educator, university dean*
Zinn, Keith Marshall *ophthalmologist, educator*
Zinsser, William Knowlton *editor, writer, educator*
Zipprodt, Patricia *costume designer*
Zirin, James David *lawyer*
Zitrin, Arthur *physician*
Zlowe, Florence Markowitz *artist*
Zoeller, Donald J. *lawyer*
Zolberg, Aristide Rodolphe *political science educator, researcher*
†Zollar, Jawole Willa Jo *art association administrator*
Zolotow, Charlotte Shapiro *author, editor*
Zoogman, Nicholas Jay *lawyer*
Zornow, David M. *lawyer*
Zox, Larry *artist*
Zschau, Marilyn *singer*
Zuccotti, John Eugene *real estate company executive*
Zuck, Alfred Christian *consulting mechanical engineer*
Zucker, Marjorie Bass *medical researcher, hematologist*
Zuckerberg, Roy J. *investment banking executive*
Zucker-Franklin, Dorothea *medical scientist, educator*
Zuckerman, Mortimer Benjamin *real estate developer, publisher, editor*
Zukerman, Michael *lawyer*
Zukerman, Morris E. *investment banker*
Zukerman, Pinchas *concert violinist, violist, conductor*
Zweibel, Joel Burton *lawyer*
Zwerling, Gary Leslie *investment bank executive*
Zylberberg, Abraham Lieb *lawyer*

Newburgh

Cloudman, Francis Harold, III *computer company executive*
Joyce, Mary Ann *principal*
Saturnelli, Annette Miele *school system administrator*
Severo, Richard *writer*
Wilcox, David Eric *educational consultant*

Newton Falls

Hunter, William Schmidt *engineering executive, environmental engineer*

Newtonville

Apostle, Christos Nicholas *social psychologist*
Weber, Barbara M. *sales executive, consultant*

Niagara Falls

Albanese, Jay Samuel *criminologist, educator*
Anton, Ronald David *lawyer*
Collins, Christopher Carl *manufacturing executive*
Dojka, Edwin Sigmund *civil engineer*
†Finan, Timothy James *health facility administrator*
Gromosiak, Paul *science and mathematics educator*
King, George Gerard *chemical company executive*
Kirchner, Bruce McHarg *manufacturing company executive*
Pillittere, Joseph T. *assemblyman*
Powers, Bruce Raymond *academic administrator, writer*

Sheeran, Thomas Joseph *education educator, consultant, judge*

Niagara University
O'Connell, Brian James *academic administrator, priest*
O'Leary, Daniel Francis *university dean*
Osberg, Timothy M. *psychologist, educator, researcher, clinician*

Niskayuna
Fitzroy, Nancy deLoye *technology executive, engineer*
Johnson, Ingolf Birger *retired electrical engineer*
Katz, Samuel *geophysics educator*
Lafferty, James Martin *physicist*
Mangan, John Leo *retired electrical manufacturing company executive, international trade and trade policy specialist*
Mihran, Theodore Gregory *retired physicist*
Whittingham, Harry Edward, Jr. *retired banker*

North Boston
Herbert, James Alan *writer*

North Salem
Larsen, Jonathan Zerbe *journalist*

North Tarrytown
Zegarelli, Edward Victor *retired dental educator, researcher*

North Tonawanda
Nadler, Sigmond Harold *physician, surgeon*

Northport
Brown, John Edward *textile company executive*
Reinertsen, Norman *retired aircraft systems company executive*
Russo, D(orothy) Christine Fiorella *elementary education and university educator*
Tsapogas, Makis J. *surgeon*

Norwich
Tecklenburg, Harry *pharmaceutical products executive*

Nyack
Degenshein, Jan *architect, planner*
Flood, (Hulda) Gay *editor, consultant*
Hendin, David Bruce *literary agent, author, consultant, numismatist*
Karp, Peter Simon *marketing executive*
Keil, John Mullan *advertising agency executive*
†Kurz, Herbert *insurance company executive*
Lehman, Paul V. *minister*
Leiser, Ernest Stern *journalist*
Mann, Kenneth Walker *retired minister, psychologist*
Penn, Lynn Sharon *materials scientist*
Rossi, Harald Hermann *retired radiation biophysicist, educator, administrator*
†Warshaw, Jerry *insurance company executive*

Oakdale
Kramer, Aaron *English educator emeritus, poet, author*
Meskill, Victor Peter *college president, educator*
Tompkins, Daniel D. *landscape architect, horticulturist*

Oceanside
Mills, James Spencer *author*
Mooney, Yvette Migdalia *health facility administrator*

Ogdensburg
Deno, Lawrence M. *academic administrator*
†Loverde, Paul S. *bishop*
Rusaw, Sally Ellen *librarian*

Old Bethpage
Dryce, H. David *accountant, consultant*
Hall, R. M. R. *historical linguist*

Old Brookville
Fairman, Joel Martin *broadcasting executive*

Old Forge
Mitchell, George Frederick *association executive*

Old Westbury
Cheek, King Virgil, Jr. *educational administrator, lawyer*
DiGiovanna, Eileen Landenberger *osteopathic physician, educator*
Ozelli, Tunch *economics educator, consultant*
Pettigrew, L. Eudora *university president*
Rabil, Albert, Jr. *humanities educator*
Schure, Alexander *retired university chancellor*
Schure, Matthew *college president*

Olean
†Godfrey, John *internist*

Oneida
Hardman, Jane McWilliams *pathologist*
Matthews, William D(oty) *lawyer, consumer products manufacturing company executive*
Muschenheim, Frederick *pathologist*
Rudnick, Marvin Jack *lawyer*

Oneonta
†Anthony, David Waller *archaeologist, anthropologist, educator*
Bergstein, Harry Benjamin *psychology educator*
Donovan, Alan Barton *college president*
Grappone, William Eugene *clinical social worker, consultant*
Hammond-Moss, Patti *nursing administrator*
Hickey, Francis Roger *physicist, educator*
Holleran, Paula Rizzo *psychology and counseling educator, researcher, consultant*
Johnson, Richard David *retired librarian*
†Knudson, Richard Lewis *editor*
Smith, Geoffrey Adams *special purpose mobile unit manufacturing executive*

Orangeburg
Brill-Edwards, Harry Walter *manufacturing executive*

Hennessy, James Ernest *telecommunications executive, retired*
Lajtha, Abel *biochemist*
Levine, Jerome *psychiatrist, educator*
Nagle, George, Jr. *state mental health administrator*
Siegel, Carole Ethel *mathematician*

Orchard Park
Bennett, Cornelius *professional football player*
Franklin, Murray Joseph *retired steel foundry executive*
Hull, Kent *professional football player*
Kelly, Jim (James Edward Kelly) *professional football player*
Levy, Marvin Daniel *professional football coach, sports team executive*
†McGroarty, Bruce James *building products manufacturing executive*
Morgan, James Durward *computer company executive*
Noll, John F. *sales and marketing executive, investment banker*
Reed, Andre Darnell *professional football player*
Reid, Thomas Fenton *minister*
Smith, Bruce *professional football player*
Sullivan, Mortimer Allen, Jr. *lawyer*
Talley, Darryl Victor *professional football player*
Tasker, Steven Jay *professional football player*
Thomas, Thurman *professional football player*

Orient
Hanson, Thor *retired health agency executive and naval officer*

Ossining
Beard, Janet Marie *health care administrator*
Carter, Richard *publisher, writer*
Chervokas, John Vincent *chamber of commerce executive*
Daly, William Joseph *lawyer*
Ravis, Howard Shepard *conference planner and publishing consultant*
Reynolds, Calvin *management consultant, business educator*
Stein, Sol *publisher, writer, editor in chief*

Oswego
Fox, Michael David *art educator, visual imagist artist*
Geisinger, Kurt Francis *academic dean, psychometrician, educator*
Gerber, Barbara Ann Witter *university dean, educator*
Gooding, Charles Thomas *psychology educator, college dean*
Gordon, Norman Botnick *psychology educator*
Moody, Florence Elizabeth *education educator, retired college dean*
Nesbitt, Rosemary Sinnett *theatre educator*
Silveira, Augustine, Jr. *chemistry educator*
Smiley, Marilynn Jean *musicologist*
Turco, Lewis Putnam *English educator*
Weber, Stephen Lewis *academic administrator*

Oyster Bay
Gable, John Allen *historian, association executive, educator*
Garone, Frank *English language educator*
Robinson, Edward T., III *lawyer*
Schwab, Hermann Caspar *banker*
Trevor, Bronson *economist*

Ozone Park
Taylor, Joyce *religious organization executive*

Painted Post
Benjamin, Keith Edward *mechanical engineer*
Hammond, George Simms *chemist*

Palisades
Berger, Thomas Louis *author*
Broecker, Wallace S. *geophysics educator*
Cane, Mark Alan *oceanography and climate researcher*
Cavett, Dick *entertainer*
Davis, Dorothy Salisbury *author*
Fairbanks, Richard G. *geological science educator*
Hayes, Dennis Edward *geophysicist, educator*
Hays, James Douglas *geologist, educator*
Kent, Dennis Vladimir *geophysicist, researcher*
Knowlton, Grace Farrar *sculptor, photographer*
Krainin, Julian Arthur *film director, producer, writer, cinematographer*
Langmuir, Charles Herbert *geology educator*
Richards, Paul Granston *geophysics educator, seismologist*
Ryan, William B. F. *geologist*
Scholz, Christopher Henry *geophysicist*
Sykes, Lynn Ray *geologist, educator*

Palmyra
Blazey, Mark Lee *management consultant*

Patchogue
Gibbard, Judith R. *library director*
Tutino, Rosalie Jacqueline *college administrator*

Pawling
Peale, Ruth Stafford (Mrs. Norman Vincent Peale) *religious leader*

Pearl River
Barik, Sudhakar *microbiologist, researcher*
Caliendo, G. D. (Jerry Caliendo) *public utility executive*
Colman, Samuel *assemblyman*
Danforth, Elliot, Jr. *medical educator*
Davis, Harold *veterinary pathologist*
Griffin, Thomas Aquinas, Jr. *utility executive*
McBennett, Robert Joseph *utility executive*
Meyer, Irwin Stephan *lawyer, accountant*
Riley, James Kevin *lawyer*
Smith, James Francis *utilities executive*

Peconic
Mitchell, Robert Everitt *lawyer*

Peekskill
Manthey, Robert Wendelin *retired educator*
Rosenberg, Marilyn Rosenthal *artist, visual poet*

Pelham
Bornand, Ruth Chaloux *small business owner*

†Conroy, Tamara Boks *artist, special education educator*
Moore, Ellis Oglesby *retired public affairs consultant*
Ralston, Lucy Virginia Gordon *artist*
Simon, Robert G. *lawyer*
Weintz, Caroline Giles *non-profit association consultant, travel writer*

Penfield
Amish, Keith Warren *retired utility executive*

Peru
Crandall, Betty C. *nephrology/transplant nurse*

Piermont
Berkon, Martin *artist*
Der Harootian, Khoren *sculptor*
Fox, Matthew Ignatius *publishing company executive*
Gussow, Alan *artist, sculptor*

Pittsford
Benson, Warren Frank *composer, educator*
†Biklen, Stephen Clinton *student loan company executive*
Dorsey, Eugene Carroll *former foundation and communications executive*
Faloon, William Wassell *physician, educator*
Gates, Martha Meyer *architect*
Herge, Henry Curtis, Jr. *consulting firm executive*
Hess, Donald K. *university administrator*
Kieffer, James Milton *lawyer*
Lyttle, Douglas Alfred *photographer, educator*
Marshall, Joseph Frank *electronic engineer*
Ouellette, Bernard Charles *pharmaceutical company executive*
Palermo, Peter M., Jr. *photography equipment company executive*
Schubert, John Edward *former banker*
Weissberger, Ruth Marion *health education company executive, psychologist*
Woodhull, Nancy Jane *publishing executive*

Plainview
Austin, Larry *travel company executive*
Brill, Steven Charles *financial advisor, lawyer*
Fulton, Richard *lecture bureau executive*
McCusker, John *financial analyst*
Meola, Tony *professional soccer player, actor*
Newman, Edwin Harold *news commentator*
Stanton, Walter Oliver *electronics company executive*

Plattsburgh
Dossin, Ernest Joseph, III *credit consulting company executive*
Graziadei, William Daniel, III *biology educator, researcher*
Heintz, Roger Lewis *biochemist, educator, researcher*
Myers, John Lytle *historian*
Smith, Noel Wilson *psychology educator*

Pleasantville
Ahrensfeld, Thomas Frederick *lawyer*
Antonecchia, Donald A. *principal*
Black, Percy *psychology educator*
†Coleman, Gregory G. *magazine publisher*
Gilmore, Kenneth Otto *editor*
Glotzer, Marilyn *principal*
Gordon, Kenneth Antony *publisher*
Jones, Ross *publishing company executive*
Joseph, Harriet *English literature educator*
Murdock, William John *librarian*
Needleman, Harry *lawyer*
Oursler, Fulton, Jr. *editor-in-chief, writer*
Pike, John Nazarian *optical engineering consultant*
Reps, David Nathan *finance educator*
Robak, Rostyslaw Wsewolod *psychologist, educator*
Schadt, James P. *publishing executive*
Schadt, James Phillip *consumer products executive*
Soden, Paul Anthony *lawyer*
Tomlinson, Kenneth Y. *periodical editor-in-chief*
Willis, William Henry *marketing executive*

Poestenkill
Radley, Virginia Louise *humanities educator*

Point Lookout
Stack, Maurice Daniel *retired insurance company executive*

Pomona
Landau, Lauri Beth *accountant, tax consultant*

Port Chester
Ailloni-Charas, Dan *marketing executive*
Blumenfeld, Seth David *communications company executive*
†Cameron, Dort *electronics executive*
Duveen, Anneta *artist*

Port Jefferson Station
Niles, Walter H. *aviation manufacturing company executive, retired*
Schlessinger, Arthur Joseph *physical education educator*
Soma, Rose Smeraldi *broadcaster, writer, women's rights activist, television and radio producer*

Port Kent
Mc Kee, James, Jr. *retired banker*

Port Washington
Anable, Anne Currier Steinert *journalist*
Blakeslee, Alton Lauren *scientific writer*
Brownstein, Martin Herbert *dermatopathologist, educator*
†Ciccariello, Priscilla Chloe *librarian*
Davidoff, Charles *chemical and metalurgical engineer, consultant*
Donohue, Peter Joseph *publishing executive*
Feldman, Jay Newman *lawyer, telecommunications executive*
Hackett, John Byron *advertising agency executive, lawyer*
†Halasz, Laszlo *musical director, conductor*
Jay, Frank Peter *writer, educator*
Johnson, Tod Stuart *market research company executive*
McGreal, Joseph A., Jr. *publishing company executive*
Otto, Terre A. *real estate executive and developer, interior designer*
Read, Frederick Wilson, Jr. *lawyer, educator*

Rough, Herbert Louis *insurance company executive*
Simmons, Lee Howard *book publishing company executive*
Sonnenfeldt, Richard Wolfgang *business educator*
Williams, George Leo *retired secondary education educator*

Potsdam
Cotellessa, Robert Francis *retired electrical engineering educator, academic administrator*
Cross, John William *foreign language educator*
Gallagher, Richard Hugo *university official, engineer*
Ha, Andrew Kwangho *education educator*
Hanson, David Justin *sociology educator, college administrator*
Harder, Kelsie Brown *retired language professional, educator*
Mackay, Raymond Arthur *chemist*
Matijevic, Egon *chemistry educator, researcher, consultant*
Merwin, William *academic administrator*
Merwin, William Charles *academic administrator*
†Sathyamoorthy, Muthukrishnan *engineering researcher, educator*
Washburn, Robert Brooks *university dean, composer*
Whelehan, Patricia Elizabeth *anthropology educator*

Poughkeepsie
Ahern, John Joseph *Italian studies educator*
Ashford, Rosalind Mary *advertising and marketing executive*
Bartlett, Lynn Conant *English literature educator*
Beck, Curt Werner *chemist, educator*
Berk, Jeremiah E. *federal judge*
Bird, Caroline *author*
Carino, Aurora Lao *psychiatrist, hospital administrator*
Chu, Richard Chao-Fan *mechanical engineer*
Conklin, D(onald) David *college president*
Daniels, Elizabeth Adams *English language educator*
Davis, Susan Lee *nurse administrator*
Deiters, Sister Joan Adele *chemistry educator, nun*
Dolan, Thomas Joseph *lawyer*
Emerson, William R. *retired library executive, historian*
Gardenier, Edna Frances *nursing educator*
Gaudieri, Alexander V. J. *museum administrator*
Glasse, John Howell *retired philosophy and theology educator*
Griffen, Clyde Chesterman *retired history educator*
Hansen, Karen Thornley *accountant*
Henley, Richard James *healthcare institution administrator and financial officer*
Henry, Charles Jay *library director*
Hytier, Adrienne Doris *French language educator*
Johnson, Lucille Lewis *anthropology educator, archaeologist*
Johnson, M(aurice) Glen *political science educator*
†Kanwit, Bert Alfred *retired surgeon*
†Kelley, David Christopher *philosopher*
Kim, David Sang Chul *publisher, evangelist, retired seminary president*
Kohl, Benjamin Gibbs *historian, educator*
Lang, William Warner *physicist*
Lipschutz, Ilse Hempel *French and Franco-Spanish relations, painting and literature educator*
Liptay, Lynne Miriam *pediatrician*
Logue, Joseph Carl *electronics engineer, consultant*
Mack, John Edward, III *utility company executive*
Maling, George Croswell, Jr. *physicist*
Marshall, Natalie Junemann *economics educator*
McEnroe, Caroline Ann *legal assistant*
Millman, Jode Susan *lawyer*
†Opdycke, Leonard Emerson *educator, publisher*
O'Shea, John P. *insurance executive*
Ostertag, Robert Louis *lawyer*
Pliskin, William Aaron *physicist*
Rosenblatt, Albert Martin *state supreme court justice*
St. John, Howard Chambers *lawyer, bank executive*
Tavel, Morton Allen *physics educator, researcher*
Van Zanten, Frank Veldhuyzen *library system director*
Willard, Nancy Margaret *writer, educator*
Wilson, Richard Edward *composer, pianist, music educator*
Winn, Otis Howard *English educator*

Pound Ridge
Bright, Craig Bartley *lawyer*
Cooper, Daniel *management consultant*
Ferro, Walter *artist*
Ostrow, Stuart *theatrical producer, educator*
Throckmorton, Joan Helen *advertising agency executive*
Webb, Richard Gilbert *financial executive*

Purchase
Akers, John Fellows *information processing company executive*
Barnes, Randall Curtis *beverage company executive*
Berman, Richard Angel *health and educational administrator*
Butler, Robert Clifton *forest products industry executive*
Calloway, D. Wayne *food and beverage products company executive*
Carleton, Robert L. *consumer products company executive*
Casebolt, Victor Alan *paper company executive*
Clark, Mary Twibill *philosopher, educator*
Deering, Allan Brooks *beverage company executive*
Dettmer, Robert Gerhart *beverage company executive*
Dillon, John T. *paper company executive*
Dwyer, Andrew T. *utility and utility service company executive*
Ehrman, Lee *geneticist*
†Fulleylove, Brian *textiles executive*
Gedeon, Lucinda Heyel *museum director*
Georges, John A. *paper company executive*
Grebstein, Sheldon Norman *university administrator*
Grendi, Ernest W. *electrical equipment and water supply company executive*
Guedry, James Walter *lawyer, paper corporation executive*
Hunziker, Robert McKee *paper company executive*
Joyce, Joseph James *lawyer, food products executive*
Kelly, Edmund Joseph *lawyer, investment banker*
Lacy, Bill *college president*
Lamagra, Anthony James *concert pianist, television host, music educator*
Lautenbach, Terry Robert *information systems and communications executive*
Lucas, Billy Joe *philosophy educator*
MacInnis, Frank T. *construction company executive, holding company executive*

McKenna, Matthew Morgan lawyer
Melican, James Patrick, Jr. lawyer
Myers, Catherine R. academic administrator
Noonan, Frank R. business executive
Oskin, David William human resources specialist
Ryan, Edward W. economics educator
Sandler, Irving Harry art critic, art historian
Siegel, Nathaniel Harold sociology educator
Sonnenberg, Hardy data processing company research and development executive, engineer
Suwyn, Mark A. paper company executive
Turk, Milan Joseph chemical company executive
Wallach, Ira David lawyer, business executive
†Welch, Patrick E. diversified financial services company executive
Wilderotter, James Arthur lawyer
Wright, David L. food and beverage company executive

Purdys
Burlingame, Edward Livermore publishing company executive

Queens Village
Corcoran, Gretchen Elizabeth nursing administrator

Queensbury
Borgos, Stephen John business educator, consultant, municipal administrator, real estate broker
Lake, William Thomas financial consultant
Mead, John Milton banker
Winsten, Archer retired newspaper and movie critic

Quogue
Cooke, Robert John history and law educator
Laurents, Arthur playwright
Macero, Teo composer, conductor

Ransomville
Mayer, George Merton elementary education educator

Rego Park
Cronyn, Hume actor, writer, director
LeFrak, Samuel J. housing and building corporation executive

Remsenburg
Billman, Irwin Edward publishing company executive
Edwards, Arthur Anderson retired mechanical engineer

Rensselaerville
Dudley, George Austin architect, planning consultant, educator

Rexford
Kirchmayer, Leon Kenneth retired electrical engineer

Rhinebeck
Clutz, William (Hartman Clutz) artist, educator
Ethan, Carol Baehr psychotherapist
McLaughlin, Dona Hougen library director
Rabinovich, Raquel artist, sculptor
Smith, Lewis Motter, Jr. advertising and direct marketing executive
Vartanian, Aram French literature educator, researcher, writer

Rhinecliff
Dierdorff, John Ainsworth retired editor

Richfield Springs
Mc Kelvey, John Jay, Jr. retired foundation executive

Richmond Hill
Scheich, John F. lawyer

Ridge
Black, Lindsay MacLeod plant virologist

Ridgewood
Jones, Harold Antony banker

Riverdale
Edelman, Samuel Irving lawyer, financial executive
Hollein, Helen Conway chemical engineer, educator
Hubley, Faith Elliott filmmaker, painter, animator
Jha, Nand Kishore engineering educator, researcher
Moss, Stanley poet
Phocas, George John international lawyer, business executive

Riverhead
Maggipinto, V. Anthony lawyer
Stark, Thomas Michael state supreme court justice
†Turner, Joseph Francis, Jr. hospital executive

Rochester
Abood, Leo George biochemistry educator
Adams, G. Rollie museum executive
Adler, Samuel Hans conductor, composer
Alling, Norman Larrabee mathematics educator
Annunziata, Frank history educator
Arden, Bruce Wesley computer science and electrical engineering educator
†Axelrod, Joel Nathan marketing executive
Balderston, William, III retired banker
Barton, Russell William psychiatrist, author
Basu, Asish Ranjan geological sciences educator, researcher
Baum, John physician
Bennett, John Morrison medical oncologist
Berg, Robert Lewis physician, educator
Berman, Howard James medical association administrator
Berman, Milton history educator
Bernstein, Paul retired academic dean
Beston, Rose Marie college president
†Bigelow, Nicholas Pierre physicist, educator
Bluhm, William Theodore political scientist, educator
Boeckman, Robert Kenneth, Jr. chemistry educator, organic chemistry researcher
†Bolger, Stuart B. museum director, architectural historian
†Bonfiglio, Thomas Albert pathologist, educator
Borch, Richard Frederic pharmacology and chemistry educator
Borgstedt, Harold Heinrich pharmacologist, toxicologist
Bouyoucos, John Vinton research and development company executive
Bowen, William Henry dental researcher, dental educator
Braunsdorf, Paul Raymond lawyer
Brennan, John Edward manufacturing company executive
Brody, Bernard B. physician, educator
Brzustowicz, Richard John neurosurgeon, educator
Buckley, Michael Francis lawyer
Burgener, Francis André radiology educator
Burns, Stephen James engineering educator, materials science researcher
Burrill, William George bishop
Burton, Richard Irving orthopedist, educator
Cain, Russell M. psychiatrist
Carlton, Charles Merritt linguistics educator
Carstensen, Edwin Lorenz biomedical engineer, biophysicist
Castle, William Eugene academic administrator
Chang, Jack Che-man photoscience research laboratory director
Chapin, Louis William, II architect
Chey, William Yoon physician
Chiarenza, Carl art historian, critic, artist, educator
Chin-Kee-Fatt, Hollis Romauld marketing professional
†Chu, Ellin Resnick librarian, consultant
Ciccone, J. Richard psychiatrist
Clark, Louis Morris, Jr. investment manager, antique dealer, innkeeper
Clark, Matthew Harvey bishop
Clark, W. Richard eyewear manufacturing company executive
Clarkson, Thomas William toxicologist, educator
Clement, Thomas Earl lawyer
Cline, Douglas physicist, educator
Coburn, Theodore James retired physicist
Cockett, Abraham T. K. urologist
Cohen, Jules academic dean, physician, educator
Cohen, Nicholas immunologist, educator
Cokelet, Giles Roy biomedical engineering educator
Coleman, Paul David neurobiology researcher, educator
Crane, Irving Donald pocket billiards player
Crino, Marjanne Helen anesthesiologist
D'Agostino, Anthony Carmen anthropologist, educator
Deci, Edward Lewis psychologist, educator
DeLeo, Dennis Michael photographic company executive
DeMarco, Roland R. foundation executive
de Papp, Elise Wachenfeld pathologist
DeToro, Irving John management consultant
Diamond, David Leo composer
Dohanian, Diran Kavork art historian, educator
Donovan, Kreag lawyer
Doty, Robert William neurophysiologist, educator
Doyle, Justin P lawyer
DuBrin, Andrew John behavioral sciences, management educator, author
Eaves, Morris Emery English language educator
Eisenberg, Richard S. chemistry educator
Elder, Fred Kingsley, Jr. physicist, educator
Engelmann, Lothar Klaus photographic science educator
Engerman, Stanley Lewis economist, educator, historian
Enyeart, James L. museum director
Everett, Claudia Kellam special education educator
Fagan, Garth choreographer, artistic director, educator
Feinberg, Martin Robert chemical engineering educator
Fenno, Richard Francis, Jr. political science educator
Ferbel, Thomas physics educator, physicist
Fink, Thomas A. lawyer
Fischer, Richard Samuel lawyer
Fisher, George Myles Cordell electronics equipment company executive, mathematician, engineer
Fisher, Robert Joseph marketing and corporate executive
Forbes, Gilbert Burnett physician, educator
Ford, Loretta C. retired university dean, nurse, educator
Fox, Edward Hanton lawyer
Frank, Irwin Norman urologist, educator
Frazer, John Paul surgeon
Freckleton, Jon Edward engineering educator, consultant, retired military officer
Freeman, Robert Schofield musicologist, educator, pianist
Frisina, Robert Dana sensory neuroscientist, educator
Fulton, Marianne curator
Gans, Roger Frederick mechanical engineering educator
Gartner, Joseph Charles business systems administrator
Gates, Marshall DeMotte, Jr. chemistry educator
Gaudion, Donald Alfred former diversified manufacturing executive
Gayle-Jones, Jewelle human services educator, school system administrator
Geertsma, Robert Henry psychologist, educator
George, Nicholas optics educator, researcher
George, Richard Neill lawyer
Giles, Peter photographic equipment manufacturing executive
Gill, Daniel E. optical manufacturing company executive
Gitler, Samuel Carlos mathematics educator, researcher
Glerum, John C. bank controller
Goldman, Joel J. lawyer
Goldsmith, Lowell Alan medical educator
Goldstein, David Arthur biophysicist, educator
†Goldstein, Stephen Barry hospital administrator
Gootnick, Margery Fischbein lawyer
Gordon, Dane Rex philosophy educator, minister
Griner, Paul Francis physician
Gumaer, Elliott Wilder, Jr. lawyer
Hai, Carol Sue interior designer
Hall, Donald S. planetarium administrator
†Hammele, Joseph Francis banker
Hampson, Thomas Meredith lawyer
Hanushek, Eric Alan economics educator
Hargrave, Alexander Davidson banker, lawyer
†Harman, Nan K. orchestra director, artistic administrator
Harris, Alfred social anthropologist, educator
Harris, Richard M., Jr. paper company executive
Harris, Wayne Manley lawyer
Harvey, Douglass Coate retired photographic company executive
Hauser, William Barry history educator, historian
Hayes, Charles Franklin, III museum research director
Hellrung, Stephen Andrew lawyer
Henderson, Robert Cameron utility executive
Herminghouse, Patricia Anne foreign language educator
Herz, Marvin Ira psychiatrist
Hilf, Russell biochemist
Hoch, Edward Dentinger author
Hodkinson, Sydney Phillip composer, educator
Hoffberg, David Lawrence lawyer
Holcomb, Grant, III museum director
Hollingsworth, Jack Waring mathematics and computer science educator
Holmes, Jay Thorpe lawyer
Holmes, Robert Lawrence philosophy educator
Hood, John B. lawyer
Hood, William Boyd, Jr. cardiologist, educator
Hoot, William John retired brewery executive
Hopkins, Thomas Duvall economics educator
Horsford, Howard Clarke English language educator
Howard, Hubert Wendell English language educator, academic administrator, choral conductor
Hoy, Cyrus Henry language professional, educator
†Hubbard, Samuel T., Jr. paper manufacturing company
Hutchins, Frank McAllister advertising executive
Hyman, Ralph Alan journalist, consultant
Iglewski, Barbara Hotham microbiologist, educator
Insel, Richard medical facility administrator/ pediatrics educator
Jackson, Thomas Humphrey university president
Jacobs, Bruce political science educator
Jacobs, Laurence Stanton physician, educator
Johnson, Bruce Marvin English language educator
Johnson, James William English educator, author
Johnson, Jean Elaine nursing educator
Jones, Ronald Winthrop economics educator
Jorne, Jacob chemical engineer, educator
Joyce, John Joseph English educator
Joynt, Robert James academic administrator
Kampmeier, Jack August Carlos chemist, educator
Kanaley, James Edward optical company executive
Kehoe, L. Paul judge
Kende, Andrew Steven chemistry educator
Khosla, Rajinder Paul physicist
Kingslake, Rudolf retired optical designer
Kinnen, Edwin electrical engineer, educator
Klimas, Antanas linguist, educator
Klinsky, Arnold communications executive
Knauer, James Philip physicist
Knox, Robert Seiple physicist, educator
Kohrt, Carl Fredrick manufacturing executive, scientist
Koret, Sydney psychologist, educator
Kowalke, Kim H. music educator, musicologist, conductor, foundation executive
Kraus, Sherry Stokes lawyer
Kreilick, Robert W. chemist, educator
Kunkel, David Nelson lawyer
Kurland, Harold Arthur lawyer
La Celle, Paul Louis biophysics educator
Laires, Fernando concert piano educator
Laniak, David Konstantyn utility company executive
Larimer, David George federal judge
Latella, Robert Natale brewing company executive, lawyer
Laties, Victor Gregory psychology educator
Law, Michael R. lawyer
LeChase, Raymond Wayne construction company executive
Lessen, Martin engineering educator, consulting engineer
†Lichtman, Marshall Albert internist
Liebert, Arthur Edgar hospital administrator
†Loewen, Erwin G. precision engineer, educator, consultant
Long, John Broaddus, Jr. economist, educator
Lundback, Staffan Bengt Gunnar lawyer
Makous, Walter Leon visual scientist, educator
Mandel, Leonard physics and optics educator
Mandt, John F. religious organization executive
Maniloff, Jack biophysicist, educator
Mann, Alfred musicology educator, choral conductor
Marcellus, John Robert, III trombonist, educator
Margolis, Richard Martin photographer, educator
Marinetti, Guido V. biochemistry educator
Matteson, Lawrence James business educator
Matzek, Richard Allan library director
May, Melanie Ann theologian
McCarthy, John Russell photographic company executive
†McClure, Lucretia Walker medical librarian
McCrory, John Brooks retired lawyer
McCrory, Robert Lee physicist, mechanical engineering educator
McCurdy, Gilbert Geier retired retailer
McDonald, David J. food products company executive
Mc Donald, Joseph Valentine neurosurgeon
McHugh, William Dennis dental educator, researcher
Mc Isaac, George Scott business policy educator, past business executive
Mc Kelvey, Jean Trepp industrial relations educator
Mc Kenzie, Lionel Wilfred economist, educator
McKie, W. Gilmore human resources executive
Mc Quillen, Michael Paul physician
McWilliams, C. Paul, Jr. engineering executive
Melissinos, Adrian Constantin physicist, educator
Meloni, Andrew P. protective services official
Menguy, Rene surgeon, educator
Merrell, Stanley Wilson manufacturing company executive
Merritt, Howard Sutermeister retired art educator
Mertin, Roger photographer
Millman, Howard J. artistic director
Mooney, Thomas T. association executive
Moore, Duncan Thomas optics educator
Morey, James Newman advertising executive
Morgan, William Lionel, Jr. physician, educator
Morrison, Patrice B. lawyer
Morrow, Paul Edward toxicology educator
Morton, John H. surgeon, educator
†Moss, Arthur Jay physician
Muchmore, William Breuleux zoologist, educator
Mueller, John Ernest political science educator, dance critic and historian
Munson, Harold Lewis education educator
†Nagano, Kent George conductor
Niemi, Richard Gene political science educator
Oberlies, John William construction company executive
Olmsted, Joanna Belle cell biology educator
Olson, Russell L. pension fund administrator
O'Mara, Robert Edmund George radiologist, educator
Orr, Jim (James D. Orr) columnist, writer
Pacala, Leon retired assocation executive
Palermo, Anthony Robert lawyer
Paley, Albert Raymond art educator, sculptor
Paley, Gerald Larry lawyer
Palmer, Harvey John chemical engineering educator, consultant
Palvino, Jack Anthony broadcasting executive
Panner, Bernard J. pathologist, educator
†Panz, Richard library director
Parsons, George Raymond, Jr. lawyer
Paterson, Eileen radiation oncologist, educator
Pearce, William Joseph public broadcasting executive
Pearse, Robert Francis psychologist, educator
Pease, Donald E. dairy farmer, food products company executive
Pettee, Daniel Starr neurologist
Pickett, William Lee academic administrator
Pitkin, Patricia Albanese library administrator
Plosser, Charles Irving dean, economics educator
Prezzano, Wilbur John photographic products company executive
Prosser, Michael Hubert communications educator
Ramsey, Jarold William English language educator, author
Reed, James Alexander, Jr. lawyer
Regenstreif, S(amuel) Peter political scientist, educator
Reifler, Clifford Bruce psychiatrist, educator
Resnick, Alan Howard health care and optics executive
†Reulecke, Heimo pharmaceutical executive
Reveal, Ernest Ira food company executive
Riley, Edward John protective services official
Robfogel, Susan Salitan lawyer
Rosenbaum, Richard Merrill lawyer
Rosett, Richard Nathaniel economist, educator
Rothberg, Abraham author, educator, editor
Rouse, Christopher Chapman, III composer
Rowley, Peter Templeton physician, educator
Saisselin, Remy Gilbert fine arts educator
Sangree, Walter Hinchman social anthropologist, educator
Sapos, Mary Ann advertising agency executive
Saunders, William Hundley, Jr. chemist, educator
Scalise, Francis Allen adminstrator, consultant
Schumacher, Jon Lee lawyer
Schwantner, Joseph composer, educator
Schwartz, Seymour Ira surgeon, educator
†Scott, Joanna Jeanne writer, English language educator
Scutt, Robert Carl lawyer
Segal, Sanford Leonard mathematics educator
Shapiro, Sidney physicist, educator
Sherman, Charles Daniel, Jr. surgeon
Sieg, Albert Louis photographic company executive
Simon, Albert physicist, engineer, educator
Simon, Leonard Samuel banker
Simon, William biomathematician, educator
Simone, Albert Joseph academic administrator
†Skupsky, Stanley laser scientist
Slattery, Paul Francis physicist, educator
Smith, John Stuart lawyer
Smith, Julia Ladd medical oncologist, hospice physician
Smith, Paul Lester photography company executive
Soures, John M. physicist, researcher
Sproull, Robert Lamb retired university president, physicist
Stapp, William Francis museum curator, photographic historian
Steamer, Robert Julius political science educator
Stewart, Sue Stern lawyer
Stonehill, Eric lawyer
Swanton, Susan Irene library director
Telesca, Michael Anthony federal judge
Thomas, Garth Johnson psychology educator emeritus
Thomas, John Howard astrophysicist, engineer, educator
Thomas, Leo J. imaging company executive
Thompson, Brian John university administrator, optics educator
Thorndike, Edward Harmon physicist
†Tipton, Paul Louis physicist, educator
Tomaino, Michael Thomas lawyer
Toohey, Margaret Louise journal editor, researcher
Toribara, Taft Yutaka radiation biologist, biophysicist, chemist, toxicologist
Trueheart, Harry Parker, III lawyer
Turri, Joseph A. lawyer
Tyler, John Randolph lawyer
Underberg, Alan J. lawyer
Van Graafeiland, Ellsworth Alfred federal judge
Van Graafeiland, Gary P. lawyer
Von Holden, Martin Harvey psychologist
Wager, Barbara headmaster
Waite, Stephen Holden lawyer
Walker, Michael Charles, Sr. retirement services executive
†Warshaw, Robert S. police chief
Watanabe, Ruth Taiko music historian, library science educator
Wayland-Smith, Robert Dean banker
Wegman, Robert B. food service executive
Wehle, John L., Jr. brewing company executive
Weiss, Howard A. violinist, concertmaster, conductor, music educator
Wey, Jong-Shinn research laboratory manager
Wheeler, Ladd psychology educator
Whitmore, Kay Rex retired photographic company executive
Whitten, David George chemistry educator, researcher
Wild, Robert Warren lawyer
Wiley, Jason LaRue, Jr. neurosurgeon
Willett, Thomas Edward lawyer
Williams, Thomas Franklin physician, educator
Witmer, George Robert, Jr. lawyer
Wolf, Emil physics educator
Woods, John Joseph executive director
Wyatt, James Franklin librarian
Wynne, Lyman Carroll psychiatrist
Young, Mary Elizabeth history educator
Zagorin, Perez historian, educator
Zax, Melvin psychologist, educator

Rock Hill
Schary, Emanuel artist

Rockville Centre
Burton, Daniel G. insurance executive
Fitzgerald, Sister Janet Anne college president
Friedman, Neil Stuart insurance company executive
Halliday, Walter John lawyer
Kivowitz, Sheila clinical social worker
McGann, John Raymond bishop
Mc Grath, John Joseph retired management consultant
Silecchia, Jerome A. mechanical engineer
Smyth, Anne elementary school educator

Rome
Coppola, Anthony *electrical engineer*
Gabelman, Irving Jacob *consulting engineering executive, retired government official*
Griffith, Emlyn Irving *lawyer*
Waters, George Bausch *newspaper publisher*

Ronkonkoma
Heiserer, Albert, Jr. *automotive educator, small business owner*
Townsend, Terry *publishing executive*

Roosevelt
Wisner, Roscoe William, Jr. *human resources executive*

Rosedale
Mindlin, Paula Rosalie *educator*

Roslyn
†Finke, Leonda Froehlich *sculptor*
Gelfand, Morris Arthur *librarian, publisher*
Risom, Ole Christian *publishing company executive*
Scollard, Patrick John *hospital executive*
†Silvestro, John Pat *hospital administrator*
Vizza, Robert Francis *hospital executive, former university administrator, marketing educator*

Roslyn Heights
Faber, Adele *author, educator*
Jaffe, Melvin *securities company executive*
Rogatz, Peter *physician*
Tully, Michael J., Jr. *state senator*

Rouses Point
Casey, William Rossiter *international transport executive*
Weierstall, Richard Paul *pharmaceutical chemist*

Rye
Anderson, Allan *architectural firm executive*
Barker, Harold Grant *surgeon*
Beldock, Donald Travis *financial executive*
Erlick, Everett Howard *broadcasting company executive*
Flanagan, Eugene John Thomas *retired lawyer*
Goldstein, Stanley P. *retail company executive*
Gurfein, Stuart James *jewelry manufacturing company executive*
Huth, Robert D. *retail company executive*
Jay, Barbara *educational consultant*
Kingsford, William Charles *retail executive*
Lehman, Lawrence Herbert *consulting engineering executive*
Metzger, Frank *management consultant*
Mintz, Stephen Allan *real estate company executive, lawyer*
Netter, Kurt Fred *building products company executive*
Newburger, Howard Martin *psychoanalyst*
Reader, George Gordon *physician, educator*
Ross, Charles Worthington, IV *metals company executive*
Savin, Robert Shevryn *health care products company executive*
Stoller, Ezra *photojournalist*
Troller, Fred *graphic designer, painter, visual consultant, educator*
Tung, David Hsi Hsin *consulting civil engineer, emeritus engineering educator*
†van Ekris, Anthonie Cornelis *trading corporation executive, retail company executive*
Varona, Daniel Robert *lawyer, insurance company executive*
Wagner, Edward Frederick, Jr. *investment management company executive*
Wessler, Stanford *physician, educator*
Wilmot, Irvin Gorsage *former hospital administrator, educator, consultant*

Rye Brook
Dangoor, David Ezra Ramsi *consumer goods company executive*
FitzSimons, Sharon Russell *international finance and treasury executive*
Masson, Robert Henry *paper company executive*

Sag Harbor
Blanc, Peter (William Peters Blanc) *sculptor, painter*
Sheed, Wilfrid John Joseph *author*
Walton, Emma *artistic director*

Sagaponack
Appleman, Marjorie (M. H. Appleman) *playwright, educator, poet*
Appleman, Philip *poet, writer, educator*
Butchkes, Sydney *artist*
Francke, Linda Bird *journalist*
Isham, Sheila Eaton *artist*

Saint Bonaventure
Dooley, Patrick Kiaran *philosopher, educator*
Doyle, Mathias Francis *university president, political scientist, educator*
Khairullah, Zahid Yahya *management sciences and marketing educator, consultant*
O'Connell, Neil James *priest, academic administrator*
Wallace, Malcolm Vincent Timothy *classics educator*

Saint James
Bigeleisen, Jacob *chemist, educator*
Irvine, Thomas Francis, Jr. *mechanical engineering educator*

Sanborn
Michalak, Janet Carol *reading education educator*

Sands Point
Lear, Erwin *anesthesiologist, educator*

Saranac Lake
North, Robert John *biologist*

Saratoga Springs
Aldrich, Alexander *lawyer*
Boyers, Margarita Anne (Peggy Boyers) *editor, periodical, writer, translator*
Boyers, Robert *English language educator*
Hall, James William *college president*
Parthasarathy, Rajagopal *writer, literature educator*
Porter, David Hugh *pianist, classicist, academic administrator, liberal arts educator*
Ratzer, Mary Boyd *secondary education educator, librarian*
Upton, Richard Thomas *artist*
Walter, Paul Hermann Lawrence *chemistry educator*

Sayville
Blume, Sheila Bierman *psychiatrist*
†Lippman, Sharon Rochelle *cultural organization educator, director*

Scarborough
Beglarian, Grant *foundation executive, composer, consultant*
Hopkins, Lee Bennett *writer, educator*
Wittcoff, Harold Aaron *chemist*

Scarsdale
Abbe, Colman *investment banker*
Bernstein, Irving *international organization executive*
Blinder, Abe Lionel *management consultant*
Blitman, Howard Norton *construction company executive*
Breinin, Raymond *painter, sculptor*
Buttinger-Fedeli, Catharine Sarina Caroline *psychiatrist*
Clark, Merrell Mays *management consultant*
Cohen, Irwin *economist*
Cox, Robert Hames *chemist, scientific consultant*
Doley, Harold Emanuel, Jr. *securities company executive*
Duncan, George Harold *broadcasting company executive*
Eforo, John Francis *financial officer*
Fendelman, Helaine *art appraiser*
Ferry, Wilbur Hugh *foundation consultant*
Frankel, Stanley Arthur *columnist, educator, business executive*
Glickenhaus, Sarah Brody *speech therapist*
Graff, Henry Franklin *historian, educator*
Hayman, Seymour *former food company executive*
Hines, William Eugene *banker*
Hoffman, Richard M. *lawyer*
Howard, John Brigham *lawyer, foundation executive*
Johnson, Boine Theodore *instruments company executive, mayor*
Johnson, Katharyn Price (Mrs. Edward F. Johnson) *civic worker*
Kaufman, Robert Jules *communications consultant, lawyer*
†Lawyer, William Grove *foundation administrator*
Lee, Robert Earl *physician*
Liston, Mary Frances *retired nursing educator*
Moser, Marvin *physician, educator, author*
O'Brien, Edward Ignatius *lawyer, private investor*
O'Neill, Michael James *editor, author*
Oswald, George Charles *advertising executive, management and marketing consultant*
Rachlin, Stephen Leonard *psychiatrist*
Ries, Martin *artist, educator*
†Rivlin, Richard Saul *physician, educator*
Rosow, Jerome Morris *institute executive*
Rubin, A. Louis *advertising executive*
Schwartz, Harry *journalist*
Shaw, Grace Goodfriend (Mrs. Herbert Franklin Shaw) *publisher, editor*
Sullivan, Adèle Woodhouse *organization official*
Topping, Seymour *publishing executive, educator*
Wertheimer, Sydney Bernard *lawyer*
Wile, Julius *former corporate executive, educator*

Schenectady
Adler, Michael S. *control systems and electronic technologies*
Alpher, Ralph Asher *physicist*
Anthony, Thomas Richard *research physicist*
Barthold, Lionel Olav *engineering executive*
†Bedard, Donna Lee *microbiologist*
Bulloff, Jack John *physical chemist, consultant*
Chestnut, Harold *foundation administrator, engineering executive*
Coffin, Louis Fussell, Jr. *mechanical engineer*
Duncan, Stanley Forbes *health care executive*
†Edelheit, Lewis S. *research physicist*
Feibes, Werner Louis *architect*
Golub, Lewis *supermarket company executive*
Golub, Neil *supermarket chain executive*
Grant, Ian Stanley *engineering company executive*
Hart, Howard Roscoe, Jr. *retired physicist*
Hebb, Malcolm Hayden *physicist*
Hedman, Dale Eugene *consulting electrical engineer*
Huening, Walter Carl, Jr. *retired consulting application engineer*
Hull, Roger Harold *college president*
Huntley, Charles William *psychology educator*
†Jonas, Manfred *historian, educator*
Kambour, Roger Peabody *polymer physical chemist, researcher*
†Kindl, Fred Henry *engineering company executive*
LaForest, James John *retired electrical engineer*
Lawrence, Albert Weaver *insurance company executive*
Lennon, Frank M. *retail executive*
Luborsky, Fred Everett *research physicist*
Mafi, Mohammad *civil engineer, educator*
Matta, Ram Kumar *aeronautical engineer*
McMurray, William *consultant, retired electrical engineer*
Milton, William Hammond, III *trust company executive*
Morris, John Selwyn *philosophy educator, college president emeritus*
Murphy, William Michael *literature educator, biographer*
†Oliker, David William *healthcare management administrator*
Pasamanick, Benjamin *psychiatrist, educator*
Peak, David *physicist, educator, researcher*
Petersen, Kenneth Clarence *chemical company executive*
Philip, A. G. Davis *astronomer, editor, educator*
Redington, Rowland Wells *physicist, researcher*
Ringlee, Robert James *consulting engineering executive*
Robb, Walter Lee *retired electric company executive, management company executive*
Rycheck, Jayne Bogus (Mrs. Roy Richard Rycheck) *retired educational administrator*
Terry, Richard Allan *consulting psychologist, former college president*
Walsh, George William *engineering executive*
Wilson, Delano Dee *consulting company executive*

Schoharie
Duncombe, Raynor Bailey *lawyer*

Schroon Lake
Swanson, Norma Frances *federal agency administrator*

Scotia
Armstrong, Karen Lee *special education educator*
Jonsson, Kjartan A. *manufacturing executive, consulting company executive, engineer*

Scottsville
Dwyer, Ann Elizabeth *equine veterinarian*

Sea Cliff
Popova, Nina *dancer, choreographer, director*

Seaford
Setzler, William Edward *chemical company executive*

Searingtown
Entmacher, Paul Sidney *insurance company executive, physician, educator*

Seneca Falls
Bradshaw, Eugene Barry *pump company executive, lawyer*
Butler, Susan Lowell *association executive, writer*
Lambertsen, Mary Ann *human resources executive*
Morphy, John *manufacturing company executive*
Tarnow, Robert L. *manufacturing corporation executive*

Setauket
Barcel, Ellen Nora *secondary education educator, free-lance writer*
Irving, A. Marshall *marine engineer*
Levine, Sumner Norton *industrial engineer, educator, editor, author, financial consultant*
MacKay, Robert Battin *museum director*
Misener, Alan Francis *science educator*
Simpson, Louis Aston Marantz *English educator, author*
Vetog, Edwin Joseph *retired gas utility executive*
Werner, Joseph *retired secondary education educator, administrator*

Shady
Ruellan, Andree *artist*

Shelter Island
Culbertson, Janet Lynn *artist*
Dowd, David Joseph *banker, builder*

Sherrill
Rosendale, Suzanne Moore *library media specialist*

Shoreham
Reynolds, Carolyn Mary *elementary educator*
Spier, Peter Edward *artist, author*

Shrub Oak
Roston, Arnold *information specialist, educator, advertising executive, artist, editor*

Sidney
Haller, Irma Tognola *secondary social studies educator*

Silver Bay
Parlin, Charles C., Jr. *retired lawyer*

Silver Creek
Schenk, Worthington George, Jr. *surgeon, educator*

Skaneateles
Pickett, Lawrence Kimball *physician, educator*
Sullivan, Walter J. *school system administrator*

Slate Hill
Reber, Raymond Andrew *chemical engineer*

Slingerlands
Ellis, David Maldwyn *history educator*
Fenton, William Nelson *anthropologist, anthropology educator emeritus*
Wilcock, Donald Frederick *mechanical engineer*

Smithtown
Artzt, Russell M. *computer software company executive*
Holland, Marvin Arthur *lawyer*
Leavy, Herbert Theodore *publisher*
Pruzansky, Joshua Murdock *lawyer*
Sporn, Stanley Robert *retired electronic company executive*
Wheatley, George Milholland *medical administrator*

Snyder
Breverman, Harvey *artist*

Somers
Abu Zayyad, Ray S. *electronics executive*
Case, Richard Paul *electronics executive*
Finnerty, Louise Hoppe *beverage and food company executive*
Lane, David Oliver *retired librarian*
Low, Paul Revere *business machine company executive*
Paxton, Dan Richards *human resources executive*
Rubin, Samuel Harold *physician, consultant*
Thoman, G. Richard *computer company executive*

South Glens Falls
Clear, Gloria Lewis *elementary education educator*

South Salem
Howard, Joan Alice *artist*
Kim, Christine S. *physician*

Southampton
Atkins, Victor Kennicott, Jr. *investment banker*
Brokaw, Clifford Vail, III *investment banker, business executive*
Brophy, James David, Jr. *humanities educator*
Fuller, Sue *artist*
Graham, Howard Barrett *publishing company executive*
Lerner, Abram *retired museum director, artist*
Lieberman, Carol Cooper *healthcare marketing communications consultant, city planning administrator*
Louchheim, Donald Harry *journalist*
Silverstein, Louis *art director, designer, editor*
Sims, Everett Martin *publishing company executive*
Smith, Dennis (Edward) *publisher, author*

Southold
Bachrach, Howard L. *biochemist*
Callis, Jerry Jackson *veterinarian*
Duffy, Eugene Henry *investor*
Mebus, Charles Albert *veterinarian*

Sparkill
Dahl, Arlene *actress, author, designer, cosmetic executive*

Spencerport
Clarke, Stephan Paul *English language educator, writer*

Spencertown
Kherdian, David *author*
Lieber, Charles Donald *publisher*

Springfield Center
Hall, Stanley Eckler *international financial consultant*

Staatsburg
Gury, Jeremy *writer, advertising executive, artist*

Stafford
Moran, John Henry, Jr. *electrical engineer, consultant*

Stamford
Bergleitner, George Charles, Jr. *investment banker*

Stanfordville
Froman, Ann *sculptor*
Owens, Mary Jo *electronic guidance services company executive*

Stanley
Jones, Gordon Edwin *horticulturist*

Staten Island
Aiken, William Eric *securities research executive*
Aronson, Marilyn Ruth *English language and literature educator*
Auh, Yang John *librarian, academic administrator*
Barton, Jerry O'Donnell *telecommunications executive*
Berger, Herbert *retired internist, educator*
Chapin, Elliott Lowell *retired bank executive*
Diamond, Richard Edward *publisher*
Didomenico, Beatrice Grillo *social worker*
†Esposito, Mario John *county clerk, association president*
Fafian, Joseph, Jr. *management consultant*
Goetz, Carol Stier *mental health nurse, educator*
Greenfield, Val Shea *ophthalmologist*
†Hartman, Hedy Ann *museum executive*
Hartman, Joan Edna *English educator*
Henry, Paul James *lawyer, health care administrator*
Johnson, Frank Corliss *psychologist*
†Jones, Eric Michael *artist, designer*
†Kastanis, John Nicholas *hospital administrator*
Laline, Brian J. *newspaper editor*
†Li, Pui-Pui *interior and graphic designer*
Lipton, Barbara *museum director, curator*
Mailman, Cynthia Marcia *artist, educator*
Mencher, Stuart Alan *sales and marketing executive*
Pennington, Catherine Ann *legal technology consultant*
Porter, Darwin Fred *writer*
Smith, Norman Raymond *college president*
Springer, Marlene *university administrator, educator*
Wisniewski, Henryk Miroslaw *pathology and neuropathology educator, research facility administrator, research scientist*

Sterling
Seawell, Thomas Robert *artist, retired educator*

Stillwater
Lindsay, W. Douglas, Jr. *historic site administrator*

Stony Brook
Abumrad, Naji N. *surgeon, educator*
Alexander, John Macmillan, Jr. *chemistry educator*
†Anderson, Michael Thomas *mathematics researcher, educator*
Aronoff, Mark H. *linguistics educator, author, consultant*
Baron, Samuel *flutist*
Bonner, Francis Truesdale *chemist, educator, university dean*
Booth, George *cartoonist*
Boucher, Louis Jack *dentist, educator*
Bouey, Ora James *nursing educator*
Carlson, Elof Axel *genetics educator*
Chen, Chi-Tsong *electrical engineering educator*
Cope, Randolph Howard, Jr. *electronic research and development executive, educator*
Davis, James Norman *neurologist, neurobiology researcher*
Douglas, Ronald George *mathematician*
Edelstein, Tilden Gerald *academic administrator, history educator*
Feinberg, Eugene Alexander *mathematics educator*
Fisher, David Woodrow *editor, publisher*
Fleagle, John Gwynn *anthropology and paleontology educator*
Fritts, Harry Washington, Jr. *physician, educator*
Glimm, James Gilbert *mathematician*
Goldberg, Homer Beryl *English language educator*
Goodman, Norman *sociologist, researcher*
Hanson, Gilbert Nikolai *geochemistry educator*
Henn, Fritz Albert *psychiatrist*
Herman, Herbert *materials science educator*
Hill, C(lyde) Denson *mathematician, educator*
Ihde, Don *philosophy educator, university administrator*
James, Estelle *economics educator*
Jonas, Steven *public health physician, medical educator, writer*
Kahn, Peter B. *physics educator*
Kaplan, Allen P. *physician, educator, academic administrator*
Katkin, Edward Samuel *psychology educator*

Kenny, Shirley Strum *college administrator*
Kim, Charles Wesley *microbiology educator*
Koppelman, Lee Edward *regional planner, educator*
Kott, Jan K. *writer, scholar*
Kuspit, Donald Burton *art historian, art critic, educator*
Lane, Dorothy Spiegel *physician*
Lawson, H(erbert) Blaine, Jr. *mathematician, educator*
Lennarz, William Joseph *research biologist, educator*
Levin, Richard Louis *English language educator*
Levinton, Jeffrey S. *biology educator, oceanographer*
Marburger, John Harmen, III *university president, physics educator*
Meyers, Morton Allen *physician, radiology educator*
Mignone, Mario B. *Italian studies educator*
Miller, Frederick *pathologist*
Neuberger, Egon *economics educator*
†Ojima, Iwao *chemistry educator*
Pekarsky, Melvin Hirsch *artist*
Pindell, Howardena Doreen *artist*
Poppers, Paul Jules *anesthesiologist, educator*
Pritchard, Donald William *oceanographer*
Rapaport, Felix Theodosius *surgeon, researcher, educator*
Rohlf, F. James *biometrician, educator*
Schneider, Mark *political science educator*
Schubel, Jerry Robert *marine science educator, scientist, university dean and official*
Shamash, Yacov *dean, electrical engineering educator*
Smith, John Brewster *dean library sciences, director*
Solomon, Philip Myron *astronomer, atmospheric scientist*
Spector, Marshall *philosophy educator*
Steigbigel, Roy Theodore *infectious disease physician and scientist, educator*
†Susman, Randall L. *anatomy educator, anthropologist*
Tanur, Judith Mark *sociologist, educator*
Travis, Martin Bice *political scientist, educator*
Tucker, Alan Curtiss *mathematics educator*
Weidner, Donald J. *geophysicist educator*
Wurster, Charles Frederick *environmental scientist, educator*
Yahil, Amos *astrophysicist, educator*
Yang, Chen Ning *physicist, educator*
Zemanian, Armen Humpartsoum *electrical engineer, mathematician*

Suffern
Monahan, Frances Donovan *nursing educator*
Schachter, Michael Ben *psychiatrist*
Sutherland, George Leslie *retired chemical company executive*
Unger, Barbara *poet, writer, educator*
Walsh, James Jerome *philosophy educator*
Zecca, John Andrew *retired association executive*

Sunnyside
Giaimo, Kathryn Ann *performing arts company executive*

Swain
Robinson, Bina Aitchison *publisher, newsletter editor*

Syosset
Bainton, Donald J. *diversified manufacturing company executive*
Barry, Richard Francis *retired life insurance company executive*
Guthart, Leo A. *electronics executive*
Hershey, Alfred Day *geneticist*
Kantor, Edwin *investment company executive*
Kata, Edward John *industrial products manufacturing company executive*
Lazor, Theodosius (His Beatitude Metropolitan Theodosius) *archbishop*
Nydick, David *school superintendent*
Rudman, Michael P. *publishing executive*
Vermylen, Paul Anthony, Jr. *oil company executive*

Syracuse
Abbott, George Lindell *librarian*
Akiyama, Kazuyoshi *conductor*
Alston, William Payne *philosophy educator*
Baldwin, John Edwin *chemistry educator*
Baldwin, Robert Frederick, Jr. *lawyer*
Balk, Alfred William *journalist*
Barclay, H(ugh) Douglas *lawyer, former state senator*
Beeching, Charles Train, Jr. *lawyer*
Bellanger, Barbara Doris Hoysak *biomedical research technologist*
Berra, P. Bruce *computer educator*
Birge, Robert Richards *chemistry educator*
Birkhead, Guthrie Sweeney, Jr. *political scientist, university dean*
Black, Lois Mae *clinical psychologist, educator*
Braungart, Richard Gottfried *sociology and international relations educator*
Brennan, Paul Joseph *civil engineer, educator*
Bunn, Timothy David *newspaper editor*
Burgess, Robert Lewis *ecologist, educator*
Burstyn, Joan Netta *educator*
Burtt, Benjamin Pickering *retired chemistry educator*
Butler, Katharine Gorrell *speech-language pathologist, educator*
Cabasso, Israel *polymer science educator*
Cargo, Gerald Thomas *mathematics educator*
Charters, Alexander Nathaniel *education educator emeritus*
Church, Philip Throop *mathematician, educator*
Cirando, John Anthony *lawyer*
Clausen, Jerry Lee *psychiatrist*
Cohen, William Nathan *radiologist*
Cole, Ned *bishop*
Collette, Alfred Thomas *biology and science education educator*
Conan, Robert James, Jr. *chemistry educator, consultant*
Cooke, Goodwin *international relations educator*
Costello, Thomas Joseph *bishop*
Crowley, John W(illiam) *English language educator*
Daly, Robert W. *psychiatrist, medical educator*
†Daniels, Bruce Eric *library director*
Davis, William E. *utility executive*
DeFrancisco, John Anthony *state senator, lawyer*
Delmar, Mario *cardiac physiology educator*
Denise, Theodore Cullom *philosophy educator*
DiLorenzo, Louis Patrick *lawyer*
Driver, Robert Baylor, Jr. *opera administrator*
Dudewicz, Edward John *statistician*
Dunham, Philip Bigelow *biology educator, physiologist*
Eisenberg, Michael Bruce *information studies educator*
Endries, John Michael *utility executive*
Eveleigh, Virgil William *electrical and computer engineering educator*
Fendler, Janos Hugo *chemistry educator*
Ferguson, Tracy Heiman *lawyer, educational administrator*
Fitzgerald, Harold Kenneth *social work educator, consultant*
Fitzpatrick, James David *lawyer*
Fleming, William Sloan *energy, environmental and technology company executive*
Fox, Geoffrey Charles *computer science and physics educator*
Fraser, Henry S. *lawyer*
Frohock, Fred Manuel *political science educator*
Gaal, John *lawyer*
Geisler, Linda Whitehead *hospital administrator, nurse*
Goetzmann, Harry Edward, Jr. *leasing company executive*
Gold, Joseph *medical researcher*
Goodman, Donald C. *university administrator*
Graver, Jack Edward *mathematics educator*
Hansen, Per Brinch *computer scientist*
Hayes, David Michael *lawyer*
Heffner, Ralph H. *agricultural products company executive*
Hennessey, John Philip *electric power industry executive*
Herzog, Peter Emilius *legal educator*
Hiemstra, Roger *adult education educator, writer*
Hoffman, Arthur Wolf *English language educator*
Hole, Richard Douglas *lawyer*
Honig, Arnold *physics educator, researcher*
Incaudo, Claude J. *food products company executive*
Jefferies, Michael John *electrical engineer*
Jensen, Robert Granville *geography educator, university dean*
Josephson, John Eric *food retail executive*
Jump, Bernard, Jr. *economics educator*
Kenna, E. Douglas *retired plastics company executive*
Ketcham, Ralph *history and political science educator*
Kieffer, Stephen Aaron *radiologist, educator*
King, Bernard T. *lawyer*
King, Chester Harding, Jr. *lawyer*
King, Robert Bainton *neurosurgeon*
Konski, James Louis *civil engineer*
Kopp, Robert Walter *lawyer*
Krathwohl, David Reading *education educator emeritus*
Kriebel, Mahlon Edward *physiology educator, inventor*
Kriesberg, Louis *sociologist, educator*
Kuchta, Ronald Andrew *art museum director, educator*
Landaw, Stephen Arthur *physician, educator*
Lanzafame, Samuel James *manufacturing company executive*
Lavine, Gary J. *utility executive*
Lawton, Joseph J., Jr. *lawyer*
Lemanski, Larry Fredrick *medical educator*
LePage, Wilbur Reed *electrical engineering educator*
†Levy, H. Richard *biochemistry educator*
Libove, Charles *mechanical and aerospace engineering educator*
Lichtblau, Myron Ivor *language educator*
Lillestol, Jane Marie *academic administrator*
Lyman, Frederic A. *mechanical and aerospace engineering educator, researcher*
Mangan, Charles Vincent *utility company executive*
Marcoccia, Louis Gary *accountant, university administrator*
Marge, Michael *disability prevention specialist*
Martonosi, Anthony Nicholas *biochemistry educator, researcher*
Mazur, Allan Carl *sociologist, engineer, educator*
McCurn, Neal Peters *federal judge*
McGraw, James L. *retired ophthalmologist, educator*
McNaughton, Samuel Joseph *ecology educator*
Meinig, Donald William *geography educator*
†Meng, Jin *educator*
Mesrobian, Arpena Sachaklian *publisher, editor, consultant*
Meyers, Peter L. *banker*
Miron, Murray Samuel *psychologist, educator*
†Mitchell, Robert Arthur *university chancellor*
Monmonier, Mark *graphics educator, geographer*
Moses, Robert Edward *lawyer*
Mower, Eric Andrew *communications and marketing executive*
Muller, Ernest H. *geology educator*
Munson, Howard G. *federal judge*
Murray, David George *orthopaedic surgeon, educator*
Murray, Raymond William, Jr. *lawyer*
Nafie, Laurence Allen *chemistry educator*
Nelli, D. James *school administrator, accountant*
Nelson, Douglas A. *pathologist, educator*
O'Day, Royal Lewis *former banker*
O'Keefe, Joseph Thomas *bishop*
Palmer, John L. *social sciences researcher, educator*
Pardee, Otway O'Meara *computer science educator*
Pellow, David Matthew *lawyer*
Pennock, Donald William *retired mechanical engineer*
†Pfeiffer, Alice Randel *business manager*
Phillips, Arthur William, Jr. *biology educator*
Phillips, Richard Hart *psychiatrist*
Powell, James Matthew *history educator*
Prucha, John James *geologist, educator*
†Rabuzzi, Daniel D. *medical educator*
Roberts, Robert *engineering organization executive, think-tank executive*
Robinson, Joseph Edward *geology educator, consulting petroleum geologist*
Rogers, Stephen *newspaper publisher*
Rosenbaum, Arthur Elihu *radiologist, educator*
†Rubardt, Peter Craig *conductor, educator*
Russell-Hunter, W(illiam) D(evigne) *zoology educator, research biologist, writer*
Samuels, Marwyn Stewart *geography educator*
Sargent, Robert George *engineering educator*
Schiess, Betty Bone *priest*
Schwartz, Richard Derecktor *sociologist, educator*
Scullin, Frederick James, Jr. *federal judge*
Serafin, John Alfred *art educator*
Shattuck, George Clement *lawyer*
Shaw, Kenneth Alan *university president*
Simmons, Roy, Jr. *university athletic coach*
Skoler, Louis *architect, educator*
Smardon, Richard Clay *landscape architecture and environmental studies educator*
Spaulding, Suzanne Marie *nursing educator*
Stam, David Harry *librarian*
Stephens, Edward Carl *communications educator, writer*
Sternlicht, Sanford *English and theater arts educator, writer*
Strait, Bradley Justus *electrical engineering educator*
Suhowatsky, Stephen Joseph *distribution company executive*
Sutton, Walter *English educator*
Szasz, Thomas Stephen *psychiatrist, educator, writer*
Tanenbaum, Stuart William *biotechnologist, educator*
Tatham, David Frederic *art historian, educator*
Taylor, Richard Fred, Jr. *lawyer*
Thomas, Sidney *fine arts educator, researcher*
Thorson, Stuart J. *political science educator*
Tully, William P. *civil engineer, academic administrator*
Verrillo, Ronald Thomas *neuroscientist*
Vook, Richard Werner *physics educator*
Wadley, Susan Snow *anthropologist*
†Wang, Chun-Juan Kao *mycology educator*
Warner, Jeffrey F. *banker*
Weiss, Volker *university administrator, educator*
Wellner, Marcel Nahum *physics educator, researcher*
Whittle, John Joseph *insurance company executive*
Wiecek, William Michael *law educator*
Wiggins, James Bryan *religion educator*
Wiley, Richard Gordon *electrical engineer*
Williams, William Joseph *physician, educator*
Wolff, Tobias (Jonathan Ansell Wolff) *author*

Tappan
Dell, Robert Christopher *geothermal sculptor, scenic artist*
Fox, Muriel *public relations executive*
Nickford, Juan *sculptor, educator*

Tarrytown
Anderson, John Erling *chemical engineer*
Ashburn, Anderson *magazine editor*
Bartoo, Richard Kieth *chemical engineer, consultant*
†Bowen, Christopher Edward *library director*
Chu, Foo *physician*
Dobkin, John Howard *art administrator*
Dorland, Byrl Brown *civic worker*
Ferrari, Robert Joseph *business educator, former banker*
Flanigen, Edith Marie *materials scientist*
Goldin, Milton *fund raising counsel, author*
†Grufferman, Barbara Hannah *publishing executive*
Gsand, William L. *computer company executive*
Hurley, William Joseph *information systems executive*
Hyman, Leonard Stephen *finanical consultant, economist, author*
Jarrett, Eugene Lawrence *chemical company executive*
Kane, Stanley Bruce *food products executive*
Kaplan, Richard *magazine editor*
Kroll, Nathan *film producer, director*
†LeGrice, Stephen *magazine editor*
Marcus, Sheldon *social sciences educator*
Neill, Richard Robert *retired publishing company executive*
Oelbaum, Harold *lawyer, corporate executive*
Rath, Bernard Emil *trade association executive*
Raymond, George Marc *city planner, educator*
†Safian, Keith Franklin *hospital administrator*
Sasayama, Takao *electronics company executive*
†Schleifer, Leonard S. *pharmaceuticals company executive*
Schmidt, Klaus Franz *advertising executive*
Toda, Keishi *electronics executive*
Vagelos, Pindaros Roy *pharmaceutical company executive*
†Weil, David S. *plastics manufacturing executive*
Whipple, Judith Roy *book editor*

Thendara
Hiltebrant-Isele, Jane *elementary education educator*

Thornwood
Bassett, Lawrence C *management consultant*
Chin, Carolyn Sue *business executive*
Douglas, Patricia Jeanne *systems designer, certification/testing consultant*

Ticonderoga
Westbrook, Nicholas Kilmer *museum administrator, historian*

Tonawanda
Browning, James Franklin *professional society executive*
†Buzzard, Clay E. *wholesale distribution executive*
Haller, Calvin John *banker*
Hettrick, John Lord *banker, manufacturer*
Miller, Robert James *fundraising company executive*

Troy
Abetti, Pier Antonio *consulting electrical engineer, technology management and entrepreneurship educator*
Ahlers, Rolf Willi *philosopher, theologian*
Anderson, John Bailey *electrical engineering educator*
Archer, Sydney *chemistry educator*
Baron, Robert Alan *psychology and business educator, author*
Bean, Charles Palmer *biophysicist*
†Belfort, Georges *chemical engineering educator, consultant*
Berg, Daniel *science and technology educator*
Bergles, Arthur Edward *mechanical engineering educator*
Block, Robert Charles *nuclear engineering and engineering physics educator*
Bonney, William Lawless *data processing and telecommunications educator*
Brazil, Harold Edmund *political science educator*
Breed, Helen Illick *ichthyologist, educator*
Brunelle, Eugene John, Jr. *mechanical engineering educator*
Buckley, J. Stephen *newspaper publisher*
Bunce, Stanley Chalmers *chemist, educator*
Chapman, Sara Simmons *academic administrator, English educator*
Cole, Julian D. *mathematician, educator*
Corelli, John Charles *physicist, educator*
Daves, Glenn Doyle, Jr. *science educator, chemist, researcher*
Desrochers, Alan Alfred *electrical engineer*
Diwan, Romesh Kumar *economics educator*
Drew, Donald Allen *mathematical sciences educator*
Duchessi, Nancy A. *manufacturing technology company administrator*
Duquette, David Joseph *materials science and engineering educator*
†Ehrlich, Henry Lutz *biology educator*
Feeser, Larry James *civil engineering educator, researcher*
Ferris, James Peter *chemist, educator*
Fleischer, Robert Louis *physics educator*
Gerhardt, Lester A. *engineering educator, dean*
Giaever, Ivar *physicist*
Gill, William Nelson *chemical engineering educator*
Glicksman, Martin Eden *materials engineering educator*
Gorenstein, Shirley Slotkin *anthropologist, educator*
Greenwood, Allan N. *engineering educator, researcher*
Gutmann, Ronald J. *electrical engineering educator*
Haviland, David Sands *architectural educator, researcher, administrator*
Hickok, Robert Lyman, Jr. *electrophysics educator*
Horton, John Tod *engineering company executive*
Jacobson, Melvin Joseph *applied mathematician, acoustician, educator*
Jones, E. Stewart, Jr. *lawyer*
Jones, Owen Craven, Jr. *nuclear and mechanical engineer, educator*
Jordan, Mark Henry *consulting civil engineer*
Judd, Gary *university administrator*
Kahl, William Frederick *retired college president*
Knoll, Bruce Evans *state agency administrator, lawyer*
Koretz, Jane Faith *biophysicist*
Krause, Sonja *chemistry educator, researcher*
Krempl, Erhard *mechanics educator, consultant*
Kroner, Walter Manfred *architect, educator*
†Lahey, Richard Thomas, Jr. *nuclear engineer, fluid mechanics engineer*
Le Maistre, Christopher William *educational director*
Levinger, Joseph Solomon *physicist, educator*
Littman, Howard *chemical engineer, educator*
McDonald, John Francis Patrick *electrical engineering educator*
McKinley, William A. *educator, physicist*
McNaughton, Robert Forbes, Jr. *computer science educator*
Medicus, Heinrich Adolf *physicist, educator*
Messler, Robert Wilmer, Jr. *materials engineering educator, consultant*
Miller, Donald Spencer *geologist, educator*
Modestino, James William *electrical engineering educator*
Nelson, John Keith *electrical engineer*
O'Neil, Mary Agnes *health science facility administrator*
Pfau, Charles Julius *biology educator, researcher*
Phelan, Thomas *clergyman, academic administrator, educator*
Pipes, Robert Byron *academic administrator, mechanical engineer*
Potts, Kevin T. *emeritus chemistry educator*
Resnick, Robert *physicist, educator*
Robinson, Sharon Pattyson *English educator*
Romond, James *principal*
Roy, Rob J. *biomedical engineer, anesthesiologist*
Rubens, Philip *communications educator, technical writer*
Sanderson, Arthur Clark *engineering educator*
Saridis, George Nicholas *electrical engineer*
†Saxena, Arjun Nath *physicist*
Schechter, Stephen L. *political scientist*
Schwartz, Robert William *management consultant*
Shephard, Mark Scott *civil and mechanical engineering educator*
Snyder, Patricia Di Benedetto *theater director and administrator*
Sperber, Daniel *physicist*
Stoloff, Norman Stanley *metallurgical engineering educator, researcher*
Wait, Samuel Charles, Jr. *academic administrator, educator*
Wentorf, Robert Henry *physical chemist*
Whitburn, Merrill Duane *English literature educator*
White, Frederick Andrew *physics educator, physicist*
Wiberley, Stephen Edward *chemistry educator, consultant*
Wilson, Jack Martin *university administrator, scientific association executive, physics educator*
Woods, John William *electrical, computer and systems engineering educator, consultant*
Zimmie, Thomas Frank *civil engineer, educator*

Trumansburg
Billings, Peggy Marie *religious organization administrator, educator*
Mc Connell, John Wilkinson *labor relations educator, labor arbitrator, former socio-economics educator*
Taylor, Richard *philosopher, educator*

Tuckahoe
Silk, Eleana S. *librarian*

Tupper Lake
Welsh, Peter Corbett *museum consultant, historian*

Tuxedo Park
Brown, Walston Shepard *lawyer*
De Main, John *conductor, music director*
Domjan, Joseph (Spiri Domjan) *artist*
Hall, Frederick Keith *chemist*
Heusser, Calvin John *biology educator, researcher*
Neblett, Carol *soprano*
Rossman, Toby Gale *genetic toxicology educator, researcher*
Shore, Howard Leslie *composer*

Unadilla
Compton, John Robinson *printing company executive*

Uniondale
Bossy, Michael *professional hockey player*
Brown, Kenneth Lloyd *lawyer*
Fortunoff, Alan Meyer *retail company executive*
Frashier, Gary Even *corporation executive*
Henning, Lorne Edward *professional hockey coach*
Mishler, Jacob *federal judge*
Pierce, Stanley *lawyer*
Platt, Thomas Collier, Jr. *federal judge*
Ray, Norretta *clinical social worker, administrator, psychotherapist, educator, consultant*
Seybert, Joanna *judge*
Shapiro, Barry Robert *lawyer*
Spatt, Arthur Donald *federal judge*
Tempest, Harrison F. *bank executive*
Waldhof, Sharka Eva *lawyer*
†Walter, Orris G., Jr. *health facilities adminstrator*

Unionville
Kemnitz, Thomas Milton *publisher*

Upton
Blume, Martin *physicist*
Bond, Peter Danford *physicist*
Casten, Richard Francis *physicist*
Chrien, Robert Edward *physicist*
Chung, Suh-Urk *physicist*
Cronkite, Eugene Pitcher *physician*
Dover, Carl Bellman *physicist, consultant*
Friedlander, Gerhart *nuclear chemist*
Goldhaber, Gertrude Scharff *physicist*
Goldhaber, Maurice *physicist*
Hamilton, Leonard Derwent *physician, molecular biologist*
Hendrie, Joseph Mallam *physicist, nuclear engineer, government official*
Holroyd, Richard Allan *researcher*
Kato, Walter Yoneo *physicist*
Lowenstein, Derek Irving *physicist*
Marr, Robert Bruce *physicist, educator*
Petrakis, Leonidas *research scientist, educator, administrator*
Radeka, Veljko *electronics engineer*
Rau, Ralph Ronald *physicist*
Samios, Nicholas Peter *physicist*
Setlow, Jane Kellock *biophysicist*
Setlow, Richard Burton *biophysicist*
†Shutt, Ralph B. *research physicist*
Souw, Bernard Eng-Kie *physicist, consultant*
Steinberg, Meyer *chemical engineer*
Studier, Frederick William *biophysicist*
Susskind, Herbert *biomedical engineer, educator*
Sutin, Norman *chemistry educator, scientist*
Wolf, Alfred Peter *chemist, educator*

Utica
Antzelevitch, Charles *research center executive*
Bloch, Milton Joseph *museum administrator*
Boyle, William Leo, Jr. *educational consultant, retired college president*
Cardamone, Richard J. *federal judge*
Donovan, Donna Mae *newspaper publisher*
Ehre, Victor Tyndall *insurance company executive*
Max, Theodore Conrad *surgeon*
McIntyre, Judith Watland *ornithologist, biology educator*
Pribble, Easton *artist*
Schrauth, William Lawrence *banker, lawyer*
Schweizer, Paul Douglas *museum director*
Simpson, Michael Kevin *college president, political science educator*
Slattery, James Arthur *electronics company executive*

Vails Gate
Fife, Betty H. *librarian*

Valatie
Opela, Marian Meade *principal, consultant*

Valhalla
Adler, Karl Paul *medical educator, academic administrator*
Carter, Anne Cohen *physician*
Christenson, William Newcome *physician*
Cimino, Joseph Anthony *physician, educator*
Del Guercio, Louis Richard Maurice *surgeon, educator, company executive*
Emerson, Rose *career consultant*
Ferrone, Soldano *microbiology and immunology educator, physician*
Fink, Raymond *medical educator*
Gross, Stanislaw *environmental sciences educator, activist*
Hodgson, W(alter) John B(arry) *surgeon*
Itskovitz, Harold David *physician*
Levin, Aaron Reuben *pediatrician, educator*
Levy, Norman B. *psychiatrist, educator*
McGiff, John C(harles) *pharmacologist*
Niguidula, Faustino Nazario *pediatric cardiothoracic surgeon*
Smythe, Sheila Mary *academic dean*
Weisburger, John Hans *medical researcher*
Williams, Gary Murray *medical researcher, pathology educator*

Valley Cottage
Atha, Stuart Kimball, Jr. *retired banker*

Valley Stream
Blakeman, Royal Edwin *lawyer*
Golden, Hyman *beverage products company executive*
Lehrer, Stanley *magazine publisher, editorial director, corporate executive*
Natow, Annette Baum *nutritionist, author, consultant*
Rachlin, Harvey Brant *author, music company executive*

Van Hornesville
Case, Everett Needham *former university president, educator*

Vestal
Koffman, Milton Aaron *corporate executive*
Piaker, Philip Martin *accountant, educator*

Waccabuc
Hall, Elizabeth *writer*
Kislik, Richard William *publishing executive*
Thompson, Edward Thorwald *magazine editor*

Wading River
Kretschmer, Ingrid Butler *elementary school educator*

Wainscott
Dubow, Arthur Myron *investor, lawyer*
Henderson, William Charles *editor*
Herzog, Arthur, III *author*
Russo, Alexander Peter *artist, educator*
Wainwright, Stuyvesant, II *lawyer*

Walden
Hanau, Kenneth John, Jr. *packaging company executive*

Wallkill
Koch, Edwin Ernest *artist, interior decorator*

Wantagh
Dawson, George Glenn *economics educator emeritus*
DeNapoli, Anthony *middle school principal*
Litman, Bernard *electrical engineer, consultant*
Ross, Sheldon Jules *dentist*
Smits, Edward John *museum consultant*
Urbaitis, Elena *artist*
Zinder, Newton Donald *stock market analyst, consultant*

Wappingers Falls
Engelman, Melvin Alkon *retired dentist, business executive, scientist*
Hogan, Edward Robert *financial services executive*
Johnson, Jeh Vincent *architect*
Maissel, Leon Israel *physicist, engineer*
Nolan, John Thomas, Jr. *retired oil industry administrator*

Warsaw
Dy-Ang, Anita C. *pediatrician*

Warwick
Franck, Frederick Sigfred *artist, author, dental surgeon*

Washingtonville
Perrego, Virginia *mathematics educator*

Water Mill
D'Urso, Joseph Paul *designer*
Mac Whinnie, John Vincent *artist*
Rosenberg, Alex Jacob *art dealer, curator, fine arts appraiser, educator*

Waterford
Gold, James Paul *museum director*

Watertown
Coe, Benjamin Plaisted *retired state official*
Johnson, John Brayton *editor, publisher*

Watervliet
Kitchens, Clarence Wesley, Jr. *physical science administrator*

Watkins Glen
Saks, William Joseph, Jr. *osteopathic physician, educator*

Wayland
Wisniewski, Joseph Michael *engineering executive*

Webster
Conwell, Esther Marly *physicist*
Duke, Charles Bryan *research and development manufacturing executive, physics educator*
Garg, Devendra *financial executive*
Johnson, Ray Clifford *mechanical engineering educator, consultant, writer*
Nicholson, Douglas Robert *accountant*
Witmer, G. Robert *retired state supreme court justice*

Weedsport
Cichello, Samuel Joseph *architect*

Wellsville
Taylor, Theodore Brewster *physicist, business executive*

West Babylon
Ziegler, Mandell Stanley *composite sheet manufacturing executive*

West Bloomfield
Charron, Helene Kay Shetler *nursing educator*

West Haverstraw
Cochran, George Van Brunt *physician, surgery educator, researcher*

West Hempstead
Brodsky, Irwin Abel *retired stockbroker*
Rothberg, June Simmonds *nursing educator emerita, psychotherapist, psychoanalyst*

West Islip
Softness, Donald Gabriel *marketing and manufacturing executive*

West Nyack
Gillespie, John Fagan *mining executive*
Hornik, Joseph William *civil engineer*
†Irwin, Ronald Gilbert *minister*
Painter, Carl Eric *manufacturing company executive*
Pringle, Laurence Patrick *writer*

West Point
Barr, Donald Roy *statistics and operations research educator, statistician*
Barrett, Lida Kittrell *mathematics educator*
Galloway, Gerald Edward, Jr. *dean*
Graves, Howard Dwayne *army officer, academic administrator, educator*
Meschutt, David Randolph *curator, historian*
†Moss, Michael Eric *museum director*
Watson, Georgianna *librarian*

West Stockholm
O'Brien, Neal Ray *geology educator*

Westbury
Barboza, Anthony *photographer, artist*
Cullen, John B. *food products company executive*
De Pauw, Gommar Albert *priest, educator*
Eisenberg, Dorothy *federal judge*
Ente, Gerald *pediatrician*
Fogg, Joseph Graham, III *investment banking executive*
Kennedy, Bernard D. *food products executive*
Martin, Daniel Richard *pharmaceutical company executive*
Olsten, Stuart *personnel services company executive*
Sandler, Gerald Howard *aerospace executive*
Sherbell, Rhoda *artist, sculptor*
Tulchin, Stanley *banker, lecturer, author, business reorganization consultant*

Westfield
Brown, Kent Louis, Sr. *surgeon*

Westhampton Beach
Maas, Jane Brown *advertising executive*

Westmoreland
Mathews, Barbara Bailey *special education educator*

White Plains
Alin, Robert David *lawyer*
†Aurichio, Joseph Louis *electrical and electronic manufacturing executive*
Beaupre, Lawrence Kenneth *newspaper editor*
†Benjamin, Colin Henry *metals company executive*
Benjamin, Theodore Simon *publishing company executive*
Berlin, Alan Daniel *lawyer, international energy and legal consultant*
Bijur, Peter I. *petroleum company executive*
Blank, H. Robert *psychiatrist*
Blass, John Paul *medical educator, physician*
Blumstein, William A. *insurance company executive*
Bober, Lawrence Harold *retired banker*
Boudreaux, John *public relations specialist*
Brazell, James Ervin *oil company executive, lawyer*
Brieant, Charles La Monte *federal judge*
Broderick, Vincent Lyons *federal judge*
Burke, Raymond F. *lawyer*
Busch, Paul Louis *engineering company executive, consultant*
Cahill, William Joseph, Jr. *utility company executive*
Carey, John *lawyer, judge*
†Chilewich, Simon *commodity trading company, cattle, meat packing company executive*
Cohen, Richard Norman *insurance executive*
Cohn, Howard *retired magazine editor*
Colwell, Howard Otis *advertising executive*
Cooke, Lloyd Miller *former organization executive*
Davidson, Carl B. *oil company executive*
DeCrane, Alfred Charles, Jr. *petroleum company executive*
Dickinson, Richard Raymond *retired oil company executive*
Dowd, Peter Jerome *public relations executive*
Doyle, William Patrick *oil company executive*
Ellenbogen, Milton Joseph *publishing executive, editor, writer*
Erla, Karen *artist, painter, collagist, printmaker*
Fjelde, Rolf Gerhard *translator, writer, educator*
Foster, John Horace *consulting environmental engineer*
Fudge, Ann Marie *marketing executive*
†Gioia, (Michael) Dana *poet, literary critic*
Gjertsen, O. Gerard *lawyer*
Glassman, George Morton *dermatologist*
Goldberg, Steven H. *law educator*
†Goodman, Walter *author, editor*
Grayson, Richard Steven (Lord of Mursley) *foreign correspondent, international legal and political management consultant, educator*
Greene, Leonard Michael *aerospace manufacturing executive, institute executive*
Gurahian, Vincent *church official, former judge*
Hardin, Adlai Stevenson, Jr. *judge*
Henningsen, Victor William, Jr. *food company executive*
†Hoffman, Milton Sills *editor*
Jensen, Eric Finn *lawyer*
Jensen, Grady Edmonds *association executive*
Johnson, Daniel Robert *lawyer*
Johnson, Janet A. *law educator, academic dean*
Johnston, Richard Boles, Jr. *pediatrician, educator, biomedical researcher*
Katz, Michael *pediatrician, educator*
Kisseberth, Paul Barto *publishing executive*
Konney, Paul Edward *consumer products company executive, lawyer*
Krowe, Allen Julian *oil company executive*
Lawrence, George Hubbard Clapp *investment company executive*
Lorelli, Michael Kevin *personal care products executive*
Lynch, Patrick *petroleum company executive*
Machover, Carl *computer graphics consultant*
Magaziner, Elliot Albert *musician, conductor, educator*
Manville, Stewart Roebling *archivist*
Manzione, Arthur P. *parochial schools administrator*
Marano, Anthony Joseph *cardiologist*
McDowell, Fletcher Hughes *physician, educator*
McQuaid, John G. *lawyer*
Merritt, Susan Mary *computer science educator, university dean*
Mitchell, Robert Dale *consulting engineer*
Monteferrante, Judith Catherine *cardiologist*
Munneke, Gary Arthur *law educator, consultant*
Nickerson, Ruth *sculptor*
O'Rourke, Andrew Patrick *lawyer, county official*
Papp, Laszlo George *architect*
Payson, Martin Fred *lawyer*
Peck, Alexander Norman *physical education educator, day camp administrator*
Peyton, Donald Leon *retired standards association executive*
Rapp, Richard Tilden *economist, consultant*
Reilly, John Lawrence *banker*
Roll, Irwin Clifford (Win Roll) *advertising, marketing and publishing executive*
Rose, William Allen, Jr. *architect*
Rosenberg, Michael *lawyer*
Samii, Abdol Hossein *physician, educator*
Schwartzberg, Howard *federal judge*
Sharp, Donald Eugene *bank consultant*
Smith, Elizabeth Patience *oil industry executive, lawyer*
Smith, Gerard Peter *neuroscientist*
Sora, Sebastian Antony *business machines manufacturing executive, educator*
Stith, Forrest Christopher *bishop*
Taylor, Judith Mundlak *neurologist*
Teitell, Conrad Laurence *lawyer, author*
Tell, William Kirn, Jr. *oil company executive, lawyer*
Tobin, Steven Michael *insurance company executive*
Triffin, Nicholas *law librarian, law educator*
Vergari, Carl Anthony *lawyer*
Wefer, Donald Peters *lawyer*
Welsh, Dennie M. *business machines company executive*
Westerhoff, Garret Peter *environmental engineer, executive*
Westerman, Gayl Shaw *law educator*
Wheaton, David *professional tennis player*

Whitesboro
Raymonda, James Earl *retired banker*

Williamsville
Danni, F. Robert *municipal official*
Paladino, Joseph Anthony *clinical pharmacist*
Reisman, Robert E. *physician, educator*

Wolcott
Anderson, Nancy Marie Greenwood *special education educator*
Bartlett, Cody Blake *lawyer, educator*

Woodbury
Agresti, Miriam Monell *psychologist*
Bell, William Joseph *cable television company executive*
Bleicher, Sheldon Joseph *endocrinologist, medical educator*
Lemle, Robert Spencer *lawyer*
Randolph, Francis Fitz, Jr. *cable television executive*
Sweeney, Daniel Thomas *cable television company executive*
†Wertheim, Harvey J. *human resource specialist*
Zirkel, Don *public information official*

Woodmere
Abramson, Martin *author, journalist*
Bobroff, Harold *lawyer*
Raab, Ira Jerry *lawyer*

Woodside
†DeFranco, Elizabeth Carol *editor*

Woodstock
Banks, Rela *sculptor*
Cox, James David *art gallery executive*
Godwin, Gail Kathleen *author*
Hoyt, Earl Edward, Jr. *industrial designer*
Ober, Stuart Alan *investment consultant, book publisher*
Smith, Albert Aloysius, Jr. *electrical engineer, consultant*

Wyandanch
Barnett, Peter John *property development executive, educator*

Yaphank
Ahern, John James *software company executive*

Yonkers
Agli, Stephen Michael *English language and literature educator*
Atkins, Leola Mae *special education educator*
Baumel, Herbert *violinist, conductor*
DeAngelis, Roger Thomas *surgeon*
Denver, Eileen Ann *magazine editor*
Drisko, Elliot Hillman *marriage and family therapist*
Eimicke, Victor W(illiam) *publishing company executive*
Foy, James E. *hospital administrator*
Gunner, Murray *Jewish organization administrator*
Karpatkin, Rhoda Hendrick *consumer information organization executive, lawyer*
Kresh, Paul *author, editor*
Landau, Irwin *magazine publishing company executive*
Liggio, Jean Vincenza *adult education educator, artist*
Miller, Jacqueline Winslow *library director*
†Petrillo, Carl Edward *construction company executive*
Robinson, Chester Hersey *retired dean*
Rosch, Paul John *physician, educator*
Varma, Baidya Nath *sociologist, broadcaster, poet*
Wolfson, Irwin M. *insurance company executive*

Yorktown Heights
Agarwal, Ramesh Chandra *applied mathematician, researcher*
Allen, Frances Elizabeth *computer scientist*
Bogdanoff, Stewart Ronald *physical education educator, coach*
Chang, Chin-An *research scientist*
†Cocke, John *computer scientist*
Dennard, Robert Heath *engineering executive, scientist*
d'Heurle, François Max *research scientist, engineering educator*
Fowler, Alan Bicksler *retired physicist*
†Garwin, Richard Lawrence *physicist*
Green, Paul Eliot, Jr. *communications scientist*
Gutzwiller, Martin Charles *theoretical physicist, research scientist*
Hoffman, Alan Jerome *mathematician, educator*
Hong, Se June *computer engineer*
Hsieh, Hazel Tseng *elementary education educator*
Jaffe, Jeffrey Martin *computer scientist*
Jones, Lauretta Marie *artist, graphic designer, computer interface designer*
Keyes, Robert William *physicist*
Kirkpatrick, Edward Scott *physicist*
Klein, Richard Stephen *internist*
Landauer, Rolf William *physicist*
Lang, Norton David *physicist*
LaRussa, Joseph Anthony *optical company executive*
Laventhol, Henry L(ee) (Hank Laventhol) *artist, etcher*
Mandelbrot, Benoit B. *mathematician, scientist, educator*
†Meyerson, Bernard Steele *physicist*
Ning, Tak Hung *physicist, microelectronic technologist*
Pugh, Emerson William *electrical engineer*
Romankiw, Lubomyr Taras *materials engineer*
Rosenblatt, Stephen Paul *marketing and sales promotion company executive*
Rosenfeld, Steven Ira *artistic director, music publisher*
Samalin, Edwin *lawyer, educator*
Sorokin, Peter Pitirimovich *physicist*
Spiller, Eberhard Adolf *physicist*
Terman, Lewis Madison *electrical engineer, researcher*
Troutman, Ronald R. *electrical engineer*
Wajda, Tadeusz *engineer*
Winograd, Shmuel *mathematician*
Wong, Chak-Kuen *computer scientist*

Youngstown
Alpert, Norman *chemical company executive*
Dunnigan, Brian Leigh *historic site administrator*

NORTH CAROLINA

Advance
Cochrane, Betsy Lane *state senator*
Huber, Thomas Martin *container company executive*
Legere, Laurence Joseph *government official*

Albemarle
Bramlett, Christopher Lewis *academic administrator*

Angier
Raynor, Wandra Adams *middle school educator*

Apex
Knapp, Richard Bruce *anesthesiologist*

Archdale
Riddick, Douglas Smith *horticultural industrialist, industrial designer*

Asheville
Annarino, Will Ray *protective services official*
Armstrong, Robert Baker *textile company executive*
Baldwin, Garza, Jr. *lawyer, manufacturing company executive*
Banks, James Barber *publishing executive*
Bissette, Winston Louis, Jr. *lawyer, mayor*
Cecil, William A. V., Sr. *landmark director*
Coli, Guido John *chemical company executive*
Conroy, David James *retired chemical and diversified manufacturing executive*
Damtoft, Walter Atkinson *editor, publisher*
Davenport, L. B. *bishop*
Davis, Roy Walton, Jr. *lawyer*
Dillon, Gary Gene *manufacturing company executive*
Etter, Robert Miller *retired consumer products executive, chemist*
Everett, Durward R., Jr. *retired banker*
Fobes, John Edwin *international organization official*
Gabriel, Robert *art association administrator*
Haggard, William Henry *meteorologist*
Hyde, Herbert Lee *lawyer*
Johnston, John Devereaux, Jr. *law educator*
Jones, J. Kenneth *art dealer, former museum administrator*
King, Joseph Bertram *architect*
Laney, Landy B. *supermarket chain executive*
Lord, Anthony *retired architect*
Merrill, Edward Clifton, Jr. *emeritus university president*
Powell, Norborne Berkeley *urologist*
Pulleyn, S(amuel) Robert *publishing company executive*
Reed, Patsy Bostick *university administrator*
Roberts, Bill Glen *retired fire chief, investor, consultant*
Rufa, Robert Henry *writer, editor, photographer, artist*
Sharpe, Keith Yount *lawyer*
Smith, Norman Cutler *geologist, business executive, educator*
Squibb, Samuel Dexter *chemistry educator*
Vander Voort, Dale Gilbert *textile company executive*
Voorhees, Richard Lesley *federal judge*
Wallin, Franklin Whittelsey *educational consultant, former college president*
Weed, Maurice James *composer, retired music educator*
Weil, Thomas P. *health services consultant*
Wilson, Lauren Ross *academic administrator*

Atlantic Beach
Barnes, James Thomas, Jr. *aquarium administrator*

Banner Elk
Isbell, Robert *writer*

Beaufort
Cullman, Hugh *retired tobacco company executive*
Hayman, Carol Bessent *poet, author*

Belmont
Stowe, Daniel Harding, Sr. *textile executive*
Stowe, Robert Lee, III *textile company executive*

Biscoe
McIlvaine, William L. *secondary school educator*

Black Mountain
Holden, Reuben Andrus *retired college president*
Ingle, Robert P. *retail groceries company executive*
Kennedy, William Bean *theology educator*
Lathrop, Gertrude Adams *chemist, consultant*
Pinkerton, Linda F. *lawyer*
Weatherford, Willis Duke, Jr. *college president emeritus*
Weinhauer, William Gillette *retired bishop*

Blowing Rock
Haley, Gail E(inhart) *author*

Boiling Springs
Lamb, Robert Lee *religious studies educator*
White, Martin Christopher *academic administrator*

Boone
Auten, Janet Sue Houck *secondary education educator*
Borkowski, Francis Thomas *university administrator*
Bowden, Elbert Victor *banking, finance and economics educator, author*
Duke, Charles Richard *academic dean*

Boonville
Reece, Joe Wilson *engineering company executive*

Brevard
Phillips, Euan Hywel *publishing executive*
Wall, Robert Wilson, Jr. *former utility executive*

Buies Creek
Davis, Ferd Leary, Jr. *law educator, lawyer, consultant*
Wiggins, Norman Adrian *university administrator, legal educator*

Burlington
†Byrd, C. R. *retail executive*
†Byrd, Jimmy L. *retail executive*
Eddins, James William, Jr. *marketing executive*
Flagg, Raymond Osbourn *biology executive*
Golden, Carole Ann *immunologist, microbiologist*
†Harris, James D. *financial executive*
Kee, Walter Andrew *former government official*
Mason, James Michael *biomedical laboratories executive*
Powell, James Bobbitt *biomedical laboratories executive, pathologist*
Tolley, Jerry Russell *clinical laboratory executive*
Weavil, David Carlton *clinical laboratory services executive*
Wilson, William Preston *psychiatrist, emeritus educator*

Burnsville
Bernstein, William Joseph *glass artist, educator*
Doyle, John Lawrence *artist*

Calabash
Strunk, Orlo Christopher, Jr. *psychology educator*

Camden
Hammond, Roy Joseph *reinsurance company executive*

Camp Lejeune
†Van Riper, Paul Kent *marine corps officer*

Canton
†Stanback, Brad *conservationist*

Carrboro
Greenslade, Forrest Charles *international health care executive*
Patterson, Neil *science publisher*

Carthage
Thomas, Carol Taylor *general services coordinator*

Cary
Andrews, John Woodhouse *newspaper publisher*
Chignell, Colin Francis *pharmacologist*
Conrad, Hans *materials engineering educator*
†Goodwin, Barry Kent *economics educator*
Jones, James Arthur *retired utilities executive*
McCarty, Thomas Joseph *publishing company executive*
Miranda, Constancio Fernandes *civil engineering educator*
Mochrie, Richard D. *physiology educator*
Reynolds, Edward *book publisher*
†Smith, Walter Sage *environmental engineer, consultant*
Sussenguth, Edward Henry *computer company executive, computer network designer*
Talbert, Luther Marcus *physician*
†Vick, Columbus Edwin, Jr. *civil engineering design firm executive*

Cashiers
Culp, Charles Allen *financial executive*
O'Connell, Edward James, Jr. *psychology educator, computer applications and data analysis consultant*

Chapel Hill
Akin, John Stephen *economics educator*
Andrews, Richard Nigel Lyon *environmental policy educator, environmental studies administrator*
Azar, Henry Amin *pathologist, medical historian*
Baerg, Richard Henry *podiatrist, surgeon, educator*
†Bailey, Donald B., Jr. *medical and special education educator*
Bain, Robert Addison *American literature educator*
Baker, Charles Ray *engineering and mathematics educator, researcher*
Baker, Ronald Dale *dental educator, surgeon, university administrator*
Barnett, Thomas Buchanan *physician, medical educator*
Baroff, George Stanley *psychologist, educator*
Baron, Samuel Haskell *historian*
Barranger, Milly Slater *performing arts company executive, writer*
Bauer, Frederick Christian *motor carrier executive*
Bawden, James Wyatt *dental educator, dental scientist*
Behrman, Jack Newton *economist*
Best, Winfield Judson *television producer, writer, public relations consultant*
Betts, Doris June Waugh *author, English language educator*
Black, Stanley Warren, III *economics educator*
Blasius, Donald Charles *appliance company executive*
Blau, Peter Michael *sociologist, educator*
Boggs, Robert Newell *editor*
Bolas, Gerald Douglas *art museum administrator, art history educator*
Bolick, Ernest Bernard, Jr. *housing administrator*
Bondurant, Stuart *physician, educational administrator*
Boone, Franklin Delanor Roosevelt, Sr. *cardiovascular perfusionist, realtor*
Bowers, Thomas Arnold *journalism educator*
Brinkhous, Kenneth Merle *pathologist, educator*
Brockington, Donald Leslie *anthropologist, archaeologist, educator*
†Brookhart, Maurice S. *chemist*
Broun, Kenneth Stanley *lawyer, educator*
Brown, Frank *social science educator*
Brownlee, Robert Calvin *pediatrician, educator*
Brummet, Richard Lee *accounting educator*
Buck, Richard Pierson *chemistry educator, researcher*
Bursey, Maurice M. *chemistry educator*
Butler, James Robert *geology educator*
Camp, Joseph Shelton, Jr. *film producer, director, writer*
Campbell, B. (Obby) Jack *university official*
Campbell, Jerry Dean *librarian*
†Cance, William George *surgeon*
Carpenter, Raymond Leonard *information science educator*
Carroll, John Bissell *psychologist, educator*
Carroll, Roy *academic administrator*
Cartwright, William Holman *education educator emeritus*
Chi, Vernon Longstreet *computer science educator, administrator*
Clark, Richard Lee *radiologist*
Clifford, Donald Francis, Jr. *law educator*
Clyde, Wallace Alexander, Jr. *pediatrics and microbiology educator*
Cobb, Henry Van Zandt *psychologist*
Cole, Richard Ray *university dean*
Collier, Albert M. *pediatric educator, child development center director*
Coulter, Elizabeth Jackson *biostatistician, educator*
Coulter, Norman Arthur, Jr. *biomedical engineering educator emeritus*
Crane, Julia Gorham *anthropology educator*
Crohn, Max Henry, Jr. *lawyer*
Cromartie, William James *medical educator, researcher*
Dahlstrom, William Grant *psychologist, educator*
Dareff, Hal *author, editor, publisher*
Davis, Morris Schuyler *astronomer*
Dearman, Henry Hursell *chemistry educator*
Debreczeny, Paul *Slavic language educator, author*
Dennison, John Manley *geologist, educator*
Denny, Floyd Wolfe, Jr. *pediatrician*
Dixon, Frederick Dail *architect*
Dixon, John Wesley, Jr. *retired religion and art educator*
Dolan, Louise Ann *physicist*
Droegemueller, William *gynecologist, obstetrician, medical educator*
Easterling, William Ewart, Jr. *obstetrician, gynecologist*
Eaton, Charles Edward *English language educator, author*
Edwards, Richard LeRoy *academic dean, social work educator, non-profit management consultant*
Eifrig, David Eric *ophthalmologist, educator*
Eisenbeis, Robert A. *business educator*
Eisenbud, Merril *environmental engineer*
Eliel, Ernest Ludwig *chemist, educator*
Ellis, Fred Wilson *pharmacology educator*
Ellis, Michael *theatrical producer*
Falk, Eugene Hannes *foreign language educator emeritus*
Farmer, Thomas Wohlsen *neurologist, educator*
Fischer, Janet Jordan *retired physician, educator, researcher*
Fischer, Newton Duchan *otolaryngologist, educator*
Flora, Joseph M(artin) *English language educator*
Fordham, Christopher Columbus, III *university dean and chancellor, medical educator*
Forman, Donald T. *biochemist*
Fox, Ronald Ernest *psychologist*
Frampton, Paul Howard *physics researcher, educator*
Frankenberg, Dirk *marine scientist*
Frelinger, Jeffrey Allen *immunologist, educator*
Friday, William Clyde *university president emeritus*
Friedman, James Winstein *economist, educator*
Fullagar, Paul David *geology educator, geochemical consultant*
Furst, Lilian Renee *language professional, educator*
Gallman, Robert Emil *economics and history educator*
Gasaway, Laura Nell *law librarian, educator*
Gil, Federico Guillermo *political science educator*
Gilbert, Lawrence Irwin *biologist, educator*
Glaze, William Howard *environmental educator*
Godschalk, David Robinson *architect, urban development planner, educator*
Goldman, Leonard Manuel *physicist, engineering educator*
Gottschalk, Carl William *physician, educator*
Goyer, Robert Andrew *pathology educator*
Graham, George Adams *political scientist, emeritus educator*
Graham, John Borden *pathologist, educator*
Gray-Little, Bernadette *psychologist*
Greganti, Mac Andrew *physician, medical educator*
Gressman, Eugene *lawyer*
Grisham, Joe Wheeler *pathologist, educator*
Gulick, John *anthropology educator*
Hairston, Nelson George *animal ecologist*
†Halverson, Paul Kenneth *hospital executive*
Hammond, David Alan *stage director, educator*
Haskell, Paul Gershon *law educator*
Hatfield, William Emerson *chemist, educator*
Hawkins, David Rollo, Sr. *psychiatrist, educator*
Hendricks, Charles Henning *retired obstetrics and gynecology educator*
Heninger, Simeon Kahn, Jr. *English language educator*
Henson, Anna Miriam *otolaryngology researcher, medical educator*
Henson, O'Dell Williams, Jr. *anatomy educator*
Hershey, H(oward) Garland, Jr. *university administrator, orthodontist*
Hirsch, Philip Francis *pharmacologist, educator*
Hitchings, George Herbert *retired pharmaceutical company executive, educator*
Hochbaum, Godfrey Martin *retired behavioral scientist*
Holley, Edward Gailon *library science educator, former university dean*
Hollister, William Gray *psychiatrist*
Hubbard, Paul Stancyl, Jr. *physics educator*
Hulka, Barbara Sorenson *epidemiology educator*
Hulka, Jaroslav Fabian *obstetrician, gynecologist*
†Ingram, James Carlton *economist, educator*
Irene, Eugene Arthur *physical chemistry educator, researcher*
Jackson, Blyden *English language educator*
Jerdee, Thomas Harlan *business administration educator, organization psychology researcher and consultant*
Johnson, George, Jr. *physician, educator*
Jones, Houston Gwynne *history educator*
Jones, Lyle Vincent *psychology educator*
Jones, Mary Ellen *biochemist*
Joyner, Leon Felix *university administrator, retired*
Judd, Burke Haycock *geneticist*
Kasarda, John Dale *business educator, researcher, administrator, consultant*
Kilgour, Frederick Gridley *librarian, educator*
Kittredge, John Kendall *retired insurance company executive*
Klarmann, Dave *university athletic coach*
Klompmaker, Jay Edward *business administration educator*
Kohn, Richard H. *historian, educator*
Kuenzler, Edward Julian *ecologist and environmental biologist*
Kusy, Robert Peter *biomedical engineering and orthodontics educator*
Langdell, Robert Dana *medical educator*
Langenderfer, Harold Quentin *accountant, educator*
Lauder, Valarie Anne *editor, educator*
Lauterborn, Robert F. *advertising educator*
Lawrence, David Michael *lawyer, educator*
†Lee, Kuo-Hsiung *medicinal chemistry educator*
Lee, Sherman Emery *art historian, curator*
Levine, Madeline Geltman *Slavic literatures educator, translator*
Loeb, Ben Fohl, Jr. *lawyer, educator*
Long, Douglas Clark *philosophy educator*
Lowman, Robert Paul *psychology educator, academic administrator*
Lucas, Carol Lee *biomedical engineer*
Ludington, Charles Townsend, Jr. *English and American studies educator*
Macdonald, James Ross *physicist, educator*
MacGillivray, Lois Ann *academic administrator*
MacRae, Duncan, Jr. *social scientist, educator*
Manire, George Philip *bacteriologist, educator*
Markham, Jordan J. *physicist, retired educator*
Martin, Harry Corpening *state supreme court justice, retired*
McBay, Arthur John *toxicologist, consultant*
Mc Curdy, Harold Grier *psychologist*
McKay, Kenneth Gardiner *physicist, electronics company executive*
McMillan, Campbell White *pediatric hematologist*
Memory, Jasper Durham *academic administrator, physics educator*
Merzbacher, Eugen *physicist, educator*
Meyer, Philip Edward *journalism educator*
Meyer, Thomas J. *chemistry educator*
Miller, C. Arden *physician, educator*
Miller, Daniel Newton, Jr. *geologist, consultant*
Mitchell, Earl Nelson *physicist, educator*
Miya, Tom Saburo *retired pharmacologist, educator*
Moran, Barbara Burns *librarian, educator*
Mueller, Nancy Schneider *retired biology educator*
Munsat, Stanley Morris *philosopher, educator*
Munson, Eric Bruce *hospital administrator*
Murphy, James Lee *college dean, economics educator*
Murray, Royce Wilton *chemistry educator*
Nelson, Philip Francis *musicology educator, consultant, choral conductor*
Ness, Albert Kenneth *artist, educator*
Neumann, Andrew Conrad *geological oceanography educator*
Newman, William Stein *music educator, author, pianist, composer*
Norwood, George Joseph *pharmacy educator*
Okun, Daniel Alexander *environmental engineering educator, consulting engineer*
Oliver, Mary Wilhelmina *law librarian, educator*
Ontjes, David Ainsworth *medicine and pharmacology educator*
Pagano, Joseph Stephen *physician, researcher, educator*
Palmer, Gary Stephen *health services administrator*
Palmer, Jeffress Gary *hematologist, educator*
Parker, Scott Jackson *theatre director*
Parr, Robert Ghormley *chemistry educator*
Pavão, Leonel Maia (Lee Pavão) *advertising executive*
Perreault, William Daniel, Jr. *business administration educator*
Pfouts, Ralph William *economist, consultant*
Pollitzer, William Sprott *anatomy educator*
Powell, Burnele Venable *law educator*
Powell, Carolyn Wilkerson *music educator*
Prange, Arthur Jergen, Jr. *psychiatrist, neurobiologist, educator*
Prather, Donna Lynn *psychiatrist*
Proffit, William Robert *orthodontics educator*
Pruett, James Worrell *librarian, musicologist*
Reisner, Howard Michael *immunologist, educator*
Richardson, Richard Judson *political science educator*
Riggs, Timothy Allan *museum curator*
Rindfuss, Ronald Richard *sociology educator*
Roberts, Harold Ross *medical educator, hematologist*
Roberts, Louis Douglas *physics educator, researcher*
Rogers, John James William *geology educator*
Rondinelli, Dennis A(ugust) *business administration educator, research center director*
Rosen, Benson *business administration educator*
Rubin, Louis Decimus, Jr. *English language and literature educator, writer, publisher*
St. Jean, Joseph, Jr. *micropaleontologist, educator*
Sanders, John Lassiter *academic administrator*
Schier, Donald Stephen *language educator*
Schopler, John Henry *psychologist, educator*
Schoultz, Lars *political scientist, educator*
Schunk, Dale Hansen *psychology educator*
Scott, Tom Keck *biologist, botanist, educator*
Shapiro, Lee Tobey *planetarium administrator, astronomer*
Sharpless, Richard Kennedy *lawyer*
Sheldon, George F. *medical educator*
Shuman, Mark Samuel *environmental and electroanalytical chemistry educator*
Simons, Gordon Donald, Jr. *statistician*
Simpson, Richard Lee *sociologist, educator*
Slack, Lewis *organization administrator*
Slifkin, Lawrence Myer *physics educator*
Smith, Dean Edwards *university basketball coach*
Smith, James Finley *economist, educator*
Smith, Sidney Rufus, Jr. *linguist, educator*
Spangler, Clemmie Dixon, Jr. *university president*
Spencer, Elizabeth *author*
Stadter, Philip Austin *classicist, educator*
Stasheff, James Dillon *mathematics educator*
Steponaitis, Vincas Petras *archaeologist, anthropologist, educator*
Stewart, Richard Edwin *insurance consulting company executive*
Stidham, Shaler, Jr. *operations research educator*
Stipe, Robert Edwin *design educator*
Stiven, Alan Ernest *population biologist, ecologist*
†Stockman, James Anthony, III *pediatrician*
Strauss, Albrecht Benno *English educator, editor*
Stumpf, Walter Erich *cell biology educator, researcher*
Sugioka, Kenneth *anesthesiologist educator*
Suzuki, Kunihiko *biomedical educator, researcher*
Thakor, Haren Bhaskerrao *manufacturing company executive*
Thomas, Colin Gordon, Jr. *surgeon, medical educator*
Tillman, Rollie, Jr. *university official*
Tindall, George Brown *historian, educator*
Tolley, Aubrey Granville *hospital administrator*
Treml, Vladimir Guy *economist, educator*
Tsiapera, Maria *linguistics educator*
Tunnessen, Walter William, Jr. *pediatrician*
Udry, J. Richard *sociology educator*
Upshaw, Harry Stephan *psychology educator*
Van Seters, John *biblical literature educator*
Van Wyk, Judson John *endocrinologist, pediatric educator*
Vogler, Frederick Wright *French language educator*
Wahl, Jonathan Michael *mathematics educator*
Warren, Donald William *physiology educator, dentistry educator*
Waud, Roger Neil *economics educator*
Wegner, Judith Welch *lawyer, educator, university dean*

Weinberg, Gerhard Ludwig history educator
Weiss, Charles Manuel environmental biologist
Weiss, Shirley F. urban and regional planner, economist, educator
Wheeler, Clayton Eugene, Jr. dermatologist, educator
White, Raymond Petrie, Jr. dentist, educator
Whybark, David Clay educator, researcher
Wilcox, Benson Reid cardiothoracic surgeon, educator
†Williams, Roberta Gay pediatric cardiologist, educator
†Williamson, Joel Rudolph humanities educator
Wilson, Glenn economist, educator
Wilson, John Eric biochemistry educator
Wilson, Robert Neal sociologist, educator
Winfield, John Buckner rheumatologist, educator
Wogen, Warren Ronald mathematics educator
Wolfenden, Richard Vance biochemistry educator
Wright, Deil Spencer political science educator
Wyrick, Priscilla Blakeney microbiologist
Yarnell, Richard Asa anthropologist
York, James Wesley, Jr. theoretical physicist, educator
Ziff, Paul philosophy educator

Charlotte

†Abercrombie, Ralph McCall hospital administrator
Abernathy, Joseph Duncan data processing executive
Anderson, Gerald Leslie financial executive
Ayscue, Edwin Osborne, Jr. lawyer
Barrows, Frank Clemence newspaper editor
Battle, George Edward, Jr. minister
Begley, Michael Joseph bishop
Belk, Irwin retail executive
Belk, Thomas Milburn apparel executive
Belthoff, Richard Charles, Jr. lawyer
Betzold, Paul Frederick, Jr. hospital administrator
Birle, James Robb investment banker
Blaschke, Robert Carvel education coordinator
Bost, Walter Lee architect, printing company executive
Bowden, James Alvin construction company financial executive
Box, Alan communications executive
Bradshaw, Howard Holt management consulting company executive
Brazeal, Donna Smith psychologist
Bristow, Allan Mercer professional basketball coach
Brown, Tony theater and dance critic
Buchan, Jonathan Edward, Jr. lawyer
Cannon, Robert Eugene librarian, public administrator, fund raiser
Carper, Barbara A. nursing educator
Citron, David Sanford physician
Clark, Ann Blakeney educational administrator
Clodfelter, Daniel Gray lawyer
Cogdell, Joe Bennett, Jr. lawyer
Colvard, Dean Wallace emeritus university chancellor
Copeland, John Wesley textile company executive
Cornell, James Fraser, Jr. entomologist, educator
Cornick, Michael F(rederick) educator
Covington, William Clyde, Jr. banker
Crosland, John, Jr. real estate developer
Crutchfield, Edward Elliott, Jr. banker
†Curlin, William G. bishop
Dagenhart, Larry Jones lawyer
Daniels, William Carlton, Jr. construction executive
Davenport, Dona Lee telecommunications consultant
Davidson, Charles Tompkins construction company executive
Davis, Jeffrey J. lawyer
Davis, William Maxie, Jr. lawyer
Dickson, Rush Stuart holding company executive
Edwards, Harold Mills government official, lawyer
Edwards, Irene Elizabeth (Libby Edwards) dermatologist, educator, researcher
†Ellison, Paul Stribling healthcare executive
†Elmore, Thomas Stephen hospital alliance executive
Ethridge, Mark Foster, III writer, publisher, newspaper consultant
Evans, Bruce Haselton art museum director
Ferebee, Stephen Scott, Jr. architect
Ferguson, James Elliot, II lawyer
Figge, Fredic J., II bank executive
Foss, Ralph Scot mechanical engineer
Freeman, Sidney Lee minister, educator
Fretwell, Elbert Kirtley, Jr. university chancellor emeritus, consultant
Gage, Gaston Hemphill lawyer
Gambrell, Sarah Belk retail executive
Georgius, John R. bank executive
†Glosson, Buster C. consulting and business development company executive, retired military officer
Goolkasian, Paula A. psychologist, educator
Goryn, Sara textiles executive, real estate developer, psychologist
Greene, William Henry L'Vel academic administrator
Grier, Joseph Williamson, Jr. lawyer
Griffith, Steve Campbell, Jr. lawyer
Grigg, William Humphrey utility executive
Gunn, Robert T. architectural firm executive
Hackler, John Byron, III architect
Hall, Peter Michael physics educator, electronics researcher
Hanna, George Verner, III lawyer
Hannah, Thomas E. textiles executive
Hardin, Thomas Jefferson, II investment counsel
Harris, Ernest Clay, Sr. marketing consultant, engineer
Harrison, J. Frank, Jr. soft drink company executive
Helms, Fred Bryan lawyer
Henson, Glenda Maria newspaper writer
Henson, Reid M. wholesale company executive
Hill, Ruth Foell language consultant
Hodges, Charles Thomas construction company executive
Holland, William Ray diversified company executive
Huberman, Jeffrey Allen architect
Hudgins, Catherine Harding business executive
Iverson, Francis Kenneth metals company executive
Johnson, Larry Demetric professional basketball player
Johnson, Phillip Eugene mathematics educator
Jones, Lewis Bevel, III bishop
Kelly, Luther Wrentmore, Jr. physician, educator
Kim, Rhyn Hyun engineering educator
King, L. Ellis civil engineer, educator and administrator
Koch, Richard Joseph publishing company executive, lawyer
Lawrence, Patricia Ann obstetrician-gynecologist
Lea, Scott Carter retired packaging company executive
Lee, William States retired utility executive
Levine, Leon retail executive
Lewis, Kenneth D. banker
Love, Franklin Sadler retired trade association executive
†Macomber, Tricia airport executive
Martin, James Grubbs medical research executive, former governor
†Maxheim, John Howard utility executive
Mazze, Edward Mark marketing consultant, business educator
McBryde, Neill Gregory lawyer
McCall, Billy Gene charitable trust executive
McColl, Hugh Leon, Jr. banker
McConnell, David Moffatt lawyer
McKeon, Robert B. textiles executive
McKeon, Robert B. retail chain stores executive
McMillan, James Bryan federal judge, retired
McVerry, Thomas Leo manufacturing company executive
Mendelsohn, Robert Victor insurance company executive
Mills, Samuel Davis, Jr. professional football player
†Montague, Edgar Burwell (Monty), III industrial designer
Moore, James L., Jr. beverage company executive
Mourning, Alonzo professional basketball player
Mullen, Graham C. federal judge
Murata, Junichi electronics company executive
Naumoff, Philip physician
Neal, William Weaver, III systems integration and software executive
Neel, Richard Eugene economics educator
Neill, Rolfe newspaper executive
Norwood, Philip Weltner lawyer
Nurkin, Harry Abraham hospital administrator
O'Connor, R. Dennis consumer products company executive
Orr, T(homas) J(erome) (Jerry Orr) airport terminal executive
Orsbon, Richard Anthony lawyer
Osborne, Richard Jay electric utility company executive
Parish, Robert Lee (Chief) professional basketball player
Patterson, Joseph H. chemical company executive
†Pehl, Glen Eugene risk and insurance consultant
†Peterson, Jim Lee food service executive
Phillips, Howard Mitchell real estate developer
†Plyler, John Laney, Jr. healthcare management professional
Porter, Gary Lynn investment manager
Potter, Robert Daniel federal judge
Powell, Charles Roland financial services company executive
Powers, Shirley Marie banker
Preyer, Norris Watson history educator
Priestley, G. T. Eric manufacturing company executive
†Priory, Richard Baldwin electric utility executive
Raper, William Cranford lawyer
Ray, Dee television executive
Regelbrugge, Roger Rafael steel company executive
Reiser, Charles Edward, Jr. hospital software company executive
Rodite, Robert R.R. engineering scientist
†Rogers, Curtis L., Jr. wholesale distribution executive
Rosamond, Patricia Ann construction company executive
Ross, David Edmond church official
Sanford, James Kenneth public relations executive
Schaffer, Eugene Carl education educator
Schmidt, Peter construction company executive
Sherman, Joseph Howard clergyman
Shinn, George professional basketball executive
Shive, Philip Augustus architect
Short, Earl de Grey, Jr. psychiatrist, consultant
Siegel, Samuel metals company executive
Singer, David Vincent bottling company executive
Sintz, Edward Francis librarian
†Smiley, E. Thomas tree pathologist
Smith, Arthur radio and television producer, composer
Smith, James Copeland controller
Stair, Frederick Rogers retired foundation executive, former seminary president
Stephens, Louis Cornelius, Jr. insurance executive
Stolpen, Spencer professional sports team executive
Taylor, David Brooke lawyer, banker
Taylor, Paul Bradford judge
Thies, Austin Cole retired utility company executive
Thigpen, Richard Elton, Jr. lawyer
Thomas, Joe Carroll human resources director
Thompson, James William banker
Tolan, David Joseph transportation executive
Turner, Thomas Patrick architect
Twisdale, Harold Winfred dentist
Ubell, Donald Paul lawyer
Van Allen, William Kent lawyer
Vane, Terence G., Jr. finance and insurance company executive, lawyer
Ver Hagen, Jan Karol manufacturing company executive
Vinroot, Richard Allen lawyer, mayor
Visser, Valya Elizabeth physician
Waldon, Grace Roberta insurance agent
Walker, Clarence Wesley lawyer
Watkins, Carlton Gunter retired pediatrician
†Watt, William G. insurance company executive
Wenner, Gene Charles arts foundation executive
Wentz, Billy Melvin, Jr. finance executive
White, David Lee journalist
Whitney, A(delbert) Grant mercantile and insurance company executive
Williams, Edwin Neel newspaper editor
Williford, Donald Bratton accounting company executive
Wireman, Billy Overton college president
Witherspoon, Jere Warthen foundation executive
Wolfe, Gary Johnson financial executive
Wood, William McBrayer lawyer
Woodward, James Hoyt university chancellor, engineer
Woolard, William Leon lawyer, electrical distributing company executive

Cherry Point

†Richwine, David Alan marine corps officer

Cherryville

Carlton, James D. trucking company executive
Huffstetler, Palmer Eugene lawyer, transportation executive
Mayhew, Kenneth Edwin, Jr. transportation company executive
Younger, Kenneth G. freight carrier corporation executive

China Grove

Baker, Ira Lee journalist, former educator

Clinton

Terry, George Marshall vocational studies educator

Columbus

Weber, Ernst engineering consultant

Concord

O'Morrow, Dianne Marie nursing administrator

Corolla

Schrote, John Ellis retired government executive

Creedmoor

Cross, June Crews music educator

Cullowhee

Blethen, Harold Tyler, III history educator
Coulter, Myron Lee retired academic administrator
Farwell, Harold Frederick, Jr. English language educator
Reed, Alfred Douglas university administrator
Willis, Ralph Houston mathematics educator

Dallas

Blanton, Robert D'Alden anthropology and history educator

Davidson

Abernethy, George Lawrence philosophy educator
Burnett, John Nicholas chemistry educator
Cole, Richard Cargill English language educator
Edmondson, Clifton Earl history educator, researcher
Jackson, Herb artist, educator
Jackson, Robert Bruce, Jr. education educator
Jacobus, Everett F., Jr. French language educator
Jones, Arthur Edwin, Jr. library administrator, English and American literature educator
Klein, Benjamin Garrett mathematics educator
Kuykendall, John Wells academic administrator, educator
Lester, Malcolm historian, educator
McKelway, Alexander Jeffrey religion studies educator
Mele, Alfred R. philosophy educator
Palmer, Edward L. social psychology educator, television researcher, writer
Park, Leland Madison librarian
Proctor, Jesse Harris, Jr. political science educator
Ratliff, Charles Edward, Jr. economics educator
Spencer, Samuel Reid, Jr. educational consultant, former university president
Stell, Lance Keith philosophy educator
Stroud, Junius Brutus, III mathematics educator
Tong, Rosemarie medical humanities and philosophy educator, consultant and researcher
Williams, Robert Chadwell history educator
Yoder, Lauren Wayne French language educator
Zimmermann, T. C. Price historian, educator

Drexel

Richetta, Fred J. manufacturing and operations executive

Dunn

Blackman, Danny religious organization administrator
Davis, Dolly religious organization administrator
Ellis, W. L. religious organization administrator
Hammond, James Thurman educator, clergyman
Heath, Preston clergy member, religious organization administrator
Muller, Donald Bruce chemical executive
Sauls, Don religious organization administrator, clergyman
Taylor, David clergy member, religious administrator

Durham

Adams, Dolph O. pathologist, educator
Aldrich, John Herbert political science educator
Allard, William Kenneth mathematician
Amos, Dennis B. immunologist
Anderson, William Banks, Jr. ophthalmology educator
Anlyan, William George surgeon, university administrator
Armstrong, Brenda Estelle pediatric cardiologist, educator
Ascher, William international policy educator
Baker, Lenox Dial orthopaedist, genealogist
Barber, James David political scientist, educator
Barrett, J. Carl cancer researcher, molecular biologist
Bartlett, Katharine Tiffany law educator
Baxter, Lawrence Gerald law educator, consultant
Beale, Sara Sun law educator
Beckum, Leonard Charles academic administrator
Behn, Robert Dietrich public policy educator, writer
Bell, Robert Maurice biochemistry educator, consultant
Bennett, Peter Brian researcher, anesthesiology educator
Bernstein, Herbert L. law educator
Bettman, James Ross management educator
Bevan, William retired foundation executive
Billings, William Dwight ecology educator
Bilpuch, Edward George nuclear physicist, educator
Biswas, Mrinmay engineering educator, consultant, researcher
†Blazer, Dan German psychiatrist, epidemiologist
Blum, Jacob Joseph physiologist, educator
Bradford, William Dalton pathologist, educator
Braibanti, Ralph John political scientist, educator
Brodie, Harlow Keith Hammond psychiatrist, educator, former university president
Bryan, Paul Robey, Jr. musician, educator
Buckley, Rebecca Hatcher physician
Budd, Louis John English language educator
Burger, Robert Mercer semiconductor device research executive
Burmeister, Edwin economics educator
Bursey, Joan Tesarek chemist
Busse, Ewald William psychiatrist, educator
Butters, Ronald Richard English language educator
Cady, Edwin Harrison English language educator, author
Caesar, Shirley gospel singer, evangelist
Campbell, Dennis Marion theology dean, educator, university administrator
Canada, Mary Whitfield librarian
Carrington, Paul DeWitt lawyer, educator
†Carter, James Harvey psychiatrist, educator
Cartmill, Matt anthropologist, anatomy educator
Casey, H(orace) Craig, Jr. electrical engineering educator
Chaddock, Jack Bartley mechanical engineering educator
Chafe, William Henry history educator
Chambers, Julius LeVonne lawyer
Chesnut, Donald Blair chemistry educator
Chilton, Mary-Dell Matchett chemical company executive
Christie, George Custis lawyer, educator, author
Christmas, William Anthony internist, educator
Clark, Arthur Watts insurance company executive
Clement, William Alexander insurance compnay executive
Clotfelter, Charles T. economics educator
Cocks, Franklin Hadley materials scientist
Cohen, Harvey Jay physician, educator
Coleman, Ralph Edward nuclear medicine physician
Collins, Bert insurance executive
Colton, Joel historian, educator
Cook, Clarence Edgar research facility executive
Cooper, Charles Howard photojournalist, newspaper publishing company executive
†Costa, Santo Joseph lawyer
Counce-Nicklas, Sheila Jean cell biology educator
Cox, James D. law educator
Cruze, Alvin M. research institute executive
Culberson, William Louis botany educator
Danner, Richard Allen law educator, dean
Davis, Calvin De Armond historian, educator
Davis, James Evans general and thoracic surgeon, parliamentarian, author
Davis, Lucy Tolbert psychologist, educator
Dawson, Jeffrey Robert immunology educator
Day, Eugene Davis, Sr. immunology educator, researcher
Dellinger, Walter Estes, III lawyer
Demott, Deborah Ann lawyer, educator
Dorfman, Ariel writer, educator
Dowell, Earl Hugh university dean, aerospace and mechanical engineering educator
Dunbar, Leslie Wallace writer, consultant
Dunteman, George Henry organizational psychologist
Durden, Robert Franklin history educator
Easterlin, Donald Jacob, III construction executive
Elliot, Jeffrey M. political science educator, author
Estes, Edward Harvey, Jr. medical educator
Evans, Ralph Aiken physicist, consultant
Fair, Richard Barton electronics executive, educator
Falletta, John Matthew pediatrician
†Feinglos, Susan Jean library director
Feldman, Jerome Myron physician
Fish, Peter Graham law educator
Fish, Stanley Eugene English language and literature educator
Fisher, Charles Page, Jr. consulting geotechnical engineer
†Fisher, Richard Wayne chemical company executive
Flanagan, Owen J. philosophy educator
Fleishman, Joel Lawrence university administrator, journalist, law educator
Fouts, James Ralph pharmacologist, educator, clergyman
Frank, Michael M. physician
Fraser-Reid, Bertram Oliver chemistry educator
Fridovich, Irwin biochemistry educator
Frothingham, Thomas Eliot pediatrician
Fulton, Katherine Nelson journalist
Gaede, Jane Taylor pathologist
Garg, Devendra Prakash mechanical engineer, educator
Georgiade, Nicholas George physician
Gillham, Nicholas Wright geneticist, educator
Gittler, Joseph Bertram sociology educator
Gleckner, Robert Francis English language professional, educator
Golding, Martin Philip law and philosophy educator
Goodwin, Frank Erik materials engineer
Gratz, Pauline former nursing science educator
Greenfield, Joseph Cholmondeley, Jr. physician, educator
Haagen, Paul Hess law educator
Hammes, Gordon G. chemistry educator
Hammond, Charles Bessellieu obstetrician-gynecologist, educator
Han, Moo-Young physicist
Handy, Rollo Leroy economics educator, research executive
Harman, Charles Morgan mechanical engineer
Harmel, Merel Hilber anesthesiologist, educator
Harris, Jerome Sylvan pediatrician, pediatrics and biochemistry educator
Hauerwas, Stanley Martin law educator, theologian
Havighurst, Clark Canfield law educator
Hawkins, William E. N. newspaper editor
Hayes, Brian Paul editor, writer
Hill, George Watts banker
Hillerbrand, Hans Joachim historian, university administrator
Hobbs, Marcus Edwin chemistry educator
Hochmuth, Robert Milo mechanical and biomedical engineer, educator
Holley, Irving Brinton, Jr. historian, educator
Holsti, Ole Rudolf political scientist, educator
Holton, Charles R. lawyer
Hopkins, Everett Harold education educator
Horowitz, Donald Leonard lawyer, educator, researcher, political scientist, arbitrator
Hough, Jerry Fincher political science educator
Hutchins, John Richard, III fiber optics electronic company executive
†Jaffe, Stephen Abram composer, music educator
Jaszczak, Ronald Jack physicist, researcher, consultant
Jennings, Robert Burgess experimental pathologist, medical educator
†Johnson, Gerald Arlen health facility executive
Johnson, Victoria Kaprielian medical educator
Johnston, William Webb pathologist, educator
Joklik, Wolfgang Karl biochemist, virologist, educator
Katz, Samuel Lawrence pediatrician, scientist
Keepler, Manuel mathematics educator, researcher
Keller, Thomas Franklin dean, management science educator
Kelley, Allen Charles economist, educator
Kempner, Walter retired physician
Keohane, Nannerl Overholser college president, political scientist
Keohane, Robert Owen political scientist, educator
Kiltzman, Bruce Maurice plastic surgery educator, researcher
King, Lowell Restell pediatric urologist
Kirk-Duggan, Michael Allan retired law and computer sciences educator

Kirshner, Norman pharmacologist, researcher, educator
Koepke, John Arthur hematologist, clinical pathologist
Krakauer, Thomas Henry museum director
Kramer, Paul Jackson plant physiologist, educator, writer, editor
†Kraus, William Erle physician, biomedical researcher
Kreps, Juanita Morris economics educator, former government official
Krzyzewski, Mike university athletic coach
Kuniholm, Bruce Robellet public policy studies institute director, history educator
Kylstra, Johannes Arnold physician
Lack, Leon pharmacology and biochemistry educator
Land, Kenneth Carl sociology educator, demographer, statistician, consultant
Lange, David L. law educator
Leach, Richard Heald political scientist, educator
Lefkowitz, Robert Joseph physician, educator
Lerner, Warren historian
Lieberman, Melvyn biology educator
Lifton, Walter M. psychology and education consultant
Lincoln, C(harles) Eric sociologist, educator, author
Little, Larry Chatmon head football coach
Livingstone, Daniel Archibald zoology educator
Llewellyn, Charles Elroy, Jr. psychiatrist
Lockhead, Gregory Roger psychology educator
Lorelli, Charles A. lawyer, chemical company executive
Loveland, Donald William computer science educator
†Lozoff, Bo nonprofit organization administrator
MacIntyre, Alasdair philosophy educator
Markham, Charles Buchanan lawyer
Matchar, David Bruce internist, educator
Mauskopf, Seymour Harold history educator
Maxwell, Richard Callender lawyer, educator
McClellan, Roger Orville toxicologist
McElhaney, James Harry biomedical engineer
McMahon, John Alexander lawyer, educator
Mc Phail, Andrew Tennent chemist, educator
Meyer, Horst physics educator
Meyers, Eric Mark religion educator
Mickiewicz, Ellen Propper political science educator
Miller, David Edmond physician
Moore, John Wilson neurophysiologist, educator
Mosteller, Robert P. law educator
Myers, George Carleton sociology and demographics educator
Naylor, Aubrey Willard botany educator
Nicklas, Robert Bruce cell biologist
Nygard, Holger Olof English and folklore educator
Oates, John Francis classics educator
O'Barr, William McAlston anthropologist, educator
Opara, Emmanuel Chukwuemeka biochemistry educator
Osterhout, Suydam physician, educator
Otterbourg, Robert Kenneth public relations consultant, writer
Page, Ellis Batten behavioral scientist, educator
Palmer, Richard Alan chemistry educator
Parker, Joseph B., Jr. psychiatrist, educator
Pearsall, George Wilbur materials scientist, mechanical engineer, educator, consultant
Pendergraft, Norman Elveis art history educator, art museum director
Perkins, Ronald Dee geologist, educator
Philyaw, A. Roger insurance company executive
Piatt, William McKinney, III consulting engineering executive
Pilkey, Orrin H. geology educator
Pilkington, Theo Clyde biomedical and electrical engineering educator
Plonsey, Robert electrical and biomedical engineer
†Powell, H. Jefferson law educator
Pratt, Philip Chase pathologist, educator
Press, Michelle editor
Preston, Richard Arthur historian
Reppy, William Arneill, Jr. law educator
Ricci, Robert Ronald manufacturing company executive
†Richardson, Curtis J. ecology educator
Richardson, Lawrence, Jr. Latin language educator, archeologist
Roberson, James O. foundation executive
Roberson, Nathan Russell physicist, educator
Robertson, Horace Bascomb, Jr. law educator
Roessler, Ernest Christian bank executive
Rogers, Mark Charles physician, educator
Rollins, Edward Tyler, Jr. newspaper executive
Rose, Donald James computer science educator
Rosenthal, Julian Bernard lawyer, association executive
Rosse, Wendell Franklyn immunology educator
Rossiter, Alexander, Jr. news service executive, editor
Rouse, Doris Jane physiologist, research administrator
Rowe, Thomas Dudley, Jr. law educator
Ryals, Clyde de Loache humanities educator
Ryan, Gerard Spencer inn executive
Sabiston, David Coston, Jr. surgeon, educator
Sanders, Charles Addison pharmaceutical company executive, physician
Sanford, David Hawley philosophy educator
Sassaman, Anne Phillips science administrator
Schanberg, Saul Murray pharmacology educator
Schiffman, Susan Stolte medical psychologist, educator
Schmalbeck, Richard Louis university dean, lawyer
Schmidt-Nielsen, Knut physiologist, educator
Schroeder, Christopher H. law educator
Scott, Anne Byrd Firor history educator
Searles, Richard Brownlee botany educator, marine biology researcher
Selkirk, James Kirkwood biochemist
†Semans, Mary Duke Biddle Trent foundation administrator
Serafin, Donald plastic surgeon
Sessoms, Stuart McGuire physician, educator, retired insurance company executive
Shimm, Melvin Gerald law educator
Smith, Grover Cleveland English language educator
Smith, Harmon Lee, Jr. clergyman, moral theology educator
Smith, Peter chemist, educator, consultant
Somjen, George Gustav physiologist
Spach, Madison Stockton cardiologist
Sparks, Bertel Milas lawyer, educator
†Speller, Benjamin Franklin, Jr. librarian, educator
Squire, Alexander management consultant
Staddon, John Eric Rayner psychology, zoology, neurobiology educator
Staelin, Richard business administration educator
Stead, Eugene Anson, Jr. physician
Steinmetz, David Curtis religion educator, publisher, minister
Strohbehn, John Walter engineering science educator
Stroscio, Michael Anthony physicist, educator
†Sumner, Gord electronics research executive
Surwit, Richard Samuel psychology educator
Taylor, Julia W. bank executive
Tebbel, John writer, educator
Thomas, Jean-Jacques Robert Romance languages educator
Thorn, Rosemary Kost librarian
Tiryakian, Edward Ashod sociology educator
Urbaniak, James Randolph orthopaedic surgeon
Utku, Senol civil engineer, computer science educator
Van Alstyne, William Warner law educator
Vitter, Jeffrey Scott computer science educator, consultant
Wainwright, Stephen A. zoology educator, design consultant
Walter, Richard Lawrence physicist, educator
Ward, Robert composer, conductor, educator
Wardropper, Bruce Wear language educator
Warner, Seth L. mathematician, educator
Warren, David Grant lawyer, educator
Watts, Charles DeWitt surgeon, corporate medical director
Weistart, John C. law educator
Welborn, Reich Lee lawyer
Werman, David Sanford psychiatrist, psychoanalyst, educator
Westbrook, Don Arlen minister
Wilbur, Karl Milton zoologist, educator
Wilbur, Robert Lynch botanist, educator
Wilder, Pelham, Jr. chemist, pharmacologist, educator
Wilkins, Robert Henry neurosurgeon, editor
Williams, George Walton English educator
Williams, Redford Brown medical educator
Willimon, William Henry minister, educator
Wilson, Ruby Leila nurse, educator
Winkler, Robert Lewis statistics educator, researcher, author, consultant
Woodbury, Max Atkin polymath, educator
Wright, Paul, Jr. banker

Eden
Bishopric, Welsford Farrell textile executive
Fraser, Kenneth William, Jr. textile company executive
Staab, Thomas Robert textile company financial executive

Edenton
Walklet, John James, Jr. publishing executive

Elizabeth City
Baker, Jean Mary cable television executive
Boyle, Terrence W. federal judge
Griffin, Gladys Bogues critical care nurse, educator
Lewis, Tola Ethridge, Jr. state agency administrator, martial arts instructor
Twiford, Travis W. school system administrator

Elizabethtown
Taylor, David Wyatt Aiken retired clergyman

Elon College
Knesel, Ernest Arthur, Jr. clinical laboratory executive
Metcalf, Corwin Moore (Mickey) business educator, businessman, consultant
Young, James Fred college president

Emerald Isle
Garvey, Robert Robey, Jr. former government official

Fairmont
Byrne, James Frederick banker

Fairview
Gaffney, Thomas Edward retired physician

Farmville
Monk, Albert C., III manufacturing executive

Fayetteville
Bowman, Charles Harwood, Jr. historian, educator
Bryant, Evelyn Christine elementary education educator
Cooke, Kenneth newspaper executive
Hackley, Lloyd Vincent university administrator, retired air force officer
Hendrick, J. R., III automotive executive
†Jansen, Michael John medical center administrator
Thrasher, Jerry Arthur library director

Fearrington Village
Doenges, Byron Frederick economist, educator, former government official

Flat Rock
Demartini, Robert John textile company executive

Forest City
Toney, Shirley Putman nursing administrator, educator

Fort Bragg
†Johnson, Julius Frank army officer
†Konitzer, Thomas Joseph military officer
Younger, Kenneth Maurice military officer

Fremont
Ackerman, Lennis Campbell management consultant retired

Fuquay Varina
Hairston, William Michael manufacturing engineer

Garner
Dobyns, Lloyd (Allen) free-lance journalist

Gastonia
Alala, Joseph Basil, Jr. lawyer, accountant
†Dickey, Crawford Marshall gas distribution executive
Jones, Terry Ray administrator
Kimbrell, Willard Duke textile company executive
Kiser, Clyde Vernon retired demographer
Lawson, William David, III cotton company executive
Stott, Grady Bernell lawyer
Stout, Richard Alan museum director
Teem, Paul Lloyd, Jr. savings and loan executive
Wall, Julia Ann Wilhite educational administrator, consultant
Williams, Raymond F. regigious organization executive
†Zeigler, Charles E., Jr. utility company executive

Gibsonville
Foster, C(harles) Allen lawyer

Gloucester
Price, Marion Woodrow journalist

Granite Falls
Humphreys, Kenneth King engineer, educator, association executive

Greensboro
Allen, Jesse Owen, III management development and organizational behavior
Bardolph, Richard historian, educator
Barker, Walter William, Jr. artist, educator
†Barry, Dennis Robert hospital administrator
†Berggren, Thage automotive executive
Blackwell, William Ernest insurance company executive, financial analyst
Bowers, Ben James editor, newspaper executive
Bryan, Joseph McKinley insurance company executive
Bullock, Frank William, Jr. federal judge
Cardwell, Jessie Womack elementary education educator
Carr, Howard Ernest retired insurance agency executive
Chappell, Fred Davis English language educator, poet
Clark, Clifton Bob physicist
Clark, Joanne school system administrator
Cline, Ned Aubrey newspaper editor
Compton, John Carroll accountant
Danahy, James Patrick textile executive
Daughtry, Sylvester protective services official
Davis, Herbert Owen lawyer
DuBuisson, Charles David newspaper editor
Eason, Robert Gaston psychology educator
Edinger, Lois Virginia education educator emeritus
Englar, John David textile company executive, lawyer
Erwin, Martin Nesbitt lawyer
Floyd, Jack William lawyer
Gill, Diane Louise psychology educator, university official
Goldman, Bert Arthur psychologist, educator
Gordon, Eugene Andrew judge
Greenberg, Frank S. textile company executive
Greenberg, George mill company executive
Griffin, Haynes Glenn telecommunications industry executive
Gumbiner, Kenneth Jay lawyer
Gutter, Robert Harold conductor, music educator
†Halstead, William B. metal products executive
Hamilton, Elizabeth Newnam credit union executive
Harllee, JoAnn Towery lawyer, educator
Hayes, Charles A. mill company executive
Helms-VanStone, Mary Wallace anthropology educator
Henderson, George, III textiles executive
Hidore, John Junior geographer, educator
Hopkins, John David lawyer
Howard, Paul Noble, Jr. retired construction company executive
Howard, Richard Turner construction company executive
Hughes, Donald R. textile executive
Hull, James Ernest religion and philosophy educator
Hunter, Bynum Merritt lawyer
Hutson, Alan Robert apparel company executive
Jellicorse, John Lee communications and theatre educator
Johnson, Andrew Myron pediatric immunologist, educator
Johnson, Marshall Hardy investment company executive
Kennedy, Charles G. wholesale distribution executive
Koonce, Neil Wright lawyer
Korb, William Brown, Jr. manufacturing company executive
Kornegay, Horace Robinson trade association executive, former congressman, lawyer
Kovacs, Beatrice library studies educator
Kretzer, William T. textile company executive
Lolley, William Randall minister
Macon, Seth Craven retired insurance company executive
Mann, Lowell Kimsey retired manufacturing executive
McCauley, Alfreda Ellis elementary school principal
McRae, Paul Anthony symphony orchestra conductor
Mebane, George Allen corporate executive, rancher
Mecimore, Charles Douglas accounting educator
Melvin, Charles Edward, Jr. lawyer
Middleton, Herman David, Sr. theater educator
Miller, Marilyn Lea library science educator
Miller, Robert Louis university dean, chemistry educator
Moore, Beverly Cooper lawyer
Morgenstern, Sheldon Jon symphony orchestra conductor
Morris, Edwin Alexander retired apparel manufacturing company executive
Nussbaum, V. M., Jr. former mayor
Osteen, William L., Sr. federal judge
Penninger, Frieda Elaine retired English language educator
Pilcher, Walter Harold apparel company executive
Polley, David E. textile manufacturing executive
Poole, Earle Gower clothing manufacturing company executive
Posey, Eldon Eugene mathematician, educator
Poteet, Daniel P(owell), II college provost
Reed, William Edward government official, educator
†Reid, Charles Murry insurance company executive
Rights, Graham Henry minister
Rogers, William Raymond college president, psychology educator
†Roland, Frank H. metal products executive, chemicals executive
Rowlenson, Richard Charles lawyer
Russell, Peggy Taylor soprano, educator
St. George, Nicholas James lawyer, manufactured housing company executive
Sanders, William Eugene marketing executive
Schappell, Lola Irene Hill school system administrator
Schell, Braxton lawyer
Schwenn, Lee William retired medical center executive
Sewell, Elizabeth author, English educator
Shelton, David Howard economics educator
Smink, Mary Jane graphic communications technology educator
Smith, John McNeill, Jr. lawyer
Smith, Lanty L(loyd) lawyer, business executive
Smith, Rebecca McCulloch human relations educator
Soles, William Roger insurance company executive
Spears, Alexander White, III tobacco company executive
Speight, Velma Ruth university administrator
†Stonecipher, David A. insurance company executive
Stoodt, Barbara Dern education educator, magazine editor
Swan, George Steven lawyer, educator
Tart, Jerry Gordon federal judge
Thompson, James Howard historian, library administrator
Tilley, Norwood Carlton, Jr. federal judge
Trogdon, Dewey Leonard, Jr. textile executive
Vetack, Richard S. textiles executive
Viele, George Brookins library executive
Watson, Robert Winthrop poet, English language educator
†Williams, Milton A. bishop
Wright, Kieth Carter librarian, educator
Yardley, Rosemary Roberts journalist, columnist
Zopf, Paul Edward, Jr. sociologist

Greenville
Bearden, James Hudson university official
†Behr, Lawrence Van Der Poel telecommunications executive
Bolande, Robert Paul pathologist, scientist, educator
Chauncey, Beatrice Arlene music educator
Clemens, Donald Faull chemistry educator
Cramer, Robert Eli geography educator
Eakin, Richard Ronald academic administrator, mathematics educator
Frisell, Wilhelm Richard biochemist, educator
Furth, Eugene David physician, educator
Hallock, James Anthony pediatrician, school dean
Hines, Danny Ray accountant, educator
Howard, Malcolm Jones federal judge
Howell, John McDade retired university chancellor, political science educator
Hudgins, Herbert Cornelius, Jr. education educator
Jackson, Bobby Rand minister
Jones, Billy Ernest dermatology educator
Laing, Penelope Gamble art educator
Laupus, William Edward physician, educator
Lee, Kenneth Stuart neurosurgeon
Lee, Tung-Kwang pathologist, cancer researcher
Leggett, Donald Yates academic administrator
Lennon, Donald Ray archivist, historian
Maier, Robert Hawthorne biology educator
Mattsson, Ake psychiatrist, physician
McRae, David Carroll hospital administrator
Norris, H. Thomas pathologist, academic administrator
Pories, Walter Julius surgeon, educator
Sanchez, Rafael Camilo physician
Sayetta, Thomas Charles physics educator
Schellenberger, Robert Earl management educator and department chairman
Snyder, Scott William geology educator
Thomas, Francis Thornton surgeon, immunologist, consultant
Thurber, Robert Eugene physiologist, researcher
Tingelstad, Jon Bunde physician
Waugh, William Howard biomedical educator
Williams, Melvin John sociologist, educator
Wrisley, Robert Lyman business educator
Zauner, Christian Walter university dean, exercise physiologist, consultant

Hampstead
Leaven, Glorious Sharpless special education educator, reading specialist
Solomon, Robert Douglas pathology educator

Henderson
Church, John Trammell retail stores company executive
Harvin, Lucius H., III department store company executive, lawyer
Jenkins, Clara Barnes psychology educator
Rose, David Cameron discount store executive

Hendersonville
Brittain, James Edward science and technology educator, researcher
Byrd, Charles L. school system administrator
Haynes, John Mabin retired utilities executive
Heltman, Robert Fairchild distribution executive
Jones, J(ohn) Charles education educator
Kehr, August Ernest geneticist, researcher
Payne, Gerald Oliver elementary education educator
Peckham, Howard Henry librarian, educator
Saby, John Sanford physicist
Schooley, Charles Earl electrical engineer, consultant
Schwarz, Richard William historian, educator
Sims, Bennett Jones minister, educator

Hickory
†Gardner, William Ronald surgeon
George, Boyd Lee consumer products company executive
Gingrich-Petersen, Carolyn Ashcraft psychologist
Knedlik, Ronald W. food wholesale and retail executive
†Loehr, Arthur William, Jr. healthcare executive, nurse
Lynn, Tony Lee import company executive
McDaniel, Michael Conway Dixon bishop, theology educator
Powell, Louise Fox real estate developer
Shuford, Harley Ferguson, Jr. furniture manufacturing executive

High Point
Brackett, Douglas Lane trade association executive
Ebeling, John Altman trucking company executive
†Ellis, Kem Byron public library administrator
Fenn, Ormon William, Jr. furniture company executive
Foscue, James E. commercial finance company executive
Howard, Lou Dean Graham elementary education educator
Huston, Fred John retired automotive engineer
Johnson, Richard Arthur factoring credit executive
Jones, Ronald Lee furniture manufacturing executive

Kleeman, Walter Benton, Jr. *interior and furniture designer, consultant, author*
Marsden, Lawrence Albert *retired textile company executive*
Martinson, Jacob Christian, Jr. *university president*
Millner, Thomas *manufacturing and holding company executive*
Phillips, Earl Norfleet, Jr. *financial services executive*
†Saxon, Franklin N. *finance executive*
Sheahan, Robert Emmett *lawyer, management employment and environment law consultant*
Wood, Stephen Wray *minister*

Highlands
Sandor, George Nason *mechanical engineer, educator*

Hillsborough
Cooley, Philip Chester *computer modeller*
Goodwin, Craufurd David *economics educator*
Stockstill, James William *secondary school educator*

Hope Mills
Windham, Cuyler LaRue *state narcotics agent*

Horse Shoe
Becker, Quinn Henderson *orthopaedic surgeon, army officer*
Howell, George Washington *lawyer, consultant*

Jackson Springs
Krebs, Max Vance *retired foreign service officer, educator*

Jacksonville
Daugherty, Robert Michael *music educator, composer*
Hutto, James Calhoun *retired financial executive*

Jefferson
Franklin, Robert McFarland *book publisher*

Kannapolis
Ridenhour, Joseph Conrad *textile company executive*
Thigpen, Alton Hill *motor transportation company executive*

Kinston
Fuchs, David *clothing manufacturing company executive*
Matthis, Eva Mildred Boney *college official*
Petteway, Samuel Bruce *college president*
Sanders, Brice Sidney *bishop*
Schechter, Sol *clothes company executive*

Kure Beach
Funk, Frank E. *retired university dean*
†Lanier, James Alfred, III *aquarium administrator*

Lake Junaluska
Bryan, Monk *retired bishop*
Hale, Joseph Rice *church organization executive*
Stokes, John Lemacks, II *clergyman, university administrator*
Tullis, Edward Lewis *retired bishop*

Lake Lure
Newbrough, Edgar Truett *retired management consultant*

Laurinburg
Nance, Tony Max-Perry *designer, illustrator*
Reuschling, Thomas Lynn *academic administrator, consultant*
Snead, Eleanor Leroy Marks *secondary school educator*

Lenoir
Carswell, Jane Triplett *family physician*

Liberty
Garner, Mildred Maxine *retired religious studies educator*
Link, Eleanor Ann *elementary education educator*

Lincolnton
Carter, John DeLaney *state senator, video producer*
Gaither, Ann Heafner *sales executive*
Saine, Betty Boston *elementary school educator*

Locust
Barbee, Bobby Harold *state legislator, insurance agency executive*

Lumberton
Lee, Elizabeth Bobbitt *architect*
MacLean, Hector *banker, lawyer*
Orr, L. Glenn, Jr. *banker*

Maiden
†Pruitt, Thomas P., Jr. *textiles executive*
†Schrum, Ed P. *manufacturing company executive*

Manteo
Hartman, Thomas *historical site administrator*
Miller, William Lee, Jr. *minister*

Mars Hill
Bentley, Fred Blake *academic administrator*

Matthews
Dunn, Edward S., Jr. *supermarket chain stores executive*
Rivenbark, Jan Meredith *food service products corporate executive*

Monroe
Griffin, Gwyn *secondary school principal*
Rorie, Nancy Katheryn *elementary and secondary school educator*

Montreat
De Jong, Arthur Jay *education consultant, former university president*
Robinson, Spencer, Jr. *retired service club executive, accountant*

Mooresville
Dausman, George Erwin *retired federal official, aeronautical engineer*

Morehead City
Williams, Winton Hugh *civil engineer*

Morganton
Ervin, Samuel James, III *federal judge*
Jokinen, John Victor *furniture company executive*
MacLeod, John Daniel, Jr. *religious organization administrator*
Simpson, Daniel Reid *lawyer*

Morrisville
Smith, Malbert, III *computer technology executive, psychologist*

Mount Airy
Rotenizer, R. Eugene *financial planner, consultant and advisor*
Woltz, Howard Osler, Jr. *steel and wire products company executive*

Mount Holly
Davis, Frank William, Jr. *elementary and secondary school educator*
†Dickson, Alan T. *mill and holding company executive*

Mount Olive
Boyd, Julia Margaret (Mrs. Shelton B. Boyd) *lay church worker*
Raper, William Burkette *retired college president*

Mount Ulla
Kluttz, Henry G. *principal*

Murfreesboro
Whitaker, Bruce Ezell *college president*

Nags Head
†Rogallo, Francis Melvin *mechanical, aeronautical engineer*

New Bern
Baughman, Fred Hubbard *aeronautical engineer, former naval officer*
Daft, Jack Robert *landscape architect, educator*
Degnan, Herbert Raymond *financial executive, lawyer, accountant*
Greer, Robert Bruce, III *orthopedic surgeon, educator*
Kellum, Norman Bryant, Jr. *lawyer*
Mack, Clifford Glenn *investment banker, management consultant*
McCotter, Charles Kennedy, Jr. *magistrate judge*
Moeller, Dade William *environmental engineer, educator*
Perdue, Beverly Moore *state legislator, geriatric consultant*
Skipper, Nathan Richard, Jr. *lawyer*
Whitehurst, Brooks Morris *chemical engineer*

Newport
Little, Loyd Harry, Jr. *author*

North Wilkesboro
Emerine, Wendell R. *retail executive*
Herring, Leonard Gray *marketing company executive*
Lovette, Blake Duane *food company executive*
Matthews, John Carroll *manufacturing executive*
Pardue, Dwight Edward *venture capitalist*
Underwood, Harry Burnham, II *financial executive, accountant*

Oxford
Pruitt, Dorothy J. Gooch *home economics educator, retired educational administrator*

Pilot Mountain
Long, James M. *judge*
Ross, Norman Alexander *retired banker*

Pine Knoll Shores
Benson, Kenneth Victor *manufacturing company executive, lawyer*
Griffin, Thomas Lee, Jr. *industrial and federal government specialist*
Lynn, Otis Clyde *former army officer*

Pinehurst
Amspoker, James Mack *retired gas company executive*
Ashby, Donald Wayne, Jr. *retired accountant*
Black, Bobby C. *chaplain*
Carroll, Kent Jean *retired naval officer*
Ellis, William Harold *former naval officer*
Gilmore, Voit *travel executive*
Henderson, Paul Audine *banker, consultant*
Huizenga, John Robert *nuclear chemist, educator*
Jacobson, Peter Lars *neurologist and educator*
Lebeck, Warren Wells *commodities consultant*
Maples, Dan *golf course designer*
Nuzzo, Salvatore Joseph *defense, electronics company executive*
O'Neill, John Joseph, Jr. *business consultant, former chemical company executive*
Owings, Malcolm William *retired management consultant*
Roberts, Francis Joseph *retired army officer, retired educational administrator, global economic advisor*
Stingel, Donald Eugene *management consultant*
Stroud, Richard Hamilton *aquatic biologist, scientist, consultant*
Twitty, James Watson *artist*

Pinetops
†Robertson, Richard Blake *management consultant*

Pisgah Forest
Albyn, Richard Keith *retired architect*

Pittsboro
Abrahamson, James Leonard *history educator*
Bailey, Herbert Smith, Jr. *retired publisher*
†Bixby, Donald Edward, Jr. *conservancy executive, veterinary consultant, rese*
Grant, Robert Erich *financial officer*
Hauser, Charles Newland McCorkle *newspaper consultant*
Lewis, Henry Wilkins *university administrator, lawyer, educator*
Magill, Samuel Hays *retired college administrator, higher education consultant*
Quinn, Jarus William *physicist, former association executive*
Robinson, Ormsbee Wright *educational consultant*
Schwinn-Jordan, Barbara (Barbara Schwinn) *painter*
Shurick, Edward Palmes *television executive, rancher*

Point Harbor
Heffernan, Phillip Thomas, Jr. *retired publisher*

Pope AFB
Conley, Raymond Leslie *English language educator*

Raleigh
Agrawal, Dharma Prakash *engineering educator*
Anderson, Glenn Elwood *investment banker*
Andrews, William Parker, Jr. *lawyer*
Aronson, Arthur Lawrence *veterinary pharmacology and toxicology educator*
Aspnes, David Erik *physicist, educator*
Atchley, William Reid *geneticist, evolutionary biologist, educator*
Baliga, Bantval Jayant *electrical engineering educator, consultant*
Barham, Charles Dewey, Jr. *electric utility executive, lawyer*
Barmore, Gregory Terhune *capital mortgage company executive*
Bass, Mary Catherine *clinical social worker, psychotherapist*
Beatty, Kenneth Orion, Jr. *chemical engineer*
Bell, Richard Chevalier *landscape architect*
†Benson, D(avid) Michael *plant pathologist*
Bergsma, Daniel *retired medical foundation executive, consultant*
Bishop, Paul Edward *microbiologist*
Bitzer, Donald Lester *electrical engineering educator, retired research laboratory administrator*
Blackmon, John (Jerry) *state senator*
Blaine, James C. *bank executive*
Bourham, Mohamed Abdelhay *nuclear and electrical engineering educator*
Boyles, Harlan Edward *state official*
Breytspraak, John, Jr. *management consultant*
Britt, W. Earl *federal judge*
Buchanan, David Royal *associate dean*
Burns, Norma DeCamp *architect*
Burns, Robert Paschal *architect, educator*
Caldwell, John Tyler *political science educator, former university administrator*
Cameron, John Lansing *retired government official*
Carlton, Alfred Pershing, Jr. *lawyer*
Case, Charles Dixon *lawyer*
Casey, Ethel Laughlin *concert and opera singer*
Champ, Raymond Lester *hospital administrator*
Church, Kern Everidge *engineer, consultant*
Clark, Roger Harrison *architect, architecture educator*
Clarke, Lewis James *landscape architect*
Cockerham, Columbus Clark *retired geneticist, educator*
Collins, Thomas Asa *minister*
Cook, Maurice Gayle *soil science educator, consultant*
Cooper, Arthur Wells *ecologist, educator*
Cox, Herbert Bartle *natural gas company executive*
†Creel, Wesley Stuart *museum executive*
Cresimore, James Leonard *food broker*
Cummings, Frances McArthur *state official, retired educational administrator*
Cummings, Ralph Waldo *soil scientist, educator, researcher*
Cuomo, Jerome John *materials scientist*
Dameron, Thomas Barker, Jr. *orthopaedic surgeon, educator*
Daniels, Frank Arthur, Jr. *newspaper publisher*
Daniels, Frank Arthur, III *publishing executive*
Dannelly, William D. *lawyer*
Davey, Charles Bingham *soil science educator*
Davis, Egbert Lawrence, III *lawyer*
Davis, James Minor, Jr. *utility company executive, mechanical engineer*
Davis, William Robert *physicist*
De Hertogh, August Albert *horticulture educator, researcher*
Denson, Alexander Bunn *federal magistrate judge*
Dixon, Wright Tracy, Jr. *lawyer*
Doherty, Robert Cunningham *advertising executive*
Dolce, Carl John *education administration educator*
Dornan, John Neill *public policy center professional*
Drew, Nancy McLaurin Shannon *counselor, consultant*
†Droessler, Earl George *geophysicist educator*
Dudziak, Donald John *nuclear engineer, educator*
Dunphy, Edward James *crop science extension specialist*
Dupree, Franklin Taylor, Jr. *federal judge*
Eagles, Sidney Smith, Jr. *judge*
Easley, Michael F. *state attorney general*
Eason, Joseph W. *lawyer*
Eberly, Harry Landis *retired communications company executive*
Ebisuzaki, Yukiko *chemistry educator*
Edmisten, Rufus Leigh *state official*
Edwards, Charles Archibald *lawyer*
Ellington, John David *state official*
Ellis, Lester Neal, Jr. *lawyer*
Estill, Robert Whitridge *retired bishop*
†Etheridge, Bob *state agency superintendant*
Exum, James Gooden, Jr. *state supreme court chief justice*
Fadum, Ralph Eigil *university dean*
Ferrell, James K. *chemical engineering educator, dean*
Fike, William T. *agricultural studies educator*
Finch, Peter W. *painter, illustrator*
Flournoy, William Louis, Jr. *landscape architect*
Foley, Peter Michael *lawyer*
†Foster, James Robert *cardiologist*
Frye, Henry E. *state supreme court justice*
Gardner, Robin Pierce *engineering educator*
Gilbert, Charles Gorman *civil engineering educator*
Glass, Margaret Smyllie *corporate treasurer, lawyer*
Godwin, James Beckham *retired landscape architect*
Goldstein, Irving Solomon *chemistry educator, consultant*
Goodman, Major Merlin *botanical sciences educator*
Gossman, Francis Joseph *bishop*
Graham, William Edgar, Jr. *lawyer, retired utility company executive*
Grubb, Donald Hartman *paper industry company executive*
Gustafson, Sarah *elementary education educator*
Hanson, John M. *civil engineering and construction educator*
Hardin, Eugene Brooks, Jr. *banker*
Hardin, James W. *botanist, herbarium curator, educator*
Harris, J. Ollie *state legislator*
Hauser, John Reid *electrical engineering educator*
Head, Allan Bruce *bar association executive*
Hodgson, Ernest *toxicology educator*
Holding, Lewis R. *banker*
Homick, Daniel John *financial executive, lawyer*
Horton, Horace Robert *biochemistry educator*
Hugus, Z Zimmerman, Jr. *chemistry educator*
Hunt, James Baxter, Jr. *governor, lawyer*
Hunter, Margaret King *architect*
Jacob, Jerry Rowland *airline executive*
Jennings, Burgess Hill *mechanical engineering educator*
Jessen, David Wayne *accountant*
Jividen, Loretta Ann Harper *secondary school educator*
Johnson, Marvin Richard Alois *architect*
Jones, Frederick Claudius *English language and linguistics educator*
Joyner, Gary Kelton *lawyer*
Joyner, Walton Kitchin *lawyer*
Kelman, Arthur *plant pathologist, educator*
Kimbrell, Odell Culp, Jr. *physician*
Klein, Verle Wesley *corporate executive, retired naval officer*
Kriz, George James *agricultural research administrator, educator*
Kuhler, Renaldo Gillet *museum official, scientific illustrator*
Leak, Robert E. *management consultant*
Leddicotte, George Comer *business executive, consultant*
Lemmond, Joseph Shawn *state legislator, insurance agent*
Levine, Ronald H. *physician, state official*
Lewis, Richard Jay *marketing educator, university dean*
Littleton, Isaac Thomas, III *retired university library administrator, consultant*
Maidon, Carolyn Howser *academic program administrator*
Malecha, Marvin John *architect, academic administrator*
Malone, Thomas Francis *university administrator, meteorologist*
Mason, David Dickenson *statistics educator*
Maupin, Armistead Jones *lawyer*
McKinney, Charles Cecil *investment company executive*
Meier, Wilbur Leroy, Jr. *industrial engineer, educator, former university chancellor*
Menius, Arthur Clayton, Jr. *former university dean*
Meyer, Lois Ann *religious school system administrator*
†Michael, Joan Yvonne Johnson *dean, psychologist*
Michael, Patricia Ann *physician, clinical systems research director*
Miller, John Henry *clergyman*
Miller, Ralph Bradley *lawyer, former state legislator*
Miller, Robert James *lawyer*
Minnick, Carlton Printess, Jr. *bishop*
Mitchell, Burley Bayard, Jr. *state supreme court chief justice*
Mitchell, Gary Earl *physicist, educator*
Monteith, Larry King *university chancellor*
Moore, Thomas Lloyd *librarian*
Moreland, Donald Edwin *plant physiologist*
Murray, Elizabeth Davis Reid *writer, lecturer*
Murray, Raymond Le Roy *nuclear engineering educator*
†Murty, Korukonda Linga *nuclear science educator*
Nagle, Hubert Troy, Jr. *electrical engineering educator*
†Nelson, Larry A. *statistics educator, consultant*
Newman, Slater Edmund *psychologist, educator*
Nickel, Donald Lloyd *engineering executive*
Ofner, J(ames) Alan *management consultant*
Overcash, Michael Ray *chemical engineering educator*
Page, Anne Ruth *gifted education educator, education specialist*
Parker, Charles Brand, Jr. *training company executive*
Parker, Joseph Mayon *printing and publishing executive*
Parramore, Barbara Mitchell *education educator*
Patterson, William S. *lawyer*
Peacock, Erle Ewart, Jr. *surgeon, lawyer, educator*
Pendleton, Gary H(erman) *life insurance agent*
Peterson, Elmor Lee *mathematical scientist, educator*
†Pope, John W. *retail executive*
Poulton, Bruce Robert *former university chancellor*
Powell, Drexel Dwane, Jr. *editorial cartoonist*
Powell, Durwood Royce *lawyer*
Poyner, James Marion *retired lawyer*
Ragsdale, George Robinson *lawyer*
Ramsey, Liston Bryan *state legislator*
Rawlings, John Oren *statistician, researcher*
Reeves, Ralph B., III *publisher, editor*
Rhodes, Donald Robert *musicologist, retired electrical engineer*
†Risher, James A. *electronics executive*
Roach, Wesley Linville *lawyer, insurance executive*
Robinson, Prezell Russell *college administrator*
Robson, Charles Baskervill, Jr. *lawyer*
Rochelle, Lugenia *academic administrator*
Rohrbach, Roger Phillip *agricultural engineer, educator*
Rosen, Lee Spencer *lawyer*
Royster, Vermont (Connecticut) *journalist*
Sanford, Terry *lawyer, educator, former U.S. senator, former governor, former university president*
Scandalios, John George *geneticist, educator*
Schneiderman, Richard Steven *museum official*
Shaw, Robert Gilbert *restaurant executive, senator*
Shaw, Talbert O. *university president*
Shih, Jason Chia-Hsing *biotechnology educator*
Shyllon, Prince E.N. *lawyer, law educator*
Skaggs, Richard Wayne *agricultural engineering educator*
Small, Alden Thomas *federal judge*
Smith, Macon Strother *architect*
Smith, Sherwood Hubbard, Jr. *utilities executive*
Smith, Stanley O'Neil, Sr. *retired military officer*
†Sneed, Ronald Ernest *engineering educator emeritus*
Speck, Marvin Luther *microbiologist, educator*
Stiles, Phillip John *physicist, educator*
Stoskopf, Michael Kerry *educator*
Stratas, Nicholas Emanuel *psychiatrist*
Stuber, Charles William *genetics educator, researcher*
Suhr, Paul Augustine *lawyer*
Sutton, Ronnie Neal *lawyer, state legislator*
Swaisgood, Harold Everett *biochemist, educator*
Tally, Lura Self *state legislator*
Timothy, David Harry *biology educator*

Tompkins, James Arthur *consulting firm executive, industrial engineer*
†Triantaphyllou, Hedwig Hirschmann *plant pathologist*
Turinsky, Paul Josef *nuclear engineer, educator*
Warren, Robert Davis *state senator*
Webb, John *state supreme court justice*
Wesler, Oscar *mathematician, educator*
Whichard, Willis Padgett *state supreme court justice*
†Whitehead, Ian *insurance company executive*
Whitten, Jerry Lynn *chemistry educator*
Wicker, Dennis A. *lieutenant governor*
Williams, Hugh Alexander, Jr. *retired mechanical engineer, consultant*
Willis, John Randolph *hospital administrator*
Wilson, Richard Ferrol *plant physiologist, educator*
Winner, Leslie Jane *state legislator, lawyer*
Winstead, Nash Nicks *university administrator, phytopathologist*
Wollum, Arthur George, II *microbiologist, researcher, educator*
Woodson, Richard Peyton, III *entrepreneur*
Wright, Thomas James *chemical company executive*
Wynne, Johnny Calvin *university dean, plant breeding researcher*
Young, James Herbert *agricultural engineer*
Zimmermann, Gerhardt *conductor*
Zorowski, Carl Frank *engineering educator, university administrator*

Randleman
Petty, Richard *retired professional race car driver*

Reidsville
Hart, Richard Wesley *religious organization administrator, pastor*

Research Triangle Park
†Barry, David Walter *infectious diseases physician, researcher*
Bursiek, Ralph David *information systems company executive*
Cipau, Gabriel *pharmaceutical executive*
Connor, Walter Robert *classics educator, humanities center administrator*
de Serres, Frederick Joseph *genetic toxicologist*
Drake, John Walter *geneticist*
Elion, Gertrude Belle *research scientist, pharmacology educator*
Gaither, John Stokes *chemical company executive*
Hagan, John Aubrey *financial executive*
†Harvey, Glenn F. *association executive*
Heck, Henry D'Arcy *toxicologist*
Holton, William Coffeen *electrical engineering executive*
Howe, Tom *broadcasting executive*
Karr, Alan Francis *statistics educator, academic administrator*
King, Theodore Matthew *obstetrician, gynecologist, educator*
Krenitsky, Thomas Anthony *biochemist, research director*
Kuhn, Matthew *engineering company executive*
Larsen, Ralph Irving *environmental research engineer*
Li, Steven Shoei-lung *geneticist, educator*
Martin, William Royall, Jr. *association executive*
†Miller, Robert Reese *trade association executive*
Niedel, James E. *pharmaceuticals executive*
Olden, Kenneth *science administrator, researcher*
Rodbell, Martin *biochemist*
†Smyth, George *electronics company executive, researcher*
Tilson, Hugh Hanna *epidemiologist*
Tracy, Philip R. *computer company executive*
Wilsnack, Roger E. *medical association administrator*
Wooten, Frank Thomas *research facility executive*

Robbinsville
Ginn, Ronn *architect, urban planner, general contractor*

Rockingham
Robertson, Ralph S. *secondary school principal*

Rocky Mount
Autry, Robert F. *restaurant chain executive*
†Boleman, Ray Judson, Jr. *banker*
Condon, Breen O'Malley *lawyer*
Cooper, Roy Asberry, III *lawyer, state senator*
Futrell, Jonas Richard, Jr. *banker*
Gibbs, V. Diane *dean*
Harrington, Jesse Moye, III *restaurant chain executive*
Laughery, Jack Arnold *restaurant chain executive*
Mauldin, Robert Ray *banker*
Parsons-Salem, Diane Lora *lawyer*
Powers, James Bascom *banker*
Simpson, Dennis Arden *lighting contracting company executive*
Wilkerson, William Holton *banker*

Salemburg
Baugh, Charles Milton *biochemistry educator, college dean*

Salisbury
Ketner, Ralph Wright *retail food company executive*
†Logan, David Bruce *health care administrator*
Shalkop, Robert Leroy *retired museum consultant*
Smith, Tom Eugene *retail food company executive*
Speaks, Ruben Lee *bishop*
†Stanback, Fred *conservationist*
Tlalka, Jacek *mathematics educator*
Trexler, Wynn Ridenhour *paralegal*

Saluda
Mowery, Bob Lee *librarian*

Sanford
Beckwith, Hugh Foster, Jr. *textile company executive*
Higgins, George Edward *sculptor*
Raisig, Paul Jones, Jr. *lawyer*
†Ward, Robert Allen *textile company executive*

Shelby
†Carver, Earl (Randy Carver) *marketing and sales consultant, video director and producer*
Edgar, Ruth R. *retired educator*
†Hudson, Mark Alan *health care executive*

Southern Pines
Lipton, Clifford Carwood *retired glass company executive*
Lowry, Charles Wesley *clergyman, lecturer*
Mataxis, Theodore Christopher *consultant, lecturer, writer, retired army officer, educator*
Ragan, Samuel Talmadge *newspaper editor, publisher, educator, poet laureate*
Toon, Malcolm *former ambassador*
Towell, William Earnest *forester, former association executive*
Vanderwoude, J. Stephen *communications company executive*
Yarborough, William Pelham *writer, lecturer, retired army officer, consultant*

Spring Hope
Hildreth, James Robert *air force officer*
Lavatelli, Leo Silvio *retired physicist, educator*

Statesville
Heymann, Hans Paulsen *community college administrator*

Swansboro
Mullikin, Thomas Wilson *mathematics educator*

Tabor City
Jorgensen, Ralph Gubler *lawyer*

Tarboro
Hopkins, Grover Prevatte *lawyer*

Thomasville
O'Brien, Charles G. *furniture manufacturing company executive*
Starr, Frederick Brown *furniture manufacturing executive*

Troy
Gasper, Theodore Howard, Jr. *college president*

Tryon
Bruce, David Lionel *retired anesthesiologist, educator*
Stinson, George Arthur *lawyer, former steel company executive*
Thayer, Lee *educator, author, consultant*

Vass
Glassman, Edward *management creativity consultant, columnist*

Wadesboro
Hightower, Foyle Robert, Jr. *state legislator, ice and fuel company executive*

Wake Forest
Binkley, Olin Trivette *clergyman, seminary president emeritus*

Warsaw
Ferrell, Rhonda Barefoot *nursing educator*

Washington
Edwards, Zeno Lester, Jr. *state legislator, retired dentist*
Hackney, James Acra, III *industrial engineer, manufacturing company executive*
Timour, John Arnold *retired librarian, medical bibliography and library science educator*

Waxhaw
Lamparter, William C. *printing and publishing consultant, digital printing and information systems specialist*

Waynesville
Matlock, Clifford Charles *retired foreign service officer*
†McKinney, Alexander Stuart *neurologist*

Weaverville
Boyce, Emily Stewart *retired library and information science educator*
Edwards, Otis Carl, Jr. *theology educator*
†Harris, Michael G. *publishing company executive*
†McGauran, Michael *manufacturing executive, light*
Parsons, Vinson Adair *retired computer software company executive*

Weldon
Barringer, Paul Brandon, II *lumber company executive*
Conger, Stephen Halsey *lumber company executive*

West End
Moncure, James Ashby *historian*

Whispering Pines
Blanchard, George Samuel *retired military officer, consultant*
Enlow, Donald Hugh *anatomist, educator, university dean*

Whiteville
†Chiusano, Michael Augustus *urologic surgeon, mechanical engineer*
Scott, Stephen Carlos *college president*

Williamston
Cowen, Robert Henry *lawyer*

Wilmington
Block, Franklin Lee *lawyer*
Brauer, Ralph Werner *physiologist, educator*
Cahill, Charles L. *university administrator, chemistry educator*
Crigler, T. P. *foreign products and investments executive*
Dewey, Ralph Jay *headmaster*
Dixon, N(orman) Rex *speech and hearing scientist, educator*
Fox, James Carroll *federal judge*
Gillen, Howard William *neurologist, medical historian*
Gottovi, Karen Elizabeth *state legislator, political consultant, researcher*
Haselden, Clyde LeRoy *librarian*
Janson, Anthony Frederick *art educator, former museum curator*
Leutze, James Richard *academic administrator, television producer and host*
Martin, Ned Harold *chemistry educator*
McManus, Hugh F. *principal*
Merritt, James Francis *biological sciences educator*
Morrison, William Fowler, Jr. *health care consultant*
Roer, Robert David *physiologist, educator*
Scheu, David Robert, Sr. *historic site director*
Seapker, Janet Kay *museum director*
Silloway, Benton, Jr. *food products executive*
Thompson, Donald Charles *electronics company executive, former coast guard officer*
Wade, James Michael *treasurer*
Wagoner, William Hampton *university chancellor*
Wilkins, Lucien Sanders *gastroenterologist*
Worzel, John Lamar *geophysicist, educator*
Wright, Thomas Henry *bishop*
Zechman, Fred William, Jr. *physiologist, educator, administrator*

Wilson
Allison, John Andrew, IV *bank executive*
Batchelor, Ruby Stephens *retired nurse*
†Coghill, Marvin W. *tobacco company executive*
†Gibbons, Larry Eugene *minister*
Hemby, James B., Jr. *college president*
Herring, Jerone Carson *lawyer, bank executive*
Kehaya, Ery W. *tobacco holding company executive*
McCain, Betty Landon Ray (Mrs. John Lewis McCain) *political party official*
Murray, J. Alec G. *manufacturing executive*
†Peters, A. Winniett *leaf tobacco merchant, exporter*
Ross, Guy Matthews, Jr. *international leaf tobacco executive*
Stewart, Burton Gloyden, Jr. *banker*
Williamson, Henry Gaston, Jr. *banker*

Winston Salem
Alderson, William Thomas *historian, consultant*
Alexander, Eben, Jr. *neurological surgeon*
Atkinson, G. Douglas, Sr. *marketing executive, consultant*
Austell, Edward Callaway *banker*
Barnett, Richard Chambers *historian, educator*
Barnhardt, Zeb Elonzo, Jr. *lawyer*
Beardsley, Charles Mitchell *retired insurance company executive*
Benfield, Marion Wilson, Jr. *lawyer, educator*
Berthrong, Merrill Gray *retired library director*
†Bittinger, Isabel *orthopedic surgeon, retired, photographer*
Black, David Charles *headmaster*
Blynn, Guy Marc *lawyer*
Bowman, Marjorie Ann *physician, academic administrator*
Brill, Frank Patrick *journalist*
Butner, Fred Washington, Jr. *architect*
Carter, Henry Moore, Jr. *foundation executive*
Cawood, Hobart Guy *historic site administrator*
Channing, Rhoda Kramer *library director*
Christopher, Floyd Hudnall, Jr. *corporate executive*
Copenhaver, W. Andrew *lawyer*
Corbett, Leon H., Jr. *lawyer, educator, university official*
Cotterill, David Lee *banker*
Covey, Cyclone *history educator*
Cowan, Robert Jenkins *radiologist, educator*
Cramer, John Scott *retired banker*
Davis, Courtland Harwell, Jr. *neurosurgeon*
Davis, Linwood Layfield *lawyer*
Davis, Thomas Henry *airline executive*
Davis, William Allison, II *lawyer*
Dean, Richard Henry *surgeon, educator*
Dodd, Virginia Marilyn *veterinarian*
Doggett, Aubrey Clayton, Jr. *real estate executive, consultant*
Donahue, Daniel William *lawyer*
Ehle, John Marsden, Jr. *writer*
Ehmann, Carl William *consumer products executive, researcher*
Eliason, Russell Allen *federal judge*
Emken, Robert Allan *diversified company executive*
Erwin, Richard Cannon *federal judge*
Ewing, Alexander Cochran *chancellor*
Faccinto, Victor Paul *artist, gallery administrator*
Farr, Henry Bartow, Jr. *lawyer*
Fitzgerald, Ernest Abner *retired bishop*
Flory, Walter S., Jr. *geneticist, botanist, educator*
Ford, Yancey William, Jr. *tobacco company executive*
Foy, Herbert Miles, III *lawyer, educator*
Gitter, Allan Reinhold *lawyer*
Gleason, Norman Dale *association executive*
Goodman, Joseph Champion *editor*
Gray, James Alexander *historic preservation official*
Greason, Murray Crossley, Jr. *lawyer*
Griscom, Thomas Cecil *presidential assistant, public relations executive*
Griswold, George *marketing, advertising and public relations executive*
Gunzenhauser, Gerard Ralph, Jr. *management consultant, investor*
Hanes, Frank Borden *author, farmer, former business executive*
Hanes, Ralph Philip, Jr. *textile company executive*
Harrelson, Walter Joseph *minister, religion educator emeritus*
Hazzard, William Russell *geriatrician, educator*
Healy, Joseph Francis, Jr. *lawyer, arbitrator, retired airline executive*
Helm, Robert Meredith *philosophy educator*
Hendricks, J(ames) Edwin *historian, educator, consultant, author*
Herndon, Claude Nash *retired geneticist, physician*
Hopkins, Judith Owen *oncologist*
Howell, Charles Maitland *dermatologist*
Janeway, Richard *university official*
Johnson, Norman *music director, opera producer, educator*
Johnston, James Wesley *tobacco company executive*
Jones, F(rancis) Whitney *fund raising executive, consultant*
Kaufman, William *internist*
Kerr, Sandria Neidus *mathematics and computer science educator*
Kohut, Robert Irwin *otolaryngologist, educator*
Lambeth, Thomas Willis *foundation executive*
Leonard, R. Michael *lawyer*
Lorentz, William Beall *pediatrician*
Mackey, Dallas L. *financial consultant, development officer*
MacKinnon, Sally Anne *retired fast food company executive*
MacKinnon, William Howard *airline executive*
Martin, James Alfred, Jr. *religious studies educator*
Maselli, John Anthony *food products company executive*
Maynard, Charles Douglas *radiologist*
†McElveen, William Henry *minister*
McNair, John Franklin, III *banker*
Medlin, John Grimes, Jr. *banker*
Mokrasch, Lewis Carl *neurochemist, educator*
Moskowitz, Jay *public health sciences educator*
Mueller-Heubach, Eberhard August *medical educator, obstetrician-gynecologist*
Newton, George Durfee, Jr. *lawyer*
Oppermann, Joseph Kay *architect*
O'Steen, Wendall Keith *neurobiology and anatomy educator*
Penry, James Kiffin *physician, neurology educator*
Perret, Peter James *symphony conductor*
†Petree, William Horton *lawyer*
Piazza, John *hosiery company executive*
Podgorny, George *emergency physician*
Preslar, Len Broughton, Jr. *hospital administrator*
Rauschenberg, Bradford Lee *museum research director*
Ray, Michael Edwin *lawyer*
Roberts, William Hugh, III *library director, consultant*
Rodgman, Alan *chemist, consultant*
Rogers, Lee Frank *radiologist*
Runnion, Howard J., Jr. *banker*
Sandridge, William Pendleton, Jr. *lawyer*
Scales, James Ralph *history educator, former university president*
Schollander, Wendell Leslie, Jr. *lawyer*
Scisco, Peter Leon *magazine editor, writer*
Shapere, Dudley *philosophy educator*
Simon, Jimmy Louis *pediatrician, educator*
Smith, Zachary Taylor, II *retired tobacco company executive*
Spach, Jule Christian *church executive*
Sparber, Gordon Mark *music journalist*
Steele, Thomas McKnight *law librarian, law educator*
Sticht, J. Paul *retired food products and tobacco company executive*
Strayhorn, Ralph Nichols, Jr. *lawyer*
Strickland, Robert Louis *business executive*
Stroupe, Henry Smith *university dean*
Sullivan, William Beaumont *lawyer*
Thompson, Cleon F., Jr. *university administrator*
†Thrift, Julianne Still *academic administrator*
Toole, James Francis *medical educator*
Trautwein, George William *conductor*
†Tursi, Frank Vincent *journalist*
Vance, Charles Fogle, Jr. *lawyer*
Walker, George Kontz *law educator*
Walter, Lloyd Guy, Jr. *architect*
Walters, Doris Lavonne *pastoral counselor*
Wanders, Hans Walter *banker*
Ward, Hiram Hamilton *federal judge*
Ward, Marvin Martin *retired state senator*
Watlington, John Francis, Jr. *banker*
Wells, Dewey Wallace *lawyer*
Wiles, Paul Martin *hospital administration executive*
†Williams, Arthur T., Jr. *gas, oil industry executive*
†Williams, Arthur T., III *oil, gas industry executive*
Williams, John Edwin *psychology educator*
Wilson, Edwin Graves *university official*
Womble, William Fletcher *lawyer*
Woods, James Watson, Jr. *cardiologist*
Worley, Bland Wallace *banker*
Zagoria, Sam D(avid) *arbitrator, author, educator*

Winterville
Myers, Robert Durant *biologist, research director, medical educator*

Wrightsville
Mc Ilwain, William Franklin *newspaper editor, writer*

NORTH DAKOTA

Ashley
Kretschmar, William Edward *state legislator, lawyer*

Bismarck
Allmaras, Lorraine *state legislator*
†Brosseau, Terrance Gene *medical center administrator*
Carlisle, Ronald Dwight *nursery owner*
Carlson, Clare *state legislator*
Carmichael, Virgil Wesly *mining, civil and geological engineer, former coal company executive*
Conmy, Patrick A. *federal judge*
Cornatzer, William Eugene *retired biochemistry educator*
Erickstad, Ralph John *judge, retired state supreme court chief justice*
Evanson, Barbara Jean *middle school education educator*
Gilmore, Kathi *state treasurer*
Heitkamp, Heidi *state attorney general*
Hook, William Franklin *radiologist*
Jaeger, Alvin A. (Al Jaeger) *secretary of state*
Joersz, Fran Woodmansee *secondary education educator*
Johnson, Judith Ekberg *broadcast executive*
Kelly, Tish *state legislator*
Kelsch, RaeAnn *state legislator*
Kinney, John Francis *bishop*
Lardy, Sister Susan Marie *prioress*
Levine, Beryl Joyce *state supreme court justice*
Maichel, Joseph Raymond *lawyer, business executive*
Meisner, Dee Dolores Annette *small business owner*
Meschke, Herbert Leonard *state supreme court justice*
Montz, Florence Stolte *church official*
Murry, Charles Emerson *lawyer, official*
Myrdal, Rosemarie Caryle *state official, former state legislator*
Nelson, Keithe Eugene *lawyer, state court administrator*
Neumann, William Allen *judge*
Newborg, Gerald Gordon *historical agency administrator*
Olson, John Michael *lawyer*
Paulson, William Lee *state justice*
Pederson, Vernon R. *judge*
Sandstrom, Dale Vernon *state supreme court judge*
Sanstead, Wayne Godfrey *state superintendent, former lieutenant governor*
Schafer, Edward T. *governor*
Schuchart, John Albert, Jr. *utility executive*
Smith, Richard Ernest *retired insurance company executive*
Solberg, Nellie Florence Coad *artist*

Sperry, James Edward *anthropologist*
Strutz, William A. *lawyer*
Torgerson, Les *bar association administrator*
VandeWalle, Gerald Wayne *state supreme court chief justice*
Van Sickle, Bruce Marion *federal judge*
Vogel, Sarah *state agency administrator, lawyer*

Bottineau
Smith, J. W. *dean*

Crosby
Andrist, John M. *state senator*

Devils Lake
Etemad, Sharon L. *dean*

Dickinson
Morud, Rollie D. *school system administrator*

Dunseith
Gorder, Steven F. *association administrator*

Fargo
Benson, Paul *federal judge*
Berg, Rick Alan *state legislator, real estate investor*
Bright, Myron H. *federal judge, educator*
Dill, William Joseph *newspaper editor*
Fairfield, Andrew H. *bishop*
Foss, Richard John *bishop*
Hill, William A(lexander) *bankruptcy judge*
†Joppa, Leonard Robert *research geneticist, agronomist, educator*
Lohman, John Frederick *editor*
†Lund, H. Roald *plant scientist, educator*
Magill, Frank John *federal judge*
Marcil, William Christ, Sr. *publisher, broadcast executive*
Mathern, Tim *state senator, social worker*
Mengedoth, Donald Roy *commercial banker*
Nickel, Janet Marlene Milton *geriatrics nurse*
Ommodt, Donald Henry *dairy company executive*
Orr, Steven R. *health facility administrator*
Ozbun, Jim L. *academic administrator*
Paulson, John Doran *newspaper editor, retired*
Query, Joy Marves Neale *medical sociology educator*
Schmidt, Claude Henri *retired research administrator*
Spaeth, Nicholas John *lawyer, former state attorney general*
Sullivan, James Stephen *bishop*
Swedback, James M. *insurance company executive*
Tallman, Robert Hall *investment company executive*
Wallwork, William Wilson, III *leasing company executive*
Webb, Rodney Scott *federal judge, lawyer*
Williams, Norman Dale *geneticist, researcher*
Zimmerman, Don Charles *plant physiologist, biochemist*

Fessenden
Streibel, Bryce *state senator*

Grafton
Tallackson, Harvey D. *real estate and insurance salesman*

Grand Forks
Baker, Kendall L. *academic administrator*
Carlson, Edward C. *anatomy educator*
Carroll, Jack Adien *hospital administrator*
Clifford, Thomas John *university president*
DeMers, Judy Lee *state legislator, dean*
Duerre, John Arden *biochemist*
Gjovig, Bruce Quentin *manufacturing consultant*
Glassheim, Eliot Alan *city manager*
†Hammen, John Leo, III *geographer, educator*
Jacobs, Francis Albin *biochemist, educator*
Kelley, Patricia Hagelin *geology educator*
Nielsen, Forrest Harold *research nutritionist*
Nordlie, Robert Conrad *biochemistry educator*
O'Kelly, Bernard *university dean*
Poolman, Jim *state legislator*
Sand, Phyllis Sue Newnam (Phyllis Sue Newnam) *retired special education educator*
Senechal, Alice R. *judge, lawyer*
Stenehjem, Wayne Kevin *state senator, lawyer*
Vogel, Robert *lawyer, educator*
Widdel, John Earl, Jr. *lawyer*
Willson, Warrack G. *physical chemist*

Jamestown
†Hall, Richard William *hospital administrator*
Hjellum, John *retired lawyer*
†Kirby, Ronald Eugene *fish and wildlife research administrator*
Walker, James Silas *college official*

Mandan
Halvorson, Ardell David *research leader, soil scientist*
Halvorson, Gary Alfred *soil scientist*

Mayville
Karaim, Betty June *librarian*

Minot
Haugland, Brynhild *retired state legislator, farmer*
Kerian, Jon Robert *judge*
Shaar, H. Erik *academic administrator*

Rugby
Axtman, Benjamin J. *farmer*

Saint Anthony
Tomac, Steven Wayne *state senator, farmer*

Turtle Lake
Grosz, Albert Mick *sales executive*

Wahpeton
Jensen, Delores (Dee Jensen) *physical education educator*

Watford City
Stenehjem, Leland Manford *banker*

Williston
Adducci, Joseph Edward *obstetrician, gynecologist*
Burdick, Eugene Allan *retired judge, lawyer, surrogate judge*
†Hedren, Paul Leslie *national park administrator, historian*
Rennerfeldt, Earl Ronald *farmer, rancher*
Stevens, Garvin L. *college dean*
Wenstrom, Frank Augustus *state senator*
Yockim, James Craig *state senator, oil and gas executive*

OHIO

Ada
Cooper, Ken Errol *management educator*
Freed, DeBow *college president*
Hanson, Eugene Nelson *judge*

Akron
Aggarwal, Sundar Lal *technology management consultant*
Albrecht, Frederick Ivan *food products executive*
Albrecht, Frederick Steven *grocery company executive, lawyer*
†Alexander, Anthony J. *electric power industry executive*
Allen, William Dale *newspaper editor*
Altenau, Alan Giles *tire and rubber company executive*
Arnett, James Edward *retired insurance company executive, retired secondary school educator*
Auburn, Norman Paul *university president*
Barker, Harold Kenneth *former university dean*
Barnett, James Wallace *manufacturing executive*
Bartlo, Sam D. *lawyer*
Bell, Samuel H. *federal judge*
Brennan, David Leo *manufacturing company executive, lawyer, developer*
Brock, James Robert *manufacturing company executive*
Brown, David Rupert *engineering executive*
Bryant, Keith Lynn, Jr. *history educator*
Calise, Nicholas James *lawyer*
Castronovo, Thomas Paul *architect, consultant*
†Cheng, Stephen Zheng Di *chemistry educator, polymeric material researcher*
Childs, James William *lawyer, legal educator*
Clapp, Joseph Mark *motor carrier company executive*
Collier, Alice Elizabeth *community organization executive*
Considine, William Howard *health care administrator*
Contie, Leroy John, Jr. *federal judge*
Coyne, Thomas Joseph *economist, finance educator*
Crawford, Robert John *credit company executive*
Culler, Eugene R. *automotive products company executive*
Dotson, John Louis, Jr. *newspaper executive*
Dowd, David D., Jr. *federal judge*
Elliott, Peggy Gordon *university president*
Ennis, Charles Roe *manufacturing company executive, lawyer*
Evans, Douglas McCullough *surgeon, educator*
Fisher, James Lee *lawyer*
†Flood, Howard L. *banker*
Frank, John V. *foundation executive*
Friedman, Richard Everett *librarian*
Gault, Stanley Carleton *manufacturing company executive*
Gent, Alan Neville *physicist, educator*
Gilbert, Albert Francis *hospital administrator*
Glass, James Richard *retired tire and rubber manufacturing company executive*
Hackbirth, David William *aluminum company executive*
Haller, Sonja Maria *lawyer*
†Hart, Karen Ann *social services administrator*
Heider, Jon Vinton *lawyer, corporate executive*
Herman, Roger Eliot *professional speaker, consultant, futurist, writer*
Holland, Willard Raymond, Jr. *electric utility executive*
Holloway, Donald Phillip *lawyer*
Jones, Robert Huhn *history educator*
Kahan, Mitchell Douglas *art museum director*
Kaufman, Donald Leroy *aluminum products company executive*
Kelley, Frank Nicholas *dean*
Kelley, John Paul *communications consultant*
Kelley, Robert W. *bishop*
Kennedy, Joseph Paul *polymer scientist, researcher*
Kirksey, Charles Ron *journalist*
Knepper, George W. *history educator*
Kodish, Arline Betty *principal*
Levy, Richard Philip *physician, educator*
†Lloyd, Philip Armour *lawyer*
LoIudice, Thomas Anthony *gastroenterologist, researcher*
Lombardi, Frederick McKean *lawyer*
MacCracken, Mary Jo *physical education educator*
Marini, Frank Nicholas *public administration and political science educator*
McCormick, William Edward *environmental consultant*
†McMillan, Robert Allan *chemical company executive*
Monacelli, Amieto *professional bowler*
Ockene, Alan L. *tire manufacturing executive*
Ong, John Doyle *lawyer*
Ozio, David *professional bowler*
Phillipson, John Samuel *retired English educator*
Piirma, Irja *chemist, educator*
Plusquellic, Donald L. *mayor*
Poll, Heinz *choreographer, artistic director*
Prus, Francis Vincent *tire company executive*
Rebenack, John Henry *retired librarian*
Reynolds, A. William *manufacturing company executive*
Richert, Paul *law educator*
Schrader, Helen Maye *retired municipal worker*
Schubert, Barbara Schuele *performing company executive*
Schulz, Mary Elizabeth *lawyer*
Seiberling, John Frederick *former congressman, law educator, lawyer*
Shaffer, Oren George *manufacturing company executive*
Shea-Stonum, Marilyn *judge*
†Sheldon, Gilbert Ignatius *clergyman*
†Smith, Terry *metal products executive*
Sonnecken, Edwin Herbert *management consultant*
Spetrino, Russell John *retired utility company executive, lawyer*
†Stefanko, Robert Allen *financial executive*
Steuert, Douglas Michael *financial executive*
Stroll, Beverly Marie *elementary school principal*
†Sullivan, Daniel Joseph, III *transportation executive*
†Taylor, Gary Lee *marketing executive*
Timmons, Gerald Dean *pediatric neurologist*
Tobler, D. Lee *chemical and aerospace company executive*
Trotter, Thomas Robert *lawyer*
Wells, Hoyt Mellor *manufacturing executive*
†Wells, Norman, Jr. *metal products executive*
Wessman, Joan Feeney *nurse administrator*
†West, Michael Alan *hospital administrator*
White, Harold F. *bankruptcy judge, retired federal judge*
Wickham, Michael W. *transportation executive*
†Wiskind, Milton I. *wholesale distribution executive, chemicals executive*

Alexandria
Palmer, Melville Louis *retired agricultural engineering educator*

Alliance
†Kitto, John Buck, Jr. *mechanical engineer*
Rockhill, Jack Kerrigan *collections company executive*
Rodman, James Purcell *astrophysicist, educator*
Weber, Ronald Gilbert *retired college president*
Woods, Rose Mary *consultant, former presidential assistant*

Alpha
James, Francis Edward, Jr. *investment counselor*

Andover
Mathay, John Preston *elementary education educator*

Ansonia
Spencer, Rex LeRoy *secondary education educator*

Ashland
Cox, Harry Seymour *financial executive*
Ford, Lucille Garber *economist, educator, college official*
†Waters, Ronald W. *church executive, pastor*

Ashtabula
Bonner, David Calhoun *chemical company executive*
Mahan, John K. *dean*
Taylor, Norman Floyd *computer educator, administrator*

Ashville
Beckman, Judith *art educator*

Athens
Beale, William Taylor *engineering company executive*
Borchert, Donald Marvin *philosopher, educator*
Bruning, James Leon *university official, educator*
Cohn, Norman Stanley *botany educator, university dean*
Crowl, Samuel Renninger *English language educator, author*
Dinos, Nicholas *engineering educator, administrator*
Eckelmann, Frank Donald *geology educator, retired*
Eckes, Alfred Edward, Jr. *historian, international trade analyst*
†Friedenberg, Walter Drew *journalist*
Gaddis, John Lewis *history educator*
Glidden, Robert Burr *university president, musician, educator*
Gustavson, Carl Gustav *historian, educator*
Hamby, Alonzo Lee *historian, educator*
Klare, George Roger *psychology educator*
Lee, Hwa-Wei *librarian, educator*
Matthews, Jack (John Harold Matthews) *English educator, writer*
Miller, Edmund Kenneth *retired electrical engineer, educator*
Miller, Peggy McLaren *management educator*
Miller, Richard Irwin *education educator, university administrator*
†Myers, Frank Wayne *osteopath, educator*
†Parmer, Jess Norman *university official, educator*
Patterson, Harlan Ray *finance educator*
Ping, Charles Jackson *university administrator, educator*
Rakes, Ganas Kaye *finance and banking educator*
Robe, Thurlow Richard *engineering educator, university dean*
Schneider, Duane Bernard *English literature educator, publisher*
Scott, Charles Lewis *photojournalist*
Stempel, Guido Hermann, III *journalism educator*
Ungar, Irwin Allan *botany educator*
Wen, Shih-Liang *mathematics educator*
Whealey, Lois Deimel *humanities scholar*

Aurora
Lawton, Florian Kenneth *artist, educator*

Barberton
Boomer, Walter Eugene *marine officer*
Moss, Robert Drexler *lawyer*
Stewart, Joe J. *manufacturing executive*

Batavia
Bower, Kenneth Francis *electrical engineer*
Rosenhoffer, Chris *lawyer*

Bay Village
Hiller, Deborah Lewis *long term care and retirement facility executive*

Beachwood
Donnem, Roland William *real estate owner and manager*
Ellett, Alan Sidney *real estate development company executive*
Lerner, Alfred *real estate and financial executive*
Seelbach, William Robert *management consultant*
Swank, Emory Coblentz *world affairs consultant, lecturer*
Wolf, Milton Albert *economist, former U.S. ambassador, investor*
Zelikow, Howard Monroe *management and financial consultant*

Beavercreek
Rodin, Alvin Eli *pathalogist, medical educator, author*

Bedford
Parch, Grace Dolores *librarian*

Bedford Heights
Moore, Dianne J. Hall *insurance claims administrator*
†Schuman, Nancy Kathleen *secondary education educator*

Bellaire
Hahn, David Bennett *hospital administrator, marketing professional*
Simpson, Daniel H. *ambassador*

Berea
Belichick, Bill *professional football coach*
Blumer, Frederick Elwin *philosophy educator*
Irwin, Richard Loren *systems management association executive*
Jensen, Adolph Robert *former chemistry educator*
Malicky, Neal *college president*
Modell, Arthur B. *professional football team executive*
Pattison, Robert Maynicke *architect*
Rison, Andre *football player*
Rypien, Mark Robert *professional football player*
Schad, Mike *professional football player*
Strew, Suzanne Claflin *choreographer, dance educator*
Thompson, Bennie *professional football player*

Blacklick
Doyle, Patrick Lee *insurance company executive*

Bluffton
Smucker, Barbara Claassen *former librarian, writer*

Bowling Green
Baird, James Abington *judge*
Brecher, Arthur Seymour *biochemistry educator*
Browne, Ray Broadus *popular culture educator*
Clark, Eloise Elizabeth *biologist, university official*
Clark, Robert King *communications educator emeritus, lecturer, consultant, actor, model*
Guthrie, Mearl Raymond, Jr. *business administration educator*
Hakel, Milton Daniel, Jr. *psychology educator, consultant, publisher*
Hanna, Martin Shad *lawyer*
Heckman, Carol A. *biology educator*
Holmes, Robert Allen *lawyer, educator, consultant, lecturer*
Lavezzi, John Charles *art history educator, archaeologist*
Lunde, Harold Irving *management educator*
McCaghy, Charles Henry *sociology educator*
Ocvirk, Otto George *artist*
Olscamp, Paul James *academic administrator*
Rockett, Carlton Lee *biological sciences educator*
Scott, John Paul *psychologist, educator, author*
Weaver, Richard L., II *speech communication educator*

Bratenahl
Jones, Trevor Owen *automobile supply company executive, management consultant*

Brecksville
Galloway, Ethan Charles *technology development executive, former chemicals executive*
Johnson, L. Neil *school system administrator*
Ludenia, Krista *psychologist, health facility administrator*
Worden, Alfred Merrill *former astronaut, research company executive*

Broadview Heights
†Hahn, Sang Ki *genetist*

Brook Park
Bluford, Guion Stewart, Jr. *engineering company executive*
Wilson, Jack *aeronautical engineer*

Brookville
Juhl, Daniel Leo *manufacturing and marketing firm executive*

Bryan
†Nelson, Sandra Kay *foundation administrator*

Bucyrus
Moore, Thomas Paul *broadcast executive*

Burbank
Koucky, Frank Louis *geology educator, archeogeology researcher*

Canal Winchester
Burrier, Gail Warren *physician*

Canfield
Bachmeyer, Robert Wesley *retired hospital administration consultant*
Itts, Elizabeth Ann Dunham *psychotherapist, consultant, designer*

Canton
Albacete, Manuel Joseph *museum director*
Ashton, P. J. *metal products executive*
Barone, Robert Paul *manufacturing company executive*
Bennington, Ronald Kent *lawyer*
Birkholz, Raymond James *metal products manufacturing company executive*
Boulton, Edwin Charles *bishop*
Carpenter, Noble Olds *banker*
Crowley, Cassandra Ann *ballet company administrator, choreographer*
Dettinger, Warren Walter *lawyer*
Dorsett, Anthony Drew (Tony Dorsett) *former professional football player*
Duncan, Joyce Louise *real estate broker*
Elliott, Peter R. *athletic organization executive*
Elsaesser, Robert James *retired manufacturing executive*
Fouts, Daniel Francis *sports announcer, former professional football player*
Grant, Bud (Harold Peter Grant) *retired professional football coach*
Heller, Charles Andrew, Jr. *electric utilities company executive*
Herritt, David R. *elementary education educator*
Hoecker, David *engineering executive*
Howland, Willard J. *radiologist, educator*

Johnson, Jimmy *former professional football player*
Kelly, Leroy *former professional football player*
Koniecko, Edward S(tanley) *biochemist*
Koontz, Raymond *retired security equipment company executive*
Lindamood, John Beyer *lawyer*
Mokodean, Michael John *lawyer, accountant*
Moorhouse, Linda Virginia *symphony orchestra administrator*
Ognibene, Andre J(ohn) *physician, army officer, educator*
Repp, Ronald Stewart *insurance company executive*
Smith, Jackie *former professional football player*
Timken, W. Robert, Jr. *manufacturing company executive*
Toot, Joseph F., Jr. *bearing manufacturing company executive*
Warner, E. John *manufacturing financial executive*
†Werstler, Richard Emerson *museum director*

Cedarville
DeWine, R. Michael *U.S. Senator, lawyer*
Gordin, Dean Lackey *retired agricultural products executive*

Celina
†Fanning, Ronald Heath *architect, engineer*

Centerville
Fulk, Paul Frederick *chiropractor*
Kelso, Harold Glen *family practice physician*
Mattia, Frank J. *secondary school principal*
Perrich, Jerry Robert *environmental consulting company executive*

Chagrin Falls
Brown, Jeanette Grasselli *university official*
Church, Irene Zaboly *personnel services company executive*
Cordes, Loverne Christian *interior designer*
Daniel, Clarence Huber *former manufacturing company executive, consultant*
Dunning, Ann Marie *architect*
Eastburn, Richard A. *retired consulting firm executive*
Fisher, Will Stratton *illumination consultant*
Frohring, Paul Robert *former business executive*
Gelb, Victor *management consultant*
Groeger, Joseph Herman *retired metal company executive*
Hawley, Richard Alan *headmaster, writer*
Lingl, Friedrich Albert *psychiatrist*
Morris, Jane Elizabeth *home economics educator*
Obert, Charles Frank *banker*
Pauly, Bruce Henry *engineering consultant*
Phillips, Dorothy Ormes *elementary education educator*
Rawski, Conrad H(enry) *humanities educator, medievalist*
Richmond, Phyllis Allen *library and information science educator*
Strachan, Donald M. *financial company executive*
Streicher, James Franklin *lawyer*
Weckesser, Elden Christian *surgery educator*

Chardon
Dietrich, Joseph Jacob *retired chemist, research executive*
Reinhard, Sister Mary Marthe *educational organization administrator*

Chesapeake
Harris, Bob L(ee) *principal*

Chesterland
Driggs, Charles Mulford *lawyer*
Durn, Raymond Joseph *lawyer*
Kancelbaum, Joshua Jacob *lawyer*

Chillicothe
New, Eloise Ophelia *special education educator*
Page, Troy Edward *health care administrator*

Cincinnati
Adams, Edmund John *lawyer*
Adams, James Louis *newspaper editor, retired*
Addison, Harry Metcalf *insurance executive*
Adolph, Robert J. *physician, medical educator*
Alexander, James Marshall, Jr. *architect, retired educator*
Alexander, James Wesley *surgeon, educator*
†Alexander, Jeffrey *performing company executive*
Alexander, John J. *chemistry educator*
Anderson, James Milton *lawyer*
Anderson, William Hopple *lawyer*
Aniskovich, Paul Peter, Jr. *insurance company executive*
Anno, James Nelson *nuclear engineering scientist, educator*
Anthony, Thomas Dale *lawyer*
Arnold, Lynn Ellis *metallurgist, consultant*
Artzt, Edwin Lewis *consumer products company executive*
Atteberry, William Duane *diversified manufacturing company executive*
Bahlman, William Thorne, Jr. *retired lawyer*
Bahr, Donald Walter *chemical engineer*
Baker, Norman Robert *education educator*
†Balistreri, William Francis *physician, pediatric gastroenterologist*
Barach, Philip G. *shoe company executive*
Barrie, Dennis Ray *museum director*
Baxter, Raoul *meat packing company executive*
Beckwith, Barbara Jean *journalist*
Beekman, Philip E. *retail company executive*
Belew, Adrian *guitarist, singer, songwriter, producer*
Bench, Johnny Lee *retired professional baseball player*
Bernstein, I. Leonard *physician, educator*
Bestehorn, Ute Wiltrud *retired librarian*
Biddinger, Paul Williams *pathologist, educator*
Bieliauskas, Vytautas Joseph *clinical psychologist, educator*
Bingham, Eula *environmental health educator*
Bishop, George Franklin *political social psychologist, educator*
Black, David deLaine *investment consultant*
Blake, George Rowell *newspaper executive*
Blanken, Sarah S. *retired foundation administrator*
Bleznick, Donald William *Romance languages educator*
Bluestein, Paul Harold *management engineer*
Bluestein, Venus Weller *retired psychology educator*
Blum, William Lee *lawyer*
Boat, Thomas Frederick *physician, educator, researcher*
Bogart, Judith Saunders *public relations executive*
Borgman, James Mark *editorial cartoonist*
Bradley, Sister Myra James *health science facility executive*
†Brandt, J. Michael *school system administrator*
†Brestel, Mary Beth *librarian*
Breth, James Raymond *scrap metals company executive*
Bridenbaugh, Phillip Owen *anesthesiologist, physician*
Bridgeland, James Ralph, Jr. *lawyer, mayor*
Briggs, Henry Payson, Jr. *headmaster*
Brod, Stanford *graphic designer, educator*
Bromberg, Barbara Schwartz *lawyer*
Bromberg, Robert Sheldon *lawyer*
Brown, Dale Patrick *advertising executive*
Brown, Mike *professional sports team executive*
Brumm, Brian Allen *accountant*
Brumm, Paul Michael *banker*
Brunner, Gordon F(rancis) *household products company executive*
Buchman, Elwood *physician, pharmaceutical company medical director*
Bullock, John McDonell *banker*
Burleigh, William Robert *newspaper executive*
Burt, David A. *grocery and drugstore company executive*
Burt, DeVere *museum administrator*
†Byer, P. Roger *holding company executive*
Byers, Kenneth Vernon *insurance company executive*
Campbell, Patricia Elaine *elementary education educator*
Cantu, John Maurice *retired insurance company executive*
Carlson, Jennie Peaslack *lawyer*
Carney, Robert Alfred *health care administrator*
Carothers, Charles Omsted *orthopedic surgeon*
Carr, Albert Anthony *organic chemist*
Carro, Jorge Luis *law librarian, educator*
Carroll, Robert Henry *accountant*
Carson, Nolan Wendell *lawyer*
Chase, William Rowell *manufacturing executive*
Chatterjee, Jayanta *educator, urban designer*
Chesley, Stanley Morris *lawyer*
Christensen, Paul Walter, Jr. *gear manufacturing company executive*
Christenson, Gordon A. *law educator*
Church, John Franklin, Jr. *paper company executive*
Ciani, Alfred Joseph *language professional, dean*
Cissell, James Charles *lawyer*
Clark, James Norman *insurance executive*
†Clark, Raymond Robert *utilities company executive*
Cody, Thomas Gerald *lawyer*
Cohen, Hirsh Joel *health care administrator*
Collins, Larry Wayne *health facility administrator*
Conaton, Michael Joseph *financial service executive*
Conley, Robert T. *educational administrator*
Cook, Jack McPherson *hospital administrator*
Coombe, V. Anderson *valve manufacturing company executive*
†Copeland, William Mack *hospital administrator, lawyer*
Coslet, Bruce N. *professional football coach*
Cowan, Jerry Louis *lawyer*
Craig, L. Clifford *lawyer*
Crowe, James Joseph *shoe company executive, lawyer*
Crumes, William Edward *bishop*
Curtin, Leah Louise *editor, author, nurse, ethician, consultant*
†Dahlman, Simon Jacques *magazine editor, minister*
de Blasis, James Michael *artistic director, producer, stage director*
DeBrunner, Gerald Joseph *accounting firm executive*
Dehner, Joseph Julnes *lawyer*
DeLeone, Carmon *conductor, musician, composer, educator*
DeLong, Deborah *lawyer*
Dember, William Norton *psychologist, educator*
Derstadt, Ronald Theodore *health care administrator*
Desmarais, Charles Joseph *museum director, writer, editor*
Devitt, John William *physicist*
Dewey, Richard Lee *telephone company executive*
Dickey, John Miller *health care facility executive*
Diller, Edward Dietrich *lawyer*
Dornette, W(illiam) Stuart *lawyer, educator*
Driehaus, Robert Joseph *financial company executive*
Dubuc, Kenneth E *management consultant*
Dunning, Thomas E. *newspaper editor*
Eager, William Earl *information systems corporation executive*
†Eaton, Edwin Harvey, Jr. *household cleaning products company executive, comptroller*
Edelstein, Chaim Y. *retail executive*
Edwards, George Clifton, Jr. *retired judge*
Ehrnschwender, Arthur Robert *former utility company executive*
Elleman, Lawrence Robert *lawyer*
Erickson, Richard J. *lawyer*
Evans, Barry Craig *financial services company exexutive*
Fagin, Richard *litigation consultant*
Faller, Susan Grogan *lawyer*
Ferriss, David Platt *advertising consultant*
Fine, Lawrence Jay *internist, occupational preventive medicine*
Fink, Jerold Albert *lawyer*
Finkelmeier, Philip Renner *law librarian, lawyer*
Flanagan, Martha Lang *corporate secretary*
Flick, Thomas Michael *mathematics educator, educational administrator*
Fokker, J. P. *waste management executive*
Ford, Emory A. *chemist, researcher*
Fowler, Noble Owen *physician, university administrator*
Francis, Marion David *consulting chemist*
Freedman, William Mark *lawyer*
Freshwater, Paul Ross *consumer goods company executive*
Gant, Ron (Ronald Edwin Gant) *professional baseball player*
Garber, Charles Nelson *financial executive*
Garfinkel, Jane E. *lawyer*
Geier, James Aylward Develin *manufacturing company executive*
Gesteland, Robert Charles *neurophysiologist*
Gettler, Benjamin *lawyer, manufacturing company executive*
Gibson, George M. *manufacturing company executive*
†Gilligan, Michael James *health care administrator*
Glendening, Everett Austin *architect*
Glenn, Jerry Hosmer, Jr. *foreign language educator*
Glover, Richard M. *manufacturing company executive*
Glueck, Helen Iglauer *physician*
Goetzman, Bruce Edgar *architecture educator*
Goodman, Bernard *physics educator*
Goodman, Stanley *lawyer*
Gosling, David *university administrator, urban design educator*
Gottschalk, Alfred *college president*
Graham, Scharleen Walker *counselor*
Gray, John Augustus *physical chemist*
Greenberg, David Bernard *chemical engineering educator*
Greenberg, Gerald Stephen *lawyer*
Greengus, Samuel *academic administrator, religion educator*
Greenwalt, Tibor Jack *physician, educator*
Griffin, William Ralph *manufacturing executive*
Guggenheim, Richard E. *lawyer, shoe company executive*
Haag, Walter M(onroe), Jr. *research institute executive, industrial engineer*
Hall, Ernest L. *electrical engineer, robotics educator*
Hardy, William Robinson *lawyer*
Harmon, Patrick *newspaperman*
Harrell, Samuel Macy *grain company executive*
Harrington, Jeremy Thomas *clergyman, publisher*
Harris, Irving *lawyer*
Harrison, Donald Carey *academic administrator, cardiologist*
Harshman, Morton Leonard *physician, business executive*
Harte, Sandra Wiswell *gifted education educator*
Harville, Thomas T. *consumer goods company executive*
Hayden, Joseph Page, Jr. *finance company executive*
Heimlich, Henry Jay *physician, surgeon*
Heineman, William Richard *chemistry educator*
Heinlen, Ronald Eugene *lawyer*
Hendricks, Harry *church administrator*
Henry, J(ohn) Porter, Jr. *sales consultant*
Hermanies, John Hans *lawyer*
Herring, Milton S. *church administrator*
Hess, Donald C. *lawyer*
Hess, Evelyn Victorine (Mrs. Michael Howett) *medical educator*
Hiatt, Marjorie McCullough *service organization executive*
†Hibbard, Dwight H. *telecommunications company executive*
Hicks, Irle Raymond *retail food chain executive*
Hill, Thomas Clark *lawyer*
Hodge, Robert Joseph *retail executive*
Hoermann, Edward Richard *urban planning educator*
Hoff, James Edwin *university president*
Hoffheimer, Daniel Joseph *lawyer*
Hoffman, Donna Coy *educator*
Hoffman, Joel Harvey *composer*
Hollerman, Charles Edward *pediatrician*
Hornbaker, Alice Joy *author*
Horwitz, Harry *radiologist, physician, educator*
Hoskins, Geraldine *hospital nursing administrator*
Houser, Dwane Russell *insurance company executive*
Hubbard, Arthur Thornton *chemistry educator, electro-surface chemist*
†Hubbard, Peter E. *transportation company executive*
Hubschman, Henry Allan *lawyer*
Hudson, Bannus B. *footwear manufacturing and apparel retail executive*
Hummel, Robert Paul *surgeon*
Hunt, James Robert *librarian*
Huron, Roderick Eugene *religious organization administrator*
Hutton, Edward Luke *diversified public corporation executive*
Huvos, Kornel *linguistics educator*
Hyre, James G. *educational administrator*
Jackobs, Miriam Ann *dietitian*
Jaffe, Murray Sherwood *surgeon*
James, Jefferson Ann *choreographer*
Johnson, C. Scott *management consultant*
Johnson, Davey (David Allen Johnson) *baseball team manager*
Johnson, James J. *lawyer*
Johnson, K(enneth) O(dell) *aerospace engineer*
Jones, Nathaniel Raphael *federal judge*
Jordan, Lorna *news director*
Joseph, David J., Jr. *trading company executive*
Kang, Mohinder Singh *biochemist*
Kaplan, Stanley Meisel *psychoanalyst*
Katz, Robert Langdon *human relations educator, rabbi*
Katzen, Raphael *consulting chemical engineer*
Kawahara, Fred Katsumi *research chemist*
Keener, C(harles) Richard *food company information systems executive*
Kehew, William James *environmental, quality assurance engineering manager*
Kellar, Lorrence Theodore *retail food and manufacturing executive*
Kelley, John Joseph, Jr. *lawyer*
Kiel, Frederick Orin *lawyer*
King, Elaine A. *curator, art historian, critic*
Kite, William McDougall *lawyer*
Klinedinst, Thomas John, Jr. *insurance agency executive*
Knipschild, Robert *artist, educator*
Knowlton, Austin E. (Dutch Knowlton) *professional football team executive*
Knue, Paul Frederick *newspaper editor*
Koebel, Sister Celestia *health care system executive*
Koepcke, F. Kristen *corporate lawyer*
Kohl, David *dean, librarian*
Kordons, Uldis *lawyer*
Krohn, Claus Dankertsen *insurance company executive*
Kroll, Robert James *aerospace engineering educator*
Kunzel, Erich, Jr. *conductor, arranger, educator*
LaBath, Octave Aaron *mechanical engineer*
†Lakey, Othal H. *bishop*
Larkin, Barry Louis *professional baseball player*
Laux, James Michael *historian, educator*
Lawrence, James Kaufman Lebensburger *lawyer*
Lawson, Randall Clayton, II *financial executive*
Leser, Lawrence A. *broadcasting company executive*
Levy, Sam Malcolm *advertising executive*
Lewis, Gene Dale *historian, educator*
Lichtin, (Judah) Leon *pharmacist*
Lienhart, David Arthur *geologist, consultant, laboratory director*
Lindberg, Charles David *lawyer*
Lindner, Keith E. *food company executive*
Lindner, Robert David *finance company executive*
Linsey, Nathaniel L. *bishop*
Lintz, Robert Carroll *financial holding company executive*
Liss, Herbert Myron *newspaper publisher, communications company executive*
Lloyd, David Livingstone, Jr. *lawyer*
Lockhart, John Mallery *management consultant*
Loggie, Jennifer Mary Hildreth *medical educator, physician*
Long, Phillip Clifford *museum director*
Longenecker, Mark Hershey, Jr. *lawyer*
Lopez-Cobos, Jesus *conductor*
Lucas, Stanley Jerome *radiologist, physician*
Lucke, Robert Vito *merger and acquisition executive*
Luckner, Herman Richard, III *interior designer*
†Lucky, Anne Weissman *dermatologist*
Lutz, James Gurney *lawyer*
Macpherson, Colin R(obertson) *pathologist, educator*
Maier, Craig Frisch *restaurant executive*
Maisel, Michael *clothing executive*
Manley, Robert Edward *lawyer, economist*
Mann, David Scott *lawyer*
Mantel, Samuel Joseph, Jr. *management educator, consultant*
Marcus, Jacob Rader *history educator*
Marcus, Leonard *retail company executive*
†Mark, James Edward *physical chemist*
Martin, Daniel William *acoustical physicist*
Martin, John Bruce *chemical engineer*
Maruska, Edward Joseph *zoo administrator*
Mattingly, Paul R. *lawyer*
Maxwell, Robert Wallace, II *lawyer*
McClain, William Andrew *lawyer*
McCoy, John Joseph *lawyer*
McDonough, James Francis *civil engineer, educator*
McDowell, John Eugene *lawyer*
McGavran, Frederick Jaeger *lawyer*
McGuire, Elaine C. *nursing administrator*
Mc Henry, Powell *lawyer*
McKenny, Collin Grad *banker*
McNulty, John William *retired public relations executive, automobile company executive*
Meal, Larie *chemistry educator, consultant*
Meisner, Gary Wayne *landscape architect*
Meranus, Leonard Stanley *lawyer*
Merchant, Mylon Eugene *physicist, engineer*
Messinger, Richard C. *engineering research and development consultant*
Meyer, Daniel Joseph *machinery company executive*
Middendorf, William Henry *electrical engineering educator*
Milligan, Lawrence Drake, Jr. *consumer products executive*
Milnes, William Robert, Jr. *insurance company executive*
Mitchell, Otis Clinton, Jr. *history educator*
†Moler, James Clark *marketing research executive*
Molitor, Sister Margaret Anne *nun, former college president*
Moll, William Gene *broadcasting company executive*
†Monder, Steven I. *orchestra executive*
†Monnig, Donna Sue *librarian*
Monroe, Murray Shipley *lawyer*
Mooney, Donald James, Jr. *lawyer*
Mooney, Timothy M. *retail executive*
Moore, Alfred Anson *corporate executive*
Moore, Michael C. *retail executive*
Moore, Thomas A. *consumer products company executive*
Morgan, John Bruce *hospital care consultant*
Morgan, Robert B. *insurance company executive*
Munn, Stephen P. *manufacturing company executive*
Muntz, Ernest Gordon *historian, educator*
Murphy, Eugene F. *aerospace, communications and electronics executive*
Naylor, Paul Donald *lawyer*
†Neale, Henry Whitehead *plastic surgery educator*
Nebert, Daniel Walter *molecular geneticist, research administrator*
Nechemias, Stephen Murray *lawyer*
Nelson, David Aldrich *federal judge*
Nester, William Raymond, Jr. *retired university chancellor and educator*
Neumark, Michael Harry *lawyer*
Nielsen, George Lee *architect*
Niemoller, Arthur B. *electrical engineer*
Nordlund, James John *dermatologist*
Norman, Peter Minert *fundraising consulting company executive*
Olson, Robert Wyrick *lawyer*
O'Reilly, James Thomas *lawyer, educator, author*
†Pancoast, Scott R. *distribution company executive*
Papadakis, Constantine N. *dean, civil engineering educator*
Parker, R. Joseph *lawyer*
Peck, Abraham Joseph *historian*
Pennacchio, Joseph *apparel executive*
Pepper, John Ennis, Jr. *consumer products company executive*
Perlman, Burton *federal judge*
Perry, Norman Robert *priest, magazine editor*
Peterson, Gale Eugene *historian*
Petry, Thomas Edwin *manufacturing company executive*
Pettengill, Kroger *investment counselor*
Phalen, Thomas Francis, Jr. *lawyer*
Phillips, T. Stephen *lawyer*
Pichler, Joseph Anton *food products executive*
Pike, Larry Ross *insurance executive*
Pilarczyk, Daniel Edward *archbishop*
Preiser, Wolfgang Friedrich Ernst *architect, educator, consultant, researcher*
Price, Thomas Emile *export and investment company executive*
Proffitt, H. Kevin *archivist*
Pruett, Samuel H. *manufacturing executive*
Puchta, Charles George *lawyer*
Qualls, Roxanne *mayor of Cincinnati*
Ralston, James Allen *lawyer*
†Ralston, Robert O. *manufacturing executive*
†Randolph, Jackson Harold *utility company executive*
Raskin, Fred Charles *transportation and utility holding company executive*
Rebar, Robert William *obstetrician, gynecologist, educator*
Reeb, Patricia A. *nursing educator, administrator*
Reichert, David *lawyer*
Rexroth, Nancy Louise *photographer*
Rich, Robert Edward *lawyer*
Roberts, Richard Stewart *lawyer*
Rockwell, R(onald) James, Jr. *laser and electro-optics consultant*
Roe, Clifford Ashley, Jr. *lawyer*
Rogers, James Eugene *electric utility executive*
Rogers, Lawrence H., II *retired television executive, investor, writer*
Rogers, Millard Foster, Jr. *art museum director*
Roomann, Hugo *architect*
Rose, Donald McGregor *lawyer*
Rubin, Carl Bernard *federal judge*

Rubin, Stanley Gerald *aerospace engineering educator*
Rudney, Harry *biochemist, educator*
†Ryan, J. Patrick *fund raising consulting company executive*
Sabin, Joan Mary *nursing executive, nurse*
Saenger, Eugene Lange *radiology educator, laboratory director*
Safferman, Robert Samuel *microbiologist*
Samuel, Gerhard *orchestra conductor, composer*
Sanders, Deion Luwynn *baseball and football player*
Santen, Ann Hortenstine *broadcasting executive*
Sawyer, John *professional football team executive*
Scarpino, Pasquale Valentine *environmental microbiologist*
Schaeter, George A., Jr. *banking executive*
Schiff, John Jefferson *insurance company executive*
Schmidt, Thomas Joseph, Jr. *lawyer*
Schneider, Harold Joel *radiologist*
Schott, Marge *professional baseball team executive*
Schottelkotte, Albert Joseph *broadcasting executive*
Schreiner, Albert William *physician, educator*
Schrier, Arnold *historian, educator*
Schubert, William Kuenneth *hospital medical center executive*
Schuck, Thomas Robert *lawyer*
Schuler, Robert Leo *appraiser, consultant*
Schwartz, Arnold (Arnie Shayne) *pharmacologist, biophysicist, biochemist, educator, actor, director, producer*
Scoggins, Samuel McWhirter *lawyer*
Scripps, Charles Edward *newspaper publisher*
Sedgwick-Hirsch, Carol Elizabeth *financial executive*
Semon, Warren Lloyd *retired computer sciences educator*
Senhauser, John Crater *architect*
Servodidio, Pat Anthony *broadcast executive*
Shenk, Richard Lawrence *real estate developer, photographer, artist*
Sherman, Jeffrey *retail executive*
†Shipley, Tony L(ee) *software company executive*
Shore, Thomas Spencer, Jr. *lawyer*
Shula, David D. *professional football team coach*
Siebenburgen, David A. *airline company executive*
Siekmann, Donald Charles *accountant*
Silbersack, Mark Louis *lawyer*
Silvers, Gerald Thomas *publishing executive*
Sjoerdsma, Albert *research institute executive*
Slater, John Greenleaf *manufacturing company executive*
Smale, John Gray *diversified industry executive*
Smith, C. LeMoyne *publishing company executive*
Smith, Gregory Allgire *academic director*
Smith, Joyce Camille *elementary education educator*
Smith, Leroy Harrington, Jr. *mechanical engineer, aerodynamics consultant*
Smith, Roger Dean *pathologist*
Smittle, Nelson Dean *electronics executive*
Snead, Richard Thomas *retail company executive*
Socol, Howard *department store executive*
Sodd, Vincent Joseph *nuclear medicine researcher, educator*
Sottile, Benjamin Joseph *greeting card company executive*
Sperelakis, Nicholas *physiology and biophysics educator, researcher*
†Sperzel, George E., Jr. *personal care industry executive*
Spiegel, S. Arthur *federal judge*
Steger, Joseph A. *university president*
Steinberg, Janet Eckstein *journalist*
†Stern, Edward *performing company executive*
Stern, Joseph Smith, Jr. *former footwear manufacturing company executive*
Sterne, Bobbie Lynn *city council member*
Stolley, Alexander *advertising executive*
Stonestreet, Robert *library director*
†Streckfuss, James Arthur *lawyer, historian*
Street, David Hargett *investment company executive*
Strubbe, John Lewis *retired food chain store executive*
†Stuhlreyer, Paul Augustus, III *cultural organization administrator*
Sullivan, Connie Castleberry *artist, photographer*
Sullivan, Dennis James, Jr. *public relations executive*
Suskind, Raymond Robert *physician, educator*
Sweeten, Gary Ray *religious counseling educator*
Swigert, James Mack *lawyer*
Tatgenhorst, (Charles) Robert *lawyer*
Taylor, Wayne Fletcher *lawyer*
Terhar, Louis F. *waste management administrator*
Terp, Thomas Thomsen *lawyer*
Thiemann, Charles Lee *banker*
†Thomas, Jeffrey Noel *aviation consulting company executive, management consultant*
Thompson, Herbert, Jr. *bishop*
Thompson, Morley Punshon *textile company executive*
Thrun, Robert Read *architect*
Tihany, Leslie Charles *retired foreign service officer, educator*
Timpano, Anne *museum director, art historian*
Tobias, Charles Harrison, Jr. *lawyer*
Tobias, Paul Henry *lawyer*
Tocco, James *pianist*
Toftner, Richard Orville *engineering executive*
Toltzis, Robert Joshua *cardiologist*
Townsend, Robert J. *lawyer*
Ullman, Louis Jay *financial executive*
Vander Laan, Mark Alan *lawyer*
Victor, William Weir *retired telephone company executive, consultant*
Vilter, Richard William *physician, educator*
Voet, Paul C. *specialty chemical company executive*
Voluse, Charles Rodger, III *education educator*
†Wachenfeld, Timothy H. *aeronautical engineering executive*
Waddell, Oliver W. *banker*
Wales, Ross Elliot *lawyer*
Walker, Michael Claude *finance educator*
Walker, Ronald F. *corporate executive*
Warden, Glenn Donald *burn surgeon*
Warnemunde, Bradley Lee *insurance company executive*
Warnken, Paula Neuman *university library director, educator*
Warrington, John Wesley *lawyer*
Watts, Barbara Gayle *law academic administrator*
Weber, Herman Jacob *federal judge*
Weed, Ithamar Dryden *life insurance company executive*
Weeks, Steven Wiley *lawyer*
Wehling, Robert Louis *household products company executive*
Weiskittel, Ralph Joseph *real estate executive*
Weisman, Joel *nuclear engineering educator, engineering consultant*
†Wellington, Jean Susorney *librarian*
Wentsler, Gertrude Josephine *secondary history educator*
Werner, Robert Joseph *college dean, music educator*
West, Clark Darwin *pediatric nephrologist, educator*
Westheimer, Ruth Welling *retired management consultant*
Whipple, Harry *newspaper publishing executive*
†White, Robert John *journalist*
White, Terry R. *hospital administrator*
Wigginton, Eugene H. *publishing executive*
†Wilburn, L. Thomas, Jr. *health facility administrator*
Williams, James Case *metallurgist*
Williams, John Pattison, Jr. *association executive*
Williams, William Joseph *insurance company executive*
Wilson, Frederic Sandford *pharmaceutical company executive*
Wilson, Lucy Jean *librarian*
Winkler, Henry Ralph *retired university president, historian*
Wiot, Jerome Francis *radiologist*
Wisler, David Charles *aerospace engineer, educator*
Witten, Louis *physics educator*
Woods, Bruce Walter *editor, poet*
Wygant, Foster Laurance *art educator*
Yocum, Ronald Harris *chemical company executive*
Yurchuck, Roger Alexander *lawyer*
Zafren, Herbert Cecil *librarian, educator*
†Zanotti, John Peter *broadcasting company executive*
Zimmerman, James M. *retail company executive*
†Zola, Gary Phillip *religious educational administrator, rabbi,*

Circleville

Norman, Jack Lee *church administrator, consultant*
Scherer, Robert Davisson *retired business and association executive*
Tipton, Daniel L. *religious organization executive*

Cleveland

Abid, Ann B. *art librarian*
Abram, Marian Christine *lawyer*
Adamo, Kenneth R. *lawyer*
Adams, Albert T. *lawyer*
Adubato, Richard Adam (Richie Adubato) *professional basketball coach*
Aikawa, Masamichi *pathologist*
Aldrich, Ann *federal judge*
Alfidi, Ralph Joseph *radiologist, educator*
Alfieri, Lisa Gwyneth *ballet dancer, teacher*
Alfred, Karl Sverre *orthopedic surgeon*
Alfred, Stephen Jay *lawyer*
Alomar, Sandy, Jr. (Santos Velazquez Alomar) *professional baseball player*
Alspaugh, Robert Odo *industrial management consultant*
Anderson, David Gaskill, Jr. *Spanish language educator*
Anderson, Harold Albert *engineering and building executive*
Anderson, James R. *engineering executive*
Andorka, Frank Henry *lawyer*
Andrews, Oakley V. *lawyer*
Andrus, Donald R. *department store company executive*
Angus, John Cotton *chemical engineering educator*
Arison, Barbara J. *lawyer*
Ashmus, Keith Allen *lawyer*
Atherton, James Dale *publishing executive*
Atkinson, William Edward *lawyer*
Ault, Charles Rollin *lawyer*
Austin, Arthur Donald, II *lawyer, educator*
Awais, George Musa *obstetrician, gynecologist*
Azoff, Elliot Stephen *lawyer*
Babin, Mara L. *lawyer*
Bacon, Brett Kermit *lawyer*
Badal, Daniel Walter *psychiatrist, educator*
Baer, Eric *engineering and science educator*
Baerga, Carlos Obed Ortiz *professional baseball player*
Bahniuk, Eugene *mechanical engineering educator*
Bailey, John Turner *public relations executive*
Baker, Saul Phillip *geriatrician, cardiologist, internist*
Ball, Robert L. *metal products company executive*
Bamberg, Barbara B. *nursing administrator*
Bamberger, David *opera company executive*
Bamberger, Richard H. *lawyer*
Banerjee, Amiya Kumar *biochemist*
Barnard, Thomas Harvie *lawyer*
Barnes, Geoffrey K. *lawyer*
Barnes de Resendiz, Susan *lawyer*
Barr, Douglas N. *lawyer*
Bartunek, Robert Richard *retired physician*
†Bassett, John E. *dean, English educator*
Bate, Brian R. *psychologist*
Bates, Walter Alan *former lawyer*
Baughman, R(obert) Patrick *lawyer*
Baumgartner, Bruce O. *lawyer*
Baxter, Howard H. *lawyer*
Baxter, Randolph *federal judge*
Beall, Cynthia *anthropologist, educator*
Beggs, Lyman M. *manufacturing executive*
Behnke, William Alfred *landscape architect, planner*
Beling, Helen *sculptor*
Bell, Edward Francis *telecommunications company executive*
Belle, Albert Jojuan *professional baseball player*
Bennett, Michael *newspaper editor*
Bennett, Paul Edward *lawyer*
Benseler, David Price *foreign language educator*
Berger, Sanford Jason *lawyer, securities dealer, real estate broker*
Bergholz, David *foundation administrator*
Bergman, Robert Paul *museum administrator, art historian, educator, lecturer*
Berick, James Herschel *lawyer*
Bernard, Lowell Francis *academic administrator, educator, consultant*
Berry, Dean Lester *lawyer*
Bersticker, Albert Charles *chemical company executive*
Besse, Ralph Moore *lawyer*
Bidelman, William Pendry *astronomer, educator*
Bilchik, Gary B. *lawyer*
Binford, Gregory Glenn *lawyer*
Bingham, Richard Donnelly *journal editor, director, educator*
Binstock, Robert Henry *public policy educator, writer, lecturer*
Bixenstine, Kim Fenton *lawyer*
Blackwell, John *polymer scientist, educator*
Blattner, Robert A. *lawyer*
Blodgett, Omer William *electric company design consultant*
Blum, Arthur *social work educator*
Bockhoff, Frank James *chemistry educator*
Bodurtha, James H. *lawyer*
Bogomolny, Richard Joseph *retail food chain executive*
Bonda, Alva Ted *electronics company executive*
Borowitz, Albert Ira *lawyer, author*
Bowen, Richard Lee *architect*
Bowerfind, Edgar Sihler, Jr. *physician, medical administrator*
†Bowman, Charles H. *petroleum company executive*
Boyd, Richard Alfred *school system administrator*
Boyle, Kammer *management psychologist*
Branagan, James Joseph *lawyer*
Brandon, Edward Bermetz *banker*
Braverman, Herbert Leslie *lawyer*
Bravo, Kenneth Allan *lawyer*
Breen, John Gerald *manufacturing company executive*
Brennan, Maureen A. *lawyer*
Brentlinger, Paul Smith *venture capital executive*
Brooks, Arthur V. N. *lawyer*
Brophy, Jere Hall *manufacturing company executive*
Brosilow, Coleman Bernard *chemical engineering educator*
Brown, Helen Bennett *biochemist*
Brown, Seymour R. *lawyer*
Brown, Troy R. *lawyer*
Brucken, Robert Matthew *lawyer*
Bryant, William H. *association executive*
Bryenton, Gary Lynn *lawyer*
Bucchieri, Stephen Joseph *architect*
Buchanan, D(aniel) Harvey *art history educator*
Buchmann, Alan Paul *lawyer*
Budd, Gene F. *finance executive*
Budd, John Henry *physician*
Buescher, Stephen L. *lawyer*
Buhrow, William Carl *religious organization administrator*
Bumpass, T. Merritt, Jr. *lawyer*
Burghart, James Henry *electrical engineer, educator*
Burke, John Francis, Jr. *economist*
Burke, Kathleen B. *lawyer*
Burke, Lillian Walker *retired judge*
Burlingame, John Hunter *lawyer*
Burns, Donald Andrew *lawyer*
Butler, William E. *manufacturing company executive*
Cairns, James Donald *lawyer*
Calfee, John Beverly *retired lawyer*
Calfee, William Lewis *lawyer*
Calkins, Hugh *foundation executive*
Campbell, Paul Barton *lawyer*
Canary, Nancy Halliday *lawyer*
Cannon, Norman Lawrence *treasurer*
†Caplan, Arnold I. *biology educator*
Cardwell, James William *business strategy consultant*
†Carestio, Ralph M., Jr. *mortgage company executive*
Carey, Paul Richard *biophysicist*
Carlson, Harry *electric company executive*
Carlson, James R. *lawyer*
Carlsson, Bo A. V. *economics educator*
Carragher, Frank Anthony *chemical company executive*
Carrick, Kathleen Michele *law librarian*
Carter, Bertha Mae *education company executive, consultant*
Carter, James Rose, Jr. *medical educator*
Carter, John Dale *organizational development executive*
Cascorbi, Helmut Freimund *anesthesiologist, educator*
Case, Betsey Brewster *lawyer*
Cassill, Herbert Carroll *artist*
Caston, J(esse) Douglas *medical educator*
†Celebrezze, Anthony *federal judge*
†Chaikin, A. Scott *public relations executive*
Chapman, Diane P. *lawyer*
Charnas, Michael (Mannie Charnas) *packaging company executive*
Chase, R. F. *oil industry executive*
Chatterjee, Pranab *social sciences educator*
Cherniack, Neil Stanley *physician, medical educator*
Clark, Gary R. *newspaper editor*
Clark, Robert Arthur *mathematician, educator*
Clarke, Charles Fenton *lawyer*
Cleary, Martin Joseph *real estate company executive*
Cligrow, Edward Thomas, Jr. *manufacturing executive*
Cline, Cathie B. *hospital administrator*
Clutter, Bertley Allen, III *management company executive*
Cochran, Earl Vernon *manufacturing executive*
Cole, Jeffrey A. *retail stores executive*
Cole, Monroe *neurologist, educator*
Collin, Robert Emanuel *electrical engineering educator*
Collin, Thomas James *lawyer*
Collinson, John Theodore *former railroad company executive*
Colombo, Louis A. *lawyer*
Conaway, Orrin Bryte *political scientist, educator*
Connelly, John James *oil company technical specialist*
Connors, Joanna *film critic*
Cooper, Hal Dean *lawyer*
Coquillette, William Hollis *lawyer*
Cornell, John Robert *lawyer*
Coughlin, Barring *lawyer*
Coulman, George Albert *chemical engineer, educator*
Courier, Jim (James Spencer Courier, Jr.) *tennis player*
Coyle, Martin Adolphus, Jr. *lawyer*
Crist, Paul Grant *lawyer*
Crosby, Fred McClellan *retail home and office furnishings executive*
Cudak, Gail Linda *lawyer*
Cullis, Christopher Ashley *dean, biology educator*
Currivan, John Daniel *lawyer*
Cutler, Alexander MacDonald *manufacturing company executive*
Daberko, David A. *banker*
Dadley, Arlene Jeanne *sleep therapist*
Dakin, Carol F. *lawyer*
Dampeer, John Lyell *lawyer*
Damsel, Richard A. *transportation company executive*
Danco, Léon Antoine *management consultant, educator*
Daniels, Anthea Rena *lawyer*
Dannemiller, John C. *transportation company executive*
Daroff, Robert Barry *neurologist*
Davis, David Aaron *journalist*
Davis, Pamela Bowes *pediatric pulmonologist*
de Acosta, Alejandro Daniel *mathematician, educator*
Deissler, Robert George *fluid dynamicist, researcher*
Dell'Osso, Louis Frank *neuroscience educator*
De Marco, Thomas Joseph *periodontist, educator*
Dempsey, James Howard, Jr. *lawyer*
Denko, Joanne D. *psychiatrist, writer*
Dewald, Ernest Leroy *landscape architect*
Diederich, Anne Marie *college president*
Dipko, Thomas E. *minister, national church executive*
Donaldson, Richard Miesse *retired oil company executive, lawyer*
Doris, Alan S(anford) *lawyer*
Dossey, Richard L. *accountant*
†Douglas, Janice Green *physician, educator*
Dowell, Michael Brendan *chemist*
Downie, John Francis *lawyer*
Downing, George *lawyer*
Drane, Walter Harding *publishing executive, business consultant*
Drinko, John Deaver *lawyer*
Drotning, John Evan *industrial relations specialist*
Duffy, John C., Jr. *lawyer*
Duncan, Ed Eugene *lawyer*
†Dunford, Edsel D. *electronics executive*
Dunn, John P. *lawyer*
Dunn, Leslie D. *lawyer*
Dupuy, William L. *public relations executive*
Durham, Mary Lynn *lawyer*
Duvin, Robert Phillip *lawyer*
Dye, Sherman *retired lawyer*
Dy Liacco, Tomas Enciso *engineering consulting executive*
Earley, Robert Wayne *labor union executive*
Easton, John Edward *accountant, financial executive*
Eastwood, Douglas William *anesthesiologist*
Eaton, Henry Felix *public relations executive*
Eberhard, William Thomas *architect*
Edelman, Murray R. *utility company executive*
Edwards, John Wesley, II *lawyer*
Eiben, Robert Michael *pediatric neurologist, educator*
Ekelman, Daniel Louis *lawyer*
Elewski, Boni Elizabeth *dermatologist, educator*
Epp, Eldon Jay *religion educator*
Epstein, Marvin Morris *retired construction executive*
Erb, Donald *composer*
Evans, Jane Keegan *opera and music theatre producer*
Every, Russel B. *business executive*
Eyre, Paul P. *lawyer*
Fabens, Andrew Lawrie, III *lawyer*
Fabris, James A. *journalist*
Fairman, Susanne Bank *hospital administrator*
Fairweather, John C. *lawyer*
†Faldo, Nick *professional golfer*
Falsgraf, William Wendell *lawyer*
Farling, Robert J. *utility company executive*
Fay, Regan Joseph *lawyer*
Fay, Robert Jesse *lawyer*
Fazio, Victor Warren *physician, colon and rectal surgeon*
Feinberg, Paul H. *lawyer*
Feliciano, José Celso *lawyer*
Fenton, Alan *artist*
Ferguson, Suzanne Carol *English educator*
Finn, Robert *writer, lecturer, broadcaster*
Fletcher, Robert *lawyer, horologist*
Foltz, Clinton Henry *advertising executive*
Fordyce, James Stuart *federal agency administrator*
†Forsythe, Frank S. *iron ore company executive*
Fountain, Ronald Glenn *bank executive*
Fratello, Michael Robert *professional basketball coach*
Friedman, Barton Robert *English educator*
Friedman, Harold Edward *lawyer*
Friedman, Hyman *lawyer*
Friedman, James Moss *lawyer*
Fruchtenbaum, Edward *greeting card company executive*
Fufuka, Natika Njeri Yaa *retail executive*
Fullmer, David R. *lawyer*
Gapen, Delores Kaye *librarian, educator*
Garner, James Parent *lawyer*
Garver, Theodore Meyer *lawyer*
Geha, Alexander Salim *cardiothoracic surgeon, educator*
Gelfand, Ivan *investment advisor*
Gerber, Carl Joseph *hospital administrator, psychiatrist*
Gerhart, Peter Milton *law educator*
Giannetti, Louis Daniel *film educator, film critic*
Gibans, James David *architect*
Gibson, Walter Samuel *humanities educator*
Gibson, Wendy Joan *lawyer*
Giesser, Nancy Lynne *nurse, academic administrator*
Gifford, Ray Wallace, Jr. *physician, educator*
Giles, Homer Wayne *lawyer*
Gillespie, Robert Wayne *banker*
Ginn, Robert Martin *retired utility company executive*
Ginsberg, Edward *lawyer*
Ginsburg, Edward S. *lawyer*
Glaser, Robert Edward *lawyer*
Gleisser, Marcus David *author, lawyer, journalist*
Glickman, Carl David *banker*
Goffman, William *mathematician, educator*
Goins, Frances Floriano *lawyer*
Gold, Gerald Seymour *lawyer*
Goldfarb, Bernard Sanford *lawyer*
Goldstein, Marvin Emanuel *aerospace scientist, research center administrator*
Goldstein, Melvyn C. *anthropologist, educator*
Goler, Michael David *lawyer*
Goodger, John Verne *electronics and computer systems executive*
Gordon, Anne Kathleen *editor*
Gorman, Joseph Tolle *corporate executive*
Grabner, George John *manufacturing executive*
Graham, Robert William *areospace research engineer*
Greer, Thomas H. *newspaper executive*
Greppin, John Aird Coutts *philologist, editor, educator*
Griswold, James B. *lawyer*
Groetzinger, Jon, Jr. *lawyer, consumer products executive*
Gronick, Patricia Ann Jacobsen *school system administrator*
Grossman, Theodore Martin *lawyer*
Gruber, Sheldon *electrical engineering educator*
Gruettner, Donald W. *lawyer*
Grundstein, Nathan David *lawyer, management science educator, management consultant*
Grundy, Kenneth William *political science educator*
Gutfeld, Norman E. *lawyer*
Haiman, Irwin Sanford *lawyer*
Hajek, Otomar *mathematics educator*
Hall, David *newspaper editor*
Hamilton, J. Richard *lawyer*

Hamilton, William Milton *retired industrial company executive*
Hammer, Daniel William *lawyer*
Hanna, Harry Adolphus *lawyer*
Hanson, Richard Winfield *biochemist, educator*
Harayda, Janice *newspaper book editor, author*
Hardesty, Hiram Haines *ophthalmologist, educator*
Harding, Frank I., III *trust banker*
Hardis, Stephen Roger *manufacturing company executive*
Hardy, Michael Lynn *lawyer*
Hardy, Richard Allen *mechanical engineer, diesel fuel engine specialist*
Hargrove, Mike (Dudley Michael Hargrove) *professional baseball team manager*
Harper, Williard Flemmett *language educator*
Harris, John William *physician, educator*
Hart, Alvin Leroy *electric manufacturing company executive*
Hartley, Robert Frank *business educator, author*
Hastings, Donald F. *electric company executive*
Hauserman, William Foley *manufacturing company executive*
Hayes, Scott Birchard *raw materials company executive*
Heald, Morrell *humanities educator*
Healy, Bernadine P. *physician, educator, federal agency administrator*
Heddesheimer, Walter Jacob *lawyer*
Heffern, Gordon Emory *banker*
Henry, Edward Frank *computer accounting service executive*
Hermann, Philip J. *lawyer*
Herndon, Charles Harbison *retired orthopaedic surgeon*
Hershiser, Orel Leonard, IV *professional baseball player*
Heuer, Arthur Harold *material science and engineering educator*
Hoag, David H. *steel company executive*
Hochman, Kenneth George *lawyer*
Hoerner, Robert Jack *lawyer*
Hokenstad, Merl Clifford, Jr. *social work educator*
Holck, Frederick H. George *priest, educator*
Holderfield, Marilyn Ida *jazz vocalist*
Holland, Darrell Wendell *newspaper religion editor*
†Holley, Brian E. *botanical garden director*
Hollington, Richard Rings, Jr. *lawyer*
Holsworth, William C. *food company executive*
Holzbach, Raymond Thomas *gastroenterologist, author, educator*
Hook, John Burney *investment company executive*
Hopkins, John S., III *lawyer*
Hopps, Sidney Bryce *lawyer*
Horvitz, Michael John *lawyer*
Hruby, Frank M. *musician, critic, educator*
†Huge, Arthur William *steel company financial executive, civil engineer*
Hushen, John W. *manufacturing company executive*
†Huston, Samuel Richard *health facility executive*
Inglis, Patricia Marcus *lawyer*
Ivy, Conway Gayle *paint company executive*
Izant, Robert James, Jr. *pediatric surgeon*
Jacobs, Leslie William *lawyer*
Jacobs, Richard E. *real estate executive, sports team owner*
Janke, Ronald Robert *lawyer*
Jeavons, Norman Stone *lawyer*
Jenkins, Thomas Llewellyn *physics educator*
Jensen, Kathryn Patricia *public broadcaster*
Jenson, Jon Eberdt *association executive*
†Jindra, Christine *editor*
Johnson, Candice Elaine Brown *pediatrics educator*
Johnson, John Frank *professional recruitment executive*
Jones, Theodore William *banker, lawyer*
Jordan, Jerry Lee *economist, banker*
Jorgenson, Mary Ann *lawyer*
Kacir, Barbara Brattin *lawyer*
Kahana, Eva Frost *sociology educator*
Kahrl, Robert Conley *lawyer*
Kaiser, Gordon S., Jr. *lawyer*
Kamm, Jacob Oswald *manufacturing executive, economist*
Kapp, C. Terrence *lawyer*
Karch, George Frederick, Jr. *lawyer*
Karch, Sargent *lawyer*
†Kass, Lawrence *hematologist*
Katcher, Richard *lawyer*
Katz, Lewis Robert *legal educator*
†Katzman, Richard A. *cardiologist, consultant*
Kellermeyer, Robert William *physician, educator*
Kelly, Dennis Michael *lawyer*
Kelly, J. Peter *steel company executive*
Kelly, John Terence *architect*
Kerr, Thomas Adolphus *retired construction company executive*
Kilbane, Thomas Stanton *lawyer*
Kirchick, Calvin B. *lawyer*
Kiser, William Sites *physician executive, urologic surgeon*
Klineberg, John Michael *federal agency administrator, aerospace researcher*
Klipfell, John Martin, III *greeting card company executive*
Klopman, Gilles *chemistry educator*
Knopp, Albert J. *lawyer*
Ko, Wen-Hsiung *electrical engineering educator*
Koch, Charles John *credit agency executive*
Koch, Charles Joseph *banker*
Koenig, Jack L. *chemist, educator*
Kola, Arthur Anthony *lawyer*
Kolb, David Allen *psychology educator*
Kordalski, Anthony Tadausz *retail department store executive*
Kosmahl, Henry G. *electron physicist*
Kovacic, Edward P. *protective services official*
Kovacs, Rosemary *newspaper editor*
Kovel, Ralph M. *author, authority on antiques*
Kovel, Terry Horvitz (Mrs. Ralph Kovel) *author, antiques authority*
Kowalski, Kenneth Lawrence *physicist, educator*
Kramer, Andrew Michael *lawyer*
Kramer, Eugene Leo *lawyer*
Krasney, Samuel Joseph *multi-industry company executive*
Krenzler, Alvin Irving *federal judge*
Krieger, Irvin Mitchell *chemistry educator, consultant*
Krulitz, Leo Morrion *financial executive*
Krupansky, Robert Bazil *federal judge*
Kuendig, William Norman, II *management consultant, actuarial consultant*
Kuhn, David Alan *lawyer*
Kundtz, John Andrew *lawyer*
Kurit, Neil *lawyer*
Lafave, Arthur J., Jr. *financial executive, lawyer*
Lambros, Thomas Demetrios *federal judge*
Lamm, Michael Emanuel *pathologist, immunologist, educator*
Lamore, George L. *manufacturing company executive*
Landau, Bernard Robert *biochemistry educator, physician*
Landis, Geoffrey Alan *physicist, writer*
Lando, Jerome Burton *macromolecular science educator*
Lang, H. Jack *advertising executive, author*
Lavelle, Michael Joseph *economist, academic administrator*
Lawniczak, James Michael *lawyer*
Lease, Robert K. *lawyer*
Leavitt, Jeffrey Stuart *lawyer*
Lebovitz, Harold Paul (Hal Lebovitz) *journalist*
Leech, John Dale *lawyer*
Lefebvre, Gabriel Felicien *retired chemical company executive*
Lefferts, William Geoffrey *physician, educator*
Leidner, Harold Edward *lawyer*
Leiken, Earl Murray *lawyer*
Lelyveld, Arthur Joseph *rabbi*
Lemke, Judith A. *lawyer*
Lenkoski, Leo Douglas *psychiatrist, educator*
Lenn, Stephen Andrew *lawyer*
Leonard, Irvin Alan *lawyer*
Leukart, Richard Henry, II *lawyer*
Lewis, John Bruce *lawyer*
Lewis, John Francis *lawyer*
Lewis, Robert Lawrence *lawyer, educator*
Liegl, Joseph Leslie *lawyer*
Lindberg, Lawrence V. *lawyer*
Litt, Morton Herbert *macromolecular science educator, researcher*
Little, Robert Andrews *architect, designer, painter*
Liu, Chung-Chiun *chemical engineering educator*
Lofton, Kenneth *professional baseball player*
Long, Kenneth Robert *natural gas company executive, lawyer*
Long, Robert M. *newspaper publishing executive*
Lopez, Nancy *professional golfer*
Lowenthal, Henry *greeting card company executive*
Lucier, P. Jeffrey *publishing executive*
Luke, Randall Dan *retired tire and rubber company executive, lawyer*
Luntz, Theodore Michael *recycling company executive*
Lynch, John Edward, Jr. *lawyer*
Lynch, Maxine *newspaper publishing executive*
Machaskee, Alex *newspaper publishing company executive*
Mac Laren, David Sergeant *manufacturing corporation executive, inventor*
Madden, James Desmond *forensic engineer*
Madison, Robert Prince *architect*
Madsen, H(enry) Stephen *retired lawyer*
Mahmoud, Adel A. F. *physician, educator, investigator*
Mandel, Jack N. *manufacturing company executive*
Mandel, Morton Leon *industrial corporation executive*
Manning, Henry Eugene *hospital administrator*
Manos, John M. *federal judge*
Marcus, Donald Howard *advertising agency executive*
Margulies, Jeffrey J. *lawyer*
Markey, Robert Guy *lawyer*
Markos, Chris *real estate company executive*
Markus, Richard M. *lawyer*
Martin, Paul Joseph *biomedical engineer, cardiology researcher, educator, consultant*
Marting, Michael G. *lawyer*
Mason, Marilyn Gell *library administrator, writer, consultant*
Mason, Robert McSpadden *technology management educator, consultant*
Mason, Thomas Albert *lawyer*
Matia, Paul Ramon *federal judge*
†Matthews, Julie *performing arts company director*
Maugans, Edgar Hurley *utility company executive*
Mawardi, Osman Kamel *plasma physicist*
Maximovich, Michael Joseph *chemist, consultant*
Mayer, Robert Anthony *college president*
Mayland, Kenneth Theodore *economist*
Mayne, Lucille Stringer *finance educator*
McAndrews, James Patrick *retired lawyer*
McArdle, Richard Joseph *academic administrator*
Mc Cartan, Patrick Francis *lawyer*
McCarthy, Mark Francis *lawyer*
Mc Clelland, James Craig *lawyer*
McConnell, Michael *opera company director*
McCullough, Joseph *college president emeritus*
Mc Elhaney, James Wilson *lawyer, educator*
McFadden, Edward Regis, Jr. *pulmonary educator*
Mc Fadden, John Volney *retired manufacturing company executive*
Mc Farlane, Karen Elizabeth *concert artists manager*
McGervey, John Donald *physics educator, researcher*
McGinty, Thomas Edward *management consultant*
McHale, Vincent Edward *political science educator*
Mc Henry, Martin Christopher *physician, educator*
McKee, Thomas Frederick *lawyer*
McLaughlin, Patrick Michael *lawyer*
Mc Murrin, Lee Ray *educational administrator*
McNamee, Bernard Joseph *lawyer*
Meaney, Michael Joseph *lawyer*
Mecredy, James R. *management consultant*
Mehlman, Maxwell Jonathan *law educator*
Meisel, George Ira *lawyer*
Melsher, Gary W. *lawyer*
Melsop, James William *architect*
Meltzer, Herbert Yale *psychiatry educator*
Mendelson, Ralph Richard *water heater manufacturing executive*
Meyer, G. Christopher *lawyer*
Milgrim, Franklin Marshall *merchant*
Milic, Louis Tonko *English educator*
Miller, Carl George *manufacturing executive*
Miller, Genevieve *retired medical historian*
Miller, Ivan Lawrence *lawyer*
Miller, John Robert *environmental recycling company executive*
Miller, Richard Hamilton *lawyer, broadcasting company executive*
†Miller, Sydell Lois *cosmetics executive, marketing professional*
Miller, Warren *bishop*
Millstone, David J. *lawyer*
Milner, Irvin Myron *lawyer*
†Minter, Steven Alan *foundation executive, social worker*
Miyares, Benjamin David *editor, publisher, consultant*
Modic, Stanley John *business editor, publisher*
Molyneaux, David Glenn *newspaper travel editor*
†Montague, Drogo K. *urologist*
Montana, Joseph C., Jr. *former professional football player*
Moody, Lizabeth Ann *law educator*
Moore, Anthony R. *lawyer*
Moore, Dan Tyler *writer*
Moore, Kenneth Cameron *lawyer*
Moore, Louis Lee *medical instrumentation company executive*
†Moore, Michael Thomas *mining executive*
Morin, Patrick Joyce *advertising executive*
Morris, Thomas William *symphony orchestra administrator*
Morrison, Donald William *lawyer*
Mortimer, J. Thomas *biomedical engineering educator*
Morway, Richard A. *newspaper publishing executive*
Moscarino, George J. *lawyer*
Moss, Thomas Henry *university dean, physicist*
Mottl, Ronald M. *state legislator, lawyer*
Murfin, Donald Leon *investment company executive*
Murray, Eddie Clarence *professional baseball player*
Murray, Thomas Henry *bioethics educator, writer*
Myers, David N. *construction executive*
Nahat, Dennis F. *artistic director, choreographer*
Naparstek, Arthur J. *social work educator*
Navratilova, Martina *former professional tennis player*
Nelson, Raymond John *mathematics and philosophy educator*
Neuhauser, Duncan von Briesen *health services educator*
Newborn, Karen B. *lawyer*
Newman, John M., Jr. *lawyer*
Newman, Joseph Herzl *advertising executive*
Nickerson, Gary Lee *secondary education educator*
Nims, Michael A. *lawyer*
Noall, Roger *bank executive*
Nolan, Cary J. *medical products manufacturer*
Norris, Dennis E. *religious organization executive*
Novatney, John F., Jr. *lawyer*
Novick, Andrew Carl *urologist*
Oakar, Mary Rose *former congresswoman*
Oberdank, Lawrence Mark *lawyer, arbitrator*
O'Brien, John Feighan *investment banker*
O'Donnell, F. Scott *banker*
O'Donnell, Thomas Michael *brokerage firm executive*
Ollinger, W. James *lawyer*
Olson, Walter Theodore *research scientist, consultant*
Olszewski, Edward John *art history educator*
Orr, Parker Murray *former lawyer*
†Ortino, Hector Ruben *chemical company executive*
Ostrach, Simon *engineering educator*
Pao, Yoh-Han *engineering educator*
Paris, Zachary T. *lawyer*
Parker, Patrick Streeter *manufacturing executive*
Parker, Robert Frederic *university dean emeritus*
Pascarella, Perry James *magazine editor*
Pataki, Andrew *bishop*
†Paul, Robert Gregory *electronic company executive*
Peckham, P. Hunter *biomedical engineer, educator*
Percy, S. W. *oil industry executive*
Perkovic, Robert Branko *international management consultant*
Perris, Terrence George *lawyer*
Perry, Chris Nicholas *advertising executive*
†Perry, George *neuroscience researcher*
Perry, George Williamson *lawyer*
Peters, James Ray *accountant*
Phillips, Lyman C. *utility company executive*
Phipps, Wilma J. *nursing educator, author*
Pianalto, Sandra *bank executive*
Pike, Kermit Jerome *library director*
Pilla, Anthony Michael *bishop*
Pilous, Betty Scheibel *medical/surgical nurse*
Pinkney, Betty Kathryn *lawyer*
Plesec, William Thomas *lawyer*
Podboy, Alvin Michael, Jr. *lawyer, law library director*
Pogue, Richard Welch *lawyer*
†Pollack, Florence Zaks *management consultant*
Porter, James Morris *state judge*
Portwood, John Harding *lawyer, electric products manufacturing executive*
Preston, Robert Bruce *retired lawyer*
Price, Charles T. *lawyer*
Price, Gordon A. *brokerage house executive*
Pringle, Barbara Carroll *state legislator*
Ptaszek, Edward Gerald, Jr. *lawyer*
Pucko, Diane Bowles *public relations executive*
Pursell, Carroll Wirth *history educator*
Putka, Andrew Charles *lawyer*
Pyke, John Secrest, Jr. *lawyer, polymers company executive*
Pytte, Agnar *university president*
Rader, Hannelore *library director, consultant*
Rains, Merritt Neal *lawyer*
Rakita, Louis *cardiologist, educator*
Ramicone, John R. *school system administrator*
Ramig, Alexander, Jr. *paint company executive, chemist*
Ransom, William Harrison *lawyer*
Rapp, Robert Neil *lawyer*
Rasmussen, Frank Morris *lawyer*
Ratner, Albert B. *building products company executive, land developer*
Ratner, Max *building products company executive, land developer*
Ratnoff, Oscar Davis *physician, educator*
Rawson, Robert H., Jr. *lawyer*
Reale, William A. *lawyer*
Redinger, James Collins *investment banker, financial consultant*
Reeves, Charles Howell *classics educator*
†Rego, Anthony C. *food products executive*
Reid, James Sims, Jr. *automobile parts manufacturer*
Reisman, Arnold *retired management science educator*
Reitman, Robert Stanley *manufacturing and marketing executive*
Rekstis, Walter J., III *lawyer*
Remington, Charles Bradford *professional services firm executive*
Renner, Simon Edward *steel company executive*
Reppert, Richard Levi *lawyer*
Reshotko, Eli *aerospace engineer, educator*
Ritchey, William Michael *chemistry educator*
Robbins, Frederick Chapman *physician, medical school dean emeritus*
Roberts, Clyde Francis *business executive*
Roberts, James Owen *financial planning executive*
Robertson, William Richard *banker, holding company executive*
Robiner, Donald Maxwell *lawyer*
Robinson, Donald Keith *physicist, educator*
†Robinson, John C. *manufacturing executive, light*
Rodewig, John Stuart *manufacturing company executive*
Rogers, Charles Edwin *physical chemistry educator*
Roj, William Henry *lawyer*
Romano, Louis, Jr. *industrial gas company executive*
Romei, Lura Knachel *magazine editor*
Roop, James John *public relations executive*
Rorimer, Louis *lawyer*
Rosegger, Gerhard *economist, educator*
Rosenbaum, Jacob I. *lawyer*
Rosenthal, Leighton A. *aviation company executive*
Ross, Ronald Jay *radiologist*
Roth, Jack Joseph *historian, educator*
Rothstein, Ronald *professional basketball coach*
Roulston, Thomas Henry *investment adviser*
Ruben, Alan Miles *lawyer, educator*
Ruflin, Paul Leroy *accountant, consultant*
Runyan, Timothy Jack *historian, educator*
Rupert, John Edward *retired savings and loan executive, business and civic affairs consultant*
Russell, Valerie Eileen *social service executive*
Ruxin, Paul Theodore *lawyer*
Rydzel, James A. *lawyer*
Saada, Adel Selim *civil engineer, educator*
Sabo, Richard Steven *electrical company executive*
Sager, John William *lawyer*
Salazar, Alberto *Olympic professional runner*
Salkind, Michael Jay *metallurgical engineer, academic administrator*
Salomon, Roger Blaine *English language educator*
Sandburg, Helga *author*
Sande, Theodore Anton *architect, educator, foundation executive*
Sargent, Noel Boyd *electrical engineer*
Savin, Samuel Marvin *geologist*
Savinell, Robert Francis *engineering educator*
Sawyer, Raymond Terry *lawyer*
Sayler, Richard H. *lawyer*
Scarpa, Antonio *medicine educator, biomedical scientist*
Schaefer, David Arnold *lawyer*
Schaut, Joseph William *banker*
Schey, Ralph Edward *manufacturing executive*
Schiller, James Joseph *lawyer*
Schloemer, Paul George *diversified manufacturing company executive*
Schlotfeldt, Rozella May *nursing educator*
Schneider, David Miller *lawyer*
Schnell, Carlton Bryce *lawyer*
Schofield, Donald Stewart *real estate investment trust executive*
†Schonberg, Alan Robert *management recruiting executive*
Schorr, Alvin Louis *social worker, educator*
Schuele, Donald Edward *physics educator*
Schurmeier, L. Jon *health care executive*
Schutter, David John *banker*
Scovil, Samuel Kingston *mining company executive*
Seaton, Robert Finlayson *retired planned giving consultant*
Seger, Thomas M. *lawyer*
Seikel, Oliver Edward *lawyer*
Seles, Monica *tennis player*
Seltzer, Phyllis Estelle *painter, printmaker*
Semelsberger, Kenneth J. *household products company executive*
Shakno, Robert Julian *hospital administrator*
Shanker, Morris Gerald *lawyer, educator*
Shapiro, Fred David *lawyer*
Sharp, Robert Weimer *lawyer*
Shaw, Russell Clyde *lawyer*
Shaw, Scott Alan *photojournalist*
Shelley, John Fletcher *lawyer*
Sherrill, Gladys Marie *elementary education educator*
Sherry, Paul Henry *minister, religious organization administrator*
Shuck, Jerry Mark *surgeon, educator*
Sibley, Willis Elbridge *anthropology educator, consultant*
Sicherman, Marvin Allen *lawyer*
Siefers, Robert George *banker*
Siegel, Robert *heat transfer engineer*
Sigalow, Steven E. *lawyer*
Simonson, John Alexander *banking executive*
Sims, J. Taylor *academic administrator*
Singer, Marcus Joseph *biologist, educator*
Skinner, Charles Scofield *technology management service executive, consultant, mechanical engineer*
Skulina, Thomas Raymond *lawyer*
Sloan, David W. *lawyer*
Smercina, Charles Joseph *mayor, accountant*
Smith, Barbara Jean *lawyer*
Smith, Charles Kent *family medicine physician*
Smith, James A. *lawyer*
†Smith, James C. *telecommunications industry executive*
Smith, Steven Ray *law educator*
Snow, David Forrest *judge*
Snyder, Kenneth F. *lawyer*
Sogg, Wilton Sherman *lawyer*
Solomon, Randall L. *lawyer*
Springel, Barry L. *lawyer*
Stadtler, Beatrice Horwitz *author*
Stanley, Hugh Monroe, Jr. *lawyer*
Stanton-Hicks, Michael D'Arcy *anesthesiologist, educator*
Stavitsky, Abram Benjamin *immunologist, educator*
Stein, Herman David *social sciences educator, past university provost*
Steinberg, Arthur G(erald) *geneticist*
Steinbrink, William H. *lawyer*
Steindler, Howard Allen *lawyer*
Sterling, Leon Samuel *computer scientist, researcher, educator*
Stevens, Edward *public relations executive*
Stevens, Thomas Charles *lawyer*
Stinchcomb, Robert G. *lawyer*
Stinson, Robert Charles *lawyer*
Stone, Harry H. *business executive*
Stone, Irving I. *greeting card company executive*
†Storey, Robert Davis *lawyer*
Straffon, Ralph Atwood *urologist*
Strang, James Dennis *editor*
Strange, Curtis Northrop *professional golfer*
Strassmeyer, Mary *newspaper columnist*
Stratton-Crooke, Thomas Edward *financial consultant*
Strauch, John L. *lawyer*
Strauss, David J. *lawyer*
Strauss, Walter Adolf *foreign languages educator*
Streeter, Richard Edward *lawyer*
Striefsky, Linda A(nn) *lawyer*
Strimbu, Victor, Jr. *lawyer*
Stuhan, Richard George *lawyer*
Sullivan, Dennis W. *power systems company executive*
Swartzbaugh, Marc L. *lawyer*
Swift, David L. *manufacturing company executive*
Szaller, James Francis *lawyer*

Szarek, Stanislaw Jerzy mathematics educator
Taft, Seth Chase retired lawyer
Taw, Dudley Joseph sales executive
Taylor, J(ocelyn) Mary museum administrator, zoologist, educator
Taylor, Philip Liddon physics educator
Taylor, Steve Henry zoologist
Thompson, Renold Durant mining and shipping executive
Thomson, Maynard F. lawyer
Tinker, H(arold) Burnham chemical company executive
Tipton-Martin, Toni newspaper editor
Toohey, Brian Frederick lawyer
Toomajian, William Martin lawyer
Traci, Donald Philip retired lawyer
Trawick, Leonard Moses English educator
Trevor, Leigh Barry lawyer
Trzcinski, Ronald E. mattress and bedding company executive
Tung, Theodore Hschum banker, economist
Turner, Evan Hopkins retired art museum director
Tuttle, Frank James bank executive
Ulchaker, Stanley Louis public relations consultant
Unger, Paul A. packaging executive
Updegraft, Kenneth E., Jr. lawyer
Urbach, Frederick Lewis chemistry educator
Urban, Richard newspaper editor
Van Ummersen, Claire A(nn) university president, biologist, educator
Vargo, Ronald Paul oil company executive
von Dohnányi, Christoph musician, conductor
von Mehren, George M. lawyer
Waldeck, John Walter, Jr. lawyer
Walker, Martin Dean specialty chemical company executive
Wallace, R. Byron lawyer
Wallach, Mark Irwin lawyer
Walters, Farah M. hospital administrator
Wamsley, James Lawrence, III lawyer
†Washington, John Augustine physician, pathologist
Watson, Richard Thomas lawyer
Watt, Ronald William public relations executive
Weaver, Robin Geoffrey lawyer, educator
Weber, Robert Carl lawyer
Webster, James Colin Eden oil company executive
Webster, Leslie Tillotson, Jr. pharmacologist, educator
Weible, Robert A. lawyer
Weidenthal, Maurice David (Bud Weidenthal) educational administrator, journalist
Weiler, Jeffry Louis lawyer
Weinberg, Helen Arnstein American art and literature educator
Weiss, Morry greeting card company executive
Wert, James William banker
Wertheim, Sally Harris academic administrator, dean, education educator
†West, Burton Carey physician
White, Fred Rollin, Jr. mining and shipping company executive
White, George W. federal judge
White, Michael Reed mayor
White, Paul Dunbar lawyer
White, Robert J. neurosurgeon, neuroscientist, educator
Whiteman, Joseph David lawyer, manufacturing company executive
Whiting, Hugh Richard lawyer
Whitney, Richard Buckner lawyer
Whittington-Gold, Iris community college educator
Wilharm, John H., Jr. lawyer
Williams, Arthur Benjamin, Jr. bishop
Williams, Clyde E., Jr. lawyer
Williams, Gordon Bretnell construction company executive
Willis, George Edmund chemical processing and electrical manufacturing executive
Winfield, David Mark professional baseball player
Wolff, Gunther Arthur physical chemist
Wolinsky, Emanuel physician, educator
Woodring, James H. lawyer
Wotman, Stephen dentistry educator
Woyczynski, Wojbor Andrzej mathematician, educator
Wright, Marshall retired manufacturing executive, former diplomat
Yeager, Ernest Bill physical chemist, electrochemist, educator
Yosowitz, Sanford lawyer, metal sales and fabricating executive
Young, Davis public relations executive
Young, James Edward lawyer
Young, Jess R. physician
Zambie, Allan John lawyer
Zangerle, John A. lawyer
Zdanis, Richard Albert academic administrator
†Zimmerman, Michael Glenn marketing/communications executive
†Zubal, John T. book exchange executive, publisher, bibliographer
Zung, Thomas Tse-Kwai architect

Columbus

Abel, Mary state legislator
Ackerman, John Henry health services consultant, physician
Ackerman, Kenneth Benjamin management consultant, writer
Adams, John Marshall lawyer
Alger, Chadwick Fairfax political scientist, educator
Alutto, Joseph Anthony university dean, management educator
†Amato, Paul H. insurance executive
Anderson, Carole Ann nursing educator
Anderson, Jon Mac lawyer
Anderson, Sandra Jo lawyer
Antler, Morton consulting engineering executive, author, educator
Armes, Walter Scott vocational school administrator
Arthur, William Edgar lawyer
†Axsmith, Brain J. botany educator
Ayers, James Cordon lawyer
Ayers, Randy university athletic coach
Baas, James William real estate developer
Babcock, Charles Luther classics educator
†Bachman, Sister Janice health care executive, vicaress
Bagby, Frederick Lair, Jr. retired research institute executive
Bahls, Steven Carl lawyer, legal educator
Bailey, Cecil Dewitt aerospace engineer, educator
Bailey, Daniel Allen lawyer
Balcerzak, Stanley Paul physician, educator
Ballou, Charles Herbert financial executive
Banasik, Robert Casmer nursing home administrator, educator
Banwart, George Junior food microbiology educator
Barker, Llyle James, Jr. journalism educator, public relations executive, former military officer
Barner, Bruce Monroe state agency administrator
Barnes, Wallace Ray lawyer
Barry, James P(otvin) writer, editor
Barth, Rolf Frederick pathologist, educator
Barthelmas, Ned Kelton investment and commercial real estate banker
Battersby, James Lyons, Jr. English language educator
Baughman, George Washington, III retired university official, financial consultant
Becher, Paul Ronald health benefits executive
Bechtel, Stephen E. mechanical engineer, educator
Beck, Paul Allen political science educator
Beckwith, Sandra Shank federal judge
Bedford, Keith Wilson civil engineering and atmospheric science educator
Behrman, Edward Joseph biochemistry educator
Beja, Morris English literature educator
Bell, George Edwin retired physician, insurance company executive
Belville, Barbara Ann lawyer
Bergansky, Suzanne Marie state legislator
Berggren, Ronald Bernard surgeon, emeritus educator
Bergstrom, Stig Magnus geology educator
Berry, Brewton writer, editor
Berry, William Lee business administration educator
Beverley, Jane Taylor artist
Beytagh, Francis Xavier, Jr. college dean, lawyer
Bhushan, Bharat mechanical engineer
Bianchine, Joseph Raymond pharmacologist
Bibart, Richard L. lawyer
Billings, Charles Edgar physician
Black, Larry David library director
Blackmore, Josiah H. university president, lawyer, educator
Blair, William Travis (Bud Blair) retired organization executive
Boardman, William Penniman lawyer, banker
†Boerner, Ralph E. J. forest soil ecologist, plant biology educator
Boh, Ivan philosophy educator
Böhm, Friedrich (Friedl) K.M. architectural firm executive
Bondurant, Byron Lee agricultural engineering educator
Bope, Edward Tharp family practitioner
Boudoulas, Harisios physician
Boulger, Francis William metallurgical engineer
Bourguignon, Erika Eichhorn anthropologist, educator
Boyd, Barbara H. state legislator
Branscomb, Lewis Capers, Jr. librarian, educator
Bridgman, G(eorge) Ross lawyer
Briggs, Marjorie Crowder lawyer
Brinkman, Dale Thomas lawyer
Brodkey, Robert Stanley chemical engineering educator
Brooks, Keith retired speech communication educator
Brooks, Richard Dickinson lawyer
Brown, Firman Hewitt, Jr. drama educator, theatrical director
Brown, Herbert Russell lawyer, writer
Brown, Philip Albert lawyer
Brown, Rowland Chauncey Widrig information systems, strategic planning and ethics consultant
†Browning, Richard Arlen air force officer
Brubaker, Robert Loring lawyer
Buchenroth, Stephen Richard lawyer
Buchsieb, Walter Charles orthodontist
Burke, Kenneth Andrew advertising executive
Burnham, John Chynoweth historian, educator
Burtch, John Hamrick lawyer
Butler, Martha L. state official, accountant
Cacioppo, John Terrance psychology educator
Cain, Madeline Ann state representative
Calhoun, Donald Eugene, Jr. federal judge
Callander, Kay Eileen Paisley business owner, retired gifted talented education educator, writer
Campbell, Richard Rice retired newspaper editor
Canzani, Joseph V. academic administrator
Capen, Charles Chabert veterinary pathology educator, researcher
Carlson, Larry Vernon insurance company executive
Carnahan, John Anderson lawyer
Carpenter, Jot David landscape architect, educator
Carpenter, Michael H. lawyer
Case, William R. lawyer
Casey, Raymond Richard agricultural business executive
Cearlock, Dennis Bill research executive
Celebrezze, Anthony J., Jr. lawyer
Chandrasekaran, Balakrishnan computer and information science educator
Chapman, Erie, III hospital administrator
Charles, Bertram radio broadcasting executive
Chester, John Jonas lawyer
Christensen, John William lawyer
Christoforidis, A. John radiologist, educator
Clovis, Albert Lee lawyer, educator
Cogan, J. Kevin lawyer
Cole, Charles Chester, Jr. educational administrator
Cole, Clarence Russell college dean
Cole, Ransey Guy, Jr. lawyer
Collier, David Alan management educator
Cook, Samuel Ronald, Jr. lawyer
Copeland, William Edgar, Sr. physician
Corbato, Charles Edward geology educator
Cornwell, David George biochemist, educator
Cottrell, David Alton school system administrator
Covault, Lloyd R., Jr. hospital administrator, psychiatrist
Cox, Mitchel Neal editor
Craig, Judith bishop
Cramblett, Henry Gaylord pediatrician, virologist, educator
Crane, Jameson plastics manufacturing company executive
Crowell, Ohmer Oreal insurance company executive
Cruz, Jose Bejar, Jr. engineering educator
Cuddihy, June Tuck pediatric nurse
Cunnyngham, Jon economist, information systems educator
Cushman, James Butler lawyer
Cvetanovich, Danny L. lawyer
Daehn, Glenn Steven materials scientist
Dawson, Virginia Sue newspaper editor
Day, Roger F. lawyer
Deep, Ira Washington plant pathology educator
De Lucia, Frank Charles physicist, educator
DeMaria, Peter James utility company executive
Dennis, Richard Irwin company executive
DeRousie, Charles Stuart lawyer
Dervin, Brenda Louise communications educator
Dillon, Merton Lynn historian, educator
Di Lorenzo, John Florio, Jr. lawyer
Disbrow, Richard Edwin retired utility executive
Disinger, John Franklin natural resources educator
Douglas, Andrew state supreme court justice
Dowling, Thomas Allan mathematics educator
Drake, Grace L. state senator
Draper, E(rnest) Linn, Jr. electric utility executive
Dreher, Darrell L. lawyer
Druen, William Sidney lawyer
Drvota, Mojmir cinema educator, author
Duckworth, Winston Howard ceramic engineer
Dugan, Charles Francis, II lawyer
Duryee, Harold Taylor insurance executive
Dwon, Larry retired electrical engineer, educator, consultant
Edwards, John White lawyer
Eggenschwiler, James E. lawyer
Eickelberg, John Edwin process control company executive
Elam, John Carlton lawyer
Elliot, David Hawksley geologist
Emanuelson, James Robert retired insurance company executive
Engdahl, Richard Bott mechanical engineer
Ensminger, Dale mechanical engineer, electrical engineer
Epstein, Arthur Joseph physics and chemistry educator
Epstein, Erwin Howard sociology educator, editor
Evans, Daniel E. sausage manufacturing and restaurant chain company executive
†Eyerly, Gloria A. lawyer
Fahey, Richard Paul lawyer
†Fan, Liang-Shih chemical engineering educator
Faure, Gunter geology educator
Fawcett, Sherwood Luther research laboratory executive
Feck, Luke Matthew utility executive
Fenton, Robert Earl electrical engineering educator
Fields, Henry William college dean
Firestone, Richard Francis chemistry educator
Fisher, John Edwin insurance company executive
Fisher, Lee I. state attorney general
Fisher, Lloyd Edison, Jr. lawyer
†Floyd, Gary Leon cell biologist, educator
Flyg, William Theodore retail executive
Foland, Kenneth A. geological sciences educator
Fornshell, Dave Lee educational broadcasting executive
Fraley, Ralph Reed hospital administrator
Franks, Richard Matthew newspaper executive
Frenzer, Peter Frederick insurance company executive
Fried, Samuel lawyer
Fry, Donald Lewis physiologist, educator
†Fu, Paul Shan law librarian, consultant
Fullerton, Charles William retired insurance company executive
Gaeth, Matthew Ben state senator
Gall, Maryann Baker lawyer
Galloway, Harvey Scott, Jr. insurance company executive
†Garrison, Lawrence Duane air force officer
Gealy, Douglas Edward television executive
Gee, Elwood Gordon university administrator
Gerber, William Kenton financial executive
Gerlach, John B. business executive
Gibson, Rankin MacDougal lawyer
Gilliom, Bonnie Lee arts educator, consultant
Gillmor, Karen Lako state legislator, strategic planner
Gilman, Kenneth B. retail executive
Glaser, Ronald microbiology educator, scientist
Goodman, Hubert Thorman psychiatrist, consultant
Goorey, Nancy Jane dentist
Gouke, Cecil Granville economist, educator
Gozon, Jozsef Stephan engineering educator
Graham, James Lowell federal judge
Grant, Dennis Duane lawyer
Grant, Michael Peter electrical engineer
Grapski, Ladd Raymond accountant
Greek, Darold I. lawyer
Gribble, Charles Edward Slavic languages educator, editor
Gross, James Howard lawyer
Grossberg, Michael Lee theater critic, writer
Gunnels, Lee O. pallet manufacturing company executive
Gunsett, Daniel J. lawyer
Habash, Stephen J. lawyer
Haddad, George Richard musician, educator
Hahm, David Edgar classics educator
Hairston, George W. lawyer
Hale, Daniel Gordon lawyer
Hamilton, Harold Philip fund raising executive
Haque, Malika Hakim pediatrician
Hardymon, David Wayne lawyer
Hare, Robert Yates music history educator
Harris, Donald composer
Haury, David Leroy science education specialist
Havens, John Franklin retired banker
Hayes, Edward F. academic administrator
Hedrick, Larry Willis airport executive
Heffner, Grover Chester retired corporate executive, retired naval officer
Hermann, Charles F. academic director, political science educator
Hermann, Margaret Gladden political science educator
Hinshaw, Virgil Goodman, Jr. philosopher, emeritus educator
Hire, Charles H. lawyer
Hoberg, John William lawyer
Hoffmann, Charles Wesley retired foreign language educator
†Hollister, Nancy state official
Holmes, Robert G. agricultural studies educator
Holschuh, John David federal judge
Hopkins, Thomas Gene retail company executive
Horton, John Edward periodontist, educator
Hoskins, W. Lee banker
Houser, Donald Russell mechanical engineering educator, consultant
Howarth, Robert F., Jr. lawyer
Howell, Norbert Allen architect
Hsu, Hsiung engineering educator
Huber, Joan Althaus sociology educator
Huff, C(larence) Ronald public administration and criminology educator
Hughes, Donald Allen, Jr. law librarian and educator
Huheey, Marilyn Jane ophthalmologist
Ichiishi, Tatsuro economics and mathematics educator
Ichino, Yoko ballet dancer
Jackson, Curtis Maitland metallurgical engineer
Jarvis, Gilbert Andrew humanities educator
Jenkins, George L. lawyer
Jenkins, John Anthony lawyer
Jennings, Edward Harrington business educator
Jezek, Kenneth Charles geophysicist, educator, researcher
Johnson, Mark Alan lawyer
†Johnston, Jeffery W. publishing executive
†Johnston, Peter osteopath, surgeon
Johnston, Philip Crater lawyer
†Jossem, Edmund Leonard physics educator
Kapral, Frank Albert medical microbiology and immunology educator
Keaney, William Regis engineering and construction services executive, consultant
Kearns, Merle Grace state senator
Kefauver, Weldon Addison publisher
Keller, John Kistler lawyer
Kendrick, Ronald Edward orthopaedic surgeon
Kennedy, James Patrick lawyer
Kessel, John Howard political scientist, educator
Kidder, C. Robert battery manufacturing company executive
Kim, Moon Hyun physician, educator
Kincaid, Robert M., Jr. lawyer
Kindig, Fred Eugene statistics educator, arbitrator
King, G. Roger lawyer
King, James R. lawyer
King, Norah McCann federal judge
Kinneary, Joseph Peter federal judge
Kirk, Ballard Harry Thurston architect
Knepper, William Edward lawyer
Knilans, Michael Jerome supermarkets executive
Kocher, Walter William lawyer, food company executive
Koenigsknecht, Roy A. university dean
Kolattukudy, Pappachan Ettoop biochemist, educator
Koncelik, Joseph Arthur industrial design educator
Kozyris, Phaedon John law educator, consultant
Krebs, Eugene Kehm, II state legislator
Ksienski, Aharon Arthur electrical engineer
Kuehn, Edmund Karl artist
Kuehnle, Kenton Lee lawyer
Kuhn, Albert Joseph English educator
Kurtz, Charles Jewett, III lawyer
Kyees, John Edward apparel company executive
Ladman, Jerry R. economist, educator
Lahey, John H. lawyer
Lal, Rattan soil scientist, researcher
LaLonde, Bernard Joseph educator
Lashutka, Gregory S. mayor, lawyer
Laufman, Leslie Rodgers hematologist, oncologist
Lazar, Theodore Aaron retired manufacturing company executive, lawyer
Leach, Russell judge
Lehiste, Ilse language educator
Lehman, Harry Jac lawyer
Leissa, Arthur William mechanical engineering educator
Leiter, William C. banking executive, controller
Leland, Henry psychology educator
Levey, Barry state senator
Lewis, Richard Phelps physician, educator
†Lhota, William J. electric company executive
Lince, John Alan pharmacist
Lipinsky, Edward Solomon chemist
Logan, Terry James soil chemist, educator
Long, Jan Michael state legislator
Long, Sarah Elizabeth Brackney physician
Long, Thomas Leslie lawyer
Lowe, Clayton Kent visual imagery, cinema, and video educator
Lucas, June H. state legislator
Luck, James I. foundation executive
Lundman, Richard Jack sociology educator
Lundstedt, Sven Bertil behavioral and social scientist, educator
Lynn, Arthur Dellert, Jr. economist, educator
Maddala, Gangadharrao Soundaryarao economics educator
Maloney, Gerald P. utility executive
Maloon, Jerry L. lawyer, physician, medicolegal consultant
Marble, Duane Francis geography educator, researcher
†Margello, Margaret Ann healthcare executive
Martin, William Giese lawyer
Marzluf, George Austin biochemistry educator
†Massey, Robert John telecommunications executive
Massie, Robert Joseph publishing company executive
Masterson, Michael Rue journalist, educator, editor
Mathews, Robert Edward banker
Mayer, Victor James earth systems science educator
Maynard, Robert Howell lawyer
Mayo, Elizabeth Broom lawyer
†Mayo, Gerald Edgar insurance company executive
Mazzaferri, Ernest Louis physician, educator
McAlister, Robert Beaton lawyer
Mc Caffrey, Thomas R. utilities company executive
McClain, Thomas E. communications executive
McConnaughey, George Carlton, Jr. lawyer
McConnell, John Henderson metal and plastic products manufacturing executive, professional sports team executive
Mc Cormac, John Waverly judge
Mc Coy, John Bonnet banker
McCoy, John Gardner banker
McCutchan, Gordon Eugene lawyer, insurance company executive
McFerson, D. Richard insurance company executive
McKenna, Alvin James lawyer
McLin, Rhine Lana state legislator, funeral service executive, educator
McMahon, John Patrick lawyer
McMaster, Robert Raymond accountant
McMorrow, Richard Mark research company executive
McNealey, J. Jeffrey lawyer, corporate executive
McWhorter, Donald Lee bank executive
Mead, Priscilla state legislator
Meider, Elmer Charles, Jr. publishing company executive
Meiling, George Robert Lucas bank holding company executive
Meshel, Harry state senator, political party official
Meuse, David Russell investment banker
Meuser, Fredrick William retired seminary president, church historian
Meyer, Donald Ray psychologist, brain researcher
Meyer, Patricia Morgan neuropsychologist, educator
Milford, Frederick John retired research company executive
Miller, Don Wilson nuclear engineering educator
Miller, Frederick Powell agronomy educator
Miller, Malcolm Lee retired lawyer
Miller, Terry Alan chemistry educator
Miller, Terry Morrow lawyer
Mills, Robert Laurence physicist, educator
Minister, Michael E. lawyer

Minor, Charles Daniel *lawyer*
Minor, Robert Allen *lawyer*
Minor, Robert Walter *lawyer*
Mirman, Joel Harvey *lawyer*
Moloney, Thomas E. *lawyer*
Mone, Robert Paul *lawyer*
Montgomery, Betty D. *state official, former state legislator*
Moody, Curtis Jerome *architect*
Moore, Donald Paul *retired electrical engineer*
Moritz, Michael Everett *lawyer*
Morrow, Grant, III *genetecist*
Moul, William Charles *lawyer*
Moulton, Edward Quentin *civil engineer, educator*
Moyer, Thomas J. *state supreme court chief justice*
Muller, Mervin Edgar *information systems educator, consultant*
Murphy, Andrew J., Jr. *newspaper editor*
Mussey, Joseph Arthur *health and medical product executive*
Namboodiri, Krishnan *sociology educator*
Naylor, James Charles *psychologist, educator*
Neckermann, Peter Josef *insurance company executive*
Neff, Joya Lee *community health nurse, administrator*
Nelson, Helaine Queen *lawyer*
Nettle, Robert Dale *state legislator, former insurance and real estate broker*
Newcomb, Lawrence Howard *agricultural educator*
Newland, Ron *airport executive*
Newman, Diana S. *community foundation executive*
Newsom, Gerald Higley *astronomy educator*
Newton, William Allen, Jr. *pediatric pathologist*
Noltimier, Hallan Costello *geology educator, researcher, consultant*
Norris, Alan Eugene *federal judge*
Nutt, Fred L., Jr. *retail store executive*
Ockerman, Herbert W. *agricultural studies educator*
O'Dorisio, Thomas Michael *internal medicine educator, researcher*
Ojalvo, Morris *civil engineer, educator*
Olesen, Douglas Eugene *research institute executive*
Oman, Richard Heer *lawyer*
Osipow, Samuel Herman *psychology educator*
Osmer, Patrick Stewart *astronomer*
Otte, Paul John *college administrator, consultant, trainer*
Ouzts, Dale Keith *broadcast executive*
Padgett, Joy *state legislator*
Page, Linda Kay *banking executive*
Pappas, Peter William *zoology educator*
†Paquette, Leo Armand *chemistry educator*
Parks, Darrell Lee *vocational education contultant*
Patil, Popat Narayan *pharmacology-pharmacy educator*
Patterson, Samuel Charles *political science educator*
Penn, Gerald Melville *pathologist*
Perkins, Robert Louis *physician, educator*
Peterle, Tony John *zoologist, educator*
Peters, Leon, Jr. *electrical engineering educator, research administ*
Petricoff, M. Howard *lawyer, educator*
Petro, James Michael *lawyer, politician*
Petty, Richard Edward *psychologist, educator, researcher*
Pfeifer, Paul E. *state supreme court justice*
Pfening, Frederic Denver, III *manufacturing company executive*
Phillips, James Edgar *lawyer*
Pieper, Heinz Paul *physiology educator*
Plagenz, George Richard *minister, journalist, columnist*
Pliskin, Marvin Robert *lawyer*
Pohlman, James Erwin *lawyer*
Pointer, Peter Leon *investment executive*
Poirier, Frank Eugene *physical anthropology educator*
Powell, Ernestine Breisch *retired lawyer*
Prentiss, C.J. *state legislator*
Pressley, Fred G., Jr. *lawyer*
Pyatt, Leo Anthony *real estate broker*
Quigley, John Bernard *law educator*
Radnor, Alan T. *lawyer*
†Rajadhyaksha, Vikram *civil engineering consulant, engineering company executive*
Rakestraw, Warren Vincent *lawyer*
Ramey, Denny L. *bar association executive director*
Rapp, Robert Anthony *metallurgical engineering educator, consultant*
Ray, Edward John *economics educator, administrator*
Ray, Frank David *government agency official*
†Rayner, John Norman *science educator*
Reasoner, Willis Irl, III *lawyer*
Redmond, Robert Francis *nuclear engineering educator*
Reece, Robert William *zoological park administrator*
Reeve, John Newton *molecular biology and microbiology educator*
Reibel, Kurt *physicist, educator*
Relle, Ferenc Matyas *chemist*
Resnick, Alice Robie *state supreme court justice*
Richardson, Laurel Walum *sociology educator*
Ridgley, Thomas Brennan *lawyer*
Ripley, Randall Butler *political scientist, educator*
†Robertson, Harry Stevens *retired mechanical engineer*
Robinson, Barry R. *lawyer*
Robol, Richard Thomas *lawyer*
Roche, Mark William *German language educator*
Rogers, Sarah Jeanne *curator*
Rose, Michael Dean *lawyer, educator*
†Rosenstock, Susan Lynn *orchestra manager*
Roth, Robert Earl *environmental educator*
Rowland, Ronald Lee *lawyer*
Royalty, Kenneth Marvin *lawyer*
Ruberg, Robert Lionel *surgery educator*
Rubin, Alan J. *environmental engineer, chemist*
Rudmann, Sally Vander Linden *medical technology educator*
Rule, John Corwin *history educator*
Rund, Douglas Andrew *emergency physician, educator*
Russell, William Fletcher, III *opera company director*
Ryan, Joseph W., Jr. *lawyer*
Ryan, Ray Darl, Jr. *academic administrator*
Ryan, Robert Seibert *consulting company executive*
Sahai, Yogeshwar *engineering educator*
St. Arnold, Dale S. *hospital administrator*
†St. Cyr, Roger Joseph *banker*
St. Pierre, George Roland, Jr. *materials science and engineering administrator, educator*
St. Pierre, Ronald Leslie *anatomy educator, university administrator*
Salgia, Tansukh Jawaharlal *academic administrator*
†Sanders, Ted *state official*
Santner, Thomas *statistician, educator*
Satyapriya, Combatore Keshavamurthy *geotechnical engineering executive*
Sawyers, Elizabeth Joan *librarian, administrator*
Sayers, Martin Peter *pediatric neurosurgeon*
Scanlan, James Patrick *philosophy and Slavic studies educator*
Schafer, William Harry *electric power industry executive*
Schermer, Harry Angus *insurance company executive*
Schlichting, Nancy Margaret *hospital administrator*
†Schlueter, Bernard Joseph *state official*
Schottenstein, Saul *retail company executive*
Schrag, Edward A., Jr. *lawyer*
Schuller, David Edward *cancer center administrator, otolaryngology*
Schwab, Glenn Orville *retired agricultural engineering educator, consultant*
Schwebel, Andrew I. *psychology educator*
Scott, Thomas Clevenger *lawyer*
Sebo, Stephen Andrew *electrical engineer, educator, researcher, consultant*
Selcer, David Mark *lawyer*
Sellers, Barbara Jackson *federal judge*
Senff, Mark D. *lawyer*
Senhauser, Donald A(lbert) *pathologist, educator*
Shamansky, Robert Norton *lawyer*
Sharp, Paul David *institute administrator*
Shayne, Stanley H. *lawyer*
Sherrill, Thomas Boykin, III *newspaper publishing executive*
Sheward, Richard S. *lawyer*
Shewmon, Paul Griffith *metallurgical engineer, educator*
†Shisler, Arden L. *insurance and transportation company executive*
Shook, Robert Louis *insurance company executive, business writer*
Sidman, Robert John *lawyer*
Siehl, Richard W. *lawyer*
Silbajoris, Frank Rimvydas *Slavic languages educator*
Silcott, James *principal*
Silverman, Jerald *veterinarian, academic administrator*
†Simms, Lowelle *synod executive*
Sims, Richard Lee *hospital administrator*
Singh, Rajendra *mechanical engineering educator*
Skillman, Thomas Grant *endocrinology consultant, former educator*
Slettebak, Arne *astronomer, educator*
Slonim, Arnold Robert *biochemist, physiologist*
Smialowska, Susan *engineering educator*
Smith, George Curtis *federal judge*
Smith, George Leonard, Jr. *industrial engineering educator*
Smith, Norman T. *lawyer*
Smith, Robert Burns *newspaper magazine executive*
Sofranko, Joel E. *pension fund administrator*
Sokol, Saul *insurance agency executive*
Soloway, Albert Herman *medicinal chemist*
Stark, Maurice Gene *research institute financial executive*
Stedman, Richard Ralph *lawyer*
Steigman, Gary *physics and astronomy educator*
Stein, Jay Wobith *legal research and education consultant*
Stephens, Thomas M(aron) *education educator*
Stern, Geoffrey *lawyer, disciplinary counsel*
Stinehart, Roger Ray *lawyer*
Strode, George K. *sports editor*
Studer, William Joseph *library director*
Sweeney, Asher William *state supreme court justice*
Sweeney, Francis E. *state supreme court justice*
Taaffe, Edward James *geography educator*
Taft, Bob *state official*
Taft, Sheldon Ashley *lawyer*
Taggart, Thomas Michael *lawyer*
Taiganides, E. Paul *agricultural-environmental engineer, consultant*
Tait, Robert Ed *lawyer*
Tarpy, Thomas Michael *lawyer*
Taylor, Celianna I. *information systems specialist*
Taylor, Joel Sanford *lawyer*
Teater, Dorothy Seath *county official*
Tell, A. Charles *lawyer*
Thomas, Duke Winston *lawyer*
Thomas, Stephen Clair *software publisher, writer, editor, consultant*
Tiefel, Virginia May *librarian*
Tilley, C. Ronald *gas company executive*
Tipton, Clyde Raymond, Jr. *communications and resources development consultant*
Todd, William Michael *lawyer*
Tomassini, Lawrence Anthony *accounting educator, consultant*
Trevor, Alexander Bruen *computer company executive*
Trimble, Marian Alice Eddy *mutual fund executive*
Triplehorn, Charles A. *entomology educator, insects curator*
Tully, Richard Lowden *architect*
Turano, David A. *lawyer*
†Turpin, Cheryl Nido *retail executive*
Tzagournis, Manuel *physician, educator, university dean and official*
Uotila, Urho Antti Kalevi *geodesist, educator*
Van Heyde, J. Stephen *lawyer*
Vassell, Gregory S. *electric utility consultant*
Voinovich, George V. *governor*
Vorys, Arthur Isaiah *lawyer*
Voss, Jerrold Richard *city planner, educator, university official*
Waldron, Acie Chandler *agronomy and entomology educator*
Wali, Mohan Kishen *environmental science and natural resources educator*
Walsh, Katherine Herald *state legislator*
Walters, Everett *retired university official, author*
Ware, Brendan John *electrical engineer, electric utility company executive*
Warmbrod, James Robert *agriculture educator, university administrator*
Warner, Charles Collins *lawyer*
Webb, Thomas Evan *biochemistry educator*
Wedge, Thomas Willim *occult consultant, criminologist*
†Wehr, Lynn *food products executive*
Weinhold, Virginia Beamer *interior designer*
Weisberg, Herbert Frank *political science educator*
Weisgerber, David Wendelin *editor, chemist*
†Wells, Richard Lewis *insurance company executive*
Wentworth, Andrew Stowell *lawyer*
Wexner, Leslie Herbert *retail executive*
Whipps, Edward Franklin *lawyer*
Wightman, Alec *lawyer*
Wigington, Ronald Lee *retired chemical information services executive*
Wilhelmy, Odin, Jr. *insurance agent*
Wilkins, John Warren *physics educator*
Williams, David Fulton *industrial distribution company executive*
Williams, Gregory Howard *lawyer, educator*
Wobst, Frank Georg *banker*
Wojcicki, Andrew Adalbert *chemist, educator*
Woodward, Robert J., Jr. *insurance executive*
Wright, Harry, III *lawyer*
Wright, J. Craig *state supreme court associate justice*
Yashon, David *neurosurgeon, educator*
Yenkin, Bernard Kalman *paint company executive*
Yoder, Amos *university research official*
Yohn, David Stewart *virologist, science administrator*
Zakin, Jacques Louis *chemical engineering educator*
†Zande, Richard Dominic *civil engineering firm executive*
Zartman, David Lester *animal sciences educator, researcher*
Zipf, William Byron *pediatric endocrinologist, educator*
Zuspan, Frederick Paul *obstetrician/gynecologist, educator*

Concord
Lenardic, Kenneth Ralph *systems architect, consultant*
Watterson, Joyce Grande *editor, publisher*
Whedon, Ralph Gibbs *manufacturing executive*

Cortland
†Evans, Ronald Leon *healthcare administrator*

Curtice
Cashen, Elizabeth Anne *elementary school educator*

Cuyahoga Falls
Haag, Everett Keith *architect*
Hooper, Blake Howard *manufacturing executive*
Jones, Wayne M. *state legislator, lawyer*
Moses, Abe Joseph *international financial consultant*

Dayton
Alexander, Roberta Sue *history educator*
Arn, Kenneth Dale *physician, city official*
Bartlett, Robert Perry, Jr. *lawyer*
Battino, Rubin *chemistry educator*
Bedell, Kenneth Berkley *computer specialist, educator*
Berrey, Robert Forrest *lawyer*
Berry, John William *investment company executive, retired telephone directory advertising company executive*
Betz, Eugene William *architect*
Bigley, Nancy Jane *microbiology educator*
†Boff, Kenneth Richard *engineering research psychologist*
Bohanon, Kathleen Sue *neonatologist, educator*
Boren, Arthur Rodney *sales management executive*
Bowman, Ed *principal*
†Breitenbach, Thomas George *health systems executive*
Bridges, Roy Dubard, Jr. *career officer*
Brown, William Milton *electrical engineering educator*
Burick, Lawrence T. *lawyer*
Cawood, Albert McLaurin (Hap Cawood) *newspaper editor*
Chait, William *librarian, consultant*
Chernesky, Richard John *lawyer*
Christensen, Julien Martin *psychologist, educator*
†Clouser, James Brady *ballet director, choreographer*
Crowe, Shelby *educational specialist, consultant*
Daley, Robert Emmett *foundation executive*
Darragh, John K. *printing company executive*
D'Azzo, John Joachim *electrical engineer, educator*
Deardorff, Darryl K. *business consultant, accountant*
DeWall, Richard Allison *retired surgeon*
Diggs, Matthew O'Brien, Jr. *air conditioning and refrigeration manufacturing executive*
Duval, Daniel Webster *manufacturing company executive*
†Eickmann, Kenneth Elmer *air force officer, engineer*
†Elliot, Ernest A. *naval officer*
Elliott, Daniel Whitacre *surgeon, retired educator*
Emrick, Donald Day *chemist, consultant*
Enouen, William Albert *paper corporation executive*
Fang, Zhaoqiang *research physicist*
Faruki, Mahmud Taji *psychiatrist, hospital administrator*
Finn, Chester Evans *lawyer*
Fitz, Brother Raymond L. *university president*
†Forster, Peter Hans *utility company executive*
Garcia, Oscar Nicolas *computer science educator*
Gies, Frederick John *education educator, university dean*
Glaser, Herbert Otto *retail executive*
Goesch, William Holbrook *aeronautical engineer*
Gottschlich, Gary William *lawyer*
Granzow, Paul H. *printing company executive*
Gray, Edman Lowell *metal distribution company executive*
Gregor, Clunie Bryan *geology educator*
Hadley, Robert James *lawyer*
Haigh, Peter Leslie *software company executive, consultant*
Halki, John Joseph *retired military officer, physician*
Hanna, Marsha L. *artistic director*
Harden, Oleta Elizabeth *English educator, university administrator*
Hartley, Milton E. *retail executive*
Hawthorne, Douglas Lawson *banker*
Hayman, Jeffrey Lloyd *corporate lawyer*
Haynes, Gerald Wayne *aerospace manufacturing administrator*
Heath, Mariwyn Dwyer *writer, legislative issues consultant*
Heft, James Lewis *academic administrator, theology educator*
Helling, James T. *library director*
Heyman, Ralph Edmond *lawyer*
†Hill, Allen M. *public utility executive*
Hilliard, Jack Briggs *museum curator*
Hitter, Joseph Ira *lawyer*
Hoge, Franz Joseph *accounting firm executive*
Holmes, David Richard *computer and business forms company executive*
Horn, Charles F. *state senator, lawyer, electrical engineer*
Houpis, Constantine Harry *electrical engineering educator*
†Huffman, Dale *journalist*
Humbert, James Ronald *pediatrician, educator*
Isaacson, Milton Stanley *research and development company executive, engineer*
James, Robert Charles *business equipment manufacturing company executive*
Janning, John Louis *research scientist, consultant*
Jenks, Thomas Edward *lawyer*
Kazimierczuk, Marian Kazimierz *electrical engineer, educator*
Kegerreis, Robert James *management consultant, marketing educator*
†Kelley, Alan Kent *newspaper editor*
Khalimsky, Efim *mathematics and computer science educator*
Kinlin, Donald James *lawyer*
Klinck, Cynthia Anne *library director*
Knapp, James Ian Keith *judge*
Kogut, Maurice David *pediatric endocrinologist*
†Koziar, Stephen Francis, Jr. *lawyer, power company executive*
Krug, Maurice F. *engineering company executive*
Ladehoff, Leo William *metal products manufacturing executive*
Langford, Roland Everett *military officer, environmental scientist, author*
Lewis, Welbourne Walker, Jr. *lawyer*
Love, Rodney Marvin *retired judge, former congressman*
Lowry, Bruce Roy *lawyer*
Macklin, Crofford Johnson, Jr. *lawyer*
†MacLeod, Thomas D. *feed company executive*
Martin, James Gilbert *university provost emeritus*
Martino, Joseph Paul *research scientist*
Mason, Steven Charles *forest products company executive*
†Massie, Lowell David *aeronautical engineer*
Matheny, Ruth Ann *editor*
Mathews, David *foundation executive*
†Mathews, John *bishop*
†Mathile, Clayton Lee *corporate executive*
†McCrabb, Donald R. *religious ministry director*
McDonnell, Sue Kartin *lawyer*
McSwiney, Charles Ronald *lawyer*
Mc Swiney, James Wilmer *retired pulp and paper manufacturing company executive*
Medford, Dale Leon *industrial company executive*
Merz, Michael *federal judge*
Mohler, Stanley Ross *physician, educator*
Morse, Kenneth Pratt *manufacturing executive*
†Murphy, Martin Joseph, Jr. *cancer research center executive*
Nam, Sang Boo *physicist*
Nevin, Robert Charles *information systems executive*
†Nix, John B. *aeronautical engineer*
Nyerges, Alexander Lee *museum director*
O'Brien, Elmer John *librarian, educator*
Office, Gerald Simms, Jr. *restaurant chain executive*
Peterson, Skip (Orley R. Peterson, III) *newspaper photographer*
†Phillips, John F. *air force officer*
Ponitz, David H. *academic administrator*
Porter, Walter Arthur *judge*
Price, Harry Steele, Jr. *construction materials company executive*
Przemieniecki, Janusz Stanislaw *college dean, engineer*
Rapp, Gerald Duane *lawyer, manufacturing company executive*
Redding, Peter Stoddard *manufacturing company executive*
Reid, Marilyn Joanne *state legislator, lawyer*
Rinzler, Allan *consulting company executive*
†Roan, James Cortland, Jr. *air force officer*
Rogers, Richard Hunter *lawyer, business executive*
Rowe, Joseph Everett *electrical engineering educator, administrator*
Ruffer, David Gray *museum director, former college president*
Schmitt, George Frederick, Jr. *materials engineer*
Schorgl, Thomas Barry *arts administrator*
Schwartz, Irving Lloyd *retired history educator*
Schwartzhoff, James Paul *foundation executive*
Scofield, Richard Melbourne *career officer*
†Shaw, George Bernard *consulting engineer, educator*
Shuey, John Henry *diversified products company executive*
Siegel, Ira T. *publishing executive*
†Soin, Rajesh K. *business executive*
Spicer, John Austin *physicist*
Stander, Joseph William *mathematics educator, former university official*
Standley, Paul Melvin *chemist*
Thomas, Donald Charles *microbiology educator, former university dean and administrator*
Thorsland, Edgar, Jr. *health facility administrator*
Tillson, John Bradford, Jr. *newspaper publisher*
Torley, John Frederic *iron and steel company executive*
Uphoff, James Kent *education educator*
†Viccellio, Henry, Jr. *career military officer*
Von Gierke, Henning Edgar *biomedical science educator, former government official, researcher*
Walden, James William *accountant, educator*
Wallach, John S(idney) *library administrator*
Walters, Jefferson Brooks *musician, retired real estate broker*
Weinberg, Sylvan Lee *cardiologist, educator, author, editor*
Wertz, Kenneth Dean *real estate executive*
Whitlock, David C. *retired military officer*
†Willett, Robert Lee *health care administrator*
Willits, Eileen Marie *medical/surgical nurse, health facility administrator*
Yates, Ronald Wilburn *air force officer*

Defiance
Elberson, Elwood L. *food company executive*
Mirchandaney, Arjan Sobhraj *mathematics educator*

Delaware
Benschneider, Donald *agricultural products company executive*
Berg, John Paul *container manufacturing company executive*
Courtice, Thomas Barr *college president*
Dempsey, John Cornelius *manufacturing company executive*
Eells, William Hastings *retired automobile company executive*
Fry, Anne Evans *zoology educator*
Mendenhall, Robert Vernon *mathematics educator*
Reitz, Elmer A. *manufacturing company executive*

Delphos
Clark, Edward Ferdnand *lawyer*
†Staup, John Gary *safety engineer*

Dresden
Reidy, Thomas Anthony *lawyer*

Dublin
Brownley, John Forrest *fast food company executive*
Casey, John K. *restaurant chain executive*
Clement, Henry Joseph, Jr. *diversified building products executive*
Felger, Ralph William *retired military officer, educator*
Freytag, Donald Ashe *management consultant*
Gores, Gary Gene *credit union executive*
Graham, Bruce Douglas *pediatrician*
Greaves, J. Randall *metals, electronics manufacturing company executive*
Haemmerle, John Martin *nursing home and retirement housing executive*
†Heffron, Robert F. *manufacturing company executive*
†Kane, John C. *health care products company executive*
Lamp, Benson J. *tractor company executive*
Madigan, Joseph Edward *financial executive, consultant, director*
Major, Coleman Joseph *chemical engineer*
Near, James W. *restaurant and franchise executive*
Ourant, Edwin L. *fast food restaurant chain executive*
Rome, John L. *restaurant chain executive*
Schauf, Lawrence E. *restaurant corporation executive*
Schinagl, Erich Friedrich *health care company executive, physician*
Smith, K(ermit) Wayne *computer company executive*
Teter, Gordon F. *fast food chain company executive*
Thomas, R. David *food services company executive*
Toller, William Robert *chemical and oil company executive*
Walter, Robert D. *wholesale pharmaceutical distribution executive*
Welter, William Michael *marketing and advertising executive*

Duncan Falls
Cooper, April Helen *nurse*

East Liverpool
Lang, Francis Harover *lawyer*

Elmore
Kaczynski, Don *metallurgical engineer*

Elyria
†Carbonari, Bruce A. *metal products executive*
Eady, Carol Murphy (Mrs. Karl Ernest Eady) *medical association administrator*
Kreighbaum, John Scott *banker*
Skillicorn, Judy Pettibone *gifted/talented education coordinator*
Ugwu, David Egbo *academic director, consulting company executive*
Uveges, George *company executive*

Englewood
Shearer, Velma Miller *clergywoman*

Fairborn
Leffler, Carole Elizabeth *mental health nurse, women's health nurse*
Martin, Donald William *psychiatrist*

Fairfield
Carr, William Anthony *retail company executive*
Goodman, Myrna Marcia *school nurse*
Murphy, Dennis F. *retail executive*
Robertson, Oscar Palmer (Big O) *former professional basketball player, chemical company executive*

Fairlawn
Bonsky, Jack Alan *chemical company executive, lawyer*
Gibson, Charles Colmery *former rubber manufacturing executive*
Isles, Marvin Lee *manufacturing executive*

Findlay
Draper, David Eugene *seminary president*
Gorr, Ivan William *retired rubber company executive*
Jetton, Girard Reuel, Jr. *lawyer, retired oil company executive*
Kremer, Fred, Jr. *manufacturing company executive*
Martin, Jim G. *church renewal consultant*
Rave, James A. *bishop*
Reinhardt, James Alec *rubber industry executive*
Teeple, Richard Duane *lawyer*
Wilkin, Richard Edwin *clergyman, religious organization executive*
Yammine, Riad Nassif *oil company executive*

Forest Park
Ashley, Lynn *educator, consultant, administrator*

Franklin
Smith, Lynn Howard *manufacturing company executive*

Fremont
Bridges, Roger Dean *historical agency administrator*

Gahanna
Chappell, Michelle R. *elementary education educator*
Myers, Phillip Fenton *financial services company executive*

Galion
Cobey, Ralph *investment company executive, industrialist*

Gallipolis
Brunner, Nancy Lee Andrew *medical center nursing administrator*
Clarke, Oscar Withers *physician*
Niehm, Bernard Frank *mental health center administrator*

Gambier
Browning, Reed S. *college official*
Gunton, James Douglas *academic administrator*
Jordan, Philip Harding, Jr. *academic administrator*
Sharp, Ronald Alan *English literature educator, author*

Gates Mills
Enyedy, Gustav, Jr. *chemical engineer*
Schanfarber, Richard Carl *real estate broker*
Veale, Tinkham, II *former chemical company executive, engineer*

Germantown
Lansaw, Charles Ray *rendering industry consultant*

Girard
Wolanin, Sophie Mae *civic worker, tutor, scholar, lecturer*

Granville
Fisher, Robert Allison *minister, church administrator*
Jacobs, Richard Allen *industrial engineer*
Myers, Michele Tolela *academic administrator*

Grove City
Black, Frances Patterson *library administrator*
Funk, John William *emergency vehicle manufacturing executive, packaging company executive, lawyer*
Kilman, James William *surgeon, educator*

Groveport
†Ricart, Paul F., Sr. *automotive retail executive*
†Ricart, Rhett C. *retail automotive executive*

Grover Hill
Harr, Joseph *religious organization administrator*

Hamilton
Belew, David Lee *retired paper manufacturing company executive*
Johnson, Pauline Benge *nurse, anesthetist*
Marcum, Joseph LaRue *insurance company executive*
Patch, Lauren Nelson *insurance company, chief executive officer*
Rorer, Leonard George *psychology educator*

Harrison
Kocher, Juanita Fay *auditor*
Stoll, Robert W. *principal*

Heath
Guthrie, Marc Dennis *former state representative*

Hilliard
Cupp, David Foster *photographer, journalist*
Keyes, James Lyman, Jr. *diesel engines distributor company owner*
†Van Fossen, Larry Jack *service company executive*

Hillsboro
Snyder, Harry Cooper *state senator*

Hiram
Jagow, Elmer *retired college president*
Oliver, G(eorge) Benjamin *academic administrator, philosophy educator*

Holland
Kennedy, James L. *accountant*
Stewart, Daniel Robert *retired glass company executive*

Holmesville
Bolender, James Henry *tire and rubber manufacturing executive*

Hubbard
Rose, Ernst *dentist*

Hudson
Griech, Frederick G. *telephone company executive*
Kirchner, James William *electrical engineer*
Monro, James Alexander, Jr. *retail executive*
Rosskamm, Alan *retail company executive*
Rosskamm, Martin *fabric manufacturing company executive*
Stec, John Zygmunt *real estate executive*
Wooldredge, William Dunbar *investment banker*

Huron
Clark, Thomas Garis *rubber products manufacturer*

Independence
Callsen, Christian Edward *medical device company executive*
Hawkinson, Gary Michael *utility holding company executive*
Linnert, Terrence Gregory *lawyer*
Meyer, Gerald Justin *energy company executive*

Ironton
Mitchell, Maurice McClellan, Jr. *chemist*
Newmark, Howard *surgeon, entrepreneur*

Jackson Center
Thompson, Wade Francis Bruce *manufacturing company executive*

Kent
Beer, Barrett Lynn *historian, educator*
Buttlar, Rudolph Otto *college dean*
Byrne, Frank Loyola *history educator*
Cartwright, Carol Ann *university president*
Cooke, G. Dennis *biological science educator*
Cooperrider, Tom Smith *botanist*
Cummins, Kenneth Burdette *retired science and mathematics educator*
Dante, Harris Loy *history educator*
†Doane, J. William *physics educator and researcher, science administrator*
Du Mont, Rosemary Ruhig *university administrator*
Giffen, Daniel Harris *lawyer, educator*
Gould, Edwin Sheldon *chemist, educator*
Hall, Bernard *retired economics educator and university official*
Harkness, Bruce *English language educator*
Hassler, Donald Mackey, II *English language educator, writer*
Heimlich, Richard Allen *geologist, educator*
James, Patricia Ann *philosophy educator*
Koller, Marvin Robert *sociology educator, writer*
Poorman, Paul Arthur *educator, media consultant*
Powell, Robert Ellis *mathematics educator, former college dean*
†Reid, Sidney Webb *English educator*
Rylant, Cynthia *author*
Schwartz, Michael *university president, sociology educator*
Stackelberg, Olaf Patrick Von *mathematician*
Tolliver, Don L. *dean library and media services*
Tuan, Debbie Fu-Tai *chemistry educator*
Varga, Richard Steven *mathematics educator*
Vars, Gordon Forrest *education educator*
Williams, Harold Roger *economist, educator*
Zornow, William Frank *historian, educator*

Kettering
Caldabaugh, Karl *holding company executive*
Taylor, Billie Wesley *secondary education educator*

Kingston
Mathew, Martha Sue Cryder *retired education educator*

Kirtland
Skerry, Philip John *English educator*

Lakewood
Berman, Phillip Lee *author, institute administrator*
Bradley, J.F., Jr. *retired manufacturing company executive*
Condon, George Edward *journalist*

Lancaster
Fox, Robert Kriegbaum *manufacturing company executive*
Hurley, Samuel Clay, III *investment company executive*
Katlic, John Edward *management consultant*
Libert, Donald Joseph *lawyer*
Phillips, Edward John *consulting firm executive*
†Varney, Richard Alan *medical office manager*
Voss, Jack Donald *international business consultant, lawyer*
Wagonseller, James Myrl *real estate executive*

Lebanon
Holtkamp, Dorsey Emil *medical research scientist*

Lima
Bassett, James H. *landscape architect*
Becker, Dwight Lowell *physician*
Borra, P. C. *health care company executive*
Collins, William Thomas *pathologist*
Cupp, Robert Richard *state senator, attorney*
Dicke, Candice Edwards *library educator*
Meek, Violet Imhof *dean*
Pranses, Anthony Louis *retired electric company executive, organization executive*
Robenalt, John Alton *lawyer*

Logan
Carmean, Jerry Richard *broadcast engineer*
Dillon, Neal Winfield *lawyer*

London
Hughes, Clyde Matthew *religious denomination executive*

Lorain
Szucs, Zoltan Daniel *religious organization executive, minister, psychologist, educator*
†Walcott, Robert *healthcare executive, priest*

Loudonville
Battison, John Henry *broadcasting executive, consulting engineer*

Lyndhurst
Sevin, Eugene *engineer, consultant, educator*

Macedonia
Baltazzi, Evan Serge *engineering research consulting company executive*
Roth, Edwin Morton *manufacturing executive*

Magnolia
Zimmerman, Judith Rose *art educator*

Mansfield
Baker, James Allan *banker*
Ellison, Lorin Bruce *management consultant*
Gorman, James Carvill *pump manufacturing company executive*
Gregory, Thomas Bradford *mathematics educator*
Houston, William Robert Montgomery *ophthalmic surgeon*
Ogden, William Michael *school system administrator*
Riedl, John Orth *university dean*
†Roesler, Karl *electronics executive*

Maple Heights
Sargent, Liz Elaine (Elizabeth Sargent) *safety consulting executive*

Marblehead
Haering, Edwin Raymond *chemical engineering educator, consultant*

Marietta
Broughton, Carl L(ouis) *food company executive*
Fields, William Albert *lawyer*
†Greene, William Maynard *hospital executive*
Hausser, Robert Louis *lawyer*
Ling, Dwight L. *college administrator, history educator*
Murdock, Eugene Converse *retired history educator*
Tipton, Jon Paul *allergist*
Wilbanks, Jan Joseph *philosopher*

Marion
Tozzer, Jack Carl *civil engineer, surveyor*

Martins Ferry
Gracey, Robert William *account executive, minister*

Marysville
Hines, Anthony Loring *automotive executive*
Rogula, James Leroy *consumer products company executive*

Mason
Clarke, W. Hall *engineer*
Clements, Michael Craig *health services consulting executive, retired renal dialysis technician*
†Soos, James E. *electronics executive*

Massillon
Dawson, Robert Earle *utilities executive*
†Fogle, Marilyn Louise Kiplinger *hospital administrator*
†Genshaft, Neil *meat packing company executive*
Glosser, James William *veterinarian*

Maumee
Allen, Darryl Frank *industrial company executive*
Anderson, Richard Paul *agricultural company executive*
Frank, Thomas Edward *food products executive*
Huffman, (Bernard) Leslie, Jr. *physician*
Kline, James Edward *lawyer*
Marsh, Benjamin Franklin *lawyer*
Selland, Howard M. *manufacturing executive*
Tigges, Kenneth Edwin *retired financial executive*
Walrod, David James *retail grocery chain executive*

Mayfield Heights
Lewis, Peter Benjamin *insurance company executive*
Marino, Michael *church administrator*
O'Brien, Frank B. *manufacturing executive*
Rankin, Alfred Marshall, Jr. *business executive*
Smith, Ward *manufacturing company executive, lawyer*

Mechanicsburg
Maynard, Joan *education educator*

Medina
Ballard, John Stuart *law educator, former mayor*
Batchelder, Alice M. *federal judge*
Gossett, Robert M. *rubber industry executive*
†Karman, James Anthony *manufacturing executive*
Matthews, Gertrude Ann Urch *retired librarian, writer*
Morris, John Hite *chemical industry executive*
Smith, Richey *chemical company executive*
Sullivan, Thomas Christopher *coatings company executive*

Mentor
Andrassy, Timothy Francis *trade association executive*
Davis, Barbara Snell *principal*
Miller, Frances Suzanne *historic site curator*

Miamisburg
Avona, Vincent Leonard *chemist*
Batista, John Veloso *wholesale food company executive*
Burshtan, Alvin *wholesale company executive*
†Byrne, John J. *manufacturing executive, light*
†Everhart, Rodney Lee *electronic publishing executive*
Mariotti, John Louis *plastics & rubber manufacturing company executive*
Northrop, Stuart Johnston *manufacturing company executive*
Robinson, Samuel L. *wholesale grocery company executive*
Simpson, Jack Ward *computer company executive*
Spicer, Harold Glenn *chemical engineer*
Twyman, Jack *wholesale grocery company executive, management services company executive*

Middleburg Heights
Hartman, Lenore Anne *physical therapist*
Maciuszko, Kathleen Lynn *librarian, educator*

Middletown
Clinton, Mariann Hancock *association executive*
Gilby, Steve *metallurgical engineering researcher*
Gilmore, June Ellen *psychologist*
Graham, Thomas Carlisle *steel company executive*
Jones, Fred E. *state judge*
Rathman, William Ernest *lawyer, minister*
Redding, Barbara J. *nursing administrator, occupational health nurse*

Milford
Fischer, Robert Andrew *computer executive*
Kenton, James Alan *healthcare products executive*
Klosterman, Albert Leonard *technical development business executive, mechanical engineer*
Vorholt, Jeffrey Joseph *lawyer, telecommunications company executive*

Millersburg
Childers, Lawrence Jeffrey *superintendent of schools*

Montpelier
Deckrosh, Hazen Douglas *retired state agency administrator, educator*

Mount Saint Joseph
Roach, Sister Jeanne, S.C. *hospital administrator*

Mount Vernon
Nease, Stephen Wesley *college president*
Turner, Harry Edward *lawyer*

Napoleon
Walker, Frank Houston, Jr. *minister*

New Albany
Kessler, John Whitaker *real estate developer*

New Bremen
Dicke, James Frederick, II *manufacturing company executive*

New Concord
Speck, Samuel Wallace, Jr. *academic administrator*

New Philadelphia
Doughten, Mary Katherine (Molly Doughten) *retired secondary education educator*
Goforth, Mary Elaine Davey *secondary education educator*

Newark
Fortaleza, Judith Ann *school system administrator*
Greenstein, Julius Sidney *academic administrator, educator*
Mantonya, John Butcher *lawyer*
McConnell, William Thompson *commercial banker*

Niles
Darlington, Oscar Gilpin *historian, educator*

Linden, Carol Marie *special education educator*
Travaglini, Raymond Dominic *corporate executive*

North Canton
Lynham, C(harles) Richard *foundry company executive*
Shadle, Donna A. Francis *elementary education educator*

North Olmsted
Lundin, Bruce Theodore *engineering and management consultant*
Tanis, John Jacob *manufacturing company executive*
Zilli, Harry Angelo, Jr. *rail transportation executive*

North Ridgeville
Haddox, Arden Ruth Stewart *automotive aftermarket manufacturing executive*
Nagy, Robert David *tenor*

Northfield
Gupta, Kishan Chand *psychologist*

Norwalk
Carpenter, Paul Leonard *lawyer*
Germann, Richard P(aul) *chemist, chemical company executive*

Novelty
Miller, Dwight Richard *cosmetologist, corporate executive, hair designer*

Oberlin
Andrews, George Harold *mathematics educator*
Arnold, Paul Beaver *artist, educator*
Blodgett, Geoffrey Thomas *history educator*
Boe, David Stephen *musician, educator, college dean*
Care, Norman Sydney *philosophy educator*
Carlton, Terry Scott *chemist, educator*
Carrier, Samuel Crowe, III *college official*
Colish, Marcia Lillian *history educator*
Distelhorst, Garis Fred *association executive*
Dye, Nancy Schrom *academic administrator, history educator*
English, Ray *library administrator*
Friedman, William John *psychology educator*
Gladieux, Bernard Louis *management consultant*
Greenberg, Nathan Abraham *classics educator*
Helm, James Joel *classicist, educator*
Layman, Emma McCloy (Mrs. James W. Layman) *psychologist, educator*
Long, Herbert Strainge *classics educator*
MacKay, Alfred F. *dean, philosophy educator*
Moore, Anne Frances *museum director*
Peterson, Carl Adrian *English language educator*
Pierce, Robert Bell *English educator*
Reinoehl, Richard Louis *writer, artist, consultant*
Simonson, Bruce Miller *geologist, educator*
Soucy, Robert Joseph *history educator*
Spear, Richard Edmund *art history educator*
Startup, Charles Harry *airline executive*
†Stinebring, Warren Richard *microbiologist, educator*
Tacha, Athena *sculptor, educator*
Williams, Eleanor Joyce *air traffic control specialist*
Wojtal, Steven Francis *geology educator, researcher*
Young, David Pollock *humanities educator, author*
Zinn, Grover Alfonso, Jr. *religion educator*

Olmsted Falls
Laessig, Robert H. *artist*

Oregon
Culver, Robert Elroy *osteopathic physician*
St. Clair, Donald David *lawyer*

Oxford
Baldwin, Arthur Dwight, Jr. *geology educator*
Brown, Edward Maurice *retired lawyer, business executive*
Dizney, Robert Edward *retired secondary education educator*
Eshbaugh, W(illiam) Hardy *botanist, educator*
Goodell, George Sidney *finance educator*
Gordon, Gilbert *chemist, educator*
Heimsch, Charles *retired botany educator*
Katon, John Edward *chemist, educator*
Kelm, Bonnie G. *art museum director, educator*
Macklin, Philip Alan *physics educator*
Miller, Harvey Alfred *botanist, educator*
Miller, Robert James *association executive*
†Park, Chull *mathematician, educator*
Paulin, Henry Sylvester *antiques dealer, emeritus educator*
Pearson, Paul Guy *university president emeritus*
Pont, John *football coach, educator*
Pratt, William Crouch, Jr. *English language educator*
Rejai, Mostafa *political science educator*
Risser, Paul Gillan *botanist, academic administrator*
Sanders, Gerald Hollie *communications educator*
Sessions, Judith Ann *librarian, university library dean*
Shriver, Phillip Raymond *university president*
Thompson, Bertha Boya *retired educator*
Throne, Marilyn Elizabeth *English educator*
Ward, Roscoe Fredrick *engineering educator*
Willeke, Gene E. *environmental engineer, educator*
Williamson, Clarence Kelly *microbiologist, educator*
Wilson, James Ray *international business educator*
Winkler, Allan Michael *history educator*

Painesville
Clement, Daniel Roy, III *accountant, assistant nurse, small business owner*
Humphrey, George Magoffin, II *plastic molding company executive*
Jayne, Theodore Douglas *technical research and development company executive*
†Kluznik, Kurt *landscape design building executive*
†Scozzie, James Anthony *chemist*

Parma
Esterhay, Judith M. *physical education educator*
Moskal, Robert M. *bishop*
Spencer, James Calvin, Sr. *humanities educator*

Peninsula
Ludwig, Richard Joseph *ski resort executive*

Pepper Pike
Bray, Pierce *business consultant*
Froelich, Wolfgang Andreas *neurologist*
Mc Call, Julien Lachicotte *banker*
Mc Innes, Robert Malcolm *lawyer, business consultant*
†Murray, Robert Eugene *coal company executive*
†Roberts, Albert George *school administrator*

Perrysburg
Autry, Carolyn *artist, art history educator*
Barbe, Betty Catherine *financial analyst*
Danford, Ardath Anne *retired librarian*
Eastman, John Richard *retired manufacturing company executive*
Khan, Amir U. *agricultural engineering consultant*
Spitzer, John Brumback *lawyer*
Williamson, John Pritchard *utility executive*
Yager, John Warren *retired banker, lawyer*

Pickerington
Zacks, Gordon Benjamin *manufacturing company executive*

Piqua
Watercutter, Jacqueline A. *health facility administrator*

Port Clinton
Subler, Edward Pierre *advertising executive*

Portsmouth
Davis, Donald W. *government official*
Horr, William Henry *lawyer*
†Rau, William Arthur *health care company financial executive*

Powell
Adeli, Hojjat *engineer, educator, computer scientist*
Hanna, Jack Bushnell *zoo director*
Kriegel, David L. *retail executive*
Lombardi, Celeste *zoological park administrator*

Randolph
Pecano, Donald Carl *truck, trailer and railcar manufacturing executive*

Reynoldsburg
Goostree, Robert Edward *political science and law educator*
Lynch, Rose Peabody *art gallery executive*
Woodward, Greta Charmaine *construction company executive*

Richfield
Price, (William) Mark *professional basketball player*

Rocky River
Castele, Theodore John *radiologist*
De Long, Erika Venta *psychiatrist*

Rootstown
Blacklow, Robert Stanley *physician, medical college administrator*
Campbell, Colin *obstetrician, gynecologist, school dean*
Gilloteaux, Jacques Jean-Marie Anthime *cell biologist, researcher*
Hutterer, Ferenc *biochemistry educator, researcher*
Saltzman, Glenn Alan *behavioral sciences educator*
Sayre, Jean Williams *librarian, educator*

Saint Clairsville
Dankworth, Margaret Anne *management consultant*

Salem
Fehr, Kenneth Manbeck *computer systems company executive*

Sandusky
Fleming, Arlene E. *health facility administrator*
Round, Alice Faye Bruce *school psychologist*
Tone, Kenneth Edward *lawyer*

Seven Hills
Stanczak, Julian *artist, educator*

Shaker Heights
Adler, Naomi Samuel *real estate counselor*
Eakin, Thomas Capper *sports promotion executive*
Held, Lila M. *art appraiser*

Shelby
Moore Moif, Florian Howard *electronics engineer*

Sidney
Laurence, Michael Marshall *magazine publisher, writer*
Lawrence, Wayne Allen *publisher*
Stevens, Robert Jay *magazine editor*

Silver Lake
Chrobak, Dennis Steven *chemical engineer*

Solon
Richard, Edward H. *manufacturing company executive, former municipal government official*
Stauffer, Thomas George *hotel executive*

South Euclid
Loehr, Marla *college president*

Spring Valley
Singhvi, Surendra Singh *finance and strategy consultant*

Springboro
Saxer, Richard Karl *metallurgical engineer, retired air force officer*

Springfield
Browne, William Bitner *lawyer*
Cantrell, John L. *secondary education educator*
Dominick, Charles Alva *college official*
Kinnison, William Andrew *university president*
Maddex, Myron Brown (Mike Maddex) *broadcasting executive*
Maki, Jerrold Alan *medical center administrator*
Montag, John Joseph, II *librarian*
Pearson, Norman Ralston *librarian*
Reck, W(aldo) Emerson *retired university administrator, public relations consultant, writer*
Rush, Kenneth G. *lawyer*

Steubenville
Corr, Sister Mary Ann *school system administrator*
Kasprzak, Lucian Alexander *physics educator, researcher*
Scanlan, Michael *priest, academic administrator*

Streetsboro
Kearns, Warren Kenneth *business executive*
Weiss, Joseph Joel *consulting company executive*

Strongsville
†Koppenhafer, Merle Edward *marketing company executive*
Oltman, C. Dwight *conductor, educator*
Opplt, Jan Jiri *clinical pathologist, educator*

Sugar Grove
Bonner, Herbert Dwight *construction management educator*
Young, Nancy Henrietta Moe *elementary education educator*

Sylvania
Heuschele, Sharon Jo *university program director*
Kneller, William Arthur *geologist, educator*
Lock, Richard William *packaging company executive*
†O'Connell, John William *health care facility administrator*
Sampson, Earldine Robison *education educator*
Verhesen, Anna Maria Hubertina *counselor*

Tiffin
Baker, David B. *environmental scientist*
Cassell, William Comyn *college president*
Davison, Kenneth Edwin *American studies educator*
Kramer, Frank Raymond *classicist, educator*
Porter, Arthur Reno *economist, arbitrator*

Tipp City
Taylor, Robert Homer *quality assurance professional, pilot*

Toledo
Anderson, Dale Kenneth *retired lawyer*
Baker, Richard Southworth *lawyer*
Bardis, Panos Demetrios *sociologist, social philosopher, historian, author, editor, poet, educator*
Batt, Nick *property and investment executive*
†Beans, Elroy William *mechanical engineering educator, administrator*
Bergsmark, Edwin Martin *mortgage bank executive*
Bick, David Greer *health care marketing executive*
Billups, Norman Fredrick *college dean, pharmacist*
Binkley, Jonathan Andrew *secondary education/junior college educator*
Block, Allan James *communications executive*
Block, John Robinson *newspaper publisher*
Block, William K., Jr. *newspaper executive*
Boeschenstein, William Wade *glass products manufacturing executive*
Boesel, Milton Charles, Jr. *lawyer, business executive*
Boggs, Ralph Stuart *lawyer*
Boller, Ronald Cecil *glass company executive*
Brockmeyer, Ann Hartmann *financial planner*
Brown, Charles Earl *lawyer*
Carson, Samuel Goodman *retired banker, company director*
Chakraborty, Joana *physiology educator, research center administrator*
Christiansen, Eric George *marketing specialist*
Colasurd, Richard Michael *lawyer*
Craig, Harald Franklin *lawyer*
Dalrymple, Thomas Lawrence *lawyer*
Dana, Charles H. *manufacturing company executive*
Depew, Charles Gardner *research company executive*
DiDio, Liberato John Alphonse *anatomist, educator*
Farison, James Blair *electrical engineer, educator*
Finkbeiner, Carleton S. (Carty) *mayor*
†Finkbeiner, Carty *mayor*
Fisher, Donald Wiener *lawyer*
Fuhrman, Charles Andrew *country club proprietor, real estate management executive, lawyer*
Gearhart, Thomas Lee *newspaper editor*
†Harold, Robert Allen *engineer*
Hauenstein, Henry William *civil engineer*
Hawkins, Donald Merton *lawyer*
Heinrichs, Mary Ann *former dean*
Hiett, Edward Emerson *retired lawyer, glass company executive*
Hills, Arthur W. *architectural firm executive*
Hiner, Glen Harold, Jr. *materials company executive*
Hirsch, Carl Herbert *manufacturing company executive*
Hoffman, James R. *bishop*
Horton, Frank Elba *university official, geography educator*
Ingle, Kay Sue *elementary education educator*
James, Harold Arthur *lawyer*
James, William *bishop*
†Kneen, James Russell *health care administrator*
Krasniewski, Walter Jacob *federal judge*
Kunze, Ralph Carl *savings and loan executive*
Laimbeer, William *manufacturing company executive*
Lanigan, Robert J. *packaging company executive*
La Rue, Carl Forman *lawyer*
Leech, Charles Russell, Jr. *lawyer*
Lemieux, Joseph Henry *manufacturing company executive*
†Lipner, William E. *information systems executive*
Mac Guidwin, Mark J. *manufacturing executive*
†Margolies, Jay Owen *transportation company executive*
Martin, Robert Edward *architect*
Massey, Andrew John *conductor, composer*
Mayhew, Harry Eugene *physician, educator*
McCormick, Edward James, Jr. *lawyer*
McGlauchlin, Tom *artist*
Morcott, Southwood J. *automotive parts manufacturing company executive*
Mulrow, Patrick Joseph *medical educator*
Northup, John David *management consultant, inventor*
O'Connell, Maurice Daniel *lawyer*
O'Gara, Patrick Denis *editor*
Paquette, Jack Kenneth *management consultant, antiques and toy soldier*
Potter, John William *federal judge*
Proefrock, Carl Kenneth *academic medical administrator*
Quick, Albert Thomas *academic law administrator, educator*
Reimer, Borge R. *motor vehicle parts manufacturer*
Richards, Raymond Sears *scientist, company executive*
Rissing, Daniel Joseph *hospital administrator*
Robb, A. M. *glass manufacturing executive*
Romanoff, Milford Martin *building contractor*
Rosenbaum, Kenneth E. *journalist, editor*
Royhab, Ronald *journalist, newspaper editor*
Rubin, Allan Maier *physician, surgeon*
Saffran, Murray *biochemist*
Saunders, Donald Herbert *utility company executive*
Saxby, Lewis Weyburn, Jr. *glass fiber manufacturing company executive*
Shelley, Walter Brown *physician, educator*
Showalter, Robert Earl *banker*
Shultz, Edward Joseph *holdings company executive*
Smart, Paul M. *utility company executive, lawyer*
Smith, Robert Freeman *history educator*
Smith, Robert Nelson *former government official, anesthesiologist*
Solari, Larry Thomas *manufacturing company executive*
Speer, Richard Lyle *federal judge*
Standaert, Frank George *medical research administrator, physician*
Stankey, Suzanne M. *editor*
Stark, Charles H., III *architectural firm executive*
Steadman, David Wilton *museum official*
Stewart, Mark Carroll *lawyer*
Strobel, Martin Jack *motor vehicle and industrial component manufacturing and distribution company executive*
Thompson, Gerald E. *historian, educator*
Tuschman, James Marshall *lawyer*
Walinski, Nicholas Joseph *federal judge*
Weber, Max O. *retired glass fiber products manufacturing company executive*
Willey, John Douglas *retired newspaper executive*
Wittmann, Otto *art museum executive*
Young, Don J. *federal judge*
Zrull, Joel Peter *psychiatry educator*
†0ichards, Raymond Sears *scientist, company executive*

Troy
Davies, Alfred Robert *physician, educator*
Deering, Joseph William *manufacturing executive*

Twinsburg
Hoven, D. Dwayne *retail executive*
Raven, Gregory Kurt *retail executive*
Solganik, Marvin *real estate executive*
†Staph, Jack A. *corporate lawyer*

University Heights
Bloch, Andrea Lynn *physical therapist*
Kelly, Joseph Francis *theology educator*

Upper Arlington
Mincy, Homer F. *school system administrator*

Valley View
Van Kirk, Robert John *nursing case manager, educator*

Van Wert
Duprey, Wilson Gilliland *retired librarian*
Liljegren, Frank Sigfrid *artist, art association official*

Vandalia
Farley, Paul Emerson *manufacturing company executive*
Smith, Marjorie Aileen Matthews *museum director*
Subotnick, Stuart *food service executive*

Vermilion
Vance, Elbridge Putnam *mathematics educator*

Walbridge
†Rudolph, Frederick William *contractor*

Wapakoneta
Brading, Charles Richard *state representative*

Warren
Alli, Richard James, Sr. *electronics executive, service executive*
†Caiazza, Donald J. *manufacturing executive heavy*
Florence, Jerry DeWayne *sales and marketing executive*
Johns, Charles Alexander *hospital administrator*
Kandrac, Jo Ann Marie *school administrator*
Nader, Robert Alexander *judge, lawyer*
Rennert, Ira Leon *heavy manufacturing executive*
Rossi, Anthony Gerald *lawyer*

Washington Court House
Fultz, Clair Ervin *former banker*
Rivers, Ronald D. *manufacturing executive*

Waterford
Montgomery, Gretchen Golzé *secondary education educator*
Riley, Nancy Mae *retired vocational home economics educator*

Waterville
Copeland, Terrilyn Denise *speech pathologist*

Wauseon
McNulty, Roberta Jo *educational administrator*

Waverly
Squire, Russel Nelson *musician, retired educator*

West Chester
Capps, Dennis William *secondary school educator*
Ofte, Donald *environmental executive, former management consultant*
Rishel, James Burton *manufacturing executive*

West Milton
†Peters, Stephen Paul *pastor*

Westerville
Booher, Charles Forest *business executive*
Conley, Sarah Ann *health facility administrator*
Dadmehr, Nahid *neurologist*
Davis, Joseph Lloyd *state council educational administrator, consultant*
DeVore, Carl Brent *college president, educator*
Kollat, David Truman *management consultant*
Paulson, Kenneth Michael *quality control executive*
Smith, C. Kenneth *corporate executive*
VanSant, Joanne Frances *academic administrator*
Willke, Thomas Aloys *university official, statistics educator*

Westfield Center
†Bosshard, Otto *insurance executive*

Westlake
Bisson, Edmond Emile *mechanical engineer*
Huff, Ronald Garland *mechanical engineer*
Myers, Ira Thomas *physicist*

Whitehouse
†Howard, John Malone *surgeon, thoracic surgeon, educator*

Wickliffe
Bardasz, Ewa Alice *chemical engineer*
Bares, William G. *chemical company executive*
Coleman, Lester Earl *chemical company executive*
Dunn, Horton, Jr. *organic chemist*
Hanzak, Janice Chrisman *accountant*
Hsu, Roger Y. K. *lawyer*
Kidder, Fred Dockstater *lawyer*
Pevec, Anthony Edward *bishop*
Rosica, Gabriel Adam *corporate executive, engineer*
Stroesenreuther, George Dale *financial executive*

Wilberforce
Gupta, Vijay Kumar *chemistry educator*

Willoughby
Abelt, Ralph William *bank executive*
Campbell, Talmage Alexander *newspaper editor*
Chiarucci, Vincent A. *diversified manufacturing company executive*
Figgie, Harry E., Jr. *corporate executive*
Grossman, Mary Margaret *elementary education educator*
Harthun, Luther Arthur *lawyer*
Kerkel, Lynn *middle school educator*
Lillich, Alice Louise *retired secondary education educator*
Manning, William Dudley, Jr. *retired specialty chemical company executive*
Pazirandeh, Mahmood *rheumatologist, consultant*

Wooster
August, Robert Olin *journalist*
Colclaser, H. Alberta *lawyer, retired government official*
Ferree, David Curtis *horticultural researcher*
Gates, Richard Daniel *manufacturing company executive*
Geho, Walter Blair *biomedical research executive*
Hickey, Damon D. *library director*
Lafever, Howard Nelson *plant breeder, geneticist, educator*
Loess, Henry Bernard *psychology educator*
Morgan, James A. *rubber products company executive*
Schmitt, Wolfgang Rudolph *consumer products executive*
Stuart, James Fortier *musician, artistic director*
Weidensaul, Thomas Craig *university administrator, researcher*
Williams, Walter W. *consumer products manufacturing executive*
Woods, Susanne *college president*

Worthington
Bernhagen, Lillian Flickinger *school health consultant*
Compton, Ralph Theodore, Jr. *electrical engineering educator*
Curtis, Nevius Minot *utility executive, retired*
Davis, Samuel Bernhard *manufacturing executive*
†Horn, Raymond Albert *school system administrator*
Idol, James Daniel, Jr. *chemist, educator, inventor, consultant*
Winter, Chester Caldwell *physician, surgery educator*

Xenia
Bigelow, Daniel James *aerospace executive*
Nutter, Zoe Dell Lantis *public relations executive, retired*

Yellow Springs
Fogarty, Robert Stephen *historian, educator, editor*
Graham, Jewel Freeman *social worker, lawyer, educator*
Guskin, Alan E. *university president*
Hamilton, Virginia (Mrs. Arnold Adoff) *author*
Lacey, Beatrice Cates *psychophysiologist*
Lacey, John Irving *psychologist, physiologist, educator*
Trolander, Hardy Wilcox *engineering executive, consultant*

Youngstown
†Allen, AndrewWuichet *hospital administrator*
Bell, Carol Willsey *genealogist*
Bowers, Bege K. *English educator*
Brothers, Barbara *English language educator*
Buchanan, C. Robert *architectural firm executive*
Butterworth, Jane Rogers Fitch *physician*
Catoline, Pauline Dessie *small business owner*
Cochran, Leslie Herschel *university administrator*
Courtney, William Francis *food and vending service company executive*
Cushwa, William Wallace *machinery parts company executive*
DeBartolo, Edward John, Jr. *professional football team owner, real estate developer*
Fok, Thomas Dso Yun *civil engineer*
Gaylord, Sanford Fred *physician*
Gillis, Bernard Thomas *chemistry educator*
Major, Richard Demarest *manufacturing company executive*
Marks, Esther L. *metals company executive*
Mastriana, Robert Alan *architect*
Mumaw, James Webster *lawyer*
Nadler, Myron Jay *lawyer*
Nunziato, Carl Anthony *lawyer, banker*
Powers, Paul J. *manufacturing company executive*
Przelomski, Anastasia Nemenyi *retired newspaper editor*
Roth, Daniel Benjamin *lawyer, business executive*
Schwartz, David *retail executive*
Sokolov, Richard Saul *lawyer*
Spector, Earl M. *lawyer, retail executive*
Stevens, Paul Edward *lawyer*
Trucksis, Theresa A. *library director*
Tucker, Don Eugene *retired lawyer*
Walton, Ralph Gerald *psychiatrist, educator*
Winkelstern, Philip Norman *financial executive*
Wolfcale, Arthur Dale *lawyer*
Wolsonovich, Nicholas *school system administrator*

Zanesville
†Barone, Thomas Anthony *hospital administration executive*
Duhs, William Andrew *banker*
Durant, Charles Edward, Jr. *medical facility administrator*
Mattingly, Robert Kerker *entrepreneur*
Micheli, Frank James *lawyer*
Ray, John Walker *otolaryngologist, educator, broadcast commentator*
Truby, John Louis *corporate executive*

OKLAHOMA

Ada
Anoatubby, Bill *governor*
Stafford, Donald Gene *chemistry educator*
Walker, Billy Kenneth *computer science educator, academic administrator*

Afton
Starbird, Lonnie Darryl *producer of custom car shows, designer and builder of custom automobiles*

Altus
Hensley, Stephen Ray *academic administrator*

Anadarko
Ellison, Rosemary *curator*
Pain, Charles Leslie *lawyer*

Antlers
Stamper, Joe Allen *lawyer*

Ardmore
Hentschel, David A. *oil company executive*
Thompson, John E. *principal*

Bartlesville
Allen, W. Wayne *oil industry executive*
Armstrong, Oliver Wendell *retired oil company executive*
Bowerman, Charles Leo *oil company executive*
Clay, Harris Aubrey *chemical engineer*
Cox, Glenn Andrew, Jr. *petroleum company executive*
Doty, Donald D. *retired banker*
Dunlap, James Robert *contractor, state legislator*
Dwiggins, Claudius William, Jr. *chemist*
Gao, Hong Wen *chemical engineer*
Hogan, J(ohn) Paul *chemistry researcher, consultant*
Johnson, Marvin Merrill *chemical engineer, chemist*
Kaiser, Jean Morgan *real estate broker*
†McGinnis, James Wesley *Petroleum company executive*
†Mulva, James Joseph *oil company executive*
Owen, Raymond Harold *minister*
Paul, William George *lawyer*
Silas, Cecil Jesse *retired petroleum company executive*
Smalley, Kenneth Lee *oil company executive*
Woodruff, William Jennings *theology educator*

Bethany
Arnold, Donald Smith *chemical engineer, consultant*
Davis, Harrison Ransom Samuel, Jr. *English language educator*
Leggett, James Daniel *church administrator*
Leupp, Edythe Peterson *retired educator, administrator*
Mercer, Ronald L. *retired manufacturing executive*
Moore, Ronald Quentin *minister*
Shelton, Muriel Moore *religious education administrator*

Bixby
Makhani, Madan Pal Singh *foundry executive*

Broken Arrow
Chambers, Richard Lee *geoscientist, researcher*
Elad, Emanuel *industrial instrumentation executive*
Janning, Sister Mary Bernadette *nun, retired association executive*
Kimbrough, James Douglas *banker*
Striegel, Peggy Simsarian *advertising executive*

Caddo
Perkins, Kent *television and movie producer*

Chandler
Mather, Stephanie J. *lawyer*

Chickasha
Beets, Freeman Haley *retired government official*
Feaver, John Clayton *philosopher, educator*
Good, Leonard Phelps *artist*

Clinton
Askew, Penny Sue *choreographer, artistic director, ballet instructor*

Collinsville
Flanagan, William Stanley, Jr. *banker, lawyer*

Duncan
Surjaatmadja, Jim Basuki *research engineer*

Durant
Garrett, Scott *vocational school administrator*
Mickle, Billy Arthur *state legislator, lawyer*
Smith, Samuel Joseph *soil scientist*
Williams, Larry Bill *university president*

Earlsboro
Duncan, Glenda Julaine *elementary education educator*

Edmond
Ashford, George Allen *investment advisor*
Brown, William Ernest *dentist*
Caire, William *biologist, educator, assistant dean*
Griggy, Kenneth Joseph *food company executive*
Loman, Mary LaVerne *retired mathematics educator*
Nelson, John Woolard *neurology educator, physician*
Nigh, George *university administrator, former governor*
Payne, William Howard *lawyer*
Raburn, Randall K. *school system administrator*
Shadid, Randel Coy *lawyer*
Zabel, Vivian Ellouise *secondary education educator*

El Reno
†Phillips, William A. *research animal scientist*

Elk City
Francis, Talton Loe *hospital administrator*

Enid
†Allen, William Richard, Jr. *finance company executive*
Jones, Stephen *lawyer*
Musser, William Wesley, Jr. *lawyer*
Taylor, Donna Lynne *adult education coordinator*
Tozzi, Richard Raymond *oil and gas company executive*
Ward, Llewellyn O(rcutt), III *oil company executive*

Fort Sill
†Dubia, John Austin *army officer*

Goodwell
Smith, Kim Lee *educator*

Guymon
Wood, Donald Euriah *lawyer*

Jenks
Wootan, Gerald Don *osteopathic physician, educator*

Kingfisher
Baker, Thomas Edward *lawyer, accountant*

Lawton
Brooks, (Leslie) Gene *cultural association administrator*
Clayton, Lawrence Otto *marriage and family therapist*
Coffey, Wallace Edward *chairman Comanche Indian tribe*
Cooke, Wanda (Cookie Cooke) *hearing aid specialist*
Davis, Don Clarence *university president*
Hooper, Roy B. *hospital administrator, insurance broker*
Moore, Roy Dean *judge*
Nalley, Elizabeth Ann *chemistry educator*
Neptune, Richard Allan (Dick Neptune) *superintendent of schools*
Reno, Jennifer *principal*
Smiley, Frederick Melvin *education educator, consultant*
Young, J. A. *bishop*

Mangum
Ford, Linda Lou *dietitian*

Mcalester
Cornish, Richard Pool *lawyer*
Reed, Walter George, Jr. *osteopath*
Smith, Dorothy Jean *principal*

Miami
Dines, James Melvin *manufacturing company executive*
Lovell, James Frederick *academic administrator*

Midwest City
Bogardus, Carl Robert, Jr. *radiologist, educator*
Folks, John M. *school system administrator*
Smith, Wayne Calvin *chemical engineer*

Moore
Harrington, Gary Burnes *retired controller*
Moore, Dalton, Jr. *petroleum engineer, scientist, geologist*

Muskogee
Kendrick, Thomas Rudolph *chemist*
Kent, Bartis Milton *physician*
Ruby, Russell (Glenn) *lawyer*
Seay, Frank Howell *federal judge*

Norman
Affleck, Marilyn *sociology educator*
Albert, Lois Eldora Wilson *archaeologist*
Atkinson, Gordon *chemistry educator*
Bauer, George W. *publishing company executive*
Bell, Robert Eugene *anthropologist educator*
Bert, Charles Wesley *mechanical and aerospace engineer, educator*
Boke, Norman Hill *botanist*
Boren, David Lyle *academic administrator*
Branch, David Reed *astrophysicist, educator*
Brown, Elvin J. *lawyer*
Brown, Sidney DeVere *history educator*
Bryant, Celia Mae Small *music educator*
Campbell, John Morgan *retired chemical engineer*
Carey, Thomas Devore *baritone, educator*
Carpenter, Charles Congden *zoologist, educator*
Carver, Charles Ray *retired information systems company executive*
Cella, Francis Raymond *economist, research consultant*
†Christian, Sherril Duane *chemistry educator*
Ciereszko, Leon Stanley *chemistry educator*
Corr, Edwin Gharst *ambassador*
Cosier, Richard A. *business educator, consultant*
Crane, Robert Kendall *engineering educator, researcher, consultant*
Cross, George Lynn *foundation administrator, former university president*
Dary, David Archie *journalism educator, author*
Dauffenbach, Robert C. *economic and management administrator, educator*
de Stwolinski, Gail Rounce Boyd *music theory and composition educator*
Dille, John Robert *physician*
Donahue, Hayden Hackney *mental health institute administrator, medical educator, psychiatric consultant*
Donahue, Patricia Toothaker *retired social worker, administrator*
Doviak, Richard James *atmospheric scientist, engineer*
Dryhurst, Glenn *chemistry educator*
Eek, Nathaniel Sisson *retired fine arts educator*
Egle, Davis Max *mechanical engineering educator*
Elkouri, Frank *legal educator*
Estes, James Russell *botanist*
Fairbanks, Robert Alvin *lawyer*
Fears, Jesse Rufus *academic dean*
Fuerbringer, Alfred Ottomar *clergyman*
Gal-Chen, Tzvi *geophysicist, meteorologist, educator*
Glad, Paul Wilbur *history educator*
Hagan, William Thomas *history educator*
Hamilton, Donna Martha *secondary education educator*
Hemingway, Richard William *lawyer, educator*
Henderson, Arnold Glenn *architect, educator*
Henderson, George *educational sociologist, educator*
Hinshaw, Lerner Brady *physiology educator*
Hodgell, Murlin Ray *university dean*
Hodges, Thompson Gene *librarian*
Hollon, William Eugene *historian, educator, author*
Huntington, Penelope Ann *educator*
Hutchison, Victor Hobbs *biologist, educator*
Kadir, Djelal *literature educator, writer, translator, editor*
Kemp, Betty Ruth *librarian*
Kessler, Edwin *meteorology educator, consultant*
Kondonassis, Alexander John *economist, educator*
Lamb, Peter James *meteorology educator, researcher, consultant*
Lee, Sul Hi *library administrator*
Leonhardt, Thomas Wilburn *librarian, technical services director*
Lis, Anthony Stanley *business administration educator*
Lowitt, Richard *history educator*
Maddox, Robert Alan *atmospheric scientist*
Mankin, Charles John *geology educator*
Mares, Michael Allen *ecologist, educator*
O'Rear, Edgar Allen, III *chemical engineering educator*
Owens, Rochelle *poet, playwright*
Pain, Betsy M. *lawyer*
Petersen, Catherine Holland *lawyer*
Ross, Allan Anderson *music educator, university official*
Schindler, Barbara Francois *school administrator*
Schnell, Gary Dean *zoology educator, administrator*
Sharp, Paul Frederick *former university president, educational consultant*
Sherman, Mary Angus *public library administrator*
†Singleton, Alma Nickell *law librarian*
Toperzer, Thomas Raymond *art museum director*
Trimble, Preston Albert *retired judge*
Van Auken, Robert Danforth *business administration educator, management consultant*
Van Horn, Richard Linley *university administrator*
Weber, Jerome Charles *education and human relations educator, former academic dean and provost*
Williams, David Samuel *insurance company executive*
Zelby, Leon Wolf *electrical engineering educator, consulting engineer*

Nowata
Osborn, Ann George *retired chemist*

Oklahoma City
Ackerman, Raymond Basil *advertising agency executive*
Alaupovic, Alexandra Vrbanic *artist, educator*
Alexander, Patrick Byron *zoological society executive*
Allen, Robert Dee *lawyer*
Alley, Wayne Edward *federal judge, retired army officer*
Anderson, Kenneth Edwin *writer, educator*
Andrews, Robert Frederick *religious organization administrator, retired bishop*
Angel, Arthur Ronald *lawyer, consultant*
Anthony, Robert Holland *state official*
Austin, Gerald Grant *wholesale food distribution company executive*
Ball, Leonard F. *lawyer, architectural firm executive*
Ball, Rex Martin *urban designer*
Barclay, Carl Archie *retired physician*
Beltran, Eusebius Joseph *archbishop*
Beutler, Randy Leon *rancher, state legislator*
Bishop, William T. *food company executive*
Blackwell, John Adrian, Jr. *computer company executive*
Bohanon, Luther L. *federal judge*
Bohanon, Richard Lee *federal judge*
Booth, Glenna Greene *genealogical researcher*
Boston, Billie *costume designer*
Boston, William Clayton *lawyer*
Boyd, Laura Wooldridge *state legislator*
Brady-Black, Wandalene *secondary school educator*
Branch, John Curtis *biology educator, lawyer*
Brandt, Edward Newman, Jr. *physician, educator*
Brawner, Lee Basil *librarian*
Bresler, Mark Irwin *rehabilitation engineer*
Brett, Thomas Marshall *judge*
Brown, Kenneth Ray *banker*
Browne, John Robinson *banker*
Buchanan, Robert Taylor *plastic surgeon*
Byers, Stansell Crawford *state agency administrator*
Caldwell, Warren A. (Tony Caldwell) *former state legislator, real estate management company executive*
Callahan, Carol B. *nursing administrator*
Cameron, Charles Metz, Jr. *physician, medical educator*
Campbell, David Gwynne *petroleum executive, geologist*
Cantrell, Charles Leonard *lawyer, educator*
Carter, L. Philip *neurosurgeon, consultant*
Cauthron, Robin J. *federal judge*
Champlin, Richard H. *lawyer, insurance company executive*
Clark, Kathryn Louise Hughes *hospital administrator*
Coats, Andrew Montgomery *lawyer, former mayor*
†Cole, Tom *state official*
Collins, William Edward *aeromedical administrator, researcher*
Comchoc, Rudolph A. *food distribution company executive*
Comp, Philip Cinnamon *medical researcher*
Couch, James Russell, Jr. *neurology educator*
Court, Leonard *lawyer*
Cunningham, Stanley Lloyd *lawyer*
Danforth, Louis Fremont *banker, educator*
Daugherty, Frederick Alvin *federal judge*
Davis, Emery Stephen *wholesale food company executive*
Deckert, Gordon Harmon *psychiatrist, educator*
†Devening, Robert Randolph *pharmaceutical company executive*
Dew, Jess Edward *chemical engineer*
Dunlap, E.T. *retired educational administrator, consultant*

Dunn, Parker Southerland *retired chemical company consultant*
Durland, Jack Raymond *lawyer*
†Edmondson, Drew *attorney general*
Emerson, Marvin Chester *legal association administrator*
England, Gary Alan *television meteorologist*
Epperson, Kraettli Quynton *lawyer, educator*
Everett, Mark Allen *dermatologist, educator*
Fair, Michael Edward *state senator*
Fallin, Mary Copeland *state official*
Fellers, James Davison *lawyer*
Felton, Warren Locker, II *surgeon*
Fishburne, John Ingram, Jr. *obstetrician-gynecologist, educator*
Ford, Charles Reed *state senator*
Ford, Michael Raye *lawyer*
Forni, Patricia Rose *nursing educator, university dean*
†Funk, Robert Allen *personnel executive*
Garrett, Sandy Langley *school system administrator*
Gaylord, Edward Lewis *publishing company executive*
Gourley, James Leland *editor, publishing executive*
Grounds, Frances Ann *cosmetics sales professional, photographer, journalist*
Gumerson, Jean Gilderhus *health foundation executive*
Hail, John Wesley *marketing professional*
Halverstadt, Donald Bruce *urologist, educator*
Hambrick, Marvin K. *energy company executive*
Hamilton, Arnold Burt *journalist, educator*
Hammons, Royce Mitchell *bank executive*
Hargrave, Rudolph *state supreme court justice*
Harlan, Ross Edgar *retired utility company executive, writer, lecturer, consultant*
Harlow, James Gindling, Jr. *utility executive*
Hartsuck, Jean Ann *chemist*
Haywood, B(etty) J(ean) *anesthesiologist*
Hemry, Jerome Eldon *lawyer*
Hendrick, Howard H. *lawyer, state senator*
Henley, Everett Scott *health care marketing firm executive*
Henry, Brad *state legislator, lawyer*
†Henry, Robert H. *federal judge, former attorney general*
Hiner, Gladys Webber *psychologist*
Hodges, Ralph B. *state supreme court justice*
Holder, Lee *educator and university dean emeritus*
Holloway, William Judson, Jr. *federal judge*
Hopkins, Robert E. *association executive, real estate and insurance broker*
Horner, Russell Grant, Jr. *diversified company executive*
†Hunter, Steven L. *medical center administrator*
Ille, Bernard Glenn *insurance company executive*
Irwin, Pat *federal magistrate judge*
Jackson, Gaines Bradford *environmental science educator*
Johnson, James Terence *college chancellor*
Jones, Robert Lee *religion educator*
Keating, Francis Anthony, II *governor, lawyer*
Keim, Robert John *otolaryngologist, educator*
Kelley, Carl Ed(win) *editor*
Kennedy, John H., Jr. *former state official*
Kent, Sherman Tecumseh *museum administrator, educator*
Kertok, Michael Bowers *architect, interior designer*
Kilbourne, Lewis Buckner *food service company executive*
Kimerer, Neil Banard, Sr. *psychiatrist, educator*
Kirkpatrick, John Elson *oil company executive, retired naval reserve officer*
Lambird, Mona Salyer *lawyer*
Lavender, Robert Eugene *state supreme court justice*
Leavitt, Joan Kazanjian *state health official, physician*
Legg, William Jefferson *lawyer*
Leonard, Sister Anne C. *superintendent, education director*
Leonard, Timothy Dwight *federal judge*
Lester, Andrew William *lawyer*
Lewis, C. A. *church administrator*
Lewis, Wilbur Curtis *surgeon*
Lhevine, Dave Bernard *radiologist, educator*
Locke, William Sweet *manufacturing executive*
Long, E(velyn) Claudine *finance planning executive, educator*
†Lopez, Francisco, IV *health care administrator*
Loving, Susan B. *lawyer, former state official*
Lynn, C(harles) Stephen *franchising company executive*
Lynn, Thomas Neil, Jr. *medical center administrator, physician*
Macer, Dan Johnstone *retired hospital administrator*
Magarian, Robert Armen *medicinal chemist, researcher, educator*
Massion, Walter Herbert *anesthesiologist, educator*
Maton, Anthea *education consultant*
McCoy, Wesley Lawrence *musician, conductor, educator*
McKenny, Jere Wesley *energy firm executive*
Mc Pherson, Frank Alfred *manufacturing corporate executive*
Mee, Herb, Jr. *natural resource/environmental services executive*
Meeks, Patricia Lowe *secondary school educator*
Meyers, Theodore A. *food products executive*
Mikkelson, Dean Harold *geological engineer*
Mildren, Jack *lieutenant governor*
Milsten, Robert B. *lawyer*
Mock, Randall Don *lawyer*
Moler, Edward Harold *lawyer*
Moll, John Edgar *wholesale grocery company executive*
Moody, Robert M. *bishop*
Moore, Joanne Iweita *pharmacologist, educator*
Murphy, Juneann Wadsworth *microbiologist, educator*
Necco, Alexander David *lawyer, educator*
Nesbitt, Charles Rudolph *lawyer, energy consultant*
Nichols, J. Larry *energy company executive, lawyer*
Noakes, Betty L. *elementary school educator*
Nokes, Mary Triplett *educator, counselor, artist*
Norick, Ronald J. *mayor of Oklahoma City*
Oehlert, William Herbert, Jr. *cardiologist, administrator, educator*
O'Keeffe, Hugh Williams *oil industry executive*
Opala, Marian P(eter) *state supreme court justice*
Painton, Ira Wayne *retired securities executive*
Parks, Ed H. *judge*
Payne, Gareld Gene *vocal music educator, medical transcriptionist*
Peace, H. W., II *oil company executive*
Pishkin, Vladimir *psychologist, educator*
Pitts, Bill *museum director*
Ponder, Alonza *church administrator*
Pope, Tim L. *state legislator, consultant*
†Porter, Don E. *sports adiministrator*
Price, B. Byron *museum director*
Rainbolt, David Eugene *banker*
Rayan, Ghazi M. *surgeon*
Raydon, Max E. *consumer products company executive*
Reynolds, Norman Eben *lawyer*
Richards, David John *food distribution company executive*
†Roach, Wayne E. *retail automotive executive*
†Roberts, Kathleen Mary *school system administrator*
Robinson, Malcolm *gastroenterologist*
Ross, William Jarboe *lawyer*
Rossavik, Ivar Kristian *obstetrician/gynecologist*
Ruhrup, Clifton Brown *sales executive*
Russell, David L. *federal judge*
Russell, Harold LeRoy *accountant*
Ryan, Patrick J. *electric utility company executive*
Schmidt, Fred C. *architect*
†Scott, Jimmie Dow *health facility administrator*
Scott, Lawrence Vernon *microbiology educator*
Scott, Willard Philip *lawyer, corporate executive*
Scribner, Ronald Kent *microbiologist*
Seideman, Ruth Evelyn Young *nurse educator*
Shorney, Margo Kay *art gallery owner*
Simmons, Jesse Doyle *minister, educator*
Smith, Clodus Ray *academic administrator*
Smith, Robert Walter *food company executive*
Smoak, David S. *food company executive*
Snider, John Joseph *lawyer*
Solomon, Dan Eugene *bishop*
Sookne, Herman Solomon (Hank Sookne) *retirement center senior executive*
Spencer, Melvin Joe *hospital administrator, lawyer*
†Stacy, Alan *gas industry executive*
†Stauth, Robert E. *food service executive*
Steinhorn, Irwin Harry *lawyer, educator, corporate executive*
†Stringer, L. E. Dean *lawyer*
Summers, Hardy *state supreme court justice*
Taylor, Stratton *state senator, lawyer*
Thompson, Guy Thomas *safety engineer*
Thompson, Ralph Gordon *federal judge*
Thurman, William Gentry *medical research foundation executive, pediatric hematology and oncology physician, educator*
Tolbert, James R., III *financial executive*
Triplett, E. Eugene *editor*
Troelstra, Arne *physics educator*
Turpen, Michael Craig *lawyer*
Underwood, Bernard Edward *religious organization administrator*
Valentine, Alan Darrell *symphony orchestra executive*
Van Rysselberge, Charles H. *organization administrator*
Verity, George Luther *lawyer*
†Walker, Bailus, Jr. *environmental scientist, dean, health facility administrator*
Walker, Clarence Eugene *psychology educator*
Walker, Jerald Carter *university administrator, minister*
Walsh, Lawrence Edward *lawyer*
Weedn, Trish *state legislator*
Weigel, Paul Henry *biochemistry educator, researcher, consultant*
Werries, E. Dean *food distribution company executive*
West, Lee Roy *federal judge*
Wheat, Willis James *university dean, management educator*
Wickens, Donald Lee *engineer executive, consultant, rancher*
Williams, George Rainey *surgeon, educator*
Williams, Richard Donald *retired wholesale food company executive*
Williams, William Ralston *retired bank and trust company executive*
Wilson, Alma *state supreme court justice*
Winn, Harry L., Jr. *food products financial executive*
Woodruff, Judson Sage *lawyer*
Woods, Pendleton *college official, author*
Worsham, Bertrand Ray *psychiatrist*
Zimmerman, Jack Wallace *newspaper editor*
Zuhdi, Nazih *surgeon*

Oktaha
Taylor, Clayton Charles *management and political legislative consultant*

Pauls Valley
Hope, Garland Howard *lawyer, retired judge*

Pawhuska
Dickerson, William Joseph *bank executive*
Strahm, Samuel Edward *veterinarian*

Perry
Beers, Frederick Gordon *writer, retired corporate communications official*

Ponca City
Bolene, Margaret Rosalie Steele *bacteriologist, civic worker*
Leonard, Samuel Wallace *oil company executive*
Northcutt, Clarence Dewey *lawyer*
Scott, Carol Lee *child care educator*

Poteau
Harper, S. Birnie *bakery executive*

Pryor
Burdick, Larry G. *school system administrator*

Purcell
Lucas, Roy Edward, Jr. *minister*

Sand Springs
Ackerman, Robert Wallace *steel company executive*

Sapulpa
Barnes, Paulette Whetstone *school system administrator*
Fletcher, Shirley Faye *counselor*
Geeslin, Robert Hawk *educational programming company executive*

Shawnee
Agee, Bob R. *university president, educator, minister*
McCaffree, Brother Benedict Bradford *historian*

Stillwater
Agnew, Theodore Lee, Jr. *historian, educator*
Ausburn, Lynna Joyce *curriculum developer, technical education specialist, consultant*
Bantle, John Albert, II *zoology educator*
†Barfield, Billy Joe *agricultural engineer, educator*
Bell, Kenneth John *chemical engineer*
Berlin, Kenneth Darrell *chemistry educator, consultant, researcher*
Boger, Lawrence Leroy *university president emeritus*
Browning, Charles Benton *university dean, agricultural educator*
Brusewitz, Gerald Henry *agricultural engineering educator, researcher*
Bynum, Jack Edward, Jr. *sociology educator*
Campbell, John Roy *animal scientist educator, academic administrator*
Case, Kenneth Eugene *industrial engineering educator*
Confer, Anthony Wayne *veterinary pathologist, educator*
Cooper, Donald Lee *physician*
Durham, Norman Nevill *microbiologist, scientist, educator*
Ewing, Sidney Alton *veterinary medical educator, parasitologist*
Fischer, LeRoy Henry *historian, educator*
Folks, J. Leroy *statistician, educator*
Gorin, George *retired chemistry educator*
Grischkowsky, Daniel Richard *research scientist, educator*
Halligan, James Edmund *university administrator, chemical engineer*
Hooper, Billy Ernest *medical association administrator*
Jadlow, Joseph Martin *economics educator*
Johnson, Edward Roy *library director*
Kamm, Robert B. *former academic administrator, educator, author, diplomat*
Langwig, John Edward *retired wood science educator*
Lawson, F. D. *bishop*
Leach, Franklin Rollin *biochemistry educator*
Lu, Huizhu *computer scientist, educator*
Luebke, Neil Robert *philosophy educator*
Maddox, Robert Nott *chemical engineer, educator*
Martin, Joel Jerome *physics educator*
Matoy, Elizabeth Anne *personnel executive*
Mc Collom, Kenneth Allen *retired university dean*
Mc Farland, Frank Eugene *university official*
Mize, Joe Henry *industrial engineer, educator*
Moomaw, Ronald Lee *economics educator*
Noyes, Ronald Tacie *agricultural engineering educator*
Owens, Fredric Newell *animal nutritionist, educator*
Ownby, Charlotte Ledbetter *anatomy educator*
Parcher, James Vernon *civil engineering educator, consultant*
Poole, Richard William *economics educator*
Quinn, Art Jay *veterinarian*
Sandmeyer, Robert Lee *university dean, economist*
Shearer, John Clyde *economics consultant, labor arbitrator, international manpower consultant*
Shirley, Glenn Dean *writer*
†Stone, John Floyd *soil physics researcher and educator*
Thompson, David Russell *agricultural engineering educator, academic dean*
Turner, Wayne Connelly *industrial engineer, educator*

Tahlequah
Mankiller, Wilma Pearl *tribal leader*
†Ross, John *cultural organization administrator*

Tinker AFB
Pray, Donald George *aerospace engineer*

Tulsa
Abbott, William Thomas *claim specialist*
Ahmadieh, Aziz *metallurgy materials science educator*
Alexander, John Robert *hospital administrator, internist*
Anderson, Peer LaFollette *petroleum corporation executive*
Arrington, John Leslie, Jr. *lawyer*
†Bailey, Keith E. *petroleum pipeline company executive*
Banker, Barbara L. *lawyer*
Barnes, James E. *energy company executive*
Beasley, William Rex *judge*
Beck, Robert James *energy economist, journal editor, consultant*
Belsky, Martin Henry *law educator, lawyer*
Berlin, Steven Ritt *oil company financial official*
Biolchini, Robert Fredrick *lawyer*
Blackstock, LeRoy *lawyer*
Bowen, William Augustus *financial consultant*
Braumiller, Allen Spooner *oil and gas exploration company executive, geologist*
Breck, Howard Rolland *geophysicist*
Brett, Thomas Rutherford *federal judge*
Brolick, Henry John *energy company executive*
Bryant, Hubert Hale *lawyer*
Buckley, Thomas Hugh *historian, educator*
Bump, Larry J. *international engineering and construction company executive*
Bynum, George T., III (Ted Bynum) *biomedical company executive*
Calvert, Delbert William *chemical company executive*
Calvert, Jon Channing *family practice physician*
†Cappy, Joseph E. *automobile company executive*
Cardwell, Sandra Gayle Bavido *real estate broker*
Cole, Clyde Curtis, Jr. *association executive*
Collins, John Roger *aerospace manufacturing company executive*
Cook, Harold Dale *federal judge*
Cooke, Marvin Lee *religious organization administrator, consultant, minister*
Cooper, Richard Casey *lawyer*
Cox, William Jackson *bishop*
Crawford, B(urnett) Hayden *lawyer*
Culp, Even Asher *communications educator*
Daniel, Samuel Phillips *lawyer*
Dickerson, Frank Secor, III *energy company executive*
Dix, Fred Andrew, Jr. *professional society executive*
Donaldson, Robert Herschel *university president*
Dotson, George Stephen *drilling company executive*
Doverspike, Terry Richard *lawyer*
Earlougher, Robert Charles, Sr. *petroleum engineer*
Eaton, Leonard James, Jr. *banker*
Elkins, Lloyd Edwin, Sr. *petroleum engineer, energy consultant*
Eriksen, Vernon Lee *manufacturing engineering executive*
Farrell, John L., Jr. *lawyer, business executive*
Fate, Martin Eugene, Jr. *utility company executive*
†Flint, Charles W., III *corporate executive*
Frey, Martin Alan *lawyer, educator*
Gaberino, John Anthony, Jr. *lawyer*
Gable, G. Ellis *lawyer*
Gaddis, Richard William *management educator*
Gentry, Bern Leon, Sr. *minority consulting company executive*
Goldthorpe, John Clifford *hospital administrator*
†Goodman, Jerry L(ynn) *judge*
Gottschalk, Sister Mary Therese *nun, hospital administrator*
Graham, Tony M. *lawyer*
†Green, Harvey Eugene *engineering executive*
Hale, Richard Lee *magazine editor*
Hall, Ronald E. *oil company executive*
†Hardman, James Reed *hospital administrator*
Haring, Robert Westing *newspaper editor*
†Harvey, James Douglas *medical foundation executive, former hospital administrator*
Hawkins, Francis Glenn *banker, lawyer*
Helmerich, Hans Christian *oil company executive*
Henderson, Robert Waugh *retired religion educator, minister*
Herbster, James Richard *information services executive, oil company executive*
Horkey, William Richard *retired diversified oil company executive*
Horn, Myron Kay *consulting petroleum geologist, author, educator*
Howard, Gene Claude *lawyer, former state senator*
Howe, Robert Melvin *oil company executive*
Howerton, Alvin *retail executive*
Huber, Fritz Godfrey *physical education educator, excercise physiologist*
Hulings, Norman McDermott, Jr. *energy consultant, former company executive*
†Huttner, Sidney Frederick *librarian*
Imel, John Michael *lawyer*
Ingram, Charles Clark, Jr. *energy company executive*
Janssen, Erwin T. *health science foundation administrator, psychiatrist*
Jatras, Stephen James *electronics company executive*
Johnson, Gerald, III *cardiovascular physiologist, researcher*
Jones, Jenk, Jr. *editor, educator*
Jones, Jenkin Lloyd *retired newspaper publisher*
Jones, Robert Lawton *architect, planner, educator*
Jones, Vernon Thomas *petrochemical company executive*
Kaefer, Gene John *manufacturing executive*
Kalbfleisch, John McDowell *cardiologist, educator*
Kennedy, Nancy Louise *retired draftsman*
Kihle, Donald Arthur *lawyer*
Killin, Charles Clark *lawyer*
King, Peter Cotterill *former utilities executive*
King, Roy Lee *computer company executive*
Kirchner, King Pouder *oil company executive*
Kitchen, Brent A. *airport executive*
†Klein, Joseph Matthew *transportation company executive*
Knaust, Clara Doss *retired elementary school educator*
Knowles, Billy C. *architect*
Kothe, Charles Aloysius *lawyer*
Kruse, David Louis, II *transportation company executive*
Langholz, Robert Wayne *lawyer, investor*
Larkin, Moscelyne *retired artistic director, dancer*
Lewis, Ceylon Smith, Jr. *physician*
Lewis, John Furman *lawyer, oil company executive*
Lowd, Judson Dean *oil and gas processing equipment manufacturing executive*
†Lunev, Aleksandr (Sasha) *dancer*
Luthey, Graydon Dean, Jr. *lawyer*
Major, John Keene *radio broadcasting executive*
†Manhart, Marcia Y(ockey) *art museum director*
†Martin, Jerry K. *engineering company executive*
Martin, Robert Finlay, Jr. *retired judge*
†Mattei, Charles A. *oil company executive*
McCalment, Raymond *junior college educator*
†McDevitt, Daniel Bernard *communications, computer and control systems application engineer*
Milsten, David Randolph *lawyer*
Mojtabai, Ann Grace *author, educator*
Morrow, Laura Annette *marketing professional*
Mourton, J. Gary *communications executive*
Narwold, Lewis Lammers *paper products manufacturer*
Neas, John Theodore *petroleum company executive*
Nero, Peter *pianist, conductor, composer, arranger*
Nettles, John Barnwell *obstetrics and gynecology educator*
Newman, Richard Oakley *utilities executive, consultant*
O'Brien, Darcy *English educator, writer*
O'Toole, Allan Thomas *electric utility executive*
Oxley, John Thurman *ranching and investments executive, former petroleum company executive*
Parker, Robert Lee, Sr. *petroleum engineer, drilling company executive*
Parker, Robert Lee, Jr. *drilling company executive*
Parr, Royse Milton *lawyer*
Payne, Christine Babcock *career psychologist*
Payne, William Haydon *broadcasting executive*
Plunket, Daniel Clark *pediatrician*
Powell, Sara Jordan *musician, religious worker*
Prayson, Alex Stephen *drafting and mechanical design educator*
Pritchard, William Winther *lawyer, drilling company executive*
Quinn, Francis Xavier *arbitrator and mediator, author, lecturer*
Rex, Lonnie Royce *religious organization administrator*
Ridenour, Windsor Allen *newspaper editor*
†Rippley, Robert *wholesale distribution executive*
Roberts, (Granville) Oral *clergyman*
Roderick, Robert Gene *accountant, chief financial officer*
Roger, Jerry Lee *school system administrator*
Rounds, Philard Leaon, Sr. *fundraiser*
Rubenstein, Bernard *orchestra conductor*
Rubottom, Donald Julian *management consultant*
Rummerfield, Benjamin Franklin *geophysicist*
Sanditen, Edgar Richard *investment company executive*
Savage, M. Susan *mayor*
Schwartz, Bernard *lawyer, educator*
Seymour, Stephanie Kulp *federal judge*
†Shane, John Marder *endocrinologist*
Slattery, Edward J. *bishop*
Smothers, William Edgar, Jr. *geophysical exploration company executive*
Sterban, Richard Anthony *singer*
Stover, Phil Sheridan, Jr. *investment consultant*
Stuart, Harold Cutliff *lawyer, business executive*
Taylor, Joe Clinton *judge*

Thomas, Robert Eggleston *former corporate executive*
Tompkins, Robert George *physician*
Troccoli, Joan Carpenter *museum director*
Upton, Howard B., Jr. *management writer, lawyer*
Wagner, John Leo *federal judge, lawyer*
Walker, Floyd Lee *lawyer*
Wesenberg, John Herman *association executive*
White, Ralph Dallas *retired health insurance executive*
White, Randall Wayne *educational development executive*
Williams, David Rogerson, Jr. *engineer, business executive*
Williams, John Horter *civil engineer, oil, gas, telecommunications and allied products distribution company executive*
Williams, Joseph Hill *retired diversified industry executive*
Williford, Richard Allen *oil executive, flight simulator company executive*
Wolking, Joseph Anthony *publishing company executive*
Wood, William Dean *accountant*
Woodrum, Patricia Ann *librarian*
†Zucconi, David G. *zoo and museum director*

Vinita
Beavers, Roy L. *retired utility executive, essayist*
Curnutte, Mark William *lawyer*
Neer, Charles Sumner, II *orthopaedic surgeon, educator*

Wanette
Thompson, Joyce Elizabeth *retired state education official*

Washington
Sliepcevich, Cedomir M. *engineering educator*

Watonga
Hoberecht, Earnest *abstract company executive, former newspaper executive*

Weatherford
Hamm, Donald Ivan *retired chemistry educator, university dean*

Webbers Falls
Evans, Karen Ruth *banker*

Wetumka
†Martin, Tony *foundation administrator*

Wewoka
Buendia, Imelda Bernardo *clinical director, physician*

Wyandotte
†Bearskin, Leaford *chief Wyandotte Nation*

Yukon
Bridges, Leroy W. *retired state agency administrator, consultant*
†Lenhart, Lowell Cordell *hospital administrator, consultant*
Somerville, Carolyn Johnson *principal*

OREGON

Albany
Bianchi, Charles Paul *technical and business executive, money manager, financial consultant*
Dooley, George Joseph, III *metallurgist*
Norman, E. Gladys *business computer educator, consultant*
Wood, Kenneth Arthur *newspaper editor emeritus, writer*
Yau, Te-Lin *corrosion engineer*

Aloha
Rojhantalab, Hossein Mohammad *chemical engineer, researcher*

Applegate
Boyle, (Charles) Keith *artist, educator*

Ashland
Abrahams, Sidney Cyril *physicist, crystallographer*
Bornet, Vaughn Davis *former history and social science educator, research historian*
Coffey, Marvin Dale *biology educator*
Farrimond, George Francis, Jr. *management educator*
Grover, James Robb *chemist, editor*
Hay, Richard Laurence *theater scenic designer*
Hemp, Ralph Clyde *retired reinsurance company executive, consultant, arbitrator, umpire*
Hirschfeld, Gerald Joseph *cinematographer*
Houston, John Albert *political science educator*
Kreisman, Arthur *higher education consultant, humanities educator emeritus*
Levy, Leonard Williams *history educator, author*
Mularz, Theodore Leonard *architect*
Smith, G(odfrey) T(aylor) *retired college president*
Walt, Harold Richard *rancher*

Astoria
Bainer, Philip La Vern *retired college president*
Foster, Michael William *librarian*
Harlan, David *reporter*
Haskell, Donald McMillan *lawyer*

Aurora
Martin, Lloyd Wayne *research agriculturist*

Baker City
Graham, Beardsley *management consultant*

Beaverton
†Boone, David Ridgway *environmental microbiology educator*
Bosch, Samuel Henry *electronics company executive*
Chang, David Ping-Chung *business consultant, architect*
†Friedley, David P. *electronics manufacturing company executive*
Hayes, Delbert J. *athletic company executive*
Henderson, George Miller *foundation executive, former banker*
Jones, Tom D. *software company executive*
Knight, Philip H(ampson) *shoe manufacturing company executive*
Long, Tom *manufacturing company executive*
Masi, Edward A. *computer company executive*
†Novy, Miles Joseph *obstetrician/gynecologist, educator*
Pond, Patricia Brown *library science educator, university administrator*
Rattner, Justin *supercomputer research manager*

Bend
Connolly, Thomas Joseph *bishop*
Hanes, Clifford Ronald *religious denomination administrator*
Kozak, Michael *real estate counselor, seminar instructor*
Luke, Dennis Robert *state legislator, home building company executive*
Mayer, Richard Dean *mathematics educator*
Wonser, Michael Dean *retired public affairs director, art educator*

Brookings
Maxwell, William Stirling *retired lawyer*
Olsen, Edward Gustave *education educator emeritus*

Cannon Beach
Greaver, Harry *artist*

Charleston
Shapiro, Lynda P. *biology educator, director*

Chiloquin
Reed, David George *entrepreneur*

Clackamas
Merrill, William Dean *architect, medical facility planning consultant*

Coquille
de Sá e Silva, Elizabeth Anne *educator*
Taylor, George Frederick *newspaper publisher, editor*

Corvallis
Arp, Daniel J. *biochemistry educator*
Becker, Boris William *business educator*
Becker, Robert Richard *biochemist, educator*
†Brown, George *research forester and educator*
Bruce, Robert Kirk *college administrator*
Byrne, John Vincent *academic administrator*
Castle, Emery Neal *agricultural and resource economist, educator*
Chambers, Kenton Lee *botany educator*
Dalrymple, Gary Brent *research geologist*
Davis, John Rowland *university administrator*
Drake, Charles Whitney *physicist*
Engelbrecht, Rudolf *electrical engineering educator*
Evans, Harold J. *plant physiologist, biochemist, educator*
†Farkas, Daniel Frederick *food science and technology educator*
Forbes, Leonard *engineering educator*
Frakes, Rod Vance *plant geneticist, educator*
Frazier, William A. *retired horticulturist*
Fuchigami, Leslie Hirao *horticulturist, researcher*
Gillis, John Simon *psychologist, educator*
Godfrey, Samuel Addison *retired telephone company executive*
Hall, Don Alan *editor, writer*
Hansen, Hugh Justin *agricultural engineer*
Harter, Lafayette George, Jr. *economics educator emeritus*
Horne, Frederick Herbert *academic administrator, chemistry educator*
Hunt, Donald R. *retired librarian*
Huyer, Adriana *oceanographer, educator*
Keller, George Henrik *marine geologist*
Knudsen, James George *chemical engineer, educator*
Koller, Loren D. *veterinary medicine educator*
Kronstad, Warren Ervind *genetics educator, researcher*
Leong, Jo-Ann Ching *microbiologist, educator*
Liston, Aaron Irving *botanist*
Mac Vicar, Robert William *retired university administrator*
Miner, John Ronald *agricultural engineer*
Mohler, Ronald Rutt *electrical engineering educator*
Moore, Thomas Carrol *botanist, educator*
Morita, Richard Yukio *microbiology and oceanography educator*
Murphy, Thomas Allen *government research administrator, scientist*
Nielson, Norma Lee *business educator*
Olleman, Roger Dean *industry consultant, former metallurgical engineering educator*
Parker, Donald Fred *college dean, human resources management educator*
Pearson, Albert Marchant *food science and nutrition educator*
Petersen, Bent Edvard *mathematician, educator*
Reed, Donald James *biochemistry educator*
Shoemaker, David Powell *chemist, educator*
Sleight, Arthur William *chemist, educator*
†Steele, Robert Edwin *orthopedic surgeon*
Tarrant, Robert Frank *soil science educator, researcher*
Temes, Gabor Charles *electrical engineering educator*
Thomas, Thomas Darrah *chemistry educator*
Towey, Richard Edward *economics educator*
Trappe, James Martin *mycologist*
Van Holde, Kensal Edward *biochemistry educator*
Westwood, Melvin Neil *horticulturist, pomologist*
†Whanger, Philip Daniel *biochemistry educator and researcher, nutrition educator*
Wilkins, Caroline Hanke *consumer agency administrator, political worker*
Willis, David Lee *radiation biology educator*
Yeats, Robert Sheppard *geologist, educator*
Young, J. Lowell *soil chemist, biologist*
Young, Roy Alton *university administrator, educator*
Zobel, Donald Bruce *botany educator*
Zwahlen, Fred Casper, Jr. *journalism educator*

Cottage Grove
Miller, Joanne Louise *middle school educator*

Eugene
Acker, Martin Herbert *psychotherapist, educator*
Aikens, C(lyde) Melvin *anthropology educator, archaeologist*
Andrews, Fred Charles *mathematics educator*
Bailey, Exine Margaret Anderson *soprano, educator*
Baker, Alton Fletcher, Jr. *newspaper editor*
†Baker, Alton Fletcher, III *newspaper editor, publishing executive*
Baker, Edwin Moody *retired newspaper publisher*
Barton, Stephen Howard *broadcast executive*
Bennett, Robert Royce *engineering and management consultant*
Birn, Raymond Francis *historian, educator*
Boekelheide, Virgil Carl *chemistry educator*
Boggs, Sam, Jr. *geology educator*
Chackel, Charles Victor *communications executive*
Chezem, Curtis Gordon *physicist, former retail executive*
Clark, Chapin DeWitt *law educator*
Coffin, Thomas M. *federal magistrate judge*
Cox, Joseph William *academic administrator*
Crasemann, Bernd *physicist, educator*
Dasso, Jerome Joseph *real estate educator, consultant*
Davis, Richard Malone *economics educator*
Dawes, Carol J. *clinical psychologist*
Decker Slaney, Mary Teresa *Olympic athlete*
Deshpande, Nilendra Ganesh *physics educator*
DeVries, Philip James *tropical field ecologist, butterfly biologist*
Donnelly, Marian Card *art historian, educator*
Donnelly, Russell James *physicist, educator*
Eisert, Debra Claire *pediatric psychologist*
Flanagan, Latham, Jr. *surgeon*
Franklin, Jon Daniel *journalist, writer, educator*
Freyd, Jennifer Joy *psychology educator*
Frohnmayer, David Braden *university president*
†Funk, David Charles *design firm executive*
Gall, Meredith Damien (Meredith Mark Damien Gall) *education educator, author*
Girardeau, Marvin Denham *physics educator*
Griffith, Osbie Hayes *chemistry educator*
Heidenheim, Roger Stewart *automotive and electronic consultant*
Higdon, Polly Susanne *federal judge*
Hildebrand, Carol Ilene *librarian*
Hildreth, Clifford *retired economist, educator*
Hogan, Michael R(obert) *federal judge*
Holser, William Thomas *geochemistry educator, geologist*
Holzapfel, Christina Marie *biologist*
Hosticka, Carl Joseph *academic administrator, educator, legislator*
†Hutchison, James E. *chemistry educator*
Ismach, Arnold Harvey *journalism educator*
Johnson, Ronald Glenn *arts administrator*
Khang, Chulsoon *economics educator*
Lemert, James Bolton *journalist, educator*
Littman, Richard Anton *psychologist, educator*
†Loescher, Richard Alvin *gastroenterologist*
Matthews, Brian W. *molecular biology educator*
Mazo, Robert Marc *chemistry educator*
McGuire, Timothy William *economics and management educator, dean*
Mikesell, Raymond Frech *economics educator*
Morrison, Perry David *librarian, educator*
Moseley, John Travis *university administrator, research physicist*
Mowday, Richard Thomas *management educator*
Mumford, William Porter, II *lawyer*
Nissel, Martin *radiologist, consultant*
Noyes, Richard Macy *physical chemist, educator*
Osborn, Ronald Edwin *minister, church history educator*
Owens, A(rnold) Dean *lawyer*
Pascal, C(ecil) Bennett *classics educator*
Peticolas, Warner Leland *physical chemistry educator*
Piele, Philip Kern *education infosystems educator*
Reinmuth, James E. *college dean*
Rendall, Steven Finlay *language educator, editor, translator, critic*
†Retallack, Gregory John *geologist educator*
Sahlstrom, E(lmer) B(ernard) *lawyer*
Sanders, Jack Thomas *religious studies educator*
Schellman, John A. *chemistry educator*
Scoles, Eugene Francis *legal educator, lawyer*
Sherriffs, Ronald Everett *communications and film educator*
Sisley, Becky Lynn *physical education educator*
Sprague, George Frederick *geneticist*
Starr, Grier Forsythe *retired pathologist*
Stirling, Isabel Ann *science librarian*
Stone, Joe Allan *economics educator*
Torrey, James D. *communications executive, consultant*
Tull, Donald Stanley *marketing educator*
Tykeson, Donald Erwin *broadcasting executive*
Upham, Steadman *anthropology educator, university dean, academic administrator*
von Hippel, Peter Hans *chemistry educator*
Wickes, George *English educator, writer*
Wiley, Carl Ross *timber company executive*
Wilhelm, Kate (Katy Gertrude) *author*

Florence
Corless, Dorothy Alice *nurse educator*
Ericksen, Jerald Laverne *educator, engineering scientist*
Gray, Augustine Heard, Jr. *computer consultant*

Forest Grove
†Coleman, Deborah Ann *electronics company executive*
Singleton, Francis Seth *dean*

Gleneden Beach
Marks, Arnold *journalist*

Grants Pass
Naylor, John Thomas *telephone company executive*
Oestmann, Irma Emma *minister, artist, educator*
Smith, Barnard Elliot *management educator*

Gresham
Caldwell, Robert John *newspaper editor*
Light, Betty Jensen Pritchett *former college dean*
Nicholson, R. Stephen *organization administrator*
Poulton, Charles Edgar *natural resources consultant*

Hillsboro
Gerlach, Robert Louis *research and development executive, physicist*
Grant, James Rusk *business owner*
Pettit, Ghery St. John *electronics engineer*
Yates, Keith Lamar *retired insurance company executive*

Klamath Falls
†Bohnen, Robert Frank *hematologist, oncologist, educator*
Ehlers, Eleanor May Collier (Mrs. Frederick Burton Ehlers) *civic worker*

La Grande
Gilbert, David Erwin *university president, physicist*
Robinson, Jens Joseph *college dean*

Lake Oswego
Gawf, John Lee *foreign service officer*
Ladehoff, Robert Louis *bishop*
Le Shana, David Charles *seminary president*
Morse, Lowell Wesley *real estate executive, banking executive*
†Philipp, Fred A. *publishing executive*
Piccard-Krone, Karen Aliotte *public relations executive, political consultant*
Pretzinger, Donald Leonard *retired insurance executive*
Thong, Tran *biomedical company executive*
Worsley, John Clayton *architect*

Lebanon
Kuntz, Joel Dubois *lawyer*

Lincoln City
Gehrig, Edward Harry *electrical engineer, consultant*
Sewell, Robert Dalton *pediatrician*

Mcminnville
Goodrich, Kenneth Paul *college dean*
McGillivray, Karen *elementary school educator*
Mc Kaughan, Howard Paul *linguistics educator*
Walker, Charles Urmston *retired university president*

Medford
Barnum, William Laird *pedodontist*
Bouquet, Francis Lester *physicist*
Bunten, John William *school system administrator*
Cutler, Kenneth Ross *investment company and mutual fund executive*
Hennion, Reeve Lawrence *communications executive*
Keener, John Wesley *management consultant*
McKinstry, Gregory John Duncan *retail executive*
O'Connor, Karl William *lawyer*
Skelton, Douglas H. *architect*
Sours, James Kingsley *association executive, former college president*
Straus, David A. *architectural firm executive*
†Wegner, Samuel Joseph *historical society executive*
†Williams, William H. *food products executive, retail executive*

Milwaukie
Jones, Alan C. *grocery company executive*
McKay, Laura L. *banker, consultant*
White, John *food marketing executive*

Monmouth
Forcier, Richard Charles *information technology educator, computer applications consultant*
Meyers, Richard Stuart *college president*
Shay, Roshani Cari *political science educator*
White, Donald Harvey *physicist, educator*

Myrtle Point
Walsh, Don *marine consultant, executive*

Newberg
Stevens, Edward Franklin *college president*

Newport
Gordon, Walter *architect*
Kennedy, Richard Jerome *writer*
Langrock, Karl Frederick *former academic administrator*
Richardson, Bruce LeVoyle *dentist*
Weber, Lavern John *marine science administrator, educator*

North Bend
Shepard, Robert Carlton *English language educator*

Oakland
Smelt, Ronald *retired aircraft company executive*

Otter Rock
Eaton, Leonard Kimball *retired architecture educator*
Kassner, Michael Ernest *materials science educator, researcher*

Pendleton
Bloom, Stephen Michael *lawyer, judge*
Kottkamp, John Harlan *lawyer*
Lund, Steve *agronomist, research administrator*
Smiley, Richard Wayne *research center administrator, researcher*

Pleasant Hill
Kesey, Ken *writer*

Port Orford
Drinnon, Richard *history educator*

Portland
Abbott, Carl John *urban studies and planning educator*
Abravanel, Allan Ray *lawyer*
Ahuja, Jagdish Chand *mathematics educator*
†Anderegg, Karen Klok *consumer products executive*
Anderson, Herbert H. *lawyer, farmer*
Artaud-Wild, Sabine Marie *retired research dietitian*
Arthur, Michael Elbert *lawyer*
Ashenden, William Joseph *broadcast executive*
Babcock, Robert Evans *lawyer*
Bailey, Robert C. *opera company executive*
Bakkensen, John Reser *lawyer*
Barham, Steven Walter *state official*
Barmack, Neal Herbert *neuroscientist*
Bates, Richard Mather *dentist*
Bauer, Louis Edward *retail bookstore executive, educator*
Beatty, John Cabeen, Jr. *judge*
Becker, Larry Wayne *property and casualty insurance company official*
Belloni, Robert Clinton *federal judge*
Bennett, Douglas Carleton *academic administrator*
Bennett, William Michael *physician*
Benson, George L. *school system administrator*
Benson, John Alexander, Jr. *physician, educator*
Berthelsdorf, Siegfried *psychiatrist*

Bhatia, Peter K. editor, journalist
Bishop, C. M., Jr. textile company executive
Blanford, J(ohn) William department store company executive
Blumel, Joseph Carlton university president
Booth, Brian Geddes lawyer
Boyman, John Edward George individual/organizational transition consultant
Bragdon, Paul Errol educator
†Breezley, Roger Lee banker
Brenneman, Delbert Jay lawyer
Brim, Armand Eugene health care executive
Browne, Joseph Peter retired librarian
Brummett, Robert Eddie pharmacology educator
Bull, Bergen Ira equipment manufacturing company executive
†Burns, Bruce food service executive
Butler, Leslie Ann advertising executive, portrait artist
Byerly, Bruce Lloyd lawyer
Cable, John Franklin lawyer
Campbell, Charles Joy fishery biologist
Campbell, John Richard pediatric surgeon
Cantlin, Richard Anthony lawyer
Carlesimo, P. J. (Peter J. Carlesimo) former college basketball coach, professional basketball coach
Carlsen, Clifford Norman, Jr. lawyer
Carmack, Mildred Jean lawyer
†Cartwright, Philip Crawford marketing executive
Carver, Loyce Cleo clergyman
Cateora, Philip Rene business educator, author
Chernoff, Daniel Paregol patent lawyer
Clarke, J(oseph) Henry dental educator, dentist
Claycomb, Cecil Keith biochemist, educator
Cohen, Norm chemist
Collins, Maribeth Wilson foundation president
Commerford, Kathleen Anne psychologist
Congdon, Marsha B. telecommunications executive
Conkling, Roger Linton consultant, business administration educator, retired utility executive
Connor, William Elliott physician, educator
Cooley, Edward H. castings manufacturing company executive
Cooper, Ginnie library director
Crabbs, Roger Alan publisher, consultant, small business owner, educator
Crawshaw, Ralph psychiatrist
Cronyn, Marshall William chemistry educator
Crosa, Jorge Homero bacterial geneticist, educator, consultant
Crow, William Beryl lawyer
Crowell, John B., Jr. lawyer, former government official
†Culver, Wesley Ellsworth relief and development organization executive
Dahl, Joyle Cochran lawyer
†Daly, Donald F. engineering company executive
Danielson, Craig wholesale grocery corporation executive
Davidson, Crow Girard lawyer
Davis, James Allan gerontologist, educator
Dean, E. Joseph lawyer
DeChaine, Dean Dennis lawyer
Deering, Thomas Phillips lawyer
DePreist, James Anderson conductor
Dew, William Waldo, Jr. bishop
Dotten, Michael Chester lawyer
Drake, Brian William photography company executive
Drummond, Gerard Kasper lawyer, retired minerals company executive
†Dunham, Tom Robert physician
Dunne, Thomas Gregory chemistry educator, researcher
Eakin, Margaretta Morgan lawyer
Edwards, Richard Alan lawyer
Eichinger, Marilynne H. museum administrator
Englert, Walter George classics and humanities educator
Epstein, Edward Louis lawyer
Ericsson Dailey, Dianne K. lawyer
Eshelman, William Robert librarian, editor
Faust, John Roosevelt, Jr. lawyer
Fell, James F. lawyer
Feuerstein, Howard M. lawyer
Findlay, Susan Halton company executive
Flowerree, Robert Edmund retired forest products company executive
Foehl, Edward Albert chemical company executive
Fogg, George Kephart lawyer
Foley, Ridgway Knight, Jr. lawyer, writer
Franz, Robert Warren banker
Franzke, Richard Albert lawyer
Frasca, Robert John architect
Fraunfelder, Frederick Theodore ophthalmologist, educator
Frazier, J(ohn) Phillip manufacturing company executive
Frisbee, Don Calvin retired utilities executive
Froebe, Gerald Allen lawyer, partner
Frolick, Patricia Mary educator, retired
Fronk, William Joseph retired machinery company executive
Frye, Helen Jackson federal judge
Gango, Jacqueline Mary publishing executive
Georges, Maurice Ostrow lawyer
Gerow, Edwin Mahaffey Indic culture educator
Gilkey, Gordon Waverly curator, artist
Gill, Rockne lawyer
Girard, Leonard Arthur lawyer
Glasgow, William Jacob lawyer
Gleason, Alfred M. telecommunications executive
Glick, Richard Myron lawyer
Glickman, Harry professional basketball team executive
Goldfarb, Timothy Moore hospital administrator
Graves, Earl William, Jr. journalist
Gray, John Delton retired manufacturing company executive
Greenlick, Merwyn Ronald health services researcher
Greenstein, Merle Edward import/export company executive
Greer, Monte Arnold physician, educator
Griffith, Stephen Loyal lawyer
Gunsul, Brooks R. W. architect
Hacker, Thomas Owen architect
Hagenstein, William David forester, consultant
Hager, Orval O. retired lawyer, consultant
Halle, John Joseph lawyer
Halverson, Gerald B. insurance company executive
Hanna, Harry Mitchell lawyer
Hardy, Randall Webster utility executive
†Harrell, Ernest James army officer
Harris, Michael Hatherly educational administrator
Haviland, John Beard anthropology and linguistics educator
Heatherington, J. Scott retired osteopathic physician and surgeon
Hebe, James L. trucking executive
Helmer, M. Christie lawyer
Hergenhan, Kenneth William lawyer
Herndon, Robert McCulloch experimental neurologist
Hess, Henry Leroy, Jr. bankruptcy judge
Hilbert, Bernard Charles retired union official
Hill, Andrew William jazz musician, composer
Hill, Ray Thomas, Jr. export and import company executive
Hill, Wilmer Bailey administrative law judge
Hinkle, Charles Frederick lawyer, clergyman, educator
Hobbs, C. D. utilities executive
Hoffman, Jack Leroy lawyer
Holman, Donald Reid lawyer
Holmes, Michael Gene lawyer
Howorth, David Bishop lawyer
Huenemann, Ruben Henry clergyman
Hutchens, Tyra Thornton physician, educator
Jacob, Stanley Wallace surgeon, educator
Jenkins, Donald John art museum administrator
Jensen, Edmund Paul bank holding company executive
Johansen, Judith A. Bearzi lawyer
Johnson, Alexander Charles lawyer, electrical engineer
Johnson, Nely Lupovici judge
Johnston, Virginia Evelyn editor
Jones, Richard Theodore biochemistry educator
Jones, Robert Edward federal judge
Josephson, Richard Carl lawyer
Juba, George E. federal judge
Jungers, Francis oil consultant
Kanter, Stephen law educator, college dean
Katz, Vera mayor, former college administrator, state legislator
Kendall, John Walker, Jr. medical educator, researcher, university dean
Kennedy, Jack Leland lawyer
Kester, Randall Blair lawyer
Kilbourn, Lee Ferris architect, specifications writer
Kilkenny, John F. federal judge, lawyer
Kinnune, William P. forest products executive
Kinzer, Donald Louis retired historian, educator
Knapp, Robert Stanley English language educator
†Koblik, Stevens S. academic administrator
Kohler, Peter Ogden physician, educator, university president
Kolde, Bert professional basketball team executive
Kristof, Ladis Kris Donabed political scientist, author
Kupel, Frederick John counselor
Lall, B. Kent civil engineering educator
Lang, Philip David former state legislator, insurance company executive
Lanz, Robert Francis corporate financial officer
Larpenteur, James Albert, Jr. lawyer
Latini, Nancy Jane special education administrator
Lawrence, Sally Clark college president
Leavy, Edward federal judge
Ledbetter, Randi Rae obstetrician/gynecologist
†Lee, John Patrick hospital administrator
Leedy, Robert Allan, Sr. retired lawyer
Lees, Martin Henry pediatrician, educator
Lendaris, George Gregory electrical educator
Levada, William Joseph archbishop
†Leyden, Norman conductor
Lim, John K. state senator, business executive
Lindley, Thomas Ernest environmental lawyer, law educator
Livingston, Louis Bayer lawyer
Lobitz, Walter Charles, Jr. physician, educator
Love, William Edward lawyer
Maclean, Charles (Bernard) transition, performance recognition and workplace violence prevention consultant
Magedanz, Dorothy C. health facility administrator, educator
Mainwaring, William Lewis publishing company executive, author
Maloney, Robert E., Jr. lawyer
Mapes, Jeffrey Robert journalist
Marandas, Susan Margaret secondary education educator
Marsh, Malcolm F. federal judge
Martin, Chrys Anne lawyer
Martin, Lucy Z. public relations executive
Marvin, Roy Mack metal products executive
Matarazzo, Joseph Dominic psychologist
Matarazzo, Ruth Gadbois psychology educator
McCall, Robert H. oil and chemical company executive
McCall, William Calder oil and chemical company executive
McCarty, Chester Earl lawyer, retired air force officer
McClave, Donald Silsbee association executive
McKennon, Keith Robert chemical company executive
McKinley, Loren Dhue museum director
Meighan, Stuart Spence hospital consultant, internist, writer
Merlo, Harry Angelo forest products executive
Michael, Gary Linn architect
Miller, Robert G. retail company executive
Miller, William Richey, Jr. lawyer
Mooney, Michael Joseph academic administrator, philosopher
Moore, Melvin G. school system administrator
Moose, Charles A. state official
Morgan, James Earl librarian, administrator
Morton, Clifford A. holding company executive
Mowe, Gregory Robert lawyer
Murphy, Francis Seward journalist
Myers, Clay retired investment management company executive
Nagel, Stanley Blair construction and investment executive
Nash, Frank Erwin lawyer
Netusil, Noelwah Rose economics educator
†Nevue, Sarah Paulson museum administrator
Nofziger, Sally Alene diversified utility company executive
Nunn, Robert Warne lawyer
O'Hanlon, James Barry retired lawyer
O'Hollaren, Paul Joseph former international fraternity administrator
Olsen, Kurt investment company executive, adviser
Olson, Donald Ernest retired physician
Olson, Roger Norman health service administrator
Orloff, Chet cultural organization administrator
O'Scannlain, Diarmuid Fionntain federal judge
Pamplin, Robert Boisseau, Sr. textile manufacturing executive
Panner, Owen M. federal judge
†Patterson, James Randolph physician
Pearson, David Petri chemist
Perris, Elizabeth L. federal judge
†Pfeifer, Larry Alan public health service coordinator
Pope, Peter T. forest products company executive
Porter, Roger Jeffrey literature educator
Porter, Terry professional basketball player
Press, Edward consulting physician
Prophet, Matthew Waller, Jr. school superintendent
Pruitt, Charles Joseph lawyer
Raaf, John Elbert neurosurgeon, educator
Ramaley, Judith Aitken university president, endocrinologist
Ramsby, Mark Delivan lighting designer and consultant
Redden, James Anthony federal judge
Reed, Gregory William broadcasting executive
Reiten, Richard G. electric power industry executive
Richards, Herbert East minister emeritus, commentator
Richardson, Campbell lawyer
Richter, Peter Christian lawyer
Ricks, Mary Frances university administrator, anthropologist
†Ridgley, Robert Louis gas company executive, lawyer
Riker, William Kay pharmacologist, educator
Ritz, Richard Ellison architect, architectural historian, writer
Roberts, Gary lawyer
Roche, David Alan accounting firm executive
Rooks, Judith Pence family planning, maternal health care, midwifery consultant
Rosenbaum, Lois Omenn lawyer
Roth, Phillip Joseph judge
Rowe, Sandra Mims newspaper editor
Roy, Richard E. lawyer
Rubin, Bruce Alan lawyer
Russell, Marjorie Rose manufacturing company executive
Rutherford, William Drake investment executive, lawyer
Rutsala, Vern A. poet, English language educator, writer
Rutzick, Mark Charles lawyer
Ryan, John Duncan lawyer
Sand, Thomas Charles lawyer
Saslow, George psychiatrist, educator
Schmidt, Waldemar Adrian pathologist, educator
Schuster, Philip Frederick, II lawyer
Scott, Brian Douglas association executive
Seil, Fredrick John neuroscientist, neurologist
Sevetson, Donald James minister, church administrator
Sheridan, Wilma Froman dean
Sherrer, Charles David college dean, clergyman
Short, Robert Henry retired utility executive
Simpson, Robert Glenn lawyer
Skopil, Otto Richard, Jr. federal judge
Smith, Milton Ray computer company executive, lawyer
Spencer, Peter Simner neurotoxicologist
Spiekerman, James Frederick lawyer
Squier, Leslie Hamilton psychology educator
Stalnaker, John Hulbert physician
Stastny, Donald Joseph architect
Staver, Leroy Baldwin banker
Steiner, Kenneth Donald bishop
Steinfeld, Ray, Jr. food products executive
Steinman, Lisa Malinowski English literature educator, writer
Sterling, Donald Justus, Jr. retired newspaper editor
Stevason, John C. lawyer
Stevens, Wendell Claire anesthesiology educator
Stewart, Milton Roy lawyer
Stickel, Frederick A. publisher
Stickel, Patrick Francis publishing executive, newspaper
Stott, Peter Walter forest products company executive
Stoyanov, Milan lumber products company executive
Strain, Douglas Campbell precision instrument company executive
Sugg, John Logan (Jack Sugg) advertising executive
Sullivan, Edward Joseph lawyer, educator
Sutter, Harvey Mack engineer,consultant
Swan, Kenneth Carl physician, surgeon
Swank, Roy Laver physician, educator, inventor
Swindells, William, Jr. lumber and paper company executive
Taylor, Carson William electrical engineer
Taylor, Robert Brown medical educator
Terkla, Louis Gabriel retired university dean
Thorpe, Otis Henry professional basketball player
Thurston, George R. lumber company executive
Tilbury, Roger Graydon lawyer, rancher
Tramposch, William Joseph museum director, consultant
Tufts, Robert B. registrar
Van Hassel, Henry John dentist, educator, university dean
Van Valkenburg, Edgar Walter lawyer
Van Valkenburg, Mac Elwyn electrical engineering educator
Vaughan, Thomas James Gregory historian
Waddingham, John Alfred artist, journalist
Waggoner, James Clyde lawyer
Walters, Stephen Scott lawyer
†Ward, C. Bruce entrepreneur
Ward, James Hubert social work educator, university dean, researcher, consultant
Warren, Robert Carlton manufacturing company executive
Weaver, Delbert Allen lawyer
Webb, Jere Michael lawyer
Weber, George Richard financial consultant, writer
Westwood, James Nicholson lawyer
Wetzel, Karl Joseph physics educator, university official and dean
Whinston, Arthur Lewis lawyer
White, Douglas James, Jr. lawyer
Whiteley, Benjamin Robert insurance company executive
Whitsell, Helen Jo lumber executive
†Wieden, Dan G. advertising executive
Wiener, Norman Joseph lawyer
Wiens, Arthur Nicholai psychology educator
Wiest, William Marvin education educator, psychologist
Williams, Charles Linwood (Buck Williams) professional basketball player
Wilson, Owen Meredith, Jr. lawyer
†Winecki, William food products executive
Winnowski, Thaddeus Richard (Ted Winnowski) bank executive
Wintermute, Marjorie McLean architect, educator
Wohler, Jeffery Wilson newspaper editor
Wood, Marcus Andrew lawyer
Woodward, Stephen Richard newspaper reporter
Wren, Harold Gwyn arbitrator, lawyer, legal educator
Wright, Charles Edward lawyer
Wyse, William Walker lawyer
Zalutsky, Morton Herman lawyer
Zimmerman, Gail Marie medical foundation executive
Zook, Ronald Z. school system administrator

Prineville
†Wick, G. Phil retail executive

Riddle
Markham, William E. timber and logging company owner

Riley
Cowan, Richard John cattle rancher

Roseburg
Plummer, Charles McDonald retired community college administrator

Saint Helens
Federici, Tony small business owner, state legislator

Salem
Archer, Stephen Hunt economist, educator
Bebe, Kathy principal
Billman, Jennifer elementsry school principal
Bradbury, William Chapman, III state senator
†Breen, Richard F., Jr. law librarian, lawyer, educator
Brown, Kate state legislator
Bunn, James Lee state senator
Carson, Wallace Preston, Jr. state supreme court chief justice
Carter, Margaret L. legislator
Cohen, Joyce E. state senator, investment executive
Elliott, Lee Ann psychologist
Fadeley, Edward Norman state supreme court justice
Gold, Shirley Jeanne state legislator, labor relations specialist
Graber, Susan P. judge
Hill, Jim state official
Hudson, Jerry E. university president
Johnson, Robert Raymond management consultant, educator
Keisling, Phillip Andrew state official
†Kitzhaber, John Albert governor, physician, former state senator
Kulongoski, Theodore R. state attorney general
Mack, Patricia secondary school principal
Mannix, Kevin Leese lawyer
Naito, Lisa Heather state legislator
Oakley, Carolyn Le state legislator, small business owner
Oberg, Larry Reynold librarian
O'Connell, Kenneth John state justice
Peterson, Edwin J. retired supreme court justice, law educator
Pierre, Joseph Horace, Jr. commercial artist
Rasmussen, Neil Woodland insurance agent
Shibley, Gail Rose state legislator
Taylor, Jacqueline Self state legislator
Thornton, Dorothy Haberlach artist, photographer
Toran, Kay Dean social services administrator
Trueblood, Paul Graham retired English educator, author, editor
Turnbaugh, Roy Carroll archivist
Unis, Richard L. state supreme court justice
Van Hoomissen, George Albert state supreme court justice
Warnath, Maxine Ammer organizational psychologist, educator
Webber, Catherine Carney state legislator, lawyer, social worker, state official
†Weide, Janice Lee librarian
Weight, George Dale banker, educator

Seaside
Sheasgreen, Betty interior designer, painter, sculptor

Siletz
Jennings, Jesse David anthropology educator
†Pigsley, Delores Ann tribal leader, educator

Sisters
Baxter, John Lincoln, Jr. manufacturing company executive

South Beach
Gilbert, David Heggie retired educational publisher, consultant

Springfield
Detlefsen, William David, Jr. research and development executive
Kimball, Reid Roberts psychiatrist
Lutes, Donald Henry architect
Walton, Ralph Ervin community mental health services adminstrator

Sunriver
Clough, Ray William, Jr. civil engineering educator
Davenport, Wilbur Bayley, Jr. electrical engineering educator
Fosmire, Fred Randall retired forest products company executive
Jamison, Harrison Clyde former oil company executive, petroleum exploration consultant

Talent
McGill, Esby Clifton former college official

Terrebonne
Siebert, Diane Dolores author, poet

Tigard
Berglund, Carl Neil electronics company executive
Nokes, John Richard retired newspaper editor, author
Replogle, William H(enry), II lawyer

Troutdale
Sizemore, Robert Dennis school counselor, educational administrator

Tualatin
Broome, John William retired architect
Brown, Robert Wallace mathematics educator

Longaker, Nancy *elementary school principal*

West Linn
Harris, Debra Coral *physical education educator*
Kane, Robert Joseph *retired floricultural company executive*
Treffinger, Karl Edward *architectural firm executive*

White City
Moore, Charles August, Jr. *psychologist*

Wilsonville
Gross, Hal Raymond *bishop*
Isberg, Reuben Albert *radio communications engineer*
Kimberley, A. G., Jr. *industrial products, factory representative, management executive*
Meyer, Jerome J. *diversified technology company executive*
†Ramadan, Sar *design automation company executive*
†Rhines, Walden C. *information system specialist*
†Richards, Waldo J. *computer software and systems company executive*

Winston
Jones, Henry Earl *dermatologist, direct patient care educator*

Woodburn
Bradley, Lester Eugene *retired steel and rubber products manufacturing executive*

Yachats
Gerdemann, James Wessel *plant pathologist, educator*

Yamhill
Kristof, Nicholas Donabet *journalist*

PENNSYLVANIA

Abington
Ayoub, Ayoub Barsoum *mathematician, educator*
Drudy, Patrick *psychologist, human relations consultant*
Dunn, Linda Kay *physician*
Lapayowker, Marc Spencer *radiologist*
Lello, David Joseph *special education educator*
Pilla, Felix Mario *hospital administrator*
Scholfield, Linda Katherine *nursing administrator*
Schuster, Ingeborg Ida *chemistry educator*

Akron
Lapp, John Allen *religious organization administrator*

Albrightsville
Wilson, George Wharton *newspaper editor*

Alexandria
Horn, John Chisolm *management consultant*

Allentown
Agger, James H. *lawyer*
Allen, Anna Foster *librarian*
Anderson, Paul Edward *cement company executive*
Armor, John N. *chemical company research manager*
Armstrong, W(illiam) Warren *advertising agency executive*
Baker, Dexter Farrington *manufacturing company executive*
Baraket, Edmund S., Jr. *general contractor, contracting consultant*
Bednar, Charles Sokol *political scientist, educator*
Berman, Muriel Mallin *civic worker*
Berman, Philip I. *foundation administrator*
Blume, Peter Frederick *museum director*
Brown, Robert Wayne *lawyer*
†Cavett, Van Andrew *journalist*
Cella, Frank G. *finance company executive*
Dent, Charles Wieder *state legislator*
†Dimechkie, Riad N. *food company executive*
Donaldson, John Anthony *manufacturing executive*
Donley, Edward *manufacturing company executive*
Doughty, George Franklin *airport administrator*
Foster, Edward Paul (Ted Foster) *process industries executive*
Frank, Bernard *lawyer*
Gabel, Ronald Glen *telecommunications executive*
Gadomski, Robert Eugene *chemical and industrial gas company executive*
Gaylor, Donald Hughes *surgeon, educator*
Gewartowski, James Walter *electrical engineer*
Goldey, James Mearns *physicist*
Graham, Kenneth Robert *psychologist, educator*
Hansel, James Gordon *engineer*
Hecht, William F. *electric power industry executive*
Heitmann, George Joseph *business educator, consultant*
Holt, Leon Conrad, Jr. *lawyer, business executive*
Jackson, William MacLeod *management consultant*
Jodock, Darrell Harland *minister, religion educator*
Kauffman, John Thomas *utility executive*
Kipa, Albert Alexander *foreign language and literature educator*
Lovett, John Robert *chemical company executive*
Lukac, George Joseph *fundraising executive*
Moller, Hans *artist*
Musselman, Jamie P. *advertising executive*
Nagel, Edward McCaul *lawyer, former utilities executive*
Parks, Jeffrey A. *lawyer*
†Pez, Guido Peter *research chemist*
Platt, William Henry *lawyer*
Reckard, Craig Reginald *physician*
Rossetti, Joseph Paul *trucking industry executive*
Samuels, Abram *stage equipment manufacturing company executive*
Shire, Donald Thomas *retired air products and chemicals executive, lawyer*
Shorts, Gary K. *newspaper publisher*
Singhal, Kishore *engineering administrator*
Smith, Warren L. *electrical engineer, physicist*
†Snyder, Frank R. *building materials manufacturing executive*
Stephanoff, Kathryn Ann *library director*
Taylor, Arthur Robert *college president, business executive*
†Tepper, Lloyd Barton *physician*
Wagner, Harold A. *industrial gas and chemical company executive*
Welsh, Thomas J. *bishop*
Winters, Arthur Ralph, Jr. *chemical and cryogenic engineer, consultant*

Allison Park
Backus, John King *former chemical company research administrator*
Craig, David W. *judge, author*
Hadidian, Dikran Yenovk *librarian, clergyman*
Herrington, John David, III *lawyer*
LaDow, C. Stuart *consultant financial services*
Miller, William Evans, Jr. *retired lawyer*
Osby, Larissa Geiss *artist*
Xu, Zhifu *chemist, researcher*

Altoona
†Duncan, David James *health services adminstrator, educator*
Meadors, Allen Coats *health administrator, educator*
Miller, Gerald E. *bishop*
Suckling, Robert McCleary *architect*
Wright, Jerry Jaye *physical education educator*

Ambler
Lengyel, Alfonz *art history, archeology and museology educator*

Ambridge
Frey, William Carl *bishop, academic administrator*

Annville
McGill, William James, Jr. *academic administrator*
Synodinos, John Anthony *academic administrator*
Verhoek, Susan Elizabeth *botany educator*

Ardmore
†Callahan, Thomas P. *wholesale distribution executive*
Chadwick, H. Beatty *lawyer*
Gutwirth, Marcel Marc *French literature educator*
Kline, George Louis *author, translator, retired philosophy and literature educator*
Scott, Bill *advertising agency executive*
Stanley, Edward Alexander *geologist, forensic scientist, technical and academic administrator*

Aston
Aldrich, Ronald Robert *health system administrator*
Barnett, Samuel Treutlen *international company executive*
Carroll, Claire Barry *special education educator*

Avondale
Friel, Daniel Denwood, Sr. *manufacturing executive*

Bala Cynwyd
Ackoff, Russell Lincoln *systems sciences educator*
Alter, Milton *neurologist, educator*
Bausher, Verne C(harles) *banker*
Benenson, James, Jr. *brokerage house executive*
Bentivegna, Peter Ignatius *architectural company executive*
Burland, J(ohn) Alexis *psychoanalyst*
Cades, Stewart Russell *lawyer, communications company executive*
Driscoll, Edward Carroll *construction management firm executive*
Elkman, Stanley *advertising executive*
Field, Joseph Myron *broadcast executive*
Furlong, Edward V., Jr. *paper company executive*
Garrity, Vincent Francis, Jr. *lawyer*
Halloran, Harry Richard *contracting company executive*
Kates, Gerald Saul *printing executive*
Katz, Julian *gastroenterologist, educator*
Lefton, Harvey Bennett *gastroenterologist, educator, author*
Lotman, Herbert *food processing executive*
Manko, Joseph Martin, Sr. *lawyer*
Marden, Philip Ayer *physician, educator*
Marinakos, Plato Anthony *medical center administrator*
McAdams, Brian *advertising executive*
McGill, Dan Mays *insurance business educator*
Miller, L. Martin *accountant, financial planning specialist*
Quay, Thomas Emery *lawyer*
Schwartz, Charles D. *broadcast executive*
Shepard, Geoffrey Carroll *insurance company executive*

Bangor
Wolf, Stewart George, Jr. *physician, medical educator*

Beaver
Dible, Dennis D. *executive editor*
Gordon, Frank Wallace *newspaper publisher*
Helmick, Gayle Johnston *elementary education educator*
Ledebur, Linas Vockroth, Jr. *lawyer*

Beaver Falls
Matchett, Janet Reedy *psychologist*
Moran, Gerald Dwight *academic librarian*

Belle Vernon
Wapiennik, Carl Francis *manufacturing firm executive, planetarium and science institute executive*

Belleville
†Cranor, John Ross *retired surgeon*

Bensalem
Bishop, Howard Stuart *management consultant*
Faijean, Francois *metal products executive*
Kang, Benjamin Toyeong *writer, clergyman*
Sidewater, Arthur *retired retail executive, consultant*
Wachs, David V. *apparel executive*

Berwyn
Brundage, Russell Archibald *retired data processing executive*
Brunner, Lillian Sholtis *nurse, author*
Burch, John Walter *mining equipment company executive*
Fry, Clarence Herbert *retail executive*
Huffaker, John Boston *lawyer*
Lund, George Edward *retired electrical engineer*
Markle, John, Jr. *lawyer*
Odell, Herbert *lawyer*
†Silverman, Stanley Wayne *chemical company executive*
Van Sant, Robert William *manufacturing company executive*
Watters, Edward McLain, III *lawyer*
†Westphal, Rainer John *software company executive*
Wood, Thomas E. *lawyer*

Bethel Park
DeMay, Helen Louise *nursing services administrator*
Korchynsky, Michael *metallurgical engineer*
Marrs, Sharon Carter *librarian*
O'Donnell, William James *engineering executive*

Bethlehem
Allen, Eugene Murray *chemist*
Anderson, David Martin *environmental engineer*
Arnot, David Sheldon *steel company executive*
Barnette, Curtis Handley *steel company executive, lawyer*
Barsness, Richard Webster *management educator, administrator*
Beedle, Lynn Simpson *civil engineering educator*
Beidler, Peter Grant *English educator*
Benz, Edward John *retired clinical pathologist*
Bergethon, Kaare Roald *retired college president*
Billingsley, Charles Edward *transportation company executive*
Boylston, Benjamin Calvin *steel company executive*
Brozek, Josef *psychology educator, scientist*
Campbell, Donald Thomas *psychologist, educator*
Church, Thomas Trowbridge *former steel company executive*
†Coleman, Steven Laurence *hospital administrator, air force officer*
Connors, Leo Gerard *former finance company executive, consultant*
Dahlke, Walter Emil *electrical engineering educator*
Dowling, Joseph Albert *historian, educator*
Durkee, Jackson Leland *civil engineer*
Fairbairn, Ursula Farrell *human resources executive*
Fisher, John William *civil engineering educator*
Frankel, Barbara Brown *cultural anthropologist*
Gaertner, Johannes Alexander *retired art history educator, author*
Gardiner, Keith Mattinson *engineering educator*
Gates, Elmer D. *business executive*
Georgakis, Christos *chemical engineer educator, consultant, researcher*
Ghosh, Bhaskar Kumar *statistics educator, researcher*
Greene, David Mason *retired English language educator*
Hartmann, Robert Elliott *manufacturing company executive*
Haynes, Thomas Morris *philosophy educator*
Hertzberg, Richard Warren *materials science and engineering educator, researcher*
Hess, Dennis William *chemical engineering educator*
Hobbs, James Beverly *business administration educator, writer*
Jordan, John Allen, Jr. *steel company executive*
Kanofsky, Alvin Sheldon *physicist*
Karakash, John J. *engineering educator*
Kerchner, Charles Frederick, Jr. *electronics executive, engineer*
Kugelman, Irwin Jay *civil engineering educator*
Lennon, Gerard Patrick *civil engineering educator, researcher*
Lewis, Andrew Lindsay, Jr. (Drew Lewis) *transportation and natural resources executive*
Likins, Peter William *university president*
Lindgren, John Ralph *philosophy educator*
Martin, Roger Harry *college president*
†Mirro, John *engineering company executive*
Moe, Alden John *university dean*
Murphy, Warren Burton *writer, screenwriter*
Penny, Roger Pratt *management executive*
Pense, Alan Wiggins *metallurgical engineer, academic administrator*
Rivlin, Ronald Samuel *mathematics educator emeritus*
Roberts, Malcolm John *steel company executive*
Roberts, Richard *mechanical engineering educator*
Rushton, Brian Mandel *chemical company executive*
Sacks, Patricia Ann *librarian, consultant*
Schwartz, Eli *economics educator, writer*
Sclar, Charles Bertram *geology educator, researcher*
Smolansky, Oles M. *humanities educator*
Smyth, Donald Morgan *chemical educator, researcher*
†Sommers, Gordon L. *religious organization administrator*
Spillman, Robert Arnold *architect*
Stuart, Gary Miller *railroad executive*
Tuzla, Kemal *mechanical engineer, scientist*
Varnerin, Lawrence John *physicist*
Viest, Ivan M(iroslav) *consulting structural engineer*
von Bernuth, Carl W. *diversified corporation executive, lawyer*
Watkins, George Daniels *physics educator*
Weidner, Richard Tilghman *physicist, educator*
Weller, Andrew Michael *steel company executive*
Wenzel, Leonard Andrew *engineering educator*
†Wickmann, David L. *clergyman*
†Wilkes, Robert Edmond *bank executive*
Williams, David Bernard *metallurgical engineer*
Williams, Walter Fred *steel company executive*

Birdsboro
Hill, Lenora Mae *astrologer*
Moyer, David Lee *veterinarian*

Bloomsburg
Loncosky, Walter Beugger *real estate manager*
Miller, David Jergen *insurance executive*
Roh, Myung Ja *social worker*
Stropnicky, Gerard Patrick *theater director, consultant*
Vann, John Daniel, III *university dean, historian*

Blue Bell
Abramson, Leonard *healthcare organization executive*
Barron, Harold Sheldon *lawyer*
Blechschmidt, Edward Allan *information services and systems executive*
Braun, Reto *computer systems company executive*
Brendlinger, LeRoy R. *college president*
Carey, Joseph A., Jr. *electronics executive*
Crawford, Christine Ann *lawyer*
Elliott, John Michael *lawyer*
Gleklen, Donald Morse *investment company executive*
Henkels, Paul MacAllister *engineering and construction company executive*
Hirsch, Robert W. *environmental consulting, engineering and construction company executive*
Keppler, William Edmund *multinational company executive*
Nardello, Robert A. *medical software company executive*
Swansen, Samuel Theodore *lawyer*
Unruh, James Arlen *business machines company executive*
Vollmar, John Raymond *electrical engineer*
Wise, Allen Floyd *insurance executive*
Young, Jere Arnold *lawyer, management consultant*
Yuhas, Alan Thomas *investment management executive*

Boiling Springs
Hoefling, John Alan *former army officer, corporation executive*

Brackenridge
Bozzone, Robert P. *steel company executive*

Braddock
Slack, Edward Dorsey, III *financial systems professional, consultant*

Bradford
†Gibson, Margaret Ferguson *poet, educator*
Rice, Lester *electronics company executive*

Bradfordwoods
Davis, Nathan Tate *musician, educator*

Bridgeville
Morgan, Joyce Elizabeth *elementary school educator*

Bristol
Arkles, Barry Charles *chemist*
Atkinson, Susan D. *producing artistic director, theatrical consultant*
Hutton, Ann Hawkes *state official*
McEwen, Joseph, Jr. *distributing company executive*

Broomall
Cohen, Philip D. *book publishing executive*
Dibianca, Joseph Philip *finance executive*
Saunders, Sally Love *poet, educator*
Stewart, Allen Warren *lawyer*

Bryn Athyn
Kintner, William Roscoe *political science educator emeritus*

Bryn Mawr
Ballam, Samuel Humes, Jr. *retired corporate director*
Barth, Charles Fredrik *aerospace engineer*
Berliner, Ernst *chemistry educator*
Bernstein, Carol Lippit *humanities educator*
Braha, Thomas I. *oil industry executive*
Brand, Charles Macy *history educator*
Broido, Arnold Peace *music publishing company executive*
Brunt, Manly Yates, Jr. *psychiatrist*
Carroll, Mary Colvert *corporate executive*
Clark, George Roberts *retired trust company executive*
Crawford, William Arthur *geologist*
Dayton, Samuel Grey, Jr. *investment banker*
de Laguna, Frederica *anthropology educator emeritus, author, consultant*
Dorian, Nancy Currier *linguistics educator*
†Drew, James Mulcro *composer*
Driskill, John Ray *association executive*
Dudden, Arthur Power *historian, educator*
Dunlop, Robert Galbraith *retired petroleum company executive*
Ellis, Richard Stephens *archaeology educator, field archaeologist, researcher, consultant*
Fanus, Pauline Rife *librarian*
Gaisser, Julia Haig *classics educator*
Goutman, Lois Clair *retired drama educator*
Hamilton, Richard *Greek language educator*
Havens, Timothy Markle *investment advisory firm executive*
Hoffman, Howard Stanley *experimental psychologist, educator*
Hoopes, Janet Louise *educator, psychologist*
Huth, Edward Janavel *physician, editor*
Kaminski, Joseph Casmir *insurance company executive*
King, Willard Fahrenkamp (Mrs. Edmund Ludwig King) *Spanish language educator*
Krausz, Michael *philosopher, educator*
Lafarge, Catherine *dean*
Lane, Barbara Miller (Barbara Miller-Lane) *humanities educator*
†Lang, Mabel Louise *classics educator*
Mallory, Frank Bryant *chemistry educator*
McCauley, Clark Richard *psychology educator*
Mc Lean, William L., III *publisher*
McPherson, Mary Patterson *academic administrator*
Moyer, F. Stanton *financial executive, advisor*
Noone, Robert Barrett *plastic surgeon*
Platt, Lucian Brewster *geology educator*
Porter, Judith Deborah Revitch *sociologist, educator*
Ridgway, Brunilde Sismondo *archaeology educator*
Rubinstein, Alvin Zachary *political science educator, author*
Salmon, John Hearsey McMillan *historian, educator*
Stapleton, Katharine Laurence *English educator, writer*
Stucky, Steven (Edward) *composer*
Tanis, James Robert *library director, history educator, clergyman*
Tidmarsh, Karen MacAusland *dean*
Turbidy, John Berry *investor, management consultant*
Walton, Clarence *political science and history educator*
Weese, Samuel H. *academic administrator*

Buck Hill Falls
Meditz, Walter Joseph *engineering consultant*

Buckingham
Altier, William John *management consultant*

Bushkill
Garretto, Leonard Anthony, Jr. *insurance company executive*

Muesing Ellwood, Edith Elizabeth *writer, researcher, publisher, editor*

Butler
†Day, Margaret Ann *research librarian, information specialist*
†Green, Charles Thomas *hardware distribution company executive*
Kane, Marilyn Elizabeth *small business owner*
Kosar, John E. *architectural firm executive*
†Rath, Frank E., Sr. *electronics executive*
†Rath, Frank E., Jr. *electronics executive*
Thomas, Russell Alvin *hardware company executive*
Zehfuss, Lawrence Thomas *hardware supply company executive*

California
Langham, Norma *playwright, educator, poet, composer, inventor*

Cambridge Springs
Hughes, William Frank *mechanical and electrical engineering educator*

Camp Hill
Bergonzi, Frank Michael *retail drug store chain executive*
Crider, Rudyard Lee *psychotherapist*
Grass, Alexander *retail company executive*
Grass, Martin Lehrman *business executive*
Johnston, Thomas McElree, Jr. *church administrator*
Keller, John Richard *insurance company executive*
Miller, Ronald Anthony *distribution company executive*
Miner, Dennis Kane *chemical engineer, consultant*
Nowak, Jacquelyn Louise *administrative officer, realtor, consultant*
†Peters, Ralph Edgar *business executive*
Robertson, James Colvert *insurance company executive*
Robinson, Ronald Michael *health care financial executive, financial consultant*
Ross, Samuel D., Jr. *insurance company executive*
†Scheiner, James Ira *engineering company executive*
Slane, Charles Joseph *chain drug store executive*
Spiers, Tomas Hoskins, Jr. *architect*
Sullivan, Barry Michael *finance executive*

Canonsburg
Harker, Joseph Edward *construction, industrial and steel company executive*
Mascetta, Joseph Anthony *principal*

Carlisle
Clarke, Walter Sheldon *federal government official, instructor*
†Dineen, Daniel Thomas *lawyer*
Fish, Chester Boardman, Jr. *publishing consultant, writer*
Fox, Arturo Angel *Spanish language educator*
Fritschler, A. Lee *college president, public policy educator*
Glenn, Peter G. *lawyer, educator*
Graham, William Patton, III *plastic surgeon, educator*
Jacobs, Norman G(abriel) *sociologist, educator*
Laws, Priscilla Watson *physics educator*
Lewis, Claude, Jr. *retired shoe company executive*
Long, Howard Charles *physics educator emeritus*
Rossbacher, Lisa Ann *dean, geology educator, writer*
Ruble, Duane Russell *retail drug store executive*
Schiffman, Joseph Harris *literary historian, educator*
†Shrader, Charles Reginald *historian*
Stachacz, John Charles *librarian*
Talley, Carol Lee *newspaper editor*

Carlisle Barracks
†Anderson, Lynn John *veterinarian, army officer*

Center Valley
Gambet, Daniel G(eorge) *college president, clergyman*

Central City
Brown, Robert Alan *retired construction materials company executive*

Chadds Ford
Duff, James Henry *museum director, environmental administrator*
Isakoff, Sheldon Erwin *chemical engineer*

Chalfont
Clifford, Maurice Cecil *physician, former college president, foundation executive*
Tomlinson, Juliette Shell *elementary school educator*

Chambersburg
Furr, Quint Eugene *marketing executive*
Gelbach, Martha Harvey *genealogist*
Rumler, Robert Hoke *agricultural consultant, retired association executive*

Cheltenham
†McGoldrick, Margaret Mary *hospital administrator*
Weinstock, Walter Wolfe *systems engineer*

Chester
Bruce, Robert James *university president*
Buck, Lawrence Paul *academic administrator*
Clark, James Edward *physician, medical educator*
Frank, Amalie Julianna *computer science, electrical engineering and mathematics educator, consultant*
Moll, Clarence Russel *university president emeritus, consultant*

Clairton
†Dick, David E. *construction company executive*
†Dick, Douglas Patrick *construction company executive*

Clarion
Foreman, Thomas Alexander *dentist*
Mc Cabe, Gerard Benedict *library administrator*

Clarks Summit
Alperin, Irwin Ephraim *clothing company executive*
Firmin, Michael Wayne *counseling educator*
Ross, Adrian E. *retired drilling manufacturing company executive*

Clearfield
Pride, Douglas Spencer *minister*
Ulerich, William Keener *publishing company executive*

Coatesville
†Ainslie, George William *psychiatrist, behavioral economist*
Bucher, John Henry *metallurgical consultant, technology manager*
Gehring, David Austin *physician, adminstrator, cardiologist*
Meyers, Frederick M. *diversified industrial products and service company executive*
Myers, Frederick M. *metal products executive*
Nocks, James Jay *psychiatrist*
Sprague, William Douglas *lawyer, company executive*

Cochranville
Sazegar, Morteza *artist*

Collegeville
Cawthorn, Robert Elston *retired health care executive*
†De Rosen, Michel *business executive*
Dupuis, Claude Paul *pharmaceutical company executive*
Farmar, Robert Melville *medical scientist, educator*
Kun, Kenneth A. *business executive*
†Perillo, Giulio *controller*
Popp, James Alan *toxicologist, toxicology executive*
Richter, Richard Paul *academic administrator*
Smalley, Christopher Joseph *pharmaceutical company professional*
Stoughton, W. Vickery *healthcare executive*
†Strassburger, John Robert *academic administrator*
Tretter, James Ray *pharmaceutical company executive*

Colmar
Weber-Roochvarg, Lynn *consultant, adult education specialist, librarian*

Conshohocken
†Benoliel, Peter Andre *chemical company executive*
Boenning, Henry Dorr, Jr. *investment banker*
Cohen, Alan *civil engineer*
Cunningham, James Gerald, Jr. *transportation company executive*
Gutkin, Arthur Lee *lawyer*
Mullen, Eileen Anne *training and development executive*
Rippel, Harry Conrad *mechanical engineer, consultant*
Rounick, Jack A. *lawyer*
Schein, Philip Samuel *physician, educator, pharmaceutical executive*
Spaeth, Karl Henry *chemical company executive, lawyer*
Tily, Stephen Bromley, III *bank executive*

Coopersburg
Eckardt, Arthur Roy *religion studies educator emeritus*
Spira, Joel Solon *electronics company executive*

Cooperstown
Hogg, James Henry, Jr. *retired education educator*

Coraopolis
Hayes, Diane Elizabeth *principal*
Koepfinger, Joseph Leo *utilities executive*
Nelson, Donald J. *engineering executive*

Cornwall
Ehrhart, Carl Yarkers *retired minister, retired college administrator*

Cranberry Township
Bashore, George Willis *bishop*
Birch, Jack Willard *psychologist, educator*

Cresson
Pierce, Edward Franklin *college president*

Dallas
Sutton, Royal Keith *marketing professional*

Danville
Ackerman, F. Kenneth, Jr. *health facility administrator*
Kazem, Ismail *radiation oncologist, educator, health science facility administrator*
Lessin, Michael Edward *oral-maxillofacial surgeon*
Morgan, Howard Edwin *physiologist*
Pierce, James Clarence *surgeon*

Darby
†Kulesher, Robert Roy *health care administrator*

Delaware Water Gap
Woods, Philip Wells (Phil Woods) *jazz musician composer*

Devon
Brody, Aaron Leo *food and packaging consultant*
Lindros, Eric Bryan *professional hockey player*
Niehaus, Robert James *investment banking executive*
O'Malley, John Edward *medical association administrator, physician*

Dillsburg
Bowers, Glenn Lee *association executive*
Jackson, George Lyman *nuclear medicine physician*

Douglassville
Burke, Peter Arthur *microbiologist, chemist*

Dover
Hayek, William Edward *investment counsel, financial consultant*

Doylestown
Brink, Frank, Jr. *biophysicst, former educator*
Cathcart, Harold Robert *hospital administrator*
Davis, Carole Joan *psychologist*
Dunn, Mignon *mezzo-soprano*
George, William Leo *plant geneticist, educator*
Holstrom, Carleton Arthur *brokerage house executive*
Long, Ronald Alex *real estate and financial consultant, educator*
Maser, Frederick Ernest *clergyman*
Mishler, John Milton (Yochanan Menashsheh ben Shaul) *natural sciences educator, academic administrator*
†Morgnanesi, Lanny M. *journalist*
Purpura, Peter Joseph *museum curator, exhibition designer*
Smith, Charles Paul *newspaper publisher*
Thomas, Ellen Louise *private school administrator*

Drexel Hill
Alexander, Lloyd Chudley *author*
Martino, Michael Charles *entertainer, musician*
McAllister, Wayne R. *principal*
Montgomery, Patricia Aline *family physician*
Perkins, Ralph Linwood *business executive, public health administration specialist*
Schiazza, Guido Domenic (Guy Schiazza) *educational association administrator*
Thompson, William David *minister, homiletics educator*

Drums
Palance, Jack *actor*

Eagles Mere
Sample, Frederick Palmer *former college president*

East Butler
Mielcuszny, Albert John *wholesale distribution executive*
Pentz, Paul *hardware company executive*

East Stroudsburg
Briggs, Philip James *political science educator, author, lecturer*
Crackel, Theodore Joseph *historian*
Gilbert, James Eastham *academic administrator*

Easton
Ashby, Richard James, Jr. *bank executive, lawyer*
Bartolacci, Guido Jamess *retail company executive*
Cooke, Jacob Ernest *history educator, author*
Grunberg, Robert Leon Willy *nephrologist*
Gurin, Richard Stephen *manufacturing company executive*
Holmes, Larry Kandy, Jr. *professional boxer*
Kincaid, John *political science educator, editor*
Mamana, Joseph *editor*
Reibman, Jeanette Fichman *retired state senator*
†Sherma, Joseph *chemistry educator*
Van Antwerpen, Franklin Stuart *federal judge*

Edinboro
Cox, Clifford Laird *university administrator, musician*
Diebold, Foster Frank *university president*
Fleischauer, John Frederick *English language educator, academic administrator*
Kemenyffy, Steven *artist, art educator*
Miller, G(erson) H(arry) *research institute director, mathematician, computer scientist, chemist*
Paul, Charlotte P. *nursing educator*

Eighty Four
Capone, Alphonse William *retired industrial executive*

Elizabethtown
Brown, Dale Weaver *clergyman, theologian, educator*
Krut, Stephen Frank *trade association administrator*
Madeira, Robert Lehman *association executive*
Mann, Lowell D. *religious organization executive*
Ritsch, Frederick Field *academic administrator, historian*

Elizabethville
†DeSoto, Pete *company executive*

Elkins Park
Bayliss, George Vincent *art educator, artist*
Davidson, Abraham A. *art historian, photographer*
Erlebacher, Martha Mayer *artist, educator*
Fussell, Catharine Pugh *biological researcher*
Madigan, Martha *photographer, artist, photography educator*
Prince, Morton Bronenberg *physicist*
†Thomas, Geoffrey C. *finance company executive*

Emmaus
Beldon, Sanford T. *publisher*
Bowers, Klaus D(ieter) *retired electronics research development company executive*
Bricklin, Mark Harris *magazine editor, publisher*
†Wallace, Ken *magazine publisher*

Erdenheim
Hargens, Charles William, III *electrical engineer, consultant*
Lantos, Peter R(ichard) *industrial consultant, chemical engineer*

Erie
Adovasio, J. M. *anthropologist, archeologist, educator*
Anderson, Cathie Kellogg *education educator*
Bentz, Warren Worthington *federal bankruptcy judge*
Boyes, Karl W. *state legislator*
Bracken, Charles Herbert *banker*
De Witt, William Gerald *retired paper company executive*
Fessler, Donald Francis *business executive*
Freeman, William A. *manufacturing company executive*
Gottschalk, Frank Klaus *real estate executive*
Gray, Robert Beckwith *engineer*
Hagen, Thomas Bailey *former insurance company executive, state official*
Hedrick, Charles Lynnwood *holding company executive*
Hendl, Walter *conductor, pianist, composer*
Hey, John Charles *electronics company executive*
Hsu, Bertrand Dahung *mechanical engineer*
Karlson, Eskil Leannart *biophysicist*
Lilley, John Mark *university provost and dean*
Mead, Edward Mathews *newspaper executive*
Mencer, Glenn Everell *federal judge*
Nash, Mary Alice *nursing educator*
Nygaard, Richard Lowell *federal judge*
Ridge, Michele Moore *librarian*

Rowley, Robert Deane, Jr. *bishop*
†Ryan, Gerald Anthony *financial advisor, venture capitalist*
Savocchio, Joyce A. *mayor*
Skonieczka, Richard Gerald *retired police chief, coroner*
Stolley, James S. *manufacturing executive*
Trautman, Donald W. *bishop*
Vanco, John L. *art museum director*
Weber, Herman C., Jr. *architect*
Zuern, David Ernest *bank executive*

Erwinna
Geldmacher, Robert Carl *software corporation executive*
Richman, Joan F. *television consultant*

Evans City
Salisbury, Judith Muriel *marketing consultant*

Exeter
Stocker, Joyce Arlene *retired secondary education educator*

Export
Andrews, Harry Nicholas *engineering executive*
Wagner, Charles Leonard *electrical engineer, consultant*

Exton
Lewis, Thomas B. *specialty chemical company executive*
†Patterson, Kent E. *environmental services consultant, hydrogeologist*
Penrose, Charles, Jr. *association executive*
Sanford, Richard D. *computer company executive*
†Woodruff, Paul Harrison *civil engineer, consultant*

Fairless Hills
Szuhy, Lawrence Gregory *automotive company executive*

Fairview
Duval, Albert Frank *paper company executive*

Farmington
Witt, Charles E. *coal company executive*

Fayetteville
Kocek, Stephanie Susan *theater executive*

Feasterville
†Liberati, Maria Theresa *fashion production company executive*
McEvilly, James Patrick, Jr. *lawyer*

Felton
Shoemaker, Eleanor Boggs *television production company executive*

Ferndale
Folk, James *sales executive*

Fleetwood
Lewis, Dana Kenneth *marketing company executive, consultant*

Flourtown
Christy, John Gilray *financial company executive*
Lambert, Joan Dorety *elementary education educator*
Lee, Adrian Iselin, Jr. *journalist*

Fogelsville
Ault, James Mase *bishop*

Fort Washington
Blumberg, Donald Freed *management consultant*
Buescher, Adolph Ernst (Dolph Buescher) *aerospace company executive*
Deric, Arthur Joseph *management consultant, lawyer*
Hague, Stephen George *museum director*
Urbach, Frederick *physician, educator*

Forty Fort
Falkowitz, Daniel *clothing manufacturing company executive*

Frazer
Godwin, Pamela June *insurance company executive*
Kennedy, Donald Davidson, Jr. *insurance company executive*

Fredericksburg
Ludwig, Edward Lee *director athletics, educator, coach*

Freeland
Rudawski, Joseph George *educational administrator*

Gaines
Beller, Martin Leonard *retired orthopaedic surgeon*

Gettysburg
Boritt, Gábor Szappanos *history educator*
Cisneros, Jose A. *historical site administrator*
Coughenour, Kavin Luther *career officer, military historian*
Hallberg, Budd Jaye *management consulting firm executive*
Mainwaring, Thomas Lloyd *motor freight company executive*
Plischke, Elmer *political science educator*
Schein, Virginia Ellen *psychologist, educator*

Gibsonia
Cauna, Nikolajs *physician, medical educator*
Heilman, Carl Edwin *lawyer*
Shoub, Earle Phelps *chemical engineer, educator*

Gladwyne
Acton, David *lawyer*
Allen, Theresa Ohotnicky *neurobiologist, consultant*
Booth, Harold Waverly *finance and investment company executive, lawyer*
†Castle, Joseph Lanktree, II *energy company executive, consultant*
Geisel, Cameron Meade, Jr. *investment professional*

Hasselman, Richard B. consultant, retired railroad executive
Mc Donald, Robert Emmett company executive
Patten, Lanny Ray industrial gas industry executive
Pettit, Horace allergist, consultant
Stick, Alyce Cushing information systems consultant

Glen Mills
Churchill, Stuart Winston chemical engineering educator

Glenside
Apperson, Jack Alfonso retired army officer, business executive
Forman, Edgar Ross mechanical engineer
Frudakis, Zenos Antonios sculptor, artist
Johnson, Waine Cecil dermatologist
Landman, Bette Emeline academic administrator

Grantham
Byers, John A. bishop
Chubb, Harold D. church official
Grannon, Charles Lee investment banking official
†Shafer, R. Donald church official
Sider, E(arl) Morris English, history educator, archivist
Sider, Harvey Ray minister, church administrator

Greensburg
Boyd, Robert Wright, III lamp company executive
Catalano, Louis William, Jr. neurologist
Duck, Patricia Mary librarian
Guyker, William Charles, Jr. electrical engineer, researcher
Harrell, Edward Harding newspaper executive
Mann, Jacinta academic administrator, mathematician, educator
McDowell, Michael David lawyer, utility executive
Winters, Sister Mary Ann religious organization administrator

Greentown
Forcheskie, Carl S. former apparel company executive

Greenville
Farina, Andrew church administrator
Stuver, Francis Edward former railway car company executive
Wilt, Sonya Anne Mugnani speech and language pathologist
Zimmer, Albert Arthur education educator

Grove City
Brenner, Frederic James biology educator, ecological consultant

Gwynedd
Bryant, Robert Parker retired food service and lodging executive
Zumeta, Bertram William retired economist

Gwynedd Valley
Feenane, Sister Mary Alice principal

Hanover
Kline, Donald food company executive
Toft, Thelma Marilyn secondary educator
†Warehime, John A. food products executive

Harleysville
Craugh, Joseph Patrick, Jr. insurance company executive, lawyer
Daller, Walter E., Jr. banking executive
Freudig, David Wayne elementary educator
McCarter, Michael G. insurance company executive
Mitchell, Bradford William insurance executive, lawyer
†Rhodes, Gary Lynn food company executive
Ruth, Alpheus Landis dairy farmer

Harrisburg
Allen, Heath Ledward lawyer
Andrezeski, Anthony (Buzz Andrezeski) state senator
Armstrong, Gibson E. state senator
Armstrong, Thomas Errol state legislator
Ball, William Bentley lawyer
Banks, Albert Victor, Jr. government administrator
Bishop, Louise Williams state legislator
Cadieux, Roger Joseph physician, mental health care executive
Caldwell, William Wilson federal judge
Campbell, Carl Lester banker
Carnahan, Frances Morris magazine editor
Cate, Donald James mechanical engineer, consultant
Cawley, James Hughes lawyer
Cline, Andrew Haley lawyer
Cramer, John McNaight lawyer
Dattilo, Nicholas C. bishop
Diehm, James Warren lawyer, educator
Dietz, John Raphael consulting engineer executive
Dorsey-Peterson, Jeanine public health administrator
Edmiston, Guy S., Jr. bishop
Fargo, Howard Lynn legislator
Farmer, Elaine Frazier state legislator
Fortier, John Bertram museum director, historian
Giusti, Joseph Paul global human resource development director, retired university chancellor
Glass, Brent D. state commission administrator
Goell, James Emanuel electronics company executive
Gover, Raymond Lewis newspaper publisher
†Grant, Robert N. state official
Gruitza, Michael legislator
Handler, Mimi editor, writer
Hanson, Robert DeLolle lawyer
Hopper, John D. state senator
Hudson, William Jeffrey, Jr. manufacturing company executive
Hughes, William Francis, Jr. education association administrator
Itkin, Ivan state legislator
Jeffries, Richard Haley physician, broadcasting company executive
Jones, Roxanne Harper state legislator
Josephs, Babette legislator
Kelly, Robert Edward, Jr. lawyer
Kimmel, Robert Irving corporate communication design consultant, former state government official
King, William J. bank executive
Klein, Michael D. lawyer
Kury, Franklin Leo lawyer
Lear, John writer, editor
Lederer, Marie A. state legislator
Loedding, Peter Alfred trade association executive
Loeper, F. Joseph state senator
Lourie, Norman Victor government official, social worker
Lucia, Philip John insurance company executive
Margo, Katherine Lane physician
Marley, James Earl manufacturing company executive
May, Felton Edwin bishop
McCormick, James Harold academic administrator
McInnes, Harold A. manufacturing company executive
McNutt, Charlie Fuller, Jr. bishop
Mead, James Matthew insurance company executive
Mitchell, Brenda K. state secretary
Moritz, Milton Edward security consultant
Narigan, Harold W. manufacturing company executive
Neilson, Winthrop Cunningham, III communications executive, financial communications consultant
Newsome, William Roy, Jr. state official
Nielsen, Edward L. medical association administrator
Nyce, Robert Eugene state legislator, tax accountant
Parker, Sara Ann librarian
Peechatka, Walter Norman government official
Preate, Ernest D., Jr. state attorney general
Raab, Walter Ferdinand manufacturing company executive
Rambo, Sylvia H. federal judge
Redmond, James Melvin medical association administrator
Ridge, Thomas Joseph governor, former congressman
Rudy, Ruth Corman state legislator
Salmon, Kathleen A. insurance company executive
Schwartz, Allyson Y. state senator
†Schweiker, Mark S. lieutenant governor
Singel, Mark Stephen state official
†Smith, Karl mortgage company executive
Souder, Robert R. personnel director
†Spector, Morton wholesale distribution executive
Stabler, Donald Billman business executive
Sturgen, Winston photographer, printmaker, artist
Termini, Roseann Bridget lawyer
Thaler, Nancy Regina state agency administrator
Tyson, Gail L. health federation administrator
Vanderveen, Peter wholesale grocery company executive
Warshaw, Allen Charles lawyer
Wei, I-Yuan research and development consultant and director
Zimmerman, LeRoy S. lawyer, former state attorney general
Zook, Merlin Wayne meteorologist

Hatboro
Hull, Lewis Woodruff manufacturing company executive

Hatfield
Garis, Mark church administrator

Haverford
Baney, John Edward insurance company executive
Bemis, Hal Lawall engineering and business executive
Bogash, Richard retired pharmaceutical company executive
Davison, John Herbert music educator, academic administrator
Frick, Sidney Wanning lawyer
Greene, Curtis mathematics educator
Heath, Douglas Hamilton psychology educator
Jorden, Eleanor Harz linguist, educator
Jurney, Dorothy Misener journalist, editor
Kessinger, Tom G. college president
Lazar, Anna chemist
McGlinn, Frank Cresson Potts lawyer
Mellink, Machteld Johanna archaeologist, educator
Merrill, Arthur Alexander financial analyst
Northrup, Herbert Roof economist, business executive
Partridge, Robert Bruce astronomy educator
Perloe, Sidney Irwin primatologist, educator
Spielman, John Philip, Jr. historian, educator
Stegeman, Charles fine arts educator, lecturer, consultant
Stroud, James Stanley retired lawyer
Szabad, George Michael lawyer, former mayor
Talucci, Samuel James retired chemical company executive
Thimann, Kenneth Vivian biology educator
Williams, William Earle artist, educator, curator
Young-Bruehl, Elisabeth philosophy educator
Zalinski, Edmund Louis Gray insurance executive, mutual funds and real estate executive, investor

Havertown
Brinker, Thomas Michael finance executive
Sheppard, Walter Lee, Jr. chemical engineer, consultant

Hawley
Conley, Clare Dean retired magazine editor

Hazleton
Denise, Robert Phillips craft company executive
Gatty, Eugene B. school system administrator
Miller, David Emanuel physics educator, researcher

Hellertown
McCullagh, James Charles publishing company executive

Herminie
McAbee, Cheryl Rosilyn lawyer

Hermitage
Havrilla, John William middle school educator

Hershey
Anderson, Allan Crosby hospital executive
Biebuyck, Julien Francois anesthesiologist, educator
Bomgardner, William Earl retired association executive, photographer
Cary, Gene Leonard psychiatrist
Davis, Dwight cardiologist, educator
Duncan, Charles Lee food products company executive
Eyster, Mary Elaine hematologist, educator
Farrell, Eugene George editor
Hopper, Anita Klein molecular genetics educator
Kauffman, Gordon Lee, Jr. surgeon, educator
Lang, Carol Max veterinarian, educator
Leaman, David Martin cardiologist
Lehman, Lois Joan medical librarian
Lindenberg, Steven Phillip counselor, consultant
Lipton, Allan medical educator
McInerney, Joseph John biomedical engineer, educator
Naeye, Richard L. pathologist, educator
Pierce, William Schuler cardiac surgeon, educator
Rapp, Fred virologist
Reynolds, Herbert Young physician, internist
Rohner, Thomas John, Jr. urologist
Schuller, Diane Ethel allergist, immunologist, educator
Severs, Walter Bruce pharmacology educator, researcher
Stump, Troy Elwood zoo director
Vesell, Elliot Saul pharmacologist, educator
Waldhausen, John Anton surgeon, educator
Wassner, Steven Joel pediatric nephrologist, educator
Wolfe, Kenneth L. food products manufacturing company executive
Zelis, Robert Felix cardiologist, educator
Zimmerman, Richard Anson food company executive
Zoumas, Barry Lee food products company executive, nutritionist

Hidden Valley
Funari, John H. editor, consultant

Highspire
†Sokol, John L. transportation executive

Holland
Umbreit, Wayne William bacteriologist, educator

Hollidaysburg
Adamec, Joseph Victor Otto bishop
Bloom, Lawrence Stephen retired clothing company executive

Honesdale
Barbe, Walter Burke education educator
Brown, Kent Louis, Jr. magazine editor
Clark, Christine May editor, author

Horsham
Alter, Dennis holding company executive
Boswell, Gary Taggart electronics company executive
Brenner, Ronald John pharmaceutical industry executive
Goff, Kenneth Wade electrical engineer
Hakimoglu, Ayhan electronics company executive
Hart, Alex Way banker
Hook, Jerry B. pharmaceutical company executive
Logue, John Joseph psychologist
McNulty, Carrell Stewart, Jr. manufacturing company executive, architect
Neff, P. Sherrill health care executive
Strock, Gerald E. school system administrator
Wesselink, David Duwayne finance company executive
Woodruff, Harrison D., Jr. principal
Zimmermann, R. Peter financial executive

Hummelstown
Bruhn, John Glyndon university official, educator
Custer, John Charles investment broker
Moffitt, Charles William insurance sales executive
Murphy, S(usan) (Jane Murphy) small business owner

Huntingdon
Durnbaugh, Donald Floyd church history educator, researcher
Murray, Andrew peace studies educator
Neff, Robert Wilbur church official, educator

Huntingdon Valley
Appell, Kathleen Marie management consultant, legal administrator
Forman, Howard Irving lawyer, former government official
Jaffe, Marvin Eugene pharmaceutical company executive, neurologist
Liberti, Paul Alfonso biotechnology executive, inventor, entrepreneur, consultant
Toll, Robert Irwin lawyer, real estate developer
West, A(rnold) Sumner chemical engineer

Indiana
Engler, W. Joseph, Jr. lawyer
Jones, Shelley Pryce chemical company executive, writer
Kegel, William George mining company executive
Mc Cauley, R. Paul criminologist, educator
Nelson, Linda Shearer child development and family relations educator
Perlongo, Daniel James composer
Pettit, Lawrence Kay university president
Thibadeau, Eugene Francis educator, consultant
†Walker, Donald Anthony economist, educator

Irvine
Koedel, John Gilbert, Jr. forge company executive

Jeannette
†Smiy, Paul R. manufacturing executive, heavy

Jenkintown
Baldwin, David Rawson retired university administrator
Beavers, Ellington McHenry chemical company executive
Clemmer, Leon architect, planner
Coccagna, Fred Joseph, Jr. flooring manufacturing executive
Colman, Wendy psychoanalyst
Driehuys, Leonardus Bastiaan conductor
Greenspan-Margolis, June E. psychiatrist
Hankin, Elaine Krieger psychologist, researcher
Haythornthwaite, Robert Morphet civil engineer, educator
Nerenberg, Aaron lawyer
Reese, Francis Edward retired chemical company executive, consultant
Sadoff, Robert Leslie psychiatrist
Seid, Ruth (Jo Sinclair) author

Jersey Shore
†Nassberg, Richard T. lawyer

Johnstown
Alcamo, Frank Paul retired principal
Antonazzo, Nicholas Orlando lawyer, corporate real estate executive
Glock, Earl Ferdinand lawyer
Glosser, William Louis lawyer
Grove, Nancy Carol academic administrator
Gunter, John Brown, Jr. retired real estate executive
†Karnes, Timothy Joseph hospital administrator, consultant
Kuhn, Howard Arthur engineering executive, educator
Menna, Christine Ann public relations executive
Miloro, Frank P. church official, religious studies educator
Nicholas, (Richard G. Smisko) bishop
Pasquerilla, Frank James real estate developer and manager
Saltz, Howard Joel newspaper editor
Simmons, Elroy, Jr. retired utility executive
†Smisko, Nicholas Richard bishop, educator
†Smith, Donald W. association executive
Wise, Robert Lester utilities executive
Yurcisin, John church official

Jones Mills
Fish, Paul Waring lawyer

Kempton
†Lenhart, Cynthia Rae conservation organization executive

Kennett Square
Allam, Mark Whittier veterinarian, former university administrator
Barr, David Charles healthcare executive
Beck, Dorothy Fahs social researcher
Bronner, Edwin Blaine history educator
Leymaster, Glen R. former medical association executive
Martin, George (Whitney) writer
May, Harold Edward chemical company executive
Naeve, Milo Merle museum curator
Nason, John William retired college president, educational consultant
Perera, George A. physician
Taylor, Bernard J., II banker
Vainstein, Rose librarian, educator
Vining, Elizabeth Gray author
Wilson, David Cartwright headmaster

Kimberton
Douglas, Bryce former pharmaceutical company executive
Williams, Lawrence Soper photographer

King Of Prussia
Bramson, Robert Sherman lawyer
Carroll, Margaret Ann chemist
Cash, Francis Winford health care executive
Dubbs, Robert Morton lawyer, health services company executive
Foster, John Hallett health facility executive
Langton, Raymond Benedict, III manufacturing company executive
Lessem, Jan Norbert medical director
Miller, Alan B. hospital management executive
Olexy, Jean Shofranko English educator
Olson, Bob Moody marketing executive
Poste, George Henry pharmaceutical company executive
†Traynor, Sean Gabrial manufacturing executive
Volpe, Ralph Pasquale insurance company executive
Wilson, Hugh Shannon retired manufacturing company executive, consultant
†Winkhaus, Hans-Dietrich chemicals executive
Wulff, Harald P. chemicals executive

Kingston
Gayeski, Alba Lori interior designer
Marko, Andrew Paul school system administrator
Weisberger, Barbara choreographer, artistic director, educator

Knox
Rupert, Elizabeth Anastasia retired university dean

Kutztown
Dougherty, Percy H. geographer, educator, politician
Ghiglia, Oscar Alberto classical guitarist
McFarland, David E. university president
Ring, Rodney Everett religion educator

Lafayette Hill
Dixon, Fitz Eugene, Jr. professional baseball team executive
Green, Rose Basile (Mrs. Raymond S. Green) poet, author, educator
King, Leon financial services executive

Lake Ariel
Massa, Conrad Harry religious studies educator
Tague, Charles Francis retired engineering, construction and real estate development company executive

Lake Harmony
Polansky, Larry Paul court administrator, consultant

Lancaster
Albright, Annarose M. secondary school educator
Brown, Joseph Allen lawyer, business executive
†Burlefinger, Erich electronics executive
Cody, William Henry journal editor
Collins, Kathleen A. artistic director
Deaver, Everette Allen diversified manufacturing company executive
Dubble, Curtis William pastor
Duroni, Charles Eugene retired lawyer, food products executive
Ebersole, Mark Chester emeritus college president
Ellis, Calvert N. former college president
Eshleman, Silas Kendrick, III psychiatrist
Filler, Mary Ann librarian
Freeman, Clarence Calvin financial executive
Gingerich, Naomi R. emergency room nurse
Glick, Garland Wayne retired theological seminary president
Hennessey, Joseph E. chemicals executive
Hess, Earl Hollinger laboratory executive, chemist
High, S. Dale diversified company executive
Joseph, John history educator
Kelly, Robert Lynn advertising agency executive

Kneedler, Alvin Richard *college president*
†Liddell, W. Kirk *specialty contracting and distribution company executive, lawyer*
Lorch, George A. *manufacturing company executive*
Nast, Dianne Martha *lawyer*
Shaw, Charles Raymond *journalist*
Shenk, Willis Weidman *newspaper executive*
Simmons, Deidre Warner *performing company executive*
Stephenson, Donald Grier, Jr. *government studies educator*
Taylor, Norman William *economics educator*
Troupe, Terry Lee *holding company banker*
Whare, Wanda Snyder *lawyer*
Zimmerman, D(onald) Patrick *lawyer, educator*

Landenberg
Aldrich, Nancy Armstrong *psychotherapist, clinical social worker*

Langhorne
Babb, Wylie Sherrill *college president*
Brafford, William Charles *lawyer*
Brennan, John James *marketing executive*
Davies, John Edward *biotechnology company executive*
Willis, Wesley Robert *college administrator*

Lansdale
Baughn, Juan R. *high school principal*
Echols, Gloria *housing service administrator*
Esterhai, John Louis *lawyer*
Fawley, John Jones *retired banker*
Lovelace, Robert Frank *health science facility administrator, researcher*
Schnable, George Luther *chemist*
Schwartz, Louis Winn *ophthalmologist*

Lansdowne
Popovics, Sandor *civil engineer, educator, researcher*
Zingraff, Michael, Jr. *magazine editor*

Latrobe
Conley, Edward Vincent, Jr. *metallurgical engineering educator*
Murtha, John Francis *priest, academic administrator, history educator*
Underwood, James Martin *business executive*
†Zanotti, Marie Louise *hospital admininstrator*

Laverock
Block, Isaac Edward *association executive*

Lebanon
Arnold, Edward Henry *transportation executive*
McMindes, Roy James *aggregate company executive*

Lehigh Valley
Kocsis, James Paul *artist, publisher*

Leola
McElhinny, Wilson Dunbar *banker*
Wedel, Paul George *retired hospital administrator*

Levittown
†Halberstein, Joseph Leonard *retired associate editor*
La Vo, Carl Palmer, Jr. *newspaper editor, author*

Lewisburg
†Adams, William D. *academic administrator*
Anderson, John Whiting *economics educator*
Candland, Douglas Keith *psychology educator*
Edgerton, Mills Fox, Jr. *foreign language educator*
Jump, Chester Jackson, Jr. *clergyman, church official*
Main, A. Donald *bishop*
Neuman, Nancy Adams Mosshammer *civic leader*
Payne, Michael David *English language educator*
Ray, David Scott *mathematics educator*
Sojka, Gary Allan *biologist, educator, university official*

Ligonier
Mellon, Seward Prosser *investment executive*
Pilz, Alfred Norman *manufacturing company executive*
Schmidt, Adolph William *retired ambassador*

Lincoln University
Gaymon, William Edward *psychology educator*
Williams, Willie, Jr. *physicist, educator*

Lititz
Acker, Raymond Abijah *minister*
Bolinger, Robert Stevens *banker*
Koch, Bruce R. *diplomat*
Smith, Thomas Clair *manufacturing company executive*

Lock Haven
Almes, June *retired education educator, librarian*
Snowiss, Alvin L. *lawyer*
Willis, Craig Dean *university president*

Loretto
Benham, Philip Owen, Jr. *business marketing educator, consultant*

Lower Burrell
Kinosz, Donald Lee *quality consultant*

Lumberville
Frank, F. Alexander *retired savings and loan executive, lawyer*
Katsiff, Bruce *artist*

Lyon Station
Bowers, Richard Philip *manufacturing executive*
Breidegam, DeLight Edgar, Jr. *battery company executive*

Macungie
Gavin, Austin *retired lawyer*

Malvern
†Bogle, John Clifton *investment company executive*
Breslin, Elizabeth Walker *biological scientist*
Cameron, John Clifford *lawyer, health science facility administrator*
Churchill, Winston John *lawyer, investment firm executive*
Dans, Peter Emanuel *medical educator*
DeHaven, Michael Allen *lawyer*
Ewing, Joseph Neff, Jr. *lawyer*
Fisher, Sallie Ann *chemist*
Frazer, Jack Winfield *chemistry researcher*
Gillespie, Mary Krempa *psychologist, consultant*
Hall, James E. *computer software executive*
Holveck, David P. *pharmaceutical company executive*
†Klapinsky, Raymond Joseph *lawyer*
McIntosh, L(orne) William *marketing executive*
Michaelis, Arthur Frederick *health care company executive*
Swymer, Stephen *principal*
Zurawski, Vincent Richard, Jr. *biotechnology company executive, research scientist*

Manchester
Owens, Marilyn Mae *art educator*

Manheim
Critz, Richard Laurens *magazine editor, architectural consultant*

Manns Choice
Jones, Oliver Hastings *consulting economist*

Maple Glen
Taddei, Edward P. *school system administrator*

Marcus Hook
†Rallis, John *manufacturing holding company*

Meadville
Adams, Earl William, Jr. *economics educator*
Cable, Charles Allen *mathematician*
Foster, Catherine Rierson *manufacturing company executive*
Hogan, James Charles *classicist, educator*
Katope, Christopher George *English language educator*
Lotze, Barbara *physicist*

Mechanicsburg
Brawner, Gerald Theodore *lawyer*
Ortenzio, Rocco Anthony *health care executive*

Mechanicsville
Bye, Ranulph DeBayeux *artist, author*

Media
Cooke, M(erritt) Todd *banker*
Dunlap, Richard Frank *school system administrator*
Elman, Gerry Jay *lawyer*
Fehnel, Edward Adam *chemist, educator*
Hand, Brian Edward *science association administrator*
Klinefelter, Hylda Catharine *obstetrician-gynecologist*
Lambert, George Robert *lawyer*
Lewandowski, Theodore Charles *psychology educator*
Peabody, William Tyler, Jr. *retired paper manufacturing company executive*
Price, Donald *retail executive*
Resnick, Stewart Allen *diversified company executive*
Reuschlein, Harold Gill *university dean*
Rothschild, Loren *toy manufacturing executive*
Salo, Harry A. *health care executive*
Smith, David Gilbert *political science educator*
Strunk, Betsy Ann Whitenight *education educator*
Sutton, Jonathan Stone *landscape architect*

Mendenhall
Elliott, R. Keith *specialty chemical company executive*
Reinert, Norbert Frederick *patent lawyer, retired chemical company executive*

Mercer
Brady, Wray Grayson *mathematician, educator*

Mercersburg
Burgin, Walter Hotchkiss, Jr. *educational administrator*

Merion Station
Lewis, Paul Le Roy *pathology educator*
Littell, Franklin Hamlin *theologian, educator*
Zaslavsky, Robert *educator*

Middleburg
Kline, David Lamar *concrete block manufacturing company executive*

Middletown
Hand, Irving *urban planning educator*
Kaynak, Erdener *marketing educator, consultant editor*

Milford
Anchel, Edward *manufacturing executive*
Gowan, Joseph Patrick, Jr. *entertainment and food services company executive*
Le Guin, Ursula Kroeber *author*
Snyder, Richard Lee *consumer products company executive*

Millersburg
Kirkwood, James Mace *pharmaceutical company executive*
Woodside, Robert Elmer *lawyer, former judge*

Millersville
Caputo, Joseph Anthony *university president*
Judge, Margaret Ann *nurse, nursing administrator*
Mallery, Anne Louise *elementary educator, consultant*
Miller, Steven Max *humanities educator*

Milton
Lu, David John *history educator, writer*

Monroeville
Carney, Ann Vincent *secondary education educator*
Creagan, Robert Joseph *consulting nuclear engineer*
†Di Gioia, Anthony Michael, Jr. *civil engineer, business executive*
†Ecklar, Julia *freelance writer, novelist*
Jacobi, William Mallett *nuclear engineer, consultant*
Maclay, William Nevin *retired manufacturing and construction company executive*
Mandel, Herbert Maurice *civil engineer*
Parker, James Roger *chemist*
Penman, Paul Duane *nuclear power laboratory executive*
Ryan, Christopher Richard *construction company executive*

Mont Alto
Russo, Peggy Anne *English language educator*

Montgomeryville
†Emory, Thomas Mercer, Jr. *data communications equipment manufacturing executive*

Montoursville
Woolever, Naomi Louise *retired editor*

Morgantown
McGraw, James Michael *manufacturing company executive*

Morrisville
Bush, Harold Ehrig *computer consultant*
Heefner, William Frederick *lawyer*
†Hemenway, Aice Pearson *museum director*
Lineberry, Paul F., Jr. *music educator*
Muth, Robert James *metal company executive, lawyer*

Mount Gretna
Cooper, Jane Todd (J. C. Todd) *poet, writer, educator*
Franklin, Al *artistic director*

Mount Joy
Dillow, G. Benjamin *human resources director, consultant*
Eichler, Franklin Roosevelt *petroleum products distributor and services company executive*

Mountainhome
Buttz, Charles William *outdoor advertising executive*

Murrysville
Colborn, Harry Walter *electrical engineering consultant*
McWhirter, James Herman *consulting engineering business executive, financial planner*

Myerstown
Robson, Barbara S. *elementary education educator*
Schock, Franklin H. *clergy member, church administrator*
Seilhamer, Ray A. *academic administrator*

Narberth
Grenald, Raymond *architectural lighting designer*
Nathanson, Neal *virologist, epidemiologist, educator*
Newhall, John Harrison *management consultant*
Strom, Brian Leslie *internist*
Wagner, Frederick Balthas, Jr. *historian, retired surgery educator*
Weisberg, Ruth Maxine *radio reporter, television talk show host*

Nazareth
Herrick, Robert Ford *personnel consultant*

New Brighton
O'Leary, John Patrick, Jr. *packaging company executive*

New Castle
Byers, Joan P. *nursing educator*

New Florence
Olson, Clinton Louis *foreign service officer, former ambassador*

New Holland
Kennedy, William T. *retail executive*
Ruggeri, Riccardo *automotive sales executive*

New Hope
Braymer, Marguerite Annetta *optical company executive*
Knight, Douglas Maitland *educational administrator, optical executive*
Williamson, Frederick Beasley, III *rubber company executive*

New Kensington
Bridenbaugh, Peter Reese *industrial research executive*
Jarrett, Noel *chemical engineer*
Lederman, Frank L. *scientist, research center administrator*
Miller, Albert Jay *retired librarian, educator*
Pien, Shyh-Jye John *mechanical engineer*

New Oxford
Frock, J. Daniel *transportation executive, retired manufacturing company executive*

New Wilmington
Deegan, John, Jr. *academic administrator, educator*
Pitman, Grover Allen *music educator*
Remick, Oscar Eugene *college president*

Newtown
Bohning, Elizabeth Edrop *foreign language educator*
Carlson, David Emil *physicist*
Cohen, Myer *former international organization official*
Denoon, Clarence England, Jr. *business executive*
Goodell, Christina Marie *human resources and employee benefit consultant*
Henshaw, Jonathan Cook *manufacturing company executive*
Keenan, Terrance *foundation executive*
Keyes, Fenton *educational consultant, writer*
Leibholz, Stephen Wolfgang *physicist, engineering company executive, entrepreneur*
Long, Harry (On-Yuen Eng) *chemist, rubber science and technology consultant*
Palmer, Robert Roswell *historian, educator*
Peroni, Peter A., II *psychologist, educator*
Pfeiffer, John Edward *author*
Selden, William Kirkpatrick *educational consultant*
Somers, Anne Ramsay *medical educator*
Thompson, Carol Lewis *editor*
Wilkinson, Harry J. *technical company executive*

Newtown Square
Bower, Ward Alan *management consultant, lawyer*
Graf, Arnold Harold *employee benefits executive, financial planner*
Magee, William H. *chemical company executive*
Maxner, Joyce Karen *family therapist, author*
Staats, Dean Roy *retired reinsurance executive*
Steinman, Robert Cleeton *accountant*
Strausz-Hupé, Robert *ambassador, author*
Turner, George Pearce *consulting company executive*
Wood, Donald W. *chemical company executive*

Norristown
Aman, George Matthias, III *lawyer*
Case, Andrew J. *educational administrator*
Clemens, Alvin Honey *insurance company executive*
Flint, Daniel Waldo Boone *lawyer*
Folmar, Larry John *lawyer*
Ganime, Peter David *psychiatrist, consultant*
Kopple, Kenneth D. *chemistry researcher, educator*
Rosenthal, David *physician*
Wetherill, Eikins *lawyer, stock exchange executive*

North East
Ayrault, Evelyn West *psychologist, writer*

North Wales
Taylor, Robert Morgan electronics company executive

Northampton
Bartholomew, Gordon Wesley *health and physical education educator*
Greenleaf, Janet Elizabeth *principal*

Oakmont
†Pruitt, Charles William, Jr. *long term health care executive, educator*

Oil City
Baum, Herbert Merrill *motor oil company executive*
†Conrad, Conrad A. *oil company executive*
Hutchinson, Scott Edward *state legislator*
Olson, Robert Edward *coal mining executive*
Wood, Quentin Eugene *oil company executive*

Oreland
Smith, Gordon Ross *retired English language educator*

Paoli
Blankley, Walter Elwood *manufacturing company executive*
Ferrell, David Lee *public relations consultant*
Gallagher, Terrence Vincent *editor*
Hedberg, Robert Daniel *venture capitalist*
Visek, Albert James *computer engineer*
Welch, Linda Ogden *sales executive*
†White, Leland I. *hospital administrator*

Parker
Meixsell, Berrae Nevin (Mike Meixsell) *retail executive*

Peach Glen
Carey, Dean Lavere *fruit canning company executive*

Penllyn
Beyer, Karl Henry, Jr. *pharmacologist*

Penn Valley
Hires, William Leland *psychologist, consultant*

Pennsburg
Shuhler, Phyllis Marie *physician*

Perkasie
Ferry, Joan Evans *school counselor*

Philadelphia
Aaron, Kenneth Ellyot *lawyer*
Abbott, Frank Harry *lawyer*
Abel, Andrew Bruce *finance and economics educator*
Abrahams, Robert David *lawyer, author*
Abramowitz, Robert Leslie *lawyer*
Abrams, Jules Clinton *psychologist*
Ackerman, Alvin S. *lawyer*
Adams, Barbara *lawyer*
Adams, F. Gerard *economist, educator*
Adom, Edwin Nii Amalai *psychiatrist*
Agersborg, Helmer Pareli K. *pharmaceutical company executive, researcher*
Agus, Zalman S. *physician, educator*
Aiken, Linda Harman *nurse, sociologist, educator*
Ajzenberg-Selove, Fay *physicist, educator*
Ake, John Notley *lawyer, former investment services executive*
Albert, Jeffrey B. *lawyer*
Albright, Hugh Norton *mathematics educator*
†Alexander, John Dewey *internist*
Alexander, William Herbert *financial business educator, former construction company executive, former army officer*
Allen, Keith *professional sports team executive*
Alter, Jean Victor *French language educator*
Amsterdam, Jay D. *psychiatry educator, researcher*
Anders, Jerrold Paul *lawyer*
Anderson, Edward Clive *lawyer*
Anderson, Rolph Ely *marketing educator*
Ando, Albert K. *economist, educator*
Andrews, Edwin Joseph *pathology educator, academic administrator*
Andrisani, Paul *business educator, management consultant*
Angell, M(ary) Faith *federal magistrate judge*
Apfel, Jerome B. *lawyer*
Aquaro, Angelo R. *architect, consultant*
Arce, A. Anthony *psychiatrist*
Armstrong, Stephen Wales *lawyer*
Arnold, Lee *library director*
Aronson, Carl Edward *pharmacology and toxicology educator*
Aronstein, Martin Joseph *lawyer, educator*
Asbury, Arthur Knight *neurologist, educator*
†Atkinson, Barbara Frajola *pathologist*
Auerbach, Nina Joan *English language educator*

Austrian, Robert *physician, educator*
Auten, David Charles *lawyer*
Auth, Tony *artist*
Avery, William Joseph *packaging manufacturing company executive*
Axam, John Arthur *library consultant*
Azoulay, Bernard *chemicals company executive*
Babbel, David Frederick *finance educator*
Baccini, Laurance Ellis *lawyer*
Bachman, Arthur *lawyer*
Bacon, Edmund Norwood *city planner*
Badler, Norman Ira *computer and information science educator*
Bailey, Elizabeth Ellery *economics educator*
Bailin, Michael A. *social research firm executive*
Baker, C. Edwin *law educator*
†Baker, Lester *physician, educator, research administrator*
Bakhru, Ashok Naraindas *paper company executive*
Bales, John Foster, III *lawyer*
Ball, Earl John, III *school administrator*
Ballengee, James McMorrow *lawyer*
Baltzell, E(dward) Digby *sociology educator*
Banerji, Ranan Bihari *mathematics and computer science educator*
Bantel, Linda Mae *art museum director*
Barchi, Robert Lawrence *neuroscience educator, clinical neurologist, neuroscientist*
†Barfield, Dede *ballerina*
Barker, Clyde Frederick *surgeon, educator*
Barlett, Donald L. *journalist*
Barrett, James Edward, Jr. *management consultant*
Barrett, John J(ames), Jr. *lawyer*
Bartle, Harvey, III *federal judge*
Bartlett, Allen Lyman, Jr. *bishop*
Bartlett, Desmond William *engineering company executive*
Bartolini, Anthony Louis *lawyer*
Baserga, Renato Luigi *pathology educator*
Bates, James Earl *college president*
Batterman, Steven Charles *engineering mechanics and bioengineering educator*
Baughman, Jon A. *lawyer*
†Baum, Stanley *radiologist, educator*
Bauman, Robert Patten *diversified company executive*
Bayer, Margret Helene Janssen *biologist, research scientist*
Beauchamp, Gary Keith *physiologist*
Bechtle, Louis Charles *federal judge*
Beck, Aaron Temkin *psychiatrist*
Becker, Edward Roy *federal judge*
Behrman, Jere Richard *economics educator*
Belinger, Harry Robert *business executive, retired*
Bell, Whitfield Jenks, Jr. *historian*
Bellack, Alan Scott *clinical psychologist*
Benfey, Otto Theodor *chemist, educator, editor, historian of science*
†Bennett, Joel S. *physician*
Benson, Morton *Slavic languages educator, lexicographer*
Berg, Ivar Elis, Jr. *social science educator*
Berger, David *lawyer*
Berger, Harold *lawyer, engineer*
Bergholtz, Norbert F. *lawyer*
Berkley, Emily Carolan *lawyer*
Berkman, Richard Lyle *lawyer*
Berlin, Norman B. *lawyer*
Bernard, John Marley *lawyer, educator*
Bernstein, George L. *lawyer, accountant*
Bershad, Jack R. *lawyer*
Bevilacqua, Anthony Joseph Cardinal *cardinal*
Bianchi, Carmine Paul *pharmacologist*
Biava, Luis *musician*
Bibbo, Marluce *physician, educator*
Bilaniuk, Larissa Tetiana *neuroradiologist, educator*
Bildersee, Robert Alan *lawyer*
Binder, David Franklin *lawyer, author*
Binder, Lucy Simpson *retired utility company executive*
Binswanger, Frank G., Jr. *realty company executive*
Binswanger, John K. *real estate company executive*
Binzen, Peter Husted *columnist*
†Birnbaum, Morris Jay *cell biology educator*
Bishop, Harry Craden *surgeon*
Bissinger, H(arry) G(erard) *journalist*
Black, Albert Pershing, Jr. *health care executive*
Black, Allen Decatur *lawyer*
Blades, Herbert William *diversified consumer products company executive*
Bloom, Michael Anthony *lawyer*
Bludman, Sidney Arnold *theoretical physicist, astrophysicist*
Bluemle, Lewis William, Jr. *medical educator*
†Blum, Michael D. *social worker*
Blumberg, Baruch Samuel *academic administrator, research scientist*
Blume, Marshall Edward *finance educator*
Boasberg, Leonard W. *reporter*
Bodine, James Forney *retired civic leader*
Boehne, Edward George *banker*
Bogutz, Jerome Edwin *lawyer*
Boldt, David Rhys *journalist*
Bonnard, Raymond *theater director*
Bookspan, Michael Lloyd *musician*
Borer, Edward Turner *investment banker*
†Borovik, Alexei Peter *ballet dancer, educator*
Boss, Amelia Helen *law educator, lawyer*
Bowditch, Nathaniel Rantoul *brokerage house executive*
Bower, John Arnold, Jr. *architect, educator*
Bowles, Lawrence Thompson *surgeon, university dean, educator*
Bowman, Edward Harry *business science educator*
Bradley, Raymond Joseph *lawyer*
Brady, John Paul *psychiatrist*
Brady, Luther W., Jr. *physician, radiation oncology educator*
Braverman, Elliott Kenneth *lawyer*
Breitenfeld, Frederick, Jr. *public broadcasting executive, educator*
Brenan, Denis V. *lawyer*
Brest, Albert N. *cardiology educator*
Breuninger, Tyrone *musician*
Bridger, Wagner H. *psychiatrist, educator*
Brier, Bonnie Susan *lawyer*
Bright, Joseph Coleman *lawyer*
Brighton, Carl Theodore *orthopedic surgery educator*
Brind'Amour, Rod Jean *professional hockey player*
Brinkworth, Donald A. *lawyer, general counsel*
Brinster, Ralph Lawrence *biologist*
Briscoe, Jack Clayton *lawyer*
Britt, Earl Thomas *lawyer*
Brobeck, John Raymond *physiology educator*
Brockman, Stanley K. *medical educator, physician, cardiothoracic surgeon*
Broderick, Gregory A. *physician, urologic surgeon, educator*
Broderick, Raymond Joseph *federal judge*
Brody, Anita Blumstein *federal judge*
Broom, William Wescott *retired newspaper executive*
Brown, Denise Scott *architect, urban planner*
Brown, Richard P., Jr. *lawyer*
Brown, Stephen D. *lawyer*
Brown, William Hill, III *lawyer*
Browne, Michael Leon *lawyer*
Browne, Stanhope Stryker *lawyer*
Brownstein, Barbara Lavin *geneticist, educator, university official*
Brucker, Paul C. *academic administrator, physician*
Bryan, Henry Collier *secondary education education, minister*
Bryan, Richard Arthur *special education educator*
Buckwalter, Ronald Lawrence *federal judge*
Buerk, Donald Gene *medical educator, biomedical engineer*
Buerkle, Jack Vincent *sociologist, educator*
†Buller, Carter R. *lawyer*
Burbank, Stephen Bradner *law educator*
Burke, Daniel William *retired college president, English educator*
†Burns, Rosalie A. *neurologist, educator*
Burstein, Elias *physicist, educator*
Butz, Geneva Mae *pastor*
†Bykofsky, Stuart Debs *newspaper columnist*
Cahn, Edward N. *federal judge*
Calabi, Eugenio *mathematician, educator*
Callé, Craig R.L. *packaging executive*
Calman, Robert Frederick *mining executive*
Calvert, Jay H., Jr. *lawyer*
Campbell, Robert H. *oil company executive*
Cander, Leon *physician, educator*
Caplan, Arthur L. *philosophy educator*
Carey, Arthur Bernard, Jr. *editor, writer, columnist*
Carmi, Shlomo *mechanical engineering educator, scientist*
Carnecchia, Baldo M., Jr. *lawyer*
Carroll, Mark Thomas *lawyer*
Carroll, Thomas Colas *lawyer, educator*
Carter, Edward Carlos, II *librarian, historian*
Casper, Charles B. *lawyer*
Cass, David *economist, educator*
Chait, Arnold *radiologist*
Chance, Britton *biophysics and physical chemistry educator emeritus*
Chance, Henry Martyn, II *engineering executive*
Cherken, Harry Sarkis, Jr. *lawyer*
Cherry, John Paul *health science association director, researcher*
Cheston, George Morris *lawyer*
Cheston, Morris, Jr. *zoological park administrator*
Cheston, Warren Bruce *research institute administrator*
Child, John Sowden, Jr. *lawyer*
Childress, Scott Julius *medicinal chemist*
Chimples, George *lawyer*
Chinsamy, Anusuya *paleobiologist, researcher*
Christman, Robert Alan *podiatric radiologist*
Chung, Edward Kooyoung *cardiologist, educator, author*
Clark, Frederic William *lawyer*
Clark, John Arthur *lawyer*
Clark, John J. *economics and finance educator*
Clark, Paul James *chemical company executive*
Clarke, Robert Earle (Bobby Clarke) *hockey executive*
Clauser, Donald Roberdeau *musician*
Clayton, Constance *school system administrator*
Clearfield, Harris Reynold *physician*
Clothier, Isaac H., IV *lawyer*
Cloues, Edward Blanchard, II *lawyer*
Cohen, David Walter *university chancellor, periodontist, educator*
Cohen, Deborah Fuchs *lawyer*
Cohen, Felix Asher *lawyer*
Cohen, Frederick *lawyer*
Cohen, Hennig *English educator*
Cohen, Ira Myron *aeronautical and mechanical engineering educator*
Cohen, Stanley *pathologist, educator*
Cohen, Sylvan Richard G. *electric power company*
Collier-Evans, Demetra Frances *veterans benefits counselor*
Collings, Robert L. *lawyer*
Collons, Rodger Duane *decision sciences educator*
Colman, Robert Wolf *physician, medical educator*
Coltoff, Beth Jamie *psychologist, small business owner*
Comer, Nathan Lawrence *psychiatrist, educator*
Comfort, Robert Dennis *lawyer*
Comisky, Hope A. *lawyer*
Comisky, Marvin *retired lawyer*
Conn, Rex Boland, Jr. *physician, educator*
Cooke, Sara Mullin Graff *daycare provider, kindergarten teacher, doctor's assistant*
Cooney, J(ohn) Gordon *lawyer*
†Cooney, Nancy *newspaper editor*
Cooper, Richard Lee *newspaper editor, journalist*
Cooperman, Barry S. *educational administrator, educator, scientist*
Coopersmith, Fran M. *foundation executive*
Copeland, Adrian Dennis *psychiatrist*
Coppock, Ada Gregory *theatre executive*
Corrigan, John Edward *government official*
Cortner, Jean Alexander *physician, educator*
Cox, Douglas Lynn *financial service executive*
Cox, Robert Harold *physiology educator*
Cox, Roger Frazier *lawyer*
Coyne, Frank J. *insurance company executive*
Cramer, Harold *lawyer*
Cramer, Richard Charles *artist, educator*
†Cramp, Donald Arthur *hospital executive*
Crawford, James Douglas *lawyer*
Creech, Hugh John *chemist*
Crough, Daniel Francis *lawyer, insurance company executive*
Crowell, Richard Lane *microbiologist*
Cruger, Lorenzo *civil engineer*
Crumb, George Henry *composer, educator*
Cullen, James G. *telecommunications industry executive*
Cummins, John David *economics educator, consultant*
Cunningham, Ann Marie *information association executive*
Cunningham, Randall *professional football player*
Curran, Stuart Alan *English language educator*
Dabby, Sabah Salman *chemical engineer*
Daemmrich, Horst Sigmund *German language and literature educator*
Dagit, Charles Edward, Jr. *architect, educator*
Dalinka, Murray Kenneth *radiologist, educator*
Daly, Charles Arthur *health services administrator*
Daly, John M. *surgeon*
Dalzell, Stewart *federal judge*
Damsgaard, Kell Marsh *lawyer*
D'Angelo, Christopher Scott *lawyer*
D'Angio, Giulio John *radiologist, educator*
Daulton, Darren Arthur *professional baseball player*
Dauth, Frances Kutcher *journalist, newspaper editor*
Davidson, Steven J. *emergency physician*
Davis, Allen Freeman *history educator, author*
Davis, Raymond, Jr. *physical chemistry researcher*
Davis, Robert Harry *physiology educator*
Dean, Michael M. *lawyer*
Dean-Zubritsky, Cynthia Marian *psychologist, reseacher*
DeBunda, Salvatore Michael *lawyer*
de Cani, John Stapley *statistician, educator*
Delacato, Carl Henry *education educator*
DeLaura, David Joseph *English language educator*
De Leon, Clark *newspaper columnist*
De Lone, H. Francis *lawyer*
Deming, Frank Stout *lawyer*
Denenberg, Herbert Sidney *journalist, lawyer, former state official*
Dennis, Edward S(pencer) G(ale), Jr. *lawyer*
Denworth, Raymond K. *lawyer*
DePace, Nicholas Louis *physician*
†de Pasquale, Joseph *musician, educator*
Depp, (O.) Richard, III *obstetrician-gynecologist, educator*
Detweiler, David Kenneth *veterinary physiologist, educator*
Devlin, Thomas McKeown *biochemist*
d'Harnoncourt, Anne *museum director*
DiBerardino, Marie Antoinette *developmental biologist, educator*
DiBona, G. Fred, Jr. *insurance company executive*
Dichter, Mark S. *lawyer*
Dicke, Arnold Arthur *insurance company executive*
Dilks, Park Bankert, Jr. *lawyer*
Dillett, Gregory Craft *finance company executive*
Dinoso, Vicente Pescador, Jr. *physician, educator*
DiPalma, Joseph Rupert *pharmacology educator*
Ditter, John William, Jr. *federal judge*
Djerassi, Isaac *physician, medical researcher*
†Dolnick, Sandy Friedman *executive*
Dolson, Franklin Robert *columnist*
Doman, Janet Joy *association executive*
Donagi, Ron *mathematics educator*
Donner, Henry Jay *lawyer*
Donoghue, Norman E., II *lawyer*
Donohue, James J. *lawyer*
Doran, Thomas E. *lawyer*
Doran, William Michael *lawyer*
Dorfman, John Charles *lawyer*
Doty, Richard Leroy *medical researcher*
Drake, Donald Charles *journalist*
Drake, William Frank, Jr. *lawyer*
Driscoll, Lee Francis, Jr. *corporate director, lawyer*
Drucker, Mindy M. *editor, writer*
Dryer, Jonathan *lawyer*
Dubin, Leonard *lawyer*
†Dubin, Stephen Victor *lawyer*
DuBois, Jan Ely *federal judge*
DuBois, Ruth Harberg *human service agency executive*
Duffy, Francis Ramon *sociology educator*
Duncan, Mariano *professional baseball player*
Dunlap, Albert John *venture capitalist*
Dunn, Wendell Earl, III *management consultant, educator*
Durham, James W. *lawyer*
Durham, John Hendrick *investment company executive*
Dworetzky, Joseph Anthony *lawyer, city official*
Dykstra, Lenny (Leonard Kyle Dykstra) *professional baseball player*
Dymicky, Michael *retired chemist*
Dyson, Robert Harris *museum director, archaeologist*
Eagleson, William Boal, Jr. *banker*
Earley, Laurence Elliott *medical educator*
Edelson, Alan Martin *medical publisher, neurophysiologist*
Edwards, Stephen Allen *lawyer*
Eichelman, Burr Simmons, Jr. *psychiatrist, researcher, educator*
Eisenstein, Bruce Allan *electrical engineering educator*
Eisenstein, Toby K. *microbiology educator*
Eiswerth, Barry Neil *architect, educator*
Eldredge, Clifford Murray *hospital administrator*
Elliott, William Homer, Jr. *lawyer*
Emerson, S. Jonathan *lawyer*
Emory, Hugh Mercer *lawyer*
Engelman, Karl *physician*
Epstein, William Eric *health facility administrator*
Erickson, Ralph O. *botany educator*
Erslev, Allan Jacob *physician, educator*
Erving, Julius Winfield, II (Dr. J.) *business executive, retired professional basketball player*
Esser, Carl Eric *lawyer*
Evan, William Martin *sociologist, educator*
Evans, Audrey Elizabeth *physician, educator*
Fader, Henry Conrad *lawyer*
Fagin, Claire Mintzer *nursing educator, administrator*
Fala, Herman C. *lawyer*
Falk, I. Lee *lawyer*
Falkie, Thomas Victor *mining engineer, natural resources company executive*
Fallon, Christopher Chaffee, Jr. *lawyer*
Fancher, Charles B. *newspaper publishing executive*
Farber, Emmanuel *pathology and biochemistry educator*
Farnam, Walter Edward *insurance company executive*
Featherman, Bernard *steel company executive*
Fegley, Kenneth Allen *systems engineering educator*
Feirson, Steven B. *lawyer*
Feldman, Albert Joseph *lawyer*
Feninger, Claude *industry management services company executive*
Ferber, Arthur Henry *engineering executive*
Ferraro, Ronald Louis *health facility administrator*
Fiebach, H. Robert *lawyer*
Fielding, Allen Fred *oral and maxillofacial surgeon, educator*
Filreis, Alan *English language educator*
Fine, Lawrence B. *lawyer*
Finet, Scott *law librarian*
Finney, Graham Stanley *management consultant*
Fisher, Aron Baer *physiology and medicine educator*
Fisher, Linda A. *lawyer*
Fisher, Marshall Lee *university decision sciences director, educator*
Fishman, Alfred Paul *physician*
Fitts, Donald Dennis *chemist, educator*
Fitts, Michael Andrew *law educator*
Flaherty, John Edward, Jr. *lawyer*
†Flamm, Eugene Somer *neurosurgeon, educator*
Flanagan, Joseph Patrick, Jr. *lawyer*
Flaxman, Howard Richard *lawyer*
Flexner, Louis Barkhouse *anatomist, educator*
Foglietta, Thomas Michael *congressman*
Foreman, Gene Clemons *newspaper editor*
Foti, Margaret Ann *association executive, editor*
Foulke, William Green *banker*
†Fox, Jonathan Charles *biomedical scientist, educator*
Fox, Lawrence J. *lawyer*
Fox, Reeder Rodman *lawyer*
Fox, Renée Claire *sociology educator*
Frank, Harvey *lawyer, writer*
Frankel, Francine Ruth *political science educator*
Frankel, Sherman *physicist*
Frankl, William Stewart *cardiologist, educator*
†Franklin, Jack T. *photographer*
Frantz, Charles *anthropology educator*
Freed, Edmond Lee *podiatrist*
Freedman, Robert Louis *lawyer*
Fregosi, James Louis *professional baseball team manager*
Freiman, David Burl *radiologist*
Frenkel, Douglas N. *law educator*
Freyd, Peter John *mathematician, computer scientist, educator*
Friedell, Ellen Silberstein *lawyer*
Friedman, Frank Bennett *lawyer*
†Friedman, Harvey Michael *infectious diseases educator*
Friedman, Murray *civil rights official, historian*
Friedman, Sidney A. *financial services executive*
Friedman, Steven Lewis *lawyer*
Friend, Theodore Wood, III *foundation executive, historian*
Frimmer, Rick Leslie *lawyer*
†Fritsch, Robert Bruce *manufacturing company executive*
Frohlich, Kenneth R. *insurance executive*
Fryman, Louis William *lawyer*
Fullam, John P. *federal judge*
Fuller, John Garsed Campbell *food and drug company executive*
Fuller, William Henry, Jr. *professional football player*
Furth, John Jacob *molecular biologist, pathologist, educator*
Fussell, Paul *author, English literature educator*
Gable, Fred Burnard *pharmacist, author*
Gabrielson, Ira Wilson *physician, educator*
Gadsden, Christopher Henry *lawyer*
Gadsden, Thomas P. *lawyer*
Gaither, William Samuel *retired college president, marine engineer, consultant*
Gamble, Harry T. *professional football team executive*
Garcia, Celso-Ramón *obstetrician and gynecologist*
†Garcia, Richard Raul *major league umpire*
Garcia, Rudolph *lawyer*
†Garfield, Bernard Howard *musician, composer*
Garfield, Eugene *information scientist, author, publisher*
Garfinkel, Judith *marketing professional*
Garonzik, Sara Ellen *stage director*
Garrison, Walter R. *corporate executive*
Gartland, John Joseph *physician, writer*
†Garvin, Vail Pryor *hospital administrator*
Gaul, Gilbert M. *reporter*
Gawthrop, Robert Smith, III *federal judge*
Gendron, Michèle Marguerite Madeleine *librarian*
Genkin, Barry Howard *lawyer*
Gerbner, George *communications educator, university dean emeritus*
Gerhart, Frederick John *lawyer*
Gerrity, Thomas P. *dean*
Gibson, JoAnn Marie *psychotherapist, consultant*
Giese, William Herbert *tax accountant*
Gilbert, Harry Ephraim, Jr. *hotel executive*
Giles, James T. *federal judge*
Giles, William Yale *professional baseball team executive*
Giordano, Nicholas Anthony *stock exchange executive*
Glanton, Richard H. *lawyer*
Glassman, Howard Theodore *lawyer*
Glassmoyer, Thomas Parvin *lawyer*
Glazer, Ronald Barry *lawyer*
Glick, Jane Mills *biochemistry educator*
Glick, John H. *oncologist, medical educator*
Gold, William Buchanan, Jr. *lawyer*
Goldberg, Jay Lenard *lawyer*
Goldberg, Martin *physician, educator*
Goldberg, Marvin Allen *lawyer, business consultant*
Goldberg, Morton Edward *pharmacologist*
Goldberg, Richard Robert *lawyer*
Golden, Gerald Samuel *national medical board executive*
Goldfarb, Stanley *internist, educator*
Goldin, Judah *Hebrew literature educator*
Goldman, Yale E. *physiologist, educator*
Goldsmith, Howard Michael *lawyer*
Goldsmith, Martin H. *health care executive*
Goldsmith, Sidney *physician, scientist, inventor*
Goldstein, William Marks *lawyer*
Goldstine, Herman Heine *mathematician, association executive*
Gonick, Paul *urologist*
Goodchild, John Charles, Jr. *advertising and public relations executive*
Goodenough, Ward Hunt *anthropologist, educator*
Goodman, Charles Schaffner *marketing educator*
Goodman, David Barry Poliakoff *physician, educator*
Goodman, Frank I. *law educator, lawyer*
Goodrich, Herbert Funk, Jr. *lawyer*
Goodyear, Frank H(enry), Jr. *art association administrator*
Goren, Denise Lynne *deputy mayor*
Gorenberg, Charles Lloyd *financial services executive*
Gorman, Robert A. *law educator*
Gornish, Gerald *lawyer*
Gossett, Joyce *religious organization administrator*
Gough, John Francis *lawyer*
Graffman, Gary *pianist*
Graham, Alexander John *classics educator*
Gralish, Tom *photographer*
Granoff, Gail Patricia *lawyer*
Grant, M. Duncan *lawyer*
Grant, Richard W. *lawyer*
Gray, Gordon L. *communications educator*
Green, Clifford Scott *federal judge*
Greenberg, Marshall Gary *marketing research consultant*

Greenberg, Peter Steven *lawyer*
†Greene, Mark Irwin *immunologist, educator*
Greenfield, Bruce Harold *lawyer, banker*
Gross, Larry Paul *communications educator*
Grossi-Tyson, Laura *lawyer*
Grossman, Sanford Jay *economics educator*
Grove, David Lavan *lawyer*
Guckes, William Ruhland, Jr. *insurance executive*
Guenther, George Carpenter *travel company executive*
†Gur, Ruben C. *psychiatry educator*
Hackney, Francis Sheldon *university president*
†Hadley, Tamara Brooke *ballet dancer*
Hagen, James Alfred *rail transportation executive*
Hale, Charles Franklin *finanical services company executive*
Haley, Vincent Peter *lawyer*
Hall, Charles P(otter), Jr. *educator consultant*
Hall, Robert J. *newspaper executive*
Halsey, Ashley, III *newspaper editor*
Hameka, Hendrik Frederik *chemist, educator*
Hamilton, Ralph West *plastic surgeon, educator*
Hamilton, Stephen David Derwent *lawyer*
Hamlin, Arthur Tenney *librarian*
Hamme, David Codrington *architect*
Hammond, Charles Ainley *clergyman*
Hand, Peter James *neurobiologist, educator*
Hangley, William Thomas *lawyer*
†Hansen-Flaschen, John Hyman *medical educator, researcher*
Harker, Robert Ian *geologist, educator*
Harkins, John Graham, Jr. *lawyer*
Harper, Edwin Leland *manufacturing executive*
Harris, Jay Terrence *newspaper editor*
Harvey, Colin Edwin *veterinary medicine educator*
Harvey, John Adriance *psychology and pharmacology educator, researcher, consultant*
Harvey, William J. *religious service organization, religious publication editor*
Haskin, Donald Lee *bank executive*
Hatoff, Howard Ira *labor lawyer*
Haugaard, Niels *pharmacologist*
Hauptfuhrer, George Jost, Jr. *lawyer*
†Haut, Michael Joel *physician*
Havard, Bernard *theatrical producer*
Havas, Peter *physicist, educator*
Haviland, Bancroft Dawley *lawyer*
Haydanek, Ronald Edward *lawyer and consultant*
†Hayden, Richard Earle *otolaryngologist*
Hayes, John Freeman *architect*
Haynes, Gary Allen *newspaper editor, journalist*
Hazard, Geoffrey Cornell, Jr. *law educator*
Heilig, William Wright *coal and manufacturing company executive*
Heilman, Wesley Marvin, III *architect*
Heim, Robert Charles *lawyer*
Helfand, Arthur E. *podiatrist*
Henderson, J(oseph) Welles *lawyer*
Hennessy, Joseph H. *lawyer*
Henrich, William Joseph, Jr. *lawyer*
Henry, Ragan A. *lawyer, broadcaster*
Herman, Charles Jacob *lawyer*
†Hershberg, Theodore *public policy and history educator*
Hess, Hans Ober *lawyer*
Hess, Sidney Wayne *management educator*
Heuser, Frederick J. *historian*
Hiesinger, Kathryn Bloom *museum curator*
Higgins, Frederick Benjamin, Jr. *environmental engineering educator, college dean*
Hildebrand, David Kent *statistics educator*
Hirschmann, Ralph Franz *chemist*
Hodavance, Robert S. *lawyer*
Hoelscher, Robert James *lawyer*
Hoenigswald, Henry Max *linguist, educator*
Hoffman, Alan Jay *lawyer*
Hoffman, Daniel (Gerard) *literature educator, poet*
Hoffman, Jerome A. *lawyer*
Hollins, David Michael *professional baseball player*
Holloman, Margaret *elementary school principal*
Holloway, Hiliary Hamilton *lawyer, banker*
†Holmes, Edward W. *physician, educator*
Holmes, Norman Leonard *lawyer*
†Holsclaw, Douglas Stanley, Jr. *pediatrics educator*
Holtzer, Howard *anatomy educator*
Honnold, John Otis, Jr. *law educator*
Horvath, Joseph John *lawyer, insurance company executive*
Humenuk, William Anzelm *lawyer*
Humes, Graham *investment banker*
Humes, James Calhoun *lawyer, communications consultant, author*
Hung, Paul Porwen *biotechnologist, educator, consultant*
Hunter, James Austen, Jr. *lawyer*
Hurst, George Cameron, III *history educator*
Hurvich, Leo Maurice *experimental psychologist, educator, vision researcher*
Hussar, Daniel Alexander *pharmacy educator*
Hutchinson, Pemberton *coal company executive*
Hutchinson, William David *federal judge*
Hutton, Herbert J. *federal judge*
Iams, David Aveling *journalist, columnist*
Iglewicz, Boris *statistician, educator*
Intemann, Robert Louis *physics educator, researcher*
Iskrant, John Dermot *lawyer*
Izenour, Steven *architect*
Jackendoff, Nathaniel *finance educator*
Jackson, Laird Gray *physician, educator*
Jaffe, Paul Lawrence *lawyer*
Jameson, Dorothea *sensory neuroscientist*
Jamieson, David Donald *lawyer*
†Jamieson, Kathleen Hall *dean, communications educator*
Janzen, Daniel Hunt *biology educator*
†Jarett, Leonard *pathologist, educator, researcher*
Jaron, Dov *biomedical engineer, educator*
Jefferies, Gregory Scott *professional baseball player*
Jellinek, Miles Andrew *lawyer*
Jennings, James Walsh *lawyer*
Jensh, Ronald Paul *anatomist, educator*
†Johnson, Alan T. *engineering educator*
Johnson, Craig Norman *investment banker*
Johnson, E(lmer) Marshall *biology educator, reproductive toxicologist*
Johnson, Joseph Eggleston, III *physician, educator*
Johnston, Francis Edward *anthropologist, educator*
Jones, Jacqueline Valarie *journalist*
Jones, Loren Farquhar *electronics executive*
Jones, O. T. *bishop*
Jones, Robert Jeffries *lawyer*
Jones, Robert Mead, Jr. *lawyer*
Jordan, Clifford Henry *management consultant*
Jordan, Joe J. *architect*
Joseph, Rosaline Resnick *hematologist/oncologist*
Joyce, Philip Halton *journalist*
Joyce, Robert Joseph *insurance executive*
Joyner, J(ames) Curtis *federal judge*
Justice, Jack Burton *lawyer*
Kadison, Richard Vincent *mathematician, educator*
Kahn, James Robert *lawyer*
Kahn, Sigmund Benham *internist, dean*
Kaji, Akira *microbiology scientist, educator*
Kaji, Hideko Katayama *pharmacologist*
Kane, Jonathan *lawyer*
Kane-Vanni, Patricia Ruth *lawyer, consultant*
Kardon, Robert *mortgage company executive*
Katherine, Robert Andrew *chemical company executive*
Katz, Harold *professional basketball team executive*
Katz, Marvin *federal judge*
Katz, Solomon Hertz *anthropologist, educator*
Kauffman, Bruce William *lawyer, former state supreme court justice*
Kaufman, David Joseph *lawyer*
Kay, Jack Garvin *chemist, educator*
Kaye, Donald *physician, educator*
Kaye, Janet Miriam *psychologist*
Kaye, Robert *pediatrics educator*
Kazazian, Haig Hagop, Jr. *medical scientist, physician, educator*
Kee, Howard Clark *religion educator*
Keenan, Mary Ann *orthopaedic surgeon, researcher*
Keene, John Clark *lawyer, educator*
†Kefalides, Nicholas Alexander *physician, educator*
Kelleher, John M. *telephone company executive*
Kellett, Morris C. *lawyer*
†Kelley, Mark Albert *internal medicine educator, university official*
†Kelley, William Nimmons *physician, educator*
Kelley, William Thomas *marketing educator*
†Kelly, Elizabeth Slusser *law librarian, educator*
Kelly, James McGirr *federal judge*
Kelly, Robert F. *federal judge*
Kempin, Frederick Gustav, Jr. *lawyer, educator*
Kendall, Robert Louis, Jr. *lawyer*
Kenty, David Earl *lawyer*
Kenworthy, Thomas Bausman *lawyer*
Kessler, Alan Craig *lawyer*
Kessler, Mark Keil *lawyer*
Keto, C. Tsehloane *historian*
Kim, Sangduk *biochemistry educator, researcher*
Kim, Synja P. *corporate business planner*
Kimball, Harry Raymond *medical association executive, educator*
Kimberly, John Robert *management educator, consultant*
Kimelman, Donald Bruce *newspaper editor*
King, Gwendolyn S. *utility company executive, former federal official*
King, Maxwell E. P. *newspaper editor*
Kise, James Nelson *architect, urban planner*
Kissick, William Lee *physician, educator*
Kittredge, Thomas M. *lawyer*
Klasko, Herbert Ronald *lawyer, law educator, writer*
Klauder, N. Jeffrey *lawyer*
Klaus, William Robert *lawyer*
Klausner, Samuel Zundel *sociologist, educator*
Klayman, Barry Martin *lawyer*
Klein, Abraham *physics educator, researcher*
Klein, Howard Bruce *lawyer, law educator*
Klein, Julia Meredith *newspaper reporter*
Klein, Lawrence Robert *economist, educator*
Klein, Michael Lawrence *research chemist, educator*
Klein, Samuel Edwin *lawyer*
Kleinzeller, Arnost *physiologist, physician, emeritus educator*
Kligerman, Morton M. *radiologist*
Kline, Thomas Richard *lawyer*
Klinghoffer, June Florence *physician, educator*
†Kluger, Joseph Harris *orchestra administrator*
Knapton, David Robert *city planner*
Knauer, Georg Nicolaus *classical philologist*
Knobler, Nathan *art educator*
Knoll, David E. *petroleum refining company executive*
Knopp, Marvin Isadore *mathematics educator*
Knudson, Alfred George, Jr. *medical geneticist*
Koelle, George Brampton *university pharmacologist, educator*
Koenig, C(arl) Frederick, III *lawyer*
Kogan, Deen *artistic director*
Kohn, Harold Elias *lawyer*
Kolansky, Harold *physician, psychiatrist, psychoanalyst*
Kopecky, Kenneth John *economics educator*
Koprowski, Hilary *medical scientist*
Kopytoff, Igor *anthropology educator*
Korsyn, Irene Hahne *marketing executive*
Kraemer, Michael Frederick *lawyer*
Kraft, Robert Alan *history of religion educator*
Kramer, Henry *metal processing executive*
Kramer, Meyer *lawyer, editor, clergyman*
Krampf, John Edward *lawyer*
Kreider, Karen Beechy *secondary education educator, language professional*
Kresh, J. Yasha *cardiovascular researcher, educator*
Kritchevsky, David *biochemist, educator*
Krol, John Cardinal *retired archbishop*
Kruk, John Martin *professional baseball player*
Krutsick, Robert Stanley *science center executive*
Krzyzanowski, Richard Lucien *lawyer, corporate executive*
Ksansnak, James E. *service management company executive*
Ku, Y. H. *engineering educator*
Kübler, Friedrich Karl *law educator*
Kundel, Harold Louis *radiologist, educator*
Kupperman, Louis Brandeis *lawyer*
Kurland, Seymour *lawyer*
Kurtz, Alfred Bernard *radiologist*
Laddon, Warren Milton *lawyer*
Ladman, A(aron) J(ulius) *anatomist, educator*
Lambertsen, Christian James *environmental physiologist, physician, educator*
Landis, Edgar David *services business company executive*
Landis, Robert M. *lawyer*
Lang, Richard Warren *economist*
Langacker, Paul George *physics educator*
Larsen, Terrance A. *bank holding company executive*
Larson, Donald Clayton *physics educator, consultant*
Larson, Ingegerd Elin *immunology/arthritis nurse*
LaValley, Frederick J. M. *lawyer*
Laverty, Bruce *curator*
Lawley, Alan *materials engineering educator*
Lawlor, Helen Anne *database publisher*
Lawson, John Quinn *architect*
Leaman, J. Richard, Jr. *paper company executive*
Leary, Michael Warren *journalist*
Leatherbee, William Bell *architect*
Le Clair, Charles George *artist, retired dean*
Ledwith, James Robb *lawyer*
Ledwith, John Francis *lawyer*
Lee, Charles *retired English language and literature educator, arts critic*
Lee, Chong-Sik *political scientist, educator*
†Lee, Joseph William *sales executive*
Leech, Noyes Elwood *lawyer, educator*
Lefer, Allan Mark *physiologist*
Lefton, Al Paul, Jr. *advertising executive*
Leibovitz, Mitchell G. *retail executive*
Leimkuhler, Gerard Joseph, Jr. *financial holding company executive*
Leiter, Robert Allen *journalist, magazine editor*
Lemaire, Jean Henri *actuarial science educator*
Lent, John Anthony *journalist, educator*
Leonard, Thomas Aloysius *lawyer*
Lesnick, Howard *legal educator*
Levin, A. Leo *law educator, retired government official*
Levin, Michael H(oward) *environmentalist*
Levin, Murray Simon *lawyer*
Levin, Susan Bass *lawyer*
Levine, Herbert Samuel *economics educator, research consultant*
Levine, Rhea Joy Cottler *anatomy educator*
Levit, Edithe Judith *physician, medical association administrator*
Levitt, Israel Monroe *astronomer*
†Levitt, Jerry David *medical educator*
Levy, Dale Penneys *lawyer*
Levy, Robert Isaac *physician, educator, research director*
Levy, Rochelle Feldman *artist*
Lewin, Moshe *historian, educator*
Lewis, Christopher Alan *lawyer*
Lewis, Claude Aubrey *columnist*
Lewis, George Withrow *business executive*
Lewis, John Hardy, Jr. *lawyer*
Lewis, Thomas John, III *hospital administrator*
Li, Weiye *ophthalmologist, biochemist, educator*
Libonati, Michael Ernest *lawyer, educator, writer*
Lichtenstein, Lawrence Jay *lawyer*
Lichtenstein, Robert Jay *lawyer*
Liebman, Paul Arno *biophysicist, educator*
Lief, Harold Isaiah *psychiatrist*
Lillie, Charisse Ranielle *lawyer, educator*
Lindsey, Jack Lee *curator*
Lipkin, Edward B. *real estate developer*
Lipman, Frederick D. *lawyer*
Lisker, Deborah J(ane) *lawyer*
Listgarten, Max Albert *periodontics educator*
Litt, Mitchell *chemical engineer, educator, bioengineer*
Litwack, Gerald *biochemistry researcher, educator, administrator*
Live, Israel *microbiologist, educator*
Llewellyn, J. Bruce *food products executive*
Lloyd, Albert Lawrence, Jr. *German language educator*
Lodish, Leonard Melvin *marketing educator, entrepreneur*
Loeb, Vernon Frederick *journalist*
Loewenstein, Benjamin Steinberg *lawyer*
Lombard, John James, Jr. *lawyer*
†Loney, Mary Rose *airport administrator*
Longnecker, David E. *anesthesiologist, educator*
LoSciuto, Leonard Anthony *psychologist, educator*
Louchheim, Frank Pfeifer *management consultant*
Lovelady, Steven M. *newspaper editor*
Loveless, George Group *lawyer*
Lowery, William Herbert *lawyer*
Lu, Ponzy *molecular biology educator*
Lucas, John Harding, Jr. *professional basketball coach*
Lucey, John David, Jr. *lawyer*
Lucid, Robert Francis *English educator*
Ludden, David *Asian studies educator*
Ludwig, Edmund Vincent *federal judge*
Lundy, Joseph E. *lawyer*
Luscombe, Herbert Alfred *physician, educator*
Lyon, William Carl *sports columnist*
MacGregor, David Bruce *lawyer*
Maclay, Donald Merle *lawyer*
†Madaio, Michael P. *medical educator*
Madeira, Edward W(alter), Jr. *lawyer*
†Madia, Giorgio *dancer, choreographer*
Madow, Leo *psychiatrist, educator*
Madva, Stephen Alan *lawyer*
Magargee, W(illiam) Scott, III *lawyer*
Magaziner, Fred Thomas *lawyer*
Magaziner, Henry Jonas *architect*
Magee, Wayne Edward *biochemistry educator, researcher*
Maguire, Henry Clinton, Jr. *dermatologist*
Mai, Elizabeth Hardy *lawyer*
Maitin, Sam(uel Calman) (Sam Maitin) *artist*
Malamud, Daniel *biochemistry educator*
Mancall, Elliott Lee *neurologist, educator*
Mangione, Jerre Gerlando *author, educator*
Mann, Bruce H. *law educator*
Mann, Theodore R. *lawyer*
Mannino, Edward Francis *lawyer*
Mansfield, Edwin *economist, educator*
Mardar, Dianna *reporter*
Marple, Dorothy Jane *retired church executive*
Marshall, Bryan Edward *anesthesiologist, educator*
Marshall, Donald Tompkins *industrial distribution executive*
Martin, Suzanne Gabrielle *health facility administrator*
Mason, Theodore W. *lawyer*
Masterson, Thomas A. *lawyer*
Mastroianni, Luigi, Jr. *physician, educator*
Mather, Barbara W. *lawyer*
Mathes, Stephen Jon *lawyer*
Matsumoto, Teruo *surgeon, educator*
Matter, Edith Ann *religion educator*
Mattoon, Peter Mills *lawyer*
Maurer, Paul Herbert *biochemist, educator*
Maxey, David Walker *lawyer*
Maxman, Susan Abel *architect*
Mayock, Robert Lee *internist*
McDougall, Walter Allan *history educator*
McGinley, Joseph Patrick *brokerage house executive*
McGlynn, Joseph Leo, Jr. *federal judge*
McHarg, Ian Lennox *landscape architect, regional planner, educator*
†McKee, Theodore A. *federal judge*
McKeever, John Eugene *lawyer*
†McKenna, Michael Joseph *manufacturing company executive*
McKenna, Thomas Morrison, Jr. *social services organization executive*
Mc Mahon, Charles Joseph, Jr. *materials science educator*
McMenamin, Richard F. *lawyer*
McNeill, Corbin Asahel, Jr. *utility executive*
McQuiston, Robert Earl *lawyer*
Means, John Barkley *foreign language educator, association executive*
Meigs, John Forsyth *lawyer*
Melinson, James Robert *judge*
Mella, Arthur John *insurance company executive*
Melnick, William *advertising executive*
Melvin, John Lewis *physical and rehabilitation physician, educator*
Menken, Jane Ava *demographer, educator*
†Mennuti, Michael Thomas *medical educator*
Merrifield, Dudley Bruce *business educator, former government official*
Merritt, John C. *investment banker*
Mesirov, Leon Isaac *lawyer*
Metzker, Ray K. *photographer*
Meyer, Leonard B. *musician, educator*
Meyer, Paul William *arboretum director, horticulturist*
Meyers, Howard L. *lawyer*
Meyerson, Martin *university executive, educator*
Mezzacappa, Dale Veronica *journalist*
Michael, Henry N. *geographer, anthropologist*
Mickens, Garfield Jones *songwriter, poet and philosopher*
Micko, Alexander S. *financial executive*
Milbourne, Walter Robertson *lawyer*
Miller, Charles Q. *engineering company executive*
Miller, Henry Franklin *lawyer*
Miller, Leonard David *surgeon*
Miller, Leslie Anne *lawyer*
Miller, Margery K. *lawyer*
Miller, Robert Wiley *educational foundation executive*
Miller, Ronald Eugene *regional science educator*
Milone, Francis Michael *lawyer*
Ming, Si-Chun *pathologist, educator*
Minisi, Anthony S. *lawyer*
Mirabello, Francis Joseph *lawyer*
Mirick, Henry Dustin *architect*
Misher, Allen *college president, retired*
Mitchell, Ehrman Burkman, Jr. *architect*
Mitchell, Howard Estill *human resources educator, consultant*
Mode, Charles J. *mathematician, educator*
Montgomery, David Paul *professional baseball team executive*
Montgomery, Edward Alembert, Jr. *not-for-profit developer*
Mooney, Charles William, Jr. *law educator*
Moore, Acel *journalist*
Morahan, Page S. *microbiologist, educator*
Morgan, Arlene Notoro *newspaper editor, reporter, recruiter*
Morikawa, Dennis J. *lawyer*
Morlok, Edward Karl *engineering educator, consultant*
Morris, George Norton *insurance company executive*
Morris, Thomas Bateman, Jr. *lawyer*
Morrison, Donald Franklin *statistician, educator*
Morse, Stephen J. *law educator*
Mosher, Paul H. *research library administrator, author, consultant*
Moss, Arthur Henshey *lawyer*
Mostovoy, Marc Sanders *conductor*
Mulholland, S. Grant *urologist*
Mulroney, John Patrick *chemical company executive*
Munch, David Edward *newspaper executive*
Murdoch, Lawrence Corlies, Jr. *retired banker, economist*
Murphey, Murray Griffin *history educator*
Murray, Terry (Terence Rodney Murray) *professional hockey team coach*
Murrell, Thomas W., III *lawyer*
Muti, Riccardo *orchestra and opera conductor*
†Myers, Allen Richard *medical school dean, rheumatologist*
Myers, James Nelson *librarian*
Myers, Kenneth Raymond *lawyer*
†Nachmias, Jacob *psychologist educator*
Nadley, Harris Jerome *accountant, educator, writer*
Nagle, Arlington, Jr. *accountant, corporate executive*
Nalle, Peter Devereux *publishing company executive*
†Naples, Ronald James *manufacturing company executive*
Narin, Stephen B. *lawyer*
Naughton, James Martin *newspaper editor*
Naylor, Robert Ernest, Jr. *chemical company executive*
†Neilson, Eric Grant *physician, educator, health facility administrator*
Nelson, Nels Robert *drama critic*
Neubauer, Joseph *food services company executive*
Newbold, Arthur *lawyer*
Newburger, Frank L., Jr. *retired investment broker*
Newcomer, Clarence Charles *federal judge*
News, Kathryn Anne *editor, educator, writer*
Niewiarowski, Stefan *physiology educator, biomedical research scientist*
Nix, Robert N(elson) C(ornelius), Jr. *state supreme court chief justice*
Nixon, Eugene Ray *chemist, educator*
Nofer, George Hancock *lawyer*
Noordergraaf, Abraham *biophysics educator*
Nowell, Peter Carey *pathologist, educator*
Nussbaum, Paul Eugene *journalist*
O'Brien, Robert Thomas *investment company executive*
O'Brien, William Jerome, II *lawyer*
O'Connor, Joseph A., Jr. *lawyer*
O'Donnell, G. Daniel *lawyer*
O'Leary, Dennis Joseph *lawyer*
Oliva, Terence Anthony *marketing educator*
Olshin, Samuel E. *architect*
Ominsky, Harris *lawyer*
O'Neill, Thomas Newman, Jr. *federal judge*
Oppenheimer, Jane Marion *biologist, historian, educator*
O'Reilly, Timothy Patrick *lawyer*
Orlando, Danielle *opera company administrator*
Osborne, Frederick Spring, Jr. *academic administrator, artist*
Oswald, Stanton S. *lawyer*
Othmer, David Artman *television and radio station executive*
Padova, John R. *federal judge*
Padulo, Louis *university administrator*
Paglia, Camille *writer, humanities educator*
Pagliaro, James Domenic *lawyer*
Pak, Hyung Woong *foundation executive, educator*
Palmer, Richard Ware *lawyer*
Palmer, Robert Bitts *banker*
Palmer, Russell Eugene *investment executive*
Panzer, Mitchell Emanuel *lawyer*
Paone, Peter *artist*
Paquette, Joseph F., Jr. *utility company executive*
Parish, Lawrence Charles *physician, editor*
Parmiter, James Darlin *safety engineer*
Parry, Lance Aaron *newspaper executive*
Patel, Ronald Anthony *newspaper editor*
Patrick, George W. *lawyer*

†Patrick, Ruth (Mrs. Charles Hodge) *limnologist, diatom taxonomist, educator*
Patterson, Donald Floyd *human, medical and veterinary genetics educator*
Peachey, Lee DeBorde *biology educator*
Pearson, Davis *architect*
†Peck, Robert McCracken *naturalist, science historian, writer*
Peirce, Donald Oluf *elementary education educator*
Pepe, Frank A. *cell and developmental biology educator*
Pepper, Jane G. *bank executive*
Percy, Ann Buchanan *museum curator*
Perkins, George Holmes *architectural educator, architect*
Perry, Robert Palese *molecular biologist, educator*
Peters, Edward Murray *history educator*
Peterson, Charles Emil *architect*
Pew, Robert Anderson *real estate corporation officer*
Phillips, Dorothy Kay *lawyer*
†Pietra, Giuseppe Giovanni *pathology educator*
Pillai, K. G. Jan *law educator, lawyer*
Pipes, Daniel *writer, editor*
Pipes, Wesley O'Feral *civil engineering educator*
Pittinger, Wilbur Barke *medical center executive*
†Poethig, Richard Scott *geneticist, biology educator*
Pokotilow, Manny David *lawyer*
Pollack, Michael *lawyer*
Pollack, Solomon Robert *bioengineering educator*
Pollak, Louis Heilprin *federal judge, educator*
Porter, Gerald Joseph *mathematician, educator*
Porter, Jill *journalist*
Porter, Roger John *medical research administrator, neurologist, pharmacologist*
Posner, Edward Martin *lawyer*
Postlewaite, Andrew William *economics and public policy educator*
Potamkin, Meyer P. *mortgage banker*
Potsic, William Paul *physician, educator*
Poul, Franklin *lawyer*
Powell, Walter Hecht *labor arbitrator*
Powers, Richard Augustine, III *federal judge*
Pratter, Gene E. K. *lawyer*
Premack, David *psychologist*
Preston, Samuel Hulse *demographer*
Prevoznik, Stephen Joseph *anesthesiologist*
Price, Robert Stanley *lawyer*
Prince, Gerald Joseph *Romance languages educator*
Pritchard, James Bennett *archaeologist, educator, author*
Prockop, Darwin Johnson *biochemist, physician*
Promislo, Daniel *lawyer*
Prowler, Donald Marc *architect*
Prywes, Noah Shmarya *computer scientist, educator*
Pugliese, Maria A. *psychiatrist*
Putney, Paul William *lawyer*
Quann, Joan Louise *English language educator, real estate broker*
Quinn, John Albert *chemical engineering educator*
Rabinowitz, Howard K. *physician, educator*
Rabinowitz, Samuel Nathan *lawyer*
Rachofsky, David J. *lawyer*
Rackow, Julian Paul *lawyer*
Rainey, Arthur H. *lawyer*
Ralph, Thomas A. *lawyer*
Rauch, John Keiser, Jr. *architect*
Reagan, Harry Edwin, III *lawyer*
Reber, Stanley Roy *insurance company executive*
Redeker, James Russell *lawyer*
Reed, Alan L. *lawyer*
Reed, Clarence Raymond *association executive*
Reed, Frank Engelhart *banker*
Reed, Lowell A., Jr. *federal judge*
Reed, Michael Haywood *lawyer*
Regan, Robert Charles *English language educator*
Reich, Abraham Charles *lawyer*
Reich, Morton Melvyn *marketing communications company executive*
Reid, John Mitchell *biomedical engineer*
Reinecke, Robert Dale *ophthalmologist*
Reinstein, Robert J. *dean, law educator*
Reiss, John Barlow *lawyer*
Reitz, Curtis Randall *lawyer, educator*
Remenick, Seymour *artist, educator*
Rendell, Edward Gene *mayor*
Rescorla, Robert Arthur *psychology educator*
Rhoads, Jonathan Evans *surgeon*
Richette, Lisa Aversa *judge*
Richetti, John Joseph *English educator, writer, editor*
Rickels, Karl *psychiatrist, physician, educator*
Rieff, Philip *sociologist*
Rima, Ingrid Hahne *economics educator*
Ripley, Edward Franklin *investment company executive*
†Ritchie, Wallace Parks, Jr. *surgeon, educator*
Ritter, Deborah Elizabeth *anesthesiologist, educator*
Rizzo, Richard C. *lawyer*
Roberts, Brian Leon *communications executive*
Roberts, Carl Geoffrey *lawyer*
Roberts, Jay *pharmacologist, educator*
Roberts, William Henry *architect*
Robinson, Robert L. *financial service company executive, lawyer*
Rocher, Ludo *humanities educator*
Rock, Milton Lee *publisher*
Rodin, Judith Seitz *academic administrator, educator*
†Roe, John Andrew (Rocky) *major league baseball umpire, consultant*
Rogers, Fred Baker *medical educator*
Rogers, Mary Martin *publishing company executive*
Rohn, Elizabeth G. *banker*
Roomberg, Lila Goldstein *lawyer*
Root, Franklin Russell *business educator*
Root, Stanley William, Jr. *lawyer*
Rorke, Lucy Balian *neuropathologist*
Rosato, Francis Ernest *surgeon*
Rose, Robert Lawrence *financial services company executive*
Rosen, Gerald Harris *physicist, consultant, educator*
Rosen, Rhoda *obstetrician-gynecologist*
Rosenberg, Charles Ernest *historian, educator*
Rosenberg, David Alan *military historian, educator*
†Rosenberg, Leroy Joseph *hospital executive, former military officer*
Rosenberg, Robert Allen *psychologist, educator, optometrist*
Rosenbleeth, Richard Marvin *lawyer*
Rosenbloom, Bert *marketing educator*
Rosenbloom, Sanford M. *lawyer*
Rosenfield, Bruce Alan *lawyer*
Rosenstein, James Alfred *lawyer*
Rosenthal, Robert Jon *newspaper editor, journalist*
Rosenzweig, Mark Richard *economist, educator*
Rosoff, William A. *lawyer*
Ross, Daniel R. *lawyer*
Ross, George Martin *investment banker*
Ross, James Francis *philosophy educator*
Ross, Leonard Lester *anatomist*
Ross, Murray Louis *lawyer, business executive*
Ross, Roderic Henry *insurance company executive*
Rossi, Steven B. *newspaper publishing executive*
Rouse, Andrew Miles *management consultant*
Rovera, Giovanni Aurelio *medical educator, scientist*
Rowan, Richard Lamar *business management educator*
Rowell, Lester John, Jr. *insurance company executive*
Rozin, Paul *psychology educator*
Rubin, Emanuel *pathologist, educator*
†Rubinstein, Robert Lawrence *anthropologist, gerontologist*
Rudolf, Max *symphony and opera director*
Rulon, Richard R. *lawyer*
Rumpf, John Louis *university official, civil engineer, educator*
Russo, Irma Haydee Alvarez de *pathologist*
Rutman, Robert Jesse *biochemist, educator*
Ryan, Desmond *film critic*
Rybczynski, Witold Marian *architect, educator, writer*
Rykwert, Joseph *architecture and art history educator*
Sabat, Richard J. *lawyer*
Sabloff, Jeremy Arac *archaeologist*
Sage, Louis E. *environmental science executive*
Saks, Stephen Howard *accountant*
Salzberg, Brian Matthew *neuroscience and physiology educator*
Samson, Peter *lawyer*
Samsot, Robert Louis *newspaper editor, consultant*
Sander, Rudolph Charles *investment banker*
Sandler, Abraham *minister*
Santomero, Anthony M. *business educator*
Santos, Adele Naude *architect, educator*
Sanyour, Michael Louis, Jr. *financial services company executive*
Sartorius, Peter S. *lawyer*
Satinsky, Barnett *lawyer*
Saul, Ralph Southey *financial service executive*
Saunders, James C. *neuroscientist, educator*
Savitz, Samuel J. *actuarial consulting firm executive*
Sawallisch, Wolfgang *conductor*
Sax, Helen Spigel *lawyer*
Saylor, Peter M. *architect*
Sayre, William Heysham *banker*
Scandura, Joseph Michael *education researcher, software engineer*
Schaedler, Russell William *microbiologist, physicians, educator*
Schaub, Harry Carl *lawyer*
Scher, Howard Dennis *lawyer*
†Scherer, Norbert Franz *chemistry educator*
Schidlow, Daniel *pediatrician, medical association administrator*
Schiffman, Harold Fosdick *Asian language educator*
Schluth, Michael Vernon *advertising executive*
Schmidt, Michael Jack *former professional baseball player*
Schneider, Adele Sandra *clinical geneticist*
Schneider, Carl W. *lawyer*
Schneider, Jan *obstetrics and gynecology educator*
Schneider, Richard Graham *lawyer*
Scholl, David Allen *federal judge*
Schotland, Donald Lewis *neurologist, educator*
Schumacher, H(arry) Ralph *internist, researcher, medical educator*
Schumann, William Henry, III *financial executive*
Schwan, Herman Paul *electrical engineering and physical science educator, research scientist*
†Schwartz, Craig *osteopath, surgeon*
†Schwartz, Elias *pediatrician*
Schwartz, Gordon Francis *surgeon, educator*
Schwartz, Robert M. *lawyer*
Schwarz, Robert Devlin *art dealer*
Scirica, Anthony Joseph *federal judge*
Scott, Donald Allison *lawyer*
Scott, Michael Timothy *lawyer*
Scott, Robert Montgomery *museum executive, lawyer*
Scott, William Proctor, III *lawyer*
Searcy, Jarrell D. (Jay) *sportswriter*
Searcy, Jay *Sportswriter*
Sebold, Russell Perry, III *Romance languages educator, author*
Segal, Bernard Gerard *lawyer*
Segal, Bernard Louis *physician, educator*
Segal, Irving Randall *lawyer*
Segal, Robert Martin *lawyer*
Segrè, Nina *lawyer*
Seiders, Joseph Robert *service company corporate executive, lawyer*
Seligman, Martin E. P. *psychologist*
Sevy, Roger Warren *retired pharmacology educator*
Sewell, Darrel Leslie *art museum curator*
Shah, Bipin Chandra *banker*
Shakow, David Joseph *law educator*
Shapiro, Cheryl Beth *lawyer*
Shapiro, Howie *newspaper editor*
Shapiro, Norma Sondra Levy *federal judge*
Shapiro, Raymond L. *lawyer*
Shapiro, Sandor Solomon *hematologist*
Sharbaugh, Thomas J. *lawyer*
Shatz, Stephen Sidney *mathematician, educator*
Shaw, Mari Gursky *lawyer*
Shecter, Howard L. *lawyer*
Sheehan, Donald Thomas *university administrator*
Shelkrot, Elliot Louis *librarian*
Shen, Benjamin Shih-Ping *scientist, engineer, educator*
Sherman, Susan Elizabeth *nursing administrator*
Sherman, Suzette *interior design consultant*
Shestack, Jerome Joseph *lawyer*
Shiekman, Laurence Zeid *lawyer*
Shields, Jerry Allen *ophthalmologist, educator*
Shields, Robert Emmet *merchant banker, lawyer*
Shils, Edward B. *management educator, lawyer*
Shipman, Lynn Karen *lawyer*
Shockman, Gerald David *microbiologist, educator*
Shoemaker, Innis Howe *art museum curator*
Shoup, Michael C. *newspaper reporter, editor*
Showers, Ralph Morris *electrical engineer educator*
Shusterman, Murray H. *lawyer*
Shuter, Bruce Donald *lawyer*
Siegman, Marion Joyce *physiology educator*
Sigmond, Robert M. *medical economist*
Silberberg, Donald H. *neurologist*
Silvers, Willys Kent *geneticist*
Sims, Armita B. *principal*
Sirkis, Robert Lane *retail industry executive*
Siskind, Ralph Walter *lawyer*
Sivin, Nathan *historian, educator*
Skalka, Anna Marie *molecular biologist, virologist*
Sloviter, Dolores Korman *federal judge*
Sloviter, Henry Allan *medical educator*
Small, Henry Gilbert *information scientist, researcher*
Smith, Donald Eugene *political science educator*
Smith, John Francis, III *lawyer*
Smith, Lloyd *musician*
Smith, Raymond W. *telecommunications company executive*
Smith, Robert Rutherford *university dean, communication educator*
Smolin, Ronald Philip *publisher*
Snider, Edward Malcolm *professional hockey club executive*
Snider, Harold Wayne *risk and insurance educator*
Snyder, Lee H. *lawyer*
Snyder, Ralph Sheldon *lawyer*
Solano, Carl Anthony *lawyer*
Solmssen, Peter *university president*
Soloff, Louis Alexander *physician, educator*
Solomon, Phyllis Linda *social work educator, researcher*
Solomon, Vita Petrosky *artist*
Somers, Hans Peter *lawyer*
Sorgenti, Harold Andrew *petroleum and chemical company executive*
Sovie, Margaret Doe *nursing administrator, college dean*
Spaeth, Edmund Benjamin, Jr. *lawyer, law educator, former judge*
Spaeth, George Link *physician, ophthalmology educator*
Spandorfer, Merle Sue *artist, educator, author*
Spector, Harvey M. *osteopathic physician*
Spector, Martin Wolf *lawyer, business executive*
Spencer, Steven D. *lawyer*
Spikol, Art *editor, writer, illustrator*
Spiro, Walter Anselm *advertising and public relations agency executive*
Spivak, Robert Elliot *financial consultant*
Spolan, Harmon Samuel *banker*
Sprague, James Mather *medical scientist, educator*
Stack, Stephen A., Jr. *lawyer*
Stakias, G. Michael *lawyer*
Stalberg, Zachary *newspaper editor*
Staloff, Arnold Fred *financial executive*
Stampone, Frederick Albert *retail executive*
Starr, Allan H. *lawyer*
Steel, Howard Haldeman *pediatric orthopaedic surgeon*
Steele, James B. *journalist*
Steinberg, Robert Philip *lawyer*
Steinhardt, Paul Joseph *physics educator, consultant*
Stern, Joan Naomi *lawyer*
Sternberg, Donna Udin *lawyer*
Stevens, Rosemary A. *academic dean, public health and social history educator*
Stewart, James Gathings *insurance company executive*
Stewart, Robert Forrest, Jr. *lawyer*
Stiller, Jennifer Anne *lawyer*
Stitt, Susan *historical society executive*
Storm, Jonathan Morris *television critic*
Stout, Juanita Kidd *judge*
Strasbaugh, Wayne Ralph *lawyer*
Strawbridge, Francis Reeves, III *department store executive*
Strawbridge, G. Stockton *retail executive*
Strawbridge, Peter S. *department store executive*
Strawbridge, Steven Lowry *retail executive*
Strickler, Matthew M. *lawyer*
Stringer, Gail Griffin *information systems administrator*
Stunkard, Albert James *physician, educator*
Stuntebeck, Clinton A. *lawyer*
Subak, John Thomas *lawyer*
Sudak, Howard Stanley *physician, psychiatry educator*
Sugarman, Robert Jay *lawyer*
Sulyk, Stephen *archbishop*
Summers, Anita Arrow *public policy and management educator*
Summers, Clyde Wilson *law educator*
Summers, Robert *economics educator*
Sunderman, Frederick William *physician, educator, author, musician*
Suplee, Dennis Raymond *lawyer*
Sutherland, Lewis Frederick *diversified services company executive*
Sutman, Francis Xavier *university dean*
Sutnick, Alton Ivan *dean, educator, researcher, physician*
†Swain, Judith Lea *cardiovascular physician, educator*
Swichar, Edward *lawyer*
Swinburne, Herbert Hillhouse *architect*
Tague, Barry Elwert *securities trader*
Taichman, Norton Stanley *pathology educator*
Tait, Elaine *restaurant critic*
Tait, John Edwin *insurance company executive*
Tarbox, Frank Kolbe *retired insurance company executive*
Tashman, Myles Richard *lawyer*
Tasman, William Samuel *ophthalmologist, medical association executive*
Taubman, Paul James *economics educator*
Taylor, Wilson H. *diversified financial company executive*
Temin, Michael Lehman *lawyer*
Thomas, Frank M., Jr. *lawyer*
Thompson, Sheldon Lee *refining company executive*
Thomson, Keith Stewart *science museum administrator, writer*
Thrower, John Eden *architectural firm executive*
Thurston, David E. *lawyer, general counsel*
Tierney, Brian Patrick *advertising and public relations executive*
Tiger, Ira Paul *lawyer*
Tise, Larry Edward *historical organization administrator, historian*
Tomazinis, Anthony Rodoflos *city planning educator*
Tomiyasu, Kiyo *consulting engineer*
Toolan, Brian Paul *newspaper editor*
Torg, Joseph Steven *orthopaedic surgeon, educator*
Torregrossa, Joseph Anthony *lawyer*
Toto, Mary *elementary and secondary education educator*
Tourtellotte, Charles Dee *physician, educator*
Tucker, Cynthia Delores Nottage (Mrs. William M. Tucker) *political party official, former state official*
Tucker, David *newspaper editor*
Turner, Franklin Delton *bishop*
Turow, Joseph Gregory *communication educator*
Tyng, Anne Griswold *architect*
Undercofler, J(onas) Clayton *lawyer*
Vaira, Peter Francis *lawyer*
Valentini, Robert M. *telecommunications industry executive*
Van Artsdalen, Donald West *federal judge*
Van der Spiegel, Jan *engineering educator*
Van De Walle, Etienne *demographer*
Van Slyke, Andrew James *professional baseball player*
van Zyl, Jacobus Lodewyk *advertising executive*
Venturi, Robert *architect*
Vernon, Shirley Jane *architect, educator*
Vinh, Binh *architect*
Vitek, Vaclav *materials scientist*
Volpicelli, Stephen L. *lawyer*
Waas, Les *advertising executive*
Wachman, Marvin *university chancellor*
Wachter, Michael L. *economics educator*
Wadden, Thomas Antony *psychologist, educator*
Wagner, Thomas Joseph *lawyer, insurance company executive*
Wald, Martin *lawyer*
Waldman, Jay Carl *federal judge*
Waldron, Ingrid Lore *biology educator*
Wales, Walter D. *physicist, educator*
Walker, Kent *lawyer*
Wallace, Anthony Francis Clarke *anthropologist, educator*
Wallace, David Alexander *architect, educator*
Wallace, Herbert William *physician, surgery educator, researcher*
Wallace, Linda Suzan *journalist*
Walls, William Walton, Jr. *helicopter company executive*
Walsh, Donald Peter *lawyer, retired oil company executive*
Walters, Christopher Kent *lawyer*
Wambold, Judson J. *lawyer*
Ward, Hiley Henry *journalist, educator*
Warner, Frank Wilson, III *mathematics educator*
Warner, Theodore Kugler, Jr. *lawyer*
Washington, Grover, Jr. *musician, producer, composer, arranger*
Waskow, Arthur Ocean *theologian, educator*
Webber, John Bentley *orthopedic surgeon*
Weber, Janet M. *nurse*
Weeks, Gerald *psychology educator*
Weidner, Roswell Theodore *artist*
Weigley, Russell Frank *history educator*
Weil, Jeffrey George *lawyer*
Wein, Alan Jerome *urologist, educator, researcher*
Weiner, Charles R. *federal judge*
Weisberg, Morris L. *retired lawyer*
Weiss, William *retired pulmonary medicine-epidemiology educator*
Weisz, Paul B(urg) *physicist, chemical engineer*
Welhan, Beverly Jean Lutz *nursing educator, administrator*
†Wender, Herbert *title company executive*
Wernick, Richard Frank *composer, conductor*
Wesler, Ken *theater company manager*
West, James Joseph *lawyer*
Wetzel, Carroll Robbins *lawyer*
Wetzel, Gilbert A. *telephone company executive*
†Whitaker, Linton Andin *plastic surgeon*
White, Albert J. *health products executive*
White, Warren Wurtele *retailing executive*
Whiteside, William Anthony, Jr. *lawyer*
Whitman, Bradford F. *lawyer*
Whybrow, Peter Charles *psychiatrist, educator*
Wiener, Ronald Martin *lawyer*
Wiener, Thomas Eli *lawyer*
Wiksten, Barry Frank *communications executive*
Wild, Richard P. *lawyer*
Wilde, Norman Taylor, Jr. *investment banking company executive*
Wilder, Robert George *advertising and public relations executive*
Wilkinson, Signe *cartoonist*
Williams, Mary Jane *fundraiser*
Williams, Robert Deland *lawyer*
†Williams, Sankey Vaughan *health services researcher, internist*
Wilson, Bruce Brighton *transportation executive*
Wilson, James Lawrence *chemical company executive*
Wilson, Marjorie Price *physician, medical commission executive*
†Wilson, Ronald D. *soft drink bottling company executive*
Winegrad, Albert Irvin *immunologist, educator*
Winfrey, Marion Lee *television critic*
Winkler, Sheldon *dentist, educator*
Witt, Thomas Powell *lawyer*
Wixon, Rufus *retired accounting educator*
Woestendiek, (William) John, Jr. *reporter*
Wolf, Robert B. *lawyer*
Wolfbein, Seymour Louis *economist, educator*
†Wolff, Deborah H(orowitz) *lawyer*
Wolfgang, Marvin Eugene *sociologist, criminologist, educator*
Wolitarsky, James William *securities industry executive*
Wolkin, Paul Alexander *lawyer, former institute executive*
Wollman, Harry *medical educator*
Wood, William Philler *lawyer*
Woods, Richard Seavey *accountant, educator*
Woodside, Lisa Nicole *academic administrator*
Wright, Minturn Tatum, III *lawyer*
Wrobleski, Jeanne Pauline *lawyer*
Wruble, Brian Frederick *investment management company executive*
Wysocki, F(elix) Michael *lawyer*
Yanoff, Myron *ophthalmologist*
†Yoh, Harold L., III *company executive*
Yohn, William Hendricks, Jr. *federal judge*
Young, Andrew Brodbeck *lawyer*
Young, Donald Stirling *clinical pathology educator*
Young, Robert Crabill *medical researcher, science facility administrator, internist*
Yunis, Jorge Jose *geneticist, pathologist, educator, poet*
Zemaitis, Thomas Edward *lawyer*
Zemel, Jay Norman *electrical engineer, educator*
Ziegler, Donald Robert *accountant*
Ziff, Lloyd Richard *lawyer*
Ziga, Kathleen *lawyer*
Ziomek, Thomas John *lawyer*
Zucchino, David Alan *newspaper journalist*
Zucker, William *retired business educator*
Zurmuhle, Robert Walter *physicist*
Zweiman, Burton *physician, scientist, educator*

Philipsburg
Reiter, Daisy K. *elementary education educator*

Phoenixville
Lukacs, John Adalbert *historian, retired educator*
Olson, James Robert *consulting engineer*
Wright, Jean Norman *elementary education educator*

Pine Grove
Hoy, Harold Joseph marketing educator, retail executive, management consultant, author, military officer

Pittsburgh
Aaron, Marcus, II lawyer
Aaronson, Joel P. lawyer
Abdelhak, Sherif Samy health science executive
Abrew, Frederick Henry utility company executive
Agnew, Franklin Ernest, III former food company executive
Alexander, James Eckert editor
Allen, Thomas E. obstetrician, gynecologist
Alstadt, Lynn Jeffery lawyer
Alvarez, Paul Hubert communications and public relations consultant
Ambrose, Donetta W. federal judge
Amon Parisi, Cristina Hortensia mechanical engineering educator, researcher
Anderson, Gary Allan professional football player
Anderson, John Robert psychology and computer science educator
Anderson, Russell Karl, Jr. physicist, horse breeder
Anderson, Thomas Caryl financial and administrative systems professional
Anthony, Edward Mason linguistics educator
Apone, Carl Anthony journalist
Aranson, Michael J. lawyer
Arkus, Leon Anthony art consultant, former museum director
Armstrong, Jack Gilliland lawyer
Aronson, Arthur H. steel company executive
Aronson, Mark Berne corporate executive
Aul, Donald J. biochemist, researcher
Baier, George Patrick lawyer, electrical engineer
Balada, Leonardo composer, educator
Balas, Egon applied mathematician, educator
Baldauf, Kent Edward lawyer
Bardyguine, Patricia Wilde ballerina, ballet theatre executive
Barone, Eugene J. medical products executive
Bartley, Burnett Graham, Jr. oil company and manufacturing executive
Basinski, Anthony Joseph lawyer
Beachley, Michael Charles radiologist
Bearman, Toni Carbo information scientist
Beck, Paul Augustine lawyer
Behrend, William Louis electrical engineer
Bell, Jay Stuart professional baseball player
Belnap, Nuel Dinsmore, Jr. philosophy educator
Bender, Charles Christian retail home center executive
Benz, Edward J., Jr. physician, educator
Berliner, Hans Jack computer scientist
Berman, Malcolm Frank health facility administrator
Bernier, George Matthew, Jr. physician, medical educator, medical school dean
Bernt, Benno Anthony financial and business executive
Berry, Guy Curtis polymer science educator, researcher
Bevan, William, III lawyer
Biondi, Manfred Anthony physicist, educator
Birks, Neil metallurgical engineering educator, consultant
Bitzer, John Frederick, Jr. diversified holding company executive
Bjorhovde, Reidar civil engineer, educator, researcher, consultant
Black, Alexander lawyer
Blaney, M. Kathleen elementary education educator
Bleil, Walter G. lawyer
Blenko, Walter John, Jr. lawyer
Bloch, Alan Neil federal judge
Bloom, William Millard furnace design engineer
Blumstein, Alfred urban and public affairs educator
Bobrow, Davis Bernard public policy educator
Bogdanovich, Joseph James food company executive
Bohlin, Peter Quarfordt architect
Bonessa, Dennis R. lawyer
Borkovic, David Allen lawyer
Borle, André Bernard physiologist
Bothner-By, Aksel Arnold chemist, horseman
†Boyce, Doreen Elizabeth education, civic development foundation executive
†Boyd, John T. engineering executive
Boyd, William, Jr. business advisor, banker
†Bozzomo, Lawrence E. superintendent of schools
Brenenborg, David C. architectural firm executive
Brennan, Carey M. lawyer
Briskman, Louis J. lawyer
Brosky, John G. judge
Broussard, Elsie Rita physician, educator, researcher
Brown, Bobby R. coal company executive
Brown, David Ronald lawyer
†Brown, Ellsworth Howard museum administrator
Brown, L. Keith anthropology educator
Bryant, Randal Everitt computer science educator, consultant
Buchanan, James Junkin classics educator
Buerger, David Bernard lawyer
Buford, Earl, Jr. protective services official
Burger, Herbert Francis advertising agency executive
†Burke, Linda Beerbower lawyer, aluminum manufacturing company executive, mining executive
Burley, Jack Lynn food products executive
Burnham, Donald Clemens manufacturing company executive
†Byham, William Clarence instructional technology company executive
Cagney, William Robert psychologist
Cahouet, Frank Vondell banker
Caldwell, Richard Clark banker
Candris, Laura A. lawyer
Capobianco, Tito opera director
Cardenes, Andres Jorge violinist, music educator
Caretto, Albert Alexander chemist, educator
Carey, John J. utilities executive
Carr, Walter James, Jr. research physicist, consultant
Carroll, Holbert Nicholson political science educator
Carter, Donald K. architectural firm executive
Casasent, David Paul electrical engineering educator, data processing executive
Casey, Robert J. international trade association executive
Cassidy, William Arthur geology and planetary science educator
Catell, Grace Louise nursing educator
Chamberlain, Denise Kay lawyer, banking counsel
Chao, Chong-Yun mathematics educator
Charap, Stanley Harvey electrical engineering educator
Cheever, George Martin lawyer
Chenery, Robin metals manufacturing executive
Chiang, Shiao-Hung chemical engineering educator
Chorazy Lyjak, Anna Julia pediatrician, medical administrator, educator
Choyke, Wolfgang Justus physicist
Christiano, Paul P. academic administrator, civil engineering educator
Christof, Joseph S. D., II lawyer
Chun, Sun W. energy technology administrator
Civello, Anthony Ned retail drug company executive, pharmacist
Clack, Jerry classics educator
Clark, Gary M. electronics executive
Clark, Richard A. lawyer
Clyde, Larry Forbes banker
Cohen, Bernard Leonard physicist, educator
Cohill, Maurice Blanchard, Jr. district court judge
Colen, Frederick Haas lawyer
Coltman, John Wesley physicist
Colville, Robert E. lawyer
Coney, Aims C., Jr. lawyer, labor-management negotiator
Connolly, Ruth Carol critical care nurse
Connors, Eugene Kenneth lawyer
Conti, Joy Flowers lawyer
Cooper, Thomas Louis lawyer
Cooper, William Marion physician
Corry, Charles Albert steel and energy company executive
Cosetti, Joseph Louis federal judge
Courtsal, Donald Preston manufacturing company executive, financial consultant
Covey, Preston King, Jr. education educator, university official
Cowan, Barton Zalman lawyer
Cowden, Jere Lee management consultant
Cowher, Bill professional football coach
Craig, Edward Armstrong, III lawyer
Craig, John Gilbert, Jr. newspaper editor
Croan, Robert James music critic, singer
Croneberger, Robert Bruce, Jr. library director
Curry, Nancy Ellen education educator, psychoanalyst, psychologist
Curtis, Gregory Dyer investment company executive, foundation administrator, lawyer, author, poet
Cutler, John Charles physician, educator
Cyert, Richard Michael former university president, economist
Dameshek, H(arold) Lee physician
Damianos, Sylvester architect, sculptor
Danforth, Douglas Dewitt manufacturing company executive
Daniel, Robert Michael lawyer
Dauler, L. Van V., Jr. chemicals executive
Davidson, George A., Jr. utility company executive
Davis, John Phillips, Jr. lawyer
Davis, Lewis U., Jr. lawyer
Davis, Otto Anderson economics educator
Dawes, Robyn Mason psychology educator
Dawson, Mary Ruth curator
Day, Maurice Jerome automobile parts distributing company executive
†DeAlmeida, Cynthia Koledo oboist
DeForest, Walter Pattison, III lawyer
deGroat, William Chesney pharmacology educator
Dehouske, Ellen Jane early childhood education educator, consultant
Deibler, William Edwin newspaper editor
Delaney, John Francis neurologist, psychiatrist
Dell, Ernest Robert lawyer
Demmler, John Henry lawyer
Demmler, Ralph Henry lawyer
Dempsey, Jerry Edward service company executive
Deskins, Wilbur Eugene mathematician, educator
Detre, Katherine Maria physician
Detre, Thomas psychiatrist, educator
Diamond, Gustave federal judge
Dimmel, Kenneth Travis cultural organization administrator, editor
DiPietro, Melanie lawyer
Director, Stephen William electrical engineering educator, researcher
Dixit, Balwant Narayan pharmacology and toxicology educator
Doerfler, Leo G. audiology educator
Doerr, Ronald H. steel company executive
Donahoe, David Lawrence state and city official
†Donahue, John Francis investment company executive
Donaldson, William Fielding, Jr. orthopaedic surgeon
Donnelly, Thomas Joseph lawyer
Doty, Robert Walter lawyer
†Dowd, Paul chemistry educator
Drake, Kingsley Dimitri professional service company executive
Drescher, Seymour history educator, writer
Duffin, Richard James mathematician, educator
Dugan, John F. lawyer
Dumbauld, Edward federal judge
Duval, Robert leasing company executive
Dybeck, Alfred Charles labor arbitrator
Eaton, Joseph W. sociology educator
Echement, John R. banker
Eckert, Jean Patricia elementary education educator
Edelman, Harry Rollings, III engineering and construction company executive
Edmonds, Mary Patricia biological sciences educator
Ehrenwerth, David Harry lawyer
Emmerich, Werner Sigmund physicist
Epperson, David Ernest dean, educator
Evans, Bruce Dwight lawyer
Evans, David Andreoff linguistics and computer science educator
Ewalt, Henry Ward lawyer
Fairbanks, Frank Bates manufacturing company executive
Fajt, Gregory Charles state legislator
Fararo, Thomas John sociologist, educator
Farley, Andrew Newell lawyer
†Faust, Charles Henry superintendent of schools
Feczko, William Albert radiologist
Feingold, David Sidney microbiology educator
Feller, Robert Livingston chemist, art conservation scientist
Fenves, Steven Joseph civil engineer
Ferguson, Mary Anne Heyward language professional, educator
Ferguson, Sanford Barnett lawyer
Fernsler, John Paul lawyer
Fienberg, Stephen Elliott statistician
Figgins, David Forrester construction company executive
Fine, Milton hotel company executive, lawyer
Finn, Frances Mary biochemistry researcher
Fireman, Philip pediatrician, allergist, immunologist, medical association executive
Fischer, Ben labor relations educator
Fischer, Richard Lawrence metal products executive
Fischhoff, Baruch psychologist, educator
Fisher, Bernard surgeon, researcher, educator
Fisher, D. Michael state senator, lawyer
Fisher, James Aiken industrial marketing executive
Fishman, Libby G. lawyer
Fitzgerald, Judith Klaswick federal judge
Flaherty, John P., Jr. state supreme court justice
Flatley, Lawrence Edward lawyer
Fletcher, Ronald Darling microbiologist educator
Flinn, Michael J. lawyer
Fort, James Tomlinson lawyer
Fox, Cyril A., Jr. law educator
Foxen, Richard William manufacturing company executive
Frank, Alan I W manufacturing company executive
Frank, Ronald W. lawyer, financier
Franklin, Kenneth Ronald franchise company executive, consultant
Fredette, Barbara Wagner art educator
Freeman, Edmund J. heavy manufacturing executive
Friday, Gilbert Anthony, Jr. pediatrician
Friede, Samuel A(rnold) health care executive
Froehlich, Fritz Edgar telecommunications educator and scientist
Frolik, Lawrence Anton law educator, lawyer, consultant
Frueh, John Curt financial executive
Gaffney, Paul Cotter physician
Gale, Robert Lee retired American literature educator and critic
Gallagher, Daniel P., Jr. lawyer
Garrett, Sylvester arbitrator
Geiger, Gene Edward engineer, educator
Genge, William Harrison advertising executive, writer
Gerhard, Harry E., Jr. counter trader, management and trade consultant
Gerjuoy, Edward physicist, lawyer
Gerlach, G. Donald lawyer
Gilbert, Ralph Whitmel, Jr. engineering company executive
†Gilbey, John Walter Guy mining company executive, geologist
Gill, Thomas James, III physician, educator
Gindroz, Raymond L. architect
Ginsburg, Mark Barry sociology of education educator
†Glaser, Robert psychology educator
Gold, Harold Arthur lawyer
Goldberg, Mark Joel lawyer
Goldstein, Gerald research psychologist
Gollin, Susanne Merle cytogeneticist, cell biologist
Gordon, Gerd Stray retired historian, educator, writer
Gottfried, Byron Stuart engineering educator
Graf, Edward Louis, Jr. lawyer, finance executive
Graham, Laurie editor
Grant, Daniel Gordon information services company executive
Gray, Charles Buffum theatrical director, producer
Green, Isaac church administrator
Grefenstette, Carl G. medical products and real estate executive
Griffin, Donald Spray mechanical engineer, consultant
Griffiths, Robert Budington physics educator
Grinberg, Meyer Stewart educational institute executive
†Grossman, Ignacio E. chemical engineering educator
Groves, Michael banker
Grunbaum, Adolf philosophy educator, author
†Guna, Edward Francis financial executive
Gurtin, Morton Edward mathematics educator
Hackney, William Pendleton lawyer
Hale, Edward Harned internist
Hall, Charles Allan numerical analyst, educator
Hallen, Philip Burgh foundation administrator
Hamburg, Lester Albert wholesale appliance company executive
Hamilton, Howard Britton electrical engineer, educator
Hammer, Harold Harlan oil company financial executive
Hammond, Paul Young political scientist, educator
Hannan, Robert William retail pharmaceutical company executive
Hardesty, Robert Lynch surgeon, educator
Hardie, James Hiller lawyer
Harff, Charles Henry lawyer, diversified industrial company executive
Harmon, Megan Elizabeth lawyer
Harris, Ann Birgitta Sutherland art historian
Harrold, Ronald Thomas research scientist
Hartkopf, Volker Hugo architect, educator
Hartman, Ronald G. lawyer
Harty, James Quinn lawyer
Harvey, Calvin Rea lawyer
Harvey, Thomas J. priest, social service organization executive
Hathaway, Alden Moinet bishop
Hayes, Ann Louise English educator, consultant, poet
†Heckler, Frederick Roger plastic surgeon
Hedquist, Jan B. advertising company executive
Heller, Lawrence Aaron business owner, association executive
Hellman, Arthur David law educator, consultant
Helwig, Gilbert John lawyer
Henry, Susan Armstrong biology educator, university dean
Herndon, James Henry orthopedic surgeon, educator
Hershey, Colin Harry management consultant
Hershey, Dale lawyer
Hershey, Nathan lawyer, educator
Hickman, Leon Edward lawyer, business executive
Higgins, James Henry retired banker
Hill, John Howard lawyer
Hillman, Henry L. investment company executive
Hingson, Robert Andrew physician, educator, inventor, farmer, poet
Hitt, Leo N. lawyer, educator
Ho, Chien biological sciences educator
Hoburg, James Frederick electrical engineering educator
Hodges, Margaret Moore author, educator
Hoffee, Patricia Anne molecular genetics educator
Hoffman, Donald Howard transportation executive
Hoffman, Ronald Robert aluminum company executive
Hoffstot, Henry Phipps, Jr. lawyer
Hollingsworth, Samuel Hawkins, Jr. bassist
Hollinshead, Earl Darnell, Jr. lawyer
Holz, Richard Lee lawyer
Holzner, Burkart sociologist, educator
Horan, Justin Thomas retired association executive
Horn, Jerry Dean health products executive
Horowitz, Don Roy instrument company executive
Hough, Thomas Henry Michael lawyer
Howard, Lawrence Cabot international affairs educator
Howland, Robert Herbert psychiatrist
Hsu, Cho-yun history educator
Humphrey, Watts Sherman technical executive, author
Hung, Tin-Kan engineering educator, researcher
Hunter, David Wittmer security brokerage executive
Huntington, James Cantine, Jr. equipment manufacturing company executive
Ijiri, Yuji accounting and economics educator
Irwin, Joe Robert banker
Isherwood, John S. beverage company executive
Ismail, Yahia Hassan dentist, educator
Janis, Allen Ira retired physicist, educator
†Jannetta, Peter Joseph neurosurgeon
Jasnow, David Michael physics educator
Jegasothy, Brian Vasanthakumar dermatology educator
Jehle, Michael Edward financial executive
Johannes, George Robert construction executive
†Johnson, Lester Deane oil and gas company executive
Johnson, Robert Alan lawyer
Johnston, Edward Joseph professional hockey team coach, former team executive, former player
Johnston, Phillip Michael museum director, curator
Jones, Craig Ward lawyer
Jones, Elizabeth Winifred biology educator
Jordan, Angel Goni electrical and computer engineering educator
Jordan, Michael Hugh electrical and electronics company executive
Josey, E(lonnie) J(unius) librarian, educator, former state administrator
Joyner, Claude Reuben, Jr. physician, medical educator
Junker, Edward P., III diversified financial services company executive
Kadane, Joseph B. statistics educator
Kanade, Takeo science educator, institute administrator
Kaplan, John photojournalist, consultant, educator
Karis, William George coal company executive
Karol, Meryl Helene immunologist
Katarincic, Joseph Anthony lawyer
Katz, Arnold economics educator
Katz, Saul Milton economist, social scientist, educator
Kaufman, William Morris research institute administrator, engineer
Keairns, Yvonne Ewing psychologist
Kearney, Hugh Francis historian, educator
Kearney, Kerry A. lawyer
Kearns, John J., III lawyer
Keefe, William Joseph political science educator
Kenkel, James Lawrence economics educator
†Kenny, Rhian Margaret musician, educator
Kenrick, Charles William lawyer
Kent, Allen library and information sciences educator
†Kent, Chester C. school system administrator
Kent, Robert Warren lawyer
Kerr, William Gregg lawyer
Ketchum, David Storey retired fundraising executive
Ketter, David Lee lawyer
Khonsari, Michael M. engineering educator
Kiger, Robert William botanist, science historian, educator
Kilmann, Ralph Herman business educator
King, James Edward museum director
King, William Richard business educator, consultant
†Kissell, Fred N. mining engineer
Kisslinger, Leonard Sol physicist, educator
Klett, Edwin Lee lawyer
Knapp, George Robert lawyer
Knox, Charles Graham lawyer
Koedel, Robert Craig minister, historian, educator
Kolodner, Ignace Izaak mathematician, educator
Krasik, Carl lawyer
Kriebel, Charles Hosey management sciences educator
Kronk, Claude F. heavy manufacturing executive
Krutz, Ronald L. computer engineer
Kryder, Mark Howard computer and electrical engineering educator, consultant
Kupfer, David J. psychiatry educator
Kushner, Robert Arnold steel company executive, lawyer
La Rue, Henry Aldred consultant, former oil company executive
Laughlin, David Eugene materials science educator, metallurgical consultant
Lauterbach, Hans pharmaceutical company executive
Lauterbach, Robert Emil steel company executive
Lave, Judith Rice economics educator
LeBoeuf, Raymond Walter manufacturing company executive
Lee, Donald John federal judge
Lego, Paul Edward retired corporation executive
Lehoczky, John Paul statistics educator
Leiter, Donald Eugene religious organization executive
LeMelle, Tilden John political science educator, editor, college official
Lemieux, Mario professional hockey player
Leo, Peter Andrew newspaper columnist
Lewis, Jessica Helen (Mrs. Jack D. Myers) physician, educator
Lewis, Richard Allan financial planner
Lewis, Timothy K. federal judge
Leyland, James Richard professional baseball team manager
Li, Ching-Chung electrical engineering, computer science educator
†Libman, Steven Bradley performing arts administrator
Lidz, Charles Wilmanns sociologist
Limbach, Walter F. construction company executive
London, Alan E. lawyer
Longest, Beaufort Brown health services administration educator, research director
Losacco, Lesley Herdt supervisor, educator
Lovett, Robert G. lawyer
Lowery, Clinton Hershey former naval officer
Ludwig, Karl David psychiatrist
†Lundquist, Dana R. health facility administrator
Luthy, Richard Godfrey environmental engineering educator
Maazel, Lorin conductor, musician
Machatzke, Heinz Wilhelm dean, chemistry educator
MacLeod, Gordon Kenneth physician, educator
Majors, Johnny (John Terrill Majors) university athletic coach
Makarewicz, Joseph Thomas research center director, historian
Mansmann, Carol Los federal judge, law educator
Mansmann, J. Jerome lawyer

Marasco, Francis Anthony *human resources executive*
Marshall, Thomas *chemical company executive*
Martin, Bruce Douglas *university official, chemist*
Masoner, Paul Henry *counseling educator*
Massalski, Thaddeus Bronislaw *material scientist, educator*
Massey, Gerald J. *philosophy educator*
Mastro, A. F. *chemical company executive*
Mathieson, Andrew Wray *investment management executive*
†Mattison, Donald Roger *dean, physician, military officer*
†Matyjaszewski, Krzysztof *chemist, educator*
Matzke, Gary Roger *pharmacologist, educator, researcher*
Maurer, Richard Michael *investment company executive*
Maximos, (Maximos Demetrios Aghiorgoussis) *bishop*
May, Charles Kent *lawyer*
Mc Anulty, Henry Joseph *university administrator*
McAvoy, Bruce Ronald *scientist, consultant*
McCall, Dorothy Kay *social worker, psychotherapist*
McCallum, Bennett Tarlton *economics educator*
Mc Cartney, Robert Charles *lawyer*
McClaran, George Joseph, Sr. *retired banker*
McClelland, James L. *psychology educator, cognitive scientist*
McCoid, Donald James *bishop*
McConomy, James Herbert *lawyer*
McConomy, Thomas Arthur *chemical company executive*
McCullough, M. Bruce *lawyer*
Mc Cune, Barron Patterson *federal judge*
McDonald, C. W. *mining executive*
Mc Dowell, John B. *bishop*
†McDuffie, Keith A. *literature educator, magazine director*
Mc Featters, Dale Stitt *retired electric company executive*
McGough, Walter Thomas *lawyer*
McGough, Walter Thomas, Jr. *lawyer*
McGovern, John Joseph *former air pollution control association executive, consultant*
McGuinn, Martin Gregory *banker, lawyer*
McIntosh, DeCourcy Eyre *museum director*
McKenna, J. Frank, III *lawyer*
Mc Kenzie, Ray *anesthesiologist, educator*
McLaughlin, John Sherman *lawyer*
McMaster, James Henry *orthopaedic surgeon*
McMichael, Francis Clay *civil engineering educator, environmental engineering consultant*
McWilliams, Betty Jane *science administrator, communication disorders educator, researcher*
Medonis, Robert Xavier *lawyer*
Meegan, Sister Elizabeth *school system administrator*
Mehrabian, Robert *academic administrator*
Meiksin, Zvi H. *electrical engineering educator*
Meisel, Alan *law educator*
Mellon, Richard Prosser *charitable foundation executive*
Mellott, Cloyd Rowe *lawyer*
Meltzer, Allan H. *economist, educator*
Mesa-Lago, Carmelo *economist, educator*
Messner, Robert Thomas *lawyer, banking executive*
Miller, David William *historian, educator*
Miller, Donald *art critic*
Miller, Harbaugh *lawyer*
Miller, James Robert *lawyer*
Miller, Mildred *opera singer, recitalist*
Miller, Patricia G. *lawyer*
Miller, Rush Glenn, Jr. *university dean, librarian*
Milnes, Arthur George *electrical engineer, educator*
Milsom, Robert Cortlandt *banker*
†Minnigh, Joel Douglas *library director*
Mitchell, Robert C. *federal judge*
Modell, John *historian, educator*
Moeller, Audrey Carolyn *energy company executive, corporate secretary*
Moore, Frederick C. *manufacturing executive*
Moore, Pearl B. *nurse*
Moore, Richard Allan *mathematics educator*
Moore, Robert Yates *neuroscience educator*
Morby, Jeffrey Lewis *banker, investment banker*
Moriarty, Richard William *pediatrician*
Morice, Joseph Richard *history educator*
Moritz, Donald I. *energy company executive*
Morton, James Davis *lawyer*
Moura, José Manuel Fonseca *electrical engineer*
Mueller, Gerd Dieter *financial and administrative executive*
Mullen, Joseph Patrick *professional hockey player*
Mulloney, Peter Black *steel, oil and gas executive*
Mulroy, Thomas Michael *lawyer*
Munsch, Martha Hartle *lawyer*
Murdoch, David Armor *lawyer*
Murdy, James L. *petroleum company executive*
Murphy, John Nolan *mining executive, researcher, electrical engineer*
Murphy, Lawrence Thomas *professional hockey player*
Murphy, Thomas J., Jr. *mayor*
Murphy, William James *materials characterization company executive, metallurgical engineer*
Murray, John Edward, Jr. *lawyer, educator, university president*
Murrin, Regis Doubet *lawyer*
†Muspratt, Kirk *conductor*
Muto, Susan Annette *religion educator, academic administrator*
Myers, Eugene Nicholas *otolaryngologist, otolaryngology educator*
Myers, Marlee S. *lawyer*
Nathanson, Harvey Charles *electrical engineer*
Needleman, Herbert Leroy *psychiatrist, pediatrician*
Neel, John Dodd *memorial park executive*
Neuman, Charles P. *electrical and computer engineering educator, consultant*
Noll, Charles Henry *former professional football coach*
Nordenberg, Mark Alan *legal educator, university administrator*
Norris, James Harold *lawyer*
Norton, Eunice *pianist*
Ober, Russell John, Jr. *lawyer*
O'Brien, Thomas Henry *bank holding company executive*
O'Connor, Donald Thomas *lawyer*
O'Connor, Edward Gearing *lawyer*
O'Connor, John Dennis *chancellor, biology educator*
Oehmler, George Courtland *corporate executive*
Ogul, Morris Samuel *political science educator, consultant*
Olson, Stephen M(ichael) *lawyer*
O'Neill, Paul Henry *aluminum company executive*
O'Reilly, Anthony John Francis *food company executive*
Ostern, Wilhelm Curt *retired holding company executive*
Owens, Gregory Randolph *physician, medical educator*
Page, Lorne Albert *physicist, educator*
Parkes, Kenneth Carroll *ornithologist*
Partanen, Carl Richard *biology educator*
Pasnick, Raymond Wallace *labor union official, editor*
Patrick, Craig *professional hockey team executive*
Patten, Charles Anthony *management consultant, arbitrator, retired manufacturing company executive, author*
Patton, Nancy Matthews *elementary education educator*
Patton, Richard Bolling *food company executive*
Patton, Robert Frederick *lawyer, banker*
Paul, John *health care executive*
Paul, Robert Arthur *steel company executive*
Paulston, Christina Bratt *linguistics educator*
Pearson, Nathan Williams *investment management executive*
Pekruhn, John Edward *retired architect, educator*
Perfido, Ruth S. *lawyer*
Perloff, Robert *psychologist, educator*
Petrov, Nicolas *dance educator, choreographer*
Pettit, Frederick Sidney *metallurgical engineering educator, researcher*
Pham, Si Mai *cadiothoracic surgeon, medical educator*
Phillips, James Macilduff *material handling company executive, engineering and manufacturing executive*
Phillips, Larry Edward *lawyer*
Plowman, Jack Wesley *lawyer*
Pohl, Paul Michael *lawyer*
Pohland, Frederick George *environmental engineering educator, researcher*
Pois, Joseph *lawyer, educator*
Pomeroy, Thomas Wilson, Jr. *lawyer, former state supreme court justice*
Popchak, Sister Barbara Jo *private school director*
Porter, Irwin W. *food store chain executive*
Porter, Milton *investment executive*
Post, Peter David *lawyer*
Powderly, William H., III *lawyer*
Prado, Gerald M. *investment banker*
Pratt, Richard Houghton *physics educator*
Price, Trevor Robert Pryce *psychiatrist, educator*
Prine, Charles W., Jr. *construction executive*
†Procyk, Judson M. *bishop*
Propst, John Leake *lawyer*
Prorok, Robert Francis *lawyer*
Prosperi, Louis Anthony *lawyer*
Pugliese, Robert Francis *lawyer, business executive*
Purdum, Robert L. *steel manufacturing company executive*
†Puskar, Milan *pharmaceuticals executive*
Quinn, John E. *lawyer*
Rabin, Bruce Stuart *immunologist, physician, educator*
Rago, Ann D'Amico *public relations professional*
Raimondi, Albert Anthony *mechanical engineer*
†Ramdin, R. H. *mining executive*
Randolph, Robert DeWitt *lawyer*
†Rangos, Alexander W. *waste management environmental services administrator*
†Rangos, John G., Sr. *waste management company executive*
Rawski, Evelyn Sakakida *history educator*
Reed, W. Franklin *lawyer*
Reif, Eric Peter *lawyer*
Rescher, Nicholas *philosophy educator*
Resnick, Lauren B. *psychology educator*
Restivo, James John, Jr. *lawyer*
Rheinboldt, Werner Carl *mathematics educator, researcher*
†Riazzi, Richard *gas industry executive*
Rimer, John Thomas *foreign language educator, academic administrator, writer, translator*
Ritchey, Patrick William *lawyer*
Robinson, William M. *lawyer*
Robitaille, Luc *professional hockey player*
Rogers, Bryan Leigh *artist, art educator*
Rogers, Fred McFeely *television producer and host*
Rogers, Robert Mark *physician*
Rohr, James Edward *banker*
Rohrer, Ronald Alan *electrical and computer engineering educator, consultant*
Romoff, Jeffrey Alan *university officer, health care executive*
Roof, Robert L. *broadcast executive, sales executive*
Rooney, Daniel M. *professional football team executive*
Rose, Evans, Jr. *lawyer*
Rosenberg, Jerome Laib *chemist, educator*
Rosenberger, Bryan David *lawyer*
Rosenkranz, Herbert S. *environmental toxicology educator*
Ross, Eunice Latshaw *judge*
Ross, Madelyn Ann *newspaper editor*
Roth, Alvin Eliot *economics educator*
Roth, Loren *psychiatrist*
Roth, William George *manufacturing company executive*
Rubin, Edward Stephen *engineering educator, mechanical engineer*
Russell, Stanley G., Jr. *accountant*
Rust, William James *retired steel company executive*
Ruttenberg, Harold Joseph *manufacturing executive*
Ryan, John Thomas, Jr. *business executive*
Ryan, John Thomas, III *safety equipment company executive*
Saalman, Howard *architectural historian, educator*
Safar, Peter *emergency health care facility administrator*
Sandman, Dan D. *lawyer*
Sante, William Arthur, II *aerospace and manufacturing company executive*
Sanzo, Anthony Michael *health care executive*
Sardi, Maurice Charles *contract furniture company executive*
Sauer, Georgia Booras *newspaper writer*
Sax, Martin *crystallographer*
Scanlon, Eugene Francis *lawyer*
Schallenberger, Carolyn *college dean*
Schaub, Marilyn McNamara *religion educator*
Scheinholtz, Leonard Louis *lawyer*
Schliebs, Charles Allan *lawyer*
Schmidt, Edward Craig *lawyer*
Schmidt, Thomas Mellon *lawyer*
Schultz, Jerome Samson *biochemical engineer, educator*
Schwab, Arthur James *lawyer*
Schwass, Gary L. *utilities executive*
Schwendeman, Paul William *lawyer*
Scorsone, Vincent Robert *aluminum company executive*
Sculley, David W. *food company executive*
Sekerka, Robert Floyd *physics educator, scientist*
Seligson, Mitchell A. *Latin American studies educator*
Sell, William Edward *legal educator*
Sensenich, Ila Jeanne *magistrate judge*
Shane, Peter Milo *law educator, lawyer*
Shapira, David S. *food chain executive*
Shapiro, Alvin Philip *physician, educator*
Shaw, Mary M. *computer science educator*
Shaw, Richard Leslie *engineering company executive*
Sheon, Aaron *art historian, educator*
Sieber, Suzanne Mahoney *sales executive*
Sieckmann, Walter *industrial manufacturing and engineering company executive*
Siewiorek, Daniel Paul *computer science educator, researcher*
Siker, Ephraim S. *anesthesiologist*
Silverman, Arnold Barry *lawyer*
Simaan, Marwan A. *electrical engineering educator*
Simmermon, James Everett *credit bureau executive*
Simmons, Richard P. *steel company executive*
Simon, Herbert A(lexander) *social scientist*
Simonds, John Ormsbee *landscape architect*
†Sinclair, Glenn Bruce *mechanical engineering educator, researcher*
Singer, Paul Meyer *lawyer*
†Smartschan, Glenn Fred *educational administrator*
Smith, Charles Raymond, Jr. *lawyer*
Smith, David Brookman *federal judge*
Smith, Phillip Hartley *steel company executive*
Smith, William J. *lawyer*
Spanovich, Milan *civil engineer*
Spina, Horacio Anselmo *physician*
Stahl, Laddie L. *electrical engineer, manufacturing company executive*
Standish, William Lloyd *federal judge*
Stargell, Willie (Wilver Dornel Stargell) *professional sports team coach, former baseball player*
Starzl, Thomas Earl *physician, educator*
Stearns, Peter Nathaniel *history educator*
Stein, Arland Thomas *lawyer*
Stephenson, Robert Clay *commercial real estate developer*
Stern, Theodore *electric company executive*
Stevens, Kevin Michael *professional hockey player*
Strader, James David *lawyer*
Strauss, Robert Philip *economics educator*
Stroyd, Arthur Heister *lawyer*
Stuckeman, Herman Campbell *architectural engineer*
†Stuenkel, William C. *airport administrator*
†Summerfield, Herbert Gibson, Jr. *bank executive*
Sussna, Edward *economist, educator*
Suzuki, Jon Byron *dean, periodontist, educator*
Swaim, Joseph Carter, Jr. *lawyer*
Swain, William Grant *landscape architect*
Swann, Lynn Curtis *sportscaster, former professional football player*
Sweeney, Clayton Anthony *lawyer, business executive*
Symons, Edward Leonard, Jr. *lawyer, educator, investment advisor*
Tarr, Joel Arthur *history and public policy educator*
Thomas, W(illiam) Bruce *retired steel, oil, gas company executive*
Thompson, Gerald Luther *operations research and applied mathematics educator*
Thompson, Thomas Martin *lawyer*
Thorne, John Reinecke *business educator, venture capitalist*
Tierney, John William *chemical engineering educator*
Tobin, William Thomas *retail executive*
†Toeplitz, Gideon *symphony society executive*
Toker, Franklin K. *art history educator, archaeologist, foundation executive*
Trapp, Frank Anderson *art educator*
Troen, Philip *physician, educator*
Trottier, Bryan John *professional sports team coach, former professional hockey player*
Tungate, David E. *lawyer, educator*
†Turbeville, Robert Morris *engineering executive*
Turnbull, Gordon Keith *metal company executive, metallurgical engineer*
Turner, Harry Woodruff *lawyer*
Ubinger, John W., Jr. *lawyer*
Udler, Rubin Jakovlevitch *linguist*
Uher, Richard A. *rail transportation executive*
Ulmer, Daniel C., Jr. *diversified financial services company executive*
Van Dusen, Albert Clarence *university official*
Van Kirk, Thomas L. *lawyer*
Vaughn, Gordon E. *bishop*
Vogeley, Clyde Eicher, Jr. *engineering educator, artist, consultant*
von Schack, Wesley W. *energy holding company executive*
Voss, James Frederick *psychologist, educator*
Wagner, Lawrence M. *diversified financial services company executive*
Wald, Niel *medical educator*
Wallace, Richard Christopher, Jr. *school system administrator, educator*
Wallace, William Edward *engineering educator, scientist*
Wallman, George *hospital and food services administrator*
Walsh, Arthur Campbell *psychiatrist*
Walsh, Michael Francis *advertising executive*
Walton, James M. *investment company executive*
Walton, Jon David *lawyer*
Wang, Allan Zuwu *cell biologist*
Ward, Thomas Jerome *lawyer*
†Warner, Richard David *research foundation executive*
Weaver, Charles Henry *business consulting executive*
Webb, William Hess *lawyer*
Weber, Alexis Kurpiewski *nursing school executive*
Weber, Gerald Joseph *federal judge*
Wedemeyer, W. Anne Little *pediatric cardiologist, educator, lawyer*
Wehmeier, Helge H. *chemical, health care and imaging technologies company executive*
Weingartner, Rudolph Herbert *philosophy educator*
Weis, Joseph Francis, Jr. *federal judge*
Weis, Konrad Max *museum administrator, retired chemical company executive*
Welfer, Thomas, Jr. *utility company executive*
Wentley, Richard Taylor *lawyer*
Werner, Gerhard *pharmacologist, psychoanalyst, educator*
Westerberg, Arthur William *chemical engineering educator*
Whetzel, Joshua Clyde, Jr. *museum executive, conservationist*
White, Richard L. *chemicals company executive*
White, Robert Marshall *physicist, educator*
Wiegand, Bruce *lawyer*
Wilcock, James William *corporation executive, retired capital equipment manufacturing company executive*
Wilde, Patricia *artistic director*
Wilkins, David George *fine arts educator*
Will, James Fredrick *steel company executive*
Williams, Charles David *oil and steel company executive*
Williams, John Wesley *fine arts educator*
Williams, Louis Stanton *glass and chemical manufacturing executive*
Williams, Lynn Russell *labor union official*
Wilson, Charles Reginald *real estate executive*
Winter, Peter Michael *physician, anesthesiologist, educator*
Wishart, Alfred W., Jr. *foundation administrator*
Wolken, Jerome Jay *biophysicist, educator*
Woo, Savio Lau-Yuen *bioengineering educator*
Woodson, Roderick Kevin *professional football player*
Woodward, Thomas Aiken *lawyer*
Woodwell, Margot Bell *broadcasting executive*
Woolls, Esther Blanche *library science educator*
Wright, Thomas David *lawyer, entrepreneur*
Wuerl, Donald W. *bishop*
Wylie, Mary Evelyn *anesthesiologist, educator*
Wynblatt, Paul Pinhas *materials science educator, researcher*
†Yang, Wen-Ching *chemical engineer*
Yasinsky, John Bernard *nuclear scientist*
Yates, John Thomas, Jr. *chemistry educator, researcher*
Yerushalmi, Joseph *chemical engineer, researcher, educator*
Yorsz, Stanley *lawyer*
Young, Hugh David *physics educator, writer, organist*
Younger, Julius Stuart *microbiologist, educator*
Yu, Victor Lin-Kai *physician, educator*
Zanardelli, John Joseph *healthcare services executive*
Zandin, Kjell Bertil *management consulting executive*
Zappala, Stephen A. *state supreme court justice*
Ziegler, Donald Emil *federal judge*
Zimmerman, Scott Franklin *lawyer*
Zoffer, H. Jerome *educator, university dean*

Plymouth Meeting
Boyer, David Scott *manufacturing company executive*
Carriker, Roy C. *physicist*
Katz, Gerald *management consultant*
Kessler, Irving Isar *epidemiologist, educator, consultant*
Kostinsky, Harvey *clinical and electrical engineer*
Levinson, Gary Howard *real estate investor*
Litman, Raymond Stephen *financial services consultant*
Nobel, Joel J. *biomedical researcher*
Siegal, Jacob J. *management and financial consultant*
Yarnall, D. Robert, Jr. *entrepreneur, investor*

Pocopson
Mulligan, James Francis *retired business executive, lawyer*

Polk
Hall, Richard Clayton *psychologist, consultant, researcher, retired*

Port Royal
Wert, Jonathan Maxwell, II *management consultant*

Pottstown
†Haratunian, Michael *engineering company executive*
Hylton, Thomas James *editorial writer*
Lenfest, Harold Fitz Gerald *cable television executive, lawyer*
Ruth, Thomas Griswold *history educator*

Pottsville
Blossey, Maureen B. *mental health administrator*
Garloff, Samuel John *psychiatrist*
†Tuley, Sister Margaret *hospital administrator*

Punxsutawney
Dinsmore, Roberta Joan Maier *library director*
Lorenzo, Nicholas Francis, Jr. *lawyer*

Quakertown
de Limantour, Clarice Barr *food scientist*

Radnor
Arader, Walter Graham *financial consultant*
Baxter, John Michael *editor*
Burtis, Theodore Alfred *oil company executive*
†Draeger, Kenneth W. *high technology company executive*
Follman, John P. *engineering comprnay executive*
Harrison, Robert Drew *management consultant*
Marland, Alkis Joseph *leasing company executive, computer science educator, financial planner*
†Nojunas, Thomas Michael *hospital executive*
Paier, Adolf Arthur *computer software and services company executive*
†Peters, Douglas Scott *health care executive*
Russell, Daniel Francis *hospital administrator*
Stearns, Milton Sprague, Jr. *financial executive*
†Stetson, John Batterson, IV *construction executive*
Wheatley, William Arthur *architect, musician*
Yoh, Harold Lionel, Jr. *engineering, construction and management company executive*
Youman, Roger Jacob *editor, writer*

Reading
Alexander, Robert William *radiologist*
Beaver, Howard Oscar, Jr. *wrought specialty alloys manufacturing company executive*
Bell, Frances Louise *medical technologist*
Cardy, Robert Willard *speciality steel company executive*
Cate, Patrick O'Hair *mission executive*
Cottrell, G. Walton *manufacturing executive*
Crain, C. William *apparel company executive*
Dersh, Rhoda E. *management consultant, business executive*
Dietrich, Bruce Leinbach *planetarium and museum administrator, astronomer, educator*
Ehlerman, Paul Michael *industrial battery manufacturing company executive*
Erdman, Carl L. N. *retired banker*
Fiore, Nicholas Francis *special alloys and materials company executive*
Hafer, Frederick Douglass *utility executive*

Harner, Paul B. gray iron foundry executive
Hawkins, Arthur battery manufacturing executive
Hawkins, Arthur Michael automotive executive
Hildreth, Eugene A. physician, educator
Hollander, Herbert I. consulting engineer
Huyett, Daniel Henry, III federal judge
Itin, James Richard financial executive
Johnson, Gerard G. apparel company executive
Ketchum, Ezekiel Sargent banker
Kevelson, Roberta philosopher, educator
Knerr, Reinhard H. communications executive
Lakin, Edwin A. retail executive
Linton, Jack Arthur lawyer
Mattern, Donald Eugene association executive
McCullough, Samuel Alexander banker
Mengel, Philip R(ichard) investment banker
Pearson, Douglas N. battery manufacturing company executive
Pugh, Lawrence R. apparel executive
†Redner, Earl W. retail executive
†Redner, Richard food products executive
Roedel, Paul Robert steel company executive
Roesch, Clarence Henry banker
Rohrer, Samuel Edward state legislator
Rothermel, Daniel Krott lawyer, holding company executive
Rowe, Jay E., Jr. research and development director
Sauer, Elissa Swisher nursing educator
Shirk, Annadora Vesper English educator
Smith, Alexander Forbes, III engineering consulting firm executive
†Smith, John Wilson, III newspaper editor, columnist, statistician
Snyder, Clair Allison banker
Sparks, David Emerson bank holding company executive
Sullivan, Charles Bernard hospital administrator
Troutman, E. Mac federal judge
Welch, Joseph F. investment company executive
Welty, John Rider lawyer
Williams, Sandra Keller postal service executive

Ridley Park
Clark, John H., Jr. lawyer

Riegelsville
Banko, Ruth Caroline library director

Robesonia
Houck, Charleen McClain educator

Rochester
LaValle, Gerald J. state senator

Rohrerstown
Stauffer, Sarah Ann political worker

Rosemont
Nixon, Agnes Eckhardt television writer, producer

Ruffs Dale
Slebodnik, Tressa Ann elementary education educator

Rydal
Black, Thomas Donald retired religious organization administrator
Kirkland, Bryant Mays clergyman

Sagamore
Cornell, William Harvey clergyman

Saint Davids
Baird, John Absalom, Jr. college official
Bertsch, Frederick Charles, III business executive
Bovaird, Brendan Peter lawyer
Heebner, Albert Gilbert economist, banker, educator
Maahs, Kenneth Henry, Sr. religion educator

Saint Marys
Brunk, Samuel Frederick oncologist
Johnson, J. M. Hamlin manufacturing company executive
Shobert, Erle Irwin, II management consultant

Saltsburg
Pidgeon, John Anderson headmaster

Sayre
Moody, Robert Adams neurosurgeon
Thomas, John Melvin surgeon

Schuylkill Haven
Loder, Michael Wescott librarian

Scottdale
Cutrell, Benjamin Elwood publisher
Miller, Levi publishing administrator

Scranton
Campion, Carol-Mae Sack librarian
Cimini, Joseph Fedele law educator, lawyer, former magistrate
Conaboy, Richard Paul federal judge
†Costello, Michael Mark hospital administrator
De Celles, Charles Edouard theologian, educator
Eagen, Jeremiah W. physician
Fusaro, Joseph A. educator
Guerrise, Patrick P. manufacturing company executive
Haggerty, James Joseph lawyer
Horton, Joseph Julian, Jr. academic dean, educator
Howley, James McAndrew lawyer
Janoski, Henry Valentine banker, former investment counselor, realtor
Jordan, John W. school system administrator
Kosik, Edwin Michael federal judge
Lynett, George Vincent newspaper publisher
Lynett, William Ruddy publishing, broadcasting company executive
Maislin, Isidore hospital administrator
Myers, Morey Mayer lawyer
Narsavage, Georgia Roberts nursing educator, researcher
Nealon, William Joseph, Jr. federal judge
Nee, Sister Mary Coleman college president emeritus
Newman, Samuel trust company executive
O'Connor, James Joseph pathologist, educator
†Olden, Peter Carter healthcare administration educator
O'Malley, Carlon Martin judge
Panuska, Joseph Allan university president
Parente, William Joseph political science educator
Passon, Richard Henry university administrator
Preate, Ernest D., Sr. lawyer
Reap, Sister Mary Margaret college administrator
†Rogers, Edwin Earl newspaper editor
Saleski, Verna Mae nursing educator
Timlin, James Clifford bishop
Turock, Jane Parsick nutritionist
†West, Daniel Jones, Jr. hospital administrator, rehabilitator counselor

Selinsgrove
Deekle, Peter Van library director
Diers, Hank H. drama educator, playwright, director

Sellersville
Loux, Norman Landis psychiatrist
Raub, Donald Wilmer minister, author

Seneca
Spring, Paull E. bishop

Sewickley
Chaplin, James Crossan, IV securities firm executive
Jones, Fred Richard financial executive
McKibbin, John Meek, III aluminum company executive
Newell, Byron Bruce, Jr. clergyman, former naval officer
Roemer, William Frederick banker
Snyder, William Penn, III manufacturing company executive
†Wedeen, Marvin Meyer hospital executive

Sharon
Epstein, Louis Ralph retired wholesale grocery executive
Rosenblum, Harold Arthur grocery distribution executive
Sheen, Martin (Ramon Estevez) actor

Shippensburg
Ceddia, Anthony Francis university administrator
Luhrs, H. Ric toy manufacturing company executive
Stone, Susan Ridgaway marketing educator
Thompson, Elizabeth Jane small business owner

Shiremanstown
Nesbit, William Terry small business owner, consultant

Sinking Spring
Wilson, Terrence Raymond manufacturing executive

Skytop
Popham, Lewis Charles, III hotel corporation director, former university dean

Slippery Rock
Aebersold, Robert Neil university president

Solebury
Anthonisen, George Rioch sculptor, artist
Valentine, H. Jeffrey legal association executive

Souderton
Hoeflich, Charles Hitschler banker

South Canaan
Herman archbishop

Southampton
DaCosta, Edward Hoban plastics and electronics manufacturing company executive
McSparran, Robert B. food products executive
Omlor, John Joseph management consultant
†Pietrzak, Leonard Walter accountant
Zocholl, Stanley Ernest electronics executive

Southeastern
Husick, Lawrence Alan lawyer
Minter, Philip Clayton retired communications company executive

Spring City
Blanchard, Norman Harris retired pharmaceutical company executive
Mayerson, Hy lawyer

Spring Grove
Curtin, Philip De Armond history educator
Helberg, Shirley Adelaide Holden artist, educator
Norris, Thomas Clayton paper company executive
Wand, Richard Walton paper company executive

Spring House
Payn, Clyde Francis technology company executive, consultant

Springfield
Ruiz, Jose Rafael podiatric surgeon
Wilkinson, William Durfee museum director

Springtown
Hunt, John Wesley English language educator

Star Junction
Baldwin, Clarence Jones, Jr. electrical engineer, manufacturing company executive

State College
Arnold, Douglas Norman mathematics educator
Asbell, Bernard English language educator, author
Bergman, Ernest L. biologist
Coppersmith Fredman, Marian Ungar magazine publisher
DeVoss, James Thomas community foundation administrator, retired
Doms, Keith retired library director
Farr, Jo-Ann Hunter psychologist
Ferguson, John Henry retired political science educator
Foderaro, Anthony Harolde nuclear engineering educator
Forth, Stuart librarian
Garrett, Steven Lurie physicist
Gould, Peter Robin geographer, educator
Haas, John C. architect
Henderson, Robert Earl mechanical engineer, educator, consultant
Hettche, L. Raymond research director
Hoffa, Harlan Edward retired university dean, art educator
Johnstone, Henry Webb, Jr. philosophy educator
Kockelmans, Joseph J. philosopher, educator
Lamb, Robert Edward diplomat
Landy, Richard Allen former geologist, consultant
Lawrence, Ken columnist
Miller, E. Willard geographer
Morrow, David Austin, III veterinary medical educator
Olson, Donald Richard mechanical engineering educator
Phillips, Janet Colleen educational association executive, editor
Remick, Forrest Jerome, Jr. former university official
Robinett, Betty Wallace linguist
†Rose, Lance Haden hospital administrator
Rusinko, Frank, Jr. fuels and materials scientist
Scott, Charles Edward philosophy educator
Thompson, Fred Clayton engineering executive, consultant
Wysk, Richard A. engineering educator, researcher

Strafford
Horwitz, Orville cardiologist, educator

Strasburg
Lindsay, George Carroll former museum director

Stroudsburg
Gasink, Warren Alfred speech communication educator

Sunbury
Weis, Sigfried supermarket chain executive

Swarthmore
Bannister, Robert Corwin, Jr. history educator
Barr, Robert Alfred, Jr. college dean
Beeman, Richard Roy historian
Bilaniuk, Oleksa Myron physicist, educator
Blackburn, Thomas Harold English language professional, educator
Bloom, Alfred Howard college president
Carey, William Bacon pediatrician, educator
Cornelsen, Rufus clergyman
Cothren, Michael Watt art educator
Devin, (Philip) Lee dramaturg, theater educator
Durkan, Michael Joseph librarian
Flemister, Launcelot Johnson physiologist, educator
Frost, Jerry William religion and history educator, library administrator
Gilbert, Scott Frederick biologist, educator, author
Hammons, James Hutchinson chemistry educator, researcher
Heaps, Marvin Dale food services company executive
Hopkins, Raymond Frederick political science educator
Hungerford, Constance Cain art educator
Kaufman, Antoinette D. business services company executive
Keith, Jennie anthropology educator/administrator, writer
Kelemen, Charles F. computer science educator
Krendel, Ezra Simon systems and human factors engineering consultant
Lacey, Hugh Matthew philosophy educator
Marecek, Jeanne Ann psychologist, educator
Morgan, Kathryn Lawson historian, educator
North, Helen Florence classicist, educator
Ostwald, Martin classics educator emeritus
Pagliaro, Harold Emil English language educator
Pasternack, Robert Francis chemistry educator
Rose, Gilbert Paul classics educator
Saffran, Bernard economist, educator
Shaull, Richard theologian, educator
Swearer, Donald Keeney Asian religions educator, writer
Swing, Peter Gram music educator
Weinstein, Philip Meyer English educator, literary critic
Wright, Harrison Morris historian, educator

Swiftwater
Woods, Walter Earl biomedical manufacturing executive

Tamaqua
Urenovitch, Joseph Victor chemical company executive

Tannersville
Moore, James Alfred ski company executive, lawyer

Tarentum
†Leonard, Richard Alan newspaper editor

Telford
Luscinski, Steven Michael corporate executive

Tidioute
†Stone, Harvey H. civil engineer, executive

Titusville
Crowe, Virginia Mary retired librarian
Peaslee, Margaret Mae Hermanek zoology educator

Topton
Farr, Lona Mae non-profit executive

Trafford
Hampton, Edward John engineering executive

Trevose
McCaughan, John F. chemical company executive

Troy
Lane, Carol Ann secondary school educator

Tunkhannock
Jones, Edward White, II lawyer

Tyrone
†Lewis, Kathryn Huxtable pediatrician
†Stoner, Philip James hospital administrator

Uniontown
Eberly, Robert Edward oil and gas production company executive
Foster, James Caldwell academic dean, historian

Unionville
De Marino, Donald Nicholson international business executive, former federal agency administrator
Forney, Robert Clyde retired chemical industry executive
Irwin, Robert Hugh Crawford manufacturing company executive

University Park
Albinski, Henry Stephen academic research center director, writer
Allcock, Harry Rex chemistry educator
Amateau, Maurice Francis materials scientist, educator
Ameringer, Charles D. history educator
Anderson, John Mueller retired philosophy educator
Andrews, George Eyre mathematics educator
Antle, Charles Edward statistics educator
Aplan, Frank Fulton metallurgical engineering educator
Askov, Eunice May education educator
Aspaturian, Vernon Varaztat political science educator, consultant, author
†Badding, John Victor chemistry educator
Baisley, Robert William music educator
Barnes, Hubert Lloyd geochemistry educator
†Benkovic, Stephen James chemist
Bennett, Peter Dunne marketing educator
Bernheim, Robert Allan chemistry educator
Bieniawski, Zdzislaw Tadeusz design engineer, educator, consultant
Blackadar, Alfred Kimball meteorologist, educator
Bollag, Jean-Marc soil biochemistry educator, consultant
Bose, Nirmal Kumar electrical engineering, mathematics educator
Brault, Gerard Joseph French language educator
Brenchley, Jean Elnora microbiologist, researcher
Brown, John Lawrence, Jr. electrical engineering educator
Brownawell, Woodrow Dale mathematics educator
Buffington, Dennis Elvin agricultural engineering educator
Buskirk, Elsworth Robert physiologist, educator
Cahir, John Joseph meteorologist, educational administrator
Castleman, Albert Welford, Jr. physical chemist, educator
Cavanagh, Peter Robert health educator, researcher, academic facility executive
Chang, Parris Hsu-cheng government official, political science educator, writer
Cline, Nancy M. librarian
Cochran, Philip Lee business educator
Coleman, Michael Murray polymer science educator
Cosgrove, Daniel Joseph biology educator
Cowen, Barrett Stickney microbiologist
Crowder, Eleanor Louise M. nursing educator
Davids, Norman engineering science and mechanics educator, researcher
De Armas, Frederick Alfred foreign language educator
Dunson, William Albert biology educator
Dupuis, Victor Lionel curriculum and instruction educator emeritus
Dutton, John Altnow meteorologist, educator
Epp, Donald James economist, educator
Feller, Irwin think-tank executive, economics educator
Feng, Tse-yun computer engineer, educator
Filippelli, Ronald Lee college dean, labor studies and industrial relations educator
Fonash, Stephen Joseph engineering educator
Ford, Donald Herbert psychologist, educator
Fowler, H(oratio) Seymour retired science educator
Fox, Richard Henry soil science educator
Frank, Robert Worth, Jr. English language educator
Frankl, Daniel Richard educator, physicist
Friedman, Robert Sidney political science educator
Garmire, Gordon Paul astronomer, educator
German, Randall Michael materials science educator, consultant
Golany, Gideon Salomon urban designer
Goldschmidt, Arthur Eduard, Jr. historian, educator
Gouran, Dennis Stephen communications educator
Guerney, Bernard Guilbert, Jr. clinical psychologist, educator
Guthrie, Helen A. nutrition educator, consultant
Hagen, Daniel Russell physiologist
†Hager, Hellmut Wilhelm art history educator
Ham, Inyong industrial engineering educator
Hammond, J. D. insurance educator
Hardy, Henry Reginald, Jr. geophysicist, educator
Helfferich, Friedrich G. chemical engineer, educator
Herman, Roger M. physicist, educator
Herrmann, Carol university adminstrator
†Hogg, Richard physical chemistry educator
Holl, John William engineering educator
Hood, Lamartine Frain college dean
Hosler, Charles Luther, Jr. meteorologist, educator
Howell, Benjamin Franklin, Jr. geophysicist, educator
Jackman, Lloyd Miles chemistry educator
Jaffe, Austin Jay business administration educator
Jordan, Bryce corporate director, retired university president
Jurs, Peter Christian chemistry educator
Kabel, Robert Lynn chemical engineering educator
Kim, Ke Chung entomology and biodiversity educator, researcher
Klein, Philip Alexander economist
Knott, Kenneth engineering educator
Koopmann, Gary Hugo educational center administrator, mechanical engineering educator
Lakshminarayana, Budugur aerospace engineering educator
Lampe, Frederick Walter chemistry educator, consultant
Larson, Russell Edward university provost emeritus, consultant agriculture research and development
Lee, Robert Dorwin public affairs educator
Leslie, Donald Wilmot landscape architecture educator
Lewis, Peirce Fee geographer, educator
Lima, Robert Hispanic studies and comparative literature educator
Lindsay, Bruce George statistics educator
Lindstrom, Eugene Shipman biologist, academic administrator
Lusht, Kenneth Michael business administration educator
Macdonald, Digby Donald scientist, science administrator
Manbeck, Harvey B. agricultural engineer, wood engineer, educator
Martorana, Sebastian Vincent educational consultant

Mathews, John David electrical engineering educator, consultant
Mayers, Stanley Penrose, Jr. public health educator
†Maynard, Julian D. acoustician, physicist, educator
McCormick, Barnes Warnock aerospace engineering educator
McDonnell, Archie Joseph environmental engineer
McKeown, James Charles accounting educator, consultant
McWhirter, John Ruben chemical engineering educator
Mentzer, John Raymond electrical engineer, educator
Michels, Joseph William anthropology and archaeology educator
Morris, Philip John aerospace engineering educator
Nelsen, Hart Michael sociologist, educator
Nelson, Paul Edward science educator
Nisbet, John Stirling electrical engineering educator
Osborn, Elburt Franklin former geochemistry educator, research scientist
Pashek, Robert Donald economics educator emeritus
Paterno, Joseph Vincent college football coach
Pazur, John Howard biochemist, educator
Porterfield, Neil Harry landscape architect, planner
Ramani, Raja Venkat mining engineering educator
Rashid, Kamal A. biotechnology training program director, educator
Ray, William Jackson psychologist
Reed, Joseph Raymond civil engineering educator, academic administrator
Rigby, Paul Herbert management educator, college dean
Rose, Adam Zachary economist, educator
Roy, Rustum interdisciplinary materials researcher, educator
Ruud, Clayton Olaf engineering educator
Scanlon, Andrew structural engineering educator
Schaie, K(laus) Warner human development and psychology educator
Schmalstieg, William Riegel Slavic languages educator
Schrader, William Joseph accountant, educator
Spanier, Graham Basil university president, family sociologist
Starling, James Lyne university administrator
Stern, Robert Morris psychology educator, researcher
Thatcher, Sanford Gray publishing executive
Thomas, Joab Langston academic administrator, biology educator
Thompson, William, Jr. engineering educator
Thuering, George Lewis industrial engineering educator
Tittmann, Bernhard Rainer engineering science and mechanics educator
Traverse, Alfred palynology educator, clergyman
Tukey, Loren Davenport pomology educator, researcher
Van Dommelen, David B. artist, educator
Vannice, M. Albert chemical engineering educator, researcher
Walden, Daniel humanities and social sciences educator
Walker, Eric Arthur consulting engineer, institute executive
Wartik, Thomas chemistry educator, former college dean
Webb, Ralph Lee mechanical engineering educator
Weintraub, Stanley arts and humanities educator, author
Wheeler, C. Herbert architect, consultant, educator
White, William Blaine geochemist, educator
Whitko, Jean Phillips academic administrator
Williams, Edward Vinson music history educator
Willumson, Glenn Gardner curator, art educator
Winograd, Nicholas chemist
Witzig, Warren Frank nuclear engineer, educator
Woodbridge, Linda English language educator
Wyand, Martin Judd economics educator, retired military officer
Yoder, Edgar Paul education educator
†Zhang, Xumu chemist, educator

Upper Darby
Apfel, Gail principal
Gasparro, Frank sculptor
Hurley, Harry James, Jr. dermatologist

Upper Saint Clair
Dunkis, Patricia B. principal

Valley Forge
Atilgan, Timur Faik structural engineer
Basile, Neal Fahr environmental consulting firm executive
Besson, Michel Louis manufacturing company executive
†Brennan, John Joseph mutual fund company executive
Buckles, Michael A. religious organization executive
Carlson, Beverly Clark historical society administrator
Collemer, Craig A. religious organization administrator
Croney, J. Kenneth lawyer
Cuzzolina, Michael Joseph financial executive
Dachowski, Peter Richard manufacturing executive
Erb, Doretta Louise Barker polymer applications scientist
Erb, Robert Allan physical scientist
Gonzales, Hector M. church administrator
González, Héctor church official
Hergert, Herbert Lawrence chemist
Hilyard, James Emerson manufacturing company executive
Kim, Jean B. religious organization executive
†Mauch, Robert Carl gas industry executive
McDermott, Dona M. historical park administrator
McNamara, John F. health services company executive
McPhee, Richard S. church administrator
Moulton, Hugh Geoffrey lawyer, business executive
Neff, John Brown financial portfolio manager
Penfield, Carole H. (Kate Penfield) minister, church official
Posner, Ernest Gary lawyer
Rassbach, Herbert David marketing executive
Renquest, Richard A. religious organization executive
Schaefer, Adolph Oscar, Jr. advertising agency executive
Smith, G. Elaine religious organization executive
†Smith, George E. chemical company executive
Smith, Gordon E. religious organization executive
Subotnick, Morton composer, clarinetist
Sundquist, John A. religious organization executive
Sutton, James Andrew diversified utility company executive
Wade, Cheryl H. church official
Weiss, Daniel Edwin clergyman, educator
Wright-Riggins, Aidsand F. religious organization executive

Vandergrift
Bullard, Ray Elva, Jr. retired psychiatrist, hospital administrator
Quader, Patricia Ann elementary education educator

Verona
†Kirchner, Louis John industrial manufacturing company executive
Matthews, Jack psychologist, speech pathologist, educator
Potts, Gerald Neal manufacturing company executive

Villanova
Alter, Maria Pospischil language educator
Beck, Robert Edward computer scientist, educator
Bergquist, James Manning history educator
Bersoff, Donald Neil lawyer, psychologist
Bush, David Frederic psychologist, educator
Caputo, John David philosophy educator
Carrasco, Gilbert Paul law educator
Cordes, Eugene Harold biochemist
Dobbin, Edmund J. university administrator
Dorian, Harry Aram financial consultant, former bank executive
Edwards, John Ralph chemist, educator
Haynor, Patricia Manzi nurse, hospital administrator
Heitzmann, Wm. Ray education educator
Helmetag, Charles Hugh foreign language educator
Hunt, John Mortimer, Jr. classical studies educator
Johannes, John Roland political science educator, college dean
Jones, Brian Joseph sociology educator
Kelley, Donald Brooks historian, educator
Kraftson, Raymond H. business executive
Lambert, William G. journalist, consultant
Langran, Robert Williams political scientist
Lesch, Ann Mosely political scientist, educator
Lewis, Wayne H. investment company executive
Malik, Hafeez political scientist, educator
McDiarmid, Lucy English educator, author
McFalls, Joseph A., Jr. sociology educator
McLaughlin, Philip VanDoren, Jr. mechanical engineering educator, researcher, consultant
Morgan, Lewis B. counseling education educator
Mulroney, Michael lawyer, law educator, graduate program director
Nolan, Patrick Joseph screenwriter, playwright, educator
Nydick, Robert Lincoln, Jr. university educator
†Palmer, Donald Curtis interdenominational missionary society executive
Perritt, Henry Hardy, Jr. law educator
Phares, Alain Joseph physicist, educator
Radan, George Tivadar art history and archaeology educator
Rudhart, Alexander H. modern European history educator
Schrems, John Joseph (Jack Schrems) political science educator
Steg, Leo research and development executive
Sullivan, Richard Cyril retired transportation executive
Thomas, Deborah Allen English educator
Tomlinson, J. Richard engineering services company executive
White, Robert Edward chemical engineering educator, consultant

Wallingford
Clauss, Alfred architect
Herpel, George Lloyd marketing educator
Parker, Jennifer Ware chemical engineer, researcher
Rice, Robert H. principal

Warminster
Tatnall, George Jacob aeronautical engineer
Whinnery, James Elliott aerospace medical scientist, flight surgeon

Warren
McComas, Murray Knabb direct mail company executive
Waterston, William King minister, educator, academic administrator

Warrendale
Hartwig, Thomas Leo civil engineer
Krysinski, Linda Ann marketing systems analyst
†Olthof, Meint engineering company executive consultant
Rumbaugh, Max Elden, Jr. professional society administrator
†Scott, Alexander Robinson engineering association executive

Warrington
Shaw, Milton Herbert conglomerate executive

Washington
Allison, Jonathan lawyer
Burnett, Howard Jerome college president
Erdner, Jon W. small business owner, securities trader
Greenlee, Gaylord W. health facility administrator
Hays, Lewis W. amateur baseball executive, writer
Kastelic, Robert Frank aerospace company executive
Piatt, Jack Boyd manufacturing executive
Richman, Stephen I. lawyer

Waverly
Matthews, Richard J. pharmaceutical research company executive

Wayne
Andes, Charles Lovett museum executive, technology association executive
Atkins, Joseph P. otorhinolaryngologist
Baldwin, Frank Bruce, III lawyer
†Bartholdson, John Robert industrial company executive
Bricklin, Patricia Ellen psychologist, educator
Brodsky, Julian A. broadcasting services, telecommunications company executive
Carroll, Robert W. retired business executive
Caruso, Richard Ernest financial company executive
Clelland, Richard Cook statistics educator, university administrator
Coane, James Edwin, III information technology executive
Curry, Thomas James manufacturers representative
DeCarlo, A. J. lumber company executive
de Rivas, Carmela Foderaro psychiatrist, hospital administrator
†Essner, Robert Alan pharmaceutical executive
Etris, Samuel Franklin association executive
Frye, Roland Mushat literary historian, theologian
Garrison, Guy Grady librarian, educator
Gozon, Richard C. paper distribution executive
Green, Norman Marston, Jr. minister
Griffith, Edward, II lawyer
Guernsey, Louis Harold retired oral and maxillofacial surgeon, educator
Hedges, Donald Walton lawyer
Henne, James Earl publisher
Hess, Eugene Lyle biologist, retired association executive
Hill, Virgil Lusk, Jr. naval officer, academic administrator
Kunkel, Russell J. bank holding company executive
Lefevre, Thomas Vernon retired utility company executive, lawyer
Lewis, James Earl investment banker
Martino, Rocco Leonard computer systems executive
Mundt, Ray B. diversified industry executive
Pearson, Willard former army officer
Peterson, Raymond A. paper company executive
Roberts, Ralph Joel cable television, telephone communications and background music company executive
Robinowitz, Joe Reece publishing executive
Russell, Kent hospital administrator
Sims, Robert John financial planner
Suer, Marvin David architect
Townsend, Philip W., Jr. library director
West, Alfred Paul, Jr. financial services executive
Wolcott, Robert Wilson, Jr. consulting company executive
Woodbury, Alan Tenney lawyer
Yoskin, Jon William, II insurance company executive

Waynesboro
Benchoff, James Martin manufacturing company executive
Holzman, Howard Eugene health services executive
Kirk, Daniel Lee physician, consultant

Wellsboro
Baker, Matthew Edward state legislator

Wernersville
Himmelberger, Richard Charles vocational school educator
Mackey, Sheldon Elias minister

West Chester
Adler, Madeleine Wing academic administrator
Bogle, Hugh Andrew chemical company executive
Diller, Barry entertainment company executive
Dwyer, Francis Gerard chemical engineer, researcher
Flood, Dorothy Garnett neuroscientist
†Garber, Charles Allen research company executive, consultant
†Gougher, Ronald Lee language educator and administrator
Gould, Irving computer company executive
Green, Andrew Wilson economist, lawyer, educator
Hajcak, Frank psychologist, cartoonist, writer, photographer, consultant
Harrington, Anne Wilson medical librarian
Hickman, Janet Susan college administrator, educator
Hipple, Walter John English language educator
Jamison, Philip artist
Judson, Franklyn Sylvanus lawyer, consultant
Kim, James Joo-Jin electronics company executive
Mahoney, William Francis editor
McKeldin, William Evans management consultant
Mecca, Joseph Nicholas logistics and manufacturing company executive
†Pepper, H. L. Perry hospital administrator
Pollock, Roy Van Horn pharmaceutical company animal health researcher
Rubin, Henri electronics executive
Schindler, Peter David child and adolescent psychiatrist
Swope, Charles Evans bank executive, lawyer
Thompson, A(nsel) Frederick, Jr. environmental engineering and consulting company executive
Tomlinson, Charles Wesley, Jr. advertising executive
Weston, Roy Francis environmental consultant

West Conshohocken
Capizzi, Robert Lawrence physician
Miller, Paul Fetterolf, Jr. investment company executive
Richard, Scott F. portfolio manager
Schumacher, Elizabeth Swisher garden ornaments shop owner

West Mifflin
Clayton, John Charles scientist, researcher

West Point
Abrams, William Bernard pharmaceutical company executive, physician
Chen, I-Wu pharmaceutical researcher
Grossman, William medical researcher, educator
Hilleman, Maurice Ralph virus research scientist
Sherwood, Louis Maier physician, scientist, pharmaceutical company executive

Westtown
Backe, John David communications corporation executive

Wexford
Hindash, Abbas Asad quality assurance and strategic analysis professional

Whitehall
Cunconan-Lahr, Robin Lynn lawyer

Wilkes Barre
Bevevino, Frank finance company executive
Hayes, Wilbur Frank biology educator
Hobbs, William Barton Rogers company executive
Johnson, Micah William television newscaster, director
Kolanowski, Ann Marie nursing educator, geriatrics nurse
Lackenmier, James Richard college president, priest
Mainwaring, William Robert bank executive
Mech, Terrence Francis library director
Musto, Joseph John lawyer
Ogren, Robert Edward biologist, educator
Polishan, Paul Frank clothing company executive
Popp, Penelope Jean health facility administrator
Rosenn, Max federal judge
Ru Dusky, Basil Michael cardiologist, consultant
Thomas, Reginald Harry, Sr. minister

Williamsport
Bryant, Martha J. accountant
Davis, William D(oyle) banker
Douthat, James Evans college administrator
Ertel, Allen Edward lawyer, former congressman
Facey, Karlyle Frank financial executive, consultant
Largen, Joseph retailer, furniture manufacturer, book wholesaler
Lattimer, Gary Lee physician
McClure, James Focht, Jr. federal judge
Muir, Malcolm federal judge
Rafferty, Michael Robert editor, columnist
Wygant, James Peter food company executive

Willow Grove
Asplundh, Christopher B. tree service company executive
Asplundh, Robert H. tree service company executive
Duff, Donald James religious organization administrator
Kulicke, C(harles) Scott business executive
Rieders, Fredric forensic toxicologist
Spikes, John Jefferson, Sr. forensic toxicologist, pharmacologist
†VanLuvanee, Donald Robert electronics executive

Willow Street
Stright, I. Leonard educational consultant

Windber
Furigay, Rodolfo Lazo surgeon

Worcester
McAdam, Will electronics consultant
Myers, Allan Ross construction executive

Wyncote
Baldridge, Robert Crary retired biochemistry educator
Bersh, Philip Joseph psychologist, educator
Burton, DeWitt A. bishop
Sasso, Sandy rabbi

Wyndmoor
Wint, Dennis Michael museum director

Wynnewood
Boyer, Vincent Saull energy consultant
Bozzelli, Andrew Joseph, Jr. valve company executive
Campbell, Alan Keith business educator
Connor, James Edward, Jr. retired chemical company executive
Doherty, Henry Joseph anesthesiologist, medical hypnotist
Flanagan, Joseph Charles ophthalmologist
Freeman, Morton S. former bar association executive, retired lawyer
Harkins, Herbert Perrin otolaryngologist, educator
Hodges, John Hendricks physician, educator
Kelly, Paul E., Jr. metal products executive
Kelly, Paul Edward, Sr. metals company executive
Khouri, Fred John political science educator
Kruger, Arthur Newman speech communication educator, author
La Blanc, Charles Wesley, Jr. financial consultant
Maxwell, John Raymond artist
Meyers, Mary Ann writer, consultant
Peskin, Matt Alan professional society administrator
Phillips, Almarin economics educator, consultant
†Sider, Ronald J. theology educator, author
Singer, Samuel L(oewenberg) journalist
Weinhouse, Sidney biochemist, educator

Wyomissing
Boyer, Robert Allen physics educator
Cellucci, Peter T. principal
Garr, Carl Robert manufacturing company executive
Moll, Lloyd Henry banker
Sidhu, Jay S. banking executive
Smith, Raymond Leigh plastic surgeon

Yardley
Crane, Barbara Joyce author, editor, publishing consulting executive
Desai, Cawas Jal distribution company executive
Elliott, Frank Nelson retired college president
Kressler, James Phillip investment and operations company executive
Newsom, Carolyn Cardall management consultant
Somma, Beverly Kathleen medical and marriage educator
Terry, John Joseph transportation investor
Zulker, Charles Bates broadcasting company executive

York
Bartels, Bruce Michael health care executive
†Borgelt, Burton C. dental and optical supply manufacturing company executive
Chronister, Virginia Ann school nurse, educator
Conway, Nancy Ann publisher, editor
Dresher, James T. manufacturing executive
Forchheimer, Otto Louis retired chemical company executive
Garner, Edward Markley, II manufacturing executive
Hamilton, Shirley Ann nursing administrator
Hetzel, Dennis Richard communications executive
†Horn, Russell Eugene engineering executive, consultant
Horn, Russell Eugene, Jr. printing executive
Jamison, Steven R. construction company executive
Keiser, Paul Harold hospital administrator
Klingaman, Robert LeRoy golf professional
Pokelwaldt, Robert N. manufacturing company executive
Rosen, Raymond health facility executive
Thornton, George Whiteley investment company executive
Waldner, George Wittman university administrator
Welber, David Alan accountant

Youngstown
Palmer, Arnold Daniel professional golfer

Zionsville
Fleming, Richard *chemical company executive*

RHODE ISLAND

Barrington
Carpenter, Charles Colcock Jones *physician, educator*
Graser, Bernice Erckert *elementary school principal*
Horton, John Alden *advertising agency executive*
O'Toole, John Dudley *retired utility executive, consultant*
Paolino, Ronald Mario *clinical psychologist, consultant, psychopharmacologist, pharmacist*

Block Island
Coxe, Weld *management consultant*
Kingsbury, Read Austin *retired journalist*

Bristol
†Esty, David Cameron *marketing and communications executive*
Wilcox, Harry Wilbur, Jr. *retired corporate executive*

Charlestown
Ungaro, Joseph Michael *newspaper publishing executive, consultant*

Coventry
Spear, Raymond E. *school system administrator*

Cranston
Crooks, W. Spencer *artist, educator*
Ferguson, Christine C. *lawyer, state agency administrator*
Gill, Carole O'Brien *family therapist*
McAulay, Dianne Lucy *gifted education educator*
Simonian, John S. *lawyer*
Thielsch, Helmut John *engineering company executive*

Cumberland
Hogan, Kenneth William *gas utility executive*

East Greenwich
Dence, Edward William, Jr. *lawyer, banker*
Deutsch, Stephen R. *real estate development executive, state senator*
Flynn, Richard James *lawyer*
Kruse, James Joseph *merchant banker*
Weiss, Alan *management consultant, author*
†Wiley, Barry Holland *marketing executive*

East Providence
DeGoes, John V. *school system administrator*
Hay, Robert J. *plastics manufacturing executive*
Mulvey, Mary C. *adult education administrator, gerontologist*

Greenville
Calo, Joseph Manuel *chemical engineering educator*

Greenwich
Valenti, Leo Frank *electronics company executive*

Harrisville
Jubinska-Christiansen, Patricia Ann *ballet instructor, choreographer*

Jamestown
Logan, Nancy Allen *library media specialist*
Potter, Clarkson Nott *publishing consultant*
Todd, Thomas Abbott *architect, urban designer*
†Wolff, Geoffrey Ansell *novelist, critic, educator*

Johnston
D'Ambra, Diane M. *nursing educator*
Martelli, Jennifer A. *social welfare administrator*
Patin, Robert White *insurance company executive*
Subramaniam, Shivan Sivaswamy *insurance company executive*

Kingston
Alexander, Lewis McElwain *geographer, educator*
Biller, Henry Burt *psychologist, educator*
Carothers, Robert Lee *academic administrator*
Cruickshank, Alexander Middleton *chemistry educator*
Driver, Rodney David *mathematics educator, former state legislator*
Gaulin, Lynn *social work educator*
Gelles, Richard James *sociology and psychology educator*
Gitlitz, David Martin *Hispanic studies educator*
Goos, Roger Delmon *mycologist*
Harlin, Marilyn Miler *marine botany educator, researcher, consultant*
Hedlund, Ronald David *academic administrator, researcher, educator*
Horn, Francis Henry *former educational administrator*
Hufnagel, Linda Ann *biology educator, researcher*
Kennard, Mary Elizabeth *lawyer*
Kim, Yong Choon *philosopher, theologian, educator*
Leete, William White *artist*
MacLaine, Allan Hugh *English language educator*
†Miller, Robert H. *soil scientist, dean*
Nixon, Scott West *oceanography science educator*
Palm, William John *mechanical engineering educator*
Pereira, Celina Antonieta *physician*
Polk, Charles *electrical engineer, educator, biophysicist*
Rohm, Robert Hermann *sculptor, educator*
Roxin, Emilio Oscar *mathematics educator*
Schmidt, Charles T., Jr. *labor and industrial relations educator*
Schwegler, Robert Andrew *English language educator*
Tufts, Donald Winston *electrical engineering educator*
Verma, Ghasi Ram *mathematics educator*
Youngken, Heber Wilkinson, Jr. *former university administrator, pharmacy educator*
Zucker, Norman Livingston *political scientist, educator, author*

Lincoln
Barr, John Douglas, II *entrepreneur, state legislator*
Brites, José Baptista *secondary education educator, writer*
Burgdoerfer, Jerry J. *marketing and distribution executive*
Carter, Wilfred Wilson *financial executive, controller*
Gulvin, David Horner *electric company executive*

Little Compton
Bullerjahn, Eduard Henri *architect*
MacKowski, John Joseph *retired insurance company executive*

Manville
Eno, Paul Frederick *editor*

Middletown
Whitman, Ruth *poet, educator, translator*

Narragansett
Leinen, Margaret Sandra *oceanographic researcher*
Pilson, Michael Edward Quinton *oceanography educator*
Pouliot, Assunta Gallucci *business school owner and director*
Sherman, Kenneth *oceanographer*
Sigurdsson, Haraldur *oceanography educator, researcher*

Newport
Baker, Winthrop Patterson, Jr. *broadcasting executive*
Brennan, Joseph Gerard *philosophy educator*
Brown, Jane G. *sports association executive*
Burgin, William Lyle *architect*
Cohen, Arthur Abram *lawyer*
Gleiman, Lubomir *philosophy educator*
Graziano, Catherine Elizabeth *nursing educator*
Hamblet, Charles Albert *educational administrator, educator*
Hayward, John Tucker *management consultant*
Holloway, Jerome Knight *publisher, former military strategy educator, retired foreign service officer*
Levie, Howard S(idney) *lawyer, educator, author*
McGann, Barbara Elizabeth *military officer*
†Schnare, Robert Edey, Jr. *library director*
Strasser, Joseph C. *career military officer, academic administrator*

North Kingstown
Kondon, E. Jane *principal*
Paolino, Richard Francis *manufacturing company executive*
Sharpe, Henry Dexter, Jr. *manufacturing company executive*

North Scituate
Stubbs, Donald Clark *secondary education educator*

Pawtucket
Carleton, Richard Allyn *cardiologist*
Davison, Charles Hamilton *financial executive*
Hassenfeld, Alan Geoffrey *toy company executive*
Heyman, Lawrence Murray *printmaker, painter*
Neff, Edward August *manufacturing company executive*
O'Neill, John T. *toy company executive*
Robbins, Donald Michael *lawyer*
Schwartz, Stephen Allan *toy company executive*
Shank, Stephen George *lawyer, toy manufacturing executive*
Tracy, Allen Wayne *manufacturing company executive*
Verrecchia, Alfred J. *toy company executive*

Portsmouth
Baker, Walter Louis *engineering company executive*
Becken, Bradford Albert *engineering executive*
Pearson, Oscar Harris *plant breeder, geneticist*

Providence
Ackerman, Felicia *philosophy educator, writer*
Adams, Thomas Randolph *bibliographer, librarian, historian*
Algiere, Dennis L. *state senator*
†Almond, Lincoln C. *governor*
Amaral, Joseph Ferreira *surgeon*
Ames, Robert San *retired manufacturing company executive*
Anderson, James Alfred *psychology educator*
Anton, Thomas Julius *political science and public policy educator, consultant*
Arant, Patricia *Slavic languages and literature educator*
Arcaro, Harold Conrad, Jr. *lawyer, educator*
Archambault, Reginald Donat *education educator*
Aronson, Stanley Maynard *physician, educator*
Avery, Donald Hills *metallurgist, educator, ethnographer*
Banchoff, Thomas Francis *mathematics educator*
Barnhill, James Orris *theater educator*
†Battaglia, Francis H. *broadcast executive*
Bensmaia, Reda *educator, researcher*
Berghahn, Volker Rolf *history educator*
Beyer, Robert Thomas *physicist, educator*
Blasing, Mutlu Konuk *English language educator*
Blough, Donald S. *psychology educator*
Blumstein, Sheila Ellen *linguistics educator*
Boegehold, Alan Lindley *classics educator*
†Boekelheide, Kim *pathologist*
Borod, Richard Melvin *lawyer*
Borts, George Herbert *economist, educator*
Bossy, Michel-Andre R. *comparative literature educator*
Boyle, Francis Joseph *federal judge*
Bray, Philip James *physicist*
Bready, Richard Lawrence *manufacturing company executive*
Briant, Clyde Leonard *metallurgist, researcher*
Bundy, Annalee Marshall *library director*
Caldwell-Wood, Naomi Rachel *library media specialist*
Campbell, Bernard Patrick *banker*
Campbell, Edwin Denton *educational administrator*
Caprio, Frank T. *lawyer, state legislator*
Carlotti, Stephen Jon *lawyer*
Carpenter, Gene Blakely *crystallography and chemistry educator*
Carreño, Antonio *humanities educator*
Casey, Brother Daniel F. *school system administrator*
Cassill, Ronald Verlin *author*
Charniak, Eugene *computer scientist, educator*
Choquette, Paul Joseph, Jr. *construction company executive*
Church, Russell Miller *psychology educator*
†Ciampa, Gail Ann *journalist*
Cianci, Vincent Albert, Jr. *lawyer, mayor*
Coffey, Sean Owen *former state senator, lawyer*
Cohen, Linda Marks *lawyer, securities negotiator*
†Coleman, Annette Wilbois *biology educator*
Cook, Albert Spaulding *comparative literature and classics educator, writer*
Cooper, Gordon Mayo *retired manufacturing company executive*
Cooper, Leon N. *physicist, educator*
Correia, John Furia *senator, plumbing supply company executive*
Courage, Thomas Roberts *lawyer*
Crooks, Bruce Philip *banker*
Cunningham, John Fabian *college president, philosophy educator*
Curran, Joseph Patrick *lawyer*
Cutts, David *physics educator*
Dafermos, Constantine Michael *applied mathematics educator*
Dahlberg, Albert Edward *biochemistry educator*
Damon, William Van Buren *developmental psychologist, educator*
Davis, Philip J. *mathematician*
Davis, Robert Paul *physician, educator*
Dickinson, Brian Ward *columnist*
Diebold, Gerald Joseph *education educator*
Dimeo, Thomas P. *construction company executive, real estate developer*
Doll, Jimmie Dave *chemistry educator*
Donnelly, Kevin William *lawyer*
Donovan, Bruce Elliot *classics educator, university dean*
Dowben, Robert Morris *physician, scientist*
Dowling, Sarah T. *lawyer, state official*
Downing, Brian Thomas *business executive*
Dujardin, Richard Charles *journalist*
Edelstein, Jerome Melvin *bibliographer*
†Egan, Patricia *theater manager*
Elbaum, Charles *physicist, educator, researcher*
Enteman, Willard Finley *philosophy educator*
Erikson, George Emil (Erik Erikson) *anatomist, archivist, historian, educator, information specialist*
Estrup, Peder Jan *physics and chemistry educator*
Farmer, Malcolm, III *lawyer*
Farmer, Susan Lawson *broadcasting executive, former secretary of state*
Farrell, Margaret Dawson *lawyer*
Feinstein, Alan Shawn *writer, financial adviser*
Feinstein, Pratarnporn *child psychiatrist*
Feldman, Walter Sidney *artist*
Field, Noel Macdonald, Jr. *lawyer*
Fiering, Norman (Sanford) *historian, library administrator*
Fitzpatrick, William Peter *computer programmer/analyst, state legislator*
Fleming, Wendell Helms *mathematician, educator*
Flynn, John William *financial services executive*
Fogarty, Charles Joseph *state senator*
Fornara, Charles William *historian, classicist, educator*
Forsyth, Donald William *geophysics educator*
Freiberger, Walter Frederick *mathematics educator, actuarial science consultant, educator*
Frerichs, Ernest Sunley *religious studies educator*
Freund, Lambert Ben *engineering educator, researcher, consultant*
Galletti, Pierre Marie *medical science educator, artificial organ scientist*
Gardner, Thomas Earle *investment banker, managment/financial consultant*
Garrison, Mark Joseph *political science educator, former diplomat*
Gasbarro, Pasco, Jr. *lawyer*
Gelineau, Louis Edward *bishop*
Gerbi, Susan Alexandra *biology educator*
Gerritsen, Hendrik Jurjen *physics educator, researcher*
Gibbs, June Nesbitt *state senator*
Gilbane, Jean Ann (Mrs. Thomas F. Gilbane) *construction company executive*
Gilbane, Thomas F., Jr. *building company executive*
Gilbane, William James *building company executive*
Gleason, Abbott *history educator*
Glicksman, Arvin S(igmund) *radiologist, physician*
Glicksman, Maurice *engineering educator, former dean and provost*
Goddard, Robert Hale Ives *investment executive*
Goldscheider, Calvin *Jewish studies educator, sociologist*
Goldscheider, Frances K. *sociologist, educator*
Goldstein, Sidney *sociology educator, demographer*
Goodman, Elliot Raymond *political scientist, educator*
Gorham, Bradford *lawyer*
Gorton, Arlene Elizabeth *physical education educator*
Goss, Richard Johnson *biologist, educator*
Graboys, George *retired bank executive*
Greene, Edward Forbes *chemistry educator*
Greer, David S. *university dean, physician, educator*
Gregorian, Vartan *academic administrator*
Grenander, Ulf *mathematics educator*
Grimm, William Richard *lawyer*
Grossman, Herschel I. *economics educator*
Gurland, Joseph *engineering educator*
Hagopian, Jacob *federal judge*
Hamblett, Stephen *newspaper publishing executive*
Hamolsky, Milton William *physician*
Hardymon, James Franklin *diversified products company executive*
Harris, Richard John *diversified holding company executive*
Hartmann, George Herman *retired manufacturing company executive*
Hawkins, Brian L. *academic administrator, educator*
Hay, Susan Stahr Heller *museum curator*
Hayes, John Edward *broadcasting executive*
Hazeltine, Barrett *electrical engineer, educator*
Heath, Dwight Braley *anthropologist, educator*
Henseler, Suzanne Marie *legislator, social studies educator, majority whip*
Higgins, Robert Joseph *banking executive*
Hitchen, Harold, Jr. *insurance company executive, treasurer, accountant*
Hitt, Mary Frances Lyster *environmentalist, deacon*
Hogan, Dennis Patrick *university educator*
Holden, Raymond Henry *clinical psychologist*
Honig, Edwin *comparative literature educator, poet*
Hopkins, Jacques Vaughn *lawyer*
Hopmann, Philip Terrence *political science educator*
Houghton, Anthony *physics educator, research scientist*
Howes, Lorraine de Wet *fashion designer, educator*
Hunt, George Nelson *bishop*
†Jaco, William H. *mathematical association executive*
Johnson, Maxine Frahm *bank executive*
Johnson, Vahe Duncan *lawyer*
Jones, Ferdinand Taylor, Jr. *psychologist, educator*
Jordy, William Henry *art history educator*
Joukowsky, Artemis A. W. *private investor*
†Juchatz, Wayne Warren *lawyer*
Kane, Agnes Brezak *pathologist, educator*
Kang, Kyungsik *physics educator*
Kean, John Vaughan *lawyer*
Kersh, DeWitte Talmadge, Jr. *lawyer*
Kilguss, George Edward, Jr. *bank executive*
Kim, Jaegwon *philosophy educator*
Klyberg, Albert Thomas *historical society administrator*
Knopf, Paul Mark *immunoparasitologist, neuroimmunologist*
Koelb, Clayton Talmadge *insurance company executive*
†Komiske, Bruce King *hospital administrator*
Konstan, David *educator, researcher*
Kreykes, William *health care management executive*
Kushner, Harold Joseph *mathematics educator*
Lagueux, Ronald Rene *federal judge*
Lancaster, Anthony *economics educator, consultant*
Landow, George Paul *English literature and art educator, writer*
Lanou, Robert Eugene, Jr. *physicist, educator*
Leis, Philip Edward *anthropologist*
Lekas, Mary Despina *otolaryngologist*
Leonard, Barbara M *former secretary of state, federal agency administrator, state agency administrator*
Lesko, Leonard Henry *Egyptologist, educator*
Levin, Frank S. *physicist, educator*
Lewis, David Carleton *medical educator, university center director*
Licht, Richard A. *lawyer*
Lipsey, Howard Irwin *lawyer*
Little, Dennis Gage *diversified business executive*
Loferski, Joseph John *electrical engineering educator*
Long, Beverly Glenn *lawyer*
Lyle, John William, Jr. *state senator, lawyer, social studies educator*
†Lynden, Frederick Charles *librarian*
Manchester, Robert D. *venture capitalist*
Mandell, Mark Steven *lawyer*
Mandle, Earl Roger *university president, former museum administrator*
Maris, Humphrey John *physicist, educator*
†Marsh, Donald Jay *college dean, medical educator*
Marsh, Robert Mortimer *sociologist, educator*
Marshall, Jean McElroy *physiologist*
Mathieu, Helen M. *state legislator*
†Mayer, Nancy J *state official*
McCann, Gail Elizabeth *lawyer*
McCartney, James Robert *psychiatrist*
Mc Donald, Charles J. *physician, educator*
McIlvane, Edward James *artist, instructor, designer*
Mc Intosh, Douglas J. *insurance company executive*
McMahon, Eleanor Marie *education educator*
McWalters, Peter *state agency administrator*
Mehlman, Edwin Stephen *endodontist*
Méras, Phyllis Leslie *journalist*
Metrey, George David *social work educator, academic administrator*
Milhaven, John Giles *religious studies educator*
Miller, Kenneth Raymond *biologist, educator*
Moffitt, Robert Allen *economics educator*
Molho, Anthony *history educator*
Monteiro, George *English educator, writer*
Monteiro, Lois Ann *medical science educator*
Mueller, Frederick *principal*
Mulvee, Robert Edward *bishop*
Murray, Florence Kerins *state supreme court justice*
Murray, Terrence *banker*
Nazarian, John *academic administrator, mathematics educator*
Needleman, Alan *mechanical engineering educator*
Nelson, Ron *composer, conductor, educator*
Neu, Charles Eric *historian, educator*
Newcomb, Martha Freeman *lawyer*
Ockerse, Thomas *graphic design educator*
O'Donnell, Charles Patrick *retired newspaper executive, consultant*
Oh, William *physician*
Olsen, Hans Peter *lawyer*
Parks, Robert Emmett, Jr. *medical science educator*
Patinkin, Mark Alan *newspaper columnist*
Pearce, George Hamilton *archbishop*
Pendergast, John Joseph, III *lawyer*
Perkins, Whitney Trow *political science educator emeritus*
Petrocelli, Americo William *higher education commissioner*
Pierce, Richard Hilton *lawyer*
Pine, Jeffrey Barry *state attorney general*
Pingree, David Edwin *ancient languages educator*
Poole, William *economics educator, consultant*
Preparata, Franco Paolo *computer science and engineering educator*
Putnam, Michael Courtney Jenkins *classics educator*
Putterman, Louis G. *economics educator*
Reed, Walter Gurnee Dyer *lawyer*
Reeder, John P., Jr. *religious studies educator*
Ribbans, Geoffrey Wilfrid *Spanish educator*
Richardson, Peter Damian *mechanical engineering educator*
Richman, Marc Herbert *forensic engineer, educator*
Rieger, Philip Henri *chemistry educator, researcher*
Risen, William Maurice, Jr. *chemistry educator*
Robinson, William Philip, III *lawyer*
Rohr, Donald Gerard *history educator*
†Rosenberg, Alan Gene *newspaper editor*
Rosenberg, Bruce Alan *English language educator, author*
Rothman, Frank George *biology educator, biochemical genetics researcher*
Roy, Norman E. *construction company executive*
Rueschemeyer, Dietrich *sociology educator*
Ryder, Harl Edgar *economist, educator*
Saint-Amand, Pierre Nemours *humanities educator*
St. Florian, Friedrich Gartler *architect, educator, university dean*
Salesses, John Joseph *university administrator*
Salter, Lester Herbert *lawyer*
Sanderson, Edward French *state official*
Sapinsley, Lila Manfield *state official*
Satterthwaite, Franklin Bache, Jr. *management educator, consultant*
†Savage, Anne *zoologist, researcher*
Savage, John Edmund *computer science educator, researcher*
Schevill, James Erwin *poet, playwright*
Schmitt, Johanna Marie *plant population biologist, educator*
Schmitt, Richard *philosopher, educator*
Schobel, George *insurance company executive*
Scholes, Robert Edward *English language educator*
Schottland, Edward Morrow *hospital adminstrator*
Schulz, Juergen *art history educator*

Selya, Bruce Marshall federal judge
Shaw, Ronald Ahrend physician, educator
Shepp, Bryan Eugene psychologist, educator
Sherman, Deming Eliot lawyer
Shu, Chi-Wang mathematics educator, researcher
Silver, Paul Allen lawyer
Silverman, Joseph Hillel mathematics educator
Simons, Thomas W., Jr. ambassador
†Simpson, Dale Arthur healthcare executive
Sinclair, Joseph Samuels broadcasting company executive, retail merchant
Siqueland, Einar psychology educator
Sizer, Theodore R. education educator
Skidmore, Thomas Elliott history educator
Smoke, Richard political scientist, political psychologist
Sosa, Ernest philosopher, educator
Soutter, Thomas D. retired lawyer
Speare, Alden, Jr. sociology educator
Spilka, Mark English educator
Staples, Richard Farnsworth lawyer
Stark, David Ethan museum curator
Stein, Jerome Leon economist, educator
Stevos, Joyce Louise education director
Stratt, Richard Mark chemist, educator
Stultz, Newell Maynard political science educator
Suuberg, Eric Michael chemical engineering educator
Svengalis, Kendall Frayne law librarian
Symonds, Paul Southworth mechanical engineering educator, researcher
Targan, David science administrator
Tauc, Jan physics educator
Taylor, Merrily Ellen university librarian
Terras, Victor Slavic languages and comparative literature educator
Thomas, John Lovell history educator
Thomson, Paul van Kuykendall priest, educator
Tillinghast, Charles Carpenter, Jr. aviation and financial consultant
Tobey, Joel Nye insurance company executive
Tobin, Bentley lawyer
Torres, Ernest C. federal judge
Trueblood, Alan Stubbs former modern language educator
Tullis, Julia Ann (Jan Tullis) geologist, educator
van Dam, Andries computer scientist, educator
Vavala, Domenic Anthony medical scientist, educator, retired air force officer
Votolato, Arthur Nicholas, Jr. federal judge
Waldrop, Bernard Keith English educator
Walker, Howard Ernest lawyer
†Wall, John W. trust company executive
Ward, Harold Roy chemist, educator
Watkins, John Chester Anderson newspaper publisher
Watkins, William, Jr. electric power industry executive
Wayland, William Francis diversified manufacturing company executive
Weaver, Barbara Frances librarian
Webb, Thompson geological sciences educator, researcher
Wegner, Peter computer science educator
Weiner, Jerome Harris mechanical engineering educator
Weisberger, Joseph Robert chief state supreme court justice
Weissfeld, Joachim Alexander lawyer
Westervelt, Peter Jocelyn physics educator
Weygand, Robert A. lieutenant governor, landscape architect
Whitcomb, Robert Bassett journalist, editor
White, Benjamin Vroom, III lawyer
White, Erskine Norman, Jr. management company executive
Widgoff, Mildred physicist, educator
Williams, Lea Everard history educator
Wilmeth, Don Burton theatre arts educator, theatre historian, administrator
Wood, Gordon Stewart historian, educator
Wooding, Peter Holden interior and industrial designer
Woolf, William Blauvelt association executive
Wrenn, James Joseph East Asian studies educator
Wunderlich, Alfred Leon artist, art educator
Wyman, James Vernon newspaper executive
Zarrella, Arthur M. superintendent
Zucchini, Michael Rinaldo banking company executive

Riverside
McElroy, Sister Maureen secondary school principal

Rumford
Cote, Louise Roseann creative director, designer
Findley, William Nichols mechanical engineering educator
†Marshall, John L., III construction company executive
Pike, Allen W. supermarket company executive
Silverman, Harvey Fox engineering educator, dean

Saunderstown
Donovan, Gerald Alton retired academic administrator, former university dean
Leavitt, Thomas Whittlesey museum director, educator

Smithfield
Haas, William Paul humanities educator, former college president
Trueheart, William E. academic administrator

South Kingstown
Berman, Allan psychologist, educator

Tiverton
Davis, Stephen Edward lawyer

Wakefield
Eddy, Edward Danforth academic administrator, educator
Fair, Charles Maitland neuroscientist, author
Mason, Scott MacGregor entrepreneur, inventor, consultant
Moore, George Emerson, Jr. geologist, educator
Morrison, Fred Beverly real estate consultant
Zuehlke, Richard William technical communications consultant, writer

Warwick
Blount, William Allan broadcasting executive
Carlin, David R., Jr. state senator
Charette, Sharon Juliette library administrator
Knowles, Charles Timothy lawyer, state legislator
Revens, John Cosgrove, Jr. state senator, lawyer
Rupley, Theodore J. insurance company executive
Sholes, David Henry lawyer, former state senator

West Greenwich
Breakstone, Robert Albert consumer products, financial computer products and services, and government executive
Markowicz, Victor video company executive

West Kingston
Abell, Paul Irving retired chemistry educator
Haring, Howard Jack magazine editor
†Landsman, Emanuel Elbert manufacturing company executive

West Warwick
Buckley, Charles E. engineering executive
Clary, Alexia Barbara management company executive
Galkin, Robert Theodore company executive

Westerly
Day, Chon cartoonist
Hennessy, Dean McDonald lawyer, multinational corporation executive
†Looper, George Kirk religious society executive
Morrone, Edward Patrick state senator, insurance and real estate company executive
Rees, Charles H. G. retired financial officer, investor, consultant
Reiland, Lowell Keith sculptor

SOUTH CAROLINA

Aiken
Alexander, Robert Earl university chancellor, educator
Buchanan, Robert Lee, Jr. lawyer
Cowan, Carolyn Cannon retired early childhood education educator
Cutting, Robert Thomas army officer, physician
Dickson, Paul Wesley, Jr. physicist
Hanna, Carey McConnell securities and investments executive
Hofstetter, Kenneth John research chemist
Kanne, Elizabeth Ann Arnold secondary school educator
Miller, Phillip Edward environmental scientist
Rudnick, Irene Krugman lawyer, state legislator, educator
Simons, Charles Earl, Jr. federal judge
Smith, Gregory White writer
Smith, Michael Howard ecologist
von Buedingen, Richard Paul urologist
Williamson, Thomas Garnett nuclear engineering and engineering physics educator

Anderson
Anderson, George Ross, Jr. federal judge
Astler, Vernon Benson surgeon
Carroll, Edward Perry instrumental music educator, conductor
Elks, William Chester, Jr. manufacturing executive
Gleason, Ralph Newton economic development consultant
Glenn, Michael Douglas lawyer
Goodner, Homer Wade process systems failure risk consultant
Hearne, Stephen Zachary minister, educator
Hendrix, James Easton textiles executive
Mitchell, Thomas Wayne newspaper editor
Watkins, William Law retired lawyer
Woodward, Karen Callison school system administrator

Arcadia
Dent, Frederick Baily mill executive, former ambassador, former secretary of commerce

Batesburg
Drafts, James Pickens, III financial and actuarial examiner

Beaufort
Day, John Sidney management sciences educator
Harvey, William Brantley, Jr. lawyer, former lieutenant governor
Jenkins, Margie Kline secondary school educator
Ogburn, Charlton writer
Pinkerton, Robert Bruce mechanical engineer

Bennettsville
Kinney, William Light, Jr. newspaper editor, publisher

Bluffton
Lowe, Felix Caleb publishing executive

Camden
†Craig, Joanna Burbank historic site director
Daniels, John Hancock agricultural products company executive
Furman, Hezekiah Wyndol Carroll lawyer

Catawba
Malenick, Donald H. metals manufacturing company executive

Cayce
Byars, Merlene Hutto accountant, visual artist
McElveen, William Lindsay broadcasting executive, lecturer

Chapin
Branham, Mack Carison, Jr. retired theological seminary executive, minister

Charleston
Addlestone, Nathan Sidney metals company executive
Adelman, Saul Joseph astronomy educator, researcher
Adelson, Gloria Ann financial executive
Anderson, Charles Roberts English language educator
Anderson, Ivan Verner, Jr. newspaper publisher
Anderson, Marion Cornelius surgeon, medical educator
Apple, David Joseph ophthalmology educator
Ashley, Franklin Bascom theater educator, writer
Austin, Charles John health services educator
Barclay, James Ralph psychologist, educator
Baron, Seymour engineering and research executive
Basler, Thomas G. librarian, administrator, educator
Belk, John M. retail company executive
Bell, Norman Howard physician, endocrinologist, educator
Berglund, Robin G. biochemist, former corporate executive
Blatt, Solomon, Jr. federal judge
Bolin, Edmund Mike electrical engineer, franchise engineering consultant
Bowman, Daniel Oliver psychologist
Brumgardt, John Raymond museum administrator
Brusca, Richard Charles zoologist, researcher, educator
Buvinger, Jan library director
Cannon, Hugh lawyer
Cantwell, Don artistic director
Carabello, Blase Anthony cardiology educator
Carek, Donald J(ohn) child psychiatry educator
Carr, Robert Stuart federal magistrate judge
†Chapin, Fred airport executive
Cheng, Thomas Clement parasitologist, immunologist, educator, author
†Cole, Douglas Wade landscape architect
Crawford, Fred Allen, Jr. cardiothoracic surgeon, educator
Creasman, William Thomas obstetrician-gynecologist, educator
Curtis, Marcia university dean
Daniell, Herman Burch pharmacologist
Delli Colli, Humbert Thomas chemist, product development specialist
†De Wolff, Louis management consultant
Dobson, Richard Lawrence dermatologist, educator
Donehue, John Douglas newspaper executive
Edwards, James Burrows university president, oral surgeon
Evans, Allen Donald investment real estate company executive
Farr, Charles Sims lawyer
†Fei, James Robert engineer
Gadsden, Richard Hamilton clinical biochemistry educator
Gaillard, John Palmer, Jr. former government official, former mayor
Gilbreth, Frank Bunker, Jr. retired communications executive, writer
Gillette, Paul Crawford pediatric cardiologist
Goff, R. Garey architect
Good, Joseph Cole, Jr. lawyer
Greenberg, Raymond Seth academic administrator, educator
†Greene, George Chester, III chemical engineer
Grimball, William Heyward lawyer
Grimsley, James Alexander, Jr. university administrator, retired army officer
†Hastie, J. Drayton plantation and garden owner, director
Hawkins, Falcon Black, Jr. federal judge
Hoel, David Gerhard statistician, scientist, educator
Hogan, Arthur James portfolio manager
Hogan, Edward Leo neurologist
Hughes, Blake retired architectural institute administrator, publisher
Hunter, Jairy C., Jr. academic administrator
Ivey, Robert Carl artistic director, educator, choreographer
Johnson, Allen Huggins physician, educator
Kent, Harry Ross construction executive, lay worker
Langley, Lynne Spencer newspaper editor, columnist
La Via, Mariano Francis physician, pathology and laboratory medicine educator
Legerton, Clarence William, Jr. gastroenterologist, educator
LeRoy, Edward Carwile rheumatologist
Lucas, Frank Edward architect
Maize, John Christopher dermatology educator
Manigault, Peter media executive
Margolius, Harry Stephen pharmacologist, physician
Martin, Roblee Boettcher retired cement manufacturing executive
Mc Devitt, Joseph Bryan retired university administrator, retired naval officer
McGee, Hall Thomas, Jr. newspaper, radio and television executive
†Meggett, Linda Linette reporter
Moore, William Vincent political science educator
Newberry, William Marcus physician, educator, university administrator
Norton, David C. federal judge
O'Brien, Paul Herbert surgeon
Ogawa, Makio physician
Othersen, Henry Biemann, Jr. pediatric surgeon, physician, educator
Pincus, Michael Stern language educator
Porter, Thomas Joseph, Jr. writer, songwriter
Purcell, Nancy Lou alcohol/drug abuse services executive
Reed, Stanley Foster editor, writer, publisher, lecturer
Reilly, David Henry university dean
Rivers, John Minott, Jr. real estate developer
Robinson, Neil Cibley, Jr. lawyer
Roof, Betty Sams internist
†Rupp, Frank A., III association executive
Salinas, Carlos Francisco dentist educator
Salmon, Edward Lloyd, Jr. bishop
Sanders, Alexander Mullings, Jr. judge
Schmitt, Robert Christian architect, interior designer
Schreadley, Richard Lee writer, retired newspaper editor
Scott, Henry Lawrence concert pianist, humorist
Simson, Jo Anne anatomy and cell biology educator
Smith, J. Roy education educator
Smith, W. Stuart hospital administrator
Swanson, Arnold Arthur retired biochemistry educator
Tarleton, Larry Wilson newspaper editor
Thompson, David B. bishop
Thompson, W(ilmer) Leigh pharmaceutical company executive, physician, pharmacologist
Watts, Claudius Elmer, III retired air force officer
†Whelan, Wayne Louis higher education administrator
Wilcox, Arthur Manigault newspaper editor
Wilson, Frederick Allen medical educator, medical center administrator, gastroenterologist
Winthrop, John investment company executive
Wyrick, Charles Lloyd, Jr. publisher, writer, editor
Young, Joseph Rutledge, Jr. lawyer

Clemson
Adams, John Quincy, III nuclear engineer
Boykin, Joseph Floyd, Jr. librarian
Bunn, Joe Millard agricultural engineering educator
Burch, Elmer Earl management educator
Calhoun, Richard James English language educator
Chisman, James Allan industrial engineering educator, consultant
Clayton, Donald Delbert astrophysicist, nuclear physicist, educator
Couch, James Houston industrial engineer, educator
Cox, Headley Morris, Jr. lawyer, educator
Curris, Constantine William university president
DesMarteau, Darryl Dwayne chemistry and geology educator
Griffin, Villard Stuart, Jr. geology educator
Han, Young Jo agricultural engineer, educator
Hays, Sidney Brooks retired entomology educator
Hicks, Edwin Hugh accountant
†Kelly, John William, Jr. head of horticulture department, botanical garden director
Kenelly, John Willis, Jr. mathematician, educator
Leonard, Michael Steven industrial engineering educator
Morr, Charles Vernon food science educator
Paul, Frank Waters mechanical engineer, educator, consultant
Pursley, Michael Bader electrical engineering educator, communications systems research and consulting
Riley, Helene Maria Kastinger Germanist
Trevillian, Wallace Dabney economics educator, retired dean
Underwood, Richard Allan English language educator
Underwood, Sandra Jane university administrator
Vogel, Henry Elliott retired university dean and physics educator
von Recum, Andreas F. bioengineer
Williamson, Robert Elmore agricultural engineering educator
Young, Joseph Laurie architecture educator
†Zumbrunnen, David Arnold mechanical engineering educator, consultant

Clinton
Cornelson, George Henry, IV retired textile company executive
Orr, Kenneth Bradley college president
Vance, Robert Mercer textile manufacturing company executive, banker

Columbia
Abel, Anne Elizabeth Sutherland pediatrician
Abel, Francis Lee physiology educator
Adams, Gregory Burke lawyer, educator
Adams, John Hurst bishop
Adams, Weston diplomat, lawyer
Adcock, David Filmore radiologist, educator
Aelion, C. Marjorie educator
Almond, Carl Herman surgeon, physician, educator
Amidon, Roger Lyman health administration educator
Anderson, Joseph Fletcher, Jr. federal judge
Aull, James Stroud bishop
Averyt, Gayle Owen insurance executive
Bagnal, Charles Wilson retired army officer, real estate broker
Bailey, George Screven lawyer
Baker, Donald lawyer
†Baum, Marsha Lynn law educator
†Beasley, David Muldrow governor
Beckham, William Arthur bishop
Belasco, Simon French language and linguistics educator
Bethea, Joseph Benjamin bishop
Bjontegard, Arthur Martin, Jr. foundation executive
Blanton, Hoover Clarence lawyer
Blount, Evelyn religious organization administrator
Boggs, Jack Aaron banker, municipal government official
Bristow, Walter James, Jr. retired state judge
Brooker, Jeff Zeigler cardiologist
Brown, Arnold health science facility administrator
Brubaker, Lauren Edgar minister, educator
Bruccoli, Matthew Joseph English educator, publisher
Callaham, Betty Elgin librarian
Carlisle, William Aiken architect
Case, George Tilden, Jr. marketing professional
Chapman, Robert Foster federal judge
†Childs, Ronald Patnode healthcare administrator
Cilella, Salvatore George, Jr. museum director
Clark, David Randolph wholesale grocer
Clifford, Amie Lois prosecutor
Coble, Bob city official
Cohn, Elchanan economics educator
Cole, Benjamin Theodore biologist
Cole, Charles Talmadge, Jr. bank executive
Collins, James Edward broadcast executive
†Condon, Charles Molony state official, lawyer
Conrad, Paul Ernest transportation consultant
Cooper, William Allen, Jr. audiologist
Cork, Holly A. state legislator
Courson, John Edward state senator, insurance company executive
Crews, Esca Holmes, Jr. utility company executive
Crim, Reuben Sidney newspaper publishing executive
Culik, Karel computer scientist, educator
Davis, Keith Eugene psychologist, educator, consultant
Dawson, Wallace Douglas, Jr. geneticist
Denton, Robert William (Pete Denton) financial executive
Dickey, James Lafayette poet, novelist, filmmaker, critic
Dixon, Albert King, II university administrator
Donald, Alexander Grant psychiatrist
Duffie, Virgil Whatley, Jr. state official
Duffy, John Joseph academic administrator, history educator
Eastman, Caroline Merriam computer science educator
Edens, Jerry Jeanne computer engineer, consultant
Edgar, Walter Bellingrath historian
Edge, Ronald Dovaston physics educator
Elliott, John Dewey lawyer
Ernst, Edward Willis electrical engineering educator
Feinn, Barbara Ann economist
Finkel, Gerald Michael lawyer
Floyd, Frank Albert, Jr. management executive
Foster, Robert Watson, Sr. legal educator
†Freeman, Kester St. Clair, Jr. hospital administrator
Friedman, Myles Ivan education educator
Fryer, John Stanley management science educator
Geckle, George Leo, III English language educator
Giese, Warren Kenneth health and physical education educator, state senator
Ginsberg, Leon Herman social work educator
Golightly, Donald Edward architect

Gray, Katherine Wilson *newspaper editor*
Gressette, Lawrence M., Jr. *utilities executive*
Haimbaugh, George Dow, Jr. *lawyer, educator*
Hallman, Harry Morgan, Jr. *retired oil company executive*
Hamilton, Clyde Henry *federal judge*
Hardin, James Neal *German and comparative literature educator, publisher*
Harvin, Charles Alexander, III *state legislator*
Hatch, David Lincoln *sociology educator*
Hatch, Mary Gies *German language educator*
Heider, Karl Gustav *anthropology educator*
Horger, Edgar Olin, III *obstetrics and gynecology educator*
Howard-Hill, Trevor Howard *English language educator*
Hultstrand, Charles John *architect*
Humphries, John O'Neal *physician, educator, university dean*
Inkley, Scott Russell, Jr. *state agency administrator*
Jervey, Harold Edward, Jr. *medical education consultant, retired*
Johnson, Herbert Alan *history and law educator, lawyer, chaplain*
Johnson, James Bek, Jr. *library director*
Johnson, Kathie Anne *nurse, administrator*
Kahn, Herman Bernard *construction company executive*
Kanes, William Henry *geology educator, research center administrator*
Kay, Carol McGinnis *literature educator*
†Kenyon, Bruce Davis *utilities executive*
Kiker, Billy Frazier *economics educator*
King, John Ethelbert, Jr. *education educator, former academic administrator*
Knight, Henry Scarborough, Jr. *lawyer*
†Krantz, Palmer Eric, III *zoo director*
Lander, James Albert *retired military officer, state senator*
Leatherman, Hugh Kenneth, Sr. *state senator, business executive*
LeFever, Michael Grant *state agency administrator*
Lindley, James Gunn *bank executive*
Long, Eugene Thomas, III *philosophy educator, administrator*
Love, Kenneth Edward *real estate, investment and business consultant*
Lumpkin, John Henderson *retired banker*
Manly, Sarah Letitia *state legislator, ophthalmic photographer, angiographer*
Marchant, Trelawney Eston *national guard officer, lawyer*
Martin, Charles Wallace *travel executive, retired university administrator*
Matthews, Steve Allen *lawyer*
Mc Cullough, Ralph Clayton, II *lawyer, educator*
McFarland, Kay Flowers *medical educator*
McGill, Jennifer Houser *non-profit association administrator*
McLean, Thomas Neil *editor*
Melton, Gary Bentley *psychology and law educator*
†Meriwether, James Babcock *English language educator*
Miles, Jim *state official*
Miller, E. Hite *banker, holding company executive*
Mishler, William, II *political science educator*
Morris, James Aloysius *economist, educator*
Muzekari, Thomasine Dabbs *educational consultant*
Myerson, Joel Arthur *English language educator, researcher*
Nelson, William Shannon, II *lawyer*
Newton, Rhonwen Leonard *writer, microcomputer consultant*
Nexsen, Julian Jacobs *lawyer*
Nielsen, Barbara Stock *state educational administrator*
Nolte, William Henry *English language educator*
Norton, Hugh Stanton *economist, educator*
†Novinger, Cathy Blackburn *utility company executive*
Ott, Jack M. *mathematics educator*
Palms, John Michael *university president*
Patterson, Grady Leslie, Jr. *state treasurer*
†Peeler, Bob *state official*
Perry, Matthew J., Jr. *federal judge*
Pritchett, Samuel Travis *finance and insurance educator, researcher*
Rawlinson, Helen Ann *librarian*
Reeves, George McMillan, Jr. *comparative literature educator, educational administrator*
Rideoutte, Joseph Green *highways and public transportation administrator*
Robinson, Christopher Thomas *artist*
Rogers, Timothy Folk *lawyer*
Rone, William Eugene, Jr. *newspaper editor*
Royall, Robert Venning, Jr. *banker*
Scarborough, Claude Mood, Jr. *lawyer*
Secor, Donald Terry, Jr. *geologist, educator*
Seigler, Ruth Queen *college nursing administrator, consultant, nurse*
Shabazz, Aiysha Muslimah *social work administrator*
Shannon, David Thomas *academic administrator*
Shedd, Dennis W. *federal judge*
Sheheen, Fred Roukos *education agency administrator*
Sigmon, Daniel Ray *foundation administrator*
Sloan, Frank Keenan *lawyer, writer*
Smith, Franklin Sumner, Jr. *retired insurance executive*
Smith, James Roland *state legislator*
Smith, J(efferson) Verne *state senator, business executive*
Spector, Joseph Robert *retired diversified manufacturing executive*
Sproat, John Gerald *historian*
Starr, Harvey *political scientist*
Synnott, Marcia Graham *history educator*
Tate, Harold Simmons, Jr. *lawyer*
Teague, Peyton Clark *chemist, educator*
†Thee, Christian *artist, designer*
Thelen, Gil *newspaper editor*
Toal, Jean Hoefer *lawyer, state supreme court justice*
Tomlin, Donald Robert, Jr. *real estate management company executive*
Tomlin, Patrick Leslie *condominium development executive*
Toombs, Kenneth Eldridge *librarian*
†Tudor, Donald Norris *state government administrator*
Vernberg, Frank John *marine and biological sciences educator*
Waites, Candy Yaghjian *former state official*
Waldron, Robert Leroy, II *physician*
Walker, Richard Louis *former ambassador, educator, author*
Warren, Charles David *library administrator*
Watabe, Norimitsu *biology and marine science educator*
Weatherbee, Donald Emery *political scientist, educator*
Wedlock, Eldon Dyment, Jr. *law educator*
Weir, Robert McColloch *history educator*
Wells, Robert Steven *law association executive*
West, Rexford Leon *banker*
Wilder, Ronald Parker *economics educator*
Willoughby, William, II *retired nuclear engineer*
Wilson, George Larry *computer software company executive*
Wolfe, George B. *lawyer*

Conway
Moore, Richard Harlan *biology educator, university official*
Sharples, D. Kent *college administrator*
Skinner, Samuel Ballou, III *physics educator, researcher*
Talbert, Roy, Jr. *history educator*
Wiseman, Dennis Gene *college dean*

Darlington
Chandler, Archie Lee *state supreme court justice*
Holt, Robert LeRoi *philosophy educator*

Dillon
Webb, Ronald Wayne *hospital administrator*

Due West
Koonts, Jones Calvin *retired education educator*
Ruble, Randall Tucker *theologian, educator, academic administrator*

Easley
Dark, Alvin Ralph *public relations executive*
Failing, George Edgar *editor, clergyman, educator*
Goldman, Joseph Elias *advertising executive*
Grantham, George Leighton *lawyer, banker, utility company executive*
Moncrief, James Loring *educational administrator*
Sundstrom, Harold Walter *public relations executive*
†Urakami, Akio *manufacturing company executive*

Estill
Eads, Albert E., Jr. *school superintendent*

Florence
Brewer, Mary Dean *medical foundation executive*
Burns, William A. *museum administrator, author*
Costa, Manuel Antone *recreational facility manager*
Dixon, Gale Harllee *drug company executive*
Houck, Charles Weston *federal judge*
Kittrell, Benjamin Upchurch *agronomist*
Sanderson, Dennis Carl *theater director, educator*
Smith, Walter Douglas *retired college president*
Strong, Roger Lee *mathematics educator*
Townsend, Nancy Christine *secondary education educator*
Wagner, John Garnet *pharmacy educator*
Wilson, L(etitia) Alexandra *elementary school educator*

Folly Beach
Overton, Marcus Lee *performing arts administrator, actor, writer*

Fort Jackson
Conrad, Paul Edward *lawyer*

Fort Mill
Bonds, C. Joseph *school system administrator*
Elisha, Walter Y. *textile manufacturing company executive*
Hodge, Bobby Lynn *mechanical engineer*
Horten, Carl Frank *textile manufacturing company executive*
Kelbley, Stephen Paul *consumer products executive*
Mantle, John Edward *newspaper publisher*
Montgomery, Terry Gray *textiles researcher*
White, James Spratt, IV *textiles executive, lawyer*

Gaffney
Griffin, Walter Roland *college president, educator, historian*
Kowalczyk, Jeanne Stuart *biology educator*
Perry, Gaylord Jackson *former professional baseball player*

Gastonia
Carson, John Little *historical theology educator, clergyman*

Georgetown
Allison, Christopher FitzSimons *bishop*
McGrath, James Charles, III *financial services company executive, lawyer, consultant*
Moore, Albert Cunningham *lawyer, insurance company executive*

Goose Creek
Johnson, Johnnie *bishop*

Greenville
Akpan, Edward *metallurgical engineer*
Alberga, Alta Wheat *artist*
†Albers, Gerald E. *aircraft parts manufacturing*
Barhyte, Donald James *newspaper executive*
Bates, George William *obstetrician, gynecologist, educator*
Bauknight, Clarence Brock *wholesale and retail company executive*
Boliek, Luther C. *bank executive*
Bonner, Jack W., III *psychiatrist, educator, administrator*
Burkhardt, J. Bland, Jr. *hospital administrator*
Carpenter, William Levy *mechanical engineer*
Chastain, Roger W. *textile company executive*
Cloer, Carl Thomas, Jr. *education educator*
Collins, Marshall J., Jr. *consumer products company executive*
Crabtree, John Henry, Jr. *retired English educator*
Dean, Warren Michael *construction company executive*
Eskew, Rhea Taliaferro *newspaper publisher*
Fayonsky, James Leon *financial planner*
Fitzgerald, Eugene Francis *management consultant*
Foulke, Edwin Gerhart, Jr. *lawyer*
Freeman, David Lynn *lawyer*
Friedman, Steven M. *textile company executive*
Frist, Thomas Ferran *philanthropic organization executive*
Gilkerson, Yancey Sherard *writer, former editor*
Grimes, J. William *cable television executive*
Hagood, William Milliken, III *lawyer*
Haskins, Terry Edward *lawyer, politician*
Henderson, James Marvin *advertising agency executive*
Herlong, Henry Michael, Jr. *federal judge*
Hill, Grace Lucile Garrison *education educator, consultant*
Hipp, Francis Moffett *insurance executive*
Hipp, William Hayne *insurance and broadcasting executive*
Hodges, Harland E. *apparel executive*
Hoffman, Michael Robert *physician*
Horton, James Wright *retired lawyer*
Hunt, Walter Kenneth, III *insurance company executive*
Hunter, Jerry E. *textile company executive*
†Inman, Thomas Patrick *newspaper editor*
Jones, Bob, Jr. *academic administrator, educator, lecturer, minister*
Kilgore, Donald Gibson, Jr. *pathologist*
Kowalski, Paul Randolph *minister*
Kuharsky, Andrew Sergius *dancer, educator*
LeBlanc, L(ouis) Christian *architect*
Leonhardt, Thomas C. *engineering company executive*
Maddrey, E. E., II *textile company executive*
Mann, James Robert *congressman*
McKnight, Edgar Vernon *religion educator*
Mebane, William deBerniere *newspaper publisher*
Morton, James Carnes, Jr. *public relations executive*
Neal, James Austin *architect*
Nemirow, Arnold Myles *manufacturing executive*
†Ogden, Ralph Lindsey *insurance company executive*
†Ornston, Darius Gray, Jr. *psychiatrist*
Pamplin, Robert Boisseau, Jr. *agricultural company executive, minister, writer*
Parente, Emil J. *chemical engineering executive*
Payne, G(eorge) Frederick *educational director*
Plumstead, William Charles *quality engineer, consultant*
†Price, Arthur D. *food products executive*
Rainsford, Bettis C. *textile company executive*
Roe, Thomas Anderson *building supply company executive*
Selvy, Barbara *dance instructor*
Shilling, Mary Emily *nursing administrator*
Smith, Morton Howison *religious organization administrator, educator*
Smith, Philip Daniel *academic administrator, education educator*
Stone, Charles Rivers *apparel manufacturing company executive*
Stultz, Thomas Joseph *newspaper executive*
Theodore, Nick Andrew *lieutenant governor*
Thompson, Robert Thomas *lawyer*
Todd, John Dickerson, Jr. *lawyer*
Traxler, William Byrd *lawyer*
Traxler, William Byrd, Jr. *federal judge*
Varin, Roger Robert *textile executive*
Walker, Wesley M. *lawyer*
Walters, Johnnie McKeiver *lawyer*
Wearn, Wilson Cannon *retired media executive*
Whitmire, John Lee *daycare provider*
Wilkins, William Walter, Jr. *federal judge*
Workman, William Douglas, III *mayor*
Young, Edwin Reynolds, Jr. *urologist, missionary*

Greenwood
Carter, Ann Keeling *nursing administrator*
Fox, Richard Shirley *zoology educator*
Jackson, Larry Artope *retired college president*
Marino, Sheila Burris *education educator*
Sigety, Charles Edward *lawyer, medical products executive*

Greer
Gallman, Clarence Hunter *textile executive*
Lane, James Garland, Jr. *diversified industry executive*
Scruggs, Jack Gilbert *retired chemical executive*

Hampton
Platts, Francis Holbrook *plastics engineer*

Hartsville
Browning, Peter Crane *packaging company executive*
Coker, Charles Westfield *diversified manufacturing company executive*
Coxe, Thomas C., III *paper and plastic products manufacturing company executive*
Daniels, James Douglas *academic administrator*
DeLoach, Harris E(ugene), Jr. *lawyer, manufacturing company executive*
Fogle, G. Lee *credit union executive, consultant*
Martin, Neal Anderson *library director*
McGee, James Gladney, Jr. *diversified products company executive*
Menius, Espie Flynn, Jr. *electrical engineer*
Shelley, James Herbert *lawyer, paper company executive*

Hilton Head Island
Adams, William Hensley *ecologist, educator*
Batten, William Milfred *retired stock exchange executive*
Becker, Karl Martin *lawyer, investment company executive*
Birk, Robert Eugene *retired physician, educator*
Brock, Karena Diane *ballerina, educator, choreographer*
Brown, Arthur Edmon, Jr. *retired army officer*
Carr, David Turner *physician*
Cunningham, William Henry *retired food products executive*
Davis, Milton Wickers, Jr. *chemical engineer, educator*
Exley, Winston Wallace *middle school educator*
†Franks, Paul Taylor *real estate executive*
Gruchacz, Robert S. *real estate executive*
Harty, James D. *former manufacturing company executive*
Hornor, Frank Berkshire *banker*
Huckins, Harold Aaron *chemical engineer*
Humphrey, Edward William *surgeon, medical educator*
Kaley, Arthur Warren *financial consulting company executive*
Little, Thomas Mayer *public relations executive*
Male, Roy Raymond *English language educator*
Margileth, Andrew Menges *physician, former naval officer*
†Marscher, Fran Heyward (Fran Smith) *editor*
McDowell, Theodore Noyes *public relations consultant*
McKinney, Donald Lee *magazine editor*
Mersereau, Hiram Stipe *wood products company consultant*
Mirse, Ralph Thomas *former college president*
Mulhollan, Paige Elliott *university president emeritus*
Owen, Warren Herbert *utility executive*
Patton, Joseph Donald, Jr. *management consultant*
Pritchard, Dalton Harold *retired electronics research engineer*
Pustilnik, Jean Todd *elementary education educator*
Radest, Howard Bernard *clergyman, educator*
Ranney, Maurice William *chemical company executive*
Rose, William Shepard, Jr. *lawyer, former federal official*
Rulis, Raymond Joseph *manufacturing company executive, consultant*
Russell, Allen Stevenson *retired aluminum company executive*
Santos, George Wesley *physician, educator*
Scarminach, Charles Anthony *lawyer*
Simpson, John Wistar *energy consultant, former manufacturing company executive*
Stoll, Richard Edmund *retired manufacturing executive*
West, John Carl *lawyer, former ambassador, former governor*
Windman, Arnold Lewis *retired mechanical engineer*

Hollywood
Hull, Edward Whaley Seabrook *freelance writer, consultant*

Hopkins
Clarkson, Jocelyn Adrene *medical technologist*

Johns Island
Behnke, Wallace Blanchard, Jr. *consultant, engineer, retired utility executive*
Cameron, Thomas William Lane *investment company executive*
Failla, Patricia McClement *biomedical and environmental research adminstrator*
Mackaness, George Bellamy *retired pharmaceutical company executive*

Kershaw
Lucas, Dean Hadden *retired educator*

Ladson
Cannon, Major Tom *special education educator*
Hyatt, David Hudson *manufacturing executive*

Lake City
TruLuck, James Paul, Jr. *dentist, vintner*

Lake Wylie
Peacock, A(lvin) Ward *textile company executive*
†Pickitt, John Leonard *retired air force officer, association executive*

Lancaster
Bundy, Charles Alan *foundation executive*

Landrum
Hilton, Ordway *document examiner*
Pauley, Robert Reinhold *broadcasting executive, financial executive*

Laurens
Bost, John Rowan *manufacturing executive, engineer*

Leesville
Crumley, James Robert, Jr. *retired clergyman*

Lexington
Gatch, Charles Edward, Jr. *middle school principal*
Miller, Ben Neely *physician*
Wilkins, Robert Pearce *lawyer*

Little River
Uzenda, Jara Carlow *technical writer*

Mauldin
Harris, Daniel Frederick *biomechanical analyst*
Phillips, James Oscar *minister*
Yingling, William E., III *retail company executive*

Moncks Corner
Morris, Henry Allen, Jr. *publisher*
Peake, Frank *middle school educator*
Rainear, Robert E. *utilities executive*

Mount Pleasant
Cooley, Kathleen Shannon *speech-language pathologist*
McConnell, John William, Jr. *lawyer*
Wohltmann, Hulda Justine *pediatric endocrinologist*

Mullins
Stonesifer, Richard James *retired humanities and social science educator*

Murrells Inlet
Noble, Joseph Veach *fine arts administrator*

Myrtle Beach
Dail, Hilda Lee *psychotherapist*
Harwell, David Walker *retired state supreme court chief justice*
Patton, Wendell Melton, Jr. *retired management educator, consulting psychologist, college president*
†Rosen, Benedict Philip *engineering executive*

Newberry
Layton, William Isaac *mathematics educator*
Logan, Sandra Jean *economics and business educator*
Pope, Thomas Harrington, Jr. *lawyer*

North
Moran, John Bernard *government official*

North Augusta
Pritchard, Constance Jenkins *human resources specialist, trainer, consultant*
†Wiser, J. W. *engineering company executive, construction executive*

North Charleston
Mc Aleece, Donald John *mechanical engineering educator*
Zucker, Jerry *energy systems manufacturing executive*

North Myrtle Beach
Atkinson, Harold Witherspoon *utilities consultant, real estate broker*

Orangeburg
Babb, Julius Wistar, III *cardiovascular surgeon*
Graule, Raymond S(iegfried) *metallurgical engineer*
Sims, Edward Howell *editor, publisher*
Thompson, Marguerite Myrtle Graming (Mrs. Ralph B. Thompson) *librarian*
†Williams, Karen Johnson *federal judge*

Parris Island
†Klimp, Jack Wilbur *marine corps officer*

Pawleys Island
Alexander, William D., III *civil engineer, consultant, former army air force officer*
Tarbox, Gurdon Lucius, Jr. *retired museum executive*

Pendleton
Spain, James Dorris, Jr. *biochemist, educator*

Ridgeland
Smart, Jacob Edward *management consultant*

Rock Hill
Bristow, Robert O'Neil *writer, educator*
Click, John William *communication educator*
Di Giorgio, Anthony J. *college president*
Du Bois, Paul Zinkhan *library director*
Viault, Birdsall Scrymser *history educator*

Saint Helena Island
Herzbrun, David Joseph *retired advertising executive, consultant*

Salem
Gentry, Robert Cecil *meteorological consultant, research scientist*
Jones, Charles Edward *mechanical engineer*
Van Buren, William Benjamin, III *retired pharmaceutical company executive*

Seneca
Clausen, Hugh Joseph *retired army officer*
Hudgin, Donald Edward *retired research company executive, editor, consultant*
Uden, David Elliott *cardiologist, educator*

Simpsonville
Drummond, Julia Elaine Butler *middle school educator*

Spartanburg
Cavin, William Pinckney *chemist, educator*
†Cogan, Jerry Albert, Jr. *chemical engineer, engineering executive*
Courtney, Charles Tyrone *state legislator, lawyer*
Fudenberg, Herman Hugh *immunologist, educator*
Glenn, Robert E. *elementary school principal*
Guthrie, John Robert *physician, health science facility administrator*
Hatley, Amy Bell *elementary education educator, broadcast journalist*
†Henson, David Leslie *hospital administrator*
†Jennings, Thomas Adolphus *hospital administrator*
Leonard, Walter Raymond *retired biology educator*
Lesesne, Joab Mauldin, Jr. *college president*
Lindsay, Bryan Eugene *humanities educator, musician, writer*
Littlejohn, Broadus Richard, Jr. *retail supermarket chain executive*
Mc Gehee, Larry Thomas *university administrator*
Owens, Hilda Faye *management/leadership development consultant, human resource trainer*
Pate, John Gillis, Jr. *financial consultant*
Patterson, Elizabeth Johnston *former congresswoman*
Russell, Donald Stuart *federal judge*
Sovey, L. Terrell, Jr. *textile executive, insurance agent*
Stephens, Bobby Gene *college administrator, consultant*
White, Robert Bruce *keyboard instruments company acoustical consultant*
Wilde, Edwin Frederick *mathematics educator*
Williams, John Cornelius *lawyer*

Sullivans Island
Romaine, Henry Simmons *investment consultant*

Summerville
Rose, Michael Thomas *state legislator, lawyer*

Sumter
Finney, Ernest Adolphus, Jr. *state supreme court chief justice*
Kieslich, Anita Frances *school system administrator*
Nock, William H. *bank executive*
Olsen, Thomas Richard, Sr. *air force officer*
Teer, Kay Stoltz *museum director*

Surfside Beach
McCrensky, Edward *international consultant, former organization executive*

Townville
Wright, George Cullen *electronics company executive*

Walterboro
Johnson, Daniel McDonald (Dan Johnson) *newspaper editor*
Marvin, Robert Earle *landscape architect*

Wellford
Stone, George Eliot *textile executive*

West Columbia
Carter, Saralee Lessman *immunologist, microbiologist*
Hand, Herbert Hensley *management educator, executive, consultant, inventor*
Ochs, Robert David *history educator*
Parker, Harold Talbot *history educator*
Wilson, Addison Graves (Joe Wilson) *lawyer, state senator*

Williamston
Davis, Michael Todd *textile company administrator*

Winnsboro
King, Robert Thomas *editor, free-lance writer*

SOUTH DAKOTA

Aberdeen
Glover, James Todd *manufacturing company executive*
Hahnemann, Barbara K. *family nurse practitioner*

Baltic
Wagner, Michael Dickman *state representative, small business owner*

Britton
Farrar, Frank Leroy *lawyer, former governor*

Brookings
Bailey, Harold Stevens, Jr. *retired educational administrator*
Duffey, George Henry *physics educator*
Gilbert, Howard Alden *economics educator*
Hugghins, Ernest Jay *biology educator*
McClure-Bibby, Mary Anne *former state legislator*
Moore, Raymond A. *agricultural educator*
Morgan, Walter *retired poultry science educator*
†Raney, Leon A. *librarian*
Storry, Junis Oliver *retired engineering educator*
Swiden, Ladell Ray *travel company executive*
Sword, Christopher Patrick *microbiologist, university dean*
Wagner, Mary Kathryn *sociology educator, former state legislator*
Wagner, Robert Todd *university president, sociology educator*

Burbank
Simmons, Joseph Thomas *accountant, educator*

Chamberlain
Gregg, Robert Lee *pharmacist*

Custer
Stofft, William A. *career officer*

Dakota Dunes
Putney, Mark William *lawyer, utility executive*

Edgemont
Bennett, Charles Leo *management consultant, rancher*

Fort Pierre
Hoyt, Irvin N. *judge*

Freeman
Waltner, John Randolph *bank executive*

Huron
Kuhler, Deborah Gail *grief counselor, former state legislator*
Reynolds, R. John *university administrator*
Wilkens, Robert Allen *utilities executive, electrical engineer*

Keystone
Wenk, Daniel N. *landmark site administrator*

Madison
Tunheim, Jerald Arden *academic administrator, physics educator*

Mitchell
Randall, Ronald Fisher *grocery store chain executive*
Shanard, George Harris *retired state senator, entrepreneur*

North Sioux City
McElroy, Edmund G., Jr. *financial executive*
Waitt, Ted W. *computer company executive*

Parker
Zimmer, John Herman *lawyer*

Pierre
Amundson, Robert A. *state supreme court justice*
Barnett, Mark William *state attorney general*
Bonaiuto, John A. *state education official*
Dunn, James Bernard *mining company executive, state legislator*
Hazeltine, Joyce *state official*
Henderson, Frank Ellis *state supreme court justice*
Hillard, Carole *state official*
Hodges, Joyce E. *state legislator*
Johnson, Julie Marie *lawyer, lobbyist, governor's cabinet*
Kundert, Alice E. *state legislator*
Miller, Robert Arthur *state supreme court chief justice*
Nicolay, Janice *state legislator*
Pederson, Gordon Roy *state legislator, retired military officer*
Porter, Donald James *federal judge*
Russell, James Donald Murray *hospital administrator*
Sabers, Richard Wayne *state supreme court justice*
Stensland, Linda L. *state senator*
Thompson, Charles Murray *lawyer*
Wuest, George W. *retired state supreme court justice*

Platte
Pennington, Beverly Melcher *financial services company executive*

Porcupine
†Tall, Joann *ecologist*

Prairie City
Wishard, Della Mae *state legislator*

Rapid City
Battey, Richard Howard *federal judge*
Bickett, Robert Winston *insurance executive*
Bogue, Andrew Wendell *federal judge*
Chaput, Charles J. *bishop*
†Clement, Dale Eugene *financial executive*
Corwin, Bert Clark *optometrist*
Erickson, John Duff *educational association adminstrator*
Foye, Thomas Harold *lawyer*
Galbraith, Jeanne Ann *nurse, administrator*
Gowen, Richard Joseph *electrical engineering educator, college president*
Gries, John Paul *geologist*
†Hersrud, James Robert *pharmacist*
Hughes, William Lewis *former university official, electrical engineer*
Jones, David L. *architect*
Lien, Bruce Hawkins *minerals and oil company executive*
Lisenbee, Alvis Lee *structural geologist, educator*
Quinn, Robert Henry *surgeon, medical school administrator*
Ramakrishnan, Venkataswamy *civil engineer, educator*
†Reiter, Richard Ronald *healthcare executive*
Riemenschneider, Albert Louis *engineering educator*
Schleusener, Richard August *college president*
Scofield, Gordon Lloyd *mechanical engineer, educator*
Smith, Paul Letton, Jr. *geophysicist*
Sykora, Harold James *military officer*
Undlin, Charles Thomas *banker*
Viken, Linda Lea Margaret *lawyer*

Selby
Akre, Donald J. *school system administrator*

Sioux Falls
Austad, Oscar *recreational supplies company executive*
Balcer, Charles Louis *college president emeritus, educator*
Billion, John Joseph *orthopedic surgeon, state representative*
†Breckenridge, James Joel *health facility administrator*
Brendtro, Larry Kay *psychologist, educator*
Carlson, Marilyn A. *English language educator*
Carlson, Robert James *bishop*
Carroll, Howard W. *school system administrator*
Christensen, David Allen *manufacturing company executive*
Cowles, Ronald Eugene *church administrator*
Dertien, James LeRoy *librarian*
Dudley, Paul V. *bishop*
Ecker, Peder Kaloides *former judge*
Eitrheim, Norman Duane *bishop*
Fenton, Lawrence Jules *pediatric educator*
Flora, George Claude *retired neurology educator, neurologist*
Fuller, Lawrence Robert *newspaper publisher*
Gibbons, Cecilia *nurse, hospital administrator*
Gibbs, Frank P. *federal judge*
Grupp, Carl Alf *art educator, artist*
Hiatt, Charles Milton *seminary president*
Hoskins, John H. *urologist, educator*
Huseboe, Arthur Robert *English language educator*
Huseboe, Doris Louise *educator, arts consultant*
†Janklow, William John *governor*
Jaqua, Richard Allen *pathologist*
Johnson, Thomas Floyd *college president, educator*
†Johnson, Warren R. *marketing executive, consultant*
Jones, John Bailey *federal judge*
Kirby, Dan Laird *lawyer*
Kirby, Joe P. *insurance company executive*
Koch, Ralph Richard *architect*
Koetzle, Gil *state legislator, fire fighter, professional association administrator*
LaFave, LeAnn Larson *lawyer*
†Marsh, John S., Jr. *newspaper editor*
Morse, Peter Hodges *ophthalmologist, educator*
Nelson, Suzanne Mosey *association executive, non-profit management consultant*
Nichol, Fred Joseph *federal judge*
Paisley, Keith W. *state senator, small business owner*
Pederson, Arnold S. *chemical company executive*
Piersol, Lawrence L. *federal judge*
†Porter, John T. *health facility administrator*
Richards, LaClaire Lissetta Jones (Mrs. George A. Richards) *social worker*
†Rykhus, David Anthony *healthcare executive*
Smith, Murray Thomas *transportation company executive*
Taplett, Lloyd Melvin *human resources management consultant*
Thompson, Ronelle Kay Hildebrandt *library director*
Tucker, William Vincent *vocational evaluator, former college president*
Van Demark, Robert Eugene, Sr. *orthopedic surgeon*
Wagoner, Ralph Howard *academic administrator, educator*
Wegner, Karl Heinrich *physician, educator*
Wiebe, Richard Herbert *reproductive endocrinologist, educator*
Wollman, Roger Leland *federal judge*
Zawada, Edward Thaddeus, Jr. *physician, educator*

Spearfish
Erickson, Richard Ames *physicist, emeritus educator*

Stratford
Gubin, Ronald *farm products association executive*

Sturgis
Ingalls, Marie Cecelie *former state legislator, retail executive*

Vermillion
Asher, Betty Turner *academic administrator*
Banks, Margaret Downie *curator, educator*
Carlson, Loren Merle *political science educator*
Clem, Alan Leland *political scientist*
Clifford, Sylvester *retired communication educator*
Dahlin, Donald C(lifford) *political science educator*
†Freeman, Jeffrey Vaughn (Jeff Freeman) *art educator, artist*
†Froberg, Brent Malcolm *classics educator*
Hagen, Arthur Ainsworth *pharmacologist*
Langworthy, Thomas Allan *microbiologist, educator*
Milton, John Ronald *English language educator, author*
Milton, Lynn Leonharda *elementary and secondary school educator*
Neuhaus, Otto Wilhelm *biochemistry educator*
Richardson, Maurine Janet *reading educator*

Volga
Moldenhauer, William Calvin *soil scientist*

Wall
Poppe, Kenneth C. *school system administrator*

Wessington
Lockner, Vera Joanne *farmer, rancher, legislator*

Wessington Springs
Burg, James Allen *state agency administrator, farmer*
Morford-Burg, JoAnn *state senator, investment company executive*

Yankton
Hirsch, Robert William *lawyer*
†Rezac, Pamela Jean *hospital executive*
Sokol, Dennis Allen *hospital administrator*

TENNESSEE

Adamsville
York, Joseph Stafford *secondary gifted and talented education educator*

Alcoa
†Piper, A. Coleman *retail executive*

Antioch
Malone, Tom *bible college president*
†Midkiff, John L., Jr. *health care administrator, retired army officer*
Reeds, Roger *church administrator*
Thomas, Roy Lee *minister*
Vallance, James *church administrator, religious publication editor*
Waddell, R. Eugene *minister*
Wisehart, Mary Ruth *academic administrator*
Worthington, Melvin Leroy *minister, writer*

Arnold AFB
†Davis, John William *engineering company executive*

Ashland City
Lindahl, Herbert Winfred *appliance manufacturing executive*

Athens
Thompson, Verdine Mae *financial planner, tax preparer*
Wilson, Ben *elementary school principal*

Brentwood
†Atchison, David Warren *church officer*
Bennett, Harold Clark *clergyman, religious organization administrator*
Bodzy, Glen Alan *lawyer*
Dalton, James Edgar, Jr. *health facility administrator*
†Duncan, John Lapsley *manufacturing company executive*
†Hearn, Billy Ray *recording industry executive*
Isom, Sam *engineer*
Ragsdale, Richard Elliot *hospital management executive*
Raskin, Edwin Berner *real estate executive*
†Spies, Robert J. *manufacturing executive, light*
Tucker, Tanya Denise *singer*
Zimmerman, Raymond *retail chain executive*

Bristol
Anderson, Jack Oland *retired college official*
Cauthen, Charles Edward, Jr. *business consultant, former retail executive*
Harkrader, Charles Johnston, Jr. *surgeon*
Riggs, Benjamin Clapp, Jr. *building products manufacturing company executive*
Stanislaw, Richard John *university program director*

Brownsville
Kalin, Robert *retired mathematics educator*

Carthage
Head, Henry Buchen *physician*

Chapel Hill
Christman, Luther Parmalee *university dean emeritus, consultant*

Chattanooga
Anderson, Lee Stratton *newspaper publisher, editor*
Ashley, Jim Ray *newspaper editor*
Bahner, Thomas Maxfield *lawyer*
Baker, Merl *engineering educator*
Bird, Suzanne Carhart *nurse, administrator*
Callahan, North *author, educator*
Charlton, Shirley Marie *instructional supervisor*
Cox, Ronald Baker *engineering and management consultant, university dean*
Cress, George Ayers *artist, educator*
Derthick, Alan Wendell *architect*
Duckworth, Jerrell James *electrical engineer*
Edgar, R(obert) Allan *federal judge*
Faires, Kurt Jeffrey *investor*
Falcon, Charles *consumer products company executive*
Feinberg, Edward Burton *ophthalmologist, educator*
Frierson, Daniel K. *textile company executive*
Fry, James C. *textile company executive*
Gore, Barry Maurice *electrical engineer*
Hall, Thor *religion educator*
Holmberg, Albert William, Jr. *publishing company executive*
Holmberg, Ruth Sulzberger *publishing company executive*
Jacobson, Katherine *nursing administrator*
Johnston, Hampton L. *photography corporation executive*
Kelley, Ralph Houston *judge*
Kiser, Thelma Kay *analytical chemist*
Kittlitz, Rudolf Gottlieb, Jr. *chemical engineer*
Knight, Ralph H. *consumer products company executive*
Long, Tom *insurance company executive*
MacManus, Yvonne Cristina *editor, videoscripter, writer, consultant*
Martin, Chester Y. *sculptor, painter*
McFarland, Jane Elizabeth *librarian*

Milburn, Herbert Theodore *federal judge*
Mills, Charles G. *photography company executive*
Mills, Olan, II *photography company executive*
Mohney, Ralph Wilson *minister*
Morton, Michael Rader *career and technology education director*
Neely, Paul *newspaper editor*
Obear, Frederick Woods *university chancellor*
Palmer, Stanton Dean *newspaper editor*
Pelletier, Charlotte M. *nurse administrator*
Porter, Dudley, Jr. *environmentalist, foundation executive, lawyer*
Powers, John Y. *federal judge*
Proctor, John Franklin *lawyer*
†Quinn, Patrick *tranportation executive*
Ragon, Robert Ronald *clergyman*
Saeger, Dixie Forester *dietitian*
St. Goar, Herbert *food corporation executive*
Scarbrough, Cleve Knox, Jr. *museum director*
Schuessler, Morgan McQueen *textile company executive*
Summitt, Robert Murray *circuit judge*
Thow, George Bruce *surgeon*
Tracy, Carol Cousins *mathematics educator*
Travis, W. Vance, Jr. *architect*
Tucker, Stanley R. *headmaster*
Walker, Winston Wakefield, Jr. *insurance company executive*
†Wheeler, Evelyn A. *communications specialist*
Witherspoon, John Knox, Jr. *investment banking executive*
Witt, Raymond Buckner, Jr. *lawyer*
Zodhiates, Spiros George *association executive*

Clarksville
Birdsong, William Herbert, Jr. *retired brigadier general*
Carlin, James Boyce *elementary education educator, consultant*
Lester, James Dudley *classicist, educator*
Smith, Gregory Dale *lawyer*

Cleveland
Albert, Leonard *religious organization executive*
Alford, Delton L. *religious organization executive*
Betancourt, Esdras *religious organization executive*
Chambers, O. Wayne *religious organization executive*
Crisp, Sam *church administrator*
Fisher, Richard Ashley *lawyer*
Fisher, Robert Elwood *minister, church official*
Gillum, Perry Eugene *college president, minister*
Goff, Nadine Farabee *elementary education educator*
Hughes, Ray Harrison *minister, church official*
Jackson, Joseph Essard *religious organization administrator*
Jones, E. L. *church admininistrator*
Lawson, Billie Katherine *elementary school educator*
Millsaps, Shelby J. *nurse, college administrator*
Moffett, B. J. *church administrator*
Murray, Billy Dwayne, Sr. *church administrator*
Nichols, John D. *church administrator*
O'Neal, Timothy D. *church administrator*
Pemberton, Donald T. *church administrator*
Rayburn, Billy J. *Church administrator*
Reyes, Jose Antonio, Sr. *minister*
Riley, Jerlena *church administrator*
Robinson, Julian B. *church administrator*
Sheeks, Bill F. *minister*
Stockburger, Harold Ellis, Jr. *state legislator, insurance agency executive*
Sustar, T. David *religious organization executive*
Taylor, William Al *church administrator*
Tomlinson, Milton Ambrose *clergyman*
Varlack, Adrian *church administrator*
Vaughan, Roland *church administrator*
Vest, R. Lamar *church administrator*
White, Robert *church administrator*

Clinton
Birdwell, James Edwin, Jr. *retired banker*

Collegedale
Bennett, Peggy Elizabeth *librarian, library director, educator*

Collierville
Cox, Terry Allen *telecommunications executive*
Shepard, Raymond Guy *purchasing executive*

Columbia
Chafin, William Vernon, Jr. *public housing manager*
Curry, Beatrice Chesrown *English educator*

Cookeville
Chowdhuri, Pritindra *electrical engineer, educator*
Coorts, Gerald Duane *horticulturist, educator, college dean*
Hearn, Edell Midgett *university dean, teacher educator*
Morton, Leland Clure *federal judge*
Peters, Ralph Martin *education educator*
Porter, Wilma Jean *university administrator*
Sissom, Leighton Esten *engineering educator, dean, consultant*
Volpe, Angelo Anthony *university administrator, chemistry educator*

Cordova
Baer, Ben Kayser *cotton merchant*
Bellantoni, Maureen Blanchfield *manufacturing executive*
Colbert, Robert B., Jr. *apparel company executive*
Cooke, Edward William *corporate executive, former naval officer*
Dean, Jimmy *meat processing company executive, entertainer*
Hunt, Gregory Lynn *writer, author*

Crossville
O'Brien, Charles H. *state supreme court chief justice*

Dandridge
Comer, Evan Philip *manufacturing company executive*

Dickson
Thomas, Janey Sue *elementary school principal*

Ducktown
Hopkins, David Lee *medical manufacturing executive*

Dyersburg
Bell, Helen Cherry *chemistry educator*

De Keyzer, Patrick Maurice *manufacturing company executive*
Nerren, George N. *school system administrator*
Taylor, Billy D. *principal*
Wiggins, Jerome Meyer *apparel textile industry financial executive*

Fayetteville
Dickey, John Harwell *public defender*

Franklin
Brophy, Jeremiah Joseph *financial company official, former army officer*
Bull, Sandy (Alexander Benjamin Bull) *musician, composer*
Guthrie, Glenda Evans *educational consultant*
O'More, Eloise Pitts *designer*

Gallatin
Brennan, Barbara Taylor *nurse administrator*
Ellis, Joseph Newlin *retired distribution company executive*
Ramer, Hal Reed *college president*

Gatlinburg
Pope, Randall Ray *retired national park superintendent*

Germantown
Ewing, William Hickman, Jr. *lawyer*
†Fischer, Paul A. *media marketing executive*
Shockley, Thomas Dewey *electrical engineering educator*

Goodlettsville
Wilkins, Rita Denise *researcher, multimedia design consultant*

Greenbrier
Newell, Paul Haynes, Jr. *engineering educator, former college president*

Greeneville
Austin, Tom Noell *retired tobacco company executive*
Hull, Thomas Gray *federal judge*
Smith, Myron John, Jr. *librarian, author*

Hendersonville
Allen, Duane David *singer*
Axton, Hoyt Wayne *singer, composer*
Bare, Robert Joseph (Bobby Bare) *country music singer, songwriter*
Cash, June Carter *singer*
Davis, Robert Norman *hospital administrator*
Hill, William Thomas *geological consultant*
Poynor, Robert Allen, Jr. *guidance counselor*
Sanders, Steve *singer*

Hermitage
Anderson, James William, III *performing artist, composer*
Chambers, Curtis Allen *clergyman, church communications executive*
Lockmiller, David Alexander *lawyer, educator*
†Willner, Robert Franklin *social health administrator*

Hixson
Sheehy, Thomas Daniel *apparel and textile manufacturing company executive*
Swafford, Cynthia Wolcott *nurse, educator*

Jacksboro
Goforth, E. Jack *security firm executive*

Jackson
Ewing, Frank Crockett *marketing entrepreneur, photographer*
Hazlewood, Judith Evans *librarian*
Lipshie, Joseph *apparel manufacturing company executive*
Maynard, Terrell Dennis *minister*
Moore, Dolores J. *nursing executive*
Moss, James Taylor *hospital administrator*
Todd, James Dale *federal judge*

Jefferson City
Bahner, Carl Tabb *retired chemistry educator, researcher*
Ball, Louis Oliver, Jr. *music educator*
Baumgardner, James Lewis *history educator*
Benson, Stanley Hugh *librarian*
Maddox, Jesse Cordell *academic administrator*
Muncy, Estle Pershing *physician*

Jellico
Hausman, Keith Lynn *hospital administrator, physical therapist*

Johnson City
Adebonojo, Festus O. *medical educator*
Alfonso, Robert John *university administrator*
Bayes, Paul Eugene *accounting educator*
Berk, Steven Lee *internist, educator*
†Conerly, Steve Garland *dairy foods company executive, economist*
Coogan, Philip Shields *pathologist*
Dyer, Allen Ralph *psychiatrist*
Edens, Myra Jim *health facility nursing administrator*
Greninger, Edwin Thomas *history educator*
Huang, Thomas Tao-shing *chemistry educator*
Paxton, J. Willene *retired university administrator*
Rasch, Ellen Myrberg *cell biology educator*
†Renzaglia, Karen Sue *botany educator*
Rider, John Allen, II *business educator, paralegal*
Roark, Edith Humphreys *private school language arts educator, reading specialist*
Schneider, Valerie Lois *speech educator*
Shaw, Angus Robertson, III *minister*
Skalko, Richard Gallant *anatomist, educator*
Stokes, Thomas Edward *librarian*
Votaw, Charles Lesley *academic dean*
Wyatt, Doris Fay Chapman *English language educator*
Yavas, Ugur *marketing educator*
Zayas-Bazan, Eduardo *foreign language educator*

Jonesborough
Weaver, Kenneth *gynecologist, researcher*

Kingsport
Coover, Harry Wesley *manufacturing company executive*
Deavenport, Earnest W., Jr. *chemical executive*
Findley, Don Aaron *manufacturing company executive*
Giggey, James Walker *chemical company executive*
Head, William Iverson, Sr. *retired chemical company executive*
Holmes, Jerry Dell *organic chemist*
Hubbard, Randall Dee *manufacturing company executive*
Kiss, Mary Catherine Clement *writer*
McKinley, John Henry *sales executive*
†Rice, Thomas James, III *health care executive, hospital administrator*
Scarff, Edward L. *diversified company executive*
Scott, H(erbert) Andrew *retired chemical engineer*
Siirola, Jeffrey John *chemical engineer*
Wolfe, Margaret Ripley *historian, educator, consultant*
Young, Howard Seth *chemist, researcher*

Kingston
Manly, William Donald *metallurgist*

Knoxville
Acker, Joseph Edington *retired cardiology educator*
Alexeff, Igor *physicist, electrical engineer, educator*
Ambrester, Marcus LaRoy *communication educator, program administrator*
Anderson, Edward Riley *state supreme court justice*
Armistead, Willis William *university administrator, veterinarian*
Arnett, Foster Deaver *lawyer*
Ashe, Victor Henderson *mayor*
Bailey, John Milton *electrical engineering educator*
†Baldonado, Orlino Castro *engineering and technical services company executive*
Bateman, Veda Mae *industrial psychologist, management consultant*
Beasley, Modena James *nursing executive*
Bell, Corinne Reed *psychologist*
Bell, H. Jenkins *clergyman, bishop*
Blake, Gerald Rutherford *banker*
Blass, William Errol *physics and astronomy educator*
Boling, Edward Joseph *university president emeritus, educator*
Bose, Bimal Kumar *electrical engineering educator*
Brady, Patrick Stephen *French literature educator*
Bressler, Marcus N. *consulting engineer*
Brockett, Ralph Grover *adult education educator*
Brott, Walter Howard *cardiac surgeon, educator, retired army officer*
Burkhart, John Henry *physician*
Christenbury, Edward Samuel *lawyer*
Cole, William Edward *economics educator, consultant*
Conger, Bob Vernon *plant and soil science educator*
Coulson, Patricia Bunker *endocrinologist*
Crowell, Craven H., Jr. *federal agency administrator*
Cutler, Everette Wayne *history educator*
Danko, Joseph Christopher *metals engineer, university official*
Dean, Charles Henry, Jr. *retired government official*
Dean, John Aurie *chemist, author, chemistry educator emeritus*
Dillard, W. Thomas *lawyer*
Donahue, Joan Elizabeth *elementary school educator*
Eisenberg, Lee B. *communications executive*
Faires, Ross N. *manufacturing company executive*
Filston, Howard Church *pediatric surgeon, educator*
Fisher, John Hurt *English language educator*
Fox, John David *educator, physicist*
Froula, James DeWayne *national honor society director, engineer*
Gonzalez, Rafael Ceferino *electrical engineering educator*
Green, Eleanor Myers *veterinarian, educator*
Griffiths, José-Marie *information science educator*
Hagood, Lewis Russell *lawyer*
Hall, O. Glen *university dean*
Hammond, Edwin Hughes *geography educator*
Harris, Charles Edgar *retired wholesale distribution company executive*
Harris, Diana Koffman *sociologist, educator*
†Harris, William Franklin, III *biologist, environmental science director and educator*
Haslam, James A., II *petroleum sales executive*
Haslam, James A., III *petroleum sales executive*
Herndon, Anne Harkness *sales executive*
Hohenberg, John *journalist, educator*
Holton, Raymond William *botanist, educator*
Howard, Lewis Spilman *lawyer*
Hughes, Karen Woodbury *botany educator, academic administrator*
Hung, James Chen *engineer, educator, consultant*
Ince, Richard W. *energy company executive*
Jacobs, Kenneth A. *composer, educator*
Jarvis, James Howard, II *federal judge*
Jenkins, Roger Lane *retail executive*
Jordan, (William) Hamilton (McWhorter) *corporate and international communications consultant*
Jordan, Robert Leon *federal judge*
Kirk, Robert H. *health and safety educator*
Kitts, Elbert Walker *minister*
Kliefoth, A(rthur) Bernhard, III *neurosurgeon*
Lange, Robert Dale *internist, educator, medical researcher*
LeVert, Francis Edward *nuclear engineer*
Lietzke, Milton Henry *chemistry educator*
Lucas, John Allen *lawyer*
Mahan, Gerald Dennis *physics educator, researcher*
Malec, William Frank *utilities company executive*
Maloney, John Alexander *retired hospital administrator*
Mamantov, Gleb *chemistry educator, consultant*
Mankel, Francis Xavier *priest*
Martin, James Robert *plastics company executive*
Maxson, Linda Ellen *biologist, educator*
Mayfield, T. Brient, IV *media and computer executive*
Mc Carty, Bruce *architect*
Mc Dow, John Jett *agricultural engineering educator*
Mc Hargue, Carl Jack *research laboratory administator*
Moser, Harold Dean *historian*
Murrian, Robert Phillip *federal judge, educator*
Nanney, Sondra Tucker *dance school executive, small business owner*
Natelson, Stephen Ellis *neurosurgeon*
Nielsen, Alvin Herborg *university dean, physicist*
O'Connell, Anthony J. *bishop*
Olmstead, Francis Henry, Jr. *plastics industry executive*
Painter, Linda Robinson *physics educator, dean*
Phillips, Jerry Juan *law educator*
Phillips, Thomas Wade *lawyer*
Prados, John William *educational administrator*
Rayson, Edwin Hope *lawyer*
Reynolds, Glenn Harlan *law educator*
Richards, Stephen Harold *engineering educator*
Richardson, Don Orland *agricultural educator*
Roth, J(ohn) Reece *electrical engineer, educator, researcher, consultant*
Roth, Stephen Evans *lawyer*
Rukeyser, William Simon *journalist, business executive*
Sanders, William Evan *bishop*
Schmidt, Benno Charles, Jr. *lawyer, educator*
Schuler, Theodore Anthony *civil engineer, city official*
Schweitzer, George Keene *chemistry educator*
Sharp, Aaron John *botanist, educator*
Sherman, Gordon Rae *computer science educator*
Simpkins, Anne Eddleman *interior designer*
Singletary, Michael Willis *journalism, educator*
Solomon, Alan *physician, medical oncologist and clinical investigator*
Soni, Kusum Kapila *mathematics educator*
Stegmayer, Joseph Henry *housing industry executive*
Stoneking, Jerry Edward *dean*
Stringfield, Hezz, Jr. *contractor, financial consultant*
Sublett, Carl Cecil *artist*
Swann, Bill *judge*
Swingle, Homer Dale *horticulturist, educator*
Teeter, Dwight Leland, Jr. *journalism educator*
Trahern, Joseph Baxter, Jr. *humanities educator*
Trevor, Kirk David Niell *orchestra conductor, cellist*
Tschantz, Bruce Allen *civil engineer, educator*
Uhrig, Robert Eugene *nuclear engineer, educator*
Vance, Stanley Charles *management educator*
Vinson, William C. *architectural firm executive*
Vogel, Howard H. *lawyer*
Walsh, Joanne Elizabeth *art educator, librarian*
Waters, John B. *lawyer*
Watson, Patricia L. *library director*
Wheeler, John Watson *lawyer*
White, David Cleaveland *microbial ecologist, environmental toxicologist*
Williams, Thomas Ffrancon *chemist, educator*
Williamson, Handy, Jr. *agricultural economist, educator*
Wilson, John Grover *securities trader*
Wisniewski, Richard *dean*
Wunderlich, Bernhard *physical chemistry educator*
Wust, Carl John *microbiology and medical biology educator*
Yates, Robert Lynn *utilities executive*

La Follette
Eads, Ora Wilbert *clergyman, church official*
McDonald, Miller Baird *management consultant, columnist, historian*

La Vergne
Findley, Charles H. *manufacturing company executive*
Forrest, Henry J. *manufacturing company executive*
Mason, Steven Jude *wholesale company executive*
Pfeffer, Philip Maurice *distribution company executive*
†Taylor, John L. *communications executive*
†Walker, Phillip R. *agricultural products supplier*

Lawrenceburg
Mauricio, Lilia D(ujua) *pathologist*

Lebanon
Daniels, Charlie *musician, songwriter*
Hubbard, Julia Faye *accountant*

Lenoir City
Breazeale, Mack Alfred *physics educator*
Gerwels, Laurenn Barker *public relations executive*

Lookout Mountain
Hardy, Thomas Cresson *insurance company executive*
Leitner, Paul R. *lawyer*
Rymer, S. Bradford, Jr. *retired appliance manufacturing company executive*
Wyeth, Andrew *artist*
Wyeth, James Browning *artist*

Loudon
Jones, Robert Gean *religion educator*

Louisville
Wheeler, George William *university provost, physicist, educator*
Williams, Timothy Wayne *finance company executive*

Luttrell
Milligan, Mancil Wood *mechanical and aerospace engineering educator*

Madison
Brannon, Rachel Ann *nurse administrator*
Kennedy, Matthew Washington *pianist, educator*
Wells, Kitty (Muriel Deason Wright) *country western singer*

Martin
Smith, Robert Mason *university dean*

Maryville
Ackerman, Ora Ray *health facility administrator*
Bradford, Tutt Sloan *retired publisher*
Brigance, Albert Henry *educational writer*
Hall, Marion Trufant *botany educator, arboretum director*
Inscho, Barbara Pickel *mathematics educator*
Koella, Carl Ohm, Jr. *lawyer, state senator*
Oakes, Lester Cornelius *retired electrical engineer, consultant*
Stone, Hubert Dean *editor, journalist*
Van Metre, Margaret Cheryl *artistic director*
Worley, Joan Hiett *library director*

Mc Minnville
Martin, Ron *adult basic education coordinator, superintendent of schools, consultant, minister*

Memphis
Abston, Dunbar, Jr. *management executive*
Adamson, John *church administrator*
Allen, James Henry *magistrate judge*
Allen, Newton Perkins *lawyer*

Allison, Beverly Gray seminary president, evangelism educator
Andrews, William Eugene construction and services company executive
Apple, John Boyd elevator company executive
Armstrong, Walter Preston, Jr. lawyer
Babin, Richard Weyro surgeon, educator
Bailey, Charles college administrator
Ballou, Howard Burgess commercial plumbing designer
Bardos, Denes Istvan research scientist, medical company executive
Battle, Allen Overton, Jr. psychologist, educator
Berry, Robert Vaughan electrical, electronic manufacturing company executive
Black, Kay Freeman public affairs administrator
Blakley, Raymond Leonard pharmacologist
Booth, Robert Lee, Jr. banker
Broadhurst, Jerome Anthony lawyer
Brode, Marvin Jay lawyer, former state legislator
†Brooks, Kathleen journalist
Brooks, P. A., II bishop
Brown, Aaron Clifton, Jr. magistrate judge
Brown, Bailey federal judge
Bruce, Marvin Ernest automotive products executive
Buchignani, Leo Joseph lawyer
Buckman, Robert Henry chemical company executive
Burch, Lucius Edward, Jr. lawyer
Burgess, Melvin protective services official
Butts, Herbert Clell dentist, educator
Caffey, Rick broadcast executive
Cannon, Robert Emmet consumer products manufacturing company executive
†Carmean, E. A., Jr. art museum director, art historian
Carroll, Billy Price artist
Carter, Michael Allen college dean, nursing educator
Carter, Sarah Anne internist, educator
Chesney, Russell Wallace pediatrician
Christopher, Robert Paul physician
Chung, King-Thom microbiologist, educator
Clark, Ross Bert, II lawyer
Clarkson, Andrew MacBeth retail executive
Cody, Walter James Michael lawyer, former state official
†Connolly, Matthew B., Jr. conservationist
†Cooper, Irby real estate development company executive
Copper, John Franklin Asian studies educator, consultant
Cox, Clair Edward, II urologist, medical educator
Cox, Larry D. airport terminal executive
Crane, Laura Jane research chemist
Crist, William Miles physician
Crump, Metcalf architect
Cunningham, Ronald M. religious education director
Daniel, Coldwell, III economist, educator
De Mere-Dwyer, Leona medical artist
Depperschmidt, Thomas Orlando economist, educator
Desiderio, Dominic Morse, Jr. chemistry and neurochemistry educator
Dickson, Alex Dockery bishop
Diggs, Walter Whitley health science facilty administrator
Donald, Bernice B. judge
Drescher, Judith Altman library director
Driscoll, James Joseph, Jr. advertising executive
Dunathan, Harmon Craig college dean
Dunavant, William Buchanan, Jr. small business owner
Dunnigan, T. Kevin electrical and electronics manufacturing company executive
Echols, James agricultural products supplier
Emery, Sue bulletin editor, owner bridge studio
Evans, James Mignon architect
Fain, John Nicholas biochemistry educator
Fondren, William Merle, Jr. hardware distribution company executive
Foote, Shelby author
Forell, David Charles financial executive
Formanek, Peter Raemin automobile parts company executive
Franklin, Stanley Phillip computer scientist, mathematician, cognitive scientist, educator
Freeman, Bob A. microbiology educator
Friedman, Robert Michael lawyer
Gates, Carolyn Helm government official
Gerald, Barry radiology educator, neuroradiologist
†Gettelfinger, Thomas Clement ophthalmologist
Gibbons, Julia Smith federal judge
Gilman, Ronald Lee lawyer
Gourley, Dick R. college dean
Granger, David Mason broadcasting and communications executive
Greenberg, Susan Lynn lawyer
Greiner, Morris Esty, Jr. broadcast executive
Griffin, Tom former editor, writer
Haizlip, Henry Hardin, Jr. real estate consultant, former banker
Hamilton, W. W. church administrator
Harpster, James Erving lawyer
Harrover, Roy Perkins architect
Harvey, Albert C. lawyer
Heimberg, Murray pharmacologist, biochemist, physician, educator
Hendren, Gary E. retail executive
Herenton, Willie W. mayor
Hodges, Velma Quinn mathematics educator
Hooks, Benjamin Lawson civil rights advocate, brokerage house executive
Horn, Ralph bank executive
Horton, Odell federal judge
Howe, Martha Morgan microbiologist, educator
Howell, Stephen Wayne church organization administrator, clergyman
Hughes, Walter Thompson physician, pediatrics educator
Hunt, James Calvin academic administrator, physician
Hyde, Joseph R., III retail auto parts executive
Ingram, Alvin John surgeon
Jenkins, Ruben Lee chemical company executive
Johnson, Harry A., III lawyer
Johnson, James Gibb physician
Johnson, Johnny research psychologist, consultant
Johnston, Archibald Currie geophysics educator, research director
Jolly, William Thomas foreign language educator
Jones, Andrewnetta county government official
Jones, Walk Claridge, III architect
Kelley, Robert C. construction industry executive
Kellogg, Frederic Hartwell civil engineer, educator
Knight, H. Stuart law enforcement official, consultant
Langford, Walter Martin retired greeting card and gift wrap manufacturing executive
Langton, Bryan D. hotel executive
Lasslo, Andrew medicinal chemist, educator
Ledsinger, Charles Albert, Jr. hotel, gaming executive
Lewin, Ann White museum director, educator
Lieberman, Phillip Louis allergist, educator
Looney, J. Carson architectural firm executive
Macklin, F. Douglas bishop
†Magrill, Joe Richard, Jr. religious organization administrator, minister
Manire, James McDonnell lawyer
Mauer, Alvin Marx physician, medical educator
McCalla, Jon P. federal judge
McCommon, Hubert benefits, training and development administrator
McEachran, Angus newspaper editor
McMinn, William A. chemicals company executive
McPherson, Larry E(ugene) photographer, educator
McRae, Robert Malcolm, Jr. federal judge
Mealor, William Theodore, Jr. geography educator, university administrator, consultant
Mendel, Maurice audiologist, educator
Merrill, J. Mark financial management executive
Miller, Neil Austin biology educator
Moore, Jackson Watts corporate executive
Mulholland, Kenneth Leo, Jr. health care facility administrator
Neely, Charles Lea, Jr. retired physician
Nesin, Jeffrey D. academic administrator
†Nienhuis, Arthur Wesley physician, researcher
Noble, Douglas Ross museum administrator
Noel, Randall Deane lawyer
Nolly, Robert J. hospital administrator, pharmaceutical science educator
Norville, Craig Hubert lawyer
O'Donnell, William Hugh English educator
Pate, James Wynford surgeon
Perry, Floyde E., Jr. bishop
Peternell, Ben Clayton hospitality company executive
Piazza, Marguerite opera singer, actress, entertainer
Pierotti, John William prosecutor
Porter, W. L. bishop
Pourciau, Lester John librarian
Powell, Joseph Herbert hospital administrator
Presley, Priscilla actress
Ramirez, Michael P. editorial cartoonist
Ramsey, Marjorie Elizabeth early childhood education educator
Ranta, Richard Robert university dean
Rawlins, Benjamin W., Jr. bank holding company executive
Reeves, Sam T. agricultural products company executive
Reynolds, Stephen Curtis hospital administrator
Rich, Charles Allan singer
Riss, Murray photographer, educator
Roberts, C. Frank broadcast executive
†Rohrbach, N. J. paper company executive
†Rose, Michael David hotel corporation executive
Runyan, John William, Jr. medical educator
Russell, James Franklin lawyer
Ryan, Kevin William research virologist, educator
Satre, Philip Glen corporate executive, lawyer
Schelp, Richard Herbert mathematics educator
Shanklin, Douglas Radford physician
†Sharpe, Robert F., Sr. writer, lecturer, educator, consultant, publisher
Shorb, Gary Seymour hospital administrator
Shugart, Cecil Glenn physics educator
†Smith, Donald N. Restaurant chain executive
Smith, Frederick Wallace transportation company executive
Smith, Whitney Bousman music and drama critic
Solomon, Solomon Sidney endocrinologist, pharmacologist, scientist
Springfield, James Francis retired lawyer, banker
Stagg, Louis Charles English language and literature educator
†Starnes, Michael S. trucking executive
†Steib, James Terry bishop
Stokes, Henry Arthur journalist
Streibich, Harold Cecil lawyer
Sullivan, Eugene Joseph food service company executive
Sullivan, Jay Michael medical educator
Summer, Harry Harmon marketing educator and consultant
Summitt, Robert Layman pediatrician, educator
Tate, Stonewall Shepherd lawyer
Terry, Ronald Anderson bank holding company executive
Thomas, Nathaniel Charles clergyman
Tibbs, Martha Jane Pullen civic worker
Todd, Virgil Holcomb clergyman, religion educator
Tucker, Jack Randolph, Jr. architectural firm executive
Turner, Jerome federal judge
Waddell, Alfred Moore, Jr. investment company executive
†Wade, Edgar L. church administrator
†Walker, Deloss advertising agency executive
†Waller, Burton Woodrow, Jr. health care executive
Wallis, Carlton Lamar librarian
Ward, Jeannette Poole psychologist, educator
†Wein, Bernard J. retail executive
†Weller, Joseph C. brokerage house executive
Wellford, Harry Walker federal judge
Werkhoven, Kathryn Regina nursing administrator
Wheeler, Orville Eugene university dean, civil and mechanical engineering educator
Whitesell, Dale Edward retired association executive, natural resources consultant
Wilcox, Harry Hammond retired medical educator
Wildman, Gary Cecil chemist
Williams, David Russell music educator
Williams, Edward F(oster), III environmental engineer
Williams, Joseph R. newspaper publishing executive
†Wilson, Charles Glen zoo administrator
Wise, George Urban botanic garden administrator, horticulturist, entomologist
Yeates, Zeno Lanier retired architect

Monteagle
Lytle, Andrew Nelson author, editor

Morristown
Cordover, Ronald Harvey business executive, venture capitalist
Johnson, Evelyn Bryan flying service executive

Mount Juliet
Kerr, Charles Randall consultant, former florist
LeDoux, Chris Lee country musician
Sweetman, Brian Jack organic, analytical chemist, educator

Mountain Home
†Fitts, Jonathan Fairfield medical center administrator
Hamdy, Ronald Charles geriatrician

Murfreesboro
Adams, W. Andrew health care executive
Aden, Robert Clark retired computer information systems educator
Berry, Mary Tom education educator
Bookner, Becci Jane school system administrator
Craig, James Donald dean
Ford, William F. banker
Hayes, Janice Cecile education educator
Huhta, James Kenneth historian, university administrator, educator, consultant
Walker, David Ellis, Jr. dean, educator, minister, consultant
Westwick, Carmen Rose nursing educator, consultant
Wyatt, Robert Odell journalism educator
Youree, Beverly B. library science educator

Nashville
Abstein, William Robert, II minister
Adkins, Cecelia N. church administrator
Alexander, Andrew Lamar (Lamar Alexander) lawyer, former secretary of education, former governor
Allbritton, Cliff publisher
Allred, Michael Sylvester lawyer
Anderson, Lynn (Rene Anderson) singer
Arnett, James William restaurant executive
Atkins, Chester Burton record company executive, guitarist, publisher
Aubrey, Roger Frederick psychology and education educator
Banks, John Houston mathematics educator
Bass, James Orin lawyer
Battle, William Robert (Bob Battle) newspaper executive
Bausman, Dennis Charles construction company executive
†Bayuzick, Robert J. material scientist, educator
Beck, Robert Beryl real estate executive
Belton, Robert law educator
Bender, Harvey W., Jr. cardiac and thoracic surgeon
Benson, Edwin Welburn, Jr. trade association executive
Bernard, Louis Joseph surgeon, educator
Berry, William Wells lawyer
Binkley, Yildiz Barlas library director
Black, Clint country singer, musician
†Blair, Joyce Allsmiller computer science educator
Bloch, Frank Samuel law educator
Blumstein, James Franklin legal educator, lawyer, consultant
Bogguss, Suzy country music singer, songwriter
Bolian, George Clement health care executive, physician
Bolinger, John C., Jr. management consultant
†Bond, Sherry Louise trade association administrator
Bonsall, Joseph Sloan, Jr. singer
Boorman, Howard Lyon history educator
Bostick, Charles Dent lawyer, educator
Bottorff, Dennis C. banker
†Bovender, Jack Oliver, Jr. health care executive
Bowen, James record company executive
Boyd, Theophilus Bartholomew, III publishing company executive
Boyer, James Floyd land surveyor, state legislator
Bradford, James C., Jr. brokerage house executive
Bragg, John Thomas state legislator, retired businessman
Brau, Charles Allen physics educator
Bredesen, Philip Norman mayor
Brodersen, Arthur James electrical engineer
Brooks, Garth (Troyal Garth Brooks) country music singer
Brooks, Kix musician
Brown, Joe Blackburn lawyer
Brown, Tommie Florence social work educator
†Brown, Tony Ersic record company executive
Brush, Clinton E., III retired architect
†Bryson, James Edward marketing professional
Buckles, Stephen Gary economist, educator
Burgess, Roger retired church official
Burnett, Lonnie Sheldon obstetrics and gynecology educator
Burson, Charles W. state attorney general
Burt, Alvin Miller, III anatomist, cell biologist, educator, writer
Buttrick, David Gardner religion educator
Byrd, Benjamin Franklin, Jr. surgeon, educator
Cadzow, James Archie engineering educator, researcher
Campbell, Gilbert R., Jr. lawyer
Cantrell, Luther E., Jr. lawyer
Carter, James McCord television producer, personality
Cawthon, William Connell operations management consultant
Chambers, James Richard banker
Chapman, John Edmon university dean, pharmacologist, physician
†Chapman, Morris Hines denominational executive
Charney, Jonathan Isa legal educator, lawyer
Chaudhuri, Dilip Kumar engineering educator
Cheek, James Howe, III lawyer
Chytil, Frank biochemist
Clark, James Hamel public relations executive, author
Clark, Roy singer, musician, recording industry executive
†Clarke, James Harold environmental scientist, educator
Clay, John W., Jr. bank executive
Clinton, Barbara Marie university health services director, social worker
Clouse, Robert Wilburn communication executive, educator
Cohen, Stanley biochemistry educator
†Collier, Simon history educator
Compton, John Joseph philosophy educator
Conkin, Paul Keith history educator
Connery, W. Hudson health facility administrator
Cook, Ann Jennalie English language educator
Cook, Charles Wilkerson, Jr. former banker, county official
Cook, George Edward electrical engineering educator, consultant
Cordaro, Matthew Charles utility executive, energy developer, engineer
Covington, Robert Newman lawyer, educator
Crabtree, Bruce Isbester, Jr. architect
Crants, R., Jr. entrepreneur
†Creasy, Charles L. creative director
Crispin, John foreign language educator
Cristina, Francis McDermott (Frank Cristina) corporate security company executive
Crofford, Oscar Bledsoe, Jr. internist, medical educator
Crooke, Philip Schuyler mathematics educator
Crowe, Dewey E., II (Rusty Crowe) state senator
Crowell, Rodney J. country music recording artist, songwriter
Culbertson, Katheryn Campbell lawyer
Cunningham, Leon William biochemist, educator
Cyrus, Billy Ray country music performer
Daane, James Dewey banker
D'Agostino, James Samuel, Jr. financial executive
Damon, William Winchell economics educator
Darnell, Riley Carlisle state government executive, lawyer
Daughtrey, Martha Craig federal judge
Davis, Danny (George Joseph Nowlan) musician
Davis, James Verlin insurance brokerage executive
Day, Mary Dean federal agency administrator
Dean, Billy (William Howard Dean) country singer, songwriter
Dedman, Bertram Cottingham retired insurance company executive
Dettbarn, Wolf-Dietrich neurochemist, pharmacologist, educator
Diffie, Joe country singer, songwriter
DiLorenzo, Joseph L. health care company executive
†Don, James K. health care company executive
Doody, Margaret Anne English educator
Doyle, Don Harrison history educator
†Dozier, Norman Buck, Jr. fire chief
Draper, James Thomas (Jimmy Draper) clergyman
Driscoll, Joseph Francis real estate executive
†Du Bois, Tim recording industry executive
Duer, Shirley Powell state legislator
Dunn, Ronnie musician
Dye, Hank public relations executive
Dykes, Archie Reece financial services executive
Echols, Robert L. federal judge
Eckenfelder, William Wesley, Jr. environmental engineer
Ellis, Weldon Thompson, Jr. management specialist, consultant, author
Ely, James Wallace, Jr. legal educator
Emans, Robert LeRoy academic administrator, education educator
Faust, A. Donovan communications executive
Feaster, Robert K. publishing company executive
Fels, Rendigs economist, educator
Fender, Freddy (Baldemar Huerta) singer
Finegan, Thomas Aldrich economist
Fischer, Patrick Carl computer scientist, educator
Fish, Donald Winston lawyer, health care company executive
Fitzgerald, Edmund Bacon electronics industry executive
Flanagan, Van Kent journalist
Fleming, Samuel M. banker
Fondaw, Elizabeth Louise vocational school educator
Ford, Jesse Hill author
Forlines, Franklin Leroy minister, educator
Forstman, Henry Jackson theology educator, university dean
Fort, Tomlinson chemist, chemical engineering educator
Fowinkle, Eugene W. physician, medical center administrator
Fowler, William Roy, Jr. anthropologist, educator
Frazier, Keith David lawyer
Frey, Herman S. publishing company executive
Frist, Thomas Fearn, Jr. hospital management company executive
Fry, Malcolm Craig clergyman
Gaultney, John Orton life insurance agent, consultant
Gavish, Bezalel computer science operations research, information systems educator
Gayle, Crystal singer
Geisel, Martin Simon college dean, educator
Gentry, Teddy country musician
Getz, Malcolm library administrator, economist, educator
Gibbs, Jack Porter sociologist, educator
Gillmor, John Edward lawyer
Girgus, Sam B. English literature educator
Gleaves, Edwin Sheffield librarian
Glenn, Wayne Eugene labor union official
Gobbell, Ronald Vance architect
Gove, Walter R. sociology educator
Graham, George J., Jr. political scientist, educator
Graham, Hugh Davis history educator
Granner, Daryl Kitley physiology and medicine educator
Grantham, Dewey Wesley historian, educator
Greenwood, Lee Melvin singer
Guengerich, Frederick Peter biochemistry educator, toxicologist, researcher
Gulmi, James Singleton apparel manufacturing company executive
Guthrie, James Williams education educator
Guy, Sharon Kaye state agency executive
Hahn, George Thomas materials engineering educator, researcher
Hall, Donald J. law educator
Hall, Douglas Scott astronomy educator
Hall, Hugh David dentist, physician, educator
Halperin, John William English literature educator
Hamilton, Joseph Hants, Jr. physicist, educater
Hamilton, Russell George, Jr. academic dean, Spanish and Portuguese language educator
Hamm, Richard L. church administrator
Hampton, Ralph Clayton, Jr. pastoral studies educator, clergyman
Hancock, M(arion) Donald political science educator
Hanselman, Richard Wilson entrepreneur
Hardin, Hal D. lawyer, former U.S. attorney, former judge
Hardman, Joel Griffeth pharmacologist
Harrawood, Paul civil engineering educator
Harris, Alice Carmichael linguist
Harris, Emmylou singer
Harris, J(acob) George health care company executive
Harris, Stacy print and broadcast journalist
Harris, Thomas Munson chemistry educator, researcher
Harrison, Clifford Joy, Jr. banker
Harrod, Howard Lee religion educator
Hart, Richard Banner lawyer
Hartford, John Cowan singer, songwriter
Harwell, Aubrey Biggs lawyer
Hassel, Rudolph Christopher English language educator
Hazelip, Herbert Harold academic administrator
Hazlehurst, Franklin Hamilton fine arts educator
†Head, Michael B. electronics company executive

Heard, (George) Alexander *retired educator and chancellor*
Hefner, James A. *academic administrator*
Heiser, Arnold Melvin *astronomer*
Henderson, Milton Arnold *association executive*
†Henry, James B. *church officer*
Henry, Taylor Hill, Jr. *restaurant executive*
Hercules, David Michael *chemistry educator, consultant*
Hieronymus, Clara Booth Wiggins *journalist*
Higgins, Thomas A. *federal judge*
Hobbs, Betty Goad *credit union executive*
Hohlfeld, Pauline *pharmaceutical executive*
Holladay, Wendell Gene *physics educator*
Holsen, Robert Charles *accountant*
†Hood, Howard Allison *law librarian*
†Hook, William John *library administrator*
House, Robert William *technology management educator*
Hummell, Burton Howard *food distribution company executive*
Inagami, Tadashi *biochemist, educator*
Ingram, E. Bronson *oil production equipment industries executive*
Ireson, Roger William *religious organization administrator, minister, educator*
Ivey, William James *foundation executive, writer, producer*
Jackson, Alan *country songwriter, singer*
Jarman, Mark Foster *poet*
Jemison, Theodore Judson *religious organization administrator*
Johnson, Hollis Eugene, III *foundation executive*
Jones, Kathryn Cherie *pastor*
Jonsson, Bjarni *mathematician, educator*
Jordan, Wrenza Lou *chamber of commerce executive*
Kaas, Jon H. *psychology educator*
Kaizaki, Yoichiro *automotive executive*
Kaludis, George *management consultant, book company executive, educator*
Kidd, Florence *principal*
Kisber, Matthew Harris *state legislator*
†Kmiec, Edward Urban *bishop*
Kono, Tetsuro *biochemist, physiologist, educator*
Krantz, Sanford Burton *physician*
Kuhn, Paul Hubert, Jr. *investment counsel*
Lachs, John *philosopher, educator*
Laczko, Brian John *theater director*
Land, Richard Dale *minister, religious organization administrator*
Langevoort, Donald Carl *law educator*
Langstaff, George Quigley, Jr. *retired footwear company executive*
Lawrence, Thomas Patterson *public relations executive*
Lazenby, Fred Wiehl *insurance company executive*
Ledyard, Robins Heard *lawyer*
Lee, Brenda (Brenda Mae Tarpley) *singer, entertainer*
Lee, Douglas A. *music educator*
Lerner, Laurence David *writer, educator*
Levinson, L(eslie) Harold *lawyer, educator*
†Loveall, Clellon Lewis *transportation administrator, civil engineer*
Lukehart, Charles Martin *chemistry educator*
Lynch, John Brown *plastic surgeon, educator*
Lyon, Philip K(irkland) *lawyer*
MacNaughton, Donald Sinclair *health care company executive*
Madden, Paul Herman *education educator*
Mahanes, David James, Jr. *retired distillery executive*
Maier, Harold Geistweit *legal educator, lawyer*
Maihafer, Harry James *retired banker, former army officer*
Mandrell, Barbara Ann *singer, entertainer*
Manning, David Lee *health care executive*
Manning, Deborah A. *physician, health facility administrator*
Martin, Charles Neil, Jr. *health care management company executive*
Martin, Henry Alan *lawyer*
Martin, James Cullen *chemistry educator*
Masters, John Christopher *psychologist, educator, writer*
Mattea, Kathy *vocalist, songwriter*
May, Joseph Leserman (Jack) *lawyer*
Mayhew, Aubrey *music business executive*
McClanahan, Larry Duncan *civil engineer, consultant*
McCoy, Thomas Raymond *lawyer, educator*
Mc Creary, James Franklin *banker, lawyer*
McMasters, Paul Kenneth *foundation executive*
McMurry, Idanelle Sam *educational consultant*
McWhorter, Ralph Clayton *health care company executive*
Meacham, William Feland *neurological surgeon, educator*
Merrills, Roy *telecommunications industry executive*
Merritt, Gilbert Stroud *federal judge*
†Miller, Calvin Francis *geology educator*
Miller, Richard L. *architectural executive*
Mills, Jon K. *psychologist, educator*
Mills, Liston Oury *theology educator*
†Moeller, Jerry G. *health care facility executive*
Monroe, William Smith *mandolin player, singer*
Moore, William Grover, Jr. *management consultant, former air freight executive, former air force officer*
Morgan, Lorrie (Loretta Lynn Morgan) *country singer*
Mosig, Gisela *molecular biology educator*
Nelson, Edward Gage *merchant banking investment company executive*
Nixon, John Trice *federal judge*
†Nunnelly, Walter Sandels, III *corporate executive*
†O'Day, Denis Michael *ophthalmologist, educator*
†O'Neill, James Anthony, Jr. *pediatric surgeon, educator*
Ono, Masatoshi *tire manufacturing executive*
Orgebin-Crist, Marie-Claire *biology educator*
Orth, David Nelson *physician, educator*
Osborne, Charles William *transportation executive*
Oslin, K. T. (Kay Toinette Oslin) *country singer*
Ossoff, Robert Henry *otolaryngological surgeon*
†Overton, Stanley Dixon *banking executive*
Page, Terry Lee *biology educator*
Panvini, Robert S. *physics educator*
Pareigis, Joyce Ann *nursing administrator*
Parker, Frank Leon *environmental engineering educator, consultant*
Partain, Clarence Leon *radiologist, nuclear medicine physician, educator, administrator*
Paschall, Douglas Duane *headmaster*
Pearl, Minnie (Sarah Ophelia Colley Cannon) *entertainer*
Peebles, James W. *publishing executive*
Pellegrino, James William *college dean, psychology educator*
Pendergrass, Henry Pancoast *physician, radiology educator*
Perry, Lewis Curtis *historian, educator*
Person, Curtis S., Jr. *lawyer, state senator*
Pichois, Claude P. *classical studies educator*
Picirilli, Robert Eugene *clergyman, college dean, writer*
Pickens, David Richard, Jr. *retired surgeon, educator*
Pincus, Theodore *microbiologist, educator*
Polley, Dale Whitcomb *bank executive*
Potter, John Leith *mechanical and aerospace engineer, educator, consultant*
†Powers, Joe L. *publishing executive*
Prine, John *singer, songwriter*
Pruett, Jeanne *singer, songwriter*
Purcell, William Paxson, III *state representative*
Rabbitt, Edward Thomas *singer, songwriter*
Rayburn, Ted Rye *newspaper editor*
Reichman, Jerome H. *law educator*
Reid, Lyle *judge*
Richards, James E. *pharmaceutical executive*
Richmond, Samuel Bernard *management educator*
Ridley, Carolyn Fludd *social studies educator*
†Riggins-Ezzell, Lois *museum administrator*
Riley, Harris DeWitt, Jr. *pediatrician*
Roaden, Arliss Lloyd *higher education executive director, former university president*
Roberts, Kenneth Lewis *investor, lawyer, foundation administrator*
Roberts, Sandra *editor*
Robertson, David *clinical pharmacologist, physician, educator*
Robinson, Roscoe Ross *nephrologist, educator*
Rogers, Roy (Leonard Franklin Slye) *country musician, actor*
Ross, Joseph Comer *physician, educator, academic administrator*
Russell, Clifford Springer *economics and public policy educator*
Russell, Fred McFerrin *journalist, author, lawyer*
Sanders, Jay William *audiology educator*
Sanders, Paul Hampton *lawyer, retired educator, arbitrator/mediator*
Sandidge, Kent, III *magistrate judge*
Sawyers, John Lazelle *surgeon*
Scheffman, David Theodore *economist, management educator, consultant*
Schnelle, Karl Benjamin, Jr. *chemical engineering educator, consultant, researcher*
Schoenblum, Jeffrey A. *law educator*
Schoggen, Phil H(oward) *psychologist, educator*
Schumaker, Larry Lee *mathematics educator*
Schweinhart, Richard Alexander *health care company executive*
Scott, Henry William, Jr. *surgeon, educator*
Seale, James Millard *religious organization administrator, clergyman*
Sharp, Bert Lavon *retired education educator, retired university dean*
Shell, Owen G., Jr. *banker*
Shelton, Larry Brandon *apparel company executive*
Shelton, Ricky Van *country music singer, songwriter*
†Sherborne, Robert *editor*
Shousha, Annette Gentry *critical care nurse*
Sims, Wilson *lawyer*
Skaggs, Ricky *country musician*
Sloan, Frank Allen *economics educator*
Smith, James Forest, Jr. *retired banker*
Smith, Samuel Boyd *history educator*
Soderquist, Larry Dean *lawyer, educator*
South, Mary Ann *pediatrics educator*
Speece, Richard Eugene *civil engineer, educator*
Spencer, Harry Chadwick *minister*
Spengler, Dan Michael *orthopedic surgery educator, researcher, surgeon*
Spiller, Hart *microbiologist*
Spinella, Judy Lynn *healthcare administrator*
Spores, Ronald Marvin *anthropology educator, ethnohistorian*
Stahlman, Mildred Thornton *pediatrics and pathology educator, researcher*
†Stark, Caroline *library director*
Stewart, David Marshall *librarian*
Stout, Lonnie James, II *restaurant operations company executive*
Stringfield, Charles David *hospital administrator*
Strupp, Hans Hermann *psychologist, educator*
Stuart, Marty *country music singer, musician, songwriter*
Stubbs, Gerald *biochemist, educator*
Stumpf, Samuel Enoch *philosophy educator*
Sullivan, Allen Trousdale *securities company executive*
Sullivan, Walter Laurence *writer, educator*
Sundquist, Donald Kenneth (Don Sundquist) *governor, former congressman, sales corporation executive*
Sutherland, Frank *publishing executive, editor*
Sutton, Barrett Boulware *former insurance company executive*
Swensson, Earl Simcox *architect*
Tarbell, Dean Stanley *chemistry educator*
†Thackston, Edward Lee *engineer, educator*
Thompson, Almose Alphonse *lawyer, educator*
Thompson, Travis *psychology educator, administrator, researcher*
Thornton, Spencer P. *ophthalmologist, educator*
Tichi, Cecelia *English language educator*
Tippin, Aaron *country music singer, songwriter*
Tolk, Norman Henry *physics educator*
Tomlinson, Gus *biology educator*
Trautman, Herman Louis *lawyer, educator*
Turner, Robby *guitarist*
Urmy, Norman B. *hospital administrator*
Van, George Paul *international money management executive*
van Eys, Jan *pediatrician, educator, administrator*
Van Mol, Louis John, Jr. *public relations executive*
Voegeli, Victor Jacque *history educator, dean*
von Raffler-Engel, Walburga *linguist, lecturer, writer*
Wagoner, Porter *country music singer, composer*
Walden, Philip Michael *recording company executive, publishing company executive*
Walker, Arthur Lonzo *religious organization administrator*
Wang, Taylor Gunjin *science administrator, astronaut, educator*
†Warren, Frank M., Jr. *construction company executive*
Weeks, Robet Andrew *materials science researcher, educator*
Weingartner, H(ans) Martin *finance educator*
Wert, James Junior *materials scientist, educator*
Westfield, Fred M. *economics educator*
Westmoreland, Barry Keith *state legislator*
Whaley, Vernon *church administrator*
Whitefield, Anne C. *secondary school principal*
Whitt, Wilby Wayne *newspaper editor*
Wilder, John Shelton *lieutenant governor, president senate*
Wilson, David James *chemistry educator*
Wire, William Shidaker, II *retired apparel and footwear manufacturing company executive*
Wiseman, Thomas Anderton, Jr. *federal judge*
Wyatt, Joe Billy *university chancellor*
Young, Tommie Morton *social psychology educator, writer*
Youree, Gene Tassey *tool design engineer*
Zibart, Michael Alan *wholesale book company executive*

Norris
Kelly, James Michael *soil scientist*

Oak Ridge
Auerbach, Stanley Irving *ecologist, environmental scientist, educator*
Beasley, Cloyd Orris, Jr. *physicist, researcher*
Boyle, William R. *science administrator*
Burtis, Carl A., Jr. *chemist*
Cain, Victor Ralph *nuclear engineer*
Cawley, Charles Nash *enviromental scientist*
Clapp, Neal Keith *experimental pathologist*
Eatherly, Walter Pasold *physicist, consultant*
†Fee, Gordon *management consulting executive*
Gardiner, Donald Andrew *statistician, consultant*
Garrett, Jerry Dale *nuclear physicist*
Gifford, Franklin Andrew, Jr. *meteorologist*
Goforth, Cheryl Clewell *medical, surgical nurse*
Gooch, Patricia Carolyn *cytogeneticist*
Hosker, Rayford Peter, Jr. *air pollution research scientist*
†Huff, Dale Duane *hydrologist, educator*
Jasny, George Roman *retired energy company executive*
Kasten, Paul Rudolph *nuclear engineer, educator*
Kliewer, Kenneth Lee *computational scientist, research administrator*
Krause, Manfred Otto *physicist*
Larson, Bennett Charles *solid state physicist, researcher*
Luxmoore, Robert John *soil and plant scientist*
Macfarlane, Alastair Iain Robert *business executive*
Maienschein, Fred C. *physicist*
Meyers, Sheldon *engineering company executive*
Plasil, Franz *physicist*
Postma, Herman *physicist, consultant*
Poutsma, Marvin L. *chemical research administration*
Raridon, Richard Jay *computer specialist*
Renshaw, Amanda Frances *physicist, nuclear engineer*
Rosenthal, Murray Wilford *chemical engineer, science administrator*
†Russell, Liane Brauch *geneticist*
Satchler, George Raymond *physicist*
Sellin, Ivan Armand *physicist, educator, researcher*
Slusher, Kimberly Goode *researcher*
Spray, Paul *surgeon*
Thomas, John Edwin *retired university administrator*
Totter, John Randolph *biochemist*
Trauger, Donald Byron *nuclear engineering laboratory administrator*
Trivelpiece, Alvin William *physicist, corporate executive*
Tyndall, Richard Lawrence *microbiologist, researcher*
Veigel, Jon Michael *corporate professional*
†Ward, Robert Cleveland *research mathematician, science administrator*
Weinberg, Alvin Martin *physicist*
Whittle, Charles Edward, Jr. *consultant, lecturer*
Wilkinson, Michael Kennerly *physicist*
Wooten, Hollis Darwin *engineer*
Zucker, Alexander *physicist, administrator*

Oliver Springs
Davis, Sara Lea *pharmacist*

Paris
Williams, Hank, Jr. *country music singer, songwriter*

Pleasant View
Davis, Alfred Lewis *manufacturing company executive*

Powell
†Gentry, Robert Vance *physicist, researcher, writer*

Pulaski
Dowdy, Ronald Raymond *academic administrator*

Sevierville
†Childress, Robert Linwood *newspaper publisher*

Sewanee
Croom, Frederick Hailey *college administrator, mathematics educator*
Croom, Henrietta Brown *biology educator*
Dunkly, James Warren *theological librarian*
Hughes, Robert Davis, III *theological educator*
Kepple, Thomas Ray, Jr. *college administrator*
Lorenz, Anne Partee *special education educator, consultant*
Puckette, Stephen Elliott *mathematics educator, mathematician*
Spears, Monroe Kirk *English educator, author*
Williamson, Samuel Ruthven, Jr. *historian, university administrator*
Yeatman, Harry Clay *biologist, educator*

Seymour
Steele, Ernest Clyde *retired insurance company executive*

Shelbyville
Cooper, James Hayes Shofner (Jim Cooper) *former congressman, lawyer*

Signal Mountain
Cooper, Robert Elbert *state supreme court justice*
Hanlin, Hugh Carey *retired life insurance company executive*

Smithville
Enoch, Leslie Blythe, II *gas industry executive, lawyer*
†Markowitz, Alan Larry *hospital administrator*

Smyrna
Moffatt, Leslie Mack *aluminum company executive*

Springfield
Fagan, A. Rudolph *minister*

Sweetwater
Johnson, Charlie James *minister*

Tullahoma
Antar, Basil Niman *engineering educator*
†Butler, R. W. *engineering company executive*
Collins, Sarah Ruth *education educator*
Franke, John Charles *human resources executive*
Gossick, Lee Van *corporate executive, retired air force officer*
†McCay, Thurman Dwayne *university administrator*
Pate, Samuel Ralph *engineering corporation executive*
Wu, Ying Chu Lin Susan *engineering company executive, engineer*

Western Institute
Wingate, Robert Lee, Jr. *internist*

TEXAS

Abilene
Boone, Billy Warren *lawyer, judge*
Boyll, David Lloyd *broadcasting company executive*
Clayton, Lawrence Ray *university dean, literary critic, biographer*
Davis, Burl Edward *social sciences research consulting company executive, communications educator*
Fleshman, Jim J. *zoological park administrator*
Fryer, William Neal *retired psychologist*
Hunter, Robert Dean (Bob Hunter) *state legislator, retired academic administrator*
Kim, Thomas Kunhyuk *college administrator*
†McCaleb, Gary Day *university administrator*
†Puckett, Frank *newspaper publisher*
Retzer, Kenneth Albert *mathematics educator*
Shimp, Robert Everett, Jr. *university administrator, historian*
Specht, Alice Wilson *library director*
Warren, Russell Glen *academic administrator*
†Waters, Michael Cooper *medical center and development corporation executive*
Wilson, Stanley P. *retired lawyer*

Alamo
McKelvy, Nicole Andrée *librarian*

Alice
Tetlie, Harold *priest*

Allen
Gilliland, Mary Margarett *healthcare consultant*
Hagar, Robert Montel *chief executive officer, business owner*
†Wynn, Robert E. *retired career officer, electronics executive*

Alpine
Morgan, Raymond Victor, Jr. *university administrator, mathematics educator*
Ortego y Gasca, Felipe de *education educator*

Alvin
Lukens, Betty Faye *health facility manager*
Oliver, Elizabeth Jeanne *nurse, educator*

Amarillo
Ayad, Joseph Magdy *psychologist*
Ball, Charles Elihue *association consultant*
Brainard, Jayne Dawson (Mrs. Ernest Scott Brainard) *civic worker*
Burgess, C(harles) Coney *banking executive*
Cox, Cheryl Craft *symphony orchestra administrator*
DeSpain, Ronald Leroy *academic administrator*
Fee, Dorothea Lillian *nurse*
Keaton, Lawrence Cluer *engineer, consultant*
†Laur, William Edward *retired dermatologist*
Madden, Wales Hendrix, Jr. *lawyer*
Marmaduke, John H. *retail executive*
Martindale, Catherine Ann *editor*
Matthiesen, Leroy Theodore *bishop*
Neal, A. Curtis *retired lawyer*
Robinson, Mary Lou *federal judge*
Setapen, James Anthony *orchestra conductor*
Smithee, John True *lawyer, state legislator*
Snelson, Pamela *health facility administrator*
Spies, Dennis J. *editor*
Sprowls, Robert Wayne *veterinarian, laboratory administrator*
Stiff, John Sterling *development company executive*
Streu, Raymond Oliver *financial planner, securities executive*
Strickland, Anita Maurine *retired business educator, librarian*
Von Eschen, Robert Leroy *electrical engineer, consultant*

Anahuac
White, Ethyle Herman (Mrs. S. Roy White) *artist*

Arlington
Anderson, Dale Arden *aerospace engineer, educator*
Brown, James Kevin *professional baseball player*
Burkart, Burke *geology educator, researcher*
Burkett, John David *professional baseball player*
Burson, Betsy Lee *librarian*
Carey, Milburn Ernest *musician, educator*
Carney, Kim *economics educator*
Clark, Will (William Nuschler Clark, Jr.) *professional baseball player*
Cole, Richard Louis *political scientist, educator*
Dickinson, Roger Allyn *business administration educator*
Elias, Harold John *artist, educator*
Farmer, James Aurther *sociology educator*
Ferrier, Richard Brooks *architecture educator, architect*
Fung, Adrian Kin-Chiu *electrical engineering educator, researcher*
Furubotn, Eirik Grundtvig *economics educator*
Gonzalez, Juan (Juan Alberto Vazquez Gonzales) *professional baseball player*
Greenspan, Donald *mathematician, educator*
Han, Chien-Pai *statistics educator*
Hunter, J(ohn) Robert *insurance consumer advocate*
Lewis-White, Linda Beth *elementary school educator*
Malone, Edwin Scott, III *radio and television producer, public relations consultant*

McCall, Tina critical care nurse
McCuistion, Peg Orem hospice administrator
McCuistion, Robert Wiley lawyer, hospital administrator, management consultant
Mc Elroy, John Harley electrical engineering educator
Meadows, Jennifer Elizabeth retired editor, tattoo artist
Miller, Darwin Leon healthcare administrator
Mullendore, Walter Edward economist
Nelson, Wallace Boyd economics and business administration educator
Oates, Johnny Lane professional baseball team manager
Payne, Fred R(ay) aerospace engineering educator, researcher
Perkins, Bob(by) F(rank) geologist, dean
Pickard, Myrna Rae college dean
Pomerantz, Martin chemistry educator, researcher
Qasim, Syed Reazul civil engineering educator, researcher
†Rajeshwar, Krishnan chemist, educator
Ramsey, Charles Eugene sociologist, educator
Rodriguez, Ivan professional baseball player
Rose, Edward W. (Rusty Rose) professional sports team executive
Russell, Andrew Milo music educator
Ryan, Nolan former professional baseball player
Sampras, Pete tennis player
†Sawyer, Raymond Lee, Jr. motel chain executive
Schieffer, J. Thomas professional baseball team executive
Schimelpfenig, C(larence) W(illiam), Jr. chemistry educator
Smith, Charles Isaac geology educator
†Snyder, Don retail automotive executive
Sobol, Harold consultant, retired dean, manufacturing executive
Stevens, Gladstone Taylor, Jr. industrial engineer
Sundel, Martin social work educator, psychologist
Tewksbury, Robert Alan professional baseball player
Thompson, Carson R. retail, manufacturing company executive
Wiig, Elisabeth Hemmersam audiologist, educator
Wright, James Edward judge
Younkin, C. George archivist

Atlanta
†Francis, Bill publishing executive

Austin
Abell, Creed W. pharmacy educator
Adams, Warren Sanford, II retired food company executive, lawyer
Adcock, Willis Alfred electrical engineer, educator
Aggarwal, Jagdishkumar Keshoram electrical and computer engineering educator, research administrator
Ahlschwede, Arthur Martin church educational official
Ahrens, Carolyn lawyer
Albin, Leslie Owens biology educator
Alexander, Drury Blakeley architectural educator
Alich, John Arthur, Jr. manufacturing company executive
Allday, Martin Lewis lawyer
Allison, John Robert lawyer, educator, author
Alofsin, Anthony architect, art historian, sculptor, educator
Alpert, Mark Ira marketing educator
Amsel, Abram experimental psychologist, educator
Anderson, David Arnold law educator
Anderson, Urton Liggett accounting educator
Antokoletz, Elliott Maxim music educator
Ardis, Susan Barber librarian, educator
Armstrong, Neal Earl civil engineering educator
Ashworth, Kenneth Hayden state educational commissioner
Austin, David Mayo social work educator
Ayres, Robert Moss, Jr. retired university president
Baade, Hans Wolfgang legal educator, law expert
Baicy, Janet Karen nursing executive
Bailey, Philip Sigmon chemistry educator
†Baird, Charles F. judge
Baker, Lee Edward biomedical engineering educator
Bard, Allen Joseph chemist, educator
Barker, Daniel Stephen geology educator
Barlow, Joel William chemical engineering educator
Barndt, Richard V. law educator
Barnes, Jay William, Jr. architect, rancher
†Barnett, Charles Joseph hospital administrator
Barr, Howard Raymond architect
Barrera, Elvira Puig counselor, therapist, educator
Bash, Frank Ness astronomer, educator
Bean, Frank D(awson) sociology and demography educator
Beard, Leo Roy civil engineer
†Benavides, Fortunato Pedro (Pete Benavides) judge
Bengtson, Roger Dean physicist
Berdahl, Robert Max academic administrator, historian educator
Bernstein, Robert retired physician, state official, former army officer
Biesele, John Julius biologist, educator
Billings, Harold Wayne librarian, editor
Binder, Bob lawyer
Bissex, Walter Earl lawyer
Black, James Sinclair architect, educator
†Blackstock, David T. mechanical engineer, educator
Blair, Calvin Patton retired business administration educator
Blake, Robert Rogers psychologist, behavioral science company executive
Bledsoe, Woodrow Wilson mathematics and computer sciences educator
Blodgett, Warren Terrell public affairs educator
Bobbitt, Philip Chase lawyer, educator, writer
Boggs, James Ernest chemistry educator
Bonjean, Charles Michael foundation executive, sociologist, educator
†Bonnecaze, Roger T. chemical engineering educator
Bordie, John George linguistics educator
Box, Barry Glenn aerospace engineer, military officer
Box, John Harold architect, educator, academic dean
†Boyd, Carolyn Patricia history educator
Boyer, Mildred Vinson retired foreign language educator
Boyer, Robert Ernst geologist, educator
Braasch, Steven Mark advertising executive
Brager, Walter S. retired food products corporation executive
Branch, Brenda Sue library director
Braybrooke, David philosopher, educator
Breen, John Edward civil engineer, educator
Brewer, Thomas Bowman retired university president
Brinkley, Fred Sinclair, Jr. state agency administrator, pharmacist
Brock, James Rush chemical engineering educator
Brockett, Oscar Gross theatre educator
Bronaugh, Edwin Lee electromagnetic compatibility engineer, consultant
Bronson, Franklin H. zoology educator
Brown, Dennis Taylor molecular biology educator
Brown, J. E. (Buster Brown) state senator, lawyer
Brown, Norman Donald history educator
Bruff, Harold Hastings law educator
Buchanan, Bruce, II political science educator
Bullock, Robert D. (Bob Bullock) state legislator, lieutenant governor, lawyer
Burnham, Walter Dean political science educator
Burns, Ned Hamilton civil engineering educator
†Bush, George W. governor
Butzer, Karl W. archaeology and geography educator
Byrd, Linward Tonnett lawyer, rancher
Cain, Sister Thecla religious schools superintendent
Campion, Alan chemistry educator
Cannon, William Bernard retired university educator
Cantilo, Patrick Herrera lawyer
Cardenas, Gilberto sociology educator, director
Cardozier, Virgus Ray higher education educator
Carey, Graham Francis engineering educator
Carleton, Don Edward history center administrator, educator, writer
Carlton, Donald Morrill research, development and engineering executive
Carpenter, Elizabeth Sutherland library consultant, author, equal rights leader, lecturer
Carrasquillo, Ramon Luis civil engineering educator, consultant
Carson, Loftus C., II law educator
Causey, Robert Louis philosopher, educator, consultant
Charbeneau, Randall J. environmental and civil engineer
Chavarria, Ernest Montes, Jr. international trade, business and finance consultant, lecturer
Christian, George Eastland political consultant
Churgin, Michael Jay law educator
Clark, Charles T(aliferro) retired business statistics educator
Cleaves, Peter Shurtleff academic administrator
Cleland, Charles Carr psychologist, educator
Cline, Clarence Lee language professional
Clinton, Sam Houston judge
Conine, Ernest newspaper commentator, writer
Cook, Chauncey William Wallace retired food products company executive
Cook, J. Rowland lawyer
Cooke, Carlton Lee, Jr. mayor
Crain, William Henry retired curator
Crenshaw, Ben professional golfer
Crosby, Alfred Worcester history educator
Croslin, Charles Wilburn, Jr. architect
Crum, Lawrence Lee banking educator
Culp, George Hart computer executive, consultant
Culp, Joe C(arl) electronics executive
Cundiff, Edward William marketing educator
Cunningham, William Hughes university chancellor, marketing educator
Dalton, Don principal
Danburg, Debra state legislator
Danielson, Wayne Allen journalism and computer science educator
Davis, Donald Gordon, Jr. librarian, educator
Davis, Edward Mott anthropology educator and researcher
Davis, Robert Larry lawyer
Dawson, Robert Oscar lawyer, educator
Deal, Ernest Linwood, Jr. banker
†Decaro, Angelo Anthony, Jr. data processing executive
Deisler, Paul Frederick, Jr. retired oil company executive
Delaney, Richard Michael broadcast executive
Delevoryas, Theodore botanist, educator
Dell, Michael S. manufacturing executive
Deming, David Lawson art educator
Denny, Mary Craver state legislator, rancher
Derounian, Steven Boghos lawyer, retired judge
de Vaucouleurs, Gerard Henri astronomer, educator
de Wette, Frederik Willem physics educator
De Witt, Bryce Seligman physics educator
De Witt-Morette, Cécile physicist
Dijkstra, Edsger Wybe computer science educator, mathematician
Divine, Robert Alexander history educator
Dodge, Joseph M. law educator
Doenges, Rudolph Conrad finance educator
Doluisio, James Thomas pharmacy educator
Dougal, Arwin Adelbert electrical engineer, educator
Dougherty, John Chrysostom, III lawyer
Douglas, James Nathaniel astronomer, educator
Dozier, Dirk A. restaurant professional
Drummond, William Eckel physics educator
Duncombe, Raynor Lockwood astronomer
Dupuis, Russell Dean electrical engineer, research scientist
Durbin, Richard Louis, Sr. healthcare administration consultant
Durden, Christopher John entomologist, paleontologist, museum curator
Dusansky, Richard economist, educator
Dzienkowski, John Stephen law educator
Edwards, Wayne Forrest paper company executive
Ellison, Samuel Porter, Jr. geologist, educator
Epstein, Jeremiah Fain anthropologist, educator
Ersek, Robert Allen plastic surgeon, inventor
Erskine, James Lorenzo physics educator
Evans, David Stanley astronomy educator
Evans, Walter Reed engineering executive, consultant
Fair, Harry David academic administrator, physicist
Fair, James Rutherford, Jr. chemical engineering educator, consultant
Farrell, Edmund James English language educator, author
Fernea, Robert Alan cultural anthropology and Middle Eastern studies educator, consultant
Finn, Patricia Gloria lawyer
Fischer, Norman, Jr. media broker
Fisher, William Lawrence geologist, educator
Fishkin, James S. law educator
Folk, Robert Louis geologist, educator
Folkers, Karl August chemistry educator
Fonken, Gerhard Joseph retired chemistry educator, academic administrator
Foss, Donald John research psychologist, educator
Fowler, David Wayne architectural engineering educator
Fowler, Nola Faye ranch owner, political consultant
Fox, Marye Anne chemistry educator
Franklin, Billy Joe international higher education specialist
Franklin, G(eorge) Charles academic administrator
Friedman, Alan Warren humanities educator
Fryxell, Greta Albrecht botany educator, oceanographer
Galinsky, Gotthard Karl classicist, educator
Gambrell, James Bruton, III lawyer, educator
Gammage, Robert Alton (Bob Gammage) state supreme court justice
Gangstad, John Erik lawyer
Gardiner, William Cecil, Jr. chemist, educator
Garner, Harvey Louis computer scientist, consultant, electrical engineering educator
Garwood, William Lockhart federal judge
Gavenda, J(ohn) David physicist
Gentle, Kenneth William physicist
George, Walter Eugene, Jr. architect
Gergen, Mark P. law educator
Gerry, Martin Hughes, IV federal agency administrator, lawyer
Getman, Julius Gerson law educator, lawyer
Gibson, William Willard, Jr. law educator
Gilbert, Lucia Albino psychology educator
Gill, Clark Cyrus retired education educator
Gillman, Leonard mathematician, educator
Girling, Robert George William, III business owner
Glade, William Patton, Jr. economics educator
Glasgow, Robert J. (Bob Glasgow) state senator, lawyer
Gleeson, Austin Michael physicist, educator
Glenn, Norval Dwight sociologist, educator
Gloyna, Earnest Frederick environmental engineer, educator
Golden, Edwin Harold insurance company executive
Goldstein, E. Ernest lawyer
Goldstein, Peggy R. sculptor
Golemon, Ronald Kinnan lawyer
Gonzales, Alexander J. lawyer
Gonzalez, Raul A. state supreme court justice
Gooch, William DeWitt librarian
Goode, Steven law educator
Goodenough, John Bannister engineering educator, research physicist
Gould, Lewis Ludlow historian
Grace, James Martin insurance company executive
Gracy, David Bergen, II archivist, information science educator, writer
Graglia, Lino Anthony lawyer, educator
Granof, Michael H. accounting educator
Grant, Verne Edwin biology educator
Gray, Kenneth Eugene petroleum engineering educator
Graydon, Frank Drake retired accounting educator, university administrator
Green, Peter Morris classics educator, writer, translator
Greene, John Joseph lawyer
Greenhill, Joe Robert former chief justice state supreme, lawyer
Greig, Brian Strother lawyer
Griffy, Thomas Alan physics educator
Guerin, John William artist
Gustafsson, Lars Erik Einar writer, educator
Haas, Joseph Marshall petroleum consultant
Hall, Beverly Adele nursing educator
Hall, Michael Garibaldi education educator
Hamermesh, Daniel Selim economics educator
Hamilton, Dagmar Strandberg lawyer, educator
Hamilton, Robert Woodruff law educator
Hancock, Ian Francis (O Yanko le Redžosko) linguistics educator
Hardin, Dale Wayne retired law educator
Harms, Robert Thomas linguist, educator
Harris, Ben Maxwell education educator
Harris, Richard Lee engineering executive, retired army officer
Harrison, Richard Wayne lawyer
Hart, Roderick P. communications educator, researcher, author
Hartshorne, Charles philosopher, retired educator
Hayes, Patricia Ann university president
Hazel, J. Patrick law educator
Hazeltine, Richard Deimel physics educator, university institute director
Hecht, Nathan Lincoln state supreme court justice
Hedrick, John Richard lawyer
Hefner, Robert Eugene technology management consultant
Helburn, Isadore B. arbitrator, mediator, educator
Heller, Adam chemist, researcher
Helmreich, Robert Louis psychologist, educator
Henderson, George Ervin lawyer
Herman, Kenneth Neil journalist
Herman, Robert physics educator
Hester, Thomas Roy anthropologist
High, Timothy Griffin artist, educator, writer
Hightower, Jack English state supreme court justice, former congressman
Himmelblau, David Mautner chemical engineer
Hinojosa-Smith, Roland English language educator, writer
Hite, Jesse Otto art gallery director
Ho, Paul Siu-Chung physics educator
Holt, David Earl librarian
Holtzman, Wayne Harold psychologist, educator
Holz, Robert Kenneth geography educator
Hopper, Robert William speech communication educator
Houston, Samuel Lee computer software company executive
Howell, John Reid mechanical engineer, educator
Hubbs, Clark zoologist, researcher
Hudspeth, Emmett LeRoy physicist, educator
Huff, David L. geography educator
Huie, William Orr legal educator
Hull, David George aerospace engineering educator, researcher
Hunter, William Morgan lawyer
Hurd, Richard Nelson pharmaceutical company executive
Hurley, Laurence Harold medicinal chemistry educator
Huston, Ted Laird psychology educator
Ikard, Frank Neville, Jr. lawyer
Ingram, Denny Ouzts, Jr. lawyer, educator
Inman, Bobby Ray investor, former electronics executive
Iscoe, Ira psychology educator, director human development institute
Ivins, Molly columnist, writer
Jackson, Eugene Bernard librarian
Jackson, William Vernon library science and Latin American studies educator
Jacobson, Antone Gardner zoology educator
Jannuzi, F. Tomasson economics educator
Jazayery, Mohammad Ali foreign languages and literature educator emeritus
Jefferys, William Hamilton, III astronomer
Jeffrey, Robert Campbell university dean
Jenkins, Marie Hooper manufacturing company executive
Jennings, Coleman Alonzo dramatics educator
Jentz, Gaylord Adair law educator
Jirsa, James Otis civil engineering educator
Johnson, Calvin Harsha law educator
Johnson, Corwin Waggoner lawyer, educator
Johnson, Lady Bird (Mrs. Lyndon Baines Johnson) widow of former President of U.S.
Johnson, Mildred Snowden nursing educator, retired
Johnson, Sam D. federal judge
Jordan, Barbara C. lawyer, educator, former congresswoman
Jordan, Terry Gilbert geography educator
Justiz, Manuel Jon educator, researcher
Kalthoff, Klaus Otto zoology educator
Katz, Michael Ray Slavic languages educator
Kelley, Henry Paul university administrator, psychology educator
Kendrick, David Andrew economist, educator
Kennamer, Lorrin Garfield, Jr. retired university dean
Kennan, Kent Wheeler composer, educator
Kilgore, Joe Madison former congressman, lawyer
King, Robert D. linguistics educator, university dean
Kinney, William Rudolph, Jr. accounting educator, researcher
Kirk, Lynda Pounds biofeedback therapist, neurotherapist
Klein, Dale Edward nuclear engineering educator
Knight, Gary lawyer, educator, publisher
Koen, Billy Vaughn mechanical engineering educator
Koros, William John chemical engineering educator
Kozmetsky, George computer science educator
Kreisle, Matthew F., III architectural firm executive
Kronkosky, Preston C. educational think-tank executive
Lagowski, J(oseph) J(ohn) chemist
LaGrone, Alfred Hall electrical engineering educator
Laine, Katie Myers communications consultant
Lake, Larry Wayne petroleum engineer
Lam, Simon Shin-Sing computer science educator
Lamb, Jamie Parker, Jr. mechanical engineer, educator
Lancaster, Tina real estate executive, small business owner, rancher
Landes, Robert Paul architect
Lariviere, Richard Wilfred Asian studies educator, consultant
Larson, Kermit Dean accounting educator
Laycock, Harold Douglas law educator, writer
Lehmann, Ruth Preston Miller literature educator
Lehmann, Winfred Philipp linguistics educator
Leiden, Carl political scientist, educator
Leon, Tomas Carlos foreign exchange broker
Levinson, Sanford Victor legal educator
Levy, Michael Richard publishing executive
Little, Emily Browning architect
Livingston, William Samuel university administrator, political scientist
Lobb, Michael Louis psychologist
Loehlin, John Clinton psychologist, educator
†Longenecker, John Bender biochemist, nutritionist, educator
López-Morillas, Juan Spanish and comparative literature educator
Lopreato, Joseph sociology educator, author
Louis, William Roger historian, educator, editor
Lundelius, Ernest Luther, Jr. vertebrate paleontologist, educator
Mackey, Louis Henry philosophy educator
Mackovic, John college football coach, athletic director
Magee, Stephen Pat economics and finance educator
Maloney, Frank judge, lawyer
Manosevitz, Martin psychologist
†Mansfield, Stephen W. judge
Marcus, Harris Leon mechanical engineering and materials science educator
Mark, Hans Michael aerospace engineering educator, physicist
Markovits, Inga law educator
Markovits, Richard Spencer lawyer, educator
Marshall, F. Ray public affairs educator
Martin, Frederick Noel audiologist
Mathias, Reuben Victor (Vic Mathias) real estate executive, investor
Matthews, Jay Arlon, Jr. publisher, editor
Matzner, Richard Alfred physicist, educator
Mauzy, Oscar Holcombe lawyer, retired state supreme court justice
Maxwell, Arthur Eugene oceanographer, marine geophysicist, educator
May, Robert George dean, accounting educator
Mayer, Susan Martin art educator
Mayers, Roy publishing executive
Mayes, Wendell Wise, Jr. broadcasting company executive
†McBee, Frank Wilkins, Jr. industrial manufacturing executive
Mc Carthy, John Edward bishop
McCormick, Michael Jerry judge
McCullough, Benjamin Franklin transportation researcher, educator
McDaniel, Myra Atwell lawyer, former state official
Mc Donald, Stephen Lee economics educator
McFadden, Dennis experimental psychology educator
McFarland, Lawrence D. photographer, educator
McGarry, William Andrew, Jr. career counselor
McGinnis, Charles Irving civil engineer
McGinnis, Robert Campbell lawyer
Mc Ketta, John J., Jr. chemical engineering educator
Meacham, Standish historian, educator
Megaw, Robert Neill Ellison English educator
Meno, Lionel R. state education official
Mercer, Melvin Ray electrical engineer, educator
Merritt, Bernard Jason architect, urban and regional planner
Mersky, Roy Martin law educator, librarian
Metcalfe, Tom Brooks chemical engineering educator
Michener, James Albert author
Middleton, Christopher Germanic languages and literature educator
Middleton, Harry Joseph library administrator
Miller, Charles E. judge
Misra, Jayadev computer science educator
Mohrmann, Leonard Edward, Jr. chemist, chemical engineer
Moore, James Robert geological oceanographer
Morales, Dan state attorney general
Moulthrop, James Sylvester research engineer, consultant
Mourelatos, Alexander Phoebus Dionysiou humanities educator
Mullen, Ron insurance company executive
Mullenix, Linda Susan lawyer, educator
Mullins, Charles Brown physician, academic administrator

Nasworthy, Carol Cantwell *education and public policy researcher*
Newton, Charles Chartier *architect*
Nichols, Steven Parks *mechanical engineer, university official*
Northington, David K. *research center director, botanist, educator*
Nowlin, James Robertson *federal judge*
Oakes, Melvin Ervin Louis *physics educator*
Oates, Carl Everette *lawyer*
Oden, John Tinsley *engineering mechanics educator, consultant*
Oram, Robert W. *library administrator*
Orr, David L. *lawyer*
Otis, Jack *social work educator*
Painton, Russell Elliott *lawyer, mechanical engineer*
Palaima, Thomas Gerard *classics educator, researcher*
Paredes, Americo *English language educator*
Park, Thomas Joseph *biology researcher, educator*
Parmer, Hugh Q. *state senator*
Paul, Donald Ross *chemical engineer, educator*
Payne, Eugene Edgar *insurance company executive*
Payne, John Ross *rare books and archives appraisal-consulting company executive, library science educator*
Payne, Tyson Elliott, Jr. *retired insurance executive*
Perry, David Brian *architect*
Peterson, Robert Allen *marketing educator*
Phillips, Frances Marie *history educator*
Phillips, Thomas Royal *judge*
Pickens, Franklin Ace *lawyer*
Pinkston, Russell Fountain *music composition educator*
Polkinghorn, James B. *architectural firm executive*
Polomé, Edgar Charles *foreign language educator*
Pope, Andrew Jackson, Jr. (Jack Pope) *retired state supreme court chief justice*
Powe, L. A. Scot, Jr. *law educator*
Powers, Pike, Jr. *lawyer*
Powers, William Charles, Jr. *law educator*
Pradzynski, Andrzej Henryk *chemist*
Preeg, William Edward *oil company executive*
Prentice, Norman Macdonald *clinical psychologist*
Preston, Jane *psychiatrist, educator*
Prigogine, Vicomte Ilya *physics educator*
Pugsley, John East *financial executive, accountant*
Rabban, David M. *law educator*
Ragsdale, Keith Ellen *nurse, educator*
†Rascoe, Paul Stephen *librarian, researcher*
Ratliff, Jack *law educator*
Rau, Alan Scott *law educator*
Ray, Cread L., Jr. *retired state supreme court justice*
Reavley, Thomas Morrow *federal judge*
Reed, Lester James *biochemist, educator*
Reid, Jackson Brock *psychologist, educator*
Rhyne, Vernon Thomas, III *electrical engineer, consultant*
Rich, John Martin *humanities educator, researcher*
Richards-Kortum, Rebecca Rae *biomedical engineering educator*
Rider, Brian Clayton *lawyer*
Rippey, Donald Taylor *education educator*
Roach, James Robert *retired political science educator*
Robertson, David Wyatt *lawyer, educator*
Robertson, Jack Clark *accounting educator*
Robertson, John A. *law educator*
Roessner, Roland Gommel *architect, educator*
Rogers, Lorene Lane *university president emeritus*
Rollins, Henry Moak *former oil drilling equipment company executive, consultant*
Rostow, Elspeth Davies *political science educator*
Rostow, Walt Whitman *economist, educator*
Roueche, John Edward, II *education educator, leadership program director*
Ruud, Millard Harrington *former legal association administrator, retired educator*
Rylander, Henry Grady, Jr. *mechanical engineering educator*
Sampson, John J. *law educator*
Sandberg, Irwin Walter *electrical and computer engineering educator*
Sapp, Mary Ellen *state official, educator*
Schapery, Richard Allan *engineering educator*
Schechter, Robert Samuel *chemical engineer, educator*
Schmandt-Besserat, Denise *archaeologist, educator*
Schmitt, Karl Michael *retired political scientist*
Schulz-Widmar, Russell Eugene *musician, educator, composer*
Schwitters, Roy Frederick *physicist, educator*
Seung, Thomas Kaehao *philosophy educator*
Shapiro, Sander Wolf *lawyer*
Sharir, Yacov *artistic director, choreographer*
Sharp, John Malcolm, Jr. *geology educator*
Shaw, James *computer systems analyst*
Sherman, Edward Francis *lawyer, educator*
Sherman, Max Ray *lawyer, academic executive, former state senator*
Short, Byron Elliott *engineering educator*
Shurley, Jay Talmadge *psychiatrist, medical educator, polar explorer, author*
Simpson, Beryl Brintnall *botany educator*
Sims, Bill *state senator, business executive*
Sims, Robert Barry *lawyer*
†Skidmore, Gary J. *marketing executive*
Slavin, Alexandra Nadal *artistic director, educator*
Smith, Alfred Goud *anthropologist, educator*
Smith, Bert Kruger *mental health services professional, consultant*
Smith, Ernest E. *lawyer, educator*
Smoluchowski, Roman *physicist, emeritus educator*
Snell, Esmond Emerson *biochemist*
Sommerfeld, Raynard Matthias *accounting educator*
Sparks, Sam *federal judge*
†Spencer, William J. *engineering executive, researcher*
Spertus, Philip *investment company executive*
Spiro, Herbert John *political scientist, politician, educator, ambassador*
Spruce, Everett Franklin *artist*
Staley, Thomas Fabian *language professional, academic administrator*
Starr, Richard Cawthon *botany educator*
Steinfink, Hugo *chemical engineering educator*
Stephen, John Erle *lawyer, consultant*
Stetson, Daniel Everett *museum director*
Stice, James Edward *chemical engineer, educator*
Stone, Leon *banker*
Stoner, James Lloyd *retired foundation executive, clergyman*
Straiton, Archie Waugh *electrical engineering educator*
Stratton, Robert *electronics company executive*
Strauser, Robert Wayne *lawyer*
Streetman, Ben Garland *electrical engineering educator*
Sturley, Michael F. *law educator*
Sullivan, Teresa Ann *law and sociology educator, academic administrator*
Summers, Edward Lee *accounting educator*
Sutherland, William Owen Sheppard *English language educator*
Sutton, Beverly Jewell *psychiatrist*
Sutton, Harry Eldon *geneticist, educator*
Sutton, John F., Jr. *law educator, university dean, lawyer*
Swartzlander, Earl Eugene, Jr. *engineering educator*
Swinney, Harry Leonard *physics educator*
Szebehely, Victor G. *aeronautical engineer*
Taber, Robert Clinton *retired army officer*
Tapley, Byron Dean *aerospace engineer, educator*
Teague, Hyman Faris *former publishing company executive*
Temple, Larry Eugene *lawyer*
Tesar, Delbert *machine systems and robotics educator, researcher, manufacturing consultant*
Thiessen, Delbert Duane *psychologist*
Thomajan, Robert *lawyer, management and financial consultant*
Thornberry, William Homer *federal judge*
Thornhill, Gabriel Felder, III *securities company executive*
Thornton, Joseph Scott *research institute executive, materials scientist*
Thurston, George Butte *mechanical and biomedical engineering educator*
Tigar, Michael Edward *lawyer, educator*
Tinic, Seha Mehmet *finance educator*
Todd, Bruce M. *mayor*
Todd, William Burton *English language and literature educator*
Topfer, Morton Louis *computer company executive*
Tottenham, Terry Oliver *lawyer*
Tucker, Richard Lee *civil engineer, educator*
Turner, Billie Lee *botanist, educator*
Tyler, Ronnie Curtis *historian*
Uhlenbeck, Karen Keskulla *mathematician, educator*
Vande Hey, James Michael *corporate executive, former air force officer*
Velz, John William *literature educator*
Vliet, Gary Clark *mechanical engineering educator*
Vykukal, Eugene Lawrence *wholesale drug company executive*
Wadlington, Warwick Paul *English language educator*
Wagner, William Bradley *lawyer*
Wahlberg, Philip Lawrence *former bishop, legislative liaison*
Walker, James Roy *microbiologist*
Walls, Carl Edward, Jr. *communications company official*
Walton, Charles Michael *civil engineering educator*
Watson, Elizabeth Marion *protective services official*
Webb, Wayne Earl, Jr. *lawyer, engineer*
Weddington, Sarah Ragle *lawyer, educator*
Wehring, Bernard William *nuclear engineering educator*
Weinberg, Louise *lawyer, educator, author*
Weintraub, Russell Jay *lawyer, educator*
Weintraub, Sidney *economist, educator*
Weismann, Donald Leroy *art educator, artist, filmmaker, writer*
Welch, Ashley James *engineering educator*
Weldon, William Forrest *electrical and mechanical engineer, educator*
Wellborn, Olin Guy, III *law educator*
Welsch, Glenn Albert *accounting educator*
Werbow, Stanley Newman *language educator*
West, Glenn Edward *business organization executive*
Westbrook, Jay Lawrence *law educator*
Wheeler, John Craig *astrophysicist, writer*
Wheeler, Marshall Ralph *zoologist, educator*
Whitbread, Thomas Bacon *English educator, author*
White, John Michael *chemistry educator*
Whitmore, Jon Scott *theater educator*
Willerman, Lee *psychologist, educator*
Williams, Mary Pearl *judge, lawyer*
Willson, C. Grant *chemistry educator, engineering educator*
Wilson, Robert Henry *English educator*
Winegar, Albert Lee *computer systems company executive*
Winfrey, Dorman Hayward *scientific society executive*
Winters, J. Sam *lawyer, federal official*
Wissler, Eugene Harley *chemical engineer, educator*
Witt, Robert Charles *finance educator*
Wolf, Harold Arthur *finance educator*
Woodson, Herbert Horace *electrical engineering educator*
Wright, Charles Alan *lawyer, educator, author*
Wright, Stephen Gailord *civil engineering educator, consultant*
Wyllys, Ronald Eugene *information science educator, dean*
Young, Harrison, II *software development and marketing executive*
Young, Phyllis Casselman *music educator*
Yudof, Mark G. *lawyer, educator, academic administrator*
Yura, Joseph Andrew *civil engineering educator, consulting structural engineer*
Ziegler, Daniel Martin *chemistry educator*
Zimmerman, Louis Seymour *lawyer*

Baird
Rodenberger, Charles Alvard *aerospace engineer, consultant*

Bangs
McDonald, Charles Eugene *lawyer*

Baytown
Leiper, Robert Duncan *protective services official*
Mendelson, Robert Allen *polymer scientist, rheologist*
Percoco, Thelma Ann *nurse, educator*
Williams, Drew Davis *surgeon*

Beaumont
†Beeler, Donald Allen *hospital administrator*
Brentlinger, William Brock *college dean*
Carron, Maudee Lilyan *painter, sculptor, writer*
Cawley, William Arthur *research educator*
Cobb, Howell *federal judge*
Coe, (Matchett) Herring *sculptor*
Dygert, William Douglas *school superintendent*
Fisher, Joseph Jefferson *federal judge*
Gagne, Mary *secondary school principal*
†Galante, Joseph A. *bishop*
Ganter, Bernard J. *bishop*
Gray, Enid Maurine *city official, director of libraries*
†Gray, Maurine *library director*
Johnson, Cecil L. *lawyer*
Long, Alfred B. *retired oil company executive, consultant*
Lord, Evelyn Marlin *former mayor*
Lozano, Jose *nephrologist*
McGary, Betty Winstead *minister, counselor, individual, marriage, and family therapist*
Schell, Richard A. *federal judge*
Smith, David Ryan *museum director*
Smith, Floyd Rodenback *utilities executive*
†Soleman, William T. *industrial services executive*
Walker, John Michael *environmental hydrogeologist, consultant*

Bedford
Lieber, David Leslie *journalist*

Bellaire
Lancaster, Carroll Townes, Jr. *corporate executive*
Mayo, Clyde Calvin *organizational psychologist*

Bellville
Bishop, James A. *architect, writer*
Dittert, J. Lee, Jr. *lawyer*

Belton
Harrison, Benjamin Leslie *retired army officer*
Parker, Bobby Eugene, Sr. *college president*
Shoemaker, Robert Morin *retired army officer, county government official*

Bertram
Albert, Susan Wittig *writer, English educator*

Big Spring
Fryrear, Donald William *agricultural engineer*
Morrison, Walton Stephen *lawyer*

Blanco
Finley, James Edward *independent oil operator*

Blue Ridge
Comola, James Paul *legislative and environmental consultant*

Boerne
Dixon, Robert James *aerospace consultant, former air force officer, former aerospace company executive*
†Price, John Randolph *writer*
Wittmer, James Frederick *preventive medicine physician, educator*

Bridge City
Smith, Phillip Carl *marine and ship pilot, rancher*

Brooks AFB
Carroll, Robert Eugene *senior flight surgeon*
Convertino, Victor Anthony *physiologist, educator, research scientist*
Cox, Ann Bruger *biological scientist, editor, researcher*
Irving, George Washington, III *military officer, research director, veterinarian*
Olsen, Richard Galen *biomedical engineer, researcher*
†Strickland, William James *air force officer, research psychologist*

Brownsville
Crum, Nancy L. *credit union executive*
Doyle, Sister Mary Dolores *academic administrator*
Farst, Don David *zoo director, veterinarian*
Fitzpatrick, John J. *bishop*
French, Bertha Doris *medical, surgical and geriatrics nurse*
Garza, Reynaldo G. *federal judge*
Garza, Roberto Jesus *education educator*
Santa-Coloma, Bernardo *secondary school educator, counselor*
Uribe, Hector R. *state senator, lawyer*
Vela, Filemon B. *federal judge*

Brownwood
DeHay, Jerry Marvin *business educator*
Jarvis, Oscar T., Jr. *dean, education educator*

Bryan
†Adam, Don A. *bank executive*
Dirks, Kenneth Ray *pathologist, medical educator, army officer*
Hubert, Frank William Rene *retired university system chancellor*
Kellett, William Hiram, Jr. *retired architect, engineer, educator*
Röller, Herbert Alfred *biology and medical scientist, educator*
Samson, Charles Harold, Jr. (Car) *retired engineering educator, consultant*
Shofstahl, Robert Maxwell *savings and loan executive*
Sulik, Edwin (Pete Sulik) *health care administrator*
Van Arsdel, Eugene Parr *tree pathologist, consultant meteorologist*

Bullard
Buckner, John Hugh *retired real estate broker, retired construction company executive, retired air force officer*

Burleson
Prior, Boyd Thelman *management consultant*
Robin, Clara Nell (Claire Robin) *English language educator*

Bushland
Howell, Terry Allen *agricultural engineer*
Unger, Paul Walter *soil scientist*

Canyon Lake
†Eberwine, James Allen *hospital and nursing home administrator, former army officer*
Phelan, Charlotte Robertson *journalist, book critic*

Carrollton
Bentley, Clarence Edward *savings and loan executive*
Butler, Abbey J. *pharmaceutical distribution company executive*
†Byrne, James J. *computer service company executive*
Gravley, Milburn Ray *mayor, investments consultant*
Grimes, Mary Woodworth *special educational consultant*
Maher, Sheila *secondary school principal*
Miller, Marvin Edward *building materials company executive*
Pasman, James S., Jr. *aluminum company executive*
Powell, Bill Jake *newspaper executive*
Schulz, Richard Burkart *electrical engineer, consultant*
Senecal, Eugene Gerald *retail executive*

Cedar Hill
Hickman, Traphene Parramore *library director, storyteller, library and library building consultant*

Chandler
Sanders, Sharon Raye (Sharri) *telecommunications executive, educator*

Channelview
Johnson, Gus LaRoy *marine chemist, safety consultant*

Chillicothe
Brock, Helen Rachel McCoy *mental health and community health nurse*

Clarendon
Chamberlain, William Rhode *county official*
Roper, Beryl Cain *library director*

Cleburne
MacLean, John Ronald *lawyer*
Urban, Carlyle Woodrow *retired lawyer*

Cleveland
Lipski, Donald G. *sculptor*

College Station
Adkisson, Perry Lee *university system chancellor*
Anderson, Aubrey Lee *oceanographer, educator*
Anderson, Duwayne Marlo *earth and polar scientist, university administrator*
Arnowitt, Richard Lewis *physics educator, researcher*
Bass, George Fletcher *archaeology educator*
Batchelor, Bill *civil engineering educator*
Beaver, Bonnie Veryle *veterinarian, educator*
Berg, Robert Raymond *geologist, educator*
Berner, Leo De Witte, Jr. *retired oceanographer*
Berthold, Dennis Alfred *English language educator*
Bhattacharyya, Shankar Prashad *electrical engineer, educator*
Black, Samuel Harold *microbiology and immunology educator*
Blakley, George Robert, Jr. *mathematician, computer scientist*
Borlaug, Norman Ernest *agricultural scientist*
Bowen, Ray Morris *academic administrator, engineering educator*
Boyer, Lester Leroy, Jr. *architecture educator, consultant*
Bradley, Walter Lee *mechanical engineer, educator, researcher, consultant*
†Brown, Robert Dale *wildlife science educator, department head*
Bryant, Vaughn Motley, Jr. *botany and anthropology educator*
Calhoun, John C., Jr. *academic administrator*
Cannon, Garland *English language educator*
Carpenter, Delbert Stanley *educational administration educator*
Carter, Neville Louis *geophysicist, educator*
Chiou, George Chung-Yih *pharmacologist, educator*
Christiansen, James Edward *agricultural educator*
Chui, Charles Kam-Tai *mathematics educator*
Cocanougher, Arthur Benton *university dean, former business administration educator*
Cochran, Robert Glenn *nuclear engineering educator*
†Cohen, Aaron *aerospace engineer*
Conole, Richard Clement *management consultant*
Conway, Dwight Colbur *chemistry educator*
Copp, James Harris *sociologist, educator*
Cotton, Frank Albert *chemist, educator*
Crumbley, Donald Larry *accounting educator, writer, consultant*
†Darensbourg, Marcetta York *chemistry educator*
Davenport, Manuel Manson *philosophy educator*
Dethloff, Henry Clay *history educator*
De Vaul, Richard Allan *medical school administrator*
†Duce, Robert Arthur *atmospheric chemist, university administrator*
Ehsani, Mehrdad (Mark) *electrical engineering educator, consultant*
Erlandson, David Alan *education administration educator*
Ewing, Richard Edward *mathematics, chemical and petroleum engineering educator*
Fackler, John Paul, Jr. *chemistry educator*
Fedorchik, Bette Joy Winter *foreign language professional*
Fisher, Richard Forrest *soils educator, academic administrator*
Fletcher, Leroy Stevenson *mechanical engineer, educator*
Friedman, Melvin *geology educator, college dean*
Gage, E. Dean *university administrator*
Godbey, Luther David *architectural and engineering executive*
Gordone, Charles *playwright*
Greenhut, Melvin Leonard *economist, educator*
Gunn, Clare Alward *consultant, writer, retired educator*
Haden, Clovis Roland *university administrator, engineering educator*
Haensly, Patricia A. *psychology educator*
Hall, Kenneth Richard *chemical engineering educator, consultant*
Hall, Timothy C. *biology educator, consultant*
Harris, William James, Jr. *research administrator, educator*
Henry, Rene Arthur, Jr. *university official*
Herbich, John Bronislaw *engineering educator*
Hiler, Edward Allan *academic administrator, agricultural engineering educator*
Hoadley, Irene Braden (Mrs. Edward Hoadley) *librarian*
Holland, Charles Donald *chemical engineer, educator*
Johnson, James Harvey *veterinary medical educator*
Jones, Bryan Davidson *political science educator*
Kennedy, Robert Alan *educational administrator*

Kern-Foxworth, Marilyn Louise *journalism educator*
Knight, James Allen *psychiatrist, educator*
Knobel, Dale Thomas *history educator, university administrator*
Knutson, Ronald Dale *economist, educator, academic adminstrator*
Kohel, Russell James *geneticist*
Kunze, Otto Robert *retired agricultural engineering educator*
Laane, Jaan *chemistry educator*
Lee, William John *petroleum engineering educator, consultant*
Lowery, Lee Leon, Jr. *civil engineer*
Lusas, Edmund William *food processing research executive*
Lytton, Robert Leonard *civil engineer, educator*
Manning, Walter Scott *accountant, former educator, consultant*
Martell, Arthur Earl *chemistry educator*
Mathewson, Christopher Colville *engineering geologist, educator*
McCrady, James David *veterinarian, educator*
Mc Dermott, John Joseph *philosophy educator*
McIntyre, John Armin *physics educator*
McIntyre, Peter Mastin *physicist, educator*
Milford, Murray Hudson *soil science educator*
Mobley, William Hodges *management educator*
Nachman, Ronald James *research chemist*
Nance, Joseph Milton *history educator*
Natowitz, Joseph B. *chemistry educator, administrator, researcher*
Neff, Ray Quinn *electric power educator, consultant*
Neill, William Harold, Jr. *biological science educator*
O'Connor, Rod *chemist, inventor*
Orville, Richard Edmonds *atmospheric science educator*
Page, Robert Henry *engineer, educator, researcher*
Painter, John Hoyt *electrical engineer*
Parzen, Emanuel *statistical scientist*
Patton, Alton DeWitt *electrical engineering educator, consultant, research administrator*
Peddicord, Kenneth Lee *academic administrator*
Pierce, Kenneth Ray *veterinary medicine educator*
Plum, Charles Walden *retired business executive and educator*
Potter, Charlotte Ann *health education educator, physical education educator*
Prescott, John Mack *biochemist, retired university administrator*
Rabins, Michael Jerome *mechanical engineer, educator*
Reddell, Donald Lee *agricultural engineer*
Reddy, J. Narasimha *mechanical engineering educator*
Reed, Raymond Deryl *architect*
Rezak, Richard *geology and oceanography educator*
Rhode, David Leland *mechanical engineering educator, consultant*
Richardson, Herbert Heath *mechanical engineer, educator, institute director*
Ringer, Larry Joel *statistics educator*
Rosberg, David William *plant sciences educator*
Rotell, Thomas M. *publishing executive*
Rowe, Gilbert Thomas *oceanography educator*
Sanchez, David Alan *science administrator*
Scott, Alastair Ian *chemistry educator*
Sis, Raymond Francis *veterinarian, educator*
Slocum, R.C. *university athletic coach*
Smith, Roberta Hawkins *plant physiologist*
Solecki, R. Stefan *anthropologist, educator*
Stanton, Robert James, Jr. *geologist, educator*
Steffy, John Richard *nautical archaeologist, educator*
Stewart, Robert Henry *oceanographer, educator*
Stipanovic, Robert Douglas *chemist, researcher*
Summers, Max (Duanne) *entomologist, scientist, educator*
Tassinary, Louis George *psychology educator, director laboratory*
Toler, Ray Edward *conductor, band director*
Trennepohl, Gary Lee *finance educator*
Unterberger, Betty Miller *history educator, writer*
Vandiver, Frank Everson *institute administrator, former university president, author, educator*
Van Riper, Paul Pritchard *political science educator*
Varner, Dickson Drew *veterinarian*
Way, James Leong *pharmacology and toxicology educator*
West, Joe Earl *veterinarian, clinical pathologist*
Wichern, Dean William *business educator*
†Wild, James Robert *biochemistry and biophysics educator*
Wilding, Lawrence Paul *pedology educator, soil science consultant*
Wilson, Don Whitman *archivist, historian*
Woodcock, David Geoffrey *architect, educator*
Wright, Nancy Jane *English language educator*
Yao, James Tsu-Ping *civil engineer*

Colleyville
Love, Ben Howard *retired organization executive*

Columbus
Hamilton, T. Earle *retired educator, honor society executive*

Comanche
Droke, Edna Faye *elementary school educator*

Comfort
DeFoore, John Norris *management consultant*

Commerce
Bell, William Jack *journalism educator*
Grimshaw, James Albert, Jr. *English language educator*
Lutz, Frank Wenzel *education administration educator*
Morris, Jerry Dean *academic administrator*
Tuerk, Richard Carl *English language educator*

Conroe
Cabaret, Joseph Ronald *defense company executive*

Converse
Vontur, Ruth Poth *elementary physical education educator*

Corpus Christi
Bateman, John Roger *investment holding company executive*
Berryhill, Henry Lee, Jr. *geologist*
Bonilla, Tony *lawyer*
Branscomb, Harvie, Jr. *lawyer*
Bucklin, Leonard Herbert *lawyer*
Canales, Herbert Glenn *librarian*
†Carey, Robert R. *electirc power industry executive*
Cockrell, William F(oster), Jr. *lawyer*
Cole, June Robertson *psychotherapist*
Cox, William Andrew *cardiovascular thoracic surgeon*
Cutlip, Randall Brower *retired psychologist, former college president*
Doty, James Edward *pastor, psychologist*
Early, William James *education educator*
Furgason, Robert Roy *university official, chemical engineering educator*
Gracida, Rene Henry *bishop*
Green, William Wells *civil engineer*
Grubbs, Donald Ray *welder, educator*
Gutierrez, Elia Garza *elementary school educator*
Haas, Paul Raymond *petroleum company executive*
Head, Hayden Wilson, Jr. *district judge*
Heinz, Walter Ernst Edward *retired chemical executive*
Hext, George D. *airport terminal executive*
House, David Augusta *newspaper editor*
Kabot, Lorraine B. *health facility executive, nursing consultant*
†Kane, Sam *meat company executive*
Lim, Alexander Rufasta *neurologist, clinical investigator, educator*
Long, Ralph Stewart *clinical psychologist*
McKinnon, Michael Dee *broadcast executive*
McMillen, James Thomas *lawyer*
Miller, Carroll Gerard, Jr. (Gerry Miller) *lawyer*
Munro, Cristina Stirling *artistic director*
Paulson, Bernard Arthur *oil company executive, consultant*
Pivonka, Leonard Daniel *priest*
Rhodes, Mary *mayor*
Roels, Oswald Albert *oceanographer, educator, business executive*
Rose, Larry Lee *newspaper executive*
Schmidt, Richard S. *federal judge*
Sisley, Nina Mae *physician, public health officer*
Sommers, Maxine Marie Bridget *writer, educator, publisher*
Stone, Rose Marie *vocational educator*
Turner, Elizabeth Adams Noble (Betty Turner) *healthcare executive, former mayor*
Ullberg, Kent Jean *sculptor*
Vanaman, Charles Arthur *lawyer*
Walraven, Joseph William (Bill Walraven) *writer, publisher*
Wood, James Allen *lawyer*
Wooster, Robert *history educator*

Corsicana
Dawson, Leighton Brooks *lawyer*

Crockett
Gibbs, James Howard *broadcast executive*
Jones, Don Carlton *insurance agent*

Crosby
Cole, Edith Fae *dietitian, consultant*
Ohsol, Ernest Osborne *consulting chemical engineer*

Crowell
Binnion, John Edward *education educator*

Crystal Beach
Dunn, Glennis Mae *writer, lyricist*

Dallas
Ablon, Arnold Norman *accountant*
Abney, Frederick Sherwood *lawyer*
Acker, Rodney *lawyer*
†Adams, John Lewis *bank executive*
Adelizzi, Robert Frederick *bank executive*
Adkins, M. Douglas *lawyer*
Admire, Ben H. *lawyer*
Agnich, Richard John *lawyer, electronics company executive*
Akin, Henry David *lawyer*
Albers, John Richard *beverage company executive*
Alford, Margaret Suzanne *lawyer*
Allen, John Carlton *minister*
Allen, Terry Devereux *urologist, educator*
†Allison, Joel Tribble *health science facility administrator*
Anders, John *newspaper columnist*
Anderson, Barbara McComas *lawyer*
Anderson, E. Karl *lawyer*
Anderson, Jack Roy *health care company executive*
Anderson, Robert Theodore *music educator, organist*
Anderson, Ron Joe *hospital administrator, physician, educator*
Anglin, Michael Williams *lawyer*
Ardoin, John Louis *music editor*
Armour, James Lott *lawyer*
Arnold, George Lawrence *advertising company executive*
†Arnold, John Hudson *bank executive*
Ash, Mary Kay Wagner *cosmetics company executive*
Aston, James William *banker*
Atkins, Samuel James, III *banker*
Ausere, Joe Morris *food manufacturing company executive*
Aylesworth, William Andrew *electronics company executive*
Babcock, Charles Lynde, IV *lawyer*
Baer, Henry *lawyer*
Baggett, W. Mike *lawyer*
Bahr, Conrad Charles, III *financial management executive, consultant*
Bailon, Gilbert *newspaper editor*
Baker, Robert Woodward *airline executive*
Ball, Charles Frederick, Jr. *banker*
Ballard, Marshall *drilling company executive*
Bangs, Nelson A. *lawyer, soft drink company executive*
Barbee, Linton E. *lawyer*
Barnes, Hershell Louis, Jr. *lawyer*
Barnes, Robert Vertreese, Jr. *masonry contractor executive*
Barnett, Patricia Ann *public relations professional*
Barrett, Colleen Crotty *airline executive*
Bartlett, Richard Chalkley *cosmetics executive, writer*
Baskin, Leland Burleson *pathologist, educator, researcher*
Bass, John Fred *lawyer*
Beane, Jerry Lynn *lawyer*
Beck, Abe Jack *retired business executive, retired air force officer*
Beck, Mary Constance *bank executive*
Bell, John Lewis McCulloch *manufacturing executive*
Berbary, Maurice Shehadeh *physician, military officer, hospital administrator, educator*
Berkeley, Marvin H. *management educator, former university dean*
Berry, Buford Preston *lawyer*
Bersano, Bob *newspaper editor*
Besing, Ray Gilbert *lawyer*
Biegler, David W. *gas company executive*
Birkeland, Bryan Collier *lawyer*
Bishop, Bryan Edwards *lawyer*
Bishop, Gene Herbert *corporate executive*
Bishop, R. Doak *lawyer*
Blachly, Jack Lee *lawyer*
Blackburn, Charles Lee *oil company executive*
Blackstone, Kevin *sports columnist*
Blattner, Wolfram Georg Michael *meteorologist*
Blau, Charles William *lawyer, former government official*
Blessen, Karen Alyce *free-lance illustrator, designer*
Blessing, Edward Warfield *petroleum company executive*
Blevins, Gary Lynn *architect, real estate broker, real estate appraiser*
Bliss, Robert Harms *lawyer*
Block, Steven Robert *lawyer*
Blomquist, Carl Gunnar *cardiologist*
Blow, Steve *newspaper columnist*
Blumenthal, Karen *newspaper executive*
Bockstruck, Lloyd DeWitt *librarian*
Bolling, Alexander Russell, Jr. *retired military officer, business executive*
Bollon, Arthur Peter *scientist, educator, biotechnology company executive*
Bonesio, Woodrow Michael *lawyer*
Bonney, Samuel Robert *lawyer*
Bonnivier, B. William *utility company executive*
Bonte, Frederick James *radiology educator, physician*
Boone, Michael Mauldin *lawyer*
Boone, Oliver Kiel *lawyer*
Boren, Benjamin N. *lawyer*
Boyce, Charles A. *oil company executive, lawyer, arbitrator*
Boyd, Dan Stewart *lawyer*
Braden, David Rice *architect*
Bradford, William Edward *oil field equipment manufacturing company executive*
Bradley, John Andrew *hospital management company executive*
Bradshaw, Lillian Moore *retired library director*
Brin, Royal Henry, Jr. *lawyer*
†Brinegar, Mary Metta *non-profit organization executive*
†Broadhead, Paul *movie theatre company executive*
Bromberg, Henri Louie, Jr. *lawyer*
Bromberg, John E. *lawyer*
Brooks, E. R. (Dick Brooks) *utility company executive*
Brooks, James Elwood *geologist, educator*
Brown, Benjamin A. *gas, oil industry executive*
Brown, Michael Stuart *geneticist*
Brown, Stephen Bryan *real estate editor*
Browne, Richard Harold *statistician, consultant*
Bruene, Warren Benz *electronic engineer*
Bryant, L. Gerald *health care administrator*
Buchholz, Donald Alden *stock brokerage company executive*
Buchmeyer, Jerry *federal judge*
Bucy, J. Fred *retired electronics company executive*
Budzinsky, Armin Alexander *investment banker*
Bumpas, Stuart Maryman *lawyer*
†Bunker, Anthony Louis *health science executive*
Burke, William Temple, Jr. *lawyer*
Burns, Scott *columnist*
Burnside, John Wayne *medical educator, university official*
Busbee, Kline Daniel, Jr. *lawyer, law educator*
Bux, William John *lawyer*
†Byerley, Robert E., Jr. *mortgage company executive*
Byrd, David Lamar *oral surgeon educator*
Cain, David *state senator, lawyer*
Caldwell, Louise Phinney *historical researcher, community volunteer*
†Cambron, Robert L. *airport terminal executive*
Campbell, Donald K. *theological seminary administrator, educator*
Campbell, Roy E. *diversified company executive*
Campfield, Regis William *law educator*
Carlton, Dean *lawyer*
Carson, Virginia Hill *oil and gas executive*
Carter, Donald *professional basketball team executive*
Carver, John W(illiam), Jr. *hospital administrator*
Casey, Albert Vincent *business policy educator, retired business executive*
Casey, John T. *medical products executive*
Castle, John Raymond, Jr. *lawyer*
Cavanagh, Harrison Dwight *ophthalmic surgeon*
Chappelear, Claude Keplar *data systems corporation executive*
Cherryholmes, James Gilbert *construction consultant, real estate agent*
Cissik, John Henry *air force career officer, medical researcher*
Clark, C. A. W. *church administrator*
Clark, John W., Jr. *lawyer*
Cline, Bobby James *insurance company executive*
Cochran, George Calloway, III *retired banker*
Cochran, Kendall Pinney *economics educator*
Coldwell, Philip Edward *financial consultant*
Coleman, Robert Winston *lawyer*
Collins, Michael Homer *lawyer*
Collins, Michael James *investment company executive*
Comini, Alessandra *art historian, educator*
Compton, Bob *newspaper editor*
Conant, Allah B., Jr. *lawyer*
Cook, Gary Raymond *university president, clergyman*
Copley, Edward Alvin *lawyer*
Copp, Emmanuel Anthony *oil company executive*
†Corbett, Roger Lee *marketing executive*
Cornwall, J(ohn) Michael *savings and loan executive*
Correu, James M. *newspaper publishing executive*
Costa, Victor Charles *fashion designer*
Costello, John Francis, Jr. (Jack Costello) *lawyer*
Countryman, Edward Francis *historian, educator*
Cowart, T(homas) David *lawyer*
Cowling, David Edward *lawyer*
Cox, James William *newspaper executive*
Cox, Rody P(owell) *medical educator, internist*
Crain, Gayla Campbell *lawyer*
Crain, John Walter *historian*
Crandall, Robert Lloyd *airline executive*
†Crawford, Joe Jay *real estate company executive*
Creany, Cathleen Annette *television station executive*
Creel, Luther Edward, III *lawyer*
Crow, F. Trammell *real estate company executive*
Crowley, James Worthington *retired lawyer, business consultant, investor*
Crowson, James Lawrence *lawyer, financial company executive*
Cruikshank, Thomas Henry *energy services and engineering executive*
†Cullum, C. Munro *psychiatry and neurology educator*
Cullum, Robert B., Jr. *retail executive, property developer*
Cummings, Brian Thomas *public relations company executive*
Cummins, James Duane *correspondant, media executive*
Cunyus, George Marvin *oil company executive*
Curran, Geoffrey Michael *lawyer*
Curtiss, Jeffrey Eugene *media company executive*
Dale, Erwin Randolph *lawyer, author*
Davis, Clarice McDonald *lawyer*
Davis, Walter Richard *lawyer*
DeBusk, Manuel Conrad *lawyer*
Decherd, Robert William *newspaper and broadcasting executive*
Dedman, Robert Henry *sales executive*
DeOre, Bill *editorial cartoonist*
DePaola, Dominick Philip *college president, dean*
Dillard, Robert Lionel, Jr. *lawyer, former life insurance executive*
Dillon, David Anthony *journalist, lecturer*
Dillon, Donald Ward *management consultant*
Doke, Marshall J., Jr. *lawyer*
Dole, S. R., Jr. *retail executive*
Dorris, Carlos E. *chemicals executive*
Dozier, David Charles, Jr. *marketing public relations and advertising executi*
Dudley, George William *behavioral scientist, writer*
Dufner, Edward Joseph *newspaper editor*
Dunlap, George Carter *lawyer*
Durham, Michael Jonathan *treasurer*
Dutton, Diana Cheryl *lawyer*
Dyess, Bobby Dale *lawyer*
Dykes, Virginia Chandler *occupational therapist*
Eberhart, Robert Clyde *biomedical engineering educator, researcher*
Eddleman, William Roseman *lawyer*
Edwards, George Alva *physician, educator*
Edwards, Marvin Earle *superintendent of schools*
Eichenwald, Heinz Felix *physician*
Einspruch, Burton Cyril *psychiatrist*
Emerson, Walter Caruth *artist, educator*
Emery, Herschell Gene *lawyer*
†Engels, Lawrence Arthur *metals company executive*
Engleman, Donald James *lawyer*
Enix, Agnes Lucille *editorial consultant*
†Ergott, Harold L., Jr. *electronics company executive*
Ericson, Ruth Ann *psychiatrist*
Erwin, O. Scott *golf recreational facility executive, consultant*
Esquivel, Agerico Liwag *research physicist*
Estabrook, Ronald Winfield *chemistry educator*
†Etgen, Ann *ballet educator*
Evans, Roger *lawyer*
Evans, William Wilson *retired newspaper editor*
Everbach, Otto George *lawyer*
Everett, C. Curtis *lawyer*
Fanning, Barry Hedges *lawyer*
Fanning, Robert Allen *lawyer*
Farrington, Jerry S. *utility holding company executive*
Faulkner, Mike *energy company executive*
†Fegan, Jeffrey P. *airport executive*
Feiner, Joel S. *psychiatrist*
Feld, Alan David *lawyer*
Feldman, H. Larry *lawyer*
Fennell, Thomas E. *lawyer*
Fenner, Suzan Ellen *lawyer*
Fenter, Felix West *aerospace company executive*
Fiddick, Paul William *broadcasting company executive*
Fielder, Charles Robert *oil industry executive*
†Fine, Kenneth Davin *gastroenterologist, researcher*
Finn, Frank *lawyer*
Finn, Peter Michael *television production executive*
Fish, A. Joe *federal judge*
Fisher, Gene Jordan *retired chemical company executive*
†Fisherkeller, Paul Francis *food service executive*
Fishman, Edward Marc *lawyer*
Fitzwater, Sidney Allen *federal judge*
Flanagan, Christie Stephen *lawyer*
Flatt, Adrian Ede *surgeon*
Flegle, Jim L. *lawyer*
Fleming, Jon Hugh *business executive, educational consultant*
Flores, Marion Thomas *advertising executive*
Flournoy, John Craig *newspaper reporter*
Fogelman, Morris Joseph *physician*
Fontana, Robert Edward *electrical engineering educator, retired air force officer*
Fordtran, John Satterfield *physician*
Fordyce, Edward Winfield, Jr. *lawyer*
Forsythe, Earl Andrew *lawyer, steel company executive*
Fortado, Michael George *lawyer*
Foster, Thomas Elmore *bank executive*
Foster, William Edwin (Bill Foster) *nonprofessional basketball coach*
Fowler, Robert Glen *exploration company executive*
Fraker, Walter Vere *oil company executive*
France, Newell Edwin *former hospital executive, businessman*
Frank, Karen Mitchell *nurse administrator*
†Frank, Richard M. *restaurant corporation executive*
Free, Mary Moore *anthropologist*
Freling, Richard Alan *lawyer*
French, Joseph Jordan, Jr. *lawyer*
Frenkel, Eugene Phillip *physician*
Friedheim, Jan V. *education administrator*
†Friedheim, Stephen Bailey *public relations executive*
Frisbie, Curtis Lynn, Jr. *lawyer*
Fulton, Duncan Thomas, III *architect*
Gage, John *opera company executive*
Gage, Tommy Wilton *pharmacologist, dentist, pharmacist, educator*
Galloway, Randy *newspaper sports columnist*
Galt, John William *actor, writer*
Galvin, Charles O'Neill *law educator*
Gandy, Dean Murray *lawyer*
Gant, Norman Ferrell, Jr. *obstetrician, gynecologist*
†Gantt, James Raiford *thoracic surgeon*
Garreans, Leonard Lansford *state court official, criminal justice professional*
Gaswirth, Ronald M. *lawyer*
Geiger, Ken *photojournalist*
George, Kenneth S. *health facility administration*
Gibbs, James Alanson *geologist*
Gibby, Mabel Enid Kunce *psychologist*
Gibson, William Edward *banker*

Gifford, Porter William retired construction materials manufacturing company executive
Gilchrist, Henry lawyer
Gill, David Brian electrical engineer, educator
Gilleland, Richard A. health care company executive
Gilley, James Ray real estate/financial services executive
Gilliam, John A. lawyer
Gillilan, William J, III construction company executive
Gilman, Alfred Goodman pharmacologist, educator
Gilmore, Jerry Carl lawyer
Ginsburg, Lawrence David lawyer
Giordano, Saverio Paul professional association executive
Glancy, Walter John lawyer
Glines, Carroll Vane, Jr. magazine editor
Godfrey, Cullen Michael lawyer
Goldstein, Joseph Leonard physician, medical educator, molecular genetics scientist
Goodell, Sol retired lawyer
Goodstein, Barnett Maurice lawyer
Goolsby, Tony state legislator
Gores, Christopher Merrel lawyer
Goss, James Walter oil company executive
Goyne, Roderick A. lawyer
Grahmann, Charles V. bishop
Green, Cecil Howard geophysicist, consultant, educator
Greenstone, James Lynn psychotherapist, mediator, consultant, author, educator
Griffith, Dotty (Dorothy Griffith Stephenson) journalist, speaker
Grimes, David Lynn communications company executive
Grissom, Gerald Homer lawyer
Grogan, Timothy James information technology executive
Gruebel, Barbara Jane internist, pulmonologist
Grundman, Valentine Rock, Jr. lawyer
Guerin, Dean Patrick food products executive
Gump, Richard Anthony lawyer
†Guthrie, M. Philip insurance company executive
Gutman, Richard Edward lawyer
Haayen, Richard Jan university official, insurance company executive
Haddock, Ronald Wayne oil company executive
Hafner, Dudley H. health agency executive
Haggar, Edmond Ralph apparel manufacturing company executive
Haire, William J. healthcare executive
Halbreich, Jeremy L. newspaper publishing executive
Hall, Cheryl newspaper editor
Hamilton, David Lee retired environmental company executive
Hamon, Richard Grady lawyer
Harasta, Cathy Ann journalist
Harbaugh, Lois Jensen secondary science educator
Harber, M(ichael) Eric manager, management consultant
Harbin, John Pickens oil well company executive
Hardy, Tom Charles, Jr. medical equipment and insurance claims management executive
†Harper, Alan G. medical center director
Harper, Harlan, Jr. lawyer
Harrell, Gwendolyn Baumann lawyer
Harrell, Morris lawyer
Harrington, Marion Ray ophthalmologist
Harris, David, Jr. minister
Harris, Leon A., Jr. writer
Harris, Lucy Brown accountant, consultant
Harrison, Frank former university president
Hart, John Clifton lawyer
Hartman, Timothy Patwill banker
Hartnett, Will Ford lawyer
Hatchell, Steven James collegiate sports association executive
Hauer, John Longan lawyer
Hauptfuhrer, Robert Paul oil company executive
Hawkins, Jack Wade lawyer
Haworth, Charles Ray lawyer
†Hay, Jess Thomas finance company executive
Haynes, J. Neauell clergyman, bishop
Hegi, Frederick B., Jr. mobile home manufacturing executive
Henkel, Kathryn G. lawyer
Hennessy, Daniel Kraft lawyer
Herbener, Mark Basil bishop
Hester, Linda Hunt university dean, counselor
Hewett, Arthur Edward real estate developer, lawyer
Hicks, Marion Lawrence, Jr. (Larry Hicks) lawyer
Higginbotham, Patrick Errol federal judge
Hill, John Rutledge, Jr. retired construction materials company executive
Hille, Robert Arthur healthcare executive
Hinshaw, Chester John lawyer
Hirl, J. Roger petrochemical company executive
Hirsch, Laurence Eliot construction executive, mortgage banker
Hirsh, Bernard supply company executive, consultant
Hitt, David Hamilton hospital executive
Hodge, George Lowrance cosmetics company executive
Hoffman, Harold Wayne advertising agency executive
Hollingsworth, John Mark lawyer
Holmes, Bert Otis E., Jr. retired newspaperman
Holsinger, W. Preston diversified holding company executive
Horchow, S(amuel) Roger theater producer
Horton, Paul Bradfield lawyer
Howie, John Robert lawyer
Howland, Grafton Dulany financial counselor
Huang, Yen Ti civil engineer
Hudspeth, Albert James biomedical researcher, educator
Huey, Ward L(igon), Jr. media executive
Huffman, Gregory Scott Combest lawyer
Hughes, Joe Kenneth retired beverage company executive
Hughes, Vester Thomas, Jr. lawyer
Humann, Walter Johann corporation executive
Humble, Monty Garfield lawyer
Hunt, David Ford lawyer
Hunt, Ray Lee petroleum company executive
Hunter, Kermit Houston writer, former university dean
Hunter, Marsha L. lawyer
Hunter, Robert Grams English language educator
†Hurford, Gary Thomas oil company executive
Hurst, John L., III (Jack Hurst) chemical company executive
Ibach, Robert Daniel, Jr. library director
Jackson, Lee Franklin judge
Jackson, Phillip Ellis lobbyist, consultant
Jacobson, Gary newspaper business editor
Jayson, Melinda Gayle lawyer
Jeffett, Frank Asbury former oil company and insurance company executive, business consultant
Jelensperger, Francis J. engineering and architectural executive
Jenkins, Chester P. religious organization, church administration
†Jenkins, Graeme James orchestra conductor
Jenkins, M. T. Pepper anesthesiologist, educator
Jennings, James Burnett oil company executive
†Jennings, Susan Jane lawyer
Jobe, Larry Alton legal association executive
Johnson, James Harold lawyer
Johnson, Judith Kay lawyer
Johnson, Richard Clayton engineer, physicist
Johnson, Richard Craig lawyer
Johnson, Robert Lee, Jr. physician, educator, researcher
Jones, Dale P. oil service company executive
†Jones, E. Edward, Sr. church officer
Jones, Everett Riley, Jr. oil company executive
Jones, James Fleming, Jr. Romance language educator, university administrator
Jones, John Gornal lawyer
Jones, Philip Davis computer service publishing consultant
Joplin, Julian Mike lawyer
Jordan, Karen Leigh travel editor
Jordan, Robert W. lawyer
Jordan, William Davis lawyer
Judy, Nancy Elizabeth county commissioner
Junkins, Jerry R. electronics company executive
Keiffer, Edwin Gene electronics industry company executive
Keiser, Robert Lee gas and oil industry executive
Keithley, Bradford Gene lawyer
Kelleher, Herbert David airline executive, lawyer
Keller, William L. lawyer
Kelly, John Price hospital administrator
Kemper, Robert Van anthropologist, educator
Kendall, Joe federal judge
Kennedy, Marc J. lawyer
Kent, David Charles lawyer
Kessler, Tom newspaper editor
Kilby, Jack St. Clair electrical engineer
Kimbrough, Allen Wayne lawyer
Kindberg, Shirley Jane pediatrician
Kinnebrew, Jackson Metcalfe lawyer
†Kirk, Ron mayor, lawyer
Kirkpatrick, Patricia Kay retail buyer
†Klehfoth, Jay Gordon publisher, writer, consultant
Kline, Harry Byrd lecture bureau executive
Kluge, John Werner broadcasting and advertising executive
Kneipper, Richard Keith lawyer
Knowles, True H. food products executive
Kolb, Nathaniel Key, Jr. architect
Konrad, Dusan chemist
Korba, Robert W. communications executive
Kramer, Robert Ivan pediatrician
Kuhn, Willis Evan, II lawyer, mediator
Kutner, Janet art critic, book reviewer
LaBrec, David John lawyer
Lacy, John Ford lawyer
Lafving, Brian Douglas lawyer
La Jone, Jay Allen lawyer
Lan, Donald Paul, Jr. lawyer
Lancaster, John Lynch, III lawyer
Lancaster, Sally Rhodus philathropy consultant
Land, Geoffrey Allison science administrator
Landers, James Michael (Jim Landers) international editor
Landry, Jane Lorenz architect
Landry, Tom (Thomas Wade Landry) former professional football coach
Lane, Alvin Huey, Jr. management consultant
Lane, Marvin Maskall, Jr. electronics company executive
Lang, Douglas Steward lawyer
Langer, Ralph Ernest journalist
Lang-Miers, Elizabeth Ann lawyer
Langston, Roy A. insurance company consultant
Lawson, Andrew Lowell, Jr. defense industry company executive
Lee, George Terry, Jr. lawyer
Leedom, John Nesbett distribution company executive, state senator
†Lehman, Donald Ray chemical company executive
Leigh-Manuell, Robert Allen training executive, educator
Lerner, Alan Burton financial service executive, lawyer
Levenson, Stanley Richard public relations and advertising executive
Levin, Richard C. lawyer
Levine, Harold lawyer
Lewis, Jerry M. psychiatrist, educator
Lewis, John P. bank executive
Leyden, Edward E. secondary school principal
Lifson, Kalman Alan management consultant, retail executive
Little, Jack Merville lawyer
Livingston, Grover D. newspaper publishing executive
Livingstone, William Edwin, III lawyer
Lo, Ronald Ping Wong banker, consultant
Lomax, John H. financial service company executive
Lombard, Richard Spencer lawyer
Longyear, Russell Hammond retail executive
Lord, Esther A. corporate executive
Low, Paul M. mortgage banking executive, food service executive
Lowden, Scott Richard lawyer
Lowenberg, Michael lawyer
Lucier, James Alfred advertising executive
Lundy, Victor Alfred architect, educator
Luther, David Gaston, Jr. lawyer
Lynch, Thomas Wimp lawyer
Lynch, William Wright, Jr. investment executive, engineer
Lysaught, Thomas Francis publishing company executive
MacMahon, Paul advertising executive
Maddrey, Willis Crocker medical educator, internist, academic administrator, consultant, researcher
Madrid, Jay Joseph lawyer
Maguire, Cary McIlwaine oil company executive
Mahoney, Margaret Ann lawyer
Mahr, George Joseph financial service executive, real estate developer
Maloney, Robert B. federal judge
Mankoff, Ronald Morton lawyer
Mantle, Mickey Charles former baseball player, marketing consultant
Margerison, Richard Wayne diversified industrial company executive
Marino, Peter Andrew electronics company executive
Maris, Stephen S. lawyer, educator
Marks, James Frederic pediatric endocrinologist, educator
Marshall, Harold D. leasing and financial services company executive
Martin, Boe Willis lawyer
Martin, Richard Kelley lawyer
Mason, Barry Jean retired banker
Massman, Richard Allan lawyer
Matthews, Clark J(io), II retail executive, lawyer
Mattingly, Patti Jane educational administrator
Mattison, Harry D. utility company executive
Maycock, Ian David oil executive
Mays, Gerald Avery (Jerry Mays) engineering executive, consultant
McAlester, Arcie Lee, Jr. geologist, educator
Mc Cann, Samuel McDonald physiologist, educator
McCarthy, Michael Joseph communications company executive
Mc Clelland, Robert Nelson surgeon, educator
McClure, Frederick Donald investment banker, lawyer
McCLure, William B., Jr. lawyer
McCord, William Charles retired diversified energy company executive
McCormack, William Arthur lawyer
McCormick, James Clarence business consultant
McCormick, James Edward oil company executive
McCormick, James Hillman retired broadcast executive
McCracken, Alexander Walker pathologist
McCullough, George Bierce oil company executive
McCune, M. Davis architect
McDonald, Gail Margaret human resources, government relations and communications executive
McDougall, Ronald Alexander restaurant executive
Mc Elhaney, John Hess lawyer
McElvain, David Plowman manufacturing company financial executive
McGlothlin, Ray, Jr. petroleum company executive
McGowan, Patrick Francis lawyer
McGregor, Martin Luther, Jr. lawyer
†McKinney, Joseph F. diversified manufacturing holding company executive
McKnight, Joseph Webb law educator, historian
McLain, Maurice Clayton lawyer, real estate executive
McLane, David Glenn lawyer
Mc Lemore, Robert Henry petroleum engineer, consultant
McMahon, Gary Francis accountant
†McNamara, Anne H. lawyer, corporate executive
McNamara, Lawrence John lawyer
McNamara, Martin Burr lawyer, oil and gas company executive
Mc Quillan, Joseph Michael finance company executive
McTeer, Robert D., Jr. bank executive
McWhorter, Kathleen orthodontist
McWilliams, Mike C. lawyer
Mears, Rona Robbins lawyer
Mebus, Robert Gwynne lawyer
Meek, Paul Derald oil and chemical company executive
Melgar, Julio retired mechanical engineer
Menges, John Kenneth, Jr. lawyer
Meyer, Richard Jonah broadcast executive, consultant
Micciche, Daniel John lawyer
Middleton, Linda Jean Greathouse lawyer
†Miercort, Clifford Roy coal mining company executive
Mighell, Kenneth John lawyer
Miller, Madelyn Sue advertising executive, food and travel writer
Miller, William Vencill medical administrator
Millican, Bill T. construction company executive
Mills, Jerry Woodrow lawyer
†Mitchell, William B. electronics company executive
Modano, Michael professional hockey player
Moneypenny, Edward William oil and gas mining executive
Mong, Robert William, Jr. managing editor
Monsees, James Eugene engineering executive, consultant
Montgomery, Edward Benjamin physicist, retired educator
Montoya, Regina T. lawyer, television and radio commentator
Moore, Robert Clay petroleum industry executive, lawyer
Moore, Stanley Ray lawyer
Moore, Thomas Joseph financial company executive
Morgan, Larry Ronald minister
Morgan, Steven Michael lawyer
Morris, Rebecca Robinson lawyer
Morrison, Lionel B. architect
Mow, Robert Henry, Jr. lawyer
Mueller, Mark Christopher lawyer
Mullinax, Otto B. lawyer
Murad, John Louis clinical microbiology educator
Murphy, John Carter economics educator
Murphy, John Joseph manufacturing company executive
†Murphy, Randall Kent training consultant
Murrell, William Ivan accountant
Neaves, William Barlow cell biologist, educator
†Neff, Howard bank executive
Nelson, Steven Douglas lawyer
New, William Neil physician, retired naval officer
Nicewander, Dan Leon lawyer, rancher
Nichols, Henry Louis lawyer
Nicholson, G. Randy petroleum company executive
Nihill, Julian Dumontiel lawyer
Nordlund, William Chalmers lawyer
†Norsworthy, Lamar petroleum company executive
Notestine, Wilbur Edmund energy company executive, lawyer
Nurenberg, David oil company executive
Nye, Erle Allen utilities executive, lawyer
O'Leary, Robert W. hospital operations company executive
Olinger, Sheff Daniel neurologist, educator
Oliver, Thomas William lawyer
Osborne, Burl newspaper publisher, editor
Owen, Robert Randolph accountant
Pace, Carolina Jolliff communications executive, commercial real estate investor
Palmer, Ronald Leigh lawyer
Parker, Angelo Pan lawyer
Parker, Barry James Charles retail executive
Parsons, Ervin Ivy, Jr. petroleum company executive
Pastine, Maureen Diane librarian
Patterson, Joseph Redwine lawyer
Patterson, Ronald Paul publishing company executive, clergyman
Paul, M(alcolm) Lee psychology educator
Pearce, Ronald retired cosmetic company executive
Peart, Sherry Hartman lawyer
Peckham, Barry newspaper publishing executive
Pederson, Rena newspaper editor
Pell, Jonathan Laurence artistic administrator
Penegar, Kenneth Lawing law educator
Perkins, Alan J. lawyer
Perley, Mary Jo health facility administrator
Perot, H. Ross investments and real estate group executive, data processing services company executive
Perry, George Wilson oil and gas company executive
Perry, Kenneth Walter integrated oil company executive
Peterson, Edward Adrian lawyer
Pettey, Walter Graves, III lawyer
Petty, Charles Sutherland pathologist
Pew, John Glenn, Jr. lawyer
Phelan, Robin Eric lawyer
Philipson, Herman Louis, Jr. investment banker
Phillips, Bettie Mae elementary school educator
Pickens, Thomas Boone, Jr. oil company executive
Pike, Kenneth Lee linguist, educator
Pingree, Bruce Douglas lawyer
Pistor, Charles Herman, Jr. former banker, academic administrator
Pleasant, James Scott lawyer
Pogue, Mack real estate company executive
Portman, Glenn Arthur lawyer
Powell, Boone, Jr. hospital administrator
Powell, Larry Randall columnist
Pratt, Edward Taylor, Jr. real estate company executive
†Pratt, Jack E., Sr. hotel executive
Price, John Aley lawyer
Price, Robert Eben judge
Pride, Charley singer
Pritzker, Jay Arthur lawyer
Prude, Elaine S. principal
Pryor, Richard Walter telecommunications executive, retired air force officer
Purnell, Maurice Eugene, Jr. lawyer
Quasha, Alan G. oil and gas company executive
Quinn, David W. building company executive
Rabin, Stanley Arthur metal products manufacturer
Race, George Justice pathology educator
Radford, Norman DePue, Jr. lawyer
Raggio, Kenneth Gaylord lawyer
Raggio, Louise Ballerstedt lawyer
Ram, Chitta Venkata physician
Randolph, James Harrison, Sr. realty company executive
Ray, Bradley Stephen petroleum geologist
Ray, George Einar lawyer
Reagan, Barbara Benton economics educator
†Reid, Jack Powell oil company executive
Reid, Langhorne, III merchant banker
Reid, Rust Endicott lawyer
Reinert, James A. entomologist, educator
Rendell, Robert Sloat lawyer
Rice, Darrel Alan lawyer
Richardi, Ralph Leonard airline executive
Richards, Jeanne Herron artist
†Richards, Stanford Harvey advertising agency executive, design studio executive
Ries, Edward Richard petroleum geologist, consultant
Riggs, Arthur Jordy retired lawyer
Ringle, Brett Adelbert lawyer
Ritchie, Robert Field lawyer
Rivera, Richard E. food products executive
Robbins, Frank Ernest linguistics educator, administrator
Robbins, Ray Charles manufacturing company executive
Roberts, Harry Morris, Jr. lawyer
Robertson, Beverly Carruth steel company executive
Robertson, Ted Zanderson judge
Robinson, Hugh Granville consulting management company executive
Robinson, Lawrence Dewitt lawyer
Roche, William Joseph lawyer
Rochon, John Philip cosmetics company executive
Rodgers, John Hunter lawyer
Roeser, Ross Joseph audiologist, educator
Roger, Richard R. personal care industry executive
Rogers, Ralph B. industrial business executive
Rogers, Robert D. steel company executive
Rone, B. J. financial executive
†Rosebery, Richard Jay electronics company executive
Rosenberg, David Howard lawyer, mediator, marketing executive
Rosenberg, Roger Newman neurologist, educator
Rosenstein, Ira M. beverage products executive
Rosson, Glenn Richard building products and furniture company executive
Roy, Clarence Leslie landscape architect
Rubottom, Roy Richard, Jr. retired diplomat and educator, consultant
Rudberg, Joe Arthur lawyer
Rundell, Thomas Gardner lawyer
St. Claire, Frank Arthur lawyer
St. James, Lyn business owner, professional race car driver
St. John, Bill Dean diversified equipment and services company executive
St. John, Bob journalist, columnist, author
Salazar, Ramiro S. library administrator
Salvaggio, Tony Joe banker
Sammons, Elaine D. corporate executive
Sanders, Harold Barefoot, Jr. federal judge
Sanderson, William Fletcher, Jr. federal judge
Sanford, Jay Philip physician, government official
†Satterwhite, William T. lawyer, energy company executive
Savage, Scott David broadcast executive
Savage, Wallace Hamilton lawyer
Schmieder, Frank Joseph banker, business executive
Schoenbrun, Larry Lynn lawyer
Schreiber, Sally Ann lawyer
Schulman, Michael Robert lawyer
†Schulze, Richard Hans engineering executive, environmental engineer
Schwartz, Charles Morris lawyer
Schwartz, Irving Donn architect
Schwartz, Marilyn columnist
Scogin, Troy Pope publishing company executive, accounts executive
Scott, Manuel church administrator
Sculley, John computer company executive
Sechrest, William B. lawyer
See, Robert Fleming, Jr. lawyer
Senkayi, Abu Lwanga environmental soil scientist
Serpan, Roger L. cement and concrete company executive
Shapiro, Robert Alan retail executive
Shaw, Dean Alvin architect
Sheeder, Robert Elwood lawyer
Sheinberg, Israel computer company executive
†Sherman, Tara S. writer

Sherrod, Blackie *mewspaper sports columnist*
Shimer, Daniel Lewis *corporate executive*
Shoup, Andrew James, Jr. *oil company executive*
Siegel, Thomas Louis *lawyer*
Siegfried, Tom *newspaper editor*
Simmons, Glenn Reuben *management executive*
Simmons, Harold C. *sugar company executive*
Simmons, James F. *textiles executive*
Singer, Sanford Robert *diversified energy company executive*
Sizer, Phillip Spelman *consultant, retired oil field services executive*
Slater, Donald J. *restaurant executive*
Slater, Oliver Eugene *bishop*
†Smith, Andrew J. *chemicals executive*
Smith, Cece *venture capitalist*
Smith, David Lee *newspaper editor*
Smith, Edwin Ide *medical educator*
Smith, Larry Van *lawyer*
Smith, Nancy Lynne *journalist, real estate agent*
Smith, Russell L. *film critic*
Smith, Sue Frances *newspaper editor*
Smith, William Randolph (Randy Smith) *health care management association executive*
Snetzer, Michael Alan *multi-industry executive*
Snyder, Leslie *newspaper editor*
Snyder, Richard Wesley *manufacturing executive*
Snyder, William D. *photojournalist*
Solender, Robert Lawrence *financial and real estate corporation officer*
Solis, Jorge Antonio *federal judge*
Sonju, Norm Arnold *professional sports team manager, executive*
Sparkman, Robert Satterfield *retired surgeon, educator*
Spiegel, Lawrence Howard *advertising executive*
Sprague, Charles Cameron *medical foundation president*
Springer, Stanley G. *lawyer*
Srere, Paul A. *biochemist, educator*
Stacy, Dennis William *architect*
Stalcup, Joe Alan *lawyer, clergyman*
Staley, Joseph Hardin, Jr. *lawyer*
Starks, Richard *newspaper publishing executive*
Staubach, Roger Thomas *real estate executive, former professional football player*
Steinberg, Lawrence Edward *lawyer*
Steinhart, Ronald G. *banker*
Stembridge, Vernie A(lbert) *pathologist, educator*
Steorts, Nancy Harvey *international management consultant*
Stewart, Robert H., III *banker*
Stilwell, John Quincy *lawyer*
Stockard, James Alfred *lawyer*
Stone, Donald James *retired retail executive*
Stone, Marvin Jules *physician, immunologist educator*
Storey, Charles Porter *lawyer*
Strange, Donald Ernest *health care company executive*
Strauss, Robert Schwarz *lawyer, former ambassador*
Stuart, Norton Arlington, Jr. *data processing manufacturing executive*
Sturns, Vernell *airport terminal executive*
Sugg, Harry Lee, Jr. *dentist*
Swanson, Wallace Martin *lawyer*
Syphers, Mary Frances *music educator*
Taylor, Ramona Garrett *executive assistant*
†Termini, Deanne Lanoix *research company executive*
Terry, Marshall Northway, Jr. *English language educator, author*
Thau, William Albert, Jr. *lawyer*
Thomas, Robert Lee *financial services company executive, consultant*
Thompson, Charles Kerry *company executive*
†Thompson, Jere William *retail food company executive*
Thompson, Jesse Eldon *vascular surgeon*
Thorson, Marcelyn Marie *applied art educator*
Thrash, Purvis James, Sr. *retired oil field equipment and service company executive*
Thurston, Stephen John *pastor*
Toohig, Timothy E. *physicist*
Trevino, Lee Buck *professional golfer*
True, Roy Joe *lawyer*
Tubb, James Clarence *lawyer*
Tucker, Laurey Dan *lawyer*
Turner, Robert Gerald *university president*
Turpin, Jack A. *electronics executive*
Tygrett, Howard Volney, Jr. *lawyer*
Utley, John M. *corporate professional*
Valentine, Foy Dan *clergyman*
Vanatta, John Crothers, III *physiologist, physician, educator*
Vanderveld, John, Jr. *waste disposal company executive*
Veach, Robert Raymond, Jr. *lawyer*
Verges, Marianne Murphree *writer*
Vestal, Tommy Ray *lawyer*
Vetter, James George, Jr. *lawyer*
Vogel, Donald Stanley *gallery executive, artist*
Vondracek, Betty Sue *interior designer, remodeling contractor, real estate agent*
Walden, Linda L. *lawyer*
†Walker, Fergus Joseph, Jr. *manufacturing company executive*
Walkowiak, Vincent Steven *lawyer*
Wall, Sidney Smith Roderick, Jr. *architectural firm executive, architect, consultant*
Wallace, William C. *airline executive*
Wallace, William Ray *fabricated steel manufacturing company executive*
Wallenstein, James Harry *lawyer*
†Walthall, David N. *advertising executive*
Walvoord, John Flipse *seminary president, chancellor, theologian*
Watson, Edward L. *electric utility executive*
Watson, John R. *landscape illuminating company executive*
Weber, William P. *electronics company executive*
Weekley, Frederick Clay, Jr. *lawyer*
Weeks, Jerome C. *writer, drama critic*
Weiland, Stephen Cass *lawyer*
Weinkauf, William Carl *communications company executive*
†Weller, Edgar O. *transportation executive*
Wells, Leonard Nathaniel David, Jr. *lawyer*
Wenrich, John William *college president*
Werner, Joseph Granberry *lawyer*
Werner, Seth Mitchell *advertising executive*
West, William Beverley, III *lawyer*
Westerman, Howard G. *oil and gas company executive*
White, James Richard *lawyer*
Whitman, Reginald Norman *railroad official*
Whitson, James Norfleet, Jr. *diversified company executive*
Wilber, Robert Edwin *corporate executive*
Wildenthal, C(laud) Kern *physician, educator*
Wiles, Charles Preston *minister*
Willey, Paul Wayne *financial executive*
Williams, Gary Alan *management consultant*
Williams, Gordon L. *aircraft manufacturing executive*
Williams, James Alexander *lawyer*
Williams, Martha Spring *psychologist*
†Williams, Sterling Lee *electronics executive*
Williamson, Walker Kendrick *insurance executive*
Willingham, Clark Suttles *lawyer*
†Wilmut, Charles Gordon *environmental engineer*
Wilson, Claude Raymond, Jr. *lawyer*
Wilson, Jean Donald *endocrinologist, educator*
Wilson, Lawrence Alexander *construction company executive*
†Wilson, Richard A. *oil/gas industry support services executive*
Wilson, Trisha *interior architectural designer*
Winborn, Terry Lee *lawyer*
Winkel, Judy Kay *lawyer*
Winn, Edward Burton *lawyer*
†Winspear, William W. *home improvement company executive*
Winters, J. Otis *oil industry consultant*
Wise, Marvin Jay *lawyer*
Witmer, John Albert *librarian*
Wright, Wallace Mathias *lawyer*
Wuntch, Philip Samuels *journalist, film critic*
Wyly, Charles Joseph, Jr. *corporate executive*
Yanagisawa, Samuel Tsuguo *electronics executive*
Yeh, Lian-Tuu *mechanical engineer*
Young, Barney Thornton *lawyer*
Youngblood, Michelle Karen Wolstein *judge*
Ytterberg, Ralph Warren *company executive*
Ziebarth, Karl Rex *international transportation consultant*
Ziff, Morris *internist, rheumatologist, educator*
Zimmerman, S(amuel) Morton (Mort Zimmerman) *electrical and electronics engineering executive*
Zisman, Barry Stuart *lawyer*
Zumwalt, Richard Dowling *flour mill executive*

De Soto
Jackson, Johnny W. *minister*
Lee, J. E. *bishop*

Decatur
Davie, Ronald B. *corporate realty executive*

Deer Park
†Stabell, Walter W. *chemicals executive*

Del Rio
Thurmond, George Murat *judge*

Denison
Farr, Reeta Rae *special education administrator*
†Hohenberger, Arthur Lee *hospital administrator*

Denton
Baier, John Leonard *university educator*
Brock, Horace Rhea *accounting educator*
Brostow, Witold Konrad *materials scientist, educator*
Brown, John Fred *steel company executive*
Brownell, Blaine Allison *university administrator, history educator*
Cissell, William Bernard *health studies educator*
Clogan, Paul Maurice *English language and literature educator*
Elder, Mark Lee *university research administrator, writer*
Golden, David Edward *physicist*
Greenlaw, Marilyn Jean *education educator, consultant, writer*
Grose, B. Donald *library administrator*
Hurley, Alfred Francis *university administrator, historian*
Jernigan, Marian Sue *fashion merchandising educator*
Kamman, William *historian, educator*
Kesterson, David Bert *English language educator*
Latham, William Peters *composer, former educator*
Lawhon, John E., III *lawyer, former county official*
Lawhon, Tommie Collins Montgomery *child development/family living educator*
Leslie, Marvin Earl *minister*
Miller, Tom Polk *retired architect*
Newell, Charldean *public administration educator*
Nichols, Irby Coghill, Jr. *historian, educator, entrepreneur*
Palermo, Judy Hancock *elementary school educator*
†Poole, Eva Duraine *librarian*
Preston, Thomas Ronald *English language educator, researcher*
Renka, Robert Joseph *computer science educator, consultant*
Rhoades, Warren A., Jr. *retired mechanical engineer*
Schwalm, Fritz Ekkehardt *biology educator*
Snapp, Elizabeth *librarian, educator*
Snapp, Harry Franklin *historian*
†Surles, Carol D. *university president*
Swigger, B. Keith *dean*
†Swigger, Keith B. *dean*
Thompson, Leslie Melvin *college dean, educator*
Toulouse, Robert Bartell *retired college administrator*
Vaughn, William Preston *historian, educator*
Vick, Frances Brannen *publishing executive*
Waage, Mervin Bernard *lawyer*
Westmoreland, Reginald Conway *journalism educator*

Diboll
Ericson, Roger Delwin *lawyer, forest resource company executive*
Grum, Clifford J. *manufacturing company executive*

Dickinson
Bush, Robert Thomas *shipping company executive*

Dripping Springs
Ballard, Mary Melinda *financial communications and investment banking firm executive*
Rios, Evelyn Deerwester *columnist, musician, artist, writer*

Early
Chapman, Dan G. *minister*

Eden
Boyd, John Hamilton *osteopath*

Edinburg
Esparza, Thomas, Sr. *academic athletics administrator*
Livas, Eduardo, Jr. *milling company executive*
Vassberg, David Erland *history educator*

El Campo
Goelzer, Ronald Eric *surgeon*

El Paso
Ainsa, Francis Swinburne *lawyer*
Bailey, Kenneth Kyle *history educator*
Blevins, Leon Wilford *political science educator, minister*
Carroll, Edwin Winford *architect*
Cassidy, Richard Thomas *hotel executive, defense industry consultant, retired army officer*
Coleman, Edmund Benedict *university dean*
Coleman, Howard S. *engineer, physicist*
Cook, Clarence Sharp *physics educator*
Crossen, John Jacob *radiologist, educator*
Day, James Milton *foundation executive, English educator*
Dell'Osso, Luino, Jr. *natural gas pipeline executive*
De Vargas, Cecilia Cordoba *psychiatrist*
Dyer, Travis Neal *defense consultant, retired army officer*
Feuille, Richard Harlan *lawyer*
Francis, Larry *mayor*
Friedkin, Joseph Frank *consulting engineering executive*
Fry, L(eo) Marcus, Jr. *hospital administrator*
Gainer, Barbara Jeanne *radiology educator*
Grieves, Robert Belanger *engineering educator*
Grimes, William Gaylord *adult education educator*
Hardaway, Robert Morris, III *physician, educator, retired army officer*
Harris, Arthur Horne *biology educator*
Heger, Herbert Krueger *education educator*
Henderson, Walter G. *utility company executive*
Hoskins, Curtis Lynn *utility executive*
Hudspeth, Harry Lee *federal judge*
Ingle, Henry Thomas *communications educator, university administrator*
Jackson, Jean Therese *surgeon*
Jurey, Wes *chamber of commerce executive*
Kelley, Sylvia Johnson *financial services firm executive*
Kidd, Gerald Steele, II *endocrinologist, educator*
Kimmel, Herbert David *psychology educator*
Leach, Joseph Lee *English language educator, author*
Maguire, Blanche Joan (Maggie) *watercolorist*
Malone, Debra Beatrice *elementary education educator*
Marshall, Richard Treeger *lawyer*
†Mason, Richard Clyde *landscape architect*
McCotter, James Rawson *lawyer*
†McLeod, Ronald *school system administrator*
Mitchell, Paula Rae *nursing educator*
Natalicio, Diana Siedhoff *university president*
Ornstein-Galicia, Jacob Leonard (Jack Ornstein-Galicia) *foreign language educator, linguist, author*
Pena, Raymundo Joseph *bishop*
Prendergast, Thomas A. *investments and management consultant*
Quevedo, Hector Adolf *operations research analyst, environmental scientist*
Ricks, Thomas Edwin *accounting executive*
Riter, Stephen *university administrator, electrical engineer*
†Roark, Charles Elvis *healthcare executive*
Roberts, Ernst Edward *marketing consultant*
Rout, Nancy Louise *health facility administrator*
Ruesch, Janet Carol *federal magistrate judge*
Schmidt, L. Lee, Jr. *university official*
Schnadig, Edgar Louis *entrepreneur, management consultant*
Shapiro, Stephen Richard *retired air force officer, physician*
Sipiora, Leonard Paul *retired museum director*
Smith, Tad Randolph *lawyer*
Stoddard, Ellwyn R. *sociology and anthropology educator*
Strait, Viola Edwina Washington *librarian*
Suissa, Mireille Renee *company executive, computer consultant*
Tackett, Stephen Douglas *education services specialist*
Treadwell, Hugh Wilson *publishing executive*
†Verghese, Abraham Cheeran *internist, writer, educator*
von Tungeln, George Robert *retired university administrator, economics consultant*
Wiggs, David Harold, Jr. *utilities company executive*
Wise, William Allan *oil company executive, lawyer*

Ennis
Mitchell, Robert Lynn *business supply company executive*

Euless
Paran, Mark Lloyd *lawyer*

Floresville
Alvarez, Olga Mendoza *elementary school educator*

Flower Mound
Gooch, Brian Eugene *health care executive, policy analyst, consultant*
Kolodny, Stanley Charles *oral surgeon, air force officer*
Morrish, Thomas Jay *golf course architect*

Forney
Cates, Don Tate *mayor, lawyer*

Fort Bliss
†Charlip, Ralph Blair *career officer*
†Cravens, James J., Jr. *military officer*

Fort Hood
Burke, Charles Michael *military officer*
Hughes, William Foster *career officer, surgeon, obstetrician, gynecologist*

Fort Sam Houston
Cameron, Richard Douglas *military officer, psychiatrist*
Pruitt, Basil Arthur, Jr. *surgeon, army officer*
†Rogers, Jody Ray *army officer*

Fort Worth
Ahmed, M. Basheer *psychiatrist, educator*
Allmand, Linda F(aith) *library director*
Anderson, John Quentin *rail transportation executive*
Appel, Bernard Sidney *electrical company executive*
Ard, Harold Jacob *library administrator*
Arena, M. Scott *pharmaceutical company executive*
Asher, Garland Parker *investment holding company executive*
Auping, Michael G. *curator*
Bagsby, N. Dionne *county commissioner, speech pathologist*
Barnes, Karen Geddes *nurse, healthcare facility executive*
Bass, Perry Richardson *oil company executive*
Battista, Orlando Aloysius *scientist, author, executive, inventor*
Becker, James William *lawyer, natural resource and transportation holding company executive*
Belew, David Owen, Jr. *judge*
Bell, David Eugene *investment company executive*
Berg, Ericson *insurance company executive*
Blazina, Janice Fay *transfusion medicine physician*
Bolen, Bob *retail merchant, university administrator*
Bousquette, William Charles *financial executive*
Boyce, Allan R. *human resources executive*
Boyd, Jeanean B. *hospital administrator*
Brandt, Roger Del *pharmaceutical company executive*
Brodale, Louise Lado *medical, post surgery and geriatrics nurse*
Brosseau, Charles Martin, Jr. *hospital administrator*
Brown, C. Harold *lawyer*
Brown, Richard Lee *lawyer*
Buckley, Betty Bob *journalist, consultant*
Calkins, Loren Gene *church executive, clergyman*
Chalk, John Allen *lawyer*
Chapman, Ira B., II *food products executive*
Clark, Emory Eugene *financial planning executive*
Cliburn, Van (Harvey Lavan Cliburn, Jr.) *concert pianist*
Collins, Whitfield James *lawyer*
Connor, Richard L. *publisher, editor*
Crane, Neal Dahlberg *manufacturing company executive*
Crumley, John Walter *lawyer*
Cunningham, Atlee Marion, Jr. *aeronautical engineer*
Cunningham, Raymond Clement *glass company executive*
Dagnon, James Bernard *human resources executive*
Davis, Jimmie Dan *newspaper editor*
Dean, Beale *lawyer*
Dean, Margo *artistic director*
Dees, Sandra Kay Martin *psychologist, research consultant*
Delaney, Joseph P. *bishop*
de Sousa, Byron Nagib *physician, anesthesiologist, clinical pharmacologist and educator*
de Tonnancour, Paul Roger Godefroy *library administrator*
Doherty, Edward J. *academic administrator*
Dominiak, Geraldine Florence *accounting educator*
Doran, Robert Stuart *mathematician, educator*
Doris Ann, (Doris Ann Scharfenberg) *producer, former broadcasting company executive*
†Edwards, Samuel Lee *religious organization executive*
Elliott, John Franklin *clergyman*
Erisman, Fred Raymond *English literature educator*
Franks, Jon Michael *lawyer, mediator*
Geren, Preston Murdoch, Jr. *architect, engineer*
Gideon, Randall Clifton *architectural firm executive*
Gilbert, James Cayce *minister*
Giordano, John Read *conductor*
Granger, Kay *mayor*
Gray, Gene *banker*
Greenhill, William Duke *lawyer*
Greenwood, William E. *rail transportation executive*
Grinstein, Gerald *transportation executive*
Gross, John Birney *retired minister*
Gutsche, Carl David *chemistry educator*
†Hammond, Wilton N. *civil engineer, consultant, architectural firm executive*
Henderson, Suzanne *county government official*
Herlihy, James Edward *retail executive*
Hicks, Maryellen Whitlock *lawyer, judge*
Hogan, Ben *former professional golfer, business executive*
Horner, Winifred Bryan *educator, researcher, consultant, writer*
Howison, George Everett *financial executive*
Hurley, Linda Kay *psychologist*
Hyde, Clarence Brodie, II *oil company executive*
Jensen, Harlan Ellsworth *veterinarian, educator*
Joe, George Washington *clinical researcher, quantitative methodologist*
Joiner, Webb Francis *helicopter manufacturing company executive*
Jurgensen, Warren Peter *psychiatrist, educator*
Kaman, Mark Joseph *health science facility administrator*
Kelly, Dee J. *lawyer*
Keltner, David E. *lawyer, judge*
Kenderdine, John Marshall *petroleum engineer, retired army officer*
Landolt, Robert George *chemistry educator*
Leone, George Frank *pharmaceutical executive*
Lorenzetti, Ole John *pharmaceutical research executive, ophthalmic research and development executive*
Mack, Theodore *lawyer*
Mahon, Eldon Brooks *federal judge*
Malone, Dan F. *journalist*
Martin, Harold Eugene *publishing executive, consultant*
McBryde, John Henry *federal judge*
McConnell, Michael Arthur *lawyer*
McGlinchey, Alexander Herbert *federal judge*
McKinney, James Carroll *baritone, educator*
McMackin, John William *lawyer*
McWhiney, Grady *history educator*
Means, Terry Robert *federal judge*
†Mejia, Paul Roman *choreographer, dancer*
†Messman, Jack L. *oil executive*
†Metzler, Thomas M. *service company executive*
Michero, William Henderson *retired retail trade executive*
Miller, Brian Keith *airline executive*
Mills, John James *research director, mechanical engineering educator*
Minton, Jerry Davis *lawyer, former banker*
Mowery, Anna Renshaw *state legislator*
Munn, Cecil Edwin *lawyer*
Murnane, Thomas George, Jr. *public health veterinarian, military*
Newport, John Paul *philosophy of religion educator, former academic administrator*
Newsom, Douglas Ann Johnson *writer, journalism educator*
Nichols, James Richard *civil engineer, consultant*
Nichols, Robert Leighton *civil engineer*

Pavony, William H. *retail executive*
Peipert, James Raymond *journalist*
Peters, Lawrence H. *management educator, consultant*
Pillsbury, Edmund Pennington *museum director*
†Pinson, Ray L. *banking services holding company executive*
Price, Debbie Mitchell *journalist, newspaper editor*
Price, Larry C. *photojournalist*
Price, Michael Howard *journalist, critic, composer, cartoonist*
Quarles, Carroll Adair, Jr. *physicist, educator*
Ratliff, William D., III *lawyer*
Ratliff, William Durrah, Jr. *lawyer*
Ravel, Dilip N. *pharmaceutical executive*
Ray, Paul Richard, Jr. *executive search consultant*
Record, Phillip Julius *newspaper executive*
Reinecke, Manfred G. *chemistry educator*
Reuter, Frank Theodore *history educator*
Rivera, Angel (Andy) Manuel *retired career officer, city official*
Roach, John Vinson, II *retail company executive*
Roberts, Leonard H. *retail executive*
Robinson, Nell Bryant *nutrition educator*
Rogers, Charles Ray *minister, religious organization administrator*
Romine, Thomas Beeson, Jr. *consulting engineering executive*
Saenz, Michael *college president*
Salih, Halil Ibrahim *political science educator*
Sasser, William Jack *government official*
Scearse, Patricia Dotson *nurse educator, college dean*
Schollmaier, Edgar H. *pharmaceutical products company executive*
Schrum, Jake Bennett *university administrator*
Sharpe, James Shelby *lawyer*
Shosid, Joseph Lewis *government official*
Smith, Thomas Hunter *ophthalmologist, ophthalmic plastic and orbital surgeon*
Smith, William Burton *chemist, educator*
†Snyder, John C. *oil and gas industry executive*
†Standifer, Monty Ray *controller*
Suggs, Marion Jack *minister, college dean*
Sullenberger, Ara Broocks *mathematics educator*
Tade, George Thomas *university dean*
Tarpley, James Merrell *utility company executive*
Teegarden, Kenneth Leroy *clergyman*
†Thompson, Douglas A. *aerospace engineer*
Thornton, Charles Victor *metals executive*
Tilley, Rice M(atthews), Jr. *lawyer*
Tinsley, Jackson Bennett *newspaper editor*
Tucker, William Edward *university chancellor, clergyman*
Turner, Loyd Leonard *advertising executive, public relations executive*
Webb, Theodore Stratton, Jr. *aerospace scientist, consultant*
Wertz, Spencer K. *philosophy educator*
Wheaton, David Joe *aerospace manufacturing company executive*
Wilkie, Valleau, Jr. *foundation executive*
†Williamson, Doug *data processing executive*
Willis, Doyle Henry *state legislator, lawyer*
Woofter, R. D. *utilities company executive*
Worcester, Donald Emmet *history educator, author*
Yarbro, James Wesley *financial executive*
Zimmerman, Bill J. *oil company executive, lawyer*

Freeport
Baskin, William Gresham *counselor*

Galveston
Arens, James F. *anesthesiologist, educator*
Bailey, Byron James *otolaryngologist, medical association executive*
Baker, Robert Ernest, Jr. *foundation executive*
Banet, Charles Henry *college president emeritus, clergyman*
Baron, Samuel *microbiologist, physician*
Barratt, Ernest Stoelting *psychologist, educator*
Bircher, Edgar Allen *lawyer*
Bonchev, Danail Georgiev *chemist, educator*
Budelmann, Bernd Ulrich *zoologist, educator*
Burns, Chester Ray *medical history educator*
Caldwell, Garnett Ernest *lawyer*
Calverley, John Robert *physician, educator*
Carrier, Warren Pendleton *retired university chancellor, writer*
Clay, Orson C. *insurance company executive*
Clayton, William Howard *retired university president*
Dawson, Earl Bliss *obstetrics and gynecology educator*
Elbert, James Peak *independent insurance agent, minister*
Ewing, George H. *pipeline company executive*
Fisher, Seymour *psychologist, educator*
Giam, Choo-Seng *marine science educator*
Gibson, Hugh *federal judge*
Gold, Daniel Howard *ophthalmologist, educator*
Goodwin, Jean McClung *psychiatrist*
Gorenstein, David G. *chemistry educator*
Grant, J(ohn) Andrew, Jr. *medical educator, allergist*
Harris, John Woods *banker, lawyer*
Hilton, James Gorton *pharmacologist*
James, Thomas Naum *cardiologist, educator*
Kent, Samuel B. *federal judge*
Koeppe, Patsy Poduska *internist, educator*
Kurosky, Alexander *biochemist, educator*
Lefeber, Edward James, Sr. *physician*
Levin, William Cohn *hematologist, former university president*
McLeod, E. Douglas *real estate developer, lawyer*
Merrell, William John, Jr. *oceanography educator*
Moore, Peter Melville *foundation adminstrator*
Norman, Dudley Kent *hospital administrator, nurse*
Ogra, Pearay L. *physician, educator*
Otis, John James *civil engineer*
Pearl, William Richard Emden *pediatric cardiologist*
Powell, Don Watson *medical educator, physiology researcher*
Powell, Leslie Charles, Jr. *obstetrics and gynecology educator*
Prakash, Satya *biology educator*
Robertson, C. R. *insurance company executive*
Russell, Attie Yvonne *academic administrator, dean, pediatrics educator*
Sandstead, Harold Hilton *medical educator*
Santschi, Peter Hans *marine sciences educator*
Schmidly, David J. *dean*
Schoenbucher, Bruce *health physicist*
Schreiber, Melvyn Hirsh *radiologist*
Schwartz, Aaron Robert *lawyer, former state legislator*
Sheppard, Louis Clarke *biomedical engineer, educator*
Shope, Robert Ellis *epidemiology educator*
Smith, David English *physician, educator*
Smith, Edgar Benton *physician*
Smith, Jerome Hazen *pathologist*
Thomas, Leelamma Koshy *women's health care nurse*
Thompson, Edward Ivins Brad *biological chemistry and genetics educator, molecular endocrinologist, department chairman*
Tyson, Kenneth Robert Thomas *surgeon, educator*
Welch, Ronald J. *actuary*
Willis, William Darrell, Jr. *neurophysiologist, educator*
Würsig, Bernd Gerhard *marine biology educator*
†Zimmerman, Roger Joseph *fisherie biologist*

Garland
Adams, Christopher Steve, Jr. *defense electronics corporation executive, former air force officer*
Driver, Joe L. *state legislator, insurance agent*
Duren, Michael *cardiologist*
Foster, Rebecca Anne Hodges *secondary school educator*
Jackson, Edwin L. *electrical engineer*
†Lindsey, Lowell L. *library director*
McGill, Maurice Leon *financial executive*
McGrath, James Thomas *real estate investment company executive*
Nicholson, Luther Beal *financial consultant*
†Ray, Richard T. *manufacturing executive, heavy*
†Ryno, Ronald Pat *business executive, chemical engineer*
Shugart, Jill *school system administrator*
Smith, Robert Hughes, Jr. (Bob Smith) *municipal official*
Stimpson, Ritchie Ples *retired United States air force officer*
Threlkeld, Mary Helen *accountant*

Gary
Speer, James *religious organization administrator*

Georgetown
Browning, Grayson Douglas *philosophy educator*
Davis, O. L., Jr. *education educator, researcher*
Gerding, Thomas Graham *medical products company executive*
Girvin, Eb Carl *biology educator*
Lord, William Grogan *financial holding company executive*
Neville, Gwen Kennedy *anthropology educator*
Rosenthal, Michael Ross *academic administrator, dean*
Shilling, Roy Bryant, Jr. *college president*
Weyrauch, Paul Turney *retired army officer*
White, Alvin Swauger *aerospace scientist, consultant*

Glen Rose
Ragan, James Otis *engineer, consultant*

Granbury
Fletcher, Riley Eugene *lawyer*
Killebrew, James Robert *architectural engineering firm executive*
McWilliams, Chris Pater Elissa *elementary school educator*
Wisler, Charles Clifton, Jr. *retired cotton oil company executive*

Grand Prairie
Childs, Hymen *broadcasting corporation executive*
Martin-Nagle, Carol Renee *lawyer*
Ritterhouse, Kathy Lee *librarian*
†Smith, G. Scott *insurance company executive*

Granger
Horton, Claude Wendell *physicist, educator*

Grapevine
Friedman, Barry *financial marketing consultant*
Hatch, John D. *lawyer, consultant*
Holley, Cyrus Helmer *management consulting service executive*
Melton, Lynda Gayle *reading specialist, educational diagnostician*
Smith, Lee Herman *business executive*

Greenville
Johnston, John Thomas *engineering executive*

Gun Barrel City
Smith, Thelma Tina Harriette *gallery owner, artist*

Hale Center
Courtney, Carolyn Ann *school librarian*

Hallettsville
Baber, Wilbur H., Jr. *lawyer*

Harlingen
Bonner, Donna Pace *real estate investments, consultant, volunteer*
Ephraim, Charles *lawyer*
Farris, Robert Gene *transportation company executive*
Glasgow, Harold Glyn *military academy administrator*
Johnson, Orrin Wendell *lawyer*
Ryall, A(lbert) Lloyd *horticulturist, refrigeration engineer*
Solis, Jim *state legislator, lawyer*

Hearne
Moore, Loretta Westbrook *banker*

Heath
Kolodey, Fred James *lawyer*

Hemphill
Boren, Hollis Grady *retired physician*

Hillsboro
Auvenshine, William Robert *academic administrator*

Hitchcock
Doyle, Charles Thomas *banker*

Horseshoe Bay
Lesikar, Raymond Vincent *business administration educator*
Moore, Lawrence Jack *lawyer*
Ramey, James Melton *chemist*

Houston
Abercia, Ralph *lawyer, financial advisor*
Able, Luke William *retired pediatric surgeon, consultant*
Ablott, Vance Randall *science foundation administrator*
†Abramson, Morrie Kaplan *electronics executive*
Adair, Red (Paul Neal Adair) *oil well problem control specialist*
Addison, Linda Leuchter *lawyer*
Adelman, Graham Lewis *lawyer*
Aguilar, Melissa Ward *newspaper editor*
Ahart, Jan Fredrick *electrical manufacturing company executive*
Akers, William Walter *chemical engineering educator*
Albrecht, Kay Montgomery *educational administrator, consultant, child advocate*
†Alderson, David P., III *oil company executive*
Alexander, Michael Lee *music educator, cellist*
Alexander, Neil Kenton *lawyer*
Alexanian, Raymond *hematologist*
Alford, Bobby Ray *physician, educator, university official*
Allen, Don Lee *dentistry educator*
Allender, John Roland *lawyer*
Allison, William V. *oil industry executive*
Amundson, Neal Russell *chemical engineer, mathematician, educator*
Anders, Milton Howard *lawyer*
Anderson, Claire W. *computer gifted and talented educator*
Anderson, D(arryl) Kent *banker*
Anderson, Eric Severin *lawyer*
Anderson, Richard Carl *geophysical exploration company executive*
Anderson, Robert Dennis *lawyer*
Anderson, Thomas Dunaway *retired lawyer*
Anderson, William (Albion), Jr. *oil and gas producer, investment banker*
Andrews, Glenn T. *oil company executive*
Andrews, Lavone D. *architect*
Anthony, Donald Barrett *engineering executive*
Appel, Stanley Hersh *neurologist*
Arnold, Daniel Calmes *finance company executive*
Arnold, Gordon Thomas *lawyer*
Ashby, Lynn Cox *newspaper editor*
Askew, William Earl *chemist, educator*
Atlas, Nancy Friedman *lawyer, mediator, arbitrator*
Atlas, Scott Jerome *lawyer*
Auchmuty, Giles *applied mathematics educator*
Austin, Harry Guiden *engineering and construction company executive*
Austin, Page Insley *lawyer*
Auston, David Henry *university administrator, educator*
Azíos, Blanca Stella *pediatrician, medical administrator, educator*
Backus, Marcia Ellen *lawyer*
†Bagwell, Jeff (Jeffrey Robert Bagwell) *professional baseball player*
Bagwell, Louis Lee *lawyer*
Bailar, Benjamin Franklin *academic administrator, administration educator*
Bailey, Charles Lyle *insurance company executive*
†Bailey, Harold Randolph *surgeon*
Bailey, Joe M. *banker*
Bair, Royden Stanley *architect*
Baker, James Addison, III *lawyer, former government official*
Baker, Stephen Denio *physics educator*
Balch, Charles M. *surgeon, educator*
Baldwin, John Charles *surgeon, researcher*
Bally, Albert W. *geology educator*
Bambace, Robert Shelly *lawyer*
Bankston, Gene Clifton *oil and gas consultant*
Baranowski, Tom *public health educator, researcher*
Barlow, Jim B. *newspaper columnist*
Barnett, Edward William *lawyer*
Barney, Charles Lester *petroleum company executive*
Barracano, Henry Ralph *retired oil company executive, consultant*
Barrett, John Adams *lawyer*
Barrett, Lyle Eugene *retail buyer, designer, artist*
Barrow, Thomas Davies *oil and mining company executive*
Barry, Allan Ronald *ship pilot, corporate executive*
Barthelme, Donald *architect*
Baskin, David Stuart *neurosurgeon*
Bast, Robert Clinton, Jr. *research scientist, medical educator*
Batsakis, John George *pathology educator*
Baugh, John Frank *wholesale company executive*
Baughn, Robert Elroy *microbiology educator*
Bean, Alan LaVern *retired astronaut, artist*
Beasley, Robert Palmer *epidemiologist, dean, educator*
Bech, Douglas York *lawyer*
Beck, John Robert *pathologist, information scientist*
Becker, Frederick Fenimore *cancer center administrator, pathologist*
Beckingham, Kathleen Mary *educator, researcher*
Beghini, Victor Gene *oil company executive*
Bell, Howard Earl *natural gas distribution executive*
Bellatti, Lawrence Lee *lawyer*
Benitez, Maurice Manuel *bishop*
Bennett, George Nelson *biochemistry educator*
Bennett, Richard Gerald *gas company executive*
Bentsen, Kenneth Edward *architect*
Berg, David Howard *lawyer*
Berra, Yogi (Lawrence Peter Berra) *professional baseball coach*
Berry, Julianne Elward *polymer and colloid chemist, researcher, inventor*
Berry, Michael A. *physician, consultant*
Berry, Thomas Eugene *lawyer*
Bethea, Louise Huffman *allergist*
†Bethune, Gordon *airline executive*
Bhandari, Arvind *oncologist*
Bickel, Stephen Douglas *insurance company executive*
Billingsley, David Stuart *chemical engineer, researcher*
†Biltz, Stuart James *health care administrator*
Bischoff, Susan Ann *newspaper editor*
Bishop, David Nolan *electrical engineer*
Bishop, Mary Lou *artist*
Bistline, F. Walter, Jr. *lawyer*
Bizzell, Bobby Gene *academic administrator*
Bjornson, Carroll Norman *business owner*
Black, Norman William *federal judge*
Blackshear, A. T., Jr. *lawyer*
†Blanton, Jack Sawtelle *oil company executive*
Bliss, Ronald Glenn *lawyer*
Bluestein, Edwin A., Jr. *lawyer*
Bodey, Gerald Paul *oncologist, educator*
Boles, John Bruce *history educator*
Bollerer, Fred L. *banker*
†Bonderman, David *airline company executive*
Bonham, Donald L. *food service executive*
Bonica, John R. *lawyer*
Bonner, Billy Edward *physics educator*
Bonnet, Beatriz Alicia *interpreter, translator, flutist*
Bonneville, Richard Briggs *petroleum exploration and production executive*
Bookout, John Frank, Jr. *oil company executive*
Boren, William Meredith *manufacturing executive*
Borget, Lloyd George *architect*
Boston, Charles D. *lawyer*
Botley, Calvin *lawyer, magistrate judge*
Boudreaux, Thomas Lee *energy company executive*
Bousquet, Thomas Gourrier *lawyer*
Bovay, Harry Elmo, Jr. *retired engineering company executive*
Bowen, W. J. *retired gas company executive*
Bowersox, Thomas H. *executive*
Boyd, Gregory *theater director*
Boyd, John E. *lawyer*
Brackley, William Lowell *aviation management consultant*
Bracy, Michael Blakeslee *energy company executive*
Brandenstein, Daniel Charles *astronaut, retired naval officer*
Brandt, I. Marvin *chemist, engineer*
Brann, Richard Roland *lawyer*
Brantley, John Randolph *lawyer*
Brents, Daniel Rugel *architectural firm executive*
Bridger, Baldwin, Jr. *electrical engineer*
Bridges, David Manning *lawyer*
Brinsmade, Lyon Louis *lawyer*
Brinson, Gay Creswell, Jr. *lawyer*
Brito, Dagobert Llanos *economics educator*
Brody, Baruch Alter *medical educator, academic center administrator*
Brooks, Philip Russell *chemistry educator, researcher*
Brotzen, Franz Richard *materials science educator*
Brouse, Michael *petroleum engineer, management consultant*
Brown, Dennison Robert *mathematician, educator*
Brown, Glenda Ann Walters *ballet director*
Brown, Jack Harold Upton *physiology educator, university official, biomedical engineer*
Brown, Jean William *advertising and public relations executive*
Brown, Karen Kennedy *federal judge*
Brown, Lewis Arnold *financial consultant*
Brown, Sara Lou *accounting firm executive*
Bryan, James Lee *oil field service company executive*
Bryan, J(ames) P(erry), Jr. *energy company executive*
Bryant, John Bradbury *economics educator, consultant*
Buchanan, Dennis Michael *manufacturing and holding company executive*
Buckingham, Edwin John, III *lawyer*
Bue, Carl Olaf, Jr. *retired federal judge*
Bui, Khoi Tien *college counselor*
Bunch, Fred *newspaper picture editor*
Bungo, Michael William *physician, educator, science administrator*
Burch, Voris Reagan *lawyer*
Burdette, Walter James *surgeon, educator*
Burdine, John A. *hospital administrator, nuclear medicine educator*
Burguieres, Philip *energy service and manufacturing company executive*
Burke, Kevin Charles Antony *geologist*
†Burrow, Harold *gas company executive*
Burrus, Charles Sidney *electrical engineering educator*
Busch, Harris *medical educator*
Bush, Barbara Pierce *volunteer, wife of former President of the United States*
Bush, George Herbert Walker *former President of the United States*
Butler, William Thomas *college president, physician, educator*
†Butters, David J. *oil industry executive*
Byars, Carlos *newspaper reporter*
Caddy, Michael Douglas *lawyer*
Cain, Gordon A. *chemicals company executive*
Caldwell, James Wiley *lawyer*
Calhoun, Frank Wayne *lawyer, former state legislator*
Calhoun, Harold *architect*
Caltrider, Thomas Lewis *environmental company executive*
Camarillo, Richard Jon *professional football player*
Cameron, Bruce Francis *data processing executive*
Cameron, William Duncan *plastics company executive*
Camfield, William Arnett *art educator*
Campbell, Bert Louis *lawyer*
Cantrell, William Allen *psychiatrist, educator*
Cantwell, Thomas *geophysicist, electrical engineer*
Capps, Ethan LeRoy *oil company executive*
Carameros, George Demitrius, Jr. *natural gas company executive*
Cardus, David *physician*
Carlquist, Robert E. *newspaper publishing executive*
†Carmichael, David M. *petroleum industry executive*
Carmody, James Albert *lawyer*
Carrington, Samuel Macon, Jr. *French language educator*
Carroll, James Vincent, III *lawyer*
†Carroll, Loren Kenneth *oil company executive*
Carroll, Michael M. *academic dean, mechanical engineering educator*
Carroll, Philip Joseph *oil company executive*
Carsey, Lamberth S. *lawyer*
Carter, John Boyd, Jr. *oil operator, bank executive*
Caskey, Charles Thomas *biology and genetics educator*
Castañeda, James Agustín *Spanish language educator, university golf coach*
Castillo, Leonel Jabier *communications and promotions executive, consultant*
Cater, James Thomas *financial and investment planner*
Catlin, Francis Irving *physician*
Caudill, William Howard *lawyer*
Cernan, Eugene A. *management company executive, former astronaut*
Chafin, James Scott *lawyer*
Chaku, Pran Nath *international consulting metallurgist*
Chalmers, David B. *petroleum executive*
Chamberlain, Joseph Wyan *astronomer, educator*
Chance, Jane *educator*
Chang, Robert Huei *library director*
Chapman, Alan Jesse *mechanical engineering educator*
Chase, John Saunders *architect*
Cheatham, John Bane, Jr. *mechanical engineering educator*
Cheavens, Joseph D. *lawyer*
Childress, Raymond Clay, Jr. *professional football player*

Christian, George Lloyd, Jr. *newspaper editor, writer*
Christopher, Socrates S. *engineering executive*
Chu, Paul Ching-Wu *physicist*
Chu, Wei-Kan *physicist, educator*
Cizik, Robert *manufacturing company executive*
Claiborn, Stephen Allan *investment banker*
Clark, John William, Jr. *electrical engineer, educator*
Clark, Letitia Z. *federal judge*
Clark, Pat English *lawyer*
Clark, Ron D(ean) *cosmetologist*
Clark, Scott *newspaper editor*
Clarke, Robert Logan *lawyer*
Clayton, William Lewis *retired utility executive*
Clemenceau, Paul B. *lawyer*
Clemons, Ralph Hardy, Jr. *diversified manufacturing company executive*
Cline, C. Bob *natural gas company executive*
Clore, Lawrence H. *lawyer*
Cochran, Les *lawyer*
Code, James Manley Wayne *manufacturing executive*
Cofran, George Lee *management consultant*
Coghlan, Kelly Jack *lawyer*
Cole, Aubrey Louis *management consultant, forest products company executive*
Coleman, Mabeth Hallmark *newspaper publishing professional*
Collins, Terry *professional baseball*
Collins, Vincent Patrick *radiologist, physician, educator*
Comer, Clarence C. *oil, gas and cement company executive*
Condit, Linda Faulkner *economist*
Conger, Franklin Barker *oil company executive*
Cook, B. Thomas *lawyer*
Cook, Eugene Augustus *lawyer*
Cooley, Denton Arthur *surgeon, educator*
Cooper, Paul *composer, educator*
Corral, Edward Anthony *fire marshal*
Corriere, Joseph N., Jr. *urologist, educator*
Couch, J. O. Terrell *lawyer, former oil company executive*
Couch, Jesse Wadsworth *retired insurance company executive, consultant*
Couch,
Crawford, David Coleman *retired diversified manufacturing company executive*
Crispin, Andre Arthur *international trading company executive*
Criswell, Ann *newspaper editor*
Crites, Omar Don, Jr. *lawyer*
Crooker, John H., Jr. *lawyer*
Crow, Michael Ray *savings and loan executive, accountant*
Crowell, Steven Galt *philosophy educator*
†Culbertson, Frank L. *astronaut*
Cullom, Hale Ellicott *investment company executive*
Cunningham, Dan *newspaper editor*
Cunningham, R. Walter *venture capitalist*
Cunningham, Tom Alan *lawyer*
Curfiss, Robert Clinton *lawyer*
Curl, Robert Floyd, Jr. *chemistry educator*
Currie, John Thornton (Jack Currie) *retired investment banker*
Curry, Alton Frank *lawyer*
Cuthbertson, Gilbert Morris *political science educator*
Cuthbertson, James *healthcare executive*
Cutler, John Earl *landscape architect*
Dack, Christopher Edward Hughes *lawyer*
Daerr, Richard Leo, Jr. *multi-services company executive, lawyer*
Dagley, Larry Jack *energy company executive*
Daily, James L., Jr. *retired financial executive*
†Dalston, Jeptha William *hospital administrator, educator*
Danburg, Jerome Samuel *oil company executive*
Dartez, Franklin *banker*
Davenport, Joseph Dale *insurance executive*
Davidson, Chandler *sociologist, educator*
Davis, Britt Duane *banker*
Davis, Leon *oil company executive*
Davis, Martha Algenita Scott *lawyer*
Davis, Rex Lloyd *insurance company executive*
Davis-Lewis, Bettye *nursing educator*
Dawn, Frederic Samuel *chemical and textile engineer*
Dawood, Mohamed Yusoff *obstetrician, gynecologist*
Dean, Robert Franklin *insurance company executive*
DeBakey, Lois *science communications educator, writer, lecturer, editor, scholar*
DeBakey, Michael Ellis *cardiovascular surgeon, educator*
DeBakey, Selma *science communication educator, writer, editor, lecturer*
De Bremaecker, Jean-Claude *geophysics educator*
Decker, Hannah Shulman *history educator*
de Kanter, Ellen Ann *English language professional, educator*
†Delehanty, Suzanne *museum director*
Del Franco, Ray *consumer products company executive*
†Del Signore, Brian A. *musician*
DeMenil, Dominique *art collector, philanthropist*
DeMent, James Alderson, Jr. *lawyer*
DeMoss, Harold R., Jr. *federal judge*
Dennis, John Emory, Jr. *mathematics educator*
Denny, Otway B., Jr. *lawyer*
Derrick, James V., Jr. *lawyer*
DesBarres, John P. *energy company executive*
Devlin, Robert Manning *financial services company executive*
Di Corcia, Edward Thomas *oil industry executive*
Dillon, Clifford Brien *retired lawyer*
Dimitry, Theodore George *lawyer*
Dinkins, Carol Eggert *lawyer*
Dishman, Cris Edward *professional football player*
Distefano, Susan Marie *nursing administrator*
Dix, Robert H. *political science educator*
Djerejian, Edward Peter *former diplomat, institute administrator*
Dodson, D. Keith *engineering and construction company executive*
Donie, Scott *Olympic athlete, platform diver*
Dosher, John Rodney *consulting management consultant*
Doughtie, Edward Orth *English language educator*
Douglas, Frank Fair *architect, graphic designer*
Douglas, James Matthew *law educator*
Douglass, John Jay *lawyer, educator*
Downes, Robin *library director*
Drabek, Doug (Douglas Dean Drabek) *baseball player*
Drexler, Clyde *professional basketball player*
Driscoll, Michael Hardee *lawyer*
Drury, Leonard Leroy *retired oil company executive*
Dubois, Jules Edward *security firm executive, consultant*
Dunbar, Burdett Sheridan *anesthesiologist, pediatrician, educator*
Duncan, Charles William, Jr. *investor, former government official*
Dunlap, James Lapham *petroleum company executive*
Dunlop, Fred Hurston *lawyer*
DuPont, Herbert Lancashire *medical educator, researcher*
Dur, Philip Alphonse *gas, oil industry executive, retired naval officer*
Dutton, Uriel Elvis *lawyer*
Dworsky, Clara Weiner *merchandise brokerage executive, lawyer*
Dykes, Osborne Jefferson, III *lawyer*
Eastland, S. Stacy *lawyer*
Ebaugh, Helen Rose *sociology educator, researcher*
Ebert, Alfred H., Jr. *lawyer*
Edens, Donald Keith *oil company executive*
Edwards, Victor Henry *chemical engineer*
Eichberger, LeRoy Carl *mechanical engineer, consultant, stress analyst*
Eisner, Diana *pediatrician*
Elers, Karl Emerson *mining company executive*
Elkins, James Anderson, Jr. *banker*
Elmer, Augustus *shipping company executive*
Engel, Paul Sanford *educator*
Engelhardt, Hugo Tristram, Jr. *physician, educator*
Englesmith, Tejas *actor, producer, curator*
Epstein, Jon David *lawyer, educator*
Estes, Carl Lewis, II *lawyer*
Estle, Thomas Leo *physicist, educator*
Eubank, J. Thomas *lawyer*
Ewell, Vincent Fletcher *lawyer*
Ewing, John Kirby *real estate, oil and investment executive*
Fabricant, Jill Diane *technology company executive*
Falick, James *architect*
Fant, Douglas Vernon *lawyer*
†Fant, Eugene Robert *steel company executive*
Fant, Patrick Joseph *radio station general manager*
Fehir, Kim Michele *oncologist, hematologist*
Feigin, Ralph David *pediatrician, educator*
Feigon, Judith Tova *ophthalmologist, surgeon, educator*
Feldcamp, Larry Bernard *lawyer*
Feldt, J(ohn) Harrell *lawyer*
Ferguson, John C. *airport terminal executive*
Ferguson, Robert R., III *airline company executive*
Ferrand, Jean C. *oil company executive*
Few, Arthur Allen, Jr. *science educator*
Finch, Michael Paul *lawyer*
Fiorenza, Joseph A. *bishop*
Fischer, Michael M. J. *anthropology educator*
Fisher, Janet Warner *secondary school educator*
Fishman, Marvin Allen *pediatrician, neurologist, educator*
Flack, Joe Fenley *county and municipal official, former insurance executive*
Focht, John Arnold, Jr. *geotechnical engineer*
Folk, Katherine Pinkston *English language educator, writer, journalist*
Foreman, George *boxer, nondenominational christian minister, boxing broadcaster*
Fort, John Franklin, III *manufacturing company executive*
Fortenbach, Ray Thomas *retired lawyer*
Foster, Charles Crawford *lawyer, educator*
Foster, Dale Warren *political scientist, educator, management consultant, real estate*
Foster, Joe B. *oil company executive*
Fowler, Robert Asa *consultant, business director, diplomat*
Foyt, A(nthony) J(oseph), Jr. *auto racing crew chief, former professional auto racer*
Frank, George Willard (Will Frank) *oil company executive, consultant*
Frank, Hilda Rhea Kaplan *dancer*
Frank, J. Louis *oil company executive*
Frankhouser, Homer Sheldon, Jr. *engineering and construction company executive*
Freeman, Marjorie Schaefer *mathematics educator*
Freireich, Emil J *hematologist, educator*
French, Arthur Leeman, Jr. *process control and instrumentation company executive*
French, Layne Bryan *lawyer, investor, community volunteer*
Friedberg, Thomas Harold *insurance company executive*
Frieden, Kit *newspaper editor*
Friedkin, Thomas H. *automotive executive*
†Frost, James Hamner *health facility administrator*
Fuchs, Bernard *apparel executive*
Fukuyama, Tohru *organic chemistry educator*
Fullenweider, Donn Charles *lawyer*
Fulwiler, Robert Neal *oil company executive*
†Funkhouser, Paul William *oil company executive, lawyer*
Gaelens, Albert Robert *educational administrator, priest*
Gagnon, Stewart Walter *lawyer*
†Gaines, Paul B. *airport executive*
Gallas, Daniel O. *oil pipeline company executive*
Gallerano, Andrew John *retail company executive*
Galt, Barry J. *diversified company executive*
Gano, John *lawyer*
Garber, Alan J(oel) *medical educator*
Gardner, Everette Shaw, Jr. *information sciences educator*
Garner, Thomas Ward *petroleum company executive*
Garrett, Jasper Patrick *lawyer*
Garrison, Martha *oil industry executive*
Garrison, Truitt B. *architect*
Garten, David B. *lawyer*
Gattis, James Ralph *oil company executive*
Gayle, Gibson, Jr. *lawyer*
Geer, Ronald Lamar *mechanical engineering consultant, retired oil company executive*
Geis, Duane Virgil *investment banker*
George, Deveral D. *editor, journalist, advertising consultant*
Georgiades, William Den Hartog *educational administrator*
Gerard, Roy Dupuy *oil company executive*
Gerraughty, David R. *newspaper editor*
Gibson, Everett Kay, Jr. *space scientist, geochemist*
Gibson, Jerry Leigh *oil company executive*
Gibson, Kathleen Rita *anatomy and anthropology educator*
Gibson, Michael Addison *chemical engineering company executive*
Gibson, Robert Lee *astronaut*
Gidley, John Lynn *engineering executive*
Gigli, Irma *physician, educator, academic administrator*
Gilbert, Harold Stanley *warehousing company executive*
Gildenberg, Philip Leon *neurosurgeon*
Gillis, (Stephen) Malcolm *academic administrator, economics educator*
Gillmore, Kathleen Cory *lawyer*
Gissel, L. Henry, Jr. *lawyer*
Glantz, Raymon M. *biochemist, biologist, educator*
Glassell, Alfred Curry, Jr. *investor*
Glassman, Armand Barry *physician, pathologist, scientist, educator, administrator*
†Gockley, (Richard) David *opera director*
Goff, Robert Burnside *retired food company executive*
†Golden, Timothy N. *foreign correspondent*
Goldsmith, Billy Joe *real estate broker*
Goldstein, Jack Charles *lawyer*
Goldstein, Margaret Ann *biologist*
Gomez, Lucas *credit manager, assistant treasurer*
Goode, James Cleveland *educational administrator*
Goodman, Herbert Irwin *petroleum company executive*
Gordon, Wendell Chaffee *economics educator*
Gordon, William Edwin *physicist, engineer, educator, university official*
Gore, Thomas Jackson *construction executive*
†Gormley, W. Clarke *lawyer*
Gorski, Daniel Alexander *art educator*
Gotto, Antonio Marion, Jr. *internist, educator*
Gottschalk, Arthur William *music company executive and educator*
Gould, Kenneth Lance *physician, educator*
Gover, Alan Shore *lawyer*
Gower, Bob G. *gas and oil industry executive*
Graham, David Yates *gastroenterologist*
Graham, Michael Paul *lawyer*
Grandy, Richard E. *philosophy educator*
Gray, Archibald Duncan, Jr. *lawyer*
Gray, Robert Steele *publishing executive, editor*
Grayson, Charles Jackson, Jr. *research association*
Griffin, Linda Gillan *fashion editor*
†Grossman, Herbert Barton *urology educator*
Grossman, Robert George *physician, educator*
Gruben, Karl Taylor *law librarian*
Gruber, Ira Dempsey *historian, educator*
Guinn, David Crittenden *petroleum engineer, drilling and exploration company executive*
Gunn, Albert Edward, Jr. *internist, educator, lawyer, hospital and university administrator*
Gunter, Joseph Clifford, III *lawyer*
Guynn, Robert William *psychiatrist, educator*
Haas, Merrill Wilber *geologist, oil company executive*
Hackerman, Norman *chemist, university president*
Hafner, Joseph A., Jr. *food company executive*
Halbouty, Michel Thomas *geologist, petroleum engineer, petroleum operator*
Hale, Leon *newspaper columnist*
Hall, Robert Joseph *physician, medical educator*
Halloran, Bernard Thorpe *lawyer*
Hamilton, Phyllis *principal*
Hammack, Gladys Lorene Mann *reading specialist, educator*
Hammond, Ken *newspaper magazine editor*
Hammond, Michael Peter *music educator, dean*
†Hanania, Nicola Alexander *physician*
Hanen, Andrew Scott *lawyer*
Hansen, Paula Renee *health care administrator*
Harasim, Paul Houck *columnist, educator*
Hardin, George Cecil, Jr. *petroleum consultant*
Hardt, Robert Miller *mathematics educator*
Hargrove, James Ward *financial consultant*
†Harle, Thomas Stanley *radiologist*
Harmon, Melinda Furche *federal judge*
Harper, Alfred John, II *lawyer*
Harper, Michael John Kennedy *obstetrics and gynecology educator*
Harrington, Bruce Michael *lawyer, investor*
Harris, Richard Foster, Jr. *insurance company executive*
Harrison, Otto R. *oil industry executive*
Hart, James Whitfield, Jr. *corporate public affairs executive, lawyer*
Hartrick, Janice Kay *lawyer*
Hartsfield, Henry Warren, Jr. *astronaut*
Harvey, F. Reese *mathematics educator*
Harvin, David Tarleton *lawyer*
Harvin, William Charles *lawyer*
Haskell, Thomas Langdon *history educator*
Hasling, Jill Freeman *meteorologist*
Haymes, Robert C. *physicist, educator*
Haymond, Paula J. *psychologist, diagnostician, hypnotherapist*
Haynes, Karen Sue *university dean, social work educator*
†Haynes, William Eli *chemical company executive*
Haynie, Thomas Powell, III *physician*
†Hayslett, Roderick James *gas company executive*
Haywood, Theodore Joseph *physician, educator*
Heckler, Walter Tim *association executive*
Hedrick, Kirby L. *petroleum company executive*
†Heiker, Vincent Edward *information systems executive*
Heimbinder, Isaac *construction company executive, lawyer*
Heinsen, Lindsay *newspaper editor*
Helland, George Archibald, Jr. *equipment manufacturing company executive, former government official, management consultant*
Hellums, Jesse David *chemical engineering educator and researcher*
Hemeyer, Terry *oil company executive*
Hempel, John P. *mathematics educator*
Henderson, Donald Blanton *lawyer, state senator*
Henderson, Nathan H. *bishop*
Hendrix, Dennis Ralph *energy company executive*
Henington, David Mead *library director*
Hennessey, Sister Colleen *academic administrator*
Henning, George Thomas, Jr. *chemical company executive*
Henning, Susan June *biomedical researcher*
Henry, John Cooper *journalist*
Hermann, Robert John *lawyer, corporate executive*
Hesse, Martha O. *natural gas company executive*
Hiatt, John David *broadcast company executive*
Hicks, Taylor M., Jr. *lawyer*
Higgs, J. Jeffrey *retired physician and medical director*
Hightower, Joe Walter *chemical engineering educator, consultant*
Hinton, Paula Weems *lawyer*
Hipple, James Blackman *financial executive*
Hirasaki, George Jiro *chemical engineer, educator*
Hirsch, Edward Mark *poet, English language educator*
Hittner, David *federal judge*
Ho, Yhi-Min *university dean, economics educator*
Hobby, William Pettus *broadcast executive*
Hodges, Ann *television editor, newspaper columnist*
Hodo, Edward Douglas *university president*
Hoffman, Philip Guthrie *former university president*
Hoglund, Forrest Eugene *petroleum company executive*
Holcomb, William A. *retired real estate broker, consultant, retired oil and gas exploration, pipeline executive*
Hollister, Leo Edward *physician, educator*
Hollyfield, John Scoggins *lawyer*
Holmes, Ann Hitchcock *journalist*
Holmes, Cecile Searson *religion editor*
Holmes, Darrell *tourism consultant*
Holmquest, Donald Lee *physician, astronaut, lawyer*
Holovak, Mike *sports association exec*
Holstead, John Burnham *lawyer*
Homeyer, Howard C. *energy consultant*
†Honea, T. Milton, Jr. *gas industry executive*
Honeycutt, George Leonard *photographer*
Hook, Harold Swanson *insurance company executive*
Hoover, Howard S., Jr. *lawyer*
Hornak, Anna Frances *library administrator*
Horning, Marjorie G. *biochemistry educator*
Horvitz, Paul Michael *finance educator*
Howard, R. L. *oil industry executive*
†Howell, Paul Neilson *oil company executive*
Hoyt, Kenneth M. *federal judge*
Hoyt, Mont Powell *lawyer*
Hsu, Thomas Tseng-Chuang *civil engineer, educator*
Huang, Elsie Lee *principal*
Huang, Huey Wen *physicist, educator*
Hudson, Frank N. *lawyer, real estate developer*
Hudspeth, Chalmers Mac *lawyer, educator*
Huelbig, Larry Leggett *lawyer*
Huff, John Rossman *oil service company executive*
Huffington, Roy Michael *ambassador*
Hughes, Lynn Nettleton *federal judge*
Hungerford, Ed Vernon, III *physics educator*
Hurwitz, Charles Edwin *manufacturing company executive*
Huston, John Dennis *English educator*
Hutcheson, Joseph Chappell, III *lawyer*
Hyman, Harold M. *history educator, consultant*
Illig, Carl *lawyer*
Irani, Katie D. *medical educator, rehabilitation services professional*
Irving, Herbert *food distribution company executive*
†Jackson, Eleanor Teddi Ross (Teddi Jackson) *health career executive*
†Jackson, Harper Scales, Jr. *healthcare executive*
Jackson, R. Graham *architect*
†Jackson, Robert Sherwood *waste management executive*
Jackson, Terrence J. *coal company executive*
Jacobus, Charles Joseph *lawyer, title company executive, author*
Jamail, Joseph Dahr, Jr. *lawyer*
Jamieson, John Kenneth *oil field services company executive*
Jankovic, Joseph *neurologist, educator, scientist*
Jansen, Donald Orville *lawyer*
Jeanneret, Paul Richard *management consultant*
Jeffires, Haywood Franklin *professional football player*
Jenkins, Daniel Edwards, Jr. *physician, educator*
Jenkins, Judith Alexander *bank consultant*
Jetton, Steve *newspaper editor*
Jewell, George Hiram *lawyer*
†Jhin, Michael Kontien *health care executive*
Johns, H. Douglas *computer company executive*
Johnson, Andrew Carey, Jr. *accountant*
Johnson, Ashmore Clark, Jr. *oil company executive*
Johnson, Frederick Dean *former food company executive*
Johnson, Kenneth Oscar *oil company executive*
Johnson, Nancy K. *judge*
Johnson, Richard James Vaughan *newspaper executive*
Johnson, Wayne D. *gas industry executive*
Johnston, Ben Earl *veterinarian*
Johnston, Marguerite *journalist, author*
†Jones, Dan B. *ophthalmologist, educator*
†Jones, Donald Drummond *financial executive*
Jones, Edith Hollan *federal judge*
Jones, Frank Griffith *lawyer*
Jones, Lincoln, III *army officer*
Jones, Samuel *conductor*
Jordan, Charles Milton *lawyer*
Jordan, Don D. *electric company executive*
Jordan, W. Carl *lawyer*
Jorden, James Roy *oil company engineering executive*
Jordon, Robert Earl *physician*
Joyce, James Daniel *clergyman*
Jurtshuk, Peter, Jr. *microbiologist, educator*
Justice, (David) Blair *psychology educator, author*
Kahan, Barry Donald *surgeon, educator*
Kaplan, Lee Landa *lawyer*
Karff, Samuel Egal *rabbi*
Katz, M. Marvin *lawyer*
Kaufman, Raymond Henry *physician*
Kay, Joel Phillip *lawyer*
Kelley, David Lee *oil company executive, petroleum engineer*
Kellison, Stephen George *insurance executive*
†Kellstrom, William A. *gas company executive*
Kelly, Dorothy Helen *pediatrician, educator*
Kelly, Hugh Rice *lawyer*
Kelly, William Franklin, Jr. *lawyer*
Kenefick, John Henry, Jr. *retired engineering company executive, consultant*
Kennedy, Ken *computer science educator*
Kerfoot, Karlene M. *health facility administrator*
Kerr, Baine Perkins *oil company executive*
Kerwin, Joseph Peter *physician, former astronaut*
Ketelsen, James Lee *diversified industry executive*
Kevan, Larry *chemistry educator*
Khoury, Raymond J. *hospital administrator*
Kientz, Renee *newspaper editor*
Kile, Darryl Andrew *professional baseball player*
Kinder, Richard Dan *natural gas pipeline, oil and gas company executive*
King, Carl B. *tool company executive*
King, Carolyn Dineen *federal judge*
King, Jonathan *architectural researcher, educator*
King, Kay Wander *design educator, fashion designer, consultant*
Kinsey, James Lloyd *chemist, educator*
Kirkland, John David *oil and gas company executive, lawyer*
Kit, Saul *biochemist, educator*

Klausmeyer, David Michael *scientific instruments manufacturing company executive*
Kline, John William *retired air force officer, management consultant*
Klingel, Martin Allen *investment company executive*
Knapp, David Hebard *banker*
Knauss, Robert Lynn *international business educator, corporate executive*
†Knight, J. Vernon *medicine and microbiology educator*
Knight, Tommy E. *civil engineer*
Knull, William H., III *lawyer*
Knull, Yolanda Chavez *lawyer*
Kobayashi, Riki *chemical engineer, educator*
Kochi, Jay Kazuo *chemist, educator*
Koenig, Rodney Curtis *lawyer, rancher*
Kollaer, Jim C. *real estate executive, architect*
Kopec, Frank John *advertising agency executive*
Kors, R. Paul *search company executive*
Kosut, Kenneth Paul *lawyer*
Kouri, Donald Jack *chemist, educator*
Kratochvil, L(ouis) Glen *lawyer*
Krause, William Austin *engineering executive*
Kraus-Friedmann, Naomi *biochemistry educator*
Krebs, Arno William, Jr. *lawyer*
Krieger, Paul Edward *lawyer*
Kripke, Margaret Louise *immunologist*
Krishen, Kumar *aerospace research technologist*
Kuntz, Edward L. *health care executive*
Kuntz, Hal Goggan *petroleum exploration company executive*
LaBoon, Robert Bruce *lawyer*
Lackey, S. Allen *petroleum company executive, corporate lawyer*
Laird, John B. *newspaper publishing executive*
Lake, Kathleen C. *lawyer*
Lake, Simeon Timothy, III *federal judge*
Lallinger, E. Michael *savings and loan association executive*
Lamb, Sydney MacDonald *linguistics and cognitive science educator*
Lane, Montague *physician, educator*
Lanier, Robert C. (Bob Lanier) *mayor*
†Lannie, Paul Anthony *lawyer*
Larkin, Lee Roy *lawyer*
Larkin, William Vincent, Jr. *oil field service company executive*
Lasseter, Charles Erwin *energy company executive*
Lassiter, Ronald Corbett *oil company executive*
Latimer, Roy Truett *museum executive*
Laughery, Kenneth Ronald *psychology educator*
Lavenant, Rene Paul, Jr. *lawyer*
Lawhon, William Griffith *lawyer*
Lawrence, Charles Edmund *architect*
Lawrie, Robert George *lawyer*
Lawson, Ben F. *lawyer, international legal consultant*
Lay, Kenneth Lee *diversified energy company executive*
LeBlanc, Rufus Joseph, Sr. *geology educator, consultant, researcher*
Lee, Janie C. *art gallery owner*
Lee, William Gentry *lawyer*
Lehrer, Kenneth Eugene *real estate advisor, economist, developer, consultant*
Le Maistre, Charles Aubrey *university official, physician*
Leonard, Gilbert Stanley *oil company executive*
†Lerup, Lars G. *architecture educator, college dean*
LeSuer, Kenneth Ray *oil company executive*
Levin, Bernard *physician*
Levit, Max *food service executive*
Levit, Milton *grocery supply company executive*
Levy, Gerard G. *industrial gases executive*
Lewis, Carl *Olympic track and field athlete*
Lewis, Edward Sheldon *chemistry educator*
Leydon, Joseph Patrick *film critic, journalist*
Liang, Edison Parktak *astrophysicist, educator, researcher*
†Lichtman, David Michael *military officer, health care administrator, orthopedist, educator*
Liddell, Leon Morris *librarian, educator*
Liedtke, John Hugh *petroleum company executive*
Lienhard, John Henry *mechanical engineering educator*
Lilienstern, O. Clayton *lawyer*
Lindsey, John Horace *insurance executive, museum official*
Lionberger, Richard Lee *lawyer*
Little, Jack Edward *oil company executive*
†Livengood, Thomas Claude *financial executive*
Loeffler, James Joseph *lawyer*
Loewenbaum, G. Walter, II *cement, oil and gas company executive*
Loftis, Jack D. *newspaper editor, newspaper executive*
Long, William Everett *retired utility executive*
Lott, Thaddeus *principal*
Love, Jeffrey Benton *lawyer*
Love, Miron Anderson *judge*
Lovelace, Byron Keith *lawyer, management consultant*
Loveland, Eugene Franklin *petroleum executive*
Low, Morton David *physician, educator*
Lowrey, E. James *food service company executive*
Ludwig, Vernell Patrick *gas pipeline company executive*
Luigs, Charles Russell *gas and oil drilling industry executive*
Lunn, Judith Saska *newspaper editor, journalist*
Luss, Dan *chemical engineering educator*
Mackey, William Sturges, Jr. *investor, consultant*
Mackie, David F. *gas company executive*
Maddox, Iris Carolyn Clark *secondary education educator*
Mai, Klaus L. *oil research company executive*
Maillard, Albert Achilles Joseph *head and neck surgeon, educator*
Malague, Marianne Tyndall *nursing educator*
Maligas, Manuel Nick *metallurgical engineer*
Maloney, James Edward *lawyer*
Mampre, Virginia Elizabeth *communications executive*
Manson, Lewis Auman *energy research executive*
Marcus, George E. *anthropologist*
Margrave, John Lee *chemist, educator, university administrator*
Marley, Everett Armistead, Jr. *lawyer*
Marr, David Francis *television announcer, former professional golfer, journalist*
†Marsh, John *research chemist*
Marshall, J. Howard, II *lawyer*
Marshall, Jane Pretzer *newspaper editor*
Marshall, Margo *artistic director*
Marshall, Thom *columnist*
Marston, Edgar Jean, III *lawyer*
Martin, J. Landis *manufacturing company executive, lawyer*
Martin, James Kirby *historian, educator*
Martin, Jerry C. *oil company executive*
Martin, Neil *lawyer*
†Martin, Randi Christine *psychology educator*
Marzio, Peter Cort *museum director*
Mason, Franklin Rogers *automotive executive*
Massad, Stephen Albert *lawyer*
Massey, Ike *newspaper publishing executive*
Mateker, Emil Joseph, Jr. *geophysicist*
Mathis, Larry Lee *health care administrator*
Mathur, Rupa Ajwani *state official, risk management consultant*
Matthews, Bruce Rankin *professional football player*
Matthews, Charles Sedwick *petroleum engineering consultant, research advisor*
Matthews, Harold Downs *author, consultant*
Matthews, Kathleen Shive *biochemistry educator*
Matthews, Thomas Michael *energy company executive*
Mattox, Kenneth Leon *surgeon, educator, medical scientist*
Matusow, Allen Joseph *history educator, academic administrator*
Mauck, William M., Jr. *executive recruiter, small business owner*
Mayer, John *lawyer*
Mayor, Heather Donald *medical educator*
Mayor, Richard Blair *lawyer*
†Mazanec, George L. *natural gas company executive*
Mc Bride, Raymond Andrew *pathologist, physician, educator*
Mc Call, Robert R. *retired oil company executive*
McClane, Drayton, Jr. *professional baseball team executive*
McCleary, Henry Glen *geophysicist*
McClelland, Bramlette *engineering executive, consultant*
McClure, Daniel M. *lawyer*
McCurdy, Larry Wayne *automotive parts company executive*
McDaniel, Jarrel Dave *lawyer*
Mc David, George Eugene (Gene Mc David) *newspaper executive*
McDonald, Gail Jacolev *lawyer*
McEvily, Daniel Vincent Sean *lawyer, author*
Mc Fadden, Joseph Michael *university president*
Mc Fedries, Robert, Jr. *power industry executive, chemical engineer*
Mc Ginty, John Milton *architect*
McGinty, Milton Bradford *architect, real estate development executive*
McIntire, Larry Vern *chemical engineering educator*
McIntosh, Susan Keech *anthropology educator*
McKim, Paul Arthur *management consultant, retired petroleum executive*
McMahon, Catherine Driscoll *lawyer*
McMillin, Jeanie Byrd *biochemist, medical educator*
McPhail, JoAnn Winstead *writer, art dealer, small business owner*
Mc Pherson, Alice Ruth *ophthalmologist*
McQuarrie, Claude Monroe, III *lawyer*
Mead, Dana George *diversified industrial manufacturing company executive*
Meeks, Herbert Lessig, III *pastor, former school system administrator*
Mehra, Jagdish *physicist*
Melo, Thomas M. *lawyer*
Mendenhall, Oniel Charles *retail executive*
Menscher, Barnet Gary *steel company executive*
Meyer, Randall *retired oil company executive*
Mian, Farouk Aslam *chemical engineer, educator*
Miele, Angelo *engineering educator, researcher, consultant, author*
Milam, John Daniel *pathologist, educator*
Millar, Jeffery Lynn *columnist*
Miller, Barry Rixmann *lawyer*
Miller, Clarence Alphonso *chemical engineering educator*
Miller, Gary Evan *psychiatrist, mental health services administrator*
Miller, Kenneth William *holding company executive, financier*
Miller, Robert Daniel *lawyer*
Minter, David Lee *English literature educator*
Mischer, Walter M. *diversified company executive, bank holding company executive*
Mischer, Walter M., Jr. *health facility administrator*
†Mitchell, David L. *phycology researcher*
Mitchell, Richard Dale *journalist, writer*
Moehlman, Michael Scott *lawyer*
Moncure, John Lewis *lawyer*
Monroe, L. A. J. *oil well drilling company executive*
Montle, Paul Joseph *entrepreneur*
Moore, Lois Jean *health science facility administrator*
Moore, Pat Howard *engineering and construction company executive*
Moore, Walter Parker, Jr. *civil engineering company executive*
Moorhead, Gerald Lee *architect*
Morehead, James Caddall, Jr. *architect, educator*
Morris, (William) Carloss *lawyer, insurance company executive*
†Morris, Malcolm Stewart *lawyer*
Morris, Owen Glenn *engineering corporation executive*
Morris, Seth Irwin *architect*
Morris, Stewart, Jr. *title insurance company executive*
Morrison, Jennifer Ann *lawyer, oil company executive*
Mosbacher, Robert Adam *oil and gas industry executive, political organization executive*
Mosher, Donald Raymond *chemical engineer, consultant*
Mottale, Mois *oil industry executive*
Mountain, Clifton Fletcher *surgeon, educator*
Mueller, Carl Gustav, Jr. *lawyer*
Munson, John Backus *computer systems consultant, retired computer engineering company executive*
Murphy, Ewell Edward, Jr. *lawyer*
†Murphy, William Alexander, Jr. *diagnostic radiologist, educator*
Murray, John A. *orthopedist, medical association executive*
†Murray, Patrick M. *oilfield service company executive*
Muse, Ewell Henderson, III *gas company executive*
Musgrave, Story *astronaut, surgeon, pilot, physiologist, educator*
Musher, Daniel Michael *physician*
Myers, Edward Wellington *hospital administrator*
Myers, Franklin *lawyer, oil service company executive*
Myers, Norman Allan *marketing professional*
Nanz, Robert Hamilton *petroleum consultant*
Nations, Howard Lynn *lawyer*
Neeld, Elizabeth Harper *author, researcher, consultant*
Nelson, Dorothy Patricia *health policy analyst, educator*
Nelson, John Robert *theology educator, clergyman*
Nestvold, Elwood Olaf *oil service company executive*
Neuhaus, Julius Victor, III *architect*
Neuhaus, Philip Ross *investment banker*
Neuhaus, William Oscar, III *architect*
Newberry, Robert Curtis, Sr. *newspaper columnist*
Newbold, Benjamin Millard, Jr. *library manager, education consultant*
Nguyen, An Duc *industrial development, consultant*
Nicandros, Constantine Stavros *oil company executive*
Nickens, Jacks Clarence *lawyer*
Niebruegge, Michael E. *lawyer*
Nielsen, Niels Christian, Jr. *theology educator*
Nimmer, Raymond T. *lawyer, law educator*
Nolen, Roy Lemuel *lawyer*
Nordgren, Ronald Paul *engineering educator, researcher*
Northrop, Monroe *lawyer*
Norton, Norman James *exploration geologist*
Nuss, Eldon Paul *casket manufacturer*
Nyberg, Donald Arvid *oil company executive*
O'Connor, Lawrence Joseph, Jr. *energy consultant*
O'Connor, Ralph Sturges *investment company executive*
O'Dell, Charles Robert *astronomer, educator*
Odhiambo, Atieno E. S. *history educator, researcher*
O'Kehie, Collins Emeka *lawyer, consultant*
Olajuwon, Hakeem Abdul (The Dream) *professional basketball player*
Oldham, Darius Dudley *lawyer*
Oliver, Rufus W., III *lawyer*
O'Malley, Bert William *cell biologist, educator, physician*
Oncken, Henry Kuck *lawyer*
O'Neal, Bob H. *utilities company executive*
O'Neil, John *artist*
Ongert, Steven Walter *lawyer, mediator*
Onstead, Randall *consumer goods company executive*
Onstead, Robert R. *consumer goods company executive*
O'Quinn, John M. *lawyer*
Ordonez, Nelson Gonzalo *pathologist*
Oren, Bruce Clifford *newspaper editor, artist*
Orloff, Gary W(illiam) *lawyer, former energy company executive*
Orme, Denis Arthur *management consultant*
Orton, Stewart *retail company executive, merchant*
Osborne, Dee S. *banker*
Ostrofsky, Benjamin *business and engineering management educator, industrial engineer*
O'Toole, Austin Martin *lawyer*
Owens, Gary Steven *architect*
Owsley, William Clinton, Jr. *radiologist*
Page, Ann *stock brokerage executive*
†Page, David Randall *hospital administrator*
Page, Thornton Leigh *astrophysicist*
Paine, Louis Burr, Jr. *lawyer*
Palacios, Ronald *immunologist*
Pallenik, Christine M. *lawyer*
Palmer, James Edward *public relations executive*
Palomo, Juan Ramón *columnist*
Panatier, M. J. *gas industry executive*
Parish, Louis Leon *oil company executive*
Parker, Jonathan Edward *beverage products company executive*
Parsley, Robert Horace *lawyer*
Pate, James Leonard *oil company executive*
Patten, Bernard Michael *neurologist, educator*
Patten, Robert Lowry *English language educator*
Patterson, Ronald R(oy) *health care systems executive*
Patterson, Steve *professional hockey team executive*
Patterson, William Wayne *electronics company executive*
Paul, Gordon Lee *behavioral scientist, psychologist*
Paul, James Robert *oil and gas mining company executive*
Pearson, James Boyd, Jr. *electrical engineering educator*
Peck, Edwin Russell *real estate management executive*
Pederson, Tony Weldon *newspaper editor*
Pelaez, Rolando Federico *economics educator, consultant,*
Penny, Charles Richard *retired advertising executive*
Perez, Francisco Ignacio *clinical psychologist, educator*
Perkins, Britten Lee *architectural firm executive*
Perry, Cynthia Norton Shepard *diplomat*
Pester, Jack Cloyd *oil company executive*
Peterkin, George Alexander, Jr. *marine transportation company executive*
Pfeiffer, Carl E. *manufacturing company executive*
Pfeiffer, Eckhard *computer company executive*
Pharis, Ruth McCalister *banker*
Pharr, George Mathews *materials science and engineering educator*
†Pianka, Uri *violinist, concertmaster*
Pickering, James Henry, III *university president*
Pickering, Robert Earl, Jr. *airline executive, consultant*
Pieper, Wylie Bernard *diversified company executive*
Pierce, George Foster, Jr. *architect*
Pinkel, Donald Paul *pediatrician*
Pinson, Artie Frances *elementary school educator*
Pitcher, Max Grow *exploration company executive, geologist*
Poindexter, John Bruce *entrepreneur*
Pomerantz, James Robert *psychology educator, academic admininstrator*
Poulos, Michael James *insurance company executive*
Powell, Alan *engineer, scientist, educator*
Powell, William Rossell, Jr. *retired judge*
Powers, Hugh William *newspaper executive*
Prats, Michael *petroleum engineer, educator*
Pravel, Bernarr Roe *lawyer*
Prentice, James Stuart *energy company executive, chemical engineer*
Presley, Brian *entrepreneur*
†Prince, Edward R., Jr. *holding company*
Proctor, Richard Owen *public health administrator, army officer*
Pryor, William Daniel Lee *humanities educator*
Pugsley, Frank Burruss *lawyer*
Quigg, Jean *principal*
Quillen, Carol E. *historian, educator*
Rabb, Carlos C., Jr. *petroleum company executive*
Rabson, Thomas Avelyn *electrical engineering educator, researcher*
Radnofsky, Barbara A. *lawyer*
Radoff, Leonard Irving *librarian, consultant*
Rainey, John David *federal judge*
Rakel, Robert Edwin *physician, educator*
Randolph, Robert Raymond *lawyer*
Ranieri, Lewis S. *financial services company executive*
Ray, Hugh Massey, Jr. *lawyer*
Read, Michael Oscar *editor, consultant*
Reasoner, Harry Max *lawyer*
Reed, Kathlyn Louise *occupational therapist, educator*
†Reeder, Jeffrey K. *retail executive*
Reiff, Patricia Hofer *space physicist, educator*
Reistle, Carl Ernest, Jr. *petroleum engineer*
Reso, Anthony *geologist, earth resources economist*
Reynolds, John Terrence *oil industry executive*
Rhoades, Floyd *real estate and property manager*
Ribble, John Charles *medical educator*
Rice, Emily Joy *retired secondary and adult educator*
Rich, Robert Regier *immunology educator, physician*
Richardson, Frank H. *retired oil industry executive*
Riedel, Alan Ellis *manufacturing company executive, lawyer*
Riley, Harold John, Jr. *manufacturing executive*
Roberts, Cecil Kenneth *lawyer*
Robertson, George Leonard *lawyer*
Robertson, James Woolsey *lawyer*
†Robertson, Joseph W., Jr. *investment company executive*
Robinson, Charles David *financial services executive*
†Rock, Douglas Lawrence *manufacturing executive*
Rockwell, Elizabeth Dennis *retirement specialist, financial planner*
Roff, J(ohn) Hugh, Jr. *energy company executive*
Rogers, Arthur Hamilton, III *lawyer*
Romsdahl, Marvin Magnus *surgeon, educator*
Roorda, John Francis, Jr. *business consultant*
Rose, Beatrice Schroeder (Mrs. William H. Rose) *harpist, educator*
†Rose, George Max *chemical company executive*
Rosenthal, Lee H. *federal judge*
Rossler, Willis Kenneth, Jr. *petroleum company executive*
Rozzell, Scott Ellis *lawyer*
Ruckelshaus, William Doyle *waste disposal services company executive*
Rudolph, Arnold Jack *pediatrician, neonatologist, medical educator*
Rudolph, Frederick Byron *biochemistry educator*
Russman, Thomas Anthony *philosophy educator*
Ryan, Cornelius O'Brien *lawyer*
Sadler, M. Whitson *petroleum company executive*
Sakowitz, Robert Tobias *investor*
Salch, Steven Charles *lawyer*
Sales, James Bohus *lawyer*
Samaan, Naguib Abdelmalik *endocrinologist*
Sampson, Franklin Delano *minister*
Sanders, John Moncrief *lawyer*
Sapp, Walter William *lawyer, energy company executive*
Sass, Ronald Lewis *biology and chemistry educator*
Saunders, Charles Albert *lawyer*
Savit, Carl Hertz *geophysicist*
†Schechter, Arthur Louis *lawyer*
Schell, William H. *oil company executive*
Schier, Mary Jane *science writer*
Schlindwein, James A. *food products company executive*
Schneider, David J. *psychology educator, academic administrator*
Schorre, Louis Charles, Jr. *artist*
Schroepfer, George John, Jr. *biochemistry educator*
Schultz, Stanley George *physiologist, educator*
Schwartz, Charles Walter *lawyer*
Schwartzel, Charles Boone *lawyer*
Scott, David Warren *statistics educator*
Scuseria, Gustavo Enrique *theoretical chemist*
Seaman, Roual Duane *data processing company executive*
Sebastian, Michael James *manufacturing company executive*
Secrest, Ronald Dean *lawyer*
Segner, Edmund Peter, III *natural gas company executive*
Selke, Charles Richard *lawyer, mediator, real estate professional*
Sellers, James Earl *theological educator*
Sewell, Ben Gardner *lawyer*
Shaddock, Carroll Sidney *lawyer*
†Shankel, Gerald Marvin *association executive*
Shaper, Stephen Jay *finance company executive*
Shapiro, Beth Janet *librarian*
Sharp, Douglas Andrew *secondary school educator*
Shearer, William Thomas *pediatrician, educator*
Sheehan, Linda Suzanne *educational administrator*
Sheffield, Don B. *wholesale distribution company executive*
Sheinfeld, Myron M. *lawyer, educator*
Sheley, Donald Ray, Jr. *manufacturing company executive*
Shen, Liang Chi *electrical engineer, educator, researcher*
Shower, Robert Wesley *financial executive*
Shulman, Robert Jay *physician*
Siegel, Milton P. *health foundation executive, international executive, educator, management consultant*
Silva, Eugene Joseph *lawyer*
Simon, Barry Philip *lawyer*
Simpson, Richard Kendall, Jr. *surgeon, physician, researcher*
Sing, William Bender *lawyer*
Singleton, John Virgil, Jr. *retired federal judge, lawyer*
Singleton, William Dean *newspaper publisher*
Sisson, Virginia Baker *geology educator*
Skalla, John Lionell *insurance agent*
Skolnick, Malcolm Harris *biophysics researcher, educator, patent lawyer, mediator*
†Slaugh, Lynn H. *chemist*
Smalley, Richard Errett *chemistry and physics educator, researcher*
Smith, Al Frederick *professional football player*
†Smith, Dan F. *oil company executive*
Smith, Frank Forsythe, Jr. *lawyer*
Smith, Jerry Edwin *federal judge*
Smith, Michael Alexis *petroleum geologist*
Smith, Richard Joseph *history educator*
†Smith, Sam K. *engineering company executive*
Smith, William Randolph *lawyer*
Smullen, James Dennis *lawyer*
Snedeker, Robert D. *air transportation executive*
Snider, Robert Larry *management consultant*
Snyder, Mike *newspaper editor*
Snyder, Robert C. *metals company executive*
Soliz, Joseph Guy *lawyer*
Sonfield, Robert Leon, Jr. *lawyer*
SoRelle, Ruth Doyle *medical writer, journalist*

Spalding, Andrew Freeman lawyer
Spanos, Pol Dimitrios engineering educator
†Speed, Stan research chemist
Spencer, W. E. oil company executive
†Spillard, Ernest John oil company executive
Spincic, Wesley James oil company executive, consultant
Spira, Melvin plastic surgeon
Squyres, Barbara Hopkins nursing administrator
Stacy, Frances H. judge
Staine, Ross lawyer
Stanley, Jack H. newspaper publishing executive
†Stanley, John R. petroleum company executive
Stapp, William Edward lawyer
Stark-Rice, Patricia Lee dean, mental health nurse
Steadman, Richard Cooke retail corporate executive
Steele, James Harlan former public health veterinarian, educator
Steen, Wesley Wilson former judge, lawyer
†Stehling, Ferdinand Christian physical chemist
Stephens, Delia Marie Lucky lawyer
Stevenson, Ben choreographer, ballet company executive
Stewart, Cornelius James, II utilities company executive
Still, Charles Henry lawyer
Stokes, Gale history educator
Stormer, John Charles, Jr. geology educator, mineralogist
Stradley, William Jackson lawyer
Stralem, Pierre retired stockbroker
Streibich, Ronald Leland fundraising executive
Streng, William Paul lawyer, educator
Strudler, Robert Jacob real estate development executive
Stryker, Steven Charles lawyer
Stuart, Walter Bynum, IV lawyer
Sudbury, John Dean religious foundation executive, petroleum chemist
Summers, Joseph Frank author, publisher
Susman, Morton Lee lawyer
Susman, Stephen Daily lawyer
Šutej, Vjekoslav conductor
Suter,school educator
Swanson, Roy Joel lawyer
Sweeney, John W., III newspaper executive
Sykes, Ruth L. special education educator
Sykora, Donald D. utility company excutive
Symons, James Martin environmental engineer, educator
Szalkowski, Charles Conrad lawyer
Talwani, Manik geophysicist, educator
Tapia, Richard Alfred mathematics educator
Tarrance, Vernon Lance, Jr. behavior research executive
Tauber, Orner J., Sr. petrochemical company executive
Taylor, James B. securities trader, financial planner
Temkin, Larry Scott philosopher, educator
Templeton, Robert Earl engineering and construction company executive
Tennant, Geraldine B. judge
Terrell, G. Irvin lawyer
Tetzlaff, Theodore R. lawyer
Thagard, Norman E. astronaut, physician, engineer
Thayer, Keith B. engineering company executive
†Thomas, Katherine Jane newspaper business columnist
Thomas, Lavon Bullock interior designer
Thomas, Marilyn Jane insurance company executive
Thomas, Orville C. physician
Thompson, Ewa M. foreign language educator
Thompson, Guy Bryan investment company executive
Thomsen, Charles Burton engineering design company executive
Thorn, Terence Hastings gas industry executive
Thorne, Joye Holley special education administrator
†Tilton, Glenn F. oil company executive
Timme, Kathryn Pearl secondary education educator
Toedt, D(ell) C(harles), III lawyer
Tomjanovich, Rudolph professional athletic coach
Tooker, Carl E. department store executive
Trammell, George Thomas physics educator
Tramuto, James Arnold utilities public affairs executive, lawyer
Travis, Andrew David lawyer
Trinh, Victor small business owner
Tronchon, Claude chemical executive
Truesdell, Carolyn Gilmour lawyer
Trusty, Roy Lee former oil company executive
Tucker, Anne Wilkes curator, photographic historian and critic, lecturer
Tucker, Randolph Wadsworth engineering executive
Tuerff, James Rodrick insurance company executive
Turner, William Wilson hospital administrator
Tyndall, Marshall Clay, Jr. banker
Uecker, Wilfred Charles accountant, educator
Urban, Stanley T. hospital administrator
Urbina, Manuel, II legal research historian, history educator
Utsey, John Blaine retail store executive
Vaden, Frank Samuel, III lawyer, engineer
Vaeth, Nancy Ann sales executive
Vail, Peter Robbins geologist
Valencia, Jaime Alfonso chemical engineer
Vallbona, Rima-Gretel Rothe Spanish language educator, writer
Van Caspel, Venita Walker financial planner
Vance, Carol Stoner lawyer
Van Fleet, George Allan lawyer
Van Horn, Verne Hile, III retail executive
Van Slyke, Paul Christopher lawyer
Varner, David Eugene lawyer, energy company executive
Vaughan, Eugene H. investment company executive
Vaughn, Donald Charles international engineering and construction company executive
von der Mehden, Fred R. political science educator
Waggoner, James Virgil chemicals company executive
Wagner, Donald Bert health care consultant
Wagner, Paul Anthony, Jr. education educator
Wainerdi, Richard Elliott medical center executive
Wakefield, Stephen Alan lawyer
Wakil, Salih Jawad biochemistry educator
Walbridge, Willard Eugene broadcasting executive
Walker, Esper Lafayette, Jr. civil engineer
Walker, Jerry Vanzant lawyer
Walker, William Easton surgeon, educator, lawyer
†Wallace, Mark Allen hospital executive
Wallingford, John Rufus lawyer
Walls, Carmage newspaper publisher
Walls, Martha Ann Williams (Mrs. B. Carmage Walls) newspaper executive
Walters, Geoffrey King physicist, educator
Waltrip, Robert L. environmentalist
Wang, Chao-Cheng mathematician, engineer
Ward, Bethea artist, small business owner
Ward, Calvin H. academic director, environmental science educator, federal agency administrator
Warner, Darrell G. petroleum company executive
†Warren, David Boardman museum director, art curator
Watson, C. L. (Chuck Watson) gas industry executive
Watson, John Allen lawyer
†Watson, Max P., Jr. computer software company executive
†Wax, David M. orchestra executive
†Waycaster, Bill chemicals executive
Weaver, Hilda counselor, psychotherapist
Webb, Jack M. lawyer
Webb, Marty Fox principal
Webb, Robert Allen lawyer, educator
Weber, Fredric Alan lawyer
Weber, Owen broadcast executive
Weber, Wilford Alexander education educator
Weinstein, Roy physics educator, researcher
Weisheit, Jon Carleton physicist, educator
Welch, Byron Eugene communications educator
Welch, Harry Scoville lawyer, retired gas pipeline company executive
Welch, Robert Morrow, Jr. lawyer
Wellin, Keith Sears investment banker
Wells, Benjamin Gladney lawyer
Wells, Damon, Jr. investment company executive
Wells, Raymond O., Jr. mathematics educator, researcher
Werlein, Ewing, Jr. federal judge, lawyer
Westmoreland, Kent Ewing lawyer
Wharton, Thomas H(eard), Jr. lawyer
Wheelan, R(ichelieu) E(dward) lawyer
White, John David lawyer
White, Robert Winslow oilfield service company executive
White, Sue Jean lawyer
Wickliffe, Jerry L. lawyer
Wiener, Martin Joel historian
†Wiese, Larry Clevenger lawyer
Wilde, Carlton D. lawyer
Wilford, Dan Sewell hospital administrator
Wilhelm, Marilyn private school administrator
†Wilkes, L. A. oil industry executive
Wilkinson, Bruce W. corporate executive, lawyer
†Wilkinson, G. Thomas gas and oil industry executive
Wilkinson, Harry Edward management educator and consultant
†Will, Edward Edmund oil company executive
Willcott, Mark Robert, III chemist, educator, researcher
Williams, Edward Earl, Jr. entrepreneur, educator
Williams, James Lee financial industries executive
Williams, Percy Don lawyer
Williams, Temple Weatherly, Jr. internist, educator
Williamson, Peter David lawyer
Williamson, Sam lawyer
Wilson, Carl Weldon, Jr. construction company executive, civil engineer
Wilson, Clarence Ivan banker
Wilson, Edward Converse, Jr. oil and natural gas production company executive
Wilson, James William lawyer
Wilson, Patricia Potter library science and reading educator, educational and library consultant
Winslow, Robert Albert gas, oil industry executive
Winton, James C. lawyer
Wold, Finn biochemist, educator
Wolf, Erving oil company executive
Wood, Ivan, Jr. lawyer
Wood, Jack Calvin health care consultant, lawyer
Woodard, Robert E. bishop
Woodhouse, John Frederick food distribution company executive
Woods, James Dudley manufacturing company executive
Woodson, Benjamin Nelson, III insurance executive
Woodward, Katherine Anne secondary education educator
Worden, Larry Lee lawyer
Wray, Marc Frederick minerals company executive
Wray, Thomas Jefferson lawyer
Wren, Robert James aerospace engineering manager
Wright, Clark Phillips computer systems specialist
Wright, Robert Payton lawyer
Wurzburg, Richard Joseph health insurance executive
Wyatt, Oscar Sherman, Jr. energy company executive
Wyschogrod, Edith philosophy educator
Yokubaitis, Roger T. lawyer
York, James Martin lawyer
Young, John Watts astronaut
†Young, Robert B., Jr. engineering company executive
Young, William John French language educator, retired university president
Youngblood, J. Craig lawyer
Youngblood, Ray Wilson publishing company executive
Yu, Aiting Tobey engineering executive
Zabcik, Daniel D. manufacturing executive
Zdobylak, Andrew Martin corporate executive, homebuilder
Zech, William Albert manufacturing company executive
Zeff, Stephen Addam accounting educator
Zerr, Emil Martin construction company executive
Zivley, Walter Perry lawyer
Zlatkis, Albert chemistry educator

Humble
Brown, Samuel Joseph, Jr. scientist, engineer
Hawk, Phillip Michael service corporation executive
Kieta, Douglas Lloyd construction company executive
†Megill, Robert Edgar retired oil company executive, consultant

Hunt
Price, Donald Albert veterinarian, consultant

Huntsville
Anisman, Martin Jay academic administrator
Biles, Robert Erle political science educator
Bruce, Amos Jerry, Jr. psychology educator
Flanagan, Timothy James criminal justice educator, university official
Gutermuth, Mary Elizabeth foreign language educator
Lea, Stanley E. artist, educator
†Smyth, Joseph Philip travel industry executive
Vick, Marie retired health science educator
Warner, Laverne education educator

Hurst
†Bishara, Amin Tawadros mechanical engineer, technical services executive
Dodd, Sylvia Bliss special education educator
†Gelinas, Marc Adrien healthcare administrator
Jackson, Donald waste management executive
Marling, Lynwood Bradley lawyer
Mc Keen, Chester M., Jr. business executive

Industry
Huitt, Jimmie L. rancher, oil, gas, real estate investor

Ingram
Hughes, David Michael oil service company executive, rancher

Irving
Aikman, Troy professional football player
†Andersen, Carsten Steen freight forwarding company executive
Auger, Harvey J. real estate executive
Baird, David Leach, Jr. lawyer, petroleum and chemical company executive
Barclay, George M. banker
Bayne, James Elwood oil company executive
Becker-Doyle, Eve trade association executive
Belknap, John Corbould financial executive
Bumpas, Scott Jackson financial executive
Callahan, Frank T. engineering executive
Cannon, Francis V., Jr. academic administrator, electrical engineer, economist
Carpenter, John W., III financial corporate executive
Cattarulla, Elliot Reynold oil company executive
Clark, Priscilla Alden elementary school educator
Collins, Stephen Barksdale health care executive
Cooper, Kathleen Bell economist
Daniel, Donald advertising executive
Dinicola, Robert consumer products company executive
Donnelly, Barbara Schettler medical technologist
Faulkner, David J. computer company executive
George, David Webster architect
Gerstein, Irving R. jewelry company executive
Gidel, Robert Hugh real estate investor
Groussman, Dean G. retail executive
Haley, Charles Lewis professional football player
Halter, Jon Charles magazine editor, writer
Hansen, Nick Dane lawyer
Hendrickson, Constance Marie McRight chemist, consultant
Hess, Edwin John oil company executive
Hughes, John Farrell finance company executive
Hughes, Keith William banking and finance company executive
Irvin, Michael Jerome professional football player
Jack, James E. financial service company executive
Jones, Jerry (Jerral Wayne Jones) professional football team executive
Judge, Stephen advertising executive
Kirkley, T. A. oil company executive
Le Vine, Duane Gilbert petroleum company executive
†Levy, Irvin L. diversified company executive
Levy, Lester A. sanitation company executive
Lindner, James D. computer company executive
Lites, James professional hockey team executive
Love, Ben F. banker
Lutz, Matthew Charles geologist, oil company executive
Martin, Kenneth Douglas consumer products company executive
Martin, Thomas Lyle, Jr. university president
Marton, Bernard Anthony headmaster, priest, educator
Metevier, James F. finance company executive
Mueller, James Bernhard anesthesiologist, pain management consultant
Munger, Sharon market research firm executive
Novacek, Jay McKinley professional football player
O'Brien, William Daniel oil industry executive
Olson, Herbert Theodore trade association executive
Perry, Charles Edward university administrator
Pickett, Edwin Gerald financial executive
Potter, Robert Joseph technical research and business executive
Rees, Frank William, Jr. architect
Robinson, Edgar Allen oil company executive
Sasseen, Robert Francis university president
Simon, Dolph B(ertram) H(irst) lawyer, jewelry company executive
Smith, Emmitt J., III professional football player
Sommerfeldt, John Robert historian
Stahl, David Edward association executive
Stepnoski, Mark Matthew professional football player
Stuckey, Scott Sherwood editor
Sullivan, Joseph Robert financial service company executive, lawyer
Switzer, Barry professional football coach, former university athletic coach
Temerlin, Liener advertising agency executive
Walwer, Frank Kurt dean, legal educator
Ward, Patrick J. oil industry executive
Wicks, William Withington retired public relations executive
Williams, Erik George professional football player
†Wilson, Sam N. transportation services executive
†Young, J. Warren magazine publisher
Zahn, Donald Jack lawyer

Jacksonville
Blaylock, James Carl clergyman, librarian
†Higgs, Grady L. religious organization administrator
Pruitt, William Charles, Jr. minister, educator

Katy
Andrews, George Arthur headmaster
Fudge, Edward William lawyer

Kerrville
Cremer, Richard Eldon marketing professional
Dozier, William Everett, Jr. newspaper editor and publisher
Frudakis, Evangelos William sculptor
Harkey, Ira Brown, Jr. newspaperman, educator, author
Holloway, Leonard Leveine former university president
Kunz, Sidney entomologist
Lich, Glen Ernst regional studies educator, ethnographer, government official, writer
Matlock, (Lee) Hudson civil engineer, educator

Kilgore
Rorschach, Richard Gordon lawyer

Killeen
Villaronga, Raul G. mayor, realtor

Kingsville
Cecil, David Rolf mathematician, educator
Ibanez, Manuel Luis university official, biological sciences educator
Morey, Philip Stockton, Jr. mathematics educator
Perez, John Carlos biology educator
Robins, Gerald Burns education educator

Kingwood
Brinkley, Charles Alexander geologist
Davies, David Keith geologist
Sale, James Prowant, Jr. lawyer

Lackland AFB
Anderson, Edgar R., Jr. career officer, hospital administrator, physician
†Carlton, Paul Kendall, Jr. air force officer, physician
†Lecholop, Stephen K. medical center administrator

Lake Jackson
Tasa, Kendall Sherwood chemistry educator

Lancaster
Fewel, Harriett lawyer
Wendorf, Denver Fred, Jr. anthropology educator

Laredo
Buckley, Esther Gonzalez-Arroyo federal commissioner, educator
Hinojosa, Sandra Joy elementary special education educator
Jacobs, Gary G. banker
Kazen, George Philip federal judge
Rodriguez, Yolanda Isabel elementary instructional administrator

Laughlin AFB
†McCarthy, Sean Michael air force pilot

League City
Ellis, Walter Leon minister
†Faget, Maxime A(llan) aeronautical engineer
†Langstaff, David Hamilton commercial industry executive
Meinke, Roy Walter electrical engineer, consultant

Levelland
Walker, James Kenneth judge

Lewisville
Bickel, Herbert Jacob, Jr. corporation executive
Downing, Clayton W. school system administrator
Vacca, John Joseph, Jr. television executive

Liberty Hill
Vance, Zinna Barth artist, writer
West, Felton newspaper writer

Lindale
Bockhop, Clarence William retired agricultural engineer
Carter, Thomas Smith, Jr. retired railroad executive
Wilson, Leland Earl petroleum engineering consultant

Livingston
†Battise, Frances Sylestine healthcare professional, tribal official
†De Revere, David Wilsen professional society administrator

Llano
Walter, Virginia Lee psychologist, educator

Longview
Beckworth, Lindley Gary, Jr. lawyer
Brannon, Clifton Woodrow, Sr. evangelist, lawyer
Crain, Bluford Walter, Jr. architect
Davis, Jimmie Mae Clayborn elementary school educator
Folzenlogen, P. D. petrochemical executive
LeTourneau, Richard Howard retired college president
McMichael, Ronald L. superintendent

Lubbock
Allison, Cecil Wayne insurance company executive
Amir-Moez, Ali Reza mathematician, educator
Archer, James Elson engineering educator
Askins, Billy Earl education educator, consultant
Bricker, Donald Lee surgeon
Buesseler, John Aure ophthalmologist, management consultant
Cartwright, Walter Joseph sociology educator
Cochran, Joseph Wesley law librarian, educator
Collins, Harker manufacturing executive, economist, publisher, marketing, financial, business and legal consultant
Connor, Seymour Vaughan historian, writer
Conover, William Jay statistics educator
Cummings, Sam R. federal judge
Curl, Samuel Everett university dean, agricultural scientist
Dregne, Harold Ernest agronomy educator
Dudek, Richard Albert engineering educator
Duncan, Robert Lloyd lawyer
Eddleman, Floyd Eugene retired English language educator
†Edson, Gary Francis museum director
Frazier, Eugene Richard designer
Gilliam, John Charles economist, educator
Glass, Carson McElyea lawyer
Haragan, Donald Robert university administrator, geosciences educator
Hartman, James Theodore physician, educator
Havens, Murray Clark political scientist, educator
Hentges, David John microbiology educator
Hulsey, Sam Byron bishop

Illner-Canizaro, Hana *physician, oral surgeon, researcher*
Jackson, Francis Charles *physician, surgeon*
Jonish, James Edward *economist, educator*
Kelsey, Clyde Eastman, Jr. *philosophy and psychology educator*
Ketner, Kenneth Laine *philosopher, educator*
Kiesling, Ernst Willie *civil engineering educator*
Kristiansen, Magne *electrical engineer, educator*
Kurtzman, Neil A. *medical educator*
Lawless, Robert William *academic administrator*
Lemley, Steven Smith *academic administrator*
Lopez, Delmira Castro *school system administrator*
Maunder, Addison Bruce *agronomic research company executive*
May, Donald Robert Lee *ophthalmologist, retina and vitreous surgeon, educator, academic administrator*
McManigal, Shirley Ann *university dean*
Messer, Robert H. *obstetrician/gynecologist, educator*
Meyer, Sister Roberta *school system administrator*
Mittemeyer, Bernhard Theodore *university official, surgeon, retired army officer*
Montford, John Thomas *lawyer, state legislator*
Murrah, David J. *archivist, historian*
Murray, Grover Elmer *geologist, educator*
Nagy, Joe Howard *lawyer*
Pasewark, William Robert *author, management consultant*
Pearce, William Martin *history educator*
Perry, Malcolm Oliver *vascular surgeon*
Portnoy, William Manos *electrical engineering educator*
Purdom, Thomas James *lawyer*
Rippel, Jeffrey Alan *library director*
Robinson, G. Wilse *molecular spectroscopist, educator*
†Rodriguez, Placido *bishop*
Rushing, Jane Gilmore *writer*
Schake, Lowell Martin *animal science educator*
Sears, Robert Stephen *finance educator*
Shine, Henry Joseph *chemistry educator*
Shires, George Thomas *surgeon, physician, educator*
Skoog, Gerald Duane *science educator*
Smith, Doris Corinne Kemp *retired nurse*
Stem, Carl Herbert *business educator*
Stuart, Frank Adell *county official*
Walker, Warren Stanley *English educator*
Watson, W. H. *bishop*
Way, Barbara Haight *dermatologist*
Wendt, Charles William *soil physicist, educator*
Williams, Darryl Marlowe *medical educator*
Wolfe, Verda Nell *pension consultant, financial planner*
Wood, Richard Courtney *library director, educator*
Woodward, Halbert Owen *federal judge*
Woolam, Gerald Lynn *surgeon*
Yoder Wise, Patricia Snyder *nurse, educator*

Lufkin
Brookshire, Wiley Eugene *consumer products company executive*
Cardwell, Horace Milton *communications company executive*
Denman, Joe Carter, Jr. *retired forest products company executive*
Hannah, John Henry, Jr. *judge*
Perry, Lewis Charles *emergency medicine physician, osteopath*
†Smith, Douglas V. *manufacturing executive, heavy*

Mabank
Beets, Hughla Fae *retired secondary school educator*

Marble Falls
Cross, Christopher *recording artist, songwriter, singer*

Marshall
Dahl, Shirley Ann *education educator*
Magrill, Rose Mary *library director*
Poindexter, Kenneth Wayne *automobile executive*

Mc Kinney
White, Nathan Emmett, Jr. *lawyer*

Mcallen
Ashley, James Thomas, III *architect*
Hinojosa, Ricardo H. *federal judge*
†McGee, William Howard John *library system coordinator*
Mittelstaedt, Gerard E. *library director*
Ramirez, Mario Efrain *physician*

Mercedes
Alaniz, Theodora Villareal *elementary education educator*

Mesquite
Bullock, Norma Kathryn Rice *chemical research professional*
Mc Gregor, Donald Thornton *newspaper editor, journalist*
Tabor, Beverly Ann *elementary school educator*
Vaughan, Joseph Lee, Jr. *education educator, consultant*
Williams, John Elbert, Jr. *library services director*

Midland
Bullock, Maurice Randolph *lawyer*
Chappell, Clovis Gillham, Jr. *lawyer*
Craddick, Thomas Russell *investor, state representative*
Grover, Rosalind Redfern *oil and gas company executive*
McAfee, John Wilson, Sr. *principal*
Morrow, William Clarence *lawyer*
Ott, Wendell Lorenz *art museum director, artist*
Reed, Joel Leston *diversified manufacturing company executive*
Roberts, James Lee *fire chief*
Smith, Robin Doyle *judge*
Sykes, Robert Reed *lawyer, former judge*
Vinson, Morty Conrad (Morty Vinson) *oil company executive, rancher*
Wagner, Cyril, Jr. *metals manufacturing company executive*
†Wegner, Sandra Sue *library director*

Midlothian
Forward, Gordon E. *cement company executive*

Missouri City
Griffin, Oscar O'Neal, Jr. *writer, former oil company executive*

Montgomery
Farmer, Joe Sam *petroleum company executive*
Holman, Charles Richardson *chemical company executive*
Tharp, Benjamin Carroll, Jr. *architect*

Mount Pleasant
Ogburn, Wayne Lee *health science facility administrator*
†Palmer, Robert Blunden *newspaper, printing executive*

Nacogdoches
Angel, Daniel Duane *university president*
Clagett, Arthur F(rank) *psychologist, sociologist, qualitative research writer, retired sociology educator*
Fish, Stewart Allison *retired obstetrician and gynecologist*
Kallsen, Theodore John *retired English language educator*
Worrell, Albert Cadwallader *forest economics educator*

Navasota
Norris, Chuck (Carlos Ray) *actor*

New Braunfels
Fomon, Samuel Joseph *physician, educator*
Oestreich, Charles Henry *college president*
Wilson, James Lee *retired geology educator, consultant*

North Richland Hills
Cunningham, Larry J. *city official*

Odessa
Bailey, Keith Stewart *insurance company executive*
Boyd, Claude Collins *education advisor*
Gilliland, William Elton *retired lawyer*
Lee, Nelda S. *artist, art appraiser and dealer, film producer*
MacDonald, Karen Hope Cowart *educator, reading specialist*
Reeves, Robert Grier LeFevre *geology educator, scientist*
Sorber, Charles Arthur *academic administrator*

Orange
Adkins, John E(arl), Jr. *chemist*
Delarue, Louis C(harles) *priest*
Eldredge, Bruce Beard *museum director*

Overton
Randel, Ronald Dean *physiologist, educator*

Palestine
Williams, Franklin Cadmus, Jr. *bibliographer*

Pampa
Cain, Donald Ezell *judge*
Warner, John William *lawyer*
Willingham, Jeanne Maggart *dance educator, ballet company executive*

Paris
Sawyer, Mary Catherine *hospital administrator*

Pasadena
Brown, Robert Griffith *chemicals executive, chemist, chemical engineer*
†Clifford, Ann Tharp *library director*
Ellis, Clarence Lee *police official*
Gilley, Mickey Leroy *musician*
Loomis, John Norman *psychiatrist*
Moon, John Henry, Sr. *banker*
Zimmerer, Ann(a) Morgan *lawyer, consulting psychologist, genealogist*

Pharr
Lindner, Kenneth Edward *academic administrator and chemistry educator emeritus*

Pittsburg
Pilgrim, Lonnie (Bo Pilgrim) *poultry production company executive*
Voss, William R. *poultry feed company executive consultant*
Galle, Richard Lynn *association executive, former municipal official*

Plano
Alberthal, Lester M., Jr. *information processing services executive*
Andrews, Judy Coker *electronics company executive*
Bain, Travis Whitsett, II *manufacturing and retail executive*
Bode, Richard Albert *retired financial executive*
Bonet, Frank Joseph *lawyer*
Brock, Dee Sala *television executive, educator, writer, consultant*
Broyles, Michael Lee *geophysics and physics educator*
Collumb, Peter John *communications company executive*
Donald, James L. *communications company executive*
Finley, Glenna *author*
Friedlander, D. Gilbert *lawyer*
Grant, Joseph Moorman *executive finance banker*
Heard, David Dennis *food products company executive*
Hinton, Norman Wayne *information services executive*
Kranzow, Ronald Roy *lawyer*
Lee, Allan Wren *clergyman*
Linderman, Dean *data processing services company executive*
Neppl, Walter Joseph *retired retail store executive*
Oesterreicher, James E. *department stores executive*
Peterson, William E. *fire chief, consultant*
Resnik, Linda Ilene *marketing and information executive, consultant*
Schuh, Frank Joseph *drilling engineering company executive, consultant*

†Scott, Terry Lee *communications company executive*
Sedei, Donald James *art director*
Senderling, Jon Townsend *journalist, public affairs specialist*
Thompson, J. Ken *gas, oil industry executive*
Wells, John Andrew *retail executive*
White, Michael Dennis *food manufacturing company executive*
Wilke, Chet *real estate executive*

Port Aransas
Lehmann, William Leonardo *electrical engineer, educator*
Wohlschlag, Donald Eugene *zoologist, marine ecologist, educator emeritus*

Port Arthur
Gipson, Robert Malone *oil industry executive*
Parker, Carl *former state senator*

Port Isabel
Smith, Mary Lou *librarian*

Portland
Cessac, Joyce Eve LaBorde *elementary school educator*

Post
Earl, Lewis Harold *economics and management consultant*

Pottsboro
Hanning, Gary William *utility executive, water company executive, consultant*
Thomas, Ann Van Wynen *lawyer, educator*

Prairie View
Boyd-Brown, Lena Ernestine *history educator, education consultant*
Clark, Sharon Enid *principal*
Coe, Elizabeth Beaubien *English language educator*
Fogarty, Thomas Nilan *electronic materials engineer*
Jones, Barbara Ann Posey *college dean*
Prestage, Jewel Limar *political science educator*
Trotty, Willie Francis *university dean*

Pyote
Trevino, Jerry Rosalez *secondary school principal*

Randolph AFB
Ryder, Gene Ed *retired United States Air Force training administrator*

Red Oak
Henderson, Edwin Harold *minister*

Rhome
Brammer, Barbara Rhudene *retired secondary education educator*

Richardson
Adamson, Dan Klinglesmith *science association executive*
Berry, Brian Joe Lobley *geographer, political economist, urban planner*
Biard, James Robert *electrical engineer*
Boyd, Joe Dan *journal editor*
Breard, Benjamin Allen *art dealer*
Brown, Ollie Dawkins *marriage, family and child therapist, scientific researcher*
Coleman, Rogers King *insurance company executive*
Conrad, Flavius Leslie, Jr. *minister*
Cordell, Robert James *retired geologist*
Dunn, David E. *university dean*
Edge, Harold Lee *manufacturing executive*
Edwards, Carl Elmo, Jr. *lawyer*
Fahrlander, Henry William, Jr. *management consultant*
Gary, John *singer*
Goldberg, Leonard *television and movie producer*
Gray, Donald Melvin *molecular and cell biology educator*
Hagan, Joseph Lawrence *communications executive*
Hiegel, James Edward *apparel executive*
Johnson, Francis Severin *physicist*
Landisman, Mark *geophysicist, educator*
Langmead, Jeffrey P. *insurance company executive*
Leach, Sheryl *television show character creator*
†Lovelace, Julianne *library director*
Lupe, John Edward, Jr. *finance executive*
Lutz, Raymond Price *industrial engineer, educator*
McDaniel, Dolan Kenneth *oil explorchemistry educator*
†Norris, John Windsor, Jr. *manufacturing company executive*
Orr, David E. *electronics executive*
Paluck, Robert John *electronics executive*
Pervin, William Joseph *computer science educator*
Putnam, Howard Dean *investor, former airline executive*
Redman, Timothy Paul *English language educator, author, chess federation administrator*
†Rogers, Gerald D. *electronics executive*
Rutford, Robert Hoxie *university educator*
Schrimsher, Jerry James *diversified financial services company executive*
Wagers, Robert Shelby *entrepreneur*
Weaver, Jo Nell *elementary school educator*
Wildenthal, Bryan Hobson *university administrator*
Young, Malcolm Eugene, Jr. *social studies secondary educator*

Richmond
Barratt, Cynthia Louise *pharmaceutical company executive*
Willis, David Edwin *retired geophysicist*

Roanoke
Bradshaw, Terry *sports announcer, former professional football player*
Steward, Jerry Wayne *air transportation executive consultant*

Rockport
Minor, Joseph Edward *civil engineer, educator*

Rockwall
Griffith, James William *engineer, consultant*
House, Robert William *music educator*
Sparks, Sherman Paul *osteopathic physician*

Wallace, Mary Elaine *opera director, author*

Round Rock
Chavez, Dorothy Vaughan *elementary school educator, environmental educator*
LaShelle, Charles Stanton *lawyer, insurance company executive*

Round Top
†Dick, James Cordell *concert pianist*

Salado
Cutler, Morene Parten *civic worker*
Parks, Lloyd Lee *oil company executive*

San Angelo
Chatfield, Mary Van Abshoven *librarian*
Coe, Robert Stanford *retired management educator*
Davison, Elizabeth Jane Linton *education educator*
Foster, Walton Arthur *broadcasting executive*
Menzies, Carl Stephen *agricultural research administrator, ruminant nutritionist*
Pfeifer, Michael David *bishop*
Torres, David *Spanish language educator*

San Antonio
Abramson, Hyman Norman *engineering and science research executive*
Adams, James R. *telecommunications executive*
Ahmad, Shair *mathematics educator*
Aldave, Barbara Bader *law educator, lawyer*
Allison, Stephen Philip *lawyer*
Anderson, George Kenneth *air force officer, physician*
Anderson, Noble *dairy products executive*
Auerbach, Ernest Sigmund *lawyer, company executive, writer*
Aust, Joe Bradley *surgeon, educator*
Baker, Floyd Wilmer *surgeon, retired army officer*
Ball, M(ary) Isabel *chemistry educator, dean*
Barnes, Gail *historic site administrator*
Barrow, Charles Wallace *university dean*
Barton, James Cary *lawyer*
Bates, David Quentin, Jr. *lawyer, pharmaceutical executive*
Beckmann, Charles Henry *cardiologist, educator*
Belgin, Harvey Harry *photojournalist*
Bellows, Thomas John *political scientist, educator*
Belzung, Paul Edward *engineering executive*
Bennett, Gerard Paul *computer scientist*
Benninger, Edward C., Jr. *petroleum and natural gas company executive*
Benz, George Albert *economic consultant, retired educator*
Berg, Thomas *manufacturing executive*
Betts, Austin Wortham *retired research company executive*
Biery, Evelyn Hudson *lawyer*
Blystone, Robert Vernon *developmental cell biologist, educator, textbook consultant*
†Bolner, Clifton Joseph *food company executive*
Bowman, Barbara Hyde *biologist, geneticist, educator*
Boyers, John Martin *principal*
Brown, Robert *manufacturing executive*
Bryan, Richard Ray *real estate development executive, construction executive*
Budalur, Thyagarajan Subbanarayan *chemistry educator*
Burch, James Leo *science research institute executive*
Burke, Michael Donald *oil and gas company executive*
Burton, Russell Rohan *aerospace scientist, researcher*
Butt, Charles C. *food service executive*
†Button, Damon *oil industry executive*
Calgaard, Ronald Keith *university president*
Carpenter, John Wilson, III *management consultant, retired air force officer, educational administrator*
Carroll, William Marion *financial services executive*
Carson, Robin D. *zoological park administrator*
Catto, Henry Edward *former government official, former ambassador*
Caudill, Howard Edwin *bishop, educator*
†Chiego, William J. *museum director*
Chong, Vernon *surgeon, physician, Air Force officer*
Clark, Leif Michael *federal judge*
Cloud, Bruce Benjamin, Sr. *construction company executive*
Compton, Clinton E. *principal*
Cook, Harold Rodney *military officer, medical facility administrator*
Coronado, Jose Ricardo Fache *hospital administrator*
Corrigan, Helen González *cytologist*
Cory, William Eugene *retired consulting company executive*
Croft, Harry Allen *psychiatrist*
Cruz-Romo, Gilda *soprano*
†Curtis, Lewis E., III *air force officer*
Davis, Walter Barry *quality assurance professional*
Dazey, William Boyd *retired lawyer*
Delmer, Merle W. *pathologist*
DeVries, Jack *engine manufacturing executive*
Dickey, John Sloan, Jr. *dean, educator, geologist, researcher*
Dobie, Robert Alan *otologist*
Dougherty, Robert James *safety consultant*
Doyle, Frank Lawrence *geologist, hydrologist, executive*
Duncan, A. Baker *investment banker*
Durbin, Richard Louis, Jr. *lawyer*
Elkin, Irvin J. *milk marketing cooperative executive*
Elliot, Sean Michael *professional basketball player*
Ellis, James D. *communications executive, corporate lawyer*
Fagan, Wayne Irwin *lawyer*
Fawcett, Leslie Clarence, Jr. *accountant*
Fawcett, Robert Earl, Jr. *retired banker*
Fink, Lyman Roger *retired manufacturing executive*
Flores, Patrick F. *archbishop*
Fox, Michael W. *lawyer*
Franklin, Larry Daniel *communications company executive*
Frazer, Robert Lee *landscape architect*
Freeman, Howard Lee, Jr. *financial executive*
Freeman, Philip Dayne *lawyer*
Fretthold, Timothy Jon *lawyer*
Frost, Thomas Clayborne *banker*
Fuhrmann, Charles J., II *investment and finance consultant*
Furino, Antonio *economist, educator*
Garcia, Hipolito Frank (Hippo Garcia) *federal judge*
Garcia, June Marie *library director*
Garcia, Linda *secondary school principal*
Garza, Emilio M(iller) *federal judge*

†Gassmann, Carl Jeffrey *oral surgeon, physician*
Gates, Mahlon Eugene *applied research executive, former government official, former army officer*
Gibbons, Robert Ebbert *university official*
Gillean, William Otho, Jr. *physician, psychiatrist*
Goelz, Paul Cornelius *university dean*
Goland, Martin *research institute executive*
†Gonzalez, Efren *airport executive*
Gonzalez, Hector Hugo *nurse, educator, consultant*
Graham, Susan Marie *nurse*
Greehey, William Eugene *energy company executive*
Green, Phillip Dale *banker*
Greenberg, Nat *orchestra administrator*
Gresham, Gary Stuart *wholesale grocery executive, accountant*
Grissom, Patsy Coleen *college administrator, English educator*
Grubb, Robert Lynn *computer system designer*
Gudinas, Donald Jerome *banker, retired army officer*
Guenther, Jack Egon *lawyer*
Hamm, William Joseph *retired physics educator*
Hanahan, Donald James *biochemist, educator*
†Hard, Robert J. *archaeology educator*
Hardberger, Phillip Duane *judge, lawyer, journalist*
Harte, Houston Harriman *newspaper, broadcasting executive*
Hauser, Victor LaVern *agricultural engineer*
Hawken, Patty Lynn *nursing educator, dean of faculty*
Haywood, Norcell Dan *architect*
Hazuda, Helen Pauline *sociologist*
Hemminghaus, Roger Roy *energy company executive, chemical engineer*
Henderson, Arvis Burl *data processing executive, biochemist*
Henderson, Dwight Franklin *dean, educator*
Hernandez, Christine *educator*
Herres, Robert Tralles *insurance company executive*
Hesson, Paul Anthony *architect*
†Hilliard, Robert Wayne *hospital administrator*
Hinojosa, Emilio Alfredo *community development director*
Holcomb, M. Staser *insurance executive*
Holguin, Alfonso Hudson *physician, educator*
Horan, James Joseph *banker*
Hornbeak, John Earl *hospital administrator*
Horner, Richard Elmer *retired telecommunications company executive*
Howard, George Salladé *conductor, music consultant, educator*
Howard, M. Francine *chemist*
Hyland, Douglas K. S. *museum administrator, educator*
†Hyslop, William Arthur *health care executive*
Iglehart, T. D. *bishop*
Issleib, Lutz E. *beverage company executive*
Jacobson, David *rabbi*
Johnson, Hansford Tillman *retired air force officer*
Johnston, Murray Lloyd, Jr. *lawyer*
Jones, Daniel Hare *librarian*
Jones, James Richard *business administration educator*
Juren, Dennis Franklin *petroleum company executive*
Kalter, Seymour Sanford *virologist, educator*
Keck, James Moulton *retired advertising and marketing executive, retired air force officer*
Keeter, James Edwin, Sr. *landscape architect*
Kellman, Steven G. *literature educator, author*
Kilpatrick, Charles Otis *newspaper editor, publisher*
King, Ronald Baker *federal judge*
Kirkpatrick, Samuel Alexander *university president, social and policy sciences educator*
Klaerner, Curtis Maurice *former oil company executive*
Klepac, Robert Karl *psychologist, consultant*
Kotas, Robert Vincent *research physician, educator*
Kozuch, Julianna Bernadette *librarian, educator*
Krier, Cynthia Taylor *lawyer, former state legislator*
Krier, Joseph Roland *chamber of commerce executive, lawyer*
Kronick, David A. *librarian*
Kutchins, Michael Joseph *airport executive*
Labay, Eugene Benedict *lawyer*
Lahourcade, John Brosius *service company executive*
Langlinais, Joseph Willis *academic administrator*
Larson, Doyle Eugene *electronics company executive, retired air force officer*
Laurence, Dan H. *author, literary and dramatic specialist*
Leavitt, Audrey Faye Cox *television programming executive*
Ledford, Frank Finley, Jr. *surgeon, army officer*
Leeper, Michael Edward *retired army officer, retired corporation executive*
Leies, John Alex *academic administrator, educator, clergyman*
Lenke, Joanne Marie *publishing executive*
†Lenschow, William *food products executive*
Leon, Robert Leonard *psychiatrist, educator*
Lindholm, Ulric Svante *engineering research institute executive, retired*
Lloyd, Susan Elaine *middle school educator*
Lowry, A. Robert *federal government railroad arbitrator*
Lyle, Robert Edward *chemist*
†Lyles, Mark Bradley *high technology company executive, dentist*
Lynch, Robert Martin *lawyer, educator*
Maas, James Weldon *psychiatrist*
Macon, Jane Haun *lawyer*
Macon, Richard Laurence *lawyer*
†Mairs, David *symphony conductor*
Manning, Noel Thomas *publishing company executive*
Marbut, Robert Gordon *communications, cable and broadcast executive*
Marek, Vladimir *ballet director, educator*
Martin, Suzanne Carole *health facility administrator*
Martinez, Pete R. *beverage company executive*
Masoro, Edward Joseph, Jr. *physiology educator*
Matthews, Dan Gus *lawyer*
Matthews, Wilbur Lee *lawyer*
Mays, L. Lowry *broadcast executive*
Mc Allister, Gerald Nicholas *retired bishop, clergyman*
McClane, Robert Sanford *bank holding company executive*
McClinton, Dorothy Hardaway *former business educator*
Mc Dermott, Robert Francis *insurance company executive*
Mc Fee, Arthur Storer *physician*
Mc Giffert, John Rutherford *retired cultural institute director, retired army officer*
†McGill, Henry Coleman, Jr. *physician, educator, researcher*
McGuire, William Dennis *health care system executive*
†McLemore, David Eugene *editor, writer*
Meyer, Alice K. *investor*
Meyer, George Gotthold *psychiatrist, educator*
Michaels, Willard A. *retired broadcasting executive*
†Michigami, Michael Masao *data processing executive*
Miles, Janice Ann *news reporter*
Miller, Larry Joseph *oil and gas company executive*
Mills, Nancy Stewart *chemistry educator*
Mitchell, George Washington, Jr. *physician, educator*
Moder, John Joseph *academic administrator, priest*
Moe, Palmer L. *gas company executive*
Montecel, Maria Robledo (Cuca Robledo Montecel) *educational association administrator*
Nance, Betty Love *librarian*
Neel, Spurgeon Hart, Jr. *physician, retired army officer*
Neiner, A(ndrew) Joseph *corporate executive*
Nix, Robert Lynn *minister*
Norwood, Carole Gene *middle school educator*
Nowak, Nancy Stein *judge*
Padgett, Shelton Edward *lawyer*
Parks, Madelyn N. *nurse, retired army officer, university official*
Parsons, Merribell Maddux *museum consultant*
Perez, Andrew, III *architect*
Persellin, Robert Harold *physician*
Pestana, Carlos *physician, educator*
Petty, Olive Scott *geophysical engineer*
†Polunsky, Bob A. *movie critic, talk show host*
Pontolillo, Brother Peter A. *school system administrator*
Post, Gerald Joseph *retired banker, retired air force officer*
Prado, Edward Charles *federal judge*
Prill, Arnold *diversified metal repair company executive*
Ranson, Guy Harvey *clergyman, religion educator*
Reuter, Stewart Ralston *radiologist, lawyer, educator*
Rhame, William Thomas *land development company executive*
Rhodes, Linda Jane *psychiatrist*
Ribble, Ronald George *psychologist, educator, writer*
Ritchie, Richard Lee *communications company executive, former railroad and forest products company executive*
Robertson, Samuel Luther, Jr. *special education educator, therapist*
Robinson, David Maurice (The Admiral) *professional basketball player*
Rodman, Dennis Keith *basketball player*
†Rodriguez, Victor *school system administrator*
†Romo, Sylvia *state legislator, accountant*
Rosoff, Leonard, Sr. *retired surgeon, medical educator*
Ross, James Ulric *lawyer, accountant, educator*
Schenker, Steven *physician, educator*
Schlueter, David Arnold *law educator*
Schulte, Josephine Helen *historian, educator*
Sessions, William Steele *former government official*
Sheerin, Maggie *small business owner, artist*
Siler-Khodr, Theresa Marie *biochemistry educator*
†Smith, Callie W. *health facility administrator*
Smith, Reginald Brian Furness *anesthesiologist, educator*
Smith, Richard Thomas *electrical engineer*
Spears, Sally *lawyer*
Stebbins, Richard Henderson *electronics engineer, peace officer, security consultant*
Steen, John Thomas, Jr. *lawyer*
Stephens, Sunny Courington *special education educator*
Stone, William Harold *geneticist, educator*
Story, Jim Lewis *neurosurgeon, educator*
†Stubblefield, James Bert, Jr. *army officer*
Sueltenfuss, Sister Elizabeth Anne *university president*
Suttle, Dorwin Wallace *federal judge*
Terracina, Roy David *food executive*
Thompson, Mary Koleta *sculptor, non-profit organization director*
†Thornton, William E. *mayor, oral surgeon*
Thornton, William James, Jr. *composer, music educator*
Townsend, Frank Marion *pathology educator*
Trench, William Frederick *mathematics educator*
Truett, Lila Flory *economics educator*
Tucker, Roy Nelson *mathematics educator, minister*
†Tucker, Stephen Lawrence *health administration educator, consultant*
Vazquez, Gilbert Falcon *lawyer*
Wagener, James Wilbur *social science educator*
†Walker, Tim *printing company executive*
Walker, William Oliver, Jr. *religion educator*
†Walsh, Nicolas Eugene *rehabilitation medicine physician, educator*
West, Robert Van Osdell, Jr. *retired petroleum executive*
Westbrook, Joel Whitsitt, III *lawyer*
Whitacre, Edward E., Jr. *telecommunications executive*
White, Mary Ruth Wathen *social services administrator*
Whitt, Robert Ampudia, III *advertising executive, marketing professional*
Whittington, Floyd Leon *economist, business consultant, retired oil company executive, foreign service officer*
Wiedeman, Geoffrey Paul *physician, air force officer*
†Willome, John *construction executive*
Willson, Robert (William) *glass sculpture and watercolor artist*
Wilson, Janie Menchaca *nursing educator, researcher*
Wimpress, Gordon Duncan, Jr. *corporate consultant, foundation executive*
Winters, Wendell Delos *microbiology educator, researcher, consultant*
†Wise, Doug *retail executive*
Witherspoon, John Marshall *advertising executive*
Wood, Frank Preuit *educator, former air force officer*
†Yerkes, Susan Gamble *newspaper columnist*
Young, James Julius *university administrator, former army officer*
Young, Olivia Knowles *retired librarian*
Zachry, Henry Bartell, Jr. *construction company executive*

San Marcos
Balanoff, Howard Richard *social sciences educator*
Barragán, Celia Silguero *elementary education educator*
Bechtol, William Milton *education educator*
Boehm, Richard Glennon *geography and planning educator, writer*
Byrom, Jack Edwards *private school administrator*
Carman, Mary Ann *special education educator*
Cassidy, Patrick Edward *chemist, educator*
†Herkimer, Allen Gillman, Jr. *health administration educator*
Longley, Glenn *biology educator, research director*
Martin, Jerri Whan *public relations executive*
Moore, Betty Jean *retired education educator*
Schultz, Clarence Carven, Jr. *sociology educator*
Supple, Jerome H. *university president*
Weinberger, George Martin *political scientist, government infosystems specialist*

Schulenburg
Clark, I. E. *publisher*

Seabrook
Earle, Kenneth Martin *retired neuropathologist*
Jacobs, Dorothy Patricia *elementary education educator*
Spears, James Grady *small business owner*
Sterling, Shirley Frampton *artist, educator*

Seagraves
McAdoo, Carolyn *secondary school business educator*

Sealy
Young, Milton Earl *retired petroleum production company executive*

Seguin
Mims, Forrest Marion, III *science writer*
Moline, Jon Nelson *philosopher, educator, college president*
Moline, Sandra Lois *librarian*

Seminole
Gremmel, Gilbert Carl *family physician*
Molinar, Lupe Rodriquez *librarian, library director*

Sherman
Brown, Paul Neeley *federal judge*
Page, Oscar C. *academic administrator*

Silsbee
Ashcraft, David Lee *forest products company executive*
White, Helen Frances Pearson *language educator, real estate broker*

Sinton
†Teer, James G. *foundation administrator*

Southlake
Norris, Richard Anthony *accountant*

Spring
Clark, Carolyn Archer *aerosopace scientist*
Cooley, Andrew Lyman *corporation executive, former army officer*
Frison, Paul Maurice *health care executive*
Hunt, T(homas) W(ebb) *retired religion educator*
Lightell, Kenneth Ray *education educator*
Riley, Arthur Roy *consulting engineer*

Springtown
Marrs, James F., Jr. *author, journalist, educator*

Stafford
Brinkley, Elise Hoffman *biofeedback counselor, marriage and family therapist, nurse*
Franks, Charles Leslie *investments executive*
Polinger, Iris Sandra *dermatologist*
Selecman, Charles Edward *business executive*

Stephenville
Christopher, Joe Randell *English language educator*
Collier, Boyd Dean *finance educator, management consultant*
King, Clyde Richard *journalism educator, writer*
†Simpson, Charles Edmond *crop science educator*
Sims, Larry Kyle *secondary school educator*

Stratford
Woods, John William *lawyer*

Sugar Land
Bartolo, Adolph Marion *food company executive*
†Brumit, Lawrence Edward, III *oil field service company executive*
Hanna, Robert C. *food products executive*
Kempner, Isaac Herbert, III *sugar company executive*
Kempner, James Carroll *sugar company executive*
McMahon, Edward Francis *oil industry executive, consultant*
Oller, William Maxwell *retired energy company executive, retired naval officer*
Preng, David Edward *management consultant*
Ramos, Rose Mary *elementary education educator*
Welch, William Henry *oil service company executive, consultant*

Sulphur Springs
McKenzie, Kenneth *retail grocery executive*
†McKenzie, Michael K. *wholesale executive*

Talpa
Russell, Nedra Joan Bibby *secondary school educator*

Temple
Dickson, Joseph M. *management consultant, former health care administrator*
Dyck, Walter Peter *gastroenterologist, educator*
Harrison, Roscoe Conklin, Jr. *special projects administrator*
Holleman, Vernon Daughty *physician, internist*
†Knudsen, Kermit Bruce *physician*
†McLane, Robert Drayton, Jr. *food products company executive*
†McLeskey, Charles Hamilton *anesthesiology educator*
Montgomery, Johnny Lester *physician, radiologist*
Morrison, Gary Brent *hospital administrator*
Pickle, Jerry Richard *lawyer*
Rajab, Mohammad Hasan *biostatistician, educator*
Rostovich, Sharon Renea *airport executive*
Skelton, Byron George *federal judge*
Swartz, Jon David *psychologist, educator*
†Sweeden, Thomas Richard *hospital administrator*

Terrell
Johnson, Doris Theressa *library director*

Texarkana
Cross, Irvie Keil *religious organization executive*
Hines, Betty Taylor *women's center administrator*
Selby, Roy Clifton, Jr. *neurosurgeon*
Silvey, James L. *religious publisher*
Tucker, Bobby Glenn *minister*

The Woodlands
Anderson, Dale *film production executive*
Ashley, Lawrence Atwell, Jr. *former construction executive, management consultant*
Clark, Bernard F. *natural gas company executive*
Connell, Joseph Edward *retired insurance executive*
Covey, F. Don *energy company executive*
Levy, Robert Edward *biotechnology company executive*
Logan, Mathew Kuykendall *journalist*
Mitchell, George P. *gas and petroleum company executive*
Neumann, W. Michael *chemicals executive*
Porter, W. Arthur *research center executive*
Sharman, Richard Lee *telecommunications executive, consultant*
Smith, Philip S. *oil and gas company executive*
Topazio, Virgil William *university official*
Williams, W. Gene *architect*

Thorndale
Fish, Howard Math *aerospace industry executive*

Tomball
Barron, Sandra McWhirter *library media specialist*

Tyler
Albertson, Christopher Adam *librarian*
Bell, Henry Marsh, Jr. *banking executive*
Blair, James Walter, Jr. *machinery company executive*
†Caldwell, Hayes *zoological park administrator*
†Carmody, Edmond *bishop*
Cleveland, Mary Louise *librarian, media specialist*
Davidson, Jack Leroy *academic administrator*
†Ellis, Elmer Gene *hospital administrator*
Frankel, Donald Leon *oil service company executive*
Gajda, Patricia Ann *history educator*
Gann, Benard Wayne *air force officer*
Guin, Don Lester *insurance company executive*
Guthrie, Judith K. *federal judge*
Justice, William Wayne *federal judge*
Kronenberg, Richard Samuel *physician, educator*
Lake, Maureen Major *nurse*
Lawson, Billy Joe *educational administrator*
†Locklin, Allen Clement *petroleum exploration geologist*
Morgan, Freeman Louis, Jr. *engineer, consultant*
Odom, Oris Leon, II *finance educator, financial consultant*
Parker, Robert M. *federal judge*
Ramirez, Enrique Rene *social sciences educator*
Robinson, Lawrence Wayne *protective services official*
Rudd, Leo Slaton *psychology educator, minister*
Smith, James Edward *petroleum engineer, consultant*
Steger, William Merritt *federal judge*
Warner, John Andrew *foundry executive*

Universal City
Atchley, Curtis Leon *mechanical engineer*

Uvalde
Ramsey, Frank Allen *veterinarian, retired army officer*

Valley Mills
Evans, Clifford Jessie *manufacturing executive, land developer*

Van
Cottrell, Ralph *religious organization executive*

Van Alstyne
Daves, Don Michael *minister*

Vega
Cook, Clayton Henry *rancher*

Victoria
Fellhauer, David E. *bishop*
Stubblefield, Page Kindred *banker*

Vidor
Stokely, Joan Barbara *elementary school educator*

Waco
Achor, Louis Joseph Merlin *psychology and neuroscience educator*
Baird, Robert Malcolm *philosophy educator, researcher*
Barcus, James Edgar *English literature educator*
Belew, John Seymour *academic administrator, chemist*
Bonnell, Pamela Gay *library administrator*
Brooks, Roger Leon *university president*
Campbell, Stanley Wallace *history educator*
Chewning, Richard Carter *religious business ethics educator*
Collmer, Robert George *English language educator*
Colvin, (Otis) Herbert, Jr. *musician, educator*
Cutter, Charles Richard, III *retired classics educator*
Flanders, Henry Jackson, Jr. *religious studies educator*
Goode, Clement Tyson *English language educator*
Gould, Loyal Norman *journalism educator*
Hair, William Bates, III *librarian*
†Hall, Joe E. *trucking company executive*
Henke, Emerson Overbeck *accountant, educator*
Herring, Jack William *English language educator*
Hillis, William Daniel *university administrator*
Kagle, Joseph Louis, Jr. *artist, arts administrator*
Lamkin, Bill Dan *psychologist, educator, consultant*
Lindsey, Jonathan Asmel *development executive, educator*
†Lott, Robert Vincent *newspaper editor*
Mann, Robert Allen *banker*
Mc Call, Abner Vernon *law educator, retired university administrator*
McClendon, Charles Youmans *nonprofessional sports association executive, coach*
Meyer, Paul James *communications company executive*

Miller, Robert T. political science educator
Mitchell, William Allen air force officer, political geography educator
Moran, Doris Ann educational consultant, mathematics educator
Odell, Patrick Lowry mathematics educator
Olson, Lyndon Lowell, Jr. insurance executive
Osborne, Harold Wayne sociology educator, consultant
Pedrotti, Leno Stephano physics educator
Preddy, Raymond Randall newspaper publisher
Progar, Dorothy retired library director
Rapoport, Bernard life insurance company executive
Rose, John Thomas finance educator
Schrupp, Walter Clair air force officer
†Sibley, David McAdams state senator, lawyer, oral surgeon
Sivam, Thangavel Parama aerospace engineer
Smith, Cullen lawyer
Smith, Walter S., Jr. federal judge
Sternberg, Daniel Arie musician, conductor, educator
Thomson, Basil Henry, Jr. lawyer, corporate
Weems, John Edward writer
Wendorf, Hulen Dee law educator, author, lecturer
Wilson, John Ross retired law educator
Wood, James E., Jr. religion educator, author
Wuebker, Virginia Ann retired elementary school educator, program director

Warda
Kunze, George William retired soil scientist

Waxahachie
†Cockerham, Sidney Joe professional society administrator
Tschoepe, Thomas bishop

Webster
Rappaport, Martin Paul internist, nephrologist, educator

Weslaco
Amador, Jose Manuel plant pathologist, research center administrator
Collins, Anita Marguerite research geneticist
King, Edgar G. agricultural researcher
Lingle, Sarah Elizabeth research scientist

Wharton
Abell, Thomas Henry judge

Whitehouse
Baker, Rebecca Louise musician, music educator, consultant

Wichita Falls
Jones, William Houston stock brokerage executive, financial consultant
Rodriguez, Louis Joseph university administrator
Sarni, Vincent Anthony manufacturing company executive
Sund, Eldon Harold chemistry educator

Wimberley
Busch, Arthur Winston environmental engineer, educator, consultant
Ellis, John small business owner
Skaggs, Wayne Gerard financial services company executive

Winnsboro
Fairchild, Raymond Eugene oil company executive

Woodsboro
Rooke, Allen Driscoll, Jr. civil engineer

Yoakum
Williams, Walter Waylon lawyer, pecan grower

UTAH

Bountiful
Beckstead, Joyce Lorraine secondary education educator
Burningham, Kim Richard former state legislator
Carter, Richard Bert retired church official, retired government official
Gutzman, Philip Charles aerospace executive, logistician
Oveson, W(ilford) Val state official, accountant

Brigham City
†Anderson, Robert Wayne oil company financial officer
Call, Osborne Jay retail executive
†Germer, Richard Eliason oil company executive

Cedar City
Fenton, Patrick H. lawyer, judge
Hunter, R. Haze state legislator
Ransom, Bill author
Sherratt, Gerald Robert college president

Corinne
Ferry, Miles Yeoman state official

Garrison
Beeston, Joseph Mack metallurgist

Hill Air Force
†Thompson, Dale Willard, Jr. career officer

Layton
Barlow, Haven J. state legislator, realtor

Logan
Anderson, Jay LaMar horticulture educator, researcher, consultant
Aust, Steven Douglas biochemistry, biotechnology and toxicology educator
Bennett, James Austin retired animal science educator
Cheng, Heng-Da computer scientist
Clark, Clayton electrical engineering educator
Ellsworth, Samuel George historian, educator
Hargreaves, George Henry civil and agricultural engineer, researcher
Hillyard, Lyle William lawyer
Keller, Jack agricultural engineering educator, consultant
Milner, Clyde A., II historian
Salisbury, Frank Boyer plant physiologist, educator
Scouten, William Henry chemistry educator, academic administrator
Shaver, James Porter education educator, university dean
Sidle, Roy Carl research hydrologist
Sigler, William Franklin environmental consultant
Steed, Allan J. physical science research administrator
Vest, Hyrum Grant, Jr. horticultural sciences educator
†Wagner, Frederic Hamilton biology educator, dean, research ecologist
†Watterson, Scott wholesale fitness equipment distribution executive
Wilkinson, Richard Francis, Jr. marketing executive
Wyse, Bonita W(ensink) nutrition educator, researcher

Murray
Goates, Delbert Tolton child psychiatrist
Volberg, Herman William electronic engineer, consultant

Ogden
†Beardall, James C. lumber company executive
Browning, Roderick Hanson banker
Buckner, Elmer La Mar insurance executive
Buss, Walter Richard geology educator
†Call, Scott Joseph insurance agent, financial planner
Corry, Lawrence Lee sugar company executive
Davidson, Thomas Ferguson chemical engineer
Dilley, William Gregory aviation company executive
†Evans, Keith Edward government official, researcher
Garrison, U. Edwin military, space and defense products manufacturing company executive
Hardy, Duane Horace federal agency administrator, educator
Harris, R. Robert lawyer
Larson, Brent T. broadcasting executive
Maughan, Willard Zinn dermatologist
†Mecham, Glenn Jefferson lawyer, mayor
†Mecham, Steven Ray school system administrator
Montgomery, Robert F. state legislator, retired surgeon, cattle rancher
†Nickerson, Guy Robert lumber company executive
Smith, Robert Bruce college administrator
Stewart, Isaac Daniel, Jr. state supreme court justice
Thompson, Paul Harold university president
Trundle, W(infield) Scott publishing executive newspaper
Welch, Garth Larry chemistry educator
Wilson, James Rigg aircraft manufacturing company executive

Orderville
Zornes, Milford artist

Orem
Ashton, Alan C. computer software company executive
Bastian, Bruce Wayne software company executive
†Bearnson, Lisa Downs editor-in-chief
Green, John Alden university director study abroad program
Jacobson, Alfred Thurl petroleum executive

Park City
Ebbs, George Heberling, Jr. management consulting company executive
Fey, John Theodore retired insurance company executive
Kennicott, James W. lawyer
Mahre, Phil alpine ski racer, race car driver
Moe, Tommy (Thomas Sven Moe) skier, former Olympic athlete
Peterson, Howard George Finnemore sports executive
Wardell, Joe Russell, Jr. pharmacologist

Provo
Abbott, Charles Favour, Jr. lawyer
Alexander, Thomas Glen history educator
Allred, Ruel Acord education educator
Arrington, Leonard James history educator
Bahr, Howard Miner sociologist, educator
Bartlett, Leonard Lee communications educator, retired advertising agency executive, advertising historian
Bergin, Allen Eric clinical psychologist, educator
Blake, George Rowland soil science educator, water resources research administrator
Bramhall, Eugene Hulbert lawyer
Buck, William Fraser, II marketing executive
Chadwick, Bruce Albert sociology educator
Christiansen, John Rees sociologist, educator
Clark, Bruce Budge humanities educator
Fleming, Joseph Clifton, Jr. university dean, law educator
Forster, Merlin Henry foreign languages educator, author, researcher
Fry, Earl Howard political scientist, educator
†Gillum, Gary Paul librarian
Hafen, Bruce Clark academic administrator
Hall, Blaine Hill librarian
Hall, Howard Tracy chemist
Harlow, LeRoy Francis organization and management educator emeritus, author
Hart, Edward LeRoy poet, educator
Hollist, William Ladd political science educator
Hunt, H(arold) Keith business management educator, marketing consultant
Jensen, Clayne R. university administrator
†Jensen, Richard Dennis librarian
†Jones, Ronald Charles hospital administrator
Jonsson, Jens Johannes electrical engineering educator
Kimball, Edward Lawrence legal educator, lawyer
Kunz, Phillip Ray sociologist, educator
Lee, Rex E. university president, lawyer
Lundberg, Constance K. law educator
Lyon, James Karl German language educator
Marchant, Maurice Peterson librarian, educator
Mason, James Albert museum director, university dean
†McArthur, Eldon Durant geneticist, researcher
Merritt, LaVere Barrus engineering educator, civil engineer
Moore, Hal G. mathematician, educator
Peer, Larry Howard literature educator
Pope, Bill Jordan chemical engineering educator, business executive
Porter, Blaine Robert Milton psychology/sociology educator
Porter, Bruce Douglas educator, federal agency administrator, writer
Robinson, Donald Wilford mathematics educator
Smith, Maurice Edward lawyer, business consultant
Smith, Nathan McKay library and information sciences educator
Smoot, Leon Douglas research director, former university dean, chemical engineering educator
Snow, Karl Nelson, Jr. public management educator, university administrator, former state senator
Stahmann, Robert F. education educator
Stanford, Melvin Joseph publisher, management consultant
Strasser, William Carl, Jr. retired college president, educator
Thomas, Darwin LaMar sociology educator
Thomas, David Albert law educator
Valentine, John Lester state legislator, lawyer
Whatcott, Marsha Rasmussen elementary educator
Whitman, Dale Alan lawyer, educator
Wilson, Ramon B. agricultural economics educator, administrator
Wilson, Richard Dale executive training, consulting company
Woodbury, Lael Jay theatre educator

Richfield
Bagley, John Neff social worker, consultant

Roy
Karras, Nolan Eldon investment advisor
Peterson, Douglas Shurtleff state legislator, packaging company official

Saint George
Beesley, H(orace) Brent savings and loan executive
Belnap, Norma Lee Madsen musician
Peterson, Steven H. school system administrator

Salt Lake City
Abildskov, J. A. cardiologist, educator
Adamson, Jack communications executive
Allison, Merle Lee geologist
Alter, Edward T. state treasurer
Anderson, Aldon J. judge
Anderson, Charles Ross civil engineer
Anderson, Grant Allen librarian
Anderson, Joseph Andrew, Jr. retired apparel company executive, retail consultant
Anderson, Stephen Hale federal judge
Baker, Charles DeWitt research and development company executive
Ballard, Melvin Russell, Jr. investment executive, church official
Bates, George Edmonds bishop
Baucom, Sidney George lawyer
Bauer, A(ugust) Robert, Jr. surgeon, educator
Beall, Burtch W., Jr. architect
Bean, Scott W. state education official
Benjamin, Lorna Smith psychologist
Bennett, Janet Huff legislative staff member
Bergeson, Scott retail executive
Berkes, Howard radio news reporter
Berman, Daniel Lewis lawyer
Bhayani, Kiran Lilachand environmental engineer, programs manager
Black, Wilford Rex, Jr. state senator
Blackner, Boyd Atkins architect
Bolinder, Robert Donald former supermarket executive
Boyd, Richard Hays chemistry educator
Bozich, Anthony Thomas transportation industry consultant, retired motor freight company executive
†Bradley, Richard dancer
Brady, Rodney Howard broadcast company executive, former college president, former government official
Bragg, David Gordon physician, radiology educator
Bremer, Ronald Allan geneologist, historian
Brems, David Paul architect
Brewer, Stanley R. wholesale grocery executive
Brierley, James Alan research administrator
Brown, Carolyn Smith communications educator, consultant
Buchi, Mark Keith lawyer
Burton, Loren G. school system administrator
†Busch, Morgan David health care executive
Buttars, Gerald Anderson librarian
†Cannon, Kent insurance company executive
Carlson, Ralph Jennings communications executive
Carmichael, Nelson skier
Carnahan, Orville Darrell state legislator, retired college president
Carroll, Karen Colleen physician, infectious disease educator, medical microbiologist
†Cash, R. D. natural gas and oil executive
Cash, R(oy) Don gas and petroleum company executive
Chase, Mary Ann physician
†Chivers, Laurie Alice state educational administrator
Chong, Richard David architect
Christensen, Ray Richards lawyer
Christiansen, Joyce L. Soelberg newspaper editor
Christopher, James Walker architect, educator
†Chummers, Paul performing company executive
Clark, Carol Lois women and children's advocate, state government agency administrator, consumer advocate, consultant, science association administrator
Clark, Deanna Dee civic leader and volunteer
Clark, Glen Edward federal judge
Cook, M(elvin) Garfield chemical company executive
Crane, Steve architectural firm executive
Creer, James Read financial officer
Dahlstrom, Donald Albert chemical and metallurgical engineering educator, former equipment manufacturing company executive
Daniels, George Nelson architect
Davis, Gene state legislator
Day, Gerald W. wholesale grocery company executive
Day, Joseph Dennis librarian
Daynes, Raymond Austin immunology educator
DeCourten, Frank L. earth science educator
De Vries, Kenneth Lawrence mechanical engineer, educator
Dick, Bertram Gale, Jr. physics educator
Drew, Clifford James university administrator, special education and educational psychology educator
Durham, Christine Meaders state supreme court justice
Eakle, Arlene H. genealogist
Eccles, Spencer Fox banker
Eernisse, Errol Peter electronics company executive, scientist
Elkins, Glen Ray service company executive
†Emerson, Sharon B. biology researcher and educator
Evans, Max Jay historical society administrator
Ewers, Anne opera company director
Eyring, Henry Bennion bishop
Faust, James E. church official
Fehr, J. Will newspaper editor
Flanagan, John Theodore language professional, educator
Foltz, Rodger Lowell chemistry educator, mass spectroscopist
Frary, Richard Spencer international consulting company executive
Frei, Michael Clark lawyer
Gale, G(len) Donald broadcast company executive
Gallivan, John William publisher
Gandhi, Om Parkash electrical engineer
Garn, Edwin Jacob (Jake Garn) former senator
Ghiselin, Brewster author, English language educator emeritus
Giddings, J. Calvin chemistry educator
Giles, Gerald Lynn psychology,learning enhancement,computer educator
Good, Rebecca Mae Wertman learning and behavior disorder counselor, hospice nurse
Goodey, Ila Marie psychologist
Graham, Jan state attorney general
Grant, David Morris chemistry educator
†Green, Sidney J. mechanical engineer, engineering executive
Greene, John Thomas, Jr. federal judge
Gregory, Herold La Mar chemical company administrator
Grosser, Bernard Irving psychiatry educator
Groussman, Raymond G. diversified utility and energy company executive, lawyer
Gunnell, Dale Ray hospital administrator
Hague, Alan Donald broadcasting executive
Hague, Donald Victor museum director
Haight, David B. church official
Hall, Gordon R. retired state supreme court chief justice
Hamill, Mark Richard actor
Hammond, M(ary) Elizabeth Hale pathologist
Hanks, Gary Arlin psychology educator
Hanson, Roger Kvamme librarian
Hart, John artistic director
Hatch, George Clinton television executive
Hatch, Wilda Gene broadcast company executive
Heiner, Clyde Mont energy company executive
Hembree, James D. retired chemical company executive
Hemingway, W(illiam) David banker
Hilbert, Robert Backus county water utility administrator
Hill, George Richard chemistry educator
Hill, Stephen D. chemical engineer, federal agency administrator
Hinckley, Gordon B. church official
Hogan, Mervin Booth mechanical engineer, educator
Holbrook, Donald Benson lawyer
Holding, R. Earl oil company executive
Holtkamp, James Arnold lawyer, legal educator
Horn, Susan Dadakis statistics educator
Hornacek, Jeffrey John professional basketball player
Howe, Richard Cuddy state supreme court justice
Huntsman, Jon M. chemical company executive
Iskander, Magdy Fahmy electrical engineering educator, consultant
Jacobsen, Stephen Charles biomedical engineer, educator
Janerich, Dwight Thomas epidemiologist, researcher
Jarvis, Joseph Boyer retired university administrator
Jenkins, Bruce Sterling federal judge
Jensen, Gordon Fred university administrator
Jensen, Willard Scott warehouse executive
Johnson, Stephen Charles exercise physiology and sport science educator
Joklik, Günther Franz mining company executive
Jones, Clark David restaurant executive, accountant
Julander, Paula Foil association administrator
Keener, Robert W. retired gas company executive
Kim, Sung Wan pharmacology educator
Kinard, J. Spencer television news executive
King, R. Peter science educator, academic center director
Knight, Joseph Adams pathologist
†Kochevar, Lewis Clayton hydraulics company executive
†Koehn, Richard Karl higher education executive, evolutionary biologist
Kolff, Willem Johan internist, educator
Layden, Francis Patrick (Frank Layden) professional basketball team executive, former coach
Lease, Ronald Charles financial economics educator
Leavitt, Michael Okerlund governor, insurance executive
Lee, Glenn Richard medical administrator, educator
†Leedom, Erin dancer
Leonard, Claire Offutt pediatric geneticist educator
Leonard, Glen M. museum administrator
Longsworth, Eileen Catherine library director
Losse, John William, Jr. mining company executive
Lueders, Edward George author, poet, educator, editor
Lund, Dale A. sociology educator
Lund, Victor L. retail food company executive
Lunt, Jack lawyer
Mabey, Ralph R. lawyer
Madsen, Brigham Dwaine history educator
†Maidon, Gilles dancer
Major, Thomas D. academic program director
Malone, Karl (The Mailman) professional basketball player
Manning, Brent V. lawyer
Mason, James Ostermann public health administrator
Matsuo, Fumisuke physician, educator
Maxwell, Neal A. church official
Mayfield, David Merkley genealogy director
McCleary, Lloyd E(verald) education educator
McIntosh, Terrie Tuckett lawyer
McKay, Monroe Gunn federal judge
McKell, Cyrus M. college dean, plant physiologist, consultant
Mc Murrin, Sterling Moss philosophy educator
Meldrum, Peter Durkee venture capital/ biotechnology company executive
Melich, Doris S. public service worker
Melich, Mitchell lawyer
Metz, Lawrence Anthony lawyer
Middleton, Anthony Wayne, Jr. urologist, educator
Miller, Jan Dean metallurgy educator
Miller, Joel Steven solid state scientist

Mirow, Susan Marilyn psychiatry educator
Mock, Henry Byron lawyer, writer, consultant
Monson, David Smith accountant, former congressman
Monson, Thomas Spencer church official, publishing company executive
Morey, Charles Leonard, III theatrical director
†Morrison, David Lee librarian, educator
Mortimer, William James newspaper publisher
Moser, Royce, Jr. physician, medical educator
Nebeker, Stephen Bennion lawyer
Nelson, Roger Hugh management educator, business executive
Nelson, Russell Marion surgeon, educator
†Niederauer, George H. bishop
Nielsen, Greg Ross lawyer
Norton, Delmar Lynn candy company executive, video executive
Norton, Howard Cherrington leasing company executive
Oaks, Dallin Harris lawyer, church official
Oblad, Alexander Golden chemistry educator, research chemist
Ockey, Ronald J. lawyer
Odell, William Douglas physician, scientist, educator
O'Halloran, Thomas Alphonsus, Jr. physicist, educator
Olpin, Robert Spencer art history educator
Olsen, Donald Bert biomedical engineer, experimental surgeon, research facility director
Oman, Richard George museum curator
Osherow, Jacqueline Sue poet, English language educator
Ottley, Jerold Don choral conductor, educator
Overall, James Carney, Jr. pediatrics laboratory medicine educator
Owen, Amy library director
Oyler, James Russell, Jr. manufacturing executive
Packer, Boyd K. church official
Paramore, James Martin church executive
†Pariseau, William G. mining engineer, educator
Parker, Scott Smith hospital administrator
Parkinson, Richard A. consumer products company executive
Parry, Robert Walter chemistry educator
Partridge, William Schaubel retired physicist, research company executive
Paulsen, Vivian magazine editor
Perry, L. Tom church official, merchant
Pershing, David Walter chemical engineering educator, researcher
Peterson, Chase N. university president
Peterson, Millie M. state legislator
Phillips, Ted Ray advertising agency executive
†Poulter, Charles Dale chemist, educator, consultant
†Qi, Jiang dancer
Renzetti, Attilio David physician
Rigdon, Imogene Stewart nursing educator, dean
Roberts, Jack Earle lawyer, ski resort operator, wood products company executive, real estate developer
†Robinson, Pamela dancer
Robison, Barbara Ann retired newspaper editor
†Rogers, Jeffrey dancer
Rogers, Vern Child engineering company executive
Roth, John Roger geneticist, biology educator
Rushforth, Craig K. electrical engineering educator, researcher
†St. John, Katherine Iva artistic director, dance educator
Sam, David federal judge
Samuelson, Cecil O. health care facility executive
Sandquist, Gary Marlin engineering educator
†Schick, Seth Harvey land resource economist
Scott, Howard Winfield, Jr. temporary help services company executive
Scott, Richard G. church official
Scowcroft, John Major petroleum refinery process development executive
Seader, Junior DeVere chemical engineering educator
Shelledy, James Edwin, III editor
Sillars, Malcolm Osgood communications educator
Silverstein, Joseph Harry conductor, musician
Simmons, Harris H. banker
Simmons, Lynda Merrill Mills educational administrator
Simmons, Roy William banker
Sinclair, Sara Voris health facility administrator, nurse
Skidmore, Rex Austin social work educator
Sloan, Jerry (Gerald Eugene Sloan) professional basketball coach
Smart, Charles Rich retired surgeon
Smith, Arthur Kittredge, Jr. university official, political science educator
Smith, Eldred Gee church leader
†Smith, Jeffrey P. supermarket chain executive
Smith, Richard D. supermarkets and drug stores executive
Snell, Ned Colwell financial planner
Sohn, Hong Yong metallurgical and chemical engineering educator
Stang, Peter John organic chemist
Steensma, Robert Charles English language educator
Steiner, Richard Russell conglomerate executive
Stockham, Thomas Greenway, Jr. electrical engineering educator
Stockton, John Houston professional basketball player
Stowe, Neal P. architect
Straight, Richard Coleman photobiologist
Stringfellow, Gerald B. engineering educator
Swensen, Laird S. orthopedic surgeon
Swenson, James Reed physician, educator
Tempest, Richard Blackett state senator, general contractor
Thurman, Samuel David legal educator
Trahant, Mark Neil newspaper editor
†van Dalen, Pieter Adriaan broadcast equipment executive
†Van Mason, Raymond dancer, choreographer
Van Treese, James Bryan book publishing and investment company executive
Velick, Sidney Frederick research biochemist, educator
Wadsworth, Harold Wayne lawyer
Walker, Olene S. lieutenant governor
Ward, John Robert physician, educator
†Warner, Bart C. retail executive
Warnick, Charles Terry research biochemist
Webb, Dean LeRoy engineering executive, consultant, civil, forensic, structural and investigative engineer
Weigand, William Keith bishop
Welch, Thomas Kenyon lawyer
White, Constance Burnham state official
†White, Victor Dea airport management executive
Wilcox, Calvin Hayden mathematics educator
Wilson, Ted Lewis educator, former mayor
Winder, David Kent federal judge
Winters, Suzanne biomedical scientist, researcher
†Wirthlin, David Bitner hospital administrator
Wirthlin, Joseph B. church official
Wolf, Harold Herbert pharmacy educator
Wong, Kuang Chung anesthesiologist
Wood, F. Russell broadcast executive
†Wood, Jane dancer
Zaharia, Eric Stafford developmental disabilities program administrator
Zeamer, Richard Jere engineer, executive
Zimmerman, Michael David state supreme court chief justice

Sandy
Bennett, Carl McGhie engineering company executive, consultant, army reserve and national guard officer
Christensen, Arnold state senator, electrical contractor
Jorgensen, Leland Howard aerospace research engineer
Pierce, Ilona Lambson educational administrator
Sabey, J(ohn) Wayne academic administrator, consultant
York, Theodore Robert consulting company executive

Sandy City Chamber
Schneiter, George Malan golf professional, development company executive

South Jordan
Bangerter, Norman Howard building contractor, developer, former governor

Tremonton
Kerr, Kleon Harding former state senator, educator

Vernal
Folks, F(rancis) Neil biologist, researcher

West Jordan
Shepherd, Paul H. elementary school educator
Sudweeks, Walter Bentley chemicals company scientist

VERMONT

Arlington
Nowicki, George Lucian retired chemical company executive

Barnard
Larson, John Hyde retired utilities executive

Barre
†Milne, James secretary of state

Bennington
Adams, Pat artist, educator
Brownell, David Wheaton editor
Coleman, Elizabeth college president
Dixon, William Robert musician, composer, educator
Gagliardi, Lee Parsons federal judge
Garret, Paula Lyn publishing company executive
Glasser, William Arnold academic administrator
Glazier, Lyle writer, educator
Kaplan, Harold humanities educator, author
Killen, Carroll Gorden electronics company executive
†Miller, Steven H. museum diector
Perin, Donald Wise, Jr. former association executive
Sandy, Stephen writer, educator

Bradford
Kaplow, Leonard Samuel pathologist, educator

Brattleboro
Akins, Zane Vernon association executive
†Cohen, Lester food products executive
Cohen, Richard grocery company executive
Cummings, Charles Rogers lawyer
Gregg, Michael B. health science association administrator, epidemiologist
Hickok, James Butler artistic director
Howland, William Stapleton anesthesiologist, educator
Lappe, Frances Moore author, lecturer
MacCormack, Charles Frederick academic administrator
Oakes, James L. federal judge
Sarle, Charles Richard health facility executive
Weigand, James Gary utility company executive, former military officer

Bristol
Kompass, Edward John consulting editor

Brookfield
Gerard, James Wilson book distributor
Newton, Earle Williams editor, museum director, library and museum consultant

Burlington
Albee, George Wilson psychology educator
Albertini, Richard Joseph molecular geneticist, educator
Anderson, Richard Louis electrical engineer
†Angell, Kenneth Anthony bishop
Bartlett, Richmond Jay soil chemistry educator, researcher
Brandenburg, Richard George university dean, management educator
Carlisle, Lilian Matarose Baker (Mrs. E. Grafton Carlisle, Jr.) author, lecturer
Carroll, John Marcus Conlon banker
Chiu, Jen-Fu biochemistry educator
Cram, Reginald Maurice retired air force officer
Cutler, Stephen Joel sociologist
Daniels, Robert Vincent history educator, former state senator
Davis, John Herschel surgeon, educator
Della Santa, Laura principal
Dinse, John Merrell lawyer
†Forcier, Lawrence Kenneth research forester
Galbraith, Richard Anthony physician, hospital administrator
Grimes, Barbara Lauritzen housing and community affairs administrator
Hall, Robert William philosophy and religion educator
Hearon, Shelby writer, lecturer, educator
Heinrich, Bernd biologist, zoology educator
Hendley, Edith Di Pasquale physiology and neuroscience educator
Hoff, Philip Henderson lawyer, state senator
Lawson, Robert Bernard psychology educator
Liggett, Lee Brown lawyer
Lucey, Jerold Francis pediatrician
Martin, Allen lawyer
Martin, Rebecca Reist librarian
McLaughlin, Kevin Michael sheriff
Pacy, James Steven political science educator
Parker, Fred I. federal judge
Pinder, George Francis engineering educator, scientist
Prentice, Frederick Sheldon lawyer
Rankin, Joanna Marie astronomy educator
Riddick, Daniel Howison obstetrics and gynecology educator, priest
Sampson, Samuel Franklin sociology educator
Scrase, David Anthony German language educator
Smallwood, Franklin political science educator
Sobel, Burton Elias physician, educator
Sullivan, Mary Margaret state legislator
Swenson, Daniel Lee bishop
Weiger, John George foreign language educator
White, William North chemistry educator
Wick, Hilton Addison lawyer

Calais
Elmslie, Kenward Gray retired publishing company executive, author

Castleton
Farmer, Martha Knight academic administrator, executive

Cavendish
Shapiro, David artist, art historian

Charlotte
Hong, Richard pediatrician, educator
Kiley, Daniel Urban landscape architect, planner
McCoubrey, R. James advertising executive
Melby, Edward Carlos, Jr. veterinarian
†Smith, Robert Pease retired physiatrist

Chester
Coleman, John Royston innkeeper, author

Chittenden
Haley, John Charles financial executive

Colchester
Green, Hope Stuart public television executive
Reiss, Paul Jacob college president

Danby
Mitchell, John McKearney manufacturing company executive

Dorset
Ketchum, Richard Malcolm editor, writer

East Calais
Gahagan, James Edward, Jr. artist
Meiklejohn, Donald philosophy educator

East Dorset
Armstrong, Jane Botsford sculptor

East Thetford
†Demarest, Chris Lynn writer, illustrator

East Wallingford
Bluhm, Norman artist

Essex Junction
Crouse, Roger Leslie information analyst, quality consultant, facilitator
Pricer, Wilbur David electrical engineer
Sweetser, Gene Gillman quality assurance professional, state legislator
Sweetser, Susan W. state legislator, lawyer, advocate

Fair Haven
Larkin, John Paul, II state legislator
Pentkowski, Raymond J. superintendent

Gaysville
Dawson, Wilfred Thomas marketing executive, consultant

Greensboro
Hill, Lewis Reuben horticulturist, nursery owner, author

Hinesburg
Ross, Charles Robert lawyer, consultant

Londonderry
Bigelow, David Skinner, III management consultant

Ludlow
Davis, Vera elementary school educator

Lyndon Center
Myers, Rex Charles academic dean

Lyndonville
Williams, Peggy Ryan academic administrator

Manchester
Freed, Walter Everett petroleum company executive, state representative
Hooper, Arthur William consultant, former association executive
Kouwenhoven, Gerrit Wolphertsen museum director
Mills, Gordon Lawrence financial executive
Wilbur, James Benjamin, III philosopher, educator
Yager, Hunter advertising executive

Marlboro
Olitski, Jules artist

Middlebury
Andrews, David Henry anthropology educator
Clifford, Nicholas Rowland history educator, college administrator
Colander, David Charles economist, educator
Ferm, Robert Livingston religion educator
Gibson, Eleanor Jack (Mrs. James J. Gibson) psychology educator
Gleason, Robert Willard chemistry educator, college dean
Hitchcock, Harold Bradford retired biology educator, zoologist
Jacobs, Travis Beal historian, educator
Lamberti, Marjorie history educator
Landgren, Craig Randall biology educator
Langrock, Peter Forbes lawyer
McCardell, John Malcolm, Jr. college administrator
O'Brien, George Dennis retired university president
†Pack, Robert M. American literature educator, poet
Palmer, Michael Paul lawyer, mediator, educator
Patterson, William Bradford surgical oncologist
†Robison, Olin Clyde political science educator, former college president
Saul, George Brandon, II biology educator
Vail, Van Horn German language educator
Wilson, George Wilton economics educator
†Winkler, Paul Frank, Jr. astrophysicist, educator

Montpelier
Allen, Frederic W. state supreme court justice
Amestoy, Jeffrey Lee state attorney general
Barbieri, Christopher George association executive
Bassett, Alice Cook state legislator
Bertrand, Frederic Howard insurance company executive
Brock, James Sidney lawyer
Campbell, Sean Patrick contractor, state legislator
Dean, Howard governor
Diamond, M. Jerome lawyer, former state official
Farmer, John Martin state senator
Guild, Alden lawyer
Harding, John Hibbard insurance company executive
Hooper, Don secretary of state
Illuzzi, Vincent state senator
Klinck, Patricia Ewasco state official
Leland, Lawrence insurance executive
McGarey Madkour, Mary Elaine Bliss state legislator
†Mills, Richard state education official
Morse, James L. state supreme court justice
Parker, Scudder Holden state senator
Slayton, Thomas Kennedy editor, writer
Snelling, Barbara state official
Steele, Karen Kiarsis state legislator
Wood, Barbara Louise Champion state legislator

Morrisville
Roberts, Carolyn C. hospital administrator
Simonds, Marshall lawyer

Newbury
McGarrell, James artist, educator

Newport
Guerrette, Richard Hector priest, management consultant

North Bennington
Belitt, Ben poet, educator
Holden, James Stuart federal judge
Kimpel, Benjamin Franklin philosophy educator emeritus, writer

North Troy
Weingart, Carol Jayne university administrator, educator, psychotherapist

Northfield
Wick, William Shinn clergyman, chaplain

Norwich
†Byrne, John J. mortgage company executive
Byrne, John Joseph, Jr. insurance executive
Drake, Charles Lum geology educator
Fitzhugh, William Wyvill, Jr. printing company executive
Naumann, Robert Bruno Alexander chemist, physicist, educator
Payson, Henry Edwards forensic psychiatrist, educator
Platto, Charles lawyer
Post, Avery Denison church official
Smith, Markwick Kern, Jr. management consultant
Snapper, Ernst mathematics educator
Stetson, Eugene William, III film and television writer and producer

Pawlet
Buechner, Carl Frederick minister, author

Peacham
Engle, James Bruce ambassador
Lederer, William Julius author

Perkinsville
Harris, Christopher publisher, designer, editor

Randolph
Angell, Philip Alvin, Jr. lawyer

Rutland
Billings, Franklin Swift, Jr. federal judge
Ferraro, Betty Ann corporate administrator, state senator
Griffin, James Edwin utilities executive
Keyser, Frank Ray, Jr. lawyer, former governor
Stafford, Robert Theodore lawyer, former senator
Wright, William Bigelow financial executive

Saint Johnsbury
Crosby, George Miner state legislator
Mayo, Bernier L. secondary school principal
Trelfa, Richard Thomas paper company executive

Shaftsbury
Bubriski, Kevin Ernest photographer, educator
Williams, Robert Joseph museum director, educator

Shelburne
Mason, Benjamin Lincoln museum director
Sawabini, Wadi Issa retired dentist
Sheldon, David Frederick museum director, headmaster

South Burlington
Hackett, Luther Frederick *insurance company executive*
Johnson, Robert Eugene *physiologist*
Kebabian, Paul Blakeslee *librarian*
Kenyon, Judith *primary school educator*
†Pizzagalli, Angelo *construction company executive*
Pizzagalli, James *construction executive*
Terris, Milton *physician, educator*

South Londonderry
Coleman, Wendell Lawrence *state legislator, farmer*
Schapiro, Meyer *retired art history educator*
Spiers, Ronald Ian *diplomat*

South Royalton
Kempner, Maximilian Walter *law school dean, lawyer*
Williams, Norman *law educator, city planner*

South Strafford
Novick, Sheldon M. *author, lawyer*

South Woodstock
Crowl, John Allen *retired publishing company executive*

Springfield
Garinger, Louis Daniel *religion educator*
Putnam, Paul Adin *retired government agency official*

Stowe
Fiddler, Barbara Dillow *sales and marketing professional*

Swanton
Wooding, William Minor *medical statistics consultant*

Thetford
Hoagland, Mahlon Bush *biochemist, educator*

Thetford Center
Brown, Robert Goodell *management consultant*

Thetford Hill
Paley, Grace *author, educator*

Vergennes
Grant, Edwin Randolph *retail and manufacturing executive*

Waitsfield
Clark, Samuel Smith *urologist*
Raphael, Albert Ash, Jr. *lawyer*

Waterbury
Adams, Charles Jairus *lawyer*
Bunting, Charles I. *academic administrator*
Cohen, Bennett R. ("Ben" Cohen) *food products executive*
Greenfield, Jerry *food products executive*
†Holland, Robert, Jr. *food products executive*
Pelton, Joan Elisabeth Mason *music company executive*

West Brattleboro
Barber, Orion Metcalf, II *publishing consultant, book packager*

West Burke
Van Vliet, Claire *artist*

Weston
Kasnowski, Chester Nelson *artist, educator*
Stettler, Stephen F. *performing company executive*

White River Junction
Barton, Gail Melinda *psychiatrist, educator*
Fayerweather, John *management and international business specialist, educator*
Halperin, George Bennett *education educator, retired naval officer*
Linnell, Robert Hartley *environment, safety consultant*
Markou, Peter John *economic developer*
Rutter, Frances Tompson *publisher*

Williston
Mc Kay, Robert James, Jr. *pediatrician, educator*
†Podhajski, Blanche Rita *language foundation administrator*

Windsor
Furnas, Howard Earl *business executive, educator, retired government official*

Winooski
Wilson, Mary Louise *learning systems company executive*

Woodstock
Blackwell, David Jefferson *insurance company executive*
Browning, Robert Masters *management consultant*

VIRGINIA

Abingdon
Graham, Howard Lee, Sr. *corporate executive*
Kinser, Cynthia D. *judge*
Widener, Hiram Emory, Jr. *federal judge*
Wilson, Samuel Grayson *federal judge*

Afton
Anderson, Donald Norton, Jr. *retired electrical engineer*

Alexandria
Abbott, Preston Sargent *psychologist*
Abell, Richard Bender *lawyer, federal official*
Abernathy, Mary Gates *elementary school educator*
Ackerman, Roy Alan *research and development executive*
Adams, Ranald Trevor, Jr. *retired air force officer*
Alderson, Margaret Northrop *arts administrator, educator, artist*
Alexander, Fred Calvin, Jr. *lawyer*
Allen, Fred Cary *retired army officer*
Arensmeyer, Robert M. *pharmaceutical company executive*
Armstrong, C(harles) Torrence *lawyer*
Babcock, Jack Emerson *retired army officer, educator, corporate executive*
Bachus, Walter Otis *retired army general, former association executive*
Baird, Charles F. *think-tank executive*
Baker, Brent Harold *foundation executive*
Baroody, Michael Elias *public policy institution executive*
Berger, Patricia Wilson *retired librarian*
Berman, Alan *physicist*
Biberman, Lucien Morton *physicist*
Birely, William Cramer *investment banker*
Blake, John Francis *former government agency official, consultant*
Blumenthal, David A. *lawyer*
†Boge, Walter Edward *army civilian official*
Bolger, Robert Joseph *retired trade association executive*
Bowman, Richard Carl *defense consultant, retired air force officer*
†Braley, George Anderson *government official*
Brenner, Alfred Ephraim *physicist*
Brickhill, William Lee *international finance consultant*
Brinkema, Leonie Milhomme *federal judge*
Brittigan, Robert Lee *lawyer*
Broide, Mace Irwin *public affairs consultant*
Brown, Ann Herrell *secondary school educator*
Brown, Frank Eugene, Jr. *lawyer*
Brown, Frederic Joseph *army officer*
Brown, Quincalee *association executive*
Brownfeld, Allan Charles *columnist*
Bryan, Albert V., Jr. *federal judge*
Budde, Mitzi Marie Jarrett *librarian*
Buhain, Wilfrido Javier *medical educator*
†Burden, Thomas William *health care executive, former naval officer*
Burke, Kelly Howard *former air force officer, business executive*
Bussler, Robert Bruce *management consultant*
Byrd-Lawler, Barbara Ann *association executive*
Byrne, John Edward *writer, retired government official*
Byrnside, Oscar Jehu, Jr. *association executive*
Cacheris, James C. *federal judge*
Campbell, Francis James *retired chemist*
Casey, Michael Kirkland *business executive, lawyer*
Chamberlain, Adrian Ramond *state agency executive*
†Chamberlin, Edward Robert *career officer, educator*
Chao, Elaine L. *philanthropic organization executive*
Choromokos, James, Jr. *consultant, former government official*
Christensen, Bruce LeRoy *public broadcasting executive*
Christie, Thomas Philip *research manager*
Clarey, Donald Alexander *government affairs consultant*
†Clark, Edwin Hill, II *state official*
Clinkscales, William Abner, Jr. *government administrator*
Clower, William Dewey *association executive*
Cohen, Bernard S. *lawyer*
Collins, Frank Charles, Jr. *industrial and service quality specialist*
Condrill, Jo Ellaresa *logistics executive, speaker*
Conger, Clement Ellis *foreign service officer, curator*
Connally, Ernest Allen *retired federal agency administrator*
Connell, John Gibbs, Jr. *former government official*
Cook, Charles William *aerospace consultant, educator*
Cooper, B. Jay *public relations executive*
Cooper, Charles Donald *association executive, editor, retired career officer*
Cooper, Kenneth Banks *business executive, former army officer*
Corson, Walter Harris *sociologist*
Covone, James Michael *automotive parts manufacturer and distribution company executive*
Cowles, Roger William *government official*
Cross, Eason, Jr. *architect*
Darling, Thomas, Jr. *retired rural electrification specialist*
Dawalt, Kenneth Francis *former army officer, former aerospace company executive*
Dawson, Samuel Cooper, Jr. *retired motel company executive*
Day, Melvin Sherman *information company executive*
DeCesare, Eileen Godoy *nurse executive, consultant, nurse entrepreneur*
Devine, Donald J. *management and political consultant*
Dicks, John G., III *lawyer*
Dies, Douglas Hilton *international trade consultant*
Dietrich, Laura Jordan *international policy advisor*
Dobson, Donald Alfred *electrical engineer*
Doeppner, Thomas Walter *electrical engineer, educator, consultant*
Donnelly, John Francis *government official*
Donohue, Thomas Joseph *transportation association executive*
Dorsey, James Francis, Jr. *naval officer*
Downs, Michael Patrick *retired marine corps officer*
Duncan, Stephen Mack *lawyer*
Eckhart, Myron, Jr. *marine engineer*
Eisenberg, David Henry *drug store executive*
Ellis, Thomas Selby, III *federal judge*
Ellison, Thorleif *consulting engineer*
Emely, Charles Harry *trade association executive*
Ensslin, Robert Frank, Jr. *retired military officer*
Evans, Grose *former curator, retired educator*
Evans, H(arold) Bradley, Jr. *lawyer*
Fahey, John M., Jr. *book publishing executive*
†Ferraez, Leon R. *charitable organization administrator*
Fichenberg, Robert Gordon *newspaper editor, consultant*
Fisher, Donald Wayne *medical association executive*
Fitzgerald, Oscar P., IV *museum administrator*
Fleming, Douglas Riley *journalist, publisher, public affairs consultant*
Foisie, Philip Manning *retired journalist, media consultant*
Forman, David C. *pharmaceutical company executive*
Foster, Luther Hilton *former university president, educational consultant*
Foster, Robert Francis *communications executive*
Fozard, John William *engineer, designer, consultant, educator*
†Gardiner, Donald Kent *professional association administrator*
Garrison, Preston Jones *association consultant*
Georges, Peter John *lawyer*
†Ginn, Richard Van Ness *army officer, health care executive*
Goldstein, Jerome Charles *professional association executive, surgeon, otolaryngologist*
Gray, John Edmund *chemical engineer*
Greenstein, Ruth Louise *research institute executive, lawyer*
Hagan, Robert Leslie *retired consulting company executive*
Hagemann, Kenneth L., Sr. *federal official, career officer*
Hampton, E. Lynn *municipal finance administrator*
Hansan, Mary Anne *marketing professional*
Harris, Thomas Everett *government official, lawyer, retired*
Hartsock, Linda Sue *educational and management development executive*
Havens, Harry Stewart *former federal assistant comptroller general, government consultant*
Helman, Gerald Bernard *government official*
†Herman, Ruth Charlene *foundation administrator*
†Hewitt, Charles C. *broadcast executive*
†Hickerson, Patricia Parsons *military officer*
Hilton, Claude Meredith *federal judge*
Hilton, Robert Parker, Sr. *national security affairs consultant, retired naval officer*
Hobbs, Michael Edwin *broadcasting company executive*
Hodder, Kenneth Lasett *social services administrator*
Holland, Dianna Gwin *real estate broker*
Hoyt, F(rank) Russell *association executive*
Huffman, Delton Cleon, Jr. *pharmaceuticals executive*
Hughes, Grace-Flores *former federal agency administrator, management consulting executive*
†Huizenga, Walter Eugene *trade association executive*
Hussey, Ward MacLean *lawyer, government official*
Irions, Charles Carter *trade association executive*
Johnson, Edgar McCarthy *psychologist*
Johnson, Robert Gerald *federal agency consultant*
Johnson, William David *retired university administrator*
Jokl, Alois Louis *electrical engineer*
†Joseph, Lennox Edmond *training and consulting company executive*
Kaff, Albert Ernest *journalist, author*
Keith, Donald Raymond *retired army officer, business executive*
Kelso, John Hodgson *government official*
Kindness, Thomas Norman *former congressman, lawyer, consultant*
Kitt, Loren Wayne *musician*
Klotz, John Wesley *electronics consultant*
Kolar, Mary Jane *association executive*
Kollander, Mel *social scientist, statistician*
Kopp, Eugene Paul *lawyer*
Lajoie, Roland *army officer*
Lancaster, Bruce Morgan *investment broker, adviser, lecturer, money manager*
†Landis, George Arthur *career officer*
Lantz, Phillip Edward *corporate executive, consultant*
Laposata, Joseph Samuel *army officer*
Lasser, Howard Gilbert *chemical engineer, consultant*
Laurent, Lawrence Bell *communications executive, former journalist*
Lenz, Edward Arnold *trade association executive, lawyer*
LLubien, Joseph Herman *psychotherapist, counselor*
Locigno, Paul Robert *public affairs executive*
Loevi, Francis Joseph, Jr. *consulting company executive*
Loving, William Rush, Jr. *public relations company executive, consultant*
Lundeberg, Philip Karl *curator*
†Majors, Steven William *director art museum, artist, art consultant*
Mandil, I. Harry *nuclear engineer*
Mann, Seymour Zalmon *political science and public administration educator emeritus, union official*
Marsh, Robert Thomas *corporate executive, retired air force general*
Masterson, Kleber Sanlin, Jr. *physicist*
Mathis, William Lowrey *lawyer*
McClure, Roger John *lawyer*
McCulloch, William Leonard *association executive*
McDaniel, William Howard Taft, Jr. *computer information systems educator*
McFarlin, Robert Paul *former army officer, consultant*
Mc Lucas, John Luther *aerospace company executive*
†McMahan, Jesse Thomas *aerospace consulting firm executive*
McMillan, Charles William *consulting company executive*
Mc Mullen, Thomas Henry *retired air force officer*
McNair, Carl Herbert, Jr. *army officer, aeronautical engineer*
Megivern, Kathleen *association director, lawyer*
Merrick, Roswell Davenport *association executive*
Messing, Frederick Andrew, Jr. *action lobbyist*
Middleton, J. Howard, Jr. *lawyer*
Miller, Martin John *lawyer*
Milling, Marcus Eugene, Sr. *geologist*
Molholm, Kurt Nelson *federal agency administrator*
Moody, W. Jarvis *think-tank executive*
Mooney, John Bradford, Jr. *oceanographer, engineer, consultant*
Moore, Jonathan *diplomat, policy analyst, advisor*
Mosely, Linda Hays *surgeon*
Muir, Warren R. *chemist, toxic substances specialist*
Mulvihill, John Gary *information services administrator*
Murray, Robert J. *think-tank executive*
Murray, Russell, II *aeronautical engineer, defense analyst, consultant*
Musselman, Norman Burkey *editor*
Myers, Denys Peter, Jr. *architectural historian*
†Natelson, Nina Beth *non-profit organization administrator*
Nelsen, Betty Jo *government administrator*
Newburger, Beth Weinstein *medical telecommunications company executive*
O'Brien, Patrick Michael *library administrator*
Olson, Warren Kinley *operations research analyst, engineer, physicist*
Osborn, William C. *personnel organization executive*
Overholt, Hugh Robert *lawyer, retired army officer*
Palma, Dolores Patricia *urban planner*
†Palmquist, Lowell Eldon *health administrator*
Parsons, Henry McIlvaine *psychologist*
Pastin, Mark Joseph *executive consultant, society administrator*
Perkins, A. William *printing executive*
Porter, Elsa Allgood *writer, lecturer*
Powell, Colin Luther *army officer*
Pringle, Robert Maxwell *diplomat*
Pulling, Ronald Wilson, Sr. *aviation systems planner, civil engineer, consultant*
Puscheck, Herbert Charles *educator*
Radewagen, Fred *publisher, organization executive*
Rall, Lloyd Louis *civil engineer*
Rayman, Russell B. *physician*
Rector, John Michael *lawyer, association executive*
†Rees, Morgan Rowlands *engineering educator*
Richardson, Robert Charlwood, III *management consultant, retired air force officer*
Ritter, James William *architect, educator*
Roberts, John Benjamin, II *public policy consultant*
Rogers, John S. *union official*
Rollins, Thomas Michieli *lawyer*
Rose, Susan Porter *federal commission administrator*
Rosenkranz, Robert Bernard *military officer*
Rowden, William Henry *naval officer*
Saint, Crosbie Edgerton *retired army officer*
Salomon, Leon Edward *career officer*
Sanfelici, Arthur H(ugo) *editor, writer*
Sava, Samuel G. *educational association administrator*
Sayre, Edward Vale *chemist*
Scheupelein, Robert John *government official*
Schultz, Franklin M. *lawyer*
Scurlock, Arch Chilton *chemical engineer*
Senese, Donald Joseph *former government official*
Shannon, Thomas Alfred *association executive*
Shapiro, Maurice Mandel *astrophysicist*
Shuster, Robert G. *electronics company executive, consultant*
Smith, Carl Richard *association executive, former air force officer*
Smith, J. Brian *advertising executive, public affairs consultant, campaign management firm executive*
Smith, Jeffrey Greenwood *industry executive, retired army officer*
Smith, William Young *consultant, former air force officer*
Spar, Edward Joel *demographer*
Spiro, Robert Harry, Jr. *foundation and business executive, educator*
Stafford, Thomas Patten *retired military officer, former astronaut*
Stempler, Jack Leon *aerospace company executive*
Straub, Peter Thornton *lawyer*
Straus, Leon Stephan *physicist*
Straw, Edward M. *naval officer*
Strickland, Nellie B. *library program director*
Sturtevant, Brereton *retired lawyer, former government official*
Swinburn, Charles *lawyer*
Thomas, Billy Marshall *retired army officer*
Thomas, William Griffith *lawyer*
Thompson, LeRoy, Jr. *radio engineer, military reserve officer*
Ticer, Patricia *mayor*
Tierney, Philip *lawyer*
Toulmin, Priestley *geologist*
Vance, Bernard Wayne *lawyer, government official*
Van Cleve, Ruth Gill *retired lawyer, government official*
Vander Myde, Paul Arthur *engineering services executive*
Vuono, Carl E. *army officer*
Wagner, Louis Carson, Jr. *retired army officer*
†Wallace, Barbara Brooks *writer*
Watson, George William *lawyer, legal consultant*
Wegner, Helmuth Adalbert *lawyer, retired chemical company executive*
Weiner, Robert Michael *engineering design company executive, consulting engineer*
Weinert, Donald G(regory) *association executive, engineer*
White, Gordon Eliot *historian*
Wilding, James Anthony *airports manager*
Williams, Cathlene Ann *association executive, researcher*
Williams, Justin W. *government official*
Wilner, Morton Harrison *retired lawyer*
Wolicki, Eligius Anthony *nuclear physicist, consultant*
Woolley, Mary Elizabeth *research administrator*
†Wurzel, Mary V. *past association executive*
Yates, Jeffrey McKee *trade association executive*
Yaworsky, George Myroslaw *physicist, technical and management consultant*
Yoder, Edwin Milton, Jr. *columnist, educator, editor, writer*
Zarro, Janice Anne *lawyer*
Ziegler, Ronald Louis *association executive, former government official*

Altavista
Moore, Robert Stuart *furniture company executive*

Amelia Court House
Wallace, John Robert *county administrator*

Amonate
†Stout, Ernest Ray *molecular biology educator, research biochemist, botanist*

Annandale
Abdellah, Faye Glenn *retired public health service executive*
Ballard, Edward Brooks *landscape architect*
Binder, Richard Allen *hematologist, oncologist*
Ernst, Richard James *academic administrator*
Faraday, Bruce John *scientific research company executive, physicist*
Galioto, Frank Martin, Jr. *pediatric cardiologist, educator*
Guthrie, Edward Everett *government executive, lawyer*
Guthrie, John Reiley *retired army officer, business executive*
Jones, David Charles *international financial and management consultant*
†Kaufmanas, Petras G. *biomedical researcher, psychologist*
Khim, Jay Wook *investment company executive*
Mandeville, Robert Clark, Jr. *former naval officer, business executive*
Matuszko, Anthony Joseph *research chemist, administrator*
McCaffree, Burnham Clough, Jr. *retired naval officer*
Mc Kee, Fran *retired naval officer*
Nowak, Jan Zdzislaw *writer, consultant*
Pollard, David Edward *editor*

†Quinn, Kenneth Michael *foreign service officer, international relations educator*
Richstein, Abraham Richard *lawyer*
Rogers, Stephen Hitchcock *former ambassador*
†Scott, Hugh Patrick *physician, naval officer*
Shamburek, Roland Howard *physician*
Simonian, Simon John *surgeon, scientist, educator*
Speakes, Larry Melvin *public relations executive*
Stage, Thomas Benton *psychiatrist*
Tontz, Robert L. *government official*
Trapnell, Christine *county official*
Williams, James Arthur *retired army officer, information systems company executive*

Appomattox
Montgomery, Jon B. *museum administrator*

Arlington
Adelman, Kenneth Lee *syndicated columnist, management consultant, former government official*
Adreon, Harry Barnes *architect*
Aggrey, Orison Rudolph *former ambassador, university administrator*
Allen, Ernest Eugene *non-profit organization executive, lawyer*
†Anderson, Maynard Carlyle *national and international security executive*
Anns, Philip Harold *international trading executive, former pharmaceutical company executive*
Anthony, Robert Armstrong *lawyer, law educator*
Ashcraft, Elizabeth Eva *lawyer, educator*
Athanas, Emanuel Stylianos *journalist, educator, radio program director*
Aukland, Elva Dayton *retired biologist, educator*
Bader, Michael Haley *lawyer, broadcasting executive*
Bailly, Henri-Claude Albert *consulting services executive*
Banister, G. Huntington *federal official*
Bannan, Kathryn E. *pharmaceutical affairs executive*
Bardon, Marcel *government official*
Barnhart, Beverly Jean *physicist*
Barrera, Manuel *foreign service officer*
Bartlett, Bruce Reeves *economist*
Bartlett, Elizabeth Susan *audio-visual specialist*
Bast, James Louis *trade association executive*
Bautz, Laura Patricia *astronomer*
Beggs, James Montgomery *former government official*
Belen, Frederick Christopher *lawyer*
Bennett, John Joseph *professional services company executive*
Berg, John Richard *chemist, former federal government executive*
Berg, Sister Marie Majella *university chancellor*
†Beyer, Barbara Lynn *aviation consultant*
Bode, Barbara *foundation executive*
Bodley, Harley Ryan, Jr. *editor, writer, broadcaster*
Boek, Walter Erwin *university president, educator, anthropologist, scientist*
Bohannon, James Everett *talk show host, newscaster, reporter*
Bolster, Archie Milburn *retired foreign service officer*
Borchers, Robert Reece *physicist and administrator*
Bordogna, Joseph *engineer, educator*
Boykin, Lykes M. *lawyer, real estate company executive*
Boyle, Robert Patrick *retired government agency consultant, lawyer*
Brandt, Werner William *federal agency official*
†Brehm, William Keith *systems company executive*
Brenner, Edgar H. *lawyer*
Bridgewater, Albert Louis *science foundation administrator*
Brown, James Harvey *neuroscientist, government research administrator*
Brown, Nicholas *retired aquarium administrator*
Brown, Robert Lyle *foreign affairs consultant*
Brunson, Burlie Allen *defense contractor executive*
Bullard, Marcia Lynn *weekly magazine editor*
Burgess, David *lawyer*
Burka, Maria Karpati *chemical engineer*
Busby, Morris D. *ambassador*
Cameron, Maryellen *science association administrator, geologist, educator*
Campanella, Anton J. *telephone company executive*
Cardwell, Nancy Lee *editor, writer*
Cargo, William Ira *ambassador, retired*
Carr, Kenneth Monroe *naval officer*
Carretta, Albert Aloysius *lawyer, educator*
Casazza, John Andrew *electrical engineer, business executive*
Case, Charles Carroll *retired army officer*
†Cavanaugh, Margaret C. *chemist*
Cetron, Marvin Jerome *management executive*
Chapman, Donald D. *retired naval officer, lawyer*
Chapple, Thomas Leslie *lawyer*
Cherniavsky, John Charles *computer scientist*
Chipman, Susan Elizabeth *psychologist*
Ciment, Melvyn *mathematician*
Clayton, James Edwin *journalist*
Clayton, William E. *naval officer*
Clements, John Brian *broadcasting executive*
†Clutter, Mary Elizabeth *federal official*
Cocklin, Robert Frank *association executive*
Coe, Paul Francis *demographer, economist*
Cohen, Ronald Eli *journalist*
Cohen, Sheldon Irwin *lawyer*
Cole, Benjamin Richason *newspaper executive*
Collins, Eileen Louise *economist*
Collins, Philip Reilly *lawyer, educator*
Corell, Robert Walden *science administration educator*
Correll, John Thomas *magazine editor*
Cox, Henry *research company executive, research engineer*
Curley, John J. *diversified media company executive*
Curley, Thomas *newspaper executive*
Curtis, Richard A. *newspaper editor*
Damich, Edward John *law educator*
DeHarde, William M. *business consultant, pension plan administrator*
Dickman, Robert Laurence *physicist, researcher*
Diggs, J(esse) Frank *retired magazine editor*
Dillaway, Robert Beacham *engineering and management consultant*
Dillon, Francis Richard *air force officer, retired*
Dolan, William David, Jr. *physician*
Doman, Elvira *science administrator*
Drayton, William *lawyer, management consultant*
Edmondson, William Brockway *retired foreign service officer*
Elliott, R Lance *lawyer*
England, Robert Stowe *writer*
Ensminger, Luther Glenn *chemist*
Entzminger, John Nelson, Jr. *government research agency executive, electronic engineer*
Erb, Karl Albert *physicist, government official*
Everett, Warren Sylvester *consultant, former government official*
Ewers, John Canfield *museum administrator*
Fabian, John McCreary *non-profit company executive, former astronaut, former air force officer*
Faris, Frank Edgar *marketing executive*
†Felton, Lewis A. *career officer*
†Fenner-Crisp, Penelope *pharmacologist, research toxicologist*
Fernandez, Henry A. *healthcare administration executive, lawyer*
Fling, Jacqueline Ann *library administrator*
Flowers, Harold Lee *aerospace engineer, consultant*
†Francis, Michael S. *military officer*
Freeman, Neal Blackwell *communications corporation executive*
Freeman, Orville Lothrop *lawyer, former governor of Minnesota*
Friedheim, Jerry Warden *museum executive*
Funseth, Robert Lloyd Eric Martin *international consultant, lecturer, retired senior foreign service officer*
Gaines, Alan McCulloch *government official, educator*
†General, John Arthur *defense intelligence systems company executive*
Gergely, Tomas *astronomer*
†Gettier, Glenn Howard, Jr. *life insurance company executive*
Gianturco, Delio E. *management consultant*
Gilbert, Arthur Charles *aerospace engineer, consulting engineer*
Gillick, John Edward *lawyer*
Giordano, Andrew Anthony *retired naval officer*
Gniewek, Raymond Louis *newspaper editor*
Goodman, Steven Mark *lawyer, journalism educator*
Gormley, Dennis Michael *consulting company executive*
Gottschalk, John Simison *biologist*
Green, Judy *mathematics educator*
Gregg, David, III *investment banker*
Greinke, Everett Donald *corporate executive, international programs consultant*
Gustafson, Richard Alexander *engineering executive*
Hagn, George Hubert *electrical engineer, researcher*
Hall, Carl William *agricultural and mechanical engineer*
Haq, Bilal Ul *national science foundation program director, researcher*
†Hartwig, Eric Owen *oceanographer*
Hatch, Monroe W., Jr. *military officer, association executive*
Haynes, Caroline Hopper *preschool administrator*
Hays, James Fred *geologist, educator*
Hazard, Neil Livingstone *corporation financial executive*
Heineken, Frederick George *biochemical engineer*
Held, Joe Roger *veterinarian, epidemiologist*
Henderson, John Brown *economist*
Hendrickson, Jerome Orland *trade association executive, lawyer*
†Hengels, Charles Francis *marketing professional, educator*
Hess, LaVerne Derryl *research laboratory scientist*
Hess, Milton Siegmund *computer company executive*
Hittle, James D. *writer, business consultant*
†Hochstein, Anatoly Boris *maritime ports and waterways educator, researcher, consultant*
†Huddle, Franklin Pierce, Jr. *diplomat*
Hugler, Edward C. *lawyer, federal and state government*
Huston, Harris Hyde *legal consultant*
Jackson, William Paul, Jr. *lawyer*
Jarvis, Elbert, II (Jay Jarvis) *human resources executive*
Johns, Michael Douglas *international affairs consultant*
†Johnson, Charles Nelson, Jr. *physicist*
†Junker, Bobby Ray *research and development executive, physicist*
Jurgensen, Karen *newspaper editor*
Kaiser, Philip Mayer *diplomat*
Katona, Peter Geza *biomedical engineer, educator*
Keating, John Richard *bishop*
Kelley, Paul Xavier *retired marine corps officer*
Kem, Richard Samuel *retired army officer*
Kilduff, Bonnie Elizabeth *director of expositions*
Kingsley, Daniel Thain *public affairs executive*
Kiraly, Karch (Charles Frederick Kiraly) *professional volleyball player*
Knipling, Edward Fred *retired research entomologist, agricultural administrator*
Knowlton, William Allen *business executive, consultant*
Korman, James William *lawyer*
Kosarin, Jonathan Henry *lawyer*
Kovacic, William Evan *law educator*
Krauss, Michael Ian *law educator*
Krys, Sheldon Jack *foreign service officer*
†Kull, Joseph *government administrator*
Lambert, Richard Bowles, Jr. *science foundation program director, oceanographer*
Lane, Neal Francis *university provost, physics researcher, federal administrator*
Langworthy, Everett Walter *association executive, natural gas exploration company executive*
Larsen-Basse, Jorn *mechanical/materials engineering educator, researcher, consultant*
Law, David Holbrook *safety engineer*
Lawrence, Ray Vance *chemist*
Lederman, Leonard Lawrence *government research executive*
Leland, Marc Ernest *trust advisor, lawyer*
Lester, Barnett Benjamin *editor, foreign affairs officer*
Levinson, Lawrence Edward *lawyer, corporation executive*
Lewis, Hunter *financial advisor, publisher*
Lisanby, James Walker *retired naval officer*
Lloyd, James T. *air carrier corporation executive, corporate lawyer*
Lloyd, Kent *education policy research and public interest executive, educator*
Lockard, John Allen *naval officer*
Loftus, William Frederick *corporate financial executive, lawyer*
London, J. Phillip *information technology company executive*
Long, Madeleine J. *mathematics and science educator*
Lorell, Monte *newspaper editor*
†Lynch, John Thomas *science foundation administrator, physicist*
MacDougall, William Lowell *magazine editor*
Malley, Robert Joseph *manufacturing company executive*
Malone, William Grady *lawyer*
Marcuccio, Phyllis Rose *association executive, editor*
Marini, Elizabeth Ann *civilian military executive*
Marshall, Charles Burton *political science consultant*
Martin, Edgar Thomas *telecommunications consultant, lawyer*
Mason, Phillip Howard *aircraft company executive, retired army officer*
Mater, Gene P. *communications consultant*
Mathis, Mark Jay *lawyer*
Matthews, Sir Stuart *aviation industry executive*
†Mazzarella, David *newspaper editor*
McCorkindale, Douglas Hamilton *publishing company executive, corporate lawyer*
McDermott, Francis Owen *lawyer*
McDonald, Bernard Robert *federal agency administrator*
McGinley, Edward Stillman, II *naval officer*
†Mc Ilhenny, James Harrison *association executive*
McNamara, Tom *newspaper editor*
McWethy, John Fleetwood *journalist*
McWethy, Patricia Joan *educational association administrator*
Melickian, Gary Edward *trade association executive*
Mense, Allan Tate *research scientist, engineer*
Merritt, Jack Neil *retired army officer*
Meyer, Richard Townsend *service company executive*
Michael, Larry Perry *broadcasting company executive*
Milburn, Richard Allan *management executive*
Miller, Loye Wheat, Jr. *journalist, corporate communications specialist*
Miller, Thomas Hulbert, Jr. *former marine corps officer*
Mirrielees, James Fay, III *publishing executive*
†Mitchell, Ralph Melvin, Jr. *naval officer*
Moore, John Hampton *academic administrator*
Moraff, Howard *science foundation program director*
Morgan, Bruce Ray *international consultant*
Morris, John Woodland *businessman, former army officer*
Muris, Timothy Joseph *law educator*
Murphy, Donn Brian *theater educator*
Murray, Jeanne Morris *computer scientist, educator, consultant*
Nalen, Craig Anthony *government official*
Neikirk, William Robert *journalist*
Nejelski, Paul Arthur *judge*
Neuharth, Allen Harold *newspaper publisher*
Nida, Jane Bolster (Mrs. Dow Hughes Nida) *retired librarian*
Nielsen, Aldon Dale *retired government agency official, economist*
Noland, Royce Paul *association executive, physical therapist*
Norwood, Janet Lippe *economist*
Oleson, Ray Jerome *computer service company executive*
O'Neill, Brian *research organization administrator*
Oren, John Birdsell *retired coast guard officer*
Paynter, Harry Alvin *retired trade association executive*
Pelaez, Marc Y.E. *federal official, career naval officer*
Peterson, Paul Quayle *retired university dean, physician*
Policinski, Eugene Francis *newspaper editor*
Prichard, Peter S. *newspaper editor*
Pyatt, Everett Arno *government official*
Quigg, Donald James *lawyer*
Quinn, John Collins *publishing executive, newspaper editor*
Rabun, John Brewton, Jr. *social services agency administrator*
Rahman, Muhammad Abdur *mechanical engineer*
Reed, Paul Allen *artist*
Rees, Clifford Harcourt, Jr. (Ted Rees) *association executive, retired air force officer*
Reynik, Robert J. *materials engineer*
Rhodes, Frank Harold Trevor *federal science agency administrator, former academic administrator, geologist*
Richtol, Herbert Harold *science foundation program director*
Riegel, Kurt Wetherhold *environmental protection, occupational safety and health*
Ritter, Hal *newspaper editor*
Roberts, James Milnor, Jr. *association executive*
Robinson, Kenneth Leonard, Jr. *trade association executive*
Rockefeller, Sharon Percy *broadcast executive*
Roco, Mihail Constantin *mechanical engineer, educator*
†Roe, David Hartley *insurance company executive, retired air force officer*
Rogers, James Frederick *banker, management consultant*
Romney, Carl F. *seismologist*
Rosenker, Mark Victor *trade association executive*
Rosenthal, Robert M. *automotive sales executive*
Rossotti, Charles Ossola *computer consulting company executive*
Saafeld, Fred Erich *naval researcher, officer*
Sancetta, Constance Antonina *oceanographer*
Sandeen, Roderick Cox *newspaper editor*
Sander, Raymond John *government executive*
Sands, Frank Melville *investment manager*
Sawhill, John Crittenden *businessman, economist, university president, government official*
Scarborough, Robert Henry, Jr. *coast guard officer*
Schaefer, Thomas J. *bank executive*
Schafer, Alice Turner *mathematics educator*
Schofield, Seth Eugene *air transport company executive*
Schwab, Michael R. *air transportation company executive*
Scott, Sally Elaine *telecommunications manager*
Scotti, Michael John, Jr. *military medical officer*
Sechrist, Chalmers Franklin, Jr. *electrical engineering educator*
Seely, James Michael *consultant, retired naval officer, small business owner*
Shalikashvili, John Malchase *military career officer*
Shamus, M. Annette *nursing administrator*
Shaud, John Albert *association executive, former air force officer*
Shoemaker, Cynthia Cavenaugh Jones *academic director*
Sielicki-Korczak, Boris Zdzislaw *political educator, investigative consultant*
Simonson, David C. *retired newspaper association executive*
Simpson, John Mathes *newspaper editor*
Sinclair, Rolf Malcolm *physicist*
Smalley, Robert Manning *government official*
Smeal, Eleanor Cutri *organization executive*
Smith, Elise Fiber *international non-profit development agency administrator*
Smith, Janet Erlene *advertising executive*
Smith, Numa Lamar, Jr. *lawyer*
Smith, Stanley Roger *retired professional tennis player*
Snow, Robert Anthony *journalist*
Stahl, O(scar) Glenn *writer, lecturer, former government official*
Stokes, B. R. *transportation consultant*
Stolgitis, William Charles *professional society executive*
Stover, David Frank *lawyer*
†Strandquist, John Herbert *association executive*
Strean, Bernard M. *retired naval officer*
†Strickland, Samuel Ray *controller*
Stuart, Charles Edward *electrical engineer, oceanographer*
Sullivan, Cornelius Wayne *marine biology researcher, educator*
†Sutton, George W. *aerospace company executive*
Sutton, George Walter *research laboratory executive, mechanical engineer*
Taggart, G. Bruce *professional society administrator*
Takeuchi, Hiroshi *investment company executive, consultant*
†Talmadge, John Barnes *science foundation administrator*
Tanzer, Lester *editor*
Taylor, Lawrence Palmer *diplomat*
Teem, John McCorkle *retired association executive, consultant*
Teichert, Curt *geologist, educator*
Thomas, Jimmy Lynn *financial executive*
Thompson, Gerald Jordan *management consultant*
Thurman, Maxwell R. *retired army officer*
Tice, Raphael Dean *army officer*
Umminger, Bruce Lynn *government official, scientist, educator*
†Van, Dirk *radio newscaster, talk show host*
Van Doren, Emerson Barclay *administrative judge*
Van Landingham, Leander Shelton, Jr. *lawyer*
Verburg, Edwin Arnold *federal agency administrator*
Vesper, Carolyn F. *newspaper publishing executive*
Voigt, Robert Gary *numerical analyst*
Volgenau, Douglas *career officer*
Wagner, George Francis Adolf *naval officer*
Wakefield, Richard Alan *energy consulting firm executive*
Walker, Walter Gray, Jr. *small business owner, program statistician*
Wall, Barbara Wartelle *lawyer*
Waring, John Alfred *former research writer, lecturer, consultant*
Wayland, Russell Gibson, Jr. *geology consultant, retired government official*
Weber, Thomas Andrew *federal agency executive*
Weidemann, Celia Jean *social scientist, international business and financial development consultant*
Weiss, Susan *newspaper editor*
Wells, Christine *foundation executive*
Wendelin, Rudolph Andrew *artist*
Whitcomb, James Hall *geophysicist, foundation administrator*
Wilkniss, Peter E. *foundation administrator, researcher*
Willenson, Kim Jeremy *publisher, journalist, author*
Williams, Luther Steward *biologist, federal agency administrator*
†Williams, Richard David, III *naval officer*
Wilson, Minter Lowther, Jr. *retired officers association executive*
Wilson, Roy Kenneth *retired education association executive, consultant*
Wodarczyk, Francis John *chemist*
Yankwich, Peter Ewald *chemistry educator*
Young, Paul Ruel *computer scientist, administrator*
Zakheim, Dov Solomon *economist, government official*
Zazulia, Irwin *retail store executive*
Zehner, Lee Randall *biotechnologist, research director*
Zirkind, Ralph *physicist*
Zorthian, Barry *communications executive*
Zumwalt, Elmo Russell, Jr. *retired naval officer*

Ashburn
Boyne, Walter James *writer, former museum director*
Cooke, John Kent *professional sports management executive*

Ashland
d'Evegnee, Charles Paul *lawyer*
Henshaw, William Raleigh *middle school educator*
Inge, Milton Thomas *American literature and culture educator, author*
Payne, Ladell *college president*
Stevenson, Carol Wells *secondary education educator*

Bassett
Spilman, Robert Henkel *furniture company executive*

Basye
Putnam, George W., Jr. *army officer*

Beaumont
Jackson, Hermoine Prestine *psychologist*

Bedford
Haymes, Harmon Hayden *economist, educator*

Berryville
White, Eugene Vaden *pharmacist*

Blacksburg
Ash, Philip *psychologist*
Barden, John Allan *horticulturist*
Batra, Romesh Chander *engineering mechanics educator, researcher*
Bauer, Henry Hermann *chemistry and science educator*
Baumgartner, Frederic Joseph *history educator*
Blackwell, William Allen *electrical engineering educator*
Bliznakov, Milka Tcherneva *architect*
Brown, Gary Sandy *electrical engineering educator*
Brown, Gregory Neil *university administrator, forest physiology educator*
Bryant, Clifton Dow *sociologist, educator*
Cairns, John, Jr. *environmental science educator, researcher*
Carlisle, Ervin Frederick *university provost*
Carter, Dean *artist*
Colmano, Germille *physiology educator, biophysics researcher*
Comparin, Robert Anton *mechanical engineering educator*

Cowles, Joe Richard *biology educator*
Currie, Leonard James *architect, planner, educator*
de Wolf, David Alter *electrical engineer, educator*
Doswald, Herman Kenneth *German language educator, academic administrator*
†Dryden, Robert D. *engineering educator*
Dukore, Bernard Frank *theatre arts and humanities educator, writer*
Fabrycky, Wolter Joseph *engineering educator, author, industrial and systems engineer*
Giovanni, Nikki *poet*
Glasser, Wolfgang Gerhard *forest products and chemical engineering researcher, educator*
Good, Irving John *statistics educator, philosopher of science*
Grover, Norman LaMotte *theologian, philosopher*
Haugh, Clarence Gene *agricultural engineering educator*
Herndon, James Francis *retired political science educator*
Hibbard, Walter Rollo, Jr. *retired engineering educator*
Jensen, Walter Edward *lawyer, educator*
Jones, James Beverly *retired mechanical engineering educator, consultant*
Killough, Larry Neil *accounting educator*
Krutchkoff, Richard Gerald *statistics educator, researcher*
Landen, Robert Geran *historian, university administrator*
Lucas, J. Richard *retired mining engineering educator*
†McGrath, James Edward *chemistry educator*
Meirovitch, Leonard *engineering educator*
Mitchell, James Kenneth *civil engineer, educator*
Mo, Luke Wei *physicist, educator*
Moore, James Mendon *industrial engineering educator, consultant*
Moore, Laurence John *business educator*
Morton, John *engineering educator, researcher*
Murray, Thomas Michael *civil engineering educator, consultant*
Musser, Stanton Richard *retired air force officer*
Nichols, James Robbs *university dean*
Ogliaruso, Michael Anthony *chemist, educator*
Olin, Robert Floyd *mathematics educator and reseacher*
Peacock, Markham Lovick, Jr. *English educator*
Pitt, Joseph Charles *philosophy educator*
Price, Dennis Lee *industrial engineer, educator*
†Purswell, Beverly Jean *veterinary medicine educator, theriogenologist*
Randall, Clifford Wendell *civil engineer*
Robertson, James Irvin, Jr. *historian, educator*
Rodriguez-Camilloni, Humberto Leonardo *architect, historian, educator*
Schneck, Daniel Julio *biomedical engineer, educator*
Sgro, Joseph Anthony *psychologist, educator*
Shepard, Jon Max *sociologist*
Siau, John Finn *wood scientist, educator*
Smeal, Paul Lester *retired horticulture educator*
Smith, Robert McNeil *university dean*
Squires, Arthur Morton *chemical engineer, educator*
Steger, Charles William *university administrator*
Stewart, Kent Kallam *analytical biochemistry educator*
Stutzman, Warren Lee *electrical engineer, educator*
Torgersen, Paul Ernest *university president*
Ulloa, Justo Celso *Spanish educator*
Weaver, Pamela Ann *hospitality research professional*
Yousten, Allan Arthur *microbiologist, educator*

Boston
Fisher, John Morris *association official, educator*

Bridgewater
Geisert, Wayne Frederick *banker, retired college president*

Brightwood
Skelton, Dorothy Geneva Simmons (Mrs. John William Skelton) *art educator*

Bristol
Byington, E(dward) L(ee), Jr. *savings and loan executive*
Deppen, Douglas *bank executive*
Jones, James Parker *lawyer*

Broad Run
Hinkle, Barton Leslie *retired electronics company executive*

Broadway
Keeler, James Leonard *food products company executive*

Brookneal
†Elson, James Martin *historic foundation director, college music educator, fine arts administrator*

Burgess
Towle, Leland Hill *government official*

Burke
Ansley, Darlene H. *communications executive*
Dean, John Wilson, Jr. *business consultant, retired army officer*
Emery, Janice Joy *obstetrician-gynecologist*
Fisher, James Burke *publishing company executive*
†Jumper, John Phillip *career officer*
Kaminski, Paul Garrett *investment banker, consultant*
O'Connor, Edward Cornelius *army officer*
Pfister, Cloyd Harry *consultant, former career officer*
Pollard, Joseph Augustine *advertising and public relations consultant*
Wood, C(harles) Norman *air force officer*

Burlington
Mead, Philip Bartlett *healthcare administrator, physician*

Castleton
Hahn, James Maglorie *former librarian, farmer*

Catlett
Scheer, Julian Weisel *business executive, author*

Centreville
†Amerault, James F. *military officer*
†Kelly, John Joseph, Jr. *career officer*

Chantilly
†Gemma, William Robert *medical association administrator, educator*
Johnson, Stuart *telecommunications industry executive*
Miller, Donald Eugene *aerospace electronics executive*
O'Brien, Robert John, Jr. *public relations executive, former government official, air force officer*
†Ramsey, Forrest G. *computer company executive*
Saunders, Norman Thomas *military officer*
Slayton, Gus *association executive*
Sroka, John Walter *trade association executive*
Stone, Thomas Edward *defense consultant, retired rear admiral*
†Winn, Paul T. *electronics executive*

Charlotte Court House
Hoffman, William *author*

Charlottesville
Abbot, William Wright *history educator*
Abraham, Henry Julian *political science educator*
Abraham, Kenneth Samuel *law educator*
Ainsworth, Mary Dinsmore Salter *psychologist, educator*
Alden, Douglas William *French language educator*
Alford, Neill Herbert, Jr. *law educator*
Allinson, Gary Dean *Japanese studies educator*
Arnold, A. James *foreign language educator*
Ayers, Carlos R. *internist, medical educator*
Aylor, James Hiram *electrical engineering educator*
Barnett, Benjamin Lewis, Jr. *physician*
Barolsky, Paul *art history educator*
Battestin, Martin Carey *English educator*
Bayston, Darwin M(erle) *professional association executive*
Bednar, Michael John *architecture educator*
Beller, George Allan *medical educator*
Bergin, Thomas Francis *lawyer*
Berkeley, Edmund, Jr. *archivist, educator*
Berkeley, Francis Lewis, Jr. *retired archivist*
Berne, Robert Matthew *physiologist, educator*
Bevier, Lillian Riemer *law educator*
Bierstedt, Robert *sociologist, author*
Biltonen, Rodney Lincoln *biochemistry and pharmacology educator*
Bonnie, Richard Jeffrey *legal educator, lawyer*
Boring, John Wayne *physicist, educator*
Bosserman, Joseph Norwood *architecture educator*
†Braciale, Thomas J. *pathologist, educator*
Bradbeer, Clive *biochemistry and microbiology educator, research scientist*
Brandt, Richard Martin *education educator*
Breneman, David Worthy *dean, educator*
Brill, Arthur Sylvan *biophysics educator*
Broome, Oscar Whitfield, Jr. *accounting educator, administrator*
Brown, Rita Mae *author*
Browne, Henry James *architect*
Brydges, David Chandos *mathematician*
Bull, George Albert *retired banker*
Bunch, John Blake *photographer, writer, educator*
Bunker, Linda Kay *dean, physical education educator*
Campbell, Stephen Donald Peter *university official*
Cano-Ballesta, Juan *Spanish language educator*
Cantrell, Robert Wendell *otolaryngologist, head and neck surgeon, educator*
Carey, Robert Munson *university dean, physician*
Cargile, James Thomas *philosophy educator*
Carpenter, Richard Amon *chemist*
Casey, John Dudley *writer, English language educator*
Casteen, John Thomas, III *university administrator*
Catlin, Avery *engineering and computer science educator, writer*
Chapel, Robert Clyde *stage director*
Chase, Karen Susan *English literature educator*
Chastain, Kenneth Duane *foreign language educator*
Cherno, Melvin *humanities educator*
Chevalier, Roger Alan *astronomy educator, consultant*
Childress, James Franklin *theology and medical educator*
Chronister, Jay Lester *education educator*
Claude, Inis Lothair, Jr. *political scientist, educator*
Cohen, Edwin Samuel *lawyer, educator*
Cohen, Ralph *English language educator*
Coleman, Almand Rouse *accounting educator*
Colker, Marvin Leonard *classics educator*
Colley, John Leonard, Jr. *educator, author, management consultant*
Collins, Richard C. *urban and environmental planning educator*
†Connor, Edward Francis *biology and ecology educator*
Cooper, James Michael *education educator*
Corse, John Doggett *university official, lawyer*
Courtney, Edward *classics educator*
Craig, James William *physician, educator, university dean*
Crigler, B. Waugh *federal judge*
Dabney, Hovey Slayton *finance company executive*
Davis, Edward Wilson *business administration educator*
Davis, John Staige, IV *physician*
Deese, James Earle *psychologist, educator*
DeMong, Richard Francis *finance and investments educator*
Denommé, Robert Thomas *foreign language educator*
Derthick, Martha Ann *political science educator*
Desjardins, Claude *physiology educator*
Detmer, Don Eugene *medical educator, administrator, surgeon*
Dodson, Claudia Lane *program supervisor*
Dooley, Michael P. *law educator*
Dorning, John Joseph *nuclear engineering, engineering physics and applied mathematics educator*
Dove, Rita Frances *poet, English language educator*
Dreifuss, Fritz Emanuel *neurologist, educator*
Du Bar, Jules Ramon *geologist, retired educator*
Dunn, Mary Jarratt *public relations executive*
Edgerton, Milton Thomas, Jr. *reconstructive and hand surgeon, educator*
Edlich, Richard French *biomedical engineering educator*
Epstein, Robert Marvin *anesthesiologist, educator*
Eustis, Albert Anthony *lawyer, diversified industry corporate executive*
Evans, Robert Henry *political science educator*
Farr, Barry Miller *physician, epidemiologist*
Fechner, Robert Eugene *pathology educator*
Ferreira, M. Jamie (Mary Ann Ferreira) *philosophy of religion educator*
Fitzgerald, Joseph Michael, Jr. *lawyer*
Fletcher, John Caldwell *religious studies educator, bioethicist*
Flickinger, Charles John *anatomist, educator*
Foard, Susan Lee *editor*
Fogarty, Gerald Philip *church history educator, priest*
Forbes, John Douglas *architectural and economic historian*
Frantz, Ray William, Jr. *retired librarian*
Fredrick, Laurence William *astronomer, educator*
Freeman, R. Edward *business educator*
Frieden, Charles Leroy *university library administrator*
Friesen, Wolfgang Otto *biology educator*
Gaden, Elmer Lewis, Jr. *chemical engineering educator*
Garrett, George Palmer, Jr. *creative writing and English language educator, writer*
Garrett, Reginald Hooker *biology educator, researcher*
Gaskin, Felicia *biochemist, educator*
Gianniny, Omer Allan, Jr. *humanities educator*
Gies, David Thatcher *language educator*
Gillenwater, Jay Young *urologist, educator*
Gilruth, Robert Rowe *aerospace consultant*
Goetz, Charles John *law educator, economic consultant*
Gold, Paul Ernest *psychology educator, behavioral neuroscience educator*
Goodell, Horace Grant *environmental sciences educator*
Gottesman, Irving Isadore *psychiatric genetics educator, consultant*
Graebner, Norman Arthur *history educator*
Greene, Virginia Carvel *chemist*
Grimes, Russell Newell *chemistry educator, inorganic chemist*
Grisham, Charles Milton *biochemist, educator*
Gross, Charles Wayne *physician, educator*
Gugelot, Piet Cornelis *physics educator*
Guiton Hill, Bonnie F. *dean*
Gwaltney, Jack Merrit, Jr. *physician, educator, scientist*
Hadden, Jeffrey Keith *sociology and religion educator*
Haigh, Robert William *business administration educator*
Haimes, Yacov Yosseph *systems and civil engineering educator, consultant*
Halseth, Michael James *medical center administrator*
Hamilton, Howard Laverne *zoology educator*
Hamner, Charles Edward, Jr. *medical center executive, research management consultant*
Handy, Alice Warner *state agency administrator*
Harbert, Guy Morley, Jr. *obstetrician-gynecologist*
Hartt, Julian Norris *religion educator*
Havran, Martin Joseph *historian, educator, author*
Healey, James Stewart *library science educator*
Heath, Peter Lauchlan *philosophy educator*
Henderson, Stanley Dale *lawyer, educator*
Henry, Laurin Luther *public affairs educator*
Herakovich, Carl Thomas *civil engineering, applied mechanics educator*
Hereford, Frank Loucks, Jr. *physicist, educator*
Hetherington, Eileen Mavis *psychologist, educator*
Hetherington, John Alan Crawford *legal educator*
Hirsch, Eric Donald, Jr. *English language educator, educational reformer*
Hodous, Robert Power *lawyer*
Hoel, Lester A. *civil engineering educator*
Holden, Matthew, Jr. *political scientist, educator, arbitrator, energy consultant*
Holt, Charles Asbury *economics educator*
Hook, Edward Watson, Jr. *physician, educator*
Hopkins, P. Jeffrey *Asian studies educator, author, translator*
Horgan, Cornelius Oliver *applied mathematics and applied mechanics educator*
Hornberger, George Milton *environmental science educator*
Hostler, Sharon Lee *pediatrics educator, rehabilitation center executive*
Howard, Arthur Ellsworth Dick *law educator*
Howards, Stuart S. *physician, educator*
Hudson, John Lester *chemical engineering educator*
Huet, Marie-Hélène Jaqueline *foreign language educator*
Humphreys, Paul William *philosophy educator, consultant*
†Hunt, Donald Frederick *chemistry educator, researcher*
Hutchinson, Thomas Eugene *biomedical engineering educator*
Hymes, Dell Hathaway *anthropologist*
Ibbeken, David H. *law educator*
Inigo, Rafael Madrigal *electrical engineering educator*
Jane, John Anthony *neurosurgeon, educator*
Jeffries, John Calvin, Jr. *law educator*
Johnson, Alex Moore *lawyer, educator*
Johnson, W(alker) Reed *nuclear engineering educator*
Johnson, William Richard *economist*
Jones, Rayford Scott *surgeon, medical educator*
Jordan, Daniel Porter, Jr. *foundation administrator, history educator*
Jordan, David Crichton *ambassador, educator*
Kadner, Robert Joseph *microbiology educator*
Kassell, Neal Frederic *neurosurgeon*
Kattwinkel, John *physician, pediatrics educator*
Keats, Theodore Eliot *physician, radiology educator*
Kellermann, Kenneth Irwin *astronomer*
Kellogg, Robert Leland *English language educator*
Kelly, Thaddeus Elliott *medical geneticist*
Kerr, Anthony Robert *scientist*
Kett, Joseph Francis *historian, educator*
Kitch, Edmund Wells *lawyer, educator, private investor*
Kitchin, James D., III *obstetrician-gynecologist, educator*
Kohler, Charlotte *language professional, educator*
Kolb, Harold Hutchison, Jr. *English language educator*
Kovacs, Paul David *classicist, educator*
Kraehe, Enno Edward *history educator*
Krzysztofowicz, Roman *systems engineering and statistical science educator, consultant*
Kubovy, Michael *psychology educator*
Kuhlmann-Wilsdorf, Doris *physics and materials science educator*
Landel, Robert Davis *business administration educator, consultant*
Landess, Fred S. *lawyer*
Lane, Ann Judith *history and women's studies educator*
Lang, Cecil Yelverton *English language educator*
Langbaum, Robert Woodrow *English language educator, author*
Lanham, Betty Bailey *anthropologist, educator*
Lankford, Francis Greenfield, Jr. *education educator emeritus*
Lasiecka, Irena M. *mathematics educator*
Lee, Jen-shih *biomedical engineering educator*
Leffler, Melvyn P. *history educator*
Leng, Shao Chuan *political science educator*
Leslie, Douglas L. *law educator*
Levenson, Jacob Clavner *English language educator*
Levmore, Saul *law educator*
Lillich, Richard B. *law educator*
Lilly, Graham C. *law educator*
Loo, Beverly Jane *publishing company executive*
Low, Peter W. *legal educator*
Lyons, John David *French, Italian and comparative literature educator*
MacAvoy, Thomas Coleman *glass manufacturing executive, educator*
Mandell, Gerald Lee *physician, medicine educator*
Mansfield, Lois Edna *mathematics educator, researcher*
Marshall, Victor Fray *physician, educator*
Martin, David Alan *law educator*
Martin, Nathaniel Frizell Grafton *mathematician, educator*
Martin, Robert Bruce *chemistry educator*
Matson, Robert Edward *leadership educator, consultant*
Mattauch, Robert Joseph *electrical engineering educator*
Mayes, Bernard Duncan *broadcast journalist, educator, dramatist*
McCallum, Richard Warwick *medical researcher, clinician, educator*
McCarty, Richard Charles *psychology educator*
McClain, Paula Denice *political scientist*
Mc Culloch, Frank W. *lawyer, government official, educator, arbitrator*
†McDuffie, Marcia Jensen *pediatrics educator, researcher*
McGann, Jerome John *English language educator*
McGee, Gary Calvin *lawyer*
McGrady, Donald Lee *Spanish language educator*
Mc Kinney, George Wesley, Jr. *banking educator*
McQueeney, Thomas A. *publisher*
McVey, Eugene Steven *electrical engineering educator, consultant*
Meador, Daniel John *lawyer, educator*
Meem, James Lawrence, Jr. *nuclear scientist*
Megill, Allan D. *historian, educator*
Meiburg, Charles Owen *business administration educator*
Menaker, Shirley Ann Lasch *psychology educator, academic administrator*
Merrill, Richard Austin *lawyer*
Mesinger, John Frederick *psychologist, special education educator*
Michael, James Harry, Jr. *federal judge*
Middleditch, Leigh Benjamin, Jr. *lawyer, educator*
Midelfort, Hans Christian Erik *history educator*
Mikalson, Jon Dennis *classics educator*
Miller, Joseph Calder *history educator, historical consultant, editor*
Miller, William Lee *writer, social ethics educator*
Monahan, John T. *law educator, psychologist*
Monroe, Brooks *investment banker*
Moore, John Norton *lawyer, diplomat, educator*
Morgan, Raymond F. *plastic surgeon*
Morton, Jeffrey Bruce *aerospace engineering educator*
Mott, William Chamberlain *lawyer, retired naval officer*
Mulder, Robert Udo *nuclear engineering educator, researcher*
Muller, William Henry, Jr. *surgeon, educator*
Murray, Joseph James, Jr. *zoologist*
†Myers, Charles *medical center director, researcher*
Nelson, Raymond John *English literature educator, university dean, author*
Nesselroade, John Richard *psychology educator*
Newman, James Wilson *business executive*
Nohrnberg, James Carson *English language educator*
Nolan, Stanton Peelle *surgeon, educator*
Norgren, C. Neil *retired manufacturing company executive*
Norton, James Adolphus *higher education administrator and consultant, retired academic administrator, political science educator*
Novak, David *Judaic studies educator, rabbi*
O'Brien, David Michael *political science educator, researcher*
O'Neil, Robert Marchant *university administrator, law educator*
Orr, Gregory Simpson *English educator, poet*
Ortega, James McDonough *mathematician, educator*
Ortiz, Daniel Roy *law educator*
Owen, John Atkinson, Jr. *physician, educator*
Paige, Eugene Carroll, Jr. *mathematics educator, consultant*
Pang, Maybeline Miusze (Chan) *software and system engineer and analyst*
Parrish, David Walker, Jr. *legal publishing company executive*
Pate, Robert Hewitt, Jr. *counselor educator*
Perdue, Charles L., Jr. *anthropology educator*
Perkins, Marvin Earl *psychiatrist, educator*
Perkins, William Allan, Jr. *retired lawyer*
Perkowski, Jan Louis *language and literature educator*
Peterson, Kent Wright *physician*
Peterson, Merrill Daniel *history educator*
Phillips, Lawrence H., II *neurologist*
Platts-Mills, Thomas Alexander E. *immunologist, educator, researcher*
Priest, Hartwell Wyse *artist*
Pullen, Edwin Wesley *anatomist, university dean*
Quandt, William Bauer *political scientist*
Rader, Louis T. *corporation executive, educator*
Ramazani, Rouhollah Karegar *government and foreign affairs educator*
Ray, Benjamin Caleb *African studies and religion educator*
Reppucci, Nicholas Dickon *psychologist, educator*
Reynolds, Albert Barnett *nuclear engineer, educator*
Reynolds, Robert Edgar *academic administrator, physician*
Rhoads, Steven Eric *political science educator*
Roberts, Morton Spitz *astronomer*
Roberts, William Woodruff, Jr. *applied mathematics educator, researcher*
Robinson, Glen O. *law educator*
Root, James Benjamin *landscape architect*
Rorty, Richard McKay *philosophy educator*
Rosenblum, John William *business educator*
Rosenblum, Marvin *mathematics educator*
Ross, Walter Beghtol *music educator, composer*
Rotch, William *business administration educator*

Rowlingson, John Clyde *anesthesiologist, educator, physician*
Ruben, Leonard *retired art educator*
Rubin, David Lee *French literature educator, critic, editor, publisher*
Rutherglen, George A. *law educator*
Sabato, Larry Joseph *political science educator*
Sachedina, Abdulaziz *religious studies educator*
Sarazin, Craig Leigh *astronomer*
Scarr, Sandra Wood *psychology educator, researcher*
Scharlemann, Robert Paul *religious studies educator, clergyman*
Schuker, Stephen Alan *historian*
Schutte, Anne Jacobson *historian, educator*
Scott, Charlotte H. *business educator*
Scott, Leonard Lewy, Jr. *mathematician, educator*
Scott, Nathan Alexander, Jr. *minister, educator, literary critic*
Sedgwick, Alexander *historian, educator*
Self, James Reed *librarian*
Shackelford, George Green *historian*
Shannon, Edgar Finley, Jr. *English language educator*
Shaw, Donald Leslie *Spanish language educator*
Shenkir, William Gary *business educator*
Sherman, Roger *economics educator*
Shugart, Herman Henry *environmental sciences educator, researcher*
Sihler, William Wooding *finance educator*
Simmonds, James Gordon *mathematician, educator*
Simmons, Alan John *philosophy educator*
Simpson, R(obert) Smith *author, retired diplomat*
Sinclair, Kent *law educator*
Slaughter, Edward Ratliff, Jr. *lawyer*
Smith, Curtis Johnston *government executive*
Snavely, William Pennington *economics educator*
Sobottka, Stanley E. *physics educator*
Sokel, Walter H. *German language and literature educator*
Somlyo, Andrew Paul *physiology, biophysics and cardiology educator*
Song, Xiaotong *physicist, educator*
Sorensen, Thomas Chaikin *financial executive*
Spacks, Patricia Meyer *English educator*
Spearing, Anthony Colin *English literature educator*
Starke, Edgar Arlin, Jr. *metallurgist, educator*
Stenberg, Carl W(aldamer), III *academic program director, educator*
Stevenson, Ian *psychiatrist, educator*
Stocker, Arthur Frederick *classics educator*
Stoner, Glenn Earl *science educator*
Stroud, Robert Edward *lawyer*
Stubbs, Kendon Lee *librarian*
Summers, John David *art history educator*
Sundberg, Richard Jay *chemistry educator*
Suratt, Paul Michael *physician, researcher*
Swofford, Donald Anthony *architect*
Sykes, Gresham M'Cready *sociologist, educator, artist*
Taylor, Alton Lee *education educator*
Taylor, Peyton Troy, Jr. *gynecologic oncologist, educator*
Taylor, Samuel James *mathematics educator*
Taylor, William B. *history educator*
Teates, Charles David *radiologist, educator*
Tewksbury, Charles G. *textiles technology executive*
Theodoridis, George Constantin *biomedical engineering educator, researcher*
Thomas, Lawrence Eldon *mathematics educator*
Thompson, Anthony Richard *electrical engineer, astronomer*
Thompson, David William *business educator*
Thompson, Kenneth W(infred) *educational director, author, editor, administrator, social science educator*
Thorner, Michael Oliver *medical educator, research center administrator*
Townsend, Miles Averill *aerospace and mechanical engineering educator*
Trent, Robert Harold *business educator*
Triggiani, Roberto *mathematics educator*
†Turner, Barry Earl *radio astronomer*
Turner, Robert Foster *lawyer, educator, former government official, writer*
Underwood, Paul Benjamin *obstetrician, educator*
Vanden Bout, Paul Adrian *astronomer, physicist, educator*
Vaughan, Joseph Lee *language educator*
Villar-Palasi, Carlos *pharmacology educator*
Wadlington, Walter James *law educator*
Wagner, Robert Roderick *microbiologist, oncology educator*
Wagner, Roy *anthropology educator, researcher*
Wagoner, Jennings Lee, Jr. *history educator*
†Watson, Linda Anne *library director*
Waxman, Ronald *computer engineer*
Weary, Peyton Edwin *medical educator*
Weber, Hans Jürgen *physics educator*
†Wenger, Larry Bruce *law librarian, law educator*
Westfall, Carroll William *architectural historian*
Whitaker, John King *economics educator*
White, George Edward *law educator, lawyer*
White, Thomas Raeburn, III *law educator, consultant*
Whitehead, John Wayne *law educator, organization administrator, author*
Wilbur, Henry Miles *zoologist*
Wilhelm, Morton *surgery educator*
Wilken, Robert Louis *historian, theologian*
Wilkinson, James Harvie, III *federal judge*
Wills, Michael Ralph *medical educator*
†Wilver, Wayne R. *electronics executive*
Wolcott, John Winthrop, III *corporate executive*
Worrell, Anne Everette Rowell *newspaper publisher*
Wright, Charles Penzel, Jr. *poet*
Wright, Theodore Robert Fairbank *biologist, educator*
Wulf, William Allan *computer information scientist, educator*
Zunz, Olivier Jean *history educator*

Chesapeake
Bateman, C. Fred *school system administrator*
Forehand Stillman, Margaret P. *library director*
Gibbs, William Eugene *scientific consultant*
Jaques, James Alfred, III *communications engineer*
Jones, John Lou *arbitrator, retired railroad executive*
Newman, W. Joe *financial planner, municipal official*
Orr, Joel Nathaniel *computer graphics consultant*

Chester
Gray, Frederick Thomas, Jr. *actor, educator*

Chesterfield
Congdon, John Rhodes *transportation executive*
Copeland, Jean Parrish *school system administrator, school board executive*
Morris, James Carl *architect*

Christiansburg
Roberts, Ruby Altizer *poet, author, fiction*

Clifton
Nong *artist, sculptor*

Colonial Heights
Bryant, Howard Louis *real estate appraiser and broker, consultant, farmer*

Covington
Grove, Jeffery Lynn *minister*

Crozet
Anderson, Robert Barber *architect*

Culpeper
Covey, Charles William *marine consultant*
Davies, John Jenkyn, III *lawyer*
Landa, William Robert *foundation executive*

Dahlgren
Evans, Alan George *electrical engineer*
Holt, William Henry *physicist, researcher*

Danville
Barker, Willie G., Jr. *agriculture executive*
Conway, French Hoge *lawyer*
Dibrell, Louis Nelson, III *tobacco company executive*
Goodson, Louie Aubrey, Jr. *retired bank executive*
Kiser, Jackson L. *federal judge*
Oakes, Timothy Wayne *tobacco import-export company executive*
Owen, Claude Bernard, Jr. *tobacco company executive*
Talbott, Frank, III *lawyer*

Dayton
†Willertsen, Steven *food products executive*

Dulles
†Thompson, David Walker *astronautics company executive*

Dumfries
Heiser, Joseph Miller, Jr. *retired army officer, business executive, author*
Mc Dowell, Charles Eager *lawyer, retired military officer*

Earlysville
Caplow, Theodore *sociologist*

East Stone Gap
Combs, Jo Karen Kobeck *artist, writer*

Emory
Dawsey, James Marshall *religious studies educator, minister*

Evington
Fortune, Laura Catherine Dawson *elementary school educator*

Faber
Friede, Eleanor Kask *editor, publisher*

Fairfax
†Acord, Herbert (Kent) *oil company executive*
Aksyonov, Vassily Pavlovich *author*
Arntson, Peter Andrew *lawyer*
Baer, Robert Jacob *retired army officer*
Bailey, Helen McShane *historian*
Barth, Michael Carl *economist*
Bausch, Richard Carl *writer, educator*
Beale, Guy Otis *engineering educator, consultant*
Beckler, David Zander *government official, science administrator*
Bennett, James Thomas *economics educator*
Bennett, Verna Green *employee relations executive*
Benton, Robert *automotive executive*
Bloomquist, Dennis Howard *lawyer*
Boneau, C. Alan *psychology educator, researcher*
Boone, James Virgil *engineering executive*
Bork, Walter Albert *oil company executive*
Boutte, David Gray *oil industry executive, lawyer*
Brown, Gary Wayne *lawyer*
†Brown, Steven Edward *hospital administrator*
Buchanan, James McGill *economist, educator*
†Burklew, Donald R. *engineering company executive*
Buzzell, Robert Dow *management educator*
Cantus, H. Hollister *engineering corporation executive*
Cary, Boyd Balford, Jr. *physicist*
Church, Randolph Warner, Jr. *lawyer*
Cook, Gerald *electrical engineering educator*
Cullison, Alexander C. (Doc Cullison) *society administrator*
Denning, Peter James *computer scientist, engineer*
Dennis, Rutledge Melvin *sociology educator, researcher*
Dettinger, Garth Bryant *surgeon, physician, retired air force officer, county health officer*
Dobson, Allen *economist*
Drenz, Charles Francis *retired army officer*
Durenberger, David Ferdinand *lawyer*
DuRocher, Frances Antoinette *physician, educator*
Edwards, James Owen *engineering and construction company executive*
Eppink, Jeffrey Francis *environmental and energy specialist*
Field, Joanne T. *school board executive*
Fink, Lester Harold *engineering company executive, educator*
Folk, Thomas Robert *lawyer*
†Forché, Carolyn Louise *poet*
†Foster, Paul Wesley, Jr. *real estate broker*
†Giuntini, Philip Merritt *management consultant, software developer*
Gollobin, Leonard Paul *chemical engineer*
Gray, Clarence Cornelius, III *international agronomist*
Gray, William H., III *association executive, former congressman*
Gross, Patrick Walter *business executive, management consultant*
Groves, Hurst Kohler *lawyer, oil company executive*
Hanuschak, George Alan *statistician*
Harlan, Stephen Donald *accountant*
Hatch, Robert Winslow *food and furniture corporation executive*
Hoenmans, Paul John *oil company executive*
Hollans, Irby Noah, Jr. *association executive*
Hopson, Everett George *retired lawyer*
Jewell-Kelly, Starla Anne *educational administrator*
Johnson, George William *university president*
Jones, Carleton Shaw *information systems company executive, lawyer*
Jones, George Fleming *diplomat*
Kash, Don Eldon *political science educator*
Kauderer, Bernard Marvin *retired naval officer*
Kennedy, Leo Raymond *engineering executive*
Kieffer, Jarold Alan *policy and management consultant, writer, editor*
King, James Cecil *academician, medievalist, German educator*
Klauberg, William Joseph *technical services company executive*
Leidinger, William John *clinic administrator*
Lipset, Seymour Martin *sociologist, political scientist, educator*
†Lipton, Eric *reporter*
Martin, George Wilbur *association executive*
McPherson, John Barkley *aerospace consultant, retired military officer*
Miller, Emilie F. *state senator*
Moore, Robert Edward *electronics executive*
Morowitz, Harold Joseph *biophysicist, educator*
Mund, Richard Gordon *foundation executive*
Murray, Allen Edward *oil company executive*
Nailor, Richard Anthony, Sr. *research company executive*
Noto, Lucio A. *gas and oil industry executive*
Nuber, Philip William *air force officer*
Otis, Glenn Kay *retired army officer, research and engineering company executive*
Ozernoy, Leonid Moissey *astrophysicist*
Palmer, James Daniel *information technology educator*
Pan, Elizabeth Lim *information systems company executive*
†Pedersen, George J. *engineering company executive, computer support company executive*
Perdue, Christine H. *lawyer*
Pitchell, Robert J. *business executive*
Pixley, John Sherman, Sr. *research company executive*
Priesman, Elinor Lee Soll *family dynamics administrator, mediator, educator*
Pugh, Arthur James *retired department store executive, consultant*
Rubin, Robert Joseph *physician, health care consultant*
Sage, Andrew Patrick, Jr. *systems information and software engineering educator*
Sanderson, Douglas Jay *lawyer*
Schrock, Simon *retail executive*
Schulman, Joseph Daniel *physician, medical geneticist, reproductive biologist, educator*
Sheehan, Edward James *technical consultant, former government official*
Shrier, Stefan *mathematician, educator*
Singer, S(iegfried) Fred *geophysicist, educator*
Spillane, Robert Richard *school system administrator*
Spitzberg, Irving Joseph, Jr. *lawyer, corporate executive*
Stitt, William C. *engineering executive*
Trefil, James S. *physicist, educator*
Uffelman, Malcolm Rucj *electronics company executive, electrical engineer*
Vaughn, Karen Iversen *economics educator*
Verheyen, Egon *art historian, educator*
Walker, Betsy Ellen *computer products and services company executive*
Ward, George Truman *architect*
Warfield, John Nelson *engineering educator, consultant*
West, Bob *pharmaceutical company executive*
Willauer, Whiting Russell *systems integration company executive*
Woodruff, C(harles) Roy *professional association executive*

Fairfax Station
Abuzaakouk, Aly Ramadan *publications director*
Jackson, Vaughn Lyle *artist, consultant*
Johansen, Eivind Herbert *special education services executive, former army officer*
Ross, Jimmy Douglas *army officer*
Scanlon, Charles Francis *army officer, retired, defense consultant*
Starry, Donn Albert *former aerospace company executive, former army officer*
Taylor, Eldon Donivan *government official*

Falls Church
†Adams, Nancy R. *nurse, military officer*
Barkley, Paul Haley, Jr. *architect*
Beach, Robert Oliver, II *computer company executive*
Benson, William Edward (Barnes) *geologist*
Block, John Rusling *former secretary of agriculture*
Boucouvalas, Marcie *adult education educator*
Braendel, Douglas Arthur *healthcare executive*
Brown, Gerald Curtis *retired army officer, engineering executive*
Bruggeman, Terrance John *financial corporate executive*
Bucur, John Charles *neurological surgeon*
Burg, Ruth Cooper (Thelma Breslauer) *administrative judge*
Calkins, Gary Nathan *lawyer, retired*
Calkins, Susannah Eby *retired economist*
†Christman, Bruce Lee *lawyer*
Cleland, Sherrill *college president*
Cohn, Samuel Maurice *economic and management consultant*
Connery, Robert Howe *author, educator*
Cooper, Arthur Irving *former association executive*
de la Colina, Rafael *diplomat*
Devaney, Everett M. *health care executive*
Diamond, Robert Michael *lawyer*
Donovan, Robert John *retired journalist*
Duesenberg, Robert H. *lawyer*
Ehrlich, Bernard Herbert *lawyer, association executive*
Ehrlich, S(aul) Paul, Jr. *physician, consultant, former government official*
Elderkin, Helaine Grace *lawyer*
†Feagles, Gail Winter *lawyer*
Feldmann, Edward George *pharmaceutical chemist*
Fink, Charles Augustin *behavioral systems scientist*
Geithner, Paul Herman, Jr. *banker*
†Gibbs, Lois Marie *environmentalist*
Gray, D'Wayne *retired marine corps officer*
Green, James Wyche *sociologist, anthropologist, psychotherapist*
Harley, William Gardner *retired communications consultant*
Hart, C(harles) W(illard), Jr. *zoologist, curator*
Hazel, John Tilghman, Jr. *lawyer, real estate developer*
Heldstab, John Christian *army officer*
†Holman, John P. *lawyer*
†Honigberg, Carol Crossman *lawyer*
Jennings, Thomas Parks *lawyer*
Kaplow, Herbert Elias *journalist*
Keesling, Karen Ruth *lawyer*
Kroesen, Frederick James *army officer*
LaNoue, Alcide Moodie *medical corps officer, health care administrator*
†Laqueur, Maria *association executive*
†Lawrence, Robert Allen *lawyer*
Layman, Lawrence *naval officer*
LeBlanc, Hugh Linus *political science educator, consultant*
Ledwig, Donald Eugene *association executive*
Leighton, Frances Spatz *writer, journalist*
†Less, Anthony Albert *retired naval officer*
Livingstone, Susan Morrisey *nonprofit administrator*
Lorenzo, Michael *engineer, government official, real estate broker*
†Lyman, Robert Howard *veterans association executive*
Masterson, Kleber Sandlin *former organization executive, retired naval officer*
†McNichols, Gerald Robert *consulting company executive*
Mellor, James Robb *electronics executive*
Morris, Robert Alan *aerospace industry executive*
Morse, Marvin Henry *judge*
Mortensen, Robert Henry *landscape architect*
Nelson, Merle Chandler *real estate executive*
Nelson, Thomas William *management consultant, former government official*
Nickle, Dennis Edwin *electronics engineer, church deacon*
Oesterling, Wendy Lee *sales and marketing executive*
Orben, Robert *editor, writer*
Palmer, Stephen Eugene, Jr. *government official*
Pendleton, Elmer Dean, Jr. *retired military officer, international consultant*
Post, Howard Allen *forest industry specialist*
Reiter, Joseph Henry *judge*
Rice, Sue Ann *dean, industrial and organizational psychologist*
Rooney, Kevin Davitt *lawyer*
Rose, Wil *foundation executive*
Rosenberg, Theodore Roy *financial executive*
Schumaker, Clarence Joseph, Jr. *sociologist, educator*
Simokaitis, Frank Joseph *air force officer, lawyer*
Spector, Louis *retired federal judge, lawyer, arbitrator, consultant*
Spindel, William *chemistry educator, scientist, educational administrator*
Stone, Marvin Lawrence *journalist, government official*
Studebaker, John Milton *utilities engineer, consultant, educator*
†Tempel, Thomas Robert *army officer, periodontist*
Theismann, Joseph Robert *former professional football player, announcer*
Villarreal, Carlos Castaneda *engineering executive*
Von Drehle, Ramon Arnold *lawyer*
Waldo, (Clifford) Dwight *political science educator*
†Walters, Victor *holding company executive*
Webb, William John *public relations counsel*
Weiss, Armand Berl *economist, association management executive*
Whitehead, Kenneth Dean *author, translator, retired federal government official*
Wright, Wiley Reed, Jr. *lawyer*
Wyczalkowski, Marcin Roman *retired economist*
Young, John Hardin *lawyer*
Zalokar, Robert H. *bank executive*

Farmville
Boyer, Calvin James *librarian*
Dorrill, William Franklin *academic administrator, political scientist, educator*

Fincastle
Crow, William Cecil *consultant, former government official*

Flint Hill
Dietel, William Moore *former foundation executive*

Fort Belvoir
Diercks, Frederick Otto *government official*
Forster, William Hull *military officer*
Scott, David Bytovetzski *dental research and forensic odontology consultant*

Fort Defiance
Livick, Malcolm Harris *school administrator*

Fort Lee
Sterling, Keir Brooks *historian, educator*
†Wakefield, Samuel Norris *army officer*

Fort Myer
Blackwell, Paul Eugene *army officer*
Hart, Herbert Michael *military officer*

Franconia
Keating, Gladys Brown *state legislator*

Franklin
Cobb, G. Elliott, Jr. *lawyer*

Fredericksburg
Dennis, Donald Daly *retired librarian*
Dorman, John Frederick *genealogist*
Farmer, James *civil rights leader, former trade union official*
Jamison, John Ambler *retired circuit court judge*
Jones, Julia Pearl *elementary school educator*
Keplinger, Duane *architectural executive*
Krick, Robert Kenneth *historian, writer*
Rowe, Charles Spurgeon *newspaper publishing and broadcasting executive*
Schmutzhart, Berthold Josef *sculptor, educator, art and education consultant*
Snapp, Roy Baker *lawyer*

Free Union
Hart, Jean Hardy *information systems specialist, consultant, editor*

Front Royal
Douglas, J(ocelyn) Fielding *toxicologist, consultant*

Gate City
Quillen, Ford Carter *state legislator, lawyer*

Glen Allen
Fife, William Franklin *retired drug company executive*
†Minor, George Gilmer, Jr. *drug and hospital supply company executive*
†Minor, George Gilmer, III *drug and hospital supply company executive*
Murphey, Robert Stafford *pharmaceutical company executive*

Gloucester
Cooke, Dorothy Helena Cosby *mathematics educator, counselor*
Donaldson, Coleman duPont *aerodynamics and aerospace consulting engineer*
Fang, Joong *mathematician, philosopher, educator*
Powell, Bolling Raines, Jr. *lawyer, educator*

Gloucester Point
Perkins, Frank Overton *marine scientist, educator*

Great Falls
Anderson, William Robert *career naval officer*
Douma, Jacob Hendrick *hydraulic engineer, consultant*
Garrett, Wilbur Eugene *magazine editor*
Hughes, Alan Richard *aerospace company executive*
Jacobson, Richard Lee *lawyer, educator*
MacGowan, Charles Frederic *retired chemical company executive*
Masters, Charles Day *geologist*
†Neidich, George Arthur *lawyer*
Railton, William Scott *lawyer*
Savage, Michael Thomas *government office executive*
Schwartz, Robert Terry *professional association executive*
Sims, John Rogers, Jr. *lawyer*
Zimmermann, Warren *former foreign service officer*

Grundy
Smith, Jack *food service executive*

Halifax
Anderson, Howard Palmer *former state senator*
Greenbacker, John Everett *lawyer*

Hampden Sydney
Arieti, James Alexander *classics educator, writer*
Bagby, George Franklin, Jr. *English language educator*
Jagasich, Paul Anthony *language educator, translator*
Joyner, Weyland Thomas *physicist, educator, business consultant*
Kniffen, Donald Avery *astrophysicist, educator, researcher*
Ortner, Donald Richard *psychology and sociology educator*
Porterfield, William Wendell *chemist, educator*
†Wilson, Samuel V. *academic adminstrator*

Hampton
Allario, Frank *aerospace science research administrator*
†Bowles, Roland L. *aeronautical engineer*
Brauer, Harrol Andrew, Jr. *broadcasting executive*
Brown, Loretta Ann Port *physician, geneticist*
Clark, Leonard Vernon *aerospace engineer*
Corlett, William Albert *aerospace engineer*
†Deepak, Adarsh *meteorologist, aerospace engineer, atmospheric scientist*
Drummond, James Everman *technology transfer company executive, former army officer*
Duberg, John Edward *aeronautical engineer, educator*
†Dwoyer, Douglas Leon *engineering executive*
Farrukh, Usamah Omar *electrical engineering educator, researcher*
Goers, Melvin Armand *retired army officer*
Harvey, William Robert *university president*
Henderson, Salathiel James *minister*
Hightower, John Brantley *arts administrator*
Holloway, Paul Fayette *aerospace executive*
Houbolt, John Cornelius *physicist*
Johnston, Ralph Thomas *museum director*
Joshi, Suresh Meghashyam *research engineering executive*
†Logeman, John Donald *air force officer*
†McCormick, Michael Patrick *optics scientist, meteorologist*
†Mehrotra, Sudhir C. *engineering company executive*
Noor, Ahmed Khairy *engineering educator, researcher*
Pandey, Dhirendra Kumar *mechanical engineer, scientist*
Patty, Anna Christine *middle school educator*
Proctor, Amelia Doleman *mathematics educator*
Sobieski, Jaroslaw *aerospace engineer*
Stern, Joseph Aaron *services contracting executive*
Tenney, Darrel R. *materials science administrator*

Harrisonburg
Arthur, Thomas Hahn *theater educator, director*
Carrier, Ronald Edwin *university administrator*
Cline, Paul Charles *political science educator, state legislator*
Dansby, Harry Bishop *lawyer*
Darazsdi, James Joseph *food processing executive*
Hodges, Ronald Dexter *lawyer*
Ivory, Ming Marie *political scientist*
Lehman, James Orten *library director*
Lemish, Donald Lee *university athletics director*
Muth, George Edward *former art and drafting supply company executive*
Palmer, Forrest Charles *librarian, educator*
Price, Charles Grattan, Jr. *retired insurance agency executive*
Ramsey, Jackson Eugene *management educator*
Rollman, Steven Allan *communication educator*

Haymarket
†Doolittle, Warren T. *retired federal official*
Moseley, Mark DeWayne *retired professional football player*

Haysi
Deel, George Moses *elementary school educator*

Heathsville
McKerns, Charles Joseph *lawyer*
Winkel, Raymond Norman *avionics manufacturing executive, retired naval officer*

Herndon
Arnberg, Robert Lewis *mathematician*
Boucher, Wayne Irving *policy analyst*
Bridges, James R. *air transportation executive*
Crossfield, Albert Scott *aeronautical science consultant, pilot*
Epstein, Samuel D. *electronics executive*
†Gorog, William Francis *corporate executive*
†Guerreri, Carl Natale *electronic company executive*
Larese, Edward John *management company executive*
†Pollard, Charles W. *transportation services executive*
Pollard, Charles William *lawyer*
Scripps, Edward Wyllis *newspaper publisher*
Spragens, William Clark *public policy educator, consultant*
Vogel, Frederick John *diplomat*

Hillsboro
Farwell, Byron Edgar *writer*

Hollins College
†O'Brien, Jane Margaret *academic administrator*

Hopewell
Connelly, Karen Whipp *nursing administrator*
Leake, Preston Hildebrand *tobacco research executive*

Hot Springs
Richey, Herbert Southall, II *coal company executive*

Huddleston
Kopp, Richard Edgar *electrical engineer*

Hume
Barr, Joseph Walker *retired corporate director*

Ivy
Selden, Richard Thomas *economist, educator*
Wilcox, Harvey John *lawyer*

Keswick
Massey, Donald Wayne *microfilm consultant, small business owner*

Kilmarnock
Maxwell, W(ilbur) Richard *management consultant*
Roberts, Austin Leonard, III *banker*

King George
Hoglund, Richard Frank *research and technical executive*
Newhall, David, III *former federal government official*

Kinsale
Gould, Gordon *physicist, retired optical communications executive*

Ladysmith
Provencher, Roger Arthur *international consultant*

Lakeridge
Bales, Richard Henry Horner *conductor, composer*
Garon, Richard Joseph, Jr. *chief of staff, political worker*

Lanexa
Kirk, Maurice Blake *lawyer, educator*

Langley AFB
†Gensler, Thomas Daniel *military officer, surgeon*
Loh, John M. *career military officer*
†Martin, Gregory S. *air force officer*
†Wolfe, Thad Allison *military officer*

Lebanon
†Spindler, G. R. *mining company executive*

Leesburg
Brown, William Holmes *government official, parliamentary consultant*
Ecker, G. T. Dunlop *hospital administration executive*
Fall, Dorothy Eleanor *librarian*
Finnegan, Edward James *lawyer*
Mims, William Cleveland *state legislator, lawyer*
Mitchell, Russell Harry *dermatologist*

Lexington
Beveridge, Albert Jeremiah, III *lawyer*
Brown, Barbara Jeanne *librarian*
Cash, Frank Errette, Jr. *foreign service officer*
DeVogt, John Frederick *management science and business ethics educator, consultant*
Elmes, David Gordon *psychologist, educator*
Elrod, John William *philosophy and religion educator, academic administrator*
Gaines, James Edwin, Jr. *retired librarian*
Gordon, Albert Claude *performing arts educator, actor*
Herrick, Bruce Hale *economics educator*
Hickman, Cleveland Pendleton, Jr. *biology educator*
Hodges, Louis Wendell *religion educator*
James, D(orris) Clayton *history educator*
Jarrard, Leonard Everett *psychologist, educator*
John, Lewis George *political science educator*
Kirgis, Frederic Lee, Jr. *legal educator*
Knapp, John Williams *college president*
Leach, Maurice Derby, Jr. *librarian*
Martin, Joseph Ramsey *philosophy educator*
McAhren, Robert Willard *history educator*
Pemberton, Harrison Joseph *educator, philosopher*
Phillips, Charles Franklin, Jr. *economist, educator*
Ray, George Washington, III *English language educator*
Read, Beverly Money *military officer*
Ryan, Halford Ross *speech educator*
Seeger, Michael *musician, singer, folklorist*
Sessions, William Lad *philosophy educator, administrator*
Simpson, Pamela Hemenway *art historian, educator*
Spencer, Edgar Winston *geology educator*
Stuart, Walker Dabney, III *poet, author, English language educator*
Sullivan, Barry *lawyer, educator*
Sundby, Scott Edwin *law educator*
Trandel, Richard Samuel *mechanical engineer, educator*
Tyree, Lewis, Jr. *retired compressed gas company executive, inventor, technical consultant*
Warner, Harry Hathaway *financial consultant*
Watt, William Joseph *academic administrator, chemistry educator*
White, Owen Kendall, Jr. *sociologist, educator*
Wiant, Sarah Kirsten *law library director, educator*
†Wilson, John D. *retired university president*
Winfrey, John Crawford *economist, educator*

Lightfoot
Morris, Robert Louis *management consultant*

Lincoln
LeSourd, Leonard Earle *publisher, editor*

Lively
Gallimore, Robert Stephenson *news service executive*

Locust Grove
Baratz, Morton Sachs *economic consultant, writer*
Featherston, Dale Marie *nursing administrator*

Lorton
Francis, Richard Haudiomont *government administrator*
Hazard, John Wharton *author, editorial consultant*

Louisa
Lanyon, Wesley Edwin *retired museum curator, ornithologist*

Lynchburg
Britton, Donald W. *insurance company executive*
Burnette, Ralph Edwin, Jr. *lawyer*
Butler, John Alden *insurance company executive*
Crow, Harold Eugene *physician, family medicine educator*
†Dodge, Lynn Louise *municipal official, librarian*
Dolan, Ronald Vincent *insurance company executive*
Duff, Ernest Arthur *political scientist, educator*
Fath, George R. *electrical engineer, communications executive*
Frazier, Robert James *small business owner*
Gilbert, Larry Alan *religious institute administrator*
Harris, Dale Hutter *judge, lecturer*
Hinnant, Hilari Anne *educator, educational consultant*
Hudson, Walter Tiree *artist*
Latimer, Paul Jerry *non-destructive testing engineer*
McRorie, William Edward *life insurance company executive*
Morgan, Evan *chemist*
Morland, John Kenneth *sociology and anthropology educator*
†Pryor, Charles Wingfield, Jr. *nuclear technology company executive*
Quillian, William Fletcher, Jr. *retired banker, former college president*
Snead, George Murrell, Jr. *army officer, scientist, consultant*
Stephens, Bart Nelson *former foreign service officer*
Stewart, George Taylor *insurance executive*
Whitman, Nancy Irene *nursing educator*

Madison
Ince, Eugene St. Clair, Jr. *cryptologist, retired naval officer*

Madison Heights
Falwell, Jerry L. *clergyman*

Manakin Sabot
Robertson, Linwood Righter *electric utility executive*

Manassas
†Foote, John Holland *lawyer*
Geerdes, James (Divine Geerdes) *chemical company executive*
Holmes, Marjorie Rose *author*
Parrish, Frank Jennings *food company executive*
Smith, Vme (Verna Mae Edom Smith) *sociology educator, freelance writer, photographer*
Tidman, Derek Albert *physics researcher*

Manassas Park
Bussard, Robert William *physicist*

Marion
Groseclose, Joanne Stowers *special education educator*
Hadley, Stanton Thomas *international manufacturing and marketing company executive, lawyer*
Peal, James Albert *psychiatrist*

Markham
Katzen, Jay Kenneth *consultant, former foreign service officer*

Marshall
Hayward, Charles Winthrop *retired railroad company executive*
Seder, Arthur Raymond, Jr. *lawyer*

Martinsville
Adams, James E. *bank executive*
McCraw, John Randolph, Jr. *assistant principal*

Maurertown
Macleod, John Amend *lawyer*

Mc Kenney
Doyle, John Robert, Jr. *writer*

Mc Lean
Adler, Larry *marketing executive*
Anderson, David Lloyd *defense industry executive*
Appler, Thomas L. *lawyer*
Bartow, Randy David *publishing executive*
Bass, Roger William *architect*
Berteau, David John *company executive*
Betsold, Robert John *federal agency administrator*
Bisbee, Gerald Elftman, Jr. *investment company executive*
Bolan, Robert S. *association executive*
Brendsel, Leland C. *federal mortgage company executive*
Brown, Billy Ross *agriculture association executive*
Brown, Thomas C., Jr. *lawyer*
Buck, Alfred Andreas *physician, epidemiologist*
†Burk, Brett J. *association executive, company executive*
Byrne, Gary Cecil *banker*
Byrnes, Arthur Francis *retired federal official*
Cabaniss, Thomas Edward *lawyer*
Cahill, Harry Amory *diplomat, educator*
Callahan, Vincent Francis, Jr. *publisher, state legislator*
Cannon, Mark Wilcox *government official, business executive*
Capone, Lucien, Jr. *management consultant, former naval officer*
†Carlucci, Frank C. *engineering company executive*
Carnicero, Jorge Emilio *aeronautical engineer, business executive*
Carter, William Walton *physicist*
Ceremsak, Karen Marie *communications executive, public relations and marketing communications executive*
Chatelain, Leon, III *architectural firm executive*
Collins, James Foster *government official*
Cooper, John Allen Dicks *medical educator*
Corson, J. Jay, IV *lawyer*
Cotterill, Carl Hayden *mineral and metals company executive*
Cowhill, William Joseph *retired naval officer, consultant*
Davis, Bennie Luke *air force officer*
Davis, William Columbus *history educator, writer, lecturer*
Deal, George Edgar *management and industrial executive*
Dean, Lydia Margaret Carter (Mrs. Halsey Albert Dean) *nutrition coordinator, author, consultant*
Deardourff, John D. *political consultant*
De Carbonnel, François Eric *management consultant*
Dempsey, James Raymon *industrial executive*
Doyle, Frederick Joseph *government research scientist*
Drummond, Carol Cramer *voice educator, singer, artist, writer*
Duncan, Robert Clifton *retired government official*
Eastman, Albert Theodore *bishop*
Enger, Walter Melvin *consulting engineer, former navy officer*
Estren, Mark James *management and media consultant, TV producer*
Finberg, Donald Richard *foundation administrator*
Foryst, Carole *mortgage broker*
Franklin, Jude Eric *electronics executive*
Friel, Thomas Patrick *association executive*
Fromm, Joseph *retired magazine editor, foreign affairs consultant*
Gammon, James Alan *lawyer*
Gardenier, John Stark, II *statistician, management scientist*
Gardenier, Turkan Kumbaraci *statistical company executive, researcher*
Gary, Charles Lester *professional association consultant, educator*
Gavazzi, Aladino A. *retired medical center administrator*
Gerson, Elliot Francis *health care and financial services executive*
Glenn, David Wright *mortgage company executive*
Gouse, S. William, Jr. *engineering executive, scientist*
Graybeal, Sidney Norman *national security executive, former government official*
Griffith, Elisabeth *headmistress*
Groennings, Sven Ole *academic administrator, higher education educator, corporate executive*
Haddock, Raymond Earl *career officer*
Halaby, Najeeb E. *financier, lawyer*
Hashim, Elinor Marie *librarian*
Healy, Theresa Ann *former ambassador*
Herge, J. Curtis *lawyer*
Hoffman, Ronald Bruce *biophysicist, life scientist, human factors consultant*
†Hollister, Cullen Agur *engineer*
Hopkins, Thomas Matthews *former naval officer*
Houley, William Purcell *federal official, career officer*
†Hwang, John Dzen *federal agency administrator*
Hyde, John Paul *retired air force officer*
James, Daniel J. *management consultant*
Jennings, Jerry D. *communications company executive*
Johnson, Frank Stanley, Jr. *communications executive, retired government official*
†Kargula, Michael R. *corporate lawyer*
Kay, Thomas Oliver *agricultural consultant*
Kennedy, Cornelius Bryant *lawyer*
Kim, Hack Hyun *telecommunications executive*
Kim, John Chan Kyu *electrical engineer*
Kimberly, William Essick *investment banker*
Kimmel, H. Steven *engineering executive*
Kiviat, Philip Jay *computer services company executive*
Klinedinst, Duncan Stewart *lawyer*
Kolombatovic, Vadja Vadim *management consulting company executive*
Laning, Robert Comegys *retired physician, former naval officer*
Layson, William McIntyre *research consulting company executive*
Leto, James J. *artificial intelligence executive*
Ling, Suilin *management consultant*
Lotz, Denton *minister, church official*
Luttig, J. Michael *federal judge*
Mahan, Clarence *retired government official, writer*
Marino, Michael Frank *lawyer*
Mars, Forrest E., Jr. *candy company executive*
Mars, John F. *candy company executive*
McCambridge, John James *civil engineer*
Mc Fate, Patricia Ann *scientist, education, foundation executive*
Mc Hugh, John Laurence *marine biologist, educator*
McInerney, James Eugene, Jr. *association executive*
Mehuron, William Otto *electronics company executive*
Mohleji, Satish Chandra *electrical engineer*
Moore, Daniel L. *architect*
Moorstein, Mark Alan *lawyer*
Murphy, Thomas Patrick *lawyer*
Nassikas, John Nicholas *lawyer*
Neel, Samuel Ellison *lawyer*
Ney, Robert Terrence *lawyer*
†Odeen, Philip A. *engineering company executive*
Parker, Scott Lane *management consultant*
Paschall, Lee McQuerter *retired communications consultant*
Perry, Charles S. *lawyer*
Prichard, Edgar Allen *lawyer*

Priem, Richard Gregory writer, systems analyst, entertainment company executive
Ramsey, Lloyd Brinkley retired savings and loan executive, retired army officer
Rau, Lee Arthur lawyer
Reswick, James Bigelow former government official, rehabilitation engineer, educator
Rhyne, Charles Sylvanus lawyer
Ring, James Edward Patrick mortgage banking consulting executive
Rogers, Alan Victor former career officer
Rogers, Thomas Francis foundation administrator
Ryan, John Franklin multinational company executive
St. Germain, Fernand Joseph congressman
†Schar, Dwight C. construction company executive
Schneck, Paul Bennett computer scientist
Schweiker, Richard Schultz trade association executive, former senator, former cabinet secretary
Searles, Dewitt Richard retired investment firm executive, retired air force officer
Shanklin, Richard Vair, III mechanical engineer
†Shenoy, Sudhakar Venkatraya computer software company executive
Silveira, Milton Anthony aerospace engineering executive
Sitkoff, Theodore public management executive
Smith, Russell Jack former intelligence official
Smith, Thomas Eugene investment company executive, financial consultant
Snyder, Franklin Farison hydrologic engineering consultant
Sollenberger, Howard Edwin retired government official
Sonnemann, Harry electrical engineer, consultant
Sowle, Donald Edgar management consultant
Stitt, David Tillman lawyer
Struelens, Michel Maurice Joseph Georges political science educator, foreign affairs consultant
Stump, John Sutton lawyer
Svahn, John Alfred government official
Talbot, Lee Merriam ecologist, environmental specialist, consultant
Tansill, Frederick Joseph lawyer
Thomas, Lydia Waters research and development executive
Topping, Peter historian, educator
Traver, Courtland Lee lawyer
Trotter, Haynie Seay lawyer
Trout, Maurice Elmore foreign service officer
Turner, Stansfield former government official, lecturer, writer, teacher
Tuttle, William G(ilbert) T(ownsend), Jr. research executive
Urquhart, Glen Taylor investment and development executive
Vandemark, Robert Goodyear retired retail company executive
†Warga, John construction company executive
Watson, Jerry Carroll advertising executive
Waylan, Cecil Jerome telecommunications executive
†Whipple, David Doty association executive
Wümpelmann, Knud Aage Abildgaard clergyman, religious organization administrator
Yager, Joseph Arthur, Jr. economist

McLean
Daub, Cindy S. federal agency administrator
Hoffmann, Martin Richard lawyer

Mechanicsville
Balser, Glennon church administrator
†Bennett, Donald Dalton grocery stores executive
Long, Patricia Gavigan elementary education educator, English language educator

Melfa
Harmon, Patricia Marie special education educator

Merrifield
Pascoe, Charles Thomas, Jr. computer systems company executive
Scott, James Martin state legislator, healthcare system executive

Middleburg
Beddall, Thomas Henry lawyer
Collins, James Lawton, Jr. retired army officer
Cooke, Jack Kent diversified company executive
Evans, John Derby telecommunications company executive
McGhee, George Crews petroleum producer, former government official
Spilhaus, Athelstan meteorologist, oceanographer
Spillane, Mickey (Frank Morrison Spillane) author

Midlothian
Jones, John Evan medical educator
Parsons, Robert Eugene transportation consultant
Rodgers, Eugene writer
Stringham, Luther Winters economist, administrator

Mineral
Donald, James Robert federal agency official, economist, outdoors writer
Speer, Jack Atkeson publisher

Moneta
Armistead, Moss William, III retired newspaper executive
Pfeuffer, Robert John musician
Singleton, Samuel Winston physician, pharmaceutical company executive
Ulmer, Walter Francis, Jr. consultant, former army officer

Montpelier Station
Southern, Hugh performing arts consultant

Montross
Fountain, Robert Roy, Jr. farmer, retired industrial executive, naval officer

Morattico
Dawson, Carol Gene former commissioner, writer, consultant

Mount Jackson
Sylvester, George Howard retired air force officer

Mount Vernon
†Rees, James Conway, IV historic site administrator

Nellysford
French, Charles Ezra economist, educational and agricultural consultant

New Market
Le Roy, L. David journalist

Newington
Foster, Eugene Lewis engineering executive
†Gageby, Stephen L. design corporation executive
Miggins, Michael Denis retired career officer, arms control analyst

Newport News
Banks, Charles A. manufacturing executive
Barnes, Myrtle Sue Snyder editor
Bateman, Fred Willom retired judge
Becker, Ivan Endre retired plastics company executive
Bernhardt, John Bowman banker
Camp, Hazel Lee Burt artist
Cantrell, Joseph Doyle newspaper company executive
Cardman, Lawrence S. physics educator
Coleman, James Eugene national laboratory administrator
Cox, Alvin Earl shipbuilding executive
Cuthrell, Carl Edward lawyer, educator, clergyman
Davis, Jack Wayne, Jr. newspaper publisher
Drummond, Neil Hiden retired secondary school educator, airman
Fisher, Timothy Scott lawyer
Fricks, William Peavy shipbuilding company executive
Giles, Glenn Ernest, Jr. nuclear engineer
Hamilton, Phillip Andrew instructional services coordinator, legislator
Harner, David Paul university administrator
Hubbard, Harvey Hart aeroacoustician, noise control engineer, consultant
Isgur, Nathan Gerald physicist, educator
Kale, Wallace Wilford, Jr. journalist, communicator, administrator
Luke, James Phillip manufacturing executive
Mazur, Rhoda Himmel federation president
Morris, James Matthew history educator
†Noland, Lloyd U., III wholesale utility supplies company executive
Peebles, David L. light manufacturing executive
Perry, Donald A. cable television consultant
Phillips, William Ray, Jr. shipbuilding executive
Polk-Matthews, Josephine Elsey school psychologist
Santoro, Anthony Richard academic administrator
Smith, Carol G. health facility administrator
Smith, Walter Tilford shipbuilding company executive
Stepnick, Arlene Alice nursing education administrator
Thomas, Dorothy Worthy English educator
†Trible, Paul Seward, Jr. former senator
Young, Maurice Isaac mechanical and aerospace engineering educator

Norfolk
Adams, David Huntington judge
Ahrari, M. Ehsan political science educator, researcher, consultant
†Alden, Raymond William, III marine biologist, laboratory director
Alessi, Keith Ernest retail executive
Allen, Russell Plowman opera company executive
Anderson, Darleen S. nursing administrator
Andrews, Mason Cooke mayor, obstetrician, gynecologist, educator
Andrews, William Cooke physician
Baird, Edward Rouzie, Jr. lawyer
Barnes, Herman Verdain internist, educator
Barry, Richard Francis, III publishing executive
Batten, Frank newspaper publisher, cable broadcaster
Bazin, Nancy Topping English language educator
†Bernd, David LeMoine multi-hospital system executive
Bernsen, Harold John political affairs consultant, retired naval officer
Blount, Robert Haddock corporate executive, retired naval officer
†Bonko, Larry Walter columnist, writer, radio personality
Bonney, Hal James, Jr. federal judge
Bullington, James R. ambassador
Campbell, Cole C. journalist, educator
Clarke, J. Calvitt, Jr. federal judge
Clemins, Archie Ray naval officer
Cooper, Deloris Louise nursing administrator
Crenshaw, Francis Nelson lawyer
Cutchins, Clifford Armstrong, III banker
Dandridge, Rita Bernice English language educator
Davey, John Michael military career officer
Devine, Charles Joseph, Jr. urologist, educator
Doumar, Robert George federal judge
Dyar, Kathryn Wilkin pediatrician
†Eisman, Dale C. journalist
El-Mahdi, Anas Morsi radiation oncologist
Etheridge, James Edward, Jr. academic administrator, pediatrics educator
Faulconer, Robert Jamieson pathologist, educator
Fitzpatrick, William Henry retired journalist
Fox, Douglas Brian newspaper publishing company executive
Frieden, Jane Heller art educator
Garlette, William Henry Lee army officer
Glickman, Albert Seymour psychologist, educator
Goldbach, Richard Albert shipyard company executive
Goode, David Ronald transportation company executive
†Grant, Walter Leroy food products executive
Greene, Douglas George humanities educator, author, publisher
Guy, Louis Lee, Jr. environmental engineer
†Hailstork, Adolphus composer
Haskins, Michael Donald naval officer
Hoffman, Walter Edward federal judge
Ives, Ronn Brian artist, educator
Jackson, Raymond A. federal judge
†Jolly, William Monroe hospital administrator
Jones, Franklin Ross education educator
Jones, Howard Wilbur, Jr. gynecologist
Jones, Leon Herbert, Jr. (Herb Jones) artist
Julian, Michael grocery company executive
Katz, Douglas Jeffrey naval officer
Kellam, Richard B. judge
Kern, Howard Paul hospital administrator
Koch, James Verch academic administrator, economist
Lefcoe, Vann H. lawyer
Lester, Richard Garrison radiologist, educator
Liles, Jack S. construction company executive
Lind, James Forest surgeon, educator
Lucking, Robert A. English literature educator
MacKenzie, John A. federal judge
Maly, Kurt John computer science educator
Marchello, Joseph Maurice mathematics and physical science educator
Mark, Peter director, conductor
Martin, Mary Coates genealogist, writer
Martin, Roy Butler, Jr. museum director, retired broker
Mc Gaughy, John Bell civil engineer
McKinnon, Arnold Borden transportation company executive
Middleton, Donald Earl transportation company executive
Miller, Yvonne Bond state senator, educator
Mitchell, Glenn R. hospital administrator
Mobley, Mark music critic, feature writer
Morgan, Henry Coke, Jr. federal judge, lawyer
Moses, Paul Davis career officer
Musgrave, Thea composer, conductor
Myers, Donald Allen university dean
Olson, Phillip Roger naval officer
†Power, Edward Francis newspaper editor
Prince, William Taliaferro federal judge
Rephan, Jack lawyer
Ritter, Alfred Francis, Jr. cable television executive
Robb, Nathaniel Heyward, Jr. national guard officer, real estate executive
†Roberts, Richard D. cable station executive
Rohn, Reuben David pediatric educator and administrator
Rose, Paul Edward publishing company executive
†Rudder, Paul R. transportation executive
Ryan, Louis Farthing lawyer
Schellenberg, Karl Abraham biochemist
Scott, Kenneth R. transportation executive
Shannon, John Sanford railway executive, lawyer
Sheetz, Richard LaTrelle retired association executive
Shuman, Deanne dental hygienist, educator
Sizemore, William Howard, Jr. newspaper editor
Smith, Rebecca Beach federal judge
Smith, Richard Muldrow lawyer
Spainhour, Tremaine Howard lawyer
†Terry, William E. rear admiral
Timms, A. Jackson lawyer
Tolmie, Donald McEachern lawyer
Train, Harry Depue, II retired naval officer
Turbyfill, John Ray railway executive
†Valentine, Herman Edward computer company executive
Vest, Frank Harris, Jr. bishop
Watts, Dave Henry corporate executive
Wei, Benjamin Min engineering educator
Wharton, Shirley Granger hospital administrator, nurse
Williams, Sue Darden library director
Wilson, Lloyd Lee organization administrator
Wiltse, James Clark civil engineer
Wynne, John Oliver newspaper, broadcast and cable executive

Norton
Earls, Donald Edward lawyer
Vest, Gayle Southworth obstetrician and gynecologist

Oakton
Curry, Thomas Fortson electronics engineer, defense industry executive
Harmon, Robert Gerald health company executive
Hu, Sue King middle school educator
Kerr, Charlotte Bowden interior designer
Wolff, Edward A. electronics engineer

Onancock
Puckorius, Theodore D. consulting company executive

Orange
Cortada, James N. mayor, former diplomat
Dunnington, Walter Grey, Jr. lawyer, retired food and tobacco executive
Soderbergh, Steven Andrew filmmaker

Orlean
Kulski, Julian Eugeniusz architect, planner, educator

Palmyra
Chapin, Suzanne Phillips retired psychologist
Leslie, William Cairns metallurgical engineering educator
Mulckhuyse, Jacob John energy conservation and environmental consultant
Ramsey, Forrest Gladstone, Jr. engineering company executive
White, Luther Wesley lawyer

Penn Laird
Wise, Charles Conrad, Jr. educator, past government official, author

Petersburg
Berry, Lemuel, Jr. academic dean, music educator
†Calkins, Christopher Miles historian
Dance, Gloria Fenderson dance studio executive, ballet administrator
Franklin, Virgil L. school administrator, education educator
Smith, Paul Edmund, Jr. philosophy and religion educator
Williams, Gertie Boothe retired home school coordinator
Young, Estelle Irene dermatologist

Poquoson
Yard, Rix Nelson former athletic director

Portsmouth
Brown, James Andrew naval architect
Burgess, Dean library director
Geib, Philip Oldham physician, retired naval officer
Mapp, Alf Johnson, Jr. writer, historian
McDaniel, William J. career military officer
Spong, William Belser, Jr. lawyer, educator
Thomas, Ted, Sr. minister

Purcellville
Conte, Joseph John, II meteorologist, management consultant
Sharples, Winston Singleton automobile importer and distributor

Quantico
Joy, James R. retail executive
Wallenborn, Janice Rae elementary education educator

Radford
James, Clarity (Carolyne Faye James) mezzo-soprano
Lamb, Lester Lewis hospital administrator
Pribram, Karl Harry psychology educator, researcher
Ross, James Barrett finance and insurance educator
Thomas, Robert Wilburn broadcasting and advertising executive
Wille, Lois Jean retired newspaper editor

Rapidan
Grimm, Ben Emmet former library director and consultant

Reston
Ackerson, Jeffrey Townsend computer systems executive
Ayers, George Edward Lewis higher education association executive
Bannister, Dan R. professional and technical services company executive
Barton, Paul Booth, Jr. geologist
†Berry Cabán, Cristóbal Santiago business executive
Black, Cathleen Prunty newspaper executive
Blanchard, Townsend Eugene service companies executive
Blum, John Curtis agricultural economist
Brett, Robin geologist
Brosseau, Irma Finn business executive, management consultant
Brown, James Robert retired air force officer
†Burton, James Samuel physical chemist
Calio, Anthony John scientist, business executive
Cannistraro, Nicholas, Jr. newspaper executive
Cerf, Vinton Gray telecommunications company executive
†Chatman, Raymond Christopher association executive
Christ, Thomas Warren electronics research and development company executive, sociologist
Clark, Sandra Helen Becker geologist
Cohen, Philip hydrogeologist, retired
Cramer, James Perry publisher, information architect
Curry, John Joseph professional organization executive
Dastur, Kersy B. real estate company executive
Doe, Bruce Roger geologist
Duggan, James H. technical services company executive
Dyer, Timothy J. educational association administrator
Eaton, Gordon Pryor geologist, research director
Fredette, Richard Chester computer specialist
†Fullagar, Paul Richard medical association administrator
Gates, James David association executive
Goldman, Ralph Morris political science educator
Goodwin, Robert Delmege retired association executive
Hamilton, Robert Morrison geophysicist
Heginbotham, Jan Sturza sculptor
Hope, Samuel Howard accreditation organization executive
Huebner, John Stephen geologist
Humphreys, David John lawyer, trade association executive
Kelly, Robert William economist
Kramish, Arnold technical consultant, author
Lewis, Arthur Dee corporation executive
Lewis, Gene Evans retired medical equipment company executive
Lowry, Frederick Sherwood minister, association director
†Mahlmann, John James educational association administrator
Mallette, Malcolm Francis newspaper editor, educator
McCartan, Lucy geologist
Metcalf, William Henry, Jr. architect
Miller, Edward David non-profit association administrator
Minton, Joseph Paul retired safety organization executive
Mumzhiu, Alexander optical and imaging processing engineer, researcher
Murdoch, Robert Waugh cement and construction materials company executive
Naeser, Nancy Dearien geologist, researcher
Payne, Roger Lee geographer
Peck, Dallas Lynn retired geologist
Piecuch, John M. manufacturing company executive
Pyle, Thomas Alton instructional television and motion picture executive
Rose, Michel construction materials company executive
Ross, Malcolm mineralogist, crystallographer
Ryan, Mary Catherine pediatrician
†Sansone, Torry Mark association executive
Sato, Motoaki geologist, researcher
Scheeler, James Arthur architect
Schelling, John Paul lawyer, consultant
Schleede, Glenn Roy energy market and policy consultant
Sherman, William Courtney foreign service officer
†Spierkel, Greg electronics executive
Walzer, William Charles church official, interdenominational religious publishing agency executive
Wilkinson, Edward Anderson, Jr. retired naval officer, business executive
Wood, Stephannie Anne lawyer
Zigel, James M. aircraft manufacturing executive

Richlands
Witten, Thomas Jefferson, Jr. mathematics educator

Richmond
Ackell, Edmund Ferris university president
Ackerly, Benjamin Clarkson lawyer
Adams, John Buchanan, Jr. advertising agency executive
Aigner, Emily Burke lay worker
Allen, George Felix governor
Alley, Robert Sutherland humanities educator, author
Alpert, Janet A(nne) title insurance company executive
Altschul, B J public relations counselor
Anderson, James Frederick clergyman
Anderson, Leonard Gustave retired lawyer, retired business executive
Aron, Mark G. transportation executive, lawyer

Ayres, Stephen McClintock *physician, educator*
Bagby, Daniel Gordon *minister*
Baker, Donald Parks *journalist, educator*
Baliles, Gerald L. *lawyer, former governor*
Baretski, Charles Allan *political scientist, librarian, educator, historian, municipal official*
Barker, Thomas Carl *health care executive*
Barry, Timothy Francis *construction company executive*
Bartell, James Elliot *oil company executive*
Batzli, Terrence Raymond *lawyer*
†Beamer, Betsy Davis *state official*
Belcher, Dennis Irl *lawyer*
Benedetti, Joseph B. *lawyer, state senator*
Berry, William Willis *retired utility executive*
Beyer, Donald Sternoff, Jr. *lieutenant governor*
Bialkowski, Diane *school system administrator*
†Billingsley, Anna Barron *journalist*
Binns, Walter Gordon, Jr. *investment company executive*
Black, Robert Perry *retired banker, executive*
Blanchard, Lawrence Eley, Jr. *lawyer, corporation executive*
Bland, Thelma Everson *state commissioner*
Blatt, Elizabeth Kempske *museum administrator*
Booker, Lewis Thomas *lawyer*
†Bosher, William Cleveland, Jr. *education educator*
Boswell, Thomas Wayne *transportation executive*
Bourke, William Oliver *retired metal company executive*
Bradley, Sterling Gaylen *microbiology and pharmacology educator*
Brame, Joseph Robert, III *lawyer*
Brandt, Yale M. *metal products executive*
Brasfield, Evans Booker *lawyer*
Brent, Andrew Jackson *lawyer*
Briggs, Edward Burton, Jr. *religion writer*
Brissette, Martha Blevins *lawyer*
Broaddus, John Alfred, Jr. *bank executive, economist*
†Broaddus, William Gray *lawyer*
Brockenbrough, Henry Watkins *lawyer*
Brooks, Robert Franklin, Sr. *lawyer*
Brown, Aubrey Neblett, Jr. *minister, editor*
Bruckart, Walter E. *electronics company executive*
Brush, Carey Wentworth *retired college administrator, history educator*
Bryan, David Tennant *media company executive*
Bryan, John Stewart, III *newspaper publisher*
Buford, Robert Pegram *lawyer*
Bunzl, Rudolph Hans *retired diversified manufacturing company executive*
Burke, John K(irkland), Jr. *lawyer*
Burrus, Robert Lewis, Jr. *lawyer*
Bush, Thomas Norman *lawyer*
Bustard, Clarke *music critic, newswriter, radio producer*
Butzner, John Decker, Jr. *federal judge*
Campbell, Thomas Corwith, Jr. *economics educator*
Capps, Thomas Edward *utilities company executive, lawyer*
†Capps, Thos E. *diversified financial services company executive*
Carrell, Daniel Allan *lawyer*
Carrico, Harry Lee *state supreme court chief justice*
Carter, Joseph Carlyle, Jr. *lawyer*
Catlett, Richard H., Jr. *retired lawyer*
Charlesworth, Arthur Thomas *mathematics and computer science educator*
Christie, Laurence Glenn, Jr. *surgeon*
Clement, Alvis Macon *former utilities executive*
Clinard, Robert Noel *lawyer*
Cohn, David Stephen *lawyer*
Compton, Asbury Christian *state supreme court justice*
Compton, Olin Randall *consulting electrical engineer, researcher*
Costa, Robert Nicholas *library director*
Cothran, Phyllis L. *personal care industry executive*
Cramer, Morgan Joseph, Jr. *international management executive*
Cutchins, Clifford Armstrong, IV *lawyer*
Dabney, Virginius *author*
Dahlenburg, Lyle Marion *investment company executive*
Daniel, Beth *professional golfer*
Davenport, Bradfute Warwick, Jr. *lawyer*
Davis, Douglas Whitfield *lawyer*
Davis, John Kennerly, Jr. *utility holding company executive*
Davis, Norwood H., Jr. *health insurance corporation executive*
Denny, Collins, III *lawyer*
Dickinson, Alfred James *realtor*
Dillon, James Lee *media company executive, newspaper publisher*
Dilworth, Robert Lexow *career officer, adult education educator*
Donnahoe, Alan Stanley *newspaper executive*
Douglass, William Birch, III *lawyer*
Downs, George Warthen *federal judge*
Dray, Mark S. *lawyer*
Dresser, Paul Alton, Jr. *paper and forest products executive*
Dunn, Leo James *obstetrician, gynecologist, educator*
Easterling, William K. *plastics and chemicals executive*
Ellis, Andrew Jackson, Jr. *lawyer*
Epps, Augustus Charles *lawyer*
Erb, James Bryan *music educator, conductor, musicologist*
Estes, Gerald Walter *newspaper executive*
Estridge, Ronald B. *paper company executive*
Evans, James Stanley *communications company executive*
Farnham, James Edward *lawyer*
Finley, Donald James *state agency administrator*
Fischer, Carl Robert *health care facility administrator*
Fishback, Patricia Davis *academic administrator*
Ford, Barbara Jean *library studies educator*
Fox, Joseph Carter *pulp and paper manufacturing company executive*
Framme, Lawrence Henry, III *lawyer*
Franko, Bernard Vincent *pharmacologist*
Freed, David Clark *artist*
Freeman, George Clemon, Jr. *lawyer*
Freeman, Robert Mallory *banker*
Freund, Emma Frances *medical technologist*
Fuller, Reginald Horace *clergyman, biblical studies educator*
Gandy, Gerald Larmon *rehabilitation counseling educator*
Gary, Richard David *lawyer*
Gasch, Manning *lawyer*
Geary, David Patrick *criminal justice educator, consultant, author*
Geisler, Ernest Keith, Jr. *lawyer*
†Gentry, Dwight Lonnie *health care administrator*
George, Lester Lee *golf course architectural firm executive*
Gewanter, Harry Lewis *pediatric rheumatologist*
Giblin, Patrick David *banker*
†Gilmore, James Stuart, III *state attourney general*
Goldman, Israel David *hematologist, oncologist*
Goodykoontz, Charles Alfred *newspaper editor, retired*
Gordon, John L., Jr. *historian, educator*
Gordon, Thomas Christian, Jr. *former justice*
Gorr, Louis Frederick *investment consultant*
Gottwald, Bruce Cobb *chemical company executive*
Gottwald, Floyd Dewey, Jr. *chemical company executive*
Gottwald, John D. *manufacturing executive*
Grandis, Leslie Allan *lawyer*
Graves, H. Brice *lawyer*
Gray, Clarence Jones *foreign language educator, dean emeritus*
Griffith, Garth Ellis *lawyer*
†Grimsley, James Edward *newspaper editor, syndicated columnist*
Gross, Paul Allan *health service executive*
Guthrie, Rebecca Claire *lawyer*
Hackney, Virginia Howitz *lawyer*
Hagan, Randall Lee *manufacturing executive*
Hall, James Curtis *business and economics educator*
Hall, Phoebe Poulterer *lawyer, judge*
Hall, Stephen Charles *lawyer*
Hamel, Dana Bertrand *academic administrator*
Hamill, A(llen) William *finance executive*
Hancock, William Glenn *lawyer*
Hanneman, Rodney Elton *metallurgical engineer*
Harbaugh, Joseph Delbert *legal educator, consultant*
Hardage, Page Taylor *health care administrator*
Hardy, Richard Earl *rehabilitation counseling educator, clinical psychologist*
Harper, James Allie, Jr. *lawyer, arbitrator, administrative hearing officer*
Harris, Henry Hiter, Jr. *banker*
Hart, Philip Ray *religion educator, minister*
Hatch, Robert Norris *banker*
Heilman, E. Bruce *academic administrator*
Hellmuth, William Frederick, Jr. *economics educator*
Helwig, Arthur Woods *chemical company executive*
Henderson, Bernard Levie, Jr. *former state official, funeral service executive*
Henderson, Nancy Carr *dietitian, medical transcriber, writer, political organization worker*
Henley, Vernard William *banker*
Hettrick, George H. *lawyer*
Hintz, Robert Louis *transportation company executive*
Holder, Richard Gibson *metal products executive*
Holton, A. Linwood, Jr. *lawyer*
Hong, James Ming *industrialist, venture capitalist*
Hoppin, Thomas Edward *transportation executive*
Horsley, Waller Holladay *lawyer*
Howell, George Cook, III *lawyer*
Howell, Janet D. *state legislator*
Hull, Rita Prizler *accounting educator*
Huntley, Robert Edward Royall *lawyer, business executive, former university president*
Jacobs, Harry Milburn, Jr. *advertising executive*
Jacobs, James Paul *retired insurance executive*
James, Allix Bledsoe *retired university president*
James, Gene Albert *farmers cooperative executive*
Jandl, Henry Anthony *architect, educator*
Jewell, Byron Frank *museum administrator*
Jezuit, Leslie James *manufacturing company executive*
Joel, William Lee, II *interior and lighting designer*
Jones, Catesby Brooke *retired banker*
Jones, David Eugene *pharmaceutical company executive*
Jordan, David Lewis *newspaper executive*
Kasen, Stewart Michael *retail executive*
Kay, John Franklin, Jr. *lawyer*
Kay, Saul *pathologist*
Kaye, Jerome *accountant*
Kearfott, Joseph Conrad *lawyer*
Kendig, Edwin Lawrence, Jr. *physician, educator*
Kevorkian, Richard *artist*
Kilpatrick, Robert Donald *retired insurance company executive*
King, Donald Edward *lawyer*
King, Robert Leroy *business administration educator*
Lambert, Benjamin Joseph, III *optometrist, state legislator*
Lanahan, John Stevenson *management consultant*
Lanam, Linda Lee *lawyer*
Landin, David Craig *lawyer*
Laskin, Daniel M. *oral and maxillofacial surgeon, educator*
Laverge, Jan *tobacco company executive*
Lawrence, Walter, Jr. *surgeon*
Leary, David Edward *university dean*
Ledbetter, David Oscar *lawyer*
†Lee, Katharine Caecilia *art museum administrator*
Lee, Peter James *bishop*
Leith, John Haddon *clergyman, theology educator*
Levit, Jay J(oseph) *lawyer*
Lewis, Frances Aaronson *retail company executive*
Lewis, Judith A. *nursing educator, women's health nurse*
Lewis, Sydney *retail company executive*
Leyden, Donald Elliott *chemist, researcher*
Ligon, William Austin *consumer products company executive*
Lindholm, John Victor *business executive*
†Mackenzie, Ross *newspaper editor*
Manning, William Raymond *retired state official*
Martenstein, Thomas Ewing *lawyer*
Mason, Vivian Lee Conway *elementary education educator*
Mathews, Roderick Bell *lawyer*
Mauck, Henry Page, Jr. *medical and pediatrics educator*
McClard, Jack Edward *lawyer*
†McCleary, Paul Frederick *voluntary agency executive*
Mc Cue, Carolyn Moore *retired pediatric cardiologist*
McDonald, Frank Albert, Jr. *personnel director*
McDonough, Reginald Milton *religious organization executive*
McElligott, James Patrick, Jr. *lawyer*
McElroy, John Lee, Jr. *brokerage house executive*
McGee, Henry Alexander, Jr. *university official*
Mc Grath, Lee Parr *author, public relations executive*
Mc Namara, Rieman, Jr. *retired banker*
McVey, George Jennings *headmaster*
McVey, Henry Hanna, III *lawyer*
Mellette, M. Susan Jackson *physician, educator, researcher*
Merhige, Robert Reynold, Jr. *federal judge*
Mezzullo, Louis Albert *lawyer*
Miller, James Christopher *paper industry information systems specialist*
Miller, Lewis Nelson, Jr. *banker*
Miller, Nan Louise *museum director*
Milmoe, Patrick Joseph *lawyer*
Modlin, George Matthews *university chancellor emeritus*
Moore, Andrew Taylor, Jr. *banker*
Moore, John Sterling, Jr. *minister*
Moore, Thurston Roach *lawyer*
Morrill, Richard Leslie *university administrator*
Morris, Dewey Blanton *lawyer*
Morris, Thomas Robbins *political science educator*
Morton, Marshall Nay *treasurer*
Munsey, Virdell Everard, Jr. *utility executive*
Neal, Marcus Pinson, Jr. *physician, medical educator*
Neathawk, Roger Delmore *marketing company executive*
Neman, Daniel Louis *movie critic*
Newbrand, Charles Michael *advertising firm executive*
Nielsen, Steven B. *medical products executive*
†Noonan, John Michael *aluminum company executive*
Norfleet, Robert F., Jr. *banking executive*
Norris, David Stuart *bank executive*
Oakey, John Martin, Jr. *lawyer*
Oken, Donald Edward *physician, educator*
Olsson, Sture Gordon *manufacturing executive*
Owen, Duncan Shaw, Jr. *physician, medical educator*
Owen, Howard Wayne *journalist, writer*
Paciocco, C. Anthony *banker*
Pasco, Hansell Merrill *retired lawyer*
Patterson, James Willis *pathology and dermatology educator*
Patterson, Robert Hobson, Jr. *lawyer*
Pauley, Stanley Frank *manufacturing company executive*
Payne, Robert E. *federal judge*
Peery, Troy Alfred, Jr. *home furnishing company executive*
Pendleton, Eugene Barbour, Jr. *business executive*
Peters, David Frankman *lawyer*
Phillips, Thomas Edworth, Jr. *investment executive, consultant*
Pinckney, C. Cotesworth *lawyer*
Plaisted, Harris Merrill, III *real estate executive*
Poff, Richard Harding *state supreme court justice*
Pollard, Overton Price *state agency executive, lawyer*
Pope, Robert Dean *lawyer*
Powell, Kenneth Edward *investment banker*
Powell, Lewis Franklin, III *lawyer*
Powell, Virginia W. *lawyer*
Puller, Linda Todd *state legislator*
Rainey, Gordon Fryer, Jr. *lawyer*
Raper, Mark Irvin *public relations executive*
Rawlings, James Scott *architect*
†Reid, Paul S. *nortgage company executive*
Reveley, Walter Taylor, III *lawyer*
Rexinger, Daniel Michael *retail company executive*
Reynolds, David Parham *metals company executive*
Reynolds, Randolph Nicklas *aluminum company executive*
Rhodes, James T. *electric power industry executive*
Richardson, David Walthall *cardiologist, educator, consultant*
Rilling, John Robert *history educator*
Roach, Edgar Mayo, Jr. *lawyer*
Robertson, William Franklin *publishing executive*
Robins, Edwin Claiborne, Sr. *retired pharmaceutical company executive*
Rogers, Isabel Wood *religious studies educator*
Rogers, James Edward *paper company executive*
Rolfe, Robert Martin *lawyer*
Roop, Ralph Goodwin *retired oil marketing company executive*
Rosbe, William Louis *lawyer*
Rowley, Frank Selby, Jr. *artist*
Rubinstein, Phyllis M. *lawyer*
Rudlin, David Alan *lawyer, educator*
Rutledge, Paul E., III *insurance company executive*
Saine, Carroll Lee *banker*
†Sauer, Conrad Frederick, IV *food products executive*
Savage, William Woodrow *education educator*
Schwarzschild, Patricia Michaelson *lawyer*
Schwarzschild, William Harry, Jr. *banker*
Self, Phyllis C. *health sciences librarian*
Seymour, Harlan Francis *healthcare industry executive*
Shands, William Ridley, Jr. *lawyer*
Shapiro, Gary Michael *philosophy educator*
Sharer, John Daniel *lawyer*
Sharp, Richard L. *retail company executive*
Shumandine, William F., Jr. *banking executive*
Simmons, S. Dallas *university president*
Simpson, John Noel *hospital administrator*
Sirica, Alphonse Eugene *pathology educator*
Slater, Thomas Glascock, Jr. *lawyer*
Slaughter, Alexander Hoke *lawyer*
Smith, R. Gordon *lawyer*
Smith, Ted Jay, III *mass communications educator*
Sniffin, John Harrison *retail executive*
†Spagnolo, Joseph A., Jr. *state agency administrator*
Spahn, Gary Joseph *lawyer*
Spain, Jack Holland, Jr. *lawyer*
Spencer, James R. *federal judge*
Spivey, Joseph M., III *lawyer*
Sprinkle, William Melvin *engineering administrator, audio-acoustical engineer*
†Stallard, Hubert R. *telecommunications industry executive*
Stallard, Hugh R. *telephone company executive*
Stephens, E. Barrie *business executive*
Stephenson, Roscoe Bolar, Jr. *state supreme court justice*
Stettinius, Wallace *communications executive*
Stockton, Thomas B. *bishop*
Strickland, William Jesse *lawyer*
Sullivan, Walter Francis *bishop*
Sweeney, Arthur Hamilton, Jr. *metal manufacturing executive, retired army officer*
Swezey, Charles Mason *Christian ethics educator, administrator*
Talley, Charles Richmond *commercial banking executive*
Taylor, Julian Howard *metals company executive*
Taylor, Welford Dunaway *English language educator*
Thomas, John Charles *lawyer, former state supreme court justice*
Thompson, Francis Neal *financial services consultant*
Thompson, Paul Michael *lawyer*
Thorp, Benjamin A., III *paper manufacturing company executive*
Tice, Douglas Oscar, Jr. *federal judge*
Tilghman, Richard Granville *banker*
Totten, Randolph Fowler *lawyer*
Trani, Eugene Paul *university president, educator*
Treadway, John David *history educator*
Trott, Sabert Scott, II *marketing professional*
Trotti, John Boone *librarian, educator*
Troy, Anthony Francis *lawyer*
Trumble, Robert Roy *business educator*
Tuck, Grayson Edwin *real estate agent, former natural gas transmission executive*
Tunner, William Sams *urological surgeon*
Twomey, Wililam Eldred, Jr. *lawyer*
Ulmer, Deborah Luxton *medical training administrator, nurse, consultant*
Urofsky, Melvin Irving *historian, educator*
Wakeham, Helmut Richard Rae *chemist, consulting company executive*
Walker, Charles B. *chemicals company executive*
Walsh, James Hamilton *lawyer*
Walsh, William Arthur, Jr. *lawyer*
Ward, John Wesley *retired pharmacologist*
Warrick, James Craig *banker*
Warthen, Harry Justice, III *lawyer*
Watkins, Hays Thomas *retired railroad executive*
Watts, Robert Glenn *retired pharmaceutical company executive*
Watts, Stephen Hurt, II *lawyer*
Wellford, Hill B., Jr. *lawyer*
Wells, James M., III *bank executive*
Wheeler, R(ichard) Kenneth *lawyer*
Whelan, Karen Mae Leppo *manufacturing executive*
White, Hugh Vernon, Jr. *lawyer*
†White, Kenneth Ray *health administration educator, consultant*
Whittemore, Anne Marie *lawyer*
Williams, Richard Leroy *federal judge*
Williams, Robert C. *paper company executive*
Wilson, James Milton, III *bank executive*
Wilson, Sara Redding *lawyer*
†Wiltshire, Richard Watkins, Sr. *insurance company executive*
†Wiltshire, Richard Watkins, Jr. *insurance company executive*
Winstead, Joy *journalist, consultant*
Wirt, John Stephen *journalist*
Witschey, Walter Robert Thurmond *science museum administrator, archaeologist, computer systems consultant*
Witt, Walter Francis, Jr. *lawyer*
Wolf, Barry *genetics, pediatric educator*
Wood, Jeanne Clarke *charitable organization executive*
Word, Thomas S., Jr. *lawyer*
Yu, Robert Kuan-jen *biochemistry educator*

Roanoke
Al-Zubaidi, Amer Aziz *physicist, educator*
Beagle, Benjamin Stuart, Jr. *columnist*
Bell, Houston Lesher, Jr. *hospital administrator*
Benedict, Linda Sherk *insurance company executive*
Berry, John Coltrin *insurance executive*
Bowers, David Allen *lawyer, mayor*
Burnette, Ollen Lawrence, Jr. *historian*
Butler, Manley Caldwell *lawyer*
Caudill, David L. *bank executive*
Conn, Thomas Finley *banker*
Dalhouse, Warner Norris *banker*
Dillard, Richard Henry Wilde *English language professional, educator, author*
Edwards, J. Randolph *medical products executive*
Ekdahl, Patricia Josephine *hospital administrator*
Fishwick, John Palmer *lawyer, retired railroad executive*
Fourcroy, Margarite *performing company executive*
Hamrick, Joseph Thomas *mechanical engineer, aerospace company executive*
Harvey, Aubrey Eaton, III *industrial engineer*
Hooper, M. David *protective services official*
Husted, John Edwin *geologist, educator*
King, Stephen Emmett *educational administrator*
Kirkwood, Richard Edwin *librarian*
Landon, Forrest M. *newspaper editor*
Layman, Mark Leslie *journalist*
Light, Arthur Heath *bishop*
Marmion, William Henry *retired bishop*
McKenna, John Dennis *environmental testing engineer*
Merker, Frank Ferdinand *retired hospital administrator*
Pearson, Henry Clyde *federal judge*
Price, Leroy Vernon *secondary school educator*
Reggia, Frank *electrical engineer*
Robertson, Thomas L. *health facility administrator*
Rugaber, Walter Feucht, Jr. *newspaper executive*
Shaffner, Patrick Noel *architectural engineering executive*
Shaftman, Fredrick Krisch *telephone communications executive*
Sowers, William Armand *civil engineer*
Stanley, Ralph *bluegrass musician*
Tota, Frank Peter *school system administrator*
Turk, James Clinton *federal judge*
Warren, William Kermit *newspaper managing editor*
Woodrum, Clifton A., III *lawyer, state legislator*

Rockbridge Baths
Patteson, Roy Kinneer, Jr. *clergyman, administrator*

Roseland
Fetter, Robert Barclay *retired administrative sciences educator*

Rosslyn
Adair, John Joseph *federal agency administrator*

Round Hill
Coll, Helen F. *banker*
Pugh, Marion Stirling *archaeologist, author*
Sadd, William Wheeler *trade association executive*

Ruckersville
†Minkle, L. Steven *manufacturing executive, light*

Salem
Bansemer, Richard Frederick *bishop*
†Boone, Charles Wimmel *healthcare executive, air force officer, writer*
Brand, Edward Cabell *retail executive*
Chakravorty, Ranes Chandra *surgeon, educator*
Fisher, Charles Harold *chemistry educator, researcher*
Gring, David M. *academic administrator*
Lane, Lawrence Jubin *electrical engineer, consultant*
Walker, Loren Haines *electrical engineer*
†Weiss, James William *healthcare executive*
Willet, Richard A. *engineering company executive*

Seaford
Hammer, Jacob Myer physicist, consultant
Jenkins, Margaret Bunting human resources executive

Smithfield
Luter, Joseph Williamson, III meat packing and processing company executive

Sperryville
Armor, David J. sociologist

Spotsylvania
Arnhoff, Franklyn Nathaniel psychologist, sociologist, educator
Hardy, Dorcas Ruth government relations and public policy consultant

Spottswood
Fredricksen, Cleve Laurance thoroughbred horse farm owner, real estate investor

Spring Grove
Daniel, Robert Williams, Jr. business executive, former congressman

Springfield
†Atkinson, Dale B. aeronautical engineering, consultant
Becton, Julius Wesley, Jr. army officer
Bradunas, Edward Terence data processing management and technology management consultant
Broome, Paul Wallace engineering research and development executive
Bruen, John Dermot computer systems company executive
Duff, William Grierson electrical engineer
Fedewa, Lawrence John information technology company executive
Finkel, Karen Evans school transportation association executive, lawyer
Gawalt, Gerard W(ilfred) historian, writer
†Gibson, Kenneth Dwight health care consultant
Larson, Reed Eugene association executive
McLaurin, Ronald De political analyst, consultant, author, journalist
Sebastian, Richard Lee physicist, executive
Singleton, John Knox hospital administrator
Steele, Lendell Eugene research scientist
Stottlemyer, David Lee government official

Stafford
Brown, Janet Louise principal
Wolle, William Down foreign service officer

Stanleytown
Stanley, Thomas Bahnson, Jr. investor

Staunton
Balsley, Philip Elwood entertainer
Cochran, George Moffett retired judge
Hammaker, Paul M. retail executive, business educator, author
†Klaffky, Susan Elizabeth museum director, consultant, researcher
Sweetman, Beverly Yarroll physical therapist

Sterling
Harris, Paul Lynwood aerospace transportation executive
LaFroscia, Ernest John business executive
Naylor, Frank Wesley, Jr. financial executive
Witek, James Eugene public relations executive

Suffolk
Birdsong, George Yancy manufacturing company executive
Carroll, George Joseph pathologist, educator
Hines, Angus Irving, Jr. petroleum marketing executive
Hope, James Franklin mayor, civil engineer, consultant
†Spain, William J., Jr. wholesale distribution executive

Susan
Ambach, Dwight Russell retired foreign service officer

Sweet Briar
Armstrong, Gregory Timon religious studies educator, minister
Hill, Barbara Ann academic administrator, consultant
Lane, Rebecca Massie museum director
McClenon, John Raymond chemistry educator
Miller, Reuben George economics educator
†Piepho, (Edward) Lee humanities educator

Tazewell
Weeks, Ross Leonard, Jr. museum foundation executive

Timberville
Barnard, Robert Edward potter, writer

University Of Richmond
Hall, James H(errick), Jr. philosophy educator, author
Terry, Robert Meredith French language educator

Upperville
di Zerega, Thomas William former energy company executive, lawyer
Smart, Stephen Bruce, Jr. business and government executive

Urbanna
Hudson, Jesse Tucker, Jr. financial executive
Salley, John Jones university administrator, oral pathologist

Verona
de Vaux, Peter Fordney advertising consultant

Vienna
Alberta, Mark Edward lawyer
Argow, Keith Angevin association executive,forester
Bartlett, John Wesley consulting firm executive
Blevins, Charles Russell publishing executive
Brandel, Ralph Edward management consultant
†Butler, Donald rental leasing company executive
†Campagna, Joseph rental, leasing company executive
Cartier, Brian Evans association executive
Chamberlain, Diane psychotherapist, author, clinical social worker
Chandler, Hubert Thomas former army officer
†Clark, Katherine Karen software company executive
Davis, Cabell Seal, Jr. naval officer
†Denman, Gary L. mechanical engineer
de Planque, Emile, III computer consultant
Dunn, Bernard Daniel former naval officer, consultant
Dupuy, Trevor Nevitt historian, research executive
Fasser, Paul James, Jr. labor arbitrator
Giovacchini, Robert Peter toxicologist, manufacturing executive, retired
Hale, Thomas Morgan professional services executive
Hatch, Harold Arthur retired military officer
Hood, William Clarence international banking official
Howard, Daggett Horton lawyer
Hughes, Thomas Joseph retired naval officer
Jackson, Dempster McKee retired naval officer
Jahn, Laurence Roy retired biologist, institute executive
Jandreau, James Lawrence program manager
Keiser, Bernhard Edward engineering company executive, consulting telecommunications engineer
Kohler, Karl Eugene architect
Kumar, Verinder accountant, financial executive
Leonard, Edward Paul naval officer, dentist, educator
Lewis, Boyd De Wolf publisher,editor, writer
Lillard, Mark Hill, III computer consulting executive, former air force officer
Lyons, Paul Michael producer, film
Mc Arthur, George journalist
McKay, Carol Ruth photographic editor
Pesner, Susan M. lawyer
Razzano, Frank Charles lawyer
Roepke, Nancy Jean investment company executive
Savoca, Antonio Litterio technology company executive
Schneider, Peter Raymond research scientist, juvenile justice consultant
†Sides, James Ralph aerospace executive
Sirpis, Andrew Paul insurance company executive
Van Stavoren, William David management consultant, retired government official
Walker, Edward Keith, Jr. business executive, retired naval officer
Webb, William Loyd, Jr. army officer
West, Richard Luther military association executive, defense consultant, retired army officer
Woodward, Kenneth Emerson retired mechanical engineer

Virginia Beach
Alexander, William Powell food products executive
Barriskill, Maudanne Kidd primary school educator
Becker, Boris professional tennis player
Brickell, Edward Ernest, Jr. management executive
El-Fayoumy, Joanne Patricia Quinn writer, poet
Farrell, Paul Edward dentist, retired naval officer, educator
Freyss, David producer, director
Green, Barbara-Marie publisher, journalist, poet
Happy, Jack Nelson oil company executive
Harrison, William Wright retired banker
Kreyling, Edward George, Jr. railroad executive
Lawrence, Joyce Wagner health facility administrator, educator
Lichtenberg, Byron K. futurist, manufacturing executive, space flight consultant
Lisota, Gary Martin business executive, retired naval officer
May, David L., Jr. architectural firm executive
Mayer, William Dixon pathologist, educator
Merchant, Donald Joseph microbiologist
Oberndorf, Meyera E. mayor
Oldfield, Edward Charles, Jr. retired naval officer, communications company executive
Richardson, Daniel Putnam headmaster, history, economics and criminal law educator
Robertson, Pat (Marion Gordon Robertson) religious broadcasting executive
†Robertson, Timothy B. cable television executive
Sanderson, James Richard naval officer, planning and investment company consultant
Sekulow, Jay Alan lawyer
Seward, William W(ard), Jr. author, educator
Sims, Martha J. library director
Smith, A. Robert editor, author
Tarbutton, Lloyd Tilghman motel executive, franchise consultant
von Braun, Peter Carl Moore Stewart company executive
Wardrup, Leo C., Jr. state legislator
Weller, Robert N(orman) hotel executive
Wick, Robert Thomas retired supermarket executive
Wiggins, Samuel Paul educator
Williams, John Rodman theologian, educator

Warm Springs
Deeds, Robert Creigh lawyer, state legislator

Warrenton
Molloy, Michael John public relations professional
Osier, William Richard school administrator
Palmer, Milton Meade landscape architect

Warsaw
Hirsch, Charles Bronislaw retired religion educator and administrator

Washingtons Birthplace
Storke, Dwight Clifton, Jr. government official

Waterford
Pollack, Reginald Murray painter, sculptor

Waynesboro
†Anderson, Judith Charlene medical record technician
†McNair, John William, Jr. civil engineer
Rippe, Peter Marquart museum administrator

West Point
†Causey, J(ohn) P(aul), Jr. lawyer

White Stone
Wroth, James Melvin former army officer, computer company executive

Williamsburg
Axtell, James Lewis history educator
Baker, Donald Scott communications executive
Ball, Donald Lewis retired English language educator
Baranowski, Frank Paul energy consultant, former government official
Becker, Lawrence Carlyle philosopher, educator, author
Birney, Robert Charles retired academic administrator, psychologist
Blouet, Brian Walter geography educator
Boatright, James Francis air force official
Braun, Richard Lane lawyer, university administrator
Brinkley, Joseph Willard association executive
Burwell, Robert Lemmon, Jr. chemist, educator
Cantlay, George Gordon retired army officer
Chappell, Miles Linwood, Jr. art history educator
Coleman, Henry Edwin art educator, artist
Coyner, Martin Boyd, Jr. history educator
Crapol, Edward P. history educator
Davis, Emma-Jo Levey retired government executive, publishing executive
Davis, Richard Bradley internal medicine, pathology educator, physician
Dittman, Duane Arthur management consultant
Edwards, Jack Donald educator
Esler, Anthony James historian, novelist
Finn, A. Michael public relations executive
Finn, Thomas Macy religion educator
Fraser, Howard Michael educator, editor
Friedman, Herbert psychology educator
Garrison, George Hartranft Haley curator of scripophily
Geddy, Vernon Meredith, Jr. lawyer
Geoffroy, Kevin Edward education educator
Godwin, R. Wayne chemicals company executive
Goodwin, Bruce Kesseli geology educator, researcher
Griffith, Melvin Eugene entomologist, public health official
Gross, Robert Alan history educator
Harris, James Franklin philosophy educator
Heller, James Stephen law librarian
Herbert, Albert Edward, Jr. interior and industrial designer
Herrmann, Benjamin Edward former insurance executive
Hornsby, Bruce Randall composer, musician
Humphreys, Homer Alexander former principal
Jacoby, William Jerome, Jr. internist, retired military officer
Johnson, Charles Royal research mathematician, educator
Johnston, Robert Atkinson educator, psychologist
Kottas, John Frederick business administration educator
Lange, Carl James psychology educator
Longsworth, Charles R. foundation administrator
Lutzer, David John college dean, mathematics professor
Maccubbin, Robert Purks literature and culture educator
Maloney, Milford Charles retired internal medicine educator
Marcus, Paul lawyer, educator
Marshall, Nancy Haig library administrator
McGiffert, Michael history educator, editor
Mc Kean, John Rosseel Overton university dean
McKenna, Virgil Vincent psychology educator, researcher
Mc Knight, John Lacy physics educator
McLane, Henry Earl, Jr. philosophy educator
Messmer, Donald Joseph business management educator, marketing consultant
Nettels, Elsa English language educator
Noël Hume, Ivor retired antiquary, consultant
O'Connell, William Edward, Jr. finance educator
Orwoll, Robert Arvid chemistry educator
Parkany, John business educator, international financial consultant
Parker, Donald Howard landscape architect
Pearson, Roy Laing business administration educator
†Pinotti, Joseph R. light manufacturing executive
Quittmeyer, Charles Loreaux business educator
Regan, Donald Thomas financier, writer, lecturer
Roberson, Robert Stephen investment company executive
Robinson, Jay (Thurston) (Thurston Robinson) artist
Rodman, Leiba mathematics educator
Roseberg, Carl Andersson sculptor, educator
Rosen, Ellen Freda psychologist, educator
Scholnick, Robert J. college dean, English language educator
Shaver, Kelly G. psychology educator
Sheppard, Thomas Frederick history educator
Sherman, Richard Beatty history educator
Siegel, Robert Ted physicist
Sipes, Larry L. lawyer
Smith, James Brown, Jr. secondary school educator
Smith, Roger Winston political theorist, educator
Smolla, Rodney Alan lawyer, educator
Spitzer, Cary Redford avionics consultant, electrical engineer
Starnes, William Herbert, Jr. chemist, educator
Strong, John Scott finance educator
Sullivan, Timothy Jackson law educator, academic administrator
Tate, Thaddeus W(ilbur), Jr. (Thad Tate) history educator, historical institute executive, historian
Van Tassel-Baska, Joyce Lenore education educator
†Verkuil, Paul Robert corporate executive
Wallach, Alan art historian, educator
Warren, William Herbert business administration educator
Whyte, James Primrose, Jr. former law educator
Wilburn, Robert Charles institute executive
Yankovich, James Michael education educator
Zamora, Mario Dimarucut anthropologist, educator

Winchester
Bechamps, Gerald J. surgeon
†Bryant, Arthur Herbert, II rubber and plastics company executive
Byrd, Harry Flood, Jr. newspaper executive, former senator
Davis, James Arnold academic administrator
Holland, James Tulley plastic products company executive
Horsburgh, Robert Laurie entomologist
Jamison, Richard Bryan airport consultant
Ludwig, George Harry physicist
Murtagh, John Edward chemist, alcohol production consultant
Pavsek, Daniel Allan banker, educator
Tisinger, Catherine Anne college dean
Whiting, Henry H. state supreme court justice

Wise
Ellsworth, Lucius Fuller academic administrator
Smiddy, Joseph Charles retired college chancellor
Yun, Peter Subueng economics educator

Woodbridge
Binder, Leonard James magazine editor, retired
Breene, Norma Wylie special education educator
Dillaber, Philip Arthur budget and resource analyst, economist, consultant
Peck, Dianne Kawecki architect
Rose, Marianne Hunt business educator
Townsend, Kenneth Ross priest
Vachher, Prehlad Singh psychiatrist

Woodstock
Walker, Charles Norman retired insurance company executive

Woodville
Mc Carthy, Eugene Joseph writer, former senator

Yorktown
Gould, Alec historic park administrator
Riggs, David Foster museum curator, historian

Zuni
Holm, Robert Arthur environmental scientist

WASHINGTON

Anacortes
Businger, Joost Alois atmospheric scientist, educator
†Collins, Thomas L. research physicist
Higgins, Robert (Walter) military officer, physician
Mc Cracken, Philip Trafton sculptor
Randolph, Carl Lowell chemical company executive
Spaulding, John Pierson public relations executive, marine consultant
Sulkin, Stephen David marine biology educator

Ashford
Briggle, William James federal agency administrator

Auburn
Bingham, Charles W. wood products company executive
Creighton, John W., Jr. forest products company executive
Lapinski, Donald elementary school principal
Sata, Lindbergh Saburo psychiatrist, physician, educator
Weyerhaeuser, George Hunt forest products company executive
Whitmore, Donald Clark retired engineer

Bainbridge Island
Bowden, William Darsie interior designer, retired
Huntley, James Robert government official, international affairs scholar and consultant
Nagle, James Francis lawyer
Randlett, Mary Willis photographer
Warns, Raymond H. judge

Battle Ground
Hansen, James Lee sculptor
Morris, William Joseph paleontologist, educator

Belfair
Walker, E. Jerry retired clergyman

Bellevue
Akutagawa, Donald psychologist, educator
Andersen, James A. state supreme court chief justice
Armstrong, Dickwin Dill chamber of commerce executive
Baker, Jackson Arnold container shipping company executive
Bergstrom, Marianne Elisabeth program coordinator, special education teacher
Berkley, James Donald clergyman
Carlson, Curtis Eugene orthodontist, periodontist
Chen, Ching-Hong medical biochemist, biotechnical company executive
Clark, Richard Walter educator, consultant
Davidson, Robert William merchant banker
Douglas, Diane Miriam museum director
Dow, Daniel Gould electrical engineering educator
Dunlap, Ron investment securities branch manager
Edde, Howard Jasper engineering executive
Eigsti, Roger Harry insurance company executive
Elliott, Richard Wayne lawyer
Faris, Charles Oren civil engineer
Fluke, John Maurice, Jr. electrical equipment manufacturing company executive
Fremouw, Edward Joseph physicist
Graham, John Robert, Jr. financial executive
Groten, Barnet energy company executive
Habbestad, Kathryn Louise writer
Hackett, Carol Ann Hedden physician
Hamachek, Tod Russell manufacturing executive
Hannah, Lawrence Burlison lawyer
Hovind, David J. manufacturing company executive
Knoepfler, Peter Tamas psychiatrist, organizational consultant
Liang, Jeffrey Der-Shing retired electrical engineer, civil worker, diplomat
Melby, Orville Erling retired banker
Metz, Marilyn Joyce bank executive
†Muhlebach, Richard Frank management and development company executive
Mutschler, Herbert Frederick retired librarian
Olson, Hilding Harold surgeon, educator
Otterholt, Barry L. technology management consultant
Phillips, Zaiga Alksnis pediatrician
Pigott, Charles McGee transportation equipment manufacturing executive
Puckett, Allen Weare health care information systems executive
Reudink, Douglas Otto John communications company executive, researcher
Roddis, Richard Stiles Law insurance company executive, consultant, legal educator
Roselle, Richard Donaldson industrial, marine and interior designer

Ryles, Gerald Fay private investor, business executive
Scaringi, Michael Joseph lawyer, consultant
Schairer, George Swift aeronautical engineer
Shih, Benedict Chesang investment company executive
Smith, George Lester lawyer
Smith, Lester Martin broadcasting executive
†Sonstelie, Richard Robert utilities executive
Stephenson, Robert Baird energy company executive
†Stevenson, Robert W. technologies company executive, financial officer
Sullivan, James Jerome lawyer, consultant
†Szablya, Helen Mary author, language professional, lecturer
Szablya, John Francis electrical engineer, consultant
Thorpe, James Alfred retired utilities executive
Wallentine, Mary Kathryn secondary educator
Walsh, John Breffni aerospace consultant
Warren, James Ronald retired museum director, author, columnist
†Weaver, William Schildecker electric power industry executive
Wright, Theodore Otis forensic engineer

Bellingham
Albrecht, Albert Pearson electronics engineer, consultant
Bestwick, Warren William retired construction company executive
Critchlow, B. Vaughn research facility administrator, researcher
DeLorme, Roland L. university provost and vice president
Diers, Carol Jean psychology educator
Doerper, John Erwin publisher, editor
Fullmer, Donald Kitchen insurance executive
Helsell, Robert M. construction executive
Jansen, Robert Bruce consulting civil engineer
Landis, Wayne G. environmental toxicologist
Morse, Karen Williams academic administrator
Naylor, Harry Brooks microbiologist
Orem, Joseph Clifton sales professional
Packer, Mark Barry lawyer, financial consultant, foundation official
Pierce, George Adams university administrator, educator
Rhoads, James Berton archivist, former government official, consultant, educator
Ross, June Rosa Pitt biologist
Self, Charles Edwin financial consultant, retail company executive
Skinner, Knute Rumsey poet, English educator
Whisenhunt, Donald Wayne history educator

Bothell
Blackburn, John Lewis consulting engineering executive
Browning, Jesse Harrison entrepreneur
Icenhower, Rosalie B. retired elementary school principal
McDonald, Michael Lee career naval officer

Bremerton
Pliskow, Vita Sari anesthesiologist

Burlington
Zeretzke, Frederick Frank H. artist, educator

Camas
Hanby, John Estes, Jr. technology management executive
Howe, Robert Wilson education educator

Centralia
Kirk, Henry Port academic administrator

Cheney
Drummond, Marshall Edward business educator, university administrator
Gerber, Sanford Edwin audiologist
Glass, James Clifford college dean, science and mathematics educator
†Hegi, Ursula writer

Colfax
Webster, Ronald B. lawyer

College Place
Jonish, Arley Duane retired bibliographer
Thompson, Alden Lloyd biblical studies educator, author

Dayton
McFarland, Jon Weldon county commissioner

Deer Harbor
Hoag, Paul Sterling architect

East Sound
Anders, William Alison aerospace and defense manufacturing executive

East Wenatchee
Bennett, Grover Bryce engineering consultant

Eatonville
Geddes, Gary Lee wildlife park director

Edmonds
Galster, Richard W. engineering geologist
†Landau, Henry Groh geoenvironmental consulting engineer
Owen, John retired newspaper editor
Paul, Ronald Stanley research institute executive
Sankovich, Joseph Bernard cemetery management consultant
Terrel, Ronald Lee civil engineer, business executive, educator
Thyden, James Eskel professional society administrator, former diplomat, educator

Ellensburg
Comstock, Dale Robert mathematics educator
Jacobs, Robert Cooper political scientist, consultant
Jones, Jerry Lynn chemistry educator
Moore, Thomas David academic administrator
Nelson, Ivory Vance university president

Enumclaw
Goff, Thomas M. secondary education educator
Vernier, Richard foreign language educator, author

Everett
King, Indle Gifford industrial designer, educator
Nelson, Gary county councilman, engineer
†Nesse, Mark A. library director
†Smith, John R. electronics executive
Toyer, Richard Henry accountant
†Wambolt, Ronald Ralph electronics company executive
†Winn, George Michael electrical equipment company executive

Fairchild AFB
†Davies, Donald Thomas hospital administrator, military officer

Federal Way
Boling, Joseph Edward numismatist, retired military officer
Curtis, Arnold Bennett lumber company executive
Hayek, Carolyn Jean retired judge
McNeese, Jack Marvin communications executive
Scott, Otto writer

Fort Lewis
Davis, Harley Cleo career officer
†Marsh, Caryl Glenn career officer

Freeland
Freehill, Maurice F. retired educational psychology educator

Friday Harbor
Blinks, John Rogers physiology and biophysics educator
Daum, David Ernest machinery manufacturing company executive
Geyman, John Payne physician, educator
Leeming, Frank, Jr. newspaper editor, publisher
MacGinitie, Walter Harold psychologist
McCreary, Dustin Campbell lawyer, arbitrator
Palmer, Norman Dunbar political scientist, educator, author
†Waite, Ric cinematographer
Willows, Arthur Owen Dennis neurobiologist, zoology educator

Gig Harbor
Canter, Ralph Raymond psychology educator, research director
Grouse, Jan Ellen physician
Huyler, Jean Wiley media and interpersonal communications consultant, hypnotherapist
Ramsey, Jerry Virgil radio broadcaster, educator, financial planner
Robinson, James William retired management consultant

Greenbank
Grant, Robert Yearington former government official
Tuell, Jack Marvin retired bishop

Hansville
Griffin, DeWitt James architect, real estate developer

Issaquah
Barchet, Stephen physician, former naval officer
Benveniste, Jacob retired physicist
Mix, Terry Platt banker
Pearson, Belinda Kemp economist, consultant
Tenenbaum, Michael steel company executive
Wainwright, Paul Edward Blech construction company executive

Kalama
Liang, Jason Chia research chemist

Kenmore
Pihl, James Melvin electrical engineer

Kennewick
Cobb, William Thompson environmental consultant
Knight, Janet Ann elementary education educator
Stevens, Henry August insurance agent, educator
Wistisen, Martin J. agricultural business executive

Kent
Goo, Abraham Meu Sen retired aircraft company executive
Hebeler, Henry Koester retired aerospace and electronics executive
Johnson, Dennis D. elementary school principal
Kelly, Patrick school system administrator
Pierce, Danny Parcel artist, educator
Soden, Ruth M. geriatrics nurse, educator
Sourapas, Steve James manufacturing executive

Kingston
Pichal, Henri Thomas electronics engineer, physicist, consultant

Kirkland
Alberg, Tom Austin communications executive, lawyer
Allen, Chuck football team executive
Ayars, Albert Lee retired school superintendent
Barto, Deborah Ann physician
Bernard, James William chemical distribution company executive
†Brotman, Jeffrey H. variety stores executive
†Craves, Robert Edward marketing professional
Dorkin, Frederic Eugene lawyer
Erickson, Dennis professional football coach, former university football coach
Flores, Thomas R. professional football team executive
Forsen, Harold Kay retired engineering executive
Gregory, Matthew James architectural firm executive
Kennedy, Cortez professional football player
Kirk, Judd real estate development executive
McCaw, Craig O. communications executive
McDonald, Joseph Lee insurance broker
Parrish, John Brett manufacturing executive
†Pugmire, Robert wholesale distribution executive
Rosett, Ann Doyle librarian
Sinegal, James D. variety store wholesale business executive
Wenk, Edward, Jr. civil engineer, policy analyst, educator

La Center
Holley, Lawrence Alvin retired labor union official

La Conner
Knopf, Kenyon Alfred economist, educator
Robbins, Tom author

Lacey
Cosand, Joseph Parker, Jr. education educator emeritus
Spangler, David Robert college administrator, engineer

Lake Stevens
Quigley, Kevin Walsh state legislator, lawyer

Langley
Bitts, Todd Michael sales and marketing consultant
Legters, Lyman Howard historian
Medlock, Ann non-profit organization executive, writer, speaker

Liberty Lake
DeMerritt, Ted C. microprocessor company executive

Longview
Kenagy, John Warner surgeon
Petersen, Michael Jon utility company executive
Wollenberg, Richard Peter paper manufacturing company executive

Lummi Island
Ewing, Benjamin Baugh environmental engineering educator, consultant

Lynnwood
Bear, Gregory Dale writer, illustrator
Benzel, Brian L. superintendent
Jenes, Theodore George, Jr. retired military officer
Lind, Gregory Alan nurse

Manchester
Fearon, Lee Charles chemist

Marrowstone Island
Klein, Lynn E. artist

Marysville
Johnson, Rob Carl insurance agent
Philpott, Larry La Fayette horn player

Mazama
Hogness, John Rusten physician, academic administrator

Medina
Schlotterbeck, Walter Albert manufacturing company executive, lawyer

Mercer Island
Bowne, Martha Hoke magazine editor, consultant
Bridgforth, Robert Moore, Jr. aerospace engineer
Coe, Robert Campbell surgeon
Elgee, Neil Johnson physician
Gould, Alvin R. international business executive
Greenwood, Wilbur Rowe, III small business owner
Haviland, James West physician
Schaumberg, William Lloyd retired banker
Spitzer, Jack J. banker
Steinhardt, Henry photographer
Vining, Glen W., Jr. insurance company executive

Mill Creek
Corbally, John Edward foundation director

Moses Lake
Leadbetter, Mark Renton, Jr. orthopaedic surgeon

Mount Vernon
Cammock, Earl E. surgeon
Hall, David Ramsay architect
Klein, Henry architect

Mountlake Terrace
Lockwood, Donald A. retired insurance company executive

Nespelem
†Palmanteer, Eddie Adrian, Jr. tribal government administrator

Nondland
Pollack, Joseph diversified company executive

Oak Harbor
Piercy, Gordon Clayton bank executive

Olympia
Alfers, Gerald Junior bank executive, retired
Belcher, Jennifer Marion state legislator, management consultant
Billings, Judith A. state education official
Blake, Ann Beth psychologist
Brachtenbach, Robert F. state supreme court justice
Cothern, Barbara Shick real estate investor, state legislator
Dolliver, James Morgan state supreme court justice
Durham, Barbara state supreme court justice
Flemming, Stanley Lalit Kumar family practice physician, state legislator
†Gardner, Booth governor
Gose, Karen Kamara state arts administrator
Gregoire, Christine O. state attorney general
Guy, Richard P. state supreme court justice
Haseltine, James Lewis artist, consultant
Haugen, Mary Margaret state legislator
Johnson, Charles William state supreme court justice
Johnson, Linda Sue state agency health administrator, former state legislator
Kessler, Lynn Elizabeth state legislator
Kohl, Jeanne Elizabeth state senator, sociologist, educator
Lind, Carl Bradley retired museum director
Long, Jeanine Hundley state legislator
Lowry, Mike governor, former congressman
Manning, Farley investment company executive
Merchant, Judith Miriam state agency administrator
Munro, Ralph Davies state government official
Mylroie, Willa Wilcox transportation engineer, regional planner
Nesbit, Robert Carrington historian
Newhouse, Irving Ralph state legislator
Norwood, Deborah Anne law librarian
O'Brien, Robert S. state official
Ogden, Valeria Juan management consultant, state representative
Pritchard, Joel state lieutenant governor
Reilly, Robert Joseph counselor
Smith, Charles Z. state supreme court justice
Smith, Linda A. congresswoman, former state legislator
Spanel, Harriet Rosa Albertsen state senator
Steiger, Gretchen Helene marine mammalogist, research biologist
Thomas, Brian Chester state legislator, engineer
Utter, Robert French state supreme court justice
Wang, Arthur C. lawyer, educator
Wojahn, R. Lorraine state legislator
Yenson, Evelyn P. lottery official
Zussy, Nancy Louise librarian

Orcas
Greever, John retired mathematics educator

Pasco
Yoshino, George food products executive

Port Angeles
Chase, John David university dean, physician
Hart, Edwin James chemist
Kilmer, Joseph Charles secondary school educator
Muller, Willard C(hester) writer
Osborne, Richard Hazelet anthropology and medical genetics educator
Ross, Robert King retired educator

Port Ludlow
Gullander, Werner Paul retired consultant, retired corporate executive
Ward, Louis Emmerson retired physician

Port Townsend
Buhler, Jill Lorie editor, writer
Harrington, LaMar curator, museum director
Warren, Patricia J. museum director

Poulsbo
Pasco, Duane Noble artist

Prosser
Miller, David Eugene soil scientist, researcher
Proebsting, Edward Louis, Jr. retired research horticulturist

Pullman
Barnes, Charles D. neuroscientist, educator
Bennett, Edward Moore historian, educator
Bertramson, B. Rodney agronomist
Bird, Robert Kenton journalist, educator
Blakeslee, Leroy Lawrence agricultural economist
Bustad, Leo Kenneth veterinary educator, college administrator
Catton, William Robert, Jr. sociology educator
Crosby, Glenn Arthur chemistry educator
Dillman, Donald Andrew sociologist, educator
Dodgen, Harold Warren chemistry and physics educator
Fowles, George Richard physicist, educator
Funk, William Henry environmental engineering educator
George, Thomas Frederick chemistry educator
Gustafsson, Borje Karl veterinarian, educator
Henson, James Bond veterinary pathologist
Hildebrandt, Darlene Myers information scientist
Hirth, John Price metallurgical engineering educator
Hosick, Howard Lawrence cell biology educator, academic administrator
Kallaher, Michael Joseph mathematics educator
Kapteyn, Henry Cornelius physics educator
Lewis, Norman G. academic administrator, researcher, consultant
Lutz, Julie Haynes astronomy and mathematics educator
McFadden, Bruce Alden biochemistry educator
McSweeney, Frances Kaye psychology educator
Murnane, Margaret Mary physics educator
Nakata, Herbert Minoru retired microbiology educator, academic administrator
Pomeranz, Yeshajahu research chemist, technologist
Randall, Linda Lea biochemist, educator
Roberts, Elizabeth Porcher library director
Ryan, Clarence Augustine, Jr. biochemistry educator
Savage, Sally P. lawyer
Sheldon, Charles Harvey political science educator
Smith, Robert Victor university administrator
Smith, Samuel Howard university president, plant pathologist
Stock, David Earl mechanical engineering educator
Warner, Dennis Allan psychology educator
Watkinson, Patricia Grieve museum director
Wilson, Robert Burton veterinary and medical educator
Young, Francis Allan psychologist

Puyallup
†Lurie, Hugh James psychiatrist, educator
Veatch, John William speech pathologist

Redmond
Beeson, Paul Bruce physician
Bingham, Robert Frederick communication company executive
†Butynski, Donald electric power industry executive
Darnell, Larry plant manager
Erxleben, William Charles lawyer, data processing executive
Gates, William Henry, III software company executive
Herres, Phillip Benjamin computer software executive
Martin, Richard Otto medical device company executive
Mollman, John Peter book publisher, consultant electronic publishing
Nagel, Daryl David retail executive
Narodick, Sally G. corporate executive
Pacholski, Richard Francis retired securities company executive, financial advisor, consultant
Rossano, August Thomas environmental engineering educator
Sargent, Murray, III physicist, educator, software engineer
Sasenick, Joseph Anthony health care company executive
Sennstrom, John Harold manufacturing company executive

†Walsh, Patrick J. medical products executive
Welke, Elton Grinnell, Jr. publisher, writer

Renton

Tajon, Encarnacion Fontecha (Connie Tajon) retired educator, association executive

Republic

Sauer, Norman Gardiner judge, attorney

Richland

Albaugh, Fred William nuclear engineer, retired research and development executive
Bair, William J. radiation biologist
Barr, Carlos Harvey lawyer
Beck, Joe Eugene environmental health scientist, educator
Bush, Spencer Harrison metallurgist
Campbell, Milton Hugh chemist
Cochran, James Alan mathematics educator
Colson, Steven Douglas research director, chemistry educator
Counsil, William Glenn electric utility executive
Elderkin, Charles Edwin meteorologist
Evans, Ersel Arthur engineering consulting executive
Jacobsen, Gerald Bernhardt biochemist
Johnson, Arnold Gordon clergyman
McDowell, Robin Scott physical chemist
Moore, Emmett Burris, Jr. physical chemist
Nolan, John Edward retired electrical corporation executive
Pippo, Steve educator
Pond, Daniel James industrial technology administrator
Rebagay, Teofila Velasco chemist, chemical engineer
Ryans, Yvonne principal
Traister, Robert Edwin naval officer, engineer
Wehner, Alfred Peter inhalation toxicologist, biomedical scientist
Wiley, William Rodney microbiologist, administrator
Zirkle, Lewis Greer physician, executive

Ritzville

Schoesler, Mark Gerald state legislator, farmer

Seattle

Aagaard, George Nelson medical educator
Abbott, Robert Dean education educator
Abelson, Herbert Traub pediatrician, educator
Ackerley, Barry professional basketball team executive, communications company executive
Adams, Hazard Simeon English educator, author
Albrecht, Richard Raymond airplane manufacturing company executive, lawyer
Aldrich, Robert Anderson physician
Alexander, Edward Russell disease research administrator
Alkire, John D. lawyer
Allen, Joanna Cowan lawyer
Allison, John Robert lawyer
Alps, Glen Earl printmaker, educator
Andersen, Niels Hjorth chemistry educator, biophysics researcher, consultant
Anderson, Arthur G., Jr. chemistry educator
Anderson, Peter MacArthur lawyer
Anderson, Richard Powell thoracic surgeon, educator
Anderson, Rick Gary newspaper columnist
Anderson, Ross columnist
Andrew, Lucius Archibald David, III bank executive
Andrews, J. David lawyer
Andrews, Richard Otis museum director
Ansell, Julian S. physician, urology educator
Aoki, John H. hotel chain executive
Armstrong, Charles G. professional baseball executive, lawyer
Aron, William marine biology administrator
Arons, Arnold Boris physicist, educator
Averill, Lloyd James, Jr. religion educator
Babb, Albert Leslie biomedical engineer, educator
Bain, William James, Jr. architect
Baker, Bruce Frederick health services association administrator
†Baker, Helen T. pediatrician, educator
Bangsund, Edward Lee aerospace company executive
Banks, James Albert educational research director, educator
Barash, David Philip psychology and zoology educator
Bargreen, Melinda Lueth music critic
Barnard, Kathryn Elaine nursing educator, researcher
Barry, Christopher John lawyer
Bassett, Edward Powers university official
Bassetti, Fred Forde architect
Bassingthwaighte, James Bucklin physiologist, educator, medical researcher
Baum, William Alvin astronomer, educator
Bayley, Christopher T. international investment banking executive
Beetham, Stanley Williams international management consultant
Beezer, Robert Renaut federal judge
Behler, Diana Ipsen Germanic language and literature educator
Behler, Ernst Heitmar comparative literature educator
Behnke, Carl Gilbert beverage franchise executive
Beighle, Douglas Paul business executive
Bell, Jeffrey Donald bank executive
Bengtson, Betty Grimes library administrator
Benirschke, Stephen Kurt orthopaedic surgeon
Bensussen, Estelle Esther writer, illustrator, artist
Berger, Paul Eric artist, photographer
Bernard, Eddie Nolan oceanographer
Bevan, Donald Edward retired marine science educator, university dean
Beyers, William Bjorn geography educator
Bierman, Charles Warren physician, educator
Bierman, Edwin Lawrence physician, educator
Bird, Thomas D. neurologist
Birmingham, Richard Joseph lawyer
Black, W. L. Rivers, III lawyer
Blagg, Christopher Robin nephrologist
Blake, Robert Wallace aeronautical engineer, consultant
Blandau, Richard Julius physician, educator
†Blase, Nancy Gross librarian
†Blethen, Frank A. newspaper publisher
Blethen, William Kingsley, Jr. newspaper publishing executive
Bliss, Lawrence Carroll botany educator
Blom, Daniel Charles lawyer, investor
Blumenfeld, Charles Raban lawyer
Boardman, David newspaper editor
Boaz, Doniella Chaves psychotherapist, consultant
Boba, Imre history educator
Bodansky, David physicist, educator
Boeder, Thomas L. lawyer
Boersma, P. Dee ecology educator
Bohm, Karl-Heinz Hermann astrophysicist, educator
Boman, Marc Allen lawyer
Bonica, John Joseph anesthesiologist, educator
Borden, Weston Thatcher chemistry educator
Borgatta, Edgar F. social psychologist, educator
Bornstein, Paul physician, biochemist
Boruchowitz, Bob lawyer
Bosmajian, Haig Aram speech communication educator
Bosworth, Thomas Lawrence architect, educator
Bounds, Christopher E. food service executive
Bourque, Philip John business economist, educator
Bowden, Douglas McHose neuropsychiatric scientist, educator, research center administrator
Bowen, Jewell Ray academic dean, chemical engineering educator
Boyko, Edward John internist, medical researcher
Boylan, Merle Nelson librarian
Brady, Viola Catt lawyer, psychologist
Brammer, Lawrence Martin psychology educator
Brandauer, Frederick Paul Asian language educator
Breslow, Norman Edward biostatistics educator, researcher
Brier, Evelyn Caroline retired investment company executive, business consultant
Brockenbrough, Edwin Chamberlayne surgeon
Bronsdon, Melinda Ann microbiologist
Brooke, Francis John, III foundation administrator
Brothers, Lynda Lee lawyer
Brown, Frederick Calvin physicist, educator
Brown, Kristi principal
Brown, Lowell Severt physicist, educator
Brown, Robert Alan atmospheric science educator, research scientist
Brownlee, Donald Eugene, II astronomer, educator
Buck, Robert Follette banker, lawyer
Buckner, Philip Franklin newspaper publisher
Burgess, Charles Orville history educator
Burkhart, William Henry lawyer
Burrows, Elizabeth MacDonald religious organization executive, educator
Butler, Timothy Harold lawyer
Butow, Robert Joseph Charles history educator
Buursma, William F. architect
Bystrom, Arne architect
Cameron, Mindy newspaper editor
Campbell, Robert Hedgcock investment banker
Cannon, James W. insurance company executive
Carlsen, James Caldwell musicologist, educator
Carlson, Dale Arvid university dean
Carlson, Stanley Andrew lawyer
Caro, Ivor dermatologist
Castanes, James Christopher architect
Cavanaugh, Michael Everett lawyer
Celentano, Francis Michael artist, art educator
Cella, John J. freight company executive
Char, Patricia Helen lawyer
Charlson, Robert Jay atmospheric sciences educator, scientist
Chihuly, Dale Patrick artist
Chirot, Daniel sociology and international studies educator
Chisholm, Margaret Elizabeth retired library education administrator
Christian, Gary Dale chemistry educator
Christiansen, Walter Henry aeronautics educator
Chu, Tony Yeling business executive, financial consultant
Cichanski, Gerald golf course architect
Claflin, Arthur Cary lawyer
†Clark, Edward Alan immunologist, microbiologist, educator
Clark, Kenneth Courtright retired physics and geophysics educator
Clark, Robert Newhall electrical and aeronautical engineering educator
Clarkson, Lawrence William airplane company executive
Cleland, Robert Erksine plant physiologist, educator
Cline, Robert Stanley air freight company executive
Clinton, Gordon Stanley lawyer
Clinton, Richard M. lawyer
Coburn, Robert Craig philosopher
Cochran, Wendell science editor
Cockburn, John F. retired banker
Coffman, Sandra Jeanne psychologist
Coldewey, John Christopher English literature educator
Coleman, Dennis G. conductor
Collett, Robert Lee financial company executive
Collins, Theodore John lawyer
Condit, Philip Murray aerospace executive, engineer
Cook, Victor physics educator, researcher
Corker, Charles Edward retired lawyer, educator
Corr, Kelly lawyer
Cosway, Richard legal educator
Coughenour, John Clare federal judge
Couser, William Griffith medical educator, academic administrator, nephrologist
Cox, Frederick Moreland retired university dean, social worker
Coyle, Marie Bridget microbiology educator, laboratory director
Cramer, John Gleason, Jr. physics educator, experimental physicist
Creager, Joe Scott geology and oceanography educator
Criminale, William Oliver, Jr. applied mathematics educator
Cross, Harry Maybury retired law educator, consultant
†Crum, Lawrence A. physicist, research educator
Cullen, James Douglas banker, finance company executive
Culp, Gordon Louis consulting engineer
Culp, Mildred Louise corporate executive
Curtis, James Austin actuary consultant
Dahl, Lance Christopher lawyer
Dale, David C. physician, medical educator
Dalton, Thomas George paralegal, social worker, legal consultant
Danelo, Peter Anthony lawyer
Dash, J. Gregory physicist, educator
Davis, Earl James chemical engineering educator
Davis, John MacDougall lawyer
Dawson, Patricia Lucille surgeon
Day, Alexandra (Sandra L. Woodward Darling) illustrator, designer
Day, Robert Winsor research administrator
De Alessi, Ross Alan lighting designer
DeBon, George A. security services company executive
Debro, Julius university dean, sociology educator
Dederer, Michael Eugene public relations company executive
Dehmelt, Hans Georg physicist
del Moral, Roger botany educator, ecologist, wetland consultant
Denniston, Martha Kent business owner, author
Denny, Brewster Castberg retired university dean
Derham, Richard Andrew lawyer
Dermanis, Paul Raymond architect
de Tornyay, Rheba nurse, university dean emeritus, educator
DeVore, Paul Cameron lawyer
Dickinson, Calhoun lawyer
Dietrich, William Alan reporter
Dillard, Marilyn Dianne property manager
Dimmick, Carolyn Reaber federal judge
Donaldson, James Adrian otolaryngology educator
Donaldson, Lauren R. fisheries biology and radiobiology educator emeritus
Dorpat, Theodore Lorenz psychoanalyst
Dubes, Michael J. insurance company executive
Duncan, Elizabeth Charlotte marriage and family therapist, educator
Dunn, Richard John English language educator
Dunne, Thomas geology educator
Dunnell, Robert Chester archaeologist, educator
Du Pen, Everett George sculptor, educator
Durham, Robert Lewis architect
Duryee, David Anthony management consultant
Dworkin, Samuel Franklin dentist, psychologist
Dwyer, William L. federal judge
Edmondson, W(allace) Thomas limnologist, educator
Edwards, John Stuart zoology educator, researcher
Ellegood, Donald Russell publishing executive
Elliott, Jeanne Marie Koreltz transportation executive
Ellis, James Reed lawyer
Ellis, Janice Rider nursing educator, consultant
Ellis, John W. professional baseball team executive, utility company executive
Ellis, Stephen D. physics educator
Ellison, Herbert Jay history educator
Engel, Thomas chemistry educator
Etcheson, Warren Wade business administration educator
Evans, Bernard William geologist, educator
Evans, Charles Albert microbiology educator
Evans, Daniel Jackson former senator, environmental consultant
Evans, Ellis Dale psychologist, educator
Evans, Trevor Heiser advertising executive
Even, Jan newspaper editor
Fancher, Michael Reilly newspaper editor, newspaper publishing executive
Farris, Jerome federal judge
Faulstich, James R. bank executive
Favorite, Felix oceanographer
Fetters, Norman Craig, II banker
Fialkow, Philip Jack academic administrator, medical educator
Fiedler, Fred Edward organizational psychology educator, consultant
Figley, Melvin Morgan radiologist, physician, educator
Finlayson, Bruce Alan chemical engineering educator
Fischer, Edmond Henri biochemistry educator
Fitzpatrick, Thomas Mark lawyer
Fix, Wilbur James department store executive
Fleagle, Robert Guthrie meteorologist, educator
Fletcher, Betty B. federal judge
Floss, Heinz G. chemistry educator, scientist
Forbes, David Craig musician
Fortson, Edward Norval physics educator
Fox, Kenneth shipbuilder, naval engineer, water transit consultant
Freed, Aaron David architect
Freeman, Antoinette Rosefeldt lawyer
Freeny, Patrick Clinton radiology educator, consultant
Funk, Robert Norris college president, lawyer
Gallagher, Marian Gould librarian, educator
Gardner, Jill Christopher neuroscientist, educator
†Gardner Karton, Ann Elizabeth visual artist
Garlid, Kermit Leroy engineering educator
†Gates, Sarah Nash costume designer, educator
Gates, William H. lawyer
Geballe, Ronald physicist, university dean
Gerberding, William Passavant university president
Gerhart, James Basil physics educator
Gerrodette, Charles Everett real estate company executive, consultant
Gerstenberger, Donna Lorine humanities educator
Gessel, Stanley Paul emeritus soil science educator
Gibaldi, Milo university dean
Giblett, Eloise Rosalie hematology educator
Gilbert, Paul H. engineering executive, consultant
Giles, Robert Edward, Jr. lawyer
Ginorio, Angela Beatriz research administrator, educator
Gittinger, D. Wayne lawyer
Givan, Boyd Eugene aircraft company executive
Glover, Karen E. lawyer
Godden, Jean W. columnist
Goeltz, Thomas A. lawyer
Goodell, Brian Wayne oncologist, medical educator
Goodlad, John Inkster education educator, author
Gorans, Gerald Elmer accountant
Gordon, Milton Paul biochemist, educator
Gordon, Patrick A. architectural firm executive
Gore, William Jay political science educator
Gouldthorpe, Kenneth Alfred Percival publisher, state official
Gouterman, Martin Paul chemistry educator
Graham, C(lyde) Benjamin, Jr. physician
Graham, Stephen Michael lawyer
Gray, Marvin Lee, Jr. lawyer
Grayston, J. Thomas medical and public health educator
Green, G. Dorsey psychologist, author
Green, Joshua, III banker
Greenan, Thomas J. lawyer
Greene, John Burkland lawyer
Gregory, Norman Wayne chemistry educator, researcher
Grenfell, Thomas Cameron geophysicist, educator
Griffey, Ken, Jr. (George Kenneth Griffey, Jr.) professional baseball player
Groman, Neal Benjamin microbiology educator
Gross, Edward retired sociologist, educator, lawyer
Grossman, Robert James architect
Guntheroth, Warren Gaden physician
Guralnick, Michael J. medical research administrator
Guy, Arthur William electrical engineering educator, researcher
Gwinn, Mary Ann newspaper reporter
Hackett, John Peter dermatologist
†Hackman, Robert Cordell pathology educator, researcher
Haggard, Joel Edward lawyer
Hague, Jane Frances county official
Hakomori, Sen-itiroh immunochemist, biochemist, researcher, educator
Hall, Benjamin Downs genetics and botany educator
Halpern, Isaac physicist, educator
Halver, John Emil nutritional biochemist
Haman, Raymond William lawyer
Hamilton, Gary Glen sociology educator
Hansen, Wayne W. lawyer
Hanson, Kermit Osmond business administration educator, university dean emeritus
Haralick, Robert Martin electrical engineering educator
Harder, Virgil Eugene business administration educator
Hargiss, James Leonard ophthalmologist
Harmon, Daniel Patrick classics educator
†Harris, Robert Myer engineer
Harrison, Don Edmunds oceanographer, educator
Hartl, John George film critic
Hartmann, Dennis Lee atmospheric science educator
†Hartwell, Leland Harrison geneticist, educator
Hastings, L(ois) Jane architect, educator
Hausam, Neal Allen civil engineer, real estate developer
Hauschka, Stephen Denison developmental biologist, educator
Haxton, Wick Christopher theoretical physicist, educator
Hazelton, Penny Ann law librarian, educator
Heath, George Ross oceanographer, university dean
Heer, Nicholas Lawson Arabist-Islamist educator
Hellmann, Donald Charles political science educator
Hellström, Ingegerd business executive
Helms, Luther Sherman, III bank executive
Henderson, Dan Fenno lawyer, retired law educator
Henderson, Maureen McGrath medical educator
Henkel, Cathy newspaper sports editor
Henley, Ernest Mark physics educator, university dean emeritus
Herring, Susan Weller anatomist
Hertzberg, Abraham aeronautical engineering educator, university research scientist
Hewitt, Edwin mathematician, educator
Hiatt, Peter library educator
Higgins, Nancy McCready lawyer, director
Hille, Bertil physiology educator
Hills, Regina J. journalist
Hilpert, Edward Theodore, Jr. lawyer
Hinshaw, Mark Larson architect, urban planner
Hirschman, Charles, Jr. sociologist, educator
Hodge, Paul William astronomer, educator
Hodson, William Alan pediatrician
Hoerni, Jean Amédée electronics consultant
Hoffman, Allan Sachs chemical engineer, educator
Hofmann, Douglas Allan lawyer
†Holbrook, Karen Ann biology educator and researcher, dean
Holtby, Kenneth Fraser aircraft manufacturing company consultant
Hood, Leroy Edward molecular biologist, educator
†Hopkins, Paul Brink chemistry educator
Hornbein, Thomas Frederic anesthesiologist
Horton, Elliott Argue, Jr. lawyer, business consultant
Houck, John Candee research facility administrator, biochemist
Houk, Benjamin Noah ballet dancer
Hudson, Leonard Dean physician
Hunkins, Francis Peter education educator
Hunt, Earl Busby psychologist
Huston, John Charles law educator
Hutcheson, Mark Andrew lawyer
Hutchinson, William Burke surgeon, research center director
Ingalls, Robert Lynn physicist, educator
Inlow, Edgar Burke political science educator
Isaki, Lucy Power Slyngstad lawyer
Ishimaru, Akira electrical engineering educator
Israel, Allen D. lawyer
Jacobson, Phillip Lee architect, educator
Jaeger, David Arnold aerospace company executive
Jameson, Henry C. lawyer
Jans, James Patrick mathematics educator
Jenkins, Speight opera company executive, writer
Jenkins, William Maxwell banker
Jennerich, Edward John university official and dean
Johnson, Bruce Edward Humble lawyer
Johnson, Randall David (Randy Johnson) professional baseball player
†Johnson, Raymond A. apparel executive
Johnson, Wayne Eaton writer, editor, former drama critic
Johnston, Norman John architecture educator
Jonassen, James O. architect
Jones, Edward Louis historian, educator
Jones, Frank Ray biotechnology company executive, researcher
Jones, Grant Richard landscape architect, planner
Jones, Johnpaul architect
Jonsen, Albert R. medical ethics educator
Joppa, Robert Glenn aeronautics educator
Judson, C(harles) James (Jim Judson) lawyer
Kalina, Robert Edward physician, educator
†Kalnasy, Glenn Bothwell investment company executive
Kane, Alan Henry lawyer
Kane, Charles A. college chancellor
Kane, Christopher lawyer
Kaplan, Barry Martin lawyer
Kapur, Kailash Chander industrial engineering educator
Kareken, Francis A. lawyer
Karl, George professional basketball coach
Karr, James Richard ecologist, researcher, educator
Katsaros, Kristina Barbro atmospheric sciences educator
Keith, Donald Malcolm physician
Kelbaugh, Douglas Stewart architect, urban designer, architecture educator
Kellogg, Kenyon P. lawyer
Kelly, Carolyn Sue newspaper executive
Kemp, Shawn T. professional basketball player
†Kendrick, William Marvin school system administrator
Kennedy, David Michael environmental scientist
Kenney, Richard Laurence poet, English language educator
Kevorkian, Jirair applied mathematics, aeronautics and astronautics educator
Keyt, David philosophy and classics educator
Killeen, Michael John lawyer
Killinger, Kerry Kent bank executive
Kippenhan, Charles Jacob mechanical engineer, retired educator
Kirby, William Murray Maurice medical educator
Kirkendall, Richard Stewart historian, educator

Klebanoff, Seymour Joseph *medical educator*
Klee, Victor La Rue *mathematician, educator*
Knechtges, David Richard *Chinese and East Asian studies educator*
†Knutson, Elliot Knut *savings and loan association executive*
Kobayashi, Albert Satoshi *mechanical engineering educator*
Koehler, Reginald Stafford, III *lawyer*
Koelsch, M. Oliver *federal judge*
Kohn, Alan J. *zoology educator*
Kolb, Keith Robert *architect, educator*
Korg, Jacob *English literature educator*
Korthuis, Kathleen E. *dean*
Kraft, George Howard *physician, educator*
†Kranda, Michael Louis *biotechnology company executive*
Krebs, Edwin Gerhard *biochemistry educator*
Krohn, Kenneth Albert *radiology educator*
Kruckeberg, Arthur Rice *botanist, educator*
Kuhrau, Edward W. *lawyer*
Kummert, Richard Osborne *lawyer, educator*
Kuvshinoff, Bertha Horne *painter, sculptor*
Kuvshinoff, Nicolai Vasily *painter, sculptor*
Kwiram, Alvin L. *physical chemistry educator, university official*
Lacitis, Erik *journalist*
Ladd, James Roger *international business consultant*
Laird, Charles David *zoology and genetics educator, researcher*
Lang, Kurt *sociologist, educator, writer*
LaPoe, Wayne Gilpin *retired business executive*
Lardy, Nicholas Richard *economics educator*
Lauritzen, Peter Owen *electrical engineering educator*
LaVeck, Gerald DeLoss *physician, educator*
Lawrence, Jacob *artist, educator*
†Ledbetter, Jeffrey A. *immunologist*
Lee, John Marshall *mathematics educator*
Leitzell, Terry Lee *lawyer*
Leland, David D. *timber company executive*
Lemly, Thomas Adger *lawyer*
Leopold, Estella Bergere *botany and environmental studies educator*
Lingafelter, Edward Clay, Jr. *chemistry educator*
Loeser, John David *neurosurgeon, educator*
†Logsdon, John *engineering consulting company executive*
Loh, Wallace D. *university dean*
Lombard, David Norman *lawyer*
†Longbrake, William Arthur *bank executive*
Loper, Robert Bruce *theater director, educator*
Lord, Jere Johns *retired physics educator*
Lovett, Wendell Harper *architect*
Lubatti, Henry Joseph *physicist, educator*
MacDonald, Andrew Stephen *management consulting firm executive*
MacKenzie, Peter Sean *writer, publications designer*
Mackey, Sally Schear *retired religious organization administrator*
MacLachlan, Douglas Lee *marketing educator*
Mah, Feng-hwa *economics educator*
Malcolm, Garold Dean *architect*
Mallory, V(irgil) Standish *geologist, educator*
Mandeville, Gilbert Harrison *consulting engineering executive*
Margon, Bruce Henry *astrophysicist, educator*
Marriott, David M. *public relations executive*
Marshall, Scott *advertising agency executive*
Martin, George Coleman *aeronautical engineer*
Martin, Joan Callaham *psychologist, educator*
Martinez, Edgar *professional baseball player*
Mason, James Tate *surgeon*
Matchett, William H(enry) *English literature educator*
Matheson, Kent D. *school system administrator*
Matthews, Donald Rowe *political scientist, educator*
Mauer, Michael Leonard *banker*
Maulding, Barry Clifford *lawyer*
Maurer, Barbara Glee *educational administrator*
McAleer, William Harrison *software company financial executive*
McAteer, James Francis *lawyer*
McCann, Richard Eugene *lawyer*
McConnell, Calvin Dale *clergyman*
Mc Donald, James Michael, Jr. *research institute consultant*
Mc Feron, Dean Earl *mechanical engineer*
McGough, Peter Myles *physician*
Mc Govern, Walter T. *federal judge*
†McHugh, Heather *poet*
McKay, John *lawyer*
McKay, Michael Dennis *lawyer*
McKeown, Mary Margaret *lawyer*
McKey, Thomas J. *lawyer*
McKinnon, James Buckner *real estate sales executive, writer, researcher*
McMillan, John A. *retail executive*
McNeely, Mark Hall *advertising executive*
McReynolds, Neil Lawrence *consultant*
Meditch, James Stephen *electrical engineering educator*
Meeuse, Bastiaan Jacob Dirk *biologist, educator, researcher*
Merendino, K. Alvin *surgical educator*
Merrill, Ronald Thomas *geophysicist, educator*
Meyer, C. Richard *architect*
Michael, Ernest Arthur *mathematics educator*
Michalik, John James *law school administrator*
Mickelwait, Lowell Pitzer *lawyer*
Miles, Don Clifford *architect*
Miles, Edward Lancelot *marine studies educator, consultant, director*
†Moberly, David Lindsey *foundation executive*
Moch, Robert Gaston *lawyer*
Monsen, Elaine Ranker *nutritionist, educator, editor*
Moore, Benjamin *theatrical producer*
Moore, Daniel Charles *physician*
Moore, James R. *lawyer*
Moore, Malcolm Arthur *lawyer*
Moore, Mary Ann *health care administrator*
Morrill, Richard Leland *geographer, educator*
Morse, John Moore *architect, planner*
Mottet, Norman Karle *pathologist, educator*
Motulsky, Arno Gunther *geneticist, physician, educator*
Moudon, Anne Vernez *urban design educator*
Mueller, Gerhard G(ottlob) *accounting educator*
Muilenburg, Robert Henry *hospital administrator*
Mullin, J(ack) Shan *lawyer*
Murphy, Thomas Joseph *archbishop*
Murray, Connel Lyle *advertising and public relations executive, consultant*
Murray, James Dickson *mathematical biology educator*
Mussehl, Robert Clarence *lawyer*
Nakatani, Roy Eiji *biologist, educator*
Nalder, Eric Christopher *investigative reporter*
Narver, John Colin *business administration educator*
Nash, Cynthia Jeanne *journalist*
Nellermoe, Leslie C. *lawyer*
Nelson, Charles Rowe *economist, educator*
Nelson, James Alonzo *radiologist, educator*
Nelson, Marshall J. *lawyer*
Nelson, Wendel Lane *medicinal chemist, educator*
Nester, Eugene William *microbiology educator*
Newmeyer, Frederick Jaret *linguist, educator*
Niemi, Janice *lawyer, former state legislator*
Nijenhuis, Albert *mathematician, educator*
Ning, Xue-Han (Hsueh-Han Ning) *physiologist, researcher*
Nishitani, Martha *dancer*
Noe, James Alva *judge*
Noe, Jerre Donald *computer science educator*
Noll, Jonathan Boyd *lawyer*
Nordstrom, Bruce A. *department store executive*
†Nordstrom, James F. *department store executive*
Nordstrom, John N. *department store executive*
†Nostrand, Howard Lee *language and literature educator*
Nudelman, Phillip M. *insurance company executive*
Odegaard, Charles Edwin *history educator*
O'Donnell, Wilson Edward *museum director*
Oehler, Richard William *lawyer*
Ojemann, George A. *neurosurgeon, medical association executive*
O'Leary, Thomas Howard *resources executive*
†Olmstead, Marjorie Ann *physics educator*
Olsen, Harold Fremont *lawyer*
Olson, David John *political science educator*
Olson, James William Park *architect*
Olstad, Roger Gale *science educator*
O'Malley, Robert Edmund, Jr. *mathematics educator*
Orians, Gordon Howell *biology educator*
Ostrom, Carol Marie *reporter*
Page, Roy Christopher *periodontist, educator*
Paine, Robert Treat *zoology educator*
Palm, Gerald Albert *lawyer*
Parker, Omar Sigmund, Jr. *lawyer*
Parks, Patricia Jean *lawyer*
Parks, Richard William *economics educator, consultant*
Parsons, A. Peter *lawyer*
Paul, Thomas Frank *lawyer*
Pawula, Kenneth John *artist, educator*
Payne, Ancil Horace *retired broadcasting executive*
Peden, Irene Carswell *electrical engineer, educator*
Perey, Ron *lawyer*
Perkin, Gordon Wesley *international health agency executive*
Perrin, Edward Burton *health services researcher, biostatistician, public health educator*
Petersdorf, Robert George *medical educator, retired association executive*
Peterson, Jane White *nursing educator, anthropologist*
Petrie, Gregory Steven *lawyer*
Phillips, Josef Clayton *insurance and investment company executive*
Pigott, George Morris *food engineering educator, consulting engineer*
Piniella, Louis Victor *professional baseball team manager*
Pinkerton, Guy Calvin *savings and loan executive*
Pitts, Barbara Towle *accountant*
Piven, Peter Anthony *architect, management consultant*
Plotnick, Robert David *academic administrator, economic consultant*
Pocker, Yeshayau *chemistry, biochemistry educator*
Polk, William Merrill *architect*
Pollack, Gerald Harvey *bioengineering educator*
Pollack, Sylvia Byrne *educator, researcher, counselor*
Polonis, Douglas Hugh *engineering educator*
Porte, Daniel, Jr. *physician, educator, health facility administrator*
Porter, Stephen Cummings *geologist, educator*
Porter, Walter Thomas, Jr. *bank executive*
Potter, Karl Harrington *philosophy educator*
Powell, George Van Tuyl *lawyer*
Pratt, David Terry *mechanical engineering educator, combustion researcher*
Prentke, Richard Ottesen *lawyer*
Pressly, Thomas James *history educator*
Prins, David *speech pathologist, educator*
Privat, Jeannette Mary *bank librarian*
Prosterman, Roy L. *law educator, development specialist*
Ptacek, William H. *library director*
Pusch, William Gerard *lawyer*
Pyke, Ronald *mathematics educator*
Pyle, Kenneth Birger *historian, educator*
Pym, Bruce Michael *lawyer*
Quimby, George Irving *anthropologist, former museum director*
Rabinovitch, Benton Seymour *chemist, educator emeritus*
Raible, Peter Spilman *minister*
Raisbeck, James David *aircraft design executive*
Ramanathan, Kavasseri Vaidianatha *accounting educator, researcher, consultant*
Ratner, Buddy Dennis *bioengineer, educator*
Ravenholt, Reimert Thorolf *epidemiologist*
Read, Charles Raymond, Sr. *business executive*
Redman, Eric *lawyer*
Reed, Richard John *retired meteorology educator*
Reed, William G., Jr. *paper company executive*
Reinhardt, William Parker *chemical physicist, educator*
Rhines, Peter Broomell *oceanographer, atmospheric scientist*
Rice, Norman B. *mayor*
Riddiford, Lynn Moorhead *zoologist, educator*
Rieke, Paul Victor *lawyer*
Rinearson, Peter Mark *journalist, author, software developer*
†Ritt, David Lawrence *symphony musician*
Ritter, Daniel Benjamin *lawyer*
Robb, Bruce *former insurance company executive*
Robb, John Wesley *religion educator*
Rockey, Jay *public relations company executive*
Ross, Austin *health care executive*
Ross, Russell *pathologist, educator*
Rothstein, Barbara Jacobs *federal judge*
†Rubbert, Paul Edward *engineering executive*
Ruddy, James W. *lawyer*
Runstad, Judith Manville *lawyer*
Rupp, John Norris *lawyer*
Russell, David Allison *aeronautical engineering educator*
Russell, Francia *ballet director, educator*
†Rutter, Deborah Frances *orchestra administrator*
Sanders, James Joseph *architect*
Sandler, Michael David *lawyer*
Sarason, Irwin G. *psychology educator*
Sateren, Terry *theater technical production*
Saunders, William Lockwood *financial consultant*
Saxberg, Borje Osvald *management educator*
Schafer, James Henry *newspaper company executive*
Schall, Lawrence Delano *economics educator, consultant*
Schaller, Joanne Frances *nursing consultant*
Scheidel, Thomas Maynard *speech communication educator*
Schellenberg, Gerard David *geneticist, researcher*
Schilling, John Albert *surgeon*
Schmidt, Peter Gustav *shipbuilding industry executive*
Schoenfeld, Walter Edwin *manufacturing company executive*
Schomaker, Verner *chemist, educator*
Scott, John Carlyle *gynecologist, oncologist*
Scribner, Belding Hibbard *medical educator, nephrologist*
Segal, Jack *mathematics educator*
†Sheng, Bright *composer, pianist, conductor*
Shepard, Thomas Hill *physician, educator*
Sherman, John Clinton *geography educator*
Shinbo, Robert *landscape architect*
Shrontz, Frank Anderson *airplane manufacturing executive*
Shulkin, Jerome *lawyer*
Silver, Michael *school superintendent*
Simcox, Craig Dennis *aeronautical engineer*
Simkin, Peter Anthony *physician, educator*
Singer, Sarah Beth *poet*
Sizemore, Herman Mason, Jr. *newspaper executive*
Skilling, John Bower *structural and civil engineer*
Sleicher, Charles Albert *chemical engineer*
Small, Robert E. *architect, architecture educator*
Smith, Andrew Vaughn *telephone company executive*
Smith, Donald William *airport manager*
Smith, Jeffrey L. (The Frugal Gourmet) *cook, writer*
Smith, Moncrieff Hynson *psychology educator*
Smith, Orville Auverne *physiology educator*
Smith, Payton *lawyer*
Smulyan, Jeffrey *radio station executive, owner pro baseball team*
Soltys, John Joseph, Jr. *lawyer*
Sontgerath, Mary *school system administrator*
Spafford, Michael Charles *artist*
Spindel, Robert Charles *electrical engineering educator*
Spinrad, Bernard Israel *physicist, educator*
Spitzer, Hugh D. *lawyer*
Springer, Floyd Ladean *architect*
Squires, William Randolph, III *lawyer*
Staley, James Trotter *microbiology educator*
Stanton, Michael John *newspaper editor*
Staryk, Steven S. *violinist, concertmaster, educator*
Stear, Edwin Byron *corporate executive*
Steele, Frank Channel *sales executive*
Steinberg, Jack *lawyer*
Steiner, Robert Alan *neuroendocrinologist, educator*
Stenchever, Morton Albert *physician, educator*
Stern, Edward Abraham *physics educator*
Stevens, Clyde Benjamin, Jr. *property manager, retired naval officer*
Stewart, Robert Andrew *lawyer*
Stowell, Kent *ballet director*
Strand, Ray Walter *general contractor*
Strandjord, Paul Edphil *physician, educator*
Strandness, Donald Eugene, Jr. *surgeon*
†Stroup, Elizabeth Faye *librarian*
Stuiver, Minze *geological sciences educator*
Su, Judy Ya Hwa Lin *pharmacologist*
Sugar, Peter Frigyes *historian*
Sullivan, Daniel J. *artistic director*
Sullivan, William James *university president*
Sundberg, Richard *architectural firm executive*
Sutter, Joseph F. *aeronautical engineer, consultant, retired aircraft company executive*
Swanson, August George *physician, retired association executive*
Swanson, Donald Alan *geologist*
Swanson, Phillip Dean *neurologist*
Sweeney, David Brian *lawyer*
Szkody, Paula *astronomy educator, researcher*
Tallman, Richard C. *lawyer*
†Talvi, Ilkka Ilari *violinist*
Teller, Davida Young *psychology, physiology and biophysics educator*
Tenney, William Frank *pediatrician*
Terrell, W(illiam) Glenn *university president emeritus*
†Thiel, Arthur Warren *journalist*
Thomas, David Phillip *forestry educator, college administrator*
Thomas, Edward Donnall *physician, researcher*
Thompson, Arlene Rita *nursing educator*
Thornton, Dean Dickson *retired airplane company executive*
Thornton, Judith Ann *economist*
Thorson, Lee A. *lawyer*
Thouless, David James *physicist, educator*
†Tomlinson, Robert John *lawyer, energy executive*
Tovar, Carole L. *real estate management administrator*
Tracy, Mary E. *principal*
†Treadway, James *hotel chain executive*
Treiger, Irwin Louis *lawyer*
Trump, Eddie *holding company executive*
Trump, Julius *holding company executive*
Trzyna, Thomas Nicholas *college dean*
Tucker, Gary Jay *physician, educator*
Tukey, Harold Bradford, Jr. *horticulture educator*
Turner, Wallace L. *reporter*
Turnovsky, Stephen John *economics educator*
van den Berghe, Pierre Louis *sociologist, anthropologist*
Van Hoosier, Gerald Leonard *veterinary science educator*
Van Orden, Phyllis Jeanne *librarian, educator*
Vecci, Raymond Joseph *airline executive*
Venkata, Subrahmanyam Saraswati *electrical engineering educator, electri energy and power researcher*
Vesper, Karl Hampton *business and mechanical engineering educator*
Voorhees, John Lloyd *columnist*
Voorhees, Lee R., Jr. *lawyer*
Wagner, Patricia H. *lawyer*
Wagoner, David Everett *lawyer*
Wagoner, David Russell *author, educator*
†Walker, Douglas *computer developement company executive*
Wall, William E. *lawyer, former utility executive*
Wallace, John Michael *meteorology educator*
Wallerstein, George *astronomy educator*
Wallis, Richard James *lawyer*
Warner, Vincent W. *bishop*
Washington, James Winston, Jr. *artist, sculptor*
Weaver, Lois Jean *physician, educator*
Webb, Eugene *English language educator*
Weinberg, John Lee *federal judge*
Weissman, Eugene Yehuda *chemical engineer*
Weitkamp, William George *retired nuclear physicist*
Wellner, Jon August *statistician, educator*
Wells, Christopher Brian *lawyer*
Wells, Judee Ann *lawyer*
West, Richard Vincent *art museum official*
Whalen, Jerome Demaris *lawyer*
Whalen, Michael P. *architect*
Wheaton, Harry James *corporate executive*
†Whitacre, John *apparel executive*
Whitford, Joseph P. *lawyer*
Whitty, Raymond John *hotel company executive*
Wiborg, James Hooker *chemicals distribution company executive*
Widener, Peri Ann *business development executive*
Wilets, Lawrence *physics educator*
Williams, J. Vernon *lawyer*
Williams, John A. (Jack Williams) *newspaper publishing executive*
Williams, Robert Walter *physics educator*
Williams, Walter Baker *mortgage banker*
Williamson, Don *newspaper columnist*
Wilske, Kenneth Ray *internist, rheumatologist, researcher*
Wilson, David Eugene *magistrate judge*
Witham, Barry Bates *drama educator*
Wolfle, Dael Lee *public affairs educator*
Wood, Stuart Kee *retired engineering manager*
Woodruff, Gene Lowry *nuclear engineer, university dean*
Wooster, Warren S(criver) *marine science educator*
Wott, John Arthur *arboretum and botanical garden executive, horticulture educator*
Wright, Eugene Allen *federal judge*
Wright, Willard Jurey *lawyer*
Yantis, Phillip Alexander *audiologist, educator*
Yarington, Charles Thomas, Jr. *surgeon, administrator*
Young, Jeffry John *psychologist, gerontologist, educator, statistician*
Yue, Agnes Kau-Wah *otolaryngologist*
Ziadeh, Farhat J. *Middle Eastern studies educator*
Zilly, Thomas Samuel *federal judge*
Zunker, Richard E. *insurance company executive*

Sequim
Barton, Jay *university administrator, biologist*
Beaton, Roy Howard *retired nuclear industry executive*
Hansey, Renee Jeanne *retired communications executive*
†McMahon, Terrence John *foreign service officer*
Meacham, Charles Harding *government official*
Ramsey, William Ray *association executive*

Shelton
Wolbrink, Donald Henry *landscape architect, city planner*

Silverdale
Walske, M(ax) Carl, Jr. *physicist*

Spanaway
Campbell, Thomas J. *legislator, chiropractor*
Westbrook, T. L. *bishop*

Spokane
Agnew, Thomas Edward *communications executive*
Aponté, Christopher Bennedettey *artistic director, choreographer, educator*
Bakker, Cornelis B. *psychiatrist, educator*
Bender, Betty Wion *librarian*
Benson, Allen B. *chemist, educator, consultant*
Bolstad, D. D. *federal agency administrator*
Burr, Robert Lyndon *library director*
Butler, Mary Latour *health facility administrator*
†Carriker, Robert Charles *history educator*
Coughlin, Bernard John *university president*
Cowles, William Stacey *publisher*
Davis, Scott Livingston *merchant banker, lawyer*
Dellwo, Dennis A. *state legislator*
Eliassen, Jon Eric *utility company executive*
Evoy, John Joseph *psychology educator*
Foley, Thomas Stephen *lawyer, former speaker House of Representatives*
Foster, Ruth Mary *dental association administrator*
Fowler, Betty Janmae *dance company director, editor*
Gibson, Melvin Roy *pharmacognosy educator*
Giller, Edward Bonfoy *retired government official, retired air force officer*
Gray, Alfred Orren *journalism educator, research and communications consultant*
Green, Dale Monte *retired judge*
Grub, Phillip Donald *business educator*
Harvey, J. R. *utilities company executive*
Hendershot, Carol Miller *physical therapist*
Herbison, John (Steve) *wholesale and retail company executive*
Herdrich, Norman Wesley *magazine editor*
Hester, Gerald LeRoy *retired school system administrator*
Imbrogno, Cynthia *judge*
Jordania, Vakhtang *conductor, educator*
Jurdana, Ernest J. *banker, accountant*
†Kafentzis, John Charles *journalist, educator*
Keller, Robert M. *bishop*
Kirschbaum, James Louis *real estate company administrator*
Klobucher, John Marcellus *federal judge*
Koegen, Roy Jerome *lawyer*
Kossel, Clifford George *retired philosophy educator, clergyman*
Kunkel, Richard Lester *public radio executive*
Lamp, John Ernest *lawyer*
Leahy, Gerald Philip *hospital administrator*
Lindsay, Donald Parker *former savings bank executive*
Matters, Clyde Burns *former college president*
McClellan, David Lawrence *physician*
†McManus, Patrick Francis *educator, writer*
McWilliams, Edwin Joseph *banker*
†Mechetti, Fabio *orchestra conductor*
Mielke, Clarence Harold, Jr. *hematologist*
Millard, James Michael *oral surgeon*
Moe, Orville Leroy *racetrack executive*
Moyer, John Arthur *obstetrician/gynecologist, state senator*
Nicolai, Eugene Ralph *public relations consultant, editor, writer*
Nielsen, William Fremming *federal judge*
Novak, Terry Lee *public adminstration educator*
Nyman, Carl John, Jr. *university dean and official*
Odegard, Richard Erwin *banker*
Polley, Harvey Lee *retired missionary and educator*
Quackenbush, Justin Lowe *chief federal judge*

Redmond, Paul Anthony *utility executive*
Robinson, Herbert Henry, III *educator, therapist*
Robinson, William P. *academic administrator, consultant, speaker*
Rowe, Marjorie Douglas *retired social services administrator*
†Schlicke, Carl Paul *retired surgeon*
Skylstad, William S. *bishop*
†Spencer, John M. *safety engineer*
Storey, Francis Harold *business consultant, retired bank executive*
Terry, Frank Jeffrey *bishop*
Van Sickle, Frederick L. *federal judge*
Wirt, Michael James *library director*
Woodard, Alva Abe *business consultant*
Yamayee, Zia Ahmad *engineering educator, dean*

Suquamish
†George, Lyle Emerson *civil service manager*

Tacoma
Alger, David Townley *religious organization director*
Anderson, Arthur Roland *engineering company executive, civil engineer*
Barna, Lillian Carattini *school system administrator*
†Belluschi, Peter Guido *retired wood products executive*
Bourgaize, Robert G. *economist*
Brevik, J. Albert *communications consultant*
†Browning, Christopher R. *historian, educator*
Bryan, Robert J. *federal judge*
Carlson, Frederick Paul *electronics executive*
Champ, Stanley Gordon *scientific company executive*
Chen, Stephen Shau-tsi *psychiatrist, physiologist*
Crisman, Mary Frances Borden *librarian*
Edington, Robert Van *university official*
Ferris, James Leonard *paper company executive*
Foley, Thomas Michael *financial executive*
Garner, Carlene Ann *orchestra administrator*
Gordon, Joseph Harold *lawyer*
Graves, Ray *lawyer*
Graybill, David Wesley *chamber of commerce executive*
Gregory, Arthur Stanley *retired chemist*
Habedank, Gary L. *brokerage house executive*
Hansen, Edward Allen *music educator, organist*
Harris, James Martin *architect*
Hawks, Katherine Anna *special education educator*
Hill, Steven Richard *business executive*
Holman, Kermit Layton *chemical engineer*
Hutchings, George Henry *food company executive*
Jasinek, Gary Donald *newspaper executive*
Johnson, Charles Robert *television news anchor, reporter*
Jungkuntz, Richard Paul *university provost emeritus*
Kaltinick, Paul R. *trust company executive*
King, Gundar Julian *retired university dean*
Lane, Robert Casey *lawyer*
Liddle, Alan Curtis *architect*
Maynard, Steven Harry *writer*
Meyer, Richard Schlomer *food company executive*
Miller, Judson Frederick *lawyer, former military officer*
Minnerly, Robert Ward *headmaster*
Odlin, Richard Bingham *retired banker*
Olson, David Mark *college dean, physical education educator*
Otten, Thomas *zoological park director*
Owen, Thomas Walker *banker, broker*
Philip, William Warren *banker*
Pierce, Susan Resneck *academic administrator, English educator*
Purnell, Carolyn Jean *lawyer*
Rieke, William Oliver *foundation director, medical educator, former university president*
Rodin, Michael F. *lawyer, corporate*
Rudolph, Wallace Morton *legal educator*
Russell, James Sargent *retired naval officer*
Schuyler, Robert Len *investment company executive*
Smith, Leo Gilbert *hospital administrator*
Steele, Anita Martin (Margaret Anne Martin) *law librarian, legal educator*
Stockdale, Ronald Allen *grocery company executive*
Sutherland, Douglass B. *tent and awning company executive, mayor*
Thompson, Ronald Edward *lawyer*
Tullis, David Allen *municipal official, safety consultant*
Walker, Sally Warden *state legislator*
Wallerich, Peter Kenneth *banker*
Watkins, Sally Marie *nursing administrator*
Wiegman, Eugene William *minister, former college administrator*
Wilson, Joan Emily *nursing education administrator*
Wold, David C. *bishop*

Taholah
Knutzen, Raymond Edward *federal official*

Toppenish
†Ross, Kathleen Anne *college president*

Vancouver
Campbell, Scott *newspaper publishing company executive*
Chartier, Vernon Lee *electrical engineer*
Ferguson, Larry Emmett *educational administrator*
Firstenburg, Edward William *banker*
Kleweno, Gilbert H. *lawyer*
Larson, Charles Lester *television writer, producer, author*
Mangino, Kristin Mikalson *secondary education educator*
†Matlock, John Hudson *science administrator, materials engineer*
Ogden, Daniel Miller, Jr. *government official, educator*
†Patella, Lawrence M. *city official*
Perlstein, Abraham Phillip *psychiatrist*

Vashon
Biggs, Barry Hugh *lawyer*
Munson, Dee Taylor Allison *food marketing executive*

Walla Walla
Corfield, Timothy Lynn *college rodeo executive, educator*
Cronin, Thomas Edward *academic administrator*
Edwards, Glenn Thomas *history educator*
Hayner, Herman Henry *lawyer*
Hayner, Jeannette Clare *state legislator*
Passmore, Michael Forrest *environmental administrator*
Perry, Louis Barnes *retired insurance company executive*
Stevens, David *economics educator*
Yaple, Henry Mack *library director*

Washougal
Schorzman, Clarice B. *principal*
Vogel, Ronald Bruce *food products executive*

Wellpinit
†Wynne, Bruce *tribal administrator, artist*

Wenatchee
†Elfving, Don C. *horticulturist, administrator*
Schrader, Lawrence Edwin *plant physiologist, educator*
†Williams, Keith Roy *museum director*

Yakima
Baker, Herbert Geoffrey *career officer*
Bruenn, Ronald Sherman *financial company executive*
Dorsett, Judith A. *elementary education educator*
George, Francis *bishop*
Grandy, Jay Franklin *fruit processing executive*
Hovis, James Brunton *federal judge*
McDonald, Alan Angus *federal judge*
Meshke, George Lewis *drama and humanities educator*
Robbins, Gary Samuel *airport manager*
Suko, Lonny Ray *lawyer*
Wright, J(ames) Lawrence *lawyer*

WEST VIRGINIA

Athens
Marsh, Joseph Franklin, Jr. *emeritus college president, educational consultant*

Barboursville
Lucas, Carol McCann *vocational education educator*

Beckley
Baligar, Virupax C. *research soil scientist*
Hallanan, Elizabeth V. *federal judge*
Voigt, Paul Warren *research geneticist*

Bethany
Cooey, William Randolph *economics educator*
Cummins, Delmer Duane *academic administrator, historian*
Sandercox, Robert Allen *college official, clergyman*

Bluefield
Blaydes, James Elliott *ophthalmologist*
Faber, David Alan *federal judge*

Bradley
Chesley, Eddie A. *librarian, educator*

Bridgeport
Timms, Leonard Joseph, Jr. *gas company executive*

Bunker Hill
Palmer, Barbara Louise Moulden *elementary education educator*

Charles Town
Layva, David *lawyer*
McDonald, Angus Wheeler *farmer*

Charleston
†Anderson, Leonard Troy *columnist*
†Arrington, Carolyn Ruth *school system administrator*
Atkinson, Robert Poland *bishop*
Basham, Debra Ann *archivist*
Bennett, Robert Menzies *retired gas pipeline company executive*
Brotherton, Ann Caskey *financial advisor*
Brotherton, William T., Jr. *state supreme court justice*
Brown, Bonnie Louise *state legislator*
Brown, James Knight *lawyer*
Burns, Thomas C. *communication company executive*
Caperton, W. Gaston *governor*
†Chilton, Elizabeth Early *newspaper executive*
Coe, Pam *educational researcher*
Conlin, Thomas (Byrd) *conductor*
Conway, Richard Ashley *environmental engineer*
Copenhaver, John Thomas, Jr. *federal judge*
Davis, James Hornor, III *lawyer*
Drennen, William Miller, Jr. *cultural administrator, film executive, producer, director, mineral resource executive*
†Eidell, Terry Lee *education research laboratory executive*
Freeman, Thomas G., II *lawyer*
Gage, Charles Quincey *lawyer*
Glazer, Frederic Jay *librarian*
Goodwin, Claude Elbert *lawyer, former gas utility executive*
Goodwin, Phillip Hugh *hospital administrator*
Grant, Richard Lee *utility company executive*
Greenfield, David Joel *editor*
Grimes, Richard Stuart *editor, writer*
Gunnoe, Nancy Lavenia *food executive, artist*
Haden, Charles H., II *federal judge*
Hall, Kenneth Keller *federal judge*
Haught, James Albert, Jr. *journalist, newspaper editor*
Hechler, Ken *state official, former congressman, political science educator, author*
Heck, Albert Frank *neurologist*
†Keith, Steven Jeffrey *newspaper editor*
Kettering, Glen Lee *utilities executive, lawyer*
Kizer, John Oscar *lawyer*
Knapp, Dennis Raymond *federal judge*
Koleske, Joseph Victor *chemical engineer, consultant*
Lawson, Robert William, Jr. *retired lawyer*
†Lilly, Peter Byron *coal company executive*
Lipton, Allen David *retail executive*
Marockie, Henry R. *state school system administrator*
Marsh, Don Seagle *retired newspaper editor*
McClaugherty, John Lewis *lawyer*
Mc Gee, John Frampton *communications company executive*
Mc Graw, Darrell Vivian, Jr. *attorney general*
McHugh, Thomas Edward *state supreme court justice*
Michael, M. Blane *federal judge*
Moore, Ruth Johnston *medical center official*
Murchison, David Roderick *lawyer*
Neely, Richard *lawyer*
†Peck, Harry *public relations executive*
†Perry, A. Michael *banker*
†Richardson, Sally Keadle *state health care administrator*
†Robinson, R. Larry *gas industry executive*
†Rogers, John Alfrod *lawyer*
†Ryan, Charles Edward *public relations executive, advertising executive*
Scott, Olof Henderson, Jr. *priest*
Seiber, William Joseph *financial and insurance consultant*
Slack, John Mark, III *lawyer*
Snyder, Giles D. H. *lawyer*
Southworth, Louis Sweetland, II *lawyer*
Stacy, Charles Brecknock *lawyer*
†Tomblin, Earl Ray *state official*
Velianoff, George D. *nursing administrator*
Wehrle, Henry Bernard, Jr. *diversified manufacturing company executive*
Wehrle, Martha Gaines *state legistator*
Welch, Edwin Hugh *academic administrator*
Whittington, Bernard Wiley *electrical engineer, consultant*
Workman, Margaret Lee *state supreme court justice*
Yoder, John Christian *state senator, lawyer, insurance company executive*

Clarksburg
Highland, Cecil Blaine, Jr. *newspaper publisher, lawyer, banker*
Keeley, Irene Patricia Murphy *federal judge*
Kidd, William Matthew *federal judge*
Kittle, Robert Earl *school system administrator*
Ona-Sarino, Milagros Felix *physician, pathologist*

Clay
Dawson, James G. *superintendent*
Gillespie, Larry *secondary school principal*

Dellslow
Allamong, Betty D. *academic administrator*

Dunbar
Russell, James Alvin, Jr. *college administrator*

Elkins
MacConkey, Dorothy I. *academic administrator*
Maxwell, Robert Earl *federal judge*
Payne, Gloria Marquette *business eductor*
Spears, Jae *state legislator*
Van Gundy, James Justin *biology educator*

Fairmont
Black, L. Alexander *bishop*
Dillman, Robert John *academic administrator*
Hardway, Wendell Gary *former college president*
Shan, Robert Kuocheng *biology educator*
Stalder, Florence Lucille *secondary education educator*
Swiger, Elizabeth Davis *chemistry educator*

Glenville
Tubesing, Richard Lee *library director*

Grafton
Harman, Charlton Newton (Bud Harman) *state senator, retired*
Poling, Kermit William *minister*

Greenville
Warner, Kenneth Wilson, Jr. *editor, association publications executive*

Harpers Ferry
Carter, Powell Frederick *retired naval officer*
Nash, Bradley DeLamater *transportation executive*
White, Thomas Edward *government park official*

Hedgesville
O'Keefe, Robert James *retired banker*

Hillsboro
Pierce, William Luther *association executive, writer*

Huntington
Barenklau, Keith Edward *safety services company executive*
Bowdler, Anthony John *physician, educator*
Cocke, William Marvin, Jr. *plastic surgeon, educator*
Davis, Donald Eugene *real estate management executive*
deBarbadillo, John Joseph *metallurgist, management executive*
Edwards, Roy Alvin *physician, psychiatrist, educator*
Esposito, Albert Charles *ophthalmologist, state legislator*
Gould, Alan Brant *academic administrator*
Hayes, Robert Bruce *former college president, educator*
Hooper, James William *educator*
Hubbard, John Lewis *chemist, educator, researcher*
Jenkins, John E., Jr. *lawyer, educator*
Kent, Calvin Albert *university administrator*
Mason, Bert E. *podiatrist*
McKernan, John Joseph *English language educator*
Mufson, Maurice Albert *physician, educator*
Polan, Nancy Moore *artist*
†Reynolds, Marshall T. *bank executive, holding company executive, investor*
Ritchie, Garry Harlan *television broadcast executive*
St. Clair, James William *lawyer*
Underwood, Cecil H. *company executive, past governor of West Virginia*

Institute
Brown, Dallas Coverdale, Jr. *history educator, retired army officer*
DasSarma, Basudeb *chemistry educator*
Scott, John Edward *librarian*
Thorn, Arline Roush *English language educator*
Wohl, David *humanities educator, theatre director*

Kearneysville
†Biggs, Alan Richard *plant pathologist, educator*

Kingwood
DeBastiani, Larue Annette *health facility director*

Lahmansville
Snyder, Robert Martin *agriculture consultant, retired government official*

Lewisburg
Cardis, Thomas Michael *chemist*
Ford, Richard Edmond *lawyer*
Seifer, Judith Huffman *sex therapist, educator*
Sprouse, James Marshall *federal judge*
Willard, Ralph Lawrence *surgery educator, physician, former college president*

Martinsburg
Malin, Howard Gerald *podiatrist*
Rice, Lacy I., Jr. *lawyer*
Yoe, Harry Warner *retired agricultural economist*

Mineral Wells
Prather, Denzil Lewis *petroleum engineer*

Morgantown
Adler, Lawrence *mining engineering consultant*
Albrink, Margaret Joralemon *medical educator*
Barba, Roberta Ashburn *social worker*
Beattie, Diana Scott *biochemistry educator*
Biddington, William Robert *university administrator, dental educator*
Blaydes, Sophia Boyatzies *English language educator*
Brooks, Dana D. *dean*
Bucklew, Neil S. *university president*
Butcher, Donald Franklin *statistics educator, computer scientist*
Chen, Ping-fan *geologist*
Colasanti, Brenda Karen *pharmacoloy and toxicology educator*
Collier, Clifford Warthen, Jr. *retired landscape architect*
Colyer, Dale Keith *agricultural economics educator*
Dadyburjor, Dady B. *chemical engineering educator, researcher*
Davis, Leonard McCutchan *speech educator*
De Vore, Paul Warren *technology educator*
Fisher, John Welton, II *law educator, magistrate judge, university official*
Fleming, William Wright, Jr. *pharmacology educator*
Fodor, Gábor Béla *chemistry educator, researcher*
Fusco, Andrew G. *lawyer*
Gagliano, Frank Joseph *playwright*
Hedge, George Albert *physiologist*
Holtan, Boyd DeVere *mathematics educator*
Jackson, Ruth Moore *academic administrator*
Keller, Edward Clarence, Jr. *foundation executive, ecologist, statistician, geneticist, educator*
Kent, James A. *consulting chemical engineer, author, consultant*
Klein, Ronald Lloyd *electrical engineer, educator*
LaBelle, Thomas Jeffrey *academic administrator*
Maxwell, Robert Haworth *agriculture educator, college dean*
McAvoy, Rogers *educational psychology educator, consultant*
Meitzen, Manfred Otto *religious studies educator*
Morris, William Otis, Jr. *lawyer, educator, author*
Nath, Joginder *genetics and biology educator, researcher*
Ong, Tong-man *microbiologist, educator*
Peterson, Sophia *international studies educator*
Pyles, Rodney Allen *archivist, county official*
Reese, Hayne Waring *psychologist*
Schroder, John L., Jr. *retired mining engineer*
†Seehra, Mohindar Singh *physics educator*
Singer, Armand Edwards *foreign language educator*
Smith, Patricia K. *reading educator*
Smith, Robert Leo *ecologist, wildlife biologist*
Snyder, Irvin Stanley *microbiologist, educator*
Stewart, Guy Harry *university dean emeritus, journalism educator*
Vest, Marvin Lewis *mathematical educator*
Warden, Herbert Edgar *surgeon, educator*
Weinstein, George William *ophthalmology educator*
Westfall, Bernard G. *university hospital executive*
†Wilt, Jeffrey Lynn *pulmonary and critical care physician*

Nitro
Lucas, Panola *elementary educator*
Magaw, Roger Wayne *construction company executive*

Parkersburg
Brum, Brenda *state legislator, librarian*
Cochran, Douglas Eugene *building products company executive*
Fahlgren, H(erbert) Smoot *advertising agency executive*
Wakley, James Turner *manufacturing company executive*
Whitsett, Kingsley P. *school administrator*

Philippi
Shearer, Richard Eugene *industrial consultant*

Poca
Ghareeb, Sami Mitri *dentist*

Powellton
†Lopez, Thomas Joseph *naval officer*

Ravenswood
Meyers, Gerald A. *metal products executive*

Salem
Ohl, Ronald Edward *academic administrator*
Raad, Virginia *pianist, lecturer*

Shenandoah Junction
Prince, Garnett B., Jr. *business executive*

Shepherdstown
Elliott, Jean Ann *library administrator*
Riccards, Michael Patrick *academic administrator*
Wilson, Miriam Janet Williams *publishing executive*

Sistersville
Wright, John Charles Young *oil and gas company executive*

Slanesville
McKee, Rae Ellen *special education educator*

Squire
Dishman, Roberta Crockett *retired educator*

Summersville
Yeager, Charles William *lawyer, newspaper publisher*

Triadelphia
Hudak, Thomas F(rancis) *finance company executive*

Weirton
Elish, Herbert *manufacturing company executive*

Wellsburg
Price, Verla Blanche *elementary education educator*

West Liberty
Campbell, Clyde Del *academic administrator*
Hunter, John Alfred *English educator*

Westover
Trythall, Harry Gilbert *music educator, composer*

Wheeling
Chbosky, Fred G. *steel company executive*
Exley, Ben, III *pharmaceutical company executive*
†Forkin, Sister Jean Louise (Sister) *healthcare administrator*
Good, Laurance Frederic *company executive*
Griffith, Mabel Maxine *education administrator*
Heceta, Estherbelle Aguilar *anesthesiologist*
Hudacek, George C. *tax specialist*
Hughes, Mary Elizabeth *interior designer*
Kirkpatrick, Forrest Hunter *management consultant*
Minear, Judith *school system administrator*
Nutting, George Ogden *newspaper publisher*
Phillips, John Davisson *retired lawyer*
Phillis, Marilyn Hughey *artist*
Ritz, Lorraine Isaacs *nursing administrator*
Robbins, William David *retired police officer*
Schmitt, Bernard W. *bishop*
Wagner, Robert Owen *association executive*
Wareham, James Lyman *steel company executive*

White Sulphur Springs
Sparrow, William Holliday *corporate financial executive*

WISCONSIN

Altoona
James, Henry Thomas *former foundation executive, educator*

Amery
Mickelson, Arnold Rust *consultant, religious denominational official*

Antigo
Tousey, LouAnn Holly *nurse administrator*

Appleton
Barlow, F(rank) John *mechanical contracting company executive*
Boldt, Oscar Charles *construction company executive*
Buchanan, Robert Campbell *corporate professional*
Chaney, William Albert *historian, educator*
Froehlich, Harold Vernon *judge, former congressman*
Goldgar, Bertrand Alvin *literary historian, educator*
Gunderson, Richard L. *insurance company executive*
Herder, Robert H. *bishop*
McManus, John Francis *association executive, writer*
Platten, Peter Michael, III *bank holding company executive*
Rankin, Arthur David *paper company executive*
†Scheig, Henry Frederick *fraternal insurance society executive*
Schumaker, Dale H. *paper manufacturing company executive*
†Spanbauer, James *chemicals executive*
Warch, Richard *university president*
†Wirth, Lawrence *chemicals executive*

Arcadia
†Wanek, Ronald G. *manufacturing executive*

Ashland
Parsonage, Robert Rue *college president*

Balsam Lake
Bergstrand, Laura Joyce *elementary education educator*

Baraboo
Brooks, Edward *dairy products company executive*
†Hartmann, Forrest D. *conservationist*
Storhoff, Donald C. *agricultural products company executive*

Beaver Dam
Butterbrodt, John Ervin *real estate executive*

Beloit
Davis, Harry Rex *political science educator*
Ferrall, Victor Eugene, Jr. *college administrator, lawyer*
Gates, Crawford Marion *conductor, composer*
Simon, Michael Alexander *photographer, educator*
Sovey, William Pierre *manufacturing company executive*

Brookfield
Corby, Francis Michael, Jr. *manufacturing company executive*
Curfman, Floyd Edwin *engineering educator*
DeLuca, Donald Paul *manufacturing company executive*
Diesem, John Lawrence *information systems executive*
Grade, Jeffery T. *manufacturing company executive*
†Grove, Richard Charles *power tool company executive*
†Haase, Bronson J. *communications company executive*
Hanson, Leila Fraser *sales and marketing executive*
Hardman, Harold Francis *pharmacology educator*
Jenkins, William Atwell *university chancellor*
Lessiter, Frank Donald *magazine editor*
McKay, John A. *mining equipment manufacturing executive*
Nelson, William George, IV *software company executive*
Payne, Howard James *insurance company executive*
†Roder, Ronald Ernest *accountant*
Schwanz, H(erman) Lee *publishing company executive*
†Smith, James R. *diversified financial services company executive*
Snyder, C(laude) Robert *insurance company executive*
†Stenicka, Charles Edward, III *professional association executive*
Welnetz, David Charles *human resources executive*
Zander, Gaillienne Glashow *psychologist*

Cable
†MacCarty, Collin S. *neurosurgeon*

Cedarburg
Clark, Harry Wilber *administrator*
Eley, Lynn W. *political science educator, former mayor*
Schaefer, Gordon Emory *food company executive*
Steffens, Donna Irene *gifted and talented education educator*

Chippewa Falls
Ewald, Robert Hansen *computer company executive*
Sazama, Thomas John *circuit judge*

Columbus
Callahan, Carroll Bernard *lawyer*

Cross Plains
Rodenschmit, Helen Juliana *elementary education educator*

Cudahy
Naimoli, Raymond Anthony *infosystems specialist, financial consultant*

De Pere
Manion, Thomas A. *college president*
†Parish, Fred *engineering company executive, architectural firm executive*

DeForest
Miller, Paul Dean *breeding company executive, geneticist*

Delavan
Donnelly, James Charles *manufacturing company executive*

Dodgeville
Comer, Gary C. *apparel company executive*

Eau Claire
Berney, Joseph Henry *appliance manufacturing company executive*
Davidson, John Kenneth, Sr. *sociologist, educator, researcher, author, consultant*
Dick, Raymond Dale *psychology educator*
Dunlap, William Phillip *dean*
Larson, Brian Foix *architect*
Marquardt, Steve Robert *library director*
†Menard, John R. *lumber company executive*
Patterson, Donald Lee *music educator*
Richards, Jerry Lee *academic administrator, religious educator*
Schenk, Quentin Frederick *retired social work educator, mayor*
Schnack, Larry Gene *university chancellor*
Shaw, Bonita Lynn *school administrator*
Thompson, Glenn Judean *library science educator*
Wantland, William Charles *bishop, lawyer*
Weil, D(onald) Wallace *business administration educator*
Zien, David Allen *state legislator*

Elkhorn
Dunn, Walter Scott, Jr. *writer, former museum director, consultant*
Reinke, Doris Marie *retired elementary education educator*

Ellison Bay
MacKinney, Arthur Clinton, Jr. *retired university official, psychologist*

Elm Grove
Gorske, Robert Herman *retired lawyer*
Halvorsen, Morrie Edward *association executive*
Headlee, Raymond *psychoanalyst, educator*

Fish Creek
Abegg, Martin Gerald *retired university president*

Fond Du Lac
Chamberlain, Robert Glenn *retired tool manfacturing executive*
Henken, Willard John *retired university dean*
Lambert, Eugene Kent *oncologist, hematologist*
Stevens, William Louis *bishop*
Treffert, Darold Allen *psychiatrist, author, hospital director*

Fort Atkinson
Albaugh, John Charles *hospital executive*
Knox, William David *publishing company executive*
Meyer, Eugene Carlton *retired editor*
Nesbitt, Arthur Wallace *mail order and manufacturing executive*
Sager, Donald Jack *publisher, former librarian*

Frederic
Rudell, Milton Wesley *aerospace engineer*

Glendale
Gefke, Henry Jerome *lawyer*
Moeser, Elliott *principal*

Grafton
Eber, Lorenz *civil engineer, inventor*

Green Bay
Backer, David F. *packing company executive*
Banks, Robert J. *bishop*
Bush, Robert G. *food service executive*
Daley, Arthur James *retired magazine publisher*
De Meuse, Donald Howard *paper products manufacturing executive*
Favre, Brett Lorenzo *professional football player*
Finesilver, Alan George *rheumatologist*
Gariepy, Corinne *elementary school principal*
Green, Mark Andrew *state legislator, lawyer*
Harlan, Robert Ernest *professional football team executive*
Heaster, Arlene L. *chemical engineer*
Hempel, Kathleen Jane *paper company executive*
Holmgren, Mike *professional football coach*
Jackson, Keith Jerome *football player*
Kemerling, James Lee *paper company executive*
Koski, Ann Louise *museum director*
Kress, George F. *packaging company executive*
Lewis, Gary *trucking executive*
McIntosh, Elaine Virginia *nutrition educator*
Meng, John C. *food service executive*
Mix, Judith Ann *nursing education administrator*
Olson, James Richard *transportation company executive*
Parins, Robert James *professional football team executive, judge*
Parkinson, Ethelyn Minerva *author*
Poppenhagen, Ronald William *newspaper editor, publishing executive*
†Resch, Richard J. *furniture manufacturing executive*
Rowley, John F. *manufacturing executive*
†Walsh, Eric *food products executive*
White, Reggie (Reginald Howard White) *professional football player*

Greendale
DeLorenzo, David Joseph *public relations executive*
Gillespie, Rory Andrew *professional association administrator*
Tucker, William Thomas, III *computer software company executive*

Hager City
Oskey, D. Beth *former banker*

Hales Corners
Hodgson, Craig Robert *radio station executive*
Laur, Bernard Paul *radio executive*
Michalski, (Żurowski) Wacław *adult education educator*

Hancock
Kostichka, Charles Joseph *agricultural studies educator, researcher*

Hartford
Lopina, Lawrence Thomas *manufacturing executive*

Hartland
Abramoff, Peter *biology educator*
Mc Neil, Donald Lewis *retired multiple association management company executive*
Stamsta, Jean F. *artist*

Hollandale
Myers, Frances *artist*

Iola
Foerster, Urban Michael, III (Trey Foerster) *newspaper owner, publisher*
Kiefer, Kit Annette *editor*
Krause, Chester Lee *publishing company executive*
Mishler, Clifford Leslie *publisher*
Rulau, Russell *numismatist, consultant*

Janesville
Diotte, Alfred Peter *investment executive, consultant*
Fitzgerald, James Francis *cable television executive*
Steil, George Kenneth, Sr. *lawyer*
Wood, Wayne W. *state legislator*

Jefferson
†Morgan, Gaylin F. *public realtions executive*

Juneau
Carpenter, David Erwin *county planner*

Kaukauna
Janssen, Gail Edwin *banking executive*

Kenosha
Adler, Seymour Jack *social services administrator*
Baker, Douglas Finley *library director*
Campbell, F(enton) Gregory *college administrator, historian*
Cornog, Robert A. *manufacturing executive*
Grover, Robert Lawrence *tool company executive*
Huml, Donald Scott *manufacturing company executive*
Jacobson, Dennis Leonard *business executive*
Kaplan, Sheila *university official*
Kolb, Vera M. *chemistry educator*
†Morrone, Frank *electronic manufacturing executive*
Smith, Eleanor Jane *academic administrator*
Steigerwaldt, Donna Wolf *clothing manufacturing company executive*
Tielke, James Clemens *retail and manufacturing executive*
†Vignieri, Charles Joseph *meat packing company executive*
†Wright, Betty Ren *children's book writer*

Kewaskum
†Peterson, Lowell N. *light manufacuring executive*
†Reigle, James D. *manufacturing executive*

Kohler
Kohler, Herbert Vollrath, Jr. *diversified manufacturing company executive*

La Crosse
Anderson, Mary Ann *hospital nursing administrator*
†Bubar, Joseph Bedell, Jr. *church official*
†Burke, Raymond L. *bishop*
Cleary, Russell George *retired brewery executive*
Corser, David Hewson *pediatrician*
Eber, David Henry *manufacturing company executive*
Gelatt, Charles Daniel *manufacturing company executive*
Klos, Jerome John *lawyer*
Kuipers, Judith L. *academic administrator*
Medland, William James *college president*
Metcalf, Jerry D. *wholesale food distribution company executive*
Nix, Edmund Alfred *lawyer*
Novotney, Donald Francis *school system administrator*
Paul, John Joseph *bishop*
Rausch, Joan Mary *art historian*
Rozelle, Lee Theodore *physical chemist*
Webster, Stephen Burtis *physician, educator*

Lake Geneva
Braden, Berwyn Bartow *lawyer*

Lake Nebagamon
Meyer, Karl William *retired university president*

Lancaster
Johnson, Hal Harold Gustav *marketing educator emeritus*

Little Chute
Rice, Ferill Jeane *writer, civic worker*

Madison
Abrahamson, Shirley Schlanger *state supreme court justice*
Adler, Julius *biochemist, biologist, educator*
Albert, Daniel Myron *ophthalmologist, educator*
Aldag, Ramon John *management and organization educator*
Ammerman, Robert Ray *philosopher, educator*
Amundson, Clyde Howard *engineering educator, researcher*
Anderson, Louis Wilmer, Jr. *physicist, educator*
Anderson, Odin Waldemar *sociologist, educator*
Andreano, Ralph Louis *economist, educator*
Armstrong, Gregory Davenport *arboretum administrator*
Arny, Deane Cedric *former plant pathology educator, researcher*
Askey, Richard Allen *mathematician*
†Atkinson, Richard Lee, Jr. *internal medicine educator*
Auen, Michael H. *lawyer*
Bablitch, William A. *state supreme court justice*
Bach-y-Rita, Paul *neurophysiologist, rehabilitation medicine specialist*
Baeumer, Max Lorenz *literature historian*
Baldwin, Gordon Brewster *lawyer, educator*
Baldwin, Robert Edward *economics educator*
Barger, Vernon Duane *physicist, educator*
Barnes, Robert F *agronomist*
Barnhill, Charles Joseph, Jr. *lawyer*
Baron, Alma Fay S. *management educator*
†Barr, Jim, III *telecommunications company executive*
Barrows, Richard Lee *economics educator, academic administrator*
Barschall, Henry Herman *physics educator*
Bartell, Jeffrey Bruce *lawyer*
Bass, Paul *pharmacology educator*
Beachley, Norman Henry *mechanical engineer, educator*
Beck, Anatole *mathematician, educator*
Beck, Stanley Dwight *retired entomology educator, researcher*
Becker, David *artist, educator*
Bell/Jackson, Marianne Jeanne *elementary education educator*
Belzer, Folkert Oene *surgeon*
Bennett, Kenneth Alan *biological anthropologist*
Bentley, Charles Raymond *geophysics educator*
Berg, William James *French language educator, writer, translator*
Berkowitz, Leonard *psychology educator*
Bernstine, Daniel O'Neal *law educator, university dean*
Berthouex, Paul Mac *civil and environmental engineer, educator*
Binning, Larry Keith *horticulture educator*
Bird, Robert Byron *chemical engineering educator, author*
Bisgard, Gerald Edwin *biosciences educator, researcher*
Bjoraker, Walter Thomas *agricultural and vocational educator emeritus*
Blaedel, Walter John *chemist, retired educator*
Blankenburg, William Burl *journalism educator*
Bloodworth, J. M. Bartow, Jr. *physician, educator*
†Bochert, Linda H. *lawyer*
Bogue, Allan G. *history educator*
†Bohnhoff, David Roy *agricultural engineer, educator*
Bollinger, John Gustave *engineering educator, college dean*
Borisy, Gary G. *molecular biology educator*
Botez, Dan *physicist*
Boutwell, Roswell Knight *oncology educator*
Boyle, William Charles *civil engineering educator*
Brembeck, Winston Lamont *retired speech communication educator*
Bretherton, Francis P. *atmospheric and oceanic sciences educator*
Brock, Thomas Dale *microbiology educator*
Brock, William Allen, III *economics educator, consultant*
Bromley, Daniel Wood *economics educator, consultant*
Brooks, Benjamin Rix *neurologist, educator*
Brown, Arnold Lanehart, Jr. *pathologist, educator, university dean*
Bruhn, Hjalmar Diehl *retired agricultural engineer, educator*
Bryson, Reid Allen *meteorology educator*
Bubenzer, Gary Dean *agricultural engineering educator, researcher*
Bugge, Lawrence John *lawyer*
Bula, Raymond J. *agronomist*
Bullock, William Henry *bishop*
Bunge, Charles Albert *library science educator*
Burgess, James Edward *newspaper publisher, executive*
Burgess, Richard Ray *oncology educator, molecular biology researcher, biotechnology consultant*
Burke, Brian B. *state senator, lawyer*
Burkholder, Wendell Eugene *entomologist*
Burris, Robert Harza *biochemist, educator*
Busby, Edward Oliver *retired dean*
Callen, James Donald *nuclear engineer, plasma physicist, educator*
Carbon, Max William *nuclear engineering educator*
Carbone, Paul Peter *oncologist, educator, administrator*
Casey, Charles Philip *organic chemist, educator*
Cassens, Robert Gene *food scientist*
Cassidy, Frederic Gomes *humanities educator*
Cassinelli, Joseph Patrick *astronomy educator*
Chang, Y. Austin *materials engineer, educator*
Chapman, Loren J. *psychology educator*

Chatterton, William Alonzo *lawyer*
†Chiarkas, Nicholas L. *lawyer, state agency administrator*
Chow, Tse-Tsung *foreign language and literature educator, author, poet*
Churchwell, Edward Bruce *astronomer, educator*
Ciplijauskaite, Birute *humanities educator*
Clark, David Leigh *marine geologist, educator*
Cleland, W(illiam) Wallace *biochemistry educator*
Cliver, Dean Otis *virologist, educator*
Coberly, Camden Arthur *chemical engineering educator*
Code, Arthur Dodd *astrophysics educator*
Coe, Christopher Lane *psychology researcher*
Cohen, Bernard Cecil *political scientist, educator*
Colás, Antonio Espada *medical educator*
Colescott, Warrington Wickham *artist, printmaker, educator*
Connors, Kenneth Antonio *chemist*
Converse, James Clarence *agricultural engineering educator*
†Conway, Robert Edward *corporate executive*
Cooper, John Milton, Jr. *history educator, author*
Cornwell, Charles Daniel *physical chemist, educator*
Couper, David Courtland *police chief*
Crabb, Barbara Brandriff *federal judge*
Craddock, (John) Campbell *geologist, educator*
Crafton, Donald Clayton *film educator*
Crandall, Lee Walter *civil and structural engineer*
Crim, Forrest Fleming, Jr. *chemist, educator*
Cronin, Patti Adrienne Wright *state agency administrator*
Cronon, E(dmund) David, Jr. *history educator, historian*
Cronon, William *history educator*
Culbertson, John Mathew *economist, educator*
Curry, Robert Lee *lawyer*
Curtiss, Charles Francis *chemist, educator*
Dahl, Lawrence Frederick *chemistry educator, researcher*
Daie, Jaleh *researcher, science educator, administrator*
Darling, Alberta Statkus *state legislator, marketing executive, former art museum executive*
Davis, Erroll Brown, Jr. *utility executive*
Davis, Richard *musician, music educator*
Day, Roland Bernard *state supreme court justice*
de Boor, Carl *mathematician*
Dembo, Lawrence Sanford *English educator*
Dembski, Stephen Michael *composer, university music composition professor*
Denevan, William Maxfield *geographer, educator*
DeNovo, John August *history educator*
Denton, Frank M. *newspaper editor*
Derzon, Gordon M. *hospital administrator*
Deutsch, Harold Francis *biochemist, researcher, educator*
DeVries, Marvin Frank *mechanical engineering educator*
DeWerd, Larry Albert *medical physicist, educator*
Dewey, Gene Lawrence *librarian*
Dick, Elliot Colter *virologist, epidemiologist, educator*
Dietmeyer, Donald Leo *electrical engineer*
Dodson, Vernon Nathan *physician, educator*
Dott, Robert Henry, Jr. *geologist, educator*
Doyle, James E(dward) *state attorney general*
Draper, Norman Richard *statistician, educator*
Duffie, John Atwater *chemical engineer, educator*
Dunwoody, Sharon Lee *science communication scholar*
DuRose, Stanley Charles, Jr. *insurance executive*
Earl, Anthony Scully *former governor*
Easterday, Bernard Carlyle *veterinary medicine educator*
Ebben, James Adrian *college president*
Ebel, Marvin Emerson *physicist,educator*
Eisinger, Peter K(endall) *political science educator*
Ellis, Arthur Baron *chemist, educator*
Emmert, Gilbert Arthur *engineer, educator*
Enslin, Jon S. *bishop*
Epstein, William *experimental psychologist*
Erhard, Michael Paul *lawyer*
Erickson, John Ronald *research administrator*
Evenson, Merle Armin *chemist, educator*
Evert, Ray Franklin *botany educator*
Fahien, Leonard August *physician, educator*
Fanlund, Paul G. *newspaper editor*
Farley, Eugene Shedden, Jr. *physician, educator*
Farrar, Thomas C. *chemist, educator*
Farrow, Margaret Ann *state legislator*
Felstehausen, Herman Henry *natural resources-land planning educator*
Felten, Edward Joseph *business executive accountant*
Fennema, Owen Richard *food chemistry educator*
Ferry, John Douglass *chemist*
Fiedler, Patrick James *circuit court judge*
Field, Henry Augustus, Jr. *lawyer*
Finman, Ted *lawyer, educator*
Fitchen, Allen Nelson *publisher*
Fitzpatrick, Mary Anne Theresa *communications educator*
Fleischman, Stephen *art center director*
Foell, Wesley Kay *engineer, energy and environmental scientist, educator, consultant*
Formisano, Roger Anthony *professor of business*
Forster, Francis Michael *physician, educator*
Foster, George William, Jr. *lawyer, educator*
Fowler, Barbara Hughes *classics educator*
Fox, Michael Vass *Hebrew educator, rabbi*
Frautschi, Walter Albert *contract and publications printing company executive*
Fritz, Bruce Morrell *photographer*
Fry, William Frederick *physics educator*
Frykenberg, Robert Eric *historian*
Gallagher, John Sill, III *astronomer*
Garver, Thomas Haskell *curator, art consultant, writer*
Gavin, Mary Jane *medical, surgical nurse*
Gaylor, Anne Nicol *editor, foundation executive*
Gehl, Eugene Othmar *power company executive, lawyer*
Gilboe, David Dougherty *physiology educator*
†Glesner, Richard Charles *lawyer, law examiner*
Goldberger, Arthur Stanley *economics educator*
Goodman, Robert Merwin *agriculturalist, plant biologist, university educator*
Gorski, Jack *biochemistry educator*
Graf, Truman Frederick *agricultural economist, educator*
Graham, Linda Kay Edwards *biology educator*
Greaser, Marion Lewis *science educator*
Green, Theodore, III *engineering and science educator*
Greenfield, Norman Samuel *psychologist, educator*
Greenwald, Caroline Meyer *artist*
Griepp, Milton Charles *distribution executive*
Grossman, Joel B(arry) *political science educator*
Gruber, John Edward *editor, railroad historian, photographer*
Gustafson, David Harold *industrial engineering and preventive medicine educator*
Hagedorn, Donald James *phytopathologist, educator, agricultural consultant*
Hall, David Charles *zoo director, veterinarian*
Haller, Archibald Orben *sociologist, educator*
Hamalainen, Pekka Kalevi *historian, educator*
Hamerow, Theodore Stephen *history educator*
†Hamers, Robert J. *chemistry educator*
Hansen, W. Lee *economics educator, author*
Harr, Lucy Loraine *association executive*
Harvey, John Grover *mathematics educator*
Haslanger, Philip Charles *journalist*
Hauser, Robert Mason *sociologist, demographer, educator*
Hearn, John Patrick *biologist, educator*
Hedden, Gregory Dexter *environmental science educator, consultant*
Heffernan, Nathan Stewart *state supreme court chief justice*
Heins, Richard M. *insurance company executive*
Helgeson, John Paul *physiologist, researcher*
Helstad, Orrin L. *lawyer, legal educator*
Herndon, Terry Eugene *insurance executive*
Hershkowitz, Noah *physicist, educator*
Hester, Donald Denison *economics educator*
Heymann, S. Richard *lawyer*
Hickman, James Charles *business and statistics educator, business school dean*
Higby, Gregory James *historical association administrator, historian*
Hildebrand, Daniel Walter *lawyer*
Hill, Charles Graham, Jr. *chemical engineering educator*
Hokin, Lowell Edward *biochemist, educator*
Holbrook, John Scott, Jr. *lawyer*
Hollingsworth, Joseph Rogers *history and sociology educator, writer*
Hopen, Herbert John *horticulture educator*
Houghton, David Drew *meteorologist, educator*
Howe, Herbert Marshall *classics educator*
Hoyt, James Lawrence *journalism educator, athletic administrator*
Huelsman, Joanne B. *state legislator*
Hunter, John Patrick *newspaper editor*
Hurst, James Willard *legal educator*
Huston, Norman Earl *nuclear engineering educator*
Ihde, Aaron John *history of science educator emeritus*
Iltis, Hugh Hellmut *plant taxonomist and evolutionist, educator*
Inman, Ross Banks *biochemistry and biophysics educator*
†Ishikawa, Jesse Steven *lawyer*
Javid, Manucher J. *neurosurgeon*
Jeanne, Robert Lawrence *entomologist, educator, researcher*
Jefferson, James Walter *psychiatry educator*
Jiao, Shou-shu *education educator, neuroscientist*
Johnson, Alton Cornelius *management educator*
Johnson, Millard Wallace, Jr. *mathematics and engineering educator*
Johnson, Richard Arnold *statistics educator, consultant*
Johnson, Roland A. *conductor, music director*
†Johnson, William Elmer, Jr. *hospital executive*
Jones, James Edward, Jr. *retired law educator*
Kaesberg, Paul Joseph *virology researcher*
Karavolas, Harry J(ohn) *biochemist, educator*
Keesey, Ulker Tulunay *retired ophthalmology and psychology educator*
Kelly, Douglas *medieval and foreign literature educator*
Kepecs, Joseph Goodman *physician, educator*
Kingdon, Robert McCune *historian, educator*
Kirk, Thomas Kent *research scientist*
Klein, Sheldon *computational linguist, educator*
Kleinhenz, Christopher *foreign language educator, researcher*
Klug, Scott Leo *congressman*
Knowles, Richard Alan John *English language educator*
Knutson, Lynn Douglas *physics educator*
Koval, Charles Francis *entomologist, agricultural administrator, educator*
Kraushaar, William Lester *physicist, educator*
Kreuter, Gretchen V. *college president*
Krusick, Margaret Ann *state legislator*
Kulcinski, Gerald LaVerne *nuclear engineer, educator*
Kumar, Anand *medical educator, researcher*
Kunicki, Walter Joseph *state legislator*
Kurtz, Thomas Gordon *mathematics educator*
Kutler, Stanley Ira *history and law educator, author*
Ladinsky, Judith Louise *preventive medicine educator*
Laessig, Ronald Harold *pathology educator, state official*
La Follette, Douglas J. *secretary of state*
Lagally, Max Gunter *physics educator*
Langer, Richard J. *lawyer*
Lardy, Henry Arnold *biochemist, biological sciences educator*
Larsen, Edwin Merritt *retired chemist, educator*
Larson, John David *life insurance company executive, lawyer*
Lautenschlager, Peggy Ann *prosecutor*
Lawler, James Edward *physics educator*
Lawson, David E. *architect*
Leavitt, Lewis A. *pediatrician, educator*
Lemberger, August Paul *university dean, pharmacy educator*
Levin, Jacob Joseph *mathematician, educator*
Levine, Solomon Bernard *business and economics educator*
Lewis, Herbert Samuel *anthropologist, educator*
†Lightfoot, Edwin Niblock, Jr. *chemical engineering ecuator*
†Linstroth, Tod B. *lawyer*
Littlefield, Vivian Moore *nursing educator, administrator*
Lobeck, Charles Champlin, Jr. *pediatrics educator*
Long, Willis Franklin *electrical engineering educator, researcher*
Lonnebotn, Trygve *battery company executive*
Loper, Carl Richard, Jr. *metallurgical engineer, educator*
Lorge, William David *state legislator, farmer*
Lovell, Edward George *engineering mechanics educator*
Luening, Robert Adami *agricultural economics educator emeritus*
Lyall, Katharine C(ulbert) *academic administrator, economics educator*
MacKendrick, Paul Lachlan *classics educator*
Mackie, Frederick David *retired utility executive*
Mac Kinney, Archie Allen, Jr. *physician*
Maher, Louis James, Jr. *geologist, educator*
Maki, Dennis G. *medical educator, researcher, clinician*
Malkus, David Starr *mechanics educator, applied mathematician*
Maloney, Michael James *research scientist*
Mare, Robert Denis *sociology educator, demography researcher*
Markley, John Lute *biochemistry educator*
Marks, Elaine *French language educator*
Marlett, Judith Ann *nutritional sciences educatr, researcher*
†Martens, Lyle Charles *state education administrator*
Marth, Elmer Herman *bacteriologist, educator*
Martin, Robert David *federal judge, law educator*
Marton, Laurence Jay *clinical pathologist, educator, researcher*
Marwell, Gerald *sociology educator, research consultant*
Mathwich, Dale F. *insurance company executive*
McBeath, Andrew Alan *orthopedic surgery educator*
McCabe, Robert Albert *wildlife ecology educator*
McCallum, James Scott *lieutenant governor, former state senator*
†McCallum, Scott *state official*
Mc Camy, James Lucian *former political science educator*
McCarty, Donald James *education educator*
McCubbin, Hamilton I. *social scientist, educator, researcher*
McGown, Wayne *academic administrator*
McLeod, Jack Myron *communications educator*
McNelly, John Taylor *journalist, educator*
McVoy, Kirk Warren *physicist, educator*
Melli, Marygold Shire *law educator*
Meloon, Robert A. *retired newspaper publisher*
Miller, Frederick William *publisher, lawyer*
Miller, James Alexander *oncologist, educator*
Miller, Richard Ulric *business and industrial relations educator*
Mitby, Norman Peter *college president*
Moen, Rodney Charles *state senator, retired naval officer*
Mohs, Frederic Edward *surgeon, educator*
Moore, Edward Forrest *computer scientist, mathematician, former educator*
Moore, John Ward *chemistry educator*
Morton, Stephen Dana *chemist*
Moses, Gregory Allen *engineering educator*
Mosse, George Lachmann *history educator, author*
Mueller, Willard Fritz *economics educator*
Mukerjee, Pasupati *chemistry educator*
Muller, H(enry) Nicholas, III *historical society director*
Mullins, Jerome Joseph *real estate developer, consulting engineer*
Murphy, Robert Brady Lawrence *lawyer*
Nelson, Oliver Evans, Jr. *geneticist, educator*
Netzer, Lanore A(gnes) *retired educational administration educator*
Nevin, John Robert *business educator, consultant*
Newcomb, Eldon Henry *retired botany educator*
Nichols, Donald Arthur *economist, educator*
Niemann, Bernard John, Jr. *land and geographical system educator, researcher, consultant*
Nordby, Eugene Jorgen *orthopedic surgeon*
Novotny, Donald Wayne *electrical engineering educator*
O'Brien, James Aloysius *foreign language educator*
Odden, Allan Robert *education educator*
Olson, Norman Fredrick *food science educator*
Otte, Clifford *state legislator*
Palmer, Robert R. *performing arts administrator*
Pampel, Roland D. *computer company executive*
†Panczenko, Russell *museum director*
Panzer, Mary E. *state legislator*
Pariza, Michael Willard *research institute executive, microbiology and toxicology educator*
Pella, Milton Orville *retired science educator*
Pellino, Charles Edward, Jr. *lawyer*
Pempel, T. J. *political science educator*
Penniman, Clara *political scientist, educator*
Perkins, Merle Lester *French language educator*
Perlman, D(avid) *biochemist, educator*
Peters, Henry Augustus *neuropsychiatrist*
Peterson, David Maurice *plant physiologist, researcher*
Pierce, Harvey R. *Insurance company executive*
Pillaert, E(dna) Elizabeth *museum curator*
Pitot, Henry Clement, III *physician, educator*
Policano, Andrew J. *university dean*
Pondrom, Lee Girard *physicist, educator*
Poniewaz, Kenneth Anthony *banker*
Porter, Andrew Calvin *educational administrator, psychology educator*
Porter, Cloyd Allen *state representative*
Powell, Barry Bruce *classicist*
Prange, Roy Leonard, Jr. *lawyer*
Pray, Lloyd Charles *geologist, educator*
Prieve, E. Arthur *arts administration educator*
Ragatz, Thomas George *lawyer*
Raushenbush, Walter Brandeis *law educator*
Ray, Dennis Jay *regulatory policy educator, researcher*
Ray, W. Harmon *chemical engineering educator, consultant, author*
†Reuhl, George *retail executive*
Reynolds, Ernest West *physician, educator*
Rice, Joy Katharine *psychologist, educational policy studies and women's studies educator*
Rich, Daniel Hulbert *chemist*
Richards, Hugh Taylor *physics educator*
Rideout, Walter Bates *English educator*
Ring, Gerald J. *real estate developer, insurance executive*
Ris, Hans *zoologist, educator*
Roberts, Leigh Milton *psychiatrist*
Robinson, Arthur Howard *geography educator*
Robinson, Stephen Michael *applied mathematician, educator*
Robson, Judith Biros *state legislator*
†Rogers, Joel *law, political science and sociology educator*
Rosser, Annetta Hamilton *composer*
Rothstein, Eric *English educator*
Rowe, George Giles *cardiologist, educator*
Rowe, John Westel *retired organic chemist*
Rowlands, Robert Edward *engineering educator*
Rudd, Dale Frederick *retired chemical engineer*
Rude, Brian David *state legislator*
Rueckert, Roland Rudyard *virologist, educator*
Rutkowski, James Anthony *state legislator*
Rutledge, Jackie Joe *genetics educator*
Ryan, Thomas Joseph *lawyer*
Sample, Nathaniel Welshire *architect*
Savage, Blair deWillis *astronomer, educator*
Schatten, Gerald Phillip *cell biologist, educator*
Schatz, Paul Frederick *laboratory director*
Schleck, Roth Stephen *banker*
Schmidt, John Richard *agricultural economics educator*
Schultz, Dale Walter *state legislator*
Schulz, Rockwell Irwin *health administration educator*
Schutta, Henry Szczesny *neurologist, educator*
Seireg, Ali A(bdel Hay) *mechanical engineer*
Sequeira, Luis *plant pathology educator*
Sewell, Richard Herbert *historian, educator*
Sewell, William Hamilton *sociologist*
Shabaz, John C. *federal judge*
Shain, Irving *retired chemical company executive and university chancellor*
Shaw, Joseph Thomas *Slavic languages educator*
Sheffield, Lewis Glosson *physiologist*
Shohet, Juda Leon *electrical and computer engineering educator, researcher, high technology company executive*
Sih, Charles John *pharmaceutical chemistry educator*
Silbaugh, Rudy Lamont *state legislator*
Simone, Beverly Sue *academic administrator*
Singer, Marcus George *philosopher, educator*
Skiles, James Jean *electrical and computer engineering educator*
Skilton, John Singleton *lawyer*
Skinner, James Lauriston *chemist, educator*
Skoog, Folke Karl *botany educator*
Slack, Jerald David *adjutant general of Wisconsin, civil engineer*
Smalley, Eugene Byron *plant pathology educator, forest pathologist, mycologist*
Smith, Michael James *industrial engineering educator*
Smith, William Leo *meteorologist, researcher, educator*
Sobkowicz, Hanna Maria *neurology researcher*
Sonnedecker, Glenn Allen *historian of pharmacy*
Spear, Thomas Turner *history educator*
Sprecher, Peter Leonard, Jr. *financial services company executive*
†Starostovic, Edward Joseph, Jr. *engineer, engineering company executive*
Stern, Steve J. *cultural organization administrator, history educator*
Stewart, Warren Earl *chemical engineer, educator*
†Still, Thomas Wayne *newspaper editor, columnist*
Strasma, John Drinan *economist, educator*
Strier, Karen Barbara *anthropology educator*
Sufit, Robert Louis *neurologist, educator*
†Suomi, Verner Edward *meteorologist, administrator, inventor*
Susman, Millard *geneticist, educator*
Swoboda, Lary Joseph *state legislator*
Swoboda, Ralph Sande *credit union official, lawyer*
Szybalski, Waclaw *molecular geneticist, educator*
Taylor, Carolyn L. *principal*
Tedeschi, John Alfred *historian, librarian*
Temkin, Harvey L. *lawyer*
Thesen, Arne *industrial engineering educator*
Thiesenhusen, William Charles *agricultural economist*
Thompson, Bjorn J. *food products company executive, mechanical engineer*
Thompson, Cliff F. *lawyer, educator*
Thompson, Howard Elliott *business educator*
Thompson, Tommy George *governor*
Tibbitts, Theodore William *horticulturist, researcher*
Tishler, William Henry *landscape architect, educator*
Tomar, Russell Herman *pathologist, educator, researcher*
Treichel, Paul Morgan, Jr. *chemistry educator*
†Tuan, Yi-Fu *geography educator*
Turner, Robert Lloyd *state legislator*
Urban, Frank Henry *dermatologist, state legislator*
Vailas, Arthur C. *biomechanics educator*
Vandell, Deborah Lowe *educational psychology educator*
Vandell, Kerry Dean *real estate and urban economics educator*
Vansina, Jan Maria Jozef *historian, educator*
Vaughan, Worth Edward *chemistry educator*
Vowles, Richard Beckman *language educator, foreign language*
Wagner, Burton Allan *lawyer*
Wahba, Grace *statistician, educator*
Waldo, Robert Leland *retired insurance company executive*
Waldron, Ellis Leigh *retired political science educator*
Walker, Duard Lee *medical educator*
Walker, William Ray *broadcasting executive*
Walsh, David Graves *lawyer*
Wang, Herbert Fan *geophysics educator*
Ward, David *academic administrator, educator*
Webster, John Goodwin *biomedical engineering educator, researcher*
Webster, Robert Loudon *banker, lawyer*
Weinbrot, Howard David *English educator*
†Weingand, Darlene Erna *librarian educator, consultant*
Weiss, Mareda Ruth *university administrator*
Welker, Wallace Irving *neurophysiologist, educator*
Wermers, Donald Joseph *registrar*
West, Robert Culbertson *chemistry educator*
Westman, Jack Conrad *child psychiatrist, educator*
Westphal, Klaus Wilhelm *university museum director*
Whiffen, James Douglass *surgeon, educator*
†White, John Graham *scientist*
White, William Fredrick *lawyer*
Whitney, Robert Michael *lawyer*
Wilcox, Jon P. *judge*
Wilcox, Michael Wing *lawyer*
Wilde, John *artist, educator*
Williams, Annette Polly *state legislator*
†Wilson, Michael Alan *health facility administrator*
†Wineke, William Robert *reporter, clergyman*
Wirtz, Virginia Haynes *nursing educator*
Wirz, George O. *bishop*
Witiak, Donald Theodore *medicinal chemistry educator*
Wolman, J. Martin *retired newspaper publisher*
†Worzala, Frank John *metallurgical engineering educator and researcher*
Wright, Erik Olin *sociology educator*
Wright, George Nelson *counselor, educator*
Young, Merwin Crawford *political science educator*
Young, Rebecca Mary Conrad *state legislator*
Yu, Hyuk *chemist, educator*
Yuill, Thomas MacKay *university administrator, microbiology educator*
Zaleski, Michael Louis *state official, lawyer*
Zimmerman, Howard Elliot *chemist, educator*
Zobel, Robert Leonard *state government official*
Zweifel, David Alan *newspaper editor*

Manitowish Waters
Laidig, William Rupert retired paper company executive

Manitowoc
†Butler, Fred M. manufacturing executive, heavy, water transportation executive
†Huss, Ronald John biochemist
Logan, Lox Albert, Jr. museum director
Muchin, Arden Archie lawyer, director
†Sfat, Michael Rudolph biochemical engineer
Trader, Joseph Edgar orthopedic surgeon

Marinette
Staudenmaier, Mary Louise banker, lawyer

Marion
Simpson, Vinson Raleigh manufacturing company executive

Marshfield
David, Barbara Marie medical, surgical nurse
Fye, W. Bruce, III cardiologist
Jaye, David Robert, Jr. retired hospital administrator
Sautter, Richard Daniel physician, administrator
Stueland, Dean Theodore emergency physician
Wrabl, Carol A. nursing administrator

Medford
Sebold, Duane David food manufacturing executive

Menasha
Aurand, Calvin W., Jr. specialized printing company executive
Baird, Roger Allen retired corporation executive
†Cianciola, Charles Sal paper manufacturing company executive
Decker, William Joseph superintendent
Gorsalitz, Jeannine Liane elementary school educator
Henseler, Gerald Anthony printing company executive

Menomonee Falls
Herma, John retail executive
Kellogg, William S. retail executive
Klug, Richard Paul financial executive
Walters, Ronald Ogden finance company executive

Mequon
Burroughs, Charles Edward lawyer
Buuck, R(oland) John university president
Dohmen, Frederick Hoeger retired wholesale drug company executive
Felde, Martin Lee advertising agency executive, accountant
Watson-Boone, Rebecca A. educator
Wray, Gail Miller environmentalist, government agency administrator

Middleton
†Clay, Clarence Samuel acoustical oceanographer
Eriksson, Larry John electrical engineer
Ferry, James Allen physicist, electrostatics company executive
Foss, Karl Robert auditor
Herb, Raymond George physicist, manufacturing company executive
Hofeldt, John W. lawyer
Ostrom, Meredith Eggers retired geologist

Milton
Hosler, Russell John retired education educator

Milwaukee
†Abdoo, Richard A. utilities company executive
†Abraham, Jeffrey L. lawyer
Abraham, William John, Jr. lawyer
†Ahrens, Gary Andrew lawyer
Aita, Carolyn Rubin physicist
Alexander, Janice Hoehner physician, educator
Alverson, William H. lawyer
Aman, Mohammed Mohammed university dean, library and information science educator
Ambrosius, Mark Ralph hospital administrator
Ament, F. Thomas county government official
Anderson, Alan R. department store executive
Arbit, Bruce direct marketing executive, consultant
Armstrong, Douglas Dean movie critic
Arreola, Philip police officer
Auer, James Matthew art critic, journalist
Babler, Wayne E., Jr. lawyer
Bacha, Diane Marie newspaper editor
Bader, Alfred Robert chemist
Balbach, George Charles technology company executive
Balinger, Louise H. artist, art educator
Bannen, John T. lawyer
Barbee, Lloyd Augustus lawyer
Barnes, Paul McClung lawyer
Barron, Russell J. lawyer
Bartel, Fred Frank consulting engineer executive
Bartels, Jean Ellen nursing educator
Bateman, C. Barry airport terminal Executive
Battocletti, Joseph Henry electrical engineer, biomedical engineer, educator
Bauer, Bruce Richard lawyer
Bauer, Chris Michael banker
Beals, Vaughn Le Roy, Jr. motorcycle and recreational vehicle manufacturing executive
Beckwith, David E. lawyer
Beglinger, Joan Ellis nursing services vice president
Behrendt, David Frogner journalist
Bell, Darryl Stephen lawyer
Berkoff, Marshall Richard lawyer
Berman, Fred Jean art educator, painter, photographer
Bero, Ronald Arthur banker
Bhore, Jay Narayan psychiatrist
Bicha, Karel Denis historian, educator
Biehl, Michael Melvin lawyer
Biller, Joel Wilson lawyer, former foreign service officer
Binder, Robert Lawrence lawyer
Bishop, Charles Joseph manufacturing company executive
Bloom, James Edward commodity trading and financial executive
Bluestone, Stanton J. department store chain executive
Blum, Lawrence Philip educational psychology educator
Boese, Gilbert Karyle cultural organization executive
Boettcher, Harold Paul engineer, educator
Bomberger, Glen R. manufacturing company executive
Bowen, Michael Anthony lawyer, writer
Braza, Mary Kathryn lawyer
Britt, Russell William utility executive
Brody, James Patrick lawyer
Brown, Edith social worker
Bruce, Jackson Martin, Jr. lawyer
Bruett, Till Arthur banker
Burgess, Richard Ball food products executive
Burkert, Robert Randall artist
Burns, Ronald James manufacturing equipment company executive
Burstein, Sol consultant, retired utility company executive, engineer
Busch, John Arthur lawyer
†Bush, Sister Lois health facilities administrator
Cannon, David Joseph lawyer
†Canter, Richard J. lawyer
Carozza, Davy Angelo Italian language educator
†Carter, Curtis Lloyd art musuem director
Case, Karen Ann lawyer
Casey, John Alexander lawyer
Casper, Richard Henry lawyer
Chait, Jon Frederick corporate executive, lawyer
Chambers, LaRoyce Francis obstetrician, gynecologist
Chan, Shih Hung mechanical engineering educator, consultant
Chapman, William Paul retired automatic control manufacturing company executive
Checota, Joseph Woodrow real estate business executive
Christiansen, Jon Peter lawyer
Christiansen, Keith Allan lawyer
Clark, James Richard lawyer
Cleary, John Washington lawyer
Coffman, Terrence J. academic administrator
†Colbert, Virgis William brewery company executive
Condon, Robert Edward surgeon, educator
Connolly, Gerald Edward lawyer
Connolly, L. William lawyer
Conrad, Kelley Allen industrial and organizational psychologist
Cooper, Richard Alan hematologist, college dean
Croak, Francis R. lawyer
Curran, Thomas J. federal judge
Cutler, Richard Woolsey lawyer
Daily, Frank J(erome) lawyer
Davis, Thomas William steel industry manufacturing executive
Davis, Walter Stewart lawyer
Dembski, Barbara newspaper editor
Demerdash, Nabeel Aly Omar electrical engineer
DiUlio, Albert Joseph university president, priest
Downey, John Wilham composer, pianist, conductor, educator
Drummond, Robert Kendig lawyer
Duback, Steven Rahr lawyer
Dunleavy, Janet Frank Egleson English language educator
Dunleavy, Michael Joseph professional basketball coach
Dupies, Donald Albert civil engineer, consultant
Dziewanowski, Marian Kamil history educator
Ehrmann, Thomas William lawyer
Eisenberg, Howard Bruce law educator
Elias, Paul S. marketing executive
Erdmann, August protective services official
Ericson, James Donald lawyer, insurance executive
Esterly, Nancy Burton physician
Evans, Terence Thomas federal judge
Farris, Trueman Earl, Jr. retired newspaper editor
Feitler, Robert shoe company executive
Fibich, Howard Raymond retired newspaper editor
Ficken, Millicent Sigler zoology educator
Fink, Jordan Norman physician, educator
Fischer, Michael Davin lawyer
Fitzsimonds, Roger Leon bank holding company executive
Florsheim, Richard Steven lawyer
Foster, Richard journalist
Frautschi, Timothy Clark lawyer
Friedman, James Dennis lawyer
Friedman, Melvin Jack language professional, literature educator
Fromstein, Mitchell S. temporary office services company executive
†Fuller, Howard school system administrator
Gaggioli, Richard Arnold mechanical engineering educator
Gallagher, Richard S. lawyer
Gallop, Jane (Anne) women's studies educator, writer
Garner, Phil professional baseball manager
Garnier, Robert Charles management consultant
Gemignani, Joseph Adolph lawyer
Gengler, Sister M. Jeanne hospital administrator
Ghiardi, James Domenic lawyer, educator
Gissler, Sigvard Gunnar, Jr. journalism educator, former newspaper editor
Goetsch, John Hubert utility company executive
Goodkind, Conrad George lawyer
Goodstein, Aaron E. federal magistrate judge
Gordon, Myron L. federal judge
Graef, Luther William civil engineer
†Granoff, Mark Howard insurance company executive
Green, Edward Anthony museum director
Greenler, Robert George physics educator, researcher
Grim, Clarence Ezra medical educator, internist, researcher
Groethe, Reed lawyer
Groiss, Fred George lawyer
Haas, George Edward lawyer
†Haberman, F. William lawyer
Habush, Robert Lee lawyer
Hachey, Thomas Eugene British and Irish history educator, consultant
†Haggerty, Nancy Leary lawyer
Halloran, William Frank English educator
†Hanson, David James lawyer
Hanthorn, Dennis Wayne performing arts association administrator
Harrington, John Timothy lawyer
Harvieux, Anne Marie psychotherapist
Hase, David John lawyer
Hassan, Ihab Habib English and comparative literature educator, author
Hatch, Michael Ward lawyer
Hatton, Janie R. Hill principal
Hawkins, Brett William political science educator
Haworth, Daniel Thomas chemistry educator
Hayes, Paul Gordon journalist
Hazelwood, John A. lawyer
Hedges, John Kim performing arts administrator, consultant
Hefty, Thomas R. insurance company executive
Heinen, James Albin electrical engineering educator
Helbert, Clifford L. graphic designer, journalism educator
Hendee, William Richard medical physics educator, university official
Hinshaw, Edward Banks broadcasting company executive
Hoelter, Timothy K. lawyer, manufacturing company executive
Hoffer, Robert Morrison retired holding company executive
Hoffman, Nathaniel A. lawyer
Hollenbach, Sister Ruth college president
Holz, Harry George lawyer
Hopkins, Edward Donald manufacturing executive
Horsman, Reginald history educator
†Hudson, Katherine Mary manufacturing company executive
Humber, Wilbur James psychologist
†Hunter, Victor Lee marketing executive, consultant
Huntington, David Mack Goode foundation administrator
†Husmann, Michael E. lawyer
Huston, Kathleen Marie library administrator
Huston, Margo journalist
Ihlenfeldt, Dale Elwood judge
Jache, Albert William retired chemistry educator, scientist
†Jackson, W. Charles lawyer
Jacobs, Burleigh Edmund foundry executive
Jaksic, Ivan A. history educator
James, Charles Franklin, Jr. engineering educator
Jansen, Daniel Ervin professional speedskater, marketing professional, former Olympic athlete
Jaques, Damien Paul theater critic
Jenkins, Louise Sherman nursing researcher
Jenkins, William Ivy hospital administrator
†Johannes, Robert J. lawyer
†Johnston, Michael Francis battery manufacturing company executive
Joseph, Jules K. retired public relations executive
Joslyn, Jay Thomas retired arts critic
Jost, Lawrence John lawyer
Joyce, Michael Stewart foundation executive, political science educator
Kahlor, Robert Arnold communications company executive
Kaiser, George Chapin investment company executive
Kamps, Charles Q. lawyer
Karl, Max Henry insurance company executive
Kelly, Francis Daniel lawyer
Kendall, Leon Thomas finance and real estate educator, retired insurance company executive
Kennedy, John Patrick lawyer, corporate executive
Kerr, Dorothy Marie Burmeister consultant, marketing executive
Kessler, Joan F. lawyer
Keuler, Roland Leo retired shoe company executive
Keulks, George William university dean, chemistry educator
Keyes, James Henry manufacturing company executive
Killian, William Paul industrial corporate executive
Kinnamon, David Lucas lawyer
Kloehn, Ralph Anthony plastic surgeon
Kochar, Mahendr Singh physician, educator, administrator, researcher, writer, consultant
Krausen, Anthony Sharnik surgeon
Kringel, Jerome Howard lawyer
Kritzer, Paul Eric media executive, communications lawyer
†Krueger, Raymond Robert lawyer
Kubale, Bernard Stephen lawyer
Kuester, Dennis J. banker
Kupst, Mary Jo psychologist, researcher
Kurtz, Harvey A. lawyer
LaBudde, Roy Christian lawyer
†Lafontsee, Dane ballet company artistic director
Landis, Fred mechanical engineering educator
Lavers, Richard Marshall lawyer
Lawrence, Willard Earl mathematics, statistics and computer science educator emeritus
Le Duc, Don Raymond lawyer, educator
Leonard, Richard Hart journalist
Levit, William Harold, Jr. lawyer
Listach, Patrick Alan professional baseball player
Loeb, Leonard L. lawyer
Long, Robert Eugene banker
Lubar, Sheldon Bernard venture capitalist
Lueders, Wayne Richard lawyer
Lydolph, Paul Edward geography educator
Macal, Zdenek conductor
MacDonald, Michael R. retail executive
MacDonough, John N. beverage company executive
MacGregor, David Lee lawyer
Machulak, Edward Leon real estate, mining and advertising company executive
MacIver, John Kenneth lawyer
Maio, F. Anthony lawyer
Manning, Kenneth Paul food company executive
Marcus, Stephen Howard hospitality and entertainment company executive
Marringa, Jacques Louis manufacturing company executive
Martin, Quinn William lawyer
Martin, Vincent Lionel manufacturing company executive
Mayer, Henry Michael mass transit consultant
Maynard, John Ralph lawyer
McCanles, Michael Frederick English language educator
McCann, Dennis John columnist
McCauley, Michael Stephen lawyer
McCollow, Thomas James communications company executive
McGaffey, Jere D. lawyer
McGinnity, Maureen Annell lawyer
McKinney, Venora Ware librarian
McSweeney, Maurice J. (Marc) lawyer
†Medved, Paul Stanley lawyer
Meisner, Mary Jo editor
Meldman, Clifford Kay lawyer
Meldman, Robert Edward lawyer
Miller, David Hewitt environmental scientist, writer
†Miller, Gordon K. lawyer
Miller, Keith insurance company executive
Moberg, David Oscar sociology educator
†Morgan, Geoffrey Richard lawyer
Morris, G. Ronald automotive executive
Mosher, George Allan manufacturing company executive
Moynihan, Michael J. artistic and producing director, writer
Moynihan, William J. museum executive
†Mueller, Wayne Dennis pastor, administrator, educator
Mulcahy, Robert William lawyer
Murphy, Judith Chisholm trust company executive
†Nagarkatti, Jai Prakash chemical company executive
Nakamoto, Kazuo chemistry educator
Namdari, Bahram surgeon
Niederjohn, Russell James electrical and computer engineering educator
Noelke, Paul lawyer
Norquist, John Olof mayor
Norris, John school system administrator
Novak, Victor Anthony semi-retired manufacturing company executive
Noyes, Anne Louise lawyer
†Obenberger, Thomas E. lawyer
†Olson, David R. lawyer
Olson, Frederick Irving retired history educator
Olson, John Marshall lawyer
Osborn, Guy A. food products company executive
O'Shaughnessy, James Patrick lawyer
O'Toole, Robert Joseph manufacturing company executive
Ovitsky, Steven Alan musician, symphony orchestra executive
Paige, Norma lawyer, corporate executive
Palay, Gilbert temporary help services company executive
Parker, Charles Walter, Jr. consultant, retired equipment company executive
Paull, Richard Allen geologist, educator
Paulson, Belden Henry political scientist
Pelisek, Frank John lawyer
Pelton, Ralph A. insurance company executive
Perlman, Richard Wilfred economist, educator
Phillips, Thomas John lawyer
Pindyck, Bruce Eben lawyer, corporate executive
Pisciotta, Anthony Vito physician, educator
Podell, Richard Jay lawyer
Poehlmann, JoAnna artist, illustrator, designer
Powell, Edmund William lawyer
Precourt, Lyman Arthur lawyer
†Prentiss, Paul E. lawyer
Quade, Quentin Lon political science educator
Randa, Rudolph Thomas federal judge
Randall, William Seymour leasing company executive
†Rao, Tanniru R. marketing educator, consultant
Raynor, John Patrick university administrator
Read, Sister Joel college administrator
Reedy, George Edward educator, author, lecturer
Reid, Robert Lelon college dean, mechanical engineer
Remsen, Charles Cornell, III microbiologist, research administrator, educator
†Rentmeester, Lawrence Raymond insurance company executive
Reynolds, John W. federal judge
†Rich, Robert C. manufacturing executive
Richman, Stephen Erik lawyer
Risch, Richard William horticultural manager
Ritz, Esther Leah civic worker, volunteer, investor
Roeming, Robert Frederick foreign language educator
†Roll, Teresa J. restaurant chain executive
†Rosen, Barry Howard museum director, history educator
Ruf, John Frederic banker
Ryan, Patrick Michael lawyer
Ryan, Thomas W. treasurer manufacturing company
Samson, Allen Lawrence bank executive
Samson, Richard Max investments and real estate executive
Sanderson, Gary Warner food company executive
Sankovitz, James Leo development director, lobbyist
Sapp, John Raymond lawyer
Schaleben, Arville newspaper editor, writer, educator
Scheinfeld, James David travel agency executive
Schenker, Eric university dean, economist
Schneider, John David theatre director, playwright, actor, jazz singer
Schnoll, Howard Manuel investment banking and managed asset consultant
Schnur, Robert Arnold lawyer
Schrader, Thomas F. utilities executive
Schroeder, John H. university administrator, history educator
Schuenke, Donald John insurance company executive
Schultz, Richard Otto ophthalmologist, educator
Schur, Leon Milton educator, economist
Schwartz, Joseph English language educator
Scrabeck, Jon Gilmen dental eductor
Scrivner, Thomas William lawyer
Selig, Allan H. (Bud Selig) professional baseball team executive
Shapiro, James Edward federal judge
†Shapiro, Robyn Sue lawyer, educator
Shea, Donald Richard political science educator
Shiely, John Stephen company executive, lawyer
Shindell, Sidney medical educator, physician
Shriner, Thomas L., Jr. lawyer
Slocum, Elizabeth newspaper editor
†Smith, David B. lawyer
†Smith, Everett G. chemicals executive
Smith, Guy W. health care executive
Smith, James John physiologist
Smith, Lois Ann real estate executive
Snyder, Marian H. nursing educator and administrator
Soergel, Konrad Hermann physician
Spann, Wilma Nadene principal
Spitzer, Robert Ralph academic administrator emeritus
Spore, Keith Kent newspaper editor
Stadtmueller, Joseph Peter federal judge
Stafl, Adolf obstetrician, gynecologist, educator
†Stein, Gerald real estate and diversified holding company executive
Steinmiller, John F. professional basketball team executive
Sterner, Frank Maurice industrial executive
Stratton, Frederick Prescott, Jr. manufacturing executive
Stromberg, Roland Nelson historian
Swanson, Roy Arthur classicist, educator
†Sykes, Leonard L., Jr. newspaper editor
†Tay, Grace So biomedical engineer, researcher
Taylor, Donald retired manufacturing company executive
Taylor, Jerry Lynn microbiologist, educator
Teerlink, Richard Francis motor company executive
Terry, Leon Cass neurologist, educator
Teschner, Richard Rewa retired lawyer
†Thompson, Basil F. ballet master
Thrall, Arthur Alvin artist
Uecker, Bob actor, radio announcer, former baseball player, TV personality
Van Antwerpen, Regina Lane underwriter, insurance company executive

Van Vugt, Eric J. *lawyer*
Vaughn, Gregory Lamont *professional baseball player*
Vespa, Ned Angelo *photographer*
Vice, Jon Earl *hospital executive*
Viets, Hermann *college president, consultant*
Wallace, Harry Leland *lawyer*
Walmer, Edwin Fitch *lawyer*
Walters, William LeRoy *physics educator*
Warren, Richard M. *experimental psychologist, educator*
Warren, Robert Willis *federal judge*
Wawrzyn, Ronald M. *lawyer*
Weakland, Rembert G. *archbishop*
Weber, Charles Edward *management educator*
Weber, Robert George *lawyer*
†Weening, Richard William, Jr. *banker, finance and communications executive, venture capitalist*
Weil, Herman *psychology educator*
Weise, Charles Martin *zoology educator*
Wells, Carolyn Cressy *social work educator*
Wenzler, William Paul *architect*
Whyte, George Kenneth, Jr. *lawyer*
Widera, Georg Ernst Otto *materials engineering educator, consultant*
Wiedenman, Jere Wayne *lawyer*
Wigdale, James B. *bank executive*
†Wighers, Arthur *real estate developer*
Wikenhauser, Charles Joseph *zoological park director*
Wiley, Edwin Packard *lawyer*
Will, Trevor Jonathan *lawyer*
Willis, William J. *lawyer*
Wills, Robert Hamilton *newspaper executive*
Wilsdon, Thomas Arthur *product development engineer, administrator*
†Winsten, Saul Nathan *lawyer*
Yontz, Kenneth Fredric *medical and chemical company executive*
Zarse, Leigh Bryant *architect, architectural engineer*
Zeidler, Frank P. *former association administrator, mayor, arbitrator, mediator, fact-finder*
Zelazo, Nathaniel K. *engineering executive*
Zigman, Robert S. *public relations executive*
Ziperski, James Richard *lawyer, trucking company executive*
Zober, Norman Alan *health facility administrator*
Zore, Edward John *insurance company investment executive*

Minocqua
Utt, Glenn S., Jr. *motel investments and biotech industry company executive*

Monroe
Brown, Sandra Lee *educational consultant, watercolorist*
Deininger, David George *state circuit court judge*
Kittelsen, Rodney Olin *lawyer*

Montello
Burns, Robert Edward *editor, publisher*

Mosinee
Janis, Donald Emil *corporate controller*

Muskego
Stefaniak, Norbert John *business administration educator*

Nashotah
Hansen, Robert Wayne *judge, editor*

Neenah
Bergstrom, Dedric Waldemar *retired paper company executive*
Brophy, George Thomas *building products company executive*
Fetzer, Edward Frank *transportation company executive*
Parker, Richard E. *building products manufacturing company executive*
Proctor, Nick Hobert *toxicologist, pharmacologist*
Shepard, D. C. *wood products manufacturing company executive*
Stanton, Thomas Mitchell *lawyer, educator*
Underhill, Robert Alan *consumer products company executive*

Neillsville
Stockwell, Richard E. *journalist, business executive*

Nekoosa
Sigler, LeRoy Walter *banker, lawyer, entrepreneur*

New Franken
Weidner, Edward William *university chancellor, political scientist*

New Glarus
Kubly, Herbert *author, educator*
Marsh, Robert Charles *writer, music critic*

New London
Fitzgerald, Laurine Elisabeth *university dean, educator*

Oak Creek
Giblin, Louis *stockbroker*
Robertson, Michael Swing *religious association administrator*

Oconomowoc
Kneiser, Richard John *accountant*
Reich, Rose Marie *retired art educator*

Oconto Falls
Schlieve, Hy C. J. *principal*

Onalaska
Wilson, Anthony Vincent *business executive, mechanical engineer*

Oregon
Dorner, Peter Paul *retired economist, educator*

Oshkosh
Barwig, Regis Norbert James *priest*
Burke, Redmond A. *priest, librarian, educator*
Burr, John Roy *philosophy educator*
Dempsey, Timothy Michael *lawyer*
Drebus, Richard William *pharmaceutical company executive*
Goodson, Raymond Eugene *automotive executive*
Gruberg, Martin *political science educator*
†Holub, Gregory Steven *medical association administrator*
Hulsebosch, Charles Joseph *truck manufacturing company executive*
Jones, Norma Louise *librarian, educator*
Kerrigan, John E. *academic administrator*
Landwehr, William Charles *museum director*
Poberezny, Thomas *museum adminstrator*
Reinke, Leonard Herman *architect*

Osseo
Wright, Rodney H. *architect*

Pewaukee
Dickson, John R. *food products company executive, dairy products company executive*
Lee, Jack (Jim Sanders Beasley) *broadcast executive*
Quadracci, Harry R. *printing company executive*
Quadracci, Harry V. *printing company executive, lawyer*
Ranus, Robert D. *food marketing executive*

Phelps
Coccia, Michel Andre *retired lawyer*

Platteville
Al Yasiri, Kahtan Abbass *college dean*
Brodbeck, William Jan *retail executive*

Plover
Peanasky, Robert Joseph *biochemist, medical educator*

Plymouth
Gentine, Lee Michael *marketing professional*

Port Edwards
Veneman, Gerard Earl *paper company executive*

Port Washington
Frazier, Warner Carlisle *manufacturing company executive*

Racine
Batten, Michael Ellsworth *manufacturing company executive*
Bernberg, Bruce Arthur *consumer products publishing, printing executive*
Boyd, William Beaty *retired foundation executive*
Bray, Charles William, III *foundation executive*
Campbell, Edward Joseph *retired machinery company executive*
Carpenter, Richard M. *chemical company executive*
Coates, Glenn Richard *lawyer*
George, William Douglas, Jr. *consumer products company executive*
Gunnerson, Robert Mark *manufacturing company executive, accountant, lawyer*
Harlan, Jean Durgin *psychologist, writer, consultant*
Hart, Robert Camillus *lawyer, company executive*
Jacobson-Wolf, Joan Elizabeth *minister*
Johnson, Samuel Curtis *wax company executive*
Karls, John B. *retired educational administrator*
Klein, Gabriella Sonja *communications executive*
Konz, Gerald Keith *manufacturing company executive*
Murphy, William Mark Hickey *headmaster*
Pavlick, Walter Eugene *lawyer, manufacturing company executive*
†Remmel, Jerry G. *utilities executive*
Richter, Earl Edward *manufacturing company executive*
Savage, Richard T. *manufacturing company executive*
†Stewart, Richard Donald *internist, educator*
Swanson, Robert Lee *lawyer*

Rhinelander
Saari, John William, Jr. *lawyer*

Rice Lake
Knutson, Gerhard I. *bishop*

Richland Center
Meyer, Edwin Dale, Sr. *school system administrator*

Ripon
Ashley, Robert Paul, Jr. *English literature educator*
Miller, George H. *historian, educator*
Northrop, Douglas Anthony *English educator, college official and dean*
Stott, William Ross, Jr. *college president*

River Falls
Johnson, James Robert *ceramic engineer, educator*
Smith, Clyde Curry *historian, educator*
Thibodeau, Gary A. *university administrator*

River Hills
Silverman, Albert A. *retired lawyer, manufacturing company executive*
Smith, Jane Farwell *civic worker*

Rothschild
Drew, Richard Allen *electrical and instrument engineer*

Sayner
Southwick, Harry Webb *surgeon*

Sheboygan
Brewer, Warren Wesley *principal*
Buchen, John Gustave *retired judge*
†Dickelman, James Howard *retail chain executive*
Gore, Donald Ray *orthopedic surgeon*
Kohler, Ruth DeYoung *arts center executive*
Longo, George P. *superintendent*
Winkle, Sharon Louise *library administrator*

Shorewood
Surridge, Stephen Zehring *lawyer, writer*

Solon Springs
Robek, Mary Frances *business education educator*

South Milwaukee
Kitzke, Eugene David *research management executive*

Spring Green
Sisson, Everett Arnold *industrial developer, business executive*

Stevens Point
Ballard, Larry Coleman *insurance company executive*
†Gaiswinkler, Robert Sigfried *savings and loan executive*
Garber, David J. *sports association executive, marketing consultant*
LeGrande, William Hunt *biology educator*
Makholm, Mark Henry *lawyer, former insurance company executive*
Paul, Justus Fredrick *historian, educator*
Sanders, Keith R. *university chancellor*
Seramur, John C. *bank executive*
Stevens, Dwight Marlyn *educational administrator*

Stone Lake
Kissinger, Harold Arthur *retired army officer*

Stoughton
Ellery, John Blaise *communications educator emeritus*
Huber, David Lawrence *physicist, educator*
Kuhn, Peter Mouat *atmospheric physicist*

Sturgeon Bay
Becker, Bettie Geraldine *artist*

Sun Prairie
Allen, Ronald Royce *communication educator*
Eustice, Francis Joseph *lawyer*
Mischke, Carl Herbert *religious association executive, retired*

Superior
Feldman, Egal *historian, educator*
Fliss, Raphael M. *bishop*
Youngblood, Betty J. *academic administrator*

Thiensville
Berry, William Martin *financial consultant*
Kostecke, B. William *utilities executive*
Lee, Tong Hun *economics educator*
Roselle, William Charles *librarian*
Williams, Maxine Eleanor *elementary education educator*

Twin Lakes
Fleischer, John Richard *retired secondary education educator*

Verona
Schroeder, Henry William *publisher*

Wales
Leekley, Marie Valpoon *secondary education educator*

Walworth
Sissons, John Roger *educational administrator*

Waterloo
Kay, Dennis Matthew *operations manager*

Watertown
Henry, Carl Ferdinand Howard *theologian*

Waukesha
DeWees, James H. *retail company executive*
Falcone, Frank S. *college president*
Huggins, Marion Dixon, Jr. *manufacturing company executive*
Larson, Russell George *magazine and book publisher*
Lusic, Ronald R. *retail company executive*
Macy, John Patrick *lawyer*
Manor, Andrea Joan *nursing administrator*
Norris, Robert F. *food products company executive*
Parsons, Virginia Mae *psychology educator*
†Platner, John Leland *process equipment company executive*
Scheving, Lawrence Einar *scientist, anatomy educator*
Scott, Rodger Gene *personnel executive*

Waunakee
Berthelsen, John Robert *printing company executive*
O'Neil, J(ames) Peter *elementary education educator, computer software designer*

Waupun
†Sperger, Courtland *food products executive*

Wausau
†Birkholz, Douglas J. *industrial designer*
Derwinski, Dennis Anthony *dentist*
Drengler, William Allan John *lawyer*
Gotham, Kathleen *college dean, human services administrator*
Orr, San Watterson, Jr. *lawyer*
Slayton, John Arthur *electric motor manufacturing executive*
Weinberger, Leon Joseph *insurance company executive*

Wauwatosa
Hollister, Winston Ned *pathologist*

West Allis
Feinsilver, Donald Lee *psychiatry educator*
Powell, Rosalie *home economist*

West Bend
Fraedrich, Royal Louis *magazine editor, publisher*
Gardner, Robert Joseph *general and thoracic surgeon*
Rodney, Joel Morris *dean*
Styve, Orloff Wendell, Jr. *electrical engineer*

Whitewater
Bhargava, Ashok *economics educator*
Carrara, Arthur Alfonso *architect, designer, painter, graphic designer*
Culbertson, Frances Mitchell *psychology educator*
Greenhill, H. Gaylon *academic administrator*
Refior, Everett Lee *labor economist, educator*
Schallenkamp, Kay *college administrator*
Verma, Krishnanand *mathematics educator, researcher, administrator, consultant*

Williams Bay
Hobbs, Lewis Mankin *astronomer*
Kron, Richard G. *astrophysicist, educator*

Wisconsin Rapids
Brennan, Patrick Francis *printing paper manufacturing executive*
Engelhardt, LeRoy A. *retired paper company executive*
Kenney, Richard John *paper company finance executive*
Mead, George Wilson, II *paper company executive*

Woodruff
Nicolette, Archie John *local government official, retired secondary education educator*
†Rosenberg, Douglas Owen *healthcare management executive*

WYOMING

Afton
Call, Reuel *corporate executive*
Call, William A. *petroleum products company executive*
Hunsaker, Floyd B. *accountant*
Lowe, James Allen *school superintendent*

Big Horn
Garry, James B. *storyteller, researcher, writer*

Bondurant
Shepard, Paul Howe *ecology educator, author, lecturer*

Casper
Bostwick, Richard Raymond *retired lawyer*
Donley, Russell Lee, III *former state representative*
Hinchey, Bruce Alan *environmental engineering company executive*
Jozwik, Francis Xavier *agricultural business executive*
Kennerknecht, Richard Eugene *sales executive*
Lowe, Robert Stanley *lawyer*
Meenan, Patrick Henry *state legislator*
Miracle, Robert Warren *retired banker*
Mobley, Karen Ruth *art gallery director*
Nagel, Patricia Jo *state legislator, consultant, lawyer*
Perkins, Dorothy A. *marketing professional*
Rosenthal, Jack *broadcasting executive*
Seeger, Sondra Joan *artist*
Stroock, Thomas Frank *manufacturing company executive*
True, Jean Durland *entrepreneur, oil company executive*
Wilde, David George *electrical engineer, consultant*
Wold, John Schiller *geologist, former congressman*

Centennial
Russin, Robert Isaiah *sculptor, educator*

Cheyenne
Barrett, James E. *federal judge*
Beaman, William Charles *magistrate judge, legal clerk*
Brimmer, Clarence Addison *federal judge*
Brorby, Wade *federal judge*
Brown, Charles Stuart *retired state supreme court justice*
Budd, Robert Wesley *trade association executive*
Cardine, Godfrey Joseph *state supreme court justice*
Drummer, Donald Raymond *financial services executive*
Freudenthal, Steven Franklin *lawyer*
†Geringer, James E. *governor*
Golden, Michael *state supreme court justice*
Hanes, John Grier *lawyer, state legislator*
Hardway, James Edward *vocational specialist*
Hart, Joseph H. *bishop*
Hirst, Wilma Elizabeth *psychologist*
Hunton, Donald Bothen *retired internist*
Johnson, Alan Bond *federal judge*
Johnson, Wayne Harold *librarian, county official*
Karpan, Kathleen Marie *former state official, lawyer, journalist*
Knight, Robert Edward *banker*
Lawes, Patricia Jean *art educator*
Laycock, Anita Simon *psychotherapist*
LeBarron, Suzanne Jane *librarian*
Macy, Richard J. *state judge*
Mc Clintock, Archie Glenn *lawyer*
Meyer, Joseph B. *state attorney general*
Mockler, Esther Jayne *political party administrator, state legislator*
†Myers, Rolland Graham *investment counselor*
Noe, Guy *social services administrator*
Ohman, Diana J. *state official, former school system administrator*
Rooney, John Joseph *lawyer, former state supreme court justice*
Rose, Robert R., Jr. *lawyer*
Schaeffer, Gary N. *mayor*
Schuman, Gerald Eugene *soil scientist*
Smith, Stanford Sidney *state treasurer*
Southworth, Rod Brand *computer science educator*
Thomas, Richard Van *state supreme court justice*
Thomson, Thyra Godfrey *former state official*
Wagner, Samuel Albin Mar *records management executive, educator*
Wittler, Shirley Joyce *former state official, state commissioner*

Cody
Hassrick, Peter Heyl *museum director*
Housel, Jerry Winters *lawyer*
Jackson, Harry Andrew *artist*
Murphy, Warren Charles *rector*
Patrick, H. Hunter *lawyer, judge*
Shreve, Peg *state legislator, retired elementary educator*

Daniel
Parker, H. Lawrence *rancher, investor, retired investment banker*

Douglas
Sanford, Leroy Leonard *rancher*

Dubois
Betts, Robert Budd, Jr. *dude ranch owner*

Fort Laramie
Hageman, James C. *rancher*

Gillette
Enzi, Michael Bradley *accountant, state legislator*

Glenrock
Marr, Jo Ann *special education educator*

Green River
Marty, Lawrence A. *lawyer, magistrate judge*

Jackson
Downer, Eugene Debs, Jr. *editor, publisher*
Gordon, Stephen Maurice *manufacturing company executive, rancher*
Hansen, Clifford Peter *rancher*
LaLonde, Robert Frederick *state senator, retired*
Law, Clarene Alta *innkeeper, state legislator*
Moeller, Robert Charles, III *fine arts consultant*
Schuster, Robert Parks *lawyer*
Thulin, Walter Willis *real estate company executive*
Watt, James Gaius *lawyer, former government official, legal consultant*

Jackson Hole
Adler, Warren *novelist, producer, playwright*
Paulson, Glenn *environmental scientist*

Kemmerer
Clark, Michael *artist, educator*

Lander
Tipton, Harry Basil, Jr. *state legislator, physician*

Laramie
Bellamy, John Cary *civil engineer, meteorologist*
Boresi, Arthur Peter *author, educator*
Caldwell, Daniel Ralston *microbiology educator*
Chai, Winberg *political science educator, foundation chair*
Chisum, Emmett Dewain *historian, archeologist, researcher*
Christensen, Martha *mycologist, educator*
Cottam, Keith M. *librarian, educator, administrator*
Cronkleton, Thomas Eugene *physician*
Dickman, Francois Moussiegt *former foreign service officer*
Dunn, Thomas Guy *biology educator, university administrator*
Ferris, Clifford Duras *electrical engineer, bioengineer, educator*
Flach, Victor Hugo *designer, educator*
Gill, George Wilhelm *anthropologist*
Grandy, Walter Thomas, Jr. *physicist*
Gressley, Gene Maurice *history educator*
Guerin, Charles Allan *museum director, artist*
Hardy, Deborah Welles *history educator*
Hartman, Ronald Lee *plant systematist*
Jones, Bob Gordon *bishop*
Kinney, Lisa Frances *lawyer*
Laman, Jerry Thomas *mining company executive*
Lillegraven, Jason Arthur *paleontologist, educator*
Long, Francis Mark *electrical engineer, educator*
Maxfield, Peter C. *state legislator, law educator, lawyer*
Meyer, Edmond Gerald *energy and natural resources educator, resources scientist, entrepreneur, former chemistry educator, university administrator*
Mingle, John Orville *engineer, educator, lawyer, consultant*
†Nord, Thomas Allison *hospital administrator*
Nye, Eric William *English language educator*
Rechard, Paul Albert *civil engineering consulting company executive*
Reif, (Frank) David *artist, educator*
Roark, Terry Paul *university president*
Smith, Thomas Shore *lawyer*
Speight, James Glassford *research company executive*
Sutherland, Robert L. *engineering company executive, educator*
Williams, Roger Lawrence *historian, educator*

Moose
Craighead, Frank Cooper, Jr. *ecologist*

Newcastle
Sample, Bette Jeane *elementary educator*

Riverton
Bebout, Eli Daniel *oil executive*
Clark, Stanford E. *accountant*
Girard, Nettabell *lawyer*
Peck, Robert A. *newspaper publisher*

Rock Springs
Baumberger, Don R. *school system administrator*
Blackwell, Samuel Eugene *state legislator*
Chadey, Henry F. *museum director*

Sheridan
Jones, Nancy C. *construction executive*
Taylor, Judith Ann *sales executive*

Story
Mc Ewan, Leonard *former judge*

Teton Village
Ellwood, Paul Murdock, Jr. *health policy analyst, consultant*

Wheatland
Bunker, John Birkbeck *cattle rancher, retired sugar company executive*
Morrison, Samuel Ferris *secondary school educator*
†Whitney, Ralph Royal, Jr. *financial executive*

Wilson
Breitenbach, Mary Louise McGraw *psychologist, drug rehabilitation counselor*
Eliot, Robert Salim *physician*
Fritz, Jack Wayne *communications and marketing company executive*
Lawroski, Harry *nuclear engineer*
Sage, Andrew Gregg Curtin, II *corporate investor, manager*

Worland
Woods, Lawrence Milton *airline company executive*

TERRITORIES OF THE UNITED STATES

AMERICAN SAMOA

Pago Pago
Kruse, F. Michael *judge*
†Lutali, A. P. *governor of American Samoa*
†Solaita, Tulafono Fuli *senator*
†Sunia, Tausese *government official*
†Togafau, Malaetasi Mauga *judge*
Varghese, Mary *secondary education educator*
Weitzel, John Quinn *bishop*

FEDERATED STATES OF MICRONESIA

Chuuk
Neylon, Martin Joseph *bishop*

Kolonia, Pohnpei
Eu, March Fong *U.S. ambassador, former state official*

Ponape
Lippwe, Esikiel *broadcast specialist*
Ramon, Kohne K. *federal official*
Weilbacher, Robert James *Micronesian goverment official*

GUAM

Agana
Apuron, Anthony Sablan *archbishop*
Bordallo, Madeleine Mary (Mrs. Ricardo Jerome Bordallo) *lieutenant governor of Guam, wife of former governor of Guam*
Crisostomo, Manny *photographer*
Cruz, Benjamin Joseph Franquez *territory judge*
Duenas, Laurent Flores *nursing administrator*
Perez, Gerald S. A. *retail executive educator*
Ruth, Martha Cruz *senator*
San Agustin, Joe Taitano *Guam senator, financial institution executive, management researcher*
Shelton, Austin James (Sonny Shelton) *territorial legislator*
Tock, Joseph *lawyer*
Udick, Robert E. *newspaper executive*
Unpingco, John Walter Sablan *federal judge*

Barrigada
Diaz, Ramon Valero *retired judge*
Uyehara, Harry Yoshimi *library educator*

Mangilao
Hamerly, Michael T. *librarian*
Lee, Chin-Tian *academic administrator, agricultural studies educator*

Talofofo
Taylor, James John *academic adminstrator*

NORTHERN MARIANA ISLANDS

Saipan
Camacho, Tomas Aguon *bishop*
Dela Cruz, Jose Santos *state supreme court chief justice*
Guerrero, Juan Tenorio *territorial senator*
Laureta, Alfred *federal judge*
†Manglona, Benjamin T. *commonwealth official*
Munson, Alex Robert *judge*

PUERTO RICO

Adjuntas
Altieri Rosado, José Aníbal *principal*

Arecibo
†Harmon, John Knud *astronomer*

Bayamon
Santacana, Guido E. *physiology educator*
Van Rooij, Vincent A. M. *university president*

Caguas
†Hernandez Rivera, Enrique *bishop*
Ortiz, Víctor Raúl *parochial school educator*

Caparra
Pont, Marisara *public relations executive*

Carolina
Figueroa, Iván *lawyer*

Catano
Behar, Abraham *construction engineer*

Corozal
Rodriguez Garcia, Jose A. *agronomist, investigator*

Coto Laurel
Basols, Jose Andres *high school director and principal, priest*

Guaynabo
Cruz Aponte, Ramón Aristides *foundation administrator, educator*

Hato Rey
Fernández Hernández, Nivia Aurora *nutrition and dietetics educator*
Ferrer, Miguel Antonio *brokerage firm and investment bank executive*

Humacao
Castrodad, Felix A. *university administrator*

Manati
Silva-Ruíz, Sergio Andrés *biochemist*

Mayaguez
†Artiles, Nemuel Othniel *hospital executive*
†Casiano Vargas, Ulises *bishop*
Collins, Dennis Glenn *mathematics educator*
Hernandez-Avila, Manuel Luis *physical oceanography educator, researcher, administrator, consultant*
Rodríguez-Arias, Jorge Herminio *retired agricultural engineering educator*

Ponce
Paracchini, Alberto M. *banker*
Sala, Luis Francisco *surgeon, educator*
Torres-Aybar, Francisco Gualberto *medical educator*
Torres Oliver, Juan Fremiot *bishop*

Rincon
Morris, Victor Franklin, Jr. *meteorology educator*

Rio Piedras
Bangdiwala, Ishver Surchand *statistician, educator*
†Maura, Mariano A. *library and information science educator*

San German
Mojica, Agnes *academic administrator*

San Juan
Acevedo, Héctor Luis *mayor*
Acevedo-Vilá, Aníbal *state legislator, lawyer*
Acosta, Raymond Luis *federal judge*
Alvarez-Pérez, Angel *bank executive*
Aponte Alsina, Marta *editor, writer, press administrator*
Behar-Ybarra, Elias *civil, structural engineer*
Bonnet, Juan Amedee *nuclear engineer, educator*
Carreras, Francisco José *retired university president, foundation executive*
Carrion, Rafael, Jr. *banker*
Carrion, Richard *bank executive*
Cerezo, Carmen Consuelo *federal judge*
Colorado, Antonio José *lawyer*
Corrada del Río, Baltasar *state official, lawyer, former mayor, former congressman*
†Crawford, William Pingree *forester*
Cruz-Velez, David Francisco *senator*
De Jesús, Nydia Rosa *physician, anesthesiologist*
del Valle, Manuel Luis *distillery executive*
Diaz-Cruz, Jorge Hatuey *lawyer, former state supreme court justice*
Fariña de Woodbury, Margarita *psychotherapist*
Fernández-Coll, Fred *microbiologist, food technology laboratory director*
Fusté, José Antonio *federal judge*
Gelabert, Pedro Antonio *federal agency administrator, geologist*
Gierbolini-Ortiz, Gilberto *federal judge*
Gonzalez, Jose Ramón *academic administrator*
González Echevarria, Amelia L. *librarian, counselor*
Hernandez-Denton, Federico *commonwealth supreme court justice*
Laffitte, Hector Manuel *federal judge*
Lugo, Ariel E. *ecologist, botanist, federal agency administrator*
Marvel, Thomas Stahl *architect*
Matheu, Federico Manuel *university chancellor*
McClintock, Kenneth Davison *state legislator*
Muñoz-Solá, Haydeé Socorro *library administrator*
Myatt, Clifford E. *federal official*
Ocasio-Melendez, Marcial Enrique *history educator*
Orkand, Richard Kenneth *neurobiologist, researcher, educator*
Ortiz Velazquez, Rolando *territory legislator, lawyer*
Perez-Gimenez, Juan Manuel *federal judge*
Pesquera Morales, Carlos I. *government official*
Pieras, Jaime, Jr. *federal judge*
Prevor, Ruth Claire *psychologist*
Quiñones, Jose Antonio *structural engineer, consultant*
Ramirez-Rivera, Jose *physician*
Rivera-Ortiz, Gilberto *senator*
Rodriguez-del Valle, Nuri *microbiology educator*
Rua, Milton Francisco *lawyer*
Sahai, Hardeo *medical statistics educator*
San Antonio Mendoza, Oscar Anibal *state legislator*
Santiago, Juan Jose *secondary school president*
Schmidt-Monge, Roberto *federal judge*
†Sierra, Roberto *composer, music educator*
Thompson, Annie Figueroa *academic director, educator*
Torruella, Juan R. *federal judge*
Trías-Monge, Jose *lawyer, former territory supreme court chief justice*
Valentin Acevedo, Freddy *senator*

Santurce
Aponte Martinez, Luis Cardinal *archbishop*
Ashby, Patricia F. *school system administrator, psychologist*
Loubriel, Tere *bank executive*

REPUBLIC OF MARSHALL ISLAND

Majuro
Fields, David Clark *diplomat*
Lemari, Kunio David *federal official*
Note, Kessai H. *federal official*

VIRGIN ISLANDS

Charlotte Amalie
Bolt, Thomas Alvin Waldrep *lawyer*
†Frazer, Victor O. *delegate, former legislator*
Moore, Thomas Kail *chief judge*
Richardson, Bingley Geraldo *territory legislator*
Scott-Williams, Stephanie *territorial legislator*
†Thomas, Elliott G. *bishop*

Christiansted
Finch, Raymond Lawrence *judge*
†Mapp, Kenneth E. *lieutenant governor*
Resnick, Jeffrey Lance *federal judge*

Cruz Bay
Blitz, Peggy Sanderfur *corporate travel management company official*

Frederiksted
O'Neal, Lilliana Belardo de *territory senator*
Pickard, Mary Ann *senator*

Saint Croix
Talbot, Frederick Hilborn *bishop, former Guyanese diplomat*

Saint Thomas
†Ballentine, Rosalie S. *attorney general*
Cockayne, Robert Barton *retail company executive*
Creque, Linda Ann *non-profit educational and research executive, former education commissioner*
Duarte, Patricia M. *real estate and insurance broker*
Feuerzeig, Henry Louis *lawyer*
Hodge, Verne Antonio *judge*
Liburd, Almando Leando *senator*
Miner, Robert Gordon *creative promotional consultant, auctioneer, writer, publisher, actor*
Silvestro, Clement Mario *museum director, historian*
Smith, Lorna Watson *accountant, environmental health administrator*

MILITARY ADDRESSES OF THE UNITED STATES

ATLANTIC

APO
Adams, Alvin Philip, Jr. *diplomat, lawyer*
Bracete, Juan Manuel *diplomat, lawyer*
Brown, Richard C. *ambassador*
Carner, George *foreign service executive, economic strategist*
†Cason, James Caldwell *diplomat*
Cheek, James Richard *ambassador*
Davidow, Jeffrey *ambassador*
de Vos, Peter Jon *ambassador*
Dyal, William M., Jr. *federal agency administrator*
†Frechette, Myles Robert Rene *ambassador*
Guinot, Luis, Jr. *lawyer, ambassador*
Hinton, Deane Roesch *ambassador*
Hobbs, Roy Jerry *military career officer, health services administrator*
†Kadunc, Edward Louis, Jr. *federal government official*
†Keane, John Francis *diplomat*
Knowlton, Nancy *biologist*
†Magruder, Lawson William, III *military officer*
Mc Afee, Marilyn *ambassador*
Melton, Richard H. *diplomat*
Pastorino, Robert Stephen *diplomat, ambassador*
Pryce, William Thornton *foreign service officer*
Romero, Peter Frank *diplomat*
Rubinoff, Ira *biologist, research administrator, conservationist*
Sanbrailo, John A. *mission director*
Taylor, Paul Daniel *ambassador*
†Taylor, Philip Bates, III *diplomat*
Walker, William Graham *ambassador*
Wetzstein, Sandra Lynne *elementary school educator*
Whitman, Gerald John *diplomat*

FPO
†Bill, David Spencer, III *naval officer*
Hyde, Jeanette W. *ambassador*
†Krekich, Alexander Joseph *naval officer*

EUROPE

APO
Aaron, David L. *diplomat*
Basora, Adrian A. *ambassador*
†Benedict, Lawrence Neal *foreign service officer*
Berry, Ann Roper *diplomat*
†Bindenagel, James Dale *diplomat*
Blinken, Donald *ambassador, investment banker*
†Bombard, Charles Frederick *nursing administrator, consultant*
Borling, John Lorin *military officer*
Boyd, Charles Graham *military officer*
†Brady, Robert Edward *career officer, dentist*
Briggs, Everett Ellis *ambassador*
Brown, William Andreas *ambassador*
†Connell, Mary Ellen *diplomat*
†Creagan, James Francis *diplomat*
†Daniel, Eugene Lee *career officer*
Davis, John Roger, Jr. *foreign service officer*
†Dickey, James Stuart *military officer*
†Downer, Lee Alan *air force officer*
Doyle, Justin Emmett *lawyer, government official*
Eizenstat, Stuart E. *ambassador, lawyer*
Elson, Edward Elliott *diplomat*
†Evans, John Marshall *diplomat*
Flynn, Raymond Leo *ambassador to the Holy See, former mayor*
†Ginsberg, Marc C. *ambassador*
†Greenlee, David Nicol *foreign service officer*
Harriman, Pamela Digby Churchill *diplomat, philanthropist*
†Harris, William Thomas, III *diplomat*
†Hennessee, James Franklin *military officer*
Hibben, Barbara Ann Pandzik *museum administrator, foreign service officer*
†Holmes, James Howard *diplomat*
Hurwitz, Edward *ambassador to Kyrgyzstan*
Johnson, Darryl Norman *ambassador*
Kennedy, Mary Virginia *diplomat*
Klosson, Michael *foreign service officer*
†Link, Charles Dale *air force officer*
Loftus, Thomas Adolph *ambassador*
†Lotzbire, Bruce John *air force officer*
Mabus, Raymond Edwin, Jr. *ambassador, former governor*
†Meigs, Montgomery Cunningham, Jr. *military officer*
Miles, Richard *diplomat*
†Montgomery, William D. *United States ambassador*
Niles, Thomas Michael Tolliver *ambassador*
Norris, James Arnold *government executive*
Oaks, Robert C. *air force officer*
Petterson, Donald K. *foreign service officer, ambassador*
Pickering, Thomas Reeve *diplomat*

Ray, Norman Wilson *career officer*
Rey, Nicholas Andrew *ambassador*
Ryerson, William Edwin *diplomat*
Secchia, Peter F. *ambassador*
Sherrill, Anita Aileen *elementary school educator, consultant, educational system administrator*
Stokes, Carl Burton *ambassador, judge, former mayor, former state legislator*
Stone, Richard B. *ambassador*
†Terry, Wayne Gilbert *healthcare executive, hospital administrator*
†Tompkins, Tain Pendleton *foreign service official*
Walker, Edward S., Jr. *diplomat*
†Wardlaw, Frank Patterson *foreign service officer*
Welch, Charles David *diplomat*
Westley, John Richard *foreign service officer*
†Witt, Buford Randolph *air force officer*
Yates, John Melvin *diplomat*
Yates, Walter Harvey, Jr. *career officer*

FPO
Allen, Lloyd Edward, Jr. *naval officer*
Boucher, Richard A. *ambassador*
Branson, Mary Lou *family therapist, military agency administrator*
Crocker, Ryan C. *ambassador*
DeMaio, Dorothy Walters *tutorial school administrator, consultant*
Picotte, Leonard Francis *naval officer*
Pletcher, John Harold, Jr. *air force officer*
†Ransom, David Michael *diplomat*
Ryan, Thomas D. *naval officer*

PACIFIC

APO
Barry, Robert Louis *diplomat*
Blackburn, Paul Pritchard *diplomat*
†Brown, Daniel G. *military officer*
Burghardt, Raymond Francis, Jr. *foreign service officer*
Chung, Tchang-Bok *management analyst, consultant*
Daly, Judith Marie *critical care nurse*
†Harvey, Barbara Sillars *foreign service officer*
†Jenkins, Robert Gordon *air force officer*
Lambertson, David Floyd *ambassador*
Mondale, Joan Adams *wife of former vice president of U.S.*
Monjo, John Cameron *ambassador*
Running, Nels *career officer*
Smith, Myron George *former government official, consultant*
Tomseth, Victor L *ambassador*
Tull, Theresa Anne *ambassador*
Wolf, John S. *ambassador*
†Yamamoto, Donald Yukio *diplomat*

FPO
Chorba, Timothy A. *ambassador to Singapore*
†Franks, Tommy Ray *army officer*
Hall, James Henry *foreign service officer*
Hickey, Robert Philip, Jr. *naval officer*
Hooley, James Robert *oral and maxillofacial surgeon, educator, university dean*
†Nance, William Bennett *economic development specialist*

CANADA

ALBERTA

Banff
Fruchtman, Milton Allen *film and television producer, director*

Bentley
Manes, John Dalton *retired hospital administrator, anaesthesiologist*

Calgary
†Adamache, Ion *engineer*
Armstrong, David Anthony *physical chemist, educator*
Ballem, John Bishop *lawyer, novelist*
Blair, Sidney Robert *petroleum company executive*
Calkin, Joy Durfée *healthcare consultant, educator*
Campbell, Finley Alexander *geologist*
Caron, Ernie Matthew *airport executive*
Cheveldae, Tim *professional hockey player*
Child, Arthur James Edward *food company executive*
Cumming, Thomas Alexander *stock exchange executive*
Curtis, John Barry *bishop*
Dixon, Gordon Henry *biochemist*
†Duerr, Alfred *mayor*
Esler, John Kenneth *artist*
Fisher, John Philip *retired printing and publishing company executive*
Forbis, Richard George *archaeologist*
Furnival, George Mitchell *petroleum and mining consultant*
Glockner, Peter G. *civil and mechanical engineering educator*
Gordon, Lorne Bertram *corporate executive*
†Graf, Hans *conductor*
Grimes, Edward Clifford *oil industry executive, consultant*
Hagerman, Allen Reid *oil and gas company executive*
Haskayne, Richard Francis *petroleum company executive*
Hay, William Charles *professional hockey team executive*
Heidemann, Robert Albert *chemical engineering educator, researcher*
Hollenberg, Morley Donald *research physician, educator*
Hopper, Wilbert Hill *retired oil industry executive*
Housley, Phil F *professional hockey player*
Hriskevich, Michael Edward *oil and gas consultant*
Hugh, George M. *pipeline company executive*
Hughes, Margaret Eileen *law educator, former dean*
†Hume, James Borden *corporate professional, foundation executive*
Hyne, James Bissett *chemistry educator, industrial scientist, consultant*
Janes, Robert Roy *museum director, archaeologist, writer*
Jenkins, Kevin J. *airline company executive*
Jones, Geoffrey Melvill *physiology research educator*
Kentfield, John Alan *mechanical engineering educator*
King, Frank *investment company executive*
King, W. David *professional hockey coach*
LaHay, David George Michael *ballet company director*
Lederis, Karolis Paul (Karl Lederis) *pharmacologist, educator, researcher*
L'Heureux, Willard John *real estate lawyer, diversified company executive*
Little, Brian F. *oil company executive*
Lougheed, Peter *lawyer, former Canadian official*
MacDonald, Alan Hugh *librarian, university administrator*
Maclagan, John Lyall *retired petroleum company executive*
Maher, Peter Michael *university dean*
Maier, Gerald James *natural gas transmission and marketing company executive*
Malik, Om Parkash *electrical engineering educator, researcher*
Matthews, Francis Richard *lawyer*
McCaig, Jeffrey James *transportation company executive*
McCaig, John Robert *transportation executive*
McCready, Kenneth Frank *electric utility executive*
McDaniel, Roderick Rogers *petroleum engineer*
McEwen, Alexander Campbell *cadastral studies educator, former Canadian government official, surveying consultant*
McIntyre, Norman F. *petroleum industry executive*
Mc Kinnon, F(rancis) A(rthur) Richard *utility executive*
Meek, Gerry *library director*
Melvill-Jones, Geoffrey *physician, educator*
Meyers, Marlene O. *hospital administrator*
†Milavsky, Harold Phillip *real estate executive*
Monk, Allan James *baritone*
†Mossop, Grant Dilworth *geological institute director*
†Mungan, Necmettin *petroleum consultant*
Neale, E(rnest) R(ichard) Ward *retired university official, consultant*
Nigg, Benno Maurus *biomechanics educator*
O'Byrne, Paul J. *bishop*
Okulitch, Vladimir Joseph *geologist, university administrator*
Paquette, Richard *airport executive*
Parkinson, Dennis *biology educator, soil biology researcher*
Perrin, Robert Maitland *solicitor, oil company executive*
Peterson, Kevin Bruce *newspaper editor, publishing executive*
Pick, Michael Claude *international exploration consultant*
Pierce, Robert Lorne *petrochemical, oil and gas company executive*
Poole, Robert Anthony *journalist*
Price, Arthur Richard *petroleum company executive*
Raeburn, Andrew Harvey *performing arts association executive, record producer*
Rasporich, Anthony Walter *university dean*
Reid, David Evans *pipeline company executive*
Rewcastle, Neill Barry *neuropathology educator*
Roberts, John Peter Lee *cultural advisor, administrator, educator, writer*
Russell, Gary *broadcast executive*
Schulz, Robert Adolph *management educator, management consultant*
Seaman, Daryl Kenneth *oil company executive*
Seaman, Donald Roy *investment company executive*
Southern, Ronald D. *diversified corporation executive*
Stanford, James M. *oil company executive*
Stebbins, Robert Alan *sociology educator*
Stell, William Kenyon *neuroscientist, educator*
ter Keurs, Henk E. D. J. *cardiologist, educator*
Thomlison, Ray J. *university dean, educator*
Thorsteinsson, Raymond *geology research scientist*
Travis, Vance Kenneth *petroleum business executive*
Wagner, Norman Ernest *former energy company executive, former university president*
Watanabe, Mamoru *former university dean, physician, researcher*
Yoon, Ji-Won *virology, immunology and diabetes educator, research administrator*
Zaruby, Walter Stephen *holding company executive*

Camrose
Campbell, John Douglas *minister*

Canmore
Wood, Sharon *mountaineer*

Carstairs
Osterman, Constantine Elaine *Canadian legislator*

Cochrane
†Schmidt, Allen Edward *religious foundation administrator*

De Winton
Shutiak, James *management consultant*

Drumheller
Naylor, Bruce Gordon *museum director*

Edmonton
Adair, James Allen *Canadian provincial government official*
Adams, Peter Frederick *university president, civil engineer*
Archer, Violet Balestreri *music educator, composer, pianist, organist, percusionist, adjudicator*
Bach, Lars *wood products engineer, researcher*
Bateman, William Maxwell *retired construction company executive*
Bellow, Donald Grant *mechanical engineering educator*
Bentley, Charles Fred *consulting agrologist*
Berg, Roy Torgny *retired university dean*
Burnett, George *professional hockey coach*
†Charlesworth, Henry A. K. *geology educator*
Clements, Patricia Dawn *English educator, university dean*
Cook, David Alastair *pharmacology educator*
Cormack, Robert George Hall *botany educator*
Cormie, Donald Mercer *investment company executive*
Cossins, Edwin Albert *biology educator, academic administrator*
Cowie, Bruce Edgar *communications executive*
Daciuk, Myron Michael *bishop*
Davis, Wayne Alton *computer science educator*
Doyle, Wilfred Emmett *retired bishop*
Eng, Howard *airport administrator*
Fenton, Terry Lynn *author, artist, consultant*
Fields, Anthony Lindsay Austin *health facility administrator, oncologist, educator*
Folinsbee, Robert Edward *retired geology educator*
Forsyth, Joseph *Canadian government official*
Fowler, Richard S. *provincial legislator*
Fraser, Catherine Anne *Canadian chief justice*
Freeman, Milton Malcolm Roland *anthropology educator*
Genge, Kenneth Lyle *bishop*
Gough, Denis Ian *geophysics educator*
Harris, Walter Edgar *chemistry educator*
Hiruki, Chuji *plant virologist, science educator*
Hislop, Mervyn Warren *health advocate administrator, psychologist*
Horton, William Russell *retired utility company executive*
Hoyt, David Lemire *musician*
Hughes, Linda J. *newspaper publisher*
†Hughes, Monica *author*
†Hutchison, Geoffrey Richard *airport general manager*
Isley, Ernest D. *Canadian provincial official*
Israel, Werner *physics educator*
James, Michael N. G. *crystallographer, educator*
Johnston, Dick *Canadian provincial government minister*
Jones, Richard Norman *physical chemist, researcher*
Jungkind, Walter *design educator, writer, consultant*
Kay, Cyril Max *biochemist*
Kebarle, Paul *chemistry educator*
Khanna, Faqir Chand *physics educator*
†Klein, Ralph *provincial legislator, former city mayor*
Koval, Don O. *electrical engineering educator*
Kratochvil, Byron George *chemistry educator, researcher*
Krotki, Karol Jozef *sociology educator, demographer*
Lechelt, Eugene Carl *psychology educator*
Lemieux, Raymond Urgel *chemistry educator*
Lock, Gerald Seymour Hunter *retired mechanical engineering educator*
†MacLean, Victoria Graham *journalist, editor*
Mac Neil, Joseph Neil *archbishop*
Main, Douglas Cameron *provincial cabinet minister*
McDougall, Donald Blake *retired government official, librarian*
McDougall, John Roland *civil engineer*
McKee, Penelope Melna *library director*
McMaster, Juliet Sylvia *English language educator*
Miller, Jack David R. *radiologist, physician, educator*
Miller, Tevie *supernumary justice, academic administrator*
†Moody, Robert Vaughan *mathematician, educator*
Morgenstern, Norbert Rubin *civil engineering educator*
O'Briain, Niall P. *wood products company executive*
Offenberger, Allan Anthony *electrical engineering educator*
†Otto, Fred Douglas *chemical engineering educator*
Patrick, Lynn Allen *lawyer, construction company executive*
Pocklington, Peter H. *business executive*
Prideaux, Gary Dean *linguistics educator*
Rajotte, Ray V. *biomedical engineer, researcher*
Roskin, Lewis Ross *broadcasting company executive*
Rostad, Kenneth Leif *provincial government official*
Rostoker, Gordon *physicist, educator*
Rutter, Nathaniel Westlund *geologist, educator*
Sather, Glen Cameron *professional hockey team executive, coach*
Schurman, Donald Peter *hospital administrator*
Shoctor, Joseph Harvey *barrister, producer, civic worker*
Smith, Peter John *geographer, educator*
Smith, Richard Carlisle *history educator*
Speaker, Ray *Canadian government official*
Spencer, Mary Eileen *biochemist, educator*
Stanway, Paul William *newspaper editor*
Stelck, Charles Richard *geology educator*
Stepney, Philip Harold Robert *museum director*
Stevenson, William Alexander *retired justice of Supreme Court of Canada*
Stollery, Robert *construction company executive*
Sykes, Brian Douglas *biochemistry educator, researcher*
Thompson, Gordon William *dentist, educator*
†Towers, Gordon Thomas *province official*
Towers, T. Gordon *Canadian lieutenant governor*
Twa, Craighton Oliver *power company executive*
Umezawa, Hiroomi *physics educator, researcher*
†Usher, W. David *earth scientist*
Vance, Dennis Edward *biochemistry educator*
Wayman, Morris *chemical engineering educator, consultant*
†Wiebe, Rudy Henry *writer*
Wood, John Denison *utility company executive*

Fort McMurray
†Hyndman, Alexander W. *earth scientist*

Fort Saskatchewan
†Masters, Ian *metallurgical engineer*
Weir, D. Robert *company executive*

Lethbridge
Cho, Hyun Ju *veterinary research scientist*
Rand, Duncan D. *librarian*
Sonntag, Bernard H. *agrologist, research executive*

McLennan
Légaré, Henri Francis *archbishop*

Red Deer
Donald, Jack C. *oil company executive*

Saint Paul
Roy, Raymond *bishop*

Sherwood Park
Finlay, James Campbell *retired museum director*

Smith
Rodnunsky, Sidney *lawyer, educator, Prince of Kiev, Prince of Trabzon, Prince and Duke of Rodari, Duke of Chernigov, Count of Riga, Count of Saint John of Alexandria*

Waterton Lakes Park
†Russell, Andrew George Alexander *author, naturalist*

BRITISH COLUMBIA

Abbotsford
Sifton, Patricia Anne *library educator*

Bamfield
Druehl, Louis Dix *biology educator*

Brentwood Bay
Carrothers, Alfred William Rooke *retired law educator*

Burnaby
Arrott, Anthony Schuyler *physics educator*
†Barth, Norman Kenneth *hospital administrator, educator*
Borden, John Harvey *entomologist, educator*
†Borwein, Peter Benjamin *mathematician*
Brandhorst, Bruce Peter *biology educator*
Brantingham, Patricia Louise *criminology educator*
Brantingham, Paul Jeffrey *criminology educator*
Buitenhuis, Peter Martinus *language professional, educator*
†Canfield, Brian A. *communications company executive*
Copes, Parzival *economist, researcher*
†Dahn, Jeff R. *physics educator*
Felter, James Warren *painter, curator*
Kitchen, John Martin *historian, educator*
Tung, Rosalie Lam *business educator, consultant*

Cobble Hill
Cox, Albert Reginald *academic administrator, physician, retired*

Duncan
Hughes, Edward John *artist*

Gibsons
Millard, Peter Tudor *English language educator*

Kaleden
Siddon, Thomas Edward *Canadian government official, environmental consultant*

Kamloops
Cruickshank, James David *bishop*
Sabatini, Lawrence *bishop*

Kelowna
Muggeridge, Derek Brian *dean, engineering consultant*

Maple Ridge
†Wainwright, David Stanley *intellectual property professional*

Nanaimo
Margolis, Leo *marine biologist*
Meadows, Donald Frederick *librarian*
Ricker, William Edwin *biologist*

Nelson
Mallon, Peter *bishop*

New Denver
†McCrory, Colleen *ecologist*

New Westminster
Fair, James Stanley *hospital administrator*
Waygood, Ernest Roy *plant physiology educator*

North Saanich
Weichert, Dieter Horst *seismologist, researcher*

North Vancouver
Gibbs, David George *retired food processing company executive*
Jarrett, Anthony *retired business executive*
Joyner, John Brooks *museum director*
Smith, Robert John *health facility administrator*

Powell River
Carsten, Arlene Desmet *financial executive*

Prince Rupert
Hannen, John Edward *bishop*

Richmond
†Halsey-Brandt, Greg *mayor*
Johnston, Rita Margaret *Canadian provincial government official*
Plomp, Teunis (Tony Plomp) *minister*

Saanichton
Crozier, Lorna *poet, educator*
Little, Carl Maurice *performing arts administrator*

Salt Spring Island
Raginsky, Nina *artist*
Shepherd, R. F. *retired bishop*

Sidney
Best, Melvyn Edward *geophysicist*
Bigelow, Margaret Elizabeth Barr *mycologist educator*
Davis, John Christopher *zoologist, aquatic toxicologist*
Irving, Edward *geophysicist, educator*
Kendrick, William Bryce *biology educator, author, publisher*
Mann, Cedric Robert *retired institute administrator, oceanographer*
Petrie, William *physicist*
van den Bergh, Sidney *astronomer*

Sooke
Booth, Andrew Donald *retired university administrator, scientist*

Summerland
†Beveridge, Herbert James Thomas *research scientist*
Dueck, John *agricultural researcher, plant pathologist*
Looney, Norman Earl *pomologist, plant physiologist*

Surrey
Farley, Lawrence *clergyman*

Kinsella, William Patrick author, educator

Vancouver

Aalto, Madeleine library director
Aberle, David Friend anthropologist, educator
†Agler, David conductor
Aguzzi-Barbagli, Danilo Lorenzo literature educator
†Alden, Thomas Hyde metallogist
Alleyne, John dancer, choreographer
Andrews, John Hobart McLean education educator
Aubke, Friedhelm chemistry educator
Baird, Patricia Ann physician, educator
Bates, David Vincent physician, medical educator
Batts, Michael Stanley German language educator
Beagrie, George Simpson dentist, educator, dean emeritus
Belzberg, Samuel real estate investment professional
Bender, Graham I. forest products executive
Bennett, Winslow Wood mechanical engineer
Bentley, Peter John Gerald forest industry company executive
Bentley, Thomas Roy literary educator, writer, consultant
Birch, Murray Patrick oil industry executive
Blair, Robert animal science administrator, educator, researcher
Bloom, Myer physicist, educator
Bonner, Robert William lawyer
Bowering, George Harry writer
Boyd, David William mathematician, educator
Buell, Thomas Allan lumber company executive
Bure, Pavel professional hockey player
Burhenne, Hans Joachim physician, radiology educator
Cairns, H. Alan C. political scientist, educator
Campbell, Bruce Alan market research consultant
Campbell, Jack James Ramsay microbiology educator
Chitty, Dennis Hubert zoology educator
Chow, Anthony Wei-Chik physician
Clark, Colin Whitcomb mathematics educator
Clarke, Garry Kenneth Connal geophysics educator
Coley, Betty librarian
Collins, Mary health association executive, former Canadian legislator
†Comisarow, Melvin B. chemist, educator
Conway, John S. history educator
Copp, Douglas Harold physiologist, educator
Craig, Kenneth Denton psychologist, educator, researcher
Crawford, Carl Benson retired civil engineer, government research administrator
Cynader, Max Sigmund psychology, physiology, brain research educator, researcher
Donald, Ian wood products company executive
Doyle, Patrick John otolaryngologist
Durrant, Geoffrey Hugh retired English language educator
Eaves, Allen Charles Edward hematologist, medical agency administrator
Elkins, David J. political science educator
Erickson, Arthur Charles architect
Ericson, Richard Victor social science and law educator, university administrator
Exner, Adam archbishop
Feaver, George A. political science educator
Feldman, Joel Shalom mathematician
†Finlay, Barton Brett science educator
Finnegan, Cyril Vincent retired university dean, zoology educator
Freeman, Hugh James gastroenterology educator
Friedman, Sydney M. anatomy educator, medical researcher
†Gallagher, Michael Francis diplomat
Gardiner, William Douglas Haig bank executive
Gilbert, John Humphrey Victor audiologist, speech scientist, educator
Goldberg, Michael Arthur land policy and planning educator
Grace, John Ross chemical engineering educator
Granirer, Edmond Ernest mathematician, educator
Griffiths, Arthur R. professional hockey team executive
Grunder, Arthur Neil forest products industry executive
Gunn, Roderick James broadcast executive
Hallam, Robert J. performing company executive, consultant
Hardwick, David Francis pathologist
Hardy, Walter Newbold physics educator, researcher
Harwood, Brian Dennis securities industry executive
Haycock, Kenneth Roy education administrator
Haysom, Ian Richard newspaper editor
Head, Ivan Leigh law educator
†Hegele, Richard G. pathologist
Hirshen, Sanford architect, educator
Ho, Samuel Pao-San economics educator
Hoar, William Stewart zoologist, educator
Holmes, Willard art gallery director
Holsti, Kalevi Jacque political scientist, educator
Holtby, Douglas Martin television executive
Howard, John Lindsay lawyer, forest industry company executive
Howard, T. E. scientific and research think-tank executive
Hudson, Donald J. stock exchange executive
Hume, Stephen writer, editor
Jackson, Stu professional sports team executive, former university basketball coach
James, Brian Robert chemistry educator
Jewesson, Peter John clinical pharmacologist, educator
Jones, David Robert zoology educator
Jordan, Robert Maynard language and literature professional, educator
Jull, Edward V. electrical engineer, radio scientist, educator
Jurock, Oswald Erich real estate executive
Keevil, Norman Bell mining executive
Kesselman, Jonathan Rhys economics educator, public policy researcher
Kieffer, Susan Werner geology educator
Klohn, Earle Jardine engineering company executive, consultant
Klonoff, Harry psychologist
Knobloch, Ferdinand J. psychiatrist, educator
Knudsen, Conrad Calvert corporate executive
Kubicek, Robert Vincent history educator
Ladner, Thomas E. lawyer
Lambert, Michael Malet hotel company executive
Langdon, Frank Corriston political science educator, researcher
Laponce, Jean Antoine political scientist
Larkin, Peter Anthony zoology educator, university dean and official
LeBlond, Paul Henri oceanographer, educator
Lindsey, Casimir Charles zoologist
Lipsey, Richard George economist, educator
Lusztig, Peter Alfred university dean, educator
Lysyk, Kenneth Martin judge
MacCrimmon, Kenneth Robert management educator
Mahler, Richard T. finance executive
March, Beryl Elizabeth animal scientist, educator
Marchak, Maureen Patricia anthropology and sociology educator
Mathews, William Henry geologist, educator
Mattessich, Richard Victor (Alvarus) business administration educator
McBride, Barry Clarke microbiology and oral biology educator, research microbiologist
†McEachern, Allan Canadian justice
McGeer, Edith Graef neurological science educator emerita
Mc Lean, Donald Millis microbiology, pathology educator, physician
McLean, Kirk professional hockey player
McNeill, John Hugh university dean
Meisen, Axel chemical engineer, university administrator
Miller, Robert Carmi, Jr. microbiology educator, university administrator
Miura, Robert Mitsuru mathematician, researcher, educator
Mizgala, Henry F. physician
Nafe, John Elliott geophysicist
Nemetz, Nathaniel Theodore lawyer, former chief justice of British Columbia
Newman, Murray Arthur aquarium administrator
Noble, Stuart Harris newspaper executive
Oberlander, Cornelia Hahn landscape architect
Overmyer, Daniel Lee Asian studies educator
†Owen, Philip Walter mayor, business owner
Ozier, Irving physicist, educator
Pacheco-Ransanz, Arsenio Hispanic and Italian studies educator
Patkau, John architect
Patkau, Patricia architect, architecture educator
Paty, Donald Winston neurologist
Pearson, Richard Joseph archaeologist, educator
Peters, Ernest metallurgy educator, consultant
Peterson, Leslie Raymond barrister
Phillips, Anthony George neurobiology educator
Phillips, Edwin Charles gas transmission company executive
Phillips, John Edward zoologist, educator
Pickard, George Lawson physics educator
Pincock, Richard Earl chemistry educator
†Pitcher, Tony John fishery science educator, author
Piternick, Anne Brearley librarian, educator
Pulleyblank, Edwin George history educator emeritus, linguist
Quinn, Pat (John Brian Patrick Quinn) professional sports team manager
Rae, Barbara Joyce employee placement company executive
Raffi, (Raffi Cavoukian) folksinger, children's entertainer
Randall, David John physiologist, zoologist, educator
†Rennie, Paul Steven science administrator, biochemist, surgeon
†Richardson, John Reginald physics educator
Riedel, Bernard Edward retired pharmaceutical sciences educator
Robinson, John Lewis geography educator
Rootman, Jack ophthalmologist, surgeon, pathologist, oncologist, artist
Rothstein, Samuel librarian, educator
Roy, Chunilal psychiatrist
Russell, Richard Doncaster geophysicist, educator, geoscientist
Saint-Jacques, Bernard linguistics educator
Salcudean, Martha Eva mechanical engineer, educator
Saunders, Peter Paul investor
Saywell, William George Gabriel foundation administrator
Seymour, Brian Richard mathematician
Shaw, Michael biologist, educator
Shearer, Ronald Alexander economics educator
Sikora, Richard Innes philosophy educator
Sinclair, Alastair James geology educator
Sion, Maurice mathematics educator
Slaymaker, H. Olav geography educator
Slonecker, Charles Edward anatomist, medical educator, author
Smethurst, Robert Guy lawyer
Smith, Michael biochemistry educator
Smith, Raymond Victor paper products manufacturing executive
Snider, Robert F. chemistry educator, researcher
Solloway, C. Robert forest products company executive
Splane, Richard Beverley social work educator
Stankiewicz, Wladyslaw Jozef political scientist, educator
Stewart, Ross chemistry educator
Stone, Robert Ryrie financial executive
Suedfeld, Peter psychologist, educator
Sutter, Morley Carman medical scientist
Swanson, Charles Andrew mathematics educator
Tees, Richard Chisholm psychology educator, researcher
Thurlbeck, William Michael retired pathologist, retired medical educator
Tingle, Aubrey James pediatric immunologist, research administrator
Tyers, Geddes Frank Owen surgeon
Underhill, Anne Barbara astrophysicist
Unger, Richard Watson history educator
Unruh, William G. physics educator, researcher
Vogt, Erich Wolfgang physicist, academic administrator
Volkoff, George Michael educational administator, former physics educator
Wakefield, Wesley Halpenny church official
Warren, Harry Verney geological sciences educator, consulting geological engineer
Webber, William Alexander university administrator, physician
Wedepohl, Leonhard M. electrical engineering educator
Wellington, William George plant science and ecology educator
Wheeler, John Oliver geologist
White, Ruth Lillian French language educator, researcher
Willson, John Michael mining company executive
Wilson, Graham McGregor energy company executive
†Yaffe, Barbara Marlene journalist
Young, Lawrence electrical engineering educator
Zidek, James Victor statistician, educator

Victoria

Antoniou, Andreas electrical engineering educator
Barber, Clarence Lyle economics educator
Barkley, William Donald museum executive director
Barnes, Christopher Richard geologist
Batten, Alan Henry astronomer
Boone, Lois Ruth legislator
Bousfield, Edward Lloyd biologist
Chard, Chester Stevens archaeologist, educator
De Roo, Remi Joseph bishop
Drew, T. John life science research administrator
Frame, John Timothy bishop
Fyke, Kenneth John hospital administrator
†Gabelmann, Colin provincial attorney general
Gardom, Garde Basil Canadian government official
Hamilton, Donald Emery librarian
Harcourt, Michael Franklin premier of Province of British Columbia
Harris, Christie Lucy author
Harvey, Donald artist, educator
Horn, Paul Joseph musician
Hutchings, John Barrie astronomer, researcher
Lam, David C. lieutenant governor
Lind, Niels Christian civil engineering educator
Mac Diarmid, William Donald physician
Manning, Eric computer science and engineering educator, university dean, researcher
Mc Carter, John Alexander biochemistry educator
McCoppin, Peter symphony orchestra conductor
McTaggart-Cowan, Ian retired university chancellor
Morton, Donald Charles astronomer
Oke, John Beverley astronomy educator
Partridge, Bruce James lawyer, educator
Payne, Robert Walter psychologist, educator
Segger, Martin Joseph museum director, art history educator
†Stetson, Peter Brailey astronomer
Strong, David F. university administrator
Tighe, James C. publisher
†Trust, Trevor John microbiology educator and researcher
Weisgerber, John Sylvester provincial legislator
Welch, S(tephen) Anthony university dean, Islamic studies and arts educator
Wiles, David McKeen chemist
Wright, Kenneth Osborne retired astronomer

West Vancouver

Bentall, Shirley Franklyn lay church leader, author
Donaldson, Edward Mossop research scientist, government official
†Pasini, Albert R. engineer
Petrina, Anthony J. mining executive, retired
Wynne-Edwards, Hugh Robert entrepreneur, scientist

White Rock

Cooke, Herbert Basil Sutton geologist, educator
Freeze, Roy Allan engineering consultant
Huntington, A. Ronald retired coal terminal executive

MANITOBA

Brandon

Robertson, John Alden agrologist, researcher

Churchill

Rouleau, Reynald bishop

Oak Hammock Marsh

Wrigley, Robert Ernest museum director, ecologist

Pinawa

Allan, Colin James nuclear research and development company executive
†Wright, Michael George science administrator, research metallurgist

Saint Boniface

Hacault, Antoine Joseph Leon archbishop

The Pas

Sutton, Peter Alfred archbishop

Winnipeg

Alexander, Norman James investment consultant
Anderson, David Trevor law educator
Angel, Aubie physician, academic administrator
Asper, Israel Harold broadcasting executive
Barber, Robert Charles physics educator
†Bentley, Jeffrey performing company executive
Bigelow, Charles Cross biochemist, university administrator
Blanchard, Robert Johnstone Weir surgeon
Bowman, John Maxwell physician, educator
Bulman, W. John A. printing company executive
Burt, Christopher Murray former newspaper editor, communications consultant
Carstairs, Sharon state legislator
Cherniack, Saul Mark retired barrister, solicitor
Cohen, Albert Diamond retail executive
Cohen, Harley civil engineer, science educator
†Connelly, Karen Marie writer
Converse, William Rawson Mackenzie librarian
Curtis, Charles Edward Canadian government official
Di Cosimo, Joanne Violet museum director
Ducharme, Gerry minister of urban affairs
Dumont, W. Yvon provincial official
Eales, John Geoffrey zoology educator
Eyre, Ivan artist
Ferguson, Robert Bury mineralogy educator
Filmon, Gary Albert Canadian provincial premier, civil engineer
Findlay, Glen Marshall agrologist
Fraser, John Foster management company executive
†Graham, Laura S.E. ballet dancer
†Haber, Steve plant pathologist, researcher
Hamerton, John Laurence geneticist, educator
Harder, Helmut George religious organization administrator
Haworth, James Chilton pediatrics educator
Hawthorne, Frank Christopher geologist, educator
†Hehn, Lorne Frederick agricultural association executive
Hermaniuk, Maxim retired archbishop
Hodne, Thomas Harold, Jr. architect, educator
Hogan, Terrence Patrick psychologist, university administrator
Israels, Lyonel Garry hematologist, medical educator
Jarmus, Stephan Onysym priest
Kaminski, John dancer
Kanfer, Julian Norman biochemist, educator
Kroetsch, Robert Paul English language educator, author
Kuffel, Edmund electrical engineering educator
†Laliberte, Garland Everett agricultural engineer
Lang, Otto E. industry executive, former Canadian cabinet minister
†Lewis, Andre Leon associate artistic director
Liba, Peter Michael communications executive
Loxley, John economics educator
Lyon, Sterling Rufus justice
MacKenzie, George Allan diversified company executive
Mantsch, Henry Horst chemistry educator
Matthews, Patrick John consumer products company executive
McGonigal, Pearl former lieutenant governor
McKie, Francis Paul journalist
Meehan, John artistic director
†Morris, Jorden Walter dancer, educator
Morrish, Allan Henry electrical engineering educator
Naimark, Arnold university president, physiologist, internist
†Oberman, Sheldon Arnold writer, educator
†Olds, Elizabeth dancer
Paddock, John professional hockey team head coach
Persaud, Trivedi Vidhya Nandan anatomy educator, researcher, consultant
Poettcker, Henry retired seminary president
†Ratmansky, Alexei dancer
Riske, William Kenneth cultural services consultant
Roblin, Duff Canadian senator
Ronald, Allan Ross internal medicine and medical microbiology educator, researcher
Ross, Robert Thomas neurologist, educator
†Rubio, Suzanne Sarah ballet dancer
†Savchenko, Alla ballet mistress
Schaefer, Theodore Peter chemistry educator
Schultz, Harry health science organization administrator
†Scott, R. J. justice
Scott, Richard Jamieson chief justice
Searle, Stewart A. transportation equipment holding company executive
†Seifert, Blair Wayne clinical pharmacist
Shenkarow, Barry L. professional hockey team executive
Shnier, Alan real estate executive
Sjoberg, Donald bishop
Smith, Ian Cormack Palmer biophysicist
Spohr, Arnold Theodore artistic director, choreographer
Stalker, Jacqueline D'Aoust academic administrator, educator
Sutherland, John Beattie radiologist, health center administrator
Suzuki, Isamu microbiology educator, researcher
Thorfinnson, A. Rodney hospital administrator
†Tipples, Keith Howard research scientist
†Tremere, Arnold Wesley agricultural institute executive
†Vodrey, Rosemary province attorney general
Wall, Leonard J. bishop
Watchorn, William Ernest diversified manufacturing executive
†Wei-Qiang, Zhang dancer
†Weismiller, David R. library administrator
Whitener, William Garnett dancer, choreographer
Wiebe, Bernie conflict resolution studies educator
Wolfart, H. C. linguistics scholar, author, editor
Wowchuk, Rosann provincial legislator
Wreford, David Mathews magazine editor

NEW BRUNSWICK

Dieppe

Finn, Gilbert lieutenant governor

Douglas

Cogswell, Frederick William English language educator, poet, editor, publisher

Fredericton

Armstrong, Robin Louis university official, physicist
†Biden, Ed biomedical engineer, educator
†Blanchard, Edmond P. Canadian provincial official and attorney general
Easterbrook, James Arthur psychology educator
Elkhadem, Saad Eldin Amin foreign language and literature educator, author, editor, publisher
Faig, Wolfgang survey engineer, engineering educator
Grotterod, Knut retired paper company executive
†Hoyt, William Lloyd Canadian chief justice
Kennedy, Richard Frederick English language educator
Kenyon, Gary Michael gerontology educator, researcher
Lemmon, George Colborne bishop
Lewell, Peter A. international technology executive, researcher
Lumsden, Ian Gordon art gallery director
†McCain, Norrie province official
McGeorge, Ronald Kenneth hospital executive
McKenna, Frank Joseph Canadian politician, lawyer
Ruthven, Douglas Morris chemical engineering educator
Valenta, Zdenek chemistry educator
Vaníček, Petr geodesist

Moncton

Albert, Elide architect
Chiasson, Donat archbishop
†Gusella, Mary Margaret deputy minister
Walker, Tennyson A. corporation executive

Rothesay

Fairweather, Robert Gordon Lee lawyer

Saint Andrews

Anderson, John Murray operations executive, former university president
Clark, David R. executive not-for-profit organization, lawyer
Scott, William Beverley ichthyologist

Saint John

Condon, Thomas Joseph university historian

Sussex

†Secord, Lloyd Douglas healthcare administrator

NEWFOUNDLAND

Corner Brook
Payne, Sidney Stewart *archbishop*
Watts, Harold Ross *hospital administrator*

Saint John's
Clark, Jack I. *civil engineer, researcher*
Coady, Larry *marine biology research administrator*
Crim, Lawrence *marine life research administrator*
Davis, Charles Carroll *aquatic biologist, educator*
Goodridge, Noel Herbert Alan *state supreme court chief justice*
Grattan, Patricia Elizabeth *art gallery director*
Harvey, Donald F. *bishop*
†Hiscock, Boyd L. *minister, religious organization administrator*
Idler, David Richard *biochemist, marine scientist, educator*
Jeffrey, N. E. *marine biology administrator*
†King, Roy D. *religious organization administrator*
Logan, Rodman Emmason *jurist*
Major, Kevin Gerald *writer*
Mate, Martin *bishop*
May, Arthur W. *former Canadian government official, educator*
Mills, David B. *museum director*
Murphy, John Joseph *city official, retail executive*
Penney, Pearce John *retired librarian*
†Roberts, Edward Moxon *Canadian government official, lawyer, politician*
Rochester, Michael Grant *geophysics educator*
Russell, Frederick William *Canadian provincial official*
Thomas, Martin Lewis H. *marine ecologist, educator*
Troy, J. Edward *bishop*
Wells, Clyde Kirby *Canadian provincial government official*
Williams, Harold *geology educator*

NORTHWEST TERRITORIES

Iqaluit
Williams, John Christopher Richard *bishop*

Yellowknife
Ballantyne, Michael Alan *legislator*
Cournoyea, Nellie J. *Canadian government official*
Croteau, Denis *bishop*
de Weerdt, Mark Murray *judge*
Kakfwi, Stephen *Canadian government official*
Patterson, Dennis Glen *Canadian government official, lawyer*

NOVA SCOTIA

Antigonish
Campbell, Colin *bishop*

Bedford
Hennigar, David J. *investment broker*

Dartmouth
Bhartia, Prakash *defense research management executive, researcher, educator*
Callaghan, J. Clair *corporate executive*
Elliott, James A. *oceanographer, researcher*
Keen, Charlotte Elizabeth *marine geophysicist, researcher*
Mann, Kenneth Henry *marine ecologist*
Needler, George Treglohan *oceanographer, researcher*
Nickerson, T. B. *think-tank organization executive*
Platt, Trevor Charles *oceanographer, scientist*

Enfield
Randell, Joseph David *airline executive*

Halifax
Amey, Lorne James *library science educator*
Birdsall, William Forest *librarian*
Borgese, Elisabeth Mann *political science educator, author*
†Burke, Austin E. *archbishop*
Carrigan, David Owen *history educator*
Carruthers, S. George *medical educator, physician*
†Clarke, Lorne O. *provincial judge*
Comeau, Louis Roland *electric power industry executive*
†Dexter, Robert Paul *lawyer*
Dickey, John Horace *lawyer*
Dykstra, Mary Elizabeth *library and information science educator*
Easterbrook, Kenneth Brian *retired microbiologist*
Fillmore, Peter Arthur *mathematician, educator*
Flint, John E. *historian, educator*
Fowler, Charles Allison Eugene *architect, engineer*
Geldart, Donald James Wallace *physics educator*
Gillis, John William *Canadian legislator, geologist*
Glube, Constance Rachelle *Canadian chief justice*
Gold, Edgar *marine affairs educator, mariner, lawyer*
Gold, Judith Hammerling *psychiatrist*
Goldbloom, Richard Ballon *pediatrics educator*
Gratwick, John *management consulting executive, writer, consultant*
Gray, James *English literature educator*
Hall, Brian Keith *biology educator, author*
Jackson, Sarah Jeanette *sculptor, graphic artist, copier artist, bookmaker*
†Kinley, John James *province official*
Langley, George Ross *medical educator*
Leffek, Kenneth Thomas *chemist, educator*
Macdonald, Joseph Albert Friel *lawyer*
MacKay-Lyons, Brian Gerald *architect, urban designer, architecture educator*
MacLean, Guy Robertson *retired university president*
Murray, Thomas John (Jock Murray) *medical humanities educator, medical researcher*
O'Dor, Ron *physiologist, marine biology educator*
Ozmon, Kenneth Lawrence *university president, educator*
†Pincock, Douglas George *electronics company executive*
Pringle, John D. *ecological research administrator*
Renouf, Harold Augustus *business consultant*
Riordon, John Bernard *museum director*
Savage, John P. *provincial official*
†Shaw, Timothy Milton *political science educator*
Smith, Ronald Emory *telecommunications executive*
Sparling, Mary Christine *foundation executive*
Stairs, Denis Winfield *political science educator*
Thompson, William Grant *management executive*
Tonks, Robert Stanley *pharmacology and therapeutics educator, former university dean*
Wilson, George Peter *industrial engineer*

Jeddore
Pottie, Roswell Francis *science and technology consultant*

Kentville
Baker, George Chisholm *engineering executive, consultant*

Liscomb
Hemlow, Joyce *language and literature educator, author*

Lunenburg
Morrow, James Benjamin *retired sea products company executive*

Mahone Bay
Tolmie, Kenneth Donald *artist, author*

North Sydney
Nickerson, Jerry Edgar Alan *manufacturing executive*

Parrsboro
Hatfield, Leonard Fraser *retired bishop*

Stellarton
Gogan, James Wilson *corporate executive*
Rowe, Allan Duncan *food products executive*
Sobey, David Frank *food company executive*
Sobey, Donald Creighton Rae *real estate developer*

Timberlea
Verma, Surjit K. *school system administrator*

Truro
Mac Rae, Herbert Farquhar *retired college president*

Wallace
Bidwell, Roger Grafton Shelford *biologist, educator*
Boyle, Willard Sterling *physicist*

Waverly
†Swan, Judith *marine lawyer*

Wolfville
Bishop, Roy Lovitt *physics and astronomy educator*
Colville, David Alexander *artist*
Elliott, Robbins Leonard *consultant*
Ogilvie, Kelvin Kenneth *chemistry educator*
Zeman, Jarold Knox *history educator*

ONTARIO

Almonte
Morrison, Angus Curran *aviation executive*
Penney, Alphonsus Liguori *archbishop*

Ancaster
†Brockhouse, Bertram Neville *physicist, retired educator*

Barrie
Clune, Robert Bell *bishop*

Blenheim
Thompson, Wesley Duncan *grain merchant*

Brampton
Bastian, Donald Noel *bishop, retired*
Beaumont, Donald A. *department store chain executive*
Greenhough, John Hardman *business forms company executive*
Prevost, Edward James *paint manufacturing executive*
†Robertson, Peter Barrie *mayor*
Toole, David George *pulp and paper products executive*

Brantford
Woodcock, Richard Beverley *health facility administrator*

Burlington
Cragg, Laurence Harold *chemist, former university president*
Donelan, Mark Anthony *physicist*
Elgersma, Ray *relief and development organization executive*
Hamilton, Donald Gordon *religious association administrator*
Harris, Philip John *engineering educator*
Jackson, Donald Kenneth *transportation company executive*
Karsten, Albert *religious organization administrator*
Krishnappan, Bommanna Gounder *fluid mechanics engineer*

Caledon
Fallis, Albert Murray *microbiology educator*

Cambridge
Hooper, Wayne Nelson *clergy member*
Turnbull, Robert Scott *manufacturing company executive*
White, Joseph Charles *manufacturing and retailing company executive*

Chalk River
Hardy, John Christopher *physicist*
Milton, John Charles Douglas *nuclear physicist*
Torgerson, David Franklyn *chemist, research facility administrator*

Chatham
McKeough, William Darcy *investment company executive*

Clarksburg
Krueger, Ralph Ray *retired geography educator*

Concord
Gingl, Manfred *manufacturing company executive*

Cornwall
Hornby, Thomas Richard *wholesale distribution executive*
La Rocque, Eugene Philippe *bishop*

Deep River
Hanna, Geoffrey Chalmers *nuclear scientist*
Newcombe, Howard Borden *biologist, consultant*

Don Mills
Applebaum, Louis *composer, conductor*
Atwood, Margaret Eleanor *author*
Budrevics, Alexander *landscape architect*
Cormack, G. J. *real estate executive*
Craig, John Grant *finance management executive*
Di Tomaso, Nick *oil industry executive*
French, William Harold *retired newspaper editor*
Glover, Donald Robert *professional association administrator, former insurance executive*
Hanna, William Brooks *book publisher*
Heisey, William Lawrence *publisher*
Hickey, Brian Edward *publishing executive*
Hurst, William Donald *civil engineer, consultant*
Koster, Emlyn Howard *geologist, educator, Canadian agency executive*
Mascitelli, Joel *oil industry executive*
Romanese, Gino *real estate executive*

Downsview
Bakht, Baidar *civil engineer, researcher, educator*
Burton, Ian *federal agency administrator, educator, environmental scientist, geographer, author, consultant*
Endler, Norman Solomon *psychology educator*
Forer, Arthur H. *biology educator, researcher, editor*
Moens, Peter B. *biology researcher and educator*
Page, Austin P. *construction technology and property development company executive*
Pritchard, Huw Owen *chemist, educator*
Ribner, Herbert Spencer *physicist, educator*
Tennyson, Roderick C. *aerospace scientist*
Thomas, Clara McCandless *retired English language educator, biographer*

Dundas
Jones, Frank Edward *sociology educator*

Dunrobin
Dickson, Brian *retired chief justice of Canada, ambassador*

Elgin
Lafave, Hugh Gordon John *medical association executive, psychiatrist, educator, consultant*

Etobicoke
Bahadur, Birendra *display specialist, liquid crystal researcher*
Beckley, Michael John *hotel executive*
†Coleman, K. Virginia *diaconal minister*
Ecroyd, Lawrence Gerald *association executive*
Graham, Allister P. *diversified company executive*
Gulden, Simon *lawyer, foods and beverages company executive*
Hyland, Geoffrey Fyfe *energy company executive*
MacKenzie, Lewis Wharton *military officer*
McGuigan, Thomas J. *engineering company executive*
Pelton, John Stafford *finance company executive*
Snedden, James Douglas *health service management consultant*
Stojanowski, Wiktor J. *mechanical engineer*

Fort Erie
Watson, Stewart Charles *construction company executive*

Galt
Dobbie, George Herbert *textile manufacturing executive*

Gloucester
Browning, Kurt *figure skating champion*
Marsters, Gerald Frederick *retired aerospace science and technology executive*

Guelph
†Benn, Denna M. *veterinarian*
Beveridge, Terrance James *microbiology educator, researcher*
Bewley, John Derek *botany researcher, educator*
†Buchanan-Smith, Jock Gordon *animal science educator*
Danby, Kenneth Edison *artist, painter, printmaker*
Dickinson, William Trevor *hydrologist, educator*
Jorgensen, Erik *forest pathologist, educator, consultant*
Karl, Gabriel *physics educator*
Kasha, Kenneth John *crop science educator*
McLeod, Norman Carl *librarian*
Oaks, B. Ann *plant physiologist, educator*
Sells, Bruce Howard *biomedical sciences educator*
Simpson, John Joseph *physics educator, researcher*
Steffer, Robert Wesley *clergyman*

Hamilton
†Asbil, Walter *bishop*
Banaschewski, Bernhard *mathematics educator*
Bandler, John William *electrical engineering educator, consultant*
Basinski, Zbigniew Stanislaw *metal physicist, educator*
Basmajian, John Varoujan *medical scientist, educator, physician*
Bienenstock, John *physician, educator*
Blewett, David Lambert *English literature educator*
Campbell, Colin Kydd *electrical and computer engineering educator, researcher*
Chadwick, Bruce Allen *advertising agency executive*
Childs, Ronald Frank *chemistry educator, science administrator*
Collins, John Alfred *obstetrician-gynecologist, educator*
Crowe, Cameron Macmillan *chemical engineering educator*
Datars, William Ross *physicist, educator*
Davies, John Arthur *physics and engineering educator, scientist*
Garland, William James *engineering physics educator*
Gillespie, Ronald James *retired chemistry educator, writer*
Hill, Graham Roderick *librarian*
King, Leslie John *geography educator*
Lee, Alvin A. *literary educator, scholar, author*
Lipton, Daniel Bernard *conductor*
MacLean, David Bailey *chemistry educator, researcher*
Marshall, Thomas David *judge*
McAnanama, Judith *library executive*
Mc Kay, Alexander Gordon *classics educator*
McMulkin, Francis John *steel company executive*
Mueller, Charles Barber *surgeon, educator*
Parnas, David Lorge *computer scientist, engineer, educator*
Pietrzak, Ted S. *art gallery director*
Preston, Melvin Alexander *physicist, educator*
Priestner, Edward Bernard *manufacturing company executive*
Roland, Charles Gordon *physician, medical historian, educator*
Ryan, Ellen Bouchard *psychology educator, gerontologist*
St. Aubin, J. Arthur *Canadian federal agency executive*
Schwarcz, Henry Philip *geologist, educator*
Shaw, Denis Martin *university dean, former geology educator*
Shaw, John Firth *orchestra administrator*
Spenser, Ian Daniel *chemist educator*
Sprung, Donald Whitfield Loyal *physics educator*
Stanbury, Robert Douglas George *lawyer, executive*
Telmer, Frederick Harold *steel products manufacturing executive*
Tonnos, Anthony *bishop*
Uchida, Irene Ayako *cytogenetics educator, researcher*
Walker, Roger Geoffrey *geology educator, consultant*
†Welch, Douglas Lindsay *physics educator*

Hawkestone
†Boville, Byron Walter *meteorologist*

Hillier
†Lunn, Janet Louise Swoboda *writer*

Islington
Foster, John Stanton *nuclear engineer*
Wykes, Edmund Harold *retired insurance company executive*

Kanata
Griffiths, Anthony F. *telecommunications industry executive*
Hunter, Edward Stewart *clergy member*

Keswick
Macdonald, John Barfoot *research foundation executive*

Kingston
Akenson, Donald Harman *historian, educator*
Bacon, David Walter *chemical engineering educator*
Batchelor, Barrington de Vere *civil engineer, educator*
Berry, John Widdup *psychologist*
Bisby, Mark Ainley *physiology educator*
Boag, Thomas Johnson *physician*
Campbell, L(ouis) Lorne *mathematics educator*
Coleman, Albert John *mathematics educator*
Dick, Susan Marie *English language educator*
Ewan, George Thomson *physicist, educator*
Furter, William Frederick *chemical engineer, university dean*
Glynn, Peter Alexander Richard *hospital administrator*
Hamilton, Albert Charles *English language educator*
Hancock, Geoffrey White *magazine editor, writer*
Kaliski, Stephan Felix *economics educator*
Kaufman, Nathan *pathology educator, physician*
Leggett, William C. *biology educator, educational administrator*
Low, James A. *physician*
Mac Kenzie, Norman Hugh *retired English educator, writer*
Manning, Charles Terrill *retired lawyer*
McDonald, Arthur Bruce *physics educator*
McGeer, James Peter *research executive, consultant*
Meisel, John *political scientist*
Read, Allan Alexander *minister*
Riley, Anthony William *German language and literature educator*
Sayer, Michael *physics educator*
Sen, Paresh Chandra *electrical engineering educator*
Spence, Francis John *archbishop*
Spencer, John Hedley *biochemistry educator*
Stanley, James Paul *printing company executive*
Stewart, Alec Thompson *physicist*
Szarek, Walter Anthony *chemist, educator*
Turpin, David Howard *biology educator, educational administrator*
Uffen, Robert James *geophysics educator, engineer*
Wyatt, Gerard Robert *biology educator, researcher*

Kitchener
Coles, Graham *conductor, composer*
Huras, William David *bishop*
MacDonald, Wayne Douglas *publisher*
†Noble, Ronald Nelson *hospital administrator*
Pollock, John Albon *broadcasting and manufacturing company executive*
Qualter, Terence Hall *retired political science educator*
Rittinger, Carolyne June *newspaper editor*
Winger, Roger Elson *church administrator*

Lions Bay
Bartholomew, Gilbert Alfred *retired physicist*

London
Allan, Ralph Thomas Mackinnon *insurance company executive*
Anderson, Oliver Duncan *consulting statistician, educator*
Bancroft, George Michael *chemical physicist, educator*
Barr, Murray Llewellyn *former anatomy educator*
Bauer, Michael Anthony *computer scientist, educator*
Bembridge, John Anthony *newspaper editor*
Borwein, David *mathematics educator*
Brooks, Vernon Bernard *neuroscientist, educator, author*
Buck, Carol Kathleen *medical educator*

Carroll, Kenneth Kitchener *biochemist, nutritionist, educator*
Collins, Thomas Joseph *English language educator*
Cornies, Larry Alan *journalist, educator*
Creighton, Dale Edward *insurance company executive*
Creighton, Douglas George *French language educator*
Crncich, Tony Joseph *retired pharmacy chain executive*
Cunningham, Gordon Ross *financial executive*
Dales, Samuel *microbiologist, virologist, educator*
Davenport, Alan Garnett *civil engineer, educator*
Davenport, Paul *university administrator, economics educator*
Desbarats, Peter Hullett *journalist, academic administrator*
Dreimanis, Aleksis *emeritus geology educator*
Dunn, Wesley John *dental educator*
Edgar, Shirley Anne *librarian, educator*
Ehrman, Joachim Benedict *mathematics educator*
Frelick, Linden Frederick *hospital executive*
Fyfe, William Sefton *geochemist, educator*
Gerber, Douglas Earl *classics educator*
Henderson, Robert Jules *food service executive*
Hennessey, Frank Martin *strategic planning executive*
Inculet, Ion I. *electrical engineering educator, consultant*
Johnston, Charles Bernie, Jr. *business educator*
Kimura, Doreen *psychology educator, researcher*
Laidler, David Ernest William *economics educator*
Lala, Peeyush Kanti *medical scientist, educator*
Livick, Stephen *fine art photographer*
Locke, Michael *zoology educator*
MacBain, William Halley *minister, theology educator, seminary chancellor*
Marotta, Joseph Thomas *medical educator*
†McInerney, Thomas Edward *financial executive*
McLeod, Philip R. *publishing executive*
McWhinney, Ian Renwick *physician, medical educator*
†O'Driscoll, Perry R. *archbishop*
Orser, Earl Herbert *insurance company executive*
Osbaldeston, Gordon Francis *business educator, former government official*
†Osborne, Reed E. *library executive*
Paivio, Allan Urho *psychology educator*
Pearson, Norman *urban and regional planner, administrator, academic and planning consultant, writer*
Peterson, Leslie Ernest *bishop*
Poole, Nancy Geddes *art gallery director, writer*
†Poznansky, Mark J. *research institute administrator, educator*
Quigley, Robert Murvin *engineering educator, research consultant*
Reaney, James Crerar *dramatist, poet, educator*
Roach, Margot Ruth *biophysicist, educator*
Scott, W. Peter *bishop*
Sherlock, John Michael *bishop*
†Stafford, Earl *conductor*
Stewart, Harold Brown *biochemist*
Stothers, John B. *chemistry educator*
Valberg, Leslie Stephen *medical educator, physician, researcher*
Weedon, Alan Charles *chemist, educator*
Widdrington, Peter Nigel Tinling *professional baseball team executive*
Wilson, Gerald Einar *mechanical and industrial engineer, business executive*
Wonnacott, Ronald Johnston *economics educator*
Zeigler, Earle Frederick *physical education-kinesiology educator*

Maberly
Kennett, William Alexander *retired Canadian government official, consultant*

Manotick
Hobson, George Donald *retired geophysicist*
Prince, Alan Theodore *former government official, engineering consultant*

Markham
Burns, H. Michael *health care company executive*
Fitzhenry, Robert Irvine *publisher*
Lewis, Michael *small business owner*
Stronach, Frank *automobile parts manufacturing executive*

Milton
Georgije, Djokic *bishop*

Mississauga
Allen, Clive Victor *lawyer, communications company executive*
Astington, John Harold *English educator*
Barkin, Martin *pharmaceutical company executive, physician*
Dallison, Frank Keith *transportation company executive*
Davies, Michael Norman Arden *lawyer, electric company executive*
†Griffin, William Arthur *clergyman, religious*

Johnson, Charles E., Jr. *paper company executive*
Kuhn, Hansjoerg Karl (George Kuhn) *transportation executive*
Leech, James William *manufacturing and technology company executive*
Lewis, William Leonard *food products executive*
MacKinnon, David Cameron *research and development company executive*
MacNaughton, John David Francis *aerospace company executive*
†McCallion, Hazel *mayor*
Mills, Donald McKenzie *librarian*
Perkin, Reginald Lewis *physician, educator*
Peterson, Oscar Emmanuel *pianist*
Ross, Thomas McCallum *association executive*
Ryan, Noel *librarian, consultant*
Sago, Anthony E.W. *financial service executive*
Strachan, Graham *pharmaceutical company executive*
Tobias, Kal *transportation executive*
Turnbull, Adam Michael Gordon *financial executive, accountant*
Williams, James B. *retail electronics company executive*

Nepean
Beare-Rogers, Joyce Louise *former research executive*
Bishop, Claude Titus *retired biological sciences research administrator, editor*
Bowness, Rick (Richard Gary Bowness) *professional hockey coach*
Cornell, Peter McCaul *economic consultant, former government official*
Kallmann, Helmut Max *music historian, retired music librarian*

Niagara Falls
Mullan, Donald William *bishop*

Niagara on the Lake
Newton, Christopher *artistic director*
Olley, Robert Edward *economist, educator*
Scott, Campbell *artist*

Nobleton
Embleton, Tony Frederick Wallace *retired Canadian government official*

North Bay
†Bell, J. Stewart *clergy member*
†Plouffe, Jean-Louis *bishop*

North York
Adelman, Howard *philosophy educator*
Arthurs, Harry William *legal educator, former university president*
Bohme, Diethard Kurt *chemistry educator*
Bryant, Josephine Harriet *library executive*
Buzacott, John Alan *engineering educator*
Carrothers, Gerald Arthur Patrick *environmental and city planning educator*
Carswell, Allan Ian *physics educator*
Castel, Jean Gabriel *lawyer*
†Coles, Don Langdon *English literature educator*
Cumming, Glen Edward *art gallery director*
Davey, Kenneth George *biologist, university official*
Davidson-Arnott, Frances E. *library science educator*
Denham, Frederick Ronald *management consultant*
Granatstein, Jack Lawrence *history educator*
Land, Reginald Brian *library administrator*
Lanthier, Ronald Ross *retired manufacturing company executive*
Lastman, Melvin D. *mayor*
Lee, Eugene *theatrical set designer*
Macdonald, Hugh Ian *university president emeritus, economist, educator*
MacDonald, Ian Duncan *commercial credit information executive*
MacKenzie, Donald Murray *hospital administrator*
Mann, Susan *university president*
Regan, David *brain researcher, educator*
Richmond, Anthony Henry *sociologist, emeritus educator*
Tulving, Endel *psychologist, educator*
Wleugel, John Peter *manufacturing company executive*
Woodruff, Laurie *oil industry executive*
Yarlow, Loretta *art museum director*

Oakville
Barlow, Kenneth James *management consultant*
Holmes, James *investment company executive*
O'Reilly, Denis *aluminum company executive, lawyer*
Wilburn, Marion Turner *library and information scientist educator, consultant*

Oshawa
†Devnich, D. D. *religious organization administrator*

Ottawa
†Alexander, Charles *geologist*
Alper, Howard *chemistry educator*
Anderson, David *Canadian government official*
Ansary, Hassan Jaber *transportation executive*
Armstrong, Henry Conner *former Canadian government official, consultant*
Augustyn, Frank Joseph *dancer, artistic director*
Austin, Jacob (Jack Austin) *Canadian senator*
†Axworthy, Chris *Canadian government official*
Axworthy, Lloyd *Canadian government official*
Babcock, Elkanah Andrew *geologist*
Barnhart, Gordon *Canadian government official*
Basken, Reginald C. *communications union executive*
†Batra, Tilak Raj *research scientist*
Beaudoin, Gérald-A(rmand) *lawyer, educator, senator*
†Beck, John Ryder *ambassador*
Beehan, Cathy *government official, lawyer*
†Bélisle, Paul *Canadian government official*
Bell, Phillip Michael *curator*
†Berry, Mike B. *federal agency administrator, geologist*
Bezanson, Keith Arthur *administrative educational executive*
Blais, Pierre *Canadian government minister*
Blanchard, James Johnston *ambassador, former governor of Michigan*
Bonin, Bernard *bank executive*
Bouchard, Lucien *Canadian legislator*
†Boudria, Don *Canadian member of parliament*
Bradford, Karleen *writer*
Brooks, David Barry *resource economist*
Brown, Jack Ernest *information scientist*

Chan, Raymond *Canadian government official*
Charest, Jean J. *Canadian government official, legislator*
Chrétien, (Joseph Jacques) Jean *prime minister of Canada, lawyer*
Clark, Charles Joseph (Joe Clark) *Canadian government official, former prime minister*
Clemenhagen, Carol Jane *health facility executive*
Clermont, Georges Charles *corporate executive*
Clever, W(arren) Glenn *editor, publishing executive, poet, writer, educator*
Cockshutt, Eric Philip *engineering executive, research scientist*
Coleman, John Morley *transportation research director*
Collenette, David M. *Canadian government official*
Collin, Arthur Edwin *Canadian government official*
Copeland, Miles Alexander *electrical engineer educator, consultant*
Copps, Sheila Maureen *Canadian government official*
Corkery, James Caldwell *Canadian government executive, mechanical engineer*
Cory, Peter de Carteret *Canadian Supreme Court justice*
†Couture, J. C. *Canadian federal judge*
Cullen, Jack Sydney George Bud *federal judge*
d'Aquino, Thomas *lawyer, business council chief executive*
Davey, Clark William *newspaper publisher*
Davis, B. *physical science administrator*
Dawson, Donald Andrew *mathematics educator, researcher*
Deacon, Paul Septimus *retired publishing, communications company executive*
de Bold, Adolfo J. *pathology and physiology educator, research scientist*
Décary, Robert *judge*
de Chastelain, A(lfred) John G(ardyne) D(rummond) *Canadian army officer, diplomat*
Dence, Michael Robert *research director*
†Desautels, L. Denis *Canadian government official, auditor*
Desjardins, Alice *federal judge*
Dlab, Vlastimil *mathematics educator, researcher*
†Dodge, David A. *Canadian government official*
Doyle, Richard James *Canadian senator, former editor*
Dray, William Herbert *philosophy educator*
†Duceppe, Gilles *Canadian House of Commons member*
Eggleton, Arthur C. *Canadian government official, member of Parliament*
Emery, Alan Roy *museum executive*
Epp, Arthur Jacob *Canadian government official*
Fairbairn, Joyce *Canadian senator*
Falconer, David Duncan *electrical engineering educator*
Fallis, Alexander Graham *chemistry educator*
†Fellegi, Ivan Peter *statistician*
Ferron, J. *mineralogy administrator*
Finestone, Sheila *Canadian government official*
Flichel, Eugene Anthony *banker*
Franca, Celia *ballet director, choreographer, dancer, narrator*
Frappier, Gilles *librarian*
Fraser, John Allen *Canadian government official*
Freedman, Charles *bank executive*
Friesen, Henry George *endocrinologist, educator*
Georganas, Nicolas D. *electrical engineering educator*
Gerrard, Jon *Canadian government official*
Gillingham, Bryan Reginald *music educator*
Giroux, Robert-Jean-Yvon *Canadian government official*
Gold, Lorne W. *Canadian government official*
Goldbloom, Victor Charles *commissioner, pediatrician*
Gonthier, Charles Doherty *Canadian supreme court justice*
Goodale, Ralph E. *Canadian government official*
Goulard, Guy Yvon *lawyer*
Grace, John William *Canadian government official*
Gravelle, Pierre *Canadian government official*
Gray, Herbert Eser *Canadian government official*
Griller, David *economics and technology consultant*
Gruchy, Charles George *conservation institute director*
Gussow, William Carruthers *petroleum engineer*
Hagen, Paul Beo *physician, medical scientist*
Halliday, Ian *astronomer*
Halstead, John G. H. *educator, diplomat, consultant*
Hamelin, Marcel *historian, educator*
Harington, Charles Richard *vertebrate paleontologist*
Haworth, Richard Thomas *geophysicist, science director*
Heald, Darrel Verner *retired Canadian federal judge*
Herzberg, Gerhard *physicist*
Himms-Hagen, Jean Margaret *biochemist*
Holmes, John Leonard *chemistry educator*
Holzman, Jacquelin *mayor*
Howe, Bruce Iver *government official*
Hughes, Stanley John *mycologist*
Hurteau, Gilles David *obstetrician, gynecologist, educator, university dean*
Iacobucci, Frank *lawyer, educator, jurist*
Ingold, Keith Usherwood *chemist, educator*
†Ingstrup, Ole Michaelsen *Canadian government agency official*
†Isaac, Julius A. *Canadian federal judge*
Itzkovitch, Irwin J. *metallurgy administrator*
Jackson, Charles Ian *writer, consultant*
Jackson, W. Bruce *ophthalmology educator, researcher*
†Jambor, John L. *mining engineer*
Jerome, James Alexander *Canadian federal justice*
Jubinville, Alain Maurice Joseph *retired economist, banker*
Karsh, Yousuf *photographer*
Kates, Morris *biochemist, educator*
Keon, Wilbert Joseph *cardiologist, surgeon, educator*
†Kilgour, David *Canadian member of parliament*
Kingsley, Jean-Pierre *government official*
Kirkwood, David Herbert Waddington *Canadian government official*
Kitchen, Paul Howard *government and association management consultant*
Kroeger, Arthur *university chancellor, former government official*
Labarge, Margaret Wade *medieval history educator*
Labbé, Paul *export corporation executive*
La Forest, Gérard Vincent *justice*
Lamer, Antonio *Canadian supreme court chief justice*
Landriault, Jacques Emile *retired bishop*
Landry, Robert Edward *public policy consultant*
†Langill, George Francis *hospital administrator, educator*

LaRocque, Judith Anne *federal official*
Lavoie, Lionel A. *physician, medical executive*
†LeBlanc, Roméo *Canadian government official*
Lewis, Douglas Grinslade *Canadian minister, parliament member*
L'Heureux-Dube, Claire *judge*
Lister, Earle Edward *animal science consultant*
Lithwick, Norman Harvey *economics educator*
Lossing, Frederick Pettit *retired chemist*
†MacDonald, Flora Isabel *Canadian government official*
MacEachen, Allan Joseph *senator*
MacFarlane, John Alexander *former federal housing agency administrator*
MacGuigan, Mark R. *Canadian federal judge*
MacKay, William Andrew *judge*
Macklem, Michael Kirkpatrick *publisher*
MacLaren, Roy *publisher, Canadian federal legislator*
MacLeod, John Munroe *radio astronomer, academic administrator*
MacNeill, James William *international government consultant*
Macphail, Moray St. John *mathematics educator emeritus*
Macquarrie, Heath Nelson *Canadian government official*
†Maheu, Shirley *Canadian legislator*
Mahoney, Patrick Morgan *retired judge*
Major, Jean-Louis *author, French literature educator*
Major, John Charles *judge*
Malouin, Jean-Louis *university dean, educator*
Manera, Anthony S. *retired broadcasting and education executive*
Manley, John *Canadian government official*
Manning, Preston *political organization worker*
Marchi, Sergio Sisto *Canadian government official*
Marleau, Diane *Canadian government official*
Marleau, Robert *parliamentary clerk*
Marmet, Paul *physicist*
Martin, Paul *Canadian government official*
Massé, Marcel *Canadian government official*
Mayman, Shlomo Alex *engineering executive*
McAvity, John Gillis *museum director, association executive, museologist*
McCabe, Michael *broadcast executive*
McGrath, James Aloysius *Canadian provincial official*
McKellar, Andrew Robert *physicist, researcher*
McLachlin, Beverley *supreme court judge*
McLaren, Digby Johns *geologist, educator*
McLellan, A. Anne *Canadian government official*
Mc Rae, Kenneth Douglas *political scientist, educator*
Mc Whinney, Edward Watson *Canadian government legislator*
Mirza, Shaukat *engineering educator, researcher, consultant*
Moore, William John Myles *electrical engineer, researcher*
Morand, Peter *research agency executive*
Morden, John Reid *Canadian government corporation administrator*
Muldoon, Francis Creighton *Canadian federal judge*
Murphy, Edmund Michael *demographer*
†Murray, J. P. R. *Canadian protective services official*
Murray, Lowell *Canadian senator*
Nordin, Vidar John *forestry educator, consultant*
Ouellet, André *Canadian government official*
Paquet, Gilles *economist, university administrator*
†Parent, Gilbert *mem. Can. Ho. of Commons*
Pepin, Jean-Luc *retired Canadian government official, political science lecturer*
Peppler, William Norman *aviation association executive*
Perrault, Raymond *Canadian legislator, senator*
†Perron, Pierre O. *science administrator*
Perry, Malcolm Blythe *biologist*
Peters, Douglas Dennison *Canadian government official, member of Parliament*
Philogene, Bernard J. R. *academic administrator, science educator*
Poulin, Marie-Paule *Canadian government official*
Pratte, Louis *Canadian federal judge*
Puddington, Ira Edwin *chemist*
Ramsay, Donald Allan *physical chemist*
Redhead, Paul Aveling *physicist*
Reid, Timothy *business organization executive*
†Rivard, Gilles *government official, lawyer*
Robertson, Robert Gordon *retired Canadian government official*
Robichaud, Fernand *Canadian government official*
Robichaud, Louis Joseph *Canadian senator*
Rock, Allan Michael *Canadian government official*
Roland, Anne *registrar Supreme Court of Canada*
Roots, Ernest Frederick *scientific advisor emeritus*
Rummery, Terrance Edward *nuclear engineering executive, researcher*
Ryan, William Francis *priest*
St-Onge, Denis Alderic *geologist, research scientist*
Schneider, William George *chemist, research consultant*
Scott, Marianne Florence *librarian, educator*
Seaden, George *civil engineer*
†Seifert, Keith Anthony *mycologist*
Sharp, Mitchell William *adviser to prime minister*
Shaw, Edgar Albert George *research association executive*
Sheflin, Michael John Edward *transportation commissioner*
Siebrand, Willem *theoretical chemist, science editor*
†Silye, Jim *member of Canadian House of Commons*
Sinha, Ramesh Chandra *plant pathologist*
Smith, Wilfred Irvin *former Canadian government official*
Soper, James Herbert *botanist, curator*
Sopinka, John *Canadian supreme court justice*
Spicer, Erik John *retired Canadian parliamentary librarian*
†Spicer, Keith *federal official, journalist, educator*
Squire, Anne Marguerite *religious leader*
Staines, David McKenzie *English educator*
Stanford, Joseph Stephen *diplomat, lawyer, educator*
Stewart, Christine Susan *Canadian government official*
Stone, Arthur Joseph *judge*
Stone, Jeffrey Jay *film critic, journalist, writer*
Storey, Kenneth Bruce *biology educator*
Suthren, Victor J. H. *museum director*
Sylvestre, Jean Guy *former national librarian*
Tait, John Charles *Canadian government official*
Tassé, Roger *lawyer, former Canadian government official*
Templeton, Ian Malcolm *retired physicist*
Thibault, J(oseph) Laurent *service company executive*
Thomson, Shirley Lavinia *museum director*

Topp, George Clarke *soil physicist*
Urie, John James *lawyer, retired Canadian federal judge*
Varshni, Yatendra Pal *physicist*
Veizer, Ján *geology educator*
Wallot, Jean-Pierre *archivist, historian*
Watt, Robert Douglas *Canadian government official*
Waugh, Douglas Oliver William *pathology educator*
Weatherill, John Frederick William *arbitrator*
Weiner, Gerry *government official*
Whitehead, J. Rennie *science consultant*
Whitham, Kenneth *science and technology consultant*
Whyte, Anne Veronica *social science researcher, educator*
Wilson, Bertha *Canadian justice*
Withers, Ramsey Muir *government consultant, former government official*
Yalden, Maxwell Freeman *Canadian diplomat*
Yeomans, Donald Ralph *Canadian government official, consultant*
Young, Douglas *Canadian government official*

Owen Sound
Adams, John David Vessot *manufacturing company executive*
Jones, Phyllis Edith *nursing educator*
Morley, Lawrence Whitaker *geophysicist, remote sensing consultant*

Pembroke
Windle, Joseph Raymond *bishop*

Peterborough
†Brown, Wendy Evelynn *library director*
Doyle, James Leonard *bishop*
Hutchinson, Thomas Cuthbert *ecology and environmental educator*
†Johnston, Julia Ann *writer*
Symons, Thomas H. B. *historian, educator*
Theall, Donald Francis *retired university president*
Young, Scott Alexander *television journalist, author*

Pontypool
Kniewasser, Andrew Graham *company director*

Port Rowan
†Francis, Charles MacKenzie *wildlife biologist*

Rexdale
Joseph, Emanuel *church administrator*
Lutgens, Harry Gerardus *food company executive*

Richmond Hill
Bolton, Charles Thomas *astronomer*
Fernie, John Donald *astronomer, educator*
Garrison, Robert Frederick *astronomer, educator*
†Gilman, Phoebe *author, illustrator*
Howe, James Tarsicius *insurance company executive*
MacRae, Donald Alexander *astronomy educator*
Marshall, Donald Stewart *computer systems company executive*
Tushingham, (Arlotte) Douglas *museum administrator*

Ridgeway
Jacobs, Eleanor Alice *retired clinical psychologist, educator*

Rockwood
Eichner, Hans *German language and literature educator*

Saint Catharines
Florio, Ermanno *conductor, music administrator*
Fulton, Thomas Benjamin *retired bishop*
O'Mara, John Aloysius *bishop*
Terasmae, Jaan *geology educator*
White, Terrence Harold *academic administrator, sociologist*

Sault Sainte Marie
Banerjee, Samarendranath *orthopedic surgeon*
Ferris, Ronald Curry *bishop*
Savoie, Leonard Norman *transportation company executive*
†Winget, Carl Henry *science administrator, forest ecologist*

Scarborough
Bassnett, Peter James *librarian*
Besse, Ronald Duncan *publishing company executive*
Campbell, E. E. *publishing executive*
†Hunter, Bernice Thurman *writer*
Isley, John Charles *publishing company executive*
Krajicek, Mark Andrew *lawyer*
†Mikloshazy, Attila *bishop*
Mitchell, Arthur Harris *newspaper columnist*
Sparshott, Francis Edward *poet, educator*

Schumacher
Lawrence, Caleb James *bishop*

Stevensville
Stevens, Sinclair McKnight *Canadian government official*
Tellier, Henri *retired Canadian military officer*

Stonbicoke
†Knipping, Hans D. *petroleum engineer*

Stoney Creek
Cowan, James Spencer *financial executive, consultant*

Sudbury
Havel, Jean Eugène Martial *author, educator*

Thornbury
Keyes, Gordon Lincoln *history educator*

Thornhill
Nimmons, Phillip Rista *composer, conductor, clarinetist, educator*

Thunder Bay
Harrison, Karen Ann *library director*
Locker, J. Gary *university official, civil engineering educator*
Masters, Jack Gerald *mayor*
Rosehart, Robert George *university president, chemical engineer*

Timmins
Cazabon, Gilles *bishop*

Toronto
Aird, John Black *lawyer, university official, former lieutenant governor*
†Akazawa-Eguchi, Miyuki Real *landscape architect, environmental artist*
Alberti, Peter William *otolaryngologist*
Alcock, Charles Benjamin *materials science consultant*
Alomar, Roberto Velazquez *professional baseball player*
Anderson, Reid Bryce *ballet company artistic director*
Apple, B. Nixon *lawyer*
Arnold, Neil David *farm and industrial equipment company executive*
Arthur, James Greig *mathematics educator*
Astman, Barbara Ann *artist, educator*
Athanassoulas, Sotirios (Sotirios of Toronto) *bishop*
Atwood, Harold Leslie *physiology and zoology educator*
†Augustine, Jerome Samuel *merchant banker*
Baillie, Alexander Charles, Jr. *banker*
Balderrama, Fernando Hiriart *electrical utility company executive*
Balmain, Keith George *electrical engineering educator, researcher*
Bandeen, Robert Angus *management corporation executive*
Barford, Ralph MacKenzie *investment executive*
Barrett, Matthew W. *bank executive*
Beckwith, John *musician, composer, educator*
Beigie, Carl Emerson *economist, research administrator, educator*
Bell, J. A. Gordon *retired banker*
Berton, Pierre *journalist, author*
Bickford, James Gordon *banker*
Birnbaum, Eleazar *language professional*
Black, Conrad Moffat *publishing corporate executive*
Blissett, William Frank *English literature educator*
Blundell, William Richard Charles *electric company executive*
Bodsworth, Fred *author, naturalist*
Boland, Janet Lang *judge*
Bone, Bruce Charles *mining and manufacturing executive*
Bonnycastle, Lawrence Christopher *retired corporate director*
†Boothroyd, Arnold Ian *astrophysicist*
Boswell, Philip John *opera administrator*
Bouissac, Paul Antoine *language professional*
Boultbee, John Arthur *publishing executive*
†Boyd, Marion *provincial attorney general*
Bradshaw, Richard James *conductor*
Braithwaite, J(oseph) Lorne *real estate executive*
Bristow, David Ian *lawyer*
Brook, Adrian Gibbs *chemistry educator*
Brooks, Robert Leslie *bank executive*
Brown, Gregory Michael *psychiatrist, educator, research director*
Brown, W. Michael *publishing company executive*
Bruce, William Robert *physician, educator*
Brumer, Paul William *chemical physicist, educator*
Bunting, Christopher Henry *public relations executive*
Burgis, Grover Cornelius *librarian*
Burns, Pat *professional hockey coach*
Bush, John Arthur Henry *mining company executive, lawyer*
Cable, Howard Reid *composer, conductor*
Cameron, Peter Alfred Gordon *corporate executive*
Campbell, Donald Graham *communications company executive*
Caplan, Elinor *Canadian provincial legislator, former cabinet minister*
Carnegie, James Gordon *association executive*
Carter, Gerald Emmett *retired archbishop*
Carter, Joe (Joseph Chris Carter) *professional baseball player*
Casson, Alan Graham *thoracic surgeon, researcher*
Chant, Dixon Samuel *company executive*
Chester, Robert Simon George *lawyer*
Ching, Julia *philosophy and religion educator*
Chodos, Robert Irwin *editor, writer*
Christopher, Raymond Joseph *computer services executive*
Cinader, Bernhard *immunologist, gerontologist, scientist, educator*
Clancy, Louis John *newspaper editor, journalist*
Clark, Samuel Delbert *sociology educator*
Clarkson, Max Boydell Elliott *printing company executive, business educator*
Cleghorn, John Edward *banker*
Cobbold, Richard Southwell Chevallier *biomedical engineer, educator*
Cockwell, Jack Lynn *financial executive*
Cohen, Marshall *diversified international corporation executive*
Coleman, John Hewson *financial consultant*
Colgrass, Michael Charles *composer*
Collins, Jerry Allan *association executive*
Colombo, John Robert *poet, editor, writer*
Conacher, Desmond John *classics educator*
Cone, David Brian *professional baseball player*
Connell, Philip Francis *food industry executive*
Cooper, Marsh Alexander *mining company executive*
Corrigan, Harold Cauldwell *accountant*
Cowan, Charles Gibbs *lawyer, corporate executive*
Coxeter, Harold Scott Macdonald *mathematician*
Crawley, Alexander Radford *performing artist, composer*
Cruickshank, John Douglas *newspaper editor*
Cullingworth, Larry Ross *residential and real estate development company executive*
Dale, Robert Gordon *business executive*
Davies, Robertson *author*
Davis, (Horace) Chandler *mathematics educator*
Davis, William Grenville *lawyer, former Canadian government official*
Davison, Edward Joseph *electrical engineering educator*
Deacon, David Emmerson *advertising executive*
Dean, William George *geography educator*
Decle, Denis Christopher *advertising executive*
Dembroski, George Steven *investment banker*
DeMone, Robert Stephen *hotel company executive*
Diamond, Abel Joseph *architect*
Dickens, Bernard Morris *law educator*
Dimma, William Andrew *real estate executive*
Dodd, Lionel G. *holding company executive*
Doherty, Tom (Thomas Storen, Jr.) *art director, set designer*
†Domb, Daniel *cellist, educator*
Donais, Gary Warren *lawyer*
Downing, John Henry *newspaper editor, journalist, columnist*
†Drabinsky, Garth Howard *entertainment company executive*
Dryer, Douglas Poole *retired philosophy educator*
Dubin, Charles Leonard *federal judge*
Dunford, Robert A. *diversified business executive*
Dunlop, David John *geophysics educator, researcher*
Eagles, Stuart Ernest *business executive*
Eastman, Harry Claude MacColl *economics educator*
Eayrs, James George *political scientist, educator*
Ediger, Nicholas Martin *energy resources company executive, consultant*
Egan, Vincent Joseph *journalist, newspaper columnist*
Egoyan, Atom *film director*
Eisen, Leonard *food and retail company executive*
Eklof, Svea Christine *ballet dancer*
Eldred, Gerald Marcus *performing arts association executive*
Elliott, R(oy) Fraser *lawyer, holding and management company executive*
Ellis, Peter Hudson *health science facility administrator*
Elting, Everett E. *advertising agency executive*
Endrenyi, Janos *research engineer*
Evans, Gregory Thomas *commissioner, retired justice*
Evans, John Robert *former university president, physician*
Eyton, John Trevor *lawyer, business executive*
Falle, Daisy Carolyne *professional society administrator*
Farquharson, Gordon MacKay *lawyer*
Fasick, Adele Mongan *library science educator*
Feldbrill, Victor *conductor*
Ferguson, Kingsley George *psychologist*
Fierheller, George Alfred *communications company executive*
Fife, Edward H. *landscape architecture educator*
Finlay, Terence Edward *bishop*
†Flanagan-Eguchi, Barbara L. *landscape architect, theme park designer*
Fletcher, Cliff *professional hockey team executive*
Flood, A. L. (Al Flood) *bank executive*
Fowke, Edith Margaret Fulton *author, English language educator emeritus*
Francis, Diane Marie *journalist*
Fraser, Donald Alexander Stuart *mathematics educator*
Fraser, William Neil *government official*
Freedman, Harry *composer*
Freedman, Theodore Jarrell *healthcare executive*
Freeman, Graham P. M. *food company executive*
Friedlander, John Benjamin *mathematics educator*
Friendly, Lynda Estelle *theatre marketing and communications executive*
Friesen, James *pediatrics research administrator*
Fullerton, R. Donald *banker*
Gairdner, John Smith *securities investment dealer*
Galloway, David Alexander *publishing company executive*
Ganczarczyk, Jerzy Jozef *civil engineering educator, wastewater treatment consultant*
Ganoza-Becker, Maria Clelia *biochemistry educator*
Gardner, John Robert *insurance company executive*
Gartner, Michael Alfred *professional hockey player*
Gaston, Cito *professional baseball manager*
†Geddes, Lorna *ballet mistress*
Gee, Gregory Williams *lawyer*
George, Peter James *economist, educator*
Gillespie, Alastair William *former Canadian government official*
Gillick, Patrick *professional baseball team executive*
Gilmour, Doug *professional hockey player*
Glasco, Kimberly *ballet dancer*
Godfrey, John Morrow *lawyer, retired Canadian government official*
Godfrey, Paul Victor *newspaper publisher*
Godsoe, Peter Cowperthwaite *banker*
Goffart, Walter André *history educator*
†Goh, Chan Hon *ballerina*
Goldberg, David Meyer *biochemistry educator*
Goldenberg, Andrew Avi *mechanical engineering educator*
Goldenberg, Gerald Joseph *physician, educator*
Goldfarb, Martin *sociologist*
†Goodenow, Robert W. *labor union administrator*
Goodrich, Maurice Keith *business forms, systems and services company executive*
Goring, David Arthur Ingham *chemical engineering educator, scientist*
Goring, Peter Allan Elliott *real estate executive*
Gotlib, Lorraine *justice, former lawyer*
Gotlieb, Allan E. *former ambassador*
Gotlieb, Calvin Carl *computer scientist, educator*
Gotlieb, Phyllis Fay Bloom *author*
Graham, James Edmund *service management executive*
Graham, John Webb *lawyer*
Graham, Kathleen Margaret (K. M. Graham) *artist*
Graham, Victor Ernest *French language educator*
Grayson, Albert Kirk *Near Eastern studies educator*
Greben, Stanley Edward *psychiatrist, educator, author, editor*
Greenwood, Lawrence George *banker*
Gregor, Tibor Philip *management consultant researcher*
Grendler, Paul Frederick *history educator*
Grier, Ruth *provincial legislator*
Griffin, Scott *manufacturing executive*
Grosland, Emery Layton *banker*
Grossman, Irving *architect*
Haeck, Christel *provincial legislator*
Halperin, John Stephen *mathematics educator*
Ham, James Milton *engineering educator*
Harrington, Margaret Helen *state legislator*
Harris, Nicholas George *publisher*
Hartley, Stuart Leslie *diversified company executive, accountant*
Harvey, George Edwin *communications company executive*
Harwood, Vanessa Clare *ballet dancer*
Hayes, Derek Cumberland *banking executive, lawyer*
Hayhurst, James Frederick Palmer *career and business consultant, inspirational speaker*
Haynes, Robert Hall *biophysicist, educator*
†Heath, Michele Christine *botany educator*
Helleiner, Gerald Karl *economics educator*
Henderson, William Boyd *engineering executive*
Hentgen, Patrick George *professional baseball player*
Herbert, Stephen W. *hospital executive*
Hirst, Peter Christopher *consulting actuary*
Hofmann, Theo *biochemist, educator*
Hollander, Samuel *economist, educator*
Honderich, Beland Hugh *publisher*
Honderich, John Allen *newspaper publisher*
Hore, John Edward *commodity futures educator*
Horsey, William Grant *corporation executive*
Houston, Stanley Dunsmore *public relations executive*
†Hubel, Vello *industrial designer, educator, artist*
Hudson, Alan Roy *neurosurgeon, medical educator, hospital administrator*
Hurlbut, Robert St. Clair *finance company executive*
Iannuzzi, Daniel Andrew *publishing and broadcasting executive*
†Illmann, Margaret Louise *ballet dancer*
Innanen, Larry John *lawyer, food products executive*
Irwin, Samuel Macdonald *toy company executive*
Israelievitch, Jacques H. *violinist, conductor*
Ivey, Donald Glenn *physics educator*
Jackman, Henry Newton Rowell *Canadian provincial official*
Jacob, Ellis *entertainment company executive*
Jagt, Jack *trading company executive*
James, Robert Scott *historic organization executive*
James, William *mining company executive*
Janischewskyj, Wasyl *electrical engineering educator*
Jay, Charles Douglas *religion educator, college administrator, clergyman*
Jervis, Robert E. *chemistry educator*
Jewison, Norman Frederick *film producer, director*
Johnson, Robert Eugene *historian, academic administrator*
Johnston, Malcolm Carlyle *bank executive*
Johnston, Robert Donaghy *cultural organization administrator*
Jolley, David *newspaper executive*
Kain, Karen Alexandria *ballet dancer*
Kaiser, Nicholas *physicist, educator*
Kalant, Harold *pharmacology educator, physician*
Kalow, Werner *pharmacologist, toxicologist*
Karakas, Rita S. *television broadcast executive*
Kay, James Fredrick *retailer*
†Keddy, Wayne Richard *university hospital administrator*
Keenan, Anthony Harold Brian *catalog company executive*
†Keenan, Patrick John *investment company executive*
†Kent, David Rowan *timpanist, symphony orchestra official*
Kerr, David Wylie *natural resource company executive*
King, John Charles Peter *newspaper editor*
Kirby, Charles William, Jr. *dancer, choreographer*
Kluge, Holger *banking executive*
Koken, Bernd Krafft *forest products company executive*
Korey-Krzeczowski, George J. M. Kniaz *university administrator, management consultant*
Korthals, Robert W. *bank executive*
Kosich, George John *retail executive*
Kossuth, Selwyn Barnett *trade association consultant*
Kramer, Burton *graphic designer, educator*
Kresge, Alexander Jerry *chemistry educator*
Kruger, Arthur Martin *economics educator, university official*
Kudelka, James *ballet dancer, choreographer*
Kuerti, Anton Emil *pianist, composer*
Kunov, Hans *biomedical and electrical engineering educator*
†Kushner, Donn Jean *microbiologist, children's author*
Kushner, Eva *academic administrator, educator, author*
Kuwabara, Bruce Bunji *architect*
†Lamy, Martine *dancer*
Landsberg, Michele *journalist*
Lane, Patrick *poet*
Lanthier, John Spencer *accounting company executive*
†Lasker, David Raymond *newspaper editor, musician*
Lasserre, Jean Paul *reinsurance company president*
Laurie, John Veldon *business financial executive, accountant*
Lavoie, Serge *principal dancer*
Lewis, Robert *periodical editor, journalist*
Light, Walter Frederick *telecommunications executive*
Lindsay, Roger Alexander *investment executive*
Lindsay, William Kerr *surgeon*
Lipowski, Zbigniew Jerzy *psychiatrist, educator*
List, Roland *physicist, educator, former UN official*
†Lister, Dianne Elizabeth *foundation administrator*
Liston, Alan A. *lawyer*
Litherland, Albert Edward *physics educator*
Livergant, Harold Leonard *health services executive*
Liversage, Richard Albert *cell biologist*
Lombardi, John Barba-Linardo *broadcasting executive*
Lowe, Donald Cameron *corporate executive*
†Lowe, Robert Edward *finance company executive*
†Lucas, Cynthia *ballet mistress, dancer*
Lyons, Joseph Chisholm *lawyer*
MacAulay, Colin Alexander *mining engineer*
Macaulay, Hugh L. *retail company executive*
Macdonald, Donald Stovel *lawyer*
MacDougall, Hartland Molson *trust company director, retired bank executive*
Mackiw, Vladimir Nicholaus *metaHerman research scientis educator*
MacLeod, William Brian *hospital executive*
Mak, Tak Wah *biochemist*
Mann, George Stanley *real estate and financial services corporation executive*
Marshall, Marvin Giffin *real estate company executive*
Marshall, Paul Macklin *oil company executive*
Martin, Robert William *former utilities company executive*
Matathia, Ira Leslie *advertising agency executive*
McAuliffe, Jane Dammen *Middle Eastern and Islamic studies educator*
McClymont, Kenneth Ross *power systems engineer, consultant*
McCoomb, Lloyd Alexander *transportation executive*
Mc Culloch, Ernest Armstrong *physician, educator*
Mc Gibbon, Pauline Mills *former Canadian government official, former university chancellor*
McGiverin, Donald Scott *retail company executive*
McKenna, Marianne *architect*
†McLean, (Andrew) Stuart *educator, journalist*
McMurtry, R. Roy *chief justice*
McNeil, John D. *insurance company executive*
McNeill, John *museum administrator*
McNeill, K(enneth) G(ordon) *medical physicist*
Meagher, George Vincent *mechanical engineer*
†Meenan, James Joseph *communications executive*
Mercier, Eileen Ann *management consultant*
Michals, George Francis *investment and business development executive*
Miller, Anthony Bernard *physician, medical researcher*
Miller, Anthony G. *advertising executive*
Miller, Kenneth Merrill *computing services company executive*
Millgate, Jane *language professional*
Millgate, Michael (Henry) *retired English educator*
Minto, Clive *retail company executive*
Moffat, John William *physics educator*
Molitor, Paul Leo *professional baseball player*
Montgomery, Donald Russell *labor consulting firm executive*
Moore, Carole Irene *librarian*
†Moore, Christopher Hugh *writer*
Morey, Carl Reginald *musicologist, academic administrator*
Morgan, Peter F. *English educator, philosophy educator*
Morgan, Wayne Philip *art and popular culture exhibition producer*
Moriyama, Raymond *architect*
Morra, Bernadette *newspaper editor, journalist*
Mowat, Farley McGill *writer*

Munk, Peter mining executive
Munro, John Henry Alexander economics educator, writer
Murasugi, Kunio mathematician, educator
Murray, Anne country singer
Mustard, James Fraser research institute executive
Naldrett, Anthony James geology educator
Nesbitt, Lloyd Ivan podiatrist
Nesbitt, Mark management consultant
Neufeld, Edward Peter retired economist
Newman, Peter Charles journalist
Nisbet, Joanne ballet mistress
Norris, Geoffrey geology educator, consultant
Nuttall, Grant retired oil company executive
Oberlander, Ronald Y. paper manufacturing company executive
Ogilvie, Richard Ian clinical pharmacologist
Oland, Sidney M. brewing and entertainment company executive
Olerud, John Garrett professional baseball player
Oliphant, Betty ballet school director
Olive, David Michael magazine writer, magazine editor
Osborne, Ronald Walter communications executive
Osler, Gordon Peter retired utility company executive
Ostry, Bernard broadcasting executive
Ostry, Sylvia academic administrator, economist
†Ottmann, Peter choreographer, ballet dancer
Owens, Joseph clergyman
Packer, Katherine Helen retired library educator
Packham, Marian Aitchison biochemistry educator
Pankratz, Henry J. management consultant
Parr, James Gordon writer
†Pawson, Anthony J. molecular biologist
Payne, Thomas Charles architect
Payton, Thomas William corporate finance consultant executive
Pedersen, Paul Richard composer, educator
Pelley, Marvin Hugh mining executive
Peterson, David Robert lawyer, former Canadian government official
Peterson, Robert Byron petroleum company executive
Petrillo, Leonard Philip corporate securities executive, lawyer
Pickard, Franklin George Thomas mining company executive
Plaut, Wolf Gunther minister, author
Polanyi, John Charles chemist, educator
Porter, Ivan company executive
Posluns, Wilfred M. manufacturing and retailing company executive
Potvin, Felix professional hockey player
Powis, Alfred natural resources company executive
Pratt, Robert Cranford political scientist, educator
Prichard, John Robert Stobo academic administrator, law educator
Prugovecki, Eduard mathematical physicist, educator, author
Pyle, Alan James trust company executive
Rae, Robert Keith Canadian premier of Ontario
Rakoff, Vivian Morris psychiatrist, writer
Ransom, Jeremy ballet dancer
Rapoport, Anatol peace studies educator, mathematical biologist
Rapson, William Howard chemical engineering educator
Rasky, Harry producer, director, writer
Rathke, Sheila Wells advertising and public relations executive
Rauhala, Ann Elaine reporter
Redford, Donald Bruce historian, archaeologist
Redway, Alan Arthur Sydney Canadian legislator, lawyer
Reid, Terence C. W. corporation executive
Rickerd, Donald Sheridan foundation executive
†Rigby, Kathryn Jill (Jill Rigby) newspaper editor, travel journalist
Rimrott, Friedrich Paul Johannes engineer, educator
Ritchie, Cedric Elmer banker
Rogers, Edward Samuel communications company executive
Rogers, Harry G. Canadian government official
Roman-Barber, Helen corporate executive
Rombout, Luke museum designer, administrator
Ronald, Thomas Iain financial services executive
Ronald, William artist
Rooney, Paul George mathematics educator
Rose, Jeffrey Raymond public servant, trade union executive, economist
Ross, Henry Raymond advertising executive and legal counsel;
Ross, Murray George social science educator, university president emeritus
Rothstein, Aser radiation biology educator
Rowe, David John physics educator
Runnalls, (Oliver) John (Clyve) nuclear engineering educator
Runte, Roseann academic administrator
Rusnell, Joanne D. brewery, entertainment business executive
Ryan, James Franklin oil company executive
Saddlemyer, Ann (Eleanor Saddlemyer) educator, critic, theater historian
Salama, C. Andre Tewfik electrical engineering educator
Sanderson, Eric George (Sandy Sanderson) broadcast executive
Scheininger, Lester lawyer, administrator religious organization
Schogt, Henry Gilius foreign language educator
Scholefield, Peter Gordon health agency executive
Schramek, Tomas ballet dancer
Schwenger, Frances library director
Scott, Steven Donald geology educator, researcher
Seagram, Norman Meredith corporate executive
Seaquist, Ernest Raymond astronomy educator
Sedra, Adel Shafeek electrical engineering educator, university administrator
Seeman, Philip pharmacology educator, neurochemistry researcher
Semak, Michael William photographer, educator
Semlyen, Adam electrical engineering educator
Sessle, Barry John university administrator, researcher
Shaffer, Donald S. retail executive
Sharpe, Charles Richard retail company executive
Shaw, Ian Alexander accountant, mining company executive
†Shearing, Clifford Denning criminology and sociology educator
Shearing, George Albert pianist, composer
Sheinin, Rose biochemist, educator
Shields, Carol Ann writer, educator
†Sigal, Israel Michael mathematics educator
Silk, Frederick C.Z. consumer products company executive
Silver, Malcolm David pathologist, educator
Singleton-Wood, Allan James publishing executive
Skinner, Alastair accountant
†Skorcz, Stephen hospital association executive
Skvorecky, Josef Vaclav English educator, novelist
Slemon, Gordon Richard electrical engineering educator
Sloan, David Edward retired corporate executive
Smith, David Todd publishing company executive
Smith, Kenneth Carless electrical engineering educator
Smith, Peter William Ebblewhite electrical engineering educator, scientist
Smith, Raymond dancer
Smith, Stephen Alexander retail and wholesale food distribution company executive
Sole, Michael Joseph cardiologist
Soler, Arthur R. food products executive
Sopko, Michael D. mining company executive
Stackhouse, Richard Gilbert retired financial company executive
Stadelman, William Ralph chemical institution executive
†Staines, Mavis Avril artistic director, ballet principal
Stavro, Steve A. professional hockey team executive
Stefanschi, Sergiu dancer
Stoicheff, Boris Peter physicist, educator
Styles, Richard Geoffrey Pentland retired banker
Synan, Edward Aloysius, Jr. clergyman, former institute president
Tall, Franklin David mathematician, neurolinguistic programming master practitioner
Taylor, Allan Richard retired banker
Taylor, Harry William physics educator
Taylor, Paul Albert banker
Ten Cate, Arnold Richard dentistry educator
†Tewsley, Robert William dancer
Thall, Burnett Murray newspaper executive
Thomas, Alan Richard natural resources products executive
Thomas, Isiah Lord, III former professional basketball player, basketball team executive
Thomas, Kenneth Glyndwr mining executive
Thomson, Kenneth R. (Lord Thomson of Fleet) publishing executive
Thomson, Richard Murray banker
Thornley, Shirley Blumberg architect
Tidwell, Thomas Tinsley chemistry educator
Till, James Edgar scientist
Tobe, Stephen Solomon zoology educator
Tremaine, Scott Duncan astrophysicist
Tsui, Lap-Chee molecular genetics educator
Turner, Craig journalist
Turner, Gerald Phillip hospital administrator
Turner, John Napier former prime minister of Canada, legislator
Turner, Peter Merrick retired manufacturing company executive
Turner, Robert Edward psychiatrist, educator
†Valdepeñas, Joaquín Mario clarinetist, conductor
Vance, James retired manufacturing company executive, lawyer
van Ginkel, Blanche Lemco architect, educator
Van Houten, Stephen H. manufacturing company executive
Venetsanopoulos, Anastasios Nicolaos electrical engineer, educator
Venter, Ronald Daniel mechanical engineering educator, researcher, administrator
Viola, Frank John, Jr. professional baseball player
Volpé, Robert endocrinologist
Walker, Ronald C. oil company executive
Ward, Duane professional baseball player
Watson, Paul photojournalist, correspondent
Webb, Anthony Allan banker
Webster, Jill Rosemary historian, educator
Weldon, David Black financial executive
Weston, Willard Galen diversified holdings executive
Wetzel, Heinz foreign language educator
Wevers, John William retired Semitic languages educator
†Wheeler, Raymond Dawson accountant
White, Adrian Michael Stephen financial executive
White, Calvin John zoo executive, financial manager, zoological association executive
White, Devon Markes professional baseball player
Whittington, Stuart Gordon chemistry educator
Wilder, Valerie ballet company director
Wilkins, Ormsby music director, conductor, pianist
Wilson, Ian Edwin cultural organization administrator, archivist
Wilson, Lois M. minister
Wilson, Thomas Arthur economics educator
Winter, Frederick Elliot fine arts educator
Witkowsky, Gizella dancer
Wolfe, Harold Joel lawyer, business executive
Wolfe, Jonathan A. food wholesaler, retailer
Wonham, Walter Murray electrical engineer, educator
Wood, Neil Roderick real estate development company executive
Worton, Ronald Gibert geneticist, educator
Yates, Keith chemistry educator, writer
Zemans, Joyce Pearl art historian, arts administrator
Zimmerman, Adam Hartley retired mining and forest industries executive

Unionville
Nichols, Harold Neil corporate executive, former pipeline company executive
Rusnak, Michael bishop
Suddick, Patrick Joseph defense systems company executive

Vanier
Davidson, Alexander T. geographer, professional society administrator

Waterloo
Aczel, Janos Dezso mathematics educator
Berczi, Andrew Stephen academic administrator
Cornell, Paul Grant history educator
Downey, James university president
Fallding, Harold Joseph sociology educator
Gladwell, Graham Maurice Leslie mathematician, civil engineering educator
Green, Arthur Nelson artist, educator
Haworth, Lawrence Lindley philosophy educator
Hynes, Hugh Bernard Noel biology educator
Kay, Jeanne dean, educator
Kraus, Michael minister
MacGregor, Kenneth Robert former insurance company executive
Masterman, Jack Verner insurance company executive
McCauley, Robert William biologist, educator
Mills (Kutz-Harder), Helga religious organization executive
Morgan, Alan Vivian geologist, educator
Nash, Peter Hugh John geographer, educator, planner
†Nelson, J. Gordon geography educator
Paldus, Josef mathematics educator
Pindera, Jerzy Tadeusz mechanical and aeronautical engineer
†Rempel, Garry Llewellyn chemical engineering educator, consultant
Rudin, Alfred chemistry educator emeritus
Sherbourne, Archibald Norbert civil engineering educator
Smith, Rowland James educational administrator
Sprott, David Arthur statistics and psychology educator
Stewart, Cameron Leigh mathematics educator
Suits, Bernard Herbert philosophy educator
Thomas, Richard Lynn geologist, researcher, educator, director university geecology center
Urquhart, Tony artist, educator
Vlach, Jiri electrical engineering educator, researcher
Warner, Barry Gregory geographer
Wright, Douglas Tyndall former university president, company director, engineering educator

Welland
Wintermans, Joseph Jack Gerard Francis financial services executive

Weston
McIntyre, John George Wallace real estate development and management consultant

Willowdale
Binder, Herbert R. drug store chain executive
Bloom, David Ronald retail drug company executive
Bulloch, John Frederick Devon association executive
Dean, Geoffrey book publisher
Hallman, H(enry) Theodore, Jr. artist, textile designer
Harris, Sydney Malcolm retired judge
Irwin, John Wesley publisher
Kerner, Fred book publisher, writer
MacDonald, Brian Scott educational administrator
McDonald, William Henry financial executive
Swartz, Malcolm Gilbert retail executive, restaurateur
Turnbull, John Cameron pharmacist, consultant

Windsor
Auld, Frank psychologist, educator
Dirksen, Jean library administrator
†Drake, Gordon F. physicist educator
Drake, Gordon William Frederic physics educator
Giffen, John A. distillery executive
Hackam, Reuben electrical engineering educator
Ianni, Ronald William university president and vice chancellor, lawyer
Israel, Fred Carl library director
Jones, William Ernest chemistry educator
Kippen, Richard Marlin wine and spirits company executive
Landry, G. Yves automotive company executive
Morgan, George Carl retired newspaper editor
Thibert, Roger Joseph clinical chemist, educator
Whitney, Barry Lyn religious studies educator

Yarker
Smallman, Beverley N. biology educator

PRINCE EDWARD ISLAND

Charlottetown
Baker, Ronald James English language educator, university administrator
†Buchanan, Alan provincial attorney general
Callbeck, Catherine S. Canadian government official
Carruthers, Norman Harry Canadian province supreme court justice
Eliot, Charles William John university president, educator
MacAulay, Lawrence A. Canadian government official
Reid, Marion L. lieutenant governor, educator
Severance, Christopher Churchill museum director

Monticello
Gingras, Gustave physician

QUEBEC

Amos
†Drainville, Gerard bishop

Athelstan
Ness, Owen McGregor retired aluminum company executive

Ayers Cliff
Beament, Thomas Harold (Tib Beament) artist, printmaker, educator

Beaconsfield
Harder, Rolf Peter graphic designer, painter

Boucherville
Martel, Jacques G. entineer, administrator

Chelsea
Warren, Jack Hamilton former trade policy advisor

Chicoutimi
Couture, Jean Guy bishop

Dorval
Bachynski, Morrel Paul physicist
Brown, Robert Ellis transportation company executive, former Canadian government official

Fleurimont
Simoneau, Normand J. hospital administrator

Hull
Blondin-Andrew, Ethel Canadian government official
†Boyer, Denis library director
Dupuy, Michel Canadian government official
Ebacher, Roger archbishop
Irwin, Ronald A. Canadian government official
†Labelle, Huguette international agency executive
MacDonald, George Frederick anthropologist, Canadian museum director

Ile des Soeurs
Dagenais, Marcel Gilles economist, educator

Ile Perrot
Tomlinson, George Herbert retired industrial company research executive

Joliette
Audet, Rene bishop
†Lussier, Gilles monsignor

Kingsbury
Blais, Marie-Claire novelist, poet, playwright

Lac Beauport
†Lane, Peter ornithologist

LaSalle
†Kristensen, John church organization administrator

Laval
David, Michel Louis geostatistician, consultant
Frisque, Gilles forestry engineer
Kluepfel, Dieter microbiologist
Pavilanis, Vytautas microbiology educator, physician
Pichette, Claude former banking executive, university rector, research executive

Leclercville
Morin, Pierre Jean retired management consultant

Lennoxville
†Deschenes, Jean-Marc agriculturist, researcher

Longueuil
Caplan, L(azarus) David manufacturing company executive
Hubert, Bernard bishop
Smith, Elvie Lawrence corporate director

Mirabel
Ginzburg, Rubin airport executive, electrical engineer

Mont Laurier
Gratton, Jean clergyman

Montpellier
Poirier, Louis Joseph neurology educator

Montreal
†Abi-Saber, Georges archbishop
Adamkiewicz, Vincent Witold microbiology and immunology educator, researcher
†Aguayo, Albert Juan neuroscientist
Alepian, Taro engineering and construction executive
Alou, Felipe Rojas professional baseball manager
Andrew, Frederick James telecommunications company executive
Ashby, Roger Arthur pulp and paper products company executive
Audet, Henri communications executive
†Bailar, John Christian, III public health educator, physician, statistician
Baxter, Donald William physician, educator
Beardmore, Harvey Ernest retired physician, educator
Beaubien, Philippe de Gaspe, II communications executive
Beauchamp, Jacques wood products executive
Beaudoin, François financial company executive
Beaudoin, Laurent industrial, recreational and transportation company executive
Beauregard, Luc public relations executive
Becklake, Margaret Rigsby physician, educator
Belanger, Pierre Rolland university dean, electrical engineering educator
Béliveau, Jules journalist
Benson, Kenneth Samuel corporate executive
Bentley, Kenneth Chessar oral and maxillofacial surgeon, educator
Bérard, André bank executive
Berube, Jacques B. communications company executive
Beugnot, Bernard Andre Henri French literature educator
Bisson, Claude retired chief justice of Quebec
Black, William Gordon transportation executive
Boucher, Raymond Gabriel advertising executive
Bougie, Jacques metal processing executive
Bourgeault, Jean-Jacques air transportation executive
Bouthillier, André public relations executive, consultant
Braide, Robert David broadcast executive
Brecher, Irving economics educator
Brecher, Michael political science educator
Brierley, John E. C. legal educator, former university dean
Brisebois, Marcel museum director
Brochu, Claude Renaud professional baseball team executive
Bronfman, Charles Rosner distillery executive
Bruemmer, Fred writer, photographer
Burgess, John Herbert physician, educator
Burns, James William business executive
Bussieres, Yvan supermarket chain executive
Caillé, André gas distribution company executive
Cameron, Alastair Duncan engineering consultant
Campeau, Jean financial executive
Carbonneau, Guy professional hockey player
Cardinal, Marcelin artist
Carroll, Robert Lynn biology educator, vertebrate paleontologist, museum curator
Castonguay, Claude former senator, corporate director, lawyer
Cedraschi, Tullio investment management company executive
Chan, Tak Hang chemist, educator
Chang, Thomas Ming Swi medical scientist, biotechnologist
Charney, Melvin artist, architect, educator
Charron, André Joseph Charles Pierre theologian, educator, former dean
Chateau, John-Peter D(avid) economics and finance educator, mining company executive
Chevrier, Jean Marc psychologist, publisher, author
Chiriaeff, Ludmilla Gorny ballet company executive, ballet dancer, choreographer

Chretien, Michel physician, educator, administrator
Clermont, Yves Wilfrid anatomy educator, researcher
Cloutier, Gilles Georges academic administrator, research executive
Corey, Ronald professional hockey team executive
Corinthios, Michael Jean George electrical engineering educator
Courtois, Edmond Jacques lawyer
Couture, Armand civil engineer
Crawford, Purdy consumer products and services company executive
Crowston, Wallace Bruce Stewart management educator
Cruess, Richard Leigh surgeon, university dean
Cuello, Augusto Claudio Guillermo medical research scientist, author
Cyr, J. V. Raymond telecommunications company executive
Daly, Gerald accountant
Damphousse, Vincent professional hockey player
†Dans, Frank performing arts executive
Dansereau, Pierre ecologist
Davidson, Colin Henry university educator
Dealy, John Michael chemical engineer, educator
Deegan, Derek James transportation executive
Demers, Jacques professional hockey team coach
De Mori, Renato computer science educator, researcher
Derome, Jacques Florian meteorology educator
Desjardins, Pierre consumer goods company executive
Desmarais, Paul holding company executive
Des Marais, Pierre, II communications holding company executive
Des Roches, Antoine newspaper executive
de Takacsy, Nicholas Benedict physicist, educator
Dingwall, David C. Canadian government official
Dubuc, Serge mathematics educator
Ducros, Pierre Y. information technology consulting and systems management executive
Dudek, Stephanie Zuperko psychology educator
Dufour, Jean-Marie economics researcher, educator
Dufresne, Guy Georges mining company executive
Duquette, Jean-Pierre French language and literature educator
Dutoit, Charles conductor
Edward, John Thomas chemist, educator
Eisenberg, Adi chemist
Elie, Jean André investment banker
Fanning, William James professional baseball team executive, radio and television broadcaster
Feindel, William Howard neurosurgeon, consultant
†Ferrabee, (Francis) James newspaper editor
Fontaine, Gilles physics educator
Freedman, Samuel Orkin university official
Freeman, Carolyn Ruth radiation oncologist
French, Stanley George university dean, philosophy educator
Fridman, Josef Josel telecommunications company executive
Gabbour, Iskandar city and regional planning educator
Gagné, Paul E. paper company executive
Gallagher, Tanya Marie speech pathologist, educator
Gardner, Richard Kent retired librarian, educator, consultant
Gaudry, Roger chemist, university official
Gaulin, Jean gas distribution company executive
Genest, Jacques physician, researcher, administrator
Gibbs, Sarah Preble biologist, educator
Gillespie, Thomas Stuart lawyer
Girard, Jacques communications executive
Gold, Alan B. former Canadian chief justice
Gold, Phil physician, educator
Goltzman, David endocrinologist, educator, researcher
Granger, Luc Andre university dean, psychologist
Guenette, Francoise legal affairs executive
Guindon, Yvan research labratory director
Gulkin, Harry arts administrator, film producer
†Hakim, Michel religious leader
Hall, Douglas John minister, educator
Hamel, Reginald history educator
Hantho, Charles Harold textile executive
Hay, Allan Stuart chemist, educator
Herling, Michael steel company executive
Herz, Carl Samuel mathematician
Hobday, John Charles foundation administrator
Hoffmann, Peter Conrad Werner history educator
†Hutchison, Andrew S. bishop
Ikawa-Smith, Fumiko anthropologist, educator
Ivanier, Paul steel products manufacturing company executive
Jacobs, Peter Daniel Alexander architecture and landscape architecture educator
Jasmin, Gaetan pathologist, educator
Johnston, David Lloyd academic administrator, lawyer
Johnstone, Rose Mamelak (Mrs. Douglas Johnstone) biochemistry educator
Jolicoeur, Paul molecular biologist
Jonas, John Joseph metallurgical engineering educator
Jonassohn, Kurt sociologist, educator
Juneau, Pierre broadcasting company executive
Kannengiesser, Charles A. theology educator
Kearney, Robert retired communications company executive
Kinsley, William Benton literature educator
Kirkpatrick, John Gildersleeve lawyer
†Kramer, Michael Stuart pediatric epidemiologist
Labelle, Eugene Jean-Marc airport director general
Lacoste, Paul lawyer, educator, university official
Ladanyi, Branko civil engineer
Lajeunesse, Marcel university administrator, educator
Lalonde, Marc lawyer, former Canadian government official
Lamarre, Bernard engineering, contracting and manufacturing advisor
Lamarre, Daniel public relations company executive
Landry, Roger D. publishing company executive
Langleben, Manuel Phillip physics educator
Lanyi, Alexander Sandor rail transportation executive
Large, John Andrew library and information service educator
Laurin, Pierre finance company executive
†Lawless, Ronald Edward transportation executive
Lawson, Jane Elizabeth bank executive
Leblanc, Hugues philosophy educator
Leblond, Charles Philippe anatomy educator, researcher
†LeClerc, Denise college dean
Lehmann, Heinz Edgar psychiatrist, consultant, researcher
Leroy, Claude physics educator, researcher
Levine, Martin David computer science and electrical engineering educator
Levitt, Brian Michael consumer products and services company executive, lawyer
Little, Alan Brian obstetrician, gynecologist, educator
Lowy, Frederick Hans university president, psychiatrist
Lussier, Jean-Paul dentistry educator
Maag, Urs Richard statistics educator
MacDonald, R(onald Angus) Neil physician, educator
MacKinnon, Rodrick Keith corporate administration executive, lawyer
Maclachlan, Gordon Alistair biology educator, researcher
Mac Lean, Lloyd Douglas surgeon
Mailhot, Louise judge
Major, André radio producer, writer, educator
Manson, Paul David retired military officer, electronics executive
Marcoux, Yvon financial executive, lawyer
Mark, Shew-Kuey Tommy physics educator
Marsan, Jean-Claude architect, urban planner, educator
Martin, Jean Claude health management educator
McEwen, Jean painter
Mc Gregor, Maurice cardiologist, medical educator
McLelland, Joseph Cumming philosophy educator, former university dean
Melzack, Ronald psychology educator
Mercier, Francois lawyer
Messier, Pierre lawyer, manufacturing company executive
Milic-Emili, Joseph physician, educator
Milner, Brenda Atkinson Langford neuropsychologist
Milner, Peter Marshall psychology educator
Mintzberg, Henry management educator, researcher, writer
Molson, Eric H. beverage company executive
Montcalm, Norman Joseph lawyer
Monty, Jean Claude telecommunications company executive
Moore, Sean pathologist, educator
Morgera, Salvatore Domenic electrical engineering educator, researcher
Morin, Yves-Charles linguistics educator, researcher
Moser, William Oscar Jules mathematics educator
Mulder, David S. cardiovascular surgeon
Mulroney, (Martin) Brian former prime minister of Canada
Murphy, Beverley Elaine Pearson scientist, administrator, physician, educator
Mysak, Lawrence Alexander oceanographer, climatologist, mathematician, educator
Nadeau, Bertin F. diversified company executive
Nattel, Stanley cardiologist, research scientist
Nault, Fernand choreographer
Nayar, Baldev Raj political science educator
Neveu, Jean printing company executive
Normandeau, Andre Gabriel criminologist, educator
Noumoff, Samuel Joseph political scientist, researcher
Obomsawin, Alanis director, producer
O'Brien, David Peter oil company executive
O'Brien, John Wilfrid economist, university president emeritus, educator
Olivella, Barry James financial executive
O'Neill, Brian Francis professional hockey executive
Orban, Edmond Henry political science educator
Ormsby, Eric Linn library administrator, researcher
Osmond, Dennis Gordon medical educator, researcher
Paidoussis, Michael Pandeli mechanical engineering educator
Paikowsky, Sandra Roslyn art historian
Pal, Prabir Kumar aluminium company executive
Panneton, Jacques librarian
†Parizeau, Jacques Canadian government official
Peladeau, Pierre publishing company executive
Pelletier, Louis Conrad surgeon, educator
Pépin, Marcel broadcast executive
Perlin, Arthur Saul chemistry educator
Pfeiffer, J(ohn) David mechanical engineering educator, consultant
Picard, Laurent A(ugustin) management educator, administrator, consultant
Pinard, Gilbert Daniel psychiatrist, educator
Pinard, Raymond R. pulp and paper consultant
Pinsky, Leonard geneticist
Plaa, Gabriel Leon toxicologist, educator
Plourde, Gerard company executive
Podgorsak, Ervin B. medical physicist, educator, administrator
Poissant, Charles-Albert paper manufacturing company executive
Popovici, Adrian law educator
Pound, Richard William Duncan lawyer, accountant
Pratte, Lise lawyer, corporate secretary
Prus, Victor Marius architect, urbanist
Purdy, William Crossley chemist, educator
Ramachandran, Venkatanarayana Deekshit electrical engineering educator
Raynauld, Andre economist, educator
Redfern, John D. manufacturing company executive
Régnier, Marc Charles lawyer, corporate executive
Rhodes, Lawrence artistic director
Richardson, Gisele management company executive
Richler, Mordecai writer
Robb, James Alexander lawyer
Romanelli, G. Jack journalist
Rothman, Melvin L. judge
Roy, Patrick professional hockey player
Royer, Raymond transportation equipment manufacturing company executive
Rugeroni, Ian aluminum company executive
Saint-Jacques Vallée, Madeleine advertising agency executive
Saint-Pierre, Guy engineering executive
Saint-Pierre, Jacques statistics educator, consultant
Sandor, Thomas biochemist
Sandorfy, Camille chemistry educator
Sattler, Rolf plant morphologist, educator
Saumier, Andre finance executive
Sauvageau, Philippe library director
Savard, Claude A. food service executive
Savard, Serge professional hockey team executive
Schuele, Alban Wilhelm chemical company executive
Schwartz, Roy Richard holding company executive
Scriver, Charles Robert medical scientist, human geneticist
Selvadurai, Antony Patrick Sinnappa civil engineering educator, applied mathematician, consultant
Shaw, Robert Fletcher retired civil engineer
Shea, William Rene historian, philosopher of science, educator
Sheppard, Claude-Armand lawyer
Silverthorne, Michael James classics educator
Silvester, Peter Peet electrical engineer, educator, consultant
Simons, John H. electronics manufacturing company executive
†Sirois, Charles communications executive
Sirois, Gerard pharmacy educator
Smith, Brian Ray Douglas rail transportation executive, lawyer
Smith, James Hamilton paper, packaging, construction material and chemicals company executive
Smith, Philip Edward Lake anthropology educator
Solomon, Samuel biochemistry educator, administrator
Somerville, Margaret Anne Ganley law educator
Sonea, Sorin I. microbiologist
Sourkes, Theodore Lionel biochemistry educator
Speirs, Derek James diversified corporation financial executive
†Spickler, Robert performing arts executive
Stanners, Clifford Paul molecular biologist, cell biologist, biochemistry educator
Stewart, Jane psychology educator
Stinson, William W. transportation executive
Stoneman, William Hambly, III professional baseball team executive
Suen, Ching Yee computer scientist and educator, researcher
Sykes, Stephanie Lynn library director, archivist, museum director
Szabo, Denis criminologist, educator
Taras, Paul physicist, educator
Tavenas, François civil engineer, educator
Taylor, Claude I. airlines executive
Tellier, Paul M. Canadian railway transportation executive
Terreault, R. Charles engineer, management educator, researcher
Thind, Tej Pal international management consultant
Thompson, John Douglas financier
Torrey, David Leonard investment banker
Tousignant, Jacques human resources executive, lawyer
Tremblay, Andre Gabriel lawyer, educator
Tremblay, Rodrigue economics educator
Trigger, Bruce Graham anthropology educator
†Trogani, Monica ballet mistress
Trudeau, Pierre Elliott lawyer, former Canadian prime minister
Turcotte, Jean-Claude Cardinal archbishop
Turmel, Jean Bernard banker
Uzan, Bernard Franck general and artistic director
Vaillancourt, Jean-Guy sociology educator
Van Vliet, Carolyne Marina physicist, educator
Vennat, Michel lawyer
Vikis-Freibergs, Vaira psychologist, educator
Wallace, Philip Russell retired physics educator
Waller, Harold M
Webster, Norman Eric journalist, charitable foundation administrator
Weir, Stephen James financial executive
Whitehead, Michael Anthony chemistry educator
Williams, Paul H. textile executive
Wilson, Lynton Ronald telecommunications company executive
Woszczyk, Wieslaw Richard audio engineering educator, researcher
†Yates, Robin David Sebastian Chinese history educator
Yong, Raymond Nen-Yiu civil engineering educator
Zakaib, Lorne industrial technology executive
Zames, George David electrical engineer, educator

Mount Royal
Chauvette, Claude R. building materials company administrator
Glezos, Matthews consumer products and services
Lessard, Michel M. finance company executive

Nemaska
†Coon Come, Matthew Native American tribal chief

North Hatley
Gustafson, Ralph Barker poet, educator
Jones, Douglas Gordon retired literature educator

Outremont
Bourassa, Robert former Premier of Québec
†Derderian, Hovnan church official
Domaradzki, Theodore Felix Slavic studies educator, editor
Gouin, Serge corporate executive
Larose, Roger former pharmaceutical company executive, former university administrator
Letourneau, Jean-Paul business association executive and consultant
Levesque, Rene Jules Albert retired physicist

Pointe Claire
Bolker, Henry Irving retired chemist, research institute director, educator
Cohen, Charles F. retail executive
Wrist, Peter Ellis pulp and paper company executive

Pontiac
Hlavina, Rasto R(astislav) sculptor

Quebec
Asselin, Martial Canadian lieutenant governor
Aubut, Marcel lawyer, sports association official
Belanger, Gerard economics educator
†Bourget, Edwin Robert marine ecologist, educator
Courtois, B. A. communications executive
Couture, Jean G. surgeon, educator
Crawford, Marc professional hockey coach
†Dinan, Robert Michael lawyer
Engel, Charles Robert chemist, educator
Gauthier, Paule lawyer
Gervais, Michel academic administrator
†Huhtala, Marie Therese diplomat
Joly, Jean Robert microbiologist, medical educator
Jovanovic, Miodrag surgeon, educator
Labrie, Fernand physician
Lafleur, Guy public relations executive, professional hockey player
Laliberté-Bourque, Andrée museum director
†L'Allier, Jean-Paul mayor
La Rochelle, Pierre-Louis civil engineering educator
Lecours, Michel electrical engineering educator
LeMay, Jacques lawyer
†Letourneau, Jocelyn history educator
Migue, Jean Luc economics educator
Normand, Robert lawyer
Page, Michel biochemist
Paradis, Andre librarian
†Parent, André neurobiology educator, researcher
Porter, John Robert art history educator, curator, writer
Potvin, Pierre physiologist, educator
Poussart, Denis Jean-Marie electrical engineering educator, consultant
Rochette, Louis shipowner
†St-Yves, Angèle agricultural engineer
Stavert, Alexander Bruce bishop
Theodorescu, Radu Amza Serban mathematician, educator
Tourigny, Christine judge
Tremblay, Marc Adélard anthropologist, educator
Trudel, Marc J. botanist
Verge, Pierre legal educator
†Villeneuve, Jean-Pierre science association director, educator

Rimouski
Blanchet, Bertrand archbishop
†Laribée, Jacques conservationist
Levesque, Louis bishop
†Rioux, Claude economics educator
Walton, Alan oceanographer

Rock Forest
Lamirande, Emilien historian, educator

Rosemere
Adrian, Donna Jean librarian

Rouyn-Noranda
Hamelin, Jean-Guy bishop

Saint Hubert
Doré, Roland dean, science association director

Saint Hyacinthe
Brouillette, Yves insurance company executive
Langevin, Louis-de-Gonzaque bishop

Saint Jean-sur-Richelieu
†Demars, Denis research institution director

Saint Jerome
Joly, Jean-Gil medical biochemist, internist, administrator, researcher, educator
Rolland, Lucien G. paper company executive
Valois, Charles bishop

Saint Lambert
Archambault, Louis sculptor
Brossard, Maurice biotechnology company executive
†Jorisch, Stéphane-Maurice illustrator

Saint Laurent
Boulet, Lionel research administrator
Harris, Hollis Loyd airline executive
Kivenko, Kenneth aerospace industry executive

Saint Luc
Marcoux, Jules Edouard physicist, educator, writer

Saint Pierre
Blanchet, Madeleine research executive

Saint Sauveur
Hanigan, Lawrence retired railway executive

Saint Sauveur des Monts
Dunsky, xecutive, communications consultant, painter

Sainte Anne de Belle
†Lawand, Thomas A. research engineer

Sainte Anne de Bellevue
Broughton, Robert Stephen irrigation and drainage engineering educator, consultant
Buckland, Roger Basil university dean, educator, vice principal
Grant, William Frederick geneticist, educator
MacLeod, Robert Angus microbiology educator, researcher
Steppler, Howard Alvey agronomist

Sainte Croix
Grenier, Fernand geographer, consultant

Sainte Foy
Boudoux, Michel environmental research executive
Cardinal, André phycologist, educator
Denis, Paul-Yves geography educator
Legendre, Louis biological oceanography educator, researcher
Maranda, Guy oral maxillofacial surgeon, Canadian health facility executive, educator
Murray, Warren James educator, philosopher
Pasquier, Joël music educator

Sherbrooke
Bureau, Michel André pediatrician, pulmonologist, faculty dean
de Margerie, Jean-M. ophthalmology educator
Deslongchamps, Pierre chemistry educator
Fortier, Jean-Marie archbishop
Tremblay, André-Marie physicist

Sillery
Couture, Maurice archbishop

Trois Rivieres
Lavallee, H.-Claude chemical engineer, researcher
Noël, Laurent bishop, educator

Valleyfield
Lebel, Robert bishop

Varennes
Bartnikas, Raymond electrical engineer, educator
Maruvada, Pereswara Sarma engineering executive, researcher
St. Jean, Guy electric power industry executive
Vijh, Ashok Kumar chemistry educator, researcher

Verdun
Delisle, Gilles Yvan *telecommunications executive*
Ferguson, Michael John *electronics and communications educator*
Paré, Jean-Jacques *civil engineer, geotechnical and dam safety consultant*

Westmount
Dunbar, Maxwell John *oceanographer, educator*
Fortier, L. Yves *barrister*
Gordonsmith, John Arthur Harold *collection agency executive*
Jasper, Herbert Henri *neuroscience researcher, consultant, writer*
Kessler, Jacques Isaac *gastroenterologist, educator*
Spalding, James Stuart *retired telecommunications company executive*

SASKATCHEWAN

Gravelbourg
Delaquis, Noel *bishop*

Prince Albert
Morand, Blaise E. *bishop*

Regina
Balfour, Reginald James *lawyer*
Barber, Lloyd Ingram *retired university president*
Bayda, Edward Dmytro *judge*
Bays, Eric *bishop*
Dalla-Vicenza, Mario Joseph *steel company financial executive*
Davis, Gordon Richard Fuerst *biologist, translator*
Driedger, Florence Gay *social agency executive, social work educator, consultant*
Fedoruk, Sylvia O. *Canadian provincial official, educator*
Holm, Roy K. *church administrator*
Hughes, Robert Lachlan *newspaper executive*
Laschuk, Roy Bogdan *lawyer*
MacKay, Harold Hugh *lawyer*
†Mitchell, Robert *province official*
Mollard, John Douglas *engineering and geology executive*
Nuttall, Richard Norris *state agency administrator*
Oko, Andrew Jan *art gallery director, curator*
Phillips, Roger *steel company executive*
Powell, Trevor John David *archivist*
Rolfes, Herman Harold *Canadian government official*
Romanow, Roy John *provincial government official, barrister, solicitor*
Sifton, Michael Clifford *broadcaster, publisher*
Teichrob, Carol *Canadian provincial official*
†Wiebe, J. E. N. *province official*

Saltcoats
Farquharson, Walter Henry *minister, church official*

Saskatoon
Babiuk, Lorne Alan *virologist, immunologist, research administrator*
Baker, Robert John *agronomy educator*
Bell, John Milton *agricultural science educator*
Belovanoff, Olga *retired health care facility administrator*
Billinton, Roy *engineering educator*
Blakeney, Allan Emrys *Canadian government official, lawyer*
Bornstein, Eli *artist, sculptor*
Brewster, Elizabeth Winifred *English language educator, poet, novelist*
Carr, Roy Arthur *agricultural products applied research, development & communication processing organization executive*
Childers, Charles Eugene *potash mining company executive*
Emson, Harry Edmund *pathology educator, bioethicist*
Filevich, Basil *bishop*
Gupta, Madan Mohan *engineering educator, researcher*
Harvey, Bryan Laurence *crop science educator*
Henry, Keith Douglas *architect*
Hirose, Akira *physics educator, researcher*
Houston, C(larence) Stuart *radiologist, educator*
Huang, Pan Ming *soil science educator*
Ish, Daniel Russell *law educator, academic adminstrator*
Jacobson, Sverre Theodore *retired minister*
Jaques, Louis Barker *pharmacologist*
Johnson, Dennis Duane *pharmacologist, educator*
Kennedy, Marjorie Ellen *librarian*
Kent, Christopher Andrew *history educator*
Knight, Arthur Robert *technical institute administrator*
Knott, Douglas Ronald *college dean, agricultural sciences educator, researcher*
Kumar, Surinder *electrical engineering educator, consultant*
Kupsch, Walter Oscar *geologist*
Mahoney, James P. *bishop*
McCallum, Kenneth James *retired university dean, chemistry and chemical engineering educator*
Morgan, Thomas Oliver *bishop*
Nikiforuk, Peter N. *university dean*
Randhawa, Bikkar Singh *psychologist, educator*
Sachdev, Mohindar Singh *engineering educator*
Shokeir, Mohamed Hassan Kamel *medical geneticist, educator*
†Steck, Warren Franklin *former entomology researcher, science administrator*
Stewart, John Wray Black *college dean*
†Vanderhaeghe, Guy Clarence *writer, creative writing educator*

YUKON TERRITORY

Whitehorse
Lobsinger, Thomas *bishop*
Ostashek, John *government leader*
Penikett, Antony David John *Canadian government official*
Phelps, Willard *Canadian government official*

MEXICO

Aristoteles
Akel, Ollie James *oil company executive*

Chihuahua
Almeida Merino, Adalberto *archbishop*

Col Tepeyac Insurgentes
Godinez Flores, Ramon *auxiliary bishop*

Cuajimalpa
†Mandri-Bellot, Jose Antonio *architect*

Cuernavaca
Mora, Francisco *artist, printmaker*

Garza Garcia
Paez, Rafael Roberto *holding company executive*

Guadalajara
Garibay-Gutierrez, Luis *physician, educator*

Juarez
Torres Medina, Emilio *oncologist, consultant*

Matamoros
Chavolla Ramos, Francisco Javier *bishop*

Mexico City
Arau, Alfonso *film producer and director, writer*
Aspe, Pedro *Mexican government official*
Azcarraga Milmo, Emilio *communication company executive*
Baer, George Martin *veterinarian, researcher*
Brown, Kenneth Charles *manufacturing company executive*
Bruton, John Macaulay *trade association executive*
del Conde, Teresa *museum director, art historian, researcher*
Diaz-Coller, Carlos *physician*
Dudley, Craig James *executive recruiter*
Ellison, Katherine Esther *journalist*
Friedeberg, Pedro *painter, sculptor, designer*
Guizar, Ricardo Diaz *clergyman*
Jones, James Robert *ambassador, former congressman, lawyer*
Lacouture, Felipe Ernesto *museum consultant*
Mendelejis, Leonardo Nierman *artist*
Paz, Octavio *poet, Mexican diplomat*
Peimbert, Manuel *astronomer*
Rajaram, Sanjaya *agricultural scientist, plant breeder*
Rodriguez, Adolfo *library director, historian*
†Ruano Angulo, Luis Carlos *secretary of Mexican navy*
Solana Morales, Fernando *diplomat, financier, educator*
Velasco, Eugenio *advertising executive*
Whitaker, Pernell (Sweet Pea) *professional boxer*
†Zedillo Ponce de León, Ernesto *president of Mexico*

Monterrey
Rizzo, Socrates *Mexican governor*
Ruiz, Othon *financial executive*

Morelia
Warren, J. Benedict *retired history educator*

Morelos
Illich, Ivan *researcher, educator*

Puebla
Zehe, Alfred Fritz Karl *physics educator*

Saltillo
Villalobos Padilla, Francisco *bishop*

Veracruz
Ranzahuer, Guillermo Gonzalez *bishop*

ARGENTINA

Bahia Blanca
Cardozo, Miguel Angel *telecommunications engineering educator*

Buenos Aires
Balve, Beba Carmen *research center administrator*
Gennadios, (Gennadios Chrysoulakis) *bishop*
Sacerdote, Manuel Ricardo *banker*

ARMENIA

Byurakan
Khachikian, Edward Yerem *astronomer*

Yerevan
Gilmore, Harry J. *ambassador*

AUSTRALIA

Adelaide
Twidale, C(harles) R(owland) *geomorphologist, educator*

Avalon
West, Morris Langlo *novelist*

Belair
Briggs, Geoffrey Hugh *retired librarian*

Bundoora
Isaac, Rhys Llywelyn *historian, educator*
James, Bruce David *chemistry educator*

Canberra
Gani, Joseph Mark *statistics educator, administrator, researcher*

Greenwich
Westerberg, Verne Edward *magazine publisher*

Hobart Tasmania
Munger, Bryce L. *physician, educator*

Kensington
Rayward, Warden Boyd *librarian, educator*

Melbourne
Lawson, Francis Colin *chemical company executive*
Mc Gimpsey, Ronald Alan *oil company executive*

Nedlands
Oxnard, Charles Ernest *anatomist, anthropologist, human biologist, educator*

New South Wales
†Davis, Judy *actress*

Norfolk Island
McCullough, Colleen *author*

Parkville
Foote, Simon James *molecular biologist*

Potts Point
Beresford, Bruce *film director*

Randwick
Hall, Peter Francis *physiologist*

Ringwood
Base, Graeme Rowland *illustrator, author*

Rockhampton
Zelmer, Amy Elliott *health science educator*

Sydney
Bleveans, John *lawyer*
Guerin, Didier *magazine executive*
Miller, George *film director*
Murdoch, (Keith) Rupert *publisher*
Salsbury, Stephen Matthew *historian, educator*

AUSTRIA

Gaz
Weisstein, Ulrich Werner *English literature educator*

Maria Enzersdorf
Vetter, Herbert *physician, educator*

Salzburg
†Mueller, Ulrich *literature educator*

Vienna
Faulkner, Julia Ellen *opera singer*
Frankl, Viktor E. *psychiatrist, author*
Hunt, Swanee G. *ambassador*
Jackovich, Victor *ambassador*
Lo Bello, Nino *author, journalist*
Ludwig, Christa *mezzo-soprano*
Niederreiter, Harald Guenther *mathematician, researcher*
Oberhuber, Konrad Johannes *art museum curator, educator*
Raimondi, Ruggero *opera singer*
Steinbruckner, Bruno Friedrich *foreign language educator*

BAHAMAS

Abaco
Goodloe, John Duncan, IV *real estate company executive*

Grand Cayman
McIntire, Jerald Gene *investment executive, former municipal official*

Nassau
Dingman, Michael David *industrial company executive*
†Ford, John Seabury *diplomat*
Templeton, John Marks *investment counsel, financial analyst*

BANGLADESH

Dhaka
†Merrill, David Nathan *ambassador*

BARBADOS

Bridgetown
Barrow, Dame Ruth Nita *governor general*
Hughes, G. Philip *diplomat*

BELARUS

Minsk
Swartz, David H. *ambassador*

BELGIUM

Antwerp
De Craene, Jacques Maria *plastics company executive, retired judge, arbitrator*

Brussels
Barnum, John Wallace *lawyer*
Branegan, James Augustus, III *journalist*
Bustin, George Leo *lawyer*
Calingaert, Michael *international consultant*
†Cornelis, François *oil industry executive*
Glazer, Barry David *lawyer*
Hunter, Robert Edwards *ambassador, diplomat*
†Ignatius, Alan (Adi) *magazine editor*
Jadot, Jean Lambert Octave *clergyman*
Janssen, Paul-Emmanuel *bank executive*
Kempe, Frederick Schumann *newspaper editor, author*
Liebman, Howard Mark *lawyer*
Loutrel, Claude Yves *corporate official*
Mestrallet, Gérard *association executive*
Oberreit, Walter William *lawyer*
Orly, Elvira Jolan *lawyer*
Portal, Gilbert Marcel Adrien *oil company executive*
Smith, Turner Taliaferro, Jr. *lawyer*

Chaumont Gistoux
Holleweg dit Wegman, Willy *management expert, educator, entrepreneurship development specialist*

Heverlee
L'abbé, Gerrit Karel *chemist*

Lens
Peat, Randall Dean *defense analysis company executive, retired air force officer*

Louvain la Neuve
Sintzoff, Michel *computer scientist, educator*

Strombeek Bever
Mancel, Claude Paul *household product company executive*

BERMUDA

Hamilton
Kramer, Donald *insurance executive*
Stempel, Ernest Edward *insurance executive*

Pembroke
Wiedemann, Joseph Robert *insurance company executive*

Tuckers Town
Heizer, Edgar Francis, Jr. *venture capitalist*

BOLIVIA

La Paz
Bowers, Charles R. *ambassador*
Kamman, Curtis Warren *ambassador*

BOTSWANA

Gaborone
Temane, Bahitik *government executive*

BRAZIL

Maceio
Fox, James Frederick *public relations counsel*

Rio de Janeiro
Costa Neto, Adelina *chemistry educator, consultant*
DaMatta, Roberto Augusto *anthropologist*
Leite, Carlos Alberto *physician, medical educator*
Sales, Eugenio de Araujo Cardinal *archbishop*

Salvador
Davidson, Ralph Kirby *economist, retired foundation executive, consultant*
Silva, Benedicto Alves de Castro *surgeon, educator*

Sao Paulo
Berman, Marcelo Samuel *mathematics and physics educator, cosmology*

BRITISH VIRGIN ISLANDS

Tortola
Green, Leon, Jr. *mechanical engineer*

CAMEROON

Yaounde
†Hughes, Morris Nelson, Jr. *foreign service officer*

CAPE VERDE

Praia
McNamara, Francis T. *ambassador*
Segars, Joseph M. *ambassador*

CAYMAN ISLAND

Grand Cayman Island
Crockett, James Grover, III *musician, former music publisher*

CENTRAL AFRICAN REPUBLIC

Bangui
Gribbin, Robert E., III *ambassador*

CHAD

N'Djamena
Pope, Laurence E., II *ambassador*
†Williams, Anne M. *diplomat, lawyer*

CHILE

Concepcion
Trzebiatowski, Gregory L. *education educator*

Santiago
Beshears, Charles Daniel *consultant, former insurance executive*
Strommen, Clifford H. *headmaster*
Whelan, James Robert *communications executive, international trade and investment consultant, author, educator*
Wilkey, Malcolm Richard *retired ambassador, former federal judge*

CHINA

Beijing
Chen, Peide *mathematics educator*
Gish, Norman Richard *oil industry executive*
Liang, Junxiang *aeronautics and astronautics engineer, educator*
Roy, J(ames) Stapleton *ambassador*

COSTA RICA

San Jose
Hoffman, Irwin *orchestra conductor*

CROATIA

Zagreb
Fertig-Dyks, Susan Beatrice *international media and business consultant*
Galbraith, Peter W. *ambassador*

CUBA

Havana
Kouri, Gustavo Pedro *virologist*

CZECH REPUBLIC

Prague
Auerbach, Stuart Charles *journalist*
Kalkus, Stanley *librarian, administrator, consultant*

DENMARK

Charlottenlund
Andreassen, Poul *business executive*

Copenhagen
Hansen, Ole *physicist*
Skylv, Grethe Krogh *rheumatologist, anthropologist*

Grasted
Wiin-Nielsen, Aksel Christopher *meteorologist educator*

Helsingør
Sørensen, Erik *international advisor*

Hoersholm
Jensen, Ole *energy researcher*

Vedbaek
Nordqvist, Erik Askbo *shipping company executive*

DOMINICAN REPUBLIC

Santo Domingo
Piantini, Carlos *conductor*

ECUADOR

Quito
†Cordero, Guido Oswaldo *banker*

EGYPT

Addis Ababa
†Hicks, Irvin *ambassador*

Cairo
El-Hamalawy, Mohamed-Younis Abd-El-Samie *computer engineering educator*
Miller, Harry George *education educator*

EL SALVADOR

San Salvador
Alfaro-Pineda, Rafael Angel *diplomat*

ENGLAND

Ascot
Grubman, Wallace Karl *chemical company executive*

Balcombe
Scofield, Paul *actor*

Berkshire
Hall, Arnold Alexander *aeronautical, mechanical and electrical executive*

Birmingham
Banowetz, Joseph Murray *musician, music educator*
Fry, Maxwell John *economist, educator*

Brentford
Wendt, Henry, III *pharmaceutical company executive*

Brighton
Watkin, David *film director, cinematographer*

Buckinghamshire
Elegant, Robert Sampson *journalist, author*

Cambridge
Acheson, Roy Malcolm *epidemiologist, educator*
Carpenter, Adelaide Trowbridge Clark *geneticist*
Hawking, Stephen W. *astrophysicist, mathematician*
Hawthorne, Sir William (Rede) *aerospace and mechanical engineer, educator*
Hogwood, Christopher Jarvis Haley *music director, educator*
Kermode, (John) Frank *literary critic, educator*
Meade, James Edward *economist*
Needham, Joseph *biochemist, historian of science, Orientalist*
Steiner, George (Francis Steiner) *author, educator*

Claverton Down
Buchanan, Robert Angus *archaeology educator*

Cornwall
Dark, Philip John Crosskey *anthropologist, educator*

Coventry
Trigg, Roger Hugh *philosophy educator*

Cranbrook
Hattersley-Smith, Geoffrey Francis *retired government research scientist*

East Sussex
Wilson, Leroy *retired glass manufacturing company executive*

Eastbourne
Baylen, Joseph O. *retired history educator*

Emsworth
Suhrbier, Klaus Rudolf *hydrodynamicist, naval architect*

Halifax
Lilly, Shannon Jeanne *dancer*

Hartlepool
Smyth, Reginald (Reggie Smythe) *cartoonist*

Hingham
Pollini, Francis *author*

Hove
Kitchin, Laurence Tyson *liberal arts and drama educator, author*

Isle of Wight
Stigwood, Robert Colin *theater, movie, television and record producer*

Iver Heath
Kubrick, Stanley *producer, director, writer*

Leicester
Harijan, Ram *technology transfer researcher*

Liverpool
Reilly, Thomas *humanities educator*

London
†Ackland-Snow, Terry *art director*
Adams, George Bell *lawyer*
Albert, Robert Alan *lawyer*
Aliki, (Aliki Liacouras Brandenberg) *author, illustrator children's books*
Ambler, Eric *writer*
Ambler, Timothy Felix John *management science researcher*
Amis, Sir Kingsley *novelist*
Ashkenazy, Vladimir Davidovich *concert pianist, conductor*
Ballard, James Graham *writer*
Band, David *investment banker*
Barnett, Bill Marvin *publishing company executive*
Barocci, Robert Louis *advertising agency executive*
Barshai, Rudolf Borisovich *conductor*
Bart, Lionel *composer, lyricist*
Bates, Malcolm Rowland *corporate director*
Batla, Raymond John, Jr. *lawyer*
Bawden, Nina (Mary) *author*
Baxendell, Sir Peter (Brian) *petroleum engineer*
Beck, Jeff *musician, composer, vocalist*
Beharrell, Steven Roderic *lawyer*
Bell, Theodore Augustus *advertising executive*
†Bennett, Richard Rodney *composer*
Berger, Andrew L. *investment banker, lawyer*
Berger, Thomas Jan *financial company executive*
Biddle, Adrian *cinematographer*
Bigbie, John Taylor *lawyer, banker*
Billings, Donald Franklin *international banking consultant*
Binney, Robert Harry *bank executive*
Bischoff, Winfried Franz Wilhelm *merchant banker*
†Biziou, Peter *cinematographer*
Blackbourn, David Gordon *history educator*
Boccardi, Louis Donald *news agency executive*
Bokaemper, Stefan *hotel executive*
Bonynge, Richard *opera conductor*
Bowie, David (David Robert Jones) *musician, actor*
Bream, Julian *classical guitarist and lutanist*
†Bridge, Andrew *theatrical lighting designer*
Brown, G(lenn) William, Jr. *investment banker*
Catto of Cairncatto, Baron Stephen Gordon *banker*
Cellan-Jones, James Gwynne *television producer, director*
Chappell, Anthony Gordon *banker*
Christie, Julie *actress*
Chubb, Joseph *lawyer*
Clarke, Arthur Charles *author*
Cleese, John Marwood *writer, businessman, comedian*
Codron, Michael Victor *theatrical producer*
Coelho, Joseph Richard *research analyst*
Cole, Richard A. *lawyer*
Collins, Paul John *banker*
Comfort, Alexander *physician, author*
Condon, Richard Thomas *author*
Conti, Tom *actor, writer, director*
Cook, Jan *recording industry executive*
Cowles, Fleur (Mrs. Tom M. Meyer) *author, artist*
Craig, Stuart N. *film production designer*
Crowe, William James, Jr. *diplomat*
Dalby, Alan James *pharmaceutical company executive*
Deal, Timothy *diplomat, government executive*
de Bellaigue, Eric *media consultant, securities analysis specialist*
Dehennin, Herman Baron *diplomat*
Deighton, Len *author*
Dibble, Gordon Lynch *engineering company executive*
Dickinson, Peter *composer*
Douglas, Mary Tew *anthropology and humanities educator*
†Doyle, Patrick *composer*
Drabble, Margaret *writer*
†Dudley, Anne *composer*
Elizabeth, Her Majesty II (Elizabeth Alexandra Mary) *Queen of United Kingdom of Great Britain and Northern Ireland, and her other Realms and Territories, head of the Commonwealth, defender of the faith*
Estes, Simon Lamont *opera singer, bass-baritone*
Ewart, Gavin Buchanan *poet, writer*
Fabricant, Arthur E. *lawyer, corporate executive*
Fine, Anne *author*
Follett, Kenneth Martin *author*
Forsyth, Frederick *author*
Foster, Lawrence *concert and opera conductor*
Foster, Sir Norman Robert *architect*
Fowles, John *author*
Fox, Hazel Mary *law educator, editor*
Francis, Freddie *film producer and director*
Fraser, Lady Antonia *writer, editor*
Freni, Mirella *soprano*
Gaines, Peter Mathew *lawyer*
†Galloway, Janice *writer, editor*
Ghiaurov, Nicolai *opera singer*
Gielgud, Sir (Arthur) John *actor, director*
Gilbert, Patrick Nigel Geoffrey *organization executive*
Gillam, Patrick John *oil company executive*
†Gleason, Howard Wesley *consulting company executive*
Gordon, Jeffrey I. *lawyer*
Grade, Lord Lew *entertainment corporation executive*
Green, Richard *psychiatrist, lawyer, educator*
Green, Richard Lancelyn (Gordon) *editor, writer*
Greener, Anthony *beverage company executive*
Gummer, Peter Selwyn *public relations executive*
Gyllenhammar, Pehr Gustaf *finance company executive, retired automobile company executive, writer*
Habgood, Anthony John *corporate executive*
Hale, Charles Martin *stockbroker*
Hall, Peter Geoffrey *urban and regional planning educator*
Hall, Sir Peter Reginald Frederick *theater opera and film director*
Hallissey, Michael *accounting company executive*
Hare, David *playwright*
Harper, Heather Mary *retired soprano*
Harris, Howard Elliott *consulting company executive*
Harris, William Cecil *insurance company consultant*
Harrison, George *musician*
Haubold, Samuel Allen *lawyer*
Hawthorne, Nigel Barnard *actor*
Hayden, Richard Michael *investment banker*
Hendricks, Barbara *opera singer, recitalist*
Higgins, Jack (Harry Patterson) *author*
Hite, Shere D. *author, cultural historian*
Hoban, Russell Conwell *author*
Holm, Ian *actor*
Hornyak, Eugene Augustine *bishop*
†Horwitz, Anthony Lander *reporter, author*
Hoskins, Bob (Robert William Hoskins) *actor*
Hudson, Manley O., Jr. *lawyer*
Hughes, Ted *poet, author*
Hughes, Winifred Shirley *writer, illustrator*
†Huismans, Sipko *diversified company executive*
Hunter Blair, Pauline Clarke *author*
Hurt, John Vincent *actor*
Idle, Eric *actor, screenwriter, producer*
Irons, Jeremy John *actor*
Irvine, Ian Alexander Noble *publishing company executive, director*
James, P(hyllis) D(orothy) (Baroness James of Holland Park of Southwold in County of Suffolk) *author*
John, Elton Hercules (Reginald Kenneth Dwight) *musician*
Johnson, Thomas Edward *lawyer*
Jones, Terry *film director, author*
Jordan, Neil Patrick *film director*
Jourdren, Marc Henri *investment banking company executive*
Junz, Helen B. *economist*
Kies, David M. *lawyer*
Kingham, Richard Frank *lawyer*
Kingsley, Ben *actor*
Kirkby, Maurice Anthony *oil company executive*
†Kissmann, Edna *communications executive*
Kitaj, R. B. *artist*
Kraus, Alfredo (Alfredo Kraus Trujillo) *tenor*
Kuper, Adam Jonathan *anthropologist, educator*
Kureishi, Hanif *author*
Lahr, John *author*
Lanigan, Denis George *retired advertising agency executive*
Laurie, James Andrew *journalist, broadcaster*
Leaf, Robert Stephen *public relations executive*
le Carré, John (David John Moore Cornwell) *author*
Lesser, Frederick Alan *mining and chemical company executive*
Lessing, Doris (May) *writer*
Le Vien, John Douglas (Jack Le Vien) *motion picture and television producer, director*
Lloyd Webber, Sir Andrew *composer*
Lynne, Gillian Barbara *choreographer, dancer, actress, director*
Mackerras, Sir (Alan) Charles (Maclaurin) *conductor*
Mackintosh, Cameron *musical theater producer*
Mallinckrodt, George W. *bank executive*
Marriner, Sir Neville *orchestra conductor*
Marsden, William *government official*
Martines, Lauro *historian, writer*
†Mathias, Sean Gerard *author, director*
Mayer, Peter *publisher*
McGinnis, Marcy Ann *television news executive producer*
McIntyre, Donald Conroy *opera singer, baritone*
McKellen, Ian *actor*
McLeod, Wilson Churchill *lawyer*
McNulty, Dermot *public relations executive*
Mellon, John *publishing executive*
Metzger, Barry *lawyer*
Miller, Jonathan Wolfe *theater and film director, physician*
Minton, Yvonne Fay *mezzo-soprano*
†Mirageas, Evans John *record company executive*
Mirren, Helen *actress*
Montero, Fernan Gonzalo *advertising executive*
Moreno, Glen Richard *banker*
Morris, Desmond *author*
Morrison, William David *lawyer*
Mulford, David Campbell *finance company executive*
Naipaul, Vidiadhar Surajprasad *author*
†Napier, John *set designer*
Nelson, Bernard Edward *lawyer*
Nelson, John Wilton *symphonic conductor*
Newburg, Andre W. G. *lawyer*
Newmarch, Michael George *insurance company executive*
Nucci, Leo *baritone*
Nunn, Trevor Robert *director*
Ogden, Peter James *investment banker*
O'Toole, Peter *actor*
Owers, Brian Charles *holding company executive*
Oxenbury, Helen *children's writer, illustrator*
Palin, Michael Edward *actor, screenwriter, author*
Paton Walsh, Jill *author*
Pennant-Rea, Rupert Lascelles *banker*
Philipsborn, John David *former banker, consultant*
Pinter, Harold *playwright*
Pleasants, Henry *music critic*
Plowright, Joan Anne *actress*
Pritchett, Sir Victor Sawdon *author*
Puttnam, Sir David Terence *film producer*
Ralston, Anthony *computer scientist, mathematician, educator*
Randour, Paul A(lfred) *lawyer*
Rattle, Simon *conductor*
Rea, Stephen *actor*
Read, Piers Paul *author*
Ricci, Ruggiero *violinist, educator*
Rice, Sir Timothy Miles Bindon *lyricist*
Rigg, Diana *actress*
Saatchi, Maurice *communications and marketing company executive*
Sainsbury of Preston Candover, Lord (Baron John Davan Sainsbury) *entrepreneur*
Salonen, Esa-Pekka *conductor*
Scardino, Albert James *journalist*
Scardino, Marjorie Morris *publishing company executive*
Schaufuss, Peter *dancer, producer, choreographer, ballet director*
Schlesinger, John Richard *film, opera and theater director*
†Secord, James Andrew *researcher, educator*
Serebrier, José *musician, conductor, composer*
Serota, Nicholas Andrew *art gallery director*
Shaw, Sir Neil McGowan *sugar, cereal and starch refining company executive*
Shaw, Richard John Gildroy *insurance executive*
Sheehy, Sir Patrick *manufacturing and service company executive*
Siepi, Cesare *opera singer*
†Slocombe, Douglas *cinematographer*
Smart, Claude Harlan, Jr. *lawyer*
Smernoff, Richard Louis *oil company executive*
Smith, Dame Maggie *actress*
Sorrell, Martin Stuart *advertising and marketing executive*
Soviero, Diana Barbara *soprano*
Spark, Dame Muriel Sarah *writer*
†Stapleton, Nigel John *finance director*
Starr, Ringo (Richard Starkey) *musician, actor*
Steen, Norman Frank *marketing executive*
Stevens, Robert Bocking *lawyer, educator*
Sting, (Gordon Matthew Sumner) *musician, songwriter, actor*
Stoppard, Tom (Tomas Straussler) *playwright*
Streator, Edward *diplomat*
Sutherland, Dame Joan *retired soprano*
Symon, Lindsay *neurological surgery educator*
Taylor, Jonathan Francis *agribusiness executive*
Tebaldi, Renata *opera singer*
Tennstedt, Klaus *conductor*
Thomas, Allen Lloyd *lawyer, private investor*
Thompson, John More *managment consultant*
Treasure, John Albert Penberthy *advertising executive*
Tuohy, William *correspondent*
Tureck, Rosalyn *concert artist, author, editor, educator*
Ustinov, Sir Peter Alexander *actor, director, writer*
Van Culin, Samuel *religious organization administrator*
Vaness, Carol *soprano*
Van Meter, John David *lawyer*
Vansittart, Peter *novelist, lecturer, critic*
Vishnevskaya, Galina Pavlovna *soprano, opera company director*
Wallis, Diana Lynn *artistic director*
Winner, Michael Robert *film director, writer, producer*
Zinnemann, Fred *film director*

Malmesbury
Shober, Edward Wharton *bioscience company executive*

Middlesex
Finlay, Robert Derek *food company executive*
Lester, Richard *film director*

Milford on Sea
Styan, John Louis *English literature and theater educator*

Milton Keynes
Daniel, John Sagar (Sir) *academic administrator, metallurgist*

Newcastle upon Tyne
Cookson, Dame Catherine Ann *author*

Oxford
Aldiss, Brian (Wilson) *writer*
Cairncross, Sir Alexander Kirkland *university chancellor, economist*
Carey, John *English language educator, literary critic*
Dawes, Geoffrey Sharman *medical researcher*
Guillery, Rainer Walter *anatomy educator*
Gulbrandsen, Natalie Webber *religious association administrator*
Hirsch, Peter Bernhard *metallurgist*
Howe, Daniel Walker *historian, educator*
May, Robert McCredie *biology educator*
Ryscavage, Richard Joseph *Jesuit priest, social services administrator*

Segal, Erich *author, educator*
Williams, William Stanley Cossom *physics educator and researcher*

Poole
Stokes, Donald Gresham *vehicle company executive*

Richmond
Attenborough, Baron Richard Samuel *actor, producer, director, goodwill ambassador*
Fraser, Campbell *business consultant*

Rottingdean
Matthews, John Floyd *writer, educator*

Saint Leonards on Sea
Holloway, Julia Bolton *retired educator*

Shepperton
Branagh, Kenneth *actor, director*

Somerset
Day-Lewis, Daniel *actor*

Stroud
Robinson, John Beckwith *development management consultant*

Suffolk
Clement, John *food products company executive*
Stauderman, Bruce Ford *advertising executive, writer*

Surrey
Diaz, Justino *bass-baritone*
Petrek, William Joseph *college president emeritus*

Warwick
Hands, Terence David (Terry Hands) *theater director*

West Sussex
Aiken, Joan (Delano) *author*

Weybridge Surrey
Olney, Robert C. *diversified products manufacturing executive*

Whitchurch
Adams, Richard George *writer*

Wiltshire
Gabriel, Peter *vocalist, composer*

Windlesham
Tarallo, Angelo Nicholas *industrial gas and health care company executive, lawyer*

FEDERATED STATES MICRONESIA

Truk
Samo, Amando *bishop*

FIJI

Suva
Usher, Sir Leonard Gray *retired news association executive*

FINLAND

Helsinki
Salonen, Heikki Olavi *corporate executive*
†Saraste, Jukka-Pekka *conductor*
Siimestö, Orvo Kalervo *financial executive*

Kuopio
Hakola, Hannu Panu Aukusti *psychiatry educator*

FRANCE

Arles
Clergue, Lucien Georges *photographer*

Beduer
Ezelle, Robert Eugene *diplomat*

Belves
Raphael, Frederic Michael *author*

Bonnes
Ogilvy, David Mackenzie *advertising executive*

Bordeaux
Gouyon, Paul Cardinal *archbishop*

Boulogne-Billancourt
Dellis, Frédy Michel *car rental company executive*

Chartres
Benoit, Jean-Pierre Robert *pneumologist, consultant*

Courbevoie
Desmarescaux, Philippe *chemical company executive, engineer*

Fontainebleu
Ayres, Robert Underwood *environmental economics and technology educator*
Churchill, Neil Center *entrepreneur, educator*

Genlis
van Raalte, John A. *research and engineering management executive*

Gouvieux
Fraser, David William *epidemiologist*

Joinville
Greer, Joseph Epps *architect*

Lauris
Spivak, Jonathan M. *journalist*

Levallois
de Pouzilhac, Alain Duplessis *advertising executive*

Marseilles
Vague, Jean Marie *endocrinologist*

Nanterre
Nguyen-Trong, Hoang *physician, consultant*

Neuilly-sur-Seine
O'Neill, Lawrence Daniel *lawyer, consultant*
Ophuls, Marcel *film director and producer*

Nice
Dickie, Brian *opera director*

Orsay
Deutsch, Claude David *physicist, educator*
Fiszer-Szafarz, Berta (Berta Safars) *research scientist*

Paris
Abboud, Ann Creelman *lawyer*
Annaud, Jean-Jacques *film director, screenwriter*
Baum, Axel Helmuth *lawyer*
Behrstock, Julian Robert *publishing consultant, writer*
Biala, Janice *artist*
Bikales, Norbert M. *chemist, science administrator*
Bommelaer, Alain *finance company executive*
Boulez, Pierre *composer, conductor*
Bourdais de Charbonniere, Eric *financial executive*
Cochran, John M., III *lawyer*
Collomb, Bertrand Pierre *cement company executive*
Cone, Sydney M., III *lawyer*
Cornell, Robert Arthur *international government official*
Cousteau, Jacques-Yves *marine explorer*
Craig, William Laurence *lawyer*
Davidson, Alfred Edward *lawyer*
Dean, John Gunther *diplomat*
de Havilland, Olivia Mary *actress*
De Lyrot, Alain Herve *editor*
†Doyle, Anne Marie *ambassador*
Dubs, Patrick Christian *publisher*
Ferriter, John Pierce *diplomat*
Gallant, Mavis *author*
†Gaultier, Jean-Paul *fashion designer*
Givenchy, Hubert James Marcel Taffin de *fashion designer*
Gontier, Jean Roger *internist, physiology educator, consultant*
Gottschalk, Charles M. *international relations consultant*
Haroche, Serge *optics scientist*
Houël, Patrick *financial executive*
Iseman, Joseph Seeman *lawyer*
Jaclot, Francois Charles *investment bank executive*
Jolas, Betsy *composer*
Konvitz, Josef Wolf *history educator, international civil servant*
Kurtz, Eugene Allen *composer, educator, consultant*
Lacroix, Christian Marie Marc *fashion designer*
Lagerfeld, Karl Otto *fashion designer*
Landers, Steven E. *lawyer*
Larson, Alan Philip *federal official*
Lecerf, Olivier Maurice Marie *construction company executive*
LeGoffic, Francois *biotechnology educator*
Levee, John Harrison *artist, designer*
Lewis, Flora *journalist*
Lubell, Harold *economic consultant*
Lubick, Donald Cyril *lawyer*
MacCrindle, Robert Alexander *lawyer*
Marceau, Marcel *pantomimist, actor, director, painter, poet*
Marcus, Claude *advertising executive*
Marton, Eva *opera singer*
Masurel, Jean-Louis Antoine Nicolas *investment company executive*
McGurn, William Barrett, III *lawyer*
Michel, James H. *ambassador, lawyer*
Mitchell, Leona Pearl *soprano*
Myerson, Jacob Myer *former foreign service officer*
†Piano, Renzo *architect*
Polanski, Roman *film director, writer, actor*
Rawlings, Boynton Mott *lawyer*
Renouf, Edda *artist*
Riggs, John Hutton, Jr. *lawyer*
Ritcheson, Charles Ray *university administrator, history educator*
Robert, Leslie Ladislas *research center administrator, consultant*
Rosenberg, Pierre Max *museum director*
Roudybush, Franklin *diplomat, educator*
Roussel, Lee Dennison *diplomat*
Roux, Ambroise Marie Casimir *business executive*
†Saint Laurent, Yves (Henri Donat Mathieu) *couturier*
Salans, Carl Fredric *lawyer*
Shapiro, Isaac *lawyer*
Suard, Pierre Henri Andre *power company executive*
†Ungaro, Emanuel Matteotti *fashion designer*
Vinciguerra, Jean-Louis *finance company executive*
Vuitton, Henry-Louis *designer*
Williams, C(harles) K(enneth) *poet, literature and writing educator*
Wolrich, Peter M. *lawyer*
Yuechiming, Roger Yue Yuen Shing *mathematics educator*

Ramatuelle
Collins, Larry *author, journalist*

Rognac
Castel, Gérard Joseph *physician*

Saint Quentin
†Poupart-LaFarge, Olivier Marie *financial executive*

Sevres
†Asscher, Jean Claude *electronic executive*

Strasbourg
Barnes, Shirley Elizabeth *foreign service officer*

Vaucluse
Pfriem, Bernard Aldine *artist*

GABON

Libreville
Wauchope, Keith L. *diplomat*

GERMANY

Berlin
Abbado, Claudio *conductor*
Anderson, David *former ambassador*
Fischer-Dieskau, Dietrich *baritone*
Iannone, Dorothy *visual artist, writer*
Palmer, R(obie Marcus Hooker) Mark *banker*

Bielefeld
Lauven, Peter Michael *anesthesiologist*

Bonn
Fleming, Joseph Benedict *newspaperman*
Redman, Charles Edgar *diplomat*

Cologne
Ungers, Oswald M. *architect, educator*

Darmstadt
Hofmann, Karl Heinrich *mathematics educator*

Dortmund
Freund, Eckhard *electrical engineering educator*

Dresden
Schreier, Peter *tenor*

Dusseldorf
Richter, Gerhard *artist*
Stuhl, Oskar Paul *scientific and regulatory consultant*

Finning
English, Charles Brand *retired lawyer*

Frankfurt
Ammann, Jean-Christophe *art director*
Simitis, Spiros *legal educator*

Godesberg
Hutton, Winfield Travis *management consultant, educator*

Gottingen
Lorenz-Meyer, Wolfgang *aeronautical engineer*
Sheldrick, George Michael *chemistry educator, crystallographer*
Tietze, Lutz Friedjan *chemist, educator*
Wedemeyer, Erich Hans *physicist*

Groebenzell
Chandrasekhar, B(ellur) S(ivaramiah) *physics educator*

Guersloh
Wössner, Mark Matthias *business executive*

Halle
Rode, Reinhard *political science educator*

Hamburg
Jensen, Elwood Vernon *biochemist*
Müller-Eberhard, Hans Joachim *medical research scientist, administrator*
Neumeier, John *choreographer, ballet company director*
Ramsey, Bill (William McCreery) *singer, actor, composer-lyricist, television executive*
Zylis-Gara, Teresa Gerarda *soprano*

Hannover
Döhler, Klaus Dieter *pharmaceutical and development company executive*

Hemsbach
Froessl, Horst Waldemar *business executive, data processing developer*

Kaiserslautern
Immesberger, Helmut *lawyer*

Katlenburg
Hagfors, Tor *institute director*

Kelkheim
Haeske, Horst *physicist*

Kussaberg
Lyndon, Maynard *architect*

Luneburg
Linde, Robert Hermann *economics educator*

Munich
Araiza, Francisco (José Francisco Araiza Andrade) *opera singer*
Berg, Jan Mikael *science educator*
Born, Gunthard Karl *aerospace executive*
Fassbaender, Brigitte *opera singer*
Fischer, Ernst Otto *chemist, educator*
Giacconi, Riccardo *astrophysicist, educator*
Goodman, Alfred *composer, musicologist*
Horak, Jan-Christopher *film studies educator, curator*
Saur, Klaus G. *publisher*
von Minckwitz, Bernhard *publishing company executive*
†von Pierer, Heinrich *manufacturing executive*
Whetten, Lawrence Lester *international relations educator*

Munster
Maltese, George John *mathematics educator*
Spevack, Marvin *English educator*

Nuremberg
Doerries, Reinhard René *modern history educator*

Paderborn
Belli, Fevzi *computing science educator, consultant*

Stuttgart
Szirmal, Endre Anreas Franz *physician, writer*

Weimar
Little, William A. *foreign language educator, researcher*

Weinheim
Köhler, Hans Dirk *publisher*

Wuppertal
Schubert, Guenther Erich *pathologist*

GHANA

Accra
Brocke, Eunice Miranda *foundation executive*
Brown, Kenneth L. *ambassador*

Kumasi
Sarpong, Peter Kwasi *bishop*

GREECE

Athens
Chytiris, Tilemachos *federal official*
Hatzakis, Michael *electrical engineer, research executive*
Iakovidis, Spyros Eustace *archaeologist*
Kalamotousakis, George John *economist*
Ligomenides, Panos Aristides *electrical and computer engineering educator, consultant*

Halandri
Dorbis, John *school system administrator*

GRENADA

Saint George's
†Anderson, Ollie Palmer, Jr. *diplomat*
Brunson, Joel Garrett *pathologist, educator*
Helgerson, John Walter *lawyer*

GUINEA

Conakry
Saloom, Joseph A., III *diplomat*

HONG KONG

Hong Kong
Allen, Richard Marlow *lawyer*
Choo, Yeow Ming *lawyer*
Chu, Franklin Dean *lawyer*
Collins, Charles Roland *lawyer*
†Gargan, Edward A. *journalist*
Halperin, David Richard *lawyer*
Kwong, Peter Kong Kit *bishop*
Larr, Peter *banker*
Lehner, Urban Charles *journalist*
Magarity, Russell Lynn *banker*
Mueller, Richard Walter *foreign service officer*
Nee, Owen D., Jr. *lawyer*
Pisanko, Henry Jonathan *command and control communications company executive*
Rowe, Kevin S. *banker*
Sherrill, Joseph Harlan, Jr. *tobacco company executive*
Tanner, Douglas Alan *lawyer*
Torres, Cynthia Ann *banker*
Tse, Edmund Sze-Wing *insurance company executive*
†Vatikiotis, Michael Richard John *journalist, writer*
Wong, Wing Keung *trading, electronics company executive, physician*

Kowloon
Burns, Robert Henry *hotel executive*
Chiang, Samuel Edward *theological educator, humanities educator*
Hsieh, Din-Yu *applied mathematics educator*
Hutt, Eric John Villette *accountant*
Kung, Shain-dow *molecular biologist, educator*
Liou, Ming-Lei *electrical engineer*

Sha Tin
Kao, Charles Kuen *electrical engineer, educator*
Lee, Tunney Fee *urban planning educator*

Wanchai
van Hoften, James Dougal Adrianus *business executive, former astronaut*

ICELAND

Reykjavik
Thorarensen, Oddur C.S. *pharmacist*

INDIA

New Delhi
Dahlburg, John-Thor Theodore *newspaper correspondent*
Gregorios, Paulos Mar *archbishop, metropolitan of Delhi*
Wisner, Frank George *ambassador*

Yavatmal
Ward, Daniel Thomas *bishop*

INDONESIA

Palembang
†Saputra, Daniel *agricultural engineering educator*

Surabaya
†Eaton, Mark Craig *diplomat*

IRAN

Tehran
Dinkha, Mar, IV *church administrator*

IRELAND

Arklow
Barber, Jerry Randel *medical device company executive*

Ballyvaughan
Wicks, Eugene Claude *college president, art educator*

Dalkey
Leonard, Hugh (John Keyes Byrne) *playwright*

Donegal
Friel, Brian (Bernard Patrick Friel) *author*

Dublin
Smith, Jean Kennedy *ambassador*

Mullingar
Donleavy, James Patrick *writer, artist*

Wicklow
McCaffrey, Anne Inez *author*

ISLE OF MAN

Peel
Wakeman, Rick *musician, composer*

ISRAEL

Haifa
Galil, Uzia *electronics company executive*
Peled, Abraham *computer company executive*

Halon
Cohen, Amram Joseph *cardiothoracic surgeon*

Herzliya
Bitan, Giora Yoav *computer systems executive*

Jerusalem
Abington, Edward Gordon, Jr. *diplomat*
Arnon, Michael *finance company executive*
Bronner, Ethan Samuel *news correspondent*
Davis, Moshe *historian*
Peleg, Bezalel *mathematician*
Rosenne, Meir *lawyer, government agency administrator*
Schindler, Pesach *rabbi, educator, author*

Ra'ananna
Hayon, Elie M. *chemist, educator*

Rehovot
†Sharon, Nathan *biochemist*

Savyon
Bushinsky, Jay (Joseph Mason) *journalist, radio/TV correspondent, columnist*

Tel Aviv
Mehta, Zubin *conductor, musician*
Melamede, Ada Karmi *architectural firm executive*
Rubin, Barry Mitchel *foreign policy analyst, writer*

ITALY

Camerino
Miyake, Akio *biologist, educator*

Florence
Cecil, Charles Harkless *artist, educator*
Kaiser, Walter *English language educator*

Milan
Calasso, Roberto *writer, publisher*
Ferré, Gianfranco *fashion designer, artistic director*
Sindoni, Elio *physics educator*

Naples
Bartoli, Cecilia *coloratura soprano, mezzo soprano*
Tarro, Giulio *virologist*

Padova
†Lalas, Alexi *professional soccer player*

Padua
Rosati, Mario *mathematician, educator*

Pontedera
Grotowski, Jerzy *theater director, acting educator*

Rome
Ahrens, William Henry *architect*
Alegi, Peter Claude *lawyer*
Antonioni, Michelangelo *film director*
Audet, Leonard *theologian*
Bafile, Corrado *cardinal*
Baum, William Wakefield Cardinal *former church official*
Bertolucci, Bernardo *film director*
Casolino, Vincenzo *library director*
Cassiers, Juan *diplomat*
Hjort, Howard Warren *international organization official, economist*
Keniaykin, Valery Fedorovich *Russian diplomat*
Loren, Sophia *actress*
Lynch, Edward Stephen *corporate executive*
Marchand, J. C. de Montigny *Canadian public servant*
Rossmiller, George Eddie *agricultural economist*
Storaro, Vittorio *cinematographer*
†Valentino, (Valentino Garavani) *fashion designer*
Wilson, George Peter *association executive*
Wynn, Coy Wilton *journalist*
Zeffirelli, Franco *theater and film director*

Turin
Agnelli, Giovanni *automotive executive*

Venice
Pasinetti, Pier Maria *author*

JAPAN

Aichi-ken
Yukei, Hasebe Yoshikazu *religious studies educator*

Chiba
Yamada, Shinichi *mathematician, computer scientist, educator*

Chikusa
Casei, Nedda *mezzo-soprano*

Ehime
Sakai, Yoshiro *chemistry educator*

Fukuoka
Aizawa, Keio *biology educator*
Shirai, Takeshi *physician*

Gotsu
Hirayama, Chisato *healthcare facility administrator, physician, educator*

Hachioji
Shimoji, Sadao *applied mathematics educator, engineer*

Hamamatsu
Aoki, Ichiro *theoretical biophysics systems science educator*

Hirakata
Nakanishi, Tsutomu *pharmaceutical science educator*

Hiroshima
Harkness, Donald Richard *hematologist, educator*

Hokkaido
Saito, Shuzo *electrical engineering educator*

Ibaraki
Ishii, Yoshinori *geophysics educator*
Yamada, Keiichi *engineering educator, university official*

Iwate
Kawauchi, Hiroshi *hormone science educator*

Kanagawa
Maeda, Toshihide Munenobu *spacecraft system engineer*
Okui, Kazumitsu *biology educator*
Saitoh, Tamotsu *pharmacology educator*
Swarz, Sahl *sculptor*

Kawasaki
Taniuchi, Kiyoshi *retired mechanical engineering educator*

Kita
Ohnami, Masateru *mechanical engineering educator*

Kitakyushu
Okubo, Toshiteru *health science facility administrator, educator*

Kobe
Yamabe, Shigeru *medical educator*

Koganei
Akiyama, Masayasu *chemistry educator*

Koriyama
Ohama, Yoshihiko *architectural engineer, educator*

Kyoto
Araki, Takeo *chemistry educator*
Shoichi, Ida *artist, printmaker, painter, sculptor*

Miyazaki
Meyer, Ruth Krueger *museum administrator, art historian*

Nagoya
Abe, Yoshihiro *ceramic engineering educator, materials scientist*
Kato, Masanobu *lawyer, educator*

Nishinomiya
Ogida, Mikio *history of religion educator*

Okayama
Oda, Takuzo *biochemistry educator*
Ubuka, Toshihiko *biochemistry educator*

Osaka
Ikeda, Kazuyosi *physicist, poet*
Kobayashi, Mitsue *chemistry educator*
Osumi, Masato *utility company executive*
Sakaguchi, Genji *food microbiologist, educator*
Solberg, Norman Robert *lawyer*
†Ueno, Hiroshi *biochemist*
Watanabe, Toshiharu *ecologist, educator*

Otsu
Matsuura, Teruo *chemistry educator*
Takemoto, Kiichi *chemistry educator*

Sakai-Gun
Ise, Norio *chemistry educator*

Sendai
Oikawa, Hiroshi *materials science educator*
Okuyama, Shinichi *physician*
Sone, Toshio *acoustical engineering educator*

Setagaya
Kurosawa, Akira *film director*

Shibuya
Torii, Shuko *psychology educator*

Shiga
Makigami, Yasuji *transportation engineering educator*

Shimizu
Uyeda, Seiya *geophysics educator*

Tenri
Miyata, Gen *history of religion educator*

Tochigi
Iida, Shuichi *physicist,educator*
Ishii, Akira *medical parasitologist, malariologist, allergologist*
Takasaki, Etsuji *urology educator*

Tokorozawa
Nakamura, Hiroshi *urology educator*

Tokyo
Akera, Tai *pharmacologist*
Aoyama, Hiroyuki *structural engineering educator*
Armacost, Michael Hayden *ambassador, government official*
Azuma, Takamitsu *architect, educator*
Drabkin, David *lawyer*
Franklin, William Emery *lumber company executive*
Hashimoto, Kunio *architect, educator*
Hori, Yukio *engineering educator, scientific association administrator*
Inagaki, Masao *advertising agency executive*
Ishikawa, Rokuro *construction company executive*
Isozaki, Arata *architect*
Ito, Masatoshi *retail executive*
Johnson, Keith Gilbert *heavy equipment company executive*
Kajima, Shoichi *general contractor executive*
Kaku, Ryuzaburo *precision instruments manufacturing company executive*
Kaneko, Hisashi *engineering executive*
Kawachi, Michael Tateo *lawyer*
Kigoshi, Kunihiko *geochemistry educator*
Kogure, Gohei *advertising executive*
Krisher, Bernard *foreign correspondent*
Kusama, Yayoi *sculptor, painter*
Makihara, Minoru *diversified corporation executive*
Makino, Shojiro (Mike Makino) *chemicals executive*
Masuda, Gohta *physician, educator*
Michaud, Michael Alan George *diplomat, writer*
Miyazawa, Akira *advertising executive*
Nakagaki, Masayuki *chemist*
Narita, Yutaka *advertising executive*
Ohe, Shuzo *chemical engineer, educator*
Ohga, Norio *electronics executive*
Ori, Kan *political science educator*
Oshita, Koji *advertising executive*
Reich, Pauline Carole *international business consultant, educator, author*
Reid, Edward Snover, III *lawyer*
Saito, Kiyomi *investment banking executive*
Simons, Lewis Martin *journalist*
Smith, Robert Lee *photographic company executive*
Taguchi, Yoshitaka *architect*
Takahashi, Keiichi *zoology educator*
Terao, Toshio *physician, educator*
Watanabe, Kouichi *pharmacologist, educator*

Tondabayashi
Nozato, Ryoichi *metallurgy educator, researcher*

Toyama
Hayashi, Mitsuhiko *physics educator*

Toyota Aichi
Toyoda, Eiji *automobile manufacturing company executive*

Tsukuba
Kobayashi, Susumu *data processing executive, super computer consultant*

Yamaguchi
Suzuki, Nobutaka *chemistry educator*

Yamashina
†Inamori, Kazuo *chemicals executive*

Yokohama
Kaneko, Yoshihiro *cardiologist, researcher*

KENYA

Nairobi
Brazeal, Aurelia Erskine *ambassador*

South Nyanza
Khan, Zeyaur Rahman *entomologist*

KOREA

Pohang
Choi, Sang-il *physics educator, researcher*

Pusan
†Kloth, Edward William, Jr. *diplomat*

Seoul
Sepulveda, Eduardo Solideo *chemical engineer*
Steinberg, David Isaac *economic development consultant, educator*

Taejon
Kim, Sung Chul *polymer engineering educator*

LATVIA

Riga
Silins, Ints M. *ambassador*

LEBANON

Beirut
Hambley, Mark Gregory *ambassador*
Jurdak, Murad Eid *mathematics educator*

LUXEMBOURG

Luxembourg
Elliott, Lawrence *writer*
Kasperczyk, Jürgen *business executive, government official, educator*

MALAYSIA

Penang
Das, Kumudeswar *food and biochemical engineering educator*

MARTINIQUE

Anses d'Arlet
Price, Richard *anthropologist, author*

MAURITANIA

Nouackchott
Brown, Gordon Stewart *diplomat*

MONACO

Monaco
Davies, Gareth John *trade association executive*

Saint-Leon
Kimmle, Manfred *investment company executive*

MOROCCO

Casablanca
Cary, Anne O. *diplomat*

MOZAMBIQUE

Maputo
Jon de Vos, Peter *former U.S. ambassador to Mozambique*

THE NETHERLANDS

Aerdenhout
Vinken, Pierre Jacques *publishing executive, neurosurgeon*

Amsterdam
Averill, Bruce Alan *chemistry educator*
Baer, Jo *painter*
Bruggink, Herman *publishing executive*
Kels, James *publishing executive*
Ostrow, Jay Donald *gastroenterology educator, researcher*
Walker, William Ross *accountant*

Goor
Bonting, Sjoerd Lieuwe *biochemist, priest*

Hilversum
De Waart, Edo *conductor*

Leiden
Banta, Henry David *physician, researcher*

Maastricht
Van Praag, Herman Meir *psychiatrist, educator, administrator*

Roosendaal
†van Deventer, Arie Pieter *agricultural engineer*

The Hague
Allison, Richard Clark *judge*
Herkstroter, Cornelius *oil industry executive*
Kylián, Jirí *choreographer*
Nones Sucre, Carlos Enrique *political organization executive*
Van Wachem, Lodewijk Christiaan *petroleum company executive*
Wilkins, C. Howard, Jr. *diplomat*

NEW CALEDONIA

Noumea
Curlook, Walter *mining company executive*

NEW ZEALAND

Bay of Islands
Veysey, Arthur Ernest *reporter, administrator, biographer*

Wellington
Newman, Della M. *ambassador*

NIGER

Niamey
Davison, John S. *ambassador*

NIGERIA

Lagos
Carrington, Walter C. *ambassador*

NORWAY

Lillestr0m
Borgen, Ole Edvard *bishop, educator*

Stavanger
Fitzpatrick, Whitfield Westfeldt *lawyer*

Trondheim
Svaasand, Lars Othar *electronics researcher*

PAKISTAN

Karachi
Shroff, Firoz Sardar *merger and acquisition professional*

Lahore
Geoffrey, Iqbal (Mohammed Jawaid Iqbal Jafree) *artist, lawyer*

Peshawar
†Smyth, Richard Henry *foreign service officer*

PANAMA

Panama City
†Fabrega P., Jorge *lawyer, writer, legal books publisher*
Thoman, Henry Nixon *food industry executive*

PERU

Lima
French, Edward Ronald *plant pathologist*

THE PHILIPPINES

Manila
Quasha, William Howard *lawyer*

Musuan
Lao, Mardonio Magadan *history educator, researcher, farmer*

Pasay
Lim, Sonia Yii *minister*

POLAND

Warsaw
Engelberg, Stephen Paul *reporter*
Koscielak, Jerzy *scientist, science administrator*
†Rader, Paul MacFarland *healthcare administrator*
Soltysinski, Stanislaw J. *law educator*

PORTUGAL

Braga
Rocha, Armandino Cordeiro Dos Santos *accountant, educator, auditor*

Funchal
Mayda, Jaro *lawyer, educator, author, consultant*

Lisbon
Berger, Jason *artist, printmaker*

REPUBLIC OF KOREA

Taejon
Lee, Choochon *physics educator, researcher*

ROMANIA

Bucharest
Moses, Alfred Henry *lawyer*

RUSSIA

Novosibirsk
Aleksandrov, Leonid Naumovitsh *physicist, educator, researcher*

SAINT LUCIA

Castries
Felix, Kelvin Edward *archbishop*

SAUDI ARABIA

Dhahran
Warne, Ronson Joseph *mathematics educator*

Jeddah
Rihani, Fuad Akil *civil engineer, researcher*

Riyadh
Chaudhary, Shaukat Ali *ecologist, plant taxonomist*
Taylor, Frederick William, Jr. *lawyer*

SCOTLAND

Aberdeen
Jones, Robert Victor *physicist, natural philosophy educator*
Rousseau, George Sebastian *eighteenth century studies educator, chamber musician*

Cellardyke
Roff, William Robert *history educator, writer*

Clydebank
Durack, David Tulloch *physician, educator*
Krakoff, Irwin Harold *pharmacology and oncology educator*

Dumfriesshire
Godden, Rumer *author*

Edinburgh
Buchan, Hamish Noble *securities analyst*
McMaster, Brian John *artistic director*
Miller, James *construction company executive*

Gifford
Menotti, Gian Carlo *composer*

Glasgow
Courtney, James McNiven *chemist*

Gullane
Collins, Jeffrey Hamilton *research facility administrator, electrical engineering educator*

Peebles
Hooper, John Edward *retired physicist, researcher*

Saint Andrews
Lenman, Bruce Philip *historian, educator*

SIERRA LEONE

Freetown
Peters, Lauralee Milberg *diplomat*
†Ray, Charles Aaron *foreign service officer*

SINGAPORE

Singapore
Burandt, Gary Edward *advertising agency executive*
McMahon, Paul Francis *international management consultant*
Reed, John G. *lawyer*
Skodon, Emil Mark *diplomat*
Wilhelm, Ralph Vincent, Jr. *electronics company executive, ceramics engineer*

SLOVENIA

Ljubljana
Sicherl, Pavle *economics educator, consultant*

SOUTH AFRICA

Johannesburg
Crockett, Phyllis Darlene *communications executive*
†McKee, Alan Reel *foreign service officer*

Klippoortjie
Els, Theodore Ernest *professional golfer*

SPAIN

Barcelona
de Larrocha, Alicia *concert pianist*
García Márquez, Gabriel José *author*
Jackson, Gabriel *historian*

Madrid
Almodóvar, Pedro *filmmaker*
Berganza Vargas, Teresa *mezzo-soprano*
Feltenstein, Harry David, Jr. *chemical executive*
Frühbeck de Burgos, Rafael *conductor*
Trueba, Fernando *film director and producer, screenwriter*

Mallorca
Raff, Joseph Allen *publishing company executive, author*
Ulbricht, John *artist*

Santander
Ballesteros, Severiano *professional golfer*

Santiago De Compostela
Balseiro Gonzalez, Manuel *management executive, consultant*

Seville
Sanchez, Leonedes Monarrize Worthington (Duke de Leonedes) *fashion designer*

Tacoronte
Kardas, Sigmund Joseph, Jr. *secondary education educator*

SRI LANKA

Colombo
Schaffer, Teresita Currie *federal official*
Spain, James William *political scientist, writer, investor*

SWEDEN

Gothenburg
Bona, Christian Johannes Maximilian *dentist, psychotherapist*

Lidingo
†Wickberg, Jens Erik *industrial executive*

Linkoping
Schröder, Harald Bertel *aerospace industry executive*

Lund
Grimmeiss, Hermann Georg *physics educator, researcher*
Welin, Walter *financial advisor*

Malmo
Cronberg, Stig *infectious diseases educator*

Stockholm
†Carlzon, Jan (Gosta) *airline company executive*
Johnson, Antonia Axson *corporate executive*
Lindberg, Helge *aviation consultant*
Meyer, Kerstin *mezzo-soprano, music educator*
Robinson, Hobart Krum *management consulting company executive*
Scharp, Anders *manufacturing company executive*
Siebert, Thomas L. *ambassador to Sweden*
Soederstrom, Elisabeth Anna *opera singer*

SWITZERLAND

Basel
†Gerber, Fritz *insurance company executive, diversified financial services company executive*
†Moret, Marc *chemicals executive*

Bern
Lawrence, M. Larry *ambassador*
Polke, Sigmar *artist*

Biel
Scheftner, Gerold *marketing executive*

Burgdorf
Haeberlin, Heinrich Rudolf *electrical engineering educator*

Busingen
Friede, Reinhard L. *neuropathologist, educator*

Chambesy
Barnes, Thomas Joseph *migration program administrator*
†Spiegel, Daniel L. *diplomat*

Fribourg
Gurley, Franklin Louis *lawyer, military historian*
Hatschek, Rudolf Alexander *electronics company executive*

Geneva
Abram, Morris Berthold *lawyer, educator, diplomat*
Ballin, William Christopher *international shipping, investments, and energy advisor*
Barenboim, Daniel *conductor, pianist*
Bogsch, Arpad *diplomat*
De Pfyffer, Andre *lawyer*
Halle, Louis Joseph *author, educator*
Harigel, Gert Günter *physicist*
Henderson, Ralph Hale *physician*
Holleran, Constance Ann *nursing association executive*
Ledogar, Stephen J. *diplomat*
O'Regan, Richard Arthur *editor, retired foreign correspondent*
Overseth, Oliver Enoch *physicist, educator*
Polunin, Nicholas *environmentalist, author, editor*
Purcell, James Nelson, Jr. *international organization administrator*

Lausanne
Bloemsma, Marco Paul *investor*
Borel, Georges Antoine *gastroenterologist, consultant*
Caste, Jean F. *financial advisor*
Stingelin, Valentin *research center director, mechanical engineer*

Lucerne
Sherwin, James Terry *lawyer, window covering company executive*

Montreux
Cronin, Robert Francis Patrick *cardiologist, educator*

Rouille
Godard, Jean-Luc *film director*

Rueschlikon
Rohrer, Heinrich *physicist*

Staad
Moore, Roger George *actor*

Valais
Chase, Morris *international management consultant*

Vaud
Joseph, Michael Anthony *marketing executive*

Zollikerberg
Bocker, Hans Jurgen *editor, analyst, consultant, management educator*

Zurich
Barnevik, Percy Nils *electrical company executive*
Gut, Rainer Emil *banker*
Jones, Gwyneth *soprano*
Lanford, Oscar Erasmus, III *mathematics educator*
Mueller, Stephan *geophysicist, educator*
Nievergelt, Jurg *computer science educator*
Panitz, Lawrence Herbert *lawyer*
Peterson, M. Roger *banker, former manufacturing executive, retired air force officer*

TAIWAN

Chung-Li
Hong, Zuu-Chang *engineering educator*

Kaohsiung
Yeh, Kung Chie *electrical engineer*

Taichung
Lee, Kuo-Chuan *horticulture educator*

Tainan
Chao, Yei-chin *aerospace engineering educator*
Huang, Ting-Chia *chemical engineering educator, researcher*

Taipei
Ch'in, Michael Kuo-hsing *international conference and travel management executive*
Pao, Yih-Hsing *engineer, educator*
Yang, Chin-Ping *chemist, engineering educator*

TAJIKISTAN

Penjikent
Arne, Kenneth George *mining executive, mineral consultant*

THAILAND

Bangkok
Carlson, Mitchell Lans *international technical advisor*
Friedman, Ronald Marvin *cellular biologist*
Ludwig, Harvey Fred *environmental engineer*
Lyman, David *lawyer*
Stueart, Robert D. *university information services director, educator*

TRINIDAD AND TOBAGO

Port of Spain
Cowal, Sally Grooms *diplomat*

TURKEY

Ankara
Inalcik, Halil *historian, educator*

Istanbul
†Rountree, George Denton *health services managemtent consultant*

TURKMENISTAN

Ashgabat
McCall, John Patrick *college president, educator*

TURKS AND CAICOS ISLANDS

Provinciales
Johnston, Samuel Thomas *entertainment company executive*

UKRAINE

Kiev
Miller, William Green *ambassador*

VATICAN CITY

Vatican City
John Paul, His Holiness Pope, II (Karol Jozef Wojtyla) *bishop of Rome*
Szoka, Edmund Casimir Cardinal *cardinal*

VENEZUELA

Caracas
Benaim-DeMan, Mireya *psychologist*
Mendelovici, Efraim Eliahu *materials chemistry researcher*
Nakano, Tatsuhiko *chemist, researcher, educator*

WEST INDIES

Grenada
Barrett, James Thomas *immunologist, educator*

ADDRESS UNPUBLISHED

Aaron, Betsy *journalist*
Aaron, Roy Henry *lawyer, business consultant*
Abadi, Fritzie *artist, educator*
Abbe, Elfriede Martha *sculptor, graphic artist*
Abel, Harold *psychologist, educator, university president*
Abell, Murray Richardson *retired medical association administrator*
Abere, Andrew Evan *economist*
Ablin, Richard Joel *immunologist, educator*
Aboody, Albert Victor *accountant*
Abramowicz, Janet *painter, print-maker*
Abzug, Bella Savitzky *lawyer, former congresswoman*
Achorn, Robert Comey *retired newspaper publisher*
Ackerman, Jack Rossin *investment banker*
Ackerman, Melvin *investment company executive*
Adam, John, Jr. *insurance company executive emeritus*
Adam, Orval Michael *retired financial executive, lawyer*

Adamovich, Shirley Gray *retired librarian, state official*
Adams, Arlin Marvin *retired judge, counsel to law firm*
Adams, Edwin Melville *former foreign service officer, actor, author, lecturer*
Adams, James Blackburn *former state government official, former federal government official, lawyer*
Adams, James Thomas *surgeon*
Adams, Jonathan L. *advertising agency executive*
Adams, Oscar William, Jr. *retired state supreme court justice*
Adams, Paul Winfrey *lawyer, business executive*
Adams, Robert McCormick *anthropologist, educator*
Adams, Rosemary *nursing educator*
Adams, William White *retired manufacturing company executive*
Adams-Leander, Sheila Elizabeth *community health nurse*
Adaskin, Murray *composer*
Adato, Perry Miller *documentary producer, director, writer*
Addiss, Susan Silliman *state government administrator*
Addy, Frederick Seale *retired oil company executive*
Adelman, Richard Charles *gerontologist, educator*
Adelman, Robert Paul *retired construction company executive, lawyer*
Adelson, Mervyn Lee *entertainment and communication industry executive*
Aden, Arthur Laverne *office systems company executive*
Adisman, I. Kenneth *prosthodontist*
Adkins, Claudia K. *nursing educator*
Adler, Gerald *retired film and television executive, lawyer*
Adler, Richard Melvin *architect, planner*
Adsit, Russell Allan *landscape designer*
Agarwal, Suman Kumar *editor*
Agnew, Spiro Theodore *former Vice President of U.S.*
Ahearne, John Francis *scientific research society administrator, researcher*
Ahlquist, Paul Gerald *molecular biology researcher, educator*
Aiken, Michael Thomas *academic administrator*
Ajemian, Robert Myron *journalist*
Akasofu, Syun-Ichi *geophysicist*
Albino, George Robert *business executive*
Alcantara, Felicisima Garcia *dietitian, nutrition consultant*
Alda, Alan *actor, writer, director*
Aldrich, Franklin Dalton *research physician*
Aldrich, Patricia Anne Richardson *retired magazine editor*
Aldrin, Buzz *former astronaut, science consultant*
Alig, Frank Douglas Stalnaker *construction company executive*
Aljian, James Donovan *investment company executive*
Alker, Hayward Rose *political science educator*
Allan, Hugh James Pearson *retired bishop*
Allen, Charles Eugene *college administrator, agriculturist*
Allen, Eric Andre *professional football player*
Allen, Kenneth Dale *insurance executive, corporate counsel*
Allen, Marilyn Myers Pool *theater director, video producer*
Allen, Theodore Earl *computer company executive*
Allen, Woody (Allen Stewart Konigsberg) *actor, filmmaker, author*
Allerton, John Stephen *association executive*
Alligood, Elizabeth H. *special education educator*
†Allison, Andrew M. *foundation administrator*
Allison, John McComb *retired aeronautical engineer*
Alm, John Richard *beverage company executive*
Almen, Louis Theodore *retired college president*
Almgren, Herbert Philip *bank executive*
Almond, Paul *film director, producer, writer*
Aloff, Mindy *writer*
Al-Sabah, Saud Nasir *diplomat, barrister*
Alsadek, Jihad Abdalla *economist*
Altan, Taylan *engineering educator, mechanical engineer, consultant*
Altekruse, Joan Morrissey *retired preventive medicine educator*
Altman, Irwin *psychology educator*
†Altman, Lyle D. *communications company executive*
Altshuler, Alan Anthony *dean, political scientist*
Altshuler, Kenneth Z. *psychiatrist*
Alvernaz, Rodrigo *insurance company executive*
Alvord, Joel Barnes *bank executive*
Amann, Charles Albert *mechanical engineer*
Ambrose, James Richard *consultant, retired government official*
Ambrozic, Aloysius Matthew *archbishop*
Ames, Donald Paul *retired aerospace company executive, researcher*
Ames, Oakes *physicist, educator*
Amini, Bijan Khajehnouri *technology company executive*
Amon, Arthur Howard, Jr. *real estate consultant, retired retailing executive*
Amstutz, Daniel Gordon *intergovernmental organization executive, former grain dealer, government official*
Anastasi, Anne (Mrs. John Porter Foley, Jr.) *psychology educator*
Anderer, Joseph Henry *textile company executive*
†Andersen, Ib Steen *ballet dancer*
†Andersen, Willem Hendrik Jan *physicist*
Anderson, Bernard E. *economist*
Anderson, Bob *state legislator, business executive*
Anderson, Charles D. *bishop*
Anderson, Diane M. *administrator*
Anderson, Elliott Van *publishing company executive*
Anderson, Fletcher Neal *chemical executive*
Anderson, Geoffrey Allen *lawyer*
Anderson, Geraldine Louise *laboratory scientist*
†Anderson, Jane Louise *education association administrator, editor*
Anderson, John Firth *church administrator, librarian*
Anderson, John Gaston *electrical engineer*
Anderson, John Rogers *Canadian diplomat*
Anderson, Joseph Norman *executive consultant, former food company executive, former college president*
Anderson, Keith *retired lawyer, retired banker*
Anderson, Michael L. *financial planning manager*
Anderson, Ned, Sr. *Apache tribal chairman*
Anderson, Nils, Jr. *former government official, retired business executive, industrial historian*
Anderson, Ross Sherwood *architect*
Anderson, Thomas Patrick *mechanical engineer, educator*
Anderson, Vernon Russell *technology company executive, entrepreneur*
Anderson, Wayne Carl *public information officer*
†Anderson, William Mills *film editor*
Anderson-Spivy, Alexandra *writer, editor*
Andersson, Craig Remington *retired chemical company executive*
Andolsek, Ludwig J. *association executive*
Andrade, Edna *artist, art educator*
Andre, (Kenneth) Michael *editor, publisher, writer*
Andreas, Dwayne Orville *investment company executive*
Andreoli, Thomas Eugene *physician*
Andretti, Mario (Gabriele) *professional race car driver*
Andretti, Michael Mario *professional race car driver*
Andreuzzi, Denis *chemical company executive*
Andrews, Jean *artist, writer*
Andrews, Julie *actress, singer*
Andrews, William Frederick *manufacturing executive*
Andriole, Stephen John *information systems executive*
Andrisani, John Anthony *editor, author, golf consultant*
Angell, Richard Bradshaw *philosophy educator*
Angelov, George Angel *pediatrician, anatomist, teratologist*
Angiuoli, Ralph *tobacco company executive*
Anglemire, Kenneth Norton *retired publishing company executive, writer, environmentalist, lawyer*
Angotti, Anthony John *advertising executive*
Anguiano, Lupe *advocate*
Angulo, Gerard Antonio *financial executive, investor, consultant*
Anker, Peter Louis *securities executive*
Annenberg, Walter H. *philanthropist, diplomat, editor, publisher, broadcaster*
Annus, John Augustus *artist*
Anselmini, Jean-Pierre *communication corporation executive*
Anspach, Herbert Kephart *retired appliance company executive, patent attorney*
Anthony, Earl Roderick *professional bowler*
Apel-Brueggeman, Myrna L. *entrepreneur*
Appelbaum, Jacob Gregory *physicist*
Appenzeller, Otto *neurologist, researcher*
Applin, Catherine Balash *primary school educator, consultant*
Apruzzi, Gene *retired stockbroker*
Apted, Michael D. *film director*
Aptheker, Herbert *historian, lecturer*
Archer, Jeffrey Howard *author, politician*
Archibald, Nolan D. *household and industrial products company executive*
Arden, Sherry W. *publishing company executive*
Arenal, Julie (Mrs. Barry Primus) *choreographer*
Arenberg, Julius Theodore, Jr. *retired accounting company executive*
Arenella, Peter Lee *law educator*
Argun, Fatima Hatice *international consultant, specialist*
Ariyoshi, George Ryoichi *lawyer, business consultant, former governor Hawaii*
Arkin, William Morris *military and political analyst, writer*
Arlen, Michael J. *writer*
Arlidge, John Walter *utility company executive*
Armacost, Mary-Linda Sorber Merriam *educational administrator*
Armistead, Thomas Boyd, III *television and film producer*
Armour, David Edward Ponton *association executive*
Armstrong, Anne Legendre (Mrs. Tobin Armstrong) *former ambassador, corporate director*
Armstrong, F(redric) Michael *retired insurance company executive*
Armstrong, John Allan *business machine company research executive*
Armstrong, Neil A. *former astronaut*
Armstrong, Thomas Newton, III *retired museum director*
Armstrong, Warren Bruce *university president, historian, educator*
Armstrong, William Henry *lawyer*
Arnaud, Claude Donald, Jr. *physician, educator*
Arnold, Duane Wade-Hampton *minister, educator*
Arnold, Henri *cartoonist*
Arnold, Jerome Gilbert *lawyer*
Arnold, Sheila *former state legislator*
Arnold, William Howard *nuclear fuel executive*
Arnoldi, Charles Arthur *painter, sculptor*
Arnott, Howard Joseph *biology educator, university dean*
Aronson, Luann Marie *actress*
Arova, Sonia *artistic director, ballet educator*
Arthur, Beatrice *actress*
Arthur, John Morrison *retired utility executive*
Arthur, Lloyd *agricultural products company executive*
Arthur, Rochelle Linda *creative director*
Aschauer, Charles Joseph, Jr. *corporate director, former company executive*
Ash, Hiram Newton *graphic designer*
Ashby, Clifford Charles *theatre arts educator, historian*
Ashcraft, Charles Olin *business educator*
Askey, William Hartman *lawyer, federal magistrate judge*
Askin, Leon *artistic director, actor, producer, writer*
Aspen, Alfred William *international trading company executive*
Assante, Armand *actor*
Atchison, Richard Calvin *trade association director*
Atherton, William *actor*
Atkins, John *concert pianist, voice teacher*
Atkinson, Bill *designer*
Atkinson, Dewey Franklin *retired educational administrator*
Atkisson, Curtis Trumbull, Jr. *auto parts company executive*
Attoe, Wayne Osborne *architecture educator, author, designer*
Atwood, Genevieve *geologist*
Au, Tung *civil engineer, educator, consultant*
Auberjonois, René Murat *actor*
Audet, Paul Andre *retired newspaper executive*
Aulbach, George Louis *property investment company executive*
Auriemma, Louis Francis *printing company executive*
Aurin, Robert James *entrepreneur*
Austin, Janet Hays *artist*
Austin, Richard H. *retired state official*
Austin, Robert Clarke *naval officer*
Autin, Ernest Anthony, II *chemist, educator*
Avalon, Frankie *singer, actor*
Aved, Barry *retail executive*
Avian, Bob *choreographer, producer*
Axelrad, Irving Irmas *lawyer, motion picture producer*
Axilrod, Stephen Harvey *investment banker, economist*
Ayres, Jayne Lynn Ankrum *community health nurse*
Azarnoff, Daniel Lester *pharmaceutical company consultant*
Baack, John Edward *publishing consultant*
Babb, Frank Edward *lawyer, executive*
Babb, Roberta J. *educational administrator*
Babbitt, Samuel Fisher *university administrator*
Bacharach, Burt *composer, conductor*
Bacharach, Melvin Lewis *venture capitalist*
Backlund, Ralph Theodore *magazine editor*
Bacon, Caroline Sharfman *investor relations consultant*
Bacon, George Edgar *retired pediatrician, educator*
Baddour, Phillip A. *lawyer, state legislator*
Badham, John MacDonald *motion picture director*
Baer, Robert J. *transportation company executive*
Baggett, Donnis Gene *journalist, editor*
Bagley, William Thompson *lawyer*
Bagwill, John Williams, Jr. *retired pension fund company executive*
Baier, Edward John *former public health official, industrial hygiene engineer, consultant*
Bailey, Francis Lee *lawyer*
Bailey, Henry John, III *retired lawyer, educator*
Bain, William Donald, Jr. *lawyer, chemical company executive*
†Baird, William David *retired anesthesiologist*
Bajcsy, Ruzena Kucerova *computer science educator*
Baker, Edward Kevin *retail executive*
Baker, Gwendolyn Calvert *United Nations official*
Baker, Henry S., Jr. *retired banker*
†Baker, Howard Henry, Jr. *former senator, lawyer*
Baker, Joe Don *actor*
Baker, Josephine L. Redenius (Mrs. Milton G. Baker) *minister, civic leader, retired career officer, former public relations company executive*
Baker, Laurence Howard *oncology educator*
Baker, Richard Hugh *congressman*
Baker, Robert M. L., Jr. *academic administrator*
†Baker, Zachary Moshe *librarian*
Balaban, Bob *actor, director*
Baldauf, Jill Christine *advertising executive*
Balding, Bruce Edward *investment executive*
Baldrige, Letitia *writer, management training consultant*
Baldwin, Alec (Alexander Rae Baldwin, III) *actor*
Baldwin, C. Andrew, Jr. *retired science educator*
Baldwin, DeWitt Clair, Jr. *physician, educator*
Baldwin, George Curriden *physicist, educator*
Baldwin, William Russell *foundation executive, optometrist*
Ball, Howard Guy *education specialist educator*
Ball, John Robert *medical association executive*
Ball, Lawrence *retired physical scientist*
Ballard, Marion Scattergood *software development professional*
Ballhaus, William Francis *retired scientific instruments company executive*
Ballou, James Howland *architect*
Balsam, Martin Henry *actor*
Balter, Alan *conductor, music director*
Bamberger, Gerald Francis *plastics marketing consultant*
Bambrick, James Joseph *labor economist, labor relations executive*
Bandeen, William Reid *retired meteorologist*
Bane, Keith James *electronics industry executive*
Bangs, John Kendrick *lawyer, foundation executive, former chemical company executive*
Banks, Jeffrey *fashion designer*
Banks, Robert Sherwood *lawyer*
Bantry, Bryan *entrepreneur*
†Banus, Peter Mario *healthcare executive*
†Baranski, Christine *actress*
Barbee, George E. L. *financial services executive*
Barca, George Gino *winery executive, finanial investor*
Barger, William James *management consultant*
Barham, Patte (Mrs. Harris Peter Boyne) *publisher, author, columnist*
†Barhydt, Sally J. *publishing company executive*
Barker, Clive *artist, screenwriter, director, producer*
Barker, Mary Katherine *retired nurse*
Barker, Peter Keefe *investment banker*
Barkley, Richard Clark *ambassador*
Barlow, Tom *congressman, sales executive*
Barnebey, Kenneth Alan *food company executive*
Barnes, Joanna *author, actress*
Barnes, Steven J. *retired food franchising company executive*
Barnett, Norman Lawrence *investment advisor*
Barnett, Vincent MacDowell, Jr. *political science educator*
Barnhart, Jo Anne B. *government official*
Barnhill, Henry Grady, Jr. *lawyer*
Barnhouse, Lillian May Palmer *retired medical, surgical nurse, researcher, civic worker*
Barone, John Anthony *university provost emeritus*
Barrack, William Sample, Jr. *petroleum company executive*
Barrett, Barbara McConnell *lawyer, ranch owner, community leader*
Barrett, Izadore *retired fisheries research administrator*
Barrett, Jane Hayes *lawyer*
Barrett, Joseph Michael *advertising and marketing consultant, actor*
Barringer, J(ohn) Paul *transportation executive, retired diplomat and career service executive*
Barron, Charles Elliott *retired electronics executive*
Barrow, Frank Pearson, Jr. *retired energy company executive*
Barry, Rick (Richard Francis Dennis Barry, III) *sportscaster, retired professional basketball player, marketing professional*
Barselou, Paul Edgar *actor, writer*
Bartels, Gerald Lee *association executive*
Bartenieff, George *producer, actor*
Barth, Frances Dorothy *artist*
Bartholomew, Donald Dekle *engineering executive, inventor*
Bartlett, James Williams *psychiatrist, educator*
Bartling, Theodore Charles *oil company executive*
Barton, Joe Linus *congressman*
Barton, Peter Richard, III *communications executive*
Bartunek, Joseph Wenceslaus *magistrate judge*
Bascom, Willard Newell *research engineer, scientist*
Basford, Robert Eugene *retired biochemistry educator, researcher*
Basham-Tooker, Janet Brooks *geropsychologist, educator*
Basia, (Basia Trzetrzelewska) *musician, vocalist*
Bass, Robert Olin *manufacturing executive*
Bassett, Barbara Wies *editor, publisher*
Bassett, Carol Ann *magazine, video, and radio documentary writer, producer, journalism educator*
Bassett, Elizabeth Ewing (Libby Bassett) *writer, editor*
Bassist, Donald Herbert *academic administrator*
Batalden, Paul Bennett *pediatrician, health care educator*
Bateman, Robert McLellan *artist*
Bates, Charles Turner *lawyer, educator*
Bates, Donald Lloyd *civil engineer, retired*
†Bates, Jared Lewis *army officer*
Bateson, Mary Catherine *anthropology educator*
Batignani, Laurie A. *communications professional*
†Battat, Felix A. *orthopedic surgeon*
Battle, Frank Vincent, Jr. *lawyer*
Bauer, Caroline Feller *author*
Bauer, Richard Carlton *nuclear engineer*
Baughman, J. Ross *photographer, writer, educator*
Bauman, Richard Arnold *coast guard officer*
Baumgartner, John H. *refining and petroleum products company executive*
Baxter, Cecil William, Jr. *retired college president*
Baxter, Stephen Bartow *retired history educator*
Baym, Gordon Alan *physicist, educator*
Beach, Edward Latimer *writer, retired military officer*
Beadle, John Grant *manufacturing company executive*
Beal, John *actor, director, narrator*
Beal, Merrill David *conservationist, museum director*
Beals, Nancy Farwell *state legislator*
Beasley, Barbara Starin *sales executive, marketing professional*
Beattie, Nora Maureen *insurance company executive, actuary*
Beatts, Anne Patricia *writer, producer*
Beatty, Michael L. *lawyer*
Beatty, Ned *actor*
†Beavers, William Reginald *financial consultant*
Becich, Raymond Brice *healthcare consultant, mediator, trainer, educator*
Beck, Isha Manna *performing company executive, actress, painter*
Beck, Jeffrey Dengler *banking executive*
Beck, John Roland *environmental consultant*
Becker, JoAnn Elizabeth *insurance company executive*
Becker, Walter Heinrich *vocational educator, planner*
Beckey, Sylvia Louise *lawyer*
Beckjord, Eric Stephen *energy researcher, nuclear engineering educator*
Bednarz, Nadine *mathematics educator, director research center*
Beebe, John Eldridge *financial service executive*
Begley, Ed, Jr. *actor*
Beighey, Lawrence Jerome *packaging company executive*
Beiser, Helen Ruth *psychiatrist*
Bejar, Jacob *physician, philosopher*
Belafonte, Harry *singer, concert artist, actor*
Beldock, Myron *lawyer*
Bell, Clarence Deshong *lawyer, state senator*
Bell, Clarence Elmo *former state senator*
Bell, Don Wayne *financial consultant*
Bell, Haney Hardy, III *lawyer*
†Bell, Michael Patrick *protective services official*
Bell, P. Jackson *computer executive*
Bell, Terrel Howard *education educator*
Bell, Thomas Rowe *retired natural gas transmission company executive*
Bellamy, James Carl *insurance company executive*
Belle Isle, Albert Pierre *electronics company executive*
Beller, Gary A. *financial services company executive, lawyer*
Belles, Anita Louise *health care safety executive*
Bellow, Saul C. *writer*
Bellum, Fred Lewis *school system administrator, retired*
Belshaw, George Phelps Mellick *bishop*
Beltz, Herbert Allison *financial consultant*
Bender, Gary Nedrow *television sportscaster*
Bender, James Frederick *psychologist, educator, university dean*
Benjamin, Edward A. *lawyer*
Benjamin, James Cover *controller, manufacturing company executive*
†Benjamin, Medea *advocate*
†Benjaminson, James A. *protective services official*
Benke, Norman R. *trucking company executive*
Benmark, Leslie Ann *chemical company executive*
Bennett, Geraldine Mae Paulette *publisher, author*
Bennett, John Roscoe *computer company executive*
Bennett, Richard Thomas *retired manufacturing executive*
Bennett, Robert John *banker*
Benney, Douglas Mabley *marketing executive, consultant*
Benton, Fletcher *sculptor*
Benton, Robert Dean *educational organization executive*
Ben Tré, Howard *artist*
Bentsen, Lloyd *former government official, former senator*
Benzle, Curtis Munhall *artist, educator*
Berdanier, Carolyn Dawson *nutrition educator, researcher*
Bergan, William Luke *lawyer*
Bergen, Candice *actress, writer, photojournalist*
Berger, Frank Stanley *consultant*
Berger, Jonathan *composer*
Berger, Lawrence Douglas *lawyer*
Berger, William Ernest *newspaper publisher*
Bergeron, Charles Edward *financial executive*
Bergman, Hermas John (Jack Bergman) *retired college administrator*
Bergman, John Hubert *fire department administrator*
Bergman, Klaus *utility executive, lawyer*
Bergson, Maria *designer*
Beringer, William Ernst *retired electrical equipment executive, lawyer*
Berkholtz, Nicholas Evald *engineering manager, consultant*
Berkley, Mary Corner *neurologist*
Berkovich, Gary A. *architect*
Berlin, Beatrice Winn *visual artist, printmaker*
Berlinger, Warren *actor*
Berlowitz Tarrant, Laurence *biotechnologist, university administrator*
Berman, Eleanore *artist*
Berman, Laura *freelance writer*
Berman, William H. *publishing company executive*
Bernard, Jami *film critic, author*
Bernard, Richard Lawson *geneticist, retired*
Bernard, Ronald Charles *entertainment company executive*

Bernhardt, Arthur Dieter building industry executive and consultant
Bernhardt, Melvin theater director
Bernstein, Alan Barry security services company executive
Bernstein, I(rving) Melvin university official and dean, materials scientist
Bernstein, Laurel publishing executive
Berra, Robert Louis chemicals consultant
Berry, Richard Lewis author, magazine editor, lecturer, programmer
Berry, Richard Stephen chemist
Berry, Robert Worth lawyer, educator, retired army officer
Bers, Abraham electrical engineering educator
Bertelsman, William Odis federal judge
Bertin, John Joseph aeronautical engineer, educator, researcher
Bertinelli, Valerie actress
Bertolett, Craig Randolph mechanical engineer consultant
Berzon, Betty psychotherapist
Bethune, Golden H. health facility administrator
Betlach, Mary Carolyn biochemist, molecular biologist
Betti, John Anso federal official, former automobile manufacturing company executive
Betts, Elaine Wiswall retired headmistress
Beveridge, James MacDonald Richardson retired college president
Beyer, Gordon Robert foreign service officer
Bhagat, Surinder Kumar environmental engineering educator
Biagi, Richard Charles retail executive, real estate consultant
Biedenharn, Lawrence C., Jr. physicist, educator
Biegel, David Eli social worker, educator
Bierbower, James J. lawyer
Bierley, Paul Edmund musician, author, publisher
Bierwirth, John Cocks retired aerospace manufacturing executive
Biesdorf, Heinz Bernard retired economist, educator
Bigelow-Lourie, Anne Edwige graphic designer
Biggs, Arthur Edward retired chemical manufacturing company executive
†Binch, Caroline Lesley illustrator, photographer
Binder, Amy Finn public relations company executive
Bingham, Jinsie Scott broadcast company executive
Birchem, Regina cell biologist, environment consultant, educator, writer
Birchfield, John Kermit, Jr. lawyer
Bird, Harrie Waldo, Jr. psychiatrist, educator
Birkenstock, James Warren business machine manufacturing company executive
Birkhoff, Garrett mathematician, educator
Bishop, Cecil bishop
Bishop, Charles Edwin university president emeritus, economist
Bishop, Raymond Holmes, Jr. physician, retired army officer
Bishop, (Ina) Sue Marquis psychiatric and mental health nurse educator, researcher, administrator
Bishop, William Squire commercial finance company executive
Bissell, Allen Morris engineer, consultant
Bissell, James Dougal, III motion picture production designer
Bistline, Stephen retired state supreme court justice
Bittke, Brian Edmund food distribution company executive
Bjerknes, Michael Leif dancer
Bjorndahl, David Lee electrical engineer
Bjornson, Maria theatrical designer
Black, Richard Bruce business executive, consultant
Black, Shirley Temple (Mrs. Charles A. Black) former ambassador, former actress
Blacker, Harriet public relations executive
Blackstone, Harry Bouton, Jr. magician, actor
Blackwell, Ronald Eugene livestock consultant
Blaine, Davis Robert valuation consultant executive
Blair, Charles Melvin manufacturing company executive, scientist
Blair, Fred Edward association executive
Blake, Joan Johnston Wallman playwright, lyricist
Blake, John Edward car rental company executive
Blanchard, Richard Frederick construction executive
Blaney, Connie Gayle importer and broker
Blank, Richard Glenn religious organization administrator, counselor
Blasco, Alfred Joseph business and financial consultant
Blatt, Harold Geller lawyer
Bliley, Thomas Jerome, Jr. congressman
Bliss, William Stanley, Jr. corporate marketing consultant
Blix, Susanne psychiatrist
Bloch, Erich electrical engineer, former science foundation administrator
Block, Barbara Ann biology educator
Block, Emil Nathaniel, Jr. military officer
Block, William newspaper publisher
Bloes, Richard Kenneth video artist
Blomgren, Bruce Holmes motivational speaker
Blood, Archer Kent retired foreign service officer
Bloom, Frank corporation executive, consultant
Bloom, Hyman artist
Bloomquist, Kenneth Gene music educator, university bands director
Blossom, Beverly choreographer, dance educator
Blow, George lawyer
Bluechel, Alan state senator, wood structural components manufacturing company executive
Bluemle, Robert Louis lawyer
Blum, Barbara Davis banker
†Blum, Bruce Alan hotel executive
Blum, Gerald Harris department store executive
†Blume, Jay Donald, Jr. air force officer
Boal, Dean arts center administrator, educator, retired
Boatright, Ann Long dancer, pianist, music educator, choreographer
Bochner, Hart actor
Bock, Jerry (Jerrold Lewis) composer
Bodanszky, Miklos chemist, educator
†Boe, Ralph Jacob carpet manufacturing executive
Boehle, William Randall music educator emeritus
Boeker, Paul Harold academic official, diplomat
Boell, Edgar John biology educator
Bogdanich, Walt journalist
Bogosian, Eric performance artist, actor
Bogue, Philip Roberts former academic administrator
Bohannan, Paul James anthropologist, writer, former university administrator
Boho, Dan L. lawyer
Bok, Sissela philosopher, writer
Boland, Margaret Frances secondary education educator
Bolen, David B. ambassador, former corporation executive
Boling, Robert Bruce physical education educator
Bolingbroke, Robert A. consumer products company executive
Bolinger, Corbin Eugene retired finance company executive
†Bolla, Karen Irene neuropsychologist, educator
Bollback, Anthony George minister
Bolliger, Eugene Frederick surgeon
Bolsterli, Margaret Jones English educator, farmer
Bondarenko, Hesperia Aura Louis entrepreneur
Bondurant, Gordon Emerson headmaster
Bonerz, Peter actor, director
Bonn, Ethel May psychiatrist, educator
Bonner, Jack public relations company executive
Bonner, John Tyler biology educator
Bonner, Patricia J. academic dean, educator
†Bonnet, John David physician, medical facility administrator
Bono, Sonny Salvatore congressman, singer, composer, former mayor
Boone, Alicia Kay Lanier marketing communications consultant, writer
Bootle, William Augustus retired federal judge
Boozer, Howard Rai state education official
Borchers, Mary Amelia middle school educator
Borda, Richard Joseph management consultant
Borden, Mark G. lawyer
Border, Pamela Ann nursing administrator, critical care nurse
Borecky, Isidore bishop
Borg, Ruth I. mental health nurse, long-term medical nurse
Borgnine, Ernest actor
Bork, Robert Heron lawyer, author, former federal judge
Borow, Richard Henry lawyer
Borten, William H. research company executive
Borton, Robert Ernest lawyer
Bortz, Paul Isaac media, sport and entertainment consultant
Borum, Rodney Lee financial business executive
†Borwein, Jonathan Michael mathematics educator
Bosco, Anthony Gerard bishop
Bosse, Malcolm Joseph, Jr. professional language educator, author
Bossier, Albert Louis, Jr. shipbuilding company executive
Bost, Raymond Morris retired college president
Boswell, Thomas Murray sports columnist, writer
Bothwell, John Charles archbishop
Boucher, Laurence James university dean, chemist
Boulden, Judith Ann federal judge
Boulet, Roger Henri art gallery director, curator
Bourdo, G. F. principal
Bourke, Dale Hanson publishing company owner
Bouton, James Alan entrepreneur, author, former sportscaster, former professional baseball player
Bova, Benjamin William author, editor, educator
Bowen, David Reece foundation director, former congressman
Bowen, J(ohn) William management consultant
Bower, Jean Ramsay court administrator, lawyer
Bowie, E(dward) J(ohn) Walter hematologist, researcher
Bowles, Barbara Landers investment company executive
Bowles, Paul Frederick composer, author
Bowman, Scotty professional hockey coach
Bowne, Shirlee Pearson credit union executive, real estate executive
Box, Dwain D. former judge
Box, George Edward Pelham statistics educator
Box, Thadis Wayne university dean emeritus, educator
Boxer, Stanley Robert artist, sculptor
†Boxleitner, Bruce actor
Boyatt, Thomas David former ambassador
†Boyce, Michael Ross inorganic chemical and mineral executive
Boyd, Alex library director
Boyd, Edward Lee financial executive
Boyd, Francis Virgil retired accounting educator
Boyd, Julianne Mamana theater director
Boyd, Liona Maria musician
Boyd, Stuart Robert military officer
Boykin, Robert Heath banker
Boyle, Peter actor
Boyle, Richard John art historian, author
Boyles, James Kenneth retired banker
†Boysen, Thomas Cyril state school system administrator
Bracken, Peg author
Brackenridge, A. Bruce trust company executive
Braden, Charles Hosea physicist, university administrator
Braden, George Walter, II (Lord of Carrigaline) company executive
Braden, Thomas Wardell news commentator
Bradford, Robert Edward supermarket executive
Bradley, Carol Ann nursing administrator
Bradley, Patricia Ellen professional golfer
Bradshaw, Dove artist
Brady, George Moore real estate executive, mortgage banker
Brady, Nicholas Frederick former secretary of treasury
Braen, Bernard Benjamin psychology educator
Bragagnolo, Julio Alfredo physicist
Brage, Carl Willis genealogist
Brain, George Bernard university dean
Brancato, Leo John manufacturing company executive
Brand, John Charles chemistry educator
Brandl, John Edward public affairs educator
Brando, Marlon, Jr. actor
Branscomb, Anne Wells communications consultant
†Brantley, Benjamin David drama critic
Brantz, George Murray retired lawyer
Branyan, Robert Lester retired university administrator
†Braswell, Arnold Webb executive consultant
Braswell, Judith F. healthcare administrator
Bratt, Nicholas investment management and research company executive
Braun, Jerome Irwin lawyer
Brazier, Don Roland retired railroad executive
Brazil, Jeff reporter
Breathed, Berkeley cartoonist
Brekke, Gail Louise broadcasting administrator
Brengel, Fred Lenhardt manufacturing company executive
Brennan, Donna Lesley public relations company executive
Brennan, Eileen Regina actress
Brennan, John A., Jr. state senator, lawyer
Brennan, Robert J. shipping company executive
Brennen, Stephen Alfred international business consultant
Brenner, Albert production designer, sculptor
Brent, Robert Leonard physician, educator
Breslin, Evalynne L. W. retired psychiatric nurse
Brett, Barbara Jeanne publisher
Brettell, Richard Robson art consultant
Brewer, Carey fund raising executive
Brewer, David Meredith retired computer company executive
Brewer, Leslie G. psychiatrist
Briccetti, Joan Therese symphony manager, arts management consultant
Brickell, Charles Hennessey, Jr. marine engineer, retired military officer
Bricken, William Marion scientist
Bricker, William Rudolph organization executive
Brickman, Ravelle public relations writer and consultant
Bright, Harold Frederick university provost emeritus, consultant
Brightmire, Paul William retired judge
Brill, Winston Jonas microbiologist, educator, research director, publisher and management consultant
Brimacombe, James Keith metallurgical engineering educator, researcher, consultant
Brinberg, Herbert Raphael information management, publishing company executive
Brinckerhoff, Richard Charles retired manufacturing company executive
Brinegar, Claude Stout retired oil company executive
Brink, Richard Edward lawyer
Brinkmann, Klaus Peter wholesale distribution executive
Britt, John Roy banker
Britton, Charles P., III banker
Broadwater, James E. publisher
Broderson, Morris artist
Brodhead, David Crawmer lawyer
Brodian, Laura broadcasting and illustration studio executive, professional illustrator
Brodie, Howard artist
Brodie, Theodore Hamilton construction company executive
†Brodkin, Alan Keith investment company executive
Brodnax, Margaret O'Bryan retired English language educator
Brodsky, David M. lawyer
Brodsky, Richard Louis state legislator
Brody, Edward Norman molecular biologist, educator
Broedling, Laurie Adele human resources executive, psychologist, educator
Brogden, Glenda Ethridge nursing administrator
Bronfman, Peter Frederick independent investor
Brooke, Ralph Ian dental educator, vice provost, university dean
Brooker, Robert Elton, Jr. manufacturing company executive
Brookner, Anita writer, educator
Brooks, Albert (Albert Einstein) actor, writer, director
Brooks, Gary management consultant
Brooks, James Sprague retired national guard officer
Brooks, Michael Paul urban planning educator
Brooks, Thomas Aloysius, III retired naval officer
Brooks, William Sidney construction executive
Brophy, Theodore Frederick telephone company executive
Brosnan, Pierce actor
Broude, Ronald music publisher
Browder, Felix Earl mathematician, educator
Brower, Charles Nelson lawyer, judge
†Brower, Forrest Allen retired health facility administrator
Brown, Bart A., Jr. consumer products company executive
Brown, Barton retired automotive company executive
Brown, Britt retired publishing company executive
Brown, Bruce Maitland philanthropy consultant
†Brown, Carol A. artist
Brown, Donald Douglas transportation company executive, retired air force officer, consultant
Brown, Earle composer, conductor
Brown, Henry Bedinger Rust financial management company executive
Brown, James Monroe, III museum administrator
Brown, Jim (James Nathaniel Brown) film actor, former professional football player
Brown, Linda Joan psychotherapist, psychoanalyst
Brown, Marcia Joan author, artist, photographer
Brown, Robert Charles college administrator
Brown, Robert Laidlaw state supreme court justice
Brown, Roberta critical care nurse
Brown, Ruth rhythm and blues singer
Brown, Sandra Jean banker
Brown, William Ferdinand artist, writer
Brown, William Houston lawyer
Browne, Cecil Thayer utility company executive
Browne, Diana Gayle artist, social services
Browne, Edmund John Phillip oil company executive
Browne, Jackson singer, songwriter
Browning, Colin Arrott retired banker
Brubaker, Crawford Francis, Jr. government official, aerospace consultant
Bruce, James Edmund retired utility company executive
Brumberg, G. David historical center administrator, history bibliographer
Brune, David Hamilton financial corporation executive, lawyer
Brune, Eva fundraiser
Brunvand, Dana Kari editor, English educator
Brustad, Wesley O. symphony executive, theater and opera director, scriptwriter
Bruzda, Francis Joseph investment executive, former banker
Bryant, Cecil Farris lawyer, retired insurance company executive
Bryant, Gail Annette Grippen nurse, educator
Bubrick, Melvin Phillip surgeon
Buchanan, Edna journalist
Buchanan, John MacLennan Canadian provincial official
Buchanan, Patrick Joseph journalist
Buchanan, Susan Shaver publishing company executive
Buck, Genevieve Carol fashion journalist
Buckels, Marvin Wayne savings and loan executive
Buckley, William Elmhirst publishing consultant
Buffkins, Archie Lee public television executive
Buffmire, Judy Ann state legislator, psychologist, consultant
Bujold, Tyrone Patrick lawyer
Buker, Robert Hutchinson, Sr. army officer, thoracic surgeon
Bulger, Roger James academic health center executive
Bulla, Ben F. retired manufacturing company executive
Bulla, Clyde Robert writer
Bullard, Helen (Mrs. Joseph Marshall Krechniak) sculptor
Bullin, Christine Neva arts administrator
Bullins, Ed author
Bullock, Theodore Holmes biologist, educator
Bullough, Bonnie nurse, educator
Bumbery, Joseph Lawrence diversified telecommunications company executive
Bunch, Franklin Swope architect
Bunch, Jennings Bryan, Jr. electrical engineer
Bunim, Mary-Ellis television producer
Bunn, George legal educator, writer
Bunning, Jim congressman, former professional baseball player
Bunton, Lucius Desha, III federal judge
Burch, Hamlin Doughty, III retired sheet metal professional
Burchman, Leonard government official
Burden, John W., III retail company executive
Burge, James Darrell personnel, government relations executive
Burge, John Wesley, Jr. management consultant
Burger, Warren Earl former chief justice of U.S. supreme court, academic administrator
Burgess, Marjorie Laura protective services official
Burk, Sylvia Joan petroleum landman, freelance writer
Burke, Edmond Wayne retired judge
Burkett, Ben Vern, Sr. aircraft support company executive
Burki, Fred Albert labor union official
Burlant, William Jack retired chemical company executive
Burlew, John Swalm research scientist
Burlingame, James Montgomery, III lawyer
Burney, Derek H. ambassador
Burns, James Francis, Jr. banker
Burns, Nancy Kay drug abuse services professional
Burns, Richard Francis mechanical engineer
Burrell, Craig Donald physician, educator
Burroughs, Franklin Troy academic administrator
Burroughs, John Townsend lawyer
Burton, Anne M. public relations professional
Burton, Joseph Alfred state legislator
Bury, John theatre designer, consultant
Bush, Charles Vernon telecommunications executive
Bush, Guy Louis biology educator
Busse, Leonard Wayne banker, financial consultant
Bussgang, Julian Jakob electronics engineer
Butkus, Dick actor, former professional football player
Butler, Eugene L. oil field equipment company executive
Butler, Jack Fairchild semiconductors company executive
Butler, Robert Leonard sales executive
Butler, Robert Thomas retired advertising executive
Butson, Alton Thomas mathematics educator
Butterfield, Alexander Porter business executive, former government official, retired air force officer
Butts, Virginia corporate public relations executive
Buxton, Winslow Hurlbert diversified manufacturing company executive
Buzard, James Albert management consultant
Byrd, Lloyd Garland civil engineer
Byrne, David musician, composer, artist, director
Byrnes, Christine Ann internist
Cachia, Pierre Jacques Middle East languages and culture educator, researcher
Cahn, Robert Nathan physicist
Caine, Raymond William, Jr. retired public relations executive
Cairns, Theodore LeSueur chemist
Calamita, Kathryn Elizabeth nursing administrator
†Calcaterra, Edward Lee construction company executive
Caldwell, Howard Bryant English language educator
Caldwell, Warren Frederick investment company executive
Calegari, Maria ballerina
Califano, Joseph Anthony, Jr. lawyer, public health policy educator, writer
Callahan, Joseph Murray magazine editor
Callahan, Richard J. communications company executive
Callander, Bruce Douglas journalist, free-lance writer
Callard, Carole Crawford librarian, educator
Callard, David Jacobus investment banker
Callender, John Hancock architect
Callow, Keith McLean judge
Callow, William Grant retired state supreme court justice
Calvert, James Francis manufacturing company executive, retired admiral
Camdessus, Michel (Jean) international organization executive
†Cameron, David Brian health service administrator
Cameron, J. Elliot retired parochial educational system administrator
Cameron, Lucille Wilson retired dean of libraries
Camisa, George Lincoln beverage company executive
Camp, Clifton Durrett, Jr. newspaper consultant, rancher
Camp, Patricia E. nursing educator
Campanelli, Pauline Eble artist
Campbell, Alice Shaw retired accountant, poet
Campbell, Arlington Fichtner military officer
Campbell, Avril Kim Canadian legislator, justice official
Campbell, Byron Chesser publishing company executive
Campbell, Craig Stewart landscape architect, town planner
Campbell, Edward Clinton small business owner, violin maker
Campbell, Henry Cummings librarian
†Campbell, John A. lumber company executive
Campbell, Patton stage designer, educator
Campbell, Richard Alden electronics company executive
Campbell, Sarah elementary education educator, special education specialist
†Campbell, Todd J. lawyer, federal official
Cane, David E. chemistry educator
Canin, Stuart Victor violinist
Canning, John J. leasing and finance company executive
Cannon, Dyan actress
Cannon, Isabella Walton mayor
Cantarella, Francesco Paquin retail executive
Cantliffe, Jeri Miller artist, art educator

Cantone, Vic political cartoonist
Cantrell, Linda Maxine counselor
Cantril, Albert H(adley) public opinion analyst
Capek, Vlastimil retired radiologist, educator
Capice, Philip Charles television production executive
Caplovitz, Coleman David physician
Caporali, Renso L. aerospace executive
Capuano, Terry Ann nursing administrator
Caray, Harry Christopher sports announcer
Carder, Paul Charles advertising executive
Cardy, Andrew Gordon hotel executive
Carey, Dennis Clarke executive search consultant
Carey, Francis James investment banker
Carey, Gerard V. banker
Carey, Mariah vocalist, songwriter
Carey, Martin Conrad gastroenterologist, molecular biophysicist, educator
†Carlin, Richard Peter editor, author
Carlquist, Sherwin biology and botany educator
Carlsen, Mary Baird clinical psychologist
Carlson, Elvin Palmer military officer
Carlson, Janet Frances psychologist, educator
Carlson, Natalie Traylor publisher
Carlyss, Earl Winston musician
Carman, George Henry retired physician
Carmody, Thomas Roswell business products company executive
Carney, Arthur William Matthew actor
Carothers, Steven Michael artist, designer, writer
Carpenter, Derr Alvin landscape architect
Carpenter, Dorothy Fulton former state legislator
Carpenter, Kenneth John nutrition educator
Carpenter, Malcolm Scott astronaut, oceanographer
Carpenter, Myron Arthur manufacturing company executive
Carr, Harold Noflet investment corporation executive
Carr, M. Robert (Bob Carr) lawyer
Carradine, Keith Ian actor, singer, composer
Carreker, John Russell retired agricultural engineer
Carroll, Bernard James psychiatrist
Carroll, Marshall Elliott architect
Carson, Johnny television personality
Carter, Elliott Cook, Jr. composer
Carter, Herbert Edmund former university official
Carter, (William) Hodding, III television and newspaper journalist
Carter, Hugh Clendenin mechanical consulting engineer
Carter, Jaine M(arie) human resources development company executive
Carter, John Swain museum administrator, consultant
Carter, Joseph Edwin former nickel company executive, writer
Carter, Nanette Carolyn artist
Carter, Richard Duane business educator
Carter, Ronald musician
Carter, Rosalynn Smith wife of former President of U.S.
Carter, Sara Kebe psychiatrist
Carter, William George, III army officer
Cartier, Celine Paule librarian, administrator, consultant
Carver, Calvin Reeve public utility company director
Carvey, Dana actor, stand up comedian
Casey, John Thomas health services agency executive
Casey, Martin M. food service executive
Casey, Robert Reisch lawyer
Cash, Carol Vivian sociologist
Cash, Johnny entertainer
Cashman, W. Timothy, II financial executive
Cashman, William James, Jr. information processing marketing executive
Cason, Nica Virginia nursing educator
Casper, Gerhard academic administrator, law educator
Casselman, William E., II lawyer
Cassidy, John Harold lawyer
Cassill, (Karilyn) Kay artist, writer
Cassini, Oleg Lolewski fashion designer, manufacturer
Casterline, Cecil W. lawyer
Castile, Jesse Randolph (Rand) retired museum director
Castle, James Cameron information systems executive
Castle, Robert Woods advertising agency executive
Caswell, Dorothy Ann Cottrell arts administrator
Catacosinos, William James utility company executive
Catlett, Elizabeth sculptor, printmaker, educator
Catlin, B. Wesley microbiologist
Cattani, Maryellen B. lawyer
Cavallaro, Mary Caroline retired physics educator
Ceci, Louis J. former state supreme court justice
Cesnik, James Michael union official, newspaperman
Chaikof, Elliot Lorne vascular surgeon
Chain, Beverly Jean communications executive
Chalfant, Richard Dewey hypnotherapist, insurance consultant
Challela, Mary Scahill maternal/child health nurse
Chamberlain, George Arthur, III manufacturing company executive, venture capitalist
Chamberlain, William Edwin, Jr. management consultant
Chamberlin, Michael Meade lawyer
Chandler, Alfred Dupont, Jr. historian, educator
Chandler, Harry Edgar author
Chandler, John Herrick college president
Chandler, John Parker Hale, Jr. state senator
Chandler, William Everett financial executive
Chandra, Pramod art history educator
Chapman, Kristin Heilig public relations consultant
Chapman, Robert L. bishop
Chapman, Tracy singer, songwriter
Chapman, William baritone
Chappell, Robert E. banker
Charlton, Betty Jo retired state legislator
Charlton, Gordon Taliaferro, Jr. retired bishop
Charlton, Jesse Melvin, Jr. management educator, lawyer
Charry, Michael R(onald) musician, conductor
Chase, Clinton Irvin psychologist, educator, business executive
Chase, James Richard retired college president
Chase, Seymour M. lawyer
Chase-Riboud, Barbara Dewayne sculptor, writer
Chawla, Krishan Kumar materials engineer, educator, consultant
Chaykin, Robert Leroy manufacturing and marketing executive
Chelberg, Bruce Stanley holding company executive
Chelberg, Robert Douglas army officer
Chellas, Brian Farrell philosophy educator
Chen, Di electro-optic company executive, consultant
Cheney, Lois Sweet infection control nurse
Chenhall, Robert Gene former museum director, consultant, author
Chepiga, Pamela Rogers lawyer
Chercover, Murray television executive
Chereskin, Alvin advertising executive
Chernichaw, Mark television, film and interactive multimedia executive producer, director, international media consultant
Chernoff, Amoz Immanuel hematologist, consultant
Cherryh, C. J. writer
Chervin, Joseph lawyer
Cheston, Theodore C. electrical engineer
Chevalier, Paul Edward retired retail executive, lawyer, art gallery executive
Cheverton, William Kearns science corporation executive, consultant
Chew, Margaret Sarah geography educator, retired
Chia, Felipe Humberto management and marketing educator
Chigier, Norman mechanical engineering educator
Childers, Pamela Barnard secondary school educator
Chin, Marjorie Scarlett Yee controller, business executive
Chinn, Thomas Wayne typographic company executive
Chinni, Peter Anthony artist
Chinoy, Helen Krich theater historian
Chisholm, Shirley Anita St. Hill former congresswoman, educator, lecturer
Chism, Linda Fay nursing educator
Chittick, David Rupert environmental management consultant
Chmielinski, Edward Alexander electronics company executive
Choi, Man-Duen mathematics educator
Chow, Rita Kathleen nursing administrator
Christensen, Albert Sherman federal judge
Christensen, Robert A. lawyer
†Christenson, Gregg Andrew bank executive
Christine, Virginia Feld actress
Christoffersen, Jon Michael bank executive
Christoffersen, Ralph Earl chemist
Christopher, Russell Lewis baritone
Christopher, Sharon A. Brown bishop
Chronley, James Andrew real estate executive
Chryssa sculptor
Chryssis, George Christopher business executive
Chu, Benjamin Thomas Peng-Nien chemistry educator
Church, Abiah A. retired broadcasting company executive, lawyer
Church, Eugene Lent physicist, consulting scientist
Church, Martha Eleanor former college president
Chyu, Chi-Oy Wei secondary school educator
Ciccone, Anne Panepinto artist
Cid Viuda de Garcia Molina, Caridad del Carmen radio producer and personality
†Cissel, John Ferrill national part superintendent
Clagett, William H., IV retired government agency administrator
Claiborne, Craig author, editor cookbooks
Claiborne, Liz (Elisabeth Claiborne Ortenberg) fashion designer
Clanon, Thomas Lawrence retired hospital administrator
Clapper, Lyle Nielsen magazine publisher
Clarizio, Josephine Delores corporate services executive, former manufacturing and engineering company executive, foundation executive
Clark, Alicia Garcia political party official
Clark, Caleb Morgan political scientist, educator
Clark, Candy actress
Clark, Claudia J. educational administration, speech, language and learning disabilities professional
Clark, Donald Otis lawyer
Clark, James Milford college president, retired
Clark, Larry photographer
Clark, Mary Higgins author, business executive
Clark, Maxine retail executive
Clark, Peter Bruce newspaper executive
Clark, Robert Phillips newspaper editor, consultant
Clark, Thomas Lloyd English linguistics educator
Clark, William, Jr. ambassador
Clarke, Edward Owen, Jr. lawyer
Clarke, Henry Lee ambassador, U.S. foreign service officer
Clarke, Hope choreographer, director, actress
Clarke, Lambuth McGeehee college president emeritus
Clarke, Malcolm filmmaker
Claver, Robert Earl television director, producer
†Claxton, Bradford Wayne professional society administrator
Claytor, Richard Anderson retired federal agency executive
Cleary, Thomas J. social worker, administrator
Clement, Hope Elizabeth Anna librarian
Clemetson, Charles Alan Blake physician
Cleveland, Charlene S. community health nurse
Cliff, Judith Anita author, biblical studies lecturer
Cliff, Ronald Laird energy company executive
Clifford, Brother Peter academic administrator, religious educator
Clifton, Russell B. banking and mortgage lending consultant, retired mortgage company executive
Closset, Gerard Paul forest products company executive
Cloud, Stanley Wills journalist, editor, writer
Clouston, Ross Neal retired food and related products company executive
Cluff, E. Dale librarian, educator, administrator
Clymer, Wayne Kenton bishop
Cobb, John Boswell, Jr. clergyman, educator
Cobb, John Cecil, Jr. (Jack Cobb) Latin America area specialist, communications specialist and executive
Cobb, Miles Alan lawyer
Cobb, Ruth artist
Cobb, Virginia Horton artist, educator
Cobham, William Emanuel, Jr. musician
Coble, Howard congressman, lawyer
Coburn, D(onald) L(ee) playwright
Coburn, Harry L. foreign service officer
Coburn, James actor
†Cochran, John Robert, III hospital administrator
Cochran, Thad senator
Cockrill, Ann Teresa lawyer
Cockrum, William Monroe, III investment banker, consultant, educator
Cody, Iron Eyes actor
Coffee, Joseph Denis, Jr. college chancellor emeritus
Coffey, John Louis federal judge
Coffman, Stanley Knight, Jr. English educator, former college president
Cogan, Ronald James editor, writer, producer
Cograve, John Edwin retired judge
Cohen, Alexander H. theatrical and television producer
Cohen, Allan Richard broadcasting executive
Cohen, B. Stanley physician
Cohen, Lita Indzel state legislator
Cohen, Mark Herbert broadcasting company executive
Cohen, Mark Steven public affairs specialist
Cohn, Avern Levin federal judge
Cohn, Leonard Allan retired chemical company executive
Coia, Robert Salvatore biology educator, consultant
Coke, Frank Van Deren museum director, photographer
Colaianni, Joseph Vincent judge
Colbert, Claudette (Lily Chauchoin) actress
Colburn, Harold Lewis dermatologist, state legislator
Cole, Brady Marshall retired naval officer
Cole, Clifford Adair clergyman
Cole, Jerome Foster research company executive
Coleman, Denis Patrick, Jr. investment banker
Coleman, John James lawyer
Coleman, Lewis Waldo bank executive
Coleman, Nancy Catherine actress
Coleman, Nancy Pees environmental toxicologist
Coleman, Robert Lee retired lawyer
Collier, Herman Edward, Jr. retired college president
Collier, Oscar literary agency consultant, writer
Collins, Jackie writer
Collins, Joan Henrietta actress
Collins, John Francis landscape architect, educator
Collins, Michael aerospace consultant, former astronaut
Collins, Robert Frederick federal judge
Collins, William Michael public relations executive
Colman, Edward Brof film director, cinematographer
Colodny, Edwin Irving lawyer, retired airline executive
†Colonna, Robert Jerome financial services consultant
Colonnier, Marc Leopold neuroanatomist, educator
Colton, Nelson Burton industrial company executive
Colvin, Burton Houston mathematician, government official
Comaneci, Nadia gymnast
Compton, Norma Haynes retired university dean
Compton, W. Dale physicist
Condayan, John foreign service officer
Condit, Doris Elizabeth historian
†Condon, Curtis Wayne magazine editor
Condry, Robert Stewart retired hospital administrator
Cone, Edward Toner composer, emeritus music educator
Conklin, Michael L. newspaper columnist
Conlon, Harry B., Jr. banking company executive
Conneally, P. Michael medical educator
Connell, George Edward former university president, scientist
Connelly, Sharon Rudolph lawyer, federal official
Connors, Mike (Krekor Ohanian) actor
Conole, Clement Vincent corporate executive
Conrad-England, Roberta Lee pathologist
Consoli, Marc-Antonio composer
Constant, Clinton chemical engineer, consultant
Constantine, Kevin professional hockey coach
Conway, James Valentine Patrick forensic document examiner, former postal service executive
Conway, Robert P. art dealer
Cook, Alexander Burns museum curator, artist, educator
Cook, Beth Marie writer, poet
Cook, Charles Beckwith, Jr. securities company executive
Cook, Charles Emerson electrical engineer
Cook, Douglas W. career officer
Cook, Fielder producer, director
Cook, Fred James journalist, author
†Cook, John Charles product designer, design consultant
Cook, Julian Abele, Jr. federal judge
Cook, Stanton R. media company executive
Cook, Steven R. financial executive
Cooke, Eileen Delores retired librarian
Cookson, Albert Ernest telephone and telegraph company executive
Cooley, James William retired executive researcher
Cooney, Barbara illustrator, author
Cooney, John Thomas retired banker
Coons, Marion McDowell retail food stores executive
Coonts, Stephen Paul novelist
Coop, Frederick Robert retired city manager
Cooper, Charles Gordon insurance consultant, former executive
Cooper, Charles Justin lawyer, former government official
Cooper, E. Camron retired oil company executive
Cooper, Francis Loren advertising executive
Cooper, Hal television director
Cooper, John Miller retired biomechanics lab director
Cooper, Sarah Jean nursing administrator
Cope, Alfred Haines political scientist, educator
Copeland, Henry Jefferson, Jr. former college president
Copes, Marcella A. nursing administrator, educator
Coplans, John Rivers artist
Coplin, Mark David lawyer
Copper, James Robert manufacturing company executive
Copperfield, David (David Kotkin) illusionist, director, producer, writer
Coppie, Comer Swift state official
Corbett, Carolyn Susanne hospital administrator, nurse
Corbin, Robert Keith lawyer, former state attorney general
Corcoran, Barbara Asenath author
Corddry, Paul I(mlay) retired food products company executive
Corey, Jeff actor, director, educator
Corey, Kenneth Edward geography and urban planning educator, researcher
Coriell, Lewis Lemon physician, research institute administrator
Cork, Edwin Kendall business and financial consultant
Cormican, M. Alma elementary education educator
Cormier, Jean G. communications company executive
Cornell, David Roger hospital administrator
Corrales, Patrick coach, former professional baseball manager
Correnti, John David steel company executive
Cortese, Richard Anthony computer company executive
Corwin, Laura J. lawyer
Cosby, Bill actor, entertainer
Coscarelli, Don film writer, film director
Cossa, Dominic Frank baritone
Costas, Robert Quinlan (Bob Costas) sportscaster
Costello, Daniel Walter retired bank executive
Costello, James Joseph retired electrical manufacturing company executive
Cotrubas, Ileana opera singer, lyric soprano, retired
Cotter, Ernest Robert, III finance company executive
Cotter, Richard Vern management consultant, author, educator
Cotton, Aylett Borel retired lawyer
Couchman, Robert George James human services consultant
Coughlan, William David association executive
†Coughlin, Sister Kathleen hospital administrator
Cougill, Roscoe McDaniel mayor, retired air force officer
Couri, John A. distribution executive
Courtney, Charles Edward government official
Coval-Apel, Naomi Miller dentist
Covalt, Genevieve corporate executive secretary
Covell, Richard Bertram bank executive
Coven, Berdeen psychotherapist
Cover, Franklin Edward actor
Cowenhoven, Garret Peter state legislator, educator
Cowles, John, Jr. publisher, women's sports promoter
Cox, David Brummal accounting firm executive
Cox, J. William physician, health services administrator
†Cox, John Curtis healthcare and educational administrator
Cox, John Francis retired cosmetic company executive
Cox, Kenneth R. state agency administrator
Cox, Wilford Donald retired food company executive
†Coyle, John J. publishing executive
Cozan, Lee clinical research psychologist
Cozen, Lewis orthopedic surgeon
Crabtree, Davida Foy minister
Crabtree, Robert Howard chemistry educator, consultant
Craft, Edmund Coleman automotive parts manufacturing company executive
Craig, William Francis banker
Cramer, Robert Vern retired college president, director scholarship program, consultant
Cramer, William F. capitol goods executive
Crampton, Esther Larson sociology and political science educator
Crandall, Albert Earl retail executive, accountant, entrepreneur
Crandles, George Marshal retired insurance company executive
Cranin, Marilyn Sunners landscape designer
Craw, Freeman (Jerry Craw) graphic artist
Crawford, Carol Tallman government executive
Crawford, Kenneth Charles educational institute executive, retired government official
Crawford, Muriel Laura lawyer, author, educator
Crawford, William Walsh retired consumer products company executive
Crean, John Gale hat manufacturer
Creech, John Lewis retired scientist, consultant
Creigh, Thomas, Jr. utility executive
Crimm, Marcy Ware Jones geritrics nurse, educator
Crippen, Robert Laurel former naval officer and astronaut
Critoph, Eugene retired physicist, nuclear research company executive
Cromwell, Florence Stevens occupational therapist
Cronkhite, Leonard Wolsey, Jr. physician, consultant, research foundation executive
Cronson, Robert Granville lawyer
Crosby, Norman Lawrence comedian
Cross, Alexander Dennis business consultant, former chemical and pharmaceutical executive
Cross, Dewain Kingsley financial executive
Cross, Elmo Garnett, Jr. lawyer, state senator
Crossley, Francis Rendel Erskine engineering educator
Crosson, John Albert advertising executive
Crouse, Lindsay actress
Crowell, Nancy Melzer investment banker
Crowther, James Earl radio and television executive
Crowther, Richard Layton architect, consultant, researcher, author, lecturer
Croxton, Fred(erick) E(mory), Jr. retired information specialist, consultant
Crudup, W. bishop
Cruise, Tom (Tom Cruise Mapother, IV) actor
Csanady, Gabriel Tibor oceanographer, meteorologist, environmental engineer
Csia, Susan Rebecca lawyer, oil company executive
Cuatrecasas, Pedro Martin research pharmacologist
Cudahy, Richard D. federal judge
Cuevas, Milton Joseph publishing company executive
Culbertson, Philip Edgar aerospace company executive
Cull, Robert Robinette electric products manufacturing company executive
Cullen, James Thaddeus, Jr. broadcast executive
Culley, June Elizabeth clinical reviewer, quality improvement specialist
Culp, William Newton retired insurance executive
Culvahouse, Arthur Boggess, Jr. lawyer
Culverwell, Albert Henry historian
Culwell, Charles Louis retired manufacturing company executive
Cummer, William Jackson former oil company executive, investor
Cumming, Robert Hugh artist, photographer
Cummings, Constance actress
Cummings, David William artist, educator
Cunnane, James Joseph manufacturing executive
Cunningham, Isabella Clara Mantovani advertising educator
†Cunningham, Ron choreographer, artistic director
Curchoe, Carl A. printing company executive
†Curlee, Jesse W. association executive
Curley, Elmer Frank librarian
Currier, Ruth dancer, choreographer and educator
Curry, Richard Orr history educator and freelance writer
Curson, Theodore musician
Curti, Merle Eugene historian, educator
Curtin, David Stephen newswriter
Curtis, James L. psychiatrist
Curtis, Mary Ellen (Mary Curtis Horowitz) publishing company executive
Curtis, Patricia nursing administrator
Curtis, Peter Campbell John retired diplomat
Cushing, Frederic Sanford publishing company executive
Cushman, Paul physician, educator
Cussler, Clive Eric author
Cutler, Winnifred Berg biologist
Cyr, Conrad Keefe federal judge
Czapor, Edward P. automobile company executive

Czarnecki, Gerald Milton *manufacturing executive*
Dabbs, Henry Erven *television and film producer, educator*
Dackow, Orest Taras *insurance company executive*
Dafoe, Willem *actor*
D'Agostino, Stephen I. *bottling company executive*
Dahl, Bren Bennington *screenwriter*
Dahlgren, Carl Herman Per *educator, arts administrator*
Dailey, Irene *actress, educator*
Dailey, Janet *novelist*
Dake, Marcia Allene *retired nursing educator, university dean*
Dale, Wesley John *chemistry educator*
Daltrey, Roger *musician*
Daly, James Joseph *bishop*
Daly, James William *physician, educator*
Daly, William James *retired health industry distributing company executive*
Dalziel, Robert David *retired telecommunications executive*
D'Amato, Alfonse M. *senator*
D'Amato, Anthony Roger *recording company executive*
d'Amboise, Christopher *ballet dancer, artistic director, choreographer*
D'Angelo, Ronald Holmes *priest, psychotherapist*
Daniel, Elbert Clifton *journalist*
Daniels, Arlene Kaplan *sociology educator*
Daniels, James Maurice *physicist*
Danilowicz, Delores Ann *pediatric cardiologist, pediatrics educator*
Danis, Peter G., Jr. *office products company executive*
Dannenberg, Martin Ernest *retired insurance company executive*
Danner, Blythe Katharine *actress*
Danoff, I. Michael *art center director, writer, educator*
Danza, Tony *actor*
Daragan, Thomas William *financial executive*
D'Arcangelo, Allan Matthew *artist*
Dasburg, John Harold *airline executive*
†Dasher-Alston, Robinette *educational organization administrator*
Dater, Judy Lichtenfeld *photographer*
Daub, Hal *mayor of Omaha, former congressman*
Daugherty, Alfred Clark *manufacturing company executive*
Daugherty, Brad(ley) (Lee) *professional basketball player*
Dauphinee, Joan Drukker *women's health educator*
Davenport, Chester *lawyer*
Davenport, Ernest Harold *university official, accountant*
Davenport, Lawrence Franklin *school system administrator*
Davidovsky, Mario *composer*
Davidsen, Arthur F. *astrophysicist, educator*
Davidson, Jeannie *costume designer*
Davidson, John *financial advisory executive*
Davidson, Mayer B. *medical educator, researcher*
Davies, Raymond Douglas *musician, songwriter*
Davies, Ronald Norwood *federal judge*
Davis, Anna Jane Ripley *elementary education educator*
Davis, Carl George *software engineer*
Davis, Darrell L. *automotive executive*
Davis, Emma R. *horticulturist*
Davis, F. Benjamin *academic administrator*
Davis, George Alfred *financial executive*
Davis, George Lynn *retired aerospace company executive*
Davis, Helen R. *elementary and middle school educator*
Davis, Henry Jefferson, Jr. *former naval officer*
Davis, Joanne Mary *advertsing service executive*
Davis, John Sidney *oil and gas company executive*
Davis, Joseph Edward *retired supermarket chain executive*
Davis, Laurence Laird *coal company executive*
Davis, Luther *writer, producer*
Davis, Mac *singer, songwriter*
†Davis, Martis James *government official*
Davis, Roger Edwin *lawyer, retired discount chain executive*
Davis, Russell Haden *association executive, pastoral psychotherapist*
Davis, Theodore Roosevelt *bishop, contractor*
Davison, Beaumont *retired university administrator*
Dawkins, Marva Phyllis *psychologist*
Dawson, Horace Greeley, Jr. *former diplomat, government official*
DeAlessandro, Joseph Paul *insurance company executive*
Dean, Dearest (Lorene Glosup) *songwriter*
Dean, Francis Hill *landscape architect, educator*
Dean, Frederick Bernard *retired holding company executive*
DeAngelis, Thomas P. *chemist*
De Antoni, Edward Paul *cancer control research scientist*
De Blasi, Tony (Anthony Armando De Blasi) *artist*
de Blij, Harm Jan *geography educator, editor*
deButts, Robert Edward Lee *corporate development and real estate executive*
DeCamp, Graydon *journalist*
Dechar, Peter Henry *artist*
†Dechario, Tony Houston *symphony orchestra executive*
Decker, Gilbert Felton *manufacturing company executive*
Decker, Hans Wilhelm *retired finance company executive*
De Concini, Dennis *former senator, lawyer*
Dees, Lynne *artist*
De Felitta, Frank Paul *producer, writer, director*
DeFleur, Melvin Lawrence *sociologist, communication educator*
De Frank, Vincent *conductor*
Deisenhofer, Johann *biochemistry educator, researcher*
de Kruif, Jack H. *manufacturing executive*
de la Garza, Eligio (Kika de la Garza) *congressman*
Delahanty, Rebecca Ann *school system administrator*
Delany, Logan Drummond, Jr. *financial consultant, investor*
Del Balzo, Joseph Michael *aviation consulting company executive*
Dell'Olio, Louis *fashion designer*
De Loach, Bernard Collins, Jr. *retired physicist*
DeLong, Norma Neill *civic association executive*
De Looper, Willem Johan *artist, museum curator*
Del Tredici, David *composer*
de Luce, Virginia *entertainer*
De Luise, Dom *actor*
Dely, Steven *aerospace company executive*
Delza-Munson, Elizabeth *dancer, choreographer, educator*
DeMark, Richard Reid *retired insurance company executive*
Dembeck, Mary Grace *artist, writer*
Demcoe, Lloyd Robert *social worker*
De Mornay, Rebecca *actress*
De Moss, Robert George *religious foundation executive*
Dempsey, Barbara Matthea *medical/surgical and critical care nurse*
De Neal, Patricia Diana *nursing administrator*
Deneuve, Catherine (Catherine Dorleac) *actress*
Denisco, Ralph Andrew *ice cream industry executive*
Denman, William Foster *retired academic administrator, educator*
Denneny, James Clinton, Jr. *business consultant*
Denny, James McCahill *retail executive*
Denton, David Edward *retired education educator*
DePalma, Ralph George *surgeon, educator*
Depkovich, Francis John *retired retail chain executive*
Derbes, Daniel William *manufacturing executive*
Derfner, Carol Ann *consultant*
Der Manuelian, Lucy *art and architecture educator*
De Salva, Salvatore Joseph *pharmacologist, toxicologist*
Detra, Ralph William *research laboratory administrator*
Detweiler, Edna J. *health facility administrator*
Devane, William *actor*
Devlin, Michael Coles *bass-baritone*
Diamond, Fred I. *electronic engineer*
Diamond, Stuart *lawyer, journalist*
Diamond, William J. *federal agency administrator*
Dibner, David Robert *architect*
Di Cicco, Joseph Nicholas, Jr. *chemical engineer*
Dicke, Robert Henry *educator, physicist*
Dickerson, James L. *writer, photographer, consultant*
Dickerson, Nancy (Whitehead) *free lance television producer, news correspondent*
Dickes, Robert *psychiatrist*
Dickinson, Angie (Angeline Brown) *actress*
Dickinson, William Richard *retired geologist and educator*
Dickman, James Bruce *photojournalist*
Dickson, James Francis, III *surgeon*
Diehl, Deborah Hilda *lawyer*
Diemer, Emma Lou *composer, music educator*
Diener, Erwin *immunologist*
Diener, Jennifer Flinton *health care services executive*
Diener, Royce *corporate director, retired health care services company executive*
Dierk, Hulda Johnson *women's health nurse*
Diffrient, Niels *industrial designer*
Di Giovanni, Anthony *retired coal mining company executive*
DiLiddo, Bart A. *chemical engineer, business executive, consultant*
Dill, Laddie John *artist*
Dille, Earl Kaye *utility company executive*
Dills, James Arlof *retired publishing company executive*
Dilworth, Ann Evans *publishing company executive*
Di Marco, Gabriel Robert *tobacco company executive*
Dinkel, John George *magazine editor*
†DiPalma, Carlo *cinematographer*
Dirks, Leslie Chant *communications and electronics company executive*
Dirksen, Richard Wayne *canon precentor, organist, choirmaster*
Dirvin, Gerald Vincent *retired consumer products company executive*
†Di Sabato, Louis Roman *zoo administrator*
Di Salvo, Arthur Francis *physician, public health official*
Disch, Thomas M(ichael) *author*
Dishman, Leland Lee *school system administrator*
Di Spigna, Tony *graphic designer*
Dixon, Ernest Thomas, Jr. *retired bishop*
Dixon, Louis Frederick *information sciences and telecommunications consulting executive*
Dobbel, Rodger Francis *interior designer*
Dobelis, George *manufacturing company executive*
Dobler, Donald William *retired college dean, consultant, corporate executive*
Dobriansky, Lev Eugene *economist, educator, diplomat*
Docker, John Thornley *religious organization administrator, minister*
Doderer, Minnette Frerichs *state legislator*
Dodson, Donald Mills *restaurant executive*
Dodson, Samuel Robinette, III *investment banker*
Dogançay, Burhan C. *artist, photographer, sculptor*
Doherty, Charles Vincent *investment counsel executive*
Dohrmann, Russell William *manufacturing company executive*
Doig, Ivan *writer*
Dolan, Edward Francis *writer*
Dolan, Peter Robert *marketing executive*
Doland, Judy Ann *administrative assistant, retired financial rating company associate*
Dole, Arthur Alexander *psychology educator*
Dole, Robert Paul *retired appliance manufacturing company executive*
Dolenz, Mickey (George Michael Dolenz) *singer, actor, television producer*
Dolin, Samuel Joseph *composer, educator*
Dolman, John Phillips (Tim), Jr. (Tim Dolman) *communications company executive*
Donahoo, Melvin Lawrence *aerospace management consultant, industrial engineer*
Donahue, Dennis Donald *foreign service officer*
Donahue, Elinor *actress*
Donath, Fred Arthur *geologist, geophysicist*
Donath, Therese *author, artist*
Donnelly, Joseph Lennon *utility company executive*
Donohue, George L. *government official, mechanical engineer*
Donovan, James Robert *business equipment company executive*
Donovan, Walter Edgar *retired mayor*
†Dooling, Richard Patrick *writer, lawyer*
Dore, Fred Hudson *retired state supreme court chief justice*
Dorman, Richard Frederick, Jr. *association executive, consultant*
Dorn, Dolores *actress*
Dorros, Irwin *retired telecommunications executive*
Dorsey, Frank James *grocery company executive*
Dorsey, Rhoda Mary *retired academic administrator*
Doskocil, Larry *food company executive*
Doty, James Robert *lawyer*
Doty, Philip Edward *accountant*
Doud, Wallace C. *retired information systems executive*
Douglas, Eileen *news broadcaster*
Douglas, Gordon Watkins *medical educator*
Douglas, James Holley *former state official*
Douglass, John Michael *internist*
Dowd, Clark Wayne *lawyer, state legislator*
Dowden, Albert Ricker *corporate executive, lawyer*
Dowie, Ian James *management consultant*
Downes, Rackstraw *artist*
Doyle, John Laurence *manufacturing company executive*
†Doyle, Tom *artist, educator*
Dozier, Glenn Joseph *medical, surgical products distribution executive*
Dozier, James Lee *former army officer*
†Dozier, O(llin) Kemp *tobacco wholesale company executive*
Drabble, Bernard James *Canadian government official*
Dragon, William, Jr. *footwear and apparel company executive*
Drake, Ervin Maurice *composer, author*
Drake, George Albert *college president, historian*
Drake, Rodman Leland *investment executive, consultant*
Draper, Line Bloom (Line B. Draper-Rubba) *artist*
Draznin, Jules Nathan *journalism and public relations educator, consultant*
Drennen, William Miller *federal judge*
Dressel, Barry *museum administrator*
Dressler, David Charles *retired aerospace company executive*
Drew, Elizabeth Heineman *publishing executive*
Drew, Walter Harlow *retired paper manufacturing company executive*
Drexler, Michael David *advertising agency executive*
Driscoll, William Michael *corporation executive*
Driskill, Clarence *publishing executive*
Driver, Lottie Elizabeth *librarian*
Drucker, Peter Ferdinand *writer, consultant, educator*
Drummond, Dorothy Weitz *geography education consultant, educator, author*
Drummond, Sally Hazelet *artist*
Dubuc, Carroll Edward *lawyer*
Dudick, Michael Joseph *bishop*
Duerr, Herman George *retired publishing executive*
Duff, John Bernard *college president, former city official*
Duffy, Martin Edward *management consultant, economist*
Dugan, Patrick Raymond *microbiologist, university dean*
Dukes, David Coleman *actor*
Dull, William Martin *engineering executive*
Dumont, Allan Eliot *physician, educator*
Duncan, Donald William *retired lawyer*
Duncan, Sandy *actress*
Dunford, David Joseph *foreign service officer, ambassador*
Dungan, Malcolm Thon *lawyer*
Dunham, Benjamin Starr *editor, arts administrator*
Dunlap, Richard Donovan *artistic director*
Dunn, Warren Howard *retired lawyer, brewery executive*
Dunne, Katherine Anne *lawyer*
Dunwiddie, Charlotte *sculptor*
Dunworth, John *retired college president*
Duppstadt, Marlyn Henry *financial executive*
Durant, John Ridgeway *physician*
Durante, Angela *university official, writer, educator*
Durden, Charles Dennis *former manufacturing company executive, consultant*
Durham, G. Robert *diversified manufacturing company executive*
Durning, Charles *actor*
Durr, Robert Joseph *construction firm executive, mechanical engineer*
Dutile, Fernand Neville *law educator*
Dutson, Thayne R. *university dean*
Duvall, Robert *actor*
Dyckman, Suzanne Barbara *secretary, administrative assistant*
Dye, Myrtice Willis *therapist, educator, children's advocate, researcher, consultant*
Dyer, Arlene Thelma *retail company owner*
Dyer, Geraldine Ann (Geri Dyer) *artist, poet*
Dyer, Ira *ocean engineering educator, consultant*
Dyer, Wayne Walter *psychologist, author, radio and television personality*
Dykhouse, David Jay *commissioner, lawyer*
Dyment, John Joseph *financial executive*
Dymond, Lewis Wandell *lawyer, mediator, educator*
Dysart, Richard A. *actor*
Dyson, Arthur Thomas *architect, educator*
Dziubla, Robert W. *lawyer*
Eagan, Sherman G. *producer, communications executive*
Eagle, Jack *commercial actor, comedian*
Eaglet, Robert Danton *electrical engineer, aerospace consultant, retired military officer*
Eagleton, William Lester, Jr. *foreign service officer*
Eaker, Ira *publishing executive*
Earle, Arthur Percival *textile executive*
Earle, Arthur Scott *retired plastic surgeon*
Earle, Steve *country rockabilly musician, songwriter*
East, Don Gaylord *computer engineer, archaeologist, writer*
Easterly, Joy Marie *health facility administrator*
Eastham, Alan Walter, Jr. *foreign service officer, lawyer*
Easton, Glenn Hanson, Jr. *management and insurance consultant, federal official, naval officer*
Easton, Michelle *foundation executive*
Eaton, Joe Oscar *federal judge*
Eaton, Merrill Thomas *psychiatrist, educator*
Eaton, William Charles *retired mechanical engineer*
Ebb, Fred *lyricist, librettist*
Ebbert, Arthur, Jr. *retired university dean*
Eberle, Charles Edward *paper and consumer products executive*
Eberly, Joseph Henry *physics educator, consultant*
Eckenhoff, James Edward *physician, educator*
†Ecton, Donna R. *business consultant*
Eddy, Don *artist*
Eddy, Esther Dewitz *retired pharmacist*
Edel, Abraham *philosophy educator*
Edgar, Thomas Flynn *chemical engineering educator*
Edmonds, Anne Carey *librarian*
Edmonds, Velma McInnis *nursing educator*
Edmunds, (Arthur) Lowell *philology educator*
Edmundson, Charles Wayne *mechanical engineer, communications executive*
Edwards, Charles *neuroscientist, educator*
Edwards, Geoffrey Hartley *newspaper publisher*
Edwards, Jerome *lawyer*
Edwards, Larry David *internist*
Edwards, Patrick Ross *former retail company executive, lawyer, management consultant*
Edwards, Ryan Hayes *baritone*
Egan, Wesley William, Jr. *ambassador*
Egelston, Roberta Riethmiller *writer*
Eglee, Charles Hamilton *television and movie writer, producer*
Ehrlich, Amy *editor, writer*
Ehrling, Sixten *orchestra conductor*
Eicher, George John *aquatic biologist*
Eischen, Michael Hugh *retired railroad executive*
Eisen, Henry *retired pharmacy educator*
Eisenberg, Morris *electronics industry executive*
Eisenhower, John Sheldon Doud *former ambassador, author*
Eitel, Dolores J. *healthcare consultant*
Ekstract, Richard Evan *publishing executive*
†Elam, Fred Eldon *career army officer*
Elder, Mark Philip *conductor*
Elders, (Minnie) Joycelyn *public health administrator, endocrinologist*
Elgart, Larry Joseph *orchestra leader*
Elikann, Lawrence S. (Larry Elikann) *television and film director*
Eliot, Theodore Lyman, Jr. *international consultant*
Elizondo, Hector *actor*
Elkind, Mort William *creative and business consultant*
Ellenberger, Jack Stuart *law librarian*
Ellerbe, Suellyn *health facility administrator*
Elliot, Jared *financial management consultant*
Elliott, David H. *insurance executive*
Elliott, David LeRoy *mathematician, educator, engineering educator*
Elliott, Lois Lawrence *audiology and otolaryngology educator*
Ellis, Anne Elizabeth *fundraiser*
Ellis, Emory Nelson, Jr. *retired lawyer*
Ellis, Harold Bernard *civil engineer*
Ellis, Howard Woodrow *evangelist, creative agent, clergyman, artist, author*
Ellis, Steven George *public relations and international political consultant*
Ellison, Eugene Curtis *radio station executive*
Ellner, Paul Daniel *clinical microbiologist*
Ellsworth, Robert F. *manufacturing executive*
Ellwanger, Mike (Cyril Albert Ellwanger) *retired utility executive*
†Else, Carolyn Joan *library system administrator*
Elsner, Sidney Edgar *journalist*
Elverum, Gerard William, Jr. *retired electronic and diversified company executive*
Ely, Joe *singer and songwriter*
Ely, Marica McCann *interior designer*
Ely, Paul C., Jr. *electronics company executive*
Embry, Carmen Dianne Wheeler *psychologist*
Embry, Wayne Richard *basketball executive*
Emerling, Carol G(reenbaum) *consumer products company executive*
Emerson, Ann Parker *dietitian, educator*
Emerson, Daniel Everett *retired communications company executive, executive advisor*
Emerson, R. Clark *priest, business administrator*
Emery, Sherman Raymond *editorial consultant*
†Emmons, Beverly *lighting designer*
Emmons, Robert Duncan *diplomat*
End, Henry *interior and industrial designer*
Engler, John *governor*
English, Bruce Vaughan *museum director and executive, environmental consultant*
English, Richard D. *lawyer, diplomat, government official*
Erb, James J. *lawyer*
Erb, Richard Louis Lundin *resort and hotel executive*
Erdeljac, Daniel Joseph *manufacturing company executive*
Erden, Sybil Isolde *artist*
Erickson, Alan Eric *librarian*
Ericson, Rolf Eric George *manufacturing company executive*
Erlenborn, John Neal *lawyer, educator, former congressman*
Erlenmeyer-Kimling, L. *psychiatric and behavior genetics researcher, educator*
Erlicht, Lewis Howard *broadcasting company executive*
Ernstthal, Henry L. *management educator*
Ersoz, Clara Jean *healthcare consultant, physician*
Erwin, Elmer Louis *vintager, cement consultant*
Erwin, Judith Ann (Judith Ann Peacock) *writer, photographer, lawyer*
Eschenbrenner, Gunther Paul *engineering consultant*
Esposito, Philip Anthony (Phil Esposito) *professional sports team executive, former hockey broadcaster, former professional hockey player*
Estés, Clarissa Pinkola *psychoanalyst, poet, writer*
Estes, Jack Charles *oil service company executive, scientist*
Estrin, Herbert Alvin *financial consultant, entertainment company executive*
Esty, John Cushing, Jr. *writer, lecturer, advisor*
Etheridge, Melissa Lou *singer, songwriter*
†Etzel, Ruth Ann *pediatrician, epidemiologist*
Eugster, Albrecht Konrad *veterinarian, laboratory director*
Evanoff, George C. *biotechnology company executive*
Evans, Geraldine Ann *academic administrator*
Evans, Marsha Johnson *naval officer*
Evans, Victor Miles *retired funeral home/cemetery company executive*
Evdokimova, Eva *prima ballerina assoluta, choreographer, director, producer*
Everdell, William *lawyer*
Everett, Donna Raney *business educator*
Everhart, Rex *actor, director, photographer*
Evstatieva, Stefka *opera singer*
Ewell, Miranda Juan *journalist*
Ewen, H.I. *physicist*
Ewing, Raymond Charles *retired ambassador*
Ewing, Wayne Turner *coal company executive*
Fabares, Shelley *actress*
Fabrick, Howard David *lawyer*
Factor, Mallory *public relations firm executive*
Fadiman, Louise *writer, consultant*
Fagerberg, Dixon, Jr. *retired accountant, weather observer*
Fahey, Joseph Francis, Jr. *banker, financial consultant*
†Fahlbeck, Douglas Alan *finance company executive*
Fahringer, Catherine Hewson *retired savings and loan executive*
Fairburn, Sandra Jean *nursing administrator*
Fajardo, Katharine Lynn *public relations and marketing executive*
Falbe, Maryann Christine *nursing administrator*
Falsey, John Henry, Jr. *television producer*
Faltings, Gerd *mathematician, educator*

Fang, Joseph Pe Yong chemistry educator
Fanwick, Ernest corporate lawyer
Farah, Joseph Francis newspaper editor, writer
Farinella, Paul James retired cultural institution executive
Fariss, Bruce Lindsay endocrinologist, educator
Farley, Lloyd Edward retired education educator
Farmakides, John Basil lawyer
Farquhar, Robin Hugh university president
Farrington, Bertha Louise nursing administrator
Farris, Robert Earl transportation consultant
Farrow, Mia Villiers actress
Fassio, Virgil newspaper publishing company executive
Faust, John Joseph, Jr. theatre educator, director
Fawcett, Farrah Leni actress, model
Fay, Conner Martindale management consultant
Fazio, Evelyn M. publisher
Feerick, John David university dean, lawyer
Fehr, Lola Mae nursing association director
Feiffer, Jules cartoonist, writer, playwright
Fein, Seymour Howard pharmaceutical executive
Feinberg, Herbert apparel and beverage executive
Feirstein, Frederick poet, playwright, psychoanalyst
Feld, Carole Leslie marketing executive
Feldman, Thomas Myron director, lighting director, director of photography, film company executive
Feldstein, Joshua academic administrator
Felix, Richard James engineering executive, consultant
Fell, James Michael Gardner mathematics educator, researcher
Feller, Robert William Andrew baseball team public relations executive, retired baseball player
Fenello, Michael John aviation consultant, retired government agency executive
Fenger, Manfred retired manufacturing executive
Fenichel, Norman Stewart public relations and advertising agency executive
Fenoglio-Preiser, Cecilia Mettler pathologist, educator
Ferguson, Glenn Walker educational consultant, lecturer
Ferguson, Maynard trumpeter, band leader
Ferguson, Robert financial services executive, writer
Ferguson, William Emmett retired securities broker
Ferlinz, Jack cardiologist, medical educator
Fernald, Anne educator
Ferrara, Diane S. critical care nurse
Ferraro, Geraldine Anne lawyer, former congresswoman
Ferre, Antonio Luis newspaper publisher
Ferris, Michael J(ames) chemical company executive
Feshbach, Norma Deitch psychologist, educator
Fetler, Andrew author, educator
Fetterly, Lynn Lawrence real estate broker/developer
Feurig, Thomas Leo health care executive
Fibiger, John Andrew life insurance company executive
Field, Arthur Norman lawyer
Field, Charles William metallurgical engineer, small business owner, consultant
Field, George Sydney retired research director
Field, Sally actress
Fielding, Harold Preston bank executive
Fields, Freddie producer, agent
Fields, Leo former jewelry company executive, investor
Fields, William Hudson, III magazine publisher
Fife, Jonathan Donald higher education educator
Fife, William J., Jr. metal products executive
Filchock, Ethel education educator, poet
Filerman, Michael Herman television producer
Finder, Theodore Roosevelt retired lawyer
Fine, Jane Madeline visual artist
Finger, Harold B. energy, space, nuclear energy and urban affairs consultant
Fink, John Francis newspaper editor
Finkel, David medical products executive
Finkelstein, Seymour business consultant
Finnegan, Sara Anne publisher
Finney, Robert G. electronics company executive
Finucane, Richard Daniel corporate medical director, retired food products executive
Fiorito, Edward Gerald lawyer
Fippinger, Grace J. retired telecommunications company executive
Firestone, Evan Richard art educator, academic administrator
Fischer, Eugene H. air force officer
Fischmar, Richard Mayer company financial executive, consultant
Fish, Janet Isobel artist
Fish, Lawrence Kingsbaker banker
Fisher, Linda Alice physician
Fishman, Bernard mechanical engineer
Fitch, Robert McLellan business and technology consultant
Fitch, Steven Joseph retired chemicals executive
Fitting-Gifford, Marjorie Ann mathematician, educator, consultant
Fitzgeorge, Harold James former oil and gas company executive
Fitzgerald, Edward Earl publishing executive, author
Fitzgerald, Geraldine actress
Fitzmaurice, Laurence Dorset banking executive
Fitzpatrick, Sean Kevin advertising agency executive
Fix, John Neilson banker
Flanders, Scott Nelson publishing company executive, lawyer, accountant
Flannery, Thomas Aquinas federal judge
Flaschen, Steward Samuel high technology company executive
Flavin, Dan artist
Fleischer, Gerald Albert industrial engineer, educator
Fleisher, David L. business communications and market research services executive
Fleming, Charles Clifford, Jr. retired airline and jet aircraft sales company executive
Fletcher, Kim savings and loan executive
Fletcher, Louise actress
Flick, John Edmond lawyer
Flinner, Beatrice Eileen library and media sciences educator
Flipse, John Edward naval architect, mechanical engineer
Flitcraft, Richard Kirby, II former chemical company executive
Florence, Paul Smith agronomist, business owner
Florescue, Barry William business executive
†Flory, Shirlene church officer
Foley, Daniel Edmund real estate development executive
Folkens, Alan Theodore clinical and pharmaceutical microbiologist
Folkman, David H. apparel wholesale executive
Fong, Wen Chih art historian, educator, author
Foote, Evelyn Patricia retired army officer, consultant
Ford, Ashley Lloyd lawyer, retired consumer products company executive
Ford, Cynthia Ann advertising executive
Ford, Ford Barney retired government official
Ford, Harrison actor
Ford, Jerry Lee products company executive
Ford, Judith Ann retired natural gas distribution company executive
Ford, Kenneth William physicist
Ford, Nancy Louise composer, scriptwriter
Ford, Wendell Hampton senator
Ford, William Francis retired bank holding company executive
Forester, Jean Martha Brouillette innkeeper, retired librarian and educator
Forester, Russell artist
Forman, Miloš film director
Forster, Ann Dorothy publicist
Forsythe, Henderson actor
Forsythe, John actor
Fort, Randall Martin corporate executive, former federal official
Forte, Craig Anthony amusement park, motion picture location executive
Fortier, D'Iberville communications consultant
Fortinberry, Glen W. advertising executive
Foss, Lukas composer, conductor, pianist
Fossier, Mike Walter consultant, retired electronics company executive
Foster, Charles Henry Wheelwright former foundation officer, consultant,author
Foster, Edson L. retired mining and manufacturing company executive, consultant
Foster, Frances actress
†Foster, Norman Holland geologist
Foster, Paul David, Jr. agribusiness executive
Foster, Robert Lawson retired judge, deacon
Foster, Stephen Kent banker
Fountain, Cornelia Wilkes special education educator
Fowler, Donald Raymond retired lawyer, educator
Fowler, John M. insurance and brokerage company executive
Fowler, Raymond David financial executive
Fowlie, Eldon Leslie retired library administrator
Fox, Edward A. retired college dean
Fox, Gerald Lynn retired oral and maxillofacial surgeon
Fox, Michael Wilson veterinarian, animal behaviorist
Foy, Charles Daley retired soil scientist
†Frailey, Stephen A. photographer
Frame, Russell William retired electronics executive
Franciosa, Anthony (Anthony Papaleo) actor
Frank, Edgar Gerald retired financial executive
Frank, Sanders Thalheimer physician, educator
Frankel, Glenn journalist
Frankenberger, Bertram, Jr. investor, consultant
Frankfurt, Stephen O. advertising agency executive
Frankish, Brian Edward film producer, director
Franklin, Barbara Kipp financial planner, investment adviser
Franklin, Jerry Forest ecologist
Franklin, Joe Hope historian, educator, author
Franklin, Kenneth L(inn) astronomer
Franklin, Margaret Lavona Barnum (Mrs. C. Benjamin Franklin) civic leader
Franklin, Michael Harold arbitrator, lawyer, consultant
Frasca, Joanne M. lawyer
Fraser, Donald C. engineering executive, educator
Fraser, Donald MacKay former mayor, former congressman
Fraser, Kathleen Joy poet, creative writing educator
Frauenfelder, Hans physicist, educator
Frawley, Patrick Joseph, Jr. health care executive
Freberg, Stan(ley) (Victor Freberg) satirist
Fredricks, Richard baritone
Fredrickson, Donald Sharp physician, scientist
Freedman, Russell Bruce author
Freeman, Arthur veterinarian, retired association administrator
Freeman, Graydon LaVerne retired publishing company executive
Freeman, Meredith Norwin former college president, education educator
Freeman, Ralph Carter management consultant
Freestone, Thomas Lawrence county government official
Frega, Patrick R. lawyer
Freilicher, Jane artist
Freitag, Harlow retired computer scientist and corporate executive
Freitag, Peter Roy transportation specialist
Freitas, Beatrice B(otty) musician, educator
French, Clarence Levi, Jr. retired shipbuilding company executive
French, Glendon Everett, Jr. health care executive
Frenkiel, Richard Henry systems engineer consultant
Freston, Thomas E. cable television programming executive
Freter, Mark Allen marketing and public relations executive, consultant
Frick, Ivan Eugene college president emeritus
Fried, Walter Rudolf engineer, aerospace scientist
Frieder, Gideon computer science and engineering educator
†Friedkin, Dawn Michele government official
†Friedlander, Charles Douglas investment company executive, space consultant
Friedman, Donald Joseph stock brokerage executive
Friedman, Emma Fleischman editor, publisher
Friedman, Eugene Warren surgeon
Friedman, Martin retired art center director
Friedman, Mildred designer, educator, curator
Frieling, Gerald Harvey, Jr. specialty steel company executive
Frierson, Jimmie Lou vocational education educator
Frisch, Robert Emile lawyer
Frith, Royce Herbert Canadian federal official, former Canadian senator, retired lawyer
Fritz, Rene Eugene, Jr. manufacturing executive
Froehlke, Robert Frederick financial services executive
Frost, Anne real estate broker, author, publisher
Frost, Sir David (Paradine) author, producer, columnist
†Frost, Everett Lloyd academic administrator
Frost, J. Ormond otolaryngologist, educator
Fry, Doris Hendricks museum curator
Fryer, Thomas Waitt, Jr. writer and editor
Fuenning, Esther Renate adult education educator
Fuentes, Carlos writer, former ambassador
†Fuerstner, Fiona Margaret Ann ballet company executive, ballet educator
Fugh, John Liu military officer, lawyer
Fuld, Richard Severin, Jr. investment banker
Fuller, James Chester Eedy retired chemical company executive
Fuller, Nancy MacMurray mathematics educator, tutor
Fuller, Robert Ferrey lawyer, investor
Fuller, Stephen Herbert business administration educator
Fulton, James Franklin industrial designer
Furley, David John classics educator
Furlong, Robert Joseph television station executive
Furman, Harry Sutton lumber distribution company executive
Gable, Carol Brignoli pharmacoeconomics researcher
Gable, Karen Elaine health occupations educator
Gaffney, Thomas banker
Gagnon, Edith Morrison ballerina, singer, actress
Gainey, Robert Michael professional hockey coach, former player
Gajdusek, Daniel Carleton pediatrician, research virologist
Galas, David John molecular biology educator, researcher
Galbraith, John Semple history educator
Galfo, Armand James statistics educator
Gallegly, Elton William congressman
Galloway, William Joyce physicist, consultant
Gamble, E. James lawyer, accountant
†Gamble, Roger R. ambassador
Gammon, Samuel Rhea, III association executive, former ambassador
Gandy, Charles David interior designer
Gannon, James Patrick newspaper editor
Gantz, Carroll Melvin industrial design consultant, consumer product designer
Ganz, Lowell screenwriter, television producer
Garcia, Alexander orthopaedic surgeon
Garcia, Edward J. federal judge
Garcia, Jerry (Jerome John Garcia) guitarist, composer
Garcia-Granados, Sergio Eduardo brokerage house executive
Gardner, James Albert investment and real estate executive
Gardner, Warner Winslow lawyer
Gardner, Wilford Robert physicist, educator
Gardner, William Michael library administrator
Garfield, Brian Wynne author
Garfield, Robert Edward newspaper columnist
Garfunkel, Art singer, actor
†Garner, Darlene C. church officer
Garner, James (James Scott Bumgarner) actor
Garrard, Don Edward Burdett operatic and concert singer
Garrett, Shirley Gene nuclear medicine technologist
Garrison, Susan Elodie hospital administrator
Garrison-Jackson, Zina tennis player
Garrity, Wendell Arthur, Jr. federal judge
Garson, Greer actress
Garten, Wayne Philip financial executive
Gartenberg, Seymour Lee retired recording company executive
Garvey, Evelyn Jewel mental health nurse
Gaspar, Anna Louise retired elementary school teacher, consultant
Gasper, Jo Ann association executive
Gates, Larry actor
Gatlin, Larry Wayne singer, songwriter
Gavin, Herbert James consultant, retired air force officer
Gay, William Ingalls veterinarian, health science administrator
Geddes, Jane professional golfer
Geddes, Robert architect, educator
Geer, Stephen DuBois retired journalist
Gehm, Denise Charlene ballerina, arts administrator
Geiselhart, Lorene Annetta English educator
Geissinger, Frederick Wallace investment banker
Geitgey, Doris Arlene retired nursing educator, dean
Gelfand, Marshall M. accountant
Geller, Seymour retired educator, researcher
Gelles, Harry P. investment banker, land investor
Gelman, Larry actor
Gemignani, Michael Caesar clergyman, retired educator
Gendell, Gerald Stanleigh retired public affairs executive
Gennaro, Antonio L. biology educator
Gens, Ralph Samuel electrical engineering consultant
Gensler, M. Arthur, Jr. architect
Gentry, Francis G. German language educator
Genung, R. K. physical sciences research administrator
Geoffroy, Charles Henry retired travel company executive
Geoghegan, John Joseph retired publisher
Geoppinger, William Anthony meat processing company executive
Georgas, John William beverage manufacturing company executive
George, Joyce Jackson lawyer, former judge
George, William Ickes manufacturing company executive
Gerald, Michael Charles pharmacy educator, college dean
Gerard, Jean Broward Shevlin former ambassador, lawyer
Gerhardt, Jon Stuart mechanical engineer, engineering educator
Germany, Daniel Monroe aerospace engineer
Gerner, Randolph Henry architect
Gers, Seymour psychiatrist
Gershel, Seth David sales executive
Gerstein, Esther sculptor
Gertenbach, Robert Frederick medical research organization executive, accountant, lawyer
Gervais, Marcel Andre bishop
Getting, Ivan Alexander physicist, former aerospace company executive
Gewecke, Thomas H. foreign service officer
Giacomini, Giuseppe tenor
Giardina, Paul Anthony environmental nuclear engineer, thoroughbred horse investment specialist
Gilb, Corinne Lathrop history educator
Gilb, Dagoberto writer, carpenter
†Gilbert, Frederick E. international development planner, consultant
Gilbert, Gayle nursing administrator
Gilbert, Kenneth Albert harpsichordist
Gilbert, Nancy Louise librarian
Gilbertz, Larry E. state legislator, entrepreneur
Gilchrest, Thornton Charles retired association executive
Gilchrist, Ellen Louise writer
Gilchrist, James Beardslee banker
Gilder, George Franklin writer
Giles, Walter Edmund alcohol and drug treatment executive
Gilford, Leon business executive and consultant
†Gilgore, Sheldon Gerald pharmaceutical products company executive
Gilinsky, Victor physicist
Gill, Henry Herr photojournalist
Gill, William Robert soil scientist
Gillam, Max Lee lawyer
Gillespie, Gerald Ernest Paul comparative literature educator, writer
Gillespie, Gwain Homer financial executive
Gillespie, Nellie Redd academic administrator, state official
Gillespie, Robert James manufacturing company executive
Gillett, George Nield, Jr. communications executive
Gillette, Stanley C. apparel manufacturing company executive
Gilliam, Terry Vance film director, actor, illustrator, writer
Gilreath, Warren Dean retired packaging company executive
Gilroy, Frank Daniel playwright
Gilson, Barbara Frances editor
Ginsburg, Iona Horowitz psychiatrist
Giordano, Richard Vincent chemicals executive
Giordano, Tony Eugene director
Girouard, Shirley Ann nurse, policy analyst
Girzone, Joseph F. retired priest, writer
Giusti, Robert George artist, educator
Giusti, William Roger lawyer
Givens, Robin actress
Gladding, Carolyn Anne nursing administrator
Gladstone, Carol Lynn assistant principal
Glasberg, Laurence Brian private investor, business executive
Glaser, Robert Leonard retired television executive
Glashow, Sheldon Lee physicist, educator
Glass, Kenneth Edward management consultant
Glassman, Jon David diplomat
†Glassman, Stanley Alan health care management consultant
Glassock, Richard James nephrologist
Gleaton, Harriet E. retired anesthesiologist
Gleijeses, Mario holding company executive
Glennon, Harrison Randolph, Jr. retired shipping company executive
Glick, J. Leslie biotechnology entrepreneur
Glick, Ruth Burtnick author, lecturer
Glover, Crispin Hellion actor
Glover, William Harper theater critic
Glower, Donald Duane university executive, mechanical engineer
Glück, Louise Elisabeth poet
Gluys, Charles Byron retired marketing management consultant
Glynn, Carlin (Carlin Masterson) actress
Gobel, John Henry lawyer
Goble, Paul author, illustrator, artist
Godino, Rino Lodovico retired petroleum and chemical company exective
Goebert, Robert J. banking executive
Goetzel, Claus Guenter metallurgical engineer
Goewey, Gordon Ira university administrator
Goffe, Esther elementary school educator
Goffe, William Arthur federal judge
Goforth, William Clements lawyer
Gogarty, William Barney oil company executive, consultant
Goin, Olive Bown biologist
Golann, Cecil P. writer, editor, researcher
†Goldberg, Danny recording industry executive
Goldberg, Samuel retired mathematician, foundation officer
Goldberg, Victor Joel retired data processing company executive
Goldberg, Whoopi (Caryn Johnson) actress
Goldberger, Arthur Earl, Jr. industrial engineer, consultant
Goldberger, Blanche Rubin sculptor, jeweler
†Goldblatt, Mark Lawrence film director
Goldblum, Jeff actor
Goldfine, Howard microbiology and biochemistry educator, researcher
Goldin, Marion Freedman television news producer, reporter
Goldman, Alan Ira investment banking executive
Goldman, Alfred Emanuel marketing research consultant
Goldman, Charles Remington environmental scientist, educator
Goldman, Gerald Hillis beverage distribution company executive
Goldner, Sheldon Herbert export-import company executive
Goldovsky, Boris musician
Goldsmith, Arthur Austin magazine editor
Goldsmith, Robert Holloway manufacturing company executive
Goldstein, Mark lawyer
Goldstein, Walter Elliott biotechnology executive
Goldston, Stephen Eugene community psychologist, educator, consultant
Goldwater, John Leonard publisher, writer
†Golightly, Cecelia King healthcare administrator, nurse
Gonsalves, Robert Arthur electrical engineering educator, consultant
†Gonzalez, William G. hospital administrator, educator
Good, Barry C. financial analyst
Good, Daniel James manufacturing executive
Good, Linda Lou elementary education educator
Good, Walter Raymond investment executive
Goode, Janet Weiss elementary school educator
Goode, Stephen Hogue publishing company executive
Goodkin, Michael Jon publishing company executive
Goodman, Erika dancer, actress
Goodwill, Margaret Jane artist
Goodwin, Barbara A. retired nurse, military officer
Gorchov, Ron artist
Gordan, Gilbert Saul physician, educator
Gordis, David Moses academic administrator, rabbi
Gordly, Avel Louise state legislator, community activist
Gordon, Bonnie Heather writer, editor
Gordon, Cyrus Herzl Orientalist, educator
Gordon, Janine M. advertising agency executive
Gordon, Richard Joseph gas distribution company executive
Gore, Sadie Lou elementary education educator, retired
Gorme, Eydie singer
Goss, Porter J. congressman
Gossett, Louis, Jr. actor
†Gostin, Judson Jacob electronics company executive
Gottlieb, Alan Merril advertising, fundraising and broadcasting executive, writer
Gottlieb, Sherry Gershon author, editor

Gould, Martha Bernice *retired librarian*
Gould, Morton *composer, conductor*
Goulet, Lorrie *sculptor*
Gounaris, Anne Demetra *biochemistry educator, researcher*
Govan, Gladys Vernita Mosley *retired critical care and medical/surgical nurse*
†Govier, George Wheeler *petroleum engineer*
Goyan, Michael Donovan *stockbroker, investment executive*
Grabemann, Karl W. *lawyer*
Grace, Marcia Bell *advertising executive*
Graebner, James Herbert *transportation executive*
Graf, Steffi *professional tennis player*
Graff, William *architect*
Grafton, Sue *novelist*
Graham, James Herbert *dermatologist*
Graham, John Darlington *financial company executive*
Grandi, Attilio *engineering consultant*
Grandy, James Frederick *retired electronics business executive, consultant*
Grant, Albert *internist*
Grant, Alexander Marshall *ballet director*
Grant, Frederick Anthony *investment banker*
Grant, Jacquelyn *minister, religion educator*
Grant, James Colin *banker*
Grant, James Francis *international business and defense consultant, retired air force officer*
Grant, Lee (Lyova Haskell Rosenthal) *actress, director*
Grant, Richard Earl *nursing administrator*
†Grant, William A., Jr. *accounting firm executive*
Granuzzo, Andrew Aloysius *career officer*
Grauman, Robert A. *healthcare executive*
Gray, David Lawrence *retired air force officer*
Gray, Donna Mae *former agricultural products executive, bookkeeper*
Gray, Francine du Plessix *author*
Gray, Harry Joshua *electrical engineer, educator*
Gray, James Peyton *computer scientist*
Gray, John Lathrop, III *retired advertising agency executive*
Gray, Patricia Ellen *psychologist*
Gray, Richard Alexander, Jr. *retired chemical company executive*
Greaves, James Louis *art conservator*
Greaves, William Garfield *film director, producer*
Greco, Joseph M *parochial school educator*
Greeley, Andrew Moran *sociologist, author*
Greeley, Gale Elizabeth *psychiatrist*
Green, Barbara Strawn *psychotherapist*
Green, David Thomas *retired surgical company research and development executive, inventor*
Green, Flora Hungerford *lactation consultant, nurse*
Green, George *radio executive*
Green, Joseph Martin *psychiatrist, educator*
Green, Mark Joseph *lawyer, author*
Green, Nancy Loughridge *higher education executive*
Green, Oliver Francis, Jr. *lawyer*
Green, Richard Calvin, Jr. *utility company executive*
Greenbaum, Lowell Marvin *pharmacologist, educator*
Greenberg, Albert *art director*
Greenberg, Arnold Elihu *water quality specialist*
Greenberg, Benjamin *physician*
Greenberg, Milton *corporation executive*
Greenblatt, Sherwin *manufacturing company executive*
Greenburg, Dan *author*
Greene, Elinore Aschah *speech and drama professional, writer*
Greene, Frank Sullivan, Jr. *investment management executive*
Greene, Laurence Whitridge, Jr. *surgical educator*
Greene, Lynne Jeannette *fashion designer*
Greenfield, Helen Meyers *inspection and testing service executive, publishing company executive, real estate executive*
Greenwald, Gerald *air transportation executive*
Greenway, John Selmes *hotel owner*
Greenwood, Frank *information scientist*
Greer, Carl Crawford *petroleum company executive*
Greer, Germaine *author*
Gregg, Michael W. *manufacturing executive*
Gregor, Dorothy Deborah *librarian*
Gregory, Eleanor Anne *artist, educator*
Gregory, Myra May *religious organization administrator, educator*
Grewe, John Mitchell *orthodontist, educator*
Griffin, Campbell Arthur, Jr. *lawyer*
Griffin, James Anthony *bishop*
Griffin, Robert Paul *former state supreme court justice*
Griffin, Suzanne Marie *medical/surgical nurse*
Griffith, Clark Calvin, II *lawyer*
Griffith, Daniel Boyd *automotive products executive*
Griffith, Melanie *actress*
Grill, Laurence Kay *molecular biologist*
Grimshaw, Paul *producer*
Grody, Donald *judge, lawyer, arbitrator, actor*
Groening, Matthew *writer, cartoonist*
Grogan, Kevin *museum director*
Grolli, Frank Thomas *pharmacist*
Gromen, Richard John *historian, educator*
Groome, Reginald Kehnroth *hotel executive*
Grooms, Red *artist*
Grosbard, Ulu *director*
Gross, Paul Randolph *biologist, academic administrator*
Gross, Ruth Taubenhaus *physician*
Gross, Terry R. *radio producer, host*
Grove, Kalvin M(yron) *lawyer*
Gruber, Fredric Francis *financial planning and investment research executive*
Gruber, Sharon Doris *former secondary educator*
Gruber, Thomas A. *marketing executive*
Grubiak, James Frank *chewing gum executive*
Grueskin, William Steven *editor*
Grund, Walter James, Jr. *retired gynecologist*
Gschwind, Donald *management and engineering consultant*
Gudenberg, Harry Richard *arbitrator, mediator*
Guild, Nelson Prescott *retired state education official*
Guillemette, Gloria Vivian *small business owner, dressmaker, designer*
Guimond, John Patrick *retired financial consultant*
Guinness, Sir Alec *actor*
Gulcher, Robert Harry *aircraft company executive*
Gullatt, Jane *state legislator*
†Gully, John Houston *research electrical engineer, engineering director*
Gummel, Hermann Karl *retired physicist, laboratory administrator*
Gummere, John *insurance company executive*
Gumpert, Gustav *public relations executive*
Gumppert, Karella Ann *federal government official*
Gund, Gordon *professional athletic teams executive*
Gundelfinger, Ralph Mellow *retired insurance company executive*
Gundersen, Wayne Campbell *management consultant, oil and gas consultant*
Gunderson, Ted Lee *security consultant*
Gunn, George R., Jr. *advertising executive*
Gunn, Michael William *airline executive*
Gunnels, Lawrence *lawyer*
Gurke, Sharon McCue *naval officer*
Gurney, Daniel Sexton *race car manufacturing company executive, racing team executive*
Gurney, James Marshall *artist, writer*
Gurwitch, Arnold Andrew *communications executive*
Gurwitz-Hall, Barbara Ann *artist*
Guthrie, Diana Fern *nursing educator*
Guthrie, Edgar King *artist*
Guthrie, Janet *professional race car driver*
Guthrie, Robert Val *psychologist*
Guthrie, Wallace Nessler, Jr. *naval officer*
†Gutierrez, Gerald Andrew *theatrical director*
Gutierrez, Lino *diplomat*
Gutsch, William Anthony, Jr. *astronomer*
Guttentag, Joseph Harris *lawyer, educator*
Guttman, Irving Allen *opera stage director*
Haas, Carolyn Buhai *publisher, writer, consultant*
Haas, Charlie *screenwriter*
Haber, Warren H. *investment company executive*
Hackel-Sims, Stella Bloomberg *lawyer, former government official*
Hackett, Robert John *lawyer*
†Hadden, Earl French *consultant, information technology*
Haddock, Harold, Jr. *retired accounting firm executive*
Haegele, John Ernest *business executive*
Haeger, Phyllis Marianna *retired association management company executive*
Haering, Rudolph Roland *retired physics educator, researcher*
Hafner, Thomas Mark *lawyer*
Haft, Gail K. *pediatrician*
Hagel, Raymond Charles *publishing company executive, educator*
Hager, Robert Worth *retired aerospace company executive*
Hahn, Helene B. *motion picture company executive*
Hahn, Mary Downing *author*
Hair, Danny G. *retail company executive*
Hairston, John Thomas, Jr. *food retail executive*
Hairston, William *author, playwright*
Halaby, Samia Asaad *artist, educator, computer artist*
Halberstam, Heini *mathematician*
Haley, George Brock, Jr. *lawyer*
Half, Robert *personnel recruiting executive, author*
Halfen, David *publishing executive*
Hall, Adrienne Ann *international marketing executive*
Hall, Anthony Robert *pharmaceuticals and consumer products company executive*
Hall, Conrad L. *cinematographer*
Hall, Donald *poet*
Hall, Jack Gilbert *lawyer, business executive*
Hall, James Stanley *jazz guitarist, composer*
Hall, Janice *soprano*
Hall, Jay *social psychologist*
Hall, John Hopkins *retired lawyer*
Hall, John Marshall *food industry consultant*
Hall, Milton Reese *retired oil company executive*
Hall, Monty *television producer, actor*
Hall, Terry Lee *accountant*
Hall, Thomas Forrest *naval officer*
Halleck, Charles White *lawyer, former judge*
Hallett, William Jared *nuclear engineer*
Halliday, William Ross *retired physician, speleologist, writer*
Halpin, Daniel William *civil engineering educator, consultant*
Halsey, James Albert *international entertainment impressario, theatrical producer, talent manager*
Hambidge, Douglas Walter *archbishop*
Hamblen, John Wesley *computer scientist, genealogist*
Hamill, Dorothy Stuart *professional ice skater*
Hamill, (William) Pete *newspaper columnist, author*
Hamilton, Allan Corning *retired oil company executive*
†Hamilton, Ann Katherine *artist*
Hamilton, Calvin Sargent *planning consultant, retired city official*
Hamilton, Donald Reed *foreign service officer*
Hamilton, Lyman Critchfield, Jr. *telecommunications industry executive*
Hamilton, Mary Lucia Kerr *retired banker, lawyer*
Hamilton, Thomas Michael *marketing executive*
Hamilton, William Frank *management educator*
Hamilton, William Howard *laboratory executive*
Hamlin, Dan William *accountant, management consultant*
Hamlin, Sonya B. *communications specialist*
Hamlisch, Marvin *composer*
Hammam, M. Shawky *electrical engineer, educator*
Hammer, Joyce Mae *gifted and talented education educator*
Hammerschmidt, John Paul *retired congressman, lumber company executive*
Hammond, Robert Lee *retired feed company executive*
Hamner, Earl Henry, Jr. *television producer, television and film writer*
Hampton, Lionel Leo *composer, conductor, entertainer*
Hancock, John Coulter *telecommunications company executive*
Handler, Harold Robert *lawyer*
Handy, Edward Otis, Jr. *financial services executive*
Handy, William Talbot, Jr. *bishop*
Hanes, John T. *food products executive*
Hanford, George Hyde *retired educational administrator*
Hankins, Mary Denman *elementary school educator*
Hanks, Robert Jack *writer, consultant, former naval officer*
Hanley, Charles *psychology educator*
Hanmer, Stephen Read, Jr. *government executive*
Hannay, N(orman) Bruce *chemist, industrial research and business consultant*
Hanners, David *journalist*
Hannigan, Maurice J. *protective services official*
Hansell, John Royer *retired physician*
Hansen, James Vear *congressman*
Hansen, Shirley Jean *energy consulting executive, professional association administrator*
Hanson, Carl Malmrose *financial company executive*
Hanson, Jo *artist*
Hanson, William Cook *judge*
Hanzlik, Rayburn DeMara *lawyer*
Harari, Hananiah *artist*
Harbison, Earle Harrison, Jr. *chemical company executive*
Harbutt, Charles *photographer*
Harden, Patrick Alan *journalist, news executive*
Harder, Robert Clarence *state official*
Hardesty, Christopher Scott *oil and mining company executive*
Hardin, Clifford Morris *retired university chancellor, cabinet member*
Hardin, Paul, III *university chancellor*
Harding, John Thomas *journalist*
†Hardwicke, Catherine Helen *motion picture production designer*
Hardy, Clarence Earl, Jr. *human resources executive*
Hardy, Gyme Dufault *social worker*
Hare, Frederick Kenneth *geography and environmental educator, university official*
Hargreaves, George Julian *landscape architect*
Harnack, Don Steger *lawyer*
Harper, Henry H. *military officer, retired*
Harper, W(alter) Joseph *financial consultant*
Harrell, Henry Howze *tobacco company executive*
Harrigan, Anthony Hart *author*
Harriman, Constance Bastine *federal official*
Harriman, John Howland *lawyer*
Harrington, Jean Patrice *former college president*
Harris, D. George *entrepreneur*
Harris, David Philip *real estate developer*
Harris, Elliott Stanley *toxicologist*
Harris, Gregory Scott *management services executive*
Harris, Howard Hunter *oil company executive*
†Harris, Jerrold B. *scientific company executive*
Harris, Jordan *record company executive*
Harris, Louis *public opinion analyst, columnist*
Harris, Marcelite Jordan *air force officer*
Harris, Margaret *pianist, conductor, composer*
Harris, Neison *manufacturing company executive*
Harris, Nell H. *retired public relations executive, real estate broker, writer*
Harris, Randy Alan *finance company executive, lawyer*
Harris, Richard (Richard St. John) *actor*
Harris, Robert Norman *advertising and communications educator*
Harris, Roy Hartley *electrical engineer*
Harris, William John *retired management holding company executive, consultant*
Harrison, Charles Maurice *lawyer, former communications company executive*
Harrison, William Burwell, Jr. *banker*
Harryhausen, Ray Frederick *special effects expert*
Harshbarger, Dwight *psychologist, management consultant*
Hart, Arthur Alvin *historian, author*
Hart, Evelyn *ballet dancer*
Hartell, John *artist, retired art educator*
Hartman, John Wheeler *publisher*
Hartman, Margaret J. *biologist, educator, university official*
Hartman, Phil Edward *actor*
Harton, John James *utility executive*
Hartsell, Samuel David *insurance agent*
Harvey, Mary Bird *retired university official*
Harza, Richard Davidson *civil engineer*
Haskew, George M., Jr. *utility executive*
Haskins, James *English language educator, writer*
Hasselmeyer, Eileen Grace *medical research administrator*
Hasselmo, Nils *university official, linguistics educator*
Hast, Adele *editor, historian*
Hatch, Kenneth L. *television executive*
Hatch, Orrin Grant *senator*
Hatchett, Edward Earl *retired aerospace manufacturing company executive*
Hauenstein, George Carey *life insurance executive*
Hausman, Arthur Herbert *electronics company executive*
Hausman, Bruce *lawyer*
Hauver, Constance Longshore *lawyer*
Havlicek, John J. (Hondo) *former professional basketball player*
Havoc, June *actress*
Hawes, Alexander Boyd, Jr. *newspaper editor, journalist*
Hawkes, John *humanities educator, author*
†Hawkes, Kevin Cliff *illustrator, author*
Hawkins, Augustus Freeman *former congressman*
Hawkins, Lawrence Charles *management consultant, educator*
Hawkins, Mary Ellen Higgins (Mary Ellen Higgins) *former state legislator, public relations consultant*
Hawkins, Michael Daly *federal judge*
Hawkins, Osie Penman, Jr. *former baritone, former performing company executive*
Hayes, Charles Raymond *utility company executive*
Hayes, David Vincent *sculptor*
Hayes, Gladys Lucille Allen *community care official, poet, writer*
Hayes, Janet Gray *retired business manager, former mayor*
Hayes, Joan Eames *state legislator*
Hayes, John Patrick *retired manufacturing company executive*
Hayes, Mary Phyllis *savings and loan association executive*
Hayes, Peter Lind *actor, writer*
Hayne, Harriet Ann *state legislator, rancher*
Hays, Thomas Chandler *holding company executive*
Hazuda, Ronald A. *church administrator*
Headley, Anne Renouf *technology commercialization financier*
Healton, Donald Carney *federal agency administrator*
Healy, Richard Joseph *lawyer*
†Healy, Sonya Ainslie *health facility administrator*
Heard, John *actor*
Hearn, J(ames) Woodrow *bishop*
Hearn, Joyce Camp *retired educator, state legislator*
Heath, Percy *jazz bassist*
Heath, Richard Eddy *lawyer*
Heath, Richard Murray *retired hospital administrator*
Heaton, Jean *early childhood educator*
Hebner, Paul Chester *retired oil company executive, consultant*
Hecht, Chic *ambassador, former senator*
Hecht, Emil *retired housing and financial company executive*
Heckart, Eileen *actress*
Heckel, John Louis (Jack Heckel) *aerospace company executive*
Heckler, John Maguire *stockbroker, investment company executive*
Hedrick, Basil Calvin *state agency administrator, ethnohistorian, educator, museum and cultural institutions consultant*
Heeschen, David Sutphin *astronomer, educator*
Hefferan, Colien Joan *economist*
Heffner, William Joseph *investment executive*
Hegarty, George John *university president, English educator*
Heggie, Robert James *steel company executive*
Heidke, Ronald Lawrence *photographic products company executive*
Heilbrun, Carolyn Gold *English literature educator*
Heilman, Marlin Grant *photographer*
Heilmann, Christian Flemming *corporate executive*
Heiman, David Gilbert *lawyer*
Heiman, Grover George, Jr. *magazine editor, author*
Heine, Ursula Ingrid *biologist, researcher, artist*
Heiney, John Weitzel *former utility executive*
Heistand, Joseph Thomas *retired bishop*
Heitz, Edward Fred *freight traffic consultant*
Helander, Bruce Paul *artist, art dealer*
Helfgott, Roy B. *economist, educator*
Helgenberger, Marg *actress*
Heller, Dorothy *artist*
Heller, Ronald Gary *manufacturing company executive, lawyer*
Hellmers, Norman Donald *historic site director*
Helm, DeWitt Frederick, Jr. *association executive*
Helman, Alfred Blair *retired college president, education consultant*
Helms, J. Lynn *former government agency administrator*
Helms, W. Richard *lawyer*
Helprin, Mark *author*
Hemann, Raymond Glenn *aerospace research company executive*
Hemmer, James Paul *lawyer*
Hemond, Roland A. *professional baseball team executive*
Henderson, Charles Brooke *research company executive*
Henes, Donna Urban Shaman *celebration artist, ritualist, writer*
Henkel, Arthur John, Jr. *investment banker*
Henle, Peter *economic consultant, arbitrator*
Henner, Marilu *actress*
Henning, Doug *illusionist*
Henry, Elizabeth Brown *medical center administrator*
Henry, John Raymond *sculptor*
Hepper, Carol *artist, educator*
Herbert, Ira C. *food processing company executive*
Herbert, John Warren *forest products executive*
Herbig, Günther *conductor*
Herbst, Jurgen *history and education educator*
Hering, Doris Minnie *dance critic*
Herington, Cecil John *classics educator*
Heris, Toni *psychologist, psychotherapist*
Herman, Chester Joseph *physician*
Herman, Hank *writer*
Herman, Joan Elizabeth *insurance company executive*
Hersey, David Kenneth *theatrical lighting designer*
Hertz, Kenneth Theodore *health care executive*
Herwitz, Carla Barron *lawyer*
Herz, George Peter *chemical engineer,industrial consultant*
Herzberg, Thomas *artist, illustrator*
Herzfeld, Charles Maria *physicist*
Herzog, Whitey (Dorrel Norman Elvert Herzog) *former professional baseball team executive*
Heskett, Luvina Hylton *elementary school educator*
Hess, David Willard *journalist*
Hess, Ulrich Edward *electrical engineer*
Hesse, Christian August *mining and tunneling industries consultant*
Hetzron, Robert *linguist, educator*
Hewes, Laurence Ilsley, III *lawyer, management and legal consultant*
Hewitt, James J. *retired credit corporation executive*
Heymann, C(lemens) David *author*
Hiatt, Arnold *shoe manufacturer, importer, retailer*
Hiatt, Robert Nelson *consumer products executive*
Hichens, Walter Wilson *former state senator*
Hickey, Joseph Michael, Jr. *investment banker*
Hicks, Sue Ann Bernard *nursing educator*
Hicks, Vicki Jean *lawyer*
Higginbotham, John Taylor *lawyer*
Hildebrandt, Theodore Ware *computer scientist*
Hilding, Jerel Lee *music and dance educator, former dancer*
Hill, Anita Carraway *retired state legislator*
Hill, John Edward, Jr. *investment banker, small business owner*
†Hill, Malcolm Kendall *library administrator*
Hill, Pamela *television executive*
†Hill, Shirley Ann *mathematics educator*
Hiller, William Arlington *agriculture executive*
Hillerman, Tony *writer, former journalism educator*
Hilliard, Sam Bowers *geography educator*
Hilton, Clifford Thomas *clergyman*
Hilty, William Jacob *retired association executive*
Himmelfarb, Milton *editor, educator*
Hinckle, Warren James, III *journalist*
Hinderliter, Richard Glenn *electrical engineer*
Hingle, Pat *actor*
Hinkley, Everett David, Jr. *scientist,business executive*
Hinson, Howard Houston *petroleum company executive*
Hirose, Teruo Terry *surgeon*
Hirsch, Horst Eberhard *business consultant*
Hirschberg, Vera Hilda *writer*
Hirsh, Norman Barry *management consultant*
Hirst, Heston Stillings *former insurance company executive*
Hitchborn, James Brian *telecommunications executive*
Hitchcock, Walter Anson *educational consultant, retired educational administrator*
Hite, Elinor Kirkland *oil company human resources manager*
Hixon, Allen Wentworth *landscape architect, land planner*
†Ho, Alexander Kitman *producer*
Ho, Michael *artistic director, choreographer, ballet teacher*
Hobbs, J. Edwin *retired utility executive*
Hoch, Frederic Louis *medical educator*
Hoch, Roland Franklin *lawyer, retired utilities corporation executive*
Hochberger, Bernadette M. *secondary education educator, counselor*
Hock, Morton *entertainment advertising executive*
Hodges, Paul Joseph *securities analyst*
Hodson, Nancy Perry *real estate agent*
Hoeg, Donald Francis *chemist, consultant, former research and development executive*
Hoeppner, David William *mechanical engineering educator*
Hoeprich, Paul Daniel *physician educator*
Hofferber, Beverly Elaine *nursing administrator*

Hoffman, Alan Craig lawyer
Hoffman, Donald Stuart music director
Hoffman, Leonard Elbert, Jr. judge
Hoffman, S. David lawyer, engineer, educator
†Hoffman, Stanley Marc composer, music engraver
Hofmann, Paul Bernard health care consultant
Hogan, Mark investment company executive
Hogan, Neville John mechanical engineering educator, consultant
Hogan, Robert Henry trust company executive, investment strategist
Hogan, Thomas Francis federal judge
Hoge, James Fulton, Jr. magazine editor
Hoggard, Lara Guldmar conductor, educator
Hoglund, William Elis retired automotive company executive
Hogue, Carol Jane Rowland epidemiologist
Hoi, Samuel Chuen-Tsung dean
Hoke, Sheila Wilder retired librarian
Holcombe, William Jones manufacturing company executive
Holiday, Edith Elizabeth former presidential adviser, cabinet secretary
Holland, David Thurston former editor
Holland, James Paul utility company executive
Holland, Randy James state supreme court justice
Holland, Robert Campbell anatomist, educator
Hölldobler, Berthold Karl zoologist, educator
Holliday, Robert Kelvin state senator, former newspaper executive
Hollis, William S. management consultant
Holloran, Thomas Edward business educator
Holloway, Robert Ross archaeologist, educator
†Holly, John Durward, III health care executive
Holm, Celeste actress
Holmer, Edwin Carl retired petrochemical company executive
Holmes, Paul Luther political scientist, educational consultant
Holster, Robert Marc health care information company executive
Holt, Douglas Eugene consulting engineer, retired business executive
Holt, Marjorie Sewell lawyer, retired congresswoman
Holt, Patricia Lester book review editor
Holt, Sandra Grace middle school educator
Holton, Robert Page publishing executive
Homestead, Susan psychotherapist
Honeystein, Karl lawyer, entertainment company executive
Hooper, Gerry Don information systems professional, consultant
Hoopes, Townsend Walter former association executive, former government official
Hoover, Francis Louis educator, gemologist, jewelry designer, appraiser fine arts and gems, writer
Hoover, John Elwood former military officer, consultant, writer
Hoover, William R(ay) computer service company executive
Horan, Hume Alexander diplomat, association executive
Horn, Todd Richard Wendell school administrator
Hornblow, Michael M. diplomat
Horner, Matina Souretis retired college president, corporate executive
Hornick, Katherine Joyce Kay artist, small business owner
Horovitz, Zola Philip pharmaceutical company executive
Horowitz, Beverly Phyllis occupational therapist
Horsburgh, Beverly law educator
Horsch, Kathleen Joanne social services administrator, educator, consultant
Horton, Robert Baynes railroad company executive
Horton, Wilfred Henry mathematics educator
Horwitz, Donald Paul lawyer
Horwitz, Larry Stuckey entrepreneur
Hostettler, Stephen John naval officer
Hottois, Lawrence Daniel retired banking executive
Houghton, Katharine actress
Houlihan, Patrick Thomas museum director
House, Charles Staver judge
Houser, William Douglas telecommunications company executive, former naval officer
Houstoun, Lawrence Orson, Jr. development consultant
Howard, Charles L. chemist, educator
Howard, Dean Denton electrical engineer, researcher, consultant
Howard, Donald Searcy banker
Howard, Jack Rohe retired newspaperman
Howard, James Joseph, III utility company executive
Howard, James Webb investment banker, lawyer, engineer
Howard, Joel L. electric power company executive
Howard, Joseph Harvey retired librarian
Howard, Matthew Aloysius retail company executive
Howard, Maureen writer
Howard, Michael Eliot historian, educator
Howard, Richard (Joseph Howard) poet, literary translator
Howe, John Perry materials science educator, research consultant
Howe, John Prentice, III health science center executive, physician
Howe, Virginia Hoffman nurse administrator
Howell, Donald Lee lawyer
Howell, William Robert retail company executive
Hoyt, Mary Finch author, editor, media consultant, former government official
Hubbard, Elizabeth actress
Hubbe, Henry Ernest financial forecaster, funds manager
Hubley, Reginald Allen publisher
Huckabee, Donna Marie nurse
Hudak, Thomas Michael plastic surgeon
Hudlin, Reginald Alan director, writer, producer
Hudnut, David Beecher retired leasing company executive, lawyer
Huerta, Mary Zapata English and foreign language educator
Huff, William Achleiss communications educator
Huffman, James Thomas William oil exploration company executive
Hufschmidt, Maynard Michael resources planning educator
Hughes, Eugene Morgan university president
Hughes, Michaela Kelly actress, dancer
Hughes, Richard Gene computer executive, consultant
Hughes, Thomas H. retired health care executive
Hughes, Thomas Parke history educator
Hughey, Richard Kohlman lawyer, author, legal publisher
Hughitt, Jeremiah Keefe utility executive
Hulbert, Bruce Walker bank executive, banker
Hull, Bobby (Robert Marvin Hull) former professional hockey player
Humes, Edward journalist, writer
Humke, Ramon L. utility executive
Hummel, Gene Maywood retired bishop
Humphrey, Arthur Earl university administrator
Humphrey, Karen Michael former mayor
Humphrey, Shirley Joy state representative, education consultant
Hungerford, Lugene Green physicist
Huning, Deborah Gray actress, dancer, audiologist
Hunt, Bryan artist
†Hunt, Donald Edward planning and engineering executive
Hunt, Joe Harold retired utility company executive
Hunt, Oliver Raymond, Jr. thoracic and cardiovascular surgeon
Hunt, Ronald Duncan veterinarian, educator, pathologist
Hunt, Ronald Forrest lawyer
Hunt, William Edward neurosurgeon, educator
Hunter, Donald utility company executive
Hunter, Duncan Lee congressman
Hunter, Holly actress
Hunter, Kim (Janet Cole) actress
Hunter, Richard Grant, Jr. neurologist, executive
Hunter, Ross film producer
Huntley, Robert Ross physician, educator
†Hurd, Joseph Elbert air force officer
Hurn, Raymond Walter religious order administrator
Hurst, John Emory, Jr. retired airline executive
Husain, Taqdir mathematics educator
Huston, Nancy Louise writer, educator
Hutcheon, Linda Ann English language educator
Hutchins, Robert Ayer architect
Hutchinson, John Woodside applied mechanics educator, consultant
†Hutchison, Kay Bailey senator
Hutner, Herbert L. financial consultant, lawyer
Huttenback, Robert Arthur academic administrator, educator
Hybl, William Joseph foundation executive, lawyer
Hyde, Robert Burke, Jr. retired oil industry executive
Hyman, Seymour Charles arbitrator
Hyman, Trina Schart illustrator
Iacocca, Lido Anthony (Lee Iacocca) former automotive manufacturing executive, venture capitalist
Idaszak, Jerome Joseph economic journalist
Iglesias, Julio (Julio Jose Iglesias De La Cueva) singer, songwriter
Iklé, Richard Adolph lawyer
Illson, James Elias management consultant
Ilutovich, Leon organization executive
Ingersoll, Paul Mills banker
Ingle, James Chesney, Jr. geology educator
Inglis, James telecommunications company executive
Inouye, David William zoology educator
Intilli, Sharon Marie television director, small business owner
Inui, Thomas Spencer physician, educator
Ipsen, Grant Ruel insurance and investments professional
Iqbal, Zafar biochemist, neurochemist
Irani, Raymond Reza electro-mechanical company executive
Ireland, Norma Olin writer, scholarly, researcher
Irey, Charlotte York dance educator
Irsay, Robert professional football team executive, construction company executive
Irvine, John Alexander lawyer
Irving, Amy actress
Irving, George Steven actor
Irving, John Winslow writer
Irving, Terry (Edward B. Irving, III) television producer
Irwin, Joseph Augustus banker
Isaac, Steven Richard advertising executive
Isaacs, Kenneth S(idney) psychoanalyst, educator
Isaacs, Susan novelist, screenwriter
Isaacson, Edith Lipsig civic leader
Isakow, Selwyn financier
Isom, Dotcy Ivertus, Jr. bishop
Israel, Robert Allan statistician
Istomin, Marta Casals performing arts administrator
Iverson, David M. church executive
Ives, Samuel Clifton minister
Ivry, Alfred Lyon foreign language and literature educator
Iyer, Ravishankar Krishnan electrical and computer engineering educator
Jackman, Jay M. psychiatrist
Jackson, Carmault Benjamin, Jr. physician
Jackson, David Gordon religious organization administrator
Jackson, Elmer Joseph lawyer, oil and gas company executive
Jackson, Lambert Blunt academic administrator
Jackson, Nagle stage director, playwright
Jackson, Rudolph Ellsworth pediatrician, educator
Jackson, Victor Louis retired naturalist
Jacobey, John Arthur, III surgeon, educator
Jacobi, Derek George actor
Jacobowitz, Ellen Sue former museum administrator
Jacobs, Abigail Conway biochemist
Jacobs, Alan lawyer
Jacobs, Herbert Howard investor
Jacobs, Hyde Spencer soil chemistry educator
Jacobs, Linda Rotroff elementary school educator
Jacobs, Wilbur Ripley writer, history educator
†Jacobs, William Jay historian, writer
Jacobsen, Arthur business and financial consultant
Jacobson, Herbert Laurence diplomat
Jacobson, James Bassett insurance executive
Jacoby, Stanley Arthur retired manufacturing executive
Jacques, Andre Charles financial consultant
Jaffe, Stanley Richard film producer, director
Jaicks, Frederick Gillies retired steel company executive
Jaicomo, Ronald James lawyer
Jakubauskas, Edward Benedict college president
Jaller, Michael M. retired orthopaedic surgeon
James, Arlo Dee state legislator, retired mining maintenance executive
James, Earl Eugene, Jr. aerospace engineering executive
Jamieson, Michael Lawrence lawyer
Jamison, John Callison business educator, investment banker
Janko, May graphic artist
Jankus, Alfred Peter retired international management and marketing consultant
Janowiak, Robert Michael engineering organization executive
Jansen, Angela Bing artist, educator
Jarrett, Keith pianist, composer
Jarvis, William Esmond Canadian government official
Jasinski, Roman Larkin artistic director
Jedenoff, George Alexander steel consultant
Jeelof, Gerrit electronics executive
Jefferies, William McKendree internist, educator
Jefferson, John Daniel political activist
Jenkins, Darrell Lee librarian
Jenkins, Lawrence Eugene retired aeronautics company executive
Jenney, Neil Franklin, Jr. artist, philosopher
Jennings, Joseph Ashby banker
Jennings, Max newspaper editor
Jennings, Waylon country musician
Jensen, Jack Michael publishing executive
Jensen, Marvin Eli retired agricultural engineer
Jensen, Robert Neal lawyer
Jensen, Robert Trygve lawyer
Jepson, Robert Scott, Jr. international investment banking specialist
Jernstedt, Richard Don public relations executive
Jessup, Harley William graphics expert, art director
†Jex, William Winkelman humanities educator and administrator
Jiang, Bai-Chuan optics researcher, educator
Jiler, William Laurence publisher
Jimenez, Luis Alfonso, Jr. sculptor
Jinks, Robert Larry retired newspaper publisher
Joanou, Phillip advertising executive
Joblove, George H. graphics and special effects expert
John, K. K. (John Kuruvilla Kaiyalethe) minister
John, Ralph Candler retired college president, educator
Johnson, Albert Wesley political science educator
Johnson, Arnold Ivan civil engineer
Johnson, (Francis) Benjamin actor
Johnson, Clifton Herman historian, archivist, former research center director
Johnson, Craig R. utilities executive
Johnson, Cyrus Edwin grain farmer, former food products executive
Johnson, Dewey E(dward) dentist
Johnson, Diane Lain novelist, critic
Johnson, Don Wayne actor
Johnson, Donald C. ambassador to Mongolia
Johnson, Everett Ramon retired college dean
Johnson, Ferd retired cartoonist, color artist
Johnson, Frank Edward newspaper editor
Johnson, Geneva Bolton retired human service organization executive
Johnson, George physician
Johnson, Harold Edward retail executive
Johnson, Irving Stanley pharmaceutical company executive, scientist
Johnson, J. J. trombonist
Johnson, Joe William engineering educator, consultant
Johnson, Malcolm Clinton, Jr. publishing consultant
Johnson, Marc corporate executive
Johnson, Marlene M. government executive
†Johnson, Marshall Wain entomologist, educator
Johnson, Mary Elizabeth Susan health care planner
Johnson, Pamela community health nurse, administrator
Johnson, Reggie professional boxer
Johnson, Rogers Bruce retired chemical company executive
Johnson, Stewart Willard civil engineer
Johnson, Sylvia Sue university administrator, educator
Johnson, Victor L. retail executive
Johnson, Warren Donald retired pharmaceutical executive, former air force officer
Johnson-Masters, Virginia E. (Mrs. William H. Masters) psychologist
Johnston, Cyrus Conrad, Jr. internist, educator
Johnston, Gerald Andrew aerospace company executive, retired
Johnston, Harry A., II congressman
Johnston, James Monroe, III air force officer
Johnston, Jerry Wilson banker
Johnston, Ralph Kennedy, Sr. aerospace engineer
Johnston, Thomas John management consultant
Jones, Anita Katherine computer scientist, educator
Jones, Anita M. medical/surgical nurse
Jones, David Charles retired air force officer, former chairman Joint Chiefs of Staff
Jones, David John aerospace executive
Jones, George country music singer, songwriter
Jones, Jack Dellis oil company executive
Jones, Jerrauld C. lawyer
Jones, Joan Megan anthropologist
Jones, Keith Alden lawyer
Jones, Lawrence Neale university dean, minister
Jones, Phyllis Gene judge
Jones, Regina Nickerson public relations executive
Jones, Richard Melvin bank executive, former retail executive
Jones, Robert Henry automotive distribution executive
Jones, Shirley actress, singer
Jones, Tommy Lee actor
Jones, Walton Linton internist, former government official
Jordan, Fred publishing company executive
Jordan, Howard Emerson retired engineering executive
Jordan, Thomas Fredrick physics educator
Jordan, William Bryan, Jr. art historian
Jorden, William John writer, retired diplomat
Josephs, Melvin Jay retired professional society administrator
Joslin, David Bruce bishop
Jourdain, Alice Marie philosopher, retired educator
Jovanovich, Peter William publishing executive
Joyce, Burton Montgomery natural resources company executive
Joye, Afrie Songco minister
Judd, Naomi country music entertainer, singer, songwriter, author
Judd, Wynonna vocalist, musician
Judelson, David N. company executive
Judge, Rosemary Ann oil company executive
Juenemann, Sister Jean hospital executive
Just, Ward Swift author
Juviler, Peter Henry political scientist, educator
Kadota, Takashi Theodore mathematician, electrical engineer
Kafes, William Owen lawyer
Kahl, John J., Jr. manufacturing executive, small business owner
Kahn, Albert Michael artist, designer
Kahn, Charles Howard architect, educator
Kahn, David dermatologist, educator
Kahn, Jenette Sarah publishing company executive
Kahn, Madeline Gail actress
Kahn, Susan Beth artist
Kalina, Richard artist
Kalish, Donald philosophy educator
Kalkwarf, Leonard V. minister
Kamen, Martin David physical biochemist
Kaminsky, Laura composer, arts presenter
Kampmeier, Curtis Neil management consultant
Kane, James Golden retired banker
Kane, Michael Joseph director
Kanin, Fay screenwriter
Kanin, Garson writer, theatrical director
Kapcsandy, Louis Endre building construction and manufacturing executive, chemical engineering consultant
Kaplan, Leonard Eugene accountant
Kapor, Mitchell David foundation executive
Kaprielian, Walter advertising executive
Karalis, John Peter computer company executive, lawyer
Karawina, Erica artist, stained glass designer
Kardos, Paul James insurance company executive
Karn, Richard Wendall civil engineer
Karnaugh, Maurice computer scientist, educator
Karp, David communications executive, writer
Karp, Sherman aerospace consultant
†Karson, Samuel psychologist, educator
Kaschak, Virginia Ruth elementary education educator
Kasem, Casey (Kemal Amin Kasem) radio and television personality
Kaser, David retired librarian, educator, consultant
Kasimer, Solomon charitable organization executive
Kaskowitz, Edwin association executive
Kaster, Laura A. lawyer
†Kastner, Marc Aaron physics educator
Kastor, Frank Sullivan English language educator
Kates, Robert William geographer, educator, independent scholar
Katz, Alan Martin secondary education educator
Katz, Anne Harris biologist, educator, writer, aviator
Katz, Leon packaging company executive
Katz, Martin Howard lawyer
Katz, Robert David architecture educator
Katzenbach, John Strong Miner author
Katzmann, Barry A. writer
Kaufman, Jane artist
Kaufman, Paula T. librarian
†Kaufman, Raymond L. energy company executive
Kauger, Yvonne state supreme court justice
Kavalek, Lubomir chess expert
Kavanagh, Kevin Patrick insurance company executive
Kavner, Julie actress
Kazan, Elia theatrical, motion picture director and producer, author
Kazmarek, Linda Adams secondary education educator
Keach, Stacy, Sr. producer, director
Keala, Francis Ahloy security executive
Kearns, James Joseph artist
Keating, Charles H., III finance company executive
Keating, Louis Jeremiah lawyer
Kebblish, John Basil retired coal company executive, consultant
Keegan, Kenneth Donald financial consultant, retired oil company executive
Keeler, William Henry cardinal
Keenan, Mike professional hockey team coach
Keiper, Marilyn Morrison educator
Keisler, H(oward) Jerome mathematics educator
Keister, Stephen Lee artist
Keith, Brian Michael actor
Kellam, Norma Dawn medical, surgical nurse
Keller, George Henry research administrator, consulting biochemist
Keller, Paul advertising agency executive
Kellerman, Faye Marder novelist, dentist
Kelley, Jackson DeForest actor
Kelley, Larry Dale retired military officer
Kellner, Jamie broadcasting executive
Kellock, Alan C(onverse) book publishing executive
Kellogg, Carol Kay neuroscientist, researcher
Kelly, Alonzo Hyatt, Jr. retired automotive company engineering executive
Kelly, Anthony Odrian flooring manufacturing company executive
Kelly, Aurel Maxey retired judge
Kelly, Ellsworth artist, sculptor
Kelly, Kevin drama critic
Kelly, Nancy Folden arts administrator
Kemnitzer, Susan Coady science foundation administrator
Kempf, Cecil Joseph naval officer
Kempfer, Homer association executive
Kendall, Christopher (Christopher Wolff) conductor, lutenist
Kendig, William L. retired government official, accountant
Kendrick, Budd Leroy psychologist
Kendrick, Joseph Trotwood former foreign service officer, writer, consultant
Kennedy, Adrienne Lita playwright
Kennedy, Harvey Edward science information publishing executive
Kennedy, William Francis lawyer
Kenner, Carol J. federal judge
Kenny, Douglas Timothy psychology educator, former university president
Kenny, Patrick Edward publishing executive
Kent, Donald Charles physician
Kent, E(verett) Allen performing arts administrator
Kent, Gary Warner film director, writer
Kent, Howard Lees obstetrician/gynecologist
Kepler, Raymond Glen physicist
Kerber, Ronald Lee industrial corporation executive
Kerins, Francis Joseph college president
Kern, Irving John retired food company executive
Kernan, Barbara Desind senior government executive
Kerr, Deborah Jane actress
Kerr, James Winslow pipe line company executive
Kerr, Leslie A. landscape architect
Kerstetter, Michael James retired manufacturing company executive
Kersting, Edwin Joseph retired university dean
Kertz, Hubert Leonard telephone company executive
Kerwin, Larkin physics educator
Kettelkamp, Donald Benjamin retired surgeon and educator
Key, Ted cartoonist
Keyes, Margaret Naumann home economics educator
Keyes, Saundra Elise newspaper editor
Keys, Jerry Malcom lawyer
Keyser, Charles Lovett, Jr. bishop
Keyserling, Harriet H. state legislator
Kezer, Pauline Ryder educational consultant
†Khaner, Jeffrey flutist, educator
Khouri, Callie Ann screenwriter

Kibler, Craig Morton *editor, columnist, poet*
Kidd, Rachel S. *nursing administrator*
Kidd, Robert Hugh *financial executive, accountant*
Kieffer, Joyce Loretta *health science facility administrator, educator*
Kiley, Richard Paul *actor*
Kilpatrick, Georgia Lee *nurse educator*
Kilpatrick, James Jackson, Jr. *columnist, author*
Kinder, James Allen *lobbyist, professional services firm executive, consultant*
King, Algin Braddy *marketing educator*
King, David Roy *lawyer*
King, Edward William *retired transportation executive*
King, Felton *bishop*
King, Imogene M. *nurse, educator*
King, James B. *federal official*
King, John Francis *lawyer*
King, John Quill Taylor *science center administrator, college administrator emeritus*
King, Larry L. *playwright, actor*
King, S(anford) MacCallum *business owner, consultant*
King, Stephen Edwin *novelist, screenwriter, director*
King, Susan Bennett *retired glass company executive, dean*
King, William Collins *oil company executive*
King, William Douglas *retired executive*
Kingsbery, Walton Waits, Jr. *retired accountant*
Kinney, Ardis *nursing administrator*
Kinsman, Frank Ellwood *engineering executive*
Kinzer, James Raymond *retired pipeline company executive*
Kipniss, Robert *artist*
Kirkendall, Donald Eugene *federal agency official*
†Kirkland, Geoffrey A. *motion picture production designer*
Kirkorian, Roy *telecommunications executive*
Kirschenmann, Henry George, Jr. *management consultant, former government official, accountant*
Kirsteuer, Ernst Karl Eberhart *biologist, curator*
Kirts, Wayne Charles *interior designer*
Kirven, Gerald *lawyer*
Kiselik, Paul Howard *manufacturing company executive*
Kisor, Manown, Jr. *banker*
Kissinger, Henry Alfred *former secretary of state, international consulting company executive*
Klapper, Carol Lorraine *magazine publisher*
Klatt, Melvin John *library consultant*
Klaus, Charles *retired lawyer*
Kleban, Kenneth A. *lawyer*
Kleiman, Alan Boyd *artist*
Kleiman, Ansel *retired electronics company executive*
Kleiman, Bernard *lawyer*
Klein, Charlotte Conrad *public relations executive*
Klein, Edward Joel *editor, author, lecturer*
Kleinberg, Howard J. *newspaper columnist*
Klett, Gordon A. *retired savings and loan association executive*
Kliebhan, Sister M(ary) Camille *academic administrator*
Klink, Robert Michael *consulting engineer, management consultant, financial consultant, property developer*
Klippstatter, Kurt L. *conductor, music director*
Klombers, Norman *association executive, retired*
Kloss, Gene (Alice Geneva Glasier) *artist*
Knauer, Virginia Harrington (Mrs. Wilhelm F. Knauer) *consumer consultant, former government official*
Knauss, Earl L. *financial executive*
Knecht, Roland Edward *retired household goods manufacturing company executive*
Knipp, Helmut *hospitality industry executive*
Knoll, Florence Schust *architect, designer*
Knowles, John *author*
Knox, Ernest Rudder *retired college president*
Kocaoglu, Dundar F. *engineering management educator, industrial and civil engineer*
Kochta, Ruth Martha *art gallery owner*
Koelling, Herbert Lee *printing company executive*
Koenig, Allen Edward *higher education consultant*
Koga, Colleen B. *critical care nurse, administrator*
Kohlmeyer, Ida Rittenberg *artist*
Kolasa, Kathryn Marianne *food and nutrition educator, consultant*
Kolb, James A. *science association director, writer*
Kolko, Gabriel *historian, educator*
Kolm, Henry Herbert *physicist, electric research company executive*
Koltai, Stephen Miklos *mechanical engineer, consultant, economist, writer, educator*
Kolton, Paul *business executive*
Komidar, Joseph Stanley *librarian*
Komisar, David Daniel *retired university provost*
Komkov, Vadim *mathematician, educator*
Kondo, Masatoshi S. *pharmaceutical executive, educator*
Koner, Pauline *dancer, choreographer*
Kongabel, H. Fred *industrial construction company executive*
Konigsburg, Elaine Lobl *author*
Koning, Hans (Hans Koningsberger) *author*
Konnyu, Ernest Leslie *former congressman*
Kontny, Vincent L. *engineering and construction company executive*
Kooken, John Frederick *retired bank holding company executive*
Koplow, David Alexander *law educator*
Koppett, Leonard *columnist, journalist, author*
Korab, Arnold Alva *corporate executive*
Korda, Reva *advertising executive, writer*
Korgaonkar, Pradeep Kashinath *marketing educator*
Kormondy, Edward John *university official, biology educator*
Korn, Peter A. *city manager, public administration educator*
Korpal, Eugene Stanley *banker, former army officer*
Korsgaard, Christine Marion *philosophy educator*
Korwek, Alexander Donald *management consultant*
Koseff, Jeffrey Russell *civil engineer, educator*
Kosheff, Martin Joel *financial executive, consultant*
Kotlarz, Shirley Ann *nursing service executive*
Kotler, Steven *investment banker*
Kozlowski, Theodore Thomas *botany educator, research director, author, editor*
Kraichnan, Robert Harry *theoretical physicist, consultant*
Kraiss, Glenn S. *retail executive*
Krakow, Amy Ginzig *advertising and marketing executive, writer*
Kramer, Dale Vernon *English language educator*
Kramer, Larry *playwright, writer*
†Kramer, Peter Robin *computer company executive*
Kramer, Reuben Robert *sculptor*
Krantz, Judith Tarcher *novelist*
Krantz, Stephen Falk *motion picture producer*
Krantz, Steven George *mathematics educator*
Kraslow, David *retired newspaper publishing executive, reporter, author, consultant*
Kratt, Peter George *lawyer*
Krause, Bernard Leo *bioacoustician, sonic artist, composer*
Krause, Werner William *plastics company executive*
Krauthammer, Charles *columnist, editor*
Kravitz, Rubin *chemist*
Kreitzer, Lois Helen *personal investor*
Krepinevich, Kevin W. *social welfare organization administrator, educator*
Kretsch, Hans Walter *retired aerospace company executive*
Kretschmer, Frank F., Jr. *electrical engineer, researcher, consultant*
Krey, Robert Dean *education educator emeritus*
†Kriegsman, Sali Ann *arts administrator, artistic director, writer, consultant*
Kristensen, Marlene *early childhood educator*
Kristofferson, Karl Eric *writer*
Kristofferson, Kris *singer, songwriter, actor*
Krogh, Lester Christensen *retired research and development executive*
Kropp, David Arthur *retired landscape architect*
Kruck, Donna Jean *special education educator, consultant*
Kruizenga, Richard John *retired energy company executive*
Krulak, Charles Chandler *marine officer*
Krumm, William Frederick *retired insurance company executive*
Krupansky, Blanche *retired judge*
Krupnick, Elizabeth Rachel *insurance company executive*
Kryza, E(lmer) Gregory *financial planner, international affairs advisor, former ambassador*
Kucera, Daniel William *bishop*
Kudrnac, Kristian Ivoj *chemical executive*
Kuehn, James Marshall *newspaper editor*
Kuehne, Richard Edward *museum administrator*
Kuennen, Thomas Gerard *journalist*
†Kuhl, Walter James, Jr. *physician*
Kuhn, James Paul *management consultant*
Kuhn, Margaret (Maggie Kuhn) *organization executive*
Kulik, Rosalyn Franta *food company executive, consultant*
Kulstad, Guy Charles *public works official*
Kumler, Kipton Cornelius *photographer, consultant*
Kump, Ernest Joseph *architect, consultant*
Kundera, Milan *writer, educator*
†Kung (Gong) Pin-Mei, Ignatius Cardinal (Ignatius Kung (Gong) Cardinal Pin-Mei) *cardinal*
Kuper, George Henry *research and development institute executive*
Kupferman, Meyer *composer*
Kurfess, Thomas Roland *mechanical engineering educator*
Kurth, Carl Ferdinand *electrical engineer, researcher*
Kurtz, Gary Douglas *film producer*
Kurtz, Lloyd Sherer, Jr. *lawyer*
Kushinka, Joyce Williams *secondary education educator, retired*
Kushner, Harvey David *management consultant*
Kuske, Edward Alan *chemical company executive*
Kusserow, Richard Phillip *government official*
Kutrzeba, Joseph S. *theatrical and film producer, director*
Kutyna, Donald Joseph *air force officer*
Kwak, Sung *conductor, music director*
Kwiat, Joseph J. *English educator, playwright*
Kyle, Henry Carper *lawyer*
Kyle, John Hamilton *publishing executive*
LaBarre, Carl Anthony *retired government official*
La Blanc, Robert Edmund *consulting company executive*
Laboda, Amy Sue *writer*
Labrecque, Richard Joseph *manufacturing company executive*
Lacey, Cloyd Eugene *retired insurance company executive*
Lacey, John William Charles *management consultant*
Lackland, John *lawyer*
Lacy, Alan Jasper *retail executive*
Lacy, Joseph Newton *architect*
Ladd, Cheryl (Cheryl Stopplemoor) *actress*
Ladd, Joseph Carroll *retired insurance company executive*
Ladly, Frederick Bernard *health services and financial services company executive*
Lafley, Alan Frederick *retired banker*
Lagos, George Peter *lawyer*
Laible, Jon Morse *retired mathematics educator, dean*
Laidlaw, Robert Richard *publishing company executive*
Laird, John Robert *finance company executive*
Laitin, Joseph *journalist, former government spokesman and public relations consultant*
Lally, Michael David *writer, actor*
LaMaina, Lawrence Joseph, Jr. *bank executive*
Lamalie, Robert Eugene *retired executive search company executive*
Lamanec, Tracy *chemist, writer*
Lamattina, Lawrence E. *advertising agency executive*
Lamb, Katie A. *nursing educator*
Lambert, Samuel Waldron, III *lawyer*
Lambro, Donald Joseph *columnist*
Lamont, Barbara *television executive*
LaMunyon, Craig Willis *biology researcher*
Lancaster, Edwin Beattie *insurance company executive*
Lancaster, John Howard *civil engineer*
Lancaster, Robert Samuel *lawyer, educator*
Landau, Kenneth Jeffrey *lawyer*
Landauer, Jeramy Lanigan *publishing company executive*
Lande, James Avra *lawyer, engineering and construction company executive*
Landel, Robert Franklin *physical chemist, rheologist*
Landes, George Miller *biblical studies educator*
Landesman, Fredric Rocco *theatre executive*
Landgren, George Lawrence *electrical engineer, consultant*
Landis, James David *publishing company executive, retired, author*
Landon, Robert Gray *retired manufacturing company executive*
Landstrom, Gay Laray *health facility administrator*
Lane, Bernard Bell *furniture company executive*
Lane, Burton (Burton Levy) *composer*
Lane, Larry *performing company executive, theater educator*
Laney, James Thomas *ambassador, educator*
Langdale, John Wesley *timber executive*
Langdon, George Dorland, Jr. *association executive*
Langenberg, Frederick Charles *business executive*
Langenfeld, Douglas Eugene *health care consultant, business advisor*
Langer, Ray Fritz *retired insurance executive*
Langerak, Esley Oren *retired research chemist*
Langley, Beverly *critical care nurse*
†Langmore, John Preston *biophysicist, educator*
Langworthy, William Clayton *college official*
Laning, J. Halcombe *retired computer scientist*
Lankford, Duane Gail *investment banker, mountaineer*
Lantz, Joanne Baldwin *university chancellor emerita*
Lantz, Kenneth Eugene *consulting firm executive*
Lanzillotti, Robert Franklin *economist, educator*
Lardner, Ring Wilmer, Jr. *author*
Larizadeh, M(ohammed) R(eza) *business educator*
Larkin, Joan *poet, English educator*
La Rocca, Isabella *artist*
Larson, George Charles *magazine editor, writer*
Larson, Mel *retired hotel facility executive, corporate executive, helicopter pilot*
Lash, Steven M. *hospital administrator*
Lasry, Jean-Michel *mathematics educator*
Lassell, Michael John *writer, editor*
Lassiter, Kenneth T. *photography educator, consultant*
Lateef, Yusef (Bill Evans) *composer, educator*
Lathlaen, Robert Frank *retired construction company executive*
Laudeman, Leslie *nursing administrator, oncological nurse*
Lauper, Cyndi *musician*
Lautenbacher, Conrad Charles, Jr. *naval officer*
Lavidge, Robert James *marketing research executive*
Lavington, Michael Richard *venture capital company executive*
Lawrence, Jerome *playwright, director, educator*
Lawrence, Linda Hiett *retired school system administrator, writer*
Lawrence, Zan *computer consultant*
Lawson, David Jerald *bishop*
Lawson Donadio, Carolina Anna *foreign language educator, translator*
Lawton, Jonathan Frederick *screenwriter*
†Laycock, Eric Paul *hospital administrator*
Laycraft, James Herbert *judge*
Lazarovic, Karen *money manager, investment consultant*
Lazarus, Margaret Louise *film producer and director*
Lazay, Paul Duane *telecommunications manufacturing company executive*
Lazechko, D. M. (Molly Lazechko) *former state legislator*
Lea, Lorenzo Bates *lawyer*
Leal, Herbert Allan Borden *former university chancellor, former government official*
Leaman, Jack Ervin *landscape architect, community/regional planner*
Leason, Jody Jacobs *newspaper columnist*
Leath, Kenneth Thomas *research plant pathologist, educator*
Leather, Victoria Potts *college librarian*
Leb, Arthur Stern *lawyer*
Lebor, John F(rancis) *retired department store executive*
Lebowitz, Catharine Koch *state legislator*
Lechevalier, Hubert Arthur *microbiology educator*
Le Dain, Gerald Eric *retired Canadian Supreme Court justice*
Leddy, Susan *nursing school educator*
Leder, Philip *geneticist, educator*
Lederman, Marie Jean *English language educator*
Ledford, Jack Clarence *retired aircraft company executive, former air force officer*
Lee, Dan M. *state supreme court justice*
Lee, Eloise R. *nursing educator and administrator*
Lee, James Matthew *Canadian politician*
Lee, John Franklin *retired lawyer, retired association executive*
Lee, Michele *actress*
Lee, Mordecai *religious agency administrator*
Lee, William Chien-Yeh *communications executive, educator*
Lee, William Saul (Bill Lee) *artist, writer*
Leff, Ilene J(oan) *management consultant, corporate and goverment executive*
Leff, Joseph Norman *yarn manufacturing company executive*
Leff, Sandra H. *gallery director, consultant*
Lefferts, George *writer, producer, director*
Leggett, Roberta Jean (Bobbi Leggett) *association executive*
Lehman, Christopher M. *international business consultant*
Lehman, Edwin *minister, head of religious organization*
Lehman, John F., Jr. *industrialist*
Lehmann, Michael Stephen *film director*
Leinart, Bonnie Katherine *nursing administrator*
Leis, Henry Patrick, Jr. *surgeon, educator*
Leith, James Clark *economics educator*
Leizear, Charles William *retired information services executive*
Lemieux, Annette Rose *artist*
Lemke, James Underwood *physicist*
Lemon, Eric V. *lawyer*
Lennon, Joseph Luke *college official, priest*
Lennox, Donald D(uane) *automotive and housing components company executive*
León, Tania Justina *composer, music director, pianist*
†Leonhard, William Edward *engineering and construction company executive*
Lerner, Harry *lawyer, consultant*
Lerner, Herbert J. *accountant*
†LeRoy, G. Palmer *publishing executive*
Lesher, John Lee, Jr. *consulting services company executive*
Lesko, Harry Joseph *transportation company executive*
Leslie, Gerrie Allen *immunologist*
Leslie, James Hill *paper company executive*
Lester, Virginia Laudano *association executive*
Levack, Arthur Paul *history educator emeritus*
Le Van, Daniel Hayden *gas industry executive*
Levenson, Harvey Stuart *manufacturing company executive*
Levenson, Marc David *optics and lasers specialist, scientist*
Leventhal, Nathan *performing arts executive, lawyer*
Leventhal, Robert Stanley *academic administrator*
Levetown, Robert Alexander *lawyer*
Levi, Barbara Goss *physicist, editor*
Levi, Josef Alan *artist*
Levi, Maurice David *economics educator*
Levin, Jack *physician, educator, biomedical investigator*
Levin, Morton D(avid) *artist, printmaker, educator*
†Levin, Robert Barry *motion picture company executive*
Levine, Meldon Edises *lawyer, former congressman*
Levinson, Herbert Sherman *civil and transportation engineer*
Levitsky, Melvyn *ambassador*
Levy, Arthur James *public relations executive, writer*
Levy, David *lawyer, insurance company executive*
Levy, David Alfred *immunology educator, physician, scientist*
Levy, Leah Garrigan *federal official*
Levy, Louis Edward *retired accounting firm executive*
Lewis, Alexander, Jr. *oil company executive*
Lewis, Charles Arlen *financial services company executive*
Lewis, Charles Leonard *psychologist*
Lewis, James Lee, Jr. *actuary*
Lewis, Martin R. *paper company executive*
Lewis, Norman *English language educator, writer*
Lewis, Rita Hoffman *plastic products manufacturing company executive*
Lewis, Samuel Winfield *retired government official, former ambassador*
Lewis, Winifred P. *nursing administrator*
†Lewison, Edward Frederick *surgeon*
†Liberman, Gail Jeanne *editor*
Lichtenstein, Roy *artist*
Liddell, Jane Hawley Hawkes *civic worker*
Liebeler, Susan Wittenberg *lawyer*
Lieberman, Louis (Karl Lieberman) *artist*
Lienhart, James Lee *graphic designer*
Liffers, William Albert *retired chemical company executive*
Lightstone, Ronald *lawyer*
Lillibridge, John Lee *retired airline executive*
Lilly, Edward Guerrant, Jr. *retired utility company executive*
Linane, William Edward *corporate real estate executive*
Lincicome, Bernard Wesley *journalist*
Linda, Gerald *advertising and marketing executive*
Lindars, Laurence Edward *retired health care products executive*
Lindbergh, Anne Spencer Morrow (Mrs. Charles Augustus Lindbergh) *author*
Linde, Hans Arthur *state supreme court justice*
Linde, Maxine Helen *lawyer, business executive, private investor*
Lindegren, Jack Kenneth *elementary and secondary education educator*
Lindfors, Viveca *actress*
Lindsay, Carol Frances Stockton *dean*
Lindsay, Dale Richard *research administrator*
Lindsay, Franklin Anthony *business executive, author*
Lindsay, John Vliet *former mayor, former congressman, author, lawyer*
Lindsay, Reginald Carl *federal judge*
Lindsey, D. Ruth *physical education educator*
Linfante, Charles Vincent *dental, medical, optical products company executive*
Ling, Deirdre Ann *headmistress*
Link, Arthur Stanley *history educator, editor*
Link, Mae Mills (Mrs. S. Gordden Link) *space medicine historian and consultant*
Link, William Theodore *television writer, producer*
Lipman, Ira Ackerman *security service company executive*
Lippincott, Philip Edward *retired paper products company executive*
Lippman, Barry *publishing executive*
Lipscomb-Brown, Edra Evadean *retired childhood educator*
Lipsey, Joseph, Jr. *water bottling company executive, retail and wholesale corporation executive*
Lipsitt, Lewis Paeff *psychology educator*
Lipsky, Janice Gwynne *nursing administrator*
Lipsky, Stephen Edward *engineering executive, electronic warfare engineer*
Lipton, Susan Lytle *investment banker, lawyer*
Lisk, Pamela Konieczka *lawyer*
Liskamm, William Hugo *architect, urban planner, educator*
Liskov, Barbara Huberman *software engineering educator*
Lister, Keith Fenimore *publishing executive*
Litherland, Kay *hospital administrator*
Litow, Joel David *controller*
Little, Loren Everton *musician, ophthalmologist*
Littler, Gene Alec *professional golfer*
Littleton, Harvey Kline *artist*
Littman, Earl *advertising and public relations executive*
Liu, Ernest K. H. *international banking executive, international financial consultant*
Lively, Edwin Lester *retired oil company executive*
Lively, H(oward) Randolph, Jr. *retail company executive*
Livingston, Thomas Mathias *advertising agency executive, writer*
Lloyd, Joseph Wesley *physicist, researcher*
Lloyd, Kate Rand *magazine editor*
Lloyd, Michael Jeffrey *recording producer*
Lo, Shui-yin *physicist*
Loach, Paul Allen *biochemist, biophysicist, educator*
Lobanov-Rostovsky, Oleg *arts association executive*
Locke, Charles Stanley *manufacturing company executive, director*
Locke, David Henry *state senator*
Locke, Norton *hotel management and construction company executive*
Locke, Virginia Otis *textbook editor, behavioral sciences writer*
Lockhart, Aileene Simpson *retired dance, kinesiology and physical education educator*
Lockwood, Robert W. *management consultant*
Lockwood, Theodore Davidge *former academic administrator*
Loder, Victoria Kosiorek *information broker*
Lodge, Arthur Scott *mechanical engineering educator*
Loeffler, David E. *transportation executive*
Loftin, Raymond Victor, Jr. *oil and gas company executive*
Logan, James Kenneth *federal judge*
Logan, John Francis *electronics company executive, management consultant*
Lohmuller, Martin Nicholas *bishop*
Lohrer, Richard Baker *investment consultant*
Lomas, Bernard Tagg *college president emeritus*
Lomax, Peggy Quarles *gifted and talented education educator*
Long, Alvin William *title insurance company executive*
†Long, Charles William *child and adolescent psychiatrist*

Long, Robert Livingston consultant, photographic equipment executive
Longnaker, John Leonard retired insurance company executive, lawyer
Longobardo, Anna Kazanjian mechanical engineer
Longstreet, Harry Stephen television producer, director, scriptwriter
Longstreet, Stephen (Chauncey Longstreet) author, painter
Longsworth, Robert Morrow English educator
Lonneke, Michael Dean radio and television marketing executive
Lopez, Barry Holstun writer
Lopez, Marlene chief executive officer, Bronx Psychiatric Center
Loppnow, Milo Alvin clergyman, former church official
Loquasto, Santo theatrical set designer
Lorant, Stefan author
Lord, Roy Alvin retired publisher
Lord, Walter author
Lord, Winston diplomat
Loring, Gloria Jean singer, actress
Loser, Joseph Carlton, Jr. dean, retired judge
Loss, John C. architect, retired educator
†Losten, Basil Harry bishop
Lotz, Arthur William retired engineering and construction company executve
Loube, Samuel Dennis physician
Loughlin, Mary Anne Elizabeth television news anchor
Loughran, James Newman philosophy educator, former university president
Lousberg, Sister Mary Clarice hospital executive
Louttit, James Russell publishing company executive
Love, Rodney J. food distribution executive
Lovell, Robert Gibson retired physician, educator
Lovell, Walter Carl engineer, inventor
Lovinger, Warren Conrad emeritus university president
Low, Emmet Francis, Jr. mathematics educator
Low, Harry William judge
Low, James Patterson professional association executive
Lowden, John L. retired corporate executive
Lowe, John, III consulting civil engineer
Lowrie, Walter Olin management consultant
Lubin, Steven concert pianist, musicologist
Lubinsky, Menachem Yechiel communications executive
Lucas, Rhett Roy artist, chemical engineer, lawyer
Lucas, William Ray aerospace consultant
Luce, Glenda L. health facility administrator
Luche, Thomas Clifford foreign service officer
†Luck, Gary Edward career officer
Ludden, John Franklin financial economist
Ludlam, James Edward, III insurance company executive
Ludwig, Allan Ira photographer, artist, author
Ludwikowski, Rett Ryszard law educator, researcher
Luecke, Joseph E. insurance company executive
Luetkehoelter, Gottlieb Werner (Lee) retired bishop, clergyman
Luger, Donald R. engineering company executive
Lukas, J. Anthony journalist
†Luke, David Lincoln, III paper company executive
Lum, Gretchen Yates poet, small business owner
Lund, David Nathan artist
Lundgren, Leonard, III retired secondary education educator
Lundy, Roland publishing executive
Lupberger, Edwin Adolph utility executive
Lupu, Radu pianist
Lurie, William L. lawyer, association executive
Luttner, Edward F. career management consultant
Lutts, Ralph Herbert museum administrator, scholar, educator
Lutz, Carl Freiheit academic administrator
Lux, John H. corporate executive
†Lux, Michael Scott federal government official
Lydford, Cynthia Winsloe nurse administrator
Lyman, Richard R. journalist
Lynch, Patricia Gates broadcasting organization executive consultant, former ambassador
Lynch, Paul Vincent safety engineer, consultant
Lynch, Peter George artist
Lynch, Thomas Francis archeologist, educator
Lynch, Thomas Peter securities executive
Lynds, Beverly Turner retired astronomer
Lyng, Richard Edmund former secretary of agriculture
Lynne, Jeff rock musician, composer
Mabry, Guy O. manufacturing company executive
Macaulay, David (Alexander) author, illustrator
MacCarthy, Talbot Leland civic volunteer
Macdonald, Donald Ian health care administrator
MacDonald, Robert Alan language educator
MacFarlane, Andrew Walker media specialist, educator
MacGregor, Donald Lane, Jr. retired banker
†Machado, Eduardo Oscar playwright
MacHovec, Frank J. psychologist
MacLachlan, Alexander chemical company executive, retired
MacLean, John Angus former premier of Prince Edward Island
MacLennan, Beryce Winifred psychologist
MacMillan, Kip Van Metre foundation executive
Macmillan, William Hooper university dean, educator
MacMinn, Aleene Merle B(arnes) newspaper editor, columnist, educator
Mac Nelly, Jeffrey Kenneth cartoonist
MacQueen, Robert Moffat solar physicist
Madden, Richard Blaine forest products executive
Maddin, Robert metallurgist educator
Madeira, Francis King Carey conductor, educator
Madera, Joseph J. bishop
Madory, James Richard hospital administrator, former air force officer
Maehl, William Harvey historian, educator
Maehl, William Henry historian, university administrator, educational consultant
Maehr, Martin Louis psychology educator
Maestrone, Frank Eusebio diplomat
Maffie, Michael Otis utility executive
Magill, Rosalind May psychotherapist
Maglich, Bogdan Cveta physicist
Magnuson, Robert Martin retired hospital administrator
Magor, Louis Roland conductor
Maguire, Maureen K. health facility administrator
Maguire, Patricia healthcare administrator
Maguire, Robert Francis, III real estate investor
Magurno, Richard Peter lawyer
Maher, Daniel Carl accountant
Mai, Chao Chen engineer
Mai, Harold Leverne retired federal judge
Maier, Alfred neuroscientist
Maillet, Antonine author, educator
Maiman, Theodore Harold physicist
†Main, Robert Peebles hospital administrator
Maitra, Subir Ranjan medical educator
Majors, Nelda Faye physical therapist
Makepeace, Darryl Lee consulting company executive
†Malakhov, Vladimir dancer
Malin, Ronald H. lawyer, real estate associate, consultant
Malkinson, Frederick David dermatologist
Mallenbaum, Allan Eliyahu marketing executive
Mallo-Garrido, Josephine Ann advertising agency owner
Mallory, Arthur Lee university dean, retired state official
Mallory, William Barton, III lawyer
Malloy, Michael Terrence retired journalist and newspaper editor
Malone, Edward H. financial executive
Malone, James William bishop
Maloney, Therese Adele insurance company executive
Malott, Adele Renee editor
Malpas, Robert company executive
Malphurs, Roger Edward insurance company executive, chiropractor, biomedical technologist, private commodity trader
Maltzan, Michael Thomas architect
Mamet, David Alan playwright, director, essayist
Mancher, Rhoda Ross federal agency administrator, strategic planner
Manchester, Kenneth Edward electronics executive, consultant
Mand, Martin G. financial executive
Mandino, Og author
Maness, Anthony Ray retired naval officer
Mangan, Frank Thomas advertising executive
Manganaro, Francis Ferdinand naval officer
Mangione, Chuck (Charles Frank Mangione) jazz musician, composer
Mangold, Sylvia Plimack artist
Mankiewicz, Frank F. journalist
Manley, Joan A(dele) Daniels retired publisher
Manley, John Hugo computing technology executive, educator
Mann, Clarence Charles real estate company official
Mann, Emily Betsy writer, artistic director, theater and film director
Mann, Jim (James William Manousos) editor, publisher
Mann, Jonathan Max international agency administrator
Mann, Robert Nathaniel violinist
Manne, Henry Girard lawyer, educator
Mannes, Elena Sabin film and television producer, director
Manning, Richard Dale writer
Mansouri, Lotfollah opera stage director
Mantzavinos, Anthony G. banker
Mapstone, Barbara J. nursing administrator
Maranda, Pierre Jean anthropologist, writer
Marca-Relli, Conrad artist
Marcinek, Margaret Ann nursing educator
Marcoux, Julia A. midwife
Marcus, Greil Gerstley critic
Marcuse, Dietrich retired physicist
†Marinaccio, Paul John, Jr. marketing executive, writer
Marinaro, Edward Francis actor
Marinis, Thomas Paul, Jr. lawyer
Marino, Joseph Anthony retired publishing executive
Mark, Mary Ellen photographer
Markinson, Martin theatre owner, producer
Markle, Roger A(llan) retired oil company executive
Markovitz, Alvin molecular biologist, geneticist
Marks, Leonard, Jr. retired corporate executive
†Marks, Richard film editor
Marks, Russell Edward, Jr. management consultant
Marlatt, Jerry Ronald lawyer
Marler, Larry John private investor
Maroni, Donna Farolino science administrator, retired
Marple, Gary Andre management consultant
Marr, Carmel Carrington lawyer, retired state official
Marrington, Bernard Harvey retired automotive company executive
Marsden, Herci Ivana classical ballet artistic director
Marsee, Susanne Irene lyric mezzo-soprano
Marsh, Ernestine Pease nursing administrator, medical-surgical nurse
Marshak, Robert Reuben former university dean, medical educator, veterinarian
Marshall, Charles Noble railroad executive
Marshall, David Lawrence freight forwarding and mining company executive
Marshall, Doyle real estate executive
Marshall, Garry film producer, director, writer
Marshall, Gerald Francis optical engineer, consultant, physicist
†Marshall, Kathryn Sue lawyer
Marshall, Richard art historian, curator
Marshall, William, Jr. architect
Martin, Albert Charles manufacturing executive, lawyer
†Martin, Charles Raymond chemist, educator
Martin, Edwin William, Jr. pharmaceutical marketing consultant, copywriter
Martin, Lee mechanical engineer
Martin, Louis Edward retired library director
†Martin, Mary secondary education educator
Martin, Murray Simpson librarian, writer, consultant
Martin, Noel graphic design consultant, educator
Martin, Robert A. electronics company executive
Martini, Robert Edward wholesale pharmaceutical and medical supplies company executive
Martyl, (Mrs. Alexander Langsdorf, Jr.) artist
Marvin, William Glenn, Jr. former foreign service officer
Marx, Anne (Mrs. Frederick E. Marx) poet
Marx, Arthur author, playwright, director
Mascotte, John Pierre insurance executive
Masiello, Rocco Joseph airlines and aerospace manufacturing executive
Masnari, Nino Antonio electrical engineer, educator
Mason, Frank Henry, III automobile company executive, leasing company executive
Mason, William Randy sales executive
Massa, Salvatore Peter psychologist
Massie, Edward Lindsey, Jr. retired publishing company executive
Massimino, Roland V. former university basketball coach
Masson, Gayl Angela airline pilot
Mast, Stewart Dale retired airport manager
Masten, Jeffrey A. English educator
Masterson, Peter actor, director
Mastrangelo, Regina Mary nursing administrator, dean
Mastroianni, Marcello actor
†Matherlee, Thomas Ray health care consultant, management executive
Mathews, Harry Burchell poet, novelist, educator
Mathis, Allen Washington, Jr. manufacturing executive
Mathis, Sharon Bell author, elementary educator, librarian
Matthei, Warren Douglas investment company executive
Matthews, Cari Pineiro lawyer, author
Matthews, James Gordon, Jr. obstetrician, gynecologist
Matthews, John Louis retired military officer, educator
Matthews, L. White, III railroad executive
Matthiessen, Peter author
Mattingly, Mack F. former US ambassador, former US senator, entrepreneur
Mattingly, William Earl lawyer
Maurer, Beverly Bennett school administrator
Maxfield, Kenneth Wayne transportation company executive
May, Kenneth Nathaniel food industry consultant
Mayer, James Joseph retired corporate lawyer
Mayeron, Carol Ann cantor
Mayfield, Robert Charles university official, geography educator
Mayo, Robert Porter banker
Mayoras, Donald Eugene corporate executive, speaker, consultant, educator
Mayron, Melanie actress, writer
Mazankowski, Donald Frank Canadian government official
Mazursky, Paul screenwriter, theatrical director and producer
McAbeer, Sara Carita school administrator
McAllister, Darrell Dean banker
McAnuff, Des artistic director
McArdle, John Edward management consultant
McBain, Diane Jean actress, writer
McBurney, Margot B. librarian
McCabe, Charles Law retired manufacturing company executive, management consultant
McCabe, David Allen lawyer
McCall, John Anthony banker
McCandless, J(ane) Bardarah retired religion educator
McCann, Elizabeth Ireland theater, television and motion picture producer, lawyer
McCarthy, J. Thomas lawyer, educator
†McCarthy, Joseph W. motel chain executive
McCarthy, Kevin Joseph academic dean, music educator
McCarthy, Vincent Paul lawyer
Mc Carthy, Walter John, Jr. retired utility executive
McCartney, (James) Paul musician
McCarty, Dennis L. insurance executive
Mc Clellan, Catharine anthropologist, educator
McClendon, Sarah Newcomb news service executive, writer
Mc Clymont, Hamilton entertainment industry executive
McColl, Hugh Leon, III investment company executive
Mc Connell, Edward Bosworth legal organization administrator, lawyer
McConnell, Elliott Bonnell, Jr. oil company executive
McConnell, James Guy lawyer
McConner, Stanley Jay, Sr. academic administrator
McCord, Alice Bird association executive
McCormick, John Owen retired comparative literature educator
McCormick, Michael D. lawyer
Mc Cormick, William Martin broadcast executive
McCown, Hale retired judge
Mc Coy, Tidal Windham former government official
McCracken, John Harvey painter, sculptor
McCullough, R. Michael management consultant
†McCurdy, Michael Charles illustrator, author
Mc Curley, Robert Lee, Jr. lawyer
McDarrah, Gloria Schoffel editor, author
McDermott, Agnes Charlene Senape philosophy educator
McDermott, Kevin J. engineering educator, consultant
McDowell, Malcolm actor
McEntire, Reba N. country singer
Mc Fadden, George Linus retired army officer
McFall, Catherine Gardner poet, critic, educator
McFarland, Gertrude Kay health scientist administrator
McFarland, Victor Alan toxicologist
McGehee, Richard Paul mathematics educator
Mc Gill, Archie Joseph venture capital and business speaker
McGillis, Kelly actress
McGillivray, Donald Dean agricultural products executive
McGinty, John B. orthopaedic surgeon, educator
McGough, John Paul conveyor and power transmission company executive
Mc Govern, George Stanley former senator
McGovern, Patricia state senator
Mc Gowan, James Atkinson business executive, financial consultant
McGraw, Warren Randolph, II state legislator, lawyer
Mc Guigan, James Edward physician, scientist, educator
McGuirk, Terrence former broadcasting company executive
McHale, Paul congressman, lawyer
McHenry, Robert (Dale) editor
McHugh, Earl Stephen dentist
McHugh, John James consultant
McIlvaine, Joseph Peter professional baseball team executive
McIntosh, Carolyn Meade retired educational administrator
McIntyre, Guy Maurice professional football player
Mc Intyre, Robert Allen, Jr. business turnaround executive
Mc Kay, Dean Raymond computer company executive
Mc Kay, Samuel Leroy clergyman
Mc Kayle, Donald Cohen choreographer, director, writer, dance educator
McKean, Robert Jackson, Jr. retired lawyer
McKenna, Quentin Carnegie tool company executive
McKenna, Richard Henry hospital consultant
McKenna, Terence Patrick insurance company executive
McKenzie, Herbert A(lonza) pharmaceutical company executive
McKinlay, Donald Carl lawyer
Mc Kinney, David E(wing) information processing products company executive
McKinney, Donald art gallery director, art dealer
McKinnon, Daniel Wayne, Jr. naval officer
McKinnon, Richard Anthony airline executive
McLarnon, Mary Frances neurologist
McLaughlin, Ann educational administrator, former federal official, lecturer, advisor
McLean, Walter Franklin international consultant, pastor, former Canadian government official
McLendon, George Leland chemistry educator, researcher
McLoone, Eugene P. education educator
Mc Mahon, George Joseph academic administrator
McMaster, Harold Ashley inventor, retired manufacturing company executive
McNeely, Donald Robert steel company executive
McNeil, Heidi Loretta lawyer
McNeil, Steven Arthur food company executive
McNulty, Henry Bryant journalist
McNutt, Suzzanne Marie lawyer
McNutt, William James consulting engineer
McPhedran, Norman Tait surgeon, educator
Mc Phee, John Angus writer
Mc Pheeters, Edwin Keith architect, educator
McPherson, James Alan writer, educator
Mc Pherson, Robert Donald retired lawyer
Mc Quade, Lawrence Carroll lawyer, corporate executive
McQuilkin, John Robertson religion educator, academic administrator, writer
McRae, Thomas Kenneth retired investment company executive
McSorley, Cisco lawyer
McSweeny, John Edward defense industry executive
McVicker, Jesse Jay artist, educator
McWilliams, Bruce Wayne marketing professional
Mead, Beverley Tupper physician, educator
Mead, Robert Norman accountant
Meade, Everard Kidder, Jr. retired broadcasting and publishing executive
Meaders, Nobuko Yoshizawa therapist, psychoanalyst
Meador, Robert Lyman dentist
Meads, Donald Edward management services company executive
Meaker, Marijane Agnes author
Meara, Anne actress, playwright, writer
Medavoy, Mike motion picture company executive
Medina, Kathryn Bach book editor
Medley, Donald Matthias retired education educator, consultant
Medlock, Donald Larson lawyer
Medlock, Thomas Travis lawyer
Mednick, Murray playwright
Mednick, Robert accountant
Medzihradsky, Fedor biochemist, educator
Meehan, John Joseph, Jr. hospital administrator
Meeker, Guy Bentley banker
Mehlfeldt, Horst K. tire manufacturing company
Meier, Gustav symphony conductor
Meier, Henry George architect
Meilman, Edward physician
Meindl, James Donald electrical engineering educator, administrator
Meister, Steven Gerard cardiologist, educator
Melady, Thomas Patrick university president, ambassador, author, public policy expert, educator
Melczek, Dale J. bishop
Melillo, Joseph Vincent producer, performing arts
Melnick, Joseph L. virologist, educator
Melody, Michael Edward publishing company executive
Melsheimer, Mel P(owell) consumer products business executive
Melsheimer, William C. principal
Melvin, Ben Watson, Jr. petroleum and chemical manufacturing executive
Melvin, Billy Alfred clergyman
Melvin, Daniel Sean radio station executive
Melvin, T. Stephen manufacturing company executive
†Menchaca, Peggy Sue Beard energy company executive
Menchel, Donald television executive
Mende, Robert Graham retired engineering association executive
Mendonsa, Arthur Adonel city official
Mendoza, George poet, author
Meneeley, Edward Sterling artist
Menendez, Carlos financial executive, banker
Menn, Julius Joel research scientist
Mercer, Edwin Wayne lawyer
Mercurio, Renard Michael real estate corporation executive
Meredith, Burgess actor
Meredith, James Howard association executive, farmer, consultant
Merlis, George television producer
Merrick, David (David Margulois) theatrical producer
Merrill, Jean Fairbanks writer
Merrill, Lindsey music educator
Merriman, Ilah Coffee financial executive
Merritt, Joshua Levering, Jr. retired engineering executive, consultant
Merseve, Walter Joseph drama studies educator, publisher
Messenkopf, Eugene John real estate and business consultant
Messmore, David William construction executive, former psychologist
Metz, Frank Andrew, Jr. data processing executive
Metzner, Charles Miller federal judge
Meyer, Frederick Jacobs architect
Meyer, Greg Charles psychiatrist
Meyer, Harry Martin, Jr. retired health science facility administrator
Meyer, Kathleen Marie college educator
Meyer, Lasker Marcel retail executive
Meyer, Louis B. superior court judge, retired state supreme court justice
Meyer, Max Earl lawyer
Meyer, Paul William biblical literature educator emeritus
Meyer, Pauline Marie retired special education educator
Meyers, Richard James landscape architect
Mezzatesta, Michael Philip art museum director
Miaskiewicz, Theresa Elizabeth secondary educator
Mich, Connie Rita mental health nurse, educator
Michael, Donald Nelson social scientist, educator
Michaelcheck, William J. investment firm executive
Michaelis, Elias K. neurochemist
Michalik, Edward Francis construction company executive
†Michelson, Harold production designer

Osbourne, Ozzy (John Osbourne) vocalist
Osimitz, Dennis Victor lawyer
Osler, Dorothy K. state legislator
†Oslin, George Poer writer, retired telegraph official
Osmer-McQuade, Margaret business executive, broadcast journalist
Osmond, Gordon Condie playwright
Osrin, Raymond Harold retired political cartoonist
Oster, Lewis Henry manufacturing executive, engineering consultant
Oster, Ludwig Friedrich physicist
Ostfeld, Leonard S. computer company executive
O'Sullivan, Paul Kevin business executive, management and instructional systems consultant
Otis, Denise Marie editor, writer
Otis, Lee Liberman lawyer, educator
Otstott, Charles Paddock army officer
Otte, Carl political cponsultant, lobbyist
Outcalt, David Lewis academic administrator, mathematician, educator
Overcash, Reece A., Jr. financial services company executive
Overfield, Ronald Edwin radiologist
Owen, John Laverty human resources executive, consultant
Owen, Suzanne retired savings and loan executive
Owens, Charles Vincent, Jr. diagnostic company executive and consultant
Owens, William Arthur military officer
Pace, Charles Robert psychologist, educator
Pace, R(alph) Wayne organizational behavior educator
Pack, Allen S. retired coal company executive
Pack, Richard Morris broadcasting executive
Pack, Susan Joan art consultant
Packard, John Mallory physician
Padberg, Harriet Ann mathematics educator
Padgett, George Arthur retired lawyer
Page, Willis conductor
Paglio, Lydia Elizabeth editor
†Paige, Woodrow Wilson columnist
Paino, Ronald Thomas education consultant
Palade, George Emil biologist, educator
Palermo, David Stuart retired psychology educator and administrator
†Palizzi, Anthony N. lawyer, retail corporation executive
Palladino, Nunzio Joseph retired nuclear engineer
Palliser, Charles writer, educator
Palmer, Dave Richard educator, military officer
Palmer, Gary Andrew portfolio manager
Palmer, Irene Sabelberg university dean and educator emeritus, nurse, researcher, historian
Palmer, James Alvin baseball commentator
Palmer, James Russworth theoretical physicist, high energy optics researcher
†Palmer, John M. medical administrator
Palmer, Langdon banker
Palmer, Raymond A. medical association administrator, librarian
Palter, Robert Monroe philosophy and history educator
Pancake, Edwina Howard science librarian
Papadakos, Nicholas Peter retired state supreme court justice
Paquin, Paul Peter retired mortgage finance executive
†Pardue, Michael Edward electronics company executive
Parent, Rodolphe Jean Canadian air force official, pilot
Parente, Michael electrical engineer
Paretsky, Sara N. writer
Parfet, William Upjohn medical supplies manufacturing company executive
Parham, Ellen Speiden nutrition educator
Pariser, Rudolph chemical company executive, consultant
Park, Charles Donald, Sr. financial executive
Park, John Thornton academic administrator
Parker, Brent Mershon retired medical educator, internist, cardiologist
Parker, Franklin writer, educator
Parker, George retired pen manufacturing company executive
Parker, Harry John retired psychologist, educator
Parker, Robert Brown novelist
Parker, Thomas Lee business executive
Parmelee, David Freeland biologist, educator
Parode, Ann banker, lawyer
Parr, Harry Edward, Jr. financial executive
Parrish, Alma Ellis elementary school educator
Parry, Atwell J., Jr. state senator, retailer
Parsegian, V. Adrian biophysicist
Parsons, Edmund Morris investment company executive
Parsons, Elmer Earl retired clergyman
†Parsons, Harry Glenwood retired surgeon
Parsons, Irene management consultant
Partington, James Wood naval officer
Parton, Dolly Rebecca singer, composer, actress
†Pascal, Francine writer
Pastorek, Norman Joseph facial plastic surgeon
Patent, Dorothy Hinshaw author, photographer
Paterson, Robert E. trading stamp company executive
Patinkin, Mandy actor
Patino, Isidro Frank law enforcement educator
Patmos, Adrian Edward university dean emeritus
Patrick, Dennis actor, director
Patrick, Deval Laurdine lawyer
Patterson, Donis Dean bishop
Patterson, Mary-Margaret Sharp writer, editor, media strategist
Patterson, Richard North writer, lawyer
Patterson, Robert Hudson library director
Patton, James Richard, Jr. lawyer
Paul, Frank retired consulting company executive
Paul, Gordon Wilbur marketing educator
Paul, Herbert Morton lawyer, accountant, taxation educator
Paul, Les entertainer, inventor
Paulino, Sister Mary McAuley principal
Paulsen, Frank Robert college dean emeritus
Paulus, Norma Jean Petersen lawyer, state school system administrator
Pauly, John Edward anatomist
Pavlick, Harvey Naylor financial executive
Paycheck, Johnny country western musician
Peacock, Mary Willa magazine editor
Pearce, Paul Francis retired aerospace electronics company executive
Pearlstein, Philip artist
Pearson, Donald Emanual chemist, educator
Pearson, John Davis naval officer
Pearson, Ralph Gottfrid chemistry educator
Peccarelli, Anthony Marando judge
Peck, Daniel Farnum chemical company executive
Peck, Gregory actor
Peckham, Donald Eugene retired utilities company executive
Pedersen, Knud George economics educator, former university president
Pedini, Kenneth physician
†Peeples, Rufus Roderick, Jr. (Roddy Peeples) farm and ranch news radio broadcaster
Peers, Michael Geoffrey archbishop
Peete, William Pettway Jones surgeon
Peiss, Clarence Norman physiology educator, college dean
Péladeau, Marius Beaudoin art consultant, retired museum director
Pelotte, Donald Edmond bishop
Peltier, Eugene Joseph civil engineer, former naval officer, business executive
Pendergrass, Teddy (Theodore D. Pendergrass) musician
Penn, Irving photographer
Pennario, Leonard concert pianist, composer
Pennington, Mary Anne art museum director, museum management consultant, art educator
Pennington, Richard Maier management consultant, retired insurance company executive, lawyer
Penrod-Hill, Barbara M. nursing administrator
Penzer, Mark lawyer, editor, corporate trainer, former publisher
Penzias, Arno Allan astrophysicist, research scientist, information systems specialist
Peoples, John Arthur, Jr. former university president, consultant
Pepper, Dorothy Mae nurse
Pepper, Jeffrey Mackenzie publishing executive
†Percy, Lee Edward motion picture film editor
Perelman, Leon Joseph paper manufacturing executive, university president
Perkins, Frederick Myers retired oil company executive
Perkins, Thomas Keeble oil company researcher
Perks, Benjamin Winwood accountant
Perle, George composer
Perlis, Michael Steven magazine publisher
Perlov, Dadie management consultant, association executive
Perman, Norman Wilford graphic designer
Perreault, Sister Jeanne college president
Perrin, Gail editor
Perrin, Robert writer, consultant
Perrot, Paul Norman museum director
Perry, J. Warren health sciences educator, administrator
Persky, Lester film producer
Peskin, Kenneth retail executive
Peter, Richard Ector zoology educator
Peters, Ralph Frew investment banker
Peters, Robert Woolsey architect
Peters, Virginia actress
Petersen, Susan Jane publishing company executive
Peterson, Ann Sullivan physician, health care consultant
Peterson, Monica (Dorothy Peterson) actress, singer, model, writer
Peterson, Roderick William television writer, producer
Peterson, Roland Oscar retired electronics company executive
Petika, David M. municipal government official, editor
Petok, Samuel retired manufacturing company executive
Petrequin, Harry Joseph, Jr. foreign service officer
Petrie, Donald Archibald lawyer, investment banker, publisher
Petrie, John Richard advertising agency executive, writer
Pettis-Roberson, Shirley McCumber former congresswoman
Pettit, Ghery DeWitt retired veterinary medicine educator
Pettitt, Jay S. architect, consultant
Petykiewicz, Sandra Dickey editor
Pew, Thomas W., Jr. advertising executive
Peyser, Joseph Leonard historical researcher, translator, author
Pflanze, Otto Paul history educator
Phelan, Ellen artist
Phelan, John J., Jr. former stock exchange executive, corporate director
Phelps, Paulding rheumatologist, internist
Philippi, Ervin William mortician
Phillips, Charles Alan accounting firm executive
Phillips, Gabrielle travel marketing executive
Phillips, George Michael communications executive
Phillips, Glynda Ann editor
Phillips, James Dickson, Jr. federal judge
Phillips, John David communications executive
Phillips, Kenneth Higbie association executive
Phillips, William George retired food products executive
Phoenix, Paul Joseph steel manufacturing company executive
Piccinini, Janice state legislator
Pick, James Block management and sociology educator
Pick, Robert Yehuda orthopedic surgeon, consultant
Pickering, Howard William metallurgy engineer, educator
Picus, Mark Anthony broadcasting executive
Piehl, Donald Herbert chemist, consultant
Pielou, Evelyn C. biologist
Pierce, Anne-Marie B. school system administrator
Pierce, David Hyde actor
Pierce, James Robert magazine executive
Pierce, Ponchitta Anne television host, producer, journalist
Pierce, Samuel Riley, Jr. government official, lawyer
Piergallini, Alfred A. food products executive
Pierluisi, Pedro Rafael lawyer
Pifer, Alan (Jay Parrish) former foundation executive
Piga, Stephen Mulry lawyer
Pilisuk, Marc community psychology educator
Pillai, A(rrackal) K(asava) B. integral development therapist, anthropology educator
†Pinckney, Darryl writer
Ping, David Thomas senior project engineer
Pinkney, D. Timothy investment company executive
Pinkney, Jerry artist, educator
Pinter, Gabriel George physiologist
Piore, Nora Kahn economist, health policy analyst
Pipal, Faustin Anthony savings bank executive
Piper, Fredessa Mary school system administrator
Pirkle, Earl Charnell geologist, educator
Pisney, Raymond Frank international consulting services executive
Pitcher, Griffith Fontaine lawyer
Pitstick, Leslie James food products company executive
Pitts, Terence Randolph curator and museum director
Pizzuro, Salvatore Nicholas special education educator
Plangere, Jules Leon, Jr. media company executive
Plank, (Ethel) Faye editor, photographer, writer
Platou, Joanne (Dode) museum director
Platti, Rita Jane educator, draftsman, author, inventor
Pleshette, Suzanne actress, writer
Pletcher, Eldon editorial cartoonist
Plimpton, Calvin Hastings physician, university president
Plumb, Pamela Pelton consulting company executive, former mayor and councilwoman
Plummer, Daniel Clarence, III insurance consultant
Poch, Stephen metallurgical engineer, consultant
Pockell, Leslie M. publishing company executive
Pocock, Frederick James scientist, consultant
Polasek, Edward John electrical engineer, consultant
†Poledouris, Basil K. composer
Polenz, Joanna Magda psychiatrist
Policano, Joseph Daniel import company executive
Polikoff, Benet, Jr. lawyer
Polk, James Ray journalist
Polk, Robert Forrest banker
Poll, Martin Harvey film producer
Pollack, Gerald Alexander economist, government official
Pollack, Joseph retired labor union official
Pollack, Ronald F(rank) foundation executive, lawyer
Pollak, Edward Barry chemical manufacturing company executive
Pollard, Henry lawyer
Pollock, Marc educational media administrator, consultant
Pomraning, Gerald Carlton engineering educator
Ponce de Leon, Michael artist, lecturer, educator
Pond, Phyllis Joan state legislator
Pool, Philip Bemis, Jr. investment banker
Pooley, Beverley John law educator, librarian
Poor, Janet Meakin landscape designer
Pope, Durand L. opera manager
Pope, Robert Glynn telecommunications executive
Popovich, Robert P. biochemical engineer, educator
Porges, Walter Rudolf television news executive
Porosky, Michael Hanny real estate and investment company executive
Porow, Marie-Carl mental health nurse
Porteous, Timothy academic administrator
Porter, Daniel Reed, III museum director
Porter, Philip Thomas retired electrical engineer
Portis, Alan Mark physicist, educator
Poser, Ernest George psychologist, educator
Posner, Kenneth Robert hotel corporation executive
Post, Markie actress
Post, Richard Bennett retired human resources executive
†Poster, Steven Barry publisher, photographer, digital imaging consultant
Poston, Tom actor
Pote, Harold William banker
Potok, Chaim author, artist, editor
Potter, James Earl retired international hotel management company executive
Potts, Douglas Gordon neuroradiologist
Potvin, Alfred Raoul engineering executive
Pouncey, Peter Richard college president, classics educator
Pound, Robert Vivian physics educator
†Pourfarrokh, Ali ballet company artistic director
Powell, Clinton Cobb radiologist, physician, former university administrator
Powell, Earl Alexander, III art museum director
†Powell, Earl W. chemicals executive
Powell, Harvard Wendell former air force officer, business executive
Powell, Thomas Edward, III biological supply company executive
Powers, Stefanie (Stefanie Federkiewicz) actress
Powledge, Fred Arlius freelance writer
Prager, David retired state supreme court chief justice
Prather, Gerald Luther management consultant, retired air force officer, judge
Pratt, Edmund Taylor, Jr. pharmaceutical company executive
Pratt, Terrence Wendall information research scientist
Preble, James J. banker
Precopio, Frank Mario chemical company executive
Press, Aida Kabatznick writer
Pressman, Thane Andrew consumer products executive
Prestera, Lauretta Anne newspaper executive
Preston, Alda S. academic administrator, nursing educator
Preston, Richard McCann creative company executive, writer
Preston, Seymour Stotler, III manufacturing company executive
Preusser, Joseph William academic administrator
Prey, Barbara Ernst artist
Priaulx, A(llan) publishing executive
Price, Paul Buford physicist, educator
Price, Phillip S. retired adult education educator
Price, Robert electronics consultant
Price, Robert Ira coast guard officer
Pridmore, Roy Davis government official
Primosch, James Thomas music educator, composer, musician
Prince, (Prince Rogers Nelson) musician, actor
Prince, Andrew Steven lawyer, former government official
Prince, Milton S. investment company executive
Prins, Robert Jack college administrator
Pritchard, Claudius Hornby, Jr. retired university president
Pritzker, Leon statistician, consultant
Procter, John Ernest former publishing company executive
Proctor, Richard J. geologist, consultant
Procunier, Richard Werner environmental scientist, administrator
Prokasy, William Frederick academic administrator
Prokopis, Emmanuel Charles communications company executive
Propst, Harold Dean retired university chancellor
Provensen, Alice Rose Twitchell artist, author
Proxmire, William former senator
Prugh, George Shipley lawyer
Pruis, John J. business executive
Prusiner, Stanley Ben neurology and biochemistry educator, researcher
Pryce, Deborah D. congresswoman
Pryor, Harold S. retired college president
Pudney, Gary Laurence television executive
Pullen, Penny Lynne non-profit administrator, former state legislator
Purcell, Philip James financial services company executive
Pursey, Derek Lindsay physics educator
Purvis, Richard George former superintendent of schools
Puryear, Alvin Nelson management educator
Pusateri, Lawrence Xavier lawyer
Pusey, William Webb, III retired dean, foreign language educator
Pustilnik, David Daniel lawyer
Putnam, Linda Lee communication educator, researcher
Quaid, Dennis actor
Quaid, Randy actor
Queenan, Joseph Martin, Jr. writer, magazine editor
Quehl, Gary Howard association executive, consultant
Quesnel, Gregory L. transportation company executive
Questrom, Allen I. retail executive
Quick, Carolyn May nurse administrator
Quick, Norman bishop
Quigley, Leonard Vincent lawyer
Quillen, Cecil Dyer, Jr. lawyer, consultant
Quillen, William Tatem state judge, lawyer, educator
Quindlen, Anna journalist, author
Quinlan, J(oseph) Michael lawyer
†Quinlan, Kathleen actress
Quinn, Charles Nicholas journalist
Quinn, Phyllis association executive
Quinnan, Edward Michael management consultant
Quirico, Francis Joseph retired state supreme court justice
Quist, Beth Dobson small business owner
Qutub, Musa Yacub hydrogeologist, educator, consultant
Raab, Herbert Norman retail executive
Rabinowitz, Mark Allan lawyer
Rabó, Jule Anthony chemical research administrator, consultant
Rabon, William James, Jr. architect
Rabson, Robert plant physiologist, administrator
Rader, Dotson Carlyle author, journalist
Radice, Anne-Imelda museum director
Radin, Norman Samuel retired biochemistry educator
Rafael, Ruth Kelson archivist, librarian, consultant
Rafelson, Bob film director
Ragsdale, Carl Vandyke motion picture producer
Raichle, Marcus Edward radiology, neurology educator
Rainey, Claude Gladwin retired health care executive
Rains, Hazel Grace curriculum director
Rajki, Walter Albert manufacturing company executive
Ralston, Joanne Smoot public relations counseling firm executive
Ramanarayanan, Madhava Prabhu science administrator, researcher, educator
Ramo, Virginia M. Smith civic worker
Rampen, Leonardus Eduard broadcasting company executive
Ramseier, Roger I. aerospace and defense products company executive
Ramsey, Claude Swanson, Jr. former industrial executive
Ramsey, Stephen Douglas lawyer
Randall, Richard Harding, Jr. art gallery director
Randall, Richard Rainier geographer
Randinelli, Tracey Anne magazine editor
Randolph, Judson Graves pediatric surgeon
Ransohoff, Martin motion picture producer
Ransome, Ernest Leslie, III transportation and retail company executive
Rapaccioli, Michel Antoine financial executive
Rappaport, Theodore Scott electrical engineering educator
Raskin, Michael A. retail company executive
Rasor, Dina Lynn investigator, journalist
Rassman, Joel H. real estate company executive, accountant
Rast, Walter, Jr. hydrologist, water quality management
Ratcliff, James Lewis administrator
Ratcliff, Sara Boney federal agency administrator
Rau, Robert Nicholas pipe distribution executive
Raucher, Herman novelist, screenwriter
Rauner, Mary Ellen nursing administrator, critical care nurse
Rawls, S(ol) Waite, III business executive
Ray, Gayle Elrod sheriff
Rayball, Sharon A. medical/surgical nurse, administrator
Raymer, Donald George utility company executive
Raymond, Lee R. oil company executive
Rayner, William Alexander retired newspaper editor
Raynolds, Harold, Jr. retired state education commissioner
Read, Paul E. horticulture educator
Reade, Robert Mellor advertising consultant, retired convenience store executive
Reath, George, Jr. lawyer
Reaves, Ray Donald civil engineer
Redbone, Leon singer, musician
Redda, Kinfe Ken chemist, educator
Reddy, Helen Maxine singer
Redford, Robert (Charles Robert Redford) actor, director
Redgrave, Vanessa actress
Redmont, Bernard Sidney university dean, journalism educator
Reed, Adam Victor psychologist, engineer
Reed, David Fredrick artist
Reeder, James Arthur lawyer
Reeder, Robert Harry retired lawyer
Reese, Harry Browne lawyer, educator
Reetz, Harold Frank, Jr. industrial agronomist
Reeves, Frank Blair architect, educator
Reeves, John Edwin, Jr. manufacturing company executive
Reeves, Keanu actor
Regalado, Raul L. airport parking executive
Regan, William Joseph, Jr. energy company executive
Regnery, Henry publisher
Rehm, Leo Frank civil engineer
Rehmus, Charles Martin law educator, arbitrator
Reich, Herb editor
Reich, Robert Bernard U.S. secretary of labor, political economics educator
Reiche, Frank Perley lawyer, former federal commissioner
Reichman, Fredrick Thomas artist
Reichstetter, Arthur Charles banker
Reid, Harry senator

Reid, Michael J. international management consultant and educator
Reidenbaugh, Lowell Henry retired sports editor
Reifsnider, Kenneth Leonard metallurgist, educator
Reilly, Edward Francis, Jr. former state senator, federal agency administrator
Reinhardt, John Edward former international affairs specialist
Reinhardt, Stephen Roy federal judge
Reinke, Ralph Louis retired academic administrator
Reisch, Michael Stewart social work educator
Reisman, Fredricka Kauffman education educator
Reiss, Jerome lawyer
Reister, Ruth Alkema lawyer, business executive
Reitan, Daniel Kinseth electrical and computer engineering educator
Reiter, Glenn Mitchell lawyer
Remer, Donald Sherwood chemical engineer, engineering economist, educator, administrator
Reminger, Richard Thomas lawyer
Renaud, Bernadette Marie Elise author
Renda, Dominic Phillip airline executive
Renkiewicz, Mary Antoinette hospital administrator
Renson, Jean Felix psychiatry educator
Reppen, Norbjorn Dag electrical engineer, consultant
Rescigno, Nicola conductor, administrator
Resnick, Myron J. insurance company executive, lawyer
Reston, James Barrett retired newspaper publishing executive, author,
Retz, William Andrew naval officer
Reuber, Grant Louis banking insurance company executive
Reuman, Robert Everett philosophy educator
Reycraft, George Dewey lawyer
Reynolds, Carl Christiansen government official
Reynolds, Jack W. retired utility company executive
Reynolds, John Charles communications company executive, management consultant
Reynolds, John Francis insurance company executive
Reynolds, Lynne Warren special education educator, speech pathologist
Reynolds, William Bradford lawyer
Rhame, Thomas Gene army officer
Rhein, Murray Harold management consultant
Rhett, John Taylor, Jr. government official, civil engineer
Rhodes, Geraldine Bryan secondary school administrator
Rhodes, Peter Edward label company executive
Riasanovsky, Nicholas Valentine historian, educator
Rice, Joseph Albert banker
Rice, Richard Campbell retired state official, retired army officer
Rice, Richard Lee retired architect
Rice, Roger Douglas television executive, artist
Rice, Stanley Travis, Jr. poet, English language educator
Rice, Stuart Alan chemist, educator
Rice, Walter Herbert federal judge
Rich, David Barry city official, auditor, accountant, entertainer
Rich, John film and television producer, director
Rich, Mary D. women's health nurse
Richard, Susan Mathis trade association executive
Richards, Paul Linford physics educator, researcher
Richards, Thomas Carl air force officer, governmental official
Richards, Vincent Philip Haslewood librarian
Richardson, Charles Clifton biochemist, educator
Richardson, Elsie Helen retired elementary educator
Richardson, Natasha Jane actress
Richardson, Robert Dale, Jr. English language educator
Richie, Lionel B., Jr. singer, songwriter, producer
Richman, Alan magazine editor
Richman, Marvin Jordan real estate developer, investor, educator
Richman, Paul semiconductor industry executive, educator
Richman, Peter electronics executive
Richmond, Julius Benjamin retired physician, health policy educator emeritus
Rickard, Ruth David retired history and political science educator
Rickards, Leonard Myron oil company executive
Rickert, Jonathan Bradley foreign service officer
Rickey, George Warren artist, sculptor, educator
Rickman, Tom screenwriter, director
Ridder, Paul Anthony newspaper executive
Riddle, Donald Husted former university chancellor
Rideout, Patricia Irene operatic, oratorio and concert singer
Ridloff, Richard real estate executive, lawyer, consultant
Riehecky, Janet Ellen writer
Rifkin, Ned museum director
Riggs, Sonya Woicinski elementary school educator
Righter, Walter Cameron bishop
Riklis, Marcia retail executive
Riley, Terry composer, musician
Rimel, Rebecca Webster foundation executive
Risebrough, Doug professional hockey team executive
Riss, Robert Bailey insurance company executive
Ritchie, Anne educational administrator
Ritter-Clough, Elise Dawn publishing company executive, consultant
Rivera, Rosalind Theresa nurse, educator
Rivers, Kenneth Jay judicial administrator, consultant
Rivkind, Perry Abbot federal railroad agency administrator
Robb, David Metheny, Jr. art historian
Robb, Lynda Johnson writer
Robbins, Frances Elaine educational administrator
Robbins, Jessie Earl metallurgist
Roberts, Alfred Wheeler, III law firm executive
Roberts, Doris actress
Roberts, Earl John carbohydrate chemist
Roberts, James G. foundation executive
Roberts, Joan I. social psychologist, educator
Roberts, John Glover, Jr. lawyer
Roberts, Julia Fiona actress
Roberts, Karlene Ann education educator
Roberts, Marie Dyer computer systems specialist
Roberts, Samuel Smith television news executive
Roberts, Thomas Morgan federal official
Robertson, A. Haeworth actuary, benefit consultant, foundation executive
Robertson, Cliff actor, writer, director
Robertson, John Archibald Law nuclear scientist
Robertson, Mary Virginia retired elementary educator
Robertson, R(ita) Kae nurse, administrator
Robins, Norman Alan strategic planning consultant, former steel company executive
Robinson, Aminah Brenda Lynn artist
Robinson, Bob Leo international investment services executive
Robinson, Bruce Butler physicist
Robinson, Charlotte Hill artist
Robinson, David Adair neurophysiologist
Robinson, David Earl pharmaceutical executive
Robinson, Edward Joseph cosmetics company executive
†Robinson, Gail Patricia mental health counselor
Robinson, James Arthur university president emeritus, political scientist
Robinson, Linda Gosden communications executive
Robinson, Marshall Alan economics educator, foundation executive
Robinson, Nina nursing administrator
Robison, James Everett management consulting company executive
Robreno, Eduardo C. federal judge
Rochberg, George composer, educator
Roche, Lisa Riley reporter
Rock, Richard Rand lawyer, former state senator
Rockburne, Dorothea G. artist
Rockefeller, Margaretta Fitler Murphy (Happy Rockefeller) widow of former vice president of U.S.
Rodbell, Clyde Armand distribution executive
†Rodgers, Bruce E. writer
†Rodgers, Fran Sussner educational development specialist
Rodgers, Lawrence Rodney physician, educator
Rodriguez, Elias C. federal judge
Rodriguez, Veronica special education educator
Roe, Thomas Coombe former utility company executive
Roeder, Mary Alice health facility administrator
Roegner, George Peter industrial designer
Roethel, David Albert Hill consultant
Roetman, Orvil M. aerospace company executive
Rogers, Bernard William military officer
Rogers, Charles Ford, II architect
Rogers, David playwright, novelist, actor
Rogers, Herbert F. manufacturing company executive
†Rogers, Jack David plant pathologist, educator
Rogers, Justin Towner, Jr. retired utility company executive
Rogers, Kate Ellen interior design educator
Rogers, Margaret Ellen Jonsson civic worker
Rogers, Nathaniel Sims banker
Rogers, Rosemary author
Rogo, Kathleen safety engineer
Rohatsch, Ralph R., Jr. (Bob Rohatsch, Jr.) career military officer
Rohlf, Robert Henry retired library director, library consultant
Rohr, Davis Charles aerospace consultant, business executive, retired air force officer
Rohrback, Robert Lee, Jr. lawyer
Roitman, Judith mathematician
†Roland, William Alfred accountant, nursing home administrator
Rolandi, Gianna coloratura soprano
Roller, Thomas Benjamin manufacturing company executive
Rollins, Alfred Brooks, Jr. historian, educator
Romans, Donald Bishop corporate executive
Romeo, Luigi linguist, educator
Rooke, David Lee retired chemical company executive
Rooks, Charles Shelby minister
Rooney, J. Patrick insurance company executive
Root, Doris Smiley portrait artist
Roper, John Lonsdale, III shipyard executive
Ropp, Ann L. nurse consultant
Rorke, Kevin Hayden broadcasting executive
Rose, Carol Marguerite law educator
Rose, Elizabeth author, satirist, poet, publisher, environmentalist
Rose, James Turner aerospace consultant
Rose, Mason H., IV psychoanalyst
Rose, Robert John bishop
Rose, Rubye Blevins (Patsy Montana) singer
Rose, T. T. bishop
Rosemberg, Eugenia physician, scientist, educator, medical research administrator
Rosemont, Norman television and feature producer
Rosen, Arthur Marvin advertising executive
Rosen, Charles Welles pianist, music educator
Rosen, Lawrence anthropology educator
Rosen, Myor harpist, educator
Rosenbaum, Irving M. retail store executive
Rosenberg, Alison P. public policy official
Rosenberg, Jerome Willard accounting and consulting company executive
Rosenberg, Sheli Zysman lawyer, financial management executive
Rosenberg, Stuart film director
†Rosenblatt, Eddie record company executive
Rosenblatt, Joseph poet, editor
Rosenblatt, Roger writer
Rosenfield, James Harold communications executive
Rosenkoetter, Gerald Edwin engineering and construction company executive
Rosenn, Harold lawyer
Rosenow, John Henry surgeon, educator
Rosenquist, James Albert artist
Rosenthal, Arnold H. film director, producer, writer, graphic designer
Rosenthal, Arthur Jesse publisher
Rosenthal, Helen Nagelberg county official, advocate
†Rosenthal, Martha Newman museum executive
Rosenthal, Sol Roy preventive medicine educator, researcher
Rosenthal, William Forshaw advertising executive
Ross, Charlotte Pack suicidologist
Ross, Donald Roe federal judge
Ross, Elinor soprano
†Ross, Gloria Frankenthaler artist, consultant
Ross, Joseph E. government official, lawyer
Ross, Robert Joseph head professional football coach
Rosselló, Pedro J. governor of Puerto Rico
Rossi, Peter Henry sociology educator
Rossman, Ruth Scharff artist, educator
Roth, Michael lawyer
Roth, Richard J. marketing and advertising consulant
Roth, Toby congressman
Rothfeld, Michael B. investment banker
Rothing, Frank John government official
Rothman, Julius Lawrence retired English language educator
Rothschild, Carolyn Anita art dealer
Rothwell, Albert Falcon retired lawyer, retired natural resource company executive
Roudybush, Alexandra novelist
Roundell, Henry J. banker
†Rounds, John Scoville, Jr. publishing executive
Rountree, Neva Dixon public relations executive
Rourke, Mickey (Philip Andre Rourke, Jr.) actor
Rouse, Roscoe, Jr. librarian, educator
Roveto, Connie Ida financial services executive
Rowe, William Davis financial services company executive
Rowlands, Gena actress
Roy, P. Norman manufacturing company executive
Royal, Darrell K. university administrator
Roychoudhuri, Chandrasekhar physicist
Royer, Donald E. lawyer
Royer, Richard Adrian hospital administrator
Ruane, Maureen Muriel labor union official
Rub, Louis John savings and loan executive
Rubello, David Jerome artist
Rubenstein, Michael Alan architect
Rubin, Larry Bruce writer, reporter
Rubin, Rick record producer
Rubin, Sandra Mendelsohn artist
Rubin, Vera Cooper research astronomer
Rubin, Zick psychology educator, lawyer, writer
Rubinstein, Eva (Anna) photographer
Ruchelman, Leonard Isadore urban studies and public administration educator
Rucker, Charles Thomas science facility administrator
Ruderman, Armand Peter health economics educator, consultant, volunteer
Rudin, Anne Noto former mayor, nurse
Rudner, Sara dancer, choreographer
Rudy, Raymond Bruce, Jr. retired food company executive
Rudzki, Eugeniusz Maciej chemical engineer, consultant
Ruegg, Donald George retired railway company executive
Rugge, Hugo Robert physicist
Ruggiero, Matthew John bassoonist
Ruland, Midlred Ardelia retail executive, retail buyer
Rundquist, Howard Irving investment banker
Runge, Donald Edward food wholesale company executive
Rupp, Glenn N. sporting goods executive
Rush, Norman author
Rush, Richard Henry financier, writer, lecturer
Russell, John Lynn, Jr. physicist
Russell, Ray author
Russell, Theresa Lynn actress
Russo, Jose pathologist
Russo, Roy Lawrence electronic design automation engineer, retired
Rutherford, John Sherman, III (Johnny Rutherford) professional race car driver
Rutledge, Kenneth Dean food company executive
Ryan, Carl Ray electrical engineer
Ryan, George H. secretary of state, pharmacist
Ryan, George William manufacturing executive
Ryan, Ione Jean Alohilani retired educator, counselor
Ryan, James insurance company executive
Ryan, John William association executive
Ryan, John William, Jr. construction-related consulting company executive
Ryan, Mary Headd nursing educator, administrator
Ryan, Robert John, Jr. agricultural cooperative executive
Ryan, Tom Kreusch cartoonist
Ryder, Georgia Atkins university dean, educator
Ryder, Jack McBride educational consultant
Rydz, John S. manufacturing executive
Ryland, G(reaner) Neal financial executive
Saar, Betye (Irene Saar) artist
Sabatini, Nelson John government official
Sabat-Rivers, Georgina Latin American literature educator
Sacha, Robert Frank osteopathic physician
Sackellares, James Chris neurology educator
Sade, (Helen Folasade Adu) singer, songwriter
Sadler, Eric recording industry executive
Sadler, Graham Hydrick library administrator
Saeks, Richard Ephraim electrical engineer
Saffir, Leonard public relations executive
Sagan, Hans mathematician, educator, author
Said, Kamal E. accounting educator
Saint, Eva Marie actress
Sajak, Pat television game show host
Sakaino, Kozo automobile company executive
Saks, Gene theater director, actor
Salathe, John, Jr. manufacturing company executive
Salatka, Charles Alexander archbishop
Salbaing, Pierre Alcee retired chemical company executive
Salhany, Lucille S. broadcast executive
Salinas de Gortari, Carlos former president of Mexico
Saliterman, Richard Arlen lawyer, educator
Sallus, Marc Leonard lawyer
Saltarelli, Eugene A. retired engineering and construction company executive, consultant
Saltzman, Philip television writer, producer
Salzman, Marilyn B. Wolfson service company executive
Samek, Michael Johann corporation executive
Sameroff, Arnold Joshua developmental psychologist, educator, research scientist
Samper, Joseph Phillip retired photographic products company executive
Sampson, Ronald Gary lawyer
Sams, John Roland retired mission executive, missionary
Samson, Alvin former distributing company executive, consultant
Samuels, Cynthia Kalish communications executive
Samuelson, Robert Jacob journalist
Sanborn, David alto saxophonist
Sanchez, Gilbert retired university president, microbiologist
Sande, Thomas Paul toy manufacturing company executive
Sanders, Aaron Perry radiation biophysics educator
Sanders, Marlene academic administrator, educator, freelance broadcast journalist
Sanders, Wayne R. manufacturing executive
Sanders, William George public relations executive
Sandor, Gyorgy pianist
Sandrich, Jay H. television director
Sands, I. Jay corporate executive, business, marketing and real estate consultant, lecturer, realtor, analyst
Saneto, Russell Patrick pediatrician, neurobiologist
Sanfelippo, Peter Michael cardiac, thoracic and vascular surgeon
Santarelli, Eugene David air force officer
Santiago-Noa, Victor Manuel psychiatrist
Santman, Leon Duane lawyer, former federal government executive
Sapsowitz, Sidney H. entertainment and media company executive
Sargent, John Turner publisher
Sarris, Andrew George film critic
Sarry, Christine ballerina
Sasdi, George P. utilities company executive
Sauer, Jane Taylor nursing administrator, medical-surgical nurse
Sauerbrey, Ellen Elaine Richmond radio talk show host
Saunby, John Brian petrochemical company executive
Saunders, Alexander Hall real estate executive
Saunders, Thomas A., III investment company executive
Sausser, Robert Gary retired army officer
Sauter, Van Gordon communications executive
Sauvage, Lester Rosaire health facility administrator, cardiovascular surgeon
Sauvey, Donald (Robert) retired musical instrument company executive
Savage, Charles Francis lawyer
Savage, Neve Richard marketing executive
Savini, Tom make-up artist, actor, director
Sax, Joseph Lawrence lawyer, educator
Saxon, John David lawyer, educator
Saxon, Virginia M. nursing administrator
Sayer, John Samuel retired information systems consultant
Sayles, Leonard Robert management educator, consultant
Sayre, David physicist
Sayre, Francis Bowes, Jr. clergyman
Scala, James health care industry consultant, author
Scandary, E. Jane special education educator, consultant
Scanlan, John Douglas foreign service officer, former ambassador
Scanlon, Edward C. clinical psychologist
Scarf, Margaret (Maggi Scarf) author
Schacht, Linda Joan broadcast journalist
Schachter, Harry biochemist, educator
Schachter, Max retired engineering services company executive
Schaefer, C. Barry railroad executive, lawyer, investment banker
Schaefer, George Louis theatrical producer and director, educator
Schafer, Raymond Murray composer, author
Scharf, Linda Margaret nursing administrator
Scharf, William artist
Schatzberg, Jerry Ned (Jerrold Schatzberg) film director
Schauf, Victoria pediatrician, educator, researcher, consultant
Schechter, Paul J. pharmacologist
Scheel, Nels Earl financial executive, accountant
Scheele, Paul Drake former hospital supply corporate executive
Schein, Harvey L. communications executive
Schell, Allan Carter electrical engineer
Schenck, Jack Lee retired electric utility executive
Schenk, Lynn congresswoman
Schenker, Leo retired utility company executive
Schenkkan, Robert Frederic writer, actor
Scheuerman, Eleanor Joyce Miller medical association administrator
Schexnayder, Brian Edward opera singer
Schey, John Anthony metallurgical engineering educator
Schiaffino, S(ilvio) Stephen retired medical society executive, consultant
Schickel, Richard writer, film critic
Schiller, Alfred George veterinarian, educator
Schiller, Lawrence Julian motion picture producer, director
Schiller, Thomas Bennett motion picture writer, director
Schleck, Thomas Todd financial executive
Schlensker, Gary Chris landscaping company executive
Schley, Reeve, III artist
Schmalz, Carl Nelson, Jr. artist, educator, printmaker
Schmergel, Gabriel pharmaceutical company executive
Schmidt, Arthur Louis retired state senator
Schmidt, Benno Charles investment company executive
Schmidt, Jean Marie microbiology educator
Schmidt, Kenneth Martin investment banker
Schmidt, Richard Edward manufacturing company executive
Schmidt, Ruth Ann retired college president
Schmitt, George Joseph chemist
Schmults, Edward Charles lawyer
Schmutz, Charles Reid university foundation executive
Schnackenberg, Roy Lee artist
Schneider, Janet M. arts administrator, curator, painter
Schneider, Phyllis Leah writer, editor
Schnucker, Robert Victor history and religion educator
Schoen, Linda Allen public affairs administrator
Schoen, William Jack financier
Schoettler, Gail Sinton state official
†Scholes, Edison Earl army officer
Scholl, Allan Henry retired school system administrator, education consultant
Schomer, Fred K. financial executive
Schonhorn, Harold chemist, researcher
Schoor, Michael Mercier lawyer, lobbyist
Schorr, Daniel Louis broadcast journalist, author, lecturer
Schrader, Harry Christian, Jr. retired naval officer
Schrader, Henry Carl civil engineer, consultant
Schrader, Martin Harry retired publisher
Schrage, Rose educational administrator
Schrager, James E. financial company executive, educator
Schreckinger, Sy Edward advertising executive, consultant
Schrempf, Detlef professional basketball player
Schroeder, Paul J., Jr. lawyer
Schroeter, Louis C. retired pharmaceutical company executive
Schuck, Joyce Haber author
Schuck, Peter Horner lawyer, educator
Schuelke, John Paul religious organization administrator
Schulberg, Jay William advertising agency executive
†Schulstad, Eugene P. computer company executive
†Schulte, Richard Frank marketing company executive
Schultz, Eileen Hedy graphic designer
Schultz, Philip poet, novelist, educator
Schulz, Ralph Richard publishing consultant

Schulze, Erwin Emil *manufacturing company executive, lawyer*
Schumacher, Robert Joseph *petroleum company executive*
Schumacher, William Jacob *retired army officer*
Schur, Susan Dorfman *state legislator*
Schurr, John Michael *chemistry educator*
†Schuster, Gary Benjamin *chemistry educator, university dean*
Schuster, Gary Francis *corporate relations specialist, former news correspondent*
Schuur, Diane Joan *vocalist*
Schwab, Eileen Caulfield *lawyer, educator*
Schwab, John Harris *microbiology and immunology educator*
Schwardt, Susan Kelly *civic organization executive*
Schwartz, Carol Levitt *former government official*
Schwartz, Doris Ruhbel *nursing educator, consultant*
Schwartz, Eleanor Brantley *academic administrator*
Schwartz, John James *association executive, consultant*
Schwartz, Lillian Feldman *artist, filmaker, art analyst, author, nurse*
Schwartz, Lloyd Marvin *newspaper and magazine correspondent, broadcaster*
†Schwartz, Michael Joel *hospital executive*
Schwartz, Robert *automotive manufacturing company executive, marketing executive*
Schwartz, Samuel *business consultant, retired chemical company executive*
Schwartz, Stephen Blair *retired information industry executive*
Schwartzberg, Martin M. *chemical company executive*
Schwary, Ronald Louis *motion picture producer*
Schwarzschild, Martin *astronomer, educator*
Schwebel, Stephen Myron *judge, arbitrator*
Schweickart, Jim *advertising executive, broadcast consultant*
†Schweig, Margaret Berris *meeting and special events consultant*
Schwier, Frederick Warren *manufacturing company executive*
Schwinn, Donald Edwin *environmental engineer*
Scoles, Clyde Sheldon *library director*
Scollard, Diane Louise *retired elementary school educator*
Scott, Amy Annette Holloway *nursing educator*
Scott, Charles David *chemical engineer*
Scott, Isadore Meyer *former energy company executive*
Scott, John Burt *life insurance executive*
Scott, Larry Marcus *aerospace engineer, mathematician*
Scott, Lorraine Ann *fraternal organization executive*
Scott, Robert Hal *minister*
Scott, Thomas Wright *jazz musician, composer*
Scott, Waldron *mission executive*
Scott, William Herbert *state agency administrator*
Scruggs, Charles G. *editor*
Scruggs, Earl Eugene *entertainer*
†Seale, John Clement *director, cinematographer*
Seamans, William *writer, commentator, former television-radio journalist*
Searle, Philip Ford *banker*
Searle, Rodney Newell *state legislator, farmer, insurance agent*
Sears, Robert Louis *industrial engineer*
Sease, Gene Elwood *public relations company executive*
Sebastian, Peter *international affairs consultant, former ambassador*
Secrest, Vickie Lynn *nursing administrator*
Seedlock, Robert Francis *engineering and construction company executive*
Seelig, Gerard Leo *management consultant*
Sefcik, John Delbert *financial services executive*
Segal, JoAn Smyth *library consultant, organization administrator*
Seidel, Frederick Lewis *poet*
Seidensticker, Edward George *Japanese language and literature educator*
Sekitani, Toru *otolaryngologist, educator*
Selby, Hubert, Jr. *writer*
Seldes, Marian *actress*
Sella, George John, Jr. *chemical company executive*
Sellars, Victor Carol Gene *lawyer*
Sello, Allen Ralph *oil company executive*
Sells, Boake Anthony *private investor*
Semerad, Roger Dale *management consultant*
Sennema, David Carl *museum consultant*
Sentenne, Justine *corporate ombudsman*
Servan-Schreiber, Jean-Jacques *engineer, author*
Servison, Roger Theodore *investment executive*
Sessions, Robert Paul *former college president and administrator, retired educator, writer*
Severinghaus, Nelson, Jr. *mining company executive*
Sewell, Phyllis Shapiro *retail chain executive*
Seymour, Dale Gilbert *publisher, author, speaker, consultant*
Seymour, Richard Kellogg *linguist, educator*
Shadbolt, Douglas *architecture educator, administrator*
Shafran, Hank *public relations agency executive*
Shamask, Ronaldus *fashion designer*
Shanas, Bert Z. *public relations executive, journalist*
Shank, Maurice Edwin *aerospace engineering executive, consultant*
Shank, Wesley Ivan *retired architect, educator*
Shannon, Iris Reed *nursing educator*
Shannon, Margaret T. *nursing administrator, educator*
Shapiro, Debbie Lynn (Lynn Shapiro) *singer, actress, dancer*
Shapiro, Karl Jay *poet, former educator*
†Shapiro, Leo J. *social researcher*
Shapiro, Michael Edward *museum administrator, curator, art historian*
Shapiro, Richard Charles *sales and marketing executive*
Shapiro, Sumner *retired naval officer, business executive*
Sharlach, Jeffrey Roy *marketing company executive*
Sharpe, Sterling *professional football player*
Sharpe, William Forsyth *economics educator*
Sharwell, William Gay *retired university president and company executive*
Shasteen, Donald Eugene *government official*
Shatin, Judith *music composing educator*
Shattuck, Cathie Ann *lawyer, former government official*
Shaver, Daniel P. *law educator, civilian military employee*
Shaw, Artie *musician, writer, lecturer*
†Shaw, David Elliot *financial executive*
Shaw, Helen Lester Anderson *nutrition educator*
Shaw, Jerome *computer executive*
Shaw, John Frederick *retired naval officer*
Shaw, Melvin Phillip *physicist, engineering educator, psychologist*
Shaw, Richard *artist*
Shea, Bernard Charles *retired pharmaceutical company executive*
Shea, Donald Francis *state supreme court justice*
Shealy, Walter Dixon, III *banker*
Shearer, Charles Livingston *academic administrator*
Sheedy, Patrick Thomas *judge*
Sheehan, James Patrick *media company executive*
Sheehy, Gail Henion *author*
Sheeline, Paul Cushing *hotel executive*
†Sheffield, Richard Lee *physicist*
Sheldon, Brooke Earle *librarian, educator*
Sheldon, Terry Edwin *lawyer, business consultant, advisor*
Sheldon, Thomas Donald *academic administrator*
Shellman-Lucas, Elizabeth C. *special education educator, researcher*
Shelton, Karl Mason *management consultant*
Shelton, Sloane *actress*
Shelton, Stephani *broadcast journalist, consultant*
Shepard, Alan Bartlett, Jr. *astronaut, real estate developer*
Shepherd, Mark, Jr. *retired electronics company executive*
Sheppard, Harold Lloyd *gerontologist, educator*
Sher, Paul Phillip *physician, pathologist*
Sheridan, Diane Frances *public policy facilitator*
Sheridan, Patrick Michael *finance company executive*
Sheridan, Sonia Landy *artist, retired art educator*
Sherin, Edwin *theatrical and film director, actor*
Sherman, John Foord *biomedical consultant*
†Sherman, Joseph Owen *pediatric surgeon*
Sherman, Richard H. *education educator*
Sherrill, Thomas Beck *financial planner, state legislator*
Sherwood, (Peter) Louis *retail executive*
Shields, H. Richard *tax consultant,business executive*
Shields, John Joseph *computer manufacturing executive*
Shillingsburg, Miriam Jones *English educator, academic administrator*
Shils, Maurice Edward *physician, educator*
Shimizu, Taisuke *bank executive*
Shimpfky, Richard Lester *bishop*
Shindler, Merrill Karsh *writer, radio personality*
Shipley, Lucia Helene *retired chemical company executive*
Shirley, David Arthur *chemistry educator, science administrator*
Shirley, George Pfeiffer *lawyer, educational consultant*
Shirley-Quirk, John *concert and opera singer*
Shockley, Edward Julian *aerospace company executive*
Shockley, James Thomas *physics educator*
Shook, Ann Jones *lawyer*
Shore, Harvey Harris *business educator*
Short, Martin *actor, comedian*
Shoulberg, Harry *artist*
Shoup, Harold Arthur *advertising executive*
Shreve, Susan Richards *author, English literature educator*
Shriber, Maurice Norden *research and manufacturing company executive*
Shughart, Donald Louis *lawyer*
Shultis, Robert Lynn *finance educator, cost systems consultant, retired professional association executive*
Shumacker, Harris B., Jr. *surgeon, educator, author*
Shur, Michael *electrical engineer, educator, consultant*
Shure, Myrna Beth *psychologist, educator*
Shute, Richard Emil *government official, engineer*
Shutler, Kenneth Eugene *lawyer*
Shyer, Charles Richard *screenwriter, film director*
Sices, David *language educator, translator*
Siddayao, Corazón Morales *economist, educator*
Siefer, Stuart B. *architect*
Siegel, Jack Morton *retired biotechnology company executive*
Siegel, Laurence Gordon *conductor*
Silberberg, Inga *dermatologist*
Silberman, Laurence Hirsch *federal judge*
Silkett, Robert Tillson *food business consultant*
Silverman, Jonathan *actor*
Silverman, Michael *manufacturing company executive*
Silverstein, Barbara Ann *conductor*
†Silvestri, Alan Anthony *film composer*
Silvius, Donald Joe *educational consultant*
Simecka, Betty Jean *convention and visitors bureau executive*
Simeral, William Goodrich *retired chemical company executive*
Simmons, Joseph Jacob, III *federal commissioner*
Simmons, Paul Allen *retired federal judge*
Simmons, Ted Conrad *writer*
Simms, Maria Ester *health services administrator*
Simms, Susan Faye *nursing administrator*
Simon, Carly *singer, composer, author*
Simon, Melvin *real estate developer, professional basketball executive*
Simon, Melvin I. *molecular biologist, educator*
Simon, Michael Paul *general contractor, realtor*
Simon, Paul *musician, composer*
Simon, Roger Lichtenberg *writer*
Simonet, John Thomas *banker*
Simonton, Robert Bennet *lawyer*
Simpson, Frederick James *retired research administrator*
Simpson, Murray *engineer, consultant*
Simpson, O. J. (Orenthal James Simpson) *former professional football player, actor, sports commentator*
Sims, Kent Otway *economist*
Sinclair, Carole *publisher, editor, author*
Sinclair, Doris Paula Gimmeson *nurse, educational administrator*
Sinclair, Virgil Lee, Jr. *lawyer, writer*
Sincoff, Michael Z. *human resources and marketing professional*
†Singer, David Michael *marketing and public relations company executive*
Singer, Markus Morton *retired trade association executive*
Sinicropi, Anthony Vincent *industrial relations and human resources educator*
†Sipple, John Harrison *physician*
Sisto, Elena *artist, educator*
Sjostrand, Fritiof Stig *biologist, educator*
Skaff, Joseph John *state agency administrator, retired army officer*
Skelton, John Edward *computer technology consultant*
Skinner, James Stanford *physiologist, educator*
Skinner, Patricia Morag *state legislator*
Skoglund, Elizabeth Ruth *marriage, child and family counselor*
Skolovsky, Zadel *concert pianist, educator*
Skov, Arlie Mason *petroleum engineer, consultant*
Skowronski, Vincent Paul *concert violinist, recording artist, executive producer, producer classical recordings*
Skratek, Sylvia Paulette *mediator, arbitrator, dispute systems designer*
Skromme, Lawrence H. *consulting agricultural engineer*
Slagle, Jacob Winebrenner, Jr. *food products executive*
Slavin, Susan Ann *secondary educator*
Slavitt, David Walton *retired lawyer*
Slayton, William Larew *planning consultant, former government official*
Slewitzke, Connie Lee *retired army officer*
Slott, Phil *advertising agency executive*
Sloyan, Gerard Stephen *religious studies educator, priest*
Small, Melvin D. *physician, educator*
Smally, Donald Jay *consulting engineering executive*
Smith, Ann C. *nursing educator*
Smith, Barbara Anne *healthcare management company consultant*
Smith, Billie M. *retired aircraft company executive*
Smith, Charles Haddon *geoscientist, consultant*
Smith, Charlotte Reed *retired music educator*
Smith, Darwin Eatna *lawyer, retired manufacturing executive*
Smith, David Callaway *retired accounting firm executive*
Smith, Donald Nickerson *food service executive*
Smith, Doris Victoria *educational agency administrator*
Smith, Edward K. *economist, consultant*
Smith, Edward Reaugh *retired lawyer, cemetery and funeral home consultant*
Smith, Fern M. *federal judge*
Smith, Floyd Leslie *insurance company executive*
Smith, Frederick Coe *manufacturing executive*
Smith, Gerald Francis *rendering company executive*
Smith, Goff *industrial equipment manufacturing executive*
Smith, Hedrick Laurence *journalist, television commentator, author, lecturer*
Smith, Howard McQueen *librarian*
Smith, Ileene Andrea *book editor*
Smith, James T. *electronics company executive*
Smith, James Thomas *food products executive*
Smith, Jean Chandler *former museum official*
Smith, Joe Mauk *chemical engineer, educator*
Smith, Kenneth Blose *former financial executive*
Smith, Lauren Ashley *lawyer, journalist, clergyman, physicist*
Smith, Laverne Byrd *educational association administrator*
Smith, Lawrence Leighton *conductor*
Smith, Lois Arlene *actress, writer*
Smith, Martin Bernhard *journalist*
Smith, Martin Cruz *author*
Smith, Martin Henry *pediatrician*
Smith, Paul James *manufacturing company executive*
Smith, Paul Vergon, Jr. *corporate executive, retired oil company executive*
Smith, Richard Anthony *investment banker*
Smith, Richard Grant *retired telecommunications executive, electrical engineer*
Smith, Robert F. *banker*
Smith, Robert Michael *lawyer*
Smith, Robert Powell *foundation executive, former ambassador*
Smith, Ronald Lynn *health system executive*
Smith, Sallye Wrye *librarian*
Smith, Seymour Maslin *financial advisor, investment banker*
Smith, Stuart Lyon *psychiatrist, corporate executive*
Smith, Thomas Winston *cotton marketing executive*
Smith, V. Kerry *economics educator*
Smith, Wilburn Jackson, Jr. *retired bank executive*
Smither, Howard Elbert *musicologist*
Smock, Raymond William *historian, government official*
Smoot, Hazel Lampkin *retired piano teacher, poet*
Smoot, Wendell McMeans, Jr. *investment counselor*
Smothers, Dick *actor, singer*
Smulyan, Lisa *educator*
Smyth, John McDonnell, III *merchant, lawyer*
Sneed, Alberta Neal *retired elementary education educator*
Snell, George Davis *geneticist*
Snelling, Robert Orren, Sr. *franchising executive*
Snelson, Kenneth Duane *sculptor*
Snetsinger, David Clarence *retired animal feed company executive*
Snider, L. Britt *government executive*
Snipes, Wesley *actor*
Snoddon, Larry Erle *public relations executive*
Snortland, Howard Jerome *educational financial consultant*
Snow, John William *railroad executive*
Snowden, Lawrence Fontaine *retired aircraft company executive, retired marine corps general officer*
Snyder, Alan Carhart *insurance company executive*
Snyder, Gary Sherman *poet*
Snyder, Susan Brooke *retired English literature educator*
Snyder, William Burton *insurance executive*
Sodolski, John *retired association administrator*
Sokal, Robert Reuven *biology educator, author*
Solarz, Stephen Joshua *congressman*
Soles, Ada Leigh *former state legislator, government advisor*
Sollender, Joel David *management consultant, financial executive*
Solomon, Robert Charles *philosopher, educator*
Solow, Herbert Franklin *film producer, writer*
Solzhenitsyn, Aleksandr Isayevich *author*
Somers, Louis Robert *retired food company executive*
Sommer, Howard Ellsworth *textile executive*
Sondheim, Stephen Joshua *composer, lyricist*
Sonnenschein, Hugo Freund *university president, economics educator*
Sorel, Edward *artist*
Sorensen, Robert Holm *diversified technology company executive, retired*
Sorensen, Sheila *state senator*
Soro, Mar Bawai *bishop*
Sorter, Bruce Wilbur *federal program administrator, educator, consultant*
Sotirhos, Michael *ambassador*
Soule, Sallie Thompson *retired state official*
Souter, David Hackett *U.S. supreme court justice*
South, Frank Edwin *physiologist, educator*
Southerland, S. Duane *manufacturing company executive*
Southwick, Charles Henry *zoologist, educator*
Souveroff, Vernon William, Jr. *corporate executive, investor, author*
†Spada, James *author, publisher*
Spadafora, David Charles *university administrator*
Spanninger, Beth Anne *lawyer*
Spatta, Carolyn Davis *education consultant*
Spaulding, Frank Henry *librarian*
Spear, Deborah *surgical nurse, administrator*
Spearman, Leonard H. O., Sr. *ambassador*
Spears, Franklin Scott *retired supreme court justice*
Spector, Michael Joseph *agribusiness executive*
Spejewski, Eugene Henry *physicist, educator*
Spence, Andrew *artist, painter*
Spence, Glen Oscar *clergyman*
†Spencer, David Mills *library administrator*
Spicer, S(amuel) Gary *lawyer, writer*
Spiesicke, Margrit Herma *counselor*
Spinelli, Jerry *writer*
Spirn, Michele Sobel *communications professional, writer*
Spittler, Jayne Zenaty *advertising executive*
Spitzer, Lyman, Jr. *astronomer*
Splietoff, William Ludwig *chemical company executive*
Splitstone, George Dale *retired hospital administrator*
Spollen, John William *lawyer*
Springer, Paul David *lawyer, motion picture company executive*
Springer, Robert Dale *retired air force officer, consultant, lecturer*
Sprinthall, Norman Arthur *psychology educator*
Srinivasan, Venkataraman *marketing and management educator*
Sroge, Maxwell Harold *marketing consultant, publishing executive*
Stabile, Benedict Louis *retired academic administrator, retired coast guard officer*
Stacy, Bill Wayne *college president*
Stadler, Craig Robert *professional golfer*
Staiger, Ralph Conrad *educational consultant, former educational association executive*
Staker, Robert Jackson *federal judge*
Stallworth-Barron, Doris A. Carter *librarian, educator*
Stalon, Charles Gary *retired economics educator, institute administrator*
Stamos, John James *judge*
Stamp, Frederick Pfarr, Jr. *federal judge*
Stamper, Malcolm Theodore *aerospace company executive*
Stanfill, Dennis Carothers *business executive*
Stanley, Margaret King *performing arts administrator*
Stanley, Scott, Jr. *editor*
Stans, Maurice Hubert *retired business consultant, former government official*
Stanton, John Jeffrey *editor, broadcast journalist, government programs director, analyst*
Stanton, Louis Lee *federal judge*
Stanton, Robert John *corporate bank executive, lawyer*
Stapleton, Maureen *actress*
Starer, Robert *composer*
Stark, Donald Gerald *pharmaceutical executive*
Stark, Nellie May *forest ecology educator*
Starr, David *newspaper editor, publisher*
Starr, Kenneth Winston *lawyer*
Starr, Leon *retired chemical research company executive*
Stavely, Keith Williams Fitzgerald *librarian*
Stearns, Carl David *architect*
Stearns, Robert Leland *curator*
Steen, Carlton Duane *private investor, former food company executive*
Stefano, Ross William *business executive*
Steffens, Dorothy Ruth *political economist*
Stegall, Daniel Richard *lawyer*
Stein, Arnold *English educator*
Stein, Dale Franklin *retired university president*
Stein, Milton Michael *lawyer*
Stein, Paul Arthur *financial services executive*
Stein, Stanley Richard *lawyer, fast food company executive*
Steinback, Kenneth B. *computer sales company executive*
Steiner, Michael *sculptor*
†Steiner, William *direct marketing advertising agency executive, consultant*
Steinhauser, Sheldon Eli *sociology and gerontology educator*
Stendahl, Krister *retired bishop*
Stengel, Ronald Francis *management consultant*
Stennett, William Clinton (Clint Stennett) *radio and television station executive, state legislator*
Stephens, Donald R(ichards) *banker*
Stephens, Elton Bryson *bank executive, service and manufacturing company executive*
Stephenson, Bette Mildred *physician, former Canadian legislator*
Stepp, James Michael *business executive*
Stern, Arthur Paul *electronics company executive, electrical engineer*
Stern, Charles *foreign trade company executive*
Stern, Daniel *author, executive, educator*
Stern, Milton *chemical company executive*
Stern, Nancy Fortgang *mathematics and computer science, educator*
†Stern, Robert Stuart *dermatologist, editor*
†Stern, Todd David *lawyer*
Sternhagen, Frances *actress*
Stetler, David J. *lawyer*
†Stevens, Berton Louis, Jr. *data processing manager*
Stevens, Lydia Hastings *civic worker*
Stevens, May *artist*
Stevens, Warren *actor*
†Stevenson, Bryan Allen *lawyer, administrator*
Stevenson, Elizabeth *author, educator*
Stevenson, Paul Michael *physics educator, researcher*
Steward, H. Leighton *oil company executive*
Stewart, Carleton M. *banker, corporate director*
Stewart, Clinton Eugene *adult education educator*
Stewart, James Maitland *actor*
Stewart, John Ezell *educational and business consultant*
Stewart, John Murray *banker*
Stewart, Marsha Beach *sales executive, entertainment executive*
Stewart, Norman Lawrence *university president*
Stewart, Peter Beaufort *retired beverage company executive*
Stewart, Richard Alfred *business executive*
Stewart, Robert Gordon *former museum curator*
Stewart, Robert William *retired physicist, government research council executive*

Stewart, Thomas James, Jr. baritone
Stewart, Thomas Simrall radio executive
Stewart, Thomas Ted real estate developer, investment banker
Stewart, Zeph classicist, educator
Stickler, Fred Charles manufacturing company executive
Stickler, Gunnar Brynolf pediatrician
Stickney, Jessica former state legislator
Stiff, Robert Martin newspaper editor
Stiller, Jerry actor
Stillings, Dennis Otto research director
Stine, R(obert) L(awrence) children's book author
Stines, Fred, Jr. publisher
Stinnett, Lee Houston newspaper association executive
Stivers, William Charles forest products company executive
Stokoe, Phillip Michael physical education educator, school board member
Stolarik, M. Mark history educator
Stolley, Richard Brockway journalist
Stone, David Deaderick physician, educator
Stone, James Robert surgeon
Stotter, Harry Shelton banker, lawyer
Strain, James Ellsworth pediatrician, retired association administrator
Strait, George country music vocalist
Strandberg, John David comparative pathologist
Strangway, David William university president
Strasser, Gabor priest, management consultant
Stratman, Joseph Lee petroleum refining company executive, consultant, chemical engineer
†Stratton, Mariann retired naval nursing administrator
Straub, Peter Francis novelist
Strauss, Simon David manufacturing executive
Strazis, Cynthia W. nurse, administrator
Stream, Arnold Crager lawyer, writer
Street, John Charles linguistics educator
Streeter, Richard Henry lawyer
Streeter, Tal sculptor
Strider, Marjorie Virginia artist, educator
Striker, Cecil Leopold archaeologist, educator
Striker, Gary E. scientist, research institution administrator
Stringham, Rene physician
Strock, William C. lawyer
Strohsahl, George Henry, Jr. retired rear admiral, consultant
†Stroman, Susan choreographer
Stromberg, Arthur Harold retired professional services company executive
Strong, William Sutherland lawyer
Strothman, James Edward editor
Struebing, Robert Virgil retired oil company executive
†Stryker, Richard Ripley, Jr. museum director
Stuart, Joseph Martin art museum administrator
Stuart, Mary actress
Stuckwisch, Clarence George university administrator
Stults, Walter Black management consultant, former trade organization executive
Stumpe, Warren Robert scientific, engineering and technical services company executive
Sturgis, William Beaufort packaging company executive
Sturtevant, Julian Munson biophysical chemist, educator
Styron, William writer
Suenholz, Herman Harry banker
Sugarman, Samuel Louis retired oil transportation and trading company executive, horse breeder
Sullivan, Daniel Joseph writer
Sullivan, George Edward author
Sullivan, James Lenox clergyman
Sullivan, Leon Howard clergyman
Sullivan, Michael Patrick marine officer
Sullivan, Nicholas G. science educator, speleologist
Sullivan, William Courtney retired communications executive
Sullivan, Woodruff Turner, III astronomy educator, science historian, researcher, gnomonicist
Sumichrast, Jozef illustrator, designer
Summerfield, John Robert textile curator
Sundaresan, Mosur Kalyanaraman physics educator
Sunderman, Duane Neuman chemist, research institute executive
Sundry, Arthur P. business executive
Sunell, Robert John retired army officer
Suppes, Patrick statistics, education, philosophy and psychology educator
Suput, Ray Radoslav librarian
Surrey, Philip Henry artist, educator
Sussman, Barry author, public opinion analyst and pollster, journalist
Sutherland, Kiefer actor
Sutton, Dolores actress, writer
Sutton, Julia Sumberg musicologist, dance historian
Sutton, Willis Anderson, Jr. sociology educator
Swanberg, Edmund Raymond investment counselor
Swanger, Sterling Orville appliance manufacturing company executive
Swango, William Franklin coal company executive
†Swanson, Dane C. navy pilot
Swanson, Dane Craig naval officer, pilot
Swanson, Paul Rubert minister
Swanson, Peter Carl editor
Swanson, Rune E. financial executive
Swanstrom, Thomas Evan economist
Sweet, Philip W. K., Jr. former banker
Swensen, Mary Jean Hamilton graphic artist
Swick, Herbert Morris medical educator, neurologist
Swihart, Jean Ogden psychoanalyst
Swihart, John Marion retired aircraft manufacturing company executive
Swindler, Daris Ray physical anthropologist, forensic anthropologist
Swing, Marce producer, publisher
Swit, Loretta actress
Switzer, Maurice Harold publisher
Switzer, Ralph Joseph, Jr. diversified industry executive
Swope, Donald Downey retired banker
Sze, Andy Hok-Fan transportation executive
Taber, Edward Albert, III investment executive
Tachmindji, Alexander John systems engineering consultant
Tagiuri, Consuelo Keller child psychiatrist, educator
Tagliattini, Maurizio construction executive, historian, writer
Takal, Peter artist
Talbot, Howard Chase, Jr. retired museum administrator
Talbot, Kathleen Mary elementary education educator
Talingdan, Arsenio Preza health science administrator
Tallchief, Maria ballerina
Tallett, Elizabeth Edith biopharmaceutical company executive
Talley, Robert Morrell aerospace company executive
Tamen, Harriet lawyer
Tan, Amy Ruth writer
Tan, Veronica Y. psychiatrist
Tancredi, Laurence Richard law and psychiatry educator, administrator
Tandler, Bernard cell biology educator
Tangney, Joseph G. insurance executive
Tanner, Laurel Nan education educator
Tansor, Robert Henry investor
Tapley, James Leroy retired lawyer, railway corporation executive
Taplin, Frank E., Jr. trustee education and arts institutions and associations
Tarr, Curtis W. business executive
Tarr, David William political scientist, educator
Tasco, Frank John insurance brokering company executive
Tashjean, Catherine Richardson librarian
Tassia, Marie C. health facility administrator
Tate, Frederick Wayne federal agency administrator
Tate, Manford Ben guided missile scientist, investor
Tatlock, Anne M. trust company executive
Tatyrek, Alfred Frank consultant, materials/ environmental engineer, analytical and research chemist
Taubman, A. Alfred real estate developer
Taylor, Allen John U.S. Coast Guard officer
Taylor, Barbara Jo Anne Harris government official, librarian, educator, civic and political worker
†Taylor, Billy (William Edward Taylor) jazz musician
Taylor, Cecil Percival pianist, composer, educator
Taylor, David George retired banker
Taylor, Gary L. federal judge
Taylor, Guy Watson symphonic conductor
Taylor, Hugh Pettingill, Jr. geologist, educator
Taylor, James E. lawyer
Taylor, John Jackson (Jay) writer, international consultant, retired foreign service officer
Taylor, Kristin Clark media specialist
Taylor, Millard Benjamin concertmaster, educator
Taylor, Richard Wirth political science educator
Teague, Wayne state education official
Teeple, Fiona Diane librarian, lawyer
Teichroew, Daniel information science educator
Teitelbaum, Irving retail executive
Temam, Roger M. mathematician
Templeton, Carson Howard engineering executive, policy analyst
Templeton, John Alexander, II coal company executive
Tenney, Stephen Marsh physiologist, educator
terHorst, Jerald Franklin public affairs counsel
Terkel, Susan Neiburg author
Terris, Susan physician, cardiologist
Terry, Clifford Lewis journalist
Terry, John Hart lawyer, former utility company executive, former congressman
Tessler, Allan Roger lawyer
Tewkesbury, Joan F. film director, writer
Textor, Robert Bayard cultural anthropology writer, consultant, educator
Thackray, Arnold Wilfrid historian, foundation executive
Thackray, Richard Irving psychologist
Thal, Herbert Ludwig, Jr. electrical engineer, engineering consultant
Thaxter, Phyllis St. Felix actress
Theno, Daniel O'Connell former state legislator
Theobald, H. Rupert retired political scientist
Theroux, Paul Edward author
Thiel, Philip design educator
Thiele, Howard Nellis, Jr. lawyer
Thiessen, Gordon George banker
Thiounn, Prasith foreign service official
Thom, Douglas Andrew paper company executive
Thomas, Franklin Augustine foundation executive
Thomas, Karen P. composer, conductor
Thomas, Martha Wetterhall advertising agency executive
Thomas, Melissa Ann lawyer
Thomas, Patricia Anne retired law librarian
Thomas, Ross Elmore author
Thomas, Tom retired plastics company executive
Thompson, Anne Marie newspaper publisher
Thompson, Charles Kevin architect, lighting designer
Thompson, Chester Franklin advertising executive
Thompson, J. Andy bank executive
Thompson, Jack Edward mining company executive
Thompson, Julia Ann physicist
Thompson, Ralph Newell former chemical corporation executive
Thompson, Richard Stephen management consultant
Thompson, Robert Elliott columnist, writer
Thompson, Robert W. theoretical physicist
Thorington, John M., Jr. computer graphics company executive
Thornburg, Frederick Fletcher diversified business executive, lawyer
Thornburg, Lacy Herman judge
Thorne, Barbara Lockwood guidance counselor, secondary education educator
Thorne, Kip Stephen physicist, educator
Thorstenberg, (John) Laurence oboe and English horn player
Threefoot, Sam Abraham physician, educator
Threet, Jack Curtis oil company executive
Threlkeld, Richard Davis broadcast journalist
Throckmorton, William Robert, Sr. sociologist
Thuillier, Richard Howard meteorologist
Tichenor, Donald Keith association executive
Tiedge-Lafranier, Jeanne Marie editor
Tiemeyer, Christian conductor
Tienken, Arthur T. retired foreign service officer
Tillman, Massie Monroe federal judge
Tillmon, Bobbi lawyer
Timmons, William Milton retired cinema arts educator, publisher, free-lance writer, film maker
Ting, Albert Chia bioengineering researcher
Tippett, Willis Paul, Jr. automotive and textile company executive, retired
Tisdale, Stuart Williams holding company executive
Tobias, Andrew Previn columnist, lecturer
Tobin, Michael Edward banker
Todd, John Odell insurance company sales professional
Todea, Rockling organizational development consultant
Toensing, Victoria lawyer
Toevs, Alden Louis management consultant
Toffler, Alvin author
Tokofsky, Jerry Herbert film producer
Toledo-Pereyra, Luis Horacio transplant surgeon, researcher, historian educator
Tolentino, Casimiro Urbano lawyer
Toll, Maynard Joy, Jr. investment banker
Tomas, Jerold F. V. business executive, management consultant
Tomasi, Donald Charles architect
Tomasko, Mark Daniel lawyer
Tombros, Peter George pharmaceutical company executive
Tomlin, Lily actress
Tompsett, Michael Francis research director
Toms, Justine Willis educational organization executive
Tomsovic, Edward Joseph college dean
Tonello-Stuart, Enrica Maria political economist
Tongue, Paul Graham financial executive
Tonjes, Marian Jeannette Benton education educator
Tonkyn, Richard George retired oil and gas company executive, researcher, consultant
Toor, Herbert Lawrence chemical engineering educator, researcher
Topaz, Muriel dance educator
Topik, Steven Curtis history educator
Topilow, Carl S. conductor
Torn, Rip (Elmore Rual Torn, Jr.) actor, director
Tourino, Ralph Gene career officer
Tovish, Harold sculptor
Towery, Matthew Allen, Sr. lawyer
Townsend, Susan Elaine social service institute administrator, hostage survival consultant
Trachta, Pamela Hale consulting executive
Transou, Lynda Lew advertising executive
Travanti, Daniel John actor
Travers, Oliver S., Jr. manufacturing company executive
Travis, Randy Bruce musician
Travisano, Frank Peter professional management consultant/business broker
Travolta, John actor
†Treat, James J. accountant, business executive
Trelease, Allen William historian, educator
Trenery, Mary Ellen librarian
Tresnowski, Bernard Richard retired health insurance company executive
Treynor, Jack Lawrence financial advisor, educator
Trigg, Paul Reginald, Jr. lawyer
Trilling, Diana writer
Trilling, Helen Regina lawyer
Trimble, Paul Joseph lawyer
Triolo, Peter advertising agency executive, marketing educator, consultant
Tripplehorn, Jeanne actress
Trombino, Roger A. investment banker
Trow, Jo Anne Johnson retired university official
Troy, B. Theodore direct mail advertising executive
Trudeau, Garretson Beekman (Garry Trudeau) cartoonist
Trueman, William Peter Main broadcaster, newspaper columnist
Truman, Margaret author
Trump, Donald John real estate developer
Trutter, John Thomas consulting company executive
Tsai, Wen-Ying sculptor, painter, engineer
Tuck, Russell R., Jr. past college president
Tucker, H. Richard oil company executive
Tucker, Hal Beall retired electric utility executive
Tucker, Jack William Andrew writer, film editor
Tucker, Paul William retired petroleum company executive
Tuft, Mary Ann former association executive
Tumbleson, Arthur Louis civil engineer, contractor
Turco, Richard Peter atmospheric scientist
†Turk, Richard Errington retired psychiatrist
Turkin, Marshall William symphony orchestra, festival and opera administrator, arranger, composer
Turnbull, Fred Gerdes electronics engineer
Turnbull, John Neil retired chemical company executive
Turner, Henry Brown finance executive
Turner, James P. lawyer
Turner, Lana (Julia Jean Mildred Frances Turner) actress
Turner, Lee S., Jr. chemical engineer,consultant, former utilities executive
†Turner, Margery Austin government agency administrator
Turner, Robert Comrie composer
Turnoff, William Charles judge
Turok, Paul Harris composer, music reviewer
Tutwiler, Margaret DeBardeleben communications executive
Twomey, Janet Louise Wilkov banker
Tyson, H. Michael bank executive
Tytler, Linda Jean communications and public affairs executive, retired state legislator
Tzimopoulos, Nicholas D. science and mathematics education specialist
Ubell, Earl television science editor
Udall, Morris King former congressman
Udcoff, George Joseph financial executive
Uehlinger, John Clark marketing executive
Ugrin, Béla video producer
Uhrich, Richard Beckley hospital executive, physician
Ullmann, Liv actress
Ulrich, Richard William finance executive
Uman, Martin Allan electrical engineering educator, researcher, consultant
Unger, Sonja Franz package company executive, travel consultant, ceramist
Unithan, Dolly visual artist
Updike, John Hoyer writer
Urdang, Laurence lexicographer, publisher
Uris, Leon Marcus author
Ussery, Luanne communications consultant
†Vachon, Louis-Albert Cardinal archbishop
Vachon, Serge Jean bank executive
Vajeeprasee Thongsak, Thomas business planning executive
Vaky, Viron Peter diplomacy educator, former foreign service officer
†Valade, Robert Charles apparel company executive
Valcic, Susan Joan lawyer
Valens, Evans Gladstone sculptor, printmaker, author, former television producer, director
Valentine, William Newton physician, educator
Vallat, Louise Marie elementary school educator, poet
†Vallone, John Charles motion picture production designer
Van Allsburg, Chris author, artist
VanButsel, Michael R. real estate developer
Vandenberg, Peter Ray magazine publisher
Vanderhoof, Irwin Thomas life insurance company executive
Vanderpool, Robert Lee, Jr. banker
Vander Wiel, Kenneth Carlton computer services company executive
Vandevender, Barbara Jewell elementary education educator, farmer
Van Dreser, Merton Lawrence ceramic engineer
Vandross, Luther singer
Van Duyn, Mona Jane poet
van Dyck, Nicholas Booraem minister, foundation official
Van Horn, Lecia Joseph legal secretary
Vanier, Jacques physicist
van Itallie, Jean-Claude playwright
Van Ness, John Ralph university foundation administrator
Van Patten, Joyce Benignia actress
Van Tassel, James Henry retired electronics executive
van't Hoff, Winfried C. J. retired diversified manufacturing executive
Van Valin, Clyde Emory bishop
Van Vinkenroye du Waysaeck, Fedia Maurice Gilles financial services executive
Varn, Richard James university administrator, lawyer, consultant
Varon, Dan electrical engineer
Vassil, Pamela graphic designer
Vaughan, John Charles, III horticultural products executive
Vega, J. William aerospace engineering executive, consultant
Velzy, Charles O. mechanical engineer
Verdecchia, Guillermo Luis playwright
Verdi, Robert William sports columnist
Vernon, Carl Atlee, Jr. retired wholesale food distributor executive
Veronis, George geophysicist, educator
Verplanck, William Samuel psychologist, educator
Verret, John Cyril advertising executive
Verwoerdt, Adriaan psychiatrist
Vickrey, Robert Edward, Jr. petroleum engineer
Vidal, Gore writer
Vila, Adis Maria corporate executive, former government official, lawyer
Villella, Edward Joseph ballet dancer, choreographer, artistic director
Vincent, Hal Wellman marine corps officer, investor
Viorst, Milton writer
Virgo, Julie Anne Carroll management consultant
Virkhaus, Taavo conductor
Voight, Elizabeth Anne lawyer
Voigt, Cynthia author
Voketaitis, Arnold Mathew bass-baritone, educator
Volcker, Paul A. economist
Volkhardt, John Malcolm food company executive
Vollmer, Richard Wade federal judge
Volpe, Edmond L(oris) college president
Voltz, Jeanne Appleton author
von Hoffman, Nicholas writer, former journalist
Voorhees, James Dayton, Jr. lawyer
Voorhees, John Schenck lawyer
Vosburg, Noble E. fur company executive
Vosburgh, Margaret Murphy nurse administrator
Voss, Omer Gerald truck company executive
Vowell, Jack C. former state legislator, investor
Waddle, John Frederick former retail chain executive
Wadley, M. Richard consumer products executive
Wagman, Robert John journalist, author
Wagner, Julia A(nne) retired editor
Wagner, Richard business executive, former baseball team executive
Wagner, Robert David, Jr. banker
Wagner, Sigurd electrical engineering educator, researcher
Wagoner, Lynda Jo pediatrics nurse
Wahl, Rosalie E. state supreme court justice
†Wahlen, Edwin Alfred, Jr. venture capitalist
Walch, W. Stanley lawyer
Waldhauser, Cathy Howard financial services executive
Waldo, Burton Corlett lawyer
Waldrop, Gideon William composer, conductor, former president music school
Waldrop, Linda M. medical administrator
Waldschutz, Gerhard corporate executive
Walker, Craig Michael lawyer
Walker, Decker Fannin education educator
Walker, Gordon Davies former government official, writer, lecturer, consultant
Walker, Henry Gilbert health care executive, consultant
Walker, James William, Jr. lawyer
Walker, John Sumpter, Jr. lawyer
†Walker, Kenneth Dale automotive parts company executive
†Walker, Leroy Tashreau university chancellor, coach
Walker, Mary L. lawyer
Walkup, John Frank electrical engineer, educator
Wall, M. Danny financial services consultant
†Wallace, Keith Alton legislator, dairy farmer
Wallace, William Augustine philosophy and history educator
Wallach, Eli actor
Wallack-Roselli, Rina Evelyn lawyer
Waller, Gary Fredric English language educator, poet
Walner, Robert Joel lawyer
Walsh, Joseph Fidler recording artist, record producer
Walsh, Kenneth Albert chemist
Walsh, William Albert management consultant, former naval officer
Walston, Ray actor
Walter, J. Jackson consultant
Walter, James W. diversified manufacturing executive
Walter, John Robert printing company executive
Walter, Martin Edward mathematician, educator
Walters, Vernon Anthony ambassador
Walthall, Lee Wade artistic director, dancer
Walton, Harold Vincent former agricultural engineering educator, academic administrator
Walton, Ronald Elwood retired school superintendent
Waltrip, Darrell Lee professional stock car driver
Wambaugh, Joseph author
Wang, James T. public planning executive
Wapenhans, Willi Adolf banking executive
†Warburton, Richard John financial executive
Ward, Elaine artist
Ward, Susan Marie cultural organization administrator
Warder, Richard Currey, Jr. mechanical aerospace engineering educator
Warfel, John Hiatt medical educator, retired
Warlick, Roger Kinney history educator, assistant dean
Warner, Jack, Jr. motion picture and television producer, writer

Warnken, Douglas Richard publishing consultant
Warren, Alfred S., Jr. automobile manufacturing company executive
Warren, Henry Clay, Jr. retired naturalist
Warson, Toby Gene retired corporate executive
Wartella, Ellen Ann communications educator, consultant
Washburn, Melinda Wall nursing administrator
Washington, Delphine Cynthia special education educator, artist
Washington, MaliVai professional tennis player
Washington, Shelley Lynne dancer
Washington, Valora foundation administrator
Washington, Walter retired college president
Wassenich, Linda Pilcher health policy analyst, fund raiser
Wasserstein, Wendy playwright
Waters, Betty Lou newspaper reporter, writer
Waters, David Rogers retail executive
Waters, John film director, writer, actor
Waters, Roger rock musician
Waters, Willie Anthony opera and orchestra conductor
Watson, James D., Jr. principal
Watson, Robert Barden physicist
Watson, W. Robert president, chief executive officer
Watt, John H. financial executive
Watts, Glenn Ellis union official
Watts, Heather ballerina
Watts, Ronald Lester retired military officer
Wayburn, Laurie Andrea environmental and wildlife foundation administrator, conservationist
Waymouth, John Francis physicist, consultant
†Weaver, Charles Horace educational administrator
Weaver, Edward T. foundation executive, educator
Weaver, Howard Cecil newspaper editor
Weber, Eugen historian, educator, author
Weber, Julian L. lawyer, former publishing and entertainment company executive
†Weber, Mary Ellen Healy economist
Webster, Robert David lawyer
Wechter, Vivienne Thaul artist, poet, educator
Weckesser, Ernest Prosper, Jr. publisher, educator
Weclew, Robert George lawyer, educator
Weddig, Lee J(ohn) trade association executive
Weertman, Johannes materials science educator
Weikart, David Powell educational research foundation administrator
Weikert, Jerard Lee real estate broker
Weil, Rolf Alfred economist, university president emeritus
Weiland, Charles Hankes lawyer
Weinberg, Robert Leonard retired lawyer
Weinberg, Steven physics educator
Weinberger, Arnold retired electrical engineer
Weinberger, Siegbert Jacob food company executive
Weiner, Louis Max retired mathematics educator
Weingarten, Joseph Leonard aerospace engineer
Weinhardt, Janice nursing educator
Weinkauf, Mary Louise Stanley clergywoman
Weinschel, Bruno Oscar engineering executive, physicist
Weinstein, Arnold Abraham playwright, theater educator
Weir, Kenneth Wynn marine corps officer, experimental test pilot
Weir, Thomas Charles banker
Weisburger, Elizabeth Kreiser chemist, editor
Weise, Theodore Louis delivery service executive
Weisman, Lorenzo David investment banker
Weismantel, Gregory Nelson management consultant and software executive
Weiss, Michael James chemistry educator
Weiss, William Lee retired communications executive
Weissman, Jack (George Anderson) editor
Weissmann, Heidi Seitelblum radiologist, educator
Weitz, Eric chemistry educator
Welch, Oliver Wendell retired pharmaceutical executive
Weld, Tuesday Ker (Susan Ker Weld) actress
Weldon, Jeffrey Alan state senator, historical research company executive
Welles, John Galt retired museum director
Welsome, Eileen journalist
Welton, Theodore Allen theoretical physics educator, consultant
Wen, Helen Hwa Jung nurse
Wendt, George Robert actor
Werman, Thomas Ehrlich record producer
Werner-Jacobsen, Emmy Elisabeth developmental psychologist
Werth, Andrew M. telecommunications executive
Wertlieb, Donald Lawrence psychologist, educator
Wesely, Marissa Celeste lawyer
Wessler, Richard Lee psychology educator, psychotherapist
Wesson, William Simpson retired paper company executive
West, Stephen Allan lawyer
Westreich, Benzion Joseph lawyer
†Westwood, Vivienne fashion designer
Wettig, Patricia actress
Wetzel, Donald Truman engineering company executive
Wexler, Jacqueline Grennan (Mrs. Paul J. Wexler) former association executive and college president
Whalen, Charles William, Jr. author, business executive, educator
Whaley, Lynne Ann senior vice president nursing
Wheaton, Warde Franklin manufacturing company executive
Wheeler, George Charles quality assurance professional
†Wheeler, Jack Cox army officer
Whistler, Roy Lester chemist, educator, industrialist
White, Augustus Aaron, III orthopaedic surgeon
White, Christine Lyons oncology nurse, nursing researcher
White, Doris Anne artist
White, Gerald Andrew chemical company executive
White, James Arthur college president
White, Loray Betty writer, actress, producer
White, Randy retired professional football player
White, Richard Clarence lawyer
White, Robb author
White, Robert Frederick landscape architect
White, Willis Sheridan, Jr. retired utilities company executive
Whitehead, Richard Lee insurance company executive
Whitehouse, Alton Winslow, Jr. retired oil company executive
Whitley, Nancy O'Neil retired radiology educator
Whitlock, Bennett Clarke, Jr. retired association executive
Whitmer, Joseph Morton benefits consulting firm executive, retired
Whitten, Dolphus, Jr. former university administrator, educational consortium executive
Wicker, Thomas Grey retired journalist
Wickman, Herbert Hollis physical chemist, condensed matter physicist
Widlus, Hannah Beverly lawyer
Widmark, Richard actor
Wiebe, Leonard Irving radiopharmacist, educator
Wiebenson, Dora Louise architectural historian, educator, author
Wien, Stuart Lewis retired supermarket chain executive
Wiesen, Donald Guy retired diversified manufacturing company executive
Wieser, Siegfried planetarium executive director
Wiesner, John Joseph retail executive
Wiessler, David Albert correspondent
Wigdor, Lawrence Allen chemical company executive
Wilder, Donny state legislator, retired newspaper publisher
Wildhack, William August, Jr. lawyer
Wiley, David Owen public relations executive
Wiley, Richard Arthur lawyer
Wilhelm, Joseph Lawrence archbishop
Wilhelmsen, Harold John accountant, operations controller
Wilke Montemayor, Joanne Marie patient care coordinator
Wilkens, Leonard Randolph, Jr. (Lenny Wilkens) professional basketball coach
Wilkerson, Charles Edward architect
Wilkins, Roger Carson retired insurance company executive
Wilkinson, Doris Yvonne medical sociology educator
Wilkinson, Stanley Ralph agronomist
Will, Joanne Marie food and consumer services executive, communications consultant, writer
Will, Mari Maseng communications consultant
Wille, Wayne Martin retired editor
Willenbecher, John artist
†Willey, Frank Patrick lawyer, insurance company executive
Willey, Gordon Randolph retired anthropologist, archaeologist, educator
William, David director, actor
Williams, Barbara Jean May state official
†Williams, Carol Joan foreign correspondent
Williams, Carolyn Elizabeth manufacturing executive
Williams, Charles Wesley technical executive, researcher
Williams, Earle Carter retired professional services company executive
Williams, Gaylen Eugene accountant
Williams, Gordon Roland librarian
Williams, Henry Stratton radiologist, educator
Williams, Joseph Theodore oil and gas company executive
Williams, Louis Clair, Jr. public relations executive
Williams, Patrick Moody composer
Williams, Raymond Crawford veterinarian anatomy educator
Williams, Richard Clarence retired librarian
Williams, Robert Leon psychiatrist, neurologist, educator
Williams, Robert Lyle corporate executive, consultant
Williams, Roger Stewart physician
Williams, Ronald Oscar systems engineer
Williams, Russell, II production sound mixer
Williams, Ted (Theodore Samuel Williams) former baseball player, former manager, consultant
Williams, Thomas Lloyd psychiatrist
Williams, Timothy James sanctuary manager, naturalist
Williams, William John, Jr. lawyer
Williamson, Fletcher Phillips real estate executive
Williamson, Laird stage director, actor
Williamson, Michael writer
Williamson, Myrna Hennrich retired army officer, lecturer, consultant
Williamson, Ronald Frank banker, former national guard official
Willig, Karl Victor computer firm executive
Willis, Bruce Walter actor, singer
Willis, Gary K. computer company executive
Wills, Charles Francis former church executive, retired career officer
Wills, William Ridley, II former insurance company executive, historian
Wilner, Judith journalist
Wilner, Thomas Bernard lawyer
Wilson, Almon Chapman surgeon, physician, retired naval officer
Wilson, Basil Wrigley oceanographic engineering consultant, artist, author
Wilson, Colin Henry writer
†Wilson, Gary Lee airline company executive
Wilson, Hugh Steven lawyer
Wilson, Jane artist
Wilson, Judy Vantrease publishing executive
Wilson, Kenneth Geddes physics research administrator, educator
Wilson, Lanford playwright
Wilson, M(athew) Kent retired chemist, researcher, educator
Wilson, Nancy singer
Wilson, Nora D. nursing administrator
Wilson, Richard Alexander career officer
Wilson, Robert James Montgomery investment company executive
Wilson, Roosevelt Ledell secondary education educator
Wilson, Roy Gardiner real estate developer
Wilson, Sheryl J. state agency administrator
Wilson, Sloan author, lecturer
Wiltbank, Joseph Kelley lawyer, university counsel, sports association executive
Winder, Robert Owen retired mathematician, computer engineer executive
†Winston, Charles David transportation company executive
Winter, Alan retired publishing company executive
Winter, John Dawson, III blues guitarist, singer
Winters, Jonathan actor
Winters, Nola Frances food company executive
Winters, Shelley (Shirley Schrift) actress
Winwood, Stephen Lawrence musician, composer
Wise, Jim Price energy company executive
Wise, Patricia lyric coloratura
Wiseman, Jay Donald photographer, mechanical contractor, designer
Witcher, Daniel Dougherty retired pharmaceutical company executive
Witt, Hugh Ernest technology consultant
Witte, Merlin Michael oil company executive
Wittich, John Jacob retired college president, educational administrator, corporation consultant
Wittner, Loren Antonow lawyer, former public relations executive
Woerner, Robert Lester landscape architect
Wofford, Harris Llewellyn former senator, lawyer
Wolf, Dale Edward state official
Wolf, Hans Abraham retired pharmaceutical company executive
Wolf, Rosalie Joyce financial executive
Wolf, William Martin computer company executive, consultant
Wolfberg, Melvin Donald company executive, optometrist, former college president, consultant
Wolfe, Gregory Baker international relations educator
Wolfe, Jean Elizabeth medical illustrator, painter
Wolff, Manfred Ernst medicinal chemist, pharmaceutical company executive
Wolff, Peter Adalbert physicist, educator
Wolfman, Ira Joel editor, writer
Wolfman Jack, (Robert Weston Smith) radio personality
Wolfson, Lawrence Aaron hospital administrator
Wollert, Gerald Dale retired food company executive, investor
Wolner, Rena Meryl publisher
Wolters, Oliver William history educator
Womach, Emily Hitch retired banker and marketing and public relations executive
Womack, Richard Marvin manufacturing company executive
Wommack, W(illiam) W(alton) retired manufacturing company executive
Wonders, William Clare geography educator
Wong, David Yue academic administrator, physics educator
Wood, Allen John electrical engineer, consultant
Wood, David Charles lawyer, finance company executive
Wood, Diane Pamela lawyer
Wood, Elwood Steven, III chemical company executive
Wood, Margaret Gray dermatologist, educator
Wood, Marian Starr publishing company executive
Wood, Presnall Hansel editor, minister
Wood, Robert Coldwell political scientist
Woodall, Jack David manufacturing company executive
Woodard, Nina Elizabeth banker
Wooden, John Robert former basketball coach
Woodhouse, Derrick Fergus ophthalmologist
Woods, Geraldine Pittman health education consultant, educational consultant
Woods, Phyllis Michalik elementary school educator
Woodward, Clinton Benjamin, Jr. civil engineering educator
Woodward, Joanne Gignilliat actress
Woodward, Thomas Morgan actor
Woosnam, Ian Harold professional golfer
Wootton, Mack Edward food products company executive
Work, William retired association executive
Worley, Gordon Roger retail chain financial executive
Worth, Gary James communications executive
Worthen, John Edward university president
Worthey, Carol composer
Wright, Ann Elizabeth physicist, consultant
Wright, Earl Jerome pastor, bishop
Wright, Gladys Stone music educator, composer, writer
Wright, James David sociology educator, writer
Wright, Linda Jean government relations executive
Wright, Sir (John) Oliver retired diplomat
Wright, Randolph Earle retired petroleum company executive
Wright, Thomas William automotive parts company executive
Wruck, Erich-Oskar German language educator, administrator
Wrucke-Nelson, Ann C. elementary school educator
Wulff, John Kenneth controller
Wussler, Robert Joseph broadcasting executive, media consultant
Wyatt, Lenore civic worker
Wyckoff, Margo Gail psychologist
Wylie, Clarence Raymond, Jr. mathematics educator
Wyman, Jane (Sarah Jane Fulks) actress
Wyman, Louis Crosby state justice, former senator, former congressman
Wymbs, Norman Elwood author, researcher
Wyngaarden, James Barnes physician
Yack, Patrick Ashley editor
Yamane, George Mitsuyoshi oral diagnosis and radiology educator
Yanagitani, Elizabeth optometrist
Yang, Xiangzhong research scientist, administrator, educator
Yarbro, Alan David lawyer
Yarbrough, Marilyn Virginia lawyer, educator
Yarrow, Peter folksinger
Yates, Charles Richardson former arts center executive
Yates, David John C. chemist, researcher
Yates, Elton G. retired petroleum industry executive
Yeager, Mark L. lawyer
Yearwood, Donald Robert oil and shipping executive
Yee, Albert Hoy retired psychologist, educator
Yellen, Linda film director, writer, producer
Yeo, Ronald Frederick librarian
Yeutter, Clayton Keith political organization executive, counselor to President of United States
Yielding, K. Lemone physician
Yntema, Mary Katherine retired mathematics educator
Yoakam, Dwight country western musician
Yocam, Delbert Wayne communication company executive
Yochelson, Bonnie Ellen museum curator, art historian
Yolton, John William philosopher, educator
York, Alexandra lawyer
Yost, William Albert psychology educator, hearing researcher
Yost, William Arthur, III lawyer
Young, John Alan electronics company executive
Young, Leo electrical engineer
Young, Margaret Buckner civic worker, author
Young, Margaret Chong elementary education educator
Young, Michael Kent lawyer, educator
Young, Peter Holden, Jr. wholesale food company executive
Young, Robert (George Young) actor
Young, Virgil M. education educator
Yovicich, George Steven Jones civil engineer
Zacks, Sumner Irwin pathologist
Zaffaroni, Alejandro C. biochemist, medical research company executive
Zaillian, Steven screenwriter, director
Zajac, Jack sculptor, painter
Zaliouk, Yuval Nathan conductor
Zander, Glenn R. airline company executive
Zanetti, Joseph Maurice, Jr. corporate executive
Zapf, Hermann book and type designer
Zayek, Francis Mansour bishop
†Zea, Kristina Gwyn costume and production designer
†Zeiger, Scott Leslie commercial theater executive
Zeigler, L(uther) Harmon political science educator
Zekman, Terri Margaret graphic designer
Zelazny, Roger Joseph author
Zeliff, William H., Jr. congressman
Zelinsky, Paul O. illustrator, painter, author
Zeller, Joseph Paul advertising executive
Zemsky, Robert educational administrator
Zhou, Ming De aeronautical scientist, educator
Zick, John Walter retired accounting company executive
Ziegler, Jack (Denmore) cartoonist
Zilkha, Ezra Khedouri banker
Zimm, Bruno Hasbrouck physical chemistry educator
Zimny, Max lawyer
Zinnen, Robert Oliver general management executive
†Zinner, Peter film editor and director, music editor
Ziock, Klaus Otto Heinrich physics educator
Zischke, Douglas Arthur foreign service officer
Zisk, Sherry health facility administrator
Zizza, Salvatore J. diversified company executive
Zoellick, Robert Bruce corporate executive, lawyer
Zuckerman, Martin Harvey personnel director
Zufryden, Fred S. academic administrator, marketing educator, researcher
†Zuiches, James Joseph academic administrator
Zweifel, Donald Edwin automobile dealer, civic affairs volunteer
Zwerver, Peter John linguistics educator
Zwislocki, Jozef John neuroscience educator, researcher

Professional Index

†New name in *Who's Who in America*, Golden 50th Edition

AGRICULTURE

UNITED STATES

ALABAMA

Anniston

Andrews, Glenn *farmer, former congressman*

ARIZONA

Green Valley

McGibbon, William Alexander *rancher, photographer*

ARKANSAS

Hot Springs National Park

Baer, Kenneth Peter *farmer cooperative executive*

CALIFORNIA

Arvin

Pankey, Edgar Edward *rancher*

Davis

Carter, Harold O. *agricultural economics educator*

Fresno

†Petrucci, Vincent Emilio *retired viticulture educator, consultant*

†Wilson, Herman T., Jr. *agricultural products supplier*

Modesto

Crawford, Charles McNeil *winery science executive*

Gallo, Ernest *vintner*

Napa

Chiarella, Peter Ralph *corporate executive*

Porterville

†Wall, Fred Willard *agricultural products supplier*

Rutherford

Eisele, Milton Douglas *viticulturist*

Sacramento

Wightman, Thomas Valentine *rancher, researcher*

San Francisco

Hills, Austin Edward *vineyard executive*

San Luis Obispo

McCorkle, Robert Ellsworth *agribusiness educator*

Sierra Madre

Whittingham, Charles Edward *thoroughbred race horse owner and trainer*

COLORADO

Denver

Foxley, William Coleman *cattleman*

Ridgway

Decker, Peter Randolph *rancher, former state official*

DELAWARE

Dover

Carey, V. George *farmer, state legislator*

DISTRICT OF COLUMBIA

Washington

Branstool, Charles Eugene *farmer, federal agency administrator*

Schmidt, Berlie Louis *agricultural research administrator*

FLORIDA

Clermont

Chandler, Robert Flint, Jr. *international agriculture consultant*

Ona

Pate, Findlay Moye *agriculture educator, university center director*

GEORGIA

Atlanta

Brooks, David William *farmer cooperative executive*

Stimpert, Michael Alan *agricultural products company executive*

Gainesville

Hatfield, Joe Sweatt, Jr. *agricultural products company executive*

HAWAII

Honolulu

Ching, Chauncey Tai Kin *agricultural economics educator*

Waialua

Singlehurst, Dona Geisenheyner *horse farm owner*

IDAHO

Boise

Hennessey, Alice Elizabeth *forest products company executive*

Simplot, John R. *agribusiness executive*

Twin Falls

Jones, Douglas Raymond *farming executive, state legislator*

ILLINOIS

Bloomington

Jones, Norman Thomas *agricultural products company executive*

Stevenson, Ernest Vail *retired farmer cooperative executive*

Stonier, Daryle L. *agricultural supplies company executive*

Webb, O. Glenn *farm supplies company executive*

Chicago

Mundlak, Yair *agriculture and economics educator*

Homewood

†Reed, Michael A. *agricultural products supplier*

Long Grove

Wilson, Stephen Ray *fertilizer manufacturing company executive*

Northfield

Bruns, Nicolaus, Jr. *retired agricultural chemicals company executive, lawyer*

Pekin

†Frison, Rick *agricultural company executive*

Urbana

Bentley, Orville George *retired agricultural educator, dean emeritus*

Cheryan, Munir *agricultural studies educator, biochemical engineering educator*

Courson, Roger Lee *agricultural educator*

Hill, Lowell Dean *agricultural marketing educator*

INDIANA

Indianapolis

French, Philip Franks *agricultural cooperative corporate executive*

Hegel, Carolyn Marie *farmer, farm bureau executive*

Lakeville

Mangus, Richard W. *farmer*

IOWA

Ames

Jacobson, Norman L. *retired agricultural educator, researcher*

Mullen, Russell Edward *agricultural studies educator*

Des Moines

Mertz, Dolores Mary *farmer, legislator*

Muscatine

Kautz, Richard Carl *chemical and feed company executive*

KANSAS

Atchison

Cray, Cloud Lanor, Jr. *grain products company executive*

Haven

Schlickau, George Hans *cattle breeder, professional association executive*

Manhattan

McKee, Richard Miles *animal studies educator*

KENTUCKY

Midway

Clay, Robert N. *thoroughbred breeder*

Port Royal

Berry, Wendell *farmer, author*

MICHIGAN

East Lansing

Paul, Eldor Alvin *agriculture, ecology educator*

†Reed, Thomas H. *livestock exchange executive*

MINNESOTA

Fridley

Rajamannan, Ambrose Harry *agriculture products supplier*

Minneapolis

Joseph, Burton M. *grain merchant*

Rosemount

Walter, Kenneth Luverne *agricultural facility director*

Saint Paul

Bertram, Jeff Nickolas *farmer, state legislator*

Dille, Stephen Everett *farmer, state legislator, veterinarian*

Zylstra, Stanley James *farmer, food company executive*

MISSOURI

Kansas City

Berg, W. Robert *agricultural products company executive*

McDowell, Robert *farmer*

Saint Louis

†Gain, Jeffrey W. *agricultural organization executive*

Springfield

Strickler, Ivan K. *dairy farmer*

NEBRASKA

Dakota City

Haines, Perry Vansant *cattle company executive*

Grand Island

Dobesh, Ernest Leonard *farmer, mayor*

Lincoln

Sheffield, Leslie Floyd *retired agricultural educator*

NEW YORK

Canandaigua

†Sands, Marvin *wine company executive*

Elmont

Stephens, Woodford Cefis (Woody Stephens) *horse trainer, breeder*

Ithaca

Bail, Joe Paul *agricultural educator emeritus*

Rochester

Pease, Donald E. *dairy farmer, food products company executive*

NORTH CAROLINA

Pittsboro

†Bixby, Donald Edward, Jr. *conservancy executive, veterinary consultant, rese*

Raleigh

Fike, William T. *agricultural studies educator*

NORTH DAKOTA

Bismarck

Carlisle, Ronald Dwight *nursery owner*

Rugby

Axtman, Benjamin J. *farmer*

Williston

Rennerfeldt, Earl Ronald *farmer, rancher*

OHIO

Columbus

Casey, Raymond Richard *agricultural business executive*

Holmes, Robert G. *agricultural studies educator*

Ockerman, Herbert W. *agricultural studies educator*

Delaware

Benschneider, Donald *agricultural products company executive*

Germantown

Lansaw, Charles Ray *rendering industry consultant*

OKLAHOMA

Oklahoma City

Beutler, Randy Leon *rancher, state legislator*

Tulsa

Oxley, John Thurman *ranching and investments executive, former petroleum company executive*

OREGON

Ashland

Walt, Harold Richard *rancher*

Riley

Cowan, Richard John *cattle rancher*

West Linn

Kane, Robert Joseph *retired floricultural company executive*

PENNSYLVANIA

Harleysville

Ruth, Alpheus Landis *dairy farmer*

SOUTH CAROLINA

Charleston

†Hastie, J. Drayton *plantation and garden owner, director*

SOUTH DAKOTA

Brookings

Moore, Raymond A. *agricultural educator*

Wessington

Lockner, Vera Joanne *farmer, rancher, legislator*

TENNESSEE

Cordova

Baer, Ben Kayser *cotton merchant*

La Vergne

†Walker, Phillip R. *agricultural products supplier*

Memphis

Echols, James *agricultural products supplier*

TEXAS

Austin

Fowler, Nola Faye *ranch owner, political consultant*

College Station

Christiansen, James Edward *agricultural educator*

Industry

Huitt, Jimmie L. *rancher, oil, gas, real estate investor*

Vega

Cook, Clayton Henry *rancher*

VIRGINIA

Burke

Dean, John Wilson, Jr. *business consultant, retired army officer*

Mc Lean

Brown, Billy Ross *agriculture association executive*

Kay, Thomas Oliver *agricultural consultant*

Montross

Fountain, Robert Roy, Jr. *farmer, retired industrial executive, naval officer*

Richmond

James, Gene Albert *farmers cooperative executive*

Spottswood

Fredricksen, Cleve Laurance *thoroughbred horse farm owner, real estate investor*

WASHINGTON

Walla Walla
Corfield, Timothy Lynn *college rodeo executive, educator*

Yakima
Grandy, Jay Franklin *fruit processing executive*

WEST VIRGINIA

Charles Town
McDonald, Angus Wheeler *farmer*

Lahmansville
Snyder, Robert Martin *agriculture consultant, retired government official*

WISCONSIN

Hancock
Kostichka, Charles Joseph *agricultural studies educator, researcher*

WYOMING

Douglas
Sanford, Leroy Leonard *rancher*

Dubois
Betts, Robert Budd, Jr. *dude ranch owner*

Fort Laramie
Hageman, James C. *rancher*

Jackson
Hansen, Clifford Peter *rancher*

Wheatland
Bunker, John Birkbeck *cattle rancher, retired sugar company executive*

CANADA

MANITOBA

Winnipeg
†Tremere, Arnold Wesley *agricultural institute executive*

ONTARIO

Blenheim
Thompson, Wesley Duncan *grain merchant*

Ottawa
Lister, Earle Edward *animal science consultant*

ADDRESS UNPUBLISHED

Aspen, Alfred William *international trading company executive*
Blackwell, Ronald Eugene *livestock consultant*
Erwin, Elmer Louis *vintager, cement consultant*
Johnson, Cyrus Edwin *grain farmer, former food products executive*
Monson, David Carl *farmer, state legislator*
Ryan, Robert John, Jr. *agricultural cooperative executive*

ARCHITECTURE AND DESIGN

UNITED STATES

ALABAMA

Auburn
Millman, Richard George *architect, educator*

Birmingham
Barrow, Richard Edward *architect*
Collier, Felton Moreland *architect, planner, developer, detention, and recreation consultant, lecturer*

Huntsville
Jones, Harvie Paul *architect*

Mobile
Winter, Arch Reese *architect*

Montgomery
Brock, Eugene C. *landscape architect*

Tuskegee
Pryce, Edward Lyons *landscape architect*

ALASKA

Anchorage
Kumin, Jonathan P. *architectural firm executive*
Maynard, Kenneth Douglas *architect*

ARIZONA

Carefree
Beadle, Alfred Newman *architect*
Robbins, Conrad W. *naval architect*

Green Valley
Schirmer, Henry William *architect*

Mesa
Shill, Victor Lamar *architect*

New River
Bruder, William Paul *architect*

Paradise Valley
Blumer, Harry Maynard *architect*

Phoenix
Adams, Gail Hayes *interior designer*
DeBartolo, Jack, Jr. *architect*
Elmore, James Walter *architect, retired university dean*
Gwozdz, Kim Elizabeth *interior designer*
Hawkins, Jasper Stillwell, Jr. *architect*
Schiffner, Charles Robert *architect*
Winslow, Paul David *architect*

Scottsdale
Douglas, John Clifton *architect*
Hill, John deKoven *architect*
Panks, Gary Allen *golf course architect*
Rutes, Walter Alan *architect*
Soleri, Paolo *architect, urban planner*

Sedona
Iverson, Wayne Dahl *landscape architect, consultant*

Sonoita
Cook, William Howard *architect*

Sun City West
Madson, John Andrew *architect*
Mc Cune, John Francis, III *retired architect*

Tempe
Abell, James Logan *architect*
Goodwin, Kemper *retired architect*
Mc Sheffrey, Gerald Rainey *architect, educator, city planner*
Thums, Charles William *designer, consultant*
Walker, Theodore Delbert *landscape architect*

Tucson
Breckenridge, Klindt Duncan *architect*
Chafee, Judith Davidson *architect*
Dinsmore, Philip Wade *architect*
Gourley, Ronald Robert *architect, educator*
Jones, Warren David *landscape architect, landscape architecture educator*
Mc Connell, Robert Eastwood *architect, educator*
Nelson, Edward Humphrey *architect*
Riggs, John B. *architect*
Wallach, Leslie Rothaus *architect*
Zube, Ervin Herbert *landscape architect, geographer, educator*

ARKANSAS

Fayetteville
Burggraf, Frank Bernard, Jr. *landscape architect, educator*
Jones, Euine Fay *architect, educator*
Jones, Fay *architect*

Little Rock
Blass, Noland, Jr. *retired architect*
Chilcote, Lugean Lester *architect*
Cromwell, Edwin Boykin *architect*
Levy, Eugene Pfeifer *architect*
Truemper, John James, Jr. *retired architect*
Wilcox, Jerry Cooper *architect*

CALIFORNIA

Altadena
Ziegler, Raymond Stewart *architect*

Bakersfield
McAlister, Michael Hillis *architect*

Berkeley
Arbegast, David Elwood *landscape architect*
Burger, Edmund Ganes *architect*
Cardwell, Kenneth Harvey *architect, educator*
Eckbo, Garrett *landscape architect, urban designer*
Hester, Randolph Thompson, Jr. *landscape architect, educator*
Hunt, Frank Bouldin *architect, water color artist*
Odermatt, Robert Allen *architect*
Paulling, John Randolph, Jr. *naval architecture educator, consultant*
Stoller, Claude *architect*

Beverly Hills
Eisenshtat, Sidney Herbert *architect*
Myers, Barton *architect*

Bodega Bay
King, Leland W. *architect*

Campbell
Richards, Lisle Frederick *architect*

Carmel
Merrill, William Dickey *architect*

Corona
Ohmert, Richard Allan *architect*

Corona Del Mar
Yeo, Ron *architect*

Coronado
Wagener, Hobart D. *retired architect*

Costa Mesa
Olson, Cal Oliver *golf architect*

Culver City
Moss, Eric Owen *architect*
Ray, Mary-Ann *architect, educator*

Dana Point
Robinson, Theodore Gould *golf course architect*

El Cerrito
Komatsu, S. Richard *architect*

Fallbrook
Burge, Henry Charles *architect*

Fresno
Darden, Edwin Speight, Sr. *architect*
Patnaude, William E. *architect*
Pings, Anthony Claude *architect*
Putman, Robert Dean *golf course architect*
Saito, Paul Makoto *landscape architect*

Glendale
Colby, Barbara Diane *interior designer, consultant*

Irvine
Dorius, Kermit Parrish *architect*
Jacobs, Donald Paul *architect*
Kraemer, Kenneth Leo *architect, urban planner, educator*
Paul, Courtland Price *landscape architect, planner*

La Jolla
Baesel, Stuart Oliver *architect*

Lafayette
Harlock, Michael J. *architect*

Laguna Hills
Burrows, Gates Wilson *retired architect*

Los Angeles
Adams, William Wesley, III *architect*
Aroni, Samuel *architecture and urban planning educator*
Axon, Donald Carlton *architect*
Berry, Richard Douglas *architectural educator, urban planner and designer*
Blankenship, Edward G. *architect*
Bobrow, Michael Lawrence *architect*
Brotman, David Joel *architectural firm executive*
DeChellis, Michael Anthony *architectural illustrator, designer*
Dworsky, Daniel Leonard *architect*
Israel, Franklin David *architect*
Jacob, Paul F., III *architectural firm executive*
Johnson, Scott *architect*
Kaliski, John *architectural firm executive*
Kline, Lee B. *architect*
Li, Gerald *architect, film producer*
†Marsh, Stephen F. *production designer*
Martin, Albert Carey *architect*
Miller, Victoria Loren *designer, art director*
Moe, Stanley Allen *architect, consultant*
Nelson, Mark Bruce *interior designer*
Neutra, Dion *architect*
†Park, Ki Su *architectural firm executive*
Phelps, Barton Chase *architect, educator*
Refuerzo, Ben J. *architectural educator, architectural firm executive*
Tanzmann, Virginia Ward *architect*
Terrell, Joseph Alcasar *interior designer*
Thoman, John Everett *architect, mediator*
Verger, Morris David *architect, planner*
Wheel, Lesley *design firm executive*

Manhattan Beach
Blanton, John Arthur *architect*

Marina Del Rey
Tanaka, Ted Tokio *architect, educator*

Marshall
Evans, Robert James *architect*

Menlo Park
Sidells, Arthur F. *architect*

Mill Valley
D'Amico, Michael *architect, urban planner*
Pflueger, John Milton *architect*

Mojave
Rutan, Elbert L. (Burt Rutan) *aircraft designer*

Mount Shasta
Anderson, Lee Roger *landscape architect, solar, environmental, recreation and site planner*

Mountain View
Kobza, Dennis Jerome *architect*

Newport Beach
Bauer, Jay S. *architect*
Dougherty, Betsey Olenick *architect*
Morgridge, Howard Henry *architect*
Richardson, Walter John *architect*
Strock, Arthur Van Zandt *architect*
Wimberly, George James *architect*

Oakland
Brocchini, Ronald Gene *architect*
Dommer, Donald Duane *architect*
Matsumoto, George *architect*
Nicol, Robert Duncan *architect*

Oxnard
O'Connell, Hugh Mellen, Jr. *architect, retired*

Palm Springs
Cordier, Herbert *interior designer*
Frey, Albert *architect*

Palo Alto
†Ivester, (Richard) Gavin *industrial designer*
Jones, Robert Trent, Jr. *golf course architect*
Knott, Donald Joseph *golf course architect*
Linn, Gary Dean *golf course architect*
†Moggridge, Bill G. *product designer, consultant*

Pasadena
Goei, Bernard Thwan-Poo (Bert Goei) *architectural and engineering firm executive*
Heaton, Culver *architect*
Thomas, Joseph Fleshman *architect*

Pleasant Hill
Hassid, Sami *architect, educator*

Pleasanton
Dunbar, Frank Rollin *landscape architect*
Fehlberg, Robert Erick *architect*

Pomona
Lyle, John Tillman *landscape architecture educator*

Rancho Cucamonga
Christopher, Gaylaird Wiley *architect*

Rancho Mirage
Chambers, Milton Warren *architect*

Redding
Buffum, Nancy Kay *interior designer*

Redondo Beach
Shellhorn, Ruth Patricia *landscape architect*

Sacramento
Cox, Whitson William *architect*
†Hallenbeck, Harry C. *architect*
Lionakis, George *architect*
Nacht, Daniel Joseph *architect*
Ross, Terence William *architect*
Wasserman, Barry L(ee) *architect*

San Diego
Blumenfeld, Alfred Morton *industrial design consultant, educator*
Delawie, Homer Torrence *architect*
Donaldson, Milford Wayne *architect, educator*
Harmon, Harry William *architect, former university administrator*
Henderson, John Drews *architect*
Holl, Walter John *architect, interior designer*
Hope, Frank Lewis, Jr. *retired architect*
Livingston, Stanley C. *architect*
Paderewski, Clarence Joseph *architect*
Stepner, Michael Jay *architect*
Wilson, Richard Allan *landscape architect*

San Francisco
Bull, Henrik Helkand *architect*
Burk, Gary Maurice *health care facility planner*
Del Campo, Martin Bernardelli *architect*
Dodge, Peter Hampton *architect*
Emmons, Donn *architect*
Esherick, Joseph *architect, educator*
Field, John Louis *architect*
Hardison, Donald Leigh *architect*
Helmich, Pamela Pence *architect*
Homsey, George W. *architectural firm executive*
Hooper, Roger Fellowes *architect*
Horan, Joseph Patrick *interior designer*
Judd, Bruce Diven *architect*
Kriken, John Lund *architect*
MacDonald, Donald William *architect*
MacLeamy, Patrick *architectural firm executive*
Mc Laughlin, Herbert E. *architect*
Moris, Lamberto Giuliano *architect*
Painter, Michael Robert *landscape architect, urban designer*
Raeber, John Arthur *architect, construction specifier consultant*
Ream, James Terrill *architect, sculptor*
Rockrise, George Thomas *architect*
Rockwell, Burton Lowe *architect*
Simon, Cathy Jensen *architect*
Sowder, Robert Robertson *architect*
†Stanton, Michael *architectural firm executive*
Thistlethwaite, David Richard *architect*
Turnbull, William, Jr. *architect*
Valentine, William Edson *architect*
Volkmann, Daniel George, Jr. *architect*

San Jose
Tanaka, Richard Koichi, Jr. *architect, planner*

San Luis Obispo
Deasy, Cornelius Michael *architect*
Fraser, Bruce Douglas, Jr. *architect, artist*
Rodman, Harry Eugene *architect, educator, acoustical and illumination consultant*

San Marino
Man, Lawrence Kong *architect*

San Rafael
†Ciampi, Mario Joseph *architect, planner*
Elliott, Edward Procter *architect*
Thompson, Peter L. H. *golf course architect*

Santa Barbara
Frizzell, William Kenneth *architect*
Kruger, Kenneth Charles *retired architect*

Santa Clara
Kwock, Royal *architect*

Santa Cruz
Oberdorfer, Jeff *architect, firm executive*

Santa Monica
Chu, Deeing *architect*
Eizenberg, Julie *architect*
Gehry, Frank Owen *architect*
Koning, Hendrik *architect*
Mayne, Thom *architect*
Miller, Leroy Benjamin *architect*
Naidorf, Louis Murray *architect*
Van Tilburg, Johannes *architectural firm executive*
Wou, Leo S. *architect, planner*

Santa Rosa
Fream, Ronald Warren *golf course architect*
Roland, Craig Williamson *architect*

Sausalito
Leefe, James Morrison *architect*
Werner, William Arno *architect*

Seal Beach
Rossi, Mario Alexander *architect*

Sherman Oaks
Thomas, Julia Dessery *space designer*

Sonoma
Allen, Rex Whitaker *architect*
Lackey, Lawrence Bailis, Jr. *retired architect, urban designer*
Woodbridge, John Marshall *architect, urban planner*

South Pasadena
Girvigian, Raymond *architect*

Stanton
Polk, Benjamin Kauffman *retired architect, composer, educator*

Sunset Beach
Faulkner, Adele Lloyd *interior designer, color consultant*

Tarzana
Smith, Mark Lee *architect*

Venice
Ehrlich, Steven David *architect*

Walnut Creek
Caddy, Edmund Harrington Homer, Jr. *architect*

West Hollywood
Luckman, Charles *architect*

COLORADO

Aspen
Caudill, Samuel Jefferson *architect*
Ensign, Donald H. *landscape architect*

Boulder
Carlson, Devon McElvin *architect, educator*

Colorado Springs
Kelsey, Floyd Lamar, Jr. *architect*
Phibbs, Harry Albert *interior designer, professional speaker, lecturer*

Denver
Abo, Ronald Kent *architect*
Anderson, John David *architect*
Berg, Karl A. *architectural firm executive*
Brownson, Jacques Calmon *architect*
Coover-Clark, Carol *architect*
Cowley, Gerald Dean *architect*
Decker, David B. *architect, educator*
Dominick, Peter Hoyt, Jr. *architect*
Fuller, Kenneth Roller *architect*
†Hatami, Marvin *architect, educator, urban designer*
Havekost, Daniel John *architect*
Hoover, George Schweke *architect*
Hornbein, Victor *architect*
Larson, Dayl Andrew *architect*
Mason, Ronald Leonard *architect*
Prosser, John Martin *architect, educator, urban design consultant*
Steenhagen, Robert Lewis *landscape architect, consultant*
Wirkler, Norman Edward *architectural, engineering, construction management firm executive*

Englewood
Eccles, Matthew Alan *golf course and landscape architect*

Evergreen
Gerou, Phillip Howard *architect*

Lakewood
Franta, Gregory Esser *architect, energy consultant*

Vail
Vosbeck, Robert Randall *architect*

CONNECTICUT

Avon
Johnson, Dean Adams *landscape architect*

Branford
Blake, Peter Jost *architect*

Cheshire
Rowland, Ralph Thomas *architect*

Cos Cob
Pomerance, Ralph *retired architect*

Darien
Spilman, Raymond *industrial designer*

Essex
Grover, William Herbert *architect*
Harper, Robert Leslie *architect, educator*
Simon, Mark *architect*

Greenwich
Barnum, William Milo *architect*
de Mar, Leoda Miller *fabric and wallcovering designer*
Hershaft, Elinor *space planner, interior designer*
Mock, Robert Claude *architect*

Hamden
Cherry, Edward Earl *architect*
Roche, (Eamonn) Kevin *architect*

Kent
Kilham, Walter H., Jr. *architect*

New Canaan
Bergmann, Richard Ronald *architect, photographer*
Risom, Jens *furniture designer, manufacturing executive*

New Haven
Clarke, Fred Webster, III *architectural firm executive*
Cosham, Don *architect*
Newick, Craig David *architect*
Newman, Herbert S. *architect, educator*
Pelli, Cesar *architect*
Platner, Warren *architect*
Roth, Harold *architect*
Woerner, Peter Kurt *architect, builder*

North Branford
Gregan, Edmund Robert *landscape architect*

North Haven
Hoffmann, John J. *architect*

Norwalk
Irving, Michael Henry *architect*

Norwich
Sharpe, Richard Samuel *architectural company executive*

Orange
Miller, Henry Forster *architect*

Ridgefield
Bye, Arthur Edwin, Jr. *landscape architect*

Southport
Parker, David Scott *architect*

Stamford
Cavallon, Betty Gabler *interior designer*
Rossman, Janet Kay *architectural interior designer*

Trumbull
Watson, Donald Ralph *architect, universiity dean, author*

Waterbury
Cohen, Andrew Stuart *architect, landscape architect*

Westport
Brown, Mona *architect*
Ferris, Roger Patrick *architect*

DELAWARE

Wilmington
Dayton, Richard Lee *architect*

DISTRICT OF COLUMBIA

Washington
Baranes, Shalom *architect*
Barr-Kumar, Raj *architect*
Bowie, Calvert S. *architect*
Britt, Stanford R. *architect*
Brodie, M. J. (Jay Brodie) *architect, city planner*
Bryant, Robert Edward *architect*
Coffin, Laurence Edmondston, Jr. *landscape architect, urban planner*
Cox, Warren Jacob *architect*
Cude, Reginald Hodgin *architect*
Czinkota, Ilona Vigh *architect*
Daileda, David Allen *architect*
Deupi, Carlos *architect*
Ensign, William Lloyd *architect*
Florance, Colden l'Hommedieu Ruggles *architect*
Fry, Louis Edwin, Jr. *architect*
Gordon, Harry Thomas *architectural firm executive*
Hartman, George Eitel *architect*
Hellmuth, George William *architect*
Jacobsen, Hugh Newell *architect*
Keune, Russell Victor *architect, architectural association executive*
Keyes, Arthur Hawkins, Jr. *architect*
Lewis, Anne McCutcheon *architect*
MacDonald, William Lloyd *architectural historian*
Mc Gaughan, Alexander Stanley *architect*
Miller, Iris Ann *landscape architect, urban designer, educator*
Moore, Arthur Cotton *architect*
Murray, Christopher Charles, III *architect*
Oehme, Wolfgang Walter *landscape architect*
Poppeliers, John Charles *architectural historian*
Ramberg, Walter Dodd *architect*
Reid, Joseph Browning *architect*
Schlesinger, B. Frank *architect, educator*
Siegel, Lloyd Harvey *architect, real estate developer, consultant*
Spreiregen, Paul David *architect, planner, author*
Wenger, Vicki *interior designer*
†White, George M. *architect, engineer, lawyer*
White, George Malcolm *architect*
Wright, Thomas William Dunstan *architect*
Yerkes, David Norton *architect*

FLORIDA

Anna Maria
Aubry, Eugene Edwards *architect*

Boca Raton
McLeod, John Wishart *architect*
Turano, Emanuel Nicolas *architect*

Bonita Springs
Trudnak, Stephen Joseph *landscape architect*

Boynton Beach
Stubbins, Hugh A(sher), Jr. *architect*

Bradenton
Keane, Gustave Robert *architect, consultant*

Clearwater
Bertram, Frederic Amos *architect*

Coral Gables
Warburton, Ralph Joseph *architect, engineer, planner, educator*

Daytona Beach
Amick, William Walker *golf course architect*
Connor, Edward Hollis, III *golf course architect*

Deland
MacMahon, Charles Hutchins, Jr. *architect*

Delray Beach
Rippeteau, Darrel Downing *architect*

Fernandina Beach
Burns, Stephen Redding *golf course architect*

Fort Lauderdale
Dickinson, Richard *landscape architect*
Singer, Donald Ivan *architect*
Stone, Edward Durell, Jr. *landscape architect*

Gainesville
Schueller, Wolfgang Augustus *architectural educator, writer*
Smith, Herrick Hayner *landscape architect, educator, consultant*

Hobe Sound
Graham, Bruce John *architect*

Hollywood
Harringer, Olaf Carl *architect, museum consultant*

Jacksonville
Barley, John McKim, II *architect*
Broward, Robert Charles *architect*
Jenkins, Leerie Thurman, Jr. *architecture engineering planning firm executive*
Morgan, William Newton *architect, educator*
Pappas, Ted Phillip *architect*
Smith, Ivan Huron *architect*
Winters, Robert Charles *architect*

Jupiter
Fazio, Tom *design firm executive, golf course designer*

Lakeland
Peterson, N. Curtis, Jr. *landscape architect, former state senator*

Maitland
Braun, Charles Stuart *architect*

Marco Island
Thorson, Oswald Hagen *architect*

Miami
Arango, Jorge Sanin *architect*
Atlas, Randall I. *architect, criminologist*
Feito, Jose *architect*
Graboski, Thomas Walter *designer, artist*
Hampton, Mark Garrison *architect*
Knight, Charles Frasuer *architect*
Lapidus, Morris *retired architect, interior designer*
Martinez, Walter Baldomero *architect*
Nicholson, William Mac *naval architect, marine engineer, consultant*
Parker, Alfred Browning *architect*
Plater-Zyberk, Elizabeth Maria *architectural educator*
Reed, George Francis *architect*
Sieger, Charles Martin *architect*
Telesca, Francis Eugene *architect*
Treister, Kenneth *architect, artist*

Miami Beach
Fort-Brescia, Bernardo *architect*
Spear, Laurinda Hope *architect*

Mount Dora
Hoag, Arthur Howard, Jr. *retired architect*

Naples
Jones, Richard Wallace *interior designer*
Lewis, Gordon Gilmer *golf course architect*

Orlando
Arnett, Warren Grant *interior designer*
Hansen, Richard Fred *architect*

Palm Beach
Wirtz, Willem Kindler *garden and lighting designer, public relations consultant*

Palm Beach Gardens
Christian, Robert Henry *architect*

Pensacola
Bullock, Ellis Way, Jr. *architect*
Woolf, Kenneth Howard *architect*

Port Saint Lucie
Clark, Harold Steve *architect*

Saint Augustine
Acito, Daniel Joseph *interior designer*
Matzke, Frank J. *architect, consultant*

Saint Petersburg
Wedding, Charles Randolph *architect*

Sarasota
Abbott, J. Carl *architect, planner, inventor, educator*
Smith, Mark Hallard *architect*

Stuart
Ankrom, Charles Franklin *golf course architect, consultant*
Jefferson, Peter Augustus *architect*

Tampa
Abell, Jan Mary *architect*
Holmes, Dwight Ellis *architect*
Howey, John Richard *architect*
Jennewein, James Joseph *architect*
Walker, H(erbert) Leslie, Jr. *architect*

Venice
Appel, Wallace Henry *retired industrial designer*

Viera
Ehrig, John Paul *architect*

Winter Haven
Burns, Arthur Lee *architect*

GEORGIA

Athens
Morrison, Darrel Gene *landscape architecture educator*

Atlanta
Amisano, Joseph *architect*
Bainbridge, Frederick Freeman, III *architect*
Balke, Robert Roy *architect*
Bowman, Juliette Joseph *interior decorator, gourmet food consultant*
Bradfield, Richard H. *architectural firm executive*
Cooper, Jerome Maurice *architect*
Diedrich, Richard Joseph *architect*
Elam, Merrill L. *architectural firm executive*
Farrington, Frank *architect*
Fash, William Leonard *retired architecture educator, college dean*
Guest, Rita Carson *interior designer*
Hoover, Ray Campbell, III *architect*
Hughes, Rufus R., II *architectural firm executive, architectural educator*
Jova, Henri Vatable *architect*
Lewcock, Ronald Bentley *architect, educator*
Mc Intosh, James Eugene, Jr. *interior designer*
Moulthrop, Edward Allen *architect, artist*
Portman, John C., Jr. *architect, developer*
Pulgram, William Leopold *architect, space designer*
Smith, Joseph Newton, III *retired architect, educator*
Surber, Eugene Lynn *architect*
Ventulett, Thomas Walker, III *architect*
Williams, Thomas Franklin *architect*

Augusta
Woodhurst, Robert Stanford, Jr. *architect*

Fayetteville
Harris, Dorothy Clark *interior architect, designer, design instructor*

Macon
Dunwody, Eugene Cox *architect*

Norcross
Crymes, Ronald Jack *draftsman, structural steel detailer*

Riverdale
Gibbs, Rose L. *interior designer*

Rome
Janowski, Thaddeus Marian *architect*

Roswell
DeVictor, D. J. *landscape architect*

HAWAII

Honolulu
Ayer, David Clay *architect*
Botsai, Elmer Eugene *architect, educator, former university dean*
Cain, Raymond Frederick *landscape architect, planning company executive*
Cruthers, Evan Douglas *architect*
Hale, Nathan Robert *architect*
Hamada, Duane Takumi *architect*
Hong, Norman G. Y. *architect*
Lau, Charles Kwok-Chiu *architect, architectural firm executive*
Sutton, Charles Richard *architect, designer*
Yeh, Raymond Wei-Hwa *architect, educator*

Kahului
Riecke, Hans Heinrich *architect*

Kaneohe
Fisette, Scott Michael *golf course designer*

IDAHO

Boise
Cline, Glen Edwin *retired architect and planner*
Hunsucker, (Carl) Wayne *architectural firm executive, educator*

Sun Valley
Bryant, Woodrow Wesley *architect*

ILLINOIS

Champaign
Baker, Jack Sherman *architect, designer, educator*

Chicago
Allan, Stanley Nance *achitect, consultant*
Amstadter, Laurence *retired architect*
Balasi, Mark Geoffrey *architect*
Barney, Carol Ross *architect*
Beeby, Thomas H. *architect*
Bellas, Jean *architect*
Belluschi, Anthony C. *architect*
Blutter, Joan Wernick *interior designer*
Bowman, John *architectural firm designer*
Brubaker, Charles William *architect*
Butler, Richard Dean *interior designer*
Campbell, Wendell Jerome *architect*
Conte, Richard Nicholas *architect*
Cook, Richard Borreson *architect*
Cooke, Robert Phillip *architect*
Curatolo, Alphonse Frank *architect*
Dubin, Arthur Detmers *architect*
Epstein, Sidney *architect and engineer*
Eyerman, Thomas Jude *architect*

†Goldberg, Bertrand *architect*
Gordon, Ezra *architect, educator*
Green, William Robert *architect*
Grunsfeld, Ernest Alton, III *architect*
Gucker, Jane Gleason *architect*
Hackl, Donald John *architect*
Hague, Richard Norris *architect*
Haymes, David Allen *architect*
Holabird, John Augur, Jr. *retired architect*
Jahn, Helmut *architect*
Keck, William *architect*
Kerbis, Gertrude Lempp *architect*
Kiel, William Frederick *architectural specifications consultant*
Kurtich, John William *architect, film-maker, educator*
Legge Kemp, Diane *architect, landscape architect*
Lohan, Dirk *architect*
Macsai, John *architect*
Manny, Carter Hugh, Jr. *architect, foundation administrator*
Matthei, Edward Hodge *architect*
McCullagh, Grant Gibson *architect*
McCurry, Margaret Irene *architect, educator*
Moses, Irving Byron *architect*
Moutoussamy, John Warren *architect*
Pappageorge, George C. *architect*
Phillips, Frederick Falley *architect*
Quebe, Jerry Lee *architect*
Schirn, Janet Sugerman *interior designer*
Schlossman, John Isaac *architect*
Schroeder, Douglas Fredrick *architect*
Smith, Adrian Devaun *architect*
Terp, Dana George *architect*
Tigerman, Stanley *architect, educator*
Tobin, Calvin Jay *architect*
Torgersen, Torwald Harold *architect, designer*
Valerio, Joseph M. *architectural firm executive, educator*
VanderBeke, Patricia K. *architect*
Vinci, John Nicholas *architect, educator*
Vrechek, George Gerald *architectural firm executive*
Weber, Hanno *architect*
Weese, Benjamin Horace *architect*
Wildermuth, Gordon Lee *architect*

Deerfield
O'Donnell, Lawrence James *architect*
Pigozzi, Raymond Anthony *architect*

Downers Grove
Kirkegaard, R. Lawrence *architectural acoustician*
Ryan, John Michael *landscape architect*

Evanston
Friedman, Hans Adolf *architect*
Salzman, Arthur George *architect*
Zolomij, Robert William *landscape architect, consultant*

Geneva
Conterato, Bruno Paul *architect*

Glenview
Bradtke, Philip Joseph *architect*
Taylor, D(arl) Coder *architect, engineer*

Hinsdale
Anderson, Harry Frederick, Jr. *architect*
Mikos, David Edward *architect*

Libertyville
Krolopp, Rudolph William *industrial designer, consultant*

Northfield
Glass, Henry Peter *industrial designer, interior architect, educator*
Otis, James, Jr. *architect*

Oak Park
Bell, Robert Alan *architect*
Worley, Marvin George, Jr. *architect*

Peoria
Kenyon, Leslie Harrison *architect*

Riverside
Potokar, Richard Albert *architect*

Rockford
Bradley, Charles MacArthur *architect*
Hill, Scott Alan *architect, farmer*

Schaumburg
Walker, Robert Giles, Jr. *architect*

Skokie
Siegal, Burton Lee *product designer, consultant, inventor*

Urbana
Poss, Jeffery Scott *architect, educator*
Replinger, John Gordon *architect*
Riley, Robert Bartlett *landscape architect*

Wilmette
Chen, Shau-Tsyh *architect*

Winnetka
Piper, Robert Johnston *architect, urban planner*
Weber, John Bertram *architect*

INDIANA

Carmel
Eden, Barbara Janiece *commercial and residential interior designer*
Mc Laughlin, Harry Roll *architect*

Evansville
Dailey, Donald Earl *industrial design consultant*

Fort Wayne
Cole, Kenneth Duane *architect*

Indianapolis
Alexander, Gary Lee *architect*
Bennett, Claire Richardson *landscape architect*
Browne, William Albert, Jr. *architectural firm executive*
Woollen, Evans *architectural firm executive*

Michigan City
Brockway, Lee J. *architect*

Mishawaka
Ponko, William Reuben *architect*
Troyer, LeRoy Seth *architect*

Muncie
Sappenfield, Charles Madison *architect, educator*

South Bend
Horsbrugh, Patrick *architect, educator*
Korbuly, Laszlo John *architect*

West Lafayette
Molnar, Donald Joseph *landscape architecture educator*

IOWA

Ames
Kainlauri, Eino Olavi *architect*
Palermo, Gregory Sebastian *architect*

Cedar Rapids
Healey, Edward Hopkins *architect*
Stone, Herbert Marshall *architect*

Davenport
Burgess, Janet Helen *interior designer*

Des Moines
Lewis, Calvin Fred *architect, educator*
Lynch, James Alexander *architect*
Vande Krol, Jerry Lee *architect*

Iowa City
Neumann, Roy Covert *architect*

Waterloo
Broshar, Robert Clare *architect*

KANSAS

Lawrence
Grabow, Stephen Harris *architecture educator*

Manhattan
Foerster, Bernd *architecture educator*
Kremer, Eugene R. *architecture educator*

Topeka
Karst, Gary Gene *architect*
Schneider, Raymond Clinton *architect, educator*

Wichita
Ellington, Howard Wesley *architect*

KENTUCKY

Lexington
Girone, Vito Anthony *architect, city planner, educator emeritus, artist*
Romanowitz, Byron Foster *architect, engineer*
Scruggs, John Dudley *landscape architect*
Wallace, Donald Querk *architect, civil engineer*

Louisville
Ward, Jasper Dudley, III *architect*

Salvisa
†Lancaster, Clay *architecture/design educator, writer*

LOUISIANA

Alexandria
Brocato, Joseph Myron *architect*

Baton Rouge
Brockway, William Robert *architect*
Desmond, John Jacob *architect*
Lee, Betty Redding *architect*
Merliss, William Sidney *retired architect, engineer*
Reich, Robert Sigmund *retired landscape architect*
Schwing, Charles E. *architect*
Williamson, William Floyd, Jr. *architect*
Zwirn, Robert *architect, architecture educator*

Lafayette
Perkins, David Layne, Sr. *architect*

Metairie
Colbert, Charles Ralph *architect*

New Orleans
Blitch, James Buchanan *architect*
Blitch, Ronald Buchanan *architect*
Filson, Ronald Coulter *architect, educator, college dean*
Frantz, Phares Albert *architect*
Klingman, John Philip *architect, educator*
Latorre, Robert George *naval architecture and engineering educator*
Steinmetz, Deborah Susan *interior designer*
Steinmetz, Robert Charles *architect*
†Verges, Ernest E. *architectural firm executive*
Waggonner, Joseph David, III *architect*

Shreveport
Elberson, Edwin Wallace *architect*
Haas, Lester Carl *architect*

MAINE

Canaan
Zikorus, Albert Michael *golf course architect*

New Harbor
Fradley, Frederick Macdonell *architect*

South Harpswell
Barnes, George William *architecture and engineering company executive*

MARYLAND

Annapolis
Jansson, John Phillip *architect, consultant*
Lee, T. Girard *architect*
Wilkes, Joseph Allen *architect*

Baltimore
Adams, Harold Lynn *architect*
Anderson, Gary Dean *architect, planner, educator*
Ayers, Richard Winston *architect*
Bridges, Leon *architect*
Donkervoet, Richard Cornelius *architect*
Ford, John Gilmore *interior designer*
Snead, James Arrington *architect*
Trostel, Michael Frederick *architect*
Ziger, Steven Gary *architect*

Bethesda
Auerbach, Seymour *architect*
Callmer, James Peter *architect*
Dawson, John Frederick *architect*
Hoenack, August Frederick *architect*
Morgan, William Bruce *naval architect*
†Mujica, Mauro E. *architect*
Spurling, Everett Gordon, Jr. *architect, construction specifications consultant*

Bowie
Stone, Edward Harris, II *landscape architect*

Calverton
Parker, Stephen L. *architectural firm executive*

Chestertown
Newlin, Peter Caverly *architect*

Chevy Chase
Freeman, Raymond Lee *landscape architect, planning consultant*
Oudens, Gerald Francis *architect, architectural firm executive*

College Park
Lewis, Roger Kutnow *architect, educator, author*

Columbia
Askew, Laurin Barker, Jr. *architect*
Slater, John Blackwell *landscape architect*

Ft Washington
Miller, John Richard *interior designer*

North Potomac
Bavier, Robert Newton, III *architect*
Passantino, Richard J. *architect*

Olney
Delmar, Eugene Anthony *architect*

Port Republic
Miller, Ewing Harry *architect*

Rockville
Elliott, Benjamin Paul *architect*
Horowitz, Harold *architect*

Salisbury
Becker, Thomas McKean *architect*

Silver Spring
Senseman, Ronald Sylvester *architect*
Ware, Thomas Earle *building consultant*

MASSACHUSETTS

Amherst
Cornish, Geoffrey St. John *golf course architect*
Rupp, William John *architect*

Belmont
Frey, John Ward *landscape architect*
Gui, James Edmund *architect*

Boston
Acton, Lloyd Phelps, Jr. *architect*
Alexander, James Garth *architect*
Bargmann, Joel David *architect*
Bertman, Richard Jay *architect*
Bourque, Michael H. *interior designer*
Clancy, John M. *architectural firm executive*
Davis, Michael Richard *architect*
Dean, Robert Charles *architect*
Elkus, Howard Felix *architect*
Finegold, Maurice Nathan *architect*
Flansburgh, Earl Robert *architect*
Forbes, Peter *architect*
Glassman, Herbert Haskel *architect*
Goody, Joan *architect*
Graham, Gary Lee *architect, facilitator*
†Gresham, David Melvin *designer, small business owner*
Heineman, Robert M. *architectural firm executive*
Koetter, Fred *architectural firm executive, educator, dean*
Manfredi, David Peter *architect*
McKinnell, Noel Michael *architect, educator*
Rawn, William Leete, III *architect*
†Rothman, Martha L. *architectural firm executive*
Shepley, Hugh *architect*
Stull, Donald LeRoy *architect*
Tappé, Albert Anthony *architect*
Wallace, David Dunsmore *architect*
†Wolf, Gary Herbert *architect*
Wood, Henry Austin *architect*

Boxboro
Gary, Benjamin Walter, Jr. *landscape architect*

Cambridge
Anderson, Stanford Owen *architect, architectural historian, educator*
Bluestone, Hugh Lawrence *architect*
Bruck, Ferdinand Frederick *architect*
Bruck, Phoebe Ann Mason *landscape architect*
Burns, Carol J. *architect, educator*
Campbell, Robert *architect, writer*
Daley, Royston Tuttle *architect*
Fletcher, Norman Collings *architect*
Green, Richard John *architect*
Hamner, W. Easley *architect*
Harkness, John Cheesman *architect*
Harris, Charles Ward *landscape architect and educator, land development consultant, editor*
Hass, Michael Shepherdson *architect*
Johnson, Carol Roxane *landscape architect*
Kobus, Richard Lawrence *architectural company executive*
Krieger, Alex *architecture and design educator*
Kruger, Kenneth *architect*
Luchetti, Robert James *architect, industrial designer*
Madsen, Peter Eric *architecture and real estate development firms executive*
McCue, Gerald Mallon *architect, educator*
Moneo, José Rafael *architecture educator*
Newman, John Nicholas *naval architect educator*
Notkin, Leonard Sheldon *architect*
Oommen, George *architect, painter*
Payne, Harry Morse, Jr. *architect*
Pollock, Wilson F. *architectural firm executive*
Porter, William Lyman *architect, educator*
Rosenfeld, Walter David, Jr. *architect, writer*
Rowe, Peter Grimmond *architecture educator, researcher*
Sekler, Eduard Franz *architect, educator*
Szabo, Albert *architect, educator*
Tsoi, Edward Tze Ming *architect, interior designer, urban planner*
Ward, Robertson, Jr. *architect*

Concord
Cutting, Heyward *designer, planner*

East Orleans
MacMillan, Douglas Clark *naval architect*

Essex
McMillen, Louis Albert *architect*

Lexington
Harkness, Sarah Pillsbury *architect*
Pierce, Walter S. *architect*

Lincoln
Merrill, Vincent Nichols *landscape architect*

Nantucket
Lethbridge, Francis Donald *architect*

Newton
Oles, Paul Stevenson (Steve Oles) *architect, perspectivist, educator*

Newton Center
Walker, Bradford C. *architect*

North Andover
Goldstein, Charles Henry *architect, consultant*

Randolph
Ross, Edward Joseph *architect*

Shirley
Field, Hermann Haviland *architect, educator*

Somerville
Korobkin, Barry Jay *architect*
Safdie, Moshe *architect*

Topsfield
Peirce, John Wentworth *architect*

Waltham
Feldman, Mark Russel *architect, policy consultant*

Watertown
Crissman, James Hudson *architect*
Dawson, Stuart Owen *landscape architect, urban designer*
Lampkin, M. Martha *architect, city planner*
Ward, Alan L. *architectural landscape designer*

Wayland
Huygens, Remmert William *architect*

West Springfield
Engebretson, Douglas Kenneth *architect*

Weston
Sturgis, Robert Shaw *architect*
Wacker, John Lee *landscape architect*

Winthrop
Costantino, Frank Mathew *architectural illustrator*

Worcester
Carlson, Suzanne Olive *architect*

MICHIGAN

Ann Arbor
Beckley, Robert Mark *architect, educator*
Benford, Harry Bell *naval architect*
Christman, James Edward *landscape architect*
Fry, Richard E. *architectural firm executive*
Marans, Robert Warren *architect, planner, educator*
Mc Gibbon, William *landscape architect*
Metcalf, Robert Clarence *architect, educator*
Paulsen, Serenus Glen *architect, educator*
Snyder, Jeanne Anne *interior designer, educator*

Birmingham
Birkerts, Gunnar *architect*
Bublys, Algimantas Vladas *architect*
Van Dine, Harold Forster, Jr. *architect*
Ziegelman, Robert Lee *architect*

Bloomfield Hills
Allen, Maurice Bartelle, Jr. *architect*
Brown, Jack Wyman *architect*

Detroit
Cox, John William *architect, educator*
Francis, Edward D. *architect*
Kessler, William Henry *architect*
Margerum, Roger Williams, Jr. *architect*
Mikon, Arnold *architect*
Roehling, Carl David *architect*
Youngren, Ralph Park *architect*

Flint
Tomblinson, James Edmond *architect*

Grand Rapids
†Bowers, Paul Duane, Jr. *architecture, engineering and planning firm executive*
Dickerson, Allen Bruce *interior designer, consultant*
Stevenson, William Alexander *architect*
Vrancken, Robert Danloy *facilities management educator*
Wold, Robert Lee *architect, engineer*

Kalamazoo
Carver, Norman Francis, Jr. *architect, photographer*
O'Boyle, Robert L. *landscape architect*

Saline
Frank, Richard Calhoun *architect*

Southfield
Redstone, Daniel Aaron *architect*
Redstone, Louis Gordon *architect*

Traverse City
Brown, Paul Bradley *architect*

Troy
Powell, Robert Barrows *architectural firm executive*

MINNESOTA

Duluth
Salmela, David Daniel *architect*
Whiteman, Richard Frank *architect*

Minneapolis
Bentz, Frederick Jacob *architect*
Carmody, John *architectural educator*
Clemence, Roger Davidson *landscape architect, educator*
Degenhardt, Robert Allan *architectural and engineering firm executive*
Eyberg, Donald Theodore, Jr. *architect*
Hargens, William Garman *architect*
Jacob, Bernard Michel *architect*
Mahaffey, Gary John *architect*
Martin, Roger Bond *landscape architect, educator*
Parker, Leonard Sam *architect, educator*
Rand, Peter Anders *architect*
Rapson, Ralph *architect, educator*
Susanka, Sarah Hills *architect*
Van Housen, Thomas Corwin, III *architect, designer, builder*

Northfield
Sovik, Edward Anders *architect, consultant*

Saint Paul
Close, Elizabeth Scheu *architect*
Close, Winston Arthur *retired architect*
Faricy, Richard Thomas *architect*
Lein, Malcolm Emil *architect*
Rafferty, Craig Elliot *architect, educator*

MISSISSIPPI

Columbus
Ivy, Robert Adams, Jr. *architect, writer*
Kaye, Samuel Harvey *architect, educator*

Hattiesburg
Traylor, Joan Sadler *interior design educator*

Jackson
Biggs, Thomas Jones *architect*
Burns, Robert, Jr. *architect, freelance writer, artist*
Harrison, Robert Vernon McElroy *architect*
Timmer, Wayne F. *architectural firm executive*

Mississippi State
Bishop, Calvin Thomas *landscape architect, educator*
Man, Cameron Robert James *landscape architect*
Martin, Edward Curtis, Jr. *landscape architect, educator*

Starkville
Ford, Robert MacDonald, III *architect, educator*

MISSOURI

Ballwin
Kern, Gary L. *golf course architect*

Clayton
Christner, Theodore Carroll *architect*
Turner, Terry Madison *architect*

Hollister
Thominet, Maurice J. *architect*

Kansas City
Baker, Robert Thomas *interior designer*
Conrad, William Merrill *architect*
†Patty, R. Bruce *architect*
Seligson, Theodore H. *architect, interior designer, art consultant*

Saint Louis
Becker, Rex Louis *architect*
Burks, Verner Irwin *architect*
Chivetta, Anthony Joseph *architect*
Cotton, W(illiam) Philip, Jr. *architect*
Hastings, Bryce *architect*
Hellmuth, George Francis *architect*
Ittner, H. Curtis *architect*
Kultermann, Udo *architectural and art historian*
Lickhalter, Merlin Eugene *architect*
Lovelace, Eldridge Hirst *retired landscape architect, city planner*
Mertz, Stuart Moulton *landscape architect*
Michaelides, Constantine Evangelos *architect, educator*
Obata, Gyo *architect*
Pickens, Buford Lindsay *architectural educator, historian*
Self, Larry Douglas *architectural firm executive*
Teasdale, Thomas Hennings *architect*
Thalden, Barry R. *architect*

Springfield
Liu, Yuan Hsiung *drafting and design educator*
Ownby, Jerry Steve *landscape architect, educator*

Webster Groves
Kramer, Gerhardt Theodore *architect*

MONTANA

Bozeman
DeHaas, John Neff, Jr. *retired architecture educator*
Mattson, George Arthur *architect*

Great Falls
Davidson, David Scott *architect*
Hoiland, Andrew Calvin *architect*

NEBRASKA

Bellevue
Hinz, Calvin L. *architectural firm executive*
Raynor, Dennis L. *architect, firm executive*

Lincoln
Gibbs, Dale L. *architect, educator*
Morrow, Andrew Nesbit *interior designer, business owner*
Stange, James Henry *architect*
Steward, Weldon Cecil *architecture educator, architect, consultant*

Omaha
Bowen, Gary Roger *architect*
Faust, Harlan R. *architect*
Polsky, Donald Perry *architect*

NEVADA

Gardnerville
Harlander, Leslie Albert *naval architectural consultant*

Reno
Hynek, Frederick James *architect*

NEW HAMPSHIRE

Fremont
Richardson, Artemas P(artridge) *landscape architect*

Hanover
Brooks, H. Allen *architectural educator, author, lecturer*
White, Cleveland Stuart, Jr. *architect*

Holderness
Cutler, Laurence Stephan *architect, urban designer, advertising executive, educator*

Jaffrey
Alderman, Bissell *architect*

Manchester
Brensinger, Barry L. *architectural firm executive*
Mires, Dennis Burnard *architect*

Meredith
Williams, Christopher Peele *architect*

Nashua
Carter, John Avery *architect*
Rudolph, John W. *architectural firm executive*

New London
Phillips, Roscoe Wendell, Jr. *architect*
Sheerr, Deirdre McCrystal *architectural firm executive*

Portsmouth
Lyman, William W., Jr. *retired architect*

NEW JERSEY

Cherry Hill
Radey, Frank Herbert, Jr. *architect*

Englewood
Schmidt, Ronald Hans *architect*

Florham Park
Bottelli, Richard *architect*

Mahwah
Hollerith, Richard, Jr. *industrial designer, consultant*

Medford
Dunn, Roy J. *landscape architect*

Montclair
Boyd, Hugh Alan *architect*
Jones, Rees Lee *golf course architect*

Moorestown
Hassinger, Herman A. *architect*

Morristown
Nadaskay, Raymond *architect*
Oishi, Satoshi *architectural and engineering executive*

Newark
Greenfield, Sanford Raymond *architect*
Horii, Howard Nobuo *architect, educator*
Mahler, Harry Bez *architect, planner*

Paramus
DiGeronimo, Suzanne Kay *architect*

Park Ridge
Wells, Peter Raymond *architect*

Princeton
Colquhoun, Alan H. *architectural educator*
Ford, Jeremiah, III *architect*
Graves, Michael *architect, educator*
Hillier, J(ames) Robert *architect*
Holt, Philetus Havens, III *architect*
Kehrt, Allan W. *architectural firm executive*
Lerner, Ralph *architect, university dean*
Mills, Michael James *architect*
Sussna, Robert Earl *architect*

Ridgefield Park
Case, Gerard Ramon *drafting technician*

Somerville
Shive, Richard Byron *architect*

South Orange
De Varis, Panayotis Eric *architect*

NEW MEXICO

Alameda
Hooker, Van Dorn *architect, artist*

Albuquerque
Campbell, C(harles) Robert *architect*
Crawford, Dale Lee *architect*
McCabe, Robert R. *architect, city planner*
Pearl, George Clayton *architect*
Sabatini, William Quinn *architect*

Placitas
Pirkl, James Joseph *industrial designer, educator*

Santa Fe
Conron, John Phelan *architect*
Leon, Bruno *architect, educator*

NEW YORK

Albany
Morgan, George Jefferson *interior designer*

Armonk
Behr, Richard Henry *architect, educator*

Bedford
Benedek, Armand *landscape architect*
Damora, Robert Matthew *architect*

Berlin
Stephens, Donald Joseph *retired architect*

Binghamton
Bearsch, Lee Palmer *architect, city planner*

Brooklyn
Delson, Sidney Leon *architect*
Ireys, Alice Recknagel *landscape architect*
Weston, I. Donald *architect*
Woolley, Margaret Anne (Margot Woolley) *architect*
†Zivari, Bashir *architect, industrial designer*

Buffalo
Coles, Robert Traynham *architect*
Freschi, Bruno Basilio *architect, educator*
Markwart, Paul Martin *architect*

Carmel
Carruth, David Barrow *landscape architect*

Cold Spring
Brill, Ralph David *architect, real estate developer, venture capitalist*

Cranberry Lake
Glavin, James Edward *landscape architect*

East Hampton
Damaz, Paul F. *architect*

Fayetteville
Sears, Bradford George *landscape architect*

Garden City
Accordino, Frank Joseph *architect, car rental company executive*

Great Neck
Turofsky, Charles Sheldon *landscape architect*

Greenlawn
Stevens, John Richard *architectural historian*

Hastings On Hudson
Weinstein, Edward Michael *architect, consultant*

Ithaca
Sims, William Riley, Jr. *design and facility management educator, consultant*

Katonah
Baker, John Milnes *architect*

Locust Valley
Bentel, Frederick Richard *architect, educator*
Bentel, Maria-Luise Ramona Azzarone (Mrs. Frederick R. Bentel) *architect, educator*
Webel, Richard Karl *landscape architect*

Long Island City
Sadao, Shoji *architect*

Malverne
Engoren, Sampson Seymour *interior designer*

Manhasset
Corva, Angelo Francis *architect*
Grossi, Olindo *architect, educator*
Schiller, Arthur A. *architect, educator*

Marcellus
Lafferty, Richard Thomas *architect*

Mount Kisco
Weiss, Caryl Shander *interior designer, educator*

New York
Abramovitz, Max *architect*
Agha, Mahmoud Fikry *architectural firm executive*
Aldea, Patricia *architect*
Annese, Domenico *landscape architect*
Arsene, Vladimir *architect*
Baker, James Barnes *architect*
Baquero, José Maria *architect, artist*
Barnes, Edward Larrabee *architect*
Barnett, Jonathan *architect, city planner*
Barratt, Michael Scott *architect*
Beckhard, Herbert *architect*
Belle, John Leighton *architect, planner*
Berg, Wayne *architect, educator*
Bland, Frederick Aves *architect*
Blinder, Richard Lewis *architect*
Bond, J. Max, Jr. *architect, educational administrator*
Bookhardt, Fred Barringer, Jr. *architect*
†Breger, William N. *architect, educator*
Breines, Simon *architect*
Brennan, Henry Higginson *architect*
Broches, Paul Elias *architect*
Buatta, Mario *interior designer*
Burgee, John Henry *architect*
Butler, Jonathan Putnam *architect*
Buttrick, Harold *architect*
Cavaglieri, Giorgio *architect*
†Chan, Eric Ping-Pang *industrial designer*
Chan, Lo-Yi Cheung Yuen *architect*
Cobb, Henry Nichols *architect*
Dattner, Richard *architect, educator*
David, Theoharis Lambros *architect, educator*
Davis, Jerry Albert *architect*
†Decker, Dennis Dale *industrial designer*
De Santo, Samuel J. *architectural firm executive, educator*
De Vido, Alfredo Eduardo *architect*
Diamond, Freda *designer, home furnishings consultant, lecturer*
Edelman, Harold *architect*
Edelman, Judith Hochberg *architect*
Eisenman, Peter David *architect, educator*
Fitch, James Marston *architectural preservationist, architectural historian, critic*
Fitzsimmons, Sophie Sonia *interior designer*
Fleischer, Joseph Linden *architect*
Fox, Robert Frederick, Jr. *architect*
Franzen, Ulrich J. *architect*
Freed, James Ingo *architect*
Friedberg, Marvin Paul *landscape architect*
Gatje, Robert Frederick *architect*
Georgopoulos, Maria *architect*
Ginsberg, David Lawrence *architect*
Glaser, Milton *interior designer*
Goldberg, Steven M. *architect*
Guise, David Earl *architect, educator*
Gwathmey, Charles *architect*
Halpin, Anna Marie *architect*
Halsband, Frances *architect*
Hardy, Hugh *architect*
Hariri, Gisue *architect, educator*
Heisel, Ralph Arthur *architect*
Hinz, Theodore Vincent *architect*
Holl, Steven Myron *architect*
Holub, Martin *architect*
Holzman, Malcolm *architect*
Hoyt, Charles King *architect, editor*
Ivanov, Lyuben Dimitrov *naval architecture researcher, educator*
Johnson, Philip Cortelyou *architect*
Kingsland, James Arthur *architect*
Kissiloff, William *industrial designer*
Kliment, Robert Michael *architect*
Kliment, Stephen Alexander *architect, editor*
Knowles, Edward F(rank) *architect*
Kohn, A. Eugene *architect*
Kondylis, Costas Andrew *architect*
Kuhn, Denis Glen *architectural firm executive*
Ladau, Robert Francis *architect, planner*
Lee, Sarah Tomerlin *design executive*
Lefferts, Gillet, Jr. *architect*
Leigh, Stephen *industrial designer*
Liebman, Theodore *architect*
Lupo, Frank Michael *architect*
Mack, Daniel Richard *furniture designer*
Masey, Jack *exhibition designer*
McCarthy, Michael Anthony *architecture executive*
Meier, Richard Alan *architect*
Owen, Sylvia *interior design executive*
Pasanella, Giovanni *architect, architectural educator*
Pasanella, Marco *furniture designer*
Pei, Ieoh Ming *architect*
Peretz, Eileen *interior designer*
Perkins, Lawrence Bradford, Jr. *architect*
†Pesce, Gaetano *architectural, interior, industrial and graphic designer*
Platt, Charles Adams *architect, planner*
Polshek, James Stewart *architect*
Pomeroy, Lee Harris *architect*
Quennell, Nicholas *landscape architect, educator*
Ricci, Kenneth *architect*
Robertson, Jaquelin Taylor *architect, educator*
Robinson, James LeRoy *architect, educator, developer*
Rosenblatt, Arthur Isaac *architect, former museum director*
Rosenblatt, Lester *naval architect*
Rossant, James Stephane *architect, artist*
Roth, Richard, Jr. *architect*
†Rowen, Daniel *architect*
Rutkin, Seymour *architect*

Saladino, John F. *architect, interior decorator, furniture designer*
Scutt, Der *architect*
Silver, Paul *architect*
Slomanson, Lloyd Howard *architect, musician*
Smith, G. E. Kidder *architect, author*
Smith-Miller, Henry Houck *architect*
Smotrich, David Isadore *architect*
Snibbe, Richard W. *architect*
Stein, Carl *architect*
Stein, Martin Donald *architect*
Stephens, Olin James, II *naval architect, yacht designer*
Stern, Robert Arthur Morton *architect, educator*
Swanke, Albert Homer *architect*
Tafel, Edgar *architect*
Todd, David Fenton Michie *architect*
Varney, Carleton Bates, Jr. *interior designer, columnist, educator, author*
†Viemeister, Tucker L. *industrial designer*
Vignelli, Massimo *architecture and design executive*
Voorsanger, Bartholomew *architect*
Walker, Kenneth Henry *architect*
White, Norval Crawford *architect*
Williams, Tod Culpan *architect*
†Willis, Beverly Ann *architect*

Nyack
Degenshein, Jan *architect, planner*

Oakdale
Tompkins, Daniel D. *landscape architect, horticulturist*

Pittsford
Gates, Martha Meyer *architect*

Rensselaerville
Dudley, George Austin *architect, planning consultant, educator*

Rochester
Chapin, Louis William, II *architect*
Hai, Carol Sue *interior designer*

Rye
Anderson, Allan *architectural firm executive*

Schenectady
Feibes, Werner Louis *architect*

Staten Island
†Li, Pui-Pui *interior and graphic designer*

Syracuse
Skoler, Louis *architect, educator*
Smardon, Richard Clay *landscape architecture and environmental studies educator*

Troy
Haviland, David Sands *architectural educator, researcher, administrator*
Kroner, Walter Manfred *architect, educator*

Wappingers Falls
Johnson, Jeh Vincent *architect*

Water Mill
D'Urso, Joseph Paul *designer*

Weedsport
Cichello, Samuel Joseph *architect*

White Plains
Papp, Laszlo George *architect*
Rose, William Allen, Jr. *architect*

Woodstock
Hoyt, Earl Edward, Jr. *industrial designer*

NORTH CAROLINA

Asheville
King, Joseph Bertram *architect*
Lord, Anthony *retired architect*

Chapel Hill
Dixon, Frederick Dail *architect*
Godschalk, David Robinson *architect, urban development planner, educator*

Charlotte
Bost, Walter Lee *architect, printing company executive*
Ferebee, Stephen Scott, Jr. *architect*
Gunn, Robert T. *architectural firm executive*
Hackler, John Byron, III *architect*
Huberman, Jeffrey Allen *architect*
†Montague, Edgar Burwell (Monty), III *industrial designer*
Shive, Philip Augustus *architect*
Turner, Thomas Patrick *architect*

High Point
Kleeman, Walter Benton, Jr. *interior and furniture designer, consultant, author*

Lumberton
Lee, Elizabeth Bobbitt *architect*

New Bern
Daft, Jack Robert *landscape architect, educator*

Pinehurst
Maples, Dan *golf course designer*

Pisgah Forest
Albyn, Richard Keith *retired architect*

Raleigh
Bell, Richard Chevalier *landscape architect*
Burns, Norma DeCamp *architect*
Burns, Robert Paschal *architect, educator*
Clark, Roger Harrison *architect, architecture educator*
Clarke, Lewis James *landscape architect*
Flournoy, William Louis, Jr. *landscape architect*
Godwin, James Beckham *retired landscape architect*
Hunter, Margaret King *architect*
Johnson, Marvin Richard Alois *architect*
Malecha, Marvin John *architect, academic administrator*
Smith, Macon Strother *architect*

Robbinsville
Ginn, Ronn *architect, urban planner, general contractor*

Winston Salem
Butner, Fred Washington, Jr. *architect*
Oppermann, Joseph Kay *architect*
Walter, Lloyd Guy, Jr. *architect*

OHIO

Akron
Castronovo, Thomas Paul *architect, consultant*

Berea
Pattison, Robert Maynicke *architect*

Celina
†Fanning, Ronald Heath *architect, engineer*

Chagrin Falls
Cordes, Loverne Christian *interior designer*
Dunning, Ann Marie *architect*

Cincinnati
Alexander, James Marshall, Jr. *architect, retired educator*
Glendening, Everett Austin *architect*
Goetzman, Bruce Edgar *architecture educator*
Luckner, Herman Richard, III *interior designer*
Meisner, Gary Wayne *landscape architect*
Nielsen, George Lee *architect*
Preiser, Wolfgang Friedrich Ernst *architect, educator, consultant, researcher*
Roomann, Hugo *architect*
Senhauser, John Crater *architect*
Thrun, Robert Read *architect*

Cleveland
Behnke, William Alfred *landscape architect, planner*
Bowen, Richard Lee *architect*
Bucchieri, Stephen Joseph *architect*
Dewald, Ernest Leroy *landscape architect*
Eberhard, William Thomas *architect*
Gibans, James David *architect*
Kelly, John Terence *architect*
Little, Robert Andrews *architect, designer, painter*
Madison, Robert Prince *architect*
Melsop, James William *architect*
Sande, Theodore Anton *architect, educator, foundation executive*
Zung, Thomas Tse-Kwai *architect*

Columbus
Böhm, Friedrich (Friedl) K.M. *architectural firm executive*
Carpenter, Jot David *landscape architect, educator*
Howell, Norbert Allen *architect*
Kirk, Ballard Harry Thurston *architect*
Koncelik, Joseph Arthur *industrial design educator*
Moody, Curtis Jerome *architect*
Tully, Richard Lowden *architect*
Weinhold, Virginia Beamer *interior designer*

Cuyahoga Falls
Haag, Everett Keith *architect*

Dayton
Betz, Eugene William *architect*

Lima
Bassett, James H. *landscape architect*

Toledo
Hills, Arthur W. *architectural firm executive*
Martin, Robert Edward *architect*
Stark, Charles H., III *architectural firm executive*

Youngstown
Buchanan, C. Robert *architectural firm executive*
Mastriana, Robert Alan *architect*

OKLAHOMA

Afton
Starbird, Lonnie Darryl *producer of custom car shows, designer and builder of custom automobiles*

Norman
Henderson, Arnold Glenn *architect, educator*

Oklahoma City
Ball, Rex Martin *urban designer*
Kertok, Michael Bowers *architect, interior designer*
Schmidt, Fred C. *architect*

Tulsa
Jones, Robert Lawton *architect, planner, educator*
Kennedy, Nancy Louise *retired draftsman*
Knowles, Billy C. *architect*

OREGON

Ashland
Mularz, Theodore Leonard *architect*

Clackamas
Merrill, William Dean *architect, medical facility planning consultant*

Lake Oswego
Worsley, John Clayton *architect*

Medford
Skelton, Douglas H. *architect*
Straus, David A. *architectural firm executive*

Newport
Gordon, Walter *architect*

Otter Rock
Eaton, Leonard Kimball *retired architecture educator*

Portland
Frasca, Robert John *architect*
Gunsul, Brooks R. W. *architect*
Hacker, Thomas Owen *architect*
Kilbourn, Lee Ferris *architect, specifications writer*
Michael, Gary Linn *architect*
Ritz, Richard Ellison *architect, architectural historian, writer*
Stastny, Donald Joseph *architect*
Wintermute, Marjorie McLean *architect, educator*

Seaside
Sheasgreen, Betty *interior designer, painter, sculptor*

Springfield
Lutes, Donald Henry *architect*

Tualatin
Broome, John William *retired architect*

West Linn
Treffinger, Karl Edward *architectural firm executive*

PENNSYLVANIA

Altoona
Suckling, Robert McCleary *architect*

Bala Cynwyd
Bentivegna, Peter Ignatius *architectural company executive*

Bethlehem
Spillman, Robert Arnold *architect*

Butler
Kosar, John E. *architectural firm executive*

Camp Hill
Spiers, Tomas Hoskins, Jr. *architect*

Erie
Weber, Herman C., Jr. *architect*

Jenkintown
Clemmer, Leon *architect, planner*

Kingston
Gayeski, Alba Lori *interior designer*

Media
Sutton, Jonathan Stone *landscape architect*

Philadelphia
Aquaro, Angelo R. *architect, consultant*
Bower, John Arnold, Jr. *architect, educator*
Brown, Denise Scott *architect, urban planner*
Dagit, Charles Edward, Jr. *architect, educator*
Eiswerth, Barry Neil *architect, educator*
Hamme, David Codrington *architect*
Hayes, John Freeman *architect*
Heilman, Wesley Marvin, III *architect*
Izenour, Steven *architect*
Jordan, Joe J. *architect*
Kise, James Nelson *architect, urban planner*
Lawson, John Quinn *architect*
Leatherbee, William Bell *architect*
Magaziner, Henry Jonas *architect*
Maxman, Susan Abel *architect*
McHarg, Ian Lennox *landscape architect, regional planner, educator*
Mirick, Henry Dustin *architect*
Mitchell, Ehrman Burkman, Jr. *architect*
Olshin, Samuel E. *architect*
Pearson, Davis *architect*
Perkins, George Holmes *architectural educator, architect*
Peterson, Charles Emil *architect*
Prowler, Donald Marc *architect*
Rauch, John Keiser, Jr. *architect*
Roberts, William Henry *architect*
Rybczynski, Witold Marian *architect, educator, writer*
Rykwert, Joseph *architecture and art history educator*
Santos, Adele Naude *architect, educator*
Saylor, Peter M. *architect*
Sherman, Suzette *interior design consultant*
Swinburne, Herbert Hillhouse *architect*
Thrower, John Eden *architectural firm executive*
Tyng, Anne Griswold *architect*
Venturi, Robert *architect*
Vernon, Shirley Jane *architect, educator*
Vinh, Binh *architect*
Wallace, David Alexander *architect, educator*

Pittsburgh
Bohlin, Peter Quarfordt *architect*
Brenenborg, David C. *architectural firm executive*
Carter, Donald K. *architectural firm executive*
Damianos, Sylvester *architect, sculptor*
Gindroz, Raymond L. *architect*
Hartkopf, Volker Hugo *architect, educator*
Pekruhn, John Edward *retired architect, educator*
Saalman, Howard *architectural historian, educator*
Simonds, John Ormsbee *landscape architect*
Swain, William Grant *landscape architect*

Radnor
Wheatley, William Arthur *architect, musician*

State College
Haas, John C. *architect*

University Park
Leslie, Donald Wilmot *landscape architecture educator*
Porterfield, Neil Harry *landscape architect, planner*
Wheeler, C. Herbert *architect, consultant, educator*

Wallingford
Clauss, Alfred *architect*

Wayne
Suer, Marvin David *architect*

RHODE ISLAND

Jamestown
Todd, Thomas Abbott *architect, urban designer*

Little Compton
Bullerjahn, Eduard Henri *architect*

Newport
Burgin, William Lyle *architect*

Providence
St. Florian, Friedrich Gartler *architect, educator, university dean*
Wooding, Peter Holden *interior and industrial designer*

SOUTH CAROLINA

Charleston
†Cole, Douglas Wade *landscape architect*
Goff, R. Garey *architect*
Lucas, Frank Edward *architect*
Schmitt, Robert Christian *architect, interior designer*

Clemson
Young, Joseph Laurie *architecture educator*

Columbia
Carlisle, William Aiken *architect*
Golightly, Donald Edward *architect*
Hultstrand, Charles John *architect*

Greenville
LeBlanc, L(ouis) Christian *architect*
Neal, James Austin *architect*

Walterboro
Marvin, Robert Earle *landscape architect*

SOUTH DAKOTA

Rapid City
Jones, David L. *architect*

Sioux Falls
Koch, Ralph Richard *architect*

TENNESSEE

Chattanooga
Derthick, Alan Wendell *architect*
Travis, W. Vance, Jr. *architect*

Knoxville
Mc Carty, Bruce *architect*
Simpkins, Anne Eddleman *interior designer*
Vinson, William C. *architectural firm executive*

Memphis
Crump, Metcalf *architect*
Evans, James Mignon *architect*
Harrover, Roy Perkins *architect*
Jones, Walk Claridge, III *architect*
Looney, J. Carson *architectural firm executive*
Tucker, Jack Randolph, Jr. *architectural firm executive*
Yeates, Zeno Lanier *retired architect*

Nashville
Brush, Clinton E., III *retired architect*
Crabtree, Bruce Isbester, Jr. *architect*
Gobbell, Ronald Vance *architect*
Miller, Richard L. *architectural executive*
Swensson, Earl Simcox *architect*

TEXAS

Arlington
Ferrier, Richard Brooks *architecture educator, architect*

Austin
Alexander, Drury Blakeley *architectural educator*
Alofsin, Anthony *architect, art historian, sculptor, educator*
Barnes, Jay William, Jr. *architect, rancher*
Barr, Howard Raymond *architect*
Black, James Sinclair *architect, educator*
Box, John Harold *architect, educator, academic dean*
Croslin, Charles Wilburn, Jr. *architect*
George, Walter Eugene, Jr. *architect*
Kreisle, Matthew F., III *architectural firm executive*
Landes, Robert Paul *architect*
Little, Emily Browning *architect*
Merritt, Bernard Jason *architect, urban and regional planner*
Newton, Charles Chartier *architect*
Perry, David Brian *architect*
Polkinghorn, James B. *architectural firm executive*
Roessner, Roland Gommel *architect, educator*

Bellville
Bishop, James A. *architect, writer*

Bryan
Kellett, William Hiram, Jr. *retired architect, engineer, educator*

College Station
Boyer, Lester Leroy, Jr. *architecture educator, consultant*
Reed, Raymond Deryl *architect*
Woodcock, David Geoffrey *architect, educator*

Dallas
Blevins, Gary Lynn *architect, real estate broker, real estate appraiser*
Braden, David Rice *architect*
Fulton, Duncan Thomas, III *architect*
Kolb, Nathaniel Key, Jr. *architect*
Landry, Jane Lorenz *architect*
Lundy, Victor Alfred *architect, educator*
McCune, M. Davis *architect*
Morrison, Lionel B. *architect*
Roy, Clarence Leslie *landscape architect*
Schwartz, Irving Donn *architect*
Shaw, Dean Alvin *architect*
Stacy, Dennis William *architect*
Vondracek, Betty Sue *interior designer, remodeling contractor, real estate agent*
Wall, Sidney Smith Roderick, Jr. *architectural firm executive, architect, consultant*
Watson, John R. *landscape illuminating company executive*
Wilson, Trisha *interior architectural designer*

Denton
Miller, Tom Polk *retired architect*

El Paso
Carroll, Edwin Winford *architect*
†Mason, Richard Clyde *landscape architect*

Flower Mound
Morrish, Thomas Jay *golf course architect*

Fort Worth
Geren, Preston Murdoch, Jr. *architect, engineer*
Gideon, Randall Clifton *architectural firm executive*

Houston
Andrews, Lavone D. *architect*
Bair, Royden Stanley *architect*
Barthelme, Donald *architect*
Bentsen, Kenneth Edward *architect*
Borget, Lloyd George *architect*
Brents, Daniel Rugel *architectural firm executive*
Calhoun, Harold *architect*
Chase, John Saunders *architect*
Cutler, John Earl *landscape architect*
Douglas, Frank Fair *architect, graphic designer*
Falick, James *architect*
Garrison, Truitt B. *architect*
Jackson, R. Graham *architect*
King, Jonathan *architectural researcher, educator*
Lawrence, Charles Edmund *architect*
†Lerup, Lars G. *architecture educator, college dean*
Mc Ginty, John Milton *architect*
McGinty, Milton Bradford *architect, real estate development executive*
Moorhead, Gerald Lee *architect*
Morehead, James Caddall, Jr. *architect, educator*
Morris, Seth Irwin *architect*
Neuhaus, Julius Victor, III *architect*
Neuhaus, William Oscar, III *architect*
Owens, Gary Steven *architect*
Perkins, Britten Lee *architectural firm executive*
Pierce, George Foster, Jr. *architect*
Thomas, Lavon Bullock *interior designer*

Irving
George, David Webster *architect*
Rees, Frank William, Jr. *architect*

Longview
Crain, Bluford Walter, Jr. *architect*

Lubbock
Frazier, Eugene Richard *designer*

Mcallen
Ashley, James Thomas, III *architect*

Montgomery
Tharp, Benjamin Carroll, Jr. *architect*

San Antonio
Frazer, Robert Lee *landscape architect*
Haywood, Norcell Dan *architect*
Hesson, Paul Anthony *architect*
Keeter, James Edwin, Sr. *landscape architect*
Perez, Andrew, III *architect*

The Woodlands
Williams, W. Gene *architect*

UTAH

Salt Lake City
Beall, Burtch W., Jr. *architect*
Blackner, Boyd Atkins *architect*
Brems, David Paul *architect*
Chong, Richard David *architect*
Christopher, James Walker *architect, educator*
Crane, Steve *architectural firm executive*
Daniels, George Nelson *architect*
Stowe, Neal P. *architect*

VERMONT

Charlotte
Kiley, Daniel Urban *landscape architect, planner*

VIRGINIA

Alexandria
Cross, Eason, Jr. *architect*
Ritter, James William *architect, educator*

Annandale
Ballard, Edward Brooks *landscape architect*

Arlington
Adreon, Harry Barnes *architect*

Blacksburg
Bliznakov, Milka Tcherneva *architect*
Currie, Leonard James *architect, planner, educator*
Rodriguez-Camilloni, Humberto Leonardo *architect, historian, educator*

Charlottesville
Bednar, Michael John *architecture educator*
Bosserman, Joseph Norwood *architecture educator*
Browne, Henry James *architect*
Root, James Benjamin *landscape architect*
Swofford, Donald Anthony *architect*

Chesterfield
Morris, James Carl *architect*

Crozet
Anderson, Robert Barber *architect*

Fairfax
Ward, George Truman *architect*

Falls Church
Barkley, Paul Haley, Jr. *architect*
Mortensen, Robert Henry *landscape architect*

Fredericksburg
Keplinger, Duane *architectural executive*

Mc Lean
Bass, Roger William *architect*
Chatelain, Leon, III *architectural firm executive*
Moore, Daniel L. *architect*

Norfolk
Goldbach, Richard Albert *shipyard company executive*

Oakton
Kerr, Charlotte Bowden *interior designer*

Orlean
Kulski, Julian Eugeniusz *architect, planner, educator*

Portsmouth
Brown, James Andrew *naval architect*

Reston
Metcalf, William Henry, Jr. *architect*
Scheeler, James Arthur *architect*

Richmond
George, Lester Lee *golf course architectural firm executive*
Jandl, Henry Anthony *architect, educator*
Joel, William Lee, II *interior and lighting designer*
Rawlings, James Scott *architect*

Vienna
Kohler, Karl Eugene *architect*

Virginia Beach
May, David L., Jr. *architectural firm executive*

Warrenton
Palmer, Milton Meade *landscape architect*

Williamsburg
Herbert, Albert Edward, Jr. *interior and industrial designer*
Parker, Donald Howard *landscape architect*

Woodbridge
Peck, Dianne Kawecki *architect*

WASHINGTON

Bellevue
Roselle, Richard Donaldson *industrial, marine and interior designer*

Deer Harbor
Hoag, Paul Sterling *architect*

Everett
King, Indle Gifford *industrial designer, educator*

Hansville
Griffin, DeWitt James *architect, real estate developer*

Kirkland
Gregory, Matthew James *architectural firm executive*

Mount Vernon
Hall, David Ramsay *architect*
Klein, Henry *architect*

Seattle
Bain, William James, Jr. *architect*
Bassetti, Fred Forde *architect*
Bosworth, Thomas Lawrence *architect, educator*
Buursma, William F. *architect*
Bystrom, Arne *architect*
Castanes, James Christopher *architect*
Cichanski, Gerald *golf course architect*
Dermanis, Paul Raymond *architect*
Durham, Robert Lewis *architect*
Freed, Aaron David *architect*
Gordon, Patrick A. *architectural firm executive*
Grossman, Robert James *architect*
Hastings, L(ois) Jane *architect, educator*
Hinshaw, Mark Larson *architect, urban planner*
Jacobson, Phillip Lee *architect, educator*
Johnston, Norman John *architecture educator*
Jonassen, James O. *architect*
Jones, Grant Richard *landscape architect, planner*
Jones, Johnpaul *architect*
Kelbaugh, Douglas Stewart *architect, urban designer, architecture educator*
Kolb, Keith Robert *architect, educator*
Lovett, Wendell Harper *architect*
Malcolm, Garold Dean *architect*
Meyer, C. Richard *architect*
Miles, Don Clifford *architect*
Morse, John Moore *architect, planner*
Olson, James William Park *architect*
Piven, Peter Anthony *architect, management consultant*
Polk, William Merrill *architect*
Sanders, James Joseph *architect*
Shinbo, Robert *landscape architect*
Small, Robert E. *architect, architecture educator*
Springer, Floyd Ladean *architect*
Sundberg, Richard *architectural firm executive*
Whalen, Michael P. *architect*

Shelton
Wolbrink, Donald Henry *landscape architect, city planner*

Tacoma
Harris, James Martin *architect*
Liddle, Alan Curtis *architect*

WEST VIRGINIA

Morgantown
Collier, Clifford Warthen, Jr. *retired landscape architect*

Wheeling
Hughes, Mary Elizabeth *interior designer*

WISCONSIN

Eau Claire
Larson, Brian Foix *architect*

Madison
Felstehausen, Herman Henry *natural resources-land planning educator*
Lawson, David E. *architect*
Niemann, Bernard John, Jr. *land and geographical system educator, researcher, consultant*
Sample, Nathaniel Welshire *architect*
Tishler, William Henry *landscape architect, educator*

Milwaukee
Wenzler, William Paul *architect*
Zarse, Leigh Bryant *architect, architectural engineer*

Oshkosh
Reinke, Leonard Herman *architect*

Osseo
Wright, Rodney H. *architect*

Wausau
†Birkholz, Douglas J. *industrial designer*

Whitewater
Carrara, Arthur Alfonso *architect, designer, painter, graphic designer*

TERRITORIES OF THE UNITED STATES

PUERTO RICO

San Juan
Marvel, Thomas Stahl *architect*

CANADA

BRITISH COLUMBIA

Vancouver
Erickson, Arthur Charles *architect*
Hirshen, Sanford *architect, educator*
Oberlander, Cornelia Hahn *landscape architect*
Patkau, John *architect*
Patkau, Patricia *architect, architecture educator*

MANITOBA

Winnipeg
Hodne, Thomas Harold, Jr. *architect, educator*

NEW BRUNSWICK

Moncton
Albert, Elide *architect*

NOVA SCOTIA

Halifax
Fowler, Charles Allison Eugene *architect, engineer*
MacKay-Lyons, Brian Gerald *architect, urban designer, architecture educator*

ONTARIO

Don Mills
Budrevics, Alexander *landscape architect*

Toronto
†Akazawa-Eguchi, Miyuki Real *landscape architect, environmental artist*
Diamond, Abel Joseph *architect*
Fife, Edward H. *landscape architecture educator*
†Flanagan-Eguchi, Barbara L. *landscape architect, theme park designer*
Grossman, Irving *architect*
†Hubel, Vello *industrial designer, educator, artist*
Kuwabara, Bruce Bunji *architect*
McKenna, Marianne *architect*
Moriyama, Raymond *architect*
Payne, Thomas Charles *architect*
Thornley, Shirley Blumberg *architect*
van Ginkel, Blanche Lemco *architect, educator*

QUEBEC

Montreal
Jacobs, Peter Daniel Alexander *architecture and landscape architecture educator*
Marsan, Jean-Claude *architect, urban planner, educator*
Prus, Victor Marius *architect, urbanist*

SASKATCHEWAN

Saskatoon
Henry, Keith Douglas *architect*

MEXICO

Cuajimalpa
†Mandri-Bellot, Jose Antonio *architect*

ENGLAND

London
Foster, Sir Norman Robert *architect*

FRANCE

Joinville
Greer, Joseph Epps *architect*

Paris
†Piano, Renzo *architect*

GERMANY

Cologne
Ungers, Oswald M. *architect, educator*

Kussaberg
Lyndon, Maynard *architect*

ISRAEL

Tel Aviv
Melamede, Ada Karmi *architectural firm executive*

ITALY

Rome
Ahrens, William Henry *architect*

JAPAN

Tokyo
Azuma, Takamitsu *architect, educator*
Hashimoto, Kunio *architect, educator*
Isozaki, Arata *architect*
Taguchi, Yoshitaka *architect*

ADDRESS UNPUBLISHED

Adler, Richard Melvin *architect, planner*
Adsit, Russell Allan *landscape designer*
Anderson, Ross Sherwood *architect*
Attoe, Wayne Osborne *architecture educator, author, designer*
Ballou, James Howland *architect*
Berkovich, Gary A. *architect*
Bunch, Franklin Swope *architect*
Callender, John Hancock *architect*
Campbell, Craig Stewart *landscape architect, town planner*
Carpenter, Derr Alvin *landscape architect*
Carroll, Marshall Elliott *architect*
Collins, John Francis *landscape architect, educator*
†Cook, John Charles *product designer, design consultant*
Cranin, Marilyn Sunners *landscape designer*
Crowther, Richard Layton *architect, consultant, researcher, author, lecturer*
Dean, Francis Hill *landscape architect, educator*
Dibner, David Robert *architect*
Diffrient, Niels *industrial designer*
Dobbel, Rodger Francis *interior designer*
Dyson, Arthur Thomas *architect, educator*
Ely, Marica McCann *interior designer*
End, Henry *interior and industrial designer*
Flipse, John Edward *naval architect, mechanical engineer*
Friedman, Mildred *designer, educator, curator*
Fulton, James Franklin *industrial designer*
Gandy, Charles David *interior designer*
Gantz, Carroll Melvin *industrial design consultant, consumer product designer*
Geddes, Robert *architect, educator*
Gensler, M. Arthur, Jr. *architect*
Gerner, Randolph Henry *architect*
Graff, William *architect*
Hargreaves, George Julian *landscape architect*
Hixon, Allen Wentworth *landscape architect, land planner*
Hutchins, Robert Ayer *architect*
Kahn, Charles Howard *architect, educator*
Katz, Robert David *architecture educator*
Kerr, Leslie A. *landscape architect*
Kirts, Wayne Charles *interior designer*
Klink, Robert Michael *consulting engineer, management consultant, financial consultant, property developer*
Knoll, Florence Schust *architect, designer*
Kropp, David Arthur *retired landscape architect*
Kump, Ernest Joseph *architect, consultant*
Lacy, Joseph Newton *architect*
Leaman, Jack Ervin *landscape architect, community/regional planner*
Liskamm, William Hugo *architect, urban planner, educator*
Loss, John C. *architect, retired educator*

Maltzan, Michael Thomas *architect*
Marshall, William, Jr. *architect*
Mc Pheeters, Edwin Keith *architect, educator*
Meier, Henry George *architect*
Meyers, Richard James *landscape architect*
Moore, Richard Alan *landscape architect*
Mumma, Albert Girard, Jr. *architect*
Murray, David George *architect*
Peters, Robert Woolsey *architect*
Pettitt, Jay S. *architect, consultant*
Poor, Janet Meakin *landscape designer*
Rabon, William James, Jr. *architect*
Reeves, Frank Blair *architect, educator*
Rice, Richard Lee *retired architect*
Roegner, George Peter *industrial designer*
Rogers, Charles Ford, II *architect*
Rogers, Kate Ellen *interior design educator*
Rubenstein, Michael Alan *architect*
Shadbolt, Douglas *architecture educator, administrator*
Shank, Wesley Ivan *retired architect, educator*
Siefer, Stuart B. *architect*
Stearns, Carl David *architect*
Thompson, Charles Kevin *architect, lighting designer*
Tomasi, Donald Charles *architect*
White, Robert Frederick *landscape architect*
Wiebenson, Dora Louise *architectural historian, educator, author*
Wilkerson, Charles Edward *architect*
Woerner, Robert Lester *landscape architect*

ARTS: LITERARY. *See also* COMMUNICATIONS MEDIA.

UNITED STATES

ALABAMA

Birmingham
Stallworth, Anne Nall *writer, writing educator*

Guntersville
Sparkman, Brandon Buster *educator, writer, consultant*

Huntsville
Smith, Philip Wayne *writer, communications company executive*

ALASKA

Fairbanks
Helmericks, Harmon *author, explorer*

Homer
†Bodett, Thomas Edward *writer, radio personality*

ARIZONA

Flagstaff
Cline, Platt Herrick *author*

Mesa
Gaylor, Walter *writer, military historian*

Paradise Valley
Carey, Ernestine Gilbreth (Mrs. Charles E. Carey) *writer, lecturer*

Scottsdale
Shreffler, Genevieve *author*

Tempe
†Alexander, Thea Ann *author, counseling psychologist*
Raby, William Louis *author*

Tucson
Ingalls, Jeremy *poet, educator*
Kingsolver, Barbara Ellen *writer*
Leydet, François Guillaume *writer*
Russ, Joanna *writer, English language educator*
Vicker, Ray *writer*

ARKANSAS

Eureka Springs
Dragonwagon, Crescent *writer*

Fayetteville
Jones, Douglas Clyde *author*
Williams, Miller *poet, translator*

Little Rock
Brown, Dee Alexander *author*

CALIFORNIA

Alamo
Bolles, Richard Nelson *author, clergyman*

Altadena
Burden, Jean (Prussing) *poet, writer, editor*

Arcadia
Sloane, Beverly LeBov *writer, consultant*

Berkeley
Burger, Robert Eugene *author, chess expert*
Callenbach, Ernest *writer, editor*
Clark, Thomas Willard *poet*
Dundes, Alan *writer, folklorist, educator*
Guest, Barbara *author, poet*
Jordan, June M. *poet, English language educator*
Kingston, Maxine Hong *author*
Meltzer, David *author, musician*
Milosz, Czeslaw *poet, author, educator*
Ogg, Wilson Reid *poet, lyricist, curator, publisher, lawyer, retired judge, educator*
Temko, Allan Bernard *writer*

Beverly Hills
Bass, Ronald *screenwriter*
Benedek, Barbara *screenwriter*
Boam, Jeffrey David *screenwriter*
Carpenter, John Howard *screenwriter, director*
Crichton, (John) Michael *author, film director*
Crowe, Cameron *screenwriter*
Curtin, Valerie *screenwriter, actress*
†Darabont, Frank *screenwriter, director*
David, Larry *television scriptwriter*
Epstein, Julius J. *screenwriter, playwright, producer*
Essex, Harry J. *screenwriter, novelist*
Eszterhas, Joseph Anthony *film scriptwriter*
Frank, Harriet, Jr. *screenwriter*
Gelbart, Larry *writer, producer*
Getchell, Robert *screenwriter*
Goldman, Bo *screenwriter, director*
Goldman, William *writer*
Koepp, David *screenwriter*
Livingston, Myra Cohn *poet, writer, educator*
Mandel, Babaloo *scriptwriter*
Meyer, Nicholas *screenwriter, director*
Meyers, Nancy Jane *screenwriter, producer*
Niven, Laurence Van Cott *author*
Pierson, Frank Romer *screenwriter, director*
Ravetch, Irving *screenwriter*
Ross, Stanley Ralph *writer, publisher, producer, software manufacturing executive*
†Roth, Eric *screenwriter*
Rudnick, Paul *playwright, screenwriter*
Schrader, Paul Joseph *film writer, director*
Schulian, John (Nielsen Schulian) *screenwriter, author*
Schulman, Tom *screenwriter*
Schumacher, Joel *film writer, director*
Shanley, John Patrick *screenwriter*
Shepard, Sam (Samuel Shepard Rogers) *playwright, actor*
Star, Darren *television writer, producer*
Towne, Robert *screenwriter*
Ward, David Schad *screenwriter, film director*
Weller, Michael *playwright, screenwriter*

Carmel
Aurner, Robert Ray *author, corporate executive*

Chico
Keithley, George *writer*

Claremont
Mezey, Robert *poet, educator*

Concord
Headding, Lillian Susan (Sally Headding) *writer, forensic clairvoyant*

Covina
Phillips, Jill Meta *novelist, critic, astrologer*

Cromberg
Kolb, Ken Lloyd *writer*

Culver City
†McNeill, Daniel Richard *writer*
Proft, Pat *screenwriter, film producer*

Cupertino
Zobel, Louise Purwin *author, educator, lecturer, writing consultant*

Cypress
Edmonds, Ivy Gordon *writer*

Dana Point
Kleiner, Richard Arthur *writer, editor*

Danville
McMillan, Terry L. *writer, educator*

Davis
Beagle, Peter Soyer *writer*
Major, Clarence Lee *novelist, poet, educator*
McPherson, Sandra Jean *poet, educator*

Fair Oaks
Inglis, Andrew Franklin *author, consultant*

Fairfax
Gores, Joseph Nicholas *novelist, scriptwriter*
Novello, Don *writer, comedian, actor*

Fieldbrook
Schaaf, Miv *writer, graphic designer, composer*

Fresno
Levine, Philip *poet, educator*

Gardena
Baker, Lillian L. *author, historian, artist, lecturer*

Georgetown
Lengyel, Cornel Adam (Cornel Adam) *author*

Healdsburg
Erdman, Paul Emil *author*

Irvine
Shusterman, Neal Douglas *author, screenwriter*

Kensington
Nathan, Leonard Edward *writer, educator*

La Jolla
Antin, David *poet, critic*

Laguna Beach
Taylor, Theodore Langhans *author*

Laguna Hills
Rabe, David William *playwright*

Landers
Landers, Vernette Trosper *writer, educator, association executive*

Los Angeles
Anderson, Jane A. *scriptwriter*
Avallone, Michael Angelo *author*
Barry, Julian *playwright, screenwriter*
Basil, Douglas Constantine *author, educator*
Blake, Michael *writer*
Bochco, Steven *screenwriter, television producer*
Brach, Gérard *screenwriter*
Branch, Taylor *writer*
Briley, John Richard *writer*
†Butler, Octavia Estelle *free-lance writer*
Carabillo, Virginia Anne (Toni Carabillo) *writer, editor, graphic designer*
Cecchetti, Giovanni *poet, Italian language educator, literary critic*
Chetwynd, Lionel *screenwriter, producer, director*
Cohen, Leonard (Norman Cohen) *poet, novelist, musician, songwriter*
Corwin, Norman *writer, director, producer*
Crow, John Armstrong *writer, educator*
Fisher, Terry Louise *television writer*
Fuller, Samuel (Michael) *scriptwriter, film director*
Highwater, Jamake *author, lecturer*
Lachman, Morton *writer, theatrical director and producer*
Launer, Dale Mark *screenwriter*
Lee, Walter William, Jr. *film writer, consultant, publishing executive*
Matheson, Richard Burton *author, scriptwriter*
Mc Kuen, Rod *poet, composer, author*
McWilliams, Peter *poet*
Miller, Jason *playwright*
Noguchi, Thomas Tsunetomi *author, forensic pathologist*
Peoples, David Webb *screenwriter*
Puzo, Mario *author*
Rayfiel, David *screenwriter*
Richter, W. D. *screenwriter, director, producer*
Robert, Patrick *playwright*
Rubin, Bruce Joel *screenwriter, director, producer*
Shagan, Steve *screenwriter, novelist, film producer*
Shapiro, Mel *playwright, director, drama educator*
Shore, Herbert *writer, poet, educator*
Steel, Ronald Lewis *author, historian, educator*
Tally, Ted *screenwriter*
Thomas, Shirley *author, educator, business executive*
Westheimer, David Kaplan *novelist*

Mariposa
Shields, Allan Edwin *writer, photographer, retired educator*

Monterey
Nowell, Elizabeth Cameron Clemons *author*

Newport Beach
Dovring, Karin Elsa Ingeborg *author, poet, playwright, communication analyst*

North Hollywood
Ribman, Ronald Burt *playwright*

Oakland
Foley, Jack (John Wayne Harold Foley) *poet, writer, editor*
†Scalapino, Leslie *poet*
Schacht, Henry Mevis *writer, consultant*
Silverberg, Robert *author*

Pacific Grove
Fleischman, Paul *children's author*

Palo Alto
Berger, Joseph *author, educator, counselor*

Petaluma
Pronzini, Bill John (William Pronzini) *author*

Piedmont
Phillips, Betty Lou (Elizabeth Louise Phillips) *author, interior designer*

Ramona
Cesinger, Joan *author*

Redondo Beach
Battles, Roxy Edith *novelist, consultant, educator*

San Diego
Boggs, Marcus Livingstone, Jr. *novelist, editor*
†Brimner, Larry Dane *author, editor, educational consultant*
Hart, Anne *author*
†Krull, Kathleen *juvenile fiction and nonfiction writer*
Linn, Edward Allen *writer*

San Francisco
Adams, Leon David *author*
Bantock, Nick *writer, illustrator*
Bowers, Edgar *poet, educator*
Ferlinghetti, Lawrence *poet*
Ferris, Russell James, II *freelance writer*
Field, Carol Hart *writer, journalist, foreign correspondent*
Gaines, Ernest James *author*
Ginsberg, Allen *poet, photographer, musician*
Gunn, Thom(son) (William) *poet*
Jundis, Orvy Lagasca *writer, consultant, educator*
Lai, Him Mark *writer*
Leonard, George Jay *author*
Olsen, Tillie *author*
Sachs, Marilyn Stickle *author, lecturer, editor*
Whalen, Philip Glenn *poet, novelist*
Wilcox, Collin M. *author*

San Jose
Loventhal, Milton *writer, playwright, lyricist*
Steele, Shelby *writer, educator*

San Marcos
Sauer, David Andrew *writer, computer consultant*

San Mateo
Korn, Walter *writer*

San Rafael
Turner, William Weyand *author*

Santa Barbara
Bock, Russell Samuel *author*
Corman, Cid (Sidney Corman) *poet, editor*
Cunningham, Julia Woolfolk *author*
Davidson, Eugene Arthur *author*
Easton, Robert (Olney) *author, environmentalist*
Jackson, Beverley Joy Jacobson *columnist, lecturer*
Smith, Michael Townsend *author, editor, stage director*

Santa Maria
Arnell, Robert Edward *technical writer*

Santa Monica
Cowan, Andrew Glenn *television writer*
Fleischman, Albert Sidney (Sid Fleischman) *writer*
Graff, Todd *screenwriter*
Stone, Oliver William *screenwriter, director*

Sherman Oaks
Ellison, Harlan Jay *author, screenwriter*
Kanter, Hal *television and film writer, producer, director*

Sonoma
Kizer, Carolyn Ashley *poet, educator*

Stanford
Conquest, (George) Robert (Acworth) *writer, historian, poet, critic, journalist*
Gardner, John William *writer, educator*
Girard, René Noel *author, educator*
Lindenberger, Herbert Samuel *writer, literature educator*
Stockdale, James Bond *writer, research scholar, retired naval officer*

Studio City
Parish, James Robert *author, cinema historian*
Pournelle, Jerry Eugene *author*
Shavelson, Melville *writer, theatrical producer and director*

Tiburon
Drury, Allen Stuart *author*

Venice
Eliot, Alexander *author, mythologist*

West Hollywood
Black, David *writer, educator, producer*
Black, Shane *screenwriter*
Dorsey, Helen Danner (Johna Blinn) *writer, author, educator*
Grasshoff, Alex *writer, producer, director*

COLORADO

Boulder
Dorn, Edward Merton *poet, educator*
Folsom, Franklin Brewster *author*
Kaye, Evelyn Patricia (Evelyn Patricia Sarson) *author, publisher, travel expert*
Metzger, H(owell) Peter *writer*
Waldman, Anne Lesley *poet, performer, editor, publisher, educational administrator*

Canon City
Bendell, Donald Ray *writer, director, poet*

Colorado Springs
†Dassanowsky-Harris, Robert von *writer, editor, educator*
Yaffe, James *author*

Denver
Ducker, Bruce *novelist, lawyer*
MacGregor, George Lescher, Jr. *freelance writer*
Mead, Beverly Mirium Anderson *writer, educator*

Estes Park
Hillway, Tyrus *author, educator*

Greeley
Willis, Connie (Constance E. Willis) *author*

Vail
Knight, Constance Bracken *writer, realtor, interior decorator, corporate executive*

CONNECTICUT

Danbury
†Weiner, Jonathan David *writer*

Essex
Keppel, John *writer, former diplomat*

Fairfield
Barone, Rose Marie Pace *writer, former educator*
Clark, Eleanor *author*

Greens Farms
St.Marie, Satenig *writer*

Greenwich
Ewald, William Bragg, Jr. *author, consultant*

Guilford
Peters, William *author, producer, director*

Hartford
†Hedrick, Joan Doran *writer*

Madison
Carlson, Dale Bick *writer*

Middletown
Manchester, William *writer*

New Canaan
Packard, Vance Oakley *writer*
Powers, Thomas Moore *author*
Prescott, Peter Sherwin *writer*

New Haven
Gallup, Donald Clifford *bibliographer, educator*

Old Lyme
St. George, Judith Alexander *author*

Old Saybrook
Hamilton, Donald Bengtsson *author*

Roxbury
Anderson, Robert Woodruff *playwright, novelist, screenwriter*
Gurney, Albert Ramsdell *playwright, novelist, educator*
Miller, Arthur *playwright, author*

Sandy Hook
Kellogg, Steven *author, illustrator*

Uncasville
Meredith, William (Morris) *poet, English language educator*

Waterford
Commire, Anne *playwright*

West Cornwall
Klaw, Spencer *writer, editor, educator*

Westbrook
Hall, Jane Anna *writer, model*

Weston
Diforio, Robert G. *literary agent*
Kilty, Jerome Timothy *playwright, stage director, actor*

Westport
Hotchner, Aaron Edward *author*
Martin, Ralph Guy *writer*
Safran, Claire *writer, editor*
Walden, Amelia Elizabeth (Mrs. John William Harmon) *author*

DISTRICT OF COLUMBIA

Washington
Abrams, Elliott *writer, foreign affairs consultant and analyst*
Alperovitz, Gar *author*
Arndt, Richard T. *writer, consultant*
Barnet, Richard Jackson *author, educator*
Black, Charlie J. *technical writer, educator, business consultant*
Bowen, Margareta Maria *interpretation and translation educator*
Burnham, David Bright *writer*
Burns, David Mitchell *writer, musician, former diplomat*
Cavnar, Samuel Melmon *author, publisher, activist*
Childs, Timothy Winston *writer*
Coffin, Tristram *writer, editor*
Dixon, Jeane *writer, lecturer, realtor, columnist*
George, Gerald William *author, administrator*
Haggerty, James Joseph *writer*
Hecht, Anthony Evan *poet*
Klay, Andor C. *author, diplomat*
Lilienthal, Alfred M(orton) *author, historian, editor*
May, Stephen *writer, former government official*
McCarthy, Abigail Quigley *writer, columnist, educator*
Merrell, Jesse Howard *writer*
Miller, Hope Ridings *author*
Naifeh, Steven Woodward *writer*
O'Doherty, Brian *playwright, filmmaker*
Ramsay, William Charles *writer*
Raskin, Marcus Goodman *writer, educator*
Richardson, David Bacon *writer, journalist*
Smith, Stuart Seaborne *writer, government official, union official*
Tannen, Deborah Frances *writer, linguist*
Taquey, Charles Henri *writer, consultant*
Viorst, Judith Stahl *author*
Weaver, Warren, Jr. *writer*
Whalen, Richard James *author, consultant*
Wouk, Herman *writer*

FLORIDA

Belleair Beach
Fuentes, Martha Ayers *playwright*

Boca Raton
Herst, Herman, Jr. *writer*
Keyes, Daniel *author*
Schaaf, Martha Eckert *author, library director, musician*

Boynton Beach
Heckelmann, Charles Newman (Charles Lawton) *author, publishing consultant*

Bradenton
Wendt, Lloyd *writer*

Captiva
Fadiman, Clifton *writer, editor, radio and television entertainer*

Clearwater
Carlson, Natalie Savage *author*
Horton, Donna Alberg *technical writer*

Coral Gables
Latham, Jean Lee *writer*
Minahan, John English *author*

Daytona Beach
Mc Collister, John Charles *writer, clergyman, educator*

Delray Beach
Coyle, William *educator*
Robinson, Richard Francis *writer, author*

Fort Myers
Powell, Richard Pitts *writer*

Gainesville
Haldeman, Joe William *novelist*

Pierce, Robert Nash *writer*
Smith, Jo Anne *writer, retired educator*

Hollywood
Blate, Michael *author, lecturer*

Indialantic
Lewis, Richard Stanley *author, former editor*

Jacksonville
Oliver, Elizabeth Kimball *writer, historian*
Slaughter, Frank Gill *author, physician*

Largo
Craft Davis, Audrey Ellen *writer*

Miami
Alschuler, Al *freelance writer, public relations counselor*
Berger, Arthur Seymour *author, lawyer, director cultural organization*
Morgan, Marabel *author*
Rockstein, Morris *science writer, editor, consultant*

Naples
Alpert, Hollis *writer*
Card, Orson Scott (Byron Walley) *writer*
Montgomery, Ruth Shick *author*

Palm Beach
Hall, Kathryn Evangeline *writer, lecturer*

Pensacola
Sargent, James O'Connor *freelance writer*

Saint Augustine
Edwards, Page Lawrence, Jr. *author, archivist, historical society administrat*

Saint Petersburg
Bryant, John *author, publisher*
Carlson, Jeannie Ann *writer*
Meinke, Peter *writer, retired educator*

Sarasota
Hayes, Joseph *author*
Irwin, Theodore *writer*
Weeks, Albert Loren *author, educator, journalist*

Stuart
Ragno, Nancy Nickell *educational writer*

Tampa
Battle, Jean Allen *writer, educator*
Dunn, Henry Hampton *writer, former television commentator, former editor*
Hanford, Grail Stevenson *writer*

Tavernier
Zim, Herbert Spencer *author, educator*

Venice
Shaw, Bryce Robert *author*

Winter Park
Balliett, Gene (Howard Eugene Balliett) *writer, lecturer*

GEORGIA

Atlanta
†Chapman, Paul H. *author*
Geigerman, Clarice Furchgott *writer, actress, consultant*
Harmer, Lee DeLoache *writer*
Horsman, David A. Elliott *writer, financial services executive, educator*
Slappey, Sterling Greene *writer, journalist, researcher*

Augusta
Taylor, Janelle Diane Williams *writer*

Decatur
Cassity, (Allen) Turner *poet*

Savannah
Hale, Charlotte *author, publishing executive*
Thomas, Dwight Rembert *writer*

HAWAII

Honolulu
Edel, (Joseph) Leon *biographer, educator*
Halloran, Richard Colby *writer, former research executive, former news correspondent*
Statler, Oliver Hadley *writer*

Kihei
Wilson, Brandon Laine *writer, advertising and public relations consultant, explorer*

ILLINOIS

Chicago
Anshaw, Carol *writer*
Brashler, William *author*
Brooks, Gwendolyn *writer, poet*
Carpenter, Allan *author, editor, publisher*
Colter, Cyrus *novelist, lawyer*
†Hoover, Paul *poet*
Lach, Alma Elizabeth *food and cooking writer, consultant*
Litweiler, John Berkey *writer, editor*
Manelli, Donald Dean *screenwriter, film producer*
Nims, John Frederick *writer, educator*
Stern, Richard Gustave *author, educator*
Terkel, Studs (Louis Terkel) *author, interviewer*
Wade, Edwin Lee *writer, lawyer*

Elburn
Etter, David Pearson *poet, editor*

Evanston
Gibbons, William Reginald, Jr. *poet, novelist, editor*

Mitchell, Kendall *writer, literary critic*
Samuels, Ernest *author, educator*

Lake Forest
Swanton, Virginia Lee *author, publisher, bookseller*

Marengo
Mrkvicka, Edward Francis, Jr. *financial writer, publisher, consultant*

Oak Park
Bowman, James Henry *writer*
Kotlowitz, Alex *writer, journalist*

Palatine
Pohl, Frederik *writer*

Park Forest
Putnam, Robert E. *writer, editor*

Urbana
Lieberman, Laurence *poet, educator*

Waukegan
Marks, Martha Alford *author*

Wilmette
Nash, Jay Robert, III *author, playwright, publisher*

INDIANA

Beverly Shores
Ruzic, Neil Pierce *author, publisher, scientist*

Bloomington
Kibbey, Hal Stephen *science writer*
Komunyakaa, Yusef (James Willie Brown, Jr.) *poet*
Mitchell, Bert Breon *literary translator*

Chesterton
Petrakis, Harry Mark *author*

Frankfort
Borland, Kathryn Kilby *author*

Muncie
Eddy, Darlene Mathis *poet, educator*

South Bend
Black, Virginia Morrow *writer*

IOWA

Ames
Smiley, Jane Graves *author, educator*

Iowa City
†Bell, Marvin Hartley *poet, English language educator*
†Graham, Jorie *author*
†Jones, Thom Douglas *writer*
Justice, Donald Rodney *poet, educator*
Stern, Gerald Daniel *poet*

KANSAS

Lawrence
Burroughs, William Seward *writer*

Manhattan
Davis, Kenneth Sidney *writer*

KENTUCKY

Lexington
Davenport, Guy Mattison, Jr. *author, retired educator*

Louisville
Davenport, Gwen (Mrs. John Davenport) *author*

LOUISIANA

Baton Rouge
Madden, David *author*

Lake Charles
Butler, Robert Olen *writer, educator*

New Orleans
Grau, Shirley Ann (Mrs. James Kern Feibleman) *writer*
Harris, Aurand *playwright*
Pizer, Donald *author, educator*

Scott
Stockton, Robert Standeford *writer, real estate development, construction, sales and management consultant*

MAINE

Bar Harbor
†Mooser, Stephen *author*

Blue Hill
Lowry, James David *author, consultant*

Brooklin
Yglesias, Helen Bassine *author, educator*

Castine
Booth, Philip *poet, educator*

East Blue Hill
Taylor, Samuel Albert *playwright*

Milbridge
Enslin, Theodore Vernon *poet*

Orono
Wilson, Dorothy Clarke *author*

Phippsburg
Mc Lanathan, Richard (Barton Kennedy) *author, consultant*

Rockland
Taylor, Roger Conant *writer*

South Berwick
Carroll, Gladys Hasty *author*

MARYLAND

Baltimore
Barth, John Simmons *writer, educator*
Epstein, Daniel Mark *poet, dramatist*
Grossman, Allen Richard *poet, educator*
†St. John, David Marshall *poet, English educator*
Truesdell, Clifford Ambrose, III *author, editor*
Tyler, Anne (Mrs. Taghi M. Modarressi) *author*

Bethesda
Clark, Blake *author, business executive*
Dyer, Frederick Charles *writer, consultant*
Free, Ann Cottrell *writer*
Hartmann, Robert Trowbridge *author, consultant*
Henze, Paul Bernard *author, former government official*
McNamara, Francis John *writer*
†Mead, Loren Benjamin *writer, consultant*
Naylor, Phyllis Reynolds *author*
Simonds, Peggy Muñoz *writer, lecturer, retired literature educator*
Vosburgh, Frederick George *writer, editor*

Brookeville
Wilson, Vincent Joseph, Jr. *writer, historian, publisher*

Burtonsville
Peck, Carol Faulkner *poet, writer, publisher, educator*

Chevy Chase
Bacon, Donald Conrad *author, editor*
Weisman, John *author*

Cockeysville
Jacobsen, Josephine *author*

College Park
†Norman, Howard A. *writer*
Whittemore, Edward Reed, II *poet, retired educator*

Fort Washington
Cameron, Rita Giovannetti *writer, publisher*

Gaithersburg
†Amato, Ivan Abel *science writer*

Garrett Park
Kornberg, Warren Stanley *science journalist*

Lanham Seabrook
Horowitz, David Joel *author*

Potomac
†Pastan, Linda Olenik *poet*

Silver Spring
Ball, Anne H. *writer, editor, public relations consultant*
Brooks, Bruce Delos *writer*
Whitten, Leslie Hunter, Jr. *author, newspaper reporter*

Upper Marlboro
Smith, Ralph Lee *author, musician*

MASSACHUSETTS

Amherst
Jenkins, Paul Randall *poet, editor*
Langland, Joseph Thomas *author, emeritus educator*
Tate, James Vincent *poet, English educator*

Bedford
Kennedy, X. J. (Joseph Kennedy) *writer*

Belmont
Cavarnos, Constantine Peter *writer, philosopher*

Boston
Andre, Rae *writer, organizational behavior educator*
Angelou, Maya *author*
Appelbaum, Diana Karter *author*
Carroll, James *author*
†Chandler, David Luscombe *science writer*
Conroy, Pat (Donald Patrick Conroy) *writer*
Davis, William Arthur *writer, editor*
Greenwald, Sheila Ellen *writer, illustrator*
Hailey, Arthur *writer*
Jones, Rodney G. *poet, English educator*
†Kindl, Patrice *writer*
Lowry, Lois (Hammersberg) *author*
Pinsky, Robert Neal *poet, educator*
Pynchon, Thomas Ruggles, Jr. *author*
Say, Allen *children's writer, illustrator*
Shattuck, Roger Whitney *author, educator*
Steig, William *author, artist*
Terrill, Ross Gladwin *author, educator*
Wakefield, Dan *author, screenwriter*
Walcott, Derek Alton *poet, playwright*
†Warren, Rosanna *poet*
Wiesel, Elie *writer, educator*

Braintree
Piraino, Thomas *writer, retired electrical engineer*

Brewster
Hay, John *writer*

Brighton
Herron, Carolivia *novelist, English educator*

Byfield
Kozol, Jonathan *writer*

Cambridge
Alfred, William *author, educator*
Bernays, Anne Fleischman *writer, educator*
Brody, Alan *playwright*
Desai, Anita *writer*
Heaney, Seamus Justin *poet, educator*
Kaplan, Justin *author*
Lamport, Felicia (Mrs. Benjamin Kaplan) *writer*
Rey, Margret Elizabeth *writer*
Yergin, Daniel Howard *writer, consultant*

Chestnut Hill
Lowell, Juliet *author*

Concord
Edmonds, Walter Dumaux *author*
Moore, Robert Lowell, Jr. (Robin Moore) *author*

Cummington
Wilbur, Richard Purdy *writer, educator*

Dover
Smith, William Henry Preston *writer, editor, former corporate executive*

Edgartown
Treat, Lawrence *author*

Gardner
Wagenknecht, Edward *author*

Gloucester
Erkkila, Barbara Howell Louise *writer, photographer*

Hatfield
Yolen, Jane *author*

Lenox
Novak, William Arnold *author, lecturer*

Leominster
Cormier, Robert Edmund *writer*

Lincoln
Donald, David Herbert *author, history educator*

Marblehead
Kemelman, Harry *author*

Needham
Walworth, Arthur *author*

Newton
Heins, Ethel L. *children's literature consultant, critic*
Porter, Jack Nusan *writer, sociologist*

North Amherst
Andersen, Richard Arnold *writer, consultant*
Lester, Julius B. *author*

North Egremont
Le Comte, Edward Semple *author, educator*

Northampton
MacLachlan, Patricia *author*

Norton
Norris, Curtis Bird *writer, journalist*

Orleans
Hughes, Libby *author*

Provincetown
Doty, Mark *poet*
Oliver, Mary *poet*

Rockport
Deedy, John Gerard, Jr. *writer*

Somerville
Wheeler, Katherine Frazier (Kate Wheeler) *writer*

South Hadley
Brodsky, Joseph (Alexandrovich) *poet, educator*
†Salter, Mary Jo *poet*
Viereck, Peter *poet, historian, educator*

South Lancaster
Chopra, Deepak *writer*

Stockbridge
Gibson, William *author*

Truro
Woolley, Catherine (Jane Thayer) *writer*

Waltham
Ellenbogen, George *poet, educator*
Hindus, Milton *writer, literature educator*
Zohn, Harry *author, educator*

Wellesley
Jacobs, Ruth Harriet *poet, playwright, sociologist, gerontologist*

Wellfleet
Piercy, Marge *poet, novelist, essayist*

West Newbury
Coit, Margaret Louise *writer*
Dooley, Ann Elizabeth *freelance writers cooperative executive, editor*

Weston
Wind, Herbert Warren *writer*

Westport
Howard, James Merriam, Jr. *education writer*

Yarmouth Port
Gorey, Edward St. John *author, artist*

MICHIGAN

Ann Arbor
Fraser, Russell Alfred *author, educator*

Battle Creek
Cline, Charles William *poet, pianist, rhetoric and literature educator*

Bloomfield Hills
Leonard, Elmore John *novelist, screenwriter*

Detroit
Madgett, Naomi Long *poet, editor, educator*
Mandel, Leon, III *author*
McWilliams, Michael G. *writer, television critic*

East Lansing
Wakoski, Diane *poet*

Kalamazoo
Light, Christopher Upjohn *writer, computer musician*

Mackinac Island
†Mc Cabe, John Charles, III *writer*

Traverse City
†Abeel, Samantha Lynn *juvenile fiction author*

Union Pier
Howland, Bette *writer*

MINNESOTA

Brooklyn Park
Spencer, LaVyrle *writer*

Duluth
Wood, Douglas *author, composer, musician*

Edina
†Esbensen, Barbara Juster *author*
Schwarzrock, Shirley Pratt *author, lecturer, educator*

Minneapolis
Baker, John Stevenson (Michael Dyregrov) *writer*
Bly, Robert *poet*
Browne, Michael Dennis *poet, educator*
Korotkin, Fred *writer, philatelist*
Teachout, Noreen Ruth *writer*

Richfield
†Thompson, Steve Allan *writer*

Saint Paul
Kenyon, Jane Jennifer *poet, writer*

Spring Grove
Hellyer, Clement David *writer*

MISSISSIPPI

Jackson
Welty, Eudora *author*

MISSOURI

Kansas City
Bombeck, Erma Louise (Mrs. William Bombeck) *author, columnist*
†MacNair, Rachel Mary *editor*
Martin-Bowen, (Carole) Lindsey *freelance writer*

Saint Charles
Castro, Jan Garden *author, arts consultant, educator*

Saint Louis
Broeg, Bob (Robert William Broeg) *writer*
†Early, Gerald *writer*
Elkin, Stanley Lawrence *author, literature educator*
Finkel, Donald *poet*
Gass, William H. *author, educator*
Long, Helen Halter *author, retired educator*
McKissack, Patricia Carwell *children's book author*
Schlafly, Phyllis Stewart *author*

Viburnum
West, Roberta Bertha *writer*

MONTANA

Livingston
Harrison, James Thomas (Jim Harrison) *author*

Mc Leod
Hjortsberg, William Reinhold *author*
McGuane, Thomas Francis, III *author, screenwriter*

NEW HAMPSHIRE

Concord
Lederer, Richard Henry *writer, educator, columnist*

Cornish
Atkinson, James Blakely *writer, editor*

Durham
Ford, Daniel (Francis) *writer*

Exeter
Slabon, Roland Michael *writer*

Hanover
Eberhart, Richard *poet*

Walpole
Gooding, Judson *writer*

NEW JERSEY

Andover
Gioseffi, Daniela *poet, author, educator*

Cape May Court House
Cohen, Daniel Edward *writer*
Cohen, Susan Lois *author*
Kurtz, James Eugene *freelance writer, minister*

Cherry Hill
†Wolff, Ferida *author*

Englewood
Gambee, Eleanor Brown *writer, lecturer, civic worker*

Hoboken
Seessel, Adam H. *writer, journalist*

Hopewell
Halpern, Daniel *poet, editor, educator*

Madison
Gibson, William Ford *author*

Millburn
Gitner, Deanne *writer*

Montclair
Alexander, Fernande Gardner *writer, photographer*

Mountainside
Horner, Shirley Jaye *writer, columnist*

New Brunswick
†Ostriker, Alicia Suskin *poet*

Newark
Dickson, Jim *playwright, stage director, arts consultant*
Hadas, Rachel *poet, educator*
Moskowitz, Sam (Sam Martin) *author, editor, publisher*

Paramus
Fader, Shirley Sloan *writer*

Pomona
†Dunn, Stephen *poet*

Princeton
Draper, Theodore *author*
Funk, Peter V. K. *writer, scholarly, lexical semanticist*
Morrison, Toni (Chloe Anthony Morrison) *novelist*
Oates, Joyce Carol *author*
Putnam, Peter Brock *author, lecturer*
Rampersad, Arnold *writer, literature educator*
Weiss, Theodore Russell *poet, editor*

Princeton Junction
Norback, Craig Thomas *writer*

Rockaway
Ruch, William Vaughn *writer, educator, consultant*

Salem
Foster, Paul *playwright*

Secaucus
†Gomes, Celeste Regina *writer, editor*

Short Hills
Middleton, Timothy George *writer*

Somerset
Plenty, Royal Homer *writer*

Somerville
Hyde, Mary Morley Crapo (Viscountess Eccles) *author*
Johnson, Nicholas *writer, lawyer, lecturer*

Stockton
Tunley, Roul *author*

West Orange
Rayfield, Gordon Elliott *playwright, political risk consultant*

NEW MEXICO

Albuquerque
Evans, Max Allen *writer, artist*
Whiddon, Carol Price *writer, editor, consultant*

Corrales
Page, Jake (James K. Page, Jr.) *writer, editor*

Las Cruces
Medoff, Mark Howard *playwright, screenwriter, novelist*

Placitas
Dunmire, William Werden *author, photographer*

Portales
Williamson, Jack (John Stewart Williamson) *writer*

Santa Fe
Bergé, Carol *author*
Connell, Evan Shelby, Jr. *author*
Tarn, Nathaniel *poet, translator, educator*

Taos
Dickey, Robert Preston *author, educator, poet*

NEW YORK

Albany
Kennedy, William Joseph *novelist, educator*

Annandale On Hudson
Kelly, Robert *poet, educator*
Manea, Norman *writer, educator*

Ballston Spa
Barba, Harry *author, educator, publisher*

Barrytown
Higgins, Dick (Richard Carter Higgins) *writer, publisher, composer, artist*

Bedford Hills
Ludlum, Robert *author*

Brewster
Barnhart, Robert Knox *writer, editor*

Bronx
Greenberg, Blu *author*

Brooklyn
Chernow, Ron *writer, columnist*
Kuskin, Karla *writer, illustrator*
†Lewin, Ted Bert *writer, illustrator*
Purdy, James *writer*
Swenson, Karen *poet, journalist*

Buffalo
Creeley, Robert White *author, English educator*
Federman, Raymond *novelist, English and comparative literature educator*
Feldman, Irving *poet*
Schatz, Lillian Lee *playwright, molecular biologist, educator*

Carmel
†Leach, William Riley *writer, historian*

Chappaqua
George, Jean Craighead *author, illustrator*
Kingsley, Emily Perl *writer*
Lundberg, Ferdinand Edgar *author*

Circleville
Hazan, Marcella Maddalena *author, educator, consultant*

Cold Spring Harbor
Freeman, Ira Henry *author, journalist*

Croton On Hudson
Henderson, Harry Brinton, Jr. *author, editor*

Dobbs Ferry
Fritz, Jean Guttery *writer*

East Hampton
Ignatow, David *poet*

Erieville
Snodgrass, W. D. *writer, educator*

Esopus
Tetlow, Edwin *author*

Flushing
Allen, Ralph Gilmore *dramatist, producer, drama educator*
Goldsmith, Howard *writer, consultant*

Franklin Square
Doyle, Will Lee *writer, editor*

Fulton
Long, Robert Emmet *author*

Garden City
De Mille, Nelson Richard *writer*

Great Neck
Hurwitz, Johanna (Frank) *author, librarian*
Mc Quade, Walter *author*

Greenfield Center
Fonseca, John dos Reis *writer, former law educator*

Guilderland
Persico, Joseph Edward *author*

Hamilton
Berlind, Bruce Peter *poet, educator*
Busch, Frederick Matthew *writer, literature educator*

Hempstead
Hijuelos, Oscar *novelist*

Hicksville
Kneitel, Thomas Stephen *writer, consultant, editor*

Hudson Falls
Bronk, William *writer, retail businessman*

Huntington
Bendiner, Robert *writer, editor*

Huntington Station
Schell, Jonathan Edward *writer*

Interlaken
Bleiler, Everett Franklin *writer, publishing company executive*

Irvington
Massie, Robert Kinloch *author*

Ithaca
Ammons, Archie Randolph *poet, English educator*
Lurie, Alison *author*

Jamaica
Paolucci, Anne Attura *playwright, poet, English and comparative literature educator*

Jamesville
Mazer, Norma Fox *writer*

Johnson City
Aswad, Betsy (Betsy Becker) *writer*
Sargent, Pamela *writer*

Keene
†Twichell, Chase *poet*

Kings Point
Bloom, Murray Teigh *author*

Larchmont
Kerr, Jean *writer*

Lockport
Cull, John Joseph *novelist, playwright*

Locust Valley
McGee, Dorothy Horton *writer, historian*

Montauk
Lavenas, Suzanne *writer, editor, consultant*

Munnsville
Carruth, Hayden *poet*

New Rochelle
Branch, William Blackwell *playwright, producer*
Saperstein, David Allan *novelist, screenwriter, film director*

New York
Adams, Alice *writer*
Adams, Douglas Noel *writer*
Akins, Ellen *writer*
Albee, Edward Franklin *author, playwright*
Allen, Jay Presson *writer, producer*
Allen, Roberta L. *fiction and nonfiction writer, conceptual artist*
Amory, Cleveland *writer*
†Anderson, Kevin James *writer*
Anderson, Poul William *author*
Angell, Roger *writer, magazine editor*
Anthony, Piers *science fiction writer*
Ashdown, Marie Matranga (Mrs. Cecil Spanton Ashdown, Jr.) *writer, lecturer*
Ashton, Dore *author, educator*
Auchincloss, Louis Stanton *writer*
Auel, Jean Marie *author*
Auster, Paul *writer*
Avi, (Avi Wortis) *author*
Baitz, Jon Robin *playwright*
Balliett, Whitney *writer, critic*
Baraka, Amiri (Everett LeRoi Jones) *author*
Barzun, Jacques *author, literary consultant*
Bauer, Marion Dane *writer*
Beattie, Ann *author*
Beim, Norman *playwright, actor, director*
Bel Geddes, Joan *writer*
Benchley, Peter Bradford *author*
Benedikt, Michael *poet, educator, author, editor, free-lance consultant*
Benn, T(heodore) Alexander (Alec Benn) *writer*
Bentley, Eric *author, playwright, comparative literature educator*
†Berendt, John Lawrence *writer, editor*
Berenstain, Janice *author, illustrator*
Berenstain, Stanley *author, illustrator*
Berg, David *author, artist*
Berkow, Ira Harvey *author, journalist*
Bernard, Kenneth (Otis Bernard) *poet, author, playwright*
Berton, Lee *writer*
Birmingham, Stephen *writer*
†Bisson, Terry Ballantine *author, editor*
Blatty, William Peter *writer*
Bliven, Bruce, Jr. *writer*
†Block, Francesca Lia *writer*
Block, Lawrence *author*
Blos, Joan W. *author, critic, lecturer*
Blume, Judy Sussman *author*
Bolt, Thomas *writer, artist*
Bourjaily, Vance *novelist*
Bradbury, Ray Douglas *author*
Bradford, Barbara Taylor *writer, journalist, novelist*
Bradford, Richard Roark *writer*
†Braudy, Susan Orr *writer*
Braun, Lilian Jackson *writer*
Brenner, Erma *author*
Breuer, Lee *playwright, theatrical director, producer, actor*
Brickman, Marshall *screenwriter, director*
Brodkey, Harold Roy *writer*
Bujold, Lois McMaster *science fiction writer*
Burland, Brian Berkeley *novelist, poet, artist, scenarist, playwright*
Burnshaw, Stanley *writer*
Calisher, Hortense (Mrs. Curtis Harnack) *writer*
Cameron, Eleanor *author*
Canin, Ethan *writer*
†Capouya, Emile *writer*
Caputo, Philip Joseph *author, journalist, screenwriter*
Caras, Roger Andrew *author, motion picture company executive, television correspondent, radio commentator*
Carlson, P(atricia) M(cElroy) *writer*
Caro, Robert Allan *author*
Cartland, Barbara *author*
†Christopher, Nicholas *poet, novelist*
†Cisneros, Sandra *poet, short story writer, essayist*
Clancy, Thomas L., Jr. *novelist*
Clark, Matt *science writer*
Cleary, Beverly Atlee (Mrs. Clarence T. Cleary) *author*
Colombo, Furio *writer, journalist*
Cook, Robin *author*
Cooper, Paulette Marcia *writer*
Coppel, Alfred *author*
Corman, Avery *author*
Corso, (Nunzio) Gregory *poet*
Coulter, Catherine *writer*
Coupland, Douglas C. *writer*
†Creech, Sharon *children's author*
Crews, Harry Eugene *author*
†Crouch, Stanley *writer, jazz musician*
Cryer, Gretchen *playwright, lyricist, actress*
Cummings, Josephine Anna *writer*
Curry, Jane Louise *writer*
Danto, Arthur Coleman *author, philosophy educator*
Danziger, Paula *author*
Davis, Lorraine Jensen *writer, editor*
Decter, Midge *writer*
de Hartog, Jan *writer*
DeLillo, Don *author*
Demaris, Ovid (Ovid Desmarais) *author*
Denker, Henry *playwright, author, director*
Deveraux, Jude (Jude Gilliam White) *writer*
Diamant, Anita *literary agent*
Diamonstein-Spielvogel, Barbaralee *writer, television interviewer/ producer*
Didion, Joan *author*
Dillard, Annie *author*
Doctorow, Edgar Lawrence *novelist, English educator*
Doerr, Harriet *writer*
Donaldson, Stephen Reeder *author*
Duffy, James Henry *writer, former lawyer*
Dunne, Dominick *writer*
Dunne, John Gregory *author*
Eckert, Allan W. *author*
Eidson, Thomas E. *writer, public relations firm executive*
†Eisner, Jack P. *writer*
Ellis, Bret Easton *author*
†Ellroy, James *writer*
Ephron, Nora *writer*
Erdrich, (Karen) Louise *fiction writer, poet*
Espy, Willard Richardson *author*
Esquivel, Laura *writer*
Fallaci, Oriana *writer, journalist*
Fast, Howard Melvin *author*
Fast, Julius *author, editor*
Fierstein, Harvey Forbes *playwright, actor*
Flanagan, Thomas James Bonner *writer, fiction, non-fiction*
Flatley, Guy *writer, magazine editor*
Fleming, Alice Carew Mulcahey (Mrs. Thomas J. Fleming) *author*
Fleming, Thomas James *writer*
Fletcher, Colin *author*
Flexner, James Thomas *author*
Foote, Horton *playwright, scriptwriter*
Fornes, Maria Irene *playwright, director*
Fox, Paula (Mrs. Martin Greenberg) *author*
Francis, Dick (Richard Stanley Francis) *novelist*
Fratti, Mario *playwright, educator*
French, Marilyn *author, critic*
Friedan, Betty Naomi *author, feminist leader*
Friedman, B(ernard) H(arper) *writer*
Friedman, Mickey (Michaele T. Friedman) *novelist*
†Fritz, Mark *reporter, journalist*
Fulghum, Robert L. *author, lecturer*
Fuller, Charles Henry, Jr. *playwright*
Furnas, Joseph Chamberlain *writer*
Gaddis, William *writer*
Gelber, Jack *playwright, director*
Giblin, James Cross *author, editor*
Gill, Brendan *writer*
Goldman, Francisco *writer*
Goldman, James *playwright, screenwriter, novelist*
Goldsmith, Barbara *author, social historian, journalist*
†Goldstein, Lisa Joy *writer*
Goodman, George Jerome Waldo (Adam Smith) *author, television journalist, editor*
Gordimer, Nadine *author*
Gordon, David *playwright, director, choreographer*
Gordon, Mary Catherine *author*
Goulden, Joseph Chesley *author*
Grant, Cynthia D. *writer*
Green, Adolph *playwright, lyricist*
Green, Gerald *author*
Greene, A(lvin) C(arl) *author*
Grimes, Martha *author*
Grisham, John *writer*
Grumbach, Doris *novelist, editor, critic, educator, bookseller*
Guare, John *playwright*
Guest, Judith Ann *author*
†Guterson, David *writer*
Hadley, Leila Eliott-Burton (Mrs. Henry Luce, III) *author*
Hall, Susan *author, film producer*
Hamburger, Philip (Paul) *writer*
Hardwick, Elizabeth *author*
Harris, Thomas *author*
Hauptman, William *playwright*
Haynes, Todd *film writer, producer, director*
Hazzard, Shirley *author*
Heller, Joseph *writer*
Hemming, Roy G. *writer, magazine editor, broadcaster*
Henley, Arthur *author, editor, television consultant*
Henley, Beth *playwright, actress*
Henry, Marguerite *author*
Hentoff, Nathan Irving *writer*
†Hesse, Karen (Sue) *writer, educator*
Heyn, Ernest V. *author, editor*
Hill, Elizabeth Starr *writer*
Hillman, Howard Budrow *author, editor, publisher, consultant*
Hines, Anna Grossnickle *author, illustrator*
Hinton, S(usan) E(loise) *author*
Hinz, Dorothy Elizabeth *writer, editor, international corporate communications and public affairs specialist*
Hoagland, Edward *author*
Hoffman, Alice *writer*
Hoffman, William M(oses) *playwright, editor*
Holabird, Katherine *children's book author*
Holroyd, Michael *author*
Holzer, Hans *author*
Horovitz, Israel Arthur *playwright*
Howe, Tina *playwright*
Hudlin, Warrington *writer, producer, director*
Hunter, Evan (Ed Mc Bain) *author*
Hwang, David Henry *playwright, screenwriter*
Hyams, Joseph *writer*
Inez, Colette *poet*
Innaurato, Albert Francis *playwright*
Jacker, Corinne Litvin *playwright*
Jaffe, Rona *author*
Jakes, John *author*
Janeway, Elizabeth Hall *author*
Jhabvala, Ruth Prawer *author*
Johnson, Angela *children's book author*
Johnson, Charles Richard *writer, teacher*
Johnson, Denis *poet, writer*
Jones, Diana Wynne *writer*
†Jones, Malcolm Wheeler *writer, editor*
Jong, Erica Mann *writer, poet*
†Joyce, William Edward *writer, illustrator*
Katz, William Loren *author*
Kauffmann, Stanley Jules *author*
Kaufman, Bel *author, educator*
Kazin, Alfred *writer*
Kehret, Peg *writer*
Kidder, (John) Tracy *writer*
Kinnell, Galway *poet, translator*
Kisner, Jacob *poet, editor*
Klein, T(heodore) E(ibon) D(onald) *writer*
Kobler, John *writer*
Koch, Kenneth *poet, playwright*
Koke, Richard Joseph *author, exhibit designer, museum curator*
Koontz, Dean Ray *writer*
Kopit, Arthur *playwright*
Kostelanetz, Richard *writer, artist*
Kotlowitz, Robert *writer,editor*
Kotzwinkle, William *author*
Kramer, Jane *writer*
Kumin, Maxine Winokur *poet, author*
Kunitz, Stanley Jasspon *poet, editor, educator*
Kuralt, Charles Bishop *writer, former television news correspondent*
Kushner, Tony *playwright*
Lader, Lawrence *writer*
Lapierre, Dominique *writer, historian, philanthropist*
Lapine, James Elliot *playwright, director*
Leavitt, David Adam *writer*
Lelchuk, Alan *author, educator*
L'Engle, Madeleine (Mrs. Hugh Franklin) *author*
Levertov, Denise *poet*
Levin, Ira *author, playwright*
Levine, Israel E. *writer*
Levoy, Myron *author*
Linney, Romulus *author, educator*
Lionni, Leonard *author, artist*
Lish, Gordon *author, educator, editor*
†Lisle, Janet Taylor *writer*
Littledale, Freya Lota Brown *writer, editor*
Lord, M. G. *writer*
Lucas, Craig *playwright, screenwriter*
Maas, Peter *writer*
Mailer, Norman *author*
Martin, Ann Matthews *writer, juvenile*
Mason, Bobbie Ann *novelist, short story writer*
Maupin, Armistead Jones, Jr. *writer*
Maxwell, William *writer*
Mayle, Peter *writer*
McCarthy, Cormac (Charles McCarthy, Jr.) *writer*
Mc Clure, Michael Thomas *poet, playwright, educator*
McCullough, David *author*
Mcdonald, Gregory Christopher *author*
Mc Ginniss, Joe *writer*
McInerney, Jay *author*
McKinley, (Jennifer Carolyn) Robin *writer*
McMeen, Albert Ralph, III *writer, lecturer*
McMurtry, Larry Jeff *author*
McNally, Terrence *playwright*
†McQuown, Judith Hershkowitz *author, financial advisor*
Mee, Charles L., Jr. *playwright, historian, editor*
Mehta, Ved (Parkash) *writer, literature and history educator*
Meltzer, Milton *author*
Merwin, William Stanley *poet*
Mitchell, Joseph (Quincy) *writer*
Mitgang, Herbert *author, journalist*
Moore, Brian *writer*
Moore, Susanna *writer*
Morgan, (George) Frederick *poet, editor*
Morgan, Robin Evonne *poet, author, journalist, activist, editor*
Morris, Wright *novelist, critic*
Morrow, Lance *writer*
Morton, Frederic *author*
†Mosley, Walter *writer*
Munro, Alice *author*
Nelson, Richard John *playwright*
Nixon, Joan Lowery *writer*
Norman, Marsha *playwright*
Offit, Sidney *writer, educator*
†Olds, Sharon *poet*
†Oppenheimer, Paul Eugene *English comparative literature educator, poet, author*
O'Rourke, P. J. (Patrick Jake O'Rourke) *writer, humorist*
Orrmont, Arthur *writer, editor*
†Osborne, Mary Pope *writer*
Ozick, Cynthia *author*
Paterson, Katherine Womeldorf *writer*
Patterson, Jerry Eugene *author*
†Peacock, Molly *poet*
Peck, Richard Wayne *novelist*
Phillips, Ethel C. (Mrs. Lloyd J. Phillips) *writer*
Philp, Richard Nilson *writer, editor*
Pirsig, Robert Maynard *author*
Plain, Belva *writer*
Plimpton, George Ames *writer, editor, television host*
Pogrebin, Letty Cottin *writer, lecturer*
†Polacco, Patricia *children's author, illustrator*
†Pollitt, Katha *writer, poet, educator*
Pomerantz, Charlotte *writer*
†Posner, Gerald *author, lawyer*
Post, Emily (Elizabeth Lindley Post) *author*
Price, Reynolds *novelist, poet, playwright, essayist, educator*
Proulx, Edna Annie *writer*
Rechy, John Francisco *author*
Reed, Ishmael Scott (Emmett Coleman) *writer*
†Reeves, Richard *writer, historian*
Regan, Sylvia *playwright*
Reig, June Wilson *writer, director, producer*
Reiss, Alvin *writer*
Rhodes, Richard Lee *writer*
Rice, Anne *author*
Rich, Adrienne *writer*
Robbins, Harold *author*
Rollin, Betty *author, television journalist*
Rooney, Andrew Aitken *writer, columnist*
Root, William Pitt *poet, educator*
Rosenthal, Macha Louis *author, educator*
Rossner, Judith *novelist*
Rosten, Leo Calvin (Leonard Q. Ross) *author, political scientist*
Roth, Henry *writer*
Roth, Philip *writer*
Rothenberg, Jerome *author*
†Rudman, Mark *poet, educator*
Sainer, Arthur *writer, theater educator*
Sale, (John) Kirkpatrick *writer*
Salinger, Jerome David *author*
Sanders, Lawrence *author*
Saul, John Woodruff, III *writer*
Saylor, Steven Warren *writer prose, fiction*
Schisgal, Murray Joseph *playwright*
Schlesinger, Arthur (Meier), Jr. *writer, educator*
Schnackenberg, Gjertrud Cecelia *poet*
Schulberg, Budd *author*
Schulman, Grace *poet, English language educator*
†Schwartz, Amy Margaret *children's book author, illustrator*
Schwartz, Arthur Robert *food writer, critic, consultant*
Schwed, Peter *author, retired editor and publisher*
Scieszka, Jon *children's author*
Seaman, Barbara (Ann Rosner) *author*
Segal, Lore *writer*
Sendak, Maurice Bernard *writer, illustrator*
Seth, Vikram *writer*
Settle, Mary Lee *author*
Shaffer, Peter Levin *playwright*
Shange, Ntozake (Paulette Williams) *playwright, poet*
Shapiro, Harvey *poet*
Shapiro, Myra Stein *poet*
Shawn, Wallace *playwright, actor*
Sheehan, Susan *writer*
Sheldon, Sidney *author*
Shepard, Elaine Elizabeth *writer, lecturer*
Shulevitz, Uri *author, illustrator*
Silverstein, Shelby (Shel Silverstein) *author, cartoonist, composer, folksinger*
Simmons, Charles *author*
Simmons, Dan *science fiction writer*
Simon, Neil *playwright, television writer*
Slade, Bernard *playwright*
Smith, Robert Kimmel *author*
Smith, William Jay *author*
Sonnenberg, Ben *playwright, poet, editor*
Sontag, Susan *writer*
Soule, Gardner Bosworth *writer*
Southall, Ivan Francis *author*
Spencer, Scott *novelist*
Spiegelman, Art *author, cartoonist*
Steel, Danielle Fernande *author*
Stein, Joseph *playwright*
Steinem, Gloria *writer, editor, lecturer*
Stevens, Shane *novelist*
Stevenson, William Henri *author*
Stewart, Mary Florence Elinor *author*
Stone, Peter *playwright, scenarist*
Stone, Robert Anthony *author*
Stowers, Carlton Eugene *writer*
Strand, Mark *poet*
Swann, Brian *writer, humanities educator*
Talese, Gay *writer*
†Taubes, Gary *scientific writer*
Taylor, Clyde Calvin, Jr. *literary agent*
Terry, Megan *playwright, performer , photographer*
Tesich, Steve *author*
Thompson, Hunter Stockton *author, political analyst, journalist*
†Toffler, Heidi *author, futurist*
Tomkins, Calvin *writer*
Trillin, Calvin Marshall *writer, columnist*
Uhry, Alfred Fox *playwright*
Ulanov, Barry *author, educator*
van Vogt, Alfred Elton *author*
Vonnegut, Kurt, Jr. *writer*
Wager, Walter Herman *author, communications director*
Walker, Alice Malsenior *author*
Wallach, Ira *writer*
Waller, Robert James *writer*
Ward, Geoffrey Champion *author, editor*
Wasserman, Albert *writer, director*
Wasserman, Dale *playwright*
Watt, Douglas (Benjamin Watt) *writer, critic*
Weidman, Jerome *author*
Wender, Phyllis Bellows *literary agent*
Weschler, Lawrence Michael *writer, journalist*
West, Paul Noden *author*
Westlake, Donald Edwin *author*
White, Edmund Valentine *author*
Wiener, Solomon *writer, consultant, former city official*
Wilson, August *playwright*
Wilson, F(rancis) Paul *novelist*
Windsor, Patricia (Katonah Summertree) *author, educator, lecturer*
Winsor, Kathleen *writer*
Wise, David *author, journalist*
Wolf, Naomi *writer*
Wolfe, Thomas Kennerly, Jr. *writer, journalist*
Wolff, Virginia Euwer *writer, secondary education educator*
Wright, Laurali R. (Bunny Wright) *writer*
Yorinks, Arthur *children's author*
Yuncker, Barbara *science writer*
Zahn, Timothy *writer*
Zara, Louis *author, editor*
Zindel, Paul *author*
Zolotow, Charlotte Shapiro *author, editor*

Newburgh
Severo, Richard *writer*

North Boston
Herbert, James Alan *writer*

Oceanside
Mills, James Spencer *author*

Palisades
Berger, Thomas Louis *author*
Davis, Dorothy Salisbury *author*

Port Washington
Blakeslee, Alton Lauren *scientific writer*

Poughkeepsie
Bird, Caroline *author*
Willard, Nancy Margaret *writer, educator*

Quogue
Laurents, Arthur *playwright*

Riverdale
Moss, Stanley *poet*

Rochester
Hoch, Edward Dentinger *author*
Rothberg, Abraham *author, educator, editor*
†Scott, Joanna Jeanne *writer, English language educator*

Roslyn Heights
Faber, Adele *author, educator*

Sag Harbor
Sheed, Wilfrid John Joseph *author*

Sagaponack
Appleman, Marjorie (M. H. Appleman) *playwright, educator, poet*
Appleman, Philip *poet, writer, educator*

Saratoga Springs
Parthasarathy, Rajagopal *writer, literature educator*

Scarborough
Hopkins, Lee Bennett *writer, educator*

Spencertown
Kherdian, David *author*

Staten Island
Porter, Darwin Fred *writer*

Stony Brook
Kott, Jan K. *writer, scholar*

Suffern
Unger, Barbara *poet, writer, educator*

Syracuse
Wolff, Tobias (Jonathan Ansell Wolff) *author*

Valley Stream
Rachlin, Harvey Brant *author, music company executive*

Waccabuc
Hall, Elizabeth *writer*

Wainscott
Herzog, Arthur, III *author*

West Nyack
Pringle, Laurence Patrick *writer*

White Plains
Fjelde, Rolf Gerhard *translator, writer, educator*
†Gioia, (Michael) Dana *poet, literary critic*

Woodmere
Abramson, Martin *author, journalist*

Woodstock
Godwin, Gail Kathleen *author*

Yonkers
Kresh, Paul *author, editor*

NORTH CAROLINA

Banner Elk
Isbell, Robert *writer*

Beaufort
Hayman, Carol Bessent *poet, author*

Blowing Rock
Haley, Gail E(inhart) *author*

Chapel Hill
Betts, Doris June Waugh *author, English language educator*
Dareff, Hal *author, editor, publisher*
Spencer, Elizabeth *author*

Durham
Dorfman, Ariel *writer, educator*
Dunbar, Leslie Wallace *writer, consultant*
Tebbel, John *writer, educator*

Greensboro
Sewell, Elizabeth *author, English educator*
Watson, Robert Winthrop *poet, English language educator*

Newport
Little, Loyd Harry, Jr. *author*

Raleigh
Murray, Elizabeth Davis Reid *writer, lecturer*

Southern Pines
Yarborough, William Pelham *writer, lecturer, retired army officer, consultant*

Winston Salem
Ehle, John Marsden, Jr. *writer*
Hanes, Frank Borden *author, farmer, former business executive*

OHIO

Cincinnati
Hornbaker, Alice Joy *author*
Steinberg, Janet Eckstein *journalist*

Cleveland
Finn, Robert *writer, lecturer, broadcaster*
Gleisser, Marcus David *author, lawyer, journalist*
Kovel, Ralph M. *author, authority on antiques*
Kovel, Terry Horvitz (Mrs. Ralph Kovel) *author, antiques authority*
Moore, Dan Tyler *writer*
Sandburg, Helga *author*
Stadtler, Beatrice Horwitz *author*

Columbus
Berry, Brewton *writer, editor*

Dayton
Heath, Mariwyn Dwyer *writer, legislative issues consultant*

Kent
Rylant, Cynthia *author*

Oberlin
Reinoehl, Richard Louis *writer, artist, consultant*

Yellow Springs
Hamilton, Virginia (Mrs. Arnold Adoff) *author*

OKLAHOMA

Norman
Owens, Rochelle *poet, playwright*

Oklahoma City
Anderson, Kenneth Edwin *writer, educator*

Perry
Beers, Frederick Gordon *writer, retired corporate communications official*

Stillwater
Shirley, Glenn Dean *writer*

Tulsa
Mojtabai, Ann Grace *author, educator*

OREGON

Eugene
Wilhelm, Kate (Katy Gertrude) *author*

Newport
Kennedy, Richard Jerome *writer*

Pleasant Hill
Kesey, Ken *writer*

Portland
Rutsala, Vern A. *poet, English language educator, writer*

Terrebonne
Siebert, Diane Dolores *author, poet*

PENNSYLVANIA

Ardmore
Kline, George Louis *author, translator, retired philosophy and literature educator*

Bethlehem
Murphy, Warren Burton *writer, screenwriter*

Bradford
†Gibson, Margaret Ferguson *poet, educator*

Broomall
Saunders, Sally Love *poet, educator*

Bushkill
Muesing Ellwood, Edith Elizabeth *writer, researcher, publisher, editor*

California
Langham, Norma *playwright, educator, poet, composer, inventor*

Drexel Hill
Alexander, Lloyd Chudley *author*

Harrisburg
Lear, John *writer, editor*

Jenkintown
Seid, Ruth (Jo Sinclair) *author*

Kennett Square
Martin, George (Whitney) *writer*
Vining, Elizabeth Gray *author*

Lafayette Hill
Green, Rose Basile (Mrs. Raymond S. Green) *poet, author, educator*

Milford
Le Guin, Ursula Kroeber *author*

Monroeville
†Ecklar, Julia *freelance writer, novelist*

Mount Gretna
Cooper, Jane Todd (J. C. Todd) *poet, writer, educator*

Newtown
Pfeiffer, John Edward *author*

Philadelphia
Fussell, Paul *author, English literature educator*
Mangione, Jerre Gerlando *author, educator*
Paglia, Camille *writer, humanities educator*
Pipes, Daniel *writer, editor*

Pittsburgh
Hodges, Margaret Moore *author, educator*

Rosemont
Nixon, Agnes Eckhardt *television writer, producer*

Villanova
Nolan, Patrick Joseph *screenwriter, playwright, educator*

Wynnewood
Meyers, Mary Ann *writer, consultant*

Yardley
Crane, Barbara Joyce *author, editor, publishing consulting executive*

RHODE ISLAND

Jamestown
†Wolff, Geoffrey Ansell *novelist, critic, educator*

Middletown
Whitman, Ruth *poet, educator, translator*

Providence
Cassill, Ronald Verlin *author*
Feinstein, Alan Shawn *writer, financial adviser*
Schevill, James Erwin *poet, playwright*

SOUTH CAROLINA

Aiken
Smith, Gregory White *writer*

Beaufort
Ogburn, Charlton *writer*

Charleston
Porter, Thomas Joseph, Jr. *writer, songwriter*

Columbia
Dickey, James Lafayette *poet, novelist, filmmaker, critic*
Newton, Rhonwen Leonard *writer, microcomputer consultant*

Greenville
Gilkerson, Yancey Sherard *writer, former editor*

Hollywood
Hull, Edward Whaley Seabrook *freelance writer, consultant*

Little River
Uzenda, Jara Carlow *technical writer*

Rock Hill
Bristow, Robert O'Neil *writer, educator*

TENNESSEE

Chattanooga
Callahan, North *author, educator*

Cordova
Hunt, Gregory Lynn *writer, author*

Kingsport
Kiss, Mary Catherine Clement *writer*

Maryville
Brigance, Albert Henry *educational writer*

Memphis
Foote, Shelby *author*
†Sharpe, Robert F., Sr. *writer, lecturer, educator, consultant, publisher*

Monteagle
Lytle, Andrew Nelson *author, editor*

Nashville
Ford, Jesse Hill *author*
Jarman, Mark Foster *poet*
Lerner, Laurence David *writer, educator*
Sullivan, Walter Laurence *writer, educator*

TEXAS

Austin
Gustafsson, Lars Erik Einar *writer, educator*
Michener, James Albert *author*

Bertram
Albert, Susan Wittig *writer, English educator*

Boerne
†Price, John Randolph *writer*

College Station
Gordone, Charles *playwright*

Corpus Christi
Sommers, Maxine Marie Bridget *writer, educator, publisher*
Walraven, Joseph William (Bill Walraven) *writer, publisher*

Crystal Beach
Dunn, Glennis Mae *writer, lyricist*

Dallas
Harris, Leon A., Jr. *writer*
Hunter, Kermit Houston *writer, former university dean*
†Sherman, Tara S. *writer*
Verges, Marianne Murphree *writer*
Weeks, Jerome C. *writer, drama critic*

Fort Worth
Newsom, Douglas Ann Johnson *writer, journalism educator*

Houston
Hirsch, Edward Mark *poet, English language educator*
Matthews, Harold Downs *author, consultant*
McPhail, JoAnn Winstead *writer, art dealer, small business owner*
Neeld, Elizabeth Harper *author, researcher, consultant*
Schier, Mary Jane *science writer*
SoRelle, Ruth Doyle *medical writer, journalist*
Summers, Joseph Frank *author, publisher*

Liberty Hill
West, Felton *newspaper writer*

Lubbock
Pasewark, William Robert *author, management consultant*
Rushing, Jane Gilmore *writer*

Plano
Finley, Glenna *author*

San Antonio
Cousins, Margaret *author, editor*
Laurence, Dan H. *author, literary and dramatic specialist*

Seguin
Mims, Forrest Marion, III *science writer*

Springtown
Marrs, James F., Jr. *author, journalist, educator*

Waco
Weems, John Edward *writer*

UTAH

Cedar City
Ransom, Bill *author*

Provo
Hart, Edward LeRoy *poet, educator*

Salt Lake City
Ghiselin, Brewster *author, English language educator emeritus*
Lueders, Edward George *author, poet, educator, editor*
Osherow, Jacqueline Sue *poet, English language educator*

VERMONT

Bennington
Glazier, Lyle *writer, educator*
Sandy, Stephen *writer, educator*

Brattleboro
Lappe, Frances Moore *author, lecturer*

Burlington
Carlisle, Lilian Matarose Baker (Mrs. E. Grafton Carlisle, Jr.) *author, lecturer*
Hearon, Shelby *writer, lecturer, educator*

East Thetford
†Demarest, Chris Lynn *writer, illustrator*

North Bennington
Belitt, Ben *poet, educator*

Norwich
Stetson, Eugene William, III *film and television writer and producer*

Peacham
Lederer, William Julius *author*

South Strafford
Novick, Sheldon M. *author, lawyer*

Thetford Hill
Paley, Grace *author, educator*

VIRGINIA

Alexandria
Porter, Elsa Allgood *writer, lecturer*
†Wallace, Barbara Brooks *writer*

Annandale
Nowak, Jan Zdzislaw *writer, consultant*

Arlington
England, Robert Stowe *writer*
Hittle, James D. *writer, business consultant*
Stahl, O(scar) Glenn *writer, lecturer, former government official*

Ashburn
Boyne, Walter James *writer, former museum director*

Blacksburg
Giovanni, Nikki *poet*

Charlotte Court House
Hoffman, William *author*

Charlottesville
Brown, Rita Mae *author*
Casey, John Dudley *writer, English language educator*
Dove, Rita Frances *poet, English language educator*
Simpson, R(obert) Smith *author, retired diplomat*
Wright, Charles Penzel, Jr. *poet*

Christiansburg
Roberts, Ruby Altizer *poet, author, fiction*

Fairfax
Aksyonov, Vassily Pavlovich *author*
Bausch, Richard Carl *writer, educator*
†Forché, Carolyn Louise *poet*

Falls Church
Connery, Robert Howe *author, educator*
Leighton, Frances Spatz *writer, journalist*
Orben, Robert *editor, writer*
Whitehead, Kenneth Dean *author, translator, retired federal government official*

Hillsboro
Farwell, Byron Edgar *writer*

Lexington
Stuart, Walker Dabney, III *poet, author, English language educator*

Lorton
Hazard, John Wharton *author, editorial consultant*

Manassas
Holmes, Marjorie Rose *author*

Mc Kenney
Doyle, John Robert, Jr. *writer*

Mc Lean
Priem, Richard Gregory *writer, systems analyst, entertainment company executive*

Middleburg
Spillane, Mickey (Frank Morrison Spillane) *author*

Midlothian
Rodgers, Eugene *writer*

Portsmouth
Mapp, Alf Johnson, Jr. *writer, historian*

Richmond
Dabney, Virginius *author*

Virginia Beach
El-Fayoumy, Joanne Patricia Quinn *writer, poet*
Seward, William W(ard), Jr. *author, educator*

Woodville
Mc Carthy, Eugene Joseph *writer, former senator*

WASHINGTON

Bellevue
Habbestad, Kathryn Louise *writer*
†Szablya, Helen Mary *author, language professional, lecturer*

Bellingham
Skinner, Knute Rumsey *poet, English educator*

Cheney
†Hegi, Ursula *writer*

Federal Way
Scott, Otto *writer*

La Conner
Robbins, Tom *author*

Lynnwood
Bear, Gregory Dale *writer, illustrator*

Port Angeles
Muller, Willard C(hester) *writer*

Seattle
Bensussen, Estelle Esther *writer, illustrator, artist*
Kenney, Richard Laurence *poet, English language educator*
†McHugh, Heather *poet*
Singer, Sarah Beth *poet*
Wagoner, David Russell *author, educator*

Tacoma
Maynard, Steven Harry *writer*

Vancouver
Larson, Charles Lester *television writer, producer, author*

WEST VIRGINIA

Morgantown
Gagliano, Frank Joseph *playwright*

WISCONSIN

Elkhorn
Dunn, Walter Scott, Jr. *writer, former museum director, consultant*

Green Bay
Parkinson, Ethelyn Minerva *author*

Kenosha
†Wright, Betty Ren *children's book writer*

Little Chute
Rice, Ferill Jeane *writer, civic worker*

New Glarus
Kubly, Herbert *author, educator*

WYOMING

Laramie
Boresi, Arthur Peter *author, educator*

CANADA

ALBERTA

Edmonton
Fenton, Terry Lynn *author, artist, consultant*
†Hughes, Monica *author*
†Wiebe, Rudy Henry *writer*

Waterton Lakes Park
†Russell, Andrew George Alexander *author, naturalist*

BRITISH COLUMBIA

Saanichton
Crozier, Lorna *poet, educator*

Surrey
Kinsella, William Patrick *author, educator*

Vancouver
Bowering, George Harry *writer*

Victoria
Harris, Christie Lucy *author*

MANITOBA

Winnipeg
†Connelly, Karen Marie *writer*
†Oberman, Sheldon Arnold *writer, educator*

NEWFOUNDLAND

Saint John's
Major, Kevin Gerald *writer*

ONTARIO

Don Mills
Atwood, Margaret Eleanor *author*

Hillier
†Lunn, Janet Louise Swoboda *writer*

London
Reaney, James Crerar *dramatist, poet, educator*

Ottawa
Bradford, Karleen *writer*
Jackson, Charles Ian *writer, consultant*
Major, Jean-Louis *author, French literature educator*

Peterborough
†Johnston, Julia Ann *writer*

Richmond Hill
†Gilman, Phoebe *author, illustrator*

Scarborough
†Hunter, Bernice Thurman *writer*
Sparshott, Francis Edward *poet, educator*

Sudbury
Havel, Jean Eugène Martial *author, educator*

Toronto
Bodsworth, Fred *author, naturalist*
Colombo, John Robert *poet, editor, writer*
Davies, Robertson *author*
Fowke, Edith Margaret Fulton *author, English language educator emeritus*
Gotlieb, Phyllis Fay Bloom *author*
Lane, Patrick *poet*
†Moore, Christopher Hugh *writer*
Mowat, Farley McGill *writer*
Parr, James Gordon *writer*
Shields, Carol Ann *writer, educator*

QUEBEC

Kingsbury
Blais, Marie-Claire *novelist, poet, playwright*

Montreal
Bruemmer, Fred *writer, photographer*
Richler, Mordecai *writer*

North Hatley
Gustafson, Ralph Barker *poet, educator*

SASKATCHEWAN

Saskatoon
†Vanderhaeghe, Guy Clarence *writer, creative writing educator*

MEXICO

Mexico City
Paz, Octavio *poet, Mexican diplomat*

AUSTRALIA

Avalon
West, Morris Langlo *novelist*

Norfolk Island
McCullough, Colleen *author*

AUSTRIA

Vienna
Lo Bello, Nino *author, journalist*

ENGLAND

Cambridge
Steiner, George (Francis Steiner) *author, educator*

Hingham
Pollini, Francis *author*

London
Aliki, (Aliki Liacouras Brandenberg) *author, illustrator children's books*
Ambler, Eric *writer*
Amis, Sir Kingsley *novelist*
Ballard, James Graham *writer*
Bawden, Nina (Mary) *author*
Clarke, Arthur Charles *author*
Cleese, John Marwood *writer, businessman, comedian*
Condon, Richard Thomas *author*
Cowles, Fleur (Mrs. Tom M. Meyer) *author, artist*
Deighton, Len *author*
Drabble, Margaret *writer*
Ewart, Gavin Buchanan *poet, writer*
Fine, Anne *author*
Follett, Kenneth Martin *author*
Forsyth, Frederick *author*
Fowles, John *author*
Fraser, Lady Antonia *writer, editor*
†Galloway, Janice *writer, editor*
Hare, David *playwright*
Higgins, Jack (Harry Patterson) *author*
Hite, Shere D. *author, cultural historian*
Hoban, Russell Conwell *author*
Hughes, Ted *poet, author*
Hughes, Winifred Shirley *writer, illustrator*
Hunter Blair, Pauline Clarke *author*
James, P(hyllis) D(orothy) (Baroness James of Holland Park of Southwold in County of Suffolk) *author*
Kureishi, Hanif *author*
Lahr, John *author*
le Carré, John (David John Moore Cornwell) *author*
Lessing, Doris (May) *writer*
†Mathias, Sean Gerard *author, director*
Morris, Desmond *author*
Naipaul, Vidiadhar Surajprasad *author*
Oxenbury, Helen *children's writer, illustrator*
Paton Walsh, Jill *author*
Pinter, Harold *playwright*
Pritchett, Sir Victor Sawdon *author*
Read, Piers Paul *author*
Spark, Dame Muriel Sarah *writer*
Stoppard, Tom (Tomas Straussler) *playwright*
Vansittart, Peter *novelist, lecturer, critic*

Newcastle upon Tyne
Cookson, Dame Catherine Ann *author*

Oxford
Aldiss, Brian (Wilson) *writer*
Segal, Erich *author, educator*

Rottingdean
Matthews, John Floyd *writer, educator*

West Sussex
Aiken, Joan (Delano) *author*

Whitchurch
Adams, Richard George *writer*

FRANCE

Belves
Raphael, Frederic Michael *author*

Paris
Gallant, Mavis *author*
Williams, C(harles) K(enneth) *poet, literature and writing educator*

Ramatuelle
Collins, Larry *author, journalist*

IRELAND

Dalkey
Leonard, Hugh (John Keyes Byrne) *playwright*

Donegal
Friel, Brian (Bernard Patrick Friel) *author*

Mullingar
Donleavy, James Patrick *writer, artist*

Wicklow
McCaffrey, Anne Inez *author*

ITALY

Milan
Calasso, Roberto *writer, publisher*

Venice
Pasinetti, Pier Maria *author*

LUXEMBOURG

Luxembourg
Elliott, Lawrence *writer*

SCOTLAND

Dumfriesshire
Godden, Rumer *author*

SPAIN

Barcelona
García Márquez, Gabriel José *author*

SWITZERLAND

Geneva
Halle, Louis Joseph *author, educator*

ADDRESS UNPUBLISHED

Aloff, Mindy *writer*
Anderson-Spivy, Alexandra *writer, editor*
Archer, Jeffrey Howard *author, politician*
Arlen, Michael J. *writer*
Baldrige, Letitia *writer, management training consultant*
Barker, Clive *artist, screenwriter, director, producer*
Barnes, Joanna *author, actress*
Bassett, Elizabeth Ewing (Libby Bassett) *writer, editor*
Bauer, Caroline Feller *author*
Beach, Edward Latimer *writer, retired military officer*
Beatts, Anne Patricia *writer, producer*
Bellow, Saul C. *writer*
Berry, Richard Lewis *author, magazine editor, lecturer, programmer*
Blake, Joan Johnston Wallman *playwright, lyricist*
Bova, Benjamin William *author, editor, educator*
Bracken, Peg *author*
Brookner, Anita *writer, educator*
Brown, Marcia Joan *author, artist, photographer*
Buck, Genevieve Carol *fashion journalist*
Bulla, Clyde Robert *writer*
Bullins, Ed *author*
Chandler, Harry Edgar *author*
Cherryh, C. J. *writer*
Claiborne, Craig *author, editor cookbooks*
Clark, Mary Higgins *author, business executive*
Coburn, D(onald) L(ee) *playwright*
Collier, Oscar *literary agency consultant, writer*
Collins, Jackie *writer*
Cook, Beth Marie *writer, poet*
Coonts, Stephen Paul *novelist*
Corcoran, Barbara Asenath *author*
Coscarelli, Don *film writer, film director*
Cussler, Clive Eric *author*
Dahl, Bren Bennington *screenwriter*
Dailey, Janet *novelist*
Davis, Luther *writer, producer*
Dickerson, James L. *writer, photographer, consultant*
Disch, Thomas M(ichael) *author*
Doig, Ivan *writer*
Dolan, Edward Francis *writer*
†Dooling, Richard Patrick *writer, lawyer*
Drucker, Peter Ferdinand *writer, consultant, educator*
Egelston, Roberta Riethmiller *writer*
Eglee, Charles Hamilton *television and movie writer, producer*
Erwin, Judith Ann (Judith Ann Peacock) *writer, photographer, lawyer*
Esty, John Cushing, Jr. *writer, lecturer, advisor*
Fadiman, Louise *writer, consultant*
Feirstein, Frederick *poet, playwright, psychoanalyst*
Fetler, Andrew *author, educator*
Fraser, Kathleen Joy *poet, creative writing educator*
Freedman, Russell Bruce *author*
Frost, Sir David (Paradine) *author, producer, columnist*
Fryer, Thomas Waitt, Jr. *writer and editor*
Fuentes, Carlos *writer, former ambassador*
Ganz, Lowell *screenwriter, television producer*
Garfield, Brian Wynne *author*
Gilb, Dagoberto *writer, carpenter*
Gilchrist, Ellen Louise *writer*
Gilroy, Frank Daniel *playwright*
Girzone, Joseph F. *retired priest, writer*
Glick, Ruth Burtnick *author, lecturer*
Glück, Louise Elisabeth *poet*
Goble, Paul *author, illustrator, artist*
Golann, Cecil P. *writer, editor, researcher*
Gordon, Bonnie Heather *writer, editor*
Gottlieb, Sherry Gershon *author, editor*
Grafton, Sue *novelist*
Gray, Francine du Plessix *author*
Greenburg, Dan *author*
Greer, Germaine *author*
Groening, Matthew *writer, cartoonist*
Haas, Charlie *screenwriter*
Hahn, Mary Downing *author*
Hairston, William *author, playwright*
Hall, Donald *poet*
Hanks, Robert Jack *writer, consultant, former naval officer*
Harrigan, Anthony Hart *author*
Helprin, Mark *author*
Herman, Hank *writer*
Heymann, C(lemens) David *author*
Hillerman, Tony *writer, former journalism educator*
Hirschberg, Vera Hilda *writer*
Howard, Maureen *writer*
Howard, Richard (Joseph Howard) *poet, literary translator*
Hoyt, Mary Finch *author, editor, media consultant, former government official*
Huston, Nancy Louise *writer, educator*
Ireland, Norma Olin *writer, scholarly, researcher*
Irving, John Winslow *writer*
Isaacs, Susan *novelist, screenwriter*
Jacobs, Wilbur Ripley *writer, history educator*
Johnson, Diane Lain *novelist, critic*
Jorden, William John *writer, retired diplomat*
Just, Ward Swift *author*
Kanin, Fay *screenwriter*
Kanin, Garson *writer, theatrical director*
Katzenbach, John Strong Miner *author*
Katzmann, Barry A. *writer*
Kellerman, Faye Marder *novelist, dentist*
Kennedy, Adrienne Lita *playwright*
Khouri, Callie Ann *screenwriter*
King, Larry L. *playwright, actor*
King, Stephen Edwin *novelist, screenwriter, director*
Knowles, John *author*
Konigsburg, Elaine Lobl *author*
Koning, Hans (Hans Koningsberger) *author*
Kramer, Larry *playwright, writer*
Krantz, Judith Tarcher *novelist*
Kristofferson, Karl Eric *writer*
Kundera, Milan *writer, educator*
Laboda, Amy Sue *writer*
Lally, Michael David *writer, actor*
Lardner, Ring Wilmer, Jr. *author*
Larkin, Joan *poet, English educator*
Lassell, Michael John *writer, editor*
Lawrence, Jerome *playwright, director, educator*
Lawton, Jonathan Frederick *screenwriter*
Lindbergh, Anne Spencer Morrow (Mrs. Charles Augustus Lindbergh) *author*
Link, William Theodore *television writer, producer*
Longstreet, Stephen (Chauncey Longstreet) *author, painter*
Lopez, Barry Holstun *writer*
Lorant, Stefan *author*
Lord, Walter *author*
Lum, Gretchen Yates *poet, small business owner*

Macaulay, David (Alexander) author, illustrator
†Machado, Eduardo Oscar playwright
Maillet, Antonine author, educator
Mamet, David Alan playwright, director, essayist
Mandino, Og author
Mann, Emily Betsy writer, artistic director, theater and film director
Marx, Anne (Mrs. Frederick E. Marx) poet
Marx, Arthur author, playwright, director
Mathews, Harry Burchell poet, novelist, educator
Mathis, Sharon Bell author, elementary educator, librarian
Matthiessen, Peter author
Mazursky, Paul screenwriter, theatrical director and producer
McFall, Catherine Gardner poet, critic, educator
Mc Phee, John Angus writer
McPherson, James Alan writer, educator
Meaker, Marijane Agnes author
Mednick, Murray playwright
Mendoza, George poet, author
Merrill, Jean Fairbanks writer
Mintz, Morton Abner author, former newspaper reporter
Mitford, Jessica author
Mogel, Leonard Henry author
Morris, Willie author, editor
Morrow, Barry Nelson screenwriter, producer
Muldoon, Thomas Lyman writer
Murdoch, (Jean) Iris author
Murray, Albert L. writer, educator
Muson, Howard Henry writer, editor
Myers, Walter Dean young adult book author
Myrer, Anton Olmstead author
Neely, Mark Edward, Jr. writer
†Nicholas, Lynn Holman writer
Nordley, Gerald David writer, investor
Norton, Andre Alice author
Nova, Craig writer
Oliansky, Joel author, director
Olsen, Jack writer
Ondaatje, (Philip) Michael author, educator
†Oslin, George Poer writer, retired telegraph official
Osmond, Gordon Condie playwright
Palliser, Charles writer, educator
Paretsky, Sara N. writer
Parker, Franklin writer, educator
Parker, Robert Brown novelist
†Pascal, Francine writer
Patent, Dorothy Hinshaw author, photographer
Patterson, Mary-Margaret Sharp writer, editor, media strategist
Patterson, Richard North writer, lawyer
Peterson, Roderick William television writer, producer
†Pinckney, Darryl writer
Potok, Chaim author, artist, editor
Press, Aida Kabatznick writer
Queenan, Joseph Martin, Jr. writer, magazine editor
Rader, Dotson Carlyle author, journalist
Raucher, Herman novelist, screenwriter
Renaud, Bernadette Marie Elise author
Rice, Stanley Travis, Jr. poet, English language educator
Riehecky, Janet Ellen writer
Robb, Lynda Johnson writer
†Rodgers, Bruce E. writer
Rogers, David playwright, novelist, actor
Rogers, Rosemary author
Rose, Elizabeth author, satirist, poet, publisher, environmentalist
Rosenblatt, Joseph poet, editor
Rosenblatt, Roger writer
Roudybush, Alexandra novelist
Rubin, Larry Bruce writer, reporter
Rush, Norman author
Russell, Ray author
Scarf, Margaret (Maggi Scarf) author
Schenkkan, Robert Frederic writer, actor
Schickel, Richard writer, film critic
Schneider, Phyllis Leah writer, editor
Schuck, Joyce Haber author
Schultz, Philip poet, novelist, educator
Seamans, William writer, commentator, former television-radio journalist
Seidel, Frederick Lewis poet
Selby, Hubert, Jr. writer
Shapiro, Karl Jay poet, former educator
Sheehy, Gail Henion author
Shindler, Merrill Karsh writer, radio personality
Shreve, Susan Richards author, English literature educator
Shyer, Charles Richard screenwriter, film director
Simmons, Ted Conrad writer
Simon, Roger Lichtenberg writer
Smith, Martin Cruz author
Snyder, Gary Sherman poet
Solzhenitsyn, Aleksandr Isayevich author
†Spada, James author, publisher
Spinelli, Jerry writer
Stern, Daniel author, executive, educator
Stevenson, Elizabeth author, educator
Stine, R(obert) L(awrence) children's book author
Straub, Peter Francis novelist
Styron, William writer
Sullivan, Daniel Joseph writer
Sullivan, George Edward author
Sussman, Barry author, public opinion analyst and pollster, journalist
Tan, Amy Ruth writer
Taylor, John Jackson (Jay) writer, international consultant, retired foreign service officer
Terkel, Susan Neiburg author
Theroux, Paul Edward author
Thomas, Ross Elmore author
Timmons, William Milton retired cinema arts educator, publisher, free-lance writer, film maker
Toffler, Alvin author
Trilling, Diana writer
Truman, Margaret author
Tucker, Jack William Andrew writer, film editor
Updike, John Hoyer writer
Uris, Leon Marcus author
Van Allsburg, Chris author, artist
Van Duyn, Mona Jane poet
van Itallie, Jean-Claude playwright
Verdecchia, Guillermo Luis playwright
Vidal, Gore writer
Viorst, Milton writer
Voigt, Cynthia author
von Hoffman, Nicholas writer, former journalist
Wambaugh, Joseph author
Wasserstein, Wendy playwright
Weinstein, Arnold Abraham playwright, theater educator
Whalen, Charles William, Jr. author, business executive, educator
White, Loray Betty writer, actress, producer
White, Robb author
Williamson, Michael writer
Wilson, Colin Henry writer
Wilson, Lanford playwright
Wilson, Sloan author, lecturer
Wymbs, Norman Elwood author, researcher
Zaillian, Steven screenwriter, director
Zelazny, Roger Joseph author

ARTS: PERFORMING

UNITED STATES

ALABAMA

Birmingham
†Gilmore, Catherine Rye ballet administrator
Polivnick, Paul conductor, music director
Sutowski, Thor Brian choreographer

Mentone
Herndon, Mark musician

Point Clear
Englund, Gage Bush dancer, educator

Troy
Moffett, Thomas Delano music educator

Tuscaloosa
Goossen, Jacob Frederic composer, educator
Rafferty, James Patrick violinist, violin educator

ALASKA

Indian
Wright, Gordon Brooks musician, conductor, educator

ARIZONA

Flagstaff
Aurand, Charles Henry, Jr. music educator

Fountain Hills
Tyl, Noel Jan baritone, astrologer

Glendale
Neff, John recording engineer, producer

Paradise Valley
Alcantara, Theo conductor

Phoenix
Aschaffenburg, Walter Eugene composer, music educator
Lambert, Dennis Alvin radio news director
Sedares, James L. conductor
Shaw, Lillie Marie King vocalist
†Uthoff, Michael dancer, choreographer, artistic director

Scottsdale
Beesemyer, Fritz Timothy radio executive
Moeck, Walter F. conductor, music director
Smith, Leonard Bingley musician
Wolfgang, Bonnie Arlene musician, bassoonist

Sedona
Gregory, James actor

Tempe
Lombardi, Eugene Patsy orchestra conductor, violinist, educator, recording artist
Nagrin, Daniel dancer, educator, choreographer, lecturer, writer

Tucson
Bernhardt, Robert music director, conductor
Cook, Gary Dennis music educator
Meyer, Eric G. orchestra administrator
Ross, Glynn opera administrator
Seaman, Arlene Anna musician, educator

CALIFORNIA

Albany
Boris, Ruthanna dancer, choreographer, dance therapist, educator

Anza
Skelton, Red (Richard Skelton) comedian, artist

Aptos
Mellenbruch, Giles (Johnny) Edward orchestra leader, lyricist

Bakersfield
Owens, Buck (Alvis Edgar, Jr.) singer, musician, songwriter

Belvedere Tiburon
Power, Jules television producer

Berkeley
Dresher, Paul Joseph composer, music educator, performer
Dugger, Edwin Ellsworth composer, educator
Hutcherson, Bobby jazz vibraphonist
Imbrie, Andrew Welsh composer, educator
†Thow, John H. music educator, composer
†Walton, Ortiz Montaigne musician, sociologist
Wood, David Kennedy Cornell choreographer, educator
Zaentz, Saul motion picture producer

Beverly Hills
†Ackerman, Thomas cinematographer
Adams, Jane actress
†Ahmad, Maher film production designer
Alexander, Jason (Jay Scott Greenspan) actor
Alice, Mary (Mary Alice Smith) actress
†Allen, Dede (Dorothea Carothers Allen) film editor
Allen, Karen Jane actress
†Anders, Allison film director, screenwriter
Anderson, Loni Kaye actress
Anderson, Richard Dean actor
Arnold, Tom actor, comedian, producer
†Arquette, Patricia actress
Arquette, Rosanna actress
August, Bille film director
†Avary, Roger Roberts film director, writer
Avildsen, John Guilbert film director
Aykroyd, Daniel Edward actor, writer
Bacon, Kevin actor
Bailey, John cinematographer
†Baird, Stuart film editor
Baker, Anita singer
Bakula, Scott actor
Baldwin, William actor
Bancroft, Anne (Mrs. Mel Brooks) actress
†Banderas, Antonio actor
Barkin, Ellen actress
Barrie, Barbara Ann actress
Barrymore, Drew actress
Bartel, Paul film director
†Bartkowiak, Andrzej cinematographer
Basinger, Kim actress
Bates, Kathy actress
Bauer, Marty agent
Baxter, Meredith actress
Beals, Jennifer actress
Beatty, (Henry) Warren actor, producer, director
Bedelia, Bonnie actress
Bellisario, Donald P. television director
Belushi, James actor
Benatar, Pat (Pat Andrzejewski) rock singer
Bening, Annette actress
Benjamin, Richard actor, director
Benson, Robby actor, director, writer, producer
Berenger, Tom (Thomas Michael Moore) actor
Bergman, Andrew motion picture director
Bernhard, Harvey producer
Berry, Halle actress
Bishop, Joey (Joseph Abraham Gottlieb) comedian
Bisset, Jacqueline actress
†Bloom, John film editor
Bolton, Michael singer, songwriter
Bracco, Lorraine actress
Brandauer, Klaus Maria actor
Bridges, Beau (Lloyd Vernet Bridges, III) actor
Bridges, Jeff actor
Bridges, Lloyd actor
Brightman, Sarah singer, actress
†Brillstein, Bernie J. producer, talent manager
Brimley, Wilford actor
Broderick, Matthew actor
Brokaw, Norman Robert talent agency executive
Bronson, Charles (Charles Buchinsky) actor
Brooks, Mel producer, director, writer, actor
†Bullock, Sandra actress
†Burgess, Don cinematographer
Burnett, Carol actress, comedienne, singer
Burstyn, Ellen (Edna Rae Gillooly) actress
Burton, Al producer, director, writer
Burton, Tim film director
†Burwell, Carter composer
Busey, Gary actor, musician
Busfield, Timothy actor
†Byrne, Gabriel actor
Caine, Michael actor
†Campion, Jane director, screenwriter
†Capshaw, Kate (Kathy Sue Nail) actress
Carrey, Jim actor
Carter, Nell actress, singer
Cates, Phoebe actress
Chamberlain, (George) Richard actor
Channing, Carol actress
Chaplin, Geraldine actress
†Chapman, Michael cinematographer, director
Cher, (Cherilyn Sarkisian) singer, actress
Chong, Thomas comedian, writer, director, musician
Chritton, George A. film producer
Cimino, Michael film director, writer
Clayburgh, Jill actress
†Clooney, George actor
Close, Glenn actress
†Coates, Anne V. film editor
Coen, Ethan film producer, writer
Coen, Joel film director, writer
Cohen, Larry film director, producer, screenwriter
Cole, Natalie Maria singer
Coleman, Dabney W. actor
Connery, Sean (Thomas Connery) actor
†Convertino, Michael composer
Coolidge, Martha film director
Corbin, Barry actor, writer
Corman, Eugene Harold motion picture producer
Costa-Gavras, (Konstaninos Gavras) director, writer
†Cox, Courteney actress
Coyote, Peter (Peter Cohon) actor
Craven, Wes film director
Crenna, Richard actor
Cronenberg, David film director
Crowe, Christopher director, screenwriter
Culkin, Macaulay actor
Cullum, John actor, singer
Culp, Robert actor, writer, director
Curry, Tim actor
Curtin, Jane Therese actress, writer
Curtis, Jamie Lee actress
Curtis, Tony (Bernard Schwartz) actor
Cusack, Joan actress
Cusack, John actor
Daly, Timothy actor
Daly, Tyne actress
D'Angelo, Beverly actress
Danson, Ted actor
Davis, Geena (Virginia Davis) actress
Davison, Bruce actor
Dawber, Pam actress
†Deakins, Roger cinematographer
Dearden, James director, screenwriter
†DeBont, Jan cinematographer, director
Delany, Dana actress
De Laurentiis, Dino motion picture producer
†Del Ruth, Thomas Anthony motion picture director of photography
De Niro, Robert actor
Dennehy, Brian actor
Depardieu, Gérard actor
Depp, Johnny actor
Dern, Bruce MacLeish actor
Dern, Laura actress
Devito, Danny Michael actor
†DiCaprio, Leonardo actor
†Dickerson, Ernest cinematographer, director
Doherty, Shannen actress
Dooley, Paul actor, writer
Douglas, Kirk (Issur Danielovitch Demsky) actor, motion picture producer
Douglas, Michael Kirk actor, film producer, director
Downey, Robert, Jr. actor
Dreyfuss, Richard Stephan actor
Duke, Patty (Anna Marie Duke) actress
Dunaway, (Dorothy) Faye actress
†Dunne, Griffin actor, producer
Duvall, Shelley actress
Eikenberry, Jill actress
Elkins, Hillard producer
Elliott, Chris actor
†Elliott, Paul cinematographer
Elliott, Robert B. comedian
Elliott, Sam actor
Elwes, Cary actor
Estevez, Emilio actor, writer, director
Evans, Linda actress
Evans, Robert J. motion picture producer, actor
Evigan, Greg actor, musician
Fahey, Jeff actor
Falk, Peter actor
†Faltermeyer, Harold composer
Farentino, James actor
Feldshuh, Tovah S. actress
Fenn, Sherilyn actress
†Ferretti, Dante production designer
†Fiennes, Ralph Nathaniel actor
†Finfer, David film editor
Finney, Albert actor, director
Fitzgerald, Ella singer
Flaum, Marshall Allen television producer, writer, director
Fleischer, Richard O. film director
Foch, Nina actress, creative consultant, educator
Fonda, Bridget actress
Fonda, Jane actress
Fox, Michael J. actor
Foxworth, Robert Heath actor, director
†Fraker, William A. cinematographer, director
Frankenheimer, John Michael film and stage director
Franklin, Aretha singer
Frears, Stephen film director
Friedkin, William film director
†Fruchtman, Lisa film editor
Furth, George actor, playwright
Gallagher, Peter actor
Garr, Teri (Ann) actress
†Garwood, Norman art director, production designer
†Gassner, Dennis production designer
Gere, Richard actor
Gilbert, Melissa actress
Gillard, Stuart Thomas film and television director, writer
Gleason, Joanna actress
Glenn, (Theodore) Scott actor
Gless, Sharon actress
Glover, Danny actor
†Goursaud, Anne Renee Mauricette Dominique film editor
Grant, Hugh actor
Graves, Peter actor
Gray, Spalding actor, writer, performance artist
†Green, Jack N. cinematographer
†Greenberg, Gerald B. film editor
Grey, Jennifer actress
Grey, Joel actor
Griffin, Merv Edward former entertainer, television producer, entrepreneur
Griffith, Andy (Andrew Samuel Griffith) actor
Grodin, Charles actor, writer, director
Guest, Christopher actor, director, screenwriter
Guttenberg, Steve actor
Hagman, Larry actor
†Hall, Roger production designer
Hallstrom, Lasse director
Hamel, Veronica actress
Hamilton, Linda actress
Hamlin, Harry Robinson actor
Hanks, Tom actor
†Hanley, Daniel film editor
Hannah, Daryl actress
Hanson, Curtis director, writer
Harmon, Mark actor
Harper, Valerie actress
Harrelson, Woody actor
Harris, Mel (Mary Ellen Harris) actress
Haskell, Peter Abraham actor
Hawke, Ethan actor
Hawn, Goldie actress
Headly, Glenne Aimée actress
Helmond, Katherine actress
Hemingway, Mariel actress
Henderson, Florence (Florence Henderson Bernstein) actress, singer
Henry, Buck actor, writer
Hepburn, Katharine Houghton actress
†Herring, Pembroke J. film editor
Herrmann, Edward Kirk actor
Hershey, Barbara (Barbara Herzstein) actress
Heston, Charlton (John Charlton Carter) actor
†Hill, Michael J. film editor
Hill, Walter film director, writer, producer
Hines, Gregory Oliver actor, dancer
†Hirsch, Paul Frederick film editor
†Hoenig, Dov film editor
Hopkins, Sir Anthony (Philip) actor
Hopper, Dennis actor, writer, photographer, film director
Howard, Ron director, actor
Hughes, John W. film producer, screenwriter, film director
Hulce, Tom actor
Hunt, Helen actress
Hunt, Linda actress
Hurd, Gale Anne film producer
Huston, Anjelica actress
†Hutshing, Joe film editor
Hutton, Timothy actor
†Isham, Mark composer, jazz musician
Jackson, Samuel L. actor
Jillian, Ann (Ann Jura Nauseda) actress, singer
†Johnson, Mark Mathis film producer
Jones, David Hugh theater, film and television director
†Jones, Robert C. film editor
Jordan, Glenn theater director
†Kahn, Michael film editor
Kasdan, Lawrence Edward film director, screenwriter
Kaufman, Philip film director
Keaton, Diane actress
Keaton, Michael actor, comedian
Keitel, Harvey actor
Kelly, Gene Curran dancer, actor, director

†Kemper, Victor J. cinematographer
Kilmer, Val actor
King, Alan entertainer television, film producer
King, Morgana jazz vocalist
Kinski, Nastassja (Nastassja Nakszynski) actress
Kirkwood, Gene motion picture producer
Kline, Kevin Delaney actor
Kravitz, Lenny singer, guitarist
Ladd, Diane actress
Landis, John David film director, writer
†Lane, Diane actress
Lane, Nathan (Joseph Lane) actor
Lange, Jessica actress
Laurie, Piper (Rosetta Jacobs) actress
Lawrence, Steve entertainer
Leachman, Cloris actress
Leary, Denis comedian
Lee, Peggy (Norma Delores Egstrom) singer, actress
Leibman, Ron actor
Leigh, Janet (Jeanette Helen Morrison) actress
Lemmon, Jack (John Uhler Lemmon, III) actor
Leonard, Robert Sean actor
†Levant, Brian film director
Levinson, Barry L. film director
Levy, Eugene actor, director, screenwriter
†Levy, Peter cinematographer
Lewis, Juliette actress
Linden, Hal actor, singer
Linkletter, Arthur Gordon radio and television broadcaster
Liotta, Ray actor
Lithgow, John Arthur actor, director
Little, Richard Caruthers (Rich Little) comedian, impressionist, actor
†Littleton, Carol film editor
Lloyd, Emily (Emily Lloyd Pack) actress
Locklear, Heather actress
Loggia, Robert actor
Loggins, Kenny (Kenneth Clarke Loggins) singer, songwriter
†Lombardo, Tony film editor
Long, Shelley actress
Loughnane, Lee David trumpeter
Louis-Dreyfus, Julia actress
†Lovejoy, Ray film editor
Lovitz, Jon actor, comedian
Lowe, Rob actor
Lynch, David K. film director, writer
MacLachlan, Kyle actor
†MacMillan, Kenneth cinematographer
Macnee, (Daniel) Patrick actor
Malkovich, John actor
Manoff, Dinah Beth actress
Manulis, Martin film producer
Marin, Cheech (Richard Anthony Marin) actor, writer, director
†Marsh, Terence production designer
Marshall, (C.) Penny actress, director
Martin, Dean (Dino Crocetti) actor, singer
Martin, Steve comedian, actor
Mason, Marsha actress, director, writer
Masterson, Mary Stuart actress
Mastrantonio, Mary Elizabeth actress
Matlin, Marlee actress
†McAlpine, Andrew production designer
McDonnell, Mary actress
McGavin, Darren actor, director, producer
Mc Kean, Michael actor
McNaughton, John D. director
Mc Tiernan, John film director
Menges, Chris cinematographer, film director
Metcalf, Laurie actress
Meyer, Ron agent
Milius, John Frederick film writer, director
Miller, Dennis comedian
Modine, Matthew Avery actor
†Moffat, Donald actor
Moloney, Jay agent
Montalban, Ricardo actor
Moore, Demi (Demi Guynes) actress
Moore, Dudley Stuart John actor, musician
†Moore, Julianne actress
Moore, Michael film director
Moranis, Rick actor
†Moriarty, Cathy actress
†Mulgrew, Katherine Kiernan actress
Mulligan, Robert Patrick film director, producer
†Musky, Jane Michelle film production designer
Nabors, James Thurston actor, singer
†Nedd-Friendly, Priscilla Anne motion picture film editor
Neeson, Liam actor
Neill, Sam actor
Nelligan, Kate (Patricia Colleen Nelligan) actress
Nelson, Judd actor
Neuwirth, Bebe dancer, actress
Newton-John, Olivia singer, actress
Nichols, Mike stage and film director
Nicita, Rick agent
Nimoy, Leonard actor, director
†Nitzsche, Jack composer
†Noble, (Terry) Thom film editor
†Noyce, Phillip film director
Nykvist, Sven Vilhem cinematographer
†O'Donnell, Chris actor
O'Donnell, Rosie comedienne, actress
O'Hara, Catherine actress, comedienne
Olin, Ken actor
Olin, Lena Maria Jonna actress
†Ondricek, Miroslav cinematographer
Ovitz, Michael S. artists agency executive
†Palminteri, Chazz actor
Pantoliano, Joe actor
Paquin, Anna actress
Parker, Alan William film director, writer
†Parker, Mary-Louise actress
†Parker, Sarah Jessica actress
†Paull, Lawrence G. production designer
†Paxton, Bill actor, writer, director
Penderecki, Krzysztof composer, conductor
Penn, Sean actor
Perez, Rosie actress, choreographer
Perkins, Elizabeth Ann actress
Perlman, Rhea actress
Perry, Luke (Coy Luther Perry, III) actor
Pesci, Joe actor
†Peterman, Donald cinematographer
Peters, Jon film producer, film company executive
Petersen, Wolfgang film director
Petrie, Daniel Mannix film, theatre and television director
Pfeiffer, Michelle actress
Pinchot, Bronson actor
Pitt, Brad actor
Plummer, Amanda actress
Plummer, (Arthur) Christopher (Orme) actor
Poitier, Sidney actor, director
Ponty, Jean-Luc violinist, composer, producer
Pop, Iggy (James Newell Osterberg) composer, singer, musician
†Pressman, Edward R. motion picture producer
Pressman, Michael film director
Ptak, John A. talent agent
†Pullman, Bill actor
Quinn, Aidan actor
Raimi, Samuel M. film director
Ramis, Harold Allen film director, screenwriter, actor
Rapke, Jack agent
Raymond, Gene actor, producer, director
Reed, Pamela actress
Reiner, Carl actor, writer, director
Reiner, Rob actor, writer, director
Reinhold, Judge (Edward Ernest Reinhold, Jr.) actor
Reiser, Paul actor, comedian
Reitman, Ivan film director, producer
Reynolds, Burt actor, director
Reynolds, Gene television producer, director
†Reynolds, William Henry film editor
Richardson, Patricia actress
Riegert, Peter actor
†Robbins, Richard composer
Robbins, Tim (Timothy Francis Robbins) actor
Roberts, Eric actor
Robinson, Phil Alden director
Roeg, Nicolas Jack film director
†Rolf, Tom film editor
Rolle, Esther actress
Rollins, Howard Ellsworth, Jr. actor
Romero, George A. film director
Ross, Herbert David film director
Roth, Tim actor
†Rotunno, Giuseppe cinematographer
†Rousselot, Philippe cinematographer
†Rubeo, Bruno production designer
Rudolph, Alan film director
Ruehl, Mercedes actress
†Russell, Charles film director, producer
Russell, Ken (Henry Kenneth Alfred Russell) film and theatre director
Russell, Kurt Von Vogel actor
Ryan, Meg actress
Rydell, Mark film director, producer, actor
Ryder, Winona (Winona Laura Horowitz) actress
Sadwith, James Steven screenwriter, director
Sager, Carole Bayer lyricist, singer
†Sakamoto, Ryuichi composer
Sarandon, Susan Abigail actress
†Scharf, William film editor
Schifrin, Lalo composer
Schlatter, George H. producer, director, writer
Schwarzenegger, Arnold Alois actor, author
Seagal, Steven actor
Seinfeld, Jerry comedian
Selleck, Tom actor
Sharif, Omar (Michael Shalhoub) actor
Sheedy, Ally (Alexandra Elizabeth Sheedy) actress
Sheen, Charlie (Carlos Irwin Estevez) actor
Sheridan, Jim director, screenwriter
Simmons, Jean actress
Singleton, John director, screenwriter
Sinise, Gary actor, director
Skerritt, Tom actor
Slater, Christian actor
†Smith, Roy Forge art director, production designer
Smith, Will actor, rapper
†Sonnenfeld, Barry cinematographer, film director
Sorvino, Paul actor
Spacek, Sissy (Mary Elizabeth Spacek) actress
Spader, James actor
Spheeris, Penelope film director
Spielberg, Steven motion picture director, producer
Stack, Robert Langford actor
Stallone, Sylvester Enzio actor, writer, director
Stamos, John actor
Steenburgen, Mary actress
Stefano, Joseph William film and television producer, author
†Steinberg, David comedian, author, actor
Stern, Daniel actor
Stewart, Patrick actor
Stockwell, Dean actor
Stoltz, Eric actor
Stone, Sharon actress
Stowe, Madeleine actress
Strasberg, Susan actress, writer, educator
Strauss, Peter actor
Streep, Meryl (Mary Louise Streep) actress
Streisand, Barbra Joan singer, actress, director
†Suschitzky, Peter cinematagrapher
Sutherland, Donald actor
Tambor, Jeffrey actor, theatre director, educator
Terry, Clark musician
Thomas, Betty actress
Thomas, Marlo (Margaret Julia Thomas) actress
Thompson, Caroline Warner film director, screenwriter
Thompson, Emma actress
Thompson, Larry Angelo producer, lawyer, personal manager
†Thorin, Donald E. cinematographer
Thurman, Uma Karuna actress
†Tilly, Meg actress
Tomei, Marisa actress
Torme, Mel(vin) (Howard Torme) musician, jazz vocalist
†Travis, Nancy actress
Trumbull, Douglas film director, writer, creator special effects
Tucker, Michael actor
Turner, Janine actress
Turner, Kathleen actress
Turner, Tina (Anna Mae Bullock) singer
Turturro, John actor
Tyson, Cicely actress
Ullman, Tracey actress, singer
Urich, Robert actor
Van Ark, Joan actress
Van Damme, Jean-Claude (Jean-Claude Van Varenberg) actor
Van Dyke, Dick actor, comedian
Van Sant, Gus, Jr. director, screenwriter
†Virkler, Dennis M. film editor
Voight, Jon actor
von Sydow, Max (Carl Adolf von Sydow) actor
Wagner, Lindsay J. actress
Wagner, Robert actor
Walken, Christopher actor
†Walker, Lesley film editor
Warren, Lesley Ann actress
Washington, Denzel actor
Wayans, Damon actor
Wayans, Keenen Ivory actor, producer
Weaver, Fritz William actor
Weaver, Sigourney (Susan Alexandra Weaver) actress
Weir, Peter Lindsay film director
Welch, Raquel actress
Weller, Peter actor
Weston, Paul composer, arranger, conductor
†Whalley-Kilmer, Joanne actress
Whitaker, Forest actor
White, Betty actress, comedienne
White, Jesse Marc actor
Williams, JoBeth actress
Williams, Treat (Richard Williams) actor
Wilson, Brian Douglas recording artist, composer, record producer
Wincer, Simon film director
Winkler, Henry Franklin actor
Winkler, Irwin motion picture producer
Wise, Robert film producer, director
Wood, Elijah actor
Woodard, Alfre actress
Woods, James Howard actor
†Wright, John film editor
†Wright, Robin actress
Yates, Peter director, producer
York, Michael (Michael York-Johnson) actor
Yorkin, Bud (Alan Yorkin) producer, director
†Young, Sean actress
Zerbe, Anthony actor
Zevon, Warren singer, songwriter
Zimmerman, Don film editor
†Zwick, Edward M. director, producer, scriptwriter

Bolinas
Murch, Walter Scott director, writer, film editor, sound designer

Burbank
Allen, Tim actor, comedian
Berman, Bruce entertainment company executive
Berry, Bill popular musician
Bruckheimer, Jerry producer
Buck, Peter musician, guitarist
†Burke, Delta actress
Burke, Michele Christine make-up artist
Clark, Dick performer, producer
Clark, Susan (Nora Goulding) actress
Clements, Ronald Francis animation director
Costello, Elvis (Declan Patrick McManus) musician, songwriter
Costner, Kevin actor
de Cordova, Frederick Timmins television producer, director
Donner, Richard film director, producer
Eastwood, Clint actor, director, former mayor
Fagen, Donald musician
†Feldman, Edward S. producer
Ferry, Bryan singer, songwriter
Flanagan, Tommy (Lee) jazz pianist
Fleetwood, Mick musician
†Frederickson, Harry Gray, Jr. motion picture producer
Gold, Jeffrey Alan record company executive
Guy, Buddy blues guitarist
†Hagar, Sammy musician, vocalist, composer
†Hall, Deidre actress
Hope, Bob actor, comedian
Ingram, James popular musician
Isaak, Chris popular musician, singer, songwriter, actor
Karras, Alex actor, former professional football player
Ketchum, Hal Michael country music singer, songwriter
Kidder, Margot actress
Lanois, Daniel record producer, musician, popular
Lawrence, Vicki Schultz singer, dancer, comedienne
Leno, Jay (James Douglas Muir Leno) comedian, writer
Mark, Laurence Maurice film producer
Marsalis, Branford musician
Mathis, Johnny singer
Mc Vie, Christine Perfect musician
Meyer, Barry Michael motion picture executive
Milchan, Arnon film producer
Nardino, Gary television and motion picture producer
Nicks, Stevie (Stephanie Nicks) singer, songwriter
Ohlmeyer, Donald Winfred, Jr. film and television producer
Pryor, Richard actor, writer
Rich, Lee entertainment industry executive
Rundgren, Todd musician, record producer
Seals, Dan Wayland country music singer
†Shuler-Donner, Lauren film producer
Silver, Joel producer
Simpson, Don film producer
Steiger, Rod actor
Stewart, Roderick David singer
Stipe, Michael musician
Tritt, Travis country music singer, songwriter
†Valdés, David Churchill motion picture producer
Weintraub, Jerry motion picture producer, executive
Wonder, Stevie (Stevland Morris) singer, musician, composer

Burlingame
Ward, William Reed composer, educator

Calabasas
Kanaly, Steven Francis actor

Carmel
Novak, Kim (Marilyn Novak) actress

Carmel Valley
Meckel, Peter Timothy arts administrator, educator

Century City
Bishop, Stephen singer, songwriter
Bogdanovich, Peter film director, writer, producer, actor

Chatsworth
Woodruff, Tom, Jr. special effects designer

Claremont
Herschensohn, Bruce film director, writer
Pronko, Leonard Cabell theater educator

Concord
Clooney, Rosemary singer
Jackson, Milton (Bags Jackson) jazz musician

Costa Mesa
Elias, Rosalind mezzo-soprano

Culver City
Abdul, Paula (Julie) singer, dancer, choreographer
Boorman, John film director, producer, screenwriter
Brooks, James L. writer, director, producer
Fetter, Trevor film executive
Gottlieb, Jerome television production company executive
Gregg, David Paul information storage media specialist
Guber, Peter producer
Levine, Alan J. entertainment company executive
Melnick, Daniel film producer
Nathanson, Michael film company executive
Stark, Ray motion picture producer
Tarantino, Quentin film director, screenwriter
†Tisch, Steven E. movie producer
Trebek, Alex television game show host
†Ziskin, Laura film producer
Zucker, David director

Davis
Swift, Richard G(ene) composer, educator

Encinitas
Peters, Leslie Ann television and radio producer

Encino
Eves, Jeffrey P. entertainment industry executive
Hubbard, Frederick Dewayne trumpeter
Nicholson, Jack actor, director, producer
Nielsen, Leslie actor
Stanton, Harry Dean actor
Zsigmond, Vilmos cinematographer, director

Fish Camp
Schneider, Arthur Paul retired videotape and film editor, author

Fresno
Gerster, Robert Gibson composer

Fullerton
Karson, Burton Lewis musician
Timm, Laurance Milo musician, educator
Walker, Mallory Elton tenor

Granada Hills
Carradine, David actor, director
†Duffield, Thomas A. art director, production designer

Hemet
Bible, Frances Lillian mezzo-soprano, educator

Hollywood
Archuletta, Patti Stolkin performing arts association administrator
Carter, Bennett Lester (Benny Carter) musician, composer, conductor
Jordan, Stanley musician
Koch, Howard Winchel film and television producer
Lewis, Huey (Hugh Anthony Cregg, III) singer, composer, bandleader
Little Richard, (Richard Wayne Penniman) recording artist, pianist, songwriter, minister
Pollack, Sydney film director
Rudin, Scott film and theatre producer
Salomon, Mikael cinematographer, director
Strock, Herbert Leonard motion picture producer, director, editor, writer
Wilder, Billy motion picture director, writer, producer

Inglewood
Rothman, Claire Lynda entertainment executive

Irvine
Cohen, Robert Stephen drama educator
Penrod, James Wilford choreographer, dancer
†Radojevic, Danilo ballet dancer
Ruyter, Nancy Lee Chalfa dance educator

Kentfield
Halprin, Anna Schuman (Mrs. Lawrence Halprin) dancer

La Jolla
Harkins, Edwin L. music educator, performer
Moore, F. Richard music educator
Ogdon, Wilbur composer, music educator
Reynolds, Roger Lee composer

Laguna Hills
Herold, Ralph Elliott motion picture arts educator

Long Beach
†Levinson, David Maynard music critic

Los Angeles
Adams, Bryan vocalist, composer
†Ahlberg, Mac cinematographer
Allen, Debbie actress, dancer, director, choreographer
Alley, Kirstie actress
†Alonzo, John A. cinematographer, director
Amos, John actor, producer, director
Anderson, Daryl actor
Anderson, Michael Joseph film director
Anderson, Richard Norman actor, film producer
Anka, Paul singer, composer
Archer, Anne actress
Ashforth, Alden musician, educator
Asner, Edward actor
Astin, John Allen actor, director, writer
Bailey, Alan J. film company executive
Bain, Conrad Stafford actor
Baker, Kathy Whitton actress
Bakshi, Ralph film and television producer, director
Banner, Bob television producer, director
Barbera, Joseph motion picture and television producer, cartoonist
Barker, Robert William television personality
Barry, Gene actor
†Barry, John composer
Barry, Philip Semple television and film producer
Bass, Barbara DeJong film assistant director, free-lance writer
Bassett, Angela actress
Bell, Lee Phillip television personality, television producer
†Belzer, Richard comedian, TV show host, actor

Bennett, Harve (Harve Fischman) television and film producer, writer
†Berger, Peter E. film editor
Bergman, Alan lyricist, writer
Bergman, (Ernst) Ingmar film director, writer
Bergman, Marilyn Keith lyricist, writer
Berle, Milton (Milton Berlinger) actor
Bernhard, Sandra actress, comedienne, singer
Bernstein, Elmer composer, conductor
Bethune, Zina actress, dancer, singer, choreographer
Blake, Robert (Michael Gubitosi) actor
Boerlage, Frans Theodoor opera director, music educator
Boone, Pat (Charles Eugene Boone) singer, actor
Bosley, Tom actor
Bostwick, Barry actor
Braun, Zev motion picture and television producer
Brest, Martin film director
†Bricmont, Wendy Greene motion picture film editor
Broccoli, Albert Romolo motion picture producer
†Brochu, Don film editor
Brolin, James (James Brunderlin) actor
Buckley, Betty Lynn actress
Burrows, James television and motion picture director, producer
Caan, James actor, director
†Cambern, Donn film editor
Campbell, Glen singer, entertainer
†Campbell, Malcolm film editor
Cannell, Stephen Joseph television writer, producer, director
Carlin, George Denis comedian
†Carpenter, Russell cinematographer
Carr, Allan film and stage producer, celebrity representative
Carroll, Pat actress
†Carter, Richard production designer
Caruso, David actor
Cates, Gilbert film, theater, television producer and director
†Chabin, James Boyd entertainment company executive
Champlin, Charles Davenport television host, book critic, writer
Charisse, Cyd (Tula Ellice Finklea) actress, dancer
Charles, Glen television producer
Charles, Les television producer
Charles, Ray (Ray Charles Robinson) musician, singer, composer
Chase, Chevy (Cornelius Crane Chase) comedian, actor, author
†Chew, Richard film editor
Chomsky, Marvin J. director
Clay, Andrew (Dice) (Andrew Clay Silverstein) comedian
Cocker, Joe popular musician
Conniff, Ray popular musician, conductor, composer, arranger
Cooder, Ry recording artist, guitarist
Corea, Chick (Armando Corea) pianist, composer
Corman, Roger William motion picture producer, director
†Crockett, Donald Harold composer, university educator
†Crow, Sheryl singer/songwriter, musician
Crystal, Billy comedian, actor
Curtis, Daniel M. film director
D'Accone, Frank Anthony music educator
Dangerfield, Rodney (Jack Roy Dangerfield) comedian, actor, author
Daniels, Jeff actor
Dante, Joe film director
Davidson, Gordon theatrical producer, director
Davis, Andrew film director, screenwriter
Davis, Ossie actor, author
Dee, Ruby (Ruby Dee Davis) actress, writer, director
†DeGovia, Jackson production designer
de Passe, Suzanne record company executive
Diamond, Matthew Philip artistic director, choreographer, dancer
Diamond, Neil Leslie singer, composer
Dillman, Bradford actor
Domino, Fats (Antoine Domino) pianist, singer, songwriter
Dr. Dre, (Andre Young) rapper, record producer
Duffy, Patrick actor
†Dunn, Andrew cinematographer
Duritz, Adam musician
†Edelman, Randy composer
Eden, Barbara Jean actress
Edwards, Blake film director
†Eidelman, Cliff composer
†Elswit, Robert cinematographer
Eno, Brian (Brian Peter George St. John De La Salle Eno) composer, musician, producer
Esposito, Giancarlo actor
Farrell, Mike actor
Ferrell, Conchata Galen actress
†Finerman, Wendy film producer
Fishburne, Laurence, III actor
Flanagan, Fionnula Manon actress, writer, producer
Fleischmann, Ernest Martin music administrator
†Folk, Robert composer
Forrest, Frederic actor
†Foster, David composer, record producer
Foster, Jodie (Alicia Christian Foster) actress
†Franke, Christopher composer
Franklin, Bonnie Gail actress
†Franz, Dennis actor
Freeman, Morgan actor
Frey, Glenn songwriter, vocalist, guitarist
†Fujimoto, Tak cinematographer
Fuller, Larry choreographer, director
Garcia, Andy actor
Getty, Estelle actress
Gibbons, Leeza television talk show host, entertainment reporter
†Gibbs, Anthony film editor
Gibbs, Marla (Margaret Gibbs) actress
Gibson, Mel actor
Giles, Anne Diener flutist
Glover, John actor
Goldberg, Gary David producer, writer
†Goldenthal, Elliot composer
Goldsmith, Jerry composer
Goldwyn, Samuel John, Jr. motion picture producer
Goodman, David Bryan musician, educator
†Goodman, Miles composer
Gordon, Lawrence film producer
Gorman, Cliff actor
Gould, Harold actor
Grammer, Kelsey actor
Grant, Amy singer, songwriter
Gray, Linda actress
†Graysmark, John production designer
Green, Guy Mervin Charles film director
Grusin, Dave film composer, record producer, pianist
†Gruska, Jay composer
Hackford, Taylor film director, producer
Hackman, Gene actor
Haden, Charles jazz bassist, composer
Haley, Jack, Jr. (John J. Haley) director, producer, writer, executive
Hall, Arsenio television talk show host, comedian
†Hallowell, Todd art director, production designer
†Halsey, Richard film editor
†Hambling, Gerald film editor
Hammer, (Stanley Kirk Burrell) musician
Hancock, Herbert Jeffrey (Herbie Hancock) composer, pianist, publisher
Hanna, William Denby motion picture and television producer, cartoonist
Harlin, Renny (Renny Lauri Mauritz Harjola) film director
Harris, Susan television producer
Hart, Mary television talk show host
Hartke, Stephen Paul composer, educator
Hartman, Lisa (Lisa Hartman Black) actress, singer
†Heim, Alan film editor
Hemion, Dwight Arlington television producer, director
Hemmings, Peter William orchestra and opera administrator
Hertzberg, Paul Stuart producer, publisher, writer
Hesseman, Howard actor
Hettler, Paul visual effects producer
Hiller, Arthur motion picture director
Holbrook, Hal (Harold Rowe Holbrook, Jr.) actor
†Horner, James composer
†Howard, James Newton composer
Howard, Sandy motion picture producer
Howe, John Thomas film director, educator
†Hoy, Maysie film editor
†Hoy, William film editor
Huddleston, David William actor, producer
Hughes, Barnard actor
Hurt, William actor
Hutton, Lauren (Mary Laurence Hutton) actress, model
†Hyman, Richard Roven composer, jazz musician
Ice Cube, (O'Shea Jackson) rap singer, actor
Ice-T, (Tracy Marrow) rap singer, actor
Iman, (Iman Abdulmajid) model
Ingels, Marty theatrical agent, television and motion picture production executive
Ireland, Kathy actress
Jackson, Isaiah conductor
Jackson, Janet Damita singer, dancer
Jackson, Mary actress
Jackson, Michael (Joseph) singer
†Jarre, Maurice Alexis composer
Jarrott, Charles film and television director
Jeter, Michael actor
Joffe, Charles motion picture producer, comedy management executive
†Johnston, P. Michael production designer, art director
Jones, Henry actor
Jones, James Earl actor
Jones, Tom singer
Kagan, Jeremy Paul director, filmmaker
†Kamen, Michael composer, musician, conductor
Kane, Carol actress
Kaneko, Mitsuru production company executive, animation producer
Kaplan, Jonathan Stewart film writer, director
Keach, Stacy, Jr. actor, director, producer, writer, musician, composer
Kellerman, Sally Claire actress
†Kempster, Victor art director, production designer
Kennedy, George actor
Kennedy, Kathleen film producer
Kidman, Nicole actress
Kirkland, Sally actress
Kleiser, (John) Randal motion picture director
Klingman, Lynzee film editor
Knotts, Don actor
Koch, Howard W., Jr. film producer
†Kopelson, Arnold film producer
Korman, Harvey Herschel actor
Kotcheff, William Theodore (Ted Kotcheff) director
Kramer, Stanley E. motion picture producer, director
Kurtz, Swoosie actress
Lahti, Christine actress
Lambro, Phillip composer, conductor, pianist
†Lamont, Peter production designer, art director
Landau, Martin actor
Langella, Frank actor
Lansing, Sherry Lee motion picture production executive
Larroquette, John Bernard actor
Lavin, Linda actress
Lear, Norman Milton producer, writer, director
†Lebenzon, Chris film editor
Lee, Christopher Frank Carandini actor, author
†Leighton, Robert film editor
Leo, Malcolm producer, director, writer
Leonard, Sheldon television producer, director
Leonetti, Matthew Frank cinematographer
†Lepine, Jean cinematographer
Levy, Norman motion picture company executive
Lewis, Shari puppeteer, entertainer
Lewitzky, Bella choreographer
Limato, Edward Frank talent agent
†Linder, Stu film editor
†Lindley, John cinematographer
Littlejohn, Bruce Every film and television producer
Lloyd, Christopher actor
†Lloyd, Walt cinematographer
Lyne, Adrian director
†Macat, Julio cinematographer
Mac Dowell, Andie (Rose Anderson MacDowell) actress
Magner, Martin theatrical producer and director
Malden, Karl (Malden Sekulovich) actor
Malone, Nancy actor, director, producer
Manilow, Barry singer, composer, arranger
Mann, Delbert film, theater, television director and producer
Marshall, E. G. actor
Marshall, Frank W. film producer, director
Martin, Ernest H. theatrical and motion picture executive
Mason, Marshall W. theater director
Matthau, Walter actor
†McAlpine, Donald cinematographer
Mc Callum, David actor
Mc Clanahan, Rue (Eddi-Rue Mc Clanahan) actress
McDonald, Jeanne Gray (Mrs. John B. McDonald) television producer
Mc Dowall, Roddy actor
†McGoohan, Patrick Joseph actor
Mc Guire, Dorothy Hackett actress
McQueen, Justice Ellis (L. Q. Jones) actor, director
Medak, Peter film director
Merkert, George visual effects producer
Michelson, Lillian motion picture researcher
†Miller, Michael Radgiff film editor
Mills, Donna actress
†Mirisch, Lawrence Alan motion picture agent
Mischer, Donald Leo television director and producer
Mitchell, Joni (Roberta Joan Anderson) singer, songwriter
Mitchum, Robert Charles Durman (Charles Mitchum) actor
Moreno, Rita actress
Morris, Garrett actor, singer
†Morriss, Frank film editor
†Morse, Susan E. film editor
Moses, Gilbert film and theatre director
Mossman, Thomas Mellish, Jr. television manager
Mueller, Carl Richard theater arts educator, author
Muldaur, Diana Charlton actress
Munzer, Cynthia Brown mezzo-soprano
Murphy, Eddie comedian, actor
†Nemec, Joseph C., III production designer
Nesmith, Michael film producer, video specialist
Neville, Aaron musician
Neville, Art musician
Neville, Charles musician
Neville, Cyril musician
†Newborn, Ira composer
Newhart, Bob entertainer
†Newman, Thomas composer
†Nichols, David production designer
†Niehaus, Lennie composer, jazz saxophonist
Noble, James Wilkes actor
Northrup, William Stephen, Jr. television producer
†Nyman, Michael Lawrence composer
O'Day, Anita Belle Colton entertainer, singer
Oldman, Gary actor
Olmos, Edward James actor
O'Neal, Tatum actress
†O'Steen, Sam film editor, director
†Pappe, Stuart H. film editor
†Peroni, Geraldine film editor
†Perrine, Valerie actress
Perry, Joe guitarist
Petty, Tom rock guitarist, band leader, composer
Phillips, Julia Miller film producer
†Pierce-Roberts, Tony cinematographer
Pollack, Daniel concert pianist
Post, Mike composer
Potts, Annie actress
Potts, Simon record company executive
Priestley, Jason actor
Principal, Victoria actress
Purcell, Lee actress
Rabinovitz, Jason film and television consultant
Rafkin, Alan television and film director
Raitt, Bonnie Lynn blues singer, guitarist
Randolph, John actor
†Random, Ida production designer
Ratzenberger, John Deszo actor, writer, director
Reaney, Gilbert musician, educator
†Rees, Roger actor, educator
†Reynolds, Norman production designer, art director
Richards, Michael actor, comedian
†Richardson, Robert cinematographer
Richman, Peter Mark actor, painter, writer
Rickles, Donald Jay comedian, actor
Rickman, Alan actor
Riley, Jack actor, writer
Ritchie, Michael Brunswick film director and producer
†Ritter, John(athan) (Southworth) actor
†Riva, J. Michael art director, production designer
Rivers, Joan entertainer
Robards, Jason Nelson, Jr. actor
Robertson, Robbie musician, popular
†Robinson, John Peter film composer, keyboardist
Robinson, Smokey singer, composer
Rogers, Kenneth Ray entertainer, recording artist
Rollins, Henry musician, author, publisher
Roos, Frederick Ried film producer
†Rosen, Charles production designer
†Rosenman, Leonard composer
Rosten, Irwin writer, producer, director
†Rotter, Stephen A. film editor
Rubin, Stanley Creamer producer
†Rubinstein, Arthur B. composer
Ruskin, Joseph Richard actor, director
†Saget, Bob actor, comedian
Sanders, Richard Kinard actor
†Sawyer, Richard art director, production designer
Sayles, John Thomas film director, writer, actor
Schell, Maximilian actor, director
Schepisi, Fred director, screenwriter
†Schmidt, Arthur film editor
†Schoonmaker Powell, Thelma film editor
Schroeder, Barbet G. director
Scott, Campbell actor
Scott, George Campbell actor, director
Scott, Ridley film director
Scott, Tony film director
Seidelman, Arthur Allan director
Seymour, Jane actress
†Seymour, Michael production designer
Shaiman, Marc composer, arranger, orchestrator
Shandling, Garry comedian, scriptwriter, actor
Shatner, William actor
Shepherd, Cybill actress, singer
Shire, David Lee composer
Shorter, Wayne musician
Skotak, Robert F. film production company executive
Slater, Helen Rachel actress
Slonimsky, Nicolas conductor, composer
†Smith, Howard film editor
Smits, Jimmy actor
Smothers, Tom actor, singer
Snyder, Allegra Fuller dance educator
†Snyder, David L. film production designer
Spelling, Aaron film and television producer, writer
†Spencer, James H. art director, production designer
Stanfill, Shelton G. performing arts administrator
Stapleton, Jean (Jeanne Murray) actress
Steel, Dawn motion picture producer
†Steinkamp, Fredric film editor
†Steinkamp, William film editor
Stevens, Andrew actor, producer, writer, director
Stevenson, Robert Murrell music educator
Stiers, David Ogden actor, conductor
†Strathairn, David actor
Swayze, Patrick actor, dancer
Taylor, Meshach actor
Tesh, John television talk show host
Thomas, Jay actor
†Thomson, Alex cinematographer
†Tilly, Jennifer actress
†Toll, John cinematographer
†Townsend, Jeffrey production designer
Townsend, Robert film director
†Travis, Neil film editor
Trembly, Dennis Michael musician
Tyler, Steven singer
Urioste, Frank J. film editor
†Vacano, Jost cinematographer
Van Patten, Dick Vincent actor
Vaughn, Robert (Francis Vaughn) actor
Vereen, Ben actor, singer, dancer
†Villalobos, Reynaldo cinematographer
Von Brandenstein, Patrizia production designer
Waits, Thomas Alan composer, actor, singer
†Walsh, Thomas A. production designer
Ward, Fred actor
Ward, Sela actress
†Warner, Mark Roy film editor
Waterston, Samuel Atkinson actor
Wedgeworth, Ann actress
†Welch, Robert W. production designer, art director
†Wellburn, Timothy film editor
Whitmore, James Allen actor
Wiatt, James Anthony theatrical agency executive
Wickes, Mary actress
Wilder, Gene actor, director, writer
Williams, John Towner composer, conductor
Williams, Paul Hamilton composer, singer
Williams, Robin actor, comedian
Winfield, Paul Edward actor
Winger, Debra actress
Winters, Barbara Jo musician
Winters, Ralph E. film editor
Wood, Karen Sue theatre manager, stage producer, consultant
Wyman, William George musician
Young, Loretta (Gretchen Young) actress
Zemeckis, Robert L. film director
†Zimmer, Hans composer
Zucker, Jerry producer, director

Malibu
Felton, Norman Francis motion picture producer
Gail, Maxwell Trowbridge, Jr. actor, director, musician
Klugman, Jack actor
Nolte, Nick actor

Marina Del Rey
†Semler, Dean cinematographer
Waite, Ralph actor

Menlo Park
Baez, Joan Chandos folk singer

Mill Valley
Padula, Fred David filmmaker

Millbrae
Li, David Wen-Chung television company executive

Mission Hills
Krieg, Dorothy Linden soprano, performing artist, educator

Newbury Park
Issari, M(ohammad) Ali film producer, educator, consultant

North Hollywood
†Badalamenti, Angelo composer
†Baker, Rick make-up artist
Buffett, Jimmy singer, songwriter, author
†Clarke, Stanley Marvin musician, composer
†Colombier, Michel composer
†Flick, Stephen Hunter sound effects artist
Fox, Charles Ira composer, conductor
Frost, Mark director, producer, writer
†Gore, Michael composer
†Laing, Robert production designer
†Lantieri, Michael special effects expert
Maltz, Jerome Paul broadcasting executive
†McMartin, John actor
Mirisch, Marvin Elliot motion picture producer
†Neill, Ve make-up artist
†Omens, Sherwood cinematographer
Reynolds, Debbie (Mary Frances Reynolds) actress
†Safan, Craig Alan film composer
†Toussieng, Yolanda make-up artist

Northridge
Molen, Gerald Robert film producer

Oakland
Cray, Robert popular blues guitarist, singer, songwriter
†Guidi, Ronn ballet company executive

Oceanside
Erickson, Frank William composer

Pacific Palisades
Albert, Eddie (Edward Albert Heimberger) actor
†Bode, Ralf D. cinematographer
†Boyd, Russell cinematographer
†Brown, Robert N. film editor
†Burum, Stephen H. cinematographer
†Butler, Wilmer C. cinematographer
Clark, Bob H. film director
†Cundey, Dean cinematographer
†Francis-Bruce, Richard film editor
†Goldblatt, Stephen cinematographer
†Gosnell, Raja film editor
Kovacs, Laszlo cinematographer
†MacDonald, Richard production designer
†Malley, William production designer
†Milsome, Douglas cinematographer
†Müller, Robby cinematographer
†Roizman, Owen cinematographer
†Rosenberg, Philip production designer
†Spinotti, Dante cinematographer
†Washington, Dennis production designer
Zipper, Herbert symphony conductor

Palm Springs
Caesar, Sid actor, comedian

Palo Cedro
Haggard, Merle Ronald songwriter, recording artist

Palos Verdes Peninsula
Ebsen, Buddy (Christian Ebsen, Jr.) actor, dancer

Giles, Allen *pianist, composer, music educator*

Pebble Beach
Cameron, JoAnna *actress, director*

Pleasanton
Goddard, John Wesley *cable television company executive*

Rancho Palos Verdes
Lima, Luis Eduardo *tenor*

Riverside
Reynolds, William Harold *music educator, choral conductor, music critic*

Sacramento
Nice, Carter *conductor, music director*

San Bernardino
Little, Thomas Warren *broadcast executive*
Robertson, Stewart *conductor*

San Diego
Burge, David Russell *concert pianist, composer, piano educator*
Campbell, Ian David *opera company director*
Flettner, Marianne *opera administrator*
†Keltner, Karen Lee *conductor*
Noehren, Robert *organist, organ builder*
Noel, Craig *performing arts company executive, producer*
Sasaki, Tatsuo *musician*
†Sidlin, Murry *conductor*
Ward-Steinman, David *composer, music educator*
Werner, Tom *television producer, professional baseball team executive*

San Francisco
†Adams, John Coolidge *composer, conductor*
Allemann, Sabina *ballet dancer*
Balin, Marty (Martyn Jerel Buchwald) *musician*
Bennett, William *oboist*
Berman, Joanna *dancer*
Blomstedt, Herbert Thorson *conductor, symphony director*
Borne, Bonita H. *ballet dancer, assistant artistic director*
Breeden, David *clarinetist*
Brubeck, David Warren *musician*
†Burr, Michael *bassist*
Caniparoli, Val William *choreographer, dancer*
Castilla, Antonio *ballet dancer*
Cisneros, Evelyn *dancer*
Collins, Jeremy *dancer*
Coppola, Francis Ford *film director, producer, writer*
†De Coteau, Denis *music director, conductor*
Eilenberg, Lawrence Ira *theater educator, artistic director*
Festinger, Richard *music educator, composer*
†Fischthal, Glenn Jay *symphony musician*
†George, Vance *conductor*
Getty, Gordon Peter *composer, philanthropist*
Haire, James *theatrical producer*
Harrington, Rex *ballet dancer*
Hastings, Edward Walton *theater director*
Hooker, John Lee *blues singer, guitarist*
†Jacobus, Arthur *dance company administrator*
†Jenkins, Margaret Ludmilla *choreographer, dancer*
Kantner, Paul *musician*
Kobler, Raymond *concertmaster*
LeBlanc, Tina *dancer*
Legate, Stephen *ballet dancer*
†Loscavio, Elizabeth *dancer*
Maffre, Muriel *ballet dancer*
†Palmer, David *dancer*
Pastreich, Peter *orchestra executive director*
Penman, Brian Edward *radio personality*
Peterson, Wayne Turner *composer, pianist*
†Posokhov, Iouri *ballet dancer, educator*
Ram, Tracy Schaefer *ballet company manager*
†Renzi, Paul *flutist*
Runnicles, Donald *conductor*
Santana, Carlos *guitarist*
†Sassoon, Janet *ballerina, educator*
Sheinfeld, David *composer*
Silver, Steve *producer, director, writer*
Smuin, Michael *choreographer, director, dancer*
Stowell, Christopher R. *dancer*
†Sullivan, John *theater administrator*
Tiano, Anthony Steven *television producer, book publishing executive*
Tomasson, Helgi *dancer, choreographer, dance company executive*
Van Dyck, Wendy *dancer*
Waldo, Katita *ballet dancer*
†Wheater, Ashley *dancer*
Zhukov, Yuri *ballet dancer*

San Jose
Dalis, Irene *mezzo-soprano, opera company administrator, music educator*

San Rafael
Brevig, Eric *special effects expert, executive*
Burtt, Ben *sound designer, director, editor*
Carson, Dave *special effects expert, executive*
Duston, Jennifer *performing arts association administrator*
Farrar, Scott *special effects expert, executive*
Goldman, Clint Paul *producer*
Gorman, Ned *film producer*
†Hall, Allen *special effects expert*
Healy, Janet *graphics expert, producer*
Kay, Douglas *graphics expert, executive*
Kennedy, Thomas *executive producer*
Lesh, Philip Chapman *musician, composer*
Lucas, George W., Jr. *film director, producer, screenwriter*
Mann, Jeff *special effects expert, executive*
†Murphy, George *special effects expert*
Nicholson, Bruce *graphics expert, executive*
Owens, Michael *camera graphics expert, executive*
Ralston, Ken *graphics expert*
Sheldon, Gary *conductor, music director*
Squires, Scott William *special effects expert, executive*

Santa Ana
St. Clair, Carl *conductor, music director*

Santa Barbara
†Anderson, Stephen Thomas *entertainment executive*
Brant, Henry *composer*
Gimbel, Norman *lyricist, music publisher, television producer*
Messick, Don *actor*
Ohyama, Heiichiro *music educator, violist, conductor*
Peterson, Gregg Lee *radio station executive*
Wayland, Newton Hart *conductor*

Santa Clarita
Powell, Mel *composer*
†Senter, Jack *art director, production designer*

Santa Cruz
Mumma, Gordon *composer, educator, author*
Winston, George *keyboardist, recording company executive*

Santa Monica
Alenikov, Vladimir *motion picture director and writer*
Allman, Gregg *musician*
Black, Noel Anthony *television and film director*
Cameron, James *film director, screenwriter, producer*
Chartoff, Robert Irwin *film producer*
Cooper, Jackie *actor, director, producer*
Daviau, Allen *cinematographer*
De Palma, Brian Russell *film director, writer*
Edwards, Sarah Anne *radio, cable television personality, clinical social worker*
Feitshans, Fred Rollin (Buzz Feitshans) *film producer*
Fogelberg, Daniel Grayling *songwriter, singer*
Jarreau, Alwyn Lopez *singer*
Leaf, Paul *producer, director, writer*
†London, Andrew Barry *film editor*
MacLaine, Shirley *actress*
Mahal, Taj (Henry St. Clair Fredericks) *composer, musician*
Mann, Michael K. *producer, director, writer*
Michael, George (Gergios Kyriakou Panayiotou) *musician, singer, songwriter*
Owens, Gary *broadcast personality, entrepreneur, author*
Pisano, A. Robert *entertainment company executive, lawyer*
Schultz, Michael *stage and film director, film producer*
Watrous, William Russell *trombonist, composer, conductor*
Watson, Doc (Arthel Lane Watson) *vocalist, guitarist, banjoist, recording artist*
Weber, Samuel Lloyd *tap dancer, choreographer*
Wexler, Haskell *film producer, cameraman*

Santa Rosa
Brown, Corrick *musician, conductor*

Sausalito
Slick, Grace Wing *singer*

Sherman Oaks
Almeida, Laurindo *guitarist, composer*
Buckingham, Lindsey *musician*
Burton, Levar (Levardis Robert Martin Burton) *actor*
Cherones, Thomas Harry, Jr. *television producer, director*
Conrad, Robert (Conrad Robert Falk) *actor, singer, producer, director*
Cossette, Pierre *agent, producer*
Easton, Sheena *rock vocalist*
Farnsworth, Richard *actor, former stuntman*
†Fenton, George *composer*
Gilmore, Art *television performer*
†Greenberg, Adam *cinematographer*
†Haigh, Nancy *set decorator*
†Jones, Trevor *composer*
Jourdan, Louis (Louis Gendre) *actor*
Kennedy, Burt Raphael *film director*
Lamas, Lorenzo *actor, race car driver*
Majors, Lee *actor*
Morse, Robert Alan *actor*
Murray, Bill *actor, writer*
Ross, Marion *actress*
Shapiro, Amy Rosemarie *film studio executive*
Silliphant, Stirling Dale *motion picture writer, producer, novelist*
Williams, Billy Dee *actor*

Simi Valley
Beck, Mat *special effects expert, photographer*
Bigelow, Michael *film director, visual effects expert*
Durst, Eric *television and commercial director*
Hoover, Richard *special effects expert, film director*
Shartle, Keith Robert *producer*
Yeatman, Hoyt *special effects expert, executive*

Stanford
Cohen, Albert *musician, educator*
Cole, Wendell Gordon *speech and drama educator*
Lyons, Charles R. *drama educator*

Stockton
Won, Kyung-Soo *symphony conductor, director*

Studio City
Autry, Gene (Orvon Gene Autry) *actor, entertainer, broadcasting executive, baseball team executive*
Bergen, Polly *actress*
Bloodworth-Thomason, Linda *television producer, writer*
†Bumstead, Henry *art director, production designer*
Carsey, Marcia Lee Peterson *television producer*
Coolidge, Rita *singer*
English, Diane *television producer, writer, communications executive*
†Galvin, Tim *art director, production designer*
Gautier, Dick *actor, writer*
Goldthwait, Bob *comedian, actor*
Goodman, John *actor*
†Guerra, Robert *art director, production designer*
†Haber, David *art director, production designer*
Harrison, Gregory *actor*
†Hasselhoff, David *actor*
†Hole, Fred *art director*
†Hutman, Jon *art director, production designer*
Kenney, H(arry) Wesley, Jr. *producer, director*
†Kenney, William *art director, production designer*
†Kilvert, Lilly *film production designer*
Leider, Gerald J. *motion picture and television company executive*
†Mansbridge, John B. *art director, production designer*
†Mansbridge, Mark *art director, production designer*
†McClellan, Bennett Earl *producer*
†McDonald, Leslie *art director, production designer*
†McShirley, Marjorie Stone *art director*
Moore, Mary Tyler *actress*
Needham, Hal *director, writer*
Peerce, Larry *film director*
Roseanne *actress, comedienne, producer, writer*
†Sandell, William *production designer*
†Scarfiotti, Ferdinando *production designer*
†Scott, Elliot *production designer*
†Smith, Peter Lansdown *art director*
†Sylbert, Paul *production designer, art director*
†Taylor, Jack G., Jr. *art director*
†Thomas, Wynn P. *art director, production designer*
†Tomkins, Alan *art director, production designer*
von Zerneck, Frank Ernest *television producer*
Westmore, Michael George *make-up artist*
†Woodruff, Donald B. *art director, production designer*

Tarzana
Abbott, Philip *actor*
†Ferguson, Jay A. *composer*
†Newman, David *composer*
†Small, Michael *composer*
†Young, Christopher *composer*

Thousand Oaks
†Miller, Jim *film editor*
Rooney, Mickey (Joe Yule, Jr.) *actor*

Topanga
Redgrave, Lynn *actress*

Torrance
Harness, William Edward *tenor*

Turlock
Goedecke, David Stewart *music educator, band educator, trumpet player*

Universal City
Day, Doris (Doris von Kappelhoff) *singer, actress*
†Kahn, Sheldon F. *film editor, producer*
LaBelle, Patti *singer*
Lansbury, Angela Brigid *actress*
Lovett, Lyle *musician*
Lynn, Loretta Webb (Mrs. Oliver Lynn, Jr.) *singer*
Meat Loaf, (Marvin Lee Aday) *popular musician, actor*
Nelson, Craig T. *actor*
Van Dyke, Jerry *actor, comedian*
Yearwood, Trisha *country music singer, songwriter*

Valley Village
Diller, Phyllis *actress, author*

Van Nuys
Allen, Stephen Valentine Patrick William *television comedian, author, pianist, songwriter*
Conway, Tim *comedian*
Gordon, Stuart *film and theater producer, director, playwright*
Ivey, Judith *actress*
Jones, Dean Carroll *actor*
Mount, David Allen *video specialist*

Venice
Bill, Tony *actor, producer, director*
†Ferry, April *costume designer*
Gould, Elliott *actor*
O'Neill, Edward *actor*

West Hills
Straight, Beatrice Whitney *actress*

West Hollywood
Benson, George *guitarist*
Bloom, Claire *actress*
Blumofe, Robert Fulton *motion picture producer, association executive*
Bogart, Paul *film director*
†Broughton, Bruce Harold *composer*
Burns, George (Nathan Birnbaum) *actor, comedian*
Cage, Nicolas (Nicolas Coppola) *actor*
Conti, Bill *film composer*
†Copeland, Stewart *composer, musician*
Denver, John (Henry John Deutschendorf, Jr.) *singer, songwriter*
Deschanel, Caleb *cinematographer, director*
Elfman, Danny *composer*
Erman, John *film director*
Fisher, Carrie Frances *actress, writer*
†Gibbs, Richard *composer*
Henley, Don *singer, drummer, songwriter*
Leblang, Steven Craig *television executive*
Leigh, Jennifer Jason (Jennifer Leigh Morrow) *actress*
Lewis, Richard *actor, comedian*
Males, William James *film producer, make-up artist*
Marsalis, Wynton *musician*
McKagan, Duff (Michael McKagan) *bassist*
Mull, Martin *comedian, singer*
†Portman, Rachel Mary Berkeley *composer*
Reid, Antonio (L. A. Reid) *musician, songwriter*
†Revell, Graeme *composer*
Ronstadt, Linda Marie *singer*
Rose, W. Axl (William Bruce Bailey) *singer*
Shaye, Robert Kenneth *cinema company executive*
Sherman, Robert B(ernard) *composer, lyricist, screenwriter*
Slash, (Saul Hudson) *guitarist*
Taylor, James Vernon *musician*
Verhoeven, Paul *film director*
Young, Neil *musician, songwriter*

Woodland Hills
Davidian, David *lighting and production designer*
Horne, Lena *singer*
Janis, Conrad *actor, jazz musician, art dealer, film producer, director*
†Nicholas, Fayard Antonio *dancer, actor, entertainer*
Perlman, Itzhak *violinist*
Scheimer, Louis *film and television producer*
Taylor, Rowan Shaw *music educator, composer, conductor*
Wester, Keith Albert *film and television recording engineer, television executive*

Yreka
Beary, Shirley Lorraine *retired music educator*

COLORADO

Aspen
Eirman, Thomas Fredrick *music festival manager*

Basalt
Feliciano, José *entertainer*
Kazan, Lainie (Lainie Levine) *singer, actress*
Puente, Tito Anthony *orchestra leader, composer, arranger*
Severinsen, Doc (Carl H. Severinsen) *conductor, musician*
Sinatra, Frank (Francis Albert Sinatra) *singer, actor*
Williams, Joe *jazz and blues singer*

Boulder
Brakhage, James Stanley *filmmaker, educator*
Duckworth, Guy *musician, educator*
Fink, Robert Russell *music theorist, university dean*
Sable, Barbara Kinsey *former music educator*
Sarson, John Christopher *television producer, director, writer*
Schwarz, Josephine Lindeman *retired ballet company director, choreographer*
Symons, James Martin *theater and dance educator*

Colorado Springs
Wilkins, Christopher Putnam *conductor*

Denver
Alsop, Marin *conductor*
Bearden, Thomas Howard *news program producer, correspondent*
Ceci, Jesse Arthur *violinist*
Fredmann, Martin *artistic director ballet, educator, choreographer*
Keats, Donald Howard *composer, educator*
Rawls, Eugenia *actress*
Rule, Daniel Rhodes *opera company executive*
Schwartz, Cherie Anne Karo *storyteller*

Loveland
Balsiger, David Wayne *television-video director, researcher, producer*

Ridgway
Weaver, Dennis *actor*

Telluride
Madonia, Valerie *dancer*

CONNECTICUT

Chester
Hays, David Arthur *theater producer, stage designer*

Cos Cob
Donahue, Barbara Lynn Sean *television producer*

Danbury
Nelson, Willie *musician, songwriter*

East Haddam
Borton, John Carter, Jr. (Terry Borton) *producer, theater*
Frost, Susan Beth *producer*

Fairfield
Mc Lean, Don *singer, instrumentalist, composer*
Wolff, Steven Alexander *arts and entertainment consultant*

Greenwich
Rutgers, Katharine Phillips (Mrs. Frederik Lodewijk Rutgers) *dancer*
Tiegs, Cheryl *model, designer*

Hartford
Lamos, Mark *artistic director, administrator, actor*
Lyman, Peggy *dancer, choreographer, educator*
Mc Lean, Jackie *jazz saxophonist, educator, composer, community activist*
Osborne, George Delano *performing arts company director*

Litchfield
Winter, Paul Theodore *musician*

Middletown
Sumarsam *music educator*

New Canaan
Richardson, Dana Roland *video producer*

New Haven
Baker, Robert Stevens *organist, educator*
Brainard, Paul Henry *musicologist, music educator*
Brown, Arvin Bragin *theater director*
French, Richard Frederic *retired music educator*
Gilman, Richard *drama educator, author*
Laderman, Ezra *composer, educator, college dean*
Morgan, Robert P. *music theorist, educator*
Nolan, Victoria Holmes *theater director*
Rosenblum, M. Edgar *theater director*
Tirro, Frank Pascale *music educator, author, composer*
Turner, Caroline *theatre manager*
†Wojewodski, Stan, Jr. *artistic director, dean*

Niantic
Bobruff, Carole Marks *radio show producer, personality*

Norwalk
Albanese, Licia *retired operatic soprano*
Bell, Martin Jay *producer, writer*
Brown, Beatrice *symphony conductor*
Caro, Warren *theatrical executive, lawyer*

Redding
Kipnis, Igor *harpsichordist, fortepianist, critic*
Mathews, Carmen Sylva *actress*

Ridgefield
Wyton, Alec *composer, organist*

Southport
Walker, Charles Dodsley *conductor, organist*

Stamford
Karp, Steve *artistic director*
Nierenberg, Roger *symphony conductor*
†Raphael, Brett *artistic director, choreographer*

Storrs
Wood, Wendy Deborah *filmmaker*

Storrs Mansfield
Birdman, Jerome Moseley *drama educator, consultant*

Thomaston
†Kirshner, Hal *cinematographer*

Washington Depot
Chase, Alison Becker *modern dancer, choreographer, teacher*
Mandler, Susan Ruth *dance company administrator*
Pendleton, Moses Robert Andrew *dancer, choreographer*
Tracy, Michael Cameron *choreographer, performer*

Waterford
White, George Cooke *theater director, foundation executive*

Weston
Bellin, Harvey Forrest *television producer, director*
Fredrik, Burry *theatrical producer, director*
Schnitzer, Robert C. *theater administrator*

Westport
Hersey, Marilyn Elaine *performing company executive*
Rose, Reginald *television writer, producer*

DELAWARE

Wilmington
Gunzenhauser, Stephen Charles *conductor*

DISTRICT OF COLUMBIA

Washington
Ames, Frank Anthony *percussionist, film producer*
Andrews, Jessica Louise *performing arts company executive*
Armstrong, Richard Burke *retired television director*
Brown, Oscar, Jr. *writer, entertainer*
Crawford-Mason, Clare Wootten *television producer, journalist*
Day, Mary *artistic director, ballet company executive*
Dukert, Betty Cole *television producer*
Farrell, Suzanne *ballerina*
Feinstein, Martin *opera director*
Flindt, Flemming *ballet master*
Forrest, Sidney *clarinetist, music educator*
†Fricke, Heinz *conductor*
Guggenheim, Charles E. *film, television producer, political media consultant*
†Hancock, Richard B. *performing company executive*
Harpham, Virginia Ruth *violinist*
Hay, George Austin *actor, producer, director, musician, artist*
Hewitt, Frankie Lea *theater producer*
Horton, John Ernest *motion picture industry consultant*
Kahn, Michael *stage director*
Kendall, Peter Landis *television news executive*
†Kennedy, Allyson Ann *television producer*
Lehrman, Margaret McBride *television news executive, producer*
Levalier, Dotian *harpist*
Makris, Andreas *composer*
†Moore, Elvi *performing company executive*
Mosettig, Michael David *television producer, writer*
†Mossel, Patricia Fleischer *opera executive*
Parris, Robert *composer*
Pasmanick, Kenneth *bassoonist*
†Ratner, Ellen Faith *radio talk show host, writer*
Russell, Mark *comedian*
Shalwitz, Howard *theater director, actor*
Sheehy, Pat Murphy *artistic director*
Silverman, Ira Norton *news producer*
Stevens, George, Jr. *film and television producer, writer, director*
Stevens, Milton Lewis, Jr. *trombonist*
Stevens, Roger Lacey *theatrical producer*
Thayer, Edwin Cabot *musician*
Thulean, Donald Myron *symphony conductor*
Wager, Douglas Charles *artistic director*
Weidenfeld, Sheila Rabb *television producer, author*
Whedon, Margaret Brunssen *television and radio producer*

FLORIDA

Boca Raton
Blanton, Jeremy *dance company director*
Fengler, John Peter *television producer, director, advertising executive*
Gold, Catherine Anne Dower *music history educator*
Gordon, Marjorie *lyric coloratura soprano, opera producer*
Wallis, John James (Jimmy Wallis) *entertainer, ventriloquist, video production executive*

Deland
Sorensen, Jacki Faye *choreographer, aerobic dance company executive*

Fort Lauderdale
Alberg, Mildred Freed *film and television producer, writer*
Gill, Richard Thomas *opera singer, economic analyst*
Holland, Beth *actress*
LeRoy, Joy *model*
Randi, James (Randall James Hamilton Zwinge) *magician, writer, educator*
Rasmussen, Geraldine Dorothy *composer, artist, musician, author*

Gainesville
Bodine, Willis Ramsey, Jr. *music educator, organist*
Kushner, David Zakeri *musicologist, educator*
White, John David *composer, theorist, cellist*

Jacksonville
Pierson, David Lowell *orchestra manager*
Swenson, Courtland Sevander *retired musician*

Lake Buena Vista
Mc Mahon, Ed *television personality*

Largo
Fournier, Serge Raymond-Jean *orchestra conductor*

Marco Island
Jones, Edward Magruder *television producer and writer, correspondent*

Miami
Allen, Charles Norman *television, film and video producer*
Brady, Alexander Childs *dancer*
Bufman, Zev *stage producer, theater chain executive*
Catanzaro, Tony *dancer*
Estefan, Gloria Maria *singer, songwriter*
Gibb, Maurice *vocalist, songwriter*
Heuer, Robert Maynard, II *opera company executive*
Reed, Alfred *retired composer, conductor*
Sandoval, Arturo *jazz musician*
Stephan, Egon, Sr. *cinematographer, film equipment company executive*

Miami Beach
Gibb, Robin *vocalist, songwriter*
†Lawson, Eve Kennedy *ballet mistress*

Naples
White, Roy Bernard *theater executive*

North Miami
Cliff, Jimmy (James Chambers) *vocalist, composer*

North Palm Beach
Hayman, Richard Warren Joseph *conductor*

Odessa
Lister, Thomas Mosie *composer, lyricist, publishing company executive, minister*

Orlando
Grant, Raymond Thomas *arts administrator*
Swedberg, Robert Mitchell *opera company director*

Pompano Beach
MacLaren, Neil Moorley, Jr. *musician, music educator*

Punta Gorda
Kavanaugh, Frank James *film producer, educator*

Saint Petersburg
Carroll, Charles Michael *music educator*
Cook, Marian Alice *musician*

Sarasota
McCollum, John Morris *tenor*
Powers, Dudley *musician*
Smith, Richard Emerson (Dick Smith) *make-up artist*

Spring Hill
Youngman, Henny *comedian*

Tallahassee
Harsanyi, Janice *soprano, educator*
Housewright, Wiley Lee *music educator*
Kirk, Colleen Jean *conductor, educator*

Tampa
Bujones, Fernando Calleiro *ballet dancer*
Hankenson, E(dward) Craig, Jr. *performing arts executive*
Ling, Jahja Wang-Chieh *conductor*

West Palm Beach
Robinson, Raymond Edwin *musician, music educator, writer*
Sennett, Henry Herbert, Jr. *theatre arts educator*

Winter Springs
Hagen, Kevin A. *performing company executive*

GEORGIA

Athens
Staub, August William *drama educator, theatrical producer*

Atlanta
†Arzewski, Cecylia *concertmaster*
Barnett, Robert James *artistic director*
†Bell, Jack Atkins *percussionist, educator*
Kamm, Laurence Richard *television producer, director*
Kennedy, Alfred Doby *performing arts administrator*
Lane, Louis *musician, conductor*
Levi, Yoel *orchestra conductor*
Love, Edith Holmes *theater producer*
†Rex, Christopher Davis *classical musician*
Shaw, Robert Lawson *symphony orchestra conductor*
†Thompson, James Wilber *symphony performer*
Turner, Ed Sims *broadcast executive, writer*

Buford
Ziegler, Delores *mezzo-soprano*

Clarkston
Downs, Jon Franklin *drama educator, director*

Columbus
Patrick, Carl Lloyd *theatre executive*
†Patrick, Michael Wynn *theatre executive*

Conyers
Smith, Michael Joseph *composer, pianist, lecturer*

Covington
Silverman, Fred *television producer*

Cumming
Pirkle, George Emory *television and film actor, director*

Decatur
Strawn-Hamilton, Frank *jazz musician, folksinger, composer and arranger, educator*

Macon
Marshall, Howard Lowen *music educator, musicologist*
Rich, Arthur Lowndes *music educator*

HAWAII

Honolulu
Ho, Donald Tai Loy *entertainer, singer*
Johanos, Donald *orchestra conductor*
†Landovsky, John *artistic director*
Langhans, Edward Allen *drama and theater educator*
McGinn, Susan Frances *musician*
Ramos, J. Mario *opera director, conductor*
Smith, Barbara Barnard *music educator*

Kula
Becker, Walter *guitarist, record producer*

IDAHO

Moscow
Bray, R(obert) Bruce *music educator*

Pocatello
Stanek, Alan Edward *music educator, performer, music administrator*

ILLINOIS

Alton
Schnabel, John Henry *music educator*

Bloomington
Brown, Jared *theater director, educator, writer*
Vayo, David Joseph *composer, music educator*

Buffalo Grove
Denov, Sam *musician*
Siegel, Sid *composer, lyricist*

Champaign
Fredrickson, L(awrence) Thomas *composer*
Garvey, John Charles *violist, conductor, retired music educator*

Chicago
Aitay, Victor *concert violinist, music educator*
Akos, Francis *violinist*
Bartoletti, Bruno *conductor*
Duell, Daniel Paul *artistic director, choreographer, lecturer*
Eaton, John C. *composer, educator*
Elliot, Willard Somers *musician, composer*
Ewen, Malcolm Dawes *stage manager*
Falls, Robert Arthur *artistic director*
Favors, Malachi *jazz musician, bassist*
Fogel, Henry *orchestra administrator*
Foldi, Andrew Harry *singer, educator*
Gonzalez, Ruben *professional musician*
Gossett, Philip *musicologist*
Hall, Tom T. *songwriter, performer*
Higgins, Ruth Ellen *theatre producer*
Hillis, Margaret *conductor, musician*
Ingram, Randy Jan *television producer*
Janson, Patrick *singer, actor, conductor, educator*
Knapp, Donald Roy *musician, educator*
Krainik, Ardis *opera company executive*
LaPointe-Peterson, Kittie Vadis *choreographer, ballet school director, educator*
Lazar, Ludmila *concert pianist, educator*
Lewis, Ramsey Emanuel, Jr. *pianist, composer*
Maggio, Michael John *artistic director*
Miller, Frederick Staten *music educator, academic administrator*
Moffatt, Joyce Anne *performing arts executive*
Mourek, Joseph Edward *musician*
Ortmann, Jeffrey *theater producer, director*
Peck, Donald Vincent *musician*
Peters, Gordon Benes *musician*
Pikler, Charles *musician*
Ragir, John Arthur *theatrical company executive*
Ran, Shulamit *composer*
†Russo, William *composer, educator*
Salenger, Lucy Lee *producer, consultant*
Schulfer, Roche Edward *theater executive director*
†Schulze, Theodora Economou *music director, educator, investment firm executive*
Schweikert, Norman Carl *musician*
Sedelmaier, John Josef *film director, cinematographer*
Shapey, Ralph *composer, conductor, educator*
Solti, Sir Georg *conductor*
Thatcher, Kristine Marie *actress, writer*
Turner, Lynne Alison (Mrs. Paul H. Singer) *harpist*
Walker, John Patrick *theater director, actor*
Wang, Albert James *violinist, educator*
Webster, Albert Knickerbocker *consultant in performing arts*
Winfrey, Oprah *television talk show host, actress, producer*
Zajicek, Jeronym *music educator*
Zlatoff-Mirsky, Everett Igor *violinist*

De Kalb
Bach, Jan Morris *composer, educator*

East Saint Louis
Dunham, Katherine *choreographer, dancer, anthropologist*

Edwardsville
Haley, Johnetta Randolph *musician, educator, university administrator*

Elk Grove Village
Sertich, Tony *artistic director*

Evanston
Collins, Rives Berryman *theater educator, artisitc director*
Eberley, Helen-Kay *opera singer, classical record company executive, poet*
Galati, Frank Joseph *stage and opera director, educator, screen writer, actor*
Giordano, August Thomas (Gus Giordano) *choreographer, dancer*
Karlins, M(artin) William *composer, educator*
Kujala, Walfrid Eugene *musician, educator*
Paynter, John Philip *conductor*
Reimer, Bennett *music educator, writer*
Vandenbroucke, Russell James *theatre director*

Highland Park
Grimmer, Margot *dancer, choreographer, director*
Mehta, Zarin *music association administrator*

Northbrook
Magad, Samuel *orchestra concertmaster, conductor*
Slattery, James Joseph (Joe Slattery) *actor*

Park Forest
Billig, Etel Jewel *theater director, actress*

Peoria
Price Boday, Mary Kathryn *choreographer, small business owner, educator*

River Forest
Columbus, Chris Joseph *film director, screenwriter*
Rimbach, Evangeline Lois *music educator*

Rockford
Larsen, Steven *orchestra conductor*
Ward, Sylvan Donald *music conductor, educator*

Skokie
Childers, John Henry *talent company executive, personality representative*

Springfield
Nanavati, Grace Luttrell *dancer, choreographer, instructor*
Thompson, Joyce Elizabeth *arts management educator*

Taylorville
Ford, Ellen Hodson *composer*

University Park
Strukoff, Rudolf Stephen *music educator*

Urbana
Boardman, Eunice *music educator*
Brün, Herbert *composer*
Elyn, Mark *opera singer, educator*
Hobgood, Burnet M. *theater educator*
Melby, John B. *composer, educator*
Warfield, William Caesar *singer, actor, educator*
Wisniewski, Thomas Joseph *music educator*

Wilmette
Merrier, Helen *actress, director*

INDIANA

Bloomington
Brown, Keith *musician, educator*
Klotman, Robert Howard *music educator*
Mac Watters, Virginia Elizabeth *singer, music educator, actress*
Orrego-Salas, Juan Antonio *composer, retired music educator*
Pagels, Jürgen Heinrich *balletmaster, dance educator, dancer, choreographer, author*
Phillips, Harvey *musician, music educator, arts consultant*
Rousseau, Eugene Ellsworth *musician, music educator, consultant*
Samuelsen, Roy *bass-baritone*
Sebok, Gyorgy *pianist, educator*
Svetlova, Marina *ballerina, choreographer, educator*
Williams, Camilla *soprano, voice educator*
Wittlich, Gary Eugene *music theory educator*

Crawfordsville
Fisher, A. James *theater educator, director, actor*

Evansville
Savia, Alfred *conductor*

Fort Wayne
Guerin, Christopher David *arts administrator*
Sack, James McDonald, Jr. *radio and television producer, marketing executive*

Indianapolis
†Bolin, Daniel Paul *music educator*
Johnson, David Allen *singer, songwriter, investor*
Jones, Robert C. *symphony orchestra administrator*
Ross, Steven Carter *entertainment executive*
Schellen, Nando *opera director*
†Stephenson, Kathryn Burg *performing company executive*
Suzuki, Hidetaro *violinist*

La Porte
Hancock, John D. *film director*

Michigan City
Musgrave, Charles Edward *music director, correctional facility official*

Muncie
Schuessler, Annemarie *pianist, educator*

South Bend
Yeh, Tsung *orchestral conductor*

Upland
Shulze, Frederick Bennett *music educator*

West Lafayette
Wright, Alfred George James *band symphony orchestra conductor, educator*

IOWA

Des Moines
Giunta, Joseph *conductor, music director*

Dubuque
Hemmer, Paul Edward *musician, broadcasting executive*

Indianola
Larsen, Robert LeRoy *artistic director*

Iowa City
Gompper, David *music educator*
Kottick, Edward Leon *music educator, harpsichord maker*
Mather, Betty Bang *musician, educator*
Mather, Roger Frederick *music educator, freelance technical writer*

Walnut
Everhart, Robert Phillip (Bobby Williams) *entertainer, songwriter, recording artist*

KANSAS

Kansas City
Stoskopf, William Howard *retired music educator*

Lawrence
Duerksen, George Louis *music educator, music therapist*
Pozdro, John Walter *music educator, composer*
Tsubaki, Andrew Takahisa *theater director, educator*

Wichita
Chen, Zuohuang *conductor*

KENTUCKY

Lexington
Zack, George J. *conductor, music director*

Louisville
Luvisi, Lee *concert pianist*
Slater, Marilee Hebert *theatre administrator, producer, director, consultant*
Smillie, Thomson John *opera producer*

LOUISIANA

Baton Rouge
Constantinides, Dinos Demetrios (Constantine Constantinides) *music educator, composer, conductor*
Mathews, Sharon Walker *artistic director, secondary school educator*
Norem, Richard Frederick, Sr. *musician, music educator*
Yarbrough, Martha Cornelia *music educator*

Franklin
Broussard, Bernard B. *social activist, publisher, writer*

Lake Charles
Hathaway, Leah *artistic director*

New Orleans
Baron, John Herschel *music educator, musicologist*
Cosenza, Arthur George *opera director*
Fountain, Peter Dewey, Jr. (Pete Fountain) *clarinetist*
Gonzales, Brother Alexis (Joseph M. Gonzales) *theater and communications educator*
Monachino, Francis Leonard *music educator*

MAINE

Bangor
†Libbey, Robert David *television producer*

Blue Hill Falls
Stookey, Noel Paul *folksinger, composer*

Boothbay Harbor
Lenthall, Franklyn *theatre historian*

Brunswick
Schwartz, Elliott Shelling *composer, author, music educator*

Castine
Davis, Peter Frank *filmmaker, author*

Gouldsboro
Wexler, Ginia Davis *singer, association executive*

Monmouth
Carlson, Marsha George *performing company executive*

Portland
Shimada, Toshiyuki *orchestra conductor, music director*
Simmonds, Rae Nichols *musician, educator*

Surry
Sopkin, George *cellist, music educator*

MARYLAND

Annapolis
Holmberg, Lawrence Oscar, Jr. *documentary film producer, photographer, writer*

Baltimore
†Gidwitz, John David *symphony orchestra executive*
Harrison, Michael *opera company executive*
Ivey, Jean Eichelberger *composer*
Yannuzzi, William A(nthony) *conductor*
Zinman, David Joel *conductor*

Bethesda
Mastny-Fox, Catherine Louise *administrator, consultant*

Chestertown
Clarke, Garry Evans *composer, educator, musician, administrator*

College Park
Moss, Lawrence Kenneth *composer, educator*

Davidsonville
Mahaffey, Redge Allan *movie producer, director, writer*

Gaithersburg
Whallon, Evan Arthur, Jr. *orchestra conductor*

Hagerstown
Tuckwell, Barry Emmanuel *musician, music educator*

Lutherville Timonium
Hambleton, Thomas Edward *theatrical producer*

Olney
Aylward, Thomas James, Jr. *communication arts and theatre educator*
Graham, William Howard *theatre producer, consultant*

Takoma Park
Carpenter, Mary Chapin *singer, songwriter*

Towson
Mark, Michael Laurence *music educator*

Wheaton
Whiddon, Jerry B. *artistic director, actor, educator*

MASSACHUSETTS

Allston
Bley, Carla Borg *jazz composer*
Metheny, Patrick Bruce *musician*
Sanders, Pharoah *saxophonist, composer*

Amherst
Bestor, Charles Lemon *composer, educator*
Brandon, Liane *filmmaker, educator*
Donohue, Therese Brady *artistic director, choreographer, designer*

Boston
Armand, Patrick *dancer*
Bauer, Elaine Louise *ballet dancer*
Cassilly, Richard *tenor, voice educator*
Cogan, Robert David *composer, school official*
Curtin, Phyllis *music educator, former dean, operatic singer*
Dana, Jerilyn *ballet company administrator*
Dederer, William Bowne *music educator, dean*
Di Domenica, Robert Anthony *musician, composer*
Gang, Stephen R. *motion picture executive, consultant*
Haas, Kenneth Gregg *orchestra executive*
Hampton, Henry Eugene *film and television producer*
Harvey, Les *composer, producer*
Hoyt, Herbert Austin Aikins *television producer*
Jochum, Veronica *pianist*
†Lockhart, Keith Alan *conductor*
MacCombie, Bruce Franklin *composer, college administrator*
Marks, Bruce *artistic director, choreographer*
†Maso, Michael Harvey *managing director*
McPhee, Jonathan *music director, conductor*
Miller, J. Philip *television producer, director, educator*
Moriarty, John *opera administrator, artistic director*
Rotenberg, Sheldon *violinist*
Row, Peter L. *musician, educator*
Totenberg, Roman *violinist, music educator*
Verrot, Pascal *conductor, educator*
Young, Laura *dance educator, choreographer*

Brookline
Blake, Ran *jazz pianist, composer*
Krasner, Louis *concert violinist*

Cambridge
Daniels, Ronald George *theater director*
de Varon, Lorna Cooke *choral conductor*
Epstein, David Mayer *composer, conductor*
Erdely, Stephen Lajos *music educator*
Harbison, John *composer*
†Jones, Cherry *actress*
Langstaff, John Meredith *musician*
Martino, Donald James *composer, educator*
†Morris, Errol M. *filmmaker*
Orchard, Robert John *theater producer, educator*
Pinkham, Daniel *composer*
Rands, Bernard *composer, educator*
Russell, George Allen *composer, musicologist*
Sims, Ezra *composer*
Wiseman, Frederick *filmmaker*
Wunderlich, Renner *film producer, cinematographer*

Charlestown
Armstrong, Nancy L. *soprano, voice coach*

Dedham
Firth, Everett Joseph *timpanist*
Magner, Jerome Allen *entertainment company executive*

Framingham
Bogard, Carole Christine *lyric soprano*

Lenox
Curtis, William Edgar *conductor, composer*

Marblehead
Zawinul, Josef *bandleader, composer, keyboardist, synthesist*

Marstons Mills
Vila, Robert Joseph *television host, designer, real estate developer*

Medford
Anderson, Thomas Jefferson, Jr. *composer, educator*
Burnim, Kalman Aaron *theatre educator emeritus*
Senelick, Laurence Philip *theatre educator, director, writer*

Nantucket
Rorem, Ned *composer, author*

Natick
Gomberg, Sydelle *dancer educator*

Newton
Caldwell, Sarah *opera producer, conductor, stage director and administrator*
Zander, Benjamin *conductor, educator*

Newton Center
Schuller, Gunther Alexander *composer*

North Dartmouth
Dace, Tish *drama educator*
Noel, Barbara Hughes McMurtry *music educator*

Northampton
Naegele, Philipp Otto *violinist, violist, music educator*

Plymouth
Gregory, Dick *comedian, civil rights activist*

Reading
McKinley, William Thomas *composer, performer, educator*

Stockbridge
Storch, Arthur *theater director*

Sudbury
Freund, Mitchell David *cable television executive, producer, director*

Truro
Falk, Lee Harrison *performing arts executive, cartoonist*

Waltham
Berger, Arthur Victor *music educator, composer, critic*
Boykan, Martin *composer, music educator*
†Shapero, Harold (Samuel) *composer, pianist, educator*
Titcomb, Caldwell *music and theatre historian*
Wyner, Yehudi *composer, pianist, conductor, educator*

Williamstown
Shainman, Irwin *music educator, musician*

MICHIGAN

Ann Arbor
Bassett, Leslie Raymond *composer, educator*
Bolcom, William Elden *musician, composer, educator, pianist*
Boylan, Paul Charles *music educator, academic administrator*
Buyse, Leone Karena *orchestral musician, educator*
Finney, Ross Lee *composer*
Lillya, Clifford Peter *musician, educator*
Nugent, Theodore Anthony *musician*
Rosseels, Gustave Alois *music educator*
Scharp-Radovic, Carol Ann *choreographer, classical ballet educator, artistic director*
Sparling, Peter David *dancer, dance educator*

Battle Creek
Starrett, Pamela Elizabeth *symphony executive director, violinist, conductor*

Bloomfield Hills
Haidostian, Alice Berberian *concert pianist, civic volunteer and fundraiser*

Coldwater
Spittle, James Pratt *arts administrator*

Detroit
Calarco, N. Joseph *theater educator*
Di Chiera, David *performing arts impresario*
DuBois, Melodee Ann *performing company executive*
Jarvi, Neeme *conductor*
Young, Gordon Ellsworth *composer, organist*

East Lansing
Johnson, Theodore Oliver, Jr. *musician, educator*
Kirk, Edgar Lee *musician, educator*

Flint
Diemecke, Enrique Arturo *conductor*

Grand Rapids
Arthur, Charthel Estner *artistic director*
Comet, Catherine *conductor*
Hardy, Michael C. *performing arts administrator*
Smith, Peter Wilson *symphony orchestra administrator*

Kalamazoo
Zupko, Ramon *composer, music professor*

Lansing
Kluge, Len H. *director, actor, theater educator*

Rochester
Daniels, David Wilder *conductor, music educator*

Saginaw
Najar, Leo Michael *conductor, arranger, educator*

Southfield
Makupson, Amyre Porter *television station executive*

MINNESOTA

Bloomington
Smith, Henry Charles, III *symphony orchestra conductor*

Duluth
Coffman, Phillip Hudson *music educator, arts administrator*

Mankato
Hustoles, Paul John *theater educator*

Minneapolis
Anderson, Clyde Bailey *musician, educator*
Busa, Stephen K. *artistic director*
Desbois, Barbra Berlovitz *artistic director, actor*
Fetler, Paul *composer*
Fleezanis, Jorja Kay *violinist, educator*
†Hyslop, David Johnson *arts administrator*
Martenson, Edward Allen *theater manager*
Miller, John William, Jr. *bassoonist*
Robins, Michael Harry *theater executive producing director*
Skrowaczewski, Stanislaw *conductor, composer*
Ware, D. Clifton *singer, educator*
Webb, Martha Jeanne *film producer*

Moorhead
Revzen, Joel *conductor*

Northfield
Sostek, Edward Leon *theater educator, director*

Saint Paul
Assink, Brent E. *performing arts executive*
Best, Eugene Crawford, Jr. *musician*
Corn, Joseph Edward, Jr. *arts management consultant*
Paulus, Stephen Harrison *composer*
Tecco, Romuald Gilbert Louis Joseph *violinist, concertmaster*

White Bear Lake
Gutchē, Gene *composer*

MISSISSIPPI

Hattiesburg
Wood, Vivian Poates *mezzo soprano, voice educator*

Jackson
Fulmer, (Mary) Jeannine *broadcasting executive*
Pearce, Colman Cormac *conductor, pianist, composer*
Reid-Petty, Jane *artistic director, actor, playwright*

MISSOURI

Arrow Rock
Bollinger, Michael *artistic director*

Branson
Tillis, Mel(vin) *musician, songwriter*
Williams, Andy *entertainer*

Columbia
Archer, Stephen Murphy *theater educator*

Joplin
Harris, Robert A. *music educator*

Kansas City
Bolender, Todd *choreographer*
†Cohen, Martin D. *ballet company administrator*
Cook, Bart R. *dancer*
Costin, James D. *performing arts company executive*
Patterson, Russell *conductor, opera executive*

Liberty
Harriman, Richard Lee *performing arts administrator, educator*

Maryland Heights
Dokoudovsky, Nina Ludmila *dance educator*

Saint Louis
Beckman, Tamela Jean (T.J. Wright) *disc jockey, entertainer*
Ehrlich, Ava *television executive producer*
Graham, Colin *stage director*
Slatkin, Leonard Edward *conductor, music director, pianist*
Stewart, John Harger *music educator*
†Vonk, Hans *conductor*

Springfield
Orms, Howard Raymond *dramatics educator*
Spicer, Holt Vandercook *speech and theater educator*

Warrensburg
Smith, Dolores Maxine Plunk *dancer, educator*

Wentzville
Berry, Chuck (Charles Edward Anderson Berry) *singer, composer*

MONTANA

Billings
Barnea, Uri N. music director, conductor, composer, violinist
Pihlaja, Maxine Muriel Mead orchestra executive

Missoula
Knowles, William Leroy (Bill Knowles) television news producer, journalism educator

NEBRASKA

Lincoln
†Dixon, Wheeler Winston film and video studies educator, writer

Omaha
Hangen, Bruce Boyer conductor, music director
Larson, Roberta M. children's theater director
Schmidman, Jo Ann artistic director

NEVADA

Las Vegas
Ann-Margret, (Ann-Margret Olsson) actress, performer
Atkins, Cholly (Charles Atkinson) choreographer, consultant
Capelle, Madelene Carole opera singer, educator, music therapist
Goulet, Robert Gerard singer, actor
Healy, Mary (Mrs. Peter Lind Hayes) singer, actress
Knight, Gladys (Maria) singer
Lewis, Jerry (Joseph Levitch) comedian
Shields, Brooke Christa Camille actress, model
Wiemer, Robert Ernest film and television producer, writer, director

NEW HAMPSHIRE

Exeter
†Saltonstall, Cecilia Drinker musician

Hanover
Dodge, Charles Malcolm composer, music educator
Hill, Errol Gaston drama educator, director, author
Sabinson, Mara Beth theatre educator, director, actress
Wolff, Christian composer, music and classics educator

Lyme
Darion, Joe librettist, lyricist

Plymouth
Swift, Robert Frederic music educator

Walpole
Burns, Kenneth Lauren filmmaker, historian

NEW JERSEY

Andover
Klein, Joseph Michelman musical director

Camden
Polin, Claire musician

Clifton
Sheehan, Deborah Ann radio station and theater executive

Denville
Fisher, Sharon Mary musician

East Brunswick
Mooney, William Piatt actor

Englewood
Bullough, John Frank organist, music educator
Zwilich, Ellen Taaffe composer

Florham Park
Aden, Laura performing arts association administrator

Fords
Brown, James singer, broadcasting executive

Fort Lee
Houston, Whitney vocalist, recording artist
Ramsey, Douglas Kenneth television anchor, journalist

Glen Ridge
Bracken, Eddie (Edward Vincent) actor, director, writer, singer, artist

Madison
Monte, Bonnie J. performing company executive
†Stotts, Michael W. theatrical producer

Maplewood
Weston, Randy (Randolph Edward Weston) pianist, composer

Medford
Sanders, Phyllis Aden retired radio and television broadcaster

Millburn
Cohen, Geoffrey Merrill theater executive

Montclair
†Griffith, Nanci singer, songwriter
Walker, George Theophilus, Jr. composer, pianist, music educator

New Brunswick
†Ferris, Harris Nichols ballet company director, dancer, educator
Hurst, Gregory Squire artistic director, director, producer
Lettvin, Theodore concert pianist
†Webre, Septime ballet company artistic director, choreographer
Yttrehus, Rolv Berger composer, educator

Newark
Jones, Etta singer
Morgenstern, Dan Michael jazz historian, educator, editor
Silipigni, Alfredo opera conductor

Newfield
McKee, Mary Elizabeth producer

Parlin
Chernow, Jay Howard music industry executive

Princeton
Estey, Audree Phipps artistic director
Levy, Kenneth music educator
Spies, Claudio composer, educator
Westergaard, Peter Talbot composer, music educator

Ridgewood
Fokine, Irine ballet educator

River Vale
Moderacki, Edmund Anthony music educator, conductor

Rockaway
Laine, Cleo (Clementina Dinah Dankworth) singer

Rutherford
Law, Janet Mary music educator

Secaucus
Pinsker, Penny Collias (Pangeota Pinsker) television producer

Trenton
Prusinowski, Julie Ellen artistic director

Warren
Maull, George Marriner music director, conductor

West Orange
Berman, Mona S. actress, playwright, theatrical director and producer

Wood Ridge
Castagnetta, Grace Sharp pianist, piano educator

NEW MEXICO

Albuquerque
Evans, Bill (James William Evans) dancer, choreographer, educator, arts administrator
Shedd, Ben Alvin film producer, director, production company executive
Stulberg, Neal Howard conductor, pianist

Corrales
Hamilton, Jerald musician

Portales
Paschke, Donald Vernon music educator

Santa Fe
Ballard, Louis Wayne composer
Baustian, Robert Frederick conductor
Brockway, Merrill LaMonte television producer and director
Crosby, John O'Hea conductor, opera manager
Gaddes, Richard performing arts administrator
Hawkanson, David Robert theater managing director
Mann, Herbie flutist

Taos
Murphey, Michael Martin country western singer, songwriter

NEW YORK

Amherst
Coover, James Burrell music educator

Astoria
Koszarski, Richard film historian, writer
McCormick, Douglas Walter cable, broadcast executive

Auburn
Sayles, Edward Thomas theatrical producer

Bayside
Zinn, William violinist, composer, business executive

Beacon
Flagello, Ezio Domenico basso

Bedford Hills
Previn, Andre composer, conductor

Bronx
Mittler, Diana (Diana Mittler-Battipaglia) music educator and administrator, pianist
Sherman, Judith Dorothy producer, recording company owner, recording engineer
Sprecher, Baron Baron William pianist, composer, conductor, diplomat

Bronxville
Biscardi, Chester composer, educator
Farber, Viola Anna dancer, choreographer, educator
Schönberg, Bessie dance educator

Brooklyn
Carter, Betty (Lillie Mae Jones) jazz singer, songwriter
Castro, Nikki Marie dancer
Hopkins, Karen art administrator
Jarman, Joseph jazz musician
Jenkins, Leroy violinist, composer
Lee, Spike (Shelton Jackson Lee) filmmaker
Lichtenstein, Harvey performing arts executive
Silver, Horace Ward Martin Tavares composer, pianist

Buffalo
Manes, Stephen Gabriel concert pianist, educator
Valdes, Maximiano conductor

Cambridge
Guma, Greg William producer, writer, administrator

Cooperstown
Evans, Abigail Winifred theatrical executive
†Jackson, Felicity Anne performing arts organization administrator

Cornwall
Gentile, Melanie Marie record producer, marketing and public relations consultant, writer

Craryville
Figols, Priscilla Gordon de soprano

Denver
Brockway, Amie artistic director

Dobbs Ferry
Kapp, Richard P. conductor, arts administrator

East Hampton
Dello Joio, Norman composer
Paxton, Tom songwriter, entertainer, author

East Setauket
Layton, Billy Jim composer

East Syracuse
Duffy, Nancy Keogh television broadcast professional

Fairport
Haylett, Margaret Wendy television director, engineer

Flushing
Grossman, Julius conductor
Moriarty, Michael actor
Smaldone, Edward Michael composer

Forest Hills
Lipkin, Seymour pianist, conductor, educator
Polakoff, Abe baritone
Prager, Alice Heinecke music company executive
Silver, Sheila Jane composer, music educator

Fredonia
Jordan, Robert concert pianist, educator

Geneva
Berta, Joseph Michel music educator, musician

Germantown
Rollins, (Theodore) Sonny composer, musician

Gilbertsville
Roos, Casper actor

Glen Head
†Sutherland, Denise Jackson ballerina

Great Neck
Brand, Oscar folksinger, author, educator
Kraft, Leo Abraham composer
Lees, Benjamin composer

Greenfield Center
Conant, Robert Scott harpsichordist, music educator

Hastings On Hudson
Wolfe, Stanley composer, educator

Hempstead
Chapman, Ronald Thomas musician, educator

Hewlett
Wolff, Eleanor Blunk actress

Hollis
Vai, Steve guitarist

Hopewell Junction
Walden, Stanley Eugene composer, clarinetist

Irvington
Angelakis, Manos G(eorge) filmmaker, communications executive

Ithaca
Hsu, John Tseng Hsin music educator, cellist, gambist, barytonist, conductor
Husa, Karel Jaroslav composer, conductor, educator

Jamaica
Desser, Maxwell Milton artist, art director, filmstrip producer

Jeffersonville
Wooddell, Philo Glenn fine arts educator, radio broadcaster and producer

Larchmont
Swire, Edith Wypler music educator, musician, violist, violinist

Lindenhurst
Farrell-Logan, Vivian actress

Long Eddy
Hoiby, Lee composer, concert pianist

Maspeth
Wykurz, Ireneusz Wojciech stage director, actor

Massapequa Park
Zizzo, Alicia concert pianist

New Kingston
Maffei, Dorothy Jean theatre manager

New Rochelle
Klein, Arthur Luce theatrical company executive
Merrill, Robert baritone

New York
Aaron, Lynn dancer
Abraham, F(ahrid) Murray actor, educator
Abrams, Muhal Richard pianist, composer
Adams, Joey comedian, author
Adler, Richard composer, lyricist
Aiello, Danny actor
Ailes, Roger Eugene television producer, consultant
Akalaitis, JoAnne theater director, writer, actress
Akiyoshi, Toshiko jazz composer, pianist
Alexopoulos, Helene ballet dancer
Allen, Betty (Mrs. Ritten Edward Lee, III) mezzo-soprano
Allen, Nancy musician, educator
Altman, Robert B. film director, writer, producer
Alvary, Lorenzo bass
Amara, Lucine opera and concert singer
Amos, Tori singer, musician
Amram, David Werner composer, conductor, musician
Anderson, Laurie performance artist
Arkin, Alan Wolf actor
Armitage, Karole dancer, choreographer
Arnold, Eddy singer
†Arnold, Skip performance artist
Arpino, Gerald Peter performing company executive
Asakawa, Takako dancer, dance teacher
Ashley, Elizabeth actress
Ashley, Merrill ballerina
†Atwood, Colleen costume designer
†Aucoin, Kevyn J. make-up artist
Ax, Emanuel pianist
†Azenberg, Emanuel theatrical producer
Babyface, (Kenny Edmunds) popular musician
Bacall, Lauren actress
Baker-Riker, Margery television executive
Barbee, Victor ballet dancer
Barber, Russell Brooks Butler television producer
Barker, Charles conductor
Barker, Edwin Bogue musician
Barsalona, Frank Samuel theatrical agent
Baryshnikov, Mikhail ballet dancer
Basden, Cameron ballet mistress, dancer
Battle, Kathleen Deanna soprano
Baudendistel, Daniel dancer
Beatty, Talley choreographer
Becofsky, Arthur Luke arts administrator, writer
Bedford, Brian actor
Bednar, Rudy Gerard television producer, director
Beeson, Jack Hamilton composer, educator, writer
Behrens, Hildegard soprano
Belkin, Boris David violinist
Belle, Regina popular musician
Bellson, Louis Paul drummer
Benichou, Pascal dancer
Bennett, Tony (Anthony Dominick Benedetto) entertainer
Benton, Nicholas theater producer
Benton, Robert film director, screenwriter
Berezin, Tanya artistic director, actress
Bergeret, Albert Hamilton artistic director, conductor, singer, theatrical technician
Bergonzi, Carlo tenor, voice educator
Berlind, Roger Stuart stage and film producer
Berman, Lazar pianist
Berman, Martin M. television producer
Bernardi, Mario conductor
Bernstein, Elliot Louis television executive
Berry, Walter baritone
Betts, Dicky (Richard Forrest Betts) guitarist, songwriter, vocalist
Bikel, Theodore actor, singer
Birkenhead, Thomas Bruce theatrical producer and manager, educator
Birnhak, Sandra Jean film company executive
Bishop, André artistic director, producer
Black, Shawn Morgado, . dancer
Blades, Ruben singer, songwriter, composer
Boal, Peter Cadbury dancer
Bocca, Julio dancer
Boelzner, Gordon orchestral conductor
Boggs, Gil principal ballet dancer
Bonazzi, Elaine Claire mezzo-soprano
Bond, Victoria Ellen conductor, composer
Bon Jovi, Jon rock singer, composer
Bono, (Paul Hewson) singer, songwriter
Borda, Deborah symphony orchestra executive
Borge, Victor entertainer, comedian, pianist
Bosco, Philip Michael actor
†Boston, Gretha mezzo-soprano, actress
Bowden, Sally Ann choreographer, teacher, dancer
Bradford, Robert Ernest motion picture producer
Braun, Craig Allen producer
Braxton, Toni popular musician
Brechner, Stanley artistic director
Bregman, Martin film producer
Brendel, Alfred concert pianist
Brewster, Robert Gene concert singer, educator
Brinkley, Christie model
Brooks, Tyrone dancer
Brothers, Joyce Diane television personality, psychologist
Brown, David motion picture producer, writer
Brown, Trisha dancer
Browning, John pianist
Bumbry, Grace soprano
Burke, Chris actor
Burrell, Kenneth Earl guitarist, composer
Bush, Kate (Catherine Bush) singer, songwriter
Button, Richard Totten television and stage producer, former figure skating champion
Byer, Diana performing arts company executive
Caldwell, Zoe actress, director
Caliban, Richard Allen artistic director
†Campbell, Alan actor
Campbell, Naomi model
Cantrell, Lana actress, singer
Capalbo, Carmen Charles director, producer
Caples, Richard James dance company executive, lawyer

Carelli, Gabor Paul opera singer
Cariou, Len Joseph actor, director
Carlson, Marvin Albert theater educator
Carpenter, Patricia music educator
Carreras, José tenor
Carver, Brent actor
Cash, Rosanne country singer, songwriter
Castel, Nico tenor, educator
Cazeaux, Isabelle Anne Marie retired musicology educator
†Chaitkin, David composer
Channing, Stockard (Susan Stockard) actress
Chapman, Wes dancer
Charnin, Martin theatrical director, lyricist, producer
†Chaya, Masazumi dancer
Checker, Chubby (Ernest Evans) musician
Chester, Giraud television executive
Christensen, Dieter ethnomusicologist
Chryst, Gary ballet dancer
Clapton, Eric musician
Clark, Joseph Gilbert opera company executive
Cohen, Selma Jeanne dance historian
Cohn, Sam motion picture and theatrical agent
Coigney, Martha Wadsworth theater executive
Cole, Vinson tenor
Coleman, Cy pianist, composer, producer
Coleman, George Edward tenor, alto and soprano saxophonist
Coleman, Ornette jazz musician
Collins, Judy Marjorie singer, songwriter
Comden, Betty writer, dramatist, lyricist, performer
Comissiona, Sergiu conductor
Como, Perry singer
Conlon, James Joseph conductor
Connick, Harry, Jr. jazz musician, actor, singer
Conway, Kevin actor, director
Cooper, Alice (Vincent Furnier) popular musician
Corigliano, John Paul composer
Corry, Carl dancer
Corsaro, Frank Andrew theater, musical and opera director
Cossotto, Fiorenza mezzo-soprano
Crawford, Cindy model
Crivello, Anthony actor
†Cruz, Celia vocalist
Crystal, Lester Martin television producer
Culhane, Shamus producer, author
Cunningham, Merce dancer
Curtis, Paul James American mime
Dakin, Christine Whitney dancer, educator
Daldry, Stephen theatrical director
Dale, Jim actor
Dalrymple, Jean Van Kirk theatrical producer, publicist, author
d'Amboise, Jacques Joseph dancer, choreographer
Danilova, Alexandra ballet dancer, choreographer
Danitz, Marilynn Patricia choreographer
Darling, Robert Edward designer, stage director
Darvarova, Elmira violinist, concertmaster
David, Hal lyricist
Davidovich, Bella pianist
Davidson, Joy Elaine mezzo-soprano
Davies, Dennis Russell conductor, music director, pianist
Davies, Martha Hill dance educator
Davis, Andrew Frank conductor
†Davis, Anthony composer, pianist, educator
Davis, Leonard violist
Dawn, Deborah dancer
de Cou, Emil conductor
De Johnette, Jack musician
de la Falaise, Lucie model
DeLay, Dorothy (Mrs. Edward Newhouse) violinist, educator
Demme, Jonathan director, producer, writer
Dempster, (Frank) Curt artistic director, producer
Dennis, Robert (Arthur) composer, educator
Diamond, David Jeremy performing arts company administrator, consultant
Dichter, Misha concert pianist
Dicterow, Glenn Eugene violinist
Di Franco, Loretta Elizabeth lyric coloratura soprano
Diggins, Peter Sheehan ballet company administrator
Dillon, Matt actor
Dispeker, Thea artists' representative
Dodson, Daryl Theodore ballet administrator, arts consultant
Domingo, Placido tenor
Donahue, Phil television personality
Dowell, Anthony James ballet dancer
Downes, Edward Olin Davenport musicologist, critic, radio broadcaster
Downs, Hugh Malcolm radio and television broadcaster
Druck, Mark David director, producer, writer
Druckman, Jacob Raphael composer
Duchin, Peter Oelrichs musician
Duddy, Joan Frances performing arts administrator, dancer
Duffy, Nicole dancer
Dufour, Val (Albert Valery Dufour) actor
Dukakis, Olympia actress
Dulaine, Pierre ballroom dancer
Dunham, Christine dancer
Dunleavy, Rosemary ballet dancer
Dunn, Susan singer
†Durang, Christopher actor, playwright
Dylan, Bob (Robert Allen Zimmerman) singer, composer
Eger, Joseph conductor, music director
Ellington, Mercer Kennedy trumpeter, conductor, composer
Emick, Jarrod actor
Englander, Roger Leslie television producer, director
Entremont, Philippe conductor, pianist
Epstein, Matthew performing company director
Eschenbach, Christoph conductor, pianist
Evangelista, Linda model
Evans, Jerry Norman television director
Everhart, Angie model
Everly, Jack conductor
Ewing, Maria Louise soprano
Fabio, (Fabio Lanzoni) model
Fairbanks, Douglas Elton, Jr. actor, producer, writer, corporation director
Falletta, Jo Ann musician
Farberman, Harold conductor, composer
Farley, Carole soprano
Farrell, Eileen soprano
Fates, Joseph Gilbert television producer
Feist, Gene theater director
Feld, Eliot dancer, choreographer
Ferra, Max stage director
Ferri, Alessandra Maria ballet dancer
Fetter, Theodore Henry entertainment consultant
Feuer, Cy motion picture and theatrical producer, director
Field, Crystal artistic director, actor
Fiorato, Hugo conductor
Fischer, Lindsay Koehler dancer
Fisher, Jules Edward producer, lighting designer, theatre consultant
Flack, Roberta singer
Flatt, Ernest Orville choreographer, director
†Fleming, Renée L. opera singer
Fodor, Eugene Nicholas concert violinist
Fontana, Thomas Michael producer, scriptwriter
Ford, Eileen Otte (Mrs. Gerard W. Ford) modeling agency executive
Foreman, Laura dancer, choreographer, conceptual artist, writer, educator
Foreman, Richard theater director, playwright
Forst, Judith Doris mezzo-soprano
Frankel, Gene theater director, author, producer, educator
Frassetto, Floriana Domina performer, choreographer, costume designer
Freizer, Louis A. radio news producer
Fricke, Janie (Jane Marie Fricke) singer
Friend, Jonathan Joseph opera administrator
Frisell-Schröder, Sonja Bettie opera producer, stage director
Fritz, Joanie M. theater director, actor
Fryer, Robert Sherwood theatrical producer
Fugate, Judith ballet dancer
Gaines, Boyd actor
Galway, James flutist
Gamson, Annabelle dancer
Gates, Jodie dancer
Gattie, Erma Charlotte opera singer
Gazzara, Ben actor
Gergiev, Valery artistic director, conductor
Gersten, Bernard theatrical producer
Giannini, Cynthia dancer
Gibb, Barry vocalist, songwriter
Gifford, Kathie Lee television personality, singer
Gilbert, Pia S. musical educator, composer
Gill, Vince country musician, singer
Glass, Philip composer, musician
Glazer, Esther violinist
Goldsmith, Merwin actor, theater director
Goodacre, Jill model
Goode, Richard Stephen pianist, educator
Gordon, David Jamieson tenor
Gottlieb, Morton Edgar theatrical and film producer
Graff, Randy actress
Graffin, Guillaume ballet dancer
Grant, Merrill Theodore producer
Grappelli, Stephane jazz violinist
Gray, Diane dancer, choreographer
Greco, Jose choreographer
Green, Al soul and gospel singer
Greene, Shecky entertainer
Grillo, Joann Danielle mezzo-soprano
Grizzard, George actor
Grose, Molly Pickering performing company executive
Grove, Barry theater executive
Guettel, Henry Arthur retired arts executive
Gurin, Meg dancer
Hackett, Buddy actor
Hadley, Jerry opera singer
Hagen, Uta Thyra actress
Hall, Daryl musician
Hancock, Gerre Edward musician
Hardy, Gordon Alfred music educator, music school president
Harkarvy, Benjamin artistic director
Harnick, Sheldon Mayer lyricist
Harrell, Lynn Morris cellist
Harris, Ed(ward Allen) actor
Harris, Julie (Ann) actress
†Harris, Rosemary Ann actress
Harrow, Nancy (Mrs. Jan Krukowski) jazz singer, songwriter, editor
Harry, Deborah Ann singer
Harth, Sidney musician, educator
Harvey, Cynthia ballet dancer
Hasso, Signe Eleonora Cecilia actress
Hastings, Baird conductor, music educator, writer
Hastings, Deborah bass guitarist
Hastings, Donald Francis actor, writer
Haubert, Alaine ballet dancer
Hayes, Isaac rhythm and blues singer, composer
†Heald, Anthony actor
†Hearn, George actor
Hebert, Bliss Edmund opera director
Hedlund, Ronald baritone
Henderson, Joe jazz tenor saxophonist
Henderson, Skitch (Lyle Russell Cedric) pianist, conductor
Herman, Jerry composer, lyricist
Herrera, Paloma dancer
Herstand, Theodore theatre artist, educator
Hetfield, James singer
Hewitt, Don S. television news producer
Heyward, Andrew John television producer
Hiatt, John musician, country, popular
Hill, George Roy film director
Hill, Robert Arthur ballet dancer
Hirsch, Judd actor
Hlinka, Nichol dancer
Hoffman, Dustin Lee actor
Holder, Geoffrey Lamont dancer, actor, choreographer, director
Hollander, Lorin pianist
Holliday, Jennifer Yvette singer, actress
Holliday, Polly Dean actress
Holloway, David baritone
Horn, Shirley vocalist, pianist
Horne, Marilyn mezzo-soprano
Houghton, Charles Norris stage director, author, educator
Howard, David ballet school administrator
Hubbe, Nikolaj dancer
Huffstodt, Karen opera singer, recitalist
Humperdinck, Engelbert (Arnold George Dorsey) singer
Hunter, Rachel model
Hupp, Robert Martin artistic director, educator
Hytner, Nicholas theatrical director
Ivory, James Francis film director
Jackson, Anne (Anne Jackson Wallach) actress
Jackson, Joe musician, singer, composer, songwriter
Jacobs, Bernard B. theater executive
Jacobs, Jim actor, playwright, composer, lyricist
Jaffe, Susan ballerina
Jagger, Mick (Michael Philip Jagger) singer, musician
Jamison, Judith dancer
Jefferson, Denise dance school director
Jenkins, Newell conductor
Joel, Billy (William Martin Joel) musician
Johansen, David (Buster Poindexter) popular musician, actor
Johnson, James M. orchestra executive
Johnson, Kate dancer
Johnson, Virginia Alma Fairfax ballerina
Jones, Bill T. dancer, choreographer
Jones, Rickie Lee singer, songwriter
Jung, Doris dramatic soprano
Kalmanoff, Martin composer
Kamlot, Robert performing arts executive
Kander, John Harold composer
Kaplan, Richard James producer, director, writer, educator, consultant
Karchin, Louis Samuel composer
Kassel, Virginia Weltmer television producer, writer
Keene, Christopher conductor, author, librettist, musician
Keeshan, Bob television producer, actor
Kellman, Barnet Kramer film, stage and television director
Kellogg, Cal Stewart, II conductor, composer
Kelm, Linda opera singer
Kent, Julie Ann ballet dancer, actress, model
Kent, Linda Gail dancer
†Kernis, Aaron Jay composer
Khan, Chaka (Yvette Marie Stevens) singer
Khanzadian, Vahan tenor
Kidd, Michael (Milton Greenwald) choreographer, director
Kinberg, Judy television producer, director
King, B. B. (Riley B. King) singer, guitarist
King, Carole songwriter, singer
King, Woodie, Jr. producer, actor, director
Kirkland, Gelsey dancer
Kirstein, Lincoln ballet promoter
Kistler, Darci Anna ballet dancer
Kitt, Eartha Mae actress, singer
Klein, Robert comedian, actor
Kness, Richard Maynard tenor
Kolpakova, Irina dancer, educator, coach
Kono, Toshihiko cellist
Kozlova, Valentina ballerina
Kramer, Jonathan Donald composer
Krawitz, Herman Everett television producer
Krone, Gerald Sidney theatrical and television producer
Krosnick, Joel cellist
Krupska, Danya (Mrs. Ted Thurston) theater director, choreographer
Kuriansky, Judy television and radio talk show host, reporter, psychologist, writer, lecturer
†Lachman, Edward cinematographer
Lacy, Steve jazz musician
La Fosse, Robert ballet dancer, choreographer
Landesman, Heidi set designer
lang, k. d. (Katherine Dawn Lang) country music singer, composer
Lang, Pearl dancer, choreographer
Langham, Michael theatrical director
Lansbury, Edgar George theatrical producer
†Larmore, Jennifer mezzo-soprano
Laufer, Beatrice composer
Leach, Robin producer, writer, television host
Lear, Evelyn soprano
Leavitt, Michael P(aul) performing arts manager and concert producer
Leber, Steven Edward film producer, corporate executive
†LeCompte, Elizabeth theater director
Lee, Dai-Keong composer
LeFrak, Francine theatre and film producer
†Legrand, Michel Jean composer
Leland, Sara ballet dancer
Lemesh, Nicholas Thomas designer, filmmaker
Lennox, Annie rock musician
Leppard, Raymond John conductor, harpsichordist
Leritz, Lawrence choreographer, dancer, actor
Letterman, David television personality, comedian, writer
†Levine, Douglas Gary music industry executive
Levine, James conductor, pianist, artistic director
Levy, Marvin David composer
Lewis, Allan conductor, ballet company music director
Lewis, Jerry Lee country-rock singer, musician
Libin, Paul theatre executive, producer
Liebermann, Lowell composer, pianist, conductor
Lightfoot, Gordon Meredith singer, songwriter
Limbaugh, Rush Hudson radio and talk show host
Lincoln, Abbey (Anna Marie Woolridge, Gaby Lee, Aminata Moseka) jazz singer, actress
Livengood, Victoria Ann opera singer
Livingston, Jay Harold composer, lyricist
LL Cool J, (James Todd Smith) rap singer, actor
Lockett, Pierre dancer
Loney, Glenn Meredith drama educator
Lopez, Lourdes ballerina
Lortel, Lucille theatrical producer
†Lottman, Evan film editor
Loudon, Dorothy actress
Louis, Murray dancer, choreographer, dance teacher
Loveless, Patty (Patty Ramey) country music singer
Lubovitch, Lar dancer, choreographer
Lucas, James E(vans) operatic director
Lucci, Susan actress
Luders, Adam ballet dancer
Ludgin, Chester Hall baritone, actor
Luening, Otto composer, conductor, flutist, educator
Lumet, Sidney film director
Lunden, Joan television personality
LuPone, Patti actress
Ma, Yo Yo cellist
Macpherson, Elle model
Macurdy, John Edward basso
Madonna, (Madonna Louise Veronica Ciccone) singer, actress
†Maher, Bill talk show host, comedian, producer
Mahoney, John actor
Malina, Judith actress, director, producer, writer
†Malkin, Barry film editor, consultant
Malle, Louis film director
Maltby, Richard Eldridge, Jr. theater director, lyricist
Mamlok, Ursula composer, educator
Mann, Theodore theatrical producer and artistic director
Mantegna, Joe Anthony actor, playwright
Maraynes, Allan Lawrence filmmaker, television producer
Marceau, Yvonne ballroom dancer
Marsh, Jean Lyndsey Torren actress, writer
†Marshall, Susan artistic director
Martin, Andrea Louise actress, comedienne, writer
Martin, Elliot Edwards theatrical producer
Martins, Nilas dancer
Martins, Peter ballet master, choreographer, dancer
Mason, Jackie comedian, actor
Masur, Kurt conductor
Matalon, Vivian theatrical director
Maxwell, Carla Lena dancer, choreographer, educator
May, Elaine actress, theatre and film director
Mayfield, Curtis Lee musician
Maynard, Parrish ballet dancer
Mazzo, Kay ballet dancer, educator
Mazzola, John William former performing arts center executive, consultant
McDonald, Audra Ann actress
McDormand, Frances actress
McFerrin, Bobby singer, musician, composer and conductor
†McKay, Craig film editor
McKenzie, Kevin Patrick ballet dancer
McKerrow, Amanda ballet dancer
McMenamy, Kristen model
Meadow, Lynne (Carolyn Meadow) theatrical producer and director
Mellencamp, John (John Cougar) singer, songwriter
Menken, Alan composer
Menuhin, Yehudi violinist
Merchant, Ismail Noormohamed film producer
Mester, Jorge conductor
Michaels, Lorne television writer, producer
Midler, Bette singer, entertainer, actress
Midori, (Midori Goto) classical violinist
Millo, Aprile Elizabeth opera singer
Milnes, Sherrill Eustace baritone
Minnelli, Liza singer, actress
Mintz, Shlomo conductor, violist, violinist
Mitchell, Arthur dancer, choreographer, educator
Mitchell, John Dietrich theatre arts institute executive
Monk, Debra actress
Monk, Meredith Jane artistic director, composer, choreographer, film maker, director
Moore, Kathleen dancer
Morris, James Peppler bass
†Morris, John composer, conductor, arranger
Morris, Mark William choreographer
Moseley, Carlos DuPre former music executive, musician
Moss, Kate model
Mossbrucker, Tom dancer
Muller, Jennifer choreographer, dancer
Mulligan, Gerald Joseph (Gerry Mulligan) composer, arranger, musician, songwriter
Muradian, Vazgen composer, viola d'amore player
Murphy, Donna actress
Murphy, Rosemary actress
Murphy, Russell Stephen theater company executive
Namath, Joseph William entertainer, former professional football player
Nash, Graham William singer, composer
Neal, Philip dancer
Nederlander, James Morton theater executive
Nichols, Kyra ballerina
Nicola, James B. stage director, composer, playwright
†Nicola, James C. theater director
Niesen, James Louis theater director
Norman, Jessye soprano
Nugent, Nelle theater, film and television producer
O'Brien, Conan writer, performer, talk show host
O'Brien, Orin Ynez musician, educator
O'Connor, Carroll actor, writer, producer
O'Connor, Sinead singer, songwriter
Ohira, Kazuto theatre company executive, writer
O'Horgan, Thomas Foster composer, director
Oliveira, Elmar violinist
O'Neal, Hank entertainment producer, business owner
Orr, Terrence S. dancer
Ostrum, Dean Gardner actor, writer, calligrapher
Owen, Michael ballet dancer
Oz, Frank (Frank Richard Oznowicz) puppeteer, film director
Ozawa, Seiji conductor, music director
Pacino, Al (Alfredo James Pacino) actor
Pakula, Alan J. producer, director
Pardo, Dominick George (Don Pardo) broadcasting announcer
Parker, Maceo jazz musician, alto saxophone
Parkinson, Georgina ballet mistress
Parks, Gordon Roger Alexander Buchanan film director, author, photographer, composer
Parseghian, Gene talent agent
Parsons, David artistic director, choreographer
Parsons, Estelle actress
Pavarotti, Luciano lyric tenor
Pellegrini, Anna Maria soprano
Penn, Arthur Hiller film and theatre producer
Perahia, Murray pianist
Peress, Maurice symphony conductor, musicologist
Perkins, Leeman Lloyd music educator, musicologist
Perlmutter, Alvin Howard television and film producer
Perry, Douglas opera singer
Peters, Bernadette (Bernadette Lazzara) actress
Peters, Roberta soprano
Peterson, Kirk Charles ballet dancer
Philbin, Regis television personality
Pirner, David musician, songwriter
†Plotnicki, Steven Joel record company executive
Plunkett, Maryann actress
Poor, Peter Varnum producer, director
Porizkova, Paulina model, actress
Porter, Karl Hampton orchestra musical director, conductor
Porter, Stephen Winthrop stage director
Poster, June performing company executive
Price, Leontyne concert and opera singer, soprano
Prince, Harold theatrical producer
Prosky, Robert Joseph actor
Protas, Ron dance company executive
Pryce, Jonathan actor
Queler, Eve conductor
Questel, Mae actress
Quilico, Louis baritone
Quinn, Anthony Rudolph Oaxaca actor, writer, artist
Quintero, Jose theatrical director
Rachleff, Owen Spencer (Owen Spencer Rackleff) actor, author
Raines, Joan Binder literary agent
Rainone, Salvatore Raffaello vocalist
†Rajski, Peggy film director, film producer
Ramey, Samuel Edward bass soloist
†Ramirez, Tina artistic director
Ramsay, Gustavus Remak actor
Ramsier, Paul composer, psychotherapist
Rand, Calvin Gordon arts and education producer and consultant
Randall, Tony (Leonard Rosenberg) actor
Randazzo, Anthony dancer
Randolph, David conductor
Raphael, Sally Jessy talk-show host
†Redden, Nigel A. performing company executive

Reeve, Christopher *actor*
Reich, Steve *composer*
Renick, Kyle *artistic director*
Renvall, Johan *ballet dancer*
Resnik, Regina *operatic singer*
Reyes, Andre *ballet dancer*
Reynolds, Brett W. *managing director, playwright*
Reznikov, Hanon *theater director, actor*
Rhodes, Samuel *violist*
Ricciarelli, Katia *soprano*
Rice, T. Walker *actor, theatre adminstrator*
Richard, Ellen *theater executive*
Richards, Keith *musician*
Richards, Lloyd George *theatrical director, university administrator*
Richardson, David John *ballet dancer, educator*
Richardson, Miranda *actress*
Rivera, Chita (Conchita del Rivero) *actress, singer, dancer*
Rivera, Geraldo *television personality, journalist*
Rizzo, Francis *arts administrator, writer, stage director*
Roach, Maxwell Lemuel *musician*
Robbins, Jerome *choreographer, director*
Roberts, Tony (David Anthony Roberts) *actor*
Robison, Paula Judith *flutist*
Rodriguez, Beatriz *ballerina*
Roerick, William (George) (William Roehrick) *actor, author*
Rollins, Jack *motion picture producer*
Roney, Wallace *musician*
Rosen, Nathaniel Kent *cellist*
Rosenberger, Carol *concert pianist*
Ross, Diana *singer, actress, entertainer, fashion designer*
Rossellini, Isabella *actress, model*
Rostropovich, Mstislav Leopoldovich *musician*
Roy, Melinda *dancer*
Ruckert, Ann Johns *musician, singer*
Rudel, Julius *conductor*
Rysanek, Leonie *soprano*
Saddler, Donald Edward *choreographer, dancer*
Sagami, Kim *dancer*
†Salerno-Sonnenberg, Nadja *violinist*
Salgado, Lissette *dancer*
Salonga, Lea *actress, singer*
Salzman, Eric *artistic director*
Sandler, Jenny *dancer*
Saunders, Arlene *opera singer*
Savich, René *broadway theater executive, producer*
Schechner, Richard *theater director, author, educator*
Scheeder, Louis *theater producer, director, educator*
Schickele, Peter *composer*
Schiffer, Claudia *model*
Schnell, Joseph *dancer*
Schorer, Suki *ballet teacher*
Schroeder, Aaron Harold *songwriter*
Schwartz, Stephen Lawrence *composer, lyricist*
Schwarz, Gerard *conductor, musician*
Sciarratta, Patrick Louis *director, educator, artistic director*
Scofield, John *jazz guitarist*
Scorsese, Martin *film director, writer*
Scott, Willard Herman *radio and television performer*
Scotto, Renata *soprano*
Sedaka, Neil *singer, songwriter*
Seeger, Pete *folk singer, songwriter*
Segal, George *actor*
Seidelman, Susan *film director*
Seltzer, Leo *filmmaker, educator, lecturer*
Seraphine, Danny Peter *drummer*
Serkin, Peter *pianist*
Shaffer, Paul *musician, bandleader*
Shane, Rita *opera singer*
Shattuck, Scott Harlan *performing company executive*
Shaw, (Francis) Harold *performing arts administrator*
Shelley, Carole Augusta *actress*
Shellman, Eddie J. *ballet dancer, teacher, choreographer*
Sherman, Arlene *television producer*
Short, Robert Waltrip (Bobby Short) *entertainer, author*
Shostakovich, Maxim Dmitriyevich *symphonic conductor*
Shull, Richard Bruce *actor*
Sidney, Sylvia (Sophia Kossow) *actress*
Siegel, Marc Monroe *television and film producer, writer, director*
Sills, Beverly (Mrs. Peter B. Greenough) *opera company director, coloratura soprano*
Silver, Joan Micklin *film director, screenwriter*
Silver, Ron *actor, director*
Silvers, Sally *choreographer, performing company executive*
Simmons, Gene *musician*
Simon, Joanna *singer*
Smith, Anna Deavere *actress, playwright*
Smith, Anna Nicole *model*
Smith, James Oscar (Jimmy Smith) *jazz organist*
Smith, Lowell *dancer*
Smith, Malcolm Sommerville *bass*
Sobel, Shepard Michael *artistic director*
Solomon, Maynard Elliott *music historian, former recording company executive*
Solomons, Gus, Jr. (Gustave Martinez) *choreographer, dancer, writer*
Solov, Zachary *choreographer, ballet artist*
Sorel, Claudette Marguerite *pianist*
Soto, Jock *dancer*
Soyer, David *cellist, music educator*
Spacey, Kevin *actor*
Spinella, Stephen *actor*
Springsteen, Bruce *singer, songwriter, guitarist*
Stapp, Olivia Brewer *opera singer*
Stern, Howard Allan *radio disc jockey, television show host*
Stern, Isaac *violinist*
Stills, Stephen *musician, vocalist, composer*
Stilwell, Richard Dale *baritone*
Stoltzman, Richard Leslie *clarinetist*
Storke, William Frederick Joseph *film producer*
Strasfogel, Ian *stage director*
Stratas, Teresa (Anastasia Strataki) *opera singer, soprano*
Stretton, Ross *ballet dancer*
†Stutzmann, Nathalie *classical vocalist*
Summers, Andy (Andrew James Somers) *popular musician*
Swados, Elizabeth A. *composer, director, writer*
Swan, William *actor*
†Sylbert, Richard *production designer, art director*
Taddei, Giuseppe *baritone*
Talmi, Yoav *conductor, composer*
Taylor, Elizabeth Rosemond *actress*
Taylor, Nicole Renée *model*
†Taylor, Patricia *theater company managing director*
Taylor, Paul *choreographer*
Taylor, Paul B. *dancer*
Taylor, Regina *actress*
Tcherkassky, Marianna Alexsavena *ballerina*
Te Kanawa, Kiri *opera and concert singer*
Terborgh, Bert *dancer*
Tetley, Glen *choreographer*
Tharp, Twyla *dancer, choreographer*
Thesing, James J. *arts organization executive*
Thomas, Richard *actor*
Thorne, Francis *composer*
Tillis, Pam *country singer, songwriter*
Tilson Thomas, Michael *symphony conductor*
Townshend, Peter *musician, composer, singer*
Tracey, Margaret *dancer*
Tree, Michael *violinist, violist, educator*
Tune, Tommy (Thomas James Tune) *musical theater director, dancer, choreographer, actor*
†Turk, Patricia Avedon *dance company executive*
Turlington, Christy *model*
Turrentine, Stanley William *musician*
Ulrich, Lars *drummer*
Upbin, Shari *theatrical producer, director, agent, educator*
Uppman, Theodor *concert and opera singer, voice educator*
Upshaw, Dawn *soprano*
Valletta, Amber *model*
Van Halen, Eddie *guitarist, rock musician*
Vedder, Eddie *singer*
Vendela *model*
Verdon, Gwen (Gwyneth Evelyn) *actress, dancer, choreographer*
†Viertel, Jack *theatrical producer, writer*
Volpe, Joseph *opera company administrator*
von Furstenberg, Betsy *actress, writer*
Von Stade, Frederica *mezzo-soprano*
Wadsworth, Charles William *pianist*
Wagner, Alan Cyril *television and film producer*
Walker, Sandra *mezzo-soprano*
Warden, Jack *actor*
Warfield, Gerald Alexander *composer, writer*
Warwick, Dionne *singer*
Waters, Sylvia *dance company artistic director*
Watts, André *concert pianist*
Webb, Veronica *fashion model, journalist*
Weisgall, Hugo David *composer, conductor*
Wenders, Wim *film director*
Wexler, Peter John *producer, director, set designer*
Whelan, Wendy *ballet dancer*
White, John Simon *opera director*
Whitehead, Robert *theatrical producer*
Wiest, Dianne *actress*
Williams, Donald Maxey *dancer, singer, actor*
Williams, Lucinda *country musician*
Williams, Stanley *ballet dancer and teacher*
Williams, Tony *jazz drummer*
Williams, Vanessa *recording artist, actress*
Willis, Gordon *cinematographer*
Wilson, Robert M. *theatrical artist*
Wincenc, Carol *concertizing flutist, educator*
Wittstein, Edwin Frank *stage and film production designer*
Woetzel, Damian Abdo *ballet dancer, educator*
Woitach, Richard *conductor, pianist*
Wolfe, George C. *theater director, producer, playwright*
Wood, Ronald *musician*
Woodman, William E. *theater, opera and television director*
Worth, Irene *actress*
Wright, Jeffrey *actor*
Wuorinen, Charles P. *composer*
Wynette, Tammy *singer*
Yellin, Victor Fell *composer, music educator*
Yeston, Maury *composer, lyricist, educator*
Zaks, Jerry *theatrical director, actor*
Zhu, Ai-Lan *opera singer*
Zschau, Marilyn *singer*
Zukerman, Pinchas *concert violinist, violist, conductor*

Nyack
Hendin, David Bruce *literary agent, author, consultant, numismatist*

Oswego
Nesbitt, Rosemary Sinnett *theatre educator*

Palisades
Cavett, Dick *entertainer*
Krainin, Julian Arthur *film director, producer, writer, cinematographer*

Pittsford
Benson, Warren Frank *composer, educator*

Port Washington
†Halasz, Laszlo *musical director, conductor*

Poughkeepsie
Wilson, Richard Edward *composer, pianist, music educator*

Pound Ridge
Ostrow, Stuart *theatrical producer, educator*

Purchase
Lamagra, Anthony James *concert pianist, television host, music educator*

Quogue
Macero, Teo *composer, conductor*

Rego Park
Cronyn, Hume *actor, writer, director*

Riverdale
Hubley, Faith Elliott *filmmaker, painter, animator*

Rochester
Adler, Samuel Hans *conductor, composer*
Diamond, David Leo *composer*
Fagan, Garth *choreographer, artistic director, educator*
†Harman, Nan K. *orchestra director, artistic administrator*
Hodkinson, Sydney Phillip *composer, educator*
Kowalke, Kim H. *music educator, musicologist, conductor, foundation executive*
Laires, Fernando *concert piano educator*
Marcellus, John Robert, III *trombonist, educator*
Millman, Howard J. *artistic director*
†Nagano, Kent George *conductor*
Rouse, Christopher Chapman, III *composer*
Schwantner, Joseph *composer, educator*
Weiss, Howard A. *violinist, concertmaster, conductor, music educator*

Sag Harbor
Walton, Emma *artistic director*

Saratoga Springs
Porter, David Hugh *pianist, classicist, academic administrator, liberal arts educator*

Sea Cliff
Popova, Nina *dancer, choreographer, director*

Sparkill
Dahl, Arlene *actress, author, designer, cosmetic executive*

Stony Brook
Baron, Samuel *flutist*

Sunnyside
Giaimo, Kathryn Ann *performing arts company executive*

Syracuse
Akiyama, Kazuyoshi *conductor*
Driver, Robert Baylor, Jr. *opera administrator*
†Rubardt, Peter Craig *conductor, educator*

Tarrytown
Kroll, Nathan *film producer, director*

Troy
Snyder, Patricia Di Benedetto *theater director and administrator*

Tuxedo Park
De Main, John *conductor, music director*
Neblett, Carol *soprano*
Shore, Howard Leslie *composer*

White Plains
Magaziner, Elliot Albert *musician, conductor, educator*

Yonkers
Baumel, Herbert *violinist, conductor*

Yorktown Heights
Rosenfeld, Steven Ira *artistic director, music publisher*

NORTH CAROLINA

Asheville
Weed, Maurice James *composer, retired music educator*

Chapel Hill
Barranger, Milly Slater *performing arts company executive, writer*
Best, Winfield Judson *television producer, writer, public relations consultant*
Camp, Joseph Shelton, Jr. *film producer, director, writer*
Ellis, Michael *theatrical producer*
Hammond, David Alan *stage director, educator*
Newman, William Stein *music educator, author, pianist, composer*
Parker, Scott Jackson *theatre director*
Powell, Carolyn Wilkerson *music educator*

Charlotte
Ray, Dee *television executive*
Smith, Arthur *radio and television producer, composer*

Durham
Bryan, Paul Robey, Jr. *musician, educator*
Caesar, Shirley *gospel singer, evangelist*
†Jaffe, Stephen Abram *composer, music educator*
Ward, Robert *composer, conductor, educator*

Greensboro
Gutter, Robert Harold *conductor, music educator*
McRae, Paul Anthony *symphony orchestra conductor*
Middleton, Herman David, Sr. *theater educator*
Morgenstern, Sheldon Jon *symphony orchestra conductor*
Russell, Peggy Taylor *soprano, educator*

Greenville
Chauncey, Beatrice Arlene *music educator*

Jacksonville
Daugherty, Robert Michael *music educator, composer*

Raleigh
Casey, Ethel Laughlin *concert and opera singer*
Rhodes, Donald Robert *musicologist, retired electrical engineer*
Zimmermann, Gerhardt *conductor*

Winston Salem
Johnson, Norman *music director, opera producer, educator*
Perret, Peter James *symphony conductor*
Trautwein, George William *conductor*

OHIO

Akron
Poll, Heinz *choreographer, artistic director*
Schubert, Barbara Schuele *performing company executive*

Berea
Strew, Suzanne Claflin *choreographer, dance educator*

Canton
Crowley, Cassandra Ann *ballet company administrator, choreographer*
Moorhouse, Linda Virginia *symphony orchestra administrator*

Cincinnati
†Alexander, Jeffrey *performing company executive*
Belew, Adrian *guitarist, singer, songwriter, producer*
de Blasis, James Michael *artistic director, producer, stage director*
DeLeone, Carmon *conductor, musician, composer, educator*
Hoffman, Joel Harvey *composer*
James, Jefferson Ann *choreographer*
Jordan, Lorna *news director*
Kunzel, Erich, Jr. *conductor, arranger, educator*
Lopez-Cobos, Jesus *conductor*
†Monder, Steven I. *orchestra executive*
Samuel, Gerhard *orchestra conductor, composer*
†Stern, Edward *performing company executive*
Tocco, James *pianist*

Cleveland
Alfieri, Lisa Gwyneth *ballet dancer, teacher*
Bamberger, David *opera company executive*
Erb, Donald *composer*
Evans, Jane Keegan *opera and music theatre producer*
Giannetti, Louis Daniel *film educator, film critic*
Holderfield, Marilyn Ida *jazz vocalist*
Hruby, Frank M. *musician, critic, educator*
†Matthews, Julie *performing arts company director*
McConnell, Michael *opera company director*
Mc Farlane, Karen Elizabeth *concert artists manager*
Morris, Thomas William *symphony orchestra administrator*
Nahat, Dennis F. *artistic director, choreographer*
von Dohnányi, Christoph *musician, conductor*

Columbus
Brown, Firman Hewitt, Jr. *drama educator, theatrical director*
Drvota, Mojmir *cinema educator, author*
Haddad, George Richard *musician, educator*
Harris, Donald *composer*
Ichino, Yoko *ballet dancer*
Lowe, Clayton Kent *visual imagery, cinema, and video educator*
†Rosenstock, Susan Lynn *orchestra manager*
Russell, William Fletcher, III *opera company director*

Dayton
†Clouser, James Brady *ballet director, choreographer*
Hanna, Marsha L. *artistic director*
Walters, Jefferson Brooks *musician, retired real estate broker*

North Ridgeville
Nagy, Robert David *tenor*

Oberlin
Boe, David Stephen *musician, educator, college dean*

Strongsville
Oltman, C. Dwight *conductor, educator*

Toledo
Massey, Andrew John *conductor, composer*

Waverly
Squire, Russel Nelson *musician, retired educator*

Wooster
Stuart, James Fortier *musician, artistic director*

OKLAHOMA

Caddo
Perkins, Kent *television and movie producer*

Clinton
Askew, Penny Sue *choreographer, artistic director, ballet instructor*

Norman
Bryant, Celia Mae Small *music educator*
Carey, Thomas Devore *baritone, educator*
de Stwolinski, Gail Rounce Boyd *music theory and composition educator*
Eek, Nathaniel Sisson *retired fine arts educator*
Ross, Allan Anderson *music educator, university official*

Oklahoma City
McCoy, Wesley Lawrence *musician, conductor, educator*
Payne, Gareld Gene *vocal music educator, medical transcriptionist*
Valentine, Alan Darrell *symphony orchestra executive*

Tulsa
Larkin, Moscelyne *retired artistic director, dancer*
†Lunev, Aleksandr (Sasha) *dancer*
Nero, Peter *pianist, conductor, composer, arranger*
Powell, Sara Jordan *musician, religious worker*
Rubenstein, Bernard *orchestra conductor*
Sterban, Richard Anthony *singer*

OREGON

Ashland
Hirschfeld, Gerald Joseph *cinematographer*

Eugene
Bailey, Exine Margaret Anderson *soprano, educator*
Johnson, Ronald Glenn *arts administrator*

Portland
Bailey, Robert C. *opera company executive*
DePreist, James Anderson *conductor*
Hill, Andrew William *jazz musician, composer*
†Leyden, Norman *conductor*

Orange
Soderbergh, Steven Andrew *filmmaker*

Petersburg
Dance, Gloria Fenderson *dance studio executive, ballet administrator*

Radford
James, Clarity (Carolyne Faye James) *mezzo-soprano*

Richmond
Erb, James Bryan *music educator, conductor, musicologist*

Roanoke
Fourcroy, Margarite *performing company executive*
Stanley, Ralph *bluegrass musician*

Staunton
Balsley, Philip Elwood *entertainer*

Vienna
Lyons, Paul Michael *producer, film*

Virginia Beach
Freyss, David *producer, director*

Williamsburg
Hornsby, Bruce Randall *composer, musician*

WASHINGTON

Friday Harbor
†Waite, Ric *cinematographer*

Gig Harbor
Ramsey, Jerry Virgil *radio broadcaster, educator, financial planner*

Marysville
Philpott, Larry La Fayette *horn player*

Seattle
Coleman, Dennis G. *conductor*
Forbes, David Craig *musician*
†Gates, Sarah Nash *costume designer, educator*
Houk, Benjamin Noah *ballet dancer*
Jenkins, Speight *opera company executive, writer*
Loper, Robert Bruce *theater director, educator*
Moore, Benjamin *theatrical producer*
Nishitani, Martha *dancer*
†Ritt, David Lawrence *symphony musician*
Russell, Francia *ballet director, educator*
†Rutter, Deborah Frances *orchestra administrator*
Sateren, Terry *theater technical production*
†Sheng, Bright *composer, pianist, conductor*
Staryk, Steven S. *violinist, concertmaster, educator*
Stowell, Kent *ballet director*
Sullivan, Daniel J. *artistic director*
†Talvi, Ilkka Ilari *violinist*
Witham, Barry Bates *drama educator*

Spokane
Aponté, Christopher Bennedettey *artistic director, choreographer, educator*
Fowler, Betty Janmae *dance company director, editor*
Jordania, Vakhtang *conductor, educator*
†Mechetti, Fabio *orchestra conductor*

Tacoma
Garner, Carlene Ann *orchestra administrator*
Hansen, Edward Allen *music educator, organist*

WEST VIRGINIA

Charleston
Conlin, Thomas (Byrd) *conductor*
Drennen, William Miller, Jr. *cultural administrator, film executive, producer, director, mineral resource executive*

Salem
Raad, Virginia *pianist, lecturer*

Westover
Trythall, Harry Gilbert *music educator, composer*

WISCONSIN

Beloit
Gates, Crawford Marion *conductor, composer*

Eau Claire
Patterson, Donald Lee *music educator*

Madison
Crafton, Donald Clayton *film educator*
Davis, Richard *musician, music educator*
Dembski, Stephen Michael *composer, university music composition professor*
Johnson, Roland A. *conductor, music director*
Palmer, Robert R. *performing arts administrator*
Rosser, Annetta Hamilton *composer*

Milwaukee
Downey, John Wilham *composer, pianist, conductor, educator*
Hanthorn, Dennis Wayne *performing arts association administrator*
Hedges, John Kim *performing arts administrator, consultant*
†Lafontsee, Dane *ballet company artistic director*
Macal, Zdenek *conductor*
Moynihan, Michael J. *artistic and producing director, writer*
Ovitsky, Steven Alan *musician, symphony orchestra executive*
Schneider, John David *theatre director, playwright, actor, jazz singer*
†Thompson, Basil F. *ballet master*
Uecker, Bob *actor, radio announcer, former baseball player, TV personality*

WYOMING

Big Horn
Garry, James B. *storyteller, researcher, writer*

Jackson Hole
Adler, Warren *novelist, producer, playwright*

TERRITORIES OF THE UNITED STATES

PUERTO RICO

San Juan
†Sierra, Roberto *composer, music educator*

CANADA

ALBERTA

Banff
Fruchtman, Milton Allen *film and television producer, director*

Calgary
†Graf, Hans *conductor*
LaHay, David George Michael *ballet company director*
Monk, Allan James *baritone*

Edmonton
Archer, Violet Balestreri *music educator, composer, pianist, organist, percussionist, adjudicator*
Hoyt, David Lemire *musician*

BRITISH COLUMBIA

Saanichton
Little, Carl Maurice *performing arts administrator*

Vancouver
†Agler, David *conductor*
Alleyne, John *dancer, choreographer*
Hallam, Robert J. *performing company executive, consultant*
Raffi, (Raffi Cavoukian) *folksinger, children's entertainer*

Victoria
Horn, Paul Joseph *musician*
McCoppin, Peter *symphony orchestra conductor*

MANITOBA

Winnipeg
†Bentley, Jeffrey *performing company executive*
†Graham, Laura S.E. *ballet dancer*
Kaminski, John *dancer*
†Lewis, Andre Leon *associate artistic director*
Meehan, John *artistic director*
†Morris, Jorden Walter *dancer, educator*
†Olds, Elizabeth *dancer*
†Ratmansky, Alexei *dancer*
Riske, William Kenneth *cultural services consultant*
†Rubio, Suzanne Sarah *ballet dancer*
†Savchenko, Alla *ballet mistress*
Spohr, Arnold Theodore *artistic director, choreographer*
†Wei-Qiang, Zhang *dancer*
Whitener, William Garnett *dancer, choreographer*

ONTARIO

Don Mills
Applebaum, Louis *composer, conductor*

Hamilton
Lipton, Daniel Bernard *conductor*
Shaw, John Firth *orchestra administrator*

Kitchener
Coles, Graham *conductor, composer*

London
†Stafford, Earl *conductor*

Mississauga
Peterson, Oscar Emmanuel *pianist*

Niagara on the Lake
Newton, Christopher *artistic director*

Ottawa
Augustyn, Frank Joseph *dancer, artistic director*
Franca, Celia *ballet director, choreographer, dancer, narrator*
Gillingham, Bryan Reginald *music educator*

Saint Catharines
Florio, Ermanno *conductor, music administrator*

Thornhill
Nimmons, Phillip Rista *composer, conductor, clarinetist, educator*

Toronto
Anderson, Reid Bryce *ballet company artistic director*
Beckwith, John *musician, composer, educator*
Boswell, Philip John *opera administrator*
Bradshaw, Richard James *conductor*
Cable, Howard Reid *composer, conductor*
Colgrass, Michael Charles *composer*
Crawley, Alexander Radford *performing artist, composer*
Doherty, Tom (Thomas Storen, Jr.) *art director, set designer*
†Domb, Daniel *cellist, educator*
†Drabinsky, Garth Howard *entertainment company executive*
Egoyan, Atom *film director*
Eklof, Svea Christine *ballet dancer*
Eldred, Gerald Marcus *performing arts association executive*
Feldbrill, Victor *conductor*
Freedman, Harry *composer*
†Geddes, Lorna *ballet mistress*
Glasco, Kimberly *ballet dancer*
†Goh, Chan Hon *ballerina*
Harwood, Vanessa Clare *ballet dancer*
†Illmann, Margaret Louise *ballet dancer*
Israelievitch, Jacques H. *violinist, conductor*
Jewison, Norman Frederick *film producer, director*
Kain, Karen Alexandria *ballet dancer*
†Kent, David Rowan *timpanist, symphony orchestra official*
Kirby, Charles William, Jr. *dancer, choreographer*
Kudelka, James *ballet dancer, choreographer*
Kuerti, Anton Emil *pianist, composer*
†Lamy, Martine *dancer*
Lavoie, Serge *principal dancer*
†Lucas, Cynthia *ballet mistress, dancer*
Murray, Anne *country singer*
Nisbet, Joanne *ballet mistress*
Oliphant, Betty *ballet school director*
†Ottmann, Peter *choreographer, ballet dancer*
Pedersen, Paul Richard *composer, educator*
Ransom, Jeremy *ballet dancer*
Rasky, Harry *producer, director, writer*
Schramek, Tomas *ballet dancer*
Shearing, George Albert *pianist, composer*
Smith, Raymond *dancer*
†Staines, Mavis Avril *artistic director, ballet principal*
Stefanschi, Sergiu *dancer*
†Tewsley, Robert William *dancer*
†Valdepeñas, Joaquín Mario *clarinetist, conductor*
Wilder, Valerie *ballet company director*
Wilkins, Ormsby *music director, conductor, pianist*
Witkowsky, Gizella *dancer*

QUEBEC

Montreal
Chiriaeff, Ludmilla Gorny *ballet company executive, ballet dancer, choreographer*
†Dans, Frank *performing arts executive*
Dutoit, Charles *conductor*
Gulkin, Harry *arts administrator, film producer*
Major, André *radio producer, writer, educator*
Nault, Fernand *choreographer*
Obomsawin, Alanis *director, producer*
Papineau-Couture, Jean *composer, educator*
Rhodes, Lawrence *artistic director*
†Spickler, Robert *performing arts executive*
†Trogani, Monica *ballet mistress*
Uzan, Bernard Franck *general and artistic director*
Woszczyk, Wieslaw Richard *audio engineering educator, researcher*

Sainte Foy
Pasquier, Joël *music educator*

MEXICO

Mexico City
Arau, Alfonso *film producer and director, writer*

AUSTRALIA

New South Wales
†Davis, Judy *actress*

Potts Point
Beresford, Bruce *film director*

Sydney
Miller, George *film director*

AUSTRIA

Vienna
Faulkner, Julia Ellen *opera singer*
Ludwig, Christa *mezzo-soprano*
Raimondi, Ruggero *opera singer*

CAYMAN ISLAND

Grand Cayman Island
Crockett, James Grover, III *musician, former music publisher*

COSTA RICA

San Jose
Hoffman, Irwin *orchestra conductor*

DOMINICAN REPUBLIC

Santo Domingo
Piantini, Carlos *conductor*

ENGLAND

Balcombe
Scofield, Paul *actor*

Birmingham
Banowetz, Joseph Murray *musician, music educator*

Brighton
Watkin, David *film director, cinematographer*

Cambridge
Hogwood, Christopher Jarvis Haley *music director, educator*

Halifax
Lilly, Shannon Jeanne *dancer*

Isle of Wight
Stigwood, Robert Colin *theater, movie, television and record producer*

Iver Heath
Kubrick, Stanley *producer, director, writer*

London
†Ackland-Snow, Terry *art director*
Ashkenazy, Vladimir Davidovich *concert pianist, conductor*
Barshai, Rudolf Borisovich *conductor*
Bart, Lionel *composer, lyricist*
Beck, Jeff *musician, composer, vocalist*
†Bennett, Richard Rodney *composer*
Biddle, Adrian *cinematographer*
†Biziou, Peter *cinematographer*
Bonynge, Richard *opera conductor*
Bowie, David (David Robert Jones) *musician, actor*
Bream, Julian *classical guitarist and lutanist*
Cellan-Jones, James Gwynne *television producer, director*
Christie, Julie *actress*
Codron, Michael Victor *theatrical producer*
Conti, Tom *actor, writer, director*
Dickinson, Peter *composer*
†Doyle, Patrick *composer*
†Dudley, Anne *composer*
Estes, Simon Lamont *opera singer, bass-baritone*
Foster, Lawrence *concert and opera conductor*
Francis, Freddie *film producer and director*
Freni, Mirella *soprano*
Ghiaurov, Nicolai *opera singer*
Gielgud, Sir (Arthur) John *actor, director*
Hall, Sir Peter Reginald Frederick *theater opera and film director*
Harper, Heather Mary *retired soprano*
Harrison, George *musician*
Hawthorne, Nigel Barnard *actor*
Hendricks, Barbara *opera singer, recitalist*
Holm, Ian *actor*
Hoskins, Bob (Robert William Hoskins) *actor*
Hurt, John Vincent *actor*
Idle, Eric *actor, screenwriter, producer*
Irons, Jeremy John *actor*
John, Elton Hercules (Reginald Kenneth Dwight) *musician*
Jones, Terry *film director, author*
Jordan, Neil Patrick *film director*
Kingsley, Ben *actor*
Kraus, Alfredo (Alfredo Kraus Trujillo) *tenor*
Le Vien, John Douglas (Jack Le Vien) *motion picture and television producer, director*
Lloyd Webber, Sir Andrew *composer*
Lynne, Gillian Barbara *choreographer, dancer, actress, director*
Mackerras, Sir (Alan) Charles (Maclaurin) *conductor*
Mackintosh, Cameron *musical theater producer*
Marriner, Sir Neville *orchestra conductor*
McIntyre, Donald Conroy *opera singer, baritone*
McKellen, Ian *actor*
Miller, Jonathan Wolfe *theater and film director, physician*
Minton, Yvonne Fay *mezzo-soprano*
Mirren, Helen *actress*
Nelson, John Wilton *symphonic conductor*
Nucci, Leo *baritone*
Nunn, Trevor Robert *director*
O'Toole, Peter *actor*
Palin, Michael Edward *actor, screenwriter, author*
Plowright, Joan Anne *actress*
Puttnam, Sir David Terence *film producer*
Rattle, Simon *conductor*
Rea, Stephen *actor*
Ricci, Ruggiero *violinist, educator*
Rice, Sir Timothy Miles Bindon *lyricist*
Rigg, Diana *actress*
Salonen, Esa-Pekka *conductor*
Schaufuss, Peter *dancer, producer, choreographer, ballet director*
Schlesinger, John Richard *film, opera and theater director*
Serebrier, José *musician, conductor, composer*
Siepi, Cesare *opera singer*
†Slocombe, Douglas *cinematographer*
Smith, Dame Maggie *actress*
Soviero, Diana Barbara *soprano*
Starr, Ringo (Richard Starkey) *musician, actor*
Sting, (Gordon Matthew Sumner) *musician, songwriter, actor*
Sutherland, Dame Joan *retired soprano*
Tebaldi, Renata *opera singer*
Tennstedt, Klaus *conductor*
Tureck, Rosalyn *concert artist, author, editor, educator*
Ustinov, Sir Peter Alexander *actor, director, writer*
Vaness, Carol *soprano*
Vishnevskaya, Galina Pavlovna *soprano, opera company director*
Wallis, Diana Lynn *artistic director*
Winner, Michael Robert *film director, writer, producer*
Zinnemann, Fred *film director*

Middlesex
Lester, Richard *film director*

Richmond
Attenborough, Baron Richard Samuel *actor, producer, director, goodwill ambassador*

Shepperton
Branagh, Kenneth *actor, director*

Somerset
Day-Lewis, Daniel *actor*

Surrey
Diaz, Justino *bass-baritone*

Warwick
Hands, Terence David (Terry Hands) *theater director*

Wiltshire
Gabriel, Peter *vocalist, composer*

FINLAND

Helsinki
†Saraste, Jukka-Pekka *conductor*

FRANCE

Neuilly-sur-Seine
Ophuls, Marcel *film director and producer*

Nice
Dickie, Brian *opera director*

Paris
Annaud, Jean-Jacques *film director, screenwriter*
Boulez, Pierre *composer, conductor*
de Havilland, Olivia Mary *actress*
Jolas, Betsy *composer*
Kurtz, Eugene Allen *composer, educator, consultant*
Marceau, Marcel *pantomimist, actor, director, painter, poet*
Marton, Eva *opera singer*
Mitchell, Leona Pearl *soprano*
Polanski, Roman *film director, writer, actor*

GERMANY

Berlin
Abbado, Claudio *conductor*
Fischer-Dieskau, Dietrich *baritone*

Dresden
Schreier, Peter *tenor*

Hamburg
Neumeier, John *choreographer, ballet company director*
Ramsey, Bill (William McCreery) *singer, actor, composer-lyricist, television executive*
Zylis-Gara, Teresa Gerarda *soprano*

Munich
Araiza, Francisco (José Francisco Araiza Andrade) *opera singer*
Fassbaender, Brigitte *opera singer*
Goodman, Alfred *composer, musicologist*
Horak, Jan-Christopher *film studies educator, curator*

ISLE OF MAN

Peel
Wakeman, Rick *musician, composer*

ISRAEL

Tel Aviv
Mehta, Zubin *conductor, musician*

ITALY

Naples
Bartoli, Cecilia *coloratura soprano, mezzo soprano*

Pontedera
Grotowski, Jerzy *theater director, acting educator*

Rome
Antonioni, Michelangelo *film director*
Bertolucci, Bernardo *film director*
Loren, Sophia *actress*
Storaro, Vittorio *cinematographer*
Zeffirelli, Franco *theater and film director*

JAPAN

Chikusa
Casei, Nedda *mezzo-soprano*

Setagaya
Kurosawa, Akira *film director*

THE NETHERLANDS

Hilversum
De Waart, Edo *conductor*

The Hague
Kylián, Jiří *choreographer*

SCOTLAND

Edinburgh
McMaster, Brian John *artistic director*

Gifford
Menotti, Gian Carlo *composer*

SPAIN

Barcelona
de Larrocha, Alicia *concert pianist*

Madrid
Almodóvar, Pedro *filmmaker*
Berganza Vargas, Teresa *mezzo-soprano*
Frühbeck de Burgos, Rafael *conductor*
Trueba, Fernando *film director and producer, screenwriter*

SWEDEN

Stockholm
Meyer, Kerstin *mezzo-soprano, music educator*
Soederstrom, Elisabeth Anna *opera singer*

SWITZERLAND

Geneva
Barenboim, Daniel *conductor, pianist*

Rouille
Godard, Jean-Luc *film director*

Staad
Moore, Roger George *actor*

Zurich
Jones, Gwyneth *soprano*

ADDRESS UNPUBLISHED

Adaskin, Murray *composer*
Adato, Perry Miller *documentary producer, director, writer*
Adelson, Mervyn Lee *entertainment and communication industry executive*
Alda, Alan *actor, writer, director*
Allen, Marilyn Myers Pool *theater director, video producer*
Allen, Woody (Allen Stewart Konigsberg) *actor, filmmaker, author*
Almond, Paul *film director, producer, writer*
†Andersen, Ib Steen *ballet dancer*
Andrews, Julie *actress, singer*
Apted, Michael D. *film director*
Arenal, Julie (Mrs. Barry Primus) *choreographer*
Armistead, Thomas Boyd, III *television and film producer*
Aronson, Luann Marie *actress*
Arova, Sonia *artistic director, ballet educator*
Arthur, Beatrice *actress*
Ashby, Clifford Charles *theatre arts educator, historian*
Askin, Leon *artistic director, actor, producer, writer*
Assante, Armand *actor*
Atherton, William *actor*
Atkins, John *concert pianist, voice teacher*
Auberjonois, René Murat *actor*
Avalon, Frankie *singer, actor*
Avian, Bob *choreographer, producer*
Bacharach, Burt *composer, conductor*
Badham, John MacDonald *motion picture director*
Baker, Joe Don *actor*
Balaban, Bob *actor, director*
Baldwin, Alec (Alexander Rae Baldwin, III) *actor*
Balsam, Martin Henry *actor*
Balter, Alan *conductor, music director*
†Baranski, Christine *actress*
Barselou, Paul Edgar *actor, writer*
Bartenieff, George *producer, actor*
Basia, (Basia Trzetrzelewska) *musician, vocalist*
Beal, John *actor, director, narrator*
Beatty, Ned *actor*
Beck, Isha Manna *performing company executive, actress, painter*
Begley, Ed, Jr. *actor*
Belafonte, Harry *singer, concert artist, actor*
Bergen, Candice *actress, writer, photojournalist*
Berger, Jonathan *composer*
Berlinger, Warren *actor*
Bernhardt, Melvin *theater director*
Bertinelli, Valerie *actress*
Bierley, Paul Edmund *musician, author, publisher*
Bjerknes, Michael Leif *dancer*
Blackstone, Harry Bouton, Jr. *magician, actor*
Bloomquist, Kenneth Gene *music educator, university bands director*
Blossom, Beverly *choreographer, dance educator*
Boatright, Ann Long *dancer, pianist, music educator, choreographer*
Bochner, Hart *actor*
Bock, Jerry (Jerrold Lewis) *composer*
Boehle, William Randall *music educator emeritus*
Bogosian, Eric *performance artist, actor*
Bonerz, Peter *actor, director*
Borgnine, Ernest *actor*
Bowles, Paul Frederick *composer, author*
†Boxleitner, Bruce *actor*
Boyd, Julianne Mamana *theater director*
Boyd, Liona Maria *musician*
Boyle, Peter *actor*
Brando, Marlon, Jr. *actor*
Brennan, Eileen Regina *actress*
Briccetti, Joan Therese *symphony manager, arts management consultant*
Brooks, Albert (Albert Einstein) *actor, writer, director*
Brosnan, Pierce *actor*
Brown, Earle *composer, conductor*
Brown, Jim (James Nathaniel Brown) *film actor, former professional football player*
Brown, Ruth *rhythm and blues singer*
Browne, Jackson *singer, songwriter*
Brustad, Wesley O. *symphony executive, theater and opera director, scriptwriter*
Bullin, Christine Neva *arts administrator*
Bunim, Mary-Ellis *television producer*
Butkus, Dick *actor, former professional football player*
Byrne, David *musician, composer, artist, director*
Calegari, Maria *ballerina*
Canin, Stuart Victor *violinist*
Cannon, Dyan *actress*
Capice, Philip Charles *television production executive*
Carey, Mariah *vocalist, songwriter*
Carlyss, Earl Winston *musician*
Carney, Arthur William Matthew *actor*
Carradine, Keith Ian *actor, singer, composer*
Carson, Johnny *television personality*
Carter, Elliott Cook, Jr. *composer*
Carter, (William) Hodding, III *television and newspaper journalist*
Carter, Ronald *musician*
Carvey, Dana *actor, stand up comedian*
Cash, Johnny *entertainer*
Caswell, Dorothy Ann Cottrell *arts administrator*
Chapman, Tracy *singer, songwriter*
Chapman, William *baritone*
Charry, Michael R(onald) *musician, conductor*
Christine, Virginia Feld *actress*
Christopher, Russell Lewis *baritone*
Cid Viuda de Garcia Molina, Caridad del Carmen *radio producer and personality*
Clark, Candy *actress*
Clarke, Hope *choreographer, director, actress*
Clarke, Malcolm *filmmaker*
Claver, Robert Earl *television director, producer*
Cobham, William Emanuel, Jr. *musician*
Coburn, James *actor*
Cody, Iron Eyes *actor*
Cohen, Alexander H. *theatrical and television producer*
Colbert, Claudette (Lily Chauchoin) *actress*
Coleman, Nancy Catherine *actress*
Collins, Joan Henrietta *actress*
Colman, Edward Brof *film director, cinematographer*
Cone, Edward Toner *composer, emeritus music educator*
Connors, Mike (Krekor Ohanian) *actor*
Consoli, Marc-Antonio *composer*
Cook, Fielder *producer, director*
Cooper, Hal *television director*
Copperfield, David (David Kotkin) *illusionist, director, producer, writer*
Corey, Jeff *actor, director, educator*
Cosby, Bill *actor, entertainer*
Cossa, Dominic Frank *baritone*
Cotrubas, Ileana *opera singer, lyric soprano, retired*
Cover, Franklin Edward *actor*
Crosby, Norman Lawrence *comedian*
Crouse, Lindsay *actress*
Cruise, Tom (Tom Cruise Mapother, IV) *actor*
Cummings, Constance *actress*
†Cunningham, Ron *choreographer, artistic director*
Currier, Ruth *dancer, choreographer and educator*
Curson, Theodore *musician*
Dabbs, Henry Erven *television and film producer, educator*
Dafoe, Willem *actor*
Dailey, Irene *actress, educator*
Daltrey, Roger *musician*
d'Amboise, Christopher *ballet dancer, artistic director, choreographer*
Danner, Blythe Katharine *actress*
Danza, Tony *actor*
Davidovsky, Mario *composer*
Davies, Raymond Douglas *musician, songwriter*
Davis, Mac *singer, songwriter*
Dean, Dearest (Lorene Glosup) *songwriter*
†Dechario, Tony Houston *symphony orchestra executive*
De Felitta, Frank Paul *producer, writer, director*
De Frank, Vincent *conductor*
Del Tredici, David *composer*
de Luce, Virginia *entertainer*
De Luise, Dom *actor*
Delza-Munson, Elizabeth *dancer, choreographer, educator*
De Mornay, Rebecca *actress*
Deneuve, Catherine (Catherine Dorleac) *actress*
Devane, William *actor*
Devlin, Michael Coles *bass-baritone*
Dickerson, Nancy (Whitehead) *free lance television producer, news correspondent*
Dickinson, Angie (Angeline Brown) *actress*
Diemer, Emma Lou *composer, music educator*
†DiPalma, Carlo *cinematographer*
Dolenz, Mickey (George Michael Dolenz) *singer, actor, television producer*
Dolin, Samuel Joseph *composer, educator*
Donahue, Elinor *actress*
Dorn, Dolores *actress*
Drake, Ervin Maurice *composer, author*
Dukes, David Coleman *actor*
Duncan, Sandy *actress*
Dunlap, Richard Donovan *artistic director*
Durning, Charles *actor*
Duvall, Robert *actor*
Dysart, Richard A. *actor*
Eagan, Sherman G. *producer, communications executive*
Eagle, Jack *commercial actor, comedian*
Earle, Steve *country rockabilly musician, songwriter*
Ebb, Fred *lyricist, librettist*
Edwards, Ryan Hayes *baritone*
Ehrling, Sixten *orchestra conductor*
Elder, Mark Philip *conductor*
Elgart, Larry Joseph *orchestra leader*
Elikann, Lawrence S. (Larry Elikann) *television and film director*
Elizondo, Hector *actor*
Ely, Joe *singer and songwriter*
†Emmons, Beverly *lighting designer*
Etheridge, Melissa Lou *singer, songwriter*
Evdokimova, Eva *prima ballerina assoluta, choreographer, director, producer*
Everhart, Rex *actor, director, photographer*
Evstatieva, Stefka *opera singer*
Fabares, Shelley *actress*
Falsey, John Henry, Jr. *television producer*
Farrow, Mia Villiers *actress*
Faust, John Joseph, Jr. *theatre educator, director*
Fawcett, Farrah Leni *actress, model*
Feldman, Thomas Myron *director, lighting director, director of photography, film company executive*
Ferguson, Maynard *trumpeter, band leader*
Field, Sally *actress*
Fields, Freddie *producer, agent*
Filerman, Michael Herman *television producer*
Fitzgerald, Geraldine *actress*
Fletcher, Louise *actress*
Ford, Harrison *actor*
Ford, Nancy Louise *composer, scriptwriter*
Forman, Miloš *film director*
Forsythe, Henderson *actor*
Forsythe, John *actor*
Forte, Craig Anthony *amusement park, motion picture location executive*
Foss, Lukas *composer, conductor, pianist*
Foster, Frances *actress*
Franciosa, Anthony (Anthony Papaleo) *actor*
Frankish, Brian Edward *film producer, director*
Freberg, Stan(ley) (Victor Freberg) *satirist*
Fredricks, Richard *baritone*
Freitas, Beatrice B(otty) *musician, educator*
Freston, Thomas E. *cable television programming executive*
†Fuerstner, Fiona Margaret Ann *ballet company executive, ballet educator*
Gagnon, Edith Morrison *ballerina, singer, actress*
Garcia, Jerry (Jerome John Garcia) *guitarist, composer*
Garfunkel, Art *singer, actor*
Garner, James (James Scott Bumgarner) *actor*
Garrard, Don Edward Burdett *operatic and concert singer*
Garson, Greer *actress*
Gates, Larry *actor*
Gatlin, Larry Wayne *singer, songwriter*
Gehm, Denise Charlene *ballerina, arts administrator*
Gelman, Larry *actor*
Giacomini, Giuseppe *tenor*
Gilbert, Kenneth Albert *harpsichordist*
Gilliam, Terry Vance *film director, actor, illustrator, writer*
Giordano, Tony Eugene *director*
Givens, Robin *actress*
Glover, Crispin Hellion *actor*
Glynn, Carlin (Carlin Masterson) *actress*
Goldberg, Whoopi (Caryn Johnson) *actress*
†Goldblatt, Mark Lawrence *film director*
Goldblum, Jeff *actor*
Goldin, Marion Freedman *television news producer, reporter*
Goldovsky, Boris *musician*
Goodman, Erika *dancer, actress*
Gorme, Eydie *singer*
Gossett, Louis, Jr. *actor*
Gould, Morton *composer, conductor*
Grant, Alexander Marshall *ballet director*
Grant, Lee (Lyova Haskell Rosenthal) *actress, director*
Greaves, William Garfield *film director, producer*
Green, George *radio executive*
Griffith, Melanie *actress*
Grimshaw, Paul *producer*
Grosbard, Ulu *director*
Gross, Terry R. *radio producer, host*
Guinness, Sir Alec *actor*
†Gutierrez, Gerald Andrew *theatrical director*
Guttman, Irving Allen *opera stage director*
Hall, Conrad L. *cinematographer*
Hall, James Stanley *jazz guitarist, composer*
Hall, Janice *soprano*
Hall, Monty *television producer, actor*
Halsey, James Albert *international entertainment impressario, theatrical producer, talent manager*
Hamlisch, Marvin *composer*
Hamner, Earl Henry, Jr. *television producer, television and film writer*
Hampton, Lionel Leo *composer, conductor, entertainer*
Harris, Margaret *pianist, conductor, composer*
Harris, Richard (Richard St. John) *actor*
Harryhausen, Ray Frederick *special effects expert*
Hart, Evelyn *ballet dancer*
Hartman, Phil Edward *actor*
Hatch, Kenneth L. *television executive*
Havoc, June *actress*
Hawkins, Osie Penman, Jr. *former baritone, former performing company executive*
Hayes, Peter Lind *actor, writer*
Heard, John *actor*
Heath, Percy *jazz bassist*
Heckart, Eileen *actress*
Helgenberger, Marg *actress*
Henes, Donna Urban Shaman *celebration artist, ritualist, writer*
Henner, Marilu *actress*
Henning, Doug *illusionist*
Herbig, Günther *conductor*
Hilding, Jerel Lee *music and dance educator, former dancer*
Hingle, Pat *actor*
†Ho, Alexander Kitman *producer*
Ho, Michael *artistic director, choreographer, ballet teacher*
†Hoffman, Stanley Marc *composer, music engraver*
Hoggard, Lara Guldmar *conductor, educator*
Holm, Celeste *actress*
Houghton, Katharine *actress*
Hubbard, Elizabeth *actress*
Hudlin, Reginald Alan *director, writer, producer*
Hughes, Michaela Kelly *actress, dancer*
Huning, Deborah Gray *actress, dancer, audiologist*
Hunter, Holly *actress*
Hunter, Kim (Janet Cole) *actress*
Hunter, Ross *film producer*
Iglesias, Julio (Julio Jose Iglesias De La Cueva) *singer, songwriter*
Intilli, Sharon Marie *television director, small business owner*
Irey, Charlotte York *dance educator*
Irving, Amy *actress*
Irving, George Steven *actor*
Irving, Terry (Edward B. Irving, III) *television producer*
Istomin, Marta Casals *performing arts administrator*
Jackson, Nagle *stage director, playwright*
Jacobi, Derek George *actor*
Jaffe, Stanley Richard *film producer, director*
Jarrett, Keith *pianist, composer*
Jasinski, Roman Larkin *artistic director*
Jennings, Waylon *country musician*
Jessup, Harley William *graphics expert, art director*
Joblove, George H. *graphics and special effects expert*
Johnson, (Francis) Benjamin *actor*
Johnson, Don Wayne *actor*
Johnson, J. J. *trombonist*
Jones, George *country music singer, songwriter*
Jones, Shirley *actress, singer*
Jones, Tommy Lee *actor*
Judd, Naomi *country music entertainer, singer, songwriter, author*
Judd, Wynonna *vocalist, musician*
Kahn, Madeline Gail *actress*
Kaminsky, Laura *composer, arts presenter*
Kane, Michael Joseph *director*
Kasem, Casey (Kemal Amin Kasem) *radio and television personality*
Kavner, Julie *actress*
Kazan, Elia *theatrical, motion picture director and producer, author*
Keach, Stacy, Sr. *producer, director*
Keith, Brian Michael *actor*
Kelley, Jackson DeForest *actor*
Kelly, Nancy Folden *arts administrator*
Kendall, Christopher (Christopher Wolff) *conductor, lutenist*
Kent, Gary Warner *film director, writer*
Kerr, Deborah Jane *actress*
†Khaner, Jeffrey *flutist, educator*
Kiley, Richard Paul *actor*
†Kirkland, Geoffrey A. *motion picture production designer*
Klippstatter, Kurt L. *conductor, music director*
Koner, Pauline *dancer, choreographer*
Krantz, Stephen Falk *motion picture producer*
Krause, Bernard Leo *bioacoustician, sonic artist, composer*
†Kriegsman, Sali Ann *arts administrator, artistic director, writer, consultant*
Kristofferson, Kris *singer, songwriter, actor*
Kupferman, Meyer *composer*
Kurtz, Gary Douglas *film producer*
Kutrzeba, Joseph S. *theatrical and film producer, director*
Kwak, Sung *conductor, music director*
Ladd, Cheryl (Cheryl Stopplemoor) *actress*
Landesman, Fredric Rocco *theatre executive*
Lane, Burton (Burton Levy) *composer*
Lane, Larry *performing company executive, theater educator*
Lateef, Yusef (Bill Evans) *composer, educator*

Lauper, Cyndi *musician*
Lazarus, Margaret Louise *film producer and director*
Lee, Michele *actress*
Lefferts, George *writer, producer, director*
Lehmann, Michael Stephen *film director*
León, Tania Justina *composer, music director, pianist*
†LeRoy, G. Palmer *publishing executive*
Leventhal, Nathan *performing arts executive, lawyer*
Lindfors, Viveca *actress*
Little, Loren Everton *musician, ophthalmologist*
Lobanov-Rostovsky, Oleg *arts association executive*
Lockhart, Aileene Simpson *retired dance, kinesiology and physical education educator*
Longstreet, Harry Stephen *television producer, director, scriptwriter*
Loring, Gloria Jean *singer, actress*
Lubin, Steven *concert pianist, musicologist*
Lupu, Radu *pianist*
Lynne, Jeff *rock musician, composer*
Madeira, Francis King Carey *conductor, educator*
Magor, Louis Roland *conductor*
†Malakhov, Vladimir *dancer*
Mangione, Chuck (Charles Frank Mangione) *jazz musician, composer*
Mann, Robert Nathaniel *violinist*
Mannes, Elena Sabin *film and television producer, director*
Mansouri, Lotfollah *opera stage director*
Marinaro, Edward Francis *actor*
Markinson, Martin *theatre owner, producer*
†Marks, Richard *film editor*
Marsden, Herci Ivana *classical ballet artistic director*
Marsee, Susanne Irene *lyric mezzo-soprano*
Marshall, Garry *film producer, director, writer*
Masterson, Peter *actor, director*
Mastroianni, Marcello *actor*
Mayeron, Carol Ann *cantor*
Mayron, Melanie *actress, writer*
McAnuff, Des *artistic director*
McBain, Diane Jean *actress, writer*
McCann, Elizabeth Ireland *theater, television and motion picture producer, lawyer*
McCartney, (James) Paul *musician*
Mc Clymont, Hamilton *entertainment industry executive*
McDowell, Malcolm *actor*
McEntire, Reba N. *country singer*
McGillis, Kelly *actress*
Mc Kayle, Donald Cohen *choreographer, director, writer, dance educator*
Meara, Anne *actress, playwright, writer*
Meier, Gustav *symphony conductor*
Melillo, Joseph Vincent *producer, performing arts*
Meredith, Burgess *actor*
Merlis, George *television producer*
Merrick, David (David Margulois) *theatrical producer*
Merrill, Lindsey *music educator*
Meserve, Walter Joseph *drama studies educator, publisher*
†Michelson, Harold *production designer*
Miller, Penelope Ann *actress*
Miller, Steve *television director, producer*
Mills, Mike *popular musician*
Minnix, Bruce Milton *television and theatre director*
Mirisch, Walter Mortimer *motion picture producer*
Mixon, Alan *actor*
Moffatt, Katy (Katherine Louella Moffatt) *musician, vocalist, songwriter*
Monty, Gloria *television producer*
Moore, Tom *film and theater director*
Morath, Max Edward *entertainer, composer*
Mordecai, Benjamin *theatrical producer, drama educator*
Morelan, Paula Kay *choreographer*
Morello, Joseph Albert *musician, educator*
Morita, (Noriyuki) Pat *actor, comedian*
Morrison, Shelley *actress*
Morrison, Van *musician, songwriter*
Morrow, Rob *actor*
Mount, Thomas H(enderson) *independent film producer*
Mulligan, Richard M. *actor, writer*
Muren, Dennis E. *visual effects director*
Murphy, Benjamin Edward *actor*
Musante, Tony (Anthony Peter Musante, Jr.) *actor*
Myers, Mike *actor, writer*
Myerson, Alan *director, film and television writer*
Narita, Hiro *cinematographer*
Naughton, James *actor*
Neame, Ronald *director, producer*
Neary, Patricia Elinor *ballet director*
Nederlander, James Laurence *theater owner, producer*
Needham, Lucien Arthur *musician, educator*
Neville, Phoebe *choreographer, dancer, educator*
Nevins, Sheila *television programmer and producer*
Newland, Larry J. *orchestra conductor*
Newman, Paul *actor, professional race-car driver, food company executive*
Newman, Randy *singer, songwriter, musician*
Newton, Wayne *entertainer, actor, recording artist*
Nilsson, Birgit *soprano*
Nissinen, Mikko Pekka *dancer*
†Nixon, David *dancer*
Nixon, Marni *singer*
Norton, Judy *actress*
O'Brien, Jack George *artistic director*
O'Neal, Ryan (Patrick Ryan O'Neal) *actor*
Oppenheim, David Jerome *musician, educational administrator*
Orbach, Jerry *actor, singer*
Osbourne, Ozzy (John Osbourne) *vocalist*
Page, Willis *conductor*
Parton, Dolly Rebecca *singer, composer, actress*
Patinkin, Mandy *actor*
Patrick, Dennis *actor, director*
Paul, Les *entertainer, inventor*
Paycheck, Johnny *country western musician*
Peck, Gregory *actor*
Pendergrass, Teddy (Theodore D. Pendergrass) *musician*
Pennario, Leonard *concert pianist, composer*
†Percy, Lee Edward *motion picture film editor*
Perle, George *composer*
Persky, Lester *film producer*
Peters, Virginia *actress*
Peterson, Monica (Dorothy Peterson) *actress, singer, model, writer*
Pierce, David Hyde *actor*
Pierce, Ponchitta Anne *television host, producer, journalist*
Pleshette, Suzanne *actress, writer*
†Poledouris, Basil K. *composer*
Poll, Martin Harvey *film producer*
Pope, Durand L. *opera manager*
Post, Markie *actress*
†Poster, Steven Barry *publisher, photographer, digital imaging consultant*
Poston, Tom *actor*
†Pourfarrokh, Ali *ballet company artistic director*
Powers, Stefanie (Stefanie Federkiewicz) *actress*
Primosch, James Thomas *music educator, composer, musician*
Prince, (Prince Rogers Nelson) *musician, actor*
Quaid, Dennis *actor*
Quaid, Randy *actor*
†Quinlan, Kathleen *actress*
Rafelson, Bob *film director*
Ragsdale, Carl Vandyke *motion picture producer*
Ransohoff, Martin *motion picture producer*
Redbone, Leon *singer, musician*
Reddy, Helen Maxine *singer*
Redford, Robert (Charles Robert Redford) *actor, director*
Redgrave, Vanessa *actress*
Reeves, Keanu *actor*
Rescigno, Nicola *conductor, administrator*
Rich, John *film and television producer, director*
Richardson, Natasha Jane *actress*
Richie, Lionel B., Jr. *singer, songwriter, producer*
Rickman, Tom *screenwriter, director*
Rideout, Patricia Irene *operatic, oratorio and concert singer*
Riley, Terry *composer, musician*
Roberts, Doris *actress*
Roberts, Julia Fiona *actress*
Roberts, Samuel Smith *television news executive*
Robertson, Cliff *actor, writer, director*
Rochberg, George *composer, educator*
Rolandi, Gianna *coloratura soprano*
Rorke, Kevin Hayden *broadcasting executive*
Rose, Rubye Blevins (Patsy Montana) *singer*
Rosemont, Norman *television and feature producer*
Rosen, Charles Welles *pianist, music educator*
Rosen, Myor *harpist, educator*
Rosenberg, Stuart *film director*
Rosenthal, Arnold H. *film director, producer, writer, graphic designer*
Ross, Elinor *soprano*
Rourke, Mickey (Philip Andre Rourke, Jr.) *actor*
Rowlands, Gena *actress*
Rudner, Sara *dancer, choreographer*
Ruggiero, Matthew John *bassoonist*
Russell, Theresa Lynn *actress*
Sade, (Helen Folasade Adu) *singer, songwriter*
Saint, Eva Marie *actress*
Sajak, Pat *television game show host*
Saks, Gene *theater director, actor*
Saltzman, Philip *television writer, producer*
Sanborn, David *alto saxophonist*
Sandor, Gyorgy *pianist*
Sandrich, Jay H. *television director*
Sarry, Christine *ballerina*
Sauerbrey, Ellen Elaine Richmond *radio talk show host*
Savini, Tom *make-up artist, actor, director*
Schaefer, George Louis *theatrical producer and director, educator*
Schafer, Raymond Murray *composer, author*
Schatzberg, Jerry Ned (Jerrold Schatzberg) *film director*
Schexnayder, Brian Edward *opera singer*
Schiller, Lawrence Julian *motion picture producer, director*
Schiller, Thomas Bennett *motion picture writer, director*
Schuur, Diane Joan *vocalist*
Schwary, Ronald Louis *motion picture producer*
Scott, Thomas Wright *jazz musician, composer*
Scruggs, Earl Eugene *entertainer*
†Seale, John Clement *director, cinematographer*
Seldes, Marian *actress*
Shapiro, Debbie Lynn (Lynn Shapiro) *singer, actress, dancer*
Shatin, Judith *music composing educator*
Shaw, Artie *musician, writer, lecturer*
Shelton, Sloane *actress*
Sherin, Edwin *theatrical and film director, actor*
Shirley-Quirk, John *concert and opera singer*
Short, Martin *actor, comedian*
Siegel, Laurence Gordon *conductor*
Silverman, Jonathan *actor*
Silverstein, Barbara Ann *conductor*
†Silvestri, Alan Anthony *film composer*
Simon, Carly *singer, composer, author*
Simon, Paul *musician, composer*
Skolovsky, Zadel *concert pianist, educator*
Skowronski, Vincent Paul *concert violinist, recording artist, executive producer, producer classical recordings*
Smith, Lawrence Leighton *conductor*
Smith, Lois Arlene *actress, writer*
Smoot, Hazel Lampkin *retired piano teacher, poet*
Smothers, Dick *actor, singer*
Snipes, Wesley *actor*
Solow, Herbert Franklin *film producer, writer*
Sondheim, Stephen Joshua *composer, lyricist*
Stanley, Margaret King *performing arts administrator*
Stapleton, Maureen *actress*
Starer, Robert *composer*
Sternhagen, Frances *actress*
Stevens, Warren *actor*
Stewart, James Maitland *actor*
Stewart, Thomas James, Jr. *baritone*
Stiller, Jerry *actor*
Strait, George *country music vocalist*
†Stroman, Susan *choreographer*
Stuart, Mary *actress*
Sutherland, Kiefer *actor*
Sutton, Dolores *actress, writer*
Swing, Marce *producer, publisher*
Swit, Loretta *actress*
Tallchief, Maria *ballerina*
†Taylor, Billy (William Edward Taylor) *jazz musician*
Taylor, Cecil Percival *pianist, composer, educator*
Taylor, Guy Watson *symphonic conductor*
Taylor, Millard Benjamin *concertmaster, educator*
Tewkesbury, Joan F. *film director, writer*
Thaxter, Phyllis St. Felix *actress*
Thomas, Karen P. *composer, conductor*
Thorstenberg, (John) Laurence *oboe and English horn player*
Tiemeyer, Christian *conductor*
Tokofsky, Jerry Herbert *film producer*
Tomlin, Lily *actress*
Topaz, Muriel *dance educator*
Topilow, Carl S. *conductor*
Torn, Rip (Elmore Rual Torn, Jr.) *actor, director*
Travanti, Daniel John *actor*
Travis, Randy Bruce *musician*
Travolta, John *actor*
Tripplehorn, Jeanne *actress*
Turkin, Marshall William *symphony orchestra, festival and opera administrator, arranger, composer*
Turner, Lana (Julia Jean Mildred Frances Turner) *actress*
Turner, Robert Comrie *composer*
Turok, Paul Harris *composer, music reviewer*
Ugrin, Béla *video producer*
Ullmann, Liv *actress*
†Vallone, John Charles *motion picture production designer*
Vandross, Luther *singer*
Van Patten, Joyce Benignia *actress*
Villella, Edward Joseph *ballet dancer, choreographer, artistic director*
Virkhaus, Taavo *conductor*
Voketaitis, Arnold Mathew *bass-baritone, educator*
Waldrop, Gideon William *composer, conductor, former president music school*
Wallach, Eli *actor*
Walsh, Joseph Fidler *recording artist, record producer*
Walston, Ray *actor*
Walthall, Lee Wade *artistic director, dancer*
Warner, Jack, Jr. *motion picture and television producer, writer*
Washington, Shelley Lynne *dancer*
Waters, John *film director, writer, actor*
Waters, Roger *rock musician*
Waters, Willie Anthony *opera and orchestra conductor*
Watts, Heather *ballerina*
Weld, Tuesday Ker (Susan Ker Weld) *actress*
Wendt, George Robert *actor*
Wettig, Patricia *actress*
Widmark, Richard *actor*
William, David *director, actor*
Williams, Patrick Moody *composer*
Williams, Russell, II *production sound mixer*
Williamson, Laird *stage director, actor*
Willis, Bruce Walter *actor, singer*
Wilson, Nancy *singer*
Winter, John Dawson, III *blues guitarist, singer*
Winters, Jonathan *actor*
Winters, Shelley (Shirley Schrift) *actress*
Winwood, Stephen Lawrence *musician, composer*
Wise, Patricia *lyric coloratura*
Wolfman Jack, (Robert Weston Smith) *radio personality*
Woodward, Joanne Gignilliat *actress*
Woodward, Thomas Morgan *actor*
Worthey, Carol *composer*
Wright, Gladys Stone *music educator, composer, writer*
Wyman, Jane (Sarah Jane Fulks) *actress*
Yarrow, Peter *folksinger*
Yellen, Linda *film director, writer, producer*
Yoakam, Dwight *country western musician*
Young, Robert (George Young) *actor*
Zaliouk, Yuval Nathan *conductor*
†Zeiger, Scott Leslie *commercial theater executive*
†Zinner, Peter *film editor and director, music editor*

ARTS: VISUAL

UNITED STATES

ALABAMA

Birmingham
Cullum, Mark Edward *editorial cartoonist*

Huntsville
Wilson, Allan Byron *graphics company executive*

Montgomery
Schwarz, Joseph Edmund *artist*

ALASKA

Anchorage
Sharp, Anne Catherine *artist, educator*

Cordova
Bugbee-Jackson, Joan *sculptor*

ARIZONA

Green Valley
Page, John Henry, Jr. *artist, educator*

Lake Montezuma
Burkee, Irvin *artist*

Oracle
Rush, Andrew Wilson *artist*

Paradise Valley
Heller, Jules *artist, writer*

Payson
Rich, Frances Luther *sculptor*

Phoenix
deMatties, Nicholas Frank *artist, art educator*
Dignac, Geny (Eugenia M. Bermudez) *sculptor*

Prescott
Farrar, Elaine Willardson *artist*
Stasack, Edward Armen *artist*

Scottsdale
Chase, James Keller *retired artist, museum director, educator*
Curtis, Philip C. *artist*
Golden, Libby *artist*
Lang, Margo Terzian *artist*
Scholder, Fritz *artist*

Tempe
Grigsby, Jefferson Eugene, Jr. *artist, educator*
Klett, Mark C. *photographer, educator*
Turk, Rudy Henry *artist, retired museum director*

Tucson
Conant, Howard Somers *artist, educator*
Flint, Willis Wolfschmidt (Willi Wolfschmidt) *artist*
Golden, Judith Greene *artist, educator*

ARKANSAS

Fayetteville
Wilson, Charles Banks *artist*

State University
Lindquist, Evan *artist, educator*

CALIFORNIA

Albion
Martin, Bill *artist, art educator*

Altadena
Ikegawa, Shiro *artist*

Aptos
Woods, Gurdon Grant *sculptor*

Aromas
Nutzle, Futzie (Bruce John Kleinsmith) *artist, author, cartoonist*

Avalon
Burns, Denise Ruth *artist*

Bakersfield
Reep, Edward Arnold *artist*

Berkeley
Abel, Ray *graphic artist*
Genn, Nancy *artist*
Hartman, Robert Leroy *artist, educator*
Kasten, Karl Albert *painter, printmaker*
Miyasaki, George Joji *artist*
Rapoport, Sonya *artist*
Simpson, David William *artist, educator*
Voulkos, Peter *artist*
Washburn, Stan *artist*

Beverly Hills
Acheson, James *costume designer*
†Allen, Marit *costume designer*
†Ballhaus, Michael *director photography*
†Cunliffe, Shay *costume designer*
†Gardiner, Lizzy *costume designer*
†Hornung, Richard *costume designer*
Klausen, Raymond *sculptor, television/theatre production designer*
†Myers, Ruth *costume designer*
†Pescucci, Gabriella *costume designer*
†Phillips, Erica Edell *costume designer*
†Scott, Deborah L. *costume designer*

Bodega
Hedrick, Wally Bill *artist*

Bolinas
Harris, Paul *sculptor*

Boonville
Hanes, John Ward *sculptor, civil engineer consultant*

Brisbane
Anargyros, Spero *sculptor*

Carmel
Kennedy, John Edward *art dealer, appraiser, curator*
Weston, Theodore Brett *photographer*

Carmichael
Sahs, Majorie Jane *art educator*

Carpinteria
Hansen, Robert William *artist, educator*

Carson
Hirsch, Gilah Yelin *artist, writer*

Claremont
Benjamin, Karl Stanley *artist, educator*
Blizzard, Alan *artist*
Casanova, Aldo John *sculptor*

Corona Del Mar
Brandt, Rexford Elson *artist*
Delap, Tony *artist*

Costa Mesa
Muller, Jerome Kenneth *editor, photographer*

Culver City
Bluth, Don *animator, director, screenwriter*

Davis
DePaoli, Geri M. *artist, art historian*

Dillon Beach
Petersen, Roland *artist, printmaker*

Escondido
Barrio, Raymond *author, artist*
Sternberg, Harry *artist*

Fallbrook
Ragland, Jack Whitney *artist*

Fullerton
Curran, Darryl Joseph *photographer, educator*

Garden Grove
Ortlieb, Robert Eugene *sculptor*

Hayward
Ramos, Melvin John *artist, educator*

Indio
Lloyd, Douglas George *watercolor artist, educator*

Inverness
Welpott, Jack Warren *photographer, educator*

Irvine
Kingman, Dong *artist, educator*

Kensington
Loran, Erle *artist*

La Jolla
Antin, Eleanor *artist*
Cuevas, Jose Luis *painter, illustrator*
Imana, Jorge Garron *artist*
Monaghan, Eileen *artist*
Whitaker, Eileen Monaghan *artist*

Lafayette
Kapp, Eleanor Jeanne *impressionistic artist, writer, researcher*

Laguna Niguel
Pierce, Hilda (Hilda Herta Harmel) *painter*

Lagunitas
Holman, Arthur Stearns *artist*

Long Beach
Dean, Charles Thomas *industrial arts educator, academic administrator*
Ferreira, Armando Thomas *sculptor, educator*

Los Angeles
†Abeles, Kim Victoria *artist*
Adam, Ken *production designer*
Bass, Saul *graphic designer, filmmaker*
Batres, Eduardo *computer model builder, animator*
Bayless, Raymond *artist*
Bothwell, Dorr *artist*
†Cox, Betsy *costume designer*
Danziger, Louis *graphic designer, educator*
Davis, Ronald *artist, printmaker*
Dillon, Paul Sanford *artist*
†Dorleac, Jean-Pierre *costume designer*
Ewing, Edgar Louis *artist, educator*
Galanos, James *fashion designer*
†Graham, Angelo *art director, production designer*
Greiman, April *graphic designer*
Hayes, Vertis Clemon *painter, sculptor, educator*
Johnston, Ynez *artist*
Kaminski, Janusz Zygmuni *photographer*
Kanemitsu, Matsumi *artist*
Ketchum, Robert Glenn *photographer, print maker*
Kienholz, Lyn Shearer *international arts projects coordinator*
†Kimball, Jeffrey L. *director of photography*
Kirschner, David *animation entertainment company executive*
Lark, Raymond *artist, art scholar*
Lem, Richard Douglas *painter*
Lewis, Samella Sanders *artist, educator*
McAuley, Skeet *artist*
Morphesis, James George *artist*
Natzler, Otto *ceramic artist*
Pederson, Con *animator*
Rankaitis, Susan *artist*
†Riggs, Rita *costume designer*
Rodgers, Aggie Guerard *costume designer*
Starr, Steven Dawson *photographer*
†Stewart, Marlene Jean *costume designer*
†van Runkle, Theadora *costume designer*
Weil, Jerry *animator*
Welch, Bo (Robert W. Welch, III) *production designer*
Welles, Melinda Fassett *artist, educator*
Woelffer, Emerson Seville *artist*
Young, Joseph Louis *artist*

Mariposa
Bruce, John Anthony *artist*
Rogers, Earl Leslie *artist, educator*

Mendocino
Alexander, Joyce Mary *illustrator*

Mill Valley
Blatt, Morton Bernard *medical illustrator*
Ihle, John Livingston *artist, educator*

Modesto
Bucknam, Mary Olivia Caswell *artist*

Monterey
Bowman, Dorothy Louise *artist*
Bradford, Howard *graphic artist, painter*

Morgan Hill
Freimark, Robert (Bob Freimark) *artist*

Napa
Garnett, William *photographer*

Newport Beach
Spitz, Barbara Salomon *artist*

Northridge
Bassler, Robert Covey *sculptor, educator*
Harden, Marvin *artist, educator*

Oakland
Beasley, Bruce Miller *sculptor*
Cook, Lia *art educator*
Dickinson, Eleanor Creekmore *artist, educator*
Leon, Dennis *sculptor*
Melchert, James Frederick *artist*
Okamura, Arthur *artist, educator, writer*
Rath, Alan T. *sculptor*

Oxnard
Perrier, Barbara Sue *artist*

Pacific Palisades
Chesney, Lee Roy, Jr. *artist*
†Norris, Patricia *costume designer*
†Norton, Rosanna *costume designer*

Palm Springs
Maree, Wendy *painter, sculptor*

Pasadena
Howe, Graham Lloyd *photographer, curator*
Newman, Joyce Kligerman *sculptor*
Zammitt, Norman *artist*

Pebble Beach
Mortensen, Gordon Louis *artist, printmaker*

Petaluma
Mc Chesney, Robert Pearson *artist*
Reichek, Jesse *artist*

Pinole
Gerbracht, Robert Thomas (Bob Gerbracht) *painter, educator*

Placentia
Galvez, William *artist*

Richmond
Wessel, Henry *photographer*

Sacramento
Dalkey, Fredric Dynan *artist*
Wallace, Patricia Jean *artist, educator, writer*

San Diego
Albuquerque, Lita *artist*
†Cannon, Janell *illustrator, writer*
Chandler, Floyd Copeland *fine arts educator*
†Diaz, David *illustrator*
Linton, Roy Nathan *graphic arts company executive*
Sorrentino, Renate Maria *illustrator*

San Francisco
Adams, Mark *artist*
Arnitz, Rick *artist*
Beall, Dennis Ray *artist, educator*
Bechtle, Robert Alan *artist, educator*
Chin, Sue Soone Marian (Suchin Chin) *conceptual artist, portraitist, photographer, community affairs activist*
Hershman, Lynn Lester *artist*
Hobbs, Carl Fredric *artist, filmmaker, author*
Holland, Tom *artist, educator*
Howard, David E. *artist*
Jones, Pirkle *photographer, educator*
Lobdell, Frank *artist*
Mach, David *artist*
Marioni, Tom *artist*
Martin, Fred *artist, college administrator*
McClintock, Jessica *fashion designer*
McNamara, John Stephen *artist, educator*
Neri, Manuel *sculptor*
Oliveira, Nathan *artist, educator*
Oropallo, Deborah *artist, educator*
Raciti, Cherie *artist*
Saunders, Raymond Jennings *artist, educator*
Van Hoesen, Beth Marie *artist, printmaker*
Wall, Brian Arthur *sculptor*
Wiley, William T. *artist*

San Jose
Estabrook, Reed *artist, educator*

San Luis Obispo
Dickerson, Colleen Bernice Patton *artist, educator*

San Marino
Medearis, Roger Norman *artist*

San Pedro
Crutchfield, William Richard *artist, educator*

San Rafael
Napoles, Veronica Kleeman *graphic designer, consultant*
Tift, Mary Louise *artist*

Santa Barbara
Eguchi, Yasu *artist*
Paradise, Phil(ip Herschel) *artist*

Santa Clarita
Fritzke, Audrey Elmere *artist*

Santa Cruz
Rydell, Amnell Roy *artist, landscape architect*
Summers, Carol *artist*

Santa Monica
†Flynt, Cynthia *costume designer*
Foulkes, Llyn *artist, educator*
Jenkins, George *stage designer, film art director*
Kauffman, Robert Craig *artist, sculptor*
†Maginnis, Molly *costume designer*
Stern, Jan Peter *sculptor*

Santa Rosa
Barr, Roger Terry *sculptor*
Rider, Jane Louise *artist, educator*

Sausalito
Glaser, Edwin Victor *rare book dealer*
Kuhlman, Walter Egel *artist, educator*

Sherman Oaks
†Beavan, Jenny *costume designer*
†Becker, Susan *costume designer*
†Bright, John *costume designer*
†Bruno, Richard *costume designer*
†Carter, Ruth E. *costume designer*
†Dalton, Phyllis *costume designer*
†Finkelman, Wayne *costume designer*
†Gresham, Gloria *costume designer*
†Heimann, Betsy Faith *costume designer*
†Hurley, Jan *costume designer*
†Jamison-Tanchuck, Francine *costume designer*
†Johnston, Joanna *costume designer*
†Jones, Gary *costume designer*
†Komarov, Shelley *costume designer*
†Kurland, Jeffrey *costume designer*
†McBride, Elizabeth *costume designer*
†Moorcroft, Judy *costume designer*
†Nadoolman, Deborah *costume designer*
†Pollack, Bernie *costume designer*
†Powell, Anthony *costume designer, set designer*
†Powell, Sandy *costume designer*
†Rand, Tom *costume designer*
†Ringwood, Bob *costume designer*
†Tompkins, Joe I. *costume designer*
†Vance-Straker, Marilyn *costume designer*
†Weiss, Julie *costume designer*

Soda Bay
Fletcher, Leland Vernon *artist*

Somis
Kehoe, Vincent Jeffré-Roux *photographer, author, cosmetic company executive*

Sonora
Price, Joe (Allen) *artist, former educator*

South Pasadena
Askin, Walter Miller *artist, educator*

Stockton
Oak, Claire Morisset *artist, educator*

Studio City
†Tavoularis, Dean *motion picture production designer*
†Wissner, Gary Charles *motion picture art director, production designer*

Summerland
Calamar, Gloria *artist*

Torrance
Everts, Connor *artist*

Valencia
Fiskin, Judith Anne *artist educator*

Venice
Bengston, Billy Al *artist*
Berlant, Anthony *artist*
Eversley, Frederick John *sculptor, engineer*

Victorville
Bascom, Earl Wesley *artist, sculptor, writer*

West Hills
Freas, Frank Kelly *illustrator*

West Hollywood
Hockney, David *artist*

Woodland Hills
Labadie, George Sherman *retired art director*

Yreka
McFadden, Leon Lambert *artist, inventor*

COLORADO

Aspen
Berkó, Ferenc *photographer*
Soldner, Paul Edmund *artist, ceramist, educator*

Aurora
Hickman, Grace Marguerite *artist*

Boulder
Balog, James Dennis *photographer*
Gough, Bryan Ray *graphic designer*
Matthews, Eugene Edward *artist*
Matthews, Wanda Miller *artist*

Brush
Cumberlin, Charles Edgar *auctioneer*

Colorado Springs
Blanchette, Jeanne Ellene Maxant *artist, educator, performer*
Goehring, Kenneth *artist*

Denver
Lawless, Sarah Madison *theatrical executive*
Norman, John Barstow, Jr. *designer, educator*

Larkspur
Bierbaum, Janith Marie *artist*

Longmont
†Adams, Robert Hickman *photographer*

Louisville
Day, Robert Edgar *retired artist, educator*
Qualley, Charles Albert *fine arts educator*

Telluride
Smith, Samuel David *artist, educator*

University Of Colorado
Chamberlin, Henry Scott *artist, educator*

CONNECTICUT

Bethel
Ajay, Abe *artist*

Bloomfield
Hammer, Alfred Emil *artist, educator*

Brookfield
Rowe, Edward Lawrence, Jr. *graphic designer*
Westermann, Horace Clifford *sculptor*
Whelan, Michael Raymond *artist, illustrator*

Cornwall Bridge
Pfeiffer, Werner Bernhard *artist, educator*

Cos Cob
Kane, Margaret Brassler *sculptor*

Danbury
Caparn, Rhys (Mrs. Herbert Johannes Steel) *sculptor*
Saghir, Adel Jamil *artist, painter, sculptor*

East Hartford
Soppelsa, George Nicholas *artist*

Essex
Curtis, Alva Marsh *artist*

Fairfield
Trager, Philip *photographer, lawyer*

Falls Village
Cronin, Robert Lawrence *sculptor, painter*

Georgetown
Roberts, Priscilla Warren *artist*

Greenwich
Neal, Irene Collins *artist, educator*
Perless, Robert L. *sculptor*
Pope, Ingrid Bloomquist *sculptor, lecturer, poet*

Hartford
Menses, Jan *artist, draftsman, etcher, lithographer, muralist*

Meriden
Bertolli, Eugene Emil *sculptor, goldsmith, designer, consultant*

Middletown
Seeley, J. *photography educator*

New Canaan
Caesar, Henry A., II *sculptor*
Kovatch, Jak Gene *artist*
Rendl-Marcus, Mildred *artist, economist*
Richards, Walter DuBois *artist, illustrator*

New Haven
Bailey, William Harrison *artist, educator*
Eisenman, Alvin *educator, graphic designer*
Johnson, Lester Fredrick *artist*
Papageorge, Tod *photographer, educator*
Pease, David Gordon *artist, educator*

Noank
Bates, Gladys Edgerly *sculptor*

Norwalk
Perry, Charles Owen *sculptor*

Old Lyme
Chandler, Elisabeth Gordon (Mrs. Laci De Gerenday) *sculptor, harpist*
de Gerenday, Laci Anthony *sculptor*

Ridgefield
Julian, Alexander, II *menswear designer*

Sherman
Goodspeed, Barbara *artist*

Stamford
Rudman, Joan Eleanor *artist, educator*
Strosahl, William Austin *artist, art director*

Storrs Mansfield
Zelanski, Paul John *art educator, author*

Voluntown
Caddell, Foster *artist*

Warren
Abrams, Herbert E. *artist*
Gray, Cleve *artist*

West Cornwall
Prentice, Tim *sculptor, architect*
Simont, Marc *artist*

West Hartford
Glasson, Lloyd *sculptor, educator*
Uccello, Vincenza Agatha *artist, director, educator emerita*

West Haven
Lee, Ming Cho *set designer*

Weston
Bleifeld, Stanley *sculptor*
Cadmus, Paul *artist, etcher*
Rand, Paul *graphic designer, educator*

Westport
†Chernow, Ann Levy *artist, art educator*
†Chernow, Burt *artist, educator, writer*
†Fisher, Leonard Everett *artist, writer, educator*
Silk, George *photographer*

Wilton
Stuart, Kenneth James *illustrator, art director*

DELAWARE

Greenville
Reynolds, Nancy Bradford duPont (Mrs. William Glasgow Reynolds) *sculptor*

Hockessin
Sawin, Nancy Churchman *educator, artist, historian*

New Castle
Almquist, Don *illustrator, artist*

Newark
Moss, Joe Francis *sculptor, painter*
Rowe, Charles Alfred *artist, designer, educator*

DISTRICT OF COLUMBIA

Washington
Blair, James Pease *photographer, retired*
Brown, John Carter *art and education consultant, federal agency administrator*
Costigan, Constance Frances *artist, educator*
Danziger, Joan *sculptor*
DiPerna, Frank Paul *photographer, educator*
Donaldson, Jeff Richardson *visual artist, educator*

†Fletcher, Carlton Henry *artist*
Gilliam, Sam *artist*
Gossage, John Ralph *photographer*
Gumpert, Gunther *artist*
Halstead, Dirck S. *photographer, journalist*
Jones, Lois Mailou (Mrs. Vergniaud Pierre-Noel) *artist, educator*
Millon, Henry Armand *fine arts educator, architectural historian*
Perlmutter, Jack *artist, lithographer*
Polan, Annette Lewis *artist*
Power, Mark *journalist, photographer, educator*
Puryear, Martin *artist*
Scorca, Marc Azzolini *arts administrator*
Stevenson, A. Brockie *artist*
Summerford, Ben Long *retired artist, educator*
Suro, Dario *artist, diplomat*
Truitt, Anne Dean *artist*

FLORIDA

Bal Harbour
Bernay, Betti *artist*

Boca Grande
Frazetta, Frank *artist*

Boca Raton
Amen, Irving *artist*
Mills, Agnes Eunice Karlin *artist, printmaker, sculptor*
Ortlip, Paul Daniel *artist*
Russo, Kathleen Marie *art educator*

Boynton Beach
Plossu, Bernard Pierre *photographer*

Bradenton
Doenecke, Carol Anne *artist*
Hodgell, Robert Overman *artist, art educator*

Coral Gables
Bannard, Walter Darby *artist, art critic*

Delray Beach
Ross, Beatrice Brook *artist*

Englewood
Sisson, Robert F. *photographer, writer, lecturer, educator*

Fernandina Beach
D'Agnese, Helen Jean *artist*

Flagler Beach
Nebil, Corinne Elizabeth *artist*

Fort Lauderdale
Bimstein, Benjamin William *ice sculptor, caterer, chef*
Friedman, Sol *inventor, writer*
Hanson, Duane Elwood *sculptor*

Fort Myers
Schwartz, Carl Edward *artist, printmaker*

Gainesville
Craven, Roy Curtis, Jr. *art educator emeritus, art gallery director*
Kerslake, Kenneth Alvin *art educator, printmaker*
Murray, Ernest Don *artist, educator*
Uelsmann, Jerry Norman *photographer*
Williams, Hiram Draper *artist, educator*

Hobe Sound
Frank, Mary *sculptor, artist*

Hollywood
Sadowski, Carol Johnson *fine artist, painter*

Holmes Beach
Neustadt, Barbara Mae *artist, illustrator, etcher*

Indian Harbour Beach
Traylor, Angelika *stained glass artist*

Jacksonville
Mikulas, Joseph Frank *graphic designer, educator, painter*

Key Largo
Fundora, Thomas *artist, journalist, composer*

Key West
Barnard, Scott *artist consultant*
Feeley, Henry Joseph, Jr. (Hank Feeley) *artist, former advertising agency executive*

Melbourne
Stark, Bruce Gunsten *artist*

Melrose
Harley, Ruth *artist, educator*

Miami
Alexenberg, Mel *artist, art educator*
Hanna, Ronald Everette *art educator, consultant*
Morgan, Andrew Wesley *artist, educator*
Strickland, Thomas Joseph *artist*

Miami Beach
Balás, Irene Barbara *artist*

Naples
Eldridge, David Carlton *art appraiser*
Hebald, Milton Elting *sculptor*
Vickrey, Robert Remsen *artist*

New Port Richey
Recchia, Susan Margaret *artist, author*

Ocala
Cini, Anthony Richard *bookbinding craftsman*

Palm Bay
Galitello-Wolfe, Jane Maryann *artist, writer*

Palm Beach
Kaplan, Muriel Sheerr *sculptor*
Wenzel, Joan Ellen *artist*

Plant City
Holland, Gene Grigsby (Scottie Holland) *artist*

Pompano Beach
Albert, Calvin *sculptor*

Quincy
Lindquist, Mark Alvin *artist*

Sarasota
Altabe, Joan Augusta Berg *artist, writer, art and architecture critic*
Chamberlain, John Angus *sculptor*
Eliscu, Frank *sculptor*
Harmon, (Loren) Foster *art consultant*
Putterman, Florence Grace *artist, printmaker*
Sawyer, Helen Alton *artist*
Sloan, Richard *artist*
Solomon, Syd *artist*
Winterhalter, Dolores August (Dee Winterhalter) *art educator*

Sebastian
Pieper, Patricia Rita *artist, photographer*

Siesta
Held, Philip *artist*

Tampa
Wilson, Wallace *art educator, artist*

Winter Park
Holt, Georgina L. *ceramic artist*

GEORGIA

Alpharetta
Byrd, Bette Jean *artist, author*

Athens
Herbert, James Arthur *artist, filmmaker*
Kent, Robert B. *artist, educator*
†Paul, William Dewitt, Jr. *artist, educator, photographer, museum director*

Atlanta
Beattie, George *artist*
Callahan, Harry Morey *photographer*
Grumet, Priscilla Hecht *fashion specialist, consultant, writer*
Guberman, Sidney Thomas *painter, writer*
McLean, James Albert *artist, educator*
Sherman, Ron *photographer*

Augusta
Rosen, James Mahlon *artist, art historian, educator*

Decatur
Loehle, Betty Barnes *artist, painter*

Mount Berry
Mew, Thomas Joseph, III (Tommy Mew) *artist, educator*

Savannah
Alley, James Pinckney, Jr. *computer art and graphic design educator*
†Aquadro, Jeana Lauren *graphic designer, educator*

HAWAII

Aiea
Monk, Gregory Brittain *artist, business owner*

Haiku
Cost, James Peter *artist*

Haleiwa
Valentine, De Wain *artist*

Honolulu
Amor, Simeon, Jr. *photographer, historian*
Betts, Barbara Stoke *artist, educator*
Kenda, Juanita Echeverria *artist, educator*

Lahaina
Sato, Tadashi *artist*

IDAHO

Saint Maries
Carlson, George Arthur *artist*

ILLINOIS

Champaign
Jackson, Billy Morrow *artist, retired art educator*
Kotoske, Roger Allen *artist, educator*

Chicago
Africano, Nicholas *artist*
Bender, Janet Pines *artist*
Boggess, Thomas Phillip, III *graphic arts company executive*
Bowman, Leah *fashion designer, consultant, photographer, educator*
Crane, Barbara Bachmann *photographer, educator*
Gehr, Mary *illustrator, painter, printmaker*
Goetz, John Bullock *graphic designer*
Gray, Richard *art dealer, consultant, holding company executive*
Greene-Mercier, Marie Zoe *sculptor*
Heinecken, Robert Friedli *art educator, artist*
Himmelfarb, John David *artist*
Jachna, Joseph D. *photographer, educator*
Josephson, Kenneth Bradley *artist, educator*
Kearney, John Walter *sculptor, painter*
King, Andre Richardson *architectural graphic designer*
Klement, Vera *artist*
Koga, Mary *artist, photographer, social worker*
Lerner, Nathan Bernard *artist*
Mintz, Harry *artist, educator*
Nutt, Jim *artist*
Paschke, Edward F. *artist, illustrator*
Paul, Arthur *artist, graphic designer, illustrator, art and design consultant*
Prekop, Martin D. *art educator, artist*
Ramberg, Christina *artist, educator*
Regensteiner, Else Friedsam (Mrs. Bertold Regensteiner) *textile designer, educator*
Saul, Peter *artist*
Skrebneski, Victor *photographer*

De Kalb
Ashmann, Jon *art professor, designer*
Even, Robert Lawrence *art educator*

Edwardsville
Malone, Robert Roy *artist, art educator*

Evanston
Conger, William Frame *artist, educator*
Sandor, Ellen Ruth *artist*
Vanderstappen, Harrie Albert *Far Eastern art educator*

Lombard
Ahlstrom, Ronald Gustin *artist*

Normal
Towner, Naomi Whiting *fiber artist, educator*

River Forest
Sloan, Jeanette Pasin *artist*
White, Philip Butler *artist*

Riverside
Howlett, Carolyn Svrluga *art educator*

Scales Mound
Lieberman, Archie *photographer, writer*

Waukegan
Bleck, Virginia Eleanore *illustrator*

Winnetka
Pattison, Abbott Lawrence *sculptor*
Plowden, David *photographer*
Sharboneau, Lorna Rosina *artist, educator, writer*

INDIANA

Anderson
Olson, Carol Lea *lithographer, educator, photographer*

Bloomington
Lowe, Marvin *artist*
Markman, Ronald *artist, educator*
O'Hearn, Robert Raymond *stage designer*
Pozzatti, Rudy Otto *artist*
†Wolin, Jeffrey Alan *artist*

Indianapolis
Block, Amanda Roth *artist*

Lowell
Boller, Carole Ann *visual artist*

Madison
Gunter, Frank Elliott *artist*

Morgantown
Boyce, Gerald G. *artist, educator*

Muncie
Connally, Sandra Jane Oppy *art educator*

Notre Dame
Lauck, Anthony Joseph *artist, retired art educator, priest*

Terre Haute
Lamis, Leroy *artist, retired educator*

West Lafayette
Ichiyama, Dennis Yoshihide *design educator, consultant*

IOWA

Davenport
Jecklin, Lois Underwood *art corporation executive, consultant*

Des Moines
Reece, Maynard Fred *artist, author*

Grinnell
Cervene, Richard T. *art educator*

Iowa City
Schmidt, Julius *sculptor*

KANSAS

Lawrence
Brawley, Robert Julius *artist, art educator*
Papanek, Victor *designer, educator, writer*

Ottawa
Howe, William Hugh *artist*

Shawnee Mission
Hershman, Mark Steven *lighting designer*

KENTUCKY

Lexington
Boyer, Lillian Buckley *artist, educator*
Henderson, Hubert Platt *fine arts association executive*

LOUISIANA

Mandeville
Rohrbough, Elsa Claire Hartman *artist*

New Orleans
Azaceta, Luis Cruz *artist*
Lovejoy, Barbara Campbell *sculptor, architectural designer*
O'Meallie, Kitty *artist*
Steg, J(ames) L(ouis) *artist*
Thornell, Jack Randolph *photographer*

MAINE

Bath
Ipcar, Dahlov *illustrator, painter, author*
Webb, Todd (Charles Clayton Webb) *photographer, writer*

Boothbay Harbor
Cavanaugh, Tom Richard *artist, antiques dealer, retired art educator*
Eames, John Heagan *etcher*
Grossman, Morton S. *artist*

Cushing
Magee, A. Alan *artist*

Damariscotta
Robinson, Walter George *arts management and funding consultant*

Gorham
Bearce, Jeana Dale *artist, educator*

Jefferson
Fiore, Joseph Albert *artist*

Kennebunk
Betts, Edward *artist*

Little Deer Isle
Mc Closkey, Robert *artist*

Monhegan Island
Hudson, Jacqueline *artist*

New Harbor
Lyford, Cabot *sculptor*

North Fryeburg
Bolomey, Roger Henry *sculptor*

Port Clyde
Thon, William *artist*

Vinalhaven
Indiana, Robert *artist*

Wiscasset
Leslie, Seaver *artist*

York Beach
Davison, Nancy Reynolds *artist*

MARYLAND

Annapolis
Koscianski, Leonard Joseph *artist*

Baltimore
Hartigan, Grace *artist*
Pittman, Carolyn *artist*
Rothschild, Amalie Rosenfeld *artist*

Bethesda
Safer, John *artist, lecturer*
Sarnoff, Lili-Charlotte Dreyfus (Lolo Sarnoff) *artist, business executive*

Brentwood
Kaskey, Raymond John *sculptor*

Centreville
Amos, James Lysle *photographer*

Chevy Chase
Asher, Lila Oliver *artist*
Calfee, William Howard *sculptor, painter*
Ginzburg, Yankel *artist*
Kainen, Jacob *artist, former museum curator*

College Park
DeMonte, Claudia Ann *artist, educator*
Lapinski, Tadeusz Andrew *artist, educator*

Columbia
Blackwell, Camellia Ann *art educator*

Denton
Doster, Rose Eleanor Wilhelm *artist*

Gaithersburg
Bochicchio, Jill Arden *photographer*

Owings
Oring, Stuart August *visual information specialist, writer/photographer*

Silver Spring
Barkin, Robert Allan *graphic designer, newspaper executive, consultant*
Peiperl, Adam *kinetic and video sculptor*

MASSACHUSETTS

Amherst
Hendricks, James Powell *artist*
Holmes, Helen Bequaert *researcher*
Liebling, Jerome *photographer, educator*

Andover
Cook, Christopher Capen *artist, educator*
Lloyd, Robert Andrew *art educator*

Ashland
Gohlke, Frank William *photographer*

Boston
Ablow, Joseph *artist, educator*
Avison, David *photographer*
Fink, Joanna Elizabeth *art dealer*
Gibran, Kahlil *sculptor*
Handford, Martin John *illustrator, author*
Isaacs, Helen Coolidge Adams (Mrs. Kenneth L. Isaacs) *artist*
Pineda, Marianna *sculptor, educator*
Preston, Malcolm *artist, art critic*
Smith, Keith A. *artist*
Stone, James J. *photographer*
Wiesner, David *illustrator, children's writer*
Yamamoto, Tamotsu *art educator, artist, architectural illustrator*

Braintree
Conlon, Eugene *artist, administrator*

Brookline
Barron, Ros *artist*
Swan, Barbara *artist*
Wilson, John *artist*

Cambridge
Ackerman, James Sloss *fine arts educator*
Alcalay, Albert S. *artist, educator*
Bapst, Sarah *artist, educator*
Feininger, Theodore Lux *artist*
Katayama, Toshihiro *artist, educator*
Koerner, Joseph Leo *art history educator*
Mazur, Michael *artist*
Mc Kie, Todd Stoddard *artist*
Piene, Otto *artist, educator*
Reimann, William Page *artist, educator*
Rosenfield, John Max *art educator*

Chilmark
Geyer, Harold Carl *artist, writer*
Low, Joseph *artist*

Concord
Ihara, Michio *sculptor*

Conway
Mallary, Robert *sculptor*

East Sandwich
Cober, Alan Edwin *artist, illustrator, printmaker, educator*

Gloucester
Curtis, Roger William *artist, educator*
Duca, Alfred Milton *artist*
Hancock, Walker Kirtland *sculptor*

Granville
†Brown, Stephen Pat *artist*

Hull
Burgess, David Lowry *artist*

Leeds
Baskin, Leonard *sculptor, graphic artist*

Lenox
LiMarzi, Joseph *artist*
Ripps, Rodney *artist*

Lowell
Sullivan, Anne Dorothy Hevner *artist*

Manchester
Lothrop, Kristin Curtis *sculptor*

Montague
Coughlin, Jack *printmaker, sculptor, art educator*

Nantucket
Holch, Eric Sanford *artist*

Natick
Geller, Esther (Bailey Geller) *artist*

Needham
Hunter, Elizabeth Ives-Valsam *consultant*

Newtonville
Polonsky, Arthur *artist, educator*

Norfolk
Beard, Carol Elaine *art educator*

North Brookfield
Neal, Avon *artist, author*
Parker, Ann (Ann Parker Neal) *photographer, graphic artist*

North Eastham
Simmel, Marianne Lenore *graphic designer*

Northampton
Rupp, Sheron Adeline *photographer, educator*

Norwell
Brett, Jan Churchill *illustrator, author*
Wentworth, Murray Jackson *artist, educator*

Orange
Bate, Judith Ellen *artist*

Orleans
Lawton, Nancy *artist*

Plymouth
Joseph, Rodney Randy *artist, arts society executive*

Rockport
Morrell, Wayne Beam, Jr. *artist*
Nicholas, Thomas Andrew *artist*
Strisik, Paul *artist*

Sherborn
Pickhardt, Carl Emile, Jr. *artist*

Somerville
Bakanowsky, Louis Joseph *visual arts educator, architect, artist*

South Hadley
Hall, Lee *artist, educator*

Sudbury
Aronson, David *artist, retired art educator*
Nyman, Georgianna Beatrice *painter*

Topsfield
Webster, Larry Russell *artist*

Waltham
Bohlen, Nina *artist*

Wellesley
O'Gorman, James Francis *art educator, writer*

West Barnstable
Bowman, George Leo *artist*

West Brookfield
Higgins, Brian Alton *art gallery executive*

Westport
Somerson, Rosanne *artist*

Westwood
Philbrick, Margaret Elder *artist*

Wilbraham
Gale, William Henry *artist*

Winchester
Neuman, Robert Sterling *art educator, artist*

MICHIGAN

Ann Arbor
Cassara, Frank *artist, printmaker*
Kamrowski, Gerome *artist*
Leonard, Joanne *photographer, educator*

Birmingham
Ortman, George Earl *artist*

Bloomfield Hills
McCoy, Katherine Braden *designer, educator*
McCoy, Michael Dale *designer, educator*

Dearborn
†Cape, James Odies E. *fashion designer*
†Telnack, John J. *automobile designer*

Detroit
Kachadoorian, Zubel *artist, educator*
Moldenhauer, Judith A. *graphic design educator*

East Lansing
Leepa, Allen *artist, educator*

Glenn
Rizzolo, Louis B. M. *artist, educator*

Grand Rapids
Blovits, Larry John *retired art educator*
Bolt, Eunice Mildred DeVries *artist*

Harsens Island
Slade, Roy *artist, college president, museum director*

Port Huron
Rowark, Maureen *fine arts photographer*

Riverdale
Kirby, Kent Bruce *artist, educator*

Royal Oak
Fredericks, Marshall Maynard *sculptor*

Troy
Avedisian, Edward *artist*

MINNESOTA

Duluth
Chee, Cheng-Khee *artist*

Edina
Saltzman, William *painter, sculptor, designer*

Minneapolis
Dugmore, Edward *artist*
Hallman, Gary L. *photographer, educator*
Larkin, Eugene David *artist, educator*
Myers, Malcolm Haynie *artist, art educator*
Preuss, Roger E(mil) *artist*
Rose, Thomas Albert *artist, art educator*

Northfield
Dittmann, Reidar *art educator*
Lloyd, Timothy L. *art educator*

MISSISSIPPI

Belzoni
Halbrook, Rita Robertshaw *artist, sculptor*

Greenville
†Carter, Peggy Wolfe *artist*

Meridian
Marshall, John Steven *artist, educator, museum administrator*

MISSOURI

Columbia
Larson, Sidney *art educator, artist, writer, painting conservator*

Des Peres
Smith, Barbara Martin *art educator*

Kansas City
Bransby, Eric James *muralist, educator*
Lee, Margaret Norma *artist*

Saint Louis
Burkett, Randy James *lighting designer*
DesRosiers, Roger I. *artist, educator*
Duhme, H(erman) Richard, Jr. *sculptor, educator*
Dunivent, John Thomas *artist, educator*
Lazorko, Anthony, Jr. *art director*
Pulitzer, Emily S Rauh (Mrs. Joseph Pulitzer, Jr.) *art consultant*
Trova, Ernest Tino *artist, sculptor*
Wandling, Marilyn Elizabeth Branson *artist, art educator*

Springfield
Delaney, Jean Marie *art educator*
King, (Jack) Weldon *photographer*

Webster Groves
Osver, Arthur *artist*

MONTANA

Browning
Scriver, Robert Macfie *sculptor*

Hot Springs
Erickson, James Gardner *retired artist, cartoonist*

Missoula
Rippon, Thomas Michael *art educator, artist*

NEVADA

Henderson
Turner, Florence Frances *ceramist*

Nellis AFB
Trippy, Donald R. *illustrator*

Reno
Harder, Kelsie T. *artist, educator*
Newberg, Dorothy Beck (Mrs. William C. Newberg) *portrait artist*

NEW HAMPSHIRE

Exeter
Dailey, Daniel Owen *artist, educator, designer*

Hanover
Boghosian, Varujan Yegan *sculptor*
Jacobus, John M., Jr. *educator, author, photographer*
Moss, Ben Frank, III *art educator, painter*

Manchester
Dobbins, James Joseph *artist*

NEW JERSEY

Asbury
Konrad, Adolf Ferdinand *artist*

Bayonne
Gorman, William David *artist, graphic artist*

Bernardsville
Coheleach, Guy Joseph *artist*
Spofford, Sally Hyslop *artist*

Blairstown
Bean, Bennett *artist*

Bridgewater
Glesmann, Sylvia-Maria *artist*
Patton, Diana Lee Wilkoc *artist*

Califon
Rosen, Carol Mendes *artist*

Cranbury
Lee-Smith, Hughie *artist, educator*

Cresskill
Smyth, Craig Hugh *fine arts educator*

Denville
Coes, Kent Day *artist*

East Brunswick
Nemser, Robert Solomon *visual communications consultant, art director, designer, educator*

Edison
Behr, Marion Ray *artist, author*

Englewood
Anuszkiewicz, Richard Joseph *artist*
Casarella, Edmond *sculptor, printmaker*

Fair Lawn
Parker, Adrienne Natalie *art educator, art historian, lecturer*

Hightstown
Howard, Barbara Sue Mesner *artist*

Iselin
Tice, George A(ndrew) *photographer*

Jersey City
Gurevich, Grigory *visual artist, educator*
Serra-Badue, Daniel Francisco *artist, educator*

Keasbey
†Hari, Kenneth Stephen *painter*

Keyport
Graupe-Pillard, Grace *artist, educator*

Milford
Carter, Clarence Holbrook *artist*

Montclair
Beerman, Miriam *artist, educator*

New Brunswick
Goffen, Rona *art educator*
Goodyear, John Lake *artist, educator*

Park Ridge
De Pol, John *artist*

Piscataway
Ortiz, Raphael Montañez *performance artist, educator*
Young, James Earl *ceramics educator, educational administrator*

Princeton
Bunnell, Peter Curtis *photography and art educator, museum curator*
Canright, Sarah Anne *artist, educator*
Carlson, Charlotte Booth *book illustrator*
George, Thomas *artist*
Grabar, Oleg *art educator*
Savage, Naomi *photographer*
Seawright, James L., Jr. *sculptor, educator*
Wilmerding, John *art history educator, museum curator*

Rockleigh
Heslin, Cathleen Jane *artist, designer, entrepreneur*

Roosevelt
Landau, Jacob *artist*

Rumson
Cocker, Barbara Joan *marine artist, interior designer*

Rutherford
Petrie, Ferdinand Ralph *illustrator, artist*

Short Hills
Good, Joan Duffey *artist*

Stillwater
Finkelstein, Louis *retired art educator*

Stockton
Mahon, Robert *photographer*
Schoenherr, John (Carl) *artist, illustrator*

Summit
Rousseau, Irene Victoria *artist, sculptor*

Tenafly
Heghinian, Elizabeth Alban Trumbower *artist, educator*
Koons, Irvin Louis *design and marketing executive, graphic artist, consultant*

Toms River
Unger, Howard Albert *artist, photographer, educator*

Trenton
Chavooshian, Marge *artist, educator*

Union
Doren, Henry Julius Thaddeus *artist, painter*

Ventnor City
Robbins, Hulda Dornblatt *artist, printmaker*

Verona
Ayaso, Manuel *artist*

Wayne
Haxton, David *computer graphics educator, computer animator, photographer*
Katz, Leandro *artist, filmmaker*

NEW MEXICO

Albuquerque
Adams, Clinton *artist, historian*
Antreasian, Garo Zareh *artist, lithographer, art educator*
Armstrong, Glenn Garnett *artist, retired postal executive*
Barrow, Thomas Francis *artist, educator*
Barry, Steve *sculptor, educator*
Hahn, Betty *artist, photographer, educator*
†Nagatani, Patrick Allan Ryoichi *artist, art educator*
Phillips, Ronald Edward *artist, sales executive*
Witkin, Joel-Peter *photographer*

Belen
Chicago, Judy *artist*

Corrales
Eaton, Pauline *artist*

Grants
Lowney, Bruce Stark *artist*

Lamy
Holt, Nancy Louise *artist*

Ranchos De Taos
Marx, Nicki D. *sculptor, painter*

Ruidoso Downs
Knapp, Thomas Edwin *sculptor, painter*

Santa Fe
Ancona, George Ephrain *photographer, film producer, author*
Clift, William Brooks, III *photographer*
Erdman, Barbara *visual artist*
Grover, Phyllis Bradman *artist, consultant*
†Handell, Albert George *artist*
Hatch, John Davis *design consultant, art historian*
Longley, Bernique *artist, painter, sculptor*
Loriaux, Maurice Lucien *artist, ecclesiologist*
Scheinbaum, David *photography educator*
Shubart, Dorothy Louise Tepfer *artist, educator*

Taos
Bell, Larry Stuart *artist*
Crespin, Leslie Ann *artist*
Ellis, Robert Malcolm *artist, foundation administrator*

NEW YORK

Afton
Schwartz, Aubrey Earl *artist*

Alfred
Billeci, Andre George *art educator, sculptor*
Higby, (Donald) Wayne *artist, educator*

Amagansett
Opper, John *painter, retired educator*

Annandale On Hudson
Sullivan, Jim *artist*

Armonk
Elson, Charles *stage designer, educator*

Babylon
Haley, Priscilla Jane *artist, printmaker*

Bayside
Goldstein, Milton *art educator, printmaker, painter*

Bearsville
Wickiser, Ralph Lewanda *painter, educator, author*

Bedford
Weinman, Robert Alexander *sculptor*

Binghamton
Ippolito, Angelo *artist, educator*

Bloomington
Ruffing, Anne Elizabeth *artist*

Bridgehampton
Jackson, Lee *artist*

Bronx
Adams, Alice *sculptor*
Kassoy, Hortense (Honey Kassoy) *artist*
Schwam, Marvin Albert *graphic design company executive*

Brooklyn
Anderson, Lennart *artist*
Artschwager, Richard Ernst *artist*
Battle, Turner Charles, III *art educator, educational association administrator*
Carlile, Janet Louise *artist, educator*
Carruthers, Walter Edward Royden (Roy Carruthers) *graphic designer, artist*
Clark, Peggy *theatrical lighting designer*
Cornell, Thomas Browne *artist, educator*
DeCarava, Roy R. *photographer, educator*
Delson, Elizabeth *artist*
Dinnerstein, Harvey *artist*
Dinnerstein, Simon Abraham *artist, educator*
Grado, Angelo John *artist*
Jones, Susan Emily *fashion educator, administrator, educator*
Lederman, Stephanie Brody *artist*
Pearlstein, Seymour *artist*
Pfaffman, William Scott *sculptor*
Rocco, Ron *artist*
Schaefer, Marilyn Louise *artist, writer, educator*
Shechter, Ben-Zion *artist, illustrator*
Shechter, Laura Judith *artist*
Sonenberg, Jack *artist*
Swirsky, Judith Perlman *arts administrator, consultant*
†von Rydingsvard, Ursula Karoliszyn *sculptor*

Buffalo
Berlin, Lorna Chumley *artist*
Piccillo, Joseph *artist*
Rogovin, Milton *photographer, retired optometrist*

Burdett
Stillman, Joyce L. *artist, educator, consultant*

Buskirk
Johanson, Patricia Maureen *artist, architect, park designer*

Campbell Hall
Greenly, Colin *artist*

Clarence
Hubler, Julius *artist*

Climax
Adler, Lee *artist, educator, marketing executive*

Corning
Buechner, Thomas Scharman *artist, retired glass manufacturing company executive, museum director*

Cornwall On Hudson
Abrams, Vivien *artist*
Grant, Joanne Catherine *auctioneer*

Cross River
Smith, Lawrence Beall *artist*

Croton On Hudson
Rubinfien, Leo H. *photographer, filmmaker*

Cutchogue
Dank, Leonard Dewey *medical illustrator, audio-visual consultant*

Douglaston
Costa, Ernest Fiorenzo *graphic designer*

East Hampton
Lassaw, Ibram *sculptor, painter*
Praetorius, William Albert, Sr. *artist, former advertising and real estate executive*
Richenburg, Robert Bartlett *artist, retired art educator*
Stein, Ronald Jay *artist, airline transport pilot*

Elmhurst
Wachsteter, George *illustrator*

Flushing
Bruder, Harold Jacob *artist, educator*
Carlson, Cynthia Joanne *artist, educator*
Laderman, Gabriel *artist*
Michael, Carola *designer, weaver*
Nicotra, Joseph Charles *artist*
Shen, Ronger *artist, Qigong educator*

Fly Creek
Dusenbery, Walter Condit *sculptor*

Forest Hills
Crystal, Boris *artist*
Gayner, Esther K. *artist*
Tewi, Thea *sculptor*

Franklin Square
Indiviglia, Salvatore Joseph *artist, retired naval officer*

Freeport
Terris, Albert *metal sculptor*

Great Neck
Seidler, Doris *artist*

Greenvale
Leipzig, Arthur *photographer, educator emeritus*

Hamilton
Loveless, James King *art educator*

Hawthorne
Sandbank, Henry *photographer, film director*

Hillsdale
Richards, Joseph Edward *artist*

Holland
Blair, Robert Noel *artist*

Hoosick Falls
Hatfield, David Underhill *artist*

Huntington
Twardowicz, Stanley Jan *artist, photographer*

Irvington
Holden, Donald *author, artist*

Ithaca
Grippi, Salvatore William *artist*
Mikus, Eleanore Ann *artist*
Poleskie, Stephen Francis *artist, educator*
Squier, Jack Leslie *sculptor, educator*

Jackson Heights
Schiavina, Laura Margaret *artist*

Jamaica
Cade, Walter, III *artist, musician, singer, actor*

Jeffersonville
Craft, Douglas Durwood *artist*
Harms, Elizabeth Louise *artist*

Katonah
Giobbi, Edward Giacchino *artist*
Toney, Anthony *artist*

Larchmont
Tobey, Alton Stanley *artist*

Locust Valley
Lippold, Richard *sculptor*

Long Island City
Di Suvero, Mark *sculptor*
Donneson, Seena Sand *artist*
Gussow, Roy *sculptor, educator*
Villinski, Paul Stephen *artist*

Mahopac Falls
Karimi, Reza *artist*

Mamaroneck
Pugh, Grace Huntley *artist*

Merrick
Cariola, Robert Joseph *artist*

Middle Village
Meyers, Edward *photographer, writer, publisher*

Middletown
Blumenthal, Fritz *printmaker, painter*

Mount Kisco
Couture, Ronald David *art administrator, design consultant*

New Paltz
Schneemann, Carolee *painter, performing artist, filmmaker, writer*

New Rochelle
Nienburg, George Frank *photographer*
Slotnick, Mortimer H. *artist*

New York
Abboud, Joseph M. *fashion designer*
Abeles, Sigmund M. *artist, printmaker*
Abish, Cecile *artist*
Abularach, Rodolfo Marco Antonio *artist*
Acconci, Vito (Hannibal) *conceptual artist*
Adams, Dennis Paul *artist*
Adams, Edward Thomas (Eddie Adams) *photographer*
Adolfo, (Adolfo F. Sardiña) *fashion designer*
Adri, (Adrienne Steckling) *fashion designer*
Adrian, Barbara (Mrs. Franklin C. Tramutola) *artist*
Aldredge, Theoni Vachliotis *costume designer*
†Alfaro, Victor *fashion designer*
Allard, Linda Marie *fashion designer*
Allner, Walter Heinz *designer, painter, art director*
Alten, Jerry *art director*
Andre, Carl *sculptor*
Anthony, William Graham *artist*
Antonakos, Stephen *sculptor*
Antupit, Samuel Nathaniel *art director*
Appel, Karel *artist, illustrator*
Archimedes, Verdun Joseph *art consultant, mental health nurse*
Arcilesi, Vincent Jasper *artist*
Arman, Armand Pierre *sculptor*
Armani, Giorgio *fashion designer*
†Aulisi, Joseph Garibaldi *costume designer*
Avedon, Richard *photographer*
Aycock, Alice *artist*
Banerjee, (Bimal) *artist, educator*
Baranik, Rudolf *artist*
Barnes, Jhane Elizabeth *fashion design company executive, designer*
Barnet, Will *artist, educator*
Barrett, Bill *sculptor*
Bartle, Annette Gruber (Mrs. Thomas R. Bartle) *artist, writer, photographer*
Bartlett, Jennifer Losch *artist*
Bartlett, John *fashion designer*
Bass, Joel Leonard *artist*
Beal, Jack *artist*
Beatty, John Lee *scenic designer*
Beck, Martha Ann *art curator, director*
Beck, Rosemarie *artist, educator*
Beene, Geoffrey *fashion designer*
Bellin, Milton Rockwell *artist*
Benglis, Lynda *artist, sculptor*
Ben-Haim, Zigi *artist*
Berger, Oscar *artist*
Berlind, Robert Elliot *artist*
Berman, Ariane R. *artist*
Bernard, Walter *art director*
Berthot, Jake *artist*
Bhavsar, Natvar Prahladji *artist*
Billian, Cathey R. *sculptor, educator*
Blaine, Nell *artist, printmaker*
Blass, Bill (William Ralph Blass) *apparel and home furnishings designer*
Blechman, R. O. *artist, filmmaker*
Block, John Douglas *auction house executive*
Boardman, Seymour *artist*
Bochner, Mel *artist*
Boley Bolaffio, Rita *artist*
Bonino, Fernanda *art dealer*
Boothe, Power *visual artist, educator, filmmaker, set designer*
Borofsky, Jonathan *artist*
Botero, Fernando *artist*
Bourgeois, Louise *sculptor*
†Bourne, Mel *production designer, art director*
Bradley, Lisa M. *artist*
Brandt, Grace Borgenicht *art dealer*
Brandt, Warren *artist*
Bricken, Barry Irwin *fashion designer*
Brooks, Diana D. *auction house executive*
Brown, Robert Delford *artist*
Bunts, Frank Emory *artist*
Burlingame, Lloyd Lamson *design instructor*
Cajori, Charles Florian *artist, educator*
Caldwell, Susan Hanes *art dealer*
Campbell, Ronald Neil *magazine designer*
†Canonero, Milena *costume designer*
Capa, Cornell *photographer, director photography museum*
Carnase, Thomas Paul *graphic designer, typographic consultant*
Carter, Kevin *photographer*
Casebere, James Edward *artist*
Cesarani, Sal *fashion designer*
Charlesworth, Sarah E. *photographer, conceptual artist*
Chen, Chi (Chen Chi) *artist*
Chermayeff, Ivan *graphic designer*
Christo, (Christo Vladimirov Javacheff) *artist*
Chwast, Seymour *graphic artist*
Clarke, John Clem *artist*
Close, Chuck (Charles Thomas Close) *artist*
Cohen, Arthur Morris *artist*
Cohen, Cora *artist*
Cole, Max *artist*
Cole, Sylvan, Jr. *art dealer*
Colker, Edward *artist, educator*
Conover, Robert Fremont *artist, educator*
Cooper, Mario *artist, educator*
Cortor, Eldzier *artist, printmaker*
Cowles, Charles *art dealer*
Crile, Susan *artist*
Cunningham, Bill *photographer*
Currie, Bruce *artist*
Dajani, Virginia *arts administrator*
Dallmann, Daniel F. *artist, educator*
Dana, F(rank) Mitchell *theatrical lighting designer*
Danne, Richard Franklin *graphic designer*
Daphnis, Nassos *artist*
Davidovich, Jaime *video artist, researcher*
Davidson, Nancy Brachman *artist, educator*
Davis, Douglas Matthew *artist, educator, author*
de Champlain, Vera Chopak *artist, painter*
Deem, George *artist*
†De Keyzer, Carl-Georges *photographer*
de Kooning, Willem *artist*
de la Renta, Oscar *fashion designer*
Demaria, Walter *sculptor*
Denes, Agnes C. *environmental artist*
Denhof, Miki *graphic designer*
Dennis, Donna Frances *sculptor, art educator*
dePaola, Thomas Anthony *illustrator, children's author*
des Rioux, Deena Victoria Coty *artist, graphics designer*
Di Meo, Dominick *artist, sculptor, painter*
Di Mitri, Piero *fashion designer*
Dine, Jim *artist*
Dintenfass, Terry *art dealer*
Dobbs, John Barnes *artist, educator*
Dodd, Lois *artist, art professor*
Donati, Enrico *artist*
Draper, William Franklin *artist, portrait and landscape painter*
Drexler, Joanne Lee *art appraiser*
Drucker, Mort *commercial artist*
Duff, John Ewing *sculptor*
Dyyon, Frazier (LeRoy Frazier) *artist*
Egielski, Richard *illustrator*
Eisen, Mark *fashion designer*
Eisenberg, Sonja Miriam *artist*
Elder, Eldon *stage designer, theatre consultant*
Eliot, Lucy Carter *artist*
Elman, Naomi Geist *artist, producer*
Enders, Elizabeth McGuire *artist*
Erwitt, Elliott Romano *photographer, cinematographer*
Estes, Richard *artist*
Evans, John *artist*
Faulkner, Frank M. *artist*
Faurer, Louis *photographer*
Federico, Gene *graphic designer*
Feigen, Richard L. *art dealer*
Feiler, Jo Alison *artist*
Feininger, Andreas Bernhard Lyonel *photographer*
Findlay, Michael Alistair *auction house executive, poet*
Fischer, Carl *photographer, graphic designer*
Fisher, Rick *lighting designer*
Fleischman, Lawrence Arthur *art dealer, publisher, consultant*
†Forbes, Colin Ames *graphic design consultant*
Frankenthaler, Helen *artist*
Freeman, Elaine Lavalle *sculptor*
Freeman, Mark *artist*
Frumkin, Allan *art dealer*
Fugate-Wilcox, Terry *artist*
Gagosian, Larry *art dealer*
Gammell, Stephen *illustrator*
Gechtoff, Sonia *artist*
Geismar, Thomas H. *graphic designer*
Geissbuhler, Stephan *graphic designer*
Georges, Paul Gordon *artist*
Gibson, Ralph H(olmes) *photographer*
Glasco, Joseph Milton *artist*
Gleason, John James *theatrical lighting designer*
Goertz, Augustus Frederick, III *artist*
Goings, Ralph *artist*
Gold, Albert *artist*
Goldberg, Michael *artist*
Goldin, Leon *artist, educator*
Golub, Leon Albert *artist*
Gottschall, Edward Maurice *graphic arts company executive*
Gramatte, Joan Helen *graphic designer, art director*
Graves, Nancy Stevenson *artist*
Gray, George *mural painter*
†Greenwood, Jane *costume designer, educator*
Griefen, John Adams *artist, educator*
Grossman, Nancy *artist*
Gutman, Robert William *retired fine arts educator*
Haacke, Hans Christoph Carl *artist, educator*
Haber, Ira Joel *artist, educator*
Hacklin, Allan *artist, art educator*
Haerer, Carol *artist*
Haessle, Jean-Marie Georges *artist*
Hallam, Beverly (Beverly Linney) *artist*
Hamilton, Patricia Rose *artist's agent*
Hardison, Ruth Inge *sculptor*
Hardy, Thomas Austin *sculptor*
Harmon, Lily *artist, author*
Hasen, Burton Stanley *artist*
Hazlitt, Donald Robert *artist*
Heiloms, May (Mrs. Samuel Heiloms) *artist*
Held, Al *artist, educator*
Heliker, John *artist*
Helioff, Anne Graile *painter*
Herrera, Carolina *fashion designer*
Hilfiger, Tommy *fashion designer*
Hill, Clinton *artist*
Hios, Theodore *painter, graphic artist*
Hirschfeld, Albert *artist*
Holland, Bradford Wayne *artist*
Holzer, Jenny *artist*
†Hopkins, Speed Elliott *art director*
Hould-Ward, Ann *theatrical costume designer*
Hull, Cathy *artist, illustrator*
Hultberg, John *artist*
Hunt, Richard *sculptor*
Incandela, Gerald Jean-Marie *artist*
Ireland, Patrick *artist*
Isley, Alexander Max *graphic designer, lecturer*
Jackson, Ward *artist*
Jacobs, Marc *fashion designer*
Jacquette, Yvonne Helene *artist*
Jampolis, Neil Peter *designer*
Jaramillo, Virginia *artist*
Jaudon, Valerie *artist*
Jenkins, Paul *artist*
Johns, Jasper *artist*
Johnson, Betsey Lee *fashion designer*
Jonas, Joan *artist*
Jones, Edward Powis *artist*
Judson, Jeannette Alexander *artist*
Kahn, Wolf *artist*
Kaish, Luise Clayborn *sculptor*
Kaish, Morton *artist, educator*
Kamali, Norma *fashion designer*
Kan, Diana Artemis Mann Shu *artist*
Kanovitz, Howard *artist*
Karan, Donna (Donna Faske) *fashion designer*
Karp, Marshall Warren *creative director, writer*
Katz, Alex *artist*
Katz, Hilda *artist*
Katzman, Herbert Henry *artist*
Kaz, Nathaniel *sculptor*
Kelly, James *artist*
Kemper, Randolph E. *fashion designer*
Kennedy, Ian Glen *art appraiser*
Kepets, Hugh Michael *artist*
Kim, Willa *costume designer*
Kinstler, Everett Raymond *artist*
Kirk, Alexis Vemian *designer*

Kirshenbaum, Richard Warren *creative director*
Klein, Calvin Richard *fashion designer*
Klotz, Florence *costume designer*
Kner, Andrew Peter *art director*
Koppelman, Chaim *artist*
Koppelman, Dorothy Myers *artist, consultant*
Kors, Michael (Karl Anderson, Jr.) *fashion designer*
Krementz, Jill *photographer, author*
Krulik, Barbara S. *director, curator*
Krushenick, Nicholas *artist*
Kushner, Robert Ellis *artist*
Lane, Kenneth Jay *jewelry designer*
Lane, Lois N. *artist*
Lang, Daniel S. *artist*
La Noue, Terence David *artist, educator*
Lanyon, Ellen (Mrs. Roland Ginzel) *artist, educator*
Lash, Stephen Sycle *auction company executive*
Lasker, Jonathan Lewis *artist*
Lasker, Joseph L. *artist, illustrator*
Lassen, Robert Maurie *graphic artist, photographer, editor*
Lauren, Ralph *fashion designer*
Lechay, James *artist, emeritus art educator*
Lee, Catherine *sculptor, painter*
Lehr, Janet *art dealer, publisher, author*
Lehrer, Leonard *artist, educator*
Leiber, Gerson August *artist*
Leiber, Judith Maria *designer, manufacturer*
Leibovitz, Annie *photographer*
Lerner, Sandy Richard *art educator, art restorer, appraiser, painter, sculptor, lithographer*
Leve, Samuel *scenic designer*
Levine, David *artist*
Levy, Benjamin *artist*
LeWitt, Sol *artist*
Liberman, Alexander *artist, editor*
Loengard, John Borg *photographer; editor*
Loring, John Robbins *artist*
Loving, Alvin Demar, Jr. *artist, educator*
Lucchesi, Bruno *sculptor*
MacIver, Loren *artist*
Mackie, Robert Gordon *costume and fashion designer*
Mackler, Tina *artist*
Madsen, Loren Wakefield *sculptor*
Mangold, Robert Peter *artist*
Manning, Jack *photographer, columnist, author*
Marion, John Louis *fine arts auctioneer and appraiser*
Marisol, (Marisol Escobar) *sculptor*
Martin, Agnes *artist*
Massey, Stephen Charles *auctioneer*
Max, Peter *artist*
McCarthy, Denis *artist, educator*
McCoy, Ann *artist*
†McCredie, James Robert *fine arts educator*
McCully, Emily Arnold *illustrator, writer*
McDarrah, Fred William *photographer, editor, writer, photography reviewer*
Mc Gowin, William Edward *artist*
McKenzie, Mary Beth *artist*
Meisel, Louis Koenig *art dealer, art historian, writer*
Meisel, Steven *advertising photographer*
Meiselas, Susan Clay *photographer*
Mendelson, Haim *artist, educator, art gallery director*
Mesches, Arnold *artist*
Meyers, Dale (Mrs. Mario Cooper) *artist*
Michals, Duane *photographer*
Miller, Harry Brill *scenic designer, director, acting instructor, lyricist, interior designer*
Miller, Lee Anne *artist, educator*
Miller, Nicole Jacqueline *fashion designer*
Miller, Richard Kidwell *artist, actor, educator*
Miller, Richard McDermott *sculptor*
Miss, Mary *artist*
Miyake, Issey *fashion designer*
Mizrahi, Isaac *fashion designer*
Moeller, Achim Ferdinand Gerd *art dealer, consultant, publisher*
Morath, Inge *photographer*
Morgan, Jacqui *illustrator, painter, educator*
Mori, Hanae *fashion designer*
Morris, Robert *artist*
Murphy, Catherine *painter*
Murphy, John Cullen *illustrator*
Murray, Elizabeth *artist*
Musser, Tharon *theatrical lighting designer, theatre consultant*
Neiman, LeRoy *artist*
Neuhaus, Max *artist, composer*
Newman, Arnold *photographer*
Newman, Elias *artist*
Norvell, Patsy *artist*
Notarbartolo, Albert *artist*
Ohlson, Douglas Dean *artist*
Oldenburg, Claes Thure *artist*
Oldham, Todd *fashion designer*
Owsley, David Thomas *art consultant, appraiser, lecturer, author*
Pace, Stephen Shell *artist, educator*
Parker, Nancy Winslow *artist, writer*
Parker, Olivia *photographer*
Parker, Robert Andrew *artist*
Pascal, David *artist*
Pearson, Henry Charles *artist*
Peckolick, Alan *graphic designer*
Pepper, Beverly *artist, sculptor*
Peress, Gilles *photographer*
Perlis, Donald M. *artist*
Phillips, Anthony Mark *auction house executive*
Pimsler, Alvin J. *artist*
Pool, Mary Jane *design consultant, author, lecturer*
Poons, Larry *artist*
Poor, Anne *artist*
Porter, Liliana Alicia *artist, printmaker*
Quackenbush, Robert Mead *artist, author, psychoanalyst*
Quaytman, Harvey *painter*
Quisgard, Liz Whitney *artist, sculptor*
Rabinowitch, David George *sculptor*
Raffael, Joseph *artist*
Rauschenberg, Robert *artist*
Reddy, Krishna Narayana *artist, educator*
†Reeves, Daniel McDonough *video artist*
Reininghaus, Ruth *artist*
Remington, Deborah Williams *artist*
Resika, Paul *artist*
Resnick, Marcia Aylene *photographic artist, educator*
Resnick, Milton *artist*
Ringgold, Faith *artist, writer*
Rodriguez, Geno (Eugene Rodriguez) *artist, arts administrator*
Roehm, Carolyne Jane *fashion designer*
Rose, Herman *artist*
Rose, Leatrice *artist, educator*
Rosenhouse, Irwin J. *artist, designer*
Rosenthal, Tony (Bernard) *sculptor*
Ross, Charles *artist*
Ross, Rhoda *artist*
†Rotan, Walter *sculptor*
Roth, Ann *costume designer*
Rothenberg, Susan *artist*
Ruscha, Edward *artist*
Ryman, Robert Tracy *artist*
†Saff, Donald Jay *artist, educator*
St. Clair, Michael *art dealer*
Sainty, Guy Stair *art dealer*
Saks, Arnold *graphic designer*
Salle, David *artist*
Savelli, Angelo *artist*
Scavullo, Francesco *photographer*
Schapiro, Miriam *artist*
Schnabel, Julian *artist*
Schneider, JoAnne *artist*
Schrag, Karl *artist*
Schwartz, Daniel Bennett *artist*
Schwartz, Eugene M. *art collector, patron*
†Scott, Michael Lester *artist, educator*
Scully, Sean Paul *artist*
Searle, Ronald *artist*
Secunda, Arthur (Holland Secunda) *artist*
Segal, George *sculptor*
Seliger, Charles *artist*
Seliger, Mark Alan *photographer*
Serra, Richard *sculptor*
Shapiro, Babe *artist*
Shapiro, Ellen Marie *graphic design company executive, writer*
Shapiro, Joel Elias *artist*
Shaw, (George) Kendall *artist, educator*
Sherman, Cindy *artist*
Shikler, Aaron *artist*
Shore, Stephen *photographer*
Shuff, Lily *artist, wood engraver*
Silverman, Burton Philip *artist*
Sis, Peter *illustrator, children's book author, artist, filmmaker*
Skupinski, Bogdan Kazimierz *artist*
Sky, Alison *artist, designer*
Slavin, Arlene *artist*
Slavin, Neal *photographer*
Sleigh, Sylvia *artist, educator*
†Smith, Lane *illustrator, author*
Smith, Leon Polk *artist*
Smith, Shirley *artist*
Smith, Vincent DaCosta *artist*
Solman, Joseph *artist*
Sonneman, Eve *artist*
Soreff, Stephen Mayer *artist*
Sperakis, Nicholas George *artist*
Sproat, Christopher Townsend *artist*
Stamos, Theodoros *artist*
Stanley, Bob *artist*
Starn, Douglas *artist, photographer*
Starn, Mike P. *artist, photographer*
Stefanelli, Joseph James (Joe Stefanelli) *artist*
Steinberg, Saul *artist*
Steir, Pat Iris *artist*
Stella, Frank Philip *artist*
Sterling, David M. *graphic designer*
Sterrett, Jane Evelyne *illustrator, artist*
Stiebel, Gerald Gustave *art dealer*
Sugarman, George *artist*
Sui, Anna *fashion designer*
Sultan, Donald Keith *artist, printmaker*
Surrey, Milt *artist*
Sutton, Pat Lipsky *artist, educator*
Swain, Robert *artist*
†Terkuhle, Abby *graphic designer*
†Thiebaud, Wayne *artist*
Thrall, Donald Stuart *artist*
Tilton, James Floyd *theatrical designer, art director*
Tipton, Jennifer *lighting designer*
Tobias, Julius *sculptor*
Tooker, George *artist*
Trigere, Pauline *fashion designer*
Tscherny, George *graphic designer*
†Twombly, Cy *artist*
Tyler, David Alan *auction house executive*
Tyler, Richard *fashion designer*
Upright, Diane Warner *auction house executive*
Vaadia, Boaz *sculptor*
van den Akker, Koos *fashion designer*
Vass, Joan *fashion designer*
Versace, Gianni *fashion designer*
Vittadini, Adrienne *fashion designer*
Viviano, Sam Joseph *illustrator*
Von Furstenberg, Diane Simone Michelle *fashion designer*
Von Ringelheim, Paul Helmut *sculptor*
Wagner, Robin Samuel Anton *stage and set designer*
Wald, Sylvia *artist*
Walton, Anthony John (Tony Walton) *theater and film designer, book illustrator*
Wang, Vera *fashion designer*
Watson, Albert MacKenzie *photographer*
Wegman, William George *artist*
Weitz, John *fashion designer, writer*
Weschler, Anita *sculptor, painter*
Wesley, John Mercer *artist*
Williams, Garth Montgomery *illustrator*
Williams, William Thomas *artist, educator*
Willis, Thornton Wilson *painter*
Winsor, Jackie *artist*
Wolins, Joseph *artist*
†Wolsky, Albert *costume designer*
Wong, Kwan Shut *art appraiser, artist*
Woodman, Timothy *artist*
Wunderman, Jan Darcourt *artist*
Wurmfeld, Sanford *artist, educator*
Yelle, Richard Wilfred *artist, product designer*
†Yohe, James Lyle *art gallery director, art dealer*
York, Richard Travis *art dealer*
Young, Ed (Tse-chun) *illustrator, children's author*
Youngerman, Jack *artist, sculptor*
Zabriskie, Virginia M. *art dealer*
Zakanitch, Robert Rahway *artist*
Zipprodt, Patricia *costume designer*
Zlowe, Florence Markowitz *artist*
Zox, Larry *artist*

Oswego
Fox, Michael David *art educator, visual imagist artist*

Palisades
Knowlton, Grace Farrar *sculptor, photographer*

Peekskill
Rosenberg, Marilyn Rosenthal *artist, visual poet*

Pelham
†Conroy, Tamara Boks *artist, special education educator*
Ralston, Lucy Virginia Gordon *artist*

Piermont
Berkon, Martin *artist*
Der Harootian, Khoren *sculptor*
Gussow, Alan *artist, sculptor*

Pittsford
Lytle, Douglas Alfred *photographer, educator*

Port Chester
Duveen, Anneta *artist*

Pound Ridge
Ferro, Walter *artist*

Rhinebeck
Clutz, William (Hartman Clutz) *artist, educator*
Rabinovich, Raquel *artist, sculptor*

Rochester
Engelmann, Lothar Klaus *photographic science educator*
Margolis, Richard Martin *photographer, educator*
Merritt, Howard Sutermeister *retired art educator*
Mertin, Roger *photographer*
Paley, Albert Raymond *art educator, sculptor*
Saisselin, Remy Gilbert *fine arts educator*

Rock Hill
Schary, Emanuel *artist*

Roslyn
†Finke, Leonda Froehlich *sculptor*

Rye
Troller, Fred *graphic designer, painter, visual consultant, educator*

Sag Harbor
Blanc, Peter (William Peters Blanc) *sculptor, painter*

Sagaponack
Butchkes, Sydney *artist*
Isham, Sheila Eaton *artist*

Saratoga Springs
Upton, Richard Thomas *artist*

Scarsdale
Breinin, Raymond *painter, sculptor*
Fendelman, Helaine *art appraiser*
Ries, Martin *artist, educator*

Shady
Ruellan, Andree *artist*

Shelter Island
Culbertson, Janet Lynn *artist*

Shoreham
Spier, Peter Edward *artist, author*

Snyder
Breverman, Harvey *artist*

South Salem
Howard, Joan Alice *artist*

Southampton
Fuller, Sue *artist*
Silverstein, Louis *art director, designer, editor*

Stanfordville
Froman, Ann *sculptor*

Staten Island
†Jones, Eric Michael *artist, designer*
Mailman, Cynthia Marcia *artist, educator*

Sterling
Seawell, Thomas Robert *artist, retired educator*

Stony Brook
Pekarsky, Melvin Hirsch *artist*
Pindell, Howardena Doreen *artist*

Syracuse
Thomas, Sidney *fine arts educator, researcher*

Tappan
Dell, Robert Christopher *geothermal sculptor, scenic artist*
Nickford, Juan *sculptor, educator*

Tuxedo Park
Domjan, Joseph (Spiri Domjan) *artist*

Utica
Pribble, Easton *artist*

Wainscott
Russo, Alexander Peter *artist, educator*

Wallkill
Koch, Edwin Ernest *artist, interior decorator*

Wantagh
Urbaitis, Elena *artist*

Warwick
Franck, Frederick Sigfred *artist, author, dental surgeon*

Water Mill
Mac Whinnie, John Vincent *artist*
Rosenberg, Alex Jacob *art dealer, curator, fine arts appraiser, educator*

Westbury
Barboza, Anthony *photographer, artist*
Sherbell, Rhoda *artist, sculptor*

White Plains
Erla, Karen *artist, painter, collagist, printmaker*
Nickerson, Ruth *sculptor*

Woodstock
Banks, Rela *sculptor*

Yorktown Heights
Jones, Lauretta Marie *artist, graphic designer, computer interface designer*
Laventhol, Henry L(ee) (Hank Laventhol) *artist, etcher*

NORTH CAROLINA

Asheville
Jones, J. Kenneth *art dealer, former museum administrator*
Rufa, Robert Henry *writer, editor, photographer, artist*

Burnsville
Bernstein, William Joseph *glass artist, educator*
Doyle, John Lawrence *artist*

Chapel Hill
Ness, Albert Kenneth *artist, educator*
Stipe, Robert Edwin *design educator*

Davidson
Jackson, Herb *artist, educator*

Greensboro
Barker, Walter William, Jr. *artist, educator*

Laurinburg
Nance, Tony Max-Perry *designer, illustrator*

Pinehurst
Twitty, James Watson *artist*

Pittsboro
Schwinn-Jordan, Barbara (Barbara Schwinn) *painter*

Raleigh
Finch, Peter W. *painter, illustrator*

Sanford
Higgins, George Edward *sculptor*

Winston Salem
Faccinto, Victor Paul *artist, gallery administrator*

NORTH DAKOTA

Bismarck
Solberg, Nellie Florence Coad *artist*

OHIO

Ashville
Beckman, Judith *art educator*

Aurora
Lawton, Florian Kenneth *artist, educator*

Bowling Green
Ocvirk, Otto George *artist*

Cincinnati
Barrie, Dennis Ray *museum director*
Brod, Stanford *graphic designer, educator*
Knipschild, Robert *artist, educator*
Rexroth, Nancy Louise *photographer*
Sullivan, Connie Castleberry *artist, photographer*
Wygant, Foster Laurance *art educator*

Cleveland
Beling, Helen *sculptor*
Cassill, Herbert Carroll *artist*
Fenton, Alan *artist*
Seltzer, Phyllis Estelle *painter, printmaker*

Columbus
Beverley, Jane Taylor *artist*
Gilliom, Bonnie Lee *arts educator, consultant*
Kuehn, Edmund Karl *artist*

Hilliard
Cupp, David Foster *photographer, journalist*

Oberlin
Arnold, Paul Beaver *artist, educator*
Tacha, Athena *sculptor, educator*

Olmsted Falls
Laessig, Robert H. *artist*

Perrysburg
Autry, Carolyn *artist, art history educator*

Seven Hills
Stanczak, Julian *artist, educator*

Shaker Heights
Held, Lila M. *art appraiser*

Toledo
McGlauchlin, Tom *artist*

Van Wert
Liljegren, Frank Sigfrid *artist, art association official*

OKLAHOMA

Chickasha
Good, Leonard Phelps *artist*

Oklahoma City
Alaupovic, Alexandra Vrbanic *artist, educator*

Boston, Billie *costume designer*

OREGON

Applegate
Boyle, (Charles) Keith *artist, educator*

Ashland
Hay, Richard Laurence *theater scenic designer*

Cannon Beach
Greaver, Harry *artist*

Eugene
†Funk, David Charles *design firm executive*

Portland
Waddingham, John Alfred *artist, journalist*

Salem
Pierre, Joseph Horace, Jr. *commercial artist*
Thornton, Dorothy Haberlach *artist, photographer*

Wilsonville
†Ramadan, Sar *design automation company executive*

PENNSYLVANIA

Allentown
Moller, Hans *artist*

Allison Park
Osby, Larissa Geiss *artist*

Cochranville
Sazegar, Morteza *artist*

Edinboro
Kemenyffy, Steven *artist, art educator*

Elkins Park
Bayliss, George Vincent *art educator, artist*
Erlebacher, Martha Mayer *artist, educator*
Madigan, Martha *photographer, artist, photography educator*

Glenside
Frudakis, Zenos Antonios *sculptor, artist*

Harrisburg
Sturgen, Winston *photographer, printmaker, artist*

Haverford
Stegeman, Charles *fine arts educator, lecturer, consultant*
Williams, William Earle *artist, educator, curator*

Kimberton
Williams, Lawrence Soper *photographer*

Lehigh Valley
Kocsis, James Paul *artist, publisher*

Lumberville
Katsiff, Bruce *artist*

Mechanicsville
Bye, Ranulph DeBayeux *artist, author*

Narberth
Grenald, Raymond *architectural lighting designer*

Philadelphia
Auth, Tony *artist*
Cramer, Richard Charles *artist, educator*
†Franklin, Jack T. *photographer*
Garonzik, Sara Ellen *stage director*
Gralish, Tom *photographer*
Knobler, Nathan *art educator*
Le Clair, Charles George *artist, retired dean*
Levy, Rochelle Feldman *artist*
Maitin, Sam(uel Calman) (Sam Maitin) *artist*
Metzker, Ray K. *photographer*
Paone, Peter *artist*
Remenick, Seymour *artist, educator*
Schwarz, Robert Devlin *art dealer*
Solomon, Vita Petrosky *artist*
Spandorfer, Merle Sue *artist, educator, author*
Weidner, Roswell Theodore *artist*

Pittsburgh
Arkus, Leon Anthony *art consultant, former museum director*
Fredette, Barbara Wagner *art educator*
Rogers, Bryan Leigh *artist, art educator*
Trapp, Frank Anderson *art educator*
Wilkins, David George *fine arts educator*
Williams, John Wesley *fine arts educator*

Solebury
Anthonisen, George Rioch *sculptor, artist*

Spring Grove
Helberg, Shirley Adelaide Holden *artist, educator*

Swarthmore
Cothren, Michael Watt *art educator*

University Park
Van Dommelen, David B. *artist, educator*

Upper Darby
Gasparro, Frank *sculptor*

West Chester
Jamison, Philip *artist*

Wynnewood
Maxwell, John Raymond *artist*

RHODE ISLAND

Cranston
Crooks, W. Spencer *artist, educator*

Kingston
Leete, William White *artist*
Rohm, Robert Hermann *sculptor, educator*

Pawtucket
Heyman, Lawrence Murray *printmaker, painter*

Providence
Feldman, Walter Sidney *artist*
Howes, Lorraine de Wet *fashion designer, educator*
McIlvane, Edward James *artist, instructor, designer*
Ockerse, Thomas *graphic design educator*
Wunderlich, Alfred Leon *artist, art educator*

Rumford
Cote, Louise Roseann *creative director, designer*

Westerly
Reiland, Lowell Keith *sculptor*

SOUTH CAROLINA

Columbia
Robinson, Christopher Thomas *artist*
†Thee, Christian *artist, designer*

Greenville
Alberga, Alta Wheat *artist*

SOUTH DAKOTA

Sioux Falls
Grupp, Carl Alf *art educator, artist*

Vermillion
†Freeman, Jeffrey Vaughn (Jeff Freeman) *art educator, artist*

TENNESSEE

Chattanooga
Cress, George Ayers *artist, educator*
Martin, Chester Y. *sculptor, painter*
Mills, Charles G. *photography company executive*
Mills, Olan, II *photography company executive*

Franklin
O'More, Eloise Pitts *designer*

Knoxville
Sublett, Carl Cecil *artist*
Walsh, Joanne Elizabeth *art educator, librarian*

Lookout Mountain
Wyeth, Andrew *artist*
Wyeth, James Browning *artist*

Memphis
Carroll, Billy Price *artist*
De Mere-Dwyer, Leona *medical artist*
McPherson, Larry E(ugene) *photographer, educator*
Riss, Murray *photographer, educator*

Nashville
†Creasy, Charles L. *creative director*
Hazlehurst, Franklin Hamilton *fine arts educator*

TEXAS

Anahuac
White, Ethyle Herman (Mrs. S. Roy White) *artist*

Arlington
Elias, Harold John *artist, educator*

Austin
Deming, David Lawson *art educator*
Goldstein, Peggy R. *sculptor*
Guerin, John William *artist*
High, Timothy Griffin *artist, educator, writer*
Hite, Jesse Otto *art gallery director*
Mayer, Susan Martin *art educator*
McFarland, Lawrence D. *photographer, educator*
Spruce, Everett Franklin *artist*
Weismann, Donald Leroy *art educator, artist, filmmaker, writer*

Beaumont
Carron, Maudee Lilyan *painter, sculptor, writer*
Coe, (Matchett) Herring *sculptor*

Cleveland
Lipski, Donald G. *sculptor*

Corpus Christi
Ullberg, Kent Jean *sculptor*

Dallas
Blessen, Karen Alyce *free-lance illustrator, designer*
Costa, Victor Charles *fashion designer*
Emerson, Walter Caruth *artist, educator*
Richards, Jeanne Herron *artist*
Thorson, Marcelyn Marie *applied art educator*

El Paso
Maguire, Blanche Joan (Maggie) *watercolorist*

Houston
Bishop, Mary Lou *artist*
Camfield, William Arnett *art educator*
DeMenil, Dominique *art collector, philanthropist*
Gorski, Daniel Alexander *art educator*
Honeycutt, George Leonard *photographer*
King, Kay Wander *design educator, fashion designer, consultant*
O'Neil, John *artist*
Schorre, Louis Charles, Jr. *artist*
Ward, Bethea *artist, small business owner*

Huntsville
Lea, Stanley E. *artist, educator*

Kerrville
Frudakis, Evangelos William *sculptor*

Liberty Hill
Vance, Zinna Barth *artist, writer*

Odessa
Lee, Nelda S. *artist, art appraiser and dealer, film producer*

Plano
Sedei, Donald James *art director*

Richardson
Breard, Benjamin Allen *art dealer*

San Antonio
Thompson, Mary Koleta *sculptor, non-profit organization director*
Willson, Robert (William) *glass sculpture and watercolor artist*

Seabrook
Sterling, Shirley Frampton *artist, educator*

Waco
Kagle, Joseph Louis, Jr. *artist, arts administrator*

UTAH

Orderville
Zornes, Milford *artist*

VERMONT

Bennington
Adams, Pat *artist, educator*

Cavendish
Shapiro, David *artist, art historian*

East Calais
Gahagan, James Edward, Jr. *artist*

East Dorset
Armstrong, Jane Botsford *sculptor*

East Wallingford
Bluhm, Norman *artist*

Marlboro
Olitski, Jules *artist*

Newbury
McGarrell, James *artist, educator*

Shaftsbury
Bubriski, Kevin Ernest *photographer, educator*

West Burke
Van Vliet, Claire *artist*

Weston
Kasnowski, Chester Nelson *artist, educator*

VIRGINIA

Alexandria
Alderson, Margaret Northrop *arts administrator, educator, artist*

Arlington
Reed, Paul Allen *artist*
Wendelin, Rudolph Andrew *artist*

Blacksburg
Carter, Dean *artist*

Brightwood
Skelton, Dorothy Geneva Simmons (Mrs. John William Skelton) *art educator*

Charlottesville
Bunch, John Blake *photographer, writer, educator*
Priest, Hartwell Wyse *artist*
Ruben, Leonard *retired art educator*

Clifton
Nong *artist, sculptor*

East Stone Gap
Combs, Jo Karen Kobeck *artist, writer*

Fairfax Station
Jackson, Vaughn Lyle *artist, consultant*

Fredericksburg
Schmutzhart, Berthold Josef *sculptor, educator, art and education consultant*

Lynchburg
Hudson, Walter Tiree *artist*

Newport News
Camp, Hazel Lee Burt *artist*

Norfolk
Frieden, Jane Heller *art educator*
Ives, Ronn Brian *artist, educator*
Jones, Leon Herbert, Jr. (Herb Jones) *artist*

Reston
Heginbotham, Jan Sturza *sculptor*

Richmond
Freed, David Clark *artist*
Kevorkian, Richard *artist*
Rowley, Frank Selby, Jr. *artist*

Timberville
Barnard, Robert Edward *potter, writer*

Waterford
Pollack, Reginald Murray *painter, sculptor*

Williamsburg
Coleman, Henry Edwin *art educator, artist*
Robinson, Jay (Thurston) (Thurston Robinson) *artist*
Roseberg, Carl Andersson *sculptor, educator*

WASHINGTON

Anacortes
Mc Cracken, Philip Trafton *sculptor*

Bainbridge Island
Randlett, Mary Willis *photographer*

Battle Ground
Hansen, James Lee *sculptor*

Burlington
Zeretzke, Frederick Frank H. *artist, educator*

Kent
Pierce, Danny Parcel *artist, educator*

Marrowstone Island
Klein, Lynn E. *artist*

Mercer Island
Steinhardt, Henry *photographer*

Olympia
Haseltine, James Lewis *artist, consultant*

Poulsbo
Pasco, Duane Noble *artist*

Seattle
Alps, Glen Earl *printmaker, educator*
Berger, Paul Eric *artist, photographer*
Celentano, Francis Michael *artist, art educator*
Chihuly, Dale Patrick *artist*
Day, Alexandra (Sandra L. Woodward Darling) *illustrator, designer*
De Alessi, Ross Alan *lighting designer*
Du Pen, Everett George *sculptor, educator*
†Gardner Karton, Ann Elizabeth *visual artist*
Kuvshinoff, Bertha Horne *painter, sculptor*
Kuvshinoff, Nicolai Vasily *painter, sculptor*
Lawrence, Jacob *artist, educator*
MacKenzie, Peter Sean *writer, publications designer*
Pawula, Kenneth John *artist, educator*
Spafford, Michael Charles *artist*
Washington, James Winston, Jr. *artist, sculptor*

Wellpinit
†Wynne, Bruce *tribal administrator, artist*

WEST VIRGINIA

Huntington
Polan, Nancy Moore *artist*

Wheeling
Phillis, Marilyn Hughey *artist*

WISCONSIN

Beloit
Simon, Michael Alexander *photographer, educator*

Hartland
Stamsta, Jean F. *artist*

Hollandale
Myers, Frances *artist*

Madison
Becker, David *artist, educator*
Colescott, Warrington Wickham *artist, printmaker, educator*
Fritz, Bruce Morrell *photographer*
Greenwald, Caroline Meyer *artist*
Wilde, John *artist, educator*

Milwaukee
Balinger, Louise H. *artist, art educator*
Berman, Fred Jean *art educator, painter, photographer*
Burkert, Robert Randall *artist*
Helbert, Clifford L. *graphic designer, journalism educator*
Poehlmann, JoAnna *artist, illustrator, designer*
Thrall, Arthur Alvin *artist*
Vespa, Ned Angelo *photographer*

Sturgeon Bay
Becker, Bettie Geraldine *artist*

WYOMING

Casper
Seeger, Sondra Joan *artist*

Centennial
Russin, Robert Isaiah *sculptor, educator*

Cheyenne
Lawes, Patricia Jean *art educator*

Cody
Jackson, Harry Andrew *artist*

Jackson
Moeller, Robert Charles, III *fine arts consultant*

Kemmerer
Clark, Michael *artist, educator*

Laramie
Flach, Victor Hugo *designer, educator*
Reif, (Frank) David *artist, educator*

MILITARY ADDRESSES OF THE UNITED STATES

EUROPE

APO
Hibben, Barbara Ann Pandzik *museum administrator, foreign service officer*

CANADA

ALBERTA

Calgary
Esler, John Kenneth *artist*

Edmonton
Jungkind, Walter *design educator, writer, consultant*

BRITISH COLUMBIA

Burnaby
Felter, James Warren *painter, curator*

Duncan
Hughes, Edward John *artist*

Salt Spring Island
Raginsky, Nina *artist*

Victoria
Harvey, Donald *artist, educator*

MANITOBA

Winnipeg
Eyre, Ivan *artist*

NOVA SCOTIA

Halifax
Jackson, Sarah Jeanette *sculptor, graphic artist, copier artist, bookmaker*

Mahone Bay
Tolmie, Kenneth Donald *artist, author*

Wolfville
Colville, David Alexander *artist*

ONTARIO

Guelph
Danby, Kenneth Edison *artist, painter, printmaker*

Hamilton
Pietrzak, Ted S. *art gallery director*

London
Livick, Stephen *fine art photographer*

Niagara on the Lake
Scott, Campbell *artist*

North York
Lee, Eugene *theatrical set designer*

Ottawa
Karsh, Yousuf *photographer*

Toronto
Astman, Barbara Ann *artist, educator*
Graham, Kathleen Margaret (K. M. Graham) *artist*
Kramer, Burton *graphic designer, educator*
Morgan, Wayne Philip *art and popular culture exhibition producer*
Ronald, William *artist*
Semak, Michael William *photographer, educator*
Winter, Frederick Elliot *fine arts educator*

Waterloo
Green, Arthur Nelson *artist, educator*
Urquhart, Tony *artist, educator*

Willowdale
Hallman, H(enry) Theodore, Jr. *artist, textile designer*

QUEBEC

Ayers Cliff
Beament, Thomas Harold (Tib Beament) *artist, printmaker, educator*

Beaconsfield
Harder, Rolf Peter *graphic designer, painter*

Montreal
Cardinal, Marcelin *artist*
Charney, Melvin *artist, architect, educator*
McEwen, Jean *painter*

Pontiac
Hlavina, Rasto R(astislav) *sculptor*

Saint Lambert
Archambault, Louis *sculptor*
†Jorisch, Stéphane-Maurice *illustrator*

SASKATCHEWAN

Saskatoon
Bornstein, Eli *artist, sculptor*

MEXICO

Cuernavaca
Mora, Francisco *artist, printmaker*

Mexico City
Friedeberg, Pedro *painter, sculptor, designer*
Mendelejis, Leonardo Nierman *artist*

AUSTRALIA

Ringwood
Base, Graeme Rowland *illustrator, author*

ENGLAND

London
†Bridge, Andrew *theatrical lighting designer*
Craig, Stuart N. *film production designer*
Kitaj, R. B. *artist*
†Napier, John *set designer*

FRANCE

Arles
Clergue, Lucien Georges *photographer*

Paris
Biala, Janice *artist*
†Gaultier, Jean-Paul *fashion designer*
Givenchy, Hubert James Marcel Taffin de *fashion designer*
Lacroix, Christian Marie Marc *fashion designer*
Lagerfeld, Karl Otto *fashion designer*
Levee, John Harrison *artist, designer*
Renouf, Edda *artist*
†Saint Laurent, Yves (Henri Donat Mathieu) *couturier*
†Ungaro, Emanuel Matteotti *fashion designer*
Vuitton, Henry-Louis *designer*

Vaucluse
Pfriem, Bernard Aldine *artist*

GERMANY

Berlin
Iannone, Dorothy *visual artist, writer*

Dusseldorf
Richter, Gerhard *artist*

Frankfurt
Ammann, Jean-Christophe *art director*

ITALY

Florence
Cecil, Charles Harkless *artist, educator*

Milan
Ferré, Gianfranco *fashion designer, artistic director*

Rome
†Valentino, (Valentino Garavani) *fashion designer*

JAPAN

Kanagawa
Swarz, Sahl *sculptor*

Kyoto
Shoichi, Ida *artist, printmaker, painter, sculptor*

Tokyo
Kusama, Yayoi *sculptor, painter*

THE NETHERLANDS

Amsterdam
Baer, Jo *painter*

PAKISTAN

Lahore
Geoffrey, Iqbal (Mohammed Jawaid Iqbal Jafree) *artist, lawyer*

PORTUGAL

Lisbon
Berger, Jason *artist, printmaker*

SPAIN

Mallorca
Ulbricht, John *artist*

Seville
Sanchez, Leonedes Monarrize Worthington (Duke de Leonedes) *fashion designer*

SWITZERLAND

Bern
Polke, Sigmar *artist*

ADDRESS UNPUBLISHED

Abadi, Fritzie *artist, educator*
Abbe, Elfriede Martha *sculptor, graphic artist*
Abramowicz, Janet *painter, print-maker*
†Anderson, William Mills *film editor*
Andrade, Edna *artist, art educator*
Andrews, Jean *artist, writer*
Annus, John Augustus *artist*
Arnoldi, Charles Arthur *painter, sculptor*
Arthur, Rochelle Linda *creative director*
Ash, Hiram Newton *graphic designer*
Atkinson, Bill *designer*
Austin, Janet Hays *artist*
Banks, Jeffrey *fashion designer*
Barth, Frances Dorothy *artist*
Bateman, Robert McLellan *artist*
Baughman, J. Ross *photographer, writer, educator*
Benton, Fletcher *sculptor*
Ben Tré, Howard *artist*
Benzle, Curtis Munhall *artist, educator*
Bergson, Maria *designer*
Berlin, Beatrice Winn *visual artist, printmaker*
Berman, Eleanore *artist*
Bigelow-Lourie, Anne Edwige *graphic designer*
†Binch, Caroline Lesley *illustrator, photographer*
Bissell, James Dougal, III *motion picture production designer*
Bjornson, Maria *theatrical designer*
Bloes, Richard Kenneth *video artist*
Bloom, Hyman *artist*
Boxer, Stanley Robert *artist, sculptor*
Bradshaw, Dove *artist*
Brenner, Albert *production designer, sculptor*
Brettell, Richard Robson *art consultant*
Broderson, Morris *artist*
Brodie, Howard *artist*
†Brown, Carol A. *artist*
Brown, William Ferdinand *artist, writer*
Browne, Diana Gayle *artist, social services*
Bullard, Helen (Mrs. Joseph Marshall Krechniak) *sculptor*
Bury, John *theatre designer, consultant*
Campanelli, Pauline Eble *artist*
Campbell, Patton *stage designer, educator*
Cantliffe, Jeri Miller *artist, art educator*
Carothers, Steven Michael *artist, designer, writer*
Carter, Nanette Carolyn *artist*
Cassill, (Karilyn) Kay *artist, writer*
Cassini, Oleg Lolewski *fashion designer, manufacturer*
Catlett, Elizabeth *sculptor, printmaker, educator*
Chase-Riboud, Barbara Dewayne *sculptor, writer*
Chinn, Thomas Wayne *typographic company executive*
Chinni, Peter Anthony *artist*
Chryssa *sculptor*
Ciccone, Anne Panepinto *artist*
Claiborne, Liz (Elisabeth Claiborne Ortenberg) *fashion designer*
Clark, Larry *photographer*
Cobb, Ruth *artist*
Cobb, Virginia Horton *artist, educator*
Conway, Robert P. *art dealer*
Cooney, Barbara *illustrator, author*
Coplans, John Rivers *artist*
Craw, Freeman (Jerry Craw) *graphic artist*
Cumming, Robert Hugh *artist, photographer*
Cummings, David William *artist, educator*
D'Arcangelo, Allan Matthew *artist*
Dater, Judy Lichtenfeld *photographer*
Davidson, Jeannie *costume designer*
De Blasi, Tony (Anthony Armando De Blasi) *artist*
Dechar, Peter Henry *artist*
Dees, Lynne *artist*
Dell'Olio, Louis *fashion designer*
De Looper, Willem Johan *artist, museum curator*
Dembeck, Mary Grace *artist, writer*
Der Manuelian, Lucy *art and architecture educator*
Dill, Laddie John *artist*
Di Spigna, Tony *graphic designer*
Doğançay, Burhan C. *artist, photographer, sculptor*
Donath, Therese *author, artist*
Downes, Rackstraw *artist*
†Doyle, Tom *artist, educator*
Draper, Line Bloom (Line B. Draper-Rubba) *artist*
Drummond, Sally Hazelet *artist*
Dunwiddie, Charlotte *sculptor*
Dyer, Geraldine Ann (Geri Dyer) *artist, poet*
Eddy, Don *artist*
Erden, Sybil Isolde *artist*
Fine, Jane Madeline *visual artist*
Firestone, Evan Richard *art educator, academic administrator*
Fish, Janet Isobel *artist*
Flavin, Dan *artist*
Forester, Russell *artist*
†Frailey, Stephen A. *photographer*
Freilicher, Jane *artist*
Gerstein, Esther *sculptor*
Giusti, Robert George *artist, educator*
Goldberger, Blanche Rubin *sculptor, jeweler*
Goodwill, Margaret Jane *artist*
Gorchov, Ron *artist*
Goulet, Lorrie *sculptor*
Greenberg, Albert *art director*
Greene, Lynne Jeannette *fashion designer*
Gregory, Eleanor Anne *artist, educator*
Grooms, Red *artist*
Gurney, James Marshall *artist, writer*
Gurwitz-Hall, Barbara Ann *artist*
Guthrie, Edgar King *artist*
Halaby, Samia Asaad *artist, educator, computer artist*
†Hamilton, Ann Katherine *artist*
Hanson, Jo *artist*
Harari, Hananiah *artist*
Harbutt, Charles *photographer*
†Hardwicke, Catherine Helen *motion picture production designer*
Hartell, John *artist, retired art educator*
†Hawkes, Kevin Cliff *illustrator, author*
Hayes, David Vincent *sculptor*
Heilman, Marlin Grant *photographer*
Helander, Bruce Paul *artist, art dealer*
Heller, Dorothy *artist*
Henry, John Raymond *sculptor*
Hepper, Carol *artist, educator*
Hersey, David Kenneth *theatrical lighting designer*
Herzberg, Thomas *artist, illustrator*
Hoover, Francis Louis *educator, gemologist, jewelry designer, appraiser fine arts and gems, writer*
Hornick, Katherine Joyce Kay *artist, small business owner*
Hunt, Bryan *artist*
Hyman, Trina Schart *illustrator*
Janko, May *graphic artist*
Jansen, Angela Bing *artist, educator*
Jenney, Neil Franklin, Jr. *artist, philosopher*
Jimenez, Luis Alfonso, Jr. *sculptor*
Kahn, Albert Michael *artist, designer*
Kahn, Susan Beth *artist*
Kalina, Richard *artist*
Karawina, Erica *artist, stained glass designer*
Kaufman, Jane *artist*
Kearns, James Joseph *artist*
Keister, Stephen Lee *artist*
Kelly, Ellsworth *artist, sculptor*
Kipniss, Robert *artist*
Kleiman, Alan Boyd *artist*
Kloss, Gene (Alice Geneva Glasier) *artist*
Kohlmeyer, Ida Rittenberg *artist*
Kramer, Reuben Robert *sculptor*
Kumler, Kipton Cornelius *photographer, consultant*
La Rocca, Isabella *artist*
Lassiter, Kenneth T. *photography educator, consultant*
Lee, William Saul (Bill Lee) *artist, writer*
Lemieux, Annette Rose *artist*
Levi, Josef Alan *artist*
Levin, Morton D(avid) *artist, printmaker, educator*
Lichtenstein, Roy *artist*
Lieberman, Louis (Karl Lieberman) *artist*
Lienhart, James Lee *graphic designer*
Littleton, Harvey Kline *artist*
Loquasto, Santo *theatrical set designer*
Lucas, Rhett Roy *artist, chemical engineer, lawyer*
Ludwig, Allan Ira *photographer, artist, author*
Lund, David Nathan *artist*
Lynch, Peter George *artist*
Mangold, Sylvia Plimack *artist*
Marca-Relli, Conrad *artist*
Mark, Mary Ellen *photographer*
Martin, Noel *graphic design consultant, educator*
Martyl, (Mrs. Alexander Langsdorf, Jr.) *artist*
McCracken, John Harvey *painter, sculptor*
†McCurdy, Michael Charles *illustrator, author*
McVicker, Jesse Jay *artist, educator*
Meneeley, Edward Sterling *artist*
Middaugh, Robert Burton *artist*
Miles, Jeanne Patterson *artist*
†Mills, Frederick VanFleet *art educator, watercolorist*
Minami, Robert Yoshio *artist, graphic designer*
†Mirojnick, Ellen *costume designer*
Misrach, Richard Laurence *photographer*
†Mollo, John *film costume designer, military historian*
Morley, Malcolm A. *artist*
Morning, John *graphic designer*
Moses, Edward Crosby *artist*
Murray, Robert Gray *sculptor*
Nakamura, Kazuo *artist*
Natkin, Robert *painter*
Newman, Muriel Kallis Steinberg *art collector*
Nichols, Iris Jean *illustrator*
Notkin, Richard T. *ceramic sculptor, educator*
Olkinetzky, Sam *artist, retired museum director and educator*
Onslow Ford, Gordon Max *painter*
Pack, Susan Joan *art consultant*
Pearlstein, Philip *artist*
Péladeau, Marius Beaudoin *art consultant, retired museum director*
Penn, Irving *photographer*
Perman, Norman Wilford *graphic designer*
Phelan, Ellen *artist*
Pinkney, Jerry *artist, educator*
Ponce de Leon, Michael *artist, lecturer, educator*
Prey, Barbara Ernst *artist*
Provensen, Alice Rose Twitchell *artist, author*
Reed, David Fredrick *artist*
Reichman, Fredrick Thomas *artist*
Rickey, George Warren *artist, sculptor, educator*
Robinson, Aminah Brenda Lynn *artist*
Robinson, Charlotte Hill *artist*
Rockburne, Dorothea G. *artist*
Root, Doris Smiley *portrait artist*
Rosenquist, James Albert *artist*
†Ross, Gloria Frankenthaler *artist, consultant*
Rossman, Ruth Scharff *artist, educator*
Rothschild, Carolyn Anita *art dealer*
Rubello, David Jerome *artist*
Rubin, Sandra Mendelsohn *artist*
Rubinstein, Eva (Anna) *photographer*
Saar, Betye (Irene Saar) *artist*
Scharf, William *artist*
Schley, Reeve, III *artist*
Schmalz, Carl Nelson, Jr. *artist, educator, printmaker*
Schnackenberg, Roy Lee *artist*
Schultz, Eileen Hedy *graphic designer*
Schwartz, Lillian Feldman *artist, filmaker, art analyst, author, nurse*
Shamask, Ronaldus *fashion designer*
Shaw, Richard *artist*
Sheridan, Sonia Landy *artist, retired art educator*
Shoulberg, Harry *artist*
Sisto, Elena *artist, educator*
Snelson, Kenneth Duane *sculptor*
Sorel, Edward *artist*
Spence, Andrew *artist, painter*
Steiner, Michael *sculptor*
Stevens, May *artist*
Streeter, Tal *sculptor*
Strider, Marjorie Virginia *artist, educator*
Sumichrast, Jozef *illustrator, designer*
Surrey, Philip Henry *artist, educator*
Swensen, Mary Jean Hamilton *graphic artist*
Takal, Peter *artist*
Thiel, Philip *design educator*
Tovish, Harold *sculptor*
Tsai, Wen-Ying *sculptor, painter, engineer*
Unithan, Dolly *visual artist*
Valens, Evans Gladstone *sculptor, printmaker, author, former television producer, director*

Vassil, Pamela *graphic designer*
Ward, Elaine *artist*
Wechter, Vivienne Thaul *artist, poet, educator*
†Westwood, Vivienne *fashion designer*
White, Doris Anne *artist*
Willenbecher, John *artist*
Wilson, Jane *artist*
Wiseman, Jay Donald *photographer, mechanical contractor, designer*
Wolfe, Jean Elizabeth *medical illustrator, painter*
Zajac, Jack *sculptor, painter*
Zapf, Hermann *book and type designer*
†Zea, Kristina Gwyn *costume and production designer*
Zekman, Terri Margaret *graphic designer*
Zelinsky, Paul O. *illustrator, painter, author*

ASSOCIATIONS AND ORGANIZATIONS. *See also* specific fields.

UNITED STATES

ALABAMA

Auburn
Teague, Sam Fuller *association executive, educator,*

Birmingham
Carter, Frances Tunnell (Fran Carter) *fraternal organization administrator*
Gross, Iris Lee *association executive*
Newton, Don Allen *association executive*
Parker, Israel Frank *national association consultant*
Rynearson, W. John *association executive*
†Slay, A. Michele *fundraiser*

Mobile
McCann, Clarence David, Jr. *special events coordinator, museum curator and director, artist*

Tuscaloosa
Summersell, Frances Sharpley *organization worker*

ALASKA

Anchorage
Strohmeyer, John *writer, former editor*

ARIZONA

Chandler
Basha, Eddie *contributor to the arts, artist*

Phoenix
Albrecht, Carol Lee *human resources consultant*
†Blake, George Alan, Jr. *non-profit association executive*
Davis, Kurt Reynolds *state government executive*
DeMenna, Kevin Bolton *lobbyist*
Haynes, James Earl, Jr. *association executive*
Lloyd, Llyn Allan *association executive*

Scottsdale
Carney, Richard Edgar *foundation executive*
Foss, Joe *association executive, speaker*
Jacobson, Frank Joel *cultural organization adminisrator*

Sedona
Keane, Mark Edward *public executive and educator*

Sun City
Jones, Alexander Elvin *retired foundation executive*

Tempe
Baker, Roland Jerald *association executive*

Tucson
Grand, Marcia *civic worker*
Riggs, Frank Lewis *foundation executive*
†Ross, Robert *health agency administrator*

Whiteriver
†Lupe, Ronnie *chairman of apache tribe*

Window Rock
Zah, Peterson *american indian tribal executive*

ARKANSAS

Camden
Smith, Judy Seriale *social services administrator, state legislator*

Fayetteville
Bell, Randall *educational association administrator*

Little Rock
Bailin, David William *educational administrator*
Busfield, Roger Melvil, Jr. *retired trade association executive, educator*

Morrilton
Havener, Robert Dale *agricultural institute administrator*

Mountain Home
Seevers, Charles Junior *foundation executive, psychologist*

CALIFORNIA

Alamo
Lee, Richard *martial arts educational executive*

Atherton
Heyns, Roger William *retired foundation executive and educator*
King, Jane Cudlip Coblentz *volunteer educator*

Bakersfield
Clark, Michal Charles *social services director*

Beaumont
†Lippert, Robert Lawrence *social services administrator*

Belvedere Tiburon
Cook, Lyle Edwards *retired fund raising executive, consultant*

Brea
Tamura, Cary Kaoru *fundraiser*

Campbell
Throndson, Edward Warner *residential association administrator*

Canoga Park
Lederer, Marion Irvine *cultural administrator*

Carlsbad
Vincent, John Graham *administrator*

Carmel
Pinkham, Frederick Oliver *foundation executive, consultant*

Chino
Johnston, Linda Joyce *educational company executive*

Claremont
†Arnn, Larry Paul *foundation executive, editor*
Rankin, Robert *retired educational foundation executive*

Covina
Jackson, John Jay *clergyman, denomination administrator*

Culver City
†Netzel, Paul Arthur *fund raising management executive, consultant*

Davis
Boulton, Lyndie McHenry *professional society administrator*
Redenbach, Sandra Irene *educational consultant*

El Portal
Medley, Steven Paul *association executive*

Fresno
Kuhlman, Josie-Lee *social work administrator*

Gardena
Crismond, Linda Fry *association executive*

Glendora
Schiele, Paul Ellsworth, Jr. *educational business owner, writer*

Irvine
Young, Robert Anthony *association director*

Keene
†Rodriguez, Arturo Salvador *labor union official*

Long Beach
Lee, Isaiah Chong-Pie *social worker, educator*
Muchmore, Don Moncrief *museum, foundation, educational, financial fund raising and public opinion consulting firm administrator*
Patino, Douglas Xavier *foundation and university administrator*

Los Alamitos
Myers, Edwin *think-tank executive*

Los Altos
Critzer, William Ernest *association executive*
Wickham, Kenneth Gregory *retired army officer, institute official*
Wilbur, Colburn Sloan *foundation administrator, chief executive officer*

Los Angeles
Caldwell-Portenier, Patty Jean Grosskopf *advocate, educator*
Chassman, Leonard Fredric *labor union administrator*
Ennis, Thomas Michael *health foundation executive*
Gumpel, Glenn J. *association executive*
Headlee, Rolland Dockeray *association executive*
Hubbs, Donald Harvey *foundation president*
Mack, J. Curtis, II *civic organization administrator*
Orsatti, Alfred Kendall *organization executive*
Reagan, Nancy Davis (Anne Francis Robbins) *volunteer, wife of former President of United States*
†Reed, Donald Anthony *executive*
Smith, Jean Webb (Mrs. William French Smith) *civic worker*

Menlo Park
†Altman, Drew E. *foundation executive*
Gardner, David Pierpont *foundation executive*
Morrison, James Ian *research institute executive*
Nichols, William Ford, Jr. *foundation executive, business executive*
Pallotti, Marianne Marguerite *foundation administrator*

Moffett Field
Scott, Donald Michael *educational association administrator, educator*

Monrovia
Seiple, Robert Allen *Christian relief organization executive*

Mountain View
Michalko, James Paul *library association administrator*

North Hollywood
Grasso, Mary Ann *theatre association administrator*

Oakland
Macmeeken, John Peebles *foundation executive, educator*
†Rosen, Corey M. *professional association executive*

Oceanside
Roberts, James McGregor *retired professional association executive*

Ojai
Mankoff, Albert William *cultural organization administrator, consultant*

Orange
Reed, David Andrew *foundation executive*

Orinda
Cooper, Clare Dunlap *civic worker, writer*

Palm Springs
Hearst, Rosalie *philanthropist, foundation executive*

Palo Alto
Duggan, Susan J. *educational administrator*
Rosenzweig, Robert Myron *educational consultant*

Pebble Beach
Gianelli, William Reynolds *foundation administrator, civil engineering consultant, former federal agency commissioner*

Pomona
Thompson, Earlene *civic volunteer*

Riverside
Pick, Arthur Joseph, Jr. *chamber of commerce executive*

Sacramento
Gray, Walter P., III *museum director, consultant*
Hay, John Thomas *trade association executive*

San Andreas
Breed, Allen Forbes *correctional administrator*

San Bernardino
Bellis, David James *public administration educator*

San Diego
Ballinger, Charles Edwin *educational association administrator*
Carleson, Robert Bazil *public policy consultant, corporation executive*
Dolan, James Michael, Jr. *zoological society executive*
†Douglas, Lee Wayland *association executive*
Grosser, T.J. *administrator, developer, fundraiser*
Lane, Gloria Julian *foundation administrator*
McCarroll, Mary Barbara *social services adminstrator, retired*
Schlotter, Wally *chamber of commerce executive, television director*
Swoap, David Bruce *children's relief administrator*

San Francisco
Collins, Dennis Arthur *foundation executive*
Du Bain, Myron *foundation administrator*
Eastham, Thomas *foundation administrator*
Fisher, Robert M. *foundation administrator, university administrator*
Giovinco, Joseph *non-profit administrator, writer*
†Harwood, Caroline Elizabeth *environmental organization administrator*
Henderson, Horace Edward *public affairs consultant, military historian*
Hickman, Maxine Viola *social services administrator*
Jacobs, John Howard *association executive*
†Milton, Catherine Higgs *public service organization executive*
Morris, Richard Ward *nonprofit organization administrator, author*
Shirpser, Clara *former Democratic national committeewoman*
Stauffer, Thomas Michael *university president*
Thelen, Max, Jr. *foundation executive, lawyer*

San Jose
Bennett, Charles Turner *social welfare administrator*

San Juan Capistrano
Horn, Deborah Sue *organization administrator, writer, editor*

San Marino
Hull, Suzanne White *retired cultural institution administrator, writer*

San Rafael
Lee, Robert *association executive, former theological educator, consultant, author*

Santa Barbara
Krieger, David Malcolm *peace foundation executive, lawyer*

Santa Monica
Abarbanel, Gail *social service administrator, educator*
†Greene, Michael C. *art association administrator*
Liddicoat, Richard Thomas, Jr. *association executive*
Rich, Michael David *research corporation executive, lawyer*
Thomson, James Alan *research company executive*
Williams, Harold Marvin *foundation official*

Scotts Valley
Bourret, Marjorie Ann *educational advocate, consultant*

Sherman Oaks
†Bruckel, Jane C. *nonprofit organization executive*
Green, Marjorie Biller *educational administrator*

Sonoma
Stadtman, Verne August *former foundation executive, editor*

South Lake Tahoe
†Nason, Rochelle *conservation organization administrator*

South Pasadena
Staehle, Robert L. *foundation executive*

Stanford
Lyman, Richard Wall *foundation and university executive, historian*
Matisoff, Susan *cultural research organization administrator*
Stone, William Edward *association executive*

Studio City
Frumkin, Simon *political activist and columnist*

Sunnyvale
Bills, Robert Howard *political party executive*
Karp, Nathan *political activist*

Trinidad
Marshall, William Edward *historical association executive*

Woodland Hills
Harris, Helen Josephine *foundation administrator*
O'Meara, Sara *foundation administrator*
Sigholtz, Sara O'Meara *non-profit organization executive*

COLORADO

Aspen
Harth, Robert James *music festival executive*

Aurora
Dye, Larry Wayne *political consultant*
Fish, Ruby Mae Bertram (Mrs. Frederick Goodrich Fish) *civic worker*
Hutchins, Charles Larry *educational association administrator, consultant*
Motz, Kenneth Lee *former farm organization official*

Boulder
†Hill, Norbert S., Jr. *executive director American Indian society*
†Jonsen, Richard Wiliam *educational administrator*
Neinas, Charles Merrill *athletic association executive*

Castle Rock
Graf, Joseph Charles *retired foundation executive*

Colorado Springs
†Flemke, Karl *economic education association executive*
Fowler, John Dale *association executive*
Killian, George Ernest *association executive*
Libby, Lauren Dean *foundation president*
†Loux, Gordon Dale *organization executive*
Rochette, Edward Charles *retired association executive*

Denver
Daley, Richard Halbert *foundation executive*
Darkey, Kermit Louis *association executive, lawyer*
Groff, JoAnn *organization administrator*
Harris, Ellen Gandy (Mrs. J. Ramsay Harris) *civic worker*
Hirschfeld, Arlene F. *civic worker, homemaker*
Hixon, Janet Kay Erickson *education specialist*
Hogan, Curtis Jule *union executive, industrial relations consultant*
Misbrener, Joseph Michael *labor union official*
Nelson, Bernard William *foundation executive, educator, physician*
†Phillips, Kay Randelle *association executive*
Reynolds, Collins James, III *association administrator*
†Smith, Rita Sue *administrator*
Sudler, Barbara Welch *retired historical society administrator*

Englewood
Chesser, Al H. *union official*
Massey, Leon R. *association executive*
†Reese, Monte Nelson *agricultural association executive*
Tanaka, Floyd Hideo *consulting firm executive*

Fort Collins
Cummings, Sharon Sue *state extension service youth specialist*
†Roberts, Archibald E. *nonprofit corporation executive*

Golden
†Shimanski, Charles Stuart *organization executive*

Grand Junction
†Morris, Rusty Lee *administrative executive*

Greenwood Village
Walker, Eljana M. du Vall *civic worker*

Lakewood
Isely, Henry Philip *association executive, integrative engineer, writer, educator*

Snowmass
Lovins, L. Hunter *public policy institute executive*

U S A F Academy
Coppock, Richard Miles *nonprofit association administrator*

CONNECTICUT

East Haven
Hegyi, Albert Paul *association executive, lawyer*

Fairfield
Polin, Jane Louise foundation official

Falls Village
Toomey, Jeanne Elizabeth animal activist

Greenwich
†Nelson, Douglas W. social service administrator
†Ramanathan, Rama foundation executive
Taylor, Sir Cyril (Julian Hebden) education association administrator, consultant

Hamden
Resnick, Idrian Navarre foundation administrator

Hartford
Bickford, Christopher Penny association executive
†Blatti, Jo historical institution administrator, historian
Connelly, William Howard retired foundation executive
Decko, Kenneth Owen association executive
Francis, Paul Wilbur, Jr. association executive

Lyme
Greene, Joseph Nathaniel, Jr. former foundation executive, former diplomat

Madison
Houghton, Alan Nourse association executive, educator, consultant

Meriden
Way, Carol Jane non-profit organization administrator

Middletown
†Sergi, Theodore S. educational administrator

Milford
Wall, Robert Emmet educational administrator, novelist

Mystic
Smith, Norman Clark fund raising consultant

New Canaan
Mountcastle, Katharine Babcock foundation executive
Thomsen, Donald Laurence, Jr. institute executive, mathematician

New Fairfield
†Meyers, Abbey S. foundation administrator

New Haven
Brewster, Carroll Worcester fund administrator
Dechant, Virgil C. fraternal organization administrator
Theodore, Eustace D. alumni association executive, management consultant

New London
Wetmore, Thomas Trask, III retired foundation administrator, retired coast guard officer

Newington
Sumner, David George association executive

North Branford
Logan, John Arthur, Jr. retired foundation executive

Norwalk
Bullard, Edward Payson, IV non-profit executive
Dresher, William Henry research association executive

Old Greenwich
Bonner, Charles William, III community services executive, newspaper writer
Scullion, Tsugiko Yamagami non-profit organization executive

Old Lyme
Bond, Niles Woodbridge cultural institute executive, former foreign service officer

Old Saybrook
Spencer, William Courtney foundation executive, international business executive

Riverside
Coulson, Robert retired association executive, lawyer

Stamford
Brakeley, George Archibald, Jr. fundraising consultant
Kaufman, John E. retired association executive
Mc Namara, Francis Joseph, Jr. foundation executive, lawyer

Westport
Levinger, Beryl Beth development specialist, organization administrator

Willimantic
Loin, E. Linnea social services administrator

Wilton
Forger, Robert Durkin retired professional association administrator

Woodmont
Frazier, Howard Thomas association executive

DELAWARE

Dover
Ornauer, Richard Lewis retired educational association administrator

Newark
†Curtis, James C. cultural organization administrator/history educator
Mitchell, Peter Kenneth, Jr. educational consultant, association administrator

Wilmington
Cartwright, Albert Thomas association executive
Peterson, Russell Wilbur former association executive, former state governor
Wheeler, M. Catherine organization executive

DISTRICT OF COLUMBIA

Washington
Able, Edward H. association executive
Ahmann, Mathew Hall social action organization administrator, consultant
Alberts, Bruce Michael foundation administrator, biochemist
Allnutt, Robert Frederick organization executive, lawyer
Ambach, Gordon Mac Kay education association executive
Anderson, Dean William educational administrator
Andrews, Laureen E. foundation administrator
Appleberry, James Bruce higher education association executive
Arnold, William Edwin foundation administrator
Atherton, Alfred Leroy, Jr. foundation executive, former foreign service officer
Atwell, Robert Herron association executive
AuCoin, Les lobbyist, former congressman
Babby, Ellen Reisman education administrator
Bagge, Carl Elmer association executive, lawyer, consultant
Bahr, Morton trade union executive
Ball, Robert M. social security, welfare and health policy specialist, writer, lecturer
Banzhaf, John F., III organization executive,lawyer
†Barach, Jeffrey Truxton trade association executive
Barbour, Haley political organization administrator, lawyer
Baroody, William Joseph, Jr. research institute executive
Barrow, Robert Earl agricultural organization administrator
Bartlett, Charles J. think-tank executive
Bartlett, Charles Leffingwell foundation executive, former newspaperman
Beazley, Hamilton Scott volunteer health organization executive
Bender, David Ray library association executive
Benjamin, Ernst professional association executive
Biller, Morris (Moe Biller) union executive
Bissell, Richard Etter association administrator
Blitzer, Charles educational administrator
Boaz, David Douglas foundation executive
Boede, Marvin J. union official
Bond, Julian civil rights leader
Bond, Richard Norman political activist
Bonosaro, Carol Alessandra professional association executive,former government official
Book, Edward R. consultant, retired association executive
Bookbinder, Hyman H(arry) public affairs counselor
Borut, Donald J. association executive
Bourne, Francis Stanley foundation administrator
Boyle, John Edward Whiteford cultural organization administrator
Boyle, Renée Kent cultural organization executive, translator, editor
Brady, Nyle C. international consultant, science educator
Brady, Sarah gun control activist
Brobeck, Stephen James consumer advocate
Brown, David R. think-tank executive
Brown, Lawrence Clifton, Jr. foundation administrator
Brown, William Robert association executive, consultant
Brownlee, Paula Pimlott association executive
Bryant, Anne Lincoln association executive
Bywater, William Harold labor union official
Cain, Becky C. association executive
Calhoun, John Alfred social services administrator
Cameron, Don R. association director
Campbell, Wallace Justin social welfare administrator, economist
Canes, Michael Edwin trade association administrator, economist
Carey, Ronald labor union leader
Carman, Anne foundation executive
Cashmore, Patsy Joy speechwriter, editor, author, consultant, educator
Cheney, Lynne V. humanities educator, writer
Chilcote, Samuel Day, Jr. association executive
Clark, Margaret Pruitt education and advocacy executive administrator
Clark, Wendell Mark travelers organization executive
Cochran, John Thomas professional association executive
Coia, Arthur A. labor union executive
†Colbert, Robert Ivan education association administrator
Collie, Homah, III trade association executive
Colton, Kent W. trade association executive
Conafay, Stephen Rogers trade association executive
Cooper, Josephine Smith trade association and public relations executive
Cope, James Dudley association executive
Crane, Edward Harrison, III institute executive
Croser, Mary Doreen educational association executive
Crutchfield, Sam Shaw, Jr. association executive, lawyer
†Cunningham, William James labor lobbyist
Dambach, Charles Frederick foundation administrator, management consultant
Damgard, John Michael trade association executive
Dando, George William professional association executive
Deets, Horace association executive
Denney, George Covert, Jr. organization administrator
DiBona, Charles Joseph association executive
†Didion, Dale Albert social services administrator
Dillon, Robert Sherwood non-profit educational organization executive
Ditlow, Clarence M. think-tank executive
Dole, Elizabeth Hanford charitable organization administrator, former secretary of labor, former secretary of transportation
†Dolibois, Robert Joseph trade association administrator
Donahue, Thomas Reilly trade union official
Dorn, Jennifer Lynn charitable organization administrator
†Dudley, Barbara environmental association executive
Eisenberg, Pablo Samuel non-profit organization executive
Elsey, George McKee association executive
Engel, Ralph manufacturers association executive
English, Glenn association executive, former congressman
Feeney, Richard Joseph trade association executive, journalist
Fink, Matthew Pollack trade association executive, lawyer
Finkle, Jeffrey Alan professional association executive
†Fisher, Sam organization administrator, consultant
†Fisher, Timothy Mark non-profit administrator
Foard, Douglas W. educational association administrator
†Fowler, Donald L. political organization leader, political science educator, retired US Army officer
†Fowler, Raymond Dalton professional association executive, psychologist
Frampton, George Thomas, Jr. conservation organization executive
Francois, Francis Bernard association executive, lawyer
†French, Catherine association executive
Friedman, Miles trade association executive, financial services company executive, university lecturer
Fritz, Thomas Vincent association and business executive, accountant
Fulbright, Harriet Mayor foundation administrator
†Fuller, Kathryn Scott environmental association executive, lawyer
Futrell, Basil Lee association executive
Futrell, Mary Alice Hatwood education association administrator
Georgine, Robert Anthony union executive
†Gershman, Carl Samuel foundation administrator
†Gilliam, Arleen Fain labor union administrator, finance executive
Goldman, Aaron foundation executive, writer
†Goldstein, Sheldon Robert professional association administrator
Golodner, Jack labor association official
Gorham, William organization executive
Goslin, David Alexander research administrator, sociologist
Gottlieb, Anita F. professional society executive
Green, Monica peace organization director
Green, Shirley Moore public affairs and communications executive
Greenburg, David Julius professional association administrator, lawyer
Griffenhagen, George Bernard trade association executive
Guenther, Kenneth Allen business association executive, economist
†Hair, Jay Dee association executive
Handelsman, M. Gene association administrator
Hanley, Edward Thomas union official
Hanley, Frank labor union official
Harbrant, Robert Francis labor union executive
Harrison, Earl Grant, Jr. educational administrator
Harrison, Monika Edwards business development executive
Hartman, Arthur A. international business consultant
Haseltine, John B. think-tank executive
Healey, John G. human services organization executive
Herbst, Robert LeRoy organization executive
†Hillman, Gracia association administrator
Hills, John Merrill public policy research center executive, former educational administrator
Hobart, Lawrence Scott service organization administrator
Hoewing, Raymond L. association executive
Holbrook, Douglas Cowen labor union administrator
†Holden, Gwen A. professional society administrator
Holloway, James Lemuel, III foundation executive, retired naval officer
Holt, Pamela Gail arts commission administrator
†Hopewell, Luz Araoz trade association executive
Howard, Jack union executive
Hoyt, John Arthur humane society executive
Huband, Frank Louis educational association executive
Hughes, Thomas Lowe foundation executive
Illig, James Michael humanitarian organization executive
Imig, David Gregg educational association executive
Ingram, Richard Thomas association executive
Ireland, Patricia association executive
Isaacs, Amy Fay political organization executive
Jacobson, Michael Faraday consumer advocate, writer
Joe, Thomas think-tank
Johnston, Laurance Scott foundation director
Joyce, John T. labor union official
Kamber, Victor Samuel political consultant
Kane, Michael Barry education research executive
Kavanaugh, Everett Edward, Jr. trade association executive
Keeny, Spurgeon Milton, Jr. association executive
†Kemp, John D. association administrator
Kempner, Jonathan L. professional society administrator
Kirkland, Joseph Lane (Lane Kirkland) labor union official
†Kirkland, Lane labor union administrator
Kleinknecht, Christian Frederick Masonic official
Knapp, Richard Maitland association executive
Kolb, Charles Chester humanities administrator
Kossak, Shelley think-tank executive
Kruse, Dennis K. think-tank executive, career officer
Kullberg, John Francis association executive
Kurth, Walter Richard association executive
Lampl, Peggy Ann association administrator
Lang, Ronald Anthony trade association executive
Langley, Chiara Maria Bini society executive, research scientist
LaPidus, Jules Benjamin association executive
Larson, Charles Fred association executive
Lawson, Richard Laverne trade association executive, retired military officer
Lesher, Richard Lee association executive
Leven, Ann Ruth arts administrator
Lewis, Ann Frank social welfare association executive
†Lewis, Green Pryor, Jr. community service administrator
Liederman, David Samuel child welfare administrator
Lilley, James Roderick foreign relations expert, former federal government official
†Limon, Lavinia social services administrator
Lively, Carol A. association executive
Low, Stephen foundation executive, educator, former diplomat
Lowe, Carol Hill social services director
Loy, Frank Ernest foundation executive
†Lucas, C. Payne development organization executive
Lucassen, Sigurd labor union administrator
Magazine, Alan Harrison association executive, consultant
Magrath, C. Peter educational association executive
Marlowe, Howard David lobbyist, public affairs company executive
†Marquardt, Sandra Mary activist, lobbyist, researcher
Masters, Edward E. association executive, former foreign service officer
†Mathews, Dan animal rights activist
McClintic, Howard Gresson foundation executive
McCloskey, J(ohn) Michael association executive
†McCloskey, Peter Francis trade association executive
†McElroy, Edward J. union officer
McEntee, Gerald W. labor union official
McGlotten, Robert Miller labor union official
Mc Kay, Emily Gantz civil and human rights professional
McLennan, Barbara Nancy trade association executive, lawyer
McNamee, Sister Catherine educational association executive
McNulty, Robert Holmes civic association executive
McSteen, Martha Abernathy organization executive
Messner, Howard Myron professional association executive
Metz, Douglas Wilber association executive, lawyer
Miller, John Francis association executive, social scientist
Mossinghoff, Gerald Joseph lawyer, association executive
Mtewa, Mekki foundation administrator
Munson, Richard Jay congressional coalition policy analyst
Murphy, Kenneth Ray non-governmental organization executive
Murphy, Patrick Vincent foundation executive
Murray, James Joseph, III association executive
Myers, Samuel Lloyd education association executive
†Myers, William Gerry, III advocate, lawyer
Nader, Ralph consumer advocate, lawyer, author
†Newkirk, Ingrid animal rights activist
Nicholson, Richard Selindh educational association administrator
Nikkel, Ronald Wilbert social services administrator
†Norris, Genie M. political organization executive
Norton, James J. union official
O'Day, Paul Thomas trade association executive
Ogilvie, Donald Gordon bankers association executive
Oliver, Daniel foundation fellow, lawyer
O'Neill, Joseph Patrick retail association executive
Onto, John think-tank executive
†Ottley, William Henry professional association director, consultant
Paulson, Stanley Fay association executive
Pearson, Roger organization executive
Peck, Robert David educational foundation administrator
Perez, Lillian non-profit association executive
Peterson, Esther consumer advocate
†Pierce, David R. educational administrator
Pings, Cornelius John educational association administrator
Pinstrup-Andersen, Per educational administrator
Porter, Elisabeth Scott (Leezee Porter) political worker
†Power, John Jay labor union official
Radin, Alex former association executive, consultant
Reger, Lawrence Lee association executive
Reich, Alan Anderson association executive
Richards, Cory demographic think-tank executive
Richardson, Ann Bishop foundation executive, lawyer
Robinson, Leonard Harrison, Jr. international government consultant, business executive
Robinson, Randall think-tank executive
Rodman, Peter Warren foreign policy specialist
Rosenberg, Sarah Zacher institute arts administration executive, humanities administration consultant
Rosenstein, Peter Daniel association executive, medical educator
Rother, John Charles association executive, lawyer
†Roush, G. Jon organization administrator
Rudder, Catherine Estelle political science association administrator
Russell, William Joseph association executive
Salvado, August J. think-tank executive
Sampson, Robert Neil association executive
Samuel, Howard David union official
Sandler, Bernice Resnick women's rights specialist
Scanlon, Patrick Michael lawyer
Scanlon, Terrence Maurice research foundation admnistrator
†Scheibel, James Allen volunteer service executive
†Schlickeisen, Rodger O. non-profit environmental organization executive
Schosberg, Paul Alan trade association executive
Schubert, Richard Francis foundation administrator
Seldman, Neil Norman cultural organization administrator
Sever, Tom labor union administrator
Sewell, John Williamson research association executive
Shanker, Albert labor union official
Shaw, Russell Burnham association executive, author
Shriver, Eunice Mary Kennedy (Mrs. Robert Sargent Shriver, Jr.) civic worker
†Shriver, Sargent organization executive, lawyer, ambassador
Siciliano, Rocco Carmine institute executive
Simmons, Caroline Thompson civic worker
Sims, Robert Bell professional society administrator, public affairs official, newspaper publisher
Skadden, Donald Harvey professional society executive, accounting educator
Slade, John Danton lobbyist, radio talk show host
Smedley, Lawrence Thomas organization executive
Spence, Sandra association executive
Splete, Allen Peterjohn association executive, educator
Staats, Elmer Boyd foundation executive, former government official
Stapleton, Jean think-tank executive
Stephens, John Frank association executive, researcher
Stern, Paula international trade advisor
†Stewart, Julie nonprofit organization executive
Stone, Jeremy Judah association executive
Strachan, David E. trade association executive
Strong, Henry foundation executive
Sugarman, Jule M. children's services consultant, former public administrator

Tanguy, Charles Reed *foundation administrator, consultant, former foreign service officer*
Tape, Gerald Frederick *former association executive*
Tarr-Whelan, Linda Jane *political organization administrator*
†Taylor, Helen Lavon Hollingshed *association executive, early childhood consultant*
Taylor, Robert William *association executive*
†Thompson, Otis Nathaniel, Jr. *executive*
Tipton, E. Linwood *trade association executive*
Tobias, Robert Max *labor leader, lawyer*
Tonkin, Leo Sampson *educational foundation administrator*
Topping, John Carruthers, Jr. *environmental organization administrator, lawyer*
Trumka, Richard Louis *labor leader, lawyer*
Ture, Norman Bernard *public policy research organization executive*
Unsell, Lloyd Neal *energy organization executive, former journalist*
Vander Horst, Kathleen Purcell *nonprofit association administrator*
Van Nelson, Nicholas Lloyd *business council executive*
Velasquez, Joe *labor union administrator*
Veliotes, Nicholas Alexander *professional association executive, former ambassador and assistant secretary of state*
Wait, Carol Grace Cox *organization administrator*
Walker, John Denley *foundation director, former government official*
Warden, Richard Dana *government labor union official*
Warren, David Liles *educational association executive*
Weber, Susan *research organization executive*
Wertheimer, Fredric Michael *association executive*
Weyrich, Paul Michael *political organizations executive*
White, Margita Eklund *television association executive*
Willging, Paul Raymond *trade association executive*
Williams, Eddie Nathan *research institution executive*
†Williams, Lawrence Floyd *conservation organization official*
Williams, Maurice Jacoutot *development organization executive*
Williams, Neville *international development organization executive*
Williams, Ronald L. *pharmaceutical association executive*
Wilson, Glen Parten *association administrator*
Wiseman, Laurence Donald *foundation executive*
Wolfe, Leslie R. *think-tank executive*
Woodall, Samuel Roy, Jr. *trade association executive*
Work, Jane Magruder *professional society administrator*
†Wynn, William Harrison *union official*
Yochim, Marie Hirst *retired association executive*
Yost, Paul Alexander, Jr. *foundation executive, retired coast guard officer*
Yzaguirre, Raul Humberto *civil rights administrator*
†Zitnay, George Albert *foundation executive*
Zuck, Alfred Miller *association executive*
Zwick, Charles J. *think-tank executive*

FLORIDA

Apopka
Shrum, Grant Arthur *non-profit organization executive*

Arcadia
Turnbull, David John (Chief Piercing Eyes-Penn) *cultural association executive*

Boca Raton
Apelian, Clover B. *non-profit management consultant*
Fey, Dorothy (Mrs. George Jay Fey) *former association executive*

Bonita Springs
Miller, Richard Dwight *professional association executive*

Boynton Beach
Falk, Bernard Henry *trade association executive*

Bradenton
†Aleppo, Joseph A. *foundation administrator*

Coral Springs
†Burg, Ralph *art association executive*

Cypress Gardens
Gobie, Henry Macaulay *philatelic researcher, retired postal executive*

Daytona Beach
Collyer, Robert B. *association executive*
Parker, Betty Morris *association administrator retired*

Delray Beach
Stewart, Patricia Carry *foundation administrator*

Englewood
Schultz, Arthur Joseph, Jr. *retired trade association executive*

Fort Lauderdale
White, Mary Lou *fundraiser, writer, educator*
Wynne, Brian James *former association executive, consultant*

Gainesville
Baughman, George Fechtig *foundation executive*
Wright, Jane Brooks *university foundation professional*

Hallandale
Contney, John Joseph *association executive*

Hollywood
Graves, Walter Albert *retired association executive, editor*

Jacksonville
†Glover, Richard Bernard *association administrator*

Lake Park
McBride, Nancy Allyson *child resource center administrator*

Lake Worth
Moore, Alderine Bernice Jennings (Mrs. James F. Moore) *association and organization administrator*

Longwood
†Dunne, Nancy Anne *retired social services administrator*
Walters, Philip Raymond *foundation executive*

Miami
Beckley, Donald K. *fundraiser*
Berger, Joyce Muriel *foundation executive, author, editor*
Brinkman, Paul Del(bert) *foundation executive*
Courshon, Carol Biel *civic worker*
Cullom, William Otis *trade association executive*
Dickason, John Hamilton *foundation executive*
Hills, Lee *foundation administrator, newspaper executive, consultant*
Rosenberg, Mark B. *think-tank executive*
VanBrode, Derrick Brent, IV *association executive*
†Walsh, Bryan Oliver *social services administrator, priest*
Weber, Nancy Walker *charitable trust administrator*

Naples
Rowe, Herbert Joseph *retired trade association executive*

Nokomis
Peters, Farnsley Lewellyn *retired association executive*

North Palm Beach
†Crawford, Roberta *association administrator*

Orlando
Ball, Joseph E. *association executive*

Osprey
Crispin, Mildred Swift (Mrs. Frederick Eaton Crispin) *civic worker, author*

Palm Beach
Chittick, Elizabeth Lancaster *association executive, women's rights activist*
Ferrin, Allan Wheeler *association executive*
†Mallardi, Vincent *organization executive*
Mandel, Carola Panerai (Mrs. Leon Mandel) *foundation trustee*
Rinker, Ruby Stewart *foundation administrator*

Patrick AFB
†Haggis, Arthur George, Jr. *retired career officer, educator, publisher*

Pensacola
Furlong, George Morgan, Jr. *retired naval officer, museum foundation executive*

Ponte Vedra Beach
Beman, Deane Randolph *association executive*

Saint Augustine
Baker, Norman Henderson *association executive*
Marsolais, Harold Raymond *association executive*

Saint Petersburg
Dickson, Suzanne Elizabeth (Sue Dickson) *educational administrator*
Shank, Clare Brown Williams *political leader*

Sanibel
Ball, Armand Baer *former association executive, consultant*

Sarasota
Balter, Frances Sunstein *civic worker*
Gerhardt, Paul Louis *professional association executive*

Tallahassee
†Manning, Altha *education commissioner*

Tampa
Zeno, Phyllis Wolfe *association executive, editor*

Tequesta
Luster, George Orchard *professional society administrator*

Vero Beach
Brim, Orville Gilbert, Jr. *former foundation administrator, author*

Wesley Chapel
Holloway, Marvin Lawrence *retired automobile club executive, rancher, vintager*

West Palm Beach
Hoewing, Mark Wesley *real estate association executive*

Winter Park
Olsson, Nils William *former association executive*

GEORGIA

Albany
Mayes, Helen *professional association administrator*

Americus
Fuller, Millard Dean *charitable organization executive, lawyer*

Atlanta
Beard, Rick *cultural organization administrator*
†Bell, Ronald Mack *university foundation administrator*
Clarke, Clifford Montreville *health foundation executive*
†DeConcini, Barbara *association executive, religious studies educator*
†Garth, Thomas G. *youth organization administrator*
Glassick, Charles Etzweiler *cultural organization administrator*
Harrison, John Raymond *foundation executive, retired newspaper executive*
Kelly, William Watkins *educational association executive*
King, Coretta Scott (Mrs. Martin Luther King, Jr.) *educational association administrator, lecturer, writer, concert singer*
†McTier, Charles Harvey *foundation administrator*
Merritt, Lynn Garnard *trade association executive*
Patterson, Anita Mattie *union administrator*
Robb, Felix Compton *association executive, consultant*
Scott, William Fred *cultural organization administrator*
Sears, Curtis Thornton, Jr. *educational administrator*
Thumann, Albert *association executive, engineer*
Tipping, William Malcolm *social services administrator*
Weltner, Betsey *state art association administrator*
Wylly, Barbara Bentley *performing arts association administrator*
Young, Andrew *clergyman, civil rights leader, former mayor, former ambassador, former congressman*

Augusta
Davison, Frederick Corbet *foundation executive*
Grier, Leamon Forest *social services administrator*

Conyers
Sheppard, Jacquelyn Smith *school system founder and administrator*

Cordele
Wade, Benny Bernar *educational administrator*

Decatur
†Davis, John M. *educational association administrator*

Macon
†Mills, Cynthia Spraker *association administrator*

Norcross
†Balestrero, Gregory *association executive*

Riverdale
Rhoden, Mary Norris *educational center director*

Roswell
†Thibaudeaux, Mary Frances *cultural organization administrator*

Savannah
Beals, L(oren) Alan *association executive*

Stone Mountain
Wingate, Henry Taylor, Jr. *foundation administrator, fundraiser*

Winterville
Shockley, W. Ray *travel trade association executive*

HAWAII

Honolulu
Jordan, Amos Azariah, Jr. *foreign affairs educator, retired army officer*
Lee, Beverly Ing *educational administrator*
Olmsted, Ronald David *foundation executive, consultant*
Robinson, Robert Blacque *association executive*

Waianae
Kanno, Brian M. *volunteer worker*

IDAHO

Boise
†Barton, Rayburn *educational administrator*

Pocatello
†Collins, Clark L. *executive*

ILLINOIS

Arlington Heights
Hoops, Donald Lee *medical association administrator*
Nerlinger, John William *association executive*

Bedford Park
Herbert, Victor James *association executive*

Buffalo Grove
Smith, Justine Townsend *recreational association executive*

Carol Stream
†Waldrop, William Thomas *executive*

Champaign
Clark, Roger Gordon *educational administrator*
Eilbracht, Lee Paul *retired association executive*

Chicago
Bailar, Barbara Ann *statistician, researcher*
Barker, Emmett Wilson, Jr. *trade association executive*
†Bloch, Ralph Jay *professional association executive*
Bottom, Dale Coyle *association executive*
†Bourdon, Cathleen Jane *executive director*
Braden, William Lou *non-profit agency manager*
†Buratto, Paddy Ann *trade association executive*
Calamaras, Louis Basil *lawyer, association executive*
†Carr, Barbara Whitney *foundation administrator*
Chacko, Samuel *association official*
Creighton, Neal *foundation administrator, retired military officer*
†Cuny, Frederick C. *disaster relief executive*
Cyr, Arthur *association executive*
Dolan, Thomas Christopher *association executive*
Donnell, Harold Eugene, Jr. *association executive*
Dykla, K.H.S. Edward George *social services administrator*
Epstein, Laura *social work educator, consultant*
Feldstein, Charles Robert *fund raising consultant*
Fetridge, Bonnie-Jean Clark (Mrs. William Harrison Fetridge) *civic volunteer*
Furman, James Merle *foundation executive*
Harvey, Katherine Abler *civic worker*
†Hayes, Patrick G. *public health administrator*
Hayes, Richard Johnson *association executive, lawyer*
Heilbrunn, Jeffrey *trade association administrator*
Heineman, Natalie (Mrs. Ben W. Heineman) *civic worker*
Henry, Patricia Jean *educational association administrator, consumer products company executive*
Hudnut, William Herbert, III *civic federation executive, political scientist*
Huston, John Leo *trade association executive*
Jackson, Jesse Louis *civic and political leader, clergyman*
Jonas, Harry S. *professional society administrator*
Jones, Barbara Loretta *social services administrator*
Koenig, Bonnie *non-profit organization administrator*
Krug, Judith Fingeret *association administrator*
†Kudo, Irma Setsuko *not-for-profit executive director*
Levitan, Valerie Fassler *fraternal organization executive*
MacDougal, Gary Edward *corporate director, foundation trustee*
Mercer, David Robinson *association executive*
Miller, Jay Alan *civil rights association executive*
Minow, Josephine Baskin *civic worker*
Murphy, Ellis *association management executive*
†Needham, George Michael *library association executive*
Olsen, Rex Norman *trade association executive*
O'Sullivan, Gerald Joseph *association executive*
Palmer, Robert Erwin *association executive*
Peterson, Mildred Othmer (Mrs. Howard R. Peterson) *lecturer, writer, librarian, civic leader*
†Pope, Steven Francois *association executive*
Richman, Harold Alan *social welfare policy educator*
Rielly, John Edward *association executive*
Rodgers, James Foster *association executive, economist*
Scalish, Frank Anthony *labor union administrator*
Seng, Ann Frances *civic organization executive*
Sigmon, Joyce Elizabeth *association executive*
Simmons, Adele Smith *foundation president, former educator*
†Viall, J(ohn) Thomas *non-profit organization executive, fundraiser*
Wardell, Jay Howard *association executive*
Wilhelm, David C. *political organization administrator*

Crystal Lake
Chamberlain, Charles James *railroad labor union executive*

De Kalb
Kleppner, Paul *social studies think-tank administrator*

Des Plaines
†Beck, Lowell Richard *lawyer, association executive*
Neel, Judy Murphy *association executive*
†Nelson, Thomas Carl *association executive*
Newman, Wade Davis *trade association executive*
Shoults, Harold E. *social services administrator*

DuQuoin
Smith, Lucius Skinner, III *educational foundation administrator*

Elgin
Kelly, Matthew Edward *association executive*

Elk Grove Village
Best, Willis D. *retired international union official*

Elmhurst
Hildreth, R(oland) James *foundation executive, economist*

Evanston
Abnee, A. Victor *trade association executive*
Bernstein, Susan Powell *development and fundraising consultant*
Gordon, Julie Peyton *foundation administrator*
Kreml, Franklin Martin *educational administrator, association executive*
Kung, Harold Hing-chuen *educational association administrator*
Thrash, Patricia Ann *association executive*
Yoder, Frederick Floyd *fraternity executive*

Flossmoor
Tiernan, James Scott, Jr. *association executive*

Galena
Hermann, Paul David *retired association executive*

Highland Park
Gordon, Edward *music association executive*

Hoffman Estates
†Biggins, James J. *fundraiser*

Lake Bluff
Schreiber, George Richard *association executive, writer*

Lake Forest
Fuhs-Smith, Wendy L. *foundation executive*

Long Grove
Connor, James Richard *foundation administrator*

Loves Park
Canova, John Richard *educational administrator*

Coldwater
Jones, Ora McConner *foundation administrator*

Dearborn
Brennan, Leo Joseph, Jr. *foundation executive*

Detroit
Bieber, Owen F. *labor union official*
†Leyh, George Francis *association executive*
†Mathieson, J. Douglas *engineering association executive*
McHugh, Richard Walker *lawyer*
Scherer, Karla *foundation executive, venture capitalist*
Schuster, Elaine *civil rights professional, state official*
Sheffield, Horace Lindsey, Jr. *union official*
Vaitkevicius, Vainutis Kazys *foundation administrator, medical educator*
Wiedyk, Gerald M. *union welfare fund administrator*

East Lansing
Munger, Benson Scott *association executive*

Farmington
Lakritz, Isaac *fundraising organization executive*

Flint
White, William Samuel *foundation executive*

Grosse Pointe
Gilbert, Ronald Rhea *organization executive, lawyer*

Hickory Corners
Brown, Norman A. *consultant*

Jackson
†Wilkinson, Howard R. *association administrator*

Madison Heights
O'Hara, Thomas Edwin *association executive*

Rochester
Packard, Sandra Podolin *association administrator*

Saint Joseph
Butt, Jimmy Lee *retired association executive*

Southfield
Fleming, Mac Arthur *labor union administrator*
†O'Donovan, Thomas Raphael *professional association administrator*

Troy
Hunia, Edward Mark *foundation executive*
Marshall, John Elbert, III *foundation executive*
Taylor, Alfred Hendricks, Jr. *former foundation executive*

University Center
Miller, Roberta Balstad *science administrator*

Ypsilanti
Corriveau, Arlene Josephine *educational specialist*
McNutt, Kristen Wallwork *consumer affairs executive*

MINNESOTA

Hopkins
Burke, Steven Francis *organization executive*

Minneapolis
Johnson, John Warren *association executive*
King, Robert Cotton *association consultant*
Kolehmainen, Jan Waldroy *association executive*
O'Keefe, Thomas Michael *foundation executive*

Rochester
†Shulman, Carole Karen *professional society administrator*
Wojcik, Martin Henry *foundation development official*

Saint Cloud
Henry, Edward LeRoy *former foundation executive, consultant, college president, public official*

Saint Paul
Archabal, Nina M(archetti) *historical society director*
Doermann, Humphrey *foundation administrator*
Fesler, David Richard *foundation director*
Goff, Lila Johnson *historical society administrator*

Saint Peter
Nelsen, William Cameron *foundation president, former college president*

Wayzata
Shannon, James Patrick *foundation consultant, retired food company executive*

MISSISSIPPI

Crenshaw
Cooke, Gloria Grayson *trust fund director*

Fayette
La Salle, Arthur Edward *historic foundation executive*

Jackson
Penick, George Dial, Jr. *foundation executive*
Thrash, Edsel E. *educational administrator*

MISSOURI

Columbia
Palo, Nicholas Edwin *professional society administrator*
Walkenbach, Ronald Joseph *foundation executive, pharmacology educator*

Earth City
Anderhalter, Oliver Frank *educational organization executive*

Hallsville
McFate, Kenneth Leverne *association administrator*

Independence
Potts, Barbara Joyce *historical society executive*

Ironton
Douma, Harry Hein *social service agency administrator*

Joplin
Williams, Rex Enoch *international union representative*

Kansas City
Bugher, Robert Dean *association executive*
Fries, James Lawrence *trade association executive*
Hartley, Richard Glendale *association executive*
Levi, Peter Steven *chamber of commerce executive, lawyer*
Wilson, Eugene Rolland *foundation executive*

Marshall
Tweito, Eleanor Marie *social services administrator, educator*

Saint Louis
Bader, Kenneth Leroy *association executive*
†Blowers, Richard M. *professional society administrator*
†Clifton, Regina Marie *health association executive*
Hunter, Earle Leslie, III *professional association executive*
Myler, Russell Clinton *social services association administrator*
†Pope, Robert Eugene *fraternal organization administrator*
Suelflow, August Robert *historical institute consultant, educator*

Springfield
Himstedt, Ronald Eugene *union official*

MONTANA

Billings
Sample, Joseph Scanlon *foundation executive*

Harrison
Jackson, Peter Vorious, III *retired association executive*

Helena
Marquardt, Kathleen Patricia *association executive*

NEBRASKA

Lincoln
Hodges, Clarence Eugene *charitable organization executive, former government official*
Rosenow, John Edward *foundation executive*
Swartz, Jack *association executive*

Omaha
Ansorge, Luella M. *retired association administrator*
Bell, C(lyde) R(oberts) (Bob Bell) *association executive*
Flickinger, Thomas Leslie *hospital alliance executive*
Monasee, Charles Arthur *healthcare foundation executive*
Roskens, Ronald William *association administrator*

Seward
Vrana, Verlon Kenneth *professional society administrator, conservationist*

NEVADA

Carson City
Ayres, Janice Ruth *social service executive*
†Sullivan, Carley Hayden *political party executive*

Henderson
Freyd, William Pattinson *fund raising executive, consultant*

Las Vegas
Horner, Lee *foundation executive, speaker, consultant, computer specialist*

Pahrump
Hersman, Marion Frank *professional administrator, lawyer*

NEW HAMPSHIRE

Concord
Crosier, John David *association administrator*
†Frisbee, John Lee *historical society director*

Dover
Trites, Donald George *human service foundation executive*

Francestown
White, Ruth O'Brien (Mrs. Wallace B. White) *civic worker*

Hancock
Carney, David Mitchel *political party official*

Hillsboro
†Gefvert, Jane V. *association executive*

Laconia
Caverly, Gardner A. *foundation executive*

Manchester
Backus, Ann Swift Newell *educator, consultant*

Marlborough
†Walton, Russell Sparey *foundation administrator*

Washington
Halverson, Wendell Quelprud *former educational association executive, clergyman, educator*

NEW JERSEY

Bernardsville
Cooperman, Saul *foundation administrator*

Bogota
Condon, Francis Edward *former foundation administrator*

Brigantine
†Schoelkopf, Robert Carl *non-profit organization administrator*

Camden
Wellington, Judith Lynn *cultural organization administrator*

Cedar Grove
Brownstein, Alan P. *health foundation executive, consultant*
Thiel, Thelma King *foundation executive*

Cherry Hill
McGuire, Mavis Louise *professional society administrator*

Cliffside Park
Pushkarev, Boris S. *research foundation director, writer*

Cranbury
Rector, Milton Gage *social work educator, former association executive*

East Rutherford
Kempner, Michael W. *public relations executive*

Edison
Maeroff, Gene I. *educational association administrator, journalist*

Englewood
Orlando, George (Joseph) *union executive*

Glen Rock
†Riggs, Gina Ginsberg *educational association administrator*

Hoboken
Buckman, Thomas Richard *foundation executive, educator*

Jersey City
Niemiec, Edward Walter *professional association executive*

Kendall Park
Goldberg, Bertram J. *social agency admininistrator*

Kinnelon
Schafer, John Stephen *foundation administrator*

Montclair
Campbell, Stewart Fred *foundation executive*
Mills, James Thoburn *association executive*
Schlesinger, Stephen Lyons *nurseryman*

Montvale
Scopes, Gary Martin *professional association executive*

Neptune
†Spencer, James Jeffrey *executive director*

New Vernon
Dugan, John Leslie, Jr. *foundation executive*

Newark
Crane, Samuel *association executive*

Passaic
†Pogorelec, Steven Martin *fraternal organization administrator*

Pennington
Calvo, Roque John *association executive*

Princeton
†Balch, Stephen Howard *association administrator*
Boyer, Ernest LeRoy *foundation executive*
Greene, Andrew Richard *foundation executive*
Hearn, Ruby Puryear *foundation executive*
Jellinek, Paul S. *foundation executive, health economist*
Kaufman, Nancy J. *health foundation executive*
Kenyon, Regan Clair *research foundation executive*
Rhett, Haskell Emery Smith *foundation executive, educator*
Stern, Gail Frieda *historical association director*

Ramsey
Eklund, Donald Arthur *trade association executive*

Red Bank
Meredith, George (Marlor) *association executive, writer*

Rumson
Brenner, Theodore Engelbert *retired trade association executive*
Freeman, David Forgan *foundation executive*
Swartz, Renee Becker *civic volunteer*

Scotch Plains
Ungar, Manya Shayon *volunteer, education consultant*

South Orange
Sontag, Frederick H. *public affairs and research consultant*

Springfield
†Stoller, Mitchell R. *non-profit organization administrator*

Trenton
Pollock, John Crothers, III *opinion research executive, educator*

Voorhees
Myslowka, Myron William (Ron Myslowka) *labor union executive*

Willingboro
Bertolino, Angela Maria *educational association administrator*

NEW MEXICO

Albuquerque
Cole, Terri Lynn *organization administrator*
Mitovich, John *association executive*
Rezac, Stephan Robert *trade association executive*
Roberts, Dennis William *association executive*

Angel Fire
Dillon, Robert Morton *retired association executive, architectural consultant*

Church Rock
Linford, Laurance Dee *cultural organization administrator*

Santa Fe
Chatfield, Cheryl Ann *nonprofit organization executive, educator*
Johnson, William Stewart *cultural arts administrator*

NEW YORK

Albany
Bellizzi, John J. *law enforcement association administrator, educator, pharmacist*
†Brown, Lester *social work educator*
Carovano, John Martin *not-for-profit adminstrator, conservationist*

Amherst
Clark, Donald Malin *association executive*

Armonk
Bergson, Henry Paul *association executive*

Ballston Lake
Lambert, Lloyd Tupper *writer, civic volunteer*

Bedford Hills
Waller, Wilhelmine Kirby (Mrs. Thomas Mercer Waller) *civic worker, organization official*

Briarcliff Manor
Luck, Edward Carmichael *association executive*

Bronx
†Biasiny-Rivera, Charles *cultural organization administrator*

Buffalo
Brandt, Barbara Berryman *cultural organization administrator*
Christopher, James Roy *executive director*
Glickman, Marlene *social organization administrator*
Serafin, James Adam *organization executive, management consultant*
Smith, Barbara *camping administrator*

Chappaqua
de Janosi, Peter Engel *research manager*

Clinton
Couper, Richard Watrous *foundation executive, educator*

Elizabethtown
Lawrence, Richard Wesley, Jr. *foundation administrator*

Flushing
Fichtel, Rudolph Robert *retired association executive*
Hoffman, Merle Holly *political activist, social psychologist, author*
Madden, Joseph Daniel *trade association executive*
Sutherland, Alan Roy *association executive*

Garrison
Pierpont, Robert *fund raising executive, consultant*

Hamilton
Appley, Lawrence A. *business executive*

Harrison
Herrick, Doris Eileen Schlesinger *sports association administrator*
Wadsworth, Frank Whittemore *foundation executive, literature educator*

Huntington
Schulz, William Frederick *human rights association executive*

Irvington
Evans, Bruce Max *foundation executive*

Larchmont
Hinerfeld, Ruth J. *civic organization executive*

Long Island City
Mojica, Aurora *association executive*
Ulrich, Werner Richard *union education administrator*

Mamaroneck
Allensworth, Dorothy Alice *education foundation administrator*

Merrick
Doyle, James Aloysius *retired association executive*

Mill Neck
Grieve, William Roy *educational administrator, researcher, consultant*

Mount Kisco
Senkier, Robert Joseph *foundation administrator, educator*

New Windsor
†Lawrence, Albert James *association executive*

New York
Allardice, Bruce *art association executive*
Allmendinger, Paul Florin *retired engineering association executive*
Aronson, Esther Leah *association administrator, psychotherapist*
Auld, Larry Elwood *foundation executive*
Barnes, Jack Whittier *political party official*
Barondess, Linda Hiddemen *professional society executive*
Bausch, James John *foundation executive*
Beardsley, Theodore S(terling), Jr. *association executive*
Beckham, Edgar Frederick *foundation administrator*
Belden, David Leigh *professional association executive, engineering educator*
Bell, Thomas Devereaux, Jr. *public affairs company executive*
Bellamy, Carol *international organization executive*
Berkman, Lillian *foundation executive, corporation executive, art collector*
Berresford, Susan Vail *philanthropic foundation executive*
Berry, Nancy Michaels *nonprofit development executive*
Bird, Mary Lynne Miller *association executive*
Braverman, Robert Jay *international consultant, public policy educator*
Brief, Henry *association executive*
Brown, Terrence Charles *art association executive, researcher, lecturer*
Burke, Mary Griggs (Mrs. Jackson Burke) *art collector*
Campbell, Colin Goetze *foundation president*
†Canada, Geoffrey *social welfare administrator*
Cantor, Alexandra *professional society administrator*
†Carton, Ellen *association executive*
Cashin, Richard Marshall *international aid official*
Cassella, William Nathan, Jr. *organization executive*
Catley-Carlson, Margaret *association executive*
Chapin, Schuyler Garrison *cultural affairs executive, university dean*
Christopher, Maurine Brooks *foundation administrator, writer, editor*
Cole, Elma Phillipson (Mrs. John Strickler Cole) *social welfare executive*
Conarroe, Joel Osborne *foundation administrator, educator, editor*
Cornez, Gerald H. *association executive*
Cross, William Redmond, Jr. *corporate director, foundation executive*
David, Miles *association and marketing executive*
Davis, Karen Padgett *fund executive*
Davis, Kathryn Wasserman *foundation executive, writer, lecturer*
Deffenbaugh, Ralston H., Jr. *immigration agency executive, lawyer*
de Menil, Lois Pattison *philanthropist*
Dennis, Everette Eugene, Jr. *foundation executive, journalism educator, media critic, author*
Diamond, Irene *foundation administrator*
Dressner, Howard Roy *foundation executive, lawyer*
Duff, Patricia *foundation administrator*
Easum, Donald Boyd *consultant, educator, former institute executive, diplomat*
Einiger, Carol Blum *foundation executive*
Eisenberg, Alan *association executive*
Ekman, Richard *foundation executive, educator*
Elam, Leslie Albert *association executive*
Emmert, Richard Eugene *professional association executive*
Engelhardt, Sara Lawrence *organization executive*
English, John Winfield *foundation administrator*
Fabian, Larry Louis *non-profit institution executive*
Fehr, Donald M. *baseball union executive*
Feist, Leonard *association executive*
Ferguson, Frances Hand *volunteer, civic worker*
Finberg, Barbara Denning *foundation executive*
†Foerst, John George, Jr. *fundraising executive*
Fox, Daniel Michael *foundation administrator, author*
†Foxman, Abraham H. *advocacy organization administrator*
Franklin, Phyllis *professional association administrator*
Freid, Jacob *association executive, educator*
Freund, Gerald *foundation administrator*
Furuhata, Taketo (Mike Furuhata) *trading company executive*
Gallagher, Edward Peter *arts association administrator*
Garrison, John Raymond *organization executive*
Gaudieri, Millicent Hall *association executive*
†Gilmore, Louise Jacobson *labor union adiministrator*
Glasser, Ira Saul *civil liberties organization executive*
Goldberg, Melvin A. *non-profit organization executive*
Goldmark, Peter Carl, Jr. *foundation executive*
Grant, Leonard Tydings *educational association president*
Gray, Arthur, Jr. *investment counselor*
Grimaldi, Nicholas Lawrence *social services administrator*
Guggenheimer, Elinor *civic leader, writer*
Guttentag, Lucas *lawyer*
Hall, Gus (Arvo Kusta Halberg) *political party official*
Halpern, Charles Robert *foundation executive, educator, lawyer*
Hammett, William M. H. *foundation executive*
Handberg, Irene Deak *educational executive*
Harris, David Alan *not-for-profit organization executive*
Harrod, B(illy) J(oe) *professional association executive*
Hart, Kitty Carlisle *arts administrator*
Hartford, Huntington *financier, art patron*
Hartley, Duncan *fundraising executive*
Hendricks, Edward David *association executive*
Heron, Nye Brian *artistic director*
Herr, Kenneth Julian *retired charitable foundation executive*
Heslin, James J. *association executive*
Hesselbein, Frances Richards *foundation executive, consultant*
Hester, James McNaughton *foundation administrator*
Holman, Margaret Mezoff *fundraising consultant*
Holtzman, Ellen A. *foundation executive*
Innis, Roy Emile Alfredo *organization executive*
Jacob, John Edward *social service agency executive*
Jacobsen, Theodore H. (Ted H. Jacobsen) *labor union official, educator*
Jacobson, Gaynor I. *retired association executive*
Janklow, Linda LeRoy *civic worker, volunteer*
Jedlicka, Judith Ann *organization executive*
Jerome, Fred Louis *science organization executive*
†Johns, William Potter *non-profit organization administrator*
†Johnston, Philip *association executive*
Jones, Elaine R. *civil rights advocate*
Kaggen, Lois Sheila *non-profit organization executive*
Kahan, Marlene *professional association executive*
Kahn, Alfred Joseph *social worker and planner, educator*
Kane, Herman William *research company executive, political scientist*
Kaplan, Robert Arthur *association executive*
Karr, Norman *association executive*
Kaskell, Peter Howard *association executive, lawyer*
Kennedy, Moorhead *foundation administrator*
†Kramberg, Ross *arts administrator*
Krasno, Richard Michael *educational organization executive, educator*
Kuh, Joyce Dattel *education administrator*
Labunski, Stephen Bronislaw *association executive*
Lamb, George Richard *foundation executive*
†Landy, Joanne Veit *foreign policy analyst*
Lawson-Johnston, Peter Orman *foundation executive*
Lee, Clement William Khan *association administrator*
Letzig, Betty Jean *association executive*
†Lewis, Sylvia Davidson *association executive*
Linder, Bertram Norman *foundation administrator, horse-breeder, actor*
Loeb, Frances Lehman *civic leader*
Lubic, Ruth Watson *association executive, nurse-midwife*
Luce, Henry, III *foundation executive*
Luckman, Sharon Gersten *arts administrator*
Mahoney, Margaret Ellerbe *foundation executive*
Mangan, Mona *association executive, lawyer*
Maraldo, Pamela Jean *nursing association executive, lecturer, consultant*
Marchi, Lorraine June *association executive*
Marks, Edward B. *international social service administrator*
Marshall, John *association administrator*
Mazur, Jay J. *trade union official*
Metcalf, Karen *foundation executive*
Michel, Harriet R. *association executive*
Milbank, Jeremiah *foundation executive*
Miller, Harvey S. Shipley *foundation trustee*
Miller, Lenore *labor union official*
†Miller, Robin Davis *professional society administrator*
Millett, Katherine Murray (Kate Millett) *political activist, sculptor, artist, writer*
Milosh, Eugene John *international trade association executive*
Moloney, Thomas Walter *consulting firm executive*
Moran, Martin Joseph *fundraising company executive*
Morrisett, Lloyd N. *foundation executive*
Muse, Martha Twitchell *foundation executive*
†Nadler, Allan Lawrence *institute director*
Neal, Leora Louise Haskett *social services administrator*
Odenweller, Robert Paul *philatelist, association executive, airline pilot*
O'Neill Bidwell, Katharine Thomas *fine arts association executive, performing arts executive*
Osborn, Frederick Henry, III *fundraiser, investment advisor*
Pace, Norma *economist, consulting firm executive*
†Peters, Robert Wayne *organization executive, lawyer*
†Pfrang, Edward Oscar *association executive*
Phillips, Russell Alexander, Jr. *foundation executive*
Piereson, James Eugene *foundation administrator*
Preston, Frances W. *performing rights organization executive*
Price, Hugh B. *foundation executive, lawyer*
Rattazzi, Serena *art museum and association administrator*
Rhodes, Milton *arts association administrator*
Robinson, David Zav *foundation administrator*
Robinson, Nan Senior *not-for-profit organization consultant*
Rockwell, John Sargent *arts administrator, music critic, writer*
Rolfe, Robin Ann *trade association executive, lawyer*
Rosoff, Jeannie I. *association administrator*
Sabinson, Harvey Barnett *cultural organiztion administrator*
Samers, Bernard Norman *fund raising organization executive*
†Sanger, Alexander Campbell *family planning executive*
Schubart, Mark Allen *arts and education executive*
Schwartz, Felice N. *social activist, educator*
Seessel, Thomas Vining *nonprofit organization executive*
Seidler, Lynn L. *foundation executive*
Sharp, Daniel Asher *foundation executive, corporate consultant*
Shea, Dion Warren Joseph *association executive*
Sheinkman, Jack *union official, lawyer*
Shelp, Ronald Kent *non-profit business and trade association executive, author, lecturer, consultant*
Sherrod, Lonnie Ray *foundation administrator, researcher, psychologist*
†Sibley, Alden Kingsland *former organization executive, retired army officer*
†Siegman, Henry *association executive*
Singer, Arthur Louis, Jr. *foundation executive*
Singh, Jyoti Shankar *political organization director*
Slater, Joseph Elliott *educational institute administrator*
Slutsky, Lorie Ann *foundation executive*
Smith, Datus Clifford, Jr. *former foundation executive, publisher*
Smith, J. Kellum, Jr. *foundation executive, lawyer*
†Sokol, Marc Jeffrey *arts administrator*
Solender, Stephen David *philanthropic organization executive*
Spira, Patricia G. *performing arts association executive*
Straus, Oscar S., II *foundation executive*
Sussman, Leonard Richard *foundation executive*
Swing, John Temple *lawyer, association executive*
Thomas, Gladys Roberts *foundation executive*
Torrence, (John) Richard *fundraising executive, special events producer*
Troubetzkoy, Alexis Serge *foundation administrator, educator*
Tudryn, Joyce Marie *professional society administrator*
Turnbaugh, Douglas Blair *arts administration executive, author*
Van Doren, Glenn Henry *professional association executive, management consultant*
†Vignola, Leonard Robert *foundation executive*
Wallach, John Paul *foundation administrator, author*
Wang, Charles Pei *social service administrator*
Wanner, Eric *foundation executive, researcher, writer, editor*
Watson, John Lawrence, III *trade association executive*
Wattleton, (Alyce) Faye *association executive*
Weeks, David Frank *foundation administrator*
Weintraub, Daniel Ralph *social welfare administrator*
Wellington, Sheila Wacks *foundation administrator, psychiatry educator*
Wohlgelernter, Beth *organization executive*
Wray, Gilda Gates *foundation administrator*
Wright, Hugh Elliott, Jr. *association executive, writer*
†Zollar, Jawole Willa Jo *art association administrator*

Old Forge
Mitchell, George Frederick *association executive*

Ossining
Chervokas, John Vincent *chamber of commerce executive*

Pelham
Weintz, Caroline Giles *non-profit association consultant, travel writer*

Pittsford
Dorsey, Eugene Carroll *former foundation and communications executive*

Richfield Springs
Mc Kelvey, John Jay, Jr. *retired foundation executive*

Rochester
DeMarco, Roland R. *foundation executive*
Mooney, Thomas T. *association executive*
Pacala, Leon *retired assocation executive*

Scarborough
Beglarian, Grant *foundation executive, composer, consultant*

Scarsdale
Bernstein, Irving *international organization executive*
Ferry, Wilbur Hugh *foundation consultant*
Johnson, Katharyn Price (Mrs. Edward F. Johnson) *civic worker*
†Lawyer, William Grove *foundation administrator*
Rosow, Jerome Morris *institute executive*
Sullivan, Adèle Woodhouse *organization official*
Wile, Julius *former corporate executive, educator*

Schenectady
Chestnut, Harold *foundation administrator, engineering executive*

Seneca Falls
Butler, Susan Lowell *association executive, writer*

Suffern
Zecca, John Andrew *retired association executive*

Tarrytown
Dobkin, John Howard *art administrator*
Dorland, Byrl Brown *civic worker*
Goldin, Milton *fund raising counsel, author*
Rath, Bernard Emil *trade association executive*

Tonawanda
Browning, James Franklin *professional society executive*
Miller, Robert James *fundraising company executive*

White Plains
Cooke, Lloyd Miller *former organization executive*
Jensen, Grady Edmonds *association executive*

Yonkers
Karpatkin, Rhoda Hendrick *consumer information organization executive, lawyer*

NORTH CAROLINA

Asheville
Fobes, John Edwin *international organization official*
Gabriel, Robert *art association administrator*

Carrboro
Greenslade, Forrest Charles *international health care executive*

Chapel Hill
Slack, Lewis *organization administrator*

Charlotte
Love, Franklin Sadler *retired trade association executive*
McCall, Billy Gene *charitable trust executive*
Stair, Frederick Rogers *retired foundation executive, former seminary president*
Wenner, Gene Charles *arts foundation executive*

Durham
Bevan, William *retired foundation executive*
†Lozoff, Bo *nonprofit organization administrator*
Roberson, James O. *foundation executive*
Rosenthal, Julian Bernard *lawyer, association executive*
†Semans, Mary Duke Biddle Trent *foundation administrator*

Greensboro
Kornegay, Horace Robinson *trade association executive, former congressman, lawyer*

High Point
Brackett, Douglas Lane *trade association executive*

Montreat
Robinson, Spencer, Jr. *retired service club executive, accountant*

Raleigh
Parker, Charles Brand, Jr. *training company executive*

Research Triangle Park
†Harvey, Glenn F. *association executive*
Martin, William Royall, Jr. *association executive*
†Miller, Robert Reese *trade assocation executive*

Wilson
McCain, Betty Landon Ray (Mrs. John Lewis McCain) *political party official*

Winston Salem
Carter, Henry Moore, Jr. *foundation executive*
Gleason, Norman Dale *association executive*
Jones, F(rancis) Whitney *fund raising executive, consultant*
Lambeth, Thomas Willis *foundation executive*

OHIO

Akron
Collier, Alice Elizabeth *community organization executive*
Frank, John V. *foundation executive*
†Hart, Karen Ann *social services administrator*

Beachwood
Swank, Emory Coblentz *world affairs consultant, lecturer*

Bryan
†Nelson, Sandra Kay *foundation administrator*

Chardon
Reinhard, Sister Mary Marthe *educational organization administrator*

Cincinnati
Blanken, Sarah S. *retired foundation administrator*
Conley, Robert T. *educational administrator*
Hiatt, Marjorie McCullough *service organization executive*
Norman, Peter Minert *fundraising consulting company executive*
†Stuhlreyer, Paul Augustus, III *cultural organization administrator*
Williams, John Pattison, Jr. *association executive*
†Zola, Gary Phillip *religious educational administrator, rabbi,*

Circleville
Scherer, Robert Davisson *retired business and association executive*

Cleveland
Bergholz, David *foundation administrator*
Bryant, William H. *association executive*
Calkins, Hugh *foundation executive*
Earley, Robert Wayne *labor union executive*
Jenson, Jon Eberdt *association executive*
Mayer, Robert Anthony *college president*
†Minter, Steven Alan *foundation executive, social worker*
Russell, Valerie Eileen *social service executive*

Columbus
Blair, William Travis (Bud Blair) *retired organization executive*
Cole, Charles Chester, Jr. *educational administrator*
Hamilton, Harold Philip *fund raising executive*
Luck, James I. *foundation executive*
Newman, Diana S. *community foundation executive*
Sharp, Paul David *institute administrator*

Dayton
Crowe, Shelby *educational specialist, consultant*
Daley, Robert Emmett *foundation executive*
Mathews, David *foundation executive*
Schwartzhoff, James Paul *foundation executive*

Girard
Wolanin, Sophie Mae *civic worker, tutor, scholar, lecturer*

Mentor
Andrassy, Timothy Francis *trade association executive*

Middletown
Clinton, Mariann Hancock *association executive*

Oberlin
Distelhorst, Garis Fred *association executive*

Oxford
Miller, Robert James *association executive*

Yellow Springs
Graham, Jewel Freeman *social worker, lawyer, educator*

OKLAHOMA

Lawton
Brooks, (Leslie) Gene *cultural association administrator*

Oklahoma City
Gumerson, Jean Gilderhus *health foundation executive*
Maton, Anthea *education consultant*
Van Rysselberge, Charles H. *organization administrator*

Tahlequah
†Ross, John *cultural organization administrator*

Tulsa
Cole, Clyde Curtis, Jr. *association executive*
Dix, Fred Andrew, Jr. *professional society executive*
†Harvey, James Douglas *medical foundation executive, former hospital administrator*
Rounds, Philard Leaon, Sr. *fundraiser*
Wesenberg, John Herman *association executive*

Wetumka
†Martin, Tony *foundation administrator*

OREGON

Beaverton
Henderson, George Miller *foundation executive, former banker*

Corvallis
Wilkins, Caroline Hanke *consumer agency administrator, political worker*

Klamath Falls
Ehlers, Eleanor May Collier (Mrs. Frederick Burton Ehlers) *civic worker*

Medford
Sours, James Kingsley *association executive, former college president*
†Wegner, Samuel Joseph *historical society executive*

Portland
Collins, Maribeth Wilson *foundation president*
†Culver, Wesley Ellsworth *relief and development organization executive*
Hilbert, Bernard Charles *retired union official*
McClave, Donald Silsbee *association executive*
O'Hollaren, Paul Joseph *former international fraternity administrator*
Orloff, Chet *cultural organization administrator*
Scott, Brian Douglas *association executive*

Salem
Toran, Kay Dean *social services administrator*

Siletz
†Pigsley, Delores Ann *tribal leader, educator*

PENNSYLVANIA

Allentown
Berman, Muriel Mallin *civic worker*
Berman, Philip I. *foundation administrator*
Lukac, George Joseph *fundraising executive*

Bryn Mawr
Carroll, Mary Colvert *corporate executive*
Driskill, John Ray *association executive*

Conshohocken
Mullen, Eileen Anne *training and development executive*

Dillsburg
Bowers, Glenn Lee *association executive*

Drexel Hill
Schiazza, Guido Domenic (Guy Schiazza) *educational association administrator*

Elizabethtown
Krut, Stephen Frank *trade association administrator*
Madeira, Robert Lehman *association executive*

Exton
Penrose, Charles, Jr. *association executive*

Harrisburg
Hughes, William Francis, Jr. *education association administrator*
Loedding, Peter Alfred *trade association executive*
Lourie, Norman Victor *government official, social worker*
Nielsen, Edward L. *medical association administrator*

Hershey
Bomgardner, William Earl *retired association executive, photographer*

Johnstown
†Smith, Donald W. *association executive*

Kempton
†Lenhart, Cynthia Rae *conservation organization executive*

Lansdale
Echols, Gloria *housing service administrator*

Laverock
Block, Isaac Edward *association executive*

Lewisburg
Neuman, Nancy Adams Mosshammer *civic leader*

Newtown
Keenan, Terrance *foundation executive*

Philadelphia
Bailin, Michael A. *social research firm executive*
Bodine, James Forney *retired civic leader*
Coopersmith, Fran M. *foundation executive*
Cunningham, Ann Marie *information association executive*
†Dolnick, Sandy Friedman *executive*
Doman, Janet Joy *association executive*
Foti, Margaret Ann *association executive, editor*
Friedman, Murray *civil rights official, historian*
Friend, Theodore Wood, III *foundation executive, historian*
Goodyear, Frank H(enry), Jr. *art association administrator*
McKenna, Thomas Morrison, Jr. *social services organization executive*
Miller, Robert Wiley *educational foundation executive*
Montgomery, Edward Alembert, Jr. *not-for-profit developer*
Pak, Hyung Woong *foundation executive, educator*
Reed, Clarence Raymond *association executive*
Stitt, Susan *historical society executive*
Tise, Larry Edward *historical organization administrator, historian*
Tucker, Cynthia Delores Nottage (Mrs. William M. Tucker) *political party official, former state official*
Williams, Mary Jane *fundraiser*

Pittsburgh
Casey, Robert J. *international trade association executive*
Dimmel, Kenneth Travis *cultural organization administrator, editor*
Dybeck, Alfred Charles *labor arbitrator*
Grinberg, Meyer Stewart *educational institute executive*
Hallen, Philip Burgh *foundation administrator*
Horan, Justin Thomas *retired association executive*
Ketchum, David Storey *retired fundraising executive*
Mellon, Richard Prosser *charitable foundation executive*
Pasnick, Raymond Wallace *labor union official, editor*
Williams, Lynn Russell *labor union official*
Wishart, Alfred W., Jr. *foundation administrator*

Reading
Mattern, Donald Eugene *association executive*

Rohrerstown
Stauffer, Sarah Ann *political worker*

State College
DeVoss, James Thomas *community foundation administrator, retired*
Phillips, Janet Colleen *educational association executive, editor*

Topton
Farr, Lona Mae *non-profit executive*

University Park
Feller, Irwin *think-tank executive, economics educator*

Valley Forge
Carlson, Beverly Clark *historical society administrator*

Warrendale
Rumbaugh, Max Elden, Jr. *professional society administrator*
†Scott, Alexander Robinson *engineering association executive*

Wayne
Etris, Samuel Franklin *association executive*

Wynnewood
Freeman, Morton S. *former bar association executive, retired lawyer*
Peskin, Matt Alan *professional society administrator*

RHODE ISLAND

Johnston
Martelli, Jennifer A. *social welfare administrator*

Kingston
Schmidt, Charles T., Jr. *labor and industrial relations educator*

Newport
Brown, Jane G. *sports association executive*

Providence
Campbell, Edwin Denton *educational administrator*
†Jaco, William H. *mathematical association executive*
Klyberg, Albert Thomas *historical society administrator*
Woolf, William Blauvelt *association executive*

SOUTH CAROLINA

Charleston
Hughes, Blake *retired architectural institute administrator, publisher*
†Rupp, Frank A., III *association executive*

Columbia
Bjontegard, Arthur Martin, Jr. *foundation executive*
McGill, Jennifer Houser *non-profit association administrator*
Shabazz, Aiysha Muslimah *social work administrator*
Sheheen, Fred Roukos *education agency administrator*
Sigmon, Daniel Ray *foundation administrator*

Easley
Moncrief, James Loring *educational administrator*

Florence
Brewer, Mary Dean *medical foundation executive*

Greenville
Frist, Thomas Ferran *philanthropic organization executive*

Lancaster
Bundy, Charles Alan *foundation executive*

Spartanburg
Owens, Hilda Faye *management/leadership development consultant, human resource trainer*

Surfside Beach
McCrensky, Edward *international consultant, former organization executive*

SOUTH DAKOTA

Rapid City
Erickson, John Duff *educational association adminstrator*

Stratford
Gubin, Ronald *farm products association executive*

TENNESSEE

Chattanooga
Morton, Michael Rader *career and technology education director*
Zodhiates, Spiros George *association executive*

Hermitage
†Willner, Robert Franklin *social health administrator*

Knoxville
Froula, James DeWayne *national honor society director, engineer*

Memphis
Hooks, Benjamin Lawson *civil rights advocate, brokerage house executive*
Tibbs, Martha Jane Pullen *civic worker*
Whitesell, Dale Edward *retired association executive, natural resources consultant*

Nashville
Benson, Edwin Welburn, Jr. *trade association executive*
†Bond, Sherry Louise *trade association administrator*
Glenn, Wayne Eugene *labor union official*
Henderson, Milton Arnold *association executive*
Ivey, William James *foundation executive, writer, producer*
Johnson, Hollis Eugene, III *foundation executive*
McMasters, Paul Kenneth *foundation executive*

TEXAS

Amarillo
Ball, Charles Elihue *association consultant*
Brainard, Jayne Dawson (Mrs. Ernest Scott Brainard) *civic worker*

Arlington
Hunter, J(ohn) Robert *insurance consumer advocate*

Austin
Bonjean, Charles Michael *foundation executive, sociologist, educator*
Kronkosky, Preston C. *educational think-tank executive*
Stoner, James Lloyd *retired foundation executive, clergyman*
West, Glenn Edward *business organization executive*
Winfrey, Dorman Hayward *scientific society executive*

College Station
Vandiver, Frank Everson *institute administrator, former university president, author, educator*

Colleyville
Love, Ben Howard *retired organization executive*

Dallas
†Brinegar, Mary Metta *non-profit organization executive*
Giordano, Saverio Paul *professional association executive*
Jackson, Phillip Ellis *lobbyist, consultant*
Lancaster, Sally Rhodus *philathropy consultant*

El Paso
Day, James Milton *foundation executive, English educator*

Fort Worth
Wilkie, Valleau, Jr. *foundation executive*

Galveston
Baker, Robert Ernest, Jr. *foundation executive*
Moore, Peter Melville *foundation adminstrator*

Houston
Albrecht, Kay Montgomery *educational administrator, consultant, child advocate*
Crispin, Andre Arthur *international trading company executive*
Grayson, Charles Jackson, Jr. *research association executive*
Heckler, Walter Tim *association executive*
†Shankel, Gerald Marvin *association executive*
Streibich, Ronald Lelad *fundraising executive*

Irving
Becker-Doyle, Eve *trade association executive*
Olson, Herbert Theodore *trade association executive*
Stahl, David Edward *association executive*

Livingston
†De Revere, David Wilsen *professional society administrator*

Plainview
Galle, Richard Lynn *association executive, former municipal official*

Richardson
Adamson, Dan Klinglesmith *science association executive*

Salado
Cutler, Morene Parten *civic worker*

San Antonio
Hinojosa, Emilio Alfredo *community development director*
Krier, Joseph Roland *chamber of commerce executive, lawyer*
Mc Giffert, John Rutherford *retired cultural institute director, retired army officer*
Montecel, Maria Robledo (Cuca Robledo Montecel) *educational association administrator*
White, Mary Ruth Wathen *social services administrator*

Sinton
†Teer, James G. *foundation administrator*

Texarkana
Hines, Betty Taylor *women's center administrator*

Waco
McClendon, Charles Youmans *nonprofessional sports association executive, coach*

Waxahachie
†Cockerham, Sidney Joe *professional society administrator*

UTAH

Salt Lake City
Clark, Carol Lois *women and children's advocate, state government agency administrator, consumer advocate, consultant, science association administrator*
Evans, Max Jay *historical society administrator*
Julander, Paula Foil *association administrator*
Melich, Doris S. *public service worker*

VERMONT

Bennington
Perin, Donald Wise, Jr. *former association executive*

Brattleboro
Akins, Zane Vernon *association executive*

Manchester
Hooper, Arthur William *consultant, former association executive*

Montpelier
Barbieri, Christopher George *association executive*

White River Junction
Linnell, Robert Hartley *environment, safety consultant*

Williston
†Podhajski, Blanche Rita *language foundation administrator*

VIRGINIA

Alexandria
Bachus, Walter Otis *retired army general, former association executive*
Baird, Charles F. *think-tank executive*
Baker, Brent Harold *foundation executive*
Bolger, Robert Joseph *retired trade association executive*
Brown, Quincalee *association executive*
Byrd-Lawler, Barbara Ann *association executive*
Byrnside, Oscar Jehu, Jr. *association executive*
Chao, Elaine L. *philanthropic organization executive*
Clower, William Dewey *association executive*
Cooper, Charles Donald *association executive, editor, retired career officer*
Dietrich, Laura Jordan *international policy advisor*
Emely, Charles Harry *trade association executive*
†Ferraez, Leon R. *charitable organization administrator*
†Gardiner, Donald Kent *professional association administrator*
Garrison, Preston Jones *association consultant*
Goldstein, Jerome Charles *professional association executive, surgeon, otolaryngologist*
Greenstein, Ruth Louise *research institute executive, lawyer*
†Herman, Ruth Charlene *foundation administrator*
Hodder, Kenneth Lasett *social services administrator*
Hoyt, F(rank) Russell *association executive*
†Huizenga, Walter Eugene *trade association executive*
Irions, Charles Carter *trade association executive*
Kolar, Mary Jane *association executive*
Lenz, Edward Arnold *trade association executive, lawyer*
McCulloch, William Leonard *association executive*
Megivern, Kathleen *association director, lawyer*
Merrick, Roswell Davenport *association executive*
Messing, Frederick Andrew, Jr. *action lobbyist*
Moody, W. Jarvis *think-tank executive*
Murray, Robert J. *think-tank executive*
†Natelson, Nina Beth *non-profit organization administrator*
Rector, John Michael *lawyer, association executive*
Rogers, John S. *union official*
Sava, Samuel G. *educational association administrator*
Shannon, Thomas Alfred *association executive*
Smith, Carl Richard *association executive, former air force officer*
Spiro, Robert Harry, Jr. *foundation and business executive, educator*
Weinert, Donald G(regory) *association executive, engineer*

Williams, Cathlene Ann *association executive, researcher*
†Wurzel, Mary V. *past association executive*
Yates, Jeffrey McKee *trade association executive*
Ziegler, Ronald Louis *association executive, former government official*

Arlington
Allen, Ernest Eugene *non-profit organization executive, lawyer*
Bailly, Henri-Claude Albert *consulting services executive*
Bast, James Louis *trade association executive*
Bode, Barbara *foundation executive*
Cocklin, Robert Frank *association executive*
Doman, Elvira *science administrator*
Fabian, John McCreary *non-profit company executive, former astronaut, former air force officer*
Hendrickson, Jerome Orland *trade association executive, lawyer*
Langworthy, Everett Walter *association executive, natural gas exploration company executive*
Lloyd, Kent *education policy research and public interest executive, educator*
Marcuccio, Phyllis Rose *association executive, editor*
†Mc Ilhenny, James Harrison *association executive*
McWethy, Patricia Joan *educational association administrator*
Melickian, Gary Edward *trade association executive*
Noland, Royce Paul *association executive, physical therapist*
Paynter, Harry Alvin *retired trade association executive*
Richtol, Herbert Harold *science foundation program director*
Roberts, James Milnor, Jr. *association executive*
Robinson, Kenneth Leonard, Jr. *trade association executive*
Rosenker, Mark Victor *trade association executive*
Shaud, John Albert *association executive, former air force officer*
Smeal, Eleanor Cutri *organization executive*
Smith, Elise Fiber *international non-profit development agency administrator*
Stolgitis, William Charles *professional society executive*
†Strandquist, John Herbert *association executive*
Taggart, G. Bruce *professional society administrator*
Teem, John McCorkle *retired association executive, consultant*
Wells, Christine *foundation executive*
Wilkniss, Peter E. *foundation administrator, researcher*
Wilson, Minter Lowther, Jr. *retired officers association executive*
Wilson, Roy Kenneth *retired education association executive, consultant*

Boston
Fisher, John Morris *association official, educator*

Brookneal
†Elson, James Martin *historic foundation director, college music educator, fine arts administrator*

Chantilly
Slayton, Gus *association executive*
Sroka, John Walter *trade association executive*

Charlottesville
Bayston, Darwin M(erle) *professional association executive*
Jordan, Daniel Porter, Jr. *foundation administrator, history educator*

Culpeper
Landa, William Robert *foundation executive*

Fairfax
Cullison, Alexander C. (Doc Cullison) *society administrator*
Gray, William H., III *association executive, former congressman*
Hollans, Irby Noah, Jr. *association executive*
Jewell-Kelly, Starla Anne *educational administrator*
Martin, George Wilbur *association executive*
Mund, Richard Gordon *foundation executive*
Woodruff, C(harles) Roy *professional association executive*

Falls Church
Cooper, Arthur Irving *former association executive*
†Laqueur, Maria *association executive*
Ledwig, Donald Eugene *association executive*
Livingstone, Susan Morrisey *nonprofit administrator*
†Lyman, Robert Howard *veterans association executive*
Masterson, Kleber Sandlin *former organization executive, retired naval officer*
Rose, Wil *foundation executive*

Flint Hill
Dietel, William Moore *former foundation executive*

Fredericksburg
Farmer, James *civil rights leader, former trade union official*

Great Falls
Schwartz, Robert Terry *professional association executive*

Lynchburg
Hinnant, Hilari Anne *educator, educational consultant*

Mc Lean
Bolan, Robert S. *association executive*
†Burk, Brett J. *association executive, company executive*
Finberg, Donald Richard *foundation administrator*
Friel, Thomas Patrick *association executive*
Gary, Charles Lester *professional association consultant, educator*
Mc Fate, Patricia Ann *scientist, education, foundation executive*
McInerney, James Eugene, Jr. *association executive*
Rogers, Thomas Francis *foundation administrator*
Schweiker, Richard Schultz *trade association executive, former senator, former cabinet secretary*
†Whipple, David Doty *association executive*

Newport News
Mazur, Rhoda Himmel *federation president*

Norfolk
Sheetz, Richard LaTrelle *retired association executive*
Wilson, Lloyd Lee *organization administrator*

Reston
Ayers, George Edward Lewis *higher education association executive*
†Chatman, Raymond Christopher *association executive*
Cramer, James Perry *publisher, information architect*
Curry, John Joseph *professional organization executive*
Dyer, Timothy J. *educational association administrator*
Gates, James David *association executive*
Goodwin, Robert Delmege *retired association executive*
Hope, Samuel Howard *accreditation organization executive*
†Mahlmann, John James *educational association administrator*
Miller, Edward David *non-profit association administrator*
Minton, Joseph Paul *retired safety organization executive*

Richmond
†McCleary, Paul Frederick *voluntary agency executive*
Wood, Jeanne Clarke *charitable organization executive*

Round Hill
Sadd, William Wheeler *trade association executive*

Spotsylvania
Hardy, Dorcas Ruth *government relations and public policy consultant*

Springfield
Larson, Reed Eugene *association executive*

Tazewell
Weeks, Ross Leonard, Jr. *museum foundation executive*

Vienna
Argow, Keith Angevin *association executive,forester*
Cartier, Brian Evans *association executive*
West, Richard Luther *military association executive, defense consultant, retired army officer*

Williamsburg
Brinkley, Joseph Willard *association executive*
Longsworth, Charles R. *foundation administrator*
Wilburn, Robert Charles *institute executive*

WASHINGTON

Edmonds
Thyden, James Eskel *professional society administrator, former diplomat, educator*

La Center
Holley, Lawrence Alvin *retired labor union official*

Langley
Medlock, Ann *non-profit organization executive, writer, speaker*

Mill Creek
Corbally, John Edward *foundation director*

Seattle
Baker, Bruce Frederick *health services association administrator*
Brooke, Francis John, III *foundation administrator*
†Moberly, David Lindsey *foundation executive*

Sequim
Ramsey, William Ray *association executive*

Spokane
Rowe, Marjorie Douglas *retired social services administrator*

Tacoma
Graybill, David Wesley *chamber of commerce executive*
Rieke, William Oliver *foundation director, medical educator, former university president*

WEST VIRGINIA

Hillsboro
Pierce, William Luther *association executive, writer*

Wheeling
Griffith, Mabel Maxine *association administrator*
Wagner, Robert Owen *association executive*

WISCONSIN

Altoona
James, Henry Thomas *former foundation executive, educator*

Brookfield
†Stenicka, Charles Edward, III *professional association executive*

Elm Grove
Halvorsen, Morrie Edward *association executive*

Greendale
Gillespie, Rory Andrew *professional association administrator*

Kenosha
Adler, Seymour Jack *social services administrator*

Madison
Gaylor, Anne Nicol *editor, foundation executive*
Harr, Lucy Loraine *association executive*
Higby, Gregory James *historical association administrator, historian*
Muller, H(enry) Nicholas, III *historical society director*
Porter, Andrew Calvin *educational administrator, psychology educator*
Stern, Steve J. *cultural organization administrator, history educator*

Milwaukee
Huntington, David Mack Goode *foundation administrator*
Joyce, Michael Stewart *foundation executive, political science educator*
Ritz, Esther Leah *civic worker, volunteer, investor*
Zeidler, Frank P. *former association administrator, mayor, arbitrator, mediator, fact-finder*

Racine
Boyd, William Beaty *retired foundation executive*
Bray, Charles William, III *foundation executive*

River Hills
Smith, Jane Farwell *civic worker*

WYOMING

Cheyenne
Budd, Robert Wesley *trade association executive*
Mockler, Esther Jayne *political party administrator, state legislator*
Noe, Guy *social services administrator*

TERRITORIES OF THE UNITED STATES

PUERTO RICO

Guaynabo
Cruz Aponte, Ramón Aristides *foundation administrator, educator*

VIRGIN ISLANDS

Saint Thomas
Creque, Linda Ann *non-profit educational and research executive, former education commissioner*

MILITARY ADDRESSES OF THE UNITED STATES

EUROPE

FPO
Branson, Mary Lou *family therapist, military agency administrator*

CANADA

ALBERTA

Calgary
Raeburn, Andrew Harvey *performing arts association executive, record producer*
Roberts, John Peter Lee *cultural advisor, administrator, educator, writer*

BRITISH COLUMBIA

Vancouver
Howard, T. E. *scientific and research think-tank executive*
Saywell, William George Gabriel *foundation administrator*

MANITOBA

Winnipeg
†Hehn, Lorne Frederick *agricultural association executive*

NEW BRUNSWICK

Fredericton
Lewell, Peter A. *international technology executive, researcher*

Saint Andrews
Clark, David R. *executive not-for-profit organization, lawyer*

NOVA SCOTIA

Dartmouth
Nickerson, T. B. *think-tank organization executive*

Halifax
Sparling, Mary Christine *foundation executive*

Wolfville
Elliott, Robbins Leonard *consultant*

ONTARIO

Don Mills
Glover, Donald Robert *professional association administrator, former insurance executive*

Etobicoke
Ecroyd, Lawrence Gerald *association executive*

Mississauga
Ross, Thomas McCallum *association executive*

Ottawa
Basken, Reginald C. *communications union executive*
Bezanson, Keith Arthur *administrative educational executive*
Landry, Robert Edward *public policy consultant*
MacNeill, James William *international government consultant*
Manning, Preston *political organization worker*
Peppler, William Norman *aviation association executive*
Reid, Timothy *business organization executive*
Shaw, Edgar Albert George *research association executive*

Pontypool
Kniewasser, Andrew Graham *company director*

Toronto
Collins, Jerry Allan *association executive*
Falle, Daisy Carolyne *professional society administrator*
†Goodenow, Robert W. *labor union administrator*
James, Robert Scott *historic organization executive*
Johnston, Robert Donaghy *cultural organization administrator*
Kossuth, Selwyn Barnett *trade association consultant*
†Lister, Dianne Elizabeth *foundation administrator*
Montgomery, Donald Russell *labor consulting firm executive*
Rickerd, Donald Sheridan *foundation executive*
Rose, Jeffrey Raymond *public servant, trade union executive, economist*
Wilson, Ian Edwin *cultural organization administrator, archivist*

Willowdale
Bulloch, John Frederick Devon *association executive*

QUEBEC

Hull
†Labelle, Huguette *international agency executive*

Montreal
Hobday, John Charles *foundation administrator*

Outremont
Letourneau, Jean-Paul *business association executive and consultant*

Saint Laurent
Boulet, Lionel *research administrator*

SASKATCHEWAN

Regina
Driedger, Florence Gay *social agency executive, social work educator, consultant*

MEXICO

Mexico City
Bruton, John Macaulay *trade association executive*

BELGIUM

Brussels
Calingaert, Michael *international consultant*
Mestrallet, Gérard *association executive*

GHANA

Accra
Brocke, Eunice Miranda *foundation executive*

ITALY

Rome
Hjort, Howard Warren *international organization official, economist*
Wilson, George Peter *association executive*

MONACO

Monaco
Davies, Gareth John *trade association executive*

THE NETHERLANDS

The Hague
Nones Sucre, Carlos Enrique *political organization executive*

SWITZERLAND

Chambesy
Barnes, Thomas Joseph *migration program administrator*

Geneva
Purcell, James Nelson, Jr. *international organization administrator*

ADDRESS UNPUBLISHED

Allerton, John Stephen *association executive*
†Allison, Andrew M. *foundation administrator*
Amstutz, Daniel Gordon *intergovernmental organization executive, former grain dealer, government official*
†Anderson, Jane Louise *education association administrator, editor*
Anderson, Ned, Sr. *Apache tribal chairman*
Andolsek, Ludwig J. *association executive*
Anguiano, Lupe *advocate*
Annenberg, Walter H. *philanthropist, diplomat, editor, publisher, broadcaster*
Armacost, Mary-Linda Sorber Merriam *educational administrator*
Armour, David Edward Ponton *association executive*
Atchison, Richard Calvin *trade association director*
Babb, Roberta J. *educational administrator*
Baldwin, William Russell *foundation executive, optometrist*
Bartels, Gerald Lee *association executive*
†Benjamin, Medea *advocate*
Benton, Robert Dean *educational organization executive*
Blair, Fred Edward *association executive*
Boal, Dean *arts center administrator, educator, retired*
Bowen, David Reece *foundation director, former congressman*
Brewer, Carey *fund raising executive*
Bricker, William Rudolph *organization executive*
Brown, Bruce Maitland *philanthropy consultant*
Brune, Eva *fundraiser*
Burki, Fred Albert *labor union official*
Camdessus, Michel (Jean) *international organization executive*
Cesnik, James Michael *union official, newspaperman*
Clark, Alicia Garcia *political party official*
†Claxton, Bradford Wayne *professional society administrator*
Coughlan, William David *association executive*
†Curlee, Jesse W. *association executive*
†Dasher-Alston, Robinette *educational organization administrator*
Davis, Russell Haden *association executive, pastoral psychotherapist*
DeLong, Norma Neill *civic association executive*
De Moss, Robert George *religious foundation executive*
Derfner, Carol Ann *consultant*
Dorman, Richard Frederick, Jr. *association executive, consultant*
Easton, Michelle *foundation executive*
Elders, (Minnie) Joycelyn *public health administrator, endocrinologist*
Eliot, Theodore Lyman, Jr. *international consultant*
Ellis, Anne Elizabeth *fundraiser*
Farinella, Paul James *retired cultural institution executive*
Farris, Robert Earl *transportation consultant*
Foster, Charles Henry Wheelwright *former foundation officer, consultant,author*
Franklin, Margaret Lavona Barnum (Mrs. C. Benjamin Franklin) *civic leader*
Gammon, Samuel Rhea, III *association executive, former ambassador*
Gasper, Jo Ann *association executive*
Gertenbach, Robert Frederick *medical research organization executive, accountant, lawyer*
Gilchrest, Thornton Charles *retired association executive*
Hanford, George Hyde *retired educational administrator*
Helm, DeWitt Frederick, Jr. *association executive*
Hilty, William Jacob *retired association executive*
Hoopes, Townsend Walter *former association executive, former government official*
Horsch, Kathleen Joanne *social services administrator, educator, consultant*
Hybl, William Joseph *foundation executive, lawyer*
Ilutovich, Leon *organization executive*
Isaacson, Edith Lipsig *civic leader*
Jefferson, John Daniel *political activist*
Johnson, Geneva Bolton *retired human service organization executive*
Josephs, Melvin Jay *retired professional society administrator*
Kapor, Mitchell David *foundation executive*
Kasimer, Solomon *charitable organization executive*
Kaskowitz, Edwin *association executive*
Kempfer, Homer *association executive*
Kent, E(verett) Allen *performing arts administrator*
Kinder, James Allen *lobbyist, professional services firm executive, consultant*
Knauer, Virginia Harrington (Mrs. Wilhelm F. Knauer) *consumer consultant, former government official*
Krepinevich, Kevin W. *social welfare organization administrator, educator*
Kuhn, Margaret (Maggie Kuhn) *organization executive*
Langdon, George Dorland, Jr. *association executive*
Lee, John Franklin *retired lawyer, retired association executive*
Leggett, Roberta Jean (Bobbi Leggett) *association executive*
Lester, Virginia Laudano *association executive*
Liddell, Jane Hawley Hawkes *civic worker*
Low, James Patterson *professional association executive*
MacCarthy, Talbot Leland *civic volunteer*
MacMillan, Kip Van Metre *foundation executive*
Mann, Jonathan Max *international agency administrator*
McCord, Alice Bird *association executive*
McLaughlin, Ann *educational administrator, former federal official, lecturer, advisor*
Mende, Robert Graham *retired engineering association executive*
Meredith, James Howard *association executive, farmer, consultant*
Migden, Chester L. *association executive*
Mitchelson, Bonnie Elizabeth *politician, nurse*
Moore, Robert William *professional organization executive*
Nardi Riddle, Clarine *association administrator, judge*
O'Connor, Doris Julia *non-profit fundraiser, consultant*
Otte, Carl *political cponsultant, lobbyist*
Phillips, Kenneth Higbie *association executive*
Pifer, Alan (Jay Parrish) *former foundation executive*
Pollack, Joseph *retired labor union official*
Pollack, Ronald F(rank) *foundation executive, lawyer*
Pullen, Penny Lynne *non-profit administrator, former state legislator*
Quehl, Gary Howard *association executive, consultant*
Quinn, Phyllis *association executive*
Ramo, Virginia M. Smith *civic worker*
Richard, Susan Mathis *trade association executive*
Rimel, Rebecca Webster *foundation executive*
Roberts, James G. *foundation executive*
Roethel, David Albert Hill *consultant*
Rogers, Margaret Ellen Jonsson *civic worker*
Rosenberg, Alison P. *public policy official*
Ross, Charlotte Pack *suicidologist*
Ruane, Maureen Muriel *labor union official*
Ryan, John William *association executive*
Schiaffino, S(ilvio) Stephen *retired medical society executive, consultant*
Schwardt, Susan Kelly *civic organization executive*
Schwartz, John James *association executive, consultant*
Scott, Lorraine Ann *fraternal organization executive*
Sheridan, Diane Frances *public policy facilitator*
Singer, Markus Morton *retired trade association executive*
Smith, Laverne Byrd *educational association administrator*
Smith, Robert Powell *foundation executive, former ambassador*
Sodolski, John *retired association administrator*
Stevens, Lydia Hastings *civic worker*
Stinnett, Lee Houston *newspaper association executive*
Taplin, Frank E., Jr. *trustee education and arts institutions and associations*
Thomas, Franklin Augustine *foundation executive*
Tichenor, Donald Keith *association executive*
Toms, Justine Willis *educational organization executive*
Townsend, Susan Elaine *social service institute administrator, hostage survival consultant*
Trachta, Pamela Hale *consulting executive*
Tuft, Mary Ann *former association executive*
Van Ness, John Ralph *university foundation administrator*
Walter, J. Jackson *consultant*
Ward, Susan Marie *cultural organization administrator*
Washington, Valora *foundation administrator*
Wassenich, Linda Pilcher *health policy analyst, fund raiser*
Watts, Glenn Ellis *union official*
Wayburn, Laurie Andrea *environmental and wildlife foundation administrator, conservationist*
Weaver, Edward T. *foundation executive, educator*
Weddig, Lee J(ohn) *trade association executive*
Weikart, David Powell *educational research foundation administrator*
Wexler, Jacqueline Grennan (Mrs. Paul J. Wexler) *former association executive and college president*
Whitlock, Bennett Clarke, Jr. *retired association executive*
Work, William *retired association executive*
Wyatt, Lenore *civic worker*
Yeutter, Clayton Keith *political organization executive, counselor to President of United States*
Young, Margaret Buckner *civic worker, author*
Zemsky, Robert *educational administrator*
Zimny, Max *lawyer*

ATHLETICS

UNITED STATES

ALABAMA

Auburn
Reeve, Thomas Gilmour *physical education educator*

Bessemer
Allison, Robert Arthur *retired professional stock car driver*

Birmingham
Starr, Bart (Bryan Bartlett Starr) *former professional football coach, former professional football player*

Talladega
Adams, James Wilson *physical education educator*

Tuscaloosa
Stallings, Gene Clifton *university athletic coach, former professional coach*

ALASKA

Wasilla
Butcher, Susan Howlet *sled dog racer, dog kennel owner*

ARIZONA

Mesa
Unser, Bobby (Robert William Unser) *professional auto racer, television commentator*

Phoenix
Barkley, Charles Wade *professional basketball player*
Berkoff, David *Olympic athlete, swimmer*
Bidwill, William V. *professional football executive*
Colangelo, Jerry John *professional basketball team executive*
Fitzsimmons, (Lowell) Cotton *professional basketball executive, broadcaster, former coach*
Johnson, Kevin Maurice *professional basketball player*
Joyner, Seth *professional football player*
Majerle, Daniel Lewis *professional basketball player, olympic athlete*
Manning, Daniel Ricardo *professional basketball player*
Ryan, Buddy (James Ryan) *professional football coach*
Simmons, Clyde *professional football player*
Van Arsdale, Dick *professional basketball team executive*
Westphal, Paul *professional basketball coach*

Tempe
Wilson, Lawrence Frank (Larry Wilson) *professional football team executive*

Tucson
Olson, Lute *university athletic coach*

ARKANSAS

Conway
Titlow, Larry Wayne *physical education and kinesiology educator*

Fayetteville
Richardson, Nolan *university athletic coach*

CALIFORNIA

Anaheim
Frontiere, Georgia *professional football team executive*
Jackson, Bo (Vincent Edward Jackson) *professional baseball, former football player*
Lachemann, Marcel *professional baseball manager*
Langston, Mark Edward *professional baseball player*
Smith, Lee Arthur *professional baseball player*
Stark, Milton Dale *sports association executive*

Bakersfield
Friedman, Gloria A. *tennis coach*

Beverly Hills
Fleming, Peggy Gale *professional ice skater*
Shoemaker, Bill (William Lee Shoemaker) *retired jockey, horse trainer*

Coronado
Axelson, Joseph Allen *professional athletics executive, publisher*

Danville
Behring, Kenneth E. *professional sports team owner*

El Dorado Hills
Mansoor, John Jirius *sports management executive*

El Segundo
Brown, Timothy Donell *professional football player*
Davis, Allen *professional football team executive*
Gossett, Jeffrey Alan *professional football player*
Herrera, John *professional football team executive*
Hostetler, Jeff W. *professional football player*
Ismail, Raghib (Rocket Ismail) *professional football player*
Jaeger, Jeff Todd *professional football player*
Mosebar, Donald Howard *professional football player*
Shell, Art *professional football team coach*
Townsend, Greg *professional football player*
Wisniewski, Stephen Adam *professional football player*

Fullerton
Garrido, Augie *university athletic coach*

Inglewood
Gretzky, WayneDouglas *professional hockey player*
Johnson, Earvin (Magic Johnson) *professional sports team executive, former professional basketball coach*
Kurri, Jari *professional hockey player*
McNall, Bruce *professional sports executive, numismatist*
Sharman, William *professional basketball team executive*
Vachon, Rogatien Rosaire (Rogie Vachon) *professional hockey team executive*
West, Jerry Alan *professional basketball team executive*
Worthy, James Ager *former professional basketball player*

Long Beach
Brisco, Valerie *track and field athlete*

Los Angeles
Baylor, Elgin Gay *professional basketball team executive*
Chamberlain, Wilton Norman *retired professional basketball player*
De La Hoya, Oscar *Olympic athlete, professional boxer*
Dismukes, Valena Grace Broussard *physical education educator*
Fitch, William C. *professional basketball coach*
Frazier, Joe *retired professional boxer, performer*
Harrick, Jim *university athletic coach*
Karros, Eric Peter *professional baseball player*
Kelly, Roberto Conrado (Bobby Kelly) *professional baseball player*
Lasorda, Thomas Charles (Tommy Lasorda) *professional baseball team manager*
Levy, Louis *chess master*
O'Malley, Peter *professional baseball club executive*
Piazza, Michael Joseph *professional baseball player*
Rothenberg, Alan I. *professional sports association executive, lawyer*
Sterling, Donald T. *professional basketball team executive*
Watts, Quincy *track and field athlete*

Malibu
Louganis, Greg E. *former Olympic athlete, actor*

Mentone
Stockton, David Knapp *professional golfer*

Napa
Miller, John Laurence *professional golfer*

Oak Park
Caldwell, Stratton Franklin *kinesiologist*

Oakland
Adelman, Rick *professional basketball coach*
Alderson, Richard Lynn (Sandy) *professional baseball team executive*
Dolich, Andrew Bruce *professional basketball team executive*
Eckersley, Dennis Lee *professional baseball player*
Finnane, Daniel F. *professional basketball team executive*
Haas, Walter J. *professional baseball team executive*
Hardaway, Timothy Duane *basketball player*
Henderson, Rickey Henley *professional baseball player*
Lanier, Bob *professional sports team executive, former basketball player*
La Russa, Tony, Jr. (Anthony La Russa, Jr.) *professional baseball manager*
McGwire, Mark David *professional baseball player*
Mullin, Chris(topher) Paul *professional basketball player*
Pierce, Ricky Charles *professional basketball player*
Sierra, Ruben Angel Garcia *professional baseball player*

Palm Springs
Jumonville, Felix Joseph, Jr. *physical education educator, realtor*

Rancho Santa Margarita
Griffith Joyner, Florence DeLorez *track and field athlete*

Sacramento
Russell, Bill *former professional basketball team executive, former professional basketball player*
St. Jean, Garry *professional basketball coach*
Thomas, Jim *professional basketball team executive*

San Diego
Benes, Andrew Charles *professional baseball player*
Freeman, Dick *professional baseball team executive*
Gwynn, Anthony Keith (Tony Gwynn) *professional baseball player*
Seau, Junior (Jr. Tiana Seau) *professional football player*
Spanos, Alexander Gus *professional football team executive*

San Francisco
Baker, Dusty (Johnnie B. Baker, Jr.) *professional baseball team manager*
Beck, Rodney Roy *professional baseball player*
Bonds, Barry Lamar *professional baseball player*
Magowan, Peter Alden *professional baseball team executive, grocery chain executive*
Mays, Willie Howard, Jr. (Say Hey Mays) *former professional baseball player*
Mc Covey, Willie Lee *former professional baseball player*
Thompson, Robert Randall (Robby Thompson) *professional baseball player*
Williams, Matt (Matthew Derrick Williams) *professional baseball player*

San Jose
Savage, Arthur L. *professional hockey team executive*

Santa Clara
Dent, Richard Lamar *professional football player*
Hanks, Merton Edward *professional football player*
Jackson, Rickey *professional football player*
McDonald, Tim *professional football player*
Rice, Jerry Lee *professional football player*
Seifert, George *professional football coach*
Young, Steven *professional football player*

Sausalito
Casals, Rosemary *professional tennis player*

Sherman Oaks
Hamilton, Scott Scovell *professional figure skater, former Olympic athlete*
Hovland, Tim (The Hov) *volleyball player*
Rock, Angela *volleyball player*
Smith, Sinjin *volleyball player*
Steffes, Kent *volleyball player*
Stoklos, Randy (Stokey) *volleyball player*
Timmons, Steve (Red) *volleyball player*

Spring Valley
Runge, Paul Edward *baseball umpire, realtor*

Stanford
Van Derveer, Tara *university athletic coach*
Walsh, William *former football coach*

Walnut
Ashford, Evelyn *track and field athlete*

Walnut Creek
Hallock, C. Wiles, Jr. *athletic official*

COLORADO

Aspen
Sullivan, Danny *professional race car driver*

Colorado Springs
Armstrong, Lance *professional cyclist*
Austin, Timothy *Olympic athlete, boxer*
Barrowman, Mike *Olympic athlete, swimmer*
Barton, Gregory Mark *Olympic athlete, kayak racer*
Bates, Michael *Olympic athlete, track and field*
Biondi, Matt *Olympic athlete, swimmer*
Burgess, Greg *Olympic athlete, swimming*
Byrd, Chris *Olympic athlete, boxer*
Conley, Mike *track and field athlete*
Dees, Tony *Olympic athlete, track and field*
Dello Joio, Norman *Olympic athlete, equestrian*
Devers, Gail *track and field athlete*
Diebel, Nelson *Olympic athlete, swimmer*
Dimas, Trent *Olympic athlete, gymnast*
Doehrin, James *Olympic athlete, track and field*
Eldredge, Todd *figure skater*
Essick, Raymond Brooke, III *amateur sports administrator*
Foth, Bob *Olympic athlete, riflery*
†Fox, James Joseph *sports executive*
Gray, Johnny *Olympic athlete, track and field*
Greene, Joe *Olympic athlete, track and field*
Groebli, Werner Fritz (Mr. Frick) *professional ice skater, realtor*
Hartwell, Erin *Olympic athlete, cycling*
Jacobi, Joe *Olympic athlete, canoeist*

Jager, Tom Olympic athlete, swimmer
Johnson, Dave Olympic athlete, track and field
Kerrigan, Nancy professional figure skater, former Olympic athlete
Lenzi, Mark Olympic athlete, springboard diver
Lewis, Steve Olympic athlete, track and field
Marsh, Michael track and field athlete
McIntyre, Elizabeth Geary Olympic athlete
Mitchell, Dennis A. Olympic athlete, track and field
Morales, Pablo Olympic athlete, swimmer
Morris, Jason Olympic athlete
Moses, Edwin former track and field athlete
Murray, Ty (The Kid) professional rodeo cowboy
Peterson, Amy Olympic athlete
Pierce, Jack Olympic athlete, track and field
Rouse, Jeff Olympic athlete, swimmer
Simpkins, Charles Olympic athlete, track and field
Stewart, Melvin Olympic athlete, swimmer
Strausbaugh, Scott David Olympic athlete, canoeist
Street, Picabo Olympic athlete
Stulce, Mike Olympic athlete, track and field
Turner, Cathy Olympic athlete
†Walker, LeRoy Olympic official
Yamaguchi, Kristi Tsuya ice skater
Young, Kevin track and field athlete

Denver
Baylor, Don Edward professional baseball manager
Bickerstaff, Bernard Tyrone, Sr. (Bernie) professional basketball team executive
Galarraga, Andres Jose professional baseball player
Gebhard, Bob professional baseball team executive
Mutombo, DiKembe (Dikembe Mutombo Mpolondo Mukamba Jean Jacque Wamutombo) professional basketball player
Swift, William Charles professional baseball player, olympic athlete

Englewood
Atwater, Stephen Dennis professional football player
Beake, John professional football team executive
Craw, Nicholas Wesson motor sports association executive
Elway, John Albert professional football player
Perry, Michael Dean professional football player
Sharpe, Shannon professional football player

Greeley
Riddoch, Gregory Lee professional baseball manager

Leadville
Gentile-Patti, Catherine Ann Olympic skier

Littleton
Kearney, Joseph Laurence athletic conference administrator

CONNECTICUT

Branford
Agassi, Andre Kirk tennis player

Bristol
Abdul-Jabbar, Kareem (Lewis Ferdinand Alcindor) retired professional basketball player, sports commentator

Hartford
Baldwin, Howard J. professional hockey team executive
Holmgren, Paul professional hockey coach

New London
Pinhey, Frances Louise physical education educator

Stamford
†Worcester, Anne Person sports association executive

Trumbull
Mazza, David Lawrence university athletic director, educator

DISTRICT OF COLUMBIA

Washington
Blair, Bonnie former professional speedskater, former Olympic athlete
Casserly, Charley professional football team executive
Fernhall, Bo physical education educator
Green, Darrell professional football player
Johnson, Tim professional football player
Lachey, James Michael professional football player
Lohmiller, John M. (Chip Lohmiller) professional football player
Thompson, John college basketball coach
Turner, Norv professional football coach
Upshaw, Gene sports association executive

FLORIDA

Boca Raton
Evert, Christine Marie (Chris Evert) retired professional tennis player

Boynton Beach
†Spannuth, John R. athletic association executive

Davie
Shula, Don Francis professional football coach

Daytona Beach
Alcott, Amy Strum professional golfer
Earnhardt, (Ralph) Dale professional race car driver
Inkster, Juli professional golfer
King, Betsy professional golfer
Mallon, Meg professional golfer
Marlin, Sterling professional race car driver
Mochrie, Dottie professional golfer
Petty, Kyle professional stock car driver
Reeves, Donna Andrews golfer
Sheehan, Patty professional golfer
Whitworth, Kathrynne Ann professional golfer
Yarborough, William Caleb former professional stock car race driver

Fort Lauderdale
Fitzpatrick, Mark professional hockey player
Holtzman, Gary Yale recreational facility executive
King, Don boxing promoter
Murray, Bryan Clarence professional sports team executive
Vanbiesbrouck, John professional hockey player

Fort Myers
Peete, Calvin professional golfer

Gainesville
Liquori, Martin William, Jr. athlete, business executive, television commentator
Lopez, Andy university athletic coach
Singer, Robert Norman motor behavior educator
Spurrier, Steve university athletic coach, former professional football player

Hobe Sound
Norman, Greg professional golfer

Hollywood
Di Maggio, Joseph Paul former professional baseball player
King, Alma Jean former health and physical education educator

Jupiter
Vanatta, Bob athletic administrator

Lakeland
Campbell, James Arthur professional baseball team executive

Miami
Carr, Charles Lee Glenn, Jr. (Chuck Carr) professional baseball player
Greene, Joe (Charles Edward Greene) former professional football player, professional football coach
Harvey, Bryan Stanley professional baseball player
Lachemann, Rene George professional sports manager
Robbie, Timothy John professional football team executive
Santiago, Benito Rivera professional baseball player
Sheffield, Gary Antonian professional baseball player
Sims, Keith professional football player
Webb, Richmond Jewel professional football player
Willis, Kevin Alvin professional basketball player

Miami Beach
Cunningham, Billy (William John Cunningham) professional basketball team executive, television sportscaster
Schaffel, Lewis professional basketball team executive

North Palm Beach
Nicklaus, Jack William professional golfer

Ocoee
Rose, Peter Edward former professional baseball player and manager

Opa Locka
Clark, Gary C. football player
Dawson, Andre Nolan professional baseball player
Kosar, Bernie, Jr. professional football player
Marino, Daniel Constantine, Jr. professional football player
Pendleton, Terry Lee baseball player

Orlando
Hill, Brian professional basketball team coach
O'Neal, Shaquille Rashaun professional basketball player
Stephenson, Jan Lynn professional golfer

Ormond Beach
Wendelstedt, Harry Hunter, Jr. umpire

Palm Beach Gardens
Awtrey, Jim L. sports association executive
Calcevecchia, Mark professional golfer
Daly, John professional golfer
Mize, Larry professional golfer
Player, Gary Jim professional golfer
Rodriguez, Chi Chi (Juan Rodriguez) professional golfer
Sabatini, Gabriela tennis player

Panama City
Green, Hubert professional golfer

Pompano Beach
Elder, Robert Lee professional golfer

Ponte Vedra Beach
Azinger, Paul professional golfer
Chang, Michael tennis player
Cook, John professional golfer
Couples, Fred professional golfer
Edberg, Stefan professional tennis player
Faxon, Brad professional golfer
Floyd, Raymond professional golfer
Forsman, Dan professional golfer
Janzen, Lee professional golfer
Kite, Thomas O., Jr. professional golfer
Love, Davis, III professional golfer
Pavin, Corey professional golfer
Price, Nick professional golfer
Stewart, Payne (William Payne Stewart) professional golfer
Wadkins, Lanny professional golfer
Zoeller, Fuzzy professional golfer

Sarasota
Graham, Otto Everett, Jr. retired athletic director

Tallahassee
Bowden, Bobby university athletic coach

Tampa
Crisp, Terry Arthur professional hockey coach
Nakamura, Yoshio professional sports team executive
Wyche, Samuel David professional football coach

West Palm Beach
Snead, Samuel Jackson former professional golfer

GEORGIA

Athens
Dooley, Vincent Joseph college athletics administrator

Atlanta
Aaron, HenryL. (Hank Aaron) professional baseball team executive
Arani, Ardy A. professional sports marketing executive, lawyer
Avery, Steven Thomas professional baseball player
Babcock, Peter Heartz professional sports executive
Blauser, Jeffrey Michael professional baseball player
Byrne, Catherine swimmer
Cox, Bobby (Robert Joe Cox) professional baseball manager
Gearon, John Michael professional basketball team executive
Glavine, Tom (Thomas Michael Glavine) professional baseball player
Grissom, Marquis Dean professional baseball player
Justice, David Christopher baseball player
Kasten, Stanley Harvey sports association executive
Maddux, Greg (Gregory Alan Maddux) professional baseball player
McGriff, Fred (Frederick Stanley McGriff) baseball player
Smith, Janet Marie professional sports team executive
Smith, Steven Delano professional basketball player
Smoltz, John Andrew professional baseball player

Marietta
Wrege, Julia Bouchelle tennis professional, physical education educator

Suwanee
Doleman, Christopher John professional football player
Hebert, Bobby Joseph, Jr. professional football player
Jones, June professional football coach
Sanders, Ricky Wayne professional football player
Shelley, Elbert Vernell professional football player
Smith, Taylor professional football team executive

ILLINOIS

Belleville
Connors, Jimmy (James Scott Connors) former professional tennis player

Carbondale
Hart, James Warren athletic director, restaurant owner, former professional football player

Centralia
Wargo, Tom professional golfer

Chicago
Abbott, Jim (James Anthony Abbott) baseball player
Amonte, Anthony Lewis professional hockey player
Belfour, Ed professional hockey player
†Bevington, Terry Paul professional baseball manager
Cannon, Bennie Marvin physical education educator
Carrier, Mark Anthony professional football player
Chelios, Christos K professional hockey player
Einhorn, Edward Martin (Eddie Einhorn) professional baseball team executive
Fisk, Carlton Ernest retired professional baseball player
Grace, Mark Eugene professional baseball player
Guillen, Oswaldo Jose Barrios (Ozzie Guillen) baseball player
Himes, Laurence Austin professional baseball executive
Ivan, Thomas Nathaniel professional hockey team executive
Jackson, Philip Douglas professional basketball coach
Johnson, Howard Michael professional baseball player
Jordan, Michael Jeffery professional basketball player, retired baseball player
King, Billie Jean Moffitt former professional tennis player
McCaskey, Edward W. professional football team executive
Meyer, Raymond Joseph former college basketball coach
Myers, Randall Kirk (Randy Myers) professional baseball player
Pippen, Scottie professional basketball player
Pizer, Howard Charles professional baseball team executive, lawyer
Raines, Timothy professional baseball player
Reinsdorf, Jerry Michael professional sports teams executive, real estate executive, lawyer, accountant
Riggleman, James David professional baseball team manager
Roenick, Jeremy professional hockey player
Savard, Denis Joseph professional hockey player
†Schwartz, Alan Gifford sport company executive
Thomas, Frank Edward professional baseball player
Ventura, Robin Mark professional baseball player
Williams, Billy Leo professional baseball coach
Wirtz, Arthur Michael, Jr. professional hockey team executive

Deerfield
Krause, Jerry (Jerome Richard Krause) professional basketball team executive

Lake Forest
Jones, Dante Delaneo professional football player
McCaskey, Michael B. professional football team executive
†Salaam, Rashaan professional football player
Singletary, Michael retired professional football player
Wannstedt, David Raymond professional football team coach
Woolford, Donnell professional football player

Rockford
Lynn, Janet (Janet Lynn Nowicki Salomon) professional figure skater

Schaumburg
Payton, Walter (Sweetness) professional race car driver, former professional football player

Urbana
Bell, Gerald Wayne physical education educator
Thompson, Margaret M. physical education educator

INDIANA

Bloomington
Counsilman, James Edward physical education educator
Knight, Bob college basketball coach

Indianapolis
Andretti, John professional race car driver
Brown, Lawrence Harvey (Larry Brown) basketball coach
Emtman, Steven Charles professional football player
Irsay, James Steven professional football team executive
Irvine, George professional basketball coach
Marchibroda, Ted (Theodore Joseph Marchibroda) professional football coach
Miller, Reginald Wayne professional basketball player
Simon, Herbert professional basketball team executive
Stark, Rohn Taylor professional football player
Walsh, Donnie sports club executive

Notre Dame
Holtz, Louis Leo college football coach

Ogden Dunes
Mulvaney, Mary Jean physical education educator

South Bend
MacLeod, John college basketball coach

Speedway
Unser, Alfred, Jr. professional race car driver

Terre Haute
Campbell, Judith May physical education educator

IOWA

Des Moines
Foster, James Franklin professional sports management executive

Iowa City
Balukas, Jean professional pocket billiard player
Fry, Hayden university athletic coach

KANSAS

Lawrence
Williams, Roy university athletic coach

Overland Park
†Dempsey, Cedric W. sports association administrator

Shawnee Mission
Byers, Walter athletic association executive
Watson, Thomas Sturges professional golfer

Westwood
Schultz, Richard Dale national athletic organizations executive

KENTUCKY

Lexington
Krone, Julie jockey
Pitino, Richard college basketball coach

Louisville
Crum, Denny (Denzel Edwin Crum) collegiate basketball coach

LOUISIANA

Baton Rouge
Brown, Dale Duward basketball coach

Grambling
Robinson, Eddie Gay college football coach

Metairie
Andersen, Morten football player
Benson, Tom professional football executive
Johnson, Vaughan professional football player
Mora, James Ernest professional football coach, professional sports team executive
Roaf, William Layton professional football player
Turnbull, Renaldo professional football player

MARYLAND

Baltimore
Baines, Harold Douglass professional baseball player
Cruz, Bobby professional boxer
Mussina, Michael Cole professional baseball player
†Regan, Philip Raymond professional baseball coach
Ripken, Calvin Edwin, Jr. (Cal Ripken) professional baseball player
Robinson, Frank professional baseball team executive, former coach, former player
Seaman, Tony university athletic coach
Taylor, Meldrick professional boxer, Olympic athlete

Bethesda
Leonard, Sugar Ray (Ray Charles Leonard) *retired professional boxer*

Landover
Lynam, Jim *professional basketball coach*
Nash, John N. *professional basketball team executive*
O'Malley, Susan *professional basketball team executive*
Patrick, Richard M. *professional hockey team executive*
Pollin, Abe *professional basketball team executive, builder*
Sachs, Jerry *professional basketball team executive*
Schoenfeld, Jim *professional hockey coach*
Unseld, Westley Sissel *professional sports team executive, former professional basketball coach, former professional basketball player*

Lutherville Timonium
Shriver, Pamela Howard *professional tennis player*

MASSACHUSETTS

Boston
Auerbach, Arnold (Red Auerbach) *professional basketball team executive*
Bird, Larry Joe *retired professional basketball player*
Bourque, Ray *professional hockey player*
Canseco, Jose *professional baseball player*
Carr, Michael Leon *professional sports team executive, former professional basketball player*
Clemens, William Roger *professional baseball player*
Gavitt, David R. (Dave Gavitt) *professional sports team executive*
Harrington, John Leo *baseball company executive*
Iafrate, Al Anthony *professional hockey player*
Johnson, Dennis *professional basketball player*
Kennedy, Kevin Curtis *professional baseball team manager*
Neely, Cameron Michael *professional hockey player*
Oates, Adam R. *professional hockey player*
Orr, Bobby (Robert Gordon Orr) *former hockey player*
Sinden, Harry *professional hockey team executive*
Vaughn, Maurice Samuel (Mo Vaughn) *professional baseball player*
Volk, Jan *professional sports team executive*
Wilkins, (Jacques) Dominique *professional basketball player*
Yastrzemski, Carl Michael *former baseball player, public relations executive*

Bridgewater
Anderson, Marcia Kay *physical education educator*

Cambridge
Parker, Harry Lambert *university rowing coach*

Foxboro
Armstrong, Bruce Charles *professional football player*
Parcells, Bill (Duane Charles Parcells) *professional football coach*
Sullivan, William Hallisey, Jr. *professional football team executive*

West Springfield
Butterfield, Jack Arlington *hockey league executive*

MICHIGAN

Auburn Hills
Dumars, Joe, III *professional basketball player*
Robertson, Alvin Cyrrale *professional basketball player*

Berrien Springs
Ali, Muhammad (Cassius Marcellus Clay) *retired professional boxer*

Detroit
Anderson, Sparky (George Lee Anderson) *professional baseball team manager*
Coffey, Paul *professional hockey player*
Davis, Eric Keith *former professional baseball player*
Devellano, James Charles *professional hockey manager*
Fielder, Cecil Grant *professional baseball player*
Fryman, David Travis *professional baseball player*
Hearns, Thomas *professional boxer*
Ilitch, Marian *professional hockey team executive*
Ilitch, Michael *professional hockey team executive*
Roberts, Peter Allen *physical education educator*
Yzerman, Steve *professional hockey player*

Pontiac
Blades, Horatio Benedict (Bennie Blades) *professional football player*
Brown, Lomas, Jr. *professional football player*
Carter, Anthony *football player*
Fontes, Wayne *professional football team head coach*
Gray, Mel *professional football player*
Sanders, Barry *football player*
Schmidt, Chuck *professional football team executive*
Spielman, Chris *professional football player*
Swilling, Pat *professional football player*

Traverse City
Howe, Gordon *former professional hockey player, sports association executive*

MINNESOTA

Bloomington
Allen, Mary Louise Hook *physical education educator*

Eden Prairie
Cooper, Adrian *football player*
Green, Dennis *professional football coach*
Headrick, Roger Lewis *professional sports executive*
Hinton, Christopher Jerrod *professional football player*
McDaniel, Randall Cornell *professional football player*
Moon, Harold Warren, Jr. *professional football player*
Skoglund, John C. *former professional football team executive*
Thomas, Henry Lee, Jr. *professional football player*

Minneapolis
Aguilera, Richard Warren (Rick Aguilera) *professional baseball player*
Bell, Jerry *professional sports team executive*
Carlton, Steven Norman *retired professional baseball player*
Fox, Howard Tall, Jr. *professional baseball team executive*
Kelly, Tom (Jay Thomas Kelly) *major league baseball club manager*
Laettner, Christian Donald *professional basketball player*
LeMond, Gregory James *former professional bicycle racer*
McHale, Kevin Edward *former professional basketball player*
Pohlad, Carl R. *professional baseball team executive, bottling company executive*
Puckett, Kirby *professional baseball player*
Ratner, Harvey *professional basketball team owner*
Stein, Bob *professional basketball team executive*
Wolfenson, Marv *professional basketball team executive*

MISSISSIPPI

Itta Bena
Ware, William Levi *physical education educator, researcher*

MISSOURI

Bridgeton
Joyner Kersee, Jacqueline *track and field athlete*

Kansas City
Allen, Marcus *professional football player*
Alt, John *football player*
Appier, (Robert) Kevin *professional baseball player*
†Boone, Robert Raymond *professional baseball coach*
Brett, George Howard *baseball executive, former professional baseball player*
Collins, Mark *professional football player*
Hunt, Lamar *professional football team executive*
Lott, Ronnie (Ronald Mandel Lott) *professional football player*
Montgomery, Jeffrey Thomas *professional baseball player*
Peterson, Carl *professional football team executive*
Robinson, Spencer T. (Herk Robinson) *professional baseball team executive*
Schottenheimer, Martin Edward *professional football coach*
Smith, Neil *professional football player*
Steadman, Jack W. *professional football team executive*

Saint Louis
Caron, Ronald Jacques *professional sports team executive*
Cooper, Scott Kendrick *professional baseball player*
Gibson, Robert *broadcaster, former baseball player*
Hull, Brett A. *professional hockey player*
Irwin, Hale S. *professional golfer*
Quinn, Jack J. *professional hockey team executive*
Schoendienst, Albert Fred (Red Schoendienst) *professional baseball coach, former baseball player*
Smith, Ozzie (Osborne Earl Smith) *professional baseball player*

NEBRASKA

Lincoln
Osborne, Tom *college football coach*

NEVADA

Las Vegas
Holmes, David Leo *recreation and leisure educator*

NEW JERSEY

East Orange
Bowe, Riddick Lamont *professional boxer*
Gibson, Althea *retired professional tennis player, golfer, state official*
Holyfield, Evander *boxer*
Moorer, Michael *professional boxer*

East Rutherford
Aufzien, Alan L. *professional sports team executive*
Beard, Alfred (Butch) *former basketball player, former commentator*
Coleman, Derrick D. *professional basketball player*
Lamoriello, Louis Anthony *professional hockey team executive*
Lemaire, Jacques *professional hockey coach*
†Lemieux, Claude *professional hockey player*
Mann, Bernard (Bernie Mann) *professional basketball team executive*
Mara, John K. *professional sports team executive*
Mara, Wellington T. *professional football team executive*
McMullen, John J. *professional hockey team executive*
Mc Nab, Maxwell Douglas *professional sports executive*
Reed, Willis *professional basketball team executive, former head coach*
Reeves, Daniel Edward *professional football coach*
Walker, Herschel *professional football player*
Young, George Bernard, Jr. *professional football team executive*

Edison
Ensor, Richard Joseph *athletic conference commissioner, lawyer*

Far Hills
Fay, David B. *sports association executive*

Jersey City
Bavasi, Peter Joseph *professional baseball team executive*

Milltown
Bradley, Edward William *sports foundation executive*

Princeton
Tierney, Bill *university athletic coach*

Union
Pasvolsky, Richard Lloyd *parks, recreation, and environment educator*

NEW MEXICO

Albuquerque
Unser, Al *professional auto racer*

NEW YORK

Bronx
Boggs, Wade Anthony *professional baseball player*
Fernandez, Tony (Octavio Antonio Castro Fernandez) *baseball player*
Hurwitz, Ted Harold *sports conference administrator*
Key, Jimmy (James Edward Key) *professional baseball player*
Lawn, John C. *professional baseball team executive, former federal government official*
Mattingly, Donald Arthur *professional baseball player*
McDowell, Jack Burns *professional baseball player*
Mulholland, Terence John (Terry Mulholland) *professional baseball player*
Richman, Arthur Sherman *sports association executive*
Showalter, Buck (William Nathaniel Showalter, III) *major league baseball team manager*
Steinbrenner, George Michael, III *professional baseball team executive, shipbuilding company executive*

Buffalo
Fuhr, Grant *professional hockey player*
Hawerchuk, Dale *professional hockey player*
Lafontaine, Pat *professional hockey player*
Meehan, Gerry *professional hockey team executive*
Muckler, John *professional hockey coach, professional team executive*

Cooperstown
Carew, Rodney Cline *batting coach, former professional baseball player*
Jenkins, Ferguson Arthur, Jr. (Fergie Jenkins) *former baseball player*

East Hampton
Jacobs, Helen Hull *former tennis player, writer*

Flushing
Bonilla, Bobby (Roberto Martin Antonio Bonilla) *professional baseball player*
Cashen, J. Frank *professional baseball team executive*
Doubleday, Nelson *professional baseball team executive*
Green, Dallas (George Dallas Green) *professional baseball team manager*
Saberhagen, Bret William *professional baseball player*

Garden City
Feingold, Ronald Sherwin *physical education educator*

Hempstead
Esiason, Boomer (Norman Julius Esiason) *professional football player*
Gutman, Steve *professional football team executive*
Hextall, Ron *professional hockey player*
Kotite, Rich *professional football coach*
Lewis, Mo *professional football player*
Lowery, Dominic Gerald (Nick) *professional football player*
Steinberg, Dick *professional football team executive*

New Hyde Park
Stevens, Gary *professional jockey*

New York
Arcaro, Eddie (George Edward) *sports broadcasting journalist, former jockey, horse trainer*
Arias, Jimmy *professional tennis player*
Austrian, Neil R. *football league executive*
Brown, Robert William *baseball league executive, physician*
Campbell, Colin (Soupy Campbell) *professional hockey coach*
Capriati, Jennifer Maria *professional tennis player*
Cauthen, Steve *former jockey, sportscaster*
Checketts, David Wayne *professional basketball team executive*
Coleman, Leonard S., Jr. *sports association executive*
Constantine, Gus *physical education educator, coach*
Cordero, Angel T., Jr. *former jockey, horse trainer*
†Evans, James Bremond (Jim Evans) *major league baseball umpire*
Ewing, Patrick Aloysius *professional basketball player*
Fires, Earlie Stancel *jockey*
Frazier, Walter, Jr. (Clyde Frazier) *radio announcer, television analyst, retired professional basketball player*
Gibbs, Joe Jackson *former professional football coach, broadcaster, professional sports team executive*
Gilbert, Bradley *professional tennis player, Olympic athlete, professional tennis coach*
Gourdine, Simon Peter *professional basketball executive*
Graves, Adam *professional hockey player*
Jackson, Reginald Martinez *former professional baseball player*
Krickstein, Aaron *professional tennis player*
Leetch, Brian Joseph *hockey player*
McClelland, Timothy Reid *baseball umpire*
McEnroe, John Patrick, Jr. *professional tennis player*
McEnroe, Patrick *professional tennis player*
Messier, Mark Douglas *professional hockey player*
Monroe, Vernon Earl, Jr. (The Pearl Monroe) *former professional basketball player*
Nelson, Donald Arvid (Nellie Nelson) *professional basketball coach*
Pelé, (Edson Arantes do Nascimento) *professional soccer player*
Pincay, Laffit, Jr. *jockey*
Powell, Mike *olympic athlete, track and field*
Reneberg, Richard (Richey Reneberg) *professional tennis player*
Richter, Michael Thomas *professional hockey player*
Riley, Patrick James *former professional basketball coach*
Rostagno, Derrick *professional tennis player*
Rozelle, Pete (Alvin Ray Rozelle) *former commissioner athletic league*
Schramm, Texas E. *football league executive*
†Scott, Dale Allan *major league umpire*
Seaver, Tom (George Thomas Seaver) *former professional baseball player*
Spinks, Michael *retired professional boxer*
Stein, Gilbert *professional hockey executive*
Stern, David Joel *basketball association executive*
Stram, Hank Louis *former professional football coach, television and radio commentator*
Tagliabue, Paul John *national football league commissioner*
Thomas, Debi (Debra J. Thomas) *ice skater*
†Tyson, Mike G. *professional boxer*
Velasquez, Jorge Luis, Jr. *jockey*
Weiss, Donald L(ogan) *retired sports association executive*
White, William Dekova (Bill White) *baseball league executive*
Zahnd, Richard Hugo *professional sports team executive, lawyer*

Orchard Park
Bennett, Cornelius *professional football player*
Hull, Kent *professional football player*
Kelly, Jim (James Edward Kelly) *professional football player*
Levy, Marvin Daniel *professional football coach, sports team executive*
Reed, Andre Darnell *professional football player*
Smith, Bruce *professional football player*
Talley, Darryl Victor *professional football player*
Tasker, Steven Jay *professional football player*
Thomas, Thurman *professional football player*

Plainview
Meola, Tony *professional soccer player, actor*

Rochester
Crane, Irving Donald *pocket billiards player*

Syracuse
†Meng, Jin *educator*
Simmons, Roy, Jr. *university athletic coach*

Uniondale
Bossy, Michael *professional hockey player*
Henning, Lorne Edward *professional hockey coach*

White Plains
Wheaton, David *professional tennis player*

Yorktown Heights
Bogdanoff, Stewart Ronald *physical education educator, coach*

NORTH CAROLINA

Chapel Hill
Klarmann, Dave *university athletic coach*
Smith, Dean Edwards *university basketball coach*

Charlotte
Bristow, Allan Mercer *professional basketball coach*
Johnson, Larry Demetric *professional basketball player*
Mills, Samuel Davis, Jr. *professional football player*
Mourning, Alonzo *professional basketball player*
Parish, Robert Lee (Chief) *professional basketball player*
Shinn, George *professional basketball executive*
Stolpen, Spencer *professional sports team executive*

Durham
Krzyzewski, Mike *university athletic coach*
Little, Larry Chatmon *head football coach*

Randleman
Petty, Richard *retired professional race car driver*

NORTH DAKOTA

Wahpeton
Jensen, Delores (Dee Jensen) *physical education educator*

OHIO

Akron
MacCracken, Mary Jo *physical education educator*
Monacelli, Amieto *professional bowler*
Ozio, David *professional bowler*

Berea
Belichick, Bill *professional football coach*
Modell, Arthur B. *professional football team executive*
Rison, Andre *football player*
Rypien, Mark Robert *professional football player*
Schad, Mike *professional football player*
Thompson, Bennie *professional football player*

Canton
Dorsett, Anthony Drew (Tony Dorsett) *former professional football player*
Elliott, Peter R. *athletic organization executive*

Grant, Bud (Harold Peter Grant) *retired professional football coach*
Johnson, Jimmy *former professional football player*
Kelly, Leroy *former professional football player*
Smith, Jackie *former professional football player*

Cincinnati
Bench, Johnny Lee *retired professional baseball player*
Brown, Mike *professional sports team executive*
Coslet, Bruce N. *professional football coach*
Gant, Ron (Ronald Edwin Gant) *professional baseball player*
Johnson, Davey (David Allen Johnson) *baseball team manager*
Knowlton, Austin E. (Dutch Knowlton) *professional football team executive*
Larkin, Barry Louis *professional baseball player*
Sanders, Deion Luwynn *baseball and football player*
Sawyer, John *professional football team executive*
Schott, Marge *professional baseball team executive*
Shula, David D. *professional football team coach*

Cleveland
Adubato, Richard Adam (Richie Adubato) *professional basketball coach*
Alomar, Sandy, Jr. (Santos Velazquez Alomar) *professional baseball player*
Baerga, Carlos Obed Ortiz *professional baseball player*
Belle, Albert Jojuan *professional baseball player*
Courier, Jim (James Spencer Courier, Jr.) *tennis player*
†Faldo, Nick *professional golfer*
Fratello, Michael Robert *professional basketball coach*
Hargrove, Mike (Dudley Michael Hargrove) *professional baseball team manager*
Hershiser, Orel Leonard, IV *professional baseball player*
Lofton, Kenneth *professional baseball player*
Lopez, Nancy *professional golfer*
Montana, Joseph C., Jr. *former professional football player*
Murray, Eddie Clarence *professional baseball player*
Navratilova, Martina *former professional tennis player*
Rothstein, Ronald *professional basketball coach*
Salazar, Alberto *Olympic professional runner*
Seles, Monica *tennis player*
Strange, Curtis Northrop *professional golfer*
Winfield, David Mark *professional baseball player*

Columbus
Ayers, Randy *university athletic coach*

Fairfield
Robertson, Oscar Palmer (Big O) *former professional basketball player, chemical company executive*

Oxford
Pont, John *football coach, educator*

Parma
Esterhay, Judith M. *physical education educator*

Richfield
Price, (William) Mark *professional basketball player*

Shaker Heights
Eakin, Thomas Capper *sports promotion executive*

Youngstown
DeBartolo, Edward John, Jr. *professional football team owner, real estate developer*

OKLAHOMA

Oklahoma City
†Porter, Don E. *sports adiministrator*

Tulsa
Huber, Fritz Godfrey *physical education educator, excercise physiologist*

OREGON

Eugene
Decker Slaney, Mary Teresa *Olympic athlete*
Sisley, Becky Lynn *physical education educator*

Portland
Carlesimo, P. J. (Peter J. Carlesimo) *former college basketball coach, professional basketball coach*
Glickman, Harry *professional basketball team executive*
Kolde, Bert *professional basketball team executive*
Porter, Terry *professional basketball player*
Thorpe, Otis Henry *professional basketball player*
Williams, Charles Linwood (Buck Williams) *professional basketball player*

PENNSYLVANIA

Altoona
Wright, Jerry Jaye *physical education educator*

Devon
Lindros, Eric Bryan *professional hockey player*

Easton
Holmes, Larry Kandy, Jr. *professional boxer*

Lafayette Hill
Dixon, Fitz Eugene, Jr. *professional baseball team executive*

Philadelphia
Allen, Keith *professional sports team executive*
Brind'Amour, Rod Jean *professional hockey player*
Clarke, Robert Earle (Bobby Clarke) *hockey executive*
Cunningham, Randall *professional football player*
Daulton, Darren Arthur *professional baseball player*
Duncan, Mariano *professional baseball player*
Dykstra, Lenny (Leonard Kyle Dykstra) *professional baseball player*
Erving, Julius Winfield, II (Dr. J.) *business executive, retired professional basketball player*
Fregosi, James Louis *professional baseball team manager*
Fuller, William Henry, Jr. *professional football player*
Gamble, Harry T. *professional football team executive*
†Garcia, Richard Raul *major league umpire*
Giles, William Yale *professional baseball team executive*
Hollins, David Michael *professional baseball player*
Jefferies, Gregory Scott *professional baseball player*
Katz, Harold *professional basketball team executive*
Kruk, John Martin *professional baseball player*
Lucas, John Harding, Jr. *professional basketball coach*
Montgomery, David Paul *professional baseball team executive*
Murray, Terry (Terence Rodney Murray) *professional hockey team coach*
†Roe, John Andrew (Rocky) *major league baseball umpire, consultant*
Schmidt, Michael Jack *former professional baseball player*
Snider, Edward Malcolm *professional hockey club executive*
Van Slyke, Andrew James *professional baseball player*

Pittsburgh
Anderson, Gary Allan *professional football player*
Bell, Jay Stuart *professional baseball player*
Cowher, Bill *professional football coach*
Johnston, Edward Joseph *professional hockey team coach, former team executive, former player*
Lemieux, Mario *professional hockey player*
Leyland, James Richard *professional baseball team manager*
Majors, Johnny (John Terrill Majors) *university athletic coach*
Mullen, Joseph Patrick *professional hockey player*
Murphy, Lawrence Thomas *professional hockey player*
Noll, Charles Henry *former professional football coach*
Patrick, Craig *professional hockey team executive*
Robitaille, Luc *professional hockey player*
Rooney, Daniel M. *professional football team executive*
Stargell, Willie (Wilver Dornel Stargell) *professional sports team coach, former baseball player*
Stevens, Kevin Michael *professional hockey player*
Trottier, Bryan John *professional sports team coach, former professional hockey player*
Woodson, Roderick Kevin *professional football player*

University Park
Paterno, Joseph Vincent *college football coach*

Washington
Hays, Lewis W. *amateur baseball executive, writer*

York
Klingaman, Robert LeRoy *golf professional*

Youngstown
Palmer, Arnold Daniel *professional golfer*

RHODE ISLAND

Providence
Gorton, Arlene Elizabeth *physical education educator*

SOUTH CAROLINA

Columbia
Giese, Warren Kenneth *health and physical education educator, state senator*

Gaffney
Perry, Gaylord Jackson *former professional baseball player*

TEXAS

Arlington
Brown, James Kevin *professional baseball player*
Burkett, John David *professional baseball player*
Clark, Will (William Nuschler Clark, Jr.) *professional baseball player*
Gonzalez, Juan (Juan Alberto Vazquez Gonzales) *professional baseball player*
Oates, Johnny Lane *professional baseball team manager*
Rodriguez, Ivan *professional baseball player*
Rose, Edward W. (Rusty Rose) *professional sports team executive*
Ryan, Nolan *former professional baseball player*
Sampras, Pete *tennis player*
Schieffer, J. Thomas *professional baseball team executive*
Tewksbury, Robert Alan *professional baseball player*

Austin
Crenshaw, Ben *professional golfer*
Mackovic, John *college football coach, athletic director*

College Station
Slocum, R.C. *university athletic coach*

Dallas
Carter, Donald *professional basketball team executive*
Foster, William Edwin (Bill Foster) *nonprofessional basketball coach*
Hatchell, Steven James *collegiate sports association executive*
Landry, Tom (Thomas Wade Landry) *former professional football coach*
Mantle, Mickey Charles *former baseball player, marketing consultant*
Modano, Michael *professional hockey player*
Sonju, Norm Arnold *professional sports team manager, executive*
Trevino, Lee Buck *professional golfer*

Fort Worth
Hogan, Ben *former professional golfer, business executive*

Houston
†Bagwell, Jeff (Jeffrey Robert Bagwell) *professional baseball player*
Berra, Yogi (Lawrence Peter Berra) *professional baseball coach*
Camarillo, Richard Jon *professional football player*
Childress, Raymond Clay, Jr. *professional football player*
Collins, Terry *professional baseball manager*
Dishman, Cris Edward *professional football player*
Donie, Scott *Olympic athlete, platform diver*
Drabek, Doug (Douglas Dean Drabek) *baseball player*
Drexler, Clyde *professional basketball player*
Foreman, George *boxer, nondenominational christian minister, boxing broadcaster*
Foyt, A(nthony) J(oseph), Jr. *auto racing crew chief, former professional auto racer*
Holovak, Mike *sports association exec*
Jeffires, Haywood Franklin *professional football player*
Kile, Darryl Andrew *professional baseball player*
Lewis, Carl *Olympic track and field athlete*
Matthews, Bruce Rankin *professional football player*
McClane, Drayton, Jr. *professional baseball team executive*
Olajuwon, Hakeem Abdul (The Dream) *professional basketball player*
Patterson, Steve *professional hockey team executive*
Smith, Al Frederick *professional football player*
Tomjanovich, Rudolph *professional athletic coach*

Irving
Aikman, Troy *professional football player*
Haley, Charles Lewis *professional football player*
Irvin, Michael Jerome *professional football player*
Jones, Jerry (Jerral Wayne Jones) *professional football team executive*
Lites, James *professional hockey team executive*
Novacek, Jay McKinley *professional football player*
Smith, Emmitt J., III *professional football player*
Stepnoski, Mark Matthew *professional football player*
Switzer, Barry *professional football coach, former university athletic coach*
Williams, Erik George *professional football player*

San Antonio
Elliot, Sean Michael *professional basketball player*
Robinson, David Maurice (The Admiral) *professional basketball player*
Rodman, Dennis Keith *basketball player*

UTAH

Park City
Mahre, Phil *alpine ski racer, race car driver*
Moe, Tommy (Thomas Sven Moe) *skier, former Olympic athlete*
Peterson, Howard George Finnemore *sports executive*

Salt Lake City
Carmichael, Nelson *skier*
Hornacek, Jeffrey John *professional basketball player*
Layden, Francis Patrick (Frank Layden) *professional basketball team executive, former coach*
Malone, Karl (The Mailman) *professional basketball player*
Sloan, Jerry (Gerald Eugene Sloan) *professional basketball coach*
Stockton, John Houston *professional basketball player*

Sandy City Chamber
Schneiter, George Malan *golf professional, development company executive*

VIRGINIA

Arlington
Kiraly, Karch (Charles Frederick Kiraly) *professional volleyball player*
Smith, Stanley Roger *retired professional tennis player*

Ashburn
Cooke, John Kent *professional sports management executive*

Charlottesville
Dodson, Claudia Lane *program supervisor*

Falls Church
Theismann, Joseph Robert *former professional football player, announcer*

Haymarket
Moseley, Mark DeWayne *retired professional football player*

Richmond
Daniel, Beth *professional golfer*

Virginia Beach
Becker, Boris *professional tennis player*

WASHINGTON

Kirkland
Allen, Chuck *football team executive*
Erickson, Dennis *professional football coach, former university football coach*
Flores, Thomas R. *professional football team executive*
Kennedy, Cortez *professional football player*

Seattle
Ackerley, Barry *professional basketball team executive, communications company executive*
Armstrong, Charles G. *professional baseball executive, lawyer*
Ellis, John W. *professional baseball team executive, utility company executive*
Griffey, Ken, Jr. (George Kenneth Griffey, Jr.) *professional baseball player*
Johnson, Randall David (Randy Johnson) *professional baseball player*
Karl, George *professional basketball coach*
Kemp, Shawn T. *professional basketball player*
Martinez, Edgar *professional baseball player*
Piniella, Louis Victor *professional baseball team manager*

Spokane
Moe, Orville Leroy *racetrack executive*

WISCONSIN

Green Bay
Favre, Brett Lorenzo *professional football player*
Harlan, Robert Ernest *professional football team executive*
Holmgren, Mike *professional football coach*
Jackson, Keith Jerome *football player*
Parins, Robert James *professional football team executive, judge*
White, Reggie (Reginald Howard White) *professional football player*

Milwaukee
Dunleavy, Michael Joseph *professional basketball coach*
Garner, Phil *professional baseball manager*
Jansen, Daniel Ervin *professional speedskater, marketing professional, former Olympic athlete*
Listach, Patrick Alan *professional baseball player*
Selig, Allan H. (Bud Selig) *professional baseball team executive*
Steinmiller, John F. *professional basketball team executive*
Vaughn, Gregory Lamont *professional baseball player*

Stevens Point
Garber, David J. *sports association executive, marketing consultant*

CANADA

ALBERTA

Calgary
Cheveldae, Tim *professional hockey player*
Hay, William Charles *professional hockey team executive*
Housley, Phil F *professional hockey player*
King, W. David *professional hockey coach*

Canmore
Wood, Sharon *mountaineer*

Edmonton
Burnett, George *professional hockey coach*
Sather, Glen Cameron *professional hockey team executive, coach*

BRITISH COLUMBIA

Vancouver
Bure, Pavel *professional hockey player*
Griffiths, Arthur R. *professional hockey team executive*
Jackson, Stu *professional sports team executive, former university basketball coach*
McLean, Kirk *professional hockey player*
Quinn, Pat (John Brian Patrick Quinn) *professional sports team manager*

MANITOBA

Winnipeg
Paddock, John *professional hockey team head coach*
Shenkarow, Barry L. *professional hockey team executive*

ONTARIO

Gloucester
Browning, Kurt *figure skating champion*

London
Widdrington, Peter Nigel Tinling *professional baseball team executive*
Zeigler, Earle Frederick *physical education-kinesiology educator*

Nepean
Bowness, Rick (Richard Gary Bowness) *professional hockey coach*

Toronto
Alomar, Roberto Velazquez *professional baseball player*
Burns, Pat *professional hockey coach*
Carter, Joe (Joseph Chris Carter) *professional baseball player*
Cone, David Brian *professional baseball player*
Fletcher, Cliff *professional hockey team executive*
Gartner, Michael Alfred *professional hockey player*
Gaston, Cito *professional baseball manager*
Gillick, Patrick *professional baseball team executive*
Gilmour, Doug *professional hockey player*
Hentgen, Patrick George *professional baseball player*
Molitor, Paul Leo *professional baseball player*
Olerud, John Garrett *professional baseball player*
Potvin, Felix *professional hockey player*
Stavro, Steve A. *professional hockey team executive*

Thomas, Isiah Lord, III former professional basketball player, basketball team executive
Viola, Frank John, Jr. professional baseball player
Ward, Duane professional baseball player
White, Devon Markes professional baseball player

QUEBEC

Montreal
Alou, Felipe Rojas professional baseball manager
Brochu, Claude Renaud professional baseball team executive
Carbonneau, Guy professional hockey player
Corey, Ronald professional hockey team executive
Damphousse, Vincent professional hockey player
Demers, Jacques professional hockey team coach
Fanning, William James professional baseball team executive, radio and television broadcaster
O'Neill, Brian Francis professional hockey executive
Roy, Patrick professional hockey player
Savard, Serge professional hockey team executive
Stoneman, William Hambly, III professional baseball team executive

Quebec
Crawford, Marc professional hockey coach

MEXICO

Mexico City
Whitaker, Pernell (Sweet Pea) professional boxer

ITALY

Padova
†Lalas, Alexi professional soccer player

SOUTH AFRICA

Klippoortjie
Els, Theodore Ernest professional golfer

SPAIN

Santander
Ballesteros, Severiano professional golfer

ADDRESS UNPUBLISHED

Allen, Eric Andre professional football player
Andretti, Mario (Gabriele) professional race car driver
Andretti, Michael Mario professional race car driver
Anthony, Earl Roderick professional bowler
Boling, Robert Bruce physical education educator
Bowman, Scotty professional hockey coach
Bradley, Patricia Ellen professional golfer
Comaneci, Nadia gymnast
Constantine, Kevin professional hockey coach
Cooper, John Miller retired biomechanics lab director
Corrales, Patrick coach, former professional baseball manager
Daugherty, Brad(ley) (Lee) professional basketball player
Embry, Wayne Richard basketball executive
Esposito, Philip Anthony (Phil Esposito) professional sports team executive, former hockey broadcaster, former professional hockey player
Gainey, Robert Michael professional hockey coach, former player
Garrison-Jackson, Zina tennis player
Geddes, Jane professional golfer
Graf, Steffi professional tennis player
Gund, Gordon professional athletic teams executive
Guthrie, Janet professional race car driver
Hamill, Dorothy Stuart professional ice skater
Havlicek, John J. (Hondo) former professional basketball player
Hemond, Roland A. professional baseball team executive
Herzog, Whitey (Dorrel Norman Elvert Herzog) former professional baseball team executive
Hull, Bobby (Robert Marvin Hull) former professional hockey player
Irsay, Robert professional football team executive, construction company executive
Johnson, Reggie professional boxer
Kavalek, Lubomir chess expert
Keenan, Mike professional hockey team coach
Lindsey, D. Ruth physical education educator
Littler, Gene Alec professional golfer
Massimino, Roland V. former university basketball coach
McIlvaine, Joseph Peter professional baseball team executive
McIntyre, Guy Maurice professional football player
Monk, Art football player
Munoz, Michael Anthony professional football player
Oates, Bart Steven professional football player
Palmer, James Alvin baseball commentator
Risebrough, Doug professional hockey team executive
Ross, Robert Joseph head professional football coach
Rutherford, John Sherman, III (Johnny Rutherford) professional race car driver
Schrempf, Detlef professional basketball player
Sharpe, Sterling professional football player
Stadler, Craig Robert professional golfer
Stokoe, Phillip Michael physical education educator, school board member
Waltrip, Darrell Lee professional stock car driver
Washington, MaliVai professional tennis player
White, Randy retired professional football player
Wilkens, Leonard Randolph, Jr. (Lenny Wilkens) professional basketball coach
Williams, Ted (Theodore Samuel Williams) former baseball player, former manager, consultant
Wooden, John Robert former basketball coach
Woosnam, Ian Harold professional golfer

BUSINESS. See **FINANCE; INDUSTRY.**

COMMUNICATIONS. See **COMMUNICATIONS MEDIA; INDUSTRY: SERVICE.**

COMMUNICATIONS MEDIA. See also **ARTS: LITERARY.**

UNITED STATES

ALABAMA

Anniston
Ayers, Harry Brandt editor, publisher, columnist

Auburn
Barker, Larry Lee communications educator

Birmingham
Bailey, Thomas Edward newspaper editor, book publisher
†Carlton, Michael magazine editor
Casey, Ronald Bruce journalist
Crichton, Douglas Bentley editor, writer
Finebaum, Paul Alan sports columnist
†Griffin, Eleanor magazine editor
Hanson, Victor Henry, II newspaper publisher
Jackson, Harold journalist
Jacobson, James Edmund newspaper editor
†Kaimann, Frederick Daniel music critic, reporter
Kennedy, Joe David, Jr. (Joey Kennedy) editor
Phillips, James Linford agricultural affairs journalist, editor
Reeves, Garland Phillip newspaper editor
Scarritt, Thomas Varnon newspaper editor
Seitz, Karl Raymond editor
†Sheppard, Scott magazine publisher
Stephens, James T. publishing executive
Walker, Evelyn retired educational television executive

Jacksonville
Merrill, Martha instructional media educator

Mobile
Hearin, William Jefferson newspaper publishing company executive
Thomson, H. Bailey editor

Monroeville
Kniskern, Maynard editor, writer

Montgomery
Amberg, Richard Hiller, Jr. newspaper executive
Brown, William Blake newspaper editor
Teague, Larry Gene editor

Red Level
Taylor, Thomas Alexander, III retired newspaper editor

Tuscaloosa
Mac Donald, Malcolm Murdoch editor, publisher
Reinhart, Kellee Connely journalist

ALASKA

Anchorage
Atwood, Robert Bruce publisher
Lindauer, John Howard, II newspaper publisher
Pearson, Larry Lester journalism educator, communication consultant
Thomas, Lowell, Jr. author, lecturer, former lieutenant governor Alaska, former state senator
Unruh, Leon Dale newspaper editor

ARIZONA

Apache Junction
Files, James Lincoln editor

Bisbee
Eppele, David Louis columnist, author

Carefree
Sackett, Susan Deanna film and television production associate, writer

Casa Grande
Kramer, Donovan Mershon, Sr. newspaper publisher

Chandler
Stellrecht, Fritz newspaper publishing executive

Flagstaff
Hammond, Howard David retired botanist and editor

Glendale
Joseph, Gregory Nelson media critic

Green Valley
Lasch, Robert former journalist
Perry, Roger Lawrence printing executive

Phoenix
Benson, Stephen R. editorial cartoonist
Bergamo, Ron broadcasting company executive
Caputo, Salvatore critic
Cheshire, William Polk newspaper columnist
DeBruhl, Richard R. television reporter
Early, Robert Joseph magazine editor
Edens, Gary Denton broadcasting executive
Ellison, Cyril Lee publisher
Genrich, Mark L. newspaper editor
Godwin, Mary Jo editor, librarian consultant
Gunty, Christopher James newspaper editor
Harelson, Hugh magazine publisher
Kolbe, John William newspaper columnist
LaFave, Kenneth John music critic, composer
Leach, John F. newspaper editor, journalism educator
Might, Thomas Owen newspaper company executive
Moyer, Alan Dean retired newspaper editor
Murian, Richard Miller book company executive
Oppedahl, John Fredrick newspaper editor
Schatt, Paul newspaper editor
Stahl, Richard G. C. journalist, editor
Steckler, Phyllis Betty publishing company executive
Weil, Louis Arthur, III newspaper publishing executive

Scottsdale
Smyth, Bernard John retired newspaper editor
Smyth, Joel Douglas newspaper executive
Walsh, Mason retired newspaperman

Sedona
Chicorel, Marietta Eva publisher
Johnson, Hoyt Charles publisher
Sasmor, James Cecil publisher representative, educator

Sun City West
Edwards, F(loyd) Kenneth journalist, educator, management consultant, marketing executive

Tempe
Frischknecht, Lee Conrad retired broadcasting executive
Galician, Mary-Lou mass media educator
Richards, Gale Lee communications educator
Sabine, Gordon Arthur educator, writer

Tucson
Hatfield, Charles Donald newspaper executive
Hutchinson, Charles Smith, Jr. book publisher
†Matthews, Mildred Shapley scientific editor, freelance writer
Neal, James Madison, Jr. editor
Peck, John Thomas newspaper editor
Roos, Nestor Robert consultant
Silva, John Philip Costa newspaper editor
†Villa, Jacqueline I. newspaper editor
Weber, Samuel editor

ARKANSAS

El Dorado
†Hogan, Robert Francis, Jr. cable company executive

Eureka Springs
Sackett, Ross DeForest publisher

Fort Smith
Flippin, Perry Welch publishing executive
Moseley, Jack Edwin newspaper editor

Little Rock
Greenberg, Paul newspaperman
†Hobbs, Ray David editor
Lutgen, Robert R. newspaper editor
Portis, Charles McColl reporter, writer
Simmons, Bill newsman
Wassell, Irene Martin food editor

Mountain Home
Anderson, Kenneth Norman retired magazine editor, author

CALIFORNIA

Agoura Hills
Chagall, David journalist, author
Teresi, Joseph publishing executive

Albany
†Sikora, Stephen Theodore publisher

Alhambra
Duke, Donald Norman publisher

Alpine
Greenberg, Byron Stanley newspaper and business executive, consultant

Avila Beach
Kamm, Herbert journalist

Bakersfield
Barro, Mary Helen broadcast executive

Belmont
†Carlson, Gary R. publishing executive
Lake, David S. publisher, lawyer

Belvedere Tiburon
Kramer, Lawrence Stephen journalist
Moffitt, Phillip William magazine editor

Berkeley
Bagdikian, Ben Haig journalist, emeritus university educator
Browne, Walter Shawn journalist, chess player
Clark, James Henry publishing company executive
Craib, Ralph Grant reporter
Drechsel, Edwin Jared retired magazine editor
Helson, Henry Berge publisher, retired mathematics educator
Lesser, Wendy literary magazine editor, writer, consultant
Light, Ken photojournalist, educator
Littlejohn, David journalism educator, writer
Weidman, Anna Kathryn publishing company financial executive

Beverly Hills
Beck, Marilyn Mohr columnist
Buyse, Emile Jules film company executive
Chernin, Peter motion picture company executive
Cort, Robert W. film company executive
Corwin, Stanley Joel book publisher
Grushow, Sandy broadcast executive
Hefner, Hugh Marston editor in chief
Heller, Paul Michael film company executive, producer
†Hill, David broadcast executive
Hinton, Leslie Frank media executive
Jenner, Bruce sportscaster, former Olympic athlete
Johnson, Jimmy sports commentator, former professional football coach
Kuhn, Michael motion picture company executive
Levy, David broadcasting executive
Lewine, Robert F. broadcasting company executive
Madden, John television sports commentator, former professional football coach
Mark, John film company executive
†Mechanic, William M. television and motion picture industry executive
Menon, Vijaya Bhaskar recording and entertainment company executive
†Pedersen, Ken recording industry executive
Pleskow, Eric Roy motion picture company executive
†Quartararo, Phil recording industry executive
†Rifkin, Arnold film company executive
†Rosenzweig, Richard Stuart publishing company executive
Rush, Herman E. television executive
Spikings, Barry Peter film company executive
Summerall, Pat (George Allan Summerall) sportscaster
Thompson, Tina Lewis Chryar publisher
Zanuck, Richard Darryl motion picture company executive

Burbank
Arkoff, Samuel Z. motion picture executive, producer
Bollenbach, Stephen Frasier entertainment executive
Brogliatti, Barbara Spencer television and motion picture executive
Daly, Robert Anthony film executive
Disney, Roy Edward broadcasting company executive
Eisner, Michael Dammann entertainment company executive
Fisher, Lucy J. motion picture company executive
†Frank, Richard H(arvey) motion picture company executive
Griffith, Robert Douglas broadcasting company executive
Hoberman, David motion picture company executive
Katzenberg, Jeffrey motion picture studio executive
†Littlefield, Warren television executive
McCann, David DeWitt motion picture company executive
Mestres, Ricardo A., III motion picture company executive
Moonves, Leslie television company executive
Robinson, James G. film production executive
Roth, Joe motion picture company executive
Semel, Terry motion picture company executive
†Waronker, Leonard record company executive
Wolper, David Lloyd motion picture and television executive

Burlingame
Mendelson, Lee M. film company executive, writer, producer, director

Camarillo
DePatie, David Hudson motion picture company executive

Cambria
Blundell, William Edward journalist, consultant

Capistrano Beach
Lewis, Jack (Cecil Paul Lewis) publishing executive, editor

Carlsbad
Brown, Jack magazine editor
Lynn, Fredric Michael sportscaster, former professional baseball player

Carmel
Koeppel, Gary Merle publisher, art gallery owner

Carson
Davidson, Mark writer, educator

Chatsworth
Rawitch, Robert Joe newspaper editor

Chico
Greb, Gordon Barry writer, educator

Claremont
Miles, Jack (John Russiano) journalist, critic

Columbia
†Maasberg, Bill Arthur publisher

Concord
Anderberg, Roy Anthony journalist

Corona Del Mar
Crump, Spencer publisher, business executive

Costa Mesa
Billiter, William Overton, Jr. journalist
†Hecht, Duvall Y. publishing industry executive
Heylin, Michael magazine editor

Culver City
†Avnet, Jonathan Michael motion picture company executive, film director
Canton, Mark motion picture company executive
Martin, Gary O. film company executive
Rosenfelt, Frank Edward motion picture company executive
Sagansky, Jeff broadcast executive
Tinker, Grant A. broadcasting executive

Danville
Reed, John Theodore publisher, writer

Del Mar
Faludi, Susan C. *journalist, scholarly writer*
Kaye, Peter Frederic *newspaper editor*

El Cajon
Fike, Edward Lake *newspaper editor*

El Centro
Lokey, Frank Marion, Jr. *broadcast executive, consultant*

Encino
Holman, Harland Eugene *retired motion picture company executive*
Karlin, Myron D. *motion picture executive*

Forestville
Benyo, Richard Stephen *magazine editor, writer*

Foster City
Goldstein, Morris *publishing company executive*

Frazier Park
Nelson, Harry *journalist, medical writer*

Fresno
†Jimenez, Edward Rucobo *editor*
Rehart, Burton Schyler *journalism educator, freelance writer*
†Setencich, Eli John *columnist*
Tatarian, Hrach Roger *journalist*

Half Moon Bay
Bonham, George Wolfgang *magazine editor, writer, foundation executive*

Hollywood
Bernstein, William *film company executive*
Israel, David *journalist, screenwriter, producer*
Miller, Betty Jean *feature film distribution company executive*
Schaefer, Carl George Lewis *writer, public relations and advertising executive*

Huntington Beach
Frye, Judith Eleen Minor *editor*

Irvine
Bartkus, Richard Anthony *magazine publisher*
Lesonsky, Rieva *editor in chief*
Power, Francis William *newspaper publisher*
Segal, D. Robert *publishing and broadcast company executive*

La Canada Flintridge
Fry, Donald Owen *broadcasting company executive*

La Jolla
Copley, David C. *newspaper publishing company executive*
Copley, Helen Kinney *newspaper publisher*
Jones, Charlie *television sports announcer*
Walker, Harold Osmonde *newspaper and cable television executive*

Lafayette
Alexander, Kenneth Lewis *editorial cartoonist*

Laguna Beach
Adler, Jeffrey D. *political consultant, public affairs consultant, crisis management expert*

Laguna Hills
James, Sidney Lorraine *television executive*

Lake Elsinore
Corral, Jeanie Beleyn *journalist, school board administrator*

Lakewood
Fenwick, James H(enry) *editor*

Long Beach
Lobdell, Robert Charles *retired newspaper executive*
Ridder, Daniel Hickey *newspaper publisher*
Ruszkiewicz, Carolyn Mae *newspaper editor*
Zappe, John Paul *city editor, educator*

Los Alamitos
Ayling, Henry Faithful *writer, editor, consultant*

Los Altos
Miller, Ronald Grant *journalist*

Los Angeles
Ansen, David B. *critic, writer*
Archerd, Army (Armand Archerd) *columnist, television commentator*
Askin, Richard Henry, Jr. *entertainment company executive*
†Barber, Gary *motion picture company executive*
Bart, Peter Benton *newspaper editor, film producer, novelist*
Belnap, David Foster *journalist*
Berger, Dan Lee *newspaper wine columnist*
Berman, Arthur Malcolm *newspaper editor*
Bernheimer, Martin *music critic*
Blackburn, Daniel M. *correspondent*
Boyarsky, Benjamin William *journalist*
Boylan, John Patrick *record producer, songwriter*
Busby, Jheryl *record company executive*
Butler, Jeffrey Sheridan *publisher*
†Cafaro, Albert *recording industry executive*
Camron, Roxanne *editor*
Cannon, Louis Simeon *journalist, author*
Cardone, Bonnie Jean *photojournalist*
Charen, Mona *syndicated columnist*
Clarke, Peter *communications and health educator*
Coffey, C. Shelby, III *newspaper editor*
†Cole, Jay N. *magazine publisher*
Cotliar, George J. *newspaper editor*
Crippens, David Lee *broadcast executive*
†Darling, Juanita Marie *correspondent*
Day, Anthony *newspaper correspondent*
Del Olmo, Frank *newspaper editor*
Delugach, Albert Lawrence *journalist*
Dolan, Mary Anne *journalist, columnist*
Dreyfuss, John Alan *journalist*
Dunnahoo, Terry (Mrs. Thomas William Dunnahoo) *editor, author*
Dwyre, William Patrick *journalist, public speaker*
Erburu, Robert F. *media and information company executive*
Falk, EuGene L. *publishing executive*
Field, Ted (Frederick Field) *film and record industry executive*
Fifield, James G. *recording industry executive*
Flanigan, James J(oseph) *journalist*
Foster, Mary Christine *motion picture and television executive*
Friedman, Arthur Meeker *magazine editor, professional motorcycle racer*
Friedman, Robert Lee *film company executive*
Garry, William James *magazine editor*
Garza, Oscar *newspaper editor*
†Gilmore, Mikal George *critic, journalist, author*
Glass, Herbert *music critic, lecturer, editor*
†Globus, Yoram *motion picture company executive*
Grad, Laurie Burrows *food editor*
Grant, David *broadcasting executive*
Grazer, Brian *film company executive*
Groves, Martha *newspaper writer*
†Haimovitz, Jules *broadcasting company executive*
Hall, Jeffrey Stuart *newspaper executive*
Handelman, David Yale *film company executive, lawyer*
Harbert, Ted *broadcast executive*
Hart, John Lewis (Johnny Hart) *cartoonist*
Hearst, George Randolph, Jr. *publishing executive, diversified ranching and real estate executive*
Hessler, Curtis Alan *newspaper publishing company executive*
†Hester, John W. *film company executive*
Hogarth, Burne *cartoonist, illustrator*
Horowitz, David Charles *consumer commentator, newspaper columnist*
†Iovine, Jimmy *recording industry executive*
Isinger, William R. *newspaper publishing executive*
Jarmon, Lawrence *developmental communications educator*
Johnson, John H. *publisher, consumer products executive, chairman*
Jones, Quincy *producer, composer, arranger, conductor, trumpeter*
Kassar, Mario F. *film production company executive*
Katleman, Harris L. *television executive*
Kaye, Jhani *radio station manager, director*
Kingsley, Walter Ingalls *television executive*
Knight, Christopher Allen *art critic*
Kobin, William H. *television station executive*
Ladd, Alan Walbridge, Jr. *motion picture company executive*
Laventhol, David Abram *newspaper editor*
Lazarus, Mell *cartoonist*
Lipstone, Howard Harold *television executive*
Lond, Harley Weldon *editor, publisher*
MacLeod, Robert Fredric *editor, publisher*
Maltin, Leonard *television commentator, writer*
Mancuso, Frank G. *entertainment company executive*
Margulies, Lee *newspaper editor*
Marion, Douglas Welch *magazine editor*
Marsh, Dave Rodney *writer, publisher, editor*
Martinez, Al *journalist, screenwriter*
Maxwell, Donald Stanley *publishing executive*
Michel, Donald Charles *editor*
Miller, Norman Charles, Jr. *newspaper editor*
Murphy, Philip Edward *broadcast executive*
Murray, James Patrick *newspaper columnist*
Neufeld, Mace *film company executive*
Newman, James Austin *financial journalist*
Nogales, Luis Guerrero *communications company executive*
Obst, Lynda Rosen *film company executive, producer, screenwriter*
O'Reilly, Richard Brooks *journalist*
Parks, Michael Christopher *journalist*
Paulson, David L. *newspaper publishing executive*
Perenchio, Andrew Jerrold *film and television executive*
Perlmutter, Donna *music and dance critic*
†Petersen, Robert E. *publisher*
Plate, Thomas Gordon *newspaper editor*
Platt, Mark E. *motion picture company executive*
Radloff, William Hamilton *editor, writer*
Ray, Kelley *production company technical director*
Rehme, Robert G. *film company executive*
Reich, Kenneth Irvin *journalist*
Rense, Paige *editor, publishing company executive*
Rice, Linda Johnson *publishing executive*
Rich, Alan *music critic, editor, author*
Rosenzweig, David *newspaper editor*
Saltzman, Joseph *journalist, producer, educator*
Salzman, David Elliot *entertainment industry executive*
Sansweet, Stephen Jay *journalist, author*
Sarnoff, Thomas Warren *television executive*
Saylor, Mark Julian *editor*
†Schifsky, Charles Mark *magazine editor*
Schlosberg, Richard T., III *newspaper publishing executive*
Schneider, Charles I. *newspaper executive*
Schneider, Wolf *magazine editor, writer*
Scott, Kelly *newspaper editor*
Scully, Vincent Edward *sports broadcaster*
Shaw, David Lyle *journalist, author*
Sigband, Norman Bruce *management communication educator*
Sinay, Hershel David *publisher*
Sloan, L. Lawrence *publishing executive*
Smith, David King *publishing executive, newspaper*
Smith, Jack Clifford *journalist, author*
†Smith, Joe *recording industry executive*
Smith, Lane Jeffrey *automotive journalist, technical consultant*
Smith, Wallace A. *radio company executive*
Spero, Stanley Leonard *broadcast executive*
Stern, Leonard Bernard *television and motion picture production company executive*
Stoddard, Brandon *film and television company executive*
Stolberg, Sheryl Gay *journalist*
Sweeney, Judith L. *newspaper publishing executive*
Tanen, Ned Stone *motion picture company executive*
Tartikoff, Brandon *broadcast executive*
Thomas, Robert Joseph *columnist, author*
Tortorici, Peter Frank *television executive*
Townley, Jon *production company creative director*
Van Dyke, David *broadcast executive*
Verdery, David Norwood *broadcast programming executive*
Ward, Leslie Allyson *journalist, editor*
White, Leonard *motion picture company executive*
Williams, Phillip L. *newspaper publishing executive*
Wilson, Charles Zachary, Jr. *newspaper publisher*
Wolinsky, Leo C. *newspaper editor*
Wright, Donald Franklin *newspaper executive*
Yablans, Frank *film company executive, motion picture producer*
Young, J. Anthony *entertainment company executive*
Zacchino, Narda *newspaper editor*
†Zimmerman, Herman F. *motion picture production designer*

Los Gatos
Meyers, Ann Elizabeth *sports broadcaster*

Marina Del Rey
Doebler, Paul Dickerson *publishing management executive*
Smith, George Drury *publisher, editor, collagist, writer*

Marysville
Hardie, Robert C. *newspaper publishing executive*

Menlo Park
Browne, Millard Child *former newspaper editor*
Litfin, Richard Albert *retired news organization executive*
Marken, William Riley *magazine editor*
Wolaner, Robin Peggy *magazine publisher*

Mill Valley
Leslie, Jacques Robert, Jr. *journalist*

Modesto
LaMont, Sanders Hickey *journalist*

Monterey
Benjamin, David Joel, III *radio broadcasting executive*
Dedini, Eldon Lawrence *cartoonist*
Ketcham, Henry King *cartoonist*
Miller, Susan Heilmann *publishing executive*

Napa
Muedeking, George Herbert *editor*

Newport Beach
Bryant, Thos Lee *magazine editor*
Dean, Paul John *magazine editor*
Homan, Rich *magazine editor*

North Hollywood
Boyle, Barbara Dorman *motion picture company executive*
Hulse, Jerry *journalist*
Loper, James Leaders *broadcasting executive*

Northridge
Boddington, Craig Thornton *magazine editor*
Devol, Kenneth Stowe *journalism educator*

Novato
Pfeiffer, Phyllis Kramer *newspaper company executive*

Oakland
†Bangs, Richard Johnston *publishing executive*
†Burt, Christopher Clinton *publisher*
Clancy, Thomas Gerald *newspaper company executive*
Haiman, Franklyn Saul *author, communications educator*
Kees, Beverly *newspaper editor*
Knight, Jeffrey William *publishing and marketing executive*
McKinney, Judson Thad *broadcast executive*
Poole, Monte LaRue *sports columnist, consultant*
Wood, Larry (Mary Laird) *journalist, author, university educator, public relations executive, environmental consultant*

Oceanside
Howard, Robert Staples *newspaper publisher*

Ontario
Ferguson, Michael Roger *newspaper executive*

Pacific Grove
Davis, Robert Edward *retired communication educator*
Roberts, William M. *publishing executive*
Verduin, Claire Leone *publishing company executive*

Pacific Palisades
Purcell, Patrick B. *motion picture company executive*

Palm Desert
Hartman, Ashley Powell *publishing executive, journalist, educator*

Palm Springs
Browning, Norma Lee (Mrs. Russell Joyner Ogg) *journalist*
Jones, Milton Wakefield *publisher*

Palmdale
Grooms, Larry Willis *newspaper editor*

Palos Verdes Peninsula
King, Nancy *communications educator*

Paradise
Fulton, Len *publisher*

Pasadena
Bergholz, Richard Cady *political writer*
Diehl, Digby Robert *journalist*
Drutchas, Gerrick Gilbert *publishing executive*
Spector, Phil *record company executive*
Wood, Nathaniel Fay *editor, writer, public relations consultant*

Paso Robles
Brown, Benjamin Andrew *journalist*

Portola Valley
Garsh, Thomas Burton *publisher*

Rancho Cordova
Wilderotter, Maggie *cable television executive*

Richmond
Doyle, William Thomas *retired newspaper editor*

Riverside
Foreman, Thomas Elton *drama critic*
Hays, Howard H. (Tim Hays) *editor, publisher*
Maas, Sally Ann *newspaper editor, journalist*
Mc Laughlin, Leighton Bates, II *journalism educator, former newspaperman*
McQuern, Marcia Alice *newspaper publishing executive*
Opotowsky, Maurice Leon *newspaper editor*
Sokolsky, Robert Lawrence *journalist, entertainment writer*

Ross
Godwin, Sara *writer*

Sacramento
Baltake, Joe *film critic*
Blum, Deborah *reporter*
Bottel, Helen Alfea *columnist, writer*
Endicott, William F. *journalist*
Glackin, William Charles *arts critic, editor*
Haugen, D. Peter *theatre critic*
Knudson, Thomas Jeffery *journalist*
Lundstrom, Marjie *newspaper editor*
McClatchy, James B. *editor, newspaper publisher*
Potts, Erwin Rea *newspaper executive*
Schrag, Peter *editor, writer*
Shaw, Eleanor Jane *newspaper editor*
Slater, Manning *broadcasting consultant*
Swatt, Stephen Benton *communications executive, consultant*
Walsh, Denny Jay *reporter*
Walters, Daniel Raymond *political columnist*
Williams, Arthur Cozad *broadcasting executive*

San Bernardino
Burgess, Mary Alice (Mary Alice Wickizer) *publisher*
Fairley Raney, Rebecca *journalist*
Garson, Arnold Hugh *newspaper editor*

San Carlos
Barnard, William Calvert *retired news service executive*

San Clemente
Singer, Kurt Deutsch *news commentator, author, publisher*

San Diego
Bell, Gene *newspaper publishing executive*
Bennett, Ronald Thomas *photojournalist*
Bolman, Pieter Simon Heinrich *publishing company executive, physicist*
Cushman, Thomas Henry *sports editor, columnist*
Freedman, Jonathan Borwick *journalist, author, lecturer*
Hope, Douglas Olerich *newspaper editor*
Jones, Welton H., Jr. *critic*
Kaufman, Julian Mortimer *broadcasting company executive, consultant*
Klein, Herbert George *newspaper editor*
Kopp, Harriet Green *communication specialist*
Krulak, Victor Harold *newspaper executive*
Lee, Marianna *editor*
Mc Kinnon, Clinton D. *editor, former congressman*
Mickelson, Sig *broadcasting executive, educator*
Morgan, Neil *author, newspaper editor, lecturer, columnist*
Pfeffer, Rubin Harry *publishing executive*
Pfeiffer, John William *publisher, management consultant*
Pincus, Robert Lawrence *art critic, cultural historian*
Quintana, Mack *newspaper publishing executive*
Rethmeier, Kenneth Wayne, Jr. *publishing company executive*
Ristine, Jeffrey Alan *reporter*
Rowe, Peter A. *newspaper columnist*
Salamone, Gary P. (Pike Salamone) *newspaper editor-in-chief, cartoonist*
Scher, Valerie Jean *music critic*
Simms, Maria Kay *publishing and computer services executive*
Steen, Paul Joseph *retired broadcasting executive*
Warren, Gerald Lee *newspaper editor*
Winner, Karin *newspaper editor*

San Francisco
Baker, Kenneth *art critic, writer*
Batlin, Robert Alfred *editor*
Bauer, Michael *newspaper editor*
Benet, Thomas Carr *journalist*
Bonetti, David *art critic*
Caen, Herb *newspaper columnist, author*
Carman, John Elwin *journalist*
Carroll, Jon *newspaper columnist*
Chapin, Dwight Allan *columnist, writer*
†Close, Sandy *journalist*
Curley, John Peter *sports editor*
†DeLuca, Nicholas Anthony *broadcasting executive*
Dewey, Phelps *publishing executive*
Dickey, Glenn Ernest, Jr. *sports columnist*
Donnally, Patricia Broderick *newspaper fashion editor*
Duscha, Julius Carl *journalist*
Eastwood, Susan *medical scientific editor*
Garchik, Leah Lieberman *journalist*
†George, Donald Warner *newspaper editor, writer, lecturer*
German, William *newspaper editor*
Graham, Robert Arlington *newspaper entertainment editor*
Graysmith, Robert *political cartoonist, author*
†Hill, Greg *newspaper bureau chief*
Hochschild, Adam *writer, commentator, journalist*
Hoppe, Arthur Watterson *columnist*
Horne, Grant Nelson *corporate communications specialist*
Hoyem, Andrew Lewison *publisher*
Hyde, Stuart Wallace *educator, author*
Jenkins, Bruce *sportswriter*
Kahn, Alice Joyce *columnist*
†Klein, Jeremy Stephen *editor*
Klein, Marc S. *newspaper editor and publisher*
Kobayashi, Tom Toru *motion picture company executive*
Lara, Adair *columnist, writer*
Luckow, Lynn D. W. *publishing executive*
Lufkin, Liz *newspaper editor*
Meyer, Thomas James *editorial cartoonist*
Nachman, Gerald Weil *columnist, critic, author*
Nichols, Robert E(dmund) *editor, writer, journalist*
O'Flaherty, Terrence *journalist*

Osterhaus, William Eric *television executive*
Ostler, Scott *newspaper sports columnist*
Perlman, David *science editor, journalist*
Reed, Robert Daniel *publisher*
Rice, Jonathan C. *educational television executive*
Roberts, Jerry *newspaper editor*
Rosenheim, Daniel Edward *journalist, newspaper editor*
Rubenstein, Steven Paul *newspaper columnist*
Rusher, William Allen *writer, commentator*
Ryan, Joan *sportswriter*
Saunders, Debra J. *columnist*
Schwarz, Glenn Vernon *editor*
Shulgasser, Barbara *writer*
Sias, John B. *multi-media company executive*
Sinton, Peter *newspaper editor, journalist*
Spander, Art *sportswriter*
Steinberg, Michael *music critic, educator*
Susskind, Teresa Gabriel *publisher*
Toms, Michael Anthony *broadcast journalist*
Tulsky, Fredric Neal *journalist*
Wilner, Paul Andrew *journalist*
Wilson, Kenneth Jay *writer*
Wilson, Matthew Frederick *newspaper editor*
Winn, Steven Jay *critic*
Wright, Rosalie Muller *newspaper and magazine editor*
†Yamamoto, Michael Toru *journalist*

San Jose
Bentel, Dwight *emeritus journalism educator*
Carey, Peter Kevin *reporter*
Ceppos, Jerome Merle *newspaper editor*
Elder, Robert Laurie *newspaper editor*
Frymer, Murry *columnist, theater critic, critic-at-large*
Ingle, Robert D. *newspaper editor, newspaper executive*
Lovell, Glenn Michael *film critic*
Migielicz, Geralyn *photojournalist*
Ritzheimer, Robert Alan *educational publishing executive*
Sumrall, Harry *journalist*
Trounstine, Philip J. *editor, journalist*
Yates, Kathleen Barrett *newspaper executive*
†Zenger, John Hancock *publishing company executive*

San Marcos
Barnes, Howard G. *film company executive, film and video producer*

San Rafael
Roffman, Howard *motion picture company executive*

Santa Ana
Cheverton, Richard E. *newspaper editor*
Katz, Tonnie *newspaper editor*
Shaw, David Allen *magazine publisher*
Stern, Sherry Ann *journalist*

Santa Barbara
Ackerman, Marshall *publishing company executive*
Brantingham, Barney *journalist, writer*
†Cameron, Heather A. *publishing executive*
Campbell, William Steen *writer, magazine publisher*
Gallagher, James Wes *journalist*
Gibney, Frank Bray *publisher, editor, writer, foundation executive*
Mitchell, Maurice B. *publishing executive, educator*
Smith, Robert Nathaniel *broadcasting executive, lawyer*
Tapper, Joan Judith *magazine editor*
Wiemann, John Moritz *communications educator, consultant*
Wright, Helene Segal *editor*

Santa Clara
Charles, Mary Louise *newspaper columnist, photographer, editor*
McVay, John Edward *professional football club executive*

Santa Monica
Alpert, Herb *musician, painter, recording artist, theatrical producer, philanthropist*
Baer, Walter S. *research executive*
Holzman, D. Keith *record company executive, producer, arts consultant*
Jacobson, Sidney *editor*
Jenest, Jeffrey Mark *video corporation executive*
Price, Frank *motion picture and television company executive*
Snedaker, Catherine Raupagh (Kit Snedaker) *editor*
Vajna, Andrew G. *film company executive*

Santa Rosa
Person, Evert Bertil *newspaper and radio executive*
Pipal, George Henry *journalist*
Schulz, Charles Monroe *cartoonist*
Swofford, Robert Lee *newspaper editor, journalist*

Sausalito
Brand, Stewart *editor, writer*

Seal Beach
Caesar, Vance Roy *newspaper executive*

Sierra Madre
Dewey, Donald William *magazine editor and publisher, writer*

Simi Valley
Killion, Jack Charles *newspaper columnist*

Somis
Gius, Julius *retired newspaper editor*

Sonoma
Beckmann, Jon Michael *publisher*

South San Francisco
Alvarez, Robert Smyth *editor, publisher*

Stanford
Barnes, Grant Alan *book publisher*
Breitrose, Henry S. *communications educator*
Chaffee, Steven Henry *communication educator*
Maharidge, Dale Dimitro *journalist, educator*
Nelson, Lyle Morgan *communications educator*
Risser, James Vaulx, Jr. *journalist, educator*
Roberts, Donald Frank, Jr. *communications educator*

Stockton
Bookman, Philip *newspaper editor*
Whittington, Robert Bruce *retired publishing company executive*

Summerland
Hall, Lee Boaz *publishing company consultant, author*

Tarzana
Lowy, Jay Stanton *music industry executive*
Shaw, Carole *editor, publisher*
Shaw-Cohen, Lori Eve *magazine editor*

Thousand Oaks
Hale, William Bryan, Jr. *newspaper editor*
Kehrer, Daniel M. *publishing executive, author, journalist*
McCune, David Franklin *publisher*
Van Mols, Brian *publishing executive*

Toluca Lake
Whitesell, John Edwin *motion picture company executive*

Torrance
Adelsman, (Harriette) Jean *newspaper editor*
Conrad, Paul Francis *editorial cartoonist*

Universal City
Horowitz, Zachary I. *entertainment company executive*
Katz, Perry Marc *motion picture company executive*
Lindheim, Richard David *television company executive*
Masket, Edward Seymour *television executive*
Paul, Charles S. *motion picture and television company executive*
Pollock, Thomas P. *motion picture company executive*
Sheinberg, Sidney Jay *recreation and entertainment company executive*
Teller, Alvin Norman *music industry executive*
Wasserman, Lew R. *film, recording and publishing company executive*

Valencia
McGlasson, James Dean *publishing executive*

Valley Village
†Stevenson, Michael Anson *motion picture film editor*

Van Nuys
Fraser, Julia Diane *publishing executive*
Frons, Brian Scott *television executive*
Sludikoff, Stanley Robert *publisher, writer*

Venice
Shapazian, Robert Michael *publishing executive*

Ventura
Greig, William Taber, Jr. *publishing company executive*
Kirman, Charles Gary *photojournalist*

Walnut Creek
Haswell, T. Clayton *newspaper editor*
Lesher, Margaret Lisco *newspaper publisher, songwriter*
Satz, Louis K. *publishing executive*

West Covina
†Pollak, Sam *sports editor, columnist*

West Hollywood
Byrne, Edward Blake *broadcasting company executive*
Fein, Irving Ashley *television and motion picture executive*
Geffen, David *recording company executive, producer*
Pasternak, Kathryn Ann *filmmaker*
Sanello, Frank Anthony *journalist, columnist*
Van Buren, Abigail (Pauline Friedman Phillips) *columnist, author, writer, lecturer*

Whittier
Loughrin, Jay Richardson *mass communications educator, consultant*

Woodland Hills
DeWitt, Barbara Jane *journalist*
Fisher, Gerald Saul *publisher, financial consultant, lawyer*
Gray, Thomas Stephen *newspaper editor*
Neill, William Alexander *magazine editor*
Rapoport, Ronald Jon *journalist*

COLORADO

Boulder
Birkenkamp, Dean Frederick *editor, publishing executive*
Bowers, John Waite *communication educator*
Davis, Donald Alan *author, news correspondent, lecturer*
Rienner, Lynne Carol *publisher*

Colorado Springs
Anderson, N. Christian, III *newspaper publisher*
Conter, Thomas Michael *publisher*
Nolan, Barry Hance *publishing company executive*
Zapel, Arthur L. *book publishing executive*

Crawford
Mosher, Lawrence Forsyth *journalist*

Denver
Barnewall, Gordon Gouverneur *news analyst, educator*
Bates, James Robert *newspaper editor*
Bradley, Jeff(rey) M. *arts critic*
Brom, Libor *journalist, educator*
Cubbison, Christopher Allen *editor*
Dallas, Sandra *correspondent, writer*
Dobbs, Gregory Allan *journalist*
Drake, Sylvie (Jurras Drake) *theater critic*
Dubroff, Henry Allen *journalist*
Engdahl, Todd Philip *newspaper editor*
Giffin, Glenn Orlando, II *music critic, writer, newspaper editor*
Green, Charles Walter *newspaper editor*
Hamblin, Kenneth Lorenzo *radio talk show host, columnist*
Hesse, Stephen Max *newspaper executive*
Hunt, Donald F. *newspaper publishing executive*
May, Clifford Daniel *newspaper editor, journalist*
McGowan, Joseph Anthony, Jr. *news executive*
McKibben, Ryan Timothy *newspaper executive*
Morgese, James N. *broadcast executive*
Movshovitz, Howard Paul *film critic, educator*
Otto, Jean Hammond *journalist*
Spencer, Frederick Gilman *newspaper editor in chief*
Stephenson, Toni Edwards *publisher, investment management executive*
Strutton, Larry D. *newspaper executive*
Udevitz, Norman *publishing executive*
Ulevich, Neal Hirsh *photojournalist*
Zeilig, Nancy Meeks *magazine editor*

Dillon
Follett, Robert John Richard *publisher*

Durango
Ballantine, Morley Cowles (Mrs. Arthur Atwood Ballantine) *newspaper editor*

Englewood
Beddow, David Pierce *broadcasting and cable executive*
†Hall, Kurt *movie theatre executive*
Schneider, Gene W. *cable television company executive, movie theater executive*

Fort Collins
Christiansen, Norman Juhl *retired newspaper publisher*
Sons, Raymond William *journalist*

Georgetown
Stern, Mort(imer) P(hillip) *journalism and communications educator, academic administrator, consultant*

Golden
Baron, Robert Charles *publishing executive*

Grand Junction
Hammer, Jan Harold *television station manager*

Lakewood
Hosokawa, William K. *newspaper columnist, author*
Myers, Harry J., Jr. *publisher*

Longmont
Stewart, William Gene *broadcast executive*

Mc Coy
Hastings, Merrill George, Jr. *publisher, marketing consultant*

Middletown
Mac Lam, Helen *editor, periodical*

Pueblo
Rawlings, Robert Hoag *newspaper publisher*

Univ Of Denver
Dance, Francis Esburn Xavier *communication educator*

Winter Park
Johnson, William Potter *newspaper publisher*

CONNECTICUT

Bridgeport
Henderson, Albert *publishing company executive, dairy executive, consultant*
Thomas, Dudley Breckinridge *newspaper pubisher*

Bristol
Melrose, Barry James *sportscaster, former professional hockey team coach*
Simms, Phillip *sports commentator, former professional football player*

Brookfield
Reynolds, Jean Edwards *publishing executive*

Chester
Cobb, Hubbard Hanford *magazine editor, writer*

Cornwall Bridge
Galazka, Jacek Michal *publishing company executive*

Cos Cob
Hauptman, Michael *broadcasting company executive*
Senter, William Joseph *publishing company executive*

Danbury
Leish, Kenneth William *publishing company executive*
Lisimachio, Jean Louis *book publishing executive*
†Primm, Earl Russell, III *publishing executive*
Toman, Stephen E. *educational publishing company executive*

Darien
Allen, Joseph Henry *retired publishing company executive*
Becker, Ralph Edward *broadcast executive, consultant*
Brooke, Avery Rogers *publisher, writer*

Durham
†Mack, Charles David *magazine educator*

Enfield
Hostetter, Amos Barr, Jr. *cable television executive*
Neher, Timothy Pyper *cable company executive*

Essex
Kenyon, Charles Moir *publishing company executive*

Fairfield
Cox, Richard Joseph *former broadcasting executive*
Limpitlaw, John Donald *retired publishing executive, clergyman*
Spence, Barbara E. *publishing company executive*

Greens Farms
Deford, Frank *sportswriter, television and radio commentator, author*

Greenwich
Bogart, Robert B. *publishing company executive*
Chapman, Gilbert Whipple, Jr. *publishing company executive*
Collins, Richard Lawrence *magazine editor, publisher, author*
Gately, George (Gallagher Gately) *cartoonist*
Goldmann, Peter D. *editor*
Hanson, Maurice Francis (Maury Hanson) *retired magazine publisher and editor*
Keogh, James *journalist*
Lurie, Ranan Raymond *political analyst, political cartoonist, artist, lecturer*
Pfeiffer, Jane Cahill *former broadcasting company executive, consultant*
Rukeyser, Louis Richard *economic commentator*
Schutz, Herbert Dietrich *publishing executive*
Shaffer, David H. *publishing company executive*
Shepard, Thomas Rockwell, Jr. *publishing consultant*

Hartford
Endrst, James Bryan *television critic, columnist*
Englehart, Robert Wayne, Jr. *cartoonist*
Golden, Louis Joseph *former business news editor, newspaper executive*
Harden, Jon Bixby *publishing executive*
Horgan, Denis Edward *journalist*
King, Richard Hood *newspaper executive*
Koupal, Raymond *newspaper publishing executive*
Lumsden, Lynne Ann *publishing company executive*
Noel, Don Obert, Jr. *newspaper columnist*
Pach, Peter Barnard *newspaper columnist and editor*
Renner, Gerald Anthony *journalist*
Roessner, Barbara *journalist*
Schweitzer, N. Tina *photojournalist, television producer, director, writer, international consultant public relations, media relations, government relations*
Zakarian, John J. *journalist*

Ivoryton
Bendig, William Charles *editor, artist, publisher*

Lakeville
Barnes, Robert Goodwin *publishing consultant*
Estabrook, Robert Harley *journalist*

Lyme
Bessie, Simon Michael *publisher*

Madison
Azarian, Martin Vartan *publishing company executive*
Egbert, Emerson Charles *publisher*
Platt, Sherman Phelps, Jr. *publishing consultant*
Purcell, Bradford Moore *publishing company executive*

Middletown
Balay, Robert Elmore *magazine editor, reference librarian*
Cumming, Robert Emil *editor*
D'Oench, Russell Grace, Jr. *publishing consultant*
Marteka, Vincent James, Jr. *magazine editor, writer*

New Canaan
Hanson, Joseph J. *publishing executive*
Thomas, Robert Dean *publisher*

New Haven
Butler, David J. *newspaper editor*
Edelson, Zelda Sarah Toll *editor*
Leeney, Robert Joseph *newspaper editor*
McClatchy, J. D. *editor, writer, educator*
McMullin, Ruth Roney *publishing company executive, management fellow*
McMunn, Richard Earl *editor, writer*
Rush, William John *newspaper executive*
Ryden, John Graham *publishing executive*

New London
MacCluggage, Reid *newspaper editor, publisher*
McGinley, Morgan *newspaper editor*

Newtown
Cayne, Bernard Stanley *editor*

North Haven
Walker, Fred Elmer *broadcasting executive*

Norwalk
Bowman, Robert Gibson *publishing company executive*
Brooks, Babert Vincent *publisher*
Howatson, Marianne *publisher*
Partch, Kenneth Paul *editor, consultant*

Old Greenwich
Islan, Gregory deFontaine *cable television executive*
Kenyon, Robert Edwin, Jr. *magazine journalist, magazine consultant, lecturer*

Old Saybrook
Jensen, Oliver Ormerod *editor, writer*

Ridgefield
Forbes, James Wendell *publishing consultant*

Riverside
Isaacson, Gerald Sidney *publishing company executive*

Rowayton
Moran, John Patrick, Jr. *publishing executive, marketing consultant*

Salem
Diamond, Sigmund *editor, educator*

Sharon
Gordon, Nicholas *broadcasting executive*

Shelton
Forbes, Richard E. *retired publishing company executive*
McCurdy, Charles Gribbel *publishing company executive*
Wham, William Neil *publisher*

Sherman
Valeriani, Richard Gerard *news broadcaster*

Stamford
Aylesworth, Thomas Gibbons *editor, author*
Bigelow, Eugene Thayer, Jr. *media company executive*
Britt, Glenn Alan *media company executive*
Chiddix, James Alan *cable television engineering executive*
Collins, Joseph J. *television services company executive*
Conover, Harvey *retired publisher*
Doolittle, James H. *cable television systems company executive*
Fossel, Peter VanBrunt *magazine editor and publisher*
Ingrum, Adrienne Gillette *book publisher*
Johnson, Martin Allen *publisher*
Lane, Hana Umlauf *editor*
O'Neill, Robert Edward *business journal editor*
Paul, Thomas A. *book publisher*
Rowe, William John *newspaper publishing executive*
Sayers, Richard James *newspaper editor*
Veronis, Peter *publisher*
Wilensky, Julius M. *publishing company executive*

Trumbull
Doherty, Donna Kathryn *editor*
Ferm, David G. *magazine publisher*
FitzGerald, James W. (Jay) *magazine publisher*
Galvin, Terry *magazine editor*
Seitz, Nicholas Joseph *magazine editor*
Tarde, Gerard *magazine editor*

Waterbury
Pape, William James, II *newspaper publisher*

West Cornwall
Klaw, Barbara Van Doren *author, editor*

West Granby
Conland, Stephen *publishing company executive*

West Hartford
Glixon, David M(orris) *editor*

West Haven
Ellis, Lynn Webster *management educator, telecommunications consultant*

Westport
Angle, Richard Warner, Jr. *not-for-profit and publishing executive*
Britt, David Van Buren *educational communications executive*
Bronson, Carole *publishing executive*
Brooks, Andrée Aelion *journalist, educator, author*
Davis, Joel *publisher*
Dunton, James Raynor *publisher*
Enos, Randall *cartoonist, illustrator*
Hagelstein, Robert Philip *publisher*
Harris, Cynthia Coolidge Mead *executive editor*
Joseph, Michael Thomas *broadcast consultant*
Knopf, Alfred, Jr. *retired publisher*
Kramer, Sidney B. *publisher, lawyer, literary agent*
McCormack, Donald Paul *newspaper consultant*
McCormack, Patricia Seger *independent press service editor, journalist*
Meckler, Alan Marshall *publisher, author*
Murphy, Thomas John *publishing executive*
Ross, John Michael *editor, magazine publisher*
Sabin, James Thomas *publisher*

Wilton
Cutler, Theodore John *cable company executive*
Joseloff, Gordon Frederic *journalist, editor*
Morris, Michael J. *book publishing executive*
Pemberton, Jeffery Kenneth *publisher*
Weissman, Robert Evan *information services company executive*

DELAWARE

New Castle
Cansler, Leslie Ervin *retired newspaper editor*

Wilmington
DeVivo, Sal J. *newspaper executive*
Kusheloff, David Leon *journalist*

DISTRICT OF COLUMBIA

Washington
Abel, Elie *reporter, broadcaster, educator*
Adams, Lorraine *reporter*
Adams, Robert Edward *journalist*
†Allen, Henry Southworth *journalist*
†Allen, William L. *editor*
Andrews, John Frank *editor, author, educator*
Andrews, Wyatt *news correspondent*
Angier, Natalie Marie *science journalist*
Anton, Frank A. *publishing executive*
Apple, Raymond Walter, Jr. *journalist*
Arnett, Peter *journalist*
Arnold, Gary Howard *film critic*
Arnovitz, Benton Mayer *editor*
Attkisson, Sharyl T. *news correspondent, writer*
Aug, Stephen M. *business journalist*
†Aukofer, Frank Alexander *journalist*
Bailey, Charles Waldo, II *journalist, author*
Baldwin, Deborah *editor*
Bancroft, Elizabeth Abercrombie *publisher, analytic chemist*
Bandow, Douglas Leighton *editor, columnist, policy consultant*
Barbash, Fred *journalist, author*
Barnes, Frederic Wood, Jr. *journalist*
Barone, Michael D. *journalist*
Barrett, Laurence Irwin *journalist*
†Bartlett, David Conant *journalist*
Beach, Walter Eggert *publishing organization executive*
Beale, Betty (Mrs. George K. Graeber) *columnist, writer*
Begleiter, Ralph J. *correspondent*
Beltz, William Albert *publisher*
Bentley, James Luther *journalist*
Bierbauer, Charles *correspondent, news analyst*
Block, Herbert Lawrence (Herblock) *editorial cartoonist*
Bradlee, Benjamin Crowninshield *executive editor*
Braestrup, Peter *editor*
Branigin, William Joseph *journalist*
Braverman, Jordan *columnist*
Brazaitis, Thomas Joseph *journalist*
Bredemeier, Kenneth Herbert *journalist*
Brinkley, David McClure *news commentator*
†Brinkley, Joel Graham *journalist*
Brock, Gerald Wayne *telecommunications educator*
Broder, David Salzer *reporter*
Brown, John Patrick *newspaper executive, financial consultant*
Brown, Richard Laurence *broadcast executive*
Bruno, Harold Robinson, Jr. *journalist*
Buchwald, Art *columnist, writer*
Burzynski, Norman Stephen *editor*
Byrd, Joann Kathleen *newswriter*
Carlson, Richard Warner *journalist, diplomat, federal agency administrator, broadcast executive*
Carmody, John *newspaper columnist*
Carto, Willis Allison *publishing executive*
Chronister, Gregory Michael *newspaper editor*
Clift, Eleanor *magazine correspondent*
Clurman, Michael *newspaper publishing executive*
Cocco, Marie Elizabeth *journalist*
Cohen, Richard Martin *journalist*
Cohn, Victor Edward *journalist*
Coll, Stephen Wilson *journalist*
Compton, Ann Woodruff *news correspondent*
Conroy, Sarah Booth *columnist, novelist, speaker, editor*
Cosgrove, John Patrick *editor*
Cowan, Edward *journalist*
Cowen, Eugene Sherman *broadcasting executive*
Crenshaw, Albert Burford *journalist*
Crewdson, John Mark *journalist, author*
Cromley, Allan Wray *journalist*
Cromley, Raymond Avolon *syndicated columnist*
Crowley, Candy Alt *news correspondent*
Curry, George Edward *journalist*
Cutler, Bernard Joseph *editor-in-chief, writer*
Dancy, John Albert *news correspondent*
Daniel, Leon *journalist, newspaper columnist, editor*
Dash, Leon DeCosta, Jr. *journalist*
Davis, Evelyn Y. *editor, writer, publisher, investor*
Davis, Garry (S. Gareth Davis) *publishing executive*
Davis, Sid *journalist*
Deane, James Garner *magazine editor, conservationist*
Dearth, Jeffrey L. *magazine publisher*
de Borchgrave, Arnaud *editor, writer, lecturer*
Denlinger, John Kenneth *journalist*
Dickinson, William Boyd, Jr. *editorial consultant*
Dillman, Grant *journalist*
Dirda, Michael *book critic*
Dixon, Phillip *newspaper editor*
Doan, Michael Frederick *editor*
Donaldson, Samuel Andrew *journalist*
Dorn, James Andrew *editor*
Downie, Leonard, Jr. *newspaper editor, author*
Drew, Elizabeth *television commentator, journalist*
†Dujack, Stephen Raymond *editor*
Dunsmore, Barrie *television news correspondent*
Edsall, Thomas Byrne *reporter*
Edwards, Bob (Robert Alan Edwards) *radio news anchor*
Edwards, Julia Spalding *journalist*
Elfin, Mel *magazine editor*
Elsasser, Glen Robert *writer, editor*
Engberg, Eric Jon *news correspondent*
Epstein, Joseph *editor, writer, educator*
Epstein, Kalman Noel *newspaper publishing company executive*
Epstein, Sidney *editor*
Evans, Rowland, Jr. *newspaper columnist*
†Evans, Thomas R. *magazine publisher*
Feld, Karen Irma *columnist, journalist, public speaker*
Felker, Alex D. *communications executive*
Felton, Gordon H. *retired publishing executive*
Ferguson, Thomas H. *newspaper executive*
Fields, Suzanne Bregman *syndicated columnist*
Foote, Timothy Gilson *editor*
Forgey, Benjamin Franklin *architecture and art critic*
†Fox, Charles Washington, III *international broadcasting executive*
Francis, Samuel Todd *columnist*
Frank, Richard Sanford *magazine editor*
Franzen, Byron T. (John Franzen) *media specialist*
†Fritts, Edward O. *broadcast executive*
Furgurson, Ernest Baker, Jr. (Pat Furgurson) *journalist*
Gart, Murray Joseph *journalist*
Geyer, Georgie Anne *syndicated columnist, educator, author, biographer*
Gilliam, Dorothy Butler *columnist*
Gilmour, Craddock Matthew, Jr. (Sandy Gilmour) *television news correspondent*
Glaser, Vera Romans *journalist*
Glass, Andrew James *newspaper editor*
Glassman, James Kenneth *editor, writer, publishing executive*
†Gonzales, Richard Steven *broadcast journalist*
Graham, Donald Edward *publisher*
Graham, Fred Patterson *journalist, lawyer*
Graham, Katharine *newspaper executive*
Graves, William P. E. *editor*
Gray, Ralph *editor, writer*
Greenfield, Meg *journalist*
Greenwood, William Warren *journalist*
Grefé, Richard *graphic design executive*
Gregory, Bettina Louise *journalist*
Griffith, Patricia King *journalist*
Grosvenor, Gilbert Melville *journalist, educator, business executive*
Gruenberg, Mark Jonathan *correspondent*
Gunther, Marc *television writer*
Gutman, Roy William *reporter*
†Guzy, Carol *photojournalist*
Gwaltney, Corbin *editor, publishing executive*
Hadar, Mary Ellen *newspaper editor*
Hager, Robert *journalist*
Hales, Linda *newspaper editor*
Hallinan, Joseph Thomas *journalist, correspondent*
Halsey, Linda *newspaper editor*
Hamachek, Ross Frank *media company executive*
Harden, Blaine Charles *journalist*
Hartman, (Howard) Carl *newspaperman*
Harwood, Richard Lee *journalist, newspaper editor*
Headden, Susan M. *editor*
Hecht, Marjorie Mazel *editor*
Herbers, Tod Arthur *publisher*
Herman, Andrea Maxine *newspaper editor*
Herman, George Edward *radio and television correspondent*
Hersh, Seymour M. *journalist*
Hey, Robert Pierpont *editor association bulletin*
Hillgren, Sonja Dorothy *journalist*
†Hilts, Philip James *correspondent*
Hinden, Stanley Jay *newspaper editor*
Hinson, Hal *film critic*
Hoagland, Jimmie Lee *newspaper editor*
†Hodgson, Frederick Kimmel *radio station executive*
Holliman, John *news broadcaster*
Horyn, Cathy *newspaper editor*
Hume, Brit (Alexander Britton Hume) *journalist*
Hume, Paul Chandler *music editor, music educator*
Hunt, Albert R. *newspaper executive*
Ignatius, David *newspaper editor*
Innerst, Preston Eugene *newspaper editor, journalist*
Irvine, Reed John *media critic, corporation executive*
Jankowski, Gene F. *broadcasting executive*
Johnson, Haynes Bonner *author, journalist*
Johnson, Robert Louis *cable television company executive*
Jones, Leonade Diane *newspaper publishing company executive*
Jones, Philip Howard *broadcast journalist*
Kaiser, Robert Greeley *newspaper editor*
Karayn, James, Jr. *broadcasting executive*
Karmin, Monroe William *senior editor*
Kaulkin, Donna Brookman *editor, writer*
Kempley, Rita A. *film critic, editor*
Kempster, Norman Roy *journalist*
Kern, Harry Frederick *editor*
Kilborn, Peter Thurston *journalist*
Kilian, Michael David *journalist, columnist, writer*
King, Larry (Larry Zeiger) *broadcaster, radio personality*
King, Nina Davis *journalist*
Kinsley, Michael E. *magazine editor*
Kiplinger, Knight A. *journalist, publisher*
Kirk, Donald *journalist*
Klass, Philip Julian *technical journalist, electrical engineer*
Knight, Athelia Wilhelmenia *journalist*
Kole, John William *writer*
Koppel, Ted *broadcast journalist*
Kornheiser, Anthony I. *journalist*
Kotz, Nathan Kallison (Nick Kotz) *news correspondent*
†Kurkjian, Stephen Anoosh *journalist*
Laden, Susan *publishing consultant*
Laessig, Walter Bruce *publishing executive*
Lanouette, William John *writer, public policy analyst*
Lardner, George, Jr. *journalist*
Lawson, Jennifer *broadcast executive*
LeBrecht, Thelma Jane Mossman *reporter*
Leeds, Charles Alan *publishing executive*
Lehrer, James Charles *television journalist*
Lepkowski, Wil (Wilbert Charles Lepkowski) *journalist*
Leubsdorf, Carl Philipp *newspaper executive*
Levey, Robert Frank *newspaper columnist*
Levine, Irving Raskin *news commentator, author, lecturer*
Lewis, Charles Joseph *journalist*
†Lewis, Delano Eugene *broadcast executive*
Limpert, John Arthur *editor*
Loker, Elizabeth St. John *newspaper executive*
Lorsung, Thomas Nicholas *editor-in-chief, director*
Lubar, Jeffrey Stuart *journalist*
Lutz, Theodore Compton *newspaper publishing executive*
Mack, Raymond Francis *newspaper executive*
Malarkey, Martin Francis, Jr. *cable television executive*
Malone, Julia Louise *news reporter, White House correspondent*
Maraniss, David *reporter*
Marquis, Christopher Holliday *newspaper correspondent*
Martin, John Joseph *journalist*
Maxa, Rudolph Joseph, Jr. *journalist*
Maynes, Charles William *editor, former government official*
McAllister, William Howard, III *newspaper reporter, columnist*
Mc Curdy, Patrick Pierre *editor, consultant*
McDowell, Charles R. *columnist, news analyst, lecturer*
Mc Grory, Mary *columnist*
McLellan, Joseph Duncan *critic, journalist*
Means, Marianne *political columnist*
Mears, Walter Robert *journalist*
Melendy, David Russell *broadcast journalist*
Merrill, Philip *publisher*
Merry, Robert William *publishing executive*
Meszar, Frank *publishing executive, former army officer*
Meyer, Lawrence Robert *journalist*
Meyerson, Adam *magazine editor, foundation executive*
Miklaszewski, James Alan *television news correspondent*
Mitchell, Andrea *journalist*
Morris, Daniel Kearns *journalist*
Moser, Donald Bruce *magazine editor*
†Moss, Madison Scott *editor*
Murphy, Caryle Marie *foreign correspondent*
Murphy, Frances Louise, II *newspaper publisher*
Murphy, Reg *publishing executive*
†Murray, Alan Stewart *publishing executive*
Naylor, Brian *news correspondent*
Neighmond, Patricia *reporter*
Nelson, John Howard (Jack Howard Nelson) *journalist*
Nelson, Lars-Erik *newspaperman*
Newman, Barbara Pollock *journalist, television writer, producer.*
Novak, Robert David Sanders *newspaper columnist, television commentator*
Nover, Naomi *journalist, editor, author*
O'Brien, Timothy Andrew *writer, journalist, lawyer*
Oppel, Richard Alfred *newspaper executive*
Orr, J. Scott *newspaper correspondent*
Parshall, Gerald *journalist*
Paxson, Richard *newspaper editor*
Peirce, Neal R. *journalist*
Pell, Ernest Eugene *broadcasting executive*
†Perkins, Lucian *photographer*
Peter, Frances Marchbank *author, editor, research agency administrator, writer, strategic planner*
Peters, Charles Given, Jr. *editor*
Pettit, William Thomas *broadcasting journalist*
†Phelps, Timothy Miller *reporter*
Phlegar, Benjamin Focht *retired magazine editor*
Pincus, Walter Haskell *editor*
Pines, Burton Yale *broadcasting executive*
Plante, William Madden *news correspondent*
Poteete, Robert Arthur *editor*
Potter, Deborah Ann *news correspondent, educator*
Povich, Shirley Lewis *columnist, former sports editor*
Powell, Anne Elizabeth *editor*
Prah, Pamela Marie *journalist*
†Price, Tom *journalist*
Prina, L(ouis) Edgar *journalist*
Pruden, James Wesley *newspaper editor, columnist*
Putzel, Michael *journalist*
Quinn, Sally *journalist*
Quinn-Judge, Paul Malachy *journalist*
Rabel, Ed *news correspondent*
Randall, Gene *news correspondent, anchor*
Rankin, Robert Arthur *journalist*
Raspberry, William James *journalist*
Richard, Paul *art critic*
†Richburg, Keith Bernard *journalist, foreign correspondent*
Richman, Phyllis Chasanow *newspaper critic*
Ridgeway, James Fowler *journalist*
Roberts, Corinne Boggs (Cokie Roberts) *correspondent, news analyst*
Rogers, Warren Joseph, Jr. *journalist*
Rooney, William Richard *magazine editor*
Roosevelt, Edith Kermit *journalist*
Rose, Lloyd *theatre critic*
Rosen, Gerald Robert *editor*
Rosenbloom, Morris Victor *author, publisher, public relations executive, government official*
Rosenfeld, Stephen Samuel *newspaper editor*
Rosenthal, Andrew *newspaper editor*
Ross, Robinette Davis *publisher*
Ross, Wendy Clucas *newspaper editor, journalist*
Rowan, Carl Thomas *columnist*
Rowson, Richard Cavanagh *publisher*
Ruby, Michael *magazine executive*
Russert, Timothy John *broadcast journalist, executive*
Safire, William *journalist, author*
Salinger, Pierre Emil George *journalist*
†Sartore, Joel *photojournalist*
Scali, John Alfred *journalist*
Scheibel, Kenneth Maynard *journalist*
Schiavone, Louise L. *political correspondent, news analyst*
Schiff, Margaret Scott *newspaper publishing executive*
Schneider, Keith Hilary *news correspondent, journalist*
Schram, Martin Jay *journalist*
Schwartz, Amy Elizabeth *editorial writer, columnist*
Seidman, L(ewis) William *television commentator*
Semas, Philip Wayne *editor*
Serafin, Barry D. *television news correspondent*
Sesno, Frank *executive editor*
Shales, Thomas William *writer, journalist, television and film critic*
Shanks, Hershel *editor, writer*
Shannon, Donald Hawkins *retired newspaperman*
Sharpe, Rochelle Phyllis *journalist*
Shaw, Bernard *television journalist*
Shaw, Gaylord *newspaper executive*
Sheehan, Neil *reporter, scholarly writer*
Sherman, Charles Edwin *broadcasting executive, educator*
Shiner, Josette Sheeran *editor*
Shogan, Robert *news correspondent*
Shribman, David Marks *editor*
Sidey, Hugh Swanson *correspondent*
Siegel, Robert Charles *broadcast journalist*
Simon, Roger *newspaper columnist, author*
Simpson, Carole Estelle *broadcast journalist*
Singer, Suzanne Fried *editor*
Skene, G(eorge) Neil *publisher, lawyer*
Sloyan, Patrick Joseph *journalist*
Smith, Dean *communications advisor, arbitrator*
Smith, Jack Prescott *journalist*
Smith, Stephen Grant *journalist*
Smith, Terence Fitzgerald *television news correspondent*
Solomon, George M. *newspaper editor*
Spears, Gregory Luttrell *journalist*
Sperling, Godfrey, Jr. *journalist*
Spoon, Alan Gary *communications and publishing executive*
Stamberg, Susan Levitt *radio broadcaster*
Steele, John Lawrence *journalist*
Stepp, Laura Sessions *journalist*
Stern, Carl Leonard *former news correspondent, federal official*
Stewart, John Daugherty *publishing company executive*
†Stout, Anthony Carder *publisher*
Sullivan, John Fox *publisher*
†Suskind, Ronald Steven *journalist*
Szulc, Tad *journalist, commentator*
Taishoff, Lawrence Bruce *publishing company executive*
Talbott, Strobe *journalist*
Terzian, Philip Henry *journalist*
Thomas, Helen A. (Mrs. Douglas B. Cornell) *newspaper bureau executive*
Thomas, Jacqueline Marie *journalist, editor*
Thompson, Edward Kramer *editor, publisher*
Thompson, Richard C. *magazine executive*
Tiede, Tom Robert *journalist*
†Tillery, Richard Lee *television executive*
Tolchin, Martin *newspaper reporter, author*
Toledano, Ralph de *columnist, author, photographer*
Tolson, John J. *editor*
Totenberg, Nina *journalist*
Toth, Robert Charles *polling consultant, journalist*
Trafford, Abigail *editor, writer, columnist*
†Trueheart, Charles *journalist, university administrator*
Tufty, Harold Guilford *editor, publisher*
†Turner, Douglas Laird *writer, editor, columnist*
Valenti, Jack Joseph *motion picture executive*
Vernon, Weston, III (Wes Vernon) *journalist*
Vise, David Allan *journalist*
Walcott, John L. *journalist*
†Walker, Ronald C. *magazine publisher*
Wallace, Christopher *broadcast television correspondent*
Warren, Albert *publishing executive*
Watson, George Henry, Jr. *broadcast executive, journalist*
Weiner, Timothy Emlyn *newspaper journalist*
West, Donald Valentine *editor, journalist*

West, Marvin Leon *managing editor*
White, Robert M., II *newspaper executive, editor, columnist*
Will, George Frederick *editor, political columnist, news commentator*
Willis, Clayton *broadcaster, corporation executive, former government official, educator, arts consultant, photojournalist, lecturer*
Wilson, Robert Spencer *magazine editor*
Winter, Thomas Swanson *editor, newspaper executive*
Witcover, Jules Joseph *newspaper columnist, author*
Woodruff, Judy Carline *broadcast journalist*
Woodward, Robert Upshur *newspaper reporter, writer*
Wooten, James Terrell *journalist*
Yardley, Jonathan *journalist, columnist*
Young, Patrick *editor*
Zelnick, Carl Robert *Congressional correspondent*
Zimmerman, Richard Gayford *journalist*

FLORIDA

Apopka
Brandner, J. William *publishing company executive, insurance company executive*

Babson Park
Morrison, Kenneth Douglas *newspaper columnist*

Bayonet Point
Smith, Frank Edward *publisher, editor*

Boca Raton
Frank, Stanley Donald *publishing company executive*
Rodman, R. Arlene *journalist*
Rukeyser, M. S., Jr. *television consultant, writer*

Boynton Beach
Beisel, Daniel Cunningham *former newspaper publisher*

Bradenton
Blancett, Suzanne Smith *editor-in-chief*
Crouthamel, Thomas Grover, Sr. *editor*
Godfrey, Paul *publisher*
McFarland, Richard Macklin *retired journalist*
Sgroi, Mario *publishing executive*
White, Dale Andrew *journalist*

Clearwater
Darack, Arthur J. *editor*
Paxson, Lowell White *television station executive*
Pinch, John G. *radio executive*

Coral Gables
Eisner, Peter Norman *reporter, correspondent*
Hertz, Arthur Herman *communications executive*

Daytona Beach
Davidson, Herbert M. (Tippen), Jr. *newspaper publisher*
Davidson, Josephine F. *newspaper editor*
Gardner, Joseph Lawrence *editor, writer*
Mechem, Charles Stanley, Jr. *former broadcasting executive, golf association executive*
O'Reilly, Don *reporter, writer, photographer*

Deerfield Beach
Hochberger, Simon *communications educator*

Delray Beach
Cary, James Donald *journalist*
Peoples, Thomas Edward *publisher, executive, writer*
Shannon, Stephen Quinby, Jr. *broadcasting and human resources executive*

Dover
Pearson, Walter Donald *editor, columnist*

Dunedin
Geer, James Hamilton *retired broadcasting company executive*

Eastpoint
Hoffer, Thomas William *communications educator*

Fort Lauderdale
Aleff, Andrea Lee (Andy Aleff) *newspaper editor*
Cryer, Eugene Edward *newspaper editor*
de Leon, Lidia Maria *magazine editor*
Doane, Harold Everett *recording executive*
Eisner, Will *publishing company executive*
Gilbert, Anne Wieland *journalist*
Greenberger, Sheldon Lee *newspaper advertising executive*
Keller, Larry Allan *reporter*
Klein, Bernard *publishing company executive*
Maucker, Earl Robert *newspaper editor, newspaper executive*
Parkyn, John William *editor, writer*
Pettijohn, Fred Phillips *retired newspaper executive, consultant*
Schulte, Frederick James *newspaper editor*
Smith, James Edward *newspaper company executive*
Soeteber, Ellen *journalist, newspaper editor*
Tenaglia, John Franc *broadcasting executive*

Fort Myers
Barbour, Hugh Revell *publisher*
Barbour, William Rinehart, Jr. *retired book publisher*

Fort Walton Beach
Phillips, Loyal *newspaper executive*

Gainesville
Barber, Charles Edward *newspaper executive, journalist*
Bedell, George Chester *retired publisher, educator, priest*
Davis, Horance Gibbs, Jr. *retired educator, journalist*
Henson, (Betty) Ann *media specialist, educator*
Hollien, Harry Francis *speech and communications scientist, educator*
Kenney, Thomas Frederick *broadcasting executive*

Goldenrod
Carmichael, William Jerome *publishing company executive*

Hollywood
Fell, Frederick Victor *publisher*
Korngold, Alvin Leonard *broadcasting company executive*
McQueen, Scott Robert *broadcasting company executive*

Homestead
Crouse, John Oliver, II *journalist*

Jacksonville
Brown, Lloyd Harcourt, Jr. *newspaper editor*
Fredrickson, Arthur Allan *retired publishing company executive*
Hartmann, Frederick William *newspaper editor*
Kress, Mary Elizabeth *newspaper editor*
Loomis, Henry *former broadcasting company executive, former government official*
Morris, William Shivers, III *newspaper executive*
Vincent, Norman Fuller *broadcasting executive*
Walters, John Sherwood *retired newspaperman*

Jupiter
Anderson, Thomas Jefferson *publisher, rancher, public speaker, syndicated columnist*

Lake Mary
Franzen, Janice Marguerite Gosnell *magazine editor*
Strang, Stephen Edward *magazine editor, publisher*

Lake Worth
Calder, Iain Wilson *publishing company executive*
†Rabinowitz, Maynard *publishing executive*

Lakeland
Perez, Louis Michael *newspaper editor*

Madeira Beach
Beckerman, Milton Bernard *media broker*

Maitland
Davis, Paul Milton *television news administrator*

Marco Island
Lavin, John Halley *editor, author*
Wheeler, Warren G(age), Jr. *retired publishing executive*

Melbourne
†Kehoe, Thomas A. *newspaper company executive*
Krieger, Robert Edward *publisher*
Spezzano, Vincent Edward *newspaper publisher*

Melrose
Burt, Alvin Victor, Jr. *journalist*

Miami
Anger, Paul *newspaper sports editor*
Balmaseda, Liz *columnist*
Barry, Dave *columnist, author*
Batten, James Knox *newspaper executive*
Black, Creed Carter *newspaper executive*
Chapman, Alvah Herman, Jr. *newspaper executive*
Clifton, Douglas C. *newspaper editor*
Cohen, Alex *retired publisher*
Dickey, Arden *newspaper publishing executive*
Dolen, Christine Arnold *theater critic*
Dubocq, Tom *newspaper reporter*
Dunaway, Victor Allan *editor*
Fichtner, Margaria *journalist*
Fontaine, John C. *newspaper company executive, corporate lawyer*
Gerber, Seymour *publishing company executive*
Hampton, John Lewis *newspaper editor*
Harris, Douglas Clay *newspaper executive*
Hoyt, Clark Freeland *journalist, newspaper editor*
Kram, Michael Arnold *magazine publisher*
Lawrence, David, Jr. *newspaper editor, publisher*
Lewis, John Milton *cable television company executive*
Miller, Gene Edward *newspaper reporter and editor*
Murphy, Stephen Edward *international media and finance consultant*
Natoli, Joe *newspaper publishing executive*
O'Bryon, Linda Elizabeth *television station executive*
Pancake, John *newspaper editor*
Pitts, Leonard Garvey, Jr. *columnist, writer*
Pope, John Edwin, III *newspaper sports editor*
Randolph, Jennings, Jr. (Jay Randolph) *sportscaster*
Reisinger, Sandra Sue *journalist, lawyer*
Russell, James Webster, Jr. *newspaper editor, columnist*
Sanchez, Robert Francis *journalist*
Savage, James Francis *editor*
Seline, Rex *reporter*
Shaklan, Allen Yale *broadcast executive*
Shoemaker, Don (Donald Cleavenger Shoemaker) *columnist*
Shroder, Tom *newspaper editor*
Smiley, Logan Henry *journalist, public concern consulant*
Sonsky, Steve *newspaper editor*
Steinback, Robert Lamont *newspaper columnist*
Suarez, Roberto *newspaper publishing executive*
Terilli, Samuel A., Jr. *newspaper publishing executive*
Verdeja, Sam *newspaper publishing executive*
Weitzel, Peter Andre *editor, newspaper*
Wickstrom, Karl Youngert *publishing company executive*
Williamson, William Paul, Jr. *journalist*

Miami Beach
Meyer, Sylvan Hugh *editor, magazine executive, author*
Wax, William Edward *photojournalist*

Mount Dora
Goodwin, Harry Eugene *journalist, educator*
Trussell, Charles Tait *columnist*

Naples
Arthur, William Bolling *retired editor*
Clapp, Roger Howland *retired newspaper executive*
Gordon, Martin *publisher, print dealer*
Hobbs, Ranald Purcell *publisher*
Kennedy, Robert Emmet *retired newspaperman*
Mc Combs, G. B. *publishing company executive*
Wodlinger, Mark Louis *broadcast executive*
Wyant, Corbin A. *newspaper publisher*

New Smyrna Beach
Makela, Benjamin R. *editor, research director*

North Fort Myers
Rogliano, Aldo Thomas *publishing executive*

North Palm Beach
Edwards, William James *broadcasting executive*

Orlando
Berry, Stephen Joseph *reporter*
†Bishop, Bill *critic*
Bollen, Roger *cartoonist*
Dunn, William Bruna, III *journalist*
Guest, Larry Samuel *newspaper columnist*
Haile, L. John, Jr. *journalist, newspaper executive*
Healy, Jane Elizabeth *newspaper editor*
Ivey, James Burnett *political cartoonist*
Maupin, Elizabeth Thatcher *theater critic*
Morgan, Richard Thomas *publishing executive*
Puerner, John *newspaper publishing executive*
Reese, Charles Edgar *columnist*
Williamson, Thomas Arnold *publishing company executive*

Osprey
Allen, George Howard *publishing management consultant*
Strongin, Theodore *journalist*

Oviedo
Linhart, Letty Lemon *columnist*

Palm Beach
Gowdy, Curtis *sportscaster*
Pryor, Hubert *editor, writer*
Roberts, Margaret Harold *editor, publisher*
Stoneman, Samuel Sidney *cinema company executive*

Palm City
Wirsig, Woodrow *magazine editor, trade organization executive, business executive*

Palm Coast
Franco, Annemarie Woletz *editor*

Pensacola
Bowden, Jesse Earle *newspaper editor, author, cartoonist, journalism educator*

Pinellas Park
†Still, Craig Russell *publishing executive*

Plant City
Tully, Darrow *newspaper publisher*

Pompano Beach
Roen, Sheldon R. *publisher, psychologist*

Port Charlotte
Flanders, Jefferson *publishing executive*

Port Saint Lucie
Sommers, Robert Thomas *editor, publisher, author*

Saint Augustine
Nolan, Joseph Thomas *journalism educator, communications consultant*

Saint Petersburg
Barnes, Andrew Earl *newspaper editor*
Belich, John Patrick, Sr. *journalist*
Benbow, Charles Clarence *retired writer, critic*
Foley, Michael Francis *newspaper executive*
†Good, Jeffrey *journalist*
Haiman, Robert James *newspaper editor, journalism educator*
Hull, Anne Victoria *journalist*
†Jenkins, Robert Norman *newswriter, editor*
Leavell, William A. *publisher, editor*
Martin, Susan Taylor *newspaper editor*
O'Hearn, John Howard *publishing company executive*
Patterson, Eugene Corbett *retired editor, publisher*
Pittman, Robert Turner *retired newspaper editor*
Schuck, Marjorie Massey *publisher, editor, consultant*
Snider, Eric Ross *music critic*
Tash, Paul C. *editor-in-chief*

Sarasota
Burket, Harriet (Mrs. Francis B. Taussig) *editor*
Estrin, Richard William *newspaper editor*
Grubbs, Elven Judson *retired newspaper publisher*
Hackl, Alphons J. *publisher*
Loomis, Wesley Horace, III *former publishing company executive*
MacDonald, Robert Taylor *newspaper executive*
Marino, Eugene Louis *publishing company executive*
McFarlin, Diane H. *newspaper editor*
North, Marjorie Mary *columnist*
Proffitt, Waldo, Jr. *newspaper editor*

Stuart
Murchake, John *publishing executive*
Slade, Gerald Jack *publishing company executive*

Sun City Center
Fleischman, Sol Joseph, Sr. *retired television broadcasting executive*

Tallahassee
Dadisman, Joseph Carrol *newspaper executive*
Heldman, Louis Marc *newspaper editor*
McBride, Donna Jannean *publisher*
Morgan, Lucy W. *journalist*

Tampa
Benjamin, Robert Spiers *foreign correspondent, writer, publicist*
Friedlander, Edward Jay *journalism educator*
Locker, Raymond Duncan *editor*
Loft, Kurt *newspaper editor, science writer, music critic*
Nevins, Albert J. *publisher, editor, author*
Pittman, Richard Frank, Jr. *newspaper publisher*
Roberts, Edwin Albert, Jr. *newspaper editor, journalist*
Ruth, Daniel John *journalist*

Venice
Corrigan, William Thomas *retired broadcast news executive*

Vero Beach
Leonsis, Theodore John *publishing company executive*
Michelson, Edward J. *journalist*
Petersmeyer, C(harles) Wrede *retired broadcasting executive, venture capitalist*

West Palm Beach
Fairbanks, Richard Monroe *broadcasting company executive*
Giuffrida, Tom A. *publisher*
†Lavine, Alan *columnist, writer*
O'Hara, Thomas Patrick *managing editor*
Passy, Charles *arts critic*
Rivers, Marie Bie *broadcasting executive*
Sears, Edward Milner, Jr. *newspaper editor*
Wright, Donald Conway *editorial cartoonist*

GEORGIA

Athens
Agee, Warren Kendall *journalism educator*
Feldman, Edmund Burke *art critic*
Fink, Conrad Charles *journalism educator, communications consultant*
Hester, Albert Lee *journalism educator*
Holder, Howard Randolph, Sr. *broadcasting company executive*

Atlanta
Berry, Dennis *newspaper publishing executive*
Bisher, James Furman *journalist, author*
Booth, Randolph Lee *broadcast executive*
Bridgewater, Herbert Jeremiah, Jr. *radio host*
Bynum, Richard Cary *publishing executive, author*
Campbell, Colin McLeod *journalist*
Chambers, Anne Cox *newspaper executive*
Cross, Joyce Annette Oscar *newscaster*
Daly, Chuck (Charles Jerome Daly) *sports commentator, former professional basketball coach*
Dobson, Bridget McColl Hursley *television executive and writer*
Dollar, Steve *music critic*
Dotson, Robert Charles *news correspondent*
Dowden, Thomas Clark *telecommunication executive*
Drennen, Eileen Moira *editor*
Easterly, David Eugene *communications executive*
Eckert, Michael Joseph *cable and broadcast television executive*
Ellis, Elmo Israel *broadcast executive, consultant, newspaper columnist*
Ezell, Reva Gross *radio station manager, writer*
Gilmer, Harry Wesley *publishing executive, educator*
Hall, Sarah E. *magazine editor, educator*
Harris, Henry Wood *cable television executive*
Holzel, David Benjamin *newspaper editor*
Hulbert, Daniel J. *theater critic, entertainment writer*
Johnson, Wyatt Thomas, Jr. (Tom Johnson) *cable news executive*
Jones, J. Kenley *journalist*
Kennedy, James C. *publishing and media executive*
Klim, Michael Stephen *legal publisher*
Kloer, Philip Baldwin *television critic*
Korn, Steven W. *broadcasting company executive, corporate lawyer*
Lamkin, William Pierce *editor*
Loory, Stuart Hugh *journalist*
†Luckovich, Mike *cartoonist*
Martin, Ron *newspaper editor in chief*
Merdek, Andrew Austin *publishing/media executive, lawyer*
Pantel, Stan Roy *newspaper publishing executive*
Pucket, Susan *newspaper editor*
Reeves, Alexis Scott *journalist*
Rierson, Robert Leak *broadcasting executive, television writer*
Ringel, Eleanor *film critic*
Rosenfeld, Arnold Solomon *newspaper editor*
Salter, Sally *reporter*
Schwartz, William A(llen) *broadcasting and cable executive*
Seabrook, Charles *reporter*
Sibley, Celestine (Mrs. John C. Strong) *columnist, reporter*
Skube, Michael *journalist, critic*
Tarver, Jackson Williams *newspaper executive*
Teepen, Thomas Henry *newspaper editor, journalist*
Tharpe, Frazier Eugene *journalist*
Tierney, Michael Stewart *newspaper editor, journalist*
Toner, Michael F. *journalist*
Tucker, Cynthia Anne *journalist*
Turner, Ted (Robert Edward Turner) *television executive*
Walter, John *newspaper editor*
Ward, Janet Lynn *magazine editor, sports wire reporter*
Whitt, Richard Ernest *reporter*
Yother, Michele *publisher*

Columbus
Watson, Billy *publishing executive, newspaper*

Decatur
Knight, Walker Leigh *editor, publisher, clergyman*
Shaw, Jeanne Osborne *editor, poet*

Juliette
Yancy, Cecil Henton, Jr. *editor*

Macon
Savage, Randall Ernest *journalist*
†Thomas, Richard D. *newspaper editor*
†Weaver, William H. *newspaper editor*

Marietta
Bemis, Royce Edwin *publishing executive*
Dunwoody, Kenneth Reed *magazine editor*

Oxford
Sitton, Claude Fox *newspaper editor*

Roswell
Peterson, Donald Robert magazine editor, vintage automobile consultant

Savannah
Coffey, Thomas Francis, Jr. editor
Tobey, Carl Wadsworth retired publisher

Sea Island
Carter, Don Earl newspaper editor, publisher

Stone Mountain
Speed, Billie Cheney (Mrs. Thomas S. Speed) retired editor, journalist

HAWAII

Honolulu
Chaplin, George newspaper editor
Chung, Kea Sung television broadcasting executive
Flanagan, John Michael editor, publisher
Jellinek, Roger editor
Keir, Gerald Janes newspaper editor
Krauss, Bob newspaper columnist, author
Luter, John news correspondent, educator
Simonds, John Edward newspaper editor
Smith, Christopher Case newspaper editor
Smyser, Adam Albert newspaper editor
Sparks, Robert William publishing executive
Twigg-Smith, Thurston newspaper publisher
Wiley, Bonnie Jean journalism educator

Lahaina
Arnold, Joan Dean publisher

IDAHO

Boise
Peterson, Curtis Gerald broadcast executive

Caldwell
Gipson, Gordon publishing company executive

Idaho Falls
Harris, Darryl Wayne publishing executive

Moscow
Anderson, Clifton Einar editor, writer

Twin Falls
Hartgen, Stephen Anthony newspaper publisher

ILLINOIS

Arlington Heights
Baumann, Daniel E. newspaper executive
†Kelson, Allen Howard consultant, writer, dining critic
Lampinen, John A. newspaper editor
Paddock, Robert Young publisher
Paddock, Stuart R., Jr. publishing executive
Ray, Douglas newspaper editor
terHorst, Cheryl Ann journalist

Barrington
Bash, Philip Edwin publishing executive

Belleville
Berkley, Gary Lee newspaper publisher

Bloomington
Merwin, Davis Underwood newspaper executive
Wills, Edgar W. (Bill) newspaper editor

Burr Ridge
Sund, Jeffrey Owen publishing company executive

Carol Stream
Coffman, Roy Walter, III publishing company executive
Myra, Harold Lawrence publisher
Shorney, George Herbert publishing executive
Taylor, Kenneth Nathaniel publishing executive, author
Yancey, Philip David editor, author

Carpentersville
Wilson, Delbert Ray publisher, author

Champaign
Foreman, John Richard newspaper editor
McCulloh, Judith Marie editor
Meyer, August Christopher, Jr. broadcasting company executive, lawyer
Sutton, Roger editor, writer, lecturer
Vedder, Byron Charles newspaper executive

Chicago
Abrams, Susan Elizabeth book editor, publisher
Allen, Richard Blose legal editor, lawyer
Anderson, Jon Stephen newswriter
Applegate, William Joseph broadcast executive
Artner, Alan Gustav art critic, journalist
Balz, Douglas Charles journalist
Beck, Joan Wagner journalist
Bell, Clark Wayne business editor, educator
Bennett, Beverly newspaper editor
Bennett, Lerone, Jr. magazine editor, author
Boers, Terry John sportswriter, radio and television personality
Bohmer, David Alan cable television executive
†Brasler, Wayne Michael journalism educator, writer
Brickhouse, John B. (Jack Brickhouse) sports broadcaster
Britton, Dennis A. newspaper editor, newspaper executive
Brotman, Barbara Louise columnist, writer
Brumback, Charles Tiedtke newspaper executive
Brummel, Mark Joseph magazine editor
Callaway, Karen A(lice) journalist
Camper, John Jacob writer, university administrator
Cappo, Joseph C. publisher
Carman, Charles Hallack legal business publisher, editor, lawyer
Champion, Charles F. newspaper publishing executive
Chapman, Stephen James columnist
Christiansen, Richard Dean newspaper editor
Ciccone, Richard newspaper editor
Coffey, Raymond Richard newspaper editor, journalist
Cohodes, Eli Aaron publisher
Connors, Dorsey television and radio commentator, newspaper columnist
Constant, Anita Aurelia publisher
Crain, Gertrude Ramsay publishing company executive
Crain, Rance publishing company executive
Crawford, William Basil, Jr. journalist
Cross, Robert Clark journalist
Curwen, Randall William journalist, editor
D'Alexander, William Joseph publishing company executive
Darby, Edwin Wheeler retired newspaper financial columnist
Davis, Andrew Bashaw publishing executive
DeBat, Donald Joseph newspaper editor
Diamond, Shari Seidman psychology educator, law researcher
Dimond, Robert Edward publisher
Dodds, Claudette La Vonn radio executive and consultant
Dold, Robert Bruce journalist
Donovan, Dianne Francys journalist
Downing, Joan Forman editor
Ebert, Roger Joseph film critic
Elleman, Barbara editor
Essex, Joseph Michael visual communication planner
Feder, Robert television and radio columnist
Fetridge, Clark Worthington publisher
Field, Marshall business executive
Figge, Frederick Henry, Jr. retired publishing executive
Fink, John editor, newspaper
Fuller, Jack William writer, newspaper executive
Gaines, William Chester journalist
Gies, Thomas Anthony publishing company executive
Goldberg, Stephanie Benson editor, magazine writer, lawyer
Goldsborough, Robert Gerald publishing executive, author
Gradowski, Stanley Joseph, Jr. publishing company executive
Graham, Jarlath John publishing executive
Granger, Bill columnist
Grant, Dennis newspaper publishing executive
Greene, Robert Bernard, Jr. (Bob Greene) broadcast television correspondent, columnist, author
Grenesko, Donald C. publishing company executive
Griffin, Jean Latz newspaper reporter
Gruber, William Paul journalist
Gwinn, Robert P. publishing executive
Haddix, Carol Ann Mighton journalist
Harvey, Paul news commentator, author, columnist
Hay, Howard newspaper publishing executive
Hefner, Christie Ann publishing executive and marketing executive
Hengstler, Gary Ardell publisher, editor, lawyer
Herguth, Robert John columnist
Hewitt, Brian journalist
Higgins, Jack editorial cartoonist
Holton, Lisa newspaper editor, journalist
Holtzman, Jerome journalist, columnist, publisher
Huntley, Robert Stephen newspaper editor
Husar, John Paul newspaper columnist, television panelist
Jefferson, Wayne broadcast executive
Kaiserlian, Penelope Jane publishing company executive
Kazik, John Stanley newspaper executive
Kelley, Michael John newspaper editor
Kennett, Robert L. publisher
Kisor, Henry Du Bois newspaper editor, critic, columnist
Klaviter, Helen Lothrop magazine editor
Koester, Robert Gregg record company executive
Kotulak, Ronald newspaper science writer
Krueger, Bonnie Lee editor, writer
Kupcinet, Irv columnist
Kyle, Robert Campbell, II publishing executive
Landers, Ann (Mrs. Esther P. Lederer) columnist
Lazarus, George Milton newspaper columnist
Leckey, Andrew A. financial columnist
Lehrman, Nat magazine editor
Lewis, Sylvia Gail journalist
Lipinski, Ann Marie newspaper editor
Locher, Richard Earl editorial cartoonist
Loesch, Katharine Taylor (Mrs. John George Loesch) communication and theatre educator
Longworth, Richard Cole journalist
Lundberg, George David, II medical editor, pathologist
Lyon, Jeffrey journalist, author
Lyons, Jeffrey film critic
Lythcott, Marcia A. newspaper editor
Madigan, John William publishing executive
†Manos, John editor-in-chief
Mariotti, Jay Anthony journalist
Markus, Robert Michael journalist
McCarron, John Francis columnist
McDaniel, Charles-Gene journalism educator, writer
McDougal, Alfred Leroy publisher
Mc Guirt, Wayne Robert publishing company executive
McIntyre, Kathryn Joan publisher, editorial director
Medved, Michael film critic, author
Migala, Lucyna Jozefa broadcast journalist, arts administrator, radio station executive
Miller, Mark newspaper editor
Nadler, Mark B. executive editor
Nault, William Henry publishing executive
Neal, Steven George journalist
Neubauer, Charles Frederick investigative reporter
Nicholls, David G. editor
Nolan, Carole Rita broadcasting executive
Nordstrand, Raymond William broadcasting company executive
Norton, Peter Bowes publishing company executive
O'Dell, James E. newspaper publishing executive
Orr, Richard Tuttle journalist
Page, Clarence E. newspaper columnist
Parisi, Joseph (Anthony) magazine editor, writer-consultant, educator
Peerman, Dean Gordon magazine editor
Peres, Judith May journalist
Petacque, Arthur M. journalist
Pierson, Don sports columnist
Plotnick, Harvey Barry publishing executive
Plotnik, Arthur publishing executive
Pope, Kerig Rodgers magazine executive
Quaal, Ward Louis broadcast executive
Quade, Victoria Catherine editor, writer
Ratny, Ruth Lucille publishing company executive, writer
Reedy, Jerry Edward editor, writer
Renshaw, Charles Clark, Jr. retired publishing executive
Rice, William Edward newspaper columnist
Rodgers, Johnathan broadcast executive
Roeper, Richard columnist
Rosenbloom, Steve sportswriter
Royko, Mike newspaper columnist
Rubin, Bonnie Miller journalist
Rynkiewicz, Stephen Michael journalist
Sachs, Lloyd Robert entertainment critic, writer
Scanlan, Thomas Cleary publishing executive, editor
Schultz, Heidi Flynn publisher
Sengstacke, John Herman Henry publishing company executive
Shere, Dennis publishing executive
Shuman, Nicholas Roman journalist, educator
Simonson, Margaret newspaper publishing executive
Siskel, Gene (Eugene Kal Siskel) film critic
†Smith, Sam P. columnist, author
Sneed, Michael (Michele) columnist
Starr, Rick broadcasting executive
Stone, Steven Michael sports announcer, former baseball player
Thomas, Leroy newspaper executive editor
Tyner, Howard A. newspaper editor, journalist
Varro, Barbara Joan editor
von Rhein, John Richard music critic, editor
Wallace, Julia Diane newspaper editor
Wasik, John Francis editor, writer, publisher
Wasiolek, Edward literary critic, language and literature educator
Weber, Arthur magazine executive
Weinberg, Lila Shaffer writer, editor
Weintraub, Joseph Barton publishing executive
Wells, Joel Freeman editor, author
Wier, Patricia Ann publishing executive, consultant
Wilkerson, Isabel journalist
Wilson, Gahan cartoonist, author
Wolfe, Sheila A. journalist
Wycliff, Noel Don journalist, newspaper editor
Youngman, Owen Ralph newspaper editor
Yuenger, James Laury journalist
Zaslow, Jeffrey Lloyd syndicated columnist
Zekman, Pamela Lois (Mrs. Fredric Soll) reporter
Zorn, Eric J. newspaper columnist

Chicago Heights
Hurd, Byron Thomas newspaper executive

Crystal Lake
Keller, William Francis publishing consultant

De Kalb
Vance Siebrasse, Kathy Ann newspaper publishing executive

Deerfield
Thorne, Oakleigh Blakeman publishing company executive

Des Plaines
Babb, Michael Paul engineering magazine editor
Clapper, Marie Anne magazine publisher
Grahn, Barbara Ascher publisher
Henrikson, Lois Elizabeth photojournalist
Hlavacek, Roy George publishing executive, magazine editor
Kelly, Timothy Michael magazine publisher
Klemens, Thomas Lloyd editor
Tory, John A. newspaper publishing executive

Dixon
Shaw, Thomas Douglas newspaper executive

Elk Grove Village
Halloran, James Joseph editor

Elmhurst
Ephland, John Russell magazine editor

Evanston
Borcover, Alfred Seymour journalist
Galvin, Kathleen Malone communications educator
Jacobs, Norman Joseph publishing company executive
Janeway, Michael Charles journalism educator, school dean
Jones, Robert Russell magazine editor
Kuenster, John Joseph magazine editor
Larson, Roy journalist, publisher
Lavine, John M. journalism educator, newspaper publisher
Otwell, Ralph Maurice retired newspaper editor
Peck, Abraham editor, writer, educator, magazine consultant
Schwarzlose, Richard Allen journalism educator
Wagner, Durrett former publisher, picture service executive
White, Willmon Lee magazine editor
Wills, Garry journalist, educator
Ziomek, Jonathan S. journalist, educator

Geneva
†Stamps, David M. publishing executive
†Whitfield, Richard publishing executive

Glen Ellyn
Crumbaugh, Lee Forrest publisher, consultant
Kirkpatrick, Clayton former newspaper executive

Glenview
Mabley, Jack newspaper columnist, communications consultant
Young, Richard Alan publishing company executive

Highland Park
Johnson, Curtis Lee publisher, editor, writer
Rutenberg-Rosenberg, Sharon Leslie journalist

Homewood
Grunwald, Arnold Paul communications executive, engineer

Itasca
†Nytko, Edward C. printing company executive

Jacksonville
Hack, Carole Mae media generalist

Lake Bluff
Felknor, Bruce Lester editorial consultant

Lake Forest
Krouse, Ann Wolk publishing executive
Schulze, Franz, Jr. art critic, educator

Lansing
†Colander, Patricia Marie newspaper publisher
†Gamble, Harry M. newspaper editor

Lincolnwood
Astrin, Marvin H. broadcasting company executive
Pattis, S. William publisher

Litchfield
Jackson, David A. retired newspaper editor

Mount Vernon
Withers, W. Russell, Jr. broadcast executive

Mundelein
Terris, William publishing executive

Naperville
Spiotta, Raymond Herman consulting editor

Normal
Mc Knight, William Warren, Jr. publisher

Northbrook
Pesmen, Sandra (Mrs. Harold William Pesmen) editor
Snader, Jack Ross publishing company executive

Northfield
Hotze, Charles Wayne publisher, printer
Tenuta, Jean Louise sports reporter, medical technologist

Oak Brook
Honeywell, Larry Gene publishing company executive, travel company executive

Oak Park
Knight, Robert Milton journalist, educator
Lyles, Jean Elizabeth Caffey journalist

Palatine
Perez, Gerard Vincent art publishing company executive

Park Ridge
Peterson, Richard Elton publisher

Peoria
Dancey, Charles Lohman newspaper executive
McConnell, John Thomas newspaper executive, publisher
Peak, William Roy newspaper editor
Slane, Henry Pindell broadcasting executive

Peru
Carus, André Wolfgang educational publishing firm executive

Quincy
Dorsey, Jeffrey Alan broadcaster

River Grove
Litzsinger, Paul Richard publishing company executive

Riverwoods
Hynes, Mary Ann publishing executive, lawyer

Rolling Meadows
Grogan, Kenneth Augustine publishing company executive

Schaumburg
Edmunds, Jane Clara communications consultant

Skokie
McNally, Andrew, III printer, publisher
McNally, Andrew, IV publishing executive
Steele, Kurt D. publishing company executive
Wildermuth, Roger Gregory publishing company executive

Springfield
Clarke, John Patrick newspaper publisher
Heintz, Jack publishing company executive
Thomas, Payne Edward Lloyd publisher

Urbana
Andersen, Kenneth Eldon speech communication educator
Helle, Steven James educator, lawyer
Littlewood, Thomas Benjamin journalism educator
Peterson, Theodore Bernard retired journalism educator

Wauconda
Bolchazy, Ladislaus Joseph publishing company executive

Wheaton
Beers, V(ictor) Gilbert publishing executive
Kelly, Robert Thomas publisher
Sweeney, Mark Owen publisher
Taylor, Mark Douglas publishing executive

Wilmette
Biedron, Theodore John newspaper executive

Winnetka
Mancuso, James Vincent automobile columnist

INDIANA

Auburn
Record, Lincoln Fredrick speech communications educator, communications consultant

Bloomington
Gough, Pauline Bjerke *magazine editor*
Jacobi, Peter Paul *journalism educator, author*
Lee, Don Yoon *publisher, academic researcher and writer*
Schurz, Scott Clark *journalist, publisher*
Weaver, David Hugh *journalism educator, communications researcher*

Evansville
Jackson, Bill D. *newspaper editor*
†Mathews, W. Garret *columnist*
Riechmann, Fred B. *retired newspaper publisher*
Ryder, Thomas Michael *newspaper editor*
Tuley, Thomas Wayne *newspaper executive*

Fort Wayne
Klugman, Stephan Craig *newspaper editor*
Lockwood, Robert Philip *publishing executive*
Pellegrene, Thomas James, Jr. *editor, researcher*
Sandeson, William Seymour *cartoonist*
Weiler, Joseph Ashby *newspaper editor*

Franklin
Jacobs, Harvey Collins *newspaper editor, writer*

Gary
Bosley, John Scott *editor*
Sutton, William Wallace, Jr. *editor, newspaper executive*

Greensburg
Small, Ralph Milton *publisher, clergyman*

Hammond
Moore, Carolyn Lannin *video specialist*

Indianapolis
Allan, Marc David *music critic*
Applegate, Malcolm W. *newspaper executive*
Birky, Nathan Dale *publishing company executive*
Born, Emily Marie *editor, association executive*
Caperton, Albert Franklin *newspaper editor*
Cohen, Gabriel Murrel *editor, publisher*
Fleming, Marcella *journalist*
Fortune, William Lemcke *journalist*
Fuson, Wayne Edward *sports editor*
Garmel, Marion Bess Simon *journalist*
Higgins, William Robert, III *journalist*
Lyst, John Henry *newspaper editor*
Phillippi, Wendell Crane *editor*
Pratt, Arthur D. *printing company executive*
Pulliam, Eugene Smith *newspaper publisher*
Pulliam, Russell Bleecker *editor, elder*
Rinck, Elizabeth Appel *editor*
Russell, Frank Eli *newspaper publishing executive*
SerVaas, Beurt Richard *corporate executive*
Staff, Charles Bancroft, Jr. *music and theater critic*
Thomas, Beth Eileen Wood (Mrs. Raymond O. Thomas) *editor*
Van Valin, John Ernest *publisher*
Werner, Charles George *cartoonist*
Wheeler, Daniel Scott *publishing executive, editor*
Wright, David Burton *retired newspaper publishing company executive*

Martinsville
Kendall, Robert Stanton *newspaper editor, journalist*

Muncie
Bell, Stephen Scott (Steve Bell) *journalist, educator*
Kumbula, Tendayi Sengerwe *journalism educator*

New Haven
Chapman, Reid Gillis *former broadcasting company executive*

Notre Dame
Langford, James Rouleau *university press administrator*
Rice, (Ethel) Ann *publishing executive, editor*

Peru
Stackhouse, John Wesley *publishing executive*

Richmond
Muzzillo, Rachel Evelyn Sheeley *reporter*
Talbot, Ardith Ann *editor*

South Bend
Schurz, Franklin Dunn, Jr. *media executive*
†Wensits, James Emrich *newspaper editor*

Terre Haute
Meany, John Joseph *newspaper publisher*

IOWA

Ames
Gartner, Michael Gay *editor, television executive*
Gerlach, Gary Gene *newspaper publisher*

Cedar Falls
Carlson, Jerry Alan *editor*

Cedar Rapids
Hladky, Joseph F., III *publishing executive*
Quarton, William Barlow *broadcasting company executive*

Davenport
Gottlieb, Richard Douglas *media executive*
†Lense, Marcia *television anchor, producer, reporter*
Schermer, Lloyd G. *publishing and broadcasting company executive*

Des Moines
Boyle, Bruce James *publisher*
Burnett, Robert A. *publisher*
Edwards, Charles C., Jr. *newspaper publisher*
Flansburg, James Sherman *editor, columnist*
Jordan, David Loran *editor*
†Kaplan, Jerry *magazine publisher*
Kerr, William T. *publishing and broadcasting executive*
Kruidenier, David *newspaper executive*
Lawless, James L. *editor, columnist*
LemMon, Jean Marie *editor-in-chief*
Little, Christopher Mark *publishing company executive, lawyer*
MacDonald, Kenneth *journalist, former editor*
Myers, Mary Kathleen *publishing executive*
Peterson, David Charles *photojournalist*
Rehm, Jack Daniel *publishing executive*
Simbro, William Charles *journalist*
Van Zante, Shirley M(ae) *magazine editor*
Witke, David Rodney *newspaper editor*
†Yepsen, David Arlon *reporter*

Dubuque
Brown, William Clifford *publishing company executive*
Kolz, Beverly Anne *publishing executive*

Iowa City
Duck, Steve Weatherill *communications educator*
Hardt, Hanno Richard Eduard *communications educator*
Keller, Eliot Aaron *broadcasting executive*
Sinicropi, Stephen Anthony *radio station executive*
Zimmer, Paul Jerome *publisher, editor, poet*

Mason City
†Collison, Jim *business executive*

Red Oak
Anderson, Ronald G. *newspaper publisher*

Spirit Lake
Hedberg, Paul Clifford *broadcasting executive*

Urbandale
Alumbaugh, JoAnn McCalla *magazine editor*

West Des Moines
Dooley, Donald John *publishing executive*

KANSAS

Coffeyville
Seaton, Richard Melvin *newspaper and broadcasting executive*

Fort Scott
Emery, Frank Eugene *publishing executive*

Hutchinson
Baumer, Beverly Belle *journalist*
Buzbee, Richard Edgar *newspaper editor*

Lawrence
Eblen, George Thomas (Tom Eblen) *journalist*
Ginn, John Charles *journalism educator, former newspaper publisher*
Levine, Stuart George *editor, English literature educator, author*
†Morgan, Scott Ellingwood *publisher, lawyer*
Orel, Harold *literary critic, educator*
Pickett, Calder Marcus *retired journalism educator*
Simons, Dolph Collins, Jr. *newspaper publisher*
Woodward, Frederick Miller *publisher*

Manhattan
Marsh, Harry Dean *journalism educator*
Seaton, Edward Lee *newspaper editor and publisher*

Marion
Meyer, Bill *newspaper publisher, editor*

Prairie Village
Franking, Holly Mae *software publisher*

Saint Marys
Latham, Dudley Eugene, III (Del Latham) *printing and paper converting executive*

Shawnee Mission
Dozois, Gardner *editor, writer*
Schweitzer, Jon Anton *broadcasting executive*
†Walsh, Robert *publishing executive*

Topeka
Peavler, Nancy Jean *editor*
Powers, Harris Pat *broadcasting executive*
Stauffer, John H. *newspaper and broadcast executive*
Stauffer, Stanley Howard *newspaper and broadcasting executive*

Wichita
Claassen, Sherida Dill *newspaper executive*
Curtright, Robert Eugene *newspaper critic and columnist*
Getz, Robert Lee *newspaper columnist*
Hatteberg, Larry Merle *photojournalist*

KENTUCKY

Covington
Clabes, Judith Grisham *newspaper editor*
Oppmann, Andrew James *newspaper editor*
Trimble, Vance Henry *retired newspaper editor*

Frankfort
Reese, Lowell D. *editor, publisher*

Goshen
Strode, William Hall, III *photojournalist, publisher*

Lexington
Allison, James Claybrooke, II *broadcasting executive*
Fox, Virginia Gaines *public broadcasting executive*
Keeling, Larry Dale *journalist*
Kelly, Timothy Michael *newspaper editor*
Owens, Lewis E. *newspaper executive*

Louisville
Bingham, George Barry, Jr. *publishing and broadcasting executive*
Bullard, Claude Earl *newspaper, commercial printing and radio and television executive*
†Crawford, Byron Garrison *newswriter, journalist*
Drury, Ralph Leon *newspaper executive*
Ellison, William Louie, Jr. *newspaper editor, journalist*
Hawpe, David Vaughn *newspaper editor, journalist*
MacKinnon, Cyrus Leland *retired newspaper executive*
Melnykovych, Andrew O. *journalist*
†Scheu, Lynn McLaughlin *scientific publication editor*
Tallichet, Leon Edgar *retired publishing executive, financial administrator*
Tinsley, Tuck, III *book publishing executive*
Towles, Donald Blackburn *retired newspaper publishing executive*
Woolsey, Frederick William *retired journalist, music critic*

Pewee Valley
Gill, George Norman *newspaper publishing company executive*

Trappist
Hart, Patrick Joseph *editor*

LOUISIANA

Alexandria
Smith, Joe Dorsey, Jr. *newspaper executive*

Baker
Roberson, Patt Foster *mass communications educator*

Baton Rouge
Giles, William Elmer *journalism educator, former newspaper editor*
Gilmore, Clarence Percy *writer, magazine editor*
Hatfield, Jack Daniel *newspaper editor*
Jenkins, Louis (Woody) *television executive, state legislator*
Manship, Douglas *broadcast and newspaper executive*
Phillabaum, Leslie Ervin *publisher*

Covington
Stroup, Sheila Tierney *columnist*

Gretna
Calhoun, Milburn *publishing executive, rare book dealer, physician*

Hammond
Kemp, John Randolph *journalist, author, academic administrator*

Lafayette
Lenox, Charles N(ewton), Jr. *newspaper editor*

Lake Charles
Beam, James C. (Jim Beam) *editor, newspaper*

Metairie
Costello, Joseph Mark, III *broadcasting and motion picture executive*

New Orleans
Amoss, Walter James, III *editor*
Ball, Millie (Mildred Porteons Ball) *editor, journalist*
Corey, Orlin Russell *publisher, editor*
†Curry, Dale B. *journalist*
Dodds, Richard Crofton *theater critic*
Ferguson, Charles Austin *retired newspaper editor*
Jimirro, James P. *broadcasting and telecommunications executive*
Phelps, Ashton, Jr. *newspaper publisher*
Pope, John M. *journalist*
Toussaint, Allen Richard *recording studio executive, composer, pianist*

Shreveport
Beaird, Charles T. *publishing executive*
Lazarus, Allan Matthew *retired newspaper editor*
Tiner, Stanley Ray *business communications executive, former editor*

MAINE

Bangor
Warren, Richard Jordan *newspaper publisher*
Warren, Richard Kearney *newspaper publisher*

Camden
Anderson, George Harding *broadcasting company executive*
Thomas, (Charles) Davis *editor*

Cape Elizabeth
Emerson, Paul Carlton *retired publishing executive*

Castine
Hall, David *sound archivist, writer*

Damariscotta
Blake, Bud (Julian Watson) *cartoonist*

Ellsworth
Dudman, Richard Beebe *communications company executive, journalist*
Wiggins, James Russell *newspaper editor*

Lincoln
Kneeland, Douglas Eugene *retired newspaper editor*

Portland
Chisholm, Colin Alexander Joseph, III *media professional*
Harte, Christopher McCutcheon *former newspaper executive, investment manager*
Neavoll, George Franklin *newspaper editor*
Ureneck, Louis Adam *newspaper editor, newspaper executive*

Rockport
Fernald, Harold Allen *publishing executive*
Jackson, David Pingree *publishing executive*

Sebago Lake
Murray, Wallace Shordon *publisher, educator*

Sedgwick
Schroth, Thomas Nolan *editor*

Thorndike
Treleaven, Phillips Albert *retired publishing company executive*

MARYLAND

Annapolis
Casey, Edward Dennis *newspaper editor*
Chambers, Ronald D. *book publishing executive*
Holmes, David Charles *broadcasting company executive*
Jackson, Elmer Martin, Jr. *newspaper executive*

Baltimore
Beckenstein, Myron *journalist*
Bor, Jonathan Steven *journalist*
Bready, James Hall *reporter*
Brunson, Dorothy Edwards *broadcasting executive*
Carroll, John Sawyer *newspaper editor*
Digges, Dudley Perkins *retired editor*
Dorsey, John Russell *art critic, journalist*
Gardner, R. H. (Rufus Hallette Gardner, III) *retired drama and film critic*
Glasgow, Jesse Edward *newspaper editor*
Goellner, Jack Gordon *publishing executive*
†Hall, Wiley A. *columnist, journalist*
Hirsh, Allan T., III *book publisher*
Hirsh, Allan Thurman, Jr. *publishing executive*
Magida, Arthur Jay *newspaper editor, writer*
Marimow, William Kalmon *journalist*
Montgomery, Paula Kay *school editor, publishing executive*
Passano, E. Magruder, Jr. *publishing executive*
Passano, Edward Magruder *printing company executive*
Rabb, Bernard Paul *book publisher, consultant*
Rodricks, Daniel John *columnist, television commentator*
Rousuck, J. Wynn *theater critic*
Scott, Frederick Isadore, Jr. *editor, business executive*
Sterne, Joseph Robert Livingston *newspaper editor*
Stevens, Elisabeth Goss (Mrs. Robert Schleussner, Jr.) *writer, journalist*
Tepper, Michael Howard *publishing company executive*
Williams, Harold Anthony *retired newspaper editor*
Woodward, Robert A. *radio broadcasting executive*

Bel Air
†Klett, Shirley Louise *columnist, writer, critic, researcher*

Bethesda
Cornish, Edward Seymour *magazine editor*
†Ford, John Bassett *broadcasting executive*
Harney, Kenneth Robert *editor, columnist*
Herman, Edith Carol *journalist*
Hoover, Roland Armitage *publisher, printer*
Iglehart, John K. *journalist*
Kamenske, Bernard Harold *journalist, communications specialist*
Kohlmeier, Louis Martin, Jr. *newspaper reporter*
Larrabee, Donald Richard *publishing company executive*
Massa, Paul Peter *publisher*
Mc Kenna, James Aloysius *broadcasting executive, former lawyer*
Morton, Herbert Charles *editor, economist*
Nessen, Ronald Harold *public affairs executive*
Otte, Ruth L. *cable television executive*
Phillips, Kevin Price *columnist, author*
Pickerell, James Howard *photojournalist*
Pratt, Dana Joseph *publishing consultant*
Roberts, Chalmers McGeagh *reporter*
Rubin, William *editor*
Shipler, David Karr *journalist, correspondent, author*
Sulkin, Sidney *editor, writer*

Bowie
Towle, Laird Charles *book publisher*

Chevy Chase
Adler, James Barron *publisher*
Chaseman, Joel *media executive*

College Park
Cleghorn, Reese *journalist, educator*
Grunig, James Elmer *communications educator, researcher, public relations consultant*
Hiebert, Ray Eldon *journalism educator, author, consultant*
Winik, Jay B. *writer, political scientist, consultant*

Columbia
Barrow, Lionel Ceon, Jr. *communications and marketing consultant*

Easton
Lockwood, Willard Atkinson *publisher*

Frederick
Beran, Denis Carl *publisher*

Gaithersburg
†Bruggeman, John Robert *publishing executive*
Deutsch, Judith Sloan *journalist, newspaper editor*
Marozsan, John Robert *publishing company executive*
Wicklein, John Frederick *journalist, educator*

Germantown
Christian, John Kenton *organization executive, publisher, writer, marketing consultant*

Grantsville
Ruddell, Gary Ronald *publisher*

Hagerstown
Fisher, Charles Worley *editor*
Warner, Harry Backer, Jr. *retired journalist, freelance writer*

Havre De Grace
Wetter, Edward *broadcasting executive*

Landover
Poile, David Robert *professional hockey team executive*

Lanham Seabrook
Connors, Maureen Stotler *publishing executive*
Fellers, Raymond *publisher*
Henry, Gisèle Byrd *publishing executive, book designer*
Nagan, Peter Seymour *publisher*

Lusby
Radcliffe, Redonia Wheeler (Donnie Radcliffe) *journalist, author*

Lutherville Timonium
Cedrone, Louis Robert, Jr. *critic*

Mitchellville
Phelps, Flora L(ouise) Lewis *editor, anthropologist, photographer*

Owings Mills
Holdridge, Barbara *book publisher*

Potomac
Fox, Arthur Joseph, Jr. *editor*
Kessler, Ronald Borek *journalist*
Munroe, Pat *retired newsman*

Rockville
Karnow, Stanley *journalist, writer*
Matthews, Daniel George *editorial consultant*
Regeimbal, Neil Robert, Sr. *retired journalist*
Schweickart, Russell Louis *communications executive, astronaut*

Salisbury
Kleiman, Gary Howard *broadcast, advertising and cellular communications consultant*

Severna Park
Moore, John Leo, Jr. *journalist, writer, editor*

Silver Spring
Barber, Ben Bernard Andrew *journalist*
Eiserer, Leonard Albert Carl *publishing executive*
Flieger, Howard Wentworth *editor*
Hegstad, Roland Rex *magazine editor*
Howze, Karen Aileen *newspaper editor, lawyer, multi-cultural communications consultant*
Mooney, James Hugh *newspaper editor*
Myers, Evelyn Stephenson *editor, writer*

Stevenson
Jacobs, Bradford McElderry *newspaper editor*

MASSACHUSETTS

Acton
Kittross, John Michael *retired communications educator*

Allston
Becton, Henry Prentiss, Jr. *broadcasting company executive*

Amherst
Wilcox, Bruce Gordon *publisher*

Arlington
O'Connell, Paul Edmund *publisher*

Bedford
Brady, Upton Birnie *editor*
Goodman, William Beehler *editor, literary agent*

Boston
Adams, Phoebe-Lou *journalist*
Ames, Damaris *publishing executive*
Bailey, Stephen *newspaper reporter*
Beatty, Jack J. *magazine editor*
Berger, Francine Ellis *radio station executive, communications executive*
Berube, Margery Stanwood *publishing executive*
Bourne, Katherine Day *journalist, educator*
Burack, Sylvia Kamerman *editor, publisher*
Caldwell, Gail *book critic*
Carr, Jay Phillip *critic*
Carroll, Matthew Shaun *reporter*
Chinlund, Christine *newspaper editor*
Christensen, Charles Harold *college publishing company executive*
Cohen, Rachelle Sharon *journalist*
Collins, Monica Ann *journalist*
Cook, David *editor*
Cousy, Bob Joseph *sports commentator*
Curtis, Christopher Michael *magazine editor*
Danziger, Jeff *political cartoonist, writer*
Darehshori, Nader Farhang *publishing sales executive*
Davison, Peter Hubert *editor, poet*
Dillin, John Woodward, Jr. *newspaper correspondent*
Dixon, Andrew Lee, Jr. *cable television company executive, lawyer*
Donovan, Helen W. *newspaper editor*
Eder, Richard Gray *newspaper critic*
Eldridge, Larry (William Lawrence Eldridge) *journalist*
Fanning, Katherine Woodruff *editor, journalism educator*
Feder, Donald Albert *syndicated columnist*
Feeney, Mark *newspaper editor*
Flint, Anthony Evans *journalist*
Gendron, George *magazine editor*
Gibson, Barry Joseph *magazine editor*
Greene, Leonard J. *newspaper columnist*
Grossfeld, Stan *newspaper photography executive, author*
Hayward, Charles E. *publishing company executive*
Higgins, George Vincent *journalist, lawyer, author, educator*
Julian, Sheryl *newspaper writer*
Katz, Larry *writer*
Kauffman, Godfrey *newspaper publishing executive*
Kimball, George Edward, III *sports columnist*
King, Nick *newspaper editor*
Klarfeld, Jonathan Michael *journalism educator*
Knight, Norman *broadcast executive*
Knox, Richard Albert *journalist*
Larkin, Michael John *newspaper editor, journalist*
Lawrence, Merloyd Ludington *editor*
Lee, Donald Young (Don Lee) *publishing executive, editor, writer*
Lewis, Anthony *newspaper columnist*
Lichtenberg, Margaret Klee *publishing company executive*
Lyman, Henry *retired publisher, marine fisheries consultant*
Manning, Robert Joseph *editor*
Manning, Thomas Allen *publishing company executive*
Manning, William Frederick *wire service photographer*
McArdle, John *publishing company executive*
Menzies, Ian Stuart *newspaper editor*
Modugno, Maria *publishing executive*
Moore, Francis Daniels *retired surgeon, educator, consultant, editor*
Morgan, Frank Brown Webb, Jr. *journalist, consultant*
Morris, Gerald Douglas *newspaper editor*
Mulvoy, Thomas F., Jr. *newspaper editor, journalist*
Newman, Richard Alan *publisher, editor and consultant*
Purcell, Patrick Joseph *newspaper publisher*
Robinson, Walter *newspaper editor*
Rodman, Oliver *newspaper publishing executive*
Sales, Robert Julian *newspaper editor*
Schwartz, Lloyd *music critic, poet*
Silvey, Anita Lynne *editor*
Skwar, Donald R. *newspaper editor*
Smyth, Peter Hayes *radio executive*
Stevens, Marilyn Ruth *editor*
Storin, Matthew Victor *newspaper editor*
Strothman, Wendy Jo *book publisher*
Szep, Paul Michael *editorial cartoonist*
Taylor, Benjamin B. *newspaper publishing executive*
Taylor, Stephen Emlyn *publishing executive*
Turek, Sonia Fay *journalist*
Utiger, Robert David *medical editor*
Wallraff, Barbara Jean *magazine editor, writer*
Walton, Bill (William Theodore Walton, III) *sportscaster, former professional basketball player*
Whitworth, William A. *magazine editor*
Yemma, John *newspaper editor*
Zellman, Ande *editor*

Brighton
Walker, Ruth Ann *journalist*

Cambridge
Aronson, Michael Andrew *editor*
Bowes, Frederick, III *publishing executive*
Donald, Aida DiPace *publishing executive*
Nordell, Hans Roderick *journalist, retired editor*
Rubin, Jerome Sanford *publishing company executive, lawyer*
Sisler, William Philip *publishing executive*
Squire, James Robert *retired publisher, consultant*
Trainor, Bernard Edmund *journalist, educator, retired marine corps officer*
Urbanowski, Frank *publishing company executive*
Wilcox, Maud *editor*

Chatham
Leighten, Edward Henry *publisher, consultant*

Chestnut Hill
Collins, Arthur Worth (Bud), Jr. *sports commentator*
Goldweitz, Saul *publishing company executive*
Levy, James Peter *publishing company executive*
Smith, Richard Alan *publishing and speciality retailing executive*
Tarr, Robert Joseph, Jr. *publishing executive, retail executive*

Dorchester
Brelis, Matthew Dean Burns *journalist*
Bruzelius, Nils Johan Axel *journalist*
Goodman, Ellen Holtz *journalist*
Greenway, Hugh Davids Scott *journalist*
Hatfield, Julie Stockwell *journalist, newspaper editor*
Huff, William Braid *publication company executive*
Kaufman, Jonathan Reed *journalist*
Larkin, Alfred Sinnott, Jr. *newspaper editor*
Leland, Timothy *newspaper executive*
Taylor, William Osgood *newspaper executive*

East Orleans
Nenneman, Richard Arthur *retired publishing executive*

Framingham
Stuart, Anne Elizabeth *journalist, freelance writer, educator*

Gloucester
Baird, Gordon Prentiss *publisher*

Groton
Smith, Alan Harvey *former editor*

Harwich
Thorndike, Joseph Jacobs, Jr. *editor*

Hingham
Replogle, David Robert *publishing company executive*

Holden
Botty, Kenneth John *editor, newspaper executive*

Holyoke
Dwight, William, Jr. *former newspaper executive, restaurateur*

Hyannis
Himstead, Scott *newspaper publisher*
White, Timothy Oliver *newspaper editor*

Ipswich
Berggren, Dick *editor*

Kingston
Stair, Gobin *publishing executive, painter, graphic designer*

Lexington
Bursma, Albert, Jr. *publishing company executive*
Korte, Loren A. *publishing company executive*

Lincoln
Adams, Thomas Boylston *journalist*
Godine, David Richard *publishing company executive*
Schwann, William Joseph *publisher, musician, discographer*

Lowell
Greenwald, John Edward *newspaper and magazine executive*
Osenton, Thomas George *publisher*

Marshfield
Mc Carthy, Thomas Patrick *magazine publisher*

Needham
Hopson, James Warren *newspaper publisher*
Lebowitz, Marshall *publishing company executive*
Sabosik, Patricia Elizabeth *publisher, editor*

New Bedford
Robbins, Orren Bourne *newspaper publisher*

Newton
Forsberg, Roy Walter *publishing company executive*
Krakoff, Robert Leonard *publishing executive*
Mason, Charles Ellis, III *magazine editor*
Rakay, William R. *publishing company executive*
Sbordon, William G. *publisher*
Stundza, Thomas John *journalist*
Thompson, Stephen Arthur *publishing executive*

Newton Center
Sandman, Peter M. *communications risk consultant*

North Adams
Thurston, Donald Allen *broadcasting executive*

North Chatham
Rowlands, Marvin Lloyd, Jr. *publishing and communications consultant*

North Quincy
Porter, John Stephen *television executive*

Norwell
Rolnik, Zachary Jacob *senior editor, publisher*

Orange
Preece, Warren Eversleigh *editor*

Orleans
Dessauer, John Phillip *publisher, financial management company executive*

Quincy
†Gorfinkle, Constance Sue *journalist*
Lippincott, Joseph P. *photojournalist, educator*

Reading
Stone, Warren R. *book publishing executive*

Richmond
Sexton, William Cottrell *journalist*

Rockport
Bissell, Phil (Charles P. Bissell) *cartoonist*

South Deerfield
Bete, Channing Lindquist, Jr. *publishing company executive*

South Harwich
Micciche, Salvatore Joseph *journalist, lawyer*

South Wellfleet
Macauley, Robie Mayhew *retired editor*

Southbridge
Ghiglione, Loren Frank *newspaper editor*

Springfield
Esposito, Joseph John *publishing company executive*
Garvey, Richard Conrad *journalist*
Gordon, Ronni Anne *journalist*
Haggerty, Thomas Francis *newspaper editor*
Long, Brian Joseph *newspaper publishing executive*
Mish, Frederick Crittenden *editor*
Morse, John M. *book publishing executive*
Norton, Peter J. *publishing executive*
Stanley, Thomas Edward *publishing company executive*

Stockbridge
Rich, Philip Dewey *publishing executive*

Sudbury
Hillery, Mary Jane Larato *columnist, producer, television host, reserve army officer*

Swansea
Holmes, Hank Eugene *broadcast journalist*

Vineyard Haven
Hough, George Anthony, III *journalism educator*

Wayland
Williams, James P., Jr. (Jay Williams) *broadcasting executive*

Wellesley
Gladstone, Richard Bennett *retired publishing company executive*
Myers, Arthur B. *journalist, author*

Wellfleet
Dugger, Ronnie E. *writer, publisher*

West Barnstable
†Breisky, William John *editor*

Weston
Oelgeschlager, Guenther Karl *publisher*
Sanzone, Donna S. *editor-in-chief*

Westwood
Borgman, George Allan *journalist*

Williamstown
Bleezarde, Thomas Warren *magazine editor*

Winchester
Ewing, David Walkley *magazine editor*
Ockerbloom, Richard C. *newspaper executive*

Woburn
Klein, Michael James *broadcast executive, engineer*

Worcester
Magiera, Frank Edward *journalist, critic*

MICHIGAN

Ann Arbor
Beaver, Frank Eugene *communication educator, film critic and historian*
Bedard, Patrick Joseph *editor, writer, consultant*
Csere, Csaba *magazine editor*
Day, Colin Leslie *publisher*
Eisendrath, Charles Rice *journalism educator, manufacturer, farmer, consultant*
Fitzsimmons, Joseph John *publishing executive*
†Martin, Bruce James *newspaper editor*
Mitzelfeld, Jim *newspaper reporter*
†Semion, A. Kay *editor*
Stowe, Leland *journalist, writer*
Yates, Brock Wendel *editor, journal*

Bay City
McDermott, Larry Arnold *newspaper publisher, newspaper editor*

Birmingham
Donald, Larry Watson *sports journalist*
McIntyre, Bruce Herbert *publishing company executive*

Bloomfield Hills
Brown, Lynette Ralya *journalist, publicist*
James, William Ramsay *cable television executive*

Detroit
Albom, Mitch David *sports columnist*
Anstett, Pat *newspaper editor*
Ashenfelter, David Louis *editor, former newspaper reporter*
Bainbridge, Leesa *newspaper editor*
Bradford, Christina *newspaper editor*
Bray, Thomas Joseph *journalist, editor*
Bryfonski, Dedria Anne *publishing company executive*
Bullard, George *newspaper editor*
Burzynski, Susan Marie *newspaper editor*
Cantor, George Nathan *journalist*
Colby, Joy Hakanson *art critic*
DeRamus, Betty Jean *columnist*
DeVine, (Joseph) Lawrence *drama critic*
Dickerson, Brian *editor, periodical*
Diebolt, Judy *newspaper editor*
†Dzwonkowski, Ronald Edward *newspaper editor*
Elsila, David August *editor*
Falls, Joseph Francis *sportswriter, editor*
Gerstel, Judith Ross *film critic*
Giles, Robert Hartmann *newspaper editor*
Givhan, Robin Deneen *journalist*
Guinn, John Rockne *music critic*
Hill, Draper *editorial cartoonist*
Hutton, Carole Leigh *newspaper editor*
Kelleher, Timothy John *publishing company executive*
Kiska, Timothy Olin *newspaper columnist*
Kushma, David William *journalist*
Laitner, Bill *reporter*
Lannon, Linnea *newspaper editor*
Laughlin, Nancy *newspaper editor*
Mathes, Caryn G. *broadcast executive*
McGruder, Robert *newspaper publishing executive*
Meriwether, Heath J. *newspaper editor*
O'Gorman, Kathleen *newspaper editor*
Olmstead, Laurence Daniel *journalist*
Parry, Dale D. *newspaper editor*
Pepper, Jonathon Lester *newspaper columnist*
Richardson, Joan *reporter*
Ross-Flanigan, Nancy *reporter*
Ruffner, Frederick G., Jr. *book publisher*
Shine, Neal James *newspaper editor*
Smith, William Huston *communication company executive*
Smyntek, John Eugene, Jr. *newspaper editor*
Spina, Anthony *photojournalist*
Stark, Susan R. *film critic*
Stroud, Joe Hinton *newspaper editor*
Sylvain, Rick *newspaper editor*
Talbert, Bob *newspaper columnist*
Teagan, John Gerard *newspaper executive*
Turnley, David Carl *photojournalist*
Vega, Frank J. *newspaper publishing executive*
Vincent, Charles Eagar, Jr. *sports columnist*
Waldmeir, Peter Nielsen *journalist*
Watson, Susan *newspaper columnist*
White, Joseph B. *reporter*

East Lansing
Greenberg, Bradley Sander *communications educator*
Johnson, J. David *communication educator*
Lowe, Kenneth Stephen *magazine editor*
Miller, Gerald Raymond *communications educator*
Ralph, David Clinton *communications educator*

Farmington Hills
Ethridge, James Merritt *editor, former publishing company executive, writer*

Grand Rapids
Baker, Richard Lee *book publishing company executive*
Bolinder, Scott W. *publishing company executive*
Gundry, Stanley N. *publishing company executive*
†Kaczmarczyk, Jeffrey Allen *journalist, classical music critic*
Lloyd, Michael Stuart *newspaper editor*
Ryskamp, Bruce E. *publishing executive*

Grosse Pointe
Christian, Edward Kieren *radio and television station executive*

McWhirter, Glenna Suzanne (Nickie McWhirter) *newspaper columnist*
Whittaker, Jeanne Evans *former newspaper columnist*

Jackson
Weaver, Franklin Thomas *newspaper executive*

Kalamazoo
Gilmore, James Stanley, Jr. *broadcast executive*

Lansing
Freedman, Eric *journalist*

Livonia
Campbell, Barbara Ann *editor*

Mount Pleasant
Orlik, Peter Blythe *media educator, author, musician*

Northville
Opre, Thomas Edward *magazine editor, film company executive, corporate travel company executive*

Plymouth
Scott, George Ernest *publisher, writer*

Saginaw
Chaffee, Paul Charles *newspaper editor*
Puravs, John Andris *journalist*
Thatcher, Rex Howard *newspaper publisher*

Southfield
Brown, June *journalist*
Nadel, Roger *radio executive*

Suttons Bay
Skinner, Thomas *broadcasting and film executive*

Troy
Fritz, Jock Thane *radio executive*
Meyers, Christine Laine *publishing and media executive, consultant*
Moore, Oliver Semon, III *publishing executive, consultant*

Whitehall
Youngquist, Alvin Menvid, Jr. *publisher, editor*

Williamston
Landis, Elwood Winton *retired newspaper editor*

Ypsilanti
Evans, Gary Lee *communications educator and consultant*

MINNESOTA

Annandale
Johnson, Jon E. *magazine editor and publisher*

Duluth
Billig, Thomas Clifford *publishing and marketing executive*
Latto, Lewis M., Jr. *broadcasting company executive*

Eagan
Opperman, Dwight Darwin *publishing company executive*

Fergus Falls
Rinden, David Lee *editor*

Mankato
Larson, Michael Len *newspaper editor*

Minneapolis
Albright, Susan *newspaper editor*
Anderson, Albert Esten *publisher*
Bisping, Bruce Henry *photojournalist*
Brings, Lawrence Martin *publisher*
Buoen, Roger *newspaper editor*
Carter, Roy Ernest, Jr. *journalist, educator*
Cope, Lewis *journalist*
Cowles, John, III *newspaper publishing executive*
Crosby, Jacqueline Garton *newspaper editor, journalist*
Dahl, Christopher T. *broadcasting executive*
Degnan, Joseph *magazine editor*
Engebrecht, Julie *newspaper sports editor*
Flanagan, Barbara *journalist*
Franklin, Robert Brewer *journalist*
Hull, William Henry *publishing company executive*
Ison, Christopher John *investigative reporter*
Johnson, Cheryl *newspaper columnist*
†Johnson, Gary Leroy *publisher*
Jones, Will (William Arnold) *writer, former newspaper columnist*
Kilzer, Louis Charles *journalist*
Kinderwater, Joseph C. (Jack Kinderwater) *publishing company executive*
Klobuchar, James John *columnist*
Kramer, Joel Roy *journalist, newspaper executive*
Laing, Karel Ann *magazine publishing executive*
Lerner, Harry Jonas *publishing company executive*
Marshall, Sherrie *newspaper editor*
McEnroe, Paul *reporter*
McGuire, Timothy James *newspaper editor, lawyer*
Meador, Ron *newspaper editor, writer*
†Mohr, L. Thomas *newspaper executive*
Moraczewski, Robert Leo *publisher*
Murphy, Joseph Edward, Jr. *broadcast executive*
Parkinson, Roger P. *publishing company executive*
Salyer, Stephen Lee *broadcast executive*
Scallen, Thomas Kaine *broadcasting executive*
Seaman, William Casper *retired news photographer*
Slovut, Gordon *reporter*
Smetanka, Mary Jane *reporter*
Strickler, Jeff *newspaper movie critic*
Swartz, Donald Everett *television executive*
Vaughan, Peter Hugh *theater critic*
Watson, Catherine Elaine *journalist*
White, Robert James *newspaper editor, columnist*
Wright, Frank Gardner *newspaper editor*
Youngblood, Richard Neil *columnist*
Ziebarth, E. William *news analyst, educator*

Minnetonka
Ehlert, John Ambrose *publisher*

Northfield
Hvistendahl, Joyce Kilmer *journalism and communications educator*

Red Wing
Seymour, Arthur Hallock *retired newspaper editor*

Saint Joseph
Rowland, Howard Ray *mass communications educator*

Saint Paul
Bremer, Victor John *broadcasting executive*
Clark, Ronald Dean *newspaper editor*
Doctor, Kenneth Jay *editor*
Elrod, Bernett Richard (Sam Elrod) *newspaper editor*
Finnegan, John Robert, Sr. *retired newspaper executive*
Fogg, James W. *printing company executive*
Fryxell, David Allen *publishing executive, newspaper editor*
Green, Philip Bevington *publishing company executive*
Hubbard, Stanley Stub *broadcast executive*
†Hudson, Gail Brown *television news producer*
Keillor, Garrison Edward *writer, radio host, storyteller*
Kling, William Hugh *broadcasting executive*
Lund, Bert Oscar, Jr. *publisher*
Lundy, Walker *newspaper editor*
Ostman, Eleanor A. *food writer*
Ridder, Bernard Herman, Jr. *newspaper publisher*

MISSISSIPPI

Biloxi
Hash, John Frank *broadcasting executive*
Weeks, Roland, Jr. *newspaper publisher*

Brandon
Buckley, Frank Wilson *newspaper executive*

Gulfport
Yeager, Andrea Wheaton *editor*

Jackson
Breese, Frank Chandler, III *newsprint company executive, lawyer*
Downing, Margaret Mary *newspaper editor*
Henderson, W. Guy *editor, minister*
Miller, Larry D. *broadcasting executive*
Saunders, Doris Evans *editor, educator, business executive*

University
Hannah, Barry *educator, writer*

Vicksburg
Briuer, Elke Moersch *editor*

Yazoo City
Brown, Marion Lipscomb, Jr. *publisher, retired chemical company executive*

MISSOURI

Columbia
Atwater, James David *journalist, educator*
†Sanders, Keith Page *journalism educator*
Taft, William Howard *journalism educator*

Joplin
Hughes, Fred George *retired newspaper publisher*

Kansas City
Anderson, David Charles *media specialist*
Anderson, James Keith *retired magazine editor*
Andrews, Kathleen W. *book publishing executive*
Batiuk, Thomas Martin *cartoonist*
Brisbane, Arthur Seward *newspaper editor*
Burg, George Roscoe *journalist*
Busby, Marjorie Jean (Marjean Busby) *journalist*
Cahill, Patricia Deal *radio station executive*
Cantrell, (Thomas) Scott *newspaper music critic*
Davis, James Robert *cartoonist*
Diuguid, Lewis Walter *editor, metrocolumnist*
Dodd, Monroe *newspaper editor*
Fox, Thomas Charles *editor, publisher, writer*
Gusewelle, Charles Wesley *journalist*
Ingram, Robert Palmer *magazine publisher*
Kipp, Robert Almy *greeting card company executive*
Larson, Gary *cartoonist*
Martin, Donna Lee *publishing company executive*
McGuff, Joe *newspaper editor*
Mc Meel, John Paul *newspaper syndicate and publishing executive*
McSweeney, William Lincoln, Jr. *publishing executive*
Myers, Wendy Suzanne *editor*
Oliphant, Patrick *editorial cartoonist*
Olson, Kay Melchisedech *magazine editor*
Palmer, Cruise *newspaper editor*
Petosa, Jason Joseph *publisher*
Piette, Edward James *television executive*
Scott, James White *newspaper editor*
Stites, C. Thomas *journalist, publisher*
Tammeus, William David *journalist, columnist*
Taylor, Jeff *reporter*
Thornton, Thomas Noel *publishing executive*
Townsend, Harold Guyon, Jr. *publishing company executive*
Watterson, Bill *cartoonist*
Wilson, Tom *cartoonist, greeting card company executive*

Liguori
O'Connor, Francine Marie *magazine editor*

Saint Joseph
Lockwood, George J. *newspaper editor*

Saint Louis
Baker, Barry *broadcast executive*
Barnes, Harper Henderson *movie critic*
Bauman, George Duncan *former newspaper publisher*
Bohle, Bruce William *editor*
Buck, Jack *sportscaster*
Christopher, Glenn A. *publishing company executive*
Dames, Joan Foster (Mrs. Urban L. Dames) *magazine editor, columnist*
Dierdorf, Daniel Lee (Dan Dierdorf) *football analyst, sports commentator, former professional football player*
Dill, John Francis *publishing company executive*
Domjan, Laszlo Karoly *newspaper executive*
Elkins, Ken Joe *broadcasting executive*
Engelhardt, Thomas Alexander *editorial cartoonist*
Freeland, A. Jerome *publishing executive*
Gauen, Patrick Emil *newspaper correspondent*
Godsey, C. Wayne *broadcasting executive*
Goldberg, Norman Albert *music publisher, writer*
Higgins, Edward Aloysius *newspaper editor*
Kanne, Marvin George *newspaper publishing executive*
Killenberg, George Andrew *newspaper consultant, former newspaper editor*
Korando, Donna Kay *journalist*
Lipman, David *multimedia company executive*
Marcus, Larry David *broadcasting executive*
Mink, Eric P. *newspaper columnist*
Norman, Charles Henry *broadcasting executive*
Olson, Clarence Elmer, Jr. *newspaper editor*
Penniman, Nicholas Griffith, IV *newspaper publisher*
Peters, Frank Lewis, Jr. *retired arts editor*
Pollack, Joe *newspaper critic and columnist, free-lance writer*
Pulitzer, Michael Edgar *publishing executive*
Richmond, Richard Thomas *journalist*
Waters, Richard *retired publishing company executive*
Wente, Patricia Ann *radio executive*
Wiley, Gregory Robert *publisher*
Woo, William Franklin *newspaper editor*

Springfield
†Booze, Joyce Wells *publishing executive*
Champion, Norma Jean *communications educator, state legislator*
Dearmore, Thomas Lee *retired journalist*
Glazier, Robert Carl *publishing executive*
Jacobi, Fredrick Thomas *newspaper publisher*
Sylvester, Ronald Charles *newspaper writer*

MONTANA

Bigfork
Blumberg, Nathan(iel) Bernard *journalist, educator, writer and publisher*

Billings
Jones, Ronald Vance *broadcast executive*

Dillon
Ross, Deborah Lynn (Debbie Ross) *reporter, photographer*

Great Falls
Kochman, Carl Jessee *media executive, consultant, educator*

Helena
Malcolm, Andrew Hogarth *journalist, writer*

Kalispell
James, Marion Ray *magazine founder, editor*
Ruder, Melvin Harvey *retired newspaper editor*

Livingston
Feldstein, Albert B. *retired editor, artist, writer*

NEBRASKA

Kearney
Wice, Paul Clinton *news director, educator*

Lincoln
Dyer, William Earl, Jr. *retired newspaper editor*
Hillegass, Clifton Keith *publisher*
Moyer, Robert Theodore *newspaper editor*
Raz, Hilda *editor-in-chief periodical, educator*
Spellman, J. R. *book publishing executive*

Omaha
Andersen, Harold Wayne *contributing editor, newspaper executive, director*
Davis, Chip *record producer, arranger*
†Donaldson, William L. *newspaper publishing company executive*
Howe, G(ary) Woodson *newspaper editor, newspaper executive*

NEVADA

Henderson
Durante, Salvatore (Rusty Durante) *broadcast executive*

Incline Village
McCartney, Patrick Kevin *newspaper reporter*

Las Vegas
†Baker, Chuck *journalist, author*
†Cling, Carol Susan *movie critic, writer*
Hill, Michael John *newspaper editor*
Kerkorian, Kirk *motion picture company executive, consultant*
Rossin, Herbert Yale *television broadcaster*
Sharits, Dean Paul *motion picture company executive*

Reno
Dalrymple, Margaret Fisher *university press editor, writer*
Miller, Newton Edd, Jr. *communications educator*
Pagliarini, James *broadcast executive*

NEW HAMPSHIRE

Alstead
Fiske, Edward Bogardus *editor, journalist, educational consultant*

Dublin
Hale, Judson Drake, Sr. *editor*

Freedom
Bickford, Gail Holmgren *publishing executive*

Goffstown
Gillmore, Robert *syndicated columnist, author, editor, publisher*

Hanover
Mc Farland, Thomas L. *book publishing executive*

Henniker
Cowan, Stuart DuBois *publisher, consultant, writer*

Hollis
Lerner, Arnold Stanley *radio station executive*

Jackson
Johnson, Ned (Edward Christopher Johnson) *publishing company executive*

Jaffrey
Schulte, Henry Frank *journalism educator*
Von Eckardt, Wolf *design critic, educator*

Lyme
Dwight, Donald Rathbun *newspaper publisher, corporate communications executive*

Manchester
Loeb, Nackey Scripps *publisher*
McQuaid, Joseph Woodbury *newspaper executive*
Perkins, Charles, III *newspaper editor*

Merrimack
Kotelly, George Vincent *editor, writer*

Nashua
Bickford, Andrew Thomas *newspaper publisher*

Portsmouth
Hopkins, Jeannette Ethel *book publisher, editor*
Silverman, George Alan *broadcasting executive*
Thornhill, Arthur Horace, Jr. *retired book publisher*

NEW JERSEY

Belle Mead
Murphy, Barry John *publishing executive*

Bloomfield
Vincent, Tony *cable television/radio executive and personality*

Bordentown
Brown, Hershel M. *newspaper publisher*

Bridgewater
Freeman, Henry McCall *newspaper publisher*
Harrigan, Laura G. *newspaper editor*
Healey, Lynne Kover *editor, broadcaster, writer, educator*

Califon
Hannigan, Frank *sportswriter, television writer and commentator, golf course design consultant*

Cedar Grove
Spagnardi, Ronald Lee *publishing executive*

Cherry Hill
Biddle, Daniel R. *reporter*
Callaway, Ben Anderson *journalist*
Rudman, Solomon Kal *magazine publisher*

Cranbury
Reichek, Morton Arthur *retired magazine editor, writer*
Yoseloff, Julien David *publishing company executive*
Yoseloff, Thomas *publisher*

Cranford
Bodian, Nat G. *publishing, marketing consultant, author, lecturer, lexicographer*

Deal
Becker, Richard Stanley *music publisher*

East Brunswick
Kabela, Frank, Jr. *broadcast executive*
Thompson, Robert McBroom *publishing executive*

East Rutherford
Taylor, Lawrence *sports commentator, former professional football player*

Edison
Comstock, Robert Ray *journalism educator, newspaper editor*
Hunter, Michael *publishing executive*

Englewood
Friedman, Emanuel *publishing company executive*
†Vane, Dena *magazine editor-in-chief*

Englewood Cliffs
Brissie, Eugene Field, Jr. *publisher*
Dojny, Richard Francis *publishing company executive*
Guiher, James Morford, Jr. *publisher*
Haltiwanger, Robert Sidney, Jr. *book publishing executive*
Hurst, Kenneth Thurston *publisher*
†Saible, Stephanie *magazine editor*
†Weiderholz, Conrad *magazine publisher*

Florham Park
Mott, Vincent Valmon *publisher, author*

Fords
†Blond, Stuart Richard *newsletter editor*

Fort Lee
Fischel, Daniel Norman *publishing consultant*
Gharib, Susie *television newscaster*
Insana, Ronald Gerard *newscaster*
Williams, Edwin William *publisher*

Hackensack
Ahearn, James *newspaper columnist*
Benfield, Richard Ernest *journalist*
Blomquist, David Wels *journalist*
†Feldberg, Robert Moses *theater critic*
Mack, Patricia Johnson *newspaper editor*
Margulies, James Howard *editorial cartoonist*
Pennington, William Mark *sportswriter*
Waixel, Vivian *journalist*

Haddonfield
Cheney, Daniel Lavern *retired magazine publisher*

Harvey Cedars
Elliott, Joseph Gordon, Jr. *retired newspaper executive*

Hoboken
Regazzi, John James, III *publishing executive*

Holmdel
Wyndrum, Ralph W., Jr. *communications company executive*

Jersey City
Ingrassia, Paul Joseph *publishing executive*
Katz, Colleen *editor in chief*
Shildneck, Barbara Jean *accounting magazine editor*
Wagner, Douglas Walker Ellyson *journal editor*

Lebanon
Goulazian, Peter Robert *retired broadcasting executive*

Linwood
McCormick, Robert Matthew, III *newspaper executive*

Litte Falls
Glasser, Lynn Schreiber *publisher*

Little Falls
Glasser, Stephen Andrew *publishing executive, lawyer*

Long Branch
Lagowski, Barbara Jean *writer, book editor*

Mahwah
Bram, Leon Leonard *publishing company executive*
Eiger, Richard William *publisher*
Hansen, Rosanna Lee *publishing executive*
Lynch, Kevin A. *book publishing executive*
Schecter, M. *book publishing executive*

Maplewood
Hammond, Caleb Dean, III *publishing executive*

Margate City
Kennedy, Berenice Connor (Mrs. Jefferson Kennedy, Jr.) *magazine executive, writer, consultant*

Marlton
Forbes, Gordon Maxwell *sports journalist, commentator*

Medford
Hogan, Thomas Harlan *publisher*

Metuchen
Horrocks, Norman *publisher*

Midland Park
Koster, John Peter, Jr. *journalist, author*

Millburn
Raff, Gilbert *publishing company executive*

Montclair
Brownrigg, Walter Grant *cartoonist, corporate executive*
Gogick, Kathleen Christine *magazine editor, publisher*
Hardin, John Alexander *retired broadcasting consultant*
Jacoby, Tamar *journalist, author*
Sabin, William Albert *editor*

Montvale
Pfister, James Joseph *publishing company executive*
Sifton, David Whittier *magazine editor*

Montville
Teubner, Ferdinand Cary, Jr. *retired publishing company executive*

Morris Plains
Krull, Kevin Charles *publishing company executive, lawyer*

Morristown
Ahl, David Howard *writer, editor*

Murray Hill
Wagner, Edward Kurt *publishing company executive*

Neptune
Clurfeld, Andrea *editor, food critic*
Lass, E(rnest) Donald *communications company executive*
Ollwerther, William Raymond *newspaper editor*
Plangere, Jules L., III *newpaper company executive*

New Brunswick
Horowitz, Irving Louis *publisher, educator*
†Reeling, Patricia Glueck *library educator, educational consultant*
Wilson, Donald Malcolm *publishing executive*

New Providence
Barnes, Sandra Henley *publishing company executive*
Cooper, Carol Diane *publishing company executive*
Walker, Stanley P. *publishing executive*

Newark
Allen, David *newspaper editor*
Aregood, Richard Lloyd *editor*
Bartner, Martin *newspaper executive*
Bishop, Gordon Bruce *journalist*
Braun, Robert *newspaper editor*
Canfield, William Newton *editorial cartoonist*
Cocchia, Neal *newspaper editor*
Everett, Richard G. *newspaper editor*
Gillett, Jonathan Newell *publishing executive*
Greendorfer, Terese Grosman *fashion editor*
Harrison, Charles *newspaper editor*
Kanzler, George *journalist, critic*
Klein, Willie *newspaper editor*
Kosof, Anna Clara *radio station executive*
Lenehan, Art *newspaper editor*
Martinez, Arturo *newspaper editor*
Maske, Monica *newspaper editor*
Newhouse, Donald E. *newspaper publishing executive*
Newhouse, Mark William *publishing executive*
†Willse, James Patrick *newspaper editor*
Wolper, Allan L. *journalist, educator*

Newton
Carstens, Harold Henry *publisher*
†Jones, Matthew T. *editorial director*

Northvale
Aronson, Jason *publisher*
Kurzweil, Arthur *publisher, writer, educator*

Oldwick
Snyder, Arthur *publishing company executive*

Oradell
Clark, Laura *magazine editor, writer*

Paramus
Kenney, Martin Edward, Jr. *publishing company executive*

Park Ridge
Noyes, Robert Edwin *publisher, writer*

Parsippany
Geyer, Thomas Powick *newspaper publisher*

Passaic
Levine, David M. *newspaper editor*
Scudder, Richard B. *newspaper executive*
†Starr, Michael Seth *critic*

Paterson
Deffaa, Chip *jazz critic*

Pennington
Harris, Frederick George *publishing company executive*

Pilesgrove
Koehler, George Applegate *broadcasting company executive*

Piscataway
Fogiel, Max *publishing executive*

Plainsboro
Talkington, William Ale *publishing company executive*

Pleasantville
Briant, Maryjane *newspaper editor*

Princeton
Buttenheim, Edgar Marion *publishing executive*
Cushmore, Carole Lee *publisher*
Doherty, Leonard Edward *financial publishing company executive*
Kull, F. Thomas, Jr. *newspaper publishing executive*
Liben, Michael Paul *magazine publisher*
Lippincott, Walter Heulings, Jr. *publishing executive*
O'Donnell, Laurence Gerard *newspaper editor*
Palsho, Dorothea Coccoli *information services executive*
Smith, Margaret Phyllis *editor, consultant*
Weiss, Renée Karol *editor, writer, musician*

Ramsey
Underwood, Steven Clark *publishing executive*

Ridgewood
Anderson, Thomas Kemp, Jr. *editor*
Economaki, Chris Constantine (Christopher Economaki) *publisher, editor*
Kiernan, Richard Francis *publisher*

Rumson
Macdonald, Donald Arthur *publishing executive*
Robinson, William Wheeler *editor*

Saddle River
Buckler, Beatrice *editor*
Caulo, Ralph Daniel *publishing executive*
Dowden, Carroll Vincent *publishing company executive*

Secaucus
Bender, Bruce F. *book publishing executive*
Thomas, Ian Leslie Maurice *publisher*

Short Hills
Winter, Ruth Grosman (Mrs. Arthur Winter) *journalist*

Sparta
Spence, Robert Leroy *publishing executive*

Springfield
Enslow, Ridley Madison, Jr. *book publisher*

Stockholm
dePaolo, Ronald Francis *editor, publisher*

Summit
Scudder, Edward Wallace, Jr. *newspaper and broadcasting executive*

Tenafly
Vinocur, M. Richard *publisher*

Trenton
Kelly, Thomas Joseph, III *photojournalist*
Stewart, Barbara Elizabeth *free-lance magazine editor, artist*
Weissman, Daniel *journalist*

Tuckerton
Egan, Roger Edward *publishing executive*

Upper Saddle River
Butterfield, Bruce Scott *publishing company executive*

Verona
Meyer, Helen (Mrs. Abraham J. Meyer) *retired editorial consultant*

NEW MEXICO

Albuquerque
Danziger, Jerry *broadcasting executive*
Goldston, Barbara M. Harral *editor*
Guthrie, Patricia Sue *newspaper reporter, free-lance writer*
Hadas, Elizabeth Chamberlayne *publisher*
Johnson, Robert Hersel *journalist*
Lang, Thompson Hughes *publishing company executive*
Looney, Ralph Edwin *newspaper editor, author, photographer*
Mc Million, John Macon *retired newspaper publisher*

Glenwood
Tackman, Arthur Lester *newspaper publisher, management consultant*

Glorieta
Mc Coy, Robert Baker *publisher*

Las Cruces
Dickinson, James Gordon *editor*

Los Alamos
Mendius, Patricia Dodd Winter *editor, educator, writer*

Santa Fe
Calloway, Larry *columnist*
Dirks, Lee Edward *newspaper executive*
Drabanski, Emily Ann *editor*
Ettinger, Richard Prentice *publishing company executive*
Forsdale, (Chalmers) Louis *education and communication educator*
Mauldin, William H. (Bill Mauldin) *cartoonist*
Mc Kinney, Robert Moody *newspaper editor and publisher*
Stieber, Tamar *writer*

Taos
Bacon, Wallace Alger *speech communications educator, author*

NEW YORK

Albany
Lynch, Daniel *newspaper editor, writer*
Morga Bellizzi, Celeste *editor*
Murray, David *journalist, author*
Ortloff, George Christian, Sr. (Chris Ortloff) *journalist, state legislator*
Reynolds, Joseph P. *publishing executive, educational consultant*
Rosenfeld, Harry Morris *editor*
Smith, Rex William *journalist*

Armonk
Sharpe, Myron Emanuel *publisher, editor, writer*
†Weber, Michael *editor*

Baldwin Place
Kurian, George Thomas *publisher*

Bangall
†Cetrone, Gene Leonard *author, producer, screenwriter*

Bayport
Poli, Kenneth Joseph *editor*

Bedford
Bowman, James Kinsey *publishing company executive, rare book specialist*

Bellport
Hughes, Elinor Lambert *drama and film critic*

Brewster
†Shepard, Jean Heck *publishing company consultant*

Briarcliff Manor
Zimmar, George Peter *publishing executive, psychology educator*

Briarwood
Danna, Jo J. *publisher, author, anthropologist*

Bridgehampton
Phillips, Warren Henry *publisher*

Bronx
Carrick, Bruce Robert *publishing company executive*
Jennings, Ralph Merwin *broadcasting executive*
Moritz, Charles Fredric *book editor*
Rizzuto, Philip Francis (Scooter) *sports broadcaster, former professional baseball player*
Weins, Leo Matthew *publishing company executive*
Zalaznick, Sheldon *editor, journalist*

Bronxville
Barnhart, Clarence Lewis *lexicographer, editor*
Lombardo, Philip Joseph *broadcasting company executive*
Noble, James Kendrick, Jr. *media industry consultant*
Shuker, Gregory Brown *publishing and production company executive*

Brooklyn
Bianco, Anthony Joseph, III *newswriter*
Bode, Walter Albert *editor*
Carlson, Ralph Lawrence *book publisher*
Federici, William Vito *newspaper reporter*
Friis, Erik Johan *editor, publisher*
Harvey, Edmund Huxley, Jr. (Tad Harvey) *editor*
Lobron, Barbara L. *writer, editor, photographer*
Moore, Arthur James *editor*
Reynolds, Nancy Remick *editor, writer*
Sanford, David Boyer *writer, editor*
Schmidt, Fred (Orval Frederick Schmidt) *editor*
Walsh, George William *publishing company executive, editor*

Brookville
Huber, Don Lawrence *publisher*

Buffalo
Brady-Borland, Karen *reporter*
Collins, J. Michael *public broadcasting executive*
Curran, Robert *columnist*
†Esmonde, Donn Patrick *newspaper columnist*
Goldhaber, Gerald Martin *communication educator, author, consultant*
Halpert, Leonard Walter *retired editor*
†Huntington, Richard (John) *art critic*
Ireland, Barbara Hennig *newspaper editor*
Light, Murray Benjamin *newspaper editor*
Okun, Janice *food editor*
Robinson, David Clinton *reporter*
Spencer, Foster Lewis *newspaper editor*
Toles, Thomas Gregory *editorial cartoonist*
Trotter, Herman Eager, Jr. (Herman Trotter) *music critic*
Urban, Henry Zeller *newspaperman*
Vogel, Michael N. *journalist, writer, historian*

Campbell Hall
Ottaway, James Haller, Jr. *newspaper publisher*

Chappaqua
Gstalder, Herbert William *publisher*

Croton On Hudson
Coleman, Earl Maxwell *publishing company executive*
Kahn, Roger *author*
Miranda, Robert Nicholas *publishing company executive*
Nelson, Charles Arthur *publisher, consultant*
Shatzkin, Leonard *publishing consultant*
Straka, Laszlo Richard *publishing consultant*
Turner, David Reuben *publisher, author*

Delmar
Mangouni, Norman *publisher*

Dobbs Ferry
Cohen, Philip Francis *publishing company executive*
Holtz, Sidney *publishing company executive*
Simon, Lothar *publishing company executive*
Whiting, John Randolph *publisher, writer, editor*

East Hampton
De Bruhl, Marshall *writer, editor, publishing consultant*

East Northport
Reed, Robert Monroe *publishing executive*

Farmingdale
Steckler, Larry *publisher, editor*

Floral Park
Chatoff, Michael Alan *legal editor*

Flushing
Cathcart, Robert Stephen *mass media consultant*
Kiner, Ralph McPherran *sports commentator, former baseball player*

Forest Hills
Stinson, Richard James *editor*

Fort Covington
Dunwich, Gerina *magazine editor, author, astrologer, witch*

Garden City
Olcott, William Alfred *magazine editor*

Goldens Bridge
Ambrose, Daniel Michael *publishing executive*

Goshen
Goodreds, John Stanton *newspaper publisher*

Grand Island
White, Ralph David *retired editor and writer*

Great Neck
Fiel, Maxine Lucille *journalist, behavioral analyst, lecturer*
Green, Dan *publishing company executive*
Panes, Jack Samuel *publishing company executive*
Roth, Harvey Paul *publisher*
Rubin, Irving *editor*
Velie, Lester *journalist*

Hamilton
Edmonston, William Edward, Jr. *publisher*

Harrison
McCaffrey, Neil *publishing executive*

Hauppauge
Reis, Don *publishing executive*

Hempstead
Adams, Robert Hugo *business news publisher, English teacher*
Masheck, Joseph Daniel *art critic, educator*

Hicksville
Salsberg, Arthur Philip *publishing company executive*
Tinghitella, Stephen *publishing company executive*

Huntington
Connor, Joseph Robert *editor*
Holahan, Richard Vincent *former magazine and book publisher*

Irvington
Lugenbeel, Edward Elmer *publisher*

Ithaca
Bourne, Russell *publisher, author*
Kendler, Bernhard *editor*
Scheuer, Katherine Dunn *editor*
Schwartz, Donald Franklin *communication educator*

Jackson Heights
Sklar, Morty E. *publisher, editor*

Jamaica
Wetherington, Roger Vincent *journalism educator, newspaper copy editor*

Jamestown
Goldman, Simon *broadcasting executive*

Katonah
Fry, John *magazine editor*
Krefting, Robert J(ohn) *publishing company executive*
Raymond, Jack *journalist, public relations executive, foundation executive*

Kinderhook
Lankhof, Frederik Jan *publishing executive*

Kings Park
Greene, Robert William *media consultant*

Lancaster
Van Nortwick, Thomas H. *radio broadcast executive*

Larchmont
Kerr, Walter F. *retired drama critic, author*

Locust Valley
Zulch, Joan Carolyn *retired medical publishing company executive, consultant*

Long Beach
Bernstein, Lester *editorial consultant*
Robbins, Jeffrey Howard *media consultant, research writer, educator*

Long Island City
Schlosser, Herbert S. *broadcasting company executive*

Manhasset
Orenstein-Bellia, Jessica *publishing company manager*
Rostky, George Harold *editor*
Wallace, Richard *editor, writer*
Wallace, Richard K. *editor, journalist*
Wettereau, Richard Bradway *editor, writer*

Maryknoll
Gormley, Robert John *book publisher*

Mattituck
Paulsen, Joanna *publishing executive*

Mechanicville
Mahoney, Michael Nicholas *newspaper owner*

Melville
Bass, Elizabeth Ruth *editor*
Brandt, Robert Frederic, III *newspaper editor, journalist*
Colen, B. D. *journalist*
Cooke, Robert William *science journalist*
†Donovan, Brian *reporter, journalist*
Dooley, James C. *newspaper editor*
Hall, Charlotte Hauch *publishing executive*
Hildebrand, John Frederick *newspaper columnist*
Isenberg, Steven Lawrence *newspaper executive*
†Jansen, Raymond A., Jr. *newspaper publishing executive*
Kahn, David *editor, author*
Klurfeld, James Michael *journalist*
Lynn, James Dougal *newspaper editor, journalist*
Marro, Anthony James *newspaper editor*
Moran, Paul James *journalist, columnist*
Payne, Leslie *newspaper editor, columnist, journalist, author*
Redder, Thomas H. *newspaper publishing executive*
Robins, Marjorie Kaplan *newspaper editor*
Roel, Ron *newspaper editor*
†Saul, Stephanie *journalist*
Sommer, Jeff *journalist*
Toedtman, James Smith *newspaper editor, journalist*
Woldt, Harold Frederick, Jr. *newspaper publishing executive*

Middle Village
Kolatch, Alfred Jacob *publisher*

Middletown
Bedell, Barbara Lee *newspaperwoman*
Sprick, Dennis Michael *critic, copy editor*

Mineola
Cirker, Hayward *publisher*

Montauk
First, Wesley *publishing company executive*

Mount Kisco
Pastorelle, Peter John *film company executive, radiological services and waste management company executive*

Mount Vernon
Mc Neill, Charles James *publishing executive*

New City
Elberg, Darryl Gerald *publisher, educator*

New Rochelle
Saunders, Rubie Agnes *former magazine editor, author*

New York
†Abatemarco, Fred *editor in chief*
Abelson, Alan *columnist*
Abercrombie, Stanley *magazine editor*
Abrahams, William Miller *editor, author*
Achtert, Walter Scott *publisher*
Addison, Herbert John *publishing executive*
Albert, Marv *sportscaster, program director*
Alexander, Shana *journalist, author, lecturer*
Alpern, David Mark *magazine editor, broadcast journalist and producer*
Alter, Jonathan Hammerman *journalist*
Amdur, Neil Lester *sports editor, writer*
Amster, Linda Evelyn *newspaper executive, consultant*
Andersen, Kurt Byars *magazine editor, critic, writer*
Anderson, Bradley Jay *cartoonist*
Anderson, David Poole *sportswriter*
Anderson, Jack Northman *newspaper columnist*
Anderson, Walter Herman *magazine editor*
Andrews, Frederick Franck *newspaper editor*
Antilla, Susan *journalist*
Antonell, Walter John *publishing executive*
Appleton, Myra *magazine editor, writer*
Arcara, James Amadeus *broadcasting company executive*
Arenson, Karen Wattel *journalist*
Arledge, Roone *television executive*
Arnold, Kenneth Lloyd *publisher, playwright*
Arnold, Martin *journalist*
Asahina, Robert James *editor, publishing company executive*
Asher, Aaron *editor, publisher*
Atkinson, Paul C. *newspaper publishing executive*
Atlas, James Robert *magazine editor, writer*
Auchincloss, Kenneth *magazine editor*
Austin, Danforth Whitley *newspaper executive*
Austin, Gabriel Christopher *publisher*
Babson, Irving K. *publishing company executive*
Bache, Theodore Stephen *recording company executive*
Bahash, Robert J. *publishing executive*
Bahr, Lauren S. *publishing company executive*
Bahrenburg, D. Claeys *publishing executive*
Bailey, Janet Dee *publishing company executive*
Bakal, Carl *writer, public relations counsel, photojournalist*
Baker, Elizabeth Calhoun *magazine editor*
Baker, Russell Wayne *columnist, author*
Baker, William Franklin *public broadcasting company executive*
Baker, William George *publishing company financial executive*
Baldassano, Corinne Leslie *radio executive*
Ball, John Paul *publishing company executive*
Bandier, Martin *music publisher*
Baranski, Joan Sullivan *publisher*
Barletta, Joseph Francis *newspaper executive, lawyer*
Barnes, Clive Alexander *drama and dance critic*
Barnes, Duncan *magazine editor, writer*
Baron, Carolyn *editor, author, publishing executive*
Baron, Maureen Walsh *editor, writer*
Barron, James Turman *journalist*
Barry, Edward William *publisher*
Barry, Lynda *cartoonist, playwright, author*
Barry, William Garrett, III *publishing company executive*
Bartley, Robert LeRoy *newspaper editor*
Baruch, Ralph M. *communications executive*
Baxter, Adrienne Marshall *art editor*
Bazell, Robert Joseph *science correspondent*
Beardsley, Charles William *engineering publisher, editor, writer*
Becker, Don Crandall *newspaper executive*
Begell, William *publisher*
Bemis, Mary Ferguson *magazine editor*
Bennack, Frank Anthony, Jr. *publishing company executive*
Bennett, Edward A. *broadcast company executive*
Bercovitch, Hanna Margareta *editor*
Berkwitt, George Joseph *editor*
Berman, Philip Averill *journalist, consultant*
Bernstein, Carl *author, journalist*
Bernstein, Richard Allen *publishing company executive*
Bernstein, Robert Louis *publishing company executive*
Berrien, James Stuart *magazine publisher*
†Berry, John Nichols, III *publishing executive, editor*
Berry, Joyce Charlotte *university press editor*
Beuth, Philip Roy *television executive*
Bewkes, Jeff *television broadcasting company executive*
Biewen, Robert L. *publishing executive*
Biondi, Frank J., Jr. *broadcast executive*
Bite-Dickson, Guna *newspaper editor*
Black, Hillel Moses *publisher*
Black, Neil Spencer *magazine publishing executive*
Black, Rosemary *newspaper editor*
Blair, William Granger *retired newspaperman*
Bleiberg, Robert Marvin *retired financial editor*
Bliven, Naomi *book reviewer*
†Bloch, Peter *editor*
Blyth, Myrna Greenstein *publishing executive, editor, author*
Blythe, William LeGette, II *editor, writer*
Boehm, David Alfred *publisher, producer*
Bonniwell, Katherine *magazine executive*
Borden, Elizabeth B. *publishing executive*
Borders, William Alexander *journalist*
Bouloukos, Don P. *broadcast company executive*
Boultinghouse, Marion Craig Bettinger *editor*
Boundas, Louise Gooch *editor*
Bourdon, David *art critic, writer*
Boyce, Joseph Nelson *journalist*
Brack, Reginald Kufeld, Jr. *publisher*
Bradford, John Carroll *retired magazine executive*
Bradley, Edward R. *news correspondent*
Brady, James Winston *writer, television commentator*
Brant, Sandra J. *magazine publisher*
Brecher, John *newspaper editor*
Breindel, Eric Marc *editor, columnist, educator*
Brennan, Timothy William *entertainment company executive*
†Brenner, Beth Fuchs *publishing executive*
Breslin, Jimmy *columnist, author*
Brewer, John Charles *journalist*
Briggs, Jean Audrey *publishing company executive*
Brill, Steven *magazine editor*
Brimelow, Peter *journalist*
Brody, Jacqueline *editor*
Brody, Jane Ellen *journalist*
Brokaw, Thomas John *television broadcast executive, correspondent*
Brooks, Geraldine *reporter, correspondent*
Brooksbank, Randolph Wood *broadcasting executive*
Brown, Helen Gurley *editor, writer*
Brown, Jeffrey Wisner *publishing company executive*
Brown, Les (Lester Louis) *journalist*
Brown, Tina *magazine editor*
Browne, Arthur *newspaper editor*
Browne, Malcolm Wilde *journalist*
Bryant, Gay *magazine editor, writer*
Brydon, Donald James *media consultant, former news service executive*
†Buckley, Kevin *magazine editor*
Buckley, Priscilla Langford *magazine editor*
Buckley, Virginia Laura *editor*
Buckley, William Frank, Jr. *magazine editor, writer*
†Buford, Bill *editor, writer*
Buhagiar, Marion *editor, author*
Burenga, Kenneth L. *publishing executive*
Burgheim, Richard Allan *magazine editor*
Burns, John F. *reporter*
Buttner, Jean Bernhard *publishing company executive*
Bylinsky, Gene Michael *magazine editor*
Byrne, Gerard Anthony *publishing company executive, marketing consultant*
Caldwell, Earl *newspaper columnist*
Callahan, Robert F., Jr. *radio network executive*
Callum, Myles *magazine editor, writer*
Campbell, Robert Chambers *critic, playwright*
Campi, John G. *newspaper publishing executive*
Campos, Fernando *editor-in-chief*
Canby, Vincent *film critic*
Cantwell, Mary *journalist*
Carr, Gladys Justin *publishing company executive*
Carroll, Kent *book publishing executive*
†Carter, Betsy L. *magazine editor*
Carter, Edward Graydon *editor*
Carter, Sylvia *journalist*
†Cassidy, John Joseph *journalist*
Chamberlin, Ward Bryan, Jr. *public broadcasting executive*
Chancellor, John William *former news correspondent*
Chandler, Kenneth A. *newspaper editor*
Chase, Sylvia B. *journalist*
Chernoff, Allan *correspondent*
Cherry, Rona Beatrice *magazine editor, writer*
Chesnutt, Jane *publishing executive*
Chiles, Nick *newspaper reporter*
Chimsky, Mark Evan *editorial executive*
Chook, Paul Howard *publishing executive*
Christian, Darrell L. *journalist*
Chung, Connie (Constance Yu-hwa Chung) *broadcast journalist*
†Church, George John *journalist*
Clabby, William Robert *editor*
Clurman, Richard Michael *journalist*
Cohl, Claudia Hope *editor*
Colasuonno, Louis Christopher *newspaper editor*
Connolly, William Gerard *newspaper editor*
Cook, James *magazine editor*
Cooke, Alfred Alistair *correspondent, broadcaster*
Cooney, Joan Ganz *broadcasting executive*
Cooper, Arthur Gerald *cable television executive*
Cooper, Arthur Martin *magazine editor*
Cooper, James H. *book publishing company executive, lawyer*
Cooper, Roger Frank *publishing company executive*
Corcoran, David *newspaper editor*
Corliss, Richard Nelson *critic, magazine editor*
Cornell, George W. *journalist*
Corporon, John Robert *broadcasting executive*
Cose, Ellis *journalist, author*
Costello, Gerald Michael *editor*
Couric, Katherine *broadcast journalist*
Court, Kathryn Diana *editor*
Cox, Winston H. *television executive*
Craig, George *publishing executive*
Crawford, Harold Bernard *publisher*
Crawley, John Boevey *publisher*
Crier, Catherine *television news correspondent*
†Crispino, Mike *sportscaster*
Crist, Judith *film and drama critic*
Croce, Arlene Louise *critic*
Cronkite, Walter *radio and television news correspondent*
Cross, Theodore Lamont *publisher, author*
Crow, Elizabeth Smith *publishing company executive*
Crowdus, Gary Alan *film company executive*
Culhane, John William *journalist, author, film historian*
Cunningham, Jeffrey Milton *publishing executive*
Cuozzo, Steven David *newspaper editor*
Curry, Ann *correspondent, anchor*
Curry, Jack *magazine editor*
Cutie, James A. *newspaper publishing executive*
Daly, Charles Patrick *publishing company executive*
Daly, Joe Ann Godown *publishing company executive*
Daly, Margaret V. *magazine editor*
Daly, Michael *newspaper columnist*
D'Angelo, Joseph Francis *publishing company executive*
Daniels, Faith *newscaster*
Daniels, Joanne D. *publisher*
Danzig, Frederick Paul *newspaper editor*
†Darnton, John Townsend *journalist*
Davis, Clive Jay *record company executive*
Davis, Orlin Ray *publisher, consultant*
Davoe, David *publishing executive*
Dedman, Bill *journalist*
Deems, Richard Emmet *magazine publisher*
Deitz, Paula *magazine editor*
Dekker, Marcel *publishing company executive*
Derow, Peter Alfred *publishing company executive*
Deutsch, Martin Bernard Joseph *editor, publisher*
Diamond, Edwin *journalism educator, editor, columnist*
Diamond, Judy Kay *publishing executive*
Diamond, Robert Stephen *publishing company executive*
Dillingham, Robert Bulger *publishing executive*
Dionne, Joseph Lewis *publishing company executive*
Disney, Anthea *editor*
†Dobbs, Lou *television executive, managing editor*
Dobell, Byron Maxwell *magazine consultant*
Doherty, Thomas *publisher*
Dolgen, Jonathan L. *motion picture company executive*
Dolger, Jonathan *editor, literary agent*
Donald, Roger Thomas *publishing executive*
Dormann, Henry O. *magazine publisher*
Dornemann, Michael *book publishing executive*
Drapkin, Arnold Howard *consulting picture editor, journalist, program director*
Drasner, Fred *newspaper publishing executive*
Drawbaugh, Kevin Alan *journalist*
Drewry, Elizabeth *newspaper publishing executive*
Duggan, Dennis Michael *newspaper editor*
Duncan, Richard *magazine editor*
Dunn, James Joseph *magazine publisher*
Dunn, Martin *newspaper editor-in-chief*
Dunne, Thomas Leo *editor, author, publisher*
Dupuy, Frank Russell, Jr. *magazine publisher*
Dutter, Andrew Allen *editor*
†Dwyer, Jim *reporter, columnist*
Dystel, Jane Dee *literary agent*
Ebersol, Dick *television broadcasting executive*
Eckman, Fern Marja *journalist*
Edmiston, Mark Morton *publishing company executive*
Eisenstaedt, Alfred *photojournalist*
Ellerbee, Linda *broadcast journalist*
Elliman, Donald *magazine company executive*
Elliott, Osborn *journalist, educator, former university dean*
Ellis, Charles Richard *publishing executive*
Ellsworth, Arthur Whitney *publishing consultant*
Emerson, Ken *newspaper editor*
Enberg, Dick *sportscaster*
†Engstrom, Erik *publishing company executive*
Epstein, Barbara *editor*
Epstein, Jason *publishing company executive*
Erbsen, Claude Ernest *journalist*
Erlanger, Steven Jay *journalist*
Ertegun, Ahmet Munir *record company executive*
Esposito, Richard Joseph *journalist, executive*
Esterow, Milton *magazine editor, publisher*
Evans, Edward Parker *former publishing company executive*
Evans, Harold M. *publishing executive, writer*
Everette, Cheryl *newspaper editor*
Fairchild, John Burr *publisher*
Faran, Ellen Webster *publishing executive*
Farber, Jackie *editor*
Fargis, Paul McKenna *publishing consultant, book developer, editor*
Farney, Dennis *journalist*
Feders, Sid *journalist, television producer*
Feinberg, Samuel *retired newspaper columnist*
Feniger, Jerome Roland, Jr. *broadcasting executive*
†Fennell, John *magazine publisher*
Fenton, Thomas Trail *journalist*
Ferber, Samuel *publishing executive*
Feretic, Eileen Susan *editor*
Ferrara, Peter Biagio, Jr. *radio broadcast executive*
Fertig, Howard *publisher, editor*
Finberg, Alan Robert *retired newspaper executive, lawyer*
Fine, Donald Irving *editor, publisher*
Fine, Michael Joseph *publishing and communications company executive*
Fiore, Mary *magazine editor*
Fish, Hamilton *public interest executive*
Fisher, Arthur *magazine editor*
Fisher, Gary Alan *publishing executive*
Fishman, James H. *magazine executive*
Fitzgerald, James E. *newspaper publishing executive*
Flagg, Jeanne Bodin *editor*
Flanagan, Bernard *newspaper publishing executive*
Flanagan, Dennis *journalist*
†Florio, Lori Zelikow *magazine publisher*
Florio, Steven T. *magazine executive*
Foley, Joseph Bernard *retired business publishing executive*
Fondiller, David Stewart *journalist*
Forbes, Christopher (Kip Forbes) *publisher*
Forbes, Malcolm Stevenson, Jr. *publishing executive*
Forbes, Timothy Carter *publisher*
Forst, Donald *newspaper editor*
†Fox, Mitchell *magazine publisher*
Fox, Stephen Cress *television correspondent, writer*
Fox, Sylvan *journalist*
Frank, James Aaron *magazine editor, author*
Frankel, Max *journalist*
Franks, Lucinda Laura *journalist*
Frawley, Sean Paul *publishing executive*
Freedgood, Anne Goodman *editor*
Freedman, Albert Z. *publishing company executive*
†Freudenheim, Milton B. *journalist*
Friedheim, Eric Arthur *publisher, editor*
Friedman, J. Roger *publisher*
Friedman, Joshua M. *journalist, educator*
Friedman, Robert *editor*
Friendly, Fred W. *journalist, educator*
Frith, Margaret *publishing company executive*
Fuchs, Joseph Louis *magazine publisher*
Fuchs, Michael Joseph *television executive*
Furlong, Charles Richard *broadcasting executive*
Gaines, James Russell *magazine editor, author*
Gainsburg, Roy Ellis *publishing executive*
Galassi, Jonathan White *book publishing company executive*
Gallo, Gregory *sports editor*
Gallo, William Victor *cartoonist*
Galotti, Donna *publishing executive*
Galotti, Ronald A. *magazine publisher*
Gandolf, Raymond L. *media correspondent*
Garagiola, Joe *sports broadcaster*
Gardino, Vincent Anthony *broadcast executive*
Garratt, Graham *publishing executive*
Gatti, Frank R. *publishing executive*
Gazouleas, Panagiotis J. *journalist*
Gehringer, Richard George *publishing executive*
Geis, Bernard *book publisher*
Geiser, Elizabeth Able *publishing company executive*
Gelb, Arthur *newspaper editor*
Gelb, Leslie Howard *organization president, lecturer*
Gerhardt, Lillian Noreen *magazine editor*
Germano, William Paul *publisher*
Gewirtz, Gerry *editor*
Gibson, Charles DeWolf *broadcast journalist*
Giddins, Gary Mitchell *music critic, columnist*
Gifford, Frank Newton *sportscaster, commentator, former professional football player*
Gilman, Richard H. *newspaper publishing executive*
Giniger, Kenneth Seeman *publisher*
Ginzburg, Ralph *editor, writer*
Giraldi, Robert Nicholas *film director*
Giroux, Robert *editor, book publisher, author*
Glass, Daniel S. *record company executive*
Gold, Sylviane *entertainment editor, writer, critic*
Goldberg, Bernard R. *news correspondent*

Goldberg, Sidney *editor*
Goldberger, Paul Jesse *architecture critic, writer, educator, editor*
Golden, Soma *newspaper editor*
Golden, Stephen *publishing executive, forest products company executive*
Goldsmith, Robert Lewis *youth association magazine executive*
Goldstein, Norm *editor, writer*
Gollin, Albert Edwin *media research executive, sociologist*
Gollob, Herman Cohen *publishing company executive, editor*
Golson, George Barry *editor*
Gooding, Richard *newspaper editor*
Goodman, Jordan Elliot *journalist*
Goodstein, Les *newspaper publishing executive*
Gordon, Elizabeth Jane *publisher*
Gorham, David L. *newspaper executive*
Gotlieb, Irwin I. *broadcast executive*
Gottlieb, Paul *publishing company executive*
Gottlieb, Robert Adams *publisher*
†Gould, Eleanor Lois (Eleanor Gould Packard) *editor, grammarian*
Gralla, Lawrence *publishing company executive*
Gralla, Milton *publisher*
Gralnick, Jeff *broadcasting company executive*
Grant, Virginia Annette *newspaper editor, journalist*
Graves, Earl Gilbert *publisher*
Gray, Barry Sherman *radio commentator*
Grebow, Edward *television executive, banker*
Green, Ashbel *publishing executive, book editor*
Green, George Joseph *publishing executive*
Greenberg, Freddi Jane *editor-in-chief, magazine*
Greenfield, (Henry) Jeff *news analyst*
Greenwald, Martin *publishing company executive*
Grenquist, Peter Carl *publishing executive*
Grey, Linda *book publisher*
Grigsby, Henry Jefferson, Jr. *editor*
Grimsley, Will Henry *author*
†Grishman, Ronnie Joyce *magazine editor*
Gropp, Louis Oliver *editor in chief*
Grose, William Rush *publishing executive*
Groseclose, Everett Harrison *editor*
Grossman, Barbara Susanne *publisher*
Grossman, Janice *publisher*
Grune, George Vincent *publishing company executive*
Guccione, Robert Charles Joseph Edward Sabatini *publisher*
†Guillermoprieto, Alma *journalist, non-fiction writer*
Gumbel, Bryant Charles *broadcaster*
Gunther, Jane Perry (Mrs. John Gunther) *editor, writer*
Gwertzman, Bernard *newspaper editor*
Hager, Larry Stanley *book editor, publishing executive*
Haiken, Leatrice Brown *periodical editor*
†Haire, Jack *magazine publisher*
Halberstam, David *journalist, author*
Hall, Nancy Christensen *publishing company executive, author, editor*
Harris, Ann S. *editor*
Harris, Charles Frederick *book publishing executive*
Harrison, Gerald *publisher*
Hartford, William H. *magazine editor, writer, lecturer*
Hauck, Marguerite Hall *broadcasting executive*
Hauser, Gustave M. *cable and electronic communications company executive*
Hayon, Jack *publishing executive*
Hearst, Randolph Apperson *publishing executive*
Hechinger, Fred Michael *newspaper editor, columnist, foundation executive*
Heckscher, August *journalist, author, foundation executive*
Heese, William John *music publishing company executive*
†Heiler, Lynn *publishing executive*
Helferich, Gerard Marion *book editor*
Heloise *columnist, lecturer, broadcaster, author*
Henley, Deborah *newspaper editor*
Henninger, Daniel Paul *editor*
Hensler, Guenter Manfred *record company executive*
Hentoff, Margot *columnist*
Herbert, Bob *newspaper columnist*
Herbst, Martin *publishing company executive*
†Herder, Gwendolin Elisabeth Maria *publishing executive*
Hertz, Leon *publishing executive*
Hertzberg, Daniel *journalist*
Hertzberg, Hendrik *magazine editor, writer*
Heuer, Kenneth John *publishing company executive*
Hewes, Henry *drama critic*
Heyworth, James O. *communications company executive*
Hills, Frederic Wheeler *editor, publishing company executive*
†Hinckley, David Malcolm *journalist, editor, critic*
Hinds, Thomas Sheldon *publisher, organization executive*
Hirsch, George Aaron *publisher*
Hirsch, Roseann Conte *publisher*
Hiss, Tony *writer*
Hockenberry, John *television journalist*
Hoeft, Julius Albert *publishing company executive*
Hoff, Syd(ney) *cartoonist, author*
Hoffman, Michael Eugene *editor, publisher, museum curator*
Hoge, Warren M. *newspaper and magazine editor*
Hollenbeck, Ralph Anthony *retired editor, book reviewer*
Hollinshead, Byron Sharpe, Jr. *publishing company executive*
Holmes, Miriam H. *publisher*
Holt, Donald Dale *magazine editor*
Honan, William Holmes *journalist, writer*
House, Karen Elliott *company executive, former editor, reporter*
Hoxter, Allegra Branson *radio news and freelance writer*
Hoyt, Seth *publisher*
Hufham, Barbara Frances *publishing executive, lawyer*
Hughes, Allen *music critic*
Hughes, Robert Studley Forrest *art critic*
Hunter-Gault, Charlayne *journalist*
Hurley, Cheryl Joyce *book publishing executive*
Hutchens, John Kennedy *journalist, editor*
Huxtable, Ada Louise *architecture critic*
Ibarguen, Alberto *newspaper executive*
Iger, Robert A. *broadcast executive*
Ingraham, David Wood *broadcast executive*
Isaacson, Walter Seff *editor*
Isay, Jane Franzblau *publisher*
Jackel, Lawrence *publishing company executive*
Jackson, David Parker *radio news anchor*
†Jackson, Kate Morgan *children's book editor*
Jackson, Keith MacKenzie *television commentator, writer, producer*
Jaffe, Andrew Mark *editor, publisher*
Jameson, Richard *magazine editor, film critic*
Jamieson, Edward Leo *magazine editor*
Jamieson, Robert John *television journalist*
†Jamison, Jayne *magazine publisher*
Janssen, Peter Anton *magazine editor and publisher*
Jaroff, Leon Morton *magazine editor*
Jarriel, Thomas Edwin *correspondent*
†Jefferson, Margo L. *theater critic*
Jellinek, George *broadcast executive, writer, music educator*
Jennings, Frank Gerard *editor*
Jennings, Peter Charles *television anchorman*
Jensen, Michael Charles *journalist, lecturer, author*
†Johnston, Catherine V. *magazine publisher*
Jones, Alex S. *reporter*
Jones, Colin Howard *publishing company executive*
Jones, David Rhodes *newspaper editor*
Jones, Gwenyth Ellen *director information systems*
Jones, Landon Y., Jr. *magazine editor*
Jones, Laurie Lynn *magazine editor*
Jones, William Randall *publisher*
Jordan, Susan *newspaper editor*
Kael, Pauline *film critic, author*
Kagan, Julia Lee *magazine editor*
Kahler, Steve Carl *publishing executive*
Kahn, Joseph Gabriel *newspaperman*
Kahn, Robert Theodore *photojournalist*
Kalech, Marc *newspaper editor*
Kaminsky, Howard *publisher*
Kann, Peter Robert *journalist, business reporting and services company executive*
Kanter, Norman A. *publishing executive*
Karpel, Craig S. *journalist, editor*
Katalinich, Peggy *magazine editor*
Katz, Phyllis Pollak *magazine publisher and editor*
Katz, Susan R. *publisher*
Kaufman, Victor A. *film company executive*
Keane, Bil *cartoonist*
Keating, Cornelius Francis *record company executive*
Keeton, Kathy Merle *publisher*
Kehr, David *film critic*
Keller, Bill *journalist*
Kellogg, David *publisher*
Keppler, Herbert *publishing company executive*
Kerrison, Ray *newspaper columnist*
Kesting, Theodore *magazine editor*
Kiechel, Walter, III *magazine editor*
Kifner, John William *journalist, newspaper correspondent*
Kirk, Susanne Smith *editor*
Kirshbaum, Laurence J. *book publishing executive*
Kismaric, Carole Lee *editor, writer, book packaging company executive*
Kissel, Howard William *drama critic*
Klein, Elaine *magazine publishing executive*
†Klinghoffer, David *journalist*
Klipper, Mitchell S. *book publishing executive*
Kluberdanz, Wallace *publishing executive*
Knell, Gary Evan *media executive, lawyer*
Knobler, Peter Stephen *magazine editor, writer*
Kolatch, Myron *magazine editor*
Koons, Linda Gleitsman *publishing executive*
Koontz, Richard Harvey *financial printing company executive*
Koppelman, Charles *record company executive*
Koren, Edward Benjamin *cartoonist, educator*
Korman, Lewis J. *film company executive, consultant, lawyer*
Korner, Anthony David *publisher*
†Koslow, Sally *editor-in-chief*
Kosner, Edward A(lan) *magazine editor and publisher*
Koster, Elaine Landis *publishing executive*
Kozodoy, Neal *magazine editor*
Kreh, Kent Q. *magazine publishing executive*
Krenek, Debby *newspaper editor*
Krents, Milton Ellis *broadcast executive*
Kriney, Marilyn Walker *publishing executive*
Kroft, Steve *news correspondent, editor*
Krzyzanowski, Eve *broadcasting executive*
Kubek, Anthony Christopher (Tony Kubek) *sports announcer*
Kurtis, William Horton (Bill Kurtis) *broadcast journalist*
Lachenbruch, David *editor, writer*
LaForce, William Leonard, Jr. *photojournalist*
Laird, Robert Winslow *journalist*
Lalli, Cele Goldsmith *editor*
Lalli, Frank *magazine editor*
Lamirande, Arthur Gordon *editor, organist*
Lamm, Donald Stephen *publishing company executive*
Lamont, Lansing *journalist, public affairs executive, author*
Landau, Peter Edward *editor*
Landau, Sidney I. *publishing executive, lexicographer*
Lane, Nancy *editor*
Lansner, Kermit Irvin *editor, consultant*
Lapham, Lewis Henry *editor, author, television host*
Larsen, Anne *editor*
Laughlin, James *publishing company executive, writer, lecturer*
Laybourne, Geraldine *broadcasting executive*
Leach, Michael Glen *publisher*
†Leahey, Lynn *editor-in-chief*
Leahy, Michael Joseph *newspaper editor*
Lederer, Edith Madelon *journalist*
LeDoux, Harold Anthony *cartoonist, painter*
†Lee, Sally A. *editor-in-chief*
Lee, Stan (Stanley Martin Lieber) *cartoon publisher, writer*
Lehmann-Haupt, Christopher Charles Herbert *book reviewer*
Lelyveld, Joseph Salem *newspaper editor, correspondent*
Leo, Jacqueline M. *publishing company executive*
Lescaze, Lee Adrien *editor*
Leser, Bernard H. *publishing executive*
Leventhal, Kathy Neisloss *magazine publisher*
Levin, Alan M. *television journalist*
Levin, Gerald Manuel *media and entertainment company executive*
Levin, Martin P. *publishing executive, lawyer*
Levine, Charles Michael *publishing company executive, consultant*
Levine, Ellen R. *magazine editor*
Levine, Richard James *publishing executive*
Levine, Suzanne Braun *magazine editor*
Levinson, Warren Mitchell *broadcast journalist*
Levitas, Mitchel Ramsey *editor*
Levitz, Paul Elliot *publishing executive*
Levy, Alain M. *record company executive*
Levy, Alan Joseph *editor, journalist, writer*
Lewis, Russell T. *newspaper publishing executive*
Lilien, Mark Ira *publishing, retailing and systems executive*
Lingeman, Richard Roberts *editor, writer*
Linz, Werner Mark *publishing executive*
†Litrell, Barbara *publishing executive*
Littlefield, Martin (Martin Kleinwald) *book publishing executive*
Loeb, Marshall Robert *journalist, magazine editor*
†Loeks, James *theater chain executive*
†Long, David L. *magazine publisher*
Long, Elizabeth Valk *magazine publisher*
Longley, Marjorie Watters *newspaper executive*
Loomis, Carol J. *journalist*
Loomis, Robert Duane *publishing company executive, author*
†Lopez, Ramon *recording industry executive*
Lorenz, Lee Sharp *cartoonist*
Losee, Thomas Penny, Jr. *publisher*
Low, Richard H. *broadcasting executive, producer*
Lund, Peter Anthony *broadcast executive*
Lupica, Michael Thomas *sports columnist*
Lynch, James C. *newspaper editor*
Lynch, William Dennis, Jr. *broadcast journalist*
Lyne, Susan *magazine editor*
Lyne, Susan Markham *magazine editor, publication director*
MacArthur, John Roderick C. G. (Rick MacArthur) *magazine publisher, journalist*
Macdonald, Clifford Palmer *editor, writer*
Machlin, Milton Robert *magazine editor, writer*
†Mack, Consuelo Cotter *news anchor and editor*
MacKenzie, John Pettibone *journalist*
MacNeil, Robert Breckenridge Ware *broadcast journalist*
Macri, Theodore William *book publisher*
Macro, Lucia Ann *editor*
Madden, John Kevin *publishing executive*
Malabre, Alfred Leopold, Jr. *journalist, author*
Malamed, Seymour H. *motion picture company executive*
Malamud, Phyllis Carole *journalist, magazine editor*
Maleska, Martin Edmund *publishing executive*
Mallardi, Michael Patrick *broadcasting company executive*
Malloy, William Michael *book editor, reviewer, writer*
Mantell, Suzanne *editor*
Mapes, Glynn Dempsey *newspaper editor*
Mapes, Pierson *broadcasting company executive*
Marchioni, Allen *publishing company executive*
Mardenborough, Leslie A. *newspaper publishing company executive*
Marella, Philip Daniel *broadcasting company executive*
Marks, Barbara Hanzel *publishing executive*
Marlette, Douglas Nigel *editorial cartoonist, comic strip creator*
†Martin, Betsy *magazine publishing executive*
Martin, Judith Sylvia *journalist, author*
Maslin, Janet *film critic*
Mastromonaco-Adler, Ellen G. *publishing company executive*
Mathews, Jack Wayne *journalist, film critic*
Mathews, Linda McVeigh *newspaper editor*
Mattson, Walter Edward *retired publishing company executive*
Maurer, Gilbert Charles *media company executive*
Mayer, Margery Weil *publishing executive*
Mazzola, Anthony Thomas *editor, art consultant, designer*
†McAniff, Nora P. *publishing executive*
†McCarrick, Edward R. *magazine publisher*
†McCarthy, Patrick *magazine publishing executive*
McCarver, James Timothy *sportscaster*
McCormack, Thomas Joseph *publishing company executive*
Mc Cormick, Kenneth Dale *retired editor*
Mc Crie, Robert Delbert *editor, publisher, educator*
McDonell, Robert Terry *magazine editor, novelist*
†McEwen, James *publishing executive*
Mc Fadden, James Patrick *publisher*
Mc Fadden, Robert Dennis *reporter*
†McFeely, William Drake *publishing company executive*
†McGill, Jay *magazine publisher*
Mc Ginnis, Arthur Joseph *publisher*
†McGrath, Judith *broadcast executive*
McGraw, Harold Whittlesey, Jr. *publisher*
McGraw, Robert Pierce *publishing executive*
Mc Guire, Alfred James *former basketball coach, sports equipment company executive, basketball commentator*
McInnis, Helen Louise *publishing company executive*
McIntyre, Douglas Alexander *magazine publisher*
†McIntyre, Thomas *recording industry executive*
Mc Kay, Jim *television sports commentator*
Mc Keown, William Taylor *magazine editor, author*
McLaughlin, Mary Rittling *magazine editor*
McManus, Jason Donald *editor*
Mc Pherson, Paul Francis *publishing and investment banking executive*
Mc Queeney, Henry Martin, Sr. *publisher*
McQuillen, Harry A. *publishing company executive*
Meagher, Mark Joseph *publishing company executive*
Medenica, Gordon *corporate planner*
Mehta, A. Sonny *publishing company executive*
Melvin, Russell Johnston *magazine publishing consultant*
Mencher, Melvin *journalist, retired educator*
Messineo, Karen *newspaper publishing executive*
Metz, Robert Roy *publisher, editor*
Meyer, Jackie Merri *publishing executive*
Meyer, Karl Ernest *journalist*
Meyer, Pucci *newspaper editor*
Meyer, Susan E. *publisher*
Meyers, John Allen *magazine publisher*
Michaels, Alan Richard *sports commentator*
Michaels, James Walker *magazine editor*
Mikita, Joseph Karl *broadcasting executive*
Millard, Wenda Harris *magazine publisher*
†Miller, Caroline *editor-in-chief*
Miller, Donald LeSessne *publishing executive*
Miller, Gerri *magazine editor, writer*
Miller, Richard B. *publishing executive*
Miller, Robert L. *publishing company executive*
Miller, Roberta Davis *editor*
Minard, Everett Lawrence, III *journalist, magazine editor*
Minick, Michael *publishing executive*
Mirabella, Grace *magazine publishing executive*
Mohler, Mary Gail *magazine editor*
Molho, Emanuel *publisher*
Montorio, John Angelo *magazine editor*
Mooney, Richard E. *editorial writer*
Moore, John Dennis *publisher*
Morgado, Robert *music company executive*
Morgan, Thomas Bruce *public affairs executive, author, editor*
Morris, Douglas Peter *recording company executive*
†Morton, Brian *writer, editor, educator*
Moskin, John Robert *editor, writer*
Moyers, Bill D. *journalist*
Muller, Henry James *journalist, magazine editor*
Mulligan, Hugh Augustine *journalist*
Mulvoy, Mark *journalist*
Munro, J. Richard *publishing company executive*
Murphy, Ann Pleshette *magazine editor-in-chief*
†Murphy, Helen *recording industry executive*
Murphy, Thomas S. *media company executive*
Muth, John Francis *newspaper editor, columnist*
Myers, William S. *magazine publishing executive*
†Nachtwey, James Alan *photojournalist*
Nagourney, Herbert *publishing company executive*
Naiburg, Irving B., Jr. *publisher*
Nathan, Paul S. *editor, writer*
Navasky, Victor Saul *magazine editor*
Nederlander, Robert E. *entertainment and television executive, lawyer*
Needham, Richard Lee *magazine editor*
Neff, Craig *periodical editor*
Neilly, Andrew Hutchinson, Jr. *publisher*
Nelson, Lindsey *sportscaster*
Neufeld, Victor *television executive*
Neuthaler, Paul David *publisher*
Newbauer, John Arthur *editor*
Newcomb, Jonathan *publishing executive*
Newfield, Jack *columnist*
Newhouse, Nancy Riley *newspaper editor*
Newhouse, Samuel I., Jr. *publishing executive*
Newman, Rachel *magazine editor*
Nibley, Andrew Mathews *editorial executive*
Nied, Thomas H. *publishing company executive*
Nielsen, Nancy *publishing executive*
Niles, Nicholas Hemelright *publisher*
Nolte, Judith Ann *magazine editor*
†Norrgard, Kristin Ann *magazine publisher*
†Norris, Floyd Hamilton *financial journalist*
Norville, Deborah *news correspondent*
Novitz, Charles Richard *television executive*
Novogrod, Nancy Ellen *editor*
Nyren, Neil Sebastian *publisher, editor*
Oakes, John Bertram *writer, editor*
Ober, Eric W. *broadcasting executive*
O'Brian, Jack *journalist*
O'Brien, Geoffrey Paul *editor*
O'Brien, John M. *newspaper publishing company executive*
Ochs, Michael *editor, librarian, music educator*
O'Connor, Robert James *publishing executive*
Ohannessian, Griselda Jackson *publishing executive*
Olafsson, Olafur J. *publishing company executive*
†Oldham, Joe *editor*
Oliver, Stephanie Stokes *magazine editor*
O'Neil, James Peter *financial printing company executive*
Oppenheim, Ellen W. *media director, advertising executive*
Oresman, Donald *entertainment and publishing company executive, corporate lawyer*
Osgood, Charles *news broadcaster, journalist*
Osnos, Peter Lionel Winston *publishing executive*
Ostling, Richard Neil *journalist, author, broadcaster*
Pace, Eric Dwight *journalist*
Pagnozzi, Amy *columnist*
†Palermo, Steve *sportscaster, color analyst, former umpire*
Pandolfi, Francis P. *publishing executive*
Paneth, Donald J. *editor, writer*
Parker, Maynard Michael *journalist, magazine executive*
Parker, Mel *editor*
Patten, John W. *magazine publisher*
Patton, Joëlle Delbourgo *publishing executive*
Paugh, Thomas Francis *magazine editor, writer, photographer*
Pauley, Jane *television journalist*
Pearlstine, Norman *editor*
Pecker, David J. *magazine publishing company executive, financial executive*
Penn, Stanley William *journalist*
Penney, Alexandra *magazine editor-in-chief, writer*
Peper, George Frederick *editor*
†Perlman, Willa M. *publishing executive*
Perry, Frank *motion picture executive, director, producer, writer*
Petersen, Raymond Joseph *publishing company executive*
Peterson, Kristina *publishing company executive*
Petzal, David Elias *editor, writer*
Peyronnin, Joseph Felix, III *network news executive*
Picower, Warren Michael *magazine editor*
Piel, Gerard *editor, publisher*
Pittman, Robert Warren *entertainment executive*
Podd, Ann *newspaper editor*
Podhoretz, Norman *magazine editor, writer*
Pollak, Richard *writer, editor*
Pollak, William L. *newspaper publishing executive*
Pomerance, Norman *publishing company executive*
Poussaint, Renee Francine *journalist*
Povich, (Maurice) Maury Richard *broadcast journalist, talk show host, television producer*
Pratt, Michael Theodore *book publishing company executive, marketing, sales and publishing specialist*
Prestbo, John Andrew *newspaper editor, journalist, author*
Priest, Aaron Mendell *publishing executive*
Primis, Lance Roy *newspaper executive*
Princz, Judith *publishing executive*
Quigley, Martin Schofield *publishing company executive, educator*
Quinn, Jane Bryant *journalist, writer*
Quinson, Bruno Andre *publishing executive*
Raab, Selwyn *journalist*
Rabiner, Susan *editor*
Ragan, David *publishing company executive*
Raines, Howell Hiram *newspaper editor, journalist*
Rainier, Robert Paul *publisher*
Rashad, Ahmad (Bobby Moore) *sports broadcaster, former professional football player*
Rasmus, John A. *magazine executive*
Rather, Dan *broadcast journalist*
Rauch, Rudolph Stewart, III *periodical editor, arts education executive*
Rawson, Eleanor S. *publishing company executive*
Reed, James Donald *journalist, author*
Reed, Rex *author, critic*
Regan, Judith Theresa *publishing executive*
Reichl, Ruth Molly *restaurant critic*
Reid-Crisp, Wendy *publishing executive*
Reidy, Carolyn Kroll *publisher*
Reilly, Edward T., Jr. *publisher*
Reilly, William Francis *publishing company executive*

Reiss, Jeffrey Charles television executive
Remnick, David J. journalist
Reuther, David Louis children's book publisher, writer
Reynolds, Warren Jay retired publisher
Rhoads, Geraldine Emeline editor
†Rhone, Sylvia recording industry executive
Rich, Frank Hart critic
Richardson, Midge Turk magazine editor
Richter, Georg book publishing executive
Ridder, Eric newspaper publisher
Rideout, Philip Munroe publishing company executive
†Rieff, David Sontag editor, writer, critic
Rigby, Paul Crispin artist, cartoonist
Riggio, Leonard book publishing executive
Riggs, Andy J., Jr. newspaper publishing executive
Riggs, Michael David magazine editor, writer
†Roberts, Eugene Leslie, Jr. newspaper executive, editor
Robertson, Nan journalist, correspondent
Robinson, Maurice Richard, Jr. publishing executive
Robinson, Richard publishing company executive
Rogalin, Roger Richard publishing executive
Rogin, Gilbert Leslie editor, author
Rollins, Sherrie Sandy television executive
Rolontz, Robert recording company executive
Ronson, Raoul R. publishing executive
Rooney, Michael Francis publisher
Rose, Charles television journalist
†Rose, Victoria Lasdon magazine publisher
†Rosen, David Paul book editor
Rosenblum, Constance newspaper editor
Rosenfield, Jay Gary publisher
Rosenthal, Jacob (Jack Rosenthal) newspaper editor
Rosenthal, Lucy Gabrielle writer, editor, educator
Ross, Brian Elliott news correspondent
Ross, Norman Alan publisher
Rosset, Barnet Lee, Jr. publisher
Rosset, Lisa Krug editor
Rothberg, Gerald editor, publisher
Rubin, Harry Meyer entertainment industry executive
Rubin, Norman Julius columnist
Rubin, Stephen Edward editor, journalist
Rushnell, Squire Derrick television executive
Russell, Charles F. newspaper publishing executive
Ryan, Regina Claire (Mrs. Paul Deutschman) editor, book packager, literary agent
Ryden, Katherine publishing executive, human resources executive
Ryder, Thomas O. magazine publishing executive
Saal, Hubert Daniel journalist
Sachs, Susan F. publishing executive
Safer, Morley journalist
Salembier, Valerie Birnbaum publishing executive
Sanders, Richard Louis assistant managing editor
Sapinsky, Joseph Charles magazine executive, photographer
Sarazen, Richard Allen media company executive
Sarnoff, William publishing company executive
†Sarris, Shirley Cornelia publishing company executive
Saunders, Dero Ames writer, editor
Sawyer, (L.) Diane television journalist
Sawyer, Forrest newscaster
Scarborough, Charles Bishop, III broadcast journalist, writer
Schaap, Richard Jay journalist
Schanberg, Sydney Hillel newspaper editor, columnist
Schieffer, Bob broadcast journalist
Schiffrin, Andre publisher
Schmemann, Serge journalist
Schmertz, Mildred Floyd editor, writer
Schmidt, Stanley Albert editor, writer
Schmitz, Robert Allen publishing executive, investor
Schneider, Martin Aaron photojournalist, ecologist, engineer, writer, artist, television director, public intervenor, educator, university instructor, lecturer
Schneiderman, David Abbott publisher, journalist
Schonberg, Harold Charles music critic, columnist
Schragis, Steven M. publisher, lawyer
Schrutt, Norman broadcast company executive
Schwartz, Jack Theodore retired publisher
Scribner, Charles, III publisher, art historian, lecturer
Seaman, Alfred Barrett journalist
Segal, Jonathan Bruce editor
Seligman, Daniel editor
Serwatka, Walter Dennis publishing executive
Settipani, Frank G. news correspondent
Seymore, James W., Jr. magazine editor
†Shain, Harold magazine publisher
Shanks, David publishing executive
Sharbel, Jean M. editor
Shepard, Stephen Benjamin journalist, magazine editor
†Shepard, Thomas Rockwell, III magazine executive
Sherak, Thomas Mitchell motion picture company executive
Sherr, Lynn Beth TV news correspondent
Shestack, Melvin Bernard editor, author, filmmaker, television producer
Shier, Shelley M. production company executive
Shnayerson, Robert Beahan editor
Shortz, Will puzzle editor
Shriver, Maria Owings news correspondent
Siegal, Allan Marshall newspaper editor
Siegel, Joel Steven television news correspondent
Siegel, Marvin newspaper editor
Sifton, Elisabeth book publisher
Silberman, Charles Eliot magazine editor, author
Silberman, James Henry editor, publisher
Silverman, Al editor
Silverman, Stephen Meredith journalist, screenwriter, producer
Silvers, Robert Benjamin editor
Simmons, Russell recording industry executive
Simon, John Ivan film and drama critic
Simonson, Lee Stuart broadcast company executive
Singerman, Martin newspaper publishing executive
Singleton, Donald Edward journalist
Sischy, Ingrid Barbara magazine editor, art critic
Skillin, Edward Simeon magazine publisher
Skinner, Peter Graeme publishing executive, lawyer
Sleed, Joel newspaper editor
†Sloan, Allan Herbert journalist
Smith, Clarence O'Farrell publishing company executive
Smith, Corlies Morgan publishing executive
Smith, Derek Armand publishing company executive
Smith, Joseph Phelan film company executive
Smith, Liz (Mary Elizabeth Smith) newspaper columnist, broadcast journalist
Smith, Richard Mills editor in chief, magazine executive
Snyder, Richard Elliott publishing company executive
Soren, Tabitha L. television newscaster, writer
Sparano, Vincent Thomas editor
Spence, James Robert, Jr. television sports executive
Spring, Michael editor, writer
Stahl, Lesley R. journalist
Stanger, Ila writer, editor
Staniar, Burton B. entertainment company executive
Steiger, Paul Ernest newspaper editor, journalist
Steinfeld, Thomas Albert publisher
Steinfels, Margaret O'Brien editor
†Steinfels, Peter Francis newspaper correspondent, writer
†Steinmetz, Sol publishing company editor
†Stepler, Richard Lewis magazine editor
Stern, Robert D. publishing executive
Stern, Roslyne Paige magazine publisher
Steves, Gale C. editor
Stewart, James B. journalist
Stossel, John news analyst
Straus, Roger W., Jr. publishing company executive
Straus, Roger W, III book publishing executive, photographer
Stringer, Howard television executive
Stuart, Carole publishing executive
Stuart, Lyle publishing company executive
Sturtevant, Peter Mann, Jr. television news executive
Subak-Sharpe, Genell Jackson editor, writer
Sugihara, Kenzi publishing executive
Sullivan, Anne Elizabeth publishing executive
Sullivan, Thomas John communications company executive
Sullivan, Walter Seager editor, author
Sulzberger, Arthur Ochs newspaper executive
Sulzberger, Arthur Ochs, Jr. newspaper publisher
Sussman, Gerald publishing company executive
Sutton, Kelso Furbush publishing executive
Sutton-Straus, Joan M. journalist
Sweezy, Paul Marlor editor, publisher
†Swenson, Emily Barron broadcast executive
Swenson, Eric Pierson publishing company executive
Swift, Isabel Davidson editorial director
Taber, Carol A. magazine publisher
Tagliaferro, John Anthony broadcasting company executive
Talese, Nan Ahearn publishing company executive
Talley, Truman Macdonald publisher
Tash, Martin Elias publishing company executive
Taylor, Humphrey John Fausitt information services executive
Taylor, Sherril Wightman broadcasting company executive
Temple, Wick journalist
Thomas, Brooks publishing company executive
Thomas, John Cox, Jr. publisher
Thompson, Martin Christian news service executive
Tigay, Alan Merrill editor
Tilberis, Elizabeth editor-in-chief
Timothy, Raymond Joseph television executive
Tisch, Laurence Alan broadcast corporation executive
Tober, Barbara D. (Mrs. Donald Gibbs Tober) editor
Todd, Patricia Anne publishing executive
Toepfer, Susan Jill editor
Toff, Nancy Ellen book editor
Tollerson, Ernest newspaper editor
Tomlinson, James Francis retired news agency executive
Townsend, Charles H. publishing executive
Traina, Albert Salvatore publishing executive
Treaster, Joseph B. (Bland) journalist
Tryhane, Gerald newspaper publishing executive
Tucker, Alan David publisher
Ubell, Robert Neil editor, publisher, consultant, literary agent
Uchitelle, Louis journalist
Ungaro, Susan Kelliher magazine editor
Urdang, Alexandra book publishing executive
Valenti, Carl M. newspaper publisher
Van Eysinga, Frans W. publisher
Van Nostrand, Morris Abbott, Jr. publisher
Van Sant, Peter Richard news correspondent
†Vaughan, Linda publishing executive
Vaughan, Samuel Snell editor, author
Vecchione, Joseph John newspaper editor
Vecsey, George Spencer sports columnist
Vega, Marylois Purdy journalist
Venza, Jac broadcast executive, cultural and arts program administrator
Verdi, David Joseph broadcast news executive
Vestal, Jeanne Marie Goodspeed book publishing company executive
Vialardi, Enzo Joseph publishing company executive
Vick, James Albert publishing executive, consultant
Vitale, Alberto Aldo publishing company executive
Vitale, Dick color commentator, sports writer
Vitt, Sam Bradshaw communications media services executive
Vittorini, Carlo publishing company executive
Vizard, Frank Joseph journalist
von Knorring, Henrik Johan publisher
†von Mehren, Jane editor
Waddell, Harry Lee editor, publisher
Wade, James O'Shea publisher
Wade, Nicholas Michael Landon journalist
Walker, Douglas Craig publishing company executive
Walker, Mort cartoonist
†Wallace, Ken magazine publisher
Wallace, Mike television interviewer and reporter
Wallace, Thomas C(hristopher) editor, literary agent
Wallace, Thomas J. magazine editor-in-chief
Wallach, Allan Henry former senior critic
Walters, Barbara television journalist
Walters, Raymond, Jr. newspaper editor, author
Walzog, Nancy Lee film and television executive
Wanek, William Charles public relations executive
Wang, Arthur Woods publisher
Warner, Peter David publishing executive
Wasserman, Steve publisher
Wattles, Joshua motion picture studio executive
Waxenberg, Alan M. publisher
Weber, Robert Maxwell cartoonist
Weeks, Brigitte publishing executive
Weill, Gus, Jr. communications consultant
Weinberger, Caspar Willard publishing executive, former secretary of defense
Weinstein, Harvey film company executive
Weinstein, Robert film company executive
Weintz, Walter Louis book publishing company executive
Wells, Linda Ann editor-in-chief
Welsh, Donald Emory publisher
Wenner, Jann Simon editor, publisher
West, Bernard investor
Westerman, Sylvia Hewitt journalist, university official
Wham, George Sims publishing executive
White, Kate editor-in-chief
White, Timothy Thomas Anthony writer, editor, broadcaster
Whiteman, Douglas E. publisher
Whitmer, Kevin newspaper sports editor
Whitney, Ruth Reinke magazine editor
Widmann, Nancy C. broadcast executive
Wiener, Hesh (Harold Frederic Wiener) publisher, editor, consultant
Wiley, Deborah E. publishing executive
Wilford, John Noble, Jr. news correspondent
Willis, John Alvin editor
Windsor, Laurence Charles, Jr. publishing executive
Winfrey, Carey Wells journalist, magazine editor
Winship, Frederick Moery journalist
Wintour, Anna editor
Wogan, Robert broadcasting company executive
Wright, Robert C. broadcasting executive
WuDunn, Sheryl journalist, correspondent
Yablon, Leonard Harold publishing company executive
Yellin, Thomas Gilmer broadcast executive
Young, Genevieve Leman publishing executive, editor
Young, Robert Francis publisher
Yunich, Peter B. publishing executive
Zacharius, Walter publishing company executive
Zackheim, Adrian Walter editor
Zahn, Paula newscaster
Zampaglione, Arturo newspaper publishing executive
Zeldin, Richard Packer publisher
Zevon, Susan Jane editor
Ziff, William Bernard, Jr. publishing executive
Zimmerman, William Edwin newspaper editor and publisher
Zinsser, William Knowlton editor, writer, educator
Zuckerman, Mortimer Benjamin real estate developer, publisher, editor

North Salem
Larsen, Jonathan Zerbe journalist

Nyack
Flood, (Hulda) Gay editor, consultant
Leiser, Ernest Stern journalist

Old Brookville
Fairman, Joel Martin broadcasting executive

Oneonta
†Knudson, Richard Lewis editor

Ossining
Carter, Richard publisher, writer
Ravis, Howard Shepard conference planner and publishing consultant
Stein, Sol publisher, writer, editor in chief

Piermont
Fox, Matthew Ignatius publishing company executive

Pittsford
Woodhull, Nancy Jane publishing executive

Plainview
Newman, Edwin Harold news commentator

Pleasantville
†Coleman, Gregory G. magazine publisher
Gilmore, Kenneth Otto editor
Gordon, Kenneth Antony publisher
Jones, Ross publishing company executive
Oursler, Fulton, Jr. editor-in-chief, writer
Schadt, James P. publishing executive
Tomlinson, Kenneth Y. periodical editor-in-chief

Port Jefferson Station
Soma, Rose Smeraldi broadcaster, writer, women's rights activist, television and radio producer

Port Washington
Anable, Anne Currier Steinert journalist
Donohue, Peter Joseph publishing executive
Jay, Frank Peter writer, educator
McGreal, Joseph A., Jr. publishing company executive
Simmons, Lee Howard book publishing company executive

Poughkeepsie
Kim, David Sang Chul publisher, evangelist, retired seminary president

Purchase
Sandler, Irving Harry art critic, art historian

Purdys
Burlingame, Edward Livermore publishing company executive

Queensbury
Winsten, Archer retired newspaper and movie critic

Remsenburg
Billman, Irwin Edward publishing company executive

Rhinecliff
Dierdorff, John Ainsworth retired editor

Rochester
Hyman, Ralph Alan journalist, consultant
Orr, Jim (James D. Orr) columnist, writer
Palvino, Jack Anthony broadcasting executive
Pearce, William Joseph public broadcasting executive
Prosser, Michael Hubert communications educator
Toohey, Margaret Louise journal editor, researcher

Rome
Waters, George Bausch newspaper publisher

Ronkonkoma
Townsend, Terry publishing executive

Roslyn
Risom, Ole Christian publishing company executive

Rye
Erlick, Everett Howard broadcasting company executive
Stoller, Ezra photojournalist

Sagaponack
Francke, Linda Bird journalist

Saratoga Springs
Boyers, Margarita Anne (Peggy Boyers) editor, periodical, writer, translator

Scarsdale
Duncan, George Harold broadcasting company executive
Frankel, Stanley Arthur columnist, educator, business executive
O'Neill, Michael James editor, author
Schwartz, Harry journalist
Shaw, Grace Goodfriend (Mrs. Herbert Franklin Shaw) publisher, editor
Topping, Seymour publishing executive, educator

Smithtown
Leavy, Herbert Theodore publisher

Southampton
Graham, Howard Barrett publishing company executive
Louchheim, Donald Harry journalist
Sims, Everett Martin publishing company executive
Smith, Dennis (Edward) publisher, author

Spencertown
Lieber, Charles Donald publisher

Staten Island
Diamond, Richard Edward publisher
Laline, Brian J. newspaper editor

Stony Brook
Booth, George cartoonist
Fisher, David Woodrow editor, publisher

Swain
Robinson, Bina Aitchison publisher, newsletter editor

Syosset
Rudman, Michael P. publishing executive

Syracuse
Balk, Alfred William journalist
Bunn, Timothy David newspaper editor
Mesrobian, Arpena Sachaklian publisher, editor, consultant
Rogers, Stephen newspaper publisher
Stephens, Edward Carl communications educator, writer

Tarrytown
Ashburn, Anderson magazine editor
†Grufferman, Barbara Hannah publishing executive
Kaplan, Richard magazine editor
†LeGrice, Stephen magazine editor
Neill, Richard Robert retired publishing company executive
Whipple, Judith Roy book editor

Troy
Buckley, J. Stephen newspaper publisher
Rubens, Philip communications educator, technical writer

Unionville
Kemnitz, Thomas Milton publisher

Utica
Donovan, Donna Mae newspaper publisher

Valley Stream
Lehrer, Stanley magazine publisher, editorial director, corporate executive

Waccabuc
Kislik, Richard William publishing executive
Thompson, Edward Thorwald magazine editor

Wainscott
Henderson, William Charles editor

Watertown
Johnson, John Brayton editor, publisher

White Plains
Beaupre, Lawrence Kenneth newspaper editor
Benjamin, Theodore Simon publishing company executive
Boudreaux, John public relations specialist
Cohn, Howard retired magazine editor
Ellenbogen, Milton Joseph publishing executive, editor, writer
†Goodman, Walter author, editor
Grayson, Richard Steven (Lord of Mursley) foreign correspondent, international legal and political management consultant, educator
†Hoffman, Milton Sills editor
Kisseberth, Paul Barto publishing executive

Woodbury
Bell, William Joseph cable television company executive
Randolph, Francis Fitz, Jr. cable television executive
Sweeney, Daniel Thomas cable television company executive

Woodside
†DeFranco, Elizabeth Carol editor

Yonkers
Denver, Eileen Ann magazine editor
Eimicke, Victor W(illiam) publishing company executive
Landau, Irwin magazine publishing company executive

NORTH CAROLINA

Asheville
Banks, James Barber *publishing executive*
Damtoft, Walter Atkinson *editor, publisher*
Pulleyn, S(amuel) Robert *publishing company executive*

Brevard
Phillips, Euan Hywel *publishing executive*

Carrboro
Patterson, Neil *science publisher*

Cary
Andrews, John Woodhouse *newspaper publisher*
McCarty, Thomas Joseph *publishing company executive*
Reynolds, Edward *book publisher*

Chapel Hill
Boggs, Robert Newell *editor*
Bowers, Thomas Arnold *journalism educator*
Lauder, Valarie Anne *editor, educator*
Meyer, Philip Edward *journalism educator*

Charlotte
Barrows, Frank Clemence *newspaper editor*
Brown, Tony *theater and dance critic*
Ethridge, Mark Foster, III *writer, publisher, newspaper consultant*
Henson, Glenda Maria *newspaper writer*
Koch, Richard Joseph *publishing company executive, lawyer*
Neill, Rolfe *newspaper executive*
White, David Lee *journalist*
Williams, Edwin Neel *newspaper editor*

China Grove
Baker, Ira Lee *journalist, former educator*

Durham
Cooper, Charles Howard *photojournalist, newspaper publishing company executive*
Fulton, Katherine Nelson *journalist*
Hawkins, William E. N. *newspaper editor*
Hayes, Brian Paul *editor, writer*
Press, Michelle *editor*
Rollins, Edward Tyler, Jr. *newspaper executive*
Rossiter, Alexander, Jr. *news service executive, editor*

Edenton
Walklet, John James, Jr. *publishing executive*

Elizabeth City
Baker, Jean Mary *cable television executive*

Fayetteville
Cooke, Kenneth *newspaper executive*

Garner
Dobyns, Lloyd (Allen) *free-lance journalist*

Gloucester
Price, Marion Woodrow *journalist*

Greensboro
Bowers, Ben James *editor, newspaper executive*
Cline, Ned Aubrey *newspaper editor*
DuBuisson, Charles David *newspaper editor*
Jellicorse, John Lee *communications and theatre educator*
Smink, Mary Jane *graphic communications technology educator*
Yardley, Rosemary Roberts *journalist, columnist*

Jefferson
Franklin, Robert McFarland *book publisher*

Pittsboro
Bailey, Herbert Smith, Jr. *retired publisher*
Hauser, Charles Newland McCorkle *newspaper consultant*
Shurick, Edward Palmes *television executive, rancher*

Point Harbor
Heffernan, Phillip Thomas, Jr. *retired publisher*

Raleigh
Daniels, Frank Arthur, Jr. *newspaper publisher*
Daniels, Frank Arthur, III *publishing executive*
Parker, Joseph Mayon *printing and publishing executive*
Powell, Drexel Dwane, Jr. *editorial cartoonist*
Reeves, Ralph B., III *publisher, editor*
Royster, Vermont (Connecticut) *journalist*

Research Triangle Park
Howe, Tom *broadcasting executive*

Southern Pines
Ragan, Samuel Talmadge *newspaper editor, publisher, educator, poet laureate*

Tryon
Thayer, Lee *educator, author, consultant*

Waxhaw
Lamparter, William C. *printing and publishing consultant, digital printing and information systems specialist*

Weaverville
†Harris, Michael G. *publishing company executive*

Winston Salem
Brill, Frank Patrick *journalist*
Goodman, Joseph Champion *editor*
Scisco, Peter Leon *magazine editor, writer*
Sparber, Gordon Mark *music journalist*
†Tursi, Frank Vincent *journalist*

Wrightsville
Mc Ilwain, William Franklin *newspaper editor, writer*

NORTH DAKOTA

Bismarck
Johnson, Judith Ekberg *broadcast executive*

Fargo
Dill, William Joseph *newspaper editor*
Lohman, John Frederick *editor*
Marcil, William Christ, Sr. *publisher, broadcast executive*
Paulson, John Doran *newspaper editor, retired*

OHIO

Akron
Allen, William Dale *newspaper editor*
Dotson, John Louis, Jr. *newspaper executive*
Herman, Roger Eliot *professional speaker, consultant, futurist, writer*
Kirksey, Charles Ron *journalist*

Athens
†Friedenberg, Walter Drew *journalist*
Scott, Charles Lewis *photojournalist*
Stempel, Guido Hermann, III *journalism educator*

Bowling Green
Clark, Robert King *communications educator emeritus, lecturer, consultant, actor, model*

Bucyrus
Moore, Thomas Paul *broadcast executive*

Canton
Fouts, Daniel Francis *sports announcer, former professional football player*

Cincinnati
Adams, James Louis *newspaper editor, retired*
Beckwith, Barbara Jean *journalist*
Blake, George Rowell *newspaper executive*
Borgman, James Mark *editorial cartoonist*
Burleigh, William Robert *newspaper executive*
†Dahlman, Simon Jacques *magazine editor, minister*
Dunning, Thomas E. *newspaper editor*
Harmon, Patrick *newspaperman*
Knue, Paul Frederick *newspaper editor*
Leser, Lawrence A. *broadcasting company executive*
Liss, Herbert Myron *newspaper publisher, communications company executive*
Moll, William Gene *broadcasting company executive*
Rogers, Lawrence H., II *retired television executive, investor, writer*
Santen, Ann Hortenstine *broadcasting executive*
Schottelkotte, Albert Joseph *broadcasting executive*
Scripps, Charles Edward *newspaper publisher*
Servodidio, Pat Anthony *broadcast executive*
Silvers, Gerald Thomas *publishing executive*
Smith, C. LeMoyne *publishing company executive*
Whipple, Harry *newspaper publishing executive*
†White, Robert John *journalist*
Wigginton, Eugene H. *publishing executive*
Woods, Bruce Walter *editor, poet*
†Zanotti, John Peter *broadcasting company executive*

Cleveland
Atherton, James Dale *publishing executive*
Bennett, Michael *newspaper editor*
Bingham, Richard Donnelly *journal editor, director, educator*
Clark, Gary R. *newspaper editor*
Connors, Joanna *film critic*
Davis, David Aaron *journalist*
Drane, Walter Harding *publishing executive, business consultant*
Fabris, James A. *journalist*
Gordon, Anne Kathleen *editor*
Greer, Thomas H. *newspaper executive*
Hall, David *newspaper editor*
Harayda, Janice *newspaper book editor, author*
Holland, Darrell Wendell *newspaper religion editor*
Jensen, Kathryn Patricia *public broadcaster*
†Jindra, Christine *editor*
Kovacs, Rosemary *newpaper editor*
Lebovitz, Harold Paul (Hal Lebovitz) *journalist*
Long, Robert M. *newspaper publishing executive*
Lucier, P. Jeffrey *publishing executive*
Lynch, Maxine *newspaper publishing executive*
Machaskee, Alex *newspaper publishing company executive*
Miyares, Benjamin David *editor, publisher, consultant*
Modic, Stanley John *business editor, publisher*
Molyneaux, David Glenn *newspaper travel editor*
Morway, Richard A. *newspaper publishing executive*
Pascarella, Perry James *magazine editor*
Romei, Lura Knachel *magazine editor*
Shaw, Scott Alan *photojournalist*
Strang, James Dennis *editor*
Strassmeyer, Mary *newspaper columnist*
Tipton-Martin, Toni *newspaper editor*
Urban, Richard *newspaper editor*
†Zubal, John T. *book exchange executive, publisher, bibliographer*

Columbus
Barker, Llyle James, Jr. *journalism educator, public relations executive, former military officer*
Barry, James P(otvin) *writer, editor*
Campbell, Richard Rice *retired newspaper editor*
Charles, Bertram *radio broadcasting executive*
Cox, Mitchel Neal *editor*
Dawson, Virginia Sue *newspaper editor*
Dervin, Brenda Louise *communications educator*
Fornshell, Dave Lee *educational broadcasting executive*
Franks, Richard Matthew *newspaper executive*
Gealy, Douglas Edward *television executive*
Grossberg, Michael Lee *theater critic, writer*
†Johnston, Jeffery W. *publishing executive*
Kefauver, Weldon Addison *publisher*
Massie, Robert Joseph *publishing company executive*
Masterson, Michael Rue *journalist, educator, editor*
Meider, Elmer Charles, Jr. *publishing company executive*
Murphy, Andrew J., Jr. *newspaper editor*
Ouzts, Dale Keith *broadcast executive*
Sherrill, Thomas Boykin, III *newspaper publishing executive*
Smith, Robert Burns *newspaper magazine executive*
Strode, George K. *sports editor*
Thomas, Stephen Clair *software publisher, writer, editor, consultant*
Weisgerber, David Wendelin *editor, chemist*

Dayton
Cawood, Albert McLaurin (Hap Cawood) *newspaper editor*
Granzow, Paul H. *printing company executive*
†Huffman, Dale *journalist*
†Kelley, Alan Kent *newspaper editor*
Matheny, Ruth Ann *editor*
Peterson, Skip (Orley R. Peterson, III) *newspaper photographer*
Siegel, Ira T. *publishing executive*
Tillson, John Bradford, Jr. *newspaper publisher*

Kent
Poorman, Paul Arthur *educator, media consultant*

Lakewood
Condon, George Edward *journalist*

Loudonville
Battison, John Henry *broadcasting executive, consulting engineer*

Miamisburg
†Everhart, Rodney Lee *electronic publishing executive*

Oxford
Sanders, Gerald Hollie *communications educator*

Sidney
Laurence, Michael Marshall *magazine publisher, writer*
Lawrence, Wayne Allen *publisher*
Stevens, Robert Jay *magazine editor*

Springfield
Maddex, Myron Brown (Mike Maddex) *broadcasting executive*

Toledo
Block, John Robinson *newspaper publisher*
Block, William K., Jr. *newspaper executive*
Gearhart, Thomas Lee *newspaper editor*
O'Gara, Patrick Denis *editor*
Rosenbaum, Kenneth E. *journalist, editor*
Royhab, Ronald *journalist, newspaper editor*
Stankey, Suzanne M. *editor*
Willey, John Douglas *retired newspaper executive*

Willoughby
Campbell, Talmage Alexander *newspaper editor*

Wooster
August, Robert Olin *journalist*

Youngstown
Przelomski, Anastasia Nemenyi *retired newspaper editor*

OKLAHOMA

Norman
Bauer, George W. *publishing company executive*
Dary, David Archie *journalism educator, author*

Oklahoma City
Gaylord, Edward Lewis *publishing company executive*
Gourley, James Leland *editor, publishing executive*
Hamilton, Arnold Burt *journalist, educator*
Kelley, Carl Ed(win) *editor*
Triplett, E. Eugene *editor*
Zimmerman, Jack Wallace *newspaper editor*

Sapulpa
Geeslin, Robert Hawk *educational programming company executive*

Tulsa
Beck, Robert James *energy economist, journal editor, consultant*
Culp, Even Asher *communications educator*
Hale, Richard Lee *magazine editor*
Haring, Robert Westing *newspaper editor*
Jones, Jenk, Jr. *editor, educator*
Jones, Jenkin Lloyd *retired newspaper publisher*
Major, John Keene *radio broadcasting executive*
Payne, William Haydon *broadcasting executive*
Ridenour, Windsor Allen *newspaper editor*
Upton, Howard B., Jr. *management writer, lawyer*
Wolking, Joseph Anthony *publishing company executive*

OREGON

Albany
Wood, Kenneth Arthur *newspaper editor emeritus, writer*

Astoria
Harlan, David *reporter*

Coquille
Taylor, George Frederick *newspaper publisher, editor*

Corvallis
Hall, Don Alan *editor, writer*
Zwahlen, Fred Casper, Jr. *journalism educator*

Eugene
Baker, Alton Fletcher, Jr. *newspaper editor*
†Baker, Alton Fletcher, III *newspaper editor, publishing executive*
Baker, Edwin Moody *retired newspaper publisher*
Barton, Stephen Howard *broadcast executive*
Franklin, Jon Daniel *journalist, writer, educator*
Ismach, Arnold Harvey *journalism educator*
Lemert, James Bolton *journalist, educator*
Sherriffs, Ronald Everett *communications and film educator*
Tykeson, Donald Erwin *broadcasting executive*

Gleneden Beach
Marks, Arnold *journalist*

Gresham
Caldwell, Robert John *newspaper editor*

Lake Oswego
†Philipp, Fred A. *publishing executive*

Portland
Ashenden, William Joseph *broadcast executive*
Bhatia, Peter K. *editor, journalist*
Crabbs, Roger Alan *publisher, consultant, small business owner, educator*
Gango, Jacqueline Mary *publishing executive*
Graves, Earl William, Jr. *journalist*
Johnston, Virginia Evelyn *editor*
Mainwaring, William Lewis *publishing company executive, author*
Mapes, Jeffrey Robert *journalist*
Murphy, Francis Seward *journalist*
Reed, Gregory William *broadcasting executive*
Rowe, Sandra Mims *newspaper editor*
Sterling, Donald Justus, Jr. *retired newspaper editor*
Stickel, Frederick A. *publisher*
Stickel, Patrick Francis *publishing executive, newspaper*
Wohler, Jeffery Wilson *newspaper editor*
Woodward, Stephen Richard *newspaper reporter*

South Beach
Gilbert, David Heggie *retired educational publisher, consultant*

Tigard
Nokes, John Richard *retired newspaper editor, author*

Yamhill
Kristof, Nicholas Donabet *journalist*

PENNSYLVANIA

Albrightsville
Wilson, George Wharton *newspaper editor*

Allentown
†Cavett, Van Andrew *journalist*
Shorts, Gary K. *newspaper publisher*

Bala Cynwyd
Field, Joseph Myron *broadcast executive*
Kates, Gerald Saul *printing executive*
Schwartz, Charles D. *broadcast executive*

Beaver
Dible, Dennis D. *executive editor*
Gordon, Frank Wallace *newspaper publisher*

Bensalem
Kang, Benjamin Toyeong *writer, clergyman*

Broomall
Cohen, Philip D. *book publishing executive*

Bryn Mawr
Broido, Arnold Peace *music publishing company executive*
Mc Lean, William L., III *publisher*

Carlisle
Fish, Chester Boardman, Jr. *publishing consultant, writer*
Talley, Carol Lee *newspaper editor*

Clearfield
Ulerich, William Keener *publishing company executive*

Doylestown
†Morgnanesi, Lanny M. *journalist*
Smith, Charles Paul *newspaper publisher*

Easton
Mamana, Joseph *editor*

Emmaus
Beldon, Sanford T. *publisher*
Bricklin, Mark Harris *magazine editor, publisher*
†Wallace, Ken *magazine publisher*

Erie
Mead, Edward Mathews *newspaper executive*

Erwinna
Richman, Joan F. *television consultant*

Felton
Shoemaker, Eleanor Boggs *television production company executive*

Flourtown
Lee, Adrian Iselin, Jr. *journalist*

Greensburg
Harrell, Edward Harding *newspaper executive*

Harrisburg
Carnahan, Frances Morris *magazine editor*
Gover, Raymond Lewis *newspaper publisher*
Handler, Mimi *editor, writer*

Haverford
Jurney, Dorothy Misener *journalist, editor*

Hawley
Conley, Clare Dean *retired magazine editor*

Hellertown
McCullagh, James Charles *publishing company executive*

Hershey
Farrell, Eugene George *editor*

Hidden Valley
Funari, John H. *editor, consultant*

Honesdale
Brown, Kent Louis, Jr. *magazine editor*
Clark, Christine May *editor, author*

Johnstown
Saltz, Howard Joel *newspaper editor*

Lancaster
Cody, William Henry *journal editor*
Shaw, Charles Raymond *journalist*
Shenk, Willis Weidman *newspaper executive*

Lansdowne
Zingraff, Michael, Jr. *magazine editor*

Levittown
†Halberstein, Joseph Leonard *retired associate editor*
La Vo, Carl Palmer, Jr. *newspaper editor, author*

Manheim
Critz, Richard Laurens *magazine editor, architectural consultant*

Montoursville
Woolever, Naomi Louise *retired editor*

Newtown
Thompson, Carol Lewis *editor*

Paoli
Gallagher, Terrence Vincent *editor*

Philadelphia
Barlett, Donald L. *journalist*
Binzen, Peter Husted *columnist*
Bissinger, H(arry) G(erard) *journalist*
Boasberg, Leonard W. *reporter*
Boldt, David Rhys *journalist*
Breitenfeld, Frederick, Jr. *public broadcasting executive, educator*
Broom, William Wescott *retired newspaper executive*
†Bykofsky, Stuart Debs *newspaper columnist*
Carey, Arthur Bernard, Jr. *editor, writer, columnist*
†Cooney, Nancy *newspaper editor*
Cooper, Richard Lee *newspaper editor, journalist*
Dauth, Frances Kutcher *journalist, newspaper editor*
De Leon, Clark *newspaper columnist*
Denenberg, Herbert Sidney *journalist, lawyer, former state official*
Dolson, Franklin Robert *columnist*
Drake, Donald Charles *journalist*
Drucker, Mindy M. *editor, writer*
Edelson, Alan Martin *medical publisher, neurophysiologist*
Fancher, Charles B. *newspaper publishing executive*
Foreman, Gene Clemons *newspaper editor*
Gaul, Gilbert M. *reporter*
Gerbner, George *communications educator, university dean emeritus*
Gray, Gordon L. *communications educator*
Gross, Larry Paul *communications educator*
Hall, Robert J. *newspaper executive*
Halsey, Ashley, III *newspaper editor*
Harris, Jay Terrence *newspaper editor*
Haynes, Gary Allen *newspaper editor, journalist*
Iams, David Aveling *journalist, columnist*
Jones, Jacqueline Valarie *journalist*
Joyce, Philip Halton *journalist*
Kimelman, Donald Bruce *newspaper editor*
King, Maxwell E. P. *newspaper editor*
Klein, Julia Meredith *newspaper reporter*
Lawlor, Helen Anne *database publisher*
Leary, Michael Warren *journalist*
Leiter, Robert Allen *journalist, magazine editor*
Lent, John Anthony *journalist, educator*
Lewis, Claude Aubrey *columnist*
Loeb, Vernon Frederick *journalist*
Lovelady, Steven M. *newspaper editor*
Lyon, William Carl *sports columnist*
Mardar, Dianna *reporter*
Mezzacappa, Dale Veronica *journalist*
Moore, Acel *journalist*
Morgan, Arlene Notoro *newspaper editor, reporter, recruiter*
Nalle, Peter Devereux *publishing company executive*
Naughton, James Martin *newspaper editor*
Nelson, Nels Robert *drama critic*
News, Kathryn Anne *editor, educator, writer*
Nussbaum, Paul Eugene *journalist*
Othmer, David Artman *television and radio station executive*
Parry, Lance Aaron *newspaper executive*
Patel, Ronald Anthony *newspaper editor*
Porter, Jill *journalist*
Rock, Milton Lee *publisher*
Rogers, Mary Martin *publishing company executive*
Rosenthal, Robert Jon *newspaper editor, journalist*
Rossi, Steven B. *newspaper publishing executive*
Ryan, Desmond *film critic*
Samsot, Robert Louis *newspaper editor, consultant*
Searcy, Jarrell D. (Jay) *sportswriter*
Searcy, Jay *Sportswriter*
Shapiro, Howie *newspaper editor*
Shoup, Michael C. *newspaper reporter, editor*
Smolin, Ronald Philip *publisher*
Spikol, Art *editor, writer, illustrator*
Stalberg, Zachary *newspaper editor*
Steele, James B. *journalist*
Tait, Elaine *restaurant critic*
Toolan, Brian Paul *newspaper editor*
Tucker, David *newspaper editor*
Turow, Joseph Gregory *communication educator*
Wallace, Linda Suzan *journalist*
Ward, Hiley Henry *journalist, educator*
Wilkinson, Signe *cartoonist*
Winfrey, Marion Lee *television critic*
Woestendiek, (William) John, Jr. *reporter*
Zucchino, David Alan *newspaper journalist*

Pittsburgh
Alexander, James Eckert *editor*
Apone, Carl Anthony *journalist*
Craig, John Gilbert, Jr. *newspaper editor*
Deibler, William Edwin *newspaper editor*
Graham, Laurie *editor*
Kaplan, John *photojournalist, consultant, educator*
Leo, Peter Andrew *newspaper columnist*
Miller, Donald *art critic*
Roof, Robert L. *broadcast executive, sales executive*
Ross, Madelyn Ann *newspaper editor*
Sauer, Georgia Booras *newspaper writer*
Swann, Lynn Curtis *sportscaster, former professional football player*
Woodwell, Margot Bell *broadcasting executive*

Pottstown
Hylton, Thomas James *editorial writer*
Lenfest, Harold Fitz Gerald *cable television executive, lawyer*

Radnor
Baxter, John Michael *editor*
Youman, Roger Jacob *editor, writer*

Reading
†Smith, John Wilson, III *newspaper editor, columnist, statistician*

Scottdale
Cutrell, Benjamin Elwood *publisher*
Miller, Levi *publishing administrator*

Scranton
Lynett, George Vincent *newspaper publisher*
Lynett, William Ruddy *publishing, broadcasting company executive*
†Rogers, Edwin Earl *newspaper editor*

State College
Coppersmith Fredman, Marian Ungar *magazine publisher*
Lawrence, Ken *columnist*

Stroudsburg
Gasink, Warren Alfred *speech communication educator*

Tarentum
†Leonard, Richard Alan *newspaper editor*

University Park
Thatcher, Sanford Gray *publishing executive*

Villanova
Lambert, William G. *journalist, consultant*

Wayne
Brodsky, Julian A. *broadcasting services, telecommunications company executive*
Henne, James Earl *publisher*
Roberts, Ralph Joel *cable television, telephone communications and background music company executive*
Robinowitz, Joe Reece *publishing executive*

West Chester
Diller, Barry *entertainment company executive*
Mahoney, William Francis *editor*

Westtown
Backe, John David *communications corporation executive*

Wilkes Barre
Johnson, Micah William *television newscaster, director*

Williamsport
Rafferty, Michael Robert *editor, columnist*

Wynnewood
Singer, Samuel L(oewenberg) *journalist*

Yardley
Zulker, Charles Bates *broadcasting company executive*

York
Conway, Nancy Ann *publisher, editor*

RHODE ISLAND

Block Island
Kingsbury, Read Austin *retired journalist*

Charlestown
Ungaro, Joseph Michael *newspaper publishing executive, consultant*

Jamestown
Potter, Clarkson Nott *publishing consultant*

Manville
Eno, Paul Frederick *editor*

Newport
Baker, Winthrop Patterson, Jr. *broadcasting executive*
Holloway, Jerome Knight *publisher, former military strategy educator, retired foreign service officer*

Providence
†Battaglia, Francis H. *broadcast executive*
†Ciampa, Gail Ann *journalist*
Dickinson, Brian Ward *columnist*
Dujardin, Richard Charles *journalist*
Farmer, Susan Lawson *broadcasting executive, former secretary of state*
Hamblett, Stephen *newspaper publishing executive*
Hayes, John Edward *broadcasting executive*
Méras, Phyllis Leslie *journalist*
O'Donnell, Charles Patrick *retired newspaper executive, consultant*
Patinkin, Mark Alan *newspaper columnist*
†Rosenberg, Alan Gene *newspaper editor*
Sinclair, Joseph Samuels *broadcasting company executive, retail merchant*
Watkins, John Chester Anderson *newspaper publisher*
Whitcomb, Robert Bassett *journalist, editor*
Wyman, James Vernon *newspaper executive*

Warwick
Blount, William Allan *broadcasting executive*

West Greenwich
Markowicz, Victor *video company executive*

West Kingston
Haring, Howard Jack *magazine editor*

Westerly
Day, Chon *cartoonist*

SOUTH CAROLINA

Anderson
Mitchell, Thomas Wayne *newspaper editor*

Bennettsville
Kinney, William Light, Jr. *newspaper editor, publisher*

Bluffton
Lowe, Felix Caleb *publishing executive*

Cayce
McElveen, William Lindsay *broadcasting executive, lecturer*

Charleston
Anderson, Ivan Verner, Jr. *newspaper publisher*
Donehue, John Douglas *newspaper executive*
Gilbreth, Frank Bunker, Jr. *retired communications executive, writer*
Langley, Lynne Spencer *newspaper editor, columnist*
Manigault, Peter *media executive*
McGee, Hall Thomas, Jr. *newspaper, radio and television executive*
†Meggett, Linda Linette *reporter*
Reed, Stanley Foster *editor, writer, publisher, lecturer*
Schreadley, Richard Lee *writer, retired newspaper editor*
Tarleton, Larry Wilson *newspaper editor*
Wilcox, Arthur Manigault *newspaper editor*
Wyrick, Charles Lloyd, Jr. *publisher, writer, editor*

Columbia
Collins, James Edward *broadcast executive*
Crim, Reuben Sidney *newspaper publishing executive*
Gray, Katherine Wilson *newspaper editor*
McLean, Thomas Neil *editor*
Rone, William Eugene, Jr. *newspaper editor*
Thelen, Gil *newspaper editor*

Easley
Failing, George Edgar *editor, clergyman, educator*
†Urakami, Akio *manufacturing company executive*

Fort Mill
Mantle, John Edward *newspaper publisher*

Greenville
Barhyte, Donald James *newspaper executive*
Eskew, Rhea Taliaferro *newspaper publisher*
†Inman, Thomas Patrick *newspaper editor*
Mebane, William deBerniere *newspaper publisher*
Stultz, Thomas Joseph *newspaper executive*
Wearn, Wilson Cannon *retired media executive*

Hilton Head Island
†Marscher, Fran Heyward (Fran Smith) *editor*
McKinney, Donald Lee *magazine editor*

Landrum
Pauley, Robert Reinhold *broadcasting executive, financial executive*

Moncks Corner
Morris, Henry Allen, Jr. *publisher*

Orangeburg
Sims, Edward Howell *editor, publisher*

Walterboro
Johnson, Daniel McDonald (Dan Johnson) *newspaper editor*

Winnsboro
King, Robert Thomas *editor, free-lance writer*

SOUTH DAKOTA

Sioux Falls
Fuller, Lawrence Robert *newspaper publisher*
†Marsh, John S., Jr. *newspaper editor*

TENNESSEE

Brentwood
†Hearn, Billy Ray *recording industry executive*

Chattanooga
Anderson, Lee Stratton *newspaper publisher, editor*
Ashley, Jim Ray *newspaper editor*
Holmberg, Albert William, Jr. *publishing company executive*
Holmberg, Ruth Sulzberger *publishing company executive*
MacManus, Yvonne Cristina *editor, videoscripter, writer, consultant*
Neely, Paul *newspaper editor*
Palmer, Stanton Dean *newspaper editor*

Goodlettsville
Wilkins, Rita Denise *researcher, multimedia design consultant*

Knoxville
Ambrester, Marcus LaRoy *communication educator, program administrator*
Hohenberg, John *journalist, educator*
Rukeyser, William Simon *journalist, business executive*
Singletary, Michael Willis *journalism, educator*
Teeter, Dwight Leland, Jr. *journalism educator*

Maryville
Bradford, Tutt Sloan *retired publisher*
Stone, Hubert Dean *editor, journalist*

Memphis
†Brooks, Kathleen *journalist*
Caffey, Rick *broadcast executive*
Emery, Sue *bulletin editor, owner bridge studio*
Greiner, Morris Esty, Jr. *broadcast executive*
Griffin, Tom *former editor, writer*
McEachran, Angus *newspaper editor*
Ramirez, Michael P. *editorial cartoonist*
Roberts, C. Frank *broadcast executive*
Smith, Whitney Bousman *music and drama critic*
Stokes, Henry Arthur *journalist*
Williams, Joseph R. *newspaper publishing executive*

Murfreesboro
Wyatt, Robert Odell *journalism educator*

Nashville
Allbritton, Cliff *publisher*
Atkins, Chester Burton *record company executive, guitarist, publisher*
Battle, William Robert (Bob Battle) *newspaper executive*
Bowen, James *record company executive*
Boyd, Theophilus Bartholomew, III *publishing company executive*
†Du Bois, Tim *recording industry executive*
Feaster, Robert K. *publishing company executive*
Flanagan, Van Kent *journalist*
Frey, Herman S. *publishing company executive*
Harris, Stacy *print and broadcast journalist*
Hieronymus, Clara Booth Wiggins *journalist*
Mayhew, Aubrey *music business executive*
Peebles, James W. *publishing executive*
†Powers, Joe L. *publishing executive*
Rayburn, Ted Rye *newspaper editor*
Roberts, Sandra *editor*
Russell, Fred McFerrin *journalist, author, lawyer*
†Sherborne, Robert *editor*
Sutherland, Frank *publishing executive, editor*
Walden, Philip Michael *recording company executive, publishing company executive*
Whitt, Wilby Wayne *newspaper editor*

Sevierville
†Childress, Robert Linwood *newspaper publisher*

TEXAS

Abilene
Boyll, David Lloyd *broadcasting company executive*
†Puckett, Frank *newspaper publisher*

Amarillo
Martindale, Catherine Ann *editor*
Spies, Dennis J. *editor*

Arlington
Meadows, Jennifer Elizabeth *retired editor, tattoo artist*

Atlanta
†Francis, Bill *publishing executive*

Austin
Conine, Ernest *newspaper commentator, writer*
Danielson, Wayne Allen *journalism and computer science educator*
Fischer, Norman, Jr. *media broker*
Herman, Kenneth Neil *journalist*
Ivins, Molly *columnist, writer*
Laine, Katie Myers *communications consultant*
Levy, Michael Richard *publishing executive*
Matthews, Jay Arlon, Jr. *publisher, editor*
Mayers, Roy *publishing executive*
Mayes, Wendell Wise, Jr. *broadcasting company executive*
Teague, Hyman Faris *former publishing company executive*

Bedford
Lieber, David Leslie *journalist*

Canyon Lake
Phelan, Charlotte Robertson *journalist, book critic*

Carrollton
Powell, Bill Jake *newspaper executive*

College Station
Kern-Foxworth, Marilyn Louise *journalism educator*
Rotell, Thomas M. *publishing executive*

Commerce
Bell, William Jack *journalism educator*

Corpus Christi
House, David Augusta *newspaper editor*
Rose, Larry Lee *newspaper executive*

Crockett
Gibbs, James Howard *broadcast executive*

Dallas
Anders, John *newspaper columnist*
Ardoin, John Louis *music editor*
Bailon, Gilbert *newspaper editor*
Bersano, Bob *newspaper editor*
Blackstone, Kevin *sports columnist*
Blow, Steve *newspaper columnist*
Blumenthal, Karen *newspaper executive*
†Broadhead, Paul *movie theatre company executive*
Brown, Stephen Bryan *real estate editor*
Burns, Scott *columnist*
Compton, Bob *newspaper editor*
Correu, James M. *newspaper publishing executive*
Cox, James William *newspaper executive*
Creany, Cathleen Annette *television station executive*
Cummins, James Duane *correspondant, media executive*
Decherd, Robert William *newspaper and broadcasting executive*
DeOre, Bill *editorial cartoonist*
Dillon, David Anthony *journalist, lecturer*
Dufner, Edward Joseph *newspaper editor*
Enix, Agnes Lucille *editorial consultant*
Evans, William Wilson *retired newspaper editor*
Fiddick, Paul William *broadcasting company executive*
Finn, Peter Michael *television production executive*
Flournoy, John Craig *newspaper reporter*

Galloway, Randy *newspaper sports columnist*
Geiger, Ken *photojournalist*
Glines, Carroll Vane, Jr. *magazine editor*
Griffith, Dotty (Dorothy Griffith Stephenson) *journalist, speaker*
Halbreich, Jeremy L. *newspaper publishing executive*
Hall, Cheryl *newspaper editor*
Harasta, Cathy Ann *journalist*
Holmes, Bert Otis E., Jr. *retired newspaperman*
Huey, Ward L(igon), Jr. *media executive*
Jacobson, Gary *newspaper business editor*
Jones, Philip Davis *computer service publishing consultant*
Jordan, Karen Leigh *travel editor*
Kessler, Tom *newspaper editor*
†Klehfoth, Jay Gordon *publisher, writer, consultant*
Kutner, Janet *art critic, book reviewer*
Landers, James Michael (Jim Landers) *international editor*
Langer, Ralph Ernest *journalist*
Livingston, Grover D. *newspaper publishing executive*
Lysaught, Thomas Francis *publishing company executive*
McCormick, James Hillman *retired broadcast executive*
Meyer, Richard Jonah *broadcast executive, consultant*
Mong, Robert William, Jr. *managing editor*
Osborne, Burl *newspaper publisher, editor*
Patterson, Ronald Paul *publishing company executive, clergyman*
Peckham, Barry *newspaper publishing executive*
Pederson, Rena *newspaper editor*
Powell, Larry Randall *columnist*
St. John, Bob *journalist, columnist, author*
Savage, Scott David *broadcast executive*
Schwartz, Marilyn *columnist*
Scogin, Troy Pope *publishing company executive, accounts executive*
Sherrod, Blackie *mewspaper sports columnist*
Siegfried, Tom *newspaper editor*
Smith, David Lee *newspaper editor*
Smith, Nancy Lynne *journalist, real estate agent*
Smith, Russell L. *film critic*
Smith, Sue Frances *newspaper editor*
Snyder, Leslie *newspaper editor*
Snyder, William D. *photojournalist*
Starks, Richard *newspaper publishing executive*
Weinkauf, William Carl *communications company executive*
Wuntch, Philip Samuels *journalist, film critic*

Denton
Vick, Frances Brannen *publishing executive*
Westmoreland, Reginald Conway *journalism educator*

Dripping Springs
Rios, Evelyn Deerwester *columnist, musician, artist, writer*

El Paso
Ingle, Henry Thomas *communications educator, university administrator*
Treadwell, Hugh Wilson *publishing executive*

Fort Worth
Buckley, Betty Bob *journalist, consultant*
Connor, Richard L. *publisher, editor*
Davis, Jimmie Dan *newspaper editor*
Malone, Dan F. *journalist*
Martin, Harold Eugene *publishing executive, consultant*
Peipert, James Raymond *journalist*
Price, Debbie Mitchell *journalist, newspaper editor*
Price, Larry C. *photojournalist*
Price, Michael Howard *journalist, critic, composer, cartoonist*
Record, Phillip Julius *newspaper executive*
Tinsley, Jackson Bennett *newspaper editor*

Grand Prairie
Childs, Hymen *broadcasting corporation executive*

Houston
Aguilar, Melissa Ward *newspaper editor*
Ashby, Lynn Cox *newspaper editor*
Barlow, Jim B. *newspaper columnist*
Bischoff, Susan Ann *newspaper editor*
Bunch, Fred *newspaper picture editor*
Byars, Carlos *newspaper reporter*
Carlquist, Robert E. *newspaper publishing executive*
Christian, George Lloyd, Jr. *newspaper editor, writer*
Clark, Scott *newspaper editor*
Coleman, Mabeth Hallmark *newspaper publishing professional*
Criswell, Ann *newspaper editor*
Cunningham, Dan *newspaper editor*
Fant, Patrick Joseph *radio station general manager*
Frieden, Kit *newspaper editor*
George, Deveral D. *editor, journalist, advertising consultant*
Gerraughty, David R. *newspaper editor*
†Golden, Timothy N. *foreign correspondent*
Gray, Robert Steele *publishing executive, editor*
Griffin, Linda Gillan *fashion editor*
Hale, Leon *newspaper columnist*
Hammond, Ken *newspaper magazine editor*
Harasim, Paul Houck *columnist, educator*
Heinsen, Lindsay *newspaper editor*
Henry, John Cooper *journalist*
Hiatt, John David *broadcast company executive*
Hobby, William Pettus *broadcast executive*
Hodges, Ann *television editor, newspaper columnist*
Holmes, Ann Hitchcock *journalist*
Holmes, Cecile Searson *religion editor*
Jetton, Steve *newspaper editor*
Johnson, Richard James Vaughan *newspaper executive*
Johnston, Marguerite *journalist, author*
Kientz, Renee *newspaper editor*
Laird, John B. *newspaper publishing executive*
Leydon, Joseph Patrick *film critic, journalist*
Loftis, Jack D. *newspaper editor, newspaper executive*
Lunn, Judith Saska *newspaper editor, journalist*
Marr, David Francis *television announcer, former professional golfer, journalist*
Marshall, Jane Pretzer *newspaper editor*
Marshall, Thom *columnist*
Massey, Ike *newspaper publishing executive*
Mc David, George Eugene (Gene Mc David) *newspaper executive*
Millar, Jeffery Lynn *columnist*
Mitchell, Richard Dale *journalist, writer*
Newberry, Robert Curtis, Sr. *newspaper columnist*
Oren, Bruce Clifford *newspaper editor, artist*
Palomo, Juan Ramón *columnist*
Pederson, Tony Weldon *newspaper editor*
Powers, Hugh William *newspaper executive*
Read, Michael Oscar *editor, consultant*
Singleton, William Dean *newspaper publisher*
Snyder, Mike *newspaper editor*
Stanley, Jack H. *newspaper publishing executive*
Sweeney, John W., III *newspaper executive*
†Thomas, Katherine Jane *newspaper business columnist*
Walbridge, Willard Eugene *broadcasting executive*
Walls, Carmage *newspaper publisher*
Walls, Martha Ann Williams (Mrs. B. Carmage Walls) *newspaper executive*
Weber, Owen *broadcast executive*
Youngblood, Ray Wilson *publishing company executive*

Irving
Halter, Jon Charles *magazine editor, writer*
Stuckey, Scott Sherwood *editor*
†Young, J. Warren *magazine publisher*

Kerrville
Dozier, William Everett, Jr. *newspaper editor and publisher*
Harkey, Ira Brown, Jr. *newspaperman, educator, author*

Lewisville
Vacca, John Joseph, Jr. *television executive*

Lufkin
Cardwell, Horace Milton *communications company executive*

Mesquite
Mc Gregor, Donald Thornton *newspaper editor, journalist*

Missouri City
Griffin, Oscar O'Neal, Jr. *writer, former oil company executive*

Mount Pleasant
†Palmer, Robert Blunden *newspaper, printing executive*

Plano
Brock, Dee Sala *television executive, educator, writer, consultant*
Senderling, Jon Townsend *journalist, public affairs specialist*

Richardson
Boyd, Joe Dan *journal editor*
Leach, Sheryl *television show character creator*

Roanoke
Bradshaw, Terry *sports announcer, former professional football player*

San Angelo
Foster, Walton Arthur *broadcasting executive*

San Antonio
Belgin, Harvey Harry *photojournalist*
Harte, Houston Harriman *newspaper, broadcasting executive*
Kilpatrick, Charles Otis *newspaper editor, publisher*
Lenke, Joanne Marie *publishing executive*
Manning, Noel Thomas *publishing company executive*
Marbut, Robert Gordon *communications, cable and broadcast executive*
Mays, L. Lowry *broadcast executive*
†McLemore, David Eugene *editor, writer*
Michaels, Willard A. *retired broadcasting executive*
Miles, Janice Ann *news reporter*
†Polunsky, Bob A. *movie critic, talk show host*
†Yerkes, Susan Gamble *newspaper columnist*

Schulenburg
Clark, I. E. *publisher*

Stephenville
King, Clyde Richard *journalism educator, writer*

The Woodlands
Anderson, Dale *film production executive*
Logan, Mathew Kuykendall *journalist*

Waco
Gould, Loyal Norman *journalism educator*
†Lott, Robert Vincent *newspaper editor*
Preddy, Raymond Randall *newspaper publisher*

UTAH

Ogden
Larson, Brent T. *broadcasting executive*
Trundle, W(infield) Scott *publishing executive newspaper*

Orem
†Bearnson, Lisa Downs *editor-in-chief*

Provo
Stanford, Melvin Joseph *publisher, management consultant*

Salt Lake City
Berkes, Howard *radio news reporter*
Brady, Rodney Howard *broadcast company executive, former college president, former government official*
Brown, Carolyn Smith *communications educator, consultant*
Christiansen, Joyce L. Soelberg *newspaper editor*
Fehr, J. Will *newspaper editor*
Gallivan, John William *publisher*
Hague, Alan Donald *broadcasting executive*
Hatch, George Clinton *television executive*
Hatch, Wilda Gene *broadcast company executive*
Mortimer, William James *newspaper publisher*
Paulsen, Vivian *magazine editor*
Robison, Barbara Ann *retired newspaper editor*
Shelledy, James Edwin, III *editor*
Trahant, Mark Neil *newspaper editor*
Van Treese, James Bryan *book publishing and investment company executive*
Wood, F. Russell *broadcast executive*

VERMONT

Bennington
Brownell, David Wheaton *editor*
Garret, Paula Lyn *publishing company executive*

Bristol
Kompass, Edward John *consulting editor*

Brookfield
Newton, Earle Williams *editor, museum director, library and museum consultant*

Calais
Elmslie, Kenward Gray *retired publishing company executive, author*

Colchester
Green, Hope Stuart *public television executive*

Dorset
Ketchum, Richard Malcolm *editor, writer*

Montpelier
Slayton, Thomas Kennedy *editor, writer*

Perkinsville
Harris, Christopher *publisher, designer, editor*

South Woodstock
Crowl, John Allen *retired publishing company executive*

West Brattleboro
Barber, Orion Metcalf, II *publishing consultant, book packager*

White River Junction
Rutter, Frances Tompson *publisher*

Winooski
Wilson, Mary Louise *learning systems company executive*

VIRGINIA

Alexandria
Brownfeld, Allan Charles *columnist*
Christensen, Bruce LeRoy *public broadcasting executive*
Fahey, John M., Jr. *book publishing executive*
Fichenberg, Robert Gordon *newspaper editor, consultant*
Fleming, Douglas Riley *journalist, publisher, public affairs consultant*
Foisie, Philip Manning *retired journalist, media consultant*
Foster, Robert Francis *communications executive*
†Hewitt, Charles C. *broadcast executive*
Hobbs, Michael Edwin *broadcasting company executive*
Kaff, Albert Ernest *journalist, author*
Musselman, Norman Burkey *editor*
Perkins, A. William *printing executive*
Radewagen, Fred *publisher, organization executive*
Sanfelici, Arthur H(ugo) *editor, writer*
Yoder, Edwin Milton, Jr. *columnist, educator, editor, writer*

Annandale
Pollard, David Edward *editor*

Arlington
Adelman, Kenneth Lee *syndicated columnist, management consultant, former government official*
Athanas, Emanuel Stylianos *journalist, educator, radio program director*
Bodley, Harley Ryan, Jr. *editor, writer, broadcaster*
Bullard, Marcia Lynn *weekly magazine editor*
Cardwell, Nancy Lee *editor, writer*
Clayton, James Edwin *journalist*
Clements, John Brian *broadcasting executive*
Cohen, Ronald Eli *journalist*
Cole, Benjamin Richason *newspaper executive*
Correll, John Thomas *magazine editor*
Curley, John J. *diversified media company executive*
Curley, Thomas *newspaper executive*
Curtis, Richard A. *newspaper editor*
Diggs, J(esse) Frank *retired magazine editor*
Gniewek, Raymond Louis *newspaper editor*
Jurgensen, Karen *newspaper editor*
Lester, Barnett Benjamin *editor, foreign affairs officer*
Lorell, Monte *newspaper editor*
MacDougall, William Lowell *magazine editor*
Mater, Gene P. *communications consultant*
†Mazzarella, David *newspaper editor*
McCorkindale, Douglas Hamilton *publishing company executive, corporate lawyer*
McNamara, Tom *newspaper editor*
McWethy, John Fleetwood *journalist*
Michael, Larry Perry *broadcasting company executive*
Miller, Loye Wheat, Jr. *journalist, corporate communications specialist*
Mirrielees, James Fay, III *publishing executive*
Neikirk, William Robert *journalist*
Neuharth, Allen Harold *newspaper publisher*
Policinski, Eugene Francis *newspaper editor*
Prichard, Peter S. *newspaper editor*
Quinn, John Collins *publishing executive, newspaper editor*
Ritter, Hal *newspaper editor*
Rockefeller, Sharon Percy *broadcast executive*
Sandeen, Roderick Cox *newspaper editor*
Simonson, David C. *retired newspaper association executive*
Simpson, John Mathes *newspaper editor*
Snow, Robert Anthony *journalist*
Tanzer, Lester *editor*
†Van, Dirk *radio newscaster, talk show host*
Vesper, Carolyn F. *newspaper publishing executive*
Weiss, Susan *newspaper editor*
Willenson, Kim Jeremy *publisher, journalist, author*

Burke
Fisher, James Burke *publishing company executive*

Charlottesville
Foard, Susan Lee *editor*
Loo, Beverly Jane *publishing company executive*
Mayes, Bernard Duncan *broadcast journalist, educator, dramatist*
McQueeney, Thomas A. *publisher*
Parrish, David Walker, Jr. *legal publishing company executive*
Worrell, Anne Everette Rowell *newspaper publisher*

Faber
Friede, Eleanor Kask *editor, publisher*

Fairfax
†Lipton, Eric *reporter*

Fairfax Station
Abuzaakouk, Aly Ramadan *publications director*

Falls Church
Donovan, Robert John *retired journalist*
Kaplow, Herbert Elias *journalist*
Stone, Marvin Lawrence *journalist, government official*

Fredericksburg
Rowe, Charles Spurgeon *newspaper publishing and broadcasting executive*

Great Falls
Garrett, Wilbur Eugene *magazine editor*

Hampton
Brauer, Harrol Andrew, Jr. *broadcasting executive*

Harrisonburg
Rollman, Steven Allan *communication educator*

Herndon
Scripps, Edward Wyllis *newspaper publisher*

Lively
Gallimore, Robert Stephenson *news service executive*

Mc Lean
Bartow, Randy David *publishing executive*
Fromm, Joseph *retired magazine editor, foreign affairs consultant*

Middleburg
Evans, John Derby *telecommunications company executive*

Mineral
Speer, Jack Atkeson *publisher*

Moneta
Armistead, Moss William, III *retired newspaper executive*

New Market
Le Roy, L. David *journalist*

Newport News
Barnes, Myrtle Sue Snyder *editor*
Cantrell, Joseph Doyle *newspaper company executive*
Davis, Jack Wayne, Jr. *newspaper publisher*
Kale, Wallace Wilford, Jr. *journalist, communicator, administrator*
Perry, Donald A. *cable television consultant*

Norfolk
Barry, Richard Francis, III *publishing executive*
Batten, Frank *newspaper publisher, cable broadcaster*
†Bonko, Larry Walter *columnist, writer, radio personality*
Campbell, Cole C. *journalist, educator*
†Eisman, Dale C. *journalist*
Fitzpatrick, William Henry *retired journalist*
Fox, Douglas Brian *newspaper publishing company executive*
Mobley, Mark *music critic, feature writer*
†Power, Edward Francis *newspaper editor*
Ritter, Alfred Francis, Jr. *cable television executive*
†Roberts, Richard D. *cable station executive*
Rose, Paul Edward *publishing company executive*
Sizemore, William Howard, Jr. *newspaper editor*
Wynne, John Oliver *newspaper, broadcast and cable executive*

Radford
Thomas, Robert Wilburn *broadcasting and advertising executive*
Wille, Lois Jean *retired newspaper editor*

Reston
Black, Cathleen Prunty *newspaper executive*
Cannistraro, Nicholas, Jr. *newspaper executive*
Mallette, Malcolm Francis *newspaper editor, educator*
Pyle, Thomas Alton *instructional television and motion picture executive*

Richmond
Baker, Donald Parks *journalist, educator*
†Billingsley, Anna Barron *journalist*
Bryan, David Tennant *media company executive*
Bryan, John Stewart, III *newspaper publisher*
Bustard, Clarke *music critic, newswriter, radio producer*
Dillon, James Lee *media company executive, newspaper publisher*
Donnahoe, Alan Stanley *newspaper executive*
Estes, Gerald Walter *newspaper executive*
Goodykoontz, Charles Alfred *newspaper editor, retired*
†Grimsley, James Edward *newspaper editor, syndicated columnist*
Jordan, David Lewis *newspaper executive*
†Mackenzie, Ross *newspaper editor*
Neman, Daniel Louis *movie critic*
Owen, Howard Wayne *journalist, writer*
Robertson, William Franklin *publishing executive*

Smith, Ted Jay, III *mass communications educator*
Winstead, Joy *journalist, consultant*
Wirt, John Stephen *journalist*

Roanoke
Beagle, Benjamin Stuart, Jr. *columnist*
Landon, Forrest M. *newspaper editor*
Layman, Mark Leslie *journalist*
Rugaber, Walter Feucht, Jr. *newspaper executive*
Warren, William Kermit *newspaper managing editor*

Vienna
Blevins, Charles Russell *publishing executive*
Lewis, Boyd De Wolf *publisher,editor, writer*
Mc Arthur, George *journalist*
McKay, Carol Ruth *photographic editor*

Virginia Beach
Green, Barbara-Marie *publisher, journalist, poet*
Robertson, Pat (Marion Gordon Robertson) *religious broadcasting executive*
†Robertson, Timothy B. *cable television executive*
Smith, A. Robert *editor, author*

Winchester
Byrd, Harry Flood, Jr. *newspaper executive, former senator*

Woodbridge
Binder, Leonard James *magazine editor, retired*

WASHINGTON

Bellevue
Berkley, James Donald *clergyman*
Smith, Lester Martin *broadcasting executive*

Bellingham
Doerper, John Erwin *publisher, editor*

Edmonds
Owen, John *retired newspaper editor*

Friday Harbor
Leeming, Frank, Jr. *newspaper editor, publisher*

Mercer Island
Bowne, Martha Hoke *magazine editor, consultant*

Port Townsend
Buhler, Jill Lorie *editor, writer*

Pullman
Bird, Robert Kenton *journalist, educator*

Redmond
Mollman, John Peter *book publisher, consultant electronic publishing*
Welke, Elton Grinnell, Jr. *publisher, writer*

Seattle
Anderson, Rick Gary *newspaper columnist*
Anderson, Ross *columnist*
Bargreen, Melinda Lueth *music critic*
†Blethen, Frank A. *newspaper publisher*
Blethen, William Kingsley, Jr. *newspaper publishing executive*
Boardman, David *newspaper editor*
Buckner, Philip Franklin *newspaper publisher*
Cameron, Mindy *newspaper editor*
Cochran, Wendell *science editor*
Culp, Mildred Louise *corporate executive*
Dietrich, William Alan *reporter*
Ellegood, Donald Russell *publishing executive*
Even, Jan *newspaper editor*
Fancher, Michael Reilly *newspaper editor, newspaper publishing executive*
Godden, Jean W. *columnist*
Gouldthorpe, Kenneth Alfred Percival *publisher, state official*
Gwinn, Mary Ann *newspaper reporter*
Hartl, John George *film critic*
Henkel, Cathy *newspaper sports editor*
Hills, Regina J. *journalist*
Johnson, Wayne Eaton *writer, editor, former drama critic*
Kelly, Carolyn Sue *newspaper executive*
Lacitis, Erik *journalist*
Nalder, Eric Christopher *investigative reporter*
Nash, Cynthia Jeanne *journalist*
Ostrom, Carol Marie *reporter*
Payne, Ancil Horace *retired broadcasting executive*
Rinearson, Peter Mark *journalist, author, software developer*
Schafer, James Henry *newspaper company executive*
Sizemore, Herman Mason, Jr. *newspaper executive*
Smulyan, Jeffrey *radio station executive, owner pro baseball team*
Stanton, Michael John *newspaper editor*
†Thiel, Arthur Warren *journalist*
Turner, Wallace L. *reporter*
Voorhees, John Lloyd *columnist*
Williams, John A. (Jack Williams) *newspaper publishing executive*
Williamson, Don *newspaper columnist*

Spokane
Cowles, William Stacey *publisher*
Gray, Alfred Orren *journalism educator, research and communications consultant*
Herdrich, Norman Wesley *magazine editor*
†Kafentzis, John Charles *journalist, educator*
Kunkel, Richard Lester *public radio executive*

Tacoma
Jasinek, Gary Donald *newspaper executive*
Johnson, Charles Robert *television news anchor, reporter*

Vancouver
Campbell, Scott *newspaper publishing company executive*

WEST VIRGINIA

Charleston
†Anderson, Leonard Troy *columnist*
†Chilton, Elizabeth Early *newspaper executive*
Greenfield, David Joel *editor*
Grimes, Richard Stuart *editor, writer*
Haught, James Albert, Jr. *journalist, newspaper editor*
†Keith, Steven Jeffrey *newspaper editor*
Marsh, Don Seagle *retired newspaper editor*

Clarksburg
Highland, Cecil Blaine, Jr. *newspaper publisher, lawyer, banker*

Greenville
Warner, Kenneth Wilson, Jr. *editor, association publications executive*

Huntington
Ritchie, Garry Harlan *television broadcast executive*

Shepherdstown
Wilson, Miriam Janet Williams *publishing executive*

Wheeling
Nutting, George Ogden *newspaper publisher*

WISCONSIN

Brookfield
Lessiter, Frank Donald *magazine editor*
Schwanz, H(erman) Lee *publishing company executive*

Fort Atkinson
Knox, William David *publishing company executive*
Meyer, Eugene Carlton *retired editor*
Sager, Donald Jack *publisher, former librarian*

Green Bay
Daley, Arthur James *retired magazine publisher*
Poppenhagen, Ronald William *newspaper editor, publishing executive*

Hales Corners
Laur, Bernard Paul *radio executive*

Iola
Foerster, Urban Michael, III (Trey Foerster) *newspaper owner, publisher*
Kiefer, Kit Annette *editor*
Krause, Chester Lee *publishing company executive*
Mishler, Clifford Leslie *publisher*

Janesville
Fitzgerald, James Francis *cable television executive*

Madison
Blankenburg, William Burl *journalism educator*
Burgess, James Edward *newspaper publisher, executive*
Denton, Frank M. *newspaper editor*
Dunwoody, Sharon Lee *science communication scholar*
Fanlund, Paul G. *newspaper editor*
Fitchen, Allen Nelson *publisher*
Fitzpatrick, Mary Anne Theresa *communications educator*
Gruber, John Edward *editor, railroad historian, photographer*
Haslanger, Philip Charles *journalist*
Hoyt, James Lawrence *journalism educator, athletic administrator*
Hunter, John Patrick *newspaper editor*
McLeod, Jack Myron *communications educator*
McNelly, John Taylor *journalist, educator*
Meloon, Robert A. *retired newspaper publisher*
Miller, Frederick William *publisher, lawyer*
†Still, Thomas Wayne *newspaper editor, columnist*
Walker, William Ray *broadcasting executive*
†Wineke, William Robert *reporter, clergyman*
Wolman, J. Martin *retired newspaper publisher*
Zweifel, David Alan *newspaper editor*

Menasha
Henseler, Gerald Anthony *printing company executive*

Milwaukee
Armstrong, Douglas Dean *movie critic*
Auer, James Matthew *art critic, journalist*
Bacha, Diane Marie *newspaper editor*
Behrendt, David Frogner *journalist*
Dembski, Barbara *newspaper editor*
Farris, Trueman Earl, Jr. *retired newspaper editor*
Fibich, Howard Raymond *retired newspaper editor*
Foster, Richard *journalist*
Gissler, Sigvard Gunnar, Jr. *journalism educator, former newspaper editor*
Hayes, Paul Gordon *journalist*
Hinshaw, Edward Banks *broadcasting company executive*
Huston, Margo *journalist*
Jaques, Damien Paul *theater critic*
Joslyn, Jay Thomas *retired arts critic*
Kritzer, Paul Eric *media executive, communications lawyer*
Leonard, Richard Hart *journalist*
McCann, Dennis John *columnist*
Meisner, Mary Jo *editor*
Reedy, George Edward *educator, author, lecturer*
Schaleben, Arville *newspaper editor, writer, educator*
Slocum, Elizabeth *newspaper editor*
Spore, Keith Kent *newspaper editor*
†Sykes, Leonard L., Jr. *newspaper editor*
Wills, Robert Hamilton *newspaper executive*

Montello
Burns, Robert Edward *editor, publisher*

Neillsville
Stockwell, Richard E. *journalist, business executive*

New Glarus
Marsh, Robert Charles *writer, music critic*

Pewaukee
Lee, Jack (Jim Sanders Beasley) *broadcast executive*

Stoughton
Ellery, John Blaise *communications educator emeritus*

Sun Prairie
Allen, Ronald Royce *communication educator*

Verona
Schroeder, Henry William *publisher*

Waukesha
Larson, Russell George *magazine and book publisher*

West Bend
Fraedrich, Royal Louis *magazine editor, publisher*

WYOMING

Casper
Rosenthal, Jack *broadcasting executive*

Jackson
Downer, Eugene Debs, Jr. *editor, publisher*

Riverton
Peck, Robert A. *newspaper publisher*

TERRITORIES OF THE UNITED STATES

FEDERATED STATES OF MICRONESIA

Ponape
Lippwe, Esikiel *broadcast specialist*

GUAM

Agana
Crisostomo, Manny *photographer*
Udick, Robert E. *newspaper executive*

PUERTO RICO

San Juan
Aponte Alsina, Marta *editor, writer, press administrator*

CANADA

ALBERTA

Calgary
Fisher, John Philip *retired printing and publishing company executive*
Peterson, Kevin Bruce *newspaper editor, publishing executive*
Poole, Robert Anthony *journalist*
Russell, Gary *broadcast executive*

Edmonton
Hughes, Linda J. *newspaper publisher*
†MacLean, Victoria Graham *journalist, editor*
Roskin, Lewis Ross *broadcasting company executive*
Stanway, Paul William *newspaper editor*

BRITISH COLUMBIA

Vancouver
Gunn, Roderick James *broadcast executive*
Haysom, Ian Richard *newspaper editor*
Holtby, Douglas Martin *television executive*
Hume, Stephen *writer, editor*
Noble, Stuart Harris *newspaper executive*
†Yaffe, Barbara Marlene *journalist*

Victoria
Tighe, James C. *publisher*

MANITOBA

Winnipeg
Asper, Israel Harold *broadcasting executive*
Burt, Christopher Murray *former newspaper editor, communications consultant*
McKie, Francis Paul *journalist*
Wreford, David Mathews *magazine editor*

ONTARIO

Don Mills
French, William Harold *retired newspaper editor*
Hanna, William Brooks *book publisher*
Heisey, William Lawrence *publisher*
Hickey, Brian Edward *publishing executive*

Kingston
Hancock, Geoffrey White *magazine editor, writer*

Kitchener
MacDonald, Wayne Douglas *publisher*
Rittinger, Carolyne June *newspaper editor*

London
Bembridge, John Anthony *newspaper editor*
Cornies, Larry Alan *journalist, educator*
Desbarats, Peter Hullett *journalist, academic administrator*
McLeod, Philip R. *publishing executive*

Markham
Fitzhenry, Robert Irvine *publisher*

Ottawa
Clever, W(arren) Glenn *editor, publishing executive, poet, writer, educator*
Davey, Clark William *newspaper publisher*
Deacon, Paul Septimus *retired publishing, communications company executive*
Macklem, Michael Kirkpatrick *publisher*
Manera, Anthony S. *retired broadcasting and education executive*
McCabe, Michael *broadcast executive*
Stone, Jeffrey Jay *film critic, journalist, writer*

Peterborough
Young, Scott Alexander *television journalist, author*

Scarborough
Besse, Ronald Duncan *publishing company executive*
Campbell, E. E. *publishing executive*
Isley, John Charles *publishing company executive*
Mitchell, Arthur Harris *newspaper columnist*

Toronto
Berton, Pierre *journalist, author*
Black, Conrad Moffat *publishing corporate executive*
Boultbee, John Arthur *publishing executive*
Clancy, Louis John *newspaper editor, journalist*
Cruickshank, John Douglas *newspaper editor*
Downing, John Henry *newspaper editor, journalist, columnist*
Egan, Vincent Joseph *journalist, newspaper columnist*
Fierheller, George Alfred *communications company executive*
Francis, Diane Marie *journalist*
Galloway, David Alexander *publishing company executive*
Godfrey, Paul Victor *newspaper publisher*
Harris, Nicholas George *publisher*
Honderich, Beland Hugh *publisher*
Honderich, John Allen *newspaper publisher*
Iannuzzi, Daniel Andrew *publishing and broadcasting executive*
Jolley, David *newspaper executive*
Karakas, Rita S. *television broadcast executive*
King, John Charles Peter *newspaper editor*
Landsberg, Michele *journalist*
†Lasker, David Raymond *newspaper editor, musician*
Lewis, Robert *periodical editor, journalist*
Lombardi, John Barba-Linardo *broadcasting executive*
†McLean, (Andrew) Stuart *educator, journalist*
Morra, Bernadette *newspaper editor, journalist*
Newman, Peter Charles *journalist*
Olive, David Michael *magazine writer, magazine editor*
Ostry, Bernard *broadcasting executive*
Rauhala, Ann Elaine *reporter*
†Rigby, Kathryn Jill (Jill Rigby) *newspaper editor, travel journalist*
Sanderson, Eric George (Sandy Sanderson) *broadcast executive*
Singleton-Wood, Allan James *publishing executive*
Smith, David Todd *publishing company executive*
Thall, Burnett Murray *newspaper executive*
Thomson, Kenneth R. (Lord Thomson of Fleet) *publishing executive*
Turner, Craig *journalist*
Watson, Paul *photojournalist, correspondent*

Willowdale
Dean, Geoffrey *book publisher*
Irwin, John Wesley *publisher*
Kerner, Fred *book publisher, writer*

Windsor
Morgan, George Carl *retired newspaper editor*

QUEBEC

Montreal
Beaubien, Philippe de Gaspe, II *communications executive*
Béliveau, Jules *journalist*
Braide, Robert David *broadcast executive*
Des Roches, Antoine *newspaper executive*
†Ferrabee, (Francis) James *newspaper editor*
Girard, Jacques *communications executive*
Juneau, Pierre *broadcasting company executive*
Landry, Roger D. *publishing company executive*
Peladeau, Pierre *publishing company executive*
Pépin, Marcel *broadcast executive*
Romanelli, G. Jack *journalist*
Webster, Norman Eric *journalist, charitable foundation administrator*

SASKATCHEWAN

Regina
Hughes, Robert Lachlan *newspaper executive*

MEXICO

Mexico City
Ellison, Katherine Esther *journalist*

AUSTRALIA

Greenwich
Westerberg, Verne Edward *magazine publisher*

Sydney
Guerin, Didier *magazine executive*
Murdoch, (Keith) Rupert *publisher*

BELGIUM

Brussels
Branegan, James Augustus, III *journalist*
†Ignatius, Alan (Adi) *magazine editor*
Kempe, Frederick Schumann *newspaper editor, author*

CROATIA

Zagreb
Fertig-Dyks, Susan Beatrice *international media and business consultant*

CZECH REPUBLIC

Prague
Auerbach, Stuart Charles *journalist*

ENGLAND

Buckinghamshire
Elegant, Robert Sampson *journalist, author*

Cambridge
Kermode, (John) Frank *literary critic, educator*

Hartlepool
Smyth, Reginald (Reggie Smythe) *cartoonist*

London
Barnett, Bill Marvin *publishing company executive*
Boccardi, Louis Donald *news agency executive*
Cook, Jan *recording industry executive*
de Bellaigue, Eric *media consultant, securities analysis specialist*
Grade, Lord Lew *entertainment corporation executive*
Green, Richard Lancelyn (Gordon) *editor, writer*
†Horwitz, Anthony Lander *reporter, author*
Irvine, Ian Alexander Noble *publishing company executive, director*
Laurie, James Andrew *journalist, broadcaster*
Mayer, Peter *publisher*
McGinnis, Marcy Ann *television news executive producer*
Mellon, John *publishing executive*
†Mirageas, Evans John *record company executive*
Pleasants, Henry *music critic*
Scardino, Albert James *journalist*
Scardino, Marjorie Morris *publishing company executive*
Tuohy, William *correspondent*

FIJI

Suva
Usher, Sir Leonard Gray *retired news association executive*

FRANCE

Lauris
Spivak, Jonathan M. *journalist*

Paris
Behrstock, Julian Robert *publishing consultant, writer*
De Lyrot, Alain Herve *editor*
Dubs, Patrick Christian *publisher*
Lewis, Flora *journalist*

GERMANY

Bonn
Fleming, Joseph Benedict *newspaperman*

Munich
Saur, Klaus G. *publisher*
von Minckwitz, Bernhard *publishing company executive*

Weinheim
Köhler, Hans Dirk *publisher*

HONG KONG

Hong Kong
†Gargan, Edward A. *journalist*
Lehner, Urban Charles *journalist*
†Vatikiotis, Michael Richard John *journalist, writer*

INDIA

New Delhi
Dahlburg, John-Thor Theodore *newspaper correspondent*

ISRAEL

Jerusalem
Bronner, Ethan Samuel *news correspondent*

Savyon
Bushinsky, Jay (Joseph Mason) *journalist, radio/TV correspondent, columnist*

ITALY

Rome
Wynn, Coy Wilton *journalist*

JAPAN

Tokyo
Krisher, Bernard *foreign correspondent*
Simons, Lewis Martin *journalist*

THE NETHERLANDS

Aerdenhout
Vinken, Pierre Jacques *publishing executive, neurosurgeon*

Amsterdam
Bruggink, Herman *publishing executive*
Kels, James *publishing executive*

NEW ZEALAND

Bay of Islands
Veysey, Arthur Ernest *reporter, administrator, biographer*

POLAND

Warsaw
Engelberg, Stephen Paul *reporter*

SPAIN

Mallorca
Raff, Joseph Allen *publishing company executive, author*

SWITZERLAND

Geneva
O'Regan, Richard Arthur *editor, retired foreign correspondent*
Polunin, Nicholas *environmentalist, author, editor*

Zollikerberg
Bocker, Hans Jurgen *editor, analyst, consultant, management educator*

TURKS AND CAICOS ISLANDS

Provinciales
Johnston, Samuel Thomas *entertainment company executive*

ADDRESS UNPUBLISHED

Aaron, Betsy *journalist*
Achorn, Robert Comey *retired newspaper publisher*
Adler, Gerald *retired film and television executive, lawyer*
Agarwal, Suman Kumar *editor*
Ajemian, Robert Myron *journalist*
Aldrich, Patricia Anne Richardson *retired magazine editor*
Anderson, Elliott Van *publishing company executive*
Andre, (Kenneth) Michael *editor, publisher, writer*
Andrisani, John Anthony *editor, author, golf consultant*
Anglemire, Kenneth Norton *retired publishing company executive, writer, environmentalist, lawyer*
Arden, Sherry W. *publishing company executive*
Arnold, Henri *cartoonist*
Audet, Paul Andre *retired newspaper executive*
Baack, John Edward *publishing consultant*
Backlund, Ralph Theodore *magazine editor*
Baggett, Donnis Gene *journalist, editor*
Barham, Patte (Mrs. Harris Peter Boyne) *publisher, author, columnist*
†Barhydt, Sally J. *publishing company executive*
Barry, Rick (Richard Francis Dennis Barry, III) *sportscaster, retired professional basketball player, marketing professional*
Bassett, Barbara Wies *editor, publisher*
Bassett, Carol Ann *magazine, video, and radio documentary writer, producer, journalism educator*
Batignani, Laurie A. *communications professional*
Bender, Gary Nedrow *television sportscaster*
Bennett, Geraldine Mae Paulette *publisher, author*
Berger, William Ernest *newspaper publisher*
Berman, Laura *freelance writer*
Berman, William H. *publishing company executive*
Bernard, Jami *film critic, author*
Bernard, Ronald Charles *entertainment company executive*
Bernstein, Laurel *publishing executive*
Bingham, Jinsie Scott *broadcast company executive*
Block, William *newspaper publisher*
Bogdanich, Walt *journalist*
Bortz, Paul Isaac *media, sport and entertainment consultant*
Boswell, Thomas Murray *sports columnist, writer*
Bourke, Dale Hanson *publishing company owner*
Braden, Thomas Wardell *news commentator*
†Brantley, Benjamin David *drama critic*
Brazil, Jeff *reporter*
Breathed, Berkeley *cartoonist*
Brekke, Gail Louise *broadcasting administrator*
Brett, Barbara Jeanne *publisher*
Brinberg, Herbert Raphael *information management, publishing company executive*
Broadwater, James E. *publisher*
Brodian, Laura *broadcasting and illustration studio executive, professional illustrator*
Broude, Ronald *music publisher*
Brown, Britt *retired publishing company executive*
Brunvand, Dana Kari *editor, English educator*
Buchanan, Edna *journalist*
Buchanan, Patrick Joseph *journalist*
Buchanan, Susan Shaver *publishing company executive*
Buckley, William Elmhirst *publishing consultant*
Buffkins, Archie Lee *public television executive*
Callahan, Joseph Murray *magazine editor*
Callander, Bruce Douglas *journalist, free-lance writer*
Camp, Clifton Durrett, Jr. *newspaper consultant, rancher*
Campbell, Byron Chesser *publishing company executive*
Cantone, Vic *political cartoonist*
Caray, Harry Christopher *sports announcer*
†Carlin, Richard Peter *editor, author*
Carlson, Natalie Traylor *publisher*
Chercover, Murray *television executive*
Chernichaw, Mark *television, film and interactive multimedia executive producer, director, international media consultant*
Church, Abiah A. *retired broadcasting company executive, lawyer*
Clapper, Lyle Nielsen *magazine publisher*
Clark, Peter Bruce *newspaper executive*
Clark, Robert Phillips *newspaper editor, consultant*
Cloud, Stanley Wills *journalist, editor, writer*
Cogan, Ronald James *editor, writer, producer*
Cohen, Allan Richard *broadcasting executive*
Cohen, Mark Herbert *broadcasting company executive*
†Condon, Curtis Wayne *magazine editor*
Conklin, Michael L. *newspaper columnist*
Cook, Fred James *journalist, author*
Cook, Stanton R. *media company executive*
Costas, Robert Quinlan (Bob Costas) *sportscaster*
Cowles, John, Jr. *publisher, women's sports promoter*
†Coyle, John J. *publishing executive*
Crowther, James Earl *radio and television executive*
Cuevas, Milton Joseph *publishing company executive*
Cullen, James Thaddeus, Jr. *broadcast executive*
Curtin, David Stephen *newswriter*
Curtis, Mary Ellen (Mary Curtis Horowitz) *publishing company executive*
Cushing, Frederic Sanford *publishing company executive*
Dahlgren, Carl Herman Per *educator, arts administrator*
D'Amato, Anthony Roger *recording company executive*
Daniel, Elbert Clifton *journalist*
DeCamp, Graydon *journalist*
Dickman, James Bruce *photojournalist*
Dills, James Arlof *retired publishing company executive*
Dilworth, Ann Evans *publishing company executive*
Dinkel, John George *magazine editor*
Douglas, Eileen *news broadcaster*
Draznin, Jules Nathan *journalism and public relations educator, consultant*
Drew, Elizabeth Heineman *publishing executive*
Driskill, Clarence *publishing executive*
Duerr, Herman George *retired publishing executive*
Dunham, Benjamin Starr *editor, arts administrator*
Eaker, Ira *publishing executive*
Edwards, Geoffrey Hartley *newspaper publisher*
Ehrlich, Amy *editor, writer*
Ekstract, Richard Evan *publishing executive*
Ellison, Eugene Curtis *radio station executive*
Elsner, Sidney Edgar *journalist*
Emery, Sherman Raymond *editorial consultant*
Erlicht, Lewis Howard *broadcasting company executive*
Ewell, Miranda Juan *journalist*
Farah, Joseph Francis *newspaper editor, writer*
Fassio, Virgil *newspaper publishing company executive*
Fazio, Evelyn M. *publisher*
Feiffer, Jules *cartoonist, writer, playwright*
Ferre, Antonio Luis *newspaper publisher*
Fields, William Hudson, III *magazine publisher*
Fink, John Francis *newspaper editor*
Finnegan, Sara Anne *publisher*
Fitzgerald, Edward Earl *publishing executive, author*
Flanders, Scott Nelson *publishing company executive, lawyer, accountant*
Frankel, Glenn *journalist*
Freeman, Graydon LaVerne *retired publishing company executive*
Friedman, Emma Fleischman *editor, publisher*
Furlong, Robert Joseph *television station executive*
Gannon, James Patrick *newspaper editor*
Garfield, Robert Edward *newspaper columnist*
Gartenberg, Seymour Lee *retired recording company executive*
Geer, Stephen DuBois *retired journalist*
Geoghegan, John Joseph *retired publisher*
Gilder, George Franklin *writer*
Gill, Henry Herr *photojournalist*
Gilson, Barbara Frances *editor*
Glaser, Robert Leonard *retired television executive*
Glover, William Harper *theater critic*
†Goldberg, Danny *recording industry executive*
Goldsmith, Arthur Austin *magazine editor*
Goldwater, John Leonard *publisher, writer*
Goode, Stephen Hogue *publishing company executive*
Goodkin, Michael Jon *publishing company executive*
Grueskin, William Steven *editor*
Haas, Carolyn Buhai *publisher, writer, consultant*
Hagel, Raymond Charles *publishing company executive, educator*
Hahn, Helene B. *motion picture company executive*
Halfen, David *publishing executive*
Hamill, (William) Pete *newspaper columnist, author*
Hanners, David *journalist*
Harden, Patrick Alan *journalist, news executive*
Harding, John Thomas *journalist*
Harris, Jordan *record company executive*
Harris, Louis *public opinion analyst, columnist*
Hartman, John Wheeler *publisher*
Hast, Adele *editor, historian*
Hawes, Alexander Boyd, Jr. *newspaper editor, journalist*
Heiman, Grover George, Jr. *magazine editor, author*
Hering, Doris Minnie *dance critic*
Hess, David Willard *journalist*
Hill, Pamela *television executive*
Himmelfarb, Milton *editor, educator*
Hinckle, Warren James, III *journalist*
Hoffman, Donald Stuart *music director*
Hoge, James Fulton, Jr. *magazine editor*
Holland, David Thurston *former editor*
Holt, Patricia Lester *book review editor*
Holton, Robert Page *publishing executive*
Howard, Jack Rohe *retired newspaperman*
Hubley, Reginald Allen *publisher*
Huff, William Achleiss *communications educator*
Humes, Edward *journalist, writer*
Idaszak, Jerome Joseph *economic journalist*
Jennings, Max *newspaper editor*
Jensen, Jack Michael *publishing executive*
Jiler, William Laurence *publisher*
Jinks, Robert Larry *retired newspaper publisher*
Johnson, Ferd *retired cartoonist, color artist*
Johnson, Frank Edward *newspaper editor*
Johnson, Malcolm Clinton, Jr. *publishing consultant*
Jordan, Fred *publishing company executive*
Jovanovich, Peter William *publishing executive*
Kahn, Jenette Sarah *publishing company executive*
Kellner, Jamie *broadcasting executive*
Kellock, Alan C(onverse) *book publishing executive*
Kelly, Kevin *drama critic*
Kennedy, Harvey Edward *science information publishing executive*
Kenny, Patrick Edward *publishing executive*
Key, Ted *cartoonist*
Keyes, Saundra Elise *newspaper editor*
Kibler, Craig Morton *editor, columnist, poet*
Kilpatrick, James Jackson, Jr. *columnist, author*
Klapper, Carol Lorraine *magazine publisher*
Klein, Edward Joel *editor, author, lecturer*
Kleinberg, Howard J. *newspaper columnist*
Koppett, Leonard *columnist, journalist, author*
Kraslow, David *retired newspaper publishing executive, reporter, author, consultant*
Krauthammer, Charles *columnist, editor*
Kuehn, James Marshall *newspaper editor*
Kuennen, Thomas Gerard *journalist*
Kyle, John Hamilton *publishing executive*
Laidlaw, Robert Richard *publishing company executive*
Laitin, Joseph *journalist, former government spokesman and public relations consultant*
Lambro, Donald Joseph *columnist*
Lamont, Barbara *television executive*
Landauer, Jeramy Lanigan *publishing company executive*
Landis, James David *publishing company executive, retired, author*
Larson, George Charles *magazine editor, writer*
Leason, Jody Jacobs *newspaper columnist*
†Levin, Robert Barry *motion picture company executive*
†Liberman, Gail Jeanne *editor*
Lincicome, Bernard Wesley *journalist*
Lippman, Barry *publishing executive*
Lister, Keith Fenimore *publishing executive*
Lloyd, Kate Rand *magazine editor*
Lloyd, Michael Jeffrey *recording producer*
Locke, Virginia Otis *textbook editor, behavioral sciences writer*
Lonneke, Michael Dean *radio and television marketing executive*
Lord, Roy Alvin *retired publisher*
Loughlin, Mary Anne Elizabeth *television news anchor*
Louttit, James Russell *publishing company executive*
Lukas, J. Anthony *journalist*
Lundy, Roland *publishing executive*
Lyman, Richard R. *journalist*
Lynch, Patricia Gates *broadcasting organization executive consultant, former ambassador*
MacFarlane, Andrew Walker *media specialist, educator*
MacMinn, Aleene Merle B(arnes) *newspaper editor, columnist, educator*
Mac Nelly, Jeffrey Kenneth *cartoonist*
Mallo-Garrido, Josephine Ann *advertising agency owner*
Malloy, Michael Terrence *retired journalist and newspaper editor*
Malott, Adele Renee *editor*
Mankiewicz, Frank F. *journalist*
Manley, Joan A(dele) Daniels *retired publisher*
Mann, Jim (James William Manousos) *editor, publisher*
Manning, Richard Dale *writer*
Marcus, Greil Gerstley *critic*
Marino, Joseph Anthony *retired publishing executive*
Massie, Edward Lindsey, Jr. *retired publishing company executive*
McClendon, Sarah Newcomb *news service executive, writer*
Mc Cormick, William Martin *broadcast executive*
McDarrah, Gloria Schoffel *editor, author*
McGuirk, Terrence *former broadcasting company executive*
McHenry, Robert (Dale) *editor*
McNulty, Henry Bryant *journalist*
Meade, Everard Kidder, Jr. *retired broadcasting and publishing executive*
Medavoy, Mike *motion picture company executive*
Medina, Kathryn Bach *book editor*
Melody, Michael Edward *publishing company executive*
Menchel, Donald *television executive*
Miles, Frank Charles *retired newspaper executive*
Miller, Robert Branson, Jr. *retired newspaper publisher*
Millett, Ralph Linwood, Jr. *retired newspaper editor*
Mills, Russell Andrew *newspaper publisher*
†Millsaps, William Hobart, Jr. *newspaper editor*
Miner, A. Bradford *journalist*
Molden, Herbert George *publisher*
Molnar, Anthony William *publishing and training company executive*
Monacelli, Gianfranco *publishing executive*
Morton, Bruce A. *news correspondent*
Mosley, Zack Terrell *cartoonist*
Mudd, Roger Harrison *news broadcaster, educator*
Mulholland, Robert Edge *broadcasting company executive*
Musburger, Brent Woody *sportscaster*
Neff, Donald Lloyd *news correspondent, writer*
Nelson, Martha Jane *magazine editor*
Nelson, Robert Charles *newspaper executive*
Nelson, William Bruce *newspaper company executive*
Novick, Julius Lerner *theater critic, educator*
†O'Boyle, Thomas Francis *editor, newspaper, writer*
Olsen, Merlin Jay *sports analyst, former professional football player, actor*
Orr, Carol Wallace *book publishing executive*
Ortner, Everett Howard *magazine editor, writer*
Osrin, Raymond Harold *retired political cartoonist*
Otis, Denise Marie *editor, writer*
Pack, Richard Morris *broadcasting executive*
Paglio, Lydia Elizabeth *editor*
†Paige, Woodrow Wilson *columnist*
Peacock, Mary Willa *magazine editor*
†Peeples, Rufus Roderick, Jr. (Roddy Peeples) *farm and ranch news radio broadcaster*
Pepper, Jeffrey Mackenzie *publishing executive*
Perlis, Michael Steven *magazine publisher*
Perrin, Gail *editor*
Petersen, Susan Jane *publishing company executive*
Petykiewicz, Sandra Dickey *editor*
Phillips, Glynda Ann *editor*
Picus, Mark Anthony *broadcasting executive*
Pierce, James Robert *magazine executive*
Plangere, Jules Leon, Jr. *media company executive*
Plank, (Ethel) Faye *editor, photographer, writer*
Pletcher, Eldon *editorial cartoonist*
Pockell, Leslie M. *publishing company executive*
Polk, James Ray *journalist*
Pollock, Marc *educational media administrator, consultant*
Porges, Walter Rudolf *television news executive*
Powledge, Fred Arlius *freelance writer*
Prestera, Lauretta Anne *newspaper executive*
Priaulx, A(llan) *publishing executive*

Pudney, Gary Laurence *television executive*
Putnam, Linda Lee *communication educator, researcher*
Quindlen, Anna *journalist, author*
Quinn, Charles Nicholas *journalist*
Randinelli, Tracey Anne *magazine editor*
Rayner, William Alexander *retired newspaper editor*
Regnery, Henry *publisher*
Reich, Herb *editor*
Reidenbaugh, Lowell Henry *retired sports editor*
Reston, James Barrett *retired newspaper publishing executive, author,*
Rice, Roger Douglas *television executive, artist*
Richman, Alan *magazine editor*
Ridder, Paul Anthony *newspaper executive*
Ritter-Clough, Elise Dawn *publishing company executive, consultant*
Roche, Lisa Riley *reporter*
†Rosenblatt, Eddie *record company executive*
Rosenthal, Arthur Jesse *publisher*
†Rounds, John Scoville, Jr. *publishing executive*
Rubin, Rick *record producer*
Ryan, Tom Kreusch *cartoonist*
Sadler, Eric *recording industry executive*
Salhany, Lucille S. *broadcast executive*
Samuelson, Robert Jacob *journalist*
Sapsowitz, Sidney H. *entertainment and media company executive*
Sargent, John Turner *publisher*
Sarris, Andrew George *film critic*
Sauter, Van Gordon *communications executive*
Schacht, Linda Joan *broadcast journalist*
Schorr, Daniel Louis *broadcast journalist, author, lecturer*
Schrader, Martin Harry *retired publisher*
Schulz, Ralph Richard *publishing consultant*
Schwartz, Lloyd Marvin *newspaper and magazine correspondent, broadcaster*
Scruggs, Charles G. *editor*
Seymour, Dale Gilbert *publisher, author, speaker, consultant*
Sheehan, James Patrick *media company executive*
Shelton, Stephani *broadcast journalist, consultant*
Simpson, O. J. (Orenthal James Simpson) *former professional football player, actor, sports commentator*
Sinclair, Carole *publisher, editor, author*
Smith, Hedrick Laurence *journalist, television comentator, author, lecturer*
Smith, Ileene Andrea *book editor*
Smith, Martin Bernhard *journalist*
Stanley, Scott, Jr. *editor*
Stanton, John Jeffrey *editor, broadcast journalist, government programs director, analyst*
Starr, David *newspaper editor, publisher*
Stennett, William Clinton (Clint Stennett) *radio and television station executive, state legislator*
Stewart, Thomas Simrall *radio executive*
Stiff, Robert Martin *newspaper editor*
Stines, Fred, Jr. *publisher*
Stolley, Richard Brockway *journalist*
Strothman, James Edward *editor*
Swanson, Peter Carl *editor*
Switzer, Maurice Harold *publisher*
Taylor, Kristin Clark *media specialist*
Terry, Clifford Lewis *journalist*
Thompson, Anne Marie *newspaper publisher*
Thompson, Robert Elliott *columnist, writer*
Threlkeld, Richard Davis *broadcast journalist*
Tiedge-Lafranier, Jeanne Marie *editor*
Tobias, Andrew Previn *columnist, lecturer*
Trudeau, Garretson Beekman (Garry Trudeau) *cartoonist*
Trueman, William Peter Main *broadcaster, newspaper columnist*
Ubell, Earl *television science editor*
Urdang, Laurence *lexicographer, publisher*
Vandenberg, Peter Ray *magazine publisher*
Verdi, Robert William *sports columnist*
Voltz, Jeanne Appleton *author*
Wagman, Robert John *journalist, author*
Wagner, Julia A(nne) *retired editor*
Warnken, Douglas Richard *publishing consultant*
Wartella, Ellen Ann *communications educator, consultant*
Waters, Betty Lou *newspaper reporter, writer*
Weaver, Howard Cecil *newspaper editor*
Weckesser, Ernest Prosper, Jr. *publisher, educator*
Weissman, Jack (George Anderson) *editor*
Welsome, Eileen *journalist*
Werman, Thomas Ehrlich *record producer*
Wicker, Thomas Grey *retired journalist*
Wiessler, David Albert *correspondent*
Wille, Wayne Martin *retired editor*
†Williams, Carol Joan *foreign correspondent*
Wilner, Judith *journalist*
Wilson, Judy Vantrease *publishing executive*
Winter, Alan *retired publishing company executive*
Wolfman, Ira Joel *editor, writer*
Wolner, Rena Meryl *publisher*
Wood, Marian Starr *publishing company executive*
Wood, Presnall Hansel *editor, minister*
Wussler, Robert Joseph *broadcasting executive, media consultant*
Yack, Patrick Ashley *editor*
Ziegler, Jack (Denmore) *cartoonist*

EDUCATION. For postsecondary education, *See also* specific fields.

UNITED STATES

ALABAMA

Anniston
Cain, William Vernon *academic administrator*

Athens
Jones, Joe Micheal *gifted education educator*
Ruth, Betty Muse *college administrator*

Auburn
Alderman, Charles Wayne *university dean*
Galbraith, Ruth Legg *retired university dean, home economist*
Muse, William Van *university president*
Owens, John Murry *dean*
Philpott, Harry Melvin *former university president*
Rouse, Roy Dennis *retired university dean*
Voitle, Robert Allen *college dean, physiologist*

Birmingham
Barker, Samuel Booth *former university dean, physiology and biology educator*
Bennett, Joe Claude *university president*
Berte, Neal Richard *college president*
Carter, John Thomas *retired educational administrator, writer*
Clarke, Juanita M. Waiters *education educator*
Corts, Thomas Edward *university president*
Fincher, John Albert *college official, consultant*
Glaze, Robert Pinckney *retired university administrator*
Goldman, Jay *university dean, industrial engineer, educator*
Gross, Michael S. *secondary school principal*
Hames, Carl Martin *educational administrator, art dealer, consultant*
Hendley, Dan Lunsford *retired university official*
Hendrick, Brice *academic administrator*
Hull, William Edward *provost, theology educator*
Lee, James Michael *religious education educator, publisher*
Left, Joan Marilyn *principal*
Mc Callum, Charles Alexander *university official*
Pewitt, James Dudley *academic administrator*
Salant, Nathan Nathaniel *athletic conference executive*
Sibley, William Arthur *academic administrator, physics educator, consultant*

Brewton
Jones, Sherman J. *academic administrator, management educator*

Decatur
Kuby, Patricia Ann Williams *early childhood educator*

Dothan
†Cross, Steven Jasper *dean, educator*
Garner, Alto Luther *retired education educator*
Harrison, Thomas E. *academic official*

Florence
Howard, G. Daniel *dean*
Potts, Robert Leslie *academic administrator*

Gadsden
Hill, Anita Griffith *principal*
Taylor, Fred M. *school system administrator*

Guntersville
Patterson, Harold Dean *superintendent of schools*

Hueytown
Gilbert, Melba Caldwell *special education and early childhood educator*

Huntsville
Billings, Nancy Carter *secondary education educator*
Elliott, Sally Ann *special education educator*
Franz, Frank Andrew *academic administrator*
Leslie, Lottie Lyle *retired secondary education educator*
Lundquist, Charles Arthur *university official*
Reaves, Benjamin F. *academic administrator*

Jacksonville
Boswell, Rupert Dean, Jr. *retired academic administrator, math educator*
Dunaway, William Preston *retired administration educator*
McGee, Harold Johnston *university president*

Jasper
Rowland, David Jack *college chancellor*

Livingston
Green, Asa Norman *university president*

Madison
Brannan, Eulie Ross *education consultant*
Stamps, Gladys A. *middle school educator*

Maxwell AFB
Kline, John Alvin *academic administrator*

Millry
Cowles, Milly *education educator*

Mobile
Baker, Amanda Sirmon *university dean, nursing educator*
Byrd, Gwendolyn Pauline *school system superintendent*
Copeland, Lewis *principal*
†Magnoli, Michael A. *academic official*
Moring, Rebecca Owen *university official*
Rewak, William John *university president, clergyman*
Vacik, James Paul *university administrator*
Volkman, Beatrice Kramer *special education educator*

Montgomery
Baker, Clifford Cornell *state educational administrator*
Bobo, Thomas *school system administrator*
Cater, Douglass *former college president, former presidential assistant, writer, editor*
†Harris, William Hamilton *academic administrator*
Johnson, Andrew Emerson, III *educational administrator*
Kurth, Ronald James *university president, retired naval officer*
Saigo, Roy H. *chancellor*
Williams, James Orrin *university administrator, educator*

Muscle Shoals
Smith, Harry Delano *educational administrator*

Normal
Henson, David B. *academic administrator*

Orange Beach
Bennett, James Jefferson *higher education consultant*

Russellville
Clemmons, Robert W. *school system administrator*

Talladega
Johnson, Joseph Benjamin *university president*

Troy
Adams, Ralph Wyatt, Sr. *university chancellor emeritus*
Hawkins, Jack, Jr. *academic administrator*
Long, John Maloy *university dean*

Tuscaloosa
Austin, Philip Edward *university chancellor*
Mitchell, Herbert Hall *former university dean, educational consultant*
Sayers, Roger *academic administrator*
Taaffe, James Griffith *university administrator, educator*
Turner, Philip Michael *university official and dean, author*

Tuskegee
Payton, Benjamin Franklin *college president*

University Of South Alabama
Whiddon, Frederick Palmer *university president*

ALASKA

Anchorage
Behrend, Donald Fraser *university administrator*
Byrd, Milton Bruce *college president, former business executive*
Davis, Bettye Jean *academic administrator, state official*
Holthouse, Rita J. *secondary school principal*
Mitchell, Michael Kiehl *elementary and secondary education educator, minister*

Barrow
Trainor, Jerry Allen *vocational education professional*

Fairbanks
Alexander, Vera *dean, marine science educator*
Doran, Timothy Patrick *educational administrator*
Drew, James Vandervort *university administrator*
Komisar, Jerome Bertram *university administrator*
Ray, Charles Kendall *retired university dean*
Reichardt, Paul Bernard *dean, chemistry educator*
Wadlow, Joan Krueger *university chancellor*
Wood, William Ransom *retired university president, city official, corporate executive*

Haines
Haas, June F. *special education educator, consultant*

Juneau
Lind, Marshall L. *academic administrator*

Tuntutuliak
Daniel, Barbara Ann *secondary education educator*

Valdez
Rogers, Harry *school system administrator*

ARIZONA

Flagstaff
Hooper, Henry Olcott *academic administrator, physicist*
Lovett, Clara Maria *university administrator, historian*

Glendale
Altersitz, Janet Kinahan *principal*
George, Gerald Eugene *high school distict administrator*
Voris, William *educational administrator*

Green Valley
Barich, Dewey Frederick *emeritus educational administrator*
Smith, Raymond Lloyd *former university president, consultant*

Marana
Sederholm, Sarah Kathleen (Kathy Sederholm) *primary education educator*

Mesa
Garwood, John Delvert *former college administrator*
Johnson, Mary Elizabeth *elementary education educator*

Page
Hart, Marian Griffith *retired educator*

Peoria
Jones, Lillie Agnes *retired educator*

Phoenix
Bylsma, Carol Ann *educational consultant, science consultant*
†Covey, Donald David *school system administrator*
Dewalt, Judith K. *elementary school principal*
Donnelly, Charles Robert *retired college president*
Ebert, Richard J. *principal*
Fitzgerald, Joan *principal*
Forsyth, Ben Ralph *academic administrator, medical educator*
Gibbs, William Harold *university administrator*
†Herbert, Victor *school system administrator*
Jones, Lucia Jean *physical education educator*
Puchi, Linda Carol *elementary school principal*
Sperling, John Glen *education company executive*
Thor, Linda Maria *college president*
Williams, Bill *academic administrator*

Prescott
Russo, Joseph Frank *former college president*

San Manuel
Hawk, Dawn Davah *secondary education educator*

Scottsdale
Hill, Louis Allen, Jr. *former university dean, consultant*

Sedona
Hoffmann, Joan Carol *retired academic dean*

Sells
Fire Thunder, Sondra Nadine *elementary educator*

Sierra Vista
Lokensgard, Jon A. *school system administrator*
Revak, JoAnn *special education educator*

Sun City
Corcoran, Eileen Lynch *special education educator emerita*

Sun City West
Cohen, Abraham J. (Al Cohen) *educational administrator*

Sun Lakes
Johnson, Marian Ilene *education educator*
Thompson, Loring Moore *retired college administrator, writer*

Tempe
Abraham, Willard B. *special education educator*
Coor, Lattie Finch *university president*
Kelly, Rita Mae *academic administrator, researcher*
Marsh, Roberta Reynolds *educator, consultant*
Overman, Glenn Delbert *college dean emeritus*
Sackton, Frank Joseph *university official, lecturer, retired army officer*
Scott, Judith Myers *elementary education educator*
Thompson, Anna Blanche *educator*
Wills, J. Robert *academic administrator, drama educator, writer*

Tolleson
Thompson, Bonnie Ransa *secondary educator, chemistry educator*

Tucson
Abrams, Eric R. *principal*
Brousseau, Georgia Cole *school principal*
Cate, Rodney Michael *academic administrator*
Chidester, Otis Holden *retired secondary education educator*
Clement, Nicholas I. *principal*
Dailey, Lynne *secondary education educator*
Harcleroad, Fred Farley *education educator*
Heins, Marilyn *college dean, pediatrics educator, author*
Hershberger, Robert Glen *dean, architect*
Humphrey, John Julius *university program director, historian, writer*
Johnson, John Gray *retired university chancellor*
Kaltenbach, C(arl) Colin *dean, educator*
Leavitt, Jerome Edward *childhood educator*
Pacheco, Manuel Trinidad *university president*
Reid, Charles Phillip Patrick *academic administrator, researcher, professor*
Smerdon, Ernest Thomas *academic administrator*
Stoffle, Carla Joy *dean university library*
Tompkins, Jeannie Kay *special education educator*
Van Kleek, Peter Eric *college dean*
Weaver, Albert Bruce *university administrator*
Wilson, John Lewis *university official*

Yuma
Young, Marilyn Rae *school system adminstrative secretary, mayor*

ARKANSAS

Arkadelphia
Dunn, Charles DeWitt *academic administrator*
Elrod, Ben Moody *academic administrator*
Grant, Daniel Ross *retired university president*
Thomas, Herman L. *school system administrator*

Batesville
Griffith, John Vincent *academic official*

Beebe
Owen, William Harold, Jr. *academic administrator*

Bella Vista
Tucker, Willis Carleton *retired academic administrator, retired journalism educator*

Camden
Brown, George J. *academic administrator*

Clarksville
Stephenson, C. Gene *academic administrator*

Conway
Bowman, Jim *university dean*
Holmes, Barbara Deveaux *college president*
Thompson, Winfred Lee *university president, lawyer*

Fayetteville
Ferritor, Daniel E. *university official*
Knowles, Malcolm Shepherd *education educator*
Madison, Bernard L. *academic dean, mathematics educator*
Oxford, Charles William *university dean, chemical engineer*
Schoppmeyer, Martin William *education educator*
Vorsanger, Fred S. *university administrator*
Williams, Doyle Z. *university dean, educator*

Fort Smith
Gooden, Benny L. *school system administrator*
Robinson, Opal Anne *secondary education educator*

Glenwood
Klopfenstein, Philip Arthur *high school educator*

Hot Springs National Park
Farris, Jefferson Davis *university administrator*
Robinson, Donald Walter *university dean*

Jonesboro
Smith, Eugene Wilson *retired university president and educator*

Little Rock
Anderson, Joel E., Jr. *university administrator*
Fribourgh, James Henry *university administrator*
Gray, John Wylie *university dean, consultant*
Hathaway, Charles E. *academic administrator*
Smith, Charles Wilson, Jr. *university dean*
Truex, Dorothy Adine *retired university administrator*
Williams, Karmen Petersen *secondary school educator*

Magnolia
Brinson, Harold Thomas *university president emeritus*
Gamble, Steven G. *academic administrator*

North Little Rock
Vogler, Diane Clark *elementary school principal*

Pine Bluff
Davis, Lawrence A. *academic administrator*

Rogers
Spainhower, James Ivan *retired college president*

Russellville
†Morris, Lois Lawson *education educator*

Searcy
Burks, David Basil *academic administrator, educator*

Springdale
Hill, Peggy Sue *principal*
Posey, Sandra Dalton *special education educator*
Rogers, Jerry *principal*
Rollins, Jimmy Don *school system administrator*

State University
Fowler, Gilbert L. *dean, educator*
Mangieri, John Nicholas *university administrator*

Walnut Ridge
Huckabay, Gary C. *academic administrator*

CALIFORNIA

Alameda
Verrill, Kathleen Wills *special education educator*

Albany
Chook, Edward Kongyen *academic administrator, disaster medicine educator*

Alhambra
Anton, William R. *retired school system administrator, consutant*

Anaheim
Balch, Glenn McClain, Jr. *academic administrator, minister, author*
†Grennan, Cynthia *school superintendent*
Grose, Elinor Ruth *retired elementary education educator*
Jackson, David Robert *school system administrator*
McGarry, Eugene L. *university official*

Angwin
Maxwell, D. Malcolm *college president*
†Maxwell, Malcolm *college president, minister*

Aptos
Bohn, Ralph Carl *educational consultant, retired educator*
Hirsch, Bette G(ross) *college administrator, foreign language educator*

Arcata
Bowker, Lee Harrington *academic administrator*
Harvey, Carol Sammons *educator*
Mc Crone, Alistair William *university president*

Artesia
Ferris, Pauline *principal*
Moffett, Kenneth Lee *superintendent schools*
Taguchi, Aileen Takayo *special education educator*

Azusa
Felix, Richard E. *academic administrator*
Gray, Paul Wesley *university dean*

Bakersfield
Arciniega, Tomas Abel *university president*
Hefner, John *principal*

Bayside
Bank, Ron *principal*

Berkeley
Bender, Richard *university dean, architect, educator*
Bowker, Albert Hosmer *retired university chancellor*
Clifford, Geraldine Joncich (Mrs. William F. Clifford) *education educator*
Cross, Kathryn Patricia *education educator*
Elberg, Sanford Samuel *university administrator*
Freedman, Sarah Warshauer *education educator*
Glenny, Lyman Albert *retired education educator*
Hardyck, Curtis Dale *psychology and education professor*
Kerr, Clark *university president emeritus*
Linn, Marcia Cyrog *educator*
Maslach, George James *former university official*
Merrill, Richard James *educational director*
Miles, Raymond Edward *former university dean, organizational behavior and industrial relations educator*
Montgomery, Roger *dean*
Rice, Robert Arnot *school administrator*
Rohwer, William D., Jr. *university dean*
Semoff, Deirdre Paula *special education administrator, academic director*
Tien, Chang-Lin *chancellor*

Blythe
Beumel, Wilford J. *college president*

Bonita
Jacobsen, Adolf M.B. *university administrator, former naval officer*

Brea
Shell, Billy Joe *retired university president*

Burbank
Godwin, Annabelle Palkes *retired early childhood education educator*
Sago, Paul Edward *college administrator*

Calabasas
Dworkoski, Robert John *headmaster*

California City
Friedl, Rick *former academic administrator, lawyer*

Cambria
Wallen, Vera S. *school superintendent*

Campo
Charles, Blanche *retired elementary education educator*
Jermini, Ellen *academic spiritual administrator*

Carlsbad
Gorsline, Samuel Gilbert, Jr. *school administrator*

Carmel
Faul, George Johnson *former college president*
Longman, Anne Strickland *educational consultant*

Carmichael
McHugh, James Joseph *retired associate dean*

Carson
Brownell, John Arnold *retired university president*
Detweiler, Robert Chester *university president, historian*

Castro Valley
Dance, Maurice Eugene *college administrator*

Cerritos
Robinson, Terence Vachel *secondary education educator*

Chico
Esteban, Manuel Antonio *university administrator, educator*

Chino
Outen, Dawn *secondary education educator*

Chula Vista
Clement, Betty Waidlich *literacy educator, consultant*

Claremont
Albrecht, Paul Abraham *dean*
Alexander, John David, Jr. *college administrator*
Bekavac, Nancy Yavor *academic administrator, lawyer*
Douglass, Enid Hart *educational program director*
Fucaloro, Anthony Frank *academic dean*
Hess, Dorothy Haldeman *college official*
Irish, Jerry Arthur *academic administrator, religion educator*
Liggett, Thomas Jackson *retired seminary president*
Maguire, John David *university administrator, educator, writer*
Massey, Marilyn Chapin *academic administrator*
Pedersen, Richard Foote *academic administrator*
Platt, Joseph Beaven *former college president*
Post, Gaines, Jr. *college educator, dean, administrator*
Riggs, Henry Earle *college president, engineering management educator*
Stanley, Peter William *college president*
Stark, Jack Lee *college president*
Tanenbaum, Basil Samuel *engineering educator*
Wettack, F. Sheldon *academic administrator*

Clovis
Bronson, George A., Jr. *school system administrator*
Driscoll, Glen Robert *former university president*

Concord
Thall, Richard Vincent *education program director*

Coronado
Trent-Ota, Jane Suzanne *elementary school educator*

Cupertino
Machamer, Sylvia Geraldine *special education educator*

Daly City
Martin, Bernard Lee *former college dean*

Davis
Greenwood, M. R. C. *college dean, biologist, nutrition educator*
Pritchard, William Roy *former university system administrator*
Smiley, Robert Herschel *university dean*
Tomlinson-Keasey, Carol Ann *university administrator*
Vanderhoef, Larry Neil *university administrator*

Downey
Brooks, Lillian Hazel Ashton *adult education educator*
†Ingwerson, Donald W. *educational administrator*

Escondido
Moore, Marc Anthony *university administrator, writer, retired military officer*

Fair Oaks
Branch, Robert Lee *retired educational administrator*

Fontana
Lardieri, Anthony J. *school system administrator*

Fortuna
Fisher, Bruce David *elementary educator*

Fullerton, Gail Jackson *university president emeritus*

Fountain Valley
Olim, August Souza *counselor*

Fremont
Brown, David Richard *school system administrator, minister*
de Roque, Barbara Penberthy *special education educator, consultant*
Ours, Marian Leah *elementary education educator*

Fresno
Andresen, Claudia *principal*
Dandoy, Maxima Antonio *education educator emeritus*
Haak, Harold Howard *university president*
Klassen, Peter James *academic administrator, history educator*
Sexton, Richard *school system administrator*
Welty, John Donald *university president*

Fullerton
Atwell, Margaret Ann *education educator*
Barchi, Barbara Ann *education and training consultant*
Borst, Philip West *academic administrator*
Donoghue, Mildred Ransdorf *education educator*
Gordon, Milton Andrew *academic administrator*
Hopping, Richard Lee *college president*
Hugstad, Paul Steven *college dean*
McGinnis, Joán Adell *secondary school educator*
Smith, Ephraim Philip *university dean, educator*

Glendale
Whalen, Lucille *academic administrator*

Glendora
Lindly, Douglas Dean *elementary school educator, administrator*

Hacienda Heights
West, Linda Lea *administrator*

Hayward
McCune, Ellis E. *retired university system chief administrator, higher education consultant*
Rees, Norma S. *university president, educator*
Resnikoff, George Joseph *university dean, mathematics and statistics educator emeritus*

Hemet
Shea, Robert Stanton *retired academic administrator*

Indian Wells
Trotter, F(rederick) Thomas *retired university president*

Inglewood
Guzy, Marguerita Linnes *educator*
Jefferson, Bernard S. *academic administrator*
Lynch, Linda Lou *reading and language arts specialist/educator*

Irvine
Fleischer, Everly Borah *academic administrator*
Garrison, Clayton *university dean*
Halm, Dennis Ray *academic administrator*
Wilkening, Laurel Lynn *university official, planetary scientist*

La Canada Flintridge
Lamson, Robert Woodrow *retired school system administrator*

La Jolla
Atkinson, Richard Chatham *university chancellor, cognitive psychologist, educator*
Chodorow, Stanley Alan *academic administrator*
Dreilinger, Charles Lewis (Chips Dreilinger) *dean*
Frieman, Edward Allan *university administrator, educator*
Masys, Daniel Richard *medical school director*
Spooner, Charles Edward *university administrator, health educator*
Stewart, John Lincoln *university administrator*
Talke, Frank Eberhard *education educator*

La Mesa
Black, Eileen Mary *elementary school educator*
Tarson, Herbert Harvey *university administrator emeritus*

La Mirada
Lingenfelter, Sherwood Galen *university provost, anthropology educator*

La Verne
Morgan, Stephen Charles *academic administrator*

Lake Elsinore
Wilson, Sonja Mary *secondary education educator, consultant, poet*

Lakewood
Bogdan, James Thomas *secondary education educator, electronics researcher and developer*

Livermore
Hazen, Judi *elementary school educator*

Loma Linda
Klooster, Judson *academic administrator, dentistry educator*

Long Beach
Anatol, Karl W. E. *provost*
Beljan, John Richard *university administrator, medical educator*
Fornia, Dorothy Louise *educator*
Giugni, Everett Thomas *school administrator*
Hobgood, E(arl) Wade *college dean*
Lathrop, Irvin Tunis *retired academic dean, educator*
Lauda, Donald Paul *university dean*
McDonough, Patrick Dennis *university executive*
Munitz, Barry *chief university administrator, English literature educator, business consultant*
Roth, Robert August *university administrator*
Thompson, William Ancker *intramural-recreational sports director, educator*

Wheeler, Diana Jean Miller *secondary education educator*

Los Altos
Drachler, Norman *retired education educator*

Los Angeles
Anastos, Rosemary Park *retired higher education educator*
Armstrong, Lloyd, Jr. *university official, physics educator*
Astin, Alexander William *education educator*
Borsting, Jack Raymond *business administration educator*
Bratt, Bengt Erik *academic administrator, consulting engineer*
Cato, Gloria Maxine *secondary education educator, school program administrator*
Cobb, Jewel Plummer *former college president, educator*
Cohen, S(tephen) Marshall *philosophy educator*
Coughlin, Sister Magdalen *college chancellor*
Dewey, Donald Odell *university dean*
Dixon, Andrew Derart *retired academic administrator*
Ellsworth, Frank L. *university administrator*
†Golub, Sidney Harris *dean, educator*
Gothold, Stuart E. *school system administrator, educator*
Hayes, Robert Mayo *university dean, library and information science educator*
Hoffman, Neil James *art school executive*
Hubbard, John Randolph *university president emeritus, history educator, diplomat*
Jackson, Kingsbury Temple *educational contract consultant*
Jensen, David Gram *university administrator*
Kennelly, Sister Karen Margaret *college administrator*
Lazzaro, Anthony Derek *university administrator*
Lieber, David Leo *university president*
Lynch, Beverly Pfeifer *education and information studies educator*
Mandel, Joseph David *university official, lawyer*
Merrifield, Donald Paul *university chancellor*
†Mitchell, Theodore R. *dean, education educator*
Patterson, Dawn Marie *dean, consultant, author, educator*
Pierskalla, William Peter *academic dean, management and engineering educator*
Prager, Susan Westerberg *dean, law educator*
Rosser, James Milton *university president*
Sample, Steven Browning *university president*
Scott, Allen John *educator*
†Shearer, Derek N. *international studies educator, diplomat, administrator*
Shutler, Mary Elizabeth *academic administrator*
Silverman, Leonard M. *university dean, electrical engineering educator*
Slaughter, John Brooks *university president*
Spitzer, William George *university dean, physicist, educator, researcher*
Steinberg, Warren Linnington *principal*
Stevens, Gerald D. *secondary education educator, consultant*
Taylor, Leigh Herbert *college dean*
Topping, Norman Hawkins *former university chancellor*
Tuckson, Reed V. *university president*
Wagner, William Gerard *university dean, physicist, consultant, information scientist, investment manager*
Wazzan, Ahmed R(assem) Frank *engineering educator, dean*
Wexler, Robert *university administrator*
Young, Charles Edward *university chancellor*
Zamir, Frances Roberta (Frances Roberta Weiss-Swede) *assistant principal*

Los Gatos
Hartinger, Patricia Bernardine Curran *elementary school educator*
Simonson, Ted *principal*

Los Olivos
Buxton, Kenneth Arthur *educator, academic dean*

Malibu
Davenport, David *university president, lawyer*
Young, Matt Norvel, Jr. *university chancellor emeritus*

Manhattan Beach
Brooks, Edward Howard *college administrator*

Mission Viejo
Hough, J. Marie *vocational education educator*
Sabaroff, Rose Epstein *retired education educator*

Modesto
Bairey, Marie *principal*
Smith, Glenda Irene *elementary school educator*

Montebello
Dible, Rose Harpe McFee *special education educator*

Monterey
Leonardich, Agnes M. *school system administrator*
Lockhart, Brooks Javins *retired college dean*

Moraga
Anderson, Brother Mel *academic administrator*

Moreno Valley
Jaynes, Cherie Lou *early childhood education educator*

Morgan Hill
Hevia, Martha *principal, educational and counseling consultant*

Mountain View
Bowler, James S. *educational administrator*

Napa
Ervin, Margaret Howie *elementary educator, special education educator*

North Hollywood
Thurston, Alice Janet *former college president*

Northridge
Bianchi, Donald Ernest *academic administrator, biology educator*
Cleary, James W. *retired university administrator*
Ellner, Carolyn Lipton *university dean, consultant*
Tanis, Norman Earl *retired university dean, library expert*
Wilson, Blenda Jacqueline *university chancellor*

Norwalk
McCamly, Jerry Allen *high school educator*

Novato
Patterson, W. Morgan *college president*

Oakland
Allen, Carole Geneva (Ward) *college administrator*
Diaz, Sharon *education administrator*
Dibble, David Van Vlack *educator of visually impaired, lawyer*
Farley, Thelma *principal*
Goldstine, Stephen Joseph *college administrator*
Gomes, Wayne Reginald *academic administrator*
Heydman, Abby Maria *academic dean*
Isaac Nash, Eva Mae *educator*
†Mesa, Richard *school superintendent*
Miller, Barry *research administrator, psychologist*
Mitrano, Joseph Charles *school principal*
Peltason, Jack Walter *university president*
Pike, Douglas Eugene *Indochina studies director*
Shoai, Elinor Josephine Kelly *elementary school educator*

Ojai
Wyman, Willard G. *headmaster*

Orange
Doti, James L. *academic administrator*
Gerhard, Nancy Lucile Dege *educator*
Hamilton, Harry Lemuel, Jr. *academic administrator*
Schrodi, Tom *instructional services director*

Orinda
Gilbert, Robert W. *secondary school principal*
Glasser, Charles Edward *academic administrator*

Oxnard
Frodsham, Olaf Milton *music educator*

Palm Desert
Sicuro, Natale Anthony *academic administrator*

Palm Springs
Aikens, Donald Thomas *educational administrator, consultant*
Fol, Monique Eliane *educator*

Palo Alto
Attig, John Clare *history educator, consultant*
†Case, Robbie *education educator, author*
Cohen, Elizabeth G. *education and sociology educator, researcher*
Gibbons, James Franklin *university dean, electrical engineering educator*

Palos Verdes Peninsula
Fischer, Robert Blanchard *university administrator, researcher*
Hurrell, Ann Patricia *assistant director, educator*

Paramount
Cook, Karla Joan *elementary education educator*

Pasadena
Everhart, Thomas Eugene *university president, engineering educator*
Freise, Earl Jerome *univeristy administrator, materials engineering educator*
Gabel, Katherine *academic administrator*
Meye, Robert Paul *retired seminary administrator, writer*
Stolper, Edward Manin *geology educator*

Pebble Beach
Sullivan, James Francis *university administrator*

Petaluma
O'Hare, Sandra Fernandez *secondary education educator*

Pinole
Grogan, Stanley Joseph *educational educator, consultant*

Point Arena
Kohl, Herbert Ralph *education educator*

Pomona
Baker, Frederick John *education educator*
Eaves, Ronald Weldon *university administrator*
Fleck, Raymond Anthony, Jr. *university administrator*
Suzuki, Bob H. *university president*

Poway
Brose, Cathy *principal*
Shippey, Lyn *reading center director*

Rancho Palos Verdes
McFadden, Thomas *academic administrator*

Redding
Treadway, Douglas Morse *academic administrator*

Redlands
Appleton, James Robert *university president, educator*

Redondo Beach
Marsee, Stuart (Earl) *educational consultant, retired*

Reseda
Anstad, Neil *director*

Richmond
Colfack, Andrea Heckelman *elementary education educator*

Riverside
Balow, Irving Henry *retired education educator*
Geraty, Lawrence Thomas *academic administrator, archaeologist*
Hodgen, Maurice Denzil *financial development administrator, educator*
Inacker, Charles John *academic dean, business educator*
Lacy, Carolyn Jean *elementary education educator, secondary education educator*
Perkins, Van L. *university administrator, educator, conservationist*
Shipley, Marilyn Elizabeth *school system administrator*
Yacoub, Ignatius I. *university dean*

Rohnert Park
Arminana, Ruben *university president, educator*
Babula, William *university dean*

Rosemead
Hansen, Robert Dennis *educational administrator*

Ross
Fitzgerald, Richard Patrick *school administrator*

Rowland Heights
Perfetti, Robert Nickolas *career education coordinator, educator*

Sacramento
Adelekan, Patricia Ann *school administrator*
Evans, James Handel *university administrator, architect, educator*
Gerth, Donald Rogers *university president*
Kerschner, Lee R(onald) *university president, political science educator*
Riles, Wilson Camanza *educational consultant*
Stegenga, Preston Jay *international education consultant*

San Andreas
Millsaps, Rita Rae *elementary school educator*

San Bernardino
Evans, Anthony Howard *university president*
Heding, Thomas John *school system administrator*

San Diego
Charles, Carol Morgan *education educator*
Day, Thomas Brennock *university president*
Feinberg, Lawrence Bernard *university dean, psychologist*
Golding, Brage *former university president*
†Hartman, Harold W. *academic admininstrator*
Hayes, Alice Bourke *university official, biology educator*
Hays, Garry D. *academic administrator*
Hughes, Author E. *university president, association executive*
Lee, Jerry Carlton *university administrator*
Lomeli, Marta *elementary education educator*
Maurer, Lawrence Michael *acting school administrator, educator*
McBrayer, Sandra L. *educational director, homeless outreach educator*
Morris, Henry Madison, Jr. *education educator*
Netter, Irene M. *secondary education educator*
Owen, Sally Ann *gifted and talented education educator*
Schade, Charlene Joanne *adult and early childhood education educator*
Schwartz, Alfred *university dean*
Trybus, Raymond J. *higher education executive, psychologist*
Wagschal, Kathleen *education educator*
Walker, Donald Ezzell *retired academic administrator*

San Dimas
Cameron, Judith Lynne *secondary education educator, hypnotherapist*

San Francisco
Ammiano, Tom *school system administrator*
Cain, Leo Francis *retired special education educator*
Corrigan, Robert Anthony *university president*
Cortines, Ramon *school superintendent*
Counelis, James Steve *education educator*
Cunningham, Arthur Francis *university dean, marketing educator*
Dullea, Charles W. *university chancellor emeritus, priest*
Fleishhacker, David *school administrator*
Gray, Frances M. *retired college president, lecturer*
Kleinberg, David Lewis *education administrator*
Kozloff, Lloyd M. *university dean, educator, scientist*
Krevans, Julius Richard *university administrator, physician*
Lo Schiavo, John Joseph *university executive*
Manson, Malcolm Hood *educational administrator*
McPhee, Sister Glenn Anne *school system administrator*
Naegele, Carl Joseph *university academic administrator, educator*
Rippel, Clarence W. *academic administrator*
†Rojas, Waldemar *school superintendent*
Schlegel, John Peter *university president*
Thê, Hoang-Dinh *middle school educator*
Wallace, Arthur, Jr. *college dean*

San Jose
Blackwell, Jacqueline Pflughoeft *school district administrator*
Caret, Robert Laurent *university president*
Collett, Jennie *principal*
Cruz, B. Robert *academic administrator*
Okerlund, Arlene Naylor *university official*
Sanders, Adrian Lionel *education consultant*
Sikora, James Robert *educational business administrator*

San Leandro
Nehls, Robert Louis, Jr. *school system administrator*

San Lorenzo
Glenn, Jerome T. *secondary school principal*

San Luis Obispo
Bailey, Philip Sigmon, Jr. *university official, chemistry educator*
Baker, Warren J(oseph) *university president*
Ericson, Jon Meyer *academic administrator, rhetoric theory educator*
Wentz, Janet *principal*

San Marcos
Lilly, Martin Stephen *university dean*

San Marino
Footman, Gordon Elliott *educational administrator*

San Mateo
Poulos, Gary Peter *school system administrator*

San Rafael
Fink, Joseph Richardson *college president*

Santa Ana
Castruita, Rudy *school system administrator*
Hernandez, Edward, Jr. *community college administrator*

Santa Barbara
Allaway, William Harris *retired university official*
Boyan, Norman J. *retired education educator*
Dahl, John Anton *education educator emeritus*
Louis, Barbra Schantz *dean*
Mac Intyre, Donald John *college president*
O'Dowd, Donald Davy *retired university administrator*
Robeck, Mildred Coen *educator*
Sinsheimer, Robert Louis *retired university chancellor and educator*
Sprecher, David A. *university administrator, mathematician*
Wilson, John Abraham Ross *academic administrator*
Yang, Henry T. *university chancellor, educator*

Santa Clara
Abdaljabbar, Abdalhameed A. *educational administrator*
Facione, Peter Arthur *dean, philosophy and education educator*
Locatelli, Paul Leo *university administrator*

Santa Clarita
Lavine, Steven David *college president*

Santa Cruz
Mc Henry, Dean Eugene *academic administrator emeritus*

Santa Maria
Dunn, Judith Louise *secondary school educator*

Santa Rosa
Christiansen, Peggy *principal*
O'Connor, Sister Ann Patricia *school system administrator*
Webb, Charles Richard *retired university president*

Seaside
Wilson, Robin Scott *university president, writer*

Sherman Oaks
Baumhoff, Walter Henry *headmaster*

Simi Valley
Brown, Melbourne Thomas, Sr. *elementary education educator*

Stanford
Baron, James Neal *organizational behavior and human resources educator, researcher*
Bridges, Edwin Maxwell *education educator*
Gross, Richard Edmund *education educator*
Henriksen, Thomas Hollinger *university official*
Jaedicke, Robert K. *university dean, accounting educator*
Kays, William Morrow *university administrator, mechanical engineer*
Kirst, Michael Weile *education educator, researcher*
Massy, William Francis *education educator, academic administrator*
Noddings, Nel *education educator, writer*
Palm, Charles Gilman *university official*
Phillips, Denis Charles *education and philosophy educator*
Reynolds, Clark Winton *principal investigator, program director, educator*
Strober, Myra Hoffenberg *education educator, consultant*
Tyack, David B. *education educator*

Stinson Beach
Metz, Mary Seawell *university dean, retired college president*

Stockton
Atchley, Bill Lee *university president*
Clancy, Sister Madeline *school system administrator*
DeRicco, Lawrence Albert *college president emeritus*
Haisley, Fay Beverley *academic dean*
Jantzen, J(ohn) Marc *retired education educator*
Klinger, Wayne Julius *secondary education educator*
Sorby, Donald Lloyd *university dean*
Thompson, Thomas Sanford *former college president*

Susanville
Blake, Larry Jay *academic administrator*

Thousand Oaks
Luedtke, Luther S. *academic administrator*

Torrance
McNamara, Brenda Norma *secondary education educator*

Tulare
Sickels, William Loyd *secondary educator*

Turlock
Amrhein, John Kilian *dean*

Twentynine Palms
Clemente, Patrocinio Ablola *psychology educator*

Vacaville
Wisneski, Mary Jo Elizabeth *reading specialist, educator*

Van Nuys
Altshiller, Arthur Leonard *physics educator*

Ventura
McElroy, Charlotte Ann *principal*

Vista
Johnson, Alan *principal*
Tiedeman, David Valentine *education educator*

Walnut Creek
Morgan, Elmo Rich *former university official*

Westlake Village
Steadman, Lydia Duff *elementary school educator, symphony violinist*

Westminster
Ryan, James Edwin *industrial arts educator*

Whittier
Ash, James Lee, Jr. *academic administrator*
Drake, E Maylon *academic administrator*
Solis, Hilda Lucia *educational administrator, state legislator*
Tunison, Elizabeth Lamb *education educator*

Woodland Hills
Swaim, Ruth Carolyn *educator*
Zeitlin, Herbert Zakary *retired college president*

Woodside
Blum, Richard Hosmer Adams *education educator, writer*
Schneider, Steven Arnold *educational administrator, consultant*

COLORADO

Aurora
Cowee, John Widmer *retired university chancellor*
Jarvis, Mary G. *principal*
Matson, Merwyn Dean *educational consultant*
Shearer, Carolyn Juanita *secondary education educator*

Bellvue
Bennett, Jim *retired university official*

Boulder
Albino, Judith E. N. *university president*
Anderson, Ronald Delaine *education educator*
Dilley, Barbara Jean *college administrator, choreographer, educator*
Ekstrand, Bruce Rowland *university administrator, psychology educator*
Enarson, Harold L. *emeritus university president*
Gabridge, Michael Gregory *university administrator, science administrator*
Johnson, Edward Alden *dean of college*
†Ko, Hon Yim *civil engineering educator, consultant*
Middleton, Charles Ronald *educator, academic dean*
Park, Roderic Bruce *university chancellor*
Sirotkin, Phillip Leonard *educational administrator*
†Thomas, Gary Edward *educator, researcher*
Williams, James Franklin, II *university dean, librarian*

Broomfield
Rodriguez, Linda Takahashi *secondary education educator*

Colorado Springs
Adams, Bernard Schroder *retired college president*
Burnley, Kenneth S. *school system administrator*
Fujimura, Robert Kiyoshi *executive director*
Mohrman, Kathryn *academic administrator*
Shaffer, Carolyn Lee (Cari Shaffer) *staffing service executive*
Waples, Eric Snowden *headmaster*
Wilcox, Rhoda Davis *elementary education educator*
Worner, Lloyd Edson *retired college president*

Denver
Antonoff, Steven Ross *educational consultant, author*
Beckman, Sister Patricia *school system administrator*
Brainard, Edward Axdal *academic administrator*
Buechner, John C. *academic administrator*
Clark, Drew *secondary education educator, state legislator*
Clarke, David Marshall *academic administrator, priest*
Craine, Thomas Knowlton *academic administrator*
†Dennis, Evie *school system administrator*
DePew, Marie Kathryn *retired secondary educator*
Dougherty, Larry W. *headmaster*
Fulginiti, Vincent *university dean*
Fulkerson, William Measey, Jr. *college president*
†Greenspahn, Barbara *dean, law educator, librarian*
Halgren, Lee A. *academic administrator*
†Hinkle, Betty Ruth *educational administator*
Jacobson, Eugene Donald *educator, administrator, researcher*
Johnston, Calvin George *secondary education educator*
Loeup, Kong *counselor*
Mc Clenney, Byron Nelson *community college administrator*
Messer, Donald Edward *theological school president*
Palmreuter, Kenneth Richard Louis *principal*
Poynter, James Morrison *travel educator, travel company executive*
Ritchie, Daniel Lee *university administrator*
Zaranka, William F. *academic administrator, author*

Durango
Jones, Joel Mackey *college president*

Englewood
DiSalle, Michael Danny *secondary education educator*
Shields, Marlene Sue *elementary school educator*

Fort Collins
Anderson, B(enard) Harold *educational administrator*
Harper, Judson Morse *university administrator, consultant, educator*
Irvine, Kevin Thomas *secondary education educator*

Jaros, Dean university official
McHugh, Helen Frances university dean, home economist
Yates, Albert Carl university administrator, chemistry educator

Fort Morgan
Bond, Richard Randolph college administrator, legislator
Perdue, James Everett university vice chancellor emeritus

Golden
Mueller, William Martin former academic administrator, metallurgical engineering educator

Grand Junction
Bergen, Virginia Louise principal, language arts educator
Kribel, Robert Edward academic administrator, physicist
Moberly, Linden Emery educational adminstrator

Greeley
Duff, William Leroy, Jr. university dean emeritus, business educator
Hause, Jesse Gilbert retired college president
Schulze, Robert Oscar university dean

Keystone
Craig, Robert Wallace educational and policy center administrator

Lakewood
Beckman, L. David university chancellor
Craig, Lexie Ferrell career development specialist, career guidance counselor, educator
Mc Bride, Guy Thornton, Jr. college president emeritus
Milan, Marjorie Lucille early childhood educator
Tucker, James Raymond elementary educator
West, Marjorie Edith elementary education educator

Leadville
McCabe, James R. school system administrator

Littleton
Ballard, Jack Stokes educator
Chavez, Cile school superintendent
Thompson, Thomas Edward educator, administrator, researcher

Pueblo
Byrnes, Lawrence William dean
Shirley, Robert Clark university president, strategic planning consultant, educator
Sisson, Ray L. dean

Rangely
Mullen, Robert Charles school system administrator

Sterling
Milander, Henry Martin community college president

Thornton
Crowley, Judith Diane secondary educator

Trinidad
Rocha, Pedro, Jr. academic administrator

U S A F Academy
†Cubero, Ruben A. dean, military officer

Univ Of Denver
†Rowe, Edward Thomas university administrator, educator

Univ Of No Colo
Lujan, Herman D. university president

Westminster
Reed, John Howard school administrator
Yocum, Charleen Elaine educational administrator, counselor

CONNECTICUT

Bloomfield
Hilsenrath, Baruch M. principal

Bridgeport
Garcia, Edna I. secondary education educator
Helfrich, Bernard D. academic administrator

Cheshire
Wallace, Ralph superintendent

Danbury
Hawkes, Carol Ann university dean
Roach, James Richard university president
Stewart, Albert Clifton college dean, marketing educator

Fairfield
Cernera, Anthony Joseph academic administrator
Kelley, Aloysius Paul university president, priest
Smith, Clifford Vaughn, Jr. academic administrator

Falls Village
Purcell, Dale college administrator, consultant

Farmington
Hartley, Harry J. academic administrator

Glastonbury
Hatch, D. Patricia P. principal
Roy, Kenneth Russell school system administrator, educator

Granby
Pestka, Stanley secondary school principal

Greenwich
Grossman, Allen, III educational administrator
Karraker, David Franklin secondary educator, reading consultant

Groton
English, James Fairfield, Jr. former college president

Hamden
Bennett, Harry Louis college educator
Norberg-Caliendo, Lynda Joy school system administrator

Hartford
Loomis, Worth (Alfred Worthington Loomis) college president, manufacturer
†Sternberg, Betty J. school system administrator
Stoker, Warren Cady university president

Kensington
Colaiacovo, Christine Mary secondary school educator

Madison
Peterkin, Albert Gordon retired education educator

Middlebury
Coleman, Robert Elliott secondary education educator

Middletown
Bennet, Douglas Joseph, Jr. university president
Creighton, Joanne Vanish academic administrator
Kerr, Clarence William retired university administrator

New Britain
Beal, Dallas Knight university president
Dethy, Ray Charles former university dean, management educator, consultant
Frost, James Arthur former university president
Jestin, Heimwarth B. retired university administrator
Judd, Richard Louis academic administrator
Shumaker, John William university president

New Canaan
Congdon, Janet Zakryk counselor

New Haven
Aaslestad, Halvor Gunerius university official
Cappelli, Mary Antoinette principal
Johnson, Eva Jo elementary education educator
Lamar, Howard Roberts educational administrator, historian
Lorimer, Linda Koch college official
Mullen, Frank Albert university official, clergyman
Wegener, Peter Paul educator, author
†Yandle, Stephen Thomas law school dean

New London
Gaudiani, Claire Lynn academic administrator

Newington
Vassar, William Gerald gifted and talented education educator

Niantic
Ashley, Eleanor Tidaback retired elementary educator

North Stonington
Keane, John Patrick retired secondary education educator

Northford
James, Virginia Stowell retired elementary education educator

Norwalk
Perschino, Arthur J. secondary school principal
Wiggins, Charles secondary education educator

Preston
Makara, Carol Pattie education educator, consultant

Ridgefield
Norman, Richard Arthur educator

Southport
Miles, Leland Weber university president

Stamford
Castrignano, Robert Anthony retired dean, retired broadcasting company executive

Storrs
†Gutteridge, Thomas G. academic administrator, consultant and labor arbitrator
Nieforth, Karl Allen university dean, educator

Storrs Mansfield
Gray, Robert Hugh college dean

Suffield
Black, Maureen McWeeny special education educator
Friedman, Dian Debra elementary education educator

Trumbull
Norcel, Jacqueline Joyce Casale educational administrator

Wallingford
Cirasuolo, Joseph J. school system administrator
Hay, Leroy E. school system administrator

Waterbury
Higgins, Dorothy Marie academic dean

West Hartford
Danker, Mervyn Kenneth director of education
Lawson, Jonathan Nevin academic administrator
Tonkin, Humphrey Richard university president

West Haven
DeNardis, Lawrence J. academic administrator

Wethersfield
Edwards, Kenneth S. principal

Willimantic
Carter, David George, Sr. university administrator
Peagler, Owen F. colege administrator

Windsor Locks
Coelho, Sandra Signorelli secondary school educator

Wolcott
Gerace, Robert F. secondary school principal

DELAWARE

Dover
Delauder, William B. academic administrator
†Lentini, James Salvatore school librarian, fraternity executive
Sorenson, Liane Beth McDowell university administrator, state legislator
Wilson, Clealyn Bullock elementary education educator

Lewes
Wilson, James L. superintendent

Milford
Moses, Charles E. superintendent

Millsboro
Derrickson, Shirley Jean Baldwin elementary school educator

Newark
Hammonds, Jay A. educator, administrator
Roselle, David Paul university administrator, mathematician
Schiavelli, Melvyn David university provost, chemistry educator, researcher

Wilmington
Desien, Mary Donna principal
Graves, Thomas Ashley, Jr. educational administrator
Olson, Leroy Calvin retired educational administration educator
Renshaw, John Hubert secondary education educator
Smith, June Ellen secondary and special education educator

DISTRICT OF COLUMBIA

Washington
Adams, Linette M. principal
Alatis, James Efstathios university dean emeritus
Alton, Bruce Taylor educational consultant
Arnez, Nancy Levi educational leadership educator
Bailey, Nancy Joyce secondary education educator
Barrett, Richard David director fundraising program, consultant
Battle, Lucius Durham retired educational institution administrator, former diplomat
Bishop, James Joseph dean
Bolling, Landrum Rymer retired academic administrator, writer, consultant
Burris, James Frederick academic dean, educator
Byrnes, Heidi academic administrator, German language educator
Chambliss, William Joseph educator, sociologist, author
Chandler, John Wesley educational consultant
Cheek, James Edward university president
Childress, Fay Alice university administrator
Collins, Herbert, Jr. retired elementary educator
Collins, Naomi F. higher education administrator
Cornett, Richard Orin research educator, consultant
Curtis, Martha Louise parochial school social studies educator, administrator
Donley, Rosemary university official
Dougherty, Jude Patrick dean
East, Maurice Alden academic dean, political scientist
Easterling, Christine Davis educational administrator
Ellis, Brother Patrick (H. J. Ellis) academic administrator
Fisher, Miles Mark, IV education educator
Fosler, R. Scott academic administrator, federal agency administrator
Gaff, Jerry Gene academic administrator
Graves, Ruth Parker educational executive
†Griffin, Elaine B. teacher
Halperin, Samuel education and training policy analyst
Harrison, Rosalie Thornton (Mrs. Porter Harmon Harrison) retired educator
†Hehir, Thomas F. educational administrator
Herbert, James Charles education executive
Herbster, William Gibson university administrator, consultant
Higgins, William Robert college administrator
Hill, Elaine Brumfield elementary education educator
Holden, John Bernard former college president, educator
Hopkinson, Shirley A. educator, consultant
Horan, Harold Eugene university administrator, former diplomat
Howard, Kenneth Lee university official, consultant
Hudson, Philip academic director
Jenkins, John Smith academic dean, lawyer
Jones, Alice Samuels elementary education educator, reading specialist
Jones-Wilson, Faustine Clarisse education educator emeritus
Jordan, Irving King academic administrator
Keeley, Robert Vossler academic administrator, retired ambassador
Kelly, Eugene Walter, Jr. counseling educator
Kent, Jill Elspeth academic administrator, lawyer, former government official
Kirkien-Rzeszotarski, Alicia Maria academic administrator, researcher, educator
Kramer, Robert dean
Krogh, Peter Frederic college dean, international affairs educator
Kupperman, Robert Harris university official
†Ladner, Joyce A. academic administrator
Leon, Donald Francis university dean, medical educator
Lieberman, Myron educational consulting firm executive
Livingston, Robert Gerald university official, political scientist
MacDonald, John Thomas educational administrator
Mattar, Philip institute director, editor
Maxwell, David E. academic administrator, educator
McGrory, Mary Kathleen university official
Melendez, Sara E. academic administrator
Mulhern, John David former academic dean, educator
Mullin, Mark Hill headmaster
Nelson, Charles J. university administrator, international consultant, diplomat, consultant
O'Donovan, Leo Jeremiah university president, theologian, priest
Ostar, Allan William higher education consultant
Packard, George Randolph journalist, educator
Parrish, Alvin Edward former university dean, medical educator
Preer, Jean Lyon university administrator, educator
Pruitt, Anne Loring university administrator, educator
Ramsey, Henry, Jr. university dean-official, lawyer, retired judge
Relic, Peter academic administrator
Riddleberger, Hugh Compton, III headmaster
Rogers, Sharon J. university administrator
Rope, William Frederick academic administrator
Rousseau, Eva Rice principal
Salamon, Linda Bradley university dean, English literature educator
Scott, Joyce Alaine university official
Short, Thomas Edward, Jr. educator
Smith, Anne Bowman academic administrator, editor
Smuckler, Ralph Herbert university dean, political science educator
Solomon, Henry university dean
Steigman, Andrew L. academic dean
†Stewart, Dorothy K. educator, librarian
Stone, Elizabeth Wenger retired dean
Sullivan, Charles university dean, educator, author
Tipton, Paul S. former college president, association executive
Trachtenberg, Stephen Joel university president
Turaj, Frank university dean, literature and film educator
Uehling, Barbara Staner academic administrator
Whitfield, Princess D. principal
Wilson, Carolyn Ross school administrator
Wolfman, Brunetta Reid education educator
Woods, Harriett Ruth academic administrator
Young, Kenneth Evans educational consultant

FLORIDA

Alachua
Marston, Robert Quarles university president
Thornton, J. Ronald university administrator

Atlantic Beach
Herge, Henry Curtis, Sr. education educator, dean emeritus

Avon Park
Cornelius, Catherine Petrey college president

Babson Park
Cloud, Linda Beal retired secondary school educator

Boca Raton
Arden, Eugene retired university provost
Arnold, Walter Martin vocational education educator
Burns, Gerald Phillip education educator
Catanese, Anthony James academic administrator
Hille, Stanley James university dean
Lampi, Juanita principal
Murray, John Ralph former college president
Ross, Donald Edward university administrator
Tennies, Robert Hunter headmaster
Turbeville, Gus emeritus college president

Bonita Springs
Johnson, Franklyn Arthur academic administrator

Brandon
Blomgren, David Kenneth dean, pastor

Cape Coral
Lane, William C., Jr. principal

Clearwater
Jacobs, Marilyn Arlene Potoker gifted education educator, consultant, author
Youngberg, Robert Stanley principal, consultant

Cocoa
Linscott, Jacqueline C. elementary school educator, consultant

Coconut Grove
Cotton, John Pierce principal

Coral Gables
Moss, Ambler Holmes, Jr. academic administrator, lawyer, former ambassador
Murfin, Ross C university dean, English educator
Yarger, Sam Jacob dean, educator

Coral Springs
Averett-Short, Geneva Evelyn college administrator
Vandiver, Frances principal

Dade City
Rine, Susan principal

Deland
Brakeman, Louis Freeman retired university administrator
Dascher, Paul Edward university dean, accounting educator
Duncan, Pope Alexander college administrator
Gill, Donald George education educator
Langston, Paul T. music educator, university dean, composer
Lee, Howard Douglas university president
Morland, Richard Boyd retired educator

Delray Beach
Terry, Margaret Smoot special education educator

Fort Lauderdale
Adams, Alfred Hugh college president

Feldman, Stephen *university president*
Fischler, Abraham Saul *university president*
Yaxley, Jack Thomas *secondary education educator*
Young, Lois Catherine Williams *university agency consultant*
Young, William Benjamin *special education educator*

Fort Myers
Adams, James Andrew *public school district official*
Cyphert, Frederick Ralph *academic administrator*
Hughes, Judi E. *principal*
Jones, Constance *principal*
Tyrer, John Lloyd *retired headmaster*

Fort Walton Beach
†Sanders, Jimmy Devon *university official*

Gainesville
Bryan, Robert Armistead *university administrator, educator*
Challoner, David Reynolds *university official, physician*
Chapin, Kenneth Lee *middle school educator*
Cheek, Jimmy Geary *university official, agricultural education and communications educator*
Clark, Elmer J. *education educator*
Davidson, James Melvin *academic administrator, researcher, educator*
Hale, James Pierce *education educator*
Lombardi, John V. *university administrator, historian*
Lowenstein, Ralph Lynn *university dean emeritus*
Neims, Allen Howard *univeristy dean, medical scientist*
Penland, Arnold Clifford, Jr. *college dean, educator*
Phillips, Winfred Marshall *dean, mechanical engineer*
Price, Donald Ray *university official, agricultural engineer*
Schwartz, Michael Averill *university dean, pharmaceutical scientist*
Smith, David C. *dean*
Sorensen, Andrew Aaron *provost*
Viessman, Warren, Jr. *academic dean, civil engineering educator, researcher*
Woeste, John Theodore *academic administrator*
York, E. Travis, Jr. *academic administrator, former university chancellor, consultant*

Goulds
Taylor, Millicent Ruth *middle school educator*

Graceville
Kinchen, Thomas Alexander *college president*

Green Cove Springs
Yelton, Eleanor O'Dell *reading specialist*

Groveland
Hamilton, Rhoda Lillian Rosen *educator, consultant*

Hollywood
Goldberg, Icchok Ignacy *retired special education educator*

Homestead
Brammer, Barbara Allison *secondary school educator, consultant*

Indian Rocks Beach
Rocheleau, James Romig *academic administrator*

Jacksonville
Barrett, S. Barre *academic administrator, art educator*
Boyles, Carol Ann Patterson *career development educator*
Brady, James Joseph *university president*
Brann, William Paul *retired university official*
Colby, Lestina Larsen *secondary education educator*
Gunning, John Thaddeus *retired superintendent*
Herbert, Adam William, Jr. *university president*
Kinne, Frances Bartlett *chancellor emeritus*
MacDonald, Carolyn Helms *gifted education educator*
Osborn, Marvin Griffing, Jr. *educational consultant*
Tierney, Patricia A. *school system administrator*

Jay
Peacock, Hugh Anthony *agricultural research director, educator*

Key West
Henriquez, Armando Joseph *superintendent*

Lady Lake
Belok, Michael Victor *education educator*

Lakeland
Davis, Robert Aldine *college president*
Wade, Ben Frank *college administrator*

Largo
Gall, Keith D. *director*
Hinesley, J. Howard *superintendent*
Shapiro, Alan B. *secondary education educator*

Maitland
MacKenzie, Charles Sherrard *college president*
Whitlock, Luder Gradick, Jr. *seminary president*

Marianna
Flowers, Virginia Anne *academic administrator emerita*

Melbourne
Barr, Constance R. *school system administrator*
Edwards, David Northrop *retired university administrator*
Hollingsworth, Abner Thomas *university dean*
Noonan, Norine Elizabeth *academic administrator, researcher*
Scheuerer, Diane Thompson *home economics educator*
Weaver, Lynn Edward *academic administrator, consultant, editor*

Melrose
Meyer, Harvey Kessler, II *retired academic administrator*

Merritt Island
McClanahan, Leland *academic adminstrator*

Miami
Bitter, John *university dean emeritus, musician, businessman, diplomat*
Breman, Joseph Eliot *school administrator, lawyer*
Brenner, Esther Hannah *elementary school educator*
Cohen, Eugene Erwin *university health institute administrator, accounting educator emeritus*
Dottin, Erskine S. *education educator*
Foote, Edward Thaddeus, II *university president, lawyer*
Frank, Walter Monroe, Jr. *media specialist*
Frei, Sister John Karen *university administrator*
Goldenberg, I. Ira *academic administrator*
Gonzales, Sylvia Alicia *academic administrator, communications executive*
Halberg, F. David *principal*
Koch, William Henry *elementary education educator*
Le Duc, Albert Louis, Jr. *computer services director*
Maidique, Modesto Alex *academic administrator*
†McCabe, Robert Howard *educator, college president*
Pyles, Carol DeLong *dean, consultant, educator*
Rosendahl, Bruce Ray *dean, geophysicist, educator*
Rossie, Carlos Enrique *computer school administrator*
Thornton, Sandi Tokoa *elementary education educator*
Williams, James A. *principal*
Young, Freddie Gilliam *educational administrator*

Miami Beach
Gitlow, Abraham Leo *retired university dean*

Miami Shores
O'Laughlin, Sister Jeanne *university administrator*

Mount Dora
Santini, John Amedeo *educational consultant*

Naples
Abbott, John Sheldon *law school dean and chancellor emeritus*
Cantelon, John Edward *academic administrator*
Mahoney, Sheila Irene *middle school educator*

North Fort Myers
Hoffman, Nelson Miles, Jr. *retired academic administrator, consultant*

North Miami Beach
Terry, Morton *academic administrator, physician*

Ocala
Phillips, Margaret Crouse *gifted and talented educator*

Opa Locka
Hopton, Janice *elementary school principal*

Orange City
Gorman, Burton William *retired education educator*

Orange Park
Ratzlaff, Judith L. *secondary school educator*

Orlando
Hitt, John Charles *university president*
Schott, James *educational administrator*

Osprey
Kern, Jean Glotzbach *elementary education educator, gifted education educator*

Oviedo
Martin, Judson Phillips *retired education educator*

Palm City
Ammarell, John Samuel *retired college president, former security services executive*

Palm Coast
Dickson, David Watson Daly *retired college president*
Godfrey, Eutha Marek *elementary school educator, consultant*

Palm Harbor
Shaneyfelt, Patricia Tharin *elementary education educator*

Penney Farms
Kimbrough, Ralph Bradley *educational administration educator emeritus*

Pensacola
Cianciolo, Sister Rosemary *school system administrator*
Marx, Morris Leon *academic administrator*

Pinellas Park
Athanson, Mary Catheryne *elementary school principal*

Placida
Schwarting, Arthur Ernest *university dean*

Plantation
Fershleiser, Steven Buckler *secondary education educator*

Ponte Vedra Beach
Hartzell, Karl Drew *retired university dean, historian*

Port Charlotte
Norris, Dolores June *elementary school educator*

Punta Gorda
Hill, Richard Earl *academic administrator*

Rockledge
Sutton, Betty Sheriff *elementary education educator*

Saint Augustine
Proctor, William Lee *college president*

Saint Leo
Mouch, Frank Messman *college president, priest*

Saint Petersburg
Allshouse, Merle Frederick *higher education executive*
Armacost, Peter Hayden *college president*
Estenes, Joseph John, Jr. *academic administrator*
Giffin, Barbara Haines *education coordinator*
Jacob, Bruce Robert *dean, academic administrator, law educator*
Kuttler, Carl Martin, Jr. *college president*
Meisels, Gerhard George *academic administrator, chemist, educator*
Nussbaum, Leo Lester *retired college president, consultant*
Peterson, Arthur Laverne *former college president*
Southworth, William Dixon *retired education educator*
Westall, Sandra Thornton *special education educator*

Sarasota
Adams, Richard Towsley *university president, educational consultant*
Christ-Janer, Arland Frederick *college president*
Downey, John Charles *university dean, zoology educator*
Felker, Ouida Jeanette Weissinger *special education educator*
Fowler, Charles William *school administrator*
Highland, Marilyn M. *principal*
Tatum, Joan Glennalyn John *secondary school educator*

Sebastian
Mauke, Otto Russell *retired college president*

Seffner
Castellano, Sandra Lorrain *curriculum director*

Spring Hill
Rojas, Victor Hugo *retired vocational education educator*

Starke
Loper, George Wilson, Jr. *physical education educator*

Tallahassee
Adams, Perry Ronald *former college administrator*
Baum, Werner A. *former academic administrator, meteorologist*
Burnette, Ada M. Puryear *educational administrator*
Bye, Raymond Erwin, Jr. *academic administrator*
Evans, Virden *educator, academic administrator*
Gil, Lazier *university dean*
Hafner, Lawrence Erhardt *education educator*
Humphries, Frederick S. *university president*
Lick, Dale Wesley *academic administrator*
McTarnaghan, Roy E. *acadamic administrator*
Morgan, Robert Marion *educational research educator*
Reed, Charles Bass *university system chancellor*
Voran, James F. *principal*

Tampa
Anderson, Robert Henry *education educator*
Bondi, Joseph Charles, Jr. *education educator, consultant*
Givens, Paul Ronald *former university chancellor*
Grady, Susanna Fenhagen *preparatory school administrator*
Heck, James Baker *university official*
Hegarty, Thomas Joseph *academic administrator, educator*
Kase-Polisini, Judith Baker *educator*
Mc Alister, Linda Lopez *educator, philosopher*
McCook, Kathleen de la Peña *university educator*
Plawecki, Judith Ann *nursing educator*
Sanchez, Mary Anne *secondary school educator*
Smith, Donn L. *university dean*
†Streeter, Richard Barry *academic official*
Weiner, Irving Bernard *university administrator, psychologist, educator*

Tarpon Springs
Byrne, Richard Hill *counselor, educator*

Tierra Verde
Schmitz, Dolores Jean *secondary education educator*

Venice
Jamrich, John Xavier *retired university administrator*
Thomas, David Ansell *retired university dean*

West Palm Beach
Corts, Paul Richard *academic administrator*

Winter Haven
Peck, Maryly VanLeer *college president, chemical engineer*

Winter Park
Bornstein, Rita *academic administrator*
Fernandez, Joseph Anthony *educational administrator*
Mc Kean, Hugh Ferguson *college president, painter, writer*
Mc Kean, Keith Ferguson *former education educator*

Zephyrhills
Jernstrom, Joan *secondary education educator*

GEORGIA

Adel
Darby, Marianne Talley *elementary school educator*

Alpharetta
Kingrea, Ann B. *principal*

Americus
Capitan, William Harry *college president*
McGrady, Clyde A. *secondary school principal*
Stanford, Henry King *college president*

Athens
Crowther, Ann Rollins *dean, political science educator*
Cutlip, Scott Munson *university dean*
†Donoho, Clive W., Jr. *dean, research horticulturalist*
Douglas, Dwight Oliver *university administrator*
Fincher, Cameron Lane *educator*
Hunt, Jacob Tate *special education educator emeritus*
Meeks, Carol Jean *educator*
Newsome, George Lane, Jr. *education educator*
Tillman, Murray Howell *instructional technology educator*
Younts, Sanford Eugene *university administrator*

Atlanta
Alexander, Cecil Abraham *college official, retired architect, consultant*
Alfred, Dewitt Clinton, Jr. *university dean, psychiatrist*
Bright, David Forbes *academic administrator, classics and comparative literature educator*
†Butts, Lester Wayne *principal*
Caprio, Anthony S. *university official*
Chace, William Murdough *university administrator*
Clough, Gerald Wayne *academic administrator*
Cole, Johnnetta Betsch *academic administrator*
Cole, Thomas Winston, Jr. *chancellor, college president, chemist*
Coleman, Mattie Jones *primary education educator*
Dees, Julian Worth *academic administrator*
Dorsey, J(onnie) Naomi *vocational education educator, consultant*
Fowler, Andrea *teachers academy administrator*
Fox, James Harold, Jr. *superintendent of schools*
Frye, Billy Eugene *university administrator, biologist*
Godard, James McFate *retired educational consultant*
Hendrix, James Paisley, Jr. *headmaster*
Henry, Ronald James Whyte *university official*
Hogan, John Donald *college dean, finance educator*
Jackson, Ernestine Hill *elementary education educator*
Jones, George Henry *university dean, research administrator, biology educator*
Keiller, James Bruce *college dean, clergyman*
Keith, Leroy, Jr. *college president*
Kelly, Michael Joseph *academic administrator, consultant*
Kraft, Arthur *academic dean*
Lewis, Larry Lynn *college official, minister, denominational official*
Matula, Richard A(llan) *academic administrator*
Parko, Edith Margaret *special education educator*
Pattillo, Manning Mason, Jr. *academic administrator*
Patton, Carl Vernon *academic administrator, educator*
Roberts, Thomasene Blount *entrepreneur*
Sink, John Davis *leadership consultant, scientist*
Stanton, Donald Sheldon *university administrator*
Suttles, William Maurrelle *university administrator, clergyman*
Tummala, Rao Ramamohana *engineering educator*
Warner, Wayne Henry *elementary and secondary educator*

Augusta
Bloodworth, William Andrew, Jr. *academic administrator*
Martin, Willie Pauline *elementary school educator, illustrator*
Puryear, James Burton *college administrator*
Tedesco, Francis Joseph *health sciences university president*

Brunswick
Harper, Janet Sutherlin Lane *educational administrator, writer*

Buford
Carswell, Virginia Colby *primary school educator, special education educator*

Carrollton
Morris, Robert Christian *education educator*
Sethna, Beheruz Nariman *college president, marketing/management educator*

Clarkston
Negron, Jaime *college biology administrator*

Cleveland
Raznoff, Beverly Shultz *education educator*

Cochran
Halaska, Thomas Edward *academic administrator, director, engineer*
Welch, Joe Ben *academic administrator*

Columbus
Averill, Ellen Corbett *science educator, administrator*
Brown, Frank Douglas *academic administrator*
Riggsby, Dutchie Sellers *education educator*
Salamanca, Merlina Espiritu *secondary education educator*

Dallas
Calhoun, Patricia Hanson *secondary education educator*

Dalton
Thomason, Frank W. *superintendent*

Decatur
Baker, Stephen M. *school system administrator*
Carey, John Jesse *academic administrator, religion educator*
Myers, Orie Eugene, Jr. *university official*
Wilkinson, Ben *chancellor, evangelist, ministry organizer, writer*

Dublin
Fatum, Delores Ruth *school counselor*
Watson, Mary Alice *academic administrator*

Duluth
Neuman, Ted R. *principal*

Elberton
Wheeler, Timothy Arneal *assistant superintendent*

Fairburn
Montague, Mary Ellen *secondary school educator*

Forsyth
Popper, Virginia Sowell *education educator*

Gainesville
Burd, John Stephen *academic administrator, music educator*

Greenville
Johnson, Hardwick Smith, Jr. *school psychologist*

Griffin
Champion, Ann Louverta *secondary school educator*

Jasper
Parrish, Carmelita *secondary school educator*

Jesup
Childers, Anita Flowers *language arts educator*

Jonesboro
Fleming, Janelle Smith *gifted and talented education educator*
Pulliam, Brenda Jane *secondary school educator*
Sprayberry, Roslyn Raye *secondary school educator*

La Fayette
Hendrix, Bonnie Elizabeth Luellen *elementary school educator*

La Grange
Ault, Ethyl Lorita *academic administrator*
Gordon, Robert Edward *university administrator*
Murphy, Walter Young *college president, clergyman*

Lilburn
Magill, Dodie Burns *early childhood education educator*
White, Jeffrey Lee *middle school educator*

Lithonia
Flanagan, James Lee *educational administrator*

Macon
Ackerman, Robert Kilgo *college president, historian*
Bayliss, Sister Mary Rosina *principal*
Dantzler, Deryl Daugherty *dean, law educator*
Godsey, R(aleigh) Kirby *university president*
Innes, David Lyn *university official, educator*
Kinnel, Mary Lou *college recruitment executive*
Mitchell, Carolyn Cochran *college official*
Steeples, Douglas Wayne *university dean, consultant, researcher*
Williamson, Christine Wilder *educational consultant, small business owner*

Marietta
Cheshier, Stephen Robert *university president, electrical engineer*
Day, Afton J. *elementary school educator, administrator*
Norman, Peggy Rocker *retired secondary school educator*
Siegel, Betty Lentz *college president*

Monroe
Lynch, Lillian *retired secondary education educator*

Mount Berry
Mathis, Luster Doyle *college administrator, political scientist*
Shatto, Gloria McDermith *college administrator, economist*

Perry
Hinnant, Tony *superintendent*

Rabun Gap
Dodd, Bruce C., Jr. *educational administrator*

Riverdale
Lambert, Ethel Gibson Clark *secondary school educator*

Rome
Hawley, Harold Patrick *educational consultant*
Perdue, Judy Clark *academic administrator*

Saint Marys
Durr, Marguerite Denise *school system administrator*

Saint Simons Island
Tomberlin, William G. *principal*

Sautee Nacoochee
Miller, Wilbur Randolph *retired university educator and administrator*

Savannah
Burnett, Robert Adair *university administrator, history educator*

Statesboro
Black, Charlene Rushton *university official, sociology educator*
Henry, Nicholas Llewellyn *college president, political science educator*

Thomson
Smith, Robert L. *principal*

Tifton
Simpson, Juliette Rich *elementary educator*

Toccoa Falls
Alford, Paul Legare *college and religious foundation administrator*

Valdosta
Bailey, Hugh Coleman *university president*
Evans, Marie Annette Lister *school system administrator*
Peace, Barbara Lou Jean *education educator*

Winterville
Anderson, David Prewitt *university dean*

Young Harris
Yow, Thomas Sidney, III *college administrator*

HAWAII

Hilo
Perrin, Kenneth Lynn *university chancellor*

Honolulu
Alm, Richard Sanford *education educator*
Aoude, Ibrahim Georges *ethnic studies educator*
Bess, Henry David *dean*
Dolly, John Patrick *university dean, educational psychologist*
Enoki, Donald Yukio *curriculum specialist*
Greenfield, David W. *academic dean, ichthyologist*
Harrison, Jeremy Thomas *dean*
Inaba, Lawrence Akio *educational director*
Jackson, Miles Merrill *university dean*
Kaiser-Botsai, Sharon Kay *early chilhood educator*
Keith, Kent Marsteller *academic administrator, corporate executive, government official, lawyer*
King, Arthur R., Jr. *education educator, researcher*
Matsuda, Fujio *institute president*
Meyer, Robert Allen *human resource management educator*
Pickens, Alexander Legrand *education educator*
Ramler, Siegfried *school administrator*
Wright, Chatt Grandison *academic administrator*

Kailua
Tam, William *secondary school principal*
Tokumaru, Roberta *principal*

Kailua Kona
Clewett, Kenneth Vaughn *college official*
Feaver, Douglas David *university dean, classics educator*

Kaneohe
Dever, Daniel *academic administrator*
Inamine, Sharon Ogawa *elementary school administrator*
Kamiyama, Linda *elementary school principal*

Kihei
Gaston, Joy Puu'olani *gifted and talented education educator*

Laie
Bradshaw, James R. *business educator*

Makawao
Mascho, George Leroy *education educator emeritus*

Waialua
Krause-Diaz, Mary Jean *educational administrator*

Waipahu
Stevens, Adele Amy Kubota *physical education educator*

IDAHO

Boise
Andrus, Cecil Dale *academic administrator*
Barr, Robert Dale *university dean, educator*
Crane, Charles Arthur *college president*
Griffin, Sylvia Gail *reading specialist*
Hollenbaugh, Kenneth M. *academic administrator, geology consultant*
Maloof, Giles Wilson *academic administrator, educator, author*
Ruch, Charles P. *university official*
Steinfort, James Richard *university program director*
Woodard, Larry L. *Bible college official*
Young, Katherine Ann *education educator*

Caldwell
Hendren, Robert Lee, Jr. *academic administrator*

Coeur D Alene
Green, Charlotte Kimball *educator*

Lewiston
Morgan, Glen D. *superintendent*

Mc Call
Evans, Darrell J. *art educator*

Moscow
Bartlett, Robert Watkins *academic dean, metallurgist*
Hendee, John Clare *college dean, natural resources educator*
Zinser, Elisabeth Ann *university president*

Nampa
Rau, Shirley A. *secondary school educator*

Pocatello
Barnett, Mary Louise *elementary education educator*
Bowen, Richard Lee *academic administrator, political science educator*
Rowe, Ernest Ras *education educator, academic administrator*
Sagness, Richard Lee *education educator, former academic dean*

ILLINOIS

Anna
Wolfe, Martha *elementary education educator*

Arlington Heights
Roderick, William Rodney *academic administrator*

Aurora
Zarle, Thomas Herbert *university president*

Barrington
Simmons, Damian *secondary education educator*

Bloomington
Gregor, Marlene Pierce *primary educator, elementary science consultant*
Myers, Minor, Jr. *college administrator, political science educator*
Watkins, Lloyd Irion *university president*

Carbondale
Casey, John P. *special education educator*
Covington, Patricia Ann *university administrator*
Dixon, Billy Gene *academic administrator*
Elkins, Donald Marcum *associate dean, agronomy educator*
Guyon, John Carl *university administrator*
Mead, John Stanley *university administrator*
Snyder, Carolyn Ann *university dean, librarian*

Carlinville
Mc Conagha, Glenn Lowery *chancellor emeritus*

Carol Stream
Choice, Priscilla Kathryn Means (Penny Choice) *gifted education educator, international consultant*

Champaign
Asaad, Kolleen Joyce *special education educator*
Cammack, Trank Emerson *retired university dean*
Dulany, Elizabeth Gjelsness *university press administrator*
Feinberg, Walter *philosophy educator*
Keen, Maria Elizabeth *retired educator*
Loeb, Jane Rupley *university administrator, educator*
Schowalter, William Raymond *college dean, educator*
Spodek, Bernard *curriculum educator*

Charleston
Buckellew, William Franklin *retired education educator*
Jorns, David Lee *university president*
Rives, Stanley Gene *university president emeritus*

Chicago
Alexandroff, Mirron (Mike Alexandroff) *academic administrator*
†Baker, Robert J. *medical academic dean, surgeon*
Begando, Joseph Sheridan *retired university chancellor, educator*
Bernadetta, Sister Maria *special education educator*
Bloom, Benjamin S. *education educator*
Bornholdt, Laura Anna *university administrator*
Bowman, Barbara Taylor *academic administrator*
Caldwell, Ethel Louise Lynch *academic administrator*
Champagne, Ronald Oscar *academic administrator, mathematics educator*
Chapman, Delores *elementary education educator*
Chippas, Denyse Leilani *secondary mathematics educator, travel agent*
Coe, Donald Kirk *university official*
Coleman, Roy Everett *secondary education educator, computer programmer*
Collens, Lewis Morton *university president, legal educator*
Crockett, George Ephriam *secondary education educator*
Cross, Dolores Evelyn *university administrator, educator*
Cummings, Maxine Gibson *elementary school educator*
Davis, Sylvester, Jr. *secondary education educator*
Dreeben, Robert *education educator*
Felton, Cynthia *principal*
Finch, Herman Manuel *academic administrator*
Freedman, Joyce Beth *academic administrator*
Fruchter, Rosalie Klausner *elementary school educator*
Gamwell, Franklin I. *dean, educator*
†Getz, Godfrey Shalom *dean, pathology educator*
Graham, Patricia Albjerg *education educator, foundation executive*
Gross, Theodore Lawrence *university administrator, author*
Henikoff, Leo M., Jr. *academic administrator, medical educator*
Hogarth, Robin Miles *academic administrator, educator*
Holland, Jean *elementary education educator*
Jegen, Sister Carol Frances *religion educator*
Johnson, Argie K. *community school district superintendent*
Johnson, Beverly June *librarian, educator*
Karlin, Bernard Richard *principal*
Kloc, Emily Alvina *elementary principal*
Lamb, Gordon Howard *academic administrator*
Lester, Robin Dale *private school educator, author, former headmaster*
Lewis, Philip *educational and technical consultant*
Long, Earline Davis *elementary education educator*
Lynn, Laurence Edwin, Jr. *university administrator, educator*
Martin, Barbara Jean *elementary school principal*
Matasar, Ann B. *former dean, business and political science educator*
Meyer, Donald Gordon *college dean, educator*
Meyers, Dorothy *adult education educator, writer*
Mindes, Gayle Dean *education educator*
Minogue, John P. *academic administrator, priest, educator*
Mosley, Elaine Christian Savage *principal, chief education officer, consultant*
†Moss, Gerald S. *dean, medical educator*
O'Reilly, Charles Terrance *university dean*
Panko, Jessie Symington *dean*
Pideritt, John J. *university educator*
Pollick, G. David *college president, philosopher*
Raven, Corinne *principal*
Reinke, John Henry *clergyman, educational administrator*
Richardson, John Thomas *university chancellor, clergyman*
Roberts, Jo Ann Wooden *school system administrator*
Schieser, Hans Alois *education educator*
Schommer, Carol Marie *principal*
Schubert, William Henry *curriculum studies educator*
Smith, Kenneth Bryant *seminary administrator*
Standberry, Herman Lee *school system administrator, consultant*
Stelmack, Gloria Joy *elementary education educator*
Stowell, Joseph, III *academic administrator*
Stukel, James Joseph *university official, mechanical engineering educator*
Sulkin, Howard Allen *college president*
Swanson, Don Richard *university dean*
Swanson, Patricia K. *university official*
Taylor, John Wilkinson *education educator*
Wasan, Darsh Tilakchand *university official, chemical engineer educator*
Watkins, Cheryl Denise *special education educator*
Yamakawa, Allan Hitoshi *university administrator*

Crystal Lake
Linklater, Isabelle Stanislawa Yarosh-Galazka (Lee Linklater) *secondary education educator*

De Kalb
La Tourette, John Ernest *academic administrator*
Monat, William Robert *university official*
Shur, George Michael *lawyer*

Decatur
McCray, Curtis Lee *university president*

Deerfield
Meyer, Kenneth Marven *academic administrator*

Des Plaines
Coburn, James LeRoy *educational administrator*
Lakier, Thelma *child development specialist, librarian*
Lee, Margaret Burke *college administrator*
Tenhoeve, Thomas *academic administrator*

Downers Grove
†Lewis, Robert J. *secondary education educator*

East Moline
Puffer, Richard Judson *retired college chancellor*

Edwardsville
Lazerson, Earl Edwin *university president emeritus*

Elgin
Didier, James William *college executive, administrator, consultant*
Weber, Harm Allen *college chancellor, former college president*

Elmhurst
Cureton, Bryant Lewis *college president, educator, political scientist*

Erie
Latham, LaVonne Marlys *physical education educator*

Eureka
Hearne, George Archer *academic administrator*

Evanston
Boye, Roger Carl *academic administrator, journalism educator, writer*
Branch, William B. *school system administrator*
Christian, Richard Carlton *university dean, former advertising agency executive*
Herron, Orley R. *college president*
Ihlanfeldt, William *university administrator, consultant*
Kern, Charles William *university official, chemistry educator*
Kerr, Thomas Jefferson, IV *academic official*
Lewis, Dan Albert *education educator*
Mack, Raymond Wright *university provost*
McCoy, Marilyn *university official*
Miller, Thomas Williams *former university dean*
Robinson, R. Clark *mathematician, educator*
Schultz, Don Edward *academic administrator*
Slaughter-Defoe, Diana Tresa *education educator*
Weber, Arnold R. *university chancellor*
Wick, John William *education educator, author*
Zarefsky, David Harris *academic administrator, communication studies educator*

Flossmoor
Ferreira, Daniel Alves *Spanish language educator*

Frankfort
Ruggles, Barbara Ann *elementary education educator*

Galesburg
Haywood, Bruce *retired college president*

Glen Ellyn
McAninch, Harold D. *college president*
Patten, Ronald James *university dean*

Glenview
Corley, Jenny Lynd Wertheim *educator*
McGrew, Jean B. *superintendent*
Traudt, Mary B. *elementary education educator*

Greenville
Stephens, William Richard *college president emeritus*

Gurnee
Meyer, Joyce *special education educator*

Highland Park
Mordini, Marilyn Heuer *physical education educator*
Moschin, Susan Kamin *school board executive*
Pokorny, Virginia Anne *elementary education educator*

Hinsdale
Burrows, Donald Albert *artist, painter, college dean*
Kalus, Richard A. *university program director*
Lynch, Charles J. *secondary school principal*
Taylor, T(homas) Roger *educational consultant, educator*

Homer
Gilhaus, Barbara Jean *home economics secondary educator*

Jacksonville
Pfau, Richard Anthony *college president*

Joliet
Caamano, Kathleen Ann Folz *gifted education professional*
†Johnson, Mary Ann *computer training/vocational school owner*
Pietak, Raymond Adam *academic administrator*

Kankakee
Bowling, John C. *academic administrator*

Knoxville
Johnson, Robert Oliver, Jr. *school system administrator*

Lake Forest
Bransfield, Joan *principal*
Hotchkiss, Eugene, III *college president emeritus*
Kreischer, Gary C. *secondary school educator*

Libertyville
Kremkau, Paul *principal*
Mraz, Alana L. *elementary school principal*

Lincolnshire
Berkey, Timothy Bruce *principal*
DuFour, Richard P. *school system administrator*

Lisle
Becker, Richard Charles *college president*

Lynwood
Dyer-Dawson, Diane Faye *educational administrator*

Macomb
Goehner, Donna Marie *university dean*
Malpass, Leslie Frederick *retired university president*
Witthuhn, Burton Orrin *university official*

Madison
Pope, Sarah Ann *elementary education educator*

Mattoon
Sherline, Harold Albert *adult education professional*

Metamora
Crow, Mary Jo Ann *elementary education educator*

Mount Prospect
Feingold, Diana *middle school educator, conservationist*
Jacobsen, Charlene Marie *music educator, band director*

Murphysboro
Brewer, Donald Louis *school superintendent*
Jacobs, Robert *education educator emeritus*

Naperville
Scullen, Thomas G. *superintendent*
Wilde, Harold Richard *college president*

Normal
Bolen, Charles Warren *university dean*
Matsler, Franklin Giles *higher education educator*
Strand, David Axel *university executive*
Wallace, Thomas Patrick *university administrator*

Northfield
Fodrea, Carolyn Wrobel *educational researcher, publisher*

Oak Forest
Hull, Charles William *special education educator*

Oak Lawn
†Gordon, Edward Earl *training company executive, educator*

Oak Park
Adelman, William John *university labor and industrial relations educator*
Davis, Christine Eurich *elementary education educator*

Oglesby
Zeller, Francis Joseph *academic administrator*

Palos Hills
Crawley, Vernon Obadiah *academic adminstrator*

Palos Park
Lawler, Susan George *elementary education educator*

Pekin
Herbstreith, Yvonne Mae *primary education educator*

Peoria
Brazil, John Russell *academic administrator*
Francis, John Elbert *university dean*
Murphy, Sharon Margaret *university official, educator*
Smith, Clyde R. *counselor educator*
Watson, Ellen I. *academic administrator*

Peru
Benning, Joseph Raymond *principal*

Poplar Grove
Hullah, Ann Marie *elementary education educator*

Quincy
Toal, James Francis *academic administrator*

River Forest
Krentz, Eugene Leo *university president, educator, minister*
Lund, Sister Candida *college chancellor*
Murray, Sister Jean Carolyn *college president*

Riverdale
Saulsbury, Ruth Eva *retired special education educator*

Rock Island
Brauch, Merry Ruth Moore *gifted education consultant*
Horstmann, James Douglas *college official*
Tredway, Thomas *college president*

Rockford
Howard, John Addison *former college president, institute executive*
Marelli, Sister M. Anthony *secondary school principal*
Steele, Carl Lavern *academic administrator*
Whitsell, Doris Benner *retired educator*

Saint Charles
Alfini, James Joseph *dean, lawyer, educator*

Schaumburg
Harmon, Nancy Jean *elementary school educator*

Skokie
Goldberg, Vicki Comm *employment services executive*

South Holland
Schaap, Marcia *special education educator*

Springfield
Layzell, Thomas D. *academic administrator*
Lynn, Naomi B. *university chancellor*
Mervis, Louis *school system administrator*
Moy, Richard Henry *academic dean, educator*
Phillips, John Robert *college dean, educator*
Poorman, Robert Lewis *education educator, consultant, academic administrator*

Sterling
Albrecht, Beverly Jean *special education educator*

Summit Argo
Urban, Patricia A. *former elementary school educator*

Sycamore
Johnson, Yvonne Amalia *elementary education educator, science consultant*

Tinley Park
Denys, Edward Paul *education educator*
Johnson, Herman *secondary education educator*

Urbana
Bloomfield, Daniel Kermit *college dean, physician*
Holt, Donald A. *university administrator, agronomist, consultant, researcher*
Ikenberry, Stanley Oliver *university president*
Mc Conkie, George Wilson *education educator*
Resek, Robert William *university administrator*
Shuman, R(obert) Baird *academic program director, writer, english educator, educational consultant*
Wedgeworth, Robert *university librarian, dean, former association executive*
Weir, Morton Webster *retired university chancellor and educator*

Venice
Purdes, Alice Marie *secondary education educator*

Villa Park
Devlin, Barbara Jo *school district administrator*
Taylor, Ronald Lee *school administrator*

Washington
McKinney-Keller, Margaret Frances *retired special education educator*

Western Springs
Mudd, Anne Chestney *small business owner, mathematics educator, real estate agent*

Wheaton
†Algeo, John Thomas *retired educator, association executive*
Sweetser, Ruth Emilie Ziemann *university administrator*
Ward, Patricia Ann *dean*

Wilmette
Beane, Marjorie Noterman *academic administrator*
Smutny, Joan Franklin *academic director, educator*

Winnetka
Lindsay, Dianna Marie *educational administrator*

INDIANA

Anderson
Edwards, James L. *university president*
Nicholson, Robert Arthur *college president*

Angola
Elliott, Carl Hartley *former university president*

Berne
Lehman, Doyle *superintendent*

Bloomington
Arnove, Robert Frederick *education educator*
Bain, Wilfred Conwell *former university dean, music educator, opera theater director*
Barnes, A. James *academic dean*
Brand, Myles *academic administrator*
†Crowe, James W. *university administrator, educator*
Gros Louis, Kenneth Richard Russell *university chancellor*
Hopkins, Jack Walker *former university administrator, environmental educator*
Johnson, Owen Verne *program director*
Mehlinger, Howard Dean *education educator*
Mobley, Tony Allen *university dean, recreation educator*
Otteson, Schuyler Franklin *former university dean, educator*
Randolph, James C. *professor*
Ryan, John William *retired university president*
Scannell, Dale Paul *dean, university educator*
Smith, Carl Bernard *education educator*
Thelin, John Robert *academic administrator, education educator, historian*
Warren, Donald *university dean, education educator*
Webb, Charles Haizlip, Jr. *university dean*
Wells, Herman B. *university chancellor*
Wentworth, Jack Roberts *business educator, consultant*
Williams, Edgar Gene *university administrator*

Carmel
Hartman, Robert D. *superintendent*

Crawfordsville
Ford, Andrew Thomas *academic administrator*

Culver
Manuel, Ralph Nixon *private school executive*

Dale
Hayes, Mary Joanne *special education educator*

East Chicago
Platis, James G. *secondary education educator*
Vis, Mary A. Murga *elementary education educator*

Elkhart
†Meyer, Albert James *educational administrator*
Preheim, John S. *secondary education educator*

Elwood
Vance, Joan Emily Jackson (Mrs. Norval E. Vance) *elementary school educator*

Evansville
Graves, Wallace Billingsley *retired university executive*
Schoffstall, Phil *school superintendent*
Vinson, James Spangler *university president*

Fishers
Gatto, Louis Constantine *retired college president*
Jontz, Polly *college official, musuem director*

Fort Branch
Bertram, Michael Wayne *secondary education educator*

Fort Wayne
Andorfer, Donald Joseph *academic administrator, educator*
Kam, Jeanette Virginia *school system administrator*
Lewark, Carol Ann *special education educator*
Pease, Ella Louise *elementary education educator*

Gary
Knight, Harriette *secondary educator*
Richards, Hilda *university administrator*
Roberts, Samuel Alden *secondary education educator*
Smith, Vernon G. *education educator, state representative*

Goshen
Stoltzfus, Victor Ezra *academic administrator*

Greencastle
Bottoms, Robert Garvin *academic administrator*
Houck, Carolyn Marie Kumpf *special education educator*

Greentown
Healy, Stephen C. *seconadry school principal*

Hammond
Delph, Donna Jean (Maroc) *education educator, consultant, university administrator*
Watson, Steven Ellis *school district administrator*

Highland
Gregory, Marian Frances *educator, counselor*

Hobart
Rajsic, Robert *secondary education educator*

Indianapolis
Alsop, Thomas Walter *secondary education educator*
Bannister, Geoffrey *university president, geographer*
Barcus, Mary Evelyn *primary school educator*
Bepko, Gerald Lewis *academic administrator, law educator, lecturer, consultant, lawyer*
†Bowes, Edward (Bud) *superintendent of schools*
Chapman, Linda Brown *school system administrator*
†Dailey, Donald Harry *adult education educator, volunteer*
Duncan-Ladd, Georgia Jones *elementary education educator*
Engledow, Jack Lee *college administrator, consultant, researcher*
Evans, Daniel Fraley *college administrator, banker, retail executive*
Felicetti, Daniel A. *academic administrator, educator*
Galbraith, Bruce W. *educational administrator*
†Gilbert, Shirl Edward *school system administrator*
Gilmore, H. William *college dean, dentistry educator*
Gould, Karen J. *elementary school principal*
Hardin, Boniface *academic administrator*
Harp, Pamela Jo *special education consultant*
Huffman-Hine, Ruth Carson *adult education administrator, educator*
Ilchman, Warren Frederick *university administrator, political science educator*
Johnstone, Joyce Visintine *education educator*
Renda, Randolph Bruce *university dean*
Shipp, Travis *education educator, author*
Silver, David Mayer *former university official*
Smith, Kathy Ann *educator, state senator*
Speth, Gerald Lennus *education and business educator*
Stern, Raymond *principal*
Stockard, Robert Thomas *secondary school administrator*
Wooden, Reba Faye Boyd *guidance counselor*
Woody, John Frederick *secondary education educator*

Kokomo
Hill, Emita Brady *academic administrator*

La Porte
Heiden, Susan Jane *elementary education educator*

Lafayette
Andrews, Frederick Newcomb *emeritus university administrator*

Linden
Lefebvre, Gren Gordon *school superintendent*

Lowell
Myers, Charlotte *secondary educator*

Marion
Barnes, James Byron *university president*

Monroeville
Geldien, Judith Ruth Motter *elementary educator*

Muncie
Marsh, Helen Unger *retired educational administrator*
Shondell, Donald Stuart *physical education educator*
Wheeler, David Laurie *university dean*

Munster
Fort, Gene *secondary educator*
Sherman, Mona Diane *school system administrator*

New Albany
Crooks, Edwin William *former academic administrator*
Rand, Leon *university administrator*

Notre Dame
Castellino, Francis Joseph *university dean*
Crosson, Frederick James *former university dean, humanities educator*
Hatch, Nathan Orr *university administrator*
O'Meara, Onorato Timothy *academic administrator, mathematician*

Pendleton
Phenis, Nancy Sue *educational administrator*

Rensselaer
Shannon, Albert Joseph *educator*

Richmond
Robinson, Dixie Faye *school system administrator*
Wood, Richard J. *college president*

Saint Mary Of The Woods
Doherty, Sister Barbara (Ann Doherty) *academic administrator*

South Bend
Charles, Isabel *university administrator*
Mills, Nancy Anne *elementary education educator*

Terre Haute
Gilman, David Alan *education educator, editor*
Grimley, Liam Kelly *special education educator*
Hulbert, Samuel Foster *college president*
Hunt, Effie Neva *former college dean, former English educator*
Jerry, Robert Howard *education educator*
Kicklighter, Clois Earl *academic administrator*
Landini, Richard George *university president, emeritus English educator*
Leach, Ronald George *university dean, librarian*
Moore, John W. *academic administrator*
Moore, John William *university administrator*
Van Til, William *education educator, writer*

Upland
Kesler, Jay Lewis *university president*

Valparaiso
Harre, Alan Frederick *university president*
Hillila, Bernhard Hugo Paul *education educator*
Miller, John Albert *university administrator, marketing consultant*
Mundinger, Donald Charles *college president retired*
Schnabel, Robert Victor *retired academic administrator*

West Lafayette
Baumgardt, Billy Ray *university official, agriculturist*
Beering, Steven Claus *university president, medical educator*
Ford, Frederick Ross *university official*
Frick, Gene Armin *university administrator*
Gappa, Judith M. *university administrator*
Gentry, Don Kenneth *academic dean*
Haring, Marilyn Joan *academic dean*
Moskowitz, Herbert *management educator*
Moyars-Johnson, Mary Annis *university administrator*
Newby, Timothy James *education educator, researcher*
Ringel, Robert Lewis *university administrator*
Shertzer, Bruce Eldon *education educator*
Stone, Beverley *former university dean, former dean of students*
Tacker, Willis Arnold, Jr. *academic administrator, medical educator, researcher*
Weidenaar, Dennis Jay *college dean*

Westville
Alspaugh, Dale William *university administrator, aeronautics and astronautics educator*

Zionsville
Hansen, Arthur Gene *former academic administrator, consultant*

IOWA

Ames
Christensen, George Curtis *university official*
Crabtree, Beverly June *college dean*
Ebbers, Larry Harold *education educator*
Jischke, Martin C. *academic administrator*
Manatt, Richard *education educator*
Rice, Ronald Max *superintendent*
†Snow, Joel Alan *research director*
Thompson, Joan Kathryn *university official*
Topel, David Glen *college dean, animal science educator*

Burlington
Brocket, Judith Ann *mathematics educator*
Longanecker, Edwin Snyder, Jr. *special education services educator*

Cedar Rapids
Brown, John Edward *college president*
Feld, Thomas Robert *college president*

Ledford, Sandra *principal*
Plagman, Ralph *principal*

Davenport
Copes, Marvin Lee *college dean*
Moeller, Donald Joseph *academic administrator, educator*
Rogalski, Edward J. *university administrator*
Schmidt, W. Robert *school system administrator*
Wenz, Richard L. *school system and church administrator*

Des Moines
Canfield, Earle Lloyd *university dean, mathematics educator*
Ferrari, Michael Richard, Jr. *university administrator*
Fitzpatrick, Sister Jude *academic administrator*
Marker, David George *university president*
Puotinen, Arthur Edwin *college president, clergyman*
Snyder, Carolyn Swick (Carrie Snyder) *special education educator, vocational program administrator*
Wegenke, Gary L. *school systems administrator*

Dubuque
Agria, John Joseph *college official*
Dunn, M. Catherine *college administrator, educator*
Peterson, Walter Fritiof *academic administrator*
Toale, Thomas Edward *school system administrator, priest*

Fort Dodge
Pratt, Diane Adele *elementary education educator*

Grinnell
Fitzgerald, Michael J. *secondary school principal*
Walker, Waldo Sylvester *academic administrator*

Indianola
Jennings, Stephen Grant *academic administrator*

Iowa City
Bruch, Delores Ruth *education educator, musician*
Dickeson, Robert Celmer *retired university president, corporation president, political science educator*
†Domsic, Dennis Michael *dean, university medical department official*
Feldt, Leonard Samuel *university educator and administrator*
MacVey, Alan Mokler *program director*
Mc Leran, James Herbert *university dean, oral surgeon*
Schulz, Rudolph Walter *university dean*
Skorton, David Jan *university official, physician, educator*
Vaughan, Emmett John *academic dean, insurance educator*

Janesville
Ehmen, James Edward *elementary educator*

Lamoni
Higdon, Barbara J. *college president*

Mount Pleasant
Haselmayer, Louis August *college president emeritus*

Oakdale
Spriestersbach, Duane Caryl *university administrator, speech pathology educator*

Ottumwa
Roseberry, Donald G. *chief administrator*

Sioux Center
Hulst, John B. *academic administrator*

Sioux City
Rants, Carolyn Jean *college official*
Rooney, Gail Schields *college administrator*
Tommeraasen, Miles *college president*
Wick, Sister Margaret *college administrator*

Storm Lake
Briscoe, Keith G. *college president*

Waterloo
Kober, Arletta Refshauge (Mrs. Kay L. Kober) *educational administrator*

Waverly
Vogel, Robert Lee *college administrator, clergyman*

West Des Moines
Barnett, Duane Alan *school system administrator*

KANSAS

Auburn
Good, Martha Gail *educational administrator*

Baldwin City
Keeling, Joe Keith *academic administrator, provost*
Lambert, Daniel Michael *academic administrator*

Burr Oak
O'Brien, Kimberly K. *secondary education educator*

Downs
La Barge, William Joseph *tutor, researcher*

El Dorado
Edwards, James Lynn *college dean*

Emporia
Glennen, Robert Eugene, Jr. *university president*

Goddard
Kastens, Beverly Ann *special and elementary education educator*

Goodland
Sharp, Glenn (Skip Sharp) *vocational education administrator*

Hays
Budke, Charles Henry *secondary education educator*
Hammond, Edward H. *university president*

Hiawatha
Pennel, Marie Lucille Hunziger *elementary education educator*

Kansas City
Coles, Anna Louise Bailey *university official, nurse*
Merritt, Carol Ruth *middle school educator*
Powell, Nancy Egan *elementary education educator*
Whelan, Richard J. *director special education and pediatrics programs, academic administrator*

Lawrence
Crowe, William Joseph *dean of libraries, educator*
Frederickson, Horace George *former college president, public administration educator*
Locke, Carl Edwin, Jr. *academic administrator, engineering educator*
Pinet, Frank Samuel *former university dean*
Turnbull, Ann Patterson *special education educator, consultant*

Manhattan
Chang, Amos Ih-Tiao *retired educator*
Coffman, James Richard *academic administrator, veterinarian*
Flaherty, Roberta D. *university official*
Kruh, Robert F. *university administrator*
Lee, William Franklin, III *association administrator*
†Oblander, Charles P. *university official*

Mc Pherson
Mason, Stephen Olin *academic administrator*

Oakley
Squibb, Sandra Hildyard *special education educator*

Olathe
Booth, Jody Shelton *executive director*

Overland Park
Cummings, Penelope Dirrig *special education educator*

Parsons
†Tignor, George *principal*

Pittsburg
Sullivan, Frank Victor *academic dean, industrial arts educator*
Wilson, Donald Wallin *university president, educator*

Salina
Stanton, Marshall P. *academic administrator, clergyman*
Tompkins, John Andrew *school system administrator*

Shawnee Mission
Kaplan, Marjorie Ann Pashkow *school district administrator*
Whitaker, Kathleen K. *gifted education facilitator*

Topeka
Shuler, Howard L. *superintendent*
Thompson, Hugh Lee *university president*

Ulysses
Palmer, Barbara Jean *special education administrator*

University Of Kansas
Hemenway, Robert E. *university administrator, language educator*

Vassar
Visser, John Evert *university president emeritus, historian*

Winfield
Willoughby, John Wallace *former college dean, provost*

KENTUCKY

Barbourville
Phillips, Jack Carter *educational administrator*

Bardstown
Carter, Carmen M. *elementary education educator, consultant*

Berea
Hager, Paul Calvin *college administrator, educator*

Bowling Green
†Daniel, Patricia Lynne *educator, consultant*
Haynes, Robert Vaughn *university administrator, historian*
Meredith, Thomas C. *academic administrator*
Murrell, Estelle C. *elementary school educator*

Covington
Bensman, Charles J. *academic administrator*

Crestwood
Upchurch, Paul *principal*

Danville
Adams, Michael F. *academic administrator, political communications specialist*
Breeze, William Hancock *college administrator*
Rowland, Robert E. *secondary school principal*
Spragens, Thomas Arthur *educational consultant*

Fairdale
Steffen, Pamela Bray *secondary school educator*

Frankfort
Wolfe, John Thomas, Jr. *university president*

Harrodsburg
Lunger, Irvin Eugene *university president emeritus, clergyman*

Highland Heights
Boothe, Leon Estel *university president*

Hopkinsville
Riley, Thomas Leslie *retired college president*

Independence
Boster, Judy Landen *primary school educator*

Lexington
Blanton, Jack Christopher *academic administrator*
Bosomworth, Peter Palliser *university medical administrator*
Flynn, Peter Francis *superintendent of schools*
Kuc, Joseph A. *educator, consultant*
Logan, Joyce Polley *education educator*
Robinson, Thomas Christopher *academic administrator, educator*
Shipley, David Elliott *university dean, lawyer*
Singletary, Otis Arnold, Jr. *university president emeritus*
Wethington, Charles T., Jr. *academic administrator*

London
Early, Jack Jones *college administrator*

Louisville
Berman, Edward Henry *education educator*
Carden, Joy Cabbage *educational consultant*
Ekstrom, William Ferdinand *college administrator*
Ferguson, Duncan Sheldon *education administrator*
Garfinkel, Herbert *university official*
Glore-Seward, Linda Jo *primary school educator*
Gummere, Walter Cooper *educator, consultant*
Hazen, Elizabeth Frances *retired special education educator*
Hoye, Robert Earl *higher education educator, health care consultant*
Kmetz, Donald R. *academic administrator*
Nystrand, Raphael Owens *university dean, educator*
Swain, Donald Christie *university president, history educator*
Taylor, Robert Lewis *academic administrator*

Madisonville
Sneed, Joanne Lawson *elementary school educator, author*

Mayfield
Harris, Isaac Henson *university dean*

Murray
Hunt, Charles Brownlow, Jr. *university dean, musician*

Owensboro
Poling, Wesley Henry *college president*

Richmond
Funderburk, H(enry) Hanly, Jr. *college president*
Kirkpatrick, Dorothy Louise *education educator, program coordinator*
Martin, Robert Richard *emeritus college president, former senator*

Saint Catherine
Collins, Martha Layne *college president, former governor*

Union
Cook, Janice Eleanor Nolan *elementary school educator*

Wilmore
McKenna, David Loren *seminary president, clergyman*

LOUISIANA

Alexandria
Mayeux, Ronald N. *school system administrator*

Arnaudville
LaGrange, Claire Mae *special education educator*

Baton Rouge
Boyce, Bert Roy *university dean, library and information science educator*
Brun, Judith *principal*
Caffey, H(orace) Rouse *academic administrator, consultant*
Copping, Allen Anthony *university president*
Davis, William Eugene *university administrator*
Hancock, Paul Byron *headmaster*
Harrison, Betty Carolyn Cook *vocational educator, administrator*
Mc Cameron, Fritz Allen *university administrator*
Prestage, James Jordan *university chancellor*
Rabideau, Peter Wayne *university dean, chemistry educator*
Soderbergh, Peter Andrew *education educator*
Walker, Florence Ann *preschool educator, insurance underwriter*
Wheeler, Otis Bullard *academic administrator, educator emeritus*
Williams, Hulen Brown *former university dean*
Woodin, Martin Dwight *retired university system president*

Covington
Bankston, Terry *school system administrator*

Deridder
Lytle, Ellen Juanita Wilson *special education educator*

Franklin
Fairchild, Phyllis Elaine *counselor*

Grambling
Smith, Betty Edmiston *university dean, nurse*

Hammond
Parker, Clea Edward *university president*
Smith, Grant Warren, II *university administrator, physical sciences educator*

Houma
Lemoine, Pamela Allyson *assistant principal*
Paisant, Sister Immaculata *school system administrator*

Independence
Vaccaro, Nick Anthony *principal*

Kenner
Cook, Willie Chunn *elementary school educator*

Lafayette
Andrew, Catherine Vige *elementary school educator*
Redding, Evelyn A. *dean, nursing educator*

Lake Charles
Cain, Sister Gloria *school system administrator*
Douglas, Wanda Sue Lenard *middle school educator*
Hebert, Robert D. *academic administrator*
Hebert, Robert D. *academic administrator*
Leder, Sandra Juanita *elementary school educator*

Leesville
Boren, Lynda Sue *educator*

Mansfield
Smelley, Joyce Marie *special education supervisor*

Metairie
Buetow, Paul Elmer *principal*
Flake, Leone Elizabeth *special education educator*
Johnson, Beth Michael *principal*
Murphy, Alvin Leo *educational administrator*

Minden
Doerge, Everett Gail *retired school system admnistrator, state rep*

Monroe
Cage, Bobby Nyle *university dean*

Napoleonville
Gunnell, William N. *school system administrator*

Natchitoches
Alost, Robert Allen *university executive*

New Iberia
Cavalier, David J. *school system administrator*

New Orleans
Abad, Rosario Dalida *elementary educator*
Berlin, Charles I. *audiologist, scientist*
Burns, Mary W. *school system administrator*
Carter, James Clarence *university administrator*
Cook, Samuel DuBois *university president, political scientist*
Gordon, Joseph Elwell *university official, educator*
Hamlin, James Turner, III *university dean, physician*
Hassenboehler, Donalyn *principal*
†Holmes, Morris L., Jr. *school superintendent*
Jefferson, Patrick O'Neal *university program director, administrative assistant*
Johnson, Lee Harnie *dean, educator*
Jones, John Anderson, Jr. *school system administrator*
Kelly, Eamon Michael *university president*
Mackin, Cooper Richerson *university chancellor*
McFarland, James W. *academic administrator*
McMahon, Maeve *principal*
Novakov, George John, Jr. *gifted and talented education educator*
Riedlinger, Brian A. *principal*
Rigby, Perry Gardner *medical center administrator, educator, former university dean, physician*
Stevenson, Bobbie Lee *education director*
Vanselow, Neal Arthur *university administrator, physician*
Walsh, John Joseph *medical school administrator, physician*
Washington, Robert Orlanda *educator, former university administrator*

Pineville
Matthews, Betty Parker *special education educator*

Ruston
Freasier, Aileen W. *special education educator*
Maxfield, John Edward *retired university dean*
Reneau, Daniel D. *university administrator*
Taylor, Foster Jay *retired university president*

Shreveport
Darling, John Rothburn, Jr. *university administrator, educator*
Schwab, Kenneth Lynn *college president*
Witt, Elizabeth Nowlin (Beth Witt) *special education educator*

Slidell
Faust, Marilyn B. *elementary school principal*

Thibodaux
Nunn, Thomas Calvin *school supervisor, retired army officer*
Worthington, Janet Evans *academic director, English language educator*

Winnsboro
Wilson, Rose Eaton *elementary education educator*

Zachary
Hull, Donnie Faye *special education director, educator*

MAINE

Bangor
Watkins, Julia M. *university dean*

Bar Harbor
Swazey, Judith Pound *institute president, sociomedical science educator*

Biddeford
Ford, Charles Willard *university administrator, educator*
Reynolds, Thomas Hedley *university president*

Bridgton
Thompson, Larry A. *principal*

Brownfield
Kloskowski, Vincent John, Jr. *educational consultant, writer*

Brunswick
Edwards, Robert Hazard *college president*
Greason, Arthur LeRoy, Jr. *university administrator*

Caribou
McElwain, Franklin Roy *educational administrator*

Cumb Foreside
Dill, William Rankin *college president*

Damariscotta
Johnson, Arthur Menzies *retired college president, historian, educator*

Farmington
Kalikow, Theodora June *university president*

Hebron
Farwell, Margaret Wheeler *elementary education educator*

Kennebunk
Dyer, Robert Darlington *elementary education educator*
McConnell, David M. *secondary school principal*

Lewiston
Harward, Donald *academic official*

Machias
Hudson, Miles *special education educator*

North Yarmouth
Fecteau, Rosemary Louise *educational consultant*

Oakland
Albanese, J. Duke *school system administrator*

Old Orchard Beach
Bartner, Jay B. *school system administrator*

Orono
Albright, Elaine McClay *dean*
Coupe, John Donald *university official, economics educator*
Hutchinson, Frederick Edward *university president*
Rauch, Charles Frederick, Jr. *academic official*
Wiersma, G. Bruce *dean, forest resources educator*

Portland
Gilmore, Roger *academic administrator*

Saint Francis
Ellwood, Stephen Charles, IV *education educator*

Spruce Head
Bird, John Adams *educational consultant*

Standish
Hart, Loring Edward *academic administrator*

Waterville
Cotter, William Reckling *college president*

MARYLAND

Adelphi
Langenberg, Donald Newton *academic administrator, physicist*

Annapolis
Brann, Eva Toni Helene *dean*
Ness, Frederic William *former academic administrator, educator, consultant*
Nuesse, Celestine Joseph *retired university official*

Baltimore
†Amprey, Walter G. *school system administrator*
Behm, Mark Edward *university administrator, consultant*
†Berger, Stuart David *school superintendent*
†Boughman, Joann Ashley *dean*
Brown, John Walter *vocational education supervisor*
Chylinski-Polubinski, Roger *academic administrator*
Delpit, Lisa D. *education educator, researcher, consultant*
Ferrara, Steven *educational administrator, researcher, consultant*
Fishbein, Estelle Ackerman *lawyer*
Fitzgerald, Thomas Rollins *university administrator*
Glynn, Edward *college administrator*
Grasmick, Nancy S. *superintendent of schools*
Hall, Merrill Souel, III *head master*
Harmening, Denise M. *academic administrator, educator*
Keller, George Charles *higher education consultant, editor*
King, Ora Sterling *education educator*
Klitzke, Theodore Elmer *former college dean, arts consultant*
Lafferty, Joyce G. Zvonar *retired educator*
Lazarus, Fred, IV *college president*
McPartland, James Michael *university official*
†Mohraz, Judy Jolley *college president*
Moreland, Ernest Ferman *dean*
Moszkowski, Lena Iggers *secondary school educator*
Reese, Errol Lynn *university administrator, dentist*
Richardson, Loretta M. *college dean, medical/surgical nurse*
Richardson, William Chase *university administrator*
Ross, Richard Starr *medical school dean emeritus, physician, cardiologist*
Schoenrich, Edyth Hull *academic administrator, physician*
Simon, David *principal*
Smith, Hoke LaFollette *university president*
Webb, Myrtle Bailey *elementary school reading teacher*

Berlin
Crawford, Norman Crane, Jr. *academic administrator, consultant*

Bethesda
Buccino, Alphonse *university dean*
Corn, Milton *academic dean, physician*
Dyer, Ann *headmistress*
Dykstra, Vergil Homer *retired academic administrator*
Gleazer, Edmund John, Jr. *retired education educator*
Lystad, Robert Arthur Lunde *retired university dean, educator*
Meltzer, Jack *consultant, retired college dean*
Reichard, John Francis *educational consultant*

Bowie
Forrester, Donald Dean *principal*

Centreville
Wharton, Kay Karole *special education educator*

Chevy Chase
Strauss, Jon Calvert *medical research administrator*

Clinton
Johns, Jayne Howell *elementary education educator, administrator, achievement specialist*

College Park
Berman, Louise Marguerite *education educator*
Birnbaum, Robert *higher education educator*
Dieter, George Elwood, Jr. *university official*
Dorsey, John Wesley, Jr. *university administrator, economist*
Ehrensberger, Ray *university chancellor*
Fallon, Daniel *university administrator*
Finkelstein, Barbara *education educator*
Hardy, Robert Charles *human development educator*
Hey, Nancy Henson *educational administrator*
Massey, Thomas Benjamin *educator*
Mayer, William Emilio *dean*
Polakoff, Murray Emanuel *university dean, economics and finance educator*
Prentice, Ann Ethelynd *academic administrator*
Seefeldt, Carol *education educator*
Stumpff, Robert Thomas *academic administrator*
Zimmerman, Mary Ann *university purchasing agent*

Columbia
Bruley, Duane Frederick *academic administrator, consultant, engineer*
Hartman, Lee Ann Walraff *educator*
Whiting, Albert Nathaniel *former university chancellor*

Crofton
Clark, Marcia Hileman *special education educator*
Eastman, John Robert *educator*

Eldersburg
Bastress, Robert Lewis *principal*

Ellicott City
Hickey, Michael E. *school system administrator*
Phelps, Catherine *elementary school principal*

Frederick
Brown, Frederick James *education educator*
Farmer, Noel T., Jr. *school system administrator*

Frostburg
Gira, Catherine Russell *university president*
Root, Edward Lakin *university dean, educator*

Gaithersburg
Brown, Dorothea Williams *technology consulting company executive*
Fleming-Durdin, Jennie *elementary school educator*
Karch, Karen Brooke *principal*

Greenbelt
Boarman, Gerald L. *principal*
Lubetzky, Carole Diane *elementary education educator, math-science specialist*

Hagerstown
Palmisano, Sister Maria Goretti *principal*

Hampstead
Staub, Martha Lou *elementary education educator*

Hyattsville
Moylan, John L. *secondary school principal*
Rodgers, Mary Columbro *university chancellor, English educator, author*

Kensington
Jackson, Mary Jane McHale Flickinger *principal*

Landover
Drahmann, Brother Theodore *academic administrator*

Laurel
Gottsman, Earl Eugene *academic administrator*
Wales, Sister Patrice *school system administrator*

Mardela Springs
Harcum, Louise Mary Davis *retired elementary education educator*

Oakland
Farrar, Richard Bartlett, Jr. *secondary education educator*

Oxford
Waetjen, Walter Bernhard *university president emeritus*

Potomac
Jung, Richard K. *headmaster*
Stupak, Ronald Joseph *dean, management educator, researcher*

Princess Anne
Hytche, William Percy *university president*

Queenstown
Mc Laughlin, David Thomas *academic administrator, business executive*

Rockville
Krear, Gail Richardson *elementary education educator, consultant*
Rosenberg, Judith Lynne *middle school educator*
Sparks, David Stanley *university administrator*
Stansfield, Charles W. *educational administrator*

Sandy Spring
Cope, Harold Cary *former university president, higher education association executive*

Severna Park
Darden, Alverta Eleanor *elementary educator*

Silver Spring
Butler, Broadus Nathaniel *retired university administrator*
Geiger, Anne Ellis *secondary educator*
Holloway, William Jimmerson *retired educator*
Pearman, Reginald James *educational administrator*
Raphael, Coleman *business school dean*
Sampugnaro, Trudy M. *principal*
Schick, Irvin Henry *educator*
Shira, Robert Bruce *university administrator, oral surgery educator*
Whalen, John Philip *retired educational administrator*

Towson
Chappell, Annette M. *university dean*
Hildebrand, Joan Martin *education educator*

Upper Marlboro
Elwood, Patricia *educator, political consultant*
Street, Patricia Lynn *secondary education educator*
Underdue, Marilyn Rosetta *special education educator*

Westminster
Chambers, Robert Hunter, III *college president, American studies educator*

MASSACHUSETTS

Agawam
Charest, Gabrielle Marya *educational administrator*

Amherst
Adrion, William Richards *academic administrator, computer and information sciences educator, author*
Anderson, Ronald Trent *art educator*
Bischoff, David Canby *university dean*
Gerety, Tom *college administrator, educator*
Marcum, James Benton *college dean*
O'Brien, Richard Desmond *university administrator, neurobiologist*
Prince, Gregory Smith, Jr. *academic administrator*
Rosbottom, Ronald Carlisle *academic administrator, French culture and literature educator*

Andover
Chase, Barbara Landis *headmistress*
Wise, Kelly *private school educator, photographer, critic*

Arlington
Fulmer, Vincent Anthony *retired college president*

Babson Park
Glavin, William Francis *academic administrator*

Bedford
Aronstein, Laurence W. *middle school principal*

Belmont
Haselkorn, David *teacher recruiting executive*

Billerica
Pike, Albert Louis, Jr. *educational administrator, consultant*

Boston
Argyris, Chris *organizational behavior educator*
Banks, Henry H. *academic dean, physician*
Chobanian, Aram Van *medical school dean, cardiologist*
Curry, John Anthony, Jr. *university administrator*
Davies, Don *education educator*
Diener, Betty Jane *university administrator*
DiFranza, Virginia *principal*
Eisner, Sister Janet Margaret *college president*
El-Baz, Farouk *program director, educator*
Estabrooks, Gordon Charles *secondary education educator*
Greene, Robert Allan *former university administrator*
†Harrison-Jones, Lois *school system administrator*
Henry, Joseph Louis *university dean*
Hooker, Michael Kenneth *college president*
Kirkpatrick, Edward Thomson *college administrator, mechanical engineer*
Lesser, Laurence *music conservatory president, cellist, educator*
Milley, Jane Elizabeth *academic administrator*
O'Connell, Kevin George *priest, fundraiser, former college president*
O'Neil, William Francis *academic administrator*
Penney, Sherry Hood *university chancellor, educator*
Rittner, Carl Frederick *educational administrator*
Roach, Sister Ann Dominic *school system administrator*
Robinson, Sumner Martin *college administrator*
Ronayne, Michael Richard, Jr. *academic dean*
Ryder, Kenneth Gilmore *university chancellor*
Sargent, David Jasper *university executive, lawyer*
Silber, John Robert *university president*
Simmons, Sylvia Jeanne Quarles (Mrs. Herbert G. Simmons, Jr.) *university administrator, educator, senior manager*
Taylor, Julius Willard *director student health services, physician*
Terry, Jannie Lee *elementary education educator*
Turlish, Molly Buffum *academic administrator*
Van Domelen, John Francis *academic administrator*
Watts, Charles Henry, II *university administrator*
Westling, Jon *university administrator*

Braintree
Gittleman, Sol *university official, humanities educator*

Bridgewater
Bardo, John William *university administrator*
Cost, Richard Willard *educator*
Rondileau, Adrian *college president*
Tinsley, Adrian *college president*

Brockton
Buote, Rosemarie Boschen *special education educator*

Brookline
Mesch, Barry *academic administrator*

Burlington
Connors, Richard J. *principal*

Byfield
Bragdon, Peter Wilkinson *headmaster*

Cambridge
Brinton, Joyce Marie *university administrator*
Bruce, James Donald *academic administrator*
†Buffa, Sebastian Joseph *art history educator, consultant*
Cavanagh, Richard Edward *university dean*
Clark, William Cummin *academic director, educator*
Clendenning, Bonnie Ryon *college administrator*
Conway, Jill Kathryn Ker *former college president*
Dickson, William Robert *academic administrator*
Emerson, Anne Devereux *university administrator*
Eurich, Nell P. *educational consultant*
Fischer, Kurt Walter *education educator*
Fox, John Bayley, Jr. *university dean*
Ganley, Oswald Harold *university official*
Gray, Paul Edward *academic official*
Hausmann, Leonard J. *academic administrator, educator*
Johnson, Howard Wesley *former university president, business executive*
McArthur, John Hector *university dean, business educator*
McKenna, Margaret Anne *college president*
McNemar, Donald William *consultant*
Ragone, David Vincent *former university president*
Rowe, Mary P. *university official, educator*
Rudenstine, Neil Leon *academic administrator, educator*
Sharp, Phillip Allen *academic administrator, biologist, educator*
Slater, Jonathan E. *director*
Smith, Ronald Lee *academic administrator, public policy educator*
Thiemann, Ronald Frank *dean, religion educator*
Vest, Charles Marstiller *university president*
Whitlock, Charles Preston *former university dean*
Wilson, Linda Smith *university administrator*

Centerville
Kiernan, Owen Burns *educational consultant*

Chestnut Hill
Altbach, Philip *higher education director, educator*
Hunt-Clerici, Carol Elizabeth *academic personnel assistant*
Monan, James Donald *college president*

Chicopee
Anderson, Nancy Elaine *home economics educator*
Fishman, Gail Barbara *special education educator*

Concord
†Howe, Harold, II *former foundation executive, educator*

Danvers
Traicoff, George *college president*

Dedham
Weiss, Bruce Jordan *academic administrator*

Dorchester
Steller, Arthur Wayne *educational administrator*

Duxbury
Mc Carthy, D. Justin *college president*

Easthampton
Grubbs, Dennis H. *secondary school principal*

Fall River
Ingles, James H. *learning resources academic director*

Fitchburg
Anderson, Charles Lee Royal *academic administrator*
Bourque, Anita Mary *school principal*
Mara, Vincent Joseph *college president*

Framingham
Atsumi, Ikuko *management school administrator, educator*
Sposato, Charles *secondary education educator*

Great Barrington
Rodgers, Bernard F., Jr. *academic administrator, dean*

Haverhill
Dimitry, John Randolph *college president*

Kingston
Rispettoso, George Alphonse *vocational educator, diesel technology consultant*
Squarcia, Paul Andrew *school superintendent*

Lee
Smith, Elske Van Panhuys *retired university administrator*

Lexington
Della Penna, Joan Frances *secondary educator*
Litchfield, Ruth France *reading, literacy specialist*

Mack, Jane Louise *early childhood educator, administrator*

Lincoln
Brown, Linda Weaver *academic administrator*

Longmeadow
Leary, Carol Ann *academic administrator*
Wright, Jeanette Tornow *college president*

Mansfield
Rosa, Edward A. *principal*

Medford
Brown, Althea T. *secondary education educator*
DiBiaggio, John A. *university administrator*
Mancke, Richard Bell *university dean, economics educator*
Mumford, George Saltonstall, Jr. *former university dean, astronomy educator*
Swap, Walter Charles *academic dean, psychology educator*

Milton
Giuliano, Frank J., Jr. *school system administrator*
Ingold, Catherine White *academic administrator*

Natick
Perrin, Stephanie B. *headmistress*

North Dartmouth
Andersen, Laird Bryce *retired university administrator*
Waxler, Robert Phillip *university educator, consultant*

Northampton
Dunn, Mary Maples *college president*
Heartt, Charlotte Beebe *university official*

Norton
†Marshall, Dale Rogers *college president, political scientist, educator*

Quincy
Hill, Kent Richmond *college president*

Rockport
Bakrow, William John *college president emeritus*

Roxbury
Short, Janet Marie *principal*

Salem
Galaris, John Daniel *director of athletics*
Harrington, Nancy D. *college president*

Saugus
Austill, Allen *dean emeritus*

Sheffield
Haworth, Donald Robert *educator, retired association executive*

South Dartmouth
Lenci, Gordon Kent *headmaster*
Ward, Richard Joseph *university official, educator, author*

South Deerfield
Fritz, Nancy *elementary education educator*

South Hadley
Kennan, Elizabeth Topham *college president*

Southwick
MacEwan, Barbara Ann *middle school educator*

Springfield
Miller, Beverly White *college president*
Negroni, Peter Joseph *school system administrator*
Riddle, James Douglass *college administrator*

Swampscott
Truog, Dean-Daniel Wesley *educator, consultant*

Taunton
Donly, Michael J. *headmaster*

Waltham
Adamian, Gregory Harry *academic administrator*
Reinharz, Jehuda *university president, history educator*

Wellesley
Auerbach, Jerold S. *university educator*
Rayen, James Wilson *art educator, artist*
†Walsh, Diana Chapman *academic administrator, social and behavioral sciences educator*

Westborough
Jackson, Frederick Herbert *educational administrator*

Westfield
Applbaum, Ronald Lee *academic administrator*

Westwood
Funkhouser, Elmer Newton, Jr. *retired academic official*

Winchester
Casey, Norine Therese *school principal*

Worcester
Berth, Donald Frank *university official, consultant*
Brooks, John Edward *college president emeritus*
Brown, John Lott *retired university president, educator*
Clements, Kevin Anthony *dean, electrical engineering educator, consultant*
Grogan, William Robert *university dean*
Hagan, Joseph Henry *college president*
Lutz, Francis Charles *university dean, civil engineering educator*
†Mattar, Edward Paul, III *academic administrator*
McManus, Charles E. *school system administrator*
Onorato, Nicholas Louis *program director, economist*

†Plummer, Edward Bruce *college librarian*
Traina, Richard Paul *university president*

Yarmouth Port
Hall, James Frederick *retired college president*

MICHIGAN

Adrian
Caine, Stanley Paul *college administrator*

Albion
Vulgamore, Melvin L. *college president*

Allendale
Lubbers, Arend Donselaar *university president*
Niemeyer, Glenn Alan *academic administrator, history educator*

Alma
Stone, Alan Jay *college administrator*
Swanson, Robert Draper *college president*

Ann Arbor
Anderson, Austin Gothard *university administrator, lawyer*
Cart, Pauline Harmon *minister, educator*
Cole, David Edward *university administrator*
Craig, Holly Kathlyn *director communicative disorders clinic*
Darwall, Stephen Leicester *educator*
Davis, Wayne Kay *university dean, educator*
Duderstadt, James Johnson *university president*
Fleming, Suzanne Marie *university official, chemistry educator*
Jelinek, Fran *school system administrator*
Kirkpatrick, Dorothy Ann *early childhood education educator*
Lewis, Robert Enzer *lexicographer, educator*
Miskel, Cecil G. *academic dean*
Paul, Ara Garo *university dean*
Paulson, William Ross *foreign language educator, researcher*
Porter, John Wilson *education executive*
Robbins, Jerry Hal *educational administration educator*
Stark, Joan Scism *education educator*
Tice, Carol Hoff *educator, consultant*
Van Houweling, Douglas Edward *university administrator, educator*
Watkins, Paul B. *academic research center administrator, medical educator*
Whitaker, Gilbert Riley, Jr. *academic administrator, business economist*
†White, B. Joseph *university dean*

Bay City
Zuraw, Kathleen Ann *special education and physical education educator*

Berrien Springs
Lesher, William Richard *retired university president*

Big Rapids
Popovich, Helen Houser *university administrator*

Bloomfield Hills
Doyle, Jill J. *elementary school principal*
Fulton, Patsy Jo *educational administrator, writer*
Hillman, Donald M. *middle school principal*

Brighton
Jensen, Baiba *principal*

Carsonville
Kummerow, Arnold A. *superintendent of schools*

Coloma
Tallman, Clifford Wayne *school system administrator, consultant*

Dearborn
Brucker, Eric *academic administrator*
Fair, Jean Everhard *education educator*
Klein, Bernard W. *academic administrator*
Morshead, Richard Williams *philosophy of education educator*

Detroit
Cortada, Rafael Leon *university president*
Cox, Clifford Ernest *deputy superintendent, chief information officer*
Ellison, James Morton *secondary education educator*
Fay, Sister Maureen A. *university president*
Hough, Leslie Seldon *educational administrator*
Lee, James Edward, Jr. *educational administrator*
McGriff, Deborah *school system administrator*
Pouncy, Marva Nell *elementary education educator*
Semanik, Anthony James *university program administrator*
Shay, John E., Jr. *college president*
Snead, David L. *superintendent*

Dowagiac
Mulder, Patricia Marie *educator*

East Lansing
Anderson, James Henry *university dean*
Bettinghaus, Erwin Paul *university dean*
Brophy, Jere Edward *education educator, researcher*
Byerrum, Richard Uglow *college dean*
Cherney, Elaine Ethel *education educator*
Honhart, Frederick Lewis, III *academic director*
Lerner, Richard M. *special education director*
Mackey, Maurice Cecil *university president, economist, lawyer*
Martin, Michael J. *university administrator, consultant*
Peterson, Penelope Loraine *education educator*
Rudman, Herbert Charles *education educator*
Saul, William Edward *academic administrator, civil engineering educator*
Snoddy, James Ernest *education educator*
van der Smissen, M. E. Betty *educator*
Wronski, Stanley Paul *education educator*

Farmington
Elder, Jean Katherine *education administrator*

Flint
Duckett, Bernadine Johnal *elementary principal*
Edson, Ray Zachariah *middle school educator*
Lorenz, John Douglas *college official*
Nelms, Charlie *academic administrator*

Frankfort
Acker, Nathaniel Hull *retired educational administrator*

Gaylord
Magsig, Judith Anne *early childhood educator*

Grand Ledge
Farnsworth, Judith Marie *elementary education educator*

Grand Rapids
Calkins, Richard W. *college president*
Deihl, Charles L. *college president*
Delnick, Martha Joyce *elementary education educator*
Diekema, Anthony J. *college president*
Gross, Michael *school system administrator*
VanHarn, Gordon Lee *college administrator and provost*

Grosse Pointe
Robie, Joan *elementary school principal*

Gwinn
Lasich, Vivian Esther Layne *secondary education educator*

Harrison Township
Suchecki, Lucy Anne *elementary education educator*

Haslett
Andrew, Gwen *university dean emerita, retired*
Hotaling, Robert Bachman *community planner, educator*

Hastings
Adrounie, V. Harry *dean, environmental scientist, educator*

Highland
Doyle, James H. *school system administrator*

Hillsdale
Roche, George Charles, III *college administrator*
Trowbridge, Ronald Lee *college admininstrator*

Holland
Jacobson, John Howard, Jr. *college president*
Van Wylen, Gordon John *former college president*

Houghton
Tompkins, Curtis Johnston *university president*

Huntington Woods
Logan, Linda Mary *art education educator*

Inkster
Ruehle, Dianne Marie *elementary education educator*

Kalamazoo
Barrett, Nancy Smith *university administrator*
Bryan, Lawrence Dow *college administrator*
Haenicke, Diether Hans *university president*
Inselberg, Rachel *education educator, researcher*
Johnson, Tom Milroy *academic dean, medical educator, physician*
†Lennon, Elizabeth M. *retired educator*
McDonald, Kenneth William *principal*
Stufflebeam, Daniel LeRoy *education educator*

Kincheloe
Light, Kenneth Freeman *college administrator*

Lansing
Brennan, Thomas Emmett *law school president*
Wotiska, Sister Dorita *school system administrator*

Livonia
Marinelli, Joseph John *educational administrator*
Van de Vyver, Sister Mary Francilene *academic administrator*

Madison Heights
Pricer, Wayne Francis *counseling administrator*

Maple City
Morris, Donald Arthur Adams *college president*

Marquette
Heldreth, Leonard Guy *university administrator*
Hill, Betty Jean *academic administator*
Vandament, William Eugene *academic administrator, educator*

Midland
Barker, Nancy Lepard *university official*
Hyde, Geraldine Veola *secondary education educator, retired*
Powell, Rebecca Ann *secondary education educator*

Monroe
Siciliano, Elizabeth Marie *secondary education educator*

Mount Clemens
Fraser, Blanche E. *school system administrator*

Mount Pleasant
Lippert, Robert J. *administrator and culinary arts educator, consultant*
Plachta, Leonard E. *academic administrator*

Muskegon
Austin, William Lamont *educational consultant, former superintendent of schools*
Hadiaris, Marie Ellen *special education educator*

Newaygo
Grodus, Edward T. *secondary school principal*

Okemos
Hickey, Howard Wesley *retired education educator*

Olivet
Bassis, Michael Steven *academic administrator*

Pontiac
Decker, Peter William *academic administrator*
McClellan, Thomas James *educator*

Port Huron
McDaniels, Peggy Ellen *special education educator*

Portland
Adams, Bill *principal*

Rochester
Polis, Michael Philip *academic administrator, electrical engineering educator*

Saginaw
Kinney, Yvonne Marie *primary grades educator*

Southfield
Chambers, Charles MacKay *university president*
Olsen, Douglas H. *superintendent*

Temperance
†Kinney, Mark B. *educator*

Traverse City
Rosser, Richard Franklin *education consultant*
Warrington, Willard Glade *former university official*
Zimmerman, Paul Albert *retired college president, minister*

University Center
Carlyon, Don J. *college president*
Gilbertson, Eric Raymond *academic administrator, lawyer*

Warren
Lorenzo, Albert L. *academic administrator*

West Bloomfield
Childress, Carl T. *principal*
Ho, Leo Chi Chien *education administrator*
Peterson, Esther *secondary school principal*

Williamsburg
Goodell, Warren Franklin *retired university administrator*

Wixom
Boynton, Irvin Parker *educational administrator*

Ypsilanti
Boone, Morell Douglas *academic administrator, information and instructional technology educator*
Goldenberg, Ronald Edwin *university dean*
Gwaltney, Thomas Marion *education educator, researcher*
Olmsted, Patricia Palmer *education educator, researcher*
Shelton, William Everett *university president*
Sullivan, Thomas Patrick *college president*

MINNESOTA

Bemidji
Martel, Petra Jean Hegstad *elementary school educator*

Bloomington
Krueger, Eugene Rex *academic program director*
Kuntz, Lila Elaine *secondary business education educator*

Circle Pines
McClellan, John R. *school system administrator*

Cokato
Thomas, Paul S. *principal*

Collegeville
Reinhart, Dietrich Thomas *university president, history educator*

Dassel
Kay, Craig *principal*

Duluth
Franks, Ronald Dwyer *university dean, psychiatrist, educator*
Ianni, Lawrence Albert *university administrator, English language educator*

Eden Prairie
McCoy, Gerald Leo *superintendent of schools*

Edina
Enger, Kathleen May *preschool administrator*

Elysian
Nickerson, James Findley *education consultant*

Grand Rapids
King, Sheryl Jayne *secondary education educator, counselor*

Hermantown
Leland, Paula Susan *educational administrator, educator*

Hopkins
Passi, Beth *school administrator*

Mankato
Rush, Richard R. *university administrator*

Maple Grove
Lamon, Beverly Ann *school system administrator*

Minneapolis
Anderson, Charles S. *college president, clergyman*

Bowie, Norman Ernest *university official, educator*
Davis, Julia McBroom *college dean, speech pathology and audiology educator*
DiGangi, Frank Edward *academic administrator*
Farber, Daniel Alan *law educator*
Ferrera, Robert James *superintendent of schools*
Gardner, William Earl *university dean*
George, Melvin Douglas *university official*
Good, David Franklin *economic historian, educator*
Hertogs, Mary Helen *educational administrator*
Hoyer, Harvey Conrad *retired college president, clergyman*
Kidwell, David Stephen *academic administrator*
Lindell, Edward Albert *former college president, religious organization administrator*
Matson, Wesley Jennings *educational administrator*
Monson, Dianne Lynn *literacy educator*
Philipson, Willard Dale *curriculum and instructional educator*
Rand, Sidney Anders *retired college administrator*
Schuh, G(eorge) Edward *university dean, agricultural economist*
Slorp, John S. *academic administrator*

Minnetonka
Vanstrom, Marilyn June *retired elementary education educator*

Moorhead
Dille, Roland Paul *college president*
Treumann, William Borgen *university dean*

Morris
Johnson, David Chester *university chancellor, sociology educator*

Northfield
Berwald, Helen Dorothy *education educator*
Bonner, Robert Elliott *dean*
†Edwards, Mark U., Jr. *college president, history educator, author*
McKinsey, Elizabeth *college dean*

Osseo
Hersch, Russell LeRoy *secondary education educator*
Ramsey, Mark *school system administrator*

Park Rapids
McNulty-Majors, Susan Rose *special education administrator*

Rosemount
Bohan, Wanda M. *secondary school educator*

Saginaw
Stauber, Marilyn Jean *educator, consultant*

Saint Cloud
Berling, John George *academic dean*
Bess, Robert O. *academic administrator*
Hofsommer, Donovan Lowell *educator, consultant*
Kallhoff, Sister Catherine *school system administrator*
Wertz, John Alan *secondary school educator*

Saint Joseph
O'Connell, Sister Colman *college president, nun*

Saint Louis Park
Dooley, David J. *elementary school principal*
Svendsbye, Lloyd August *college president, clergyman, educator*

Saint Paul
Brushaber, George Karl *academic president, minister*
Buckheit, James E. *primary and secondary education administrator*
Gavin, Robert Michael, Jr. *college president*
Graham, Charles John *university educator, former university president*
Huber, Sister Alberta *college president*
Janavaras, Basil John *business consultant, business educator*
Keffer, Charles Joseph *academic administrator*
Kerr, Sylvia Joann *educator*
MacTaggart, Terrence Joseph *academic administrator*
Osnes, Larry G. *academic administrator*
Pampusch, Anita Marie *academic administrator*
†Perry, James Alfred *natural resources and policy management educator, researcher, consultant*
Sullivan, Alfred Dewitt *university administrator*

Spring Park
Nelson, Craig Wayne *academy administrator*

Stillwater
Anderson, Burnell *principal*

Waseca
Frederick, Edward Charles *university official*

Wayzata
Fish, James Stuart *college dean, advertising consultant*

White Bear Lake
Gabrick, Robert William *secondary education educator*

Winona
DeThomasis, Brother Louis *college president*
Krueger, Darrell William *academic administrator*
Preska, Margaret Louise Robinson *education educator, institute executive*
Towers, James Mc *education educator*

MISSISSIPPI

Ackerman
Coleman, Frances McLean *secondary school educator*

Biloxi
Cozzi, Sister Joanne *school system administrator*

Cleveland
Wyatt, Forest Kent *university president*

Clinton
Eichelberger, Lisa Wright *academic administrator, nursing educator*
Nobles, Lewis *college president*

Columbus
Fant, Joseph Lewis, III *retired army officer, educator*
Rent, Clyda Stokes *university president*

Gulfport
Daffron, Martha *retired education educator*

Hattiesburg
Lucas, Aubrey Keith *university president*
Noonkester, James Ralph *retired college president*
Saucier Lundy, Karen *college dean, educator*

Holly Springs
Beckley, David Lenard *academic administrator*

Jackson
Burnham, Tom *state school system administrator*
Christ, Mary Ann *academic administrator, nursing educator*
Cullen, William *school system administrator*
Dodson, William H. *school system administrator*
Harmon, George Marion *college president*
Williams, William Lane *university administrator, anatomist*

Laurel
Masters, Beda Doris *elementary educator*

Meridian
Drawdy, Larry A. *school system administrator*
Phillips, Patricia Jeanne *retired school administrator, consultant*

Mississippi State
Hawkins, Merrill Morris *college administrator*
Lee, John Edward, Jr. *university administrator*
Mabry, Donald Joseph *university administrator, history educator*
McRae, John Malcolm *college dean, architect*
Powe, Ralph Elward *university administrator*
Zacharias, Donald Wayne *university president*

Oxford
Moorhead, Sylvester Andrew *education educator retired*

Perkinston
Parker, Ora Dean Simmons *elementary school educator*

Starkville
Martin, Theodore Krinn *former university administrator (deceased)*
Palmertree, Ruth Godron *counselor*

Tupelo
Johnson, Ruth Allen *elementary school educator*

University
Cottle, Rex L. *college dean*
Ferris, William Reynolds *folklore educator*
Leary, William James *educational administrator*
Meador, John Milward, Jr. *university dean*
Sam, Joseph *retired university dean*
Smith, Allie Maitland *university dean*

MISSOURI

Blue Springs
Hatley, Patricia Ruth *school system administrator*

Boonville
Cline, Dorothy May Stammerjohn (Mrs. Edward Wilburn Cline) *vocational school educator*

California
Wood, Mary Marie *secondary education educator*

Cape Girardeau
Stroup, Kala Mays *university president*

Clayton
Bartlett, Joe Michael *school system administrator*
Kohm, Barbara *principal*
Zimmerman, Harold Seymour *elementary school educator*

Clinton
Deskins, Gary *school system administrator*

Columbia
Adams, Algalee Pool *college dean, art educator*
Burchett, Betty Martela *science education educator*
Dyrenfurth, Michael John *vocational technical and industrial arts educator, consultant*
Gysbers, Norman Charles *education educator*
Hatley, Richard V(on) *education educator*
Keith, Everett Earnest *educator, education administrator*
Lenox, Mary Frances *academic dean*
McCollum, Clifford Glenn *college dean emeritus*
Miller, Paul Ausborn *adult education educator*
Monroe, Haskell M., Jr. *university educator*
Russell, George Albert *university president*
†Smith, Bruce L. *secondary education educator*
Wheeler, Otis V., Jr. *public school principal*

Fenton
Korn, Irene Elizabeth *elementary education educator, consultant*

Florissant
Bartlett, Robert James *principal*

Fulton
Barnett, Jahnae Harper *academic administrator*
Davidson, Robert Laurenson Dashiell *college president emeritus, philatelist*
Remley, Audrey Wright *educational administrator, psychologist*

Gallatin
Wilsted, Joy *elementary education educator, reading specialist, parenting consultant*

Hillsboro
Adkins, Gregory D. *academic administrator*

Independence
Henley, Robert Lee *school system administrator*

Jefferson City
Rayburn, Wendell Gilbert *college president*
Scott, Gary Kuper *academic administrator*

Joplin
Pulliam, Frederick Cameron *educational administrator*

Kansas City
Doyle, Wendell E. *retired educator*
Durig, James Robert *college dean*
Eubanks, Eugene Emerson *education educator, consultant*
Harvey, Thomas D. *headmaster*
Hoffer, Sharon Marie *educator*
Horsely, Willie Woodruff *educational administrator*
Isler, Mamie *secondary school principal*
Kramer, Lawrence John *college president*
†Marks, Walter *school system administrator*
†Martin, Deanna Coleman *university director*
Perkins, Sister Victoria Marie *school system administrator*
Savage, Thomas Joseph *college president, governance and planning consultant, educator, priest*
Van Ackeren, Maurice Edward *college administrator*

Liberty
Sizemore, William Christian *college president*
Tanner, Jimmie Eugene *college dean*

Manchester
Warner, Vinnie *principal*

Mansfield
Wallace, Dorothy Alene *special education administrator*

Marshall
Wymore, Luann Courtney *elementary education educator*

Maryville
Hubbard, Dean Leon *university president*
Jonagan, Glenn E. *principal*
Strating, Sharon L. *elementary school educator*

Moberly
Pelfrey, Lloyd Marvin *college president*

Normandy
Meyer, Ruth Ann *physical education and dance educator*

Parkville
Breckon, Donald John *academic administrator*

Point Lookout
Klinefelter, Sarah Stephens *division dean, radio station manager*

Richmond Heights
Chandler, James Barton *international education consultant*

Rolla
Warner, Don Lee *dean emeritus*

Saint Charles
Porterfield, Patricia Rough *education educator*

Saint Joseph
†Murphy, Janet Gorman *college president*

Saint Louis
Allen, Renee *principal*
Barth, Karl Luther *retired seminary president*
Biondi, Lawrence *university administrator, priest*
Bloomberg, Terry *early childhood education administrator*
Bohne, Jeanette Kathryn *mathematics and science educator*
Burke, Mary Leyhe *school administrator*
Byrnes, Christopher Ian *academic dean, researcher*
Cain, James Nelson *arts school administrator*
Conaway, Mary Ann *professional counselor, educator*
Danforth, William Henry *academic administrator, physician*
Deal, Joseph Maurice *university dean, art educator, photographer*
Earle, James A. *educational administrator*
Eckhoff, Sister Mary Ann *academic administrator*
Ellis, Dorsey Daniel, Jr. *dean*
Gerdine, Leigh *retired academic administrator*
Gilligan, Sandra Kaye *private school director*
Hasl, Rudolph Carl *university dean, law educator, lawyer*
Henle, Robert John *former university president*
Hunter, Thom Hugh *seminary administrator*
King, Morris Kenton *medical school dean*
Koff, Robert Hess *program director*
Krekorian, Elizabeth Anne *nursing college administrator*
Lovin, Keith Harold *university administrator, philosophy educator*
Marsh, James C., Jr. *secondary school principal*
McFarland, Mary A. *elementary/secondary school educator/administrator*
Morgan, Lawrence Allison *headmaster, educational administrator*
Mulligan, Robert William *university official, clergyman*
O'Neill, Sheila *principal*
Patton, Thomas F. *college administrator, pharmaceutical chemist*
Pfefferkorn, Michael Gene, Sr. *secondary education educator, writer*
Pfefferkorn, Sandra J. *secondary education educator*
Pflueger, M(elba) Lee *academic administrator*
Ramming, Michael Alexander *school system administrator*

Reinert, Paul Clare *university chancellor emeritus*
Schoeneberg, Joyce Eileen *secondary school biology educator*
†Stodghill, Ronald *school system administrator*
Touhill, Blanche Marie *university chancellor, history-education educator*
Truitt, William Harvey *private school educator*
Turner, Harold Edward *education educator*
Watkins, Hortense Catherine *middle school educator*
Weiss, Robert Francis *former academic administrator, religious organization administrator, consultant*

Sedalia
Noland, Gary Lloyd *vocation educational administrator*

Springfield
Ames, Jimmy Ray *education educator*
Groves, Sharon Sue *elementary education educator*
Hagerty, Paul James *school superintendent*
Moore, John Edwin, Jr. *college president*
Stovall, Richard L. *academic administrator*

University City
Flanagan, Joan Wheat (Maggie Flanagan) *educational therapist*

Warrensburg
Elliott, Eddie Mayes *college president*
Limback, E(dna) Rebecca *vocational education educator*

Webster Groves
Schenkenberg, Mary Martin *principal*

MONTANA

Antelope
Olson, Betty-Jean *elementary education educator*

Arlee
Gregory, Russell Arthur *education and training consultant*

Bigfork
Keller, Barbara Lynn *special education educator*

Billings
Carpenter, Bruce H. *academic administrator*
DeRosier, Arthur Henry, Jr. *college president*
Heiny, Robert Wayne *special education educator*
McCracken, Joe C. *school system administrator*
Surwill, Benedict Joseph, Jr. *college dean, educator*
Williams, Judy Carol *teacher*

Bozeman
Characklis, William Gregory *university research center director, engineering educator*
Goering, Kenneth Justin *college administrator*
Malone, Michael Peter *academic administrator, historian*
Pagenkopf, Andrea LeSuer *university official*
Ratliff, Gerald Lee *dean, speech and theatre educator*

Dayton
Catalfomo, Philip *university dean*

Gallatin Gateway
Monaco, Paul *academic administrator, educator, artist, writer*

Havre
Leeds, Debra Ann *primary school educator*
Windel, Robert Eugene *school system administrator*

Kalispell
Ormiston, Patricia Jane *elementary education educator*

Missoula
Dennison, George Marshel *academic administrator*
Fisher, William Henry *education educator*
Kindrick, Robert LeRoy *academic administrator, dean, English educator*
Kraft, Dennis *school system administrator*
Stevenson, Marolane *counselor*
Winston, Bente *academic administrator*

Victor
Stewart, JoAnne *secondary school educator*

NEBRASKA

Auburn
Winegardner, Rose Mary *special education educator*

Bellevue
Muller, John Bartlett *university president*

Boys Town
Peter, Val Joseph *social service administrator, educator, priest*

Gering
Harvey, Karon Lee *secondary education educator*

Grand Island
Ryan, Thomas A. *school system administrator*
Zichek, Shannon Elaine *secondary school educator*

Gretna
Riley, Kevin M. *principal*

Hartington
Meyer, Betty Jean *physical education educator*

Hastings
Larsen, Glen L. *school system administrator*

Lincoln
Bradley, Richard Edwin *retired university president*
Childs, Gayle B(ernard) *retired education educator*

Grew, Priscilla Croswell *university official, geology educator*
Hendrickson, Kent Herman *dean, librarian*
Hermance, Lyle Herbert *college official*
Janzow, Walter Theophilus *retired college administrator*
Laursen, Paul Herbert *retired university educator*
Nelson, Darrell Wayne *university administrator, scientist*
Powers, David Richard *educational administrator*
Rogers, Vance Donald *former university president*
Smith, Lewis Dennis *academic administrator*
White, John Wesley, Jr. *university president*

Madison
Mortensen-Say, Marlys (Mrs. John Theodore Say) *school system administrator*

Norfolk
Kubik, James Donald *educator*

Omaha
Banville, Guy Rene *academic dean*
Bauer, Otto Frank *university official, communication educator*
Fjell, Mick *principal*
Garofolo, Ronald Joseph *drafting and architecture education educator*
Haselwood, Eldon LaVerne *education educator*
McEniry, Robert Francis *education educator*
Morrison, Michael Gordon *university president, clergyman, history educator*
Mulcahey, Sister Patricia *school system administrator*
Newton, John Milton *acadmeic administrator, psychology educator*
O'Brien, Richard L(ee) *academic administrator, physician, cell biologist*
Peck, Ernest James, Jr. *academic administrator*
Schlessinger, Bernard S. *retired university dean*
†Schuerman, Norbert Joel *school superintendent*
Tucker, Michael *elementary school principal*
Weber, Delbert Dean *university administrator*

Plainview
Mauch, Jeannine Ann *elementary education educator*

Scottsbluff
Weichenthal, Burton A. *educational administrator, beef specialist*

Valley
Lerew, Everett Duane *special education administrator*

Wayne
Mash, Donald J. *college president*

NEVADA

Battle Mountain
Hensley, E. Leon *school system administrator*

Dyer
Howard, Sherwin Ward *college president*

Fallon
Plants, Walter Dale *elementary education educator, minister*

Glenbrook
Buscaglia, (Felice) Leo(nardo) *special education educator, author*

Hawthorne
Graham, Lois Charlotte *retired educator*
Sortland, Trudith Ann *educator, speech and language therapist*

Henderson
Benson, James DeWayne *university administrator*

Incline Village
Hiatt, Robert Worth *former university president*

Incline Vlg
White, Richard Hugh *dean student affairs*

Las Vegas
Brown, Lori Lipman *secondary school educator*
†Cram, Brian Manning *school system administrator*
Cwerenz-Maxime, Virginia Margaret *secondary education educator*
Harter, Carol Clancey *university president, English language educator*
Iorio, John Emil *retired education educator*
McDonald, Malcolm Gideon *education educator*
Sestini, Virgil Andrew *secondary education educator*
Zehm, Stanley James *education educator*

Lovelock
Kiley, James P. *retired school system administrator*

North Las Vegas
Regan, John Bernard (Jack Regan) *community relations executive, assemblyman*
Williams, Mary Irene *college administrator*

Reno
Cain, Edmund Joseph *education educator, emeritus dean*
Clarke, Janice Cessna *principal*
Crowley, Joseph Neil *academic administrator*
Daugherty, Robert Melvin, Jr. *university dean, medical educator*
Gifford, Gerald Frederic *education educator*
Humphrey, Neil Darwin *university president, retired*
Loveless, Edward Eugene *education educator, musician*
Perry, Jean Louise *dean*

NEW HAMPSHIRE

Amherst
Collins, Paul D. *principal*
Lalley, Richard A. *school system administrator*

Chester
Preston, Faith *college president*

Durham
Farrell, William Joseph *university chancellor*
Lawson, John H. *university official*
Nitzschke, Dale Frederick *university president*
Palmer, Stuart Hunter *academic dean, sociology educator*
Perry, Bradford Kent *academic administrator*
Powers, John H. *school system administrator*
Ritvo, Roger Alan *university dean, health management-policy educator*

Exeter
Erickson, Raymond Leroy *dean, psychologist*
McLaughlin, Anne Elizabeth *secondary education educator*
O'Donnell, Kendra Stearns *principal*

Goffstown
Glines, Jon Malcolm *secondary education educator*

Greenfield
†Wheelock, Major William, Jr. *college administrator*

Hancock
Brown, David Warfield *retired academic administrator*

Hanover
Birnie, Richard Williams *graduate studies dean*
Blaydon, Colin Campbell *university professor*
Freedman, James Oliver *university president, lawyer*
Hennessey, John William, Jr. *academic administrator*
Hutchinson, Charles Edgar *engineering educator, dean emeritus*
Rieser, Leonard Moos *college administrator, physics educator*
Wright, James Edward *dean, history educator*

Henniker
Arnesen, Deborah Arnie *educator*
Cummiskey, J. Kenneth *former college president*
O'Connell, William Raymond, Jr. *college president*

Hudson
Blanchard, Glenn Robert *principal*

Keene
Hickey, Delina Rose *education educator*
Yarosewick, Stanley J. *academic administrator, physicist*

Kingston
Curtis, Staton Russell *university dean*

Lebanon
Jillette, Arthur George, Jr. *school system administrator*

Manchester
Comeau, Reginald Alfred *academic administrator, consultant*
DeFelice, Jonathan Peter *college president, priest*
Gustafson, Richard Alrick *college president*

Pelham
Holmes, Richard Dale *secondary educator, historical consultant*

NEW JERSEY

Atlantic City
Stuart, Eve Lynne *elementary education educator*

Atlantic Highlands
Crowley, Cynthia Johnson *secondary school educator*
Fink, Dolores Hesse *special education educator*

Beachwood
Newman, Justina Anne *nursery school administrator, consultant*

Belleville
Pincus, George *university dean, engineering educator*

Bellmawr
Wilke, Constance Regina *elementary education educator*

Brick
Gluck, Lucille Gindoff *educator*

Camden
Gordon, Walter Kelly *provost, English language educator*
Peacock, Patricia Anne *academic program director*

Cedar Grove
Nash, Annamarie *secondary education educator*

Cliffside Park
Jaspen, Nathan *educational statistics educator*

Clifton
Petrucelli, Frank *school system administrator*
Roberts, Robert Charles *secondary education educator*

Columbus
Sikora, Jane Ann *secondary education educator, reference librarian*

East Brunswick
Candelmo, Lee France *special education educator*
Fisher, Lucille *principal*
Haupin, Elizabeth Carol *retired secondary school educator*
King, Charles M. *principal*
Lund, Daryl Bert *college dean*

East Hanover
Morris, Patricia Smith *media specialist, author, educator*

Edison
Danzis, Rose Marie *emeritus college president*

Elmer
Slavoff, Harriet Emonds *learning disabilities teacher, consultant*

Elmwood Park
Blume, Paula Jollin *special education educator*

Englewood
Jones, Stephen Powell *school administrator*

Fair Lawn
Panella, Elizabeth M. *secondary school principal*

Fort Lee
Huppuch, Winfield Adelbert, III *secondary education educator, publishing executive*
Sugarman, Alan William *educational administrator*

Glassboro
Gephardt, Donald Louis *college official*
James, Herman Delano *college administrator*

Haddon Heights
Gwiazda, Stanley John *university dean*

Highland Lakes
Ansorge, Helen J. *retired elementary school educator*

Highland Park
Broggi, Barbara Ann *elementary education educator, staff developer*

Hoboken
Raveché, Harold Joseph *university administrator, physical chemist*

Howell
Borowick, Bernadine Ann *supervisor of instruction*

Jersey City
Foster, Delores Jackson *elementary school principal*
Fox, Thomas George *academic adminstrator, healthscience educator*
Means, Fred Ernest *dean*
Reynolds, Scott Walton *academic administrator*

Lake Hiawatha
Schonfeld, Rudolf Leopold *secondary school educator*

Lakewood
Williams, Barbara Anne *college president*

Lawrenceville
Stehle, Edward Raymond *secondary education educator, school system administrator*
Tharney, Leonard John *education educator, consultant*

Lincroft
Pollock, William John *secondary school administrator*
Sullivan, Brother Jeremiah Stephen *former college president*

Linden
Hart, Paul *dean, poet, educator*
Malec, Ruth Ellen *special services director*

Lindenwold
Tucker-Keto, Claudia A. *academic administrator*

Little Falls
Nash, James John *superintendent*

Little Ferry
Barbarow, Thomas Steven *public school system administrator*

Madison
Kean, Thomas H. *academic administrator, former governor*

Mahwah
Scott, Robert Allyn *college administrator*

Margate City
Weiss, Mordechai *principal*

Medford
Konstantinos, K. Kiki *school system administrator*

Mendham
Posunko, Barbara *elementary education educator*
Posunko, Linda Mary *elementary education educator*

Montclair
Strobert, Barbara *principal*

Neshanic Station
Weicksel, Charlene Marie *principal*

New Brunswick
Carman, John Herbert *elementary education educator*
Dill, Ellis Harold *university dean*
Garner, Charles William *educational administration educator, consultant*
Nelson, Jack Lee *education educator*
Reock, Ernest C., Jr. *retired government services educator and academic director*
Tanner, Daniel *curriculum theory educator*
Wheeler, Kenneth William *historian, educator*

Newark
Abrams, Roger I. *academic dean, labor arbitrator*
Bergen, Stanley Silvers, Jr. *university president, physician*
Chagnon, Joseph V. *school system administrator*
Covington-Winrow, Carolyn *school administrator*
Fenster, Saul K. *university president*
Hollander, Toby Edward *education educator*
Lanzoni, Vincent *medical school dean*
Murray, Constance Ann *college dean*

Pfeffer, Edward Israel *educational administrator*
Starks, Florence Elizabeth *special education educator*
Thomas, Gary L. *academic administrator*

North Branch
Gartlan, Philip M. *secondary school director*

Old Bridge
Swett, Stephen Frederick, Jr. *principal*

Paramus
Plucinsky, Constance Marie *school counselor, supervisor*

Paterson
Pulhamus, Marlene Louise *elementary school educator*

Perth Amboy
DeFiore, Leonard F. *academic administrator*

Phillipsburg
Stull, Frank Walter *educator*

Piscataway
Colaizzi, John Louis *college dean*
Rudczynski, Andrew B. *academic administrator, medical researcher*

Pomona
Farris, Vera King *college president*
Gasbarro, Norman John, Jr. *educational administrator*

Princeton
Gillespie, Thomas William *theological seminary administrator, religion educator*
Howarth, William (Louis) *education educator, writer*
Jahn, Robert George *university dean, engineering educator*
Labalme, Patricia Hochschild *educational administrator*
Malkiel, Nancy Weiss *college dean, history educator*
Shapiro, Harold Tafler *university president, economist*
Timpane, Philip Michael *educator, foundation official*
Williams, Bertha Elizabeth Griffin *elementary education educator*

Ridgefield Park
Ranone, John Louis *school board executive*

Rockaway
Allen, Dorothea *secondary education educator*

Roselle Park
Zahumeny, Janet Mae *secondary education educator*

Rutherford
Barzanti, Sergio *educator*

Saddle River
Lehmann, Doris Elizabeth *elementary education educator*

Scotch Plains
Johnson, Valerie Anne *elementary education educator*

Skillman
Messner, Richard Stephen *school system administrator*

Somerdale
Morgan, Mary Anne *secondary education educator*

South Orange
Harahan, Robert E. *rector*

South Plainfield
Goode, Bobby Claude *secondary education educator*

Sparta
Harrison, Alice Kathleen *retired elementary educato*
Saxe, Thelma Richards *secondary education educator, consultant*

Springfield
Merachnik, Donald *superintendent of schools*

Summit
Rossey, Paul William *school superintendent, university president*

Teaneck
Mertz, Francis James *academic administrator*
Pischl, Adolph John *school administrator*

Tenafly
Gerst, Elizabeth Carlsen (Mrs. Paul H. Gerst) *university dean, researcher, educator*

Titusville
†Swissler, Robert *educational consultant*

Trenton
Eickhoff, Harold Walter *college president, humanities educator*
Losty, Barbara Paul *college official*
Megna, Jerome Francis *academic administrator, educator*
Pruitt, George Albert *college president*
Stein, Sandra Lou *educational psychologist, educator*

Union
Hennings, Dorothy Grant (Mrs. George Hennings) *educational educator*

Union City
Bozoyan, Sylvia *elementary school educator*

Upper Montclair
Coffin, Charlsa Lee *Montessori educator, writer, artist*
Reid, Irvin D. *academic official*

Washington
De Sanctis, Vincent *college president*

Wayne
Benedict, Theresa Marie *mathematics educator*
Speert, Arnold *college president, chemistry educator*

West Long Branch
Rouse, Robert Sumner *former college official*
Stafford, Rebecca *college president, sociologist*

West New York
Aquino, Felix John *college administrator*

Westfield
McDevitt, Brian Peter *educational consultant*

Westmont
Danner, Charles L. *elementary education educator*

Westwood
Cullen, Ruth Enck *reading specialist, elementary education educator*

NEW MEXICO

Albuquerque
Anaya, Rudolfo *educator, writer*
Caplan, Edwin Harvey *university dean, accounting educator*
Drummond, Harold Dean *education educator*
Garcia, F. Chris *academic administrator, political science educator, public opinion researcher*
Lattman, Laurence Harold *retired academic administrator*
May, Gerald William *university administrator, educator, civil engineering consultant*
Norman, Ralph David *consulting psychologist, former university administrator*
Peck, Richard Earl *academic administrator, playwright, novelist*
Travelstead, Chester Coleman *former educational administrator*
Zink, Lee B. *academic administrator, economist, educator*

Artesia
Sarwar, Barbara Duce *school system administrator*

Crownpoint
Tolino, Arlene Becenti *elementary education educator*

Cuba
Lopez, Joe A. *school system administrator*

Gallup
Maikowski, Thomas Robert *priest, educational director*

Las Cruces
Easterling, Kathy *elementary school principal*
Elliott, Richard L. *school administrator*
Gale, Thomas Martin *university dean*

Los Alamos
Engel, Emily Flachmeier *school administrator*

Mesilla
Willey, Darrell S. *education educator*

Mesilla Park
Shutt, Frances Barton *special education educator*

Montezuma
Geier, Philip Otto, III *college president*

Raton
Robinson, Janie Monette *education educator*

Ruidoso
Coe, Elizabeth Ann *elementary education educator*

Santa Fe
Agresto, John *college president*
Bond, Thomas Alden *university president*
Kasbeer, Stephen Frederick *university official*

Silver City
Paez, Carolyn Jean *secondary education educator*
Snedeker, John Haggner *university president*

Univ Of New Mexico
Hull, McAllister Hobart, Jr. *retired university administrator*

NEW YORK

Albany
Burke, Joseph C. *university administrator*
Hughs, Richard Earl *business school dean*
†Kadamus, James A. *educational administrator*
Kiepper, James Julius *education educator*
Kinney, Thomas J. *adult education educator*
†Prieto, Claudio R. *academic administrator, lawyer*
Robbins, Cornelius (Van Vorse) *education administration educator*
Thornton, Maurice *university administrator*
Vaccaro, Louis Charles *college president*

Alfred
Coll, Edward Girard, Jr. *university president*
Ott, Walter Richard *academic administrator*

Alfred Station
Love, Robert Lyman *educational consulting company executive*

Amenia
Gilbert, Linda Johanna *special education administrator*

Annandale On Hudson
†Botstein, Leon *college president, historian, conductor, music critic*

Auburn
Eldred, Thomas Gilbert *secondary education educator, historian*

Batavia
Steiner, Stuart *college president*

Bellmore
Schlossberg, Fred Paul *elementary education educator*

Binghamton
Defleur, Lois B. *university president, sociology educator*
Feisel, Lyle Dean *university dean, electrical engineering educator*

Briarcliff Manor
Radandt, Friedhelm K. *college president*

Bridgehampton
Edwards, John W. *school superintendent*

Brockport
Harter, Michael Thomas *college dean, health sciences consultant*
Studer, Ginny *college dean*
Van de Wetering, John E(dward) *college president*

Bronx
Fernandez, Ricardo R. *university administrator*
Iazetti, Anthony M. *school system administrator*
Nathanson, Melvyn Bernard *university provost, mathematician*
Rothstein, Anne Louise *education educator, college official*
Scanlan, Thomas Joseph *college president, educator*
Smith, Sharon Patricia *university dean*

Bronxville
Ilchman, Alice Stone *college president, former government official*
Kaplan, Barbara *college dean*
Mau, Dwayne Holger *minister*

Brooklyn
Alfano, Edward Charles, Jr. *elementary education educator*
Barabash, Claire *special education administrator, psychologist*
Birenbaum, William M. *former university president*
Bugliarello, George *university president*
Comer, John F. *superintendent*
Edelstein, Brenda *school administrator*
Gresser, Carol A. *school system administrator*
Handlin, James Patrick *headmaster*
Kaplan, Frada M. *principal, special education educator*
Kimmich, Christoph Martin *academic administrator, educator*
O'Connor, Sister George Aquin (Margaret M. O'Connor) *college president, sociology educator*
Sullivan, Donald *college president*
Wasserman, Arnold Saul *academic dean, industrial design executive*
Williams, Emma Louise *elementary education educator*
Williams, William Magavern *headmaster*
Wolfe, Ethyle Renee (Mrs. Coleman Hamilton Benedict) *college administrator*

Brookville
Woodsworth, Anne *university dean, librarian*

Buchanan
Somerstein, Aurora Abrera *educator*

Buffalo
Birch, David William *college official*
Gemmett, Robert James *university dean, English language educator*
Greiner, William Robert *university administrator, educator, lawyer*
Johnstone, D. Bruce *university administrator*
Ottenbacher, Kenneth John *dean, educator*
Richardson, F. C. *academic administrator*
Seidl, Fredrick William *dean, social work educator*
Stull, G. Alan *university dean, health professions educator*
Triggle, David John *university dean, consultant*
Wiesen, Richard A. *academic administrator, educator*

Canton
Fleming, Barbara Joan *university administrator*
Peterson, Patti McGill *college president*

Castleton On Hudson
Lanford, Oscar Erasmus, Jr. *retired university vice chancellor*

Centereach
McAllister, Dee Theresa *elementary education educator*

Centerport
Mallett, Helene Gettler *elementary education educator*

Chittenango
Schultz, Ruth Anne *home economics educator, parenting educator, consultant*

Clifton Park
Schmitt, Roland Walter *retired academic administrator*

Clinton
Fuller, Ruthann *principal*

Cold Spring Harbor
Huffman, Carol Koster *middle school educator*
Roberts, Francis Joy *secondary education educator, journalist*

Corona
Cole, Donald H. *middle school educator*

De Witt
Ball, Baxter Fenton, Jr. *secondary school administrator*

Delmar
Quackenbush, Roger E. *secondary education educator*

Dix Hills
Murphy, Edward J. *school system administrator*

Dobbs Ferry
Clarke, Pamela Jones *headmaster*
Moore, Sandra M. *director of admissions*

Dunkirk
Smith, Claire Laremont *language educator*

East Aurora
Spahn, Mary Attea *retired educator*
Woodard, Carol Jane *educational consultant*

East Islip
Somerville, Daphine Holmes *elementary education educator*

East Meadow
Beyer, Norma Warren *secondary education educator*

Elmhurst
Lester, Lance Gary *education educator, researcher*

Elmira
Burke, Rita Hoffmann *educational administrator*
Meier, Thomas Keith *college president, English educator*

Farmingdale
Cipriani, Frank Anthony *college president*

Floral Park
Goldstein, George A. *school system administrator*
Scricca, Diane Bernadette *principal*

Flushing
Brush, George W. *college president*
Chabora, Peter Christian *academic administrator, researcher, educator*
Sessoms, Allen Lee *academic administrator, former diplomat, physicist*

Forest Hills
Pinto, Rosalind *retired educator, civic volunteer*
Rogers, Philip Virgilius, Jr. *headmaster*

Fredonia
MacPhee, Donald Albert *academic administrator*
Mac Vittie, Robert William *retired college administrator*

Friendship
Kingdon, Mary Oneida Grace *elementary education educator*

Garden City
Kane, Jeffrey *academic dean*
Okulski, John Allen *principal*
Webb, Igor Michael *university administrator*

Geneva
Hersh, Richard H. *academic administrator*

Glen Head
Boyrer, Elaine M. *principal*

Glenmont
Block, Murray Harold *educational consultant*
Robillard, Donald J. *elementary school principal*

Greece
Ryan-Johnson, Deborah *principal*

Greenvale
Cook, Edward Joseph *college president*
Gillespie, John Thomas *university administrator*
Steinberg, David Joel *academic administrator, historian, educator*

Greenwood
Rollins, June Elizabeth *elementary education educator*

Hamilton
Cappeto, Michael Arnold *educator*
DeBoer, George Edward *education educator*
†Grabois, Neil Robert *college president*
Jones, Howard Langworthy *educational administrator, consultant*

Hauppauge
Oschmann, Joan Edythe *gifted and elementary education educator*

Hempstead
Berliner, Herman Albert *university provost and dean, economics educator*
Haynes, Ulric St. Clair, Jr. *university dean*
Shuart, James Martin *university president*

Hicksville
O'Flaherty, Lucy Louise *secondary education educator*

Hilton
Scutt, Ed *English language educator*

Horseheads
Cusimano, Adeline Mary *educational administrator*
Mortimer, Garth Eugene *mathematics educator*

Houghton
Chamberlain, Daniel Robert *college president*
Luckey, Robert Reuel Raphael *retired academic administrator*

Huntington
D'Addario, Alice Marie *school administrator*

Huntington Station
Braun, Ludwig *educational technology consultant*

Ithaca
Ben Daniel, David Jacob *entrepreneurship educator, consultant*
Cooke, William Donald *university administrator, chemistry educator*
Corson, Dale Raymond *retired university president, physicist*
Cotton, Dorothy Foreman *former director student activities, consultant*
Craft, Harold Dumont, Jr. *university official, radio astronomer*
Firebaugh, Francille Maloch *university official*
Hopcroft, John Edward *dean, computer science educator*
Kubiak, John Michael *academic administrator*
Longin, Thomas Charles *academic administrator*
Merten, Alan Gilbert *university dean*
Nesheim, Malden C. *university administrator*
Oblak, John Byron *academic administrator*
Phemister, Robert David *college dean*
Rawlings, Hunter Ripley, III *university administrator*
Rhodin, Thor Nathaniel *educational administrator*
Scott, Norman Roy *academic administrator, agricultural engineering educator*
Seibert, Mary Lee *college official*
Streett, William Bernard *university dean, engineering educator*
Tynes, Theodore Archibald *educational administrator*
Weinstein, Leonard Harlan *institute program director*
Whalen, James Joseph *college president*

Jamaica
Bartilucci, Andrew Joseph *university administrator*
Cline, Janice Claire *education educator*
Harrington, Donald James *university president*
Melton, Marie Frances *university dean*
Sciame, Joseph *university administrator*

Jamestown
Benke, Paul Arthur *college president*

Jericho
Mandery, Mathew M. *principal*
Martin, David S. *educator, administrator*

Kenmore
Vienne, Dorothy Titus *school principal*

Kings Park
LoPresti, Marilyn Angela *school system administrator*
Smith, Norma Jane *elementary education educator*

Kings Point
Matteson, Thomas T. *academic administrator*
Mazek, Warren F(elix) *academic administrator, economics educator*

Larchmont
Gallaher, Carolyn Combs *secondary education educator*

Lindenhurst
Gentile, Patricia M. *elementary education educator*

Liverpool
Sharp, Walter Len *secondary educator*

Long Beach
Thompson, Dorothy Barnard *elementary school educator*

Loudonville
McConville, William *academic administrator*

Mahopac
Gould, Sandra M. *elementary school principal*
†Silbert, Alvin Jay *secondary physics educator*
Silbert, Linda Bress *educational counselor, therapist*

Middle Island
Mastrion, Guy *secondary school principal*

Mineola
Salten, David George *university administrator, educator*

Moriches
Casciano, Paul *principal*

Nanuet
Gold, Arline *educational administrator*

New Paltz
Chandler, Alice *university president, educator*

New Rochelle
Gallagher, John Francis *academic administrator, education educator*
Kelly, Sister Dorothy Ann *college president*
Sweeny, Stephen Jude *academic administrator*
Wolotsky, Hyman *retired college dean*

New York
Bloom, David E. *university educator*
Brademas, John *retired university president, former congressman*
Brenner, Egon *university official, education consultant*
Burton, John Campbell *university dean, educator, consultant*
Campbell, Mary Schmidt *dean art school*
Caputo, David Armand *university president, political scientist educator*
Carey, James William *university dean, educator, researcher*
Claster, Jill Nadell *university administrator, history educator*
†Cohen, Audrey C. *college president*
Cohen, Saul Bernard *former college president, geographer*
Consagra, Sophie Chandler *academy administrator*
Conyard, Shirley Jean *college dean*
Daly, George Garman *college dean, educator*
Duggan, Rosemary H. *vocational administrator*

Laing, Penelope Gamble *art educator*
Leggett, Donald Yates *academic administrator*
Zauner, Christian Walter *university dean, exercise physiologist, consultant*

Hampstead
Leaven, Glorious Sharpless *special education educator, reading specialist*

Hendersonville
Byrd, Charles L. *school system administrator*
Jones, J(ohn) Charles *education educator*
Payne, Gerald Oliver *elementary education educator*

High Point
Howard, Lou Dean Graham *elementary education educator*
Martinson, Jacob Christian, Jr. *university president*

Hillsborough
Stockstill, James William *secondary school educator*

Kinston
Matthis, Eva Mildred Boney *college official*
Petteway, Samuel Bruce *college president*

Kure Beach
Funk, Frank E. *retired university dean*

Laurinburg
Reuschling, Thomas Lynn *academic administrator, consultant*
Snead, Eleanor Leroy Marks *secondary school educator*

Liberty
Link, Eleanor Ann *elementary education educator*

Lincolnton
Saine, Betty Boston *elementary school educator*

Mars Hill
Bentley, Fred Blake *academic administrator*

Monroe
Griffin, Gwyn *secondary school principal*
Rorie, Nancy Katheryn *elementary and secondary school educator*

Montreat
De Jong, Arthur Jay *education consultant, former university president*

Mount Holly
Davis, Frank William, Jr. *elementary and secondary school educator*

Mount Olive
Raper, William Burkette *retired college president*

Mount Ulla
Kluttz, Henry G. *principal*

Murfreesboro
Whitaker, Bruce Ezell *college president*

Oxford
Pruitt, Dorothy J. Gooch *home economics educator, retired educational administrator*

Pittsboro
Lewis, Henry Wilkins *university administrator, lawyer, educator*
Magill, Samuel Hays *retired college administrator, higher education consultant*
Robinson, Ormsbee Wright *educational consultant*

Raleigh
Buchanan, David Royal *associate dean*
Dolce, Carl John *education administration educator*
Dornan, John Neill *public policy center professional*
Fadum, Ralph Eigil *university dean*
Gustafson, Sarah *elementary education educator*
Jividen, Loretta Ann Harper *secondary school educator*
Maidon, Carolyn Howser *academic program administrator*
Malone, Thomas Francis *university administrator, meteorologist*
McKinney, Charles Cecil *investment company executive*
Menius, Arthur Clayton, Jr. *former university dean*
Meyer, Lois Ann *religious school system administrator*
†Michael, Joan Yvonne Johnson *dean, psychologist*
Monteith, Larry King *university chancellor*
Page, Anne Ruth *gifted education educator, education specialist*
Parramore, Barbara Mitchell *education educator*
Poulton, Bruce Robert *former university chancellor*
Robinson, Prezell Russell *college administrator*
Rochelle, Lugenia *academic administrator*
Shaw, Talbert O. *university president*
Winstead, Nash Nicks *university administrator, phytopathologist*
Wynne, Johnny Calvin *university dean, plant breeding researcher*

Rockingham
Robertson, Ralph S. *secondary school principal*

Rocky Mount
Gibbs, V. Diane *dean*

Shelby
Edgar, Ruth R. *retired educator*

Statesville
Heymann, Hans Paulsen *community college administrator*

Troy
Gasper, Theodore Howard, Jr. *college president*

Whiteville
Scott, Stephen Carlos *college president*

Wilmington
Cahill, Charles L. *university administrator, chemistry educator*
Dewey, Ralph Jay *headmaster*
Leutze, James Richard *academic administrator, television producer and host*
McManus, Hugh F. *principal*
Wagoner, William Hampton *university chancellor*

Wilson
Hemby, James B., Jr. *college president*

Winston Salem
Black, David Charles *headmaster*
Ewing, Alexander Cochran *chancellor*
Janeway, Richard *university official*
Stroupe, Henry Smith *university dean*
Thompson, Cleon F., Jr. *university administrator*
†Thrift, Julianne Still *academic administrator*
Wilson, Edwin Graves *university official*

NORTH DAKOTA

Bismarck
Evanson, Barbara Jean *middle school education educator*
Joersz, Fran Woodmansee *secondary education educator*

Bottineau
Smith, J. W. *dean*

Devils Lake
Etemad, Sharon L. *dean*

Dickinson
Morud, Rollie D. *school system administrator*

Fargo
Ozbun, Jim L. *academic administrator*

Grand Forks
Baker, Kendall L. *academic administrator*
Clifford, Thomas John *university president*
O'Kelly, Bernard *university dean*
Sand, Phyllis Sue Newnam (Phyllis Sue Newnam) *retired special education educator*

Jamestown
Walker, James Silas *college official*

Minot
Shaar, H. Erik *academic administrator*

Williston
Stevens, Garvin L. *college dean*

OHIO

Ada
Freed, DeBow *college president*

Akron
Auburn, Norman Paul *university president*
Barker, Harold Kenneth *former university dean*
Elliott, Peggy Gordon *university president*
Kelley, Frank Nicholas *dean*
Kodish, Arline Betty *principal*
Seiberling, John Frederick *former congressman, law educator, lawyer*
Stroll, Beverly Marie *elementary school principal*

Alliance
Weber, Ronald Gilbert *retired college president*

Andover
Mathay, John Preston *elementary education educator*

Ansonia
Spencer, Rex LeRoy *secondary education educator*

Ashtabula
Mahan, John K. *dean*

Athens
Bruning, James Leon *university official, educator*
Glidden, Robert Burr *university president, musician, educator*
Miller, Richard Irwin *education educator, university administrator*
†Parmer, Jess Norman *university official, educator*
Ping, Charles Jackson *university administrator, educator*

Bedford Heights
†Schuman, Nancy Kathleen *secondary education educator*

Berea
Malicky, Neal *college president*

Bowling Green
Olscamp, Paul James *academic administrator*

Brecksville
Johnson, L. Neil *school system administrator*

Canton
Herritt, David R. *elementary education educator*

Centerville
Mattia, Frank J. *secondary school principal*

Chagrin Falls
Brown, Jeanette Grasselli *university official*
Hawley, Richard Alan *headmaster, writer*
Phillips, Dorothy Ormes *elementary education educator*

Chesapeake
Harris, Bob L(ee) *principal*

Chillicothe
New, Eloise Ophelia *special education educator*

Cincinnati
Baker, Norman Robert *education educator*
†Brandt, J. Michael *school system administrator*
Briggs, Henry Payson, Jr. *headmaster*
Campbell, Patricia Elaine *elementary education educator*
Gosling, David *university administrator, urban design educator*
Gottschalk, Alfred *college president*
Greengus, Samuel *academic administrator, religion educator*
Harrison, Donald Carey *academic administrator, cardiologist*
Harte, Sandra Wiswell *gifted education educator*
Hoff, James Edwin *university president*
Hoffman, Donna Coy *educator*
Hyre, James G. *educational administrator*
Kohl, David *dean, librarian*
Nester, William Raymond, Jr. *retired university chancellor and educator*
Papadakis, Constantine N. *dean, civil engineering educator*
Smith, Gregory Allgire *academic director*
Smith, Joyce Camille *elementary education educator*
Steger, Joseph A. *university president*
Voluse, Charles Rodger, III *education educator*
Wentsler, Gertrude Josephine *secondary history educator*
Werner, Robert Joseph *college dean, music educator*
Winkler, Henry Ralph *retired university president, historian*

Cleveland
†Bassett, John E. *dean, English educator*
Bernard, Lowell Francis *academic administrator, educator, consultant*
Boyd, Richard Alfred *school system administrator*
Carter, Bertha Mae *education company executive, consultant*
Cullis, Christopher Ashley *dean, biology educator*
Diederich, Anne Marie *college president*
Gronick, Patricia Ann Jacobsen *school system administrator*
McArdle, Richard Joseph *academic administrator*
McCullough, Joseph *college president emeritus*
Mc Murrin, Lee Ray *educational administrator*
Moss, Thomas Henry *university dean, physicist*
Nickerson, Gary Lee *secondary education educator*
Parker, Robert Frederic *university dean emeritus*
Pytte, Agnar *university president*
Ramicone, John R. *school system administrator*
Sherrill, Gladys Marie *elementary education educator*
Sims, J. Taylor *academic administrator*
Van Ummersen, Claire A(nn) *university president, biologist, educator*
Weidenthal, Maurice David (Bud Weidenthal) *educational administrator, journalist*
Wertheim, Sally Harris *academic administrator, dean, education educator*
Whittington-Gold, Iris *community college educator*
Zdanis, Richard Albert *academic administrator*

Columbus
Alutto, Joseph Anthony *university dean, management educator*
Armes, Walter Scott *vocational school administrator*
Baughman, George Washington, III *retired university official, financial consultant*
Beytagh, Francis Xavier, Jr. *college dean, lawyer*
Blackmore, Josiah H. *university president, lawyer, educator*
Canzani, Joseph V. *academic administrator*
Cole, Clarence Russell *college dean*
Cottrell, David Alton *school system administrator*
Fields, Henry William *college dean*
Gee, Elwood Gordon *university administrator*
Hayes, Edward F. *academic administrator*
Hermann, Charles F. *academic director, political science educator*
Koenigsknecht, Roy A. *university dean*
Meuser, Fredrick William *retired seminary president, church historian*
Otte, Paul John *college administrator, consultant, trainer*
Parks, Darrell Lee *vocational education contultant*
Ryan, Ray Darl, Jr. *academic administrator*
Salgia, Tansukh Jawaharlal *academic administrator*
Silcott, James *principal*
Stephens, Thomas M(aron) *education educator*
Walters, Everett *retired university official, author*
Yoder, Amos *university research official*

Concord
Watterson, Joyce Grande *editor, publisher*

Curtice
Cashen, Elizabeth Anne *elementary school educator*

Dayton
Bowman, Ed *principal*
Fitz, Brother Raymond L. *university president*
Gies, Frederick John *education educator, university dean*
Heft, James Lewis *academic administrator, theology educator*
Martin, James Gilbert *university provost emeritus*
Ponitz, David H. *academic administrator*
Przemieniecki, Janusz Stanislaw *college dean, engineer*
Rowe, Joseph Everett *electrical engineering educator, administrator*
Uphoff, James Kent *education educator*

Delaware
Courtice, Thomas Barr *college president*

Dublin
Felger, Ralph William *retired military officer, educator*

Elyria
Skillicorn, Judy Pettibone *gifted/talented education coordinator*
Ugwu, David Egbo *academic director, consulting company executive*

Findlay
Draper, David Eugene *seminary president*

Forest Park
Ashley, Lynn *educator, consultant, administrator*

Gahanna
Chappell, Michelle R. *elementary education educator*

Gambier
Browning, Reed S. *college official*
Gunton, James Douglas *academic administrator*
Jordan, Philip Harding, Jr. *academic administrator*

Granville
Myers, Michele Tolela *academic administrator*

Harrison
Stoll, Robert W. *principal*

Hiram
Jagow, Elmer *retired college president*
Oliver, G(eorge) Benjamin *academic administrator, philosophy educator*

Kent
Buttlar, Rudolph Otto *college dean*
Cartwright, Carol Ann *university president*
Du Mont, Rosemary Ruhig *university administrator*
Schwartz, Michael *university president, sociology educator*
Tolliver, Don L. *dean library and media services*
Vars, Gordon Forrest *education educator*

Kettering
Taylor, Billie Wesley *secondary education educator*

Kingston
Mathew, Martha Sue Cryder *retired education educator*

Lima
Meek, Violet Imhof *dean*

Magnolia
Zimmerman, Judith Rose *art educator*

Mansfield
Ogden, William Michael *school system administrator*
Riedl, John Orth *university dean*

Marietta
Ling, Dwight L. *college administrator, history educator*

Mechanicsburg
Maynard, Joan *education educator*

Mentor
Davis, Barbara Snell *principal*

Millersburg
Childers, Lawrence Jeffrey *superintendent of schools*

Mount Vernon
Nease, Stephen Wesley *college president*

New Concord
Speck, Samuel Wallace, Jr. *academic administrator*

New Philadelphia
Doughten, Mary Katherine (Molly Doughten) *retired secondary education educator*
Goforth, Mary Elaine Davey *secondary education educator*

Newark
Fortaleza, Judith Ann *school system administrator*
Greenstein, Julius Sidney *academic administrator, educator*

Niles
Linden, Carol Marie *special education educator*

North Canton
Shadle, Donna A. Francis *elementary education educator*

Oberlin
Carrier, Samuel Crowe, III *college official*
Dye, Nancy Schrom *academic administrator, history educator*
MacKay, Alfred F. *dean, philosophy educator*

Oxford
Dizney, Robert Edward *retired secondary education educator*
Pearson, Paul Guy *university president emeritus*
Shriver, Phillip Raymond *university president*
Thompson, Bertha Boya *retired educator*

Pepper Pike
†Roberts, Albert George *school administrator*

South Euclid
Loehr, Marla *college president*

Springfield
Cantrell, John L. *secondary education educator*
Dominick, Charles Alva *college official*
Kinnison, William Andrew *university president*
Reck, W(aldo) Emerson *retired university administrator, public relations consultant, writer*

Steubenville
Corr, Sister Mary Ann *school system administrator*

Sugar Grove
Young, Nancy Henrietta Moe *elementary education educator*

Sylvania
Heuschele, Sharon Jo *university program director*
Sampson, Earldine Robison *education educator*

Tiffin
Cassell, William Comyn *college president*

Toledo
Billups, Norman Fredrick *college dean, pharmacist*
Binkley, Jonathan Andrew *secondary education/junior college educator*
Heinrichs, Mary Ann *former dean*

Horton, Frank Elba *university official, geography educator*
Ingle, Kay Sue *elementary education educator*
Proefrock, Carl Kenneth *academic medical administrator*
Quick, Albert Thomas *academic law administrator, educator*

Upper Arlington
Mincy, Homer F. *school system administrator*

Warren
Kandrac, Jo Ann Marie *school administrator*

Waterford
Montgomery, Gretchen Golzé *secondary educator*

West Chester
Capps, Dennis William *secondary school educator*

Westerville
DeVore, Carl Brent *college president, educator*
VanSant, Joanne Frances *academic administrator*
Willke, Thomas Aloys *university official, statistics educator*

Willoughby
Grossman, Mary Margaret *elementary education educator*
Kerkel, Lynn *middle school educator*
Lillich, Alice Louise *retired secondary education educator*

Wooster
Weidensaul, Thomas Craig *university administrator, researcher*
Woods, Susanne *college president*

Worthington
†Horn, Raymond Albert *school system administrator*

Yellow Springs
Guskin, Alan E. *university president*

Youngstown
Cochran, Leslie Herschel *university administrator*
Wolsonovich, Nicholas *school system administrator*

OKLAHOMA

Altus
Hensley, Stephen Ray *academic administrator*

Ardmore
Thompson, John E. *principal*

Bethany
Leupp, Edythe Peterson *retired educator, administrator*

Durant
Garrett, Scott *vocational school administrator*
Williams, Larry Bill *university president*

Earlsboro
Duncan, Glenda Julaine *elementary education educator*

Edmond
Nigh, George *university administrator, former governor*
Raburn, Randall K. *school system administrator*
Zabel, Vivian Ellouise *secondary education educator*

Enid
Taylor, Donna Lynne *adult education coordinator*

Lawton
Davis, Don Clarence *university president*
Neptune, Richard Allan (Dick Neptune) *superintendent of schools*
Reno, Jennifer *principal*
Smiley, Frederick Melvin *education educator, consultant*

Mcalester
Smith, Dorothy Jean *principal*

Miami
Lovell, James Frederick *academic administrator*

Midwest City
Folks, John M. *school system administrator*

Norman
Boren, David Lyle *academic administrator*
Fears, Jesse Rufus *academic dean*
Hamilton, Donna Martha *secondary education educator*
Hodgell, Murlin Ray *university dean*
Huntington, Penelope Ann *educator*
Schindler, Barbara Francois *school administrator*
Sharp, Paul Frederick *former university president, educational consultant*
Van Horn, Richard Linley *university administrator*

Oklahoma City
Brady-Black, Wandalene *secondary school educator*
Dunlap, E.T. *retired educational administrator, consultant*
Garrett, Sandy Langley *school system administrator*
Holder, Lee *educator and university dean emeritus*
Johnson, James Terence *college chancellor*
Leonard, Sister Anne C. *superintendent, education director*
Meeks, Patricia Lowe *secondary school educator*
Noakes, Betty L. *elementary school educator*
†Roberts, Kathleen Mary *school system administrator*
Smith, Clodus Ray *academic administrator*
Walker, Jerald Carter *university administrator, minister*
Wheat, Willis James *university dean, management educator*
Woods, Pendleton *college official, author*

Ponca City
Scott, Carol Lee *child care educator*

Pryor
Burdick, Larry G. *school system administrator*

Sapulpa
Barnes, Paulette Whetstone *school system administrator*
Fletcher, Shirley Faye *counselor*

Shawnee
Agee, Bob R. *university president, educator, minister*

Stillwater
Ausburn, Lynna Joyce *curriculum developer, technical education specialist, consultant*
Boger, Lawrence Leroy *university president emeritus*
Browning, Charles Benton *university dean, agricultural educator*
Halligan, James Edmund *university administrator, chemical engineer*
Kamm, Robert B. *former academic administrator, educator, author, diplomat*
Mc Collom, Kenneth Allen *retired university dean*
Mc Farland, Frank Eugene *university official*
Sandmeyer, Robert Lee *university dean, economist*

Tulsa
Donaldson, Robert Herschel *university president*
Knaust, Clara Doss *retired elementary school educator*
McCalment, Raymond *junior college educator*
Roger, Jerry Lee *school system administrator*
White, Randall Wayne *educational development executive*

Yukon
Somerville, Carolyn Johnson *principal*

OREGON

Ashland
Kreisman, Arthur *higher education consultant, humanities educator emeritus*
Smith, G(odfrey) T(aylor) *retired college president*

Astoria
Bainer, Philip La Vern *retired college president*

Bend
Wonser, Michael Dean *retired public affairs director, art educator*

Brookings
Olsen, Edward Gustave *education educator emeritus*

Coquille
de Sá e Silva, Elizabeth Anne *educator*

Corvallis
Bruce, Robert Kirk *college administrator*
Byrne, John Vincent *academic administrator*
Davis, John Rowland *university administrator*
Horne, Frederick Herbert *academic administrator, chemistry educator*
Mac Vicar, Robert William *retired university administrator*
Parker, Donald Fred *college dean, human resources management educator*
Young, Roy Alton *university administrator, educator*

Cottage Grove
Miller, Joanne Louise *middle school educator*

Eugene
Cox, Joseph William *academic administrator*
Frohnmayer, David Braden *university president*
Gall, Meredith Damien (Meredith Mark Damien Gall) *education educator, author*
Hosticka, Carl Joseph *academic administrator, educator, legislator*
Moseley, John Travis *university administrator, research physicist*
Reinmuth, James E. *college dean*

Forest Grove
Singleton, Francis Seth *dean*

Gresham
Light, Betty Jensen Pritchett *former college dean*

La Grande
Gilbert, David Erwin *university president, physicist*
Robinson, Jens Joseph *college dean*

Lake Oswego
Le Shana, David Charles *seminary president*

Mcminnville
Goodrich, Kenneth Paul *college dean*
McGillivray, Karen *elementary school educator*
Walker, Charles Urmston *retired university president*

Medford
Bunten, John William *school system administrator*

Monmouth
Meyers, Richard Stuart *college president*

Newberg
Stevens, Edward Franklin *college president*

Portland
Bennett, Douglas Carleton *academic administrator*
Benson, George L. *school system administrator*
Blumel, Joseph Carlton *university president*
Frolick, Patricia Mary *educator, retired*
Harris, Michael Hatherly *educational administrator*
†Koblik, Stevens S. *academic administrator*
Latini, Nancy Jane *special education administrator*
Lawrence, Sally Clark *college president*
Marandas, Susan Margaret *secondary education educator*
Mooney, Michael Joseph *academic administrator, philosopher*
Moore, Melvin G. *school system administrator*
Prophet, Matthew Waller, Jr. *school superintendent*

Ramaley, Judith Aitken *university president, endocrinologist*
Ricks, Mary Frances *university administrator, anthropologist*
Sheridan, Wilma Froman *dean*
Sherrer, Charles David *college dean, clergyman*
Terkla, Louis Gabriel *retired university dean*
Tufts, Robert B. *registrar*
Ward, James Hubert *social work educator, university dean, researcher, consultant*
Wiest, William Marvin *education educator, psychologist*
Zook, Ronald Z. *school system administrator*

Roseburg
Plummer, Charles McDonald *retired community college administrator*

Salem
Bebe, Kathy *principal*
Billman, Jennifer *elementsry school principal*
Hudson, Jerry E. *university president*
Mack, Patricia *secondary school principal*

Talent
McGill, Esby Clifton *former college official*

Troutdale
Sizemore, Robert Dennis *school counselor, educational administrator*

Tualatin
Longaker, Nancy *elementary school principal*

West Linn
Harris, Debra Coral *physical education educator*

PENNSYLVANIA

Abington
Lello, David Joseph *special education educator*

Allentown
Taylor, Arthur Robert *college president, business executive*

Annville
McGill, William James, Jr. *academic administrator*
Synodinos, John Anthony *academic administrator*

Aston
Carroll, Claire Barry *special education educator*

Beaver
Helmick, Gayle Johnston *elementary education educator*

Bethlehem
Bergethon, Kaare Roald *retired college president*
Likins, Peter William *university president*
Martin, Roger Harry *college president*
Moe, Alden John *university dean*

Bloomsburg
Vann, John Daniel, III *university dean, historian*

Blue Bell
Brendlinger, LeRoy R. *college president*

Bridgeville
Morgan, Joyce Elizabeth *elementary school educator*

Bryn Mawr
Lafarge, Catherine *dean*
McPherson, Mary Patterson *academic administrator*
Tidmarsh, Karen MacAusland *dean*
Weese, Samuel H. *academic administrator*

Canonsburg
Mascetta, Joseph Anthony *principal*

Carlisle
Fritschler, A. Lee *college president, public policy educator*
Rossbacher, Lisa Ann *dean, geology educator, writer*

Center Valley
Gambet, Daniel G(eorge) *college president, clergyman*

Chalfont
Tomlinson, Juliette Shell *elementary school educator*

Chester
Bruce, Robert James *university president*
Buck, Lawrence Paul *academic administrator*
Moll, Clarence Russel *university president emeritus, consultant*

Collegeville
Richter, Richard Paul *academic administrator*
†Strassburger, John Robert *academic administrator*

Colmar
Weber-Roochvarg, Lynn *consultant, adult education specialist, librarian*

Cooperstown
Hogg, James Henry, Jr. *retired education educator*

Coraopolis
Hayes, Diane Elizabeth *principal*

Cresson
Pierce, Edward Franklin *college president*

Doylestown
Thomas, Ellen Louise *private school administrator*

Drexel Hill
McAllister, Wayne R. *principal*

Eagles Mere
Sample, Frederick Palmer *former college president*

East Stroudsburg
Gilbert, James Eastham *academic administrator*

Edinboro
Cox, Clifford Laird *university administrator, musician*
Diebold, Foster Frank *university president*

Elizabethtown
Ritsch, Frederick Field *academic administrator, historian*

Erie
Anderson, Cathie Kellogg *education educator*
Lilley, John Mark *university provost and dean*

Exeter
Stocker, Joyce Arlene *retired secondary education educator*

Flourtown
Lambert, Joan Dorety *elementary education educator*

Fredericksburg
Ludwig, Edward Lee *director athletics, educator, coach*

Freeland
Rudawski, Joseph George *educational administrator*

Glenside
Landman, Bette Emeline *academic administrator*

Greensburg
Mann, Jacinta *academic administrator, mathematician, educator*

Greenville
Zimmer, Albert Arthur *education educator*

Gwynedd Valley
Feenane, Sister Mary Alice *principal*

Hanover
Toft, Thelma Marilyn *secondary educator*

Harleysville
Freudig, David Wayne *elementary educator*

Harrisburg
McCormick, James Harold *academic administrator*

Haverford
Kessinger, Tom G. *college president*

Hazleton
Gatty, Eugene B. *school system administrator*

Hermitage
Havrilla, John William *middle school educator*

Honesdale
Barbe, Walter Burke *education educator*

Horsham
Strock, Gerald E. *school system administrator*
Woodruff, Harrison D., Jr. *principal*

Hummelstown
Bruhn, John Glyndon *university official, educator*

Huntingdon
Neff, Robert Wilbur *church official, educator*

Indiana
Pettit, Lawrence Kay *university president*
Thibadeau, Eugene Francis *educator, consultant*

Jenkintown
Baldwin, David Rawson *retired university administrator*

Johnstown
Alcamo, Frank Paul *retired principal*
Grove, Nancy Carol *academic administrator*

Kennett Square
Nason, John William *retired college president, educational consultant*
Wilson, David Cartwright *headmaster*

King Of Prussia
Olexy, Jean Shofranko *English educator*

Kingston
Marko, Andrew Paul *school system administrator*

Knox
Rupert, Elizabeth Anastasia *retired university dean*

Kutztown
McFarland, David E. *university president*

Lancaster
Albright, Annarose M. *secondary school educator*
Ebersole, Mark Chester *emeritus college president*
Ellis, Calvert N. *former college president*
Kneedler, Alvin Richard *college president*

Langhorne
Babb, Wylie Sherrill *college president*
Willis, Wesley Robert *college administrator*

Lansdale
Baughn, Juan R. *high school principal*

Lewisburg
†Adams, William D. *academic administrator*

Lock Haven
Almes, June *retired education educator, librarian*
Willis, Craig Dean *university president*

Malvern
Swymer, Stephen *principal*

Manchester
Owens, Marilyn Mae *art educator*

Maple Glen
Taddei, Edward P. *school system administrator*

Media
Dunlap, Richard Frank *school system administrator*
Reuschlein, Harold Gill *university dean*
Strunk, Betsy Ann Whitenight *education educator*

Mercersburg
Burgin, Walter Hotchkiss, Jr. *educational administrator*

Merion Station
Zaslavsky, Robert *educator*

Millersville
Caputo, Joseph Anthony *university president*
Mallery, Anne Louise *elementary educator, consultant*

Monroeville
Carney, Ann Vincent *secondary education educator*

Morrisville
Lineberry, Paul F., Jr. *music educator*

Myerstown
Robson, Barbara S. *elementary education educator*
Seilhamer, Ray A. *academic administrator*

New Hope
Knight, Douglas Maitland *educational administrator, optical executive*

New Wilmington
Deegan, John, Jr. *academic administrator, educator*
Remick, Oscar Eugene *college president*

Newtown
Selden, William Kirkpatrick *educational consultant*

Norristown
Case, Andrew J. *educational administrator*

Northampton
Bartholomew, Gordon Wesley *health and physical education educator*
Greenleaf, Janet Elizabeth *principal*

Perkasie
Ferry, Joan Evans *school counselor*

Philadelphia
Ball, Earl John, III *school administrator*
Bates, James Earl *college president*
Blumberg, Baruch Samuel *academic administrator, research scientist*
Brucker, Paul C. *academic administrator, physician*
Bryan, Henry Collier *secondary education education, minister*
Bryan, Richard Arthur *special education educator*
Clayton, Constance *school system administrator*
Cohen, David Walter *university chancellor, periodontist, educator*
Collier-Evans, Demetra Frances *veterans benefits counselor*
Cooke, Sara Mullin Graff *daycare provider, kindergarten teacher, doctor's assistant*
Cooperman, Barry S. *educational administrator, educator, scientist*
Delacato, Carl Henry *education educator*
Fisher, Marshall Lee *university decision sciences director, educator*
Gerrity, Thomas P. *dean*
Hackney, Francis Sheldon *university president*
Holloman, Margaret *elementary school principal*
†Jamieson, Kathleen Hall *dean, communications educator*
Kim, Sangduk *biochemistry educator, researcher*
Kreider, Karen Beechy *secondary education educator, language professional*
Meyerson, Martin *university executive, educator*
Misher, Allen *college president, retired*
†Myers, Allen Richard *medical school dean, rheumatologist*
Osborne, Frederick Spring, Jr. *academic administrator, artist*
Padulo, Louis *university administrator*
Peirce, Donald Oluf *elementary education educator*
Reinstein, Robert J. *dean, law educator*
Rodin, Judith Seitz *academic administrator, educator*
Rumpf, John Louis *university official, civil engineer, educator*
Sheehan, Donald Thomas *university administrator*
Sims, Armita B. *principal*
Smith, Robert Rutherford *university dean, communication educator*
Solmssen, Peter *university president*
Stevens, Rosemary A. *academic dean, public health and social history educator*
Sutman, Francis Xavier *university dean*
Sutnick, Alton Ivan *dean, educator, researcher, physician*
Toto, Mary *elementary and secondary education educator*
Wachman, Marvin *university chancellor*
Woodside, Lisa Nicole *academic administrator*

Philipsburg
Reiter, Daisy K. *elementary education educator*

Phoenixville
Wright, Jean Norman *elementary education educator*

Pittsburgh
Blaney, M. Kathleen *elementary education educator*
†Boyce, Doreen Elizabeth *education, civic development foundation executive*
†Bozzomo, Lawrence E. *superintendent of schools*
Christiano, Paul P. *academic administrator, civil engineering educator*
Covey, Preston King, Jr. *education educator, university official*
Curry, Nancy Ellen *education educator, psychoanalyst, psychologist*
Cyert, Richard Michael *former university president, economist*
Dehouske, Ellen Jane *early childhood education educator, consultant*
Eckert, Jean Patricia *elementary education educator*
Epperson, David Ernest *dean, educator*
†Faust, Charles Henry *superintendent of schools*
†Kent, Chester C. *school system administrator*
Losacco, Lesley Herdt *supervisor, educator*
Machatzke, Heinz Wilhelm *dean, chemistry educator*
Makarewicz, Joseph Thomas *research center director, historian*
Martin, Bruce Douglas *university official, chemist*
†Mattison, Donald Roger *dean, physician, military officer*
Mc Anulty, Henry Joseph *university administrator*
†McDuffie, Keith A. *literature educator, magazine director*
Meegan, Sister Elizabeth *school system administrator*
Mehrabian, Robert *academic administrator*
Miller, Rush Glenn, Jr. *university dean, librarian*
O'Connor, John Dennis *chancellor, biology educator*
Patton, Nancy Matthews *elementary education educator*
Popchak, Sister Barbara Jo *private school director*
Schallenberger, Carolyn *college dean*
†Smartschan, Glenn Fred *educational administrator*
Suzuki, Jon Byron *dean, periodontist, educator*
Van Dusen, Albert Clarence *university official*
Wallace, Richard Christopher, Jr. *school system administrator, educator*
Zoffer, H. Jerome *educator, university dean*

Robesonia
Houck, Charleen McClain *educator*

Ruffs Dale
Slebodnik, Tressa Ann *elementary education educator*

Saint Davids
Baird, John Absalom, Jr. *college official*

Saltsburg
Pidgeon, John Anderson *headmaster*

Scranton
Fusaro, Joseph A. *educator*
Horton, Joseph Julian, Jr. *academic dean, educator*
Jordan, John W. *school system administrator*
Nee, Sister Mary Coleman *college president emeritus*
Panuska, Joseph Allan *university president*
Passon, Richard Henry *university administrator*
Reap, Sister Mary Margaret *college administrator*

Shippensburg
Ceddia, Anthony Francis *university administrator*

Slippery Rock
Aebersold, Robert Neil *university president*

State College
Hoffa, Harlan Edward *retired university dean, art educator*
Remick, Forrest Jerome, Jr. *former university official*

Swarthmore
Barr, Robert Alfred, Jr. *college dean*
Bloom, Alfred Howard *college president*

Troy
Lane, Carol Ann *secondary school educator*

Uniontown
Foster, James Caldwell *academic dean, historian*

University Park
Albinski, Henry Stephen *academic research center director, writer*
Askov, Eunice May *education educator*
Dupuis, Victor Lionel *curriculum and instruction educator emeritus*
Filippelli, Ronald Lee *college dean, labor studies and industrial relations educator*
Herrmann, Carol *university adminstrator*
Hood, Lamartine Frain *college dean*
Koopmann, Gary Hugo *educational center administrator, mechanical engineering educator*
Larson, Russell Edward *university provost emeritus, consultant agriculture research and development*
Martorana, Sebastian Vincent *educational consultant*
Rashid, Kamal A. *biotechnology training program director, educator*
Spanier, Graham Basil *university president, family sociologist*
Starling, James Lyne *university administrator*
Thomas, Joab Langston *academic administrator, biology educator*
Wartik, Thomas *chemistry educator, former college dean*
Whitko, Jean Phillips *academic administrator*
Yoder, Edgar Paul *education educator*

Upper Darby
Apfel, Gail *principal*

Upper Saint Clair
Dunkis, Patricia B. *principal*

Vandergrift
Quader, Patricia Ann *elementary education educator*

Villanova
Dobbin, Edmund J. *university administrator*
Heitzmann, Wm. Ray *education educator*
Morgan, Lewis B. *counseling education educator*

Wallingford
Rice, Robert H. *principal*

Washington
Burnett, Howard Jerome *college president*

Wernersville
Himmelberger, Richard Charles *vocational school educator*

West Chester
Adler, Madeleine Wing *academic administrator*
Hickman, Janet Susan *college administrator, educator*

Wilkes Barre
Lackenmier, James Richard *college president, priest*

Williamsport
Douthat, James Evans *college administrator*

Willow Street
Stright, I. Leonard *educational consultant*

Wyomissing
Cellucci, Peter T. *principal*

Yardley
Elliott, Frank Nelson *retired college president*

York
Waldner, George Wittman *university administrator*

RHODE ISLAND

Barrington
Graser, Bernice Erckert *elementary school principal*

Coventry
Spear, Raymond E. *school system administrator*

Cranston
McAulay, Dianne Lucy *gifted education educator*

East Providence
DeGoes, John V. *school system administrator*
Mulvey, Mary C. *adult education administrator, gerontologist*

Kingston
Carothers, Robert Lee *academic administrator*
Hedlund, Ronald David *academic administrator, researcher, educator*
Horn, Francis Henry *former educational administrator*
Youngken, Heber Wilkinson, Jr. *former university administrator, pharmacy educator*

Lincoln
Brites, José Baptista *secondary education educator, writer*

Narragansett
Pouliot, Assunta Gallucci *business school owner and director*

Newport
Hamblet, Charles Albert *educational administrator, educator*

North Kingstown
Kondon, E. Jane *principal*

North Scituate
Stubbs, Donald Clark *secondary education educator*

Providence
Archambault, Reginald Donat *education educator*
Bensmaia, Reda *educator, researcher*
Casey, Brother Daniel F. *school system administrator*
Cunningham, John Fabian *college president, philosophy educator*
Diebold, Gerald Joseph *education educator*
Greer, David S. *university dean, physician, educator*
Gregorian, Vartan *academic administrator*
Grenander, Ulf *mathematics educator*
Hawkins, Brian L. *academic administrator, educator*
Konstan, David *educator, researcher*
Mandle, Earl Roger *university president, former museum administrator*
†Marsh, Donald Jay *college dean, medical educator*
McMahon, Eleanor Marie *education educator*
Mueller, Frederick *principal*
Nazarian, John *academic administrator, mathematics educator*
Salesses, John Joseph *university administrator*
Sizer, Theodore R. *education educator*
Stevos, Joyce Louise *education director*
Targan, David *science administrator*
Zarrella, Arthur M. *superintendent*

Riverside
McElroy, Sister Maureen *secondary school principal*

Saunderstown
Donovan, Gerald Alton *retired academic administrator, former university dean*

Smithfield
Trueheart, William E. *academic administrator*

SOUTH CAROLINA

Aiken
Alexander, Robert Earl *university chancellor, educator*
Cowan, Carolyn Cannon *retired early childhood education educator*
Kanne, Elizabeth Ann Arnold *secondary school educator*

Anderson
Woodward, Karen Callison *school system administrator*

Beaufort
Jenkins, Margie Kline *secondary school educator*

Chapin
Branham, Mack Carison, Jr. *retired theological seminary executive, minister*

Charleston
Curtis, Marcia *university dean*
Edwards, James Burrows *university president, oral surgeon*
Greenberg, Raymond Seth *academic administrator, educator*
Grimsley, James Alexander, Jr. *university administrator, retired army officer*
Hunter, Jairy C., Jr. *academic administrator*
Mc Devitt, Joseph Bryan *retired university administrator, retired naval officer*
Reilly, David Henry *university dean*
Smith, J. Roy *education educator*
†Whelan, Wayne Louis *higher education administrator*

Clemson
Curris, Constantine William *university president*
†Kelly, John William, Jr. *head of horticulture department, botanical garden director*
Underwood, Sandra Jane *university administrator*
Vogel, Henry Elliott *retired university dean and physics educator*

Clinton
Orr, Kenneth Bradley *college president*

Columbia
Aelion, C. Marjorie *educator*
Dixon, Albert King, II *university administrator*
Duffy, John Joseph *academic administrator, history educator*
Friedman, Myles Ivan *education educator*
Kay, Carol McGinnis *literature educator*
King, John Ethelbert, Jr. *education educator, former academic administrator*
Muzekari, Thomasine Dabbs *educational consultant*
Palms, John Michael *university president*
Shannon, David Thomas *academic administrator*

Conway
Sharples, D. Kent *college administrator*
Wiseman, Dennis Gene *college dean*

Due West
Koonts, Jones Calvin *retired education educator*

Estill
Eads, Albert E., Jr. *school superintendent*

Florence
Smith, Walter Douglas *retired college president*
Townsend, Nancy Christine *secondary education educator*
Wilson, L(etitia) Alexandra *elementary school educator*

Fort Mill
Bonds, C. Joseph *school system administrator*

Gaffney
Griffin, Walter Roland *college president, educator, historian*

Greenville
Cloer, Carl Thomas, Jr. *education educator*
Hill, Grace Lucile Garrison *education educator, consultant*
Jones, Bob, Jr. *academic administrator, educator, lecturer, minister*
Payne, G(eorge) Frederick *educational director*
Smith, Philip Daniel *academic administrator, education educator*
Whitmire, John Lee *daycare provider*

Greenwood
Jackson, Larry Artope *retired college president*
Marino, Sheila Burris *education educator*

Hartsville
Daniels, James Douglas *academic administrator*

Hilton Head Island
Exley, Winston Wallace *middle school educator*
Mirse, Ralph Thomas *former college president*
Mulholland, Paige Elliott *university president emeritus*
Pustilnik, Jean Todd *elementary education educator*

Kershaw
Lucas, Dean Hadden *retired educator*

Ladson
Cannon, Major Tom *special education educator*

Lexington
Gatch, Charles Edward, Jr. *middle school principal*

Moncks Corner
Peake, Frank *middle school educator*

Rock Hill
Di Giorgio, Anthony J. *college president*

Simpsonville
Drummond, Julia Elaine Butler *middle school educator*

Spartanburg
Glenn, Robert E. *elementary school principal*
Hatley, Amy Bell *elementary education educator, broadcast journalist*
Lesesne, Joab Mauldin, Jr. *college president*
Mc Gehee, Larry Thomas *university administrator*
Stephens, Bobby Gene *college administrator, consultant*

Sumter
Kieslich, Anita Frances *school system administrator*

SOUTH DAKOTA

Brookings
Bailey, Harold Stevens, Jr. *retired educational administrator*
Wagner, Robert Todd *university president, sociology educator*

Huron
Reynolds, R. John *university administrator*

Madison
Tunheim, Jerald Arden *academic administrator, physics educator*

Rapid City
Hughes, William Lewis *former university official, electrical engineer*
Schleusener, Richard August *college president*

Selby
Akre, Donald J. *school system administrator*

Sioux Falls
Balcer, Charles Louis *college president emeritus, educator*
Carroll, Howard W. *school system administrator*
Hiatt, Charles Milton *seminary president*
Huseboe, Doris Louise *educator, arts consultant*
Johnson, Thomas Floyd *college president, educator*
Tucker, William Vincent *vocational evaluator, former college president*
Wagoner, Ralph Howard *academic administrator, educator*

Vermillion
Asher, Betty Turner *academic administrator*
Milton, Lynn Leonharda *elementary and secondary school educator*
Richardson, Maurine Janet *reading educator*

Wall
Poppe, Kenneth C. *school system administrator*

TENNESSEE

Adamsville
York, Joseph Stafford *secondary gifted and talented education educator*

Antioch
Malone, Tom *bible college president*
Wisehart, Mary Ruth *academic administrator*

Athens
Wilson, Ben *elementary school principal*

Bristol
Anderson, Jack Oland *retired college official*
Stanislaw, Richard John *university program director*

Chapel Hill
Christman, Luther Parmalee *university dean emeritus, consultant*

Chattanooga
Charlton, Shirley Marie *instructional supervisor*
Obear, Frederick Woods *university chancellor*
Tucker, Stanley R. *headmaster*

Clarksville
Carlin, James Boyce *elementary education educator, consultant*

Cleveland
Gillum, Perry Eugene *college president, minister*
Goff, Nadine Farabee *elementary education educator*
Lawson, Billie Katherine *elementary school educator*

Cookeville
Hearn, Edell Midgett *university dean, teacher educator*
Peters, Ralph Martin *education educator*
Porter, Wilma Jean *university administrator*
Volpe, Angelo Anthony *university administrator, chemistry educator*

Dickson
Thomas, Janey Sue *elementary school principal*

Dyersburg
Nerren, George N. *school system administrator*
Taylor, Billy D. *principal*

Franklin
Guthrie, Glenda Evans *educational consultant*

Gallatin
Ramer, Hal Reed *college president*

Hendersonville
Poynor, Robert Allen, Jr. *guidance counselor*

Jefferson City
Maddox, Jesse Cordell *academic administrator*

Johnson City
Alfonso, Robert John *university administrator*
Paxton, J. Willene *retired university administrator*
Roark, Edith Humphreys *private school language arts educator, reading specialist*
Votaw, Charles Lesley *academic dean*

Knoxville
Armistead, Willis William *university administrator, veterinarian*
Boling, Edward Joseph *university president emeritus, educator*
Brockett, Ralph Grover *adult education educator*
Donahue, Joan Elizabeth *elementary school educator*
Hall, O. Glen *university dean*
Mankel, Francis Xavier *priest*
Nielsen, Alvin Herborg *university dean, physicist*
Prados, John William *educational administrator*
Stoneking, Jerry Edward *dean*
Wisniewski, Richard *dean*

Louisville
Wheeler, George William *university provost, physicist, educator*

Martin
Smith, Robert Mason *university dean*

Mc Minnville
Martin, Ron *adult basic education coordinator, superintendent of schools, consultant, minister*

Memphis
Allison, Beverly Gray *seminary president, evangelism educator*
Bailey, Charles *college administrator*
Carter, Michael Allen *college dean, nursing educator*
Dunathan, Harmon Craig *college dean*
Gourley, Dick R. *college dean*
Hunt, James Calvin *academic administrator, physician*
Nesin, Jeffrey D. *academic administrator*
Ramsey, Marjorie Elizabeth *early childhood education educator*
Ranta, Richard Robert *university dean*
Wheeler, Orville Eugene *university dean, civil and mechanical engineering educator*

Murfreesboro
Berry, Mary Tom *education educator*
Bookner, Becci Jane *school system administrator*
Craig, James Donald *dean*
Hayes, Janice Cecile *education educator*
Walker, David Ellis, Jr. *dean, educator, minister, consultant*

Nashville
Chapman, John Edmon *university dean, pharmacologist, physician*
Clinton, Barbara Marie *university health services director, social worker*
Emans, Robert LeRoy *academic administrator, education educator*
Fondaw, Elizabeth Louise *vocational school educator*
Geisel, Martin Simon *college dean, educator*
Guthrie, James Williams *education educator*
Hamilton, Russell George, Jr. *academic dean, Spanish and Portuguese language educator*
Hazelip, Herbert Harold *academic administrator*
Hefner, James A. *academic administrator*
Kidd, Florence *principal*
Madden, Paul Herman *education educator*
McMurry, Idanelle Sam *educational consultant*
Paschall, Douglas Duane *headmaster*
Pellegrino, James William *college dean, psychology educator*
Ridley, Carolyn Fludd *social studies educator*
Sharp, Bert Lavon *retired education educator, retired university dean*
Whitefield, Anne C. *secondary school principal*
Wyatt, Joe Billy *university chancellor*

Oak Ridge
Thomas, John Edwin *retired university administrator*

Pulaski
Dowdy, Ronald Raymond *academic administrator*

Sewanee
Croom, Frederick Hailey *college administrator, mathematics educator*
Kepple, Thomas Ray, Jr. *college administrator*
Lorenz, Anne Partee *special education educator, consultant*

Tullahoma
Collins, Sarah Ruth *education educator*
†McCay, Thurman Dwayne *university administrator*

TEXAS

Abilene
Clayton, Lawrence Ray *university dean, literary critic, biographer*
Kim, Thomas Kunhyuk *college administrator*
†McCaleb, Gary Day *university administrator*
Shimp, Robert Everett, Jr. *university administrator, historian*
Warren, Russell Glen *academic administrator*

Alpine
Morgan, Raymond Victor, Jr. *university administrator, mathematics educator*
Ortego y Gasca, Felipe de *education educator*

Amarillo
DeSpain, Ronald Leroy *academic administrator*

Arlington
Lewis-White, Linda Beth *elementary school educator*
Pickard, Myrna Rae *college dean*
Sobol, Harold *consultant, retired dean, manufacturing executive*

Austin
Ayres, Robert Moss, Jr. *retired university president*
Barrera, Elvira Puig *counselor, therapist, educator*
Berdahl, Robert Max *academic administrator, historian educator*
Brewer, Thomas Bowman *retired university president*
Cain, Sister Thecla *religious schools superintendent*
Cannon, William Bernard *retired university educator*
Cardozier, Virgus Ray *higher education educator*
Cleaves, Peter Shurtleff *academic administrator*
Cunningham, William Hughes *university chancellor, marketing educator*
Dalton, Don *principal*
Fair, Harry David *academic administrator, physicist*
Franklin, Billy Joe *international higher education specialist*
Franklin, G(eorge) Charles *academic administrator*
Gill, Clark Cyrus *retired education educator*
Hall, Michael Garibaldi *education educator*
Harris, Ben Maxwell *education educator*
Hayes, Patricia Ann *university president*
Jeffrey, Robert Campbell *university dean*
Justiz, Manuel Jon *educator, researcher*
Kelley, Henry Paul *university administrator, psychology educator*
Kennamer, Lorrin Garfield, Jr. *retired university dean*
Livingston, William Samuel *university administrator, political scientist*
May, Robert George *dean, accounting educator*
McGarry, William Andrew, Jr. *career counselor*
Rippey, Donald Taylor *education educator*
Rogers, Lorene Lane *university president emeritus*
Roueche, John Edward, II *education educator, leadership program director*

Beaumont
Brentlinger, William Brock *college dean*
Cawley, William Arthur *research educator*
Dygert, William Douglas *school superintendent*
Gagne, Mary *secondary school principal*

Belton
Parker, Bobby Eugene, Sr. *college president*

Brownsville
Doyle, Sister Mary Dolores *academic administrator*
Garza, Roberto Jesus *education educator*
Santa-Coloma, Bernardo *secondary school educator, counselor*

Brownwood
DeHay, Jerry Marvin *business educator*
Jarvis, Oscar T., Jr. *dean, education educator*

Bryan
Hubert, Frank William Rene *retired university system chancellor*

Carrollton
Grimes, Mary Woodworth *special educational consultant*
Maher, Sheila *secondary school principal*

College Station
Adkisson, Perry Lee *university system chancellor*
Bowen, Ray Morris *academic administrator, engineering educator*
Calhoun, John C., Jr. *academic administrator*
Carpenter, Delbert Stanley *educational administration educator*
Cocanougher, Arthur Benton *university dean, former business administration educator*
Erlandson, David Alan *education administration educator*
Gage, E. Dean *university administrator*
Haden, Clovis Roland *university administrator, engineering educator*
Henry, Rene Arthur, Jr. *university official*
Hiler, Edward Allan *academic administrator, agricultural engineering educator*
Kennedy, Robert Alan *educational administrator*
Peddicord, Kenneth Lee *academic administrator*

Comanche
Droke, Edna Faye *elementary school educator*

Commerce
Lutz, Frank Wenzel *education administration educator*
Morris, Jerry Dean *academic administrator*

Converse
Vontur, Ruth Poth *elementary physical education educator*

Corpus Christi
Early, William James *education educator*
Furgason, Robert Roy *university official, chemical engineering educator*
Gutierrez, Elia Garza *elementary school educator*
Stone, Rose Marie *vocational educator*

Crowell
Binnion, John Edward *education educator*

Dallas
Berkeley, Marvin H. *management educator, former university dean*
Campbell, Donald K. *theological seminary administrator, educator*
Cook, Gary Raymond *university president, clergyman*
DePaola, Dominick Philip *college president, dean*
Edwards, Marvin Earle *superintendent of schools*
Fleming, Jon Hugh *business executive, educational consultant*
Friedheim, Jan V. *education administrator*
Haayen, Richard Jan *university official, insurance company executive*
Harrison, Frank *former university president*
Hester, Linda Hunt *university dean, counselor*
Leyden, Edward E. *secondary school principal*
Mattingly, Patti Jane *educational administrator*
Phillips, Bettie Mae *elementary school educator*
Prude, Elaine S. *principal*
Syphers, Mary Frances *music educator*
Turner, Robert Gerald *university president*
Walvoord, John Flipse *seminary president, chancellor, theologian*
Wenrich, John William *college president*

Denison
Farr, Reeta Rae *special education administrator*

Denton
Baier, John Leonard *university educator*
Brownell, Blaine Allison *university administrator, history educator*
Elder, Mark Lee *university research administrator, writer*
Greenlaw, Marilyn Jean *education educator, consultant, writer*
Hurley, Alfred Francis *university administrator, historian*
Palermo, Judy Hancock *elementary school educator*
†Surles, Carol D. *university president*
Swigger, B. Keith *dean*
†Swigger, Keith B. *dean*
Thompson, Leslie Melvin *college dean, educator*
Toulouse, Robert Bartell *retired college administrator*

Edinburg
Esparza, Thomas, Sr. *academic athletics administrator*

El Paso
Coleman, Edmund Benedict *university dean*
Grimes, William Gaylord *adult education educator*
Heger, Herbert Krueger *education educator*
Malone, Debra Beatrice *elementary education educator*
†McLeod, Ronald *school system administrator*
Natalicio, Diana Siedhoff *university president*
Riter, Stephen *university administrator, electrical engineer*
Schmidt, L. Lee, Jr. *university official*
Tackett, Stephen Douglas *education services specialist*
von Tungeln, George Robert *retired university administrator, economics consultant*

Floresville
Alvarez, Olga Mendoza *elementary school educator*

Fort Worth
Doherty, Edward J. *academic administrator*
Horner, Winifred Bryan *educator, researcher, consultant, writer*
Mills, John James *research director, mechanical engineering educator*
Saenz, Michael *college president*
Schrum, Jake Bennett *university administrator*
Tade, George Thomas *university dean*
Tucker, William Edward *university chancellor, clergyman*

Galveston
Banet, Charles Henry *college president emeritus, clergyman*
Carrier, Warren Pendleton *retired university chancellor, writer*
Clayton, William Howard *retired university president*
Russell, Attie Yvonne *academic administrator, dean, pediatrics educator*
Schmidly, David J. *dean*

Garland
Foster, Rebecca Anne Hodges *secondary school educator*
Shugart, Jill *school system administrator*

Georgetown
Davis, O. L., Jr. *education educator, researcher*
Rosenthal, Michael Ross *academic administrator, dean*
Shilling, Roy Bryant, Jr. *college president*

Granbury
McWilliams, Chris Pater Elissa *elementary school educator*

Grapevine
Melton, Lynda Gayle *reading specialist, educational diagnostician*

Hale Center
Courtney, Carolyn Ann *school librarian*

Harlingen
Glasgow, Harold Glyn *military academy administrator*

Hillsboro
Auvenshine, William Robert *academic administrator*

Houston
Anderson, Claire W. *computer gifted and talented educator*
Auston, David Henry *university administrator, educator*
Bailar, Benjamin Franklin *academic administrator, administration educator*
Beckingham, Kathleen Mary *educator, researcher*
Bizzell, Bobby Gene *academic administrator*
Bui, Khoi Tien *college counselor*
Butler, William Thomas *college president, physician, educator*
Carroll, Michael M. *academic dean, mechanical engineering educator*
Chance, Jane *educator*
Djerejian, Edward Peter *former diplomat, institute administrator*
Fisher, Janet Warner *secondary school educator*
Gaelens, Albert Robert *educational administrator, priest*
Georgiades, William Den Hartog *educational administrator*
Gillis, (Stephen) Malcolm *academic administrator, economics educator*
Goode, James Cleveland *educational administrator*
Hamilton, Phyllis *principal*
Hammack, Gladys Lorene Mann *reading specialist, educator*
Haynes, Karen Sue *university dean, social work educator*
Hennessey, Sister Colleen *academic administrator*
Ho, Yhi-Min *university dean, economics educator*
Hodo, Edward Douglas *university president*
Hoffman, Philip Guthrie *former university president*
Huang, Elsie Lee *principal*
Le Maistre, Charles Aubrey *university official, physician*
Lott, Thaddeus *principal*
Maddox, Iris Carolyn Clark *secondary education educator*
Mc Fadden, Joseph Michael *university president*
Pickering, James Henry, III *university president*
Pinson, Artie Frances *elementary school educator*
Quigg, Jean *principal*
Rice, Emily Joy *retired secondary and adult educator*
Sharp, Douglas Andrew *secondary school educator*
Sheehan, Linda Suzanne *educational administrator*
Stark-Rice, Patricia Lee *dean, mental health nurse*
Sykes, Ruth L. *special education educator*
Thorne, Joye Holley *special education administrator*
Timme, Kathryn Pearl *secondary education educator*
Wagner, Paul Anthony, Jr. *education educator*
Ward, Calvin H. *academic director, environmental science educator, federal agency administrator*
Webb, Marty Fox *principal*
Weber, Wilford Alexander *education educator*
Wilhelm, Marilyn *private school administrator*
Woodward, Katherine Anne *secondary education educator*

Huntsville
Anisman, Martin Jay *academic administrator*
Warner, Laverne *education educator*

Hurst
Dodd, Sylvia Bliss *special education educator*

Irving
Cannon, Francis V., Jr. *academic administrator, electrical engineer, economist*
Clark, Priscilla Alden *elementary school educator*
Martin, Thomas Lyle, Jr. *university president*
Marton, Bernard Anthony *headmaster, priest, educator*
Perry, Charles Edward *university administrator*
Sasseen, Robert Francis *university president*
Walwer, Frank Kurt *dean, legal educator*

Katy
Andrews, George Arthur *headmaster*

Kerrville
Holloway, Leonard Leveine *former university president*

Kingsville
Ibanez, Manuel Luis *university official, biological sciences educator*
Robins, Gerald Burns *education educator*

Laredo
Condon, Maria del Carmen *retired elementary school educator*
Hinojosa, Sandra Joy *elementary special education educator*
Rodriguez, Yolanda Isabel *elementary instructional administrator*

Lewisville
Downing, Clayton W. *school system administrator*

Longview
Davis, Jimmie Mae Clayborn *elementary school educator*
LeTourneau, Richard Howard *retired college president*
McMichael, Ronald L. *superintendent*

Lubbock
Askins, Billy Earl *education educator, consultant*
Curl, Samuel Everett *university dean, agricultural scientist*
Haragan, Donald Robert *university administrator, geosciences educator*
Lawless, Robert William *academic administrator*
Lemley, Steven Smith *academic administrator*
Lopez, Delmira Castro *school system administrator*
McManigal, Shirley Ann *university dean*
Meyer, Sister Roberta *school system administrator*
Mittemeyer, Bernhard Theodore *university official, surgeon, retired army officer*

Mabank
Beets, Hughla Fae *retired secondary school educator*

Marshall
Dahl, Shirley Ann *education educator*

Mercedes
Alaniz, Theodora Villarreal *elementary education educator*

Mesquite
Tabor, Beverly Ann *elementary school educator*
Vaughan, Joseph Lee, Jr. *education educator, consultant*

Midland
McAfee, John Wilson, Sr. *principal*

Nacogdoches
Angel, Daniel Duane *university president*

New Braunfels
Oestreich, Charles Henry *college president*

Odessa
Boyd, Claude Collins *education advisor*
MacDonald, Karen Hope Cowart *educator, reading specialist*
Sorber, Charles Arthur *academic administrator*

Pharr
Lindner, Kenneth Edward *academic administrator and chemistry educator emeritus*

Portland
Cessac, Joyce Eve LaBorde *elementary school educator*

Prairie View
Clark, Sharon Enid *principal*
Jones, Barbara Ann Posey *college dean*
Trotty, Willie Francis *university dean*

Pyote
Trevino, Jerry Rosalez *secondary school principal*

Rhome
Brammer, Barbara Rhudene *retired secondary education educator*

Richardson
Dunn, David E. *university dean*
Rutford, Robert Hoxie *university educator*
Weaver, Jo Nell *elementary school educator*
Wildenthal, Bryan Hobson *university administrator*
Young, Malcolm Eugene, Jr. *social studies secondary educator*

Round Rock
Chavez, Dorothy Vaughan *elementary school educator, environmental educator*

San Angelo
Davison, Elizabeth Jane Linton *education educator*

San Antonio
Barrow, Charles Wallace *university dean*
Boyers, John Martin *principal*
Calgaard, Ronald Keith *university president*
Compton, Clinton E. *principal*
Dickey, John Sloan, Jr. *dean, educator, geologist, researcher*
Garcia, Linda *secondary school principal*
Gibbons, Robert Ebbert *university official*
Goelz, Paul Cornelius *university dean*
Grissom, Patsy Coleen *college administrator, English educator*
Henderson, Dwight Franklin *dean, educator*
Hernandez, Christine *educator*
Kirkpatrick, Samuel Alexander *university president, social and policy sciences educator*
Langlinais, Joseph Willis *academic administrator*
Leies, John Alex *academic administrator, educator, clergyman*
Lloyd, Susan Elaine *middle school educator*
Moder, John Joseph *academic administrator, priest*
Norwood, Carole Gene *middle school educator*
Pontolillo, Brother Peter A. *school system administrator*
Robertson, Samuel Luther, Jr. *special education educator, therapist*
†Rodriguez, Victor *school system administrator*
Stephens, Sunny Courington *special education educator*
Sueltenfuss, Sister Elizabeth Anne *university president*
Wood, Frank Preuit *educator, former air force officer*
Young, James Julius *university administrator, former army officer*

San Marcos
Barragán, Celia Silguero *elementary education educator*
Bechtol, William Milton *education educator*
Byrom, Jack Edwards *private school administrator*
Carman, Mary Ann *special education educator*
Moore, Betty Jean *retired education educator*
Supple, Jerome H. *university president*

Seabrook
Jacobs, Dorothy Patricia *elementary education educator*

Seagraves
McAdoo, Carolyn *secondary school business educator*

Sherman
Page, Oscar C. *academic administrator*

Spring
Lightell, Kenneth Ray *education educator*

Stephenville
Sims, Larry Kyle *secondary school educator*

Sugar Land
Ramos, Rose Mary *elementary education educator*

Talpa
Russell, Nedra Joan Bibby *secondary school educator*

The Woodlands
Topazio, Virgil William *university official*

Tomball
Barron, Sandra McWhirter *library media specialist*

Tyler
Davidson, Jack Leroy *academic administrator*
Lawson, Billy Joe *educational administrator*

Vidor
Stokely, Joan Barbara *elementary school educator*

Waco
Belew, John Seymour *academic administrator, chemist*
Brooks, Roger Leon *university president*
Hillis, William Daniel *university administrator*
Moran, Doris Ann *educational consultant, mathematics educator*
Wuebker, Virginia Ann *retired elementary school educator, program director*

Wichita Falls
Rodriguez, Louis Joseph *university administrator*

UTAH

Bountiful
Beckstead, Joyce Lorraine *secondary education educator*

Cedar City
Sherratt, Gerald Robert *college president*

Logan
Shaver, James Porter *education educator, university dean*

Ogden
†Mecham, Steven Ray *school system administrator*
Smith, Robert Bruce *college administrator*
Thompson, Paul Harold *university president*

Orem
Green, John Alden *university director study abroad program*

Provo
Allred, Ruel Acord *education educator*
Fleming, Joseph Clifton, Jr. *university dean, law educator*
Hafen, Bruce Clark *academic administrator*
Jensen, Clayne R. *university administrator*
Lee, Rex E. *university president, lawyer*
Stahmann, Robert F. *education educator*
Strasser, William Carl, Jr. *retired college president, educator*
Whatcott, Marsha Rasmussen *elementary educator*

Saint George
Peterson, Steven H. *school system administrator*

Salt Lake City
Burton, Loren G. *school system administrator*
†Chivers, Laurie Alice *state educational administrator*
Drew, Clifford James *university administrator, special education and educational psychology educator*
Jarvis, Joseph Boyer *retired university administrator*
Jensen, Gordon Fred *university administrator*
†Koehn, Richard Karl *higher education executive, evolutionary biologist*
Major, Thomas D. *academic program director*
McCleary, Lloyd E(verald) *education educator*
McKell, Cyrus M. *college dean, plant physiologist, consultant*
Peterson, Chase N. *university president*
Simmons, Lynda Merrill Mills *educational administrator*
Smith, Arthur Kittredge, Jr. *university official, political science educator*
Wilson, Ted Lewis *educator, former mayor*

Sandy
Pierce, Ilona Lambson *educational administrator*
Sabey, J(ohn) Wayne *academic administrator, consultant*

West Jordan
Shepherd, Paul H. *elementary school educator*

VERMONT

Bennington
Coleman, Elizabeth *college president*
Glasser, William Arnold *academic administrator*

Brattleboro
MacCormack, Charles Frederick *academic administrator*

Burlington
Brandenburg, Richard George *university dean, management educator*
Della Santa, Laura *principal*

Castleton
Farmer, Martha Knight *academic administrator, executive*

Colchester
Reiss, Paul Jacob *college president*

Fair Haven
Pentkowski, Raymond J. *superintendent*

Ludlow
Davis, Vera *elementary school educator*

Lyndon Center
Myers, Rex Charles *academic dean*

Lyndonville
Williams, Peggy Ryan *academic administrator*

Middlebury
McCardell, John Malcolm, Jr. *college administrator*
O'Brien, George Dennis *retired university president*

North Troy
Weingart, Carol Jayne *university administrator, educator, psychotherapist*

Saint Johnsbury
Mayo, Bernier L. *secondary school principal*

South Burlington
Kenyon, Judith *primary school educator*

South Royalton
Kempner, Maximilian Walter *law school dean, lawyer*

Waterbury
Bunting, Charles I. *academic administrator*

White River Junction
Halperin, George Bennett *education educator, retired naval officer*

VIRGINIA

Alexandria
Abernathy, Mary Gates *elementary school educator*
Brown, Ann Herrell *secondary school educator*
Foster, Luther Hilton *former university president, educational consultant*
Johnson, William David *retired university administrator*
Puscheck, Herbert Charles *educator*

Annandale
Ernst, Richard James *academic administrator*

Arlington
Bartlett, Elizabeth Susan *audio-visual specialist*
Berg, Sister Marie Majella *university chancellor*
Boek, Walter Erwin *university president, educator, anthropologist, scientist*
Haynes, Caroline Hopper *preschool administrator*
Lane, Neal Francis *university provost, physics researcher, federal administrator*
Moore, John Hampton *academic administrator*
Peterson, Paul Quayle *retired university dean, physician*
Shoemaker, Cynthia Cavenaugh Jones *academic director*

Ashland
Henshaw, William Raleigh *middle school educator*
Payne, Ladell *college president*
Stevenson, Carol Wells *secondary education educator*

Blacksburg
Brown, Gregory Neil *university administrator, forest physiology educator*
Carlisle, Ervin Frederick *university provost*
Nichols, James Robbs *university dean*
Smith, Robert McNeil *university dean*
Steger, Charles William *university administrator*
Torgersen, Paul Ernest *university president*

Bridgewater
Geisert, Wayne Frederick *banker, retired college president*

Charlottesville
Brandt, Richard Martin *education educator*
Breneman, David Worthy *dean, educator*
Bunker, Linda Kay *dean, physical education educator*
Campbell, Stephen Donald Peter *university official*
Carey, Robert Munson *university dean, physician*
Casteen, John Thomas, III *university administrator*
Chronister, Jay Lester *education educator*
Cooper, James Michael *education educator*
Corse, John Doggett *university official, lawyer*
Guiton Hill, Bonnie F. *dean*
Lankford, Francis Greenfield, Jr. *education educator emeritus*
Norton, James Adolphus *higher education administrator and consultant, retired academic administrator, political science educator*
O'Neil, Robert Marchant *university administrator, law educator*
Reynolds, Robert Edgar *academic administrator, physician*
Stenberg, Carl W(aldamer), III *academic program director, educator*
Taylor, Alton Lee *education educator*
Thompson, Kenneth W(infred) *educational director, author, editor, administrator, social science educator*

Chesapeake
Bateman, C. Fred *school system administrator*

Chesterfield
Copeland, Jean Parrish *school system administrator, school board executive*

Evington
Fortune, Laura Catherine Dawson *elementary school educator*

Fairfax
Field, Joanne T. *school board executive*
Johnson, George William *university president*
Spillane, Robert Richard *school system administrator*

Falls Church
Boucouvalas, Marcie *adult education educator*
Cleland, Sherrill *college president*
Rice, Sue Ann *dean, industrial and organizational psychologist*

Farmville
Dorrill, William Franklin *academic administrator, political scientist, educator*

Fort Defiance
Livick, Malcolm Harris *school administrator*

Fredericksburg
Jones, Julia Pearl *elementary school educator*

Hampden Sydney
†Wilson, Samuel V. *academic adminstrator*

Hampton
Harvey, William Robert *university president*
Hightower, John Brantley *arts administrator*
Patty, Anna Christine *middle school educator*

Harrisonburg
Carrier, Ronald Edwin *university administrator*
Lemish, Donald Lee *university athletics director*

Haysi
Deel, George Moses *elementary school educator*

Hollins College
†O'Brien, Jane Margaret *academic administrator*

Lexington
Knapp, John Williams *college president*
Watt, William Joseph *academic administrator, chemistry educator*
†Wilson, John D. *retired university president*

Marion
Groseclose, Joanne Stowers *special education educator*

Martinsville
McCraw, John Randolph, Jr. *assistant principal*

Mc Lean
Griffith, Elisabeth *headmistress*
Groennings, Sven Ole *academic administrator, higher education educator, corporate executive*

Mechanicsville
Long, Patricia Gavigan *elementary education educator, English language educator*

Melfa
Harmon, Patricia Marie *special education educator*

Newport News
Drummond, Neil Hiden *retired secondary school educator, airman*
Harner, David Paul *university administrator*
Polk-Matthews, Josephine Elsey *school psychologist*
Santoro, Anthony Richard *academic administrator*
Stepnick, Arlene Alice *nursing education administrator*

Norfolk
Etheridge, James Edward, Jr. *academic administrator, pediatrics educator*
Jones, Franklin Ross *education educator*
Koch, James Verch *academic administrator, economist*
Myers, Donald Allen *university dean*

Oakton
Hu, Sue King *middle school educator*

Petersburg
Berry, Lemuel, Jr. *academic dean, music educator*
Franklin, Virgil L. *school administrator, education educator*

Poquoson
Yard, Rix Nelson *former athletic director*

Quantico
Wallenborn, Janice Rae *elementary education educator*

Richmond
Ackell, Edmund Ferris *university president*
Bialkowski, Diane *school system administrator*

†Bosher, William Cleveland, Jr. *education educator*
Brush, Carey Wentworth *retired college administrator, history educator*
Fishback, Patricia Davis *academic administrator*
Hamel, Dana Bertrand *academic administrator*
Heilman, E. Bruce *academic administrator*
James, Allix Bledsoe *retired university president*
Leary, David Edward *university dean*
Mason, Vivian Lee Conway *elementary education educator*
McGee, Henry Alexander, Jr. *university official*
McVey, George Jennings *headmaster*
Modlin, George Matthews *university chancellor emeritus*
Morrill, Richard Leslie *university administrator*
Savage, William Woodrow *education educator*
Simmons, S. Dallas *university president*
Trani, Eugene Paul *university president, educator*

Roanoke
King, Stephen Emmett *educational administrator*
Price, Leroy Vernon *secondary school educator*
Tota, Frank Peter *school system administrator*

Salem
Gring, David M. *academic administrator*

Stafford
Brown, Janet Louise *principal*

Sweet Briar
Hill, Barbara Ann *academic administrator, consultant*

Urbanna
Salley, John Jones *university administrator, oral pathologist*

Virginia Beach
Barriskill, Maudanne Kidd *primary school educator*
Richardson, Daniel Putnam *headmaster, history, economics and criminal law educator*
Wiggins, Samuel Paul *educator*

Warrenton
Osier, William Richard *school administrator*

Williamsburg
Birney, Robert Charles *retired academic administrator, psychologist*
Edwards, Jack Donald *educator*
Fraser, Howard Michael *educator, editor*
Geoffroy, Kevin Edward *education educator*
Humphreys, Homer Alexander *former principal*
Lutzer, David John *college dean, mathematics professor*
Mc Kean, John Rosseel Overton *university dean*
Scholnick, Robert J. *college dean, English language educator*
Smith, James Brown, Jr. *secondary school educator*
Van Tassel-Baska, Joyce Lenore *education educator*
Yankovich, James Michael *education educator*

Winchester
Davis, James Arnold *academic administrator*
Tisinger, Catherine Anne *college dean*

Wise
Ellsworth, Lucius Fuller *academic administrator*
Smiddy, Joseph Charles *retired college chancellor*

Woodbridge
Breene, Norma Wylie *special education educator*

WASHINGTON

Auburn
Lapinski, Donald *elementary school principal*

Bellevue
Bergstrom, Marianne Elisabeth *program coordinator, special education teacher*
Clark, Richard Walter *educator, consultant*
Wallentine, Mary Kathryn *secondary educator*

Bellingham
DeLorme, Roland L. *university provost and vice president*
Morse, Karen Williams *academic administrator*
Pierce, George Adams *university administrator, educator*

Bothell
Icenhower, Rosalie B. *retired elementary school principal*

Camas
Howe, Robert Wilson *education educator*

Centralia
Kirk, Henry Port *academic administrator*

Cheney
Glass, James Clifford *college dean, science and mathematics educator*

Ellensburg
Moore, Thomas David *academic administrator*
Nelson, Ivory Vance *university president*

Enumclaw
Goff, Thomas M. *secondary education educator*

Kennewick
Knight, Janet Ann *elementary education educator*

Kent
Johnson, Dennis D. *elementary school principal*
Kelly, Patrick *school system administrator*

Kirkland
Ayars, Albert Lee *retired school superintendent*

Lacey
Cosand, Joseph Parker, Jr. *education educator emeritus*
Spangler, David Robert *college administrator, engineer*

Lynnwood
Benzel, Brian L. *superintendent*

Port Angeles
Chase, John David *university dean, physician*
Kilmer, Joseph Charles *secondary school educator*
Ross, Robert King *retired educator*

Pullman
Lewis, Norman G. *academic administrator, researcher, consultant*
Smith, Robert Victor *university administrator*
Smith, Samuel Howard *university president, plant pathologist*

Renton
Tajon, Encarnacion Fontecha (Connie Tajon) *retired educator, association executive*

Richland
Piippo, Steve *educator*
Ryans, Yvonne *principal*

Seattle
Abbott, Robert Dean *education educator*
Banks, James Albert *educational research director, educator*
Bassett, Edward Powers *university official*
Bowen, Jewell Ray *academic dean, chemical engineering educator*
Brown, Kristi *principal*
Carlson, Dale Arvid *university dean*
Cook, Victor *physics educator, researcher*
Cox, Frederick Moreland *retired university dean, social worker*
Debro, Julius *university dean, sociology educator*
Denny, Brewster Castberg *retired university dean*
Fialkow, Philip Jack *academic administrator, medical educator*
Funk, Robert Norris *college president, lawyer*
Gerberding, William Passavant *university president*
Gibaldi, Milo *university dean*
Ginorio, Angela Beatriz *research administrator, educator*
Goodlad, John Inkster *education educator, author*
Hunkins, Francis Peter *education educator*
Jennerich, Edward John *university official and dean*
Kane, Charles A. *college chancellor*
†Kendrick, William Marvin *school system administrator*
Korthuis, Kathleen E. *dean*
Loh, Wallace D. *university dean*
Matheson, Kent D. *school system administrator*
Maurer, Barbara Glee *educational administrator*
Michalik, John James *law school administrator*
†Olmstead, Marjorie Ann *physics educator*
Plotnick, Robert David *academic administrator, economic consultant*
Silver, Michael *school superintendent*
Sontgerath, Mary *school system administrator*
Sullivan, William James *university president*
Terrell, W(illiam) Glenn *university president emeritus*
Tracy, Mary E. *principal*
Trzyna, Thomas Nicholas *college dean*

Sequim
Barton, Jay *university administrator, biologist*

Spokane
Coughlin, Bernard John *university president*
Hester, Gerald LeRoy *retired school system administrator*
Matters, Clyde Burns *former college president*
†McManus, Patrick Francis *educator, writer*
Nyman, Carl John, Jr. *university dean and official*
Robinson, Herbert Henry, III *educator, therapist*
Robinson, William P. *academic administrator, consultant, speaker*

Tacoma
Barna, Lillian Carattini *school system administrator*
Edington, Robert Van *university official*
Hawks, Katherine Anna *special education educator*
Jungkuntz, Richard Paul *university provost emeritus*
King, Gundar Julian *retired university dean*
Minnerly, Robert Ward *headmaster*
Olson, David Mark *college dean, physical education educator*
Pierce, Susan Resneck *academic administrator, English educator*

Toppenish
†Ross, Kathleen Anne *college president*

Vancouver
Ferguson, Larry Emmett *educational administrator*
Mangino, Kristin Mikalson *secondary education educator*

Walla Walla
Cronin, Thomas Edward *academic administrator*

Washougal
Schorzman, Clarice B. *principal*

Yakima
Dorsett, Judith A. *elementary education educator*

WEST VIRGINIA

Athens
Marsh, Joseph Franklin, Jr. *emeritus college president, educational consultant*

Barboursville
Lucas, Carol McCann *vocational education educator*

Bethany
Cummins, Delmer Duane *academic administrator, historian*
Sandercox, Robert Allen *college official, clergyman*

Bunker Hill
Palmer, Barbara Louise Moulden *elementary education educator*

Charleston
†Arrington, Carolyn Ruth *school system administrator*
Coe, Pam *educational researcher*
†Eidell, Terry Lee *education research laboratory executive*
Welch, Edwin Hugh *academic administrator*

Clarksburg
Kittle, Robert Earl *school system administrator*

Clay
Dawson, James G. *superintendent*
Gillespie, Larry *secondary school principal*

Dellslow
Allamong, Betty D. *academic administrator*

Dunbar
Russell, James Alvin, Jr. *college administrator*

Elkins
MacConkey, Dorothy I. *academic administrator*

Fairmont
Dillman, Robert John *academic administrator*
Hardway, Wendell Gary *former college president*
Stalder, Florence Lucille *secondary education educator*

Huntington
Gould, Alan Brant *academic administrator*
Hayes, Robert Bruce *former college president, educator*
Hooper, James William *educator*
Kent, Calvin Albert *university administrator*

Morgantown
Biddington, William Robert *university administrator, dental educator*
Brooks, Dana D. *dean*
Bucklew, Neil S. *university president*
Jackson, Ruth Moore *academic administrator*
LaBelle, Thomas Jeffrey *academic administrator*
Maxwell, Robert Haworth *agriculture educator, college dean*
Stewart, Guy Harry *university dean emeritus, journalism educator*

Nitro
Lucas, Panola *elementary educator*

Parkersburg
Whitsett, Kingsley P. *school administrator*

Salem
Ohl, Ronald Edward *academic administrator*

Shepherdstown
Riccards, Michael Patrick *academic administrator*

Slanesville
McKee, Rae Ellen *special education educator*

Squire
Dishman, Roberta Crockett *retired educator*

Wellsburg
Price, Verla Blanche *elementary education educator*

West Liberty
Campbell, Clyde Del *academic administrator*

Wheeling
Minear, Judith *school system administrator*

WISCONSIN

Appleton
Warch, Richard *university president*

Ashland
Parsonage, Robert Rue *college president*

Balsam Lake
Bergstrand, Laura Joyce *elementary education educator*

Beloit
Ferrall, Victor Eugene, Jr. *college administrator, lawyer*

Brookfield
Jenkins, William Atwell *university chancellor*

Cedarburg
Steffens, Donna Irene *gifted and talented education educator*

Cross Plains
Rodenschmit, Helen Juliana *elementary education educator*

De Pere
Manion, Thomas A. *college president*

Eau Claire
Dunlap, William Phillip *dean*
Richards, Jerry Lee *academic administrator, religious educator*
Schnack, Larry Gene *university chancellor*
Shaw, Bonita Lynn *school administrator*

Elkhorn
Reinke, Doris Marie *retired elementary education educator*

Fish Creek
Abegg, Martin Gerald *retired university president*

Fond Du Lac
Henken, Willard John *retired university dean*

Glendale
Moeser, Elliott *principal*

Green Bay
Gariepy, Corinne *elementary school principal*

Hales Corners
Michalski, (Żurowski) Wacław *adult education educator*

Kenosha
Campbell, F(enton) Gregory *college administrator, historian*
Kaplan, Sheila *university official*
Smith, Eleanor Jane *academic administrator*

La Crosse
Kuipers, Judith L. *academic administrator*
Medland, William James *college president*
Novotney, Donald Francis *school system administrator*

Lake Nebagamon
Meyer, Karl William *retired university president*

Madison
Bell/Jackson, Marianne Jeanne *elementary education educator*
Bernstine, Daniel O'Neal *law educator, university dean*
Busby, Edward Oliver *retired dean*
Ebben, James Adrian *college president*
Jiao, Shou-shu *education educator, neuroscientist*
Kreuter, Gretchen V. *college president*
Lemberger, August Paul *university dean, pharmacy educator*
Lyall, Katharine C(ulbert) *academic administrator, economics educator*
†Martens, Lyle Charles *state education administrator*
McCarty, Donald James *education educator*
McGown, Wayne *academic administrator*
Mitby, Norman Peter *college president*
Netzer, Lanore A(gnes) *retired educational administration educator*
Odden, Allan Robert *education educator*
Policano, Andrew J. *university dean*
Prieve, E. Arthur *arts administration educator*
Ray, Dennis Jay *regulatory policy educator, researcher*
Simone, Beverly Sue *academic administrator*
Taylor, Carolyn L. *principal*
Ward, David *academic administrator, educator*
Weiss, Mareda Ruth *university administrator*
Wermers, Donald Joseph *registrar*
Witiak, Donald Theodore *medicinal chemistry educator*
Yuill, Thomas MacKay *university administrator, microbiology educator*

Menasha
Decker, William Joseph *superintendent*
Gorsalitz, Jeannine Liane *elementary school educator*

Mequon
Buuck, R(oland) John *university president*
Watson-Boone, Rebecca A. *educator*

Milton
Hosler, Russell John *retired education educator*

Milwaukee
Aman, Mohammed Mohammed *university dean, library and information science educator*
Coffman, Terrence J. *academic administrator*
DiUlio, Albert Joseph *university president, priest*
†Fuller, Howard *school system administrator*
Hatton, Janie R. Hill *principal*
Hollenbach, Sister Ruth *college president*
Keulks, George William *university dean, chemistry educator*
Norris, John *school system administrator*
†Rao, Tanniru R. *marketing educator, consultant*
Raynor, John Patrick *university administrator*
Read, Sister Joel *college administrator*
Reid, Robert Lelon *college dean, mechanical engineer*
Sankovitz, James Leo *development director, lobbyist*
Schenker, Eric *university dean, economist*
Schroeder, John H. *university administrator, history educator*
Spann, Wilma Nadene *principal*
Spitzer, Robert Ralph *academic administrator emeritus*
Viets, Hermann *college president, consultant*

Monroe
Brown, Sandra Lee *educational consultant, watercolorist*

New Franken
Weidner, Edward William *university chancellor, political scientist*

New London
Fitzgerald, Laurine Elisabeth *university dean, educator*

Oconomowoc
Reich, Rose Marie *retired art educator*

Oconto Falls
Schlieve, Hy C. J. *principal*

Oshkosh
Kerrigan, John E. *academic administrator*

Platteville
Al Yasiri, Kahtan Abbass *college dean*

Racine
Karls, John B. *retired educational administrator*
Murphy, William Mark Hickey *headmaster*

Richland Center
Meyer, Edwin Dale, Sr. *school system administrator*

Ripon
Stott, William Ross, Jr. *college president*

River Falls
Thibodeau, Gary A. *university administrator*

Sheboygan
Brewer, Warren Wesley *principal*
Longo, George P. *superintendent*

Stevens Point
Sanders, Keith R. *university chancellor*
Stevens, Dwight Marlyn *educational administrator*

Superior
Youngblood, Betty J. *academic administrator*

Thiensville
Williams, Maxine Eleanor *elementary education educator*

Twin Lakes
Fleischer, John Richard *retired secondary education educator*

Wales
Leekley, Marie Valpoon *secondary education educator*

Walworth
Sissons, John Roger *educational administrator*

Waukesha
Falcone, Frank S. *college president*

Waunakee
O'Neil, J(ames) Peter *elementary education educator, computer software designer*

Wausau
Gotham, Kathleen *college dean, human services administrator*

West Bend
Rodney, Joel Morris *dean*

Whitewater
Greenhill, H. Gaylon *academic administrator*
Schallenkamp, Kay *college administrator*

WYOMING

Afton
Lowe, James Allen *school superintendent*

Glenrock
Marr, Jo Ann *special education educator*

Laramie
Roark, Terry Paul *university president*

Newcastle
Sample, Bette Jeane *elementary educator*

Rock Springs
Baumberger, Don R. *school system administrator*

Wheatland
Morrison, Samuel Ferris *secondary school educator*

TERRITORIES OF THE UNITED STATES

AMERICAN SAMOA

Pago Pago
Varghese, Mary *secondary education educator*

GUAM

Mangilao
Lee, Chin-Tian *academic administrator, agricultural studies educator*

Talofofo
Taylor, James John *academic adminstrator*

PUERTO RICO

Adjuntas
Altieri Rosado, José Aníbal *principal*

Bayamon
Van Rooij, Vincent A. M. *university president*

Caguas
Ortiz, Víctor Raúl *parochial school educator*

Coto Laurel
Basols, Jose Andres *high school director and principal, priest*

Humacao
Castrodad, Felix A. *university administrator*

San German
Mojica, Agnes *academic administrator*

San Juan
Carreras, Francisco José *retired university president, foundation executive*
Gonzalez, Jose Ramón *academic administrator*
Matheu, Federico Manuel *university chancellor*
Santiago, Juan Jose *secondary school president*
Thompson, Annie Figueroa *academic director, educator*

Santurce
Ashby, Patricia F. *school system administrator, psychologist*

MILITARY ADDRESSES OF THE UNITED STATES

ATLANTIC

APO
Wetzstein, Sandra Lynne *elementary school educator*

EUROPE

APO
Sherrill, Anita Aileen *elementary school educator, consultant, educational system administrator*

FPO
DeMaio, Dorothy Walters *tutorial school administrator, consultant*

PACIFIC

APO
Mondale, Joan Adams *wife of former vice president of U.S.*

CANADA

ALBERTA

Calgary
Maher, Peter Michael *university dean*
Neale, E(rnest) R(ichard) Ward *retired university official, consultant*
Rasporich, Anthony Walter *university dean*
Thomlison, Ray J. *university dean, educator*
Watanabe, Mamoru *former university dean, physician, researcher*

Edmonton
Adams, Peter Frederick *university president, civil engineer*
Berg, Roy Torgny *retired university dean*

BRITISH COLUMBIA

Cobble Hill
Cox, Albert Reginald *academic administrator, physician, retired*

Kelowna
Muggeridge, Derek Brian *dean, engineering consultant*

Sooke
Booth, Andrew Donald *retired university administrator, scientist*

Vancouver
Andrews, John Hobart McLean *education educator*
Finnegan, Cyril Vincent *retired university dean, zoology educator*
Haycock, Kenneth Roy *education administrator*
Lusztig, Peter Alfred *university dean, educator*
McNeill, John Hugh *university dean*
Webber, William Alexander *university administrator, physician*

Victoria
McTaggart-Cowan, Ian *retired university chancellor*
Strong, David F. *university administrator*
Welch, S(tephen) Anthony *university dean, Islamic studies and arts educator*

MANITOBA

Winnipeg
Naimark, Arnold *university president, physiologist, internist*
Poettcker, Henry *retired seminary president*
Stalker, Jacqueline D'Aoust *academic administrator, educator*

NEW BRUNSWICK

Fredericton
Armstrong, Robin Louis *university official, physicist*

NOVA SCOTIA

Halifax
MacLean, Guy Robertson *retired university president*
Murray, Thomas John (Jock Murray) *medical humanities educator, medical researcher*
Ozmon, Kenneth Lawrence *university president, educator*

Timberlea
Verma, Surjit K. *school system administrator*

Truro
Mac Rae, Herbert Farquhar *retired college president*

ONTARIO

Hamilton
Shaw, Denis Martin *university dean, former geology educator*

London
Davenport, Paul *university administrator, economics educator*

North York
Macdonald, Hugh Ian *university president emeritus, economist, educator*
Mann, Susan *university president*

Ottawa
Kroeger, Arthur *university chancellor, former government official*
Labarge, Margaret Wade *medieval history educator*
Malouin, Jean-Louis *university dean, educator*
Philogene, Bernard J. R. *academic administrator, science educator*

Peterborough
Theall, Donald Francis *retired university president*

Saint Catharines
White, Terrence Harold *academic administrator, sociologist*

Thunder Bay
Locker, J. Gary *university official, civil engineering educator*
Rosehart, Robert George *university president, chemical engineer*

Toronto
Evans, John Robert *former university president, physician*
Hayhurst, James Frederick Palmer *career and business consultant, inspirational speaker*
Korey-Krzeczowski, George J. M. Kniaz *university administrator, management consultant*
Kushner, Eva *academic administrator, educator, author*
Ostry, Sylvia *academic administrator, economist*
Prichard, John Robert Stobo *academic administrator, law educator*
Runte, Roseann *academic administrator*
Sessle, Barry John *university administrator, researcher*

Waterloo
Berczi, Andrew Stephen *academic administrator*
Downey, James *university president*
Kay, Jeanne *dean, educator*
Smith, Rowland James *educational administrator*
Wright, Douglas Tyndall *former university president, company director, engineering educator*

Willowdale
MacDonald, Brian Scott *educational administrator*

Windsor
Ianni, Ronald William *university president and vice chancellor, lawyer*

PRINCE EDWARD ISLAND

Charlottetown
Eliot, Charles William John *university president, educator*

QUEBEC

Montreal
Belanger, Pierre Rolland *university dean, electrical engineering educator*
Cloutier, Gilles Georges *academic administrator, research executive*
Davidson, Colin Henry *university educator*
Freedman, Samuel Orkin *university official*
French, Stanley George *university dean, philosophy educator*
Granger, Luc Andre *university dean, psychologist*
Johnston, David Lloyd *academic administrator, lawyer*
Lajeunesse, Marcel *university administrator, educator*
†LeClerc, Denise *college dean*
Lowy, Frederick Hans *university president, psychiatrist*

Quebec
Gervais, Michel *academic administrator*

Saint Hubert
Doré, Roland *dean, science association director*

Sainte Anne de Bellevue
Buckland, Roger Basil *university dean, educator, vice principal*

Sainte Foy
Murray, Warren James *educator, philosopher*

SASKATCHEWAN

Regina
Barber, Lloyd Ingram *retired university president*

Saskatoon
Knight, Arthur Robert *technical institute administrator*
Knott, Douglas Ronald *college dean, agricultural sciences educator, researcher*
McCallum, Kenneth James *retired university dean, chemistry and chemical engineering educator*
Nikiforuk, Peter N. *university dean*
Stewart, John Wray Black *college dean*

CHILE

Concepcion
Trzebiatowski, Gregory L. *education educator*

Santiago
Strommen, Clifford H. *headmaster*

EGYPT

Cairo
Miller, Harry George *education educator*

ENGLAND

Milton Keynes
Daniel, John Sagar (Sir) *academic administrator, metallurgist*

Oxford
Cairncross, Sir Alexander Kirkland *university chancellor, economist*

Surrey
Petrek, William Joseph *college president emeritus*

GERMANY

Frankfurt
Simitis, Spiros *legal educator*

GREECE

Halandri
Dorbis, John *school system administrator*

IRELAND

Ballyvaughan
Wicks, Eugene Claude *college president, art educator*

ITALY

Florence
Kaiser, Walter *English language educator*

SPAIN

Tacoronte
Kardas, Sigmund Joseph, Jr. *secondary education educator*

TURKMENISTAN

Ashgabat
McCall, John Patrick *college president, educator*

ADDRESS UNPUBLISHED

Aiken, Michael Thomas *academic administrator*
Allen, Charles Eugene *college administrator, agriculturist*
Alligood, Elizabeth H. *special education educator*
Almen, Louis Theodore *retired college president*
Altshuler, Alan Anthony *dean, political scientist*
Applin, Catherine Balash *primary school educator, consultant*
Armstrong, Warren Bruce *university president, historian, educator*
Atkinson, Dewey Franklin *retired educational administrator*
Babbitt, Samuel Fisher *university administrator*
Baker, Robert M. L., Jr. *academic administrator*
Baldwin, C. Andrew, Jr. *retired science educator*
Ball, Howard Guy *education specialist educator*
Barone, John Anthony *university provost emeritus*
Bassist, Donald Herbert *academic administrator*
Baxter, Cecil William, Jr. *retired college president*
Becker, Walter Heinrich *vocational educator, planner*
Bell, Terrel Howard *education educator*
Bellum, Fred Lewis *school system administrator, retired*
Bergman, Hermas John (Jack Bergman) *retired college administrator*
Bernstein, I(rving) Melvin *university official and dean, materials scientist*
Betts, Elaine Wiswall *retired headmistress*
Beveridge, James MacDonald Richardson *retired college president*
Bishop, Charles Edwin *university president emeritus, economist*
Boeker, Paul Harold *academic official, diplomat*
Bogue, Philip Roberts *former academic administrator*
Boland, Margaret Frances *secondary education educator*
Bondurant, Gordon Emerson *headmaster*
Bonner, Patricia J. *academic dean, educator*
Borchers, Mary Amelia *middle school educator*
Bost, Raymond Morris *retired college president*
Boucher, Laurence James *university dean, chemist*
Bourdo, G. F. *principal*
Box, Thadis Wayne *university dean emeritus, educator*
Brain, George Bernard *university dean*
Branyan, Robert Lester *retired university administrator*
Bright, Harold Frederick *university provost emeritus, consultant*
Brown, Robert Charles *college administrator*
Bulger, Roger James *academic health center executive*
Burroughs, Franklin Troy *academic administrator*
Caldwell, Howard Bryant *English language educator*
Cameron, J. Elliot *retired parochial educational system administrator*
Cameron, Lucille Wilson *retired dean of libraries*
Campbell, Sarah *elementary education educator, special education specialist*
Carter, Herbert Edmund *former university official*
Casper, Gerhard *academic administrator, law educator*
Chandler, John Herrick *college president*
Chase, James Richard *retired college president*
Childers, Pamela Barnard *secondary school educator*
Church, Martha Eleanor *former college president*
Chyu, Chi-Oy Wei *secondary school educator*

Clark, Claudia J. educational administration, speech, language and learning disabilities professional
Clark, James Milford college president, retired
Clarke, Lambuth McGeehee college president emeritus
Clifford, Brother Peter academic administrator, religious educator
Coffee, Joseph Denis, Jr. college chancellor emeritus
Collier, Herman Edward, Jr. retired college president
Compton, Norma Haynes retired university dean
Connell, George Edward former university president, scientist
Copeland, Henry Jefferson, Jr. former college president
Cormican, M. Alma elementary education educator
Cramer, Robert Vern retired college president, director scholarship program, consultant
Crawford, Kenneth Charles educational institute executive, retired government official
Davenport, Ernest Harold university official, accountant
Davenport, Lawrence Franklin school system administrator
Davis, Anna Jane Ripley elementary education educator
Davis, F. Benjamin academic administrator
Davis, Helen R. elementary and middle school educator
Davison, Beaumont retired university administrator
Delahanty, Rebecca Ann school system administrator
Denman, William Foster retired academic administrator, educator
Denton, David Edward retired education educator
Dishman, Leland Lee school system administrator
Dobler, Donald William retired college dean, consultant, corporate executive
Dorsey, Rhoda Mary retired academic administrator
Drake, George Albert college president, historian
Duff, John Bernard college president, former city official
Dunworth, John retired college president
Durante, Angela university official, writer, educator
Dutson, Thayne R. university dean
Ebbert, Arthur, Jr. retired university dean
Evans, Geraldine Ann academic administrator
Everett, Donna Raney business educator
Farley, Lloyd Edward retired education educator
Farquhar, Robin Hugh university president
Feerick, John David university dean, lawyer
Feldstein, Joshua academic administrator
Ferguson, Glenn Walker educational consultant, lecturer
Fernald, Anne educator
Fife, Jonathan Donald higher education educator
Filchock, Ethel education educator, poet
Fountain, Cornelia Wilkes special education educator
Fox, Edward A. retired college dean
Freeman, Meredith Norwin former college president, education educator
Frick, Ivan Eugene college president emeritus
Frierson, Jimmie Lou vocational education educator
†Frost, Everett Lloyd academic administrator
Fuenning, Esther Renate adult education educator
Gaspar, Anna Louise retired elementary school teacher, consultant
Gillespie, Nellie Redd academic administrator, state official
Gladstone, Carol Lynn assistant principal
Glower, Donald Duane university executive, mechanical engineer
Goewey, Gordon Ira university administrator
Goffe, Esther elementary school educator
Good, Linda Lou elementary education educator
Goode, Janet Weiss elementary school educator
Gordis, David Moses academic administrator, rabbi
Gore, Sadie Lou elementary education educator, retired
Greco, Joseph M parochial school educator
Green, Nancy Loughridge higher education executive
Gruber, Sharon Doris former secondary educator
Hammer, Joyce Mae gifted and talented education educator
Hankins, Mary Denman elementary school educator
Hardin, Clifford Morris retired university chancellor, cabinet member
Hardin, Paul, III university chancellor
Harrington, Jean Patrice former college president
Harvey, Mary Bird retired university official
Hasselmo, Nils university official, linguistics educator
Heaton, Jean early childhood educator
Hegarty, George John university president, English educator
Helman, Alfred Blair retired college president, education consultant
Heskett, Luvina Hylton elementary school educator
Hitchcock, Walter Anson educational consultant, retired educational administrator
Hochberger, Bernadette M. secondary education educator, counselor
Hoi, Samuel Chuen-Tsung dean
Holt, Sandra Grace middle school educator
Horn, Todd Richard Wendell school administrator
Horner, Matina Souretis retired college president, corporate executive
Hughes, Eugene Morgan university president
Humphrey, Arthur Earl university administrator
Huttenback, Robert Arthur academic administrator, educator
Jackson, Lambert Blunt academic administrator
Jacobs, Linda Rotroff elementary school educator
Jakubauskas, Edward Benedict college president
John, Ralph Candler retired college president, educator
Johnson, Everett Ramon retired college dean
Johnson, Sylvia Sue university administrator, educator
Jones, Lawrence Neale university dean, minister
Kaschak, Virginia Ruth elementary education educator
Katz, Alan Martin secondary education educator
Kazmarek, Linda Adams secondary education educator
Keiper, Marilyn Morrison educator
Kerins, Francis Joseph college president
Kersting, Edwin Joseph retired university dean
Kezer, Pauline Ryder educational consultant
Kliebhan, Sister M(ary) Camille academic administrator
Knox, Ernest Rudder retired college president
Koenig, Allen Edward higher education consultant
Komisar, David Daniel retired university provost
Kormondy, Edward John university official, biology educator
Krey, Robert Dean education educator emeritus
Kristensen, Marlene early childhood educator
Kruck, Donna Jean special education educator, consultant
Kushinka, Joyce Williams secondary education educator, retired
Laible, Jon Morse retired mathematics educator, dean
Langworthy, William Clayton college official
Lantz, Joanne Baldwin university chancellor emerita
Lawrence, Linda Hiett retired school system administrator, writer
Leal, Herbert Allan Borden former university chancellor, former government official
Leddy, Susan nursing school educator
Lennon, Joseph Luke college official, priest
Leventhal, Robert Stanley academic administrator
Lindegren, Jack Kenneth elementary and secondary education educator
Lindsay, Carol Frances Stockton dean
Ling, Deirdre Ann headmistress
Lipscomb-Brown, Edra Evadean retired childhood educator
Lockwood, Theodore Davidge former academic administrator
Lomas, Bernard Tagg college president emeritus
Lomax, Peggy Quarles gifted and talented education educator
Loser, Joseph Carlton, Jr. dean, retired judge
Lovinger, Warren Conrad emeritus university president
Lundgren, Leonard, III retired secondary education educator
Luttner, Edward F. career management consultant
Lutz, Carl Freiheit academic administrator
Macmillan, William Hooper university dean, educator
Mallory, Arthur Lee university dean, retired state official
Marshak, Robert Reuben former university dean, medical educator, veterinarian
†Martin, Mary secondary education educator
Maurer, Beverly Bennett school administrator
Mayfield, Robert Charles university official, geography educator
McAbeer, Sara Carita school administrator
McCarthy, Kevin Joseph academic dean, music educator
McConner, Stanley Jay, Sr. academic administrator
McIntosh, Carolyn Meade retired educational administrator
McLoone, Eugene P. education educator
Mc Mahon, George Joseph academic administrator
Medley, Donald Matthias retired education educator, consultant
Melady, Thomas Patrick university president, ambassador, author, public policy expert, educator
Melsheimer, William C. principal
Meyer, Kathleen Marie college educator
Meyer, Pauline Marie retired special education educator
Miaskiewicz, Theresa Elizabeth secondary educator
Miller, Arjay retired university dean
Miller, James Vince university president
Miller, Jerry Huber retired university chancellor
Mills, Eugene Sumner college president
Mills, Robert Lee president emeritus
Moeckel, Bill Reid retired university dean
Monahan, Edward Charles academic administrator, marine science educator
Morgan, Ruth Prouse academic administrator, educator
Morris, Bevan Howell university official
Mortola, Edward Joseph emeritus university chancellor
Myers, Harold Mathews academic administrator
Nelson, Edwin Clarence academic administrator, emeritus
Neunzig, Carolyn Miller middle school educator
Norris, Alfred Lloyd theological seminary president, clergyman
†Null, Jack Elton schools superintendent
O'Donnell, Brother Frank Joseph principal
O'Malley, Thomas Patrick university president
Outcalt, David Lewis academic administrator, mathematician, educator
Paino, Ronald Thomas education consultant
Palmer, Irene Sabelberg university dean and educator emeritus, nurse, researcher, historian
Park, John Thornton academic administrator
Parrish, Alma Ellis elementary school educator
Patmos, Adrian Edward university dean emeritus
Paulino, Sister Mary McAuley principal
Paulsen, Frank Robert college dean emeritus
Peoples, John Arthur, Jr. former university president, consultant
Perreault, Sister Jeanne college president
Pierce, Anne-Marie B. school system administrator
Piper, Fredessa Mary school system administrator
Pizzuro, Salvatore Nicholas special education educator
Platti, Rita Jane educator, draftsman, author, inventor
Porteous, Timothy academic administrator
Pouncey, Peter Richard college president, classics educator
Preston, Alda S. academic administrator, nursing educator
Preusser, Joseph William academic administrator
Price, Phillip S. retired adult education educator
Prins, Robert Jack college administrator
Pritchard, Claudius Hornby, Jr. retired university president
Prokasy, William Frederick academic administrator
Propst, Harold Dean retired university chancellor
Pryor, Harold S. retired college president
Purvis, Richard George former superintendent of schools
Pusey, William Webb, III retired dean, foreign language educator
Rains, Hazel Grace curriculum director
Ratcliff, James Lewis administrator
Redmont, Bernard Sidney university dean, journalism educator
Reinke, Ralph Louis retired academic administrator
Reisman, Fredricka Kauffman education educator
Reynolds, Lynne Warren special education educator, speech pathologist
Rhodes, Geraldine Bryan secondary school administrator
Richardson, Elsie Helen retired elementary educator
Riddle, Donald Husted former university chancellor
Riggs, Sonya Woicinski elementary school educator
Ritchie, Anne educational administrator
Robbins, Frances Elaine educational administrator
Roberts, Karlene Ann education educator
Robertson, Mary Virginia retired elementary educator
Robinson, James Arthur university president emeritus, political scientist
†Rodgers, Fran Sussner educational development specialist
Rodriguez, Veronica special education educator
Royal, Darrell K. university administrator
Ryan, Ione Jean Alohilani retired educator, counselor
Ryder, Georgia Atkins university dean, educator
Ryder, Jack McBride educational consultant
Sanchez, Gilbert retired university president, microbiologist
Sanders, Marlene academic administrator, educator, freelance broadcast journalist
Scandary, E. Jane special education educator, consultant
Schmidt, Ruth Ann retired college president
Scholl, Allan Henry retired school system administrator, education consultant
Schrage, Rose educational administrator
Schwartz, Eleanor Brantley academic administrator
Scollard, Diane Louise retired elementary school educator
Sessions, Robert Paul former college president and administrator, retired educator, writer
Sharwell, William Gay retired university president and company executive
Shaw, Helen Lester Anderson nutrition educator
Shearer, Charles Livingston academic administrator
Sheldon, Thomas Donald academic administrator
Shellman-Lucas, Elizabeth C. special education educator, researcher
Sherman, Richard H. education educator
Silvius, Donald Joe educational consultant
Slavin, Susan Ann secondary educator
Smulyan, Lisa educator
Sneed, Alberta Neal retired elementary education educator
Snortland, Howard Jerome educational financial consultant
Sonnenschein, Hugo Freund university president, economics educator
Spadafora, David Charles university administrator
Spatta, Carolyn Davis education consultant
Spiesicke, Margrit Herma counselor
Stabile, Benedict Louis retired academic administrator, retired coast guard officer
Stacy, Bill Wayne college president
Staiger, Ralph Conrad educational consultant, former educational association executive
Stein, Dale Franklin retired university president
Stewart, Clinton Eugene adult education educator
Stewart, John Ezell educational and business consultant
Stewart, Norman Lawrence university president
Strangway, David William university president
Stuckwisch, Clarence George university administrator
Talbot, Kathleen Mary elementary education educator
Tanner, Laurel Nan education educator
Thorne, Barbara Lockwood guidance counselor, secondary education educator
Tomsovic, Edward Joseph college dean
Tonjes, Marian Jeannette Benton education educator
Trow, Jo Anne Johnson retired university official
Tuck, Russell R., Jr. past college president
Vallat, Louise Marie elementary school educator, poet
Vandevender, Barbara Jewell elementary education educator, farmer
Varn, Richard James university administrator, lawyer, consultant
Volpe, Edmond L(oris) college president
Walker, Decker Fannin education educator
†Walker, Leroy Tashreau university chancellor, coach
Walton, Ronald Elwood retired school superintendent
Washington, Delphine Cynthia special education educator, artist
Washington, Walter retired college president
Watson, James D., Jr. principal
†Weaver, Charles Horace educational administrator
Wilson, Roosevelt Ledell secondary education educator
White, James Arthur college president
Whitten, Dolphus, Jr. former university administrator, educational consortium executive
Wittich, John Jacob retired college president, educational administrator, corporation consultant
Wong, David Yue academic administrator, physics educator
Woods, Phyllis Michalik elementary school educator
Worthen, John Edward university president
Wrucke-Nelson, Ann C. elementary school educator
Young, Margaret Chong elementary education educator
Young, Virgil M. education educator
Zufryden, Fred S. academic administrator, marketing educator, researcher
†Zuiches, James Joseph academic administrator

ENGINEERING

UNITED STATES

ALABAMA

Auburn
Aldridge, Melvin Dayne electrical engineering educator
Cochran, John Euell, Jr. aerospace engineer, educator, lawyer
Crocker, Malcolm John mechanical engineer, noise control engineer, educator
Irwin, John David electrical engineering educator
Jaeger, Richard Charles electrical engineer, educator, science center director
Rainer, Rex Kelly civil engineer, educator
Schafer, Robert Louis agricultural engineer, researcher
Siginer, Dennis Aydeniz mechanical engineering educator, researcher
Turnquist, Paul Kenneth agricultural engineer, educator

Birmingham
Appleton, Joseph Hayne civil engineer, educator
Edmonds, William Fleming retired engineering and construction company executive
Gilbert, Rodney C. engineering executive
Goodrich, Thomas Michael engineering and construction executive
Kennedy, Theodore Clifford engineering and construction company executive, consultant
Miller, Edmond Trowbridge civil engineer, educator, consultant

Daphne
Jeffreys, Elystan Geoffrey geological engineer, petroleum consultant and appraiser

Huntsville
Costes, Nicholas Constantine aerospace technologist, government official
Dannenberg, Konrad K. aeronautical engineer
Daussman, Grover Frederick electrical engineer, consultant
Douillard, Paul Arthur engineering and financial executive, consultant
Emerson, William Kary engineering company executive
Hung, Ru J. engineering educator, research scientist
Joner, Bruno aeronautical engineer
Kowel, Stephen Thomas electrical engineer, educator
Mc Donough, George Francis, Jr. aerospace engineer
Moore, Fletcher Brooks engineering company executive
Pittman, William Claude electrical engineer
Polites, Michael Edward aerospace research engineer
Potate, John Spencer, Sr. engineering company executive, consultant
Ritter, Alfred aerospace consultant
Russell, Lynn Darnell engineering educator
†Schonberg, William Peter mechanical and civil engineering educator
Schroer, Bernard Jon industrial engineering educator
†Simmons, Jennings (Jay) aerospace engineer
Vinz, Frank Louis electrical engineer
Wessling, Francis Christopher mechanical engineer, educator

Madison
Hawk, Clark Wiliams mechanical engineering educator

Mobile
Hamid, Michael electrical engineering educator, consultant

Montgomery
Paddock, Austin Joseph engineering executive

Orange Beach
Brennan, Lawrence Edward electronics engineer

Point Clear
Ferguson, Joseph Gantt chemical engineer

Tuscaloosa
Barfield, Robert F. retired mechanical engineer, educator, dean
Bryan, Colgan Hobson aerospace engineering educator
Doughty, Julian Orus mechanical engineer, educator
Frye, John H., Jr. metallurgical engineering educator
Griffin, Marvin Anthony industrial engineer, educator
Morley, Lloyd Albert mining engineering educator

ALASKA

Anchorage
Johnson, Eric Gordon geotechnical engineer
Leman, Loren Dwight civil engineer
Thomas, Howard Paul civil engineer, consultant

Fairbanks
Behlke, Charles Edward civil engineer, former university dean
Bennett, Fred Lawrence engineering educator
Sengupta, Mritunjoy mining engineer, educator
Tilsworth, Timothy retired environmental/civil engineering educator

ARIZONA

Carefree
Bergstrom, Richard Norman civil engineer

Chandler
Ratkowski, Donald J. mechanical engineer, consultant

Flagstaff
Somerville, Mason Harold mechanical engineering educator, university dean

Green Valley
Peterson, Harold Albert electrical engineer, educator

Mesa
Fairbanks, Harold Vincent metallurgical engineer, educator
Rummel, Robert Wiland aeronautical engineer, author

Paradise Valley
Russell, Paul Edgar electrical engineering educator

Phoenix
Bachus, Benson Floyd mechanical engineer, consultant
†Baltes, Robert Thomas electrical engineer
Burchard, John Kenneth chemical engineer
Chisholm, Tom Shepherd environmental engineer
Faul, Gary Lyle electrical engineering supervisor
Freyermuth, Clifford L. structural engineering consultant
Jorgensen, Gordon David engineering company executive
Miller, Michael Jon survey engineer, local government manager
Stine, George Harry consulting engineer, author
Thomas, Harold William avionics systems engineer, flight instructor
Watson, Harold George engineering executive, mechanical engineer
Zeilinger, Philip Thomas aeronautical engineer
Zweifel, Terry L. aeronautical engineer, researcher

Prescott
Chesson, Eugene, Jr. *civil engineering educator, consultant*
Hasbrook, A. Howard *aviation safety engineer, consultant*
Kahne, Stephen James *systems engineer, educator, academic administrator, engineering executive*

Rio Verde
Jordan, Richard Charles *engineering executive*

Scottsdale
Aadland, Donald Ingvald *engineering executive*
Blackburn, Jack Bailey *retired civil engineering educator*
Fisher, John Richard *engineering consultant, former naval officer*
Kline, Arthur Jonathan *electronics engineer*
Leeser, David O. *materials engineer, metallurgist*

Sun City West
Woodruff, Neil Parker *agricultural engineer*

Tempe
Akers, Lex A. *engineering educator*
Backus, Charles Edward *engineering educator, researcher*
Balanis, Constantine Apostle *electrical engineering educator*
Berman, Neil Sheldon *chemical engineering educator*
Carpenter, Ray Warren *materials scientist and engineer, educator*
Ferry, David Keane *electrical engineering educator*
†Guilbeau, Eric J. *biomedical engineer, electrical engineer, educator*
Karady, George Gyorgy *electrical engineering educator, consultant*
Kaufman, Irving *retired engineering educator*
Schroder, Dieter Karl *electrical engineering educator*
Shaw, Milton Clayton *mechanical engineering educator*
Singhal, Avinash Chandra *engineering administrator, educator*
†Wood, Byard Dean *mechanical engineering educator and researcher*

Tonopah
Brittingham, James Calvin *nuclear engineer*

Tucson
Arnell, Walter James William *mechanical engineering educator, consultant*
Battistelli, Joseph John *electronics executive*
Chen, Chuan Fang *mechanical engineering educator*
Davidson, Lacinda Susan *materials engineer, chemist*
Desai, Chandrakant S. *civil engineering and engineering mechanics educator*
Freeh, Edward James *chemical engineer*
Galloway, Kenneth Franklin *electrical engineering educator*
Ganapol, Barry Douglas *nuclear engineering educator, consultant*
Gross, Joseph Francis *retired bio-engineering educator*
Harrington, Roger Fuller *electrical engineering educator, consultant*
Hunt, Bobby Ray *electrical engineering educator, consultant*
Jones, Roger Clyde *retired electrical engineering educator*
Kececioglu, Dimitri Basil *reliability engineering educator*
Kerwin, William James *electrical engineering educator, consultant*
Kinney, Robert Bruce *mechanical engineering educator*
Korn, Granino Arthur *engineer*
Nordby, Gene Milo *engineering educator*
Porcello, Leonard Joseph *engineering research and development executive*
Prince, John Luther, III *engineering educator*
†Randolph, Alan Dean *chemical engineering educator*
Renard, Kenneth George *civil engineer*
Sears, William Rees *engineering educator*
Speas, Robert Dixon *aeronautical engineer, aviation company executive*
Wait, James Richard *electrical engineering educator, scientist*
Wygnanski, Israel Jerzy *aerospace engineering educator*
Zeigler, Bernard Phillip *electrical and computer engineering educator*

Youngtown
Gross, Al *electrical engineer, consultant*

ARKANSAS

Conway
Holt, Frank Ross *retired aerospace engineer*

Fayetteville
Andrews, John Frank *civil and environmental engineering educator*
Gaddy, James Leoma *chemical engineer, educator*
LeFevre, Elbert Walter, Jr. *civil engineering educator*
Schmitt, Neil Martin *biomedical engineer, electrical engineering educator*

CALIFORNIA

Agoura Hills
Chang, Chong Eun *chemical engineer*

Alameda
Klehs, Henry John Wilhelm *civil engineer*

Alta Loma
Cooper, George Robert *electrical engineer, educator*

Anaheim
Hubbard, Charles Ronald *engineering executive*
Prince, Warren Victor *mechanical engineer*
Rivera, Armando Remonte *utilities engineer*

Arcadia
Broderick, Donald Leland *electronics engineer*

Belvedere Tiburon
Elder, Rex Alfred *civil engineer*

Berkeley
Angelakos, Diogenes James *electrical engineering educator*
Berger, Stanley Allan *mechanical engineering educator*
Birdsall, Charles Kennedy *electrical engineer*
Bogy, David B(eauregard) *mechanical engineering educator*
Cairns, Elton James *chemical engineering educator*
Chopra, Anil Kumar *civil engineering educator*
Chua, Leon O. *electrical engineering and computer science educator*
Denn, Morton Mace *chemical engineering educator*
Desoer, Charles Auguste *electrical engineer*
Dornfeld, David Alan *engineering educator*
Evans, James William *metallurgical educator*
Fatt, Irving *optometry and bioengineering educator*
Finnie, Iain *mechanical engineer, educator*
Frisch, Joseph *mechanical engineer, educator, consultant*
Fuerstenau, Douglas Winston *mineral engineering educator*
Garrison, William Louis *civil engineering educator*
Goldsmith, Werner *mechanical engineering educator*
Gray, Paul Russell *educator*
Grossman, Lawrence Morton *nuclear engineering educator*
Harris, Guy Hendrickson *chemical research engineer*
Hodges, David Albert *electrical engineering educator*
Hsu, Chieh Su *applied mechanics engineering educator, researcher*
Hu, Chenming *electrical engineering educator*
Jewell, William Sylvester *engineering educator*
Kastenberg, William Edward *engineering and applied science educator*
Kuh, Ernest Shiu-Jen *electrical engineering educator*
Leitmann, George *mechanical engineering educator*
Lewis, Edwin Reynolds *biomedical engineering educator*
May, Adolf Darlington *civil engineering educator*
Mei, Kenneth K. *electrical engineering and computer sciences educator*
Messerschmitt, David Gavin *engineering educator*
Monismith, Carl Leroy *civil engineering educator*
Mote, Clayton Daniel, Jr. *mechanical engineer, educator, administrator*
Muller, Richard Stephen *electrical engineer, educator*
Newman, John Scott *chemical engineer, educator*
Oldham, William George *electrical engineering and computer science educator*
Ott, David Michael *engineering company executive*
Pagni, Patrick John *mechanical and fire safety engineering science educator* ,
Pask, Joseph Adam *ceramic engineering educator*
Penzien, Joseph *structural engineering educator*
Pigford, Thomas Harrington *nuclear engineering educator*
Polak, Elijah *engineering educator, computer scientist*
Popov, Egor Paul *engineering educator*
Prausnitz, John Michael *chemical engineer, educator*
Sangiovanni-Vincentelli, Alberto Luigi *electrical engineering and computer science educator, consultant*
Schrock, Virgil Edwin *mechanical and nuclear engineer*
Scordelis, Alexander Costicas *civil engineering educator*
Susskind, Charles *engineering educator, author, publishing executive*
Tobias, Charles William *chemical engineer, educator*
Turin, George Lewis *electrical engineering educator, university dean*
Whinnery, John Roy *electrical engineering educator*
White, Richard Manning *electrical engineering educator*
Wiegel, Robert Louis *consulting engineering executive*
†Witherspoon, Paul Adams, Jr. *geological engineer, petroleum engineer*
Wong, Eugene *engineering educator*
Zwoyer, Eugene Milton *consulting engineering executive*

Campbell
Ross, Hugh Courtney *electrical engineer*

Canoga Park
Norman, Arnold McCallum, Jr. *engineering specialist*

Carmel
Alsberg, Dietrich Anselm *electrical engineer*
Brahtz, John Frederick Peel *civil engineering educator*

Carmel Valley
Lorenzen, Coby *emeritus engineering educator*

Chico
Allen, Charles William *mechanical engineering educator*

Chula Vista
Wolk, Martin *electronic engineer, physicist*

Claremont
Dym, Clive Lionel *engineering educator*
Molinder, John Irving *engineering educator, consultant*
Monson, James Edward *electrical engineer, educator*
Phillips, John Richard *engineering educator*

Concord
†Cassidy, John Joseph *hydraulic and hydrologic engineer*
Lee, Low Kee *electronics engineer, consultant*

Corona
Tillman, Joseph Nathaniel *engineering executive*

Corona Del Mar
Richmond, Ronald LeRoy *aerospace engineer*

Culver City
Sensiper, Samuel *consulting electrical engineer*

Cupertino
Fenn, Raymond Wolcott, Jr. *retired metallurgical engineer*
Lindsay, Leslie *packaging engineer*
†Lundgren, David Albert *product design engineer*
†Starkweather, Gary Keith *optical engineer, computer company executive*

Danville
Maninger, R(alph) Carroll *engineering executive, consultant*
Trezek, George James *mechanical engineer*

Davis
Akesson, Norman Berndt *agricultural engineer, emeritus educator*
Beadle, Charles Wilson *retired mechanical engineering educator*
Brandt, Harry *mechanical engineering educator*
Chancellor, William Joseph *agricultural engineering educator*
Cheney, James Addison *civil engineering educator*
Dorf, Richard Carl *electrical engineering and management educator*
Fridley, Robert Bruce *agricultural engineering educator*
Gardner, William Allen *electrical engineering educator*
Gates, Bruce Clark *chemical engineer, educator*
Ghausi, Mohammed Shuaib *electrical engineering educator, university dean*
Giedt, Warren Harding *mechanical engineer, educator*
Hakimi, S. Louis *electrical and computer engineering educator*
Kemper, John Dustin *mechanical engineering educator*
Kepner, Robert Allen *agricultural engineering researcher, educator*
Larock, Bruce Edward *civil engineering educator*
Tchobanoglous, George *civil engineering educator*
Wang, Shih-Ho *electrical engineer, educator*

Del Mar
Cutrona, Louis John *engineering executive*
Wilkinson, Eugene Parks *nuclear engineer*

Dinuba
Leps, Thomas MacMaster *civil engineer, consultant*

Downey
Baumann, Theodore Robert *aerospace engineer, consultant, army officer*
Brofman, Woody *astronautical engineer, educator*
Demarchi, Ernest Nicholas *aerospace company executive*

Duarte
Chou, Chung-Kwang *bio-engineer*

Edwards
Deets, Dwain Aaron *aeronautical research engineer*
†Fugate, Robert Q. *optical engineer*

El Segundo
Gupta, Madhu Sudan *electrical engineering educator*
Lantz, Norman Foster *electrical engineer*
Mo, Roger Shih-Yah *electronics engineering manager*
Ricardi, Leon Joseph *electrical engineer*
Tamrat, Befecadu *aeronautical engineer*

Encinitas
Morrow, Charles Tabor *aerospace consulting engineer*

Encino
Acheson, Louis Kruzan, Jr. *aerospace engineer and systems analyst*
Friedman, George Jerry *aerospace company executive, engineer*
Knuth, Eldon Luverne *engineering educator*

Fair Oaks
Agerbek, Sven *mechanical engineer*
Smiley, Robert William *industrial engineer*

Folsom
Ettlich, William F. *electrical engineer*

Foster City
Ham, Lee Edward *civil engineer*

Fresno
Brahma, Chandra Sekhar *civil engineering educator*

Fullerton
Begovich, Nicholas Anthony *electrical engineer, consultant*

Gardena
Kucij, Timothy Michael *engineer, composer, organist, pianist, conductor, minister, theologian*

Glendale
Knoop, Vern Thomas *civil engineer, consultant*
Vilnrotter, Victor Alpár *research engineer*

Granite Bay
Crossley, Frank Alphonso *former metallurgical engineer*

Hacienda Heights
Love, Daniel Joseph *consulting engineer*

Half Moon Bay
Hidy, George Martel *chemical engineer, executive*

Hawthorne
Ashkenas, Irving Louis *aerospace executive*
†McRuer, Duane Torrance *aerospace engineering executive*

Hermosa Beach
McDowell, Edward R. H. *chemical engineer*

Hillsborough
Blume, John August *consulting civil engineer*

Huntington Beach
Anderson, Raymond Hartwell, Jr. *metallurgical engineer*
Falcon, Joseph A. *mechanical engineering consultant*
Hildebrant, Andy McClellan *retired electrical engineer*

Indian Wells
Pace, Stanley Carter *retired aeronautical engineer*

Irvine
Ang, Alfredo Hua-Sing *civil engineering educator*
Bershad, Neil Jeremy *electrical engineering educator*
Griffin, Gerald D. *engineering company executive*
Guymon, Gary LeRoy *civil engineering educator, consultant*
Hess, Cecil F. *engineering executive*
Korb, Robert William *former materials and processes engineer*
McCraw, Leslie G. *engineering and construction company executive*
Sirignano, William Alfonso *aerospace and mechanical engineer, educator*
Sklansky, Jack *electrical and computer engineering educator, researcher*
Stubberud, Allen Roger *electrical engineering educator*
†Yamano, Donald *engineering executive*

Kensington
Oppenheim, Antoni Kazimierz *mechanical engineer*

La Jolla
†Asaro, Robert J. *engineering educator*
Breitwieser, Charles John *engineer, educator*
Chang, William Shen Chie *electrical engineering educator*
Chien, Shu *physiology and bioengineering educator*
Conn, Robert William *engineering science educator*
Counts, Stanley Thomas *aerospace consultant, retired naval officer, retired electronics company executive*
Fung, Yuan-Cheng Bertram *bioengineering educator, author*
Goldman, Stanford *electrical engineer, scientist*
Helstrom, Carl Wilhelm *electrical engineering educator*
Intaglietta, Marcos *bioengineering educator*
Levy, Ralph *engineering executive, consultant*
Milstein, Laurence Bennett *electrical engineering educator, researcher*
Nelles, Maurice *mechanical engineer, author*
Penner, Stanford Solomon *engineering educator*
Rudee, Mervyn Lea *engineering educator, researcher*
Schmid-Schoenbein, Geert Wilfried *biomedical engineer, educator*
Skalak, Richard *engineering mechanics educator, researcher*
Williams, Forman Arthur *engineering science educator, combustion theorist*
Wolf, Jack Keil *electrical engineer, educator*

La Selva
Brown, Alan Charlton *retired aeronautical engineer*

Lafayette
Laird, Alan Douglas Kenneth *mechanical engineering educator*
Peirano, Lawrence Edward *civil engineer*

Laguna Hills
Larson, Harry Thomas *electronics engineer*
Lederer, Jerome *aerospace safety engineer, educator*

Lancaster
Hodges, Vernon Wray *mechanical engineer*

Livermore
Carley, James French *chemical and plastics engineer*
†Dane, Paul Nelson *communication engineer, retired*
Johnson, Roy Ragnar *electrical engineer*
King, Ray John *electrical engineer*
Sheem, Sang Keun *fiber optics engineering professional*

Long Beach
Brent, Paul Leslie *mechanical engineering educator*
de Soto, Simon *mechanical engineer*
Dillon, Michael Earl *engineering executive, mechanical engineer, educator*
Donald, Eric Paul *aeronautical engineer, inventor*
Kumar, Rajendra *electrical engineering educator*

Los Alamitos
Iceland, William Frederick *engineering consultant*

Los Altos
Besser, Les *electrical engineer*
Fondahl, John Walker *civil engineering educator*
Ginzton, Edward Leonard *retired engineering company executive*
Kazan, Benjamin *research engineer*
Peterson, Victor Lowell *aerospace engineer, management consultant*
Sharpe, Roland Leonard *retired engineering company executive, earthquake and structural engineering consultant*

Los Angeles
Ayres, James Marx *mechanical engineer*
Blackwelder, Ron Forest *engineering educator, consultant, researcher*
Breuer, Melvin Allen *electrical engineering educator*
Bucy, Richard Snowden *aerospace engineering and mathematics educator, consultant*
Catton, Ivan *mechanical engineer*
Charwat, Andrew Franciszek *engineering educator*
Cheng, Hsien Kei *aeronautics educator*
Cheng, Tsen-Chung *electrical engineering educator*
Chilingarian, George Varos *petroleum, environmental and civil engineering educator*
Chobotov, Vladimir Alexander *aerospace engineer, educator*
Crombie, Douglass Darnill *aerospace communications engineer, former government official*
Cross, Glenn Laban *engineering executive, development planner*
Dhir, Vijay K. *mechanical engineering educator*
Dorman, Albert A. *consulting engineer executive, architect*
Dougherty, Elmer Lloyd, Jr. *chemical engineering educator, consultant*
Friedlander, Sheldon Kay *chemical engineering educator*
Friedmann, Peretz Peter *aerospace engineer, educator*
Galloway, Arnold John *aerospace engineer*

Gaspari, Russell Arthur *electrical engineer*
†Goulding, Merrill Keith *engineer, consultant*
Habeishi, Fred Gabriel *engineering and construction services executive*
Handy, Lyman Lee *petroleum engineer, chemist, educator*
Holman, Tomlinson *engineer, film educator*
Hovanessian, Shahen Alexander *electrical engineer, educator*
Incaudo, Joseph August *engineering company executive*
Itoh, Tatsuo *engineering educator*
Johnston, Roy G. *consulting structural engineer*
Karplus, Walter J. *engineering educator*
Kashar, Lawrence Joseph *metallurgical engineer, consultant*
Kuehl, Hans Henry *electrical engineering educator*
Leal, George D. *engineering company executive*
Lin, Tung Hua *civil engineering educator*
MacKenzie, John Douglas *engineering educator*
†Martin, John A. *engineering company executive*
Martin, J(ohn) Edward *architectural engineer*
Masri, Sami F(aiz) *civil and mechanical engineering educator, consultant*
Maxworthy, Tony *mechanical and aerospace engineering educator*
Meecham, William Corvell *engineering educator*
Mendel, Jerry Marc *electrical engineering educator*
Monkewitz, Peter Alexis *mechanical and aerospace engineer, educator*
Mortensen, Richard Edgar *engineering educator*
Muntz, Eric Phillip *aerospace engineering and radiology educator, consultant*
Nadler, Gerald *engineering educator, management consultant*
Newman, Richard *engineering executive*
Nobe, Ken *chemical engineering educator*
Okrent, David *engineering educator*
O'Neill, Russell Richard *engineering educator*
Orchard, Henry John *electrical engineer*
Perrine, Richard Leroy *environmental engineering educator*
Perry, Robert Michael *consulting engineering company executive*
Portenier, Walter James *aerospace engineer*
Puckett, Allen Emerson *aeronautical engineer*
Purcell, Arthur Henry *environmental engineering educator, consultant*
Ramo, Simon *engineering executive*
Rauch, Lawrence Lee *aerospace and electrical engineer, educator*
†Raymond, Arthur Emmons *aerospace engineer*
†Rogoway, Lawrence Paul *civil engineer, consultant*
Rubinstein, Moshe Fajwel *engineering educator*
Safonov, Michael George *electrical engineering educator, consultant*
Schmit, Lucien André, Jr. *structural engineer*
Scholtz, Robert Arno *electrical engineering educator*
Schumacher, Joseph Charles *chemical engineer*
Seide, Paul *civil engineering educator*
Speyer, Jason Lee *engineer, educator*
Udwadia, Firdaus Erach *engineering educator, consultant*
Wagner, Christian Nikolaus Johann *materials engineering educator*
Welch, Lloyd Richard *electrical engineering educator, communications consultant*
Willner, Alan Eli *electrical engineer, educator*
Willson, Alan Neil, Jr. *engineering educator, dean*
Yeh, William Wen-Gong *civil engineering educator*
Yen, Teh Fu *civil engineering and environmental educator*
Yue, Alfred Shui-choh *metallurgical engineer, educator*

Los Gatos
Leverett, Miles Corrington *retired nuclear power consultant*
Naymark, Sherman *consulting nuclear engineer*

Los Osos
Cloonan, Clifford B. *electrical engineer, educator*

Malibu
Widmann, Glenn Roger *electrical engineer*

Manhattan Beach
Bradburn, David Denison *engineer,retired air force officer*

Menlo Park
Duda, Richard Oswald *electrical engineering educator, researcher*
Edson, William Alden *electrical engineer*
Honey, Richard Churchill *retired electrical engineer*
Kohne, Richard Edward *retired engineering executive*
Leadabrand, Ray L. *engineering executive, defense industry consultant*
McCarthy, Roger Lee *mechanical engineer*
Szentirmai, George *electrical engineer, corporate executive*

Mission Hills
Cramer, Frank Brown *engineering executive, combustion engineer, systems consultant*

Mission Viejo
Pohl, John Henning *chemical engineer, consultant*

Moffett Field
Kerr, Andrew W. *aerodynamics researcher*
McCroskey, William James *aeronautical engineer*
Park, Chul *aerospace engineer*
Statler, Irving Carl *aerospace engineer*

Monrovia
Mac Cready, Paul Beattie *aeronautical engineer*

Monterey
Butler, Jon Terry *computer engineering educator, researcher*
Marto, Paul James *mechanical engineering educator, researcher*
Newberry, Conrad Floyde *aerospace engineering educator*
Newton, Robert Eugene *mechanical engineering educator*
Sarpkaya, Turgut *mechanical engineering educator*

Mountain View
Johnson, Noel Lars *biomedical engineer*
Marple, Stanley Lawrence, Jr. *electrical engineer, signal processing researcher*

Peters, Stanley Thomas *materials engineer, consultant, educator*

Napa
Folsom, Richard Gilman *retired mechanical engineer and academic administrator, consultant*

Newport Beach
Lurie, Harold *engineer, lawyer*
†Maddock, Thomas Smothers *engineering company executive, civil engineer*

Northridge
Bradshaw, Richard Rotherwood *engineering executive*
Jakobsen, Jakob Knudsen *mechanical engineer*
Kiddoo, Robert James *engineering service company executive*
Stout, Thomas Melville *control system engineer*
Torgow, Eugene N. *electrical engineer*

Novato
Harding, Richard Swick *engineering executive*

Oakland
Ambrose, Tommy W. *chemical engineer, executive*
Borum, William Donald *engineer*
King, Cary Judson, III *chemical engineer, educator, university official*
List, Raymond Edward *engineering and construction executive, management consultant*
†O'Brien, George Donoghue, Jr. *engineering consultant company executive*

Occidental
Rumsey, Victor Henry *electrical engineering educator emeritus*

Ontario
Johnson, Maurice Verner, Jr. *agricultural research and development executive*

Orange
Fisk, Edward Ray *retired civil engineer, author, educator*
Toeppe, William Joseph, Jr. *retired aerospace engineer*

Palmdale
Harsha, Philip Thomas *aerospace engineer*
Rich, Ben Robert *aerospace executive, aero-thermodynamicist*

Palo Alto
Baldwin, Gary Lee *electronics engineer, research laboratory administrator*
Brown, David Randolph *electrical engineer*
Childs, Wylie Jones *metallurgical engineer*
Cohen, Karl Paley *nuclear energy consultant*
Friedlander, Benjamin *electrical and computer engineering educator*
†Giffard, Robin P. *computer engineer, industrial physicist*
Hodge, Philip Gibson, Jr. *mechanical and aerospace engineering educator*
Johnson, Conor Deane *mechanical engineer*
Kino, Gordon Stanley *electrical engineering educator*
Kiremidjian, Anne Aghavny *civil engineering educator*
Lender, Adam *electrical engineer*
Luenberger, David Gilbert *electrical engineer, educator*
Moll, John Lewis *electronics engineer*
Oliver, Bernard More *electrical engineer, technical consultant*
Partain, Larry Dean *solar research engineer*
Taylor, John Joseph *nuclear engineer*
†Thacker, Charles P. *computer engineer, engineering executive*
Thompson, David Alfred *industrial engineer*
Yuan, Sidney Wei Kwun *cryogenic engineer, consultant*

Palos Verdes Estates
Rechtin, Eberhardt *retired aerospace educator*

Palos Verdes Peninsula
Mirels, Harold *aerospace engineer*
Raue, Jorg Emil *electrical engineer*
Spinks, John Lee *engineering executive*
Weiss, Herbert Klemm *aeronautical engineer*

Pasadena
†Bailey, James Edwin *chemical engineer*
†Barney, Kline Porter, Jr. *engineering company executive, consultant*
Boulos, Paul Fares *civil and environmental engineer*
Brady, John Francis *chemical engineering educator*
Bridges, William Bruce *electrical engineer, researcher, educator*
Brooks, Norman Herrick *environmental and civil engineer, educator*
Carroll, William Jerome *civil engineer*
Coles, Donald Earl *aeronautics educator*
†Dallas, Saterios (Sam) *aerospace engineer, researcher, consultant*
Flagan, Richard Charles *chemical engineering educator*
Gavalas, George R. *chemical engineering educator*
Gould, Roy Walter *engineering educator*
Hall, William E. *engineering and construction company executive*
Hatheway, Alson Earle *mechanical engineer*
Hilbert, Robert S(aul) *optical engineer*
Hornung, Hans Georg *aeronautical engineering educator, science facility administrator*
Housner, George William *civil engineering educator, consultant*
Hudson, Donald Ellis *civil engineering educator*
Iwan, Wilfred Dean *engineering educator*
Jacobs, Joseph Donovan *engineering firm executive*
Jacobs, Joseph John *engineering company executive*
Jennings, Paul Christian *civil engineering educator, academic administrator*
†Knauss, Wolfgang Gustav *engineering educator*
Knowles, James Kenyon *applied mechanics educator*
List, Ericson John *environmental engineering science educator, engineering consultant*
Loven, Andrew Witherspoon *environmental engineering company executive*
Martin, Craig Lee *engineering company executive*
McEliece, Robert James *electrical engineering educator, author, consultant*

†McLaughlin, William Irving *aerospace engineer*
Middlebrook, Robert David *electronics educator*
Morari, Manfred *chemical engineer, educator*
Nothmann, Gerhard Adolf *retired engineering executive, research engineer*
Presecan, Nicholas Lee *civil, environmental engineer, consultant*
†Raichlen, Fredric *civil engineering educator, consultant*
Sabersky, Rolf Heinrich *mechanical engineer*
Schlinger, Warren Gleason *retired chemical engineer*
Scott, Ronald Fraser *civil engineering educator, engineering consultant*
Seinfeld, John Hersh *chemical engineering educator*
Simon, Marvin Kenneth *electrical engineer, consultant*
Slater, Richard James *engineering company executive*
†Spear, Anthony J. *aerospace engineer*
Springer, Edwin Kent *mechanical engineer*
Stewart, Homer Joseph *engineering educator*
Vanoni, Vito August *hydraulic engineer*
Weisbin, Charles Richard *nuclear engineer*
Wu, Theodore Yao-Tsu *engineer*
Yamarone, Charles Anthony, Jr. *aerospace engineer, consultant*
Yariv, Amnon *electrical engineering educator, scientist*
Yeh, Paul Pao *electrical and electronics engineer, educator*

Penn Valley
Throner, Guy Charles, Jr. *engineering executive, scientist, engineer, inventor, consultant*

Pismo Beach
Saveker, David Richard *naval and marine architectural engineering executive*

Playa Del Rey
Copperman, William H *value engineer, consultant*

Pomona
Kauser, Fazal Bakhsh *aerospace engineer, educator*

Port Hueneme
Chapla, P.A. *civil engineering research administrator*

Rancho Santa Fe
Gunness, Robert Charles *chemical engineer*

Redondo Beach
Buchta, Edmund *engineering executive*
Chazen, Melvin Leonard *chemical engineer*
Cohen, Clarence Budd *aerospace engineer*
Heller, Anthony Ferdinand *electronics engineer*
Sackheim, Robert Lewis *aerospace engineer, educator*

Redwood City
Eliassen, Rolf *environmental engineer, emeritus educator*

Richmond
Bertero, Vitelmo Victorio *civil engineer*
Moehle, Jack P. *civil engineer, engineering executive*

Ridgecrest
Pearson, John *mechanical engineer*

Riverside
Beni, Gerardo *electrical and computer engineering educator, robotics scientist*
Carrillo, Gilberto *engineer*
Gerdel, Miguel Antonio *manufacturing research engineer, researcher*
Hackwood, Susan *electrical and computer engineering educator*

Rohnert Park
Lord, Harold Wilbur *electrical engineer, electronics consultant*

Ross
Scott, John Walter *chemical engineer, research management executive*

Sacramento
Bezzone, Albert Paul *structural engineer*
Cavigli, Henry James *petroleum engineer*
Collins, William Leroy *telecommunications engineer*
Crimmins, Philip Patrick *metallurgical engineer, lawyer*
Forsyth, Raymond Arthur *civil engineer*
†Hartman, Howard Levi *mining engineering educator, consultant*
Lagarias, John Samuel *engineering executive*
Mujumdar, Vilas Sitaram *structural engineer, management executive*

San Bernardino
Holtz, Tobenette *aerospace engineer*

San Carlos
Symons, Robert Spencer *electronics engineer*

San Clemente
White, Stanley Archibald *research electrical engineer*

San Diego
Anderson, Paul Maurice *electrical engineering educator, researcher, consultant*
Beyster, John Robert *engineering company executive*
†Bucker, Homer Park, Jr. *acoustical engineer*
Chen, Kao *consulting electrical engineer*
Conly, John Franklin *engineering educator, researcher*
Fernandez, Fernando Lawrence *research company executive, aeronautical engineer*
Huang, Chien Chang *electrical engineer*
†Huston, William Alvin *engineering executive*
Normandy, George Mitchell, Jr. *electrical engineer*
St. Clair, Hal Kay *electrical engineer*
Sesonske, Alexander *nuclear and chemical engineer*
Slate, John Butler *biomedical engineer*
Su, Shiaw-Der *nuclear engineer*
Tricoles, Gus Peter *electromagnetics engineer, physicist, consultant*
Verbeke, Frank Girard, Jr. *mechanical engineer*
Viterbi, Andrew James *electrical engineering and computer science educator, business executive*

San Francisco
Angell, James Browne *electrical engineering educator*
Bechtel, Riley Peart *engineering company executive*
Bechtel, Stephen Davison, Jr. *engineering company executive*
Brand, Donald A. *electrical engineer*
Brooks, William George *aeronautical engineer*
Cheng, Wan-Lee *mechanical engineer, industrial technology educator*
Chu, Kuang-Han *structural engineer, educator*
Dolby, Ray Milton *engineering company executive, electrical engineer*
Gerwick, Ben Clifford, Jr. *construction engineer, educator*
Gulbenkian, Paul *civil engineer, inventor*
†Harrison, Blaine L. *engineering consulting company executive*
Hotchkiss, Ralf David *engineer, educator*
Johnstone, R. C., Jr. *engineering company executive*
Keller, Edward Lowell *electrical engineer, educator*
Koffel, Martin M. *engineering company executive*
Lin, Tung Yen *civil engineer, educator*
Lolli, Andrew Ralph *industrial engineer, retired army officer*
Luft, Rene Wilfred *civil engineer*
Marshall, John Paul *broadcast engineer*
Morrin, Thomas Harvey *engineering research company executive*
†Price, Jim *engineering company executive, earth scientist*
Sarsten, Gunnar Edward *mechanical engineer, construction executive*
Shor, Samuel Wendell Williston *naval engineer*
Yuan, Shao Wen *aerospace engineer, educator*

San Jose
Adams, William John, Jr. *mechanical engineer*
Chen, Wen H. *engineering executive, educator*
†Heneghan, John James *geotechnical engineer*
Huang, Francis Fu-Tse *mechanical engineering educator*
Hucker, Robert Joseph *software engineer*
Levy, Salomon *mechanical engineer*
†Markle, David A. *optical engineer*
McCarthy, Mary Ann Bartley *electrical engineer*
Montgomery, Leslie David *biomedical engineer, cardiovascular physiologist*
Moody, Frederick Jerome *mechanical engineer, consultant thermal hydraulics*
Morimoto, Carl Noboru *computer system engineer, crystallographer*
†Rao, Atambir Singh *nuclear engineer*
Rosenheim, Donald Edwin *electrical engineer*
Valentine, Ralph Schuyler *chemical engineer, research director*

San Luis Obispo
Blattner, Ernest Willi *mechanical engineering educator*
Hasslein, George Johann *architectural educator*
Mc Donald, Henry Stanton *electrical engineer*

San Marcos
Dhawan, Gulshan Kumar *chemical engineer*

San Marino
Smith, Apollo Milton Olin *retired aerodynamics engineer*

San Pedro
Ellis, George Edwin, Jr. *chemical engineer*
McCarty, Frederick Briggs *electrical engineer*

Santa Ana
†Amoroso, Frank *retired communication system engineer, consultant*
Idriss, Izzat M. *civil engineer, consultant*
Jacobsen, Eric Kasner *consulting engineer*
Kelly, James Patrick, Jr. *retired engineering and construction executive*
Zabsky, John Mitchell *engineering executive*

Santa Barbara
†Chmelka, Bradley Floyd *chemical engineering educator*
Fredrickson, Glenn Harold *chemical engineering and materials educator*
†Hedgepeth, John M(ills) *aerospace engineer, mathematician, engineering executive*
Iselin, Donald Grote *civil engineering and management consultant*
Laub, Alan John *engineering educator*
Lawrance, Charles Holway *civil and sanitary engineer*
Leal, Leslie Gary *chemical engineering educator*
Leckie, Frederick Alexander *mechanical engineer, educator*
Lick, Wilbert James *mechanical engineering educator*
Mitra, Sanjit Kumar *electrical and computer engineering educator*
Russell, Charles Roberts *chemical engineer*
Wade, Glen *electrical engineer, educator*
†Weinberg, William Henry *chemical engineer, chemical physicist, educator*
Wooldridge, Dean Everett *engineering executive, scientist*

Santa Clara
Chan, Shu-Park *electrical engineering educator*
Hoagland, Albert Smiley *electrical engineer*
Parden, Robert James *engineering educator, management consultant*
Siljak, Dragoslav D. *engineering educator*
Yin, Gerald Zheyao *technology and engineering executive*

Santa Clarita
Lieberman, Paul *aeronautical engineer, engineering research company executive*

Santa Cruz
Langdon, Glen George, Jr. *electrical engineer*
Pister, Karl Stark *engineering educator*

Santa Margarita
Thomas, John Bowman *educator, electrical engineer*

Santa Monica
Bedrosian, Edward *electrical engineer*
Crain, Cullen Malone *electrical engineer*
Gritton, Eugene Charles *nuclear engineer*
Hammond, R. Philip *chemical engineer*
Kayton, Myron *engineering company executive*

Roney, Robert Kenneth *retired aerospace company executive*
Weingarten, Victor I. *engineering educator*

Santa Rosa
Rancourt, James Daniel *optical engineer*

Saratoga
Cooper, George Emery *aerospace consultant*
Syvertson, Clarence Alfred *aerospace engineering consultant*
Wenzel, James Gottlieb *ocean engineering executive, consultant*

Seal Beach
†Robinson, Michael R. *aeronautical engineer*

Sierra Madre
†O'Neil, William J. *aerospace engineer*

Simi Valley
Deisenroth, Clinton Wilbur *electrical engineer*

Sonoma
Muchmore, Robert Boyer *engineering consultant executive*

Sonora
Walasek, Otto Frank *chemical engineer, biochemist, photographer*

South Pasadena
Glad, Dain Sturgis *retired aerospace engineer, consultant*
Kopp, Eugene Howard *electrical engineer*

South San Francisco
Swanson, Robert A. *genetic engineering company executive*

Spring Valley
Gardner, Leonard Burton, II *industrial automation engineer*

Stanford
Aziz, Khalid *petroleum engineering educator*
Barkan, Philip *mechanical engineer*
Boudart, Michel *chemical engineer, chemist, educator*
Bracewell, Ronald Newbold *electrical engineering educator*
Bradshaw, Peter *engineering educator*
Brigham, William Everett *petroleum engineering educator*
Bryson, Arthur Earl, Jr. *retired engineering educator*
Cannon, Robert Hamilton, Jr. *aerospace engineering educator*
Carlson, Robert Codner *industrial engineering educator*
Carter, Dennis Robert *biomechanical engineer, educator*
Cox, Donald Clyde *electrical engineering educator*
DeBra, Daniel B. *mechanical engineering educator*
Dutton, Robert Wilbur *electrical engineering educator*
Eaton, John Kelly *mechanical engineering educator*
Eshleman, Von Russel *electrical engineering educator*
Eustis, Robert Henry *mechanical engineer*
Ferziger, Joel Henry *mechanical engineering educator, mathematician*
Franklin, Gene Farthing *electrical engineering educator, consultant*
Gere, James Monroe *civil engineering educator*
Goodman, Joseph Wilfred *electrical engineering educator*
Gray, Robert M(olten) *electrical engineering educator*
Harris, James Stewart, Jr. *engineering educator, researcher*
Harris, Stephen Ernest *electrical engineering and applied physics educator*
Herrmann, George *mechanical engineering educator*
†Hesselink, Lambertus *aeronautics, astronautics and electrical engineering educator*
Hewett, Thomas Avery *petroleum engineer, educator*
Hoff, Nicholas John *mechanical and aerospace engineer*
Hughes, Thomas Joseph *mechanical engineering educator, consultant*
Inan, Umran Savas *electrical engineering educator, researcher*
Jadvar, Hossein *biomedical engineer, physician*
Kailath, Thomas *electrical engineer, educator*
Kane, Thomas Reif *engineering educator*
Kline, Stephen Jay *mechanical engineer, educator*
Kruger, Charles Herman, Jr. *mechanical engineering educator*
Leckie, James Oliver *engineering educator*
Leifer, Larry John *mechanical engineering design educator, health science facility administrator*
Levitt, Raymond Elliot *civil engineering educator*
Linvill, John Grimes *engineering educator*
Macovski, Albert *electrical engineering educator*
Madix, Robert James *chemical engineer, educator*
McCluskey, Edward Joseph *engineering educator*
Orr, Franklin Mattes, Jr. *petroleum engineering educator*
Ortolano, Leonard *civil engineering educator, water resources planner*
Ott, Wayne Robert *environmental engineer*
Parkinson, Bradford W. *aeronautical engineering educator*
Paté-Cornell, Marie-Elisabeth Lucienne *industrial engineering educator*
Paulson, Boyd Colton, Jr. *civil engineering educator*
Pease, Roger Fabian Wedgwood *electrical engineering educator*
Pierce, John Robinson *electrical engineer, educator*
Plummer, James D. *electrical engineering educator*
Pratt, Vaughan Ronald *computer engineering educator*
Quate, Calvin Forrest *engineering educator*
Reynolds, William Craig *mechanical engineer, educator*
Roth, Bernard *mechanical engineering educator, researcher*
Rott, Nicholas *fluid mechanics educator*
Shah, Haresh C. *civil engineering educator*
Siegman, Anthony Edward *electrical engineer, educator*
Spreiter, John Robert *engineering educator, space physics scientist*
Springer, George Stephen *mechanical engineering educator*
Street, Robert Lynnwood *civil and mechanical engineer*
Sweeney, James Lee *engineering and economic systems educator*
Teicholz, Paul M. *civil engineering educator, administrator*
†Tyler, G. Leonard *electrical engineering educator*
Van Dyke, Milton Denman *aeronautical engineering educator*
Vincenti, Walter Guido *aeronautical engineer, emeritus educator*
White, Robert Lee *electrical engineer, educator*
Widrow, Bernard *electrical engineering educator*
Wooley, Bruce Allen *electronics engineer, educator*

Stockton
Heyborne, Robert Linford *electrical engineering educator*

Sunnyvale
†Araki, Minoru S. *aerospace engineer*
Kim, Wan Hee *electrical engineering educator, business executive*
Ma, Fengchow Clarence *agricultural engineering consultant*
Omura, Jimmy Kazuhiro *electrical engineer*
Schubert, Ronald Hayward, Sr. *retired aerospace engineer*
Zebroski, Edwin Leopold *nuclear engineer consultant*

Tarzana
Hansen, Robert Clinton *electrical engineering consultant*
Macmillan, Robert Smith *electronics engineer*

Temecula
Minogue, Robert Brophy *retired nuclear engineer*

Thousand Oaks
Krumm, Charles Ferdinand *electrical engineer*

Tiburon
Heacox, Russel Louis *mechanical engineer*

Torrance
Brodsky, Robert Fox *aerospace engineer*
Mason, John Latimer *engineering executive*
Sheh, Robert Bardhyl *environmental management company executive*

Ventura
Gaynor, Joseph *technical and management consultant*
Matley, Benvenuto Gilbert (Ben Matley) *computer engineer, educator, consultant*
Wheeler, Harold Alden *retired radio engineer*

Walnut Creek
Crandall, Ira Carlton *consulting electrical engineer*
Woodward, Richard Joseph, Jr. *geotechnical engineer*

Westlake Village
Caligiuri, Joseph Frank *retired engineering executive*

Westminster
Armstrong, Gene Lee *systems engineering consultant, retired aerospace company executive*

Whittier
Lillevang, Omar Johansen *civil engineer*

Wilmington
Hatch, Ronald Ray *engineer*

Woodland Hills
Higginbotham, Lloyd William *mechanical engineer*
Oltman, Henry George, Jr. *retired engineering executive*

COLORADO

Boulder
Avery, Susan Kathryn *electrical engineering educator, researcher*
Barnes, Frank Stephenson *electrical engineer, educator*
Beckmann, Petr *electrical engineer, educator*
†Born, George H. *aerospace engineer, educator*
Cathey, Wade Thomas *electrical engineering educator*
Corotis, Ross Barry *civil engineering educator, academic administrator*
Fuller, Jackson Franklin *electrical engineering educator*
Geers, Thomas Lange *mechanical engineering educator*
Gerstle, Kurt Herman *retired civil engineering educator, consultant*
Gupta, Kuldip Chand *electrical and computer engineering educator, researcher*
Hanna, William Johnson *electrical engineering educator*
†Hauser, Ray Louis *research engineer, entrepreneur*
Hill, David Allan *electrical engineer*
Kanda, Motohisa *electronics engineer*
Maley, Samuel Wayne *electrical engineering educator*
†Reitsema, Harold James *aerospace engineer*
Rodriguez, Juan Alfonso *technology corporation executive*
Sani, Robert LeRoy *chemical engineering educator*
Smith, Ernest Ketcham *electrical engineer*
Sodal, Ingvar Edmund *electrical engineer, scientist*
Timmerhaus, Klaus Dieter *chemical engineering educator*
Uberoi, Mahinder Singh *aerospace engineering educator*
Utlaut, William Frederick *electrical engineer*

Canon City
Mc Bride, John Alexander *retired chemical engineer*

Colorado Springs
Allen, J. Lamar *engineering company executive, educator*
Anderson, Lawrence Keith *electrical engineer*
Kohlman, David Leslie *engineering executive, consultant*
Watts, Oliver Edward *engineering consultancy company executive*
Ziemer, Rodger Edmund *electrical engineering educator, consultant*

Conifer
Powers, Edwin Malvin *consulting engineer*

Denver
Ballhaus, William Francis, Jr. *aerospace industry executive, research scientist*
Chmelir, John David *engineer, consultant*
†East, Donald Robert *civil engineer*
Evans, Ginger Sunday *civil engineer*
Ferguson, Lloyd Elbert *manufacturing engineer*
Haddon, Timothy John *mining engineer*
Krill, Arthur Melvin *engineering, architectural and planning company executive*
†Longwell, John Dorney *petroleum engineer*
Mc Candless, Bruce, II *engineer, former astronaut*
Mehring, Clinton Warren *engineering executive*
Perez, Jean-Yves *engineering company executive*
Poirot, James Wesley *engineering company executive*
Pollard, William Sherman, Jr. *civil engineer, educator*
†Waller, Frank S. *engineering company executive*
Yamamoto, Kaoru *psychology, education educator*

Englewood
†Aguirre, Vukoslav Eneas *soils engineer*
†Schirmer, Howard August, Jr. *civil engineer*

Estes Park
Webb, Richard C. *engineering company executive*

Evergreen
Jesser, Roger Franklyn *former brewing company engineering executive, consultant*
Newkirk, John Burt *metallurgical engineer, administrator*

Fort Collins
Boyd, Landis Lee *agricultural engineer, educator*
Cermak, Jack Edward *engineer, educator*
Frasier, Gary W. *hydraulic engineer*
Garvey, Daniel Cyril *mechanical engineer*
Heermann, Dale Frank *agricultural engineer*
Kaufman, Harold Richard *mechanical engineer and physics educator*
Medearis, Kenneth Gordon *engineering research consultant, educator*
Richardson, Everett Vern *hydraulic engineer, educator, administrator*
Sandborn, Virgil Alvin *civil engineer, educator*
Woolhiser, David Arthur *hydraulic engineer*

Golden
Ansell, George Stephen *metallurgical engineering educator, academic administrator*
Danzberger, Alexander Harris *chemical engineer, consultant*
Hager, John Patrick *metallurgy engineering educator*
Johnstone, James George *engineering educator*
Poettmann, Frederick Heinz *retired petroleum engineering educator*
Salamon, Miklos Dezso Gyorgy *mining educator*
Yarar, Baki *metallurgical engineering educator*

Lakewood
Elkins, Lincoln Feltch *petroleum engineering consultant*
Lu, Paul Haihsing *mining engineer, geotechnical consultant*

Littleton
Kazemi, Hossein *petroleum engineer*
Kullas, Albert John *management and systems engineering consultant*
Ulrich, John Ross Gerald *aerospace engineer*

Pueblo West
Giffin, Walter Charles *retired industrial engineer, educator, consultant*

Wheat Ridge
Barrett, Michael Henry *civil engineer*
Scherich, Erwin Thomas *civil engineer, consultant*

CONNECTICUT

Bloomfield
Leonberger, Frederick John *electrical engineer, photonics manager*

Branford
Cohen, Myron Leslie *mechanical engineer, business executive*
Izenour, George Charles *mechanical, electrical engineering educator*

Bridgeport
Brunale, Vito John *aerospace engineer*

Cheshire
Fuller, Jack Glendon, Jr. *retired plastics engineer*

Danbury
Rubin, Jacob Carl *mechanical research engineer*

Darien
Bays, John Theophanis *consulting engineering executive*
Forman, J(oseph) Charles *chemical engineer, consultant, writer*
Glenn, Roland Douglas *chemical engineer*
McCurdy, Richard Clark *engineering consultant*

East Hartford
Foyt, Arthur George *electronics research administrator*

Ellington
Setzer, Herbert John *chemical engineer*

Farmington
Maranzano, Miguel Franscisco *engineer*

Greenwich
Marchand, Nathan *electrical engineer, corporation president*

Groton
Sheets, Herman Ernest *marine engineer*

Hamden
Walker, Charles Allen *chemical engineer, educator*

Hartford
Bronzino, Joseph Daniel *electrical engineer*
Smith, Donald Arthur *mechanical engineer, researcher*

Manchester
†Reuter, James D. *aeronautical engineering manager*
Slaiby, Theodore George *aeronautical engineer, consultant*

Mansfield Center
Aldrich, Robert Adams *agricultural engineer*

Middlefield
Thermenos, Nicholas *engineering company executive*

Middletown
Day, William Hudson *mechanical engineer, turbomachinery company executive*

New Canaan
Halverstadt, Robert Dale *mechanical engineer, metals manufacturing company executive*
O'Neill, Patrick Henry *consulting mining engineer*

New Hartford
Hall, Newman A. *retired mechanical engineer*

New Haven
Apfel, Robert Edmund *mechanical engineering educator, applied physicist, research scientist*
Barker, Richard Clark *electrical engineering educator*
Cunningham, Walter Jack *electrical engineering educator*
Haller, Gary Lee *chemical engineering educator*
Horváth, Csaba *chemical engineering educator, researcher*
Ma, Tso-Ping *electrical engineering educator, researcher, consultant*
Narendra, Kumpati Subrahmanya *electrical engineer, educator*
Sreenivasan, Katepalli Raju *mechanical engineering educator*

New London
Owsley, Norman Lee *electrical engineer, educator*

North Stonington
Mollegen, Albert Theodore, Jr. *engineering company executive*

Norwich
Meseha, George Mansour *mechanical engineer*

Old Saybrook
Elrod, Harold Glenn *retired engineering science educator, consultant*

Rocky Hill
Chuang, Frank Shiunn-Jea *engineering executive, consultant*

Stamford
Deneberg, Jeffrey N. *engineering executive*
Gupta, Dharam V. *chemical engineer*

Storrs
De Maria, Anthony John *electrical engineer*
Long, Richard Paul *civil engineering educator, geotechnical engineering consultant*
Pitkin, Edward Thaddeus *aerospace engineer, consultant*

Storrs Mansfield
DiBenedetto, Anthony Thomas *engineering educator*
Howes, Trevor Denis *metallurgical engineering educator, researcher*
McFadden, Peter William *mechanical engineering educator*
Shaw, Montgomery Throop *chemical engineering educator*

Tariffville
Johnson, Loering M. *design engineer, historian, consultant*

Tolland
Wilde, Daniel Underwood *computer engineering educator*

Trumbull
Gladki, Hanna Zofia *civil engineer, hydraulic mixer specialist*

Vernon Rockville
†Sturgess, Geoffrey J. *aeronautical research engineer*

Waterford
Hinkle, Muriel Ruth Nelson *naval warfare analysis company executive*
Kandetzki, Carl Arthur *engineer*
†Markowicz, John C. *engineering consulting company executive*

West Hartford
†Cornell, Robert Witherspoon *engineering consultant*

Weston
Offenhartz, Edward *aerospace executive*

Wilton
Juran, Joseph Moses *engineer*
Martimucci, Richard Anthony *engineering company executive*

Windsor
Rocco, Vincent Anthony *consulting firm executive*
Scherer, A. Edward *nuclear engineering executive*

DELAWARE

Greenville
†Dombeck, Harold Arthur *engineering company executive*

Hockessin
Bischoff, Kenneth Bruce *chemical engineer, educator*
Sciance, Carroll Thomas *chemical engineer*

Newark
Allen, Herbert Ellis *environmental chemistry educator*
Barteau, Mark Alan *chemical engineering and chemistry educator*
Beris, Antony Nicolas *chemical engineer, educator*
Cooper, Stuart Leonard *chemical engineering educator, researcher, consultant*
Ih, Charles Chung Sen *electrical engineering educator, researcher*
Jones, Russel Cameron *civil engineering educator*
Kennedy, Christopher Robin *ceramist*
Klein, Michael Tully *chemical engineering educator, consultant*
McCullough, Roy Lynn *chemical engineering educator*
Nye, John Calvin *agricultural engineer, educator*
†Reid, Stephen Robert *power generation engineer, consultant*
Russell, Thomas William Fraser *chemical engineering educator*
Sandler, Stanley Irving *chemical engineering educator*
Szeri, Andras Z. *engineering educator*
Urquhart, Andrew Willard *engineering and business executive*

Wilmington
Huang, Hua-Feng *electrical engineer, researcher*
Murphy, Arthur Thomas *systems engineer*
Salzstein, Richard Alan *biomedical engineer, researcher*

DISTRICT OF COLUMBIA

Washington
Aein, Joseph Morris *electrical engineer*
Aggarwal, Satish Kumar *electrical engineer, government official*
Arkilic, Galip Mehmet *mechanical engineer, educator*
Bainum, Peter Montgomery *aerospace engineer, consultant*
†Baublitz, John Eberhart *chemical engineer*
†Bowes, William C. *aerospace engineer*
Brahms, Thomas Walter *engineering institute executive*
Briskman, Robert David *engineering executive*
Cambel, Ali Bulent *engineering educator*
Campbell, Nancy Edinger *nuclear engineer*
Cerny, Louis Thomas *civil engineer, association executive*
Chalmers, Franklin Stevens, Jr. *engineering consultant*
Chen, Ho-Hong H. H. *industrial engineering executive, educator*
Coyne, James Kitchenman, III *engineering executive*
Dinberg, Michael David *industrial engineer, uniformed services officer*
Dinneen, Gerald Paul *electrical engineer, former government official*
†Divone, Louis Vincent *aerospace engineer, educator, author*
†Durocher, Cort Louis *aerospace engineer, association executive*
Eisner, Howard *engineering educator, engineering executive*
†Elms, Charles Patrick *engineering company executive*
Flax, Alexander Henry *aeronautical engineer, federal science agency administrator*
†Foley, Gary J. *research chemical engineer, computer scientist, federal agency administrator*
Friedman, Arthur Daniel *electrical engineering and computer science educator, investment management company executive*
Giallorenzi, Thomas Gaetano *optical engineer*
†Hampton, Delon *engineering consulting company executive*
†Hawksworth, K. J. *engineering company executive*
Hazelrigg, George Arthur, Jr. *engineer*
Hershey, Robert Lewis *mechanical engineer, management consultant*
Hollister, Floyd Hill *electrical engineer, engineering executive*
Husemann, Robert William *mechanical engineer*
Jones, Howard St. Claire, Jr. *electronics engineering executive*
Kahn, Walter Kurt *engineering and applied science educator*
†Kappaz, Michael H. *engineering company executive*
Kaufman, John Gilbert, Jr. *materials engineer*
Kiper, Ali Muhlis *mechanical engineering educator, consultant*
Kirkbride, Chalmer Gatlin *chemical engineer*
Liebowitz, Harold *aeronautical engineering educator, dean emeritus*
Lynch, Charles Theodore, Sr. *materials science engineering researcher, administrator, educator*
Lynn, Larry *engineering executive*
McCarthy, Wilbert Alan *mechanical engineer*
†McCoy, John J. *engineering educator*
†Menendez, Adofo *engineering company executive*
Monroe, Robert Rawson *engineering construction executive*
Montgomery, G(eorge) Franklin *electrical engineer, consultant*
Nichols, Kenneth David *consulting engineer*
Ochs, Walter J. *civil engineer, drainage adviser*
Page, Robert Wesley *engineering and construction company executive, federal official*
Pickholtz, Raymond Lee *electrical engineering educator, consultant*
Reck, Gregory Milton *aerospace engineer*
Reis, Victor H. *mechanical engineer, government official*
Russell, Ted McKinnies *electronics technician*
Salmon, William Cooper *mechanical engineer, engineering academy executive*
Shalowitz, Erwin Emmanuel *civil engineer*
Shon, Frederick John *nuclear engineer*
Skolnik, Merrill I. *electrical engineer*
Sorensen, John Noble *mechanical and nuclear engineer*
Stanwick, Tad *systems engineering and business management executive*
Stever, Horton Guyford *aerospace scientist and engineer, educator, consultant*
Townsend, Marjorie Rhodes *aerospace engineer, business executive*
Walker, M. Lucius, Jr. *mechanical engineer*
Walters, John Linton *electronics engineer, consultant*
Wang, John Cheng Hwai *communications engineer*
Warnick, Walter Lee *mechanical engineer*
†Webb, David Owen *petroleum engineer, association executive*
White, Robert Roy *chemical engineer*
Willenbrock, Frederick Karl *engineer, educator*
Wisniewski, John William *mining engineer, bank engineering executive*
Yang, Tony Tien Sheng *engineering educator*

FLORIDA

Atlantic Beach
Engelmann, Rudolph Herman *electronics consultant*
Wheeler, William Crawford *agricultural engineer, educator*

Boca Raton
Arockiasamy, Madasamy *engineering educator*
Chryssafopoulos, Nicholas *civil engineer*
Lin, Y. K. *engineer, educator*
Rosenthal, Myron Martin *retired electrical engineer, educator, author*

Boynton Beach
Cross, Ralph Emerson *mechanical engineer*
Turner, William Benjamin *electrical engineer*

Bradenton
Friedrich, Robert Edmund *retired electrical engineer, corporate consultant*

Cape Canaveral
†Block, David L. *solar engineering executive*
Clark, John F. *aerospace research and engineering educator*

Cape Coral
Purdy, Alan Harris *biomedical engineer*

Coral Gables
Baddour, Raymond Frederick *chemical engineer, educator, entrepreneur*
Fung, Kee-Ying *engineer, educator, researcher*
Jury, Eliahu Ibraham *electrical engineer, research educator*
Kline, Jacob *biomedical engineering educator*
Saffir, Herbert Seymour *structural engineer, consultant*
Sumanth, David Jonnakoty *industrial engineer, educator*
Young, Tzay Y. *electrical and computer engineering educator*

Coral Springs
Elmore, Walter A. *electrical engineer, consultant*

Crystal River
Black, Charles Alvin *consulting engineering executive*

Daytona Beach
Geier, George *optical engineering consultant*
Haviland, Robert Paul *engineering executive, author*
Millar, Gordon Halstead *mechanical engineer, agricultural machinery manufacturing executive*
Sliwa, Steven Mark *engineering executive, academic administrator*

Dundee
Johnson, Gordon Selby *consulting electrical engineer*

Englewood
Suiter, John William *industrial engineer, consultant*

Fort Myers
Mergler, Harry Winston *engineering educator*
Moeschl, Stanley Francis *electrical engineer, management consultant*
Ölling, Edward Henry *aerospace engineer, consulting firm executive*
Scott, Kenneth Elsner *mechanical engineering educator*

Fort Myers Beach
Arneson, Harold Elias Grant *manufacturing engineer, consultant*

Gainesville
Abbaschian, Reza *materials science and engineering educator*
†Anderson, Timothy J. *chemical engineering educator*
Anghaie, Samim *nuclear engineer, educator*
Block, Seymour Stanton *chemical engineering educator, consultant, writer*
Capehart, Barney Lee *industrial and systems engineer*
Childers, Donald Gene *electrical engineering educator, researcher*
Couch, Leon Worthington *electrical engineering educator*
Delfino, Joseph John *environmental engineering sciences educator*
Drucker, Daniel Charles *engineer, educator*
Elzinga, Donald Jack *industrial engineering researcher, educator*
Fossum, Jerry George *electrical engineering educator*
Isaacs, Gerald William *agricultural engineer, educator*
†Issacs, Gerald William *retired agricultural engineering educator, consultant*
Kurzweg, Ulrich Hermann *engineering science educator*
†Law, Mark Edward *electrical engineer, educator*
Lindholm, Fredrik Arthur *electrical engineering educator, researcher*
Malvern, Lawrence Earl *engineering educator, researcher*
Neugroschel, Arnost *electrical engineering educator*
Ohanian, Mihran Jacob *engineering educator*
Peebles, Peyton Zimmerman, Jr. *electrical engineer, educator*
Schaub, James Hamilton *engineering educator*
Schmertmann, John Henry *civil engineer, educator, consultant*
Shyy, Wei *aerospace, mechanical engineering researcher and educator*
Singley, John Edward, Jr. *environmental engineer, consultant*
Smith, John James, Jr. *environmental engineering laboratory executive*
Tou, Julius T. *electrical and computer engineering educator*
Verink, Ellis Daniel, Jr. *metallurgical engineering educator, consultant*
Wethington, John Abner, Jr. *retired nuclear engineering educator*

Hollywood
Nusim, Stanley Herbert *chemical engineer, consultant*

Indian Harbour Beach
Denaburg, Charles Robert *metallurgical engineer, retired government official*

Jacksonville
Joyce, Edward Rowen *chemical engineer, educator*
Klabosh, Charles Joseph *aerospace research and development executive*
†Liebtag, Benford Gustav, III (Ben Liebtag) *engineer, consultant*
Mueller, Edward Albert *transportation engineer executive*
Russell, David Emerson *mechanical engineer, consultant*
Shivler, James Fletcher, Jr. *retired civil engineer*
Tsai, James Tarng *chemical and plastics company executive*

Jensen Beach
Kirjassoff, Gordon Louis *consulting civil engineer*

Juno Beach
Migliaro, Marco William *electrical engineer*

Lady Lake
Dore, Stephen Edward, Jr. *retired civil engineer*

Lighthouse Point
Farho, James Henry, Jr. *mechanical engineer, consultant*

Maitland
†Galloway, Robert Thomas *aerospace engineer*

Melbourne
Lewis, Bernard Leroy *electronic scientist, consultant*
Swalm, Thomas Sterling *aerospace executive, retired military officer*
Van Arsdall, Robert Armes *engineer, retired air force officer*

Miami
Ajamil, Luis *civil engineer*
de la Guardia, Mario Francisco *electrical engineer*
Dye, H. Michael *engineering executive*
Le Mehaute, Bernard Jean *marine physics educator*
Lindquist, Claude S. *electrical and computer engineering educator*
Nagel, Joachim Hans *biomedical engineer, educator*
Schuetzenduebel, Wolfram Gerhard *engineering executive*
Torres, Milton John *industrial engineering educator*
Veziroglu, Turhan Nejat *mechanical engineering educator, energy researcher*
Wolfenson, Azi U. *electrical engineer*

Mulberry
Carrier, W(illiam) David, III *geotechnical engineer*

Naples
Benedict, Manson *chemical engineer, educator*
Suziedelis, Vytautas A. *engineering corporation executive*
Tanner, Robert Hugh *engineer, consultant*
Widman, Richard Gustave *engineering and construction company executive*
Williams, George Earnest *engineer, retired business executive*

Nokomis
Cather, Donald Warren *civil engineer*

Orlando
Buchanan, Walter Woolwine *engineering educator, electrical engineer*
Rice, Stephen Landon *engineering educator*
Roesner, Larry August *civil engineer*
Soileau, Marion Joseph *engineering and physics educator*

Ormond Beach
Jacobson, Ira David *aerospace engineer, educator, researcher*
†Wild, Harry E. *engineering company executive*

Osprey
Coates, Clarence Leroy, Jr. *research engineer, educator*

Palm Harbor
Curreri, John Robert *mechanical engineer, consultant*

Panama City
D'Arcy, Gerald Paul *engineering executive, consultant*

Pensacola
McSwain, Richard Horace *materials engineer, consultant*
Watt, Stuart George *engineering contracting company executive*

Ponte Vedra Beach
Schultz, Andrew Schultz, Jr. *industrial engineering educator*

Port Charlotte
Munger, Elmer Lewis *civil engineer, educator*

Saint Cloud
Everett, Woodrow Wilson *electrical engineer, educator*

Saint Petersburg
Collins, Carl Russell, Jr. *architectural engineer*
Donaldson, Merle Richard *electrical engineering educator, consultant*

Sarasota
Beck, George William *retired industrial engineer*
Hrones, John Anthony *mechanical engineering educator*
Long, Robert Radcliffe *fluid mechanics educator*
Ross, Gerald Fred *engineering executive, researcher*
Veinott, Cyril George *electrical engineer, consultant*
Weeks, Walter LeRoy *electrical engineering educator*

Stuart
Morena, John Joseph *manufacturing engineer, executive*

Sun City Center
Jeffries, Robert Joseph *retired engineering educator, business executive*

Tallahassee
Braswell, Robert Neil *scientist, engineer, educator*
Chen, Ching Jen *mechanical engineering educator, research scientist*
Coloney, Wayne Herndon *civil engineer*
De Forest, Sherwood Searle *agricultural engineer, agribusiness services executive*
Hall, Houghton Alexander *engineering professional*
Harrison, Thomas James *electrical engineer, educator*

Tampa
Deutsch, Sid *bioengineer, educator*
Givens, Paul Edward *industrial engineer, educator*
Gregg, Charles Wayne *engineering executive*
Henning, Rudolf Ernst *electrical engineer, educator, consultant*
Miller, Charles Leslie *civil engineer, planner, consultant*
Wade, Thomas Edward *electrical engineering educator, university research administrator*

Tarpon Springs
Scala, Sinclaire Maximilian *aerospace engineer, retired*

Venice
Concordia, Charles *consulting engineer*
Hays, Herschel Martin *electrical engineer*

Vero Beach
Haywood, Oliver Garfield *engineer*

West Palm Beach
Aaron, M. Robert *electrical engineer*
Coar, Richard John *mechanical engineer, aerospace consultant*
Gillette, Frank C., Jr. *aeronautical engineer*
Koff, Bernard Louis *engineering executive*
Olsak, Ivan Karel *civil engineer*

Winter Park
Flick, Carl *electrical engineer, consultant, free-lance author*

GEORGIA

Albany
Marbury, Ritchey McGuire, III *engineering executive, surveyor*

Athens
Kraszewski, Andrzej Wojciech *electrical engineer, researcher*
Nelson, Stuart Owen *agricultural engineer, researcher, educator*

Atlanta
Abdel-Khalik, Said Ibrahim *nuclear and mechanical engineering educator*
Akers, Sheldon Buckingham, Jr. *electrical and computer engineering educator*
†Atluri, Satya N(adham) *aerospace engineering educator*
Bacon, Louis Albert *retired consulting civil engineer*
Barksdale, Richard Dillon *civil engineer, educator*
Barnwell, Thomas Pinkney, III *electrical engineering educator, business executive*
†Bates, Valentino Travis *engineering executive*
Black, Kirby Samuel *biomedical engineer, immunologist, biologist, educator*
Bourne, Henry Clark, Jr. *electrical engineering educator, former academic official*
Brighton, John Austin *mechanical engineer, educator*
Carlson, Robert Lee *engineering educator*
Dahlke, Wayne Theodore *civil engineer, corporate executive*
Dalrymple, Gordon Bennett *former engineering company executive*
Durbetaki, Pandeli *mechanical engineer, educator, researcher*
Eckert, Charles Alan *chemical engineering educator*
Fitzgerald, John Edmund *civil engineering educator, dean*
Grace, Donald J. *engineering researcher*
Griffin, Clayton Houstoun *retired power company engineer, lecturer*
†Haddad, Wassim Michael *aerospace engineer, educator*
Hatch, Henry J. *engineering executive*
Higgins, Richard J. *microelectronics research administrator, educator*
Hodges, Dewey Harper *aerospace engineer, educator*
Joy, Edward Bennett *electrical engineer, educator*
McClellan, James Harold *electrical engineering educator*
Moore, Henry Rogers *consulting engineer, retired railroad executive*
Nemhauser, George L. *industrial, systems engineer, operations research educator*
Nerem, Robert Michael *engineering educator, consultant*
Paris, Demetrius Theodore *electrical engineering educator*
Pence, Ira Wilson, Jr. *material handling research executive, engineer*

Poehlein, Gary Wayne *chemical engineering educator*
Porter, Alan Leslie *industrial and systems engineering educator*
Reedy, Edward K. *system engineer administrator*
Richards, Robert Wadsworth *civil engineer, consultant*
Rodrigue, George Pierre *electrical engineering educator, consultant*
Rousseau, Ronald William *chemical engineering educator, researcher*
Saxena, Ashok *materials engineering educator, consultant*
Schafer, Ronald William *electrical engineering educator*
Scovil, Roger Morris *engineering company executive*
Smith, Glenn Stanley *electrical engineering educator*
Stacey, Weston Monroe, Jr. *nuclear engineer, educator*
Su, Kendall Ling-Chiao *engineering educator*
Teja, Amyn Sadrudin *chemical engineering educator, consultant*
Thuesen, Gerald Jorgen *industrial engineer, educator*
Toler, James C. *electrical engineer*
Tucker, Robert Arnold *electrical engineer*
Vanegas, Jorge Alberto *civil engineering educator*
Webb, Roger Paul *electrical engineer, educator*
White, John Austin, Jr. *engineering educator, dean, consultant*
Wiedeman, John Herman *civil engineer*
Winer, Ward Otis *mechanical engineer, educator*
Wu, James Chen-Yuan *aerospace engineering educator*
Wyvill, J. Craig *research engineer, program director*
Yoganathan, Ajit Prithiviraj *biomedical engineer, educator*

Carrollton
Johnson, Harris Tucker *engineering educator, university administrator*

Dahlonega
Jones, William Benjamin, Jr. *electrical engineering educator*

Doraville
Wempner, Gerald Arthur *engineering educator*

Grovetown
Baldwin, James Edwin *civil engineer, land development executive*

Jersey
Batchelor, Joseph Brooklyn, Jr. *electronics engineer, consultant*

Kennesaw
Rusche, Benard C. *engineering executive*

Lilburn
Bristow, Preston Abner, Jr. *civil engineer, environmental engineer*

Marietta
Hayes, Robert Deming *electrical engineer, consultant*
Ranu, Harcharan Singh *biomedical scientist, administrator, orthopaedic biomechanics educator*

Norcross
Adams, Dee Briane *hydrologist, civil engineer*
Harrison, Gordon Ray *engineering executive, consultant, research scientist*
Rouse, William Bradford *systems engineering executive, researcher, educator*

Roswell
Dickens, Gordon Lee, III *engineer, data processing company executive*

Savannah
Hsu, Ming-Yu *engineer, educator*

Tifton
Butler, James Lee *agricultural engineer, researcher*

HAWAII

Honolulu
Abramson, Norman *electronics executive*
Antal, Michael Jerry, Jr. *mechanical engineering educator*
Cox, Richard Horton *civil engineering executive*
Craven, John Piña *civil engineering and law educator, lawyer*
Kohloss, Frederick Henry *consulting engineer*
Koide, Frank Takayuki *electrical engineer*
Krock, Hans-Jurgen *civil engineer*
†Sato, Richard Michio *consulting engineering company executive*
Tanio, Tony *electrical engineer, hotel executive*
Wang, Jaw-Kai *agricultural engineering educator*
Yee, Alfred Alphonse *structural engineer, consultant*

Kaneohe
Hanson, Richard Edwin *civil engineer*

Kapaau
McFee, Richard *electrical engineer, physicist*

IDAHO

Boise
McKee, Joseph Fulton *engineering and construction executive*
Slavich, Denis Michael *engineering and construction company executive*
True, Leland Beyer *civil engineer, consultant*
Wilbur, Lyman Dwight *consulting engineering executive*

Idaho Falls
Riemke, Richard Allan *mechanical engineer*

Island Park
Stratford, Ray Paul *electrical engineer, consultant*

Moscow
DeShazer, James Arthur *agricultural engineer, educator, administrator*

Jackson, Melbourne Leslie *chemical engineering educator and administrator, consultant*
Jacobsen, Richard T. *mechanical engineering educator*
Peterson, Charles Loren *agricultural engineer, educator*
Woodall, David Monroe *research engineer*

Pocatello
Wilson, Albert Eugene *retired nuclear engineering educator*

Rigby
Peterson, Erle Vidaillet *retired metallurgical engineer*

ILLINOIS

Argonne
Braun, Joseph Carl *nuclear engineer, scientist*
Chang, Yoon Il *nuclear engineer*
Kumar, Romesh *chemical engineer*

Arlington Heights
Jenny, Daniel P. *retired engineer*

Barrington
Francis, Philip Hamilton *engineering executive, mechanical engineer*

Bartlett
†Khan, Kalim Ullah *metallurgical engineer, consultant*

Buffalo Grove
Kaplan, Mitchell Philip *consulting engineer, marketing executive*

Carbondale
Orthwein, William Coe *mechanical engineer*
Smith, James Gilbert *electrical engineer*

Champaign
Khan, Latif Akbar *mineral engineer*
Kruger, William Arnold *consulting civil engineer*
†O'Connor, John T. *civil engineering educator*
Puckett, Hoyle Brooks *agricultural engineer, research scientist, consultant*

Chicago
Acs, Joseph Steven *transportation engineering consultant*
Agarwal, Gyan Chand *engineering educator*
Babcock, Lyndon Ross, Jr. *environmental engineer, educator*
Biljetina, Richard *chemical engineering researcher*
Breyer, Norman Nathan *metallurgical engineering educator, consultant*
Budenholzer, Roland Anthony *mechanical engineering educator*
Camras, Marvin *electrical and computer engineering educator, inventor*
Chen, Wai-Kai *electrical engineering and computer science educator, consultant*
Chung, Paul Myungha *mechanical engineer, educator*
Dix, Rollin C(umming) *mechanical engineering educator, consultant*
Epstein, Raymond *engineering and architectural executive*
Fahnestock, Jean Howe *retired civil engineer*
Gerstner, Robert William *structural engineering educator, consultant*
Graupe, Daniel *electrical and computer engineering educator, systems and biomedical engineer*
Gupta, Krishna Chandra *mechanical engineering educator*
Guralnick, Sidney Aaron *civil engineering educator*
Hartnett, James Patrick *engineering educator*
Hobbs, Marvin *engineering executive*
Kim, H. J. (Shaun Kim) *engineer*
Koncel, James E. *electrical engineer*
Kupperman, Melvin *civil engineer, construction and development company executive*
Lin, James Chih-I *biomedical and electrical engineer, educator*
Linden, Henry Robert *chemical engineering research executive*
McLaughlin, John Michael, Jr. *engineer, engineering company executive*
Michelson, Irving *aerospace engineer*
Miller, Irving Franklin *chemical engineering educator, academic administrator*
Minkowycz, W. J. *mechanical engineering educator*
Murata, Tadao *engineering and computer science educator*
Nelson, Kenneth Edward *consulting engineer*
Nickel, Melvin Edwin *metallurgical engineer*
Novick, David *civil engineer, educator*
†Powers, James *engineering company executive*
†Raczkiewicz, Maciej A. *engineering company executive*
Riddell, Matthew Donald Rutherford *consulting environmental engineer*
Rikoski, Richard Anthony *engineering executive, electrical engineer*
†Sandberg, Harold Raymond *civil engineer*
†Shah, Manu Hirachand *civil and structural engineer*
Smith, Spencer Bailey *engineering and business educator*
Stone, Daniel Hunter *metallurgical engineer, researcher*
Swanson, Bernet Steven *consulting engineer, former educator*
Tijunelis, Donatas *engineering executive*
Todd Copley, Judith Ann *materials and metallurgical engineering educator*

Clarendon Hills
Moritz, Donald Brooks *mechanical engineer, consultant*

Decatur
Graf, Karl Rockwell *nuclear engineer*
Koucky, John Richard *metallurgical engineer, manufacturing executive*

Des Plaines
Dlouhy, Phillip Edward *engineering, construction executive*
†Winfield, Michael D. *engineering company executive*

Downers Grove
†Dietz, Charles Kenneth *chemical engineer*

Dunlap
Bailey, John Maxwell *retired mechanical engineer, consultant*

Elmhurst
Balcerzak, Marion John *mechanical engineer*
Burton, Darrell Irvin *engineering executive*
Grisim, J. Terrence *safety consulting company executive*

Evanston
Achenbach, Jan Drewes *engineer and scientist*
Bankoff, Seymour George *chemical engineer, educator*
Bazant, Zdenek Pavel *structural engineering educator, scientist, consultant*
Belytschko, Ted Bohdan *civil, mechanical engineering educator*
Brazelton, William Thomas *chemical engineering educator*
Butt, John Baecher *chemical engineering educator*
Carr, Stephen Howard *materials engineer, educator*
Cheng, Herbert Su-Yuen *mechanical engineering educator*
Chung, Yip-Wah *engineering educator*
Daniel, Isaac Mordochai *mechanical engineering educator*
Daskin, Mark Stephen *civil engineering educator*
Ehmann, Kornel F. *mechanical engineering educator*
Epstein, Max *electrical engineering educator*
Fine, Morris Eugene *materials engineer, educator*
†Fourer, Robert H. *industrial engineering educator, consultant*
Frey, Donald Nelson *industrial engineer, educator, manufacturing company executive*
Goldstick, Thomas Karl *biomedical engineering educator*
Haddad, Abraham Herzl *electrical engineering educator, researcher*
Keer, Leon Morris *engineering educator*
Kistler, Alan Lee *engineering educator*
Kliphardt, Raymond A. *engineering educator*
Kovitz, Arthur A. *mechanical engineering educator*
Krizek, Raymond John *civil engineering educator, consultant*
Liu, Wing Kam *mechanical and civil engineering educator*
Mah, Richard Sze Hao *chemical engineering educator*
Marhic, Michel Edmond *engineering educator, entrepreneur, consultant*
Mura, Toshio *civil engineering educator*
Murphy, Gordon John *engineering educator*
Ottino, Julio Mario *chemical engineering educator, scientist*
Plonus, Martin Algirdas *electrical engineering educator*
Rath, Gustave J(oseph) *industrial engineering educator, psychologist*
Rubenstein, Albert Harold *industrial engineering and management sciences educator*
Rudnicki, John Walter *engineering educator*
Shah, Surendra Poonamchand *engineering educator, researcher*
Sobel, Alan *electrical engineer, physicist*
Taflove, Allen *electrical engineer, educator, researcher, consultant*
Tankin, Richard Samuel *fluid dynamics engineer, educator*
Van Ness, James Edward *electrical engineering educator*
Walker, John Andrew *mechanical engineer, educator*

Evergreen Park
Ephraim, Max, Jr. *mechanical engineer*

Flossmoor
Ripling, Edward Joseph *metallurgical engineer, researcher*

Gilman
Ireland, Herbert Orin *engineering educator*

Glenview
Adler, Robert *electronics engineer*
Harris, Ronald David *chemical engineer*
Panarese, William C. *civil engineer*
Russell, Henry George *structural engineer*
Van Zelst, Theodore William *civil engineer, natural resource exploration company executive*

Hartford
Christian, Nelson Frederick *chemical engineer*

Joliet
McCullough, Henry G(lenn) L(uther) *nuclear engineer*

Lake Forest
Lambert, John Boyd *chemical engineer, consultant*

Lemont
Chen, Shoei-Sheng *mechanical engineer*

Lincolnshire
Kotynek, George Roy *mechanical engineer, educator, marketing executive*
Speer, David Blakeney *industrial executive*

Lisle
Melsa, James Louis *electrical engineer*

Lombard
Branum, William Howell *engineering company executive*

Moline
Harrington, Roy Edwards *agricultural engineer, author*

Mount Prospect
Basar, Ronald John *research engineer, engineering executive*
†Lo, Robert *process engineering company executive, computer support company executive*
Scott, Norman Laurence *engineering consultant*

Naperville
Crawford, Raymond Maxwell, Jr. *nuclear engineer*

Oxenreiter, Maurice Frank *chemical engineer*
†Patel, Ramanlal L. *engineering executive*
†Vora, Manu Kishandas *chemical engineer, quality consultant*

Northfield
Fraenkel, Stephen Joseph *engineering and research executive*

Oak Brook
†Akin, Lewis E. *mechanical engineer*
Degerstrom, James Marvin *engineering manager*

Oak Park
Clark, John Peter, III *engineering consultant*

Orland Park
Dyott, Richard Burnaby *research engineering executive*

Palatine
Novak, Robert Louis *civil engineer, pavement management consultant*

Park Ridge
Bridges, Jack Edgar *electronics engineer*
Ellis, Robert Griswold *engineering executive*

Peoria
Doyle, Richard Lee *architect, engineer*
Rainson, Ronald Lee *engineering executive, consultant*

Plainfield
Chakrabarti, Subrata Kumar *marine research engineer*

Rock Island
Mulich, Steve Francis *safety engineer*

Rockford
Eliason, Jon Tate *electrical engineer*
†Hess, George J. *electrical engineer, consultant*
†Vincenti-Brown, Crispin Rufus William *engineering executive*

Schaumburg
Wyslotsky, Ihor *engineering company executive*

Skokie
Corley, William Gene *engineering research executive*
Hognestad, Eivind *retired civil engineer*
Siegal, Rita Goran *engineering company executive*

Springfield
Hahn, Ralph Crane *structural engineer, consultant*
Hanson, Walter Edmund *consulting civil engineer*
Lyons, J. Rolland *civil engineer*
†Thompson, Donald Edward *engineering company executive*

Urbana
Addy, Alva Leroy *mechanical engineer*
Alkire, Richard Collin *chemical engineering educator*
Axford, Roy Arthur *nuclear engineering educator*
Basar, Tamer *electrical engineering educator*
Bayne, James Wilmer *mechanical engineering educator*
Beck, Paul Adams *metallurgist, educator*
Bergeron, Clifton George *ceramic engineer, educator*
Blahut, Richard Edward *electrical and computer engineering educator*
Chao, Bei Tse *mechanical engineering educator*
Chato, John Clark *mechanical engineering educator*
Clausing, Arthur M. *mechanical engineering educator*
Coleman, Paul Dare *electrical engineering educator*
Conry, Thomas Francis *mechanical engineering educator, consultant*
Cusano, Cristino *mechanical engineer, educator*
Dobrovolny, Jerry Stanley *engineering educator*
Economy, James *polymer researcher, consultant*
Eden, James Gary *electrical engineering and physics educator, researcher*
Engelbrecht, Richard Stevens *environmental engineering educator*
Gaddy, Oscar Lee *electrical engineering educator*
Goering, Carroll E. *agricultural engineering educator*
Hajj, Ibrahim Nasri *electrical and computer engineering educator*
Hall, William Joel *civil engineer, educator*
Hannon, Bruce Michael *engineer, educator*
Hanratty, Thomas Joseph *chemical engineer, educator*
Herrin, Moreland *civil engineering educator, consultant*
Hess, Karl *electrical and computer engineering educator*
Holonyak, Nick, Jr. *electrical engineering educator*
Huang, Thomas Shi-Tao *electrical engineering educator, researcher*
Hunt, Donnell Ray *agricultural engineering educator*
Jenkins, William Kenneth *electrical engineering educator*
Jones, Benjamin Angus, Jr. *retired agricultural engineering educator, administrator*
Kang, Sung-Mo (Steve Kang) *electrical engineering educator*
Kesler, Clyde Ervin *engineering educator*
Kumar, Panganamala Ramana *electrical and computer engineering educator*
Maxwell, William Hall Christie *civil engineering educator*
May, Walter Grant *chemical engineer*
Mayes, Paul Eugene *engineering educator, technical consultant*
Mazumder, Jyotirmoy *mechanical and industrial engineering educator*
Miley, George Hunter *nuclear engineering educator*
Miller, Robert Earl *engineer, educator*
†Morkoç, Hadis *electrical engineer, educator*
Ormsbee, Allen Ives *aeronautical and astronautical engineering educator, researcher, consultant*
Pai, Anantha Mangalore *electrical engineering educator, consultant*
Perkins, William Randolph *electrical engineer, educator*
Rao, Nannapaneni Narayana *electrical engineer*
†Shaffer, Louis Richard *engineering research administrator, civil engineering educator*
Siess, Chester Paul *civil engineering educator*
Socie, Darrell Frederick *mechanical engineering educator*

Soo, Shao Lee mechanical engineer, educator
Stallmeyer, James Edward engineer, educator
Swenson, George Warner, Jr. electronics engineer, radio astronomer, educator
Tang, Wilson Hon-chung engineering educator
Trick, Timothy Noel electrical and computer engineering educator, researcher
Trigger, Kenneth James manufacturing engineering educator
Wert, Charles Allen metallurgical and mining engineering educator
Westwater, James William chemical engineering educator
Yoerger, Roger Raymond agricultural engineer, educator

Wilmette
Barnett, Ralph Lipsey engineering educator
Muhlenbruch, Carl W. civil engineer

INDIANA

Bloomington
Harder, John E. electrical engineer

Carmel
Monical, Robert Duane consulting structural engineer

Chesterfield
Fry, Meredith Warren civil engineer, consultant

Columbus
Kamo, Roy engineering company executive
Kubo, Isoroku mechanical engineer

Evansville
Gerhart, Philip Mark mechanical engineering educator
Hartsaw, William O. mechanical engineering educator

Fort Wayne
Lyons, Jerry Lee mechanical engineer
Mahmoud, Aly Ahmed electrical engineering educator
Mills, Rodney Daniel engineering company executive
Quinn, C. Jack mechanical engineering educator, consultant
Weatherford, George Edward civil engineer
Williams, Walter Jackson, Jr. electrical engineer, consultant

Hammond
Neff, Gregory Pall manufacturing engineering educator, consultant
Pierson, Edward Samuel engineering educator, consultant

Indianapolis
Brannon-Peppas, Lisa chemical engineer, researcher
Cones, Van Buren electronics engineer, consultant
Gable, Robert William, Jr. aerospace engineer

Lafayette
Bement, Arden Lee, Jr. engineering educator
Emery, Alden Hayes, Jr. chemical engineer, educator
Etzel, James Edward environmental engineering educator
Fox, Robert William mechanical engineering educator
Geddes, Leslie Alexander bioengineer, physiologist, educator
Gustafson, Winthrop Adolph aeronautical and astronautical engineering educator
Mc Laughlin, John Francis civil engineer, educator
Ott, Karl Otto nuclear engineering educator, consultant

Muncie
Bennon, Saul electrical engineer, transformer consultant

Notre Dame
Gray, William Guerin civil engineering educator
Jerger, Edward William mechanical engineer, university dean
Kohn, James Paul engineering educator
Merz, James Logan electrical engineering and materials educator, researcher
Michel, Anthony Nikolaus electrical engineering educator, researcher
Sain, Michael Kent electrical engineering educator
Schmitz, Roger Anthony chemical engineering educator, academic administrator
Sweeney, Thomas Leonard chemical engineering educator, researcher
Szewczyk, Albin Anthony engineering educator
Varma, Arvind chemical engineering educator, researcher

Orleans
Keys, Steven Franklin chemical engineer

Princeton
Mullins, Richard Austin chemical engineer

Terre Haute
Smith, Charles Oliver engineer
Wheelock, Larry Arthur engineer, consultant

West Lafayette
Albright, Lyle Frederick chemical engineering educator
Altschaeffl, Adolph George civil engineering educator
Andres, Ronald Paul chemical engineer, educator
Barany, James Walter industrial engineering educator
Bogdanoff, John Lee aeronautical engineering educator
Cohen, Raymond mechanical engineer, educator
Cooper, James Albert, Jr. electrical engineering educator
Dayananda, Mysore Ananthamurthy materials engineering educator
Delleur, Jacques William civil engineering educator
Dolch, William Lee retired engineering materials educator
Drnevich, Vincent Paul civil engineering educator
Eckert, Roger E(arl) chemical engineering educator
Farris, Thomas N. engineering educator, researcher
Friedlaender, Fritz Josef electrical engineering educator
Fukunaga, Keinosuke engineering educator
Grace, Richard Edward engineering educator
Greenkorn, Robert Albert chemical engineering educator
Harr, Milton Edward civil engineering professor, engineering consultant
Herrick, Robert James electrical engineering technology educator, electronics engineer
Hillberry, Ben(ny) M(ax) mechanical engineering educator
Hinkle, Charles Nelson retired agricultural engineering educator
Incropera, Frank Paul mechanical engineering educator
Kashyap, Rangasami Lakshmi Narayan electrical engineering educator
Landgrebe, David Allen electrical engineer
Leimkuhler, Ferdinand Francis industrial engineering educator
Liley, Peter Edward mechanical engineering educator
Lin, Pen-Min electrical engineer, educator
Marshall, Francis Joseph aerospace engineer
Mc Gillem, Clare Duane electrical engineering educator
Michael, Harold Louis civil engineering educator
Monke, Edwin John agricultural engineering educator
Neudeck, Gerold Walter electrical engineering educator
Ong, Chee-Mun engineering educator
Peppas, Nikolaos Athanassiou chemical engineering educator, consultant
Pritsker, A. Alan B. engineering executive, educator
Richey, Clarence Bentley agricultural engineering educator
Salvendy, Gavriel industrial engineer
Schuhmann, Reinhardt, Jr. metallurgical engineering educator, consultant
Schwartz, Richard John electrical engineering educator, researcher
Skelton, Robert Eugene aeronautics and astronautics educator
Solberg, James Joseph industrial engineering educator
Sozen, Mete Avni civil engineering educator
Stevenson, Warren Howard mechanical engineering educator
Taber, Margaret Ruth electrical engineering technology educator, electrical engineer
Taylor, Raymond Ellory mechanical engineering researcher
Thomas, Marlin Uluess industrial engineering educator
Vest, Robert Wilson ceramic engineering educator
Viskanta, Raymond mechanical engineering educator
Wankat, Phillip Charles chemical engineering educator
Williams, Theodore Joseph engineering educator
Wright, Jeff Regan civil engineering educator

IOWA

Ames
Anderson, Robert Morris, Jr. electrical engineer
Basart, John Philip electrical engineering and radio astronomy researcher, educator
Baumann, Edward Robert sanitary engineering educator
Boylan, David Ray retired chemical engineer, educator
Brown, Robert Grover engineering educator
Buchele, Wesley Fisher agricultural engineering educator, consultant
Burnet, George, Jr. engineering educator
Cleasby, John LeRoy civil engineer, educator
Colvin, Thomas Stuart agricultural engineer, farmer
Curry, Norval Herbert retired agricultural engineer
Ekberg, Carl Edwin, Jr. civil engineering educator
Inger, George Roe aerospace engineering educator
Iversen, James Delano aerospace engineering educator, consultant
Johnson, Howard Paul agricultural engineering educator
Jones, Edwin Channing, Jr. electrical engineering educator
Larsen, William Lawrence materials science and engineering educator
Larson, Maurice Allen chemical engineer, educator
Maze, Thomas H. engineering educator
Mischke, Charles Russell mechanical engineering educator
Okiishi, Theodore Hisao mechanical engineering educator
Porter, Max L. engineering educator
Riley, William Franklin mechanical engineering educator
Sanders, Wallace Wolfred, Jr. civil engineer
Tannehill, John C. aerospace engineer, educator
Wilder, David Randolph materials engineer, consultant
Wilson, Lennox Norwood aeronautical engineering educator
Young, Donald Fredrick engineering educator

Davenport
Kanzaki, George Akaki industrial engineer, educator

Decorah
Erdman, Lowell Paul civil engineer, land surveyor

Iowa City
Arora, Jasbir Singh engineering educator
Carmichael, Gregory Richard chemical engineering educator
Chen, Lea D. engineering educator, researcher
Eyman, Earl Duane electrical science educator, consultant
Haug, Edward Joseph, Jr. mechanical engineering educator, simulation research engineer
Hering, Robert Gustave mechanical engineer, educator, university administrator
Korpel, Adrian electrical and computer engineering educator, consultant
Kusiak, Andrew manufacturing engineer, educator
Lance, George Milward mechanical engineering educator
Lonngren, Karl Erik electrical and computer engineering educator
Madsen, Donald Howard engineering educator, consultant
Marshall, Jeffrey Scott mechanical engineer, educator
Patel, Virendra Chaturbhai mechanical engineering educator

Madrid
Handy, Richard Lincoln civil engineer, educator

Mason City
Wallace, Ralph Howes retired engineering company executive

Muscatine
Fosholt, Sanford Kenneth consulting engineer
Stanley, Richard Holt consulting engineer
Thomopulos, Gregs G. consulting engineering company executive

Sioux City
Walker, Jimmie Kent mechanical engineer

KANSAS

Lawrence
Benjamin, Bezaleel Solomon architecture and architectural engineering educator
Darwin, David civil engineering educator, researcher, consultant
Farokhi, Saeed aerospace engineering educator, consultant
Forman, George Whiteman mechanical design consultant
Green, Don Wesley chemical and petroleum engineering educator
Holtzman, Julian Charles electrical engineer
Leonard, Roy Junior civil engineering educator
Lucas, William Max, Jr. structural engineer, university dean
Mc Kinney, Ross Erwin civil engineering educator
Moore, Richard Kerr electrical engineering educator
Muirhead, Vincent Uriel aerospace engineer
Rolfe, Stanley Theodore civil engineer, educator
Roskam, Jan aerospace engineer
Rowland, James Richard electrical engineering educator
Smith, Howard Wesley engineering educator
Smith, Robert Lee retired civil engineering educator
Zerwekh, Robert Paul engineering administrator, engineering management educator, researcher, consultant, artist

Manhattan
Appl, Fredric Carl retired mechanical engineering educator
Cogley, Allen C. mechanical engineering educator, administrator
Erickson, Larry Eugene chemical engineering educator
Fenton, Donald Lee mechanical engineering educator, consultant
Hagen, Lawrence Jacob agricultural engineer
Johnson, William Howard agricultural engineer, educator
Kirmser, Philip George engineering educator
Lee, E(ugene) Stanley industrial engineer, mathematician, educator
Simons, Gale Gene nuclear engineering educator, university administrator

Overland Park
Baker, Charles H. engineering company executive

Salina
Crawford, Lewis Cleaver engineering executive

Shawnee Mission
Callahan, Harry Leslie civil engineer
Robinson, Thomas Bullene retired civil engineer

Topeka
Comstock, Glen David civil engineer
Metzler, Dwight Fox civil engineer, retired state official

University Of Kansas
Kraft, David Christian civil engineering educator

Wichita
Egbert, Robert Iman electrical engineering educator, academic administrator
Gosman, Albert Louis mechanical engineering educator
Mc Kee, George Moffitt, Jr. civil engineer, consultant
Wentz, William Henry, Jr. aerospace engineer, educator
Wilhelm, William Jean civil engineering educator

KENTUCKY

Lexington
Caroland, William Bourne structural engineer
Cremers, Clifford John mechanical engineering educator
†Ely, George Melvin, Jr. civil engineer
†Foree, Edward Golden environmental engineer, consultant
Grimes, Dale Mills electrical engineering educator
Hanson, Mark Tod engineering mechanics educator
Nasar, Syed Abu electrical engineering educator
Shuler, Scott civil engineer
Steele, Earl Larsen electrical engineering educator
Tauchert, Theodore Richmond mechanical engineer, educator
Traynor, Harry Sheehy engineering consultant
Turner, Larry William agricultural engineer, educator
Walker, John Neal agricultural engineering educator

Louisville
Clark, John Hallett, III consulting engineering executive
Cornelius, Wayne Anderson engineering technology educator, consultant
†Corradino, Joseph Carmen civil engineer
Garcia, Rafael Jorge chemical engineer
Hanley, Thomas Richard engineering educator
Krainer, Edward Frank engineering executive
Ward, Thomas Leon engineering educator

LOUISIANA

Baker
Moody, Lamon Lamar, Jr. retired civil engineer

Baton Rouge
Acar, Yalcin Bekir civil engineer, soil remediation technology executive, educator
Aghazadeh, Fereydoun industrial engineer, educator
Arman, Ara civil engineering educator
Chen, Peter Pin-Shan electrical engineering and computer science educator, data processing executive
Constant, William David chemical engineer, educator
Desbrandes, Robert petroleum engineering educator, consultant
Gernon, Clarke Joseph, Sr. mechanical and forensic engineering consultant
Gopu, Vijaya K.A. engineer, consultant
Marshak, Alan Howard electrical engineer, educator
McLaughlin, Edward chemical engineering educator, dean
Moody, Gene Byron engineering executive, small business owner
Parish, Richard Lee engineer, consultant
Pike, Ralph Webster chemical engineer, educator, university official
Stopher, Peter Robert civil and transportation engineering educator, consultant
Tipton, Kenneth Warren agricultural administrator, researcher
Tumay, Mehmet Taner geotechnical consultant, educator, research administrator

Kenner
Siebel, Mathias Paul mechanical engineer

Lafayette
Domingue, Emery consulting engineering company executive
Leon, Benjamin Joseph electrical engineering educator, consultant

Natchitoches
Christensen, Raymond Lyle electrical engineer, educator

New Orleans
Crisp, John N. engineering educator
Lannes, William Joseph, III electrical engineer
Lee, Griff Calicutt civil engineer
†Nelson, Waldemar Stanley civil engineer, consultant
Quirk, Peter Richard engineering company executive
Tewell, Joseph Robert, Jr. electrical engineer
Walk, Frank Humphrey consulting engineer

Ruston
Barron, Randall Franklin mechanical engineer, educator, consultant
Painter, Jack Timberlake civil engineer
Warrington, Robert O'Neil, Jr. mechanical engineering educator and administrator, researcher

Saint Gabriel
Das, Dilip Kumar chemical engineer

Shreveport
Demopulos, Chris engineering company executive

MAINE

East Boothbay
Smith, Merlin Gale engineering executive, researcher

New Harbor
Brown, Donald Vaughn technical educator, engineering consultant

Oakland
Poulin, Thomas Edward marine engineer, state legislator, retail business owner

Orono
Rivard, William Charles mechanical engineering educator

Portland
Raisbeck, Gordon systems engineer

Prospect Harbor
Shipman, Charles William chemical engineer

MARYLAND

Aberdeen Proving Ground
Paules, Palmer L. engineering director

Annapolis
Allen, John Loyd technical engineering consultant
DiAiso, Robert Joseph civil engineer
Granger, Robert Alan aerospace engineer
Henderson, William Boyd engineering consulting company executive
Ho, Louis Ting mechanical engineer
Johnson, Bruce engineering educator
Kapland, Mitchell Arthur engineering firm executive
†Pierce, James Lee engineering and information systems company executive

Baltimore
Brush, Lucien Munson, Jr. hydrologist, educator
Chapanis, Alphonse human factors engineer, ergonomist
Corn, Morton environmental engineer, educator
Degenford, James Edward electrical engineer, educator
Donohue, Marc David chemical engineering educator
Ellingwood, Bruce Russell structural engineering researcher
Fisher, Jack Carrington environmental engineering educator
Giddens, Don Peyton engineering educator, researcher
Hirsch, Richard Arthur mechanical engineer
Huggins, William Herbert electrical engineering educator
Jelinek, Frederick electrical engineer, educator

Joseph, Richard Isaac *electrical engineering and computer science educator*
Katz, Joseph Louis *chemical engineer, educator*
Knoedler, Elmer L. *retired chemical engineer*
Lemer, Andrew Charles *engineer, economist*
Maslen, Stephen Harold *research engineer, consultant*
Mc Cord, Kenneth Armstrong *consulting engineer*
Popel, Aleksander S. *engineering educator*
Prince, Jerry Ladd *engineering educator*
ReVelle, Charles S. *environmental engineer, geophysicist, systems analysis and economics educator*
Rugh, Wilson John, II *electrical engineering educator*
Sharpe, William Norman, Jr. *mechanical engineer, educator*

Bel Air
Powers, Doris Hurt *engineering company executive*

Bethesda
Bosnak, Robert John *mechanical engineer, federal agency administrator*
†Burdeshaw, William Brooksbank *engineering executive*
Cottony, Herman Vladimir *electronic engineer, consultant*
Eden, Murray *electrical engineer, emeritus educator*
Freedman, Joseph *sanitary and public health engineering consultant*
Koltnow, Peter Gregory *engineering consultant*
Kynoch, James Brent *environmental engineering executive*
†Mann, Gary T. *engineering company executive*
Saville, Thorndike, Jr. *coastal engineer, consultant*
Sevik, Maurice *engineer*

Burtonsville
Yang, Jackson *aerospace engineering company executive*

Catonsville
Cadman, Theodore Wesley *chemical engineering educator*

Chevy Chase
Edelson, Burton Irving *electrical engineering educator*
Mayers, Jean *aeronautical engineering educator*
Rockwell, Theodore *nuclear engineer*

Clarksburg
Arnold, Jay *engineering executive*
Bargellini, Pier Luigi *electrical engineer*
Mahle, Christoph Erhard *electrical engineer*

Clarksville
Brancato, Emanuel Leonard *electrical engineering consultant*

College Park
Anderson, John David, Jr. *aerospace engineer*
Barbe, David Franklin *electrical engineer, educator*
Blankenship, Gilmer Leroy *electrical engineering educator, engineering company executive*
Cunniff, Patrick Francis *mechanical engineer*
Dally, James William *mechanical engineering educator, consultant*
Ephremides, Anthony *electrical engineering educator*
Gentry, James Walter *chemical engineer, educator*
Gessow, Alfred *aerospace engineer, educator*
Granatstein, Victor Lawrence *electrical engineer, educator*
Gupta, Ashwani Kumar *mechanical engineering educator*
Levine, William Silver *electrical engineering educator*
Marcus, Steven Irl *electrical engineering educator*
Newcomb, Robert Wayne *electrical engineer*
Pai, Shih I. *aeronautical engineer*
Singh, Amarjit *engineering executive, scientist, management consultant*
Smith, Theodore Goodwin *chemical engineering educator*
Taylor, Leonard Stuart *engineering educator, consultant*

Columbia
Hegedus, L. Louis *chemical engineer, research and development executive*

Frederick
Bryan, John Leland *retired engineering educator*

Gaithersburg
Arrowsmith, Peter D. *engineering executive*
Cookson, Alan Howard *electrical engineer, researcher*
Fuhrman, Ralph Edward *civil and environmental engineer*
Levine, Robert Sidney *chemical engineer*
Mathias, Joseph Simon *metallurgical engineer, consultant*
Nayyar, Mohinder Lal *mechanical engineer*
Rabinow, Jacob *electrical engineer, consultant*
Wright, Richard Newport, III *civil engineer, government official*

Glen Arm
Mc Cord, Marshal *civil engineer*

Greenbelt
Cooper, Robert Shanklin *engineering executive, former government official*
O'Mara, Arthur James *civil engineer*

Hunt Valley
Kinstlinger, Jack *engineer executive, consultant*
McKay, Jack Alexander *electronics engineer, physicist*

Kingsville
Pullen, Keats A., Jr. *electronics engineer*

Landover
Freeman, Ernest Robert *engineering executive*

Lanham Seabrook
Blanchard, David Lawrence *aerospace executive, real estate developer*

Laurel
Billig, Frederick Stucky *mechanical engineer*
Dallman, Paul Jerald *engineer, writer*
Eaton, Alvin Ralph *aeronautical and systems engineer, research and development administrator*
Halushynsky, George Dobroslav *systems engineer*
Perrone, Nicholas *mechanical engineer, business executive*
Sherwood, Aaron Wiley *aerodynamics educator*
Westhaver, Lawrence Albert *electronics engineer, consultant*

Linthicum Heights
Skillman, William Alfred *consulting engineering executive*

Owings Mills
†Parviainen, Asko *engineering company executive, consultant*

Potomac
Peters, Frank Albert *retired chemical engineer*

Rockville
†Abron, Lilia A. *chemical engineer*
Bell, William Coleman *agricultural engineer, consultant*
†Campbell, Barry G. *engineering company executive*
†Chang, Kung-Li (Charlie) *engineering consulting firm executive*
Foa, Joseph Victor *aeronautical engineer, educator*
†Freiman, StephenWeil *ceramic engineering researcher*
McDonald, Capers Walter *biomedical engineer, corporate executive*
McMahon, Edward Peter *systems engineer, consultant*
†Minor, Marilyn T. *engineering company executive*
†Motayed, Asok K. *engineering company executive*
†Ramsey, James P. *marine engineering consultant, computer services company consultant*
†Scearce, P. Jennings, Jr. *engineering executive*
Ulbrecht, Jaromir Josef *chemical engineer*
Weinberger, Leon Walter *sanitary engineer*

Seabrook
Durrani, Sajjad Haidar *space communications engineer*
Laurenson, Robert Mark *mechanical engineer*

Severna Park
Davis, John Adams, Jr. *electrical engineer, roboticist, corporate research executive*
Retterer, Bernard Lee *electronic engineering consultant*

Silver Spring
Blake, Lamont Vincent *electronics consultant*
Eades, James Beverly, Jr. *aeronautical engineer*
Foresti, Roy, Jr. *chemical engineer*
Glenn, Robert Edward *industrial hygienist, trade association executive, former government research administrator*
Hermach, Francis Lewis *consulting engineer*
†Johnson, Charles Christopher, Jr. *consulting environmental engineer*
Mundel, Marvin Everett *industrial engineer*
Scipio, L(ouis) Albert, II *aerospace science engineering educator, architect, military historian*
Shames, Irving Herman *engineering educator*

Sparks
Barr, Irwin Robert *retired aeronautical engineer*

MASSACHUSETTS

Acton
Lee, Shih-Ying *mechanical engineering educator*
Peterson, Bob *environmental company executive, consultant*
†Ziminski, Richard William *engineering executive*

Amherst
Abbott, Douglas Eugene *engineering educator*
Berger, Bernard Ben *environmental and civil engineer, former educator and public health officer*
Franks, Lewis E. *electrical and computer engineering educator, researcher*
Haensel, Vladimir *chemical engineering educator*
Laurence, Robert Lionel *chemical engineering educator*
McIntosh, Robert Edward, Jr. *electrical engineering educator, consultant, electronics executive*
Menon, Premachandran Rama *electrical engineering educator*
Motherway, Joseph Edward *mechanical engineer, educator*
Nash, William Arthur *civil engineer, educator*
Schaubert, Daniel Harold *electrical engineering educator*
Swift, Calvin Thomas *electrical and computer engineering educator*

Andover
Jakes, William Chester *electrical engineer*

Arlington
Gumpertz, Werner Herbert *structural engineering company executive*

Ashfield
Nye, Edwin Packard *mechanical engineering educator*

Bedford
Cronson, Harry Marvin *electronics engineer*
Dill, Melville Reese, Jr. *industrial engineering consultant*
Fante, Ronald Louis *engineering scientist*
Hicks, Walter Joseph *electrical engineer, consultant*
Jelalian, Albert V. *electrical engineer*
Kovaly, John Joseph *consulting engineering executive, educator*
Ren, Chung-Li *engineer*
Winter, David Louis *systems engineer, human factors scientist, retired*
Zraket, Charles Anthony *systems research and engineering company executive*

Belmont
Haralampu, George Stelios *electric power engineer, former engineering executive electric utility company*
Keil, Alfred Adolf Heinrich *marine engineering educator*
Merrill, Edward Wilson *chemical engineering educator*
Seifert, William Walther *electrical engineering educator*

Billerica
Brebbia, Carlos Alberto *educator, engineering consultant*
Schmidt, James Robert *facilities engineer*

Bolton
Kadak, Andrew C. *engineering company executive*

Boston
†Callahan, James T. *engineering company executive*
Cravalho, Ernest George *biomedical engineering educator*
De Luca, Carlo John *biomedical engineer*
Felsen, Leopold B. *engineer, educator*
Fine, Samuel *biomedical engineering educator, consultant*
Harrington, Joseph John *environmental engineering educator*
Hines, Marion Ernest *electronic engineering consultant*
Langer, Robert Martin *retired chemical engineering company executive, consultant*
McCluskey, Jean Louise *civil and consulting engineer*
Moore, Richard Lawrence *structural engineer, consultant*
Pierce, Allan Dale *engineering educator, researcher*
Raemer, Harold Roy *electrical engineering educator*
Reinschmidt, Kenneth Frank *engineering and construction executive*
Saleh, Bahaa E. A. *electrical engineering educator*
Tierney, Robert Thomas *civil engineer*
Vershbow, Arthur Emmanuel *mechanical engineer*

Braintree
Davis, Robert Jocelyn *engineering executive*
Foster, Arthur Rowe *mechanical engineering educator*

Brookline
Katz, Israel *engineering educator, retired*

Cambridge
Abernathy, Frederick H. *mechanical engineering educator*
Akylas, Triantaphyllos R. *mechanical engineering educator*
Allen, Samuel Miller *metallurgical engineer*
Antoniadis, Dimitri Alexander *electrical engineering educator*
Argon, Ali Suphi *mechanical engineering educator*
Athans, Michael *electrical engineering educator, consultant*
Baron, Judson Richard *aerospace educator*
Baron, Sheldon *research and development company executive*
Battin, Richard Horace *astronautical engineer*
Beér, János Miklós *engineering educator*
Ben-Akiva, Moshe Emanuel *civil engineering educator*
Bowen, H. Kent *engineering educator, consultant*
Braida, Louis Benjamin Daniel *electrical engineering educator*
Bras, Rafael Luis *engineering educator*
Brenner, Howard *chemical engineering educator*
Brown, Robert Arthur *chemical engineering educator*
Budiansky, Bernard *engineering educator*
Carmichael, Alexander Douglas *engineering educator*
Chen, Sow-Hsin *nuclear engineering educator, researcher*
Clark, Joel Phillip *engineering educator, consultant*
†Clark, Peter P. *optical engineer*
Cohen, Morris *engineering educator*
Cohen, Robert Edward *chemical engineering educator, consultant*
Colton, Clark Kenneth *chemical engineering educator*
Counselman, Charles Claude, III *electrical engineering educator*
Crandall, Stephen Harry *engineering educator*
Crawley, Edward Francis *aerospace engineering educator*
de Neufville, Richard Lawrence *engineering educator*
Dewey, Clarence Forbes, Jr. *engineering educator*
Drake, Elisabeth Mertz *chemical engineer*
Dubowsky, Steven *mechanical engineering educator*
Duffy, Robert Aloysius *aeronautical engineer*
Dugundji, John *aeronautical engineer*
†Durlach, Nathaniel I. *acoustical engineering educator*
Elias, Peter *electrical engineering educator*
Emmons, Howard Wilson *engineer, educator, consultant, researcher*
Fano, Robert Mario *electrical engineering educator*
Fay, James Alan *mechanical engineering educator*
Flemings, Merton Corson *engineering educator, materials scientist*
†Flowers, Woodie Claude *mechanical engineering educator and researcher, engineering director*
Fortmann, Thomas Edward *research and development company executive*
Fujimoto, James G. *electrical engineering educator*
†Furman, Thomas D., Jr. *engineering company executive*
Gallager, Robert Gray *electrical engineering educator*
Gatos, Harry Constantine *engineering educator*
Glaser, Peter Edward *mechanical engineer, consultant*
Golay, Michael Warren *nuclear engineering educator*
Greitzer, Edward Marc *aeronautical engineering educator, consultant*
Griffith, Peter *mechanical engineering educator, researcher*
†Guerra, John Michael *optical engineer*
Gyftopoulos, Elias Panayiotis *mechanical and nuclear engineering educator*
Hansen, Kent Forrest *nuclear engineering educator*
Hansman, Robert John, Jr. *aeronautics and astronautics educator*
Harleman, Donald Robert Fergusson *environmental engineering educator*
Harling, Otto Karl *nuclear engineering educator, researcher*
Haus, Hermann Anton *electrical engineering educator*
Heney, Joseph Edward *environmental engineer*
Henry, Allan Francis *nuclear engineering educator, consultant, researcher*
Heywood, John Benjamin *mechanical engineering educator*
Ho, Yu-Chi *electrical engineering educator*
Hoag, David Garratt *aerospace engineer*
Howard, Jack Benny *chemical engineer, educator, researcher*
Ippen, Erich Peter *electrical engineering educator*
Jensen, Klavs Fleming *chemical engineering educator*
Kamm, Roger Dale *biomedical engineer, educator*
†Kassakian, John Gabriel *research electrical engineer, engineering director*
Kazimi, Mujid Suliman *nuclear engineer, educator*
Kennedy, Robert Spayde *electrical engineering educator*
Kerrebrock, Jack Leo *aeronautics and astronautics engineering educator*
Kong, Jin Au *electrical engineering educator*
Kung, H. T. *computer science and engineering educator, consultant*
Kyhl, Robert Louis *electrical engineering educator*
Ladd, Charles Cushing, III *civil engineering educator*
†Laibinis, Paul Edward *chemical engineering educator*
Langer, Robert Samuel *chemical, biomedical engineering educator*
Latanision, Ronald Michael *materials science and engineering educator, consultant*
Lee, Thomas Henry *electrical engineer, educator*
Leehey, Patrick *mechanical and ocean engineering educator*
†LeMessurier, William James *structural engineer*
Longwell, John Ploeger *chemical engineering educator*
Makhoul, John Ibrahim *electrical engineer, researcher*
Mann, Robert Wellesley *biomedical engineer, educator*
Marini, Robert Charles *environmental engineering executive*
Markey, Winston Roscoe *aeronautical engineering educator*
Marks, David Hunter *civil engineering educator*
McGarry, Frederick Jerome *civil engineering educator*
Meyer, John Edward *nuclear engineering educator*
Milgram, Jerome H. *marine and ocean engineer, educator*
Miller, Rene Harcourt *aerospace engineer, educator*
Mitter, Sanjoy K. *electrical engineering educator*
†Moran, W. Dennis *engineering consulting executive*
Murman, Earll M. *aeronautics and astronautics educator*
Ogilvie, T(homas) Francis *engineer, educator*
Oppenheim, Alan Victor *electrical engineering educator*
Owen, Walter Shepherd *materials science and engineering educator*
Parthum, Charles Albert *civil engineer*
Pelloux, Regis Marc Noel *materials engineering educator*
Penfield, Paul Livingstone, Jr. *electrical engineering educator*
†Peterson, Carl Richard *mechanical engineering educator, consultant*
Pian, Theodore Hsueh-Huang *engineering educator, consultant*
Powers, Michael Kevin *architectural and engineering executive*
Preston, John Thomas *engineering executive*
Probstein, Ronald Filmore *mechanical engineering educator*
Rabinowicz, Ernest *mechanical engineer, tribologist, educator*
Rasmussen, Norman Carl *nuclear engineer*
Reid, Robert Clark *chemical engineering educator*
Rogers, Peter Philips *environmental engineering educator, city planner*
Rohsenow, Warren Max *retired mechanical engineer, educator*
Roos, Daniel *civil engineering educator*
Ruina, Jack Philip *electrical engineer, educator*
Russell, Kenneth Calvin *metallurgical engineer, educator*
Saltzer, Jerome Howard *computer science educator*
Satterfield, Charles Nelson *chemical engineer, educator*
Schreiber, William Francis *electrical engineering educator*
Seamans, Robert Channing, Jr. *astronautical engineering educator*
†Shea, Joseph F. *aeronautical engineering educator*
Sheridan, Thomas Brown *mechanical engineering and applied psychology educator, researcher, consultant*
Siebert, William McConway *electrical engineering educator*
Smith, Kenneth Alan *chemical engineer, educator*
Sonin, Ain A. *mechanical engineering educator, consultant*
Staelin, David Hudson *electrical engineering educator, consultant*
Stephanopoulos, Gregory *chemical engineering educator, consultant, researcher*
Stevens, Kenneth Noble *electrical engineering educator*
Suh, Nam Pyo *mechanical engineering educator*
†Tassell, Jon Van *optical engineer*
Thomas, Edwin L. *materials engineering educator*
Thomas, Harold Allen, Jr. *civil engineer, educator*
Todreas, Neil Emmanuel *nuclear engineering educator*
Trilling, Leon *aeronautical engineering educator*
Troxel, Donald Eugene *electrical engineering educator*
Tuller, Harry Louis *materials science and engineering educator*
Ungar, Eric Edward *mechanical engineer*
Vander Velde, Wallace Earl *aeronautical and astronautical educator*
†Vér, István László *acoustical consultant*
Vivian, Johnson Edward *retired chemical engineering educator*
Wechsler, Alfred Elliot *engineering executive, consultant, chemical engineer*
Weiss, Stanley Irwin *engineering executive, aeronautical engineer*
Weiss, Thomas Fischer *electrical engineering educator, biophysicist*
White, David Calvin *electrical engineer, energy educator, consultant*
Whitman, Robert Van Duyne *civil engineer, educator*

Williams, James Henry, Jr. *mechanical engineer, educator, consultant*
Wilson, David Gordon *mechanical engineering educator*
Wilson, Gerald Loomis *electrical engineer, college dean*
Wuensch, Bernhardt John *ceramic engineering educator*
Yannas, Ioannis Vassilios *polymer science and engineering educator*
Zahn, Markus *electrical engineering educator*

Chelmsford
Fulks, Robert Grady *engineering computer executive*

Concord
Drew, Philip Garfield *consultant engineering company executive*
Villers, Philippe *mechanical engineer*
Woll, Harry J. *electrical engineer*

Dedham
†Maloof, Richard C. *engineering executive*

Dighton
Chu, David Yuk *chemical engineer*

East Falmouth
George, M(erton) Baron T(isdale) *aerospace researcher, aviation artist*

Foxboro
Bowditch, Hoel Lawrence *design engineer inventor, consultant*
Ghosh, Asish *control engineer*
Pierce, Francis Casimir *civil engineer*

Framingham
Bose, Amar Gopal *electrical engineering educator*

Harwich
Bush, Richard James *engineering executive, lay church worker*

Holbrook
†Crandlemere, Robert Wayne *engineering executive*

Holyoke
†Parent, Mark *engring company executive, computer support company executive*

Hopkinton
Leamon, Tom B. *industrial engineer, educator*
Novich, Bruce Eric *materials engineer*

Jamaica Plain
Shapiro, Ascher Herman *mechanical engineer, educator, consultant*

Lenox
Krofta, Milos *engineer*

Lexington
Bailey, Fred Coolidge *retired engineering consulting company executive*
Barton, David Knox *engineering executive, radar engineer*
Brookner, Eli *electrical engineer*
Cooper, William Eugene *consultant engineer*
Freed, Charles *engineering consultant, researcher*
Kingston, Robert Hildreth *engineering educator*
McWhorter, Alan Louis *electronics researcher, engineering educator*
Morrow, Walter Edwin, Jr. *electrical engineer, university laboratory administrator*
O'Donnell, Robert Michael *electrical engineering executive*
Osepchuk, John Moses *engineering physicist, consultant*

Lincoln
Eschenroeder, Alan Quade *environmental scientist*

Littleton
Fuller, Samuel Henry, III *computer engineer*
Mikes, Thomas Louis *optical design engineer*

Longmeadow
Ferris, Theodore Vincent *chemical engineer, consulting technologist*
Hopfe, Harold Herbert *chemical engineer*

Lowell
Kumnick, Albert Joseph *engineering executive*
Reinisch, Bodo Walter *electrical engineering educator*

Lynn
Kercher, David Max *mechanical engineer*

Marblehead
Ehrich, Fredric F. *aeronautical engineer*

Marlborough
Bennett, C. Leonard *consulting engineer*
Stiffler, Jack Justin *electrical engineer*

Medford
Astill, Kenneth Norman *mechanical engineering educator*
Balabanian, Norman *electrical engineering educator*
Garrelick, Joel Marc *acoustical scientist, consultant*
Greif, Robert *mechanical engineering educator*
Howell, Alvin Harold *engineer*
Manno, Vincent Paul *mechanical engineer*
Nelson, Frederick Carl *mechanical engineering educator*
Noonan, Joseph Patrick *engineering educator*
Sussman, Martin Victor *chemical engineering educator, inventor, consultant*
Uhlir, Arthur, Jr. *electrical engineer, university administrator*

Milford
Carson, Charles Henry *electronics engineer*
Gliksberg, Alexander David *engineering executive*

Millbury
Pan, Coda H. T. *mechanical engineering educator, consultant, researcher*

Nantucket
Jesser, Benn Wainwright *chemical engineering and construction company executive*

Needham
Toner, Walter Joseph, Jr. *transportation engineer, financial consultant*

New Bedford
Chang, Robin *engineering executive*

Newton
Barclay, Stanton Dewitt *engineering executive, consultant*
†Marram, Edward P. *engineering company executive*
Saffran, Kalman *engineering consulting company executive, entrepreneur*

Newton Center
Mark, Melvin *consulting mechanical engineer, educator*

North Chatham
Hiscock, Richard Carson *marine safety investigator*

North Dartmouth
Law, Frederick Masom *engineering educator, structural engineering firm executive*

Northampton
Vesely, Alexander *civil engineer*

Northborough
Jeas, William C. *electronics and aerospace engineering executive*

Norwood
Imbault, James Joseph *engineering executive*
Sheingold, Daniel H. *electrical engineer*

Osterville
Old, Bruce Scott *chemical and metallurgical engineer*

Peabody
Goldberg, Harold Seymour *electrical engineer, academic administrator*
†Peters, Leo Francis *environmental engineer*

Pittsfield
Feigenbaum, Armand Vallin *systems engineer, systems equipment executive*
Shammas, Nazih Kheirallah *environmental engineering educator, consultant*

Quincy
Mancini, Rocco Anthony *civil engineer*

Rockland
Campbell, David Stetson *civil engineer, engineering executive*

South Yarmouth
McIlveen, Edward E. *electrical engineer, association executive*

Springfield
Koeninger, Edward Calvin *chemical engineer*

Stow
Shrader, William Whitney *radar consulting scientist*

Sudbury
Fowler, Charles Albert *electronics engineer*

Vineyard Haven
Porter, James H. *chemical engineering executive*

Wakefield
†Paltiel, A. Robert *engineering consulting company executive*

Waltham
†Ellenbogen, S. David *electronics company executive*
Hatsopoulos, George Nicholas *mechanical engineer, thermodynamicist, educator*
Kern, Fred Robert, Jr. *engineer*

Watertown
Katz, William Emanuel *chemical engineer*
True, Edward Keene *architectural engineer*

Wayland
Weil, Thomas Alexander *electronics engineer*

Wellesley
Farnham, Sherman Brett *retired electrical engineer*
Reiss, Martin Harold *engineering executive*

West Roxbury
Wiegner, Allen Walter *biomedical engineering educator, researcher*

Westborough
Gionfriddo, Maurice Paul *research and development manager, aeronautical engineer*

Westford
Dennison, Byron Lee *electrical engineering educator, consultant*

Weston
Anthony, Michael Thomas *consulting engineering firm executive*
Kendall, Julius *consulting engineer*
Resden, Ronald Everette *medical devices product development engineer*

Weymouth
Connor, Jerome Joseph *civil engineering educator*

Wilmington
Faccini, Ernest Carlo *mechanical engineer*
Reeves, Barry Lucas *aerophysics research engineer*

Winchester
Hansen, Robert Joseph *civil engineer*
Hirschfeld, Ronald Colman *retired consulting engineering executive*
Hottel, Hoyt Clarke *consulting chemical engineer*

Woburn
Donadio, Robert Nicholas *mechanical engineer*
†Ginwala, Kymus *engineering executive*

Worcester
Biederman, Ronald R. *mechanical engineer, educator*
Clarke, Edward Nielsen *engineering science educator*
DeFalco, Frank Damian *civil engineering educator*
Sioui, Richard Henry *chemical engineer*
Weiss, Alvin Harvey *chemical engineering educator, catalysis researcher and consultant*
Wilbur, Leslie Clifford *mechanical engineering educator*
Zwiep, Donald Nelson *mechanical engineering educator, administrator*

Yarmouth Port
Stott, Thomas Edward, Jr. *engineering executive*

MICHIGAN

Ann Arbor
Adamson, Thomas Charles, Jr. *aerospace engineering educator, consultant*
Akcasu, Ahmet Ziyaeddin *nuclear engineer, educator*
Assanis, Dennis N. (Dionissios Assanis) *mechanical engineering educator*
Banks, Peter Morgan *electrical engineering educator*
Becher, William Don *electrical engineering educator, engineering consultant*
Bhattacharya, Pallab Kumar *electrical engineering educator, researcher*
Bilello, John Charles *materials science and engineering educator*
Bitondo, Domenic *engineering executive*
Cain, Charles Alan *electrical engineering educator, researcher*
Calahan, Donald Albert *electrical engineering educator*
Clark, John Alden *mechanical engineering educator*
Dow, William Gould *electrical engineer, educator*
England, Anthony Wayne *electrical engineering and computer science educator, astronaut, geophysicist*
Enns, Mark Kynaston *electrical engineer*
Faeth, Gerard Michael *aerospace engineering educator, researcher*
Fogler, Hugh Scott *chemical engineer, educator, consultant*
Gibala, Ronald *metallurgical engineering educator*
Gilbert, Elmer Grant *aerospace engineering educator, control theorist*
Gillespie, Thomas David *mechanical engineer, researcher*
Gomberg, Henry Jacob *nuclear engineer*
Haddad, George Ilyas *engineering educator, research scientist*
Haddox, Mark *electronic engineer*
Hansen, Will *civil engineer, educator, consultant*
Hanson, Robert Duane *civil engineering educator*
Hayes, John Patrick *electrical engineering and computer science educator, consultant*
Kauffman, Charles William *aerospace engineer*
Kerr, William *nuclear engineering educator*
Knoll, Glenn Frederick *nuclear engineering educator*
Kozma, Adam *electrical engineer*
Leith, Emmett Norman *electrical engineer, educator*
Liu, Vi-Cheng *aerospace engineering educator*
Macnee, Alan Breck *electrical engineer, educator*
Martin, William Russell *nuclear engineering educator*
McClamroch, N. Harris *aerospace engineering educator, consultant, researcher*
Merte, Herman, Jr. *educator, mechanical engineer*
Meyer, John Frederick *engineering and computer science educator, researcher, consultant*
Morakinyo, Akinbola Oluwole *mechanical, energy engineer*
Nagy, Andrew Francis *engineering educator*
O'Brien, William Joseph *educator, consultant*
Pehlke, Robert Donald *materials and metallurgical engineering educator*
Petrick, Ernest Nicholas *mechanical engineer*
Pollock, Stephen Michael *industrial engineering educator, consultant*
Root, William Lucas *electrical engineering educator*
Rumman, Wadi (Saliba Rumman) *civil engineer*
Schultz, Albert Barry *engineering educator*
Schwank, Johannes Walter *chemical engineering educator*
Scott, Norman Ross *electrical engineering educator*
Senior, Thomas Bryan A. *electrical engineering educator, researcher, consultant*
Solomon, David Eugene *engineering company executive*
Tai, Chen-To *electrical engineering educator*
Ulaby, Fawwaz Tayssir *electrical engineering and computer science educator, research center administrator*
Upatnieks, Juris *optical engineer, researcher, educator*
†Vinh, Nguyen Xuan *aerospace engineer, educator*
†Wang, Henry Y. *chemical engineering educator*
Weber, Walter Jacob, Jr. *engineering educator*
Wight, James K. *civil engineer, research scientist, educator*
Williams, William James *electrical engineering educator*
Willmarth, William Walter *aerospace engineering educator*
Wilson, Richard Christian *engineering firm executive*
Wineman, Alan Stuart *mechanical engineering and applied mechanics educator*
Wylie, Evan Benjamin *civil engineering educator, consultant, researcher*
Yang, Ralph Tzu-bow *chemical engineer*
Yeh, Chai *electrical engineer, educator*
Yih, Chia-Shun *fluid mechanics educator*
Young, Edwin Harold *chemical and metallurgical engineering educator*

Big Rapids
Thapa, Khagendra *survey engineering educator*

Bingham Farms
†McKeen, Alexander C. *engineering consulting company owner*

Bloomfield Hills
Klingler, Eugene Herman *consulting engineer, educator*
Kollins, Michael Jerome *automotive engineer, historian, writer*
Stivender, Donald Lewis *mechanical engineering consultant*

Clarkston
Erkfritz, Donald Spencer *mechanical engineer*

Dearborn
Cairns, James Robert *mechanical engineering educator*
†Ghafari, Yousif Butrus *chemical engineer*
Little, Robert Eugene *mechanical engineering educator, materials behavior researcher, consultant*
†Manoogian, John A. *manufacturing engineer*
Meitzler, Allen Henry *electrical engineering educator, automotive scientist*

Detroit
Beaufait, Frederick W(illiam) *civil engineering educator*
Brammer, Forest Evert *electrical engineering educator*
Holness, Gordon Victor Rix *engineering executive, mechanical engineer*
Kline, Kenneth Alan *mechanical engineering educator*
Kummler, Ralph H. *chemical engineering educator*
Meisel, Jerome *electrical engineer*
Schmidt, Robert *mechanics and civil engineering educator*
Sengupta, Dipak Lal *electrical engineering and physics educator, researcher*
Stynes, Stanley Kenneth *retired chemical engineer, educator*
Uicker, James Leo *mechanical engineer*
Uicker, Joseph Bernard *engineering company executive*
Wagner, Harvey Arthur *nuclear engineer*

East Lansing
Andersland, Orlando Baldwin *civil engineering educator*
Asmussen, Jes, Jr. *electrical engineer*
Bickart, Theodore Albert *electrical and computer engineering educator, university dean*
Chen, Kun-Mu *electrical engineering educator*
Cutts, Charles Eugene *civil engineering educator*
Foss, John Frank *mechanical engineering educator*
Goodman, Erik David *engineering educator*
Lloyd, John Raymond *mechanical engineering educator*
Merva, George Ellis *agricultural engineer, educator, researcher*
Mukherjee, Kalinath *materials science and engineering educator, researcher*
Snell, John Raymond *civil engineer*
Soutas-Little, Robert William *mechanical engineer, educator*
von Bernuth, Robert Dean *agricultural engineering educator, consultant*
Von Tersch, Lawrence Wayne *electrical engineering educator, university dean*

Farmington
†Neyer, Jerome Charles *consulting civil engineer*

Flint
Gratch, Serge *mechanical engineering educator*

Grand Blanc
Tomlinson, James Lawrence *mechanical engineer*

Greenbush
Paulson, James Marvin *engineering educator*

Grosse Pointe
Beltz, Charles Robert *engineering executive*

Houghton
Heckel, Richard Wayne *metallurgical engineering educator*
Huang, Eugene Yuching *civil engineer, educator*
Lumsdaine, Edward *mechanical engineering educator, university dean*
Pelc, Karol I. *engineering management educator, researcher*
Smith, Darrell Wayne *metallurgical engineering educator, consultant*

Kalamazoo
Fitch, W. Chester *industrial engineer*

Madison Heights
Jeffe, Sidney David *automotive engineer*
†Keisoglou, Abraham Nikolaos *engineering company executive*

Midland
Carson, Gordon Bloom *engineering executive*
Meister, Bernard John *chemical engineer*
†Schrenk, Walter John *research chemical engineer*

Novi
Singh, Jaswant *environmental company executive*

Okemos
Giacoletto, Lawrence Joseph *electronics engineering educator, researcher, consultant*

Plymouth
Grannan, William Stephen *safety engineer, consultant*
†Trim, Donald Roy *consulting engineer*

Rochester
Hovanesian, Joseph Der *mechanical engineering educator*

Romulus
Archer, Hugh Morris *consulting engineer, manufacturing professional*

Saint Joseph
Castenson, Roger R. *agricultural engineer, association executive*
Maley, Wayne Allen *engineering consultant*

Southfield
Ellis, Robert William *engineering educator*

Sturgis
Mackay, Edward *engineer*

Tecumseh
Hood, Douglas Crary *retired electronics educator*

Troy
†Milidrag, George D. *engineering company executive*

Warren
Brayer, Robert Marvin *program manager, engineer*
Gallopoulos, Nicholas Efstratios *chemical engineer*
Jacovides, Linos Jacovou *electrical engineering research manager*
†Kirby, Patrick G. *engineering executive*
Lau, Ian Van *safety research engineer, biomechanics expert*
Nagy, Louis Leonard *engineering executive, researcher*

Waterford
Hampton, Phillip Michael *consulting engineering company executive*

West Bloomfield
†Di Pietro, Frank Anthony *manufacturing engineer*

MINNESOTA

Brooklyn Park
Peterson, Donn Neal *forensic engineer*

Chanhassen
Thorson, John Martin, Jr. *electrical engineer, consultant*

Eden Prairie
Higgins, Robert Arthur *electrical engineer, educator, consultant*

Lutsen
Napadensky, Hyla Sarane *engineering consultant*

Madison
Husby, Donald Evans *engineering company executive*

Minneapolis
Albertson, Vernon Duane *electrical engineering educator*
Anderson, John Edward *mechanical engineering educator*
Arndt, Roger Edward Anthony *hydraulic engineer, educator*
Baker, Michael Harry *chemical engineer*
Bakken, Earl Elmer *electrical engineer, bioengineering company executive*
Caretta, Raul Alberto *chemical engineering educator*
Cohen, Arnold A. *electrical engineer*
Davis, Howard Ted *chemical engineering educator*
Eckert, Ernst R. G. *mechanical engineering educator*
Fairhurst, Charles *civil and mining engineering educator*
Fletcher, Edward Abraham *engineering educator*
Frame, J. Leonard *engineering company executive, retail company executive*
Galambos, Theodore Victor *civil engineer, educator*
Gerberich, William Warren *engineering educator*
Goldstein, Richard Jay *mechanical engineer, educator*
Gopinath, Anand *electrical engineer, research scientist*
†Hoelscher, Douglas Richard *engineering company executive, educator*
Isbin, Herbert Stanford *chemical engineering educator*
Johnson, Walter Kline *civil engineer*
Joseph, Daniel Donald *aeronautical engineer, educator*
Kain, Richard Yerkes *electrical engineer, researcher, educator*
Kvalseth, Tarald Oddvar *mechanical engineer, educator*
Lambert, Robert Frank *electrical engineer, educator*
Lee, E. Bruce *electrical engineering educator*
Liu, Benjamin Young-hwai *engineering educator*
†McMurry, Peter Howard *mechanical engineer, educator*
Nathan, Marshall Ira *electrical engineering educator*
Ogata, Katsuhiko *engineering educator*
Oriani, Richard Anthony *metallurgical engineering educator*
Persson, Erland Karl *electrical engineer*
Pfender, Emil *mechanical engineering educator*
†Pilgrim, Richard D. *engineering company executive*
Porter, William L. *electrical engineer*
†Schmidt, Lanny D. *chemical engineering educator and researcher, physical chemist*
Scriven, L. E(dward) *chemical engineering educator, scientist*
Shulman, Yechiel *engineering educator*
Sparrow, Ephraim Maurice *mechanical engineering scientist, educator*
Sterling, Raymond Leslie *civil engineering educator, researcher, consultant*
†Tirrell, Matthew *chemical engineering/materials science educator*
Weisberg, Leonard R. *research and engineering executive, retired*

New Brighton
†Sharma, Raghu Nandan *engineering executive*

Osseo
Haun, James William *chemical engineer, retired food company executive, consultant*

Rochester
Huffine, Coy Lee *retired chemical engineer, consultant*

Saint Paul
Fingerson, Leroy Malvin *engineering executive, mechanical engineer*
Goodman, Lawrence Eugene *structural analyst, educator*
Tuominen, F(rancis) William *research and engineering company executive*

Stillwater
Sowman, Harold Gene *ceramic engineer, researcher*

Woodbury
Benforado, David M. *environmental engineer*

MISSISSIPPI

Hazlehurst
Lowenkamp, William Charles, Jr. *medical device engineer, researcher, consultant*

Jackson
Pearce, David Harry *biomedical engineer*

Mississippi State
Cliett, Charles Buren *aeronautical engineer, educator, academic administrator*
Jacob, Paul Bernard, Jr. *electrical engineering educator*
Taylor, Clayborne Dudley *engineering educator*
Thompson, Joe Floyd *aerospace engineer, research director*

Oxford
Meyer, L. Donald *agricultural engineer, researcher, educator*

Starkville
Carley, Charles Team, Jr. *mechanical engineer*
Priest, Melville Stanton *retired consulting hydraulic engineer*

University
Horton, Thomas Edward, Jr. *mechanical engineering educator*

Vicksburg
Albritton, Gayle Edward *structural engineer*
Herrmann, Frank Adolph, Jr. *hydraulics laboratory director, researcher*

MISSOURI

Ballwin
Cornell, William Daniel *mechanical engineer*

Centralia
Harmon, Robert Wayne *electrical engineering executive*

Chesterfield
Yardley, John Finley *aerospace engineer*

Columbia
Day, Cecil LeRoy *agricultural engineering educator*
El-Gizawy, Ahmed Sherif *mechanical and aerospace engineering educator, manufacturing engineer, consultant*
Frisby, James Curtis *agricultural engineering educator*
Heldman, Dennis Ray *engineering educator*
Pringle, Oran Allan *mechanical and aerospace engineering educator*
Viswanath, Dabir Srikantiah *chemical engineer*
Yasuda, Hirotsugu Koge *chemical engineering professor*

Fenton
Richardson, Thomas Hampton *design consulting engineer*

Florissant
Martin, Edward Brian *electrical engineer*

Fortuna
Ramer, James LeRoy *civil engineer*

Kansas City
Acheson, Allen Morrow *retired engineering executive*
Adam, Paul James *engineering company executive, mechanical engineer*
Ayres, John Samuel *retired chemical engineer*
Boyd, John Addison, Jr. *civil engineer*
Davis, F(rancis) Keith *civil engineer*
Karmeier, Delbert Fred *consulting engineer*
McGarry, Robert George *safety engineer*
†Nofsinger, William Morris *engineering executive*
Robinson, John Hamilton *civil engineer*
Stewart, Albert Elisha *safety engineer, industrial hygienist*

Kirkwood
Holsen, James Noble, Jr. *retired chemical engineer*

Lake Lotawana
Heineman, Paul Lowe *consulting civil engineer*

Lake Saint Louis
Czarnik, Marvin Ray *retired aerospace engineer*

Lees Summit
Puglisi, Philip James *electrical engineer*

Maryland Heights
Beumer, Richard Eugene *engineer, architect, construction firm executive*
Schwartz, Henry Gerard, Jr. *consulting engineering company executive*
Smith, Brice Reynolds, Jr. *engineering company executive*
Uselton, James Clayton *engineering executive*

Rolla
Babcock, Daniel Lawrence *chemical engineer, educator*
Barr, David John *civil, geological engineering educator*
Crosbie, Alfred Linden *mechanical engineering educator*
Day, Delbert Edwin *ceramic engineering educator*
Johnson, James Winston *chemical engineering educator*
Munger, Paul R. *civil engineering educator*
Omurtag, Yildirim (Bill) *engineering educator*
Rao, Vittal Srirangam *electrical engineering educator*
Saperstein, Lee Waldo *mining engineering educator*
Sarchet, Bernard Reginald *retired chemical engineering educator*
Sauer, Harry John, Jr. *mechanical engineering educator, university administrator*
†Scott, James J. *retired mining engineer*
†Summers, David Archibald *research mining engineer, engineering educator and director*
Tsoulfanidis, Nicholas *nuclear engineering educator*

Saint Joseph
Johnson, Marvin Melrose *industrial engineer, consultant*

Saint Louis
Brasunas, Anton de Sales *metallurgical engineering educator*
Breihan, Erwin Robert *civil engineer, consultant*
Briggs, William Benajah *aeronautical engineer*
Cairns, Donald Fredrick *engineering educator, management consultant*
Cox, Jerome Rockhold, Jr. *electrical engineer*
Dreifke, Gerald Edmond *electrical engineering educator*
†Dudukovic, Milorad P. *chemical engineering educator, consultant*
Fascia, Remo Mario *aviation consultant, airplane manufacturing company executive*
Gould, Phillip L. *civil engineering educator, consultant*
Howard, Walter Burke *chemical engineer*
Husar, Rudolf Bertalan *mechanical engineering educator*
Kirberg, Leonard Carl *engineering executive*
†Kowalskey, Zygmont John, Jr. *aerospace executive*
McKelvey, James Morgan *chemical engineering educator*
Morgan, Robert Peter *engineering educator*
Muller, Marcel W(ettstein) *electrical engineering educator*
Nathanson, Wayne Richard *aerospace company executive*
Orton, George Frederick *aerospace engineer*
Paris, Paul Croce *mechanics educator, engineering consultant, researcher*
Peters, David Allen *mechanical engineering educator, consultant*
†Peterson, T. Roger *engineering company executive*
Prickett, Gordon Odin *mining, mineral and energy engineer*
Ross, Donald Kenneth *consulting engineering executive*
Ross, Monte *electrical engineer*
Ryckman, DeVere Wellington *consulting environmental engineer*
Shipton, Harold William *biomedical engineering educator, researcher*
Shrauner, Barbara Wayne Abraham *electrical engineering educator*
†Smith, Gene R. *engineering company executive*
Sparks, Robert Edward *chemical engineering educator*
Staley, Robert W. *mechanical engineer, electric company executive*
Sutera, Salvatore Philip *mechanical engineering educator*
Szabo, Barna Aladar *mechanical engineering educator, mining engineer*
West, Robert C. *engineering company executive*
Winter, David Ferdinand *electrical engineering educator, consultant*
Wolfe, Charles Morgan *electrical engineering educator*
Zurheide, Charles Henry *consulting electrical engineer*

Springfield
Hansen, John Paul *metallurgical engineer*
Nuccitelli, Saul Arnold *civil engineer, consultant*

MONTANA

Bozeman
Berg, Lloyd *chemical engineering educator*
Cundy, Vic Arnold *mechanical engineer, educator*
Sanks, Robert Leland *environmental engineer, emeritus educator*
Stanislao, Joseph *consulting engineer, educator*

Butte
Studebaker, Irving Glen *engineering educator, researcher*

Great Falls
Walker, Leland Jasper *civil engineer*

Helena
Johnson, David Sellie *civil engineer*

NEBRASKA

Clay Center
Hahn, George LeRoy *agricultural engineer, biometeorologist*

Lincoln
Bahar, Ezekiel *electrical engineering educator*
Edison, Allen Ray *electrical engineer, educator*
Edwards, Donald Mervin *biological systems engineering educator, university dean*
Elias, Samy E. G. *engineering executive*
†Margolis, Stuart W. *computer science and engineering educator*
Nelson, Don Jerome *electrical engineering and computer science educator*
Splinter, William Eldon *agricultural engineering educator*
Ullman, Frank Gordon *electrical engineering educator*
Woollam, John Arthur *electrical engineering educator*

Omaha
Ben-Yaacov, Gideon *computer system designer*
Coy, William Raymond *civil engineer*
Hultquist, Paul Fredrick *electrical engineer, educator*
Matthies, Frederick John *architectural engineer*
Tunnicliff, David George *civil engineer*

Valley
Chapman, John Arthur *agricultural engineering executive*

NEVADA

Boulder City
Wyman, Richard Vaughn *engineering educator, exploration company executive*

Incline Village
Merdinger, Charles John *civil engineer, naval officer, academic adminstrator*

Las Vegas
Boehm, Robert Foty *mechanical engineer, educator, researcher*
Haas, Robert John *aerospace engineer*
Herzlich, Harold J. *chemical engineer*
Messenger, George Clement *engineering executive, consultant*

Reno
Krenkel, Peter Ashton *engineer, educator*
Middlebrooks, Eddie Joe *environmental engineer*

Sparks
Kleppe, John Arthur *electrical engineering educator, business executive*

NEW HAMPSHIRE

Amherst
†Morley, Richard E. *manufacturing engineer*

Center Sandwich
Simmons, Alan Jay *electrical engineer, consultant*

Hanover
Browning, James Alexander *engineering company executive,inventor*
Dean, Robert Charles, Jr. *mechanical engineer, entrepreneur, innovator*
Ermenc, Joseph John *mechanical engineering educator*
Long, Carl Ferdinand *engineering educator*
Marvin, Eugene L. *civil engineer*
Queneau, Paul Etienne *metallurgical engineer, educator*
Stearns, Stephen Russell *civil engineer, forensic engineer, educator*
Wallis, Graham Blair *engineer, educator*

Hollis
Wright, George Walter *aeronautical engineer, state legislator*

Merrimack
Hower, Philip Leland *semiconductor device engineer*
Malley, James Henry Michael *industrial engineer*

Nashua
Lee, Paul King-lung *electronics engineer, researcher*
Woodruff, Thomas Ellis *electronics consulting executive*

Stratham
Bjorkman, Gordon Stuart, Jr. *structural engineer, consultant*

Warner
Hunt, Everett Clair *engineering educator, researcher, consultant*

West Lebanon
MacAdam, Walter Kavanagh *consulting engineering executive*

NEW JERSEY

Allendale
Birdsall, Blair *consulting engineering executive*

Annandale
†Milner, Scott T. *chemical engineer*

Barnegat
Hawk, Frank Carkhuff, Sr. *industrial engineer*

Bedminster
David, Edward Emil, Jr. *electrical engineer, business executive*

Belle Mead
Singley, Mark Eldridge *agricultural engineering educator*

Bellmawr
Hughes, James Sinclair *electronic engineer, executive*

Bergenfield
Pei, Ming L. *civil engineering educator*

Berkeley Heights
Rabiner, Lawrence Richard *electrical engineer*

Bloomfield
Hutcheon, Forbes Clifford Robert *engineer*
Martel, Eugene Harvey *engineering company executive*
Solomon, Stephen Michael *chemical engineer, company executive*

Caldwell
Stanton, George Basil, Jr. *engineering executive, chemical engineer, consultant*

Cherry Hill
Getz, Solomon *defense consulting executive, aerospace engineer*
†Singh, Krishna Pal *mechanical engineer*

Clifton
Srinivasachari, Samavedam *chemical engineer*

Clinton
Atwater, N. William *engineering and construction executive*
Newman, Stephen Alexander *chemical engineer, thermodynamicist*
†Swift, Richard J. *engineering company executive*
Winkin, Justin Philip *engineering executive*

Cranbury
Wang, Chih Chun *material scientist, business executive*

Cranford
Schink, Frank Edward *electrical engineer*
Sommerlad, Robert Edward *environmental research engineer*

Egg Harbor City
Melick, George Fleury *mechanical engineer, educator*

Englewood
Deresiewicz, Herbert *mechanical engineering educator*

Fairfield
Finn, James Francis *consulting engineering executive*

Florham Park
Lieberman, Lester Zane *engineering company executive*

Fort Monmouth
Lymberis, Costas Triantafillos *environmental engineer*
Perlman, Barry Stuart *electrical engineer, researcher*

Green Village
Castenschiold, René *engineering company executive, author, consultant*

Hackensack
Mavrovic, Ivo *chemical engineer*
Michel, Robert Charles *retired engineering company executive*
†Yagoda, Harry Nathan *system engineering executive*

Haddonfield
Siskin, Edward Joseph *engineering and construction company executive*

Hewitt
Selwyn, Donald *engineering administrator, researcher, inventor, educator*

Hoboken
Boesch, Francis Theodore *electrical engineer, educator*
Gans, Manfred *chemical engineer*
Griskey, Richard George *chemical engineering educator*
Savitsky, Daniel *engineer, educator*
Sisto, Fernando *mechanical engineering educator*
Swern, Frederic Lee *engineering educator*

Holmdel
Abate, John E. *electrical and electronic engineer, communications consultant*
Boyd, Gary Delane *electro-optical engineer, researcher*
Johannes, Virgil Ivancich *electrical engineer*
Li, Tingye *electrical engineer*
Meadors, Howard Clarence, Jr. *electrical engineer*
Opie, William Robert *retired metallurgical engineer*
Ross, Ian Munro *electrical engineer*
Tien, Ping King *electronics engineer*

Jamesburg
Maxwell, Bryce *engineer,educator*

Jersey City
Chatterjee, Amit *structural engineer*
Hernon, Richard Francis *engineer*

Kinnelon
Haller, Charles Edward *engineering consultant*

Lawrenceville
Kihn, Harry *electronics engineer, manufacturing company executive*

Little Falls
Dohr, Donald R. *metallurgical engineer, researcher*

Little Silver
Fleischer, Paul E. *electrical engineer*

Livingston
Daman, Ernest Ludwig *mechanical engineer*
Heilmeier, George Harry *electrical engineer, researcher*
†Jacobs, Richard Moss *consulting engineer*
†Pai, David H(sien)-C(hung) *research engineer*

Long Branch
Nahavandi, Amir Nezameddin *retired engineering firm executive*

Maplewood
Lev, Alexander Shulim *mechanical engineer*

Marlboro
Schwartz, Perry Lester *information systems engineer, consultant*

Mendham
Kaprelian, Edward K. *mechanical engineer, physicist*

Middletown
O'Neill, Eugene Francis *communications engineer*

Morristown
Kurtz, Bruce Edward *chemical engineer, research and development executive*
Personick, Stewart David *electrical engineer*
†Urban, John S. *engineering company executive*

Mount Laurel
†Barba, Evans Michael *civil engineer*
†Vidas, Vincent George *engineering executive*

Mountain Lakes
Mattes, Hans George *communications system design scientist, researcher*

Murray Hill
Cho, Alfred Yi *electrical engineer*
Johnson, David Wilfred, Jr. *ceramic scientist, researcher*
†Kurkjian, Charles R(obert) *ceramic engineer, researcher*
Murthy, Srinivasa K. *engineering corporation executive*

New Brunswick
Eager, George Sidney, Jr. *electrical engineer, business executive*
Katz, Carlos *electrical engineer*
Mc Laren, Malcolm Grant, IV *ceramic engineering educator*
Nawy, Edward George *civil engineer, educator*
Vieth, Wolf Randolph *chemical engineering educator*
Wolfe, Robert Richard *bioresource engineer, educator*

Newark
Bar-Ness, Yeheskel *electrical engineer, educator*
Bigley, William Joseph, Jr. *control engineer*
Friedland, Bernard *engineer, educator*
Guenzel, Frank Bernhard *chemical engineer*
Hanesian, Deran *chemical engineer, chemistry and environmental science educator, consultant*
Henderson, Dorland John *retired electrical engineer*
Hrycak, Peter *mechanical engineer, educator*
Hsieh, Jui Sheng *mechanical engineer, educator*
Hsu, Cheng-Tzu Thomas *civil engineering educator*
Pfeffer, Robert *chemical engineer, academic administrator, educator*
Pignataro, Louis James *engineering educator*
Spillers, William Russell *civil engineering educator*
Yu, Yi-Yuan *mechanical engineering educator*

North Brunswick
Awan, Ahmad Noor *civil engineer*

North Caldwell
Stevens, William Dollard *consulting mechanical engineer*

Oakland
Bacaloglu, Radu *chemical engineer*

Ocean City
Speitel, Gerald Eugene *consulting environmental engineer*

Oradell
Roe, Kenneth Keith *power and industrial engineering/construction company executive*

Paramus
Balter, Leslie Marvin *business communications educator*
†Samuels, Reuben *engineering consultant*

Passaic
Lindholm, Clifford Falstrom, II *engineering executive, mayor*

Pennsauken
Alday, Paul Stackhouse, Jr. *mechanical engineer*

Phillipsburg
Cooper, Paul *mechanical engineer, research director*

Piscataway
Flanagan, James Loton *electrical engineer, educator*
Freeman, Herbert *computer engineering educator*
Hidalgo, Alberto F. *chemical engineering executive*
Salkind, Alvin J. *electrochemical engineer, educator*
Sannuti, Peddapullaiah *electrical engineering educator*
Shanefield, Daniel Jay *ceramics engineering educator*
Welkowitz, Walter *biomedical engineer, educator*
Williams, James Richard *human factors engineering psychologist*

Plainfield
Granstrom, Marvin Leroy *civil and sanitary engineering educator*

Princeton
Axtmann, Robert Clark *nuclear and chemical engineering educator*
Ayers, William McLean *electrochemical engineering company executive*
Bartolini, Robert Alfred *electrical engineer, researcher*
Bergman, Richard Isaac *engineering executive, consultant*
Billington, David Perkins *civil engineering educator*
Bogdonoff, Seymour Moses *aeronautical engineer*
Bracco, Frediano Vittorio *mechanical engineering educator*
Cakmak, Ahmet Sefik *civil engineering educator*
Cinlar, Erhan *engineering educator*
Curtiss, Howard Crosby, Jr. *mechanical engineer, educator*
Denlinger, Edgar Jacob *electronics engineering research executive*
Dickinson, Bradley William *electrical engineering educator*
Durbin, Enoch Job *aeronautical engineering educator*
File, Joseph *research physics engineer*
Gibson, James John *electronics engineer, consultant*
Gillham, John Kinsey *chemical engineering educator*
Glassman, Irvin *mechanical and aeronautical engineering educator, consultant*
Graessley, William Walter *chemical engineering educator*
†Jackson, Roy *chemical engineering educator*
Johnson, Ernest Frederick *chemical engineer, educator*
Johnson, Walter Curtis *electrical engineering educator*
Karol, Reuben Hirsh *civil engineer, sculptor*
†Kessel, Charles *plasma engineer, research physicist*
Kung, Sun-Yuan *electrical engineering educator*
Law, Chung King *aerospace engineering educator, researcher*
Lechner, Bernard Joseph *consulting electrical engineer*
Liu, Bede *electrical engineering educator*
Lopresti, Philip Vincent *electrical engineer, researcher, consultant*
Miles, Richard Bryant *mechanical and aerospace engineering educator*
Morel, François Marie Michel *environmental geology educator*
Patel, Mukund Ranchhodlal *electrical engineer, researcher*
Poor, Harold Vincent *electrical engineering educator*
Prud'homme, Robert Krafft *chemical engineering educator*
Rosen, Arye *microwave, optoelectronics and medicine researcher*
Saville, Dudley Albert *chemical engineering educator*
Schoen, Alvin E., Jr. *environmental engineer*
Schroeder, Alfred Christian *electronics research engineer*
Schwartz, Stuart Carl *electrical engineering educator*
Shinozuka, Masanobu *civil engineer, educator*
Smith, Michael A. *aerospace engineer, engineering executive*
Socolow, Robert Harry *engineering educator, scientist*
Stengel, Robert Frank *mechanical and aerospace engineering educator*
Tarbox, Dick *communications engineering executive*
Vahaviolos, Sotirios John *electrical engineer, scientist, corporate executive*
Vanmarcke, Erik Hector *civil engineering educator*
Wei, James *chemical engineering educator, academic dean*
Weimer, Paul K(essler) *electrical engineer*

Princeton Junction
Haddad, James Henry *chemical engineering consultant*

Red Bank
Hollywood, John Matthew *electronics consultant*
Lucky, Robert Wendell *electrical engineer*
Schneider, Sol *electronic engineer, consultant, researcher*

Ridgewood
Abplanalp, Glen Harold *civil engineer*

Riverside
Gouda, Moustafa Abdel-Hamid *geotechnical engineer consultant*

Robbinsville
Goldstein, Norman Robert *safety engineer*

Rumson
Rosen, Bernard H. *chemical engineer*

Sea Bright
Plummer, Dirk Arnold *electrical engineer*

Short Hills
Kaye, Jerome R. *retired engineering and construction company executive*
Moore, Robert Condit *civil engineer*
Wharton, Lennard *engineering company executive*

Shrewsbury
Reich, Bernard *telecommunications engineer*

Skillman
Brill, Yvonne Claeys *engineer, consultant*

Somerville
Beck, Eckardt C. *engineering executive*
Cirello, John *environmental management and engineering company executive*
Glenn, Arthur L. *engineering company executive*

Summit
Fukui, Hatsuaki *electrical engineer, art historian*

Swedesboro
Lovell, Theodore *electrical engineer, consultant*

Teaneck
Borg, Sidney Fred *mechanical engineer, educator*
Ehrlich, Ira Robert *mechanical engineering consultant*

Tenafly
Lang, Hans Joachim *engineering company executive*

Toms River
Fanuele, Michael Anthony *electronics engineer, research engineer*

Trenton
Crom, William Hampton *engineer*
Giddings, S. Arthur *chemical engineer*
Jester, Roberts Charles, Jr. *engineering services company executive*

Upper Montclair
Aronson, David *chemical and mechanical engineer*

Upper Saddle River
Wallace, William, III *engineering executive*

Warren
Salem, Eli *chemical engineer*
Sartor, Anthony Joseph *environmental engineer*

Wayne
Benjamin, James Anthony *electrical engineer, educator*
Cheng, David Hong *mechanical engineering educator*

Whippany
Colmenares, Narses Jose *electrical engineer*
Michaelis, Paul Charles *engineering physicist executive*

Willingboro
Schnapf, Abraham *aerospace engineer, consultant*

NEW MEXICO

Albuquerque
Austin, Edward Marvin *mechanical engineer, researcher, consultant*
Bolie, Victor Wayne *electrical and computer engineering educator*
Carrick, David Stanley *electrical engineer*
Dorato, Peter *electrical and computer engineering educator*
Eaton, George Wesley, Jr. *petroleum engineer, oil company executive*
Haddad, Edward Raouf *civil engineer, consultant*
Hall, Jerome William *research engineering educator*
Howard, William Jack *mechanical engineer, retired*
Karni, Shlomo *electrical engineering educator*
Kramarsic, Roman Joseph *engineering consultant*
McKiernan, John William *mechanical engineer*
Molzen, Dayton Frank *consulting engineering executive*
Peck, Ralph Brazelton *civil engineering educator, consultant*
Westwood, Albert Ronald Clifton *engineer*
Wildin, Maurice Wilbert *mechanical engineering educator*

Belen
Toliver, Lee *mechanical engineer*

Farmington
Garretson, Owen Loren *engineer*

Kirtland AFB
†Anderson, Christine Marlene *software engineer*
Baum, Carl Edward *electromagnetic theorist*

Las Cruces
Ford, Clarence Quentin *mechanical engineer, educator*
Matthews, Larryl Kent *mechanical engineering educator*
Morgan, John Derald *electrical engineer*
Thode, Edward Frederick *chemical engineer, educator*
Weigle, Robert Edward *mechanical engineer, research director*

Los Alamos
Andrews, Andrew Edward *nuclear engineer*
Jackson, James F. *nuclear engineer*
Nunz, Gregory Joseph *program manager, aerospace engineer, educator*
Stoddard, Stephen Davidson *ceramic engineer, former state senator*

Santa Fe
Moellenbeck, Albert John, Jr. *engineering executive*
Phister, Montgomery, Jr. *computer engineering consultant, writer*

Socorro
†Lyons, William Claypool *engineering educator and consultant*

Tijeras
Vizcaino, Henry P. *mining engineer, consultant*

White Sands Missle Range
Arthur, Paul Keith *electronic engineer*

NEW YORK

Albany
Happ, Harvey Heinz *electrical engineer, educator*

Alfred
Frechette, Van Derck *ceramic engineer*
McCauley, James Weymann *ceramics engineer, educator*
Spriggs, Richard Moore *ceramic engineer, research center administrator*

Amherst
Reinhorn, Andrei M. *civil engineering educator, consultant*

Amityville
†Gordon, Saul Wolfe *technology educator*

Ballston Lake
Fiedler, Harold Joseph *electrical engineer, consultant*

Bethpage
Melnik, Robert Edward *aeronautical engineer*
Rockensies, John William *mechanical engineer*

Binghamton
Cornacchio, Joseph Vincent *engineering educator, computer researcher, consultant*
Jennings, Frank Louis *engineering company executive, engineer*
Lowen, Walter *mechanical engineering educator*
Schwartz, Richard Frederick *electrical engineering educator*

Bohemia
Kern, Harry *developmental engineer*

Bronx
Hovnanian, H. Philip *biomedical engineer*
Linden, Barnard Jay *electrical engineer*

Brooklyn
Bertoni, Henry Louis *electrical engineering educator*
†Falcocchio, John Carlo *civil engineer*
Giordano, Anthony Bruno *electrical engineering educator, retired college dean*
Goodman, Alvin S. *engineering educator, consultant*
Helly, Walter Sigmund *engineering educator*
Karamouz, Mohammad *engineering educator*
Kempner, Joseph *aerospace engineering educator*
Margolin, Harold *metallurgical educator*
Pan, Huo-Hsi *mechanical engineer, educator*
Rice, John Thomas *architecture educator*
Roess, Roger Peter *engineering educator*
Shaw, Leonard Glazer *electrical engineering educator, consultant*
Shooman, Martin Lawrence *electrical engineer, computer scientist, educator*

Buffalo
Abate, Ralph Francis *structural engineer*
Anderson, Wayne Arthur *electrical engineering educator*
Ashgriz, Nasser *mechanical and aerospace engineer, educator*
Benenson, David Maurice *engineering educator*
†Drury, Colin Gordon *engineering consultant, educator*
Kinzly, Robert Edward *engineering company executive*
Kiser, Kenneth M(aynard) *chemical engineering educator*
Landi, Dale Michael *industrial engineer, academic administrator*
Lee, George C. *civil engineer, university administrator*
Liew, Fah Pow *mechanical engineer*
Meredith, Dale Dean *civil engineering educator*
Metzger, Ernest Hugh *aerospace engineer, scientist*
Reismann, Herbert *engineer, educator*
Ruckenstein, Eli *chemical engineering educator*
Rumer, Ralph Raymond, Jr. *civil engineer, educator*
Sarjeant, Walter James *electrical and computer engineering educator*
Shaw, David Tai-Ko *electrical and computer engineering educator, university administrator*
Weber, Thomas William *chemical engineering educator*
Weller, Sol William *chemical engineering educator*

Centerport
Caputi, William James, Jr. *engineering consultant*

Chappaqua
O'Neill, Robert Charles *consultant, inventor*
Pomerene, James Herbert *retired computer engineer*

Clarence
Greatbatch, Wilson *biomedical engineer*

Clifton Park
Panek, Jan *electrical power engineer, consultant*

Corning
†Beall, George Halsey *ceramic engineer*

Deer Park
Taub, Jesse J. *electrical engineering researcher*

Delmar
Birdsey, Anna Campas *civil engineer, architect*

East Amherst
Soong, Tsu-Teh *engineering science educator*

East Syracuse
Landsberg, Dennis Robert *engineering executive, consultant*

Elmira
Orsillo, James Edward *computer systems engineer, company executive*

Endwell
Wagner, Peter Ewing *physics and electrical engineering educator*

Fairport
Oldshue, James Y. *chemical engineering consultant*

Farmingdale
Bolle, Donald Martin *engineering educator*
Bongiorno, Joseph John, Jr. *electrical engineering educator*
Klosner, Jerome Martin *mechanical engineer, educator*
LaTourrette, James Thomas *retired electrical engineering and computer science educator*

Fayetteville
Dosanjh, Darshan S(ingh) *aeronautical engineer, educator*

Flushing
Birnstiel, Charles *consulting engineer*
Stahl, Frank Ludwig *civil engineer*

Garden City
Fleisig, Ross *aeronautical engineer, engineering manager*

Glen Cove
Casem, Conrado Sibayan *civil, structural engineer*
Conti, James Joseph *chemical engineer, educator*

Glenham
Douglas, Fred Robert *cost engineering consultant*

Glens Falls
Allard, Edward F. *engineering company executive*

Glenville
Anderson, Roy Everett *electrical engineering consultant*

Great Neck
Shaffer, Bernard William *mechanical and aerospace engineering educator*

Greenlawn
Bachman, Henry Lee *electrical engineer, engineering executive*
†Newman, Edward M. *engineering executive*

Hauppauge
†Costa, Pat Vincent *automation sciences executive*
Miller, Kenneth Allen *electrical engineer*

Hawthorne
†Batstone, Joanna L. *computer scientist*
McConnell, John Edward *electrical engineer, company executive*

Hempstead
Goldstein, Stanley Philip *engineering educator*
Maier, Henry B. *environmental engineer*

Hopewell Junction
†Mohammad, Shaikh Noor *electronics engineer, educator*

Huntington
Christiansen, Donald David *engineer, editor, publishing consultant*
Papoulis, Athanasios *electrical engineering educator*

Huntington Station
Agosta, Vito *mechanical/aerospace engineering educator*
Lanzano, Ralph Eugene *civil engineer*

Ithaca
Berger, Toby *electrical engineer*
Booker, John Franklin *mechanical engineer, educator*
Carlin, Herbert J. *electrical engineering educator, researcher*
Caughey, David Alan *engineering educator, researcher*
Dalman, Gisli Conrad *electrical engineering educator*
De Boer, Pieter Cornelis Tobias *mechanical and aerospace engineering educator*
Dick, Richard Irwin *environmental engineer, educator*
Dworsky, Leonard B. *civil and environmental engineer, educator*
Eastman, Lester Fuess *electrical engineer, educator*
Fine, Terrence Leon *electrical engineering and statistics educator*
George, Albert Richard *aerospace and mechanical engineering educator*
Gubbins, Keith Edmund *chemical engineering educator*
Kramer, Edward John *materials science and engineering educator*
Leibovich, Sidney *engineering educator*
Loucks, Daniel Peter *environmental systems engineer*
Lynn, Walter Royal *civil engineering educator, university administrator*
Maxwell, William Laughlin *industrial engineering educator*
Mc Guire, William *civil engineer, educator*
McIsaac, Paul Rowley *electrical engineer, educator*
Meyburg, Arnim Hans *transportation engineer, educator, consultant*
O'Rourke, Thomas Denis *civil engineer, educator*
Parks, Thomas W. *electrical engineering educator, consultant*
Phelan, Richard Magruder *mechanical engineer*
Pope, Stephen Bailey *engineering educator*
Rehkugler, Gerald Edwin *agricultural engineering educator, consultant*
Rodríguez, Ferdinand *chemical engineer, educator*
Shuler, Michael Louis *biochemical engineering educator, consultant*
Smith, Julian Cleveland, Jr. *chemical engineering educator*
Sudan, Ravindra Nath *electrical engineer, physicist, educator*
Thorp, James Shelby *electrical engineering educator*
Torng, Hwa C. *engineering educator, researcher*
Wang, Kuo-King *manufacturing engineer, educator*
White, Richard Norman *civil and environmental engineering educator*
Wolf, Edward Dean *electrical engineering educator*

Jamaica
Vasilopoulos, Athanasios V. *engineering educator*

Jericho
Shinners, Stanley Marvin *electrical engineer*

Katonah
Bashkow, Theodore Robert *electrical engineering consultant, former educator*

Levittown
Rubin, Arnold Jesse *aeronautical engineer*

Locust Valley
Schaffner, Charles Etzel *consulting engineering executive*

Long Beach
†Sherman, Zachary *civil and aerospace engineer, consultant*

Long Island City
Jablowsky, Albert Isaac *civil engineer*

Massapequa Park
Plotkin, Martin *retired electrical engineer*

Melville
Marchesano, John Edward *electro-optical engineer*

Millbrook
Johnston, Robert Cossin *consulting engineer executive*

Mineola
Newman, Malcolm *civil engineering consultant*

New Hartford
Maurer, Gernant Elmer *metallurgical executive, consultant*

New Rochelle
Lulla, Jack David *polymer engineer*

New York
Acampora, Anthony Salvator *electrical engineer, educator*
Acrivos, Andreas *chemical engineering educator*
Ahmad, Jameel *civil engineer, researcher, educator*
Aktar, A.S. (Art Aktar) *civil engineer, consultant*
Alexander, Harold *bioengineer, educator*
Allen, William Frederick, Jr. *mechanical engineer*
Augeri, Joseph Leonard *packaging engineer*
Bardin, Clyde Wayne *biomedical researcher and developer of contraceptives*
Baron, Melvin Leon *civil engineer, consultant*
Baum, Eleanor *electrical engineering educator, academic administrator*
Bendelius, Arthur George *engineering firm executive*
Binger, Wilson Valentine *civil engineer*
Boley, Bruno Adrian *engineering educator*
Boshkov, Stefan Hristov *mining engineer, educator*
Bove, John Louis *chemistry and environmental engineering educator, researcher*
Brazinsky, Irving *chemical engineering educator*
Brown, Seymour William *engineering executive, consultant*
Cantilli, Edmund Joseph *safety engineering educator, writer*
Cheh, Huk Yuk *engineering educator, electrochemist*
Cohen, Edward *civil engineer*
Coler, Myron A(braham) *chemical engineer, educator*
†Coles, Bruce C. *engineering company executive*
Cowin, Stephen Corteen *biomedical engineering educator, consultant*
Danziger, Bruce Edward *structural engineer*
De Gaster, Zachary *engineering company executive*
Diament, Paul *electrical engineering educator, consultant*
DiMaggio, Frank Louis *civil engineering educator*
Eberstein, Arthur *biomedical engineering educator, researcher*
Fink, Donald Glen *engineering executive, editor*
Fogel, Irving Martin *consulting engineering company executive*
Freudenstein, Ferdinand *mechanical engineering educator*
Goldfarb, Donald *industrial engineering educator*
Gordon, Roy Harris *engineering design firm executive*
Grace, E. *engineering executive*
Greenfield, Seymour Stephen *mechanical engineer*
Grossman, Jacob S. *structural engineer*
Grunes, Robert Lewis *engineering consulting firm executive*
Happel, John *chemical engineer, researcher*
Harris, Colin Cyril *mineral engineer, educator*
†Hennessy, John Francis, III *engineering executive, mechanical engineer*
Hoberman, Charles Steven *mechanical engineer, inventor*
Keller, Kenneth Harrison *engineering educator, science policy analyst*
Klein, Morton *industrial engineer, educator*
Knobler, Alfred Everett *ceramic engineer, manufacturing company executive, publisher*
Kok, Hans Gebhard *consulting engineer*
Koshar, Louis David *civil engineer*
Lai, W(ei) Michael *mechanical engineer, educator*
Landau, Ralph *chemical engineer*
Lee, Martin Yongho (Kyung-Joo Lee) *mechanical engineer*
Lee, Sidney Phillip *chemical engineer, state senator*
Leonard, Edward F. *chemical engineer, educator*
Lewis, William Scheer *electrical engineer*
Longman, Richard Winston *mechanical engineering educator*
Low, Dana Evarts *consulting engineer*
Lowen, Gerard Gunther *mechanical engineering educator*
Luo, Gangming *mechanical engineer*
McAward, Patrick Joseph, Jr. *architectural and engineering company executive*
Michel, Henry Ludwig *civil engineer*
Miele, Joel Arthur, Sr. *civil engineer*
Mow, Van C. *engineering educator, researcher*
†O'Neill, Thomas J. *engineering company executive*
Ozero, Brian John *chemical engineer*
Paaswell, Robert Emil *civil engineer, educator*
Robertson, Leslie Earl *structural engineer*
Ross, Donald Edward *engineering company executive*
Sadegh, Ali M. *mechanical engineering educator, researcher, consultant*
Salvadori, Mario *mathematical engineer*
Schwartz, Mischa *electrical engineering educator*
Schwarz, Ralph Jacques *engineering educator*
†Servedio, Dominick Michael *engineering executive*
Shapiro, Murray *structural engineer*
Shinnar, Reuel *chemical engineering educator, industrial consultant*
Smith, Gordon H. *civil engineer*
Somasundaran, Ponisseril *surface and colloid engineering, applied science educator*
Sookram, Atma Ram *transportation engineer*
Stasior, William F. *engineering company executive*
Subak-Sharpe, Gerald Emil *electrical engineer, educator*
Teich, Malvin Carl *electrical engineering educator*
Themelis, Nickolas John *metallurgical and chemical engineering educator*
Tsividis, Yannis P. *electrical engineering educator*
Unger, Stephen Herbert *electrical engineer, computer scientist*
Vaicaitis, Rimas *civil engineering and engineering mechanics educator*
Vogelman, Joseph Herbert *scientific engineering company executive*
Watkins, Charles Booker, Jr. *mechanical engineering educator*
Weidlinger, Paul *civil engineer*
Weinstein, Herbert *chemical engineer, educator*
Wheeler, Wesley Dreer *marine engineer, naval architect, consultant*
Yang, Edward S. *electrical engineering educator*
Yao, David Da-Wei *engineering science educator*
Yegulalp, Tuncel M. *mining engineer, educator*
Young, Morris *electrical engineering consultant*
Zakkay, Victor *aeronautical engineering educator, scientist*
Zuck, Alfred Christian *consulting mechanical engineer*

Newton Falls
Hunter, William Schmidt *engineering executive, environmental engineer*

Niagara Falls
Dojka, Edwin Sigmund *civil engineer*

Niskayuna
Johnson, Ingolf Birger *retired electrical engineer*

Painted Post
Benjamin, Keith Edward *mechanical engineer*

Pittsford
Marshall, Joseph Frank *electronic engineer*

Pleasantville
Pike, John Nazarian *optical engineering consultant*

Port Washington
Davidoff, Charles *chemical and metalurgical engineer, consultant*

Potsdam
Cotellessa, Robert Francis *retired electrical engineering educator, academic administrator*
†Sathyamoorthy, Muthukrishnan *engineering researcher, educator*

Poughkeepsie
Chu, Richard Chao-Fan *mechanical engineer*
Logue, Joseph Carl *electronics engineer, consultant*

Remsenburg
Edwards, Arthur Anderson *retired mechanical engineer*

Rexford
Kirchmayer, Leon Kenneth *retired electrical engineer*

Riverdale
Hollein, Helen Conway *chemical engineer, educator*
Jha, Nand Kishore *engineering educator, researcher*

Rochester
Bouyoucos, John Vinton *research and development company executive*
Burns, Stephen James *engineering educator, materials science researcher*
Carstensen, Edwin Lorenz *biomedical engineer, biophysicist*
Cokelet, Giles Roy *biomedical engineering educator*
Feinberg, Martin Robert *chemical engineering educator*
Freckleton, Jon Edward *engineering educator, consultant, retired military officer*
Gans, Roger Frederick *mechanical engineering educator*
Jorne, Jacob *chemical engineer, educator*
Kinnen, Edwin *electrical engineer, educator*
Lessen, Martin *engineering educator, consulting engineer*
†Loewen, Erwin G. *precision engineer, educator, consultant*
McWilliams, C. Paul, Jr. *engineering executive*
Palmer, Harvey John *chemical engineering educator, consultant*

Rockville Centre
Silecchia, Jerome A. *mechanical engineer*

Rome
Coppola, Anthony *electrical engineer*
Gabelman, Irving Jacob *consulting engineering executive, retired government official*

Rye
Lehman, Lawrence Herbert *consulting engineering executive*
Tung, David Hsi Hsin *consulting civil engineer, emeritus engineering educator*

Saint James
Irvine, Thomas Francis, Jr. *mechanical engineering educator*

Schenectady
Barthold, Lionel Olav *engineering executive*
Coffin, Louis Fussell, Jr. *mechanical engineer*
Hedman, Dale Eugene *consulting electrical engineer*
Huening, Walter Carl, Jr. *retired consulting application engineer*
†Kindl, Fred Henry *engineering company executive*
LaForest, James John *retired electrical engineer*
Mafi, Mohammad *civil engineer, educator*
Matta, Ram Kumar *aeronautical engineer*
McMurray, William *consultant, retired electrical engineer*
Ringlee, Robert James *consulting engineering executive*
Walsh, George William *engineering executive*

Setauket
Irving, A. Marshall *marine engineer*
Levine, Sumner Norton *industrial engineer, educator, editor, author, financial consultant*

Slate Hill
Reber, Raymond Andrew *chemical engineer*

Slingerlands
Wilcock, Donald Frederick *mechanical engineer*

Stafford
Moran, John Henry, Jr. *electrical engineer, consultant*

Stony Brook
Chen, Chi-Tsong *electrical engineering educator*
Cope, Randolph Howard, Jr. *electronic research and development executive, educator*
Zemanian, Armen Humpartsoum *electrical engineer, mathematician*

Syracuse
Brennan, Paul Joseph *civil engineer, educator*
Cabasso, Israel *polymer science educator*
Eveleigh, Virgil William *electrical and computer engineering educator*
Jefferies, Michael John *electrical engineer*
Konski, James Louis *civil engineer*
LePage, Wilbur Reed *electrical engineering educator*
Libove, Charles *mechanical and aerospace engineering educator*
Lyman, Frederic A. *mechanical and aerospace engineering educator, researcher*
Pennock, Donald William *retired mechanical engineer*
Roberts, Robert *engineering organization executive, think-tank executive*
Sargent, Robert George *engineering educator*
Strait, Bradley Justus *electrical engineering educator*
Tully, William P. *civil engineer, academic administrator*
Wiley, Richard Gordon *electrical engineer*

Tarrytown
Anderson, John Erling *chemical engineer*
Bartoo, Richard Kieth *chemical engineer, consultant*

Thornwood
Douglas, Patricia Jeanne *systems designer, certification/testing consultant*

Troy
Abetti, Pier Antonio *consulting electrical engineer, technology management and entrepreneurship educator*
Anderson, John Bailey *electrical engineering educator*
†Belfort, Georges *chemical engineering educator, consultant*
Bergles, Arthur Edward *mechanical engineering educator*
Block, Robert Charles *nuclear engineering and engineering physics educator*
Brunelle, Eugene John, Jr. *mechanical engineering educator*
Desrochers, Alan Alfred *electrical engineer*
Duquette, David Joseph *materials science and engineering educator*
Feeser, Larry James *civil engineering educator, researcher*
Gerhardt, Lester A. *engineering educator, dean*
Gill, William Nelson *chemical engineering educator*
Glicksman, Martin Eden *materials engineering educator*
Greenwood, Allan N. *engineering educator, researcher*
Gutmann, Ronald J. *electrical engineering educator*
Horton, John Tod *engineering company executive*
Jones, Owen Craven, Jr. *nuclear and mechanical engineer, educator*
Jordan, Mark Henry *consulting civil engineer*
Krempl, Erhard *mechanics educator, consultant*
†Lahey, Richard Thomas, Jr. *nuclear engineer, fluid mechanics engineer*
Littman, Howard *chemical engineer, educator*
McDonald, John Francis Patrick *electrical engineering educator*
Messler, Robert Wilmer, Jr. *materials engineering educator, consultant*
Modestino, James William *electrical engineering educator*
Nelson, John Keith *electrical engineer*
Roy, Rob J. *biomedical engineer, anesthesiologist*
Sanderson, Arthur Clark *engineering educator*
Saridis, George Nicholas *electrical engineer*
Shephard, Mark Scott *civil and mechanical engineering educator*
Stoloff, Norman Stanley *metallurgical engineering educator, researcher*
Woods, John William *electrical, computer and systems engineering educator, consultant*
Zimmie, Thomas Frank *civil engineer, educator*

Upton
Radeka, Veljko *electronics engineer*
Steinberg, Meyer *chemical engineer*
Susskind, Herbert *biomedical engineer, educator*

Wantagh
Litman, Bernard *electrical engineer, consultant*

Watervliet
Kitchens, Clarence Wesley, Jr. *physical science administrator*

Wayland
Wisniewski, Joseph Michael *engineering executive*

Webster
Johnson, Ray Clifford *mechanical engineering educator, consultant, writer*

West Nyack
Hornik, Joseph William *civil engineer*

Westbury
Sandler, Gerald Howard *aerospace executive*

White Plains
Busch, Paul Louis *engineering company executive, consultant*
Foster, John Horace *consulting environmental engineer*
Mitchell, Robert Dale *consulting engineer*
Westerhoff, Garret Peter *environmental engineer, executive*

Woodstock
Smith, Albert Aloysius, Jr. *electrical engineer, consultant*

Yorktown Heights
Dennard, Robert Heath *engineering executive, scientist*
Hong, Se June *computer engineer*
Pugh, Emerson William *electrical engineer*
Romankiw, Lubomyr Taras *materials engineer*
Terman, Lewis Madison *electrical engineer, researcher*
Troutman, Ronald R. *electrical engineer*
Wajda, Tadeusz *engineer*

NORTH CAROLINA

Boonville
Reece, Joe Wilson *engineering company executive*

Cary
Conrad, Hans *materials engineering educator*
Miranda, Constancio Fernandes *civil engineering educator*
†Smith, Walter Sage *environmental engineer, consultant*
†Vick, Columbus Edwin, Jr. *civil engineering design firm executive*

Chapel Hill
Baker, Charles Ray *engineering and mathematics educator, researcher*
Coulter, Norman Arthur, Jr. *biomedical engineering educator emeritus*
Eisenbud, Merril *environmental engineer*
Kusy, Robert Peter *biomedical engineering and orthodontics educator*
Lucas, Carol Lee *biomedical engineer*
Okun, Daniel Alexander *environmental engineering educator, consulting engineer*
Stidham, Shaler, Jr. *operations research educator*

Charlotte
Foss, Ralph Scot *mechanical engineer*
Kim, Rhyn Hyun *engineering educator*
King, L. Ellis *civil engineer, educator and administrator*
Rodite, Robert R.R. *engineering scientist*

Columbus
Weber, Ernst *engineering consultant*

Durham
Biswas, Mrinmay *engineering educator, consultant, researcher*
Casey, H(orace) Craig, Jr. *electrical engineering educator*
Chaddock, Jack Bartley *mechanical engineering educator*
Fisher, Charles Page, Jr. *consulting geotechnical engineer*
Garg, Devendra Prakash *mechanical engineer, educator*
Goodwin, Frank Erik *materials engineer*
Harman, Charles Morgan *mechanical engineer*
Hochmuth, Robert Milo *mechanical and biomedical engineer, educator*
McElhaney, James Harry *biomedical engineer*
Piatt, William McKinney, III *consulting engineering executive*
Pilkington, Theo Clyde *biomedical and electrical engineering educator*
Plonsey, Robert *electrical and biomedical engineer*
Strohbehn, John Walter *engineering science educator*
Utku, Senol *civil engineer, computer science educator*

Fuquay Varina
Hairston, William Michael *manufacturing engineer*

Granite Falls
Humphreys, Kenneth King *engineer, educator, association executive*

Hendersonville
Schooley, Charles Earl *electrical engineer, consultant*

High Point
Huston, Fred John *retired automotive engineer*

Highlands
Sandor, George Nason *mechanical engineer, educator*

Morehead City
Williams, Winton Hugh *civil engineer*

Nags Head
†Rogallo, Francis Melvin *mechanical, aeronautical engineer*

New Bern
Baughman, Fred Hubbard *aeronautical engineer, former naval officer*
Moeller, Dade William *environmental engineer, educator*
Whitehurst, Brooks Morris *chemical engineer*

Raleigh
Agrawal, Dharma Prakash *engineering educator*
Baliga, Bantval Jayant *electrical engineering educator, consultant*
Beatty, Kenneth Orion, Jr. *chemical engineer*
Bitzer, Donald Lester *electrical engineering educator, retired research laboratory administrator*
Bourham, Mohamed Abdelhay *nuclear and electrical engineering educator*
Church, Kern Everidge *engineer, consultant*
Dudziak, Donald John *nuclear engineer, educator*
Ferrell, James K. *chemical engineering educator, dean*
Gardner, Robin Pierce *engineering educator*
Gilbert, Charles Gorman *civil engineering educator*
Hanson, John M. *civil engineering and construction educator*
Hauser, John Reid *electrical engineering educator*
Jennings, Burgess Hill *mechanical engineering educator*
Kriz, George James *agricultural research administrator, educator*
Meier, Wilbur Leroy, Jr. *industrial engineer, educator, former university chancellor*
Murray, Raymond Le Roy *nuclear engineering educator*
Nagle, Hubert Troy, Jr. *electrical engineering educator*
Nickel, Donald Lloyd *engineering executive*
Overcash, Michael Ray *chemical engineering educator*
Rohrbach, Roger Phillip *agricultural engineer, educator*
Skaggs, Richard Wayne *agricultural engineering educator*
†Sneed, Ronald Ernest *engineering educator emeritus*
Turinsky, Paul Josef *nuclear engineer, educator*
Williams, Hugh Alexander, Jr. *retired mechanical engineer, consultant*
Young, James Herbert *agricultural engineer*
Zorowski, Carl Frank *engineering educator, university administrator*

Research Triangle Park
Holton, William Coffeen *electrical engineering executive*
Kuhn, Matthew *engineering company executive*
Larsen, Ralph Irving *environmental research engineer*

Washington
Hackney, James Acra, III *industrial engineer, manufacturing company executive*

NORTH DAKOTA

Bismarck
Carmichael, Virgil Wesly *mining, civil and geological engineer, former coal company executive*

OHIO

Akron
Brown, David Rupert *engineering executive*

Alexandria
Palmer, Melville Louis *retired agricultural engineering educator*

Alliance
†Kitto, John Buck, Jr. *mechanical engineer*

Athens
Beale, William Taylor *engineering company executive*
Dinos, Nicholas *engineering educator, administrator*
Miller, Edmund Kenneth *retired electrical engineer, educator*
Robe, Thurlow Richard *engineering educator, university dean*

Batavia
Bower, Kenneth Francis *electrical engineer*

Brook Park
Bluford, Guion Stewart, Jr. *engineering company executive*
Wilson, Jack *aeronautical engineer*

Canton
Hoecker, David *engineering executive*

Chagrin Falls
Pauly, Bruce Henry *engineering consultant*

Cincinnati
Anno, James Nelson *nuclear engineering scientist, educator*
Arnold, Lynn Ellis *metallurgist, consultant*
Bahr, Donald Walter *chemical engineer*
Bluestein, Paul Harold *management engineer*
Greenberg, David Bernard *chemical engineering educator*
Hall, Ernest L. *electrical engineer, robotics educator*
Johnson, K(enneth) O(dell) *aerospace engineer*
Katzen, Raphael *consulting chemical engineer*
Kehew, William James *environmental, quality assurance engineering manager*
Kroll, Robert James *aerospace engineering educator*
LaBath, Octave Aaron *mechanical engineer*
Martin, John Bruce *chemical engineer*
McDonough, James Francis *civil engineer, educator*
Messinger, Richard C. *engineering research and development consultant*
Middendorf, William Henry *electrical engineering educator*
Niemoller, Arthur B. *electrical engineer*
Rubin, Stanley Gerald *aerospace engineering educator*
Smith, Leroy Harrington, Jr. *mechanical engineer, aerodynamics consultant*
Toftner, Richard Orville *engineering executive*
†Wachenfeld, Timothy H. *aeronautical engineering executive*
Weisman, Joel *nuclear engineering educator, engineering consultant*
Wisler, David Charles *aerospace engineer, educator*

Cleveland
Anderson, James R. *engineering executive*
Angus, John Cotton *chemical engineering educator*
Baer, Eric *engineering and science educator*
Bahniuk, Eugene *mechanical engineering educator*
Brosilow, Coleman Bernard *chemical engineering educator*
Burghart, James Henry *electrical engineer, educator*
Collin, Robert Emanuel *electrical engineering educator*
Coulman, George Albert *chemical engineer, educator*
Dy Liacco, Tomas Enciso *engineering consulting executive*
Goldstein, Marvin Emanuel *aerospace scientist, research center administrator*
Graham, Robert William *areospace research engineer*
Gruber, Sheldon *electrical engineering educator*
Hardy, Richard Allen *mechanical engineer, diesel fuel engine specialist*
Ko, Wen-Hsiung *electrical engineering educator*
Liu, Chung-Chiun *chemical engineering educator*
Madden, James Desmond *forensic engineer*
Martin, Paul Joseph *biomedical engineer, cardiology researcher, educator, consultant*
Mortimer, J. Thomas *biomedical engineering educator*
Ostrach, Simon *engineering educator*
Pao, Yoh-Han *engineering educator*
Peckham, P. Hunter *biomedical engineer, educator*
Reisman, Arnold *retired management science educator*
Reshotko, Eli *aerospace engineer, educator*
Saada, Adel Selim *civil engineer, educator*
Salkind, Michael Jay *metallurgical engineer, academic administrator*
Sargent, Noel Boyd *electrical engineer*
Savinell, Robert Francis *engineering educator*
Siegel, Robert *heat transfer engineer*

Columbus
Antler, Morton *consulting engineering executive, author, educator*
Bailey, Cecil Dewitt *aerospace engineer, educator*
Bechtel, Stephen E. *mechanical engineer, educator*
Bedford, Keith Wilson *civil engineering and atmospheric science educator*
Bhushan, Bharat *mechanical engineer*
Bondurant, Byron Lee *agricultural engineering educator*
Boulger, Francis William *metallurgical engineer*
Brodkey, Robert Stanley *chemical engineering educator*
Cearlock, Dennis Bill *research executive*
Cruz, Jose Bejar, Jr. *engineering educator*
Duckworth, Winston Howard *ceramic engineer*
Dwon, Larry *retired electrical engineer, educator, consultant*
Engdahl, Richard Bott *mechanical engineer*
Ensminger, Dale *mechanical engineer, electrical engineer*
†Fan, Liang-Shih *chemical engineering educator*
Fenton, Robert Earl *electrical engineering educator*
Gozon, Jozsef Stephan *engineering educator*
Grant, Michael Peter *electrical engineer*
Houser, Donald Russell *mechanical engineering educator, consultant*
Hsu, Hsiung *engineering educator*
Jackson, Curtis Maitland *metallurgical engineer*
Keaney, William Regis *engineering and construction services executive, consultant*
Ksienski, Aharon Arthur *electrical engineer*
Leissa, Arthur William *mechanical engineering educator*
Miller, Don Wilson *nuclear engineering educator*
Moore, Donald Paul *retired electrical engineer*
Moulton, Edward Quentin *civil engineer, educator*
Ojalvo, Morris *civil engineer, educator*
Peters, Leon, Jr. *electrical engineering educator, research administ*
†Rajadhyaksha, Vikram *civil engineering consulant, engineering company executive*
Rapp, Robert Anthony *metallurgical engineering educator, consultant*
Redmond, Robert Francis *nuclear engineering educator*
†Robertson, Harry Stevens *retired mechanical engineer*
Rubin, Alan J. *environmental engineer, chemist*
Sahai, Yogeshwar *engineering educator*
St. Pierre, George Roland, Jr. *materials science and engineering administrator, educator*
Satyapriya, Combatore Keshavamurthy *geotechnical engineering executive*
Schwab, Glenn Orville *retired agricultural engineering educator, consultant*
Sebo, Stephen Andrew *electrical engineer, educator, researcher, consultant*
Shewmon, Paul Griffith *metallurgical engineer, educator*
Singh, Rajendra *mechanical engineering educator*
Smialowska, Susan *engineering educator*
Smith, George Leonard, Jr. *industrial engineering educator*
Taiganides, E. Paul *agricultural-environmental engineer, consultant*
Uotila, Urho Antti Kalevi *geodesist, educator*
Ware, Brendan John *electrical engineer, electric utility company executive*
Zakin, Jacques Louis *chemical engineering educator*
†Zande, Richard Dominic *civil engineering firm executive*

Concord
Lenardic, Kenneth Ralph *systems architect, consultant*

Dayton
Brown, William Milton *electrical engineering educator*
D'Azzo, John Joachim *electrical engineer, educator*
Goesch, William Holbrook *aeronautical engineer*
Haigh, Peter Leslie *software company executive, consultant*
Houpis, Constantine Harry *electrical engineering educator*
Kazimierczuk, Marian Kazimierz *electrical engineer, educator*
Krug, Maurice F. *engineering company executive*
†Massie, Lowell David *aeronautical engineer*
†Nix, John B. *aeronautical engineer*
Schmitt, George Frederick, Jr. *materials engineer*
†Shaw, George Bernard *consulting engineer, educator*

Delphos
†Staup, John Gary *safety engineer*

Dublin
Major, Coleman Joseph *chemical engineer*

Elmore
Kaczynski, Don *metallurgical engineer*

Gates Mills
Enyedy, Gustav, Jr. *chemical engineer*

Granville
Jacobs, Richard Allen *industrial engineer*

Hudson
Kirchner, James William *electrical engineer*

Logan
Carmean, Jerry Richard *broadcast engineer*

Lyndhurst
Sevin, Eugene *engineer, consultant, educator*

Macedonia
Baltazzi, Evan Serge *engineering research consulting company executive*

Marblehead
Haering, Edwin Raymond *chemical engineering educator, consultant*

Marion
Tozzer, Jack Carl *civil engineer, surveyor*

Mason
Clarke, W. Hall *engineer*

Miamisburg
Spicer, Harold Glenn *chemical engineer*

Middletown
Gilby, Steve *metallurgical engineering researcher*

North Olmsted
Lundin, Bruce Theodore *engineering and management consultant*

Oxford
Ward, Roscoe Fredrick *engineering educator*
Willeke, Gene E. *environmental engineer, educator*

Painesville
Jayne, Theodore Douglas *technical research and development company executive*

Perrysburg
Khan, Amir U. *agricultural engineering consultant*

Powell
Adeli, Hojjat *engineer, educator, computer scientist*

Shelby
Moore Moif, Florian Howard *electronics engineer*

Silver Lake
Chrobak, Dennis Steven *chemical engineer*

Springboro
Saxer, Richard Karl *metallurgical engineer, retired air force officer*

Toledo
†Beans, Elroy William *mechanical engineering educator, administrator*
Farison, James Blair *electrical engineer, educator*
†Harold, Robert Allen *engineer*
Hauenstein, Henry William *civil engineer*
Richards, Raymond Sears *scientist, company executive*

Westlake
Bisson, Edmond Emile *mechanical engineer*
Huff, Ronald Garland *mechanical engineer*

Wickliffe
Bardasz, Ewa Alice *chemical engineer*

Worthington
Compton, Ralph Theodore, Jr. *electrical engineering educator*

Yellow Springs
Trolander, Hardy Wilcox *engineering executive, consultant*

Youngstown
Fok, Thomas Dso Yun *civil engineer*

OKLAHOMA

Bartlesville
Clay, Harris Aubrey *chemical engineer*
Gao, Hong Wen *chemical engineer*
Johnson, Marvin Merrill *chemical engineer, chemist*

Bethany
Arnold, Donald Smith *chemical engineer, consultant*

Duncan
Surjaatmadja, Jim Basuki *research engineer*

Midwest City
Smith, Wayne Calvin *chemical engineer*

Moore
Moore, Dalton, Jr. *petroleum engineer, scientist, geologist*

Norman
Bert, Charles Wesley *mechanical and aerospace engineer, educator*
Campbell, John Morgan *retired chemical engineer*
Crane, Robert Kendall *engineering educator, researcher, consultant*
Egle, Davis Max *mechanical engineering educator*
O'Rear, Edgar Allen, III *chemical engineering educator*
Zelby, Leon Wolf *electrical engineering educator, consulting engineer*

Oklahoma City
Dew, Jess Edward *chemical engineer*
Mikkelson, Dean Harold *geological engineer*
Thompson, Guy Thomas *safety engineer*
Wickens, Donald Lee *engineer executive, consultant, rancher*

Stillwater
†Barfield, Billy Joe *agricultural engineer, educator*
Bell, Kenneth John *chemical engineer*
Brusewitz, Gerald Henry *agricultural engineering educator, researcher*
Case, Kenneth Eugene *industrial engineering educator*
Maddox, Robert Nott *chemical engineer, educator*
Mize, Joe Henry *industrial engineer, educator*
Noyes, Ronald Tacie *agricultural engineering educator*
Parcher, James Vernon *civil engineering educator, consultant*
Thompson, David Russell *agricultural engineering educator, academic dean*
Turner, Wayne Connelly *industrial engineer, educator*

Tinker AFB
Pray, Donald George *aerospace engineer*

Tulsa
Earlougher, Robert Charles, Sr. *petroleum engineer*
Elkins, Lloyd Edwin, Sr. *petroleum engineer, energy consultant*
Eriksen, Vernon Lee *manufacturing engineering executive*
†Green, Harvey Eugene *engineering executive*
†Martin, Jerry K. *engineering company executive*
†McDevitt, Daniel Bernard *communications, computer and control systems application engineer*
Parker, Robert Lee, Sr. *petroleum engineer, drilling company executive*
Prayson, Alex Stephen *drafting and mechanical design educator*
Williams, David Rogerson, Jr. *engineer, business executive*
Williams, John Horter *civil engineer, oil, gas, telecommunications and allied products distribution company executive*

Washington
Sliepcevich, Cedomir M. *engineering educator*

OREGON

Albany
Yau, Te-Lin *corrosion engineer*

Aloha
Rojhantalab, Hossein Mohammad *chemical engineer, researcher*

Corvallis
Engelbrecht, Rudolf *electrical engineering educator*
Forbes, Leonard *engineering educator*
Hansen, Hugh Justin *agricultural engineer*
Knudsen, James George *chemical engineer, educator*
Miner, John Ronald *agricultural engineer*
Mohler, Ronald Rutt *electrical engineering educator*
Olleman, Roger Dean *industry consultant, former metallurgical engineering educator*
Temes, Gabor Charles *electrical engineering educator*

Florence
Ericksen, Jerald Laverne *educator, engineering scientist*

Hillsboro
Pettit, Ghery St. John *electronics engineer*

Lincoln City
Gehrig, Edward Harry *electrical engineer, consultant*

Myrtle Point
Walsh, Don *marine consultant, executive*

Portland
†Daly, Donald F. *engineering company executive*
Lall, B. Kent *civil engineering educator*
Lendaris, George Gregory *electrical educator*
Sutter, Harvey Mack *engineer,consultant*
Taylor, Carson William *electrical engineer*
Van Valkenburg, Mac Elwyn *electrical engineering educator*

Sunriver
Clough, Ray William, Jr. *civil engineering educator*
Davenport, Wilbur Bayley, Jr. *electrical engineering educator*

Wilsonville
Isberg, Reuben Albert *radio communications engineer*

PENNSYLVANIA

Allentown
Gewartowski, James Walter *electrical engineer*
Hansel, James Gordon *engineer*
Singhal, Kishore *engineering administrator*
Smith, Warren L. *electrical engineer, physicist*
Winters, Arthur Ralph, Jr. *chemical and cryogenic engineer, consultant*

Berwyn
Lund, George Edward *retired electrical engineer*

Bethel Park
Korchynsky, Michael *metallurgical engineer*
O'Donnell, William James *engineering executive*

Bethlehem
Anderson, David Martin *environmental engineer*
Beedle, Lynn Simpson *civil engineering educator*
Dahlke, Walter Emil *electrical engineering educator*
Durkee, Jackson Leland *civil engineer*
Fisher, John William *civil engineering educator*
Gardiner, Keith Mattinson *engineering educator*
Georgakis, Christos *chemical engineer educator, consultant, researcher*
Hess, Dennis William *chemical engineering educator*
Karakash, John J. *engineering educator*
Kugelman, Irwin Jay *civil engineering educator*
Lennon, Gerard Patrick *civil engineering educator, researcher*
†Mirro, John *engineering company executive*
Pense, Alan Wiggins *metallurgical engineer, academic administrator*
Roberts, Richard *mechanical engineering educator*
Tuzla, Kemal *mechanical engineer, scientist*
Viest, Ivan M(iroslav) *consulting structural engineer*
Wenzel, Leonard Andrew *engineering educator*
Williams, David Bernard *metallurgical engineer*

Blue Bell
Hirsch, Robert W. *environmental consulting, engineering and construction company executive*
Vollmar, John Raymond *electrical engineer*

Bryn Mawr
Barth, Charles Fredrik *aerospace engineer*

Buck Hill Falls
Meditz, Walter Joseph *engineering consultant*

Cambridge Springs
Hughes, William Frank *mechanical and electrical engineering educator*

Camp Hill
Miner, Dennis Kane *chemical engineer, consultant*
†Scheiner, James Ira *engineering company executive*

Chadds Ford
Isakoff, Sheldon Erwin *chemical engineer*

Cheltenham
Weinstock, Walter Wolfe *systems engineer*

Conshohocken
Cohen, Alan *civil engineer*
Rippel, Harry Conrad *mechanical engineer, consultant*

Coraopolis
Nelson, Donald J. *engineering executive*

Erdenheim
Hargens, Charles William, III *electrical engineer, consultant*
Lantos, Peter R(ichard) *industrial consultant, chemical engineer*

Erie
Gray, Robert Beckwith *engineer*
Hsu, Bertrand Dahung *mechanical engineer*

Export
Andrews, Harry Nicholas *engineering executive*
Wagner, Charles Leonard *electrical engineer, consultant*

Exton
†Woodruff, Paul Harrison *civil engineer, consultant*

Fort Washington
Buescher, Adolph Ernst (Dolph Buescher) *aerospace company executive*

Gibsonia
Shoub, Earle Phelps *chemical engineer, educator*

Glen Mills
Churchill, Stuart Winston *chemical engineering educator*

Glenside
Forman, Edgar Ross *mechanical engineer*

Greensburg
Guyker, William Charles, Jr. *electrical engineer, researcher*

Harrisburg
Cate, Donald James *mechanical engineer, consultant*
Dietz, John Raphael *consulting engineer executive*
Giusti, Joseph Paul *global human resource development director, retired university chancellor*

Haverford
Bemis, Hal Lawall *engineering and business executive*

Havertown
Sheppard, Walter Lee, Jr. *chemical engineer, consultant*

Hershey
McInerney, Joseph John *biomedical engineer, educator*

Horsham
Goff, Kenneth Wade *electrical engineer*

Huntingdon Valley
West, A(rnold) Sumner *chemical engineer*

Jenkintown
Haythornthwaite, Robert Morphet *civil engineer, educator*

Johnstown
Kuhn, Howard Arthur *engineering executive, educator*

Lake Ariel
Tague, Charles Francis *retired engineering, construction and real estate development company executive*

Lansdowne
Popovics, Sandor *civil engineer, educator, researcher*

Latrobe
Conley, Edward Vincent, Jr. *metallurgical engineering educator*

Monroeville
Creagan, Robert Joseph *consulting nuclear engineer*
†Di Gioia, Anthony Michael, Jr. *civil engineer, business executive*
Jacobi, William Mallett *nuclear engineer, consultant*
Mandel, Herbert Maurice *civil engineer*

Murrysville
Colborn, Harry Walter *electrical engineering consultant*

New Kensington
Jarrett, Noel *chemical engineer*
Pien, Shyh-Jye John *mechanical engineer*

Paoli
Visek, Albert James *computer engineer*

Philadelphia
Bartlett, Desmond William *engineering company executive*
Batterman, Steven Charles *engineering mechanics and bioengineering educator*
Carmi, Shlomo *mechanical engineering educator, scientist*
Chance, Henry Martyn, II *engineering executive*
Cohen, Ira Myron *aeronautical and mechanical engineering educator*
Cruger, Lorenzo *civil engineer*
Dabby, Sabah Salman *chemical engineer*
Eisenstein, Bruce Allan *electrical engineering educator*
Falkie, Thomas Victor *mining engineer, natural resources company executive*
Fegley, Kenneth Allen *systems engineering educator*
Gaither, William Samuel *retired college president, marine engineer, consultant*
Higgins, Frederick Benjamin, Jr. *environmental engineering educator, college dean*
Jaron, Dov *biomedical engineer, educator*
†Johnson, Alan T. *engineering educator*
Ku, Y. H. *engineering educator*
Lawley, Alan *materials engineering educator*
Litt, Mitchell *chemical engineer, educator, bioengineer*
Mc Mahon, Charles Joseph, Jr. *materials science educator*
Miller, Charles Q. *engineering company executive*
Morlok, Edward Karl *engineering educator, consultant*
Parmiter, James Darlin *safety engineer*
Pipes, Wesley O'Feral *civil engineering educator*
Quinn, John Albert *chemical engineering educator*
Reid, John Mitchell *biomedical engineer*
Schwan, Herman Paul *electrical engineering and physical science educator, research scientist*
Showers, Ralph Morris *electrical engineer educator*
Tomiyasu, Kiyo *consulting engineer*
Van der Spiegel, Jan *engineering educator*
Zemel, Jay Norman *electrical engineer, educator*

Phoenixville
Olson, James Robert *consulting engineer*

Pittsburgh
Amon Parisi, Cristina Hortensia *mechanical engineering educator, researcher*
Behrend, William Louis *electrical engineer*
Birks, Neil *metallurgical engineering educator, consultant*
Bjorhovde, Reidar *civil engineer, educator, researcher, consultant*
Bloom, William Millard *furnace design engineer*
†Boyd, John T. *engineering executive*
Casasent, David Paul *electrical engineering educator, data processing executive*
Charap, Stanley Harvey *electrical engineering educator*
Chiang, Shiao-Hung *chemical engineering educator*
Director, Stephen William *electrical engineering educator, researcher*
Fenves, Steven Joseph *civil engineer*
Geiger, Gene Edward *engineer, educator*
Gilbert, Ralph Whitmel, Jr. *engineering company executive*
Gottfried, Byron Stuart *engineering educator*
Griffin, Donald Spray *mechanical engineer, consultant*
†Grossman, Ignacio E. *chemical engineering educator*
Hamilton, Howard Britton *electrical engineer, educator*
Hoburg, James Frederick *electrical engineering educator*
Hung, Tin-Kan *engineering educator, researcher*
Jordan, Angel Goni *electrical and computer engineering educator*
Khonsari, Michael M. *engineering educator*
†Kissell, Fred N. *mining engineer*
Krutz, Ronald L. *computer engineer*
Kryder, Mark Howard *computer and electrical engineering educator, consultant*
Li, Ching-Chung *electrical engineering, computer science educator*
Luthy, Richard Godfrey *environmental engineering educator*
McAvoy, Bruce Ronald *scientist, consultant*
McMichael, Francis Clay *civil engineering educator, environmental engineering consultant*
Meiksin, Zvi H. *electrical engineering educator*
Milnes, Arthur George *electrical engineer, educator*
Moura, José Manuel Fonseca *electrical engineer*
Murphy, William James *materials characterization company executive, metallurgical engineer*
Nathanson, Harvey Charles *electrical engineer*
Neuman, Charles P. *electrical and computer engineering educator, consultant*
Pettit, Frederick Sidney *metallurgical engineering educator, researcher*
Pohland, Frederick George *environmental engineering educator, researcher*
Raimondi, Albert Anthony *mechanical engineer*
Rohrer, Ronald Alan *electrical and computer engineering educator, consultant*
Rubin, Edward Stephen *engineering educator, mechanical engineer*
Schultz, Jerome Samson *biochemical engineer, educator*
Shaw, Richard Leslie *engineering company executive*
Simaan, Marwan A. *electrical engineering educator*
†Sinclair, Glenn Bruce *mechanical engineering educator, researcher*
Spanovich, Milan *civil engineer*
Stuckeman, Herman Campbell *architectural engineer*
Tierney, John William *chemical engineering educator*
†Turbeville, Robert Morris *engineering executive*
Vogeley, Clyde Eicher, Jr. *engineering educator, artist, consultant*
Wallace, William Edward *engineering educator, scientist*
Westerberg, Arthur William *chemical engineering educator*
Woo, Savio Lau-Yuen *bioengineering educator*
†Yang, Wen-Ching *chemical engineer*
Yerushalmi, Joseph *chemical engineer, researcher, educator*

Plymouth Meeting
Kostinsky, Harvey *clinical and electrical engineer*

Pottstown
†Haratunian, Michael *engineering company executive*

Radnor
Follman, John P. *engineering comprnay executive*

Reading
Hollander, Herbert I. *consulting engineer*
Smith, Alexander Forbes, III *engineering consulting firm executive*

Star Junction
Baldwin, Clarence Jones, Jr. *electrical engineer, manufacturing company executive*

State College
Foderaro, Anthony Harolde *nuclear engineering educator*
Henderson, Robert Earl *mechanical engineer, educator, consultant*
Olson, Donald Richard *mechanical engineering educator*
Thompson, Fred Clayton *engineering executive, consultant*
Wysk, Richard A. *engineering educator, researcher*

Swarthmore
Krendel, Ezra Simon *systems and human factors engineering consultant*

Tidioute
†Stone, Harvey H. *civil engineer, executive*

Trafford
Hampton, Edward John *engineering executive*

University Park
Aplan, Frank Fulton *metallurgical engineering educator*
Bieniawski, Zdzislaw Tadeusz *design engineer, educator, consultant*
Bose, Nirmal Kumar *electrical engineering, mathematics educator*
Brown, John Lawrence, Jr. *electrical engineering educator*
Buffington, Dennis Elvin *agricultural engineering educator*
Davids, Norman *engineering science and mechanics educator, researcher*
Feng, Tse-yun *computer engineer, educator*
Fonash, Stephen Joseph *engineering educator*
Ham, Inyong *industrial engineering educator*
Helfferich, Friedrich G. *chemical engineer, educator*
Holl, John William *engineering educator*
Kabel, Robert Lynn *chemical engineering educator*
Knott, Kenneth *engineering educator*

Lakshminarayana, Budugur *aerospace engineering educator*
Mathews, John David *electrical engineering educator, consultant*
McCormick, Barnes Warnock *aerospace engineering educator*
McDonnell, Archie Joseph *environmental engineer*
McWhirter, John Ruben *chemical engineering educator*
Mentzer, John Raymond *electrical engineer, educator*
Morris, Philip John *aerospace engineering educator*
Nisbet, John Stirling *electrical engineering educator*
Ramani, Raja Venkat *mining engineering educator*
Reed, Joseph Raymond *civil engineering educator, academic administrator*
Ruud, Clayton Olaf *engineering educator*
Scanlon, Andrew *structural engineering educator*
Thompson, William, Jr. *engineering educator*
Thuering, George Lewis *industrial engineering educator*
Tittmann, Bernhard Rainer *engineering science and mechanics educator*
Vannice, M. Albert *chemical engineering educator, researcher*
Walker, Eric Arthur *consulting engineer, institute executive*
Webb, Ralph Lee *mechanical engineering educator*
Witzig, Warren Frank *nuclear engineer, educator*

Valley Forge
Atilgan, Timur Faik *structural engineer*

Villanova
McLaughlin, Philip VanDoren, Jr. *mechanical engineering educator, researcher, consultant*
Tomlinson, J. Richard *engineering services company executive*
White, Robert Edward *chemical engineering educator, consultant*

Wallingford
Parker, Jennifer Ware *chemical engineer, researcher*

Warminster
Tatnall, George Jacob *aeronautical engineer*

Warrendale
Hartwig, Thomas Leo *civil engineer*
†Olthof, Meint *engineering company executive consultant*

West Chester
Dwyer, Francis Gerard *chemical engineer, researcher*
Thompson, A(nsel) Frederick, Jr. *environmental engineering and consulting company executive*

York
†Horn, Russell Eugene *engineering executive, consultant*

RHODE ISLAND

Cranston
Thielsch, Helmut John *engineering company executive*

Greenville
Calo, Joseph Manuel *chemical engineering educator*

Kingston
Palm, William John *mechanical engineering educator*
Polk, Charles *electrical engineer, educator, biophysicist*
Tufts, Donald Winston *electrical engineering educator*

Portsmouth
Baker, Walter Louis *engineering company executive*
Becken, Bradford Albert *engineering executive*

Providence
Freund, Lambert Ben *engineering educator, researcher, consultant*
Glicksman, Maurice *engineering educator, former dean and provost*
Gurland, Joseph *engineering educator*
Hazeltine, Barrett *electrical engineer, educator*
Loferski, Joseph John *electrical engineering educator*
Needleman, Alan *mechanical engineering educator*
Preparata, Franco Paolo *computer science and engineering educator*
Richardson, Peter Damian *mechanical engineering educator*
Richman, Marc Herbert *forensic engineer, educator*
Suuberg, Eric Michael *chemical engineering educator*
Symonds, Paul Southworth *mechanical engineering educator, researcher*
Weiner, Jerome Harris *mechanical engineering educator*

Rumford
Findley, William Nichols *mechanical engineering educator*
Silverman, Harvey Fox *engineering educator, dean*

West Warwick
Buckley, Charles E. *engineering executive*

SOUTH CAROLINA

Aiken
Williamson, Thomas Garnett *nuclear engineering and engineering physics educator*

Anderson
Goodner, Homer Wade *process systems failure risk consultant*

Beaufort
Pinkerton, Robert Bruce *mechanical engineer*

Charleston
Baron, Seymour *engineering and research executive*
Bolin, Edmund Mike *electrical engineer, franchise engineering consultant*
†Fei, James Robert *engineer*
†Greene, George Chester, III *chemical engineer*

Clemson
Adams, John Quincy, III *nuclear engineer*
Bunn, Joe Millard *agricultural engineering educator*
Chisman, James Allan *industrial engineering educator, consultant*
Couch, James Houston *industrial engineer, educator*
Han, Young Jo *agricultural engineer, educator*
Leonard, Michael Steven *industrial engineering educator*
Paul, Frank Waters *mechanical engineer, educator, consultant*
Pursley, Michael Bader *electrical engineering educator, communications systems research and consulting*
von Recum, Andreas F. *bioengineer*
Williamson, Robert Elmore *agricultural engineering educator*
†Zumbrunnen, David Arnold *mechanical engineering educator, consultant*

Columbia
Edens, Jerry Jeanne *computer engineer, consultant*
Ernst, Edward Willis *electrical engineering educator*
Willoughby, William, II *retired nuclear engineer*

Fort Mill
Hodge, Bobby Lynn *mechanical engineer*

Greenville
Akpan, Edward *metallurgical engineer*
Carpenter, William Levy *mechanical engineer*
Leonhardt, Thomas C. *engineering company executive*
Plumstead, William Charles *quality engineer, consultant*

Hampton
Platts, Francis Holbrook *plastics engineer*

Hartsville
Menius, Espie Flynn, Jr. *electrical engineer*

Hilton Head Island
Davis, Milton Wickers, Jr. *chemical engineer, educator*
Huckins, Harold Aaron *chemical engineer*
Windman, Arnold Lewis *retired mechanical engineer*

Laurens
Bost, John Rowan *manufacturing executive, engineer*

Myrtle Beach
†Rosen, Benedict Philip *engineering executive*

North Augusta
†Wiser, J. W. *engineering company executive, construction executive*

North Charleston
Mc Aleece, Donald John *mechanical engineering educator*

Orangeburg
Graule, Raymond S(iegfried) *metallurgical engineer*

Pawleys Island
Alexander, William D., III *civil engineer, consultant, former army air force officer*

Salem
Jones, Charles Edward *mechanical engineer*

Spartanburg
†Cogan, Jerry Albert, Jr. *chemical engineer, engineering executive*

SOUTH DAKOTA

Brookings
Storry, Junis Oliver *retired engineering educator*

Rapid City
Gowen, Richard Joseph *electrical engineering educator, college president*
Ramakrishnan, Venkataswamy *civil engineer, educator*
Riemenschneider, Albert Louis *engineering educator*
Scofield, Gordon Lloyd *mechanical engineer, educator*

TENNESSEE

Arnold AFB
†Davis, John William *engineering company executive*

Brentwood
Isom, Sam *engineer*

Chattanooga
Baker, Merl *engineering educator*
Cox, Ronald Baker *engineering and management consultant, university dean*
Duckworth, Jerrell James *electrical engineer*
Gore, Barry Maurice *electrical engineer*
Kittlitz, Rudolf Gottlieb, Jr. *chemical engineer*

Cookeville
Chowdhuri, Pritindra *electrical engineer, educator*
Sissom, Leighton Esten *engineering educator, dean, consultant*

Germantown
Shockley, Thomas Dewey *electrical engineering educator*

Greenbrier
Newell, Paul Haynes, Jr. *engineering educator, former college president*

Kingsport
Scott, H(erbert) Andrew *retired chemical engineer*
Siirola, Jeffrey John *chemical engineer*

Knoxville
Bailey, John Milton *electrical engineering educator*
Bose, Bimal Kumar *electrical engineering educator*
Bressler, Marcus N. *consulting engineer*
Danko, Joseph Christopher *metals engineer, university official*
Gonzalez, Rafael Ceferino *electrical engineering educator*
Hung, James Chen *engineer, educator, consultant*
LeVert, Francis Edward *nuclear engineer*
Mc Dow, John Jett *agricultural engineering educator*
Richards, Stephen Harold *engineering educator*
Richardson, Don Orland *agricultural educator*
Roth, J(ohn) Reece *electrical engineer, educator, researcher, consultant*
Schuler, Theodore Anthony *civil engineer, city official*
Tschantz, Bruce Allen *civil engineer, educator*
Uhrig, Robert Eugene *nuclear engineer, educator*

Luttrell
Milligan, Mancil Wood *mechanical and aerospace engineering educator*

Maryville
Oakes, Lester Cornelius *retired electrical engineer, consultant*

Memphis
Kellogg, Frederic Hartwell *civil engineer, educator*
Williams, Edward F(oster), III *environmental engineer*

Nashville
Brodersen, Arthur James *electrical engineer*
Cadzow, James Archie *engineering educator, researcher*
Chaudhuri, Dilip Kumar *engineering educator*
Cook, George Edward *electrical engineering educator, consultant*
Eckenfelder, William Wesley, Jr. *environmental engineer*
Hahn, George Thomas *materials engineering educator, researcher*
Harrawood, Paul *civil engineering educator*
House, Robert William *technology management educator*
McClanahan, Larry Duncan *civil engineer, consultant*
Parker, Frank Leon *environmental engineering educator, consultant*
Potter, John Leith *mechanical and aerospace engineer, educator, consultant*
Schnelle, Karl Benjamin, Jr. *chemical engineering educator, consultant, researcher*
Speece, Richard Eugene *civil engineer, educator*
†Thackston, Edward Lee *engineer, educator*
Youree, Gene Tassey *tool design engineer*

Oak Ridge
Cain, Victor Ralph *nuclear engineer*
Kasten, Paul Rudolph *nuclear engineer, educator*
Meyers, Sheldon *engineering company executive*
Rosenthal, Murray Wilford *chemical engineer, science administrator*
Trauger, Donald Byron *nuclear engineering laboratory administrator*
Wooten, Hollis Darwin *engineer*

Tullahoma
Antar, Basil Niman *engineering educator*
†Butler, R. W. *engineering company executive*
Pate, Samuel Ralph *engineering corporation executive*
Wu, Ying Chu Lin Susan *engineering company executive, engineer*

TEXAS

Amarillo
Keaton, Lawrence Cluer *engineer, consultant*
Von Eschen, Robert Leroy *electrical engineer, consultant*

Arlington
Anderson, Dale Arden *aerospace engineer, educator*
Fung, Adrian Kin-Chiu *electrical engineering educator, researcher*
Mc Elroy, John Harley *electrical engineering educator*
Payne, Fred R(ay) *aerospace engineering educator, researcher*
Qasim, Syed Reazul *civil engineering educator, researcher*
Stevens, Gladstone Taylor, Jr. *industrial engineer*

Austin
Adcock, Willis Alfred *electrical engineer, educator*
Aggarwal, Jagdishkumar Keshoram *electrical and computer engineering educator, research administrator*
Armstrong, Neal Earl *civil engineering educator*
Baker, Lee Edward *biomedical engineering educator*
Barlow, Joel William *chemical engineering educator*
Beard, Leo Roy *civil engineer*
†Blackstock, David T. *mechanical engineer, educator*
†Bonnecaze, Roger T. *chemical engineering educator*
Box, Barry Glenn *aerospace engineer, military officer*
Breen, John Edward *civil engineer, educator*
Brock, James Rush *chemical engineering educator*
Bronaugh, Edwin Lee *electromagnetic compatibility engineer, consultant*
Burns, Ned Hamilton *civil engineering educator*
Carey, Graham Francis *engineering educator*
Carlton, Donald Morrill *research, development and engineering executive*
Carrasquillo, Ramon Luis *civil engineering educator, consultant*
Charbeneau, Randall J. *environmental and civil engineer*
Dougal, Arwin Adelbert *electrical engineer, educator*
Dupuis, Russell Dean *electrical engineer, research scientist*
Evans, Walter Reed *engineering executive, consultant*
Fair, James Rutherford, Jr. *chemical engineering educator, consultant*
Fowler, David Wayne *architectural engineering educator*
Gloyna, Earnest Frederick *environmental engineer, educator*
Goodenough, John Bannister *engineering educator, research physicist*
Gray, Kenneth Eugene *petroleum engineering educator*
Harris, Richard Lee *engineering executive, retired army officer*
Himmelblau, David Mautner *chemical engineer*
Howell, John Reid *mechanical engineer, educator*
Hull, David George *aerospace engineering educator, researcher*
Jirsa, James Otis *civil engineering educator*
Klein, Dale Edward *nuclear engineering educator*
Koen, Billy Vaughn *mechanical engineering educator*
Koros, William John *chemical engineering educator*
LaGrone, Alfred Hall *electrical engineering educator*
Lake, Larry Wayne *petroleum engineer*
Lamb, Jamie Parker, Jr. *mechanical engineer, educator*
Marcus, Harris Leon *mechanical engineering and materials science educator*
Mark, Hans Michael *aerospace engineering educator, physicist*
McGinnis, Charles Irving *civil engineer*
Mc Ketta, John J., Jr. *chemical engineering educator*
Mercer, Melvin Ray *electrical engineer, educator*
Metcalfe, Tom Brooks *chemical engineering educator*
Moulthrop, James Sylvester *research engineer, consultant*
Nichols, Steven Parks *mechanical engineer, university official*
Oden, John Tinsley *engineering mechanics educator, consultant*
Paul, Donald Ross *chemical engineer, educator*
Rhyne, Vernon Thomas, III *electrical engineer, consultant*
Richards-Kortum, Rebecca Rae *biomedical engineering educator*
Rylander, Henry Grady, Jr. *mechanical engineering educator*
Sandberg, Irwin Walter *electrical and computer engineering educator*
Schapery, Richard Allan *engineering educator*
Schechter, Robert Samuel *chemical engineer, educator*
Short, Byron Elliott *engineering educator*
†Spencer, William J. *engineering executive, researcher*
Steinfink, Hugo *chemical engineering educator*
Stice, James Edward *chemical engineer, educator*
Straiton, Archie Waugh *electrical engineering educator*
Streetman, Ben Garland *electrical engineering educator*
Swartzlander, Earl Eugene, Jr. *engineering educator*
Szebehely, Victor G. *aeronautical engineer*
Tapley, Byron Dean *aerospace engineer, educator*
Tesar, Delbert *machine systems and robotics educator, researcher, manufacturing consultant*
Thurston, George Butte *mechanical and biomedical engineering educator*
Tucker, Richard Lee *civil engineer, educator*
Vliet, Gary Clark *mechanical engineering educator*
Walton, Charles Michael *civil engineering educator*
Wehring, Bernard William *nuclear engineering educator*
Welch, Ashley James *engineering educator*
Weldon, William Forrest *electrical and mechanical engineer, educator*
Wissler, Eugene Harley *chemical engineer, educator*
Woodson, Herbert Horace *electrical engineering educator*
Wright, Stephen Gailord *civil engineering educator, consultant*
Yura, Joseph Andrew *civil engineering educator, consulting structural engineer*

Baird
Rodenberger, Charles Alvard *aerospace engineer, consultant*

Big Spring
Fryrear, Donald William *agricultural engineer*

Boerne
Dixon, Robert James *aerospace consultant, former air force officer, former aerospace company executive*

Brooks AFB
Olsen, Richard Galen *biomedical engineer, researcher*

Bryan
Samson, Charles Harold, Jr. (Car) *retired engineering educator, consultant*

Bushland
Howell, Terry Allen *agricultural engineer*

Carrollton
Schulz, Richard Burkart *electrical engineer, consultant*

Channelview
Johnson, Gus LaRoy *marine chemist, safety consultant*

College Station
Batchelor, Bill *civil engineering educator*
Bhattacharyya, Shankar Prashad *electrical engineer, educator*
Bradley, Walter Lee *mechanical engineer, educator, researcher, consultant*
Cochran, Robert Glenn *nuclear engineering educator*
†Cohen, Aaron *aerospace engineer*
Ehsani, Mehrdad (Mark) *electrical engineering educator, consultant*
Fletcher, Leroy Stevenson *mechanical engineer, educator*
Godbey, Luther David *architectural and engineering executive*
Hall, Kenneth Richard *chemical engineering educator, consultant*
Herbich, John Bronislaw *engineering educator*
Holland, Charles Donald *chemical engineer, educator*
Kunze, Otto Robert *retired agricultural engineering educator*
Lee, William John *petroleum engineering educator, consultant*
Lowery, Lee Leon, Jr. *civil engineer*
Lytton, Robert Leonard *civil engineer, educator*
Mathewson, Christopher Colville *engineering geologist, educator*
Page, Robert Henry *engineer, educator, researcher*
Painter, John Hoyt *electrical engineer*
Patton, Alton DeWitt *electrical engineering educator, consultant, research administrator*

Rabins, Michael Jerome *mechanical engineer, educator*
Reddell, Donald Lee *agricultural engineer*
Reddy, J. Narasimha *mechanical engineering educator*
Rhode, David Leland *mechanical engineering educator, consultant*
Richardson, Herbert Heath *mechanical engineer, educator, institute director*
Yao, James Tsu-Ping *civil engineer*

Corpus Christi
Green, William Wells *civil engineer*

Crosby
Ohsol, Ernest Osborne *consulting chemical engineer*

Dallas
Bruene, Warren Benz *electronic engineer*
Eberhart, Robert Clyde *biomedical engineering educator, researcher*
Fontana, Robert Edward *electrical engineering educator, retired air force officer*
Gill, David Brian *electrical engineer, educator*
Huang, Yen Ti *civil engineer*
Jelensperger, Francis J. *engineering and architectural executive*
Kilby, Jack St. Clair *electrical engineer*
Mays, Gerald Avery (Jerry Mays) *engineering executive, consultant*
Mc Lemore, Robert Henry *petroleum engineer, consultant*
Melgar, Julio *retired mechanical engineer*
Monsees, James Eugene *engineering executive, consultant*
†Schulze, Richard Hans *engineering executive, environmental engineer*
†Wilmut, Charles Gordon *environmental engineer*
Yeh, Lian-Tuu *mechanical engineer*

Denton
Rhoades, Warren A., Jr. *retired mechanical engineer*

El Paso
Coleman, Howard S. *engineer, physicist*
Friedkin, Joseph Frank *consulting engineering executive*
Grieves, Robert Belanger *engineering educator*

Fort Worth
Cunningham, Atlee Marion, Jr. *aeronautical engineer*
†Hammond, Wilton N. *civil engineer, consultant, architectural firm executive*
Kenderdine, John Marshall *petroleum engineer, retired army officer*
Nichols, James Richard *civil engineer, consultant*
Nichols, Robert Leighton *civil engineer*
Romine, Thomas Beeson, Jr. *consulting engineering executive*
†Thompson, Douglas A. *aerospace engineer*

Galveston
Otis, John James *civil engineer*
Sheppard, Louis Clarke *biomedical engineer, educator*

Garland
Jackson, Edwin L. *electrical engineer*
†Ryno, Ronald Pat *business executive, chemical engineer*

Glen Rose
Ragan, James Otis *engineer, consultant*

Granbury
Killebrew, James Robert *architectural engineering firm executive*

Greenville
Johnston, John Thomas *engineering executive*

Houston
Akers, William Walter *chemical engineering educator*
Amundson, Neal Russell *chemical engineer, mathematician, educator*
Anthony, Donald Barrett *engineering executive*
Billingsley, David Stuart *chemical engineer, researcher*
Bishop, David Nolan *electrical engineer*
Bovay, Harry Elmo, Jr. *retired engineering company executive*
Bridger, Baldwin, Jr. *electrical engineer*
Brouse, Michael *petroleum engineer, management consultant*
Burrus, Charles Sidney *electrical engineering educator*
Chapman, Alan Jesse *mechanical engineering educator*
Cheatham, John Bane, Jr. *mechanical engineering educator*
Christopher, Socrates S. *engineering executive*
Clark, John William, Jr. *electrical engineer, educator*
Dawn, Frederic Samuel *chemical and textile engineer*
Edwards, Victor Henry *chemical engineer*
Eichberger, LeRoy Carl *mechanical engineer, consultant, stress analyst*
Focht, John Arnold, Jr. *geotechnical engineer*
Frankhouser, Homer Sheldon, Jr. *engineering and construction company executive*
Geer, Ronald Lamar *mechanical engineering consultant, retired oil company executive*
Gibson, Michael Addison *chemical engineering company executive*
Gidley, John Lynn *engineering executive*
Guinn, David Crittenden *petroleum engineer, drilling and exploration company executive*
Hellums, Jesse David *chemical engineering educator and researcher*
Hightower, Joe Walter *chemical engineering educator, consultant*
Hirasaki, George Jiro *chemical engineer, educator*
Hsu, Thomas Tseng-Chuang *civil engineer, educator*
Kenefick, John Henry, Jr. *retired engineering company executive, consultant*
Knight, Tommy E. *civil engineer*
Kobayashi, Riki *chemical engineer, educator*
Krause, William Austin *engineering executive*
Krishen, Kumar *aerospace research technologist*
Lienhard, John Henry *mechanical engineering educator*
Luss, Dan *chemical engineering educator*
Maligas, Manuel Nick *metallurgical engineer*
Matthews, Charles Sedwick *petroleum engineering consultant, research advisor*
McClelland, Bramlette *engineering executive, consultant*
McIntire, Larry Vern *chemical engineering educator*
Mian, Farouk Aslam *chemical engineer, educator*
Miele, Angelo *engineering educator, researcher, consultant, author*
Miller, Clarence Alphonso *chemical engineering educator*
Moore, Pat Howard *engineering and construction company executive*
Moore, Walter Parker, Jr. *civil engineering company executive*
Morris, Owen Glenn *engineering corporation executive*
Mosher, Donald Raymond *chemical engineer, consultant*
Nordgren, Ronald Paul *engineering educator, researcher*
Ostrofsky, Benjamin *business and engineering management educator, industrial engineer*
Pearson, James Boyd, Jr. *electrical engineering educator*
Pharr, George Mathews *materials science and engineering educator*
Powell, Alan *engineer, scientist, educator*
Prats, Michael *petroleum engineer, educator*
Rabson, Thomas Avelyn *electrical engineering educator, researcher*
Reistle, Carl Ernest, Jr. *petroleum engineer*
Shen, Liang Chi *electrical engineer, educator, researcher*
†Smith, Sam K. *engineering company executive*
Spanos, Pol Dimitrios *engineering educator*
Symons, James Martin *environmental engineer, educator*
Thayer, Keith B. *engineering company executive*
Thomsen, Charles Burton *engineering design company executive*
Tucker, Randolph Wadsworth *engineering executive*
Valencia, Jaime Alfonso *chemical engineer*
Walker, Esper Lafayette, Jr. *civil engineer*
Wilkinson, Bruce W. *corporate executive, lawyer*
Wren, Robert James *aerospace engineering manager*
†Young, Robert B., Jr. *engineering company executive*
Yu, Aiting Tobey *engineering executive*

Humble
Brown, Samuel Joseph, Jr. *scientist, engineer*

Hurst
†Bishara, Amin Tawadros *mechanical engineer, technical services executive*

Irving
Callahan, Frank T. *engineering executive*

Kerrville
Matlock, (Lee) Hudson *civil engineer, educator*

League City
†Faget, Maxime A(llan) *aeronautical engineer*
Meinke, Roy Walter *electrical engineer, consultant*

Lindale
Bockhop, Clarence William *retired agricultural engineer*
Wilson, Leland Earl *petroleum engineering consultant*

Lubbock
Archer, James Elson *engineering educator*
Dudek, Richard Albert *engineering educator*
Kiesling, Ernst Willie *civil engineering educator*
Kristiansen, Magne *electrical engineer, educator*
Portnoy, William Manos *electrical engineering educator*

Port Aransas
Lehmann, William Leonardo *electrical engineer, educator*

Prairie View
Fogarty, Thomas Nilan *electronic materials engineer*

Richardson
Biard, James Robert *electrical engineer*
Lutz, Raymond Price *industrial engineer, educator*

Rockport
Minor, Joseph Edward *civil engineer, educator*

Rockwall
Griffith, James William *engineer, consultant*

San Antonio
Abramson, Hyman Norman *engineering and science research executive*
Belzung, Paul Edward *engineering executive*
Dougherty, Robert James *safety consultant*
Hauser, Victor LaVern *agricultural engineer*
Petty, Olive Scott *geophysical engineer*
Smith, Richard Thomas *electrical engineer*
Stebbins, Richard Henderson *electronics engineer, peace officer, security consultant*

Spring
Riley, Arthur Roy *consulting engineer*

Tyler
Morgan, Freeman Louis, Jr. *engineer, consultant*
Smith, James Edward *petroleum engineer, consultant*

Universal City
Atchley, Curtis Leon *mechanical engineer*

Waco
Sivam, Thangavel Parama *aerospace engineer*

Wimberley
Busch, Arthur Winston *environmental engineer, educator, consultant*

Woodsboro
Rooke, Allen Driscoll, Jr. *civil engineer*

UTAH

Bountiful
Gutzman, Philip Charles *aerospace executive, logistician*

Logan
Clark, Clayton *electrical engineering educator*
Hargreaves, George Henry *civil and agricultural engineer, researcher*
Keller, Jack *agricultural engineering educator, consultant*

Murray
Volberg, Herman William *electronic engineer, consultant*

Ogden
Davidson, Thomas Ferguson *chemical engineer*

Provo
Jonsson, Jens Johannes *electrical engineering educator*
Merritt, LaVere Barrus *engineering educator, civil engineer*
Pope, Bill Jordan *chemical engineering educator, business executive*
Smoot, Leon Douglas *research director, former university dean, chemical engineering educator*

Salt Lake City
Anderson, Charles Ross *civil engineer*
Bhayani, Kiran Lilachand *environmental engineer, programs manager*
Dahlstrom, Donald Albert *chemical and metallurgical engineering educator, former equipment manufacturing company executive*
De Vries, Kenneth Lawrence *mechanical engineer, educator*
Eernisse, Errol Peter *electronics company executive, scientist*
Gandhi, Om Parkash *electrical engineer*
†Green, Sidney J. *mechanical engineer, engineering executive*
Hill, Stephen D. *chemical engineer, federal agency administrator*
Hogan, Mervin Booth *mechanical engineer, educator*
Iskander, Magdy Fahmy *electrical engineering educator, consultant*
Jacobsen, Stephen Charles *biomedical engineer, educator*
†Kochevar, Lewis Clayton *hydraulics company executive*
Olsen, Donald Bert *biomedical engineer, experimental surgeon, research facility director*
†Pariseau, William G. *mining engineer, educator*
Pershing, David Walter *chemical engineering educator, researcher*
Rogers, Vern Child *engineering company executive*
Rushforth, Craig K. *electrical engineering educator, researcher*
Sandquist, Gary Marlin *engineering educator*
Seader, Junior DeVere *chemical engineering educator*
Sohn, Hong Yong *metallurgical and chemical engineering educator*
Stockham, Thomas Greenway, Jr. *electrical engineering educator*
Stringfellow, Gerald B. *engineering educator*
Webb, Dean LeRoy *engineering executive, consultant, civil, forensic, structural and investigative engineer*
Zeamer, Richard Jere *engineer, executive*

Sandy
Bennett, Carl McGhie *engineering company executive, consultant, army reserve and national guard officer*
Jorgensen, Leland Howard *aerospace research engineer*

VERMONT

Burlington
Anderson, Richard Louis *electrical engineer*
Pinder, George Francis *engineering educator, scientist*

Essex Junction
Pricer, Wilbur David *electrical engineer*

VIRGINIA

Afton
Anderson, Donald Norton, Jr. *retired electrical engineer*

Alexandria
Ackerman, Roy Alan *research and development executive*
Cook, Charles William *aerospace consultant, educator*
Darling, Thomas, Jr. *retired rural electrification specialist*
Dobson, Donald Alfred *electrical engineer*
Doeppner, Thomas Walter *electrical engineer, educator, consultant*
Eckhart, Myron, Jr. *marine engineer*
Ellison, Thorleif *consulting engineer*
Fozard, John William *engineer, designer, consultant, educator*
Gray, John Edmund *chemical engineer*
Jokl, Alois Louis *electrical engineer*
Klotz, John Wesley *electronics consultant*
Lasser, Howard Gilbert *chemical engineer, consultant*
Mandil, I. Harry *nuclear engineer*
Murray, Russell, II *aeronautical engineer, defense analyst, consultant*
Rall, Lloyd Louis *civil engineer*
†Rees, Morgan Rowlands *engineering educator*
Scurlock, Arch Chilton *chemical engineer*
Thompson, LeRoy, Jr. *radio engineer, military reserve officer*
Weiner, Robert Michael *engineering design company executive, consulting engineer*

Arlington
Bordogna, Joseph *engineer, educator*
Burka, Maria Karpati *chemical engineer*
Casazza, John Andrew *electrical engineer, business executive*
Dillaway, Robert Beacham *engineering and management consultant*
Flowers, Harold Lee *aerospace engineer, consultant*
Gilbert, Arthur Charles *aerospace engineer, consulting engineer*
Gustafson, Richard Alexander *engineering executive*
Hagn, George Hubert *electrical engineer, researcher*
Hall, Carl William *agricultural and mechanical engineer*
Katona, Peter Geza *biomedical engineer, educator*
Larsen-Basse, Jorn *mechanical/materials engineering educator, researcher, consultant*
Law, David Holbrook *safety engineer*
Rahman, Muhammad Abdur *mechanical engineer*
Reynik, Robert J. *materials engineer*
Roco, Mihail Constantin *mechanical engineer, educator*
Sechrist, Chalmers Franklin, Jr. *electrical engineering educator*
Stuart, Charles Edward *electrical engineer, oceanographer*
Sutton, George Walter *research laboratory executive, mechanical engineer*

Blacksburg
Batra, Romesh Chander *engineering mechanics educator, researcher*
Blackwell, William Allen *electrical engineering educator*
Brown, Gary Sandy *electrical engineering educator*
Comparin, Robert Anton *mechanical engineering educator*
de Wolf, David Alter *electrical engineer, educator*
†Dryden, Robert D. *engineering educator*
Fabrycky, Wolter Joseph *engineering educator, author, industrial and systems engineer*
Glasser, Wolfgang Gerhard *forest products and chemical engineering researcher, educator*
Haugh, Clarence Gene *agricultural engineering educator*
Hibbard, Walter Rollo, Jr. *retired engineering educator*
Jones, James Beverly *retired mechanical engineering educator, consultant*
Lucas, J. Richard *retired mining engineering educator*
Meirovitch, Leonard *engineering educator*
Mitchell, James Kenneth *civil engineer, educator*
Moore, James Mendon *industrial engineering educator, consultant*
Morton, John *engineering educator, researcher*
Murray, Thomas Michael *civil engineering educator, consultant*
Price, Dennis Lee *industrial engineer, educator*
Randall, Clifford Wendell *civil engineer*
Schneck, Daniel Julio *biomedical engineer, educator*
Squires, Arthur Morton *chemical engineer, educator*
Stutzman, Warren Lee *electrical engineer, educator*

Charlottesville
Aylor, James Hiram *electrical engineering educator*
Dorning, John Joseph *nuclear engineering, engineering physics and applied mathematics educator*
Edlich, Richard French *biomedical engineering educator*
Gaden, Elmer Lewis, Jr. *chemical engineering educator*
Gilruth, Robert Rowe *aerospace consultant*
Haimes, Yacov Yosseph *systems and civil engineering educator, consultant*
Herakovich, Carl Thomas *civil engineering, applied mechanics educator*
Hoel, Lester A. *civil engineering educator*
Hudson, John Lester *chemical engineering educator*
Hutchinson, Thomas Eugene *biomedical engineering educator*
Inigo, Rafael Madrigal *electrical engineering educator*
Johnson, W(alker) Reed *nuclear engineering educator*
Krzysztofowicz, Roman *systems engineering and statistical science educator, consultant*
Lee, Jen-shih *biomedical engineering educator*
Mattauch, Robert Joseph *electrical engineering educator*
McVey, Eugene Steven *electrical engineering educator, consultant*
Morton, Jeffrey Bruce *aerospace engineering educator*
Mulder, Robert Udo *nuclear engineering educator, researcher*
Reynolds, Albert Barnett *nuclear engineer, educator*
Theodoridis, George Constantin *biomedical engineering educator, researcher*
Thompson, Anthony Richard *electrical engineer, astronomer*
Townsend, Miles Averill *aerospace and mechanical engineering educator*
Waxman, Ronald *computer engineer*

Chesapeake
Jaques, James Alfred, III *communications engineer*

Dahlgren
Evans, Alan George *electrical engineer*

Fairfax
Beale, Guy Otis *engineering educator, consultant*
Boone, James Virgil *engineering executive*
†Burklew, Donald R. *engineering company executive*
Cantus, H. Hollister *engineering corporation executive*
Cook, Gerald *electrical engineering educator*
Fink, Lester Harold *engineering company executive, educator*
Gollobin, Leonard Paul *chemical engineer*
Kennedy, Leo Raymond *engineering executive*
McPherson, John Barkley *aerospace consultant, retired military officer*
Nailor, Richard Anthony, Sr. *research company executive*
†Pedersen, George J. *engineering company executive, computer support company executive*
Stitt, William C. *engineering executive*
Warfield, John Nelson *engineering educator, consultant*

Falls Church
Lorenzo, Michael *engineer, government official, real estate broker*
Nickle, Dennis Edwin *electronics engineer, church deacon*
Studebaker, John Milton *utilities engineer, consultant, educator*

Villarreal, Carlos Castaneda *engineering executive*

Gloucester
Donaldson, Coleman duPont *aerodynamics and aerospace consulting engineer*

Great Falls
Douma, Jacob Hendrick *hydraulic engineer, consultant*

Hampton
†Bowles, Roland L. *aeronautical engineer*
Clark, Leonard Vernon *aerospace engineer*
Corlett, William Albert *aerospace engineer*
Duberg, John Edward *aeronautical engineer, educator*
†Dwoyer, Douglas Leon *engineering executive*
Farrukh, Usamah Omar *electrical engineering educator, researcher*
Joshi, Suresh Meghashyam *research engineering executive*
†Mehrotra, Sudhir C. *engineering company executive*
Noor, Ahmed Khairy *engineering educator, researcher*
Pandey, Dhirendra Kumar *mechanical engineer, scientist*
Sobieski, Jaroslaw *aerospace engineer*

Huddleston
Kopp, Richard Edgar *electrical engineer*

King George
Hoglund, Richard Frank *research and technical executive*

Lexington
Trandel, Richard Samuel *mechanical engineer, educator*

Lynchburg
Fath, George R. *electrical engineer, communications executive*
Latimer, Paul Jerry *non-destructive testing engineer*

Mc Lean
†Carlucci, Frank C. *engineering company executive*
Carnicero, Jorge Emilio *aeronautical engineer, business executive*
Enger, Walter Melvin *consulting engineer, former navy officer*
Gouse, S. William, Jr. *engineering executive, scientist*
†Hollister, Cullen Agur *engineer*
Kim, John Chan Kyu *electrical engineer*
Kimmel, H. Steven *engineering executive*
McCambridge, John James *civil engineer*
Mohleji, Satish Chandra *electrical engineer*
†Odeen, Philip A. *engineering company executive*
Shanklin, Richard Vair, III *mechanical engineer*
Silveira, Milton Anthony *aerospace engineering executive*
Snyder, Franklin Farison *hydrologic engineering consultant*
Sonnemann, Harry *electrical engineer, consultant*
Thomas, Lydia Waters *research and development executive*

Newington
Foster, Eugene Lewis *engineering executive*
†Gageby, Stephen L. *design corporation executive*

Newport News
Giles, Glenn Ernest, Jr. *nuclear engineer*
Hubbard, Harvey Hart *aeroacoustician, noise control engineer, consultant*
Young, Maurice Isaac *mechanical and aerospace engineering educator*

Norfolk
Guy, Louis Lee, Jr. *environmental engineer*
Mc Gaughy, John Bell *civil engineer*
Wei, Benjamin Min *engineering educator*
Wiltse, James Clark *civil engineer*

Oakton
Curry, Thomas Fortson *electronics engineer, defense industry executive*
Wolff, Edward A. *electronics engineer*

Palmyra
Leslie, William Cairns *metallurgical engineering educator*
Ramsey, Forrest Gladstone, Jr. *engineering company executive*

Reston
Kramish, Arnold *technical consultant, author*
Mumzhiu, Alexander *optical and imaging processing engineer, researcher*

Richmond
Compton, Olin Randall *consulting electrical engineer, researcher*
Hanneman, Rodney Elton *metallurgical engineer*
Sprinkle, William Melvin *engineering administrator, audio-acoustical engineer*

Roanoke
Hamrick, Joseph Thomas *mechanical engineer, aerospace company executive*
Harvey, Aubrey Eaton, III *industrial engineer*
McKenna, John Dennis *environmental testing engineer*
Reggia, Frank *electrical engineer*
Shaffner, Patrick Noel *architectural engineering executive*
Sowers, William Armand *civil engineer*

Salem
Lane, Lawrence Jubin *electrical engineer, consultant*
Walker, Loren Haines *electrical engineer*
Willet, Richard A. *engineering company executive*

Springfield
†Atkinson, Dale B. *aeronautical engineering, consultant*
Broome, Paul Wallace *engineering research and development executive*
Duff, William Grierson *electrical engineer*

Vienna
†Denman, Gary L. *mechanical engineer*
Keiser, Bernhard Edward *engineering company executive, consulting telecommunications engineer*
Woodward, Kenneth Emerson *retired mechanical engineer*

Waynesboro
†McNair, John William, Jr. *civil engineer*

WASHINGTON

Auburn
Whitmore, Donald Clark *retired engineer*

Bellevue
Dow, Daniel Gould *electrical engineering educator*
Edde, Howard Jasper *engineering executive*
Faris, Charles Oren *civil engineer*
Liang, Jeffrey Der-Shing *retired electrical engineer, civil worker, diplomat*
Schairer, George Swift *aeronautical engineer*
Szablya, John Francis *electrical engineer, consultant*
Walsh, John Breffni *aerospace consultant*
Wright, Theodore Otis *forensic engineer*

Bellingham
Albrecht, Albert Pearson *electronics engineer, consultant*
Jansen, Robert Bruce *consulting civil engineer*

Bothell
Blackburn, John Lewis *consulting engineering executive*

East Wenatchee
Bennett, Grover Bryce *engineering consultant*

Edmonds
Galster, Richard W. *engineering geologist*
†Landau, Henry Groh *geoenvironmental consulting engineer*
Terrel, Ronald Lee *civil engineer, business executive, educator*

Kenmore
Pihl, James Melvin *electrical engineer*

Kennewick
Cobb, William Thompson *environmental consultant*

Kingston
Pichal, Henri Thomas *electronics engineer, physicist, consultant*

Kirkland
Forsen, Harold Kay *retired engineering executive*
Wenk, Edward, Jr. *civil engineer, policy analyst, educator*

Lummi Island
Ewing, Benjamin Baugh *environmental engineering educator, consultant*

Mercer Island
Bridgforth, Robert Moore, Jr. *aerospace engineer*

Olympia
Mylroie, Willa Wilcox *transportation engineer, regional planner*

Pullman
Funk, William Henry *environmental engineering educator*
Hirth, John Price *metallurgical engineering educator*
Stock, David Earl *mechanical engineering educator*

Redmond
Rossano, August Thomas *environmental engineering educator*

Richland
Albaugh, Fred William *nuclear engineer, retired research and development executive*
Evans, Ersel Arthur *engineering consulting executive*
Pond, Daniel James *industrial technology administrator*

Seattle
Babb, Albert Leslie *biomedical engineer, educator*
Bangsund, Edward Lee *aerospace company executive*
Blake, Robert Wallace *aeronautical engineer, consultant*
Christiansen, Walter Henry *aeronautics educator*
Clark, Robert Newhall *electrical and aeronautical engineering educator*
Culp, Gordon Louis *consulting engineer*
Davis, Earl James *chemical engineering educator*
Finlayson, Bruce Alan *chemical engineering educator*
Fox, Kenneth *shipbuilder, naval engineer, water transit consultant*
Garlid, Kermit Leroy *engineering educator*
Gilbert, Paul H. *engineering executive, consultant*
Guy, Arthur William *electrical engineering educator, researcher*
Haralick, Robert Martin *electrical engineering educator*
†Harris, Robert Myer *engineer*
Hausam, Neal Allen *civil engineer, real estate developer*
Hertzberg, Abraham *aeronautical engineering educator, university research scientist*
Hoffman, Allan Sachs *chemical engineer, educator*
Ishimaru, Akira *electrical engineering educator*
Joppa, Robert Glenn *aeronautics educator*
Kapur, Kailash Chander *industrial engineering educator*
Kippenhan, Charles Jacob *mechanical engineer, retired educator*
Kobayashi, Albert Satoshi *mechanical engineering educator*
Lauritzen, Peter Owen *electrical engineering educator*
†Logsdon, John *engineering consulting company executive*
Mandeville, Gilbert Harrison *consulting engineering executive*
Martin, George Coleman *aeronautical engineer*
Mc Feron, Dean Earl *mechanical engineer*
Meditch, James Stephen *electrical engineering educator*
Peden, Irene Carswell *electrical engineer, educator*
Pollack, Gerald Harvey *bioengineering educator*
Polonis, Douglas Hugh *engineering educator*
Pratt, David Terry *mechanical engineering educator, combustion researcher*
†Rubbert, Paul Edward *engineering executive*
Russell, David Allison *aeronautical engineering educator*
Simcox, Craig Dennis *aeronautical engineer*
Skilling, John Bower *structural and civil engineer*
Sleicher, Charles Albert *chemical engineer*
Spindel, Robert Charles *electrical engineering educator*
Sutter, Joseph F. *aeronautical engineer, consultant, retired aircraft company executive*
Venkata, Subrahmanyam Saraswati *electrical engineering educator, electri energy and power researcher*
Vesper, Karl Hampton *business and mechanical engineering educator*
Weissman, Eugene Yehuda *chemical engineer*
Wood, Stuart Kee *retired engineering manager*
Woodruff, Gene Lowry *nuclear engineer, university dean*

Spokane
†Spencer, John M. *safety engineer*
Yamayee, Zia Ahmad *engineering educator, dean*

Tacoma
Anderson, Arthur Roland *engineering company executive, civil engineer*
Holman, Kermit Layton *chemical engineer*

Vancouver
Chartier, Vernon Lee *electrical engineer*

WEST VIRGINIA

Charleston
Conway, Richard Ashley *environmental engineer*
Koleske, Joseph Victor *chemical engineer, consultant*
Whittington, Bernard Wiley *electrical engineer, consultant*

Huntington
deBarbadillo, John Joseph *metallurgist, management executive*

Mineral Wells
Prather, Denzil Lewis *petroleum engineer*

Morgantown
Adler, Lawrence *mining engineering consultant*
Dadyburjor, Dady B. *chemical engineering educator, researcher*
Kent, James A. *consulting chemical engineer, author, consultant*
Klein, Ronald Lloyd *electrical engineer, educator*
Schroder, John L., Jr. *retired mining engineer*

WISCONSIN

Brookfield
Curfman, Floyd Edwin *engineering educator*

De Pere
†Parish, Fred *engineering company executive, architectural firm executive*

Frederic
Rudell, Milton Wesley *aerospace engineer*

Grafton
Eber, Lorenz *civil engineer, inventor*

Green Bay
Heaster, Arlene L. *chemical engineer*

Madison
Amundson, Clyde Howard *engineering educator, researcher*
Beachley, Norman Henry *mechanical engineer, educator*
Berthouex, Paul Mac *civil and environmental engineer, educator*
Bird, Robert Byron *chemical engineering educator, author*
†Bohnhoff, David Roy *agricultural engineer, educator*
Bollinger, John Gustave *engineering educator, college dean*
Boyle, William Charles *civil engineering educator*
Bretherton, Francis P. *atmospheric and oceanic sciences educator*
Bruhn, Hjalmar Diehl *retired agricultural engineer, educator*
Bubenzer, Gary Dean *agricultural engineering educator, researcher*
Callen, James Donald *nuclear engineer, plasma physicist, educator*
Carbon, Max William *nuclear engineering educator*
Chang, Y. Austin *materials engineer, educator*
Coberly, Camden Arthur *chemical engineering educator*
Converse, James Clarence *agricultural engineering educator*
Crandall, Lee Walter *civil and structural engineer*
DeVries, Marvin Frank *mechanical engineering educator*
Dietmeyer, Donald Leo *electrical engineer*
Duffie, John Atwater *chemical engineer, educator*
Emmert, Gilbert Arthur *engineer, educator*
Foell, Wesley Kay *engineer, energy and environmental scientist, educator, consultant*
Green, Theodore, III *engineering and science educator*
Gustafson, David Harold *industrial engineering and preventive medicine educator*
Hill, Charles Graham, Jr. *chemical engineering educator*
Huston, Norman Earl *nuclear engineering educator*
Kulcinski, Gerald LaVerne *nuclear engineer, educator*
†Lightfoot, Edwin Niblock, Jr. *chemical engineering ecuator*
Long, Willis Franklin *electrical engineering educator, researcher*
Loper, Carl Richard, Jr. *metallurgical engineer, educator*
Lovell, Edward George *engineering mechanics educator*
Malkus, David Starr *mechanics educator, applied mathematician*
Moses, Gregory Allen *engineering educator*
Novotny, Donald Wayne *electrical engineering educator*
Ray, W. Harmon *chemical engineering educator, consultant, author*
Rowlands, Robert Edward *engineering educator*
Rudd, Dale Frederick *retired chemical engineer*
Seireg, Ali A(bdel Hay) *mechanical engineer*
Shohet, Juda Leon *electrical and computer engineering educator, researcher, high technology company executive*
Skiles, James Jean *electrical and computer engineering educator*
Smith, Michael James *industrial engineering educator*
†Starostovic, Edward Joseph, Jr. *engineer, engineering company executive*
Stewart, Warren Earl *chemical engineer, educator*
Thesen, Arne *industrial engineering educator*
Webster, John Goodwin *biomedical engineering educator, researcher*
†Worzala, Frank John *metallurgical engineering educator and researcher*

Manitowoc
†Sfat, Michael Rudolph *biochemical engineer*

Middleton
Eriksson, Larry John *electrical engineer*

Milwaukee
Bartel, Fred Frank *consulting engineer executive*
Battocletti, Joseph Henry *electrical engineer, biomedical engineer, educator*
Boettcher, Harold Paul *engineer, educator*
Chan, Shih Hung *mechanical engineering educator, consultant*
Demerdash, Nabeel Aly Omar *electrical engineer*
Dupies, Donald Albert *civil engineer, consultant*
Gaggioli, Richard Arnold *mechanical engineering educator*
Graef, Luther William *civil engineer*
Heinen, James Albin *electrical engineering educator*
James, Charles Franklin, Jr. *engineering educator*
Landis, Fred *mechanical engineering educator*
Niederjohn, Russell James *electrical and computer engineering educator*
†Tay, Grace So *biomedical engineer, researcher*
Widera, Georg Ernst Otto *materials engineering educator, consultant*
Wilsdon, Thomas Arthur *product development engineer, administrator*
Zelazo, Nathaniel K. *engineering executive*

River Falls
Johnson, James Robert *ceramic engineer, educator*

Rothschild
Drew, Richard Allen *electrical and instrument engineer*

West Bend
Styve, Orloff Wendell, Jr. *electrical engineer*

WYOMING

Casper
Donley, Russell Lee, III *former state representative*
Hinchey, Bruce Alan *environmental engineering company executive*
Wilde, David George *electrical engineer, consultant*

Laramie
Bellamy, John Cary *civil engineer, meteorologist*
Ferris, Clifford Duras *electrical engineer, bioengineer, educator*
Long, Francis Mark *electrical engineer, educator*
Mingle, John Orville *engineer, educator, lawyer, consultant*
Rechard, Paul Albert *civil engineering consulting company executive*
Sutherland, Robert L. *engineering company executive, educator*

Wilson
Lawroski, Harry *nuclear engineer*

TERRITORIES OF THE UNITED STATES

PUERTO RICO

Catano
Behar, Abraham *construction engineer*

Mayaguez
Rodríguez-Arias, Jorge Herminio *retired agricultural engineering educator*

San Juan
Behar-Ybarra, Elias *civil, structural engineer*
Bonnet, Juan Amedee *nuclear engineer, educator*
Quiñones, Jose Antonio *structural engineer, consultant*

CANADA

ALBERTA

Calgary
†Adamache, Ion *engineer*
Glockner, Peter G. *civil and mechanical engineering educator*
Heidemann, Robert Albert *chemical engineering educator, researcher*
Kentfield, John Alan *mechanical engineering educator*
Malik, Om Parkash *electrical engineering educator, researcher*
McDaniel, Roderick Rogers *petroleum engineer*

Edmonton
Bach, Lars *wood products engineer, researcher*

Bellow, Donald Grant *mechanical engineering educator*
Koval, Don O. *electrical engineering educator*
Lock, Gerald Seymour Hunter *retired mechanical engineering educator*
McDougall, John Roland *civil engineer*
Morgenstern, Norbert Rubin *civil engineering educator*
Offenberger, Allan Anthony *electrical engineering educator*
†Otto, Fred Douglas *chemical engineering educator*
Rajotte, Ray V. *biomedical engineer, researcher*
Wayman, Morris *chemical engineering educator, consultant*

Fort Saskatchewan
†Masters, Ian *metallurgical engineer*

BRITISH COLUMBIA

Vancouver
Bennett, Winslow Wood *mechanical engineer*
Crawford, Carl Benson *retired civil engineer, government research administrator*
Grace, John Ross *chemical engineering educator*
Jull, Edward V. *electrical engineer, radio scientist, educator*
Klohn, Earle Jardine *engineering company executive, consultant*
Meisen, Axel *chemical engineer, university administrator*
Peters, Ernest *metallurgy educator, consultant*
Salcudean, Martha Eva *mechanical engineer, educator*
Wedepohl, Leonhard M. *electrical engineering educator*
Young, Lawrence *electrical engineering educator*

Victoria
Antoniou, Andreas *electrical engineering educator*
Lind, Niels Christian *civil engineering educator*

West Vancouver
†Pasini, Albert R. *engineer*

White Rock
Freeze, Roy Allan *engineering consultant*

MANITOBA

Winnipeg
Cohen, Harley *civil engineer, science educator*
Kuffel, Edmund *electrical engineering educator*
†Laliberte, Garland Everett *agricultural engineer*
Morrish, Allan Henry *electrical engineering educator*

NEW BRUNSWICK

Fredericton
†Biden, Ed *biomedical engineer, educator*
Faig, Wolfgang *survey engineer, engineering educator*
Ruthven, Douglas Morris *chemical engineering educator*

NEWFOUNDLAND

Saint John's
Clark, Jack I. *civil engineer, researcher*

NOVA SCOTIA

Halifax
Wilson, George Peter *industrial engineer*

Kentville
Baker, George Chisholm *engineering executive, consultant*

ONTARIO

Burlington
Harris, Philip John *engineering educator*
Krishnappan, Bommanna Gounder *fluid mechanics engineer*

Don Mills
Hurst, William Donald *civil engineer, consultant*

Downsview
Bakht, Baidar *civil engineer, researcher, educator*

Etobicoke
McGuigan, Thomas J. *engineering company executive*
Stojanowski, Wiktor J. *mechanical engineer*

Hamilton
Bandler, John William *electrical engineering educator, consultant*
Campbell, Colin Kydd *electrical and computer engineering educator, researcher*
Crowe, Cameron Macmillan *chemical engineering educator*

Islington
Foster, John Stanton *nuclear engineer*

Kingston
Bacon, David Walter *chemical engineering educator*
Batchelor, Barrington de Vere *civil engineer, educator*
Furter, William Frederick *chemical engineer, university dean*
Sen, Paresh Chandra *electrical engineering educator*

London
Davenport, Alan Garnett *civil engineer, educator*
Inculet, Ion I. *electrical engineering educator, consultant*
Quigley, Robert Murvin *engineering educator, research consultant*

Wilson, Gerald Einar *mechanical and industrial engineer, business executive*

North York
Buzacott, John Alan *engineering educator*

Ottawa
Cockshutt, Eric Philip *engineering executive, research scientist*
Copeland, Miles Alexander *electrical engineer educator, consultant*
Falconer, David Duncan *electrical engineering educator*
Georganas, Nicolas D. *electrical engineering educator*
Gussow, William Carruthers *petroleum engineer*
†Jambor, John L. *mining engineer*
Mayman, Shlomo Alex *engineering executive*
Mirza, Shaukat *engineering educator, researcher, consultant*
Moore, William John Myles *electrical engineer, researcher*
Rummery, Terrance Edward *nuclear engineering executive, researcher*
Seaden, George *civil engineer*

Stonbicoke
†Knipping, Hans D. *petroleum engineer*

Toronto
Balmain, Keith George *electrical engineering educator, researcher*
Cobbold, Richard Southwell Chevallier *biomedical engineer, educator*
Davison, Edward Joseph *electrical engineering educator*
Endrenyi, Janos *research engineer*
Ganczarczyk, Jerzy Jozef *civil engineering educator, wastewater treatment consultant*
Goldenberg, Andrew Avi *mechanical engineering educator*
Goring, David Arthur Ingham *chemical engineering educator, scientist*
Ham, James Milton *engineering educator*
Henderson, William Boyd *engineering executive*
Janischewskyj, Wasyl *electrical engineering educator*
Kunov, Hans *biomedical and electrical engineering educator*
MacAulay, Colin Alexander *mining engineer*
Mackiw, Vladimir Nicholaus *metallurgical consultant*
McClymont, Kenneth Ross *power systems engineer, consultant*
Meagher, George Vincent *mechanical engineer*
Rapson, William Howard *chemical engineering educator*
Rimrott, Friedrich Paul Johannes *engineer, educator*
Runnalls, (Oliver) John (Clyve) *nuclear engineering educator*
Salama, C. Andre Tewfik *electrical engineering educator*
Sedra, Adel Shafeek *electrical engineering educator, university administrator*
Semlyen, Adam *electrical engineering educator*
Slemon, Gordon Richard *electrical engineering educator*
Smith, Kenneth Carless *electrical engineering educator*
Smith, Peter William Ebblewhite *electrical engineering educator, scientist*
Venetsanopoulos, Anastasios Nicolaos *electrical engineer, educator*
Venter, Ronald Daniel *mechanical engineering educator, researcher, administrator*
Wonham, Walter Murray *electrical engineer, educator*

Waterloo
Pindera, Jerzy Tadeusz *mechanical and aeronautical engineer*
†Rempel, Garry Llewellyn *chemical engineering educator, consultant*
Sherbourne, Archibald Norbert *civil engineering educator*
Vlach, Jiri *electrical engineering educator, researcher*

Windsor
Hackam, Reuben *electrical engineering educator*

QUEBEC

Boucherville
Martel, Jacques G. *entineer, administrator*

Montreal
Alepian, Taro *engineering and construction executive*
Cameron, Alastair Duncan *engineering consultant*
Corinthios, Michael Jean George *electrical engineering educator*
Couture, Armand *civil engineer*
Dealy, John Michael *chemical engineer, educator*
Haccoun, David *electrical engineering educator*
Jonas, John Joseph *metallurgical engineering educator*
Ladanyi, Branko *civil engineer*
Lamarre, Bernard *engineering, contracting and manufacturing advisor*
Morgera, Salvatore Domenic *electrical engineering educator, researcher*
Paidoussis, Michael Pandeli *mechanical engineering educator*
Pfeiffer, J(ohn) David *mechanical engineering educator, consultant*
Ramachandran, Venkatanarayana Deekshit *electrical engineering educator*
Saint-Pierre, Guy *engineering executive*
Selvadurai, Antony Patrick Sinnappa *civil engineering educator, applied mathematician, consultant*
Shaw, Robert Fletcher *retired civil engineer*
Silvester, Peter Peet *electrical engineer, educator, consultant*
Tavenas, François *civil engineer, educator*
Terreault, R. Charles *engineer, management educator, researcher*
Yong, Raymond Nen-Yiu *civil engineering educator*
Zames, George David *electrical engineer, educator*

Quebec
La Rochelle, Pierre-Louis *civil engineering educator*
Lecours, Michel *electrical engineering educator*
Poussart, Denis Jean-Marie *electrical engineering educator, consultant*

†St-Yves, Angèle *agricultural engineer*

Sainte Anne de Belle
†Lawand, Thomas A. *research engineer*

Sainte Anne de Bellevue
Broughton, Robert Stephen *irrigation and drainage engineering educator, consultant*

Trois Rivieres
Lavallee, H.-Claude *chemical engineer, researcher*

Varennes
Bartnikas, Raymond *electrical engineer, educator*
Maruvada, Pereswara Sarma *engineering executive, researcher*

Verdun
Paré, Jean-Jacques *civil engineer, geotechnical and dam safety consultant*

SASKATCHEWAN

Regina
Mollard, John Douglas *engineering and geology executive*

Saskatoon
Billinton, Roy *engineering educator*
Gupta, Madan Mohan *engineering educator, researcher*
Kumar, Surinder *electrical engineering educator, consultant*
Sachdev, Mohindar Singh *engineering educator*

ARGENTINA

Bahia Blanca
Cardozo, Miguel Angel *telecommunications engineering educator*

BRITISH VIRGIN ISLANDS

Tortola
Green, Leon, Jr. *mechanical engineer*

CHINA

Beijing
Liang, Junxiang *aeronautics and astronautics engineer, educator*

EGYPT

Cairo
El-Hamalaway, Mohamed-Younis Abd-El-Samie *computer engineering educator*

ENGLAND

Cambridge
Hawthorne, Sir William (Rede) *aerospace and mechanical engineer, educator*

Emsworth
Suhrbier, Klaus Rudolf *hydrodynamicist, naval architect*

London
Baxendell, Sir Peter (Brian) *petroleum engineer*
Dibble, Gordon Lynch *engineering company executive*

GERMANY

Dortmund
Freund, Eckhard *electrical engineering educator*

Gottingen
Lorenz-Meyer, Wolfgang *aeronautical engineer*

GREECE

Athens
Hatzakis, Michael *electrical engineer, research executive*
Ligomenides, Panos Aristides *electrical and computer engineering educator, consultant*

HONG KONG

Kowloon
Liou, Ming-Lei *electrical engineer*

Sha Tin
Kao, Charles Kuen *electrical engineer, educator*

INDONESIA

Palembang
†Saputra, Daniel *agricultural engineering educator*

JAPAN

Hokkaido
Saito, Shuzo *electrical engineering educator*

Ibaraki
Yamada, Keiichi *engineering educator, university official*

Kanagawa
Maeda, Toshihide Munenobu *spacecraft system engineer*

Kawasaki
Taniuchi, Kiyoshi *retired mechanical engineering educator*

Kita
Ohnami, Masateru *mechanical engineering educator*

Koriyama
Ohama, Yoshihiko *architectural engineer, educator*

Nagoya
Abe, Yoshihiro *ceramic engineering educator, materials scientist*

Sendai
Sone, Toshio *acoustical engineering educator*

Shiga
Makigami, Yasuji *transportation engineering educator*

Tokyo
Aoyama, Hiroyuki *structural engineering educator*
Hori, Yukio *engineering educator, scientific association administrator*
Kaneko, Hisashi *engineering executive*
Ohe, Shuzo *chemical engineer, educator*

KOREA

Seoul
Sepulveda, Eduardo Solideo *chemical engineer*

Taejon
Kim, Sung Chul *polymer engineering educator*

MALAYSIA

Penang
Das, Kumudeswar *food and biochemical engineering educator*

THE NETHERLANDS

Roosendaal
†van Deventer, Arie Pieter *agricultural engineer*

NORWAY

Trondheim
Svaasand, Lars Othar *electronics researcher*

SAUDI ARABIA

Jeddah
Rihani, Fuad Akil *civil engineer, researcher*

SWITZERLAND

Burgdorf
Haeberlin, Heinrich Rudolf *electrical engineering educator*

TAIWAN

Chung-Li
Hong, Zuu-Chang *engineering educator*

Kaohsiung
Yeh, Kung Chie *electrical engineer*

Tainan
Chao, Yei-chin *aerospace engineering educator*
Huang, Ting-Chia *chemical engineering educator, researcher*

Taipei
Pao, Yih-Hsing *engineer, educator*

THAILAND

Bangkok
Ludwig, Harvey Fred *environmental engineer*

ADDRESS UNPUBLISHED

Allison, John McComb *retired aeronautical engineer*
Altan, Taylan *engineering educator, mechanical engineer, consultant*
Amann, Charles Albert *mechanical engineer*
Anderson, John Gaston *electrical engineer*
Anderson, Thomas Patrick *mechanical engineer, educator*
Au, Tung *civil engineer, educator, consultant*
Bartholomew, Donald Dekle *engineering executive, inventor*
Bascom, Willard Newell *research engineer, scientist*
Bates, Donald Lloyd *civil engineer, retired*
Bauer, Richard Carlton *nuclear engineer*
Beck, John Roland *environmental consultant*
Beckjord, Eric Stephen *energy researcher, nuclear engineering educator*
Berkholtz, Nicholas Evald *engineering manager, consultant*
Bers, Abraham *electrical engineering educator*
Bertin, John Joseph *aeronautical engineer, educator, researcher*
Bertolett, Craig Randolph *mechanical engineer consultant*

Bhagat, Surinder Kumar *environmental engineering educator*
Bissell, Allen Morris *engineer, consultant*
Bjorndahl, David Lee *electrical engineer*
Bloch, Erich *electrical engineer, former science foundation administrator*
Brickell, Charles Hennessey, Jr. *marine engineer, retired military officer*
Brimacombe, James Keith *metallurgical engineering educator, researcher, consultant*
Brooks, Michael Paul *urban planning educator*
Bunch, Jennings Bryan, Jr. *electrical engineer*
Burns, Richard Francis *mechanical engineer*
Bussgang, Julian Jakob *electronics engineer*
Byrd, Lloyd Garland *civil engineer*
Carreker, John Russell *retired agricultural engineer*
Carter, Hugh Clendenin *mechanical consulting engineer*
Chawla, Krishan Kumar *materials engineer, educator, consultant*
Cheston, Theodore C. *electrical engineer*
Chigier, Norman *mechanical engineering educator*
Collins, Michael *aerospace consultant, former astronaut*
Constant, Clinton *chemical engineer, consultant*
Cook, Charles Emerson *electrical engineer*
Crossley, Francis Rendel Erskine *engineering educator*
Davis, Carl George *software engineer*
Diamond, Fred I. *electronic engineer*
Di Cicco, Joseph Nicholas, Jr. *chemical engineer*
Donahoo, Melvin Lawrence *aerospace management consultant, industrial engineer*
Dull, William Martin *engineering executive*
Dyer, Ira *ocean engineering educator, consultant*
Eaglet, Robert Danton *electrical engineer, aerospace consultant, retired military officer*
East, Don Gaylord *computer engineer, archaeologist, writer*
Eaton, William Charles *retired mechanical engineer*
Edgar, Thomas Flynn *chemical engineering educator*
Edmundson, Charles Wayne *mechanical engineer, communications executive*
Eisenberg, Morris *electronics industry executive*
Ellis, Harold Bernard *civil engineer*
Eschenbrenner, Gunther Paul *engineering consultant*
Felix, Richard James *engineering executive, consultant*
Field, Charles William *metallurgical engineer, small business owner, consultant*
Finger, Harold B. *energy, space, nuclear energy and urban affairs consultant*
Fishman, Bernard *mechanical engineer*
Fleischer, Gerald Albert *industrial engineer, educator*
Fraser, Donald C. *engineering executive, educator*
Frenkiel, Richard Henry *systems engineer consultant*
Fried, Walter Rudolf *engineer, aerospace scientist*
Gens, Ralph Samuel *electrical engineering consultant*
Gerhardt, Jon Stuart *mechanical engineer, engineering educator*
Germany, Daniel Monroe *aerospace engineer*
Giardina, Paul Anthony *environmental nuclear engineer, thoroughbred horse investment specialist*
Goetzel, Claus Guenter *metallurgical engineer*
Goldberger, Arthur Earl, Jr. *industrial engineer, consultant*
Gonsalves, Robert Arthur *electrical engineering educator, consultant*
†Govier, George Wheeler *petroleum engineer*
Grandi, Attilio *engineering consultant*
Gray, Harry Joshua *electrical engineer, educator*
†Gully, John Houston *research electrical engineer, engineering director*
Hallett, William Jared *nuclear engineer*
Halpin, Daniel William *civil engineering educator, consultant*
Hammam, M. Shawky *electrical engineer, educator*
Harris, Roy Hartley *electrical engineer*
Harza, Richard Davidson *civil engineer*
Henderson, Charles Brooke *research company executive*
Herz, George Peter *chemical engineer,industrial consultant*
Hess, Ulrich Edward *electrical engineer*
Hinderliter, Richard Glenn *electrical engineer*
Hoeppner, David William *mechanical engineering educator*
Hogan, Neville John *mechanical engineering educator, consultant*
Holt, Douglas Eugene *consulting engineer, retired business executive*
Howard, Dean Denton *electrical engineer, researcher, consultant*
†Hunt, Donald Edward *planning and engineering executive*
Hutchinson, John Woodside *applied mechanics educator, consultant*
Iyer, Ravishankar Krishnan *electrical and computer engineering educator*
James, Earl Eugene, Jr. *aerospace engineering executive*
Janowiak, Robert Michael *engineering organization executive*
Jensen, Marvin Eli *retired agricultural engineer*
Johnson, Arnold Ivan *civil engineer*
Johnson, Joe William *engineering educator, consultant*
Johnson, Stewart Willard *civil engineer*
Johnston, Ralph Kennedy, Sr. *aerospace engineer*
Jordan, Howard Emerson *retired engineering executive*
Karn, Richard Wendall *civil engineer*
Karp, Sherman *aerospace consultant*
Kinsman, Frank Ellwood *engineering executive*
Kocaoglu, Dundar F. *engineering management educator, industrial and civil engineer*
Koltai, Stephen Miklos *mechanical engineer, consultant, economist, writer, educator*
Kontny, Vincent L. *engineering and construction company executive*
Korab, Arnold Alva *corporate executive*
Koseff, Jeffrey Russell *civil engineer, educator*
Kretsch, Hans Walter *retired aerospace company executive*
Kretschmer, Frank F., Jr. *electrical engineer, researcher, consultant*
Kurfess, Thomas Roland *mechanical engineering educator*
Kurth, Carl Ferdinand *electrical engineer, researcher*
Lancaster, John Howard *civil engineer*
Landgren, George Lawrence *electrical engineer, consultant*
†Leonhard, William Edward *engineering and construction company executive*
Levinson, Herbert Sherman *civil and transportation engineer*
Lipsky, Stephen Edward *engineering executive, electronic warfare engineer*
Lodge, Arthur Scott *mechanical engineering educator*
Longobardo, Anna Kazanjian *mechanical engineer*
Lovell, Walter Carl *engineer, inventor*
Lowe, John, III *consulting civil engineer*
Luger, Donald R. *engineering company executive*
Lynch, Paul Vincent *safety engineer, consultant*
Mai, Chao Chen *engineer*
Marshall, Gerald Francis *optical engineer, consultant, physicist*
Martin, Lee *mechanical engineer*
Masnari, Nino Antonio *electrical engineer, educator*
McDermott, Kevin J. *engineering educator, consultant*
McNutt, William James *consulting engineer*
Meindl, James Donald *electrical engineering educator, administrator*
Merritt, Joshua Levering, Jr. *retired engineering executive, consultant*
Meyer, Frederick Jacobs *architect*
Mitzner, Kenneth Martin *electrical engineer*
Mokhayesh, Carl *retired electrical engineer*
Moore, James Allan *agricultural engineering educator*
Morgan, James John *environmental engineering educator*
Myers, Phillip Samuel *mechanical engineering educator*
Nadel, Norman Allen *civil engineer*
Nahman, Norris Stanley *electrical engineer*
Norris, Michael R. *engineering administrator*
Olstowski, Franciszek *chemical engineer, consultant*
Ortolano, Ralph J. *engineering consultant*
Palladino, Nunzio Joseph *retired nuclear engineer*
Parente, Michael *electrical engineer*
Peltier, Eugene Joseph *civil engineer, former naval officer, business executive*
Pickering, Howard William *metallurgy engineer, educator*
Ping, David Thomas *senior project engineer*
Poch, Stephen *metallurgical engineer, consultant*
Polasek, Edward John *electrical engineer, consultant*
Pomraning, Gerald Carlton *engineering educator*
Popovich, Robert P. *biochemical engineer, educator*
Porter, Philip Thomas *retired electrical engineer*
Potvin, Alfred Raoul *engineering executive*
Rabó, Jule Anthony *chemical research administrator, consultant*
Rappaport, Theodore Scott *electrical engineering educator*
Reaves, Ray Donald *civil engineer*
Rehm, Leo Frank *civil engineer*
Reifsnider, Kenneth Leonard *metallurgist, educator*
Reitan, Daniel Kinseth *electrical and computer engineering educator*
Remer, Donald Sherwood *chemical engineer, engineering economist, educator, administrator*
Reppen, Norbjorn Dag *electrical engineer, consultant*
Roetman, Orvil M. *aerospace company executive*
Rogo, Kathleen *safety engineer*
Rohr, Davis Charles *aerospace consultant, business executive, retired air force officer*
Rosenkoetter, Gerald Edwin *engineering and construction company executive*
Rudzki, Eugeniusz Maciej *chemical engineer, consultant*
Russo, Roy Lawrence *electronic design automation engineer, retired*
Ryan, Carl Ray *electrical engineer*
Saeks, Richard Ephraim *electrical engineer*
Schachter, Max *retired engineering services company executive*
Schell, Allan Carter *electrical engineer*
Schey, John Anthony *metallurgical engineering educator*
Schrader, Henry Carl *civil engineer, consultant*
Schwinn, Donald Edwin *environmental engineer*
Scott, Charles David *chemical engineer*
Scott, Larry Marcus *aerospace engineer, mathematician*
Sears, Robert Louis *industrial engineer*
Seedlock, Robert Francis *engineering and construction company executive*
Servan-Schreiber, Jean-Jacques *engineer, author*
Shank, Maurice Edwin *aerospace engineering executive, consultant*
Shur, Michael *electrical engineer, educator, consultant*
Simpson, Murray *engineer, consultant*
Skov, Arlie Mason *petroleum engineer, consultant*
Skromme, Lawrence H. *consulting agricultural engineer*
Smally, Donald Jay *consulting engineering executive*
Smith, Joe Mauk *chemical engineer, educator*
Stumpe, Warren Robert *scientific, engineering and technical services company executive*
Tatyrek, Alfred Frank *consultant, materials/ environmental engineer, analytical and research chemist*
Templeton, Carson Howard *engineering executive, policy analyst*
Thal, Herbert Ludwig, Jr. *electrical engineer, engineering consultant*
Ting, Albert Chia *bioengineering researcher*
Toor, Herbert Lawrence *chemical engineering educator, researcher*
Tumbleson, Arthur Louis *civil engineer, contractor*
Turnbull, Fred Gerdes *electronics engineer*
Turner, Lee S., Jr. *chemical engineer,consultant, former utilities executive*
Uman, Martin Allan *electrical engineering educator, researcher, consultant*
Van Dreser, Merton Lawrence *ceramic engineer*
Varon, Dan *electrical engineer*
Vega, J. William *aerospace engineering executive, consultant*
Velzy, Charles O. *mechanical engineer*
Vickrey, Robert Edward, Jr. *petroleum engineer*
Wagner, Sigurd *electrical engineering educator, researcher*
Walkup, John Frank *electrical engineer, educator*
Walton, Harold Vincent *former agricultural engineering educator, academic administrator*
Warder, Richard Currey, Jr. *mechanical aerospace engineering educator*
Weinberger, Arnold *retired electrical engineer*
Weingarten, Joseph Leonard *aerospace engineer*
Weinschel, Bruno Oscar *engineering executive, physicist*
Wetzel, Donald Truman *engineering company executive*
Williams, Charles Wesley *technical executive, researcher*
Williams, Ronald Oscar *systems engineer*
Wilson, Basil Wrigley *oceanographic engineering consultant, artist, author*
Wood, Allen John *electrical engineer, consultant*
Woodward, Clinton Benjamin, Jr. *civil engineering educator*
Young, Leo *electrical engineer*
Yovicich, George Steven Jones *civil engineer*

FINANCE: BANKING SERVICES. *See also* FINANCE: INVESTMENT SERVICES.

UNITED STATES

ALABAMA

Birmingham
Banton, Julian Watts *banker*
Brock, Harry Blackwell, Jr. *banker*
Gilbert, Roy W., Jr. *banker*
Horsley, Richard D. *banker*
Jones, D. Paul, Jr. *banker, lawyer*
Mackin, J. Stanley *banker*
Malone, Wallace D., Jr. *bank executive*
Moor, Manly Eugene, Jr. *retired banker*
Morgan, Hugh Jackson, Jr. *bank executive*
Nichol, Victor E., Jr. *banking executive*
Northen, Charles Swift, III *banker*
Powell, William Arnold, Jr. *retired banker*
Sellers, Fred Wilson *banker*
Stone, Edmund Crispen, III *banker*
Weatherly, Robert Stone, Jr. *banker*
Woodall, Norman Eugene *banker*
Woods, John Witherspoon *banker*

Dothan
Martin, Winn Farrar *banking executive*

Huntsville
Boykin, Betty Ruth Carroll *mortgage loan officer, bank executive*

Jasper
Oliver, John Thomason, Jr. *commercial bank executive*

Mobile
Crow, James Sylvester *retired banker, railway executive*

Montgomery
Frazer, Nimrod Thompson *investment banker, financial services executive*
Gorland, Ronald Kent *bank executive*
Hoffman, Richard William *banker*
Holleman, John Albert *mortgage company executive*
†Williams, Vicki *mortgage company executive*

ALASKA

Anchorage
Cuddy, Daniel Hon *bank executive*
Harris, Roger J. *mortgage company executive, entrepreneur*
Rasmuson, Elmer Edwin *banker, former mayor*
Sorvoja, Markku *banker, accountant*

ARIZONA

Carefree
Craft, Robert Homan *banker, corporate executive*

Green Valley
Miner, Earl Howard *retired trust banker*

Phoenix
Bimson, Carl Alfred *bank executive*
Bradley, Gilbert Francis *retired banker*
Houseworth, Richard Court *banker*
Huck, Leonard William *retired banker*
Maas, Terry Leo *investment banker*
Middleton, Lowell Glenn *bank executive*

Scottsdale
Howe, H(ugh) Philip *banker*

Tubac
Miller, Frederick Robeson *banker*

Tucson
Gisi, John Joseph *banker*

ARKANSAS

Barling
Francis, Darryl Robert *former banker*

Conway
Daugherty, Billy Joe *banker*

Little Rock
Bisno, Alison Peck *investment banker*
Bowen, William Harvey *banker, lawyer*
Bradbury, Curt *bank executive*
Butler, Richard Colburn *banker, lawyer*
Gulley, Wilbur Paul, Jr. *former savings and loan executive*
Hatcher, Joe Branch *banker*
McAdams, Herbert Hall, II *banker*
Stephens, Warren A. *banking executive*

CALIFORNIA

Aptos
Dobey, James Kenneth *banker*

Arcadia
Baillie, Charles Douglas *banker*

Baldwin Park
Swartz, Stephen Arthur *banker, lawyer*

Beverly Hills
Davis, Stuart *savings and loan association executive*
Goldsmith, Bram *banker*

Burbank
Miller, Clifford Albert *merchant banker, business consultant*

Burlingame
Souter, Robert Taylor *retired banker*

Chatsworth
Montgomery, James Fischer *savings and loan association executive*

Costa Mesa
Riordan, George Nickerson *investment banker*

Escondido
Newman, Barry Ingalls *retired banker, lawyer*
O'Meara, David Collow *retired banker*

Glendale
Cross, Richard John *banker*
Trafton, Stephen J. *banking executive*

Irvine
Butler, Merrill *bank executive*
De Roes, Nanda Yvonne *banker*
Jamshidipour, Yousef *bank executive, financial consultant, financial planner and advisor*
Rady, Ernest S. *thrift and loan association executive*

Irwindale
Rinehart, Charles R. *savings and loan association executive*

La Jolla
Robbins, John Michael, Jr. *mortgage company executive*

La Mesa
Schmidt, James Craig *retired bank executive, bankruptcy examiner*

La Puente
Perret, Joseph Aloysius *banker, consultant*

Lafayette
Dethero, J. Hambright *banker*

Laguna Hills
Luhring, John William *former bank executive*

Long Beach
Hancock, John Walker, III *banker*

Los Angeles
Badie, Ronald Peter *banker*
Buchman, Mark Edward *banker*
Callender, William Lacey *savings and loan executive, lawyer*
Carson, Edward Mansfield *banker*
Cecil, John Lamont *retired bank executive, lawyer*
Dockson, Robert Ray *savings and loan executive*
†Lenard, Michael Barry *merchant banker, lawyer*
Manning, Whipple Hall *savings and loan executive, real estate finance consultant*
Marrie, Thomas Phillip *bank executive*
Martin, Ray *banker*
McKee, Kathryn Dian Grant *banker*
McLarnan, Donald Edward *banker, corporation executive*
Mc Namar, Richard Timothy *merchant banker*
Mullane, Donald A. *banker*
Siart, William Eric Baxter *banker*
Van Asperen, Morris Earl *banker*
Willison, Bruce Gray *banker*
Wu, Li-Pei *banker*

Monterey
Spitler, Lee William *banker*

Napa
Hill, Orion Alvah, Jr. *retired banker*

Newport Beach
Frederick, Dolliver H. *merchant banker*
McAlister, Maurice L. *savings and loan association executive*
†Prince, Thomas E. *bank executive*
†Prough, Stephen W. *savings and loan executive*
Rehfeldt, David John *savings and loan executive*

Oakland
Judd, James Thurston *savings and loan executive*
Kingman, Alton (Hayward), Jr. *banker*
†McCarthy, Michael Andrew *banker, lawyer*
Sandler, Herbert M. *savings and loan association executive*
Sandler, Marion Osher *savings and loan association executive*

Orange
Smith, Philip Walter *savings and loan association executive, real estate consultant*
†Sneed, Gail *mortgage company executive*
Starr, Richard William *retired banker*

Pacific Palisades
Kridel, James S. *banker*
Rode, James Dean *banker*

Palos Verdes Estates
Yamaguchi, Tamotsu *bank executive*

Pasadena
Deihl, Richard Harry *savings and loan association executive*
Patton, Richard Weston *mortgage company executive*
Smith, Richard Howard *banker*
Ulrich, Peter Henry *banker*
Vaughn, John Vernon *banker, industrialist*

Pebble Beach
Burkett, William Andrew *banker*

Piedmont
Hoover, Robert Cleary *retired bank executive*

Rancho Cordova
Ling, Robert Malcolm *banker, publishing executive*

Redwood City
Russell, Charles T. *bank executive*

Riverside
†Crebs, Raymond Lee *mortgage banking executive*

Sacramento
†Cirona, James Michael *banker*
Cox, David W. *bank executive*
Hoagland, Dennis Roy *trust banker, financial consultant*

San Bernardino
MacCauley, Hugh Bournonville *banker*

San Diego
Binkley, Nicholas Burns *banking executive*
Blakemore, Claude Coulehan *banker*
Kendrick, Ronald H. *banker*
Mills, Lorna Henrietta *banker*
Moody, Rhea Phenon *banking executive*
Reinhard, Christopher John *merchant banking company executive*
Villani, Kevin Emil *banker*
Wiesler, James Ballard *retired banker*
Yacovone, Ellen Elaine *banker*

San Francisco
August-deWilde, Katherine *banker*
Barron, Patrick Kenneth *bank executive*
Baumhefner, Clarence Herman *banker*
Bee, Robert Norman *banker*
Bloch, Julia Chang *bank executive, former government official*
Bolin, William Harvey *banker*
Coombe, George William, Jr. *banker, lawyer*
Demarest, David Franklin, Jr. *banker, former government official*
Eckersley, Norman Chadwick *banker*
Gomi, Yasumasa *bank executive*
Gordon, Roger L. *savings and loan association executive*
Hazen, Paul Mandeville *banker*
Ikagawa, Tadaichi *banking executive*
†Larrouilh, Michel *banker*
Lindh, Patricia Sullivan *banker, former government official*
Luikart, John Ford *investment banker*
McLin, Stephen T. *investment banker*
†Mehta, Shailesh J. *banker*
Meyer, Donald Robert *banker, lawyer*
Otto, George John *investment banker*
Parry, Robert Troutt *bank executive, economist*
Peterson, Rudolph A. *banker*
Readmond, Ronald Warren *investment banking firm executive*
Rosenberg, Richard Morris *banker*
Schmidt, Chauncey Everett *banker*
Stewart, Samuel B. *banker, lawyer*
Taylor, Glenhall E. *banker*
Trowbridge, Thomas, Jr. *mortgage banking company executive*
Warner, Harold Clay, Jr. *banker, investment management executive*
Williams, Morgan Lloyd *retired investment banker*
Young, William Victor *banker*

San Mateo
Balles, John Joseph *banker, business consultant*
Brubaker, John E. *bank executive*

Santa Ana
Potter, Charles Arthur, Jr. *trust company executive*

Santa Barbara
Anderson, Donald Meredith *bank executive*
Tilton, David Lloyd *savings and loan association executive*

Santa Fe Springs
Popejoy, William J. *savings and loan association executive*

Santa Monica
Barren, Bruce Willard *merchant banker*
†Heimbuch, Babette E. *bank executive*
Morgan, Monroe *retired savings and loan executive*
Mortensen, William S. *banking executive*
Weil, Leonard *banker*

Stockton
Antoci, Mario *savings and loan company executive*
Barnum, Robert T. *bank executive*

Walnut Creek
McGrath, Don John *banker*
Rhody, Ronald Edward *banker, communications executive*

COLORADO

Boulder
Martin, Phillip Dwight *banking consulting company executive, mayor*

Colorado Springs
Gillaspie, Richard C. *banker*
Olin, Kent Oliver *banker*

Denver
Grant, William West, III *banker*
Krane, Robert Alan *banker*
Malone, Robert Joseph *bank executive*
†Moore, Ronald L. *bank executive*
Nicholson, Will Faust, Jr. *bank holding company executive*
Rockwell, Bruce McKee *retired banker, retired foundation executive*
Sanders-Childears, Linda *banker*
Silburn, Elaine Gwendolyn *banker*

Englewood
Rosser, Edwin Michael *mortgage company executive*
Sims, Doug *bank executive*

Fowler
Fox, Maxine Randall *banker*

Lakewood
Orullian, B. LaRae *bank executive*

Pueblo
Horn, Thomas Carl *retired banker*

CONNECTICUT

Avon
Rutland, George Patrick *banker*

Bridgeport
Carson, David Ellis Adams *banker*
DelGrego, Andrew August *banker*
Goodspeed, Norwick Royall Givens *banker*
Jacobsen, Daniel Tower *banker*

Darien
Mapel, William Marlen Raines *retired banking executive*

Fairfield
Brett, Arthur Cushman, Jr. *banker*
Jewitt, David Willard Pennock *retired banker*

Greenwich
Dianis, Walter Joseph *retired banker*
Egbert, Richard Cook *retired banker*
Massey, James L. *investment banker*
Moller, William Richard, Jr. *banker*
Woelflein, Kevin Gerard *banker*

Hamden
Williams, Edward Gilman *retired banker*

Hartford
Knisel, Russell H. *banker*
Kraus, Eileen S. *bank executive*
Lipp, Robert I. *bank holding company executive*
Overstrom, Gunnar S., Jr. *banker*

Middletown
Stevens, Robert Edwin *bank executive, former insurance company executive*

New Canaan
de Selding, Edward Bertrand *retired banker*
Dillon, James McNulty *retired banker*

New Haven
Behan, Robert Francis *bank executive*
Cottrell, Mary-Patricia Tross *banker*
Morriss, George W. *banking executive*

New London
Creviston, Richard L. *banker*

Newtown
Verano, Anthony Frank *retired banker*

Norfolk
Vagliano, Alexander Marino *banker*

Stamford
Philipps, Edward William *banker, real estate appraiser*
Verrico, Ernest Joseph *banker*

Washington Depot
Hardee, William Covington *banker, lawyer*

Waterbury
Narkis, Robert Joseph *bank executive, lawyer*

West Hartford
Miller, Elliott Cairns *retired bank executive, lawyer*
Newell, Robert Lincoln *retired banker*

Weston
Lindsay, Charles Joseph *banker*

Whitneyville
Miller, Walter Richard, Jr. *banker*

DELAWARE

Dover
Moran, Joseph Milbert *retired banker*

Newark
Cawley, Charles M. *banker*
Cochran, John R. *bank executive*
Enlow, Fred Clark *banker*
Kaufman, M(ichael) Scot *bank executive*
Wright, Vernon Hugh Carroll *bank executive*

Wilmington
Cecala, Ted Thomas, Jr. *banker, accountant*
Porter, John Francis, III *banker*
†Quill, Leonard Walter *banker*
St. Clair, Jesse Walton, Jr. *retired savings and loan executive*

DISTRICT OF COLUMBIA

Washington
Adams, Paul G. *bank executive*
†Aguirre-Sacasa, Francisco Xavier *international banker*
Andringa, Calvin Bruce *investment banker*
Applegarth, Paul Vollmer *investment banking and finance executive*
†Baxter, Nevins Dennis *bank consultant*
Bibby, Douglas Martin *mortgage association executive*
Coreth, Joseph Herman *bank executive*
Coughlin, Timothy Crathorne *bank executive*
Dame, William Page, III *bank executive, educational administrator*
D'Aniello, Daniel *merchant banker*
DuCran, Claudette Deloris *bank officer*
Fitts, C. Austin *investment banker, former federal agency administrator*
Fitz-Hugh, Glassell Slaughter, Jr. *bank executive*
Gilbert, Jackson B. *banker*
Hawley, Frederick William, III *bank executive, former federal official*
Iglesias, Enrique V. *bank executive, former government minister*
Jaycox, Edward Van Kleeck *bank executive*
Kesterman, Frank Raymond *investment banker*
Lasko, Warren Anthony *mortgage banker, economist*
Marsh, Quinton Neely *banker*
Mathias, Edward Joseph *merchant banker*
Mc Namara, Robert Strange *former banking executive, cabinet member*
†Meehan, John J. *mortgage company executive*
Miller, G(eorge) William *merchant banker, business executive*
Petty, John Robert *banker*
Preston, Lewis Thompson *banker*
Raines, Franklin Delano *investment banker*
Riley, Joseph Harry *retired banker*
Robinson, Daniel Baruch *banker*
Rodriguez, Rita Maria *bank executive*
Roley, Jerry *bank executive*
Rotberg, Eugene Harvey *investment banker, lawyer*
Seelig, Steven Alfred *government financial executive*
Smilow, Michael A. *mortgage company excecutive*
Stevenson, Eric Van Cortlandt *mortgage banker, real estate executive, lawyer*

FLORIDA

Boca Raton
Cannon, Herbert Seth *investment banker*

Bonita Springs
Birky, John Edward *banker, consultant, financial advisor*

Boynton Beach
Jacobs, C. Bernard *banker*

Clearwater
Gilgar, Arthur Emery *bank executive*

Coral Gables
Gutierrez, Jose Ramon *bank executive*

Dunedin
Rosa, Raymond Ulric *retired banker*

Fort Lauderdale
Levi, Kurt *retired banker*
†Waters, M. Jean *mortgage company executive*
†Waters, Richard W., Sr. *mortgage company executive*

Fort Myers
Idelson, Charles K. *bank executive*

Holmes Beach
Browning, Henry Prentice *banker*

Jacksonville
Ernest, Albert Devery, Jr. *banker*
Lane, Edward Wood, Jr. *retired banker*
Lastinger, Allen Lane, Jr. *banker*
Rice, Charles Edward *banker*
Rishel, Richard Clinton *banker*
Watford, John Hardin *bank executive*

Jupiter
Holbert, Theodore Frank *banker*

Lake Worth
Finch, Ronald M., Jr. *savings bank executive*

Maitland
Fichthorn, Luke Eberly, III *investment banker*

Miami
Barnes, Donald Winfree *banker*
Brownell, Edwin Rowland *banker, civil engineer, land surveyor and mapper*
Cooper, Thomas Astley *banking executive*
Courshon, Arthur Howard *banker, lawyer*
Giller, Norman Myer *banker, architect, author*
Holtz, Abel *bank executive*
Holtz, Daniel Martin *banker*
Kanter, Joseph Hyman *banker, community developer*
Ream, John K. *banker*
Rebozo, Charles Gregory *banker*
Scheinberg, Steven Eliot *investment banker*
Smathers, Frank, Jr. *banker, horticulturist*
Stuzin, Charles Bryan *savings and loan association executive*
Taylor, Stephen Dewitt *savings and loan association executive*
Weiner, Morton David *banker, insurance agent*
Wessel, Jeffrey Hall *bank executive*
Wilson, Milner Bradley, III *banker*

Naples
Craighead, Rodkey *banker*
Hooper, John Allen *retired banker*
Kley, John Arthur *banker*
Martinuzzi, Leo Sergio, Jr. *banker*

North Palm Beach
Connor, John Thomas *retired bank and corporate executive, lawyer*

Ocala
Andrews, Richard L. *bank executive*

Orange Park
Kirkwood, Maurice Richard *banker*

Orlando
Hoepner, Theodore John *banker*
McNulty, Chester Howard *bank holding company executive*

Palm Beach
Curry, Bernard Francis *former banker, consultant*
Levine, Laurence Brandt *investment banker*

Pompano Beach
Kester, Stewart Randolph *banker*

Ponte Vedra Beach
McMullan, William Patrick, Jr. *banker*
O'Brien, Raymond Vincent, Jr. *banker*

Saint Petersburg
Ogletree, Thomas Vincent *savings and loan association executive*
Zahorian, Stephen Glen *banker*

Santa Rosa Beach
Wright, John Peale *retired banker*

Sarasota
Angelotti, Richard H. *science administrator, banker*
Jacobs, Debra McQuaig *banker*
Page, George Keith *banker*

South Miami
Benbow, John Robert *banker*

Sun City Center
Sevold, Gordon James *savings and loan executive*

Tampa
Koehn, George Waldemar *bank executive*
Mirro, Richard Allen *bank executive*

Temple Terrace
Rink, Wesley Winfred *banker*

Tequesta
Turrell, Richard Horton, Sr. *retired banker*

Vero Beach
Berkovitch, Boris S. *retired trust company executive*
Riley, Randy James *banker*
Sheehan, Charles Vincent *investment banker*
Slater, George Richard *retired banker*

West Palm Beach
Lynch, William Walker *savings and loan association executive*
O'Brien, Robert Brownell, Jr. *investment banker, consultant, savings bank executive, yacht broker*
†Strickland, R. Michael *bank executive*

GEORGIA

Atlanta
†Ash, Thomas Gray *banker*
Boland, Thomas Edwin *banker*
Brandt, Harry *federal reserve bank executive*
Brown, Bennett Alexander *former banker*
†Carothers, Rick *mortgage company executive*
Chapman, Hugh McMaster *banker*
Flinn, Patrick L. *bank executive*
Forrestal, Robert Patrick *banker, lawyer*
Hall, Jesse Seaborn *banker*
Hollis, Charles Eugene, Jr. *savings and loan association executive*
Hutchins, Ralph Edwin, Jr. *banker*
McIntyre, John William *banker*
Miller, William Frederick *trust company executive*
Snelling, George Arthur *banker*
Spiegel, John William *banker*
Tschinkel, Sheila Lerner *banker, economist*
VanLandingham, William Jennings *banker*
Williams, James Bryan *banker*
Williams, John Young *merchant banker*

Decatur
Mc Mahan, Robert Chandler *savings and loan association executive*

Douglas
Palmer, Timothy Jackson *bank executive*

Savannah
Bell, William Henry, Jr. *banker*

Sea Island
LaWare, John Patrick *retired banker, federal official*

Smyrna
†Rineheart, Gary *mortgage company executive*

Snellville
Carlson, Roy Perry Merritt *retired banker*

Tucker
Smith, Leroy, Jr. *bank executive*

HAWAII

Honolulu
Dods, Walter Arthur, Jr. *bank executive*
Hoag, John Arthur *retired bank executive*
Horner, Donald Gordon *banker*
Johnson, Lawrence M. *banker*
Midkiff, Robert Richards *financial and trust company executive, consultant*
Stephenson, Herman Howard *banker*
Wolff, Herbert Eric *banker, former army officer*
Wong, Henry Li-Nan *bank executive, economist*

IDAHO

Boise
Jones, D. Michael *banker*
Keane, Edmund J., Jr. *banker*
Speer, William Thomas, Jr. *banker, investor, consultant, rancher*

ILLINOIS

Batavia
Schilling, Arlo Leonard *bank executive*

Blue Island
Kollmann, Hilda Hanna *banker*

Champaign
Froom, William Watkins *banker*

Chicago
Bakwin, Edward Morris *banker*
Barrow, Charles Herbert *investment banker*
Bartter, Brit Jeffrey *investment banker*
Bouchard, Craig Thomas *international banker*
Brennan, Richard Snyder *bank executive, lawyer*
Croisant, Eugene R. *banker*
Dancewicz, John Edward *investment banker*
Darr, Milton Freeman, Jr. *banker*
deGrijs, Leo Charles *banker*
Doyle, Daniel M. *bank executive*
Eddy, David Latimer *banker*
Finch, David S. *banker*
Finley, Harold Marshall *investment banker*
Fox, David Wayne *banker*
Franke, Richard James *investment banker*
Ginley, Thomas J. *banker*
Goldberg, Sherman I. *banking company executive*
Heagy, Thomas Charles *banker*
Hollis, Donald Roger *banker*
Huber, Richard Leslie *banker*
Jahns, Adam A. *banking executive*
Johnson, Chauncey Paul *banker*
Keehn, Silas *retired bank executive*
Kinzie, Raymond Wyant *banker, lawyer*
Klapperich, Frank Lawrence, Jr. *investment banker*
Lecker, Abraham *former banker*
Lorenz, Katherine Mary *banker*
Massolo, Arthur James *banker*
Mc Kay, Neil *banker*
Mitchell, Douglas Farrell *trust company executive, lawyer*
Montgomery, Charles Howard *retired bank executive*
Morgan, Howard Campbell *banker*
Mullin, Leo Francis *banker*
Murray, Michael J. *bank executive*
Neal, John Eric *banking executive*
O'Connell, Harold Patrick, Jr. *banker*
Pollock, Alexander John *banker*
Rahe, Maribeth Sembach *bank executive*
Roberts, Theodore Harris *banker*
Rowen, Robert G. *savings and loan executive*
Schroeder, Charles Edgar *banker, investment management executive*
Scully, Joseph C. *bank executive*
Shanahan, Edmond Michael *savings and loan executive*
Socolofsky, Jon Edward *banker*
Stirling, James Paulman *investment banker*
Theobald, Thomas Charles *banker*
Thomas, Richard Lee *banker*
Trukenbrod, William Sellery *banker*
Ulbricht, Robert E. *savings and loan executive, lawyer*
Vander Wilt, Carl Eugene *banker*
West, Byron Kenneth *banker*
Williams, Edward Joseph *banker*

Deerfield
Foght, James Loren *banker*

Des Plaines
Kubalanza, Ronald J. *bank executive*

Fox River Grove
Abboud, Alfred Robert *banker, consultant, investor*

Glenview
Kramer, Ferdinand *mortgage banker*

Highwood
Brown, Lawrence Haas *banker*

Hinsdale
Kinney, Kenneth Parrish *banker, retired*

Hoffman Estates
Weston, Roger Lance *banker*

Joliet
Barber, Andrew Bollons *bank executive*

Kenilworth
Corrigan, John Edward, Jr. *banker, lawyer*

Lake Bluff
Anderson, Roger E. *bank executive*

Matteson
Yager, Vincent Cook *banker*

Northbrook
Gardner, Marshall Allen *merchant banker*

Northfield
Edelson, Ira J. *venture banker*

Palatine
Fitzgerald, Gerald Francis *retired banker*

Rockford
Meuleman, Robert Joseph *banker*

Springfield
Ferguson, Mark Harmon *banker, lawyer*
Hudson, Claude Earl *banker*
Lohman, Walter Rearick *banker*

INDIANA

Columbus
Abts, Henry William *banker*
Nash, John Arthur *bank executive*

Evansville
Hargrave, Robert Webb *banker*
†Mitchell, Daniel Wertz *banking executive*

Fort Wayne
Bender, Linda Arlene *bank officer*
Shaffer, Paul E. *banker*
†Waterfield, Richard Dallas *bank executive, mortgage company executive*

Indianapolis
Dietz, William Ronald *financial services executive*
Frenzel, Otto N., III *banker*
Givens, David W. *banker*
Heger, Martin L. *bank executive*
Massey, James D. *bank holding company executive*
Paine, Andrew J., Jr. *banker*
Risk, John Fred *banker, investment banker*

Lafayette
Howarth, David H. *retired bank executive*

Muncie
Anderson, Stefan Stolen *bank executive*
Sursa, Charles David *banker*

Portage
Gasser, Wilbert (Warner), Jr. *retired banker*

South Bend
Raclin, Ernestine Morris *banker*

Terre Haute
Smith, Donald Eugene *banker*

Vincennes
Rose, Robert Carlisle *banker*

Zionsville
Meyer, William Michael *mortgage banking executive*

IOWA

Adel
Garst, Elizabeth *bank executive*

Bettendorf
Shenk, John Christian, Jr. *retired savings bank executive*

Burlington
Grinde, Douglas *banker*

Cedar Rapids
Wax, Nadine Virginia *retired banker*

Clinton
Weil, Myron *retired banker*

Johnston
Steele, Betty Louise *retired banker*

Schaller
Currie, James Morton *bank executive*

Sioux City
Hagen, R. E. *bank executive*

KANSAS

Leawood
Ballard, John William, Jr. *banker*

Manhattan
Stolzer, Leo William *bank executive*

Overland Park
†Browning, Roy Wilson, III *mortgage banking executive*
Dore, James Francis *financial services executive*
Linn, James Herbert *retired banker*

Pratt
Loomis, Howard Krey *banker*

Shawnee Mission
McEachen, Richard Edward *banker, lawyer*
†Reichert, Patricia *mortgage company executive*
Widder, Willard Graves *retired banker*

Topeka
Dicus, John Carmack *savings and loan association executive*
Johnson, Arnold William *mortgage company executive*

Wichita
Bunten, William Daniel *banker*
Jabara, Francis Dwight *merchant banker, educator, entrepreneur*
†Rhodes, Darryl W. *bank executive*

KENTUCKY

Lexington
Nyere, Robert Alan *banker*

Louisville
†Boyd, Morton *banker*
Chancey, Malcolm B., Jr. *bank executive*
Davis, Harry Scott, Jr. *banker*
†Guillaume, Raymond Kendrick *banker*
Hower, Frank Beard, Jr. *retired banker*
Phelps, Joseph William *banker*
Tyrrell, Gerald Gettys *banker*

Marrowbone
Clark, Betty Pace *banking executive*

LOUISIANA

Alexandria
Bolton, Robert Harvey *banker*

Baton Rouge
Griffin, G. Lee *banker*
Moyse, Hermann, Jr. *banker*
Urban, Gilbert William *banker*
Watson, J(ames) Hugh *banker*

Covington
Blossman, Alfred Rhody, Jr. *banker*

Lafayette
Stuart, Walter Bynum, III *banker*

Lake Charles
Lawton, William Burton *bank executive*

New Orleans
Arnof, Ian *banker*
Beason, Amos Theodore *banker*
Clayton, Paul David *savings and loan executive*
Milling, R(oswell) King *bank executive, lawyer*
Wakefield, Benton McMillin, Jr. *banker*

MAINE

Andover
Ellis, George Hathaway *retired banker and utility company executive*

Bangor
Bullock, William Clapp, Jr. *banker*

Bristol
Schmidt, Thomas Carson *international development banker*

Cumb Foreside
Harper, Ralph Champlin *retired banker*

Portland
Bonney, Weston Leonard *bank executive*
†Burns, Robert E. *bank executive*
Grosset, Alexander Donald, Jr. *banker*
Ryan, William J. *bank executive*
Saufley, William Edward *banker, lawyer*

MARYLAND

Annapolis
Schleicher, Nora Elizabeth *banker, treasurer, accountant*
Weitzel, Harry John, Jr. *banker*

Baltimore
Baldwin, Henry Furlong *banker*
Barber, John Merrell *banker*
Bramble, Frank P. *bank executive*
Cole, Charles W., Jr. *bank holding company executive*
Couper, William *banker*
Dodge, Douglas Walker *banker*
Graham, Jerry Fisher *bank executive, accountant*
Hale, Danny Lyman *bank executive*
Harvey, Robert Dixon Hopkins *banker*
Liberto, Joseph Salvatore *banker*
McGuire, Charles Carroll, Jr. *banking executive*
McGuirk, Ronald Charles *banker*
Morrel, William Griffin, Jr. *banker*
Murray, Joseph William *banker*
Peck, James Stevenson *banker*
Price, Leigh *banker*
Rank, Larry Gene *executive director*
Ray, Robert Franklin *banker*
Schaefer, Robert Wayne *banker*
Shattuck, Mayo Adams, III *investment banking executive*
†Williams, Richard F. *banker*
Wood, Howard Graham *banker*

Bethesda
Comings, William Daniel, Jr. *mortgage banker, housing development executive*

Chestertown
Williams, Henry Thomas *retired banker, real estate agent*

Cheverly
Lockyer, Charles Warren, Jr. *corporate executive*

Chevy Chase
Broumas, John George *retired banker, retired theatre owner*
Saul, B. Francis, II *bank executive*

Columbia
†Potts, Thomas H. *trust company executive*

Crownsville
Wright, Harry Forrest, Jr. *retired banker*

Easton
Belmont, August *investment banker*

Elkton
Harrington, Benjamin Franklin, III *business consultant*

Ellicott City
Faulstich, Albert Joseph *banking consultant*

Frederick
Hoff, Charles Worthington, III *banker*

Laurel
†Springer, Jeffrey R. *bank officer*
†Ward, James D. *bank executive building material executive*

Potomac
Schonholtz, Joan Sondra Hirsch *banker, civic worker*

Rockville
Meyer, F. Weller *bank executive*

Sparks Glencoe
†Swackhamer, Gene L. *bank executive*

Stevenson
Schnering, Philip Blessed *investment banker*

MASSACHUSETTS

Boston
Alden, Vernon Roger *corporate director, trustee*
Beal, Ilene *bank executive*
Beinhocker, Gilbert David *investment banker*
Berg, Warren Stanley *retired banker*
Blampied, Peter J. *banker*
Breitman, Leo R. *banker*
Brown, William L. *banker*
Costellese, Linda E. Grace *banker*
Crozier, William Marshall, Jr. *bank holding company executive*
Curry, John Michael *investment banker*
Driver, William Raymond, Jr. *banker*
Fesus, George John *banker*
Finnegan, Neal Francis *banker*
Gifford, Charles Kilvert *banker*
Gordon, Ralph Dearing *bank executive*
Gulley, Joan Long *banker*
Hamill, John P. *bank executive*
Harrison, Carter Henry *banker*
Hill, Richard Devereux *retired banker*
Laine, Richard R. *banking executive*
Little, Arthur Dehon *investment banker*
Lonkart, Georgia Faith *banker*
Maher, Peter Sutton *banker*
Mc Kinnon, Alan Leo *banker*
Monrad, Ernest Ejner *trust company executive*
Mulligan, Gerald Thomas *banker*
Nutt, William James *investment, management and mutual funds company executive*
Phillips, Daniel Anthony *trust company executive*
Ray, William F. *banker*
Regan, Peter John *banker*
Schrader, William Cutler *banker*
†Solomon, David *investment banker*
Stepanian, Ira *banker*
Tempel, Jean C. *bank executive*
Vermilye, Peter Hoagland *banker*
Vineburgh, James Hollander *banking executive*
Williams, Charles Marvin *commercial banking educator*

Burlington
Mosher, Giles Edmund, Jr. *banker*

Cambridge
Edgerly, William Skelton *banker*
Holmes, Michael Denison *trust company executive*

Cohasset
Sewall, Tingey Haig *banker*

Dover
Aldrich, Frank Nathan *bank executive*
Crittenden, Gazaway Lamar *retired banker*
Stockwell, Ernest Farnham, Jr. *banker*

Lexington
Fallon, John Golden *banker*
Lawton, Eugene Alfred *banking executive*

Longmeadow
Lo Bello, Joseph David *banking executive*

Lynn
Lukowski, Stanley J. *banker*
Stark, Dennis Edwin *banker*

Manchester
Bundy, Harvey Hollister *retired bank executive*

Marstons Mills
Wheeler, Richard Warren *banker*

Medford
Sloane, Marshall M. *banker*

New Bedford
McCarter, Robert *banking executive*

North Quincy
Allinson, A. Edward *banking executive*

Richmond
Curtiss, Trumbull Cary *banker*

Rockport
Cotter, Joseph Francis *bank officer*

Waltham
Riley, Henry Charles *banker*

Weston
Aquilino, Daniel *banker*

Winchester
Brennan, Francis Patrick *banker*

Worcester
Cabot, Harold *banker*
Hunt, John David *retired banker*
Spencer, Harry Irving, Jr. *retired banker*

MICHIGAN

Ann Arbor
Delonis, Robert Joseph *bank executive*
Freeth, Douglas Duncan *banker*
†Weber, Roy Edwin *savings and loan association executive*

Bay City
Van Dyke, Clifford Craig *retired banker*

Bloomfield Hills
Colladay, Robert S. *trust company executive, consultant*
Houston, E. James, Jr. *bank officer*

Rusin, Edward A. *bank executive*

Detroit
Betanzos, Louis *banker*
Fisher, Charles Thomas, III *banker*
Harling, Carlos Gene *savings and loan executive*
Istock, Verne George *banker*
Jeffs, Thomas Hamilton, II *banker*
Miller, Eugene Albert *banker*
Surdam, Robert McClellan *retired banker*
Walton, Jonathan Taylor *banker*

Elk Rapids
Briggs, Robert Peter *banker*

Farmington
†Booth, Eric D. *bank executive*
Mylod, Robert Joseph *banker*
†Richards, Robert W. *mortgage company executive*

Farmington Hills
Heiss, Richard Walter *banker, consultant*

Flint
Piper, Mark Harry *retired banker*

Frankfort
Foster, Robert Carmichael *banker*

Grand Rapids
Canepa, John Charles *banking executive*
Sadler, Robert Livingston *banker*
†Wagner, David James *banker*

Grosse Pointe
Couzens, Frank, Jr. *banker*
Richardson, Dean Eugene *retired banker*
Thurber, Cleveland, Jr. *trust banker*

Kalamazoo
Holland, Harold Herbert *banker*
Klein, Richard Dean *banker*
McCarty, Theodore Frederick *banker*
Smith, Daniel R. *bank holding company executive*

Monroe
Keck, Merel Fogg *bank executive*

Saginaw
Evans, Harold Edward *banker*

Southgate
Brodhun, Andrew R. *banker*

Suttons Bay
Whitney, William Chowning *retired banker, financial consultant*

Troy
Fellingham, David Andrew *mortgage banker*
Leach, Ralph F. *banker*
Ricketts, Thomas Roland *bank executive*

MINNESOTA

Chanhassen
Severson, Roger Allan *bank executive*

Eden Prairie
Hanson, Dale S. *banker*

Excelsior
Rich, Willis Frank, Jr. *banker*

Minneapolis
Andreas, David Lowell *banker*
Campbell, James Robert *banker*
Cooper, William Allen *banking executive*
Deming, Frederick Lewis *banker*
Dove, William Edwin *banker*
Gainor, Thomas Edward *banker*
Grundhofer, John F. *banker*
Hetland, James Lyman, Jr. *banker, lawyer, educator*
Huston, Beatrice Louise *banker*
†Jensen, Robert P. *investment banking executive*
Johnson, Lloyd Peter *banker*
Kovacevich, Richard M. *banker*
Morrison, Clinton *banker*
Rahn, Alvin Albert *former banker*
Rohr, Daniel C. *banker*
Swanson, Lloyd Oscar *former savings and loan association executive*
Walters, Glen Robert *banker*
Walters, Jay B. *banker*
Webster, Melville Jay, III *bank executive*

Saint Paul
Bjorklund, Frederick *savings and loan association executive*
†White, Duane E. *mortgage company executive*

MISSISSIPPI

Gulfport
Hinkle, Walter C., Jr. *banker*
Pickering, Shelbie Jean *mortgage loan executive*
Schloegel, George Anthony *banker*
Seal, Leo William, Jr. *banker*
Thatcher, George Robert *banker*

Jackson
†Day, Frank R. *bank executive*
McMillan, Howard Lamar, Jr. *banker*
Robinson, E. B., Jr. *bank executive*
Sewell, Charles Haslett *banker*
Tullos, John Baxter *banker*
†Wilder, Margaret T. *bank holding company executive*

Monticello
Allen, Frank Carroll *retired banker*

Tupelo
Patterson, Aubrey Burns, Jr. *banker*
Smith, John Willis *banker*

MISSOURI

Jefferson City
Cook, Sam B. *banker*

Kansas City
Aslin, M. M. *banker*
Brown, John O. *banker*
Crider, Stephen Wayne *banker, lawyer*
†Genovese, Peter J. *banker*
Hendrickson, Marshall David *banker*
Hoenig, Thomas M. *bank executive*
Kemper, David Woods, II *banker*
Kemper, James Madison, Jr. *banker*
Kemper, Rufus Crosby, Jr. *banker*
Murdock, Stuart Laird *banker, investment adviser*
Pendleton, Barbara Jean *retired banker*
Reiter, Robert Edward *banker*
Skahan, Paul L(aurence) *bank executive, lawyer*
Vaughan, Kirk William *banker*
†Wells, J. Lyle, Jr. *bank executive*

Nevada
Morton, John, III *banker*

Saint Joseph
Sprong, Gerald Rudolph *banker*

Saint Louis
Andes, G. Thomas *banker*
Babb, Ralph Wheeler, Jr. *banker*
Badgley, William S. *multi-bank holding company executive*
Barksdale, Clarence Caulfield *banker*
Bealke, Linn Hemingway *bank executive*
Bowen, James Ronald *banker*
Bryant, Ruth Alyne *banker*
Craig, Andrew Billings, III *bank holding company executive*
Farrell, Neal Joseph *banker*
†Gilcrest, James P. *mortgage banker*
Gray, Walter Franklin *retired banker*
Hayes, Samuel Banks, III *banking company executive*
†Horner, Robert David *mortgage banking executive*
Jacobsen, Thomas H(erbert) *banker*
James, William W. *banker*
Kling, S(tephen) Lee *banker*
Leonard, Eugene Albert *banker*
MacCarthy, John Peters *banker*
†Rosenberg, Kim David *banker*
Siteman, Alvin Jerome *banker*
Stoecker, David Thomas *banker*
Walker, Dale Rush *banker*

Springfield
McCartney, N.L. *investment banker*

Warrensburg
Harmon, Lynn Adrian *banker*

NEBRASKA

Lincoln
Stuart, James *banker, broadcaster*
Young, Dale Lee *banker*

Omaha
Fitzgerald, William Allingham *savings and loan association executive*
†Giltner, F. P. *bank executive*
Lauritzen, John Ronnow *banker*
Miller, Morris Folsom *banker*

NEVADA

Las Vegas
Mack, Jerome D. *banker*
†Randall, William *bank executive*
Troidl, Richard John *banker*

Reno
Binns, James Edward *banker*
Day, Kevin Thomas *banker, community services director*

NEW HAMPSHIRE

Concord
Rogers, David H. *banker*

Hanover
Paganucci, Paul Donnelly *banker, lawyer, former college official*
Weiss, Ira Francis *retired banker*

Lancaster
Drapeau, Phillip David *banking executive*

Manchester
†O'Brien, L. Douglas *banking executive*
Thurber, Cleveland, Jr. *trust banker*

NEW JERSEY

Bordentown
Walther, John Henry *banker*

Bridgewater
Lewis, Donald Emerson *banker*

Chatham
Feeney, John Robert *banker*
Sayles, Thomas Dyke, Jr. *banker*

Cherry Hill
Simmerman, Gary F. *bank executive*

Cinnaminson
Johnson, Victor Lawrence *banker*

Clifton
Magnus, Frederick Samuel *investment banker*

Colts Neck
French, Charles Ferris, Jr. *banker*

East Brunswick
Georgantas, Aristides William *banking executive*

East Windsor
Phelan, Richard Paul *trust company executive*

Edison
Parker, Barbara Z. *bank executive*
†Peraino, Roy T. *banker*
Scheuring, Garry Joseph *banker*
Silberstein, Alan Mark *banker*
Sullivan, Cornelius Francis, Jr. *banking executive*

Egg Harbor City
Dittenhafer, Brian Douglas *banker, economist*
Hamilton, Thomas Herman *savings and loan association executive*

Elizabeth
Leonett, Anthony Arthur *banker*

Florham Park
Monks, Donald Richard *banker*

Glen Rock
Blackin, Jack Milton *banker*
Shell, Glenn Harmen *bank executive*

Jersey City
Howard, Stanley Louis *investment banker*
Nash, Lee J. *banker*
Tugwell, John *bank executive*
Tymon, Leo F., Jr. *banker*

Lawrenceville
Terracciano, Anthony Patrick *banker*

Livingston
Zappulla, Lawrence Joseph *bank executive*

Montclair
Pierson, Robert David *banker*

Montvale
Sbarbaro, Robert Arthur *banker*

Morristown
Simon, William Edward *investment banker, former secretary of treasury*

Mountain Lakes
Turnheim, Palmer *banker*

Newark
Knapp, Edward D. *banker*
Quinn, John Joseph *bank executive*

Paramus
Birchby, Kenneth Lee *banker*

Parsippany
Olsen, Robert John *savings and loan association executive*
Singleterry, Gary Lee *investment banker*

Pennington
Wallace, John Duncan *banker*

Perth Amboy
Gemmell, Joseph Paul *banker*

Plainfield
Turnbull, Kenneth W. *bank executive*

Point Pleasant
Feeks, J. Michael *bank executive*

Princeton
de Vries, Jacobus E. *investment banker*
Ganoe, Charles Stratford *banker*
Haggerty, John Richard *banker*
Holzinger, James Jay *bank executive*
Mills, Bradford *merchant banker*
Paneyko, Stephen Hobbs *banker*
Roberts, Peter A. *banker*
Semrod, T. Joseph *banker*

Red Bank
Dale, Madeline Houston McWhinney *banker*

Roseland
Costanzo, Hilda Alba *retired banker*

Short Hills
Klemme, Carl William *banker*

Shrewsbury
Jones, Charles Hill, Jr. *banker*

Summit
Moore, Milo Anderson *banker*
Mueller, Paul Henry *retired banker*

Tenafly
Levy, Norman Jay *investment banker, financial consultant*

Totowa
Jelliffe, Charles Gordon *banker*

Trenton
Meyer, Robert *bank executive*

Wayne
Haswell, Carleton Radley *banker*
†Southway, Peter *bank holding company executive*

NEW MEXICO

Alamogordo
Hawkins, James Lowell, Jr. *bank executive*

Albuquerque
Clark, James A. *banker*

Las Cruces
Papen, Frank O'Brien *banker, former state senator*

Santa Fe
Koessel, Donald Ray *retired banker*

NEW YORK

Albany
Brown, Albert Joseph, Jr. *banker*
Chorbajian, Herbert G. *bank executive*
MacFarland, Robert Frederick *bank executive*
Robinson, John Bowers, Jr. *bank holding company executive*
Shea, Maurice P., III *bank executive*
Ward, Frank Jay *banker*

Babylon
Keane, Daniel J. *banker*

Bay Shore
Merolla, Carmine Ralph *banker*

Bedford
Philip, Peter Van Ness *former trust company executive*

Bedford Hills
Nichols, C. Walter, III *retired trust company executive*

Briarcliff Manor
Carey, James Henry *banker*

Bronx
Howell, Alfred Hunt *former banker*

Bronxville
Arndt, Kenneth Eugene *banker*
Wilson, John Donald *banker, economist*

Brooklyn
Dellomo, Frank A. *banker*
Hamm, Charles John *banker*
Hohenrath, William Edward *retired banker*
Pollack, Bruce *banker, real estate consultant*
Reissman, Maurice L. *bank executive*

Buffalo
Cleave, James H. *bank executive*
Kenzie, Ross Bruce *retired banker*
Knox, Northrup Rand *banker*
Lucey, Thomas William *banker*
Pett, John Lyman *banker*
Rappolt, William Carl *banker*
Ruch, Paul Edward *banker*
Shanahan, Robert B. *banker*
Stainrook, Harry Richard *banker*
Vardon, James Lewes *bank executive*
Wilmers, Robert George *banker*

Cold Spring Harbor
Hargraves, Gordon Sellers *banker*

Elmont
Cusack, Thomas Joseph *banker*

Flushing
Diehl, Stephen Anthony *banker*
Johnson, Thomas Stephen *banker*
Lee, Paul Ching-Lai *banker, real estate developer*

Garden City
Desch, Carl William *banker, consultant*
Lovely, Thomas Dixon *banker*
Marlin, Jenesta *banker*

Geneseo
Hickman, John Hampton, III *entrepreneurial investment banker, industrialist, educator*

Great Neck
Katz, Edward Morris *banker*

Hawthorne
Hooley, Robert Childs *banker*

Hewlett
Dalrymple, Richard William *banker*
Large, James Mifflin, Jr. *banker*

Hicksville
Walsh, Charles Richard *banker*

Ithaca
Smith, Robert Samuel *banker, former agricultural finance educator*

Jamesville
Morton, William Gilbert *banker*

Larchmont
Aburdene, Odeh Felix *banker*
Kaufmann, Henry Mark *mortgage banker*

Locust Valley
Davison, Daniel Pomeroy *retired banking executive*

Manhasset
Lindow, John Wesley *banker, corporate executive*

Melville
Olson, Gary Robert *banker*
Viklund, William Edwin *banker*

Nanuet
Burden, Ordway Partridge *investment banker*

New Hyde Park
†Redman, Monte N. *bank executive*

New York
Agostinelli, Robert Francesco *investment banker*
Aisenbrey, Stuart Keith *trust company official*
Albright, Harry Wesley, Jr. *banking executive, former government official, lawyer*
Altschul, Arthur Goodhart *investment banker*
Ardrey, Rushton Leigh, Jr. *banker*
Bacot, John Carter *banker*
Bains, Leslie Elizabeth *banker*
Barkhorn, Henry Charles, III *investment banker*
Barksdale, Phillip Dunlap, Jr. *banker*
Bartlett, C(raig) Scott, Jr. *banker*
Baylis, Robert Montague *investment banker*
Beim, David Odell *investment banker, educator*
Bellanger, Serge René *banker*
Benedetto, M. William *investment banker*
Berens, Rodney Bristol *investment banker*
Biggs, Jeremy Hunt *trust company executive*
Bland, Peter George *bank executive*
Blum, Howard Louria, Jr. *investment banking executive*
Bohn, John Augustus, Jr. *banker, lawyer*
Bolebruch, John J. *investment banking company executive*
Boothby, Willard Sands, III *bank executive*
Bravmann, Ludwig *investment banker*
Brenner, Howard Martin *banker*
Bruckmann, Donald John *investment banker*
Butcher, Willard Carlisle *banker*
Cajigal, Joseph A. *financial services executive*
Calise, Ronald Jan *investment banking executive*
Campbell, Douglass *banker*
Cardew, William Joseph *bank executive*
Carlson, Loren Dale *finance executive*
Carter, Marshall Nichols *banker*
Caruso, Victor Guy *investment banker*
Castle, John Krob *merchant banker*
Cayne, James E. *investment banker*
Chevalier, Samuel Fletcher *banker*
Childs, John Farnsworth *investment banker*
Ciechanover, Joseph *banker, lawyer*
Clark, Thomas Carlyle *banker*
Clayton, Jonathan Alan *banker*
Clifford, Stewart Burnett *banker*
Comfort, William Twyman, Jr. *banker*
Corcoran, Robert Lee, Jr. *banker*
Corley, Leslie M. *investment banker*
Corrigan, E. Gerald *investment banker*
Cory, Charles Robinson *investment banker*
Crevier, Roger L. *banker*
Cromwell, Oliver Dean *investment banker*
Crosby, John Griffith *investment banker*
Croy, Sandra Lee *bank officer*
Darst, David Martin *investment banking company executive, writer, educator*
David-Weill, Michel Alexandre *investment banker*
Davis, George Linn *banker*
Debs, Richard A. *investment banker, government official*
DeGroff, Ralph Lynn, Jr. *retired investment banker*
Dempsey, Louis F(rancis), III *banker*
deVeer, Robert Kipp, Jr. *investment banker*
Douglass, Robert Royal *banker, lawyer*
Doyle, L. F. Boker *trust company executive*
Druker, Henry Leo *investment banker*
Dugan, Edward Francis *bank executive*
du Vair, Pierre Henri Serge Marie *banker*
Dwek, Cyril S. *banker*
Edelstein, Haskell *banker, tax lawyer*
Elliott, A. Wright *banker*
Enders, Anthony Talcott *banker*
Esposito, Michael Patrick, Jr. *banker*
Farley, Terrence Michael *banker*
Feldberg, Chester Ben *banker, lawyer*
Finocchiaro, Alfonso G. *bank executive*
Fisher, Bennett Lawson *investment executive*
Flynn, James T. *banker*
Foulke, William Green, Jr. *banker*
Frangopoulos, Zissimos A. *banker*
Franz, Donald Eugene, Jr. *merchant banker, security analyst*
Friedberg, Barry Sewell *investment banker*
Gale, John *banker*
Gallagher, Thomas Joseph *banker*
Galleno, Anthony Massimo *bank executive*
Garver, Robert S. *banker*
George, David Alan *investment banker*
Gerry, Elbridge Thomas, Jr. *banker*
Giaquinto, Philip M. *banker*
Gibson, William Francis *investment banking executive*
Gillham, Robert *bank executive*
Goldberg, Arthur Abba *merchant banker, financial advisor*
Goldberg, Samuel *holding company executive*
Goodchild, Robert Marshall *trust company executive*
Goodwin, Todd *banker*
Gossett, Robert Francis, Jr. *merchant banker*
Greenstein, Abraham Jacob *mortgage company executive, accountant*
Griffith, Alan Richard *banker*
Gruver, William Rolfe *investment banker*
Guenther, Jack Donald *banker*
Guldimann, Till M. *banker*
Hampton, Philip McCune *banker*
Harlan, Leonard Morton *merchant banker*
Hartman, Stephen Jennings, Jr. *banker*
Hayne, Thomas Arthur *banker*
Heard, Edwin Anthony *banker*
Hedstrom, Mitchell Warren *banker*
Hellmold, Ralph O. *investment banker*
Herregat, Guy-Georges Jacques *banker*
Hertz, Rudolf Heinrich *banker*
Hilliard, Landon *banker*
Hoch, Frank William *banker*
†Hoover, James Bentley *private investor*
Hover, John Calvin, II *banker*
Hunnewell, Francis O. *bank executive*
Huntington, Lawrence Smith *investment banker*
Ingraham, John Wright *banker*
Jaffe, Suzanne Denbo *investment banker, entrepreneur*
Joseph, Frederick Harold *investment banker*
Kahana, Aron *bank executive*
Kane, Jay Brassler *banker*
Kaufmann, Mark Steiner *banker*
Kearney, Michael John *banker*
Keegan, Gerard C. *bank executive*
Keilin, Eugene Jacob *investment banker, lawyer*
Keller, Richard Charles *banker*
Kilburn, H(enry) T(homas), Jr. *investment banker*
Killefer, Tom *banker*
Kirsch, Arthur William *investment banker*
Klein, Robert Majer *retired bank executive*
Kole, Adrian G. *banker*
Kopech, Robert Irving *banker*
Kretschmer, Paul Robert *investment banker*
Kroll, Arnold Howard *investment banker*
Kruech, Paul C. *bank executive*
Labrecque, Thomas G. *banker*
Lang, Theresa *investment banker*
Lattin, Albert Floyd *banker*
Lavin, Thomas J. A. *investment banker*
Layton, Donald Harvey *banker*
Lear, Robert William *holding company executive*
LeBlond, Richard Knight, II *banker*
Lengyel, Peter Emery *banker*
Lesser, Edward Arnold *banker*
Leute, William Russell, III *bank executive*
Levin, Neil D. *bank executive*
Lincoln, Edmond Lynch *investment banker*
Lindsay, Robert Van Cleef *trust company executive*
Lissack, Michael Robert *investment banker*
Lockhart, James Bicknell, III *investment banker*
Loeb, John Langeloth *banker, broker*
Lohse, Austin Webb *banker*
Londoner, David Jay *investment banker, analyst*
MacEwan, Nigel Savage *merchant banker*
Magdol, Michael Orin *bank executive*
Manges, James Horace *investment banker*
Matsakis, Steven C. *bank executive, retail executive*
McCarty, Michiel Cleve *investment banker*
†McCree, Donald Hanna, Jr. *banker*
McDonough, William J. *banker*
Mc Gillicuddy, John Francis *retired banker*
McKnew, Robert David *banker*
Meachin, David James Percy *investment banker, import-export executive*
†Menaker, Ronald Herbert *banking executive*
Mendell, Oliver M. *banking executive*
Menschel, Robert Benjamin *investment banker*
Merriss, Philip Ramsay, Jr. *banker*
Mesznik, Joel R. *investment banker*
Meyer, Sandra W(asserstein) *bank executive, management consultant*
Miller, Edward Daniel *banker*
Miller, Raymond F. *banker*
Miller, Richard Jerome *bank executive*
Mintz, Norman Nelson *investment banker, educator*
Moore, Andrew Given Tobias, II *investment banker, educator*
Murphy, Charles Joseph *investment banker*
Myerberg, Marcia *investment banker*
Newbold, John Lowe *banker*
Nolan, William Joseph, III *banker*
Nuzum, John M., Jr. *banker*
Olds, John Theodore *banker*
Oliver, Steven Wiles *banker*
Ostergard, Paul Michael *bank executive*
Pados, Frank John, Jr. *trust company executive*
Palermo, Nicholas J. *banker*
Palmer, Edward Lewis *banker*
Parsons, Richard Dean *banker, lawyer*
Patterson, Ellmore Clark *banker*
Peterson, Peter G. *banker*
Petrie, Donald Joseph *banker*
Pettus, Barbara Wyper *bank executive*
Pincus, Lionel Irwin *venture banker*
Pirie, Robert S. *investment banker, lawyer*
Poll, Robert Eugene, Jr. *bank executive*
Porretta, Emanuele Peter *banker*
Potter, Cary Nicholas *banker*
Prizzi, Jack Anthony *investment banking executive*
Prouty, Norman R. *investment banker*
Pryor, Alan Mark *banker*
Pyne, Eben Wright *banker*
Ramsey, Peter Christie *bank executive*
Reed, John Shepard *banker*
Rendino, Anthony *trust company executive*
Repko, William Clarke *banker*
†Rhodes, William Reginald *banker*
Rimerman, Ira Stephen *banker*
Rines, S. Melvin *investment banker*
Roach, John Hendee, Jr. *bank executive, investment banker*
Roberts, Donald Munier *banker, trust company executive*
Roche, John J. *banking company executive, corporate lawyer*
Rockefeller, David *banker*
Rogers, Arthur Merriam, Jr. *banker*
Ruding, Herman Onno *banker, former Dutch government official*
Ruffle, John Frederick *banker*
Ryan, Thomas Timothy, Jr. *banker, lawyer, government official*
Salmans, Charles Gardiner *banker*
Sanford, Charles Steadman, Jr. *banker*
Schlein, Dov C. *banker*
Schneider, Donald Frederic *banker*
Schumacher, Robert Denison *banker*
Schwarz, H. Marshall *trust company executive*
Scopaz, John Matthew *banker*
Scowcroft, John Arthur *portfolio manager*
Segalas, Hercules Anthony *investment banker*
Seligson, Carl H. *investment banker*
Sendrovic, Israel *bank executive*
Shanks, Eugene B., Jr. *banker*
Shipley, L. Parks, Jr. *banker*
Shipley, Walter Vincent *banker*
Shuman, Stanley S. *investment banker*
Sim, Craig Stephen *investment banker*
Simmons, John Derek *investment banker*
Slusser, William Peter *investment banker*
Small, Elaine Luchak *banker*
Smith, Kathleen Tener *bank executive*
Smith, Peter Bennett *banker*
Smith, Phillips Guy *banker*
Solar, Richard Leon *banker*
Spaeh, Winfried Heinrich *banker*
Spangler, Arnold Eugene *investment banker*
Speciale, Richard *bank executive*
Spelker, Arnold William *banker*
Steffen, Christopher J. *bank executive*
Stein, Howard S. *banker*
Stephens, Lester John, Jr. *banker*
Stewart, James M. *merchant banker*
Stewart, James Montgomery *banker*
Strong, Robert S. *banker*
Tarnopol, Michael L. *bank executive*
Tauber, Ronald Steven *investment banker*
Tetzeli, Frederick Edward *banker*
Torell, John Raymond, III *banker*
Trachtenberg, Matthew J. *bank holding company executive*
Urkowitz, Michael *banker*
van Hengel, Maarten *banker*
Viermetz, Kurt F. *banker*
Vona, Carmine *banker*
Von Fraunhofer-Kosinski, Katherina *bank executive*
Wallace, Robert Fergus *banker*
Warner, Douglas Alexander, III *banker*
Wasserman, Charles *banker*
Weare, Ashley *banker*
Weatherstone, Dennis *trust company executive*
Weil, Frank A. *investment banker, lawyer*
Weill, Sanford I. *banker*
Weiner, Walter Herman *banker, lawyer*
Whitcraft, Edward C. R. *investment banker*
Whiteman, H(orace) Clifton *banker*
Whitmore, John Rogers *banker*
Whittemore, Laurence Frederick *private banker*
Wilson, John Hill Tucker *investment banker*
Wirz, Pascal Francois *trust company executive*
Wolfensohn, James David *bank executive*
Wolff, William F., III *investment banker*
Woods, Rodney Ian *banker*
Wriston, Walter Bigelow *retired banker*
Yeo, Edwin Harley, III *bank executive*
Young, Harrison Hurst, III *banker*
Zukerman, Morris E. *investment banker*
Zwerling, Gary Leslie *investment bank executive*

Niskayuna
Whittingham, Harry Edward, Jr. *retired banker*

Oyster Bay
Schwab, Hermann Caspar *banker*

Pittsford
†Biklen, Stephen Clinton *student loan company executive*
Schubert, John Edward *former banker*

Port Kent
Mc Kee, James, Jr. *retired banker*

Queensbury
Mead, John Milton *banker*

Ridgewood
Jones, Harold Antony *banker*

Rochester
†Hammele, Joseph Francis *banker*
Hargrave, Alexander Davidson *banker, lawyer*
Simon, Leonard Samuel *banker*
Wayland-Smith, Robert Dean *banker*

Scarsdale
Hines, William Eugene *banker*

Schenectady
Milton, William Hammond, III *trust company executive*

Shelter Island
Dowd, David Joseph *banker, builder*

Stamford
Bergleitner, George Charles, Jr. *investment banker*

Staten Island
Chapin, Elliott Lowell *retired bank executive*

Syracuse
Meyers, Peter L. *banker*
O'Day, Royal Lewis *former banker*
Warner, Jeffrey F. *banker*

Tonawanda
Haller, Calvin John *banker*
Hettrick, John Lord *banker, manufacturer*

Uniondale
Tempest, Harrison F. *bank executive*

Utica
Schrauth, William Lawrence *banker, lawyer*

Valley Cottage
Atha, Stuart Kimball, Jr. *retired banker*

Westbury
Tulchin, Stanley *banker, lecturer, author, business reorganization consultant*

White Plains
Bober, Lawrence Harold *retired banker*
Reilly, John Lawrence *banker*

Whitesboro
Raymonda, James Earl *retired banker*

NORTH CAROLINA

Asheville
Everett, Durward R., Jr. *retired banker*

Charlotte
Birle, James Robb *investment banker*
Covington, William Clyde, Jr. *banker*
Crutchfield, Edward Elliott, Jr. *banker*
Figge, Fredic J., II *bank executive*
Georgius, John R. *bank executive*
Lewis, Kenneth D. *banker*
McColl, Hugh Leon, Jr. *banker*
Powers, Shirley Marie *banker*
Thompson, James William *banker*

Durham
Hill, George Watts *banker*
Roessler, Ernest Christian *bank executive*
Taylor, Julia W. *bank executive*
Wright, Paul, Jr. *banker*

Fairmont
Byrne, James Frederick *banker*

Gastonia
Teem, Paul Lloyd, Jr. *savings and loan executive*

Lumberton
MacLean, Hector *banker, lawyer*
Orr, L. Glenn, Jr. *banker*

Pilot Mountain
Ross, Norman Alexander *retired banker*

Pinehurst
Henderson, Paul Audine *banker, consultant*

Raleigh
Barmore, Gregory Terhune *capital mortgage company executive*
Blaine, James C. *bank executive*
Hardin, Eugene Brooks, Jr. *banker*
Holding, Lewis R. *banker*

Rocky Mount
†Boleman, Ray Judson, Jr. *banker*
Futrell, Jonas Richard, Jr. *banker*
Mauldin, Robert Ray *banker*
Powers, James Bascom *banker*
Wilkerson, William Holton *banker*

Wilson
Allison, John Andrew, IV *bank executive*
Stewart, Burton Gloyden, Jr. *banker*
Williamson, Henry Gaston, Jr. *banker*

Winston Salem
Austell, Edward Callaway *banker*
Cotterill, David Lee *banker*
Cramer, John Scott *retired banker*
McNair, John Franklin, III *banker*
Medlin, John Grimes, Jr. *banker*
Runnion, Howard J., Jr. *banker*
Wanders, Hans Walter *banker*
Watlington, John Francis, Jr. *banker*
Worley, Bland Wallace *banker*

NORTH DAKOTA

Fargo
Mengedoth, Donald Roy *commercial banker*

Watford City
Stenehjem, Leland Manford *banker*

OHIO

Akron
†Flood, Howard L. *banker*

Canton
Carpenter, Noble Olds *banker*

Chagrin Falls
Obert, Charles Frank *banker*

Cincinnati
Brumm, Paul Michael *banker*
Bullock, John McDonell *banker*
McKenny, Collin Grad *banker*
Schaeter, George A., Jr. *banking executive*
Thiemann, Charles Lee *banker*
Waddell, Oliver W. *banker*

Cleveland
Brandon, Edward Bermetz *banker*
†Carestio, Ralph M., Jr. *mortgage company executive*
Daberko, David A. *banker*
Fountain, Ronald Glenn *bank executive*
Gillespie, Robert Wayne *banker*
Glickman, Carl David *banker*
Harding, Frank I., III *trust banker*
Heffern, Gordon Emory *banker*
Jones, Theodore William *banker, lawyer*
Koch, Charles Joseph *banker*
Noall, Roger *bank executive*
O'Donnell, F. Scott *banker*
Pianalto, Sandra *bank executive*
Robertson, William Richard *banker, holding company executive*
Rupert, John Edward *retired savings and loan executive, business and civic affairs consultant*
Schaut, Joseph William *banker*
Schutter, David John *banker*
Siefers, Robert George *banker*
Simonson, John Alexander *banking executive*
Tung, Theodore Hschum *banker, economist*
Tuttle, Frank James *bank executive*
Wert, James William *banker*

Columbus
Havens, John Franklin *retired banker*
Hoskins, W. Lee *banker*
Leiter, William C. *banking executive, controller*
Mathews, Robert Edward *banker*
Mc Coy, John Bonnet *banker*
McCoy, John Gardner *banker*
McWhorter, Donald Lee *bank executive*
Meiling, George Robert Lucas *bank holding company executive*
Page, Linda Kay *banking executive*
†St. Cyr, Roger Joseph *banker*
Wobst, Frank Georg *banker*

Dayton
Hawthorne, Douglas Lawson *banker*

Dublin
Gores, Gary Gene *credit union executive*

Elyria
Kreighbaum, John Scott *banker*

Hudson
Wooldredge, William Dunbar *investment banker*

Mansfield
Baker, James Allan *banker*

Newark
McConnell, William Thompson *commercial banker*

Pepper Pike
Mc Call, Julien Lachicotte *banker*

Perrysburg
Yager, John Warren *retired banker, lawyer*

Toledo
Bergsmark, Edwin Martin *mortgage bank executive*
Carson, Samuel Goodman *retired banker, company director*
Kunze, Ralph Carl *savings and loan executive*

Showalter, Robert Earl *banker*

Washington Court House
Fultz, Clair Ervin *former banker*

Willoughby
Abelt, Ralph William *bank executive*

Zanesville
Duhs, William Andrew *banker*

OKLAHOMA

Bartlesville
Doty, Donald D. *retired banker*

Broken Arrow
Kimbrough, James Douglas *banker*

Collinsville
Flanagan, William Stanley, Jr. *banker, lawyer*

Oklahoma City
Brown, Kenneth Ray *banker*
Browne, John Robinson *banker*
Danforth, Louis Fremont *banker, educator*
Hammons, Royce Mitchell *bank executive*
Rainbolt, David Eugene *banker*
Williams, William Ralston *retired bank and trust company executive*

Pawhuska
Dickerson, William Joseph *bank executive*

Tulsa
Eaton, Leonard James, Jr. *banker*
Hawkins, Francis Glenn *banker, lawyer*

Webbers Falls
Evans, Karen Ruth *banker*

OREGON

Milwaukie
McKay, Laura L. *banker, consultant*

Portland
†Breezley, Roger Lee *banker*
Franz, Robert Warren *banker*
Jensen, Edmund Paul *bank holding company executive*
Staver, Leroy Baldwin *banker*
Winnowski, Thaddeus Richard (Ted Winnowski) *bank executive*

Salem
Weight, George Dale *banker, educator*

PENNSYLVANIA

Bala Cynwyd
Bausher, Verne C(harles) *banker*

Bethlehem
†Wilkes, Robert Edmond *bank executive*

Bryn Mawr
Clark, George Roberts *retired trust company executive*

Conshohocken
Boenning, Henry Dorr, Jr. *investment banker*
Tily, Stephen Bromley, III *bank executive*

Easton
Ashby, Richard James, Jr. *bank executive, lawyer*

Erie
Bracken, Charles Herbert *banker*
Zuern, David Ernest *bank executive*

Gladwyne
Geisel, Cameron Meade, Jr. *investment professional*

Harleysville
Daller, Walter E., Jr. *banking executive*

Harrisburg
Campbell, Carl Lester *banker*
King, William J. *bank executive*
†Smith, Karl *mortgage company executive*

Horsham
Hart, Alex Way *banker*

Kennett Square
Taylor, Bernard J., II *banker*

Lancaster
Troupe, Terry Lee *holding company banker*

Lansdale
Fawley, John Jones *retired banker*

Leola
McElhinny, Wilson Dunbar *banker*

Lititz
Bolinger, Robert Stevens *banker*

Lumberville
Frank, F. Alexander *retired savings and loan executive, lawyer*

Media
Cooke, M(erritt) Todd *banker*

Philadelphia
Boehne, Edward George *banker*
Eagleson, William Boal, Jr. *banker*
Foulke, William Green *banker*
Haskin, Donald Lee *bank executive*
Kardon, Robert *mortgage company executive*
Larsen, Terrance A. *bank holding company executive*
Murdoch, Lawrence Corlies, Jr. *retired banker, economist*
Palmer, Robert Bitts *banker*
Pepper, Jane G. *bank executive*
Potamkin, Meyer P. *mortgage banker*
Reed, Frank Engelhart *banker*
Rohn, Elizabeth G. *banker*
Ross, George Martin *investment banker*
Sayre, William Heysham *banker*
Shah, Bipin Chandra *banker*
Shields, Robert Emmet *merchant banker, lawyer*
Spolan, Harmon Samuel *banker*

Pittsburgh
Cahouet, Frank Vondell *banker*
Caldwell, Richard Clark *banker*
Clyde, Larry Forbes *banker*
Echement, John R. *banker*
Groves, Michael *banker*
Higgins, James Henry *retired banker*
Irwin, Joe Robert *banker*
McClaran, George Joseph, Sr. *retired banker*
McGuinn, Martin Gregory *banker, lawyer*
Milsom, Robert Cortlandt *banker*
Morby, Jeffrey Lewis *banker, investment banker*
O'Brien, Thomas Henry *bank holding company executive*
Ostern, Wilhelm Curt *retired holding company executive*
Pearson, Nathan Williams *investment management executive*
Rohr, James Edward *banker*
†Summerfield, Herbert Gibson, Jr. *bank executive*

Reading
Erdman, Carl L. N. *retired banker*
Ketchum, Ezekiel Sargent *banker*
McCullough, Samuel Alexander *banker*
Mengel, Philip R(ichard) *investment banker*
Roesch, Clarence Henry *banker*
Snyder, Clair Allison *banker*
Sparks, David Emerson *bank holding company executive*

Scranton
Janoski, Henry Valentine *banker, former investment counselor, realtor*
Newman, Samuel *trust company executive*

Sewickley
Roemer, William Frederick *banker*

Souderton
Hoeflich, Charles Hitschler *banker*

Wayne
Kunkel, Russell J. *bank holding company executive*

West Chester
Swope, Charles Evans *bank executive, lawyer*

Wilkes Barre
Mainwaring, William Robert *bank executive*

Williamsport
Davis, William D(oyle) *banker*

Wyomissing
Moll, Lloyd Henry *banker*
Sidhu, Jay S. *banking executive*

RHODE ISLAND

East Greenwich
Kruse, James Joseph *merchant banker*

Providence
Campbell, Bernard Patrick *banker*
Crooks, Bruce Philip *banker*
Gardner, Thomas Earle *investment banker, managment/financial consultant*
Graboys, George *retired bank executive*
Higgins, Robert Joseph *banking executive*
Johnson, Maxine Frahm *bank executive*
Kilguss, George Edward, Jr. *bank executive*
Murray, Terrence *banker*
†Wall, John W. *trust company executive*
Zucchini, Michael Rinaldo *banking company executive*

SOUTH CAROLINA

Columbia
Boggs, Jack Aaron *banker, municipal government official*
Cole, Charles Talmadge, Jr. *bank executive*
Lindley, James Gunn *bank executive*
Lumpkin, John Henderson *retired banker*
Miller, E. Hite *banker, holding company executive*
Royall, Robert Venning, Jr. *banker*
West, Rexford Leon *banker*

Greenville
Boliek, Luther C. *bank executive*

Hilton Head Island
Hornor, Frank Berkshire *banker*

Sumter
Nock, William H. *bank executive*

SOUTH DAKOTA

Freeman
Waltner, John Randolph *bank executive*

Rapid City
Undlin, Charles Thomas *banker*

TENNESSEE

Clinton
Birdwell, James Edwin, Jr. *retired banker*

Knoxville
Blake, Gerald Rutherford *banker*

Memphis
Booth, Robert Lee, Jr. *banker*
Horn, Ralph *bank executive*
Rawlins, Benjamin W., Jr. *bank holding company executive*
Terry, Ronald Anderson *bank holding company executive*

Murfreesboro
Ford, William F. *banker*

Nashville
Bottorff, Dennis C. *banker*
Chambers, James Richard *banker*
Clay, John W., Jr. *bank executive*
Cook, Charles Wilkerson, Jr. *former banker, county official*
Daane, James Dewey *banker*
Fleming, Samuel M. *banker*
Harrison, Clifford Joy, Jr. *banker*
Maihafer, Harry James *retired banker, former army officer*
Mc Creary, James Franklin *banker, lawyer*
†Overton, Stanley Dixon *banking executive*
Polley, Dale Whitcomb *bank executive*
Shell, Owen G., Jr. *banker*
Smith, James Forest, Jr. *retired banker*

TEXAS

Amarillo
Burgess, C(harles) Coney *banking executive*

Austin
Deal, Ernest Linwood, Jr. *banker*
Stone, Leon *banker*

Bryan
†Adam, Don A. *bank executive*
Shofstahl, Robert Maxwell *savings and loan executive*

Carrollton
Bentley, Clarence Edward *savings and loan executive*

Dallas
†Adams, John Lewis *bank executive*
Adelizzi, Robert Frederick *bank executive*
†Arnold, John Hudson *bank executive*
Aston, James William *banker*
Atkins, Samuel James, III *banker*
Ball, Charles Frederick, Jr. *banker*
Beck, Mary Constance *bank executive*
Bishop, Gene Herbert *corporate executive*
†Byerley, Robert E., Jr. *mortgage company executive*
Cochran, George Calloway, III *retired banker*
Cornwall, J(ohn) Michael *savings and loan executive*
Foster, Thomas Elmore *bank executive*
Gibson, William Edward *banker*
Hartman, Timothy Patwill *banker*
Lewis, John P. *bank executive*
Lo, Ronald Ping Wong *banker, consultant*
Low, Paul M. *mortgage banking executive, food service executive*
Mason, Barry Jean *retired banker*
McTeer, Robert D., Jr. *bank executive*
†Neff, Howard *bank executive*
Pistor, Charles Herman, Jr. *former banker, academic administrator*
Reid, Langhorne, III *merchant banker*
Salvaggio, Tony Joe *banker*
Schmieder, Frank Joseph *banker, business executive*
Steinhart, Ronald G. *banker*
Stewart, Robert H., III *banker*

Fort Worth
Gray, Gene *banker*
†Pinson, Ray L. *banking services holding company executive*

Galveston
Harris, John Woods *banker, lawyer*

Hearne
Moore, Loretta Westbrook *banker*

Hitchcock
Doyle, Charles Thomas *banker*

Houston
Anderson, D(arryl) Kent *banker*
Bailey, Joe M. *banker*
Bollerer, Fred L. *banker*
Crow, Michael Ray *savings and loan executive, accountant*
Dartez, Franklin *banker*
Davis, Britt Duane *banker*
Elkins, James Anderson, Jr. *banker*
Geis, Duane Virgil *investment banker*
Knapp, David Hebard *banker*
Lallinger, E. Michael *savings and loan association executive*
Osborne, Dee S. *banker*
Pharis, Ruth McCalister *banker*
Tyndall, Marshall Clay, Jr. *banker*
Wilson, Clarence Ivan *banker*

Irving
Barclay, George M. *banker*
Hughes, Keith William *banking and finance company executive*
Love, Ben F. *banker*

Laredo
Jacobs, Gary G. *banker*

Pasadena
Moon, John Henry, Sr. *banker*

Plano
Grant, Joseph Moorman *executive finance banker*

San Antonio
Fawcett, Robert Earl, Jr. *retired banker*
Frost, Thomas Clayborne *banker*
Green, Phillip Dale *banker*
Gudinas, Donald Jerome *banker, retired army officer*
Horan, James Joseph *banker*
McClane, Robert Sanford *bank holding company executive*
Post, Gerald Joseph *retired banker, retired air force officer*

Tyler
Bell, Henry Marsh, Jr. *banking executive*

Victoria
Stubblefield, Page Kindred *banker*

Waco
Mann, Robert Allen *banker*

UTAH

Ogden
Browning, Roderick Hanson *banker*

Saint George
Beesley, H(orace) Brent *savings and loan executive*

Salt Lake City
Eccles, Spencer Fox *banker*
Hemingway, W(illiam) David *banker*
Simmons, Harris H. *banker*
Simmons, Roy William *banker*

VERMONT

Norwich
†Byrne, John J. *mortgage company executive*

VIRGINIA

Alexandria
Birely, William Cramer *investment banker*
Lancaster, Bruce Morgan *investment broker, adviser, lecturer, money manager*

Arlington
Leland, Marc Ernest *trust advisor, lawyer*
Rogers, James Frederick *banker, management consultant*
Schaefer, Thomas J. *bank executive*

Bristol
Byington, E(dward) L(ee), Jr. *savings and loan executive*
Deppen, Douglas *bank executive*

Charlottesville
Bull, George Albert *retired banker*

Danville
Goodson, Louie Aubrey, Jr. *retired bank executive*

Falls Church
Geithner, Paul Herman, Jr. *banker*
Zalokar, Robert H. *bank executive*

Kilmarnock
Roberts, Austin Leonard, III *banker*

Lynchburg
Quillian, William Fletcher, Jr. *retired banker, former college president*

Martinsville
Adams, James E. *bank executive*

Mc Lean
Byrne, Gary Cecil *banker*
Forsyt, Carole *mortgage broker*
Glenn, David Wright *mortgage company executive*
Kimberly, William Essick *investment banker*
Ramsey, Lloyd Brinkley *retired savings and loan executive, retired army officer*
Ring, James Edward Patrick *mortgage banking consulting executive*

Newport News
Bernhardt, John Bowman *banker*

Norfolk
Cutchins, Clifford Armstrong, III *banker*

Richmond
Black, Robert Perry *retired banker, executive*
Broaddus, John Alfred, Jr. *bank executive, economist*
Freeman, Robert Mallory *banker*
Giblin, Patrick David *banker*
Harris, Henry Hiter, Jr. *banker*
Hatch, Robert Norris *banker*
Henley, Vernard William *banker*
Jones, Catesby Brooke *retired banker*
Mc Namara, Rieman, Jr. *retired banker*
Miller, Lewis Nelson, Jr. *banker*
Moore, Andrew Taylor, Jr. *banker*
Norfleet, Robert F., Jr. *banking executive*
Norris, David Stuart *bank executive*
Paciocco, C. Anthony *banker*
†Reid, Paul S. *nortgage company executive*
Saine, Carroll Lee *banker*
Schwarzschild, William Harry, Jr. *banker*
Shumandine, William F., Jr. *banking executive*
Talley, Charles Richmond *commercial banking executive*
Tilghman, Richard Granville *banker*
Warrick, James Craig *banker*
Wells, James M., III *bank executive*
Wilson, James Milton, III *bank executive*

Roanoke
Caudill, David L. *bank executive*
Conn, Thomas Finley *banker*
Dalhouse, Warner Norris *banker*

Round Hill
Coll, Helen F. *banker*

Vienna
Hood, William Clarence *international banking official*

Virginia Beach
Harrison, William Wright *retired banker*

Winchester
Pavsek, Daniel Allan *banker, educator*

WASHINGTON

Bellevue
Davidson, Robert William *merchant banker*
Melby, Orville Erling *retired banker*
Metz, Marilyn Joyce *bank executive*

Issaquah
Mix, Terry Platt *banker*

Mercer Island
Schaumberg, William Lloyd *retired banker*
Spitzer, Jack J. *banker*

Oak Harbor
Piercy, Gordon Clayton *bank executive*

Olympia
Alfers, Gerald Junior *bank executive, retired*

Seattle
Andrew, Lucius Archibald David, III *bank executive*
Bell, Jeffrey Donald *bank executive*
Buck, Robert Follette *banker, lawyer*
Campbell, Robert Hedgcock *investment banker*
Cockburn, John F. *retired banker*
Cullen, James Douglas *banker, finance company executive*
Faulstich, James R. *bank executive*
Fetters, Norman Craig, II *banker*
Green, Joshua, III *banker*
Helms, Luther Sherman, III *bank executive*
Jenkins, William Maxwell *banker*
Killinger, Kerry Kent *bank executive*
†Knutson, Elliot Knut *savings and loan association executive*
†Longbrake, William Arthur *bank executive*
Mauer, Michael Leonard *banker*
Pinkerton, Guy Calvin *savings and loan executive*
Porter, Walter Thomas, Jr. *bank executive*
Williams, Walter Baker *mortgage banker*

Spokane
Davis, Scott Livingston *merchant banker, lawyer*
Jurdana, Ernest J. *banker, accountant*
Lindsay, Donald Parker *former savings bank executive*
McWilliams, Edwin Joseph *banker*
Odegard, Richard Erwin *banker*

Tacoma
Kaltinick, Paul R. *trust company executive*
Odlin, Richard Bingham *retired banker*
Owen, Thomas Walker *banker, broker*
Philip, William Warren *banker*
Wallerich, Peter Kenneth *banker*

Vancouver
Firstenburg, Edward William *banker*

WEST VIRGINIA

Charleston
†Perry, A. Michael *banker*

Hedgesville
O'Keefe, Robert James *retired banker*

Huntington
†Reynolds, Marshall T. *bank executive, holding company executive, investor*

WISCONSIN

Appleton
Platten, Peter Michael, III *bank holding company executive*

Hager City
Oskey, D. Beth *former banker*

Kaukauna
Janssen, Gail Edwin *banking executive*

Madison
Poniewaz, Kenneth Anthony *banker*
Schleck, Roth Stephen *banker*
Webster, Robert Loudon *banker, lawyer*

Marinette
Staudenmaier, Mary Louise *banker, lawyer*

Milwaukee
Bauer, Chris Michael *banker*
Bero, Ronald Arthur *banker*
Bruett, Till Arthur *banker*
Fitzsimonds, Roger Leon *bank holding company executive*
Kuester, Dennis J. *banker*
Long, Robert Eugene *banker*
Murphy, Judith Chisholm *trust company executive*
Ruf, John Frederic *banker*
Samson, Allen Lawrence *bank executive*
†Weening, Richard William, Jr. *banker, finance and communications executive, venture capitalist*
Wigdale, James B. *bank executive*

Nekoosa
Sigler, LeRoy Walter *banker, lawyer, entrepreneur*

Stevens Point
†Gaiswinkler, Robert Sigfried *savings and loan executive*
Seramur, John C. *bank executive*

WYOMING

Casper
Miracle, Robert Warren *retired banker*

Cheyenne
Knight, Robert Edward *banker*

TERRITORIES OF THE UNITED STATES

PUERTO RICO

Ponce
Paracchini, Alberto M. *banker*

San Juan
Alvarez-Pérez, Angel *bank executive*
Carrion, Rafael, Jr. *banker*
Carrion, Richard *bank executive*

Santurce
Loubriel, Tere *bank executive*

CANADA

BRITISH COLUMBIA

Vancouver
Gardiner, William Douglas Haig *bank executive*

ONTARIO

Ottawa
Bonin, Bernard *bank executive*
Flichel, Eugene Anthony *banker*
Freedman, Charles *bank executive*

Toronto
†Augustine, Jerome Samuel *merchant banker*
Baillie, Alexander Charles, Jr. *banker*
Barrett, Matthew W. *bank executive*
Bell, J. A. Gordon *retired banker*
Bickford, James Gordon *banker*
Brooks, Robert Leslie *bank executive*
Cleghorn, John Edward *banker*
Flood, A. L. (Al Flood) *bank executive*
Fullerton, R. Donald *banker*
Godsoe, Peter Cowperthwaite *banker*
Greenwood, Lawrence George *banker*
Grosland, Emery Layton *banker*
Hayes, Derek Cumberland *banking executive, lawyer*
Johnston, Malcolm Carlyle *bank executive*
Kluge, Holger *banking executive*
Korthals, Robert W. *bank executive*
MacDougall, Hartland Molson *trust company director, retired bank executive*
Pyle, Alan James *trust company executive*
Ritchie, Cedric Elmer *banker*
Styles, Richard Geoffrey Pentland *retired banker*
Taylor, Allan Richard *retired banker*
Taylor, Paul Albert *banker*
Thomson, Richard Murray *banker*
Webb, Anthony Allan *banker*

QUEBEC

Chelsea
Warren, Jack Hamilton *former trade policy advisor*

Montreal
Bérard, André *bank executive*
Lawson, Jane Elizabeth *bank executive*
Turmel, Jean Bernard *banker*

ARGENTINA

Buenos Aires
Sacerdote, Manuel Ricardo *banker*

BELGIUM

Brussels
Janssen, Paul-Emmanuel *bank executive*

ECUADOR

Quito
†Cordero, Guido Oswaldo *banker*

ENGLAND

London
Band, David *investment banker*
Billings, Donald Franklin *international banking consultant*
Binney, Robert Harry *bank executive*
Bischoff, Winfried Franz Wilhelm *merchant banker*
Brown, G(lenn) William, Jr. *investment banker*
Catto of Cairncatto, Baron Stephen Gordon *banker*
Chappell, Anthony Gordon *banker*
Collins, Paul John *banker*
Mallinckrodt, George W. *bank executive*
Moreno, Glen Richard *banker*
Ogden, Peter James *investment banker*
Philipsborn, John David *former banker, consultant*

GERMANY

Berlin
Palmer, R(obie Marcus Hooker) Mark *banker*

HONG KONG

Hong Kong
Larr, Peter *banker*
Magarity, Russell Lynn *banker*
Rowe, Kevin S. *banker*
Torres, Cynthia Ann *banker*

JAPAN

Tokyo
Saito, Kiyomi *investment banking executive*

SWITZERLAND

Zurich
Gut, Rainer Emil *banker*
Peterson, M. Roger *banker, former manufacturing executive, retired air force officer*

ADDRESS UNPUBLISHED

Ackerman, Jack Rossin *investment banker*
Almgren, Herbert Philip *bank executive*
Alvord, Joel Barnes *bank executive*
Axilrod, Stephen Harvey *investment banker, economist*
Baker, Henry S., Jr. *retired banker*
Barker, Peter Keefe *investment banker*
Beck, Jeffrey Dengler *banking executive*
Bennett, Robert John *banker*
Blum, Barbara Davis *banker*
Boykin, Robert Heath *banker*
Boyles, James Kenneth *retired banker*
Britt, John Roy *banker*
Britton, Charles P., III *banker*
Brown, Sandra Jean *banker*
Browning, Colin Arrott *retired banker*
Buckels, Marvin Wayne *savings and loan executive*
Burns, James Francis, Jr. *banker*
Busse, Leonard Wayne *banker, financial consultant*
Carey, Francis James *investment banker*
Carey, Gerard V. *banker*
Chappell, Robert E. *banker*
†Christenson, Gregg Andrew *bank executive*
Christoffersen, Jon Michael *bank executive*
Clifton, Russell B. *banking and mortgage lending consultant, retired mortgage company executive*
Coleman, Denis Patrick, Jr. *investment banker*
Coleman, Lewis Waldo *bank executive*
Conlon, Harry B., Jr. *banking company executive*
Cooney, John Thomas *retired banker*
Costello, Daniel Walter *retired bank executive*
Covell, Richard Bertram *bank executive*
Craig, William Francis *banker*
Crowell, Nancy Melzer *investment banker*
Dodson, Samuel Robinette, III *investment banker*
Fahey, Joseph Francis, Jr. *banker, financial consultant*
Fahringer, Catherine Hewson *retired savings and loan executive*
Fielding, Harold Preston *bank executive*
Fish, Lawrence Kingsbaker *banker*
Fitzmaurice, Laurence Dorset *banking executive*
Fix, John Neilson *banker*
Fletcher, Kim *savings and loan executive*
Ford, William Francis *retired bank holding company executive*
Foster, Stephen Kent *banker*
Gaffney, Thomas *banker*
Gilchrist, James Beardslee *banker*
Goebert, Robert J. *banking executive*
Grant, James Colin *banker*
Hamilton, Mary Lucia Kerr *retired banker, lawyer*
Harrison, William Burwell, Jr. *banker*
Hayes, Mary Phyllis *savings and loan association executive*
Hogan, Robert Henry *trust company executive, investment strategist*
Hottois, Lawrence Daniel *retired banking executive*
Howard, Donald Searcy *banker*
Hulbert, Bruce Walker *bank executive, banker*
Ingersoll, Paul Mills *banker*
Irwin, Joseph Augustus *banker*
Jennings, Joseph Ashby *banker*
Johnston, Jerry Wilson *banker*
Jones, Richard Melvin *bank executive, former retail executive*
Kane, James Golden *retired banker*
Kisor, Manown, Jr. *banker*
Klett, Gordon A. *retired savings and loan association executive*
Kooken, John Frederick *retired bank holding company executive*
Korpal, Eugene Stanley *banker, former army officer*
Lafley, Alan Frederick *retired banker*
LaMaina, Lawrence Joseph, Jr. *bank executive*
Lankford, Duane Gail *investment banker, mountaineer*
Linane, William Edward *corporate real estate executive*
Liu, Ernest K. H. *international banking executive, international financial consultant*
MacGregor, Donald Lane, Jr. *retired banker*
Mantzavinos, Anthony G. *banker*
Mayo, Robert Porter *banker*
McAllister, Darrell Dean *banker*
McCall, John Anthony *banker*
Meeker, Guy Bentley *banker*
Milligan, Arthur Achille *banker*
Montgomery, Parker Gilbert *investment banker*
Moriarty, Donald William, Jr. *banker*
Morris, Frank Eugene *banker*
Morrison, James R. *retired banker*
Morrison, John Washburn *banker*
Mortensen, Peter *banker*
Moss, John Emerson *banker, former congressman*
Muñoz, Carlos Ramón *bank executive*
Nelson, Clifford Arnold *retired bank executive*
Newman, Denis *merchant banker*
Nicholson, Richard Joseph *trust banking executive*
North, Phil Record *retired banker*
Norton, George Dawson *retired banker*
O'Brien, Thomas Henry, Jr. *banker*
Odell, Frank Harold *banker*
Osborn, William George *savings and loan executive*
Owen, Suzanne *retired savings and loan executive*
Palmer, Langdon *banker*
Paquin, Paul Peter *retired mortgage finance executive*
Parode, Ann *banker, lawyer*
Pipal, Faustin Anthony *savings bank executive*
Polk, Robert Forrest *banker*
Pote, Harold William *banker*
Preble, James J. *banker*
Reichstetter, Arthur Charles *banker*
Reuber, Grant Louis *banking insurance company executive*
Rice, Joseph Albert *banker*
Rogers, Nathaniel Sims *banker*
Roundell, Henry J. *banker*
Rub, Louis John *savings and loan executive*
Rundquist, Howard Irving *investment banker*
Searle, Philip Ford *banker*
Shealy, Walter Dixon, III *banker*
Shimizu, Taisuke *bank executive*
Simonet, John Thomas *banker*
Smith, Richard Anthony *investment banker*
Smith, Robert F. *banker*
Smith, Wilburn Jackson, Jr. *retired bank executive*
Stanton, Robert John *corporate bank executive, lawyer*
Stephens, Donald R(ichards) *banker*
Stephens, Elton Bryson *bank executive, service and manufacturing company executive*
Stepp, James Michael *business executive*
Stewart, Carleton M. *banker, corporate director*
Stewart, John Murray *banker*
Stotter, Harry Shelton *banker, lawyer*
Suenholz, Herman Harry *banker*
Sweet, Philip W. K., Jr. *former banker*
Swope, Donald Downey *retired banker*
Tatlock, Anne M. *trust company executive*
Taylor, David George *retired banker*
Thiessen, Gordon George *banker*
Thompson, J. Andy *bank executive*
Tobin, Michael Edward *banker*
Toll, Maynard Joy, Jr. *investment banker*
Trombino, Roger A. *investment banker*
Twomey, Janet Louise Wilkov *banker*
Tyson, H. Michael *bank executive*
Vachon, Serge Jean *bank executive*
Vanderpool, Robert Lee, Jr. *banker*
Wagner, Robert David, Jr. *banker*
†Wahlen, Edwin Alfred, Jr. *venture capitalist*
Wapenhans, Willi Adolf *banking executive*
Weir, Thomas Charles *banker*
Williamson, Ronald Frank *banker, former national guard official*
Womach, Emily Hitch *retired banker and marketing and public relations executive*
Woodard, Nina Elizabeth *banker*
Zilkha, Ezra Khedouri *banker*

FINANCE: FINANCIAL SERVICES

UNITED STATES

ALABAMA

Auburn
Barth, James Richard *finance educator*

Birmingham
Clemens, Peter John, III *manufacturing company financial executive*
Powers, Edward Latell *accountant*
Vogelsang, John Martin *financial executive*

Huntsville
Graves, Benjamin Barnes *business administration educator*

Tuscaloosa
Garner, Samuel Paul *accounting educator, author*
Gup, Benton Eugene *banking educator*
Lee, Thomas Alexander *accountant, educator*
Mayer, Morris Lehman *marketing educator*
Penz, Anton Jacob *retired accounting educator*

ALASKA

Anchorage
Rose, David Allan *investment manager*

Fairbanks
Rice, Michael Lewis *business educator*

Juneau
†Pihl, Martin *trust fund adminstrator*

ARIZONA

Phoenix
Bumpers, W. Carroll *finance corporation executive*
Burg, Jerome Stuart *financial planning consultant*
Chrisman, William Herring *property tax consultant*
Daniel, James Richard *accountant, computer company financial executive*
Feldman, Ira S. *accountant*
†Fitzsimmons, Robert James *finance company executive*
Fulk, Roscoe Neal *retired accountant*
Halliday, Keith *finance company executive*
Holloway, Edgar Austin *retired diversified business executive*
Khan, Ahmed Mohiuddin *finance, insurance executive*
Leonard, George Edmund *finance company executive, consultant*
Linxwiler, Louis Major, Jr. *retired finance company executive*
Mullen, Daniel Robert *finance company executive*
Stern, Richard David *investment company executive*

Scottsdale
Hansen, Donald W. *insurance and financial services executive*
Huizingh, William *former accounting educator*
Kosick, Howard Allen *accountant, finance executive*

Peyton, William Maupin *treasurer, management educator*

Sun City West
Person, Robert John *financial management consultant*
Schrag, Adele Frisbie *business education educator*

Tempe
Files, L(awrence) Burke *financial consultant*
†Manz, Charles C. *management educator*
Pany, Kurt Joseph *accounting educator, consultant*
Poe, Jerry B. *financial educator*
Upson, Donald V. *financial executive*

Tucson
Brasswel, Kerry *tax accountant, horsewoman*
Carleton, Willard Tracy *finance educator*
Nixon, Robert Obey, Sr. *business educator*

ARKANSAS

Fayetteville
Cook, Doris Marie *accountant, educator*
Hay, Robert Dean *retired management educator*
Rosenberg, Leon Joseph *marketing educator*

Hot Springs National Park
Wallace, William Hall *economic and financial consultant*

Little Rock
Bethea, William C. *financial administrator, lawyer*

State University
Ruby, Ralph, Jr. *vocational business educator*

CALIFORNIA

Alameda
Taveggia, Thomas Charles *management educator*

Alhambra
Siler, Walter Orlando, Jr. *retired business executive*

Alta Loma
Wu, Seng-Chai *financial planner, life insurance agency official*

Anaheim
Lano, Charles Jack *management auditor*
†Steel, Alan Richard *financial executive*

Atherton
†Barker, Robert Jeffery *financial executive*
Chetkovich, Michael N. *accountant*

Belvedere Tiburon
Cook, Robert Donald *financial service executive*

Berkeley
Blume, James Beryl *financial advisor*
Bucklin, Louis Pierre *business educator, consultant*
Lev, Baruch Itamar *business administration educator, consultant*
Staubus, George Joseph *accounting educator*
Vogel, David Jay *business educator*

Beverly Hills
LaScala, Anthony Charles *financial company executive*
McGagh, William Gilbert *financial consultant*

Brea
Engleman, David S. *diversified financial services executive*

Burbank
Marinace, Kenneth Anthony *financial advisor*
Peterson, Ralph *financial executive*
Shao, Shiu *financial executive*

Carlsbad
Peasland, Bruce Randall *financial executive*

Carmel
Steele, Charles Glen *retired accountant*

Carmichael
Areen, Gordon E. *finance company executive*

Chatsworth
Palko, Michael James *finance company executive*

Compton
Bogdan, Carolyn Louetta *financial specialist*
Briskin, Bernard *finance executive*

Corona Del Mar
Helphand, Ben J. *actuary*

Coronado
Allen, Charles Richard *retired financial executive*

Costa Mesa
Pearson, William James *finance company executive*

Culver City
Eckel, James Robert, Jr. *financial planner*

Cypress
Lowell, Wayne Brian *financial officer*

Dana Point
Kesselhaut, Arthur Melvyn *financial consultant*

Danville
Amon, William Frederick, Jr. *finance company executive*

Davis
Yang, Linda Tsao *financial consultant*

Del Mar
Jeub, Michael Leonard *financial executive*

El Segundo
Neal, Jerry Eugene *controller*

Encino
Dragutsky, Howard William *estate planner*

Fallbrook
Freeman, Harry Lynwood *accountant*

Foster City
MacNaughton, Angus Athole *finance company executive*
Paterson, Richard Denis *financial executive*

Fremont
†Harms, Ralph John *financial executive*

Fresno
Emrick, Terry Lamar *financial business consultant*
Tellier, Richard Davis *management educator*

Fullerton
Axelson, Charles Frederic *retired accounting educator*

Glendale
Greenwood, Richard M. *finance company executive, bank executive*
Howell, Jack Lynn *financial executive*

Glendora
Christofi, Andreas Charalambos *finance educator*

Irvine
Feldstein, Paul Joseph *management educator*
Peterson, Arthur Jack *finance company executive*
Stolz, Neil N. *financial services company executive*

Irwindale
DeKruif, Robert M. *financial services company executive*

La Jolla
Dorsey, Dolores Florence *corporate treasurer, business executive*
Dunn, David Joseph *financial executive*
Simon, Ronald I. *financial consultant*

Laguna Beach
Garfin, Louis *actuary*
Warner, Robert S. *company director, former accountant*

Los Altos
Hinckley, Gregory Keith *financial executive*

Los Angeles
†Allison, Laird Burl *business educator*
Anderson, George Edward *financial services company executive*
Bennis, Warren Gameliel *business administration educator, author, consultant*
Broad, Eli *financial services executive*
Brockett, Peter Charles *financial executive*
Cohen, William Alan *marketing educator, author, consultant*
Coombs, John Wendell *financial service executive*
Cummings, Thomas Gerald *management educator, consultant*
DeBard, Roger *investment executive*
Engler, George Nichols *financial consultant, educator*
Feiman, Thomas E. *accounting company executive*
Freer, James Lewis *accounting company executive*
Frisch, Robert A. *financial planning company executive*
Gailys, John M. *finance and operations executive*
†Goldstein, Harvey A. *accountant*
Gooch, Lawrence Boyd *accounting executive*
Hein, Leonard William *accounting educator*
Kahn, Roger Charles *investment banker*
King, Joseph Paul *finance executive*
Kleingartner, Archie *business educator, academic administrator*
Knapp, Cleon Talboys *business executive*
Lane, Marilyn Edith *treasurer, corporate executive*
Leach, Anthony Raymond *financial executive*
Lewin, David *management educator*
Magner, Fredric Michael *financial services executive*
Meloan, Taylor Wells *marketing educator*
Miech, Allen C. *financial services company executive*
Mock, Theodore Jaye *accounting educator*
Morrison, Donald Graham *business educator, consultant*
Morrow, Winston Vaughan *financial executive*
Mosich, Anelis Nick *accountant, author, educator, consultant*
Nanus, Burton Benjamin *management educator, researcher*
†Ross, Stan *accounting firm executive*
Ross, William H. *accountant*
Roussey, Robert Stanley *accountant, educator*
Stancill, James McNeill *finance educator, consultant*
Stern, Marc Irwin *financial services executive*
Thune, Dale Gene *financial executive, appraiser*
Weston, John Frederick *business educator, consultant*
Williams, Julie Ford *mutual fund specialist*

Malibu
Baskin, Otis Wayne *business educator*
Yates, Jere Eugene *business educator, management consultant*

Manhattan Beach
Anderson, Charles Michael *accountant*

Menlo Park
Fassett, Hugh Gardner *investment counselor*
McDonald, Warren George *accountant, former savings and loan executive*

Monrovia
Breen, Thomas Albert *financial services executive*

Morro Bay
Lanser, Herbert Raymond *financial planner*

Mountain View
Benham, James Mason *mutual fund executive*
†North, Daniel Warner *consulting analyst*

Newport Beach
Gross, William H. *financial analyst, insurance company executive*
Indiek, Victor Henry *finance corporation executive*
Masotti, Louis Henry *management educator, consultant*
Panetti, Ramon Stanley *investment company executive, consultant, lawyer*
Plat, Richard Vertin *corporate finance executive*
Schroeder, Charles Henry *corporate treasurer*
Wood, George H. *investment executive*

Oakland
Barlow, William Pusey, Jr. *accountant*
Helvey, Julius Louis, II *finance company executive*
Lee, Jong Hyuk *accountant*
Schwyn, Charles Edward *accountant*

Orange
Fipps, Michael W. *corporate executive*

Palo Alto
Horngren, Charles Thomas *accounting educator*
Ivy, Benjamin Franklin, III *financial and real estate investment advisor*
Roberts, Frank Emmett *financial executive*

Pollock Pines
Johnson, Stanford Leland *marketing educator*

Pomona
Collins, Catherine Clay *finincial consultant*
Patten, Thomas Henry, Jr. *management, human resources educator*

Portola Valley
Berghold, Joseph Philip *finance company executive*

Rancho Mirage
Buskirk, Richard Hobart *marketing educator*
Kocen, Joel Evan *financial planner*

Redwood City
Elkus, Richard J. *finance and industrial company executive*

Sacramento
Herman, Irving Leonard *business administration educator*

Salinas
Stevens, Wilbur Hunt *accountant*

San Diego
Bateman, Giles Hirst Litton *finance executive*
Brimble, Alan *business executive*
Brown, Robert John *accountant*
Pierson, Albert Chadwick *business management educator*
Riedy, Mark Joseph *finance educator*
Spanos, Dean A. *business executive*
Tennent, Valentine Leslie *accountant*
West, James Harold *accounting company executive*

San Dimas
Johnson, Richard M. *not-for-profit financial cooperative executive*

San Francisco
†Alderson, Gerald Robert *finance company executive*
Brandin, Mark Semple *financial services executive*
Buckner, John Knowles *pension administrator*
Carniglia, Stephen Davis *accountant, real estate consultant, lawyer*
Case, Daniel Hibbard, III *investment banker*
†Dachs, Alan Mark *investment company executive*
Duff, James George *financial services executive*
Fuller, James William *financial director*
Greeley, Robert Emmett *financial analyst*
Gund, George, III *financier*
Harvey, James Ross *finance company executive*
Herringer, Frank Casper *diversified financial services company executive*
Kahn, Paul Markham *actuary*
Kingsley, Leonard Edward *financial services executive*
Krause, Lawrence Allen *financial adviser, financial planner*
Kuhns, Craig Shaffer *business educator*
Mayer, Patricia Jayne *financial officer, management accountant*
Mumford, Christopher Greene *corporate financial executive*
Nord, Paul Elliott *accountant*
Palmer, William Joseph *accountant*
Peterson, Harries-Clichy *financial consultant*
Quiban, Estelita Cabrera *controller*
Scholz, Garret Arthur *financial executive*
Schultz, Dean M. *finance company executive*
Silverman, Alan *accounting firm partner*
Simini, Joseph Peter *accountant, financial consultant, author, former educator*
Stumbo, Richard William, Jr. *mining company financial executive*
Uri, George Wolfsohn *accountant*
Weihrich, Heinz *management educator*
Whitney, David Clay *business educator, consultant, writer*

San Jose
Belluomini, Frank Stephen *accountant*
Halverson, George Clarence *business administration educator*
Slayen, Howard Theo *accounting company executive*
Smith, David Eugene *business administration educator*

San Luis Obispo
Buxbaum, James Monroe *business administration educator*
Stream, Jay Wilson *financial consultant*

San Marcos
Melcher, Trini Urtuzuastegui *accounting educator*

San Mateo
Johnson, Charles Bartlett *mutual fund executive*
Silver, William Robert *corporate finance executive*

Santa Ana
Hickson, Ernest Charles *financial executive*
Seoane, Emilio *accountant*

Santa Barbara
Mehra, Rajnish *finance educator*

Santa Clara
Delucchi, George Paul *accountant*
Martin, Joseph Robert *financial executive*

Santa Monica
Mc Intyre, James A. *diversified financial services executive*

Santa Rosa
Lee, Young Woo *financial executive*

Sausalito
Lamoreaux, Phillip Addison *investment management company executive*

South San Francisco
Leylegian, Jack H., II *investment management company executive*

Springs
Olofson, Roy Leonard *financial executive, accountant*

Stanford
Baron, David P. *business educator*
Beaver, William Henry *accounting educator*
Davis, Robert T. *marketing educator*
Germane, Gayton Elwood *business educator*
Holloway, Charles Arthur *public and private management educator*
Leavitt, Harold Jack *management educator*
Martin, Joanne *business educator*
McDonald, John Gregory *financial investment educator*
Miller, James Rumrill, III *finance educator*
Montgomery, David Bruce *marketing educator*
Pfeffer, Jeffrey *business educator*
Porterfield, James Temple Starke *business administration educator*
Saloner, Garth *management educator*
Serbein, Oscar Nicholas *business educator, consultant*
†Spence, Michael *finance educator, dean*
Wolfson, Mark Alan *accounting and finance educator*

Thousand Oaks
Sherman, Gerald *financial estate planner, nuclear physicist*

Tiburon
Heller, H(einz) Robert *financial executive*

Torrance
O'Connor, William Charles *automobile agency finance executive*
Sakai, Shinji *finance company executive*
†Whitley, Ralph C. *diversified financial services company executive*

Universal City
Baker, Richard Eugene *controller, corporate executive*
Boulanger, Donald Richard *financial services executive*

Upland
Jones, Nancy Langdon *financial planner, investment advisor*

Victorville
Caldwell, Patricia Frances *management consultant, lecturer*

Vista
†Ferguson, Margaret Ann *tax consultant*

Walnut Creek
Hamilton, Allen Philip *financial advisor*

Whittier
Maxwell, Raymond Roger *accountant*

Woodland Hills
Anaya, Richard Alfred, Jr. *accountant, investment banker*
Robison, Frederick Mason *financial executive*
Taubitz, Fredricka *financial executive*

COLORADO

Aspen
O'Toole, James Joseph *business educator*

Aurora
Bauman, Earl William *accountant, government official*

Boulder
Bangs, F(rank) Kendrick *former business educator*
Baughn, William Hubert *former business educator and academic administrator*
Buchanan, Dodds Ireton *business educator, consultant*
Mason, Leon Verne *financial planner*
Melicher, Ronald William *finance educator*
Stanton, William John, Jr. *marketing educator, author*

Castle Rock
Eppler, Jerome Cannon *private financial advisor*

Columbine Valley
Wittbrodt, Edwin Stanley *consultant, former bank executive, former air force officer*

Denver
Berger, William Merriam Bart *finance company executive*
Bracken, Gary K. *controller*
Cook, Albert Thomas Thornton, Jr. *financial advisor*
Edwards, Phyllis Mae *accountant, graphologist*
Fernandez, Tomas Isidro *accountant*
Gillis, Paul Leonard *accountant*
Herz, Leonard *financial consultant*
Jensen, Peter L. *accounting company executive*
Sandler, Thomas R. *accountant*
Schulzetenberg, John Martin *finance company executive, accountant*
Sullivan, Claire Ferguson *marketing educator*

Englewood
Gimbel, Alfred Adolf *employee benefits professional*
Harding, W. M. *cooperative financial institution executive*

Golden
Eaton, Mark Rayner *financial executive*

Grand Junction
McDonald, Barbara Ann *marketing educator*

Greeley
†Thiesen, Gregory Alan *accountant*

Littleton
Barnard, Rollin Dwight *retired financial executive*
†Bass, Charles Morris *financial and systems consultant*
Hadley, Marlin LeRoy *direct sales financial consultant*
Hansen, Bruce Whipple *financial consultant*
Snyder, William Harry *financial advisor*

CONNECTICUT

Bloomfield
Desautelle, William Peter *financial executive*

Danbury
Goldstein, Joel *management science educator, researcher*
Holzman, Robert Stuart *tax consultant*

Darien
Hart, Eric Mullins *finance company executive*
Nava, Eloy Luis *financial consultant*
Owen, Robert Vaughan *financial company executive*
Schell, James Munson *financial executive*

East Hartford
Mordo, Jean Henri *financial executive*

Fairfield
Cion, Richard M. *financial executive, lawyer*
Dammerman, Dennis Dean *financial executive*
Golub, Stephen Bruce *accountant, consultant, educator*

Farmington
Johnson, Robert E. *financial executive*

Greenwich
Gabelli, Mario J. *diversified financial services company executive*
Horton, Jared Churchill *retired corporation executive*
Howard, John Arnold *marketing educator*
Long, James Alfred *financial services company executive*
Maroni, Paul L. *finance executive*
McLaughlin, Michael John *financial executive*
Miles, Jesse Mc Lane *retired accounting company executive*
Moonie, Clyde Wickliffe *financial consultant*
Ordway, John Danton *pension administrator, lawyer, accountant*
Richards, Fred Tracy *finance company executive*
Smith, Rodger Field *financial executive*
Springsteen, David Folger *financial consultant*

Hartford
Gorvett, Robert L. *accountant*
†Weintraub, Allen *diversified financial services executive*

Middlebury
Todt, Malcolm S. *company finance executive*

Middletown
Francisco, William H. *accounting educator*

Milford
Madigan, Michael Scott *financial executive, treasurer*

New Haven
Buck, Donald Tirrell *finance educator*
Deese, James LaMotte *financial executive*
French, Kenneth Ronald *finance educator*
Fried, Charles A. *accountant,financial executive*
Malkin, Moses Montefiore *employee benefits administration company executive*
Vroom, Victor Harold *management consultant, educator*

North Stonington
Nolf, David Manstan *financial executive*

Norwalk
Foster, John McNeely *accounting standards executive*
Heeb, Louis F. *diversified corporation executive*
Mosso, David *accountant*
Payne, Paul D. *finance company executive*
Schmalzried, Marvin Eugene *financial consultant*

Old Lyme
Volland, Robert Stephen *financial executive*

Ridgefield
Finneran, Thomas Aquinas *finance company executive*

Shelton
Stauff, Michael Frederick *financial manager*

Stamford
Fillet, Mitchell Harris *financial services executive*
Frank, Charles Raphael, Jr. *financial executive*
Higgins, Jay Francis *financial service executive*
Howard, Melvin *financial executive*
James, John Whitaker, Sr. *financial services executive*
Marsden, Charles Joseph *financial executive*
McCain, Arthur Williamson, Jr. *pension investment consultant*
McNear, Barbara Baxter *financial communications executive, consultant*
Morgan, William J. *accounting company executive*
Norman, Geoffrey Robert *financial executive*
Ozanne, James Herbert *financial services executive*
Pacter, Paul Allan *accounting educator*
Pollack, Gerald J. *financial executive*
†Rabey, T. W., Jr. *financial company executive*
Reynolds, Robert Louis *financial services executive*
Riggs, James Arthur *financial executive*
Ross, Stuart B. *corporate financial executive*
Sharp, Edgar E. *diversified corporation executive*

Thompson
Fisher, William Thomas *business administration educator*

Waterbury
Hamilton, John Ross *financial consultant, educator*

West Hartford
Generas, George Paul, Jr. *accounting educator*
Kramer, Karen Lee Van Brunt *business administration educator*
Mason, George H. *business educator, consultant*

West Simsbury
Barney, Austin Cornelius Dunham, II *estate planner*

Westport
Chang, Robert Timothy *financial products company executive*
Ready, Robert James *financial company executive*

Wilton
Billings, Edward Robert *accountant*
Campbell, Robert Ayerst *accounting company executive*
Cook, Jay Michael *accounting company executive*
Kangas, Edward A. *accounting firm executive*

DELAWARE

New Castle
†Freytag, Richard Arthur *finance executive*

Newark
Davies, Ronald Wynn *financial services executive*

Wilmington
Bloch, Thomas Morton *tax company executive*
Caspersen, Finn Michael Westby *diversified financial services company executive*
Lukens, Paul Bourne *financial executive*
MacKenzie, George *controller, manufacturing executive*
Rogoski, Patricia Diana *financial executive*
Schofield, Paul Michael *finance company executive*
Slook, George Francis *finance company executive*
Tucker, Keith E. *pension fund executive, portfolio manager*

DISTRICT OF COLUMBIA

Washington
Allbritton, Joe Lewis *diversified holding company executive*
Arnold, G. Dewey, Jr. *accountant*
Bloom, Thomas Richard *accountant*
Byron, William James *management educator, former university president*
Calhoun, John Cozart *financial services marketing executive*
De La Torre-Leano, Jose Adolfo *financial advisor, lawyer*
de Saint Phalle, Thibaut *investment banker, educator, lawyer, financial consultant*
Droms, William George *finance educator*
Edwards, Bert Tvedt *accountant*
Ewing, Samuel Daniel, Jr. *financial executive*
Fischetti, Michael Joseph *accounting educator*
Frank, Victor H., Jr. *international financial consultant*
Frankel, Michael Henry *accountant, lawyer*
Hough, Lawrence A. *financial organization executive*
Johnson, James A. *financial organization executive*
Kanter, Arnold Lee *policy analyst*
Larsen, Richard Gary *accounting firm executive*
Linowes, Harry Michael *accountant*
Litke, Arthur Ludwig *business executive*
MacLaury, Bruce King *research institution executive*
Malek, Frederic Vincent *finance company executive*
McCarten, William Weisel *financial executive*
McKinless, Kathy Jean *accountant*
Nason, Charles Tuckey *financial services executive*
Naughton, Paul Francis *financial executive*
Page, Harry Robert *business administration educator*
Parrish, Edgar Lee *financial services executive*
Pivik, Robert William *accounting executive*
Seale, William Edward *finance educator*
Silver, David *financial executive, lawyer*
†Slate, Martin Ira *pension benefit executive*
Small, Lawrence M. *financial organization executive*
Sockwell, Oliver R., Jr. *financial services company executive*
Taylor, David Kerr *international business educator, consultant*
Tuggle, Francis Douglas *management educator*
Walker, David A(lan) *finance educator*
Waterfield, Randolph Hearst, Jr. *accountant*
West, Emery Joseph *financial analyst, investment portfolio manager*
West, J. Robinson *petroleum finance company executive, former government official*
Wyatt, Wilson Watkins, Jr. *finance association and public relations executive*
Zoeller, Jack Carl *financial executive*

FLORIDA

Apopka
Rufenacht, Roger Allen *accounting educator*

Arcadia
Davis, Bruce Livingston, Jr. *retired accountant*

Aventura
Kliger, Milton Richard *financial services executive*

Boca Raton
Broich, William John, Jr. *financial executive*
Jaffe, Leonard Sigmund *financial executive*
Jessup, Joe Lee *business educator, management consultant*
Kelley, Eugene John *business educator*
Miller, Eugene *business educator, university official*
Shane, Ronald *financial company executive*
Sigel, Marshall Elliot *financial consultant*

Boynton Beach
Bartholomew, Arthur Peck, Jr. *accountant*

Clearwater
Leeds, Robert Lewis, Jr. *marketing and management educator*
Pendleton, Sumner Alden *financial consultant*

Coral Springs
Luing, Gary Alan *financial management educator*
Sommerer, John *accountant*

Deerfield Beach
Bernstein, Stanley Robert *financial consultant, mortgage broker and banker*

Deland
Horton, Thomas R. *business advisor*

Delray Beach
Bryan, Robert Fessler *former investment analyst*

Englewood
Defliese, Philip Leroy *accountant, educator*

Fort Lauderdale
Becker, Edward A. *accounting educator, consultant*
Shoemaker, William Edward *financial executive*

Gainesville
†Hammer, Russell J. *corporate financial executive*
Simmons, John Kaul *accounting educator*
Stone, Williard Everard *accountant, educator*

Hernando
Bell, Philip Wilkes *accounting and economics educator*

Hialeah
Heimbuch, Joseph William *marketing educator*
Kennedy, Thomas Patrick *financial executive*
Shaw, Steven John *retired marketing educator, academic administrator*

Hobe Sound
DeHority, Edward Havens, Jr. *retired accountant, lawyer*
Vanderbilt, Oliver Degray *financier*

Hollywood
Sim, Robert Wilson *accountant*

Jacksonville
El-Ansary, Adel Ibrahim *business educator*
Frankland, G. Thomas *accountant, finance company executive*
Lindner, Carl Henry, Jr. *financial holding company executive*
Singleton, Larry William *financial officer*
Tomlinson, William Holmes *management educator, retired army officer*

Jupiter
Danforth, Arthur Edwards *finance executive*

Largo
Criqui, William Edmund *lighting company financial executive*

Manalapan
Doherty, Thomas Joseph *financial services industry consultant*

Melbourne
Canfield, Constance Dale *accountant, nurse*
Fay, Robert Woods *financial executive*
Roub, Bryan R(oger) *financial executive*
Sottile, James *financier*

Miami
Berkman, Harold William *marketing educator*
Capraro, Franz *investment management executive*
Coton, Carlos David *finance manager*
Ehrlich, Morton *international finance executive*
Hendrickson, Harvey Sigbert *accounting educator*
O'Rourke, Jack *financial company administrator*
Pomeranz, Felix *accounting educator*
Wolper, Marshall *insurance and financial consultant*

Naples
Fess, Philip Eugene *accountant, educator*

Nokomis
Meyerhoff, Jack Fulton *financial executive*

North Miami Beach
Fishel, Peter Livingston *accounting business executive*

Orlando
Abbott, Edward Leroy *finance executive*
Gray, Anthony Rollin *capital management company executive*
Miller, Charles Edward, Jr. *financial executive*

Palm Beach
Barness, Amnon Shemaya *financial service executive*
Bishop, Warner Bader *finance company executive*
Cook, Edward Willingham *diversified industry executive*
Fitilis, Theodore Nicholas *portfolio manager*
Riefler, Donald Brown *financial consultant*

Palm Beach Gardens
Herrick, John Dennis *financial consultant, former law firm executive, retired food products executive*

Panama City Beach
Miller, Robert William *personal property appraiser, writer*

Pensacola
Usry, Milton Franklin *accounting educator*

Pompano Beach
Heir, Kal M. *financial executive*

Punta Gorda
Bulzacchelli, John G. *financial executive*

Saint Petersburg
Blumenthal, Herman Bertram *accountant*
Freeman, Corinne *financial services, former mayor*
Gonzalez, Hernan *accountant, lawyer*
†Keller, Richard Donald *accountant*
McMurray, Joseph Patrick Brendan *financial consultant*
Putnam, J. Stephen *financial executive*
†Shuck, Robert F. *financial executive*
†Wandler, Leslie Roy *financial executive*

Sarasota
Arreola, John Bradley *diversified financial service company executive, financial planner*
Bailey, Robert Elliot *financial executive*
Bewley, David Charles *financial planner*
Lambert, John Phillip *financial executive, consultant*
Miles, Arthur J. *financial planner, consultant*
Vestal, Lucian LaRoe *financier*

Tallahassee
Anthony, William Philip *management educator*

Tampa
Alexander, William Olin *finance company executive*
Hernandez, Gilberto Juan *accountant, auditor, management consultant*
Homan, Paul M. *financial consultant*
Nord, Walter Robert *business administration educator, researcher, consultant*
Wissman, Jack Paul *financial executive*

Tequesta
Stanger, John William *finance company executive*

Vero Beach
Hill, Henry Parker *accountant*
Kinard, Hargett Yingling *financial consultant*
Koontz, Alfred Joseph, Jr. *financial and operating management executive, consultant*

West Palm Beach
Eppley, Roland Raymond, Jr. *retired financial services executive*
Hamilton, Neil Alfred *financial executive*
Livingstone, John Leslie *accountant, management consultant, business economist, educator*

Winter Park
Plane, Donald Ray *management science educator*
Richards, Max De Voe *management educator, consultant, researcher, author*
Rogers, Donald Patrick *business administration educator*

GEORGIA

Alpharetta
Zimmermann, John *financial consultant*

Athens
Horton, Gerald Talmadge *educator, public relations executive*
Miller, Herbert Elmer *accountant*

Atlanta
Baxter, Arthur Pearce *financial services marketing company executive*
Benston, George James *accountant, economist*
Bragg, John Mackie *actuarial consultant*
Chalmers, Alan Knight *financial corporation executive*
Cotton, James Perry, Jr. *holding company executive*
Dykes, John Henry, Jr. *finance executive*
†Ellis, David Oliver *merchant banker*
Frank, Ronald Edward *marketing educator*
Hawkins, Robert Garvin *management educator, consultant*
Henry, William Ray *business administration educator*
Herold, David Mark *management educator*
Lobb, William Atkinson *financial services executive*
Manners, George Emanuel *business educator, emeritus dean*
McGovern, John Francis *financial executive*
Merrigan, Eugene T. *financial company executive, marketing specialist*
Nelson, Robert Earl, Jr. *financial services company executive*
†Pannone, Richard R. *treasurer*
Parsons, Leonard Jon *marketing educator, consultant*
†Patterson, Solon P. *investment counselor*
Phillips, Herbert Alvin, Jr. *retired financial executive*
Reichardt, Delbert Dale *financial executive*
Ryan, J. Bruce *financial consulting company*
Seto, William Roderick *public accounting company executive*
Sheth, Jagdish Nanchand *business administration educator*
Sinanian, Loris R. *financial consultant, deacon*
Stubbs, Thomas Hubert *company executive*
Thompson, James David *financial services company executive, lawyer*
Walker, David Michael *compensation and benefits consultant, accountant*
Whittington, Frederick Brown, Jr. *business administration educator*
Winter, Wilburn Jackson, Jr. *financial executive*

Columbus
Blanchard, James Hubert *finance company executive*

Dalton
†Norris, Kenneth L. *accountant*

Decatur
Myers, Clark Everett *retired business administration educator*

Macon
Owens, Garland Chester *accounting educator*

Marietta
Aronoff, Craig Ellis *management educator, consultant*
†Dewberry, James Terry *business executive*
Kiger, Ronald Lee *price analyst*
North, John Adna, Jr. *accountant, real estate appraiser*
O'Haren, Thomas Joseph *financial services executive*

Milledgeville
Engerrand, Doris Dieskow *business educator*

Norcross
Wagner, Harvey Alan *finance executive*

Peachtree City
Thompson, Claude M. *finance officer, pharmacy consultant*

Roswell
Richkin, Barry Elliott *financial services executive*

Savannah
Sortor, Harold Edward *financial executive*

Statesboro
Murkison, Eugene Cox *business educator*

Watkinsville
Tate, Curtis E. *management educator*

West Point
Sauers, Clayton Henry *financial executive*

Woodstock
Austin, John David *financial executive*

HAWAII

Honolulu
†Cassiday, Paul Richard *estate administrator*
Cotlar, Morton *organizational scientist, educator*
Hook, Ralph Clifford, Jr. *business educator*
Miccio, Joseph V. *business educator, consultant*
Nakagawa, Jean Harue *diversified corporation executive*
Slain, George Cedric *finance executive*
Solidum, James *finance and insurance executive*

IDAHO

Boise
Ingram, Cecil D. *accountant, state legislator*
Kayser, Donald Robert *financial executive*
Pomeroy, Horace Burton, III *accountant, corporate executive*

ILLINOIS

AMF Ohare
Fisher, Patricia Sweeney *business executive, lawyer*

Aurora
Halloran, Kathleen L. *financial executive, accountant*

Bannockburn
Zorio, John William *financial services executive*

Belleville
Fietsam, Robert Charles *accountant*

Bloomington
Beernink, Darrell Wayne *actuary, life insurance company executive*

Calumet City
Edwards, James Clifford *finance company executive*

Champaign
Bailey, Andrew Dewey, Jr. *accounting educator*
Brighton, Gerald David *accounting educator*
Bryan, William Royal *finance educator*
Neumann, Frederick Loomis *accounting educator, academic administrator, consultant*
Perry, Kenneth Wilbur *accounting educator*
Schoenfeld, Hanns-Martin Walter *accounting educator*

Chicago
Allgyer, Robert Earl *accounting company executive*
Almeida, Richard J. *finance company executive*
Blum, Michael Stephen *financial services executive*
Bohne, Carl John, Jr. *accountant*
Bott, Harold Sheldon *accountant, management consultant*
Brice, James John *retired accounting firm executive*
Caccamo, Nicholas James *financial executive*
Canning, John Anthony, Jr. *venture capital company executive*
Center, Robert A. *accounting firm executive*
Chapman, Alger Baldwin *finance executive, lawyer*
Chlebowski, John Francis, Jr. *financial executive*
Chookaszian, Dennis Haig *financial executive*
Ciccarone, Richard Anthony *financial executive*
Ciotola, Nicholas Anthony *financial executive*
Cloonan, James Brian *investment executive*
Cotner, C(arol) Beth *financial services company executive*
†Dunn, E(dward) Paul, Jr. *treasurer*
Eppen, Gary Dean *business educator*
Fiorentino, Leon Francis *holding company executive*
Fitzgerald, Robert Maurice *financial executive*
Flanagan, Thomas Patrick *accountant*
†Fleming, Richard H. *finance executive*
†Gale, Neil Jan *finance company executive, consultant*
Garrigan, Richard Thomas *finance educator, consultant, editor*
Hansen, Claire V. *financial executive*
Harding, James Warren *finance company executive*
†Hillman, Lee Scott *financial executive*
Kierscht, Charles M. *financial company executive*
†Kleckner, Robert A. *accounting firm executive*
Koltin, Allan David *accountant*
Krupnik, Vee M. *financial company executive*
Kuchta, Thomas Walter *accountant, tax consultant*
Kudish, David J. *financial executive*
Kullberg, Duane Reuben *accounting firm executive*
Langbaum, Gary Alan *financial executive*
Lennes, Gregory *manufacturing and financing company executive*
Lewis, John D. *financial services company executive*
Longman, Gary Lee *accountant*
Lorie, James Hirsch *business administration educator*
Love, Clinton Kenneth *finance company executive*
Lyman, Arthur Joseph *financial executive*
Mallory, Robert Mark *controller, finance executive*
Mayer, Raymond Richard *business administration educator*
McCormack, Robert Cornelius *investment banker*
Measelle, Richard L. *accountant*
Medvin, Harvey Norman *financial executive, treasurer*
Miller, Merton Howard *finance educator*
Moor, Roy Edward *finance educator*
Morisato, Susan Cay *actuary*
Nason, Robert E. *accountant*
Neuhausen, Benjamin Simon *auditor, accountant*
Pitts, Robert Eugene, Jr. *marketing educator, consultant*
Rachwalski, Frank Joseph, Jr. *financial executive*
Reiss, Dale Anne *accounting executive*
Robertson, Sara Stewart *portfolio manager*
Rohlin, Diane Elizabeth *financial public relations executive*
Rosenbaum, Michael A. *investor relations consultant*
Ryan, Leo Vincent *business educator*
Schornack, John James *accountant*
Sexton, Carol Burke *financial institution executive*
Smith, Freddye L(ee) *financial planner*
Stearns, Neele Edward, Jr. *diversified holding company executive*
Stelzel, Walter Tell, Jr. *accountant, financial company executive*
Sullivan, Bernard James *accountant*
Thornton, Theodore Kean *investment advisor*
Verschoor, Curtis Carl *business educator, consultant*
Ward, James Frank *pension fund administrator*
Weil, Roman Lee *accounting educator*
Wing, John Adams *financial services executive*
Wishner, Maynard Ira *finance company executive, lawyer*
Yacktman, Donald Arthur *financial executive, investment counselor*
Zimmerman, Martin E. *financial executive*

De Kalb
Hanna, Nessim *marketing educator*

Decatur
Decker, Charles Richard *business educator*

Deerfield
Boyd, Joseph Don *financial services executive*
†Chromizky, William Rudolph *accountant*
Heiman, Marvin Stewart *financial services company executive*
Van Sickle, Paul Brunton *financial executive*

Elk Grove Village
†Dzurinko, Joseph J. *corporate executive, controller*

Evanston
Balachandran, Bala Venkataraman *accounting systems educator*
Cassell, Frank Hyde *business educator*
Catlett, George Roudebush *accountant*
Corey, Gordon Richard *financial advisor, former utilities executive*
Duncan, Robert Bannerman *strategy and organizations educator*
Jacobs, Donald P. *banking and finance educator*
Prince, Thomas Richard *accountant, educator*
Revsine, Lawrence *accounting educator, consultant*
Scott, Walter Dill *management educator*
Stern, Louis William *marketing educator, consultant*

Gays
Finley, Gary Roger *financial company executive*

Geneva
Young, Jack Allison *financial executive*

Hinsdale
Urbik, Jerome Anthony *financial consultant*

Homewood
Brunst-May, Lois *accounting & association management firm executive*

La Grange
Norby, William Charles *financial consultant*

Lake Bluff
Ott, James Forgan *finance company executive*

Lake Forest
Reichert, Norman Vernon *financial services consultant*
Van Gorkom, Jerome William *financial executive*

Lincolnshire
O'Connell, Edward Joseph, III *financial executive, accountant*

Long Grove
Mathis, David B. *financial services and insurance company executive*
Timbers, Stephen Bryan *financial services company executive*

Naperville
Dranias, Dean Anthony *financial and sports marketing executive*

Normal
Williams, Michael Roy *marketing research, management educator*

Northbrook
Afterman, Allan B. *accountant, educator, researcher*
Cunningham, R. John *financial consultant*
†Lane, William Noble, III *financial executive*
†Newman, Lawrence William *financial executive*
Russell, William Steven *finance executive*

Oak Brook
Schueppert, George Louis *financial executive*
Stonich, Timothy Whitman *financial executive*

Okawville
Schmale, Allen Lee *financial services company executive*

Palatine
Butler, John Musgrave *business financial consultant*
Kasten, Richard John *accountant*

Peoria
Poupard, James J. *controller*

Prospect Heights
Clark, Donald Cameron *financial services company executive*

Riverdale
Hoekwater, James Warren *treasurer*

Riverside
Fleck, Gordon Pierce *accounting firm executive*
Perkins, William H., Jr. *finance company executive*

Rockford
DeLuca, August Frank, Jr. *financial executive*

Schaumburg
Geiger, Joseph Francis *financial planner*

Skokie
†Bielinski, Donald Edward *financial executive*
Dishman, Leonard I. *accountant*
Pappano, Robert Daniel *financial company executive*

Springfield
Travis, Lawrence Allan *accountant*

Urbana
Bedford, Norton Moore *accounting educator*

Vernon Hills
Donovan, Nancy S. *financial services executive*

Wilmette
Stipp, John Edgar *financial consultant, lawyer*

INDIANA

Beech Grove
Clapper, George Raymond *accountant, computer consultant*

Bloomington
Belth, Joseph Morton *retired business educator*
DeHayes, Daniel Wesley *management executive, educator*
Dieterle, Donald Lyle *accountant, educator*
Swanson, Robert Mclean *retired business educator*

Carmel
Pickens, Robert Bruce *accountant*

Columbus
Berman, Lewis Paul *financial executive*
Sales, A. R. *financial executive*

Evansville
Gaither, John Francis *accountant, consultant*

Fort Wayne
Graf, Robert Arlan *financial services executive*

Goshen
Lehman, Karl Franklyn *accountant*

Indianapolis
Brinkerhoff, Tom J. *financial services executive*
Carey, Edward Marshel, Jr. *accounting company executive*
Fisher, Gene Lawrence *financial executive*
Furlow, Mack Vernon, Jr. *financial executive, treasurer*
Goodwin, William Maxwell *financial executive*
Helmkamp, John G. *accounting educator, consultant*
Israelov, Rhoda *financial planner, writer, entrepreneur*
Kaufman, Barton Lowell *financial services company executive*
Khalil, Michael O. *actuary*
Long, Clarence William *accountant*
Neal, Richard Edward *finance company executive*

Notre Dame
Reilly, Frank Kelly *business educator*
Shannon, William Norman, III *marketing and international business educator, food service executive*
Tavis, Lee A. *business educator*
Vecchio, Robert Peter *business management educator*

South Bend
Cohen, Ronald S. *accountant*
Harriman, Gerald Eugene *retired business administrator, economics educator*
Murphy, Christopher Joseph, III *financial executive*
†Naus, James H. *accountant*

Wabash
Curless, Larry Dean *tax consultant, farm manager*

West Lafayette
Lewellen, Wilbur Garrett *management educator, consultant*

IOWA

Des Moines
Smith, Diana Marie *business educator*
Young, Dennis Eugene *financial services executive*

Independence
Handy, Charles Brooks *accountant, educator*

Iowa City
Collins, Daniel W. *accountant, educator*
Riesz, Peter Charles *marketing educator, consultant*

Keokuk
Atterberg, Douglas Keith *financial planner*

Muscatine
Dvorchak, Thomas Edward *financial executive*
McMains, Melvin L(ee) *controller*

Sioux City
Hansen, Doris Anne *accountant*
Silverberg, David S. *financial consultant*

Storm Lake
Shafer, Everett Earl *business administration educator*

Waterloo
Taylor, Lyle Dewey *economic development company executive*

West Des Moines
Sather, Everett Norman *accountant*

KANSAS

Emporia
Hashmi, Sajjad Ahmad *business educator, university dean*

Kansas City
†Cargin, Thomas C. *controller*
†Reed, V. Keith *pension fund administrator*

Lawrence
Beedles, William LeRoy *finance educator, financial consultant*

Lecompton
Conard, John Joseph *financial official*

Mc Pherson
Hull, Robert Glenn *retired financial administrator*

Shawnee Mission
Boysen, Melicent Pearl *finance company executive*
Hechler, Robert Lee *financial services company executive*
Howard, Theodore Walter *mutual fund corporation executive*
Mitlyng, Errol Paul *financial executive*
Stevens, James Hervey, Jr. *financial advisor*

South Hutchinson
Myers, Theodore Ash *financial executive*

Topeka
McCandless, Barbara J. *auditor*

Wichita
Knudsen, Darrell G. *diversified financial services company executive*
Pohlman, Randolph Allen *business administration educator, dean*
Redman, Peter *finance company executive*

KENTUCKY

Goshen
Mc Clinton, Donald G. *diversified holding company executive*

Louisville
Bryant, Oscar Sims, Jr. *investment advisor*
Daulton, David Coleman *actuary*
†Winters, Donald *finance company executive*

LOUISIANA

Baton Rouge
Bedeian, Arthur George *business educator*
Booth, George Geoffrey *finance educator*
Kendrick, Brian Edward *financial executive*
†Redman, Dale E. *diversified financial services company executive, title company executive*

Covington
Files, Mark Willard *business and financial consultant*

Grambling
Fields, Hall Ratcliff *finance educator*

Kenner
Scherich, Edward Baptiste *retired diversified company executive*

Lafayette
Burnam, Paul Wayne *accountant, educator*
Castellini, Patricia Bennett *business management educator*

Metairie
McShan, Clyde Griffin, II *financial executive*

Monroe
Wall, Jerry Leon *management educator, university administrator*

New Orleans
Berger, Walter Jasper, Jr. *financial executive*
Hansel, Stephen Arthur *holding company executive*
Peyroux, Robert Albert *accounting company executive*

Ruston
Posey, Clyde Lee *business administration and accounting educator*

Thibodaux
Fairchild, Joseph Virgil, Jr. *accounting educator*

MAINE

Bangor
Albrecht, Ronald Lewis *financial services executive*

Friendship
MacIlvaine, Chalmers Acheson *retired financial executive, former association executive*

MARYLAND

Annapolis
McAfee, Lawrance Wiley *finance executive*

Baltimore
Ambler, Bruce Melville *finance company executive*
†Ballantyne, Harry Clay *actuary*
Beasley, Robert Scott *financial executive*
Blake, Norman Perkins, Jr. *finance company executive*
Colhoun, Howard Post *financial executive*
Eanes, Joseph Cabel, Jr. *surety company executive*
Gray, Dahli *accounting educator and administrator*
Jacobs, Richard James *banker, educator*
Killebrew, Robert Sterling, Jr. *investment manager*
Kues, Irvin William *health care financial executive*
Quinn, Michael Desmond *diversified financial services executive*
Thalheimer, Louis B. *diversified corporation executive*
Thomas, Gary Lynn *financial executive*

Beltsville
Carroll, Stephen John, Jr. *business educator*

Berlin
Howarth, Thomas *tax consultant*

Bethesda
Castelli, Alexander Gerard *accountant*
Kamerow, Martin Laurence *accountant*
Wolfsheimer, Ronald Milton *financial services executive*

Cockeysville Hunt Valley
Simms, Charles Averill *environmental management company executive*

College Park
Gordon, Lawrence Allan *accounting educator*
Kolodny, Richard *finance educator*
Lamone, Rudolph Philip *business educator*
†Sims, Henry P. *management educator*

Columbia
Hotchkies, Barry *financial executive*

Gaithersburg
Lee, John Chonghoon, Sr. *financial executive, international laywer*
Ruth, James Perry *financial planning executive*

Hyattsville
Lovick, Norman *accountant*

Landover
McClelland, W. Clark *retail company financial executive*

Owings Mills
Kershaw, Robert Alan *corporate treasurer*

Potomac
Lemley, Barbara Wink *business educator*

Rockville
Graff, Stuart Leslie *accounting executive*
Milan, Thomas Lawrence *accountant*

Silver Spring
DeMartini, Richard Michael *financial services company executive*
Grubbs, Donald Shaw, Jr. *actuary*
Simon, Donald John *financial planner, insurance and investment broker*
Wood, Robert Elkington, II *financial services company executive*
Yasher, Michael *accountant*

Woodstock
Price, John Roy, Jr. *financial executive*

Wye Mills
Schnaitman, William Kenneth *finance company executive*

MASSACHUSETTS

Allston
Mills, Daniel Quinn *business educator, consultant, author*
Silk, Alvin John *business educator*

Attleboro
DeWerth, Gordon Henry *corporate finance executive*

Bedford
Kouyoumjian, Charles H. *diversified financial services company executive*

Boston
Akin, Steven Paul *financial company executive*
Baker, Charles Duane *business administration educator, former management executive*
Benning, John Alan *financial services executive*
Berg, Norman Asplund *management educator*
Bower, Joseph Lyon *business administration educator*
Bruns, William John, Jr. *business administration educator*
Cariseo, David Joseph *financial services executive*
Christensen, Carl Roland *business administration educator*
Christenson, Charles John *business educator*
Clapp, Eugene Howard, II *financial executive*
Crook, Robert Wayne *mutual funds executive*
D'Alessandro, David Francis *financial services company executive*
DiStasio, James Shannon *accountant*
Dooley, Arch Richard *business administration educator*
Eastman, Thomas George *investment management executive*
Elfner, Albert Henry, III *mutual fund management company executive*
Gardner, Dorsey Robertson *finance company executive*
Gifford, Nelson Sage *financial company executive*
Gould, James Spencer *financial consultant*
Haber, Robert J. *mutual fund manager*
Hayes, Robert Herrick *technology management educator*
Hayes, Samuel Linton, III *business educator*
Hjerpe, Edward Alfred, III *finance and banking executive*
Johnson, Edward Crosby, III *financial company executive*
Kanter, Rosabeth Moss *management educator, consultant, writer*
†Karelitz, Richard Alan *financial executive, lawyer*
Kingman, William Lockwood *financial consultant*
Kotter, John Paul *organizational behavior educator, management consultant*
Lane, Harold Edwin *retired management educator, consultant*
Lawrence, Paul Roger *retired organizational behavior educator*
Lee, Jonathan Owen *financial services company executive, lawyer*
Leibler, Kenneth Robert *financial service executive*
Liukkonen, Karen Elaine *financial company executive*
Lodge, George C(abot) *business administration educator*
Love, David *accountant*
Lovett, Miller Currier *management educator, clergyman*
Lynch, Peter S. *retired portfolio manager*
Marshall, Martin Vivan *business administration educator, business consultant*
McCraw, Thomas Kincaid *business history educator, editor, author*
McFarlan, Franklin Warren *business administration educator*
Mills, Andrew Geoffrey *financial executive*
Park, William H(erron) *financial executive*
Pratt, Albert *financial consultant, trustee*
Provost, David Emile *financial services executive*
Reiling, Henry Bernard *business educator*
Riley, Robert Edward *financial services company executive*
Schnitzer, Iris Taymore *financial management executive*
Schwartz, Jules Jacob *management educator*
Skinner, Wickham *business administration educator*
Sloane, Carl Stuart *business educator, management consultant*
Stevenson, Howard Higginbotham *business educator*
Stobaugh, Robert Blair *business educator, business executive*
Temkin, Robert Harvey *accountant*
Tucker, Richard Lee *financial executive*
Uyterhoeven, Hugo Emil Robert *business educator and consultant*
Vatter, Paul August *business administration educator, dean*
Walton, Richard Eugene *business educator*
Wheatland, Richard, II *fiduciary services executive, museum executive*
Young, David William *accounting educator*

Braintree
†Remondi, John F. *student aid administrator*

Brighton
Bernstein, Emil Steven *financial executive*

Brockton
Clark, Carleton Earl *tax consultant*

Cambridge
Freund, Robert Michael *management science educator*
†Greenberg, Arthur Wayne *financial executive*
Hauser, John Richard *marketing and management science educator*
Hax, Arnoldo Cubillos *management educator, industrial engineer*
Kelley, Albert Joseph *management educator, executive consultant*
Leonard, Herman Beukema (Dutch Leonard) *public finance and management educator*
Lessard, Donald Roy *management educator*
Little, John Dutton Conant *management scientist, educator*
Magnanti, Thomas L. *management and engineering educator*
O'Neil, William Francis *financial executive*
Parker, Sam *finance company executive*
†Pettinella, Nicholas Anthony *financial executive*
Pounds, William Frank *management educator*
Rosenbloom, Richard Selig *business administration educator*
Safran, Edward Myron *financial service company executive*
Schein, Edgar Henry *management educator*
Scott Morton, Michael Stewart *business management educator*
Shapiro, Jeremy Frank *management educator*

Canton
Tockman, Ronald Chester *accountant*

Chatham
Miles, Robert Henry *management educator, university dean, consultant*

Chestnut Hill
Glynn, Arthur Lawrence *business administration and accounting educator*

Concord
Smith, Peter Walker *finance executive*

Dartmouth
Kahalas, Harvey *business educator*

Dedham
Russo, Peter Francis *financial executive, accountant*

Everett
Jenkins, Alexander, III *financial business executive*

Falmouth
Mitchell, Charles Archie *financial planning consultant, engineer*

Foxboro
Bush, Raymond T. *accountant, corporate professional*

Hanover
Hart, Richard Nevel, Jr. *financial exective, consultant*

Hingham
†Kutsch, Michael R. *oil company financial executive, finance company executive*

Hyannis Port
Ludtke, James Buren *business and finance educator*

Lexington
Deitcher, Herbert *financial executive*
†Moren, Nicholas Charles *investment and holding company executive*
Wyss, David Alen *financial service executive*

Longmeadow
Skelton, Don Richard *consulting actuary, retired insurance company executive*

Mansfield
Khan, Gordon Simeon *financial executive*

Millbury
Noonan, Stephen Joseph *accounting firm executive*

Monson
Krach, Mitchell Peter *retired financial services executive*

Natick
Babson, Arthur Clifford *financial executive*

Needham
Tarsky, Eugene Stanley *accountant, management and systems consultant*

Pittsfield
Gregware, James Murray *financial planner*

Quincy
Pitts, James Atwater *financial executive*

South Orleans
Hickok, Richard Sanford *accountant*

South Yarmouth
Arthur, George Roland *accountant, engineer, mathematician*

Springfield
Woods, David Fitzwilliam *insurance, estate and financial planner*

Sudbury
Meltzer, Donald Richard *treasurer*

Taunton
Iannoni, F. Joseph, Jr. *finance executive, hospital executive*

Waltham
Pantazelos, Peter George *financial executive*

Wellesley
Siskind, Paul M. *retired executive*

Weston
Clayton, Richard Reese *holding company executive*
El-Hage, Nabil Nazih *financial company executive*
Ives, J. Atwood *financial executive*
Rockwell, George Barcus *financial consultant*

Wilmington
Bartlett, John Bruen *financial executive*

Worcester
Greenberg, Nathan *accountant*

MICHIGAN

Ann Arbor
Cornelius, Kenneth Cremer, Jr. *finance executive*
Crawford, Charles Merle *business administration educator*
Foster, Alan Herbert *financial consultant*
Griffin, Carleton Hadlock *accountant, educator*
Huntington, Curtis Edward *actuary*
Kim, E. Han *finance and business administration educator*
Pierpont, Wilbur K. *retired accounting educator*

Battle Creek
Fritz, William Warren *accountant, foundation executive*

Benton Harbor
LeBlanc, James E. *financial services company executive*

Bingham Farms
Garpow, James Edward *financial executive*

Birmingham
McCuen, John Joachim *financial company executive*

Bloomfield Hills
Cooper, John Arnold *financial analyst*
Forrester, Alan McKay *capital company executive*
Marks, Craig *management educator, consultant, engineer*
Poth, Stefan Michael *retired sales financing company executive*
Sillman, Herbert Phillip *accounting firm executive*

Dearborn
Bobb, Richard Allen *credit company executive*
Czarnecki, Richard Edward *business educator*
Odom, William E. *automobile finance company executive*

Detroit
Adams, William Johnston *financial and tax consultant*
Bergeron, Jeffrey David *accountant*
Clarke, Edwin Richards, III *financial executive*
Dunham, Frank L. *accounting company executive*
Halperin, Jerome Yale *accountant, consultant*
Krauss, Charles A(nthony), Jr. *finance company executive*
Massura, Edward Anthony *accountant*
Patton, George Thomas, Jr. *credit agency executive*

Farmington Hills
Fox, Dean Frederick *coporate executive*

Flint
Rappleye, Richard Kent *financial executive, consultant, educator*

Grand Rapids
†Marchido, William F. *finance executive, accountant*

Grosse Pointe
Nicholson, George Albert, Jr. *financial analyst*

Ishpeming
Cope, Robert Gary *management educator, author, consultant*

Kalamazoo
Salisbury, Robert Cameron *financial executive*

Lansing
DeHaven, Clark Edwin *business educator*

Marquette
Camerius, James Walter *marketing educator, corporate researcher*

Monroe
Mlocek, Sister Frances Angeline *financial executive*

Mount Pleasant
Zimmerman, Helene Loretta *business educator*

Okemos
Oberg, Roger Winston *management educator*

Orchard Lake
Haven, Thomas Kenneth *financial consultant*

Portland
Rich, Joseph John *accountant*

Rochester
Horwitz, Ronald M. *business administration educator*

Saginaw
Doud, Kenneth Eugene, Jr. *accountant*
Kern, Franklin Lorenz *auditor*

Southfield
Cantwell, Dennis Michael *finance company executive*
Moran, Frank Sullivan *accounting executive*

Stanwood
Cawthorne, Kenneth Clifford *financial planner*

Traverse City
Taylor, Donald Arthur *marketing educator*

Troy
Wetstein, Gary M. *accountant, company executive*

Warren
Valerio, Michael Anthony *financial executive*

Ypsilanti
Duncan, Charles Howard *business education educator*

MINNESOTA

Hopkins
Haugen, Gerald Alan *financial consultant*

Maple Plain
Larson, Mark Allan *financial executive*

Minneapolis
Amdahl, Byrdelle John *business consulting executive*
Berry, David J. *financial services company executive*
Berryman, Robert Glen *accounting educator, consultant*
Buckley, John William *financial company executive*
Diracles, John Michael, Jr. *financial executive*
Falker, John Richard *investor relations counsel*
Hoffmann, Thomas Russell *business management educator*

Hubers, David Ray *financial services company executive*
Jones, Norman M. *finance executive*
King, Richard Harding *financial consultant, retired food processing company executive*
Kinney, Earl Robert *mutual funds company executive*
Kling, Richard William *financial services executive*
†Koschinska, Gregory Don *accountant*
†Martin, Le Roy *accounting firm executive*
Miller, Donald Muxlow *accountant, administrator*
Montgomery, Henry Irving *financial planner*
Pillsbury, George Sturgis *investment adviser*
Rudelius, William *marketing educator*
Saunders, R. Reed *financial services company executive*
Shipp, Roger Lee *finance company executive*
Sorbo, Allen Jon *actuary, consultant*
Thornton, John T. *corporate financial executive*
Viera, James Joseph *financial executive*
†Weber, Don *finance company executive*
Weiss, James Michael *financial analyst, portfolio manager*

Minnetonka
Sorensen, Stuart L. *actuary*

Nisswa
Marmas, James Gust *retired businees educator, retired college dean*

Ottertail
†Hanson, Al *financial newsletter editor and publisher*

Saint Paul
Bothun, Donald Dean *controller*
Brink, John William *financial corporation executive*
Dalton, Howard Edward *accounting executive*
Halverson, Richard Paul *investment management company executive*
†Heasley, Philip *financial services company executive*
Olson, Sigmund Lars *corporate finance executive*
Palmer, Roger Raymond *accounting educator*
Vaughn, John Rolland *auditor*

MISSISSIPPI

Bay Saint Louis
Sidders, Patrick Michael *financial executive*

Biloxi
Young, Walter Richard *controller*

Jackson
Watts, John McCleave *financial services executive*

Mississippi State
Nash, Henry Warren *marketing educator*

Ocean Springs
Morrison, Mable Johnson *business technology educator*

MISSOURI

Blue Springs
Foudree, Charles M. *financial executive*

Chesterfield
Bradshaw, Stanley J. *financial holding company executive*
Henry, Roy Monroe *financial planner*
Liggett, Hiram Shaw, Jr. *retired diversified industry financial executive*
Turley, Clarence M., Jr. *finance company executive*
Unterreiner, C. Martin *financial advisor*

Columbia
Geiger, Mark Watson *management educator*
Nikolai, Loren Alfred *accounting educator, author*
Silvoso, Joseph Anton *accounting educator*
Wagner, William Burdette *business educator*

Crestwood
Reitter, Charles Andrew *personal financial planner*

Jefferson City
Kelly, Margaret Blake *auditor, state official*

Kansas City
Bloch, Henry Wollman *tax preparation company executive*
Hoffman, Alfred John *retired mutual fund executive*
Hunerberg, David W. *accounting firm executive*
Sexton, Donald Lee *business administration educator*

Saint Louis
Baloff, Nicholas *business educator, consultant*
Bloemer, Rosemary Celeste *bookkeeper*
Butler, James Lawrence *financial planner*
†Carlson, Arthur Eugene *accounting educator*
Cooper, David Booth, Jr. *financial executive*
Dill, Virginia S. *accountant*
Frederick, William Sherrad *manufacturing and retailing company executive*
Hewitt, Thomas Edward *financial executive*
Jones, Wilbur Boardman, Jr. *trust company executive*
Kniffen, Jan Rogers *finance executive*
Lamoreux, Frederick Holmes *financial executive*
Maguire, John Patrick *investment company executive*
†Melnuk, Paul D. *diversified financial services company executive*
Mueller, David Brian *accountant, chief financial officer*
Nemanick, Richard Charles *business executive*
Peiser, Robert Alan *financial executive*
Roberts, Hugh Evan *business investment services company executive*
Schmidt, Robert Charles, Jr. *finance company executive*
Walsh, John E., Jr. *business educator, consultant*
Wilson, Betty May *finance company executive*

Springfield
Abraham, Yohannan *management educator*

MONTANA

Bozeman
Davis, Nicholas Homans Clark *finance company executive*

Great Falls
Christiaens, Chris (Bernard Francis Christiaens) *financial analyst, state senator*

NEBRASKA

Fremont
Dunklau, Rupert Louis *personal investments consultant*

Gibbon
Wiley, Ronald LeRoy *financial executive*

Lincoln
Broman, Keith Leroy *finance educator, financial planner*
Cederberg, John Edwin *accountant*
Digman, Lester Aloysius *management educator*
Johnson, Margaret Kathleen *business educator*
Schwendiman, Gary *business administration educator*
†Smith, Donald Eugene *financial analyst*

Norfolk
Wehrer, Charles Siecke *business educator*

Omaha
Erickson, James Paul *financial service company executive*
Krogstad, Jack Lynn *accounting educator*
Munger, Charles T. *diversified company executive*

NEVADA

Carson City
Larson, Gerald Lee *auditor*

Incline Village
Diederich, J(ohn) William *financial consultant*
Henderson, Paul Bargas, Jr. *economic development consultant*

Las Vegas
Rogers, David Hughes *finance executive*

Reno
Neidert, Kalo Edward *accountant, educator*

NEW HAMPSHIRE

Concord
Currie, Glenn Kenneth *financial consultant*
Hayes, Robert Cunningham *financial executive*

Gilmanton
Osler, Howard Lloyd *controller*

Hanover
Anthony, Robert Newton *management educator emeritus*
Deshpandé, Rohit *marketing educator*
Montgomery, William J. *finance company executive*

Nashua
†Magnano, Salvatore Paul *financial executive, treasurer*

NEW JERSEY

Avon By The Sea
Bruno, Grace Angelia *accountant, educator*

Bay Head
Benning, Joseph Francis, Jr. *portfolio manager, financial analyst*

Bedminster
Darr, John Keith *finance executive*

Camden
Rapaport, Robert M. *financial executive*

Cherry Hill
Newell, Eric James *financial planner, tax consultant, former insurance executive*

Clinton
Boyland, Joseph Francis *corporate controller*

Convent Station
Wright, Robert Burroughs *financial consultant*

Eatontown
Dalton, John Joseph *healthcare consultant*

Edison
†Berg, Carol Scherer *financial executive*
†Bonini, Victor *accountant*
Cangemi, Michael Paul *accountant, financial executive*

Glen Rock
Fine, Seymour Howard *marketing educator, lecturer, author, consultant*

Hackensack
Mehta, Jay *financial executive*

Haddonfield
LaBarge, Richard Allen *financial analyst, educator*

Harrington Park
†McKelvey, Don Richard *finance company executive*

Hoboken
Jurkat, Martin Peter *management educator*

Holmdel
Ayub, Yacub *financial consultant*

Iselin
Hecht, William David *accountant*

Jackson
Hagberg, Carl Thomas *financial executive*

Jersey City
Dubin, Michael *financial services executive*
Fortune, Robert Russell *financial consultant*
Tognino, John Nicholas *financial services executive*

Lakewood
Nolan, Harold Joseph, Jr. *marketing educator*

Lawrenceville
†Farrar, Donald Keith *financial executive*

Liberty Corner
Rajani, Prem Rajaram *transportation company financial executive*

Lincroft
Keenan, Robert Anthony *financial services company executive, educator, consultant*

Little Falls
Armellino, Michael Ralph *retired asset management executive*

Monmouth Beach
Herbert, LeRoy James *retired accounting firm executive*

Montvale
Brecht, Warren Frederick *business executive*
Moritz, James R. *financial executive*

Montville
Klapper, Byron D. *financial company executive*

Morristown
Cregan, Frank Robert *financial executive, consultant*
Hesselink, Ann Patrice *financial executive, lawyer*
O'Connor, Francis X. *financial executive*

Mount Laurel
Laubach, Roger Alvin *accountant*

Murray Hill
Rayner, Robert Martin *financial executive*

Netcong
Sekula, Edward Joseph, Jr. *financial executive*

New Brunswick
Johnson, Clark Hughes *financial executive*

New Providence
Symanski, Robert Anthony *treasurer*

Newark
Arabie, Phipps *marketing educator, researcher*
Contractor, Farok *business and management educator*
Rosenberg, Jerry Martin *business administration educator*

North Bergen
Kelly, Thomas James *finance executive*

North Brunswick
Mills, George Marshall *insurance and financial consultant*

Old Bridge
†Meisel, Robert P. *financial company executive*

Paramus
Ross, William *financial planner*
Salizzoni, Frank Louis *financial executive*

Phillipsburg
Paige, Richard Bruce *financial information executive*

Point Pleasant
Albano, Pasquale Charles *management educator, management and organization development consultant*

Princeton
Appelbaum, Michael Arthur *finance company executive*
Goldman, Clifford Alan *financial advisor*
Harvey, Norman Ronald *finance company executive*
Henkel, William *financial services executive*
Kemmerer, Peter Ream *financial executive*
Tabell, Anthony *financial analyst*

Red Bank
McCann, John Francis *financial services company executive*

Ridgewood
Geraghty, Margaret Karl *financial consultant, portfolio manager*
McBride, William Bernard *treasurer*

River Edge
Gass, Manus M. *accountant, business executive*

Robbinsville
Moustafa, Fikry Sayed *accountant*

Roseland
McElwee, Andrew Allison *finance executive, lawyer*

Rutherford
Liptak, Irene Frances *retired business executive*

Short Hills
Mebane, William Black *controller, financial consultant*
Soderlind, Sterling Eugene *newspaper industry consultant*

Somerville
Cohen, Walter Stanley *accountant, financial consultant*

Southampton
Knortz, Walter Robert *accountant, former insurance company executive*

Summit
Batzer, R. Kirk *accountant*
Vogel, Julius *consulting actuary, former insurance company executive*

Teaneck
Forson, Norman Ray *controller*

Tenafly
Lilley, Theodore Robert *financial executive*

Tinton Falls
Van Winkle, William *financial planner*

Waldwick
Surdoval, Donald James *accounting and management consulting company executive*

Wall
†Downes, Laurence M. *treasurer*

Warren
Hartman, David Gardiner *actuary*

West New York
Rolston, Robert John *accountant, consultant*

West Paterson
Kaufman, Allan M. *actuary, consultant*

Westfield
Boutillier, Robert John *accountant*
Connolly, Ronald Cavanagh *financial services executive*

Whitehouse Station
Atieh, Michael Gerard *accountant*

Wyckoff
Abdelrahman, Talaat Ahmad Mohammad *financial executive*

NEW MEXICO

Albuquerque
Strati, Tony J. *accountant*

Las Cruces
Peterson, Robin Tucker *marketing educator*

Santa Fe
Watkins, Stephen Edward *accountant*

NEW YORK

Albany
Blount, Stanley Freeman *marketing educator*
Holstein, William Kurt *business administration educator*
Langlitz, Harold N. *pension fund administrator*
Riley, Victor J., Jr. *financial services company executive*
Wierzbicki, Ronald Gerard *auditor*

Amherst
Jen, Frank Chifeng *finance and management educator*

Amityville
Linehan, Patrick Francis, Jr. *financial planner*

Armonk
Godfrey, Robert R. *financial services executive*

Bedford
Ruppel, George Robert *accountant*

Bethpage
Freese, Robert Gerard *financial executive*

Binghamton
Shillestad, John Gardner *financial services company executive*

Briarcliff Manor
†McLeish, David James Dow *employee benefits consulting executive, actuary*

Bronx
Aiken, William *accountant*
Stuhr, David Paul *business educator, consultant*

Bronxville
Martin, R. Keith *business and information systems educator, consultant*

Brooklyn
DeBock, Florent Alphonse *controller*
Gordon, Conrad J. *financial executive*
Lebouitz, Martin Frederick *financial services industry executive, consultant*
Sands, Edith Sylvia Abeloff (Mrs. Abraham M. Sands) *finance educator, author*

Buffalo
Draper, Verden Rolland *accountant*
Eagan, John Gayle *business educator*
Flint, Mark Addison *financial executive*
Gruen, David Henry *financial executive, consultant*

Jacobs, Jeremy M. *diversified holding company executive, hockey team owner*
Kellner, Douglas Ernest *financial executive*
Layton, Rodney Eugene *controller, newspaper executive*

Canton
Pollard, Fred Don *finance company executive*

Cedarhurst
Cohen, Philip Herman *accountant*

Chappaqua
Cronin, Raymond Valentine *financial executive*

Chittenango
Cassell, William Walter *retired accounting operations consultant*

College Point
Hegarty, Michael John *financial officer*

Commack
Nelson, Marvin Bernard *financial executive*

East Garden City
Baker, J. A., II *monetary architect, financial engineer*

East Hampton
Dalzell, Fred Briggs *financial consultant*

East Rochester
Murray, James Doyle *accountant*

Elmira
Kintz, Ronald Joseph *hospital financial executive, treasurer*

Floral Park
Moskowitz, Stanley Alan *financial executive*

Flushing
Curzio, Francis Xavier *finance company executive*

Forest Hills
Phelan, Arthur Joseph *financial executive*

Garden City
†Covich, Frank J. *business transfer consultant*

Glens Falls
Bitner, William Lawrence, III *retired banker, educator*

Great Neck
Levy, Joel N. *financial executive*

Hampton Bays
Yavitz, Boris *business educator and dean emeritus*

Harrison
Serenbetz, Warren Lewis *financial management company executive*

Hartsdale
Gillingham, Stephen Thomas *financial planner*

Hastings On Hudson
Shillinglaw, Gordon *accounting educator, consultant, writer*

Hempstead
Montana, Patrick Joseph *management educator*
Roble, Carole Marcia *accountant*

Horseheads
Huffman, Patricia Joan *accounting coordinator*

Huntington
Hayden, Ralph Frederick *accountant, financial consultant*

Ithaca
Brunk, Max Edwin *marketing educator emeritus*
Dyckman, Thomas Richard *accounting educator*
Elliot, John *accountant, educator*
Geller, A. Neal *business educator, financial consultant*
Lesser, William Henri *marketing educator*
Van Houtte, Raymond A. *financial executive*

Kew Gardens
Schnakenberg, Donald G. *financial administrator*

Larchmont
Fletcher, Denise Koen *strategic and financial consultant*

Long Island City
Brustein, Lawrence *financial executive*

Massapequa
Hughes, Spencer Edward, Jr. *financial executive, consultant*

Merrick
Beckman, Judith Kalb *financial counselor and planner, educator, writer*

Mount Kisco
Keesee, Thomas Woodfin, Jr. *financial consultant*

New Hyde Park
Chafitz, Alan Herbert *financial services company executive*
Richards, Bernard *investment company executive*

New Rochelle
Brodie, Norman *retired financial actuary*
Dobrin, Bernard Robert *financial executive*

New York
Alexander, Barbara Toll *investment banker*
Ali, Mehdi *financial services company executive*
Allardice, Robert B., III *financial services company executive*
Alper, Merlin Lionel *financial executive*
Altfest, Lewis Jay *financial and investment advisor*
Anderson, Theodore Wellington *portfolio strategist*
Anshen, Melvin *business educator*
Appel, Michael R(obert) *corporation treasurer*
Assael, Henry *marketing educator*
Atwater, Verne Stafford *finance educator*
Auriemmo, Frank Joseph, Jr. *financial holding company executive*
Bains, Harrison MacKellar, Jr. *financial executive*
Baldasaro, P. Michael *tax consultant*
Barnett, Bernard *accountant*
Basile, Thomas J. *accountant*
Baumann, Gary Joseph *accountant*
Berg, Jonathan Albert *investment company executive*
Berger, Stephen *financial services company executive*
Berliner, William Michael *business educator*
Bernstein, Zalman C. *research and money management executive*
Betley, John Robert *accountant*
†Bibliowicz, Jessica M. *financial analyst*
Bolter, Eugene P. *investment counselor*
†Bonmati, Reynald G. *investment banking executive*
Borelli, Francis J(oseph) (Frank Borelli) *insurance brokerage and consulting firm financial executive*
Bovin, Denis Alan *finance company executive*
Boyarski, Joel I. *financial executive*
Brennan, Daniel L. *accounting, consulting firm executive*
Brocksmith, James G., Jr. *accounting, management consulting firm executive*
Brofman, Lance Mark *portfolio manager, mutual fund executive*
Brooke, Paul Alan *finance company executive*
Butterfield, R. Keith *financial company executive*
Byington, Homer Morrison, III *financial consultant*
Caldwell, Philip *financial services company executive, retired automobile manufacturing company executive*
Campbell, Timothy Reid *financial services company executive*
Cantor, Bernard Gerald *financial executive*
Carroll, Thomas Joseph *investment services company executive*
Carthaus, James Arthur *financial service company executive*
Chenault, Kenneth Irvine *financial services company executive*
Chenok, Philip Barry *accountant, association executive*
Clark, Howard Longstreth, Jr. *finance company executive*
Clauson, James Wilson *accountant*
Clayton, Jon Kerry *holding company executive*
Cohen, Burton Jerome *financial service executive*
Cohen, Irving I. *finance company executive*
Colby, Marvelle Seitman *business management educator, administrator*
Connor, Joseph E. *accountant*
Cornstein, David B. *finance executive*
Corr, Gary Alan *finance company executive*
Craig, Charles Samuel *marketing educator*
Cumming, Ian M. *holding company executive*
Daley, James E. *accounting firm executive*
Dawson, Thomas Cleland, II *financial executive*
Deupree, Marvin Mattox *accountant, business consultant*
Dewing, Merlin Eugene *diversified financial services company executive*
Dimon, James *financial services executive*
Dirks, Dennis John *financial services executive*
Donaldson, William Henry *financial executive*
Edwards, James D. *accounting company executive*
Eig, Norman *investment company executive*
Eisner, Richard Alan *accountant*
Emmerman, Michael N *financial analyst*
Erosh, William Daniel *financial services company executive*
Eveillard, Jean-Marie *financial company executive*
Farley, James Bernard *retired financial services company executive*
Farley, Peggy Ann *finance company executive*
†Fernando, Lakshman G. *accountant*
Fishman, Jay Steven *financial services executive*
Foresman, Bruce Chalfin *treasurer*
Frank, David Abraham *finance executive*
Freeburg, Richard Gorman *financial derivatives company executive*
Freedman, Eugene M. *accounting firm executive*
Freiberg, Lowell Carl *financial executive*
Frimerman, Leslie *financial services company executive*
Froewiss, Kenneth Clark *corporate finance executive*
Frommer, Henry *financial executive*
Frost, Robert *financial consulting firm executive*
Frye, Clayton Wesley, Jr. *financial executive*
†Gantcher, Nathan *financial services company executive*
Garba, Edward Aloysius *financial executive*
Garrett, Robert *financial advisory executive*
Gaughan, Eugene Francis *accountant*
Geraghty, Kenneth George *financial services company executive*
Gill, Ardian C. *actuary*
Gladstone, William Louis *accountant*
†Glover, Ron K. *business information services company executive*
Glynn, Gary Allen *pension fund executive*
Goldberg, Edward L. *financial services executive*
Golden, William Theodore *corporate trustee, director*
†Goldman, James M. *financial executive*
Goldman, Robert Irving *financial services company executive*
Goldschmidt, Robert Alphonse *financial executive*
Goldstein, Fred *accountant*
Gollin, Stuart Allen *accountant*
Golub, Harvey *financial services company executive*
Graf, Peter Gustav *accountant, lawyer*
Green, David O. *accounting educator, educational administrator*
Greenberg, Robert A. *financial consultant*
Grisi, Jeanmarie Conte *finance executive*
Groves, Ray John *accountant*
Guth, William Donald *business educator*
Hajim, Edmund A. *financial services executive*
Halloran, Leo Augustine *retired financial executive*
Harfst, Jeffrey Loren *accountant*
Harrison, John Alexander *financial executive*
†Hauck, Mary Elizabeth *portfolio manager*
Hazen, William Harris *finance executive*
Herrera, Paul Fredrick *accountant*
Hewitt, Dennis Edwin *financial executive*
Hibel, Bernard *financial consultant, former apparel company executive*
Hickman, J. Kenneth *accounting company executive*
Horner, Larry Dean *retired accounting firm executive, brokerage firm executive*
Jacey, Charles Frederick, Jr. *accounting company executive, consultant*
Jacobs, Mark Neil *financial services corporation executive, lawyer*
Johnson, Clarke Courtney *finance educator*
Johnson, Freda S. *public finance consultant*
Johnson, J. Chester *financial executive, poet*
Jones, Thomas Wade *financial services executive*
Joseph, Michael Sarkies *accountant*
Karpen, Marian Joan *financial executive*
Kaye, Walter *financial executive*
Kelly, Robert J. *accounting firm executive*
Kenney, Jerome P. *finance company executive*
†Kirsch, Donald *financial consultant, author*
Klausmann, Walter Joseph *financial executive*
Kobayashi, Hisao *financial company executive*
Koeppel, Noel Immanuel *financial planner, securities and real estate broker*
Kohn, Stephen Jerome *accounting company executive*
Kolesar, Peter John *business and engineering educator*
Kolmer, John H., Jr. *banker*
†Komansky, David H. *financial services executive*
Kopelman, Richard Eric *management educator*
Kotecha, Mahesh Kanjibhai *financial guarantee insurance company executive*
Kovalcik, Kenneth John *accountant*
Kravis, Henry R. *venture financier*
Kvint, Vladimir Lev *finance educator, mining engineer*
Ladjevardi, Hamid *fund manager*
Langer, Horst *financial corporate executive*
Lappin, Joan E. *financial executive*
†Laskawy, Philip A. *accounting and management consulting firm executive*
Leaf, Roger Warren *business consultant*
Lewins, Steven *security analyst, investment advisor, corporate executive*
Libby, John Kelway *financial services company executive*
Lieberman, Gail Forman *finance executive*
Lipton, William James *accountant, lawyer*
Livnat, Joshua *accounting educator, consultant*
Loeb, Peter Kenneth *money manager*
Long, Robert Douglas *financial service executive*
Loss, Stuart Harold *financial executive*
Lowenthal, Jacob *finance executive*
Lucido, Louis Charles *finance company executive*
†Lynch, Ronald P. *financial manager*
Lynn, Evadna Saywell *investment analyst*
MacHale, Joseph P. *financial executive*
Madden, Michael Daniel *finance company executive*
Madonna, Jon C. *accounting firm executive*
Maffei, Gregory B. *investment banker*
Mankin, Robert Stephen *financial executive*
Mantell, Lester J. *financial business executive*
Margolis, Louis Irving *financial executive*
Martinez, Roman, IV *financial executive*
Mathes, Sorrell Mark *investment banker*
Matthews, Westina L. *finance and banking executive*
Maurer, Jeffrey Stuart *finance executive*
McCaffrey, William Thomas *financial services company executive*
McCandless, Stephen Porter *financial executive*
McCarthy, Bryant *accounting firm executive*
McDonald, James L. *accounting firm executive*
McDowell, Robert Neil *accounting company executive*
Mc Gruder, Stephen Jones *portfolio manager*
McKessy, Stephen W. *accounting firm executive*
Merrill, Newton Phelps Stokes *financial executive*
Merz, Carl Allen *financial services company executive*
Miller, Joel E. *accountant, finance company executive*
Miller, Neil S. *financial officer, advertising executive*
Monaco, Michael P. *finance company executive*
Morrow, E. Frederic *financial consultant, retired banker*
Mortimer, Henry Tilford, Jr. *financial assurance executive*
Mosse, Peter John Charles *financial services executive*
Murchie, Edward Michael *accountant*
Nagle, Arthur Joseph *investment banker*
Nagy, Stephen Felsobuki *investment company executive*
Nayden, Denis J. *diversified financial services company executive*
†Neary, Robert D. *accounting firm executive*
Neff, Walter Perry *financial consultant*
Norman, Stephen Peckham *financial services company executive*
O'Brien, William K. *accounting firm executive*
O'Malley, Shaun F. *accounting firm executive*
†O'Reilly, Vincent M. *accounting firm executive*
Palitz, Bernard G. *finance company executive*
Peppet, Russell Frederick *accountant*
Peritz, Abraham Daniel *business executive*
Peters, Ronald George *investment banker*
Pitti, Donald Robert *financial service company executive*
Posner, Roy Edward *finance executive*
†Potter, Delcour S. *finance company executive*
Powers, Richard F., III *finance company executive*
Prendergast, John Patrick *accounting company executive*
Presby, J. Thomas *financial advisor*
Pyle, Robert Milner, Jr. *financial services company executive*
Rappaport, Steven N. *financial information services executive*
Reese, Ann N. *financial executive*
Rein, Catherine Amelia *financial services executive, lawyer*
Rinaldini, Luis Emilio *investment banker*
Ritch, Herald LaVern *finance company executive*
Ritch, Kathleen *diversified company executive*
Roberts, John J. *accounting firm executive*
Robinson, James Dixon, III *corporate executive*
Robinson, Robert Armstrong *pension fund executive*
Roche, Kevin Joseph *finance executive*
Roethenmund, Otto Emil *financial and banking executive*
Rosenberg, Michael Joseph *financial executive*
Rosenthal, Charles Michael *financial executive*
Rosenthal, Imre *financial company executive*
Ross, Coleman DeVane *accountant, insurance company consultant*
Salomon, Robert S., Jr. *portfolio manager*
Salzman, Robert Jay *accountant*
Sandalls, William Thomas, Jr. *financial services company executive*
Sarver, Eugene *finance educator*
Scanlon, Peter Redmond *accountant*
Schmidt, Richard Frederick *business executive*
Segal, Martin Eli *retired actuarial and consulting company executive*
†Sellers, Wallace Osborne *financial services company executive*
Shapoff, Stephen H. *financial executive*
Shaw, Alan Roger *financial executive, educator*
Siguler, George William *financial services executive*
Silber, William L. *finance educator*
Silverman, Herbert R. *corporate financial executive*
Skomorowsky, Peter P. *accounting company executive*
Skwiersky, Paul *accountant*
†Smith, Harold Charles *private pension fund executive*
Smith, Paul Thomas *financial services company executive*
Smith, Winthrop Hiram, Jr. *financial services executive*
Soldatos, Paul W. *holding company executive*
Sompolski, Timothy Andrew *benefits compensation executive*
Soros, George *fund management executive*
Sorrentino, Ralph Joseph *controller*
Sorter, George Hans *accounting and law educator, consultant*
Starr, Martin Kenneth *management educator*
Stein, Howard *mutual fund executive*
Stein, Robert William *actuary, accountant*
Stiefler, Jeffrey E. *financial services executive*
Stockman, David Allen *former federal official, congressman, financier*
Stone, David Kendall *financial executive*
Stovall, Robert H(enry) *money management company executive*
Stux, Ivan Ernest *financial executive*
Syron, Richard Francis *financial services executive, economist*
Tarantino, Dominic A. *accounting firm executive*
Tarbox, Katharine Riggs *investor relations executive*
Tavel, Mark Kivey *money management company executive, economist*
Tisch, Preston Robert *finance executive*
Tobin, Peter J. *financial executive*
Trager, Alan Martin *financial services company executive*
Treuhold, Charles Richard *investment banker*
Tully, Daniel Patrick *financial services executive*
Tushman, Michael *business educator*
Twell, Nicholas J. *financial analyst*
Valles, Jean-Paul *finance company executive*
Volk, Norman Hans *financial executive*
Volney, Taylor *financial executive*
Walsh, Thomas Gerard *actuary*
†Wankel, Robert E. *financial executive*
Waters, William Francis *financial services executive*
Weinbach, Lawrence Allen *accounting executive*
Weiner, Ronald Gary *accounting executive*
Weingrow, Howard L. *financial executive, investor*
Weiss, Myrna Grace *business consultant*
Wiener, Robert Alvin *accountant*
Wilby, William Langfitt *international portfolio manager, economist*
Woodward, M. Cabell, Jr. *financial executive*
Wright, Richard John *business executive*
Zand, Dale Ezra *business management educator*

Old Bethpage
Dryce, H. David *accountant, consultant*

Pittsford
Herge, Henry Curtis, Jr. *consulting firm executive*

Plainview
Brill, Steven Charles *financial advisor, lawyer*
McCusker, John *financial analyst*

Plattsburgh
Dossin, Ernest Joseph, III *credit consulting company executive*

Pleasantville
Reps, David Nathan *finance educator*

Pomona
Landau, Lauri Beth *accountant, tax consultant*

Port Washington
Sonnenfeldt, Richard Wolfgang *business educator*

Poughkeepsie
Hansen, Karen Thornley *accountant*

Pound Ridge
Webb, Richard Gilbert *financial executive*

Purchase
Noonan, Frank R. *business executive*
†Welch, Patrick E. *diversified financial services company executive*

Queensbury
Borgos, Stephen John *business educator, consultant, municipal administrator, real estate broker*
Lake, William Thomas *financial consultant*

Rochester
Balderston, William, III *retired banker*
Glerum, John C. *bank controller*
Matteson, Lawrence James *business educator*
Olson, Russell L. *pension fund administrator*

Rye
Beldock, Donald Travis *financial executive*

Rye Brook
FitzSimons, Sharon Russell *international finance and treasury executive*

Scarsdale
Eforo, John Francis *financial officer*

Springfield Center
Hall, Stanley Eckler *international financial consultant*

Syracuse
Marcoccia, Louis Gary *accountant, university administrator*
†Pfeiffer, Alice Randel *business manager*

Tarrytown
Ferrari, Robert Joseph *business educator, former banker*

Vestal
Piaker, Philip Martin *accountant, educator*

Wappingers Falls
Hogan, Edward Robert *financial services executive*

Webster
Garg, Devendra *financial executive*
Nicholson, Douglas Robert *accountant*

White Plains
Sharp, Donald Eugene *bank consultant*

NORTH CAROLINA

Boone
Bowden, Elbert Victor *banking, finance and economics educator, author*

Burlington
†Harris, James D. *financial executive*

Chapel Hill
Brummet, Richard Lee *accounting educator*
Kasarda, John Dale *business educator, researcher, administrator, consultant*
Langenderfer, Harold Quentin *accountant, educator*
Perreault, William Daniel, Jr. *business administration educator*
Rosen, Benson *business administration educator*

Charlotte
Anderson, Gerald Leslie *financial executive*
Powell, Charles Roland *financial services company executive*
Smith, James Copeland *controller*
Vane, Terence G., Jr. *finance and insurance company executive, lawyer*
Wentz, Billy Melvin, Jr. *finance executive*
Williford, Donald Bratton *accounting company executive*
Wolfe, Gary Johnson *financial executive*

Durham
Bettman, James Ross *management educator*
Staelin, Richard *business administration educator*

Elon College
Metcalf, Corwin Moore (Mickey) *business educator, businessman, consultant*

Greensboro
Compton, John Carroll *accountant*
Hamilton, Elizabeth Newnam *credit union executive*
Mecimore, Charles Douglas *accounting educator*

Greenville
Hines, Danny Ray *accountant, educator*
Schellenberger, Robert Earl *management educator and department chairman*
Wrisley, Robert Lyman *business educator*

Hickory
Knedlik, Ronald W. *food wholesale and retail executive*

High Point
Foscue, James E. *commercial finance company executive*
Johnson, Richard Arthur *factoring credit executive*
†Saxon, Franklin N. *finance executive*

Jacksonville
Hutto, James Calhoun *retired financial executive*

Mount Airy
Rotenizer, R. Eugene *financial planner, consultant and advisor*

New Bern
Degnan, Herbert Raymond *financial executive, lawyer, accountant*

North Wilkesboro
Underwood, Harry Burnham, II *financial executive, accountant*

Pinehurst
Ashby, Donald Wayne, Jr. *retired accountant*

Pittsboro
Grant, Robert Erich *financial officer*

Raleigh
Glass, Margaret Smyllie *corporate treasurer, lawyer*
Homick, Daniel John *financial executive, lawyer*
Jessen, David Wayne *accountant*

Research Triangle Park
Hagan, John Aubrey *financial executive*

Weaverville
Boyce, Emily Stewart *retired library and information science educator*

Wilmington
Wade, James Michael *treasurer*

Winston Salem
Mackey, Dallas L. *financial consultant, development officer*

OHIO

Ada
Cooper, Ken Errol *management educator*

Akron
†Stefanko, Robert Allen *financial executive*
Steuert, Douglas Michael *financial executive*

Ashland
Cox, Harry Seymour *financial executive*

Athens
Miller, Peggy McLaren *management educator*
Patterson, Harlan Ray *finance educator*
Rakes, Ganas Kaye *finance and banking educator*

Canton
Warner, E. John *manufacturing financial executive*

Chagrin Falls
Strachan, Donald M. *financial company executive*

Cincinnati
Black, David deLaine *investment consultant*
Brumm, Brian Allen *accountant*
Carroll, Robert Henry *accountant*
Conaton, Michael Joseph *financial service executive*
DeBrunner, Gerald Joseph *accounting firm executive*
Driehaus, Robert Joseph *financial company executive*
Evans, Barry Craig *financial services company exexutive*
Garber, Charles Nelson *financial executive*
Hayden, Joseph Page, Jr. *finance company executive*
Lawson, Randall Clayton, II *financial executive*
Lindner, Robert David *finance company executive*
Lintz, Robert Carroll *financial holding company executive*
Mantel, Samuel Joseph, Jr. *management educator, consultant*
Sedgwick-Hirsch, Carol Elizabeth *financial executive*
Siekmann, Donald Charles *accountant*
Ullman, Louis Jay *financial executive*
Walker, Michael Claude *finance educator*
Watts, Barbara Gayle *law academic administrator*

Cleveland
Budd, Gene F. *finance executive*
Cannon, Norman Lawrence *treasurer*
Dossey, Richard L. *accountant*
Easton, John Edward *accountant, financial executive*
Gelfand, Ivan *investment advisor*
Hartley, Robert Frank *business educator, author*
Koch, Charles John *credit agency executive*
Krulitz, Leo Morrion *financial executive*
Lafave, Arthur J., Jr. *financial executive, lawyer*
Mayne, Lucille Stringer *finance educator*
Peters, James Ray *accountant*
Roberts, James Owen *financial planning executive*
Ruflin, Paul Leroy *accountant, consultant*
Seaton, Robert Finlayson *retired planned giving consultant*
Stratton-Crooke, Thomas Edward *financial consultant*

Columbus
Ballou, Charles Herbert *financial executive*
Berry, William Lee *business administration educator*
Collier, David Alan *management educator*
Gerber, William Kenton *financial executive*
Grapski, Ladd Raymond *accountant*
Kyees, John Edward *apparel company executive*
McMaster, Robert Raymond *accountant*
Sofranko, Joel E. *pension fund administrator*
Stark, Maurice Gene *research institute financial executive*
Tomassini, Lawrence Anthony *accounting educator, consultant*
Trimble, Marian Alice Eddy *mutual fund executive*

Cuyahoga Falls
Moses, Abe Joseph *international financial consultant*

Dayton
Hoge, Franz Joseph *accounting firm executive*
Walden, James William *accountant, educator*

Dublin
Madigan, Joseph Edward *financial executive, consultant, director*

Harrison
Kocher, Juanita Fay *auditor*

Holland
Kennedy, James L. *accountant*

Kettering
Caldabaugh, Karl *holding company executive*

Lancaster
Voss, Jack Donald *international business consultant, lawyer*

Maumee
Tigges, Kenneth Edwin *retired financial executive*

North Canton
Lynham, C(harles) Richard *foundry company executive*

Oxford
Goodell, George Sidney *finance educator*
Wilson, James Ray *international business educator*

Painesville
Clement, Daniel Roy, III *accountant, assistant nurse, small business owner*

Perrysburg
Barbe, Betty Catherine *financial analyst*

Portsmouth
†Rau, William Arthur *health care company financial executive*

Spring Valley
Singhvi, Surendra Singh *finance and strategy consultant*

Toledo
Brockmeyer, Ann Hartmann *financial planner*
Shultz, Edward Joseph *holdings company executive*

Wickliffe
Hanzak, Janice Chrisman *accountant*
Stroesenreuther, George Dale *financial executive*

Youngstown
Winkelstern, Philip Norman *financial executive*

OKLAHOMA

Edmond
Ashford, George Allen *investment advisor*

Enid
†Allen, William Richard, Jr. *finance company executive*

Moore
Harrington, Gary Burnes *retired controller*

Norman
Cosier, Richard A. *business educator, consultant*
Lis, Anthony Stanley *business administration educator*
Van Auken, Robert Danforth *business administration educator, management consultant*

Oklahoma City
Long, E(velyn) Claudine *finance planning executive, educator*
Russell, Harold LeRoy *accountant*
Tolbert, James R., III *financial executive*

Tulsa
Bowen, William Augustus *financial consultant*
Gaddis, Richard William *management educator*
Roderick, Robert Gene *accountant, chief financial officer*
Wood, William Dean *accountant*

OREGON

Albany
Bianchi, Charles Paul *technical and business executive, money manager, financial consultant*

Corvallis
Becker, Boris William *business educator*
Nielson, Norma Lee *business educator*

Eugene
Mowday, Richard Thomas *management educator*

Grants Pass
Smith, Barnard Elliot *management educator*

Portland
Cateora, Philip Rene *business educator, author*
Lanz, Robert Francis *corporate financial officer*
Roche, David Alan *accounting firm executive*
Weber, George Richard *financial consultant, writer*

PENNSYLVANIA

Allentown
Cella, Frank G. *finance company executive*
Heitmann, George Joseph *business educator, consultant*

Allison Park
LaDow, C. Stuart *consultant financial services*

Bala Cynwyd
McGill, Dan Mays *insurance business educator*
Miller, L. Martin *accountant, financial planning specialist*

Bethlehem
Barsness, Richard Webster *management educator, administrator*
Connors, Leo Gerard *former finance company executive, consultant*
Hobbs, James Beverly *business administration educator, writer*

Blue Bell
Yuhas, Alan Thomas *investment management executive*

Braddock
Slack, Edward Dorsey, III *financial systems professional, consultant*

Broomall
Dibianca, Joseph Philip *finance executive*

Bryn Mawr
Moyer, F. Stanton *financial executive, advisor*

Camp Hill
Robinson, Ronald Michael *health care financial executive, financial consultant*
Sullivan, Barry Michael *finance executive*

Collegeville
†Perillo, Giulio *controller*

Dover
Hayek, William Edward *investment counsel, financial consultant*

Elkins Park
†Thomas, Geoffrey C. *finance company executive*

Flourtown
Christy, John Gilray *financial company executive*

Gladwyne
Booth, Harold Waverly *finance and investment company executive, lawyer*

Haverford
Merrill, Arthur Alexander *financial analyst*

Havertown
Brinker, Thomas Michael *finance executive*

Horsham
Alter, Dennis *holding company executive*
Wesselink, David Duwayne *finance company executive*
Zimmermann, R. Peter *financial executive*

Lafayette Hill
King, Leon *financial services executive*

Lancaster
Freeman, Clarence Calvin *financial executive*

Loretto
Benham, Philip Owen, Jr. *business marketing educator, consultant*

Murrysville
McWhirter, James Herman *consulting engineering business executive, financial planner*

Newtown Square
Graf, Arnold Harold *employee benefits executive, financial planner*
Steinman, Robert Cleeton *accountant*

Philadelphia
Abel, Andrew Bruce *finance and economics educator*
Alexander, William Herbert *financial business educator, former construction company executive, former army officer*
Anderson, Rolph Ely *marketing educator*
Andrisani, Paul *business educator, management consultant*
Babbel, David Frederick *finance educator*
Blume, Marshall Edward *finance educator*
Bowman, Edward Harry *business science educator*
Cox, Douglas Lynn *financial service executive*
Dillett, Gregory Craft *finance company executive*
Friedman, Sidney A. *financial services executive*
Giese, William Herbert *tax accountant*
Goodman, Charles Schaffner *marketing educator*
Gorenberg, Charles Lloyd *financial services executive*
Hale, Charles Franklin *finanical services company executive*
Hess, Sidney Wayne *management educator*
Jackendoff, Nathaniel *finance educator*
Kelley, William Thomas *marketing educator*
Kim, Synja P. *corporate business planner*
Kimberly, John Robert *management educator, consultant*
Ksansnak, James E. *service management company executive*
Leimkuhler, Gerard Joseph, Jr. *financial holding company executive*
Lemaire, Jean Henri *actuarial science educator*
Lodish, Leonard Melvin *marketing educator, entrepreneur*
Merrifield, Dudley Bruce *business educator, former government official*
Micko, Alexander S. *financial executive*
Nadley, Harris Jerome *accountant, educator, writer*
Nagle, Arlington, Jr. *accountant, corporate executive*
Robinson, Robert L. *financial service company executive, lawyer*
Root, Franklin Russell *business educator*
Rose, Robert Lawrence *financial services company executive*
Rosenbloom, Bert *marketing educator*
Rowan, Richard Lamar *business management educator*
Saks, Stephen Howard *accountant*
Santomero, Anthony M. *business educator*
Sanyour, Michael Louis, Jr. *financial services company executive*
Saul, Ralph Southey *financial service executive*
Savitz, Samuel J. *actuarial consulting firm executive*
Schumann, William Henry, III *financial executive*
Shils, Edward B. *management educator, lawyer*
Spivak, Robert Elliot *financial consultant*
Staloff, Arnold Fred *financial executive*
Sutherland, Lewis Frederick *diversified services company executive*
Taylor, Wilson H. *diversified financial company executive*
Wixon, Rufus *retired accounting educator*
Woods, Richard Seavey *accountant, educator*
Ziegler, Donald Robert *accountant*
Zucker, William *retired business educator*

Pine Grove
Hoy, Harold Joseph *marketing educator, retail executive, management consultant, author, military officer*

Pittsburgh
Anderson, Thomas Caryl *financial and administrative systems professional*
Bernt, Benno Anthony *financial and business executive*
Franklin, Kenneth Ronald *franchise company executive, consultant*
Frueh, John Curt *financial executive*
†Guna, Edward Francis *financial executive*
Ijiri, Yuji *accounting and economics educator*
Jehle, Michael Edward *financial executive*
Junker, Edward P., III *diversified financial services company executive*
Kilmann, Ralph Herman *business educator*
King, William Richard *business educator, consultant*
Kriebel, Charles Hosey *management sciences educator*
Lewis, Richard Allan *financial planner*
Russell, Stanley G., Jr. *accountant*
Thorne, John Reinecke *business educator, venture capitalist*
Ulmer, Daniel C., Jr. *diversified financial services company executive*
Wagner, Lawrence M. *diversified financial services company executive*

Plymouth Meeting
Litman, Raymond Stephen *financial services consultant*

Radnor
Arader, Walter Graham *financial consultant*
Stearns, Milton Sprague, Jr. *financial executive*

Reading
Itin, James Richard *financial executive*

Saint Davids
Bertsch, Frederick Charles, III *business executive*

Sewickley
Jones, Fred Richard *financial executive*

Southampton
†Pietrzak, Leonard Walter *accountant*

University Park
Bennett, Peter Dunne *marketing educator*
Cochran, Philip Lee *business educator*
Jaffe, Austin Jay *business administration educator*
Lusht, Kenneth Michael *business administration educator*
McKeown, James Charles *accounting educator, consultant*
Schrader, William Joseph *accountant, educator*

Valley Forge
Cuzzolina, Michael Joseph *financial executive*
Neff, John Brown *financial portfolio manager*

Villanova
Dorian, Harry Aram *financial consultant, former bank executive*

Wallingford
Herpel, George Lloyd *marketing educator*

Wayne
Caruso, Richard Ernest *financial company executive*
Sims, Robert John *financial planner*
West, Alfred Paul, Jr. *financial services executive*

West Conshohocken
Richard, Scott F. *portfolio manager*

Wilkes Barre
Bevevino, Frank *finance company executive*

Williamsport
Bryant, Martha J. *accountant*
Facey, Karlyle Frank *financial executive, consultant*

Wynnewood
Campbell, Alan Keith *business educator*
La Blanc, Charles Wesley, Jr. *financial consultant*

York
Welber, David Alan *accountant*

RHODE ISLAND

Lincoln
Carter, Wilfred Wilson *financial executive, controller*

Pawtucket
Davison, Charles Hamilton *financial executive*

Providence
Downing, Brian Thomas *business executive*
Flynn, John William *financial services executive*
Harris, Richard John *diversified holding company executive*
Satterthwaite, Franklin Bache, Jr. *management educator, consultant*
Tillinghast, Charles Carpenter, Jr. *aviation and financial consultant*

Westerly
Rees, Charles H. G. *retired financial officer, investor, consultant*

SOUTH CAROLINA

Batesburg
Drafts, James Pickens, III *financial and actuarial examiner*

Cayce
Byars, Merlene Hutto *accountant, visual artist*

Charleston
Adelson, Gloria Ann *financial executive*
Hogan, Arthur James *portfolio manager*

Clemson
Hicks, Edwin Hugh *accountant*

Columbia
Denton, Robert William (Pete Denton) *financial executive*
Fryer, John Stanley *management science educator*
Pritchett, Samuel Travis *finance and insurance educator, researcher*

Georgetown
McGrath, James Charles, III *financial services company executive, lawyer, consultant*

Greenville
Fayonsky, James Leon *financial planner*

Hilton Head Island
Kaley, Arthur Warren *financial consulting company executive*

Myrtle Beach
Patton, Wendell Melton, Jr. *retired management educator, consulting psychologist, college president*

Spartanburg
Pate, John Gillis, Jr. *financial consultant*

West Columbia
Hand, Herbert Hensley *management educator, executive, consultant, inventor*

SOUTH DAKOTA

Burbank
Simmons, Joseph Thomas *accountant, educator*

Platte
Pennington, Beverly Melcher *financial services company executive*

Rapid City
†Clement, Dale Eugene *financial executive*

TENNESSEE

Athens
Thompson, Verdine Mae *financial planner, tax preparer*

Franklin
Brophy, Jeremiah Joseph *financial company official, former army officer*

Johnson City
Bayes, Paul Eugene *accounting educator*
Rider, John Allen, II *business educator, paralegal*

Lebanon
Hubbard, Julia Faye *accountant*

Louisville
Williams, Timothy Wayne *finance company executive*

Memphis
Forell, David Charles *financial executive*
Merrill, J. Mark *financial management executive*

Nashville
D'Agostino, James Samuel, Jr. *financial executive*
Dykes, Archie Reece *financial services executive*
Holsen, Robert Charles *accountant*
Richmond, Samuel Bernard *management educator*
Van, George Paul *international money management executive*
Weingartner, H(ans) Martin *finance educator*

TEXAS

Allen
Hagar, Robert Montel *chief executive officer, business owner*

Amarillo
Streu, Raymond Oliver *financial planner, securities executive*
Strickland, Anita Maurine *retired business educator, librarian*

Arlington
Dickinson, Roger Allyn *business administration educator*

Austin
Alpert, Mark Ira *marketing educator*
Anderson, Urton Liggett *accounting educator*
Blair, Calvin Patton *retired business administration educator*
Crum, Lawrence Lee *banking educator*
Cundiff, Edward William *marketing educator*
Doenges, Rudolph Conrad *finance educator*
Granof, Michael H. *accounting educator*
Graydon, Frank Drake *retired accounting educator, university administrator*
Kinney, William Rudolph, Jr. *accounting educator, researcher*
Larson, Kermit Dean *accounting educator*
Peterson, Robert Allen *marketing educator*
Pugsley, John East *financial executive, accountant*
Robertson, Jack Clark *accounting educator*
Sommerfeld, Raynard Matthias *accounting educator*
Summers, Edward Lee *accounting educator*
Tinic, Seha Mehmet *finance educator*
Welsch, Glenn Albert *accounting educator*
Witt, Robert Charles *finance educator*
Wolf, Harold Arthur *finance educator*

Brownsville
Crum, Nancy L. *credit union executive*

College Station
Crumbley, Donald Larry *accounting educator, writer, consultant*
Manning, Walter Scott *accountant, former educator, consultant*
Mobley, William Hodges *management educator*
Plum, Charles Walden *retired business executive and educator*
Trennepohl, Gary Lee *finance educator*
Wichern, Dean William *business educator*

Dallas
Ablon, Arnold Norman *accountant*
Casey, Albert Vincent *business policy educator, retired business executive*
Coldwell, Philip Edward *financial consultant*
Durham, Michael Jonathan *treasurer*
Harris, Lucy Brown *accountant, consultant*
†Hay, Jess Thomas *finance company executive*
Holsinger, W. Preston *diversified holding company executive*
Howland, Grafton Dulany *financial counselor*
Lerner, Alan Burton *financial service executive, lawyer*
Lomax, John H. *financial service company executive*
Mahr, George Joseph *financial service executive, real estate developer*
Marshall, Harold D. *leasing and financial services company executive*
McCormick, James Clarence *business consultant*
McElvain, David Plowman *manufacturing company financial executive*
McMahon, Gary Francis *accountant*
Mc Quillan, Joseph Michael *finance company executive*
Moore, Thomas Joseph *financial company executive*
Murrell, William Ivan *accountant*
Owen, Robert Randolph *accountant*
Rone, B. J. *financial executive*
Shimer, Daniel Lewis *corporate executive*
Solender, Robert Lawrence *financial and real estate corporation officer*
Thomas, Robert Lee *financial services company executive, consultant*
Willey, Paul Wayne *financial executive*

Denton
Brock, Horace Rhea *accounting educator*

El Paso
Kelley, Sylvia Johnson *financial services firm executive*
Ricks, Thomas Edwin *accounting executive*

Fort Worth
Bell, David Eugene *investment company executive*
Bousquette, William Charles *financial executive*
Clark, Emory Eugene *financial planning executive*
Dominiak, Geraldine Florence *accounting educator*
Howison, George Everett *financial executive*
†Standifer, Monty Ray *controller*
Yarbro, James Wesley *financial executive*

Galveston
Welch, Ronald J. *actuary*

Garland
McGill, Maurice Leon *financial executive*
Nicholson, Luther Beal *financial consultant*
Threlkeld, Mary Helen *accountant*

Georgetown
Lord, William Grogan *financial holding company executive*

Houston
Arnold, Daniel Calmes *finance company executive*
Brown, Lewis Arnold *financial consultant*
Brown, Sara Lou *accounting firm executive*
Cater, James Thomas *financial and investment planner*
Daily, James L., Jr. *retired financial executive*
Gomez, Lucas *credit manager, assistant treasurer*
Hargrove, James Ward *financial consultant*
Hipple, James Blackman *financial executive*
Horvitz, Paul Michael *finance educator*
Jenkins, Judith Alexander *bank consultant*
Johnson, Andrew Carey, Jr. *accountant*
†Jones, Donald Drummond *financial executive*
Knauss, Robert Lynn *international business educator, corporate executive*
†Livengood, Thomas Claude *financial executive*
Miller, Kenneth William *holding company executive, financier*
Ranieri, Lewis S. *financial services company executive*
Robinson, Charles David *financial services executive*
Rockwell, Elizabeth Dennis *retirement specialist, financial planner*
Shaper, Stephen Jay *finance company executive*
Shower, Robert Wesley *financial executive*
Uecker, Wilfred Charles *accountant, educator*
Van Caspel, Venita Walker *financial planner*
Wells, Damon, Jr. *investment company executive*
Wilkinson, Harry Edward *management educator and consultant*
Williams, James Lee *financial industries executive*
Zeff, Stephen Addam *accounting educator*

Irving
Belknap, John Corbould *financial executive*
Carpenter, John W., III *financial corporate executive*
Hughes, John Farrell *finance company executive*
Jack, James E. *financial service company executive*
Metevier, James F. *finance company executive*
Pickett, Edwin Gerald *financial executive*
Sullivan, Joseph Robert *financial service company executive, lawyer*

Lubbock
Sears, Robert Stephen *finance educator*
Stem, Carl Herbert *business educator*
Wolfe, Verda Nell *pension consultant, financial planner*

Plainview
Duvall, Wallace Lee *management educator, consultant*

Plano
Bode, Richard Albert *retired financial executive*

Richardson
Lupe, John Edward, Jr. *finance executive*
Schrimsher, Jerry James *diversified financial services company executive*

San Antonio
Carroll, William Marion *financial services executive*
Fawcett, Leslie Clarence, Jr. *accountant*
Freeman, Howard Lee, Jr. *financial executive*
Fuhrmann, Charles J., II *investment and finance consultant*
Jones, James Richard *business administration educator*
Neiner, A(ndrew) Joseph *corporate executive*

Southlake
Norris, Richard Anthony *accountant*

Stephenville
Collier, Boyd Dean *finance educator, management consultant*

Tyler
Odom, Oris Leon, II *finance educator, financial consultant*

Waco
Henke, Emerson Overbeck *accountant, educator*
Rose, John Thomas *finance educator*

Wimberley
Skaggs, Wayne Gerard *financial services company executive*

UTAH

Provo
Hunt, H(arold) Keith *business management educator, marketing consultant*

Roy
Karras, Nolan Eldon *investment advisor*

Salt Lake City
Creer, James Read *financial officer*
Monson, David Smith *accountant, former congressman*
Nelson, Roger Hugh *management educator, business executive*
Snell, Ned Colwell *financial planner*

VERMONT

Chittenden
Haley, John Charles *financial executive*

Manchester
Mills, Gordon Lawrence *financial executive*

Rutland
Wright, William Bigelow *financial executive*

VIRGINIA

Alexandria
Brickhill, William Lee *international finance consultant*
Pastin, Mark Joseph *executive consultant, society administrator*

Annandale
Jones, David Charles *international financial and management consultant*

Arlington
Hazard, Neil Livingstone *corporation financial executive*
Lewis, Hunter *financial advisor, publisher*
Loftus, William Frederick *corporate financial executive, lawyer*
Sands, Frank Melville *investment manager*
†Strickland, Samuel Ray *controller*
Thomas, Jimmy Lynn *financial executive*

Blacksburg
Killough, Larry Neil *accounting educator*
Moore, Laurence John *business educator*

Charlottesville
Broome, Oscar Whitfield, Jr. *accounting educator, administrator*
Coleman, Almand Rouse *accounting educator*
Dabney, Hovey Slayton *finance company executive*
Davis, Edward Wilson *business administration educator*
DeMong, Richard Francis *finance and investments educator*
Matson, Robert Edward *leadership educator, consultant*
Mc Kinney, George Wesley, Jr. *banking educator*
Rosenblum, John William *business educator*
Scott, Charlotte H. *business educator*
Shenkir, William Gary *business educator*
Sihler, William Wooding *finance educator*
Sorensen, Thomas Chaikin *financial executive*
Thompson, David William *business educator*
Trent, Robert Harold *business educator*

Chesapeake
Newman, W. Joe *financial planner, municipal official*

Fairfax
Buzzell, Robert Dow *management educator*
Harlan, Stephen Donald *accountant*

Falls Church
Bruggeman, Terrance John *financial corporate executive*
Rosenberg, Theodore Roy *financial executive*

Lexington
DeVogt, John Frederick *management science and business ethics educator, consultant*
Warner, Harry Hathaway *financial consultant*

Mc Lean
Halaby, Najeeb E. *financier, lawyer*

Radford
Ross, James Barrett *finance and insurance educator*

Richmond
†Capps, Thos E. *diversified financial services company executive*
Hamill, A(llen) William *finance executive*
Hull, Rita Prizler *accounting educator*
Kaye, Jerome *accountant*
King, Robert Leroy *business administration educator*
Morton, Marshall Nay *treasurer*
Thompson, Francis Neal *financial services consultant*
Trumble, Robert Roy *business educator*

Roseland
Fetter, Robert Barclay *retired administrative sciences educator*

Sterling
Naylor, Frank Wesley, Jr. *financial executive*

Upperville
Smart, Stephen Bruce, Jr. *business and government executive*

Urbanna
Hudson, Jesse Tucker, Jr. *financial executive*

Vienna
Kumar, Verinder *accountant, financial executive*

Virginia Beach
von Braun, Peter Carl Moore Stewart *company executive*

Williamsburg
Kottas, John Frederick *business administration educator*
Messmer, Donald Joseph *business management educator, marketing consultant*
O'Connell, William Edward, Jr. *finance educator*

Parkany, John *business educator, international financial consultant*
Pearson, Roy Laing *business administration educator*
Quittmeyer, Charles Loreaux *business educator*
Regan, Donald Thomas *financier, writer, lecturer*
Roberson, Robert Stephen *investment company executive*
Strong, John Scott *finance educator*
Warren, William Herbert *business administration educator*

Woodbridge
Dillaber, Philip Arthur *budget and resource analyst, economist, consultant*
Rose, Marianne Hunt *business educator*

WASHINGTON

Bellevue
Dunlap, Ron *investment securities branch manager*
Graham, John Robert, Jr. *financial executive*
†Stevenson, Robert W. *technologies company executive, financial officer*

Bellingham
Self, Charles Edwin *financial consultant, retail company executive*

Cheney
Drummond, Marshall Edward *business educator, university administrator*

Everett
Toyer, Richard Henry *accountant*

Longview
Petersen, Michael Jon *utility company executive*

Redmond
Narodick, Sally G. *corporate executive*

Seattle
Chu, Tony Yeling *business executive, financial consultant*
Collett, Robert Lee *financial company executive*
Curtis, James Austin *actuary consultant*
Etcheson, Warren Wade *business administration educator*
Gorans, Gerald Elmer *accountant*
Hanson, Kermit Osmond *business administration educator, university dean emeritus*
Harder, Virgil Eugene *business administration educator*
MacLachlan, Douglas Lee *marketing educator*
Mueller, Gerhard G(ottlob) *accounting educator*
Pitts, Barbara Towle *accountant*
Ramanathan, Kavasseri Vaidianatha *accounting educator, researcher, consultant*
Saunders, William Lockwood *financial consultant*
Saxberg, Borje Osvald *management educator*
Trump, Eddie *holding company executive*
Trump, Julius *holding company executive*

Spokane
Grub, Phillip Donald *business educator*

Tacoma
Foley, Thomas Michael *financial executive*

Yakima
Bruenn, Ronald Sherman *financial company executive*

WEST VIRGINIA

Charleston
Brotherton, Ann Caskey *financial advisor*
Seiber, William Joseph *financial and insurance consultant*

Triadelphia
Hudak, Thomas F(rancis) *finance company executive*

Wheeling
Hudacek, George C. *tax specialist*

White Sulphur Springs
Sparrow, William Holliday *corporate financial executive*

WISCONSIN

Brookfield
†Roder, Ronald Ernest *accountant*
†Smith, James R. *diversified financial services company executive*

Eau Claire
Weil, D(onald) Wallace *business administration educator*

Madison
Aldag, Ramon John *management and organization educator*
Baron, Alma Fay S. *management educator*
Nevin, John Robert *business educator, consultant*
Sprecher, Peter Leonard, Jr. *financial services company executive*
Swoboda, Ralph Sande *credit union official, lawyer*

Menomonee Falls
Klug, Richard Paul *financial executive*
Walters, Ronald Ogden *finance company executive*

Middleton
Foss, Karl Robert *auditor*

Milwaukee
Kaiser, George Chapin *investment company executive*
Kendall, Leon Thomas *finance and real estate educator, retired insurance company executive*
Ryan, Thomas W. *treasurer manufacturing company*

Mosinee
Janis, Donald Emil *corporate controller*

Muskego
Stefaniak, Norbert John *business administration educator*

Oconomowoc
Kneiser, Richard John *accountant*

Solon Springs
Robek, Mary Frances *business education educator*

Thiensville
Berry, William Martin *financial consultant*

Waterloo
Kay, Dennis Matthew *operations manager*

Wisconsin Rapids
Kenney, Richard John *paper company finance executive*

WYOMING

Afton
Hunsaker, Floyd B. *accountant*

Cheyenne
Drummer, Donald Raymond *financial services executive*

Gillette
Enzi, Michael Bradley *accountant, state legislator*

Riverton
Clark, Stanford E. *accountant*

Wheatland
†Whitney, Ralph Royal, Jr. *financial executive*

TERRITORIES OF THE UNITED STATES

VIRGIN ISLANDS

Saint Thomas
Smith, Lorna Watson *accountant, environmental health administrator*

CANADA

ALBERTA

Calgary
Schulz, Robert Adolph *management educator, management consultant*

BRITISH COLUMBIA

Burnaby
Tung, Rosalie Lam *business educator, consultant*

Powell River
Carsten, Arlene Desmet *financial executive*

Vancouver
MacCrimmon, Kenneth Robert *management educator*
Mahler, Richard T. *finance executive*
Mattessich, Richard Victor (Alvarus) *business administration educator*
Stone, Robert Ryrie *financial executive*

MANITOBA

Winnipeg
Watchorn, William Ernest *diversified manufacturing executive*

NEW BRUNSWICK

Saint Andrews
Anderson, John Murray *operations executive, former university president*

ONTARIO

Don Mills
Craig, John Grant *finance management executive*

Etobicoke
Pelton, John Stafford *finance company executive*

London
Cunningham, Gordon Ross *financial executive*
Johnston, Charles Bernie, Jr. *business educator*
†McInerney, Thomas Edward *financial executive*
Osbaldeston, Gordon Francis *business educator, former government official*

Mississauga
Sago, Anthony E.W. *financial service executive*
Turnbull, Adam Michael Gordon *financial executive, accountant*

North York
MacDonald, Ian Duncan *commercial credit information executive*

Stoney Creek
Cowan, James Spencer *financial executive, consultant*

Toronto
Cockwell, Jack Lynn *financial executive*
Coleman, John Hewson *financial consultant*
Corrigan, Harold Cauldwell *accountant*
Dodd, Lionel G. *holding company executive*
Greig, Thomas Currie *retired financial executive*
Hartley, Stuart Leslie *diversified company executive, accountant*
Hirst, Peter Christopher *consulting actuary*
Hurlbut, Robert St. Clair *finance company executive*
Jagt, Jack *trading company executive*
†Keenan, Patrick John *investment company executive*
Lanthier, John Spencer *accounting company executive*
Laurie, John Veldon *business financial executive, accountant*
†Lowe, Robert Edward *finance company executive*
Mann, George Stanley *real estate and financial services corporation executive*
Payton, Thomas William *corporate finance consultant executive*
Ronald, Thomas Iain *financial services executive*
Skinner, Alastair *accountant*
Sloan, David Edward *retired corporate executive*
Stackhouse, Richard Gilbert *retired financial company executive*
Weldon, David Black *financial executive*
†Wheeler, Raymond Dawson *accountant*
White, Adrian Michael Stephen *financial executive*

Welland
Wintermans, Joseph Jack Gerard Francis *financial services executive*

QUEBEC

Laval
Pichette, Claude *former banking executive, university rector, research executive*

Montreal
Beaudoin, François *financial company executive*
Campeau, Jean *financial executive*
Crowston, Wallace Bruce Stewart *management educator*
Daly, Gerald *accountant*
Desmarais, Paul *holding company executive*
Laurin, Pierre *finance company executive*
Marcoux, Yvon *financial executive, lawyer*
Mintzberg, Henry *management educator, researcher, writer*
Olivella, Barry James *financial executive*
Picard, Laurent A(ugustin) *management educator, administrator, consultant*
Saumier, Andre *finance executive*
Speirs, Derek James *diversified corporation financial executive*
Thompson, John Douglas *financier*
Weir, Stephen James *financial executive*

Mount Royal
Lessard, Michel M. *finance company executive*

MEXICO

Monterrey
Ruiz, Othon *financial executive*

ENGLAND

London
Berger, Thomas Jan *financial company executive*
Gyllenhammar, Pehr Gustaf *finance company executive, retired automobile company executive, writer*
Hallissey, Michael *accounting company executive*
†Stapleton, Nigel John *finance director*

FINLAND

Helsinki
Siimestö, Orvo Kalervo *financial executive*

FRANCE

Paris
Bommelaer, Alain *finance company executive*
Bourdais de Charbonniere, Eric *financial executive*
Houël, Patrick *financial executive*
Vinciguerra, Jean-Louis *finance company executive*

HONG KONG

Kowloon
Hutt, Eric John Villette *accountant*

JAPAN

Tokyo
Makihara, Minoru *diversified corporation executive*
Reich, Pauline Carole *international business consultant, educator, author*

THE NETHERLANDS

Amsterdam
Walker, William Ross *accountant*

PORTUGAL

Braga
Rocha, Armandino Cordeiro Dos Santos *accountant, educator, auditor*

SWEDEN

Lund
Welin, Walter *financial advisor*

SWITZERLAND

Lausanne
Caste, Jean F. *financial advisor*

ADDRESS UNPUBLISHED

Aboody, Albert Victor *accountant*
Adam, Orval Michael *retired financial executive, lawyer*
Anderson, Michael L. *financial planning manager*
Angulo, Gerard Antonio *financial executive, investor, consultant*
Arenberg, Julius Theodore, Jr. *retired accounting company executive*
Ashcraft, Charles Olin *business educator*
Barbee, George E. L. *financial services executive*
†Beavers, William Reginald *financial consultant*
Beebe, John Eldridge *financial service executive*
Bell, Don Wayne *financial consultant*
Beller, Gary A. *financial services company executive, lawyer*
Beltz, Herbert Allison *financial consultant*
Benjamin, James Cover *controller, manufacturing company executive*
Bergeron, Charles Edward *financial executive*
Bishop, William Squire *commercial finance company executive*
Bolinger, Corbin Eugene *retired finance company executive*
Borum, Rodney Lee *financial business executive*
Bowne, Shirlee Pearson *credit union executive, real estate executive*
Boyd, Edward Lee *financial executive*
Boyd, Francis Virgil *retired accounting educator*
Brackenridge, A. Bruce *trust company executive*
Brown, Henry Bedinger Rust *financial management company executive*
Brune, David Hamilton *financial corporation executive, lawyer*
Bulla, Ben F. *retired manufacturing company executive*
Campbell, Alice Shaw *retired accountant, poet*
Carter, Richard Duane *business educator*
Cashman, W. Timothy, II *financial executive*
Chandler, William Everett *financial executive*
Charlton, Jesse Melvin, Jr. *management educator, lawyer*
Chelberg, Bruce Stanley *holding company executive*
Chia, Felipe Humberto *management and marketing educator*
Chin, Marjorie Scarlett Yee *controller, business executive*
†Colonna, Robert Jerome *financial services consultant*
Conole, Clement Vincent *corporate executive*
Cook, Steven R. *financial executive*
Cotter, Ernest Robert, III *finance company executive*
Cox, David Brummal *accounting firm executive*
Cross, Dewain Kingsley *financial executive*
Daragan, Thomas William *financial executive*
Davidson, John *financial advisory executive*
Davis, George Alfred *financial executive*
Dean, Frederick Bernard *retired holding company executive*
Decker, Hans Wilhelm *retired finance company executive*
Delany, Logan Drummond, Jr. *financial consultant, investor*
Doty, Philip Edward *accountant*
Duppstadt, Marlyn Henry *financial executive*
Dyment, John Joseph *financial executive*
Ernstthal, Henry L. *management educator*
Estrin, Herbert Alvin *financial consultant, entertainment company executive*
Fagerberg, Dixon, Jr. *retired accountant, weather observer*
†Fahlbeck, Douglas Alan *finance company executive*
Ferguson, Robert *financial services executive, writer*
Fowler, John M. *insurance and brokerage company executive*
Fowler, Raymond David *financial executive*
Frank, Edgar Gerald *retired financial executive*
Franklin, Barbara Kipp *financial planner, investment adviser*
Fuller, Stephen Herbert *business administration educator*
Garten, Wayne Philip *financial executive*
Gelfand, Marshall M. *accountant*
Gillespie, Gwain Homer *financial executive*
Gleijeses, Mario *holding company executive*
Good, Barry C. *financial analyst*
Graham, John Darlington *financial company executive*
Grant, James Francis *international business and defense consultant, retired air force officer*
†Grant, William A., Jr. *accounting firm executive*
Gruber, Fredric Francis *financial planning and investment research executive*
Guimond, John Patrick *retired financial consultant*
Haddock, Harold, Jr. *retired accounting firm executive*
Hall, Terry Lee *accountant*
Hamilton, William Frank *management educator*
Hamlin, Dan William *accountant, management consultant*
Handy, Edward Otis, Jr. *financial services executive*
Hanson, Carl Malmrose *financial company executive*
Harper, W(alter) Joseph *financial consultant*
Harris, Randy Alan *finance company executive, lawyer*
Hecht, Emil *retired housing and financial company executive*
Hodges, Paul Joseph *securities analyst*
Holloran, Thomas Edward *business educator*
Hubbe, Henry Ernest *financial forecaster, funds manager*
Hutner, Herbert L. *financial consultant, lawyer*
Isakow, Selwyn *financier*
Jacques, Andre Charles *financial consultant*
Jamison, John Callison *business educator, investment banker*
Kaplan, Leonard Eugene *accountant*
Keating, Charles H., III *finance company executive*
Keegan, Kenneth Donald *financial consultant, retired oil company executive*
Kidd, Robert Hugh *financial executive, accountant*
King, Algin Braddy *marketing educator*

Kingsbery, Walton Waits, Jr. *retired accountant*
Knauss, Earl L. *financial executive*
Kolton, Paul *business executive*
Kosheff, Martin Joel *financial executive, consultant*
Kreitzer, Lois Helen *personal investor*
Kryza, E(lmer) Gregory *financial planner, international affairs advisor, former ambassador*
La Blanc, Robert Edmund *consulting company executive*
Laird, John Robert *finance company executive*
Larizadeh, M(ohammed) R(eza) *business educator*
Lazarovic, Karen *money manager, investment consultant*
Lerner, Herbert J. *accountant*
Lesher, John Lee, Jr. *consulting services company executive*
Levy, Louis Edward *retired accounting firm executive*
Lewis, Charles Arlen *financial services company executive*
Lewis, James Lee, Jr. *actuary*
Litow, Joel David *controller*
Maher, Daniel Carl *accountant*
Malone, Edward H. *financial executive*
Mand, Martin G. *financial executive*
Mayoras, Donald Eugene *corporate executive, speaker, consultant, educator*
Mc Gowan, James Atkinson *business executive, financial consultant*
Mead, Robert Norman *accountant*
Mednick, Robert *accountant*
Menendez, Carlos *financial executive, banker*
Merriman, Ilah Coffee *financial executive*
Miller, Robert Stevens, Jr. *finance professional*
Morgan, Robert Arthur *accountant*
Mosler, John *retired financial planner*
Nair, Raghavan D. *accountant, educator*
Neelankavil, James Paul *marketing educator, researcher and consultant*
Nehrt, Lee Charles *management educator*
Neimark, Philip John *financial consultant, editor*
Newman, Dennis Collins, Sr. *accountant*
Norris, Stephen Leslie *merchant banking, tax and finance executive*
Overcash, Reece A., Jr. *financial services company executive*
Palmer, Gary Andrew *portfolio manager*
Park, Charles Donald, Sr. *financial executive*
Parr, Harry Edward, Jr. *financial executive*
Pennington, Richard Maier *management consultant, retired insurance company executive, lawyer*
Perks, Benjamin Winwood *accountant*
Phillips, Charles Alan *accounting firm executive*
Pick, James Block *management and sociology educator*
Purcell, Philip James *financial services company executive*
Rapaccioli, Michel Antoine *financial executive*
Rawls, S(ol) Waite, III *business executive*
Robertson, A. Haeworth *actuary, benefit consultant, foundation executive*
†Roland, William Alfred *accountant, nursing home administrator*
Rosenberg, Jerome Willard *accounting and consulting company executive*
Roveto, Connie Ida *financial services executive*
Rowe, William Davis *financial services company executive*
Rush, Richard Henry *financier, writer, lecturer*
Ryland, G(reaner) Neal *financial executive*
Said, Kamal E. *accounting educator*
Sayles, Leonard Robert *management educator, consultant*
Scheel, Nels Earl *financial executive, accountant*
Schleck, Thomas Todd *financial executive*
Schoen, William Jack *financier*
Sefcik, John Delbert *financial services executive*
†Shaw, David Elliot *financial executive*
Sheridan, Patrick Michael *finance company executive*
Shields, H. Richard *tax consultant,business executive*
Shore, Harvey Harris *business educator*
Shultis, Robert Lynn *finance educator, cost systems consultant, retired professional association executive*
Smith, David Callaway *retired accounting firm executive*
Smith, Gerald Francis *rendering company executive*
Smith, Kenneth Blose *former financial executive*
Smith, Seymour Maslin *financial advisor, investment banker*
Snelling, Robert Orren, Sr. *franchising executive*
Srinivasan, Venkataraman *marketing and management educator*
Stein, Paul Arthur *financial services executive*
Swanson, Rune E. *financial executive*
Tongue, Paul Graham *financial executive*
†Treat, James J. *accountant, business executive*
Treynor, Jack Lawrence *financial advisor, educator*
Turner, Henry Brown *finance executive*
Udcoff, George Joseph *financial executive*
Ulrich, Richard William *finance executive*
Van Vinkenroye du Waysaeck, Fedia Maurice Gilles *financial services executive*
Waldhauser, Cathy Howard *financial services executive*
Wall, M. Danny *financial services consultant*
†Warburton, Richard John *financial executive*
Watson, W. Robert *president, chief executive officer*
Watt, John H. *financial executive*
Wilhelmsen, Harold John *accountant, operations controller*
Williams, Gaylen Eugene *accountant*
Wolf, Rosalie Joyce *financial executive*
Wulff, John Kenneth *controller*
Zick, John Walter *retired accounting company executive*

FINANCE: INSURANCE

UNITED STATES

ALABAMA

Birmingham
Dover, James Burrell *insurance executive*
Nabers, Drayton, Jr. *insurance company executive*
Pope, G. Phillip *insurance company executive*
Renneker, Frederick Weyman, III *insurance executive*
Richey, Ronald Kay *insurance company executive, lawyer*
Rushton, William James, III *insurance company executive*
Truitt, John H. *insurance agency executive*
Williams, Phillip Adger *insurance company executive*

Fairhope
Boyington, James Jerry *former state senator, insurance executive, restaurateur*

ARIZONA

Carefree
Wise, Paul Schuyler *insurance company executive*

Chandler
Daniels, Lori S. *insurance agent*

Flagstaff
Mullens, William Reese *retired insurance company executive*

Green Valley
Brissman, Bernard Gustave *insurance company executive*

Phoenix
†Foley, William Patrick, II *title insurance company executive*
Melner, Sinclair Lewis *insurance company executive*

Scottsdale
Burr, Edward Benjamin *life insurance company executive, financial executive*
Prisbrey, Rex Prince *insurance agent, underwriter, financial consultant*
Vairo, Robert John *insurance company executive*

Tempe
Christie, Clarence J. *insurance brokerage executive*
Oxford, Sharon M. *insurance company executive*

Tucson
Martin, Paul Edward *retired insurance company executive*
Ziehler, Tony Joseph *insurance agent*

ARKANSAS

Fayetteville
Dulan, Harold Andrew *former insurance company executive, educator*

Pine Bluff
Bradford, Jay Turner *insurance executive, state legislator*

CALIFORNIA

Auburn
Jeske, Howard Leigh *life insurance company executive, lawyer*

Burlingame
Bell, Herbert Aubrey Frederick *life insurance company executive*

Chatsworth
†Southan, Arthur *insurance company executive*

Costa Mesa
Gore, Thomas Gavin *insurance and securities broker*

Danville
Frederickson, John Marcus *insurance executive*

Diamond Bar
Fisher, Louis Raymond *insurance executive*

Encino
Webster, David Arthur *life insurance company executive*

Garden Grove
Williams, J(ohn) Tilman *insurance executive, real estate broker, city official*

Hemet
Treece, Joseph Charles *insurance broker*

La Jolla
Jeffers, Donald E. *retired insurance executive, consultant*

Livermore
Dyer, Richard Hutchins *risk management executive*

Los Angeles
Baker, Lawrence Colby, Jr. *insurance company executive*
Carpenter, David Roland *life insurance executive*
Denlea, Leo Edward, Jr. *insurance company executive*
Faulwell, Gerald Edward *insurance company executive*
Gelfand, Leonard H. *insurance company executive*
Gingrich, Harold *insurance executive*
Gurash, John Thomas *insurance company executive*
Houston, Ivan James *insurance company executive*
Nikolai, James A. *insurance executive*
Rinsch, Charles Emil *insurance company executive*
Rosner, T. *insurance executive*
Seebart, George E. *insurance executive*

Menlo Park
†Crall, Michael J. *insurance executive*

Newport Beach
†Cvengros, William D. *insurance company executive*
Gerken, Walter Bland *insurance company executive*
Marcoux, Carl Henry *former insurance executive, writer, historian*
Sutton, Thomas C. *insurance company executive*

Northridge
Norris, Darell Forest *retired insurance company executive*

Novato
Hansmeyer, Herbert *insurance company executive*
Meyer, John F. *insurance company executive*

Oakland
Skinner, Clifford *insurance company executive*

Pasadena
Bare, Bruce *life insurance company executive*
Bourdeau, Paul Turgeon *insurance company executive*

Rancho Cordova
Alenius, John Todd *insurance executive*

Roseville
Singer, Frank J. *insurance company executive, lawyer*

Sacramento
Gray, Myles McClure *insurance company executive*

Saint Helena
Hayes, James Edward *retired insurance executive*

San Diego
Albritton, Robert Sanford *life insurance executive*
Hayes, Robert Emmet *retired insurance company executive*
Hill, Frank Whitney, Jr. *insurance company executive*
Ross, Vonia Pearl *insurance agent, small business owner*
Rotter, Paul Talbott *retired insurance executive*

San Francisco
Broome, Burton Edward *insurance company executive*
Clark, Edgar Sanderford *insurance broker, consultant*
Djordjevich, Michael *insurance company executive*
Drexler, Fred *insurance executive*
Enfield, D(onald) Michael *insurance executive*
Hatfield, Dale Charles *insurance company executive, banker*
Hill, Arthur Brian *auto insurance company executive*
Jaeger, Joseph C. *insurance company executive*
Lamberson, John Roger *insurance company executive*
Levine, Norman Gene *insurance company executive*
Murrin, Thomas Edward *insurance company executive*
Nevins, Robert Charles *insurance broker*
Ward, William T. *insurance company executive*
Webb, J. A. *insurance company executive*
Williford, Lawrence Harding *public relations company executive*

San Marcos
Reed, H(orace) Curtis *insurance company executive, management consultant*

Santa Ana
Kennedy, Donald Parker *title insurance company executive*

Santa Barbara
Terry, John Timothy *insurance company executive*

Spring Valley
Peterson, Donald Curtis *life care executive, consultant*

Tarzana
Braun, Stanley *insurance company executive*

Thousand Oaks
Gregory, Calvin *insurance service executive*

Torrance
Westover, Samuel Lee *insurance company executive*

Whittier
Davidson, Alan Charles *insurance executive*

Woodland Hills
Weinberg, D. Mark *health insurance company executive*

COLORADO

Aurora
Huff, Paul Emlyn *insurance executive*

Denver
Conroy, Thomas Francis *insurance company executive*
Deering, Fred Arthur *insurance company executive*
Hardy, Wayne Russell *insurance broker*
†Kikumoto, Charles David *health insurance marketing executive*
Robinson, Carole Ann *insurance executive, retired*
Shulkin, Jerome Robert *insurance brokerage executive*
Sutton, Robert Edward *investment company executive*

Englewood
Manley, Richard Walter *insurance executive*
O'Bryan, William Hall *insurance executive*
†Ware, Roger B. *insurance company executive*

Golden
Lewis, Charles D. *insurance executive, rancher*

Parker
Nelson, Marvin Ray *retired life insurance company executive*

CONNECTICUT

Avon
Jarvis, Ronald Dean *life insurance company executive*

Bloomfield
Dooley, Thomas Howard *insurance company executive*
English, Lawrence P. *insurance company executive*

Collinsville
Ford, Dexter *retired insurance company executive*

Cos Cob
Woodman, Harry Andrews *retired life insurance company executive, consultant*

East Hartford
Campbell, Jerry F. *insurance company executive*

Fairfield
O'Connell, Robert John *insurance company executive*

Farmington
Paul, Christian Thomas *retired insurance company executive*

Glenbrook
Schofield, Herbert Spencer, III *insurance executive*

Greenwich
Berkley, William Robert *insurance holding company executive*
Clements, Robert *insurance brokerage executive*
Fuller, Theodore *retired insurance executive*
Heer, Edwin LeRoy *insurance executive*
Lederman, Ira Seth *insurance executive, lawyer*

Hartford
Baird, Zoë *insurance company executive, lawyer*
Benanav, Gary G. *insurance company counsel*
Booth, Richard H. *insurance company executive*
Budd, Edward Hey *insurance company executive*
Compton, Ronald E. *insurance and financial services executive*
Conrad, Donald Glover *insurance executive*
Fiondella, Robert William *insurance company executive*
Frahm, Donald Robert *insurance company executive*
Gingold, George Norman *insurance company executive, lawyer*
Hamilton, James Carl *insurance company executive*
Hess, Wheeler Herdman *insurance executive*
Hickey, Kevin Francis *insurance company executive*
Holt, Timothy Arthur *insurance company executive*
Jones, Thomas Chester *insurance company executive*
Lautzenheiser, Barbara Jean *insurance executive*
Marrs, Richard E. *insurance company executive*
McLane, James Woods *insurance executive*
McLoughlin, Philip Robert *insurance company executive*
Messmore, Thomas Ellison *insurance company executive*
Mueller, Marnie Wagstaff *insurance company executive, economist*
Murphy, Ann Burke *insurance company executive, computer engineer*
Nicholas, Robert B. *insurance executive*
Paydos, Charles J. *insurance company executive*
Petry, Paul E. *insurance company executive*
Randall, Gerald J. *insurance company executive*
Sargent, Joseph Denny *insurance executive*
Scott, Brian E. *insurance company executive*
Scully, John Carroll *life insurance marketing research company executive*
Stephen, Michael Anthony *insurance company executive*
Westervelt, James Joseph *insurance company executive*
Wilde, Wilson *insurance company executive*
Wilder, Michael Stephen *insurance company executive*
†Williams, Sandra *insurance company executive*

Madison
Anderson, Roy Ryden *former insurance executive, consultant*

Simsbury
Krisher, William K. *former insurance company executive*
Lance, Larry Kent *insurance company executive*
†Vander Putten, LeRoy Andrew *insurance company executive*

Stamford
Block, Ruth *retired insurance company executive*
Ferguson, Ronald Eugene *reinsurance company executive*
Hudson, Harold Jordon, Jr. *retired insurance executive*
Kellogg, Tommy Nason *reinsurance corporation executive*
Rondepierre, Edmond Francois *insurance company executive*

Vernon Rockville
Wolff, Thomas John *insurance company executive, consultant, author*

West Hartford
Abbot, Quincy Sewall *retired insurance executive*
Mullane, Denis Francis *insurance executive*
Reynolds, Philip Reeves *insurance company executive*

Weston
Thompson, N(orman) David *insurance company executive*

DELAWARE

Wilmington
Nottingham, Robinson Kendall *life insurance company executive*

DISTRICT OF COLUMBIA

Washington
Browne, Ray *insurance broker*
Canapary, Herbert Carton *insurance company executive*
Ellis, Rudolph Lawrence *insurance company executive*
Fowler, Caleb L. *insurance company executive, lawyer*
Freeman, Robert Turner, Jr. *insurance executive*
Hohlt, Deborah M. *insurance company executive*
Howes, Theodore Clark *claims examiner*
Lewin, George Forest *former insurance company executive*
Lynn, James Thomas *investment banker, insurance company executive, government executive, lawyer*
Meyung, Eugene J. *insurance company executive*
Oakley, Diane *insurance executive, benefit consultant*
Simpson, Louis A. *insurance company executive*
Sormani, Charles Robert *insurance company executive, actuary*
Stark, Nathan Julius *association administrator, lawyer*
†Utley, Edward H. *insurance company executive*
Vagley, Robert Everett *insurance association executive*

FLORIDA

Boca Raton
Deppe, Henry Adolph *insurance company executive*
Leahy, William F. *insurance company executive, lawyer*
Lipsey, John C. (Jack Lipsey) *insurance company executive*
Lynn, Eugene Matthew *insurance company executive*
Napsky, Martin Ben *insurance executive*
Richardson, R(oss) Fred(erick) *insurance executive*

Boynton Beach
Bryant, Donald Loyd *insurance company executive*
Caras, Joseph Sheldon *life insurance company executive*

Bradenton
Phelan, John Densmore *insurance executive, consultant*

Clearwater
Caronis, George John *insurance executive*

Delray Beach
Sibigtroth, Joseph Clarence *insurance company executive*

Jacksonville
Gibbons, G. Hunter *insurance executive*
Howell, John Floyd *insurance company executive*
Lyon, Wilford Charles, Jr. *insurance executive*
McCullough, Ray Daniel, Jr. *insurance company executive*
†Morehead, Charles Richard *insurance company executive*
Purcifull, Robert Otis *insurance company executive*

Key Largo
Daenzer, Bernard John *insurance company executive, legal consultant*

Largo
Alpert, Barry Mark *insurance company and banking executive*

Marathon
Kolker, Roger Russell *insurance executive*

Miami
Denison, Floyd Gene *insurance executive*
†Heggen, Arthur William *insurance company executive*
Johnson, Glendon E. *insurance company executive*
Landon, Robert Kirkwood *insurance company executive*
Mandine, Salvador G. *insurance executive*
Schonbrun, Michael Keith *health care executive*
Toro, Carlos Hans *insurance/financial products marketing executive*
Van Wyck, George Richard *insurance company executive*

Murdock
Cross, George R. *insurance consultant*

Naples
Duff, Daniel Vincent *former insurance company executive, former mayor*
Mc Queen, Robert Charles *retired insurance executive*
Moorefield, James Lee *retired insurance executive, lawyer*
Parish, John Cook *insurance executive*

Orlando
Kovaleski, Charles J. *title insurance company official, lawyer*

Osprey
Woodall, William Leon *retired insurance executive*

Palm Beach Gardens
Lebed, Hartzel Zangwill *insurance company executive*

Pensacola
DeBardeleben, John Thomas, Jr. *retired insurance company executive*

Pompano Beach
Zinman, Jacques *former insurance agency executive*

Ponte Vedra Beach
Hanigan, Marvin Frank *insurance executive*

Port Saint Lucie
Rhodes, Alfred William *former insurance company executive*

Sarasota
Gervais, Darwin *banker, insurance executive*
†Neff, Ray *insurance company executive*

Tallahassee
Gunter, William Dawson, Jr. (Bill Gunter) *insurance company executive*
Hunt, John Edwin *insurance company executive, consultant*

Tampa
Poe, William Frederick *insurance agency executive, former mayor*

Tequesta
Holmes, Melvin Almont *insurance company executive*

Vero Beach
Burton, Arthur Henry, Jr. *insurance company executive*
Feagles, Robert West *insurance company executive*

Village Of Golf
Bates, Edward Brill *retired insurance company executive*

Winter Park
Hoche, Philip Anthony *life insurance company executive*

GEORGIA

Atlanta
Baxter, Robert Hampton, III *insurance executive*
Black, Kenneth, Jr. *insurance executive, educator, author*
Boyko, Gregory Andrew *insurance company executive*
Buck, Lee Albert *retired insurance company executive, evangelist*
Burns, Carroll Dean *insurance company executive*
Cooper, Keith Harvey *insurance consultant*
Dodge, William Douglas *risk management, insurance, benefits consultant*
Gregory, Mel Hyatt, Jr. *retired insurance company executive*
Hilliard, Robert Glenn *insurance company executive, lawyer*
Huntley, William Thomas, III *insurance agent, consultant*
Johnston, Lynn Henry *insurance company executive*
Peacock, George Rowatt *retired life insurance company executive*
Shirk, Richard D. *insurance company executive*

Augusta
Miller, Charles F. *insurance executive*

Columbus
Amos, Daniel Paul *insurance executive*
Amos, Paul Shelby *insurance company executive*
Cloninger, Kriss, III *insurance company executive*

La Grange
Hudson, Charles Daugherty *insurance executive*

Savannah
Innes, John Phythian, II *insurance company executive*

HAWAII

Honolulu
Kanehiro, Kenneth Kenji *insurance educator, risk analyst, consultant*
Kiessling, Ralph J. *health insurance company executive*

IDAHO

Boise
Black, Max C. *insurance agent*

ILLINOIS

Barrington
Flieder, John Joseph *insurance consultant, marketing professional*

Bloomington
Bower, Marvin D. *insurance company executive*
Callis, Bruce *insurance company executive*
Curry, Alan Chester *insurance company executive*
Edmondson, James William (Jay Edmondson) *insurance company executive*
Engelkes, Donald John *insurance company executive*
Johnson, Earle Bertrand *insurance executive*
Joslin, Roger Scott *insurance company executive*
Miller, Duane Leon *insurance company executive*
Rood, Don D *insurance executive*
Rust, Edward Barry, Jr. *insurance company executive, lawyer*
Shelley, Edward Herman, Jr. *retired insurance company executive*
Trosino, Vincent Joseph *insurance company executive*
Vincent, Norman L. *insurance company executive*
White, John, Jr. *insurance company executive, farm organization executive*
Wright, Charles Richard *insurance executive*

Champaign
Peterson, Roger Lyman *insurance company executive*

Chicago
Bartholomay, William C. *insurance brokerage company executive, professional baseball team executive*
Berkery, Michael John *insurance company executive*
Bolnick, Howard Jeffrey *insurance company executive*
DeMoss, Jon W. *insurance company executive, lawyer*
Desch, Theodore Edward *health insurance company executive, lawyer*
Dunphy, Thomas *insurance company executive*
Gill, William Haywood *insurance broker*
Hinkelman, Ruth Amidon *insurance company executive*
Holmberg, Ronald K. *insurance company executive*
†Howard, Vance Francis *insurance company executive*
Jerome, Jerrold V. *insurance company executive*
Kendrick, William Monroe *insurance company executive*
Lorenz, Hugo Albert *insurance executive*
Manning, Frederick James *insurance company executive*
Mc Caskey, Raymond F. *insurance company executive*
Murphy, Barth T. *insurance company executive*
Noha, Edward J. *insurance company executive*
†Rabin, Paul *insurance company executive*
Ryan, Patrick G. *insurance company executive*
Rycroft, Donald Cahill *insurance executive*
Shanks, Gerald Robert *insurance company executive*
†Toft, Richard P(aul) *title insurance executive*
Vie, Richard Carl *insurance company executive*
Zucaro, Aldo Charles *insurance company executive*

Decatur
Braun, William Joseph *underwriter*
Strong, John David *insurance company executive*

Deerfield
Cruikshank, John W., III *life insurance underwriter*
Halaska, Robert H. *health care executive*

Des Moines
Kelley, Bruce Gunn *insurance company executive, lawyer*

Evanston
Pabst, Edmund G. *retired insurance company executive, lawyer*

Geneva
Goulet, Charles Ryan *retired insurance company executive*

Glencoe
Webb, James Okrum, Jr. *insurance company executive*

Goreville
Fosse, E(rwin) Ray *insurance company executive*

Highland Park
Boruszak, James Martin *insurance company executive*

Itasca
Grue, Howard Wood *former insurance company executive*

Lake Forest
Brown, Cameron *insurance company consultant*
Eckert, Ralph John *insurance company executive*
Ford, Donald James *retired insurance company executive, consultant, lawyer*
O'Loughlin, John Kirby *retired insurance executive*
Peterson, Donald Matthew *insurance company executive*

Libertyville
Kummer, Daniel William *insurance executive*

Long Grove
Fitzpatrick, John Henry *insurance company executive*
Hayes, Percy B. *retired insurance company training executive*
Maatman, Gerald Leonard *insurance company executive*
Standbridge, Peter Thomas *insurance company executive*

Morrison
French, Raymond Douglas *insurance agent, realtor,*

Northbrook
Lower, Louis Gordon, II *insurance company executive*
McFadden, Joseph Patrick *insurance company executive*
Saunders, Kenneth D. *insurance company executive, consultant, arbitrator*

Orland Park
Schultz, Barbara Marie *insurance company executive*

Pekin
Scheffler, Robert W. *insurance company executive*

Peoria
Michael, Jonathan Edward *insurance company executive*
Stephens, Gerald D. *insurance company executive*

Prospect Heights
Clark, Donald Robert *retired insurance company executive*

Rock Island
Cheney, Thomas Ward *insurance company executive*
Lardner, Henry Petersen (Peter Lardner) *insurance company executive*

Schaumburg
Bolinder, William Howard *insurance company executive*
†Nauert, Robert F. *insurance company executive*

Skokie
Hedien, Wayne Evans *retired insurance company executive*

Springfield
Budinger, Charles Jude *state agency insurance analyst*
Humphrey, Howard C. *insurance company executive*
Tarr, Paul Cresson, III *insurance company executive*

Vernon Hills
Skidmore, Paul Harold *insurance broker*

Waukegan
†Stover, William Ruffner *insurance company executive, retired*

Wheaton
Flynn, James Rourke *retired insurance company executive*

INDIANA

Bloomington
Long, John D. *retired insurance educator*

Carmel
Dick, Rollin Merle *insurance company executive*
Gongaware, Donald Francis *insurance company executive*
Hilbert, Stephen C. *insurance company executive*

Fort Wayne
Anker, Robert Alvin *insurance company executive*
Clarke, Kenneth Stevens *insurance company executive*
Dunsire, P(eter) Kenneth *insurance company executive*
Edris, Charles Lawrence *insurance company executive*
Lupke, Duane Eugene *insurance company executive*
Robertson, Richard Stuart *insurance holding company executive*
Rolland, Ian McKenzie *insurance executive*
Vachon, Marilyn Ann *retired insurance company executive*
West, Thomas Meade *insurance company executive*

Indianapolis
Bash, James Francis *insurance company executive*
Christenson, Le Roy Howard *insurance company officer*
Cramer, Betty F. *life insurance company executive*
Heard, William Robert *retired insurance company executive*
Huber, Richard C. *insurance company executive*
Husman, Catherine Bigot *insurance company executive, actuary*
Lytle, L(arry) Ben *insurance company executive, lawyer*
Mc Carthy, Harold Charles *retired insurance company executive*
McGowan, Hugh Barry *insurance agency executive*
McKinney, E. Kirk, Jr. *retired insurance company executive*
Norman, LaLander Stadig *insurance company executive*
†Prible, Larry R. *insurance company executive*
Reich, Jack Egan *insurance company executive*
Robinson, Larry Robert *insurance company executive*
Semler, Jerry D. *insurance company executive*
Whelan, John Martin *insurance executive*
Wolsiffer, Patricia Rae *insurance company executive*

Jasper
Fleck, Albert Henry, Jr. *insurance agency executive*

Lafayette
Hobbs, James Allen *insurance executive*
Whitsel, Robert Malcolm *insurance company executive*

Leo
Worman, Richard W. *insurance company executive, state senator*

Pendleton
Kischuk, Richard Karl *insurance company executive*

IOWA

Cedar Rapids
†Blankenship, David Lynn *insurance company executive*
Falconio, Patrick E. *insurance company executive*
Fick, E(arl) Dean *insurance executive*

Council Bluffs
Nelson, H. H. Red *insurance company executive*

Des Moines
†Butkiewicz, Ronald M. *insurance company executive*
Ehrle, Roy W. *insurance company executive*
Ellis, Mary Louise Helgeson *insurance company executive*
†Evans, John Erik *insurance company executive*
Hennesy, Craig *insurance company executive*
Hubbell, James Windsor, Jr. *retired insurance company executive*
Hurd, G. David *insurance company executive*
Hutchison, Theodore Murtagh *insurance company executive*
Kalainov, Sam Charles *insurance company executive*
Kelley, Robb Beardsley *insurance company executive*
Newsome, Jon P. *insurance company executive*
†Powell, Watson (Scot) W., III *insurance company executive*
†Powell, Watson W., Jr. *insurance executive*
Ray, Robert D. *health insurance company executive*
Richards, Riley Harry *insurance company executive*
Rohm, Charles Edward *insurance company executive*
Schneider, William George *former life insurance company executive*
Schroeder, Jack Walter *insurance executive, lawyer*
Speas, Raymond Aaron *retired insurance company executive*
Stauffer, William Albert *insurance company executive*
Wells, Samuel Joseph *insurance company executive*

West Des Moines
Brooks, Roger Kay *insurance company executive*
Davis, Ronald Arthur *life insurance brokerage executive*
†Plunk, Robert Malcome *insurance company executive*

Westerbeck, Kenneth Edward *retired insurance company executive*

KANSAS

Merriam
Miller, Stanford *reinsurance executive, arbitrator, lawyer*

Overland Park
Burton, Delmar Lee *insurance company executive*
Neal, Louise Kathleen *life insurance company executive, accountant*
Oldham, Dale Ralph *life insurance company executive, actuary*
Shipman, David Norval *healthcare consultant*
Walter, Alan Stuart *crop insurance industry association executive*

Shawnee Mission
Barton, C. Robert *insurance company executive*
Holliday, John Moffitt *insurance company executive*

Topeka
Abrahams, John Hambleton *life insurance company executive*
Eisenbarth, Gary *insurance company executive*
Fricke, Howard R. *insurance company executive*
Heitz, Mark V. *insurance company executive*
Laster, Ralph William, Jr. *insurance company executive, accountant*
Miller, Thomas L. *insurance company executive*

Wichita
Durst, Martha Lynn *insurance agent*

KENTUCKY

Lexington
Gunn, Wendell Lavelle *insurance company executive*
Kissling, Fred Ralph, Jr. *insurance agency executive*

Louisville
Allen, Phillip E. *insurance company executive*
Bailey, Irving Widmer, II *insurance holding company executive*
Baxter, James William, III *insurance and investment executive*
Bow, Stephen Tyler, Jr. *insurance company executive*
McCormick, Steven Thomas *insurance company executive*
Pollard, Carl F. *health insurance company executive*
Rice, Jerry W. *insurance company executive*
Rosky, Theodore Samuel *insurance company executive*
Shaw, Robert T. *life insurance holding company executive*
Speed, John Sackett *insurance company executive*
†Sprague, William *insurance company executive, farmer*

LOUISIANA

Baton Rouge
Greer, Robert Stephenson *insurance company executive*

New Orleans
Marks, Charles Dennery *insurance salesman*
Purvis, George Frank, Jr. *life insurance company executive*
Roberts, John Kenneth, Jr. *life insurance company executive*
Trapolin, Frank Winter *retired insurance executive*

MAINE

Portland
Freilinger, James Edward *insurance and investments company executive*
Orr, James F., III *insurance company executive*
Politis, Timothy Jude *insurance company executive*

South Portland
Dalbeck, Richard Bruce *insurance executive*

MARYLAND

Baltimore
Bradley, Thomas Andrew *insurance company executive*
Dailey, George R., Jr. *insurance company executive*
Hayes, Charles Lawton *insurance company executive, holding company executive*
Hecht, Alan Dannenberg *insurance executive*
Jenkins, Benjamin Larry *insurance company executive*
Meehan, David Howard *insurance company executive*

Chester
Dabich, Eli, Jr. *insurance company executive*

Gaithersburg
Boddiger, George Cyrus *insurance corporate executive, consultant*

Hunt Valley
Yow, Raymond Murray *insurance company executive, retired physician*

Kensington
Clarke, Frederic B., III *risk analysis consultant*

Lutherville
Morgan, James Gilmor *insurance executive*

Mount Airy
Collins, Henry James, III *insurance company executive*

Owings Mills
Disharoon, Leslie Benjamin *retired insurance executive*
Gloth, Fred M., Jr. *insurance company executive*
Walsh, Semmes Guest *retired insurance company executive*
Wieczynski, Frank Robert *insurance brokerage executive*

Oxford
Radcliffe, George Grove *retired life insurance company executive*

Rockville
†Canter, Mark A. *insurance company executive*

Silver Spring
Jaskot, John Joseph *insurance company executive*

MASSACHUSETTS

Andover
Fitzgerald, Michael Anthony *insurance company executive*
Sullivan, John Vincent *life insurance company executive*

Beverly
†St. Laurent, David Francis *insurance company executive*

Boston
Aborn, Foster Litchfield *insurance company executive*
Atherton, William *insurance company executive*
Bissell, George S. *insurance company executive*
Boyan, William L., Jr. *insurance company executive*
Brown, Michael *information technology executive*
Brown, Stephen Lee *insurance company executive*
Buckley, Joseph W. *insurance company executive*
Chilvers, Derek *insurance company executive*
Conners, John Brendan *insurance company executive*
Countryman, Gary Lee *insurance company executive*
Duffy, Kenneth J. *insurance company executive*
Fish, David Earl *insurance company executive*
Hirtle, Richard C. *insurance company executive*
Kamer, Joel Victor *insurance company executive, actuary*
†Kelley, Kevin H. *insurance company executive*
Kelly, Edmund F. *insurance company executive*
King, Kernan Francis *insurance company executive, lawyer*
King, Robert David *insurance company executive*
La Fontaine, Raymond M. *insurance company executive*
Lykins, Marshall Herbert *insurance company executive*
Mansfield, Christopher Charles *insurance company legal executive*
Morton, Edward James *insurance company executive*
Nashe, Carol *association executive, public relations consultant*
Roffey, Robert C., Jr. *insurance company executive*
Rohda, Rodney Raymond *insurance company executive*
Rosensteel, John William *insurance company executive*
Scipione, Richard Stephen *insurance company executive, lawyer*
Shafto, Robert Austin *insurance company executive*
Shaw, Henry D. *insurance company executive*
Shemin, Barry L. *insurance company executive*
Toran, Daniel James *insurance executive*
Worthen, John A. *insurance executive*

Brookline
Shaw, Samuel Ervine, II *retired insurance company executive, consultant*

Duxbury
Wangler, William Clarence *retired insurance company executive*

Eastham
McLaughlin, Richard Warren *retired insurance company executive*

Framingham
Oleskiewicz, Francis Stanley *retired insurance executive*

Great Barrington
Schenck, Benjamin Robinson *insurance consultant*

Lynnfield
Gianino, John Joseph *former insurance executive*

Needham
Carey, Robert Williams *retired insurance company executive*
Cowens, David William (Dave Cowens) *insurance executive, retired professional basketball player, basketball school executive*

Newton
Rodman, Sumner *insurance executive*

Pittsfield
Cornelio, Albert Carmen *insurance executive*

Salem
O'Brien, Robert Kenneth *insurance company executive*

Springfield
Bixby, Allan Barton *insurance company executive*
Clark, William James *insurance company executive*
Dooley, Richard Gordon *insurance company executive*
Finnegan, Thomas Joseph, Jr. *insurance executive, lawyer*
Johnson, Robert Allison *life insurance company executive*
Naughton, John M. *insurance company executive*
Wheeler, Thomas Beardsley *insurance company executive*
†Whitt, David Virgel *insurance company executive*

Waltham
Bumpus, Frederick Joseph *insurance company executive*

Weston
Mc Elwee, John Gerard *retired life insurance company executive*

Winchester
Cowgill, F(rank) Brooks *retired insurance company executive*

Worcester
O'Brien, John F. *insurance company executive*
Olson, Robert Leonard *retired insurance company executive*
Quinlan, John Michael *insurance company executive*
Soule, Charles Everett *insurance executive*

Yarmouth Port
Teague, Edward B., III *insurance and investment broker*

MICHIGAN

Battle Creek
Hutson, Don D. *insurance company executive*

Bloomfield Hills
Pero, Joseph John *retired insurance company executive*

Detroit
Buselmeier, Bernard Joseph *insurance company executive*
Lindow, Donald August *insurance company executive*

Farmington
Headlee, Richard Harold *insurance company executive*

Lansing
Arends, Herman Joseph *insurance company executive*
Saltzman, Robert Paul *insurance company executive*

Midland
†Roels, Philip *insurance company executive*

Southgate
Torok, Margaret Louise *insurance company executive*

Tecumseh
Taylor, Robert Lee *financial services and sales executive, information systems account executive, educator*

Traverse City
Chang, Ching-I Eugene *insurance executive*

MINNESOTA

Bemidji
Bridston, Paul Joseph *insurance company executive, consultant*

Ivanhoe
Hoversten, Ellsworth Gary *insurance executive, producer*

Lake Elmo
Shervheim, Lloyd Oliver *insurance company executive, lawyer*

Minneapolis
Anderson, Lowell Carlton *insurance company executive*
Barnhill, Howard Eugene *insurance company executive*
Blomquist, Robert Oscar *insurance company executive*
Flittie, John Howard *insurance company executive*
Gandrud, Robert P. *insurance company executive*
Guillaume, Marnix Leo Karl *insurance company executive*
McErlane, Joseph James *insurance company executive*
Mitchell, James Austin *insurance company executive*
Nicholson, Bruce J. *insurance company executive*
Thompson, Leonard Allen *insurance sales and marketing specialist, consultant*
Turner, John Gosney *insurance company executive*

Minnetonka
Maxwell, Robert Oliver *insurance company executive*
Robbins, Orem Olford *insurance company executive*

Owatonna
Buxton, Charles Ingraham, II *insurance company executive*
Nelson, Kirk N. *insurance company executive*

Saint Paul
Bloomfield, Coleman *insurance company executive*
Boudreau, James Lawton *insurance company executive*
Kane, Stanley Phillip *insurance company executive*
Leatherdale, Douglas West *insurance company executive*
Williams, Chester Arthur, Jr. *insurance educator*

Woodbury
Clancy, Robert J. *insurances company executive*

MISSISSIPPI

Clinton
Montgomery, Keith Norris, Sr. *insurance executive, state legislator*

Gulfport
Hewes, William Gardner, III *insurance executive, real estate agent, legislator*

Inverness
Pratt, William Hunter *insurance agent, small business owner*

Jackson
Dean, Jack Pearce *retired insurance company executive*
Stovall, Jerry (Coleman Stovall) *insurance company executive*

Summit
Jones, Lawrence David *insurance and medical consultant*

MISSOURI

Columbia
Holden, Sandra S(ue) *insurance executive*
Sphar, Gail Ellen *insurance company executive*

Eagle Rock
Rowan, Gerald Burdette *insurance company executive, lawyer*

Kahoka
Huffman, Robert Merle *insurance company executive*

Kansas City
Bixby, Walter E. *insurance company executive*
Bradshaw, William David *insurance company executive*
Chastain, Larry Kent *insurance company executive*
Hazlett, James Arthur *insurance administrator*
Malacarne, C. John *insurance company executive, lawyer*
Mc Gee, Joseph John, Jr. *former insurance company executive*
Merriman, Joe Jack *insurance company executive*
Reaves, Charles William *insurance company executive, writer, educator, investment advisor*
Sayler, J. W., Jr. *insurance company executive*

Lees Summit
Timmons, Joseph Dean *insurance company executive*

Saint Louis
†Craib, Donald Forsyth, Jr. *insurance company executive*
Dressel, Roy Robert *insurance company executive*
Haberstroh, Richard David *insurance agent*
Liddy, Richard A. *insurance company executive*
Schumacher, Frederick Carl *former insurance company executive*
Trusheim, H. Edwin *insurance executive*
Winer, Warren James *insurance executive*
Wolzenski, Ben H. *insurance company executive*

Springfield
Ostergren, Gregory Victor *insurance company executive*

MONTANA

Helena
†Cain, Alan F. *insurance company executive*

NEBRASKA

Holdrege
Hendrickson, Bruce Carl *life insurance company executive*

Lincoln
Angle, John Charles *retired life insurance company executive*
Arth, Lawrence Joseph *insurance executive*
Day, Richard Putnam *marketing and employee benefits consultant*
Louis, Kenneth Clair *insurance company executive*
Tyner, Neal Edward *retired insurance company executive*

Omaha
Ames, George Ronald *insurance marketing executive*
Barrett, Frank Joseph *insurance company executive*
Bookout, John G. *insurance company executive*
Conley, Eugene Allen *retired insurance company executive*
Crummer, Murray Thomas, Jr. *insurance company executive*
Gano, Clifton Wayne, Jr. *risk management executive*
Goaley, Donald Joseph *insurance company executive, accountant*
Graham, Wayne *insurance company executive*
Haney, J. Terrence *insurance consultant*
Jay, Burton Dean *insurance actuary*
Maginn, John Leo *insurance company executive*
Myers, Herman E., Jr. *life insurance company executive*
Skutt, Thomas James *insurance company executive*
Weekly, John William *insurance company executive*

NEVADA

Reno
Delaney, William Francis, Jr. *reinsurance broker*

NEW HAMPSHIRE

Concord
Swope, John Franklin *retired insurance executive*

Grantham
Boothroyd, Herbert J. *insurance company executive*

Keene
Colby, Kenneth Poole *insurance company executive*

Portsmouth
Smith, Stanton Thomas *insurance company executive*

Rochester
†Dworkin, Gary Steven *insurance company executive*

Sunapee
MacKinnon, Malcolm D(avid) *retired insurance company executive*

Wolfeboro
Murphy, Gordon Laurence *insurance company executive*

NEW JERSEY

Berkeley Heights
Gottheimer, George Malcolm, Jr. *insurance executive, educator*

Branchville
Hallowell, Walter Henry *insurance company executive*

Cherry Hill
Beebe, Leo Clair *industrial equipment executive, former educator*

Cranbury
Boulanger, Robert N. *insurance company executive*

East Orange
Green, David *insurance company executive*

Florham Park
Bossen, Wendell John *insurance company executive*
Erickson, Charles Edward *insurance company executive*
Marshall, Philips Williamson *insurance agency executive*
Smith, Robert William *former insurance company executive, lawyer*

Jersey City
Sanders, Franklin D. *insurance company executive*

Liberty Corner
Stoll, Roger G. *health insurance company executive*

Madison
Calligan, William Dennis *retired life insurance company executive*
Leak, Margaret Elizabeth *insurance company executive*

Morristown
Munson, William Leslie *insurance company executive*
Newhouse, Robert J., Jr. *insurance executive*

Mount Tabor
Lender, Herman Joseph *reinsurance company executive*

Mountain Lakes
Cook, Charles Francis *insurance executive*

Neptune
Suozzo, Frank Vincent *insurance company executive*

New Brunswick
Nelson, Douglas Lee *insurance company executive*

Newark
Beck, Robert Arthur *insurance company executive*
Clark, Dewey P. *insurance company executive*
D'Uva, Robert Carmen *insurance and real estate broker*
Dwane, James E. *insurance company executive*
Gerathy, E. Carroll *former insurance executive, real estate developer*
Keith, Garnett Lee, Jr. *insurance company investment executive*
Latini, Anthony A. *insurance company financial executive*
Light, Dorothy Kaplan *insurance executive, lawyer*
Link, William P. *insurance company executive*
Murray, John Peter *insurance company executive*
†Ostroff, Allen J. *insurance company executive*
Ralson, Lesley Lloyd *insurance company executive*
†Ryan, Arthur Frederick *insurance company executive*
Tremayne, William Howard *insurance company executive*
Winters, Robert Cushing *insurance company executive*
Zinbarg, Edward Donald *insurance company executive*

Ocean City
Brown, Frederick Harold *insurance company executive*

Parsippany
†Simon, Richard A. *insurance company executive*
Waggoner, Leland Tate *insurance company executive*

Plainsboro
Jones, Allen N. *insurance company executive*

Princeton
Goldsholle, Gerry H(arvey) *insurance executive, lawyer*
Inderbitzin, Paul Herold *reinsurance company executive*
Jobe, Edward B. *insurance company executive*
Wentz, Sidney Frederick *insurance company executive, foundation executive*

Ridgewood
Knies, Paul Henry *former life insurance company executive*

Rumson
Creamer, William Henry, III *insurance company executive*

Somerset
Brophy, Joseph Thomas *insurance company executive*

Warren
Chubb, Percy, III *insurance company executive*
Norton, Donn H. *insurance company executive*
O'Hare, Dean Raymond *insurance company executive*
Parker, Henry Griffith, III *insurance executive*
Smith, Dudley Renwick *insurance company executive*
Smith, Richard D. *insurance holding company executive*

Wyckoff
Miller, Walter Neal *insurance company consultant*

NEW MEXICO

Albuquerque
Rotherham, Larry Charles *insurance executive*

Las Cruces
Cochrun, John Wesley *insurance agent*

NEW YORK

Albany
Brantlinger, Frank Herbert *insurance company executive*

Armonk
Bailey, William O. *retired insurance company executive*
Elliott, David H. *insurance company executive*

Binghamton
†Atkin, William Walter *insurance company executive*
Best, Robert Mulvane *insurance company executive*
Dalke, Robert Lynn *insurance company executive*
Dunn, Melvin Bernard *insurance company executive*
Pearson, Paul Holding *insurance company executive*

Briarcliff Manor
Pruitt, Peter Taliaferro *insurance company executive*

Bronxville
Knapp, George Griff Prather *insurance consultant, arbitrator*

Brooklyn
Faison, Seth Shepard *retired insurance broker*

Edmeston
†Robinson, D. Theodore *insurance company executive*
†Robinson, Van Ness D. *insurance company executive*

Fayetteville
Sager, Roderick Cooper *retired life insurance company executive*

Flushing
Sanborn, Anna Lucille *pension and insurance consultant*

Jericho
Spivack, Henry Archer *life insurance company executive*

Locust Valley
Sunderland, Ray, Jr. *retired insurance company executive*

Malverne
Knight, John Francis *insurance company executive*

Merrick
Cherry, Harold *insurance company executive*
O'Brien, Kenneth Robert *life insurance company executive*

New York
Athanassiades, Ted *insurance company executive*
Bartlett, Dwight Kellogg, III *insurance company executive*
Benjamin, George David *retired insurance company executive, risk consultant*
Biggs, John Herron *insurance company executive*
†Blondeau, Jacques Patrick Adrien *reinsurance company executive*
Briggs, Philip *insurance company executive*
Bundschuh, George August William *insurance company executive*
Bushey, Alan Scott *insurance holding company executive*
Caouette, John Bernard *insurance company executive*
Clapman, Peter Carlyle *insurance company executive, lawyer*
Comey, Dale Raymond *insurance company executive*
Conklin, Thomas J. *insurance company executive*
Crane, Stephen Andrew *insurance company executive*
Creedon, John J. *insurance company executive*
Crimmins, Robert John *insurance company executive*
Crosby, Gordon Eugene, Jr. *insurance company executive*
Crystal, James William *insurance company executive*
Decaminada, Joseph Pio *insurance company executive, educator*
Dolan, Raymond Bernard *insurance executive*
Ehlers, Walter George *retired insurance executive*
Ercklentz, Alexander Tonio *insurance company executive*
Ferrara, Arthur Vincent *insurance company executive*
Forte, Wesley Elbert *insurance company executive, lawyer*
Futia, Leo Richard *former insurance company executive*
Gammill, Lee Morgan, Jr. *insurance company executive*
Gamper, Albert R., Jr. *insurance executive*
Garber, Harry Douglas *life insurance executive*
Gavrity, John Decker *insurance company executive*
Gibson, William Shepard *insurance executive*
Gilmore, Robert Gordon *insurance company executive*
Glidden, Allan Hartwell *insurance company executive*
Goodstone, Edward Harold *retired insurance company executive*
Greenberg, Maurice Raymond *insurance company executive*
Gruber, Alan Richard *insurance company executive*
Hansen, Richard Arthur *insurance company executive, psychologist*
Harnedy, Edmund Richard *insurance executive*
Harris, David Henry *retired life insurance company executive*
Hauser, Fred P. *insurance company executive*
†Heck, Warren W. *insurance company executive*
Hohn, Harry George *insurance company executive, lawyer*
Hutchings, Peter Lounsbery *insurance company executive*
Irvin, Tinsley Hoyt *insurance broker*
Kamen, Harry Paul *life insurance company executive, lawyer*
Karter, Jerome *reinsurance company executive*
Kavee, Robert Charles *insurance company executive*
King, Douglas Lohr *insurance executive, lawyer*
Klein, Paul E. *insurance company executive, lawyer*
Knudsen, Rudolph Edgar, Jr. *insurance company executive*
Kornreich, Morton Alan *insurance brokerage company executive*
Lamel, Linda Helen *insurance company executive, college president, lawyer*
Lassiter, Phillip B. *insurance company executive*
Leaf, Robert Jay *dental insurance consultant*
Lee, J. Daniel, Jr. *insurance company executive*
Lowry, William Ketchin, Jr. *insurance company executive*
Lynch, Frank Joseph *insurance company executive*
Mangino, Robert *insurance company executive*
Manton, Edwin Alfred Grenville *insurance company executive*
Martin, James Smith *insurance executive*
Martin, Richard L. *insurance executive*
Matthews, Edward E. *insurance company executive*
McCormack, John Joseph, Jr. *insurance executive*
Mc Elrath, Richard Elsworth *insurance company executive*
McKillop, Daniel James *insurance company real estate executive*
McLaughlin, Michael John *insurance company executive*
Melone, Joseph James *insurance company executive*
Meyer, Richard E. *insurance agent*
Morrison, Michael Ian Donald *insurance company executive*
Morrissey, Dolores Josephine *insurance executive*
Moynahan, John Daniel, Jr. *insurance executive*
†Murphy, George William *insurance executive*
Murray, Richard Maximilian *insurance executive*
Nagler, Stewart Gordon *insurance company executive*
Neeck, Bernard J. *insurance company executive*
Norton, Paul Allen *insurance executive*
O'Healy, Quill *insurance company executive*
Olsen, David Alexander *insurance executive*
Osterhout, Dan Roderick *insurance executive*
Papa, Vincent T. *insurance company executive*
Parker, Charles A. *insurance company executive*
Paul, Douglas Allan *insurance executive*
†Peugeot, Patrick *insurance executive*
Putney, John Alden, Jr. *insurance company executive*
Reuter, Carol Joan *insurance company executive*
Ricker, John Boykin, Jr. *insurance counselor*
Roberts, John Joseph *insurance company executive*
Ross, Donald Keith *retired insurance company executive*
Rotenstreich, Jon W. *insurance company executive*
Sandler, Robert Michael *insurance company executive, actuary*
†Satz, Michael Ellis *insurance executive*
Schwartz, Robert George *retired insurance company executive*
Seippel, Thomas J. *insurance executive*
Shinn, Richard Randolph *former insurance executive, former stock exchange executive*
Shur, Walter *retired insurance company executive*
Sienkiewicz, John Casimir *insurance company executive*
Simpson, William Arthur *insurance company executive*
Smith, Alexander John Court *insurance executive*
Smith, John Matthew *insurance company executive*
Smith, Steven James *insurance company executive*
Somers, John Arthur *insurance company executive*
Spencer, Henry Benning *insurance industry investment advisor*
Spooner, Forrest Allen *insurance company executive*
Sternberg, Seymour *insurance company executive*
Sullivan, Joseph Peter *insurance broker*
Tirakis, Judith Angelina *financial company executive*
Tocklin, Adrian Martha *insurance company executive, lawyer*
†Trowbridge, Edward Kenneth *insurance executive*
Tse, Stephen Yung Nien *insurance executive*
Typermass, Arthur G. *insurance company executive*
Underhill, Jacob Berry, III *retired insurance company executive*
Wolf, James Anthony *insurance company executive*
Woodbury, Marion A. *insurance company executive*
Yalen, Gary N. *insurance company executive*
Zarb, Frank Gustave *insurance brokerage executive*

Nyack
†Kurz, Herbert *insurance company executive*
†Warshaw, Jerry *insurance company executive*

Point Lookout
Stack, Maurice Daniel *retired insurance company executive*

Port Washington
Rough, Herbert Louis *insurance company executive*

Poughkeepsie
O'Shea, John P. *insurance executive*

Rockville Centre
Burton, Daniel G. *insurance executive*
Friedman, Neil Stuart *insurance company executive*

Schenectady
Lawrence, Albert Weaver *insurance company executive*

Searingtown
Entmacher, Paul Sidney *insurance company executive, physician, educator*

Syosset
Barry, Richard Francis *retired life insurance company executive*

Syracuse
Marge, Michael *disability prevention specialist*
Whittle, John Joseph *insurance company executive*

Utica
Ehre, Victor Tyndall *insurance company executive*

White Plains
Blumstein, William A. *insurance company executive*
Cohen, Richard Norman *insurance executive*
Tobin, Steven Michael *insurance company executive*

Yonkers
Wolfson, Irwin M. *insurance company executive*

NORTH CAROLINA

Camden
Hammond, Roy Joseph *reinsurance company executive*

Chapel Hill
Kittredge, John Kendall *retired insurance company executive*
Stewart, Richard Edwin *insurance consulting company executive*

Charlotte
Mendelsohn, Robert Victor *insurance company executive*
†Pehl, Glen Eugene *risk and insurance consultant*
Stephens, Louis Cornelius, Jr. *insurance executive*
Waldon, Grace Roberta *insurance agent*
†Watt, William G. *insurance company executive*
Whitney, A(delbert) Grant *mercantile and insurance company executive*

Durham
Clark, Arthur Watts *insurance company executive*
Clement, William Alexander *insurance compnay executive*
Collins, Bert *insurance executive*
Philyaw, A. Roger *insurance company executive*

Greensboro
Blackwell, William Ernest *insurance company executive, financial analyst*
Bryan, Joseph McKinley *insurance company executive*
Carr, Howard Ernest *retired insurance agency executive*
Macon, Seth Craven *retired insurance company executive*
†Reid, Charles Murry *insurance company executive*
Soles, William Roger *insurance company executive*
†Stonecipher, David A. *insurance company executive*

Raleigh
Pendleton, Gary H(erman) *life insurance agent*
†Whitehead, Ian *insurance company executive*

Winston Salem
Beardsley, Charles Mitchell *retired insurance company executive*

NORTH DAKOTA

Bismarck
Smith, Richard Ernest *retired insurance company executive*

Fargo
Swedback, James M. *insurance company executive*

OHIO

Akron
Arnett, James Edward *retired insurance company executive, retired secondary school educator*

Bedford Heights
Moore, Dianne J. Hall *insurance claims administrator*

Blacklick
Doyle, Patrick Lee *insurance company executive*

Canton
Repp, Ronald Stewart *insurance company executive*

Cincinnati
Addison, Harry Metcalf *insurance executive*
Aniskovich, Paul Peter, Jr. *insurance company executive*
Byers, Kenneth Vernon *insurance company executive*
Cantu, John Maurice *retired insurance company executive*
Clark, James Norman *insurance executive*
Houser, Dwane Russell *insurance company executive*
Klinedinst, Thomas John, Jr. *insurance agency executive*
Krohn, Claus Dankertsen *insurance company executive*
Milnes, William Robert, Jr. *insurance company executive*
Morgan, Robert B. *insurance company executive*
Pike, Larry Ross *insurance executive*
Schiff, John Jefferson *insurance company executive*
Warnemunde, Bradley Lee *insurance company executive*
Weed, Ithamar Dryden *life insurance company executive*
Williams, William Joseph *insurance company executive*

Columbus
†Amato, Paul H. *insurance executive*
Carlson, Larry Vernon *insurance company executive*
Crowell, Ohmer Oreal *insurance company executive*
Duryee, Harold Taylor *insurance executive*

Emanuelson, James Robert *retired insurance company executive*
Fisher, John Edwin *insurance company executive*
Frenzer, Peter Frederick *insurance company executive*
Fullerton, Charles William *retired insurance company executive*
Galloway, Harvey Scott, Jr. *insurance company executive*
†Mayo, Gerald Edgar *insurance company executive*
McFerson, D. Richard *insurance company executive*
Neckermann, Peter Josef *insurance company executive*
Schermer, Harry Angus *insurance company executive*
†Shisler, Arden L. *insurance and transportation company executive*
Shook, Robert Louis *insurance company executive, business writer*
Sokol, Saul *insurance agency executive*
†Wells, Richard Lewis *insurance company executive*
Wilhelmy, Odin, Jr. *insurance agent*
Woodward, Robert J., Jr. *insurance executive*

Hamilton
Marcum, Joseph LaRue *insurance company executive*
Patch, Lauren Nelson *insurance company, chief executive officer*

Mayfield Heights
Lewis, Peter Benjamin *insurance company executive*

Westerville
Booher, Charles Forest *business executive*

Westfield Center
†Bosshard, Otto *insurance executive*

OKLAHOMA

Norman
Williams, David Samuel *insurance company executive*

Oklahoma City
Ille, Bernard Glenn *insurance company executive*

Tulsa
Abbott, William Thomas *claim specialist*
White, Ralph Dallas *retired health insurance executive*

OREGON

Ashland
Hemp, Ralph Clyde *retired reinsurance company executive, consultant, arbitrator, umpire*

Hillsboro
Yates, Keith Lamar *retired insurance company executive*

Lake Oswego
Pretzinger, Donald Leonard *retired insurance executive*

Portland
Becker, Larry Wayne *property and casualty insurance company official*
Halverson, Gerald B. *insurance company executive*
Lang, Philip David *former state legislator, insurance company executive*
Whiteley, Benjamin Robert *insurance company executive*

Salem
Rasmussen, Neil Woodland *insurance agent*

PENNSYLVANIA

Bloomsburg
Miller, David Jergen *insurance executive*

Blue Bell
Wise, Allen Floyd *insurance executive*

Bryn Mawr
Kaminski, Joseph Casmir *insurance company executive*

Bushkill
Garretto, Leonard Anthony, Jr. *insurance company executive*

Camp Hill
Keller, John Richard *insurance company executive*
Robertson, James Colvert *insurance company executive*
Ross, Samuel D., Jr. *insurance company executive*

Erie
Hagen, Thomas Bailey *former insurance company executive, state official*

Frazer
Godwin, Pamela June *insurance company executive*
Kennedy, Donald Davidson, Jr. *insurance company executive*

Harleysville
Craugh, Joseph Patrick, Jr. *insurance company executive, lawyer*
McCarter, Michael G. *insurance company executive*
Mitchell, Bradford William *insurance executive, lawyer*

Harrisburg
Lucia, Philip John *insurance company executive*
Mead, James Matthew *insurance company executive*
Salmon, Kathleen A. *insurance company executive*

Haverford
Baney, John Edward *insurance company executive*
Zalinski, Edmund Louis Gray *insurance executive, mutual funds and real estate executive, investor*

Hummelstown
Moffitt, Charles William *insurance sales executive*

King Of Prussia
Volpe, Ralph Pasquale *insurance company executive*

Newtown Square
Staats, Dean Roy *retired reinsurance executive*

Norristown
Clemens, Alvin Honey *insurance company executive*

Philadelphia
Coyne, Frank J. *insurance company executive*
DiBona, G. Fred, Jr. *insurance company executive*
Dicke, Arnold Arthur *insurance company executive*
Farnam, Walter Edward *insurance company executive*
Frohlich, Kenneth R. *insurance executive*
Guckes, William Ruhland, Jr. *insurance executive*
Joyce, Robert Joseph *insurance executive*
Mella, Arthur John *insurance company executive*
Morris, George Norton *insurance company executive*
Reber, Stanley Roy *insurance company executive*
Ross, Roderic Henry *insurance company executive*
Rowell, Lester John, Jr. *insurance company executive*
Snider, Harold Wayne *risk and insurance educator*
Stewart, James Gathings *insurance company executive*
Tait, John Edwin *insurance company executive*
Tarbox, Frank Kolbe *retired insurance company executive*

Pittsburgh
Duval, Robert *leasing company executive*

University Park
Hammond, J. D. *insurance educator*

Wayne
Yoskin, Jon William, II *insurance company executive*

RHODE ISLAND

Johnston
Patin, Robert White *insurance company executive*
Subramaniam, Shivan Sivaswamy *insurance company executive*

Little Compton
MacKowski, John Joseph *retired insurance company executive*

Providence
Hitchen, Harold, Jr. *insurance company executive, treasurer, accountant*
Koelb, Clayton Talmadge *insurance company executive*
Mc Intosh, Douglas J. *insurance company executive*
Schobel, George *insurance company executive*
Tobey, Joel Nye *insurance company executive*

Warwick
Rupley, Theodore J. *insurance company executive*

SOUTH CAROLINA

Columbia
Averyt, Gayle Owen *insurance executive*
Smith, Franklin Sumner, Jr. *retired insurance executive*

Greenville
Hipp, Francis Moffett *insurance executive*
Hipp, William Hayne *insurance and broadcasting executive*
Hunt, Walter Kenneth, III *insurance company executive*
†Ogden, Ralph Lindsey *insurance company executive*

SOUTH DAKOTA

Rapid City
Bickett, Robert Winston *insurance executive*

Sioux Falls
Kirby, Joe P. *insurance company executive*

TENNESSEE

Chattanooga
Long, Tom *insurance company executive*
Walker, Winston Wakefield, Jr. *insurance company executive*

Lookout Mountain
Hardy, Thomas Cresson *insurance company executive*

Nashville
Davis, James Verlin *insurance brokerage executive*
Dedman, Bertram Cottingham *retired insurance company executive*
Gaultney, John Orton *life insurance agent, consultant*
Lazenby, Fred Wiehl *insurance company executive*
Sutton, Barrett Boulware *former insurance company executive*

Seymour
Steele, Ernest Clyde *retired insurance company executive*

Signal Mountain
Hanlin, Hugh Carey *retired life insurance company executive*

TEXAS

Austin
Golden, Edwin Harold *insurance company executive*
Grace, James Martin *insurance company executive*
Mullen, Ron *insurance company executive*
Payne, Eugene Edgar *insurance company executive*
Payne, Tyson Elliott, Jr. *retired insurance executive*

Crockett
Jones, Don Carlton *insurance agent*

Dallas
Cline, Bobby James *insurance company executive*
†Guthrie, M. Philip *insurance company executive*
Hardy, Tom Charles, Jr. *medical equipment and insurance claims management executive*
Langston, Roy A. *insurance company consultant*
Williamson, Walker Kendrick *insurance executive*

Fort Worth
Berg, Ericson *insurance company executive*

Galveston
Clay, Orson C. *insurance company executive*
Elbert, James Peak *independent insurance agent, minister*
Robertson, C. R. *insurance company executive*

Grand Prairie
†Smith, G. Scott *insurance company executive*

Houston
Bailey, Charles Lyle *insurance company executive*
Bickel, Stephen Douglas *insurance company executive*
Couch, Jesse Wadsworth *retired insurance company executive, consultant*
Davenport, Joseph Dale *insurance executive*
Davis, Rex Lloyd *insurance company executive*
Dean, Robert Franklin *insurance company executive*
Devlin, Robert Manning *financial services company executive*
Farr, Walter Emil, Jr. *insurance agent*
Friedberg, Thomas Harold *insurance company executive*
Harris, Richard Foster, Jr. *insurance company executive*
Hook, Harold Swanson *insurance company executive*
Kellison, Stephen George *insurance executive*
Lindsey, John Horace *insurance executive, museum official*
Morris, Stewart, Jr. *title insurance company executive*
Poulos, Michael James *insurance company executive*
Skalla, John Lionell *insurance agent*
Thomas, Marilyn Jane *insurance company executive*
Tuerff, James Rodrick *insurance company executive*
Woodson, Benjamin Nelson, III *insurance executive*
Wurzburg, Richard Joseph *health insurance executive*

Lubbock
Allison, Cecil Wayne *insurance company executive*

Odessa
Bailey, Keith Stewart *insurance company executive*

Richardson
Coleman, Rogers King *insurance company executive*
Langmead, Jeffrey P. *insurance company executive*

San Antonio
Herres, Robert Tralles *insurance company executive*
Holcomb, M. Staser *insurance executive*
Mc Dermott, Robert Francis *insurance company executive*

The Woodlands
Connell, Joseph Edward *retired insurance executive*

Tyler
Guin, Don Lester *insurance company executive*

Waco
Olson, Lyndon Lowell, Jr. *insurance executive*
Rapoport, Bernard *life insurance company executive*

UTAH

Ogden
Buckner, Elmer La Mar *insurance executive*
†Call, Scott Joseph *insurance agent, financial planner*

Park City
Fey, John Theodore *retired insurance company executive*

Salt Lake City
†Cannon, Kent *insurance company executive*

VERMONT

Montpelier
Bertrand, Frederic Howard *insurance company executive*
Harding, John Hibbard *insurance company executive*
Leland, Lawrence *insurance executive*

Norwich
Byrne, John Joseph, Jr. *insurance executive*

South Burlington
Hackett, Luther Frederick *insurance company executive*

Woodstock
Blackwell, David Jefferson *insurance company executive*

VIRGINIA

Abingdon
Graham, Howard Lee, Sr. *corporate executive*

Alexandria
Casey, Michael Kirkland *business executive, lawyer*

Arlington
DeHarde, William M. *business consultant, pension plan administrator*
†Gettier, Glenn Howard, Jr. *life insurance company executive*
†Roe, David Hartley *insurance company executive, retired air force officer*

Harrisonburg
Price, Charles Grattan, Jr. *retired insurance agency executive*

Lynchburg
Britton, Donald W. *insurance company executive*
Butler, John Alden *insurance company executive*
Dolan, Ronald Vincent *insurance company executive*
McRorie, William Edward *life insurance company executive*
Stewart, George Taylor *insurance executive*

Richmond
Alpert, Janet A(nne) *title insurance company executive*
Davis, Norwood H., Jr. *health insurance corporation executive*
Jacobs, James Paul *retired insurance executive*
Kilpatrick, Robert Donald *retired insurance company executive*
Rutledge, Paul E., III *insurance company executive*
†Wiltshire, Richard Watkins, Sr. *insurance company executive*
†Wiltshire, Richard Watkins, Jr. *insurance company executive*

Roanoke
Benedict, Linda Sherk *insurance company executive*
Berry, John Coltrin *insurance executive*

Vienna
Sirpis, Andrew Paul *insurance company executive*

Williamsburg
Herrmann, Benjamin Edward *former insurance executive*

Woodstock
Walker, Charles Norman *retired insurance company executive*

WASHINGTON

Bellevue
Eigsti, Roger Harry *insurance company executive*
Roddis, Richard Stiles Law *insurance company executive, consultant, legal educator*

Bellingham
Fullmer, Donald Kitchen *insurance executive*

Kennewick
Stevens, Henry August *insurance agent, educator*

Kirkland
McDonald, Joseph Lee *insurance broker*

Marysville
Johnson, Rob Carl *insurance agent*

Mercer Island
Vining, Glen W., Jr. *insurance company executive*

Mountlake Terrace
Lockwood, Donald A. *retired insurance company executive*

Seattle
Cannon, James W. *insurance company executive*
Dubes, Michael J. *insurance company executive*
LaPoe, Wayne Gilpin *retired business executive*
Nudelman, Phillip M. *insurance company executive*
Phillips, Josef Clayton *insurance and investment company executive*
Robb, Bruce *former insurance company executive*
Zunker, Richard E. *insurance company executive*

Walla Walla
Perry, Louis Barnes *retired insurance company executive*

WISCONSIN

Appleton
Gunderson, Richard L. *insurance company executive*
†Scheig, Henry Frederick *fraternal insurance society executive*

Brookfield
Payne, Howard James *insurance company executive*
Snyder, C(laude) Robert *insurance company executive*

Madison
DuRose, Stanley Charles, Jr. *insurance executive*
Heins, Richard M. *insurance company executive*
Herndon, Terry Eugene *insurance executive*
Larson, John David *life insurance company executive, lawyer*
Mathwich, Dale F. *insurance company executive*
Pierce, Harvey R. *Insurance company executive*
Waldo, Robert Leland *retired insurance company executive*

Milwaukee
†Granoff, Mark Howard *insurance company executive*
Hefty, Thomas R. *insurance company executive*
Karl, Max Henry *insurance company executive*
Miller, Keith *insurance company executive*
Pelton, Ralph A. *insurance company executive*
†Rentmeester, Lawrence Raymond *insurance company executive*
Schuenke, Donald John *insurance company executive*
Van Antwerpen, Regina Lane *underwriter, insurance company executive*

Zore, Edward John *insurance company investment executive*

Stevens Point
Ballard, Larry Coleman *insurance company executive*

Wausau
Weinberger, Leon Joseph *insurance company executive*

CANADA

ONTARIO

Islington
Wykes, Edmund Harold *retired insurance company executive*

London
Allan, Ralph Thomas Mackinnon *insurance company executive*
Creighton, Dale Edward *insurance company executive*
Orser, Earl Herbert *insurance company executive*

Richmond Hill
Howe, James Tarsicius *insurance company executive*

Toronto
Chant, Dixon Samuel *company executive*
Gardner, John Robert *insurance company executive*
Lasserre, Jean Paul *reinsurance company president*
McNeil, John D. *insurance company executive*
Nesbitt, Mark *management consultant*

Waterloo
MacGregor, Kenneth Robert *former insurance company executive*
Masterman, Jack Verner *insurance company executive*

QUEBEC

Saint Hyacinthe
Brouillette, Yves *insurance company executive*

BERMUDA

Hamilton
Kramer, Donald *insurance executive*
Stempel, Ernest Edward *insurance executive*

Pembroke
Wiedemann, Joseph Robert *insurance company executive*

ENGLAND

London
Harris, William Cecil *insurance company consultant*
Newmarch, Michael George *insurance company executive*
Shaw, Richard John Gildroy *insurance executive*

HONG KONG

Hong Kong
Tse, Edmund Sze-Wing *insurance company executive*

SWITZERLAND

Basel
†Gerber, Fritz *insurance company executive, diversified financial services company executive*

ADDRESS UNPUBLISHED

Adam, John, Jr. *insurance company executive emeritus*
Allen, Kenneth Dale *insurance executive, corporate counsel*
Alvernaz, Rodrigo *insurance company executive*
Armstrong, F(redric) Michael *retired insurance company executive*
Beattie, Nora Maureen *insurance company executive, actuary*
Becker, JoAnn Elizabeth *insurance company executive*
Bellamy, James Carl *insurance company executive*
Cooper, Charles Gordon *insurance consultant, former executive*
Crandles, George Marshal *retired insurance company executive*
Culp, William Newton *retired insurance executive*
Dackow, Orest Taras *insurance company executive*
Dannenberg, Martin Ernest *retired insurance company executive*
DeAlessandro, Joseph Paul *insurance company executive*
DeMark, Richard Reid *retired insurance company executive*
Elliott, David H. *insurance executive*
Fibiger, John Andrew *life insurance company executive*
Gummere, John *insurance company executive*
Gundelfinger, Ralph Mellow *retired insurance company executive*
Hartsell, Samuel David *insurance agent*
Hauenstein, George Carey *life insurance executive*
Herman, Joan Elizabeth *insurance company executive*
Hirst, Heston Stillings *former insurance company executive*
Ipsen, Grant Ruel *insurance and investments professional*
Jacobson, James Bassett *insurance executive*
Kardos, Paul James *insurance company executive*
Kavanagh, Kevin Patrick *insurance company executive*
Krumm, William Frederick *retired insurance company executive*
Krupnick, Elizabeth Rachel *insurance company executive*
Lacey, Cloyd Eugene *retired insurance company executive*
Ladd, Joseph Carroll *retired insurance company executive*
Lancaster, Edwin Beattie *insurance company executive*
Langer, Ray Fritz *retired insurance executive*
Long, Alvin William *title insurance company executive*
Longnaker, John Leonard *retired insurance company executive, lawyer*
Ludlam, James Edward, III *insurance company executive*
Luecke, Joseph E. *insurance company executive*
Maloney, Therese Adele *insurance company executive*
Malphurs, Roger Edward *insurance company executive, chiropractor, biomedical technologist, private commodity trader*
Mascotte, John Pierre *insurance executive*
McCarty, Dennis L. *insurance executive*
McHugh, John James *consultant*
McKenna, Terence Patrick *insurance company executive*
Moreland, Ronald William *insurance company executive*
Morrill, Thomas Clyde *insurance company executive*
Murdock, Mickey Lane *insurance company executive*
Nelson, Walter Gerald *retired insurance company executive*
†Newman, Steven Harvey *insurance company executive*
Plummer, Daniel Clarence, III *insurance consultant*
Resnick, Myron J. *insurance company executive, lawyer*
Reynolds, John Francis *insurance company executive*
Riss, Robert Bailey *insurance company executive*
Rooney, J. Patrick *insurance company executive*
Ryan, James *insurance company executive*
Scott, John Burt *life insurance executive*
Smith, Floyd Leslie *insurance company executive*
Snyder, Alan Carhart *insurance company executive*
Snyder, William Burton *insurance executive*
Tangney, Joseph G. *insurance executive*
Tasco, Frank John *insurance brokering company executive*
Todd, John Odell *insurance company sales professional*
Tresnowski, Bernard Richard *retired health insurance company executive*
Vanderhoof, Irwin Thomas *life insurance company executive*
Whitehead, Richard Lee *insurance company executive*
Wilkins, Roger Carson *retired insurance company executive*
Wills, William Ridley, II *former insurance company executive, historian*

FINANCE: INVESTMENT SERVICES

UNITED STATES

ALABAMA

Birmingham
Comer, Donald, III *investment company executive*
Marks, Charles Caldwell *retired investment banker, retired industrial distribution company executive*
Massey, Richard Walter, Jr. *investment counselor*
Tucker, Thomas James *investment manager*

Gadsden
†Weaver, Jerry *entrepreneur, holding company executive*

Huntsville
Rhett, Harry Moore, Jr. *investment executive*
Spencer, Guy J., Jr. *entrepreneur*

Montgomery
Blount, Winton Malcolm, III *investment executive*
Folsom, James, Jr. *investment company executive, consultant, former governor*

Mountain Brook
Haworth, Michael Elliott, Jr. *investor, former aerospace company executive*

ALASKA

Anchorage
Hickel, Walter Joseph *investment firm executive, forum administrator*
Woodworth, Harry Eades, III *brokerage house executive*

Juneau
Bushre, Peter Alvin *investment company executive*

ARIZONA

Phoenix
Bansak, Stephen A., Jr. *investment banker, financial consultant*
Quinsler, William Thomson *retired investment advisor*
†Sargent, Henry Barry, Jr. *holding company executive*
Zoller, Richard Bernard *investment counsel consultant*

Scottsdale
Kahn, Jeffrey Hay *retired investment banker*
Rizzo, Mary Ann Frances *international trade executive, former educator*

Sierra Vista
Dinges, Richard Allen *entrepreneur*

Tucson
Schannep, John Dwight *brokerage firm executive*

Vail
Maierhauser, Joseph George *entrepreneur*

ARKANSAS

Fort Smith
Hembree, Hugh Lawson, III *diversified holding company executive*

Little Rock
McGowan, Michael Benedict *investment banker*
Morris, Walter Scott *investment company executive*
Reeves, Rosser Scott, III *retired investment company executive*
Stephens, Jackson Thomas *investment executive*
Wilbourn, Gordon Gene *investment banker*

CALIFORNIA

Beverly Hills
Mc Kenna, William Edward *entrepreneur*
Walker, William Tidd, Jr. *investment banker*

Burlingame
Holmes, Richard Hugh Morris *investment management executive*

Carmel
Jordan, Edward George *business investor, former college president, former railroad executive*
Stratton, Thomas Oliver *investment banker*

Coronado
Grant, Alan J. *business executive*

Cupertino
Horn, Christian Friedrich *venture capital company executive*
Markkula, A. C., Jr. *entrepreneur, computer company executive*
Perkins, Thomas James *venture capital company executive*

Escondido
Allen, Donald Vail *investment executive, author, concert pianist*

Foster City
Turner, Ross James *investment corporation executive*

Fresno
Buzick, William Alonson, Jr. *investor, lawyer, educator*
Dauer, Donald Dean *investment executive*

Goleta
Bartlett, James Lowell, III *investment banker*

Hayward
Morgan, Joe Leonard *investment company executive, former professional baseball player*

Hollywood
Marshall, Conrad Joseph *entrepreneur*

Irvine
Burns, Donald Snow *registered investment advisor, financial and business consultant*
Cowart, Jim Cash *business executive*

Larkspur
Kirk, Gary Vincent *investment advisor*

Long Beach
Schinnerer, Alan John *entrepreneur*

Los Altos
Carsten, Jack Craig *venture capitalist*

Los Angeles
Angeloff, Dann V. *investment banking executive*
Baker, William Garrett, Jr. *investment banker*
†Baxter, Frank Edward *brokerage executive*
Bernstein, Arthur Harold *venture capital executive*
Campbell, Douglas Argyle *securities broker*
Drew, Paul *entrepreneur*
Dunton, James Kegebein *investment management company executive*
Emmeluth, Bruce Palmer *investment banker, venture capitalist*
Galef, Andrew Geoffrey *investment and manufacturing company executive*
Gebhart, Carl Grant *security broker*
Gordy, Berry *entrepreneur, record company executive, motion picture executive*
Greenstadt, Melvin *investor, retired educator*
Hurt, William Holman *investment management company executive*
Hurwitz, Lawrence Neal *investment banking company executive*
†Kaye, Barry *investment company executive*
Kelly, Raymond Francis *commodity company executive*
Koffler, Stephen Alexander *investment banker*
Mann, Nancy Louise (Nancy Louise Robbins) *entrepreneur*
Morgan, Todd Michael *investment advisor*
Nilles, John Mathias (Jack Nilles) *entrepreneur*
Ogle, Edward Proctor, Jr. *investment counseling executive*
†Roath, Kenneth B. *investment company executive*
Tennenbaum, Michael Ernest *investment banker*
Terry, Thomas Edward *investment company executive, lawyer*
Wedbush, Edward William *investment banker*
Winkler, Howard Leslie *investment banker, stockbroker, business consultant*
Wiseley, Richard Eugene *securities corporation executive*

Menlo Park
Bissell, Betty Dickson *retired stockbroker*
Hoagland, Laurance Redington, Jr. *investment executive*
Lucas, Donald Leo *private investor*
McCown, George E. *venture banking company executive*
McMurtry, Burton John *venture capital investor, electrical engineer*
Roberts, George R. *venture capital company executive*
Walsh, William Desmond *investor*

Napa
Strock, David Randolph *brokerage house executive*

Newport Beach
Albright, Archie Earl, Jr. *investment banker*
Fletcher, Douglas Baden *investment company executive*
Giannini, Valerio Louis *investment banker*
Solberg, Ronald Louis *investment manager, international economist*

Palm Desert
Budge, Hamer Harold *mutual fund company executive*
Krallinger, Joseph Charles *entrepreneur, business advisor, author*

Palm Springs
Yantis, Richard William *investments executive*

Palos Verdes Estates
Mennis, Edmund Addi *investment management consultant*

Pasadena
Arnott, Robert Douglas *investment company executive*
Baum, Dwight Crouse *investment banking executive*
Howes, Benjamin Durward, III *mergers and acquisitions executive*
Lauter, James Donald *stockbroker*

Riverside
Walter-Robinson, Carol Sue *investment executive*

San Francisco
Apatoff, Michael John *finance executive*
Bertelsen, Thomas Elwood, Jr. *investment banker*
†Brandford, Napoleon *securities firm executive*
Dellas, Robert Dennis *investment banker*
De Lutis, Donald Conse *investment manager, consultant*
deWilde, David Michael *executive search consultant, financial services executive, lawyer*
Dunn, Richard Joseph *investment counselor*
Gardner, James Harkins *venture capitalist*
Greber, Robert Martin *financial investments executive*
Halliday, John Meech *investment company executive*
Hambrecht, William R. *venture capitalist*
Hellman, F(rederick) Warren *investment advisor*
Korins, Leopold *stock exchange executive*
Latzer, Richard Neal *investment company executive*
Martin, Paul Egley *investment banker*
McGettigan, Charles Carroll, Jr. *investment banker*
Nodelman, Jared Robert *investment advisor*
Pfau, George Harold, Jr. *stockbroker*
Pottruck, David Steven *brokerage house executive*
Ratzlaff, James W. *investment company executive*
Redo, David Lucien *investment company executive*
Rock, Arthur *venture capitalist*
Rosenberg, Claude Newman, Jr. *investment adviser*
Ross, Sue *entrepreneur, author, fundraising executive*
Rowen, Harvey Allen *investment company executive*
Seip, Tom Decker *securities executive*
Shansby, John Gary *investment banker*
Shelton, Richard Fottrell *investment executive*
Stein, Alan L. *investment banker*
Stupski, Lawrence J. *investment company executive*
Turner, Marshall Chittenden, Jr. *venture capitalist*
Veitch, Stephen William *investment counselor*
Wiley, Thomas Glen *retired investment company executive*
Wolfe, Barbara Ahmajan *stock brokerage executive, administrator*

San Jose
Hall, Robert Emmett, Jr. *investment banker, realtor*

San Juan Capistrano
Robinson, Daniel Thomas *brokerage company executive*

San Leandro
Pansky, Emil John *entrepreneur*

San Marino
Zimmerman, William Robert *entrepreneur, engineering based manufacturing company executive*

San Mateo
†Burns, Harmon E. *investment company executive*
Fenton, Noel John *venture capitalist*

San Ysidro
Holderman, John Loran *financial broker*

Santa Clara
Lynch, Charles Allen *investment executive, corporate director*

Santa Monica
Lovelace, Jon B. *investment management company executive*
Richards, David Kimball *investor*
Sher, Allan L. *retired brokerage company executive*

Sausalito
Blunt, Peter Howe *capital company executive, lawyer*

Solana Beach
Beare, Bruce Riley *trading company and sales executive*

Westlake Village
Fredericks, Ward Arthur *venture capitalist, food industry consultant*

COLORADO

Denver
Butler, Owen Bradford securities advisor
Holte, Debra Leah investment executive, financial analyst
Imhoff, Walter Francis investment banker
†Marcum, Walter Phillip investment banker
Stephenson, Arthur Emmet, Jr. investment company executive, banker
Wagner, Judith Buck investment firm executive
†Weiman, Stephen L. investment company executive

Englewood
Van Loucks, Mark Louis venture capitalist, business advisor

Evergreen
Jackson, William Richard entrepreneur

Grand Junction
Sewell, Beverly Jean financial executive

CONNECTICUT

Bridgeport
Wetzel, Edward Thomas investment company executive

Darien
Lewis, A. Duff, Jr. investment executive
Morse, Edmond Northrop investment management executive

Farmington
Bailey, Samuel, Jr. investment advisor, lawyer
Bigler, Harold Edwin, Jr. investment company executive
Halligan, Howard Ansel investment management company executive

Greenwich
Baker, Charles Ernest stockbroker
Foley, Thomas Coleman investor
Grabe, William O. investment company executive
Jordan, Jerry Neville investment company executive
Kopp, W. Brewster corporate director, advisor
Larned, William Edmund, Jr. international development and venture capital company executive
Lewis, Perry Joshua investment banker
Nevin, Crocker investment banker
Pringle, Lewis Gordon international trade and investment company executive

Guilford
Boyle, Helen D. entrepreneur

Hartford
Carpenter, Michael Alan securities firm executive
O'Keefe, James William, Jr. investment manager and banker

Litchfield
Booth, John Thomas investment banker

Lyme
Friday, John Ernest, Jr. retired securities company executive

New Canaan
Jennings, William Christopher securities industry executive
Mendez, Albert Orlando industrialist, financier
Pike, William Edward business executive
Snyder, Nathan entrepreneur

Norwalk
Hathaway, Carl Emil investment management company executive
Maisano, Phillip Nicholas investment company executive

Old Greenwich
Maher, Stephen Albert investment banker

Old Saybrook
Schneider, John Arnold business investor

Southbury
Fabiani, Dante Carl industrialist

Southport
Wilbur, E. Packer investment company executive

Stamford
Alley, William Jack holding company executive
Beyman, Jonathan Eric information officer
Ekernas, Sven Anders investment company executive
Frey, Dale Franklin financial investment company executive, manufacturing company executive
Hawley, Frank Jordan, Jr. venture capital executive
Maxwell, Anders John corporate executive
Prindiville, Robert Andrew investment executive

Westport
Kalan, George Richard venture capitalist
Kelly, Paul Knox investment banker
O'Keefe, John David investment specialist
Scheinman, Stanley Bruce venture capital executive, lawyer
Walton, Alan George venture capitalist

Wilton
Finlayson, John L. commodities company executive
Finn, Daniel R., Jr. investment company executive
†Godfrey, Albert Blanton research and management consulting company executive, writer, educator
Ritter, Bruce Commodities Company executive

DELAWARE

Wilmington
Boyer, David Creighton stockbroker
Dewees, Donald Charles securities company executive

DISTRICT OF COLUMBIA

Washington
Ansary, Cyrus A. investment company executive, lawyer
Bonde, Count Peder Carlsson investment company executive
Brody, Kenneth David investment banker
Carley, L. David investment consultant, former college administrator
Countryman, John Russell business executive, former ambassador
Cusick, Ralph A., Jr. investment banking company executive
Douglas, Leslie investment banker
Ellsworth, Robert Fred investment executive, former government official
Farrar, Donald Eugene capital markets advisor
Ferris, George Mallette, Jr. investment banker
Fisher, Robert Dale stockbroker, retired naval officer
Fleming, Robert Wright investment banker
Gaines, Ludwell Ebersole investment executive
Gibson, Paul Raymond international trade and investment development executive
Hardiman, Joseph Raymond securities industry executive
Hartwell, Stephen investment company executive
Isaac, William Michael investment firm executive, former government official
Kelly, Charles J., Jr. investment company executive
Lackritz, Marc E. securities trade association executive
Levitt, Arthur, Jr. securities and publishing executive, federal agency administrator
Lister, Harry Joseph financial company executive, consultant
Lurton, Horace VanDeventer brokerage house executive
Macomber, John D. industrialist
†Miller, Robert J. financial executive
Niehoff, Karl Richard Besuden financial executive
Peterson, Charles Hayes trading company executive
Sethness, Charles Olin international financial official
Shrier, Adam Louis investment firm executive
Silby, Donald Wayne investment executive, entrepreneur
Spangler, Scott Michael private investor
Stearns, James Gerry retired securities company executive
Thompson, Bruce Edward, Jr. brokerage house executive, former government official
Tomlinson, Alexander Cooper investment banker, consultant
Tucker, Howard McKeldin investment banker, consultant
Wortley, George Cornelius business consultant, investor

FLORIDA

Boca Raton
Garzarelli, Elaine Marie brokerage house executive, economist

Boynton Beach
Allison, Dwight Leonard, Jr. investor
Davant, James Waring investment banker

Clearwater
Brown, Herbert Graham entrepreneur

Coral Gables
Nunez-Portuondo, Ricardo investment company executive

Daytona Beach
Locke, Edwin Allen, Jr. investment banker

Delray Beach
Holmes, Walter Stephen, Jr. retired financial executive

Englewood
Simis, Theodore Luckey investment banker, information technology executive

Fort Lauderdale
Huizenga, Harry Wayne entrepreneur, entertainment corporation executive, professional sports team executive
Sanders, Howard investment company executive
Shaw, Bryan P. H. retired investment company executive
Thayer, Charles J. investment banker

Hobe Sound
Fiske, Guy Wilbur investment company executive
Hotchkiss, Winchester Fitch retired investment banker

Jacksonville
Monsky, John Bertrand investment banking executive
Schultz, Frederick Henry investor, former government official
Travis, Forrest investment firm executive

Marco Island
Pettersen, Kjell Will stockbroker, consultant

Miami
Bishopric, Karl investment banker, real estate executive, advertising executive
Bradley, Ronald Calvin investment company executive
Dorion, Robert Charles entrepreneur, investor
Garner, John Michael investment company executive
Gittlin, Arthur Sam industrialist, banker
Stoller, Eric Chester stockbroker

Naples
Dover, Clarence Joseph entrepreneur, public and employee relations executive, educator, consultant, communication director
Elliott, Edward investment executive, financial planner
Guarino, Roger Charles consulting company executive
Harvey, Curran Whitthorne, Jr. investment management executive
Oliver, Robert Bruce retired investment company executive
Osias, Richard Allen international financier, investor, real estate investment executive, corporate investor
Perry, Jesse Laurence, Jr. investment manager, financier

North Palm Beach
Doede, John Henry investment company executive
Gray, Harry Jack investment executive

Palm Beach
Adduci, Vincent James investment company executive
Bagby, Joseph Rigsby financial investor
Gundlach, Heinz Ludwig investment banker, lawyer
Halmos, Peter investment company executive
Korn, David investment company executive
Rudolph, Malcolm Rome investment banker

Palm Beach Gardens
Mergler, H. Kent investment counselor

Pompano Beach
Rifenburgh, Richard Philip investment company executive

Ponte Vedra Beach
Krusen, Henry Stanley investment banker
Thorndike, Richard King former brokerage company executive

Saint Petersburg
Emerson, William Allen retired investment company executive
Galbraith, John William securities company executive
Godbold, Francis Stanley investment banker, real estate executive
Mosby, John Davenport, III investment banking executive
Scott, Lee Hansen retired holding company executive

Sarasota
Cox, Houston Abraham, Jr. futures markets consultant
Levitt, Irving Francis investment company executive

Tampa
Crowe, Eugene Bertrand retired investment counselor
Holder, Harold Douglas, Sr. investor, industrialist

Tierra Verde
Gaffney, Thomas Francis investment company executive

Vero Beach
Clawson, John Addison financier, investor
Ebbitt, Kenneth Cooper investor
Glassmeyer, Edward investment banker
†Ludwig, William Frank retired investment banker, lawyer
Thompson, William David investment banking executive

West Palm Beach
Price, William James, IV investment banker

GEORGIA

Albany
Greene, William Joshua, III investment executive and consultant

Athens
Holcomb, Alice Willard Power diversified investments executive

Atlanta
Dowling, Roderick Anthony investment banker
Green, Holcombe Tucker, Jr. investment executive
Keough, Donald Raymond investment company executive
McMahon, Donald Aylward investor, corporate director
Tracy, Thomas Kit investment company executive
Warren, Edus Houston, Jr. investment management executive
Whitman, Homer William, Jr. investment counseling company executive
Williams, Ralph Watson, Jr. retired securities company executive
Winship, Wadleigh Chichester holding company executive

Cleveland
Lewis, Richard, Sr. securities broker, consultant

Columbus
Diaz-Verson, Salvador, Jr. investment advisor

Sea Island
Brown, Ann Catherine investment company executive
Brown, George Hay investment counselor

HAWAII

Honolulu
Behnke, Richard Frederick investment banking executive
Ho, Stuart Tse Kong investment company executive
McCready, William Floyd venture capitalist, entrepreneur

ILLINOIS

Barrington
Baxter, Reginald Robert investment company executive
Farina, Nick Charles investor relations consultant

Chicago
Bergonia, Raymond David venture capitalist
Blair, Bowen investment banker
Blair, Edward McCormick investment banker
Block, Philip Dee, III investment counselor
Brodsky, William J. futures options exchange executive
Buckle, Frederick Tarifero international holding company executive, political and business intelligence analyst
Chaleff, Carl Thomas brokerage house executive
Clarke, Philip Ream, Jr. investment banker
Cole, Franklin Alan investment company executive
Cone, Joseph Jay investment banking officer
Donovan, Thomas Roy futures exchange executive
Ender, Jon T. investment management executive, banker
Fenton, Clifton Lucien investment banker
Foster, James Reuben investment company executive
Freehling, Stanley Maxwell investment banker
Freehling, Willard Maxwell stockbroker
Gorter, James Polk investment banker
Hawkinson, John former investment management company executive
Henry, Charles Joseph options exchange board executive
Ishikawa, Kozo securities executive
Kahn, Herta Hess (Mrs. Howard Kahn) retired stockbroker
Kaufman, Ira Jeffrey investment banker
Kelly, Arthur Lloyd management and investment company executive
Knox, Lance Lethbridge venture capital executive
Kunkle, Sandra Lee brokerage house executive, sales executive
Larson, Harry Robert investment banking executive
Lewis, Charles A. investment company executive
Lincoln, Sandy investment management executive
Livingston, Homer J., Jr. stock exchange executive
Loucks, Ralph Bruce, Jr. investment company executive
McCausland, Thomas James, Jr. brokerage house executive
McConahey, Stephen George securities company executive
McNeill, Robert Patrick investment counselor
Meers, Henry W. investment banker
Melamed, Leo investment company executive
Miner, Thomas Hawley international entrepreneur
Mukoyama, James Hidefumi, Jr. securities executive
Mulvihill, Terence Joseph investment banking executive
Nash, Donald Gene commodities specialist
Oliver, Harry Maynard, Jr. retired brokerage house executive
Phillips, Donald Wright investment company executive
Podesta, Robert Angelo investment banker
Pritzker, Nicholas J. diversified services corporation executive
Rasin, Rudolph Stephen corporate executive
Rogers, John Washington, Jr. investment management company executive
Sandner, John Francis commodity futures broker, lawyer
Schulte, David Michael investment banker
Slansky, Jerry William investment company executive
Stead, James Joseph, Jr. securities company executive
Swift, Edward Foster, III investment banker
Waite, Dennis Vernon investor relations consultant
Weitzman, Robert Harold investment company executive
Wilmouth, Robert K. commodities executive
Wirsching, Charles Philipp, Jr. brokerage house executive, investor
Woods, Robert Archer investment counsel
Young, Ronald Faris commodity trader

Danville
Burnside, William Charles investment company executive

Deerfield
Howell, George Bedell equity investing and managing executive

Evanston
Downen, David Earl investment banking executive

Highland Park
Uhlmann, Frederick Godfrey commodity and securities broker
Weinberg, Michael, Jr. commodities broker

Jacksonville
Olinger, Glenn Slocum entrepreneur, consultant, investor

Northbrook
Searle, William Louis investment company executive

Oak Brook
Kelly, Donald Philip entrepreneur

Palatine
Flavin, Patrick Brian investment company executive, securities analyst

Princeton
Schultz, Robert Vernon entrepreneur

Riverwoods
Leatham, John Tonkin business executive

Villa Park
McDonnell, Dennis J. securities industry executive

Wheeling
Saranow, Mitchell Harris investment banker, financial consultant

Wilmette
Albright, Townsend Shaul investment banker, government benefits consultant

Winnetka
Mathers, Thomas Nesbit financial consultant
Sick, William Norman, Jr. investment company executive

INDIANA

Evansville
Brill, Alan Richard *entrepreneur*

Indianapolis
Fritz, Cecil Morgan *investment company executive*
Grube, Elizabeth *investment company executive*
Peterson, John Dwight *investment company executive*

Richmond
Passmore, Jan William *investment company executive*

IOWA

Cedar Falls
Oster, Merrill James *entrepreneur, publisher, author, lecturer*

KANSAS

Kansas City
Olofson, Tom William *private investor, business executive*

KENTUCKY

Harrods Creek
Chandler, James Williams *retired securities company executive*

Lexington
Wagner, Alan Burton *entrepreneur*

Louisville
Dabney, Watson Barr *investment banker*
Lomicka, William Henry *investor*
Porter, Henry Homes, Jr. *investor*
Ready, William Andrew *mergers/acquisitions and management consultant*

LOUISIANA

New Orleans
Copelin, Sherman Nathaniel, Jr. *state legislator, enterpreneur, business executive*
Levert, John Bertels, Jr. *investment executive*
Welch, Robert Ballinger *investment planner*

MAINE

Augusta
Moody, Stanley Alton *entrepreneur, financial consultant*

Bryant Pond
Conary, David Arlan *investment company executive*

Portland
Crispin, Robert William *investment company executive*
Powell, Larson Merrill *investment advisory service executive*

Southwest Harbor
Delehanty, Edward John *investment company executive*

Waterville
Ezhaya, Joseph Bernard *brokerage house executive*

MARYLAND

Baltimore
Bacigalupo, Charles Anthony *brokerage company executive*
Brinkley, James Wellons *investment company executive*
Byrnes, William Gerard *investment banker*
Cashman, Edmund Joseph, Jr. *investment banker*
Collins, George Joseph *investment counselor*
Curley, John Francis, Jr. *securities company executive*
Franyo, Richard Louis *investment banker*
Griswold, Benjamin Howell, IV *investment banker*
Hebb, Donald Bruce, Jr. *investment banker*
Himelfarb, Richard Jay *securities firm executive*
Hopkins, Samuel *retired investment banker*
Hyman, Harris, IV *investment banker*
Kent, Edgar Robert, Jr. *investment banker*
Mason, Raymond Adams *brokerage company executive*
McManus, Walter Leonard *investment executive*
Newhall, Charles Watson, III *venture capitalist*
Ober, Douglas Gary *investment company executive*
Paternotte, William Leslie *brokerage house executive*
Preston, Mark I. *investment company executive*
Richlin, W. Gar *investment banking executive, lawyer*
Riepe, James Sellers *investment company executive*
Semans, Truman Thomas *investment company executive*
Shaeffer, Charles Wayne *investment counselor*

Bethesda
Bailey, William Wesley *insurance company executive*
Corbett, Jack Elliott *mutual fund officer, clergyman, author*

Chestertown
Sener, Joseph Ward, Jr. *securities company executive*

Chevy Chase
Freeman, Harry Louis *investment executive*

Lutherville Timonium
Cappiello, Frank Anthony, Jr. *investment advisor*

Potomac
Proffitt, John Richard *investment banking executive*

Queenstown
Bancroft, Paul, III *investment company executive, venture capitalist*

Riverside
Guetzkow, Daniel Steere *technology company entrepreneur*

Rockville
Christie, R(obert) Brent *entrepreneur, real estate and hotel executive*
Tripp, Frederick Gerald *investment advisor*

MASSACHUSETTS

Boston
Aikman, William Francis *venture capitalist*
Bailey, Richard Briggs *investment company executive*
Bennett, George Frederick *investment manager*
Burgess, R. William, Jr. *investment banking executive*
Calderwood, Stanford Matson *investment management executive*
Cantella, Vincent Michele *stockbroker*
Cole, Carolyn Jo *brokerage company executive*
Cox, Howard Ellis, Jr. *venture capitalist*
Crofwell, James B. *stock exchange executive*
de Burlo, Comegys Russell, Jr. *investment advisor, educator*
Drohan, Thomas H. *investment management executive*
Elfers, William *retired investment company director*
Estin, Hans Howard *investment executive*
Glazer, Donald Wayne *business executive, lawyer, educator*
Greeley, Walter Franklin *management and acquisition corporation executive, lawyer*
Griswold, Frank Matthew, Jr. *investment executive*
Hagler, Jon Lewis *investment executive*
Hobbs, Matthew Hallock *investment banker*
Langermann, John W. R. *institutional equity salesperson*
Lee, David Stoddart *investment counselor*
Leonard, Laurence Barberie, Jr. *investment company executive*
Loring, Caleb, Jr. *investment company executive*
Lovell, Francis Joseph, III *investment company executive*
Mc Carthy, Denis Michael *investment executive*
Mc Neice, John Ambrose, Jr. *investment company executive*
Meister, Doris Powers *investment management executive*
Morby, Jacqueline *venture capitalist*
Morrison, Gordon Mackay, Jr. *investment company executive*
Morton, William Gilbert, Jr. *stock exchange executive*
Moseley, Frederick Strong, III *investment banker*
Oates, William Armstrong, Jr. *investment company executive*
Paladino, Albert Edward *venture capitalist*
Peckham, John Munroe, III *investment executive, author*
Pierce, Daniel *investment company executive*
Piret, Marguerite Alice *investment banker*
Rice, William Phipps *investment counselor*
Rieper, Alan George *brokerage company executive*
Romney, W. Mitt *investment company executive*
Sobin, Julian Melvin *international consultant*
Stone, David Barnes *investment advisor*
Tempel, Jean Curtin *venture capitalist*
Thorndike, John Lowell *investment executive*
Towles, Stokley Porter *commercial and investment banking executive*
Vinik, Jeffrey *investment portfolio manager*
Webb, Alexander, III *investment company executive*

Cambridge
Babson, David Leveau *retired investment counsel*
Bedrosian, Edward Robert *investment management company executive*
Lloyd, Boardman *investment executive*

Carlisle
Fohl, Timothy *consulting and investment company executive*

Concord
Lombardo, Gaetano (Guy) *venture capitalist*
Schiller, Pieter Jon *venture capital executive*

Lexington
Colburn, Kenneth Hersey *investment banker*

Milton
Kennedy, Thomas Leo *investment management company executive*

Newton
Henderson, Kenneth Atwood *investment counseling executive*

Reading
Burbank, Nelson Stone *investment banker*

Stoneham
Mc Donald, Andrew Jewett *securities firm executive*

Waltham
Wallace, John *investment company executive*

Wellesley
Anthony, Edward Lovell, II *retired investments executive*
Beckedorff, David Lawrence *investment manager, computer scientist*
Valente, Louis Patrick (Dan Valente) *technical corporation executive*

Westwood
Gillette, Hyde *investment banker*

Woburn
Eddison, Elizabeth Bole *entrepreneur, information specialist*

MICHIGAN

Beulah
Auch, Walter Edward *securities company executive*

Bloomfield Hills
Benton, Robert Austin, Jr. *investment banker, broker*
Rom, (Melvin) Martin *securities executive*
Winograd, Bernard *financial adviser*

Detroit
Brown, William Paul *investment executive*
Callaway, David Henry, Jr. *investment banker*
Lane, James McConkey *investment executive*
Martin, John Gustin *investment banker*
Mengden, Joseph Michael *investment banker*

Oak Park
Novick, Marvin *investment company executive, former automotive supplier executive, accountant*

Traverse City
LeJeune, Dennis Edward *investment counsel*

MINNESOTA

Minneapolis
Gallagher, Gerald Raphael *venture capitalist*
Goldberg, Luella Gross *business executive*
Horsch, Lawrence Leonard *venture capitalist, corporate revitalization executive*
Kraut, Gerald Anthony *investment banker*
Lindau, James H. *grain exchange executive*
Piper, Addison Lewis *securities executive*
Ross, Percy Nathan *business executive, newspaper columnist*
Ruvelson, Alan Kenneth *investment company executive*

Saint Paul
Brooks, Conley, Jr. *investment management executive*
Rothmeier, Steven George *merchant banker, investment manager*

South Saint Paul
Kampmeier, Donald George *livestock association executive*

Waubun
Christensen, Marvin Nelson *venture capitalist*

MISSISSIPPI

Jackson
Burwell, Dudley Sale *retired investment executive and food executive*

MISSOURI

Kansas City
Braude, Michael *commodity exchange executive*
Latshaw, John *entrepreneur*
Rowland, Landon Hill *diversified holding company executive*
Stowers, James Evans, Jr. *investment company executive*

Lees Summit
Korschot, Benjamin Calvin *investment executive*

Saint Louis
Avis, Robert Grier *investment company executive, civil engineer*
Bachmann, John William *securities firm executive*
Bernstein, Donald Chester *brokerage company executive, lawyer*
Clement, Richard Francis *retired investment company executive*
Costigan, Edward John *investment banker*
Frager, Norman *stockbroker*
Marsh, Miles L. *holding company executive*
Newton, George Addison *investment banker, lawyer*
O'Neill, Eugene Milton *mergers and acquisitions consultant*
Walker, George Herbert, III *investment banking company executive, lawyer*

NEBRASKA

Dakota City
Tinstman, Dale Clinton *investment company executive*

Omaha
Buffett, Warren Edward *entrepreneur*
Greer, Randall Dewey *investment company executive*
Sawtell, Stephen M. *private investor, lawyer*
Sokolof, Phil *industrialist, consumer advocate*
Soshnik, Joseph *investment banking consultant*
Velde, John Ernest, Jr. *business executive*

NEVADA

Glenbrook
Jabara, Michael Dean *investment banker*

Incline Village
Dale, Martin Albert *investment banking executive*
Johnson, James Arnold *business consultant, venture capitalist*

Las Vegas
Di Palma, Joseph Alphonse *brokerage house executive, lawyer*
Kornstein, Don Robert *investment banker*

Logandale
Smiley, Robert William, Jr. *investment banker*

Smith
Weaver, William Merritt, Jr. *investment banker*

NEW HAMPSHIRE

Concord
Levins, John Raymond *investment advisor, management consultant, educator*

Manchester
Ryan, Philip Browne *investment banker*

Portsmouth
Morin, Carlton Paul *private investments executive*

Wolfeboro
Meredith, David Robert *investor*

NEW JERSEY

Bloomfield
Stella, John Anthony *investment company executive*

Cranford
Bardwil, Joseph Anthony *investments consultant*

East Orange
Howe, James Everett *investment company executive*

Fairfield
Oolie, Sam *investment company executive*

Florham Park
Clayton, William L. *investment banking executive*
Lovell, Robert Marlow, Jr. *investment company executive*

Fort Lee
Lippman, William Jennings *investment company executive*

Gladstone
Detwiler, Peter Mead *investment banker*

Hackensack
Delaney, Patrick James *investment company executive*

Jersey City
Dreman, David Nasaniel *investment counselor, security analyst*
Smith, James Frederick *securities executive*

Madison
Johnson, William Joseph *stockbroker*

Mendham
Kirby, Allan Price, Jr. *investment company executive*

Montclair
Richart, John Douglas *investment banker*

Morristown
Kearns, William Michael, Jr. *investment banker*
Warlick, Robert Patterson *investment management company executive*

Mountain Lakes
Wolff, Ivan Lawrence *venture capitalist*

New Vernon
Le Buhn, Robert *investment executive*

Newark
Hannon, John Robert *investment company executive*
O'Leary, Paul Gerard *investment executive*

Parsippany
Bean, Bruce Winfield *investment banker, lawyer*

Plainsboro
†Glenn, Terry Kimball *investment management executive, lawyer*
Hewitt, N. J. *investment company executive*
Schreyer, William Allen *retired investment firm executive*
Urciuoli, J. Arthur *investment executive*

Princeton
Chamberlin, John Stephen *investor, former cosmetics company executive*
Dilworth, Joseph Richardson *investment banker*
Ehrenberg, Edward *executive, investor*
Johnston, Robert Fowler *venture capitalist*
Schafer, Carl Walter *investment executive*
†Treu, Jesse Isaiah *venture capitalist*

Red Bank
Weiant, William Morrow *investment banking executive*

Ringoes
Price, Liza *entrepreneur*

Rockleigh
Heslin, John Thomas *entrepreneur, historic preservationist*

Scotch Plains
Bishop, Robert Milton *former stock exchange official*

Short Hills
Bartels, Stanley Leonard *investment banker*
Yorks, Richard Alan *investment banker*

South Plainfield
Kopley, Catherine S. *investment company executive*

Summit
Geiger, Richard Lawrence *entrepreneur*

Teaneck
Palitz, Clarence Yale, Jr. *commercial finance executive*

Upper Montclair
Kidde, John Lyon *investment manager*

Weehawken
Hess, Dennis John *investment banker*

Westfield
Priest, William Wallace, Jr. *investment counselor*
Simon, Martin Stanley *commodity marketing company executive, economist*

Wyckoff
Bucko, John Joseph *investment corporation executive*

NEW MEXICO

Albuquerque
Malina, Robert S. *investment company executive*

Corrales
Eisenstadt, Pauline Doreen Bauman *investment company executive*

Santa Fe
Davis, Shelby M. C. *investment executive, consultant*
Dreisbach, John Gustave *investment banker*
Duval, Michael Raoul *investment banker*
Nurock, Robert Jay *investment analysis company executive*

NEW YORK

Ardsley
Sanders, Robert Martin *commodity trader*

Bedford
Clifford, Lawrence M. *investment company executive*

Bedford Corners
Singer, Craig *broker, consultant, investor*

Bedford Hills
Fissell, William Henry *investment advisor*

Bronxville
Penisten, Gary Dean *entrepreneur*

Brooklyn
Leyh, Richard Edmund, Sr. *retired investment executive*

Buffalo
Irwin, Robert James Armstrong *investment company executive*
Littlewood, Douglas Burden *business brokerage executive*

Dobbs Ferry
Grunebaum, Ernest Michael *investment banker*

Garden City
Gordon, Barry Joel *investment advisor*

Glen Head
Sutherland, Donald James *investment company executive*

Glendale
Hess, Karsten *trading company executive*

Great Neck
Fialkov, Herman *investment banker*
Hampton, Benjamin Bertram *brokerage house executive*

Hartsdale
Katz, John *investment banker, business consultant, lawyer*

Jamestown
Bargar, Robert Sellstrom *investor*

Locust Valley
Benson, Robert Elliott *investment banker, consultant*

Mount Kisco
Wood, James *broker*

Mount Vernon
†Wasserspring, Fredric R. *securities trader*

New York
Acampora, Ralph Joseph *brokerage firm executive*
Albers, Charles Edgar *investment manager, insurance executive*
Allen, Herbert *investment banker*
Allison, Herbert Monroe, Jr. *investment firm executive*
Alworth, Sandra Ann *municipal bond salesperson, brokerage house executive*
Ames, George Joseph *investment banker*
Andersen, K(ent) Tucker *investment executive*
Arnhold, Henry H. *investment banker*
Aronson, Edgar David *venture capitalist*
Bach, Arthur James *investment banker*
Ball, George L. *securities company executive*
Ballard, Charles Alan *investment banker*
†Ballard, Claude Mark, Jr. *real estate investment executive*
Barr, Michael Charles *securities analyst, investment banker*
Barrett, Richard James *investment banker*
Barry, Thomas Corcoran *investment counsellor*
Beale, Christopher William *investment banker*
Beard, Anson McCook, Jr. *investment banker*
Beinecke, Frederick William *investment company executive*
Bell, Martin Allen *investment company executive*
Bellas, Albert Constantine *investment banker, advisor*
Belson, Jerome *investment company executive, real estate developer*
Berlin, Howard Richard *investment advisory company executive*
Berlin, Jordan Stuart *investment company executive*
Bernard, Lewis W. *foundation executive*
Berry, Joseph John *brokerage house executive*
Bewkes, Eugene Garrett, Jr. *investment company executive, consultant*
Bickford, Jewelle Wooten *investment banker*
Biderman, Mark Charles *investment banker*
Biggs, Barton Michael *investment company executive*
Birkelund, John Peter *investment banking executive*
Blackwell, John Wesley *securities industry executive, consultant*
Blalock, Sherrill *investment advisor*
Borenstein, Abe Isaac *securities industry executive*
Boulanger, Jacques Pierre *investment banker*
Boyd, Michael Alan *investment banking company executive, lawyer*
Brennan, Donald P. *investment company executive*
Brigstocke, David Hugh Charles *investment banker*
Brinker, Robert J. *investment company executive, radio talk show host*
Brittenham, Raymond Lee *investment company executive*
Brody, Alan Jeffrey *investment company executive*
Brody, Eugene David *investment company executive*
Brown, Fred Elmore *investment executive*
Brown, Ronald *stockbroker*
Bruce, Duncan Archibald *financier*
Brunie, Charles Henry *investment manager*
Buck, James E. *financial exchange executive*
Buckles, Robert Howard *investment company executive*
Bullock, Hugh *investment banker*
Burke, James Joseph, Jr. *investment banker*
Caggiano, Michael Vincent *financial services company executive*
Cannaliato, Vincent, Jr. *investment banker, mathematician*
Carey, William Polk *investment banker*
Carter, Cary Warren *investment banking executive*
Chalsty, John Steele *investment banker*
Chammah, Walid A. *investment banker*
Chapman, Peter Herbert *investment company executive*
Charrier, Michael Edward *investment banker*
†Chazanoff, Jay David *investment company executive*
Chefitz, Harold Neal *investment banker*
†Chen, Philip Minkang *investment banker, corporate executive, lawyer, engineer*
Chu, Richard Shao-hung *investment banker*
Claire, Thomas Andrew *business executive, writer*
Clarens, John Gaston *investment executive*
Cogan, Marshall S. *entrepreneur*
Cohen, Abby Joseph *securities analyst*
†Cohen, Claire Gorham *investors service company executive*
Cohen, Fred Howard *investment banker*
Cohen, Jonathan Little *investment banker*
Cohn, Bertram Josiah *investment banker*
Coles, Michael H. *investment banker*
Colombo, Frank V. *securities company executive*
Corn, Bennett Julian *commodity exchange executive*
Corzine, Jon Stevens *investment banker*
Cox, Archibald, Jr. *investment banker*
Crowley, Mark *investment company executive*
Culp, Michael *securities company executive, research director*
Cushing, Harry Cooke, IV *investment banker*
Daly, John Neal *investment company executive*
DaPuzzo, Peter James *investment banker, trader, financial consultant*
Darlington, Henry, Jr. *investment broker*
Davis, Martin S. *investment company executive*
Davis, Richard Bruce *investment banker*
DeBusschere, David Albert *brokerage executive, retired professional basketball player and team executive*
de la Gueronniere, Raphael *securities firm executive*
DeMarco, Robert Thomas *investment company executive*
Dempsey, Edward A. *securities company executive*
DeNunzio, Ralph Dwight *investment banker*
Derchin, Michael Wayne *research director, investment banker, financial analyst*
DeRoma, Leonard James *securities firm executive*
Dewey, Robert Manson, Jr. *investment company executive*
Dillon, Clarence Douglas *retired investment company executive*
Doyle, William Stowell *venture capitalist*
Dritz, Michael A. *securities company executive*
Dudack, Gail Marie *brokerage house executive*
DuGan, Gordon F. *investment banker*
Dyson, Robert R. *investment company executive*
Ebbitt, Kenneth Cooper, Jr. *investment company executive*
Edlow, Kenneth Lewis *securities brokerage official*
Ehinger, Albert Louis, Jr. *securities trader*
Einbender, Alvin H. *securities dealer*
Einiger, Roger W. *brokerage house executive*
Eisenberg, Steven *securities analyst*
Eisenstadt, Samuel *investment company executive*
Elrod, James Lake, Jr. *investment banker*
Emmons, Delia McQuade *investment industry executive*
Eppley, Stephen Clyde *investment banker*
Evnin, Anthony Basil *venture capital investor*
Fahey, Peter M(atthew) *investment banker*
Fein, Bernard *investments executive*
Fensterstock, Lee *securities firm executive*
Ferris, Barton Purdy, Jr. *investment banker*
Fetscher, Paul George William *brokerage house executive*
Fidanza, Giovanni *securities broker, dealer, executive*
Fisher, Richard B. *investment banker*
Fiumefreddo, Charles A. *investment management company executive*
Flanigan, Peter Magnus *investment banker*
Fogarty, John Thomas *business executive, former association executive*
Forlano, Anthony *retired investment company executive*
Fowler, Henry Hamill *investment banker*
Frackman, Richard Benoit *investment banker*
France, Joseph David *securities analyst*
Frank, Frederick *investment banker*
Franklin, Edward Ward *international investment consultant, lawyer, actor*
Frantzen, Henry Arthur *investment company executive*
Fried, Albert, Jr. *investment banker*
Friedenberg, Daniel Meyer *financial investor*
Friedman, Alvin Edward *investment executive*
Friedman, Howard Martin *financial executive*
Fritzlen, Thomas L., Jr. *investment banker and broker*
Furman, Roy L. *investment banker*
Galbraith, Evan Griffith *investment banker*
Gambee, Robert Rankin *investment banker*
Gant, Donald Ross *investment banker*
Garner, Albert Headden *investment banker*
Geduld, Emanuel Edward *equity trading company executive*
Gelb, Harold Seymour *investor*
Gellert, Michael Erwin *investment banker*
Gerard, Emanuel *investment banking executive*
†Giakas, Wallace Martin *investment banker*
Gilbert, Thomas Strong *investment banker, venture capitalist*
Glick, Allan H. *business executive*
Gold, Jeffrey Mark *investment banker, financial adviser*
Goldberg, David Alan *investment banker, lawyer*
Golden, Robert Charles *brokerage executive*
Gonzalez, Eugene Robert *investment banker*
Goodman, Stuart Franklyn *brokerage house executive*
Gordon, Albert Hamilton *investment banker*
Gottesman, David Sanford *investment executive*
Granger, David *investment banker*
Grano, Joseph J., Jr. *securities industry executive*
Grant, William Robert *investment banker*
Grasso, Richard A. *stock exchange executive*
Greenberg, Alan Courtney (Ace Greenberg) *stockbroker*
Greenhill, Robert Foster *investment banker*
Gruss, Martin David *private investor*
Guenther, Paul Bernard *securities company executive*
Guttman, Zoltan Lou *exchange executive*
Hackett, Bruce Clayton *investment banking company executive*
Haire, John Russell *corporate executive, lawyer*
Hallingby, Paul, Jr. *investment banker*
Hanemann, John H. *commodity exchange executive*
Hansmann, Ralph Emil *investment executive*
Harmon, James Allen *investment banker*
Hart, Gurnee Fellows *investment counselor*
Haskell, John Henry Farrell, Jr. *investment banking company executive*
Hedley, David Van Houten *investment banker*
Heimann, John Gaines *investment banker*
Helwig, George James *securities trader, dealer*
Hennessy, John M. *brokerage house executive*
†Herbst, Edward Ian *brokerage firm executive*
Herkness, Lindsay Coates, III *securities broker*
†Hero, Byron A. *investment banker, lawyer*
Herrmann, Lacy Bunnell *investment company executive, financial entrepreneur, venture capitalist*
Heyman, George Harrison, Jr. *securities company executive*
Heyman, William Herbert *securities firm executive*
Higgins, Harrison Scott *investment company executive*
Hill, J(ames) Tomilson *investment banker*
Hobbs, Franklin Warren, IV *investment banker*
Holland, Michael Francis *investment company executive*
Horowitz, Gedale Bob *investment banker*
Horowitz, Lewis Jay *stock exchange executive*
Hotz, Robert Henry *investment banking executive*
Howard, Nathan Southard *investment banker, lawyer*
Hu, Joseph Chi-Ping *mortgage securities analyst*
Hultquist, Timothy Allen *investment banker*
Hurford, John Boyce *investment counselor*
Hurst, Robert Jay *securities company executive*
Hyman, Seymour *capital and product development company executive*
Idleman, Lee Hillis *investment company executive*
Jacoby, A. James *securities brokerage firm executive*
Jaffee, Sandra Schuyler *financial executive*
James, Frank Munger *brokerage house executive*
James, Hamilton Evans *investment banking firm executive*
Janiak, Anthony Richard, Jr. *investment banker*
Janney, Stuart Symington, III *investment company executive*
Jenrette, Richard Hampton *investment and insurance company executive*
Jepson, Hans Godfrey *investment company executive*
Johnston, Michael J. *brokerage house executive*
Jones, Abbott C. *investment banking executive*
Jones, Barclay Gibbs, III *investment banker*
†Jones, Paul Tudor, II *investment executive*
Jones, Robert Quince *securities company executive*
Jordan, John W., II *holding company executive*
Kautz, James Charles *investment banker*
Kealy, William James *investment executive*
Keevil, Philip Clement *investment banker*
Kellen, Stephen Max *investment banker*
Kellogg, Peter R. *securities dealer*
Kerschner, Edward *brokerage house executive*
Khayatt, Shaker Albert *investment banker*
Kingsberg, Harold Joseph *investment management company executive*
Kittell, Donald D. *investment firm executive*
Klemm, Richard Henry *investment company executive*
Klingenstein, Frederick Adler *investment banking executive*
Knight, Howard Atwood *investment banking executive, consultant*
Kretschmer, Keith Hughes *stockbroker*
Krimendahl, Herbert Frederick, II *investment banker*
Krueger, Harvey Mark *investment banker, lawyer*
Lane, Frederick Carpenter *investment banker*
Lane, Jeffrey Bruce *financial services company executive*
Laren, Kuno *investment banker*
Lasser, Joseph Robert *investment company executive*
Lavine, Lawrence Neal *investment banker*
Lavitt, Mel S. *investment banking professional*
Lawrence, Bryan Hunt *investment banking executive*
Lebec, Alain *investment banker*
Le Fevre, William Mathias, Jr. *brokerage company executive*
Leighton, Lawrence Ward *investment banker*
Levine, Gerald Richard *investment banker, finanical advisor, estate planning and philanthropy specialist*
Levitan, Dan *investment banker*
Levy, Leon *investment company executive*
Lewis, Sherman Richard, Jr. *investment banker*
Liddell, Donald Macy, Jr. *retired investment counsellor*
Loeb, John Langeloth, Jr. *investment counselor*
Logan, J. Murray *investment manager*
Long, Thomas Michael *investment banker*
Loomis, Philip Clark *investment executive*
Ludovici, Anthony *security investment executive*
Lyons, Laurence *securities executive*
Madoff, Bernard Lawrence *investment dealer*
Mager, Ezra Pascal *automobile dealership group executive*
Malin, Robert Abernethy *investment management executive*
Maloney, William Gerard *retired investment company executive*
Mangold, Glenn E. *securities industry executive*
†Manuel, Bernard M. *investment banker*
Marcus, James Stewart *investment banker*
Marks, Edwin S. *investment company executive*
Marlas, James Constantine *holding company executive*
Marron, Donald Baird *investment banker*
Matthews, Gilbert Elliott *investment banker*
Mattone, Vincent J. *investment banker*
Maughan, Deryck C. *investment banker*
Mazzilli, Paul John *investment banker*
McBride, Rodney Lester *investment counselor*
Mc Carter, Thomas N., III *investment counseling company executive*
McCleary, Benjamin Ward *investment banker*
McGirr, David William John *investment banker*
Mc Lendon, Heath Brian *securities investment company executive*
McMullan, William Patrick, III *investment banker*
Meehan, John Joseph *brokerage house executive*
Menges, Carl Braun *investment banker*
Menschel, Richard Lee *investment banker*
Metz, Emmanuel Michael *investment company executive, lawyer*
Miller, B. Jack *investment company executive*
Miller, Donald Keith *venture capitalist, asset management executive*
Miller, Paul Lukens *investment banker*
Minard, Frank Pell Lawrence *investment manager*
Minikes, Michael *investment banker*
Mintz, Walter *investment company executive*
Moak-Mazur, Connie J. *investment consultant, marketing professional*
Moltz, James Edward *brokerage company executive*
Morahan, Matthew Joseph *investment banker*
Moran, Charles A. *securities executive*
Moran, John A. *investment company executive*
Morosani, John Warrington *brokerage house executive*
Morris, William Charles *investor*
Morrissey, Thomas Jerome *investment banker*
Most, Nathan *securities exchange executive*
Mountcastle, Kenneth Franklin, Jr. *stockbroker*
Muratore, Peter Frederick *securities executive*
Nabi, Stanley Andrew *investment executive*
Nadel, Elliott *investment firm executive*
†Nash, Jack *investment banker*
Nazem, Fereydoun F. *venture capitalist, financier*
Neal, James Weatherly *investment banker*
Necarsulmer, Henry *investment banker*
Needham, George Austin *investment banker*
Neuberger, Roy R. *investment counselor*
Niemiec, David Wallace *investment company executive*
Nussbaum, Mark Stephen *securities trader*
Obernauer, Marne, Jr. *investment company executive*
Obolensky, Ivan *investment banker, foundation consultant, writer, publisher*
O'Connell, Daniel S. *private investments and management buyouts*
O'Donnell, Richard Walter *lawyer, accountant, brokerage company executive*
Offensend, David Glenn *investment executive*
Offit, Morris Wolf *investment management executive*
O'Neill, George Dorr *business executive*
Orben, Jack Richard *investment company executive*
Osborne, Stanley de Jongh *investment banker*
Ostrander, Thomas William *investment banker*
Overlock, Willard Joseph, Jr. *investment banker*
Owen, Thomas Llewellyn, Sr. *investment executive*
†Page, Jonathan Roy *investment analyst*
Pampel, Joseph Philip Stevenson *investment executive*
Panitch, Michael B. *brokerage house executive*
Pardee, Scott Edward *securities dealer*
Paton, Leland B. *investment banker*
Patrick, Thomas H. *brokerage house executive*
†Paul, Andrew Mitchell *venture capitalist*
Paumgarten, Nicholas Biddle *investment banker*
Peet, Creighton Houck *brokerage firm executive*
Perlmutter, Louis *investment banker, lawyer*
Phillips, Howard William *investment banker*
Piper, Thomas Laurence, III *investment banker*
Pittaway, David Bruce *investment banker, lawyer*
Pollack, Stephen J. *stockbroker*
Pollicino, Joseph Anthony *investment company executive*
Posner, Edward Mark *brokerage company executive*
Potter, William James *investment banker*
Pulling, Thomas Leffingwell *investment advisor*
Quain, Mitchell I. *investment executive*
†Quick, Leslie Charles, III *brokerage house executive*
Quick, Thomas Clarkson *brokerage house executive*
Quirk, John James *investment company executive*
Rafferty, Brian Joseph *investor relations consultant*
Rainis, Eugene Charles *brokerage house executive*
Rand, Lawrence Anthony *investor and financial relations executive*
Rattner, Steven Lawrence *investment banker*
Reis, Judson Patterson *investment banker*
†Relkin, Allen *commodities executive*
Rice, James A. *investment company executive*
Riley, Ivers Whitman *stock exchange executive*
†Robert, Stephen *investment firm executive*
Roby, Joe Lindell *investment banker*
Roehm, MacDonell, Jr. *investment firm executive*
Rogers, Eugene Charles *investment firm executive*
Rogers, Theodore Courtney *investment company executive*
Rohatyn, Felix George *investment company executive*
Roosevelt, Theodore, IV *investment banker*
Rose, Robert Neal *brokerage house executive*
Rosen, Benjamin Maurice *venture capitalist, computer company executive*
Rosenberg, Judith Meta *brokerage executive*
Rosenbloom, Daniel *investment banker, lawyer*
Rosenwald, E. John, Jr. *brokerage house executive, investment banker*
Rosenwald, William *investment executive, philanthropist*
Rothstein, Gerald Alan *investment company executive*
Rubin, Robert Samuel *investment banker*
Sacerdote, Peter M. *investment banker*
Salomon, Richard *investor*
Samuels, Nathaniel *business executive, government administrator*
†Sanders, Lewis A. *investment research and management executive*
Sardanis, Andrew S. *investment company executive*

Scaturro, Philip David *investment banker*
Schaffran, Charles Brad *investment company executive*
Schapiro, Morris A. *investment banker*
Schick, Harry Leon *investment company executive*
Schiff, David Tevele *investment banker*
Schless, Phyllis Ross *investment banker*
Seff, Leslie S. *securities trader*
Seidman, Samuel Nathan *investment banker, economist*
Senior, Enrique Francisco *investment banker*
Sepahpur, Hayedeh C(hristine) *investment executive*
Shapiro, Robert Frank *investment banking company executive*
Shaykin, Leonard P. *investor*
Shen, Theodore Ping *investment banker*
Sheppard, William Stevens *investment banker*
Sherrill, H. Virgil *securities company executive, manufacturing company executive*
Sherva, Dennis G. *investment company executive*
Shinn, George Latimer *investment banker, consultant, educator*
Siebert, Muriel *brokerage house executive, former state banking official*
Siegler, Thomas Edmund *investment banking executive*
Siemer, Fred Harold *securities analyst*
Silfen, David M. *investment banker*
Silverman, Henry Richard *diversified business executive, lawyer*
Silverstein, Howard Alan *investment banker*
Simmons, Hardwick *investment banker*
Simons, Kent Cobb *mutual fund executive*
Sloan, Stephen Stehly *investment banker*
Smethurst, E(dward) William, Jr. *brokerage house executive*
Smith, Hilary Cranwell Bowen *investment banker*
Smith, Malcolm Bernard *investment company executive*
Smith, Pierce Reiland *stock brokerage, investment banking executive*
Sorensen, Burton Erhard *investment banker*
Spielvogel, Sidney Meyer *investment banker*
Stamas, Stephen *investment executive*
Steffens, John Laundon *brokerage house executive*
Steiger, Heidi Schwarzbauer *investment executive*
Stein, Bernard *stockbroker*
Stein, David Fred *investment executive*
Steinberg, Joseph Saul *investment company executive*
Steinberg, Robert M. *holding company executive*
Steinberg, Saul Phillip *holding company executive*
Sterling, Robert Lee, Jr. *investment company executive*
Stern, James Andrew *investment banker*
Stern, Stanley B. *investment banker*
†Stern, Walter Phillips *investment executive*
Stiles, Thomas Beveridge, II *investment banking executive*
Stoddard, George Earl *investment company financial executive*
Straton, John Charles, Jr. *investment banker*
Straus, Melville *investment company executive*
Strong, William L., III *investment executive*
Sulimirski, Witold Stanislaw *investment company executive*
Suskind, Dennis A. *investment banker*
Suzuki, Ryosuke *securities firm executive*
Svenson, Charles Oscar *investment banker*
Tagliaferri, Lee Gene *investment banker*
Tanner, Harold *investment banker*
Taylor, Richard William *investment banker, securities broker*
Terry, F. Davis, Jr. *investment company executive*
Tierney, Paul E., Jr. *investment company executive*
Tizzio, Thomas Ralph *brokerage executive*
Topol, Robert Martin *financial services executive, securities trader*
Towbin, A(braham) Robert *investment banker*
Tozer, W. James, Jr. *investment company executive*
Train, John *investment counselor, writer, government official*
Treadway, James Curran *investment company executive, lawyer, former government official*
Treadway, Stephen Joseph *investment banking and brokerage executive*
Tufts, David Albert, Jr. *securities company executive*
Tyson, Harry James *investment banker*
Underwood, Paul *brokerage house executive*
Van Dine, Vance *investment banker*
Walters, Milton James *investment banker*
Wareham, Raymond Noble *investment banker*
†Warner, Miner Hill *investment banker*
Wasserstein, Bruce *investment banker*
Watts, Henry Miller, Jr. *stockbroker*
Weathersby, George Byron *investment management executive*
Webster, John Kimball *investment executive*
Weinberg, John Livingston *investment banker*
Weiss, Charles Stanard *investment banker*
Weiss, Stephen Henry *investment firm executive*
Weissman, Paul Marshall *investment company executive*
Wendel, Thomas Michael *financial services company executive*
Whitehead, John Cunningham *investment executive*
Whiting, Richard Brooke *retired investment banker*
Whitney, Edward Bonner *investment banker*
Wiegers, George Anthony *investment banker*
Wiener, Malcolm Hewitt *investment management company executive*
Wigmore, Barrie Atherton *investment banker*
Williams, Dave Harrell *investment executive*
Wilson, Edgar Byron *business executive*
Wit, Harold Maurice *investment banker, lawyer, investor*
Wolcott, Samuel H., III *investment banker*
Wolitzer, Steven Barry *investment banker*
Yancey, Richard Charles *investment banker*
Zeikel, Arthur *investment company executive*
Zeisler, Richard Spiro *investor*
Zeuschner, Erwin Arnold *investment advisory company executive*
Zuckerberg, Roy J. *investment banking executive*

Rochester
Clark, Louis Morris, Jr. *investment manager, antique dealer, innkeeper*

Roslyn Heights
Jaffe, Melvin *securities company executive*

Rye
†van Ekris, Anthonie Cornelis *trading corporation executive, retail company executive*
Wagner, Edward Frederick, Jr. *investment management company executive*

Scarsdale
Abbe, Colman *investment banker*
Doley, Harold Emanuel, Jr. *securities company executive*

Southampton
Atkins, Victor Kennicott, Jr. *investment banker*
Brokaw, Clifford Vail, III *investment banker, business executive*

Southold
Duffy, Eugene Henry *investor*

Staten Island
Aiken, William Eric *securities research executive*

Syosset
Kantor, Edwin *investment company executive*

Wainscott
Dubow, Arthur Myron *investor, lawyer*

Wantagh
Zinder, Newton Donald *stock market analyst, consultant*

West Hempstead
Brodsky, Irwin Abel *retired stockbroker*

Westbury
Fogg, Joseph Graham, III *investment banking executive*

White Plains
Lawrence, George Hubbard Clapp *investment company executive*

Woodstock
Ober, Stuart Alan *investment consultant, book publisher*

NORTH CAROLINA

Cashiers
Culp, Charles Allen *financial executive*

Charlotte
Hardin, Thomas Jefferson, II *investment counsel*
Porter, Gary Lynn *investment manager*

Greensboro
Johnson, Marshall Hardy *investment company executive*

High Point
Phillips, Earl Norfleet, Jr. *financial services executive*

North Wilkesboro
Pardue, Dwight Edward *venture capitalist*

Pinehurst
Lebeck, Warren Wells *commodities consultant*

Raleigh
Anderson, Glenn Elwood *investment banker*
Woodson, Richard Peyton, III *entrepreneur*

Winston Salem
Strickland, Robert Louis *business executive*

NORTH DAKOTA

Fargo
Tallman, Robert Hall *investment company executive*

OHIO

Alpha
James, Francis Edward, Jr. *investment counselor*

Cincinnati
Joseph, David J., Jr. *trading company executive*
Lucke, Robert Vito *merger and acquisition executive*
Pettengill, Kroger *investment counselor*
Street, David Hargett *investment company executive*

Cleveland
Brentlinger, Paul Smith *venture capital executive*
Hook, John Burney *investment company executive*
Murfin, Donald Leon *investment company executive*
O'Brien, John Feighan *investment banker*
O'Donnell, Thomas Michael *brokerage firm executive*
Price, Gordon A. *brokerage house executive*
Redinger, James Collins *investment banker, financial consultant*
Roulston, Thomas Henry *investment adviser*

Columbus
Barthelmas, Ned Kelton *investment and commercial real estate banker*
Jennings, Edward Harrington *business educator*
Meuse, David Russell *investment banker*
Pointer, Peter Leon *investment executive*

Dayton
Berry, John William *investment company executive, retired telephone directory advertising company executive*

Galion
Cobey, Ralph *investment company executive, industrialist*

Lancaster
Hurley, Samuel Clay, III *investment company executive*

Martins Ferry
Gracey, Robert William *account executive, minister*

Zanesville
Mattingly, Robert Kerker *entrepreneur*

OKLAHOMA

Oklahoma City
Painton, Ira Wayne *retired securities executive*

Tulsa
Sanditen, Edgar Richard *investment company executive*
Stover, Phil Sheridan, Jr. *investment consultant*

OREGON

Chiloquin
Reed, David George *entrepreneur*

Medford
Cutler, Kenneth Ross *investment company and mutual fund executive*

Portland
Myers, Clay *retired investment management company executive*
Olsen, Kurt *investment company executive, adviser*
Rutherford, William Drake *investment executive, lawyer*
†Ward, C. Bruce *entrepreneur*

PENNSYLVANIA

Bala Cynwyd
Benenson, James, Jr. *brokerage house executive*

Blue Bell
Gleklen, Donald Morse *investment company executive*

Bryn Mawr
Dayton, Samuel Grey, Jr. *investment banker*
Havens, Timothy Markle *investment advisory firm executive*
Turbidy, John Berry *investor, management consultant*

Devon
Niehaus, Robert James *investment banking executive*

Doylestown
Holstrom, Carleton Arthur *brokerage house executive*

Erie
†Ryan, Gerald Anthony *financial advisor, venture capitalist*

Grantham
Grannon, Charles Lee *investment banking official*

Hummelstown
Custer, John Charles *investment broker*

Ligonier
Mellon, Seward Prosser *investment executive*

Malvern
†Bogle, John Clifton *investment company executive*

Newtown Square
Turner, George Pearce *consulting company executive*

Paoli
Hedberg, Robert Daniel *venture capitalist*

Philadelphia
Borer, Edward Turner *investment banker*
Bowditch, Nathaniel Rantoul *brokerage house executive*
Dunlap, Albert John *venture capitalist*
Durham, John Hendrick *investment company executive*
Giordano, Nicholas Anthony *stock exchange executive*
Humes, Graham *investment banker*
Johnson, Craig Norman *investment banker*
McGinley, Joseph Patrick *brokerage house executive*
Merritt, John C. *investment banker*
Newburger, Frank L., Jr. *retired investment broker*
O'Brien, Robert Thomas *investment company executive*
Palmer, Russell Eugene *investment executive*
Ripley, Edward Franklin *investment company executive*
Sander, Rudolph Charles *investment banker*
Tague, Barry Elwert *securities trader*
Wilde, Norman Taylor, Jr. *investment banking company executive*
Wolitarsky, James William *securities industry executive*
Wruble, Brian Frederick *investment management company executive*

Pittsburgh
Bitzer, John Frederick, Jr. *diversified holding company executive*
Curtis, Gregory Dyer *investment company executive, foundation administrator, lawyer, author, poet*
†Donahue, John Francis *investment company executive*
Hillman, Henry L. *investment company executive*
Hunter, David Wittmer *security brokerage executive*
Mathieson, Andrew Wray *investment management executive*
Maurer, Richard Michael *investment company executive*
Porter, Milton *investment executive*
Prado, Gerald M. *investment banker*
Walton, James M. *investment company executive*

Plymouth Meeting
Yarnall, D. Robert, Jr. *entrepreneur, investor*

Reading
Welch, Joseph F. *investment company executive*

Sewickley
Chaplin, James Crossan, IV *securities firm executive*

Valley Forge
†Brennan, John Joseph *mutual fund company executive*

Villanova
Lewis, Wayne H. *investment company executive*

Wayne
Lewis, James Earl *investment banker*

West Conshohocken
Miller, Paul Fetterolf, Jr. *investment company executive*

Yardley
Kressler, James Phillip *investment and operations company executive*

York
Thornton, George Whiteley *investment company executive*

RHODE ISLAND

Lincoln
Barr, John Douglas, II *entrepreneur, state legislator*

Providence
Goddard, Robert Hale Ives *investment executive*
Joukowsky, Artemis A. W. *private investor*
Manchester, Robert D. *venture capitalist*

Wakefield
Mason, Scott MacGregor *entrepreneur, inventor, consultant*

SOUTH CAROLINA

Aiken
Hanna, Carey McConnell *securities and investments executive*

Charleston
Winthrop, John *investment company executive*

Hilton Head Island
Batten, William Milfred *retired stock exchange executive*

Johns Island
Cameron, Thomas William Lane *investment company executive*

Sullivans Island
Romaine, Henry Simmons *investment consultant*

SOUTH DAKOTA

North Sioux City
McElroy, Edmund G., Jr. *financial executive*

TENNESSEE

Chattanooga
Faires, Kurt Jeffrey *investor*
Witherspoon, John Knox, Jr. *investment banking executive*

Knoxville
Wilson, John Grover *securities trader*

Memphis
Waddell, Alfred Moore, Jr. *investment company executive*
†Weller, Joseph C. *brokerage house executive*

Nashville
Bradford, James C., Jr. *brokerage house executive*
Crants, R., Jr. *entrepreneur*
Hanselman, Richard Wilson *entrepreneur*
Kuhn, Paul Hubert, Jr. *investment counsel*
Nelson, Edward Gage *merchant banking investment company executive*
Roberts, Kenneth Lewis *investor, lawyer, foundation administrator*
Sullivan, Allen Trousdale *securities company executive*

TEXAS

Austin
Inman, Bobby Ray *investor, former electronics executive*
Leon, Tomas Carlos *foreign exchange broker*
Spertus, Philip *investment company executive*
Thornhill, Gabriel Felder, III *securities company executive*

Corpus Christi
Bateman, John Roger *investment holding company executive*

Dallas
Buchholz, Donald Alden *stock brokerage company executive*
Budzinsky, Armin Alexander *investment banker*
Collins, Michael James *investment company executive*
Lynch, William Wright, Jr. *investment executive, engineer*
McClure, Frederick Donald *investment banker, lawyer*
Perot, H. Ross *investments and real estate group executive, data processing services company executive*
Philipson, Herman Louis, Jr. *investment banker*
Smith, Cece *venture capitalist*

Whitson, James Norfleet, Jr. diversified company executive

El Paso
Prendergast, Thomas A. investments and management consultant
Schnadig, Edgar Louis entrepreneur, management consultant

Fort Worth
Asher, Garland Parker investment holding company executive

Garland
McGrath, James Thomas real estate investment company executive

Houston
Claiborn, Stephen Allan investment banker
Cullom, Hale Ellicott investment company executive
Cunningham, R. Walter venture capitalist
Currie, John Thornton (Jack Currie) retired investment banker
Duncan, Charles William, Jr. investor, former government official
Dworsky, Clara Weiner merchandise brokerage executive, lawyer
Glassell, Alfred Curry, Jr. investor
Klingel, Martin Allen investment company executive
Mackey, William Sturges, Jr. investor, consultant
Mischer, Walter M. diversified company executive, bank holding company executive
Montle, Paul Joseph entrepreneur
Neuhaus, Philip Ross investment banker
O'Connor, Ralph Sturges investment company executive
Page, Ann stock brokerage executive
Poindexter, John Bruce entrepreneur
Presley, Brian entrepreneur
†Robertson, Joseph W., Jr. investment company executive
Sakowitz, Robert Tobias investor
Stralem, Pierre retired stockbroker
Taylor, James B. securities trader, financial planner
Thompson, Guy Bryan investment company executive
Vaughan, Eugene H. investment company executive
Wellin, Keith Sears investment banker
Williams, Edward Earl, Jr. entrepreneur, educator

Irving
Bumpas, Scott Jackson financial executive

Richardson
Putnam, Howard Dean investor, former airline executive

San Antonio
Duncan, A. Baker investment banker
Meyer, Alice K. investor

Stafford
Franks, Charles Leslie investments executive

Wichita Falls
Jones, William Houston stock brokerage executive, financial consultant

UTAH

Salt Lake City
Ballard, Melvin Russell, Jr. investment executive, church official
Meldrum, Peter Durkee venture capital/ biotechnology company executive

VIRGINIA

Annandale
Khim, Jay Wook investment company executive

Arlington
Anns, Philip Harold international trading executive, former pharmaceutical company executive
Gregg, David, III investment banker
Takeuchi, Hiroshi investment company executive, consultant

Burke
Kaminski, Paul Garrett investment banker, consultant

Charlottesville
Monroe, Brooks investment banker
Newman, James Wilson business executive

Mc Lean
Bisbee, Gerald Elftman, Jr. investment company executive
Searles, Dewitt Richard retired investment firm executive, retired air force officer
Smith, Thomas Eugene investment company executive, financial consultant
Urquhart, Glen Taylor investment and development executive

Richmond
Binns, Walter Gordon, Jr. investment company executive
Dahlenburg, Lyle Marion investment company executive
Gorr, Louis Frederick investment consultant
Hong, James Ming industrialist, venture capitalist
McElroy, John Lee, Jr. brokerage house executive
Phillips, Thomas Edworth, Jr. investment executive, consultant

Stanleytown
Stanley, Thomas Bahnson, Jr. investor

Vienna
Roepke, Nancy Jean investment company executive

WASHINGTON

Bellevue
Ryles, Gerald Fay private investor, business executive
Shih, Benedict Chesang investment company executive

Bothell
Browning, Jesse Harrison entrepreneur

Olympia
Manning, Farley investment company executive

Redmond
Pacholski, Richard Francis retired securities company executive, financial advisor, consultant

Seattle
Bayley, Christopher T. international investment banking executive
Brier, Evelyn Caroline retired investment company executive, business consultant
†Kalnasy, Glenn Bothwell investment company executive

Tacoma
Habedank, Gary L. brokerage house executive
Schuyler, Robert Len investment company executive

WISCONSIN

Janesville
Diotte, Alfred Peter investment executive, consultant

Milwaukee
Bloom, James Edward commodity trading and financial executive
Lubar, Sheldon Bernard venture capitalist
Samson, Richard Max investments and real estate executive
Schnoll, Howard Manuel investment banking and managed asset consultant

Oak Creek
Giblin, Louis stockbroker

WYOMING

Casper
True, Jean Durland entrepreneur, oil company executive

Cheyenne
†Myers, Rolland Graham investment counselor

Daniel
Parker, H. Lawrence rancher, investor, retired investment banker

Wilson
Sage, Andrew Gregg Curtin, II corporate investor, manager

TERRITORIES OF THE UNITED STATES

PUERTO RICO

Hato Rey
Ferrer, Miguel Antonio brokerage firm and investment bank executive

CANADA

ALBERTA

Calgary
Cumming, Thomas Alexander stock exchange executive
King, Frank investment company executive
Seaman, Donald Roy investment company executive

Edmonton
Cormie, Donald Mercer investment company executive
Pocklington, Peter H. business executive

BRITISH COLUMBIA

Vancouver
Harwood, Brian Dennis securities industry executive
Hudson, Donald J. stock exchange executive
Saunders, Peter Paul investor

MANITOBA

Winnipeg
Alexander, Norman James investment consultant

NOVA SCOTIA

Bedford
Hennigar, David J. investment broker

ONTARIO

Chatham
McKeough, William Darcy investment company executive

Oakville
Holmes, James investment company executive

Toronto
Barford, Ralph MacKenzie investment executive
Dembroski, George Steven investment banker
Dunford, Robert A. diversified business executive
Gairdner, John Smith securities investment dealer
Hore, John Edward commodity futures educator
Lindsay, Roger Alexander investment executive
Michals, George Francis investment and business development executive
Petrillo, Leonard Philip corporate securities executive, lawyer
Weston, Willard Galen diversified holdings executive

QUEBEC

Montreal
Cedraschi, Tullio investment management company executive
Elie, Jean André investment banker
Schwartz, Roy Richard holding company executive
Torrey, David Leonard investment banker

BAHAMAS

Grand Cayman
McIntire, Jerald Gene investment executive, former municipal official

Nassau
Templeton, John Marks investment counsel, financial analyst

BERMUDA

Tuckers Town
Heizer, Edgar Francis, Jr. venture capitalist

ENGLAND

London
Berger, Andrew L. investment banker, lawyer
Hale, Charles Martin stockbroker
Hayden, Richard Michael investment banker
Jourdren, Marc Henri investment banking company executive
Mulford, David Campbell finance company executive
Sainsbury of Preston Candover, Lord (Baron John Davan Sainsbury) entrepreneur

FRANCE

Fontainebleu
Churchill, Neil Center entrepreneur, educator

Paris
Jaclot, Francois Charles investment bank executive
Masurel, Jean-Louis Antoine Nicolas investment company executive

ISRAEL

Jerusalem
Arnon, Michael finance company executive

MONACO

Saint-Leon
Kimmle, Manfred investment company executive

PAKISTAN

Karachi
Shroff, Firoz Sardar merger and acquisition professional

SCOTLAND

Edinburgh
Buchan, Hamish Noble securities analyst

SWITZERLAND

Lausanne
Bloemsma, Marco Paul investor

ADDRESS UNPUBLISHED

Ackerman, Melvin investment company executive
Aljian, James Donovan investment company executive
Andreas, Dwayne Orville investment company executive
Anker, Peter Louis securities executive
Apel-Brueggeman, Myrna L. entrepreneur
Apruzzi, Gene retired stockbroker
Aurin, Robert James entrepreneur
Bacharach, Melvin Lewis venture capitalist
Bacon, Caroline Sharfman investor relations consultant
Bagwill, John Williams, Jr. retired pension fund company executive
Balding, Bruce Edward investment executive
Bantry, Bryan entrepreneur
Barnett, Norman Lawrence investment advisor
Black, Richard Bruce business executive, consultant
Bondarenko, Hesperia Aura Louis entrepreneur
Bouton, James Alan entrepreneur, author, former sportscaster, former professional baseball player
Bowles, Barbara Landers investment company executive
Bratt, Nicholas investment management and research company executive
†Brodkin, Alan Keith investment company executive
Bronfman, Peter Frederick independent investor
Bruzda, Francis Joseph investment executive, former banker
Caldwell, Warren Frederick investment company executive
Callard, David Jacobus investment banker
Carr, Harold Noflet investment corporation executive
Cockrum, William Monroe, III investment banker, consultant, educator
Cook, Charles Beckwith, Jr. securities company executive
Doherty, Charles Vincent investment counsel executive
Drake, Rodman Leland investment executive, consultant
Ferguson, William Emmett retired securities broker
Frankenberger, Bertram, Jr. investor, consultant
†Friedlander, Charles Douglas investment company executive, space consultant
Friedman, Donald Joseph stock brokerage executive
Froehlke, Robert Frederick financial services executive
Fuld, Richard Severin, Jr. investment banker
Garcia-Granados, Sergio Eduardo brokerage house executive
Gardner, James Albert investment and real estate executive
Geissinger, Frederick Wallace investment banker
Gelles, Harry P. investment banker, land investor
Glasberg, Laurence Brian private investor, business executive
Goldman, Alan Ira investment banking executive
Good, Walter Raymond investment executive
Goyan, Michael Donovan stockbroker, investment executive
Grant, Frederick Anthony investment banker
Greene, Frank Sullivan, Jr. investment management executive
Haber, Warren H. investment company executive
Harris, D. George entrepreneur
Hays, Thomas Chandler holding company executive
Headley, Anne Renouf technology commercialization financier
Heckler, John Maguire stockbroker, investment company executive
Heffner, William Joseph investment executive
Henkel, Arthur John, Jr. investment banker
Hickey, Joseph Michael, Jr. investment banker
Hill, John Edward, Jr. investment banker, small business owner
Hogan, Mark investment company executive
Horwitz, Larry Stuckey entrepreneur
Howard, James Webb investment banker, lawyer, engineer
Jacobs, Herbert Howard investor
Jepson, Robert Scott, Jr. international investment banking specialist
Kotler, Steven investment banker
Lipton, Susan Lytle investment banker, lawyer
Lohrer, Richard Baker investment consultant
Lynch, Thomas Peter securities executive
Marks, Leonard, Jr. retired corporate executive
Marler, Larry John private investor
Matthei, Warren Douglas investment company executive
McColl, Hugh Leon, III investment company executive
Mc Gill, Archie Joseph venture capital and business speaker
McMaster, Harold Ashley inventor, retired manufacturing company executive
McRae, Thomas Kenneth retired investment company executive
Michaelcheck, William J. investment firm executive
Mikitka, Gerald Peter investment banker, financial consultant
Miller, Alan Jay financial consultant, author
Millsaps, Fred Ray investor
Morosky, Robert Harry private investor, operator
Myers, John Herman investment management executive
Nilsson, A. Kenneth investor
Parsons, Edmund Morris investment company executive
Pavlick, Harvey Naylor financial executive
Peters, Ralph Frew investment banker
Petrie, Donald Archibald lawyer, investment banker, publisher
Phelan, John J., Jr. former stock exchange executive, corporate director
Pinkney, D. Timothy investment company executive
Pool, Philip Bemis, Jr. investment banker
Prince, Milton S. investment company executive
Robinson, Bob Leo international investment services executive
Rothfeld, Michael B. investment banker
Saunders, Thomas A., III investment company executive
Schmidt, Benno Charles investment company executive
Schmidt, Kenneth Martin investment banker
Sells, Boake Anthony private investor
Servison, Roger Theodore investment executive
Smoot, Wendell McMeans, Jr. investment counselor
Stanfill, Dennis Carothers business executive
Steen, Carlton Duane private investor, former food company executive
Swanberg, Edmund Raymond investment counselor
Taber, Edward Albert, III investment executive
Tansor, Robert Henry investor
Weisman, Lorenzo David investment banker
Wilson, Robert James Montgomery investment company executive

FINANCE: REAL ESTATE

UNITED STATES

ALABAMA

Abbeville
Rane, Michael Gregory preservation company executive

Arab
Hammond, Ralph Charles real estate executive

Birmingham
Copeland, Hunter Armstrong *real estate executive*

Florence
Mullins, Betty Johnson *realtor*

ALASKA

Anchorage
Faulkner, Sewell Ford *real estate executive*

ARIZONA

Bullhead City
Jones, Vernon Quentin *surveyor*

Mesa
Bell, Daniel Carroll *realtor, ranch and land manager*

Peoria
Morrison, Manley Glenn *real estate investor, former army officer*

Phoenix
Donaldson, Wilburn Lester *property management corporation executive*
Lewis, Orme, Jr. *real estate company executive, land use adviser*
†Pond, Kenneth W. *title company executive*
Rau, David Edward *real estate company executive*
†Schrader, William P. *organization executive, farmer*
Spencer, John Andrew *real estate development corporation executive*
Tatz, Paul H. *real estate executive*

Prescott
Broadston, Donald Andrew *real estate broker*

Sedona
Preston, Edgar Harlan *real estate broker*

Sierra Vista
Morrison, Francis Martin *real estate broker*

Tucson
Best, Gary Thorman *real estate broker*
Longan, George Baker, III *real estate executive*

West Sedona
Lane, Margaret Anna Smith *property manager developer*

ARKANSAS

Bella Vista
†Cooper, John Alfred, Jr. *community development company executive*
†McMennamy, Roger Neal *community development company executive*

Little Rock
McCarley, Robert Edward *real estate executive, real estate appraiser*
McConnell, John Wesley *real estate-resort developer, corporate executive*
Shults, Robert Lee *real estate executive, airline executive*

CALIFORNIA

Agoura Hills
†Scardina, Frank Joseph *real estate executive*

Belvedere Tiburon
Caselli, Virgil P. *real estate executive*

Berkeley
Catlin, James C. *conservationist, land use planner, electrical engineer*

Beverly Hills
Bergman, Nancy Palm *real estate investment company executive*
Shapell, Nathan *financial and real estate executive*
Victor, Robert Eugene *real estate corporation executive, lawyer*
Winthrop, John *real estate executive, lawyer*

Big Sur
Cross, Robert Louis *realtor, land use planner, writer*
Owings, Margaret Wentworth *conservationist, artist*

Bonita
Dresser, Jesse Dale *real estate investor*

Campbell
Nicholson, Joseph Bruce *real estate developer*

Carmel
Barton, Gerald Gaylord *land development company executive*

Citrus Heights
†Richards, Tom, III *real estate manager*

Costa Mesa
Argyros, George L. *development company executive, former professional sports team owner*
†Reppert, Joseph R. *title company executive*

Danville
Plummer, Marcie Stern *real estate broker*

El Macero
Wheeler, Douglas Paul *conservationist, government official, lawyer*

Foster City
Meredith, Allen Kent *real estate developer*

Glendale
Beban, Gary Joseph *real estate corporation officer*

Inglewood
Buss, Jerry Hatten *real estate executive, sports team owner*

Irvine
Stack, Geoffrey Lawrence *real estate developer*

La Jolla
Anthony, Harry Antoniades *city planner, architect, educator*
Foley, L(ewis) Michael *real estate executive*

Laguna Beach
Hanauer, Joe Franklin *real estate executive*

Laguna Niguel
York, James Orison *real estate executive*

Larkspur
Roulac, Stephen E. *real estate consultant*

Lompoc
Woodberry, Paul Francis *real estate executive*

Los Alamitos
Spiegel, Marilyn Harriet *real estate executive*

Los Angeles
Abernethy, Robert John *real estate developer*
Didion, James J. *real estate company executive*
Gordon, Milton G. *real estate counselor, consultant*
Grantham, Richard Robert *real estate company executive*
Linsk, Michael Stephen *real estate executive*
Martin, Vincent Francis, Jr. *real estate investment executive*
Mitchell, Joseph Nathan *retired real estate executive*
Nelson, James Augustus, II *real estate executive, architect, banker*
†Souza, Anthony P. *real estate developer, wholesale distribution services executive, finance company executive*
†Surace, Ronald J. *real estate executive*
Tornek, Terry E. *real estate executive*
Wachs, Martin *urban planning educator*

Manhattan Beach
Krienke, Carol Belle Manikowske (Mrs. Oliver Kenneth Krienke) *realtor*

Mission Viejo
†Smith, William K. *real estate developer*

National City
Potter, J(effrey) Stewart *property manager*

Newbury Park
Fredericks, Patricia Ann *real estate executive*
Guggenheim-Boucard, Alan Andre Albert Paul Edouard *business executive, international consultant*

Newport Beach
Kenney, William John, Jr. *real estate development executive*
Warren, William Robinson *real estate broker*
†Wirta, Ray *real estate developer*

North Hollywood
Milner, Howard M. *real estate developer, international real estate financier*

Oakland
Fischer, Michael Ludwig *environmental executive*

Palm Desert
Wiedle, Gary Eugene *real estate management company executive*

Palmdale
Anderson, R(obert) Gregg *real estate company executive*

Palo Alto
†Marcus, George Mathew *real estate executive*
Warne, William Elmo *irrigationist*

Placerville
Craib, Kenneth Bryden *resource development executive, physicist, economist*

Portola Valley
†Litton, Martin *conservationist*

Rancho Cucamonga
†Rankin, Jim *real estate developer*

Rancho Mirage
Gardner, Donald LaVere *development company executive*

Rosemead
†Pollay, Richard L. *title company executive*

Sacramento
Lukenbill, Gregg *sports promoter, real estate developer*

San Diego
Mc Comic, Robert Barry *real estate development company executive, lawyer*

San Francisco
Brower, David Ross *conservationist*
Colwell, Kent Leigh *real estate executive*
Freund, Fredric S. *real estate broker, property manager*
Humphrey, Jayne Hulbert *real estate development and financial consultant*
Lynch, Timothy Jeremiah-Mahoney *realty holding company executive, author, lawyer, theologian, law educator*
Mc Mahan, John William *real estate investment advisor*
Pendleton, Alan R. *conservation agency executive*
Shorenstein, Walter Herbert *commercial real estate development company executive*
†Smith, David A. *real estate developer*

San Jose
Rothblatt, Donald Noah *urban and regional planner, educator*

San Mateo
Bohannon, David D. *community planner and developer*
Leeder, Stuart L. Sandy *real estate financial executive*

Santa Cruz
Dilbeck, Charles Stevens, Jr. *real estate company executive*

Santa Rosa
Brunner, Howard William *professional land surveyor*

Thousand Oaks
Fore, Richard Lewis *real estate development company executive*

Torrance
Alter, Gerald L. *real estate executive*

Twain Harte
Kinsinger, Robert Earl *property company executive, educational consultant*

Upland
Lewis, Goldy Sarah *real estate developer, corporation executive*
Lewis, Ralph Milton *real estate developer*

Vista
Cavanaugh, Kenneth Clinton *retired housing consultant*

Walnut Creek
†Wentzel, Dan R. *title company executive*

COLORADO

Boulder
McCabe, Richard Lee *real estate developer*

Denver
Antonoff, Gary L. *real estate executive*
Howlett, John David *urban planner, consultant*
Lochmiller, Kurtis L. *real estate entrepreneur*
†Mandarich, David D. *real estate corporation executive*
†Post, Richard *real estate company executive*

Englewood
Crowley, John Robert *real estate development company executive*
Fisher, Bob *real estate broker, franchisor*

Fort Collins
Frink, Eugene Hudson, Jr. *business and real estate consultant*

Grand Junction
Nelson, Paul William *real estate broker*

Vail
Kelton, Arthur Marvin, Jr. *real estate developer*

CONNECTICUT

Greenwich
Badman, John, III *real estate developer, architect, construction executive*

New Britain
Adams, John Francis, Jr. *real estate executive*

New Haven
Harrison, Henry Starin *real estate educator, appraiser, entrepreneur*

DELAWARE

Dover
Cohen, William John *urban and environmental planner, educator, photographer*

Newark
Byrne, John Michael *energy and environmental policy educator, researcher*

Wilmington
Bredin, J(ohn) Bruce *retired real estate executive*
Gilman, Marvin Stanley *real estate developer, educator*

DISTRICT OF COLUMBIA

Washington
Berg, Norman Alf *conservation consultant*
Blackwelder, Brent Francis *environmentalist*
Glogower, Michael Howard *housing program specialist, business and real estate consultant*
Golden, Terence C. *realty corporation executive, former government official*
Hanke, Byron Reidt *residential land planning and community associations consultant*
Hollander, Richard Edward *real estate executive*
Meyer, Alden Merrill *environmental association executive*
†Pritchard, Paul Clement *conservation association executive*
Reardon, Pearl Rance *real estate executive, writer*
Rumford, Lewis, III *real estate company executive*
Stollman, Israel *city planner*
Stone, Roger David *environmentalist*

FLORIDA

Arcadia
Schmidt, Harold Eugene *real estate company executive*

Boca Raton
Lagin, Neil *property management executive*
Mandor, Leonard Stewart *real estate company executive*

Cedar Key
Starnes, Earl Maxwell *urban and regional planner, architect*

Clearwater
Glindeman, Henry Peter, Jr. *real estate developer*

Coral Gables
Blumberg, David *builder, developer*

Deland
Tedros, Theodore Zaki *educator, real estate broker, appraiser*

Fort Lauderdale
Cummings, Virginia J(eanne) *former real estate company executive*
Hirshson, William Roscoe *real estate consultant*
Paulauskas, Edmund Walter *real estate broker*
Sutte, Donald T., Jr. *real estate executive*

Fort Walton Beach
Cooke, Fred Charles *real estate broker*

Gainesville
Feiss, Carl Lehman *retired urban planning educator*
Stein, Jay M. *planning and design educator, consultant*

Hollywood
Burton, John Jacob *real estate company executive, appraiser*

Jacksonville
Lovett, Radford Dow *real estate and investment company executive*
†Osteen, H(oward) Kenneth, Jr. *real estate developer, hotel management executive*
Parker, David Forster *real estate development consultant*

Lakeland
Smith, Levie David, Jr. *real estate appraiser, consultant*

Maitland
Vallee, Judith Delaney *environmentalist, fundraiser*

Melbourne
Michalski, Thomas Joseph *city planner, developer*
†Pruitt, J. Michael *real estate company executive*
†Pruitt, James H. *real estate company executive*

Miami
Mozian, Gerard Paul *real estate company executive, business consultant*
Parker, Ree *real estate investor*
Raffel, Leroy B. *real estate development company executive*
Roemer, Elaine Sloane *real estate broker*
Salvaneschi, Luigi *real estate and development executive, business educator*
Stover, James Howard *real estate executive*

Micco
Muller, Henry John *real estate developer*

Mount Dora
Adams, Carl Morgan, Jr. *real estate appraiser, mortgage banker*

Naples
Evans, Elizabeth Ann West *real estate agent*

New Port Richey
Rhodes, Eric Foster *real estate and insurance executive, consultant*

Palm Beach
†Bagby, Martha L. Green *real estate holding company, novelist, publisher*
Bonan, Seon Pierre *real estate developer*

Ponte Vedra Beach
Moore, Philip Walsh *appraisal company executive*

Saint Petersburg
Rummel, Harold Edwin *real estate developing executive*

Saint Petersburg Beach
Hurley, Frank Thomas, Jr. *realtor*

Sanibel
Courtney, James Edmond *real estate development*

Sarasota
Pillot, Gene Merrill *retired superintendent of schools*

Sebring
Sherrick, Daniel Noah *real estate broker*

Sunrise
Cronin, Mary Haag *real estate referral agent*

Tallahassee
Avant, David Alonzo, Jr. *realty company executive, photographer*
Johnson, Benjamin F., VI *real estate developer, consulting economist*

Tampa
Corbitt, Doris Orene *real estate agent, dietitian*

Vero Beach
Dillard, Rodney Jefferson *real estate company executive*

West Palm Beach
Wilensky, Alvin *real estate investment trust executive*

GEORGIA

Atlanta
Charania, Barkat *real estate consultant*
Cupp, Robert Erhard *golf course designer, land use planner*
†Glover, John Trapnell *real estate executive*
Regenstein, Lewis Graham *conservationist, author, lecturer, speech writer*
†Williams, John A. *real estate developer, property manger*
Wolbrink, James Francis *real estate investor*

Augusta
Mayberry, Julius Eugene *realty company owner, investor*

Folkston
Crumbley, Esther Helen Kendrick *realtor, retired educator*

Macon
Jones, John Ellis *real estate broker*

Toccoa
Maypole, John Floyd *real estate holding company executive*

HAWAII

Honolulu
Albano, Andres, Jr. *real estate developer, real estate broker*
Levine, Aaron *city planner*

Lihue
Cobb, Rowena Noelani Blake *real estate broker*

IDAHO

Boise
†Burnham, William A. *wildlife protection society administrator*
Reuling, Michael Frederick *supermarket company, real estate executive*

Idaho Falls
Thorsen, Nancy Dain *real estate broker*
Williams, Phyllis Cutforth *retired realtor*

Payette
Jones, Donna Marilyn *real estate broker, legislator*

Stanley
Kimpton, David Raymond *natural resource consultant, writer*

ILLINOIS

Champaign
Guttenberg, Albert Ziskind *planning educator*

Chicago
†Ady, Robert *relocation consulting firm executive*
Amato, Isabella Antonia *real estate executive*
Beitler, J. Paul *real estate developer*
Bluhm, Neil Gary *real estate company executive*
Bynoe, Peter Charles Bernard *real estate developer, legal consultant*
Claeys, Jerome Joseph, III *real estate company executive*
Eubanks-Pope, Sharon G. *real estate entrepreneur*
Gerst, C(ornelius) Gary *real estate executive*
Glass, Ronald Lee *real estate executive*
Gordon, Jacques Nicholas *real estate economist*
Grabowski, Roger J. *business, intangible assets, real estate appraiser*
Greenberg, Arthur A. *diversified real estate and financial services executive, manufacturing company executive*
Hill, Arthur J. *real estate company executive*
†Kateley, Richard *real estate consultant*
Levy, Arnold S(tuart) *real estate company executive*
McFarland, Claudette *real estate executive*
Pezzella, Jerry James, Jr. *investment and real estate corporation executive*
†Pollay, Richard L. *real estate title insurance company executive*
Reschke, Michael W. *real estate executive*
Sen, Ashish Kumar *urban planner, educator*
Stein, Paula Jean Anne Barton *hotel real estate consultant*
Stein, Richard Allen *real estate developer*
Totlis, Gust John *title insurance company executive*
Travis, Dempsey Jerome *real estate executive, mortgage banker*
†Warshauer, Myron C. *land use planner*
Wirtz, William Wadsworth *real estate and sports executive*

Edwardsville
Ottwein, Merrill William George *real estate company executive, veterinarian*

Flossmoor
Wagner, Alvin Louis, Jr. *real estate appraiser, consultant*

Glenview
Groh, Thomas Joseph *real estate executive*

Hinsdale
Wheeler, Paul James *real estate executive*

Itasca
Bingham, Bruce Bryan *real estate developer*
Sheridan, James Leslie *real estate developer*

Lake Zurich
Schultz, Carl Herbert *real estate management and development company executive*

Oak Brook
Cosenza, G. Joseph *real estate executive*
Goodwin, Daniel L. *real estate company executive*

Oswego
Stephens, Steve Arnold *real estate broker*

Saint Charles
Urhausen, James Nicholas *real estate developer, construction executive*

Urbana
Blair, Lachlan Ferguson *urban planner, educator*
Goodman, William I. *urban planner, educator*

INDIANA

Elkhart
Vite, Frank Anthony *realtor*

Fort Wayne
Hirschy, Gordon Harold *real estate agent*

Indianapolis
Jewett, John Rhodes *real estate executive*
Mullen, Thomas Edgar *real estate consultant*

Jeffersonville
Reisert, Charles Edward, Jr. *real estate executive*

Montpelier
Neff, Kenneth D. *realtor, mayor*

Newburgh
Tierney, Gordon Paul *real estate broker, genealogist*

Terre Haute
Perry, Eston Lee *real estate and equipment leasing company executive*

West Lafayette
Curtis, Kenneth Stewart *land surveyor*

IOWA

Des Moines
Bucksbaum, Martin *real estate developer*
Bucksbaum, Matthew *real estate development company president*

West Des Moines
Schroder, Andrea Ruth Lundeen *realtor*

Windsor Heights
Ansorge, Iona Marie *retired real estate agent, musician, high school and college instructor*

KANSAS

Concordia
Casado, Antonio Francisco *retired real estate executive*

Liberal
Holmes, Carl Dean *landowner, state legislator*

Westwood
Buckner, William Claiborne *real estate broker*

KENTUCKY

Lexington
Gable, Robert Elledy *real estate investment company executive*

LOUISIANA

Baton Rouge
McLindon, Gerald Joseph *planning and environmental design consultant, university dean emeritus*

Harvey
Chee, Shirley *real estate broker*

Metairie
†Derbes, Max Joseph, Jr. *real estate appraiser*
Myers, Iona Raymer *real estate and property manager*

New Orleans
†Stanback, Lawrence *conservationist*
Villavaso, Stephen Donald *urban planner, lawyer*

MAINE

Augusta
Richard, Debrah Jane *environmental planner*

Lincolnville
Williams, Robert Luther *city planning consultant*

MARYLAND

Baltimore
Apgar, Mahlon, IV *real estate management counselor*
Bart, Polly Turner *commercial real estate developer*
Frank, Robert Allen *real estate securities investment analyst*
Lavin, Charles Blaise, Jr. *realtor, association executive*
†Pinkard, Walter Devier, Jr. *real estate executive*

Berlin
Passwater, Barbara Gayhart *real estate broker*

Bethesda
†Chappell, Raymond Edward *real estate company executive*
Lee, Edward Brooke, Jr. *real estate executive, fund raiser*
Sams, James Farid *real estate development company executive*
Walker, Mallory *real estate executive*

Chevy Chase
Blair, William Draper, Jr. *conservationist*

Columbia
Alexander, Bruce Donald *real estate executive*
Cook, Stephen Bernard *homebuilding company executive*
Deering, Anthony Wayne Marion *real estate developer*
DeVito, Mathias Joseph *real estate executive*
Hilderbrandt, Donald Franklin, II *urban designer, landscape architect, artist*
McCauley, Richard Gray *real estate developer, lawyer*
McCuan, William Patrick *real estate company executive*
Millspaugh, Martin Laurence *real estate developer, urban development consultant*

Gaithersburg
Watkins, Michael Dean *town planner*

Lutherville
Barton, Meta Packard *property management executive, financial planner*

Lutherville Timonium
Kerr, Patrick Corbitt *real estate appraiser, consultant*

Rockville
Dockser, William Barnet *real estate management and mortgages executive*
Lee, James Jieh *environmental educator, computer specialist*

Silver Spring
Humphries, Weldon R. *real estate/hotel executive*
Kronstadt, Arnold Mayo *community and architectural planner*
Ventre, Francis Thomas *environmental design and policy educator*

MASSACHUSETTS

Amherst
Bentley, Richard Norcross *regional planner, educator*
Larson, Joseph Stanley *environmentalist, educator, researcher*

Boston
Beal, Robert Lawrence *real estate executive*
Cervieri, John Anthony, Jr. *real estate company officer*
Colloredo-Mansfeld, Ferdinand *real estate company executive*
Logue, Edward Joseph *development company executive*
Morse, Garlan, Jr. *real estate investment counseling officer*
Radloff, Robert Albert *real estate executive*
Thibedeau, Richard Herbert *environmental planner, administrator*

Boylston
Brazelton, Roy Dale *real estate executive*

Cambridge
Fagans, Karl Preston *real estate facilities administration executive*
Fleming, Ronald Lee *urban designer, administrator, preservation planner, environmental educator*
Gakenheimer, Ralph Albert *urban planning educator, consultant*
Spunt, Shepard Armin *real estate executive, management and financial consultant*
Susskind, Lawrence Elliott *urban and environmental planner, educator, mediator*
Vigier, François Claude Denis *city planning educator*

Franklin
Bonin, Paul Joseph *real estate and banking executive*

Hanover
Fantozzi, Peggy Ryone *environmental planner*

Longmeadow
Louargand, Marc Andrew *real estate executive, financial consultant*

Natick
Strauss, Harlee Sue *environmental consultant*

Newburyport
Howard, John Tasker *city planner*

Newton
Bernard, Michael Mark *city planning consultant, lawyer*
Frieden, Bernard Joel *urban studies educator*

North Reading
Dolan, Edward Corcoran *real estate developer and investor*

Peabody
Wood, Richard Robinson *real estate executive*

Waltham
Nelson, Arthur Hunt *real estate management development company executive*

Winchester
Blackham, Ann Rosemary (Mrs. J. W. Blackham) *realtor*

MICHIGAN

Ann Arbor
Clark, Thomas Bertram, Sr. *real estate broker*
Duke, Richard De La Barre *urban planner, educator*
Rycus, Mitchell Julian *urban planning educator, urban security and energy planning consultant*
Surovell, Edward David *real estate company executive*

Dearborn
†Werling, Donn Paul *environmental educator*

East Lansing
Hamlin, Roger Eugene *urban planning educator, economic and financial analyst*

Grosse Ile
Smith, Veronica Latta *real estate corporation officer*

Kalamazoo
Taborn, Jeannette Ann *real estate investor*

Novi
†Kowalski, Thomas P. *environmental consulting executive*

Saginaw
Cline, Thomas William *real estate leasing company executive, management consultant*

West Bloomfield
Colton, Victor Robert *real estate developer, investor,*

MINNESOTA

Bloomington
Dahlberg, Burton Francis *real estate corporation executive*

Duluth
Bowman, Roger Manwaring *real estate executive*

Faribault
Turnbull, Charles Vincent *real estate broker*

Minneapolis
Bolan, Richard Stuart *urban planner, educator, researcher*
Stuebner, James Cloyd *real estate developer, contractor*

Minnetonka
Johnson, Kay Durbahn *real estate manager, consultant*

MISSISSIPPI

Meridian
Church, George Millord *real estate executive*

Mississippi State
Parsons, George William *city planner, educator*

MISSOURI

Chesterfield
Thomas, Violeta de los Angeles *real estate broker*

Kansas City
Cohen, Roger L. *real estate executive*
Dumovich, Loretta *real estate and transportation company executive*
Shutz, Byron Christopher *real estate executive*

Lake Saint Louis
Royal, William Henry *real estate developer, architect*

Saint Joseph
Miller, Lloyd Daniel *real estate agent*

Saint Louis
†Davis, Stuart Alan *real estate company executive*
Fleming, Richard Carl Dunne *city planner, business executive*
Loomstein, Arthur *real estate company executive*
Meissner, Edwin Benjamin, Jr. *real estate broker*
Morley, Harry Thomas, Jr. *real estate executive*
†Riley, Joe *real estate executive*
Schierholz, William Francis, Jr. *real estate developer*
†Spehr, Steven *real estate company executive*

Stockton
Jackson, Betty L. Deason *real estate developer*

MONTANA

Darby
Brandborg, Stewart Monroe *conservationist, government official*

Great Falls
Stevens, George Alexander *realtor*

NEBRASKA

Norfolk
Wozniak, Richard Michael, Sr. *city and regional planner*

NEVADA

Carson City
McLain, John Lowell *resource specialist, consultant*

Henderson
McKinney, Sally Vitkus *realty company executive, business owner*

Las Vegas
†Canarelli, Lawrence D. *real estate developer*
Thomas, Peter M. *real estate developer*

Reno
Dulgar, Pam *realtor*

NEW HAMPSHIRE

Concord
†Bofinger, Paul O. *conservationist*

Hanover
†Meadows, Donella *environmentalist*

Hinsdale
Smith, Edwin O. *real estate executive, state legislator*

NEW JERSEY

Bound Brook
Chandler, Marguerite Nella *real estate corporation executive*

Colts Neck
Rode, Leif *real estate personal computer consultant*

Haworth
Stokvis, Jack Raphael *urban planner and developer, government agency administrator*

Hightstown
Arnold, Matthew Charles *real estate corporation officer*

Imlaystown
Richardson, Donald Campbell *land planner, landscape architect*

Mercerville
†Kraus, Ted Richard *real estate consultant*

Morristown
Booth, Albert Edward, II *real estate executive*

Mount Laurel
Buchan, Alan Bradley *land planner, consultant, civil engineer*

Newark
Simmons, Peter *urban planning educator*

Paramus
Gingras, Paul Joseph *real estate management company executive*

Princeton
Baker, Richard Wheeler, Jr. *real estate executive*
Wood, Eric Franklin *earth and environmental sciences educator*

Red Bank
Hovnanian, Kevork S. *real estate developer*
Schimpf, John Joseph *real estate developer*

Rochelle Park
Mack, Earle Irving *real estate company executive*

Rumson
†Bryan, Richard D.S. *conservationist*

Short Hills
Good, Allen Hovey *acquisitions broker, real estate broker*

Summit
Natkin, Alvin Martin *environmental company executive*

Westwood
Andolsek, Charles Merrick *land development consultant*

NEW MEXICO

Albuquerque
Liberman, Ira L. *real estate broker*
Stahl, Jack Leland *real estate company executive*

Santa Fe
Pearson, Margit Linnea *real estate company executive*

NEW YORK

Albany
Picotte, Michael Bernard *real estate developer*
†Roberts, Hugh D. *real estate company executive*
†Roberts, Katherine Christina *real estate executive*

Bloomingdale
†Ketchledge, Edwin H. *conservationist*

Brasher Falls
Patterson, Florence Ghoram *real estate broker*

Bronx
Pearl, Mary Corliss *wildlife conservationist*
†Robinson, John Gwilym *conservationist*

Brooklyn
Blackman, Robert Irwin *real estate developer and investor, lawyer, accountant*

Buffalo
Wirth, Sandra Lee *real estate company owner*

Cambridge
Sullivan, Patricia W. (Terry Sullivan) *real estate trainer*

Central Islip
McGowan, Harold *real estate developer, investor, scientist, author, philanthropist*

Elizabethtown
Davis, George Donald *land use policy consultant*

Flushing
Wilpon, Fred *real estate developer, baseball team executive*

Forest Hills
LeFrak, Richard Stone *real estate developer*

Goshen
Ward, William Francis, Jr. *real estate investment banker*

Great Neck
Zirinsky, Daniel *real estate investor and photographer*

Ithaca
Goldsmith, William Woodbridge *city and regional planning educator*
Parsons, Kermit Carlyle *urban planning educator, former university dean*
Saltzman, Sidney *city and regional planning educator*

Jericho
Axinn, Donald Everett *real estate investor, developer*

Larchmont
Levi, James Harry *real estate executive, investment banker*

Locust Valley
Devendorf, Barbara Lancaster (Bonnie Lancaster Devendorf) *real estate broker*

Mount Vernon
Rossini, Joseph *contracting and development corporate executive*

New Hyde Park
Cooper, Milton *real estate investment trust executive*
Jacob, Gary Steven *real estate developer*

New York
Benenson, Edward Hartley *realty company executive*
Berliner, Ruth Shirley *real estate company executive*
Brown, Thomas J. *real estate syndication company executive*
Cohen, Irving Elias *real estate executive*
Cohen, Lawrence Alan *real estate executive*
Fiedler, Lawrence Elliot *real estate investment company executive*
Friedman, Howard W. *retired real estate company executive*
Gellman, Isaiah *environmental consultant*
Gochberg, Thomas *real estate investor, financial executive*
Goddess, Lynn Barbara *commercial real estate broker*
Goldenberg, Charles Lawrence *real estate company executive*
†Helmsley, Harry B. *real estate company executive*
Hemmerdinger, H. Dale *real estate executive*
Hernstadt, Judith Filenbaum *city planner, real estate executive, broadcasting executive*
Hutton, Ernest Watson, Jr. *urban designer, city planner*
Jenkins, Robert Nesbit *real estate executive*
Kalikow, Peter Stephen *real estate developer, former newspaper owner, publisher*
Katz, Daniel Roger *conservation executive*
Keith, John Pirie *urban planner*
Kent, Barbara *real estate investor*
Lachman, Marguerite Leanne *real estate investment advisor*
Licari, Joseph *real estate company executive*
Malino, John Gray *real estate executive*
Marder, John G. *real estate investor, marketing consultant, corporate director*
Marshall, Alton Garwood *real estate counselor*
McClellan, Anne Starr *environmentalist*
†Mirante, Arthur J., II *real estate company executive*
Moody, John Stephen *real estate executive*
Morris, Kenneth Baker *mergers, acquisition and real estate executive*
Moss, Mitchell Lawrence *urban planning educator*
Murray, Thomas Francis *real estate executive*
Newman, William *real estate executive*
Nichols, Carol D. *real estate professional, association executive*
Pasquarelli, Joseph J. *real estate, engineering and construction executive*
Petz, Edwin V. *real estate executive, lawyer*
Purse, Charles Roe *real estate company executive*
†Rose, Daniel *real estate company executive, consultant*
Rose, Elihu *real estate executive*
Roskind, E. Robert *real estate company executive*
Ruben, Lawrence *real estate developer, building company executive, lawyer*
Schwerin, Warren Lyons *real estate developer*
Scroggins, Richard Muir *real estate executive*
Scurry, Richardson Gano, Jr. *real estate company financial executive*
Stemmer, Wayne J. *real estate and financial services company executive*
Strum, Brian J. *real estate executive*
Tishman, John L. *realty and construction company executive*
Tishman, Robert V. *real estate and construction company executive*
Toote, Gloria E. A. *developer, lawyer, columnist*
Urstadt, Charles Jordan *real estate executive*
Voell, Richard Allen *real estate services company executive*
†Wallace, Paul F. *real estate company officer*
†Ward, Robert *property manager*
Warsawer, Harold Newton *real estate appraiser and consultant*
Weiss, Ronald Whitman *real estate executive, lawyer*
Weston, M. Moran, II *educator, real estate developer, banker, clergyman*
Widney, Marilyn Edith (Marilyn Perry) *international finance and real estate executive, television producer*
Wolf, Petér Michael *investment and land planning consultant, educator, author*
Wood, Christopher L. J. *real estate consulting firm executive*
Zeckendorf, William, Jr. *real estate developer*
Zuccotti, John Eugene *real estate company executive*

Port Washington
Otto, Terre A. *real estate executive and developer, interior designer*

Rye
Mintz, Stephen Allan *real estate company executive, lawyer*

Stony Brook
Koppelman, Lee Edward *regional planner, educator*

Tarrytown
Raymond, George Marc *city planner, educator*

Wyandanch
Barnett, Peter John *property development executive, educator*

NORTH CAROLINA

Canton
†Stanback, Brad *conservationist*

Chapel Hill
Weiss, Shirley F. *urban and regional planner, economist, educator*

Charlotte
Crosland, John, Jr. *real estate developer*
Phillips, Howard Mitchell *real estate developer*

Hickory
Powell, Louise Fox *real estate developer*

Salisbury
†Stanback, Fred *conservationist*

Winston Salem
Doggett, Aubrey Clayton, Jr. *real estate executive, consultant*

NORTH DAKOTA

Grafton
Tallackson, Harvey D. *real estate and insurance salesman*

OHIO

Beachwood
Donnem, Roland William *real estate owner and manager*
Ellett, Alan Sidney *real estate development company executive*
Lerner, Alfred *real estate and financial executive*

Canton
Duncan, Joyce Louise *real estate broker*

Cincinnati
Chatterjee, Jayanta *educator, urban designer*
Hoermann, Edward Richard *urban planning educator*
Schuler, Robert Leo *appraiser, consultant*
Shenk, Richard Lawrence *real estate developer, photographer, artist*
Weiskittel, Ralph Joseph *real estate executive*

Cleveland
Cleary, Martin Joseph *real estate company executive*
Jacobs, Richard E. *real estate executive, sports team owner*
Markos, Chris *real estate company executive*
Schofield, Donald Stewart *real estate investment trust executive*

Columbus
Baas, James William *real estate developer*
Pyatt, Leo Anthony *real estate broker*
Voss, Jerrold Richard *city planner, educator, university official*

Dayton
Wertz, Kenneth Dean *real estate executive*

Gates Mills
Schanfarber, Richard Carl *real estate broker*

Hudson
Stec, John Zygmunt *real estate executive*

Lancaster
Wagonseller, James Myrl *real estate executive*

New Albany
Kessler, John Whitaker *real estate developer*

Painesville
†Kluznik, Kurt *landscape design building executive*

Shaker Heights
Adler, Naomi Samuel *real estate counselor*

Toledo
Batt, Nick *property and investment executive*

Twinsburg
Solganik, Marvin *real estate executive*

OKLAHOMA

Bartlesville
Kaiser, Jean Morgan *real estate broker*

Tulsa
Cardwell, Sandra Gayle Bavido *real estate broker*

Watonga
Hoberecht, Earnest *abstract company executive, former newspaper executive*

OREGON

Bend
Kozak, Michael *real estate counselor, seminar instructor*

Eugene
Dasso, Jerome Joseph *real estate educator, consultant*

Lake Oswego
Morse, Lowell Wesley *real estate executive, banking executive*

Portland
Abbott, Carl John *urban studies and planning educator*

PENNSYLVANIA

Bloomsburg
Loncosky, Walter Beugger *real estate manager*

Doylestown
Long, Ronald Alex *real estate and financial consultant, educator*

Erie
Gottschalk, Frank Klaus *real estate executive*

Johnstown
Gunter, John Brown, Jr. *retired real estate executive*

Middletown
Hand, Irving *urban planning educator*

Philadelphia
Bacon, Edmund Norwood *city planner*
Binswanger, Frank G., Jr. *realty company executive*
Binswanger, John K. *real estate company executive*
Lipkin, Edward B. *real estate developer*
†Peck, Robert McCracken *naturalist, science historian, writer*
Pew, Robert Anderson *real estate corporation officer*
Tomazinis, Anthony Rodoflos *city planning educator*
†Wender, Herbert *title company executive*

Pittsburgh
Stephenson, Robert Clay *commercial real estate developer*
Wilson, Charles Reginald *real estate executive*

Plymouth Meeting
Levinson, Gary Howard *real estate investor*

University Park
Golany, Gideon Salomon *urban designer*

Valley Forge
Basile, Neal Fahr *environmental consulting firm executive*

RHODE ISLAND

East Greenwich
Deutsch, Stephen R. *real estate development executive, state senator*

Providence
Hitt, Mary Frances Lyster *environmentalist, deacon*

Wakefield
Morrison, Fred Beverly *real estate consultant*

SOUTH CAROLINA

Charleston
Evans, Allen Donald *investment real estate company executive*
Rivers, John Minott, Jr. *real estate developer*

Columbia
Love, Kenneth Edward *real estate, investment and business consultant*
Tomlin, Donald Robert, Jr. *real estate management company executive*

Hilton Head Island
†Franks, Paul Taylor *real estate executive*
Gruchacz, Robert S. *real estate executive*

TENNESSEE

Brentwood
Raskin, Edwin Berner *real estate executive*

Chattanooga
Porter, Dudley, Jr. *environmentalist, foundation executive, lawyer*

Memphis
†Connolly, Matthew B., Jr. *conservationist*

†Cooper, Irby *real estate development company executive*
Haizlip, Henry Hardin, Jr. *real estate consultant, former banker*

Nashville
Beck, Robert Beryl *real estate executive*
Boyer, James Floyd *land surveyor, state legislator*
Driscoll, Joseph Francis *real estate executive*

TEXAS

Amarillo
Stiff, John Sterling *development company executive*

Austin
Lancaster, Tina *real estate executive, small business owner, rancher*
Mathias, Reuben Victor (Vic Mathias) *real estate executive, investor*

Blue Ridge
Comola, James Paul *legislative and environmental consultant*

Bullard
Buckner, John Hugh *retired real estate broker, retired construction company executive, retired air force officer*

Dallas
†Crawford, Joe Jay *real estate company executive*
Crow, F. Trammell *real estate company executive*
Gilley, James Ray *real estate/financial services executive*
Hamilton, David Lee *retired environmental company executive*
Hewett, Arthur Edward *real estate developer, lawyer*
Pogue, Mack *real estate company executive*
Pratt, Edward Taylor, Jr. *real estate company executive*
Randolph, James Harrison, Sr. *realty company executive*
Staubach, Roger Thomas *real estate executive, former professional football player*

Decatur
Davie, Ronald B. *corporate realty executive*

Galveston
McLeod, E. Douglas *real estate developer, lawyer*

Harlingen
Bonner, Donna Pace *real estate investments, consultant, volunteer*

Houston
Ewing, John Kirby *real estate, oil and investment executive*
Goldsmith, Billy Joe *real estate broker*
Holcomb, William A. *retired real estate broker, consultant, retired oil and gas exploration, pipeline executive*
Kollaer, Jim C. *real estate executive, architect*
Lehrer, Kenneth Eugene *real estate advisor, economist, developer, consultant*
Nguyen, An Duc *industrial development, consultant*
Peck, Edwin Russell *real estate management executive*
Rhoades, Floyd *real estate and property manager*
Strudler, Robert Jacob *real estate development executive*
Waltrip, Robert L. *environmentalist*

Irving
Auger, Harvey J. *real estate executive*
Gidel, Robert Hugh *real estate investor*

Plano
Wilke, Chet *real estate executive*

San Antonio
Bryan, Richard Ray *real estate development executive, construction executive*
Rhame, William Thomas *land development company executive*

UTAH

Logan
Sigler, William Franklin *environmental consultant*

VIRGINIA

Alexandria
Holland, Dianna Gwin *real estate broker*
Palma, Dolores Patricia *urban planner*

Charlottesville
Collins, Richard C. *urban and environmental planning educator*

Colonial Heights
Bryant, Howard Louis *real estate appraiser and broker, consultant, farmer*

Fairfax
Eppink, Jeffrey Francis *environmental and energy specialist*
†Foster, Paul Wesley, Jr. *real estate broker*

Falls Church
†Gibbs, Lois Marie *environmentalist*
Nelson, Merle Chandler *real estate executive*

Palmyra
Mulckhuyse, Jacob John *energy conservation and environmental consultant*

Reston
Dastur, Kersy B. *real estate company executive*

Richmond
Dickinson, Alfred James *realtor*
Plaisted, Harris Merrill, III *real estate executive*

Tuck, Grayson Edwin *real estate agent, former natural gas transmission executive*

WASHINGTON

Bellevue
†Muhlebach, Richard Frank *management and development company executive*

Kirkland
Kirk, Judd *real estate development executive*

Olympia
Cothern, Barbara Shick *real estate investor, state legislator*

Seattle
Dillard, Marilyn Dianne *property manager*
Gerrodette, Charles Everett *real estate company executive, consultant*
McKinnon, James Buckner *real estate sales executive, writer, researcher*
Moudon, Anne Vernez *urban design educator*
Stevens, Clyde Benjamin, Jr. *property manager, retired naval officer*
Tovar, Carole L. *real estate management administrator*

Spokane
Kirschbaum, James Louis *real estate company administrator*

WEST VIRGINIA

Huntington
Davis, Donald Eugene *real estate management executive*

WISCONSIN

Baraboo
†Hartmann, Forrest D. *conservationist*

Beaver Dam
Butterbrodt, John Ervin *real estate executive*

Madison
Mullins, Jerome Joseph *real estate developer, consulting engineer*
Ring, Gerald J. *real estate developer, insurance executive*
Vandell, Kerry Dean *real estate and urban economics educator*

Milwaukee
Checota, Joseph Woodrow *real estate business executive*
Machulak, Edward Leon *real estate, mining and advertising company executive*
Smith, Lois Ann *real estate executive*
†Stein, Gerald *real estate and diversified holding company executive*
†Wighers, Arthur *real estate developer*

Minocqua
Utt, Glenn S., Jr. *motel investments and biotech industry company executive*

WYOMING

Jackson
Thulin, Walter Willis *real estate company executive*

TERRITORIES OF THE UNITED STATES

VIRGIN ISLANDS

Saint Thomas
Duarte, Patricia M. *real estate and insurance broker*

CANADA

ALBERTA

Calgary
L'Heureux, Willard John *real estate lawyer, diversified company executive*
McEwen, Alexander Campbell *cadastral studies educator, former Canadian government official, surveying consultant*
†Milavsky, Harold Phillip *real estate executive*

BRITISH COLUMBIA

Vancouver
Belzberg, Samuel *real estate investment professional*
Goldberg, Michael Arthur *land policy and planning educator*
Jurock, Oswald Erich *real estate executive*

MANITOBA

Winnipeg
Shnier, Alan *real estate executive*

NOVA SCOTIA

Stellarton
Sobey, Donald Creighton Rae *real estate developer*

ONTARIO

Don Mills
Cormack, G. J. *real estate executive*
Romanese, Gino *real estate executive*

Downsview
Page, Austin P. *construction technology and property development company executive*

London
Pearson, Norman *urban and regional planner, administrator, academic and planning consultant, writer*

North York
Carrothers, Gerald Arthur Patrick *environmental and city planning educator*

Toronto
Braithwaite, J(oseph) Lorne *real estate executive*
Cullingworth, Larry Ross *residential and real estate development company executive*
Dimma, William Andrew *real estate executive*
Goring, Peter Allan Elliott *real estate executive*
Marshall, Marvin Giffin *real estate company executive*
Wood, Neil Roderick *real estate development company executive*

Weston
McIntyre, John George Wallace *real estate development and management consultant*

QUEBEC

Montreal
Gabbour, Iskandar *city and regional planning educator*

Rimouski
†Laribée, Jacques *conservationist*

BAHAMAS

Abaco
Goodloe, John Duncan, IV *real estate company executive*

ENGLAND

London
Hall, Peter Geoffrey *urban and regional planning educator*

HONG KONG

Sha Tin
Lee, Tunney Fee *urban planning educator*

ADDRESS UNPUBLISHED

Amon, Arthur Howard, Jr. *real estate consultant, retired retailing executive*
Aulbach, George Louis *property investment company executive*
Beal, Merrill David *conservationist, museum director*
Bernhardt, Arthur Dieter *building industry executive and consultant*
Brady, George Moore *real estate executive, mortgage banker*
Burk, Sylvia Joan *petroleum landman, freelance writer*
Chronley, James Andrew *real estate executive*
Corey, Kenneth Edward *geography and urban planning educator, researcher*
deButts, Robert Edward Lee *corporate development and real estate executive*
Fetterly, Lynn Lawrence *real estate broker/developer*
Foley, Daniel Edmund *real estate development executive*
Frost, Anne *real estate broker, author, publisher*
†Gilbert, Frederick E. *international development planner, consultant*
Hamilton, Calvin Sargent *planning consultant, retired city official*
Harris, David Philip *real estate developer*
Hodson, Nancy Perry *real estate agent*
Houstoun, Lawrence Orson, Jr. *development consultant*
Hufschmidt, Maynard Michael *resources planning educator*
Maguire, Robert Francis, III *real estate investor*
Mann, Clarence Charles *real estate company official*
Marshall, Doyle *real estate executive*
Mercurio, Renard Michael *real estate corporation executive*
Messenkopf, Eugene John *real estate and business consultant*
Mitchell, Robert Edward *urban planner, international development specialist, educator*
Porosky, Michael Hanny *real estate and investment company executive*
Rassman, Joel H. *real estate company executive, accountant*
Richman, Marvin Jordan *real estate developer, investor, educator*
Ridloff, Richard *real estate executive, lawyer, consultant*
Saunders, Alexander Hall *real estate executive*
Simon, Melvin *real estate developer, professional basketball executive*
Slayton, William Larew *planning consultant, former government official*
Stewart, Thomas Ted *real estate developer, investment banker*
Taubman, A. Alfred *real estate developer*
Trump, Donald John *real estate developer*
VanButsel, Michael R. *real estate developer*
Wang, James T. *public planning executive*
Weikert, Jerard Lee *real estate broker*
Williamson, Fletcher Phillips *real estate executive*
Wilson, Roy Gardiner *real estate developer*

GOVERNMENT: AGENCY ADMINISTRATION

UNITED STATES

ALABAMA

Clanton
Williams, Paulette W. *state agency administrator*

Mobile
Lager, Robert John *state agency administrator*

Montgomery
Bass, Ray Dean *state highway director*
Gainous, Fred Jerome *state agency administrator*
Wilson, John *protective services official*

Tuscaloosa
Flinn, David R. *federal agency research director*

ALASKA

Akiachak
†Kasayulie, Willie *trial government official*

Anchorage
Porter, Brian Stanley *police chief*

Juneau
Deihl, Michael Allen *federal agency administrator*
Nordlund, James Robert *state agency administrator*

ARIZONA

Glendale
North, Warren James *government official*

Phoenix
Bishop, C. Diane *state agency administrator, educator*
Brunacini, Alan Vincent *fire chief*
Garrett, Dennis Andrew *police official*
Nielson, Theo Gilbert *law enforcement official, university official*

Sun City West
De Layo, Leonard Joseph *former state education official*

Tucson
Isenhower, Eleanor Anne Hexamer *state government administrator*

ARKANSAS

Mountain Home
Saltzman, Benjamin Nathan *retired state health administrator, physician*

CALIFORNIA

Anaheim
Bowman, Jeffrey R. *protective services official*

Castro Valley
Palmer, James Daniel *inspector*

Cupertino
Compton, Dale Leonard *retired space agency executive*

Dana Point
Lacy, James Vincent *government official*

Fresno
Rank, Everett George *government official*

Fullerton
Coleman, Ronny Jack *fire chief*

La Jolla
Knauss, John Atkinson *federal agency administrator, oceanographer, educator, former university dean*

Long Beach
Jeffery, James Nels *protective services official*

Los Angeles
†Davis, Gray *state controller*
Ellingwood, Herbert E. *government official, lawyer*
Manning, Donald O. *protective services official*
Montoya Thompson, Velma *federal agency administrator*
Williams, Willie *protective services official*

Rocklin
Ha, Chong Wan *state government executive*

Roseville
Simms, Thomas Haskell *chief of police*

Sacramento
Muehleisen, Gene Sylvester *retired law enforcement officer, state official*
Strock, James Martin *state agency administrator, lawyer, conservationist*
†Venegas, Arturo, Jr. *chief police*

San Diego
Osby, Robert Edward *protective services official*

San Francisco
Draper, William Henry, III *business executive*
Honig, Bill *state educational administrator*

COLORADO

Aurora
†Montgomery, John E. *federal medical association administrator*

Boulder
Birmingham, Bascom Wayne *retired government official*
Chinnery, Michael Alistair *federal government official, geophysicist*
Gilman, Peter A. *national laboratory administrator, scientist*

Colorado Springs
Leuver, Robert Joseph *former government official, association executive*

Denver
Berger, John Milton *state agency administrator*
†Downing, Sybil S. *state agency administrator*
McGraw, Jack Wilson *government official*
Nash, Stella B. *government nutrition administrator*
Randall, William Theodore *state official*
Simons, Lynn Osborn *state education official*

Englewood
McBeth, Ruben Jose, Jr. *retired criminal justice administrator*

Estes Park
Thompson, James Bruce *national park administrator*

Fort Collins
Eberhart, Steve A. *federal agency administrator, research geneticist*

Golden
Baumgart, Norbert K. *retired government official*
Olson, Marian Katherine *emergency management executive, consultant, publisher*
Stewart, Frank Maurice, Jr. *federal agency administrator*
Toll, Jack Benjamin *government official*

Grand Junction
Olson, Sylvester Irwin *government official*

Lakewood
Horn, Steven Walter *state agency official*

Longmont
Kaminsky, Glenn Francis *deputy chief of police retired, business owner, teacher*

Monument
Miele, Alfonse Ralph *former government official*

CONNECTICUT

Cheshire
McKee, Margaret Jean *federal agency executive*

Hartford
†Ferrandino, Vincent L. *stage agency administrator*
Piotrowski, Richard Francis *state agency administrator, council chairman*
Shimelman, Susan Fromm *state administrator*

New Canaan
Bosworth, Stephen Warren *foundation executive*

Riverside
Powers, Claudia McKenna *state government official*

Stamford
Schilling, Albert Henry *former government agency administrator, corporate environmental consultant*

Suffield
Hanzalek, Astrid Teicher *public policy consultant*

Wethersfield
Tanguay, Norbert Arthur *municipal police training officer*

DELAWARE

Dover
Forgione, Pascal D., Jr. *state superintendent*
Kern, John Rudolph *government administrator, historian*
Lowell, Howard Parsons *government records administrator*

Newark
Keene, William Blair *state education official*

Wilmington
Benson, Barbara Ellen *state agency administrator*
delTufo, Theresa Lallana Izon *state official*
Eichler, Thomas P. *state agency administrator*

DISTRICT OF COLUMBIA

Washington
Adams, Gordon Merritt *federal agency administrator*
Aikens, Joan Deacon *government official*
Alexander, Jane *arts endowment administrator, actress, producer*
Allen, Frederick Warner *federal agency executive*
Anderson, David Turpeau *government official, judge*
Anfinson, Thomas Elmer *government financial administrator*
Apfel, Kenneth S. *federal government official*
†Aponte-Lebrón, Nilda I. *government executive, lawyer*
Armstrong, David Andrew *federal agency official, retired army officer*
†Bacon, Kenneth H. *federal agency administrator, editor, journalist*
Bailey, John E. *federal agency administrator*
Baker, D(onald) James *government official, oceanographer*
Bane, Mary Jo *federal agency administrator*
Baquet, Charles R., III *federal agency administrator*
Barrett, Andrew *federal agency administrator*
Barton, William Russell *government official*
Bateman, Paul William *government official, business executive*
Batjargal, Zambyn *Mongolian government official*
†Bayer, Robert Edward *defense department official*
Beaumont, Enid Franklin *public administration executive*
Beebe, Cora Prifold *government official*
Beecher, William Manuel *government official*
†Behney, Clyde Joseph *technology assessment manager*
Berget, Grete Anni *federal agency administrator*
Bernthal, Frederick Michael *association executive*
Bertini, Judith Emerline *government agency administrator*
Berube, Raymond P. *federal agency administrator*
Biddle, Livingston Ludlow, Jr. *former government official, author*
Bigelow, Donald Nevius *educational administrator, historian, consultant*
†Billingsley, Karen Anne *federal agency administrator*
Breger, Marshall J. *government official, legal educator*
Bresee, James Collins *federal agency administrator*
Britten, Gerald Hallbeck *government official*
Broderick, Anthony James *federal government administrator*
Brown, Dale Susan *government administrator, writer*
Brown, Harold *corporate director, former secretary of defense*
Buffum, Elizabeth V. *federal agency administrator*
Bullard, John Kilburn *federal agency administrator*
†Burnett, Michael A. *federal agency administrator*
Burt, John Alan *federal agency administrator*
Campbell, Donald Alfred *government official*
†Card, Andrew H., Jr. *government official*
Carlson, William Dwight *government agency administrator*
Carney, Nell Cardwell *federal agency executive*
Carrier, Joyce H. *federal agency administrator*
†Chesser, Judy Lee *federal agency administrator, lawyer*
Clark, Ian Douglas *international agency official*
Clarke, Richard A. *national security specialist*
Colton, Deborah G. *federal government official*
Congel, Frank Joseph *federal agency administrator, physicist*
Conway, John Thomas *government official, lawyer, engineer*
Cooper, Benita Ann *federal agency administrator*
Cooper, Susan Louise *government agency executive*
†Corlett, Cleve Edward *government administrator*
Cotruvo, Joseph Alfred *federal agency administrator*
†Coyle, Philip E. *federal agency administrator, engineer*
Cremona, Vincent Anthony *federal agency administrator*
†Crunican, Grace *federal agency administrator*
Cunningham, George Woody *federal official, metallurgical engineer*
Curran, Donald Charles *federal agency administrator, government librarian*
Danaher, James William *federal government executive*
Daniels, Stephen M. *government official*
Davies, Tudor Thomas *federal agency administrator*
Dawson, Robert Kent *government relations expert*
Dean, Alan Loren *government official*
Deer, Ada E. *federal agency official, social worker, educator*
†DeLong, James Bradford *government official, economics educator*
DeMars, Bruce *naval administrator*
†Derby, Adele *government agency administrator*
Detchon, Bryan Reid *federal agency administrator*
DiMario, Michael Francis *federal agency official, lawyer*
Donahue, John David *federal official*
Donley, Michael Bruce *federal government executive, financial manager*
Duggan, Ervin S. *federal agency administrator*
†Dunn, Michael V. *federal agency administrator*
†Eggenberger, Andrew Jon *federal agency administrator*
Elliott, Emerson John *federal agency administrator, policy analyst*
Erdreich, Ben Leader *federal agency executive*
Ericsson, Sally Claire *federal agency adminstrator*
†Esserman, Susan Gayle *government official administrator*
Fell, James Carlton *scientific and technical affairs executive, consultant*
†Finch, Johnny Charles *government agency executive*
Fingerhut, Marilyn Ann *federal agency administrator*
†Fischer, Dennis J. *government official*
Fishbaugh, Franklin James *government intelligence officer, researcher, weapons specialist*
Fisher, Farley *chemist, federal agency administrator*
Fletcher, Arthur A. *federal official*
Flint, Myles Edward *federal agency administrator, lawyer*
†Flynn, Nancy Marie *government executive*
†Force, Charles Thomas *government executive*
Fox, Lynn Smith *federal government official*
Frazier, Henry Bowen, III *government official, lawyer*
Freeh, Louis J. *federal agency administrator*
Freeman, Chas. W., Jr. *government official, ambassador*
Fried, Edward R. *government official*
Frohnmayer, John Edward *legal scholar, ethicist, writer*
Frost, Ellen Louise *federal agency administrator*
†Furiga, Richard Daniel *government official*
Gauldin, Michael Glen *federal agency administrator*
Gibson, Thomas Fenner, III *public affairs consultant, political cartoonist*
Gillingham, Robert Fenton *federal agency administrator, economist*
Gilliom, Judith Carr *government official*
Glynn, Thomas P. *federal agency administrator*
Gober, Hershel W. *government official*
Goldin, Daniel S. *government agency administrator*
Golding, Carolyn May *government administrator*
†Goldman, Lynn Rose *federal agency administrator*
Good, Mary Lowe (Mrs. Billy Jewel Good) *government official*
Goodman, Margaret Gertrude *government administrator*
†Goodwin, Larry Kenneth *federal government official*
Gordon, Nancy M. *congressional administrator*
Gorn, Janet Marie *government official*
Gould, William Benjamin, IV *federal official, lawyer, educator*
Grayson, Lawrence Peter *federal educational administrator*
Green, Richard James *federal agency administrator, aerospace engineer*
Guimond, Richard Joseph *federal agency executive, environmental scientist*
Gulya, Brigitta Rianna *federal government official*
Haas, Ellen *federal agency administrator*
Haass, Richard Nathan *federal agency administrator*
Hagenstad, M. Thomas *federal government administrator*
†Hale, Robert Fargo *government official*
†Hall, James Evan *federal agency administrator, lawyer*
Haller, Ralph A. *federal agency administrator*
Hallett, Carol Boyd *government official*
Hammond, Jerome Jerald *government program administrator, agricultural economist*
Hannigan, Vera Simmons *federal agency administrator*
Hansen, Frederic J. *state environmental agency director*
†Harkin, Ruth R. *federal agency administrator, lawyer*
Harris, David Ford *federal agency administrator*
Harris, Wesley L. *federal agency administrator*
Hathaway, William Dodd *federal agency administrator*
†Haughton, Claiborne Douglass, Jr. *government official*
†Hayes, Nancy Keir *government agency administrator*
Hayes, Paula Freda *governmental official*
Hedrick, Floyd Dudley *government official, author*
†Helfer, Ricki Tigert *federal agency administrator*
†Herberger, Albert J. *federal agency administrator, retired naval officer*
Hervey, Homer Vaughan *federal agency administrator*
Heumann, Judith *federal agency administrator*
Hill, Jimmie Dale *government official*
†Hilton, Steven Michael *federal agency administrator*
Hitz, Frederick Porter *federal agency administrator, lawyer*
Hogan, John P. *federal agency official*
†Hollis, Walter W. *government official*
Holum, John D. *government official*
†Horner, Constance J. *federal agency administrator*
Hove, Andrew Christian *federal agency administrator*
Howerton, Helen Veronica *federal agency administrator*
Hoyt, David Richard *federal agency official*
Hsu, Ming Chen *federal agency administrator*
†Huerta, Michael Peter *government official*
Hughes, Ann Hightower *economist, government official*
Hundt, Reed Eric *federal official, lawyer*
Hunkele, Lester Martin, III *federal agency administrator*
Iklé, Fred Charles *former federal agency administrator, policy advisor, defense expert*
Itteilag, Anthony Louis *government official*
†Jansen, Bonnie *federal agency administrator*
†Jaramillo, Mari-Luci *federal agency administrator*
†Jeff, Gloria Jean *federal government administrator*
Jewett, David Stuart *federal agency administrator*
Johnson, Arlene Lytle *government agency official*
Johnson, Ralph Raymond *ambassador, federal agency administrator*
Johnson, Roger W. *federal official, computer manufacturing company executive*
Johnson, Stephen L. *federal agency administrator*
Jordan, John Patrick *government agency executive, research scientist, educator*
†Kaplan, Stephen H. *federal agency administrator, lawyer*
†Karp, Naomi Katherine *United States government administrator*
Katz, Jonathan Garber *federal agency executive, lawyer*
Kearney, Stephen Michael *government official*
Kelley, Edward Watson, Jr. *federal agency administrator*
Kilgore, Edwin Carroll *retired government official, consultant*
Kinghorn, Charles Morgan, Jr. *federal agency administrator*
Kinlow, Eugene *federal agency executive*
Kitzmiller, William Michael *government official*
†Klein, Leonard Robert *government official*
Klepner, Jerry D. *federal agency administrator*
Kline, Jerry Robert *government official, ecologist*
Knoll, Jerry *former government official*
Koskinen, John Andrew *federal government executive*
Kropp, Arthur John *public interest organization executive*
Kruesi, Frank Eugene *federal agency administrator*
†Kruvant, William *federal agency administrator*
Kunin, Madeleine May *federal agency administrator, former governor*
Kutscher, Ronald Earl *federal government executive*
Lachance, Janice Rachel *federal agency administrator, lawyer*
†Lakshmanan, T.R. *federal agency administrator, geography and environmental engineering educator, writer*
†Laws, Elliott Pearson *federal agency administrator*
Layton, John C. *federal agency administrator*
†Leestma, Robert *federal agency administrator, educator*
†Lieberman, James *federal agency administrator*
Logue-Kinder, Joan *government official*
Lord, Jerome Edmund *federal education administrator, writer*
†Lynn, William J., III *federal agency administrator*
Maas, Joe (Melvin Joseph Maas) *federal agency administrator*
Mack, Ronald J. *park superintendent*
†Mackie, Bert H. *postal service administrator*
†Mader, David A. *federal agency executive*
Martin, Jerry L. *federal agency administrator*
Marzetti, Loretta A. *government agency executive, policy analyst*
†Massey, William Lloyd *federal agency administrator, lawyer*
Masten, Charles C. *federal agency administrator*
Maxwell, David Ogden *government official, financial executive*
Mc Afee, William *government official*
McCahill, Barry Winslow *federal public affairs official*
McCollum, Gary Wayne *federal agency administrator*
McCormick, Robert Junior *government official*
McDonald, Gail Clements *government official*
Mc Fee, Thomas Stuart *government agency administrator*
McGarry, John Warren *government official*
McLaughlin, Maureen A. *federal agency administrator*
McLucas, William Robert *federal agency director*
McNeill, John Henderson *government official, lawyer*
Meikle, Philip G. *government agency executive*
†Metzler, Cynthia A. *federal agency administrator, lawyer*
Miller, Stephanie Lee *federal agency administrator*
Millhone, John Paul *federal laboratory administrator*
Mlay, Marian *government official*
Moler, Elizabeth Anne *federal agency administrator, lawyer*
†Moore, Richard Thomas *federal agency administrator*
Moos, Eugene *federal agency administrator*
Moose, George E. *government official*
Mosemann, Lloyd Kenneth, II *government official*
Nash, Bob J. (Bob Nash) *under-secretary agriculture rural and small development*
Neal, Darwina Lee *government official*
Nethery, John Jay *government official*
Newhouse, Alan Russell *federal government executive*
Newman, Don Melvin *federal agency administrator*
Newquist, Don *federal agency administrator*
Nichols, Mary D. *federal agency administrator, lawyer*
Nitze, William Albert *lawyer, government official*
†Nussbaum, Karen *federal agency administrator*
Palast, Geri D. *federal agency administrator*
Patron, June Eileen *former government official*
Pettengill, Harry Junior *federal agency administrator*
Pincus, Ann Terry *federal agency administrator*
Plowman, R. Dean *federal agriculture agency administrator*
Pulliam, Howard Ronald *federal agency administrator*
Quello, James Henry *government official*
Reed, Vincent Emory *federal education official*
Reidy, Gerald Patrick *federal organization executive, arbitrator, mediator, fact-finder*
†Reinsch, William Alan *government executive, educator*
Richardson, Margaret Milner *federal agency administrator, lawyer*
Rieke, Elizabeth Ann *federal agency administrator*
†Roberts, Richard Y. *federal agency administrator*
Rogers, Jerry L. *federal agency administrator*
Rogers, Raymond Jesse *federal railroad associate administrator*
Rominger, Richard *federal agency administrator*
Rosendhal, Jeffrey David *federal science agency administrator, astronomer*
Rothkopf, David Jochanan *federal official*
Rottman, Ellis *public information officer*
†Rubinoff, Roberta Wolff *government administrator*
†Sahli, Nancy Ann *government agency administrator*
Savage, Phillip Hezekiah *federal agency administrator*
Savage, Xyla Ruth *government official*
Schapiro, Mary *federal agency administrator, lawyer*
Schenkel, Suzanne Chance *natural resource specialist*
Schneider, Mark Lewis *government official*
Schoenberg, Mark George *government agency administrator*
Schoenberger, James Edwin *federal agency administrator*
Scott, Audrey Ebba *federal agency administrator*
Searing, Marjory Ellen *government official, economist*
Seidel, Milton Joseph *government administrator*
Shank, Fred Ross *federal agency administrator*
Shapiro, Michael Henry *government executive*
Shearer, P. Scott *government relations professional*
Sherman, Wendy Ruth *federal agency administrator*
Sherwin, Michael Dennis *government official*
Siegel, Richard David *lawyer, former government official*
Sieverts, Frank Arne *government official*
Slater, Rodney E. *federal administrator*
Smith, Richard Melvyn *government official*
Soderberg, Nancy *federal agency administrator*
Spector, Eleanor Ruth *government executive*
Spero, Joan Edelman *federal agency administrator*
†Springer, Fred Everett *federal agency administrator*
Springer, Michael Louis *federal agency administrator*
Stanley, William Robert *federal agency official*
Steele, Ana Mercedes *government official*
Stephens, James M. *federal agency administrator*
Stewart, Ruth Ann *public policy analyst, library administrator*
†Stillman, Robert Donald *government official*
Stonehill, Robert Michael *federal agency administrator*
Stoner, John Richard *federal government executive*
†Straub, Chester John, Jr. *government official*
Stuntz, Linda Gillespie *government official, lawyer*
Summers, Lawrence *under secretary treasury department*
Sweedler, Barry Martin *federal agency administrator*
†Taft, Robert Anthony *government official, educator*
Tarnoff, Peter *governmental official*
Tarrants, William Eugene *government official*
†Tate, Daniel Clyde, Jr. *federal agency administrator*
Taylor, Christopher Andrew *securities industry regulation executive*
Taylor, Harold Allen, Jr. *federal agency administrator*
Tetelman, Alice Fran *city government official*
Thomas, Fred *police chief*
Thomas, James Bert, Jr. *government official*
†Thompson, Lawrence Leonard *federal agency administrator*
Tippeconnic, John W., III *federal agency administrator*
†Tipton, Whitney Hord *federal agency administrator*
Townsend, Wardell C., Jr. *federal agency administrator*
Trilling, Donald R. *federal agency administrator*
Trodden, Stephen Anthony *federal agency administrator*
Truesdale, John Cushman *government executive*
Tuck, John Chatfield *former federal agency administrator, public policy advisor*
†Twiss, John R., Jr. *federal government agency executive*
†Tyler, George Randolph *government official*
Ulsamer, Andrew George *federal agency manager*
Vanderveen, John E. *federal agency administrator*
Verhalen, Robert Donald *federal agency executive*
†Verstandig, Toni Grant *federal agency administrator*
Vogt, Carl William *federal official, lawyer*

†Voles, Lorraine Ann *government administrator*
†Wallerstein, Mitchel Bruce *government official*
Walsh, Edward Patrick *federal agency administrator*
Watson, Harlan L(eroy) *federal official, physicist, economist*
†Webb, Ali *federal agency administrator*
Weiner, Robert Stephen *federal agency administrator*
†Weirich, Richard Denis *government official*
Weisberg, Stuart Elliot *federal official, lawyer*
†Weiss, Jeffrey L. *federal agency director*
Weiss, Paul Thomas *federal agency executive*
Wells, Linton, II *federal official*
West, Togo Dennis, Jr. *secretary of Army, former aerospace executive*
White, George *government official, physical scientist*
†White, Robert M. *federal engineering agency administrator, engineer*
Wilkinson, John Burke *former government official, novelist, biographer*
Williams, Arthur E. *federal agency administrator*
Williams, Paul *federal agency administrator*
Wince-Smith, Deborah L. *federal agency administrator*
Winter, Roger Paul *government official*
Witt, James Lee *federal agency administrator*
†Wolanin, Thomas Richard *federal government official*
Wolfe, Janice E. *business development executive*
†Yager, Milan P. *government agency administrator*
Yancik, Joseph John *government official*
†Yim, Joan B. *federal agency administrator*
Zenowitz, Allan Ralph *government official*
†Zonana, Victor F. *government agency official, writer, communications executive*

FLORIDA

Bradenton
Thompson, Barbara Storck *state official*

Fort Lauderdale
Cicora, Kenneth Allan *public information officer*

Fort Myers
Nottingham, James (Leroy Nottingham) *retired protective services official, professional society administrator*

Fort Pierce
Boucher, Mildred Eileen *state agency administrator*

Hollywood
Ward, James Theron *protective services official*

Jupiter
Komarek, Thomas Charles *retired government official*

Melbourne
Cockriel, Russell George, Sr. *crime investigation official*

Miami
†Gimenez, Carlos Antonio *fire chief*

North Palm Beach
Oleksiw, Daniel Philip *former foreign service officer, consultant*

Palm Beach
Asencio, Diego C. *state agency administrator, former federal commission administrator, consultant, business executive*

Palm City
Pepitone, Byron Vincent *former government official*

Pensacola
Dixon, James Andrew, Jr. *protective services official*
Hass, Charles John William *criminal justice program coordinator*

Saint Augustine
Gillilland, Thomas *consultant*

Saint Petersburg
Barca, James Joseph *fire department administrative services executive*

Tallahassee
Durrence, James Larry *state executive, history educator*
Mann, Marcia L. *state agency administrator*
Milligan, Robert F. *state agency administrator*

GEORGIA

Athens
Carter, Mary Eddie *government administrator*

Atlanta
Benson, Ronald Edward *state humanities program executive, clergyman, educator*
Collins, Marcus E., Sr. *state agency administrator*
Creed, Thomas Wayne *retired federal executive*
Ebneter, Stewart Dwight *federal agency administrator*
Hinman, Alan Richard *public health administrator, epidemiologist*
Larche, James Clifford, II *state agency administrator*
Ledford, Hanna May *state official*
Millar, John Donald *occupational and environmental health consultant, educator*

Brunswick
Rinkevich, Charles Francis *federal official*

Columbus
Collins, Wayne Winford *protective services official*

Midway
Cobb, John Anthony *retired state veterinarian*

Warm Springs
†Barnes, Charles Gerald *historic site administrator*

HAWAII

Honolulu
Gibb, Douglas Glenn *police chief*
Miyamoto, Owen *state agency administrator*
Nakashima, Mitsugi *state agency administrator*
Saiki, Patricia (Mrs. Stanley Mitsuo Saiki) *former federal agency administrator, former congresswoman*

Kaneohe
Ikeda, Moss Marcus Masanobu *retired state education official, lecturer, consultant*

IDAHO

Boise
Evans, Jerry Lee *school system administrator*
Ferrell, Yvonne Signe *state recreation commission administrator*
Humpherys, A. Rich *state police administrator*
Ryals, Connie *state government department administrator*
Wood, Jeannine Kay *state official*

Moscow
Butterfield, Samuel Hale *former government official and educator*

ILLINOIS

Chicago
Anderson, Douglas Charles *juvenile probation administrator*
Clark, Jeanne (Barbara) *police commander*
Moskow, Michael H. *federal official*
Orozco, Raymond E. *protective services official*
Prochnow, Herbert Victor *former government official, banker, author*
Rodriguez, Matt L. *protective services professional*
Rogers, Desiree Glapion *state official*
Rumsfeld, Donald Henry *former government official, corporate executive*
Wilson, Richard Harold *government official*

Hoffman Estates
Laubenstein, Vernon Alfred *state agency administrator*

Springfield
Mogerman, Susan *state agency administrator*
Shim, Sang Koo *state mental health official*
Zollar, Nikki Michelle *state agency administrator*

INDIANA

Fort Wayne
Brown, Ronald Wayne *fire chief*
Riemen, David Clarence *chief of police*

Indianapolis
Harden, Mary Louise *human resources management specialist*
Kaufman, Karl Lincoln *consultant, former state agency administrator*
Kirk, Carol *state official, lawyer*
†Reed, Suellen Kinder *state education administrator*
†Rump, Erwin Elmer *state agency administrator*
Smith, Keith *protective services official*

La Porte
Hiler, John Patrick *former government official, former congressman, business executive*

Notre Dame
Kmiec, Douglas William *government official, law educator*

IOWA

Cedar Rapids
Hinzman, Gerald Richard *chief of police*

Des Moines
Lepley, William *state education official*
Moulder, William H. *chief of police*

Mc Callsburg
Lounsberry, Robert Horace *former state government administrator*

KANSAS

Colby
Finley, Philip Bruce *retired state adjutant general*

Topeka
Blackburn, Harold Lee, Jr. *state agency administrator*
Douglas, Joe J., Jr. *fire chief*
Droegmueller, Lee *state education official*
†Freden, Sharon Elsie Christman *state education agency administrator*

KENTUCKY

Frankfort
Brown, Viola Davis *state agency administrator*
McDonald, Alice Coig *state education official*

Hopkinsville
Watson, Roger Elton *human resources administrator*

Lexington
Calvert, C(lyde) Emmett *state agency adminstrator, retired*
†King, James Orell *public administrator*

Louisville
Adams, Robert Waugh *state agency administrator, economics educator*

Madisonville
Veazey, Doris Anne *field office administrator*

LOUISIANA

Baton Rouge
Arveson, Raymond G. *state superintendent*
Brickman, Kenneth Alan *state lottery executive*

Kenner
Zito, Michael Steven *protective services official*

Lafayette
Benoit, Robert Patrick *protective services official*

Monroe
Stewart, Joe R. *law enforcement official*

Shreveport
Greene, Dallas Whorton, Jr. *fire chief*

MAINE

Augusta
†Martin, Leo G. *educational administrator*
Sewell, Dwight A. *state government official*

MARYLAND

Adelphi
Lyons, John W(inship) *government agency administrator, chemist*

Annapolis
Aery, Shaila Rosalie *state educational administrator*
Taussig, Joseph Knefler, Jr. *retired government official, lawyer*

Baltimore
Abato, F. Rozann *federal government administrator, nurse*
Abrams, Rosalie Silber *state agency administrator*
Anderson, John William *protective services official*
DiPentima, Renato Anthony *government agency official*
Guest, James Alfred *public service official*
Hart, Robert Gordon *federal agency administrator*
Hilgenberg, Eve Brantly Handy *government official*
Martin, George Reilly *federal agency administrator*
†Pierce, Ruth A. *federal agency administrator*
Smith, Elmer W. *federal government administrator*
Thompson, Lawrence Hyde *federal agency official*
Wilzack, Adele *state health official*

Beltsville
Tso, Tien Chioh *federal agency official, plant physiologist*
van Schilfgaarde, Jan *agricultural engineer, government agricultural service administrator*

Bethesda
Brown, Ann *federal agency administrator*
Burton, Benjamin Theodore *government official*
Campbell, Arthur Andrews *government official*
Chen, Philip S., Jr. *government official*
Dunning, Herbert Neal *government official, physical chemist*
†Gorden, Phillip *federal agency administrator*
Gutheim, Robert Julius *government official*
†Howard, Frances Estella Humphrey *government official*
Lee, Young Jack *federal agency administrator*
O'Callaghan, Jerry Alexander *government official*
Parkman, Paul Douglas *federal agency administrator*
Peterson, Shirley D. *federal agency administrator*
Reeves, Richard Allen *government aerospace program executive, lawyer*
Richardson, John *retired international relations executive*
Schambra, Philip Ellis *federal agency administrator, radiobiologist*
Sprott, Richard Lawrence *government official, researcher*
Varmus, Harold Eliot *government health institutes administrator*
Walleigh, Robert Shuler *consultant*
Whaley, Storm Hammond *retired government official, consultant*

Bowie
Sullivan, Francis Edward *research administrator*

Chevy Chase
Hudson, Anthony Webster *retired federal agency administrator*
Mulligan, James Kenneth *government official*
Quinn, Eugene Frederick *government official, clergyman*

Fort George G Meade
McConnell, John Michael *federal agency administrator*

Fort Washington
Stiver, William Earl *retired government administrator*

Gaithersburg
Ambler, Ernest *government official*
Hertz, Harry Steven *government official*
Kammer, Raymond Gerard, Jr. *government official*
Prabhakar, Arati *federal administration research director, electrical engineer*
Snell, Jack Eastlake *federal agency administrator*

Greenbelt
O'Sullivan, Judith Roberta *state administrator, author*
Rothenberg, Joseph Howard *federal agency administrator*

Kensington
Suraci, Charles Xavier, Jr. *retired federal agency administrator, aerospace education consultant*

Oxon Hill
Boerrigter, Glenn Charles *educational administrator*

Potomac
Frey, James McKnight *government official*
Rotberg, Iris Comens *social scientist*

Rockville
Aamodt, Roger Louis *federal agency administrator*
†Chavez, Nelba *federal agency administrator*
Fouchard, Joseph James *retired government agency administrator*
Hoffman, C. Michael *federal agency administrator*
Johnson, Elaine McDowell *federal government administrator*
Kawazoe, Robin Inada *federal official*
Kelsey, Frances Oldham (Mrs. Fremont Ellis Kelsey) *government official*
Kessler, David A. *health services commissioner*
†Millstein, Richard Allen *federal agency administrator*
Rheinstein, Peter Howard *government official, physician, lawyer*
†Stoiber, Carlton Ray *government agency official*
†Taylor, Michael R. *federal agency administrator, lawyer*
†Vollmer, Richard Henry *federal agency administrator*

Silver Spring
Attaway, David Henry *federal research administrator, oceanographer*
Carnell, Paul Herbert *federal education official*
Day, Daniel Edgar *government information officer*
Friday, Elbert Walter, Jr. *federal agency administrator, meteorologist*
†Hall, J. Michael *federal agency administrator, meteorologist*
Haynes, Leonard L., III *government official, consultant, educator*
Telesetsky, Walter *government official*

Sykesville
Enoff, Louis D. *international consultant*

Upper Marlboro
Aluisi, James Vincent *protective services official, security specialist*

Woodbine
Brush, Peter Norman *federal agency administrator, lawyer*

MASSACHUSETTS

Boston
Goodman, Abbie Rebecca *state agency executive*
Mason, Nancy Tolman *state agency director*
Pierce, Martin E., Jr. *fire commissioner*
Roache, Francis Michael *law enforcement official*
Whitburn, Gerald *state agency administrator*

Bridgewater
†Heffernan, Peter John *state official*

Dorchester
Garrison, Althea *goverment official*

New Bedford
Benoit, Richard Armand *police chief, lawyer*

Plymouth
Forman, Peter *sheriff, former state legislator*

MICHIGAN

Belding
Mason, Donald Roger *protective services official, city official*

Detroit
McKinnon, Isaiah *police chief*
Moss, Leslie Otha *court administrator*
Ryan, Earl M. *public affairs analyst*

Flint
Duncan, Clydell *police chief, educator*

Lansing
Beardmore, Dorothy *state education administrator*
Braunstein, Diane Karen *state agency administrator*
Kindinger, Paul Eugene *state director of agriculture*
Perry, Maxine Lewis *state official*

MINNESOTA

Arden Hills
Lindmark, Ronald Dorance *retired federal agency administrator*

International Falls
Clary, Ben *park superintendent*

Minneapolis
Carlson, Norman A. *government official*

Saint Paul
McCoy, Mary Ann *state official*
Todd, Henry Reynolds, Jr. *director state tourism office*

MISSOURI

Jefferson City
Bartman, Robert E. *state education official*
Karll, Jo Ann *state agency administrator, lawyer*
McClain, Charles James *state educational administrator*
Parr, Lloyd Byron *state official*

Peeno, Larry Noyle *state agency administrator, consultant*
Waters, Stephen Russell *state agency administrator*

Kansas City
Getty, Carol Pavilack *government official*

Lambert Airport
Griggs, Leonard LeRoy, Jr. *federal agency administrator*

Springfield
Gruhn, Robert Stephen *parole officer*

NEBRASKA

Lincoln
Liggett, Twila Marie Christensen *public television company executive, academic administrator*

NEVADA

Carson City
Paslov, Eugene T. *state education official*

Las Vegas
†Aquilina, Nick C. *government agency administrator*
Broadbent, Robert N. *government official, pharmacist*

North Las Vegas
Marchand, Russell David, II *fire chief*

NEW HAMPSHIRE

Concord
Brunelle, Robert L. *retired state education director*
Day, Russell Clover *federal agency administrator*
Marston, Charles *state education official*
Mevers, Frank Clement *state archivist, historian*

Exeter
Boggess, Jerry Reid *protective services official*

NEW JERSEY

Atlantic City
Tucci, Mark A. *state agency administrator*

Barrington
Florio, Maryanne J. *state health research scientist*

Fort Monmouth
Kalwinsky, Charles Knowlton *government official*

Long Branch
Caron, Patrick Edward *protective services official*

Morristown
DeLury, Bernard E. *vice president labor relations*

Newark
Silverman, A(lan) Jared *state agency administrator, lawyer*

Pennsauken
Connor, Wilda *government health agency administrator*

Trenton
Wolfe, Deborah Cannon Partridge *government education consultant*

NEW MEXICO

Albuquerque
Gordon, Larry Jean *public health administrator and educator*

Roswell
Lewis, George Raymond *clinical social worker*

Santa Fe
Curran, Neil Willis *state police chief*
Espinosa, Judith M. *state agency administrator*
Humphries, William R. *state land commissioner*
Knapp, Edward Alan *scientist, government administrator*
Morgan, Alan D. *state education official*

NEW YORK

Albany
†Meader, John Daniel *state agency administrator, judge*

Brooklyn
Safir, Howard *fire commissioner*

Greenport
Breeze, Roger Gerrard *federal agency administrator*

Islip
Muuss, John *public safety and emergency management executive*

Lewiston
Kennedy, G. Alfred *federal agency administrator*

New York
Brezenoff, Stanley *bi-state agency administrator*
†Fasullo, Eugene Jack *state official*
Gelb, Bruce S. *city commissioner*
Gregg, Donald Phinney *federal agency administrator, lecturer*
Ink, Dwight A. *government agency administrator*
Mahon, John Joseph *federal agency administrator*
†Maple, John E. *protective services official*
Murphy, Eugene Francis *consultant, retired government official*
Parker, Susan Brooks *rehabilitation administrator*
Samuels, Leslie B. *federal agency administrator, lawyer*
Sorensen, Gillian Martin *United Nations official*
Talbot, Phillips *Asian affairs specialist*

Orangeburg
Nagle, George, Jr. *state mental health administrator*

Rochester
Meloni, Andrew P. *protective services official*
Riley, Edward John *protective services official*
†Warshaw, Robert S. *police chief*

Schroon Lake
Swanson, Norma Frances *federal agency administrator*

Troy
Knoll, Bruce Evans *state agency administrator, lawyer*

Woodbury
Zirkel, Don *public information official*

NORTH CAROLINA

Asheville
Annarino, Will Ray *protective services official*
Roberts, Bill Glen *retired fire chief, investor, consultant*

Burlington
Kee, Walter Andrew *former government official*

Corolla
Schrote, John Ellis *retired government executive*

Elizabeth City
Lewis, Tola Ethridge, Jr. *state agency administrator, martial arts instructor*

Emerald Isle
Garvey, Robert Robey, Jr. *former government official*

Greensboro
Daughtry, Sylvester *protective services official*
Reed, William Edward *government official, educator*

Mooresville
Dausman, George Erwin *retired federal official, aeronautical engineer*

Raleigh
†Etheridge, Bob *state agency superintendant*

Winston Salem
Griscom, Thomas Cecil *presidential assistant, public relations executive*

NORTH DAKOTA

Bismarck
Sanstead, Wayne Godfrey *state superintendent, former lieutenant governor*
Vogel, Sarah *state agency administrator, lawyer*

Williston
†Hedren, Paul Leslie *national park administrator, historian*

OHIO

Alliance
Woods, Rose Mary *consultant, former presidential assistant*

Cleveland
Fordyce, James Stuart *federal agency administrator*
Klineberg, John Michael *federal agency administrator, aerospace researcher*
Kovacic, Edward P. *protective services official*

Columbus
Barner, Bruce Monroe *state agency administrator*
Butler, Martha L. *state official, accountant*
Ray, Frank David *government agency official*
†Schlueter, Bernard Joseph *state official*

Dayton
Schorgl, Thomas Barry *arts administrator*

Montpelier
Deckrosh, Hazen Douglas *retired state agency administrator, educator*

Toledo
Smith, Robert Nelson *former government official, anesthesiologist*

Westerville
Davis, Joseph Lloyd *state council educational administrator, consultant*

OKLAHOMA

Chickasha
Beets, Freeman Haley *retired government official*

Oklahoma City
Byers, Stansell Crawford *state agency administrator*
Collins, William Edward *aeromedical administrator, researcher*
Leavitt, Joan Kazanjian *state health official, physician*

Wanette
Thompson, Joyce Elizabeth *retired state education official*

Yukon
Bridges, Leroy W. *retired state agency administrator, consultant*

OREGON

Portland
Barham, Steven Walter *state official*

PENNSYLVANIA

Erie
Skonieczka, Richard Gerald *retired police chief, coroner*

Harrisburg
Glass, Brent D. *state commission administrator*
Peechatka, Walter Norman *government official*
Thaler, Nancy Regina *state agency administrator*

Pittsburgh
Buford, Earl, Jr. *protective services official*

Reading
Williams, Sandra Keller *postal service executive*

University Park
Lee, Robert Dorwin *public affairs educator*

RHODE ISLAND

Providence
McWalters, Peter *state agency administrator*
Sapinsley, Lila Manfield *state official*

SOUTH CAROLINA

Charleston
Gaillard, John Palmer, Jr. *former government official, former mayor*

Columbia
Inkley, Scott Russell, Jr. *state agency administrator*
LeFever, Michael Grant *state agency administrator*
Nielsen, Barbara Stock *state educational administrator*

Greenville
Theodore, Nick Andrew *lieutenant governor*

North
Moran, John Bernard *government official*

SOUTH DAKOTA

Pierre
Bonaiuto, John A. *state education official*

Wessington Springs
Burg, James Allen *state agency administrator, farmer*

TENNESSEE

Knoxville
Crowell, Craven H., Jr. *federal agency administrator*
Dean, Charles Henry, Jr. *retired government official*

Memphis
Black, Kay Freeman *public affairs administrator*
Burgess, Melvin *protective services official*
Knight, H. Stuart *law enforcement official, consultant*

Nashville
Day, Mary Dean *federal agency administrator*
Guy, Sharon Kaye *state agency executive*
Roaden, Arliss Lloyd *higher education executive director, former university president*

TEXAS

Austin
Ashworth, Kenneth Hayden *state educational commissioner*
Brinkley, Fred Sinclair, Jr. *state agency administrator, pharmacist*
Gerry, Martin Hughes, IV *federal agency administrator, lawyer*
Meno, Lionel R. *state education official*
Sapp, Mary Ellen *state official, educator*
Watson, Elizabeth Marion *protective services official*
Winters, J. Sam *lawyer, federal official*

Baytown
Leiper, Robert Duncan *protective services official*

Dallas
Garreans, Leonard Lansford *state court official, criminal justice professional*

Fort Worth
Sasser, William Jack *government official*

Houston
Corral, Edward Anthony *fire marshal*

Midland
Roberts, James Lee *fire chief*

Pasadena
Ellis, Clarence Lee *police official*

San Antonio
Sessions, William Steele *former government official*

Tyler
Robinson, Lawrence Wayne *protective services official*

UTAH

Ogden
Hardy, Duane Horace *federal agency administrator, educator*

Provo
Porter, Bruce Douglas *educator, federal agency administrator, writer*

VERMONT

Burlington
Grimes, Barbara Lauritzen *housing and community affairs administrator*
McLaughlin, Kevin Michael *sheriff*

Springfield
Putnam, Paul Adin *retired government agency official*

VIRGINIA

Alexandria
Blake, John Francis *former government agency official, consultant*
Chamberlain, Adrian Ramond *state agency executive*
Choromokos, James, Jr. *consultant, former government official*
Christie, Thomas Philip *research manager*
Clinkscales, William Abner, Jr. *government administrator*
Connally, Ernest Allen *retired federal agency administrator*
Connell, John Gibbs, Jr. *former government official*
Cowles, Roger William *government official*
Harris, Thomas Everett *government official, lawyer, retired*
Hughes, Grace-Flores *former federal agency administrator, management consulting executive*
Johnson, Robert Gerald *federal agency consultant*
Kelso, John Hodgson *government official*
Molholm, Kurt Nelson *federal agency administrator*
Nelsen, Betty Jo *government administrator*
Senese, Donald Joseph *former government official*
Williams, Justin W. *government official*

Annandale
Guthrie, Edward Everett *government executive, lawyer*

Arlington
Bardon, Marcel *government official*
Beggs, James Montgomery *former government official*
Boyle, Robert Patrick *retired government agency consultant, lawyer*
Brandt, Werner William *federal agency official*
†Clutter, Mary Elizabeth *federal official*
Entzminger, John Nelson, Jr. *government research agency executive, electronic engineer*
Johns, Michael Douglas *international affairs consultant*
Lederman, Leonard Lawrence *government research executive*
McDonald, Bernard Robert *federal agency administrator*
Nalen, Craig Anthony *government official*
Nielsen, Aldon Dale *retired government agency official, economist*
Rhodes, Frank Harold Trevor *federal science agency administrator, former academic administrator, geologist*
Sander, Raymond John *government executive*
Verburg, Edwin Arnold *federal agency administrator*
Weber, Thomas Andrew *federal agency executive*

Burgess
Towle, Leland Hill *government official*

Charlottesville
Handy, Alice Warner *state agency administrator*
Smith, Curtis Johnston *government executive*

Fairfax Station
Taylor, Eldon Donivan *government official*

Lorton
Francis, Richard Haudiomont *government administrator*

Mc Lean
Betsold, Robert John *federal agency administrator*
Brendsel, Leland C. *federal mortgage company executive*
Collins, James Foster *government official*
Duncan, Robert Clifton *retired government official*
†Hwang, John Dzen *federal agency administrator*
Mahan, Clarence *retired government official, writer*
Reswick, James Bigelow *former government official, rehabilitation engineer, educator*
Svahn, John Alfred *government official*
Turner, Stansfield *former government official, lecturer, writer, teacher*

McLean
Daub, Cindy S. *federal agency administrator*

Mineral
Donald, James Robert *federal agency official, economist, outdoors writer*

Richmond
Finley, Donald James *state agency administrator*
Pollard, Overton Price *state agency executive, lawyer*
†Spagnolo, Joseph A., Jr. *state agency administrator*

Roanoke
Hooper, M. David *protective services official*

Rosslyn
Adair, John Joseph *federal agency administrator*

Williamsburg
Davis, Emma-Jo Levey *retired government executive, publishing executive*

WASHINGTON

Ashford
Briggle, William James *federal agency administrator*

Greenbank
Grant, Robert Yearington *former government official*

Olympia
Billings, Judith A. *state education official*
Gose, Karen Kamara *state arts administrator*
Johnson, Linda Sue *state agency health administrator, former state legislator*
Merchant, Judith Miriam *state agency administrator*
Yenson, Evelyn P. *lottery official*

Sequim
Meacham, Charles Harding *government official*

Spokane
Bolstad, D. D. *federal agency administrator*

Suquamish
†George, Lyle Emerson *civil service manager*

Taholah
Knutzen, Raymond Edward *federal official*

Walla Walla
Passmore, Michael Forrest *environmental administrator*

WEST VIRGINIA

Charleston
Marockie, Henry R. *state school system administrator*
†Richardson, Sally Keadle *state health care administrator*

Harpers Ferry
White, Thomas Edward *government park official*

Wheeling
Robbins, William David *retired police officer*

WISCONSIN

Madison
Couper, David Courtland *police chief*
Cronin, Patti Adrienne Wright *state agency administrator*
Fiedler, Patrick James *circuit court judge*

Mequon
Wray, Gail Miller *environmentalist, government agency administrator*

Milwaukee
Arreola, Philip *police officer*
Erdmann, August *protective services official*

WYOMING

Cheyenne
Karpan, Kathleen Marie *former state official, lawyer, journalist*

TERRITORIES OF THE UNITED STATES

PUERTO RICO

San Juan
Gelabert, Pedro Antonio *federal agency administrator, geologist*

MILITARY ADDRESSES OF THE UNITED STATES

ATLANTIC

APO
Dyal, William M., Jr. *federal agency administrator*
†Kadunc, Edward Louis, Jr. *federal government official*

CANADA

NEW BRUNSWICK

Fredericton
†Blanchard, Edmond P. *Canadian provincial official and attorney general*
McKenna, Frank Joseph *Canadian politician, lawyer*

Moncton
†Gusella, Mary Margaret *deputy minister*

NORTHWEST TERRITORIES

Yellowknife
Patterson, Dennis Glen *Canadian government official, lawyer*

NOVA SCOTIA

Jeddore
Pottie, Roswell Francis *science and technology consultant*

ONTARIO

Downsview
Burton, Ian *federal agency administrator, educator, environmental scientist, geographer, author, consultant*

Ottawa
†Berry, Mike B. *federal agency administrator, geologist*
Blais, Pierre *Canadian government minister*
Collin, Arthur Edwin *Canadian government official*
Epp, Arthur Jacob *Canadian government official*
Gravelle, Pierre *Canadian government official*
†Ingstrup, Ole Michaelsen *Canadian government agency official*
MacFarlane, John Alexander *former federal housing agency administrator*
Macquarrie, Heath Nelson *Canadian government official*
Morden, John Reid *Canadian government corporation administrator*
Murphy, Edmund Michael *demographer*
†Murray, J. P. R. *Canadian protective services official*
†Rivard, Gilles *government official, lawyer*

Toronto
Fraser, William Neil *government official*
Gillespie, Alastair William *former Canadian government official*
Rogers, Harry G. *Canadian government official*

SASKATCHEWAN

Regina
Fedoruk, Sylvia O. *Canadian provincial official, educator*
Nuttall, Richard Norris *state agency administrator*
Teichrob, Carol *Canadian provincial official*

ADDRESS UNPUBLISHED

Anderson, Wayne Carl *public information officer*
†Bell, Michael Patrick *protective services official*
†Benjaminson, James A. *protective services official*
Bergman, John Hubert *fire department administrator*
Boozer, Howard Rai *state education official*
†Boysen, Thomas Cyril *state school system administrator*
Brubaker, Crawford Francis, Jr. *government official, aerospace consultant*
Burgess, Marjorie Laura *protective services official*
Clagett, William H., IV *retired government agency administrator*
Claytor, Richard Anderson *retired federal agency executive*
Conway, James Valentine Patrick *forensic document examiner, former postal service executive*
Courtney, Charles Edward *government official*
Cox, Kenneth R. *state agency administrator*
Crawford, Carol Tallman *government executive*
Diamond, William J. *federal agency administrator*
Guild, Nelson Prescott *retired state education official*
Hannigan, Maurice J. *protective services official*
Harder, Robert Clarence *state official*
Harriman, Constance Bastine *federal official*
Healton, Donald Carney *federal agency administrator*
Hedrick, Basil Calvin *state agency administrator, ethnohistorian, educator, museum and cultural institutions consultant*
Helms, J. Lynn *former government agency administrator*
Johnson, Marlene M. *government executive*
Keala, Francis Ahloy *security executive*
Kirkendall, Donald Eugene *federal agency official*
Kusserow, Richard Phillip *government official*
LaBarre, Carl Anthony *retired government official*
Lewis, Samuel Winfield *retired government official, former ambassador*
Mancher, Rhoda Ross *federal agency administrator, strategic planner*
Mc Coy, Tidal Windham *former government official*
Morales, Diane K. *government official*
Murr, James Coleman *federal government official*
Narramore, Randy Earl *protective services official*
Patino, Isidro Frank *law enforcement educator*
Perrin, Robert *writer, consultant*
Ratcliff, Sara Boney *federal agency administrator*
Ray, Gayle Elrod *sheriff*
Rhett, John Taylor, Jr. *government official, civil engineer*
Rivkind, Perry Abbot *federal railroad agency administrator*
Ross, Joseph E. *government official, lawyer*
Scott, William Herbert *state agency administrator*
Shasteen, Donald Eugene *government official*
Shute, Richard Emil *government official, engineer*
Skaff, Joseph John *state agency administrator, retired army officer*
Smith, Doris Victoria *educational agency administrator*
Sorter, Bruce Wilbur *federal program administrator, educator, consultant*
Tate, Frederick Wayne *federal agency administrator*
Teague, Wayne *state education official*
†Turner, Margery Austin *government agency administrator*
Walker, Gordon Davies *former government official, writer, lecturer, consultant*
Williams, Barbara Jean May *state official*
Wilson, Sheryl J. *state agency administrator*

GOVERNMENT: EXECUTIVE ADMINISTRATION

UNITED STATES

ALABAMA

Bessemer
Bains, Lee Edmundson *lawyer, state official*

Birmingham
Arrington, Richard, Jr. *mayor*
Bennett, James Ronald *secretary of state*
Boomershine, Donald Eugene *bureau executive, development official*
Brewer, Albert Preston *lawyer, former governor, law and government educator*
Dentiste, Paul George *city and regional planning executive*
Weems, Frances Elizabeth *lawyer, county official*

Gadsden
Hudgins, Don Franklin *city official*

Huntsville
Hettinger, Steve *mayor*

Mobile
Delaney, Thomas Caldwell, Jr. *city official*

Montgomery
Bridges, Edwin Clifford *state official*
Camp, Billy Joe *state official*
Evans, James Harold *state attorney general*
†James, Forrest Hood, Jr. (Fob James) *governor*
Latham, Larry Lee *state administrator, psychologist*
†Siegelman, Don Eugene *state official*
Sizemore, James Middleton, Jr. *state commissioner, lawyer*

ALASKA

Anchorage
Brown, Dean Naomi *state official, geologist*

Barrow
†Stalker, Annie Eleanor *borough official*

Fairbanks
Smith, Robert London *commissioner, retired air force officer, political scientist, educator*
Wolting, Robert Roy *city official*

Juneau
Botelho, Bruce Manuel *state official, mayor*
Coghill, John Bruce *state official*
Meacham, Charles P. *president, capital consulting*
Ulmer, Fran *state official*

Kodiak
Selby, Jerome M. *mayor*

Mekoryuk
†Williams, Solomon *Indian organization executive*

Ninilchik
†Oskolkoff, Grassim *Native American Indian tribal chief*

ARIZONA

Chinle
Yazhe, Herbert *national monument superintendent*

Davis Monthan AFB
†Monk, Richard Francis *air force officer, health care administrator*

Gilbert
Carrico, Donald Jefferson *public transit system manager*

Green Valley
Egger, Roscoe L., Jr. *consultant, former federal commissioner*

Mesa
†Wong, Willie *mayor, automotive executive*

Phoenix
Breen, John *government official*
Cordova, Alexander M. *city clerk*
Frank, Anthony Melchior *federal official, former financial executive*
Hull, Jane Dee *state official, former state legislator*
Mahoney, Richard *state official*
†Rimsza, Skip *mayor*
Symington, J. Fife, III *governor*
Woods, Grant *state attorney general*
Woods, Joel Grant *state attorney general*

Scottsdale
Hannah, Norman Britton *former foreign service officer*

Sun City
Farwell, Albert Edmond *retired government official, consultant*

Tempe
Tambs, Lewis Arthur *diplomat, historian, educator*

Tucson
Miller, George *mayor*
Williams, Ben Franklin, Jr. *mayor, lawyer*

ARKANSAS

Bella Vista
Medin, Myron James, Jr. *city manager*

Little Rock
Ahlen, John William, III *state official, scientist, educator*
Bryant, Winston *state attorney general*
†Elliott, Burton *state education official*
Fisher, Jimmie Lou *state official*
Goss, Kay Gentry Collett *state official*
Huckabee, Michael Dale *state official, minister*
Jones, Beverly Ward *state official*
Jones, Julia Hughes *state official*
McCuen, William James (Bill McCuen) *state official*
†Priest, Sharon Devlin *state official*
Tucker, Jim Guy, Jr. *governor*

CALIFORNIA

Anaheim
†Daly, Tom *mayor*

Bakersfield
†Price, Robert O. *mayor*
Shell, Mary Katherine Jaynes Hosking (Mrs. Joseph C. Shell) (Mrs. Joseph C. Shell) *county official*

Berkeley
Rice, Edward Earl *former government official, author*

Beverly Hills
Covitz, Carl D. *state official, real estate and investment executive*

Concord
Davis, Robert Leach *retired government official, consultant*

Coronado
Hostler, Charles Warren *international affairs consultant*

Costa Mesa
Hugo, Nancy *county official, alcohol and drug addiction professional*

Downey
Schoettger, Theodore Leo *city official*

El Cajon
Shoemaker, Joan *mayor*

Encinitas
Hano, E. Gail *mayor*

Felicity
Istel, Jacques Andre *mayor*

Fresno
Patterson, James *mayor*

Fullerton
†Sa, Julie *mayor, restaurant chain owner*

Glendale
Day, John Francis *city official, former savings and loan executive, former mayor*

La Jolla
Klein, David *foreign service officer*
Shakespeare, Frank *ambassador*

Lafayette
Uilkema, Gayle Burns *mayor, councilwoman, business educator*

Laguna Hills
Hussey, William Bertrand *retired foreign service officer*

Lemoore
†Atwell, Clarence, Jr. *Indian tribal leader*

Livermore
Brown, Cathie *city official*

Long Beach
†O'Neill, Beverly Lewis *mayor, former college president*
Sato, Eunice Noda *former mayor, consultant*

Los Altos
Gray, Robert Donald *mayor*

Los Angeles
Peters, Aulana Louise *government agency commissioner, lawyer*
Reagan, Ronald Wilson *former President of United States*
Remy, Ray *chamber of commerce official*
Rice, Donald Blessing *former secretary of air force, corporate executive*
Riordan, Richard J. *mayor*
Schnabel, Rockwell Anthony *ambassador*
Shelton, Turner Blair *diplomat*
Zolin, Frank Stanley *county administrator*

Los Gatos
Farley, Philip Judson *former government official*

Marina
Myers, James David *municipal government official*

Menlo Park
Lane, Laurence William, Jr. *retired U.S. ambassador, publisher*

Mission Viejo
Small, Richard F. *mechanical engineer, consultant*

Modesto
†Lang, Richard Arthur *mayor, educator*
Mensinger, Peggy Boothe *retired mayor*

Monterey
Wright, Mary R. state park superintendent

Napa
Battisti, Paul Oreste county supervisor

Oakland
Harris, Elihu Mason mayor

Oceanside
Lyon, Richard mayor, retired naval officer

Orinda
Conran, James Michael state government official

Pasadena
Bean, Maurice Darrow retired diplomat

Placerville
McIntosh, Paul Eugene county government official

Rancho Mirage
Ford, Gerald Rudolph, Jr. former President of United States

Rancho Santa Fe
Capen, Richard Goodwin, Jr. ambassador

Richmond
Corbin, Rosemary Mac Gowan mayor

Riverside
Brown, Albert Clarence former mayor
Steckel, Barbara Jean city financial officer

Sacramento
Betts, Bert A. former state treasurer, accountant
Brown, Kathleen state treasurer, lawyer
Grissom, Lee Alan state official
Lungren, Daniel Edward state attorney general
McCarthy, Leo Tarcisius state lieutenant governor
Nelson, Alan Curtis government official, lawyer
Peck, Ellie Enriquez retired state administrator
Serna, Joe, Jr. mayor
Takasugi, Nao state official, business developer
Toman, Mary Ann federal official
Walston, Roderick Eugene state attorney general
Whiteside, Carol Gordon state official, former mayor
Wilson, Pete governor of California

San Bernardino
Turoci, Marsha May county official

San Diego
Bliesner, James Douglas municipal/county official, consultant
Freeman, Myrna Faye county schools official
Golding, Susan mayor
Kenneally, Dennis Michael government official

San Francisco
Jordan, Frank M. mayor
Migden, Carole county official
Rosenthal, James D. former ambassador, government and foundation executive
Stone, Michael P. W. former federal official
Taylor, John Lockhart city official

San Jose
Gonzales, Ron county supervisor
Hammer, Susan W. mayor

San Leandro
†Bohne, David Rees city government administrator

Santa Ana
Vasquez, Gaddi county official

Santa Clarita
†Pederson, George Ludvig mayor, retired law enforcer

Santa Rosa
Frowick, Robert Holmes retired diplomat

Solana Beach
Ernst, Roger Charles former government official, natural resources consultant, association executive
Gildred, Theodore Edmonds ambassador

Stanford
Raisian, John public policy institute executive, economist
Shultz, George Pratt former secretary of state, economics educator

Yuba City
Kemmerly, Jack Dale retired state official, aviation consultant

COLORADO

Colorado Springs
Isaac, Robert Michael mayor, lawyer
Milton, Richard Henry retired diplomat

Denver
Brown, Keith Lapham retired ambassador
†Buckley, Vikki state official
Callihan, C. Michael lieutenant governor, former state senator
Norton, Gale A. state attorney general
Romer, Roy R. governor
Webb, Wellington E. mayor
Zakhem, Sam Hanna diplomat

Grand Junction
Achen, Mark Kennedy city manager

Pueblo
Casey, William Robert, Jr. ambassador, mining engineer
Occhiato, Michael Anthony city official

CONNECTICUT

Bloomfield
Houston, Howard Edwin retired government official

Bristol
Moffitt, George, Jr. foreign service officer

Easton
Meyer, Alice Virginia state official

Hamden
Clayman, Lillian Dudkiewicz mayor

Hartford
Blumenthal, Richard state attorney general
†Burnham, Christopher Bancroft state treasurer, investment banker
De Rocco, Andrew Gabriel state commissioner, educator
Groark, Eunice state official
Harris, James George, Jr. social services administrator, consultant
Kee Borges, Saundra Alice city manager, lawyer
Killian, Robert Kenneth former lieutenant governor
Milner, Thirman L. state senator
Polinsky, Janet Naboicheck state official, former state legislator
†Rapoport, Miles S. state official
†Rell, M. Jodi state official

Middlebury
†Rowland, John G. governor, former congressman

New Haven
Piscottano, Ann Uscilla city official

Northford
James, William Hall former state official, educator

West Hartford
Farren, J. Michael former government official, lawyer

Wethersfield
Precourt, George Augustine government official

DELAWARE

Dover
Bookhammer, Eugene Donald state government official
†Brady, M. Jane state official
Carper, Thomas Richard governor
Minner, Ruth Ann state official

Newark
Woo, S. B. (Shien-Biau Woo) former lieutenant governor, physics educator

Wilmington
Ianni, Francis Alphonse state official, former army officer
Oberly, Charles Monroe, III state attorney general

DISTRICT OF COLUMBIA

Washington
Abshire, David Manker diplomat, research executive
Achtenberg, Roberta federal official
Adoum, Mahamat Ali minister of foreign relations
Albornoz, Francisco government executive, urban planner, civil engineer
Albright, Raymond Jacob government official
†Alexander, Dawn Alicia government official
Allison, Graham Tillett, Jr. federal government official
Al-Saud, Prince Ibn Abdulaziz government official
Altman, Roger C. former federal official
Andersen, Robert Allen government official
Angula, Helmut Kangulohi government executive
Anschuetz, Norbert Lee retired diplomat, banker
Anthony, Sheila F. federal official
Archard, Douglas Bruce foreign service officer
†Argrett, Loretta Collins assistant attorney general, educator
†Arietti, Michael Ray diplomat
Atherton, Charles Henry federal commission administrator
Atwood, John Brian federal official, foundation administrator
Auten, John Harold government official
Ayres, Mary Ellen government official
Azcuenaga, Mary Laurie government official
Babbitt, Bruce Edward U.S. secretary of the interior
Bachula, Gary R. federal official
Baena Soares, João Clemente ambassador
Bair, Sheila Colleen commissioner
Baldyga, Leonard J. diplomat, international consultant, retired
Ballantyne, Robert Jadwin former foreign service officer, consultant
Baltimore, Richard Lewis, III foreign service officer
Barnett, Robert Warren diplomat, author
Barram, David J. federal official
†Barreda, William E. government executive
Barrett, Dennis P. ambassador to Madagascar
Barringer, Philip E. government official
†Barry, Marion Shepilov, Jr. mayor
Bartholomew, Reginald diplomat
Bassin, Jules foreign service officer
†Battle, Dolores state official
Bauer, Gary Lee government official
†Beard, Daniel P. federal government executive
Bell, Robert G. federal agency official
Bellinger, John B., Jr. federal official
Bellows, Michael Donald foreign service officer
Benedick, Richard Elliot diplomat
Berg, Olena federal official
Berger, Samuel R. federal official
Berlincourt, Marjorie Alkins government official
†Biles, Brian Lewis government official
†Binnendijk, Johannes Albert institute administrator
†Blickstein, Irving N. defense department executive
Bodde, William, Jr. foreign service officer
Boehm, Richard Wood ambassador
Bogosian, Richard Wayne diplomat
Bolino, John Vincent federal agency administrator
Borg, Parker Webb ambassador
†Bouchey, L. Francis diplomat
Bowles, Erskine White House staff member
Bowsher, Charles Arthur government official
Boyd, Thomas Marshall federal official, lawyer
†Boykin, Keith O. government official
†Bragg, Lynn Munroe commissioner
Brewster, Robert Charles diplomat, consultant
Broadnax, Walter D. federal official
Bromwich, Michael Ray federal official
Brotzman, Donald Glenn government official, lawyer
Brown, Elizabeth Ann foreign service officer
Brown, Jesse federal official
Brown, June Gibbs government official
Brown, Kent Newville ambassador
Brown, Lee Patrick federal official, law enforcement educator
Brown, Ronald Harmon U.S. secretary of commerce, political organization administrator, lawyer
Browner, Carol federal official
†Browning, Stephen Carroll government official
Brynn, Edward Paul ambassador
†Burleigh, A. Peter ambassador
Calderhead, William Dickson former foreign service officer
Camp, Donald A. diplomat
Cantú, Norma V. federal official
†Caplan, Phillip M. government official
Carlucci, Frank Charles, III former secretary of defense
Carnes, Bruce M. federal official
Carozza, Shirley Caviness government department administrator
Carson, Johnnie ambassador
Casey, Mary Ann diplomat
Casstevens, Kay L. federal official
Catlett, D. Mark federal official
Charles, Kathleen J. federal agency official
Chavez, Linda government official
Cheatham, Linda Moye city manager
Cheney, Dick (Richard Bruce Cheney) former secretary of defense, former congressman
Cheshes, Martin L. ambassador
Chrétien, Raymond A. J. ambassador
Christensen, Sally Hayden government executive
Christopher, Warren U.S. secretary of state
Cisneros, Henry G. U.S. secretary of housing and urban development
Cleveland, Paul Matthews diplomat
Clinton, Bill (William Jefferson Clinton) President of the United States
Cohen, Bonnie R. government official
†Cole, Kenneth J. federal commissioner
Colon, Gilbert federal official
Constable, Elinor Greer federal official, diplomat
Cook, Frances D. diplomat
Cook, Michael Blanchard government executive
Cooke, David Ohlmer government official
Courtney, William Harrison diplomat
Covington, Pamela Jean government official
Crawford, William Rex, Jr. former ambassador
Creekmore, Marion Virgil, Jr. diplomat
Crocker, Chester Arthur diplomat, scholar
Crowder, Richard Thomas federal government official
Crowley, John Joseph, Jr. ambassador
Crutcher, John William federal agency commissioner
Cutler, Walter Leon diplomat, foundation executive
Dabengwa, Dumiso foreign government official
Dalton, John Howard Secretary of the Navy, financial consultant
Dameron, William H., III ambassador
Danescu, George Ioan government official
†D'Anna, Vincent P. federal commissioner
Danzig, Richard Jeffrey government official, lawyer
Dapice, Ronald R. government official
Darman, Richard G. investor, former government official, former investment banker, former educator
Davis, Marilynn A. housing agency administrator
De Alwis, Susantha diplomat
Dean, Edwin Robinson government official, economist
Dean, Leslie Alan foreign service officer
DeGeorge, Francis Donald federal official
DeJarnette, Edmund ambassador
deLaski, Kathleen M. federal official
DeSeve, G. Edward federal official
Deutch, John Mark federal official, chemist, academic administrator
Dewhurst, Stephen B. government official, lawyer
DeWitt, Charles Barbour federal government official
Dickey, George Edward federal government executive
Dobbins, James Francis, Jr. foreign service officer
Dodd, Thomas J. ambassador, educator
Donilon, Thomas E. federal official
Dreyer, David E. federal official
Duemling, Robert Werner diplomat, museum director
Duffey, Joseph Daniel federal official
Dulles, Eleanor Lansing diplomatic consultant, retired diplomat, educator
Dunbar, Charles Franklin diplomat
Durham, Archer L. federal official, retired career officer
Dyvig, Peter P. ambassador
Dziewanowski, Kazimierz diplomat, journalist
†Ebbitt, James Roger government official
Eddy, John Joseph diplomat
Ehrlich, Everett Michael federal official, computer company executive
Ein, Melvin Bennett government official
Einaudi, Luigi Roberto federal official, educator
Eller, Jeff media affairs director, assistant to President
Elliott, Lee Ann federal official
Ellwood, David T. federal agency administrator
Ely-Raphel, Nancy diplomat
Escudero, Stanley ambassador
Espy, Mike (Alphonso Michael Espy) U.S. secretary of agriculture
Faleomavaega, Eni F. H. territorial diplomat
Feinberg, Richard E. federal official
Ferrara, Peter Joseph federal official, lawyer, author, educator
Fielek, Etta state official
†Fitzgerald, Joseph Edward, Jr. government official
FitzGerald, William Henry G. diplomat, corporation executive
Fitzwater, (Max) Marlin former government official, press secretary, advertising executive
Flanigan, Alan H. ambassador
Ford, Charles A. federal official
†Fowler, Mary Emily federal agency administrator
Franklin, Barbara Hackman former goverment official
Frasure, Robert Conway diplomat
Freitag, Robert Frederick government official
Friedman, Townsend B., Jr. ambassador
Fry, Tom federal official
Gaffney, Susan federal official
Galloway, William Jefferson former foreign service officer
Gallucci, Robert Louis diplomat, federal government official
Gati, Toby T. federal official
Gearan, Mark D. federal official
Geisel, Harold Walter diplomat
Gergen, David Richmond federal official, editor
†Gessaman, Donald Eugene government executive
Gibbons, John Howard (Jack Gibbons) government official, physicist
Gildenhorn, Joseph Bernard businessman, diplomat, lawyer
Glauthier, T. James federal official
†Golden, Myron government official, diplomat
Gore, Albert Vice President of the United States
Gosnell, Jack Leslie diplomat
Green, Marshall former ambassador, consultant
†Gregg, Richard Leo federal commissioner
Gribbin, David James, III federal official
Grimmett, Richard Fieldon government official
†Grossman, Marc ambassador
Grove, Brandon Hambright, Jr. diplomat
Haig, Alexander Meigs, Jr. former secretary of state, former army officer, business executive
Hale, Marcia L. federal official
Hall, Douglas K. federal official
Hall, Keith R. federal official
Hamilton, Milton Holmes, Sr. government executive, politic-military analyst
Harrop, William Caldwell retired ambassador, foreign service officer
Hart, John P. federal official
Hawk, Kathleen M. federal official
Hawkins, Wilbur federal official
Heaphy, Eileen Michele diplomat
Henderson, Donald Ainslie government science administrator
Hennemeyer, Robert Thomas diplomat
Herman, Alexis M. federal official
High, George Borman executive director, research organization
†Hobbs, David L. foreign service officer
Holden, Glen A. ambassador
Holmes, Genta Hawkins diplomat
Holmes, Henry Allen government official
Houdek, Robert G. diplomat
Howard, Robert Elliott federal official
†Huddleston, Vicki Jean diplomat
Hughes, Arthur H. ambassador to Yemen
Hulings, Joseph Simpson diplomat
Huntress, Wesley Theodore, Jr. government official
Hyun, Hong Choo ambassador
Ingersoll, John Joseph retired foreign service officer
Irving, Clarence L., Jr. (Larry Irving) federal official
Isom, Harriet Winsar ambassador
Jackson, Karl Dion government official business executive, scholar
Jacobsen, William Ludwig, Jr. ambassador
Janis, Michael B. federal official
Jesseramsing, Chitmansing ambassador
Jeter, Howard F. ambassador
Jett, Dennis Coleman ambassador
Johnson, U. Alexis diplomat
Kakish, Bassam Eid ambassador
Kalnay, Eugenia government official, meteorologist
Kampelman, Max M. former ambassador, lawyer
Kantor, Michael (Mickey Kantor) federal trade representative
Kappner, Augusta Souza government official
Karelis, Charles Howard government official
Kauzlarich, Richard Dale U.S. ambassador, foreign service officer
Keating, Robert B. ambassador
Keel, Alton Gold, Jr. ambassador
Keevey, Richard Francis government official, educator
Keith, Kenton W. ambassador to Qatar
Kelley, Wayne Plumbley, Jr. federal official
Kelly, John Hubert diplomat, business executive
Kelman, Steven Jay government official
Kemp, Jack French association director, former U.S. secretary of housing and urban development, former congressman
Kennedy, Patrick F. federal official
Kennedy, Richard Thomas government official
Kerber, Frank John diplomat
Kidd, Charles Vincent former civil servant, educator
Killgore, Andrew Ivy former ambassador
†Kimbrough, Kenneth R. commisioner public buildings service
Kirby, Harmon E. ambassador
Knisely, Robert August government official, lawyer
Komer, Robert William government official, consultant
Kornblum, John Christian foreign service officer
Korth, Penne Percy ambassador
†Kott, Robert Joseph diplomat
Kovach, Eugene George government official, consultant
Kristol, William public policy activist
Kuchel, Roland Karl ambassador
†Kursch, Donald Bowman foreign service officer
†LaGamma, Robert Ronald diplomat
Laird, Melvin Robert former secretary of defense
Lake, Anthony federal official
Lake, Joseph Edward ambassador
Lalley, Frank Edward federal government official
Lanpher, E. Gibson ambassador to Zimbabwe
Lastowka, James Anthony former federal agency executive, lawyer
Lau, Cheryl A. former state official
LaVelle, Avis federal administration official
Le Baron, Joseph Evan diplomat
Lee, Chester Maurice government official
Leetsar, Jaan government official
Lenahan, Walter Clair retired foreign service officer
Leonard, Michael federal official
†Lese, William G(eorge), Jr. government official
Levy, Michael B. federal official
Lilly, William Eldridge government official
Longanecker, David A. federal official
Longstreet, Victor Mendell government official
Lovell, Malcolm Read, Jr. public policy institute executive, educator, former government official, former trade association executive
Lowe, Mary Frances federal government official
Lowenstein, James Gordon former diplomat, international consultant
Lucas, James Walter federal government official
Ludwig, Eugene Allan U.S. comptroller of the currency, lawyer
†Lufrano, Michael Richard federal government official
Lyman, Princeton Nathan ambassador

Lyons, James Robert *federal official*
Magaw, John W. *federal law enforcement official*
Magaziner, Ira *federal official*
Maisto, John F. *ambassador*
Maldon, Alphonso, Jr. *federal official, retired military officer*
Malott, Frank Stephen *foreign service officer*
Malott, John Raymond *foreign service officer*
Mansfield, Michael Joseph *former ambassador, former senator*
†Marshall, Andrew Walter *federal official*
†Martin, William Edwin *government official*
Mathews, Jessica Tuchman *policy researcher, columnist*
Mbila, Simon *government official, accountant*
Mbumba, Nangolo *government executive*
McCaffrey, Shellyn Gae *federal official*
McCallie, Marshall F. *ambassador*
McCammon, Helen Mary *government administrator*
McCargar, James Goodrich *diplomat, writer*
McCarthy, John Thomas *diplomat*
McConnell, Donald J. *ambassador*
McConnell, James Michael *federal official*
McCormack, Richard Thomas Fox *government official*
McCurry, Michael Demaree *government spokesman, press secretary*
Mc Donald, John Warlick *diplomat, global strategist*
McGue, Christie *federal official*
McGuire, Roger Alan *foreign service officer*
McHenry, Donald F. *former diplomat, international affairs consultant, educator*
McKinley, Brunson *diplomat*
†McKune, Elizabeth D. *diplomat*
McLarty, Thomas F., III (Mack McLarty) *federal official*
McMichael, Guy H., III *federal official*
McMillen, (Charles) Thomas *federal official*
McNamara, Thomas Edmund *diplomat*
McNicol, David Leon *federal official*
Meissner, Doris *federal commissioner*
Meyer, Armin Henry *retired diplomat, author, educator*
Milam, William Bryant *diplomat, economist*
Miller, William Lawrence *government official*
Mintz, Richard I. *federal official*
Mohler, Brian Jeffery *diplomat*
Moore, Richard Anthony *diplomat, lawyer*
Moose, Richard M. *federal official*
Morgan, John Davis *government official*
Morris, Stanley E. *federal official*
Morrison, James William, Jr. *lobbyist and government relations consultant*
Moscato, Anthony Charles *federal official*
Murata, Ryohei *diplomat*
Murphy, Gerald *government official*
Myers, Dee Dee (Margaret Jane Myers) *former press secretary*
†Nach, James Peter *foreign service officer*
Natter, Robert, Jr. *federal official, military career officer*
Newman, Frank Neil *federal official*
Nitze, Paul Henry *international studies educator*
Noble, Ronald K. *government official, lawyer*
Nolan, Jean *federal agency official*
Norland, Donald Richard *retired foreign service officer*
†Oakley, Phyllis Elliott *diplomat*
Obee, Kent *foreign service officer*
O'Brien, William Vincent *government educator*
O'Bryon, James Fredrick *defense executive*
†Ochmanek, David Alan *government official*
†O'Connor, Jennifer *public administrator*
O'Leary, Hazel R. *U.S. secretary of energy, former power company executive, lawyer*
O'Toole, Tara J. *federal official*
Owen, Henry *former ambassador, consultant*
Oxman, Stephen A. *federal official*
Page, Marcus William *federal official*
Palmer, Ronald DeWayne Faisal *retired diplomat, educator, consultant*
Palmer, Steven O. *federal official*
Panetta, Leon Edward *federal official, former congressman*
Pang, Frederick F. Y. *federal official*
Partridge, William Russell *federal executive*
Patrick, Sue Ford *diplomat*
†Payzant, Thomas *government official*
Pelaez, Emmanuel N. *ambassador*
Pelletreau, Robert Halsey *diplomat*
Peña, Federico Fabian *federal official*
Pendleton, Mary Catherine *foreign service officer*
Perkins, Edward J. *diplomat*
Perle, Richard Norman *government official*
Philbin, Edward James *federal agency commissioner, military officer, legal educator, engineer*
Phillips, Christopher Hallowell *diplomat*
Phillips, James D. *retired diplomat*
Pierce, Margaret Hunter *government official*
Piroumian, Felix Ashot *Armenian government official*
Placke, James A(nthony) *foreign service officer, international affairs consultant*
Plaisted, Joan M. *diplomat*
Poneman, Daniel Bruce *federal official*
Quainton, Anthony Cecil Eden *diplomat*
Ramsey, William C. *ambassador*
Rankin, Haywood Forney *diplomat*
Raphel, Robin *federal official*
Rasco, Carol Hampton *federal official*
Rawson, David P. *ambassador*
Reade, Lewis Pollock *diplomat, engineer*
Rechcigl, Miloslav, Jr. *government official*
Reed, John Hathaway *former ambassador*
Reeder, Joe Robert *federal official*
Reilly, William Kane *former government official, educator, lawyer, conservationist*
Render, Arlene *ambassador*
Reno, Janet *U.S. attorney general*
Retsinas, Nicolas P. *federal official*
†Richard, Mark M. *government official, lawyer*
†Richards, Charles A. *government official*
Ridgway, Rozanne LeJeanne *government executive, former diplomat*
†Riley, Michael Joseph *government official*
Riley, Richard Wilson *U.S. secretary of education*
Rivas-Vazquez, Ana Victoria *federal official*
Robinson, Sharon Porter *federal official*
†Rogowsky, Robert A. *trade commission director*
Rohr, David Baker *federal agency commissioner*
Rollwagen, John A. *federal official*
Romero-Barceló, Carlos Antonio *resident commissioner, former chairman New Progressive Party, former governor, lawyer, real estate agent*
†Roque, Margarita *government administrator*
Rosenthal, Alan Sayre *government official*
Ross, Christopher Wade Stelyan *diplomat*
Ross, Thomas Bernard *federal government official*
Rubin, Robert Edward *U.S. secretary of the treasury*
Rugh, William Arthur *diplomat*
Ruhfus, Jürgen *ambassador*
Runyon, Marvin Travis *postmaster general*
†Russell, Theodore Emery *diplomat*
Ryan, Mary A. *diplomat*
Sacksteder, Frederick Henry *former foreign service officer*
Safarian, Ashot Andraniki *Armenian government official*
Sam, Pierre Desforges *ambassador*
Sampas, Dorothy M. *government official*
San Martin, Robert L. *federal official*
†Saxon, Janet D. *federal government official*
Sayre, Robert Marion *ambassador*
Scarbrough, Frank Edward *government official*
Scassa, Eugene L. *ambassador*
Schiavo, A. Mary Fackler *federal official, lawyer*
Schley, Wayne A. *postal rate commissioner*
Schroeter, Richard B. *federal official*
†Schuker, Jill Anita *federal official, consultant*
Seidman, Ricki *federal official*
Selin, Ivan *federal official*
Sellin, Theodore *foreign service officer, consultant*
Seymour, Jon *federal government official*
Shafer, Jeffrey Richard *federal official*
Shalala, Donna Edna *federal official, political scientist, educator, university chancellor*
Shattuck, John H. F. *federal official*
Shelly, Christine Deborah *foreign service officer*
Sherifis, Michael Eleftheriou *ambassador*
Shinn, David Hamilton *diplomat*
Shlaudeman, Harry Walter *retired ambassador*
Shumate, John Page *diplomat*
Shurtleff, Leonard Grant *ambassador*
Siegel, Jack S. *federal official*
Silberman, Rosalie Gaull *federal official*
†Silver, Jonathan Moses *government official*
†Simon, Gregory *advisor to the Vice President*
Simon, Jeanne Hurley *federal commissioner*
Skol, Michael *diplomat*
†Skolfield, Melissa T. *government official*
Smith, Dallas R. *federal official*
Smith, Elaine Diana *foreign service officer*
Smith, Marshall Savidge *government official, academic dean, educator*
Smith, Patricia Grace *government official*
Somerville, Walter Raleigh, Jr. *government official*
Sommerfelt, Soren Christian *foreign affairs, international trade consultant, former Norwegian diplomat, lawyer*
Sonnenfeldt, Helmut *former government official, educator, consultant, author*
Sprott, John T. *ambassador*
†Stauber, Karl Neill *federal executive*
†Stayman, Allen Paul *government executive*
Steiger, Janet Dempsey *government official*
Stephanopoulos, George Robert *federal official*
Stoll, Louise Frankel *federal official*
Storing, Paul Edward *foreign service officer*
Stuart, Sandra Kaplan *federal official*
Sundquist, Maria Alexandra *diplomat*
†Suttenfield, Nancy Dezort *financial executive*
†Sutter, Eleanor Bly *diplomat*
Swihart, James W., Jr. *diplomat*
†Swimmer, Ross Owen *federal agency administrator*
Swing, William Lacy *ambassador*
Tarullo, Daniel K. *federal official*
Taylor, William James, III *federal official*
Teare, Richard Wallace *ambassador*
Thomas, Charles Howard, II *federal official*
Thomas, Ralph Charles, III *federal official*
Thomas, Scott E. *federal government executive, lawyer*
Thomasson, Patsy *federal official*
Thunborg, Anders Ingemar *ambassador*
Tierney, Susan Fallows *federal official*
Todman, Terence A. *diplomat*
Torres-Gil, Fernando M. *federal official*
Trezise, Philip Harold *government official*
Tucker, Alvin Leroy *federal government executive*
Turner, Leslie Marie *federal official*
Tuthill, John Wills *former diplomat, educator*
Twaddell, William Hartsthorne *diplomat*
Underwood, Robert A. *congressional delegate, university official*
Upadhyay, Yog Prasad *former diplomat*
Varney, Christine A. *federal official*
Verville, Elizabeth Giavani *federal official*
Wachtmeister, Count Wilhelm H. F. *diplomat*
Walker, Howard Kent *diplomat*
†Walter, Judith Anne *government executive*
Ward, George Frank, Jr. *foreign service officer*
Ward, Jennifer C. *diplomat*
Ware, Thaddeus Van *government official*
Warshaw, Stanley Irving *government official*
Watkins, Birge Swift *real estate investment executive*
†Watkins, Calvin W. *government executive*
Watkins, David *federal official*
Watson, Alexander Fletcher *ambassador*
Watson, Arthur Dennis *government official*
†Watson, Jennifer Darrow *foreign service and political officer, researcher*
Wayne, Stephen J. *government educator, academic director, writer*
Weise, George J. *commissioner*
†Weiss, Marina *government official*
Wendt, E. Allan *ambassador*
Widnall, Sheila Evans *federal official, air force officer, former aeronautical educator, former university official*
Wiedemann, Kent M. *federal official*
Wilcox, Philip Connacher, Jr. *foreign service officer*
Williams, Margaret *federal official*
Williams, Richard Llewellyn *diplomat*
Williamson, Richard Hall *association executive*
Wilson, Joseph Charles, IV *ambassador*
Winter, Andrew J. *ambassador*
Winter, Harvey John *government official*
Wirth, Timothy Endicott *federal official, former senator*
Withrow, Mary Ellen *treasurer of United States*
Wolters, Curt Cornelis Frederik *foreign service officer*
Woods, Millicent Wasell *federal official*
Woodward, Robert Forbes *retired government official, consultant*
Woolsey, R. James, Jr. *federal agency administrator*
Worthy, Patricia Morris *municipal official, lawyer*
†Yellen, Janet Louise *government official, economics educator*
†Young, Loretta *government official*
Ziglar, James W. *former federal official, lawyer, investment banker*

FLORIDA

Bal Harbour
Horton, Jeanette *municipal government official*

Brooksville
Anderson, Richard Edmund *city manager, management consultant*
Hetrick, Charles Brady *county official*

Clearwater
Parks, Sallie Ann *county official, public relations executive, marketing professional*
Todd, Barbara Sheen *county commissioner*

Coral Gables
Arcos, Cresencio S. *ambassador*

Fort Lauderdale
Adams, Damon R. *city official*
Gunzburger, Suzanne Nathan *county commissioner, social worker*
Hanbury, George Lafayette, II *city manager*

Gainesville
Heflin, Martin Ganier *foreign service officer, international political economist*
Jones, Elizabeth Nordwall *county government official*

Green Cove Springs
Lee, Ruth Davidson *tax collector*

Hialeah
Martinez, Julio J. *mayor*
Martinez, Raul L. *mayor, publisher*

Hollywood
Giulianti, Mara Selena *mayor, civic worker*

Jacksonville
Austin, T. Edward (Ed Austin) *mayor*

Lakeland
Hollis, Mark D. *federal official*

Leesburg
Houston, John Coates, Jr. *consultant*

Mac Dill AFB
Passage, David *diplomat*

Miami
†Avino, Joaquin G. *county official*
Clark, Stephen P. *mayor*

North Palm Beach
Fauver, John William *mayor, retired business executive*

Ocala
Lewis, Richard Knox *assitant city manager*

Ormond Beach
Nasser, Joseph Yousef *public safety adminstrator, consultant*

Palm City
Henry, David Howe, II *former diplomat and international organization official*

Saint Petersburg
Fischer, David J. *mayor*
Mc Connell, Robert Chalmers *former city official*

Sarasota
Connor, Robert T. *former government official*
Yordan, Carlos Manuel *foreign service officer*

Sun City Center
Weatherbee, Artemus Edwin *former federal government official*

Tallahassee
Butterworth, Robert A. *state attorney general*
Chiles, Lawton Mainor *governor, former senator*
Clark, Herbert Forrester *state commissioner*
MacKay, Kenneth Hood (Buddy MacKay) *state official, former congressman*
Mortham, Sandra Barringer *state official*
†Parker, Herbert Gerald *state official*
Smith, James Cloudis *secretary of state, former state attorney general*

Tampa
Freedman, Sandra Warshaw *mayor*
†Greco, Dick A. *mayor, hardware company executive*
Platt, Jan Kaminis *former county official*
Richardson, Edward James *federal government agency official*
Studer, William Allen *county official*

Vero Beach
White, Thomas Patrick *county official, small business owner*

West Palm Beach
Roberts, Carol Antonia *county commissioner, real estate associate*

Winter Park
Hawkins, Paula *federal official, former senator*

GEORGIA

Athens
Hillenbrand, Martin Joseph *diplomat, educator*

Atlanta
Bell, Griffin B. *lawyer, former attorney general*
Bowers, Michael Joseph *state attorney general*
Campbell, Bill *mayor, broadcasting executive*
Carter, Jimmy (James Earl Carter, Jr.) *former President of United States*
Cleland, Joseph Maxwell (Max Cleland) *state official*
Malone, Perrillah Atkinson (Pat Malone) *retired state official*
Miller, Zell Bryan *governor*
Nethercut, Philip Edwin *honorary consul*
Poythress, David Bryan *state commissioner, lawyer*
Rogers, Werner *state superintendent schools*
Schwartz, William B., Jr. *ambassador*
Streeb, Gordon Lee *diplomat, economist*
Sullivan, Louis Wade *former secretary health and human services, physician*

Carrollton
Harrison, Earle *former county official*

Cartersville
Harris, Joe Frank *former governor*

Columbus
†Martin, Frank Kieffer *mayor, lawyer*

Decatur
Gay, Robert Derril *county official*
Howard, Pierre *lieutenant governor, president senate*

Midland
Hadden, Mayo Addison *chamber of commerce executive, military officer, educator*

Saint Simons Island
Douglas, William Ernest *retired government official*

Savannah
Rousakis, John Paul *former mayor*

Smyrna
Wallace, Clifford Noble, III *public assembly facility management executive*

HAWAII

Honolulu
Cayetano, Benjamin Jerome *governor, former state senator and representative*
†Harris, Jeremy *mayor*
Hirono, Mazie Keiko *state official*
†Marks, Robert Arthur *lawyer*
Salmon, Charles B., Jr. *diplomat*

IDAHO

Boise
†Batt, Philip E. *governor*
Cenarrusa, Pete T. *secretary of state*
EchoHawk, Larry *state attorney general*
Hawkins, James Victor *state official*
Otter, Clement Leroy *lieutenant governor*
Wilson, Jack Fredrick *retired federal government official*

ILLINOIS

Champaign
Semonin, Richard Gerard *state official*

Chicago
Bishop, Oliver Richard *state official*
Daley, Richard Michael *mayor*
Lafontant-Mankarious, Jewel (Mrs. Naguib S. Mankarious) *diplomat, lawyer*
Levi, Edward Hirsch *former attorney general, university president emeritus*
Mosena, David R. *aviation commissioner*
Phelan, Richard John *county administrator, lawyer*
Roque, Roberto Dizon *city official*
†Ryan, James E. *attorney general*
Topinka, Judy Baar *state official*

Evanston
Ingersoll, Robert Stephen *former diplomat, federal agency administrator*

Hudson
Mills, Lois Jean *legislative aide, former education educator*

Joliet
O'Connell, James Joseph *port official*

Northfield
Louis, John (Jeffry), Jr. *former ambassador*

Peoria
Maloof, James A(loysius) *mayor, real estate company executive*
Mikulecky, Thomas J. *city manager*

Quincy
Points, Roy Wilson *municipal official*

Springfield
Burris, Roland Wallace *state attorney general*
Edgar, Jim *governor*
†Kustra, Robert W. (Bob Kustra) *lieutenant governor, political scientist, educator*

Urbana
Prussing, Laurel Lunt *state official, economist*

Wheaton
Bellock, Patricia Rigney *county government official*
Stone, Irene Mildred *county commissioner*

INDIANA

Bloomington
Allison, Tomilea *mayor*

Carmel
Quayle, J(ames) Danforth *former vice president of United States, investment company executive*

Evansville
Vandeveer, Michael D. *city official*

Fort Wayne
Helmke, (Walter) Paul, Jr. *mayor, lawyer*

Gary
Barnes, Thomas Vernon *mayor, lawyer*

Indianapolis
Bayh, Evan *governor*
Carter, Pamela Lynn *state attorney general*
†Gilroy, Sue Anne *state official*
Goldsmith, Stephen *mayor*
Hogsett, Joseph H. *state official*
O'Bannon, Frank Lewis *state official, lawyer*
Prosser, Kathy *state official*
†Rieck, Theodore J. *city official*
†Usher, Phyllis Land *state official*

Notre Dame
Wadsworth, Michael A. *ambassador, director of athletics, former professional football player*

Terre Haute
†Ralston, Patrick Robert *state government official*

IOWA

Cedar Rapids
Novetzke, Sally Johnson *former ambassador*

Des Moines
Baxter, Elaine *state government official*
Branstad, Terry Edward *governor, lawyer*
Campbell, Bonnie Jean *former state attorney general*
Corning, Joy Cole *state official*
Fitzgerald, Michael Lee *state official*
†Miller, Thomas J. *state attorney general*
Odell, Mary Jane *former state official*

Oelwein
McFarlane, Beth Lucetta Troester *former mayor*

Sioux City
Juon, Lester Allen *utility executive*

Steamboat Rock
Taylor, Ray *state senator*

KANSAS

Colby
Frahm, Sheila *lieutenant governor, former state legislator*

Kansas City
Hollenbeck, Marynell *municipal government official*

Lenexa
Stephan, Robert Taft *state attorney general*

Mc Pherson
Steffes, Don Clarence *state senator*

Shawnee Mission
Kemp, John Bernard *retired state secretary of transportation*

Topeka
Francisco, James L. *lieutenant governor*
Graves, William Preston *governor*
†Stovall, Carla Jo *state official, lawyer*
Thompson, Sally Engstrom *state official*

Wichita
Knight, Robert G. *mayor, investment banker*

KENTUCKY

Burkesville
Smith, Paul Traylor *mayor, former business executive, former army officer*

Frankfort
Babbage, Robert A. *state official*
Gorman, Chris *state attorney general*
Jones, Brereton C. *governor*
Miller, Mary Helen *public administrator*
Mills, Frances Jones *state official*
Patton, Paul E. *state official*
†Reidy, Edward, Jr. *state official*
Wallace, Peggy Marie *state commissioner*

Hebron
Holscher, Robert F. *county official*

Lexington
Miller, Pamela Gundersen *mayor*

LOUISIANA

Baton Rouge
Brown, James H., Jr. *state official, lawyer*
Edwards, Edwin Washington *state governor*
Hunter, Kim Antoinette *state official*
Ieyoub, Richard Phillip *state attorney general*
McKeithen, Walter Fox *secretary of state*
Schwegmann, Melinda *state official*

Lake Charles
Mount, Willie Landry *mayor*

New Orleans
Dixon, Irma Muse *state commissioner, former state legislator, social worker*
Levell, Edward, Jr. *city official*
Morial, Marc Haydel *mayor*
Ortique, Revius Oliver, Jr. *city official*
Roesler, Robert Harry *city official*
†Simms, Ellenese Brooks *civic leader, retired school system administrator*

Wilson, Peggy Henican *city official*

MAINE

Augusta
†Butland, Jeffrey H. *president of senate, customer service representative*
Carpenter, Michael E. *state attorney general*
Diamond, G. William *secretary of state*
Scribner, Rodney Latham *state official*

Belfast
Worth, Mary Page *mayor*

Springvale
Eastman, Harland Horace *former foreign service officer*

Topsham
Tierney, James Edward *attorney general*

MARYLAND

Annapolis
†Athey, Tyras S. *state official*
Brock, William Emerson *former secretary of labor*
Coulter, James Bennett *state official*
†Glendening, Parris Nelson *governor, political science educator*
Goldstein, Louis Lazarus *state official*
Maurer, Lucille Darvin *state treasurer*
Meima, Ralph Chester, Jr. *corporate execuitve, former foreign service officer*
Papet, Louis M. *federal official, civil engineer*
†Russell, William T. *government executive, nuclear engineer*
Steinberg, Melvin Allen *lieutenant governor, lawyer*
†Townsend, Kathleen Kennedy *state official*

Baltimore
Chater, Shirley Sears *federal commissioner*
Curran, J. Joseph, Jr. *state attorney general*
Jones, Raymond Moylan *strategy and public policy educator*
O'Hare, Thomas J(ames), Jr. *federal commissioner*
Schmoke, Kurt L. *mayor*

Bethesda
Clark, William Doran *former government official*
Gallagher, Hubert R. *governmental consultant*
Goldberg, Herman Raphael *government agency official, educator*
Green, Jerome George *federal government official*
Hempstone, Smith, Jr. *diplomat, journalist*
Hill, Hugh Kenneth *retired diplomat, former ambassador*
Ingraham, Edward Clarke, Jr. *foreign service officer*
Jones-Smith, Jacqueline *federal commission administrator, lawyer*
Laingen, Lowell Bruce *diplomat*
Lewis, James Histed *retired foreign service officer*
McManus, Edward Hubbard *government official*
Neill, Denis Michael *government relations consulting executive*
Neumann, Robert Gerhard *ambassador, consultant*
Newsom, David Dunlop *foreign service officer, educator*
North, William Haven *foreign service officer*
Peck, Edward Lionel *retired foreign service officer, corporate executive*
Rowell, Edward Morgan *retired foreign service officer, lecturer*
Ruppe, Loret Miller *former ambassador*
Vest, George Southall *diplomat*
Walker, Lannon *foreign service officer*

Braddock Heights
Wirths, Theodore William *public policy consultant*

Burkittsville
Aughenbaugh, Deborah Ann *mayor, retired educator*

Chevy Chase
Bush, Frederick Morris *federal official*
Lukens, Alan Wood *retired ambassador and foreign service officer*
Mc Closkey, Robert James *former diplomat*
Pancoast, Edwin C. *retired foreign service officer, writer, researcher*
Prince, Julius S. (Bud) *retired foreign service reserve officer*

College Park
Peterson, David Frederick *government agency executive*

Dunkirk
Ewing, Richard Tucker *diplomat, educator, publisher*

Ellicott City
†Longuemare, R. Noel, Jr. *federal official*

Gaithersburg
French, Judson Cull *government official*
Mills, Kevin Lee *government executive*
Rollow, Thomas A. *federal official*

Grasonville
Andrews, Archie Moulton *government official*

Kensington
Rogers, Kenneth Norman *retired foreign service officer, lawyer, international political and commercial consultant*
Root, William Alden *export control consultant*

Laurel
Sharpless, Joseph Benjamin *former county official*

Potomac
Nichol, Henry Ferris *former government official, environment consultant*
Shepard, William Seth *government official, diplomat*

Rockville
Chiogioji, Melvin Hiroaki *government official*
†Holston, Sharon Smith *government official*

Hoobler, James Ferguson *federal executive*
†Hubbard, William Keith *government executive*
Krahnke, Betty Ann *county official*
Pagan Martinez, Juan *administrative corps officer*
Sacchet, Edward M. *foreign service officer*
Szabo, Daniel *government official*

Silver Spring
Ahmad, Mirza Muzaffar *economic advisor*
Gott, Daniel *government official, consultant*
Manduley, Jose Carlos *government official*
Popkin, Roy Sandor *emergency management consultant, writer, researcher*

Westminster
Cueman, Edmund Robert *county planner*

MASSACHUSETTS

Boston
Cellucci, Argeo Paul *state official*
Connolly, Michael Joseph *state official*
Crane, Andrew B. *state official*
†Galvin, William Francis *secretary of state, lawyer*
Harshbarger, Scott *state attorney general*
Malone, Joseph D. *state treasurer*
Menino, Thomas M. *mayor*
Weld, William Floyd *governor, lawyer*

Brewster
Hemsing, Albert E. *public affairs adviser*

Cambridge
Heymann, Philip B. *law educator, academic director*
Porter, Roger Blaine *government official, educator*

Concord
Cavazos, Lauro Fred *former U.S. secretary of education, former university president, educator*
Rathore, Naeem Gul *United Nations official, retired*

Falmouth
Brewer, William Dodd *former ambassador, political science educator emeritus*

Lowell
Natsios, Nicholas Andrew *retired foreign service officer*

New Bedford
Tierney, Rosemary *mayor*

Sherborn
Kennedy, Chester Ralph, Jr. *former state official, art director*

Springfield
Markel, Robert Thomas *mayor*

Taunton
Lopes, Maria Fernandina *commissioner*

Waltham
Fuchs, Lawrence Howard *government official, educator*

Wellesley
Levin, Burton *diplomat*
Parker, William H., III *federal official*

Worcester
Sharp, Joann M. *county official*

MICHIGAN

Ann Arbor
Sheldon, Ingrid Kristina *mayor*

Detroit
Archer, Dennis Wayne *mayor*
Martin, Fred *retired municipal official*
McNamara, Edward Howard *county official, former mayor*
Worden, William Michael *city agency administrator, preservation consultant*

Grand Rapids
Logie, John Hoult *mayor, lawyer*

Lansing
Binsfeld, Connie Berube *lieutenant governor*
†Hawks, Gary D. *state education official*
Kelley, Frank Joseph *state attorney general*
Miller, Candice S. *state official*
†Schiller, Robert E. *state official*

Mount Clemens
Kolakowski, Diana Jean *county commissioner*

Muskegon
Roy, Paul Emile, Jr. *county official*

Negaunee
Friggens, Thomas George *state official, historian*

Pontiac
Huntoon, Donna R. *commissioner*

Sterling Heights
Duchane, Stephen Michael *city manager*

Troy
Stine, Jeanne M. *mayor, educator*

Warren
Bonkowski, Ronald Lawrence *mayor*

MINNESOTA

Babbitt
†de Marcken, Baudouin François *foreign service officer*

Minneapolis
Belton, Sharon Sayles *mayor*
Fraser, Arvonne Skelton *former United Nations ambassador*
Joseph, Geri Mack (Geraldine Joseph) *former ambassador, educator*

Moorhead
Sinner, George Albert *former state governor, farmer, corporate executive*

Northfield
Flaten, Robert Arnold *ambassador, retired*

Saint Paul
Benson, Joanne *lieutenant governor*
Carlson, Arne Helge *governor*
†Coleman, Norm *mayor*
Dyrstad, Joanell M. *former lieutenant governor*
Growe, Joan Anderson *state official*
Humphrey, Hubert Horatio, III *state attorney general*
McGrath, Michael Alan *state government officer*
Powell, Linda *state education official*
Thomas, Brenda C. *county official*

MISSISSIPPI

Carrollton
McConnell, David Stuart *insurance agent, retired federal executive*

Hattiesburg
Rawlings, Paul C. *retired government official*

Jackson
Briggs, Eddie J. *state official*
Ditto, (John) Kane *mayor*
Fordice, Daniel Kirkwood, Jr. (Kirk Fordice) *governor, construction company executive, engineer*
Molpus, Dick *state official*
Moore, Mike *state attorney general*
Ray, H. M. *lawyer*
Winter, William Forrest *former governor, lawyer*

Madison
Hays, Donald Osborne *retired government official*

Natchez
Parker, Mary Evelyn *former state treasurer*

Ridgeland
Dye, Bradford Johnson, Jr. *former lieutenant governor, lawyer, partner*

Stennis Space Center
Blair, Ruth Reba *government official*
Mc Call, Jerry Chalmers *government official*

MISSOURI

Independence
Kaufman, Lawrence Clark *city official*

Jefferson City
Blunt, Roy D. *state official*
Carnahan, Mel *governor, lawyer*
Holden, Bob *state official*
Moriarty, Judith Kay Spry *state official*
Nixon, Jeremiah W. (Jay Nixon) *state attorney general*
Wilson, Roger B. *lieutenant governor, school administrator*

Kansas City
Davis, Richard Francis *city government official*
Edwards, Horace Burton *former state official, former oil pipeline company executive, management consultant*
Price, Charles H., II *former ambassador*
Steele, Kathleen Frances *federal official*

Saint Joseph
Kelly, Glenda Marie *former mayor*

Saint Louis
Bosley, Freeman Robertson, Jr. *mayor*
Farris, Charles Lowell *city official*
Osterloh, Everett William *county official*
Schoemehl, Vincent Charles, Jr. *mayor*
Winter, William Earl *mayor, retired beverage company executive*

MONTANA

Billings
Larsen, Richard Lee *former city manager, business, municipal and labor relations consultant, arbitrator*

Helena
†Cooney, Mike *state official*
†Keenan, Nancy A. *state agency administrator*
Marks, Robert L. (Bob Marks) *treasurer ex-officio, rancher*
Mazurek, Joseph P. *state attorney general*
Racicot, Marc F. *governor*
Rehberg, Dennis R. *state official*

Missoula
Kemmis, Daniel Orra *mayor, author*
Turman, George *former lieutenant governor*

NEBRASKA

Lincoln
Beermann, Allen J. *state official*
Johnson, Raymond Allen Constan *state auditor of public accounts, accountant*
Lutjeharms, Joseph Earl *commissioner*
†Moore, Scott *state official*
Moul, Maxine Burnett *state official*
Nelson, E. Benjamin *governor*

Robak, Kim M. *state official*
Stenberg, Donald B. *state attorney general*
Vicary, Duane S. *chamber of commerce executive*

North Bend
Johnson, Lowell C. *commissioner*

Omaha
Bechtel, James M. *retired civil servant*
Cunningham, Glenn Clarence *government official*

Wood River
Bish, Milan David *former ambassador, consultant*

NEVADA

Carson City
Del Papa, Frankie Sue *state attorney general*
†Hammargren, Lonnie *lieutenant governor*
†Heller, Dean *state official*
Miller, Robert Joseph *governor, lawyer*
Santor, Ken *state treasurer*
Seale, Robert L. *state treasurer*
Wagner, Sue Ellen *former state official*

Las Vegas
Jones, Jan Laverty *mayor*
Lurie, Ron *mayor*

NEW HAMPSHIRE

Concord
Gardner, William Michael *state official*
Merrill, Stephen *governor*
Randlett, Gloria *clerk of the New Hampshire Senate*

Grantham
Feldman, Roger Bruce *government official*

Lancaster
Pratt, Leighton Calvin *state legislator*

Salem
Sununu, John H. *former chief of staff President of U.S., former governor*

NEW JERSEY

Elizabeth
Stender, Linda de Milt *county official*

Millville
†Johnson, James Robert *county agricultural official, educator*

Newark
Foushee, Geraldine George *municipal county government official, detective*
James, Sharpe *mayor*

Secaucus
Donovan, Raymond James *U.S. secretary of labor*

Trenton
Clymer, Brian William *state official*
Dalton, Daniel J. *secretary of state*
Haberle, Joan Baker *state official*
Kirk, Dolores Ann *government administrative assistant*
Trainor, Lillian (Midge Trainor) *elections official*
Whitman, Christine Todd *governor*

NEW MEXICO

Albuquerque
Chavez, Martin Joseph *mayor, attorney*
Clark, Alan Barthwell *city administrator*
Lujan, Manuel, Jr. *former U.S. secretary of the interior, former congressman*

Carlsbad
Ricer, N. Dean *park superintendent*

Los Alamos
Keene, Douglas Ralph *diplomat*

Santa Fe
†Bradley, Walter D. *lieutenant governor, real estate broker*
Gonzales, Stephanie *state official*
†Johnson, Gary Earl *governor*
Udall, Thomas *state attorney general*

NEW YORK

Albany
Bradford, Peter Amory *state official*
Cotter, William Donald *state commissioner, former newspaper editor*
Coughlin, Thomas A., III *state official*
Haydock, Michael Damean *commissioner*
Herman, Robert S. *former state official, economist, educator*
Lundine, Stanley Nelson *state government official, former congressman, lawyer*
†McCaughey, Elizabeth P. (Betsy McCaughey) *state official*
O'Connell, George Edward *state official*
†Pataki, George E. *governor*
Shaffer, Gail S. *state government official*
Sobol, Thomas *state education commissioner*
†Walton, Arthur L. *state education official*

Bridgehampton
Needham, James Joseph *consultant*

Brooklyn
Garcia, Marc Anthony *diplomat*

Buffalo
Marinelli, Lynn M. *county official*

†Masiello, Anthony M. (Tony Masiello) *mayor*
Millane, Lynn *town official*
Rochwarger, Leonard *former ambassador*

Chappaqua
Laun, Louis Frederick *government official*

Delhi
MacDonald, Robert Bruce *county official*

Hamilton
†Blackton, John Stuart *diplomat*

Homer
†Twentyman, Lee *foreign service officer, economist*

Hyde Park
Dayson, Diane Harris *superintendent, park ranger*

Jamaica
Trepel, Mindy J. *county official, lawyer*

Mineola
Rozzi, Santa Caputo *county official*

Nedrow
†Lyons, Oren *Native American chieftain, conservationist*

New York
Abrams, Robert *former state attorney general*
Aksin, Mustafa *diplomat*
Albright, Madeleine Korbel *diplomat, political scientist*
Baker, James Estes *foreign service officer*
Boutros-Ghali, Boutros *United Nations official*
†Bratton, William J. *police commissioner*
Brown, Carroll *diplomat, association executive*
Bundy, McGeorge *former government official, history educator*
Bushnell, John Alden *diplomat, economist*
Chaves, Jose Maria *diplomat, foundation administrator, lawyer, educator*
Cohn, David Herc *retired foreign service officer*
Curley, Walter Joseph Patrick *diplomat, investment banker*
Duke, Angier Biddle *retired diplomat*
Dunham, Donald Carl *diplomat*
Eisenstadt, G. Michael *diplomat, author, lecturer, research scholar*
Fleming, Charles Stephen *ambassador*
Fowler, Robert Ramsay *Canadian deputy defence minister*
†Fréchette, Louise *Canadian diplomat*
Gardner, Richard Newton *diplomat, lawyer, educator*
Gelber, Herbert Donald *diplomat*
Giuliani, Rudolph W. *mayor, former lawyer*
Gnehm, Edward W., Jr. *ambassador*
Katz, Abraham *retired foreign service officer*
Koch, Edward I. *former mayor, lawyer*
Lehman, Orin *retired state official*
Matlock, Jack Foust, Jr. *diplomat*
Messinger, Ruth W. *borough president*
Murphy, Richard William *retired foreign service officer, Middle East specialist, consultant*
Ney, Edward N. *ambassador, advertising and public relations company executive*
Novello, Antonia Coello *United Nations official, former U.S. surgeon general*
Okun, Herbert Stuart *ambassador, international executive*
Pease, Denise Louise *state bank regulator*
Platt, Nicholas *Asian affairs specialist, ambassador*
Rabetafika, Joseph Albert Blaise *UN representative*
†Ranadive, Prakash Kamlakant *government official, diplomat*
Rao, Sethuramiah Lakshminarayana *United Nations official*
Reed, Joseph Verner, Jr. *diplomat*
Rogers, Elizabeth Barlow *municipal park administrator*
Schweitzer, Melvin L. *commissioner, lawyer*
Segesváry, Victor Gyözö *retired diplomat*
Sutresna, Nana S. *ambassador*
Weil, Leon Jerome *diplomat*
Wells, Melissa Foelsch *foreign service officer*

Niagara Falls
Pillittere, Joseph T. *assemblyman*

Plainview
Fulton, Richard *lecture bureau executive*

Staten Island
†Esposito, Mario John *county clerk, association president*

Watertown
Coe, Benjamin Plaisted *retired state official*

White Plains
O'Rourke, Andrew Patrick *lawyer, county official*

Williamsville
Danni, F. Robert *municipal official*

NORTH CAROLINA

Advance
Legere, Laurence Joseph *government official*

Chapel Hill
Bolick, Ernest Bernard, Jr. *housing administrator*

Charlotte
Edwards, Harold Mills *government official, lawyer*

Greensboro
Nussbaum, V. M., Jr. *former mayor*

Hope Mills
Windham, Cuyler LaRue *state narcotics agent*

Jackson Springs
Krebs, Max Vance *retired foreign service officer, educator*

Raleigh
Boyles, Harlan Edward *state official*
Cameron, John Lansing *retired government official*
Cummings, Frances McArthur *state official, retired educational administrator*

Easley, Michael F. *state attorney general*
Edmisten, Rufus Leigh *state official*
Ellington, John David *state official*
Hunt, James Baxter, Jr. *governor, lawyer*
Wicker, Dennis A. *lieutenant governor*

Southern Pines
Toon, Malcolm *former ambassador*

Waynesville
Matlock, Clifford Charles *retired foreign service officer*

NORTH DAKOTA

Bismarck
Gilmore, Kathi *state treasurer*
Heitkamp, Heidi *state attorney general*
Jaeger, Alvin A. (Al Jaeger) *secretary of state*
Myrdal, Rosemarie Caryle *state official, former state legislator*
Schafer, Edward T. *governor*

Fargo
Spaeth, Nicholas John *lawyer, former state attorney general*

Grand Forks
Glassheim, Eliot Alan *city manager*

OHIO

Akron
Plusquellic, Donald L. *mayor*
Schrader, Helen Maye *retired municipal worker*

Bellaire
Simpson, Daniel H. *ambassador*

Cincinnati
Qualls, Roxanne *mayor of Cincinnati*
Tihany, Leslie Charles *retired foreign service officer, educator*

Cleveland
Smercina, Charles Joseph *mayor, accountant*
White, Michael Reed *mayor*

Columbus
Fisher, Lee I. *state attorney general*
†Hollister, Nancy *state official*
Lashutka, Gregory S. *mayor, lawyer*
Montgomery, Betty D. *state official, former state legislator*
†Sanders, Ted *state official*
Taft, Bob *state official*
Teater, Dorothy Seath *county official*
Voinovich, George V. *governor*

Portsmouth
Davis, Donald W. *government official*

Toledo
Finkbeiner, Carleton S. (Carty) *mayor*
†Finkbeiner, Carty *mayor*

Wauseon
McNulty, Roberta Jo *educational administrator*

OKLAHOMA

Ada
Anoatubby, Bill *governor*

Lawton
Coffey, Wallace Edward *chairman Comanche Indian tribe*

Norman
Corr, Edwin Gharst *ambassador*

Oklahoma City
Anthony, Robert Holland *state official*
†Cole, Tom *state official*
†Edmondson, Drew *attorney general*
Fallin, Mary Copeland *state official*
Keating, Francis Anthony, II *governor, lawyer*
Kennedy, John H., Jr. *former state official*
Mildren, Jack *lieutenant governor*
Norick, Ronald J. *mayor of Oklahoma City*

Tahlequah
Mankiller, Wilma Pearl *tribal leader*

Tulsa
Savage, M. Susan *mayor*

Wyandotte
†Bearskin, Leaford *chief Wyandotte Nation*

OREGON

Corvallis
Murphy, Thomas Allen *government research administrator, scientist*

Lake Oswego
Gawf, John Lee *foreign service officer*

Portland
Katz, Vera *mayor, former college administrator, state legislator*
Moose, Charles A. *state official*

Salem
Hill, Jim *state official*
Keisling, Phillip Andrew *state official*
†Kitzhaber, John Albert *governor, physician, former state senator*
Kulongoski, Theodore R. *state attorney general*

PENNSYLVANIA

Bristol
Hutton, Ann Hawkes *state official*

Carlisle
Clarke, Walter Sheldon *federal government official, instructor*

Erie
Savocchio, Joyce A. *mayor*

Harrisburg
Banks, Albert Victor, Jr. *government administrator*
†Grant, Robert N. *state official*
Mitchell, Brenda K. *state secretary*
Newsome, William Roy, Jr. *state official*
Preate, Ernest D., Jr. *state attorney general*
Ridge, Thomas Joseph *governor, former congressman*
†Schweiker, Mark S. *lieutenant governor*
Singel, Mark Stephen *state official*

Ligonier
Schmidt, Adolph William *retired ambassador*

Lititz
Koch, Bruce R. *diplomat*

New Florence
Olson, Clinton Louis *foreign service officer, former ambassador*

Newtown
Cohen, Myer *former international organization official*

Newtown Square
Strausz-Hupé, Robert *ambassador, author*

Philadelphia
Corrigan, John Edward *government official*
Goren, Denise Lynne *deputy mayor*
Knapton, David Robert *city planner*
Rendell, Edward Gene *mayor*

Pittsburgh
Donahoe, David Lawrence *state and city official*
Murphy, Thomas J., Jr. *mayor*

State College
Lamb, Robert Edward *diplomat*

University Park
Chang, Parris Hsu-cheng *government official, political science educator, writer*

RHODE ISLAND

Providence
†Almond, Lincoln C. *governor*
Leonard, Barbara M *former secretary of state, federal agency administrator, state agency administrator*
†Mayer, Nancy J. *state official*
Petrocelli, Americo William *higher education commissioner*
Pine, Jeffrey Barry *state attorney general*
Sanderson, Edward French *state official*
Simons, Thomas W., Jr. *ambassador*
Weygand, Robert A. *lieutenant governor, landscape architect*

SOUTH CAROLINA

Columbia
Adams, Weston *diplomat, lawyer*
†Beasley, David Muldrow *governor*
Coble, Bob *city official*
†Condon, Charles Molony *state official, lawyer*
Duffie, Virgil Whatley, Jr. *state official*
Miles, Jim *state official*
Patterson, Grady Leslie, Jr. *state treasurer*
†Peeler, Bob *state official*
Rideoutte, Joseph Green *highways and public transportation administrator*
†Tudor, Donald Norris *state government administrator*
Waites, Candy Yaghjian *former state official*
Walker, Richard Louis *former ambassador, educator, author*

Greenville
Workman, William Douglas, III *mayor*

Hilton Head Island
West, John Carl *lawyer, former ambassador, former governor*

SOUTH DAKOTA

Pierre
Barnett, Mark William *state attorney general*
Hazeltine, Joyce *state official*
Hillard, Carole *state official*

Sioux Falls
†Janklow, William John *governor*

TENNESSEE

Columbia
Chafin, William Vernon, Jr. *public housing manager*

Knoxville
Ashe, Victor Henderson *mayor*

Memphis
Gates, Carolyn Helm *government official*
Herenton, Willie W. *mayor*
Jones, Andrewnetta *county government official*

Nashville
Bredesen, Philip Norman *mayor*
Burson, Charles W. *state attorney general*
Darnell, Riley Carlisle *state government executive, lawyer*
†Dozier, Norman Buck, Jr. *fire chief*
Jordan, Wrenza Lou *chamber of commerce executive*
Sundquist, Donald Kenneth (Don Sundquist) *governor, former congressman, sales corporation executive*
Wilder, John Shelton *lieutenant governor, president senate*

TEXAS

Austin
†Bush, George W. *governor*
Cooke, Carlton Lee, Jr. *mayor*
Johnson, Lady Bird (Mrs. Lyndon Baines Johnson) *widow of former President of U.S.*
Morales, Dan *state attorney general*
Todd, Bruce M. *mayor*

Beaumont
Gray, Enid Maurine *city official, director of libraries*
Lord, Evelyn Marlin *former mayor*

Carrollton
Gravley, Milburn Ray *mayor, investments consultant*

Clarendon
Chamberlain, William Rhode *county official*

Corpus Christi
Rhodes, Mary *mayor*

Dallas
Judy, Nancy Elizabeth *county commissioner*
†Kirk, Ron *mayor, lawyer*
Rubottom, Roy Richard, Jr. *retired diplomat and educator, consultant*

El Paso
Dyer, Travis Neal *defense consultant, retired army officer*
Francis, Larry *mayor*
Jurey, Wes *chamber of commerce executive*

Forney
Cates, Don Tate *mayor, lawyer*

Fort Worth
Bagsby, N. Dionne *county commissioner, speech pathologist*
Granger, Kay *mayor*
Henderson, Suzanne *county government official*
Shosid, Joseph Lewis *government official*

Garland
Smith, Robert Hughes, Jr. (Bob Smith) *municipal official*

Houston
Bush, Barbara Pierce *volunteer, wife of former President of the United States*
Bush, George Herbert Walker *former President of the United States*
Flack, Joe Fenley *county and municipal official, former insurance executive*
Fowler, Robert Asa *consultant, business director, diplomat*
Huffington, Roy Michael *ambassador*
Lanier, Robert C. (Bob Lanier) *mayor*
Mathur, Rupa Ajwani *state official, risk management consultant*
Perry, Cynthia Norton Shepard *diplomat*

Killeen
Villaronga, Raul G. *mayor, realtor*

Laredo
Buckley, Esther Gonzalez-Arroyo *federal commissioner, educator*

Lubbock
Stuart, Frank Adell *county official*

North Richland Hills
Cunningham, Larry J. *city official*

Plano
Peterson, William E. *fire chief, consultant*

San Antonio
Catto, Henry Edward *former government official, former ambassador*
†Thornton, William E. *mayor, oral surgeon*

UTAH

Bountiful
Oveson, W(ilford) Val *state official, accountant*

Ogden
†Evans, Keith Edward *government official, researcher*

Salt Lake City
Alter, Edward T. *state treasurer*
Bean, Scott W. *state education official*
Clark, Deanna Dee *civic leader and volunteer*
Graham, Jan *state attorney general*
Hilbert, Robert Backus *county water utility administrator*
Leavitt, Michael Okerlund *governor, insurance executive*
Walker, Olene S. *lieutenant governor*
White, Constance Burnham *state official*
†White, Victor Dea *airport management executive*

VERMONT

Barre
†Milne, James *secretary of state*

Montpelier
Amestoy, Jeffrey Lee *state attorney general*
Dean, Howard *governor*
Hooper, Don *secretary of state*
Klinck, Patricia Ewasco *state official*
†Mills, Richard *state education official*
Snelling, Barbara *state official*

Peacham
Engle, James Bruce *ambassador*

South Londonderry
Spiers, Ronald Ian *diplomat*

VIRGINIA

Alexandria
Baroody, Michael Elias *public policy institution executive*
†Braley, George Anderson *government official*
Clarey, Donald Alexander *government affairs consultant*
†Clark, Edwin Hill, II *state official*
Conger, Clement Ellis *foreign service officer, curator*
Donnelly, John Francis *government official*
Hagemann, Kenneth L., Sr. *federal official, career officer*
Hampton, E. Lynn *municipal finance administrator*
Havens, Harry Stewart *former federal assistant comptroller general, government consultant*
Helman, Gerald Bernard *government official*
Hilton, Robert Parker, Sr. *national security affairs consultant, retired naval officer*
Moore, Jonathan *diplomat, policy analyst, advisor*
Pringle, Robert Maxwell *diplomat*
Rose, Susan Porter *federal commission administrator*
Scheupelein, Robert John *government official*
Ticer, Patricia *mayor*

Amelia Court House
Wallace, John Robert *county administrator*

Annandale
†Quinn, Kenneth Michael *foreign service officer, international relations educator*
Rogers, Stephen Hitchcock *former ambassador*
Tontz, Robert L. *government official*
Trapnell, Christine *county official*

Arlington
Aggrey, Orison Rudolph *former ambassador, university administrator*
Banister, G. Huntington *federal official*
Barrera, Manuel *foreign service officer*
Bolster, Archie Milburn *retired foreign service officer*
Busby, Morris D. *ambassador*
Cargo, William Ira *ambassador, retired*
Edmondson, William Brockway *retired foreign service officer*
Everett, Warren Sylvester *consultant, former government official*
Fernandez, Henry A. *healthcare administration executive, lawyer*
†Huddle, Franklin Pierce, Jr. *diplomat*
Kaiser, Philip Mayer *diplomat*
Krys, Sheldon Jack *foreign service officer*
†Kull, Joseph *government administrator*
Pyatt, Everett Arno *government official*
Smalley, Robert Manning *government official*
Taylor, Lawrence Palmer *diplomat*
Umminger, Bruce Lynn *government official, scientist, educator*

Charlottesville
Jordan, David Crichton *ambassador, educator*

Fairfax
Beckler, David Zander *government official, science administrator*
Jones, George Fleming *diplomat*

Falls Church
Block, John Rusling *former secretary of agriculture*
de la Colina, Rafael *diplomat*
Palmer, Stephen Eugene, Jr. *government official*

Fincastle
Crow, William Cecil *consultant, former government official*

Fort Belvoir
Diercks, Frederick Otto *government official*

Great Falls
Savage, Michael Thomas *government office executive*
Zimmermann, Warren *former foreign service officer*

Haymarket
†Doolittle, Warren T. *retired federal official*

Herndon
Vogel, Frederick John *diplomat*

King George
Newhall, David, III *former federal government official*

Ladysmith
Provencher, Roger Arthur *international consultant*

Leesburg
Brown, William Holmes *government official, parliamentary consultant*

Lexington
Cash, Frank Errette, Jr. *foreign service officer*

Lynchburg
†Dodge, Lynn Louise *municipal official, librarian*
Stephens, Bart Nelson *former foreign service officer*

Markham
Katzen, Jay Kenneth *consultant, former foreign service officer*

Mc Lean
Berteau, David John *company executive*
Byrnes, Arthur Francis *retired federal official*
Cahill, Harry Amory *diplomat, educator*
Cannon, Mark Wilcox *government official, business executive*
Healy, Theresa Ann *former ambassador*
Houley, William Purcell *federal official, career officer*
Smith, Russell Jack *former intelligence official*
Sollenberger, Howard Edwin *retired government official*
Trout, Maurice Elmore *foreign service officer*

Morattico
Dawson, Carol Gene *former commissioner, writer, consultant*

Norfolk
Andrews, Mason Cooke *mayor, obstetrician, gynecologist, educator*
Bullington, James R. *ambassador*

Orange
Cortada, James N. *mayor, former diplomat*

Reston
Sherman, William Courtney *foreign service officer*

Richmond
Allen, George Felix *governor*
†Beamer, Betsy Davis *state official*
Beyer, Donald Sternoff, Jr. *lieutenant governor*
Bland, Thelma Everson *state commissioner*
†Gilmore, James Stuart, III *state attourney general*
Henderson, Bernard Levie, Jr. *former state official, funeral service executive*
Manning, William Raymond *retired state official*

Springfield
Stottlemyer, David Lee *government official*

Stafford
Wolle, William Down *foreign service officer*

Suffolk
Hope, James Franklin *mayor, civil engineer, consultant*

Susan
Ambach, Dwight Russell *retired foreign service officer*

Virginia Beach
Oberndorf, Meyera E. *mayor*

Washingtons Birthplace
Storke, Dwight Clifton, Jr. *government official*

WASHINGTON

Bainbridge Island
Huntley, James Robert *government official, international affairs scholar and consultant*

Bellevue
Armstrong, Dickwin Dill *chamber of commerce executive*

Dayton
McFarland, Jon Weldon *county commissioner*

Nespelem
†Palmanteer, Eddie Adrian, Jr. *tribal government administrator*

Olympia
†Gardner, Booth *governor*
Gregoire, Christine O. *state attorney general*
Lowry, Mike *governor, former congressman*
Munro, Ralph Davies *state government official*
O'Brien, Robert S. *state official*
Pritchard, Joel *state lieutenant governor*

Seattle
Hague, Jane Frances *county official*
Rice, Norman B. *mayor*

Sequim
†McMahon, Terrence John *foreign service officer*

Spokane
Giller, Edward Bonfoy *retired government official, retired air force officer*

Tacoma
Tullis, David Allen *municipal official, safety consultant*

Vancouver
Ogden, Daniel Miller, Jr. *government official, educator*
†Patella, Lawrence M. *city official*

WEST VIRGINIA

Charleston
Caperton, W. Gaston *governor*
Hechler, Ken *state official, former congressman, political science educator, author*
Mc Graw, Darrell Vivian, Jr. *attorney general*
†Tomblin, Earl Ray *state official*

Shenandoah Junction
Prince, Garnett B., Jr. *business executive*

WISCONSIN

Juneau
Carpenter, David Erwin *county planner*

Madison
Doyle, James E(dward) *state attorney general*
Earl, Anthony Scully *former governor*
La Follette, Douglas J. *secretary of state*
McCallum, James Scott *lieutenant governor, former state senator*
†McCallum, Scott *state official*
Thompson, Tommy George *governor*
Zaleski, Michael Louis *state official, lawyer*
Zobel, Robert Leonard *state government official*

Milwaukee
Ament, F. Thomas *county government official*
Norquist, John Olof *mayor*

Woodruff
Nicolette, Archie John *local government official, retired secondary education educator*

WYOMING

Cheyenne
†Geringer, James E. *governor*
Meyer, Joseph B. *state attorney general*
Ohman, Diana J. *state official, former school system administrator*
Schaeffer, Gary N. *mayor*
Smith, Stanford Sidney *state treasurer*
Thomson, Thyra Godfrey *former state official*
Wittler, Shirley Joyce *former state official, state commissioner*

Laramie
Dickman, Francois Moussiegt *former foreign service officer*

TERRITORIES OF THE UNITED STATES

AMERICAN SAMOA

Pago Pago
†Lutali, A. P. *governor of American Samoa*
†Sunia, Tausese *government official*

FEDERATED STATES OF MICRONESIA

Kolonia, Pohnpei
Eu, March Fong *U.S. ambassador, former state official*

Ponape
Ramon, Kohne K. *federal official*
Weilbacher, Robert James *Micronesian goverment official*

GUAM

Agana
Bordallo, Madeleine Mary (Mrs. Ricardo Jerome Bordallo) *lieutenant governor of Guam, wife of former governor of Guam*
Shelton, Austin James (Sonny Shelton) *territorial legislator*

NORTHERN MARIANA ISLANDS

Saipan
Guerrero, Juan Tenorio *territorial senator*
†Manglona, Benjamin T. *commonwealth official*

PUERTO RICO

San Juan
Acevedo, Héctor Luis *mayor*
Corrada del Río, Baltasar *state official, lawyer, former mayor, former congressman*
Cruz-Velez, David Francisco *senator*
Myatt, Clifford E. *federal official*
Pesquera Morales, Carlos I. *government official*

REPUBLIC OF MARSHALL ISLAND

Majuro
Fields, David Clark *diplomat*
Lemari, Kunio David *federal official*
Note, Kessai H. *federal official*

VIRGIN ISLANDS

Christiansted
†Mapp, Kenneth E. *lieutenant governor*

Saint Thomas
†Ballentine, Rosalie S. *attorney general*

MILITARY ADDRESSES OF THE UNITED STATES

ATLANTIC

APO
Adams, Alvin Philip, Jr. *diplomat, lawyer*
Bracete, Juan Manuel *diplomat, lawyer*
Brown, Richard C. *ambassador*
Carner, George *foreign service executive, economic strategist*
†Cason, James Caldwell *diplomat*
Cheek, James Richard *ambassador*
Davidow, Jeffrey *ambassador*
de Vos, Peter Jon *ambassador*
†Frechette, Myles Robert Rene *ambassador*
Hinton, Deane Roesch *ambassador*
†Keane, John Francis *diplomat*
Mc Afee, Marilyn *ambassador*
Melton, Richard H. *diplomat*
Pastorino, Robert Stephen *diplomat, ambassador*
Pryce, William Thornton *foreign service officer*

Romero, Peter Frank *diplomat*
Sanbrailo, John A. *mission director*
Taylor, Paul Daniel *ambassador*
†Taylor, Philip Bates, III *diplomat*
Walker, William Graham *ambassador*
Whitman, Gerald John *diplomat*

FPO
Hyde, Jeanette W. *ambassador*

EUROPE

APO
Aaron, David L. *diplomat*
Basora, Adrian A. *ambassador*
†Benedict, Lawrence Neal *foreign service officer*
Berry, Ann Roper *diplomat*
†Bindenagel, James Dale *diplomat*
Blinken, Donald *ambassador, investment banker*
Briggs, Everett Ellis *ambassador*
Brown, William Andreas *ambassador*
†Connell, Mary Ellen *diplomat*
†Creagan, James Francis *diplomat*
Davis, John Roger, Jr. *foreign service officer*
Eizenstat, Stuart E. *ambassador, lawyer*
Elson, Edward Elliott *diplomat*
†Evans, John Marshall *diplomat*
Flynn, Raymond Leo *ambassador to the Holy See, former mayor*
†Ginsberg, Marc C. *ambassador*
†Greenlee, David Nicol *foreign service officer*
Harriman, Pamela Digby Churchill *diplomat, philanthropist*
†Harris, William Thomas, III *diplomat*
†Holmes, James Howard *diplomat*
Hurwitz, Edward *ambassador to Kyrgyzstan*
Johnson, Darryl Norman *ambassador*
Kennedy, Mary Virginia *diplomat*
Klosson, Michael *foreign service officer*
Loftus, Thomas Adolph *ambassador*
Mabus, Raymond Edwin, Jr. *ambassador, former governor*
Miles, Richard *diplomat*
†Montgomery, William D. *United States ambassador*
Niles, Thomas Michael Tolliver *ambassador*
Norris, James Arnold *government executive*
Petterson, Donald K. *foreign service officer, ambassador*
Pickering, Thomas Reeve *diplomat*
Rey, Nicholas Andrew *ambassador*
Ryerson, William Edwin *diplomat*
Secchia, Peter F. *ambassador*
Stokes, Carl Burton *ambassador, judge, former mayor, former state legislator*
Stone, Richard B. *ambassador*
†Tompkins, Tain Pendleton *foreign service official*
Walker, Edward S., Jr. *diplomat*
†Wardlaw, Frank Patterson *foreign service officer*
Welch, Charles David *diplomat*
Westley, John Richard *foreign service officer*
Yates, John Melvin *diplomat*

FPO
Boucher, Richard A. *ambassador*
Crocker, Ryan C. *ambassador*
†Ransom, David Michael *diplomat*

PACIFIC

APO
Barry, Robert Louis *diplomat*
Blackburn, Paul Pritchard *diplomat*
Burghardt, Raymond Francis, Jr. *foreign service officer*
†Harvey, Barbara Sillars *foreign service officer*
Lambertson, David Floyd *ambassador*
Monjo, John Cameron *ambassador*
Smith, Myron George *former government official, consultant*
Tomseth, Victor L *ambassador*
Tull, Theresa Anne *ambassador*
Wolf, John S. *ambassador*
†Yamamoto, Donald Yukio *diplomat*

FPO
Chorba, Timothy A. *ambassador to Singapore*
Hall, James Henry *foreign service officer*

CANADA

ALBERTA

Calgary
†Duerr, Alfred *mayor*

Carstairs
Osterman, Constantine Elaine *Canadian legislator*

Edmonton
Forsyth, Joseph *Canadian government official*
Isley, Ernest D. *Canadian provincial official*
Johnston, Dick *Canadian provincial government minister*
Main, Douglas Cameron *provincial cabinet minister*
Rostad, Kenneth Leif *provincial government official*
Speaker, Ray *Canadian government official*
†Towers, Gordon Thomas *province official*
Towers, T. Gordon *Canadian lieutenant governor*

BRITISH COLUMBIA

Kaleden
Siddon, Thomas Edward *Canadian government official, environmental consultant*

Richmond
†Halsey-Brandt, Greg *mayor*
Johnston, Rita Margaret *Canadian provincial government official*

Vancouver
†Gallagher, Michael Francis *diplomat*
†Owen, Philip Walter *mayor, business owner*

Victoria
†Gabelmann, Colin *provincial attorney general*
Gardom, Garde Basil *Canadian government official*
Harcourt, Michael Franklin *premier of Province of British Columbia*
Lam, David C. *lieutenant governor*

MANITOBA

Winnipeg
Curtis, Charles Edward *Canadian government official*
Ducharme, Gerry *minister of urban affairs*
Dumont, W. Yvon *provincial official*
Filmon, Gary Albert *Canadian provincial premier, civil engineer*
McGonigal, Pearl *former lieutenant governor*
†Vodrey, Rosemary *province attorney general*

NEW BRUNSWICK

Dieppe
Finn, Gilbert *lieutenant governor*

Fredericton
†McCain, Norrie *province official*

NEWFOUNDLAND

Saint John's
May, Arthur W. *former Canadian government official, educator*
Murphy, John Joseph *city official, retail executive*
†Roberts, Edward Moxon *Canadian government official, lawyer, politician*
Russell, Frederick William *Canadian provincial official*
Wells, Clyde Kirby *Canadian provincial government official*

NORTHWEST TERRITORIES

Yellowknife
Cournoyea, Nellie J. *Canadian government official*
Kakfwi, Stephen *Canadian government official*

NOVA SCOTIA

Halifax
†Kinley, John James *province official*
Savage, John P. *provincial official*

ONTARIO

Brampton
†Robertson, Peter Barrie *mayor*

Hamilton
St. Aubin, J. Arthur *Canadian federal agency executive*

Maberly
Kennett, William Alexander *retired Canadian government official, consultant*

Manotick
Prince, Alan Theodore *former government official, engineering consultant*

Mississauga
†McCallion, Hazel *mayor*

Nobleton
Embleton, Tony Frederick Wallace *retired Canadian government official*

North York
Lastman, Melvin D. *mayor*

Ottawa
Anderson, David *Canadian government official*
Armstrong, Henry Conner *former Canadian government official, consultant*
†Axworthy, Chris *Canadian government official*
Axworthy, Lloyd *Canadian government official*
Barnhart, Gordon *Canadian government official*
†Beck, John Ryder *ambassador*
Beehan, Cathy *government official, lawyer*
†Bélisle, Paul *Canadian government official*
Blanchard, James Johnston *ambassador, former governor of Michigan*
Bouchard, Lucien *Canadian legislator*
Chan, Raymond *Canadian government official*
Charest, Jean J. *Canadian government official, legislator*
Chrétien, (Joseph Jacques) Jean *prime minister of Canada, lawyer*
Clark, Charles Joseph (Joe Clark) *Canadian government official, former prime minister*
Collenette, David M. *Canadian government official*
Copps, Sheila Maureen *Canadian government official*
Corkery, James Caldwell *Canadian government executive, mechanical engineer*
†Desautels, L. Denis *Canadian government official, auditor*
†Dodge, David A. *Canadian government official*
Finestone, Sheila *Canadian government official*
Fraser, John Allen *Canadian government official*
Gerrard, Jon *Canadian government official*
Giroux, Robert-Jean-Yvon *Canadian government official*
Gold, Lorne W. *Canadian government official*
Goldbloom, Victor Charles *commissioner, pediatrician*
Goodale, Ralph E. *Canadian government official*
Grace, John William *Canadian government official*
Gray, Herbert Eser *Canadian government official*
Halstead, John G. H. *educator, diplomat, consultant*
Holzman, Jacquelin *mayor*
Howe, Bruce Iver *government official*
Kingsley, Jean-Pierre *government official*
Kirkwood, David Herbert Waddington *Canadian government official*
†Lanthier, Claude *Canadian government official*
LaRocque, Judith Anne *federal official*
†LeBlanc, Roméo *Canadian government official*
Lewis, Douglas Grinslade *Canadian minister, parliament member*
†MacDonald, Flora Isabel *Canadian government official*
MacLaren, Roy *publisher, Canadian federal legislator*
Manley, John *Canadian government official*
Marchi, Sergio Sisto *Canadian government official*
Marleau, Diane *Canadian government official*
Martin, Paul *Canadian government official*
Massé, Marcel *Canadian government official*
McGrath, James Aloysius *Canadian provincial official*
McLellan, A. Anne *Canadian government official*
Ouellet, André *Canadian government official*
Pepin, Jean-Luc *retired Canadian government official, political science lecturer*
Peters, Douglas Dennison *Canadian government official, member of Parliament*
Poulin, Marie-Paule *Canadian government official*
Robertson, Robert Gordon *retired Canadian government official*
Robichaud, Fernand *Canadian government official*
Rock, Allan Michael *Canadian government official*
Roland, Anne *registrar Supreme Court of Canada*
Smith, Wilfred Irvin *former Canadian government official*
†Spicer, Keith *federal official, journalist, educator*
Stanford, Joseph Stephen *diplomat, lawyer, educator*
Stewart, Christine Susan *Canadian government official*
Tait, John Charles *Canadian government official*
Tobin, Brian *Canadian government official*
Watt, Robert Douglas *Canadian government official*
Weiner, Gerry *government official*
Withers, Ramsey Muir *government consultant, former government official*
Yalden, Maxwell Freeman *Canadian diplomat*
Yeomans, Donald Ralph *Canadian government official, consultant*
Young, Douglas *Canadian government official*

Stevensville
Stevens, Sinclair McKnight *Canadian government official*

Thunder Bay
Masters, Jack Gerald *mayor*

Toronto
†Boyd, Marion *provincial attorney general*
Caplan, Elinor *Canadian provincial legislator, former cabinet minister*
Carnegie, James Gordon *association executive*
Evans, Gregory Thomas *commissioner, retired justice*
Gotlieb, Allan E. *former ambassador*
Jackman, Henry Newton Rowell *Canadian provincial official*
Mc Gibbon, Pauline Mills *former Canadian government official, former university chancellor*
Rae, Robert Keith *Canadian premier of Ontario*
Redway, Alan Arthur Sydney *Canadian legislator, lawyer*
Turner, John Napier *former prime minister of Canada, legislator*

PRINCE EDWARD ISLAND

Charlottetown
†Buchanan, Alan *provincial attorney general*
Callbeck, Catherine S. *Canadian government official*
MacAulay, Lawrence A. *Canadian government official*
Reid, Marion L. *lieutenant governor, educator*

QUEBEC

Hull
Blondin-Andrew, Ethel *Canadian government official*
Dupuy, Michel *Canadian government official*
Irwin, Ronald A. *Canadian government official*

Montreal
Dingwall, David C. *Canadian government official*
Mulroney, (Martin) Brian *former prime minister of Canada*
†Parizeau, Jacques *Canadian government official*

Nemaska
†Coon Come, Matthew *Native American tribal chief*

Outremont
Bourassa, Robert *former Premier of Québec*

Quebec
Asselin, Martial *Canadian lieutenant governor*
†Huhtala, Marie Therese *diplomat*
†L'Allier, Jean-Paul *mayor*

SASKATCHEWAN

Regina
†Mitchell, Robert *province official*
Rolfes, Herman Harold *Canadian government official*
Romanow, Roy John *provincial government official, barrister, solicitor*
†Wiebe, J. E. N. *province official*

Saskatoon
Blakeney, Allan Emrys *Canadian government official, lawyer*

YUKON TERRITORY

Whitehorse
Ostashek, John *government leader*
Penikett, Antony David John *Canadian government official*
Phelps, Willard *Canadian government official*

MEXICO

Mexico City
Aspe, Pedro *Mexican government official*
Jones, James Robert *ambassador, former congressman, lawyer*
†Ruano Angulo, Luis Carlos *secretary of Mexican navy*
Solana Morales, Fernando *diplomat, financier, educator*
†Zedillo Ponce de León, Ernesto *president of Mexico*

Monterrey
Rizzo, Socrates *Mexican governor*

ARMENIA

Yerevan
Gilmore, Harry J. *ambassador*

AUSTRIA

Vienna
Hunt, Swanee G. *ambassador*
Jackovich, Victor *ambassador*

BAHAMAS

Nassau
†Ford, John Seabury *diplomat*

BANGLADESH

Dhaka
†Merrill, David Nathan *ambassador*

BARBADOS

Bridgetown
Barrow, Dame Ruth Nita *governor general*
Hughes, G. Philip *diplomat*

BELARUS

Minsk
Swartz, David H. *ambassador*

BELGIUM

Brussels
Hunter, Robert Edwards *ambassador, diplomat*

BOLIVIA

La Paz
Bowers, Charles R. *ambassador*
Kamman, Curtis Warren *ambassador*

BOTSWANA

Gaborone
Temane, Bahitik *government executive*

CAMEROON

Yaounde
†Hughes, Morris Nelson, Jr. *foreign service officer*

CAPE VERDE

Praia
McNamara, Francis T. *ambassador*
Segars, Joseph M. *ambassador*

CENTRAL AFRICAN REPUBLIC

Bangui
Gribbin, Robert E., III *ambassador*

CHAD

N'Djamena
Pope, Laurence E., II *ambassador*
†Williams, Anne M. *diplomat, lawyer*

CHILE

Santiago
Wilkey, Malcolm Richard *retired ambassador, former federal judge*

CHINA

Beijing
Roy, J(ames) Stapleton *ambassador*

CROATIA

Zagreb
Galbraith, Peter W. *ambassador*

EGYPT

Addis Ababa
†Hicks, Irvin *ambassador*

EL SALVADOR

San Salvador
Alfaro-Pineda, Rafael Angel *diplomat*

ENGLAND

London
Crowe, William James, Jr. *diplomat*
Deal, Timothy *diplomat, government executive*
Dehennin, Herman Baron *diplomat*
Elizabeth, Her Majesty II (Elizabeth Alexandra Mary) *Queen of United Kingdom of Great Britain and Northern Ireland, and her other Realms and Territories, head of the Commonwealth, defender of the faith*
Marsden, William *government official*
Streator, Edward *diplomat*

FRANCE

Beduer
Ezelle, Robert Eugene *diplomat*

Paris
Cornell, Robert Arthur *international government official*
Dean, John Gunther *diplomat*
†Doyle, Anne Marie *ambassador*
Ferriter, John Pierce *diplomat*
Larson, Alan Philip *federal official*
Michel, James H. *ambassador, lawyer*
Myerson, Jacob Myer *former foreign service officer*
Roudybush, Franklin *diplomat, educator*
Roussel, Lee Dennison *diplomat*

Strasbourg
Barnes, Shirley Elizabeth *foreign service officer*

GABON

Libreville
Wauchope, Keith L. *diplomat*

GERMANY

Berlin
Anderson, David *former ambassador*

Bonn
Redman, Charles Edgar *diplomat*

GHANA

Accra
Brown, Kenneth L. *ambassador*

GREECE

Athens
Chytiris, Tilemachos *federal official*

GRENADA

Saint George's
†Anderson, Ollie Palmer, Jr. *diplomat*

GUINEA

Conakry
Saloom, Joseph A., III *diplomat*

HONG KONG

Hong Kong
Mueller, Richard Walter *foreign service officer*

INDIA

New Delhi
Wisner, Frank George *ambassador*

INDONESIA

Surabaya
†Eaton, Mark Craig *diplomat*

IRELAND

Dublin
Smith, Jean Kennedy *ambassador*

ISRAEL

Jerusalem
Abington, Edward Gordon, Jr. *diplomat*

ITALY

Rome
Cassiers, Juan *diplomat*
Keniaykin, Valery Fedorovich *Russian diplomat*
Marchand, J. C. de Montigny *Canadian public servant*

JAPAN

Tokyo
Armacost, Michael Hayden *ambassador, government official*
Michaud, Michael Alan George *diplomat, writer*

KENYA

Nairobi
Brazeal, Aurelia Erskine *ambassador*

KOREA

Pusan
†Kloth, Edward William, Jr. *diplomat*

LATVIA

Riga
Silins, Ints M. *ambassador*

LEBANON

Beirut
Hambley, Mark Gregory *ambassador*

MAURITANIA

Nouackchott
Brown, Gordon Stewart *diplomat*

MOROCCO

Casablanca
Cary, Anne O. *diplomat*

MOZAMBIQUE

Maputo
Jon de Vos, Peter *former U.S. ambassador to Mozambique*

THE NETHERLANDS

The Hague
Wilkins, C. Howard, Jr. *diplomat*

NEW ZEALAND

Wellington
Newman, Della M. *ambassador*

NIGER

Niamey
Davison, John S. *ambassador*

NIGERIA

Lagos
Carrington, Walter C. *ambassador*

PAKISTAN

Peshawar
†Smyth, Richard Henry *foreign service officer*

SIERRA LEONE

Freetown
Peters, Lauralee Milberg *diplomat*
†Ray, Charles Aaron *foreign service officer*

SINGAPORE

Singapore
Skodon, Emil Mark *diplomat*

SOUTH AFRICA

Johannesburg
†McKee, Alan Reel *foreign service officer*

SRI LANKA

Colombo
Schaffer, Teresita Currie *federal official*

SWEDEN

Stockholm
Siebert, Thomas L. *ambassador to Sweden*

SWITZERLAND

Bern
Lawrence, M. Larry *ambassador*

Chambesy
†Spiegel, Daniel L. *diplomat*

Geneva
Bogsch, Arpad *diplomat*
Ledogar, Stephen J. *diplomat*

THAILAND

Bangkok
Carlson, Mitchell Lans *international technical advisor*

TRINIDAD AND TOBAGO

Port of Spain
Cowal, Sally Grooms *diplomat*

UKRAINE

Kiev
Miller, William Green *ambassador*

ADDRESS UNPUBLISHED

Adams, Edwin Melville *former foreign service officer, actor, author, lecturer*
Adams, James Blackburn *former state government official, former federal government official, lawyer*
Addiss, Susan Silliman *state government administrator*
Agnew, Spiro Theodore *former Vice President of U.S.*
Al-Sabah, Saud Nasir *diplomat, barrister*
Anderson, John Rogers *Canadian diplomat*
Anderson, Nils, Jr. *former government official, retired business executive, industrial historian*
Argun, Fatima Hatice *international consultant, specialist*
Armstrong, Anne Legendre (Mrs. Tobin Armstrong) *former ambassador, corporate director*
Austin, Richard H. *retired state official*
Baker, Gwendolyn Calvert *United Nations official*
Barkley, Richard Clark *ambassador*
Bentsen, Lloyd *former government official, former senator*
Betti, John Anso *federal official, former automobile manufacturing company executive*
Beyer, Gordon Robert *foreign service officer*
Black, Shirley Temple (Mrs. Charles A. Black) *former ambassador, former actress*
Blood, Archer Kent *retired foreign service officer*
Bolen, David B. *ambassador, former corporation executive*
Boyatt, Thomas David *former ambassador*
Brady, Nicholas Frederick *former secretary of treasury*
Buchanan, John MacLennan *Canadian provincial official*
Burchman, Leonard *government official*
Burney, Derek H. *ambassador*
Campbell, Avril Kim *Canadian legislator, justice official*
Cannon, Isabella Walton *mayor*
Carter, Rosalynn Smith *wife of former President of U.S.*
Clark, William, Jr. *ambassador*
Clarke, Henry Lee *ambassador, U.S. foreign service officer*
Coburn, Harry L. *foreign service officer*
Condayan, John *foreign service officer*
Coop, Frederick Robert *retired city manager*
Coppie, Comer Swift *state official*
Cougill, Roscoe McDaniel *mayor, retired air force officer*
Curtis, Peter Campbell John *retired diplomat*
Daub, Hal *mayor of Omaha, former congressman*
†Davis, Martis James *government official*
Dawson, Horace Greeley, Jr. *former diplomat, government official*
Donahue, Dennis Donald *foreign service officer*
Donohue, George L. *government official, mechanical engineer*
Donovan, Walter Edgar *retired mayor*
Douglas, James Holley *former state official*
Drabble, Bernard James *Canadian government official*
Dunford, David Joseph *foreign service officer, ambassador*
Dykhouse, David Jay *commissioner, lawyer*
Eagleton, William Lester, Jr. *foreign service officer*
Eastham, Alan Walter, Jr. *foreign service officer, lawyer*
Egan, Wesley William, Jr. *ambassador*
Eisenhower, John Sheldon Doud *former ambassador, author*
Emmons, Robert Duncan *diplomat*
Engler, John *governor*
Ewing, Raymond Charles *retired ambassador*
Ford, Ford Barney *retired government official*
Fraser, Donald MacKay *former mayor, former congressman*
Freestone, Thomas Lawrence *county government official*
†Friedkin, Dawn Michele *government official*
Frith, Royce Herbert *Canadian federal official, former Canadian senator, retired lawyer*
Fugh, John Liu *military officer, lawyer*
†Gamble, Roger R. *ambassador*
Gerard, Jean Broward Shevlin *former ambassador, lawyer*
Gewecke, Thomas H. *foreign service officer*
Glassman, Jon David *diplomat*
Gumppert, Karella Ann *federal government official*
Gutierrez, Lino *diplomat*
Hamilton, Donald Reed *foreign service officer*
Hanmer, Stephen Read, Jr. *government executive*
Hecht, Chic *ambassador, former senator*
Holiday, Edith Elizabeth *former presidential adviser, cabinet secretary*
Horan, Hume Alexander *diplomat, association executive*
Hornblow, Michael M. *diplomat*
Humphrey, Karen Michael *former mayor*
Jacobson, Herbert Laurence *diplomat*
Jarvis, William Esmond *Canadian government official*
Johnson, Donald C. *ambassador to Mongolia*
Kendig, William L. *retired government official, accountant*
Kendrick, Joseph Trotwood *former foreign service officer, writer, consultant*
Kernan, Barbara Desind *senior government executive*
King, James B. *federal official*
Kissinger, Henry Alfred *former secretary of state, international consulting company executive*
Korn, Peter A. *city manager, public administration educator*
Kulstad, Guy Charles *public works official*
Laney, James Thomas *ambassador, educator*
Lee, James Matthew *Canadian politician*
Levitsky, Melvyn *ambassador*
Levy, Leah Garrigan *federal official*
Lindsay, John Vliet *former mayor, former congressman, author, lawyer*
Lord, Winston *diplomat*
Luche, Thomas Clifford *foreign service officer*
†Lux, Michael Scott *federal government official*
Lyng, Richard Edmund *former secretary of agriculture*
MacLean, John Angus *former premier of Prince Edward Island*
Maestrone, Frank Eusebio *diplomat*
Marvin, William Glenn, Jr. *former foreign service officer*
Mattingly, Mack F. *former US ambassador, former US senator, entrepreneur*
Mazankowski, Donald Frank *Canadian government official*
McLean, Walter Franklin *international consultant, pastor, former Canadian government official*
Medlock, Thomas Travis *lawyer*
Mendonsa, Arthur Adonel *city official*
Millson, John Arthur *former mayor*
Mondale, Walter Frederick *former vice president of United States, diplomat, lawyer*
Moore, Powell Allen *former government official, consultant*
Morgan, William Douglass *diplomat*
Morris, Robert G(emmill) *retired foreign service officer*
Neff, Francine Irving (Mrs. Edward John Neff) *former federal government official*
Negroponte, John Dimitri *diplomat*
Nelson, Harvey Frans, Jr. *retired foreign service officer*
Nightingale, Retha Lee *federal agency administrator*
Ogg, George Wesley *retired foreign service officer*
Orr, Robert Dunkerson *diplomat, former governor*
Ortiz, Francis Vincent, Jr. *retired ambassador*
Petika, David M. *municipal government official, editor*
Petrequin, Harry Joseph, Jr. *foreign service officer*
Pierce, Samuel Riley, Jr. *government official, lawyer*
Pridmore, Roy Davis *government official*
Raynolds, Harold, Jr. *retired state education commissioner*
Reich, Robert Bernard *U.S. secretary of labor, political economics educator*
Reinhardt, John Edward *former international affairs specialist*
Reynolds, Carl Christiansen *government official*
Rice, Richard Campbell *retired state official, retired army officer*
Rich, David Barry *city official, auditor, accountant, entertainer*
Rickert, Jonathan Bradley *foreign service officer*
Roberts, Thomas Morgan *federal official*
Rockefeller, Margaretta Fitler Murphy (Happy Rockefeller) *widow of former vice president of U.S.*
Rohatsch, Ralph R., Jr. (Bob Rohatsch, Jr.) *career military officer*
Rosenthal, Helen Nagelberg *county official, advocate*
Rossellō, Pedro J. *governor of Puerto Rico*
Rothing, Frank John *government official*
Rudin, Anne Noto *former mayor, nurse*
Ryan, George H. *secretary of state, pharmacist*
Sabatini, Nelson John *government official*
Salinas de Gortari, Carlos *former president of Mexico*
Scanlan, John Douglas *foreign service officer, former ambassador*
Schoettler, Gail Sinton *state official*
Sentenne, Justine *corporate ombudsman*
Simmons, Joseph Jacob, III *federal commissioner*
Snider, L. Britt *government executive*
Sotirhos, Michael *ambassador*
Soule, Sallie Thompson *retired state official*
Spearman, Leonard H. O., Sr. *ambassador*
Taylor, Barbara Jo Anne Harris *government official, librarian, educator, civic and political worker*
Thiounn, Prasith *foreign service official*
Tienken, Arthur T. *retired foreign service officer*
Vaky, Viron Peter *diplomacy educator, former foreign service officer*
Walters, Vernon Anthony *ambassador*
Wolf, Dale Edward *state official*
Wright, Sir (John) Oliver *retired diplomat*
Zischke, Douglas Arthur *foreign service officer*

GOVERNMENT: LEGISLATIVE ADMINISTRATION

UNITED STATES

ALABAMA

Birmingham
Allen, Maryon Pittman *former senator, journalist, lecturer, interior and clothing designer*

Mobile
Bedsole, Ann Smith *state senator*
Callahan, H. L. (Sonny Callahan) *congressman*
Edwards, Jack *former congressman, lawyer*

Montgomery
Clark, James S. *state legislator*
Dixon, Larry Dean *state legislator*
Langford, Charles Douglas *state legislator, lawyer*
Mitchell, Alfred Henry *state government official*
Walker, Claud Ladale, Sr. *state representative*

Phenix City
Corbett, James Daniel (Danny) *state senator*

Selma
Goodwin, Earl *state senator*
Sanders, Hank *state senator, lawyer*

ALASKA

Anchorage
Barnes, Ramona *state legislator*
Hensley, William L. *state senator, corporate executive*
Toohey, Cynthia D. *state legislator*

Eagle River
Cotten, Samuel Richard *former state legislator, fisherman*
Willis, Edward Charles *legislator*

Fairbanks
Brice, Tom Luther *state legislator*

Homer
Phillips, Gail *state legislator*

Juneau
Grussendorf, Benjamin Franklin, Jr. *state house speaker*
Kelly, Timothy Donahue *state senator*
Mulder, Eldon Paul *state legislator, real estate agent*
Pearce, Drue *state legislator*
Rieger, Steven Arthur *state legislator, business consultant*

North Pole
James, Jeannette Adeline *state legislator, accountant*

ARIZONA

Phoenix
Aguirre, Linda G. *state legislator*
Alston, Lela *state senator*
Brewer, Janice Kay *state legislator*
Burns, Brenda *state legislator*
Cajero, Carmen *state legislator*
Kyle, Richard Daniel *state legislator, fundraising consultant*
Pena, Manuel, Jr. *state senator*
Preble, Lou-Ann M. *state legislator*
Turner, Warren Austin *state legislator*

Queen Creek
Sossaman, James J. *state legislator*

Scottsdale
Goldwater, Barry Morris *former senator*
Pritzlaff, John Charles, Jr. *former state senator*
Rudd, Eldon *retired congressman*

Sun City West
Smith, Virginia Dodd (Mrs. Haven Smith) *congresswoman*

Tucson
Bartlett, David Carson *state legislator*

ARKANSAS

Dumas
Schexnayder, Charlotte Tillar *state legislator*

Fayetteville
Malone, David Roy *university administrator, state senator*

Fort Smith
Pollan, Carolyn Joan *state legislator, job research administrator*

Greenwood
Walters, Bill *state senator, lawyer*

Hamburg
Murphy, N. B. (Nap Murphy) *state congressman, automobile dealer*

Little Rock
Brandon, Doug *state senator*
Hinshaw, Jerrold Eldon *state legislator*
Roberts, Jacqueline *state legislator, political consultant*

Malvern
Hopkins, George *senator*

Russellville
Hardin, Luther *state senator*

Searcy
Beebe, Mike *state senator, lawyer*

Sherwood
Wood, Marion Douglas *state legislator, lawyer*

CALIFORNIA

Balboa Island
Badham, Robert E. *former congressman*

Fresno
Krebs, John H. *former congressman*

Glendale
Russell, Newton Requa *state senator*

Inglewood
Dymally, Mervyn Malcolm *retired congressman, international business executive*

Los Angeles
Hayden, Tom *state legislator, author*

Modesto
Snyder, Margaret Elizabeth *assemblywoman, paralegal*

Newport Beach
Cox, Christopher *congressman*

Palm Desert
Hunter, Patricia Rae *state legislator, nurse*

Roseville
Leslie, (Robert) Tim *state legislator*

Sacramento
Boatwright, Daniel E. *state legislator*
Brown, Valerie *state legislator*
Brown, Willie Lewis, Jr. *state legislator, lawyer*
Connolly, Tom M. *state legislator, lawyer*
Cortese, Dominic L. *state legislator, farmer*
Holmes, Robert Eugene *state legislative consultant, journalist*
Hughes, Teresa P. *state legislator*
Knight, William J. (Pete Knight) *state legislator, retired military officer*
Napolitano, Grace F. *state legislator*
Presley, Robert Buel *state senator*

San Diego
Alpert, Deirdre Whittleton *state legislator*

San Francisco
Cranston, Alan *former senator*

COLORADO

Colorado Springs
Wells, Jeffrey M. *state senator, lawyer, judge*

Denver
Adkins, Jeanne M. *state legislator*
Allen, Deborah Colleen *state legislator*
Berry, Charles Eugene (Chuck Berry) *state legislator*
Bishop, Tilman Malcolm *state senator, retired college administrator*
Faatz, Jeanne Ryan *state legislator*
Gallagher, Dennis Joseph *state senator, educator*
Lyle, Glenda Swanson *state legislator*
Meiklejohn, Alvin J., Jr. *state senator, lawyer, accountant*
Morrison, Marcy *state legislator*
Norton, Thomas Edmond *state senator, engineer*
Schaffer, Robert Warren *state senator*
Tanner, Gloria Geraldine *state legislator*
Taylor-Little, Carol J(oyce) *legislator*
Wham, Dorothy Stonecipher *state legislator*

Englewood
Hart, Gary W. *former senator, lawyer*

Golden
Hopper, Sally *state legislator*

CONNECTICUT

Bristol
Krawiecki, Edward C., Jr. *state legislator, lawyer*

Glastonbury
Googins, Sonya Forbes *state legislator, retired banker*

Hartford
DePino, Chris Anthoney *state legislator*
Flaherty, Patrick John *state legislator, economist*
Gill, Margaret S. *state legislator*
Gunther, George Lackman *state senator, natureopathic physician, retired*
Hess, Marilyn Ann *state legislator*
Joyce, Raymond M. H. *state legislator*
Maloney, James Henry *state senator, lawyer*
Mattiello, Brian Edward *state legislator*
Meotti, Michael Patrick *state legislator, lawyer*
Mushinsky, Mary M. *state legislator*
Simmons, Robert Ruhl *state legislator, educator*
Upson, Thomas Fisher *state legislator, lawyer*
Young, Leslie Towner *state legislator, stockbroker*

New Haven
Krevit, Rita Recha *alderwoman, retired business owner*
Stolberg, Irving J. *state legislator, consultant*

Southbury
O'Neill, Arthur Julius *state legislator, lawyer*

Stratford
Chase, J. Vincent *state legislator, shopping center executive*

Vernon Rockville
Herbst, Marie Antoinette *former state senator*

Wallingford
Fritz, Mary G. *state legislator*

West Hartford
Streeter, Anne Paul *state senator*

Westport
Freedman, Judith Greenberg *state senator, importer*

DELAWARE

Dover
Hedrick, JoAnn M. *legislative staff member*
Vaughn, James T. *former state police officer, state senator*

Newark
Neal, James Preston *state senator, project engineer*

Wilmington
Amick, Steven Hammond *lawyer, senator*

DISTRICT OF COLUMBIA

Washington
Abercrombie, Neil *congressman*
†Abraham, Spencer *senator*
Ackerman, Gary Leonard *congressman*
Akaka, Daniel Kahikina *senator*
Allard, Wayne A. *congressman, veterinarian*
Anderson, Debra R. *state representative*
Andrews, Robert E. *congressman*
Archer, William Reynolds, Jr. (Bill Reynolds) *congressman*
Armey, Richard Keith *congressman*
†Ashcroft, John David *senator*
†Baca, Polly *state senator*
Bachus, Spencer T., III *congressman, lawyer*
Baesler, Scotty *congressman*
Baker, William P. (Bill Baker) *congressman*
†Baldacci, John Elias *congressman*
Ballenger, Thomas Cass *congressman*
Barcia, James A. *congressman*
†Barr, Robert Laurence, Jr. *congressman, lawyer*
Barrett, Thomas M. *congressman*
Barrett, William E. *congressman*
Bartlett, Roscoe G. *congressman*
†Bass, Charles F. *congressman*
Bateman, Herbert Harvell *congressman*
Baucus, Max S. *senator*
Baumgartner, Eileen Mary *government official*
Becerra, Xavier *congressman, lawyer*
Beilenson, Anthony Charles *congressman*
Bennett, Robert F. *senator*
†Bentsen, Ken, Jr. *congressman*
Bereuter, Douglas Kent *congressman*
Berman, Howard Lawrence *congressman*
Bevill, Tom *congressman, lawyer*
Biden, Joseph Robinette, Jr. *senator*
†Bilbray, Brain P. *congressmant*
Bilirakis, Michael *congressman, lawyer, business executive*
Bingaman, Jeff *senator*
Bishop, Sanford Dixon, Jr. *congressman*
Blute, Peter I. *congressman*
Boehlert, Sherwood Louis *congressman*
Boehner, John A. *congressman*
Bond, Christopher Samuel (Kit Bond) *senator, lawyer*
Bonilla, Henry *congressman, broadcast executive*
Bonior, David Edward *congressman*
Borski, Robert Anthony *congressman*
Boucher, Frederick C. *congressman, lawyer*
Boxer, Barbara *senator*
Bradley, Bill *senator*
Breaux, John B. *senator, former congressman*
Brewster, Bill K. *congressman*
Browder, John Glen *congressman, educator*
Brown, Corrine *congresswoman*
Brown, George Edward, Jr. *congressman*
Brown, Hank *senator*
Brown, Sherrod *congressman, former state official*
†Brownback, Sam *congressman*
Bryan, Richard H. *senator*
†Bryant, Edward *congressman*
Bryant, John Wiley *congressman*
Bumpers, Dale L. *senator, former governor*
†Bunn, Jim *congressman*
Burns, Conrad Ray *senator*
†Burr, Richard M. *congressman*
Burton, Danny Lee *congressman*
Buyer, Steve E. *congressman, lawyer*
Byrd, Robert Carlyle *senator*
Calvert, Ken *congressman*
Camp, Dave *congressman*
Campbell, Ben Nighthorse *senator*
Canady, Charles T. *congressman, lawyer*
Cannon, Howard Walter *former senator*
Caputo, Lisa M. *White House staff member*
Cardin, Benjamin Louis *congressman*
Carlisle, Margo Duer Black *chief senatorial staff*
Castle, Michael N. *congressman, former governor of Delaware, lawyer*
†Chabot, Steven J. *congressman*
Chafee, John Hubbard *senator*
†Chambliss, Saxby *congressman*
Chapman, James L. (Jim Chapman) *congressman*
†Chenoweth, Helen *congresswoman*
†Christensen, Jon *congressman*
†Christianson, Geryld B. *Senate committee staff*
†Chrysler, Richard R. *congressman*
Clark, Dick *former senator, ambassador, foreign affairs specialist*
Clay, William Lacy *congressman*
Clayton, Eva M. *congresswoman, former county commissioner*
Clement, Bob *congressman*
Clinger, William Floyd, Jr. *congressman*
Clyburn, James E. *congressman*
Coats, Daniel Ray *senator*
Cobb, Jane Overton *legislative staff member*
†Coburn, Tom A. *congressman*
Cohen, William Sebastian *senator*
Coleman, Ronald D. (Ron Coleman) *congressman*
Collins, Barbara-Rose *congresswoman*
Collins, Cardiss *congresswoman*
Collins, Michael A. (Mac Collins) *congressman*
Combest, Larry Ed *congressman*
Condit, Gary A. *congressman*
Conrad, Kent *senator*
Conyers, John, Jr. *congressman*
†Cooley, Wes *Congressman*
Costello, Jerry F., Jr. *congressman, former county official*
Coverdell, Paul Douglas *senator*
Coyne, William Joseph *congressman*
Craig, Larry Edwin *senator*
Cramer, Robert E., Jr. (Bud Cramer) *congressman*
Crane, Philip Miller *congressman*
Crapo, Michael Dean *congressman, lawyer*
†Cremeans, Frank A. *congressman*
Cunningham, Randy *congressman*
Danner, Patsy Ann (Mrs. C. M. Meyer) *congresswoman*
Daschle, Thomas Andrew *senator*
†Davis, Thomas M., III *congressman*
Deal, Nathan J. *congressman, lawyer*
DeFazio, Peter A. *congressman*
DeLauro, Rosa L. *congresswoman*
DeLay, Thomas D. (Tom DeLay) *congressman*
Dellums, Ronald V. *congressman*
Derrick, Butler Carson, Jr. *congressman*
Deutsch, Peter R. *congressman, lawyer*
Diaz-Balart, Lincoln *congressman*
Dickey, Jay W., Jr. *congressman, lawyer*
Dicks, Norman De Valois *congressman*
Dingell, John David, Jr. *congressman*
Dixon, Julian Carey *congressman*
Dodd, Christopher J. *senator*
Doggett, Lloyd *congressman, former state supreme court justice*
Dole, Robert J. *senator*
Domenici, Pete (Vichi Domenici) *senator*
Dooley, Calvin Millard *congressman*
Doolittle, John Taylor *congressman*
Dorgan, Byron Leslie *senator*
Dornan, Robert Kenneth *congressman*
Dougherty, Charlene *legislative staff member*
†Doyle, Michael F. *congressman*
Dreier, David Timothy *congressman*
Duncan, John J., Jr. *congressman*
Dunn, Jennifer Blackburn *congresswoman*
Durbin, Richard Joseph *congressman*
Edwards, Chet *congressman*
Ehlers, Vernon James *congressman*
†Ehrlich, Robert L., Jr. *congressman*
Emerson, William *congressman*
Engel, Eliot L. *congressman*
†English, Philip S. *congressman*
†Ensign, John E. *congressman*
Eshoo, Anna Georges *congresswoman*
Evans, Lane *congressman*
Everett, R. Terry *congressman, farmer, newspaper executive, bank executive*
Ewing, Thomas W. *congressman, lawyer*
Exon, J(ohn) James *senator*
Faircloth, Duncan McLauchlin (Lauch Faircloth) *senator, businessman, farmer*
Farr, Sam Sharon *congressman*
†Fattah, Chaka *congressman, former state legislator*
Fawell, Harris W. *congressman*
Fazio, Vic *congressman*
Feingold, Russell Dana *senator*
†Feinstein, Dianne *senator*
†Feltus, William James *legislative staff member*
Fields, Cleo *congressman*
Fields, Jack Milton, Jr. *congressman*
Filner, Bob *congressman*
†Fisher, Joseph A. *legislative official*
Flake, Floyd Harold *congressman*
†Flanagan, Michael Patrick *congressman, lawyer*
†Foley, Mark Adam *congressman*
†Forbes, Michael P. *congressman*
Ford, Harold Eugene *congressman*
Fowler, Tillie Kidd *congresswoman*
†Fox, Jon D. *congressman*
Frank, Barney *congressman*
Franks, Gary Alvin *congressman, real estate professional*
†Frelinghuysen, Rodney P. *congressman*
†Frisa, Daniel *congressman*
†Frist, William H. *senator, surgeon*
Frost, Jonas Martin, III *congressman*
Funderburk, David B. *congressman, history educator, former ambassador*
Furse, Elizabeth *congresswoman, small business owner*
†Ganske, Greg *congressman*
Gejdenson, Sam *congressman*
Gekas, George William *congressman*
Gephardt, Richard Andrew *congressman*
Geren, Preston (Pete Geren) *congressman*
Gest, Kathryn Waters *press secretary*
Gibbons, Samuel Melville (Sam Gibbons) *congressman*
Gilchrest, Wayne Thomas *congressman, former high school educator*
Gillmor, Paul E. *congressman, lawyer*
Gilman, Benjamin Arthur *congressman*
Gingrich, Newt (Newton Leroy Gingrich) *congressman*
Glenn, John Herschel, Jr. *senator*
Glickman, Daniel Robert *federal agency administrator*
Gonzalez, Henry Barbosa *congressman*
Goodlatte, Robert William *congressman, lawyer*
Goodling, William F. *congressman*
Gordon, Barton Jennings (Bart Gordon) *congressman, lawyer*
Gorton, Slade *senator*
†Gradison, Willis David, Jr. *congressman, investment broker*
Graham, D. Robert (Bob Graham) *senator, former governor*
†Graham, Lindsey O. *congressman*
Gramm, William Philip (Phil Gramm) *senator, economist*
Grams, Rodney D. *congressman, construction executive, television producer and anchor*
Grassley, Charles Ernest *senator*
Greenwood, James Charles *congressman*
Gregg, Judd *senator, former governor*
Gunderson, Steve Craig *congressman*
Gutierrez, Luis V. *congressman, elementary education educator*
Gutknecht, Gilbert William, Jr. *congressman, former state legislator, auctioneer*
Hall, Gerri Lynn *legislative staff member*
Hall, Ralph Moody *congressman*
Hall, Tony P. *congressman*
Hamilton, Lee Herbert *congressman*
†Hamre, John J. *legislative official*
Hancock, Mel *congressman*
Harkin, Thomas Richard *senator*
Harman, Jane Frank *congresswoman, lawyer*
Hastert, (J.) Dennis *congressman*
Hastings, Alcee Lamar *congressman, former federal judge*
†Hastings, Richard (Doc) *congressmant*
Hatfield, Mark O. *senator*
Hayes, James Alison *congressman*
†Hayworth, John David, Jr. *congressman, sportscaster, commentator, broadcaster*
Hefley, Joel M. *congressman*
Heflin, Howell Thomas *senator, lawyer, former state supreme court chief justice*
Hefner, W. G. (Bill) *congressman*
†Heineman, Frederick K. (Fred Heineman) *congressman*
Helms, Jesse *senator*
Herger, Wally W. *congressman*
†Hilleary, W. Van *congressman*

Hilliard, Earl Frederick *congressman, former state senator*
Hinchey, Maurice D., Jr. *congressman*
Hoagland, Peter Jackson *former congressman, lawyer*
Hobson, David Lee *congressman, lawyer*
Hoehn, William Edwin *federal goverment official*
Hoekstra, Peter *congressman, manufacturing executive*
Hoke, Martin Rossiter *congressman*
Holden, Tim *congressman, protective official*
Hollings, Ernest Frederick *senator*
Horn, (John) Stephen *congressman, political science educator*
†Hostettler, John N. *congressman*
Houghton, Amory, Jr. *congressman*
Hoyer, Steny Hamilton *congressman*
Hughes, William John *congressman*
Hutchinson, Tim *congressman*
Hyde, Henry John *congressman*
Inglis, Robert D (Bob Inglis) *congressman, lawyer*
Inhofe, James M. *U.S. Senator*
Inouye, Daniel Ken *senator*
Istook, Ernest James, Jr. (Jim Istook) *congressman, lawyer*
†Jackson-Lee, Sheila *congresswoman*
Jacobs, Andrew, Jr. *congressman*
James, Julie Ann *congressional staff member*
Jefferson, William L. (Jeff Jefferson) *congressman*
Jeffords, James Merrill *senator*
Johnson, Eddie Bernice *congresswoman*
Johnson, Nancy Lee *congresswoman*
Johnson, Samuel (Sam Johnson) *congressman*
Johnson, Timothy Peter *congressman*
Johnston, John Bennett, Jr. *senator*
†Jones, Walter B., Jr. *congressman*
Kanjorski, Paul Edmund *congressman, lawyer*
Kaptur, Marcia Carolyn *congresswoman*
Kasich, John R. *congressman*
Kassebaum, Nancy Landon *senator*
Kasten, Robert W., Jr. *former senator*
†Kelly, Sue W. *congresswoman*
Kempthorne, Dirk Arthur *senator*
Kennedy, Edward Moore *senator*
†Kennedy, James Keith *senate staff member*
Kennedy, Joseph Patrick, II *congressman*
†Kennedy, Patrick J. *congressman*
Kennelly, Barbara B. *congresswoman*
Kerrey, Bob (J. Robert Kerrey) *senator*
Kerry, John Forbes *senator*
Kildee, Dale Edward *congressman*
Kim, Jay *congressman*
King, Peter T. *congressman, lawyer*
Kingston, Jack *congressman*
Kleczka, Gerald D. *congressman*
Klink, Ron *congressman, reporter, newscaster*
Knollenberg, Joseph (Joe Knollenberg) *congressman*
Kohl, Herbert *senator, professional sports team owner*
Kolbe, James Thomas *congressman*
†Kundanis, George *congressional aide*
Kyl, Jon *senator*
La Falce, John Joseph *congressman, lawyer*
†LaHood, Ray *congressman*
Lambert Lincoln, Blanche M. *congresswoman*
Lancaster, H(arold) Martin *congressman*
Lantos, Thomas Peter *congressman*
†Largent, Steve *congressman, former professional football player*
†Latham, Tom *congressman*
†LaTourette, Steven C. *congressman*
Laughlin, Gregory H. (Greg Laughlin) *congressman*
Lautenberg, Frank R. *senator*
†Lawrence, John Alan *legislative staff director*
Lazio, Rick A. *congressman, lawyer*
Leach, James Albert Smith *congressman*
Leahy, Patrick Joseph *senator*
Lent, Norman Frederick, Jr. *former congressman*
Levin, Carl *senator*
Levin, Sander M. *congressman*
Lewis, Jerry *congressman*
Lewis, John R. *congressman*
†Lewis, Ron *congressman*
Lieberman, Joseph I. *senator*
Lightfoot, James Ross *congressman*
Linder, John E *congressman, dentist*
Lipinski, William Oliver *congressman*
Livingston, Robert Linlithgow, Jr. (Bob Livingston, Jr.) *congressman*
†LoBiondo, Frank A. *congressman*
†Lofgren, Zoe *congresswoman, former county government official*
Lott, Trent *senator*
Lowey, Nita M. *congresswoman*
Lucas, Frank D. *congressman*
Lugar, Richard Green *senator*
†Luther, William P. *congressman*
Mack, Connie, III (Cornelius Mack) *senator*
Manton, Thomas Joseph *congressman*
Manzullo, Donald A *congressman, lawyer*
Markey, Edward John *congressman*
Martinez, Matthew Gilbert *congressman*
†Martini, William J. *congressman*
†Mascara, Frank *congressman*
Matsui, Robert Takeo *congressman*
May, Edgar *former state legislator, nonprofit administrator*
McCain, John Sidney, III *senator*
McCarthy, Karen P. *congresswoman, former state representative*
Mc Collum, Ira William, Jr. (Bill Mc Collum) *congressman*
McConnell, Addison Mitchell, Jr. (Mitch McConnell, Jr.) *senator, lawyer*
McCrery, James (Jim McCrery) *congressman*
McDade, Joseph Michael *congressman*
McDermott, James A. *congressman, psychiatrist*
McHugh, John Michael *congressman, former state senator*
McInnis, Scott Steve *congressman, lawyer*
†McIntosh, David M. *congressman*
McKeon, Howard P. (Buck McKeon) *congressman, former mayor*
McKinney, Cynthia Ann *congresswoman*
McNulty, Michael Robert *congressman*
Meehan, Martin Thomas *congressman, lawyer*
Meek, Carrie P. *congresswoman*
Menendez, Robert *congressman, lawyer*
†Metcalf, Jack *congressman, retired state senator*
Metz, Craig Huseman *legislative staff*
Metzenbaum, Howard Morton *senator*
Meyers, Jan *congresswoman*
Mfume, Kweisi *congressman*
Miller, Dan *congressman*
Miller, George *congressman*
Mineta, Norman Yoshio *congressman*
Minge, David *congressman, lawyer, law educator*
Mink, Patsy Takemoto *congresswoman*
Moakley, John Joseph *congressman*
Molinari, Susan K. *congresswoman*
Mollohan, Alan B. *congressman, lawyer*
Montgomery, Gillespie V. (Sonny Montgomery) *congressman*
Moorhead, Carlos J. *congressman*
Moran, James Patrick, Jr. *congressman, stockbroker*
Morella, Constance Albanese *congresswoman*
Moseley-Braun, Carol *senator*
Moynihan, Daniel Patrick *senator, educator*
Murkowski, Frank Hughes *senator*
Murray, Patty *senator*
Murtha, John Patrick *congressman*
Myers, John Thomas *congressman*
Myrick, Sue *congresswoman, former mayor*
Nadler, Jerrold Lewis *congressman, lawyer*
Neal, Richard Edmund *congressman, former mayor*
Nelson, Gaylord Anton *former senator, association executive*
†Nethercutt, George Rector, Jr. *congressman, lawyer*
†Neumann, Mark W. *congressman*
†Ney, Robert W. *congressman*
Nickles, Donald (Don Nickles) *senator*
Nintemann, Terri *legislative staff member*
Norton, Eleanor Holmes *congresswoman, lawyer, educator*
†Norwood, Charles W., Jr. *congressman*
Nunn, Samuel (Sam Nunn) *senator*
Nussle, James Allen *congressman*
Oberstar, James L. *congressman*
Obey, David Ross *congressman*
†O'Donnell, Lawrence Francis, Jr. *legislative staff administrator, author*
Olver, John Walter *congressman*
Ortiz, Solomon P. *congressman*
Orton, William H. (Bill Orton) *congressman, lawyer*
Owens, Major Robert Odell *congressman*
Oxley, Michael Garver *congressman*
Packard, Ronald *congressman*
Packwood, Bob *senator*
Pallone, Frank, Jr. *congressman*
Parker, Michael (Mike Parker) *congressman*
†Parris, Stanford E. *congressman*
Pastor, Ed *congressman*
Paxon, L. William *congressman*
Payne, Donald M. *congressman*
Payne, Lewis Franklin, Jr. (L.F. Payne) *congressman*
Pell, Claiborne *senator*
Pelosi, Nancy *congresswoman*
Penny, Timothy Joseph *congressman*
Peterson, Collin C. *congressman*
Peterson, Douglas Pete (Pete Peterson) *congressman*
Petri, Thomas Evert *congressman*
Pickett, Owen B. *congressman*
Pombo, Richard *congressman, rancher, farmer*
Pomeroy, Earl R. *congressman, former state insurance commissioner*
Porter, John Edward *congressman*
Portman, Rob *congressman*
Poshard, Glenn W. *congressman*
Pressler, Larry *senator*
Pryor, David Hampton *senator*
Quillen, James Henry (Jimmy Quillen) *congressman*
Quinn, Jack *congressman, English language educator, sports coach*
†Radanovich, George P. *congressman*
Rahall, Nick Joe, II (Nick Rahall) *congressman*
Ramstad, Jim *congressman, lawyer*
Rangel, Charles Bernard *congressman*
Reed, John Francis (Jack Reed) *congressman, lawyer*
Regula, Ralph *congressman, lawyer*
Reynolds, Melvin J. (Mel Reynolds) *congressman*
Richardson, William Blaine *congressman*
†Riggs, Frank *congressman*
†Rivers, Lynn N. *congresswoman*
Robb, Charles Spittal *senator, lawyer*
Roberts, Charles Patrick *congressman*
Rockefeller, John Davison, IV (Jay Rockefeller) *senator, former governor*
Roemer, Timothy J. *congressman*
Rogers, Harold Dallas (Hal Rogers) *congressman*
Rohrabacher, Dana *congressman*
Rose, Charles Grandison, III (Charlie Rose) *congressman*
Ros-Lehtinen, Ileana *congresswoman*
Roth, William V., Jr. *senator*
Roukema, Margaret Scafati *congresswoman*
Rowland, (James) Roy *congressman*
Roybal-Allard, Lucille *congresswoman*
Royce, Edward R. (Ed Royce) *congressman*
Rudman, Warren Bruce *former senator, lawyer*
Rush, Bobby L. *congressman*
Sabo, Martin Olav *congressman*
Salmon, Matt *congressman*
Sanders, Bernard (Bernie Sanders) *congressman*
†Sanford, Marshall (Mark Sanford) *congressman*
Santorum, Rick *U.S. Senator*
Sarbanes, Paul Spyros *senator*
Sawyer, Thomas C. *congressman*
Saxton, H. James *congressman*
†Saxton, James *congressman*
†Scarborough, Joe *congressman*
Schaefer, Dan L. *congressman*
Schiff, Steven Harvey *congressman, lawyer*
Schroeder, Patricia Scott (Mrs. James White Schroeder) *congresswoman*
Schumer, Charles Ellis *congressman*
Scott, Robert Cortez *congressman, lawyer*
†Seastrand, Andrea H. *congresswoman*
Sensenbrenner, Frank James, Jr. *congressman, lawyer*
Serrano, Jose E. *congressman*
†Shadegg, John B. *congressman*
Shaw, E. Clay, Jr. (Clay Shaw) *congressman*
Shays, Christopher *congressman*
Shelby, Richard Craig *senator, former congressman*
Shepherd, Karen *congresswoman*
Shuster, Bud *congressman*
Simon, Paul *senator, educator, author*
Simpson, Alan Kooi *senator*
Sisisky, Norman *congressman, soft drink bottler*
Skaggs, David E. *congressman*
Skeen, Joseph Richard *congressman*
Skelton, Isaac Newton, IV (Ike Skelton) *congressman*
Slaughter, Louise McIntosh *congresswoman*
Smeeton, Thomas Rooney *congressional staff director*
Smith, Christopher Henry *congressman*
Smith, Lamar Seeligson *congressman*
Smith, Nick *congressman, farmer*
Smith, Robert Clinton *senator*
Snowe, Olympia J. *senator*
Solomon, Gerald Brooks Hunt *congressman*
†Souder, Mark Edward *congressman*
Specter, Arlen *senator*
Spence, Floyd Davidson *congressman*
Spratt, John McKee, Jr. *congressman, lawyer*
Stark, Fortney Hillman (Pete Stark) *congressman*
Stearns, Clifford Bundy *congressman, business executive*
Stenholm, Charles W. *congressman*
Stevens, Theodore Fulton *senator*
†Stockman, Stephen E. *congressman*
Stokes, Louis *congressman*
Studds, Gerry Eastman *congressman*
Stump, Bob *congressman*
Stupak, Bart T. *congressman, lawyer*
Talent, James M. *congressman, lawyer*
Tanner, John S. *congressman, lawyer*
†Tate, Randall J. (Randy) *congressman*
Tauzin, W. J. Billy, II (Wilbert J. Tauzin) *congressman*
Taylor, Charles H. *congressman*
Taylor, Gene *congressman*
Tejeda, Frank *congressman*
Thomas, Craig *senator*
Thomas, William Marshall *congressman*
Thompson, Bennie G. *congressman*
†Thompson, Fred Dalton *senator*
†Thornberry, William M. (Mac Thornberry) *congressman*
Thornton, Ray *congressman*
Thurman, Karen L. *congresswoman*
Thurmond, Strom *senator*
Tiahrt, W. Todd *congressman, former state senator*
Torkildsen, Peter G. *congressman*
Torres, Esteban Edward *congressman, business executive*
Torricelli, Robert G. *congressman*
Towns, Edolphus *congressman*
Traficant, James A., Jr. *congressman*
Tucker, Walter Rayford, III *congressman, lawyer, former mayor*
Upton, Frederick Stephen *congressman*
Velazquez, Nydia M. *congresswoman*
Vento, Bruce Frank *congressman*
Visclosky, Peter John *congressman, lawyer*
Volkmer, Harold L. *congressman*
Vucanovich, Barbara Farrell *congresswoman*
Wainman, Barbara Walden *legislative staff member*
†Waldholtz, Enid Greene *congresswoman*
Walker, Robert Smith *congressman*
Walsh, James Thomas *congressman*
†Wamp, Zach P. *congressman*
Ward, Michael Delavan *congressman, former state legislator*
Warner, John William *senator*
Washington, Craig A. *congressman*
Waters, Maxine *congresswoman*
Watt, Melvin L. *congressman, lawyer*
†Watts, J. C., Jr. *congressman*
Waxman, Henry Arnold *congressman*
Weiss, Gail Ellen *legislative staff director*
Weldon, W(ayne) Curtis *congressman*
†Weller, Gerald C. *congressman*
Wellstone, Paul *senator*
†White, Richard A. *congressman*
†Whitfield, Edward *congressman*
†Wicker, Roger F. *congressman*
Williams, Pat *congressman*
Wilson, Charles (Charlie Wilson) *congressman*
Wise, Robert Ellsworth, Jr. (Bob Ellsworth) *congressman*
Wolf, Frank R. *congressman, lawyer*
Woolsey, Lynn *congresswoman*
Wyden, Ronald Lee *congressman*
Wynn, Albert Russell *congressman*
Yates, Sidney Richard *congressman, lawyer*
Young, C. W. (Bill Young) *congressman*
Young, Donald E. *congressman*
Zimmer, Richard Alan *congressman, lawyer*

FLORIDA

Bradenton
Woodson-Howard, Marlene Erdley *former state legislator*

Fort Lauderdale
Dawson, Muriel Amanda *legislator*

Jacksonville
Bennett, Charles Edward *former congressman, educator*
Lee, E. Denise *council woman*

Melbourne
†Weldon, David Joseph, Jr. *congressman, physician*

Miami
Cosgrove, John Francis *state legislator, lawyer*
Fascell, Dante B. *lawyer, congressman*
Gordon, Jack David *senator, foundation executive*

Orlando
†Sublette, William Edward *state representative*

Pensacola
Hutto, Earl *retired congressman*

Tallahassee
Brennan, Mary M. *state legislator*
Sindler, Robert Brian *state legislator, veterinarian*

Tampa
Davis, Helen Gordon *former state senator*
Glickman, Ronnie Carl *state official, lawyer*
Grant, John Audley, Jr. *state senator, lawyer*
Miller, Lesley James, Jr. *state representative*

Winter Park
Mica, John L. *congressman*

GEORGIA

Atlanta
Martin, James Francis *state legislator, lawyer*
McBee, Mary Louise *state legislator, former academic administrator*
Murphy, Thomas Bailey *state legislator*
Purcell, Ann Rushing *state legislator, office manager medical business*
Slotin, Ronald David *state legislator*

Augusta
Barnard, Druie Douglas, Jr. *former congressman, former bank executive*

Columbus
Harbison, Ed *state senator, broadcast journalist*

Gainesville
Hemmer, Jane Reynolds *state senator, real estate executive*

Lawrenceville
Wall, Clarence Vinson *congressman*

Milledgeville
Kidd, E. Culver, Jr. *state senator, management professional*

Riverdale
King, Glynda B. *state legislator*

Smyrna
Atkins, William A. (Bill) *state legislator*

Washington
McGill, Sam Peyton *state senator*

HAWAII

Hilo
Ushijima, John Takeji *state senator, lawyer*

Honolulu
Baker, Rosalyn *state legislator*
Beirne, Danielle Ululani *state legislator*
Cachola, Romy Munoz *state representative*
Chun Oakland, Suzanne Nyuk Jun *state legislator*
Fasi, Frank Francis *state senator*
Fong, Hiram L. *former senator*
Ikeda, Donna Rika *state senator*
Iwase, Randall Yoshio *state senator*
Takumi, Roy Mitsuo *state representative*

Kailua
George, Mary Shannon *state senator*

IDAHO

Boise
Aherns, Pamela Bengson *state legislator*
Barrett, Lenore Hardy *state legislator, mining and investment consultant*
Black, Pete *state legislator, educator*
Blackbird, Mike *state senator, sales representative*
Gurnsey, Kathleen Wallace *state legislator*
Hartung, Mary *state legislator*
McLaughlin, Marguerite P. *state senator, logging company executive*
Nafziger, Pattie Lois *state legislator*
Taylor, W.O. (Bill) *state legislator, business consultant*

Caldwell
Kerrick, David Ellsworth *state senator, lawyer*

Jerome
Bell, Maxine Toolson *state legislator, librarian*

Pocatello
Hofman, Elaine D. *state legislator*

Rupert
Antone, Steve *state legislator, farmer*

Twin Falls
McRoberts, Joyce *state legislator*

ILLINOIS

Aurora
Etheredge, Forest DeRoyce *former state senator, university administrator*
Lindner, Patricia Reid *state representative, lawyer*

Buffalo Grove
Clayton, Verna Lewis *state legislator*

Chicago
Berman, Arthur Leonard *state senator*
Bugielski, Robert Joseph *state legislator*
Jones, Emil, Jr. *state senator*
Marovitz, William A. *state senator, lawyer*
Munizzi, Pam *state senator*
Rostenkowski, Dan *congressman*
Stevenson, Adlai Ewing, III *lawyer, former senator*

Hinsdale
Dyer, Goudyloch Erwin *state legislator*

Jacksonville
Findley, Paul *former congressman, author, educator*

Lake Forest
Frederick, Virginia Fiester *state legislator*

Mokena
Sangmeister, George Edward *congressman, lawyer*

Naperville
Cowlishaw, Mary Lou *state legislator*

Northfield
Stern, Grace Mary *former state legislator*

Palatine
Fitzgerald, Peter Gosselin *state senator, lawyer*

Schaumburg
Wojcik, Kathleen Louise *state representative*

Springfield
Currie, Barbara Flynn *state legislator*
Hughes, Ann *state legislator*
Madigan, Michael Joseph *state legislator*
Moore, Andrea S. *state legislator*
Netsch, Dawn Clark *state official, law educator*
Philip, James (Pate Philip) *state senator*

Ronen, Carol *state legislator*
Satterthwaite, Helen Foster *state legislator*
Severns, Penny L. *state legislator*
Welch, Patrick Daniel *state senator*

Sterling
von Bergen Wessels, Pennie Lea *state legislator*

Westchester
Walsh, Thomas James *state senator*

Wheaton
Fawell, Beverly Jean *state legislator*
Roskam, Peter James *state legislator, lawyer*

INDIANA

Attica
Harrison, Joseph William *state senator*

Columbus
Garton, Robert Dean *state senator*

Fort Wayne
Goeglein, Gloria J. *state legislator*

Indianapolis
Antich, Rose Ann *state legislator*
Becker, Vaneta G. *state representative*
Budak, Mary Kay *state legislator*
Engle, Barbara Louise *state legislator*
Henderson, Linda Kay *state legislator*
Miller, Patricia Louise *state legislator, nurse*
Scholer, Sue Wyant *state legislator*
Simpson, Vi *state senator*
Tinkle, Carolyn J. *state legislative staff member*
Vobach, William H. *state senator*

Monticello
Wolf, Katie Louise *state legislator*

IOWA

Ames
Rosenberg, Ralph *former state senator, lawyer, consultant, educator*

Cedar Rapids
Chapman, Kathleen Halloran *state legislator, lawyer*
Nielsen, Joyce *former state legislator*

Davenport
Tinsman, Margaret Neir *state senator*

Davis City
Boswell, Leonard L. *state senator*

Des Moines
Beatty, Linda L. *state legislator*
Daggett, Horace Clinton *state legislator*
Drake, Richard Francis *state senator*
Garman, Teresa Agnes *state legislator*
Grubbs, Steven Eric *state representative*
Grundberg, Betty *state legislator, property manager*
Harper, Patricia M. *state legislator*
Lundby, Mary A. *state legislator*
Murphy, Patrick Joseph *state representative*
Rittmer, Sheldon *farmer, senator*
Szymoniak, Elaine Eisfelder *state senator*

KANSAS

Clay Center
Braden, James Dale *former state legislator*

Coffeyville
Garner, Jim David *state legislator, lawyer*

Hutchinson
Kerr, David Mills *state legislator*
O'Neal, Michael Ralph *state legislator, lawyer*

Iola
Talkington, Robert Van *state senator*

Kansas City
Jones, Sherman Jarvis *state senator*

Lawrence
Winter, Winton Allen, Jr. *lawyer, state senator*

Lenexa
Parkinson, Mark Vincent *state legislator, lawyer*

Mc Pherson
Nichols, Richard Dale *former congressman, banker*

Olathe
Burke, Paul E., Jr. *state senator, investment banker*
Hackler, Ruth Ann *state legislator*
O'Connor, Kay *state legislator*

Shawnee Mission
Bogina, August, Jr. *state senator*
Langworthy, Audrey Hansen *state legislator*
Sader, Carol Hope *former state legislator*

Topeka
Benlon, Lisa L. *state legislator*
Chronister, Rochelle Beach *state legislator*
Gannon, Richard Galen *state senator, rancher, farmer*
Lynch, Eloise *state legislator*
Mays, M. Douglas *state legislator, financial consultant*
McClure, Janice Lee *state legislator, farmer, graphic designer*
Oleen, Lana *state legislator*
Petty, Marge *state senator*
Praeger, Sandy *state legislator*
Salisbury, Alicia Laing *state legislator*
Samuelson, Ellen Banman *state legislator*
Sebelius, Kathleen Gilligan *state legislator*
Standifer, Sabrina *state legislator*
Tillotson, Carolyn *state legislator*
Wagle, Susan *state legislator, small business owner*
Wagnon, Joan *former state legislator, association executive*
Welshimer, Gwen R. *state legislator, real estate broker, appraiser, tax consultant*

University Of Kansas
Ballard, Barbara W. *state legislator*

Wichita
Pottorff, Jo Ann *state legislator*

KENTUCKY

Covington
Harper, Kenneth Franklin *state legislator, retired, real estate broker*

Frankfort
Northup, Anne Meagher *state legislator*
†Trapp, Leslie Combs *state legislator*

LOUISIANA

Baton Rouge
Flournoy, Melissa *state legislator*
Rayburn, B. B. *state senator, farmer*

Grambling
Wilkerson, Pinkie Carolyn *state legislator, lawyer*

Harahan
Bowler, Shirley *state legislator*

Marksville
Riddle, Charles Addison, III *state legislator, lawyer*

Shreveport
Nelson, Sydney B. *lawyer, state senator*

MAINE

Augusta
Barth, Alvin Ludwig *state legislator*
Brawn, Linda Curtis *state legislator*
Bustin, Beverly Miner *state legislator*
Kilkelly, Marjorie Lee *state legislator*
Martin, John L. *state legislator*
Saxl, Jane Wilhelm *state legislator*
Winn, Julie *state representative*

Brunswick
Pfeiffer, Sophia Douglass *state legislator, lawyer*

Cape Elizabeth
Simonds, Stephen Paige *former state legislator*

Fairfield
Gwadosky, Dan A. *state legislator*

Freeport
Clark, Nancy Randall *former state legislator*

Hallowell
Treat, Sharon Anglin *state legislator*

Pejepscot
Chonko, Lorraine Nancy *state legislator*

Presque Isle
Donnelly, James Owen *state legislator, bank executive*

MARYLAND

Aberdeen
Bonsack, Rose Mary Hatem *state legislator, physician*

Annapolis
Boergers, Mary H. *senator*
Cade, John A. *state senator*
Forehand, Jennie Meador *state legislator*
Hixson, Sheila Ellis *state legislator*
Hollinger, Paula Colodny *state senator*
Hutchinson, Leslie E *state legislator, fiscal programs manager, consultant*
Kelley, Delores Goodwin *state legislator*
Klima, Martha Scanlan *state legislator*
Lapides, Julian Lee *state senator, lawyer*
Madden, Martin Gerard *state legislator, insurance agent*
Maloney, Timothy Francis *state legislator, lawyer*
Menes, Pauline H. *state legislator*
Mitchell, R. Clayton, Jr. *state legislator*
Montague, Kenneth Charles *congressman*
Morgan, John Stephen *state representative, materials science researcher*
Perry, Marsha Gratz *legislator, professional skating coach*
Roesser, Jean Wolberg *state legislator*
Ruben, Ida Gass *state senator*
Winegrad, Gerald William *lawyer, state senator, educator*

Baltimore
Marriot, Salima Siler *state legislator, social work educator*
Stone, Norman R., Jr. *state legislator*

Bethesda
Gude, Gilbert *former state and federal legislator, nurseryman, writer*

Bowie
Green, Leo Edward *lawyer, state legislator*

Denton
Thornton, Robert Alan, Jr. *state legislator, lawyer*

Riverdale
O'Reilly, Thomas Patrick *state senator, lawyer*

Rockville
Petzold, Carol Stoker *state legislator*

MASSACHUSETTS

Boston
Bertonazzi, Louis Peter *state senator*
Brenton, Marianne Webber *state legislator, technical librarian*
Cleven, Carol Chapman *state legislator*
Cronin, Bonnie Kathryn Lamb *legislative staff executive*
Donovan, Carol Ann *state legislator*
Doris, Francis D. *state senator*
Durand, Robert Alan *state senator*
Harkins, Lida E. *state legislator, educator*
Harold, Paul Dennis *state senator*
Hawke, Robert Douglas *state legislator*
Melconian, Linda Jean *state senator, lawyer*
Murphy, Dennis Michael *state legislator*
Pines, Lois G. *state legislator*
Rogeness, Mary Speer *state legislator*
Rushing, Byron Douglas *state legislator*
Swift, Jane Maria *state senator*
Walrath, Patricia A. *state legislator*

East Weymouth
Hedlund, Robert L. *state senator, automobile executive*

Fall River
Correia, Robert *state legislator*

Springfield
Lees, Brian Paul *state senator*

Westfield
Hahn, Celia Ferner *state legislator, broadcaster*

MICHIGAN

Grand Blanc
Corbin, Gary George *state legislator*

Kalamazoo
Welborn, John Alva *former state senator, small business owner*

Lansing
Barns, Justine *state legislator*
Bullard, Willis Clare, Jr. *state legislator*
Cropsey, Alan Lee *state legislator, lawyer*
Dobronski, Agnes Marie *state legislator*
Dolan, Jan Clark *state legislator*
Emmons, Joanne *state senator*
Geake, Raymond Robert *state senator*
Hammerstrom, Beverly Swoish *state representative*
Hoffman, Philip Edward *state legislator*
Kaza, Greg John *state representative, economist*
Kilpatrick, Carolyn Cheeks *state legislator, educator*
Pitoniak, Gregory Edward *state representative*
Schroer, Mary *state legislator*
Schwarz, John J.H. *state senator, surgeon*
Smith, Virgil Clark *state legislator*
Vaughn, Jackie, III *state legislator*

Mount Pleasant
McBryde, James Edward *state legislator*

Onondaga
Byrum, Dianne *state legislator*

MINNESOTA

Anoka
Sekhon, Kathleen *state legislator*

Lakeville
Krueger, Richard Arnold *state legislator*

Mankato
Hottinger, John Creighton *state legislator, lawyer*

Minneapolis
Hilary, Sandra Marie *councilwoman*
Oliver, Edward Carl *state senator, retired investment executive*
Reichgott Junge, Ember D. *state legislator, lawyer*

Saint Paul
Asch, Marc *consultant*
Berglin, Linda *state senator*
Betzold, Donald Richard *state senator*
Brown, Kay *state legislator*
Carlson, Lyndon Richard *state legislator, educator*
Clark, Karen *state legislator*
Frederickson, Dennis Russel *state legislator, farmer*
Hanson, Paula E. *state legislator*
Haukoos, Melvin Robert *state representative*
Hughes, Jerome Michael *state senator, educator*
Kelso, Becky *state legislator*
Kiscaden, Sheila M. *state legislator*
Leppik, Margaret White *state legislator*
Long, Dee *state legislator*
Lourey, Becky J. *state legislator*
Luther, Darlene *state legislator*
Lynch, Teresa Ann *state legislator*
Marty, John *state senator, writer*
McCollum, Betty *state legislator*
McGuire, Mary Jo *state legislator*
Molnau, Carol *state legislator*
Mondale, Theodore Adams *state senator*
Murphy, Mary C. *state legislator*
Murphy, Steven Leslie *state senator, utilities company official*
Neary, Pamela *state legislator*
Olson, Katy *state legislator, farmer*
Orfield, Myron Willard, Jr. *state legislator, educator*
Pappas, Sandra Lee *state senator*
Piper, Pat Kathryn *state senator*
Robertson, Martha Rappaport *state senator, consultant*
Seagren, Alice *state legislator*
Solberg, Loren Albin *state legislator, secondary education educator*
Spear, Allan Henry *state senator, historian, educator*
Tompkins, Eileen *state legislator*
Vellenga, Kathleen Osborne *former state legislator*
Wagenius, Jean *state representative*

Saint Peter
Ostrom, Don *state legislator, political science educator*

MISSISSIPPI

Amory
Bryan, Hob *lawyer, state senator*

Clarksdale
Williams, Kenneth Ogden *farmer*

Columbia
Simmons, Miriam Quinn *state legislator*

Gulfport
Guice, Daniel Dicks, Jr. *state legislator*

Jackson
Bourdeaux, Norma Sanders *state legislator*
Green, Tomie Turner *lawyer, state legislator*
Hall, Dick *state legislator*
Rayborn, William Lee *state senator*
Woodfield, Clyde Vernon *senator*

MISSOURI

Cameron
Griffin, Bob Franklin *state legislator, lawyer*

Cassville
Melton, Emory Leon *state legislator, lawyer, publisher*

Eminence
Staples, Danny Lew *state senator*

Hale
Danner, Steve *senator*

Hattiesburg
Saucier, Gene Duane *state legislator, import/export company executive*

Jefferson City
Backer, Gracia Yancey *state legislator*
Bray, Joan *state legislator*
Clay, William Lacy, Jr. *state legislator*
Goode, Wayne *state senator, corporate executive*
Griesheimer, John Elmer *state representative*
Hale, David Clovis *former state representative*
Kauffman, Sandra Daley *state legislator*
Lumpe, Sheila *state legislator*
Maxwell, Joe *state representative, lawyer*
Mays, Carol Jean *state legislator*
McClelland, Emma L. *state legislator*
Morgan, Annette N. *state legislator*
Park, Carole Roper *state legislator*
Steinmetz, Kaye H. *state legislator*
Treppler, Irene Esther *state senator*
Wiggins, Harry *state senator, lawyer*

Saint Louis
Danforth, John Claggett *senator, lawyer, clergyman*
Hoblitzelle, George Knapp *former state legislator*
Shelton, O. L. *state legislator*

MONTANA

Anaconda
McCarthy, Bea *state legislator*

Billings
Russell, Angela Veta *state legislator, social worker*

Cascade
Mesaros, Kenneth Lee *rancher, state senator*

Dutton
DeBruycker, Jane Crystal *state legislator*

Great Falls
Ryan, William Matthew *lineman, state legislator*

Helena
Bartlett, Sue *state legislator*
Brooke, Vivian M. *state legislator*
Cocchiarella, Vicki Marshall *state legislator*
Hanson, Marian W. *state legislator*
Jacobson, Judith Helen *state senator*
Kasten, Betty Lou *state legislator*
Swanson, Emily *state legislator*
Vaughn, Eleanor *state legislator*

Wibaux
Bruski-Maus, Betty Jean *state legislator*

NEBRASKA

Lincoln
Curtis, Carl Thomas *former senator*
Landis, David Morrison *state legislator*
Marsh, Frank (Irving) *former state official*
Pedersen, Dwite A. *state senator, alcohol/drug abuse counselor*
Pirsch, Carol McBride *state senator, community relations manager*
Schimek, DiAnna Ruth Rebman *state legislator*
Wesely, Donald Raymond *state senator*
Will, Eric John *state senator*

Malcolm
Hudkins, Carol L. *state legislator*

Omaha
Abboud, Christopher William *state senator*

NEVADA

Carson City
Lowden, Suzanne *state legislator*
O'Connell, Mary Ann *state senator, business owner*
Tiffany, Sandra L. *state legislator*
Titus, Alice Cestandina (Dina Titus) *state legislator*

Las Vegas
Bilbray, James Hubert *former congressman, lawyer, consultant*

Reno
Raggio, William John *state senator*

Yerington
Dini, Joseph Edward, Jr. *state legislator*

NEW HAMPSHIRE

Concord
Arnold, Thomas Ivan, Jr. *legislator*
Bagley, Amy L. *state legislator*
Bartlett, William Stuart, Jr. *state legislator, realtor*
Chambers, Mary Peyton *state legislator*
Cote, David Edward *state legislator*
Delahunty, Joseph Lawrence *state senator, business investor*
Dunn, Miriam D. *legislative research firm executive*
Foss, Patricia Howland *state legislator, insurance agency manager*
Hager, Elizabeth Sears *state legislator*
Hurst, Sharleene Page *state legislator*
McRae, Karen K. *state legislator*
Newland, Matthew John *state legislator*
O'Rourke, Joanne A. *state legislator*
Packard, Bonnie Bennett *state legislator*
Pearson, Gertrude Booth *state legislator*
Pignatelli, Debora Becker *state legislator*
Podles, Eleanor Pauline *state senator*
Preston, Robert Francis *state legislator*
Shaw, Randall Francis *state legislator*
Teschner, Douglass Paul *state legislator*

Derry
Aranda, Mary Kathryn *state legislator*
Katsakiores, George Nicholas *state legislator, retired restauranteur*

Dover
Merritt, Deborah Foote *state legislator, counselor*
Parks, Joe Benjamin *state legislator*
Pelletier, Arthur Joseph *state legislator, industrial arts and computer programming educator*
Pelletier, Marsha Lynn *state legislator, secondary school educator*

Durham
Wheeler, Katherine Wells *state legislator*

Franklin
Asplund, Bronwyn Lorraine *state legislator*

Hanover
Crory, Elizabeth L. *state legislator*
Guest, Robert Henry *state legislator, management educator*

Loudon
Heath, Roger Charles *state senator, writer*

Manchester
Arnold, Barbara Eileen *state legislator*

Nashua
Nelson, Mary S. *former state legislator*
Pressly, Barbara *state legislator*

Newport
Stamatakis, Carol Marie *state legislator, lawyer*

Plaistow
Senter, Merilyn P(atricia) *state legislator, retired freelance reporter*

Raymond
Warburton, (Nathaniel) Calvin, Jr. *state legislator, retired clergyman*

Rochester
Bickford, Drucilla *state legislator*
Hambrick, Patricia *state legislator*

Rumney
King, Wayne Douglas *state senator*

NEW JERSEY

Edison
Warsh, Jeffrey Alan *state legislator, lawyer*

Emerson
Rooney, John Edward *state legislator, electrical company executive*

Flemington
Lance, Leonard *assemblyman*

Glassboro
Marcus, Laurence Richard *state official*

Millburn
Ogden, Maureen Black *state legislator*

New Brunswick
Lynch, John A. *lawyer, state senator*

Trenton
Bakelaar, Donna *state assembly staff member*
DiFrancesco, Donald T. *state senator*

Union
Bassano, C. Louis *state senator, fuel oil company executive*
Franks, Robert D. (Bob Franks) *congressman*

Woodbury
Zane, Raymond J. *lawyer, state senator*

NEW MEXICO

Albuquerque
Carraro, Joseph John *senator, small business owner, consultant*
Riley, Ann J. *state legislator, technology specialist*
Rutherford, Thomas Truxtun, II *state senator, lawyer*
Schmitt, Harrison Hagan *former senator, geologist, astronaut, consultant*

Corrales
Tice, Clifford Ray *state legislator, oil company executive*

Hobbs
Reagan, Gary Don *state legislator, lawyer*

Las Cruces
Porter, William Emme *state legislator, small business owner*

Los Alamos
Wallace, Jeannette Owens *state legislator*

New Mexico State Capitol
Lambert, Martha Lowery *state legislator*
Morgan, Lynda M. *state legislator*
Nava, Cynthia D. *state legislator*
Stefanics, Elizabeth T. (Liz Stefanics) *state legislator*

Roswell
Casey, Barbara A. Perea *state representative, educator*
Knowles, Richard Thomas *state legislator, retired army officer*

NEW YORK

Albany
Calhoun, Nancy *state legislator*
Connelly, Elizabeth Ann *state legislator*
Farley, Hugh Thomas *state senator, law educator*
Galiber, Joseph Lionel *state senator*
Gottfried, Richard Norman *state legislator*
Harenberg, Paul E. *state legislator*
Hill, Earlene Hooper *state legislator*
Holland, Joseph Robert *state senator*
Lack, James J. *state senator, lawyer*
Leichter, Franz S. *state senator*
Luster, Martin Arnold *state legislator*
Marchi, John Joseph *state senator, lawyer*
Miller, Melvin Howard *state legislator*
O'Neil, Chloe Ann *state legislator*
Santiago, Nellie *state legislator*
Singer, Cecile Doris *state legislator*
Skelos, Dean G. *senator*
Smith, Ada L. *state legislator*
Solomon, Martin M. *state senator*
Stachowski, William T. *state senator*
Vitaliano, Eric Nicholas *state legislator, lawyer*
Volker, Dale Martin *state senator, lawyer*

Ballston Lake
Proskin, Arnold W. *state assemblyman, lawyer*

Binghamton
Libous, Thomas William *state senator*

Brooklyn
Montgomery, Velmanette *state legislator*

East Setauket
Englebright, Steven Cale *assemblyman*

Glendale
Maltese, Serphin Ralph *state senator, lawyer*

Herkimer
Mitchell, Donald J. *former congressman*

Kenmore
Schimminger, Robin *state legislator*

Montauk
Duryea, Perry Belmont, Jr. *former state legislator, business executive*

New City
Gromack, Alexander Joseph *state legislator*

New York
†Goodman, Roy Matz *senator, business executive*
Ohrenstein, Manfred *state senator, lawyer*
Silver, Sheldon *lawyer, state legislator*
Speth, James Gustave *United Nations executive, lawyer*

Pearl River
Colman, Samuel *assemblyman*

Roslyn Heights
Tully, Michael J., Jr. *state senator*

Syracuse
DeFrancisco, John Anthony *state senator, lawyer*

NORTH CAROLINA

Advance
Cochrane, Betsy Lane *state senator*

Lincolnton
Carter, John DeLaney *state senator, video producer*

Locust
Barbee, Bobby Harold *state legislator, insurance agency executive*

New Bern
Perdue, Beverly Moore *state legislator, geriatric consultant*

Raleigh
Blackmon, John (Jerry) *state senator*
Harris, J. Ollie *state legislator*
Lemmond, Joseph Shawn *state legislator, insurance agent*
Ramsey, Liston Bryan *state legislator*
Sutton, Ronnie Neal *lawyer, state legislator*
Tally, Lura Self *state legislator*
Warren, Robert Davis *state senator*
Winner, Leslie Jane *state legislator, lawyer*

Wadesboro
Hightower, Foyle Robert, Jr. *state legislator, ice and fuel company executive*

Washington
Edwards, Zeno Lester, Jr. *state legislator, retired dentist*

Wilmington
Gottovi, Karen Elizabeth *state legislator, political consultant, researcher*

Winston Salem
Ward, Marvin Martin *retired state senator*

NORTH DAKOTA

Ashley
Kretschmar, William Edward *state legislator, lawyer*

Bismarck
Allmaras, Lorraine *state legislator*
Carlson, Clare *state legislator*
Kelly, Tish *state legislator*
Kelsch, RaeAnn *state legislator*

Crosby
Andrist, John M. *state senator*

Fargo
Berg, Rick Alan *state legislator, real estate investor*
Mathern, Tim *state senator, social worker*

Fessenden
Streibel, Bryce *state senator*

Grand Forks
DeMers, Judy Lee *state legislator, dean*
Poolman, Jim *state legislator*
Stenehjem, Wayne Kevin *state senator, lawyer*

Minot
Haugland, Brynhild *retired state legislator, farmer*

Saint Anthony
Tomac, Steven Wayne *state senator, farmer*

Williston
Wenstrom, Frank Augustus *state senator*
Yockim, James Craig *state senator, oil and gas executive*

OHIO

Cedarville
DeWine, R. Michael *U.S. Senator, lawyer*

Cincinnati
Sterne, Bobbie Lynn *city council member*

Cleveland
Mottl, Ronald M. *state legislator, lawyer*
Oakar, Mary Rose *former congresswoman*
Pringle, Barbara Carroll *state legislator*

Columbus
Abel, Mary *state legislator*
Bergansky, Suzanne Marie *state legislator*
Boyd, Barbara H. *state legislator*
Cain, Madeline Ann *state representative*
Drake, Grace L. *state senator*
Gaeth, Matthew Ben *state senator*
Gillmor, Karen Lako *state legislator, strategic planner*
Kearns, Merle Grace *state senator*
Krebs, Eugene Kehm, II *state legislator*
Levey, Barry *state senator*
Long, Jan Michael *state legislator*
Lucas, June H. *state legislator*
McLin, Rhine Lana *state legislator, funeral service executive, educator*
Mead, Priscilla *state legislator*
Meshel, Harry *state senator, political party official*
Nettle, Robert Dale *state legislator, former insurance and real estate broker*
Padgett, Joy *state legislator*
Prentiss, C.J. *state legislator*
Walsh, Katherine Herald *state legislator*

Cuyahoga Falls
Jones, Wayne M. *state legislator, lawyer*

Dayton
Horn, Charles F. *state senator, lawyer, electrical engineer*
Reid, Marilyn Joanne *state legislator, lawyer*

Heath
Guthrie, Marc Dennis *former state representative*

Hillsboro
Snyder, Harry Cooper *state senator*

Lima
Cupp, Robert Richard *state senator, attorney*

Wapakoneta
Brading, Charles Richard *state representative*

OKLAHOMA

Durant
Mickle, Billy Arthur *state legislator, lawyer*

Oklahoma City
Boyd, Laura Wooldridge *state legislator*
Caldwell, Warren A. (Tony Caldwell) *former state legislator, real estate management company executive*
Fair, Michael Edward *state senator*
Ford, Charles Reed *state senator*
Henry, Brad *state legislator, lawyer*
Hopkins, Robert E. *association executive, real estate and insurance broker*
Pope, Tim L. *state legislator, consultant*
Taylor, Stratton *state senator, lawyer*
Weedn, Trish *state legislator*

OREGON

Bend
Luke, Dennis Robert *state legislator, home building company executive*

Portland
Lim, John K. *state senator, business executive*

Salem
Bradbury, William Chapman, III *state senator*
Brown, Kate *state legislator*
Bunn, James Lee *state senator*
Carter, Margaret L. *legislator*
Cohen, Joyce E. *state senator, investment executive*
Gold, Shirley Jeanne *state legislator, labor relations specialist*
Naito, Lisa Heather *state legislator*
Oakley, Carolyn Le *state legislator, small business owner*
Shibley, Gail Rose *state legislator*
Taylor, Jacqueline Self *state legislator*
Webber, Catherine Carney *state legislator, lawyer, social worker, state official*

PENNSYLVANIA

Allentown
Dent, Charles Wieder *state legislator*

Easton
Reibman, Jeanette Fichman *retired state senator*

Erie
Boyes, Karl W. *state legislator*

Harrisburg
Andrezeski, Anthony (Buzz Andrezeski) *state senator*
Armstrong, Gibson E. *state senator*
Armstrong, Thomas Errol *state legislator*
Bishop, Louise Williams *state legislator*
Fargo, Howard Lynn *legislator*
Farmer, Elaine Frazier *state legislator*
Gruitza, Michael *legislator*
Hopper, John D. *state senator*
Itkin, Ivan *state legislator*
Jones, Roxanne Harper *state legislator*
Josephs, Babette *legislator*
Lederer, Marie A. *state legislator*
Loeper, F. Joseph *state senator*
Nyce, Robert Eugene *state legislator, tax accountant*
Rudy, Ruth Corman *state legislator*
Schwartz, Allyson Y. *state senator*

Oil City
Hutchinson, Scott Edward *state legislator*

Philadelphia
Foglietta, Thomas Michael *congressman*

Pittsburgh
Fajt, Gregory Charles *state legislator*
Fisher, D. Michael *state senator, lawyer*

Reading
Rohrer, Samuel Edward *state legislator*

Rochester
LaValle, Gerald J. *state senator*

Wellsboro
Baker, Matthew Edward *state legislator*

RHODE ISLAND

Providence
Algiere, Dennis L. *state senator*
Coffey, Sean Owen *former state senator, lawyer*
Correia, John Furia *senator, plumbing supply company executive*
Fogarty, Charles Joseph *state senator*
Gibbs, June Nesbitt *state senator*
Henseler, Suzanne Marie *legislator, social studies educator, majority whip*
Lyle, John William, Jr. *state senator, lawyer, social studies educator*
Mathieu, Helen M. *state legislator*

Warwick
Carlin, David R., Jr. *state senator*
Revens, John Cosgrove, Jr. *state senator, lawyer*

Westerly
Morrone, Edward Patrick *state senator, insurance and real estate company executive*

SOUTH CAROLINA

Aiken
Rudnick, Irene Krugman *lawyer, state legislator, educator*

Columbia
Cork, Holly A. *state legislator*
Courson, John Edward *state senator, insurance company executive*
Harvin, Charles Alexander, III *state legislator*
Leatherman, Hugh Kenneth, Sr. *state senator, business executive*
Manly, Sarah Letitia *state legislator, ophthalmic photographer, angiographer*
Smith, James Roland *state legislator*
Smith, J(efferson) Verne *state senator, business executive*

Greenville
Mann, James Robert *congressman*

Spartanburg
Courtney, Charles Tyrone *state legislator, lawyer*
Patterson, Elizabeth Johnston *former congresswoman*

Summerville
Rose, Michael Thomas *state legislator, lawyer*

West Columbia
Wilson, Addison Graves (Joe Wilson) *lawyer, state senator*

SOUTH DAKOTA

Baltic
Wagner, Michael Dickman *state representative, small business owner*

Brookings
McClure-Bibby, Mary Anne *former state legislator*

Mitchell
Shanard, George Harris *retired state senator, entrepreneur*

Pierre
Hodges, Joyce E. *state legislator*
Kundert, Alice E. *state legislator*
Nicolay, Janice *state legislator*
Pederson, Gordon Roy *state legislator, retired military officer*
Stensland, Linda L. *state senator*

Prairie City
Wishard, Della Mae *state legislator*

Sioux Falls
Koetzle, Gil *state legislator, fire fighter, professional association administrator*
Paisley, Keith W. *state senator, small business owner*

Sturgis
Ingalls, Marie Cecelie *former state legislator, retail executive*

Wessington Springs
Morford-Burg, JoAnn *state senator, investment company executive*

TENNESSEE

Cleveland
Stockburger, Harold Ellis, Jr. *state legislator, insurance agency executive*

Maryville
Koella, Carl Ohm, Jr. *lawyer, state senator*

Nashville
Bragg, John Thomas *state legislator, retired businessman*
Crowe, Dewey E., II (Rusty Crowe) *state senator*
Duer, Shirley Powell *state legislator*
Kisber, Matthew Harris *state legislator*
Person, Curtis S., Jr. *lawyer, state senator*
Purcell, William Paxson, III *state representative*
Westmoreland, Barry Keith *state legislator*

Shelbyville
Cooper, James Hayes Shofner (Jim Cooper) *former congressman, lawyer*

TEXAS

Abilene
Hunter, Robert Dean (Bob Hunter) *state legislator, retired academic administrator*

Austin
Brown, J. E. (Buster Brown) *state senator, lawyer*
Bullock, Robert D. (Bob Bullock) *state legislator, lieutenant governor, lawyer*
Danburg, Debra *state legislator*
Denny, Mary Craver *state legislator, rancher*
Glasgow, Robert J. (Bob Glasgow) *state senator, lawyer*
Kilgore, Joe Madison *former congressman, lawyer*
Parmer, Hugh Q. *state senator*
Sims, Bill *state senator, business executive*

Brownsville
Uribe, Hector R. *state senator, lawyer*

Dallas
Cain, David *state senator, lawyer*
Goolsby, Tony *state legislator*
Leedom, John Nesbett *distribution company executive, state senator*

Fort Worth
Mowery, Anna Renshaw *state legislator*
Willis, Doyle Henry *state legislator, lawyer*

Garland
Driver, Joe L. *state legislator, insurance agent*

Harlingen
Solis, Jim *state legislator, lawyer*

Houston
Green, Gene *congressman*
Henderson, Donald Blanton *lawyer, state senator*

Lubbock
Montford, John Thomas *lawyer, state legislator*

Midland
Craddick, Thomas Russell *investor, state representative*

Port Arthur
Parker, Carl *former state senator*

San Antonio
†Romo, Sylvia *state legislator, accountant*

Waco
†Sibley, David McAdams *state senator, lawyer, oral surgeon*

UTAH

Bountiful
Burningham, Kim Richard *former state legislator*

Cedar City
Hunter, R. Haze *state legislator*

Corinne
Ferry, Miles Yeoman *state official*

Layton
Barlow, Haven J. *state legislator, realtor*

Ogden
Montgomery, Robert F. *state legislator, retired surgeon, cattle rancher*

Provo
Valentine, John Lester *state legislator, lawyer*

Roy
Peterson, Douglas Shurtleff *state legislator, packaging company official*

Salt Lake City
Bennett, Janet Huff *legislative staff member*
Black, Wilford Rex, Jr. *state senator*
Carnahan, Orville Darrell *state legislator, retired college president*
Davis, Gene *state legislator*
Garn, Edwin Jacob (Jake Garn) *former senator*
Peterson, Millie M. *state legislator*
Tempest, Richard Blackett *state senator, general contractor*

Sandy
Christensen, Arnold *state senator, electrical contractor*

Tremonton
Kerr, Kleon Harding *former state senator, educator*

VERMONT

Burlington
Carroll, John Marcus Conlon *banker*
Hoff, Philip Henderson *lawyer, state senator*
Sullivan, Mary Margaret *state legislator*

Essex Junction
Sweetser, Susan W. *state legislator, lawyer, advocate*

Fair Haven
Larkin, John Paul, II *state legislator*

Montpelier
Bassett, Alice Cook *state legislator*
Campbell, Sean Patrick *contractor, state legislator*
Farmer, John Martin *state senator*
Illuzzi, Vincent *state senator*
McGarey Madkour, Mary Elaine Bliss *state legislator*
Parker, Scudder Holden *state senator*
Steele, Karen Kiarsis *state legislator*
Wood, Barbara Louise Champion *state legislator*

Saint Johnsbury
Crosby, George Miner *state legislator*

South Londonderry
Coleman, Wendell Lawrence *state legislator, farmer*

VIRGINIA

Alexandria
Kindness, Thomas Norman *former congressman, lawyer, consultant*

Fairfax
Miller, Emilie F. *state senator*

Franconia
Keating, Gladys Brown *state legislator*

Gate City
Quillen, Ford Carter *state legislator, lawyer*

Halifax
Anderson, Howard Palmer *former state senator*

Lakeridge
Garon, Richard Joseph, Jr. *chief of staff, political worker*

Leesburg
Mims, William Cleveland *state legislator, lawyer*

Mc Lean
Callahan, Vincent Francis, Jr. *publisher, state legislator*
St. Germain, Fernand Joseph *congressman*

Merrifield
Scott, James Martin *state legislator, healthcare system executive*

Newport News
Hamilton, Phillip Andrew *instructional services coordinator, legislator*
†Trible, Paul Seward, Jr. *former senator*

Norfolk
Miller, Yvonne Bond *state senator, educator*

Richmond
Howell, Janet D. *state legislator*
Puller, Linda Todd *state legislator*

Virginia Beach
Wardrup, Leo C., Jr. *state legislator*

WASHINGTON

Everett
Nelson, Gary *county councilman, engineer*

Lake Stevens
Quigley, Kevin Walsh *state legislator, lawyer*

Olympia
Belcher, Jennifer Marion *state legislator, management consultant*
Haugen, Mary Margaret *state legislator*
Kessler, Lynn Elizabeth *state legislator*
Kohl, Jeanne Elizabeth *state senator, sociologist, educator*
Long, Jeanine Hundley *state legislator*
Newhouse, Irving Ralph *state legislator*
Smith, Linda A. *congresswoman, former state legislator*
Spanel, Harriet Rosa Albertsen *state senator*
Thomas, Brian Chester *state legislator, engineer*
Wang, Arthur C. *lawyer, educator*
Wojahn, R. Lorraine *state legislator*

Ritzville
Schoesler, Mark Gerald *state legislator, farmer*

Seattle
Evans, Daniel Jackson *former senator, environmental consultant*

Spanaway
Campbell, Thomas J. *legislator, chiropractor*

Spokane
Dellwo, Dennis A. *state legislator*

Tacoma
Walker, Sally Warden *state legislator*

Walla Walla
Hayner, Jeannette Clare *state legislator*

WEST VIRGINIA

Charleston
Brown, Bonnie Louise *state legislator*
Wehrle, Martha Gaines *state legistator*
Yoder, John Christian *state senator, lawyer, insurance company executive*

Elkins
Spears, Jae *state legislator*

Grafton
Harman, Charlton Newton (Bud Harman) *state senator, retired*

Parkersburg
Brum, Brenda *state legislator, librarian*

WISCONSIN

Eau Claire
Zien, David Allen *state legislator*

Green Bay
Green, Mark Andrew *state legislator, lawyer*

Janesville
Wood, Wayne W. *state legislator*

Madison
Burke, Brian B. *state senator, lawyer*
Darling, Alberta Statkus *state legislator, marketing executive, former art museum executive*
Farrow, Margaret Ann *state legislator*
Huelsman, Joanne B. *state legislator*
Klug, Scott Leo *congressman*
Krusick, Margaret Ann *state legislator*
Kunicki, Walter Joseph *state legislator*
Lorge, William David *state legislator, farmer*
Moen, Rodney Charles *state senator, retired naval officer*
Otte, Clifford *state legislator*
Panzer, Mary E. *state legislator*
Porter, Cloyd Allen *state representative*
Robson, Judith Biros *state legislator*
Rude, Brian David *state legislator*
Rutkowski, James Anthony *state legislator*
Schultz, Dale Walter *state legislator*
Silbaugh, Rudy Lamont *state legislator*
Swoboda, Lary Joseph *state legislator*
Turner, Robert Lloyd *state legislator*
Williams, Annette Polly *state legislator*
Young, Rebecca Mary Conrad *state legislator*

WYOMING

Casper
Meenan, Patrick Henry *state legislator*
Nagel, Patricia Jo *state legislator, consultant, lawyer*

Cody
Shreve, Peg *state legislator, retired elementary educator*

Jackson
LaLonde, Robert Frederick *state senator, retired*

Lander
Tipton, Harry Basil, Jr. *state legislator, physician*

Laramie
Maxfield, Peter C. *state legislator, law educator, lawyer*

Rock Springs
Blackwell, Samuel Eugene *state legislator*

TERRITORIES OF THE UNITED STATES

AMERICAN SAMOA

Pago Pago
†Solaita, Tulafono Fuli *senator*

GUAM

Agana
Ruth, Martha Cruz *senator*
San Agustin, Joe Taitano *Guam senator, financial institution executive, management researcher*

PUERTO RICO

San Juan
Acevedo-Vilá, Aníbal *state legislator, lawyer*
McClintock, Kenneth Davison *state legislator*
Ortiz Velazquez, Rolando *territory legislator, lawyer*
Rivera-Ortiz, Gilberto *state senator*
San Antonio Mendoza, Oscar Anibal *state legislator*
Valentin Acevedo, Freddy *senator*

VIRGIN ISLANDS

Charlotte Amalie
†Frazer, Victor O. *delegate, former legislator*
Richardson, Bingley Geraldo *territory legislator*
Scott-Williams, Stephanie *territorial legislator*

Frederiksted
O'Neal, Lilliana Belardo de *territory senator*
Pickard, Mary Ann *senator*

Saint Thomas
Liburd, Almando Leando *senator*

CANADA

ALBERTA

Edmonton
Adair, James Allen *Canadian provincial government official*
Fowler, Richard S. *provincial legislator*
†Klein, Ralph *provincial legislator, former city mayor*

BRITISH COLUMBIA

Victoria
Boone, Lois Ruth *legislator*
Weisgerber, John Sylvester *provincial legislator*

MANITOBA

Winnipeg
Carstairs, Sharon *state legislator*
Roblin, Duff *Canadian senator*
Wowchuk, Rosann *provincial legislator*

NORTHWEST TERRITORIES

Yellowknife
Ballantyne, Michael Alan *legislator*

NOVA SCOTIA

Halifax
Gillis, John William *Canadian legislator, geologist*

ONTARIO

Ottawa
Austin, Jacob (Jack Austin) *Canadian senator*
†Boudria, Don *Canadian member of parliament*
Doyle, Richard James *Canadian senator, former editor*
†Duceppe, Gilles *Canadian House of Commons member*
Eggleton, Arthur C. *Canadian government official, member of Parliament*
Fairbairn, Joyce *Canadian senator*
†Kilgour, David *Canadian member of parliament*
MacEachen, Allan Joseph *senator*
†Maheu, Shirley *Canadian legislator*
Marleau, Robert *parliamentary clerk*
Mc Whinney, Edward Watson *Canadian government legislator*

Murray, Lowell *Canadian senator*
†Parent, Gilbert *mem. Can. Ho. of Commons*
Perrault, Raymond *Canadian legislator, senator*
Robichaud, Louis Joseph *Canadian senator*
†Silye, Jim *member of Canadian House of Commons*

Toronto
Grier, Ruth *provincial legislator*
Haeck, Christel *provincial legislator*
Harrington, Margaret Helen *state legislator*

QUEBEC

Montreal
Castonguay, Claude *former senator, corporate director, lawyer*

ADDRESS UNPUBLISHED

Anderson, Bob *state legislator, business executive*
Arnold, Sheila *former state legislator*
†Baker, Howard Henry, Jr. *former senator, lawyer*
Baker, Richard Hugh *congressman*
Barlow, Tom *congressman, sales executive*
Barnhart, Jo Anne B. *government official*
Barton, Joe Linus *congressman*
Beals, Nancy Farwell *state legislator*
Bell, Clarence Deshong *lawyer, state senator*
Bell, Clarence Elmo *former state senator*
Bliley, Thomas Jerome, Jr. *congressman*
Bluechel, Alan *state senator, wood structural components manufacturing company executive*
Bono, Sonny Salvatore *congressman, singer, composer, former mayor*
Brennan, John A., Jr. *state senator, lawyer*
Brodsky, Richard Louis *state legislator*
Buffmire, Judy Ann *state legislator, psychologist, consultant*
Bunning, Jim *congressman, former professional baseball player*
Burton, Joseph Alfred *state legislator*
Carpenter, Dorothy Fulton *former state legislator*
Carr, M. Robert (Bob Carr) *lawyer*
Chandler, John Parker Hale, Jr. *state senator*
Charlton, Betty Jo *retired state legislator*
Chisholm, Shirley Anita St. Hill *former congresswoman, educator, lecturer*
Coble, Howard *congressman, lawyer*
Cochran, Thad *senator*
Cohen, Lita Indzel *state legislator*
Cowenhoven, Garret Peter *state legislator, educator*
D'Amato, Alfonse M. *senator*
De Concini, Dennis *former senator, lawyer*
de la Garza, Eligio (Kika de la Garza) *congressman*
Doderer, Minnette Frerichs *state legislator*
Ford, Wendell Hampton *senator*
Gallegly, Elton William *congressman*
Gilbertz, Larry E. *state legislator, entrepreneur*
Gordly, Avel Louise *state legislator, community activist*
Goss, Porter J. *congressman*
Gullatt, Jane *state legislator*
Hammerschmidt, John Paul *retired congressman, lumber company executive*
Hansen, James Vear *congressman*
Hatch, Orrin Grant *senator*
Hawkins, Augustus Freeman *former congressman*
Hawkins, Mary Ellen Higgins (Mary Ellen Higgins) *former state legislator, public relations consultant*
Hayes, Joan Eames *state legislator*
Hayne, Harriet Ann *state legislator, rancher*
Hearn, Joyce Camp *retired educator, state legislator*
Hichens, Walter Wilson *former state senator*
Hill, Anita Carraway *retired state legislator*
Holliday, Robert Kelvin *state senator, former newspaper executive*
Humphrey, Shirley Joy *state representative, education consultant*
Hunter, Duncan Lee *congressman*
†Hutchison, Kay Bailey *senator*
James, Arlo Dee *state legislator, retired mining maintenance executive*
Johnston, Harry A., II *congressman*
Keyserling, Harriet H. *state legislator*
Konnyu, Ernest Leslie *former congressman*
Lazechko, D. M. (Molly Lazechko) *former state legislator*
Lebowitz, Catharine Koch *state legislator*
Locke, David Henry *state senator*
Mc Govern, George Stanley *former senator*
McGovern, Patricia *state senator*
McGraw, Warren Randolph, II *state legislator, lawyer*
McHale, Paul *congressman, lawyer*
Mikulski, Barbara Ann *senator*
Nielsen, Glade Benjamin *mayor, former state senator*
Nielson, Howard Curtis *former congressman, retired educator*
Oppenheimer, Suzi *state senator*
Osler, Dorothy K. *state legislator*
Parry, Atwell J., Jr. *state senator, retailer*
Pettis-Roberson, Shirley McCumber *former congresswoman*
Piccinini, Janice *state legislator*
Pond, Phyllis Joan *state legislator*
Proxmire, William *former senator*
Pryce, Deborah D. *congresswoman*
Reid, Harry *senator*
Reilly, Edward Francis, Jr. *former state senator, federal agency administrator*
Roth, Toby *congressman*
Schenk, Lynn *congresswoman*
Schmidt, Arthur Louis *retired state senator*
Schur, Susan Dorfman *state legislator*
Schwartz, Carol Levitt *former government official*
Searle, Rodney Newell *state legislator, farmer, insurance agent*
Sherrill, Thomas Beck *financial planner, state legislator*
Skinner, Patricia Morag *state legislator*
Solarz, Stephen Joshua *congressman*
Soles, Ada Leigh *former state legislator, government advisor*
Sorensen, Sheila *state senator*
Stickney, Jessica *former state legislator*
Theno, Daniel O'Connell *former state legislator*
Udall, Morris King *former congressman*
Vowell, Jack C. *former state legislator, investor*
†Wallace, Keith Alton *legislator, dairy farmer*
Weldon, Jeffrey Alan *state senator, historical research company executive*
Wilder, Donny *state legislator, retired newspaper publisher*
Wofford, Harris Llewellyn *former senator, lawyer*
Zeliff, William H., Jr. *congressman*

HEALTHCARE: DENTISTRY

UNITED STATES

ALABAMA

Birmingham
Alling, Charles Calvin, III *oral-maxillofacial surgeon, educator, writer*
Fullmer, Harold Milton *dentist, educator*
Manson-Hing, Lincoln Roy *dental educator*

Lillian
Shory, Naseeb Lein *dentist, retired state official*

ARIZONA

Flagstaff
Ririe, Craig Martin *periodontist*

Phoenix
Fournier, Donald Frederick *dentist*

Tucson
Eshelman, Enos Grant, Jr. *prosthodontist*
Hawke, Robert Francis *dentist*
Nadler, George L. *orthodontist*

CALIFORNIA

Arcadia
Gamboa, George Charles *oral surgeon, educator*

Burlingame
Truta, Marianne Patricia *oral and maxillofacial surgeon, educator, author*

La Jolla
Silverstone, Leon Martin *pedodontist, cariologist, neuroscientist, educator, researcher*

La Mesa
Williams, Carlton Hinkle *dentist*

Long Beach
Domondon, Oscar *dentist*

Los Angeles
Dummett, Clifton Orrin *dentist, educator*
Yagiela, John Allen *dental educator*

Manteca
Tonn, Elverne Meryl *pediatric dentist, dental insurance consultant*

Pasadena
Mc Carthy, Frank Martin *surgical sciences educator*

Sacramento
Redig, Dale Francis *dentist, association executive*

San Diego
Ingle, John Ide *dental educator*

San Francisco
Bensinger, David August *dentist, university dean*
Dugoni, Arthur A. *orthodontics educator, university dean*
Greene, John Clifford *dentist, former university dean*
Greenspan, Deborah *oral medicine educator*
Khosla, Ved Mitter *oral and maxillofacial surgeon, educator*

San Jose
Higgins, James Bradley *dentist*
Yoshizumi, Donald Tetsuro *dentist*

San Rafael
Gryson, Joseph Anthony *orthodontist*

Thousand Palms
Smith, Charles Thomas *retired dentist, educator*

Torrance
Leake, Donald Lewis *oral and maxillofacial surgeon, oboist*

West Hollywood
Etessami, Rambod *endonontist*

COLORADO

Arvada
Ingalls, Gegory Kent *oral and maxillofacial sugeon*

Aurora
Eames, Wilmer Ballou *dental educator*

Denver
Bomberg, Thomas James *dental educator*
DiGiorgio, Robert Michael *dentist*
Doida, Stanley Y. *dentist*
Martin, William Truett *oral surgeon, state legislature*

CONNECTICUT

Farmington
Löe, Harald *dentist, educator, researcher*

New Canaan
Gottlieb, Arnold *dentist*

Norwalk
Brod, Morton Shlevin *oral surgeon*

DISTRICT OF COLUMBIA

Bolling AFB
Gardner, Jerry Dean *dentist, military officer*

Washington
Calhoun, Noah Robert *oral maxillofacial surgeon, educator*
Gardner, Alvin Frederick *oral pathologist, government official*
Lorton, Lewis *dentist, researcher, computer scientist*
Sazima, Henry John *oral and maxillofacial surgery educator*
Sinkford, Jeanne Craig *dentist, educator*

FLORIDA

Bal Harbour
Rosenbluth, Morton *periodontist, educator*

Boynton Beach
Kronman, Joseph Henry *orthodontist*

Fort Myers
Laboda, Gerald *oral and maxillofacial surgeon*

Gainesville
Legler, Donald Wayne *university dean, dentist*
Medina, Jose Enrique *dentist, educator*

Miami
Gittess, Ronald Marvin *dentist*
Higley, Bruce Wadsworth *orthodontist*
Hyman, Milton *dental educator*

Palm Beach
Tiecke, Richard William *pathologist, educator, association executive*

Pensacola
Hamilton, Robert Edward *oral and maxillofacial surgeon, naval officer*
Shows, Clarence Oliver *dentist*

Tamarac
Fish, Robert Jay *dental surgeon, lawyer, medico-legal consultant, diversified entrepreneur*

West Palm Beach
Elder, Stewart Taylor *dentist, retired naval officer*

Winter Haven
Turnquist, Donald Keith *orthodontist*

Winter Park
McKean, Thomas Wayne *dentist, retired naval officer*

GEORGIA

Atlanta
Neaverth, Elmer Joseph, Jr. *dentist, endodontist, educator*

Augusta
Hammer, Wade Burke *oral and maxillofacial surgeon, educator*

Evans
Beaudreau, David Eugene *dentist, educator*

Macon
Holliday, Peter Osborne, Jr. *dentist*
Walton, DeWitt Talmage, Jr. *dentist*

HAWAII

Honolulu
George, Peter T. *orthodontist*
Nishimura, Pete Hideo *oral surgeon*
Scheerer, Ernest William *dentist*

Pearl City
Sue, Alan Kwai Keong *dentist*

IDAHO

Boise
Mulick, Edward James *orthodontist*

ILLINOIS

Alton
†Dickey, Keith Winfield *dentist, dental educator*
Heuertz, Sarah Jane *dentist*
King, Ordie Herbert, Jr. *oral pathologist*

Chicago
†Bogert, John Alden, II *dental association executive*
Buckner, James Lowell *dentist*
Diefenbach, Viron Leroy *dental, public health educator, university dean*
Driskell, Claude Evans *dentist*
†Eisenmann, Dale Richard *dental educator*
Goepp, Robert August *dental educator, oral pathologist*
Graber, Thomas M. *orthodontist*
Heuer, Michael Alexander *dentist, educator*
Ouzounian, Armenuhi *dentist*
Santangelo, Mario Vincent *dental association executive, educator*
Scholle, Roger Hal *dentist*
Weclew, Victor T. *dentist*
Yale, Seymour Hershel *dental radiologist, educator, university dean, gerontologist*
Zaki, Abdelmoneim Emam *dental educator*

Libertyville
Goodman, Evan Besey *dentist*

Naperville
Grimley, Jeffrey Michael *dentist*

Pekin
Bell, John Richard *dentist*

Riverwoods
Douglas, Bruce Lee *oral and maxillofacial surgeon, educator, health consultant, gerontology consultant*

INDIANA

Carmel
Roche, James Richard *pediatric dentist, university dean*

Clinton
Cloyd, George Thomas *dentist*

Dyer
Teuscher, George William *dental educator*

Indianapolis
Standish, Samuel Miles *oral pathologist, college dean*

IOWA

Iowa City
Bishara, Samir Edward *orthodontist*
Jacobs, Richard Matthew *dentist, orthodontics educator*
Olin, William Harold *orthodontist, educator*

KENTUCKY

Lexington
Mink, John Robert *dental educator*

Louisville
Parkins, Frederick Milton *dental educator, university dean*

West Liberty
Blevins, Walter, Jr. *dentist, state legislator*

LOUISIANA

New Orleans
Rayson, Jack Henry *dentist, educator, retired*

MARYLAND

Bethesda
Kruger, Gustav Otto, Jr. *oral surgeon, educator*

Potomac
Cotton, William Robert *dentist*

MASSACHUSETTS

Boston
Frankl, Spencer Nelson *dentist, university dean*
Hein, John William *dentist, educator*
Shklar, Gerald *oral pathologist, periodontist, educator*

Dorchester
Lee, June Warren *dentist*

Hanover
Lonborg, James Reynold *dentist, former professional baseball player*

Milton
Dunn, Martin Joseph *dentist*

Wellesley
Doku, Hristo Chris *dental educator*

MICHIGAN

Ann Arbor
Ash, Major McKinley, Jr. *dentist, educator*
Avery, James Knuckey *dental educator*
Christiansen, Richard Louis *orthodontics educator, research director, former dean*
Craig, Robert George *dental science educator*
Striffler, David Frank *dental public health educator*

Detroit
Dziuba, Henry Frank *dental school administrator*

MINNESOTA

Minneapolis
Doroschak, John Z. *dentist*
Elzay, Richard Paul *dental school administrator*
Geistfeld, Ronald Elwood *dental educator*
Shapiro, Burton Leonard *experimental pathologist, geneticist, educator*
Wolff, Larry F. *dental educator, researcher*

Saint Paul
Jensen, James Robert *dentist, educator*

MISSOURI

Kansas City
Burk, Norman *oral surgeon*

Moore, David Lowell *dentist*
Moore, Dorsey Jerome *dentistry educator, maxillofacial prosthetist*

Lees Summit
Waite, Daniel Elmer *retired oral surgeon*

Saint Louis
Isselhard, Donald Edward *dentist*
Selfridge, George Dever *dentist, retired naval officer*

NEBRASKA

Omaha
Lynch, Benjamin Leo *oral surgeon educator*

NEVADA

Las Vegas
Rawson, Raymond D. *dentist*

NEW HAMPSHIRE

Manchester
Bryan, Roland Henry *dentist*

NEW JERSEY

Clifton
Swystun-Rives, Bohdana Alexandra *dentist*

Fort Lee
Kiriakopoulos, George Constantine *dentist*

Montclair
Bolden, Theodore Edward *dentist, educator*

Morris Plains
Picozzi, Anthony *dentistry educator, educational administrator*

Ridgewood
Lucca, John James *retired dental educator*

Tinton Falls
Furman, Samuel Elliott *dentist*

Westfield
Feret, Adam Edward, Jr. *dentist*

NEW YORK

Bronx
Friedman, Joel Matthew *oral and maxillofacial surgeon, educator*

Buffalo
Ciancio, Sebastian Gene *periodontist, educator*
Drinnan, Alan John *oral pathologist*

Great Neck
Elkowitz, Lloyd Kent *dental anesthesiologist, dentist, pharmacist*
Wank, Gerald Sidney *periodontist*

Island
Kaslick, Ralph Sidney *dentist, educator*

Massena
Pellegrino, James Martin *dentist*

New Hyde Park
Mulvihill, James Edward *periodontist, university administrator, educator, health care executive*

New York
Arvystas, Michael Geciauskas *orthodontist, educator*
Ashkinazy, Larry Robert *dentist*
Brzustowicz, Stanislaw Henry *clinical dentistry educator*
Di Salvo, Nicholas Armand *dental educator, orthodontist*
Klatell, Jack *dentist*
Mandel, Irwin Daniel *dentist*
Marder, Michael Zachary *dentist, researcher, educator*
Sendax, Victor Irven *dentist, educator, dental implant researcher*

North Tarrytown
Zegarelli, Edward Victor *retired dental educator, researcher*

Rochester
Bowen, William Henry *dental researcher, dental educator*
McHugh, William Dennis *dental educator, researcher*

Stony Brook
Boucher, Louis Jack *dentist, educator*

Wantagh
Ross, Sheldon Jules *dentist*

Wappingers Falls
Engelman, Melvin Alkon *retired dentist, business executive, scientist*

NORTH CAROLINA

Chapel Hill
Baker, Ronald Dale *dental educator, surgeon, university administrator*
Bawden, James Wyatt *dental educator, dental scientist*
Hershey, H(oward) Garland, Jr. *university administrator, orthodontist*
Proffit, William Robert *orthodontics educator*
White, Raymond Petrie, Jr. *dentist, educator*

Charlotte
Twisdale, Harold Winfred *dentist*

OHIO

Cleveland
De Marco, Thomas Joseph *periodontist, educator*
Wotman, Stephen *dentistry educator*

Columbus
Buchsieb, Walter Charles *orthodontist*
Goorey, Nancy Jane *dentist*
Horton, John Edward *periodontist, educator*

Hubbard
Rose, Ernst *dentist*

OKLAHOMA

Edmond
Brown, William Ernest *dentist*

OREGON

Medford
Barnum, William Laird *pedodontist*

Newport
Richardson, Bruce LeVoyle *dentist*

Portland
Bates, Richard Mather *dentist*
Clarke, J(oseph) Henry *dental educator, dentist*
Van Hassel, Henry John *dentist, educator, university dean*

PENNSYLVANIA

Clarion
Foreman, Thomas Alexander *dentist*

Danville
Lessin, Michael Edward *oral-maxillofacial surgeon*

Philadelphia
Fielding, Allen Fred *oral and maxillofacial surgeon, educator*
Listgarten, Max Albert *periodontics educator*
Winkler, Sheldon *dentist, educator*

Pittsburgh
Ismail, Yahia Hassan *dentist, educator*

Wayne
Guernsey, Louis Harold *retired oral and maxillofacial surgeon, educator*

RHODE ISLAND

Providence
Mehlman, Edwin Stephen *endodontist*

SOUTH CAROLINA

Charleston
Salinas, Carlos Francisco *dentist educator*

Lake City
TruLuck, James Paul, Jr. *dentist, vintner*

TENNESSEE

Memphis
Butts, Herbert Clell *dentist, educator*

Nashville
Hall, Hugh David *dentist, physician, educator*

TEXAS

Dallas
Byrd, David Lamar *oral surgeon educator*
McWhorter, Kathleen *orthodontist*
Sugg, Harry Lee, Jr. *dentist*

Flower Mound
Kolodny, Stanley Charles *oral surgeon, air force officer*

Houston
Allen, Don Lee *dentistry educator*

San Antonio
†Gassmann, Carl Jeffrey *oral surgeon, physician*

VERMONT

Shelburne
Sawabini, Wadi Issa *retired dentist*

VIRGINIA

Fort Belvoir
Scott, David Bytovetzski *dental research and forensic odontology consultant*

Norfolk
Shuman, Deanne *dental hygienist, educator*

Richmond
Laskin, Daniel M. *oral and maxillofacial surgeon, educator*

Virginia Beach
Farrell, Paul Edward *dentist, retired naval officer, educator*

WASHINGTON

Bellevue
Carlson, Curtis Eugene *orthodontist, periodontist*

Seattle
Dworkin, Samuel Franklin *dentist, psychologist*
Page, Roy Christopher *periodontist, educator*

Spokane
Foster, Ruth Mary *dental association administrator*
Millard, James Michael *oral surgeon*

WEST VIRGINIA

Poca
Ghareeb, Sami Mitri *dentist*

WISCONSIN

Milwaukee
Scrabeck, Jon Gilmen *dental eductor*

Wausau
Derwinski, Dennis Anthony *dentist*

MILITARY ADDRESSES OF THE UNITED STATES

PACIFIC

FPO
Hooley, James Robert *oral and maxillofacial surgeon, educator, university dean*

CANADA

ALBERTA

Edmonton
Thompson, Gordon William *dentist, educator*

BRITISH COLUMBIA

Vancouver
Beagrie, George Simpson *dentist, educator, dean emeritus*

ONTARIO

London
Dunn, Wesley John *dental educator*

Toronto
Ten Cate, Arnold Richard *dentistry educator*

QUEBEC

Montreal
Bentley, Kenneth Chessar *oral and maxillofacial surgeon, educator*
Lussier, Jean-Paul *dentistry educator*

Sainte Foy
Maranda, Guy *oral maxillofacial surgeon, Canadian health facility executive, educator*

SWEDEN

Gothenburg
Bona, Christian Johannes Maximilian *dentist, psychotherapist*

ADDRESS UNPUBLISHED

Adisman, I. Kenneth *prosthodontist*
Brooke, Ralph Ian *dental educator, vice provost, university dean*
Coval-Apel, Naomi Miller *dentist*
Fox, Gerald Lynn *retired oral and maxillofacial surgeon*
Grewe, John Mitchell *orthodontist, educator*
Johnson, Dewey E(dward) *dentist*
McHugh, Earl Stephen *dentist*
Meador, Robert Lyman *dentist*

HEALTHCARE: HEALTH SERVICES

UNITED STATES

ALABAMA

Auburn
Barker, Kenneth Neil *pharmacy administration educator*
Vaughan, John Thomas *veterinarian, educator, university dean*

Birmingham
Booth, Rachel Zonelle *nursing educator*
†Callaway, Warren Eugene *hospital administrator*
Caplan, Lester *optometrist, educator*
Devane, Denis James *health care company executive*
†Faulkner, Charles Addison *health care administrator*
†Glasscock, Gary M. *health care administrator*
Grant, Phyllis Hunt *hospital administrator*
†Hall, Dennis A. *hospital administrator*
Johnson, Emmett Raymond *hospital administrator*
Lee, James A. *health facility finance executive*
Lewis, James Eldon *health care executive*
Loftin, Sister Mary Frances *health facility administrator*
Miller, Dennis Edward *corporate executive*
Peters, Henry Buckland *optometrist, educator*
Quintana, Jose Booth *health care executive*
Richards, J. Scott *rehabilitation medicine professional*
Stelling, Joan Donna *rehabilitation nurse*
†Weinsier, Roland Louis *nutrition educator and director*

Cherokee
†Oliver, Gerald Clifford *hospital administrator*

Daphne
Gettig, Carl William *optometrist*

Dothan
Inscho, Jean Anderson *social worker*

Florence
†Collins, Byron Griggs *hospital administrator*

Gadsden
†Williams, Walter Abner, Jr. *healthcare administrator, realtor*

Hartselle
Slate, Joe Hutson *psychologist, educator*

Huntsville
Boston, Edward Dale *hospital administrator*

Lillian
Moyer, Kenneth Evan *psychologist, educator*

Mobile
Clark, Jack *retired hospital company executive, accountant*
Johnson, David Pittman *psychotheraphy consultant, social work educator*
Shepherd, Linda Pace *nurse, educator, administrator*
Vitulli, William Francis *psychology educator*

Montgomery
Barnes, Robert E. *health care company executive*
Hornsby, Andrew Preston, Jr. *human services administrator*
Myers, Ira Lee *physician*
Rowan, John Robert *medical center director*

Normal
Okezie, B. Onuma *food scientist, nutritionist, educator*

Opelika
Knecht, Charles Daniel *veterinarian*

Pell City
Passey, George Edward *psychology educator*

Tuscaloosa
Cooper, Eugene Bruce *speech-language pathologist, educator*
Doerr, Robert Wayne *nursing administrator*
Ford, James Henry, Jr. *hospital executive*
Prigmore, Charles Samuel *social work educator*
Shellhase, Leslie John *social work educator*
†Thomas, Jerry *pharmacist*

Valley
†Humphrey, Robert Jennings *hospital executive*

ALASKA

Anchorage
Henderson-Dixon, Karen Sue *psychologist*
†Meddleton, Daniel Joseph *health facility administrator*
Risley, Todd Robert *psychologist, educator*

Juneau
Nord, Elfrida *community health nurse*

Sitka
Willman, Arthur Charles *healthcare executive*

Soldotna
Franzmann, Albert Wilhelm *wildlife veterinarian, consultant*

ARIZONA

Mesa
Boyd, Leona Potter *retired social worker*
†Evans, Don A. *healthcare company executive*
Roe, Carolyn *nursing educator*

Paradise Valley
Timmons, Evelyn Deering *pharmacist*

Phoenix
Ballantyne, Reginald Malcolm, III *healthcare executive*
Binnie, Nancy Catherine *nurse, educator*
Bonny, Mary Cleinmark *nurse*
Cheifetz, Lorna Gale *psychologist*
Crews, James Cecil *hospital administrator*
DeSilva, Joseph J. *hospital administrator*

†Harrington, John Leonard, Jr. *hospital administrator*
Rodgers, Anthony D. *hospital administrator*
Ryan, Tula Fleshman *health service consultant and nursing facility administrator*
Seiler, Steven Lawrence *health facility administrator*
†Wellinger, Charles H. *health services company executive*
†Welliver, Charles Harold *hospital administrator*
†Zobell, Gregory Grant *hospital administrator*

Prescott
Longfellow, Layne Allen *psychologist, educator*
Markham, Richard Glover *research executive*
Mc Cormack, Fred Allen *state social services administrator*

Scottsdale
Gordon, Rena Joyce *health services researcher, educator*
Jenkins, William Walter *psychologist, consultant*
Kizziar, Janet Wright *psychologist, author, lecturer*
†Poll, Max Henry *hospital administrator*

Sonoita
Scott, William Coryell *medical executive*

Sun City
Peterson, Leland Wilmer *health facility administrator*

Sun City West
Becker, Wesley Clemence *psychology educator emeritus*

Tempe
Uttal, William R(eichenstein) *psychology and engineering educator, research scientist*
Wesbury, Stuart Arnold, Jr. *health administration and policy educator*

Tucson
Beach, Lee Roy *psychologist, educator*
Kirk, Samuel Alexander *psychologist, educator*
Morford, James Warren *international health care executive*
Nation, James Edward *speech pathologist*
Pearson, Paul Brown *nutritionist, educator*
Shropshire, Donald Gray *hospital executive*
Smith, David Wayne *psychologist*
Tang, Esther Don *development consultant, retired social worker*
Weber, Charles Walter *nutrition educator*

ARKANSAS

Conway
†Summersett, James A., III *health care executive, hospital administrator*

El Dorado
Hopson, Brenda *nursing administrator*

Forrest City
Brown, Patricia Ann *child health nurse*

Fort Smith
Banks, David Russell *health care executive*
Ellis, Mary Calline *nursing administrator*
Stephens, Bobby Wayne *nursing home administrator*

Hot Springs National Park
Farley, Roy C. *rehabilitation researcher, educator*
Phelps, Charlotte Mae *health educator*

Little Rock
Berube, Michael Edward *nursing administrator*
Blandford, Sister Margaret Vincent *infirmary executive*
†Harrington, Russell Doyne, Jr. *hospital administrator*
Pierson, Richard Allen *hospital administrator*
Wolfe, Jonathan James *pharmacy educator*
Woodruff, John Douglas *non-profit association administrator, retired air force officer*

Mabelvale
Larch, Billie Bentley *nursing administrator*

Springdale
Sword, Russ Donald *hospital administrator*

State University
Whitis, Grace Ruth *nursing educator*

CALIFORNIA

Agoura Hills
Merchant, Roland Samuel, Sr. *hospital administrator, educator*

Aliso Viejo
Sanford, Sarah J. *nurse, health care executive*

Arcadia
Horner, Althea Jane *psychologist*

Bakersfield
Decker, James Thomas *psychotherapist*
Frankel, Helen Bruce *county executive*
Murillo, Velda Jean *social worker, counselor*

Berkeley
Baumrind, Diana *research psychologist*
Calloway, Doris Howes *nutrition educator*
Clausen, John Adam *social psychologist*
Enoch, Jay Martin *vision scientist, educator*
Fleming, Scott *retired health services executive*
Gilbert, Neil Robin *social work educator, author, consultant*
Greene, Albert Lawrence *hospital administrator*
Hafey, Joseph Michael *health association executive*
†Hafter, Ervin R. *psychology educator*
Hancock, Emily Stone *psychologist*
Holder, Harold D. *public health administrator, communications specialist, educator*
Jensen, Arthur Robert *psychology educator*
Lambert, Nadine Murphy *psychologist, educator*
Lashof, Joyce C. *public health educator*
Lazarus, Richard Stanley *psychology educator*
Lubin, Mary Luella *nursing home administrator*
Maslach, Christina *psychology educator*
Maurer, Adah Electra *psychologist*
Nemeth, Charlan Jeanne *psychology educator*
Rosenzweig, Mark Richard *psychology educator*
Staw, Barry Martin *business and psychology educator*
Tannenbaum, Percy H. *psychology educator*
Westheimer, Gerald *optometrist, educator*

Beverly Hills
Aguilera, Donna Conant *psychologist, researcher*
Evans, Louise *psychologist, investor, philanthropist*
Simmons, Richard Milton Teagle *physical fitness specialist, television personality*

Bishop
Haber, Ralph Norman *psychology consultant, researcher, educator*

Brea
Dyer, Alice Mildred *psychotherapist*

Burbank
Hartshorn, Terry O. *health facility administrator*
†LaLanne, Jack (François Henri LaLanne) *physical fitness specialist, entrepreneur*

Burlingame
Castetter, Sandra Lea *nursing executive*
Crawford, William Richard *psychologist*

Calabasas
†Bastone, Peter Francis *hospital administrator*

Canoga Park
Taylor, Edna Jane *employment program counselor*

Carmel
Parker, Donald Henry *psychologist, author*

Carson
Palmer, Beverly Blazey *psychologist, educator*

Cayucos
Hedlund, James Lane *retired psychologist, educator*

Chico
†Hartman, Andrew Paul, Jr. *hospital association administrator*

Chula Vista
Schorr, Martin Mark *forensic psychologist, educator, writer*

Corona Del Mar
Davis, Arthur David *psychology educator, musician*

Costa Mesa
Crinella, Francis Michael *neuropsychologist, science foundation director*

Culver City
Maltzman, Irving Myron *psychology educator*

Cupertino
Norman, Donald Arthur *cognitive scientist*

Cypress
Hoops, Alan *health care company executive*

Daly City
Mullins, Anna Carrolle *hospital administrator*

Danville
Davis, James Ivey *company president, laboratory associate*

Davis
Ardans, Alexander Andrew *veterinarian, laboratory director, educator*
Biberstein, Ernst Ludwig *veterinary medicine educator*
Harper, Lawrence Vernon *human development educator*
Hawkes, Glenn Rogers *psychology educator*
Mason, William A(lvin) *psychologist, educator, researcher*
Owings, Donald Henry *psychology educator*
Rhode, Edward Albert *veterinary medicine educator, veterinary cardiologist*
Schneeman, Barbara Olds *nutrition educator, dean*
Schwabe, Calvin Walter *veterinarian, medical historian, medical educator*
Steffey, Eugene Paul *veterinary medicine educator*
Theilen, Gordon Henry *veterinary surgery educator*

Downey
Schroeder, Robert J. *veterinarian, association executive*

Duarte
Shapero, Sanford Marvin *hospital executive, rabbi*

El Cajon
Colling, Kenneth Frank *hospital administrator*

El Cerrito
Conti, Isabella *psychologist, consultant*

Escondido
Damsbo, Ann Marie *psychologist*
Harper, Lilah Marie *nursing service administrator*

Eureka
†Kriger, Peter Wilson *healthcare administrator*

Fountain Valley
Gumbiner, Robert *health services executive*
Jessup, R. Judd *managed care executive*

Fresno
Coe, William Charles *psychology educator*
†O'Connor, Kevin John *psychologist*
Ogle, Mary Ellen *nursing and surgical services executive*
Stude, Everett Wilson, Jr. *rehabilitation counselor, educator*

Fullerton
Cole, Sherwood Orison *psychologist*
Hershey, Gerald Lee *psychologist*

Granada Hills
Aller, Wayne Kendall *psychology educator, researcher, computer education company executive, property manager*

Grass Valley
Cartwright, Mary Lou *laboratory scientist*

Hayward
Meyer, Ann Jane *human development educator*
Whalen, Thomas Earl *psychology educator*

Hemet
Hall, John Thomas, Jr. *patient care services administrator, consultant*

Huntington Beach
Martin, Wilfred Wesley Finny *psychologist, property owner and manager*

Inglewood
Epstein, Marsha Ann *public health administrator, physician*
†Long, Ophelia *hospital administrator*

Irvine
Greenberger, Ellen *psychologist, educator*
Jones, Joie Pierce *acoustician, educator, writer, scientist*
Knight, Patricia Marie *eye care company executive*
Luce, R(obert) Duncan *psychology educator*
Martin, Jay Herbert *psychoanalysis and English educator*
Mc Gaugh, James Lafayette *psychobiologist*
Sperling, George *cognitive scientist, educator*

La Honda
Waldhauer, Fred Donald *health care executive*

La Jolla
Arnold, Jean Ann *health science facility administrator*
Cain, William Stanley *psychologist, educator*
Cornette, William Magnus *scientist, research director, company executive*
†Ewell, Charles Muse *health care industry executive, consultant, educator*
Farson, Richard Evans *psychologist*
Harris, Philip Robert *management and space psychologist*
†Hudson, Richard Earl *hospital administrator*
Kaplan, Robert Malcolm *health researcher, educator*
Lakier, Nancy S. *health facility administrator*
Maher, James R. *laboratory administrator*
Mandler, George *psychologist*
Mandler, Jean Matter *psychologist, educator*
Spinweber, Cheryl Lynn *research psychologist*

La Quinta
Hartley, Celia Love *nursing educator, nursing administrator*

Laguna Beach
Arterburn, Stephen Forrest *health care company executive*
Banuelos, Betty Lou *rehabilitation nurse*
Smith, Leslie Roper *hospital administrator*

Laguna Niguel
Carr, Bernard Francis *hospital administrator*

Loma Linda
Hinshaw, David B., Sr. *hospital administrator*
Moss, Susan Linda *nurse*
Register, Ulma Doyle *nutrition educator*
Zolber, Kathleen Keen *nutrition educator*

Long Beach
Harmon Brown, Valarie Jean *hospital laboratory director, information systems executive*
Kohn, Gerhard *psychologist, educator*
Kokaska, Charles James *educational psychologist*
Mullins, Ruth Gladys *pediatrics nurse*
Talmadge, Mary Christine *nursing educator*

Los Angeles
Andersen, Ronald Max *health services educator, researcher*
†Boswell, James Douglas *medical research executive*
†Caldwell, Alethea Otti *health care systems executive*
Eamer, Richard Keith *health care company executive, lawyer*
Feshbach, Seymour *psychology educator*
Floyd, Anne Marie Daze *neonatology nurse, administrator*
Forness, Steven Robert *educational psychologist*
Gallistel, Charles Ransom *psychology educator*
Gates, Robert C. *health system administrator*
Gilman, John Joseph *research scientist*
Greenberg, Ira Arthur *psychologist*
Gunn, Karen Sue *psychologist*
Holmes, Gene L. *social services professional, child care specialist*
Hopkins, Carl Edward *public health educator*
Horowitz, Ben *medical center executive*
Hummel, Joseph William *hospital administrator*
Jacobs, Marilyn Susan *psychologist, author*
Jacobs, Marion Kramer *psychologist*
Kelley, Harold Harding *psychology educator*
King, Sheldon Selig *medical center administrator, educator*
Lasswell, Marcia Lee *psychologist, educator*
†Lavond, David G. *psychology educator*
Leary, Timothy *psychologist, author*
Lien, Eric Jung-chi *pharmacist, educator*
Lindsley, Donald Benjamin *physiological psychologist, educator*
Lyman, John *psychology and engineering educator*
Michael, William Burton *psychologist, educator*
Miller, Norman *psychology educator, researcher*
Neumann, Alfred Kurt *public health physician, educator*
Noce, Walter William, Jr. *hospital administrator*
Okeh, Samson Ewruje *psychiatric nurse*
Park, Chui Suh *pharmacist*
Perkins, William Hughes *speech pathologist, educator*
Phinney, Jean Swift *psychology educator*
Raven, Bertram H(erbert) *psychology educator*
†Renford, Edward J. *hospital administrator*
Roberts, Robert Winston *social work educator, dean*
Rodnick, Eliot Herman *psychologist, educator*
Shneidman, Edwin S. *psychologist, educator, thanatologist, suicidologist*
Sinay, Ruth Doris *psychologist*
Sloane, Robert Malcolm *hospital administrator*
Song, Moon Ki *biomedical research scientist*
Thompson, Richard Frederick *psychologist, neuroscientist, educator*
Utz, Sarah Winifred *nursing educator*
Watson, Sharon Gitin *psychologist, executive*
†Williams, Richard T. *hospital administrator*
Wittrock, Merlin Carl *educational psychologist*
Wood, Nancy Elizabeth *psychologist, educator*

Los Gatos
Olender, Beatrijs Tobi *psychologist, marriage and family therapist*

Los Osos
Brown, Mary Eleanor *physical therapist, educator*
Thomas, Robert Murray *educational psychology educator*

Malibu
Aiken, Lewis Roscoe, Jr. *psychologist, educator*
Palacio, June Rose Payne *professor of nutritional science*
Reres, Mary Epiphany *health care and administration consultant*

Menlo Park
Salmon, Vincent *acoustical consultant*
Speidel, John Joseph *physician, foundation officer*

Mill Valley
Benezet, Louis Tomlinson *retired psychology educator, former college president*

Mission Viejo
Milunas, J. Robert *health care organization executive*

Moffett Field
Cohen, Malcolm Martin *psychologist, researcher*
Haines, Richard Foster *psychologist*
Lauber, John K. *research psychologist*

Monrovia
Salaman, Maureen Kennedy *nutritionist*

Moraga
Allen, Richard Garrett *health care and education consultant*

Moss Landing
†Johnston, Gail Liragis *laboratory director*

Newbury Park
†Bullock, Gayle Nelson *healthcare executive*

Newport Beach
†Haskins, Larry Wayne *health care administrator*
Stephens, Michael Dean *hospital administrator*
†Teslow, Paul Andre *retired health executive*

Norco
Parmer, Dan Gerald *veterinarian*

Northridge
Butler, Karla *psychologist*

Oakhurst
Bonham, Clifford Vernon *social worker, educator*

Oakland
Bangham, Robert Arthur *orthotist*
Caulfield, W. Harry *health care industry executive, physician*
Gardner, Robert Alexander *career counselor, career management consultant*
Lawrence, David M. *health facility administrator*
Moon, Wayne *health facility administrator*
Sargent, Arlene Hondl *nursing educator*
Vohs, James Arthur *health care program executive*

Oceanside
Hertweck, E. Romayne *psychology educator*
Ladley, Karen J. *nursing administrator, nurse*

Orange
Levine, Howard Harris *health facility executive*

Oroville
Ward, Chester Lawrence *physician, county health official, retired military officer*

Oxnard
Dimitriadis, Andre C. *health care executive*
Herlinger, Daniel Robert *hospital administrator*

Palo Alto
†Goff, James Albert *medical center administrator*
Hammett, Benjamin Cowles *psychologist*
Lindzey, Gardner *psychologist, educator*

Pasadena
Buckingham, Jerry L. *hospital administrator*
Cole, Roberta Carley *nursing educator*
Messenger, Ron J. *health facility administrator*
Nackel, John George *health care consulting director*
†Sauer, James Edward, Jr. *hospital administrator*

Pauma Valley
Dooley, George Elijah *health facility administrator*

Pebble Beach
Keene, Clifford Henry *medical administrator*

Petaluma
Carr, Les *psychologist, educator*

Piedmont
Daniels, Lydia M. *health care administrator*

Pleasant Hill
Gomez, Edward Casimiro *physician, educator*

Pleasanton
Shen, Mason Ming-Sun *medical center administrator*

Poway
Buncher, James Edward *healthcare management executive*

Rancho Mirage
Deiter, Newton Elliott *clinical psychologist*
Ford, Betty Bloomer (Elizabeth Ford) *health facility executive, wife of former President of United States*
†Wiskowski, Eugene *health facility administrator*

Rancho Santa Fe
Trout, Monroe Eugene *hospital systems executive*

Redding
Wilson, David Lee *clinical psychologist*

Reseda
Hoover, Pearl Rollings *nurse*

Riverside
Bowers, Norene A. *nursing administrator, critical care nurse*
Chang, Sylvia Tan *health facility administrator, educator*
Cohen, Kenneth Bruce *health agency director*
Eyman, Richard Kenneth *psychologist, educator*
Hadfield, Tomi Senger *hospital administrator*
Ham, Gary Martin *psychologist*
Petrinovich, Lewis F. *psychology educator*
Warren, David Hardy *psychology educator*
†White, Thomas Jeffrey *healthcare management educator*

Roseville
Dupper, Frank Floyd *health care facility executive*

Sacramento
†Beckwith, Charles Allan *healthcare administrator, consultant*
Bennett, Lawrence Allen *psychologist, criminal justice researcher*
Chapman, Loring *psychologist, educator, neuroscientist*
Farrell, Francine Annette *psychotherapist, educator*
Greenfield, Carol Nathan *psychotherapist*
Hays, Patrick Gregory *health care executive*
Loge, Frank Jean, II *hospital administrator*
†Majesty, Melvin Sidney *psychologist, consultant*
Merwin, Edwin Preston *health care consultant, educator*

Salinas
Eifler, Carl Frederick *retired psychologist*
Francis, Alexandria Stephanie *psychologist*

San Bernardino
Timmreck, Thomas C. *health sciences and health administration educator*

San Diego
†Aden, Gary Dee *healthcare company executive*
Bakko, Orville Edwin *retired health care executive, consultant*
Doyle, Thomas J. *healthcare administrator, consultant, educator*
Early, Ames S. *health facility administrator*
Ellsworth, Peter Kennedy *health care executive*
Heuschele, Werner Paul *veterinary researcher*
Johnson, Kenneth Owen *retired audiologist*
Kayler, Robert Samuel *hospital administrator*
Kent, Theodore Charles *psychologist*
Keyser, Richard Lee *hospital executive*
Klausmeier, Herbert John *psychologist, educator*
Koch, Charles Stephen *hospital executive, economist*
Litrownik, Alan Jay *psychologist, educator*
†Maguire, Edward Francis *hospital administrator*
Mc Guigan, Frank Joseph *psychologist, educator*
Roy, Catherine Elizabeth *physical therapist*
Schmidt, Patricia Fain *nurse educator*
Schmidt, Terry Lane *health care executive*
Storms, Lowell Hanson *psychologist*
Weisman, Irving *social worker, educator*

San Dimas
Flores, Frank Cortez *health sciences administrator, public health educator*

San Francisco
Alderman, Margaret C. *nursing administrator*
Calvin, Allen David *psychologist, educator*
Eng, Catherine *health care facility administrator, physician, medical educator*
Freedman, Mervin Burton *psychologist, educator*
Gortner, Susan Reichert *nursing educator*
Green, Robert Leonard *hospital management company executive*
Howatt, Sister Helen Clare *human services director*
Johnson, Herman Leonall *research nutritionist*
Krippner, Stanley Curtis *psychologist*
Malin, Harold Martin, Jr. *sexologist, educator*
Martinson, Ida Marie *nurse, physiologist, educator*
Meleis, Afaf Ibrahim *nurse sociologist, educator, clinician*
Nafziger, Dean H. *special education research executive*
Ripple, Helen Bernice *nursing administrator*
†Silverman, Mervyn F. *health science association administrator, consultant*
Styles, Margretta Madden *nursing educator*
†Turnlund, Judith Rae *nutrition scientist*
Underwood, Patricia Ruth *clinical nursing educator, consultant*
Westerdahl, John Brian *nutritionist, health educator*
†Young, Lowell Sung-yi *medical administrator, educator*

San Jose
Cedoline, Anthony John *psychologist*
Pellegrini, Robert J. *psychology educator*
Smith, Joan Petersen *nursing administrator, educator*

San Lorenzo
Lantz, Charles Alan *chiropractor, researcher*

San Luis Obispo
Holder, Elaine Edith *psychologist, educator*
Smith, Joey Spauls *mental health nurse, biofeedback therapist, bodyworker, hypnotist*

San Marcos
Knight, Edward Howden *retired hospital administrator*
Liggins, George Lawson *microbiologist-diagnostic company executive*

San Ramon
Weil, Jon David *psychologist, geneticist, administrator*

Santa Barbara
Blum, Gerald Saul *psychologist, educator*
Edwardsen, Kenneth Robert *administrator*
Kendler, Howard H(arvard) *psychologist, educator*
Mayer, Richard Edwin *psychology educator*
Narayanamurti, Venkatesh *research administrator*
Sherman, Alan Robert *psychologist, educator*
†Wilde, Gary Kezerian *hospital administrator, business educator*

Santa Cruz
Henderson, Ronald Wilbur *psychology educator*
Pettigrew, Thomas Fraser *social psychologist, educator*
Smith, M(ahlon) Brewster *psychologist, educator*
Tharp, Roland George *psychology, education educator*

Santa Monica
Barbakow, Jeffrey *health facility administrator*
Bedrosian, John C. *health care executive*
Brook, Robert Henry *physician, educator, health services researcher*
Cohen, Leonard *hospital management company executive*
Focht, Michael Harrison *health care industry executive*
Kahan, James Paul *psychologist*
Nizze, Judith Anne *physician assistant*
Pettit, John W. *hospital administrator*

Santa Rosa
Eilerman, Betty Jean *marriage and family counselor*

Sherman Oaks
Azpeitia, Lynne Marie *psychotherapist, educator, trainer, consultant*
Peplau, Hildegard Elizabeth *nursing educator*

Solvang
Hegarty, William Kevin *medical center executive*

Sonoma
Markey, William Alan *health care administrator*

Stanford
Bandura, Albert *psychologist*
Basch, Paul Frederick *international health educator, parasitologist*
Calfee, Robert Chilton *psychologist, educational researcher*
Carlsmith, James Merrill *psychologist, educator*
Flavell, John Hurley *psychologist, educator*
Gage, Nathaniel Lees *psychologist, educator*
Hilgard, Ernest Ropiequet *psychologist*
Krumboltz, John Dwight *psychologist, educator*
Lepper, Mark Roger *psychology educator*
Maccoby, Eleanor Emmons *psychology educator*
Mc Namara, Joseph Donald *researcher, retired police chief, novelist*
Rosenhan, David L. *psychologist, educator*
Shepard, Roger Newland *psychologist, educator*
†Skeff, Kelley Michael *health facility administrator*
Zajonc, Robert B(oleslaw) *psychology educator*
Zimbardo, Philip George *psychologist, educator, writer*

Stockton
Matuszak, Alice Jean Boyer *pharmacy educator*

Susanville
†Bateson, Clarence Owen *chiropractor*

Tarzana
†Michaelson, Richard Aaron *health science facility administrator*

Torrance
Foley, Edward Joseph *hospital administrator*
Prell, Joel James *medical group administrator*

Turlock
Ahlem, Lloyd Harold *psychologist*

Tustin
London, Ray William *clinical and forensic psychologist*

Van Nuys
Brock, Richard Barrett *hospital nursing administrator*
Rosen, Alexander Carl *psychologist, consultant*

Walnut Creek
Zander, Alvin Frederick *social psychologist*

West Covina
†Makowski, Peter Edgar *hospital executive*

Winters
Low, Donald Gottlob *retired veterinary medicine educator*

Woodland
†Marler, Phillip Lynn *healthcare administrator*

Woodland Hills
Schaeffer, Leonard David *health care executive*

Yountville
Helzer, James Dennis *hospital executive*

COLORADO

Aurora
Fedak, Barbara Kingry *technical center administrator*

Boulder
Anderson, Robert K. *health care company executive*
Bourne, Lyle Eugene, Jr. *psychology educator*
Healy, Alice Fenvessy *psychology educator, researcher*
Holdsworth, Janet Nott *women's health nurse*
Jessor, Richard *psychologist, educator*
Katz, Phyllis Alberts *developmental research psychologist*
Kintsch, Walter *psychology educator, director*

Colorado Springs
†Cameron, Paul Drummond *research facility administrator*
Farr, Leonard Alfred *hospital administrator*
†Hamilton, James Milton *veterinarian*
Rooney, Margaret Elaine *nurse, educator*
Shafer, Dallas Eugene *psychology gerontology educator, minister*
Vayhinger, John Monroe *psychotherapist, minister*
West, Ralph Leland *veterinarian*

Denver
Albrecht, Duane Taylor *veterinarian*
Bauder, Sister Marianna *hospital administrator*
Berland, Karen Ina *psychologist*
Brimhall, Dennis C. *hospital executive*
Chinn, Peggy Lois *nursing educator, editor*
Clough, Nadine Doerr *school psychologist, psychotherapist*
Conger, John Janeway *psychologist, educator*
Doran, Maureen O'Keefe *psychotherapist, psychiatric nursing consultant*
Hill, Diane Seldon *corporate psychologist*
Kirkpatrick, Charles Harvey *physician, immunology researcher*
Lockwood, Barbara Jordan *nurse administrator*
Markman, Howard J. *psychology educator*
Parker, Catherine Susanne *psychotherapist*
Purcell, Kenneth *psychology educator, university dean*
Rael, Henry Sylvester *health administrator*
Scherer, Ronald Callaway *voice scientist, educator*
†Sparkman, Cathryn *health facility administrator, lawyer*
Zimet, Carl Norman *psychologist, educator*
Zook, Kay Marie *nursing administrator*

Englewood
Busse, Lu Ann *audiologist*
Edelman, Joel *medical center executive*

Fort Collins
Bennett, Thomas LeRoy, Jr. *clinical neuropsychology educator*
Gubler, Duane J. *research scientist, administrator*
†Lauri, John Peter *hospital administrator*
Suinn, Richard Michael *psychologist*
Voss, James Leo *veterinarian*

Grand Junction
Pantenburg, Michel *hospital administrator, health educator, holistic health coordinator*
Zumwalt, Roger Carl *hospital administrator*

Greenwood Village
†Haymons, Dan Lester, Jr. *hospital administrator*

Lakewood
Wellisch, William Jeremiah *social psychology educator*

Littleton
Cabell, Elizabeth Arlisse *psychologist*
Vail, Charles Daniel *veterinarian, consultant*

Longmont
Melendez, Joaquin *orthopedic assistant*

Pueblo
Post-Gorden, Joan Carolyn *psychology educator*

Wheat Ridge
LaMendola, Walter Franklin *huamn services, information technology consultant*

CONNECTICUT

Avon
Patricelli, Robert E. *health care company executive*

Bridgeport
†Trefry, Robert J. *healthcare administrator*

Cromwell
Bushnell, Clarence William *retired hospital consultant*

Danbury
†Robilotti, Gerard Daniel *hospital administrator*
Tolor, Alexander *psychologist, educator*

Derby
Brassil, Jean Ella *psychologist*

Farmington
Kegeles, S. Stephen *behavioral science educator*

Glastonbury
Bruner, Robert B. *hospital consultant*

Greenwich
Sheppard, Posy (Mrs. Jeremiah Milbank) *social worker*

Guilford
Hayes, Michael Ernest *psychotherapist, educator*

Hartford
D'Eramo, David *hospital administrator*
Hamilton, Thomas Stewart *physician, hospital administrator*
†Himmelsbach, William Anthony, Jr. *healthcare executive*
Ivey, Elizabeth S. *acoustician, physicist*
Lewis, Lois A. *health services administrator*
O'Malley, Marjorie Glaubach *health care executive*
†Rosenberg, Steven H. *health facility administrator*
Springer, John Kelley *hospital administrator*

Manchester
Chung, Douglas Chu *pharmacist, consultant*
Richard, Ann Bertha *nursing administrator*

Mansfield Center
Liberman, Alvin Meyer *psychology educator*

Middletown
Adams, David Bachrach *psychology educator*
Bailey, Debra Sue *psychologist, neuropsychologist*
Harris, Dale Benner *psychology educator*
Scheibe, Karl Edward *psychology educator*
Steele, Robert Steven *psychology educator*

Milford
Muth, Eric Peter *ophthalmic optician, consultant*
Taylor, Charles Henry *psychoanalyst, educator*

New Britain
Tanner, Laurence Aram *hospital administrator*

New Haven
Abelson, Robert Paul *psychologist, educator*
Ames, Louise Bates *child psychologist*
Beauchesne, Karen Sue *nurse, administrator*
Blatt, Sidney Jules *psychology educator, psychoanalyst*
Brownell, Kelly David *psychologist, educator*
Child, Irvin Long *psychologist, educator*
Clizbe, John Anthony *psychologist*
Crowder, Robert George *psychology educator*
De Rose, Sandra Michele *psychotherapist, educator, supervisor, administrator*
Doob, Leonard William *psychology educator, academic administrator*
Garner, Wendell Richard *psychology educator*
†Gray, Bradford Hitch *medical educator*
Jekel, James Franklin *physician, public health educator*
Kessen, William *psychologist, educator*
Krauss, Judith Belliveau *nursing educator*
Marks, Lawrence Edward *psychologist*
Mc Guire, William James *social psychology educator*
Meyer, Patricia Ann *veterinarian*
Miller, Neal Elgar *psychologist, emeritus educator*
Schmeer, Arline Catherine *cancer research development chemotherapy scientist*
Sparrow, Sara S. *psychology educator, psychologist*
Sternberg, Robert Jeffrey *psychology educator*
Stevens, Joseph Charles *psychology educator*
Wagner, Allan Ray *psychology educator, experimental psychologist*
Weaver, Diana Jane *nursing administrator*
Zaccagnino, Joseph Anthony *hospital administrator*
†Zigler, Edward Frank *educator, psychologist*

North Haven
Mahl, George Franklin *psychoanalyst, psychologist, educator*

Putnam
Desaulniers, Rene Gerard Lesieur *optometrist*

Redding
Benyei, Candace Reed *psychotherapist*

Riverside
Otto, Charles Edward *health care administrator*

South Windsor
Bapat, Vijaya *pediatrician, educator*

Stamford
Fein, Leah Gold *psychologist*
Haber, Judith Ellen *nursing educator*

Storrs
Allen, George James *psychologist, educator*
Anderson, Stephen Alan *family psychology educator*
†Katz, Leonard *psychology educator*

Storrs Mansfield
Denenberg, Victor Hugo *psychology educator*
Schwarz, J(ames) Conrad *psychology educator*

Wallingford
Spero, Barry Melvin *medical center executive*

Waterbury
Oliver, Eugene Alex *speech and language pathologist*
†Waite, Marguerite Frances *hospital administrator*

Weston
Laikind, Donna *psychotherapist, consultant*

Willimantic
Diehl, Lesley Ann *psychologist*

Woodbridge
Womer, Charles Berry *retired hospital executive, management consultant*

DELAWARE

Hockessin
Herzog, Kathryn Wedel *health care administrator, hospice consultant*

Lewes
Fried, Jeffrey Michael *health care administrator*

Newark
Caffo, Betty Jane *nursing educator, medical/surgical nurse*
Doberenz, Alexander R. *nutrition educator, chemist*
Graham, Frances Keesler (Mrs. David Tredway Graham) *psychologist, educator*
Gulick, Walter Lawrence *psychologist, former college president*
Hurst, Christina Marie *respiratory therapist*

Sheer, Barbara Lee *nursing educator*

Smyrna
†Mays, William Fritz *health facility regional administrator, retired military career officer*

Wilmington
Adams, Wayne Verdun *pediatric psychologist, educator*
Johnson, Allen Leroy *hospital administrator*

DISTRICT OF COLUMBIA

Washington
Arbelbide, Cindy Lea *victim advocate, librarian, educator*
Barton, Jean Marie *psychologist, educator*
Basseches, Harriet Itkin *psychoanalyst, clinical psychologist*
Beale, Susan Yates *social worker*
Bentley, James Daniel *medical association executive*
Blanck, Ronald Ray *hospital administrator, internist, career officer*
†Brown, Donald Lee *hospital administrator*
Buckalew, Judith Adele *nurse, pharmaceutical industry executive*
†Chapman, Thomas William *hospital executive*
Chilman, Catherine Earles Street *social welfare educator, author*
Crawford, Lester Mills, Jr. *veterinarian*
Davis, Carolyne Kahle *health care consultant*
Eckenhoff, Edward Alvin *health care administrator*
Falter, Robert Gary *correctional health care administrator*
Feingold, S. Norman *psychologist*
Filerman, Gary Lewis *health education executive*
Francke, Gloria Niemeyer *pharmacist, editor, publisher*
†Garfunkel, Sanford M. *medical administrator*
Gaull, Gerald Edward *nutritionist, scientist, educator, food company executive*
Greenwood, Janet Kae Daly *psychologist, educational administrator*
Hanft, Ruth S. Samuels (Mrs. Herbert Hanft) *health care consultant, educator, economist*
Harper, Robert Allan *consulting psychologist*
Hudec, Mary Suzanne *nursing and patient services administrator*
Jones, Stanley Boyd *health policy analyst, priest*
†Kawata, Paul Akio *health association administrator*
Lash, Myles Perry *hospital administrator*
Littig, Lawrence William *psychologist, educator*
Majors, Richard George *psychology educator*
Masi, Dale A. *research company executive, social work educator*
May, Sterling Randolph *health association executive*
McCarthy, John B. *veterinarian, veterinary association executive*
McDaniel, John Perry *health care company executive*
McGeein, Mary Martha *health care organization executive*
McGinnies, Elliott Morse *psychologist, educator*
Menning, Edward Lee *veterinarian*
Moore, Julia Alice *non-profit executive*
Nef, Evelyn Stefansson *psychotherapist, author, editor, specialist polar regions*
Norby, Ronald Brandon *nurse executive*
Norcross, Marvin Augustus *veterinarian, government agency official*
O'Connell, Daniel Craig *psychology educator*
Peele, Roger *hospital administrator*
Raphael-Howell, Frances Jayne *clinical psychologist*
Riecken, Henry William *psychologist, research director*
Robinson, Daniel N. *psychology educator*
†Samet, Andrew *government official*
Samet, Kenneth Alan *hospital administrator*
Schorr, Lisbeth Bamberger *child and family policy analyst, author, educator*
†Seelman, Katherine Dolores *institute administrator*
Shaw, Sallye Brown *women's health nurse*
Shinn, Linda Jane *nurse, association executive*
Smits, Helen Lida *public adminstrator, physician, educator*
Tracy, Thomas Miles *international health organization official*
VandenBos, Gary Roger *psychologist, publisher*
Woteki, Catherine Ellen *nutritionist*

FLORIDA

Bal Harbour
Radford, Linda Robertson *psychologist*

Bay Pines
Weaver, Thomas Harold *health facility administrator*

Boca Raton
Baumgarten, Diana Virginia *geriatrics nurse*
Latané, Bibb *social psychologist*
Wolgin, David Lewis *psychology educator*

Boynton Beach
Peltzie, Kenneth Gerald *hospital administrator, educator*

Bradenton
†Tague, Karl Raymond *health care executive*

Brandon
Applegate, Minerva Irons *nursing educator, nurse*
Mussenden, Gerald *psychologist*

Brooksville
†Leftwich, Hal West *health facility administrator*

Chattahoochee
Ivory, Peter B. C. B. *medical administrator*

Clearwater
De Lara, Mario, Jr. *psychologist, psychometrician, behavioral analyst*
Gibson, Barbara Arlene *nurse, writer*
Graves, Robert Lee *hospital administration*
Houtz, Duane Talbott *hospital administrator*

Daytona Beach
Elliott, Carol Harris *nutrition counselor, dietitian*
McCoy, Edward Fitzgerald *social services facility administrator*

Wehner, Henry Otto, III *pharmacist, consultant*

Destin
†Levin, Peter J. *hospital administrator, public health professor*

Dunnellon
Dixon, W(illiam) Robert *retired educational psychology educator*

Fernandina Beach
Kurtz, Myers Richard *hospital administrator*

Fort Lauderdale
Andrews, John Harold *health care administrator*
Azrin, Nathan Harold *psychologist*
Campbell, Donna Grayce *nursing administrator*
†Peluso, David Anthony *clinical pharmacist, consultant*
†Solomon, Barry Jason *healthcare administrator, consultant*
Turner, Richard Stanley *health care financial executive*
Wallace, Joan Scott *psychologist, social worker, international consultant*

Fort Myers
Harmer, Rose *marriage and family therapist, mental health counselor*
Kelly, William E. *psychoanalyst*
Mainous, Theresa Lei *nursing administrator*
Nathan, James Robert *hospital administrator*
Rollason, Wendell Norton *social services administrator*

Gainesville
Brown, William Samuel, Jr. *communication processes and disorders educator*
Burridge, Michael John *veterinarian, educator, academic administrator*
Capaldi, Elizabeth Ann Deutsch *psychological sciences educator*
Dewsbury, Donald Allen *historian of psychology, comparative psychologist*
Dierks, Richard Ernest *veterinarian, educational administrator*
Green, David Marvin *psychology educator, researcher, consultant*
Himes, James Albert *veterinary medicine educator emeritus*
Jaeger, Boi Jon *health administrator educator*
†Kiehne, Lynn Sheree *hospital administrator*
McKnew, Linda Alexander *health facility administrator*
Nicoletti, Paul Lee *veterinarian, educator*
Randall, Malcom *health care administrator*
Severy, Lawrence James *psychologist, educator*
Teitelbaum, Philip *psychologist*
Thompson, Neal Philip *food science and nutrition educator*
Wass, Hannelore Lina *educational psychology educator emeritus*
Watson, Robert Joe *hospital administrator, retired career officer*

Gulf Breeze
Lankton, Stephen Ryan *family therapist, management consultant*

High Springs
Eaton, Wayne Carl *chiropractic physician*

Hollywood
Bujnicki, Sharon A. *health facility administrator*
Sacco, Frank Vincent *hospital administrator*

Homosassa
Acton, Norman *international organization executive*

Jacksonville
†Cuny, John Dana *health care system executive*
Gregg, John Franklin *hospital administrator*
Mason, William Cordell, III *hospital administrator*
Monroe, Helen Leola *nurse, consultant, educator*
Wilson, C. Nick *health educator, consultant, researcher, lecturer*
Yamane, Stanley Joel *optometrist*

Jensen Beach
Gamble, Raymond Wesley *marriage and family therapist, clergyman*

Jupiter
Mc Call, Charles Barnard *health facility executive, educator*

Lake City
Welborn, Elsie Elender Jenkins *nurse executive, nurse*

Lakeland
Smith, Sherwood Draughon *retired hospital administrator*

Largo
Haile, James Francis *hospital administrator*
Hamlin, Robert Henry *public health educator, management consultant*

Lutz
Garcia, Sandra Joanne Anderson *law and psychology educator*

Melbourne
Means, Michael David *hospital administrator*

Miami
Barritt, Evelyn Ruth Berryman *nurse, educator, university dean*
†Bernstein, Stephen *healthcare executive*
Burkett, Marjorie Theresa *nursing educator, gerontology nurse*
Cherry, Andrew Lawrence, Jr. *social work educator, researcher*
Clark, Ira C. *hospital association administrator, educator*
Clot, Archlyn Ann *medical technologist*
Desautel, Helen Craig *health facility administrator*
Glaskowsky, Elizabeth Pope *nutritionist, dietitian*
Huysman, Arlene Weiss *psychologist, educator*
Keeley, Brian E. *hospital administrator*

Kunce, Avon Estes *senior vocational rehabilitation counselor*
Marano, Angeline Marie *hospital administrator*
†Messing, Fred M. *health care executive*
†Noriega, Rudy Jorge *hospital administrator*
Plungis, Barbara Marie *health facility nursing administrator*
Routh, Donald K(ent) *psychology educator*
Russell, Elbert Winslow *neuropsychologist*
Sims, James Larry *hospital administrator, healthcare consultant*
Stuchins, Carol Mayberry *nursing executive*
Teicher, Morton Irving *social worker, educator*

Miami Shores
Boyle, Judith Pullen *clinical psychology, professor*

Micanopy
Cripe, Wyland Snyder *veterinary medicine educator, consultant*

Naples
Clark, Kenneth Edwin *psychologist, former university dean*
Crone, William Gerald *hospital administrator*
Dion, Nancy Logan *health care administrator, management consultant*
Gilman, John Richard, Jr. *organization behavior consultant*
Terenzio, Peter Bernard *hospital administrator*

Orange Park
Rice, Ronald James *hospital administrator*

Orlando
Blair, Mardian John *hospital management executive*
Gonong, Zoila Obmana *medical, surgical nurse*
Harvill-Dickson, Clara Gean *medical facility administrator*
Salmons, Joanna *health facility administrator*
Strack, J. Gary *hospital administrator*
Strifler, Susan Victoria *nursing administrator*
Ward, Sharon Polk *nursing administrator*
Werner, Thomas Lee *hospital administrator*

Osprey
Ward, Jacqueline Ann Beas *nurse, healthcare administrator*

Panama City
Childers, Perry Robert *psychology educator*

Panama City Beach
Nelson, Edith Ellen *dietitian*

Pembroke Pines
Armstrong, Ivy Claudette *nursing administrator*

Pensacola
Caton, Betty Ann *health science administrator*
Groner, Pat Neff *health care executive*
Loesch, Mabel Lorraine *social worker*
Maygarden, Jerry Louis *health care foundation executive*
VanSlyke, Robert Emmett *health care executive*
Yoder, Ronda Elaine *nursing educator*

Pineland
Doherty, Michel George *alcohol and drug treatment facility administrator*

Plantation
Baez, Manuel *health care executive*
Buck, Thomas Randolph *business executive*

Pompano Beach
Ayres, John Cecil *retired public health executive*

Port Charlotte
Ward-Presson, Kathryn M. *health facility administrator*

Saint Petersburg
Clark, Carolyn Chambers *nurse, author, educator*
Harrington, Joan Kathryn *counselor*
Jordan, William Reynier Van Evera, Sr. *therapist, poet*
McIntyre, Deborah *psychotherapist, author*
Wisler, Willard Eugene *health care management executive*

Sanford
Osborne-Popp, Glenna Jean *health services administrator*
San Miguel, Sandra Bonilla *social worker*

Sarasota
Byron, H. Thomas, Jr. *veterinarian, educator*
Covert, Michael Henri *healthcare facility administrator*
Dearden, Robert James *pharmacist*
Gurvitz, Milton Solomon *psychologist*

South Miami
Bruel, Iris Barbara *psychologist*

Sun City Center
Hall, John Fry *psychologist, educator*
Parsons, George Williams *retired medical center administrator, cattle rancher*

Sunrise
McBride, Wanda Lee *psychiatric nurse*

Tallahassee
Kenshalo, Daniel Ralph *psychologist, educator*
Mc Knight, Paul James, Jr. *hospital corporate executive*
Moore, Duncan *healthcare executive*
Mustian, Middleton Truett *hospital administrator*
Tuckman, Bruce Wayne *educational psychologist, educator, researcher*

Tamarac
Krause, John L. *optometrist*

Tampa
Bice, Michael O. *health science association administrator*
Bussone, David Eben *hospital administrator*

Ferlita, Theresa Ann *clinical social worker*
†Hoard, Jack Dale *hospital administrator*
Kimmel, Ellen Bishop *psychologist, educator*
Kozlowski, Donna Maureen *hospital administrator*
Molnar, Lewis K. *health facility administrator*
Porter, Nicolas Christopher *healthcare executive*
Read, Peter Kip *health care administrator*
Ritterman, Stuart I. *speech pathologist, educator*
Silver, Richard Abraham *hospital administrator*

West Palm Beach
Kaslow, Florence W. *psychologist*
Katz, William David *psychologist, psychoanalytic psychotherapist, educator, mental health consultant*
Vanek, Cynthia Wilkinson *administrator*

Winter Garden
Clifford, Margaret Louise *psychologist*

GEORGIA

Albany
†Norwood, Geoffrey Alexander *hospital administrator*

Americus
Gray, Margaret Edna *nursing educator, dean*

Athens
Ansel, Howard Carl *pharmacist, educator*
Barry, John Reagan *psychology educator*
Levine, David Lawrence *social work educator*
Pavlik, William Bruce *psychologist, educator*
Peacock, Lelon James *psychologist, educator*
Tesser, Abraham *social psychologist*
Torrance, Ellis Paul *psychologist, educator*
Trim, Cynthia Mary *veterinarian, educator*
Tyler, David Earl *veterinary medical educator*

Atlanta
Banks, Bettie Sheppard *psychologist*
Barker, William Daniel *hospital administrator*
†Chandler, Robert Charles *hospital administrator*
Drucker, Melvin Bruce *psychology educator*
Eber, Herbert Wolfgang *psychologist*
Garland, LaRetta Matthews *educational psychologist, nursing educator*
Gayer, Alan J. *hospital administrator*
Henry, John Dunklin *hospital administrator*
Honaman, J. Craig *health facility administrator*
Hopkins, Donald Roswell *public health physician*
†Hutton, Donald Henry *hospital administrator*
Iodice, Joanna DiMeno (Jody Iodice) *psychotherapist*
†Karahalis, George Gregory *healthcare management consultant*
Kerr, Nancy Helen *psychology educator*
Koplan, Jeffrey Powell *physician*
Marr, David Franklin *nurse, administrator*
Martin, David Edward *health sciences educator*
Neisser, Ulric *psychology educator*
Nichols, William Curtis *psychologist, family therapist, consultant*
†Oakley, Godfrey Porter, Jr. *health facility administrator, medical educator*
Panlilio, Adelisa Lorna *public health physician*
Patti, Sister Josephine Marie *health science facility administrator*
Payne, Maxwell Carr, Jr. *retired psychology educator*
†Rosenthal, Mark Elliott *hospital administrator*
Satcher, David *public health service officer, federal official*
Shepherd, James Harold, Jr. *hospital administrator, contruction executive*
Weiss, Jay M(ichael) *psychologist, educator*
Wells, Donald Eugene *hospital administrator*
Woody, Mary Florence *nursing educator, university administrator*

Augusta
Bray, Donald Claude *hospital administrator*
Feldman, Elaine Bossak *medical nutritionist, educator*
Gillespie, Edward Malcolm *hospital administrator*
Peloquin, Garry Wayne *retired hospital executive*
Richie, Sharon I. *army nursing officer*
Zachert, Virginia *psychologist, educator*

Brunswick
Hammill, R. Joseph *health facility administrator*

Clarkston
Valenti, Rita *critical care nurse*

Clayton
†Knepp, Gerald Everett *hospital director*

Columbus
Brabson, Max LaFayette *health care executive*
†Keaton, Charles Howard *health care administrator*
McIntosh, Joseph William *health administration consultant*

Doraville
Yancey, Eleanor Margaret Garrett *crisis intervention clinician*

Dunwoody
Bartolo, Donna Marie *hospital administrator, nurse*

Evans
Fournier, Joseph Andre Alphonse *nurse, social worker, psychotherapist*

Fort Oglethorpe
Stutz, Angela Lynn *health facility administrator*

Greensboro
†Kuntz, Louis Edward *health science facility administrator*

Macon
Crawford, Edwin Mack *health facilities executive*
Fickling, William Arthur, Jr. *health care manager*
Landry, Sara Griffin *social worker*
Laughlin, James Rodney *health care company executive*
Mac Crawford, Edwin *health facility administrator*

Murdoch, Bernard Constantine *psychology educator*

Marietta
Petit, Parker Holmes *health care corporation executive*

Milledgeville
Osborne, Paul Douglas *hospital administrator*

Morrow
Samson, Linda Forrest *nursing educator and administrator*

Norcross
Milum-Wood, Joan *hospital administrator*

Rome
Papp, Leann Ilse Kline *respiratory therapy educator*

Saint Simons Island
Edwards, Brenda Faye *counselor*

Savannah
Ives, John Elway *hospital administrator*

Snellville
†Maxwell, Clyde Edwin, Jr. *hospital administrator*

Sparta
†Holtz, Daniel Dwight *hospital administrator, retired air force officer*

Tifton
Thomas, Adrian Wesley *laboratory director*

Valdosta
Branan, John Maury *psychology educator, counselor*

HAWAII

Hilo
Dixon, Paul William *psychology educator*
Werner, Marlin Spike *speech pathologist and audiologist*

Honolulu
Bitterman, Morton Edward *psychologist, educator*
Corsini, Raymond Joseph *psychologist*
Fischer, Joel *social work educator*
Fullmer, Daniel Warren *psychologist, educator*
Hanson, Dennis Michael *medical imaging executive*
Hatfield, Elaine Catherine *psychology educator*
Holland, Charles Malcolm, Jr. *retired health care executive, development corporation executive, retired banker*
Lum, Jean Loui Jin *nurse educator*
Michael, Jerrold Mark *public health specialist, former university dean, educator*
†Thompson, Henry Nainoa *hospital administrator*
†Waterhouse, Blake E. *health facility administrator*

Kailua
†White, Terry Wayne *hospital administration executive*

Kailua Kona
Ashley, Darlene Joy *psychologist*

Kaneohe
Winters-Maloney, Carol Emerson *nursing educator, academic administrator*

Mililani
Kiley, Thomas *rehabilitation counselor*

Waianae
Pinckney, Neal Theodore *psychologist, educator*

IDAHO

Blackfoot
†Peterson, Robert Marcellus *hospital and nursing home administrator*

Bonners Ferry
McClintock, William Thomas *health care administrator*

ILLINOIS

Abbott Park
McIntyre, John Duncan *health care executive*

Alton
†Kessler, William Eugene *health care executive*

Anna
†Livengood, Joanne Desler *healthcare administrator*

Belleville
Eichelberger, Geralyn Mary *nursing administrator, critical care nurse*

Bolingbrook
Price, Theodora Hadzisteliou *individual and family therapist*

Burr Ridge
Hatch, Edward William (Ted Hatch) *health care executive*

Carbondale
Buckley, John Joseph, Jr. *health care executive*
Rubin, Harris B. *psychology educator*

Carol Stream
Cook, Jeanette E. *nursing administrator*

Champaign
Birdzell, Samuel Henry *hospital administrator*
Davis, James Henry *psychology educator*
Eriksen, Charles Walter *psychologist, educator*
Humphreys, Lloyd Girton *research psychologist, educator*
Kanfer, Frederick H. *psychologist, educator*
†Taylor, James David *health care executive*

Chicago
Andreoli, Kathleen Gainor *nurse, educator, administrator*
Baptist, Allwyn J. *health care consultant*
Bolger, Anne Margaret *hospital administrator*
Burger, Mary Louise *psychologist, educator*
Butler, Robert Allan *psychologist, educator*
Campbell, Bruce Crichton *hospital administrator*
†Carlson, Rolland S. *health facility adminstrator*
Carney, Jean Kathryn *psychologist*
Cohen, Jerome *psychology educator, electrophysiologist*
Conibear, Shirley Ann *occupational health consultant, physician*
Connors, Mary Eileen *psychologist*
Csikszentmihalyi, Mihaly *psychology educator*
Duncan, Starkey Davis, Jr. *behavioral sciences educator*
Esmond, Truman H., Jr. *health facility administrator*
Farran, Carol J. *nursing educator*
Fiorella, Beverly Jean *medical technologist, educator*
Fromm, Erika (Mrs. Paul Fromm) *clinical psychologist*
Getzels, Jacob Warren *psychologist, educator*
Goldiamond, Israel *experimental psychologist, educator*
†Goldmann, James A. *healthcare consultant*
Gutmann, David Leo *psychology educator*
Hannan, C(hristie) Phillip *health facility administrator*
Hunt, Roger Schermerhorn *hospital administrator*
Kennedy, Eugene Cullen *psychology educator, writer*
Kopel, David *psychologist, educator*
Logemann, Jerilyn Ann *speech pathologist, educator*
Lubawski, James Lawrence *health care administrator*
Maltz, J. Herbert *physician, hospital director*
Marston-Scott, Mary Vesta *nurse, educator*
†McKinney, William T. *psychiatrist, educator*
McNeill, G. David *psychologist, educator*
Mecklenburg, Gary Alan *hospital executive*
Muller, Ralph W. *hospital administrator*
Newsome, Mary de Sévigné *psychoanalyst*
Pugh, Roderick Wellington *psychologist, educator*
Rosenheim, Margaret Keeney *social welfare policy educator*
Rothstein, Ruth M. *hospital adminstrator*
Russell, Lillian *medical, surgical nurse*
Rychlak, Joseph Frank *psychology educator, theoretician*
Sanders, Jacquelyn Seevak *psychologist, educator*
Sarchi, Bernard *healthcare administrator*
†Schoeller, Dale Alan *nutrition research educator*
Schuerman, John Richard *social work educator*
Schwartz, John Norman *health care executive*
Simon, Bernece Kern *social work educator*
Simons, Helen *school psychologist, psychotherapist*
Spivey, Bruce E. *integrated delivery systems management executive*
Walberg, Herbert John *psychologist, educator, consultant*
Walker, Ronald Edward *psychologist, educator*
Weimer, Jean Elaine *nursing educator*
Wilson, Ruby Lee *nurse, director*
Wright, Benjamin Drake *psychology, statistics, education educator*

Danville
Kettling, Virginia *administrator*

De Kalb
Buckner, Kathleen E. *nursing educator, maternal-child health nurse*

Decatur
Perry, Anthony John *retired hospital executive*

Des Plaines
Saporta, Jack *psychologist, educator*

Dixon
Belcher-Redebaugh-Levi, Caroline Louise *nursing home administrator, nurse*

Downers Grove
Gioioso, Joseph Vincent *psychologist*

East Peoria
Walker, Philip Chamberlain, II *health care executive*

Elgin
Hoeft, Elizabeth Bayless *speech and language pathologist*
Nelson, John Thilgen *hospital administrator, physician*

Evanston
Eagly, Alice Hendrickson *social psychology educator*
Hill, Winfred Farrington *psychology educator*
Howard, Kenneth Irwin *psychology educator*
Mineka, Susan *psychology educator*
†Neaman, Mark A. *health facility administrator*
Neaman, Mark Robert *hospital administrator*
Revelle, William Roger *psychology educator*
Rosenbaum, James Edward *psychologist, educator*
Wilber, Laura Ann *audiologist*

Frankfort
Pearson, Gerald P. *hospital administrator*

Galesburg
Kowalski, Richard Sheldon *hospital administrator*

Glen Ellyn
Wilhoit, Carol Lynn *physician*

Glencoe
Grabow, Beverly *learning disability therapist*

Glenview
†Hillebrand, Jeffrey Henry *hospital executive*

Godfrey
Harner, Linda Jeane *allied health educator*

Granite City
†Raczkiewicz, Paul Edward *hospital administrator*

Great Lakes
Andrews, Carolyn Fraser *psychologist*

Highland Park
Friend, Peter Michael *hospital executive*

Hines
Daane, Kathryn D. *nursing administrator*

Hoffman Estates
Pasen, Robert Martin *psychologist*

Joliet
Benfer, David William *hospital administrator*
Sova, Rita Wolz *community health nurse, educator*

Kankakee
†Feth, Joseph S. *healthcare administrator*
Schroeder, David Harold *health care facility executive*

Kenilworth
Frederick, Earl James *healthcare consultant*

Macomb
Hopper, Stephen Rodger *hospital administrator*

Marion
Livengood, Richard Vaughn *healthcare executive*

Maywood
Cera, Lee Marie *veterinarian*
†Cohen, Elliot Gene *hospital administrator*

Mc Henry
Duel, Ward Calvin *health care consultant*

Mokena
Janssen, Sister Norma *hospital administrator*

Moline
Larson, Sandra Mae *nursing educator*

Morton Grove
Farber, Isadore E. *psychologist, educator*

Naperville
†Hannon, Steven Kevin *hospital administrator*
†Marion, Daniel J(oseph) *hospital executive*
Thomas, Joseph Erumappettical *psychologist*

North Chicago
Kringel, John G. *health products company executive*

Northbrook
Lever, Alvin *health science association administrator*
Rudnick, Ellen Ava *health care executive*

Oak Brook
Baker, Robert J(ohn) *hospital administrator*
Risk, Richard R. *health facility administrator*
Wardell, Kevin Stuart *hospital administrator*

Oak Brook Mall
†Peterson, Allen Kenneth *healthcare administrator*

Oak Lawn
Massura, Eileen Kathleen *family therapist*

Oak Park
Edwards, Linda H. *public health professional*
Varchmin, Thomas Edward *environmental health administrator*

Olympia Fields
Haley, David Alan *preferred provider organization executive*

Park Forest
McDonald, Stanford Laurel *clinical psychologist*
Steinmetz, Jon David *mental health facility administrator, psychologist*

Park Ridge
Boe, Gerard Patrick *health science association administrator*
Casten, Carol Elizabeth *nursing administrator*
McCarthy, Michael Shawn *health care company executive, lawyer*
Ryan, Judith Andre *health care executive, hospital administrator, nurse*
Ummel, Stephen L. *health facility administrator*

Peoria
McCollum, Jean Hubble *medical assistant*

Plainfield
Schinderle, Robert Frank *hospital administrator*

Riverwoods
Kirby, Emily Baruch *psychologist, writer*

Rockford
Maysent, Harold Wayne *hospital administrator*

Roscoe
Dorsey-Wong, Kathleen M. *critical care nurse, administrator*

Schaumburg
Wagner, Betty Valiree *medical organization executive*

Springfield
Laabs, Allison C. *hospital administrator*
Trstensky, Sister Jomary *hospital administrator*

University Park
Wentz, Walter John *health administration educator*

Urbana
Gabriel, Michael *psychology educator*
Parker, Alan John *veterinary neurologist, educator, researcher*
Siedler, Arthur James *nutrition and food science educator*
Small, Erwin *veterinarian, educator*
Visek, Willard James *nutritionist, animal scientist, physician, educator*
Wagner, William Charles *veterinarian*

Villa Park
Evans, Austin James *hospital administrator*
†Kay, Robert Lee *hospital administrator*

Westchester
Clarke, Richard Lewis *health science association administrator*
†Weinstein, Alan *health care management executive*

Western Springs
Tiefenthal, Marguerite Aurand *school social worker*

Wheaton
Loebig, Wilfred F. *health care executive*

Wilmette
Gary, James Francis *mental health counselor, educational counselor*
Randolph, Lillian Larson *medical association executive*

Winfield
Calvin, Patricia Lynn *hospital administrator*

Wood Dale
Thompson, John Henry *consulting executive*

INDIANA

Bloomington
Dinsmoor, James Arthur *psychology educator*
Guth, Sherman Leon (S. Lee Guth) *psychologist, educator*
Heise, George Armstrong *psychologist, educator*
Hofstadter, Douglas Richard *cognitive, computer scientist, educator*
Ingersoll, Gary Michael *educational psychologist*
Kohr, Roland Ellsworth *hospital administrator*
Schroeder, Henry J. *health science organization administrator*

Bluffton
Brockmann, William Frank *medical facility administrator*

Carmel
Chittenden, Michael Dennis *hospital administrator*
†Magliery, Frank Thomas *hospital administrator*

Crawfordsville
Michal, Philip Quentin *veterinarian, mayor*

East Chicago
Papachronis, Darlene R. *hospital administrator*

Elwood
†Baer, James Edward *hospital administrator*

Evansville
Prybil, Lawrence Dewey *health system executive*
White, Linda Elaine *nursing administrator*
Young Lively, Sandra Lee *nurse*

Fort Wayne
Dax, Janice M. *nursing administrator*
Flynn, Pauline T. *speech pathologist, educator*
Hoffer, Alma Jeanne *nursing educator*
Kerr, Frederick Hohmann *hospital administrator, college president*
Labernik, Mary Sue *nurse*
Ridderheim, David Sigfrid *hospital administrator*

Goshen
Gunden, Elizabeth Ann *nursing administrator*

Hammond
Diamond, Eugene Christopher *lawyer, hospital administrator*
Gerard, Peggy S. *critical care nurse, researcher*
Marshall, Philomena Ann *health care administration*

Hope
Golden, Eloise Elizabeth *community health nurse*

Indianapolis
Allerheiligen, Sandra Renee *pharmacokineticist*
Brashear, Diane Lee *marital and sex therapist*
Corley, William Edward *hospital administrator*
Das, Eula *hospital administrator*
Farris, Bain Joseph *health care executive*
Gray, Mary Jo Zimmer *medical/surgical nurse*
Grossman, Elizabeth Korn *nursing administrator, retired college dean*
Handel, David Jonathan *health care administrator*
†Hayes, John Robert *health care executive, psychiatrist*
Herman, Barbara F. *psychologist*
†Hicks, Allen Morley *hospital administrator*
Hingtgen, Joseph Nicholas *psychologist, neuroscientist, educator*
Loveday, William John *hospital administrator*
McBride, Angela Barron *nursing educator*
McIntyre, Rita Ann *nursing consultant*
Riegsecker, Marvin Dean *pharmacist, state senator*
†Smith, Donald Eugene *healthcare facility management administrator owner*

La Porte
Morris, Leigh Edward *hospital executive officer*

Lafayette
Claflin, Robert Malden *veterinary educator, university dean*
Coburn, Patricia Ellen *oncological nurse*
Geddes, LaNelle Evelyn *nursing educator, physiologist*
Sperandio, Glen Joseph *pharmacy educator*
Veenker, Claude Harold *health education educator*

Lanesville
Cleveland, Peggy Rose Richey *cytotechnologist*

Liberty Mills
Gross, Rachel Ann *human services coordinator*

Mishawaka
Goebel, Richard Alan *veterinarian*
Scott, Darrel Joseph *healthcare executive*

New Castle
Walburn, John Clifford *mental health services professional*

Notre Dame
Howard, George Stephen *psychology educator*

Reelsville
Powell, Audrey Lee *nursing administrator, critical care nurse*

South Bend
Ecker, Carol Adele *veterinarian*

Valparaiso
Carr, Wiley Nelson *hospital administrator*

West Lafayette
Albright, Jack Lawrence *animal science and veterinary educator*
Amstutz, Harold Emerson *veterinarian, educator*
Belcastro, Patrick Frank *pharmaceutical scientist*
Brown, Donald Ray *psychologist, university administrator*
Christian, John Edward *health science educator*
Cicirelli, Victor George *psychologist*
Feldhusen, John Frederick *educational psychology educator*
Gruen, Gerald Elmer *psychologist, educator*
Haelterman, Edward Omer *veterinary microbiologist, educator*
King, Donald C. *psychologist, educator*
Kirksey, Avanelle *nutrition educator*
Knevel, Adelbert Michael *pharmacy educator*
Peck, Garnet Edward *pharmacist, educator*
Schönemann, Peter Hans *psychology educator*
Shell, Kevin Duane *human services researcher, psychologist*
Stump, John Edward *veterinary anatomy educator, ethologist*
Swensen, Clifford Henrik, Jr. *psychologist, educator*

IOWA

Ames
Ahmann, John Stanley *psychology educator*
Ahrens, Franklin Alfred *veterinary pharmacology educator*
Benbow, Camilla Persson *psychology educator, researcher*
Beran, George Wesley *veterinary microbiology educator*
Brown, Frederick Gramm *psychology educator*
Edwards, David Charles *psychology educator*
Ghoshal, Nani Gopal *veterinary anatomist, educator*
Greve, John Henry *veterinary parasitologist, educator*
Mengeling, William Lloyd *veterinarian, virologist, researcher*
Moon, Harley William *veterinarian*
O'Berry, Phillip Aaron *veterinarian*
†Osweiler, Gary Douglas *veterinary medicine educator, toxicologist*
Pearson, Phillip Theodore *veterinary clinical sciences and biomedical engineering educator*
Ross, Richard Francis *veterinarian, microbiologist, educator*
Seaton, Vaughn Allen *veterinary pathology educator*
Wass, Wallace Milton *veterinarian, clinical science educator*

Cedar Rapids
Bowers, M. Joan *nursing administrator*
Kasparek, Ann Janine *health facility administrator*
Wallace, Samuel Taylor *hospital administrator*

Coon Rapids
Shirbroun, Richard Elmer *veterinarian, cattleman*

Davenport
Bhatti, Iftikhar Hamid *chiropractic educator*

Des Moines
Fox, Marcia Helen *nursing administrator, medical-surgical nurse*
Goldsmith, Janet Jane *pediatric nurse practitioner*
Kramer, Mary Elizabeth *health services executive, state legislator*
Lund, Doris Hibbs *dietitian*
Ramsey, David Selmer *hospital executive*
†Reitinger, Thomas Anthony *hospital administrator*
Sullivan, Patricia Clare *hospital administrator*

Forest City
Vammen, James Oliver *human services administrator*

Glenwood
Campbell, William Edward *state hospital school administrator*

Iowa City
Aydelotte, Myrtle Kitchell *nursing administrator, educator, consultant*
Banker, Gilbert Stephen *industrial and physical pharmacy educator, administrator*
Brennan, Robert Lawrence *psychometrician*
Coffman, William Eugene *educational psychologist*
Colloton, John William *university health care executive*
Hardy, James Chester *speech pathologist, educator*
Knutson, John Franklin *psychology educator, clinical psychologist*
Levey, Samuel *health care administration educator*
Lopes, Lola Lynn *psychologist, educator*
Nathan, Peter E. *psychologist, educator*
Obermann, C. Esco *psychologist, rehabilitation consultant*
Small, Arnold McCollum *psychologist, educator*
Wasserman, Edward Arnold *psychology educator*
Wurster, Dale Erwin *pharmacy educator, university dean*

Knoxville
Joslyn, Wallace Danforth *psychologist*

Larchwood
Onet, Virginia C(onstantinescu) *research scientist, educator, writer*

Mason City
Rosenberg, Dale Norman *psychology educator*
Schumacher, Larry P. *health facility administrator*

Sioux City
†Biorn, David Olaf *hospital administrator*

West Des Moines
Zimmerman, Jo Ann *health services and educational consultant, former lieutenant governor*

Windsor Heights
Demorest, Allan Frederick *psychologist, consultant*

KANSAS

Bonner Springs
Elliott-Watson, Doris Jean *psychiatric, mental health and gerontological nursing educator*

Chanute
Mitchell, Donald E. *rehabilitation counselor, transition counselor*

Derby
†Guntly, Gregory G. *health facility administrator*

Emporia
Christiansen, David K. *hospital administrator*

Fort Leavenworth
Oliver, Thornal Goodloe *health care executive*

Fort Riley
†Gorsline, Stephen Paul *medical technician*

Hays
Lee, Carla Ann Bouska *nursing educator*

Hutchinson
Schmidt, Gene Earl *hospital administrator*

Kansas City
Godwin, Harold Norman *pharmacist, educator*
Jerome, Norge Winifred *nutritionist, anthropologist*
Maher, Sylvia Arlene *nurse administrator*
Potter, Glenn Edward *hospital administrator*

Lake Quivira
Hall, R. Vance *psychology researcher, educator, administrator, consultant, business executive*

Lawrence
Baumgartel, Howard J., Jr. *psychology educator, academic administrator*
Martin, Edwin J(ohn) *psychologist*
†Ohlen, Robert Bruce *hospital executive*
Schroeder, Stephen Robert *psychology researcher*

Leavenworth
Glatt, Sister Marie Damian *healthcare corporation executive*

Manhattan
Erickson, Howard Hugh *veterinarian*
Lorenz, Michael Duane *veterinary medicine educator*
Murray, John Patrick *psychologist, educator, researcher*
Parish, Thomas Scanlan *human development educator*
Phares, E. Jerry *psychology educator*
Setser, Carole Sue *food science educator*
Spears, Marian Caddy *dietetics and institutional management educator*
Vorhies, Mahlon Wesley *veterinary pathologist, educator*

Shawnee Mission
†Boyle, James Wilbur *hospital administrator*

Topeka
†Chase, Howard Marion *hospital administrator*
Mara, John Lawrence *veterinarian, consultant*
Samuelson, Marvin Lee *veterinarian*
Sheffel, Irving Eugene *psychiatric institution executive*
Spohn, Herbert Emil *psychologist*
Varner, Charleen LaVerne McClanahan (Mrs. Robert B. Varner) *nutritionist, educator, administrator, dietitian*

University Of Kansas
†Turnbull, H. Rutherford, III *law educator, lawyer*

Wichita
†Banks, Michael A. *hospital administrator*
Biltz, Jim *hospital administrator*
Clark, Susan Matthews *psychologist*
Denger, Elsie Sue *nursing administrator*
Egan, Sister M. Sylvia *hospital administrator*
Hicks, M. Elizabeth *pharmacist*
Reed, Darwin Cramer *health care consultant*

Winfield
Crowley, Marilyn *critical care nurse, educator*

KENTUCKY

Bowling Green
Cangemi, Joseph Peter *psychologist, consultant, educator*

Covington
Gross, Joseph Wallace *hospital administrator*

Elizabethtown
Modderman, Melvin Earl *health administrator*

Fort Thomas
Gooch, Deborah Ann Grimme *medical/surgical nurse, administrator*

†Hoyle, John Douglas *hospital administrator*

Lexington
Butler, Frank Anthony *hospital administrator*
†Calico, Forrest W. *health facility administrator*
Cole, Henry Philip *educational psychologist*
DeLuca, Patrick Phillip *pharmaceutical scientist, educator, administrator*
Dittert, Lewis William *pharmacy educator*
Timoney, Peter Joseph *veterinarian, virologist, educator, consultant*
Worell, Judith P. *psychologist, educator*

Louisville
Baron, Martin Raymond *psychology educator*
Coggins, Homer Dale *retired hospital administrator*
Cybulski, Joanne Karen *nutritionist, diabetes educator*
Ehrlich, Virginia Lee *nursing administrator*
Eighmey, Douglas Joseph, Jr. *hospital administrator*
Hockenberger, Susan Jane *nurse educator*
Jones, David Allen *health facility executive*
Kelley, Noble Henry *former psychologist, educator*
Lonergan, Jeanette Nancy *nurse*
Marvin, Oscar McDowell *retired hospital administrator*
Mather, Elizabeth Vivian *health care executive*
Pickle, James C. *hospital administrator*
Potvin, Suzanne Hilda *chief nurse*
†Smith, R. Gene *health facility administrator*
Vandewater, David *hospital administrator*
†Wagner, Henry Carrh, III *health care executive*
†Williams, Steven A. *hospital administrator*

Nazareth
Dundon, Mark Walden *hospital administrator*

Paducah
Brown, Laverne Kindred *health facility administrator, nurse*

Russellville
Harper, Shirley Fay *nutritionist, educator, consultant*

LOUISIANA

Alexandria
Sneed, Ellouise Bruce *nursing educator*

Baton Rouge
Berg, Irwin August *psychology educator*
Besch, Everett Dickman *veterinarian, university dean emeritus*
†Chandler, Bruce Stanhope, III *hospital administrator*
Cox, Hollis Utah *veterinarian*
Geiselman, Paula Jeanne *psychologist*
Ropielle, Arthur Jean *psychologist*
Sawyer, Thomas Harry *health care facility administrator*
Timmons, Edwin O'Neal *psychologist*

Deville
McCann, Norma Reed *health facility administrator*

Kenner
Treuting, Edna Gannon *retired nursing administrator*

Lafayette
Bertrand, Harry C. *health facility administrator*
Kline, Roger V. *health science facility adminstrator*

Leesville
Russell, Gerald Edward *social worker, retired army officer*

Metairie
Brisolara, Ashton *substance abuse and employee assistance programs consultant*
†Holland, Jeffrey Stuart *hospital executive*

Monroe
Marsala, Theresa Clark *nurse, adminstrator*

Natchitoches
Egan, Shirley Anne *retired nursing educator*

New Orleans
Campbell, Margaret M. *social work educator*
Fine, David Jeffrey *hospital executive, educator, consultant, lecturer*
Moely, Barbara E. *psychology educator*
Olson, Richard David *psychology educator*
O'Neal, Edgar Carl *psychology educator*
Paradise, Louis Vincent *psychology educator, university provost*
Pittman, Jacquelyn *mental health nurse, nursing educator*
Remley, Theodore Phant, Jr. *counselor, educator and lawyer*
Roberts, Elliott C., Sr. *hospital administrator*

Shreveport
Kelley, Marie Nichols *hospital administrator*
Preston, Loyce Elaine *retired social work educator*
†Schneider, Thomas Richard *hospital administrator*
Winham, George Keeth *mental health nurse*

Slaughter
Gremillion, Curtis Lionel, Jr. *psychologist, hospital administrator, musician*

Slidell
Hall, Ogden Henderson *allied health educator*

West Monroe
Rentfro, Larry Dean *hospital administrator*

MAINE

Augusta
Kany, Judy C(asperson) *health policy analyst, former state senator*
Sotir, Thomas Alfred *healthcare executive, retired shipbuilder*

Bangor
Mills, David Harlow *psychologist, association executive*

Brunswick
Fuchs, Alfred Herman *psychologist, college dean, educator*

East Boothbay
Eldred, Kenneth McKechnie *acoustical consultant*

Lewiston
†Cassidy, James Edward *hospital executive*

Orono
Goldstone, Sanford *psychology educator*

Portland
DiMatteo, John R. *health facility administrator*
McDowell, Donald L. *hospital administrator*
Zieff, Ralph Morrison *psychologist*

Rockland
McGuigan, Charles James *rehabilitation therapist*

Surry
Pickett, Betty Horenstein *psychologist*

MARYLAND

Baltimore
Abeloff, Martin David *medical administrator, educator, researcher*
Alliker, Stanford Arnold *hospital administrator*
†Applebaum, Gary E. *medical director, executive*
Block, James A. *hospital administrator, pediatrician*
Brieger, Gert Henry *medical historian, educator*
Cain, Rosa Marie *nurse, educator*
Carlton, Sara Boehlke *rehabilitation services administrator*
Catania, A(nthony) Charles *psychology educator*
†Cunningham, Terence Thomas, III *hospital administrator*
Davis, Ada Romaine *nursing educator*
Desoto, Clinton Burgel *psychologist, educator*
Ebinger, Mary Ritzman *pastoral counselor*
Engel, Bernard Theodore *psychologist, educator*
Gaver, Barbara Anne *child and adolescent psychotherapist*
Goldstein, Gary W. *rehabilitation research administrator*
Graves, Pirkko Maija-Leena *clinical psychologist, psychoanalyst*
Gray, Carol Joyce *nurse, educator*
Green, Bert Franklin, Jr. *psychologist*
†Guggino, William Biagio *medical administrator, physiology educator*
Hansen, Jeanne Bodine *retired counselor*
†Henderson, Robin *pediatrics educator, pediatric nutritionist*
Hulse, Stewart Harding, Jr. *educator, experimental psychologist*
Jacox, Ada Kathryn *nurse, educator*
Knapp, David Allan *pharmaceutical educator, researcher*
Kowal, Robert Paul *hospital administrator*
Kumin, Libby Barbara *speech language pathologist, educator*
†Loftus, Donald Gregory *hospital administrator*
Mallette, Phyllis Cooper Spencer *medical/surgical nurse*
Merritt, Betty L. *medical/surgical and mental health nurse*
Money, John William *psychologist*
Nathanson, Constance A. *health science organization administrator, sociology educator*
Piotrow, Phyllis Tilson *public health educator, international development specialist*
Redman, Barbara Klug *nursing educator*
†Rose, Sister Cecilia *healthcare management administrator*
Ryan, Judith W. *geriatrics nurse, adult nurse practitioner, educator, researcher*
Shapiro, Sam *health care analyst, biostatistician*
Sharfstein, Steven Samuel *health care executive, medical director*
Sommer, Alfred *public health professional, ophthalmologist, epidemiologist*
Stanley, Julian Cecil, Jr. *psychology educator*
Steinwachs, Donald Michael *public health educator*
†Turnock, James McClymonds *healthcare executive*
Vasile, Gennaro James *health care executive*

Beltsville
Levin, Gilbert Victor *health information, bioengineering and environmental control company executive*

Bethesda
Atwell, Constance Woodruff *health services executive, researcher*
Banik, Sambhu Nath *psychologist*
Bryant, Bertha Estelle *retired nurse*
Cooper, Merri-Ann *psychologist*
Dogoloff, Lee Israel *clinical social worker, psychotherapist, consultant*
Fauci, Anthony Stephen *health facility administrator, physician*
Gaarder, Marie *speech pathologist*
Gallin, John Isaac *health science association administrator*
†Geller, Ronald Gene *health administrator*
Gluckstein, Fritz Paul *veterinarian, biomedical information specialist*
Hurd, Suzanne Sheldon *federal agency health science director*
Jonas, Gary Fred *health care center executive*
†Kalt, Marvin Robert *health organization administrator, cell biologist*
Malouff, Frank Joseph *health care association executive*
McKeon, Kathryn Lothschuetz *nursing administrator*
Metzger, Henry *federal research institution administrator*
Mishkin, Mortimer *neuropsychologist*
Notkins, Abner Louis *physician, researcher*
Obrams, Gunta Iris *research administrator*
O'Donnell, James Francis *health science administrator*
Onufrock, Richard Shade *pharmacist, researcher*
Ory, Marcia Gail *social science researcher*

Quraishi, Mohammed Sayeed *health scientist, administrator*
Roberts, Doris Emma *epidemiologist, consultant*
Schneider, John Hoke *health science administrator*
Talbot, Bernard *government medical research facility official, physician*
Trumbull, Richard *psychologist*
Vaitukaitis, Judith Louise *medical research administrator*
Vickers, James Hudson *veterinarian, research pathologist*
Winkler, James B. *health care consultant*

Chevy Chase
Crawford, Meredith Pullen *research psychologist*
Walk, Richard David *retired psychology educator*

Clinton
Sizemore, Carolyn Lee *nuclear medicine technologist*
Ward, Sue Elleanore Fryer *social worker, state agency administrator*

College Park
Gaylin, Ned L. *psychology educator*
Greenberg, Jerrold Selig *health education educator*
Hill, Clara Edith *psychology educator*
Locke, Edwin Allen, III *psychologist, educator*
Michels, Eugene *physical therapist*
Schneider, Benjamin *psychology educator*
Sigall, Harold Fred *psychology educator*

Columbia
†Northrop, Thomas Webster *health care facility administrator*

Ellicott City
Robison, Susan Miller *psychologist, educator, consultant*
Tillman, Elizabeth Carlotta *nurse, educator*

Gaithersburg
McShefferty, John *research company executive*
Ross, Sherman *psychologist, educator*

Greenbelt
†Emerson, Jeff Douglas *healthcare executive*

Hagerstown
Harrison, Lois Smith *hospital executive, educator*

Hunt Valley
Parker, Lewis E. S. *orthopedic company executive, commercial vineyard operator*

Hyattsville
Herrmann, Douglas J. *psychology educator, researcher*

Kensington
Braden, Joan Kay *mental health counselor*

La Plata
Galvin, Noreen Ann *nurse, educator*

Landover
Colyer, Sheryl Lynn *psychologist*

Largo
Isom, Virginia Annette Veazey *nursing educator*

Lutherville
Corcoran, Loma M. *hospital administrator*

Lutherville Timonium
†Thompson, Wayne Paul *healthcare executive*

Marriottsville
Fitzgerald, John L. *hospital administrator*

Olney
Pines, Nancy Freitag *psychotherapist*

Owings Mills
†Elkins, Robert N. *association executive*

Potomac
Brewer, Nathan Ronald *veterinarian, consultant*
Evans, Christine Burnett *health care executive*
Heller, Peggy Osna *poetry therapist, psychotherapist*
Reynolds, Frank Miller *retired government administrator*

Riva
Powers, Margaret A. *nursing administrator*

Rockville
Arnstein, Sherry Phyllis *health care executive*
Brumback, Gary Bruce *industrial and organizational psychologist*
†Gabelnick, Henry Lewis *medical research director*
Howard, Lee Milton *international health consultant*
Koslow, Stephen Hugh *science administrator, pharmacologist*
McCormick, Kathleen Ann Krym *geriatrics nurse, computer information specialist, federal agency administrator*
Milner, Max *food and nutrition consultant*
†Nightingale, Stuart Lester *physician, public health officer*
Nora, Audrey Hart *physician*
†Robinson, William Andrew *health service executive, physician*
†Smith, Vivian Louise *substance abuse prevention professional, social worker*
Snyder, Marvin *neuropsychologist*
Teske, Richard Henry *veterinarian*
Whitney, Robert A., Jr. *veterinarian, government public health executive*

Salisbury
Poisker, Karen Coons *nursing administrator*

Silver Spring
Gilbert, Arthur Charles Francis *psychologist*
Hamill, James Paul *hospital administrator*
Milligan, Glenn Ellis *psychologist*
Munson, John Christian *acoustician*
Rayburn, Carole (Mary Aida) Ann *psychologist, researcher, writer*

Towson
Irwin, Sister Marie Cecilia *hospital administrator*
Muuss, Rolf Eduard *psychologist, educator*

Woodstock
Fitzgerald, John *health facility executive*

MASSACHUSETTS

Amherst
Averill, James Reed *psychology educator*
Berger, Seymour Maurice *social psychologist*
Fox, Thomas Walton *veterinary science educator*
Grose, Robert Freeman *psychology educator*
Strickland, Bonnie Ruth *psychologist, educator*

Andover
Anderson, Amelia E. *nursing administrator, geriatrics nurse*

Belmont
Levendusky, Philip George *clinical psychologist, administrator*
Levine, Sarah Loewenberg *developmental psychologist, school director*

Boston
Ansin, Betsey Iris *psychotherapist, clinical social worker*
Blendon, Robert Jay *health policy educator*
†Carton, Lonnie Caming *educational psychologist*
Copeland, Anne Pitcairn *psychologist*
†Druhot, Theodore J(oseph) *hospital admintrator*
†Gaintner, J(ohn) Richard *health facility executive, medical educator*
Gleason, Jean Berko *psychology educator*
Golomb, Claire *psychology educator*
Goodglass, Harold *psychologist, neurology educator*
Grossman, Frances Kaplan *psychologist*
†Holick, Michael Francis *nutritionist*
Kubzansky, Philip Eugene *environmental and organizational psychologist*
Liang, Matthew H. *medical director*
Lorsch, Jay William *business educator*
Macdonald, Mary Elizabeth *nursing administrator, educator*
Martin, Dale *vocational rehabilitation executive*
Millar, Sally Gray *nurse*
Murphy, Evelyn Frances *healthcare administrator, former lieutenant governor*
Nesson, H. Richard *medical administrator, physician*
O'Hern, Jane Susan *psychologist, educator*
Page, Patricia M. *health science association administrator*
†Purvis, George Porter, III *health services company executive, consultant*
Reinherz, Helen Zarsky *social services educator*
†Robinson, William R. *health facility adminstrator*
Scrimshaw, Nevin Stewart *physician, nutrition and health educator*
Shaw, James Headon *nutritionist, educator*
Stare, Fredrick John *nutritionist, biochemist, physician*
Wechsler, Henry *research psychologist*
Weinstein, Milton Charles *health policy educator*
Winkelman, James Warren *hospital administrator, pathology educator*

Boxford
Siegert, Barbara (Marie) *health care administrator*

Brookline
Kibrick, Anne *nursing educator, university dean*

Burlington
Freeman, Donald Chester, Jr. *health care company executive*

Cambridge
Appley, Mortimer Herbert *psychologist, university president emeritus*
Bailyn, Lotte *psychology and management educator*
Brown, Roger William *psychologist, educator*
Burlage, Dorothy Dawson *clinical psychologist*
Caramazza, Alfonso *psychology educator*
Castaldi, David Lawrence *health care company executive*
Chall, Jeanne Sternlicht *psychologist, educator*
Colby, Anne *psychologist*
Collins, Allan Meakin *cognitive scientist, psychologist, educator*
Davis, Edgar Glenn *science and health policy executive*
Estes, William Kaye *psychologist, educator*
Gardner, Howard Earl *psychologist, author*
Gilligan, Carol F. *psychologist, writer*
Herrnstein, Richard Julius *psychology educator*
Holzman, Philip Seidman *psychologist, educator*
Kagan, Jerome *psychologist, educator*
Kelman, Herbert Chanoch *psychology educator*
Kosslyn, Stephen M. *psychologist educator*
Langer, Ellen Jane *psychologist, educator, writer*
Levinson, Harry *psychologist, educator*
Maher, Brendan Arnold *psychology educator, editor*
Nakayama, Ken *psychology educator*
Rosenthal, Robert *psychology educator*
Rubin, Jeffrey Zachary *psychologist, educator*
Swets, John Arthur *psychologist, scientist*
Wexler, Kenneth Norman *psychology educator*

Canton
Bihldorff, John Pearson *hospital director*

Chestnut Hill
Hawkins, Joellen Margaret Beck *nursing educator*

Danvers
Manganello, James Angelo *psychologist*

Fitchburg
†Cronin, Francis Joseph, Jr. *hospital administrator*
†Fredette, Raymond David *healthcare executive*

Framingham
Vermette, Raymond Edward *clinical laboratories administrator*

Greenfield
Curtiss, Carol Perry *nursing consultant*

Halifax
Fanning, Margaret Beverly *psychotherapist*

Hanson
Norris, John Anthony *health sciences executive, lawyer, educator*

Harvard
†Larson, Roland Elmer *health care executive*

Haverhill
Haritos, Dolores Jean *nursing educator*

Lawrence
Mosca, Anthony John *substance abuse professional*

Lexington
Chaskelson, Marsha Ina *neuropsychologist*
Wathne, Carl Norman *hospital administrator*

Lincoln
Barrett, Beatrice Helene *psychologist*

Marlborough
Bethel, Tamara Ann *psychiatric nurse, consultant*

Medford
DeBold, Joseph Francis *psychology educator*
Elkind, David *psychology educator*
Junger, Miguel Chapero *acoustics researcher*
Kanarek, Robin Beth *psychology educator, nutrition educator, researcher*
Luria, Zella Hurwitz *psychology educator*
Miczek, Klaus Alexander *psychology educator*

Melrose
Gibbons, Patrice Ellen *critical care nurse*

Milton
Berzon, Faye Clark *retired nursing educator*

Nantucket
Murray, Caroline Fish *psychologist*

Natick
Bensel, Carolyn Kirkbride *psychologist*

Needham
Cantor, Pamela Corliss *psychologist*

New Bedford
Merolla, Michele Edward *chiropractor*

Newton
White, Burton Leonard *educational psychologist, author*

North Grafton
Loew, Franklin Martin *medical and biological scientist*
Ross, James Neil, Jr. *veterinary educator*
Schwartz, Anthony *veterinary surgeon, educator*

Northampton
Crosby, Faye Jacqueline *psychology educator, author*
Volkmann, Frances Cooper *psychologist, educator*

Orleans
Russell, David L(awson) *psychology educator*

Roxbury
Jacobs, Annette *health facilities administrator*

Sandwich
Terrill, Robert Carl *hospital administrator*

Southbridge
Mangion, Richard Michael *health care executive*

Springfield
Bode, Susan Mary *nursing administrator*
Daly, Michael Joseph *hospital administrator*
Winder, Alvin Eliot *public health educator, clinical psychologist*

Stoughton
Amirault, Carol Jean *nurse*

Waltham
Kunkel, Barbara *psychologist, consultant, educator*
Mitchell, Janet Brew *health services researcher*
Morant, Ricardo Bernardino *psychology educator*
Nogelo, Anthony Miles *health care company executive*
Sekuler, Robert William *psychology educator, scientist*
†Wallack, Stanley S. *healthcare administrator*
†Wilczek, Joseph *health facilities administrator*

Ware
Shirtcliff, Christine Fay *healthcare facility executive*

Watertown
Pellegrom, Daniel Earl *international health and development executive*

Wayland
Wolf, Irving *clinical psychologist*

Wellesley
Giddon, Donald B(ernard) *psychologist, educator*
Montague, Joel Gedney *public health consultant*

West Tisbury
Smith, Henry Clay *retired psychology educator*

Westfield
Ashley, Cynthia Elizabeth *psychotherapist, human service administrator*

Weston
Bales, Robert Freed *social psychologist, educator*
Fine, Bernard J. *retired psychologist, consultant*

Westwood
Donahue, Charles Lee, Jr. *health network executive*

Williamstown
Conklin, Susan Joan *psychotherapist*
Cramer, Phebe *psychologist*
Crider, Andrew Blake *psychologist*
Goethals, George R., II *psychology educator*
Hastings, Philip Kay *psychology educator*
McGill, Thomas Emerson *psychology educator*
Solomon, Paul Robert *neuropsychologist, educator*

Wilmington
Foster, Henry Louis *veterinarian, laboratory executive*

Woburn
Breazeale, Kelly Wade *health care association executive, consultant*

Worcester
Bourgeois, Anne Mary *nursing administrator*
Dorman, Harry Gaylord, III *hospital administrator*
Mancini, Valerie *health facility administrator*
Wapner, Seymour *psychologist, educator, administrator*

Wrentham
Brown, Millie Louise *mental health nurse*

MICHIGAN

Ann Arbor
Apperson, Jean *psychologist*
Barbarin, Oscar Anthony *psychologist*
Brown, Donald Robert *psychology educator*
Cain, Albert Clifford *psychology educator*
Cannell, Charles Frederick *psychologist, educator*
Clark, Noreen Morrison *behavioral science educator, researcher*
Douvan, Elizabeth *social psychologist, educator*
Drach, John Charles *researcher, dental basic science educator*
Ellsworth, Phoebe Clemencia *psychology educator*
Eron, Leonard David *psychology educator*
Finch, Debra Ann *registered nurse*
Forsyth, John D. *hospital administrator*
Gomberg, Edith S. Lisansky *psychologist, educator*
Griffith, John Randall *health services administrator, educator*
Hagen, John William *psychology educator*
House, James Stephen *social psychologist, educator*
Jackson, James Sidney *psychology educator*
Jones, Beverly Ann *critical care and pediatrics nurse*
Kalisch, Beatrice Jean *nursing educator, consultant*
Ketefian, Shaké *nursing educator*
Manis, Melvin *psychologist, educator*
McKeachie, Wilbert James *psychologist, educator*
Nisbett, Richard Eugene *psychology educator*
Oakley, Deborah Jane *researcher, educator*
†Olson, Gary Monroe *psychology educator*
Pender, Nola J. *community health nursing educator, researcher*
Powell, Linda Rae *educational healthcare consultant*
Ringler, Daniel Howard *lab animal medicine educator*
Romani, John Henry *health administration educator*
Rupp, Ralph Russell *audiologist, educator, author*
Smith, J(ames) E(verett) Keith *psychologist, educator*
Stevenson, Harold William *psychology educator*
Sullivan, Donald John *health care corporation executive*
Warner, Kenneth E. *public health educator, consultant*
Zucker, Robert A(lpert) *psychologist*

Benton Harbor
Rasmussen, Alice Call *nursing educator*

Big Rapids
Weinlander, Max Martin *retired psychologist*

Croswell
Anderson, Sandy Fay *healthcare executive, nurse*

Dearborn
Fitzgerald, Gerald Dennis *hospital administrator*

Detroit
Barr, Martin *health care and higher education admnistrator*
Bennett, Margaret Ethel Booker *psychotherapist*
†Broughton, Paul Laurence *hospital administrator*
Campbell, David James *hospital administrator*
Cantoni, Louis Joseph *psychologist, poet, sculptor*
†Eustis, Mark Arthur *hospital administrator*
Heppner, Gloria Hill *science administrator*
Housley, Charles Edward *hospital system executive*
Iacobell, Frank Peter *hospital administrator*
Johnson, Robert Bertram *hospital administrator*
†Lee, André Lafayette *hospital administrator*
Leininger, Madeleine Monica *nurse, anthropologist, administrator, consultant, editor*
Mack, Robert Emmet *hospital administrator*
†Mirer, Franklin Emanuel *industrial hygienist*
Prasad, Ananda Shiva *medical educator*
Rintelmann, William Fred *audiology educator*
†Schaengold, Phillip S. *hospital adiministrator*
Thomas, Edward St. Clair *hospital administrator*
Warden, Gail Lee *health care executive*
Wesselmann, Glenn Allen *hospital executive*
Wittrup, Richard Derald *health care executive*

East Lansing
Abeles, Norman *psychologist, educator*
Courtney, Gladys (Atkins) *nursing educator, former dean*
Ilgen, Daniel Richard *psychology educator*
Tasker, John Baker *veterinary medical educator, college dean*
Winder, Clarence Leland *psychologist, educator*
Witter, Richard Lawrence *veterinarian, educator*

Farmington
Baker, Edward Martin *engineering and industrial psychologist*
Burns, Sister Elizabeth Mary *hospital administrator*
†Haydon, Glen Edgar *healthcare administrator*
Schwartz, Michael Robinson *health administrator*

Farmington Hills
Abrams, Roberta Busky *hospital administrator, nurse*

Heid, Sister Mary Corita *hospital administrator*
Pelham, Judith *hospital administrator*

Flint
Campbell, Phyllis *nursing administrator*
†Incarnati, Philip Anthony *hospital administrator*
†Reetz, Gary *medical facility administrator*

Grand Haven
Anderson, Cynthia Finkbeiner Sjoberg *speech and language pathologist*

Grand Rapids
Brent, Helen Teressa *mental health nurse*
Emery, Marcia Rose *parapsychologist, psychologist, consultant*
Jackson, Beth Ann *nursing administrator*
†Nadel, Mark Alan *hospital executive*
Viehl, Marjorie Alice *nursing educator*

Grosse Pointe Farms
Cartmill, George Edwin, Jr. *retired hospital administrator*

Holland
Hountras, Peter Timothy *psychologist, educator*

Jackson
Genyk, Ruth Bel *psychotherapist*

Kalamazoo
Fredericks, Sharon Kay *nurses aide*
†Ludwig, Patric E. *health care group executive*
†Stack, R. Timothy *health facility administrator*
†Stasik, Randy *health facility administrator*

Lansing
Anthony, Vernice Davis *public health officer*
Crandall, Nancy Lee *geriatrics service professional, nurse*
†McRee, Edward Barxdale *hospital administrator*
†Neumann, Forrest Karl *hospital administrator*

Livonia
Needham, Kathleen Ann *gerontology educator, consultant*

Madison Heights
†Tersigni, Anthony *health science facility administrator*

Monroe
Heselton, Patricia Ann *clinical psychologist*

Mount Pleasant
Lovinger, Sophie Lehner *child psychologist*

Plymouth
McClendon, Edwin James *health science educator*

Pontiac
Wilcox, Joann Rose Court *hospital administrator*

Royal Oak
Karavite, Carlene Marie *psychologist, real estate property manager*
Klosinski, Deanna Dupree *medical laboratory sciences educator*
Matzick, Kenneth John *hospital administrator*
Myers, Kenneth Ellis *hospital administrator*

Southfield
†Barrett, John Eugene, Jr. *health care administrator*
†Beuerlein, Sister Juliana *hospital administrator*
Thimotheose, Kadakampallil George *psychologist*

Traverse City
†Bay, John Cantrell *retired hospital administrator*

Troy
†Haven, Carl Ole *hospital adminstrator*

Union Lake
Boulos, Nadia Ebid *medical/surgical nurse*

University Center
Lange, Crystal Marie *nursing educator*

West Bloomfield
Green, Shirley Laak *nursing administrator*

Ypsilanti
Holland, Joy *health care facility executive*
Williams, Regina Marion *nursing educator*
Wilson, Lorraine M. *medical, surgical nurse, nursing educator*

MINNESOTA

Cloud
Holthaus, Thomas Anthony *hospital administrator*

Cottage Grove
Glazebrook, Rita Susan *nursing educator*

Duluth
Gallinger, Lois Mae *medical technologist*

Eden Prairie
Schaeffer, Brenda Mae *psychologist*

Faribault
Saufferer, William Charles *health center executive*

Golden Valley
Van Hauer, Robert *former health care company executive*

Mankato
Zeller, Michael James *psychologist, educator*

Minneapolis
Appel, William Frank *pharmacist*
Baum, David Roy *research psychologist*
Berscheid, Ellen S. *psychology educator, author, researcher*
Bouchard, Thomas Joseph, Jr. *psychology educator, researcher*
Corcoran, Mary Elizabeth *educational psychology educator emeritus*
Cummings, Larry Lee *psychologist, educator*
Dawis, René V. *psychology educator, research consultant*
Garmezy, Norman *psychology educator*
Grant, David James William *pharmacy educator*
Hansen, Jo-Ida Charlotte *psychology educator, researcher*
Hanson, A. Stuart *medical foundation executive, physician*
Johnson, David Wolcott *psychologist, educator*
Konopka, Gisela Peiper (Mrs. Erhardt Paul Konopka) *social worker, author, lecturer, educator*
Kralewski, John Edward *health service administration educator*
Manning, Patrick James *veterinarian, experimental pathologist, educator*
Marks, Florence Carlin Elliott *nursing informaticist*
Meehl, Paul Everett *psychologist, educator*
Morath, Julianne Mollie *nursing administrator*
Newman, Margaret Ann *nursing educator*
Patterson, Joan Marie *maternal/child health educator, psychologist*
Pitt, Helen K. *nurse, hospital administrator*
Sawchuk, Ronald John *pharmaceutical scientist, educator*
Schofield, William *psychologist, educator*
Spinner, Robert Keith *hospital administrator*
Sprenger, Gordon M. *hospital administrator*
†Tibbetts, Pamela Lee *health facility administrator*
Toscano, James Vincent *medical institute administration*
Walker, Elva Mae Dawson *health consultant*
Walter, Frank Sherman *retired health care corporation executive*
Weinberg, Richard Alan *psychologist*
Wiener, Daniel Norman *psychologist*
†Yonas, Albert *psychology educator*
Ysseldyke, James Edward *psychology educator, research center administrator*
†Ziegenhagen, David M. *healthcare company executive*

Morris
Kemble, Ernest Dell *psychology educator*

Redlake
Ceterski, Dorothy *nutritionist*

Robbinsdale
Anderson, Scott Robbins *hospital administrator*

Rochester
Anderson, James Gerard *hospital administrator*
Gervais, Sister Generose *hospital consultant*
Leonard, David Arthur *hospital executive emeritus*

Saint Louis Park
Gerike, Ann Elizabeth *psychologist*

Saint Paul
Ashton, Sister Mary Madonna *healthcare administrator*
†Aune, R. Benjamin *healthcare alliance administrator*
Czarnecki, Caroline MaryAnne *veterinary anatomy educator*
Diesch, Stanley La Verne *veterinarian, educator*
Dunlop, Robert Hugh *veterinary medicine educator*
†Fetrow, John Patrick *veterinary medicine educator*
†Francis, D. Max *healthcare management executive*
†Garland, Robert Field *health facility executive*
Johnson, Kenneth Harvey *veterinary pathologist*
†Lawton, Lois *health facility administrator*
Mrkonich, Dorothy Evanson *nursing educator*
†Perryman, Margaret E. *hospital executive*
Rossmann, Jack Eugene *psychology educator*

White Bear Lake
Williams, Julie Belle *psychiatric social worker*

MISSISSIPPI

Carriere
Wilson, Raymond Clark *former hospital executive*

Cleveland
Thornton, Larry Lee *psychotherapist, author, educator*

Columbus
†Duke, Lance Brittain *hospital administrator*

Gulfport
Brignac, Wanda Anne *nursing educator*

Hattiesburg
Woodall, Lowery A. *hospital administrator*

Jackson
Baltz, Richard Jay *health care company executive*
Bender, Kaye W. *nursing administrator*
Dubbert, Patricia Marie *psychologist*
Malloy, James Matthew *managed care executive, health care consultant*
Stubbs, James Carlton *retired hospital administrator*
Woodrell, Frederick Dale *health care executive*
Wright, Maria Gloria *nursing administrator*

Mississippi State
Khatena, Joe *psychology educator*

Ocean Springs
McNulty, Matthew Francis, Jr. *health sciences and health services administrator, educator, university administrator, consultant, horse and cattle breeder*

Pascagoula
McIlwain, Thomas David *fishery administrator, marine biologist, educator*

Southaven
Utroska, William Robert *veterinarian*

Tupelo
†Hicks, John David *hospital administrator*

University
Cooker, Philip George *psychology educator*

Whitfield
Morton, James Irwin *hospital administrator*

MISSOURI

Cape Girardeau
Southard-Ritter, Marcia *nursing administrator*

Chesterfield
Humphreys, James Burnham *hospital administrator*

Columbia
Biddle, Bruce Jesse *social psychologist, educator*
Blaine, Edward H. *health science association administrator*
Dolliver, Robert Henry *psychology educator*
Hensley, Elizabeth Catherine *nutritionist, educator*
Kausler, Donald Harvey *psychology educator*
Kiesler, Charles Adolphus *psychologist, academic administrator*
LoPiccolo, Joseph *psychologist, educator, author*
Morehouse, Lawrence Glen *veterinarian, educational administrator*
†Thomas, Thomas Stanton *health system executive*
Thompson, Warren A. *mental health services educator, director*
Wagner, Joseph Edward *veterinarian, educator*

Florissant
Betts, Warren R. *retired health facility administrator*

Grandview
Justesen, Don Robert *psychologist*

Hamilton
Esry, Cordelia Cochran *community health nurse*

Independence
Lammers, Joseph Edwin *hospital executive*
Vigen, Kathryn L. Voss *nursing administrator, educator*

Jefferson City
Dey, Charlotte Jane *community health nurse*

Kansas City
Couch, Daniel Michael *healthcare executive*
†Doughty, Clark Ronald *healthcare executive, government official*
Eddy, William Bahret *psychology educator, university dean*
Hasting, Glen Richard, II *health care executive, educator*
Kingsley, James Gordon *health care executive*
†Lindstrom, Charles Clifford *hospital administrator*
Lubin, Bernard *psychologist, educator*
Piepho, Robert Walter *pharmacy educator, researcher*
Presson, Ellis Wynn *health services executive*
Quirk, Barbara Long *medical center executive, nurse*
Samuel, Robert Thompson *optometrist*
†Weathers, K. Russell *hospital foundation executive, mayor*
†Wiener, Mark Seth *health facility administrator*

Rolla
Irion, Arthur Lloyd *psychologist, educator*

Saint Louis
†Brown, Frederick Lee *health care executive*
Carey, Patricia Elaine Stedman *hospital administrator*
†Carr, Julian Lanier, Jr. *healthcare and educational services industries executive*
Cobb, Donna Deanne Hill *physical therapist*
†Cook, Patricia Florence *nursing administrator*
Du Bois, Philip Hunter *psychologist, educator*
Farrell, John Timothy *hospital administrator*
Finan, John Joseph *hospital administrator*
Folk, Roger Maurice *laboratory director*
Hirsh, Ira Jean *psychology educator, researcher*
Ihde, Daniel Carlyle *health science executive*
Jobe, Muriel Ida *medical technologist*
Mattson, William Royce, Jr. *health care consulting company executive*
†Mazzotta, Bruno Robert *hospital administrator, former military officer*
Merbaum, Michael *psychology educator, clinical psychologist*
Myers, Raymond Irvin *optometrist, researcher*
Rosenzweig, Saul *psychologist, educator, administrator*
†Schneiderman, Herbert Barry *hospital administrator*
Schoenhard, William Charles, Jr. *health care executive*
†Sikorski, James Alan *research chemist*
Storandt, Martha *psychologist*
Stretch, John Joseph *social work educator, management and evaluation consultant*
Van Bokkelen, William Requa *health facility administrator*
†Wetzel, Sister Damian *health care administrator*

Sparta
Madore, Joyce Louise *gerontology nurse*

Springfield
Edwards, Charles M. *hospital administrator*
Swift, James William *health care executive*
Westphal, Leonard Wyrick *health care executive, consultant*

Valley Park
Benedict, Gary Clarence *psychotherapist*

MONTANA

Bozeman
Gray, Philip Howard *psychologist, educator*

Forsyth
Smith, Jeffry Alan *health administrator, physician, consultant*

Great Falls
Downer, William John, Jr. *retired hospital administrator, consultant*
†Wilson, Kirk George *medical service executive*

Missoula
Strobel, David Allen *psychology educator*
Watkins, John Goodrich *psychologist, educator*
Wollersheim, Janet Puccinelli *psychology educator*

NEBRASKA

Grand Island
Etheridge, Margaret Dwyer *medical center director*

Lincoln
Bleich, Michael Robert *nursing administrator and consultant*
Hamilton, David Wendell *medical services executive*
Nolte, Walter Eduard *retired retirement home executive, foundation counsel, former banker*
Schmitz, John Albert *veterinary pathologist*
Sonderegger, Theo Brown *psychology educator*

Omaha
†Fraser, John Martin *hospital administrator*
Hachten, Richard Arthur, II *hospital administrator*
Moeller, A. Diane *health facility administrator*
†Moriarty, Jeanne Marie *medical center administrator*
Omer, Robert Wendell *hospital administrator*
Schwartz, C. Edward *hospital administrator*

NEVADA

East Ely
Alderman, Minnis Amèlia *psychologist, educator, small business owner*

Incline Village
Cordingley, Mary Jeanette Bowles (Mrs. William Andrew Cordingley) *social worker, psychologist, artist, writer*

Las Vegas
Brandsness, David R. *hospital administrator*
Gowdy, Miriam Betts *nutritionist*
Law, Flora Elizabeth (Libby Law) *retired community health and pediatrics nurse*
Michel, Mary Ann Kedzuf *nursing educator*
Ogren, Carroll Woodrow *retired hospital administrator*
Wilson, Warner Rushing *psychology educator*

Reno
Bijou, Sidney William *psychology educator*
Cummings, Nicholas Andrew *psychologist*
Guinn, Janet Martin *psychologist, consultant*
Larwood, Laurie *psychologist*
Locke, William Louis *pharmacist*
May, Jerry Russell *psychologist*
Pinson, Larry Lee *pharmacist*
Smith, Aaron *research director, clinical psychologist*

Sparks
Allen, Judith Martha *nursing administrator, career officer*

NEW HAMPSHIRE

Bedford
Collins, Diana Josephine *psychologist*

Concord
Dupuis, Sylvio Louis *optometrist, educator, administrator*
Kalipolites, June E. Turner *rehabilitation professional*

Conway
Solomon, Richard Lester *retired psychology educator*

Hanover
Kleck, Robert Eldon *psychology educator*
Riggs, Lorrin Andrews *psychologist, educator*

Keene
Baldwin, Peter Arthur *psychologist, educator, minister*

Lebanon
Emery, Virginia Olga Beattie *psychologist, researcher*
†Silberfarb, Peter Michael *psychiatrist, educator*
Varnum, James William *hospital administrator*

Manchester
Blake, Jeannette Belisle *psychotherapist*

Sanbornton
Meader, Ralph Gibson *medical administrator*

Sandown
Densen, Paul Maximillian *former health administrator, educator*

West Peterborough
Dyer, Merton S. *pharmacist, state legislator*

NEW JERSEY

Atlantic Highlands
Royce, Paul Chadwick *medical administrator*

Belle Mead
Evans, Frederick John *psychologist*

Bridgewater
Hillegass, Christine Ann *psychologist*

Brielle
Palisi, Anthony Thomas *psychologist, educator*

Camden
†Abbott, Ann Augustine *social worker, educator*
†Halpern, Kevin Gregg *hospital administrator*
Mancini, Nicholas Angelo *psychologist*
Wood, Martha Oakwell *obstetrics-gynecology nurse practitioner*

Cherry Hill
Iglewicz, Raja *state agency administrator, researcher, industrial hygienist*
Israelsky, Roberta Schwartz *speech pathologist, audiologist*

Clark
Kinley, David *physical therapist, acupuncturist*

Clifton
Adelsberg, Harvey *hospital administrator*

East Brunswick
Johnson, Edward Elemuel *psychologist, educator*

Elizabeth
Buonanni, Brian Francis *health care facility administrator, consultant*

Englewood
Kane, Daniel A. *hospital administrator*
Mc Mullan, Dorothy *nurse educator*

Englewood Cliffs
†Farrell, Patricia Ann *psychologist, educator*

Florham Park
Perham, Roy Gates, III *industrial psychologist*

Fort Lee
Roglieri, John Louis *health facility administrator*

Franklin Lakes
Hegelmann, Julius *retired pharmacy educator*

Hackensack
Baker, Andrew Hartill *clinical laboratory executive*
Ferguson, John Patrick *medical center executive*
Fiore, Antoinette *nursing administrator*

Haddon Heights
O'Toole, Marie Theresa *rehabilitation nursing educator*

Haddonfield
†Carter, Joan Pauline *medical services company executive*

Hoboken
Johnson, James Myron *psychologist, educator*

Jersey City
Collins, Doris L. *nursing educator, psychiatric-mental health nurse*
Holmes, Aline MacDonnell *nursing administrator*
Metsch, Jonathan Martin *health facility executive*
Mortensen, Eugene Phillips *hospital administrator*
†Welfeld, Joseph Alan *healthcare consultant*

Kinnelon
Davis, Dorinne Sue Taylor Lovas *audiologist*
Preston, Andrew Joseph *pharmacist, drug company executive*
Richardson, Irene M. *health facility administrator*

Lakewood
Shawl, S. Nicole *counseling psychologist*

Livingston
Del Mauro, Ronald *hospital administrator*

Long Branch
†Dadlez, Christopher M. *hospital administrator*

Lyons
Kidd, A. Paul *hospital administrator, government official*

Madison
Ellenbogen, Leon *nutritionist, pharmaceutical company executive*

Medford
Katzell, Raymond A. *psychologist, educator*
Klugman, Peter Jay *psychologist, consultant*
Wallis, Robert Ray *psychologist, entrepreneur*

Montclair
Tonges, Mary Crabtree *nurse executive*

Morristown
†Oths, Richard Philip *hospital administrator, insurance firm executive*

Mount Holly
Tiedeken, Kathleen Helen *health facilities administrator*

Murray Hill
Atal, Bishnu Saroop *speech research executive*

Neptune
Lloyd, John Koons *hospital administrator*

New Brunswick
Boehm, Werner William *social work educator*
Dinerman, Miriam *social work educator*
Flaherty, Charles Foster, Jr. *psychology educator, researcher*
Glass, David Carter *psychology educator*
Holzberg, Harvey Alan *hospital administrator*
Kovach, Barbara Ellen *management and psychology educator*
Matuska, John E. *hospital administrator*
Peterson, Donald Robert *psychologist, educator, university administrator*
Rosenberg, Seymour *psychologist, educator*
Wilkinson, Louise Cherry *psychology educator, dean*

Newark
Bornstein, Lester Milton *medical center executive*
Carroll, John Douglas *mathematical and statistical psychologist*
Cheng, Mei-Fang *psychobiology educator, neuroethology researcher*
De Lisa, Joel Alan *rehabilitation physician*
Gossett, George Boyd *human service executive*
Lory, Marc H. *hospital administrator*
Samojlik, Eugeniusz *administrator, medical educator*
Stein, Donald Gerald *psychology educator*

Nutley
Drews, Jürgen *pharmaceutical researcher*

Ocean Gate
Campbell, Edward Wallace *nutritionist*

Paramus
Adams, Eda Ann Fischer *nursing educator*
Machlin, Lawrence J. *nutritionist, biochemist, educator*

Parsippany
Agostini, Rosemarie Coniglio *human services administrator*

Paterson
†Duffy, Joseph Frederick *hospital administrator*

Pequannock
MacMurren, Harold Henry, Jr. *psychologist, lawyer*

Piscataway
Alderfer, Clayton Paul *organizational psychologist, educator, author, administrator*
Chien, Yie W. *pharmaceutics educator*
Goldstein, Bernard David *physician, educator*
Julesz, Bela *experimental psychologist, educator, electrical engineer*
Lazarus, Arnold Allan *psychologist, educator*
McCrady, Barbara Sachs *psychologist, educator*
Schwebel, Milton *psychologist, educator*
Spence, Donald Pond *psychologist, psychoanalyst*

Plainfield
Kopicki, John R. *hospital administrator*

Pomona
Bukowski, Elaine Louise *physical therapist*

Pottersville
Goodenough, Marion P. *nursing administrator*

Princeton
Cooper, Joel *psychology educator*
Darley, John McConnon *psychologist*
Ekstrom, Ruth Burt *psychologist*
Emmerich, Walter *psychologist*
Girgus, Joan Stern *psychologist, university administrator*
Glucksberg, Sam *psychology educator*
Greenberg, Herbert M(arvin) *psychologist, corporate executive*
Gross, Charles Gordon *psychology educator, neuroscientist*
Hawver, Dennis Arthur *psychological consultant*
Hoebel, Bartley Gore *psychology educator*
Manning, Winton Howard *psychologist, educational administrator*
†Meade, Dale Michael *laboratory director*
Miller, George Armitage *psychologist, educator*
Nadler, Georgia Jane *nursing administrator*
Willingham, Warren Willcox *psychologist, testing service executive*

Raritan
†Goldstein, Jack *health science executive, microbiologist*

Red Bank
Trofino, Joan Alhanati *health care facility administrator*

Ridgewood
Azzara, Michael William *hospital administration executive*
Clements, Lynne Fleming *family therapist, programmer*

Roseland
Malafronte, Donald *health executive*

Secaucus
Newton, V. Miller *medical psychotherapist, neuropsychologist, writer*

Somerset
DeVaris, Jeannette Mary *psychologist*
Nemeth, Patricia A. *school nurse*

South Plainfield
Borah, Kripanath *pharmacist*

Sparta
Buist, Jean Mackerley *veterinarian*

Summit
†Earle, Jean Buist *hospital administrator*
Sniffen, Michael Joseph *hospital administrator*

Teaneck
Fairfield, Betty Elaine Smith *psychologist*
Gordon, Jonathan David *psychologist*
Herman, Kenneth *psychologist*

Toms River
Pilla, Mark Domenick *hospital administrator*

Trenton
Schirber, Annamarie Riddering *speech and language pathologist, educator*

Union
Kaplan, Doris Weiler *social worker*

Ventnor City
Panico, Elaine Hartman *nurse*

Vineland
Hunt, Howard F(rancis) *psychologist, educator*

Voorhees
Hutchinson, Susan Elaine *hospital administrator*

Warren
Cohen, Bertram David *psychologist, educator*

Wayne
Wendowski, Kathleen Cecelia *hospital administrator*

West New York
Kelly, Lucie Stirm Young *nursing educator*

Whitehouse Station
Gilmartin, Raymond V. *health care products company executive*

NEW MEXICO

Albuquerque
Anderson, Darrell Edward *psychologist, educator*
Cofer, Charles Norval *psychologist, educator*
Johnson, William Hugh, Jr. *hospital administrator*
Levin, Thomas Augustus *health care corporation executive*
Mauderly, Joe Lloyd *pulmonologist*
Solomon, Arthur Charles *pharmacist*

Clovis
Rehorn, Lois Marie Smith *nursing administrator*

Corrales
Adams, James Frederick *psychologist, educational administrator*

Gallup
Crouch, Altha Marie *health educator, consultant*

Las Cruces
Ketchum, Rhonda J. *hospital administrator*
Roscoe, Stanley Nelson *psychologist, aeronautical engineer*

Las Tablas
Laos, Jeffery Baffert *health services specialist*

Los Alamos
Bame, Samuel Jarvis, Jr. *research scientist*
Thompson, Lois Jean Heidke Ore *industrial psychologist*

Los Lunas
Mateju, Joseph Frank *hospital administrator*

Santa Fe
Abeyta, Santiago Audoro (Jim Abeyta) *human services administrator*
Candelaria, Judith (Watt) *nursing administrator*
Noble, Merrill Emmett *retired psychology educator, psychologist*
Nuckolls, Leonard Arnold *retired hospital administrator*
Phipps, Claude Raymond *research scientist*

Univ Of New Mexico
Sarto, Gloria Elizabeth *obstetrician/gynecologist, educator*

Wagon Mound
Abeyta, Jose Reynato *retired pharmacist, state legislator, cattle rancher*

NEW YORK

Albany
Biggs, Donald Anthony *psychologist, educator*
Csiza, Charles Karoly *veterinarian, microbiologist*
DeNuzzo, Rinaldo Vincent *pharmacy educator*
Furlong, Patrick Louis *health science association administrator*
Giblin, Mary Ellen *mental health professional*
Ley, Ronald *psychologist, educator*
Margolis, Natalie *nursing administrator, educator*
McCarthy, Mary Lynn *social work educator*
Reid, William James *social work educator*
Tedeschi, James Theodore, Jr. *psychologist educator*
Teevan, Richard Collier *psychology educator*

Alfred
Keith, Timothy Zook *psychology educator*
Rand, Joella Mae *nursing educator*

Amherst
Cramer, Stanley Howard *psychology educator, author*
Rossberg, Robert Howard *psychology educator, former university dean*

Apalachin
Linder, Fannie Ruth *psychotherapist, concert soprano*

Ardsley
Mohl, Allan S. *social worker*
Ricklin, Arthur H. *hospital administrator*

Astoria
Fox, R. Steven *psychotherapist, theologian*

Binghamton
Babb, Harold *psychology educator*
Brehm, Sharon Stephens *psychology educator, university administrator*
Feldsine, Frances Teresa *nursing administrator*
Isaacson, Robert Lee *psychology educator, researcher*
Levis, Donald James *psychologist, educator*

Bronx
Gootzeit, Jack Michael *rehabilitation institute executive*
Heath, Cedric Alexander *nurse, health services administrator*
Martinez-Tabone, Raquel *school psychologist supervisor*
Ottenberg, James Simon *hospital executive*
Tregde, Lorraine C. *hospital administrator*

Bronxville
Dvorak, Roger Gran *health facility executive*
Franklin, Margery Bodansky *psychology educator, researcher*
Graham, Nancy O. *nurse, administrator*

Brooklyn
Adams, George Harold *hospital and health executive*
Adasko, Mary *speech pathologist*
Agard, Emma Estornel *psychotherapist*
Allen, Percy, II *hospital administrator*
Alley, Frederick Don *hospital executive*
†Broas, Donald Sanford *hospital executive*
Costantino, Giuseppe *psychologist, researcher, administrator, educator*
Eschen, Albert Herman *optometrist*
Ford, Vandelette *mental health educator*
Gross, Stephen Mark *pharmacist, academic dean*
†Gustin, Mark Douglas *hospital administrator*
Heidtmann, Susan Ann *nursing administrator*
Jones, Blanche *nursing administrator, orthopaedic and gerontology consultant*
Kippel, Gary M. *psychologist*
Klainberg, Marilyn Blau *community health educator*
†Light, Harold L. *health care facility executive*
Maddalena, Frank Joseph *health care executive*
Marcus, Harold *physician, health facility administrator*
Marsala-Cervasio, Kathleen Ann *medical/surgical nurse*
Mundy, Mark James *hospital administrator*
Murillo-Rohde, Ildaura Maria *marriage and family therapist, consultant, educator, dean*
†Nelson, Karl Emil *hospital administrator, healthcare consultant*
Phillips, Gretchen *clinical social worker*
†Primm, Beny Jene *addiction treatment foundation administrator*
†Puccio, John *hospital administrator*
Reinisch, June Machover *psychologist, educator*
Spivack, Frieda Kugler *psychologist, administrator, educator, academician*

Buffalo
Allen, Barbara Jo *health facility administrator*
Behling, Charles Frederick *psychology educator*
Blane, Howard Thomas *research institute administrator*
Friedlander, John Eastburn *health facility administrator*
Fung, Ho-Leung *pharmacy educator, researcher, consultant*
Hull, Elaine Mangelsdorf *psychology educator*
Katz, Jack *audiology educator*
Kelley, Sister Helen *hospital executive*
Levy, Kenneth Jay *psychology educator, academic administrator*
Pruitt, Dean Garner *psychologist, educator*
Schentag, Jerome John *pharmacy educator*
Sharma, Sushil Chandra *hospital administrator*
Solo, Alan Jere *medicinal chemistry educator, consultant*

Carmel
†Gosline, Peter Lawrence *hospital administrator*
Huckabee, Carol Brooks *psychologist*

Central Islip
Finnin, Mary Josephine *nurse, consultant*

Chappaqua
Boal, Lyndall Elizabeth *social worker*

Cohoes
Kennedy, Kathleen Ann *nursing administrator*

Cooperstown
Hermann, William Henry *retired hospital administrator, consultant*

Dobbs Ferry
Perelle, Ira B. *psychologist, educator*

Douglaston
Helfat, Lucile *social services professional*

East Meadow
Albert, Gerald *clinical psychologist*

Elmira
Farley, H. Fred *nursing educator*

Elmsford
Bostin, Marvin Jay *hospital and health services consultant*

Farmingdale
Lamberg, Stanley Lawrence *medical technologist, educator*

Feura Bush
Byrne, Donn Erwin *psychologist, educator*

Floral Park
Weinrib, Sidney *retired optometric and optical products and services executive*

Flushing
Dubocq, Carole Ann *nursing administrator*
Kaplan, Stephen *parapsychologist*

Garden City
Harr, Alma Elizabeth Tagliabue *nursing educator*
Nicklin, George Leslie, Jr. *psychoanalyst, educator, physician*
Vigilante, Joseph Louis *social worker, social policy educator*

Glen Head
Cohen, Lawrence N. *health care management consultant*

Glen Oaks
Ryan, Therese Eileen *nursing administrator*

Goshen
Hall, Wanda Jean *mental health professional, consultant*

Great Neck
Harris, Rosalie *psychotherapist, clinical counselor, Spanish language professional and multi-linguist, English as second language educator*

Greenvale
Araoz, Daniel Leon *psychologist, educator*

Guilderland
Gordon, Leonard Victor *psychologist, educator emeritus*

Hamilton
Dovidio, John Francis *psychology educator*

Hastings On Hudson
Clark, Kenneth Bancroft *psychologist, educator*

Hempstead
Block, Jules Richard *psychologist, educator, university official*

Hicksville
Calabrese, Alphonse Francis Xavier *psychotherapist*

Holbrook
Lissman, Barry Alan *veterinarian*

Howard Beach
Berliner, Patricia Mary *psychologist*

Ithaca
Bronfenbrenner, Urie *psychologist*
Darlington, Richard Benjamin *psychology educator*
Dobson, Alan *veterinary physiology educator*
Fox, Francis Henry *veterinarian*
Gilbert, Robert Owen *veterinary educator, researcher*
Gillespie, James Howard *veterinary microbiologist, educator*
Glock, Marvin David *retired psychology educator*
†Haas, Jere Douglas *nutritional sciences educator, researcher*
Habicht, Jean-Pierre *public health researcher, educator, consultant*
†Howell, Bonnie Howard *hospital administrator*
Isen, Alice M. *experimental social psychologist, behavioral science educator*
Kallfelz, Francis A. *veterinary medicine educator*
Lambert, William Wilson *psychology educator*
Lust, Barbara C. *psychology and linguistics educator*
Maas, James Beryl *psychology educator, lecturer, filmmaker*
Mueller, Betty Jeanne *social work educator*
Poppensiek, George Charles *veterinary scientist, educator*
Schlafer, Donald Hughes *veterinary pathologist*
Scott, Fredric Winthrop *veterinarian*
Williams, David Vandergrift *organizational psychologist*
Zall, Robert Rouben *food scientist, educator*

Jamaica
Conway, Alvin James *hospital administrator*
Etzel, Joseph Vincent *pharmacy educator*
Geffner, Donna Sue *speech pathologist, audiologist*
Kay, Mary Ellen *nurse*

Lake Placid
†Caguiat, Carlos Jose *health care administrator, episcopal priest*

Little Falls
Barlow, Phyllis L. *nurse manager, coordinator*
Feeney, Mary Katherine O'Shea *retired public health nurse*

Mahopac
Richards, Edgar Lester *psychologist, educator*

Malverne
Ryan, Suzanne Irene *nursing educator*

Manhasset
Croce, Anne Lally *nurse, commissioner*
Gallagher, John S. T. (Jack Gallagher) *hospital administrator*

Melville
Krueger, Gerald Peter *psychologist*

Mineola
Delaney, Martin Joseph *hospital administrator*
Hankin, Errol Patrick *hospital administrator*
Yeh, James Kuen-Jann *nutritionist*

Monsey
Schore, Robert *social worker, educator*

Mount Kisco
Schwarz, Wolfgang *psychologist*

Mount Vernon
Camerano, Franklin *medical center administrator*

Nanuet
Vamvaketis, Carole *nursing educator*

New Hyde Park
Fink, Martin Neil *hospital administrator*
Pappas, Christine Ann *nursing administrator*

New Rochelle
Golub, Sharon Bramson *psychologist, educator*
†Mamangakis, John Paul *health facility administrator*

New York
Akabas, Sheila Helene *social work educator*
Allison, David Bradley *psychologist*
Antrobus, John Simmons *psychologist, educator*
Baker, Elmer Elias, Jr. *speech pathology and communication educator*
Bardach, Joan Lucile *clinical psychologist*
Barron, Susan *clinical psychologist*
Bernard, Viola Wertheim *psychiatrist*
Bessey, Edward Cushing *health care company executive*
Binkert, Alvin John *hospital administrator*
†Bischoff, Theresa *medical center administrator*
Brier, Pamela Sara *health facility administrator*
Buck, Louise Zierdt *psychologist*
Bundy, Mary Lothrop *social worker*
Caroff, Phyllis M. *social work educator*
Carr, Arthur Charles *psychologist, educator*
Chamson, Sandra Potkorony *psychologist*
Channing, Alan Harold *hospital administrator*
Clamar, Aphrodite J. *psychologist*
Cloward, Richard Andrew *social work educator*
Connolly, John Joseph *health care company executive*
Cooke, Mary A. *hospice director*
Core, Mary Carolyn W. Parsons *radiologic technologist*
Costa, Max *health facility administrator, pharmacology educator, environmental medicine educator*
Coté, Anne Alexis *hospital nursing administrator*
Cox, Darlene Louise *health care executive, nurse*
Cutler, Rhoda *psychologist*
Davis, Samuel *hospital administrator, educator, consultant*
deMause, Lloyd *psychohistorian*
Dimen, Muriel Vera *psychoanalyst*
Dobrof, Rose Wiesman *geriatric services professional*
†Dorn, Sue Bricker *hospital and medical school administrator*
Ellis, Albert *clinical psychologist, educator, author*
Feinberg, Mortimer Robert *psychologist, educator*
Feldman, Ronald Arthur *social work educator, researcher*
Feldmann, Shirley Clark *psychology educator*
Ferrari, Alberto Mario *health care company executive*
Fewell, Christine Huff *psychoanalyst, alchohol counselor*
Filer, Elizabeth Ann *psychotherapist*
Fiorillo, John A(nthony) *health care executive*
Freudenberger, Herbert Justin *psychoanalyst*
Galanter, Eugene *psychologist, educator*
Gambuti, Gary *hospital administrator*
George, Gladys *hospital administrator*
Gitterman, Alex *social work educator*
Goldman, George David *psychologist, psychoanalyst*
Goldman, Leo *psychologist, educator*
Grant, James Deneale *health care company executive*
Haber, Pierre Claude *psychologist*
Hammer, Emanuel Frederick *clinical psychologist, psychoanalyst*
Haywood, H(erbert) Carl(ton) *psychologist, educator*
Heber, Ruth R. *psychologist, consultant*
Heyde, Martha Bennett (Mrs. Ernest R. Heyde) *psychologist*
Hochberg, Irving *audiologist, educator*
Hochberg, Julian *psychologist*
Hoffman, Martin Leon *psychology educator*
Hollander, Edwin Paul *psychologist, educator*
Israel, Margie Olanoff *psychotherapist*
Jacoby, Jacob *consumer psychology educator*
Jonas, Ruth Haber *psychologist*
Kamerman, Sheila Brody *educator, social worker*
Koppenaal, Richard John *psychology educator*
Kramer, Marc B. *forensic audiologist*
Krauss, Herbert Harris *psychologist*
Lantay, George Charles (Wagner) *psychologist, psychotherapist, consultant*
Lee, Robert Sanford *psychologist*
Levinson, Rascha *psychotherapist*
Markle, Cheri Virginia Cummins *nurse*
Mattson, Marlin Roy Albin *health facility administrator, psychiatry educator*
Mc Fadden, G. Bruce *hospital administrator*
Meyer-Bahlburg, Heino F. L. *psychologist*
Mintz, Donald Edward *psychologist, educator*
Morris, Thomas Quinlan *hospital administrator, physician*
Nauert, Roger Charles *health care executive*
Nidetch, Jean *health service executive*
Papalia, Diane Ellen *human development educator*
Piemonte, Robert Victor *association executive*
Pilcz, Maleta *psychotherapist*
Pulitzer, Roslyn K. *social worker, psychotherapist*
Ringler, Lenore *educational psychologist*
Riss, Eric *psychologist*
Rosenbluth, Lucille Maxine *health research facility administrator*
Sackeim, Harold *psychologist, educator*
Saxe, Leonard *social psychologist, educator*
Schachter, Stanley *psychology educator*
Scott, Mimi Koblenz *actress, psychotherapist*
Simon, Norma Plavnick *psychologist*
Singer-Magdoff, Laura Joan Silver (Mrs. Samuel Magdoff) *psychotherapist*
Solender, Sanford *social worker*
†Speck, William T. *health facility administrator*
Sperry, Sandra Phillips *nursing administrator*
Stone, Bonnie Carol *healthcare executive*
Straus, Donald Blun *retired company executive*
Sweeney, Sister Margaret Mary *hospital administrator, nun*
Tallmer, Margot Sallop *psychologist, psychoanalyst, gerontologist*
Terenzio, Joseph Vincent *hospital administrator*
Terrace, Herbert S(ydney) *psychologist, educator*
Turo, Joann K. *psychoanalyst, psychotherapist, consultant*
Vitz, Paul Clayton *psychologist, educator*
Watson, Anthony L. *health facility executive*
Weiner, Max *educational psychology educator*
Weiss, Lewis Stephen *pharmaceutical executive*
Weissman, Gail Kuhn *nursing administrator*
Wessler, Sheenah Hankin *psychotherapist, consultant*
Westheimer, Ruth Siegel (Karola Ruth Siegel Westheimer) *psychologist, television personality*
†Wexler, Nancy Sabin *clinical neuropsychology educator*
Witkin, Georgia Hope *clinical psychologist*
Witkin, Mildred Hope Fisher *psychotherapist, educator*
Wood, Paul F. *national health agency executive*
Yankelovich, Daniel *social researcher, public opinion analyst*
Zawistowski, Stephen Louis *psychologist, educator*
Zucker-Franklin, Dorothea *medical scientist, educator*

Newtonville
Apostle, Christos Nicholas *social psychologist*

Niagara Falls
†Finan, Timothy James *health facility administrator*

Niagara University
Osberg, Timothy M. *psychologist, educator, researcher, clinician*

Oceanside
Mooney, Yvette Migdalia *health facility administrator*

Oneonta
Bergstein, Harry Benjamin *psychology educator*
Grappone, William Eugene *clinical social worker, consultant*
Hammond-Moss, Patti *nursing administrator*
Holleran, Paula Rizzo *psychology and counseling educator, researcher, consultant*

Ossining
Beard, Janet Marie *health care administrator*

Oswego
Gooding, Charles Thomas *psychology educator, college dean*
Gordon, Norman Botnick *psychology educator*

Peru
Crandall, Betty C. *nephrology/transplant nurse*

Pittsford
Weissberger, Ruth Marion *health education company executive, psychologist*

Plattsburgh
Smith, Noel Wilson *psychology educator*

Pleasantville
Black, Percy *psychology educator*
Robak, Rostyslaw Wsewolod *psychologist, educator*

Poughkeepsie
Carino, Aurora Lao *psychiatrist, hospital administrator*
Davis, Susan Lee *nurse administrator*
Gardenier, Edna Frances *nursing educator*
Henley, Richard James *healthcare institution administrator and financial officer*

Purchase
Berman, Richard Angel *health and educational administrator*

Queens Village
Corcoran, Gretchen Elizabeth *nursing administrator*

Rhinebeck
Ethan, Carol Baehr *psychotherapist*

Riverhead
†Turner, Joseph Francis, Jr. *hospital executive*

Rochester
Deci, Edward Lewis *psychologist, educator*
DuBrin, Andrew John *behavioral sciences, management educator, author*
Gayle-Jones, Jewelle *human services educator, school system administrator*
Geertsma, Robert Henry *psychologist, educator*
†Goldstein, Stephen Barry *hospital administrator*
Insel, Richard *medical facility administrator/ pediatrics educator*
Johnson, Jean Elaine *nursing educator*
Koret, Sydney *psychologist, educator*
Laties, Victor Gregory *psychology educator*
Liebert, Arthur Edgar *hospital administrator*
Moore, Duncan Thomas *optics educator*
Pearse, Robert Francis *psychologist, educator*
Thomas, Garth Johnson *psychology educator emeritus*
Von Holden, Martin Harvey *psychologist*
Walker, Michael Charles, Sr. *retirement services executive*
Wey, Jong-Shinn *research laboratory manager*
Wheeler, Ladd *psychology educator*
Zax, Melvin *psychologist, educator*

Rockville Centre
Kivowitz, Sheila *clinical social worker*

Roslyn
Scollard, Patrick John *hospital executive*
†Silvestro, John Pat *hospital administrator*

Rye
Newburger, Howard Martin *psychoanalyst*

Scarsdale
Glickenhaus, Sarah Brody *speech therapist*
Liston, Mary Frances *retired nursing educator*

Schenectady
Duncan, Stanley Forbes *health care executive*
Huntley, Charles William *psychology educator*
Terry, Richard Allan *consulting psychologist, former college president*

Scottsville
Dwyer, Ann Elizabeth *equine veterinarian*

Smithtown
Wheatley, George Milholland *medical administrator*

Southold
Callis, Jerry Jackson *veterinarian*
Mebus, Charles Albert *veterinarian*

Staten Island
Didomenico, Beatrice Grillo *social worker*
Goetz, Carol Stier *mental health nurse, educator*
Johnson, Frank Corliss *psychologist*
†Kastanis, John Nicholas *hospital administrator*

Stony Brook
Bouey, Ora James *nursing educator*
Katkin, Edward Samuel *psychology educator*

Suffern
Monahan, Frances Donovan *nursing educator*

Syracuse
Black, Lois Mae *clinical psychologist, educator*
Butler, Katharine Gorrell *speech-language pathologist, educator*
Fitzgerald, Harold Kenneth *social work educator, consultant*
Geisler, Linda Whitehead *hospital administrator, nurse*
Miron, Murray Samuel *psychologist, educator*
Spaulding, Suzanne Marie *nursing educator*

Tarrytown
†Safian, Keith Franklin *hospital administrator*

Troy
Baron, Robert Alan *psychology and business educator, author*
O'Neil, Mary Agnes *health science facility administrator*

Uniondale
Ray, Norretta *clinical social worker, administrator, psychotherapist, educator, consultant*
†Walter, Orris G., Jr. *health facilities administrator*

Valley Stream
Natow, Annette Baum *nutritionist, author, consultant*

West Bloomfield
Charron, Helene Kay Shetler *nursing educator*

West Hempstead
Rothberg, June Simmonds *nursing educator emerita, psychotherapist, psychoanalyst*

Williamsville
Paladino, Joseph Anthony *clinical pharmacist*

Woodbury
Agresti, Miriam Monell *psychologist*

Yonkers
Drisko, Elliot Hillman *marriage and family therapist*
Foy, James E. *hospital administrator*

NORTH CAROLINA

Asheville
Weil, Thomas P. *health services consultant*

Burlington
Mason, James Michael *biomedical laboratories executive*
Powell, James Bobbitt *biomedical laboratories executive, pathologist*

Calabash
Strunk, Orlo Christopher, Jr. *psychology educator*

Cashiers
O'Connell, Edward James, Jr. *psychology educator, computer applications and data analysis consultant*

Chapel Hill
Baroff, George Stanley *psychologist, educator*
Carroll, John Bissell *psychologist, educator*
Cobb, Henry Van Zandt *psychologist*
Dahlstrom, William Grant *psychologist, educator*
Fox, Ronald Ernest *psychologist*
Gray-Little, Bernadette *psychologist*
†Halverson, Paul Kenneth *hospital executive*
Hochbaum, Godfrey Martin *retired behavioral scientist*
Jones, Lyle Vincent *psychology educator*
Lowman, Robert Paul *psychology educator, academic administrator*
Mc Curdy, Harold Grier *psychologist*
Munson, Eric Bruce *hospital administrator*
Norwood, George Joseph *pharmacy educator*
Palmer, Gary Stephen *health services administrator*
Schopler, John Henry *psychologist, educator*
Schunk, Dale Hansen *psychology educator*
Tolley, Aubrey Granville *hospital administrator*
Upshaw, Harry Stephan *psychology educator*

Charlotte
†Abercrombie, Ralph McCall *hospital administrator*
Betzold, Paul Frederick, Jr. *hospital administrator*
Brazeal, Donna Smith *psychologist*
Carper, Barbara A. *nursing educator*
†Ellison, Paul Stribling *healthcare executive*
†Elmore, Thomas Stephen *hospital alliance executive*
Goolkasian, Paula A. *psychologist, educator*
Martin, James Grubbs *medical research executive, former governor*
Nurkin, Harry Abraham *hospital administrator*
Witherspoon, Jere Warthen *foundation executive*

Concord
O'Morrow, Dianne Marie *nursing administrator*

Davidson
Palmer, Edward L. *social psychology educator, television researcher, writer*

Durham
Davis, Lucy Tolbert *psychologist, educator*
Dunteman, George Henry *organizational psychologist*
Gratz, Pauline *former nursing science educator*
†Johnson, Gerald Arlen *health facility executive*
Lifton, Walter M. *psychology and education consultant*
Lockhead, Gregory Roger *psychology educator*
Page, Ellis Batten *behavioral scientist, educator*
Schiffman, Susan Stolte *medical psychologist, educator*
Staddon, John Eric Rayner *psychology, zoology, neurobiology educator*
Surwit, Richard Samuel *psychology educator*
Wilson, Ruby Leila *nurse, educator*

Elizabeth City
Griffin, Gladys Bogues *critical care nurse, educator*

Elon College
Knesel, Ernest Arthur, Jr. *clinical laboratory executive*

Fayetteville
†Jansen, Michael John *medical center administrator*

Forest City
Toney, Shirley Putman *nursing administrator, educator*

Gastonia
Jones, Terry Ray *administrator*

Greensboro
†Barry, Dennis Robert *hospital administrator*
Eason, Robert Gaston *psychology educator*
Gill, Diane Louise *psychology educator, university official*
Goldman, Bert Arthur *psychologist, educator*
Schwenn, Lee William *retired medical center executive*
Smith, Rebecca McCulloch *human relations educator*

Greenville
McRae, David Carroll *hospital administrator*

Henderson
Jenkins, Clara Barnes *psychology educator*

Hickory
Gingrich-Petersen, Carolyn Ashcraft *psychologist*
†Loehr, Arthur William, Jr. *healthcare executive, nurse*

Raleigh
Aronson, Arthur Lawrence *veterinary pharmacology and toxicology educator*
Bass, Mary Catherine *clinical social worker, psychotherapist*
Champ, Raymond Lester *hospital administrator*
Drew, Nancy McLaurin Shannon *counselor, consultant*
Newman, Slater Edmund *psychologist, educator*
Willis, John Randolph *hospital administrator*

Research Triangle Park
Olden, Kenneth *science administrator, researcher*

Salisbury
†Logan, David Bruce *health care administrator*

Shelby
†Hudson, Mark Alan *health care executive*

Warsaw
Ferrell, Rhonda Barefoot *nursing educator*

Wilmington
Dixon, N(orman) Rex *speech and hearing scientist, educator*
Morrison, William Fowler, Jr. *health care consultant*

Wilson
Batchelor, Ruby Stephens *retired nurse*

Winston Salem
Dodd, Virginia Marilyn *veterinarian*
Moskowitz, Jay *public health sciences educator*
Preslar, Len Broughton, Jr. *hospital administrator*
Walters, Doris Lavonne *pastoral counselor*
Wiles, Paul Martin *hospital administration executive*
Williams, John Edwin *psychology educator*

NORTH DAKOTA

Bismarck
†Brosseau, Terrance Gene *medical center administrator*

Fargo
Nickel, Janet Marlene Milton *geriatrics nurse*
Orr, Steven R. *health facility administrator*

Grand Forks
Carroll, Jack Adien *hospital administrator*
Nielsen, Forrest Harold *research nutritionist*

Jamestown
†Hall, Richard William *hospital administrator*

OHIO

Akron
Considine, William Howard *health care administrator*
Gilbert, Albert Francis *hospital administrator*
Wessman, Joan Feeney *nurse administrator*
†West, Michael Alan *hospital administrator*

Athens
Klare, George Roger *psychology educator*

Bay Village
Hiller, Deborah Lewis *long term care and retirement facility executive*

Bellaire
Hahn, David Bennett *hospital administrator, marketing professional*

Bowling Green
Hakel, Milton Daniel, Jr. *psychology educator, consultant, publisher*
Scott, John Paul *psychologist, educator, author*

Brecksville
Ludenia, Krista *psychologist, health facility administrator*

Canfield
Itts, Elizabeth Ann Dunham *psychotherapist, consultant, designer*

Centerville
Fulk, Paul Frederick *chiropractor*

Chillicothe
Page, Troy Edward *health care administrator*

Cincinnati
Bieliauskas, Vytautas Joseph *clinical psychologist, educator*
Bluestein, Venus Weller *retired psychology educator*
Bradley, Sister Myra James *health science facility executive*
Carney, Robert Alfred *health care administrator*
Cohen, Hirsh Joel *health care administrator*
Collins, Larry Wayne *health facility administrator*
Cook, Jack McPherson *hospital administrator*
†Copeland, William Mack *hospital administrator, lawyer*
Curtin, Leah Louise *editor, author, nurse, ethician, consultant*
Dember, William Norton *psychologist, educator*
Dickey, John Miller *health care facility executive*
†Gilligan, Michael James *health care administrator*
Graham, Scharleen Walker *counselor*
Haag, Walter M(onroe), Jr. *research institute executive, industrial engineer*
Hoskins, Geraldine *hospital nursing administrator*
Jackobs, Miriam Ann *dietitian*
Koebel, Sister Celestia *health care system executive*
Lichtin, (Judah) Leon *pharmacist*
McGuire, Elaine C. *nursing administrator*
Morgan, John Bruce *hospital care consultant*
Reeb, Patricia A. *nursing educator, administrator*
Sabin, Joan Mary *nursing executive, nurse*
Schubert, William Kuenneth *hospital medical center executive*
White, Terry R. *hospital administrator*
†Wilburn, L. Thomas, Jr. *health facility administrator*

Cleveland
Bamberg, Barbara B. *nursing administrator*
Bate, Brian R. *psychologist*
Blum, Arthur *social work educator*
Boyle, Kammer *management psychologist*
Cline, Cathie B. *hospital administrator*
Dadley, Arlene Jeanne *sleep therapist*
†Douglas, Janice Green *physician, educator*
Fairman, Susanne Bank *hospital administrator*
Gerber, Carl Joseph *hospital administrator, psychiatrist*
Giesser, Nancy Lynne *nurse, academic administrator*
Hokenstad, Merl Clifford, Jr. *social work educator*
†Huston, Samuel Richard *health facility executive*
Kolb, David Allen *psychology educator*
Manning, Henry Eugene *hospital administrator*
Naparstek, Arthur J. *social work educator*
Neuhauser, Duncan von Briesen *health services educator*
Phipps, Wilma J. *nursing educator, author*
Pilous, Betty Scheibel *medical/surgical nurse*
Schlotfeldt, Rozella May *nursing educator*
Schorr, Alvin Louis *social worker, educator*
Schurmeier, L. Jon *health care executive*
Shakno, Robert Julian *hospital administrator*
Walters, Farah M. *hospital administrator*

Columbus
Anderson, Carole Ann *nursing educator*
Banasik, Robert Casmer *nursing home administrator, educator*
Cacioppo, John Terrance *psychology educator*
Capen, Charles Chabert *veterinary pathology educator, researcher*
Chapman, Erie, III *hospital administrator*
Covault, Lloyd R., Jr. *hospital administrator, psychiatrist*
Cuddihy, June Tuck *pediatric nurse*
Fraley, Ralph Reed *hospital administrator*
Leland, Henry *psychology educator*
Lince, John Alan *pharmacist*
†Margello, Margaret Ann *healthcare executive*
Meyer, Donald Ray *psychologist, brain researcher*
Meyer, Patricia Morgan *neuropsychologist, educator*
Naylor, James Charles *psychologist, educator*
Neff, Joya Lee *community health nurse, administrator*
Osipow, Samuel Herman *psychology educator*
Petty, Richard Edward *psychologist, educator, researcher*
Rudmann, Sally Vander Linden *medical technology educator*
St. Arnold, Dale S. *hospital administrator*
Schlichting, Nancy Margaret *hospital administrator*
Schuller, David Edward *cancer center administrator, otolaryngology*
Schwebel, Andrew I. *psychology educator*
Silverman, Jerald *veterinarian, academic administrator*
Sims, Richard Lee *hospital administrator*

Cortland
†Evans, Ronald Leon *healthcare administrator*

Dayton
†Boff, Kenneth Richard *engineering research psychologist*
Christensen, Julien Martin *psychologist, educator*
†Murphy, Martin Joseph, Jr. *cancer research center executive*
Thorsland, Edgar, Jr. *health facility administrator*
†Willett, Robert Lee *health care administrator*
Willits, Eileen Marie *medical/surgical nurse, health facility administrator*

Dublin
Haemmerle, John Martin *nursing home and retirement housing executive*
†Kane, John C. *health care products company executive*

Duncan Falls
Cooper, April Helen *nurse*

Fairborn
Leffler, Carole Elizabeth *mental health nurse, women's health nurse*

Fairfield
Goodman, Myrna Marcia *school nurse*

Gallipolis
Brunner, Nancy Lee Andrew *medical center nursing administrator*

Niehm, Bernard Frank *mental health center administrator*

Hamilton
Johnson, Pauline Benge *nurse, anesthetist*
Rorer, Leonard George *psychology educator*

Lancaster
†Varney, Richard Alan *medical office manager*

Lorain
†Walcott, Robert *healthcare executive, priest*

Marietta
†Greene, William Maynard *hospital executive*

Mason
Clements, Michael Craig *health services consulting executive, retired renal dialysis technician*

Massillon
†Fogle, Marilyn Louise Kiplinger *hospital administrator*
Glosser, James William *veterinarian*

Middleburg Heights
Hartman, Lenore Anne *physical therapist*

Middletown
Gilmore, June Ellen *psychologist*
Redding, Barbara J. *nursing administrator, occupational health nurse*

Mount Saint Joseph
Roach, Sister Jeanne, S.C. *hospital administrator*

Northfield
Gupta, Kishan Chand *psychologist*

Oberlin
Friedman, William John *psychology educator*
Layman, Emma McCloy (Mrs. James W. Layman) *psychologist, educator*

Piqua
Watercutter, Jacqueline A. *health facility administrator*

Sandusky
Fleming, Arlene E. *health facility administrator*
Round, Alice Faye Bruce *school psychologist*

Springfield
Maki, Jerrold Alan *medical center administrator*

Sylvania
†O'Connell, John William *health care facility administrator*
Verhesen, Anna Maria Hubertina *counselor*

Toledo
Depew, Charles Gardner *research company executive*
†Kneen, James Russell *health care administrator*
Rissing, Daniel Joseph *hospital administrator*

University Heights
Bloch, Andrea Lynn *physical therapist*

Valley View
Van Kirk, Robert John *nursing case manager, educator*

Warren
Johns, Charles Alexander *hospital administrator*

Waterville
Copeland, Terrilyn Denise *speech pathologist*

Westerville
Conley, Sarah Ann *health facility administrator*

Wooster
Loess, Henry Bernard *psychology educator*

Worthington
Bernhagen, Lillian Flickinger *school health consultant*

Yellow Springs
Lacey, John Irving *psychologist, physiologist, educator*

Youngstown
†Allen, AndrewWuichet *hospital administrator*

Zanesville
†Barone, Thomas Anthony *hospital administration executive*
Durant, Charles Edward, Jr. *medical facility administrator*

OKLAHOMA

Elk City
Francis, Talton Loe *hospital administrator*

Lawton
Clayton, Lawrence Otto *marriage and family therapist*
Cooke, Wanda (Cookie Cooke) *hearing aid specialist*
Hooper, Roy B. *hospital administrator, insurance broker*

Mangum
Ford, Linda Lou *dietitian*

Norman
Dille, John Robert *physician*
Donahue, Hayden Hackney *mental health institute administrator, medical educator, psychiatric consultant*
Donahue, Patricia Toothaker *retired social worker, administrator*
Weber, Jerome Charles *education and human relations educator, former academic dean and provost*

Oklahoma City
Bresler, Mark Irwin *rehabilitation engineer*
Callahan, Carol B. *nursing administrator*
Clark, Kathryn Louise Hughes *hospital administrator*
Forni, Patricia Rose *nursing educator, university dean*
Henley, Everett Scott *health care marketing firm executive*
Hiner, Gladys Webber *psychologist*
†Hunter, Steven L. *medical center administrator*
†Lopez, Francisco, IV *health care administrator*
Lynn, Thomas Neil, Jr. *medical center administrator, physician*
Macer, Dan Johnstone *retired hospital administrator*
Nokes, Mary Triplett *educator, counselor, artist*
Pishkin, Vladimir *psychologist, educator*
†Scott, Jimmie Dow *health facility administrator*
Seideman, Ruth Evelyn Young *nurse educator*
Sookne, Herman Solomon (Hank Sookne) *retirement center senior executive*
Spencer, Melvin Joe *hospital administrator, lawyer*
Walker, Clarence Eugene *psychology educator*

Pawhuska
Strahm, Samuel Edward *veterinarian*

Stillwater
Confer, Anthony Wayne *veterinary pathologist, educator*
Ewing, Sidney Alton *veterinary medical educator, parasitologist*
Quinn, Art Jay *veterinarian*

Tulsa
Alexander, John Robert *hospital administrator, internist*
Goldthorpe, John Clifford *hospital administrator*
†Hardman, James Reed *hospital administrator*
Janssen, Erwin T. *health science foundation administrator, psychiatrist*
Payne, Christine Babcock *career psychologist*

Wewoka
Buendia, Imelda Bernardo *clinical director, physician*

Yukon
†Lenhart, Lowell Cordell *hospital administrator, consultant*

OREGON

Corvallis
Gillis, John Simon *psychologist, educator*
Koller, Loren D. *veterinary medicine educator*

Eugene
Acker, Martin Herbert *psychotherapist, educator*
Dawes, Carol J. *clinical psychologist*
Eisert, Debra Claire *pediatric psychologist*
Freyd, Jennifer Joy *psychology educator*
Littman, Richard Anton *psychologist, educator*

Florence
Corless, Dorothy Alice *nurse educator*

Portland
Artaud-Wild, Sabine Marie *retired research dietitian*
Brim, Armand Eugene *health care executive*
Commerford, Kathleen Anne *psychologist*
Goldfarb, Timothy Moore *hospital administrator*
Greenlick, Merwyn Ronald *health services researcher*
†Lee, John Patrick *hospital administrator*
Magedanz, Dorothy C. *health facility administrator, educator*
Matarazzo, Joseph Dominic *psychologist*
Matarazzo, Ruth Gadbois *psychology educator*
Meighan, Stuart Spence *hospital consultant, internist, writer*
Olson, Roger Norman *health service administrator*
†Pfeifer, Larry Alan *public health service coordinator*
Rooks, Judith Pence *family planning, maternal health care, midwifery consultant*
Squier, Leslie Hamilton *psychology educator*
Wiens, Arthur Nicholai *psychology educator*

Salem
Elliott, Lee Ann *psychologist*
Warnath, Maxine Ammer *organizational psychologist, educator*

Springfield
Walton, Ralph Ervin *community mental health services adminstrator*

White City
Moore, Charles August, Jr. *psychologist*

PENNSYLVANIA

Abington
Drudy, Patrick *psychologist, human relations consultant*
Pilla, Felix Mario *hospital administrator*
Scholfield, Linda Katherine *nursing administrator*

Allentown
Graham, Kenneth Robert *psychologist, educator*

Altoona
Meadors, Allen Coats *health administrator, educator*

Aston
Aldrich, Ronald Robert *health system administrator*

Bala Cynwyd
Marinakos, Plato Anthony *medical center administrator*

Beaver Falls
Matchett, Janet Reedy *psychologist*

Berwyn
Brunner, Lillian Sholtis *nurse, author*

Bethel Park
DeMay, Helen Louise *nursing services administrator*

Bethlehem
Brozek, Josef *psychology educator, scientist*
Campbell, Donald Thomas *psychologist, educator*

Birdsboro
Moyer, David Lee *veterinarian*

Bloomsburg
Roh, Myung Ja *social worker*

Blue Bell
Abramson, Leonard *healthcare organization executive*

Bryn Mawr
Hoffman, Howard Stanley *experimental psychologist, educator*
Hoopes, Janet Louise *educator, psychologist*
McCauley, Clark Richard *psychology educator*

Camp Hill
Crider, Rudyard Lee *psychotherapist*
Nowak, Jacquelyn Louise *administrative officer, realtor, consultant*

Carlisle Barracks
†Anderson, Lynn John *veterinarian, army officer*

Cheltenham
†McGoldrick, Margaret Mary *hospital administrator*

Clarks Summit
Firmin, Michael Wayne *counseling educator*

Collegeville
Cawthorn, Robert Elston *retired health care executive*
Stoughton, W. Vickery *healthcare executive*

Cranberry Township
Birch, Jack Willard *psychologist, educator*

Danville
Ackerman, F. Kenneth, Jr. *health facility administrator*

Darby
†Kulesher, Robert Roy *health care administrator*

Doylestown
Cathcart, Harold Robert *hospital administrator*
Davis, Carole Joan *psychologist*

Edinboro
Paul, Charlotte P. *nursing educator*

Erie
Nash, Mary Alice *nursing educator*

Gettysburg
Schein, Virginia Ellen *psychologist, educator*

Greenville
Wilt, Sonya Anne Mugnani *speech and language pathologist*

Harrisburg
Dorsey-Peterson, Jeanine *public health administrator*
Tyson, Gail L. *health federation administrator*

Haverford
Heath, Douglas Hamilton *psychology educator*

Hershey
Anderson, Allan Crosby *hospital executive*
Lang, Carol Max *veterinarian, educator*
Lindenberg, Steven Phillip *counselor, consultant*

Horsham
Logue, John Joseph *psychologist*
Neff, P. Sherrill *health care executive*

Indiana
Nelson, Linda Shearer *child development and family relations educator*

Jenkintown
Colman, Wendy *psychoanalyst*
Hankin, Elaine Krieger *psychologist, researcher*

Johnstown
†Karnes, Timothy Joseph *hospital administrator, consultant*

Kennett Square
Allam, Mark Whittier *veterinarian, former university administrator*
Barr, David Charles *healthcare executive*
Beck, Dorothy Fahs *social researcher*

King Of Prussia
Cash, Francis Winford *health care executive*
Foster, John Hallett *health facility executive*
Miller, Alan B. *hospital management executive*

Lancaster
Gingerich, Naomi R. *emergency room nurse*

Landenberg
Aldrich, Nancy Armstrong *psychotherapist, clinical social worker*

Lansdale
Lovelace, Robert Frank *health science facility administrator, researcher*

Latrobe
†Zanotti, Marie Louise *hospital admininstrator*

Leola
Wedel, Paul George *retired hospital administrator*

Lewisburg
Candland, Douglas Keith *psychology educator*

Lincoln University
Gaymon, William Edward *psychology educator*

Malvern
Gillespie, Mary Krempa *psychologist, consultant*
Michaelis, Arthur Frederick *health care company executive*

Media
Lewandowski, Theodore Charles *psychology educator*
Salo, Harry A. *health care executive*

Millersville
Judge, Margaret Ann *nurse, nursing administrator*

New Castle
Byers, Joan P. *nursing educator*

Newtown
Peroni, Peter A., II *psychologist, educator*

Newtown Square
Maxner, Joyce Karen *family therapist, author*

North East
Ayrault, Evelyn West *psychologist, writer*

Paoli
†White, Leland I. *hospital administrator*

Penn Valley
Hires, William Leland *psychologist, consultant*

Philadelphia
Abrams, Jules Clinton *psychologist*
Aiken, Linda Harman *nurse, sociologist, educator*
Bellack, Alan Scott *clinical psychologist*
†Blum, Michael D. *social worker*
Cherry, John Paul *health science association director, researcher*
Coltoff, Beth Jamie *psychologist, small business owner*
†Cramp, Donald Arthur *hospital executive*
Daly, Charles Arthur *health services administrator*
Dean-Zubritsky, Cynthia Marian *psychologist, reseacher*
Detweiler, David Kenneth *veterinary physiologist, educator*
Doty, Richard Leroy *medical researcher*
Eldredge, Clifford Murray *hospital administrator*
Epstein, William Eric *health facility administrator*
Fagin, Claire Mintzer *nursing educator, administrator*
Ferraro, Ronald Louis *health facility administrator*
Gable, Fred Burnard *pharmacist, author*
†Garvin, Vail Pryor *hospital administrator*
Gibson, JoAnn Marie *psychotherapist, consultant*
Goldsmith, Martin H. *health care executive*
Harvey, Colin Edwin *veterinary medicine educator*
Harvey, John Adriance *psychology and pharmacology educator, researcher, consultant*
Hurvich, Leo Maurice *experimental psychologist, educator, vision researcher*
Hussar, Daniel Alexander *pharmacy educator*
Kaye, Janet Miriam *psychologist*
Larson, Ingegerd Elin *immunology/arthritis nurse*
Lewis, Thomas John, III *hospital administrator*
LoSciuto, Leonard Anthony *psychologist, educator*
Martin, Suzanne Gabrielle *health facility administrator*
†Nachmias, Jacob *psychologist educator*
Pittinger, Wilbur Barke *medical center executive*
Premack, David *psychologist*
Rescorla, Robert Arthur *psychology educator*
†Rosenberg, Leroy Joseph *hospital executive, former military officer*
Rosenberg, Robert Allen *psychologist, educator, optometrist*
Rozin, Paul *psychology educator*
Seligman, Martin E. P. *psychologist*
Sherman, Susan Elizabeth *nursing administrator*
Solomon, Phyllis Linda *social work educator, researcher*
Sovie, Margaret Doe *nursing administrator, college dean*
Wadden, Thomas Antony *psychologist, educator*
Weber, Janet M. *nurse*
Welhan, Beverly Jean Lutz *nursing educator, administrator*
Whybrow, Peter Charles *psychiatrist, educator*
†Williams, Sankey Vaughan *health services researcher, internist*

Pittsburgh
Abdelhak, Sherif Samy *health science executive*
Anderson, John Robert *psychology and computer science educator*
Berman, Malcolm Frank *health facility administrator*
Cagney, William Robert *psychologist*
Catell, Grace Louise *nursing educator*
Connolly, Ruth Carol *critical care nurse*
Dawes, Robyn Mason *psychology educator*
Doerfler, Leo G. *audiology educator*
Fischhoff, Baruch *psychologist, educator*
Friede, Samuel A(rnold) *health care executive*
†Glaser, Robert *psychology educator*
Goldstein, Gerald *research psychologist*
Keairns, Yvonne Ewing *psychologist*
Longest, Beaufort Brown *health services administration educator, research director*
†Lundquist, Dana R. *health facility administrator*
Masoner, Paul Henry *counseling educator*
McCall, Dorothy Kay *social worker, psychotherapist*
McClelland, James L. *psychology educator, cognitive scientist*
Moore, Pearl B. *nurse*
Paul, John *health care executive*
Perloff, Robert *psychologist, educator*
Resnick, Lauren B. *psychology educator*
Romoff, Jeffrey Alan *university officer, health care executive*
Safar, Peter *emergency health care facility administrator,*
Sanzo, Anthony Michael *health care executive*
Voss, James Frederick *psychologist, educator*

Wallman, George *hospital and food services administrator*
Weber, Alexis Kurpiewski *nursing school executive*
Zanardelli, John Joseph *healthcare services executive*

Polk
Hall, Richard Clayton *psychologist, consultant, researcher, retired*

Pottsville
Blossey, Maureen B. *mental health administrator*
†Tuley, Sister Margaret *hospital administrator*

Radnor
†Nojunas, Thomas Michael *hospital executive*
Russell, Daniel Francis *hospital administrator*

Reading
Bell, Frances Louise *medical technologist*
Sauer, Elissa Swisher *nursing educator*
Sullivan, Charles Bernard *hospital administrator*

Scranton
†Costello, Michael Mark *hospital administrator*
Maislin, Isidore *hospital administrator*
Narsavage, Georgia Roberts *nursing educator, researcher*
†Olden, Peter Carter *healthcare administration educator*
Saleski, Verna Mae *nursing educator*
Turock, Jane Parsick *nutritionist*
†West, Daniel Jones, Jr. *hospital administrator, rehabilitator counselor*

State College
Farr, Jo-Ann Hunter *psychologist*
Morrow, David Austin, III *veterinary medical educator*
†Rose, Lance Haden *hospital administrator*

Swarthmore
Marecek, Jeanne Ann *psychologist, educator*

Tyrone
†Stoner, Philip James *hospital administrator*

University Park
Cavanagh, Peter Robert *health educator, researcher, academic facility executive*
Crowder, Eleanor Louise M. *nursing educator*
Ford, Donald Herbert *psychologist, educator*
Guerney, Bernard Guilbert, Jr. *clinical psychologist, educator*
Guthrie, Helen A. *nutrition educator, consultant*
Mayers, Stanley Penrose, Jr. *public health educator*
Ray, William Jackson *psychologist*
Schaie, K(laus) Warner *human development and psychology educator*
Stern, Robert Morris *psychology educator, researcher*

Valley Forge
McNamara, John F. *health services company executive*

Verona
Matthews, Jack *psychologist, speech pathologist, educator*

Villanova
Bush, David Frederic *psychologist, educator*
Haynor, Patricia Manzi *nurse, hospital administrator*

Washington
Greenlee, Gaylord W. *health facility administrator*

Wayne
Bricklin, Patricia Ellen *psychologist, educator*
Russell, Kent *hospital administrator*

West Chester
Hajcak, Frank *psychologist, cartoonist, writer, photographer, consultant*
†Pepper, H. L. Perry *hospital administrator*

West Point
Chen, I-Wu *pharmaceutical researcher*

Wilkes Barre
Kolanowski, Ann Marie *nursing educator, geriatrics nurse*
Popp, Penelope Jean *health facility administrator*

Wyncote
Bersh, Philip Joseph *psychologist, educator*

York
Bartels, Bruce Michael *health care executive*
Chronister, Virginia Ann *school nurse, educator*
Hamilton, Shirley Ann *nursing administrator*
Keiser, Paul Harold *hospital administrator*
Rosen, Raymond *health facility executive*

RHODE ISLAND

Barrington
Paolino, Ronald Mario *clinical psychologist, consultant, psychopharmacologist, pharmacist*

Cranston
Gill, Carole O'Brien *family therapist*

Johnston
D'Ambra, Diane M. *nursing educator*

Kingston
Biller, Henry Burt *psychologist, educator*
Gaulin, Lynn *social work educator*

Newport
Graziano, Catherine Elizabeth *nursing educator*

Providence
Anderson, James Alfred *psychology educator*
Blough, Donald S. *psychology educator*
†Boekelheide, Kim *pathologist*
Church, Russell Miller *psychology educator*
Damon, William Van Buren *developmental psychologist, educator*
Holden, Raymond Henry *clinical psychologist*
Jones, Ferdinand Taylor, Jr. *psychologist, educator*
†Komiske, Bruce King *hospital administrator*
Metrey, George David *social work educator, academic administrator*
Schottland, Edward Morrow *hospital adminstrator*
Shepp, Bryan Eugene *psychologist, educator*
†Simpson, Dale Arthur *healthcare executive*
Siqueland, Einar *psychology educator*
Vavala, Domenic Anthony *medical scientist, educator, retired air force officer*

South Kingstown
Berman, Allan *psychologist, educator*

SOUTH CAROLINA

Charleston
Austin, Charles John *health services educator*
Barclay, James Ralph *psychologist, educator*
Bowman, Daniel Oliver *psychologist*
Purcell, Nancy Lou *alcohol/drug abuse services executive*
Smith, W. Stuart *hospital administrator*

Columbia
Amidon, Roger Lyman *health administration educator*
Brown, Arnold *health science facility administrator*
†Childs, Ronald Patnode *healthcare administrator*
Cooper, William Allen, Jr. *audiologist*
Davis, Keith Eugene *psychologist, educator, consultant*
†Freeman, Kester St. Clair, Jr. *hospital administrator*
Ginsberg, Leon Herman *social work educator*
Johnson, Kathie Anne *nurse, administrator*
Melton, Gary Bentley *psychology and law educator*
Seigler, Ruth Queen *college nursing administrator, consultant, nurse*

Dillon
Webb, Ronald Wayne *hospital administrator*

Greenville
Burkhardt, J. Bland, Jr. *hospital administrator*
Shilling, Mary Emily *nursing administrator*

Greenwood
Carter, Ann Keeling *nursing administrator*

Hopkins
Clarkson, Jocelyn Adrene *medical technologist*

Mauldin
Harris, Daniel Frederick *biomechanical analyst*

Mount Pleasant
Cooley, Kathleen Shannon *speech-language pathologist*

Myrtle Beach
Dail, Hilda Lee *psychotherapist*

Spartanburg
†Henson, David Leslie *hospital administrator*

SOUTH DAKOTA

Aberdeen
Hahnemann, Barbara K. *family nurse practitioner*

Chamberlain
Gregg, Robert Lee *pharmacist*

Huron
Kuhler, Deborah Gail *grief counselor, former state legislator*

Pierre
Russell, James Donald Murray *hospital administrator*

Rapid City
Corwin, Bert Clark *optometrist*
Galbraith, Jeanne Ann *nurse, administrator*
†Hersrud, James Robert *pharmacist*
†Reiter, Richard Ronald *healthcare executive*

Sioux Falls
†Breckenridge, James Joel *health facility administrator*
Brendtro, Larry Kay *psychologist, educator*
Gibbons, Cecilia *nurse, hospital administrator*
†Porter, John T. *health facility administrator*
Richards, LaClaire Lissetta Jones (Mrs. George A. Richards) *social worker*
†Rykhus, David Anthony *healthcare executive*

Yankton
Sokol, Dennis Allen *hospital administrator*

TENNESSEE

Antioch
†Midkiff, John L., Jr. *health care administrator, retired army officer*

Brentwood
Dalton, James Edgar, Jr. *health facility administrator*
Ragsdale, Richard Elliot *hospital management executive*

Chattanooga
Bird, Suzanne Carhart *nurse, administrator*
Jacobson, Katherine *nursing administrator*
Pelletier, Charlotte M. *nurse administrator*
Saeger, Dixie Forester *dietitian*

Cleveland
Millsaps, Shelby J. *nurse, college administrator*

Burlington
Albee, George Wilson *psychology educator*
Lawson, Robert Bernard *psychology educator*

Charlotte
Melby, Edward Carlos, Jr. *veterinarian*

Middlebury
Gibson, Eleanor Jack (Mrs. James J. Gibson) *psychology educator*

Morrisville
Roberts, Carolyn C. *hospital administrator*

VIRGINIA

Alexandria
Abbott, Preston Sargent *psychologist*
†Burden, Thomas William *health care executive, former naval officer*
DeCesare, Eileen Godoy *nurse executive, consultant, nurse enterpreneur*
Fisher, Donald Wayne *medical association executive*
Johnson, Edgar McCarthy *psychologist*
LLubien, Joseph Herman *psychotherapist, counselor*
†Palmquist, Lowell Eldon *health administrator*
Parsons, Henry McIlvaine *psychologist*

Annandale
Abdellah, Faye Glenn *retired public health service executive*

Arlington
Chipman, Susan Elizabeth *psychologist*
Held, Joe Roger *veterinarian, epidemiologist*
Rabun, John Brewton, Jr. *social services agency administrator*
Shamus, M. Annette *nursing administrator*

Beaumont
Jackson, Hermoine Prestine *psychologist*

Berryville
White, Eugene Vaden *pharmacist*

Blacksburg
Ash, Philip *psychologist*
†Purswell, Beverly Jean *veterinary medicine educator, theriogenologist*
Sgro, Joseph Anthony *psychologist, educator*

Burlington
Mead, Philip Bartlett *healthcare administrator, physician*

Charlottesville
Ainsworth, Mary Dinsmore Salter *psychologist, educator*
Deese, James Earle *psychologist, educator*
Gold, Paul Ernest *psychology educator, behavioral neuroscience educator*
Halseth, Michael James *medical center administrator*
Hamner, Charles Edward, Jr. *medical center executive, research management consultant*
Hetherington, Eileen Mavis *psychologist, educator*
McCarty, Richard Charles *psychology educator*
Menaker, Shirley Ann Lasch *psychology educator, academic administrator*
Mesinger, John Frederick *psychologist, special education educator*
†Myers, Charles *medical center director, researcher*
Nesselroade, John Richard *psychology educator*
Pate, Robert Hewitt, Jr. *counselor educator*
Reppucci, Nicholas Dickon *psychologist, educator*
Scarr, Sandra Wood *psychology educator, researcher*

Fairfax
Boneau, C. Alan *psychology educator, researcher*
†Brown, Steven Edward *hospital administrator*
Leidinger, William John *clinic administrator*
Priesman, Elinor Lee Soll *family dynamics administrator, mediator, educator*

Fairfax Station
Johansen, Eivind Herbert *special education services executive, former army officer*

Falls Church
†Adams, Nancy R. *nurse, military officer*
Braendel, Douglas Arthur *healthcare executive*
Devaney, Everett M. *health care executive*
Fink, Charles Augustin *behavioral systems scientist*

Hampden Sydney
Ortner, Donald Richard *psychology and sociology educator*

Hopewell
Connelly, Karen Whipp *nursing administrator*

Lexington
Elmes, David Gordon *psychologist, educator*
Jarrard, Leonard Everett *psychologist, educator*

Locust Grove
Featherston, Dale Marie *nursing administrator*

Lynchburg
Whitman, Nancy Irene *nursing educator*

Mc Lean
Dean, Lydia Margaret Carter (Mrs. Halsey Albert Dean) *nutrition coordinator, author, consultant*
Gavazzi, Aladino A. *retired medical center administrator*

Newport News
Coleman, James Eugene *national laboratory administrator*
Smith, Carol G. *health facility administrator*

Norfolk
Anderson, Darleen S. *nursing administrator*
†Bernd, David LeMoine *multi-hospital system executive*
Cooper, Deloris Louise *nursing administrator*
Glickman, Albert Seymour *psychologist, educator*
†Jolly, William Monroe *hospital administrator*
Kern, Howard Paul *hospital administrator*
Mitchell, Glenn R. *hospital administrator*
Wharton, Shirley Granger *hospital administrator, nurse*

Palmyra
Chapin, Suzanne Phillips *retired psychologist*

Radford
Lamb, Lester Lewis *hospital administrator*
Pribram, Karl Harry *psychology educator, researcher*

Richmond
Barker, Thomas Carl *health care executive*
Fischer, Carl Robert *health care facility administrator*
Freund, Emma Frances *medical technologist*
Gandy, Gerald Larmon *rehabilitation counseling educator*
†Gentry, Dwight Lonnie *health care administrator*
Hardage, Page Taylor *health care administrator*
Hardy, Richard Earl *rehabilitation counseling educator, clinical psychologist*
Henderson, Nancy Carr *dietitian, medical transcriber, writer, political organization worker*
Lambert, Benjamin Joseph, III *optometrist, state legislator*
Lewis, Judith A. *nursing educator, women's health nurse*
Seymour, Harlan Francis *healthcare industry executive*
Simpson, John Noel *hospital administrator*
Ulmer, Deborah Luxton *medical training administrator, nurse, consultant*
†White, Kenneth Ray *health administration educator, consultant*

Roanoke
Bell, Houston Lesher, Jr. *hospital administrator*
Ekdahl, Patricia Josephine *hospital administrator*
Merker, Frank Ferdinand *retired hospital administrator*
Robertson, Thomas L. *health facility administrator*

Salem
†Boone, Charles Wimmel *healthcare executive, air force officer, writer*
†Weiss, James William *healthcare executive*

Spotsylvania
Arnhoff, Franklyn Nathaniel *psychologist, sociologist, educator*

Springfield
†Gibson, Kenneth Dwight *health care consultant*
Singleton, John Knox *hospital administrator*

Staunton
Sweetman, Beverly Yarroll *physical therapist*

Vienna
Chamberlain, Diane *psychotherapist, author, clinical social worker*

Virginia Beach
Lawrence, Joyce Wagner *health facility administrator, educator*

Williamsburg
Friedman, Herbert *psychology educator*
Johnston, Robert Atkinson *educator, psychologist*
Lange, Carl James *psychology educator*
McKenna, Virgil Vincent *psychology educator, researcher*
Rosen, Ellen Freda *psychologist, educator*
Shaver, Kelly G. *psychology educator*

WASHINGTON

Bellevue
Akutagawa, Donald *psychologist, educator*

Bellingham
Diers, Carol Jean *psychology educator*

Cheney
Gerber, Sanford Edwin *audiologist*

Fairchild AFB
†Davies, Donald Thomas *hospital administrator, military officer*

Freeland
Freehill, Maurice F. *retired educational psychology educator*

Friday Harbor
MacGinitie, Walter Harold *psychologist*

Gig Harbor
Canter, Ralph Raymond *psychology educator, research director*

Kent
Soden, Ruth M. *geriatrics nurse, educator*

Lynnwood
Lind, Gregory Alan *nurse*

Olympia
Blake, Ann Beth *psychologist*
Reilly, Robert Joseph *counselor*

Pullman
Bustad, Leo Kenneth *veterinary educator, college administrator*
Gustafsson, Borje Karl *veterinarian, educator*
Henson, James Bond *veterinary pathologist*
McSweeney, Frances Kaye *psychology educator*
Warner, Dennis Allan *psychology educator*
Wilson, Robert Burton *veterinary and medical educator*
Young, Francis Allan *psychologist*

Puyallup
Veatch, John William *speech pathologist*

Redmond
Sasenick, Joseph Anthony *health care company executive*

Seattle
Barash, David Philip *psychology and zoology educator*
Barnard, Kathryn Elaine *nursing educator, researcher*
Boaz, Doniella Chaves *psychotherapist, consultant*
Brammer, Lawrence Martin *psychology educator*
Coffman, Sandra Jeanne *psychologist*
Day, Robert Winsor *research administrator*
de Tornyay, Rheba *nurse, university dean emeritus, educator*
Duncan, Elizabeth Charlotte *marriage and family therapist, educator*
Ellis, Janice Rider *nursing educator, consultant*
Evans, Ellis Dale *psychologist, educator*
Fiedler, Fred Edward *organizational psychology educator, consultant*
Green, G. Dorsey *psychologist, author*
Hellström, Ingegerd *business executive*
Hunt, Earl Busby *psychologist*
Martin, Joan Callaham *psychologist, educator*
Monsen, Elaine Ranker *nutritionist, educator, editor*
Moore, Mary Ann *health care administrator*
Muilenburg, Robert Henry *hospital administrator*
Perkin, Gordon Wesley *international health agency executive*
Perrin, Edward Burton *health services researcher, biostatistician, public health educator*
Peterson, Jane White *nursing educator, anthropologist*
Prins, David *speech pathologist, educator*
Sarason, Irwin G. *psychology educator*
Schaller, Joanne Frances *nursing consultant*
Smith, Moncrieff Hynson *psychology educator*
Teller, Davida Young *psychology, physiology and biophysics educator*
Thompson, Arlene Rita *nursing educator*
Van Hoosier, Gerald Leonard *veterinary science educator*
Yantis, Phillip Alexander *audiologist, educator*
Young, Jeffry John *psychologist, gerontologist, educator, statistician*

Spokane
Butler, Mary Latour *health facility administrator*
Evoy, John Joseph *psychology educator*
Hendershot, Carol Miller *physical therapist*
Leahy, Gerald Philip *hospital administrator*

Tacoma
Smith, Leo Gilbert *hospital administrator*
Watkins, Sally Marie *nursing administrator*
Wilson, Joan Emily *nursing education administrator*

WEST VIRGINIA

Charleston
Goodwin, Phillip Hugh *hospital administrator*
Moore, Ruth Johnston *medical center official*
Velianoff, George D. *nursing administrator*

Kingwood
DeBastiani, Larue Annette *health facility director*

Lewisburg
Seifer, Judith Huffman *sex therapist, educator*

Morgantown
Barba, Roberta Ashburn *social worker*
McAvoy, Rogers *educational psychology educator, consultant*
Reese, Hayne Waring *psychologist*
Westfall, Bernard G. *university hospital executive*

Wheeling
†Forkin, Sister Jean Louise (Sister) *healthcare administrator*
Ritz, Lorraine Isaacs *nursing administrator*

WISCONSIN

Antigo
Tousey, LouAnn Holly *nurse administrator*

Brookfield
Zander, Gaillienne Glashow *psychologist*

Eau Claire
Dick, Raymond Dale *psychology educator*
Schenk, Quentin Frederick *retired social work educator, mayor*

Ellison Bay
MacKinney, Arthur Clinton, Jr. *retired university official, psychologist*

Elm Grove
Headlee, Raymond *psychoanalyst, educator*

Fort Atkinson
Albaugh, John Charles *hospital executive*

Green Bay
McIntosh, Elaine Virginia *nutrition educator*
Mix, Judith Ann *nursing education administrator*

La Crosse
Anderson, Mary Ann *hospital nursing administrator*

Madison
Berkowitz, Leonard *psychology educator*
Chapman, Loren J. *psychology educator*
Coe, Christopher Lane *psychology researcher*
Derzon, Gordon M. *hospital administrator*
Easterday, Bernard Carlyle *veterinary medicine educator*
Epstein, William *experimental psychologist*
Gavin, Mary Jane *medical, surgical nurse*
Greenfield, Norman Samuel *psychologist, educator*
†Johnson, William Elmer, Jr. *hospital executive*
Littlefield, Vivian Moore *nursing educator, administrator*
Maloney, Michael James *research scientist*
Marlett, Judith Ann *nutritional sciences educatr, researcher*
Rice, Joy Katharine *psychologist, educational policy studies and women's studies educator*
Schulz, Rockwell Irwin *health administration educator*
Vandell, Deborah Lowe *educational psychology educator*
†Wilson, Michael Alan *health facility administrator*
Wirtz, Virginia Haynes *nursing educator*
Wright, George Nelson *counselor, educator*

Marshfield
David, Barbara Marie *medical, surgical nurse*
Jaye, David Robert, Jr. *retired hospital administrator*
Wrabl, Carol A. *nursing administrator*

Milwaukee
Ambrosius, Mark Ralph *hospital administrator*
Bartels, Jean Ellen *nursing educator*
Beglinger, Joan Ellis *nursing services vice president*
Blum, Lawrence Philip *educational psychology educator*
Brown, Edith *social worker*
†Bush, Sister Lois *health facilities administrator*
Conrad, Kelley Allen *industrial and organizational psychologist*
Gengler, Sister M. Jeanne *hospital administrator*
Harvieux, Anne Marie *psychotherapist*
Humber, Wilbur James *psychologist*
Jenkins, Louise Sherman *nursing researcher*
Jenkins, William Ivy *hospital administrator*
Kupst, Mary Jo *psychologist, researcher*
Smith, Guy W. *health care executive*
Snyder, Marian H. *nursing educator and administrator*
Vice, Jon Earl *hospital executive*
Warren, Richard M. *experimental psychologist, educator*
Weil, Herman *psychology educator*
Wells, Carolyn Cressy *social work educator*
Zober, Norman Alan *health facility administrator*

Racine
Harlan, Jean Durgin *psychologist, writer, consultant*

Waukesha
Manor, Andrea Joan *nursing administrator*
Parsons, Virginia Mae *psychology educator*

Whitewater
Culbertson, Frances Mitchell *psychology educator*

Woodruff
†Rosenberg, Douglas Owen *healthcare management executive*

WYOMING

Cheyenne
Hardway, James Edward *vocational specialist*
Hirst, Wilma Elizabeth *psychologist*
Laycock, Anita Simon *psychotherapist*

Laramie
†Nord, Thomas Allison *hospital administrator*

Teton Village
Ellwood, Paul Murdock, Jr. *health policy analyst, consultant*

Wilson
Breitenbach, Mary Louise McGraw *psychologist, drug rehabilitation counselor*

TERRITORIES OF THE UNITED STATES

GUAM

Agana
Duenas, Laurent Flores *nursing administrator*

PUERTO RICO

Hato Rey
Fernández Hernández, Nivia Aurora *nutrition and dietetics educator*

Mayaguez
†Artiles, Nemuel Othniel *hospital executive*

San Juan
Fariña de Woodbury, Margarita *psychotherapist*
Prevor, Ruth Claire *psychologist*

MILITARY ADDRESSES OF THE UNITED STATES

EUROPE

APO
†Bombard, Charles Frederick *nursing administrator, consultant*
†Terry, Wayne Gilbert *healthcare executive, hospital administrator*

PACIFIC

APO
Daly, Judith Marie *critical care nurse*

CANADA

ALBERTA

Bentley
Manes, John Dalton *retired hospital administrator, anaesthesiologist*

Calgary
Calkin, Joy Durfée *healthcare consultant, educator*
Meyers, Marlene O. *hospital administrator*

Edmonton
Fields, Anthony Lindsay Austin *health facility administrator, oncologist, educator*
Hislop, Mervyn Warren *health advocate administrator, psychologist*
Lechelt, Eugene Carl *psychology educator*
Schurman, Donald Peter *hospital administrator*

Lethbridge
Cho, Hyun Ju *veterinary research scientist*

BRITISH COLUMBIA

Burnaby
†Barth, Norman Kenneth *hospital administrator, educator*

New Westminster
Fair, James Stanley *hospital administrator*

North Vancouver
Smith, Robert John *health facility administrator*

Vancouver
Collins, Mary *health association executive, former Canadian legislator*
Craig, Kenneth Denton *psychologist, educator, researcher*
Cynader, Max Sigmund *psychology, physiology, brain research educator, researcher*
Gilbert, John Humphrey Victor *audiologist, speech scientist, educator*
Klonoff, Harry *psychologist*
Riedel, Bernard Edward *retired pharmaceutical sciences educator*
Splane, Richard Beverley *social work educator*
Suedfeld, Peter *psychologist, educator*
Tees, Richard Chisholm *psychology educator, researcher*

Victoria
Fyke, Kenneth John *hospital administrator*
Payne, Robert Walter *psychologist, educator*

MANITOBA

Winnipeg
Hogan, Terrence Patrick *psychologist, university administrator*
Schultz, Harry *health science organization administrator*
†Seifert, Blair Wayne *clinical pharmacist*
Thorfinnson, A. Rodney *hospital administrator*

NEW BRUNSWICK

Fredericton
Easterbrook, James Arthur *psychology educator*
McGeorge, Ronald Kenneth *hospital executive*

Sussex
†Secord, Lloyd Douglas *healthcare administrator*

NEWFOUNDLAND

Corner Brook
Watts, Harold Ross *hospital administrator*

ONTARIO

Brantford
Woodcock, Richard Beverley *health facility administrator*

Downsview
Endler, Norman Solomon *psychology educator*

Elgin
Lafave, Hugh Gordon John *medical association executive, psychiatrist, educator, consultant*

Guelph
†Benn, Denna M. *veterinarian*

Hamilton
Ryan, Ellen Bouchard *psychology educator, gerontologist*

Keswick
Macdonald, John Barfoot *research foundation executive*

Kingston
Berry, John Widdup *psychologist*
Glynn, Peter Alexander Richard *hospital administrator*
McGeer, James Peter *research executive, consultant*

Kitchener
†Noble, Ronald Nelson *hospital administrator*

London
Kimura, Doreen *psychology educator, researcher*
Paivio, Allan Urho *psychology educator*

Nepean
Beare-Rogers, Joyce Louise *former research executive*

North York
MacKenzie, Donald Murray *hospital administrator*
Tulving, Endel *psychologist, educator*

Ottawa
Clemenhagen, Carol Jane *health facility executive*
†Langill, George Francis *hospital administrator, educator*

Owen Sound
Jones, Phyllis Edith *nursing educator*

Ridgeway
Jacobs, Eleanor Alice *retired clinical psychologist, educator*

Toronto
Ellis, Peter Hudson *health science facility administrator*
Ferguson, Kingsley George *psychologist*
Freedman, Theodore Jarrell *healthcare executive*
Herbert, Stephen W. *hospital executive*
†Keddy, Wayne Richard *university hospital administrator*
MacLeod, William Brian *hospital executive*
Scholefield, Peter Gordon *health agency executive*
Turner, Gerald Phillip *hospital administrator*

Windsor
Auld, Frank *psychologist, educator*

QUEBEC

Fleurimont
Simoneau, Normand J. *hospital administrator*

Montreal
†Bailar, John Christian, III *public health educator, physician, statistician*
Chevrier, Jean Marc *psychologist, publisher, author*
Dudek, Stephanie Zuperko *psychology educator*
Gallagher, Tanya Marie *speech pathologist, educator*
Martin, Jean Claude *health management educator*
Melzack, Ronald *psychology educator*
Milner, Brenda Atkinson Langford *neuropsychologist*
Milner, Peter Marshall *psychology educator*
Scriver, Charles Robert *medical scientist, human geneticist*
Sirois, Gerard *pharmacy educator*
Stewart, Jane *psychology educator*
Vikis-Freibergs, Vaira *psychologist, educator*

Saint Pierre
Blanchet, Madeleine *research executive*

SASKATCHEWAN

Saskatoon
Belovanoff, Olga *retired health care facility administrator*
Randhawa, Bikkar Singh *psychologist, educator*

MEXICO

Mexico City
Baer, George Martin *veterinarian, researcher*

Morelos
Illich, Ivan *researcher, educator*

AUSTRALIA

Rockhampton
Zelmer, Amy Elliott *health science educator*

DENMARK

Helsingør
Sørensen, Erik *international advisor*

ICELAND

Reykjavik
Thorarensen, Oddur C.S. *pharmacist*

JAPAN

Gotsu
Hirayama, Chisato *healthcare facility administrator, physician, educator*

Hirakata
Nakanishi, Tsutomu *pharmaceutical science educator*

Kitakyushu
Okubo, Toshiteru *health science facility administrator, educator*

Shibuya
Torii, Shuko *psychology educator*

POLAND

Warsaw
†Rader, Paul MacFarland *healthcare administrator*

SWITZERLAND

Geneva
Holleran, Constance Ann *nursing association executive*

TURKEY

Istanbul
†Rountree, George Denton *health services managemtent consultant*

VENEZUELA

Caracas
Benaim-DeMan, Mireya *psychologist*

ADDRESS UNPUBLISHED

Abel, Harold *psychologist, educator, university president*
Adams, Rosemary *nursing educator*
Adams-Leander, Sheila Elizabeth *community health nurse*
Adkins, Claudia K. *nursing educator*
Alcantara, Felicisima Garcia *dietitian, nutrition consultant*
Altman, Irwin *psychology educator*
Anastasi, Anne (Mrs. John Porter Foley, Jr.) *psychology educator*
Anderson, Diane M. *administrator*
Anderson, Geraldine Louise *laboratory scientist*
Ayres, Jayne Lynn Ankrum *community health nurse*
Baier, Edward John *former public health official, industrial hygiene engineer, consultant*
Barker, Mary Katherine *retired nurse*
Barnhouse, Lillian May Palmer *retired medical, surgical nurse, researcher, civic worker*
Barrett, Barbara McConnell *lawyer, ranch owner, community leader*
Basham-Tooker, Janet Brooks *geropsychologist, educator*
Batalden, Paul Bennett *pediatrician, health care educator*
Becich, Raymond Brice *healthcare consultant, mediator, trainer, educator*
Belles, Anita Louise *health care safety executive*
Bender, James Frederick *psychologist, educator, university dean*
Berdanier, Carolyn Dawson *nutrition educator, researcher*
Berzon, Betty *psychotherapist*
Bethune, Golden H. *health facility administrator*
Biegel, David Eli *social worker, educator*
Bishop, (Ina) Sue Marquis *psychiatric and mental health nurse educator, researcher, administrator*
Blomgren, Bruce Holmes *motivational speaker*
†Bolla, Karen Irene *neuropsychologist, educator*
Border, Pamela Ann *nursing administrator, critical care nurse*
Borg, Ruth I. *mental health nurse, long-term medical nurse*
Bradley, Carol Ann *nursing administrator*
Braen, Bernard Benjamin *psychology educator*
Braswell, Judith F. *healthcare administrator*
Breslin, Evalynne L. W. *retired psychiatric nurse*
Brogden, Glenda Ethridge *nursing administrator*
†Brower, Forrest Allen *retired health facility administrator*
Brown, Linda Joan *psychotherapist, psychoanalyst*
Brown, Roberta *critical care nurse*
Bryant, Gail Annette Grippen *nurse, educator*
Bullough, Bonnie *nurse, educator*
Burns, Nancy Kay *drug abuse services professional*
Calamita, Kathryn Elizabeth *nursing administrator*
†Cameron, David Brian *health service administrator*
Camp, Patricia E. *nursing educator*
Cantrell, Linda Maxine *counselor*
Capuano, Terry Ann *nursing administrator*
Carlsen, Mary Baird *clinical psychologist*
Carlson, Janet Frances *psychologist, educator*
Carpenter, Kenneth John *nutrition educator*
Casey, John Thomas *health services agency executive*
Cason, Nica Virginia *nursing educator*
Chalfant, Richard Dewey *hypnotherapist, insurance consultant*
Challela, Mary Schaill *maternal/child health nurse*
Chase, Clinton Irvin *psychologist, educator, business executive*
Cheney, Lois Sweet *infection control nurse*
Chism, Linda Fay *nursing educator*
Chow, Rita Kathleen *nursing administrator*
Clanon, Thomas Lawrence *retired hospital administrator*
Cleary, Thomas J. *social worker, administrator*
Cleveland, Charlene S. *community health nurse*
†Cochran, John Robert, III *hospital administrator*
Condry, Robert Stewart *retired hospital administrator*
Cooper, Sarah Jean *nursing administrator*
Copes, Marcella A. *nursing administrator, educator*
Corbett, Carolyn Susanne *hospital administrator, nurse*
Cornell, David Roger *hospital administrator*
Couchman, Robert George James *human services consultant*
†Coughlin, Sister Kathleen *hospital administrator*
Coven, Berdeen *psychotherapist*
Cox, J. William *physician, health services administrator*
†Cox, John Curtis *healthcare and educational administrator*
Cozan, Lee *clinical research psychologist*
Crimm, Marcy Ware Jones *geritrics nurse, educator*
Cromwell, Florence Stevens *occupational therapist*
Culley, June Elizabeth *clinical reviewer, quality improvement specialist*
Curtis, Patricia *nursing administrator*
Dake, Marcia Allene *retired nursing educator, university dean*
Dauphinee, Joan Drukker *women's health educator*
Dawkins, Marva Phyllis *psychologist*
Demcoe, Lloyd Robert *social worker*
Dempsey, Barbara Matthea *medical/surgical and critical care nurse*
De Neal, Patricia Diana *nursing administrator*
Detweiler, Edna J. *health facility administrator*
Diener, Jennifer Flinton *health care services executive*
Dierk, Hulda Johnson *women's health nurse*
Dole, Arthur Alexander *psychology educator*
Dye, Myrtice Willis *therapist, educator, children's advocate, researcher, consultant*
Dyer, Wayne Walter *psychologist, author, radio and television personality*
Easterly, Joy Marie *health facility administrator*
Eddy, Esther Dewitz *retired pharmacist*
Edmonds, Velma McInnis *nursing educator*
Eisen, Henry *retired pharmacy educator*
Eitel, Dolores J. *healthcare consultant*
Ellerbe, Suellyn *health facility administrator*
Elliott, Lois Lawrence *audiology and otolaryngology educator*
Embry, Carmen Dianne Wheeler *psychologist*
Emerson, Ann Parker *dietitian, educator*
Ersoz, Clara Jean *healthcare consultant, physician*
Estés, Clarissa Pinkola *psychoanalyst, poet, writer*
Eugster, Albrecht Konrad *veterinarian, laboratory director*
Fairburn, Sandra Jean *nursing administrator*
Falbe, Maryann Christine *nursing administrator*
Farrington, Bertha Louise *nursing administrator*
Fehr, Lola Mae *nursing association director*
Ferrara, Diane S. *critical care nurse*
Feshbach, Norma Deitch *psychologist, educator*
Feurig, Thomas Leo *health care executive*
Finucane, Richard Daniel *corporate medical director, retired food products executive*
Fox, Michael Wilson *veterinarian, animal behaviorist*
Freeman, Arthur *veterinarian, retired association administrator*
French, Glendon Everett, Jr. *health care executive*
Garrett, Shirley Gene *nuclear medicine technologist*
Garrison, Susan Elodie *hospital administrator*
Garvey, Evelyn Jewel *mental health nurse*
Gay, William Ingalls *veterinarian, health science administrator*
Geitgey, Doris Arlene *retired nursing educator, dean*
Gerald, Michael Charles *pharmacy educator, college dean*
Gilbert, Gayle *nursing administrator*
Giles, Walter Edmund *alcohol and drug treatment executive*
Girouard, Shirley Ann *nurse, policy analyst*
Gladding, Carolyn Anne *nursing administrator*
Goldston, Stephen Eugene *community psychologist, educator, consultant*
†Golightly, Cecelia King *healthcare administrator, nurse*
†Gonzalez, William G. *hospital administrator, educator*
Goodwin, Barbara A. *retired nurse, military officer*
Govan, Gladys Vernita Mosley *retired critical care and medical/surgical nurse*
Grant, Richard Earl *nursing administrator*
Gray, Patricia Ellen *psychologist*
Green, Barbara Strawn *psychotherapist*
Green, Flora Hungerford *lactation consultant, nurse*
Griffin, Suzanne Marie *medical/surgical nurse*
Grolli, Frank Thomas *pharmacist*
Guthrie, Diana Fern *nursing educator*
Guthrie, Robert Val *psychologist*
Hall, Jay *social psychologist*
Hanley, Charles *psychology educator*
Hardy, Gyme Dufault *social worker*
Harshbarger, Dwight *psychologist, management consultant*
Hasselmeyer, Eileen Grace *medical research administrator*
†Healy, Sonya Ainslie *health facility administrator*
Heath, Richard Murray *retired hospital administrator*
Henry, Elizabeth Brown *medical center administrator*
Heris, Toni *psychologist, psychotherapist*
Hertz, Kenneth Theodore *health care executive*
Hicks, Sue Ann Bernard *nursing educator*
Hofferber, Beverly Elaine *nursing administrator*
Hofmann, Paul Bernard *health care consultant*
†Holly, John Durward, III *health care executive*
Homestead, Susan *psychotherapist*
Horowitz, Beverly Phyllis *occupational therapist*
Howe, John Prentice, III *health science center executive, physician*
Howe, Virginia Hoffman *nurse administrator*
Huckabee, Donna Marie *nurse*
Hunt, Ronald Duncan *veterinarian, educator, pathologist*
Isaacs, Kenneth S(idney) *psychoanalyst, educator*
Johnson, Pamela *community health nurse, administrator*
Johnson-Masters, Virginia E. (Mrs. William H. Masters) *psychologist*
Jones, Anita M. *medical/surgical nurse*
Juenemann, Sister Jean *hospital executive*
†Karson, Samuel *psychologist, educator*
Kellam, Norma Dawn *medical, surgical nurse*
Keller, George Henry *research administrator, consulting biochemist*
Kendrick, Budd Leroy *psychologist*
Kenny, Douglas Timothy *psychology educator, former university president*
Kidd, Rachel S. *nursing administrator*
Kieffer, Joyce Loretta *health science facility administrator, educator*
Kilpatrick, Georgia Lee *nurse educator*
King, Imogene M. *nurse, educator*
Kinney, Ardis *nursing administrator*
Koga, Colleen B. *critical care nurse, administrator*
Kolasa, Kathryn Marianne *food and nutrition educator, consultant*
Kotlarz, Shirley Ann *nursing service executive*
Ladly, Frederick Bernard *health services and financial services company executive*
Lamb, Katie A. *nursing educator*
Landstrom, Gay Laray *health facility administrator*
Langenfeld, Douglas Eugene *health care consultant, business advisor*
Langley, Beverly *critical care nurse*
Lash, Steven M. *hospital administrator*
Laudeman, Leslie *nursing administrator, oncological nurse*
†Laycock, Eric Paul *hospital administrator*
Lee, Eloise R. *nursing educator and administrator*
Leinart, Bonnie Katherine *nursing administrator*
Lewis, Charles Leonard *psychologist*
Lewis, Winifred P. *nursing administrator*
Lipsitt, Lewis Paeff *psychology educator*
Lipsky, Janice Gwynne *nursing administrator*
Litherland, Kay *hospital administrator*
Lousberg, Sister Mary Clarice *hospital executive*
Luce, Glenda L. *health facility administrator*
Lydford, Cynthia Winsloe *nurse administrator*
Macdonald, Donald Ian *health care administrator*
MacHovec, Frank J. *psychologist*
MacLennan, Beryce Winifred *psychologist*
Madory, James Richard *hospital administrator, former air force officer*
Maehr, Martin Louis *psychology educator*
Magill, Rosalind May *psychotherapist*
Magnuson, Robert Martin *retired hospital administrator*
Maguire, Maureen K. *health facility administrator*
Maguire, Patricia *healthcare administrator*
†Main, Robert Peebles *hospital administrator*
Majors, Nelda Faye *physical therapist*
Mapstone, Barbara J. *nursing administrator*

Marcinek, Margaret Ann nursing educator
Marcoux, Julia A. midwife
Marsh, Ernestine Pease nursing administrator, medical-surgical nurse
Massa, Salvatore Peter psychologist
Mastrangelo, Regina Mary nursing administrator, dean
†Matherlee, Thomas Ray health care consultant, management executive
McFarland, Gertrude Kay health scientist administrator
McKenna, Richard Henry hospital consultant
Meaders, Nobuko Yoshizawa therapist, psychoanalyst
Meehan, John Joseph, Jr. hospital administrator
Meyer, Harry Martin, Jr. retired health science facility administrator
Mich, Connie Rita mental health nurse, educator
Milewski, Barbara Anne pediatrics nurse, neonatal intensive care nurse
Miller, Lillie M. nursing educator
Miller, Mary Alice nursing educator
Mills, Celeste Louise hypnotherapist, professional magician
Mitchell, Carol Ann nursing educator
Mitchell, Nancy K. nurse
Moffatt, Hugh McCulloch, Jr. hospital administrator, physical therapist
Mooneyhan, Esther Louise retired nurse, educator
Moreira, Martha critical care nurse
Moreland, Alvin Franklin veterinarian
Morey, Sharon Lynn psychotherapist, mediator
Morris, Carol Ann nursing educator
Morrison, Linda L. women's health nurse, medical/surgical nurse
Moses, Beth Herman psychiatric-mental health nurse, nursing educator
Muller, Frederica Daniela psychology educator
Munro, Barbara Hazard nursing educator, researcher
Murphree, Tammy Marie hospital administrator
Nakagawa, Allen Donald radiologic technologist
Newell, William Talman, Jr. hospital administrator
Nichols, Elizabeth Grace nursing educator, administrator
Nitta, Diane E. nursing administrator
Noffsinger, Anne-Russell L. former nursing administrator, educator
Nosek, Laura J. health facility administrator
†Nussbaum, Stephen health care executive
O'Keefe, Karen health facility administrator
Olson, Marteen Leslie nurse
O'Neill, Donald Edmund health science executive
Pace, Charles Robert psychologist, educator
Palermo, David Stuart retired psychology educator and administrator
†Palmer, John M. medical administrator
Parham, Ellen Speiden nutrition educator
Parker, Harry John retired psychologist, educator
Penrod-Hill, Barbara M. nursing administrator
Pepper, Dorothy Mae nurse
Perry, J. Warren health sciences educator, administrator
Pettit, Ghery DeWitt retired veterinary medicine educator
Pilisuk, Marc community psychology educator
Porow, Marie-Carl mental health nurse
Poser, Ernest George psychologist, educator
Quick, Carolyn May nurse administrator
Rainey, Claude Gladwin retired health care executive
Rauner, Mary Ellen nursing administrator, critical care nurse
Rayball, Sharon A. medical/surgical nurse, administrator
Reed, Adam Victor psychologist, engineer
Reisch, Michael Stewart social work educator
Renkiewicz, Mary Antoinette hospital administrator
Rich, Mary D. women's health nurse
Rivera, Rosalind Theresa nurse, educator
Roberts, Joan I. social psychologist, educator
Robertson, R(ita) Kae nurse, administrator
†Robinson, Gail Patricia mental health counselor
Robinson, Nina nursing administrator
Roeder, Mary Alice health facility administrator
Ropp, Ann L. nurse consultant
Rose, Mason H., IV psychoanalyst
Royer, Richard Adrian hospital administrator
Rubin, Zick psychology educator, lawyer, writer
Ryan, Mary Headd nursing educator, administrator
Sameroff, Arnold Joshua developmental psychologist, educator, research scientist
Sauer, Jane Taylor nursing administrator, medical-surgical nurse
Sauvage, Lester Rosaire health facility administrator, cardiovascular surgeon
Saxon, Virginia M. nursing administrator
Scala, James health care industry consultant, author
Scanlon, Edward C. clinical psychologist
Scharf, Linda Margaret nursing administrator
Schiller, Alfred George veterinarian, educator
Schwartz, Doris Ruhbel nursing educator, consultant
†Schwartz, Michael Joel hospital executive
Scott, Amy Annette Holloway nursing educator
Secrest, Vickie Lynn nursing administrator
Shannon, Iris Reed nursing educator
Shannon, Margaret T. nursing administrator, educator
Shure, Myrna Beth psychologist, educator
Simms, Maria Ester health services administrator
Simms, Susan Faye nursing administrator
Sinclair, Doris Paula Gimmeson nurse, educational administrator
Skoglund, Elizabeth Ruth marriage, child and family counselor
Smith, Ann C. nursing educator
Smith, Ronald Lynn health system executive
Spear, Deborah surgical nurse, administrator
Splitstone, George Dale retired hospital administrator
Sprinthall, Norman Arthur psychology educator
†Stratton, Mariann retired naval nursing administrator
Strazis, Cynthia W. nurse, administrator
Swihart, Jean Ogden psychoanalyst
Talingdan, Arsenio Preza health science administrator
Tassia, Marie C. health facility administrator
Thackray, Richard Irving psychologist
Uhrich, Richard Beckley hospital executive, physician
Verplanck, William Samuel psychologist, educator
Vosburgh, Margaret Murphy nurse administrator
Wagoner, Lynda Jo pediatrics nurse
Waldrop, Linda M. medical administrator
Washburn, Melinda Wall nursing administrator
Weinhardt, Janice nursing educator
Wen, Helen Hwa Jung nurse
Werner-Jacobsen, Emmy Elisabeth developmental psychologist
Wertlieb, Donald Lawrence psychologist, educator
Wessler, Richard Lee psychology educator, psychotherapist
Whaley, Lynne Ann senior vice president nursing
White, Christine Lyons oncology nurse, nursing researcher
Wiebe, Leonard Irving radiopharmacist, educator
Wilke Montemayor, Joanne Marie patient care coordinator
Williams, Raymond Crawford veterinarian anatomy educator
Wilson, Nora D. nursing administrator
Wolfson, Lawrence Aaron hospital administrator
Woods, Geraldine Pittman health education consultant, educational consultant
Wyckoff, Margo Gail psychologist
Yanagitani, Elizabeth optometrist
Yee, Albert Hoy retired psychologist, educator
Yost, William Albert psychology educator, hearing researcher
Zisk, Sherry health facility administrator

HEALTHCARE: MEDICINE

UNITED STATES

ALABAMA

Anniston
Albritton, William Leonard physician, microbiologist

Birmingham
Allen, James Madison family practice physician, lawyer, consultant
†Avent, Charles Kirk medical educator
Bridgers, William Frank physician, educator
Bueschen, Anton Joslyn physician, educator
Caulfield, James Benjamin pathologist, educator
Cooper, Max Dale physician, medical educator, researcher
Curtis, John J. medical educator
Diethelm, Arnold Gillespie surgeon
†Fallon, Harold Joseph physician, pharmacology and biochemistry educator
Finley, Wayne House medical educator
Foft, John William physician, educator
Fraser, Robert Gordon diagnostic radiologist
Friedel, Robert Oliver physician
Friedlander, Michael J. neuroscientist, animal physiologist, medical educator
Geer, Jack Charles retired pathology educator
Herrera, Guillermo Antonio pathologist
Hill, Samuel Richardson, Jr. medical educator
Hirschowitz, Basil Isaac physician
Kirklin, John Webster surgeon
Kochakian, Charles Daniel endocrinologist, educator
Lloyd, Lewis Keith, Jr. surgery and urology educator
Meezan, Elias pharmacologist, educator
Mowry, Robert Wilbur pathologist, educator
Nuckols, Frank Joseph psychiatrist
Oakes, Walter Jerry pediatric neurosurgeon
Omura, George Adolf medical oncologist
Oparil, Suzanne cardiologist, educator, researcher
Pacifico, Albert Dominick cardiovascular surgeon
Pfister, Roswell Robert ophthalmologist
Pittman, James Allen, Jr. endocrinologist, dean emeritus, educator
Russell, Richard Olney, Jr. cardiologist, educator
Skalka, Harold Walter ophthalmologist, educator
Tieszen, Ralph Leland, Sr. internist
Vinik, H(ymie) Ronald anesthesiologist, physician
Warnock, David Gene nephrologist

Huntsville
Tietke, Wilhelm gastroenterologist

Mobile
Anderson, Lewis Daniel medical educator, orthopaedic surgeon
Brogdon, Byron Gilliam physician, radiology educator
Conrad, Marcel Edward hematologist, educator
DeBakey, Ernest George physician, surgeon
Eichold, Samuel medical educator, medical museum curator
Gardner, William Albert, Jr. pathologist, medical foundation executive
Littleton, Jesse Talbot, III radiology educator
Parmley, Loren Francis, Jr. medical educator
Pitcock, James Kent head and neck surgical oncologist
Smith, Jesse Graham, Jr. dermatologist, educator
White, Lowell E., Jr. medical educator

Montgomery
Givhan, Edgar Gilmore physician
Yow, John Stuart, Jr. retired internist

Opelika
Brown, Robert Glenn plastic surgeon

Tuscaloosa
Coggins, Wilmer Jesse physician, medical school administrator
Mozley, Paul David obstetrics and gynecology educator

ALASKA

Anchorage
†Archer, Gary William cardiologist
Mala, Theodore Anthony physician, consultant

Fairbanks
Doolittle, William Hotchkiss internist

Valdez
Todd, Kathleen Gail physician

ARIZONA

Green Valley
Wasmuth, Carl Erwin physician, lawyer

Mesa
Thompson, Ronald MacKinnon family physician, artist, writer

Peoria
Palmer, Alice Eugenia retired physician, educator

Phoenix
Bower, Willis Herman retired psychiatrist, former medical administrator
Calkins, Jerry Milan anesthesiologist, educator, administrator, biomedical engineer
Charlton, John Kipp pediatrician
Cozzi, Hugo Louis psychiatrist
Griffith, Ernest Ralph physician, educator
†Johnson, Peter Charles neuropathologist
Kurtz, Joan Helene pediatrician
Lawrence, William Doran physician
Lorenzen, Robert Frederick ophthalmologist
Reed, Wallace Allison physician
Rowley, Beverley Davies medical sociologist
Schiller, William Richard surgeon
Sellers, Joel Scott sports medicine physician
Zerella, Joseph T. pediatric surgeon

Scottsdale
Clement, Richard William plastic and reconstructive surgeon
DeHaven, Kenneth Le Moyne retired physician
Evans, Tommy Nicholas physician, educator
Friedman, Shelly Arnold cosmetic surgeon
Furman, Robert Howard physician, educator
Harrison, Harold Henry physician, scientist, educator
Kübler-Ross, Elisabeth physician
Osborn, Leslie Andrewartha psychiatrist
Pomeroy, Kent Lytle physical medicine and rehabilitation physician
Sanderson, David R. physician
Simon, Ernest Robert physician, business executive

Sedona
Hawkins, David Ramon psychiatrist, writer, researcher
Shors, Clayton Marion cardiologist

Sun City
Pallin, Irving M. anesthesiologist

Sun Lakes
Houser, Harold Byron epidemiologist

Tempe
Anand, Suresh Chandra physician
Noce, Robert Henry neuropsychiatrist, educator

Tucson
Abrams, Herbert Kerman physician, educator
Alpert, Joseph Stephen physician, educator
Beigel, Allan psychiatry educator
Boyse, Edward Arthur research physician
Brosin, Henry Walter psychiatrist, educator
Bryant, Charles Austin, IV pediatrician, medical facility director
Burrows, Benjamin physician, educator
Capp, Michael Paul physician, educator
Cisler, Theresa Ann osteopath
Cremer, Mabelle A. obstetrician, gynecologist
Dalen, James Eugene physician, educator
David, Ronald Sigmund psychiatrist
Drach, George Wisse urology educator
Ewy, Gordon Allen cardiologist, educator
Halonen, Marilyn Jean immunologist, pharmacologist, educator
Hildebrand, John G(rant) neurobiologist, educator
Houle, Joseph Adrien orthopaedic surgeon
Kaszniak, Alfred Wayne neuropsychologist
Klotz, Arthur Paul physician, educator
Lebowitz, Michael David epidemiologist
Levenson, Alan Ira psychiatrist, physician, educator
Marcus, Frank Isadore physician, educator
McCuskey, Robert Scott anatomy educator, researcher
Meislin, Harvey Warren emergency healthcare physician, professional society administrator
Nugent, Charles Arter physician
Reinmuth, Oscar MacNaughton physician, educator
Sibley, William Austin neurologist, educator
Smith, Josef Riley internist
†Stearns, Elliott Edmund, Jr. retired surgeon
†Woolfenden, James Manning nuclear medicine physician, educator
†Zukoski, Charles F. surgeon, educator

Vail
Reichlin, Seymour physician, educator

Yuma
Martin, James Franklin physician, lawyer

ARKANSAS

Clarksville
Pennington, Donald Harris physician

El Dorado
Tommey, Charles Eldon surgeon

Fort Smith
Crow, Neil Edward radiologist
Hoge, Marlin Boyd surgeon
Snider, James Rhodes radiologist

Jefferson
Hart, Ronald Wilson radiobiologist, toxicologist, government research executive

Little Rock
Campbell, Gilbert Sadler surgery educator, surgeon
Cave, Mac Donald anatomy educator
Diner, Wilma Canada radiologist, educator
Doherty, James Edward, III physician, educator
Doyle, Lee Lee research scientist, educator
Ferris, Ernest Joseph radiology educator
Garcia-Rill, Edgar Enrique neuroscientist
Goss, Kenneth George physician, educator
Guggenheim, Frederick Gibson psychiatry educator
Hough, Aubrey Johnston, Jr. pathologist, physician, educator
Jansen, G. Thomas dermatologist
Lucy, Dennis Durwood, Jr. neurologist
Maloney, Francis Patrick physiatrist
McMillan, Donald Edgar pharmacologist
Stead, William White physician, educator, public health administrator
Suen, James Yee otolaryngologist, educator
Ward, Harry Pfeffer physician, university chancellor

North Little Rock
Griffith, Jack William medical librarian

Roland
Ebert, Richard Vincent physician, educator

Scranton
Uzman, Betty Geren pathologist, retired educator

CALIFORNIA

Agoura Hills
deCiutiis, Alfred Charles Maria medical oncologist, television producer

Alameda
Whorton, M. Donald occupational and environmental health physician, epidemiologist

Alamo
Burchell, Mary Cecilia surgeon

Apple Valley
Win, Khin Swe anesthesiologist

Atascadero
Eggertsen, Paul Fred psychiatrist

Bakersfield
Badgley, Theodore McBride psychiatrist, neurologist
Corder, Michael Paul physician, educator
Izenstark, Joseph Louis radiologist, physician, educator

Balboa Island
Daughaday, William Hamilton retired physician

Bellflower
Gillman, Greta Joanne physician

Belvedere Tiburon
Behrman, Richard Elliot pediatrician, neonatologist, university dean

Berkeley
Abel, Carlos Alberto immunologist
Allison, James Patrick immunology educator, medical association administrator
Budinger, Thomas Francis radiologist, educator
†Caetano, Raul epidemiologist, educator
Castro, Joseph Ronald physician, oncology researcher, educator
Diamond, Marian Cleeves anatomy educator
Duhl, Leonard psychiatrist, educator
Falkner, Frank Tardrew physician, educator
Grossman, Elmer Roy pediatrician
Holmes, James Gordon retired vascular surgeon, medical educator
Hurst, Deborah pediatric hematologist
Koshland, Marian Elliott immunologist, educator
Kretchmer, Norman obstetrics, pediatrics and nutritional science educator
Policoff, Leonard David physician, educator
Roller, Robert Douglas, III psychiatrist
Seitz, Walter Stanley cardiovascular research consultant
Srebnik, Herbert Harry retired anatomy educator
Superko, H. Robert research physician
Syme, Sherman Leonard epidemiology educator
Tempelis, Constantine Harry immunologist, educator

Beverly Hills
Allen, Howard Norman cardiologist, educator
Bao, Katherine Sung pediatric cardiologist
Fein, William ophthalmologist
Gilberg, Arnold L. psychiatrist and psychoanalyst
Giorgi, Elsie Agnes physician
Karpman, Harold Lew cardiologist, educator, author
Klein, Arnold William dermatologist
Menkes, John Hans pediatric neurologist
Stein, Myron internist, educator
Towers, Bernard Leonard medical educator

Brawley
Jaquith, George Oakes ophthalmologist

Burlingame
Gradinger, Gilbert Paul plastic surgeon

Camarillo
Street, Dana Morris orthopedic surgeon

Campbell
Wu, William Lung-Shen (You-Ming Wu) aerospace medical engineering design specialist, foreign intelligence analyst

Capistrano Beach
Roemer, Edward Pier neurologist

Carmel
Felch, William Campbell internist, editor

Carmichael
Bromberg, Walter psychiatrist
Wagner, Carruth John physician

Chula Vista
Allen, Henry Wesley biomedical researcher
Cohen, Elaine Helena pediatrician, pediatric cardiologist

Coronado
Mock, David Clinton, Jr. internist

Corte Madera
Epstein, William Louis dermatologist, educator

Covina
Schneider, Calvin physician

Takei, Toshihisa otolaryngologist

Culver City
Rose, Margarete Erika pathologist

Dana Point
Bruggeman, Lewis LeRoy radiologist

Davis
Enders, Allen Coffin anatomy educator
Fowler, William Mayo, Jr. rehabilitation medicine physician
Gardner, Murray Briggs pathologist, educator
Halsted, Charles Hopkinson internist
Hendrickx, Andrew George anatomy educator
Jasper, Donald Edward clinical pathology educator
Lazarus, Gerald Sylvan physician
Lipscomb, Paul Rogers orthopaedic surgeon, educator
Overstreet, James Wilkins obstetrics and gynecology educator, administrator
Palmer, Philip Edward Stephen radiologist
Plopper, Charles George anatomist, cell biologist
Schenker, Marc Benet medical educator
Stowell, Robert Eugene pathologist, retired educator
Tupper, Charles John physician, educator
Williams, Hibbard Earl medical educator, physician
Youmans, Julian Ray neurosurgeon, educator

Downey
Gong, Henry, Jr. physician, researcher
Hackney, Jack Dean physician
Perry, Jacquelin orthopedic surgeon
Redeker, Allan Grant physician, medical educator
Sapico, Francisco Lejano internist, educator
Shapiro, Richard Stanley physician

Duarte
Comings, David Edward physician, medical genetics scientist
Kovach, John Stephen oncologist, research center administrator
Levine, Rachmiel physician

El Macero
Raventos, Antolin radiology educator

Encinitas
Dennish, George William, III cardiologist
Satur, Nancy Marlene dermatologist

Encino
†King, Peter DeWitt psychiatrist, educator, real estate developer

Escondido
Everton, Marta Ve ophthalmologist

Fairfield
Martin, Clyde Verne psychiatrist

Fresno
Falcone, Alfonso Benjamin physician
Holmes, Albert William, Jr. physician
Leigh, Hoyle psychiatrist, educator, writer

Glendale
Dent, Ernest DuBose, Jr. pathologist
Kernen, Jules Alfred pathologist

Greenbrae
Levy, S. William dermatologist
Parnell, Francis William, Jr. physician

Half Moon Bay
Robertson, Abel L., Jr. pathologist

Hemet
Kopiloff, George psychiatrist

Hillsborough
†Kraft, Robert Arnold retired medical educator, physician

Hollywood
Bessman, Samuel Paul biochemist, pediatrician

Indian Wells
Carter, Paul Richard physician

Indio
Fischer, Craig Leland physician

Inglewood
Jobe, Frank Wilson orthopedic surgeon

Irvine
Charles, M. Arthur endocrinologist, educator
Connolly, John Earle surgeon, educator
Felton, Jean Spencer physician
Friedenberg, Richard Myron radiology educator, physician
Friou, George Jacob immunologist, physician, educator
George, Kattunilathu Oommen homoeopathic physician, educator
Gottschalk, Louis August neuropsychiatrist, psychoanalyst
Gupta, Sudhir immunologist, educator
†Henry, Walter L. cardiologist, educator
Jones, Edward George anatomy and neurobiology professor, department chairman
Miledi, Ricardo neurobiologist
Morrison, Gilbert Caffall psychiatrist
Mosier, Harry David, Jr. physician, educator
Phalen, Robert F. community and environmental medicine educator, occupational health educator, research scientist
Starr, Arnold neurologist, educator
Tobis, Jerome Sanford physician
van-den-Noort, Stanley physician, educator
Waitzkin, Howard Bruce physician, sociologist, educator

La Canada Flintridge
Byrne, George Melvin physician

La Habra
Barnett, Albert E. physician

La Jolla
Anderson, Richard William retired psychiatrist, educator
Barrett-Connor, Elizabeth Louise epidemiologist, educator
Bergan, John Jerome vascular surgeon
Bernstein, Eugene Felix vascular surgeon, medical educator
Beutler, Ernest physician, research scientist
Block, Melvin August surgeon, educator
Carmichael, David Burton physician
Carson, John Congleton cardiologist, educator
Cheney, Carol endocrinologist
Dalessio, Donald John physician, neurologist, educator
Dixon, Frank James medical scientist, educator
Edwards, Charles Cornell physician, research administrator
Farr, Richard Studley immunologist, educator, physician
Fosburg, Richard Garrison cardiothoracic surgeon
Friedman, Paul Jay radiologist, chest radiologist, educator
†Garland, Cedric Frank epidemiologist, educator
Gittes, Ruben Foster urological surgeon
Hench, Philip Kahler physician
Hofmann, Alan Frederick biomedical educator, researcher
†Horres, Mary Milon medical librarian
Johnson, Allen Dress cardiologist
Karten, Harvey Jules neurosciences educator
Keeney, Edmund Ludlow physician
Klinman, Norman Ralph immunologist, medical educator
Lele, Padmakar Pratap physician, educator
Mathews, Kenneth Pine physician, educator
Nakamura, Robert Motoharu pathologist
Nyhan, William Leo pediatrician, educator
†Pierce, John Patrick epidemiology educator
Steinberg, Daniel preventive medicine physician, educator
Tan, Eng Meng immunologist, rheumatologist, biomedical scientist
Terry, Robert Davis neuropathologist, educator
Weigle, William Oliver immunologist, educator
Yen, Samuel S(how)-C(hih) obstetrics and gynecology educator, reproductive endocrinologist

La Quinta
Boysen, Harry obstetrician, gynecologist

Loma Linda
Adey, William Ross physician
Bailey, Leonard Lee surgeon
Behrens, Berel Lyn physician, academic administrator
Bull, Brian Stanley pathology educator, medical consultant, business executive
Coggin, Charlotte Joan cardiologist, educator
Condon, Stanley Charles gastroenterologist
Hinshaw, David B., Jr. radiologist
Johns, Varner Jay, Jr. medical educator
Kuhn, Irvin Nelson hematologist, oncologist
Llaurado, Josep G. nuclear medicine physician, scientist
Mace, John Weldon pediatrician
Peterson, John Eric physician, educator
Rendell-Baker, Leslie anesthesiologist, educator
Roberts, Walter Herbert Beatty anatomist
Slater, James Munro radiation oncologist
Stilson, Walter Leslie radiologist, educator

Long Beach
Alkon, Ellen Skillen physician
Kurnick, Nathaniel Bertrand oncology educator, researcher
†Light, Richard Wayne medical educator
Loganbill, G. Bruce logopedic pathologist
Mills, Don Harper pathology and psychiatry educator
Snape, William John, Jr. physician
Todd, Malcolm Clifford surgeon

Los Angeles
Apt, Leonard physician
Ashley, Sharon Anita pediatric anesthesiologist
Askanas-Engel, Valerie neurologist, educator, researcher
Bao, Joseph Yue-Se orthopaedist, microsurgeon, educator
Barker, Wiley Franklin surgeon, educator
Barrio, Jorge Raul medical educator
†Beart, Robert W., Jr. surgeon, educator
Beck, John Christian physician, educator
Bernstein, Sol cardiologist, educator
Biles, John Alexander pharmacology educator, chemistry educator
Blahd, William Henry physician
Boak, Ruth Alice physician, educator
Bondareff, William psychiatry educator
Breslow, Lester physician, educator
Buchwald, Nathaniel Avrom neurophysiologist
Chandor, Stebbins Bryant pathologist
Cherry, James Donald physician
Cicciarelli, James Carl immunology educator
Clemente, Carmine Domenic anatomist, educator
Cochran, Sachiko Tomie radiologist
Cooper, Edwin Lowell anatomy educator
Crandall, Edward David medical educator
Danoff, Dudley Seth surgeon, urologist
Davidson, Ezra C., Jr. physician, educator
Davis, Sybil Alicia obstetrician gynecologist
Detels, Roger epidemiologist, physician, former university dean
Dignam, William Joseph obstetrician, gynecologist, educator
Edgerton, Bradford Wheatly plastic surgeon
†Ettenger, Robert Bruce physician, nephrologist
Fahey, John Leslie immunologist
Feig, Stephen Arthur pediatrics educator, hematologist, oncologist
Fish, Barbara psychiatrist, educator
Fonkalsrud, Eric Walter pediatric surgeon, educator
†Fox, Saul Laurie physician, researcher
Gale, Robert Peter physician, scientist, researcher
Gambino, Jerome James nuclear medicine educator
Gold, Richard Horace radiologist
Gonick, Harvey Craig nephrologist, educator
Gorney, Roderic psychiatry educator
Gorski, Roger Anthony neuroendocrinologist, educator
Grinnell, Alan Dale neurobiologist, educator, researcher
Harold, John Gordon cardiologist, internist
Haskell, Charles Mortimer medical oncologist, educator
Haywood, L. Julian physician, educator
Hoang, Duc Van theoretical pathologist, educator
Horwitz, David A. medicine and microbiology educator
House, John William otologist
Hughes, Everett Clark otolaryngology educator
Jarvik, Lissy F. psychiatrist
Jarvik, Murray Elias psychiatry, pharmacology educator
Jenden, Donald James pharmacologist, educator
Johnson, Cage Saul hematologist, educator
Kagan, Benjamin M. pediatrician
Kambara, George Kiyoshi retired ophthalmologist, educator
Kaplan, Samuel pediatric cardiologist
Katz, Ronald Lewis physician, educator
Kelly, Arthur Paul physician
Kilburn, Kaye Hatch medical educator
Koch, Richard pediatrician, educator
Korenman, Stanley George medical investigator, educator
Krim, Mathilde medical educator
Kruger, Lawrence neuroscientist
Lane, Joseph M. orthopaedic surgeon, oncologist
Lawrence, Sanford Hull physician, immunochemist
Lehman, Robert Nathan ophthalmologist, educator
Lewin, Klaus J. pathologist, educator
Lewis, Charles Edwin physician, educator
Liberman, Robert Paul psychiatry educator, researcher, writer
Longmire, William Polk, Jr. physician, surgeon
Looney, Gerald Lee medical educator, administrator
Marmor, Judd psychiatrist, educator
Maronde, Robert Francis internist, clinical pharmacologist, educator
Mellinkoff, Sherman Mussoff medical educator
Metzner, Richard Joel psychiatrist, psychopharmacologist, educator
Mihan, Richard dermatologist
Miles, Samuel Israel psychiatrist
Miller, Timothy Alden plastic and reconstructive surgeon
Mishell, Daniel R., Jr. physician, educator
Moxley, John Howard, III physician
Mulder, Donald Gerrit surgeon, educator
Noble, Ernest Pascal physician, biochemist, educator
Paredes, Alfonso psychiatrist
Parker, John William pathology educator, investigator
Parker, Robert George radiation oncology educator, academic administrator
Parmelee, Arthur Hawley, Jr. pediatric medical educator
Perloff, Joseph Kayle cardiologist
Pettit, Thomas Henry ophthalmologist
Pitkin, Roy Macbeth physician, educator
Rachelefsky, Gary S. medical educator
Rangell, Leo psychiatrist, psychoanalyst
Rimoin, David Lawrence physician, geneticist
Ritvo, Edward Ross psychiatrist
Roemer, Milton Irwin physician, educator
Ross, Joseph Foster physician, educator
Ryan, Stephen Joseph, Jr. ophthalmology educator, university dean
Saad, Mohammed Fathy medical educator
Sarnat, Bernard George plastic surgeon, educator, researcher
Savage, Edward Warren, Jr. physician
Sawyer, Charles Henry anatomist, educator
Scheibel, Arnold Bernard psychiatrist, educator, researcher
Schiff, Martin physician, surgeon
Schneider, Edward Lewis medicine educator, research administrator
Schwabe, Arthur David physician, educator
†Siegel, Michael Elliot nuclear medicine physician, educator
Siegel, Sheldon C. physician
Solomon, David Harris physician, educator
Solomon, George Freeman academic psychiatrist
Sprague, Norman Frederick, Jr. surgeon, educator
Steckel, Richard J. radiologist, academic administrator
Stern, Walter Eugene neurosurgeon, educator
Stiehm, E. Richard pediatrician, educator
Straatsma, Bradley Ralph ophthalmologist, educator
Sullivan, Stuart Francis anesthesiologist, educator
†Tashkin, Donald P. physician
Tischler, Gary Lowell psychiatrist, educator
Titus, Edward Depue psychiatrist, administrator
Tompkins, Ronald K. surgeon
Tranquada, Robert Ernest medical educator, physician
van Dam, Heiman psychoanalyst
Van Der Meulen, Joseph Pierre neurologist
Verity, Maurice Anthony pathologist, neuropathologist, educator, consultant
Villablanca, Jaime Rolando medical scientist, educator
Vredevoe, Donna Lou research immunologist, microbiologist, educator
Walsh, John Harley medical educator
Watring, Watson Glenn gynecologic oncologist, educator
Weiner, Leslie Philip neurology educator, researcher
Weinstein, Irwin Marshall internist, hematologist
Weiss, Martin Harvey neurosurgeon, educator
Wilson, Miriam Geisendorfer physician, educator
Wincor, Michael Z. psychopharmacology educator, clinician, researcher
Yamamoto, Joe psychiatrist, educator
†Zawacki, Bruce E. surgeon, ethicist

Los Gatos
Lorincz, Albert Bela physician, educator

Malibu
Lilly, John Cunningham medical scientist, author
Morgenstern, Leon surgeon

Martinez
Efron, Robert neurology educator, research institute administrator
Geokas, Michael C. gastroenterologist

Marysville
Hamilton, Richard Daniel neurosurgeon

Menlo Park
Glaser, Robert Joy physician, foundation executive
Sparks, Robert Dean medical administrator, physician

Merced
Maytum, Harry Rodell retired physician

Mill Valley
Newman, Nancy Marilyn ophthalmologist, educator, consultant, inventor, entrepreneur
Wallerstein, Robert Solomon psychiatrist

Monterey
Black, Robert Lincoln pediatrician
Mushkin, Leonard Barton podiatrist

Moraga
†Frey, William Rayburn healthcare educator, consultant

Mountain View
†Gelpi, Armand Philippe hemotologist/oncologist

Napa
Francis, Marc Baruch pediatrician
†Zimmermann, John Paul plastic surgeon

Newport Beach
Kahn, Douglas Gerard psychiatrist

Nipomo
Brantingham, Charles Ross podiatrist, ergonomics consultant

North Hollywood
Gregorius, Beverly June retired obstretician-gynecologist

Northridge
Davidson, Sheldon Jerome hematologist
Madison, Roberta Eleanor epidemiologist, educator, consultant

Novato
Bozdech, Marek Jiri physician
Franklin, Robert Blair cardiologist

Oakland
†Barricks, Michael Eli retinal surgeon
Collen, Morris Frank physician
Fink, Diane Joanne physician
Friedman, Gary David epidemiologist, research facility administrator
†Sass, Donald Jay anesthesiologist
Weinmann, Robert Lewis neurologist

Orange
Anzel, Sanford Harold orthopaedic surgeon
Armentrout, Steven Alexander oncologist
†Barr, Ronald Jeffrey dermatologist, pathologist
Berk, Jack Edward physician, educator
Braunstein, Phillip radiologist, educator
Crumley, Roger Lee surgeon, educator
Dana, Edward Runkle physician, educator
Dietrich, Rosalind radiology educator
DiSaia, Philip John gynecologist, obstetrician, radiology educator
Furnas, David William plastic surgeon
Lott, Ira Totz pediatric neurologist
†MacArthur, Carol Jeanne pediatric otolaryngology educator
Morgan, Beverly Carver physician, educator
Quilligan, Edward James obstetrician/gynecologist, educator
Rowen, Marshall radiologist
Thompson, William Benbow, Jr. obstetrician/ gynecologist, educator
Yu, Jen medical educator

Pacific Palisades
Claes, Daniel John physician
Dignam, Robert Joseph retired orthopaedic surgeon

Palm Desert
McKissock, Paul Kendrick plastic surgeon

Palm Springs
Kroger, William Saul obstetrician-gynecologist
Weil, Max Harry physician, medical educator, medical scientist

Palo Alto
Adamson, Geoffrey David reproductive endocrinologist, surgeon
Agras, William Stewart psychiatry educator
Amylon, Michael David physician, educator
Bagshaw, Malcolm A. radiation therapist, educator
†Basso, Lawrence Vincent physician
Bhatt, Kiran physician, educator
Blau, Helen Margaret molecular pharmacology educator
Britton, M(elvin) C(reed), Jr. physician, rheumatologist
Carlson, Robert Wells physician, educator
Chase, Robert Arthur surgeon, educator
Cooper, Allen David research scientist, educator
Dement, William Charles sleep researcher, medical educator
Farber, Eugene Mark psoriasis research institute administrator
Farquhar, John William physician, educator
Fries, James Franklin internal medicine educator
Furthmayr, Heinz pathologist, researcher
Goldstein, Avram pharmacology educator
Hays, Marguerite Thompson physician
Holman, Halsted Reid medical educator
Jamison, Rex Lindsay medical educator
Jamplis, Robert Warren surgeon, medical foundation executive
Knudsen, Eric Ingvald neuroscientist
Lane, William Kenneth physician
Linna, Timo Juhani immunologist, researcher, educator
†Matthews, Zakee psychiatrist, educator
Morris, Randall Ellis immunologist, university program director
Remington, Jack Samuel physician
Robinson, Thomas Nathaniel pediatrician, educator, researcher
Sawyer, Wilbur Henderson pharmacologist, educator
Schrier, Stanley Leonard physician, educator
Strober, Samuel immunologist, educator
Urquhart, John medical researcher, educator

Palos Verdes Peninsula
Haynes, Moses Alfred physician
Thomas, Claudewell Sidney psychiatry educator

Panorama City
Bass, Harold Neal *pediatrician, medical geneticist*

Pasadena
Caillouette, James Clyde *physician*
Harvey, Joseph Paul, Jr. *orthopedist, educator*
Konishi, Masakazu *neurobiologist*
MacLaren, Walter Rogers *allergist, educator*
Mathies, Allen Wray, Jr. *physician, hospital administrator*
Yeager, Caroline Hale *radiologist, consultant*

Philo
Hill, Rolla B. *pathologist*

Piedmont
Cuttle, Tracy Donald *physician, former naval officer*
Hughes, James Paul *physician*
Montgomery, Theodore Ashton *physician*

Pinole
Harvey, Elinor B. *child psychiatrist*

Pomona
†Pumerantz, Philip *medical school president*

Portola Valley
Creevy, Donald Charles *obstetrician-gynecologist*

Rancho Mirage
Cone, Lawrence Arthur *research medicine educator*

Rancho Santa Fe
Affeldt, John Ellsworth *physician*

Redlands
Skoog, William Arthur *retired oncologist*

Redwood City
Seltzer, Ronald Anthony *radiologist, educator*
Wong, Nancy L. *dermatologist*

Richmond
Rubanyi, Gabor Michael *medical research company executive*

Riverside
Jukkola, George Duane *obstetrician-gynecologist*

Rolling Hills Estates
Bellis, Carroll Joseph *surgeon*

Roseville
Hendricks, Ed Jerald *physician*

Ross
Way, Walter Lee *anesthetist, pharmacologist, educator*

Sacramento
Benfield, John Richard *surgeon*
Bogren, Hugo Gunnar *radiology educator*
Chapman, Michael William *orthopedist, educator*
Cunningham, Mary Elizabeth *physician*
Deitch, Arline Douglis *cell biologist*
Dorn, Robert Murray *physician, psychiatrist, educator, psychoanalyst*
Dreyfus, Pierre Marc *neurologist, educator*
Evrigenis, John Basil *obstetrician-gynecologist*
Frey, Charles Frederick *surgeon, educator*
Lake, Carol Lee *anesthesiologist, educator*
Lynch, Peter John *dermatologist*
Richman, David Paul *neurologist, researcher*
Stabenau, James Raymond *research psychiatrist, educator*
Wolfman, Earl Frank, Jr. *surgeon, educator*

Salinas
†Kellogg, Donald Ray *surgeon, plastic surgeon*

San Bernardino
Nies, Boyd Arthur *hematologist, oncologist*

San Bruno
Bradley, Charles William *podiatrist, educator*

San Clemente
Kim, Edward William *ophthalmic surgeon*

San Diego
Akeson, Wayne Henry *orthopedic surgeon, orthopedic educator*
Bailey, David Nelson *pathologist, educator*
Benirschke, Kurt *pathologist, educator*
Blum, John Alan *urologist, educator*
Bradley, John Edmund *physician, emeritus educator*
Crutchfield, Susan Ramsey *neurophysiologist*
DeMaria, Anthony Nicholas *cardiologist, educator*
Dziewanowska, Zofia Elizabeth *neuropsychiatrist, pharmaceutical executive, physician*
Goltz, Robert William *physician, educator*
Griffin, Herschel Emmett *epidemiology educator, administrator*
Halasz, Nicholas Alexis *surgeon*
Hamburg, Marian Virginia *health science educator*
Harwood, Ivan Richmond *pediatric pulmonologist*
Henderson, Brian Edmond *physician, educator*
Isenberg, Jon Irwin *gastroenterologist, educator*
Jacoby, Irving *physician*
Jeste, Dilip Vishwanath *psychiatrist, researcher*
†Kaback, Michael *medical educator*
Kaplan, George Willard *urologist*
Kidokoro, Yasuko *physician*
Lewis, Gregory Williams *scientist*
Magnuson, Harold Joseph *physician*
Moossa, A. R. *surgery educator*
Moser, Kenneth Miles *physician*
Nadler, Henry Louis *pediatrician, geneticist, medical educator*
Neuman, Tom S. *emergency medical physician, educator*
O'Malley, Edward *physician, consultant*
Owsia, Nasrin Akbarnia *pediatrician*
Ranney, Helen Margaret *physician, educator*
Resnik, Robert *medical educator*
Saidman, Lawrence Jay *anesthesiologist*
Salk, Jonas Edward *physician, scientist*
†Stein, Robert Benjamin *biomedical researcher, physician*
Turrell, Eugene Snow *psychiatrist*
Wallace, Helen Margaret *physician, educator*
Wasserman, Stephen Ira *physician, educator*
Wight, Nancy Elizabeth *neonatologist*

San Fernando
Chiu, Dorothy *pediatrician*

San Francisco
Aird, Robert Burns *neurologist, educator*
Amend, William John Conrad, Jr. *physician, educator*
Arieff, Allen Ives *physician*
Asling, Clarence Willet *anatomist, educator*
Auerback, Alfred *psychiatrist*
Barondes, Samuel Herbert *psychiatrist, educator*
Benet, Leslie Zachary *pharmacokineticist*
Biglieri, Edward George *physician*
Bishop, John Michael *biomedical research scientist, educator*
Boles, Roger *otolaryngologist*
†Bradford, David S. *surgeon*
†Brandborg, Lloyd Leon *retired medical educator*
Bredt, David Scott *neuroscience and physiology educator*
†Cleaver, James Edward *radiologist, educator*
Clever, Linda Hawes *physician*
Crede, Robert Henry *physician, educator*
Cunningham, Emmett Thomas, Jr. *physician, researcher*
Curry, Francis John *physician*
†Curtis, David Lambert *rheumatologist, educator*
Dawson, Chandler R. *ophthalmologist, educator*
Debas, Haile T. *gastrointestinal surgeon, physiologist, educator*
Epstein, Charles Joseph *physician, medical geneticist, pediatrics and biochemistry educator*
Epstein, John Howard *dermatologist*
Epstein, Leon Joseph *psychiatrist*
Erskine, John Morse *surgeon*
†Faden, Alan Ira *neurology educator*
Farber, Seymour Morgan *physician, university administrator*
Fielder, David R. *medical research administrator*
Finberg, Laurence *pediatrician, educator, college dean*
Foye, Laurance Vincent *physician, hospital administrator*
Fraser, Cosmo Lyle *medical educator, researcher*
Frick, Oscar Lionel *physician, educator*
Friedman, Meyer *physician*
Fu, Karen King-Wah *radiation oncologist*
Goode, Erica Tucker *internist*
Gooding, Charles Arthur *radiologist, physician, educator*
Gooding, Gretchen Ann Wagner *physician, educator*
Gottfried, Eugene Leslie *physician, educator*
Greenspan, Francis S. *physician*
Grumbach, Melvin Malcolm *physician, educator*
Havel, Richard Joseph *physician, educator*
Henry, Margaret Elizabeth *physician, surgeon*
Herbert, Chesley C. *psychiatrist*
Heyman, Melvin Bernard *pediatric gastroenterologist*
Hinman, Frank, Jr. *urologist, educator*
Hoffman, Arlene Faun *podiatric medicine educator, physiologist*
Hoffman, Julien Ivor Ellis *pediatric cardiologist, educator*
†Hsu, John Chao-Chun *retired pediatrician*
Jacobs, Edwin Max *oncologist, consultant*
Jaffe, Robert Benton *obstetrician-gynecologist, reproductive endocrinologist*
Kan, Yuet Wai *physician, investigator*
Katz, Hilliard Joel *physician*
Kilgore, Eugene Sterling, Jr. *surgeon*
†Kolb, Felix Oscar *physician*
†Kramer, Steven G. *opthalmologist, educator*
Kuzell, William Charles *physician, instrument company executive*
LaVail, Jennifer Hart *neurobiologist, educator, researcher*
Levin, Alan Scott *pathologist, allergist, immunologist*
Lim, Robert Cheong, Jr. *surgeon, educator*
Maibach, Howard I. *dermatologist*
Margulis, Alexander Rafailo *physician, educator*
Martin, Joseph Boyd *neurologist, educator*
Mason, Dean Towle *cardiologist*
Mathes, Stephen John *plastic and reconstructive surgeon, educator*
†McAninch, Jack Weldon *urological surgeon, educator*
McCorkle, Horace Jackson *physician, educator*
Murray, John Frederic *physician, educator*
Mustacchi, Piero *physician, educator*
Myers, Howard Milton *pharmacologist, educator*
O'Connor, G(eorge) Richard *ophthalmologist*
Perkins, Herbert Asa *physician*
Petrakis, Nicholas Louis *physician, medical researcher, educator*
Phillips, Theodore Locke *radiation oncologist, educator*
Piel, Carolyn Forman *pediatrician, educator*
Ralston, Henry James, III *neurobiologist, anatomist, educator*
Risse, Guenter Bernhard *physician, historian, educator*
Roe, Benson Bertheau *surgeon, educator*
Rosinski, Edwin Francis *health sciences educator*
Rudolph, Abraham Morris *physician, educator*
Schiller, Francis *neurologist, medical historian*
Schmid, Rudi (Rudolf Schmid) *internist, educator, university official*
Schmidt, Robert Milton *physician, scientist, educator*
Scholten, Paul *obstetrician-gynecologist, educator*
Seebach, Lydia Marie *physician*
Shapiro, Larry Jay *pediatrician, scientist, educator*
Shinefield, Henry Robert *pediatrician*
Shumate, Charles Albert *retired dermatologist*
Skinner, Harry Bryant *orthopaedic surgery educator*
Smith, David Elvin *physician*
Sokolow, Maurice *physician, educator*
†Spencer, William H. *ophthalmologist*
†Stamper, Robert Lewis *opthalmologist, educator*
Szabo, Zoltan *medical science educator, medical institute administrator*
Terr, Lenore Cagen *psychiatrist, writer*
Veith, Ilza *retired psychiatric history educator*
Volpe, Peter Anthony *surgeon*
Wallerstein, Ralph Oliver *physician*
Watts, Malcolm S(tuart) M(cNeal) *physician, medical educator*
Way, E(dward) Leong *pharmacologist, toxicologist, educator*
Wilson, Charles B. *neurosurgeon, educator*
Wintroub, Bruce Urich *dermatologist, educator, researcher*
Wolff, Sheldon *radiobiologist, educator*
Zippin, Calvin *epidemiologist*

San Jose
Boldrey, Edwin Eastland *retinal surgeon, educator*
Johnson, Allen Halbert *surgeon*
Kramer, Richard Jay *gastroenterologist*
Lippe, Philipp Maria *neurosurgeon, educator*
Okita, George T. *pharmacologist, educator*

San Juan Capistrano
Braunstein, Herbert *pathologist, educator*
Fisher, Delbert Arthur *physician, educator*

San Leandro
Leighton, Joseph *pathologist*

San Marino
Benzer, Seymour *neurosciences educator*

San Mateo
Goble, Elise Joan H. *pediatric ophthalmologist*
Kidera, George Jerome *physician*
Van Kirk, John Ellsworth *cardiologist*

San Pablo
Bristow, Lonnie Robert *physician*
†Woodruff, Kay Herrin *pathologist, educator*

San Rafael
Bruyn, Henry Bicker *physician*
Danse, Ilene Homnick Raisfeld *physician, educator, toxicologist*
Hinshaw, Horton Corwin *physician*
Shepard, James Edward *physician*

San Ramon
Litman, Robert Barry *physician, author, television and radio commentator*

Santa Ana
Abbruzzese, Carlo Enrico *physician, writer, educator*
Pratt, Lawrence Arthur *thoracic surgeon, foreign service officer*

Santa Barbara
Bischel, Margaret DeMeritt *physician, managed care consultant*
Carleton, John Lowndes *psychiatrist*
†Corman, Marvin Leonard *surgeon*
Enelow, Allen Jay *psychiatrist, educator*
Fisher, Steven Kay *neurobiology eductor*
Mathews, Barbara Edith *gynecologist*
†Prager, Elliot David *surgeon, educator*
Preston, Frederick Willard *surgeon*
Riemenschneider, Paul Arthur *physician, radiologist*
Rockwell, Don Arthur *psychiatrist*
Taylor, Dermot Brownrigg *pharmacology researcher*
Wayland, L. C. Newton *public health pediatrician*

Santa Clara
†Fernbach, Stephen A. *pediatrician*

Santa Cruz
Magid, Gail Avrum *neurosurgery educator*
Shorenstein, Rosalind Greenberg *physician*

Santa Monica
Gupta, Rishab Kumar *medical association administrator, educator, researcher*
Marrs, Richard Preston *gynecologist, obstetrician*
McGuire, Michael Francis *plastic and reconstructive surgeon*
Rand, Robert Wheeler *neurosurgeon, educator*
Singer, Frederick Raphael *medical researcher, educator*
Thompson, Dennis Peters *plastic surgeon*

Sepulveda
Costea, Nicolas Vincent *physician, researcher*

Sherman Oaks
Zemplenyi, Tibor Karol *cardiologist*

Sierra Madre
Nation, Earl F. *retired urologist, educator*

Somerset
Collier, Clarence Robert *physician, educator*

Stanford
Abrams, Herbert LeRoy *radiologist, educator*
Bauer, Eugene Andrew *dermatologist, educator*
Baylor, Denis Aristide *neurobiology educator*
Beard, Rodney Rau *physician, educator*
Bensch, Klaus George *pathology educator*
†Blaschke, Terrence F. *medicine and molecular pharmacology educator*
Brown, J. Martin *oncologist, educator*
†Cohen, Harvey Joel *pediatric hematology and oncology educator*
†Dafoe, Donald Cameron *surgeon, educator*
†Date, Elaine Satomi *physician*
†Egbert, Peter R. *ophthalmologist, educator*
Gibson, Count Dillon, Jr. *physician, educator*
†Glazer, Gary Mark *radiology educator*
Goldstein, Dora Benedict *pharmacologist, educator*
Harris, Edward D., Jr. *physician*
†Hlatky, Mark Andrew *cardiologist, health services researcher*
Hubert, Helen Betty *epidemiologist*
Jardetzky, Oleg *medical educator, scientist*
Kendig, Joan Johnston *neurobiology educator*
Korn, David *educator, pathologist*
Krensky, Alan Michael *pediatrician, educator*
†Levy, Ronald *medical educator, researcher*
Litt, Iris Figarsky *pediatrics educator*
Maffly, Roy Herrick *medical educator*
Mansour, Tag Eldin *pharmacologist*
Mark, James B. D. *surgeon*
Marmor, Michael Franklin *ophthalmologist, educator*
McDevitt, Hugh O'Neill *immunology educator, physician*
McDougall, Iain Ross *nuclear medicine educator*
Melmon, Kenneth Lloyd *physician, biologist, pharmacologist, consultant*
Merigan, Thomas Charles, Jr. *physician, medical researcher, educator*
Niederhuber, John Edward *surgical oncologist and molecular immunologist, university educator and administrator*
†Oberhelman, Harry Alvin, Jr. *surgeon, educator*
Paffenbarger, Ralph Seal, Jr. *epidemiologist*
Payne, Anita Hart *reproductive endocrinologist, researcher*
†Polan, Mary Lake *obstetrics and gynecology educator*
Raffin, Thomas A. *physician*
†Reitz, Bruce Arnold *cardiac surgeon, educator*
Rosenberg, Saul Allen *oncologist, educator*
Rubenstein, Edward *physician, educator*
Schatzberg, Alan Frederic *psychiatrist, researcher*
†Schendel, Stephen Alfred *plastic surgery educator, oral surgeon*
†Schurman, David Jay *orthopaedic surgeon, educator*
Shortliffe, Edward Hance *internist, medical information science educator*
†Shuer, Lawrence Mendel *neurosurgery educator*
Silverman, Frederic Noah *physician*
†Stamey, Thomas Alexander *physician, urology educator*
Stinson, Edward Brad *surgery educator*
†Tune, Bruce M. *pediatrics educator, renal toxicologist*
Warnke, Roger Allen *pathology educator*

Sylmar
Tully, Susan Balsley *pediatrician, educator*

The Sea Ranch
Resch, Joseph Anthony *neurologist*

Torrance
Ananth, Jambur *psychiatrist, educator*
Brasel, Jo Anne *physician*
Emmanouilides, George Christos *physician, educator*
Gurevitch, Arnold William *dermatology educator*
Itabashi, Hideo Henry *neuropathologist, neurologist*
Krout, Boyd Merrill *psychiatrist*
Lin, Keh-Ming *psychiatrist, researcher*
Miller, Milton Howard *psychiatrist*
Myhre, Byron Arnold *pathologist, educator*
Narasimhan, Padma Mandyam *physician*
Prakash, Ravi *physician, educator*
Swerdloff, Ronald S. *medical educator, researcher*
Tanaka, Kouichi Robert *physician, educator*

Visalia
Riegel, Byron William *ophthalmologist*

Volcano
Prout, Ralph Eugene *physician*

Walnut Creek
Acosta, Julio Bernard *obstetrician, gynecologist*
Farr, Lee Edward *physician*
Seegers, Walter Henry *hematology educator emeritus*

West Hollywood
Brunell, Philip A. *physician*
Wilson, Myron Robert, Jr. *former psychiatrist*

Whittier
Arcadi, John Albert *urologist*
Arenowitz, Albert Harold *psychiatrist*
†Briney, Allan King *radiologist*

Woodland Hills
Chernof, David *internist*
Fricker, John Arthur *pediatrician, educator*
†Greaves, Roger F. *health maintenance organization executive*
†Hasan, Malik M. *health maintenance organization executive*

COLORADO

Boulder
Dubin, Mark William *educator, neuroscientist*

Castle Rock
Thornbury, John Rousseau *radiologist, physician*

Colorado Springs
Anderson, Paul Nathaniel *oncologist, educator*
Halling, Leonard William *retired pathologist, laboratory administrator*

Denver
Adler, Charles Spencer *psychiatrist*
Aikawa, Jerry Kazuo *physician, educator*
Atkins, Dale Morrell *physician*
Barkin, Roger Michael *pediatrician, emergency physician, educator*
Battaglia, Frederick Camillo *physician*
Blager, Florence Berman *voice pathology educator*
†Bloor, John Holt *gastroenterologist, educator*
Bunn, Paul A., Jr. *oncologist, educator*
†Chase, H. Peter *medical educator*
†Clayton, Mack Louis *surgery professor, educator*
Deitrich, Richard Adam *pharmacology educator*
†Dempsey, Edward Charles *thoracic surgeon*
Eickhoff, Theodore Carl *physician*
Firminger, Harlan Irwin *pathologist, educator*
Friedman, H. Harold *cardiologist, internist*
Golitz, Loren Eugene *dermatologist, pathologist, clinical administrator, educator*
Green, Larry Alton *physician, educator*
Iseman, Michael Dee *medical educator*
Jafek, Bruce William *otolaryngologist, educator*
Kauvar, Abraham J. *gastroenterologist, medical administrator*
Kern, Fred, Jr. *physician, educator*
Krikos, George Alexander *pathologist, educator*
Larsen, Gary Loy *physician, researcher*
Lilly, John Russell *surgeon, educator*
Lubeck, Marvin Jay *ophthalmologist*
Makowski, Edgar Leonard *obstetrician and gynecologist*
Martin, Richard Jay *medical educator*
McAtee, Patricia Anne Rooney *medical educator*
Moore, Ernest Eugene, Jr. *surgeon, educator*
Moore, George Eugene *surgeon*
Nakakuki, Masafumi *physician, psychiatry educator*
Nelson, Nancy Eleanor *pediatrician, educator*
†Novins, Douglas K. *psychiatrist, educator*
Petty, Thomas Lee *physician, educator*
†Pomerantz, Marvin *thoracic surgeon*
Rainer, William Gerald *cardiac surgeon*
Repine, John E. *internist, educator*
Ruge, Daniel August *retired neurosurgeon, educator*
Rutherford, Robert Barry *surgeon*
Schiff, Donald Wilfred *pediatrician, educator*

Schneck, Stuart Austin *neurologist, educator*
Shore, James H(enry) *psychiatrist*
Silverman, Arnold *physician*
Sondheimer, Judith M. *pediatrician, educator*
Szefler, Stanley James *pediatrics and pharmacology educator*
Taylor, Edward Stewart *physician, educator*
Tormey, Douglass Cole *medical oncologist*
Washington, Reginald Louis *pediatric cardiologist*
†Weatherley-White, Roy Christopher Anthony *surgeon, consultant*
Weston, William Lee *dermatologist*
Wiggs, Eugene Overbey *ophthalmologist, educator*

Durango
Moore, John George, Jr. *medical educator*

Englewood
†Arenberg, Irving Kaufman *ear surgeon, educator*
English, Gerald Marion *otolaryngologist*
Pearlman, David Samuel *allergist*

Fort Collins
Gillette, Edward LeRoy *radiation oncology educator*

Grand Junction
Sadler, Theodore R., Jr. *thoracic and cardiovascular surgeon*

Greeley
Cook, Donald E. *pediatrician*

Lakewood
†Swan, Henry *retired surgeon*

Littleton
Bachman, David Christian *orthopedic surgeon*

Snowmass Village
Diamond, Edward *gynecologist, infertility specialist, clinician*

Westminster
Silverberg, Stuart Owen *obstetrician, gynecologist*

Wheat Ridge
Hashimoto, Christine L. *physician*
Straits, Beverly Joan *gynecologist*

CONNECTICUT

Ansonia
Yale, Jeffrey Franklin *podiatrist*

Avon
Smith, Leonard Kelley *former plastic and reconstructive surgeon, consultant*

East Haven
Conn, Harold O. *physician, educator*

Farmington
†Besdine, Richard William *medical educator*
Cooperstein, Sherwin Jerome *medical educator*
Donaldson, James Oswell, III *neurology educator*
Escobar, Javier Ignacio *psychiatrist*
Gossling, Harry Robert *orthopaedic surgeon, educator*
Hinz, Carl Frederick, Jr. *physician, educator*
Katz, Arnold Martin *medical educator*
Massey, Robert Unruh *physician, university dean*
Raisz, Lawrence Gideon *medical educator, consultant*
Rothfield, Naomi Fox *physician*
Schenkman, John Boris *pharmacologist, educator*
Walker, James Elliot Cabot *physician*

Greenwich
Foraste, Roland *psychiatrist*
Kopenhaver, Patricia Ellsworth *podiatrist*
Randt, Clark Thorp *physician, educator*

Guilford
Warshaw, Joseph Bennett *pediatrician, educator*

Hamden
Nuland, Sherwin *surgeon, author*

Hartford
Brauer, Rima Lois *psychiatrist*
Donnelly, John *psychiatrist, educator*
†Gibbons, John Martin, Jr. *physician, educator*
Jones, Richard F., III *obstetrician/gynecologist*
Kang, Juliana Haeng-Cha *anesthesiologist*
Roberts, Melville Parker, Jr. *neurosurgeon, educator*
Tingley, Floyd Warren *physician*
Trowbridge, Phillip Edmund *surgeon, educator*
Welch, John Paton *surgeon, educator*

Lyme
Bloom, Barry Malcolm *medical consultant*

Madison
Snell, Richard Saxon *anatomist*

Middletown
Brewer, Timothy Francis, III *cardiologist*

New Canaan
Coughlin, Francis Raymond, Jr. *surgeon, educator, lawyer*

New Haven
Aghajanian, George Kevork *medical educator*
†Askenase, Philip W. *medicine and pathology educator*
Barash, Paul George *anesthesiologist, educator*
†Beardsley, G(eorge) Peter *pediatric oncologist, biochemical pharmacologist*
Behrman, Harold Richard *endocrinologist, physiologist, educator*
Berliner, Robert William *physician, medical educator*
Boyer, James Lorenzen *physician, educator*
Braverman, Irwin Merton *dermatologist, educator*
Brown, Thomas Huntington *neuroscientist*
Bunney, Benjamin Stephenson *psychiatrist*
Burrow, Gerard Noel *physician, educator*
Byck, Robert Samuel *psychiatrist, educator*
Cohen, Donald Jay *pediatrics, psychiatry and psychology educator, administrator*
Cohen, Lawrence Sorel *physician, educator*
Cohen, Melvin Joseph *neuroscientist*
†Cole, Laurence Anthony *reproductive biology and cancer biology educator*
Collins, William F., Jr. *neurosurgery educator*
Comer, James Pierpont *psychiatrist*
†Cooney, Leo Mathias, Jr. *geriatrician, educator*
Cooper, Jack Ross *pharmacology educator, researcher*
Davey, Lycurgus Michael *neurosurgeon*
Davis, Michael *medical educator*
Dolan, Thomas F., Jr. *pediatrician, educator*
Donaldson, Robert Macartney, Jr. *physician*
Edelson, Marshall *psychiatry educator, psychoanalyst*
†Edelson, Richard L. *dermatology educator*
†Elias, Jack Angel *physician, educator*
Evans, Alfred Spring *physician, educator*
Feinstein, Alvan Richard *physician*
Friedlaender, Gary Elliott *orthopedist, educator*
Genel, Myron *pediatrician, educator*
Gillis, C. Norman *anesthesiology and pharmacology educator*
Glaser, Gilbert Herbert *neuroscientist, physician, educator*
†Gross, Ian *academic pediatrician, neonatologist*
†Haddad, Gabriel G. *physician, pediatrics educator*
Hayslett, John Paul *physician, medical educator, researcher*
Heninger, George Robert *psychiatry educator, researcher*
Herbert, Peter Noel *physician, medical educator*
Horstmann, Dorothy Millicent *physician, educator*
Jackson, Stanley Webber *psychiatrist, medical historian*
Jacoby, Robert Ottinger *comparative medicine educator*
Jatlow, Peter I. *pathologist, medical educator, researcher*
Kashgarian, Michael *pathologist, physician*
Katz, Jay *psychiatry and law educator*
Kirchner, John Albert *retired otolaryngology educator*
†Kleinman, Charles Stephan *physician, medical educator*
Komp, Diane Marilyn *pediatric oncologist, hematologist, writer*
Kushlan, Samuel Daniel *physician, educator, hospital administrator*
†Leffell, David Joel *surgeon, dermatologist, educator, researcher*
Lentz, Thomas Lawrence *biomedical educator, dean, researcher*
Levine, Robert John *physician, educator*
Lewis, Melvin *psychiatrist, pediatrician, psychoanalyst*
†McCarthy, Paul Louis *pediatrics educator*
†Mermann, Alan Cameron *pediatrics educator, chaplain*
†Merritt, John Augustus *geriatrician, educator*
Miller, I. George *physician, educator, researcher*
†Morrow, Jon Stanley *pathology educator, medical scientist*
Musto, David Franklin *physician, historian, consultant*
Naftolin, Frederick *physician, reproductive biologist educator*
Newman, Harry Rudolph *urologist, educator*
Niederman, James Corson *physician, educator*
Ostfeld, Adrian Michael *physician*
Polayes, Irving Marvin *plastic surgeon*
Pruett, Kyle Dean *psychiatrist, writer, educator*
Prusoff, William Herman *biochemical pharmacologist, educator*
Rakic, Pasko *neuroscientist, educator*
Redmond, Donald Eugene, Jr. *neuroscientist, educator*
Reiser, Morton Francis *psychiatrist, educator*
†Reiss, Michael *medical oncologist, researcher*
Ritchie, J. Murdoch *pharmacologist*
Sartorelli, Alan Clayton *pharmacology educator*
Sasaki, Clarence Takashi *surgeon, medical educator*
Schowalter, John Erwin *psychiatrist, educator*
Schwartz, Ilsa Roslow *neuroscientist*
Schwartz, Peter Edward *physician, gynecologic oncology educator*
†Sears, Marvin *ophthalmologist, educator*
Seashore, Margretta Reed *physician*
†Siegel, Norman Joseph *pediatrician, educator*
Silver, George Albert *physician, educator*
Solnit, Albert Jay *commissioner, physician, educator*
Spiro, Howard Marget *physician, educator*
Stenn, Kurt S. *dermatology and pathology educator*
†Tamborlane, William V., Jr. *physician, biomedical researcher, pediatrics educator*
Taylor, Kenneth John W. *physician of diagnostic imagery*
Waxman, Stephen George *neurologist, researcher*
Weiss, Robert M. *urologist, educator*
Wessel, Morris Arthur *pediatrician*
Wright, Hastings Kemper *surgeon, educator*
Zaret, Barry Lewis *cardiologist, medical educator*

New London
Bobruff, Jerome *physician*

Newington
Fleeson, William *psychiatry educator*

Norwalk
Floch, Martin Herbert *physician*
Needham, Charles William *neurosurgeon*
Tracey, Edward John *physician, surgeon*

Old Lyme
Cook, Charles Davenport *pediatrician, educator*

Ridgefield
Margolis, George *pathologist, medical educator*

Sharon
†Gottlieb, Richard Matthew *psychiatrist, consultant*

Stamford
Epstein, Simon Jules *psychiatrist*
Gefter, William Irvin *physician, educator*
Rosenberg, Charles Harvey *otorhinolaryngologist*
Walsh, Thomas Joseph *neuro-ophthalmologist*

Storrs
Dardick, Kenneth Regen *physician, educator*

Storrs Mansfield
†Kerr, Kirklyn M. *veterinary pathologist, researcher*

Trumbull
Bravo, Anthony John *radiologist*

Vernon Rockville
Marmer, Ellen Lucille *pediatrician*

Waterbury
Dudrick, Stanley John *surgeon, scientist, educator*

West Hartford
Hickcox, Curtiss Bronson *anesthesiologist*
McCawley, Austin *psychiatrist, educator*

West Simsbury
Morest, Donald Kent *neuroscientist*

Westport
Clausman, Gilbert Joseph *medical librarian*
Densen-Gerber, Judianne *psychiatrist, lawyer, educator*
Sacks, Herbert Simeon *psychiatrist, educator, consultant*
Sarn, James *physician, health association administrator*
Satinover, Jeffrey Burke *psychiatrist, health science facility administrator, lecturer, author*
Tec, Leon *psychiatrist*

Woodbridge
Bondy, Philip Kramer *physician, educator*

DELAWARE

New Castle
Mac Ewen, George Dean *physician, medical institute executive*

Newark
Dow, Lois Weyman *physician*
Graff, Harold *psychiatrist, psychoanalyst, hospital administrator*
Graham, David Tredway *medical educator, physician*
Lemole, Gerald Michael *surgeon*
McNicholas, Kathleen Winifred *cardiac surgeon*

Rockland
Levinson, John Milton *obstetrician-gynecologist*

Wilmington
Carson, James Elijah *psychiatrist*
Cornelison, Floyd Shovington, Jr. *retired psychiatrist, former educator*
Doughty, Robert Allen *medical institute director*
Harley, Robison Dooling *physician, educator*
Inselman, Laura Sue *pediatrician*
Kay, Jerome *psychiatrist, educator*
Nelson, Dewey Allen *neurologist, educator*
Nwe, Khin May *physician, educator*
Pan, Henry Yue-Ming *clinical pharmacologist*

DISTRICT OF COLUMBIA

Washington
Adamson, Richard Henry *pharmacologist*
Anthony, Virginia Quinn Bausch *medical association executive*
Arling, Bryan Jeremy *internist*
Armaly, Mansour F(arid) *ophthalmologist, educator*
Avery, Gordon Bennett *medical educator, neonatologist*
Bachman, Leonard *physician, retired federal official*
Beary, John Francis, III *physician, pharmaceutical executive*
Belman, A. Barry *pediatric urologist*
Berman, Sidney *psychiatrist*
Blum, Robert Allan *psychiatrist*
Blumenthal, Susan Jane *physician*
Bourne, Peter Geoffrey *physician, educator, author*
Callaway, Clifford Wayne *physician*
Callender, Clive Orville *surgeon*
Canter, Jerome Wolf *surgeon, educator*
Catoe, Bette Lorrina *physician, health educator*
Cheng, Tsung O. *cardiologist, educator*
Chester, Alexander Campbell, III *physician*
†Cohen, Jordan Jay *medical association executive*
Coleman, Roy Melvin *psychiatrist*
Connell, Alastair McCrae *physician*
Cornely, Paul Bertau *physician, educator*
†Cowdry, Rex William *physician, researcher*
Cummings, Martin Marc *medical educator, physician, scientific administrator*
Curfman, David Ralph *neurological surgeon, musician*
Cytowic, Richard Edmund *neurologist*
Davis, David Oliver *radiologist, educator*
Deutsch, Stanley *anesthesiologist, educator*
De Vault, Virgil Thomas *physician*
Dublin, Thomas David *physician*
Earll, Jerry Miller *internist, educator*
Ein, Daniel *allergist*
Eisenberg, John Meyer *physician, educator*
Elgart, Mervyn L. *dermatologist*
Elliott, Larry Paul *cardiac radiologist, educator*
Epps, Charles H., Jr. *medical educator, college dean*
Feldman, Bruce Allen *otolaryngologist*
Felts, William Robert, Jr. *physician*
Finkelstein, James David *physician*
†Fox, Harold Edward *obstetrician/gynecologist, educator, researcher*
Fox, Samuel Mickle, III *physician, educator*
Gary, Nancy Elizabeth *nephrologist, academic administrator*
Gehrig, Leo Joseph *surgeon*
Gilbert, Charles Richard Alsop *physician, medical educator*
Goldson, Alfred Lloyd *oncologist, educator*
Gray, Sheila Hafter *psychiatrist, psychoanalyst*
Grossman, John Henry, III *obstetrician, gynecologist, educator*
†Gulbrandsen, Patricia Hughes *physician*
Harvey, John Collins *physician, educator*
Hein, Karen Kramer *pediatrician, epidemiologist*
Henry, Walter Lester, Jr. *physician, educator*
Herman, Mary Margaret *pathologist*
Hicks, Jocelyn Muriel *laboratory medicine specialist*
Higginbotham, Edith Arleane *radiologist, researcher*
Holden, Raymond Thomas *physician, educator*
Hollinshead, Ariel Cahill *research oncologist*
Hudgins, Michael Pharr *internist*
†Hussain, Syed Taseer *anatomy educator, researcher*
Irey, Nelson Sumner *pathologist*
Kahler, Elizabeth Sartor (Mrs. Ervin Newton Chapman) *physician*
Kant, Gloria Jean *neuroscientist, researcher*
Kassebaum, Donald Gene *medical association administrator, physician, medical educator*
Katz, Sol *physician*
Kaufman, Paul *physician, former naval officer, association executive*
Kent, Kenneth Mitchell *medical educator*
Kind, Phyllis Dawn *immunologist*
Kobrine, Arthur *neurosurgeon*
Koering, Marilyn Jean *anatomy educator, researcher*
Kurtzke, John Francis, Sr. *neurologist, epidemiologist*
Law, David Hillis *physician*
Lee, Philip Randolph *medical educator*
Lessin, Lawrence Stephen *hematologist, oncologist, educator*
Lippman, Marc Estes *pharmacology educator*
Little, John William *plastic surgeon, educator*
†Lynn, D. Joanne *physician, ethicist, health services researcher*
MacLean, Paul Donald *government institute medical research official*
Majd, Massoud *radiology and nuclear medicine educator*
Mandel, H(arold) George *pharmacologist*
Manley, Audrey Forbes *physician*
Mann, Marion *physician, educator*
Mann, Oscar *physician, internist, educator*
Mc Ginnis, James Michael *physician*
†McGrath, Mary Helena *plastic surgeon, educator*
†Meyerhoff, James Lester *medical researcher*
Miller, Harry Charles, Jr. *physician, urologist, educator*
Moritsugu, Kenneth Paul *physician, government official*
Murray, Robert Fulton, Jr. *physician*
Nelson, Alan Ray *internist, medical assocation executive*
Neviaser, Robert Jon *orthopedic surgeon, educator*
Noshpitz, Joseph Dove *child and adolescent psychiatrist*
Novitch, Mark *physician, educator, retired pharmaceutical executive*
Olsen, Kathie Lynn *neuroscientist, administrator*
Parker, Gerald William *physician, medical center administrator, retired air force officer*
Parrott, Robert Harold *pediatrician, educator*
Pawlson, Leonard Gregory *physician*
Pearse, Warren Harland *association executive, obstetrician and gynecologist*
†Peck, Gary Lawrence *dermatologist, researcher*
Pellegrino, Edmund Daniel *physician, educator, former university president*
Perlin, Seymour *psychiatrist, educator*
Perry, Seymour Monroe *physician*
Potter, John Francis *surgical oncologist, educator*
Queenan, John Thomas *obstetrician, gynecologist, educator*
Rall, David Platt *pharmacologist, environmentalist*
Rockoff, S. David *radiologist, physician, educator*
Rosenquist, Glenn Carl *pediatrician*
Ross, Allan Michael *physician, medical educator*
Rowley, William Robert *surgeon*
Sabshin, Melvin *psychiatrist, educator, medical association administrator*
Samman, George *obstetrician, gynecologist*
Sandler, Sumner Gerald *medical educator*
Schechter, Geraldine Poppa *hematologist*
Schreiner, George E. *nephrologist, educator, writer*
Schwartz, Marshall Zane *pediatric surgeon*
Shine, Kenneth Irwin *cardiologist, educator*
Short, Elizabeth M. *physician, educator, federal agency administrator*
Sidransky, Herschel *pathologist*
Silva, Omega Logan *physician*
Simopoulos, Artemis Panageotis *physician, educator*
Sivasubramanian, Kolinjavadi Nagarajan *neonatologist, educator*
Sly, Ridge Michael *physician, educator*
Smith, Lee Elton *surgery educator, retired military officer*
†Spagnolo, Samuel Vincent *medical educator*
Sphar, Raymond Leslie, Jr. *physician, research administator*
Stemmler, Edward Joseph *physician, retired association executive, retired academic dean*
Telford, Ira Rockwood *anatomist, educator*
Wallace, Robert Bruce *surgeon*
Warchol, Richard James *physician*
Webster, Thomas Glenn *psychiatrist*
Weinberger, Daniel R. *psychiatrist, neurologist*
Werbos, Paul John *neural research director*
Werkman, Sidney Lee *psychiatry educator*
Werner, Mario *pathology educator*
†Wilson, Norman Louis *psychiatrist, educator*
Wyatt, Richard Jed *psychiatrist, educator*
†Yoshikawa, Thomas T. *internist*
Young, Donald Alan *physician*
Zimmerman, Hyman Joseph *internist, educator*

FLORIDA

Alachua
Gifford, George E. *immunology and medical microbiology educator*

Atlantis
Newmark, Emanuel *ophthalmologist*

Bay Pines
†Johnson, David Porter *infectious diseases physician*
Keskiner, Ali *psychiatrist*
Robson, Martin Cecil *surgery educator, plastic surgeon*
†Stewart, Jonathan Taylor *psychiatrist, educator*

Belleair
Dexter, Helen Louise *dermatologist, consultant*

Boca Grande
VanItallie, Theodore Bertus *physician*

Boca Raton
Bressler, Steven L. *cognitive neuroscientist*
Cohn, Jess Victor *psychiatrist*
Kramer, Cecile E. *retired medical librarian*
Mirkin, Abraham Jonathan *surgeon*
Stein, Irvin *orthopaedic surgeon, educator*

Bradenton
†Klopp, Calvin Trexler *surgeon, educator*

Bradenton Beach
Vega, Mario *family practice physician*

Brandon
Lafferty, Beverly Lou Brookover *physician*

Clearwater
Fromhagen, Carl, Jr. *obstetrician and gynecologist*
Horowitz, Harry I. *podiatrist*
Lansky, Zena *surgeon*
Wheat, Myron William, Jr. *cardiothoracic surgeon*

Coral Gables
Perez, Josephine *psychiatrist, educator*
†Quillian, Warren Wilson, II *pediatrician, educator*

Dade City
McBath, Donald Linus *osteopathic physician*

Dunedin
Bradley, Robert Lee *surgeon*

Fernandina Beach
Barlow, Anne Louise *pediatrician, medical research administrator*

Fort Lauderdale
Lodwick, Gwilym Savage *radiologist, educator*
Lyons, Richard Chapman *former urologist*
Smolar, Edward Nelson *physician, consultant*

Fort Myers
Aleo, Joseph John *pathology scientist, educator, academic research administrator*
Conger, Kyril B. *urologist*
Ferguson, James A. *surgeon*
Grove, William Johnson *physician, surgery educator*
Simmons, Vaughan Pippen *medical consultant*
Sypert, George Walter *neurosurgery educator, clinical neurosurgeon, research neurophysiologist*

Fort Walton Beach
Gates, Philip Don *anesthesiologist*

Gainesville
Behnke, Marylou *neonatologist, educator*
Cluff, Leighton Eggertsen *physician*
Copeland, Edward Meadors, III *surgery educator*
Gravenstein, Joachim Stefan *anesthesiologist, educator*
Greer, Melvin *medical educator*
Grundy, Betty Lou Bottoms *anesthesiology and pharmaceutics educator*
Modell, Jerome Herbert *anesthesiologist, educator, dean*
Pepine, Carl John *physician, educator*
Pfaff, William Wallace *physician, educator*
Rhoton, Albert Loren, Jr. *neurological surgery educator*
Rosenbloom, Arlan Lee *physician, educator*
Rubin, Melvin Lynne *ophthalmologist, educator*
Schiebler, Gerold Ludwig *physician, educator*
Small, Parker Adams, Jr. *pediatrician, educator*
Suzuki, Howard Kazuro *retired anatomist, educator*
Talbert, James Lewis *pediatric surgeon, educator*
Taylor, William Jape *physician*
†Toskes, Phillip Paul *physician, educator, clinical researcher*
Vaughn, Rufus Mahlon *psychiatrist*
Vierck, Charles John, Jr. *neuroscience educator, scientist*
Walker, Robert Dixon, III *surgeon, urologist, educator*
Williams, Ralph Chester, Jr. *physician, educator*

Hallandale
Haspel, Arthur Carl *podiatrist, surgeon*

Hawthorne
Fackler, Martin L(uther) *surgeon*

Hialeah
Economides, Christopher George *pathologist*

Hollywood
Bergman, Harry *urologist*
Weinberg, Harry Bernard *cardiologist*

Jacksonville
Bosworth, William Posey *physician, physical education educator*
Bremer, Alfonso M. *neurosurgeon, neuro-oncologist*
Carithers, Hugh Alfred *physician*
Groom, Dale *physician, educator*
Hrachovina, Frederick Vincent *osteopathic physician and surgeon*
Jeanes, Lincoln Douglas, Jr. *neurosurgeon*
Kelalis, Panayotis *pediatric urologist*
Mass, M. F. *allergist, immunologist*
Nicolitz, Ernst *ophthalmologist, educator*
Prempree, Thongbliew *oncology radiologist*
Stephenson, Samuel Edward, Jr. *physician*
Toker, Karen Harkavy *physician*

Key Biscayne
Palmer, Roger Farley *pharmacology educator*

Lake City
†Wheaton, T. Frederic, III *psychiatrist, retired naval officer*

Largo
Brown, Warren Joseph *physician*

Marathon
Calvert, William Preston *radiologist*

Marco Island
Sundberg, R. Dorothy *physician, educator*

Melbourne
Baney, Richard Neil *physician, internist*

Miami
Anderson, Douglas Richard *ophthalmologist, educator, scientist, researcher*
Bolooki, Hooshang *cardiac surgeon*
Casariego, Jorge Isaac *psychiatrist, psychoanalyst, educator*
Cohen, Sanford Irwin *physician, educator*
Daughtry, DeWitt Cornell *surgeon, physician*
†Davis, Richard Edmund *plastic surgeon*
Dean, Stanley Rochelle *psychiatrist*
Eaglstein, William Howard *dermatologist, educator*
Flynn, John T. *ophthalmology educator*
Freshwater, Michael Felix *hand surgeon, educator*
Gelband, Henry *pediatric cardiologist*
Ginsberg, Myron David *neurologist*
Howell, Ralph Rodney *pediatrician, educator*
Jude, James Roderick *cardiac surgeon*
Ketcham, Alfred Schutt *surgeon, educator*
Lasseter, Kenneth Carlyle *pharmacologist*
Lemberg, Louis *cardiologist, educator*
Manov, Leslie Joan Boyle *radiologist, medical administrator*
Martínez, Luís Osvaldo *radiologist, educator*
Mc Kenzie, John Maxwell *physician*
Mettinger, Karl Lennart *neurologist*
Nisonson, Ian *urologist*
Page, Larry Keith *neurosurgeon, educator*
Papper, Emanuel Martin *anesthesiologist*
Politano, Victor Anthony *urology educator, physician*
Postel, Joachim Michael *cardiac surgeon*
Potter, James Douglas *pharmacology educator*
Prineas, Ronald James *epidemiologist, educator*
Quencer, Robert Moore *neuroradiologist, researcher*
Ripstein, Charles Benjamin *surgeon*
Sackner, Marvin Arthur *physician*
Scheinberg, Peritz *neurologist*
Schiff, Eugene Roger *medical educator, hepatologist*
Sussex, James Neil *psychiatrist, educator*
Tejada, Francisco *physician, educator*
Valdes-Dapena, Marie Agnes *pediatric pathologist, educator*

Miami Beach
Goldstein, Burton Jack *psychiatrist*

Miami Lakes
Getz, Morton Ernest *medical facility director, gastroenterologist*

Naples
Gahagan, Thomas Gail *obstetrician, gynecologist*
Gross, Paul *pathologist, educator*
Levitt, LeRoy Paul *psychiatrist, psychoanalyst*
Robinson, Nathaniel David *physician*

Ocala
Cabrera-Mendez, Fabio *psychiatrist*
Corwin, William *psychiatrist*

Orlando
Cary, Freeman Hamilton *physician*
Hall, Richard C. Winton *psychiatrist*
Hornick, Richard Bernard *physician*
Norris, Franklin Gray *thoracic and cardiovascular surgeon*

Osprey
Gross, James Dehnert *pathologist*

Palm Beach
Alpert, Seymour *anesthesiologist, educator*

Pensacola
Dillard, Robert Perkins *pediatrician, educator*
Lautier, Yves Laurent *physician*
Love, Robert William, Jr. *retired physician, government administrator*

Pinellas Park
†Morris, Daniel *osteopath*

Pompano Beach
Bliznakov, Emile George *biomedical research scientist*
Patterson, Alan Bruce *obstetrician, gynecologist*

Ponte Vedra Beach
ReMine, William Hervey, Jr. *surgeon*

Port Richey
Radomski, Jack London *pharmacologist, consultant*

Saint Petersburg
†Bercu, Barry B. *pediatric endocrinologist*
Good, Robert Alan *physician, educator*
Root, Allen William *pediatrician, educator*
Sibley, Mark Anderson *ophthalmologist*

Sanibel
Adair, Charles Valloyd *retired physician*

Sarasota
Friedberg, Harold David *cardiologist*
Giordano, David Alfred *internist, gastroenterologist*
Keitel, Hans George *pediatrician*
Kiplinger, Glenn Francis *pharmacologist, medical-legal consultant*
Radnay, Paul Andrew *physician*
Welch, John Dana *urologist, performing arts association executive*

Seminole
Nesbitt, Robert Edward Lee, Jr. *physician, educator*

Spring Hill
Finney, Roy Pelham, Jr. *urologist, surgeon, inventor*

Stuart
Haserick, John Roger *retired dermatologist*
Pisani, Joseph Michael *physician*
Westlake, Robert Elmer, Sr. *physician*

Surfside
Prystowsky, Harry *physician, educator*

Tallahassee
Brodsky, Lewis *psychiatrist, educator*
Maguire, Charlotte Edwards *retired physician*
Penrod, Kenneth Earl *medical education consultant*

Tampa
Afield, Walter Edward *psychiatrist, service executive*
Barness, Lewis Abraham *physician*
Behnke, Roy Herbert *physician, educator*
Bowen, Thomas Edwin *cardiothoracic surgeon, retired army officer*
Branch, William Terrell *urologist, educator*
Bukantz, Samuel Charles *physician, educator*
Carey, Larry Campbell *surgeon*
Cavanagh, Denis *physician, educator*
del Regato, Juan Angel *radio-therapeutist and oncologist, educator*
Farrior, Joseph Brown *otologist*
Frias, Jaime Luis *pediatrician, educator*
Gilbert-Barness, Enid F. *pathologist, pathology and pediatrics educator*
Glasser, Stephen Paul *cardiologist*
Greenfield, George B. *radiologist*
Hartmann, William Herman *pathologist, educator*
Jacobson, Howard Newman *obstetrics/gynecology educator, researcher*
Kaufman, Ronald Paul *physician, school official*
Krzanowski, Joseph John, Jr. *pharmacology educator*
Lockey, Richard Funk *allergist, educator*
Martin, Robert Leslie *physician*
McIntosh, Henry Deane *cardiologist*
McMillan, Donald Ernest *internal medicine educator, state program director*
Muroff, Lawrence Ross *nuclear medicine physician*
Nagera, Humberto *psychiatrist, psychoanalyst, educator, author*
Olson, Robert Eugene *physician, biochemist, educator*
Pfeiffer, Eric Armin *psychiatrist, gerontologist*
Pollara, Bernard *immunologist, pediatrician*
Reading, Anthony John *physician*
Richardson, Sylvia Onesti *physician*
†Rogal, Philip James *physician*
Rowlands, David Thomas *pathology educator*
Schmidt, Paul Joseph *physician, educator*
Schnitzlein, Harold Norman *anatomy educator*
Schonwetter, Ronald Scott *physician, educator*
Shively, John Adrian *pathologist*
Sodeman, William Anthony, Sr. *cardiologist*
Spellacy, William Nelson *obstetrician-gynecologist, educator*
Sullivan, Sister Marie Celeste *health care executive*
Watkins, Joan Marie *osteopath, occupational medicine physician*

Tequesta
Ruoff, Andrew Christian, III *orthopedic surgeon, educator, consultant*
Seaman, William Bernard *physician, radiology educator*

Venice
Kinney, Michael James *physician*

Vero Beach
Christy, Nicholas Pierson *physician*
Lawrence, Merle *medical educator*
Schulman, Harold *obstetrician, gynecologist, perinatologist*

West Palm Beach
Brumback, Clarence Landen *physician*
MacDonald, Richard Annis *pathologist, physician, educator*
Pottash, A. Carter *psychiatrist, hospital executive*
Roberts, Hyman Jacob *internist, researcher, author, historian, publisher*
Sokmensuer, Adil *physician, educator*
Upledger, John Edwin *osteopath, physician*

GEORGIA

Athens
Bowen, John Metcalf *pharmacologist, toxicologist, educator*
Norred, William Preston, Jr. *pharmacologist, educator*

Atlanta
Ambrose, Samuel Sheridan, Jr. *urologist*
Bakay, Roy Arpad Earle *neurosurgeon, educator*
†Baker, Edward L. *physician, science facility executive*
Barnett, Crawford Fannin, Jr. *internist, educator, cardiologist*
†Barrow, Daniel Louis *neurosurgeon*
Broome, Claire Veronica *epidemiologist, researcher*
Byrd, Larry Donald *behavioral pharmacologist*
Carpenter, Charles Bernard *medical educator*
Clements, James David *psychiatry educator, physician*
Connell-Tatum, Elizabeth Bishop *physician*
Davis, Lawrence William *radiation oncologist*
Elsas, Louis Jacob, II *medical educator*
Elsner, Carlene W. *reproductive endocrinologist*
Evans, Edwin Curtis *internist, educator, geriatrician*
†Falk, Henry *pediatrician, research epidemiologist*
Foster, Roger Sherman, Jr. *surgeon, educator, health facility administrator*
Galambos, John Thomas *medical educator, internist*
Gayles, Joseph Nathan, Jr. *medical educator, administrator*
Guinan, Mary Elizabeth *physician, research scientist*
Hall, Wilbur Dallas, Jr. *medical educator*
Hanson, Victor Arthur *surgeon*
Hatcher, Charles Ross, Jr. *cardiothoracic surgeon, medical center executive*
Haverty, John Rhodes *physician, former university dean*
Houpt, Jeffrey Lyle *psychiatrist, educator*
Huber, Douglas Crawford *pathologist*
Huddleston, John Franklin *obstetrics and gynecology educator*
Hug, Carl Casmir, Jr. *pharmacology and anesthesiology educator*
Hughes, James Mitchell *epidemiologist*
Israili, Zafar Hasan *scientist, clinical pharmacologist, educator*
Jurkiewicz, Maurice John *surgeon, educator*
Karp, Herbert Rubin *neurologist, educator*
Kaufmann, James A. *internist, educator*
King, Frederick Alexander *neuroscientist, educator*
Klein, Luella Voogd *obstetrics-gynecology educator*
Lemen, Richard Alan *epidemiologist, medical administrator*
Letton, Alva Hamblin *surgeon, educator*
Lipman, Bernard *internist, cardiologist*
Lubin, Michael Frederick *physician, educator*
Lybarger, Jeffrey Allen *epidemiology research administrator*
Margolis, Harold Stephen *epidemiologist*
McDuffie, Frederic Clement *physician*
Murphy, Gerald Patrick *urologist, educator*
Nahmias, André Joseph *physician, educator, scientist*
Nemeroff, Charles Barnet *neurobiology and psychiatry educator*
O'Brien, Mark Stephen *pediatric neurosurgeon*
O'Shea, Patricia A. *physician, educator*
Owings, Francis Barre *surgeon*
†Parks, John Scott *pediatric endocrinologist*
Peacock, Lamar Batts *retired physician*
Perdue, Garland Day *surgeon, educator, hospital director*
Reed, James Whitfield *physician, educator*
Rock, John Aubrey *gynecologist and obstetrician, educator*
Seffrin, John Reese *medical society executive*
Sexson, Sandra Griffin Bishop *child psychiatrist, educator*
Sherman, Roger Talbot *surgeon, educator*
Smith, Robert Boulware, III *vascular surgeon, educator*
Steinhaus, John Edward *physician, medical educator*
†Thomas, Kenneth Eastman *cardiothoracic surgeon*
Tindall, George Taylor *neurosurgeon, educator*
Turner, John Sidney, Jr. *otolaryngologist, educator*
Tyler, Carl Walter, Jr. *physician, health research administrator*
Waller, John Louis *anesthesiology educator*
Ward, Richard Storer *child psychiatrist, educator emeritus*
White, Perry Merrill, Jr. *orthopedic surgeon*
Woodard, John Roger *urologist*
Yeargin-Allsopp, Marshalyn *epidemiologist, pediatrician*
Zumpe, Doris *psychiatry researcher, educator*

Augusta
Chandler, Arthur Bleakley *pathologist, educator*
Colborn, Gene Louis *anatomy educator, researcher*
Cundey, Paul Edward, Jr. *cardiologist*
Gambrell, Richard Donald, Jr. *endocrinologist, educator*
Given, Kenna Sidney *surgeon, educator*
Luxenberg, Malcolm Neuwahl *ophthalmologist, educator*
Mahesh, Virendra Bhushan *endocrinologist*
Mansberger, Arlie Roland, Jr. *surgeon*
Parrish, Robert Alton *retired pediatric surgeon, educator*
Pryor, Carol Graham *obstetrician-gynecologist*
Puchtler, Holde *histochemist, pathologist, educator*
Rasmussen, Howard *medical educator, medical institute executive*
Ryan, James Walter *physician, medical researcher*
Solursh, Lionel Paul *psychiatrist*

Dahlonega
Allen, Delmas James *anatomist, educator, university administrator*

Dalton
Clark, Winston Craig *neurosurgeon*

Decatur
Bain, James Arthur *pharmacologist, educator*
Hill, Thomas Glenn, III *dermatologist*
Martinez-Maldonado, Manuel *medical service administrator, physician*
Whitesides, Thomas Edward, Jr. *orthopaedic surgeon*

Evans
Hartlage, Lawrence Clifton *neuropsychologist, educator*

Fort Gordon
†Duffy, Walter James *psychiatrist*
Xenakis, Stephen Nicholas *psychiatrist, army officer*

Griffin
Gillaspie, Athey Graves, Jr. *pathologist, researcher*

Hinesville
Gennrich, Robert Paul, II *radiologic technologist*

La Grange
Copeland, Robert Bodine *internist, cardiologist*
West, John Thomas *surgeon*

Lawrenceville
Fetner, Robert Henry *radiation biologist*

Macon
Swartwout, Joseph Rodolph *obstetrics and gynecology educator, university administrator*

Milledgeville
Evans, Frank Owen, Jr. *physician*

Norcross
Nardelli-Olkowska, Krystyna Maria *ophthalmologist, educator*

Quitman
Baum, Joseph Herman *retired biomedical educator*

Savannah
Horan, Leo Gallaspy *physician, educator*
Krahl, Enzo *retired surgeon*
†Wirth, Fremont Philip *neurosurgeon, educator*

Stone Mountain
Gotlieb, Jaquelin Smith *pediatrician*
Rogers, James Virgil, Jr. *retired radiologist and educator*

Thomasville
†Watt, William Vance *surgeon*

Valdosta
Beal, John M. *surgeon, medical educator*

Warner Robins
Charkatz, Harry Marvin *psychiatrist*

HAWAII

Hilo
Taniguchi, Tokuso *surgeon*

Honolulu
Chee, Percival Hon Yin *ophthalmologist*
Fong, Bernard W. D. *physician, educator*
Ho, Reginald Chi Shing *medical educator*
Kolonel, Laurence Norman *epidemiologist, public health educator*
†Lau, H. Lorrin *physician, inventor*
Linman, James William *retired physician, educator*
Marvit, Robert Charles *psychiatrist*
Mc Dermott, John Francis, Jr. *psychiatrist, physician*
Meagher, Michael *radiologist*
Pang, Herbert George *ophthalmologist*
Person, Donald Ames, Sr. *pediatrician, rheumatologist*
†Pien, Francis D. *internist, microbiologist*
Schatz, Irwin Jacob *cardiologist*
Sharma, Santosh Devraj *obstetrician and gynecologist, educator*
Shibata, Shoji *pharmacology educator, researcher*
†Smith, Thomas Kent *radiologist*

Mililani
Gardner, Sheryl Paige *obstetrician/gynecologist*

Waikoloa
Copman, Louis *radiologist*

IDAHO

Boise
Daniels, Christopher Kent *pharmacologist, researcher*
Nyborg, Lester Phil *physician*
Olson, Richard Dean *researcher, pharmacology educator*
Schwartz, Theodore B. *physician, educator*

Emmett
Holverson, Harmon Elmer *family practice physician*

Lewiston
Chinchinian, Harry *pathologist, educator*

Nampa
Botimer, Allen Ray *retired surgeon, retirement center owner*

Pocatello
Hillyard, Ira William *pharmacologist, educator*

Twin Falls
†Katz, Edward Lyle *neurosurgeon*

ILLINOIS

Abbott Park
Sasahara, Arthur Asao *cardiologist, educator, researcher*

Arlington Heights
Pochyly, Donald Frederick *physician, hospital administrator*
Shetty, Mulki Radhakrishna *oncologist, consultant*

Aurora
Ball, William James *pediatrician*

Belleville
Cagas, Cosme Ralota *pediatrician, endocrinologist*

Carol Stream
Schmerold, Wilfried Lothar *dermatologist*

Chicago
Abcarian, Herand *surgeon, educator*
Adams, John Richard *psychiatrist, educator*
Albrecht, Ronald Frank *anesthesiologist*
Andersen, Burton Robert *physician, educator*
†Andersen, Dana Kimball *surgeon, educator*
Applebaum, Edward Leon *otolaryngologist, educator*
Arnason, Barry Gilbert Wyatt *neurologist, educator*
Arnsdorf, Morton Frank *cardiologist, educator*
Baffes, Thomas Gus *cardiac surgeon, lawyer*
Bailey, Orville Taylor *neuropathologist*
Barker, Walter Lee *thoracic surgeon*
Barton, Evan Mansfield *physician*
Batlle, Daniel *nephrologist*
Beatty, William Kaye *medical bibliography educator*
Beaty, Harry Nelson *internist, educator, university dean*
Beck, Robert N. *nuclear medicine educator*
†Becker, Michael A. *physician, educator*
Beigl, William *physician, naturopath, hypnotist, acupuncturist, consultant*
Berry, Leonidas Harris *gastroenterologist, internist*
Betts, Henry Brognard *physician, health facility administrator, educator*
Boggs, Joseph Dodridge *pediatric pathologist, educator*
Boshes, Louis D. *physician, scientist, educator*
Bowman, James Edward *physician, educator*
†Brasitus, Thomas Albert *gastroenterologist, educator*
Bresnahan, James Francis *medical ethics educator*
Brewer, John Isaac *obstetrician, gynecologist*
Brown, Rowine Hayes *physician, former medical administrator*
Brueschke, Erich Edward *physician, researcher, educator*
Calenoff, Leonid *radiologist*
Carnow, Bertram Warren *occupational and environmental health consultant*
Caro, William Allan *physician*
Carone, Frank *medical educator, pathologist*
Casper, Regina Claire *physician, researcher*
Charles, Allan G. *physician, educator*
Chatterton, Robert Treat, Jr. *reproductive endocrinology educator*
Clark, John Whitcomb *diagnostic radiologist*
Coe, Fredric L. *physician, educator, researcher*
Cohen, Melvin R. *physician, educator*
Conway, James Joseph *physician*
Coopersmith, Bernard Ira *obstetrician/gynecologist, educator*
Cotsonas, Nicholas John, Jr. *physician, medical educator*
†Daum, Robert Steven *pediatrics educator*
Davies, Peter Francis *pathology educator, medical educator*
Davison, Richard *physician, educator*
De Costa, Edwin J. *physician, surgeon*
Degroot, Leslie Jacob *medical educator*
del Greco, Francesco *physician, educator*
Derlacki, Eugene L(ubin) *otolaryngologist, physician*
Diamond, Seymour *physician*
Dunea, George *nephrologist, educator*
Dyrud, Jarl Edvard *psychiatrist*
Ebert, Paul Allen *surgeon, educator*
Eisenman, Trudy Fox *dermatologist*
Erdos, Ervin George *pharmacology and biochemistry educator*
Evans, Thelma Jean Mathis *internist*
Fennessy, John James *radiologist, educator*
Ferguson, Donald John *surgeon, educator*
Fierer, Joshua Allan *pathology educator*
Fitch, Frank Wesley *pathologist, immunologist, educator, administrator*
Flaherty, Emalee Gottbrath *pediatrician*
Frederiksen, Marilynn Elizabeth Conners *physician*
Freedman, Philip *physician, educator*
Fried, Walter *hematologist, educator*
Frohman, Lawrence Asher *endocrinology educator, scientist*
Gartner, Lawrence Mitchel *pediatrician, medical college educator*
Gecht, Martin Louis *physician, bank executive*
Gerbie, Albert Bernard *obstetrician, gynecologist, educator*
Gewertz, Bruce Labe *surgeon, educator*
Giovacchini, Peter Louis *psychoanalyst*
Gladstone, Lee *psychiatrist, addictionist*
Golomb, Harvey Morris *oncologist, educator*
†Gould, Samuel Halpert *pediatrics educator*
Graettinger, John Sells *physician, educator*
Grayhack, John Thomas *urologist, educator*
†Griffin, Andrew Joseph *pediatrician*
Griffith, B(ezaleel) Herold *physician, educator, plastic surgeon*
Grimes, Hugh Gavin *physician*
Haber, Meryl Harold *physician, educator, author*
Hambrick, Ernestine *colon and rectal surgeon*
Hand, Roger *physician, educator*
Haring, Olga Munk *medical educator, physician*
Harris, Jules Eli *medical educator, physician, clinical scientist, administrator*
Hart, Cecil William Joseph *otolaryngologist, head and neck surgeon*
Hast, Malcolm Howard *medical educator, scientist*
Havdala, Henri Salomon *anesthesiologist, educator, consultant*
Heller, Paul *medical educator*
Hellman, Samuel *radiologist, physician, educator*
Herbolsheimer, Henrietta *physician, consultant*
Herbst, Arthur Lee *obstetrician-gynecologist*
Hines, James Rodger *surgeon*
Hinojosa, Raul *physician, ear pathology researcher*
Honig, George Raymond *pediatrician*
Horwitz, Irwin Daniel *otolaryngologist, educator*
Huckman, Michael Saul *neuroradiologist, educator*
Huggins, Charles Brenton *surgical educator*
Hughes, John Russell *physician, educator*
Hunter, James Alexander *surgeon, educator*
†Huttenlocher, Peter Richard *child neurologist*
Jonasson, Olga *surgeon, educator*
Jordan, V. Craig *endocrine pharmacologist, educator*
Kark, Robert M. *physician, educator*
Karp, Robert *surgeon, educator*
Katz, Adrian Izhack *physician, educator*
Katz, Robert Stephen *rheumatologist, educator*
Kent, Geoffrey *pathology educator, physician*
Kirschner, Barbara Starrels *pediatric gastroenterologist*
Kirsner, Joseph Barnett *physician, educator*
Kittle, Charles Frederick *surgeon*
Koehler, Irmgard Kilb *dermatologist, educator*
Kohrman, Arthur Fisher *pediatric educator*
Kornel, Ludwig *medical educator, physician, scientist*
Kraft, Sumner Charles *physician, educator*
Landau, Richard L. *physician, educator*
Landsberg, Lewis *endocrinologist, medical researcher*
Langsley, Donald Gene *psychiatrist, medical board executive*
LaVelle, Arthur *anatomy educator*
†Lee, Raphael Carl *plastic surgeon*
Leff, Alan Richard *medical educator*
†Leventhal, Bennett Lee *psychiatry and pediatrics educator, administrator*
Lichter, Edward Arthur *physician, educator*
Lin, Chin-Chu *physician, educator, researcher*
Lorincz, Allan Levente *physician, educator*
Lumpkin, John Robert *public health physician, state official*
Marcus, Joseph *child psychiatrist*
Metz, Charles Edgar *radiology educator*
Meyer, Paul Reims, Jr. *orthopedic surgeon*
†Miller, Sheldon Irvin *psychiatrist, educator*
Millichap, Joseph Gordon *neurologist, educator*
Mirkin, Bernard Leo *clinical pharmacologist, pediatrician*
Moawad, Atef *obstetrician-gynecologist, educator*
Morris, Ralph William *chronopharmacologist*
Mullan, John Francis (Sean Mullan) *neurosurgeon, educator*
Musa, Mahmoud Nimir *psychiatry educator*
Nahrwold, David Lange *surgeon, educator*
Narahashi, Toshio *pharmacology educator*
Newell, Frank William *ophthalmologist, educator*
Nyhus, Lloyd Milton *surgeon, educator*
Offer, Daniel *psychiatrist*
Oryshkevich, Roman Sviatoslav *physician, physiatrist, dentist, educator*
Osiyoye, Adekunle *obstetrician/gynecologist, educator*
Pachman, Daniel J. *physician, educator*
Page, Ernest *medical educator*
†Page, John Arthur *professional association executive, educator*
Pappas, George Demetrios *anatomy and cell biology educator, scientist*
Perlman, Robert L. *pediatrics, pharmacology, and physiology educator*
Polley, Edward Herman *anatomist, educator*
Pollock, George Howard *psychiatrist, psychoanalyst*
Pomerantz, Rhoda Silverstein *geriatrician, internist, health center executive*
Pope, Richard M. *rheumatologist*
Poznanski, Andrew Karol *pediatric radiologist*
Ramsey-Goldman, Rosalind *physician*
Rhone, Douglas Pierce *pathologist, educator*
†Robinson, June Kerswell *dermatologist, educator*
Rosen, Steven Terry *oncologist, hematologist*
Rosenfield, Robert Lee *pediatric endocrinologist, educator*
Rosenthal, Ira Maurice *pediatrician, educator*
Roth, Sanford Irwin *pathologist, educator*
Rotman, Carlotta J. H. *physician*
Rowley, Janet Davison *physician*
Rubenstein, Arthur Harold *physician, educator*
Rudy, Lester Howard *psychiatrist*
†Sandlow, Leslie J. *physician, educator*
Scarse, Olivia Marie *cardiologist, consultant*
Schafer, Michael Frederick *orthopedic surgeon*
Schild, Joyce Anna *otolaryngologist, surgeon*
Schilsky, Richard Lewis *oncologist, researcher*
†Schoenberg, Harry W. *urologic surgeon*
Schulman, Sidney *neurologist, educator*
Schumer, William *surgeon, educator*
Senturia, Yvonne Dreyfus *pediatrician, epidemiologist*
Shambaugh, George Elmer, III *internist*
Shields, Thomas William *surgeon, educator*
Siegler, Mark *internist, educator*
Singh, Manmohan *orthopedic surgeon, educator*
†Skom, Joseph Harry *medical educator*
Smith, David Waldo Edward *pathology educator, physician*
Sorensen, Leif Boge *physician, educator*
Sparberg, Marshall Stuart *gastroenterologist, educator*
Speigel, I. Joshua *neurosurgery educator*
Sternberg, Paul *retired ophthalmologist*
Storb, Ursula Beate *molecular genetics and cell biology educator*
Strauch, Gerald Otto *surgeon*
Swerdlow, Martin Abraham *physician, pathologist*
Tardy, Medney Eugene, Jr. *otolaryngologist*
Taswell, Howard Filmore *pathologist, blood bank specialist, educator*
Tatooles, Constantine John *cardiovascular and thoracic surgeon*
Todd, James S. *surgeon, educator, medical association administrator*
Todd, James Stiles *surgeon, professional executive association*
Tulsky, Alex Sol *physician*
Ultmann, John Ernest *physician, educator*
Vanecko, Robert Michael *surgeon, educator*
Waldstein, Sheldon Saul *physician, educator*
Waxler, Beverly Jean *anesthesiologist, physician*
Webster, James Randolph, Jr. *physician*
†Weichselbaum, Ralph R. *oncologist chairman*
†Weir, Bryce K. A. *neurosurgeon, neurology educator*
†Whitington, Peter Frank *pediatrics educator, pediatric hepatologist*
Wied, George Ludwig *physician*
Willoughby, William Franklin, II *physician, researcher*
Winnie, Alon Palm *anesthesiologist, educator*
Wolpert, Edward Alan *psychiatrist*
Yarkony, Gary Michael *physician, researcher*
Zatuchni, Gerald Irving *physician, educator*

Danville
Prabhudesai, Mukund M. *pathology educator, laboratory director, researcher, administrator*

Decatur
Requarth, William Henry *surgeon*

Deerfield
Scheiber, Stephen Carl *psychiatrist*

Des Plaines
Sisson, George Allen, Sr. *physician, educator*

Downers Grove
Colbert, Marvin Jay *retired internist, educator*
Fruin, Robert Cornelius *physician, hospital administrator*

Elmhurst
Blain, Charlotte Marie *physician, educator*
Fornatto, Elio Joseph *otolaryngologist, educator*

Evanston
Bashook, Philip G. *medical association executive, educator*
Crawford, James Weldon *psychiatrist, educator, administrator*
Dockery, J. Lee *medical school administrator*
Enroth-Cugell, Christina Alma Elisabeth *neurophysiologist, educator*
Huff, Stanley Eugene *dermatologist*
Hughes, Edward Francis Xavier *physician, educator*
Khandekar, Janardan Dinkar *oncologist, educator*
Mc Nerney, Walter James *health policy educator, consultant*
Plaut, Eric Alfred *psychiatrist, educator*
†Quigley, Robert Lawrence *cardiothoracic surgeon, educator*
Samter, Max *physician, educator*
Schwartz, Neena Betty *endocrinologist, educator*
Sprang, Milton LeRoy *obstetrician, gynecologist, educator*
†Takahashi, Joseph S. *neuroscientist*
Traisman, Howard Sevin *pediatrician*

Flossmoor
Lis, Edward Francis *pediatrician, consultant*

Galesburg
Tourlentes, Thomas Theodore *psychiatrist*

Glen Ellyn
Dieter, Raymond Andrew, Jr. *physician, surgeon*
Egan, Richard Leo *medical association administrator, medical educator*
Temple, Donald *allergist, dermatologist*

Glencoe
Fenninger, Leonard Davis *medical educator, consultant*

Glenview
Ampel, Leon Louis *anesthesiologist*
Hafner, Arthur Wayne *author, information scientist, medical librarian*

Gurnee
†Funk, Carla Jean *medical librarian*

Harvey
Jensen, Harold Leroy *physician*

Hickory Hills
Johnson, (Mary) Anita *physician, medical service administrator*

Highland Park
Bluefarb, Samuel Mitchell *physician*
Hirsch, Jay G. *psychiatrist, educator*

Hines
Green, Joseph Barnet *neurologist, educator*
Mason, George Robert *surgeon, educator*
Zvetina, James Raymond *pulmonary physician*

Hinsdale
Birnholz, Jason Cordell *radiologist, consultant, educator*
Paloyan, Edward *physician, educator, reseacher*

Homewood
Schumacher, Gebhard Friederich Bernhard *obstetrician-gynecologist*

Joliet
Ring, Alvin Manuel *pathologist*

Lake Bluff
Kelly, Daniel John *physician*

Lake Forest
Levy, Nelson Louis *physician, scientist, corporate executive*
Murad, Ferid *physician*
Salter, Edwin Carroll *physician*
Vuckovich, Dragomir Michael *neurologist, educator*
Wilbur, Richard Sloan *physician, foundation executive*

Lincolnshire
Hughes, William Franklin, Jr. *ophthalmologist, emeritus educator*

Long Grove
Ausman, Robert K. *surgeon, research executive*

Macomb
Dexter, Donald Harvey *surgeon*

Maywood
Canning, John Rafton *urologist*
Celesia, Gastone Guglielmo *neurologist, neurophysiologist, researcher*
Freeark, Robert James *surgeon, educator*
Gamelli, Richard Louis *surgeon, educator*
Greenlee, Herbert Breckenridge *surgeon, educator*
Hanin, Israel *pharmacologist, educator*
†Radke, Jan Rodger *pulmonologist, hospital program administrator*
Slogoff, Stephen *anesthesiologist, educator*
†Winship, Daniel Holcomb *medicine educator, university dean*

Moline
Arnell, Richard Anthony *radiologist*

Mount Prospect
Cucco, Ulisse P. *obstetrician, gynecologist*

Naperville
Schwab, Paul Josiah *psychiatrist educator*

Niles
Chertack, Melvin M. *internist*

North Chicago
Beer, Alan Earl *physician, medical educator*
Ehrenpreis, Seymour *pharmacology educator*
Freese, Uwe Ernest *physician, educator*
Gall, Eric Papineau *physician educator*
Hawkins, Richard Albert *medical educator, administrator*
Kim, Yoon Berm *immunologist, educator*
Morris, Charles Elliot *neurologist*
Nair, Velayudhan *pharmacologist, medical educator*
Rogers, Eugene Jack *medical educator*
Rudy, David Robert *physician, educator*
Schneider, Arthur Sanford *physician, educator*
Sierles, Frederick Stephen *psychiatrist, educator*
Sladek, Celia Davis *neuroscientist, educator*
Taylor, Michael Alan *psychiatrist*

Northbrook
Day, Emerson *physician*
Hirsch, Lawrence Leonard *physician, retired educator*
Mc Laren, John Alexander *retired physician*
Rodriguez-Erdmann, Franz *physician*
Scanlon, Edward F. *surgeon, educator*

Northfield
Cutler, Robert Porter *psychiatrist, psychoanalyst*
Giffin, Mary Elizabeth *psychiatrist, educator*

Oak Brook Mall
Christian, Joseph Ralph *physician*
O'Leary, Dennis Sophian *medical organization executive*

Oak Lawn
Rathi, Manohar Lal *pediatrician, neonatologist*

Oak Park
Brackett, Edward Boone, III *orthopedic surgeon*
Schultz, Bryan Christopher *dermatologist, educator*
Valinsky, Mark Steven *podiatrist*

Olney
Edwards, Ian Keith *obstetrician, gynecologist*

Park Ridge
Schultz, Richard Carlton *plastic surgeon*
Weinberg, Milton, Jr. *cardiovascular-thoracic surgeon*

Peoria
Meriden, Terry *physician*

Princeville
Erickson, Marianna Cuany *family physician*

Prospect Heights
Hindo, Walid Afram *radiology educator, researcher*

River Grove
Hillert, Gloria Bonnin *anatomist, educator*

Rock Island
Forlini, Frank John, Jr. *cardiologist*

Rockford
Heerens, Robert Edward *physician*
Olson, Stanley William *physician, educator, medical school dean*
Pritikin, Roland I. *opthalmologic surgeon, writer, lecturer*

Round Lake
Kingdon, Henry Shannon *physician, biochemist, educator, executive*

Saint Charles
McCartney, Charles Price *retired obstetrician-gynecologist*

Schiller Park
Ring, Alice Ruth Bishop *physician*

Skokie
Bellows, Randall Trueblood *ophthalmologist, educator*
Boxer, Robert William *allergist*
Goldmann, Morton Aaron *cardiologist*
Olwin, John Hurst *surgeon*

Springfield
Dodd, Robert Bruce *physician, educator*
Frank, Stuart *cardiologist*
Holland, John Madison *family practice physician*
Myers, Phillip Ward *otolaryngologist*
Rabinovich, Sergio *physician, educator*
†Rockey, Paul Henry *physician, medical educator, university official*
Zook, Elvin Glenn *plastic surgeon, educator*

Urbana
Greenwold, Warren Eldon *retired physician, medical educator*
Nelson, Ralph Alfred *physician*
O'Morchoe, Charles Christopher Creagh *administrator, anatomical sciences educator*
O'Morchoe, Patricia Jean *pathologist, educator*
Voss, Edward William, Jr. *immunologist, educator*

Villa Park
Becker, Robert Jerome *allergist, health care consultant*

Wheaton
Bogdonoff, Maurice Lambert *physician*
Haenszel, William Manning *epidemiologist, educator*
Maibenco, Helen Craig *anatomist, educator*

Winnetka
Carrow, Leon Albert *physician*
dePeyster, Frederic Augustus *surgeon*
Earle, David Prince, Jr. *physician, educator*
Jones, Philip Newton *physician, medical educator*

INDIANA

Anderson
King, Charles Ross *physician*

Bloomington
Bishop, Michael D. *emergency physician*
Moore, Ward Wilfred *medical educator*
Rebec, George Vincent *neuroscience researcher, educator, administrator*
Rink, Lawrence Donald *cardiologist*

Chesterton
Martino, Robert Salvatore *orthopedic surgeon*

Evansville
Anderson, Milton Henry *psychiatrist*
Faw, Melvin Lee *retired physician*
Penkava, Robert Ray *radiologist, educator*

Fort Wayne
Donesa, Antonio Braganza *neurosurgeon*
Lee, Shuishih Sage *pathologist*
Richardson, Joseph Hill *physician, medical educator*

Hammond
Steen, Lowell Harrison *physician*

Huntington
Doermann, Paul Edmund *retired surgeon*

Indianapolis
Allen, Stephen D(ean) *pathologist, microbiologist*
Besch, Henry Roland, Jr. *pharmacologist, educator*
Brady, Mary Sue *pediatric dietitian, educator*
Brandt, Ira Kive *pediatrician, medical geneticist*
Brickley, Richard Agar *retired surgeon*
Brown, Edwin Wilson, Jr. *physician, educator*
Broxmeyer, Hal Edward *medical educator*
Campbell, Judith Lowe *child psychiatrist*
Chernish, Stanley Michael *physician*
Cohen, Marlene Lois *pharmacologist*
Daly, Walter Joseph *physician, educator*
†De Rosa, Guy Paul *orthopedic surgery educator*
Eigen, Howard *pediatrician, educator*
Einhorn, Lawrence Henry *medical educator*
Faulk, Ward Page *immunologist*
Feigenbaum, Harvey *cardiologist, educator*
Fisch, Charles *physician*
Gabovitch, Edward Robert *internist*
Geisler, Hans Emanuel *gynecologic oncologist*
Ghetti, Bernardino Francesco *neuropathologist, neurobiology researcher*
Green, Morris *physician, educator*
Greist, Mary Coffey *dermatologist*
Grosfeld, Jay Lazar *pediatric surgeon, educator*
Hamburger, Richard James *physician, educator*
Helveston, Eugene McGillis *pediatric ophthalmologist, educator*
Hubbard, Jesse Donald *pathology educator*
Irwin, Glenn Ward, Jr. *medical educator, physician, university official*
Jackson, Valerie Pascuzzi *radiologist, educator*
Joyner, John Erwin *medical educator, neurological surgeon*
†Klug, Michael Gregory *physician*
Knoebel, Suzanne Buckner *cardiologist, medical educator*
Lemberger, Louis *pharmacologist, physician*
Lindseth, Richard Emil *orthopedic surgeon*
Manders, Karl Lee *neurosurgeon*
Merritt, Doris Honig *pediatrics educator*
Miyamoto, Richard Takashi *otolaryngologist*
Myers, Woodrow Augustus, Jr. *physician, corporate medical director*
Norins, Arthur Leonard *physician, educator*
Pless, John Edward *forensic pathologist, educator*
Richter, Judith Anne *pharmacology educator*
Rogers, Robert Ernest *medical educator*
Ross, Edward *cardiologist*
Roth, Lawrence Max *pathologist, educator*
†Sherman, Stuart *physician*
Small, Joyce Graham *psychiatrist, educator*
Stoelting, Robert K. *anesthesiologist, medical association executive*
Watanabe, August Masaru *physician, scientist, medical educator, corporate executive*
Weber, George *oncology and pharmacology researcher, educator*
Weinberger, Myron Hilmar *medical educator*
Wellman, Henry Nelson *nuclear medicine specialist*
White, Arthur Clinton *physician*
†Wilson, Fred M., II *ophthalmologist, educator*
Zipes, Douglas Peter *cardiologist, researcher*

Lafayette
Gordon, Irene Marlow *radiology educator*
Maickel, Roger Philip *pharmacologist, educator*

Marion
Fisher, Pierre James, Jr. *physician*

Monrovia
Bennett, James Edward *retired plastic surgeon, educator*

Nappanee
Borger, Michael Hinton Ivers *osteopathic physician, educator*

Terre Haute
Kunkler, Arnold William *surgeon*

Walton
Chu, Johnson Chin Sheng *physician*

Warsaw
†McCaffrey, R. Michael *orthopedic company executive*

West Lafayette
Borowitz, Joseph Leo *pharmacologist*
Byrn, Stephen R. *medical educator*
Hem, Stanley Lawrence *pharmacy educator, researcher*
Kessler, Wayne Vincent *health sciences educator, researcher, consultant*
O'Connor, Ruth Susan *physician, educator*
Robinson, Farrel Richard *pathologist, toxicologist*
Rutledge, Charles Ozwin *pharmacologist, educator*
Shaw, Stanley Miner *nuclear pharmacy scientist*

IOWA

Bettendorf
Edgerton, Winfield Dow *gynecologist*

Cedar Rapids
Norris, Albert Stanley *psychiatrist, educator*

Davenport
Rohlf, Paul Leon *urologist*

Des Moines
de Gravelles, William Decatur, Jr. *physician*
Elmets, Harry Barnard *osteopath, dermatologist*
Glomset, Daniel Anders *physician*
Neis, Arthur Veral *healthcare and development company executive*
Thoman, Mark Edward *pediatrician*

Dubuque
Herzberger, Eugene E. *retired neurosurgeon*

Iowa City
Abboud, Francois Mitry *physician, educator*
Afifi, Adel Kassim *physician*
Andreasen, Nancy Coover *psychiatrist, educator*
Bar, Robert S. *endocrinologist*
Baron, Jeffrey *pharmacologist, educator*
Bedell, George Noble *physician, educator*
Bergman, Ronald Arly *anatomist, educator*
Bonfiglio, Michael *surgeon, educator*
†Buckwalter, Joseph Addison *orthopaedic surgeon, educator*
Burns, C(harles) Patrick *hematologist-oncologist*
Clifton, James Albert *physician*
Cooper, Reginald Rudyard *orthopedic surgeon, educator*
Damasio, Antonio R. *physician, neurologist*
Eckhardt, Richard Dale *physician, educator*
Eckstein, John William *physician, educator*
Ehrenhaft, Johann Leo *surgeon*
Fellows, Robert Ellis *medical educator, medical scientist*
Filer, Lloyd Jackson, Jr. *pediatric educator, clinical investigator*
Fitz, Annette Elaine *physician, educator*
Franken, Edmund Anthony, Jr. *radiologist, educator*
Galask, Rudolph Peter *obstetrician-gynecologist*
†Galbraith, William Bruce *physician, educator*
Gantz, Bruce Jay *otolaryngologist, educator*
Gergis, Samir Danial *anesthesiologist, educator*
Hammond, Harold Logan *pathology educator, oral pathologist*
Hoffmann, Louis Gerhard *immunologist, educator, sex therapist*
January, Lewis Edward *physician, educator*
Kelch, Robert Paul *pediatric endocrinologist*
Kirchner, Peter Thomas *physician nuclear medicine, educator, consultant*
Long, John Paul *pharmacologist, educator*
Mason, Edward Eaton *surgeon*
Morriss, Frank Howard, Jr. *pediatrics educator*
Nelson, Herbert Leroy *psychiatrist*
Ponseti, Ignacio Vives *orthopaedic surgery educator*
Richerson, Hal Bates *physician, internist, allergist, immunologist, educator*
Strauss, John Steinert *dermatologist, educator*
Tephly, Thomas Robert *pharmacologist, toxicologist, educator*
Thompson, Herbert Stanley *neuro-ophthalmologist*
Van Gilder, John Corley *neurosurgeon, educator*
Weinberger, Miles M. *physician, pediatric educator*
Weingeist, Thomas Alan *ophthalmology educator*
Williams, Richard Dwayne *physician, educator*
Winokur, George *psychiatrist, educator*
Ziegler, Ekhard Erich *pediatrics educator*

Sioux City
Spellman, George Geneser, Sr. *internist*

West Des Moines
Alberts, Marion Edward *physician*

KANSAS

Great Bend
Jones, Edward *physician, pathologist*

Kansas City
Anderson, Harrison Clarke *pathology educator, biomedical researcher*
Arakawa, Kasumi *physician, educator*
Cho, Cheng Tsung *pediatrician, educator*
Dunn, Marvin Irvin *physician*
Godfrey, Robert Gordon *physician*
Goodwin, Donald William *psychiatrist, educator*
Grantham, Jared James *nephrologist, educator*
Greenberger, Norton Jerald *physician*
Hollander, Daniel *gastroenterologist, medical educator*
Hudson, Robert Paul *medical educator*
Krantz, Kermit Edward *physician, educator*
Mathews, Paul Joseph *allied health educator*
Mathewson, Hugh Spalding *anesthesiologist, educator*
Mohn, Melvin Paul *anatomist, educator*
Moore, Wayne V. *pediatrician, educator, endocrinologist*
Morrison, David Campbell *immunology educator*
Robinson, David Weaver *surgeon, educator*
Samson, Frederick Eugene, Jr. *neuroscientist, educator*
Schloerb, Paul Richard *surgeon, educator*
Walaszek, Edward Joseph *pharmacology educator*
Waxman, David *physician, university consultant*
Ziegler, Dewey Kiper *neurologist*

Kingman
Burket, George Edward, Jr. *family physician*

Lawrence
Miller, Don Robert *surgeon*
Ross, Jack Lewis *psychiatrist*

Leavenworth
Mengel, Charles Edmund *physician, medical educator*

Manhattan
Durkee, William Robert *retired physician*
Oehme, Frederick Wolfgang *medical researcher and educator*

Mission
Thomas, Christopher Yancey, III *surgeon, educator*

Shawnee Mission
Bell, Deloris Wiley *physician*
Dockhorn, Robert John *physician*
Fairchild, Robert Charles *pediatrician*
Nauer, Paula Lou *physician*
Price, James Gordon *physician*
Wenner, Herbert Allan *pediatrician*

Topeka
Conroy, Robert Warren *psychiatrist*
Gabbard, Glen Owens *psychiatrist, psychoanalyst*
Harper, Patricia Nelsen *psychiatrist*
Menninger, William Walter *psychiatrist*
Simpson, William Stewart *retired psychiatrist, sex therapist*
Swogger, Glenn, Jr. *psychiatrist*
Ware, Lucile Mahieu *child psychiatrist, educator, researcher*

Wichita
Dyck, George *psychiatry educator*
Guthrie, Richard Alan *physician*
Manning, Robert Thomas *physician, educator*
North, Doris Griffin *physician, educator*
†Oxley, Dwight K(ahala) *pathologist*
Reals, William Joseph *pathologist, academic administrator, educator*

Winfield
Miller, Franklin Rush *retired internist, educator*

KENTUCKY

Berea
Lamb, Irene Hendricks *medical researcher*

Bowling Green
Dewhurst, William Harvey *psychiatrist*
Tapp, John Cecil *physician, educator, futures trader*

Hopkinsville
Freer, John Herschel *psychiatrist*

Lexington
Avant, Robert Frank *physician, educator*
Baumann, Robert Jay *child neurology educator*
Clawson, David Kay *orthopedic surgeon*
David, Miriam Lang *physician*
Diedrich, Donald Frank *pharmacology educator*
Friedell, Gilbert Hugo *pathologist, hospital administrator, educator, cancer center director*
Gilliam, M(elvin) Randolph *urologist, educator*
Glenn, James Francis *urologist, educator*
Griffen, Ward O., Jr. *surgeon, educator, medical board executive*
Hagen, Michael Dale *medical educator, family practice researcher*
Hamburg, Joseph *physician, educator*
Holsinger, James Wilson, Jr. *physician*
Markesbery, William R. *neurology and pathology educator, physician*
Noonan, Jacqueline Anne *pediatrics educator*
Parks, Harold Francis *anatomist, educator*
Vittetoe, Marie Clare *retired medical technology educator*
Vore, Mary Edith *pharmacology educator, researcher*
Young, Paul Ray *medical board executive, physician*

Louisville
Adams, Christine Beate Lieber *psychiatrist, educator*
Andrews, Billy Franklin *pediatrician, educator*
Aronoff, George Rodger *medicine and pharmacology educator*
Callen, Jeffrey Phillip *dermatologist, educator*
Danzl, Daniel Frank *emergency physician*
DeVries, William Castle *surgeon, educator*
Garretson, Henry David *neurosurgeon*
Haynes, Douglas Martin *physician, educator*
Huang, Kee Chang *pharmacology educator, physician*
Keeney, Arthur Hail *physician, educator*
Kleinert, Harold Earl *plastic surgery educator*
Lansing, Allan Meredith *cardiovascular surgeon, educator*
Neustadt, David Harold *physician*
Polk, Hiram Carey, Jr. *surgeon, educator*
Schwab, John Joseph *psychiatrist, educator*
Scott, Ralph Mason *physician, radiaiton oncology educator*
†Tanguay, Peter Eugene *child and adolescent psychiatry educator*
Tsai, Tsu-Min *surgeon*
Uhde, George Irvin *physician*
Waddell, William Joseph *pharmacologist, toxicologist*
Weisskopf, Bernard *pediatrician, child behavior, development and genetics specialist, educator*
Zimmerman, Thom Jay *ophthalmologist, educator*

Owensboro
Neal, Wilmer Lewis *clinical neurophysiologist*

Somerset
Jasper, Patrick Lee *pediatrician, medical association executive*

LOUISIANA

Baton Rouge
Bray, George August *physician, scientist, educator*
Cherry, William Ashley *surgeon, state health officer*
Hill, Ralph Kelly *physician*
Krotoski, Wojciech Antoni *research physician, educator*
Le Vine, Jerome Edward *retired ophthalmologist, educator*
Lucas, Fred Vance *pathology educator, university administrator*

Benton
Dunnihoo, Dale Russell *physician, medical educator*

Covington
Roberts, James Allen *urologist*

Gretna
Lupin, Ellis Ralph *physician, lawyer, coroner*

Hammond
Hejtmancik, Milton Rudolph *medical educator*

Lake Charles
Drez, David Jacob, Jr. *orthopaedic surgeon, educator*

Metairie
Bower, Philip Jeffrey *cardiologist, administrator*
Carter, Rebecca Davilene *general surgeon, surgical oncology educator*
Spruiell, Vann *psychoanalyst*

New Orleans
Agrawal, Krishna Chandra *pharmacology educator*
Beckerman, Robert Cy *pediatrician, educator*
Berenson, Gerald Sanders *physician*
Bertrand, William Ellis *public health educator, international health center administrator*
Brannan, William *urologist, educator*
Cohn, Isidore, Jr. *surgeon, educator*
Connolly, Edward S. *neurological surgeon*
Corrigan, James John, Jr. *pediatrician*
D'Ambrosia, Robert Dominick *orthopaedic educator*
Daniels, Robert Sanford *psychiatrist, medical school dean*
Domer, Floyd Ray *pharmacologist, educator*
Domingue, Gerald James *medical scientist, microbiology, immunology and urology educator, researcher, clinical bacteriologist*
Duffy, John Charles *psychiatrist, physician*
Duncan, Margaret Caroline *physician*
Easson, William McAlpine *psychiatrist*
†Edisen, Clayton Byron *physician*
Epstein, Arthur William *physician, educator*
Ewin, Dabney Minor *surgeon*
Fisher, James William *medical educator, pharmacologist*
Friedlander, Miles Herbert *ophthalmologist*
Frohlich, Edward David *physician*
García Oller, José Luis *neurosurgeon*
Gathright, John Byron, Jr. *colon and rectal surgeon, educator*
Gerber, Michael Albert *pathologist, researcher*
Gottlieb, A(braham) Arthur *medical educator, biotechnology corporate executive*
Hewitt, Robert Lee *surgeon, educator*
Hyman, Albert Lewis *cardiologist*
Jaffe, Bernard Michael *surgeon*
Jung, Rodney C. *internist, academic administrator*
†Kaufman, Herbert Edward *ophthalmologist, educator*
Kline, David Gellinger *neurosurgery educator*
Krementz, Edward Thomas *surgeon*
Lang, Erich Karl *physician, radiologist*

Le Jeune, Francis Ernest, Jr. *otolaryngologist*
Lewy, John Edwin *pediatric nephrologist*
Litwin, Martin Stanley *surgeon*
Locke, William *endocrinologist*
†Lopez, Manuel *immunology and allergy educator*
Low, Frank Norman *anatomist, educator*
†Martin, David Hubert *physician, educator*
†Massare, John Steve *medical association administrator, educator*
Mickal, Abe *retired physician*
†Miller, Robert Harold *otolaryngologist, educator*
Mogabgab, William Joseph *epidemiologist, educator*
Nelson, James Smith *pathologist, educator*
Nice, Charles Monroe, Jr. *physician, educator*
Nichols, Ronald Lee *surgeon, educator*
Ochsner, John Lockwood *thoracic-cardiovascular surgeon*
Pankey, George Atkinson *physician, educator*
Pfister, Richard Charles *physician, radiology educator*
Plavsic, Branko Milenko *radiology educator*
Puyau, Francis Albert *physician, radiology educator*
†Re, Richard N. *endocrinologist*
Reisin, Efrain *nephrologist, researcher, educator*
Richardson, Donald Edward *neurosurgery educator*
†Riddick, Frank Adams, Jr. *physician, health care facility administrator*
Salvaggio, John Edmond *physician, educator*
Schally, Andrew Victor *endocrine oncologist, researcher*
Schneider, George T. *obstetrician-gynecologist*
Straumanis, John Janis, Jr. *psychiatry educator*
Usdin, Gene Leonard *physician, psychiatrist*
Waring, William Winburn *pediatric pulmonologist, educator*
Webb, Watts Rankin *surgeon*
Weill, Hans *physician, educator*
Weiss, Thomas Edward *physician*
Welsh, Ronald Arthur *physician, educator*
White, Charles Albert, Jr. *medical educator, obstetrician-gynecologist*
Yates, Robert Doyle *anatomy educator*
Young, Lucy Cleaver *physician*
Zimny, Marilyn Lucile *anatomist, educator*

Pineville
Swearingen, David Clarke *general practice physician, musician*

Saint Bernard
Gilbert, Norman Sutcliffe *research physician*

Shreveport
Boyd, Clarence Elmo *retired surgeon*
Bradley, Ronald James *neuroscientist*
Breffeilh, Louis Andrew *ophthalmologist, educator*
Crissinger, Karen Denise *pediatric gastroenterologist, physiologist*
Dilworth, Edwin Earle *obstetrician, gynecologist*
Fort, Arthur Tomlinson, III *physician*
Ganley, James Powell *ophthalmologist, educator*
George, Ronald Baylis *physician*
McDonald, John Clifton *surgeon*
Misra, Raghunath Prasad *physician, educator*
Reddy, Pratap Chandupatla *cardiologist, educator, researcher*
Schober, Charles Coleman, III *psychiatrist, psychoanalyst*
Shelby, James Stanford *cardiovascular surgeon*
Thurmon, Theodore Francis *medical educator*

MAINE

Augusta
Cheng, Hsueh Ching *physician*

Bar Harbor
Green, Earl Leroy *retired biomedical research administrator, geneticist*

Camden
Spock, Benjamin McLane *physician, educator*

Friendship
†Walker, Douglass Willey *retired pediatrician-medical center administrator*

Hampden
Brown, Robert Horatio *retired orthopedic surgeon*

Oxford
Bensen, Pamela Parke *emergency medicine physician, educator*

Rockport
Swenson, Orvar *surgeon*

South Portland
Katz, Steven Edward *psychiatrist, state health official*

Surry
Whitcomb, Benjamin Bradford, Jr. *neurosurgeon*

Union
Buchan, Ronald Forbes *preventive medicine physician*

York Beach
Dutton, Robert Edward, Jr. *medical educator*

MARYLAND

Annapolis
†Holtgrewe, Henry Logan *urologist*

Baltimore
†Adkinson, N. Franklin, Jr. *clinical immunologist*
Andres, Reubin *gerontologist*
†August, Joseph Thomas *pharmacology educator*
Bachur, Nicholas Robert, Sr. *research physician*
Baker, R. Robinson *surgeon*
Baker, Susan P. *public health educator*
Baker, Timothy Danforth *physician, educator*
Bayless, Theodore M(orris) *gastroenterologist, educator, researcher*
Bereston, Eugene Sydney *dermatologist*
Berlin, Fred Saul *psychiatrist*
Berman, Barnett *internist, educator*
Bigelow, George E. *psychology and pharmacology scientist*
Borden, Ernest Carleton *physician, educator*
Breitenecker, Rudiger *pathologist*
Brody, Eugene B. *psychiatrist, educator*
Brusilow, Saul *pediatrics educator*
†Cameron, John Lemuel *general surgeon*
Campazzi, Earl James *physician*
Charache, Samuel *hematologist*
Childs, Barton *physician, educator*
Chisolm, James Julian, Jr. *pediatrics educator*
Clements, Mary Lou *epidemiologist, educator*
†Colombani, Paul Michael *general pediatric and transplant surgeon*
Conley, Carroll Lockard *physician, emeritus educator*
Connaughton, James Patrick *psychiatrist*
Cornblath, Marvin *pediatrician, educator*
Crenshaw, Marion Carlyle, Jr. *obstetrician, educator*
Cummings, Charles William *physician, educator*
Dannenberg, Arthur Milton, Jr. *experimental pathologist, immunologist, educator*
Dorst, John Phillips *physician, radiology and pediatrics educator*
Eisenberg, Howard Michael *neurosurgeon*
†Eleff, Scott Marshall *anesthesiology educator, brain damage researcher*
†Fantry, George Thomas *gastroenterologist*
Fedoroff, Nina Vsevolod *research scientist, consultant*
Felsenthal, Gerald *physiatrist, educator*
Fishman, Jacob Robert *psychiatrist, educator, corporate executive, investor*
Frank, Jerome David *psychiatrist, educator*
Freeman, John Mark *pediatric neurologist*
Godenne, Ghislaine Dudley *physician, psychoanalyst*
Goldberg, Morton Falk *ophthalmologist, educator*
Gordis, Leon *physician*
Graham, George Gordon *physician*
Greenough, William Bates, III *medical educator*
Griffin, Diane Edmund *research physician, virologist, educator*
Griffith, Lawrence Stacey Cameron *cardiologist*
†Handelsman, Jacob Charles *surgeon*
Harvey, Abner McGehee *physician, educator*
Helrich, Martin *anesthesiologist, educator*
Heptinstall, Robert Hodgson *physician*
Hungerford, David Samuel *orthopaedic surgeon, educator*
Hussels Maumenee, Irene E. *ophthalmology educator*
Hutchins, Grover MacGregor *pathologist, educator*
Johns, Carol Johnson *physician, educator*
Johns, Michael Marieb Edward *otolaryngologist, university dean*
Johns, Richard James *physician*
Johnson, Kenneth Peter *neurologist, medical researcher*
Kastor, John Alfred *cardiologist, educator*
Kidd, Langford *pediatrician, cardiologist, educator*
Kinnard, William James, Jr. *pharmacy educator*
Kowarski, Allen Avinoam *endocrinologist, educator*
Kwiterovich, Peter Oscar, Jr. *medical science educator, researcher, physician*
†Lakatta, Edward Gerard *biomedical researcher*
Lawrence, Robert Swan *physician, educator, academic administrator*
Lichtenstein, Lawrence Mark *allergy, immunology educator, physician*
Long, Donlin Martin *surgeon, educator*
Massof, Robert William *neuroscientist, educator*
McDowell, Elizabeth Mary *pathology educator*
Mc Hugh, Paul R. *psychiatrist, neurologist, educator*
McKhann, Guy Mead *physician, educator*
Medani, Charles Richard *pediatric nephrology educator*
Migeon, Claude Jean *pediatricics educator*
Miller, Edward Doring, Jr. *anesthesiologist*
Milnor, William Robert *physician*
Monroe, Russell Ronald *psychiatrist, educator*
Moser, Hugo Wolfgang *physician*
†Mulholland, John Henry *physician, educator*
Munster, Andrew Michael *surgeon, educator*
Norman, Philip Sidney *physician*
Oski, Frank Aram *physician, educator*
Owens, Albert Henry, Jr. *oncologist, educator*
Patz, Arnall *physician*
Platt, William Rady *pathology educator*
Prendergast, Robert A. *pathologist educator*
Price, Thomas Ransone *neurologist, educator*
Proctor, Donald Frederick *otolaryngology educator, physician*
†Provost, Thomas Taylor *dermatology educator, researcher*
Rayson, Glendon Ennes *internist, preventive medicine specialist, writer*
Rennels, Marshall Leigh *neuroanatomist, biomedical scientist, educator*
Rose, Noel Richard *immunologist, microbiologist, educator*
Rosenstein, Beryl Joel *physician*
†Sanfilippo, Alfred Paul *pathologist, educator*
Schimpff, Stephen Callender *internist, oncologist*
Silbergeld, Ellen Kovner *environmental epidemiologist and toxicologist*
Silverstein, Arthur Matthew *ophthalmic immunologist, educator, historian*
†Simpson, Thomas William *physician*
Smith, Gardner Watkins *physician*
Smith, Julian Payne *gynecological oncologist, educator*
Snyder, Solomon Halbert *psychiatrist, pharmacologist*
Starfield, Barbara Helen *physician, educator*
Sternberger, Ludwig Amadeus *neurologist, educator*
Stobo, John David *physician, educator*
Stolley, Paul David *medical educator, researcher*
Strickland, George Thomas, Jr. *physician, researcher, educator*
Tabatznik, Bernard *physician, educator*
Talalay, Paul *pharmacologist, physician*
Taylor, Carl Ernest *physician, educator*
†Van Metre, Thomas Earle *physician, allergist*
Vogelstein, Bert *oncology educator*
Wagner, Henry Nicholas, Jr. *physician*
Wallach, Edward Eliot *physician, educator*
Walser, Mackenzie *physician, educator*
†Walsh, Patrick Craig *urologist*
†Weiss, James Lloyd *cardiology educator*
Welch, Robert Bond *ophthalmologist, educator*
Whelton, Paul K. *medical educator, researcher*
Wilson, Donald Edward *physician, educator*
†Woods, Alan Churchill, Jr. *retired surgery educator*
Woodward, Theodore Englar *medical educator, internist*
Young, Barbara *psychiatrist, psychoanalyst, psychiatry educator, photographer*
Zassenhaus, Hiltgunt Margret *physician*
Zizic, Thomas Michael *physician, educator*

Beltsville
Lincicome, David Richard *biomedical and animal scientist*
†Palm, Mary Egdahl *mycologist*

Bethesda
Abbrecht, Peter Herman *medical educator*
Alexander, Duane Frederick *pediatrician, research administrator*
Axelrod, Julius *pharmacologist, biochemist*
Barter, Robert Henry *physician, retired educator*
Berendes, Heinz Werner *medical epidemiologist, pediatrician*
Breggin, Peter Roger *psychiatrist, author*
Brodine, Charles Edward *physician*
Brown, Dudley Earl, Jr. *psychiatrist, educator, health executive, former federal agency administrator, former naval officer*
†Brownstein, Michael Jay *pharmacologist, neuroscientist*
Cath, Stanley Howard *psychiatrist, psychoanalyst*
Chase, Thomas Newell *neurologist, researcher, educator*
Cheever, Allen Williams *pathologist*
Cohen, Max Harry *surgeon*
Cohen, Robert Abraham *retired physician*
Cohen, Sheldon Gilbert *physician, historian*
Cowie, Catherine Christine *epidemiologist*
Crout, J(ohn) Richard *physician, pharmaceutical researcher*
Cummings, Nancy Boucot *nephrologist*
Decker, John Laws *physician*
Dietrich, Robert Anthony *pathologist, medical administrator, consultant*
Drucker, William Richard *surgeon*
Elin, Ronald John *pathologist*
Epps, Roselyn Elizabeth Payne *pediatrician, educator*
Evans, Charles Hawes, Jr. *immunologist, medical researcher*
Farmer, Richard Gilbert *physician, foundation administrator, medical advisor*
Feller, William Frank *surgery educator*
†Fleisher, Thomas Arthur *physician*
†Fratantoni, Joseph Charles *medical researcher, hematologist, medical association administrator*
Frommer, Peter Leslie *physician, medical institute administrator*
Gallin, John I. *physician/scientist/medical research administrator*
Gershon, Elliot Sheldon *psychiatrist*
Gibson, Sam Thompson *internist, educator*
Gohagan, John Kenneth *medical institute administrator, educator*
Gold, Philip William *neurobiologist*
Goldstein, Robert Arnold *physician*
Greenwald, Peter *physician, government medical research director*
Hallett, Mark *physician, neurologist, health research institute administrator*
Harlan, William Robert, Jr. *physician, educator, researcher*
Haseltine, Florence Pat *research administrator, obstetrician, gynecologist*
Helke, Cinda Jane *pharmacology and neuroscience educator, researcher*
Hersh, Stephen Peter *psychiatrist, educator*
Hoak, John Charles *physician, educator*
Hoth, Daniel Floyd *infectious diseases administrator*
Hughes, Carl Wilson *physician*
Hutcheson, Janet Reid *radiologist*
Hutton, John Evans, Jr. *surgery educator, retired military officer*
Johnson, Joyce Marie *psychiatrist, epidemiologist*
Joy, Robert John Thomas *medical history educator*
Kapikian, Albert Zaven *physician, epidemiologist*
Keiser, Harry Robert *physician*
Kirschstein, Ruth Lillian *physician*
Kopin, Irwin Jerome *physician, pharmacologist*
Krause, Richard Michael *medical scientist, government official, educator*
Kupfer, Carl *ophthalmologist, science administrator*
Lenfant, Claude Jean-Marie *physician*
Leonard, James Joseph *physician, educator*
Leventhal, Carl M. *neurologist, government official*
Levine, Arthur Samuel *physician, scientist*
Liotta, Lance Allen *pathologist*
†Lockshin, Michael Dan *rheumatologist*
Macnamara, Thomas Edward *physician, educator*
Mansfield, Carl Major *radiation oncology educator*
McAfee, John Gilmour *nuclear medicine physician*
McCurdy, Harry Ward *otolaryngologist*
Nelson, Karin Becker *child neurologist*
Neva, Franklin Allen *physician, educator*
Nyirjesy, Istvan *obstetrician, gynecologist*
Okunieff, Paul *radiation oncologist, physician*
Ommaya, Ayub Khan *neurosurgeon*
Paul, William Erwin *immunologist, researcher*
Pollard, Harvey B. *physician, neuroscientist*
Post, Robert M. *psychiatrist*
Quinnan, Gerald Vincent, Jr. *medical educator*
†Rabson, Alan Saul *physician, educator*
Rall, Joseph Edward *physician*
Rapoport, Judith *psychiatrist*
Reese, Thomas Sargent *neurobiology educator and researcher*
†Reid, Clarice Delores *physician*
Reighard, Homer Leroy *physician*
Resnik, Harvey Lewis Paul *psychiatrist*
Rosenberg, Steven Aaron *surgeon, medical researcher*
Roth, Harold Philmore *physician*
Saffiotti, Umberto *pathologist*
Sausville, Edward Anthony *medical oncologist*
Schlom, Jeffrey Bert *research scientist*
Sheridan, Philip Henry *pediatrician, neurologist*
Sindelar, William Francis *surgeon, researcher*
Snow, James Byron, Jr. *physician, research administrator*
Sontag, James Mitchell *cancer researcher*
Stewart, Harold Leroy *physician, educator*
Sturtz, Donald Lee *physician, naval officer*
†Tabor, Edward *physician, researcher*
Thorgeirsson, Snorri Sveinn *physician, pharmacologist*
Waldmann, Thomas Alexander *medical research scientist, physician*
Walter, William Arnold, Jr. *physician*
Walters, Judith Richmond *neuropharmacologist*
Webster, Henry deForest *neuroscientist*
Wehr, Thomas A. *psychiatrist, researcher*
Wolffe, Alan Paul *molecular embryologist, molecular biologist*
Wong, Ma-Li *psychiatrist*
Work, Henry Harcus *physician, educator*
Yaffe, Sumner Jason *pediatrician, research center administrator, educator*

Cabin John
Sewell, Winifred *pharmaceutical librarian*

Chevy Chase
Crain, Darrell Clayton, Jr. *physician*
Dyer, Robert Francis, Jr. *internist, educator*
Ellis, Sydney *pharmacological scientist, former pharmacology educator*
Ferguson, James Joseph, Jr. *researcher, educator*
Greenberg, Robert Milton *retired psychiatrist*
Oler, Wesley Marion, III *physician, educator*
Romansky, Monroe James *physician, educator*
Rose, John Charles *physician, educator*
Welch, Arnold DeMerritt *pharmacologist, biochemist*
Williams, Charles Laval, Jr. *physician, international organization official*

Clinton
Cruz, Wilhelmina Mangahas *nephrologist, educator*

Cockeysville
Futcher, Palmer Howard *physician, educator*

Columbia
Carr, Charles Jelleff *pharmacologist, educator, toxicology consultant*
Harrison, Elza Stanley *medical association executive*
Hyman, Lawrence Robert *psychiatrist*

Easton
Engle, Mary Allen English *physician*
Engle, Ralph Landis, Jr. *internist, educator*

Gaithersburg
Crisp, Elizabeth Amanda *physician*
Hegyeli, Ruth Ingeborg Elisabeth Johnsson *pathologist, government official*
Schwartzberg, Allan Zelig *psychiatrist, educator*

Garrett Park
Silbergeld, Sam *psychiatrist*

Grasonville
Prout, George Russell, Jr. *medical educator, urologist*

Hollywood
Hertz, Roy *physician, educator, researcher*

Lusby
Howell, James Theodore *medical consultant, internist*

Lutherville
Sanders, Roger Cobban *radiologist*

Lutherville Timonium
Bundick, William Ross *dermatologist*
Park, Lee Crandall *psychiatrist*

Mitchellville
Bever, Christopher Theodore *psychiatrist*

Monkton
Mountcastle, Vernon Benjamin *neurophysiologist*

Parkville
Munson, Paul Lewis *pharmacologist*

Perry Point
Peszke, Michael Alfred *psychiatrist, educator*

Potomac
Antoniou, Lucy D. *internist, nephrologist*
Bradley, Mark Edmund *physician, consultant*
Evanega, George Ronald *medical company executive*
Haddy, Francis John *physician, educator*

Rockville
Akhter, Mohammad Nasir *physician, government public health administrator*
Birns, Mark Theodore *physician*
DuPont, Robert Louis *psychiatrist, physician*
Fenton, Wayne S. *psychiatrist*
Forbes, Allan Louis *physician, foods and nutrition consultant*
Geier, Mark Robin *obstetrical genetics and infertility physician*
Haffner, Marlene Elisabeth *internist, health care administrator*
Hanna, Michael George, Jr. *immunologist, institute administrator*
†Hardegree, Mary Carolyn *medical association administrator, pediatrician, immunologist*
Haudenschild, Christian Charles *pathologist, educator*
Henderson, Edward Shelton *oncologist*
Hoyer, Leon William *physician, educator*
Johnson, Emery Allen *physician*
Ley, Herbert Leonard, Jr. *retired epidemiologist*
Liard, Jean-Francois *cardiovascular physiologist, researcher, educator*
Lim, David Jong-Jai *otolaryngology educator, researcher*
Lloyd, Douglas Seward *physician, public health administrator*
Lutwak, Leo *physician, educator*
Naunton, Ralph Frederick *surgeon, educator*
Nora, James Jackson *physician, author, educator*
Rosenstein, Marvin *public health administrator*
Seltser, Raymond *epidemiologist, educator*
Sumaya, Ciro Valent *pediatrician, educator*
†Waugaman, Richard Merle *psychiatrist*

Saint Michaels
Rever, George Wright *psychiatrist, health facility administrator*

Salisbury
Houlihan, Hilda Imelio *physician*

Severna Park
Greulich, Richard Curtice *anatomist, gerontologist*

Silver Spring
Berger, Allan Sidney *psychiatrist*

Waldrop, Francis Neil *physician*

Stevenson
Hendler, Nelson Howard *physician, medical clinic director*

Towson
Mc Indoe, Darrell Winfred *nuclear medicine physician, former air force officer*
Spodak, Michael Kenneth *forensic psychiatrist*
Udvarhelyi, George Bela *neurosurgery educator emeritus, cultural affairs administrator*

Union Bridge
Laughlin, Henry Prather *physician, psychiatrist, educator, author, editor*

MASSACHUSETTS

Amherst
Fleischman, Paul R. *psychiatrist, writer*

Attleboro
†King, Melvin James *internist*

Bedford
Alarcon, Rogelio Alfonso *physician, researcher*
†Elkinton, Joseph Russell *medical educator*
Volicer, Ladislav *physician, educator*

Belmont
Bird, Edward Dennis *physician*
Cohen, Bruce Michael *psychiatrist, educator, scientist*
†Coyle, Joseph Thomas *psychiatrist*
de Marneffe, Francis *psychiatrist, hospital administrator*
Nixon, Ralph Angus *psychiatrist, educator, research neuroscientist*
Onesti, Silvio Joseph *psychiatrist*
Pope, Harrison Graham, Jr. *psychiatrist, educator*
Sifneos, Peter Emanuel *psychiatrist*

Boston
Adams, Douglass Franklin *radiologist, educator*
Adams, John Randolph *neurologist, educator*
Adelstein, S(tanley) James *physician, educator*
Adler, David Avram *psychiatrist*
Aisenberg, Alan C. *physician, educator, researcher*
Alpert, Joel Jacobs *medical educator, pediatrician*
Angelo, E. Joanne *child, adolescent and adult psychiatrist*
Arias, Irwin Monroe *physician, educator*
Arky, Ronald Alfred *medical educator*
Austen, K(arl) Frank *physician*
Austen, W(illiam) Gerald *surgeon, educator*
Avery, Mary Ellen *pediatrician, educator*
Barlow, Charles Franklin *physician, educator*
Barlow, John Sutton *neurophysiologist, electroencephalographer*
Barry, Patricia Pound *physician, educator*
Beck, William Samson *physician, educator, biochemist*
Berenberg, William *physician, educator*
Bernfield, Merton Ronald *pediatrician, scientist, educator*
Bernhard, William Francis *thoracic and cardiovascular surgeon*
Berson, Eliot Lawrence *ophthalmologist, medical educator*
Biederman, Joseph *psychiatrist*
Blau, Monte *radiology educator*
Bloch, Kurt Julius *physician*
Bondoc, Conrado Cervania *surgeon, educator*
Brain, Joseph David *biomedical scientist*
Braunwald, Eugene *physician, educator*
Brazelton, Thomas Berry *pediatrician, educator*
Brenner, Barry Morton *physician*
†Brooke, Marvin McClatchey *rehabilitative medicine physician, educator*
Buckley, Mortimer Joseph *physician*
Burakoff, Steven James *immunologist, educator*
Burke, John Francis *surgeon, educator, researcher*
Burns, Padraic *physician, psychiatrist, psychoanalyst, educator*
†Buxbaum, Robert C. *internist*
Callow, Allan Dana *surgeon*
Caplan, Louis Robert *neurology educator*
Cassidy, Carl Eugene *physician*
†Castaneda, Aldo R. *pediatric cardiac surgeon*
Chen, Lincoln Chin-ho *medical educator*
Cleveland, Richard Joseph *surgeon*
Coffman, Jay Denton *physician, educator*
†Coggins, Cecil Hammond *physician, educator*
Cohen, Alan Seymour *internist*
Coleman, C. Norman *radiologist, oncologist, researcher, educator*
Collins, John Joseph, Jr. *cardiac and thoracic surgeon*
Corcoran, Paul John *physician*
Cotran, Ramzi S. *pathologist, educator*
†Cotton, Deborah Jean *physician*
Crocker, Allen Carrol *pediatrician*
De Cherney, Alan Hersh *obstetrics and gynecology educator*
Delbanco, Thomas Lewis *medical educator, researcher*
DeSanctis, Roman William *cardiologist*
Desforges, Jane Fay *medical educator, physician*
†Dluhy, Robert George *physician*
Dvorak, Harold F. *pathologist, educator, scientist*
Eckstein, Marlene R. *vascular radiologist*
Egdahl, Richard Harrison *surgeon, medical educator, health science administrator*
Eisenberg, Leon *psychiatrist, educator*
Ellis, Franklin Henry, Jr. *surgeon, educator*
Epstein, Franklin Harold *physician, educator*
†Federman, Daniel David *medical educator, educational administrator, endocrinologist*
Feldman, Robert George *neurologist, medical educator*
Ferris, Benjamin Greeley, Jr. *retired physician, environmental researcher, educator*
Field, James Bernard *internist, educator*
Fineberg, Harvey Vernon *physician, educator*
†Fischbach, Gerald D. *neurobiology educator*
Fitzpatrick, Thomas Bernard *dermatologist, educator*
Fletcher, Robert Hillman *medical educator*
Fletcher, Suzanne Wright *physician, educator*
Folkman, Moses Judah *surgeon*
Fox, Bernard Hayman *cancer epidemiologist, educator*
Freedberg, A. Stone *physician*
Frei, Emil, III *physician, medical researcher, educator*
Freiman, David Galland *pathologist, educator*
Frigoletto, Fredric David, Jr. *physician*
Galaburda, Albert Mark *neurologist, researcher, educator*
Gellis, Sydney Saul *physician*
Gimbrone, Michael Anthony, Jr. *research scientist, pathologist, educator*
†Glickman, Robert Morris *physician, educator*
Glimcher, Melvin Jacob *orthopedic surgeon*
Goldberg, Irving Hyman *molecular pharmacology and biochemistry educator*
Goldsmith, Harry Sawyer *surgeon, educator*
Gottlieb, Leonard Solomon *pathology educator*
Goyal, Raj Kumar *medical educator*
Graham, John David *public health educator*
Green, Gareth Montraville *physician, educator, scientist*
Greenblatt, David J. *pharmacologist, educator*
Grillo, Hermes Conrad *surgeon*
Haber, Edgar *physician, educator*
Hall, John Emmett *orthopedic surgeon, educator*
Harris, Burton Henry *surgeon*
Harris, William Hamilton *orthopedic surgeon*
Hay, Elizabeth Dexter *embryology researcher, educator*
Hedley-Whyte, Elizabeth Tessa *neuropathologist*
Hennekens, Charles Henry *physician, epidemiologist*
Heros, Roberto Cosme *neurosurgeon*
Hiatt, Howard H. *physician, educator*
Hingson, Ralph W. *medical educator*
Hobson, John Allan *psychiatrist, researcher, educator*
†Holman, B. Leonard *radiology educator, researcher*
†Howley, Peter Maxwell *pathology educator*
Hutchinson, Bernard Thomas *ophthalmologist*
Hutter, Adolph Matthew, Jr. *cardiologist, educator*
Jandl, James Harriman *physician, educator*
†Jellinek, Michael Steven *psychiatrist, pediatrician*
†Kaplan, Marshall Myles *gastroenterologist, researcher, educator*
Karnovsky, Morris John *pathologist, biologist*
Kazemi, Homayoun *physician, medical educator*
Kieff, Elliott Dan *medical educator*
Kim, Ducksoo *radiologist and educator*
Kimura, Robert Shigetsugu *otologic researcher*
Kitz, Richard John *anesthesiologist, educator*
Klempner, Mark Steven Joel *physician, research scientist, educator*
Krane, Stephen Martin *physician, educator*
Lasagna, Louis Cesare *medical educator*
Leaf, Alexander *physician, educator*
Lee, Robin S. *surgeon, researcher*
Leeman, Susan Epstein *neuroscientist, educator*
Levine, Ruth Rothenberg *biomedical science educator*
Levinsky, Norman George *physician, educator*
Libby, Peter *cardiologist, medical researcher*
Lipton, Stuart Arthur *neuroscientist*
Little, John Bertram *physician, radiobiology educator, researcher*
Livingston, David Morse *biomedical scientist, physician, internist*
Madara, James L. *epitheliologist, pathologist, educator*
Mankin, Henry Jay *physician, educator*
Mannick, John Anthony *surgeon*
May, James Warren, Jr. *plastic surgeon, medical association executive*
Mc Arthur, Janet Ward *endocrinologist, educator*
McCluskey, Robert Timmons *physician*
McCormick, Marie Clare *pediatrician, educator*
Mc Dermott, William Vincent, Jr. *physician, educator*
McDougal, William Scott *urology educator*
McNeil, Barbara Joyce *radiologist*
Medearis, Donald Norman, Jr. *physician, educator*
Mellins, Harry Zachary *radiologist, educator*
Messerle, Judith Rose *medical librarian, public relations director*
†Michel, Thomas Mark *internal medicine educator*
Miller, Keith Wyatt *pharmacology educator*
Moellering, Robert Charles, Jr. *internist, educator*
Monaco, Anthony Peter *surgery educator, medical institute administrator*
Montgomery, William Wayne *surgeon*
Morgan, James Philip *pharmacologist, cardiologist, educator*
Morgentaler, Abraham *urologist, researcher*
Munsat, Theodore L. *neurologist, researcher*
Nadas, Alexander Sandor *pediatric cardiologist*
Naimi, Shapur *cardiologist, educator*
Nathan, David Gordon *physician, educator*
Nichols, David Harry *gynecologic surgeon, obstetrics and gynecology educator, author*
Ojemann, Robert Gerdes *neurosurgeon*
†Ostheimer, Gerard William *anesthesiology educator*
†Parrish, John Albert *dermatologist, research administrator*
Paul, Oglesby *physician*
†Paulin, Sven Josef Karl *radiologist, educator*
Peppercorn, Mark Allen *gastroenterologist, educator*
Pochi, Peter Ernest *physician*
Poser, Charles Marcel *neurology educator*
†Potts, John Thomas, Jr. *physician, educator*
Poussaint, Alvin Francis *psychiatrist, educator*
Quickel, Kenneth Elwood, Jr. *physician, medical center executive*
Rabkin, Mitchell Thornton *physician, hospital administrator, educator*
Reid, Lynne McArthur *pathologist*
Relman, Arnold Seymour *physician, educator, editor*
Reppert, Steven Marion *pediatrician, educator*
Richie, Jerome Paul *surgeon, educator*
Richter, James Michael *physician, clinical investigator*
†Rockoff, Mark Alan *anesthesiologist*
Roehrig, C(harles) Burns *internist, health policy consultant, editor*
Rosen, Fred Saul *pediatrics educator*
Rosenblatt, Michael *medical researcher, educator*
†Ruby, Leonard Kenneth *hand surgeon, orthopaedic surgeon, educator*
Rush, David *medical investigator, epidemiologist*
Russell, Paul Snowden *surgeon, educator*
Ryan, Kenneth John *physician, educator*
Sandson, John I. *physician, educator, retired university dean*
Saper, Clifford Baird *neurobiology and neurology educator*
Schlossman, Stuart Franklin *physician, educator, researcher*
†Schnitzer, Jan Eugeniusz *medical educator, scientist*
Schuknecht, Harold Frederick *physician, educator*
Schwartz, Bernard *physician*
Seddon, Johanna Margaret *ophthalmologist, epidemiologist*
Selkoe, Dennis Jesse *neurologist, researcher, educator*
Shader, Richard Irwin *psychiatrist, educator*
Shapiro, Jerome Herbert *radiologist, educator*
Shields, Lawrence Thornton *orthopedic surgeon, educator*
Short, Marion Priscilla *neurologist*
Shucart, William Arthur *neurosurgeon*
†Silen, William *physician, surgery educator*
†Sledge, Clement Blount *orthopedic surgeon, educator*
Smith, Thomas Woodward *cardiologist, educator*
Steele, Glenn Daniel, Jr. *surgical oncologist*
Steere, Allen Caruthers, Jr. *physician, educator*
Stollerman, Gene Howard *physician, educator*
Strom, Terry Barton *immunologist*
Summerville, David *pediatrician, chemist*
Swartz, Morton Norman *medical educator*
Tauber, Alfred Imre *hematologist, immunologist, philosopher of science*
Taubman, Martin Arnold *immunologist*
Taveras, Juan Manuel *physician, educator*
Thorn, George Widmer *physician, educator*
†Thrall, James Hunter *radiology educator*
†Tompkins, Ronald Gary *surgeon, educator, biomedical investigator*
Trier, Jerry Steven *gastroenterologist, educator*
Vaillant, George Eman *psychiatrist*
Volpe, Joseph John *pediatric neurologist, educator*
†Wang, Timothy C. *gastroenterologist*
Warshaw, Andrew Louis *surgeon, researcher*
Weiss, Earle Burton *physician*
Welch, Claude Emerson *surgeon*
†Williams, Gordon Harold *medical educator, researcher*
Willock, Marcelle Monica *medical educator*
†Wood, Lawrence Crane *medical association administrator, educator*
Wyman, Stanley Moore *radiologist*
Zaleznik, Abraham *psychoanalyst, management specialist, educator*
Zarins, Bertram *orthopaedic surgeon*
Zervas, Nicholas Themistocles *neurosurgeon*
Zinner, Michael Jeffrey *surgeon, educator*

Brockton
Carlson, Desiree Anice *pathologist*

Brookline
Ames, Adelbert, III *neurophysiologist, educator*
Blom, Gaston Eugene *psychiatrist*
Brooks, Joae Graham *psychiatrist, educator*
Gray, Seymour *medical educator, author*
Jakab, Irene *psychiatrist*
Kadin, Marshall Edward *hematopathologist, educator*
Nadelson, Carol Cooperman *psychiatrist, educator*
Tyler, H. Richard *physician*

Burlington
Clerkin, Eugene Patrick *physician*
Fager, Charles Anthony *physician, neurosurgeon*
Moschella, Samuel L. *dermatology educator*
Schoetz, David John, Jr. *colon and rectal surgeon*
Seckel, Brooke Rutledge *plastic surgeon*
Veidenheimer, Malcolm Charles *surgeon*
Wise, Robert Edward *radiologist*

Cambridge
Anderson, William Henry *psychobiologist, educator*
Bartus, Raymond Thomas *neuroscientist, pharmaceutical executive, writer*
Bizzi, Emilio *neurophysiologist, educator*
Brusch, John Lynch *physician*
Buchanan, John Robert *physician, educator*
†Buttenwieser, Paul Arthur *writer, psychiatrist*
Coles, Robert *child psychiatrist, educator, author*
Davidson, Charles Sprecher *physician*
Davie, Joseph Myrten *physician, pathology and immunology educator, science administrator*
Eisen, Herman Nathaniel *immunology educator, medical researcher*
Eisenberg, Carola *psychiatry educator*
Goldman, Laura Nan *physician*
†Grotzinger, John P. *surgeon*
Havens, Leston Laycock *psychiatrist, educator*
†Heifetz, Ronald Abadian *psychiatrist, educator*
Homburger, Freddy *physician, scientist, artist*
Kiang, Nelson Yuan-sheng *medical educator*
†Nadol, Joseph B., Jr. *otolaryngologist, educator*
†Ris, Howard C., Jr. *nonprofit public policy organization administrator*
Shore, Miles Frederick *psychiatrist, educator*
Steiner, Lisa A(melia) *immunologist, educator*
Wacker, Warren Ernest Clyde *physician, educator*
Wilson, Mary Elizabeth *physician*
Wurtman, Richard Jay *physician, educator*

Charlestown
Bonventre, Joseph Vincent *physician, scientist, medical educator*
Isselbacher, Kurt Julius *physician, educator*
Lamont-Havers, Ronald William *physician, research administrator*
Moskowitz, Michael Arthur *neuroscientist, neurologist*

Chelmsford
†Howard, Terry Thomas *obstetrician/gynecologist*

Chestnut Hill
Baum, Jules Leonard *ophthalmologist, educator*
Courtiss, Eugene Howard *plastic surgeon, educator*
Knapp, Robert Charles *retired obstetrics and gynecology educator*
Kosasky, Harold Jack *gynecologist*
Meissner, William Walter *psychiatrist, clergyman*
Stanbury, John Bruton *physician, educator*
Thier, Samuel Osiah *physician, educator*

Concord
Meistas, Mary Therese *endocrinologist, diabetes researcher*
Palay, Sanford Louis *retired scientist, educator*

Danvers
†Rubinstein, Sidney Jacob *orthopaedic technologist*

Dover
Buyse, Marylou *pediatrician, clinical geneticist, medical administrator*

Falmouth
Gilmour, Edward Ellis *psychiatrist*

Fitchburg
Bogdasarian, John Robert *otolaryngologist*

Framingham
†Castelli, William Peter *cardiovascular epidemiologist, educator*
Hoffer, Edward Peter *physician*

Harwich
Rigg, Charles Andrew *pediatrician*

Haverhill
Ehrig, Ulrich *physician*
Niccolini, Drew George *gastroenterologist*

Hyannis
Chiotellis, Philip Nicos *cardiologist*

Jamaica Plain
Pierce, Chester Middlebrook *psychiatrist, educator*
Snider, Gordon Lloyd *physician*

Lincoln
Cannon, Bradford *surgeon*

Medford
Burke, Edward Newell *radiologist*

Needham
Chattoraj, Aparna *gynecologist, educator*
Weller, Thomas Huckle *physician, emeritus educator*

New Bedford
Shapiro, Gilbert Lawrence *orthopedist*

New Salem
Lenherr, Frederick Keith *neurophysiologist, computer scientist*

Newton
Blacher, Richard Stanley *psychiatrist*
Gill, Benjamin Franklin *physician*
Myerson, Paul Graves *psychiatrist, educator*
Rogoff, Jerome Howard *psychiatrist, psychoanalyst, forensic expert*
Simon, Harold *radiologist*
Young, James Morningstar *physician, naval officer*

North Andover
Scully, Stephen J. *plastic surgeon*

North Attleboro
†Friend, Dale Gilbert *retired medical educator*

North Dighton
Cserr, Robert *psychiatrist, physician, hospital administrator*

North Falmouth
Bass, Norman Herbert *physician, scientist, university and hospital administrator, health care executive*

Northampton
Dashef, Stephen Sewell *psychiatrist*

Northborough
Fulmer, Hugh Scott *physician, educator*

Norwood
Berliner, Allen Irwin *dermatologist*
Florian, Agustin Max *thoracic and cardiovascular surgeon*

Roxbury
Berman, Marlene Oscar *neuropsychologist, educator*
Caldini, Maria Pia *physician*
Peters, Alan *anatomy educator*

Salem
Piro, Anthony John *radiologist*

Shrewsbury
Zamecnik, Paul Charles *oncologist, medical research scientist*

Southborough
Dews, P(eter) B(ooth) *medical scientist, educator*

Springfield
Dastgeer, Ghulam Mohammad *surgeon*
Frankel, Kenneth Mark *thoracic surgeon*
Liptzin, Benjamin *psychiatrist*
McGee, William Tobin *intensivist*
†Navab, Farhad *medical educator*

Stockbridge
Shapiro, Edward Robert *psychiatrist, educator, psychoanalyst*

Stoneham
Igou, Raymond Alvin, Jr. *orthopedic surgeon*

Vineyard Haven
Jacobs, Gretchen Huntley *psychiatrist*

Walpole
Dexter, Lewis *physician*
Warthin, Thomas Angell *physician, educator*

Waltham
Lackner, James Robert *aerospace medicine educator*
Leach, Robert Ellis *physician, educator*
Reilly, Philip Raymond *medical research administrator*

Watertown
Loney, Linda Christine *pediatrician*

Wayland
Ebert, Robert Higgins *physician, educator, foundation consultant*
Freed, Murray Monroe *physician, medical educator*

Wellesley
Coyne, Mary Downey *biologist, endocrinologist, educator*
Murray, Joseph Edward *plastic surgeon*

West Roxbury
Hedley-Whyte, John *anesthesiologist, educator*

Westborough
Strauss, Judith Feigin *physician*

Weston
Brooks, John Robinson *surgeon, educator*

Williamstown
Wilkins, Earle Wayne, Jr. *surgery educator emeritus*

Winchester
Smith, Robert Moors *anesthesiologist*

Woods Hole
Rafferty, Nancy Schwarz *anatomy educator*

Worcester
Appelbaum, Paul Stuart *psychiatrist, educator*
Bonkovsky, Herbert Lloyd *gastroenterologist, educator*
Brill, A. Bertrand *nuclear medicine educator*
Charney, Evan *pediatrician, educator*
Drachman, David Alexander *neurologist*
Dunlop, George Rodgers *surgeon*
Hanshaw, James Barry *physician, educator*
Hunter, Richard Edward *physician*
Kaplan, Melvin Hyman *immunology, rheumatology, medical educator*
Laster, Leonard *physician, consultant, author*
Levine, Peter Hughes *physician, health facility administrator*
Ludlum, David Blodgett *pharmacologist, educator*
Menon, Mani *urological surgeon, educator*
Smith, Edward Herbert *radiologist, educator*
Tonkonogy, Joseph Moses *physician, neuropsychiatrist, researcher*
Townes, Philip Leonard *pediatrician, educator*
Wheeler, Hewitt Brownell *surgeon, educator*
Wilkinson, Harold Arthur *neurosurgeon*
Zurier, Robert Burton *medical educator, clinical investigator*

MICHIGAN

Alma
Sanders, Jack Ford *physician*

Ann Arbor
Abrams, Gerald David *physician, educator*
Ansbacher, Rudi *physician*
Bole, Giles G. *physician, researcher, medical educator*
Burdi, Alphonse Rocco *anatomist*
†Cameron, Oliver Gene *psychiatrist, educator psychobiology reseacher*
Casey, Kenneth Lyman *neurologist*
Castor, C. William, Jr. *physician, educator*
Christensen, A(lbert) Kent *anatomy educator*
Coran, Arnold Gerald *pediatric surgeon, educator*
Counsell, Raymond Ernest *pharmacology educator*
Curtis, George Clifton *psychiatry educator, clinical research investigator*
De La Iglesia, Felix Alberto *pathologist, toxicologist*
DeWeese, Marion Spencer *educator, surgeon*
Domino, Edward Felix *pharmacologist, educator*
Donabedian, Avedis *physician*
Dubin, Howard Victor *dermatologist*
†Dunnick, N. Reed *physician, radiologist, educator*
Fajans, Stefan Stanislaus *internist, retired educator*
†Fekety, Robert *physician, educator*
†Frueh, Bartley Richard *surgeon*
Gikas, Paul William *medical educator*
Gilman, Sid *neurologist*
Goldstein, Irwin Joseph *medical research executive*
Goldstein, Steven Alan *medical and engineering educator*
Greden, John Francis *psychiatrist, educator*
Greene, Douglas A. *internist, educator*
†Greenfield, Lazar John *surgeon, educator*
†Halter, Jeffrey B. *internal medicine educator, geriatrician*
Hawthorne, Victor Morrison *epidemiologist, educator*
Heidelberger, Kathleen Patricia *physician*
Henderson, John Woodworth *ophthalmologist, educator*
Hiss, Roland Graham *physician, medical educator*
Hoff, Julian Theodore *physician, educator*
Howell, Joel DuBose *physician, educator*
Huelke, Donald Fred *anatomy and cell biology educator, research scientist*
†Julius, Stevo *physician, educator, physiologist*
Kimbrough, William Walter, III *psychiatrist*
Kramer, Charles Henry *psychiatrist*
Krause, Charles Joseph *otolaryngologist*
Kuhl, David Edmund *physician, nuclear medicine educator*
La Du, Bert Nichols, Jr. *pharmacology educator, physician*
Lapides, Jack *urologist, medical educator*
Lichter, Paul Richard *ophthalmology educator*
Lopatin, Dennis Edward *immunologist, educator*
Margolis, Philip Marcus *psychiatrist, educator*
Martel, William *radiologist, educator*
Midgley, A(lvin) Rees, Jr. *reproductive endocrinology educator, researcher*
†Monto, Arnold S. *epidemiology educator*
Morley, George William *gynecologist*
Nelson, Virginia Simson *pediatrician, educator*
Newman, Sarah Winans *neuroanatomist, educator*
Oliver, William John *pediatrician, educator*
Orringer, Mark B. *thoracic surgeon*
Osborn, June Elaine *pediatrician, microbiologist, educator*
Pitt, Bertram *cardiologist, consultant*
Rosenthal, Amnon *pediatric cardiologist*
Schenck, John Frederic *physician*
Schottenfeld, David *epidemiologist, educator*
†Schteingart, David Eduardo *internist*
Shayman, James Alan *nephrologist, educator*
Silverman, Albert Jack *psychiatrist, educator*
Smith, David John, Jr. *plastic surgeon*
Strang, Ruth Hancock *pediatric educator, pediatric cardiologist, priest*
Stross, Jeoffrey Knight *physician, educator*
Tandon, Rajiv *psychiatrist, educator*
Taren, James Arthur *neurosurgeon, educator*
Taylor, William Brooks, II *retired dermatologist*
Thompson, Norman Winslow *surgeon, educator*
†Tremper, Kevin K. *anesthesiologist, educator*
Turcotte, Jeremiah George *physician, surgery educator*
†Voorhees, John James *dermatologist*
Waggoner, Raymond Walter *neuropsychiatrist*
Wahl, Richard Leo *radiology educator, nuclear medicine cancer researcher*
Ward, Peter Allan *pathologist, educator*
Watson, Andrew Samuel *psychiatry and law educator*
Weber, Wendell William *pharmacologist*
Weg, John Gerard *physician*
Wegman, Myron Ezra *physician, educator*
Wicha, Max S. *oncologist, educator*
Zarafonetis, Chris John Dimiter *physician, emeritus educator*

Battle Creek
Bruce, Thomas Allen *physician, philanthropic administrator*

Birmingham
Chodorkoff, Bernard *psychoanalyst, psychiatrist*

Bloomfield Hills
Ball, Patricia Ann *physician*
Chason, Jacob (Leon Chason) *neuropathologist*
Hsu, John J. *psychiatrist*
Rosenfeld, Joel *ophthalmologist, lawyer*

Clinton Township
†Brown, Ronald Delano *endocrinologist*

Copemish
Wells, Herschel James *physician, former hospital administrator*

Dearborn
Coburn, Ronald Murray *ophthalmic surgeon, researcher*
Hirsch, Lore *psychiatrist*
Joseph, Ramon Rafael *physician, educator*

Detroit
Abramson, Hanley Norman *pharmacy educator*
†Anderson, John Albert *physician*
Blain, Alexander, III *surgeon, educator*
Brown, Eli Matthew *anesthesiologist*
Cerny, Joseph Charles *urologist, educator*
Cohen, Sanford Ned *pediatrics educator, academic administrator*
Diamond, Michael P. *obstetrician-gynecologist, educator*
Ernst, Calvin Bradley *vascular surgeon, surgery educator*
†Evans, Mark Ira *obstetrician, geneticist*
Fitzgerald, Robert Hannon, Jr. *orthopedic surgeon*
Fromm, David *surgeon*
Garcia, Julio Hernan *pathology educator*
Kantrowitz, Adrian *surgeon, educator*
Krull, Edward Alexander *dermatologist*
Lesch, Michael *cardiologist*
Livingood, Clarence S. *dermatologist*
Lupulescu, Aurel Peter *medical educator, researcher, physician*
Lusher, Jeanne Marie *pediatric hematologist, educator*
Miller, Orlando Jack *physician, educator*
Ownby, Dennis Randall *pediatrician, allergist, educator, researcher*
Peters, William P. *oncologist, science administrator, educator*
Porter, Arthur T. *oncologist, educator*
†Powsner, Edward Raphael *physician*
†Sokol, Robert James *obstetrician, gynecologist, educator*
Stein, Paul David *cardiologist*
Szilagyi, D(esiderius) Emerick *surgeon, researcher, educator*
Walt, Alexander Jeffrey *surgeon, educator*
Whitehouse, Fred Waite *endocrinologist, researcher*
Wiener, Joseph *pathologist*

East Lansing
Beckmeyer, Henry Ernest *anesthesiologist, medical educator*
Brody, Theodore Meyer *pharmacologist, educator*
Gottschalk, Alexander *radiologist, diagnostic radiology educator*
Johnson, John Irwin, Jr. *neuroscientist*
Kay, Bernard Melvin *osteopathic pediatrician, educational administrator*
Krecke, Charles Francis *radiologist, educator*
Moore, Kenneth Edwin *pharmacology educator*
Murray, Raymond Harold *physician*
Netzloff, Michael Lawrence *pediatric educator, endocrinologist*
Potchen, E. James *radiology educator*
Reinhart, Mary Ann *medical board executive*
Ristow, George Edward *neurologist, educator*
Rovner, David Richard *endocrinology educator*
Walker, Bruce Edward *anatomy educator*
Williams, Donald Herbert *psychiatric education administrator*
†Wood, Douglas L. *medical educator*

Flint
Farrehi, Cyrus *cardiologist, educator*
Himes, George Elliott *pathologist*
Jayabalan, Vemblaserry *nuclear medicine physician, radiologist*
Tauscher, John Walter *retired pediatrician, emeritus educator*

Flushing
Schriner, Jon Leslie *sports medicine physician*

Franklin
Adler, Philip *osteopathic physician*
Zylanoff, Phillipa Louise *anesthesiologist*

Grand Rapids
Andrews, Alice French *neonatologist educator*
Bartek, Gordon Luke *radiologist*
Daniels, Joseph *neuropsychiatrist*

Grosse Pointe
Beierwaltes, William Henry *physician, educator*
Sphire, Raymond Daniel *anesthesiologist*

Harper Woods
DeGiusti, Dominic Lawrence *medical science educator, academic administrator*

Kalamazoo
Aladjem, Silvio *obstetrician, gynecologist, educator*
Chodos, Dale David Jerome *physician, consumer advocate*
Gladstone, William Sheldon, Jr. *radiologist*
Smith, Robert James *immunopharmacologist*

Lake Angelus
Kresge, Bruce Anderson *retired physician*

Lansing
Wiegenstein, John Gerald *physician*

Livonia
Sobel, Howard Bernard *osteopath*

Mancelona
Whelan, Joseph L(eo) *neurologist*

Northville
Lockett, Harold James *physician, psychiatrist*

Okemos
Ochberg, Frank Martin *psychiatrist, health science facility administrator, author*

Pleasant Ridge
Krabbenhoft, Kenneth Lester *radiologist, educator*

Port Huron
Coury, John, Jr. *surgeon*

Royal Oak
Bernstein, Jay *pathologist, researcher, educator*
Dworkin, Howard Jerry *nuclear physician, educator*
LaBan, Myron Miles *physician, administrator*
Proctor, Conrad Arnold *physician*
Walker, Richard Harold *pathologist, educator*

Saginaw
†Manning, John Warren, III *retired surgeon, medical educator*

Saint Clair Shores
Walker, Frank Banghart *pathologist*

Southfield
Hammel, Ernest Martin *medical educator, academic administrator*
Kevorkian, Jack *pathologist*
Mathog, Robert Henry *otolaryngologist, educator*
Rosenzweig, Norman *psychiatry educator*

Sterling Heights
†Frank, Michael Sanford *dermatologist*

Troy
Schafer, Sharon Marie *anesthesiologist*

West Bloomfield
Sarwer-Foner, Gerald Jacob *physician, educator*
Sawyer, Howard Jerome *physician*

Ypsilanti
Ritter, Frank Nicholas *otolaryngologist, educator*

MINNESOTA

Bloomington
Lakin, James Dennis *allergist, immunologist*

Detroit Lakes
Eginton, Charles Theodore *surgeon, educator*

Duluth
Aufderheide, Arthur Carl *pathologist*
Eisenberg, Richard Martin *pharmacology educator*

Excelsior
Bilka, Paul Joseph *physician*
French, Lyle Albert *surgeon*

Fridley
Vernier, Robert Lawrence *physician, educator*

Mendota Heights
Dennis, Clarence *surgeon, educator*

Minneapolis
Balfour, Henry Hallowell, Jr. *medical educator, researcher, physician, writer*
Blackburn, Henry Webster, Jr. *physician*
Brown, David M. *physician, educator, dean*
Buchwald, Henry *surgeon, educator, researcher*
Burton, Charles Victor *physician, surgeon, inventor*
Cavert, Henry Mead *physician, retired educator*
Chavers, Blanche Marie *pediatrician, educator, reseacher*
Chisholm, Tague Clement *pediatric surgeon, educator*
Chou, Shelley Nien-chun *neurosurgeon, university official, educator*
Clinton, Joseph Edward *emergency physician*
Craig, James Lynn *physician, consumer products company executive*
Etzwiler, Donnell Dencil *pediatrician*
Fisch, Robert Otto *medical educator*
Gault, N. L., Jr. *physician, educator*
Gedgaudas, Eugene *radiologist, educator*
Gorlin, Robert James *medical educator*
Gullickson, Glenn, Jr. *physician, educator*
Harris, Jean Louise *physician*
Holter, Arlen Rolf *cardiothoracic surgeon*
Horns, Howard Lowell *physician, educator*
Joseph, Marilyn Susan *gynecologist*
Kane, Robert Lewis *public health educator*
Kaplan, Manuel E. *physician, educator*
Keane, William Francis *nephrology educator, research foundation executive*
Kennedy, B(yrl) J(ames) *medicine and oncology educator*
Knopman, David S. *neurologist*
Langer, Leonard O., Jr. *radiologist, educator*
Leon, Arthur Sol *research cardiologist, exercise physiologist*
Levitt, Seymour Herbert *physician, radiology educator*
Loh, Horace H. *pharmacology educator*
Luepker, Russell Vincent *epidemiology educator*
Mazze, Roger Steven *medical educator, researcher*
McQuarrie, Donald Gray *surgeon, educator*
Michael, Alfred Frederick, Jr. *physician, medical educator*
Najarian, John Sarkis *surgeon, educator*
Oppenheimer, Jack Hans *internist, scientist, educator*
Paparella, Michael M. *otolaryngologist*
Payne, Elizabeth Eleanore *surgeon, otolaryngologist*
Phibbs, Clifford Matthew *surgeon, educator*
Prem, Konald Arthur *physician, educator*
Quie, Paul Gerhardt *physician, educator*
Sabath, Leon David *internist, educator*
Shapiro, Fred Louis *physician, educator*
Staba, Emil John *pharmacognosy and medicinal chemistry educator*
Stenwick, Michael William *internist, geriatric medicine consultant*
Swaiman, Kenneth Fred *pediatric neurologist, educator*
Tagatz, George Elmo *obstetrician, gynecologist, educator*
Thompson, Theodore Robert *pediatric educator*
Thompson, William Moreau *radiologist, educator*
Ward, Wallace Dixon *medical educator*
Warwick, Warren J. *pediatrics educator*
Weir, Edward Kenneth *cardiologist*
White, James George *pediatrician, hematologist, pathologist, educator*
Wild, John Julian *physician, director medical research institute*
Wilson, Leonard Gilchrist *history of medicine educator*
Winter, Robert Bruce *orthopaedic surgeon, educator*
Wood, Joseph George *neurobiologist, educator*

Rochester
Bartholomew, Lloyd Gibson *physician*
Beahrs, Oliver Howard *surgeon*
†Beckett, Victoria Ling *physician*
Berge, Kenneth George *retired internist, educator*
Bisel, Harry Ferree *oncologist*
Brimijoin, William Stephen *pharmacology educator, neuroscience researcher*
Bulbulian, Arthur H. *biomedical scientist, medical graphics and facial prosthetics specialist*
Butt, Hugh Roland *gastroenterologist, educator*
Corbin, Kendall Brooks *physician, scientist*
Danielson, Gordon Kenneth, Jr. *cardiovascular surgeon, educator*
DeRemee, Richard Arthur *physician, educator, researcher*
†Dickson, Edgar Rolland *gastroenterologist*
Douglass, Bruce E. *physician*
Du Shane, James William *physician, educator*
Engel, Andrew George *neurologist*
Feldt, Robert Hewitt *pediatric cardiologist, educator*
Gastineau, Clifford Felix *retired physician*
Gilchrist, Gerald Seymour *pediatric hematologist, oncologist, educator*
Gomez, Manuel Rodriguez *physician*
Gracey, Douglas Robert *physician, physiologist, educator*
Hattery, Robert R. *radiologist, educator*
Kempers, Roger Dyke *obstetrics and gynecology educator*
Keys, Thomas Edward *medical library consultant*
Krom, Ruud Arne Finco *surgeon*
Kurland, Leonard Terry *epidemiologist educator*
Kyle, Robert Arthur *medical educator, oncologist*
Lofgren, Karl Adolph *surgeon*
Lucas, Alexander Ralph *child psychiatrist, educator*
Malkasian, George Durand, Jr. *physician, educator*
Martin, Gordon Mather *physician, educator, administrator*
Martin, Maurice John *psychiatrist*
Mc Conahey, William McConnell, Jr. *physician, educator*
Mc Goon, Dwight Charles *retired surgeon, educator*
Michenfelder, John Donahue *anesthesiology educator*
Morlock, Carl Grismore *physician, medical educator*
Mulder, Donald William *physician, educator*
Muller, Sigfrid Augustine *dermatologist, educator*
Neel, Harry Bryan, III *surgeon, scientist, educator*
Nichols, Donald Richardson *medical educator*
Olsen, Arthur Martin *physician, educator*
†Opitz, Joachim Ludwig *physiatrist*
Payne, W(illiam) Spencer *retired surgeon*
Perry, Harold Otto *dermatologist*
Phillips, Sidney Frederick *gastroenterologist*
Pittelkow, Mark Robert *dermatology educator, researcher*
Polley, Howard Freeman *physician*
Pratt, Joseph Hyde, Jr. *surgeon*
Reitemeier, Richard Joseph *physician*
Riggs, Byron Lawrence, Jr. *physician, educator*
Rosenow, Edward Carl, III *medical educator*
Siekert, Robert George *neurologist*
Stillwell, G(eorge) Keith *physician*
Symmonds, Richard Earl *gynecologist*
Waller, Robert Rex *ophthalmologist, educator, foundation executive*
Whisnant, Jack Page *neurologist*
Woods, John Elmer *plastic surgeon*

Saint Cloud
Gruys, Robert Irving *physician, surgeon*

Saint Louis Park
Knighton, David Reed *vascular surgeon, educator*

Saint Paul
Burchell, Howard Bertram *retired physician, educator*
Edwards, Jesse Efrem *physician, educator*
Fuller, Benjamin Franklin *physician, educator*
Lillehei, Clarence Walton *surgeon*
Rowe, Clarence John *psychiatrist*
Titus, Jack L. *pathologist, educator*
Zander, Janet Adele *psychiatrist*

Spicer
Wescoe, W(illiam) Clarke *physician*

Spring Grove
Roverud, Eleanor *pathologist, neuropathologist*

Stillwater
Asch, Susan McClellan *pediatrician*

Virginia
Knabe, George William, Jr. *pathologist, educator*

MISSISSIPPI

Brandon
Nelson, Norman Crooks *surgeon, academic administrator, educator*

Jackson
Achord, James Lee *gastroenterologist, educator*
Ball, Carroll Raybourne *anatomist, medical educator, researcher*
Batson, Blair Everett *pediatrician, educator*
Bloom, Sherman *pathologist, educator*
Brooks, Thomas Joseph, Jr. *preventive medicine educator*
Cruse, Julius Major, Jr. *pathologist*
Currier, Robert David *neurologist*
Das, Suman Kumar *plastic surgeon, researcher*
Draper, Edgar *psychiatrist*
Forks, Thomas Paul *osteopathic physician*
Freeland, Alan Edward *orthopedic surgery educator, physician*
Guyton, Arthur Clifton *physician, educator*
Halaris, Angelos *psychiatrist, educator*
Houston, Gerry Ann *oncologist*
Lewis, Robert Edwin, Jr. *pathology immunology educator, researcher*
Seltzer, Ada May *librarian, medical library director*
Vance, Ralph Brooks *oncologist and educator*

Ridgeland
Morrison, Francis Secrest *physician*

MISSOURI

Chesterfield
Hunter, Harlen Charles *orthopedic surgeon*
Levin, Marvin Edgar *physician*
Payne, Meredith Jorstad *physician*

Columbia
Allen, William Cecil *physician, educator*
Bryant, Lester R. *surgeon, educator*
Colwill, Jack Marshall *physician, educator*
Cunningham, Milamari Antoinella *anesthesiologist*
Eggers, George William Nordholtz, Jr. *anesthesiologist, educator*
Hillman, Richard Ephraim *pediatrician, educator*
Kashani, Javad Hassan-Nejad *physician*
Long, Edwin Tutt *surgeon*
Perkoff, Gerald Thomas *physician, educator*
Perry, Michael Clinton *physician, medical educator, academic administrator*
Puckett, C. Lin *plastic surgeon, educator*
Silver, Donald *surgeon, educator*
Stephenson, Hugh Edward, Jr. *retired physician, educator*
Weiss, James Moses Aaron *psychiatrist, educator*
Witten, David Melvin *radiology educator*

Florissant
Tanphaichitr, Kongsak *rheumatologist, allergist, immunologist, internist*

Fulton
Gish, Edward Rutledge *surgeon*

Independence
Smith, Wallace Bunnell *physician, church official*

Joplin
Singleton, Marvin Ayers *otolaryngologist, senator*

Kansas City
Abdou, Nabih I. *physician, educator*
Blim, Richard Don *pediatrician*
Dimond, Edmunds Grey *medical educator*
Ellfeldt, Howard James *orthopedic surgeon*
Graham, James Robert, III *physician, medical society administrator*
Grunt, Jerome Alvin *pediatric endocrinologist*
Hartzler, Geoffrey Oliver *cardiologist*
Holder, Thomas Martin *physician*
Hunzicker, Warren John *research consultant, physician, cardiologist*
Huston, Kent Allen *rheumatologist*
Mc Coy, Frederick John *retired plastic surgeon*
Mebust, Winston Keith *surgeon, educator*
Moffatt, David John *anatomy educator*
Mongan, James John *physician*
Noback, Richardson Kilbourne *medical educator*
O'Hearne, John Joseph *psychiatrist*
Perrin, John Paul *medical school president*
Sauer, Gordon Chenoweth *physician, educator*
Schoolman, Arnold *neurological surgeon*
Wheeler, Charles Bertan *pathologist*

North Kansas City
Hagan, John Charles, III *ophthalmologist*

Poplar Bluff
Alexander, C. Alex *physician*

Saint Charles
Dieterich, Russell Burks *obstetrician/gynecologist*

Saint Louis
Agrawal, Harish Chandra *neurobiologist, researcher, educator*
Alpers, David Hershel *physician, educator*
Anderson, Charles Bernard *surgeon, educator*
†Arrington, Barbara *public health educator*
Backer, Matthias, Jr. *obstetrician-gynecologist*
Ballinger, Walter Francis *surgeon, educator*
Baue, Arthur Edward *surgeon, educator, administrator*
Berg, Leonard *neurologist, educator, researcher*
Bowen, Stephen Francis, Jr. *ophthalmic surgeon*
Brodeur, Armand Edward *pediatric radiologist*
Chaplin, Hugh, Jr. *physician, educator*
Cloninger, Claude Robert *psychiatric researcher, educator, genetic epidemiologist*
Cole, Barbara Ruth *pediatrician, nephrologist*
Colten, Harvey Radin *pediatrician, educator*
Cryer, Philip Eugene *medical educator, scientist, endocrinologist*
†Cummings, James M. *urology educator*
Dewald, Paul Adolph *psychiatrist*
Dodge, Philip Rogers *physician, educator*
Drews, Robert Carrel *physician*
Evens, Ronald Gene *radiologist, medical center administrator*
Ferrendelli, James Anthony *neurologist, educator*
Fischer, Harry William *radiologist, educator*
Fitch, Coy Dean *physician, educator*
Fletcher, James Warren *physician*
Flye, M. Wayne *surgeon, immunologist, educator*
Fogarty, William Martin, Jr. *physician*
Frawley, Thomas Francis *physician*
Fredrickson, John Murray *otolaryngologist*
Friedman, William Hersh *otolaryngologist, educator*
Goldberg, Anne Carol *physician, educator*
Guze, Samuel Barry *psychiatrist, educator, university official*
Hershey, Falls Bacon *surgeon, educator*
†Hirsch, Ira Jean *otolaryngologist, educator*
Hofstatter, Leopold *psychiatrist, researcher*
Holmes, Nancy Elizabeth *pediatrician*
Hsu, Chung Yi *neurologist*
Joist, Johann Heinrich *hematologist, medical researcher, educator*
Kaplan, Henry Jerrold *ophthalmologist, educator*
Keltner, Raymond Marion, Jr. *surgeon, educator*
Kimmey, James Richard, Jr. *medical educator, consultant*
Kinsella, Ralph Aloysius, Jr. *physician*
Kipnis, David Morris *physician, educator*
Klahr, Saulo *physician, educator*
Kodner, Ira J. *surgeon, educator*
Kolker, Allan Erwin *ophthalmologist*
Kouchoukos, Nicholas Thomas *surgeon*
Lacy, Paul Eston *pathologist*
Lagunoff, David *physician, educator*
Landau, William Milton *neurologist*
Loeb, Virgil, Jr. *oncologist, hematologist*
Luther, George Aubrey *orthopedic surgeon*
Majerus, Philip Warren *physician*
Manske, Paul Robert *orthopedic hand surgeon, educator*
Masters, William Howell *physician, educator*
Mattison, Richard *psychiatry educator*
Middelkamp, John Neal *pediatrician, educator*
Minnich, Virginia *retired medical researcher, educator*
Murphy, George Earl *psychiatrist, educator*
Myerson, Robert J. *radiologist, educator*
Owens, William Don *anesthesiology educator*
Peck, William Arno *physician*
Perez, Carlos A. *radiation oncologist, educator*
Petrie, Roy H. *obstetrician, gynecologist, educator*
Prensky, Arthur Lawrence *pediatric neurologist, educator*
Price, Joseph Levering *neuroscientist, educator*
Robins, Lee Nelken *medical educator*
Ryall, Jo-Ellyn M. *psychiatrist*
Santiago, Julio Victor *medical educator, researcher and administrator*
Schonfeld, Gustav *medical educator, researcher*
Schwartz, Alan Leigh *pediatrician, educator*
Schwartz, Henry Gerard *surgeon, educator*
Shank, Robert Ely *physician, preventive medicine educator emeritus*
Slatopolsky, Eduardo *nephrologist, educator*
Slavin, Raymond Granam *allergist, immunologist*
†Smith, Morton Edward *ophthalmology educator, dean*
Spector, Gershon Jerry *physician, educator, researcher*
†Stoneman, William, III *physician, educator*
Strunk, Robert Charles *physician*
Suba, Antonio Ronquillo *surgeon*
Sutter, Richard Anthony *physician*
Teitelbaum, Steven Lazarus *pathology educator*
Ternberg, Jessie Lamoin *pediatric surgeon*
Thomas, Lewis Jones, Jr. *anesthesiology educator, biomedical researcher*
†Thompson, Robert W. *surgeon*
Ulett, George Andrew *psychiatrist*
Walentik, Corinne Anne *pediatrician*
Walz, Bruce James *radiation oncologist*
Weeks, Paul Martin *plastic surgeon, educator*
Wells, Samuel Alonzo, Jr. *surgeon, educator*
Whyte, Michael Peter *medicine and pediatrics educator, research director*
Wickline, Samuel Alan *cardiologist, educator*
Willman, Vallee Louis *physician, surgery educator*
Wissner, Seth Ernst *gynecologist, educator*
Young, Paul Andrew *anatomist*

Springfield
Hackett, Earl Randolph *neurologist*
H'Doubler, Francis Todd, Jr. *surgeon*
Shealy, Clyde Norman *neurosurgeon*

University City
Shen, Jerome Tseng Yung *pediatrician*

MONTANA

Billings
†Hylton, Robert Ralph *anesthesiologist*

Great Falls
Day, James Lawrence *psychiatrist*

Livingston
†LeBlond, Richard Foard *internist, educator*

Missoula
Fawcett, Don Wayne *anatomist*

Whitefish
Miller, Ronald Alfred *family physician*

Wolf Point
Listerud, Mark Boyd *retired surgeon*

NEBRASKA

Kearney
De Los Angeles, Reynaldo Adrillana *psychiatrist, consultant*

Lincoln
Fuenning, Samuel Isaiah *sports medicine research director*
Hirai, Denitsu *surgeon*
Koszewski, Bohdan Julius *internist, medical educator*

Omaha
Aschenbrener, Carol Ann *pathologist, educator*
Brody, Alfred Walter *pulmonologist*
Casey, Murray Joseph *physician*
Cox, Robert Sayre, Jr. *pathologist, researcher, educator*
Davis, John Byron *surgeon*
Fusaro, Ramon Michael *dermatologist, researcher*
Gardner, Paul Jay *anatomist, educator*
Gordon, John Leo *anesthesiologist*
Harned, Roger Kent *radiology educator*
Harter, David John *radiation oncologist*
Heaney, Robert Proulx *physician, educator*
Hodgson, Paul Edmund *surgeon*
Imray, Thomas John *radiologist, educator*
Klassen, Lynell W. *rheumatologist, transplant immunologist*
Korbitz, Bernard Carl *oncologist, hematologist, educator, consultant*
Lemon, Henry Martyn *physician, educator*
Maurer, Harold Maurice *pediatrician*
Mohiuddin, Syed Maqdoom *cardiologist, educator*
O'Donohue, Walter John, Jr. *medical educator*
Pearson, Paul Hammond *physician*
Rikkers, Layton F. *surgeon*
†Rikkers, Layton Frederick *surgeon*
Rogan, Eleanor Groeniger *cancer researcher, educator*
Ruddon, Raymond Walter, Jr. *pharmacology educator*
Rupp, Mark Edmund *medical educator*
Sanders, W(illiam) Eugene, Jr. *physician, educator*
Sheehan, John Francis *cytopathologist, educator*
Skoog, Donald Paul *retired physician, educator*
†Townley, Robert Gordon *medical educator*
Truhlsen, Stanley Marshall *physician, educator*
Waggener, Ronald Edgar *radiologist*

Papillion
Dvorak, Allen Dale *radiologist*

NEVADA

Las Vegas
Bandt, Paul Douglas *physician*
Barger, James Daniel *physician*
Brown, Brice Norman *surgeon, educator*
Fortier, Quincy Ernest *obstetrician, gynecologist*
Hamilton, Richard Lee *surgeon*
Herte, Mary Charlotte *plastic surgeon*
Lazerson, Jack *pediatrician, educator*
Shettles, Landrum Brewer *obstetrician-gynecologist*

Reno
Barnet, Robert Joseph *cardiologist*
Small, Elisabeth Chan *psychiatrist, educator*

NEW HAMPSHIRE

Canterbury
†Chamberlin, Robert West *medical educator*

Etna
Ferm, Vergil Harkness *anatomist, embryologist*

Exeter
†Weeder, Dana Nixon *surgeon*

Grantham
Knights, Edwin Munroe *pathologist*
MacNeill, Arthur Edson *physician, science consultant*
Wells, Edward Phillips *radiologist*

Hanover
Almy, Thomas Pattison *physician, educator*
Cahill, George Francis, Jr. *physician, educator*
Chapman, Carleton Burke *physician*
Koop, Charles Everett *surgeon, government official*
McCollum, Robert Wayne *physician, educator*
Rawnsley, Howard Melody *physician, educator*
Staples, O. Sherwin *orthopaedic surgeon*
Wallace, Andrew Grover *physician*

Hooksett
Bagan, Merwyn *neurological surgeon*

Keene
Fachada, Ederito Paul *podiatrist*

Lebanon
Clendenning, William Edmund *dermatologist*
Cornwell, Gibbons Gray, III *physician, medical educator*
Galton, Valerie Anne *endocrinology educator*
†Glass, D. David *anesthesiologist*
Kelley, Maurice Leslie, Jr. *gastroenterologist, educator*
Morain, William Douglas *surgeon, educator*
Myers, Warren Powers Laird *physician, educator*
Rolett, Ellis Lawrence *medical educator, cardiologist*
Rous, Stephen Norman *urologist, educator*
Smith, Barry David *obstetrician-gynecologist, educator*
Sox, Harold Carleton, Jr. *physician, educator*
Wallace, Harold James, Jr. *physician*

Lyme
McIntyre, Oswald Ross *physician*

Manchester
†Angoff, Gerald Harvey *cardiologist*
DesRochers, Gerard Camille *surgeon*
Emery, Paul Emile *psychiatrist*
Kissmeyer-Nielsen, Perla M.S. *psychiatrist*

New London
Foote, Robert Stephens *physician*

West Lebanon
Chalmers, Thomas Clark *physician, educational and research administrator*

NEW JERSEY

Bayonne
Pelosi, Marco Antonio *obstetrician/gynecologist*

Beach Haven
Brunt, Harry Herman, Jr. *psychiatrist*

Boonton
Ahmad, Mehmood Riaz *cardiologist*

Bridgewater
Bernson, Marcella Shelley *psychiatrist*

Camden
Ances, I. G(eorge) *obstetrician/gynecologist, educator*
Morrison, Ashton Byrom *pathologist, medical school official*

Cherry Hill
Margolis, Gerald Joseph *psychiatrist, educator*
Olearchyk, Andrew S. *cardiothoracic surgeon, educator*
Werbitt, Warren *gastroenterologist, educator*

Clifton
Silber, Judy G. *dermatologist*

Cresskill
Gardner, Richard Alan *psychiatrist, writer*

East Brunswick
Rosenberg, Norman *surgeon*

East Hanover
Anderson, Gary William *physician*
Finkel, Marion Judith *physician*

East Orange
Brundage, Gertrude Barnes *pediatrician*

Englewood
Chiorazzi, Mary Lorraine *psychiatrist*

Flemington
Accettola, Albert Bernard *orthopedic surgeon, educator*
Katcher, Avrum L. *pediatrician*

Florham Park
McDonagh, Thomas Joseph *physician*

Franklin Lakes
Ginsberg, Barry Howard *physician, researcher*

Glen Ridge
Clemente, Celestino *physician, surgeon*

Hackensack
Gross, Peter Alan *epidemiologist, researcher*
Spackman, Thomas James *radiologist*

Haddonfield
Capelli, John Placido *nephrologist*

Hanover
Salans, Lester Barry *physician, scientist, educator*

Hoboken
Gerstein, Richard *medical research executive*

Jamesburg
Miller, Theodore Robert *surgeon, educator*

Jersey City
Melnick, Gilbert Stanley *radiologist, educator*

Lakewood
Bowers, John Zimmerman *physician, educator*

Lawrenceville
Moser, Robert Lawrence *pathologist, health facility administrator*

Leonia
Hollinshead, May Block *anatomist, educator*

Livingston
Barlotta, Flora Maria *hematologist*
Caballes, Romeo Lopez *pathologist, bone tumor researcher*
Keswani, Satty Gill *reproductive endocrinologist*
Krieger, Abbott Joel *neurosurgeon*
Kuzmak, Lubomyr Ihor *surgeon*

Long Branch
Arvanitis, Cyril Steven *surgeon, educator*
Barnett, Lester Alfred *surgeon*
†Fox, Howard Alan *physician, medical educator*
Makhija, Mohan *nuclear medicine physician*

Long Valley
Levich, Cecilia Cortes *psychiatrist*

Manalapan
Harrison-Johnson, Yvonne Elois *pharmacologist*

Marlton
Byerly, LeRoy James *psychiatrist, educator*

Maywood
Fitzpatrick, Judith *immunochemist*

Mendham
Desjardins, Raoul *medical association administrator, financial consultant*

Millburn
†Duberstein, Joel Lawrence *physician*

Montclair
Behrle, Franklin Charles *retired pediatrician and educator*
Fleming, Thomas Crawley *physician, medical director, former editor*

Morris Plains
Fielding, Stuart *psychopharmacologist*

Morristown
Granet, Roger B. psychiatrist, educator
Lindner, Joseph, Jr. physician, medical administrator
Parr, Grant Van Siclen surgeon

Mountainside
Lissenden, Carolkay pediatrician

Neptune
Harrigan, John Thomas, Jr. physician, obstetrician-gynecologist

New Brunswick
Aisner, Joseph oncologist, physician
†Eisinger, Robert Peter nephrologist, educator
Ettinger, Lawrence Jay pediatric hematologist-oncologist, educator
Gocke, David Joseph immunology educator, physician, medical scientist
Greco, Ralph Steven surgeon, researcher, medical educator
Laraya-Cuasay, Lourdes Redublo pediatric pulmonologist, educator
Scully, John Thomas obstetrician, gynecologist, educator
Seibold, James Richard physician, researcher
Snyderman, Reuven Kenneth plastic surgeon, educator
Walters, Arthur Scott neurologist, educator, clinical research scientist

Newark
Baker, Herman vitaminologist
Ben-Menachem, Yoram radiologist
Cinotti, Alfonse Anthony ophthalmologist, educator
Cook, Stuart Donald physician, educator
Eslami, Hossein Hojatol surgeon, educator
Evans, Hugh E. pediatrician
Feldman, Susan Carol neurobiologist, anatomy educator
Gardner, Bernard surgeon, educator
Goldenberg, David Milton experimental pathologist, oncologist
Hill, George James surgeon, educator
Hobson, Robert Wayne, II surgeon
Hutcheon, Duncan Elliot physician, educator
Iffy, Leslie medical educator
Layman, William Arthur psychiatrist, educator
Ledeen, Robert Wagner neurochemist, educator
Leevy, Carroll Moton medical educator, hepatology researcher
Materna, Thomas Walter ophthalmologist
Reichman, Lee Brodersohn physician
Tallal, Paula cognitive neuroscientist
Weiss, Gerson physician, educator

Nutley
Burns, John Joseph pharmacology educator
Kuntzman, Ronald pharmacology research executive
Mostillo, Ralph medical association executive

Oldwick
Blewitt, George Augustine physician, pharmaceutical company executive

Paramus
Bagli, Vincent Joseph plastic surgeon
†Liva, Edward Louis eye surgeon

Parsippany
Winters, Robert W. medical educator, pediatrician

Passaic
Haddad, Jamil Raouf physician

Phillipsburg
Rosenthal, Marvin Bernard pediatrician, educator

Piscataway
Bretschneider, Ann Margery histotechnologist
Conney, Allan Howard pharmacologist
Edelman, Norman H. medical educator
Murphree, Henry Bernard Scott psychiatry educator, consultant
Pollack, Irwin William psychiatrist, educator
Rhoads, George Grant medical epidemiologist
Shea, Stephen Michael physician, educator

Plainfield
†Eisenstat, Theodore Ellis colon and rectal surgeon, educator
Yood, Harold Stanley internist

Point Pleasant Beach
Motley, John Paul psychiatrist, consultant

Pomona
Sung, Edward physician

Princeton
Bunn, William Bernice, III physician, lawyer, epidemiologist
Carver, David Harold physician, educator
Chandler, James John surgeon
Conn, Hadley Lewis, Jr. physician, educator
Hathaway, David Roger physician, medical educator, scientist
Khachadurian, Avedis physician
Mueller, Peter Sterling psychiatrist, educator
Napoliello, Michael John psychiatrist
Reynolds, Richard Clyde physician, foundation administrator
Rosenberg, Leon Emanuel medical educator, geneticist, university dean
Schroeder, Steven Alfred medical educator, researcher, foundation executive
Weiss, Robert Jerome psychiatrist, educator

Roselle Park
Wilchins, Sidney A. gynecologist

Short Hills
Aviado, Domingo M. pharmacologist, toxicologist

Stratford
Mendels, Joseph psychiatrist, educator

Summit
Pincus, Jillian Ruth physician

Teaneck
Churg, Jacob pathologist
Lehrer, Joel Fredric otolaryngologist
Ngai, Shih Hsun physician

Tenafly
Cosgriff, Stuart Worcester internist, consultant
Katzman, Merle Hershel orthopaedic surgeon

Tinton Falls
Orlando, Carl medical research and development executive

Trenton
Weinberg, Martin Herbert psychiatrist

Ventnor City
Zuckerman, Stuart psychiatrist, educator

Voorhees
Barone, Donald Anthony neurologist, educator
Swiecicki, Martin neurosurgeon

Wayne
†Gollance, Robert Barnett ophthalmologist

West Caldwell
Chun, Edward Hong Yun psychiatrist

West Orange
Brodkin, Roger Harrison dermatologist, educator
Ghali, Anwar Youssef psychiatrist, educator
Wu, Nan Faion pediatrician

Whitehouse Station
Douglas, Robert Gordon, Jr. physician

Whiting
Williams, Roger Wright public health educator

Wyckoff
Bauer, Theodore James physician
Stahl, Alice Slater psychiatrist

NEW MEXICO

Alamogordo
Stapp, John Paul surgeon, former air force officer

Albuquerque
Ballard, David Eugene anesthesiologist
Barbo, Dorothy Marie obstetrician-gynecologist, educator
Buss, William Charles research pharmacology educator
Dixon, George Lane, Jr. orthopaedic surgeon
Edwards, William Sterling, III cardiovascular surgeon
Kelley, Robert Otis medical science educator
Knospe, William Herbert medical educator
McCarty, W(illard) Duane obstetrician-gynecologist, physician executive
†Mora, Federico neurosurgeon
Napolitano, Leonard Michael anatomist, university administrator
Neidhart, James Allen physician, educator
Omer, George Elbert, Jr. orthopaedic surgeon, hand surgeon, educator
Ottensmeyer, David Joseph neurosurgeon, health care executive
Saland, Linda Carol anatomy educator
†Simpson, Steven Quentin physician, researcher
Tatum, Ronald Winston physician, endocrinologist
Uhlenhuth, Eberhard Henry psychiatrist, educator
Winslow, Walter William psychiatrist
Worrell, Audrey Martiny geriatric psychiatrist
Worrell, Richard Vernon orthopedic surgeon, educator
†Zumwalt, Ross Eugene forensic pathologist, educator

Carlsbad
Markle, George Bushar, IV surgeon

Chama
Moser, Robert Harlan physician, educator, writer

Corrales
†Cobb, John Candler medical educator

Las Cruces
Jacobs, Kent Frederick dermatologist
Reeves, Billy Dean obstetrics/gynecology educator emeritus

Los Alamos
Smith, Fredrica Emrich rheumatologist, internist

Roswell
Jennings, Emmit M. surgeon

Santa Fe
Frenkel, Jacob Karl physician, consultant, researcher
Schwartz, George R. physician
†Spencer, Steven Sears medical consultant
Upton, Arthur Canfield experimental pathologist, educator

Univ Of New Mexico
Goodin, Julia C. medical investigator, state official, educator

NEW YORK

Albany
Arseneau, James Charles physician
Beebe, Richard Townsend physician
Bradley, Wesley Holmes physician
Davis, Paul Joseph endocrinologist
DeFelice, Eugene Anthony physician, medical educator, consultant, magician
Dougherty, James orthopedic surgeon, educator
Doyle, Joseph Theobald physician, educator
Gellhorn, Alfred physician, educator
Gruber, Scott Alan medical educator
Han, Jaok cardiologist, researcher, educator
Hoffmeister, Jana Marie cardiologist
Kaye, Gordon Israel pathologist, anatomist, educator
Lumpkin, Lee Roy dermatologist, educator
Macario, Alberto Juan Lorenzo physician
Mihm, Martin Charles, Jr. pathologist, educator
Swartz, Donald Percy physician

Armonk
Mellors, Robert Charles physician scientist

Bath
Sandt, John Joseph psychiatrist, educator

Bay Shore
Pinsker, Walter allergist, immunologist

Beacon
Garell, Paul Charles family physician

Bellmore
Crouch, Howard Earle health service organization executive

Binghamton
Michael, Sandra Dale reproductive endocrinology educator, researcher

Briarcliff Manor
Gaylin, Willard physician, educator
Glassman, Jerome Martin clinical pharmacologist, educator
Weintraub, Michael Ira neurologist

Bronx
Bhalodkar, Narendra Chandrakant cardiologist
Blaufox, Morton Donald physician, educator
Brescia, Michael Joseph nephrologist, educator
Bruenn, Howard Gerald physician
Burde, Ronald Marshall neuro-ophthalmologist
Buschke, Herman neurologist
Cimino, James Ernest physician
Cohen, Herbert Jesse physician, educator
DeMartino, Anthony Gabriel cardiologist, internist
Duncalf, Deryck anesthesiologist
Edelmann, Chester Monroe, Jr. pediatrician, medical school dean
Eder, Howard Abram physician
Eliasoph, Joan radiologist, educator
Elkin, Milton radiologist, physician, educator
Foreman, Spencer pulmonary specialist, hospital executive
Frater, Robert William Mayo surgeon, educator
Freeman, Leonard Murray radiologist, nuclear medicine physician, educator
Fulop, Milford physician
Gandhi, Bhanumati Bhagwandas anesthesiologist
Gerst, Paul Howard physician
Gliedman, Marvin L. surgeon, educator
Gross, Ludwik physician
Hait, Gershon pediatric cardiologist
Hirano, Asao neuropathologist
Jacobson, Harold Gordon radiologist, educator
Jaffé, Ernst Richard medical educator and administrator
Kahn, Thomas medical educator
Karasu, T(oksoz) Byram psychiatry educator
Karmen, Arthur physician, science administrator, educator
Koss, Leopold G. pathologist, educator, physician
Lieber, Charles Saul physician, educator
Marx, Gertie Florentine anesthesiologist
Michelsen, W(olfgang) Jost neurosurgeon, educator
Muschel, Louis Henry immunologist, educator
Nagler, Arnold Leon pathologist, scientist, educator
Nathenson, Stanley Gail immunology educator
Orkin, Louis Richard physician, educator
Pitchumoni, Capecomorin Sankar gastroenterologist, educator
Purpura, Dominick P. neuroscientist, university dean
Rapin, Isabelle physician
Reynolds, Benedict Michael surgeon
Romney, Seymour Leonard physician, educator
Ruben, Robert Joel physician, educator
Scharff, Matthew Daniel immunologist, cell biologist, educator
Scharrer, Berta Vogel anatomy and neuroscience educator
Schaumburg, Herbert Howard neurology educator
Shafritz, David Andrew physician, research scientist
Shinnar, Shlomo child neurologist, educator
Spitzer, Adrian pediatrician, medical educator
Stein, Ruth Elizabeth Klein physician
Surks, Martin I. medical educator, endocrinologist
Waltz, Joseph McKendree neurosurgeon, educator
Wiernik, Peter Harris oncologist, educator
Williams, Marshall Henry, Jr. physician, educator

Bronxville
Barkhuus, Arne physician
Levitt, Miriam pediatrician
Lukash, Barbara Lynne dermatologist

Brooklyn
Alfonso, Antonio Escolar surgeon
Barth, Robert Henry nephrologist
Bergeron, R. Thomas radiologist, educator
Biro, Laszlo dermatologist
Cracco, Roger Quinlan medical educator, neurologist
Crum, Albert Byrd psychiatrist, consultant
Edemeka, Udo Edemeka surgeon
†Erber, William Franklin gastroenterologist
Fodstad, Harald neurosurgeon
Friedman, Eli Arnold nephrologist
Friedman, Howard Samuel cardiologist, educator
Gintautas, Jonas physician, scientist, administrator
Glickman, Franklin Sheldon dermatologist, educator
Gotta, Alexander Walter anesthesiologist, educator
Holden, David Morgan medical educator
Imperato, Pascal James physician, health administrator, author, editor, medical educator
Jindrak, Karel Francis pathologist, researcher, educator
Kamholz, Stephan L. physician
Kravath, Richard Elliot pediatrician, educator
Lee, Stanley physician, educator
Leeman, Cavin Philip psychiatrist, educator
Levere, Richard David physician, academic administrator, educator
Lindo, J. Trevor psychiatrist, consultant
Malach, Monte physician
Milhorat, Thomas Herrick neurosurgeon
Milman, Doris Hope pediatrics educator, psychiatrist
Mohaideen, A. Hassan surgeon, healthcare consultant
Namba, Tatsuji physician, medical researcher
Norstrand, Iris Fletcher psychiatrist, neurologist, educator
Nurhussein, Mohammed Alamin internist, geriatrician, educator
Plotz, Charles Mindell physician
Ravitz, Leonard J., Jr. physician, scientist, consultant
Reich, Nathaniel Edwin physician, poet, author, artist, educator
Shalita, Alan Remi dermatologist
Sher, Norman psychiatrist, child psychiatrist
Sullivan, Colleen Anne physician, educator
Weiner, Irwin M. medical educator, college dean, researcher
Wise, Leslie surgeon, educator
Wolintz, Arthur Harry physician, neuro-ophthalmologist
Wollman, Leo physician

Buffalo
Ambrus, Clara Maria physician
Ambrus, Julian L. physician, medical educator
Ament, Richard anesthesiologist, educator
Bakay, Louis neurosurgeon
†Ballow, Mark physician, educator
Brody, Harold neuroanatomist, gerontologist
Brooks, John Samuel Joseph pathologist, researcher
Calkins, Evan physician, educator
Chu, Tsann Ming immunochemist, educator
Chutkow, Jerry Grant neurologist, educator
Creaven, Patrick Joseph physician, research oncologist
Genco, Robert Joseph scientist, immunologist, periodontist, educator
Glasauer, Franz Ernst neurosurgeon
Gona, M. Jayakumari nuclear medicine physician
Graham, (Lloyd) Saxon epidemiology educator
Gresham, Glen Edward physician
Halbreich, Uriel Morav psychiatrist, educator
Hare, Daphne Kean medical association director, educator
Helm, Frederick dermatology educator
Horoszewicz, Juliusz Stanislaw oncologist, cancer researcher, laboratory administrator
Katz, Leonard Allen medical director, educator
Kurlan, Marvin Zeft surgeon
Lee, Richard Vaille physician, educator
Middleton, Elliott, Jr. physician
Mihich, Enrico medical researcher
Milgrom, Felix immunologist, educator
Mindell, Eugene Robert surgeon, educator
Mirand, Edwin Albert medical scientist
Naughton, John Patrick cardiologist, medical school administrator
Panaro, Victor Anthony radiologist
Piver, M. Steven gynecologic oncologist
Regan, Peter Francis, III physician, psychiatry educator
Rekate, Albert C. physician
Richmond, Allen Martin speech pathologist, educator
Seller, Robert Herman cardiologist, family physician
Shedd, Donald Pomroy surgeon
Small, S(aul) Mouchly psychiatrist, educator
Stoll, Howard Lester, Jr. dermatologist
Voorhess, Mary Louise pediatric endocrinologist
Wright, John Robert pathologist
Zaleski, Marek Bohdan immunologist

Canaan
Bell, James Milton psychiatrist
Rothenberg, Albert psychiatrist, educator

Carle Place
Linchitz, Richard Michael pain medicine specialist, psychiatrist, physician

Castle Point
Greene, Jerry George physician

Cedarhurst
Cohen, Harris L. diagnostic radiologist, consultant

Centerport
Fischel, Edward Elliot physician

Chestnut Ridge
Day, Stacey Biswas physician, educator

Chucktowaga
Howland, Murray Shipley, Jr. gastroenterologist

Cooperstown
†Bordley, James, IV surgeon
†Franck, Walter Alfred rheumatologist, medical administrator, educator
Pearson, Thomas Arthur epidemiologist, educator

Croton On Hudson
†Wandel, Thaddeus ophthalmologist

East Islip
Fleishman, Philip Robert internist

Eatons Neck
Altner, Peter Christian orthopedic surgeon, medical educator

Edmeston
Price, James Melford physician

Flushing
Dubov, Spencer Floyd podiatrist, educator
Ellis, John Taylor pathologist, educator
Kornhauser, Stanley Henry medical administrator, educator, consultant

Glenmont
Kolb, Lawrence Coleman psychiatrist

Great Neck
Arlow, Jacob A. psychiatrist, educator
Simon, Arthur pharmacologist, research laboratory executive

Hawthorne
Swift, Michael Ronald physician, scientist, educator

Hempstead
Laano, Archie Bienvenido Maaño *cardiologist*

Huntington
Vale, Margo Rose *physician*

Ithaca
Dietert, Rodney Reynolds *immunology/toxicology educator*
Moore, Norman Slawson *physician*
Whitaker, Susanne Kanis *veterinary medical librarian*

Jamaica
Rosner, Fred *physician, educator*

Jericho
†Harris, Elaine K. *medical consultant*
Khan, Arfa *radiologist, educator*

Larchmont
Bellak, Leopold *psychiatrist, psychoanalyst, psychologist*
Gillman, Arthur Emanuel *psychiatrist*
Holleb, Arthur Irving *surgeon*

Lawrence
Sklarin, Burton S. *endocrinologist*

Liverpool
†Kark, Pieter Robert Adriaan *neurologist*

Lockport
Carr, Edward Albert, Jr. *medical educator, physician*

Lowville
Becker, Robert Otto *orthopedic surgery educator*

Mamaroneck
Halpern, Abraham Leon *psychiatrist*

Manhasset
Arnold, Charles Burle, Jr. *psychiatric resident, epidemiologist, writer*
Enquist, Irving Fridtjof *surgeon*
Fenton, Arnold N. *obstetrician, gynecologist, educator*
Kreis, Willi *physician*
Scherr, Lawrence *physician, educator*
Warren, Kenneth S. *medical educator, physician*

Massapequa
Aiello-Contessa, Angela Marie *physician*

Merrick
Copperman, Stuart Morton *pediatrician*

Mineola
Shperling, Irena *internist*
Twist, Paul Francis, Jr. *neonatologist*

Monroe
Werzberger, Alan *pediatrician*

Monticello
Lauterstein, Joseph *cardiologist*

Nanuet
Savitz, Martin Harold *neurosurgeon*

Naples
Beal, Myron Clarence *osteopathic physician*

New City
Esser, Aristide Henri *psychiatrist*

New Hyde Park
Biddle, David *neurologist*
Koplewicz, Harold Samuel *child and adolescent psychiatrist*
Seltzer, Vicki Lynn *obstetrician-gynecologist*
Shenker, Ira Ronald *pediatrician*
Wolf, Julius *medical educator*

New Rochelle
Golub, James Robert *internist, allergist*
Hayes, Arthur Hull, Jr. *physician, clinical pharmacology educator, medical school dean, business executive, consultant*
Petrucelli, R(occo) Joseph, II *nephrologist*
Rovinsky, Joseph Judah *obstetrician, gynecologist*

New York
Abrahamsen, David *psychiatrist, psychoanalyst, author*
Abramson, Sara Jane *radiologist, educator*
Adamson, John William *hematologist*
Ahrens, Edward Hamblin, Jr. *physician*
Alderson, Philip Otis *radiologist, educator*
Altman, Lawrence Kimball *physician, journalist*
Altman, Roy Peter *pediatric surgeon*
Ames, Richard Pollard *physician, author, educator*
Archibald, Reginald Mac Gregor *physician, chemist, educator*
Arnot, Bob *physician, medical correspondent*
Aron, Alan Milford *pediatric neurology educator*
Aronoff, Michael Stephen *psychiatrist*
Asanuma, Hiroshi *physician, educator*
Atkinson, Holly Gail *physician, journalist, author, lecturer*
Aufses, Arthur H(arold), Jr. *surgeon, medical educator*
Axel, Richard *pathology and biochemistry educator*
Baden, Michael M. *pathologist, educator*
Baer, Rudolf Lewis *dermatologist, educator*
Baldwin, David Shepard *physician*
Barker, Barbara Ann *ophthalmologist*
Barnett, Henry Lewis *medical educator, pediatrician*
Barondess, Jeremiah Abraham *physician*
Bearn, Alexander Gordon *physician scientist, former pharmaceutical company executive*
Beattie, Edward James *surgeon, educator*
Beck, Adrian Robert *surgeon, educator*
Bellin, Howard Theodore *plastic surgeon*
Bendixen, Henrik Holt *physician, educator, dean*
Berger, Frank Milan *biomedical researcher, scientist, former pharmaceutical company executive*
Berk, Paul David *physician, scientist, educator*
Berns, Kenneth Ira *physician*
Bernstein, Anne Elayne *psychoanalyst*
Bertino, Joseph Rocco *physician, educator*
Bertles, John Francis *physician, educator*
Betcher, Albert Maxwell *anesthesiologist*
Bickers, David Rinsey *physician, educator*
Bigger, John Thomas, Jr. *physician, educator*
Biller, Hugh Frederick *medical educator*
Blank, Marion Sue *psychologist*
Blitzer, Andrew *otolaryngologist, educator*
Bogdonoff, Morton David *physician, educator*
Borer, Jeffrey Stephen *cardiologist*
Bosniak, Morton Arthur *physician, educator*
Brand, Leonard *physician, educator*
Braude, Robert Michael *medical library administrator*
Breinin, Goodwin M. *physician*
Breslow, Jan Leslie *scientist, educator, physician*
Brook, David William *psychiatrist*
Brown, Arthur Edward *physician*
Brown, Jason Walter *neurologist, educator, researcher*
†Bush, Harry Leonard, Jr. *surgery educator*
Butler, Robert Neil *gerontologist, psychiatrist, writer, educator*
Butler, Vincent Paul, Jr. *physician, educator*
Buxton, Jorge Norman *ophthalmologist*
Bystryn, Jean-Claude *dermatologist, educator*
Cahan, William George *surgeon, educator*
Calder, Kenneth Thomas *psychiatrist, psychoanalyst, educator*
Cancro, Robert *psychiatrist*
Candia, Oscar A. *ophthalmologist, physiology educator*
Cantor, Richard Ira *physician, corporate health executive*
Carr, Ronald Edward *ophthalmologist, educator*
Casals-Ariet, Jordi *physician*
Cassell, Eric Jonathan *physician*
Castellino, Ronald Augustus Dietrich *radiologist*
Chahinian, Aram Philippe *oncologist*
Chan, W. Y. *pharmacologist, educator*
Chaney, Verne Edward, Jr. *surgeon, foundation executive, educator*
Chase, Merrill Wallace *immunologist, educator*
Chiu, David Tak Wai *surgeon*
†Christian, Charles Leigh *physician, educator*
Clark, William Stratton *physician*
Cohen, David Harris *neurobiology educator, university official*
Cohen, Noel Lee *otolaryngologist, educator*
Coleman, Lester Laudy *otolaryngologist*
Coleman, Morton *oncologist, hematologist, educator*
Cooper, Norman Streich *pathologist, medical educator*
Crain, Irving Jay *psychiatrist, educator*
Cramer, Marjorie *plastic surgeon*
Curtin, Brian Joseph *ophthalmologist*
Daniel, Gerard Lucian *physician, pharmaceutical company executive*
Davis, Kenneth Leon *psychiatrist, pharmacologist, medical educator*
Dell, Ralph Bishop *pediatrician, researcher*
DeVita, Vincent Theodore, Jr. *oncologist*
Dohrenwend, Bruce Philip *psychiatric epidemiologist, social psychologist, educator*
Dole, Vincent Paul *medical research executive, educator*
Dolgin, Martin *cardiologist*
Downey, John Alexander *physician, educator*
Doyle, Eugenie Fleri *pediatric cardiologist, educator*
Drusin, Lewis Martin *physician, educator*
Dworetzky, Murray *physician, educator*
Edmunds, Robert Thomas *retired surgeon*
Ego-Aguirre, Ernesto *surgeon*
Ehlers, Kathryn Hawes (Mrs. James D. Gabler) *physician*
Ellis, Kent *radiologist, consultant*
Ergas, Enrique *orthopedic surgeon*
Esman, Aaron H. *physician, psychiatrist*
Estabrook, Alison *breast surgeon, surgical oncologist, educator*
Fahn, Stanley *neurologist, educator*
Fair, William Robert *physician*
Farber, Saul Joseph *physician, educator*
Feldman, Samuel Mitchell *neuroscientist, educator*
Fellner, Michael Josef *dermatologist*
Ferrer, Marie Irene *physician*
†Fleiss, David Jonathan *orthopedist*
Foley, Kathleen M. *neurologist, educator, researcher*
Fortner, Joseph Gerald *surgeon, educator*
Fox, Arthur Charles *physician, educator*
†Frangione, Blas *physician*
Frankel, Alice Kross *physician, director*
Frantz, Andrew Gibson *physician, educator*
Freedberg, Irwin Mark *dermatologist*
Freedman, Alfred Mordecai *psychiatrist, educator*
Friedewald, William Thomas *physician*
Friedhoff, Arnold J. *psychiatrist, medical scientist*
Friedlander, Ralph *thoracic and vascular surgeon*
Friedman, Alan Herbert *ophthalmologist*
Friedman, Emanuel A. *medical educator*
Friedman, Ira Hugh *surgeon*
Fuchs, Anna-Riitta *medical educator, scientist*
Fuks, Zvi Y. *medical educator*
Furmanski, Philip *cancer research scientist*
Fuster, Valentin *cardiologist, educator*
Gabrilove, Jacques Lester *physician*
Galanter, Marc *psychiatrist, educator*
Galin, Miles A. *ophthalmologist, educator*
Gebbie, Kristine Moore *health science educator, health official*
Geiger, H. Jack *medical educator*
Genkins, Gabriel *physician*
Gershengorn, Marvin Carl *physician, scientist, educator*
†Gershon, Michael David *anatomist, educator*
Gersony, Welton Mark *physician, pediatric cardiologist, educator*
Gertler, Menard M. *physician, educator*
Gertner, Joseph Michael *physician, educator*
Ginsberg-Fellner, Fredda *pediatric endocrinologist, researcher*
Glassman, Alexander Howard *psychiatrist, researcher*
Godman, Gabriel Charles *pathology educator*
Golde, David William *physician, educator*
Goldsmith, Stanley Joseph *nuclear medicine physician, educator*
Goldstein, Marc *microsurgeon, urology educator, academic administrator*
Golomb, Frederick Martin *surgeon, educator*
Gorlin, Richard *physician, educator*
Graber, Edward Alex *obstetrician, gynecologist, educator*
Grant, Alfred David *orthopaedic surgeon, educator*
Graziano, Joseph Harold *scientist, educator*
Green, Jack Peter *pharmacology educator, medical scientist*
Green, Maurice Richard *neuropsychiatrist*
Greene, Lloyd Asher *pathology educator*
Greengard, Paul *neuroscientist*
Griffiths, Sylvia Preston *physician*
Guida, Peter Matthew *surgeon, educator*
Gusberg, Saul Bernard *physician, educator*
Guthrie, Randolph Hobson, Jr. *plastic surgeon*
Haddad, Heskel Marshall *ophthalmologist*
Haggerty, Robert Johns *physician, educator*
Halberg, G. Peter *ophthalmologist*
Hambrick, George Walter, Jr. *dermatologist, educator*
Hamburg, Beatrix Ann *medical educator, researcher*
Hamburg, David A. *psychiatrist, foundation executive*
Han, Yingshi *medical educator and medical researcher*
Harley, Naomi Hallden *radiation specialist, environmental medicine educator*
Harris, Henry William *physician*
Hashim, George A. *immunologist, biomedical researcher, educator*
Hawkins, Katherine Ann *hematologist, educator*
Heimarck, Gregory James *psychoanalyst, child psychiatrist*
Hilgartner, Margaret Wehr *pediatric hematologist, educator*
Hirsch, Jules *physician, scientist*
Hirschhorn, Kurt *pediatrics educator*
Hirschman, Shalom Zarach *physician*
Hofer, Myron A(rms) *psychiatrist, researcher*
Hogan, Charles Carlton *psychiatrist*
Holt, Peter Rolf *physician, educator*
Hoskins, William John *obstetrician and gynecologist, educator*
Howard, Clifton Merton, Jr. *psychiatrist*
Hugo, Norman Eliot *plastic surgeon, medical educator*
Hurvitz, Arthur Isaac *pathologist, researcher*
Hyman, Bruce Malcolm *ophthalmologist*
Hymes, Norma *internist*
Imparato, Anthony Michael *vascular surgeon, medical educator, researcher*
†Imperato-McGinley, Julianne L. *endocrinologist, educator*
Isay, Richard Alexander *psychiatrist*
Janowitz, Henry David *physician, researcher, medical educator*
Jarecki, Henry George *physician, financial executive*
Jelinek, Josef Emil *dermatologist*
Johnson, Horton Anton *pathologist*
†Johnson, Warren Douglas *infectious diseases physician, researcher*
Jonas, Saran *neurologist, educator*
Jurka, Edith Mila *psychiatrist, researcher*
Kabat, Elvin Abraham *immunochemist, biochemist, educator*
Kahn, Norman *pharmacology and dentistry educator*
Kalsner, Stanley *pharmacologist, physiologist, educator*
Kanick, Virginia *radiologist*
Kaplan, Harold Irwin *psychiatrist, psychoanalyst, educator*
Kappas, Attallah *physician, medical scientist*
Katz, Jose *cardiologist, theoretical physicist, educator*
Keill, Stuart Langdon *psychiatrist*
Kellerman, Jonathan Seth *pediatric psychologist, writer*
Kelman, Charles D. *ophthalmologist, educator*
King, Thomas Creighton *thoracic surgeon, educator*
Klein, Donald Franklin *scientist, psychiatrist, educator*
†Klein, Harvey *physician, educagtor*
Kligfield, Paul David *physician, medicine educator*
Kolodny, Edwin Hillel *neurologist, geneticist, medical administrator*
Komisar, Arnold *otolaryngologist, educator*
Kosovich, Dushan Radovan *psychiatrist*
Krown, Susan Ellen *physician, researcher*
Krugman, Saul *physician, educator, researcher*
Kupfer, Sherman *physician, educator, researcher*
Kwa, Raymond Pain-Boon *cardiologist*
Landrigan, Philip John *epidemiologist*
Laragh, John Henry *physician, scientist, educator*
Lattes, Raffaele *physician, educator*
Lattimer, John Kingsley *physician, educator*
Lauersen, Niels Helth *physician, educator*
Laufman, Harold *surgeon*
Laurence, Jeffrey Conrad *immunologist*
Lawrence, Henry Sherwood *physician, educator*
Lawry, Sylvia (Mrs. Stanley Englander) *association executive*
Ledger, William Joe *physician, educator*
Lefkovits, Albert Meyer *dermatologist*
Leiter, Elliot *urologist*
Lepore, Michael Joseph *gastroenterologist, educator*
Lewis, John Leeman, Jr. *obstetrician, gynecologist*
Lifton, Robert Jay *psychiatrist, author*
Lin, Joseph Pen-Tze *neuroradiologist, clinical administrator, educator*
Lipkin, Martin *physician, scientist*
Liu, Brian Cheong-Seng *urology and oncology educator, researcher*
Localio, S. Arthur *retired surgeon, educator*
Lubkin, Virginia Leila *ophthalmologist*
MacKinnon, Roger Alan *psychiatrist*
Malis, Leonard Irving *neurosurgeon*
Malitz, Sidney *psychiatrist, educator, researcher*
Malkin, Stanley Lee *neurologist*
Malm, James Royal *surgeon*
Manger, William Muir *internist*
Marcus, Eric Robert *psychiatrist*
Marks, Paul Alan *oncologist, cell biologist, educator*
Marsh, William Laurence *retired research pathology executive*
Maslow, Melanie Jane *physician*
Masterson, James Francis *psychiatrist*
Matz, Robert *physician, educator*
Mazzia, Valentino Don Bosco *physician, educator, lawyer*
McCall, Marsh *cardiologist*
McCarthy, Joseph Gerald *plastic surgeon, educator*
McCarty, Maclyn *medical scientist*
Mc Crory, Wallace Willard *pediatrician, educator*
McGovern, John Hugh *urologist, educator*
Mc Murtry, James Gilmer, III *neurosurgeon*
Meikle, Thomas Harry, Jr. *foundation administrator, neuroscientist, educator*
Mellins, Robert B. *pediatrician, educator*
Mendelsohn, John *oncologist, hematologist, educator*
Mesnikoff, Alvin Murray *psychiatry educator*
Michels, Robert *psychiatrist*
Michelsen, Christopher Bruce Hermann *surgeon*
Mildvan, Donna *infectious diseases physician*
Millman, Robert Barnet *psychiatry and public health educator*
Mohr, Jay Preston *neurologist*
Montemayor, Jesus Samson *physician*
Moore, Malcolm Andrew Stephen *cancer researcher*
Moss, Melvin Lionel *anatomist*
†Moss-Salentijn, Letty (Aleida Moss-Salentijn) *anatomist*
†Murray, Henry Wilke *physician, educator*
Myers, Wayne Alan *psychiatrist, educator*
Nabatoff, Robert Allan *vascular surgeon, educator*
†Nachman, Ralph Louis *physician, educator*
Nahas, Gabriel Georges *pharmacologist, educator*
Nathan, Carl Francis *medical educator*
†Nay, Howard Riley *surgeon, educator*
Neu, Harold Conrad *physician, educator*
Neubauer, Peter Bela *psychoanalyst*
Neuwirth, Robert Samuel *obstetrician, gynecologist*
New, Maria Iandolo *physician, educator*
Newman, Robert Gabriel *physician*
Noback, Charles Robert *anatomist, educator*
Novick, Nelson Lee *dermatologist, internist, writer*
Oettgen, Herbert Friedrich *physician*
Old, Lloyd John *cancer biologist*
Oldham, John Michael *physician, psychiatrist, educator*
Olsson, Carl Alfred *urologist*
Pacella, Bernard Leonardo *psychiatrist*
Pardes, Herbert *psychiatrist, educator*
Parker, Lynda Michele *psychiatrist*
Patterson, Russel Hugo, Jr. *neurosurgeon, educator*
Peck, M(organ) Scott *psychiatrist, writer*
Phillips, Gerald Baer *internal medicine educator, scientist*
Pierson, Richard Norris, Jr. *medical educator*
Pirani, Conrad Levi *pathologist, educator*
Pi-Sunyer, F. Xavier *medical educator, medical investigator*
†Plum, Fred *neurologist*
Posner, Jerome Beebe *neurologist, educator*
Potter, Guy Dill *radiologist, educator*
Quraishi, Nisar Ali *internist*
Rabinowitz, Jack Grant *radiologist, educator*
†Rafii, Shahin *medicine educator*
Rainer, John David *psychiatrist*
Rainess, Alan Edward *psychiatrist*
Raynor, Richard Benjamin *neurosurgeon, educator*
Redo, S(averio) Frank *surgeon*
†Reemtsma, Keith *surgeon, educator*
Reidenberg, Marcus Milton *physician, educator*
Reis, Donald Jeffery *neurologist, neurobiologist, educator*
Reisberg, Barry *geropsychiatrist, neuropsychopharmacologist*
Reisner, Milton *psychiatrist, psychoanalyst*
Richman, Howard *surgeon*
Rifkin, Harold *physician, educator*
Rifkind, Arleen B. *physician, researcher*
Riker, Walter F., Jr. *pharmacologist, physician*
†Roen, Philip Ruben *urologist, surgeon, medical educator*
Roman, Stanford Augustus, Jr. *medical educator, dean*
Rosenfield, Allan *physician*
Rothenberg, Robert Edward *physician, surgeon, author*
Rowland, Lewis Phillip *neurologist, medical editor, educator*
Rubin, Albert L. *physician, educator*
Rubin, Gustav *orthopedic surgeon, consultant, researcher*
Rubin, Theodore Isaac *psychiatrist*
Sachar, David Bernard *gastroenterologist, medical educator*
Sachdev, Ved Parkash *neurosurgeon*
Sacks, Oliver Wolf *neurologist, writer*
Sadock, Benjamin James *psychiatrist, educator*
Sager, Clifford J(ulius) *psychiatrist, educator*
Santulli, Thomas Vincent *surgeon*
Sawyer, William Dale *physician, educator, university dean, foundation administrator*
†Schaffner, Bertram Henry *psychiatrist*
Scheinberg, Labe Charles *physician, educator*
Schiavi, Raul Constante *psychiatrist, educator, researcher*
Schlesinger, David Harvey *medical educator, researcher*
Schlesinger, Edward Bruce *neurological surgeon*
Schlessinger, Joseph *pharmacology educator*
†Schley, William Shain *otorhinolaryngologist*
Schneck, Jerome M. *psychiatrist, medical historian, educator*
Schneier, Harvey Allen *physician, pharmaceutical researcher*
Schwartz, Irving Leon *physician, scientist, educator*
Schwartz, Roselind Shirley Grant *podiatrist*
Schwarz, Richard Howard *obstetrician/gynecologist, educator*
Sedlin, Elias David *physician, orthopedic researcher, educator*
Seely, Robert Daniel *physician, medical educator*
Shaffer, David *psychiatrist*
Shainess, Natalie *psychiatrist, educator*
Shapiro, Theodore *psychiatrist, educator*
Shapley, Robert Martin *neurophysiology and perception educator*
Siffert, Robert Spencer *orthopedic surgeon*
Silver, Richard Tobias *physician, educator*
†Siris, Ethel Silverman *endocrinologist*
Sitarz, Anneliese Lotte *pediatrics educator, physician*
†Skinner, David Bernt *surgeon, educator*
Sorrel, William Edwin *psychiatrist, educator, psychoanalyst*
Spiegel, Herbert *psychiatrist, educator*
Stark, Richard Boies *surgeon, artist*
Stein, Bennett Mueller *neurosurgeon*
Stein, Marvin *psychiatrist, educator*
Stenzel, Kurt Hodgson *physician, nephrologist, educator*
Stern, Marvin *psychiatrist, educator*
†Stevenson, Nikolai *medical association executive*
Stimmel, Barry *cardiologist, internist, educator, university dean*
Susser, Mervyn Wilfred *epidemiologist, educator*
Thompson, David Duvall *physician*
Tilson, M(artin) David *surgeon, scientist*
†Torman, Howard Alan *cardiologist, medical correspondent*
Torre, Douglas Paul *dermatologist*
Turino, Gerard Michael *physician, medical scientist, educator*
Tzimas, Nicholas Achilles *orthopedic surgeon, educator*
Vaughan, Edwin Darracott, Jr. *urologist, surgeon*
†Vaughan, Susan Carole *psychiatrist, psychoanalyst*
Vilcek, Jan Tomas *medical educator*
Waksman, Byron Halsted *neuroimmunologist, experimental pathologist, educator, medical association administrator*
Wallach, Stanley *medical educator, consultant, administrator*
†Walther, Robert R. *physician, educator*
Warshaw, Leon J(oseph) *physician*

Wasserman, Louis Robert *physician, educator*
Watanabe, Kyoichi A(loysius) *chemist, researcher, pharmacology educator*
Waugh, Theodore Rogers *orthopedic surgeon*
Wecker, William A. *preventive medicine physician, neuropsychiatrist*
Weinstein, I. Bernard *physician*
Weisfeldt, Myron Lee *physician, educator*
Weissmann, Gerald *medical educator, researcher, writer, editor*
†Weksler, Marc Edward *physician, educator*
Whelan, Elizabeth Ann Murphy *epidemiologist*
White, Kerr Lachlan *physician, foundation director*
Whitehead, E. Douglas *urology educator*
Wiesel, Torsten Nils *neurobiologist, educator*
Winawer, Sidney Jerome *physician, clinical investigator, educator*
Winick, Myron *educator, physician*
Winikoff, Beverly *physician*
Wishnick, Marcia Margolis *pediatrician, geneticist, educator*
†Wolff, William I. *surgeon, educator*
Worman, Howard Jay *physician, educator*
Wright, Irving Sherwood *physician, retired educator*
Wright, Jane Cooke *physician, educator, consultant*
Yahr, Melvin David *physician*
†Yurt, Roger William *surgeon, educator*
Zinn, Keith Marshall *ophthalmologist, educator*
Zitrin, Arthur *physician*
Zucker, Marjorie Bass *medical researcher, hematologist*

North Tonawanda
Nadler, Sigmond Harold *physician, surgeon*

Northport
Tsapogas, Makis J. *surgeon*

Nyack
Rossi, Harald Hermann *retired radiation biophysicist, educator, administrator*

Old Westbury
DiGiovanna, Eileen Landenberger *osteopathic physician, educator*

Olean
†Godfrey, John *internist*

Oneida
Hardman, Jane McWilliams *pathologist*
Muschenheim, Frederick *pathologist*

Orangeburg
Levine, Jerome *psychiatrist, educator*

Pearl River
Danforth, Elliot, Jr. *medical educator*
Davis, Harold *veterinary pathologist*

Pittsford
Faloon, William Wassell *physician, educator*

Port Washington
Brownstein, Martin Herbert *dermatopathologist, educator*

Poughkeepsie
†Kanwit, Bert Alfred *retired surgeon*
Liptay, Lynne Miriam *pediatrician*

Rochester
Barton, Russell William *psychiatrist, author*
Baum, John *physician*
Bennett, John Morrison *medical oncologist*
Berg, Robert Lewis *physician, educator*
Berman, Howard James *medical association administrator*
†Bonfiglio, Thomas Albert *pathologist, educator*
Borch, Richard Frederic *pharmacology and chemistry educator*
Borgstedt, Harold Heinrich *pharmacologist, toxicologist*
Brody, Bernard B. *physician, educator*
Brzustowicz, Richard John *neurosurgeon, educator*
Burgener, Francis André *radiology educator*
Burton, Richard Irving *orthopedist, educator*
Cain, Russell M. *psychiatrist*
Chey, William Yoon *physician*
Ciccone, J. Richard *psychiatrist*
Cockett, Abraham T. K. *urologist*
Cohen, Nicholas *immunologist, educator*
Crino, Marjanne Helen *anesthesiologist*
de Papp, Elise Wachenfeld *pathologist*
Doty, Robert William *neurophysiologist, educator*
Forbes, Gilbert Burnett *physician, educator*
Frank, Irwin Norman *urologist, educator*
Frazer, John Paul *surgeon*
Frisina, Robert Dana *sensory neuroscientist, educator*
Goldsmith, Lowell Alan *medical educator*
Griner, Paul Francis *physician*
Herz, Marvin Ira *psychiatrist*
Hood, William Boyd, Jr. *cardiologist, educator*
Jacobs, Laurence Stanton *physician, educator*
†Lichtman, Marshall Albert *internist*
†McClure, Lucretia Walker *medical librarian*
Mc Donald, Joseph Valentine *neurosurgeon*
Mc Quillen, Michael Paul *physician*
Menguy, Rene *surgeon, educator*
Morgan, William Lionel, Jr. *physician, educator*
Morton, John H. *surgeon, educator*
†Moss, Arthur Jay *physician*
O'Mara, Robert Edmund George *radiologist, educator*
Panner, Bernard J. *pathologist, educator*
Paterson, Eileen *radiation oncologist, educator*
Pettee, Daniel Starr *neurologist*
Reifler, Clifford Bruce *psychiatrist, educator*
Rowley, Peter Templeton *physician, educator*
Schwartz, Seymour Ira *surgeon, educator*
Sherman, Charles Daniel, Jr. *surgeon*
Smith, Julia Ladd *medical oncologist, hospice physician*
Toribara, Taft Yutaka *radiation biologist, biophysicist, chemist, toxicologist*
Wiley, Jason LaRue, Jr. *neurosurgeon*
Williams, Thomas Franklin *physician, educator*
Wynne, Lyman Carroll *psychiatrist*

Roslyn Heights
Rogatz, Peter *physician*

Rye
Barker, Harold Grant *surgeon*
Reader, George Gordon *physician, educator*
Wessler, Stanford *physician, educator*
Wilmot, Irvin Gorsage *former hospital administrator, educator, consultant*

Sands Point
Lear, Erwin *anesthesiologist, educator*

Sayville
Blume, Sheila Bierman *psychiatrist*

Scarsdale
Buttinger-Fedeli, Catharine Sarina Caroline *psychiatrist*
Lee, Robert Earl *physician*
Moser, Marvin *physician, educator, author*
Rachlin, Stephen Leonard *psychiatrist*
†Rivlin, Richard Saul *physician, educator*

Schenectady
†Oliker, David William *healthcare management administrator*
Pasamanick, Benjamin *psychiatrist, educator*

Silver Creek
Schenk, Worthington George, Jr. *surgeon, educator*

Skaneateles
Pickett, Lawrence Kimball *physician, educator*

Somers
Rubin, Samuel Harold *physician, consultant*

South Salem
Kim, Christine S. *physician*

Staten Island
Berger, Herbert *retired internist, educator*
Greenfield, Val Shea *ophthalmologist*

Stony Brook
Abumrad, Naji N. *surgeon, educator*
Davis, James Norman *neurologist, neurobiology researcher*
Fritts, Harry Washington, Jr. *physician, educator*
Henn, Fritz Albert *psychiatrist*
Jonas, Steven *public health physician, medical educator, writer*
Kaplan, Allen P. *physician, educator, academic administrator*
Lane, Dorothy Spiegel *physician*
Meyers, Morton Allen *physician, radiology educator*
Miller, Frederick *pathologist*
Poppers, Paul Jules *anesthesiologist, educator*
Rapaport, Felix Theodosius *surgeon, researcher, educator*
†Susman, Randall L. *anatomy educator, anthropologist*

Suffern
Schachter, Michael Ben *psychiatrist*

Syracuse
Bellanger, Barbara Doris Hoysak *biomedical research technologist*
Clausen, Jerry Lee *psychiatrist*
Cohen, William Nathan *radiologist*
Daly, Robert W. *psychiatrist, medical educator*
Gold, Joseph *medical researcher*
Kieffer, Stephen Aaron *radiologist, educator*
King, Robert Bainton *neurosurgeon*
Landaw, Stephen Arthur *physician, educator*
Lemanski, Larry Fredrick *medical educator*
McGraw, James L. *retired ophthalmologist, educator*
Murray, David George *orthopaedic surgeon, educator*
Nelson, Douglas A. *pathologist, educator*
Phillips, Richard Hart *psychiatrist*
†Rabuzzi, Daniel D. *medical educator*
Rosenbaum, Arthur Elihu *radiologist, educator*
Szasz, Thomas Stephen *psychiatrist, educator, writer*
Verrillo, Ronald Thomas *neuroscientist*
Williams, William Joseph *physician, educator*

Tarrytown
Chu, Foo *physician*

Upton
Cronkite, Eugene Pitcher *physician*
Hamilton, Leonard Derwent *physician, molecular biologist*
Holroyd, Richard Allan *researcher*

Utica
Max, Theodore Conrad *surgeon*

Valhalla
Adler, Karl Paul *medical educator, academic administrator*
Carter, Anne Cohen *physician*
Christenson, William Newcome *physician*
Cimino, Joseph Anthony *physician, educator*
Del Guercio, Louis Richard Maurice *surgeon, educator, company executive*
Fink, Raymond *medical educator*
Hodgson, W(alter) John B(arry) *surgeon*
Itskovitz, Harold David *physician*
Levin, Aaron Reuben *pediatrician, educator*
Levy, Norman B. *psychiatrist, educator*
McGiff, John C(harles) *pharmacologist*
Niguidula, Faustino Nazario *pediatric cardiothoracic surgeon*
Weisburger, John Hans *medical researcher*
Williams, Gary Murray *medical researcher, pathology educator*

Warsaw
Dy-Ang, Anita C. *pediatrician*

Watkins Glen
Saks, William Joseph, Jr. *osteopathic physician, educator*

West Haverstraw
Cochran, George Van Brunt *physician, surgery educator, researcher*

Westbury
Ente, Gerald *pediatrician*

Westfield
Brown, Kent Louis, Sr. *surgeon*

White Plains
Blank, H. Robert *psychiatrist*
Blass, John Paul *medical educator, physician*
Glassman, George Morton *dermatologist*
Johnston, Richard Boles, Jr. *pediatrician, educator, biomedical researcher*
Katz, Michael *pediatrician, educator*
Marano, Anthony Joseph *cardiologist*
McDowell, Fletcher Hughes *physician, educator*
Monteferrante, Judith Catherine *cardiologist*
Samii, Abdol Hossein *physician, educator*
Smith, Gerard Peter *neuroscientist*
Taylor, Judith Mundlak *neurologist*

Williamsville
Reisman, Robert E. *physician, educator*

Woodbury
Bleicher, Sheldon Joseph *endocrinologist, medical educator*

Yonkers
DeAngelis, Roger Thomas *surgeon*
Rosch, Paul John *physician, educator*

Yorktown Heights
Klein, Richard Stephen *internist*

NORTH CAROLINA

Apex
Knapp, Richard Bruce *anesthesiologist*

Asheville
Powell, Norborne Berkeley *urologist*

Burlington
Golden, Carole Ann *immunologist, microbiologist*
Wilson, William Preston *psychiatrist, emeritus educator*

Cary
Chignell, Colin Francis *pharmacologist*
Talbert, Luther Marcus *physician*

Chapel Hill
Azar, Henry Amin *pathologist, medical historian*
Baerg, Richard Henry *podiatrist, surgeon, educator*
†Bailey, Donald B., Jr. *medical and special education educator*
Barnett, Thomas Buchanan *physician, medical educator*
Bondurant, Stuart *physician, educational administrator*
Boone, Franklin Delanor Roosevelt, Sr. *cardiovascular perfusionist, realtor*
Brinkhous, Kenneth Merle *pathologist, educator*
Brownlee, Robert Calvin *pediatrician, educator*
†Cance, William George *surgeon*
Clark, Richard Lee *radiologist*
Clyde, Wallace Alexander, Jr. *pediatrics and microbiology educator*
Collier, Albert M. *pediatric educator, child development center director*
Cromartie, William James *medical educator, researcher*
Denny, Floyd Wolfe, Jr. *pediatrician*
Droegemueller, William *gynecologist, obstetrician, medical educator*
Easterling, William Ewart, Jr. *obstetrician, gynecologist*
Eifrig, David Eric *ophthalmologist, educator*
Ellis, Fred Wilson *pharmacology educator*
Farmer, Thomas Wohlsen *neurologist, educator*
Fischer, Janet Jordan *retired physician, educator, researcher*
Fischer, Newton Duchan *otolaryngologist, educator*
Frelinger, Jeffrey Allen *immunologist, educator*
Gottschalk, Carl William *physician, educator*
Goyer, Robert Andrew *pathology educator*
Graham, John Borden *pathologist, educator*
Greganti, Mac Andrew *physician, medical educator*
Grisham, Joe Wheeler *pathologist, educator*
Hawkins, David Rollo, Sr. *psychiatrist, educator*
Hendricks, Charles Henning *retired obstetrics and gynecology educator*
Henson, Anna Miriam *otolaryngology researcher, medical educator*
Henson, O'Dell Williams, Jr. *anatomy educator*
Hirsch, Philip Francis *pharmacologist, educator*
Hollister, William Gray *psychiatrist*
Hulka, Barbara Sorenson *epidemiology educator*
Hulka, Jaroslav Fabian *obstetrician, gynecologist*
Johnson, George, Jr. *physician, educator*
Langdell, Robert Dana *medical educator*
McMillan, Campbell White *pediatric hematologist*
Miller, C. Arden *physician, educator*
Miya, Tom Saburo *retired pharmacologist, educator*
Ontjes, David Ainsworth *medicine and pharmacology educator*
Pagano, Joseph Stephen *physician, researcher, educator*
Palmer, Jeffress Gary *hematologist, educator*
Pollitzer, William Sprott *anatomy educator*
Prange, Arthur Jergen, Jr. *psychiatrist, neurobiologist, educator*
Prather, Donna Lynn *psychiatrist*
Reisner, Howard Michael *immunologist, educator*
Roberts, Harold Ross *medical educator, hematologist*
Sheldon, George F. *medical educator*
†Stockman, James Anthony, III *pediatrician*
Sugioka, Kenneth *anesthesiologist educator*
Suzuki, Kunihiko *biomedical educator, researcher*
Thomas, Colin Gordon, Jr. *surgeon, medical educator*
Tunnessen, Walter William, Jr. *pediatrician*
Van Wyk, Judson John *endocrinologist, pediatric educator*
Wheeler, Clayton Eugene, Jr. *dermatologist, educator*
Wilcox, Benson Reid *cardiothoracic surgeon, educator*
†Williams, Roberta Gay *pediatric cardiologist, educator*
Winfield, John Buckner *rheumatologist, educator*

Charlotte
Citron, David Sanford *physician*
Edwards, Irene Elizabeth (Libby Edwards) *dermatologist, educator, researcher*
Kelly, Luther Wrentmore, Jr. *physician, educator*
Lawrence, Patricia Ann *obstetrician-gynecologist*
Naumoff, Philip *physician*
†Plyler, John Laney, Jr. *healthcare management professional*
Short, Earl de Grey, Jr. *psychiatrist, consultant*
Visser, Valya Elizabeth *physician*
Watkins, Carlton Gunter *retired pediatrician*

Durham
Adams, Dolph O. *pathologist, educator*
Amos, Dennis B. *immunologist*
Anderson, William Banks, Jr. *ophthalmology educator*
Anlyan, William George *surgeon, university administrator*
Armstrong, Brenda Estelle *pediatric cardiologist, educator*
Baker, Lenox Dial *orthopaedist, genealogist*
Bennett, Peter Brian *researcher, anesthesiology educator*
†Blazer, Dan German *psychiatrist, epidemiologist*
Bradford, William Dalton *pathologist, educator*
Brodie, Harlow Keith Hammond *psychiatrist, educator, former university president*
Buckley, Rebecca Hatcher *physician*
Busse, Ewald William *psychiatrist, educator*
†Carter, James Harvey *psychiatrist, educator*
Cartmill, Matt *anthropologist, anatomy educator*
Christmas, William Anthony *internist, educator*
Cohen, Harvey Jay *physician, educator*
Coleman, Ralph Edward *nuclear medicine physician*
Davis, James Evans *general and thoracic surgeon, parliamentarian, author*
Dawson, Jeffrey Robert *immunology educator*
Day, Eugene Davis, Sr. *immunology educator, researcher*
Estes, Edward Harvey, Jr. *medical educator*
Falletta, John Matthew *pediatrician*
Feldman, Jerome Myron *physician*
Fouts, James Ralph *pharmacologist, educator, clergyman*
Frank, Michael M. *physician*
Frothingham, Thomas Eliot *pediatrician*
Gaede, Jane Taylor *pathologist*
Georgiade, Nicholas George *physician*
Greenfield, Joseph Cholmondeley, Jr. *physician, educator*
Hammond, Charles Bessellieu *obstetrician-gynecologist, educator*
Harmel, Merel Hilber *anesthesiologist, educator*
Harris, Jerome Sylvan *pediatrician, pediatrics and biochemistry educator*
Jennings, Robert Burgess *experimental pathologist, medical educator*
Johnson, Victoria Kaprielian *medical educator*
Johnston, William Webb *pathologist, educator*
Katz, Samuel Lawrence *pediatrician, scientist*
Kempner, Walter *retired physician*
Kiltzman, Bruce Maurice *plastic surgery educator, researcher*
King, Lowell Restell *pediatric urologist*
Kirshner, Norman *pharmacologist, researcher, educator*
Koepke, John Arthur *hematologist, clinical pathologist*
†Kraus, William Erle *physician, biomedical researcher*
Kylstra, Johannes Arnold *physician*
Lack, Leon *pharmacology and biochemistry educator*
Lefkowitz, Robert Joseph *physician, educator*
Llewellyn, Charles Elroy, Jr. *psychiatrist*
Matchar, David Bruce *internist, educator*
Miller, David Edmond *physician*
Moore, John Wilson *neurophysiologist, educator*
Osterhout, Suydam *physician, educator*
Parker, Joseph B., Jr. *psychiatrist, educator*
Pratt, Philip Chase *pathologist, educator*
Rogers, Mark Charles *physician, educator*
Rosse, Wendell Franklyn *immunology educator*
Sabiston, David Coston, Jr. *surgeon, educator*
Schanberg, Saul Murray *pharmacology educator*
Serafin, Donald *plastic surgeon*
Sessoms, Stuart McGuire *physician, educator, retired insurance company executive*
Spach, Madison Stockton *cardiologist*
Stead, Eugene Anson, Jr. *physician*
Urbaniak, James Randolph *orthopaedic surgeon*
Watts, Charles DeWitt *surgeon, corporate medical director*
Werman, David Sanford *psychiatrist, psychoanalyst, educator*
Wilkins, Robert Henry *neurosurgeon, editor*
Williams, Redford Brown *medical educator*

Fairview
Gaffney, Thomas Edward *retired physician*

Greensboro
Johnson, Andrew Myron *pediatric immunologist, educator*

Greenville
Bolande, Robert Paul *pathologist, scientist, educator*
Furth, Eugene David *physician, educator*
Hallock, James Anthony *pediatrician, school dean*
Jones, Billy Ernest *dermatology educator*
Laupus, William Edward *physician, educator*
Lee, Kenneth Stuart *neurosurgeon*
Lee, Tung-Kwang *pathologist, cancer researcher*
Mattsson, Ake *psychiatrist, physician*
Norris, H. Thomas *pathologist, academic administrator*
Pories, Walter Julius *surgeon, educator*
Sanchez, Rafael Camilo *physician*
Thomas, Francis Thornton *surgeon, immunologist, consultant*
Tingelstad, Jon Bunde *physician*
Waugh, William Howard *biomedical educator*

Hampstead
Solomon, Robert Douglas *pathology educator*

Hickory
†Gardner, William Ronald *surgeon*

Horse Shoe
Becker, Quinn Henderson *orthopaedic surgeon, army officer*

Lenoir
Carswell, Jane Triplett *family physician*

New Bern
Greer, Robert Bruce, III *orthopedic surgeon, educator*

Pinehurst
Jacobson, Peter Lars *neurologist and educator*

Raleigh
Dameron, Thomas Barker, Jr. *orthopaedic surgeon, educator*
†Foster, James Robert *cardiologist*
Kimbrell, Odell Culp, Jr. *physician*
Levine, Ronald H. *physician, state official*
Michael, Patricia Ann *physician, clinical systems research director*
Peacock, Erle Ewart, Jr. *surgeon, lawyer, educator*
Stratas, Nicholas Emanuel *psychiatrist*

Research Triangle Park
†Barry, David Walter *infectious diseases physician, researcher*
Elion, Gertrude Belle *research scientist, pharmacology educator*
King, Theodore Matthew *obstetrician, gynecologist, educator*
Tilson, Hugh Hanna *epidemiologist*
Wilsnack, Roger E. *medical association administrator*

Tryon
Bruce, David Lionel *retired anesthesiologist, educator*

Waynesville
†McKinney, Alexander Stuart *neurologist*

Whispering Pines
Enlow, Donald Hugh *anatomist, educator, university dean*

Whiteville
†Chiusano, Michael Augustus *urologic surgeon, mechanical engineer*

Wilmington
Gillen, Howard William *neurologist, medical historian*
Wilkins, Lucien Sanders *gastroenterologist*

Winston Salem
Alexander, Eben, Jr. *neurological surgeon*
†Bittinger, Isabel *orthopedic surgeon, retired, photographer*
Bowman, Marjorie Ann *physician, academic administrator*
Cowan, Robert Jenkins *radiologist, educator*
Davis, Courtland Harwell, Jr. *neurosurgeon*
Dean, Richard Henry *surgeon, educator*
Hazzard, William Russell *geriatrician, educator*
Hopkins, Judith Owen *oncologist*
Howell, Charles Maitland *dermatologist*
Kaufman, William *internist*
Kohut, Robert Irwin *otolaryngologist, educator*
Lorentz, William Beall *pediatrician*
Maynard, Charles Douglas *radiologist*
Mueller-Heubach, Eberhard August *medical educator, obstetrician-gynecologist*
O'Steen, Wendall Keith *neurobiology and anatomy educator*
Penry, James Kiffin *physician, neurology educator*
Podgorny, George *emergency physician*
Rogers, Lee Frank *radiologist*
Simon, Jimmy Louis *pediatrician, educator*
Toole, James Francis *medical educator*
Woods, James Watson, Jr. *cardiologist*

NORTH DAKOTA

Bismarck
Hook, William Franklin *radiologist*

Grand Forks
Carlson, Edward C. *anatomy educator*

Williston
Adducci, Joseph Edward *obstetrician, gynecologist*

OHIO

Akron
Evans, Douglas McCullough *surgeon, educator*
Levy, Richard Philip *physician, educator*
LoIudice, Thomas Anthony *gastroenterologist, researcher*
Timmons, Gerald Dean *pediatric neurologist*

Athens
†Myers, Frank Wayne *osteopath, educator*

Beavercreek
Rodin, Alvin Eli *pathalogist, medical educator, author*

Canal Winchester
Burrier, Gail Warren *physician*

Canton
Howland, Willard J. *radiologist, educator*
Ognibene, Andre J(ohn) *physician, army officer, educator*

Centerville
Kelso, Harold Glen *family practice physician*

Chagrin Falls
Lingl, Friedrich Albert *psychiatrist*
Weckesser, Elden Christian *surgery educator*

Cincinnati
Adolph, Robert J. *physician, medical educator*
Alexander, James Wesley *surgeon, educator*
†Balistreri, William Francis *physician, pediatric gastroenterologist*
Bernstein, I. Leonard *physician, educator*
Biddinger, Paul Williams *pathologist, educator*
Bingham, Eula *environmental health educator*
Boat, Thomas Frederick *physician, educator, researcher*
Bridenbaugh, Phillip Owen *anesthesiologist, physician*
Buchman, Elwood *physician, pharmaceutical company medical director*
Carothers, Charles Omsted *orthopedic surgeon*
Fine, Lawrence Jay *internist, occupational preventive medicine*
Fowler, Noble Owen *physician, university administrator*
Gesteland, Robert Charles *neurophysiologist*
Glueck, Helen Iglauer *physician*
Greenwalt, Tibor Jack *physician, educator*
Harshman, Morton Leonard *physician, business executive*
Heimlich, Henry Jay *physician, surgeon*
Hess, Evelyn Victorine (Mrs. Michael Howett) *medical educator*
Hollerman, Charles Edward *pediatrician*
Horwitz, Harry *radiologist, physician, educator*
Hummel, Robert Paul *surgeon*
Jaffe, Murray Sherwood *surgeon*
Kaplan, Stanley Meisel *psychoanalyst*
Loggie, Jennifer Mary Hildreth *medical educator, physician*
Lucas, Stanley Jerome *radiologist, physician*
†Lucky, Anne Weissman *dermatologist*
Macpherson, Colin R(obertson) *pathologist, educator*
†Neale, Henry Whitehead *plastic surgery educator*
Nordlund, James John *dermatologist*
Rebar, Robert William *obstetrician, gynecologist, educator*
Saenger, Eugene Lange *radiology educator, laboratory director*
Schneider, Harold Joel *radiologist*
Schreiner, Albert William *physician, educator*
Schwartz, Arnold (Arnie Shayne) *pharmacologist, biophysicist, biochemist, educator, actor, director, producer*
Smith, Roger Dean *pathologist*
Sodd, Vincent Joseph *nuclear medicine researcher, educator*
Suskind, Raymond Robert *physician, educator*
Toltzis, Robert Joshua *cardiologist*
Vilter, Richard William *physician, educator*
Warden, Glenn Donald *burn surgeon*
West, Clark Darwin *pediatric nephrologist, educator*
Wiot, Jerome Francis *radiologist*

Cleveland
Aikawa, Masamichi *pathologist*
Alfidi, Ralph Joseph *radiologist, educator*
Alfred, Karl Sverre *orthopedic surgeon*
Awais, George Musa *obstetrician, gynecologist*
Badal, Daniel Walter *psychiatrist, educator*
Baker, Saul Phillip *geriatrician, cardiologist, internist*
Bartunek, Robert Richard *retired physician*
Bowerfind, Edgar Sihler, Jr. *physician, medical administrator*
Budd, John Henry *physician*
Carter, James Rose, Jr. *medical educator*
Cascorbi, Helmut Freimund *anesthesiologist, educator*
Caston, J(esse) Douglas *medical educator*
Cherniack, Neil Stanley *physician, medical educator*
Cole, Monroe *neurologist, educator*
Daroff, Robert Barry *neurologist*
Davis, Pamela Bowes *pediatric pulmonologist*
Dell'Osso, Louis Frank *neuroscience educator*
Denko, Joanne D. *psychiatrist, writer*
Eastwood, Douglas William *anesthesiologist*
Eiben, Robert Michael *pediatric neurologist, educator*
Elewski, Boni Elizabeth *dermatologist, educator*
Fazio, Victor Warren *physician, colon and rectal surgeon*
Geha, Alexander Salim *cardiothoracic surgeon, educator*
Gifford, Ray Wallace, Jr. *physician, educator*
Hardesty, Hiram Haines *ophthalmologist, educator*
Harris, John William *physician, educator*
Healy, Bernadine P. *physician, educator, federal agency administrator*
Herndon, Charles Harbison *retired orthopaedic surgeon*
Holzbach, Raymond Thomas *gastroenterologist, author, educator*
Izant, Robert James, Jr. *pediatric surgeon*
Johnson, Candice Elaine Brown *pediatrics educator*
†Kass, Lawrence *hematologist*
†Katzman, Richard A. *cardiologist, consultant*
Kellermeyer, Robert William *physician, educator*
Kiser, William Sites *physician executive, urologic surgeon*
Lamm, Michael Emanuel *pathologist, immunologist, educator*
Lefferts, William Geoffrey *physician, educator*
Lenkoski, Leo Douglas *psychiatrist, educator*
Mahmoud, Adel A. F. *physician, educator, investigator*
McFadden, Edward Regis, Jr. *pulmonary educator*
Mc Henry, Martin Christopher *physician, educator*
Meltzer, Herbert Yale *psychiatry educator*
†Montague, Drogo K. *urologist*
Novick, Andrew Carl *urologist*
†Perry, George *neuroscience researcher*
Rakita, Louis *cardiologist, educator*
Ratnoff, Oscar Davis *physician, educator*
Robbins, Frederick Chapman *physician, medical school dean emeritus*
Ross, Ronald Jay *radiologist*
Scarpa, Antonio *medicine educator, biomedical scientist*
Shuck, Jerry Mark *surgeon, educator*
Smith, Charles Kent *family medicine physician*
Stanton-Hicks, Michael D'Arcy *anesthesiologist, educator*
Stavitsky, Abram Benjamin *immunologist, educator*
Straffon, Ralph Atwood *urologist*
†Washington, John Augustine *physician, pathologist*
Webster, Leslie Tillotson, Jr. *pharmacologist, educator*
†West, Burton Carey *physician*
White, Robert J. *neurosurgeon, neuroscientist, educator*
Wolinsky, Emanuel *physician, educator*
Young, Jess R. *physician*

Columbus
Ackerman, John Henry *health services consultant, physician*
†Bachman, Sister Janice *health care executive, vicaress*
Balcerzak, Stanley Paul *physician, educator*
Barth, Rolf Frederick *pathologist, educator*
Bell, George Edwin *retired physician, insurance company executive*
Berggren, Ronald Bernard *surgeon, emeritus educator*
Bianchine, Joseph Raymond *pharmacologist*
Billings, Charles Edgar *physician*
Bope, Edward Tharp *family practitioner*
Boudoulas, Harisios *physician*
Christoforidis, A. John *radiologist, educator*
Copeland, William Edgar, Sr. *physician*
Cramblett, Henry Gaylord *pediatrician, virologist, educator*
Goodman, Hubert Thorman *psychiatrist, consultant*
Haque, Malika Hakim *pediatrician*
Huheey, Marilyn Jane *ophthalmologist*
†Johnston, Peter *osteopath, surgeon*
Kendrick, Ronald Edward *orthopaedic surgeon*
Kim, Moon Hyun *physician, educator*
Laufman, Leslie Rodgers *hematologist, oncologist*
Lewis, Richard Phelps *physician, educator*
Long, Sarah Elizabeth Brackney *physician*
Mazzaferri, Ernest Louis *physician, educator*
Newton, William Allen, Jr. *pediatric pathologist*
O'Dorisio, Thomas Michael *internal medicine educator, researcher*
Patil, Popat Narayan *pharmacology-pharmacy educator*
Penn, Gerald Melville *pathologist*
Perkins, Robert Louis *physician, educator*
Ruberg, Robert Lionel *surgery educator*
Rund, Douglas Andrew *emergency physician, educator*
St. Pierre, Ronald Leslie *anatomy educator, university administrator*
Sayers, Martin Peter *pediatric neurosurgeon*
Senhauser, Donald A(lbert) *pathologist, educator*
Skillman, Thomas Grant *endocrinology consultant, former educator*
Tzagournis, Manuel *physician, educator, university dean and official*
Yashon, David *neurosurgeon, educator*
Zipf, William Byron *pediatric endocrinologist, educator*
Zuspan, Frederick Paul *obstetrician/gynecologist, educator*

Dayton
Arn, Kenneth Dale *physician, city official*
Bohanon, Kathleen Sue *neonatologist, educator*
DeWall, Richard Allison *retired surgeon*
Elliott, Daniel Whitacre *surgeon, retired educator*
Faruki, Mahmud Taji *psychiatrist, hospital administrator*
Humbert, James Ronald *pediatrician, educator*
Kogut, Maurice David *pediatric endocrinologist*
Mohler, Stanley Ross *physician, educator*
Von Gierke, Henning Edgar *biomedical science educator, former government official, researcher*
Weinberg, Sylvan Lee *cardiologist, educator, author, editor*

Dublin
Graham, Bruce Douglas *pediatrician*

Elyria
Eady, Carol Murphy (Mrs. Karl Ernest Eady) *medical association administrator*

Fairborn
Martin, Donald William *psychiatrist*

Gallipolis
Clarke, Oscar Withers *physician*

Grove City
Kilman, James William *surgeon, educator*

Ironton
Newmark, Howard *surgeon, entrepreneur*

Lebanon
Holtkamp, Dorsey Emil *medical research scientist*

Lima
Becker, Dwight Lowell *physician*
Collins, William Thomas *pathologist*

Mansfield
Houston, William Robert Montgomery *ophthalmic surgeon*

Marietta
Tipton, Jon Paul *allergist*

Maumee
Huffman, (Bernard) Leslie, Jr. *physician*

Novelty
Miller, Dwight Richard *cosmetologist, corporate executive, hair designer*

Oregon
Culver, Robert Elroy *osteopathic physician*

Pepper Pike
Froelich, Wolfgang Andreas *neurologist*

Rocky River
Castele, Theodore John *radiologist*
De Long, Erika Venta *psychiatrist*

Rootstown
Blacklow, Robert Stanley *physician, medical college administrator*
Campbell, Colin *obstetrician, gynecologist, school dean*
Saltzman, Glenn Alan *behavioral sciences educator*

Strongsville
Opplt, Jan Jiri *clinical pathologist, educator*

Toledo
Chakraborty, Joana *physiology educator, research center administrator*
DiDio, Liberato John Alphonse *anatomist, educator*
Mayhew, Harry Eugene *physician, educator*
Mulrow, Patrick Joseph *medical educator*
Rubin, Allan Maier *physician, surgeon*
Shelley, Walter Brown *physician, educator*
Standaert, Frank George *medical research administrator, physician*
Zrull, Joel Peter *psychiatry educator*

Troy
Davies, Alfred Robert *physician, educator*

Westerville
Dadmehr, Nahid *neurologist*

Whitehouse
†Howard, John Malone *surgeon, thoracic surgeon, educator*

Willoughby
Pazirandeh, Mahmood *rheumatologist, consultant*

Wooster
Geho, Walter Blair *biomedical research executive*

Worthington
Winter, Chester Caldwell *physician, surgery educator*

Yellow Springs
Lacey, Beatrice Cates *psychophysiologist*

Youngstown
Butterworth, Jane Rogers Fitch *physician*
Gaylord, Sanford Fred *physician*
Walton, Ralph Gerald *psychiatrist, educator*

Zanesville
Ray, John Walker *otolaryngologist, educator, broadcast commentator*

OKLAHOMA

Edmond
Nelson, John Woolard *neurology educator, physician*

Jenks
Wootan, Gerald Don *osteopathic physician, educator*

Mcalester
Reed, Walter George, Jr. *osteopath*

Midwest City
Bogardus, Carl Robert, Jr. *radiologist, educator*

Muskogee
Kent, Bartis Milton *physician*

Oklahoma City
Barclay, Carl Archie *retired physician*
Brandt, Edward Newman, Jr. *physician, educator*
Buchanan, Robert Taylor *plastic surgeon*
Cameron, Charles Metz, Jr. *physician, medical educator*
Carter, L. Philip *neurosurgeon, consultant*
Comp, Philip Cinnamon *medical researcher*
Couch, James Russell, Jr. *neurology educator*
Deckert, Gordon Harmon *psychiatrist, educator*
Everett, Mark Allen *dermatologist, educator*
Felton, Warren Locker, II *surgeon*
Fishburne, John Ingram, Jr. *obstetrician-gynecologist, educator*
Halverstadt, Donald Bruce *urologist, educator*
Haywood, B(etty) J(ean) *anesthesiologist*
Keim, Robert John *otolaryngologist, educator*
Kimerer, Neil Banard, Sr. *psychiatrist, educator*
Lewis, Wilbur Curtis *surgeon*
Lhevine, Dave Bernard *radiologist, educator*
Massion, Walter Herbert *anesthesiologist, educator*
Moore, Joanne Iweita *pharmacologist, educator*
Oehlert, William Herbert, Jr. *cardiologist, administrator, educator*
Rayan, Ghazi M. *surgeon*
Robinson, Malcolm *gastroenterologist*
Rossavik, Ivar Kristian *obstetrician/gynecologist*
Thurman, William Gentry *medical research foundation executive, pediatric hematology and oncology physician, educator*
Williams, George Rainey *surgeon, educator*
Worsham, Bertrand Ray *psychiatrist*
Zuhdi, Nazih *surgeon*

Stillwater
Cooper, Donald Lee *physician*
Hooper, Billy Ernest *medical association administrator*

Tulsa
Calvert, Jon Channing *family practice physician*
Kalbfleisch, John McDowell *cardiologist, educator*
Lewis, Ceylon Smith, Jr. *physician*
Nettles, John Barnwell *obstetrics and gynecology educator*
Plunket, Daniel Clark *pediatrician*
†Shane, John Marder *endocrinologist*
Tompkins, Robert George *physician*

Vinita
Neer, Charles Sumner, II *orthopaedic surgeon, educator*

OREGON

Beaverton
†Novy, Miles Joseph *obstetrician/gynecologist, educator*

Corvallis
†Steele, Robert Edwin *orthopedic surgeon*
Willis, David Lee *radiation biology educator*

Eugene
Flanagan, Latham, Jr. *surgeon*
†Loescher, Richard Alvin *gastroenterologist*
Nissel, Martin *radiologist, consultant*
Starr, Grier Forsythe *retired pathologist*

Klamath Falls
†Bohnen, Robert Frank *hematologist, oncologist, educator*

Lake Oswego
Thong, Tran *biomedical company executive*

Lincoln City
Sewell, Robert Dalton *pediatrician*

Portland
Barmack, Neal Herbert *neuroscientist*
Bennett, William Michael *physician*
Benson, John Alexander, Jr. *physician, educator*
Berthelsdorf, Siegfried *psychiatrist*
Brummett, Robert Eddie *pharmacology educator*
Campbell, John Richard *pediatric surgeon*
Connor, William Elliott *physician, educator*
Crawshaw, Ralph *psychiatrist*
†Dunham, Tom Robert *physician*
Fraunfelder, Frederick Theodore *ophthalmologist, educator*
Greer, Monte Arnold *physician, educator*
Heatherington, J. Scott *retired osteopathic physician and surgeon*
Herndon, Robert McCulloch *experimental neurologist*
Hutchens, Tyra Thornton *physician, educator*
Jacob, Stanley Wallace *surgeon, educator*
Kendall, John Walker, Jr. *medical educator, researcher, university dean*
Kohler, Peter Ogden *physician, educator, university president*
Ledbetter, Randi Rae *obstetrician/gynecologist*
Lees, Martin Henry *pediatrician, educator*
Lobitz, Walter Charles, Jr. *physician, educator*
Olson, Donald Ernest *retired physician*
†Patterson, James Randolph *physician*
Press, Edward *consulting physician*
Raaf, John Elbert *neurosurgeon, educator*
Riker, William Kay *pharmacologist, educator*
Saslow, George *psychiatrist, educator*
Schmidt, Waldemar Adrian *pathologist, educator*
Seil, Fredrick John *neuroscientist, neurologist*
Stalnaker, John Hulbert *physician*
Stevens, Wendell Claire *anesthesiology educator*
Swan, Kenneth Carl *physician, surgeon*
Swank, Roy Laver *physician, educator, inventor*
Taylor, Robert Brown *medical educator*
Zimmerman, Gail Marie *medical foundation executive*

Springfield
Kimball, Reid Roberts *psychiatrist*

Winston
Jones, Henry Earl *dermatologist, direct patient care educator*

PENNSYLVANIA

Abington
Dunn, Linda Kay *physician*
Lapayowker, Marc Spencer *radiologist*

Allentown
Gaylor, Donald Hughes *surgeon, educator*
Reckard, Craig Reginald *physician*
†Tepper, Lloyd Barton *physician*

Bala Cynwyd
Alter, Milton *neurologist, educator*
Burland, J(ohn) Alexis *psychoanalyst*
Katz, Julian *gastroenterologist, educator*
Lefton, Harvey Bennett *gastroenterologist, educator, author*
Marden, Philip Ayer *physician, educator*

Bangor
Wolf, Stewart George, Jr. *physician, medical educator*

Belleville
†Cranor, John Ross *retired surgeon*

Bethlehem
Benz, Edward John *retired clinical pathologist*

Bryn Mawr
Brunt, Manly Yates, Jr. *psychiatrist*
Huth, Edward Janavel *physician, editor*
Noone, Robert Barrett *plastic surgeon*

Carlisle
Graham, William Patton, III *plastic surgeon, educator*

Chalfont
Clifford, Maurice Cecil *physician, former college president, foundation executive*

Chester
Clark, James Edward *physician, medical educator*

Coatesville
†Ainslie, George William *psychiatrist, behavioral economist*
Gehring, David Austin *physician, adminstrator, cardiologist*
Nocks, James Jay *psychiatrist*

Collegeville
Farmar, Robert Melville *medical scientist, educator*

Conshohocken
Schein, Philip Samuel *physician, educator, pharmaceutical executive*

Danville
Kazem, Ismail *radiation oncologist, educator, health science facility administrator*
Pierce, James Clarence *surgeon*

Devon
O'Malley, John Edward *medical association administrator, physician*

Dillsburg
Jackson, George Lyman *nuclear medicine physician*

Drexel Hill
Montgomery, Patricia Aline *family physician*

Easton
Grunberg, Robert Leon Willy *nephrologist*

Fort Washington
Urbach, Frederick *physician, educator*

Gaines
Beller, Martin Leonard *retired orthopaedic surgeon*

Gibsonia
Cauna, Nikolajs *physician, medical educator*

Gladwyne
Pettit, Horace *allergist, consultant*

Glenside
Johnson, Waine Cecil *dermatologist*

Greensburg
Catalano, Louis William, Jr. *neurologist*

Harrisburg
Cadieux, Roger Joseph *physician, mental health care executive*
Jeffries, Richard Haley *physician, broadcasting company executive*
Margo, Katherine Lane *physician*
Redmond, James Melvin *medical association administrator*

Hershey
Biebuyck, Julien Francois *anesthesiologist, educator*
Cary, Gene Leonard *psychiatrist*
Davis, Dwight *cardiologist, educator*
Eyster, Mary Elaine *hematologist, educator*
Kauffman, Gordon Lee, Jr. *surgeon, educator*
Leaman, David Martin *cardiologist*
Lehman, Lois Joan *medical librarian*
Lipton, Allan *medical educator*
Naeye, Richard L. *pathologist, educator*
Pierce, William Schuler *cardiac surgeon, educator*
Reynolds, Herbert Young *physician, internist*
Rohner, Thomas John, Jr. *urologist*
Schuller, Diane Ethel *allergist, immunologist, educator*
Severs, Walter Bruce *pharmacology educator, researcher*
Vesell, Elliot Saul *pharmacologist, educator*
Waldhausen, John Anton *surgeon, educator*
Wassner, Steven Joel *pediatric nephrologist, educator*
Zelis, Robert Felix *cardiologist, educator*

Jenkintown
Greenspan-Margolis, June E. *psychiatrist*
Sadoff, Robert Leslie *psychiatrist*

Kennett Square
Leymaster, Glen R. *former medical association executive*
Perera, George A. *physician*

King Of Prussia
Lessem, Jan Norbert *medical director*

Lancaster
Eshleman, Silas Kendrick, III *psychiatrist*

Lansdale
Schwartz, Louis Winn *ophthalmologist*

Malvern
Dans, Peter Emanuel *medical educator*

Mechanicsburg
Ortenzio, Rocco Anthony *health care executive*

Media
Klinefelter, Hylda Catharine *obstetrician-gynecologist*

Merion Station
Lewis, Paul Le Roy *pathology educator*

Narberth
Strom, Brian Leslie *internist*

Newtown
Somers, Anne Ramsay *medical educator*

Norristown
Ganime, Peter David *psychiatrist, consultant*
Rosenthal, David *physician*

Penllyn
Beyer, Karl Henry, Jr. *pharmacologist*

Pennsburg
Shuhler, Phyllis Marie *physician*

Philadelphia
Adom, Edwin Nii Amalai *psychiatrist*
Agus, Zalman S. *physician, educator*
†Alexander, John Dewey *internist*
Amsterdam, Jay D. *psychiatry educator, researcher*
Andrews, Edwin Joseph *pathology educator, academic administrator*
Arce, A. Anthony *psychiatrist*
Aronson, Carl Edward *pharmacology and toxicology educator*
Asbury, Arthur Knight *neurologist, educator*
†Atkinson, Barbara Frajola *pathologist*
Austrian, Robert *physician, educator*
†Baker, Lester *physician, educator, research administrator*
Barchi, Robert Lawrence *neuroscience educator, clinical neurologist, neuroscientist*
Barker, Clyde Frederick *surgeon, educator*
Baserga, Renato Luigi *pathology educator*
†Baum, Stanley *radiologist, educator*
Beck, Aaron Temkin *psychiatrist*
†Bennett, Joel S. *physician*
Bianchi, Carmine Paul *pharmacologist*
Bibbo, Marluce *physician, educator*
Bilaniuk, Larissa Tetiana *neuroradiologist, educator*
Bishop, Harry Craden *surgeon*
Bluemle, Lewis William, Jr. *medical educator*
Bowles, Lawrence Thompson *surgeon, university dean, educator*
Brady, John Paul *psychiatrist*
Brady, Luther W., Jr. *physician, radiation oncology educator*
Brest, Albert N. *cardiology educator*
Bridger, Wagner H. *psychiatrist, educator*
Brighton, Carl Theodore *orthopedic surgery educator*
Brockman, Stanley K. *medical educator, physician, cardiothoracic surgeon*
Broderick, Gregory A. *physician, urologic surgeon, educator*
Buerk, Donald Gene *medical educator, biomedical engineer*
†Burns, Rosalie A. *neurologist, educator*
Cander, Leon *physician, educator*
Chait, Arnold *radiologist*
Chinsamy, Anusuya *paleobiologist, researcher*
Christman, Robert Alan *podiatric radiologist*
Chung, Edward Kooyoung *cardiologist, educator, author*
Clearfield, Harris Reynold *physician*
Cohen, Stanley *pathologist, educator*
Colman, Robert Wolf *physician, medical educator*
Comer, Nathan Lawrence *psychiatrist, educator*
Conn, Rex Boland, Jr. *physician, educator*
Copeland, Adrian Dennis *psychiatrist*
Cortner, Jean Alexander *physician, educator*
Dalinka, Murray Kenneth *radiologist, educator*
Daly, John M. *surgeon*
D'Angio, Giulio John *radiologist, educator*
Davidson, Steven J. *emergency physician*
DePace, Nicholas Louis *physician*
Depp, (O.) Richard, III *obstetrician-gynecologist, educator*
Dinoso, Vicente Pescador, Jr. *physician, educator*
DiPalma, Joseph Rupert *pharmacology educator*
Djerassi, Isaac *physician, medical researcher*
Earley, Laurence Elliott *medical educator*
Ehrlich, George Edward *rheumatologist, international pharmaceutical consultant*
Eichelman, Burr Simmons, Jr. *psychiatrist, researcher, educator*
Engelman, Karl *physician*
Erslev, Allan Jacob *physician, educator*
Evans, Audrey Elizabeth *physician, educator*
Fishman, Alfred Paul *physician*
†Flamm, Eugene Somer *neurosurgeon, educator*
Flexner, Louis Barkhouse *anatomist, educator*
Frankl, William Stewart *cardiologist, educator*
Freed, Edmond Lee *podiatrist*
Freiman, David Burl *radiologist*
†Friedman, Harvey Michael *infectious diseases educator*
Gabrielson, Ira Wilson *physician, educator*
García, Celso-Ramón *obstetrician and gynecologist*
Gartland, John Joseph *physician, writer*
Glick, John H. *oncologist, medical educator*
Goldberg, Martin *physician, educator*
Goldberg, Morton Edward *pharmacologist*
Golden, Gerald Samuel *national medical board executive*
Goldfarb, Stanley *internist, educator*
Goldsmith, Sidney *physician, scientist, inventor*
Gonick, Paul *urologist*
Goodman, David Barry Poliakoff *physician, educator*
†Greene, Mark Irwin *immunologist, educator*
†Gur, Ruben C. *psychiatry educator*
Hamilton, Ralph West *plastic surgeon, educator*
†Hansen-Flaschen, John Hyman *medical educator, researcher*
Haugaard, Niels *pharmacologist*
†Haut, Michael Joel *physician*
†Hayden, Richard Earle *otolaryngologist*
Helfand, Arthur E. *podiatrist*
†Holmes, Edward W. *physician, educator*
†Holsclaw, Douglas Stanley, Jr. *pediatrics educator*
Holtzer, Howard *anatomy educator*
Jackson, Laird Gray *physician, educator*
Jameson, Dorothea *sensory neuroscientist*
†Jarett, Leonard *pathologist, educator, researcher*
Jensh, Ronald Paul *anatomist, educator*
Johnson, Joseph Eggleston, III *physician, educator*
Joseph, Rosaline Resnick *hematologist/oncologist*
Kahn, Sigmund Benham *internist, dean*
Kaji, Hideko Katayama *pharmacologist*
Kaye, Donald *physician, educator*
Kaye, Robert *pediatrics educator*
Kazazian, Haig Hagop, Jr. *medical scientist, physician, educator*
Keenan, Mary Ann *orthopaedic surgeon, researcher*
†Kefalides, Nicholas Alexander *physician, educator*
†Kelley, Mark Albert *internal medicine educator, university official*
†Kelley, William Nimmons *physician, educator*
Kimball, Harry Raymond *medical association executive, educator*
Kissick, William Lee *physician, educator*
Kligerman, Morton M. *radiologist*
Klinghoffer, June Florence *physician, educator*
Koelle, George Brampton *university pharmacologist, educator*
Kolansky, Harold *physician, psychiatrist, psychoanalyst*
Kresh, J. Yasha *cardiovascular researcher, educator*
Kundel, Harold Louis *radiologist, educator*
Kurtz, Alfred Bernard *radiologist*
Ladman, A(aron) J(ulius) *anatomist, educator*
Lambertsen, Christian James *environmental physiologist, physician, educator*
Levine, Rhea Joy Cottler *anatomy educator*
Levit, Edithe Judith *physician, medical association administrator*
†Levitt, Jerry David *medical educator*
Levy, Robert Isaac *physician, educator, research director*
Li, Weiye *ophthalmologist, biochemist, educator*
Lief, Harold Isaiah *psychiatrist*
Longnecker, David E. *anesthesiologist, educator*
Luscombe, Herbert Alfred *physician, educator*
†Madaio, Michael P. *medical educator*
Madow, Leo *psychiatrist, educator*
Maguire, Henry Clinton, Jr. *dermatologist*
Mancall, Elliott Lee *neurologist, educator*
Marshall, Bryan Edward *anesthesiologist, educator*
Mastroianni, Luigi, Jr. *physician, educator*
Matsumoto, Teruo *surgeon, educator*
Mayock, Robert Lee *internist*
Melvin, John Lewis *physical and rehabilitation physician, educator*
†Mennuti, Michael Thomas *medical educator*
Miller, Leonard David *surgeon*
Ming, Si-Chun *pathologist, educator*
Mulholland, S. Grant *urologist*
†Neilson, Eric Grant *physician, educator, health facility administrator*
Nowell, Peter Carey *pathologist, educator*
Parish, Lawrence Charles *physician, editor*
†Pietra, Giuseppe Giovanni *pathology educator*
Potsic, William Paul *physician, educator*
Prevoznik, Stephen Joseph *anesthesiologist*
Pugliese, Maria A. *psychiatrist*
Rabinowitz, Howard K. *physician, educator*
Reinecke, Robert Dale *ophthalmologist*
Rhoads, Jonathan Evans *surgeon*
Rickels, Karl *psychiatrist, physician, educator*
†Ritchie, Wallace Parks, Jr. *surgeon, educator*
Ritter, Deborah Elizabeth *anesthesiologist, educator*
Roberts, Jay *pharmacologist, educator*
Rogers, Fred Baker *medical educator*
Rorke, Lucy Balian *neuropathologist*
Rosato, Francis Ernest *surgeon*
Rosen, Rhoda *obstetrician-gynecologist*
Ross, Leonard Lester *anatomist*
Rovera, Giovanni Aurelio *medical educator, scientist*
Rubin, Emanuel *pathologist, educator*
Russo, Irma Haydee Alvarez de *pathologist*
Salzberg, Brian Matthew *neuroscience and physiology educator*
Saunders, James C. *neuroscientist, educator*
Schidlow, Daniel *pediatrician, medical association administrator*
Schneider, Jan *obstetrics and gynecology educator*
Schotland, Donald Lewis *neurologist, educator*
Schumacher, H(arry) Ralph *internist, researcher, medical educator*
†Schwartz, Craig *osteopath, surgeon*
†Schwartz, Elias *pediatrician*
Schwartz, Gordon Francis *surgeon, educator*
Segal, Bernard Louis *physician, educator*
Sevy, Roger Warren *retired pharmacology educator*
Shapiro, Sandor Solomon *hematologist*
Shields, Jerry Allen *ophthalmologist, educator*
Silberberg, Donald H. *neurologist*
Sloviter, Henry Allan *medical educator*
Soloff, Louis Alexander *physician, educator*
Spaeth, George Link *physician, ophthalmology educator*
Spector, Harvey M. *osteopathic physician*
Sprague, James Mather *medical scientist, educator*
Steel, Howard Haldeman *pediatric orthopaedic surgeon*
Stunkard, Albert James *physician, educator*
Sudak, Howard Stanley *physician, psychiatry educator*
Sunderman, Frederick William *physician, educator, author, musician*
†Swain, Judith Lea *cardiovascular physician, educator*
Taichman, Norton Stanley *pathology educator*
Tasman, William Samuel *ophthalmologist, medical association executive*
Torg, Joseph Steven *orthopaedic surgeon, educator*
Tourtellotte, Charles Dee *physician, educator*
Wallace, Herbert William *physician, surgery educator, researcher*
Webber, John Bentley *orthopedic surgeon*
Wein, Alan Jerome *urologist, educator, researcher*
Weiss, William *retired pulmonary medicine-epidemiology educator*
†Whitaker, Linton Andin *plastic surgeon*
Wilson, Marjorie Price *physician, medical commission executive*
Winegrad, Albert Irvin *immunologist, educator*
Wollman, Harry *medical educator*
Yanoff, Myron *ophthalmologist*
Young, Donald Stirling *clinical pathology educator*
Zweiman, Burton *physician, scientist, educator*

Pittsburgh
Allen, Thomas E. *obstetrician, gynecologist*
Beachley, Michael Charles *radiologist*
Benz, Edward J., Jr. *physician, educator*
Bernier, George Matthew, Jr. *physician, medical educator, medical school dean*
Broussard, Elsie Rita *physician, educator, researcher*
Chorazy Lyjak, Anna Julia *pediatrician, medical administrator, educator*
Cooper, William Marion *physician*
Cutler, John Charles *physician, educator*
Dameshek, H(arold) Lee *physician*
deGroat, William Chesney *pharmacology educator*
Delaney, John Francis *neurologist, psychiatrist*
Detre, Katherine Maria *physician*
Detre, Thomas *psychiatrist, educator*
Dixit, Balwant Narayan *pharmacology and toxicology educator*
Donaldson, William Fielding, Jr. *orthopaedic surgeon*
Feczko, William Albert *radiologist*
Fireman, Philip *pediatrician, allergist, immunologist, medical association executive*
Fisher, Bernard *surgeon, researcher, educator*
Friday, Gilbert Anthony, Jr. *pediatrician*
Gaffney, Paul Cotter *physician*
Gill, Thomas James, III *physician, educator*
Hale, Edward Harned *internist*
Hardesty, Robert Lynch *surgeon, educator*
Harrold, Ronald Thomas *research scientist*
†Heckler, Frederick Roger *plastic surgeon*
Herndon, James Henry *orthopedic surgeon, educator*
Hingson, Robert Andrew *physician, educator, inventor, farmer, poet*
Howland, Robert Herbert *psychiatrist*
†Jannetta, Peter Joseph *neurosurgeon*
Jegasothy, Brian Vasanthakumar *dermatology educator*
Joyner, Claude Reuben, Jr. *physician, medical educator*
Karol, Meryl Helene *immunologist*
Kupfer, David J. *psychiatry educator*
Lewis, Jessica Helen (Mrs. Jack D. Myers) *physician, educator*
Ludwig, Karl David *psychiatrist*
MacLeod, Gordon Kenneth *physician, educator*
Matzke, Gary Roger *pharmacologist, educator, researcher*
Mc Kenzie, Ray *anesthesiologist, educator*
McMaster, James Henry *orthopedic surgeon*
Moore, Robert Yates *neuroscience educator*
Moriarty, Richard William *pediatrician*
Myers, Eugene Nicholas *otolaryngologist, otolaryngology educator*
Needleman, Herbert Leroy *psychiatrist, pediatrician*
Owens, Gregory Randolph *physician, medical educator*
Pham, Si Mai *cadiothoracic surgeon, medical educator*
Price, Trevor Robert Pryce *psychiatrist, educator*
Rabin, Bruce Stuart *immunologist, physician, educator*
Rogers, Robert Mark *physician*
Roth, Loren *psychiatrist*
Shapiro, Alvin Philip *physician, educator*
Siker, Ephraim S. *anesthesiologist*
Spina, Horacio Anselmo *physician*
Starzl, Thomas Earl *physician, educator*
Troen, Philip *physician, educator*
Wald, Niel *medical educator*
Walsh, Arthur Campbell *psychiatrist*
Wedemeyer, W. Anne Little *pediatric cardiologist, educator, lawyer*

Werner, Gerhard *pharmacologist, psychoanalyst, educator*
Winter, Peter Michael *physician, anesthesiologist, educator*
Wylie, Mary Evelyn *anesthesiologist, educator*
Yu, Victor Lin-Kai *physician, educator*

Plymouth Meeting
Kessler, Irving Isar *epidemiologist, educator, consultant*
Nobel, Joel J. *biomedical researcher*

Pottsville
Garloff, Samuel John *psychiatrist*

Reading
Alexander, Robert William *radiologist*
Hildreth, Eugene A. *physician, educator*

Saint Marys
Brunk, Samuel Frederick *oncologist*

Sayre
Moody, Robert Adams *neurosurgeon*
Thomas, John Melvin *surgeon*

Scranton
Eagen, Jeremiah W. *physician*
O'Connor, James Joseph *pathologist, educator*

Sellersville
Loux, Norman Landis *psychiatrist*

Springfield
Ruiz, Jose Rafael *podiatric surgeon*

Strafford
Horwitz, Orville *cardiologist, educator*

Swarthmore
Carey, William Bacon *pediatrician, educator*

Tyrone
†Lewis, Kathryn Huxtable *pediatrician*

Upper Darby
Hurley, Harry James, Jr. *dermatologist*

Vandergrift
Bullard, Ray Elva, Jr. *retired psychiatrist, hospital administrator*

Warminster
Whinnery, James Elliott *aerospace medical scientist, flight surgeon*

Wayne
Atkins, Joseph P. *otorhinolaryngologist*
de Rivas, Carmela Foderaro *psychiatrist, hospital administrator*

Waynesboro
Kirk, Daniel Lee *physician, consultant*

West Chester
Flood, Dorothy Garnett *neuroscientist*
Harrington, Anne Wilson *medical librarian*
Schindler, Peter David *child and adolescent psychiatrist*

West Conshohocken
Capizzi, Robert Lawrence *physician*

West Point
Grossman, William *medical researcher, educator*
Sherwood, Louis Maier *physician, scientist, pharmaceutical company executive*

Wilkes Barre
Ru Dusky, Basil Michael *cardiologist, consultant*

Williamsport
Lattimer, Gary Lee *physician*

Windber
Furigay, Rodolfo Lazo *surgeon*

Wynnewood
Doherty, Henry Joseph *anesthesiologist, medical hypnotist*
Flanagan, Joseph Charles *ophthalmologist*
Harkins, Herbert Perrin *otolaryngologist, educator*
Hodges, John Hendricks *physician, educator*

Wyomissing
Smith, Raymond Leigh *plastic surgeon*

RHODE ISLAND

Barrington
Carpenter, Charles Colcock Jones *physician, educator*

Kingston
Pereira, Celina Antonieta *physician*

Pawtucket
Carleton, Richard Allyn *cardiologist*

Providence
Amaral, Joseph Ferreira *surgeon*
Aronson, Stanley Maynard *physician, educator*
Davis, Robert Paul *physician, educator*
Dowben, Robert Morris *physician, scientist*
Erikson, George Emil (Erik Erikson) *anatomist, archivist, historian, educator, information specialist*
Feinstein, Pratarnporn *child psychiatrist*
Galletti, Pierre Marie *medical science educator, artificial organ scientist*
Glicksman, Arvin S(igmund) *radiologist, physician*
Hamolsky, Milton William *physician*
Kane, Agnes Brezak *pathologist, educator*
Lekas, Mary Despina *otolaryngologist*
Lewis, David Carleton *medical educator, university center director*
McCartney, James Robert *psychiatrist*
Mc Donald, Charles J. *physician, educator*
Monteiro, Lois Ann *medical science educator*
Oh, William *physician*
Parks, Robert Emmett, Jr. *medical science educator*
Shaw, Ronald Ahrend *physician, educator*

Wakefield
Fair, Charles Maitland *neuroscientist, author*

SOUTH CAROLINA

Aiken
von Buedingen, Richard Paul *urologist*

Anderson
Astler, Vernon Benson *surgeon*

Charleston
Anderson, Marion Cornelius *surgeon, medical educator*
Apple, David Joseph *ophthalmology educator*
Bell, Norman Howard *physician, endocrinologist, educator*
Carabello, Blase Anthony *cardiology educator*
Carek, Donald J(ohn) *child psychiatry educator*
Crawford, Fred Allen, Jr. *cardiothoracic surgeon, educator*
Creasman, William Thomas *obstetrician-gynecologist, educator*
Daniell, Herman Burch *pharmacologist*
Dobson, Richard Lawrence *dermatologist, educator*
Gillette, Paul Crawford *pediatric cardiologist*
Hogan, Edward Leo *neurologist*
Johnson, Allen Huggins *physician, educator*
La Via, Mariano Francis *physician, pathology and laboratory medicine educator*
Legerton, Clarence William, Jr. *gastroenterologist, educator*
LeRoy, Edward Carwile *rheumatologist*
Maize, John Christopher *dermatology educator*
Margolius, Harry Stephen *pharmacologist, physician*
Newberry, William Marcus *physician, educator, university administrator*
O'Brien, Paul Herbert *surgeon*
Ogawa, Makio *physician*
Othersen, Henry Biemann, Jr. *pediatric surgeon, physician, educator*
Roof, Betty Sams *internist*
Simson, Jo Anne *anatomy and cell biology educator*
Wilson, Frederick Allen *medical educator, medical center administrator, gastroenterologist*

Columbia
Abel, Anne Elizabeth Sutherland *pediatrician*
Adcock, David Filmore *radiologist, educator*
Almond, Carl Herman *surgeon, physician, educator*
Brooker, Jeff Zeigler *cardiologist*
Donald, Alexander Grant *psychiatrist*
Horger, Edgar Olin, III *obstetrics and gynecology educator*
Humphries, John O'Neal *physician, educator, university dean*
Jervey, Harold Edward, Jr. *medical education consultant, retired*
McFarland, Kay Flowers *medical educator*
Waldron, Robert Leroy, II *physician*

Florence
Wagner, John Garnet *pharmacy educator*

Greenville
Bates, George William *obstetrician, gynecologist, educator*
Bonner, Jack W., III *psychiatrist, educator, administrator*
Hoffman, Michael Robert *physician*
Kilgore, Donald Gibson, Jr. *pathologist*
†Ornston, Darius Gray, Jr. *psychiatrist*
Young, Edwin Reynolds, Jr. *urologist, missionary*

Hilton Head Island
Birk, Robert Eugene *retired physician, educator*
Carr, David Turner *physician*
Humphrey, Edward William *surgeon, medical educator*
Margileth, Andrew Menges *physician, former naval officer*
Santos, George Wesley *physician, educator*

Lexington
Miller, Ben Neely *physician*

Mount Pleasant
Wohltmann, Hulda Justine *pediatric endocrinologist*

Orangeburg
Babb, Julius Wistar, III *cardiovascular surgeon*

Seneca
Uden, David Elliott *cardiologist, educator*

Spartanburg
Fudenberg, Herman Hugh *immunologist, educator*
Guthrie, John Robert *physician, health science facility administrator*

West Columbia
Carter, Saralee Lessman *immunologist, microbiologist*

SOUTH DAKOTA

Rapid City
Quinn, Robert Henry *surgeon, medical school administrator*

Sioux Falls
Billion, John Joseph *orthopedic surgeon, state representative*
Fenton, Lawrence Jules *pediatric educator*
Flora, George Claude *retired neurology educator, neurologist*
Hoskins, John H. *urologist, educator*
Jaqua, Richard Allen *pathologist*
Morse, Peter Hodges *ophthalmologist, educator*
Van Demark, Robert Eugene, Sr. *orthopedic surgeon*
Wegner, Karl Heinrich *physician, educator*
Wiebe, Richard Herbert *reproductive endocrinologist, educator*
Zawada, Edward Thaddeus, Jr. *physician, educator*

Vermillion
Hagen, Arthur Ainsworth *pharmacologist*

TENNESSEE

Bristol
Harkrader, Charles Johnston, Jr. *surgeon*

Carthage
Head, Henry Buchen *physician*

Chattanooga
Feinberg, Edward Burton *ophthalmologist, educator*
Thow, George Bruce *surgeon*

Jefferson City
Muncy, Estle Pershing *physician*

Johnson City
Adebonojo, Festus O. *medical educator*
Berk, Steven Lee *internist, educator*
Coogan, Philip Shields *pathologist*
Dyer, Allen Ralph *psychiatrist*
Skalko, Richard Gallant *anatomist, educator*

Jonesborough
Weaver, Kenneth *gynecologist, researcher*

Knoxville
Acker, Joseph Edington *retired cardiology educator*
Brott, Walter Howard *cardiac surgeon, educator, retired army officer*
Burkhart, John Henry *physician*
Coulson, Patricia Bunker *endocrinologist*
Filston, Howard Church *pediatric surgeon, educator*
Kliefoth, A(rthur) Bernhard, III *neurosurgeon*
Lange, Robert Dale *internist, educator, medical researcher*
Natelson, Stephen Ellis *neurosurgeon*
Solomon, Alan *physician, medical oncologist and clinical investigator*

Lawrenceburg
Mauricio, Lilia D(ujua) *pathologist*

Memphis
Babin, Richard Weyro *surgeon, educator*
Blakley, Raymond Leonard *pharmacologist*
Carter, Sarah Anne *internist, educator*
Chesney, Russell Wallace *pediatrician*
Christopher, Robert Paul *physician*
Cox, Clair Edward, II *urologist, medical educator*
Crist, William Miles *physician*
Gerald, Barry *radiology educator, neuroradiologist*
†Gettelfinger, Thomas Clement *ophthalmologist*
Heimberg, Murray *pharmacologist, biochemist, physician, educator*
Hughes, Walter Thompson *physician, pediatrics educator*
Ingram, Alvin John *surgeon*
Johnson, James Gibb *physician*
Lieberman, Phillip Louis *allergist, educator*
Mauer, Alvin Marx *physician, medical educator*
Neely, Charles Lea, Jr. *retired physician*
†Nienhuis, Arthur Wesley *physician, researcher*
Pate, James Wynford *surgeon*
Runyan, John William, Jr. *medical educator*
Shanklin, Douglas Radford *physician*
Solomon, Solomon Sidney *endocrinologist, pharmacologist, scientist*
Sullivan, Jay Michael *medical educator*
Summitt, Robert Layman *pediatrician, educator*
Wilcox, Harry Hammond *retired medical educator*

Mountain Home
Hamdy, Ronald Charles *geriatrician*

Nashville
Bender, Harvey W., Jr. *cardiac and thoracic surgeon*
Bernard, Louis Joseph *surgeon, educator*
Burnett, Lonnie Sheldon *obstetrics and gynecology educator*
Burt, Alvin Miller, III *anatomist, cell biologist, educator, writer*
Byrd, Benjamin Franklin, Jr. *surgeon, educator*
Crofford, Oscar Bledsoe, Jr. *internist, medical educator*
Fowinkle, Eugene W. *physician, medical center administrator*
Hardman, Joel Griffeth *pharmacologist*
Krantz, Sanford Burton *physician*
Lynch, John Brown *plastic surgeon, educator*
Manning, Deborah A. *physician, health facility administrator*
Meacham, William Feland *neurological surgeon, educator*
†O'Day, Denis Michael *ophthalmologist, educator*
†O'Neill, James Anthony, Jr. *pediatric surgeon, educator*
Orth, David Nelson *physician, educator*
Ossoff, Robert Henry *otolaryngological surgeon*
Partain, Clarence Leon *radiologist, nuclear medicine physician, educator, administrator*
Pendergrass, Henry Pancoast *physician, radiology educator*
Pickens, David Richard, Jr. *retired surgeon, educator*
Riley, Harris DeWitt, Jr. *pediatrician*
Robertson, David *clinical pharmacologist, physician, educator*
Robinson, Roscoe Ross *nephrologist, educator*
Ross, Joseph Comer *physician, educator, academic administrator*
Sawyers, John Lazelle *surgeon*
Scott, Henry William, Jr. *surgeon, educator*
South, Mary Ann *pediatrics educator*
Spengler, Dan Michael *orthopedic surgery educator, researcher, surgeon*
Stahlman, Mildred Thornton *pediatrics and pathology educator, researcher*
Thornton, Spencer P. *ophthalmologist, educator*
van Eys, Jan *pediatrician, educator, administrator*

Oak Ridge
Clapp, Neal Keith *experimental pathologist*
Spray, Paul *surgeon*

Western Institute
Wingate, Robert Lee, Jr. *internist*

TEXAS

Amarillo
†Laur, William Edward *retired dermatologist*

Austin
Bernstein, Robert *retired physician, state official, former army officer*
Ersek, Robert Allen *plastic surgeon, inventor*
Mullins, Charles Brown *physician, academic administrator*
Preston, Jane *psychiatrist, educator*
Shurley, Jay Talmadge *psychiatrist, medical educator, polar explorer, author*
Sutton, Beverly Jewell *psychiatrist*

Baytown
Williams, Drew Davis *surgeon*

Beaumont
Lozano, Jose *nephrologist*

Boerne
Wittmer, James Frederick *preventive medicine physician, educator*

Brooks AFB
Carroll, Robert Eugene *senior flight surgeon*

Bryan
Dirks, Kenneth Ray *pathologist, medical educator, army officer*

College Station
Chiou, George Chung-Yih *pharmacologist, educator*
De Vaul, Richard Allan *medical school administrator*
Knight, James Allen *psychiatrist, educator*
Way, James Leong *pharmacology and toxicology educator*

Corpus Christi
Cox, William Andrew *cardiovascular thoracic surgeon*
Lim, Alexander Rufasta *neurologist, clinical investigator, educator*
Sisley, Nina Mae *physician, public health officer*

Dallas
Allen, Terry Devereux *urologist, educator*
Baskin, Leland Burleson *pathologist, educator, researcher*
Berbary, Maurice Shehadeh *physician, military officer, hospital administrator, educator*
Blomquist, Carl Gunnar *cardiologist*
Bonte, Frederick James *radiology educator, physician*
Burnside, John Wayne *medical educator, university official*
Cavanagh, Harrison Dwight *ophthalmic surgeon*
Cox, Rody P(owell) *medical educator, internist*
†Cullum, C. Munro *psychiatry and neurology educator*
Edwards, George Alva *physician, educator*
Eichenwald, Heinz Felix *physician*
Einspruch, Burton Cyril *psychiatrist*
Ericson, Ruth Ann *psychiatrist*
Feiner, Joel S. *psychiatrist*
†Fine, Kenneth Davin *gastroenterologist, researcher*
Flatt, Adrian Ede *surgeon*
Fogelman, Morris Joseph *physician*
Fordtran, John Satterfield *physician*
France, Newell Edwin *former hospital executive, businessman*
Frenkel, Eugene Phillip *physician*
Gage, Tommy Wilton *pharmacologist, dentist, pharmacist, educator*
Gant, Norman Ferrell, Jr. *obstetrician, gynecologist*
†Gantt, James Raiford *thoracic surgeon*
Gilman, Alfred Goodman *pharmacologist, educator*
Goldstein, Joseph Leonard *physician, medical educator, molecular genetics scientist*
Gruebel, Barbara Jane *internist, pulmonologist*
Harrington, Marion Ray *ophthalmologist*
Jenkins, M. T. Pepper *anesthesiologist, educator*
Johnson, Robert Lee, Jr. *physician, educator, researcher*
Kindberg, Shirley Jane *pediatrician*
Kramer, Robert Ivan *pediatrician*
Lewis, Jerry M. *psychiatrist, educator*
Maddrey, Willis Crocker *medical educator, internist, academic administrator, consultant, researcher*
Marks, James Frederic *pediatric endocrinologist, educator*
Mc Clelland, Robert Nelson *surgeon, educator*
McCracken, Alexander Walker *pathologist*
Miller, William Vencill *medical administrator*
New, William Neil *physician, retired naval officer*
Olinger, Sheff Daniel *neurologist, educator*
Petty, Charles Sutherland *pathologist*
Race, George Justice *pathology educator*
Ram, Chitta Venkata *physician*
Rosenberg, Roger Newman *neurologist, educator*
Sanford, Jay Philip *physician, government official*
Smith, Edwin Ide *medical educator*
Sparkman, Robert Satterfield *retired surgeon, educator*
Sprague, Charles Cameron *medical foundation president*
Stembridge, Vernie A(lbert) *pathologist, educator*
Stone, Marvin Jules *physician, immunologist educator*
Thompson, Jesse Eldon *vascular surgeon*
Wildenthal, C(laud) Kern *physician, educator*
Wilson, Jean Donald *endocrinologist, educator*
Ziff, Morris *internist, rheumatologist, educator*

Eden
Boyd, John Hamilton *osteopath*

El Campo
Goelzer, Ronald Eric *surgeon*

El Paso
Crossen, John Jacob *radiologist, educator*
De Vargas, Cecilia Cordoba *psychiatrist*
Gainer, Barbara Jeanne *radiology educator*
Jackson, Jean Therese *surgeon*

Kidd, Gerald Steele, II *endocrinologist, educator*
†Verghese, Abraham Cheeran *internist, writer, educator*

Fort Sam Houston
Pruitt, Basil Arthur, Jr. *surgeon, army officer*

Fort Worth
Ahmed, M. Basheer *psychiatrist, educator*
Blazina, Janice Fay *transfusion medicine physician*
de Sousa, Byron Nagib *physician, anesthesiologist, clinical pharmacologist and educator*
Joe, George Washington *clinical researcher, quantitative methodologist*
Jurgensen, Warren Peter *psychiatrist, educator*
Lorenzetti, Ole John *pharmaceutical research executive, ophthalmic research and development executive*
Smith, Thomas Hunter *ophthalmologist, ophthalmic plastic and orbital surgeon*

Galveston
Arens, James F. *anesthesiologist, educator*
Bailey, Byron James *otolaryngologist, medical association executive*
Burns, Chester Ray *medical history educator*
Calverley, John Robert *physician, educator*
Dawson, Earl Bliss *obstetrics and gynecology educator*
Gold, Daniel Howard *ophthalmologist, educator*
Goodwin, Jean McClung *psychiatrist*
Grant, J(ohn) Andrew, Jr. *medical educator, allergist*
Hilton, James Gorton *pharmacologist*
James, Thomas Naum *cardiologist, educator*
Koeppe, Patsy Poduska *internist, educator*
Lefeber, Edward James, Sr. *physician*
Levin, William Cohn *hematologist, former university president*
Ogra, Pearay L. *physician, educator*
Pearl, William Richard Emden *pediatric cardiologist*
Powell, Don Watson *medical educator, physiology researcher*
Powell, Leslie Charles, Jr. *obstetrics and gynecology educator*
Sandstead, Harold Hilton *medical educator*
Schreiber, Melvyn Hirsh *radiologist*
Shope, Robert Ellis *epidemiology educator*
Smith, David English *physician, educator*
Smith, Edgar Benton *physician*
Smith, Jerome Hazen *pathologist*
Tyson, Kenneth Robert Thomas *surgeon, educator*
Willis, William Darrell, Jr. *neurophysiologist, educator*

Garland
Duren, Michael *cardiologist*

Hemphill
Boren, Hollis Grady *retired physician*

Houston
Able, Luke William *retired pediatric surgeon, consultant*
Alexanian, Raymond *hematologist*
Alford, Bobby Ray *physician, educator, university official*
Appel, Stanley Hersh *neurologist*
Azios, Blanca Stella *pediatrician, medical administrator, educator*
†Bailey, Harold Randolph *surgeon*
Balch, Charles M. *surgeon, educator*
Baldwin, John Charles *surgeon, researcher*
Baskin, David Stuart *neurosurgeon*
Bast, Robert Clinton, Jr. *research scientist, medical educator*
Batsakis, John George *pathology educator*
Beasley, Robert Palmer *epidemiologist, dean, educator*
Beck, John Robert *pathologist, information scientist*
Berry, Michael A. *physician, consultant*
Bethea, Louise Huffman *allergist*
Bhandari, Arvind *oncologist*
Bodey, Gerald Paul *oncologist, educator*
Brody, Baruch Alter *medical educator, academic center administrator*
Bungo, Michael William *physician, educator, science administrator*
Burdette, Walter James *surgeon, educator*
Busch, Harris *medical educator*
Cantrell, William Allen *psychiatrist, educator*
Cardus, David *physician*
Catlin, Francis Irving *physician*
Collins, Vincent Patrick *radiologist, physician, educator*
Cooley, Denton Arthur *surgeon, educator*
Corriere, Joseph N., Jr. *urologist, educator*
Couch, Robert Barnard *physician, educator*
Dawood, Mohamed Yusoff *obstetrician, gynecologist*
DeBakey, Michael Ellis *cardiovascular surgeon, educator*
Dunbar, Burdett Sheridan *anesthesiologist, pediatrician, educator*
DuPont, Herbert Lancashire *medical educator, researcher*
Eisner, Diana *pediatrician*
Engelhardt, Hugo Tristram, Jr. *physician, educator*
Fehir, Kim Michele *oncologist, hematologist*
Feigin, Ralph David *pediatrician, educator*
Feigon, Judith Tova *ophthalmologist, surgeon, educator*
Fishman, Marvin Allen *pediatrician, neurologist, educator*
Freireich, Emil J *hematologist, educator*
Garber, Alan J(oel) *medical educator*
Gibson, Kathleen Rita *anatomy and anthropology educator*
Gigli, Irma *physician, educator, academic administrator*
Gildenberg, Philip Leon *neurosurgeon*
Glassman, Armand Barry *physician, pathologist, scientist, educator, administrator*
Gotto, Antonio Marion, Jr. *internist, educator*
Gould, Kenneth Lance *physician, educator*
Graham, David Yates *gastroenterologist*
†Grossman, Herbert Barton *urology educator*
Grossman, Robert George *physician, educator*
Gunn, Albert Edward, Jr. *internist, educator, lawyer, hospital and university administrator*
Guynn, Robert William *psychiatrist, educator*
Hall, Robert Joseph *physician, medical educator*
†Hanania, Nicola Alexander *physician*
†Harle, Thomas Stanley *radiologist*
Harper, Michael John Kennedy *obstetrics and gynecology educator*
Haynie, Thomas Powell, III *physician*
Haywood, Theodore Joseph *physician, educator*
Henning, Susan June *biomedical researcher*
Higgs, J. Jeffrey *retired physician and medical director*
Hollister, Leo Edward *physician, educator*
Holmquest, Donald Lee *physician, astronaut, lawyer*
Irani, Katie D. *medical educator, rehabilitation services professional*
Jankovic, Joseph *neurologist, educator, scientist*
Jenkins, Daniel Edwards, Jr. *physician, educator*
†Jones, Dan B. *ophthalmologist, educator*
Jordon, Robert Earl *physician*
Kahan, Barry Donald *surgeon, educator*
Kaufman, Raymond Henry *physician*
Kelly, Dorothy Helen *pediatrician, educator*
Kerwin, Joseph Peter *physician, former astronaut*
†Knight, J. Vernon *medicine and microbiology educator*
Kripke, Margaret Louise *immunologist*
Lane, Montague *physician, educator*
Levin, Bernard *physician*
Low, Morton David *physician, educator*
Maillard, Albert Achilles Joseph *head and neck surgeon, educator*
Mattox, Kenneth Leon *surgeon, educator, medical scientist*
Mayor, Heather Donald *medical educator*
Mc Bride, Raymond Andrew *pathologist, physician, educator*
Mc Pherson, Alice Ruth *ophthalmologist*
Milam, John Daniel *pathologist, educator*
Miller, Gary Evan *psychiatrist, mental health services administrator*
Mountain, Clifton Fletcher *surgeon, educator*
†Murphy, William Alexander, Jr. *diagnostic radiologist, educator*
Murray, John A. *orthopedist, medical association executive*
Musher, Daniel Michael *physician*
Ordonez, Nelson Gonzalo *pathologist*
Owsley, William Clinton, Jr. *radiologist*
Palacios, Ronald *immunologist*
Patten, Bernard Michael *neurologist, educator*
Pinkel, Donald Paul *pediatrician*
Rakel, Robert Edwin *physician, educator*
Ribble, John Charles *medical educator*
Rich, Robert Regier *immunology educator, physician*
Romsdahl, Marvin Magnus *surgeon, educator*
Rudolph, Arnold Jack *pediatrician, neonatologist, medical educator*
Samaan, Naguib Abdelmalik *endocrinologist*
Shearer, William Thomas *pediatrician, educator*
Shulman, Robert Jay *physician*
Simpson, Richard Kendall, Jr. *surgeon, physician, researcher*
Spira, Melvin *plastic surgeon*
Thomas, Orville C. *physician*
Walker, William Easton *surgeon, educator, lawyer*
Williams, Temple Weatherly, Jr. *internist, educator*

Irving
Mueller, James Bernhard *anesthesiologist, pain managememt consultant*

Lubbock
Bricker, Donald Lee *surgeon*
Buesseler, John Aure *ophthalmologist, management consultant*
Hartman, James Theodore *physician, educator*
Illner-Canizaro, Hana *physician, oral surgeon, researcher*
Jackson, Francis Charles *physician, surgeon*
Kurtzman, Neil A. *medical educator*
May, Donald Robert Lee *ophthalmologist, retina and vitreous surgeon, educator, academic administrator*
Messer, Robert H. *obstetrician/gynecologist, educator*
Perry, Malcolm Oliver *vascular surgeon*
Shires, George Thomas *surgeon, physician, educator*
Way, Barbara Haight *dermatologist*
Williams, Darryl Marlowe *medical educator*
Woolam, Gerald Lynn *surgeon*

Lufkin
Perry, Lewis Charles *emergency medicine physician, osteopath*

Mcallen
Ramirez, Mario Efrain *physician*

Nacogdoches
Fish, Stewart Allison *retired obstetrician and gynecologist*

New Braunfels
Fomon, Samuel Joseph *physician, educator*

Pasadena
Loomis, John Norman *psychiatrist*

Rockwall
Sparks, Sherman Paul *osteopathic physician*

San Antonio
Aust, Joe Bradley *surgeon, educator*
Baker, Floyd Wilmer *surgeon, retired army officer*
Beckmann, Charles Henry *cardiologist, educator*
Chong, Vernon *surgeon, physician, Air Force officer*
Croft, Harry Allen *psychiatrist*
Delmer, Merle W. *pathologist*
Dobie, Robert Alan *otologist*
Gillean, William Otho, Jr. *physician, psychiatrist*
Kotas, Robert Vincent *research physician, educator*
Ledford, Frank Finley, Jr. *surgeon, army officer*
Leon, Robert Leonard *psychiatrist, educator*
Maas, James Weldon *psychiatrist*
Mc Fee, Arthur Storer *physician*
†McGill, Henry Coleman, Jr. *physician, educator, researcher*
Meyer, George Gotthold *psychiatrist, educator*
Mitchell, George Washington, Jr. *physician, educator*
Neel, Spurgeon Hart, Jr. *physician, retired army officer*
Persellin, Robert Harold *physician*
Pestana, Carlos *physician, educator*
Reuter, Stewart Ralston *radiologist, lawyer, educator*
Rhodes, Linda Jane *psychiatrist*
Rosoff, Leonard, Sr. *retired surgeon, medical educator*
Schenker, Steven *physician, educator*
Smith, Reginald Brian Furness *anesthesiologist, educator*
Story, Jim Lewis *neurosurgeon, educator*
Townsend, Frank Marion *pathology educator*
†Walsh, Nicolas Eugene *rehabilitation medicine physician, educator*
Wiedeman, Geoffrey Paul *physician, air force officer*

Seabrook
Earle, Kenneth Martin *retired neuropathologist*

Seminole
Gremmel, Gilbert Carl *family physician*

Stafford
Polinger, Iris Sandra *dermatologist*

Temple
Dyck, Walter Peter *gastroenterologist, educator*
Holleman, Vernon Daughty *physician, internist*
†Knudsen, Kermit Bruce *physician*
†McLeskey, Charles Hamilton *anesthesiology educator*
Montgomery, Johnny Lester *physician, radiologist*

Texarkana
Selby, Roy Clifton, Jr. *neurosurgeon*

Tyler
Kronenberg, Richard Samuel *physician, educator*

Webster
Rappaport, Martin Paul *internist, nephrologist, educator*

UTAH

Murray
Goates, Delbert Tolton *child psychiatrist*

Ogden
Maughan, Willard Zinn *dermatologist*

Park City
Wardell, Joe Russell, Jr. *pharmacologist*

Salt Lake City
Abildskov, J. A. *cardiologist, educator*
Bauer, A(ugust) Robert, Jr. *surgeon, educator*
Bragg, David Gordon *physician, radiology educator*
Carroll, Karen Colleen *physician, infectious disease educator, medical microbiologist*
Chase, Mary Ann *physician*
Daynes, Raymond Austin *immunology educator*
Grosser, Bernard Irving *psychiatry educator*
Hammond, M(ary) Elizabeth Hale *pathologist*
Janerich, Dwight Thomas *epidemiologist, researcher*
Kim, Sung Wan *pharmacology educator*
Knight, Joseph Adams *pathologist*
Kolff, Willem Johan *internist, educator*
Matsuo, Fumisuke *physician, educator*
Middleton, Anthony Wayne, Jr. *urologist, educator*
Mirow, Susan Marilyn *psychiatry educator*
Moser, Royce, Jr. *physician, medical educator*
Nelson, Russell Marion *surgeon, educator*
Odell, William Douglas *physician, scientist, educator*
Overall, James Carney, Jr. *pediatrics laboratory medicine educator*
Renzetti, Attilio David *physician*
Smart, Charles Rich *retired surgeon*
Swensen, Laird S. *orthopedic surgeon*
Swenson, James Reed *physician, educator*
Ward, John Robert *physician, educator*
Winters, Suzanne *biomedical scientist, researcher*
Wong, Kuang Chung *anesthesiologist*

VERMONT

Bradford
Kaplow, Leonard Samuel *pathologist, educator*

Brattleboro
Howland, William Stapleton *anesthesiologist, educator*

Burlington
Davis, John Herschel *surgeon, educator*
Galbraith, Richard Anthony *physician, hospital administrator*
Lucey, Jerold Francis *pediatrician*
Riddick, Daniel Howison *obstetrics and gynecology educator, priest*
Sobel, Burton Elias *physician, educator*

Charlotte
Hong, Richard *pediatrician, educator*
†Smith, Robert Pease *retired physiatrist*

Middlebury
Patterson, William Bradford *surgical oncologist*

Norwich
Payson, Henry Edwards *forensic psychiatrist, educator*

South Burlington
Terris, Milton *physician, educator*

Swanton
Wooding, William Minor *medical statistics consultant*

Waitsfield
Clark, Samuel Smith *urologist*

White River Junction
Barton, Gail Melinda *psychiatrist, educator*

Williston
Mc Kay, Robert James, Jr. *pediatrician, educator*

VIRGINIA

Alexandria
Buhain, Wilfrido Javier *medical educator*
Mosely, Linda Hays *surgeon*
Rayman, Russell B. *physician*

Annandale
Binder, Richard Allen *hematologist, oncologist*
Galioto, Frank Martin, Jr. *pediatric cardiologist, educator*
†Kaufmanas, Petras G. *biomedical researcher, psychologist*
†Scott, Hugh Patrick *physician, naval officer*
Shamburek, Roland Howard *physician*
Simonian, Simon John *surgeon, scientist, educator*
Stage, Thomas Benton *psychiatrist*

Arlington
Brown, James Harvey *neuroscientist, government research administrator*
Dolan, William David, Jr. *physician*
†Fenner-Crisp, Penelope *pharmacologist, research toxicologist*

Burke
Emery, Janice Joy *obstetrician-gynecologist*

Chantilly
†Gemma, William Robert *medical association administrator, educator*

Charlottesville
Ayers, Carlos R. *internist, medical educator*
Barnett, Benjamin Lewis, Jr. *physician*
Beller, George Allan *medical educator*
†Braciale, Thomas J. *pathologist, educator*
Cantrell, Robert Wendell *otolaryngologist, head and neck surgeon, educator*
Craig, James William *physician, educator, university dean*
Davis, John Staige, IV *physician*
Detmer, Don Eugene *medical educator, administrator, surgeon*
Dreifuss, Fritz Emanuel *neurologist, educator*
Edgerton, Milton Thomas, Jr. *reconstructive and hand surgeon, educator*
Epstein, Robert Marvin *anesthesiologist, educator*
Farr, Barry Miller *physician, epidemiologist*
Fechner, Robert Eugene *pathology educator*
Flickinger, Charles John *anatomist, educator*
Gillenwater, Jay Young *urologist, educator*
Gross, Charles Wayne *physician, educator*
Gwaltney, Jack Merrit, Jr. *physician, educator, scientist*
Harbert, Guy Morley, Jr. *obstetrician-gynecologist*
Hook, Edward Watson, Jr. *physician, educator*
Hostler, Sharon Lee *pediatrics educator, rehabilitation center executive*
Howards, Stuart S. *physician, educator*
Jane, John Anthony *neurosurgeon, educator*
Jones, Rayford Scott *surgeon, medical educator*
Kassell, Neal Frederic *neurosurgeon*
Kattwinkel, John *physician, pediatrics educator*
Keats, Theodore Eliot *physician, radiology educator*
Kitchin, James D., III *obstetrician-gynecologist, educator*
Mandell, Gerald Lee *physician, medicine educator*
Marshall, Victor Fray *physician, educator*
McCallum, Richard Warwick *medical researcher, clinician, educator*
†McDuffie, Marcia Jensen *pediatrics educator, researcher*
Morgan, Raymond F. *plastic surgeon*
Muller, William Henry, Jr. *surgeon, educator*
Nolan, Stanton Peelle *surgeon, educator*
Owen, John Atkinson, Jr. *physician, educator*
Perkins, Marvin Earl *psychiatrist, educator*
Peterson, Kent Wright *physician*
Phillips, Lawrence H., II *neurologist*
Platts-Mills, Thomas Alexander E. *immunologist, educator, researcher*
Pullen, Edwin Wesley *anatomist, university dean*
Rowlingson, John Clyde *anesthesiologist, educator, physician*
Stevenson, Ian *psychiatrist, educator*
Suratt, Paul Michael *physician, researcher*
Taylor, Peyton Troy, Jr. *gynecologic oncologist, educator*
Teates, Charles David *radiologist, educator*
Thorner, Michael Oliver *medical educator, research center administrator*
Underwood, Paul Benjamin *obstetrician, educator*
Villar-Palasi, Carlos *pharmacology educator*
Weary, Peyton Edwin *medical educator*
Wilhelm, Morton *surgery educator*
Wills, Michael Ralph *medical educator*

Fairfax
Dettinger, Garth Bryant *surgeon, physician, retired air force officer, county health officer*
DuRocher, Frances Antoinette *physician, educator*
Rubin, Robert Joseph *physician, health care consultant*
Schulman, Joseph Daniel *physician, medical geneticist, reproductive biologist, educator*

Falls Church
Bucur, John Charles *neurological surgeon*
Ehrlich, S(aul) Paul, Jr. *physician, consultant, former government official*

Hampton
Brown, Loretta Ann Port *physician, geneticist*

Leesburg
Mitchell, Russell Harry *dermatologist*

Lynchburg
Crow, Harold Eugene *physician, family medicine educator*

Marion
Peal, James Albert *psychiatrist*

Mc Lean
Buck, Alfred Andreas *physician, epidemiologist*
Cooper, John Allen Dicks *medical educator*
Gerson, Elliot Francis *health care and financial services executive*
Laning, Robert Comegys *retired physician, former naval officer*

Midlothian
Jones, John Evan *medical educator*

Moneta
Singleton, Samuel Winston *physician, pharmaceutical company executive*

Norfolk
Andrews, William Cooke *physician*
Barnes, Herman Verdain *internist, educator*
Devine, Charles Joseph, Jr. *urologist, educator*
Dyar, Kathryn Wilkin *pediatrician*
El-Mahdi, Anas Morsi *radiation oncologist*
Faulconer, Robert Jamieson *pathologist, educator*
Jones, Howard Wilbur, Jr. *gynecologist*
Lester, Richard Garrison *radiologist, educator*
Lind, James Forest *surgeon, educator*
Rohn, Reuben David *pediatric educator and administrator*

Norton
Vest, Gayle Southworth *obstetrician and gynecologist*

Oakton
Harmon, Robert Gerald *health company executive*

Petersburg
Young, Estelle Irene *dermatologist*

Portsmouth
Geib, Philip Oldham *physician, retired naval officer*

Reston
†Fullagar, Paul Richard *medical association administrator*
Ryan, Mary Catherine *pediatrician*
†Sansone, Torry Mark *association executive*

Richmond
Ayres, Stephen McClintock *physician, educator*
Christie, Laurence Glenn, Jr. *surgeon*
Dunn, Leo James *obstetrician, gynecologist, educator*
Franko, Bernard Vincent *pharmacologist*
Gewanter, Harry Lewis *pediatric rheumatologist*
Goldman, Israel David *hematologist, oncologist*
Kay, Saul *pathologist*
Kendig, Edwin Lawrence, Jr. *physician, educator*
Lawrence, Walter, Jr. *surgeon*
Mauck, Henry Page, Jr. *medical and pediatrics educator*
Mc Cue, Carolyn Moore *retired pediatric cardiologist*
Mellette, M. Susan Jackson *physician, educator, researcher*
Neal, Marcus Pinson, Jr. *physician, medical educator*
Oken, Donald Edward *physician, educator*
Owen, Duncan Shaw, Jr. *physician, medical educator*
Patterson, James Willis *pathology and dermatology educator*
Richardson, David Walthall *cardiologist, educator, consultant*
Self, Phyllis C. *health sciences librarian*
Sirica, Alphonse Eugene *pathology educator*
Tunner, William Sams *urological surgeon*
Ward, John Wesley *retired pharmacologist*

Salem
Chakravorty, Ranes Chandra *surgeon, educator*

Suffolk
Carroll, George Joseph *pathologist, educator*

Virginia Beach
Mayer, William Dixon *pathologist, educator*

Waynesboro
†Anderson, Judith Charlene *medical record technician*

Williamsburg
Davis, Richard Bradley *internal medicine, pathology educator, physician*
Jacoby, William Jerome, Jr. *internist, retired military officer*
Maloney, Milford Charles *retired internal medicine educator*

Winchester
Bechamps, Gerald J. *surgeon*

Woodbridge
Vachher, Prehlad Singh *psychiatrist*

WASHINGTON

Auburn
Sata, Lindbergh Saburo *psychiatrist, physician, educator*

Bellevue
Hackett, Carol Ann Hedden *physician*
Knoepfler, Peter Tamas *psychiatrist, organizational consultant*
Olson, Hilding Harold *surgeon, educator*
Phillips, Zaiga Alksnis *pediatrician*

Bremerton
Pliskow, Vita Sari *anesthesiologist*

Friday Harbor
Geyman, John Payne *physician, educator*

Gig Harbor
Grouse, Jan Ellen *physician*

Issaquah
Barchet, Stephen *physician, former naval officer*

Kirkland
Barto, Deborah Ann *physician*

Longview
Kenagy, John Warner *surgeon*

Mazama
Hogness, John Rusten *physician, academic administrator*

Mercer Island
Coe, Robert Campbell *surgeon*
Elgee, Neil Johnson *physician*
Haviland, James West *physician*

Moses Lake
Leadbetter, Mark Renton, Jr. *orthopaedic surgeon*

Mount Vernon
Cammock, Earl E. *surgeon*

Olympia
Flemming, Stanley Lalit Kumar *family practice physician, state legislator*

Port Ludlow
Ward, Louis Emmerson *retired physician*

Pullman
Barnes, Charles D. *neuroscientist, educator*

Puyallup
†Lurie, Hugh James *psychiatrist, educator*

Redmond
Beeson, Paul Bruce *physician*

Richland
Bair, William J. *radiation biologist*
Zirkle, Lewis Greer *physician, executive*

Seattle
Aagaard, George Nelson *medical educator*
Abelson, Herbert Traub *pediatrician, educator*
Aldrich, Robert Anderson *physician*
Anderson, Richard Powell *thoracic surgeon, educator*
Ansell, Julian S. *physician, urology educator*
†Baker, Helen T. *pediatrician, educator*
Bassingthwaighte, James Bucklin *physiologist, educator, medical researcher*
Benirschke, Stephen Kurt *orthopaedic surgeon*
Bierman, Charles Warren *physician, educator*
Bierman, Edwin Lawrence *physician, educator*
Bird, Thomas D. *neurologist*
Blagg, Christopher Robin *nephrologist*
Blandau, Richard Julius *physician, educator*
Bonica, John Joseph *anesthesiologist, educator*
Bornstein, Paul *physician, biochemist*
Bowden, Douglas McHose *neuropsychiatric scientist, educator, research center administrator*
Boyko, Edward John *internist, medical researcher*
Brockenbrough, Edwin Chamberlayne *surgeon*
Caro, Ivor *dermatologist*
Couser, William Griffith *medical educator, academic administrator, nephrologist*
Dale, David C. *physician, medical educator*
Dawson, Patricia Lucille *surgeon*
Donaldson, James Adrian *otolaryngology educator*
Dorpat, Theodore Lorenz *psychoanalyst*
Figley, Melvin Morgan *radiologist, physician, educator*
Freeny, Patrick Clinton *radiology educator, consultant*
Gardner, Jill Christopher *neuroscientist, educator*
Giblett, Eloise Rosalie *hematology educator*
Goodell, Brian Wayne *oncologist, medical educator*
Graham, C(lyde) Benjamin, Jr. *physician*
Grayston, J. Thomas *medical and public health educator*
Guntheroth, Warren Gaden *physician*
Guralnick, Michael J. *medical research administrator*
Hackett, John Peter *dermatologist*
†Hackman, Robert Cordell *pathology educator, researcher*
Hargiss, James Leonard *ophthalmologist*
Henderson, Maureen McGrath *medical educator*
Herring, Susan Weller *anatomist*
Hodson, William Alan *pediatrician*
Hornbein, Thomas Frederic *anesthesiologist*
Hudson, Leonard Dean *physician*
Hutchinson, William Burke *surgeon, research center director*
Jonsen, Albert R. *medical ethics educator*
Kalina, Robert Edward *physician, educator*
Keith, Donald Malcolm *physician*
Kirby, William Murray Maurice *medical educator*
Klebanoff, Seymour Joseph *medical educator*
Kraft, George Howard *physician, educator*
Krohn, Kenneth Albert *radiology educator*
LaVeck, Gerald DeLoss *physician, educator*
†Ledbetter, Jeffrey A. *immunologist*
Loeser, John David *neurosurgeon, educator*
Mason, James Tate *surgeon*
McGough, Peter Myles *physician*
Merendino, K. Alvin *surgical educator*
Moore, Daniel Charles *physician*
Mottet, Norman Karle *pathologist, educator*
Nelson, James Alonzo *radiologist, educator*
Ojemann, George A. *neurosurgeon, medical association executive*
Petersdorf, Robert George *medical educator, retired association executive*
Porte, Daniel, Jr. *physician, educator, health facility administrator*
Ravenholt, Reimert Thorolf *epidemiologist*
Ross, Russell *pathologist, educator*
Schilling, John Albert *surgeon*
Scott, John Carlyle *gynecologist, oncologist*
Scribner, Belding Hibbard *medical educator, nephrologist*
Shepard, Thomas Hill *physician, educator*
Simkin, Peter Anthony *physician, educator*
Steiner, Robert Alan *neuroendocrinologist, educator*
Stenchever, Morton Albert *physician, educator*
Strandjord, Paul Edphil *physician, educator*
Strandness, Donald Eugene, Jr. *surgeon*
Su, Judy Ya Hwa Lin *pharmacologist*
Swanson, August George *physician, retired association executive*
Swanson, Phillip Dean *neurologist*
Tenney, William Frank *pediatrician*
Thomas, Edward Donnall *physician, researcher*
Weaver, Lois Jean *physician, educator*
Wilske, Kenneth Ray *internist, rheumatologist, researcher*
Yarington, Charles Thomas, Jr. *surgeon, administrator*
Yue, Agnes Kau-Wah *otolaryngologist*

Spokane
Bakker, Cornelis B. *psychiatrist, educator*
Gibson, Melvin Roy *pharmacognosy educator*
McClellan, David Lawrence *physician*
Mielke, Clarence Harold, Jr. *hematologist*
Moyer, John Arthur *obstetrician/gynecologist, state senator*
†Schlicke, Carl Paul *retired surgeon*

Tacoma
Chen, Stephen Shau-tsi *psychiatrist, physiologist*

Vancouver
Perlstein, Abraham Phillip *psychiatrist*

WEST VIRGINIA

Bluefield
Blaydes, James Elliott *ophthalmologist*

Charleston
Heck, Albert Frank *neurologist*

Clarksburg
Ona-Sarino, Milagros Felix *physician, pathologist*

Huntington
Bowdler, Anthony John *physician, educator*
Cocke, William Marvin, Jr. *plastic surgeon, educator*
Edwards, Roy Alvin *physician, psychiatrist, educator*
Esposito, Albert Charles *ophthalmologist, state legislator*
Mason, Bert E. *podiatrist*
Mufson, Maurice Albert *physician, educator*

Lewisburg
Willard, Ralph Lawrence *surgery educator, physician, former college president*

Martinsburg
Malin, Howard Gerald *podiatrist*

Morgantown
Albrink, Margaret Joralemon *medical educator*
Colasanti, Brenda Karen *pharmacoloy and toxicology educator*
Fleming, William Wright, Jr. *pharmacology educator*
Warden, Herbert Edgar *surgeon, educator*
Weinstein, George William *ophthalmology educator*
†Wilt, Jeffrey Lynn *pulmonary and critical care physician*

Wheeling
Heceta, Estherbelle Aguilar *anesthesiologist*

WISCONSIN

Brookfield
Hardman, Harold Francis *pharmacology educator*

Cable
†MacCarty, Collin S. *neurosurgeon*

Fond Du Lac
Lambert, Eugene Kent *oncologist, hematologist*
Treffert, Darold Allen *psychiatrist, author, hospital director*

Green Bay
Finesilver, Alan George *rheumatologist*

La Crosse
Corser, David Hewson *pediatrician*
Webster, Stephen Burtis *physician, educator*

Madison
Albert, Daniel Myron *ophthalmologist, educator*
†Atkinson, Richard Lee, Jr. *internal medicine educator*
Bach-y-Rita, Paul *neurophysiologist, rehabilitation medicine specialist*
Bass, Paul *pharmacology educator*
Belzer, Folkert Oene *surgeon*
Bloodworth, J. M. Bartow, Jr. *physician, educator*
Boutwell, Roswell Knight *oncology educator*
Brooks, Benjamin Rix *neurologist, educator*
Brown, Arnold Lanehart, Jr. *pathologist, educator, university dean*
Burgess, Richard Ray *oncology educator, molecular biology researcher, biotechnology consultant*
Carbone, Paul Peter *oncologist, educator, administrator*
Colás, Antonio Espada *medical educator*
Dodson, Vernon Nathan *physician, educator*
Fahien, Leonard August *physician, educator*
Farley, Eugene Shedden, Jr. *physician, educator*
Forster, Francis Michael *physician, educator*
Javid, Manucher J. *neurosurgeon*
Jefferson, James Walter *psychiatry educator*
Keesey, Ulker Tulunay *retired ophthalmology and psychology educator*
Kepecs, Joseph Goodman *physician, educator*
Kumar, Anand *medical educator, researcher*
Ladinsky, Judith Louise *preventive medicine educator*
Laessig, Ronald Harold *pathology educator, state official*
Leavitt, Lewis A. *pediatrician, educator*
Lobeck, Charles Champlin, Jr. *pediatrics educator*
Mac Kinney, Archie Allen, Jr. *physician*
Maki, Dennis G. *medical educator, researcher, clinician*
Marton, Laurence Jay *clinical pathologist, educator, researcher*
McBeath, Andrew Alan *orthopedic surgery educator*
Miller, James Alexander *oncologist, educator*
Mohs, Frederic Edward *surgeon, educator*
Nordby, Eugene Jorgen *orthopedic surgeon*
Peters, Henry Augustus *neuropsychiatrist*
Pitot, Henry Clement, III *physician, educator*
Reynolds, Ernest West *physician, educator*
Roberts, Leigh Milton *psychiatrist*
Rowe, George Giles *cardiologist, educator*
Schutta, Henry Szczesny *neurologist, educator*
Sobkowicz, Hanna Maria *neurology researcher*
Sonnedecker, Glenn Allen *historian of pharmacy*
Sufit, Robert Louis *neurologist, educator*
Tomar, Russell Herman *pathologist, educator, researcher*
Urban, Frank Henry *dermatologist, state legislator*
Westman, Jack Conrad *child psychiatrist, educator*
Whiffen, James Douglass *surgeon, educator*

Manitowoc
Trader, Joseph Edgar *orthopedic surgeon*

Marshfield
Fye, W. Bruce, III *cardiologist*
Sautter, Richard Daniel *physician, administrator*
Stueland, Dean Theodore *emergency physician*

Milwaukee
Alexander, Janice Hoehner *physician, educator*
Bhore, Jay Narayan *psychiatrist*
Chambers, LaRoyce Francis *obstetrician, gynecologist*
Condon, Robert Edward *surgeon, educator*
Cooper, Richard Alan *hematologist, college dean*
Esterly, Nancy Burton *physician*
Fink, Jordan Norman *physician, educator*
Grim, Clarence Ezra *medical educator, internist, researcher*
Kloehn, Ralph Anthony *plastic surgeon*
Kochar, Mahendr Singh *physician, educator, administrator, researcher, writer, consultant*
Krausen, Anthony Sharnik *surgeon*
Namdari, Bahram *surgeon*
Pisciotta, Anthony Vito *physician, educator*
Schultz, Richard Otto *ophthalmologist, educator*
Shindell, Sidney *medical educator, physician*
Soergel, Konrad Hermann *physician*
Stafl, Adolf *obstetrician, gynecologist, educator*
Terry, Leon Cass *neurologist, educator*

Oshkosh
†Holub, Gregory Steven *medical association administrator*

Racine
†Stewart, Richard Donald *internist, educator*

Sayner
Southwick, Harry Webb *surgeon*

Sheboygan
Gore, Donald Ray *orthopedic surgeon*

Waukesha
Scheving, Lawrence Einar *scientist, anatomy educator*

Wauwatosa
Hollister, Winston Ned *pathologist*

West Allis
Feinsilver, Donald Lee *psychiatry educator*

West Bend
Gardner, Robert Joseph *general and thoracic surgeon*

WYOMING

Cheyenne
Hunton, Donald Bothen *retired internist*

Laramie
Cronkleton, Thomas Eugene *physician*

Wilson
Eliot, Robert Salim *physician*

TERRITORIES OF THE UNITED STATES

PUERTO RICO

Ponce
Sala, Luis Francisco *surgeon, educator*
Torres-Aybar, Francisco Gualberto *medical educator*

San Juan
De Jesús, Nydia Rosa *physician, anesthesiologist*
Ramirez-Rivera, Jose *physician*
Sahai, Hardeo *medical statistics educator*

CANADA

ALBERTA

Calgary
Hollenberg, Morley Donald *research physician, educator*
Lederis, Karolis Paul (Karl Lederis) *pharmacologist, educator, researcher*
Melvill-Jones, Geoffrey *physician, educator*
Rewcastle, Neill Barry *neuropathology educator*
Stell, William Kenyon *neuroscientist, educator*
ter Keurs, Henk E. D. J. *cardiologist, educator*

Edmonton
Cook, David Alastair *pharmacology educator*
Miller, Jack David R. *radiologist, physician, educator*

BRITISH COLUMBIA

Vancouver
Baird, Patricia Ann *physician, educator*
Bates, David Vincent *physician, medical educator*
Burhenne, Hans Joachim *physician, radiology educator*
Chow, Anthony Wei-Chik *physician*
Doyle, Patrick John *otolaryngologist*
Eaves, Allen Charles Edward *hematologist, medical agency administrator*
Freeman, Hugh James *gastroenterology educator*
Friedman, Sydney M. *anatomy educator, medical researcher*
Hardwick, David Francis *pathologist*
†Hegele, Richard G. *pathologist*
Jewesson, Peter John *clinical pharmacologist, educator*
Knobloch, Ferdinand J. *psychiatrist, educator*
McGeer, Edith Graef *neurological science educator emerita*

Mizgala, Henry F. *physician*
Paty, Donald Winston *neurologist*
Rootman, Jack *ophthalmologist, surgeon, pathologist, oncologist, artist*
Roy, Chunilal *psychiatrist*
Slonecker, Charles Edward *anatomist, medical educator, author*
Sutter, Morley Carman *medical scientist*
Thurlbeck, William Michael *retired pathologist, retired medical educator*
Tingle, Aubrey James *pediatric immunologist, research administrator*
Tyers, Geddes Frank Owen *surgeon*

Victoria
Mac Diarmid, William Donald *physician*

MANITOBA

Winnipeg
Angel, Aubie *physician, academic administrator*
Blanchard, Robert Johnstone Weir *surgeon*
Bowman, John Maxwell *physician, educator*
Haworth, James Chilton *pediatrics educator*
Israels, Lyonel Garry *hematologist, medical educator*
Persaud, Trivedi Vidhya Nandan *anatomy educator, researcher, consultant*
Ronald, Allan Ross *internal medicine and medical microbiology educator, researcher*
Ross, Robert Thomas *neurologist, educator*
Sutherland, John Beattie *radiologist, health center administrator*

NOVA SCOTIA

Halifax
Carruthers, S. George *medical educator, physician*
Gold, Judith Hammerling *psychiatrist*
Goldbloom, Richard Ballon *pediatrics educator*
Langley, George Ross *medical educator*
Tonks, Robert Stanley *pharmacology and therapeutics educator, former university dean*

ONTARIO

Hamilton
Basmajian, John Varoujan *medical scientist, educator, physician*
Bienenstock, John *physician, educator*
Collins, John Alfred *obstetrician-gynecologist, educator*
Mueller, Charles Barber *surgeon, educator*
Roland, Charles Gordon *physician, medical historian, educator*
Uchida, Irene Ayako *cytogenetics educator, researcher*

Kingston
Boag, Thomas Johnson *physician*
Kaufman, Nathan *pathology educator, physician*
Low, James A. *physician*

London
Barr, Murray Llewellyn *former anatomy educator*
Brooks, Vernon Bernard *neuroscientist, educator, author*
Buck, Carol Kathleen *medical educator*
Frelick, Linden Frederick *hospital executive*
Lala, Peeyush Kanti *medical scientist, educator*
Marotta, Joseph Thomas *medical educator*
McWhinney, Ian Renwick *physician, medical educator*
Valberg, Leslie Stephen *medical educator, physician, researcher*

Mississauga
Perkin, Reginald Lewis *physician, educator*

North York
Regan, David *brain researcher, educator*

Ottawa
de Bold, Adolfo J. *pathology and physiology educator, research scientist*
Friesen, Henry George *endocrinologist, educator*
Hagen, Paul Beo *physician, medical scientist*
Hurteau, Gilles David *obstetrician, gynecologist, educator, university dean*
Jackson, W. Bruce *ophthalmology educator, researcher*
Keon, Wilbert Joseph *cardiologist, surgeon, educator*
Lavoie, Lionel A. *physician, medical executive*
Waugh, Douglas Oliver William *pathology educator*

Sault Sainte Marie
Banerjee, Samarendranath *orthopedic surgeon*

Toronto
Alberti, Peter William *otolaryngologist*
Brown, Gregory Michael *psychiatrist, educator, research director*
Bruce, William Robert *physician, educator*
Casson, Alan Graham *thoracic surgeon, researcher*
Cinader, Bernhard *immunologist, gerontologist, scientist, educator*
Friesen, James *pediatrics research administrator*
Goldenberg, Gerald Joseph *physician, educator*
Greben, Stanley Edward *psychiatrist, educator, author, editor*
Hudson, Alan Roy *neurosurgeon, medical educator, hospital administrator*
Kalant, Harold *pharmacology educator, physician*
Kalow, Werner *pharmacologist, toxicologist*
Lindsay, William Kerr *surgeon*
Lipowski, Zbigniew Jerzy *psychiatrist, educator*
Mc Culloch, Ernest Armstrong *physician, educator*
Miller, Anthony Bernard *physician, medical researcher*
Nesbitt, Lloyd Ivan *podiatrist*
Ogilvie, Richard Ian *clinical pharmacologist*
Rakoff, Vivian Morris *psychiatrist, writer*
Rothstein, Aser *radiation biology educator*
Seeman, Philip *pharmacology educator, neurochemistry researcher*
Silver, Malcolm David *pathologist, educator*
†Skorcz, Stephen *hospital association executive*
Sole, Michael Joseph *cardiologist*
Till, James Edgar *scientist*
Turner, Robert Edward *psychiatrist, educator*
Volpé, Robert *endocrinologist*

Willowdale
Turnbull, John Cameron *pharmacist, consultant*

PRINCE EDWARD ISLAND

Monticello
Gingras, Gustave *physician*

QUEBEC

Montpellier
Poirier, Louis Joseph *neurology educator*

Montreal
†Aguayo, Albert Juan *neuroscientist*
Baxter, Donald William *physician, educator*
Beardmore, Harvey Ernest *retired physician, educator*
Becklake, Margaret Rigsby *physician, educator*
Burgess, John Herbert *physician, educator*
Chretien, Michel *physician, educator, administrator*
Clermont, Yves Wilfrid *anatomy educator, researcher*
Cruess, Richard Leigh *surgeon, university dean*
Cuello, Augusto Claudio Guillermo *medical research scientist, author*
Feindel, William Howard *neurosurgeon, consultant*
Freeman, Carolyn Ruth *radiation oncologist*
Genest, Jacques *physician, researcher, administrator*
Gold, Phil *physician, educator*
Goltzman, David *endocrinologist, educator, researcher*
Jasmin, Gaetan *pathologist, educator*
†Kramer, Michael Stuart *pediatric epidemiologist*
Leblond, Charles Philippe *anatomy educator, researcher*
Lehmann, Heinz Edgar *psychiatrist, consultant, researcher*
Little, Alan Brian *obstetrician, gynecologist, educator*
MacDonald, R(onald Angus) Neil *physician, educator*
Mac Lean, Lloyd Douglas *surgeon*
Mc Gregor, Maurice *cardiologist, medical educator*
Milic-Emili, Joseph *physician, educator*
Moore, Sean *pathologist, educator*
Mulder, David S. *cardiovascular surgeon*
Nattel, Stanley *cardiologist, research scientist*
Osmond, Dennis Gordon *medical educator, researcher*
Pelletier, Louis Conrad *surgeon, educator*
Pinard, Gilbert Daniel *psychiatrist, educator*

Quebec
Couture, Jean G. *surgeon, educator*
Jovanovic, Miodrag *surgeon, educator*
Labrie, Fernand *physician*
†Parent, André *neurobiology educator, researcher*

Sherbrooke
Bureau, Michel André *pediatrician, pulmonologist, faculty dean*
de Margerie, Jean-M. *ophthalmology educator*

Westmount
Jasper, Herbert Henri *neuroscience researcher, consultant, writer*
Kessler, Jacques Isaac *gastroenterologist, educator*

SASKATCHEWAN

Saskatoon
Emson, Harry Edmund *pathology educator, bioethicist*
Houston, C(larence) Stuart *radiologist, educator*
Jaques, Louis Barker *pharmacologist*
Johnson, Dennis Duane *pharmacologist, educator*

MEXICO

Guadalajara
Garibay-Gutierrez, Luis *physician, educator*

Juarez
Torres Medina, Emilio *oncologist, consultant*

Mexico City
Diaz-Coller, Carlos *physician*

AUSTRALIA

Hobart Tasmania
Munger, Bryce L. *physician, educator*

Nedlands
Oxnard, Charles Ernest *anatomist, anthropologist, human biologist, educator*

AUSTRIA

Maria Enzersdorf
Vetter, Herbert *physician, educator*

Vienna
Frankl, Viktor E. *psychiatrist, author*

BRAZIL

Rio de Janeiro
Leite, Carlos Alberto *physician, medical educator*

Salvador
Silva, Benedicto Alves de Castro *surgeon, educator*

DENMARK

Copenhagen
Skylv, Grethe Krogh *rheumatologist, anthropologist*

ENGLAND

Cambridge
Acheson, Roy Malcolm *epidemiologist, educator*

London
Comfort, Alexander *physician, author*
Green, Richard *psychiatrist, lawyer, educator*
Symon, Lindsay *neurological surgery educator*

Oxford
Dawes, Geoffrey Sharman *medical researcher*
Guillery, Rainer Walter *anatomy educator*

FINLAND

Kuopio
Hakola, Hannu Panu Aukusti *psychiatry educator*

FRANCE

Chartres
Benoit, Jean-Pierre Robert *pneumologist, consultant*

Gouvieux
Fraser, David William *epidemiologist*

Marseilles
Vague, Jean Marie *endocrinologist*

Nanterre
Nguyen-Trong, Hoang *physician, consultant*

Paris
Gontier, Jean Roger *internist, physiology educator, consultant*

Rognac
Castel, Gérard Joseph *physician*

GERMANY

Bielefeld
Lauven, Peter Michael *anesthesiologist*

Stuttgart
Szirmal, Endre Anreas Franz *physician, writer*

Wuppertal
Schubert, Guenther Erich *pathologist*

GRENADA

Saint George's
Brunson, Joel Garrett *pathologist, educator*

ISRAEL

Halon
Cohen, Amram Joseph *cardiothoracic surgeon*

JAPAN

Fukuoka
Shirai, Takeshi *physician*

Hiroshima
Harkness, Donald Richard *hematologist, educator*

Kanagawa
Saitoh, Tamotsu *pharmacology educator*

Kobe
Yamabe, Shigeru *medical educator*

Sendai
Okuyama, Shinichi *physician*

Tochigi
Takasaki, Etsuji *urology educator*

Tokorozawa
Nakamura, Hiroshi *urology educator*

Tokyo
Akera, Tai *pharmacologist*
Masuda, Gohta *physician, educator*
Terao, Toshio *physician, educator*
Watanabe, Kouichi *pharmacologist, educator*

Yokohama
Kaneko, Yoshihiro *cardiologist, researcher*

THE NETHERLANDS

Amsterdam
Ostrow, Jay Donald *gastroenterology educator, researcher*

Leiden
Banta, Henry David *physician, researcher*

Maastricht
Van Praag, Herman Meir *psychiatrist, educator, administrator*

SCOTLAND

Clydebank
Durack, David Tulloch *physician, educator*
Krakoff, Irwin Harold *pharmacology and oncology educator*

SWEDEN

Malmo
Cronberg, Stig *infectious diseases educator*

SWITZERLAND

Busingen
Friede, Reinhard L. *neuropathologist, educator*

Geneva
Henderson, Ralph Hale *physician*

Lausanne
Borel, Georges Antoine *gastroenterologist, consultant*

Montreux
Cronin, Robert Francis Patrick *cardiologist, educator*

WEST INDIES

Grenada
Barrett, James Thomas *immunologist, educator*

ADDRESS UNPUBLISHED

Abell, Murray Richardson *retired medical association administrator*
Ablin, Richard Joel *immunologist, educator*
Adams, James Thomas *surgeon*
Aldrich, Franklin Dalton *research physician*
Altekruse, Joan Morrissey *retired preventive medicine educator*
Altshuler, Kenneth Z. *psychiatrist*
Andreoli, Thomas Eugene *physician*
Angelov, George Angel *pediatrician, anatomist, teratologist*
Appenzeller, Otto *neurologist, researcher*
Arnaud, Claude Donald, Jr. *physician, educator*
Bacon, George Edgar *retired pediatrician, educator*
†Baird, William David *retired anesthesiologist*
Baker, Laurence Howard *oncology educator*
Baldwin, DeWitt Clair, Jr. *physician, educator*
Ball, John Robert *medical association executive*
Bartlett, James Williams *psychiatrist, educator*
†Battat, Felix A. *orthopedic surgeon*
Beiser, Helen Ruth *psychiatrist*
Bejar, Jacob *physician, philosopher*
Berkley, Mary Corner *neurologist*
Bird, Harrie Waldo, Jr. *psychiatrist, educator*
Bishop, Raymond Holmes, Jr. *physician, retired army officer*
Blix, Susanne *psychiatrist*
Bolliger, Eugene Frederick *surgeon*
Bonn, Ethel May *psychiatrist, educator*
†Bonnet, John David *physician, medical facility administrator*
Bowie, E(dward) J(ohn) Walter *hematologist, researcher*
Brent, Robert Leonard *physician, educator*
Brewer, Leslie G. *psychiatrist*
Bubrick, Melvin Phillip *surgeon*
Burrell, Craig Donald *physician, educator*
Byrnes, Christine Ann *internist*
Capek, Vlastimil *retired radiologist, educator*
Caplovitz, Coleman David *physician*
Carey, Martin Conrad *gastroenterologist, molecular biophysicist, educator*
Carman, George Henry *retired physician*
Carroll, Bernard James *psychiatrist*
Carter, Sara Kebe *psychiatrist*
Chaikof, Elliot Lorne *vascular surgeon*
Chernoff, Amoz Immanuel *hematologist, consultant*
Clemetson, Charles Alan Blake *physician*
Cohen, B. Stanley *physician*
Colburn, Harold Lewis *dermatologist, state legislator*
Colonnier, Marc Leopold *neuroanatomist, educator*
Conneally, P. Michael *medical educator*
Conrad-England, Roberta Lee *pathologist*
Coriell, Lewis Lemon *physician, research institute administrator*
Cozen, Lewis *orthopedic surgeon*
Cronkhite, Leonard Wolsey, Jr. *physician, consultant, research foundation executive*
Cuatrecasas, Pedro Martin *research pharmacologist*
Curtis, James L. *psychiatrist*
Cushman, Paul *physician, educator*
Daly, James William *physician, educator*
Danilowicz, Delores Ann *pediatric cardiologist, pediatrics educator*
Davidson, Mayer B. *medical educator, researcher*
DePalma, Ralph George *surgeon, educator*
De Salva, Salvatore Joseph *pharmacologist, toxicologist*
Dickes, Robert *psychiatrist*
Dickson, James Francis, III *surgeon*
Diener, Erwin *immunologist*
Di Salvo, Arthur Francis *physician, public health official*
Douglas, Gordon Watkins *medical educator*
Douglass, John Michael *internist*
Dumont, Allan Eliot *physician, educator*
Durant, John Ridgeway *physician*
Earle, Arthur Scott *retired plastic surgeon*
Eaton, Merrill Thomas *psychiatrist, educator*
Eckenhoff, James Edward *physician, educator*
Edwards, Charles *neuroscientist, educator*
Edwards, Larry David *internist*
†Etzel, Ruth Ann *pediatrician, epidemiologist*
Fariss, Bruce Lindsay *endocrinologist, educator*
Fenoglio-Preiser, Cecilia Mettler *pathologist, educator*
Ferlinz, Jack *cardiologist, medical educator*
Fisher, Linda Alice *physician*
Frank, Sanders Thalheimer *physician, educator*
Fredrickson, Donald Sharp *physician, scientist*
Friedman, Eugene Warren *surgeon*
Frost, J. Ormond *otolaryngologist, educator*
Gable, Carol Brignoli *pharmacoeconomics researcher*

Gable, Karen Elaine health occupations educator
Gajdusek, Daniel Carleton pediatrician, research virologist
Garcia, Alexander orthopaedic surgeon
Gers, Seymour psychiatrist
Ginsburg, Iona Horowitz psychiatrist
Glassock, Richard James nephrologist
Gleaton, Harriet E. retired anesthesiologist
Gordan, Gilbert Saul physician, educator
Graham, James Herbert dermatologist
Grant, Albert internist
Greeley, Gale Elizabeth psychiatrist
Green, Joseph Martin psychiatrist, educator
Greenbaum, Lowell Marvin pharmacologist, educator
Greenberg, Benjamin physician
Greene, Laurence Whitridge, Jr. surgical educator
Gross, Ruth Taubenhaus physician
Grund, Walter James, Jr. retired gynecologist
Haft, Gail K. pediatrician
Halliday, William Ross retired physician, speleologist, writer
Hansell, John Royer retired physician
Herman, Chester Joseph physician
Hirose, Teruo Terry surgeon
Hoch, Frederic Louis medical educator
Hoeprich, Paul Daniel physician educator
Hogue, Carol Jane Rowland epidemiologist
Holland, Robert Campbell anatomist, educator
Hudak, Thomas Michael plastic surgeon
Hunt, Oliver Raymond, Jr. thoracic and cardiovascular surgeon
Hunt, William Edward neurosurgeon, educator
Hunter, Richard Grant, Jr. neurologist, executive
Huntley, Robert Ross physician, educator
Inui, Thomas Spencer physician, educator
Iqbal, Zafar biochemist, neurochemist
Jackman, Jay M. psychiatrist
Jackson, Carmault Benjamin, Jr. physician
Jackson, Rudolph Ellsworth pediatrician, educator
Jacobey, John Arthur, III surgeon, educator
Jaller, Michael M. retired orthopaedic surgeon
Jefferies, William McKendree internist, educator
Johnson, George physician
Johnston, Cyrus Conrad, Jr. internist, educator
Jones, Walton Linton internist, former government official
Kahn, David dermatologist, educator
Kellogg, Carol Kay neuroscientist, researcher
Kent, Donald Charles physician
Kent, Howard Lees obstetrician/gynecologist
Kettelkamp, Donald Benjamin retired surgeon and educator
Klombers, Norman association executive, retired
†Kuhl, Walter James, Jr. physician
Leis, Henry Patrick, Jr. surgeon, educator
Leslie, Gerrie Allen immunologist
Levin, Jack physician, educator, biomedical investigator
Levy, David Alfred immunology educator, physician, scientist
†Lewison, Edward Frederick surgeon
†Long, Charles William child and adolescent psychiatrist
Lopez, Marlene chief executive officer, Bronx Psychiatric Center
Loube, Samuel Dennis physician
Lovell, Robert Gibson retired physician, educator
Maier, Alfred neuroscientist
Maitra, Subir Ranjan medical educator
Malkinson, Frederick David dermatologist
Matthews, James Gordon, Jr. obstetrician, gynecologist
McGinty, John B. orthopaedic surgeon, educator
Mc Guigan, James Edward physician, scientist, educator
McLarnon, Mary Frances neurologist
McPhedran, Norman Tait surgeon, educator
Mead, Beverley Tupper physician, educator
Meilman, Edward physician
Meister, Steven Gerard cardiologist, educator
Meyer, Greg Charles psychiatrist
Michaelis, Elias K. neurochemist
†Milde, Leslie Newberg anesthesiologist, educator
Miller, Ross Hays retired neurosurgeon
Millikan, Clark Harold physician
Moffet, Hugh Lamson pediatrician
Montgomery, John Richard pediatrician, educator
Moossy, John neuropathologist, neurologist, consultant
Morgan, Elizabeth plastic and reconstructive surgeon
Morwood, Betty Jo psychiatrist, physician
Motto, Jerome Arthur psychiatry educator
Napodano, Rudolph Joseph internist, medical educator
Nelson, Erland Randall educator, neurologist
Nelson, William Rankin surgeon
Novack, Alvin John physician
O'Leary, Denis Joseph retired physician, insurance company executive
Overfield, Ronald Edwin radiologist
Packard, John Mallory physician
Palmer, Raymond A. medical association administrator, librarian
Pancake, Edwina Howard science librarian
Parker, Brent Mershon retired medical educator, internist, cardiologist
†Parsons, Harry Glenwood retired surgeon
Pastorek, Norman Joseph facial plastic surgeon
Pauly, John Edward anatomist
Pedini, Kenneth physician
Peete, William Pettway Jones surgeon
Peterson, Ann Sullivan physician, health care consultant
Phelps, Paulding rheumatologist, internist
Pick, Robert Yehuda orthopedic surgeon, consultant
Plimpton, Calvin Hastings physician, university president
Polenz, Joanna Magda psychiatrist
Potts, Douglas Gordon neuroradiologist
Powell, Clinton Cobb radiologist, physician, former university administrator
Prusiner, Stanley Ben neurology and biochemistry educator, researcher
Raichle, Marcus Edward radiology, neurology educator
Randolph, Judson Graves pediatric surgeon
Renson, Jean Felix psychiatry educator
Richmond, Julius Benjamin retired physician, health policy educator emeritus
Robinson, David Adair neurophysiologist
Rodgers, Lawrence Rodney physician, educator
Rosemberg, Eugenia physician, scientist, educator, medical research administrator
Rosenow, John Henry surgeon, educator
Rosenthal, Sol Roy preventive medicine educator, researcher
Russo, Jose pathologist
Sacha, Robert Frank osteopathic physician
Sackellares, James Chris neurology educator
Sanders, Aaron Perry radiation biophysics educator
Saneto, Russell Patrick pediatrician, neurobiologist
Sanfelippo, Peter Michael cardiac, thoracic and vascular surgeon
Santiago-Noa, Victor Manuel psychiatrist
Schauf, Victoria pediatrician, educator, researcher, consultant
Schechter, Paul J. pharmacologist
Scheuerman, Eleanor Joyce Miller medical association administrator
Sekitani, Toru otolaryngologist, educator
Sher, Paul Phillip physician, pathologist
Sherman, John Foord biomedical consultant
†Sherman, Joseph Owen pediatric surgeon
Shils, Maurice Edward physician, educator
Shumacker, Harris B., Jr. surgeon, educator, author
Silberberg, Inga dermatologist
†Sipple, John Harrison physician
Small, Melvin D. physician, educator
Smith, Martin Henry pediatrician
Smith, Stuart Lyon psychiatrist, corporate executive
Stephenson, Bette Mildred physician, former Canadian legislator
†Stern, Robert Stuart dermatologist, editor
Stickler, Gunnar Brynolf pediatrician
Stillings, Dennis Otto research director
Stone, David Deaderick physician, educator
Stone, James Robert surgeon
Strain, James Ellsworth pediatrician, retired association administrator
Strandberg, John David comparative pathologist
Stringham, Rene physician
Swick, Herbert Morris medical educator, neurologist
Tagiuri, Consuelo Keller child psychiatrist, educator
Tan, Veronica Y. psychiatrist
Terris, Susan physician, cardiologist
Threefoot, Sam Abraham physician, educator
Toledo-Pereyra, Luis Horacio transplant surgeon, researcher, historian educator
†Turk, Richard Errington retired psychiatrist
Valentine, William Newton physician, educator
Verwoerdt, Adriaan psychiatrist
Warfel, John Hiatt medical educator, retired
Weissmann, Heidi Seitelblum radiologist, educator
White, Augustus Aaron, III orthopaedic surgeon
Whitley, Nancy O'Neil retired radiology educator
Williams, Henry Stratton radiologist, educator
Williams, Robert Leon psychiatrist, neurologist, educator
Williams, Roger Stewart physician
Williams, Thomas Lloyd psychiatrist
Wilson, Almon Chapman surgeon, physician, retired naval officer
Wolfberg, Melvin Donald company executive, optometrist, former college president, consultant
Wood, Margaret Gray dermatologist, educator
Woodhouse, Derrick Fergus ophthalmologist
Wyngaarden, James Barnes physician
Yamane, George Mitsuyoshi oral diagnosis and radiology educator
Yielding, K. Lemone physician
Zacks, Sumner Irwin pathologist
Zwislocki, Jozef John neuroscience educator, researcher

HUMANITIES: LIBERAL STUDIES

UNITED STATES

ALABAMA

Auburn
Amacher, Richard Earl literature educator
Andelson, Robert Vernon social philosopher, educator
Lewis, Walter David historian
Littleton, Taylor Dowe humanities educator
Skelton, Robert Beattie language educator

Birmingham
Allen, Lee Norcross historian, educator
Benditt, Theodore Matthew humanities educator
Hamilton, Virginia Van der Veer historian, educator
Irons, George Vernon history educator
Morton, Marilyn Miller genealogy and history educator, lecturer, researcher, travel executive, director
Roberts, David Harrill English language educator

Huntsville
Mercieca, Charles philosophy and political science educator
Roberts, Frances Cabaniss history educator
White, John Charles historian

Montgomery
Cornett, Lloyd Harvey, Jr. retired historian
Gribben, Alan English language educator, research consultant

Troy
McPherson, Milton Monroe history educator

Tuscaloosa
Bell, Robert Fred German language educator
Hocutt, Max Oliver philosophy educator
McDonald, Forrest historian, educator

ALASKA

Fairbanks
Krauss, Michael Edward linguist

ARIZONA

Apache Junction
Bracken, Harry McFarland philosophy educator

Bisbee
Hagstrum, Jean Howard language professional, educator

Flagstaff
Brown, Burton Ross humanities educator, university administrator
Hallowell, Robert Edward French language educator
Poen, Monte M. history educator, researcher

Green Valley
Dmytryshyn, Basil historian, educator

Peoria
Bergmann, Fredrick Louis English language educator, theater historian

Phoenix
Land, George A. philosopher, writer, educator, consultant

Scottsdale
Donaldson, Scott English language educator, writer

Sun City
Oppenheimer, Max, Jr. foreign language educator, consultant

Surprise
Clark, Lloyd historian, educator

Tempe
Brack, O. M., Jr. English language educator
Harris, Mark English educator, author
Iverson, Peter James historian, educator
MacKinnon, Stephen R. Asian studies administrator, educator
Ney, James Walter Edward Colby English language educator
Rios, Alberto Alvaro English educator
Ruiz, Vicki Lynn history educator

Tucson
Austin, John Norman classics educator
Birkinbine, John, II philatelist
Briggs, Peter Stromme art historian, curator
Dinnerstein, Leonard historian, educator
Dufner, Max retired German language educator
Lamb, Ursula Schaefer history educator
Langendoen, Donald Terence linguistics educator
Momaday, Navarre Scott English educator, author

ARKANSAS

Conway
Kearns, Terrance Brophy English language educator
Stiritz, Marette McCauley English language educator, consultant

Fayetteville
Faulkner, Claude Winston language professional
Gatewood, Willard Badgett, Jr. historian
Levine, Daniel Blank classical studies educator

Jonesboro
Elkins, Francis Clark history educator, university official

Little Rock
Ferguson, John Lewis state historian
Williams, C(harles) Fred history professor

Magnolia
Davis, Elizabeth Hawk English language educator

Monticello
Babin, Claude Hunter history educator

Searcy
Organ, Dennis Michael English educator

CALIFORNIA

Atherton
Bales, Royal Eugene philosophy educator

Bakersfield
Boyd, William Harland historian
Kegley, Jacquelyn Ann philosophy educator

Balboa Island
Abramson, Albert television historian, consultant

Berkeley
Alter, Robert B. comparative literature educator and critic
Anderson, William Scovil classics educator
Baas, Jacquelynn art historian, museum administrator
Barish, Jonas Alexander English language educator
Bouwsma, William James history educator
Bronstein, Arthur J. linguistics educator
Cahill, James Francis art history educator
Calame, Alexandre Emile retired French literature educator
Chapman, G. Arnold Romance languages educator
Costa, Gustavo Italian language educator
Crews, Frederick Campbell humanities educator, writer
Davidson, Donald Herbert philosophy educator
Greenblatt, Stephen J. English language educator
Grossman, Joan Delaney language and literature educator
Gruen, Erich Stephen classics educator
Heilbron, John L. historian
Herr, Richard history educator
Jordan, John Emory language professional, educator
Karlinsky, Simon language educator, author
Kay, Paul de Young linguist
Kerman, Joseph Wilfred musicologist, critic
Lichterman, Martin history educator
Litwack, Leon Frank historian, educator
Long, Anthony Arthur classics educator
Maron, Melvin Earl philosopher, educator
Mc Cullough, Helen Craig Oriental languages educator
Merchant, Carolyn environmental history educator
Middlekauff, Robert Lawrence history educator, administrator
Muscatine, Charles English educator, author
Nagler, Michael Nicholas classics and comparative literature educator
Ohala, John Jerome linguistics educator
Penzl, Herbert German language and linguistics educator
Rauch, Irmengard linguist, educator
Sealey, B. Raphael classicist, educator
Seeba, Hinrich Claassen foreign language educator
Selz, Peter Howard art historian, educator
Shannon, Thomas Frederic German language educator
Sloane, Thomas O. speech educator
Tracy, Robert (Edward) English educator, poetry translator
Wakeman, Frederic Evans, Jr. historian
Wang, William Shi-Yuan linguistics educator
Zwerdling, Alex English educator

Beverly Hills
Kravitz, Ellen King musicologist, educator

Carmel
Chung, Kyung Cho Korean specialist, scholar, educator, author

Chico
Moore, Brooke Noel philosophy educator

Claremont
Ackerman, Gerald Martin art historian, consultant
Atlas, Jay David philosopher, consultant, linguist
Barnes, Richard Gordon English educator, poet
Beckman, Tad Alan philosophy educator
Burns, Richard Dean history educator, publisher, author
Davis, Nathaniel humanities educator
Dunbar, John Raine retired English educator
Elsbree, Langdon English language educator
Erickson, Stephen A. philosophy and humanities educator, programs director
Goodrich, Norma Lorre (Mrs. John H. Howard) French and comparative literature educator
Lofgren, Charles Augustin legal and constitutional historian
Macaulay, Ronald Kerr Steven linguistics educator, former college dean
McGaha, Michael Dennis Spanish educator
McKirahan, Richard Duncan, Jr. classics and philosophy educator
Moss, Myra Ellen (Myra Moss Rolle) philosophy educator
Neumann, Harry philosophy educator
Olson, Richard George historian, educator
Pinney, Thomas Clive English language educator
Roth, John King philosopher, educator
Sellery, J'nan Morse English and American literature educator
Smith, Steven Albert philosophy educator
Sontag, Frederick Earl philosophy educator
Young, Howard Thomas foreign language educator

Culver City
Clodius, Albert Howard history educator

Davis
Crummey, Robert Owen history educator, university dean
Forbes, Jack D. ethnohistorian, educator, writer
Gullón, Germán Spanish educator
Hayden, John Olin English literature educator, author
Hays, Peter L. English language and literature educator
Hoffman, Michael Jerome humanities educator
Jackson, William Turrentine history educator
Rothstein, Morton historian, retired educator
Waddington, Raymond Bruce, Jr. English language educator
Williamson, Alan Bacher English literature educator, poet, writer
Willis, Frank Roy history educator
Woodress, James Leslie, Jr. English language educator

Duarte
Smith, Hallett Darius retired English literature educator

El Cerrito
Kuo, Ping-chia historian, educator

Fresno
Flores, William Vincent Latin American studies educator
Kouymjian, Dickran art historian, Orientalist, educator

Gualala
Gaustad, Edwin Scott historian

Hayward
Mayers, Eugene David philosopher, educator

Irvine
Clark, Michael Phillip English educator
Hine, Robert Van Norden, Jr. historian, educator
Key, Mary Ritchie (Mrs. Audley E. Patton) linguist, author, educator
Kluger, Ruth German language educator, editor
Krieger, Murray English educator, author
Lehnert, Herbert Hermann foreign language educator
Lillyman, William John German language educator
Maddy, Penelope Jo philosopher
Mc Culloch, Samuel Clyde history educator
Miller, Joseph Hillis comparative literature educator
Navajas, Gonzalo foreign language educator
Sutton, Dana Ferrin classics educator
Wiener, Jon history educator

Kensington
Malkiel, Yakov linguistics educator

La Canada Flintridge
Dales, Richard Clark history educator

La Jolla
Langacker, Ronald Wayne linguistics educator
McDonald, Marianne classicist
Newmark, Leonard Daniel linguistics educator
Olafson, Frederick Arlan philosophy educator
Ruiz, Ramon Eduardo history educator
Wesling, Donald Truman English literature educator

Wright, Andrew *English literature educator*

Laguna Beach
Calderwood, James Lee *former English literature educator, writer*

Long Beach
Beebe, Sandra E. *retired English language educator, artist, writer*
Polakoff, Keith Ian *historian, university administrator*
Stetler, Charles Edward *English language educator*
Tang, Paul Chi Lung *philosophy educator*

Los Angeles
Alkon, Paul Kent *English language educator*
Allen, Michael John Bridgman *English educator*
Alpers, Edward Alter *history educator*
Amneus, D. A. *English language educator*
Andersen, Henning *linguistics educator*
Appleby, Joyce Oldham *historian*
Arora, Shirley Lease *Spanish language educator*
Bahr, Ehrhard *Germanic languages and literature educator*
Bauml, Franz Heinrich *German language educator*
Beckwith, Charles Emilio *English educator*
Birnbaum, Henrik *Slavic languages and literature educator*
Boime, Albert Isaac *art history educator*
Bradshaw, Murray Charles *musicologist*
Braudy, Leo Beal *English language educator, author*
Burns, Robert Ignatius *historian, educator, clergyman*
Dallek, Robert *history educator*
Davidson, Herbert Alan *Near Eastern languages and cultures educator*
Dearing, Vinton Adams *retired English language educator*
Dyck, Andrew Roy *philologist*
Fromkin, Victoria Alexandra *linguist, phonetician, educator*
Fry, Michael Graham *historian, educator*
Göllner, Marie Louise *musicologist, educator*
Greene, Donald Johnson *retired English language educator, author*
Hadda, Janet Ruth *Yiddish language educator, lay psychoanalyst*
Hospers, John *philosophy educator*
Hovannisian, Richard G. *Armenian and Near East history educator*
Hundley, Norris Cecil, Jr. *history educator*
Jorgensen, Paul Alfred *English language educator emeritus*
Kaplan, Robert B. *linguistics educator, consultant, researcher*
Kelly, Henry Ansgar *English language educator*
Kolve, V. A. *English literature educator*
Ladefoged, Peter Nielsen *phonetician*
Laird, David *humanities educator emeritus*
Lehan, Richard D'Aubin *English language educator, writer*
Levine, Philip *classics educator*
Löfstedt, Bengt Torkel Magnus *classics educator*
MacGregor, Geddes *author, philosophy educator*
†McClary, Susan *musicology educator, writer*
Nakanishi, Don Toshiaki *Asian American studies educator, writer*
Nunis, Doyce Blackman, Jr. *historian, educator*
Puhvel, Jaan *philologist, educator*
Rathbun, John Wilbert *American studies educator*
Rogger, Hans Jack *history educator*
Rouse, Richard Hunter *historian, educator*
Sanjian, Avedis Krikor *Armenian studies educator*
Schaefer, William David *English educator*
Schutz, John Adolph *historian, educator, former university dean*
Schwartz, Leon *foreign language educator*
†See, Carolyn *English educator, book critic*
Shideler, Ross Patrick *foreign language and comparative literature educator, author, translator, poet*
Stockwell, Robert Paul *linguist, educator*
Tennyson, G(eorg) B(ernhard) *English educator*
Toulmin, Stephen Edelston *humanities educator*
Wills, John Elliot, Jr. *history educator, writer*
Winterowd, Walter Ross *English educator*
Wortham, Thomas Richard *English language educator*

Menlo Park
Craig, Gordon Alexander *historian, educator*
Storer, Morris Brewster *retired philosophy educator*

Mission Viejo
Teitelbaum, Harry *English educator*

Montclair
Haage, Robert Mitchell *retired history educator, organization leader*

Montecito
Atkins, Stuart (Pratt) *German language and literature educator*
Rose, Mark Allen *humanities educator*

Monterey
Kennedy-Minott, Rodney *international relations educator, former ambassador*

Moorpark
Hall, Elton A. *philosophy educator*

Newport Beach
Brown, Giles Tyler *history educator, lecturer*

Northridge
Chen, Joseph Tao *historian, educator*

Oxnard
Cathcart, Linda *art historian*
Hill, Alice Lorraine *history, geneology, and social researcher, educator*

Pacific Palisades
Garwood, Victor Paul *retired speech communication educator*
Nash, Gary Baring *historian, educator*

Palo Alto
Buss, Claude Albert *history educator*
Dallin, Alexander *history and political science educator*
Guerard, Albert Joseph *retired modern literature educator, author*
Knoles, George Harmon *history educator*

Pasadena
Elliot, David Clephan *historian, educator*
Fay, Peter Ward *history educator*
Graham, Lanier *art and architecture historian, cultural planner*
Kevles, Daniel Jerome *history educator, writer*
Kousser, J(oseph) Morgan *history educator*
Mandel, Oscar *literature educator, writer*
Searle, Eleanor Millard *history educator*

Piedmont
Putter, Irving *French language educator*

Redondo Beach
Ilie, Paul *foreign language educator*

Riverside
Elliott, Emory Bernard *English language educator, educational adminstrator*
Fagundo, Ana Maria *creative writing and Spanish literature educator*
Hanna, Ralph, III *English educator, author*
Ravitch, Norman *history educator*
Ross, Delmer Gerrard *historian, educator*
Snyder, Henry Leonard *history educator, bibliographer*

Rohnert Park
Grivas, Theodore *retired historian, educator*

Sacramento
Meindl, Robert James *English language educator*
Schmitz, Dennis Mathew *English language educator*

San Diego
Brandes, Raymond Stewart *history educator*
Coox, Alvin David *history educator*
Daley, Arthur Stuart *retired humanities educator*
Feinberg, Leonard *English language educator*
Gregor, Mary Jeanne *educator*
Lauer, Jeanette Carol *history educator, author*
Vanderbilt, Kermit *English language educator*

San Francisco
Brown, H. Douglas *English educator*
Cherny, Robert Wallace *history educator*
Edwards, John Hamilton *language professional*
Gregory, Michael Strietmann *English language educator*
Hale, Cecil *communications educator*
Needleman, Jacob *philosophy educator, writer*
Satin, Joseph *language professional, university administrator*
Thompson, William Irwin *humanities educator, author*
Wilczek, John Franklin *history educator*

San Jose
Melendy, Howard Brett *historian, educator*

San Luis Obispo
Riedlsperger, Max Ernst *history educator*

San Marino
Karlstrom, Paul Johnson *art historian*
Ridge, Martin *historian, educator*
Rolle, Andrew F. *historian, educator, author*
Steadman, John Marcellus, III *English educator*
Thorpe, James *humanities scholar*
Zall, Paul Maxwell *retired English language educator, consultant*

San Rafael
Eekman, Thomas Adam *Slavic languages educator*

Santa Barbara
Avalle-Arce, Juan Bautista *language educator*
Brownlee, Wilson Elliot, Jr. *history educator*
Chafe, Wallace LeSeur *linguist, educator*
Collins, Robert Oakley *history educator*
Crawford, Donald Wesley *philosophy educator, university official*
Dauer, Francis Watanabe *philosophy educator*
Del Chiaro, Mario Aldo *art historian, archeologist, etruscologist, educator*
Djordjevic, Dimitrije *historian, educator*
Fingarette, Herbert *philosopher, educator*
Fleming, Brice Noel *retired philosophy educator*
Graham, Otis Livinston, Jr. *history educator*
Gunn, Giles Buckingham *English educator, religion educator*
Hay, Eloise Knapp *English language educator*
†Helgerson, Richard *English language educator*
Hollister, Charles Warren *history educator, author*
Hsu, Immanuel Chung Yueh *history educator*
McGee, James Sears *historian*
Moir, Alfred Kummer *art history educator*
Renehan, Robert Francis Xavier *Greek and Latin educator*
Russell, Jeffrey Burton *historian, educator*
Sears, Joanne Lewis *retired educator, author*
Wilkins, Burleigh Taylor *philosophy educator*
Zimmerman, Everett Lee *English educator, academic administrator*

Santa Clara
Gordon, Mary McDougall *history educator*
Meier, Matthias S(ebastian) *historian*

Santa Cruz
Dizikes, John *American studies educator*
Ellis, John Martin *German literature educator*
Lieberman, Fredric *ethnomusicologist, educator*
Lynch, John Patrick *classics educator, university official*
†Stevens, Stanley David *local history researcher, retired librarian*
Suckiel, Ellen Kappy *philosophy educator*

Santa Monica
Abrams, Irwin *historian, educator, consultant*
Schipper, Merle *art historian and critic, exhibition curator*

Santa Rosa
Aman, Reinhold Albert *philologist, publisher*

Stanford
Baker, Keith Michael *history educator*
Baugh, John *linguistics and anthropology educator, researcher*
Carnochan, Walter Bliss *retired English educator*
Degler, Carl Neumann *history educator*
Dekker, George Gilbert *literature educator, literary scholar, writer*
Dunlop, John Barrett *foreign language educator, research institution scholar*
Duus, Peter *history educator*
Eitner, Lorenz Edwin Alfred *art historian, educator*
Fehrenbacher, Don Edward *retired history educator*
Follesdal, Dagfinn *philosophy educator*
Frank, Joseph Nathaniel *comparative literature educator*
Fredrickson, George Marsh *history educator*
Gelpi, Albert Joseph *English educator, literary critic*
Giraud, Raymond Dorner *retired language professional*
Hilton, Ronald *international studies educator*
Johnson, John J. *historian, educator*
Kennedy, David Michael *historian, educator*
L'Heureux, John Clarke *English language educator*
Loftis, John (Clyde), Jr. *English language educator*
Lohnes, Walter F. W. *German language and literature educator*
Middlebrook, Diane Wood *English language educator*
Mommsen, Katharina *German language and literature educator*
Moravcsik, Julius Matthew *philosophy educator*
Newman-Gordon, Pauline *French language and literature educator*
Nivison, David Shepherd *Chinese and philosophy educator*
Perloff, Marjorie Gabrielle *English and comparative literature educator*
Perry, John Richard *philosophy educator*
Robinson, Paul Arnold *historian, educator, author*
Sheehan, James John *historian, educator*
Sorrentino, Gilbert *English language educator, novelist, poet*
Spitz, Lewis William *historian, educator*
Stansky, Peter David Lyman *historian*
Traugott, Elizabeth Closs *linguistics educator and researcher*
Van Slyke, Lyman Page *history educator*
Watt, Ian Pierre *retired English literature educator*

Stockton
Limbaugh, Ronald Hadley *history educator, history center director*

Sylmar
Hoggatt, Clela Allphin *English language educator*

Van Nuys
Zucker, Alfred John *English educator, academic administrator*

Wilmington
Smith, June Burlingame *English educator*

COLORADO

Arvada
Elrick, Billy Lee *English language educator*

Boulder
Bright, William Oliver *linguistics educator*
Brutus, Dennis Vincent *African literature, poetry, creative writing educator*
Fest, Thorrel Brooks *former speech educator, consultant*
†Frey, Julia Bloch *French language educator*
Hawkins, David Cartwright *philosophy and history of science, educator*
Hill, Boyd H., Jr. *medieval history educator*
†Limerick, Patricia Nelson *history educator*
Main, Jackson Turner *history educator*
Rood, David S. *linguistics educator*
Taylor, Allan Ross *linguist, educator*

Colorado Springs
Cramer, Owen Carver *classics educator*
Hallenbeck, Kenneth Luster *numismatist*
Stavig, Mark Luther *English language educator*

Denver
Breck, Allen du Pont *historian, educator*
Hamilton, William T. *English educator, former academic administrator*
Pfnister, Allan Orel *humanities educator*
Storey, Brit Allan *historian*
Sullivan, Mary Rose *English educator*

Dolores
Kreyche, Gerald Francis *retired philosophy educator*

Fort Collins
Gilderhus, Mark Theodore *historian, educator*
Kennedy, George Alexander *classicist, educator*
Rock, Kenneth Willett *history educator*
Rollin, Bernard Elliot *philosophy educator, consultant on animal ethics*

Golden
Eckley, Wilton Earl, Jr. *humanities educator*
Pegis, Anton George *English educator*
Sneed, Joseph Donald *philosophy educator, author*

Greeley
Worley, Lloyd Douglas *English educator*

Pueblo
Farwell, Hermon Waldo, Jr. *parliamentarian, educator, former speech communication educator*

CONNECTICUT

Ansonia
Mendyk, Sandra L. *English educator*

Bridgeport
Allen, Richard Stanley (Dick Allen) *English language educator, author*

Brooklyn
Meigs, Joseph Carl, Jr. *retired English language educator*

Colebrook
Mc Neill, William Hardy *retired history educator, writer*

Danbury
Edelstein, David Simeon *historian, educator*
Toland, John Willard *historian, writer*

Deep River
Hieatt, Allen Kent *language professional, educator*
Hieatt, Constance Bartlett *English language educator*

East Windsor
Folmsbee, Patricia Hurley *reading consultant*

Fairfield
Lachowicz, Franciszek *foreign language educator*
Newton, Lisa Haenlein *philosophy educator*

Goshen
Berleant, Arnold *philosopher*

Greenwich
Pope, Marvin Hoyle *language educator, writer*

Guilford
Whitaker, Thomas Russell *English literature educator*

Hamden
Gay, Peter *history educator, author*
McClellan, Edwin *language educator*
Rosenthal, Franz *language educator*
Woodward, C. Vann *historian*

Hartford
†Carroon, Robert Girard *historian, clergyman*
Cooper, George Brinton *historian, educator*
Mahoney, Michael Robert Taylor *art historian, educator*

Ivoryton
Osborne, John Walter *historian, educator, author*

Mansfield Center
Butler, Francelia McWilliams *retired English language educator, writer*

Middletown
Arnold, Herbert Anton *German language educator*
†Braxton, Anthony *musicologist*
Briggs, Morton Winfield *Romance language educator*
Buel, Richard Van Wyck, Jr. *history educator, writer, editor*
Gillmor, Charles Stewart *history and science educator, researcher*
Gourevitch, Victor *philosophy educator*
Lensing, Leo A. *foreign language and humanities educator*
Meyer, Priscilla Ann *Russian language and literature educator*
Pomper, Philip *history educator*
Reed, Joseph Wayne *American studies educator*
Reeve, Franklin D. *literature educator, writer*
Rose, Phyllis *English language professional, author*
Schwarcz, Vera *East Asian studies educator, history educator*
Shapiro, Norman Richard *Romance languages and literatures educator*
Slotkin, Richard Sidney *American studies educator, writer*
Stowe, William Whitfield *English language educator*
Turco, Alfred, Jr. *English language educator*
Wensinger, Arthur Stevens *German language and literature educator, author*
Winston, Krishna Ricarda *foreign language professional*

New Britain
Gallo, Donald Robert *English educator*

New Haven
Alexandrov, Vladimir Eugene *Russian literature educator*
Bers, Victor *classics educator*
Bloom, Harold *humanities educator*
Blum, John Morton *historian*
Böowering, Gerhard H. *Islamic studies educator*
Borroff, Marie *English language educator*
Brooks, Peter (Preston) *French and comparative literature educator, writer*
Cahn, Walter B. *art history educator*
Culler, Arthur Dwight *English language educator*
Davis, David Brion *historian, educator*
Demos, John Putnam *history educator, writer, consultant*
Dupré, Louis *philosopher, educator*
Erlich, Victor *Slavic languages educator*
Geanakoplos, Deno John *history educator*
†Gilbert, Creighton Eddy *art historian*
Glier, Ingeborg Johanna *German language and literature educator*
Greene, Liliane *French educator, editor*
Greene, Thomas McLernon *language professional, educator*
Guicharnaud, Jacques E. H. *language educator*
Hallo, William Wolfgang *Assyriologist*
Hanson, Anne Coffin *art historian*
Harries, Karsten *philosophy educator, researcher*
Hartman, Geoffrey H. *language professional, educator*
Hersey, George Leonard *art history educator*
Hollander, John *humanities educator, poet*
Holmes, Frederic Lawrence *science historian*
Holquist, James Michael *Russian and comparative literature educator*
Hyman, Paula E(llen) *history educator*
Insler, Stanley *philologist, educator*
Kagan, Donald *historian, educator*
Kazemzadeh, Firuz *history educator*
Kennedy, Paul Michael *history educator*
Kleiner, Diana Elizabeth Edelman *art history educator, administrator*
Lord, George deForest *English educator*
MacMullen, Ramsay *retired history educator*
Marcus, Ruth Barcan *philosopher, educator, writer, lecturer*

Martin, Samuel Elmo *linguistics educator*
Martz, Louis Lohr *English literature educator*
Mazzotta, Giuseppe Francesco *Italian language and literature educator*
Miskimin, Harry Alvin *history educator*
Natanson, Maurice Alexander *philosopher, educator*
Newman, Sasha Mary *art historian, curator*
Nochlin, Linda *art history educator*
Outka, Gene Harold *philosophy and Christian ethics educator*
Palisca, Claude Victor *musicologist, educator*
Pelikan, Jaroslav Jan *history educator*
Peterson, Linda H. *English language and literature educator*
Poirion, Daniel *foreign language educator*
Pollitt, Jerome Jordan *art history educator*
Porter, Charles Allan *French language educator, educational administrator*
†Prown, Jules David *art historian educator*
Rawson, Claude Julien *English educator*
Robinson, Fred Colson *English language educator*
Sammons, Jeffrey Leonard *foreign language educator*
Schenker, Alexander Marian *Slavic linguistics educator*
Scully, Vincent *art historian, retired educator, writer*
Smith, John Edwin *philosophy educator*
Spence, Jonathan Dermot *historian, educator*
Totman, Conrad Davis *history educator*
Underdown, David Edward *historian, educator*
Valesio, Paolo *Italian language and literature educator, writer*
Wandycz, Piotr Stefan *history educator*
Winks, Robin William *history educator*
Yeazell, Ruth Bernard *English educator*

New London
Mulvey, Helen Frances *retired history educator*
Rice, Argyll Pryor *Hispanic studies and Spanish language educator*

Old Greenwich
Baritz, Loren *history educator*

Storrs
Charters, Ann *biographer, editor, educator*
Coons, Ronald Edward *historian, educator*
Greene, John Colton *retired history educator*
Rosen, William *English language educator*
Shaffer, Jerome Arthur *philosophy educator*

Storrs Mansfield
Abramson, Arthur Seymour *linguistics educator, researcher*
Reed, Howard Alexander *historian, educator*

Washington Depot
Leab, Daniel Josef *history educator*

West Hartford
Chiarenza, Frank John *English language educator*

West Haven
Turner, Frank Miller *historian, educator*

Willimantic
Philips, David Evan *English language educator*

Windsor
Auten, Arthur Herbert *history educator*

Woodbridge
Ecklund, Constance Cryer *French language educator*

DELAWARE

Dover
Lahvis, Sylvia Leistyna *art historian, educator, curator*

Newark
Allmendinger, David Frederick, Jr. *history educator*
Bohner, Charles Henry *English language educator*
Capek, Milic *retired philosophy educator*
Day, Robert Androus *English language educator, former library director, editor, publisher*
Halio, Jay Leon *language professional, educator*
Homer, William Innes *art history educator, art expert, author*
McLaren, James Clark *French educator*
Steiner, Roger Jacob *linguistics educator, author, researcher*
Tolles, Bryant Franklin, Jr. *history and art history educator*
Valbuena-Briones, Angel Julian *language educator, author*
Venezky, Richard Lawrence *English educator*
Weslager, Clinton Alfred *historian, writer*
Wolters, Raymond *historian, educator*

DISTRICT OF COLUMBIA

Bolling AFB
†Hallion, Richard Paul *aerospace historian, museum consultant*

Washington
Allard, Dean Conrad *historian, naval history center director*
Ashkenazi, Elliott Uriel *historian, lawyer*
Atil, Esin *Islamic art historian, researcher*
Bearss, Edwin C(ole) *historian*
Beauchamp, Tom L. *philosophy educator*
Bedini, Silvio A. *historian, author*
Bennett, Betty T. *English educator, university dean, writer*
Berry, Mary Frances *history and law educator*
Billington, James Hadley *historian, librarian*
Bloomfield, Maxwell Herron, III *historian, educator*
Boorstin, Daniel J. *historian, lector, educator, author, editor*
Broun, Elizabeth *art historian, museum administrator*
Burgan, Mary Alice *English language educator*
Caws, Peter James *philosopher, educator*
Cook, Walter Anthony *linguist, educator*
Cua, Antonio S. *philosophy educator*
Davidson, Dan Eugene *language educator, educational exchange administrator*
Davison, Roderic Hollett *historian, educator*
De Pauw, Linda Grant *history educator*
Durfee, Harold Allen *philosophy educator*
†Dyson, Lowell Keith *historian*
Farr, Judith Banzer *writer, literature educator*
Fern, Alan Maxwell *art historian, museum director*
Fink, Lois Marie *art historian*
Goode, James Moore *historian*
Hamarneh, Sami Khalaf *historian of medicine and science, author*
Hammond, Deanna Lindberg *linguist*
Heelan, Patrick Aidan *philosophy educator*
Hill, Bennett David *history educator, Benedictine monk, priest*
Irizarry, Estelle Diane *foreign language educator, author, editor*
Kennedy, Robert Emmet, Jr. *history educator*
Kreidler, Charles W(illiam) *linguist, educator*
Laiou, Angeliki Evangelos *history educator*
Langan, John Patrick *philosophy educator*
Laqueur, Walter *history educator*
Lewis, Douglas *art historian*
Lewis, Emanuel Raymond *historian, librarian, psychologist*
Lucas, George Ramsdell, Jr. *philosophy educator*
Menard, Edith *English language educator, artist, poet, actress*
Miles, Ellen Gross *art historian, museum curator*
Miller, Jeanne-Marie Anderson (Mrs. Nathan J. Miller) *English language educator, academic administrator*
Minnich, Nelson Hubert Joseph *historian, educator*
Morse, Richard McGee *historian*
Mujica, Barbara Louise *foreign language educator, author*
Myers, Robert Manson *English educator, author*
Nisbet, Robert A. *historian, sociologist*
Pfordresher, John Charles *English educator*
Raaflaub, Kurt A. *classics educator*
Rand, Harry Zvi *art historian, poet*
Reingold, Nathan *historian*
Robb, James Willis *Romance languages educator*
Roberts, Jeanne Addison *literature educator*
Rodrigues, Eusebio L. *humanities educator*
Rosenblatt, Jason Philip *English language educator*
Rothenberg, Marc *historian*
Sachar, Howard Morley *history educator*
Schlagel, Richard H. *philosophy educator*
Schoenbaum, Samuel *English educator*
Schwartz, Richard Brenton *English language educator, university dean, writer*
Severino, Roberto *foreign language educator, academic administration executive*
Shih, J. Chung-wen *Chinese language educator*
Simko, Jan *English and foreign language literature educator*
Smith, Bruce R. *English language educator*
Snowden, Frank Martin, Jr. *classics educator*
Taylor, Estelle Wormley *English educator, college dean*
Taylor, Henry Splawn *literature educator, poet, writer*
Van Cleve, John Vickrey *history educator*
Vaslef, Irene *historian, librarian*
Veatch, Robert Marlin *philosophy educator, medical ethics researcher*
Ver Eecke, Wilfried Camiel *philosopher, educator*
Walker, Robert Harris *historian, author, editor*
Washburn, Wilcomb Edward *historian, educator*
Webb, Robert Kiefer *history educator*
Weiss, Paul *philosopher, educator*
Wheelock, Arthur Kingsland, Jr. *art historian*

FLORIDA

Beverly Hills
Larsen, Erik *art history educator*

Clearwater
Tutton, Betty Jane *humanities educator*

Coral Gables
Kirsner, Robert *language educator*
Lemos, Ramon Marcelino *philosophy educator*
McCarthy, Patrick A. *English educator*

Crescent City
Garcia, Mary Elizabeth *Spanish and English as second languages educator*

Daytona Beach
Osterholm, J(ohn) Roger *humanities educator*

Dunedin
Espy, Charles Clifford *English language educator, author, consultant, lecturer, administrator*

Englewood
Marchand, Leslie Alexis *language educator, writer*

Fort Lauderdale
Maher, Kim Leverton *museum administrator*
Van Alstyne, Judith Sturges *English language educator*

Fort Myers
Brown, Earl Kent *historian, clergyman*
Solomon, Irvin D. *history educator, author*

Fort Pierce
Bynum, Henri Sue *education and French educator*

Gainesville
Abbott, Thomas Benjamin *speech educator*
Der-Houssikian, Haig *linguistics educator*
Emch-Dériaz, Antoinette Suzanne *historian*
Goldhurst, William *retired humanities and English educator, writer*
Haring, Ellen Stone (Mrs. E. S. Haring) *philosophy educator*
Harrison, John Armstrong *historian, university dean*
Hartigan, Karelisa Dorothy *classics educator*
Holland, Norman Norwood *English language educator*
Proctor, Samuel *history educator*
Schmeling, Gareth *classics educator*
Stephan, Alexander F. *German language and literature educator*
Wyatt-Brown, Bertram *historian, educator*

Highland Beach
Stimson, Frederick Sparks *Hispanist, educator*

Homestead
Reeder, Cecelia Painter *English educator*

Jacksonville
Harmon, Gary Lee *language professional, educator*

Key Biscayne
Markell, Alan William *linguistic company executive*

Lakeland
Fadley, Ann Miller *English language and literature educator, writer*
Peeler, Scott Loomis, Jr. *foreign language educator*

Lecanto
Brogan, Howard Oakley *English language educator*

Maitland
Nash, Ronald Herman *philosophy educator*

Marathon
Mc Cormick, Edward Allen *foreign language educator*
Wiecha, Joseph Augustine *linguist, educator*

Miami
Jones y Diez Arguelles, Gastón Roberto *language educator*
Leeder, Ellen Lismore *language and literature educator, literary critic*
Schwartz, Kessel *modern language educator*

Naples
Griffin, Linda L. *English language and speech educator*
Waller, George Macgregor *historian, educator*

Oldsmar
Thompson, Mack Eugene *history educator*

Orlando
Pauley, Bruce Frederick *history educator*

Palm Beach
Artinian, Artine *French literature scholar, collector*

Pensacola
Smith, Jody Brant *philosophy and humanities educator*

Saint Augustine
Adams, William Roger *historian*
Russell, Josiah Cox *historian, educator*

Saint Petersburg
†Hinz, John *English and American literature educator*
Sherburne, Donald Wynne *philosopher, educator*
Walker, Brigitte Maria *translator, linguistic consultant*

Sarasota
Ebitz, David MacKinnon *art historian, museum director*
Hansen, Elisa Marie *art historian*
Hoover, Dwight Wesley *history educator*
Noether, Emiliana Pasca *historian, educator*
Taplin, Winn Lowell *historian, retired senior intelligence operations officer*

Tallahassee
Bartlett, Richard Adams *American history educator, history consultant*
Beck, Earl Ray *historian, educator*
Burroway, Janet G. *English language educator, novelist*
Davis, Bertram Hylton *retired English educator*
Dillingham, Marjorie Carter *foreign language educator*
Dorn, Charles Meeker *art education educator*
Frechette, Ernest Albert *foreign language educator emeritus*
Golden, Leon *classicist, educator*
Harper, George Mills *English language educator*
Kaelin, Eugene Francis *philosophy educator*
McCrimmon, James McNab *language educator*
Moore, John Hebron *history educator*
Oldson, William Orville *history educator*

Tampa
Anton, John Peter *philosopher, educator*
Cundiff, Paul Arthur *English language educator*
Perry, James Frederic *philosophy educator, author*
Preto-Rodas, Richard Anthony *foreign language educator*

Venice
Palermo, Joseph *language educator*

Winter Haven
Love, John Wesley, Jr. *English language and reading educator*

Winter Park
Sedwick, (Benjamin) Frank *language educator*
Seymour, Thaddeus *English educator*

GEORGIA

Andersonville
Boyles, Frederick Holdren *historian*

Athens
Anderson, James L. *history educator, business developer*
Dickie, Margaret McKenzie *English language educator*
Freer, Coburn *English language educator*
Kretzschmar, William Addison, Jr. *English language educator*
Lindberg, Stanley William *English language educator, editor*
Mamatey, Victor Samuel *history educator*
Mc Feely, William Shield *historian, writer*
Miller, Ronald Baxter *English language educator, author*
Moore, Rayburn Sabatzky *American literature educator*
Nute, Donald E., Jr. *philosophy educator*
Rosenberg, Alexander *philosophy educator, author*
Steer, Alfred Gilbert, Jr. *foreign language educator*
Wall, Bennett Harrison *history educator*

Atlanta
Bakewell, Peter John *history educator*
Benario, Herbert William *classics educator*
Burns, Thomas Samuel *history educator*
Carter, Dan T. *history educator*
Dillingham, William Byron *literature educator, author*
Fox-Genovese, Elizabeth Ann *humanities educator*
Genovese, Eugene Dominick *historian, educator*
Hartle, Robert Wyman *retired foreign language and literature educator*
Kranzberg, Melvin *history educator*
Kuntz, Marion Lucile Leathers *classicist, historian, educator*
†Kuntz, Paul Grimley *philosopher, educator*
Mafico, Temba Levi Jackson *Old Testament and Semitic languages educator, clergy*
Manley, Frank *English language educator*
Rojas, Carlos *Spanish literature educator*
Sitter, John Edward *English literature educator*
Spivey, Ted Ray *English educator*
Williams, Emily Allen *English language educator*

Augusta
Cashin, Edward Joseph *history educator*
Puryear, Joan Copeland *English language educator*

Decatur
†Major, James Russell Richards *historian, educator*
Pepperdene, Margaret Williams *English educator*
Young, James Harvey *historian, educator*

Gainesville
Wagner, Clarence *historian*

Macon
Cockfield, Jamie Hartwell *history educator*

Marietta
Rainey, Kenneth Tyler *English language educator*

Valdosta
McClain, Benjamin Richard *music educator, educational administrator*

HAWAII

Honolulu
Bender, Byron Wilbur *linguistics educator*
Copi, Irving Marmer *philosophy educator*
Dyen, Isidore *linguistic scientist, educator*
Knowlton, Edgar Colby, Jr. *linguist, educator*
Nunn, G. Raymond *history educator*
Peterson, Barbara Ann Bennett *history educator*
Rapson, Richard L. *history educator*
Rehg, Kenneth Lee *linguistics educator*
Stephan, John Jason *historian, educator*
Varley, Herbert Paul *Japanese language and cultural history educator*

IDAHO

Boise
Knight, Margot Haliday *oral historian*
Nguyen, King Xuan *language educator*
Wells, Merle William *historian, state archivist*

Caldwell
Attebery, Louie Wayne *English language educator, folklorist*

Emmett
Farnham, Wallace Dean *historian*

ILLINOIS

Alton
Hodgson, Peter John *music educator*

Bloomington
Bray, Robert C. *literature educator*

Carbondale
Ammon, Harry *history educator*
Brown, James Montgomery *retired English language and literature educator, academic administrator*
Fladeland, Betty *historian, educator*
Gilbert, Glenn Gordon *linguistics educator*
Hahn, Lewis Edwin *philosopher, retired educator*
Spees, Emil Ray *philosophy educator*
Webb, Howard William, Jr. *humanities educator, university official*
Woodbridge, Hensley Charles *retired foreign languages educator, librarian*

Champaign
Crummey, Donald Edward *history educator*
Friedberg, Maurice *Russian literature educator*
Koenker, Diane P. *history educator*
Love, Joseph L. *history educator, cultural studies center administrator*
O'Neill, John Joseph *speech educator*
Smith, Ralph Alexander *cultural and educational policy educator*
Spence, Clark Christian *history educator*

Chicago
Adkins, Arthur William Hope *humanities educator*
Adler, Mortimer Jerome *philosopher, author*
Aronson, Howard Isaac *linguist, educator*
Bevington, David Martin *English literature educator*
Biggs, Robert Dale *Near Eastern studies educator*
Booth, Wayne Clayson *English literature and rhetoric educator, author*
Brinkman, John Anthony *historian, educator*
Chappell, Sally *art historian*
Cohen, Ted *philosophy educator*
Cullen, Charles Thomas *historian, librarian*
Debus, Allen George *history educator*
Dembowski, Peter Florian *foreign language educator*
Erlebacher, Albert *history educator*
Fleischer, Cornell Hugh *history educator*

Frings, Manfred Servatius philosophy educator
Gannon, Sister Ann Ida retired philosophy educator, former college administrator
Garber, Daniel Elliot philosophy educator
Gilman, Sander Lawrence German language educator
Goldsmith, John Anton linguist, educator
Grant, Robert McQueen humanities educator
Gray, Hanna Holborn history educator
Grove, Helen Harriet historian, artist
Haley, George Romance languages educator
Hamp, Eric Pratt linguist
Harris, Neil history educator
Harvanek, Robert Francis philosophy educator, clergyman
Headrick, Daniel Richard history and social sciences educator
Heller, Reinhold August art educator, consultant
Hellie, Richard Russian history educator, researcher
Helmbold, Nancy Pearce classical languages educator
Holt, Thomas Cleveland history educator, consultant, writer, lecturer
Hunter, J(ames) Paul English language educator, literary critic, historian
Hurley, William James, Jr. English language educator
Ingham, Norman William Russian literature educator, genealogist
Jones, Peter d'Alroy history educator, author
Karanikas, Alexander English language educator, author, actor
Karl, Barry Dean historian, educator
Kazazis, Kostas linguist, educator
Keenan, James George classics educator
Khalidi, Rashid Ismail history educator
Kolb, Gwin Jackson language professional, educator
Lawler, James Ronald French language educator
Lieb, Michael English educator, humanities educator
Marshall, Donald Glenn English language and literature educator
Miller, James Edwin, Jr. English language educator
Mitchell, W. J. T. English language, literature and visual arts educator, editor
Najita, Tetsuo history educator
Newman, Ralph Geoffrey literary scholar historian
Novick, Peter historian, educator
Nussbaum, Martha Craven philosophy and classics educator
Pestureau, Pierre Gilbert literature educator, literary critic, editor
Pollock, Sheldon Ivan language professional, educator
Rosenheim, Edward Weil English educator
Rosenthal, Earl Edgar art history educator
Roy, David Tod Chinese literature educator
Saller, Richard Paul classics educator
Sochen, June history educator
Tanner, Helen Hornbeck historian
Thaden, Edward Carl history educator
Weinberg, Meyer humanities educator
Weintraub, Karl Joachim history educator

De Kalb
Aung-Thwin, Michael Arthur history educator
Hagelman, Charles William, Jr. language professional, educator

Des Plaines
Krupa, John Henry English language educator

Edwardsville
Going, William Thornbury English educator

Evanston
†Breslin, Paul English language educator
Buchbinder-Green, Barbara Joyce art and architectural historian
Cole, Douglas English literature educator
Condit, Carl Wilbur history educator
De Coster, Cyrus Cole Spanish language and literature educator
Fine, Arthur I. philosopher
Fox, Edward Inman education administrator and Spanish educator
†Greenberg, Douglas Stuart history educator
Heyck, Bill historian
Perkin, Harold James social historian
Sheridan, James Edward history educator
Ver Steeg, Clarence Lester historian, educator
Weil, Irwin Slavic languages and literature educator
Weil, Irwin language educator
Werckmeister, Otto Karl art historian and educator
Wilks, Ivor Gordon Hughes historian, educator
Wright, John classics educator

Galesburg
Hane, Mikiso history educator

Glenview
Levine, Edwin Burton retired classics educator

Joliet
Marion, Marjorie Anne English educator

Macomb
Brown, Spencer Hunter historian
Spencer, Donald Spurgeon historian, academic administrator
Vos, Morris foreign languages educator, language services consultant

Monmouth
Johnson, John Prescott philosophy educator

Mount Prospect
Stamper, James M. retired English language educator

Normal
Shields, John Charles American studies and African American studies and literature educator

Palatine
Hull, Elizabeth Anne English language educator
Smith-Pierce, Patricia A. speech professional

Palos Heights
Higgins, Francis Edward history educator

Peoria
Ballowe, James English educator, author

Romeoville
Lifka, Mary Lauranne history educator

Springfield
†Davis, George Cullom, Jr. history educator
Fischoff, Ephraim humanities educator, sociologist, social worker
Temple, Wayne Calhoun historian

Urbana
Aldridge, Alfred Owen English language educator
Antonsen, Elmer Harold Germanic languages and literature educator
Arnstein, Walter Leonard historian, educator
Bateman, John Jay classics educator
Bates, James Leonard historian
Baym, Nina English educator
Broudy, Harry Samuel retired philosophy educator
Cheng, Chin-Chuan linguistics educator
Dawn, Clarence Ernest history educator
Gaeng, Paul Ami foreign language educator
Garfield, Evelyn Picon Spanish educator
Haile, H. G. German language and literature educator
Hendrick, George English language educator
Hurt, James Riggins English language educator
Jacobson, Howard classics educator
Kachru, Braj Behari linguist
Kachru, Yamuna linguist
Kim, Chin-Woo linguist, educator
Mainous, Bruce Hale foreign language educator
Manning, Sylvia English studies educator
Marcovich, Miroslav classics educator
McColley, Robert McNair history educator
Newman, John Kevin classics educator
Queller, Donald Edward historian, educator
Scanlan, Richard Thomas classics educator
Schacht, Richard Lawrence philosopher, educator
Solberg, Winton Udell history educator
Spence, Mary Lee historian
Stillinger, Jack Clifford English educator
Talbot, Emile Joseph French language educator
Watts, Emily Stipes English educator

Westchester
Masterson, John Patrick retired English language educator

Wilmette
Fries, Robert Francis historian, educator

INDIANA

Bloomington
Anderson, Judith Helena English language educator
Barnstone, Willis (Robert Barnstone) language literature educator, poet, scholar
Battenhouse, Roy Wesley English educator
Baxter, Maurice Glen historian, educator
Boerner, Peter language and literature educator
Bonser, Charles Franklin public administration educator
Bregel, Yuri history educator
Buelow, George John musicologist, educator
Byrnes, Robert Francis history educator
Cohen, William Benjamin historian, educator
Cole, Bruce Milan art historian
Dunn, Jon Michael philosophy educator
Edgerton, William B. foreign language educator
Eisenberg, Paul David philosophy educator
Ferrell, Robert Hugh historian, educator
Foster, Kathleen Adair art historian, museum curator
†Gubar, Susan (David) English educator, writer
Hanson, Karen philosopher, educator
Hodge, Carleton Taylor linguist, educator
Johnson, Sidney Malcolm foreign language educator
Juergens, George Ivar history educator
Lebano, Edoardo Antonio foreign language educator
Martins, Heitor Miranda foreign language educator
McDowell, John Holmes folklore educator, institute director
Nordloh, David Joseph English language educator
Oinas, Felix Johannes foreign language educator
Pletcher, David Mitchell history educator
Remak, Henry H.H. foreign language educator
Rosenberg, Samuel Nathan French and Italian language educator
Salmon, Russell Owen, II Latin American studies educator, academic administrator
Sebeok, Thomas Albert linguistics educator
Simmons, Merle Edwin foreign language educator
Sinor, Denis Orientalist, educator
Sperling, Elliot Harris history educator
Westfall, Richard Samuel historian
Wilson, George Macklin history educator, cultural studies center administrator

Charlestown
Schmidt, Jakob Edward medical and medicolegal lexicographer, physician, author, inventor

Crawfordsville
Barnes, James John history educator

Culver
Holaday, Allan Gibson English educator

Fort Wayne
Fairchild, David Lawrence philosophy educator
Scheetz, Sister Mary JoEllen English language educator

Greencastle
DiLillo, Leonard Michael Spanish educator, researcher, academic administrator
†Dittmer, John Avery history educator
Phillips, Clifton J. history educator
Weiss, Robert Orr speech educator

Greenfield
Bettler, Janet Louise Bell foreign language educator

Indianapolis
Baetzhold, Howard George English language educator
Casebeer, Edwin Frank, Jr. English language educator
Krasean, Thomas Karl historian
Plater, William Marmaduke English language educator, academic administrator

Muncie
†Hayashi, Tetsumaro English educator, author, editor
†Rippy, Frances Marguerite Mayhew English educator

Notre Dame
Bruns, Gerald L. English literature educator
Burrell, David Bakewell philosophy educator
Delaney, Cornelius Francis philosophy educator
De Santis, Vincent Paul historian, educator
Dougherty, James Patrick English language educator
Gabriel, Astrik Ladislas medieval studies educator, scholar
Gutting, Gary Michael philosophy educator
Jemielity, Thomas John English educator
Lanzinger, Klaus language educator
Loux, Michael Joseph philosophy educator
Manier, August Edward philosophy of biology educator
Matthias, John Edward English literature educator
McInerny, Ralph Matthew philosophy educator, author
Mc Mullin, Ernan Vincent philosophy educator
Nugent, Walter Terry King historian
O'Rourke, William Andrew English language educator, author
Plantinga, Alvin philosophy educator, author
Quinn, Philip Lawrence philosophy educator
Rosenberg, Charles Michael art historian, educator
Sayre, Kenneth Malcolm philosophy educator
Walicki, Andrzej Stanislaw history educator

South Bend
Costello, Donald Paul English educator
van Inwagen, Peter Jan philosophy educator

Terre Haute
Baker, Ronald Lee English educator
Carmony, Marvin Dale linguist, educator
De Marr, Mary Jean English language educator

Valparaiso
Peters, Howard Nevin foreign language educator

West Lafayette
Broden, Thomas Francis, III French educator
Contreni, John Joseph, Jr. humanities educator
Garfinkel, Alan Spanish language and education educator
Gottfried, Leon Albert English language educator
Leitch, Vincent Barry literary studies educator
Mc Bride, William Leon philosopher, educator
Reichard, Hugo Manley English literature educator
Rothenberg, Gunther Erich history educator
Woodman, Harold David historian

IOWA

Ames
Bruner, Charlotte Hughes French language educator
Dobson, John McCullough historian
Herrnstadt, Richard Lawrence American literature educator
Wilt, Alan Freese history educator

Cedar Falls
Maier, Donna Jane-Ellen history educator
Thompson, Thomas Henry philosophy educator
Wilson, Robley Conant, Jr. English educator, editor, author

Cedar Rapids
Lisio, Donald John historian, educator

Davenport
Luzkow, Jack Lawrence history educator, writer, consultant

Grinnell
Kaiser, Daniel Hugh historian, educator
Kintner, Philip L. history educator
Kissane, James Donald English literature educator
Leggett, Glenn former English language educator, academic administrator
Michaels, Jennifer Tonks foreign language educator
Wall, Joseph Frazier historian, educator

Iowa City
Addis, Laird Clark, Jr. philosopher, educator, musician
Andrews, Clarence Adelbert historian, educator, writer, publisher
Butchvarov, Panayot Krustev philosophy educator
Deligiorgis, Stavros G. literature educator
DiPardo, Anne English language and education educator
Gelfand, Lawrence Emerson historian, educator
Gerber, John Christian English language educator
Goldstein, Jonathan Amos ancient history and classics educator
Hanley, Sarah history educator
Hawley, Ellis Wayne historian, educator
Hornsby, Roger Allen classics educator
Kelley, Robert E. English language educator
Kerber, Linda Kaufman historian, educator
Percas de Ponseti, Helena foreign language and literature educator
Persons, Stow Spaulding historian, educator
Raeburn, John Hay English language educator
Ringen, Catherine Oleson linguistics educator
Sayre, Robert Freeman English language educator
Schoenbaum, David Leon historian
Solbrig, Ingeborg Hildegard German literature educator, author
Steele, Oliver English educator
Trank, Douglas Monty rhetoric and speech communications educator
Wachal, Robert Stanley linguistics educator, consultant

KANSAS

Dighton
Stanley, Ellen May historian, consultant

Lawrence
Alexander, John Thorndike historian, educator
Andrews, William Leake English educator
Cherniss, Michael David English educator
Debicki, Andrew Peter foreign language educator
De George, Richard Thomas philosophy educator
Eldredge, Charles Child, III art history educator
Genova, Anthony Charles philosophy educator
Gunn, James E. English educator
Li, Chu-Tsing art history educator
Mc Coy, Donald Richard historian
Phillips, Oliver C. classics educator
Quinn, Dennis B. English language and literature educator
Robinson, Walter Stitt, Jr. historian
Saul, Norman Eugene history educator
Schoeck, Richard Joseph English and humanities scholar
Seaver, James Everett historian, educator
Spires, Robert Cecil foreign language educator
Stokstad, Marilyn Jane art history educator, curator
Tuttle, William McCullough, Jr. history educator
Vincent, Jon Stephen foreign language educator
Woelfel, James Warren philosophy educator
Worth, George John English literature educator
Young, J(ohn) Michael philosophy educator

Manhattan
Higham, Robin historian, editor, publisher
McCulloh, John Marshall historian

Topeka
Wagnon, William Odell, Jr. history educator

University Of Kansas
Kuznesof, Elizabeth Anne history educator

KENTUCKY

Bowling Green
Constans, Henry Philip, Jr. philosopher, educator
Minton, John Dean historian, educator

Danville
Newhall, David Sowle history educator

Frankfort
Gale, Steven Hershel humanities educator
Geddes, LaDonna McMurray speech educator

Highland Heights
Wallace, Harold Lew historian, educator

Lexington
Bryant, Joseph Allen, Jr. English language educator
Coffman, Edward McKenzie history educator
Eller, Ronald D historian, educator
Madden, Edward Harry philosopher, educator
Perdue, Theda history educator, author
Warth, Robert Douglas history educator

Louisville
Brockwell, Charles Wilbur, Jr. history educator
Ford, Gordon Buell, Jr. English language and linguistics educator, author, retired hospital industry financial management executive
Garcia-Varela, Jesus language educator, literature educator
Miller, Robert Henry English educator
St. Clair, Robert Neal English language and linguistics educator

Midway
Minister, Kristina speech communication educator

Murray
Pogue, Forrest Carlisle retired historian

Pleasureville
O'Nan, Martha foreign language educator

Richmond
Burkhart, Robert Edward English language educator
Shearon, Forrest Bedford humanities educator
Witt, Robert Wayne English educator

Versailles
Freehling, William Wilhartz historian, educator

Wilmore
†Kuhn, Anne Naomi Wicker (Mrs. Harold B. Kuhn) foreign language educator

LOUISIANA

Baton Rouge
Arceneaux, William historian, educator, association official
Cooper, William James, Jr. history educator
Duffy, John history educator
Edgeworth, Robert Joseph classical languages educator
Hardy, John Edward English language educator, author
Haynes, Leonard L., Jr. philosophy educator, clergyman
Olney, James English language educator
Smith, David Jeddie American literature educator
Stanford, Donald Elwin English educator, editor, poet, critic

Eunice
Rogers, Donald Onis language educator

Hammond
Jackson, Joy Juanita history educator
Thorburn, James Alexander humanities educator

Lafayette
Nolan, Paul Thomas retired English and humanities educator
Poe, (Lydia) Virginia reading educator

New Orleans
Ambrose, Stephen Edward history educator, author
Cohen, Joseph English literature educator, writer, business owner
Cummings, Anthony Michael music historian, educator, academic administrator

Greenleaf, Richard Edward *Latin American history educator*
†Kukla, Jon (Keith) *historian, museum director*
Luza, Radomir Vaclav *historian, educator*
Paolini, Gilbert *literature and science educator*
Poesch, Jessie Jean *art historian*
Reck, Andrew Joseph *philosophy educator*
Roberts, Louise Nisbet *philosopher*
Sellin, Eric *linguist, poet, educator*
Thompson, Annie Laura *foreign language educator*
Woodward, Ralph Lee, Jr. *historian, educator*

Pineville
Howell, Thomas *history educator*
Tapley, Philip Allen *English language and literature educator*

Ruston
Halliburton, Lloyd *Romance philology educator*

Thibodaux
Swetman, Glenn Robert *English language educator, poet*

MAINE

Brunswick
Hodge, James Lee *German language educator*

Falmouth
Sadik, Marvin Sherwood *art consultant, former museum director*

Orono
Hatlen, Burton Norval *English educator*
Ives, Edward Dawson *folklore educator*

Portland
Schwanauer, Francis *philosopher, educator*

Waterville
Bassett, Charles Walker *English language educator*
Hudson, Yeager *philosophy educator, minister*

MARYLAND

Annapolis
†Hagan, Kenneth James *historian, museum director*

Baltimore
Achinstein, Peter Jacob *philosopher, educator*
Anderson, Wilda Christine *French literature educator*
Badder, Susan Stevenson *art historian, educator*
Baldwin, John Wesley *history educator*
Barker, Stephen Francis *philosophy educator*
Cacossa, Anthony Alexander *Romance languages educator*
Castro-Klaren, Sara *Latin American literature educator*
Cohen, Warren I. *history educator*
Cooper, Jerrold Stephen *historian, educator*
Cropper, M. Elizabeth *art history educator*
Dempsey, Charles Gates *art historian, educator*
Ditz, Toby Lee *history educator*
Fleishman, Avrom Hirsch *English educator*
Forster, Robert *history educator*
Goldberg, Jonathan *English literature educator*
Greene, Jack Phillip *historian, educator*
Higham, John *history educator*
Hillers, Delbert Roy *Near East language educator*
Irwin, John Thomas *humanities educator*
Johnson, Michael Paul *history educator*
Judson, Horace Freeland *history of science, writer, educator*
Kagan, Richard Lauren *history educator*
Kessler, Herbert Leon *art historian, educator*
Knight, Franklin W. *history educator*
Kurth, Lieselotte *foreign language educator*
Lidtke, Vernon LeRoy *history educator*
Luck, Georg Hans Bhawani *classics educator*
McCarter, P(ete) Kyle, Jr. *Near Eastern studies educator*
McKinney, Richard Ishmael *philosophy educator*
Nägele, Rainer *German and comparative literary educator*
Nichols, Stephen George *Romance languages educator*
Paulson, Ronald Howard *English and humanities educator*
Peirce, Carol Marshall *English educator*
Pocock, John Greville Agard *historian, educator*
Ranum, Orest Allen *historian, educator*
Ross, Dorothy *history educator*
Russell-Wood, Anthony John R. *history educator*
Schneewind, Jerome Borges *philosophy educator*
Terborg-Penn, Rosalyn Marian *historian, educator*
Walker, Mack *historian, educator*
Ziff, Larzer *English language educator*

Bethesda
Benson, Elizabeth Polk *Pre-Columbian art specialist*
Duncan, Francis *historian, government official*
Highfill, Philip Henry, Jr. *retired language educator*

Bowie
Sterling, Richard Leroy *English and foreign language educator*

Catonsville
Loerke, William Carl *art history educator*

Chestertown
Trout, Charles Hathaway *historian, educator*

Chevy Chase
Durant, Frederick Clark, III *aerospace history and space art consultant*
Goodwin, Ralph Roger *historian, editor*
Key, Kerim Kami *historian, educator*

Cockeysville Hunt Valley
Peirce, Brooke *English language educator*

College Park
Brown, Peter Gilbert *philosopher, educator*
Dietrich, Martha Jane (Martha Jane Shultz) *genealogist*
Fuegi, John *comparative literature educator, author, filmmaker*
Harlan, Louis Rudolph *history educator, writer*
Holton, William Milne *English language and literature educator*
Lightfoot, David William *linguistics educator*
Olson, Keith Waldemar *history educator*
Oster, Rose Marie Gunhild *foreign language professional, educator*
Pasch, Alan *philosophy educator*
Russell, John David *English literature educator*
Sagoff, Mark *philosopher, educator, academic administrator*
†Weart, Spencer Richard *historian*
Yaney, George *history educator*

Columbia
Butcher, (Charles) Philip *English language educator, author*
†Wright, Abraham *English language educator, college lecturer*

Darnestown
Knox, Bernard MacGregor Walker *retired classics educator*

Frederick
Pyne, Frederick Wallace *genealogist, clergyman, retired civil engineer, retired mathematics educator*

Lusby
Eshelman, Ralph Ellsworth *historian, consultant*

Myersville
Blake, John Ballard *retired historian*

Pocomoke City
Kerbin, Diane Leithiser *history educator*

Rockville
Hewlett, Richard Greening *historian*

Saint Michaels
Marshall, Robert Gerald *language educator*

Severna Park
Schick, Edgar Brehob *German literature educator*

Silver Spring
†Borkovec, Vera Z. *Russian studies educator*
Calinger, Ronald Steve *historian*
Cole, Wayne Stanley *historian, educator*
Doherty, William Thomas, Jr. *historian, retired educator*
Morrison, Roy Dennis, II *philosophy, religion and science educator emeritus*

Solomons
Samuels, Sheldon Wilfred *philosophy educator, writer*

Sparks
Suarez-Murias, Marguerite C. *retired language and literature educator*

Towson
Baker, Jean Harvey *history educator*

Williamsport
Chesnut, Nondis Lorine *English language educator, writer, consultant*

MASSACHUSETTS

Amesbury
Labaree, Benjamin Woods *history educator*

Amherst
Bagg, Robert Ely *English educator, poet*
Baker, Lynne Rudder *philosophy educator*
†Benitez-Rojo, Antonio *Romance languages educator*
Bezucha, Robert Joseph *history educator*
Chappell, Vere Claiborne *philosophy educator*
Creed, Robert Payson, Sr. *literature educator*
Gibson, Walker *retired English language educator, poet, writer*
Hernon, Joseph Martin, Jr. *history educator*
Kinney, Arthur Frederick *literary history educator, author, editor*
Oates, Stephen Baery *history educator*
Partee, Barbara Hall *linguist, educator*
Porter, Dennis Dudley *foreign language educator*
Tager, Jack *historian, educator*
Taubman, Jane Andelman *Russian literature educator*
Wideman, John Edgar *English literature educator, novelist*
Wolff, Robert Paul *philosophy educator*
Wyman, David Sword *historian, educator*

Belmont
Buckley, Jerome Hamilton *English language educator*

Boston
Brandt, Allan M. *medical history educator*
Bromsen, Maury Austin *historian, bibliographer, antiquarian bookseller*
Cardona, Rodolfo *Spanish language and literature educator*
Foss, Clive Frank Wilson *history educator*
Hartmann, Edward George *historian, educator*
Henry, DeWitt Pawling, II *creative writing educator, writer, arts administrator*
Hintikka, Jaakko *philosopher, educator*
Kleiner, Fred Scott *art history and archaeology educator, editor*
Langer, Lawrence Lee *English educator, writer*
Lowry, Bates *art historian, museum director*
Lyons, David Barry *philosophy and law educator*
Mc Carthy, Joseph Michael *historian*
Menyuk, Paula *developmental psycholinguistics educator*
Miller, Naomi *art historian*
Naeser, Margaret Ann *linguist, medical researcher*
Neville, Robert Cummings *philosophy and religion educator*
Phillips, William *English language educator, editor, author*
Riley, Stephen Thomas *historian, librarian*
Rosen, Stanley Howard *humanities educator*
†Sanborn, George Freeman, Jr. *genealogist*
Scanlon, Dorothy Therese *history educator*
†Smith, Louise Zandberg *English studies educator, writer*
Weitzman, Arthur Joshua *English educator*
Wermuth, Paul Charles *retired English educator*
Wiseman, James Richard *classicist, archaeologist, educator*

Brookline
Mc Cormick, Thomas Julian *art history educator*

Cambridge
Alexiou, Margaret Beatrice *Greek studies educator*
Anderson-Imbert, Enrique *retired Hispanic literature educator, author*
Appiah, Kwame Anthony *philosophy educator*
Badian, Ernst *history educator*
Bailyn, Bernard *historian, educator*
Barnet, Sylvan *English literature educator*
Bate, Walter Jackson *English literature educator*
Block, Ned *philosophy educator*
Bol, Peter Kees *Chinese history educator*
Bolster, Arthur Stanley, Jr. *history educator*
Boolos, George Stephen *philosophy educator*
Bottiglia, William Filbert *humanities educator*
Brustein, Robert Sanford *English language educator, theatre director, author*
Buell, Lawrence Ingalls *English language educator*
Cavell, Stanley *philosophy educator, writer*
Chomsky, Avram Noam *linguistics and philosophy educator*
Chvany, Catherine Vakar *foreign language educator*
Clausen, Wendell Vernon *classics educator*
Craig, Albert Morton *Asian studies educator*
Cross, Frank Moore, Jr. *foreign language educator*
Donoghue, Daniel Gerard *English language educator*
Dreben, Burton Spencer *philosopher,educator*
Dunn, Charles William *Celtic languages and literature educator, author*
Dupree, Anderson Hunter *historian, educator*
Dyck, Arthur James *ethicist, educator*
Dyck, Martin *literary theorist, mathematics historian*
Engell, James Theodore *English educator*
Fanger, Donald Lee *Slavic language and literature educator*
Fernandez-Cifuentes, Luis I. *foreign language educator, researcher*
Fisher, Philip J. *English language and literature educator*
Fleming, Donald Harnish *historian, educator*
Flier, Michael Stephen *Slavic languages educator*
Ford, Franklin Lewis *history educator, historian*
Ford, Patrick Kildea *Celtic studies educator*
Frye, Richard Nelson *historian, educator*
Gates, Henry Louis, Jr. *English language educator*
Gienapp, William Eugene *history educator*
Goldfarb, Warren (David) *philosophy educator*
Graham, Loren Raymond *historian, educator*
Graubard, Stephen Richards *history educator, editor*
Guthke, Karl Siegfried *foreign language educator*
Halle, Morris *linguist, educator*
Hanan, Patrick Dewes *foreign language professional, educator*
Handlin, Oscar *historian, educator*
Heimert, Alan Edward *humanities educator*
Henrichs, Albert Maximinus *classicist, educator*
Huehnergard, John *semitic philology educator*
Iriye, Akira *historian, educator*
Jones, Christopher Prestige *classicist, historian, educator, consultant*
Jones, Robert Emmet *French language educator*
Kalb, Marvin *public policy and government educator*
Keenan, Edward Louis *history educator*
Keyser, Samuel Jay *linguistics educator, university official*
Kugel, James Lewis *Hebrew literature educator*
Ladjevardi, Habib *historian*
Lee, Leo Ou-fan *Far Eastern languages educator*
Lunt, Horace Gray *linguist, educator*
MacMaster, Robert Ellsworth *historian, educator*
Mahoney, Thomas Henry Donald *historian, educator, government official*
Maier, Charles Steven *history educator*
Maier, Pauline *history educator*
Malmstad, John Earl *Slavic languages and literatures, educator*
Marx, Leo *retired American cultural history educator*
May, Ernest Richard *historian, educator*
Mazlish, Bruce *historian, educator*
McCormick, Michael *history educator*
Nozick, Robert *philosophy educator, author*
Nykrog, Per *French literature educator*
O'Neil, Wayne *linguist, educator*
Owen, Stephen *Chinese literature educator*
Ozment, Steven *historian, educator*
Paradis, James Gardiner *historian*
Parsons, Charles Dacre *philosophy educator*
Perkins, David *English language educator*
Pian, Rulan Chao *musicologist, scholar*
Pipes, Richard *historian, educator*
Preyer, Robert Otto *English literature educator*
Quine, Willard Van Orman *philosophy educator*
Rosenkrantz, Barbara Gutmann *retired history educator*
Ryan, Judith Lyndal *German language and literature educator*
Scheffler, Israel *philosopher, educator*
Segal, Charles Paul *classics educator, author*
Sevcenko, Ihor *history and literature educator*
Shinagel, Michael *English literature educator*
Simon, Eckehard (Peter) *foreign language educator*
Singer, Irving *philosopher*
Smith, Merritt Roe *history educator*
Sollors, Werner *English language, literature and American studies educator*
Striedter, Jurij *foreign language educator*
Striker, Gisela *philosophy educator*
Sulloway, Frank Jones *historian*
Tarrant, R(ichard) J(ohn) *classicist, educator*
Tayler, Irene *English educator*
Teeter, Karl van Duyn *retired linguistic scientist, educator*
Thernstrom, Stephan Albert *historian, educator*
Thorburn, David *literature educator*
Ulrich, Laurel Thatcher *historian, educator*
Vanger, Milton Isadore *history educator*
Vendler, Helen Hennessy *literature educator, poetry critic*
Vermeule, Emily Townsend (Mrs. Cornelius C. Vermeule, III) *classicist, educator*
Ward, John Milton *music educator*
Weiner, Charles *historian, educator*
West, Cornel *philosopher, writer*
Winner, Thomas G. *foreign literature educator*
Wolff, Christoph Johannes *music historian, educator*
Wolff, Cynthia Griffin *humanities educator, author*
Zerner, Henri Thomas *art historian*
Ziolkowski, Jan M. *English educator*

Chestnut Hill
Barth, John Robert *English educator, priest*
Blanchette, Oliva *philosophy educator*
Casper, Leonard Ralph *American literature educator*
Duhamel, Pierre Albert *English language professional*
Mahoney, John L. *English literature educator*
McAleer, John Joseph *English literature educator*
Valette, Rebecca Marianne *Romance languages educator*

East Longmeadow
Cushman, Elizabeth *English educator*

Framingham
Lipton, Leah *art historian, educator, museum curator*

Harwich Port
Mc Cormick, Richard Patrick *history educator*

Longmeadow
Cobbs, Russell L(ewis) *English language educator*

Lowell
Shirvani, Hamid *philosophy educator, university dean, critic*

Medford
Bedau, Hugo Adam *philosophy educator*
†Brooke, John L. *history educator*
Cartwright, Helen Morris *philosophy educator, writer*
Caviness, Madeline Harrison *art history educator, researcher*
Cavitch, David *English language educator*
Daniels, Norman *philosopher, educator*
Dennett, Daniel Clement *philosopher, author, educator*
Fyler, John Morgan *English language educator*
Laurent, Pierre-Henri *history educator*
Marcopoulos, George John *history educator*
Romero, Christiane *German language educator*
Simches, Seymour Oliver *language educator*
Wechsler, Judith Glatzer *art historian, filmmaker, educator*

Natick
Current, Richard Nelson *historian, educator*

Needham
Burrell, Sidney Alexander *history educator*

North Dartmouth
Yoken, Mel B. *French language educator, author*

Northampton
Elkins, Stanley Maurice *historian, educator*
Ellis, Frank Hale *English literature professional*
Hoyt, Nelly Schargo (Mrs. N. Deming Hoyt) *history educator*
Little, Lester Knox *historian, educator*
Pickrel, Paul *English educator*
Smith, Malcolm Barry Estes *philosophy educator, lawyer*
Vaget, Hans Rudolf *language professional, educator*
von Klemperer, Klemens *historian, educator*

Norton
Dahl, Curtis *English literature educator*
Olson, Roberta Jeanne Marie *art historian, author, educator*
Taylor, Robert Sundling *English educator, art critic*

Randolph
Morrissey, Edmond Joseph *classical philologist*

Rockport
Delakas, Daniel Liudviko *retired foreign language educator*
Walen, Harry Leonard *historian, lecturer, author*

South Hadley
Berek, Peter *English educator*
Brownlow, Frank Walsh *English language educator*
Ciruti, Joan Estelle *Spanish language and literature educator*
Farnham, Anthony Edward *English language educator*
Herbert, Robert Louis *art history educator*
Johnson, Richard August *English language educator*
Mazzocco, Angelo *language educator*
Quinn, Betty Nye *former classics educator*
Robin, Richard Shale *philosophy educator*

South Yarmouth
Benoit, Leroy James *language educator*

Springfield
Porter, Burton Frederick *philosophy educator, author*

Waltham
Black, Eugene Charlton *historian, educator*
Engelberg, Edward *comparative literature educator*
Harth, Erica *French language and comparative literature educator*
Jackendoff, Ray Saul *linguistics educator*
Marshall, Robert Lewis *musicologist, educator*
Staves, Susan *English educator*
Wasserstein, Bernard Mano Julius *historian*
Young, Dwight Wayne *ancient civilization educator*

Watertown
Goodheart, Eugene *English language educator*
Rivers, Wilga Marie *foreign language educator*

Wellesley
Jacoff, Rachel *Italian language and literature educator*
Lefkowitz, Mary Rosenthal *Greek literature educator*
Ma, Jing-Heng Sheng *East Asian languages educator*
Mistacco, Vicki E. *foreign language educator*

Piper, Adrian Margaret Smith *philosopher, artist, educator*
Putnam, Ruth Anna *philosopher, educator*
Ruiz-de-Conde, Justina *retired foreign language educator*

West Barnstable
Corsa, Helen Storm *language professional*

Weston
Higgins, Sister Therese *English educator, former college president*

Williamstown
Bahlman, Dudley Ward Rhodes *history educator*
Bell, Michael Davitt *history and literature educator*
Bell-Villada, Gene H. *literature educator, writer*
Dalzell, Robert Fenton, Jr. *historian*
Dew, Charles Burgess *historian, educator*
Dickerson, Dennis Clark *history educator*
Dunn, Susan *literature and history educator*
Edgerton, Samuel Youngs, Jr. *art historian, educator*
Filipczak, Zirka Zaremba *art historian, educator*
Fuqua, Charles John *classics educator*
Graver, Lawrence Stanley *English language professional*
Graver, Suzanne Levy *English language educator*
Hyde, John Michael *history educator*
Johnson, Eugene Joseph, III *art historian, educator*
Norton, Glyn Peter *French literature educator*
Oakley, Francis Christopher *history educator, former college president*
Payne, Harry Charles *historian, educator*
Pistorius, George *language educator*
Raab, Lawrence Edward *English educator*
Rudolph, Frederick *history educator*
Stamelman, Richard Howard *French and humanities educator*
Waite, Robert George Leeson *history educator*

Worcester
Billias, George Athan *history educator*
Vaughan, Alden True *history educator*
Von Laue, Theodore Herman *historian, educator*
Zeugner, John Finn *history educator, writer*

MICHIGAN

Ann Arbor
Aldridge, John Watson *English language educator, author*
Amann, Peter Henry *historian, educator*
Arthos, John *English language educator*
Bailey, David Roy Shackleton *classics educator*
Bailey, Richard Weld *English educator*
Baker, Sheridan *English educator, author*
Becker, Marvin Burton *historian*
Blotner, Joseph Leo *English language educator*
Blouin, Francis Xavier, Jr. *history educator*
Bornstein, George Jay *literary educator*
Brandt, Richard Booker *former philosophy educator*
Brown, Deming Bronson *Slavic languages and literature educator*
Burbank, Jane Richardson *Russian and European studies educator*
Chambers, Leigh Ross *French language educator*
Cole, Juan R.I. *history educator*
Cowen, Roy Chadwell, Jr. *German language educator*
Curley, Edwin Munson *philosophy educator*
Danly, Robert Lyons *Japanese studies educator, author, translator*
D'Arms, John Haughton *classics educator, university dean*
Eby, Cecil DeGrotte *English language educator, writer*
Eisenberg, Marvin Julius *art history educator*
Eisenstein, Elizabeth Lewisohn *historian, educator*
Fader, Daniel Nelson *English language educator*
Feuerwerker, Albert *history educator*
Forsyth, Ilene Haering *art historian*
Gomez, Luis Oscar *Asian and religious studies educator*
Hackett, Roger Fleming *history educator*
Knott, John Ray, Jr. *language professional, educator*
Koenen, Ludwig *classical studies educator*
Konigsberg, Ira *film and literature educator, writer*
McCarus, Ernest Nasseph *language educator*
McDougal, Stuart Yeatman *comparative literature educator, author*
Mersereau, John, Jr. *Slavic languages and literatures educator*
Morgan, Raleigh, Jr. *linguistics educator*
Morris, Phyllis Sutton *philosophy educator*
Munro, Donald Jacques *philosopher, educator*
Murphey, Rhoads *history educator*
Pulgram, Ernst *linguist, philologist, Romance and classical linguistics educator, writer*
Starr, Chester G. *history educator*
Steinhoff, William Richard *English literature educator*
Stolz, Benjamin Armond *foreign language educator*
Super, Robert Henry *English educator*
Trautmann, Thomas Roger *history and anthropology educator*
Weisbuch, Robert Alan *English educator*
Woodcock, Leonard *humanities educator, former ambassador*

Berrien Springs
Waller, John Oscar *English language educator*

Bloomfield Hills
Bonner, Thomas Neville *history and higher education educator*

Detroit
Abt, Jeffrey *art and art history educator*
Kowalczyk, Richard Leon *English language educator, technical writing consultant*
Schindler, Marvin Samuel *foreign language educator*
Small, Melvin *history educator*
van der Marck, Jan *art historian*
Williamson, Marilyn Lammert *English educator, university adminstrator*

East Lansing
Anderson, David Daniel *retired humanities educator, writer, editor*
Appel, John J. *history educator*
Eadie, John William *history educator*
Eulenberg, John Bryson *artificial languages educator, administrator*
Falk, Julia S. *linguist, educator*
Fisher, Alan Washburn *historian, educator*
Greer, Thomas Hoag *historian, educator*
Grimes, Margaret Whitehurst *medievalist, educator*
Huzar, Eleanor Goltz *history educator*
Kronegger, Maria Elisabeth *French and comparative literature educator*
Mansour, George P. *Spanish language and literature educator*
Paananen, Victor Niles *English educator*
Platt, Franklin Dewitt *history educator*
Pollack, Norman *history educator*
Silverman, Henry Jacob *history educator*
Whallon, William *literature educator*

Grand Rapids
Hoekema, David Andrew *philosophy educator, academic administrator*

Grosse Pointe
Peters, Thomas Robert *English educator, writer*

Harbert
Morrissette, Bruce Archer *Romance languages educator*

Hillsdale
Castel, Albert Edward *history educator*

Holland
Quimby, Robert Sherman *retired humanities educator*

Huntington Woods
Gutmann, Joseph *art history educator*

Jackson
Feldmann, Judith G. *language professional, educator*

Kalamazoo
Breisach, Ernst A. *historian, educator*
†Dybek, Stuart *English educator, writer*
Gordon, Jaimy *English educator*
Gregory, Ross *history educator, author*
Light, Timothy *linguistics, religious and Asian studies educator, academic administrator*
Maier, Paul Luther *history educator, author, chaplain*
Moritz, Edward *historian, educator*
Ruoff, Cynthia Osowiec *foreign language educator*
Waring, Walter Weyler *English language educator*

Lansing
Harvey, Joanne H. *genealogist*

Livonia
Holtzman, Roberta Lee *French and Spanish language educator*

Okemos
Huddleston, Eugene Lee *retired American studies educator*

Rochester
Thomas, S. Bernard *history educator*

Rochester Hills
Matthews, George Tennyson *history educator*

Southfield
Papazian, Dennis Richard *history educator, political commentator*
Stern, Guy *German language educator, writer*

Sterling Heights
Ice, Orva Lee, Jr. *history educator*

Ypsilanti
Norton, Jody (John Douglas Norton) *English language educator*
Perkins, Bradford *history educator*

MINNESOTA

Bemidji
Paul, Sherman *retired English language educator*

Duluth
Fischer, Roger Adrian *history educator*
Jankofsky, Klaus Peter *medieval studies educator*
Schroeder, Fred Erich Harald *humanities educator*

Minneapolis
Anderson, Chester Grant *English educator*
Bales, Kent Roslyn *English language educator*
Browne, Donald Roger *speech communication educator*
Campbell, Karlyn Kohrs *speech and communication educator*
Conley, Tom Clark *literature educator*
Erickson, Gerald Meyer *classical studies educator*
Farah, Caesar Elie *Middle Eastern and Islamic studies educator*
Firchow, Evelyn Scherabon *German educator, author*
Firchow, Peter Edgerly *language professional, educator, author*
Garner, Shirley Nelson *English language educator*
Griffin, Edward Michael *language professional, educator*
Kohlstedt, Sally Gregory *history educator*
Layton, Edwin Thomas, Jr. *science and technology history educator, writer*
Lehmberg, Stanford Eugene *historian, educator*
Leppert, Richard David *humanities educator*
McDonald, William Andrew *classics educator*
Nagel, Paul Chester *historian, writer, lecturer*
Noonan, Thomas Schaub *history educator, Russian studies educator*
Norberg, Arthur Lawrence, Jr. *historian, physicist educator*
Pazandak, Carol Hendrickson *liberal arts educator*
Rath, R. John *historian, educator*
Ross, Donald, Jr. *English language educator, university administrator*
Scott, Robert Lee *speech educator*
Sonkowsky, Robert Paul *classicist, educator, actor*
Tracy, James Donald *historian*
Vecoli, Rudolph John *history educator*
Weiss, Gerhard Hans *German language educator*

Moorhead
Anderson, Jerry Maynard *speech educator*
Coomber, James Elwood *English language educator*

Northfield
Clark, Clifford Edward, Jr. *history educator*
Haworth, Dale Keith *art history educator, gallery director*
Iseminger, Gary H. *philosophy educator*
Mason, Perry Carter *philosophy educator*
McDonnell, James *English educator*
Morral, Frank Rolf *English educator, psychologist*
†Paas, John Roger *German language educator*
Sipfle, David Arthur *philosophy educator*
Soth, Lauren *art history educator*
Soule, George Alan *literature educator*
Yandell, Cathy Marleen *foreign language educator*
Zelliot, Eleanor Mae *history educator*

Saint Paul
Kane, Patricia Lanegran *language professional, educator*
Mather, Richard Burroughs *retired Chinese language and literature educator*
Murray, Peter Bryant *English language educator*
Stewart, James Brewer *historian, author, college administrator*
Weiner, Carl Dorian *historian*

MISSISSIPPI

Biloxi
Hagood, Annabel Dunham *speech communication educator, communication consultant*

Cleveland
Cash, William McKinley *history educator*

Clinton
Bigelow, Martha Mitchell *retired historian*

Columbus
Stringer, Mary Evelyn *art historian, educator*

Hattiesburg
Gonzales, John Edmond *history educator*
Sims, James Hylbert *English educator, former university administrator*

Mississippi State
Crowell, Lorenzo Mayo *historian, educator*
Donaghy, Henry James *English literature educator, academic administrator*
Lowery, Charles Douglas *history educator, academic administrator*
Parrish, William Earl *history educator*
Shillingsburg, Peter LeRoy *English language educator*
Wiltrout, Ann Elizabeth *foreign language educator*

Rose Hill
Young, Thomas Daniel *retired humanities educator, author*

Starkville
Wolverton, Robert Earl *classics educator*

University
Jordan, Winthrop Donaldson *historian, educator*
Kiger, Joseph Charles *history educator*
†Landon, Michael de Laval *historian, educator*
Walton, Gerald Wayne *English educator, university officiala*

MISSOURI

Chesterfield
Bowling, William Glasgow *English educator*

Columbia
Alexander, Thomas Benjamin *history educator*
Anderson, Donald Kennedy, Jr. *English educator*
Bien, Joseph Julius *philosophy educator*
Fulweiler, Howard Wells *language professional*
Geiger, Louis George *historian*
Goodrich, James William *historian, association executive*
Jones, William McKendrey *language professional, educator*
Lago, Mary McClelland *English language educator, author*
Mullen, Edward John, Jr. *Spanish language educator*
Overby, Osmund Rudolf *art historian, educator*
Reid, Loren Dudley *speech educator*
Strickland, Arvarh Eunice *history educator*
Timberlake, Charles Edward *history educator*

Jefferson City
Hearn, Rosemary *English language educator*

Kansas City
Cappon, Alexander Patterson *English language educator*
Hoffmann, Donald *architectural historian*

Marshall
Gruber, Loren Charles *English language educator, writer*

Rolla
†Allison, Sandy *genealogist, appraiser, political consultant*

Saint Charles
Barnett, Howard Albert *English language educator*

Saint Louis
Bagley, Mary Carol *literature educator, writer, broadcaster*
Barmann, Lawrence Francis *history educator*
Benberry, Cuesta Ray *historian*
Berthoff, Rowland Tappan *historian, educator*
Bourke, Vernon Joseph *philosophy educator*
Boyd, Robert Cotton *English educator*
Herbert, Kevin Barry John *classics educator*
Hexter, Jack H. *historian, educator*
Krukowski, Lucian *philosophy educator, artist*
Lacy, Norris Joiner *French language and literature educator*
Loewenstein, Joseph F. *English literature educator*
Morrow, Ralph Ernest *historian, educator*
Ruland, Richard Eugene *English and American literature educator, critic, literary historian*
Sale, William Merritt *classicist, comparatist, educator*
Schwarz, Egon *humanities and German language educator, author, literary critic*
Shea, Daniel Bartholomew, Jr. *English language educator, actor*
Smith, Jeffrey E. *historian, educator*
Spector, Stanley *foreign language educator*
Ullian, Joseph Silbert *philosophy educator*
Watson, Richard Allan *philosophy educator, writer*
Wellman, Carl Pierce *philosophy educator*
Wheeler, Burton M. *literature educator, higher education consultant, college dean*
Wu, Nelson Ikon *art history educator, author, artist*

MONTANA

Billings
Small, Lawrence Farnsworth *history educator*

NEBRASKA

Hastings
McEwen, Larry Burdette *retired English and theater arts educator, author*

Kearney
Young, Ann Elizabeth O'Quinn *historian, educator*

Lincoln
Bailey, Dudley *English educator*
Crompton, Louis William *English literature educator*
Leinieks, Valdis *classicist, educator*
Rawley, James Albert *history educator*
Sawyer, Robert McLaran *history educator*
Stover, John Ford *railroad historian, educator*

Omaha
Bergquist, Gordon Neil *English educator*
Cunningham, William Francis, Jr. *English language educator, university administrator*
Dougherty, Charles John *philosophy and medical ethics educator*
Horning, Ross Charles, Jr. *historian, educator*

NEVADA

Las Vegas
Adams, Charles Lynford *English language educator*
Stevens, Arthur Wilber, Jr. *English literature educator, writer, editor*

NEW HAMPSHIRE

Alstead
Lyon, Bryce Dale *historian, educator*

Center Sandwich
Folch-Pi, Willa Babcock *Romance language educator*

Durham
Hapgood, Robert Derry *English educator*
Rouman, John Christ *classics educator*
Voll, John Obert *history educator*

Freedom
Kucera, Henry *linguistics educator*

Hanover
Arndt, Walter Werner *Slavic scholar, linguist, writer, translator*
Bien, Peter Adolph *English language educator, author*
Daniell, Jere Rogers, II *history educator, consultant, public lecturer*
Doenges, Norman Arthur *classics educator*
Doney, Willis Frederick *philosophy educator*
Duncan, Bruce *foreign language educator*
†Fogelin, Robert John *philosophy educator*
Garthwaite, Gene Ralph *historian, educator*
Gert, Bernard *philosopher, educator*
Green, Mary Jean Matthews *foreign language educator*
Heffernan, James Anthony Walsh *English language and literature educator*
Kritzman, Lawrence David *humanities educator*
Loseff, Lev Lifschutz *Russian educator*
Mansell, Darrel Lee, Jr. *English educator*
Oxenhandler, Neal *language educator, writer*
Parton, James *historian*
Penner, Hans Henry *historian*
Russell, Robert Hilton *Romance languages and literature educator*
Scher, Steven Paul *literature educator*
Scherr, Barry Paul *foreign language educator*
Sheldon, Richard Robert *Russian language and literature educator*
Shewmaker, Kenneth Earl *history educator*
Spitzer, Leo *historian, educator*
Wood, Charles Tuttle *history educator*
Wykes, David *English educator*

Laconia
Heald, Bruce Day *English and music educator, historian*

Madbury
Bruce, Robert Vance *historian, educator*

Nashua
Light, James Forest *English educator*

New Castle
Silva, Joseph Donald *English language educator*

Strafford
Simic, Charles *English language educator, poet*

NEW JERSEY

Camden
Showalter, English, Jr. *French language educator*

Cape May
Lassner, Franz George *historian, educator*

Englewood
Beer, Jeanette Mary Scott *foreign language educator*

Fort Monmouth
Ignoffo, Matthew Frederick *English language educator, writer, counselor*

Frenchtown
Scaglione, Aldo Domenico *language educator*

Highland Lakes
†Kiraly, Bèla Kàlmàn *retired history educator, Hungarian army officer*

Highland Park
Pane, Remigio Ugo *Romance languages educator*

Madison
Knox, John, Jr. *philosopher, educator*
Mc Mullen, Edwin Wallace, Jr. *English language educator*

Mahwah
Weinberg, Sydney Stahl *historian*

New Brunswick
Gardner, Lloyd Calvin, Jr. *history educator*
Gillette, William *historian, educator*
Grob, Gerald N. *historian, educator*
Hartman, Mary S. *historian*
Kelley, Donald Reed *historian*
Levine, George Lewis *English language educator, literature critic*
Lewis, David Levering *history educator*
Morrison, Karl Frederick *history educator*
O'Neill, William Lawrence *history educator*
Poirier, Richard *English educator, literary critic*
Reed, James Wesley *social historian, educator*
Stimpson, Catharine Roslyn *English language educator, writer*
Wasson, Richard Howard *English language educator*

Newark
Crew, Louie (Li Min Hua) *language professional, educator*
Estrin, Herman Albert *English language educator*
Schweizer, Karl Wolfgang *historian, writer*
Vevier, Charles *historian, educator, consultant, university administrator*

Princeton
Aandahl, Fredrick *historian, editor*
Aarsleff, Hans *linguistics educator*
Beeners, Wilbert John *speech professional, minister*
Benacerraf, Paul Joseph Salomon *philosophy educator*
Bowersock, Glen Warren *historian*
Brombert, Victor Henri *literature educator, author*
Brown, Leon Carl *history educator*
Cassidy, Brendan Francis *art educator and director*
Champlin, Edward James *classics educator*
Coffin, David Robbins *art historian, educator*
Cooper, John Madison *philosophy educator*
Corngold, Stanley Alan *German and comparative literature educator, writer*
Curschmann, Michael Johann Hendrik *German language and literature educator*
Danson, Lawrence Neil *English language educator*
Darnton, Robert Choate *history educator*
Davis, Natalie Zemon *history educator*
de Grazia, Sebastian *political philosopher, author*
Ermolaev, Herman Sergei *Slavic languages educator*
Finch, Jeremiah Stanton *English language educator*
Fleming, John Vincent *humanities educator*
Forcione, Alban Keith *language educator*
Goheen, Robert Francis *classicist, educator, former ambassador*
Goldman, Michael Paul *language professional, educator, writer*
†Grafton, Anthony Thomas *history educator*
Habicht, Christian Herbert *history educator*
Harman, Gilbert Helms *philosophy educator*
Hollander, Robert B., Jr. *Romance languages educator*
Hynes, Samuel *English language educator, author*
Itzkowitz, Norman *history educator*
Jansen, Marius Berthus *historian, educator*
Jeffery, Peter Grant *musicologist, fine arts educator*
Jeffrey, Richard Carl *philosophy educator*
Jordan, William Chester *history educator*
Kaufmann, Thomas DaCosta *art history educator*
Keaney, John Joseph *classics educator*
Keeley, Edmund LeRoy *English, creative writing and modern Greek studies educator, author*
Kennan, George Frost *historian, educator, former ambassador,*
Knoepflmacher, Ulrich Camillus *literature educator*
Lange, Victor *language educator, author*
Lewis, Bernard *Near Eastern studies educator*
Lewis, David Kellogg *philosopher, educator*
Litz, Arthur Walton, Jr. *English language educator*
Ludwig, Richard Milton *English literature educator, librarian*
Mahoney, Michael Sean *history educator*
Marks, John Henry *Near Eastern studies educator*
Mayer, Arno Joseph *history educator*
Mc Pherson, James Munro *history educator*
Miner, Earl Roy *English educator*
Moote, A. Lloyd *history educator*
Moynahan, Julian Lane *English language educator, author*
Nehamas, Alexander *philosophy educator*
Ober, Josiah *history educator*
Painter, Nell Irvin *historian, educator*
Paret, Peter *historian*
Peterson, Willard James *Chinese history educator*
Rabb, Theodore K. *historian, educator*
Rigolot, François *French literature educator, literary critic*
Rodgers, Daniel Tracy *history educator*
Schofield, Robert E(dwin) *history educator, academic administrator*
Schorske, Carl Emil *historian, educator*
Shimizu, Yoshiaki *art historian, educator*
Showalter, Elaine *humanities educator*
Soames, Scott *philosophy educator*
Steiner, Robert Lisle *language consultant*
Stone, Lawrence *historian*
Tignor, Robert Lee *historian, educator*
Townsend, Charles Edward *Slavic languages educator*
†Udovitch, Abraham Labe *historian, educator*
Uitti, Karl David *language educator*
White, Morton Gabriel *philosopher, author*
Wilentz, Robert Sean *history educator, author*
Wilson, Margaret Dauler *philosophy educator*
Wolfson, Susan Jean *English literature educator*
Woolf, Harry *historian, educator*
Yu, Ying Shih *history educator, researcher*
Zeitlin, Froma I. *classics educator*
Ziolkowski, Theodore Joseph *comparative literature educator*

Ridgewood
Molnar, Thomas *philosophy of religion educator, author*

Scotch Plains
Edwards, Thomas Robert, Jr. *language professional, investment company executive*

Short Hills
Broder, Patricia Janis *art historian, writer*

South Orange
Reilly, George Love Anthony *history educator*

Teaneck
Fatemi, Faramarz Saifpour *history and political science educator, consultant*
Gordon, Lois Goldfein *English language educator*
Rudy, Willis *historian*
Williams, John A. *English language educator, author*

Trenton
George, Emery Edward *foreign language and studies educator*

Wayne
O'Connor, John Morris, III *philosophy educator*

NEW MEXICO

Albuquerque
Bahm, Archie John *philosophy educator*
Fuller, Anne Elizabeth Havens *English educator, consultant*
Hutton, Paul Andrew *history educator, writer*
Kutvirt, Duda Chytilova (Ruzena) *scientific translator*
MacCurdy, Raymond Ralph, Jr. *modern language educator*
Nash, Gerald David *historian*
Sturm, Fred Gillette *philosopher, educator*

Corrales
Martin, Harold Clark *humanities educator*

Las Cruces
Bloom, John Porter *historian, editor, administrator, archivist*

Placitas
Forrest, Suzanne Sims *research historian*

Portales
Matheny, Robert Lavesco *history educator, former university president*

Santa Fe
McLaughlin, Ted John *speech educator*

Univ Of New Mexico
Thorson, James Llewellyn *English language educator*

NEW YORK

Albany
Beharriell, Frederick John *German and comparative literature educator*
Creegan, Robert Francis *philosophy educator*
Donovan, Robert Alan *English educator*
Eckstein, Jerome *philosopher, educator*
Kekes, John *philosopher, educator*
Lenardon, Robert Joseph *classics educator*
Moelleken, Wolfgang Wilfried *Germanic languages and literature educator*
Pohlsander, Hans Achim *classics educator*
Purves, Alan Carroll *English language educator, education educator*
Reese, William Lewis *philosophy educator*
Roberts, Warren Errol *history educator*
Zacek, Joseph Frederick *history educator, international studies consultant, East European affairs specialist*

Alfred
Potter, Barrett George *historian, educator*

Amherst
Gracia, Jorge Jesus Emiliano *philosopher, educator*
Kurtz, Paul *publisher, philosopher, educator*

Annandale On Hudson
Achebe, Chinua *humanist, humanities educator*
Ashbery, John Lawrence *language educator, poet, playwright*
Frank, Elizabeth *English literature educator, author*

Astoria
†See Fong Chan *retired linguist, composer*

Binghamton
Block, Haskell Mayer *humanities educator*
Gaddis Rose, Marilyn *comparative literature educator, translator*
Kessler, Milton *English language educator, poet*
Sklar, Kathryn Kish *historian, educator*
Stein, George Henry *historian, educator, administrator*

Briarcliff Manor
Leiser, Burton Myron *philosophy and law educator*

Brockport
Leslie, William Bruce *history educator*
Marcus, Robert D. *historian, educator*
Stack, George Joseph *philosophy educator*

Bronx
Ansbro, John Joseph *philosophy educator*
Bowers, Francis Robert *literature educator*
Hallett, Charles Arthur, Jr. *English and humanities educator*
Himmelberg, Robert Franklin *historian, educator*
Karp, Abraham Joseph *historian, rabbi, educator*
Macklin, Ruth *bioethics educator*
Maddox, Utricia Antoinette *English educator, communications educator*
Tusiani, Joseph *foreign language educator, author*
Ultan, Lloyd *historian*
Zeichner, Oscar *historian, educator*

Bronxville
Forester, Erica Simms *decorative arts historian, consultant, educator*
Krupat, Arnold *English educator, writer*
Peters, Sarah Whitaker *art historian, writer, lecturer*
Randall, Francis Ballard *historian, educator, writer*

Brooklyn
Ashley, Leonard Raymond Nelligan *English language educator*
Blasi, Alberto *Romance languages educator, writer*
Brownstone, Paul Lotan *retired speech communications and drama educator*
Contino, Rosalie Helene *English educator, costume designer*
Everdell, William Romeyn *humanities educator*
Flam, Jack Donald *art historian, educator*
Hoogenboom, Ari Arthur *historian, educator*
Jofen, Jean *foreign language educator*
King, Margaret Leah *history educator*
†La Corte, John J. *philososhy educator, historical society executive*
Olson, Robert Goodwin *philosophy educator*
Slade, Rejane De Oliveira *Portuguese language educator*
Spector, Robert Donald *language professional, educator*

Buffalo
Allen, William Sheridan *history educator*
Drew, Fraser Bragg Robert *English language educator*
Fiedler, Leslie Aaron *English educator, actor, author*
Hare, Peter Hewitt *philosophy educator*
Iggers, Georg Gerson *history educator*
Levine, George Richard *English language educator*
Milligan, John Drane *historian, educator*
Payne, Frances Anne *literature educator, researcher*
Peradotto, John Joseph *classics educator, editor*
Richards, David Gleyre *German language educator*
Riepe, Dale Maurice *philosopher, writer, illustrator, educator, Asian art dealer*
Saveth, Edward Norman *history educator*
Siedlecki, Peter Anthony *English educator*
Wolck, Wolfgang Hans-Joachim *linguist, educator*

Canton
Goldberg, Rita Maria *foreign language educator*

Clinton
Blackwood, Russell Thorn, III *philosophy educator*
Rupprecht, Carol Schreier *comparative literature educator, dream researcher*
Wagner, Frederick Reese *language professional*

Cortland
Anderson, Donna Kay *musicologist, educator*
Kaminsky, Alice Richkin *English language educator*

Delmar
Odenkirchen, Carl Josef *Romance languages and literatures educator*

Dobbs Ferry
Panitz, Esther Leah *English language educator*

East Berne
Grenander, M. E. *English language educator, critic*

Flushing
Hirshson, Stanley Philip *history educator*
Lamont, Rosette Clementine *Romance languages educator, theatre journalist, translator*
Parmet, Herbert Samuel *historian, educator*
Rabassa, Gregory *Romance languages educator, translator*
Tytell, John *humanities educator, writer*
Wolz, Henry George *philosophy educator*

Fredonia
Sonnenfeld, Marion *linguist, educator*

Garden City
Diamandopoulos, Peter *philosopher, educator*
Jenkins, Kenneth Vincent *literature educator, writer*
Korshak, Yvonne *art historian*
Makapela, Alven *history educator*
Shirk, Evelyn Urban *retired philosophy educator*
Shneidman, J. Lee *historian, educator*

Gardiner
Mabee, Carleton *historian, educator*

Geneseo
Edgar, William John *philosophy educator*
Fausold, Martin Luther *history educator*

Geneva
Caponegro, Mary *English language educator*

Hamilton
Blackton, Charles S(tuart) *history educator*
Busch, Briton Cooper *historian*
Garland, Robert Sandford John *classical studies educator*
Hathaway, Robert Lawton *Romance languages educator*
Hoffmann, Dierk Otto *German language educator*
Jones, Frank William *language educator*
Levy, Jacques *educator, theater director, lyricist, writer*
Little, Daniel Eastman *philosophy educator, associate dean*
Nakhimovsky, Alice Stone *foreign language educator*
Staley, Lynn *English educator*
Van Schaack, Eric *art historian, educator*

Ithaca
Abrams, Meyer Howard *English language educator*
Brazell, Karen Woodard *Japanese literature educator*
Brown, Theodore Morey *art history educator*
Caputi, Anthony *comparative literature educator*
Colby-Hall, Alice Mary *Romance studies educator*
Culler, Jonathan Dwight *English language educator*
Eddy, Donald Davis *English language educator*
Elledge, Scott Bowen *language professional, educator*
Gibian, George *Russian and comparative literature educator*
Groos, Arthur Bernhard, Jr. *German literature educator*
Hohendahl, Peter Uwe *German language and literature educator*
Kammen, Michael *historian, educator*
Kronik, John William *Romance studies educator*
LaCapra, Dominick Charles *historian*
LaFeber, Walter Frederick *history educator, author*
McConkey, James Rodney *English educator, writer*
Norton, Mary Beth *history educator, author*
Polenberg, Richard *history educator*
Porte, Joel Miles *English educator*
Radzinowicz, Mary Ann *language educator*
Rossiter, Margaret Walsh *history of science educator*
Scammell, Michael *foreign language educator, translator, writer*
Shoemaker, Sydney S. *philosophy educator*
Silbey, Joel Henry *history educator*
Strout, Sewall Cushing, Jr. *humanities educator*
Williams, Leslie Pearce *history educator*

Jamaica
Fay, Thomas A. *philosopher, educator*
Harmond, Richard Peter *historian, educator*

Jericho
Astuto, Philip Louis *retired Spanish educator*

Lockwood
Keating, Keith Anthony *English language educator*

Massapequa
Vaccaro, Nicholas Carmine *English language and media educator*

New Paltz
Hathaway, Richard Dean *language professional, educator*
Ryan, Marleigh Grayer *Japanese language educator*

New York
Abel, Reuben *humanities educator*
Alazraki, Jaime *Romance languages educator*
Anderson, Quentin *English language educator, critic*
Apple, Max Isaac *English educator*
Austerlitz, Robert Paul *linguistics educator*
Bagnall, Roger Shaler *history educator*
Baker, Paul Raymond *history educator*
Balakian, Anna *foreign language educator, scholar, critic, writer*
Balbin, Julius *foreign language educator, poet, translator*
Barolini, Teodolinda *foreign language educator*
Barzilay, Isaac Eisenstein *historian*
Beck, James (Henry) *art historian, author*
Belknap, Robert Lamont *Slavic language educator*
Bender, Thomas *history and humanities educator, writer*
Bent, Ian David *musicologist*
Bonfante, Larissa *classics educator*
Brilliant, Richard *art history educator*
Brody, Saul Nathaniel *English literature educator*
Brooks, Jerome Bernard *English and Afro-American literature educator*
Brown, Jonathan *art historian, fine arts educator*
Brown, Milton Wolf *art historian, educator*
Brush, Craig Balcombe *French language and computer educator*
Bulliet, Richard Williams *history educator, novelist*
Burrill, Kathleen R. F. (Kathleen R. F. Griffin-Burrill) *Turkologist, educator*
Bushman, Richard L. *history educator, writer, consultant*
Cahn, Steven M. *philosopher, educator*
Cantor, Norman Frank *history educator, writer*
Castronovo, David *English language educator*
Caws, Mary Ann *French language and comparative literature educator, critic*
†Cohen, Naomi Wiener *historian, educator*
Compagnon, Antoine Marcel *French language educator*
Cook, Blanche Wiesen *history educator, journalist*
Costello, John Robert *linguistics educator*
Cullen, Patrick Colborn *English educator*
Czerwinski, Edward Joseph *foreign language educator*
Dauben, Joseph Warren *history educator*
Davies, Jane B(adger) (Mrs. Lyn Davies) *architectural historian*
Deak, Istvan *historian, educator*
de Bary, William Theodore *Asian studies educator*
Diver, William *linguistics educator*
Duberman, Martin *historian*
Eisler, Colin Tobias *art historian, curator*
Elderfield, John *art historian, museum curator*
Embree, Ainslie Thomas *history educator*
Ferrante, Joan Marguerite *English and comparative literature educator*
Foner, Eric *historian, educator*
Franco, Jean *Spanish language educator*
Freedberg, David Adrian *art educator, historian*
Garrow, David Jeffries *historian, author*
Gerdts, William Henry *art history educator*
Ginter, Valerian Alexius *urban historian*
Glissant, Edouard Mathieu *French language educator, writer*
Gluck, Carol *history educator*
†Goodwin, Doris Helen Kearns *history educator, writer*
Grele, Ronald John *historian*
†Gromada, Thaddeus V. *historian, administrator*
Harrington, John Patrick *English language educator, college dean*
Harris, William Vernon *history educator*
Harter, Hugh Anthony *foreign language educator*
Hartman-Goldsmith, Joan *art historian*
Harvey, Donald Joseph *history educator*

Heffner, Richard Douglas historian, educator, communications consultant, television producer
Held, Virginia philosophy educator
Hoeflin, Ronald Kent philosopher, test designer, newsletter publisher
Hovde, Carl Frederick language professional, educator
Howe, Florence English educator, writer, publisher
Hunter-Stiebel, Penelope art historian, art dealer
Huyssen, Andreas German literature educator
Jackson, Kenneth Terry historian, educator
Karsen, Sonja Petra retired Spanish educator
Kivette, Ruth Montgomery English language educator
Klein, Herbert Sanford historian
Kneller, John William French language educator
Kortepeter, Carl Max history educator, columnist
Kra, Pauline Skornicki French language educator
Krinsky, Carol Herselle art history educator
Kristeller, Paul Oskar former philosophy educator
Kroeber, Karl English language educator
Lamont, Corliss philosopher, educator, author
La Rue, (Adrian) Jan (Pieters) musicologist, educator, author
Leavitt, Charles Loyal English language educator, administrator
Leibowitz, Herbert Akiba English language educator, author
Lencek, Rado L. Slavic languages educator
Levi, Isaac philosophy educator
London, Herbert Ira humanities educator
Lorch, Maristella De Panizza (Mrs. Inama von Brunnenwald) Romance languages educator, writer, lecturer
Low, Anthony English language educator
Lowenthal, Constance art historian
Lynch, Hollis Ralph history educator
Maguire, Robert Alan Slavic languages and literatures educator
Malefakis, Edward E. history educator
Malin, Irving English educator, literary critic
Malone, Joseph Lawrence linguistics educator
Matthews, William Procter English educator
May, Gita French language and literature educator
Mayerson, Philip classics educator
Maynard, John Rogers English educator
Mc Kitrick, Eric Louis historian, educator
Meier, August historian, educator
Meisel, Martin English and comparative literature educator
Meisel, Perry English educator
Mendelson, Edward James English literature educator
Middendorf, John Harlan English literature educator
Morris, Robert C. historian, archivist, educator
Mundy, John Hine history educator
Myers, Gerald E. humanities educator
Novak, Barbara art history educator
†Ochs, Carol Rebecca philosophy and religion educator, writer
Paxton, Robert Owen historian, educator
Plottel, Jeanine Parisier foreign language educator
Posner, Donald art historian
Potoker, Edward Martin English language educator, author
Prince, Carl E. historian, educator
Quigley, Austin Edmund literature and language educator
Ragusa, Olga Maria Italian language educator
Ravitch, Diane Silvers historian, educator, author, government official
Rebay, Luciano Italian literature educator, literary critic
Reff, Theodore art historian
Reiman, Donald Henry English language educator
Reiss, Timothy James comparative literature educator, writer
Reynolds, Donald Martin art historian, foundation administrator, educator
Rice, Eugene Franklin, Jr. history educator
Riffaterre, Michael foreign language educator, writer
Rosand, David art history educator
Rosenberg, John David English educator, literary critic
Rosenblum, Robert art historian, educator
Rothman, David J. history and medical educator
Rowen, Ruth Halle musicologist, educator
Said, Edward W. English language and literature educator
Sandler, Lucy Freeman art history educator
Schama, Simon historian, educator, author
Scheindlin, Raymond Paul Hebrew literature educator, translator
Seigel, Jerrold Edward historian, writer
Selig, Karl-Ludwig language and literature educator
Semmel, Bernard historian, educator
Shenton, James Patrick history educator
Silver, Philip Warnock Spanish language educator
Silverman, Kenneth Eugene English educator, writer
Sisman, Elaine Rochelle musicology educator
Somerville, Robert Eugene historian
Stade, George Gustav humanities educator
Steinberg, Leo art historian, educator
Stephens, Gary Ralph American literature and journalism educator
Stern, Fritz Richard historian, educator
Stevens, Martin English educator
Tanselle, George Thomas English language educator, foundation executive
Taran, Leonardo classicist, educator
Tayler, Edward William English language educator
Tilly, Louise Audino history and sociology educator
Tison-Braun, Micheline Lucie French language educator
Treitler, Leo musicologist, educator
Turner, Almon Richard art historian, educator
Tuttleton, James Wesley English educator
Unger, Irwin historian, educator
Unger, Peter Kenneth philosophy educator
Vai, Marjorie Theresa language educator, university administrator, author
Valenstein, Suzanne Gebhart art historian
Walkowitz, Daniel J. historian, filmmaker, educator
Wardwell, Allen art historian
Wasser, Henry retired English educator
Weaver, Martin Edward historic conservation educator, administrator
Weil-Garris Brandt, Kathleen art historian
Weinberg, H. Barbara art historian, educator, curator paintings and sculpture
Wilson, Fredric Woodbridge musicologist, library curator
Wittreich, Joseph Anthony, Jr. English language educator, author
Wixom, William David art historian, museum administrator, educator
Wortman, Richard S. historian, educator
Yerushalmi, Yosef Hayim historian, educator
Yurchenco, Henrietta Weiss ethnomusicologist, writer

Oakdale
Kramer, Aaron English educator emeritus, poet, author

Old Bethpage
Hall, R. M. R. historical linguist

Old Westbury
Rabil, Albert, Jr. humanities educator

Oswego
Smiley, Marilynn Jean musicologist
Turco, Lewis Putnam English educator

Oyster Bay
Gable, John Allen historian, association executive, educator
Garone, Frank English language educator

Plattsburgh
Myers, John Lytle historian

Pleasantville
Joseph, Harriet English literature educator

Poestenkill
Radley, Virginia Louise humanities educator

Potsdam
Cross, John William foreign language educator
Harder, Kelsie Brown retired language professional, educator

Poughkeepsie
Ahern, John Joseph Italian studies educator
Bartlett, Lynn Conant English literature educator
Daniels, Elizabeth Adams English language educator
Griffen, Clyde Chesterman retired history educator
Hytier, Adrienne Doris French language educator
†Kelley, David Christopher philosopher
Kohl, Benjamin Gibbs historian, educator
Lipschutz, Ilse Hempel French and Franco-Spanish relations, painting and literature educator
Winn, Otis Howard English educator

Purchase
Clark, Mary Twibill philosopher, educator
Lucas, Billy Joe philosophy educator

Quogue
Cooke, Robert John history and law educator

Rhinebeck
Vartanian, Aram French literature educator, researcher, writer

Rochester
Annunziata, Frank history educator
Berman, Milton history educator
Carlton, Charles Merritt linguistics educator
Chiarenza, Carl art historian, critic, artist, educator
Dohanian, Diran Kavork art historian, educator
Eaves, Morris Emery English language educator
Freeman, Robert Schofield musicologist, educator, pianist
Gordon, Dane Rex philosophy educator, minister
Hauser, William Barry history educator, historian
Herminghouse, Patricia Anne foreign language educator
Holmes, Robert Lawrence philosophy educator
Horsford, Howard Clarke English language educator
Howard, Hubert Wendell English language educator, academic administrator, choral conductor
Hoy, Cyrus Henry language professional, educator
Johnson, Bruce Marvin English language educator
Johnson, James William English educator, author
Joyce, John Joseph English educator
Klimas, Antanas linguist, educator
Mann, Alfred musicology educator, choral conductor
Ramsey, Jarold William English language educator, author
Watanabe, Ruth Taiko music historian, library science educator
Young, Mary Elizabeth history educator
Zagorin, Perez historian, educator

Saint Bonaventure
Dooley, Patrick Kiaran philosopher, educator
Wallace, Malcolm Vincent Timothy classics educator

Saratoga Springs
Boyers, Robert English language educator

Scarsdale
Graff, Henry Franklin historian, educator

Schenectady
†Jonas, Manfred historian, educator
Morris, John Selwyn philosophy educator, college president emeritus
Murphy, William Michael literature educator, biographer

Setauket
Simpson, Louis Aston Marantz English educator, author

Slingerlands
Ellis, David Maldwyn history educator

Southampton
Brophy, James David, Jr. humanities educator

Spencerport
Clarke, Stephan Paul English language educator, writer

Staten Island
Aronson, Marilyn Ruth English language and literature educator
Hartman, Joan Edna English educator

Stony Brook
Aronoff, Mark H. linguistics educator, author, consultant
Goldberg, Homer Beryl English language educator
Ihde, Don philosophy educator, university administrator
Kuspit, Donald Burton art historian, art critic, educator
Levin, Richard Louis English language educator
Mignone, Mario B. Italian studies educator
Spector, Marshall philosophy educator

Suffern
Walsh, James Jerome philosophy educator

Syracuse
Alston, William Payne philosophy educator
Crowley, John W(illiam) English language educator
Denise, Theodore Cullom philosophy educator
Hoffman, Arthur Wolf English language educator
Ketcham, Ralph history and political science educator
Lichtblau, Myron Ivor language educator
Powell, James Matthew history educator
Sternlicht, Sanford English and theater arts educator, writer
Sutton, Walter English educator
Tatham, David Frederic art historian, educator

Troy
Ahlers, Rolf Willi philosopher, theologian
Robinson, Sharon Pattyson English educator
Whitburn, Merrill Duane English literature educator

Trumansburg
Taylor, Richard philosopher, educator

Yonkers
Agli, Stephen Michael English language and literature educator

NORTH CAROLINA

Chapel Hill
Bain, Robert Addison American literature educator
Baron, Samuel Haskell historian
Debreczeny, Paul Slavic language educator, author
Eaton, Charles Edward English language educator, author
Falk, Eugene Hannes foreign language educator emeritus
Flora, Joseph M(artin) English language educator
Furst, Lilian Renee language professional, educator
Heninger, Simeon Kahn, Jr. English language educator
Jackson, Blyden English language educator
Jones, Houston Gwynne history educator
Kohn, Richard H. historian, educator
Lee, Sherman Emery art historian, curator
Levine, Madeline Geltman Slavic literatures educator, translator
Long, Douglas Clark philosophy educator
Ludington, Charles Townsend, Jr. English and American studies educator
Munsat, Stanley Morris philosopher, educator
Nelson, Philip Francis musicology educator, consultant, choral conductor
Rubin, Louis Decimus, Jr. English language and literature educator, writer, publisher
Schier, Donald Stephen language educator
Smith, Sidney Rufus, Jr. linguist, educator
Stadter, Philip Austin classicist, educator
Strauss, Albrecht Benno English educator, editor
Tindall, George Brown historian, educator
Tsiapera, Maria linguistics educator
Vogler, Frederick Wright French language educator
Weinberg, Gerhard Ludwig history educator
†Williamson, Joel Rudolph humanities educator
Ziff, Paul philosophy educator

Charlotte
Hill, Ruth Foell language consultant
Preyer, Norris Watson history educator

Cullowhee
Blethen, Harold Tyler, III history educator
Farwell, Harold Frederick, Jr. English language educator

Davidson
Abernethy, George Lawrence philosophy educator
Cole, Richard Cargill English language educator
Edmondson, Clifton Earl history educator, researcher
Jacobus, Everett F., Jr. French language educator
Lester, Malcolm historian, educator
Mele, Alfred R. philosophy educator
Stell, Lance Keith philosophy educator
Tong, Rosemarie medical humanities and philosophy educator, consultant and researcher
Williams, Robert Chadwell history educator
Yoder, Lauren Wayne French language educator
Zimmermann, T. C. Price historian, educator

Durham
Budd, Louis John English language educator
Butters, Ronald Richard English language educator
Cady, Edwin Harrison English language educator, author
Chafe, William Henry history educator
Colton, Joel historian, educator
Davis, Calvin De Armond historian, educator
Durden, Robert Franklin history educator
Fish, Stanley Eugene English language and literature educator
Flanagan, Owen J. philosophy educator
Gleckner, Robert Francis English language professional, educator
Golding, Martin Philip law and philosophy educator
Hillerbrand, Hans Joachim historian, university administrator
Holley, Irving Brinton, Jr. historian, educator
Lerner, Warren historian
MacIntyre, Alasdair philosophy educator
Mauskopf, Seymour Harold history educator
Nygard, Holger Olof English and folklore educator
Oates, John Francis classics educator
Pendergraft, Norman Elveis art history educator, art museum director
Preston, Richard Arthur historian
Richardson, Lawrence, Jr. Latin language educator, archeologist
Ryals, Clyde de Loache humanities educator
Sanford, David Hawley philosophy educator
Scott, Anne Byrd Firor history educator
Smith, Grover Cleveland English language educator
Thomas, Jean-Jacques Robert Romance languages educator
Wardropper, Bruce Wear language educator
Williams, George Walton English educator

Fayetteville
Bowman, Charles Harwood, Jr. historian, educator

Greensboro
Bardolph, Richard historian, educator
Chappell, Fred Davis English language educator, poet
Penninger, Frieda Elaine retired English language educator
Thompson, James Howard historian, library administrator

Hendersonville
Schwarz, Richard William historian, educator

Pittsboro
Abrahamson, James Leonard history educator

Pope AFB
Conley, Raymond Leslie English language educator

Raleigh
Jones, Frederick Claudius English language and linguistics educator

Research Triangle Park
Connor, Walter Robert classics educator, humanities center administrator

West End
Moncure, James Ashby historian

Winston Salem
Alderson, William Thomas historian, consultant
Barnett, Richard Chambers historian, educator
Covey, Cyclone history educator
Helm, Robert Meredith philosophy educator
Hendricks, J(ames) Edwin historian, educator, consultant, author
Scales, James Ralph history educator, former university president
Shapere, Dudley philosophy educator

NORTH DAKOTA

Bismarck
Newborg, Gerald Gordon historical agency administrator

OHIO

Akron
Bryant, Keith Lynn, Jr. history educator
Jones, Robert Huhn history educator
Knepper, George W. history educator
Phillipson, John Samuel retired English educator

Athens
Borchert, Donald Marvin philosopher, educator
Crowl, Samuel Renninger English language educator, author
Eckes, Alfred Edward, Jr. historian, international trade analyst
Gaddis, John Lewis history educator
Gustavson, Carl Gustav historian, educator
Hamby, Alonzo Lee historian, educator
Matthews, Jack (John Harold Matthews) English educator, writer
Schneider, Duane Bernard English literature educator, publisher
Whealey, Lois Deimel humanities scholar

Berea
Blumer, Frederick Elwin philosophy educator

Bowling Green
Browne, Ray Broadus popular culture educator
Lavezzi, John Charles art history educator, archaeologist
Weaver, Richard L., II speech communication educator

Chagrin Falls
Rawski, Conrad H(enry) humanities educator, medievalist

Cincinnati
Bleznick, Donald William Romance languages educator
Ciani, Alfred Joseph language professional, dean
Glenn, Jerry Hosmer, Jr. foreign language educator
Huvos, Kornel linguistics educator
Laux, James Michael historian, educator
Lewis, Gene Dale historian, educator
Marcus, Jacob Rader history educator
Mitchell, Otis Clinton, Jr. history educator
Muntz, Ernest Gordon historian, educator
Peck, Abraham Joseph historian
Peterson, Gale Eugene historian
Schrier, Arnold historian, educator

Cleveland
Anderson, David Gaskill, Jr. Spanish language educator
Benseler, David Price foreign language educator
Buchanan, D(aniel) Harvey art history educator
Ferguson, Suzanne Carol English educator
Friedman, Barton Robert English educator
Gibson, Walter Samuel humanities educator
Greppin, John Aird Coutts philologist, editor, educator
Harper, Williard Flemmett language educator
Heald, Morrell humanities educator
Milic, Louis Tonko English educator
Miller, Genevieve retired medical historian
Olszewski, Edward John art history educator
Pursell, Carroll Wirth history educator
Reeves, Charles Howell classics educator
Roth, Jack Joseph historian, educator
Runyan, Timothy Jack historian, educator
Salomon, Roger Blaine English language educator
Strauss, Walter Adolf foreign languages educator
Trawick, Leonard Moses English educator

Weinberg, Helen Arnstein *American art and literature educator*

Columbus
Babcock, Charles Luther *classics educator*
Battersby, James Lyons, Jr. *English language educator*
Beja, Morris *English literature educator*
Boh, Ivan *philosophy educator*
Brooks, Keith *retired speech communication educator*
Burnham, John Chynoweth *historian, educator*
Dillon, Merton Lynn *historian, educator*
Gribble, Charles Edward *Slavic languages educator, editor*
Hahm, David Edgar *classics educator*
Hare, Robert Yates *music history educator*
Hinshaw, Virgil Goodman, Jr. *philosopher, emeritus educator*
Hoffmann, Charles Wesley *retired foreign language educator*
Jarvis, Gilbert Andrew *humanities educator*
Kuhn, Albert Joseph *English educator*
Lehiste, Ilse *language educator*
Roche, Mark William *German language educator*
Rule, John Corwin *history educator*
Scanlan, James Patrick *philosophy and Slavic studies educator*
Silbajoris, Frank Rimvydas *Slavic languages educator*

Dayton
Alexander, Roberta Sue *history educator*
Harden, Oleta Elizabeth *English educator, university administrator*
Schwartz, Irving Lloyd *retired history educator*

Gambier
Sharp, Ronald Alan *English literature educator, author*

Kent
Beer, Barrett Lynn *historian, educator*
Byrne, Frank Loyola *history educator*
Dante, Harris Loy *history educator*
Harkness, Bruce *English language educator*
Hassler, Donald Mackey, II *English language educator, writer*
James, Patricia Ann *philosophy educator*
†Reid, Sidney Webb *English educator*
Zornow, William Frank *historian, educator*

Kirtland
Skerry, Philip John *English educator*

Marietta
Murdock, Eugene Converse *retired history educator*
Wilbanks, Jan Joseph *philosopher*

Niles
Darlington, Oscar Gilpin *historian, educator*

Oberlin
Blodgett, Geoffrey Thomas *history educator*
Care, Norman Sydney *philosophy educator*
Colish, Marcia Lillian *history educator*
Greenberg, Nathan Abraham *classics educator*
Helm, James Joel *classicist, educator*
Long, Herbert Strainge *classics educator*
Peterson, Carl Adrian *English language educator*
Pierce, Robert Bell *English educator*
Soucy, Robert Joseph *history educator*
Spear, Richard Edmund *art history educator*
Young, David Pollock *humanities educator, author*

Oxford
Pratt, William Crouch, Jr. *English language educator*
Throne, Marilyn Elizabeth *English educator*
Winkler, Allan Michael *history educator*

Parma
Spencer, James Calvin, Sr. *humanities educator*

Tiffin
Davison, Kenneth Edwin *American studies educator*
Kramer, Frank Raymond *classicist, educator*

Toledo
Smith, Robert Freeman *history educator*
Thompson, Gerald E. *historian, educator*

Yellow Springs
Fogarty, Robert Stephen *historian, educator, editor*

Youngstown
Bell, Carol Willsey *genealogist*
Bowers, Bege K. *English educator*
Brothers, Barbara *English language educator*

OKLAHOMA

Bethany
Davis, Harrison Ransom Samuel, Jr. *English language educator*

Chickasha
Feaver, John Clayton *philosopher, educator*

Goodwell
Smith, Kim Lee *educator*

Norman
Brown, Sidney DeVere *history educator*
Glad, Paul Wilbur *history educator*
Hagan, William Thomas *history educator*
Hollon, William Eugene *historian, educator, author*
Kadir, Djelal *literature educator, writer, translator, editor*
Lowitt, Richard *history educator*

Oklahoma City
Booth, Glenna Greene *genealogical researcher*

Stillwater
Agnew, Theodore Lee, Jr. *historian, educator*
Fischer, LeRoy Henry *historian, educator*
Luebke, Neil Robert *philosophy educator*

Tulsa
Buckley, Thomas Hugh *historian, educator*
O'Brien, Darcy *English educator, writer*

OREGON

Ashland
Bornet, Vaughn Davis *former history and social science educator, research historian*
Levy, Leonard Williams *history educator, author*

Eugene
Birn, Raymond Francis *historian, educator*
Donnelly, Marian Card *art historian, educator*
Pascal, C(ecil) Bennett *classics educator*
Rendall, Steven Finlay *language educator, editor, translator, critic*
Wickes, George *English educator, writer*

Mcminnville
Mc Kaughan, Howard Paul *linguistics educator*

North Bend
Shepard, Robert Carlton *English language educator*

Port Orford
Drinnon, Richard *history educator*

Portland
Englert, Walter George *classics and humanities educator*
Gerow, Edwin Mahaffey *Indic culture educator*
Kinzer, Donald Louis *retired historian, educator*
Knapp, Robert Stanley *English language educator*
Porter, Roger Jeffrey *literature educator*
Steinman, Lisa Malinowski *English literature educator, writer*
Vaughan, Thomas James Gregory *historian*

Salem
Trueblood, Paul Graham *retired English educator, author, editor*

PENNSYLVANIA

Allentown
Kipa, Albert Alexander *foreign language and literature educator*

Ambler
Lengyel, Alfonz *art history, archeology and museology educator*

Ardmore
Gutwirth, Marcel Marc *French literature educator*

Bethlehem
Beidler, Peter Grant *English educator*
Dowling, Joseph Albert *historian, educator*
Gaertner, Johannes Alexander *retired art history educator, author*
Greene, David Mason *retired English language educator*
Haynes, Thomas Morris *philosophy educator*
Lindgren, John Ralph *philosophy educator*
Smolansky, Oles M. *humanities educator*

Bryn Mawr
Bernstein, Carol Lippit *humanities educator*
Brand, Charles Macy *history educator*
Dorian, Nancy Currier *linguistics educator*
Dudden, Arthur Power *historian, educator*
Gaisser, Julia Haig *classics educator*
Hamilton, Richard *Greek language educator*
King, Willard Fahrenkamp (Mrs. Edmund Ludwig King) *Spanish language educator*
Krausz, Michael *philosopher, educator*
Lane, Barbara Miller (Barbara Miller-Lane) *humanities educator*
†Lang, Mabel Louise *classics educator*
Salmon, John Hearsey McMillan *historian, educator*
Stapleton, Katharine Laurence *English educator, writer*

Carlisle
Fox, Arturo Angel *Spanish language educator*
Schiffman, Joseph Harris *literary historian, educator*
†Shrader, Charles Reginald *historian*

Chambersburg
Gelbach, Martha Harvey *genealogist*

East Stroudsburg
Crackel, Theodore Joseph *historian*

Easton
Cooke, Jacob Ernest *history educator, author*

Edinboro
Fleischauer, John Frederick *English language educator, academic administrator*

Elkins Park
Davidson, Abraham A. *art historian, photographer*

Gettysburg
Boritt, Gábor Szappanos *history educator*

Grantham
Sider, E(arl) Morris *English, history educator, archivist*

Haverford
Jorden, Eleanor Harz *linguist, educator*
Spielman, John Philip, Jr. *historian, educator*
Young-Bruehl, Elisabeth *philosophy educator*

Kennett Square
Bronner, Edwin Blaine *history educator*

Lancaster
Joseph, John *history educator*

Lewisburg
Edgerton, Mills Fox, Jr. *foreign language educator*
Payne, Michael David *English language educator*

Meadville
Hogan, James Charles *classicist, educator*
Katope, Christopher George *English language educator*

Millersville
Miller, Steven Max *humanities educator*

Milton
Lu, David John *history educator, writer*

Mont Alto
Russo, Peggy Anne *English language educator*

Narberth
Wagner, Frederick Balthas, Jr. *historian, retired surgery educator*

Newtown
Bohning, Elizabeth Edrop *foreign language educator*
Palmer, Robert Roswell *historian, educator*

Oreland
Smith, Gordon Ross *retired English language educator*

Philadelphia
Alter, Jean Victor *French language educator*
Auerbach, Nina Joan *English language educator*
Bell, Whitfield Jenks, Jr. *historian*
Benson, Morton *Slavic languages educator, lexicographer*
Burke, Daniel William *retired college president, English educator*
Caplan, Arthur L. *philosophy educator*
Cohen, Hennig *English educator*
Curran, Stuart Alan *English language educator*
Daemmrich, Horst Sigmund *German language and literature educator*
Davis, Allen Freeman *history educator, author*
DeLaura, David Joseph *English language educator*
Filreis, Alan *English language educator*
Graham, Alexander John *classics educator*
†Hershberg, Theodore *public policy and history educator*
Heuser, Frederick J. *historian*
Hoenigswald, Henry Max *linguist, educator*
Hoffman, Daniel (Gerard) *literature educator, poet*
Hurst, George Cameron, III *history educator*
Keto, C. Tsehloane *historian*
Knauer, Georg Nicolaus *classical philologist*
Lee, Charles *retired English language and literature educator, arts critic*
Lewin, Moshe *historian, educator*
Lloyd, Albert Lawrence, Jr. *German language educator*
Lucid, Robert Francis *English educator*
Ludden, David *Asian studies educator*
McDougall, Walter Allan *history educator*
Means, John Barkley *foreign language educator, association executive*
Murphey, Murray Griffin *history educator*
Peters, Edward Murray *history educator*
Prince, Gerald Joseph *Romance languages educator*
Quann, Joan Louise *English language educator, real estate broker*
Regan, Robert Charles *English language educator*
Richetti, John Joseph *English educator, writer, editor*
Rocher, Ludo *humanities educator*
Rosenberg, Charles Ernest *historian, educator*
Rosenberg, David Alan *military historian, educator*
Ross, James Francis *philosophy educator*
Schiffman, Harold Fosdick *Asian language educator*
Sebold, Russell Perry, III *Romance languages educator, author*
Sivin, Nathan *historian, educator*
Weigley, Russell Frank *history educator*

Phoenixville
Lukacs, John Adalbert *historian, retired educator*

Pittsburgh
Anthony, Edward Mason *linguistics educator*
Belnap, Nuel Dinsmore, Jr. *philosophy educator*
Buchanan, James Junkin *classics educator*
Clack, Jerry *classics educator*
Drescher, Seymour *history educator, writer*
Evans, David Andreoff *linguistics and computer science educator*
Ferguson, Mary Anne Heyward *language professional, educator*
Gale, Robert Lee *retired American literature educator and critic*
Gordon, Gerd Stray *retired historian, educator, writer*
Grunbaum, Adolf *philosophy educator, author*
Harris, Ann Birgitta Sutherland *art historian*
Hayes, Ann Louise *English educator, consultant, poet*
Hsu, Cho-yun *history educator*
Kearney, Hugh Francis *historian, educator*
Massey, Gerald J. *philosophy educator*
Miller, David William *historian, educator*
Modell, John *historian, educator*
Morice, Joseph Richard *history educator*
Paulston, Christina Bratt *linguistics educator*
Rawski, Evelyn Sakakida *history educator*
Rescher, Nicholas *philosophy educator*
Rimer, John Thomas *foreign language educator, academic administrator, writer, translator*
Seligson, Mitchell A. *Latin American studies educator*
Sheon, Aaron *art historian, educator*
Stearns, Peter Nathaniel *history educator*
Tarr, Joel Arthur *history and public policy educator*
Toker, Franklin K. *art history educator, archaeologist, foundation executive*
Udler, Rubin Jakovlevitch *linguist*
Weingartner, Rudolph Herbert *philosophy educator*

Pottstown
Ruth, Thomas Griswold *history educator*

Reading
Kevelson, Roberta *philosopher, educator*
Shirk, Annadora Vesper *English educator*

Spring Grove
Curtin, Philip De Armond *history educator*

Springtown
Hunt, John Wesley *English language educator*

State College
Asbell, Bernard *English language educator, author*
Johnstone, Henry Webb, Jr. *philosophy educator*
Kockelmans, Joseph J. *philosopher, educator*
Robinett, Betty Wallace *linguist*
Scott, Charles Edward *philosophy educator*

Swarthmore
Bannister, Robert Corwin, Jr. *history educator*
Beeman, Richard Roy *historian*
Blackburn, Thomas Harold *English language professional, educator*
Hungerford, Constance Cain *art educator*
Lacey, Hugh Matthew *philosophy educator*
Morgan, Kathryn Lawson *historian, educator*
North, Helen Florence *classicist, educator*
Ostwald, Martin *classics educator emeritus*
Pagliaro, Harold Emil *English language educator*
Rose, Gilbert Paul *classics educator*
Weinstein, Philip Meyer *English educator, literary critic*
Wright, Harrison Morris *historian, educator*

University Park
Ameringer, Charles D. *history educator*
Anderson, John Mueller *retired philosophy educator*
Brault, Gerard Joseph *French language educator*
De Armas, Frederick Alfred *foreign language educator*
Frank, Robert Worth, Jr. *English language educator*
Goldschmidt, Arthur Eduard, Jr. *historian, educator*
†Hager, Hellmut Wilhelm *art history educator*
Lima, Robert *Hispanic studies and comparative literature educator*
Schmalstieg, William Riegel *Slavic languages educator*
Weintraub, Stanley *arts and humanities educator, author*
Woodbridge, Linda *English language educator*

Villanova
Alter, Maria Pospischil *language educator*
Bergquist, James Manning *history educator*
Caputo, John David *philosophy educator*
Helmetag, Charles Hugh *foreign language educator*
Hunt, John Mortimer, Jr. *classical studies educator*
Kelley, Donald Brooks *historian, educator*
McDiarmid, Lucy *English educator, author*
Radan, George Tivadar *art history and archaeology educator*
Rudhart, Alexander H. *modern European history educator*
Thomas, Deborah Allen *English educator*

Wayne
Frye, Roland Mushat *literary historian, theologian*

West Chester
†Gougher, Ronald Lee *language educator and administrator*
Hipple, Walter John *English language educator*

Wynnewood
Kruger, Arthur Newman *speech communication educator, author*

RHODE ISLAND

Kingston
Gitlitz, David Martin *Hispanic studies educator*
Kim, Yong Choon *philosopher, theologian, educator*
MacLaine, Allan Hugh *English language educator*
Schwegler, Robert Andrew *English language educator*

Newport
Brennan, Joseph Gerard *philosophy educator*
Gleiman, Lubomir *philosophy educator*

Providence
Ackerman, Felicia *philosophy educator, writer*
Arant, Patricia *Slavic languages and literature educator*
Berghahn, Volker Rolf *history educator*
Blasing, Mutlu Konuk *English language educator*
Blumstein, Sheila Ellen *linguistics educator*
Boegehold, Alan Lindley *classics educator*
Bossy, Michel-Andre R. *comparative literature educator*
Carreño, Antonio *humanities educator*
Cook, Albert Spaulding *comparative literature and classics educator, writer*
Donovan, Bruce Elliot *classics educator, university dean*
Enteman, Willard Finley *philosophy educator*
Fiering, Norman (Sanford) *historian, library administrator*
Fornara, Charles William *historian, classicist, educator*
Gleason, Abbott *history educator*
Honig, Edwin *comparative literature educator, poet*
Jordy, William Henry *art history educator*
Kim, Jaegwon *philosophy educator*
Landow, George Paul *English literature and art educator, writer*
Lesko, Leonard Henry *Egyptologist, educator*
Molho, Anthony *history educator*
Monteiro, George *English educator, writer*
Neu, Charles Eric *historian, educator*
Pingree, David Edwin *ancient languages educator*
Putnam, Michael Courtney Jenkins *classics educator*
Ribbans, Geoffrey Wilfrid *Spanish educator*
Rohr, Donald Gerard *history educator*
Rosenberg, Bruce Alan *English language educator, author*
Saint-Amand, Pierre Nemours *humanities educator*
Schmitt, Richard *philosopher, educator*
Scholes, Robert Edward *English language educator*
Schulz, Juergen *art history educator*
Skidmore, Thomas Elliott *history educator*
Sosa, Ernest *philosopher, educator*
Spilka, Mark *English educator*
Terras, Victor *Slavic languages and comparative literature educator*
Thomas, John Lovell *history educator*
Trueblood, Alan Stubbs *former modern language educator*
Waldrop, Bernard Keith *English educator*
Williams, Lea Everard *history educator*

Wood, Gordon Stewart historian, educator
Wrenn, James Joseph East Asian studies educator

Smithfield
Haas, William Paul humanities educator, former college president

SOUTH CAROLINA

Charleston
Anderson, Charles Roberts English language educator
Pincus, Michael Stern language educator

Clemson
Calhoun, Richard James English language educator
Riley, Helene Maria Kastinger Germanist
Underwood, Richard Allan English language educator

Columbia
Belasco, Simon French language and linguistics educator
Bruccoli, Matthew Joseph English educator, publisher
Edgar, Walter Bellingrath historian
Geckle, George Leo, III English language educator
Hardin, James Neal German and comparative literature educator, publisher
Hatch, Mary Gies German language educator
Howard-Hill, Trevor Howard English language educator
Johnson, Herbert Alan history and law educator, lawyer, chaplain
Long, Eugene Thomas, III philosophy educator, administrator
†Meriwether, James Babcock English language educator
Myerson, Joel Arthur English language educator, researcher
Nolte, William Henry English language educator
Reeves, George McMillan, Jr. comparative literature educator, educational administrator
Sproat, John Gerald historian
Synnott, Marcia Graham history educator
Weir, Robert McColloch history educator

Conway
Talbert, Roy, Jr. history educator

Darlington
Holt, Robert LeRoi philosophy educator

Greenville
Crabtree, John Henry, Jr. retired English educator

Hilton Head Island
Male, Roy Raymond English language educator

Mullins
Stonesifer, Richard James retired humanities and social science educator

Rock Hill
Viault, Birdsall Scrymser history educator

Spartanburg
Lindsay, Bryan Eugene humanities educator, musician, writer

West Columbia
Ochs, Robert David history educator
Parker, Harold Talbot history educator

SOUTH DAKOTA

Sioux Falls
Carlson, Marilyn A. English language educator
Huseboe, Arthur Robert English language educator

Vermillion
†Froberg, Brent Malcolm classics educator
Milton, John Ronald English language educator, author

TENNESSEE

Clarksville
Lester, James Dudley classicist, educator

Columbia
Curry, Beatrice Chesrown English educator

Jefferson City
Baumgardner, James Lewis history educator

Johnson City
Greninger, Edwin Thomas history educator
Schneider, Valerie Lois speech educator
Wyatt, Doris Fay Chapman English language educator
Zayas-Bazan, Eduardo foreign language educator

Kingsport
Wolfe, Margaret Ripley historian, educator, consultant

Knoxville
Brady, Patrick Stephen French literature educator
Cutler, Everette Wayne history educator
Fisher, John Hurt English language educator
Moser, Harold Dean historian
Trahern, Joseph Baxter, Jr. humanities educator

Memphis
Copper, John Franklin Asian studies educator, consultant
Jolly, William Thomas foreign language educator
O'Donnell, William Hugh English educator
Stagg, Louis Charles English language and literature educator

Murfreesboro
Huhta, James Kenneth historian, university administrator, educator, consultant

Nashville
Boorman, Howard Lyon history educator
†Collier, Simon history educator
Compton, John Joseph philosophy educator
Conkin, Paul Keith history educator
Cook, Ann Jennalie English language educator
Crispin, John foreign language educator
Doody, Margaret Anne English educator
Doyle, Don Harrison history educator
Girgus, Sam B. English literature educator
Graham, Hugh Davis history educator
Grantham, Dewey Wesley historian, educator
Halperin, John William English literature educator
Harris, Alice Carmichael linguist
Hassel, Rudolph Christopher English language educator
Lachs, John philosopher, educator
Perry, Lewis Curtis historian, educator
Pichois, Claude P. classical studies educator
Smith, Samuel Boyd history educator
Stumpf, Samuel Enoch philosophy educator
Tichi, Cecelia English language educator
Voegeli, Victor Jacque history educator, dean
von Raffler-Engel, Walburga linguist, lecturer, writer

Sewanee
Spears, Monroe Kirk English educator, author
Williamson, Samuel Ruthven, Jr. historian, university administrator

TEXAS

Austin
Bordie, John George linguistics educator
†Boyd, Carolyn Patricia history educator
Boyer, Mildred Vinson retired foreign language educator
Braybrooke, David philosopher, educator
Brown, Norman Donald history educator
Carleton, Don Edward history center administrator, educator, writer
Causey, Robert Louis philosopher, educator, consultant
Cline, Clarence Lee language professional
Crosby, Alfred Worcester history educator
Divine, Robert Alexander history educator
Farrell, Edmund James English language educator, author
Friedman, Alan Warren humanities educator
Galinsky, Gotthard Karl classicist, educator
Gould, Lewis Ludlow historian
Green, Peter Morris classics educator, writer, translator
Hancock, Ian Francis (O Yanko le Redžosko) linguistics educator
Harms, Robert Thomas linguist, educator
Hartshorne, Charles philosopher, retired educator
Hinojosa-Smith, Roland English language educator, writer
Hopper, Robert William speech communication educator
Jazayery, Mohammad Ali foreign languages and literature educator emeritus
Katz, Michael Ray Slavic languages educator
King, Robert D. linguistics educator, university dean
Lehmann, Ruth Preston Miller literature educator
Lehmann, Winfred Philipp linguistics educator
López-Morillas, Juan Spanish and comparative literature educator
Louis, William Roger historian, educator, editor
Mackey, Louis Henry philosophy educator
Meacham, Standish historian, educator
Megaw, Robert Neill Ellison English educator
Middleton, Christopher Germanic languages and literature educator
Mourelatos, Alexander Phoebus Dionysiou humanities educator
Palaima, Thomas Gerard classics educator, researcher
Paredes, Americo English language educator
Phillips, Frances Marie history educator
Polomé, Edgar Charles foreign language educator
Rich, John Martin humanities educator, researcher
Seung, Thomas Kaehao philosophy educator
Staley, Thomas Fabian language professional, academic administrator
Sutherland, William Owen Sheppard English language educator
Todd, William Burton English language and literature educator
Tyler, Ronnie Curtis historian
Velz, John William literature educator
Wadlington, Warwick Paul English language educator
Werbow, Stanley Newman language educator
Whitbread, Thomas Bacon English educator, author
Wilson, Robert Henry English educator

Burleson
Robin, Clara Nell (Claire Robin) English language educator

College Station
Berthold, Dennis Alfred English language educator
Cannon, Garland English language educator
Davenport, Manuel Manson philosophy educator
Dethloff, Henry Clay history educator
Fedorchik, Bette Joy Winter foreign language professional
Knobel, Dale Thomas history educator, university administrator
Mc Dermott, John Joseph philosophy educator
Nance, Joseph Milton history educator
Unterberger, Betty Miller history educator, writer
Wright, Nancy Jane English language educator

Columbus
Hamilton, T. Earle retired educator, honor society executive

Commerce
Grimshaw, James Albert, Jr. English language educator
Tuerk, Richard Carl English language educator

Corpus Christi
Wooster, Robert history educator

Dallas
Caldwell, Louise Phinney historical researcher, community volunteer
Comini, Alessandra art historian, educator
Countryman, Edward Francis historian, educator
Crain, John Walter historian
Hunter, Robert Grams English language educator
Jones, James Fleming, Jr. Romance language educator, university administrator
Pike, Kenneth Lee linguist, educator
Robbins, Frank Ernest linguistics educator, administrator
Terry, Marshall Northway, Jr. English language educator, author

Denton
Clogan, Paul Maurice English language and literature educator
Kamman, William historian, educator
Kesterson, David Bert English language educator
Nichols, Irby Coghill, Jr. historian, educator, entrepreneur
Preston, Thomas Ronald English language educator, researcher
Snapp, Harry Franklin historian
Vaughn, William Preston historian, educator

Edinburg
Vassberg, David Erland history educator

El Paso
Bailey, Kenneth Kyle history educator
Leach, Joseph Lee English language educator, author
Ornstein-Galicia, Jacob Leonard (Jack Ornstein-Galicia) foreign language educator, linguist, author

Fort Worth
Erisman, Fred Raymond English literature educator
McWhiney, Grady history educator
Reuter, Frank Theodore history educator
Wertz, Spencer K. philosophy educator
Worcester, Donald Emmet history educator, author

Georgetown
Browning, Grayson Douglas philosophy educator

Houston
Boles, John Bruce history educator
Bonnet, Beatriz Alicia interpreter, translator, flutist
Carrington, Samuel Macon, Jr. French language educator
Castañeda, James Agustín Spanish language educator, university golf coach
Crowell, Steven Galt philosophy educator
Decker, Hannah Shulman history educator
de Kanter, Ellen Ann English language professional, educator
Doughtie, Edward Orth English language educator
Folk, Katherine Pinkston English language educator, writer, journalist
Grandy, Richard E. philosophy educator
Gruber, Ira Dempsey historian, educator
Haskell, Thomas Langdon history educator
Huston, John Dennis English educator
Hyman, Harold M. history educator, consultant
Lamb, Sydney MacDonald linguistics and cognitive science educator
Martin, James Kirby historian, educator
Matusow, Allen Joseph history educator, academic administrator
Minter, David Lee English literature educator
Odhiambo, Atieno E. S. history educator, researcher
Patten, Robert Lowry English language educator
Pryor, William Daniel Lee humanities educator
Quillen, Carol E. historian, educator
Russman, Thomas Anthony philosophy educator
Smith, Richard Joseph history educator
Stokes, Gale history educator
Temkin, Larry Scott philosopher, educator
Thompson, Ewa M. foreign language educator
Urbina, Manuel, II legal research historian, history educator
Vallbona, Rima-Gretel Rothe Spanish language educator, writer
Wiener, Martin Joel historian
Wyschogrod, Edith philosophy educator
Young, William John French language educator, retired university president

Huntsville
Gutermuth, Mary Elizabeth foreign language educator

Irving
Sommerfeldt, John Robert historian

Kerrville
Lich, Glen Ernst regional studies educator, ethnographer, government official, writer

Lubbock
Connor, Seymour Vaughan historian, writer
Eddleman, Floyd Eugene retired English language educator
Kelsey, Clyde Eastman, Jr. philosophy and psychology educator
Ketner, Kenneth Laine philosopher, educator
Pearce, William Martin history educator
Walker, Warren Stanley English educator

Nacogdoches
Kallsen, Theodore John retired English language educator

Prairie View
Boyd-Brown, Lena Ernestine history educator, education consultant
Coe, Elizabeth Beaubien English language educator

Richardson
Redman, Timothy Paul English language educator, author, chess federation administrator

San Angelo
Torres, David Spanish language educator

San Antonio
Kellman, Steven G. literature educator, author
Schulte, Josephine Helen historian, educator

Seguin
Moline, Jon Nelson philosopher, educator, college president

Silsbee
White, Helen Frances Pearson language educator, real estate broker

Stephenville
Christopher, Joe Randell English language educator

Tyler
Gajda, Patricia Ann history educator

Waco
Baird, Robert Malcolm philosophy educator, researcher
Barcus, James Edgar English literature educator
Campbell, Stanley Wallace history educator
Collmer, Robert George English language educator
Cutter, Charles Richard, III retired classics educator
Goode, Clement Tyson English language educator
Herring, Jack William English language educator

UTAH

Logan
Ellsworth, Samuel George historian, educator
Milner, Clyde A., II historian

Provo
Alexander, Thomas Glen history educator
Arrington, Leonard James history educator
Clark, Bruce Budge humanities educator
Forster, Merlin Henry foreign languages educator, author, researcher
Lyon, James Karl German language educator
Peer, Larry Howard literature educator

Salt Lake City
Bremer, Ronald Allan geneologist, historian
Eakle, Arlene H. genealogist
Flanagan, John Theodore language professional, educator
Madsen, Brigham Dwaine history educator
Mayfield, David Merkley genealogy director
Mc Murrin, Sterling Moss philosophy educator
Olpin, Robert Spencer art history educator
Sillars, Malcolm Osgood communications educator
Steensma, Robert Charles English language educator

VERMONT

Bennington
Kaplan, Harold humanities educator, author

Burlington
Daniels, Robert Vincent history educator, former state senator
Hall, Robert William philosophy and religion educator
Scrase, David Anthony German language educator
Weiger, John George foreign language educator

East Calais
Meiklejohn, Donald philosophy educator

Manchester
Wilbur, James Benjamin, III philosopher, educator

Middlebury
Clifford, Nicholas Rowland history educator, college administrator
Jacobs, Travis Beal historian, educator
Lamberti, Marjorie history educator
†Pack, Robert M. American literature educator, poet
Vail, Van Horn German language educator

North Bennington
Kimpel, Benjamin Franklin philosophy educator emeritus, writer

South Londonderry
Schapiro, Meyer retired art history educator

VIRGINIA

Alexandria
Byrne, John Edward writer, retired government official
Myers, Denys Peter, Jr. architectural historian
White, Gordon Eliot historian

Ashland
Inge, Milton Thomas American literature and culture educator, author

Blacksburg
Baumgartner, Frederic Joseph history educator
Doswald, Herman Kenneth German language educator, academic administrator
Landen, Robert Geran historian, university administrator
Peacock, Markham Lovick, Jr. English educator
Pitt, Joseph Charles philosophy educator
Robertson, James Irvin, Jr. historian, educator
Ulloa, Justo Celso Spanish educator

Charlottesville
Abbot, William Wright history educator
Alden, Douglas William French language educator
Allinson, Gary Dean Japanese studies educator
Arnold, A. James foreign language educator
Barolsky, Paul art history educator
Battestin, Martin Carey English educator
Cano-Ballesta, Juan Spanish language educator
Cargile, James Thomas philosophy educator
Chase, Karen Susan English literature educator
Chastain, Kenneth Duane foreign language educator
Cherno, Melvin humanities educator
Cohen, Ralph English language educator
Colker, Marvin Leonard classics educator
Courtney, Edward classics educator
Denommé, Robert Thomas foreign language educator
Ferreira, M. Jamie (Mary Ann Ferreira) philosophy of religion educator
Forbes, John Douglas architectural and economic historian
Garrett, George Palmer, Jr. creative writing and English language educator, writer
Gianniny, Omer Allan, Jr. humanities educator
Gies, David Thatcher language educator
Graebner, Norman Arthur history educator
Havran, Martin Joseph historian, educator, author
Heath, Peter Lauchlan philosophy educator

Hirsch, Eric Donald, Jr. *English language educator, educational reformer*
Hopkins, P. Jeffrey *Asian studies educator, author, translator*
Huet, Marie-Hélène Jaqueline *foreign language educator*
Humphreys, Paul William *philosophy educator, consultant*
Kellogg, Robert Leland *English language educator*
Kett, Joseph Francis *historian, educator*
Kohler, Charlotte *language professional, educator*
Kolb, Harold Hutchison, Jr. *English language educator*
Kovacs, Paul David *classicist, educator*
Kraehe, Enno Edward *history educator*
Lane, Ann Judith *history and women's studies educator*
Lang, Cecil Yelverton *English language educator*
Langbaum, Robert Woodrow *English language educator, author*
Leffler, Melvyn P. *history educator*
Levenson, Jacob Clavner *English language educator*
Lyons, John David *French, Italian and comparative literature educator*
McGann, Jerome John *English language educator*
McGrady, Donald Lee *Spanish language educator*
Megill, Allan D. *historian, educator*
Midelfort, Hans Christian Erik *history educator*
Mikalson, Jon Dennis *classics educator*
Miller, Joseph Calder *history educator, historical consultant, editor*
Nelson, Raymond John *English literature educator, university dean, author*
Nohrnberg, James Carson *English language educator*
Orr, Gregory Simpson *English educator, poet*
Perkowski, Jan Louis *language and literature educator*
Peterson, Merrill Daniel *history educator*
Ray, Benjamin Caleb *African studies and religion educator*
Rorty, Richard McKay *philosophy educator*
Rubin, David Lee *French literature educator, critic, editor, publisher*
Schuker, Stephen Alan *historian*
Schutte, Anne Jacobson *historian, educator*
Sedgwick, Alexander *historian, educator*
Shackelford, George Green *historian*
Shannon, Edgar Finley, Jr. *English language educator*
Shaw, Donald Leslie *Spanish language educator*
Simmons, Alan John *philosophy educator*
Sokel, Walter H. *German language and literature educator*
Spacks, Patricia Meyer *English educator*
Spearing, Anthony Colin *English literature educator*
Stocker, Arthur Frederick *classics educator*
Summers, John David *art history educator*
Vaughan, Joseph Lee *language educator*
Wagoner, Jennings Lee, Jr. *history educator*
Westfall, Carroll William *architectural historian*
Wilken, Robert Louis *historian, theologian*
Zunz, Olivier Jean *history educator*

Fairfax
Bailey, Helen McShane *historian*
King, James Cecil *academician, medievalist, German educator*
Verheyen, Egon *art historian, educator*

Fort Lee
Sterling, Keir Brooks *historian, educator*

Fredericksburg
Dorman, John Frederick *genealogist*
Krick, Robert Kenneth *historian, writer*

Gloucester
Fang, Joong *mathematician, philosopher, educator*

Hampden Sydney
Arieti, James Alexander *classics educator, writer*
Bagby, George Franklin, Jr. *English language educator*
Jagasich, Paul Anthony *language educator, translator*

Lexington
Elrod, John William *philosophy and religion educator, academic administrator*
James, D(orris) Clayton *history educator*
Martin, Joseph Ramsey *philosophy educator*
McAhren, Robert Willard *history educator*
Pemberton, Harrison Joseph *educator, philosopher*
Ray, George Washington, III *English language educator*
Ryan, Halford Ross *speech educator*
Sessions, William Lad *philosophy educator, administrator*
Simpson, Pamela Hemenway *art historian, educator*

Mc Lean
Davis, William Columbus *history educator, writer, lecturer*
Topping, Peter *historian, educator*

Newport News
Morris, James Matthew *history educator*
Thomas, Dorothy Worthy *English educator*

Norfolk
Bazin, Nancy Topping *English language educator*
Dandridge, Rita Bernice *English language educator*
Greene, Douglas George *humanities educator, author, publisher*
Lucking, Robert A. *English literature educator*
Martin, Mary Coates *genealogist, writer*

Petersburg
†Calkins, Christopher Miles *historian*
Smith, Paul Edmund, Jr. *philosophy and religion educator*

Richmond
Alley, Robert Sutherland *humanities educator, author*
Gordon, John L., Jr. *historian, educator*
Gray, Clarence Jones *foreign language educator, dean emeritus*
Rilling, John Robert *history educator*
Shapiro, Gary Michael *philosophy educator*
Taylor, Welford Dunaway *English language educator*
Treadway, John David *history educator*
Urofsky, Melvin Irving *historian, educator*

Roanoke
Burnette, Ollen Lawrence, Jr. *historian*
Dillard, Richard Henry Wilde *English language professional, educator, author*

Sweet Briar
†Piepho, (Edward) Lee *humanities educator*

University Of Richmond
Hall, James H(errick), Jr. *philosophy educator, author*
Terry, Robert Meredith *French language educator*

Vienna
Dupuy, Trevor Nevitt *historian, research executive*

Williamsburg
Axtell, James Lewis *history educator*
Ball, Donald Lewis *retired English language educator*
Becker, Lawrence Carlyle *philosopher, educator, author*
Chappell, Miles Linwood, Jr. *art history educator*
Coyner, Martin Boyd, Jr. *history educator*
Crapol, Edward P. *history educator*
Esler, Anthony James *historian, novelist*
Gross, Robert Alan *history educator*
Harris, James Franklin *philosophy educator*
Maccubbin, Robert Purks *literature and culture educator*
McGiffert, Michael *history educator, editor*
McLane, Henry Earl, Jr. *philosophy educator*
Nettels, Elsa *English language educator*
Sheppard, Thomas Frederick *history educator*
Sherman, Richard Beatty *history educator*
Tate, Thaddeus W(ilbur), Jr. (Thad Tate) *history educator, historical institute executive, historian*
Wallach, Alan *art historian, educator*

WASHINGTON

Bellingham
Whisenhunt, Donald Wayne *history educator*

Enumclaw
Vernier, Richard *foreign language educator, author*

Federal Way
Boling, Joseph Edward *numismatist, retired military officer*

Langley
Legters, Lyman Howard *historian*

Olympia
Nesbit, Robert Carrington *historian*

Pullman
Bennett, Edward Moore *historian, educator*

Seattle
Adams, Hazard Simeon *English educator, author*
Behler, Diana Ipsen *Germanic language and literature educator*
Behler, Ernst Heitmar *comparative literature educator*
Boba, Imre *history educator*
Bosmajian, Haig Aram *speech communication educator*
Brandauer, Frederick Paul *Asian language educator*
Burgess, Charles Orville *history educator*
Butow, Robert Joseph Charles *history educator*
Carlsen, James Caldwell *musicologist, educator*
Coburn, Robert Craig *philosopher*
Coldewey, John Christopher *English literature educator*
Dunn, Richard John *English language educator*
Ellison, Herbert Jay *history educator*
Gerstenberger, Donna Lorine *humanities educator*
Harmon, Daniel Patrick *classics educator*
Heer, Nicholas Lawson *Arabist-Islamist educator*
Jones, Edward Louis *historian, educator*
Keyt, David *philosophy and classics educator*
Kirkendall, Richard Stewart *historian, educator*
Knechtges, David Richard *Chinese and East Asian studies educator*
Korg, Jacob *English literature educator*
Matchett, William H(enry) *English literature educator*
Newmeyer, Frederick Jaret *linguist, educator*
†Nostrand, Howard Lee *language and literature educator*
Odegaard, Charles Edwin *history educator*
Potter, Karl Harrington *philosophy educator*
Pressly, Thomas James *history educator*
Pyle, Kenneth Birger *historian, educator*
Scheidel, Thomas Maynard *speech communication educator*
Sugar, Peter Frigyes *historian*
Webb, Eugene *English language educator*
Ziadeh, Farhat J. *Middle Eastern studies educator*

Spokane
†Carriker, Robert Charles *history educator*
Kossel, Clifford George *retired philosophy educator, clergyman*

Tacoma
†Browning, Christopher R. *historian, educator*

Walla Walla
Edwards, Glenn Thomas *history educator*

Yakima
Meshke, George Lewis *drama and humanities educator*

WEST VIRGINIA

Huntington
McKernan, John Joseph *English language educator*

Institute
Brown, Dallas Coverdale, Jr. *history educator, retired army officer*
Thorn, Arline Roush *English language educator*
Wohl, David *humanities educator, theatre director*

Morgantown
Blaydes, Sophia Boyatzies *English language educator*
Davis, Leonard McCutchan *speech educator*
Singer, Armand Edwards *foreign language educator*
Smith, Patricia K. *reading educator*

West Liberty
Hunter, John Alfred *English educator*

WISCONSIN

Appleton
Chaney, William Albert *historian, educator*
Goldgar, Bertrand Alvin *literary historian, educator*

Iola
Rulau, Russell *numismatist, consultant*

La Crosse
Rausch, Joan Mary *art historian*

Madison
Ammerman, Robert Ray *philosopher, educator*
Baeumer, Max Lorenz *literature historian*
Berg, William James *French language educator, writer, translator*
Bogue, Allan G. *history educator*
Brembeck, Winston Lamont *retired speech communication educator*
Cassidy, Frederic Gomes *humanities educator*
Chow, Tse-Tsung *foreign language and literature educator, author, poet*
Ciplijauskaite, Birute *humanities educator*
Cooper, John Milton, Jr. *history educator, author*
Cronon, E(dmund) David, Jr. *history educator, historian*
Cronon, William *history educator*
Dembo, Lawrence Sanford *English educator*
DeNovo, John August *history educator*
Fowler, Barbara Hughes *classics educator*
Frykenberg, Robert Eric *historian*
Hamalainen, Pekka Kalevi *historian, educator*
Hamerow, Theodore Stephen *history educator*
Hollingsworth, Joseph Rogers *history and sociology educator, writer*
Howe, Herbert Marshall *classics educator*
Ihde, Aaron John *history of science educator emeritus*
Kelly, Douglas *medieval and foreign literature educator*
Kingdon, Robert McCune *historian, educator*
Klein, Sheldon *computational linguist, educator*
Kleinhenz, Christopher *foreign language educator, researcher*
Knowles, Richard Alan John *English language educator*
Kutler, Stanley Ira *history and law educator, author*
MacKendrick, Paul Lachlan *classics educator*
Marks, Elaine *French language educator*
Mosse, George Lachmann *history educator, author*
O'Brien, James Aloysius *foreign language educator*
Perkins, Merle Lester *French language educator*
Powell, Barry Bruce *classicist*
Rideout, Walter Bates *English educator*
Rothstein, Eric *English educator*
Sewell, Richard Herbert *historian, educator*
Shaw, Joseph Thomas *Slavic languages educator*
Singer, Marcus George *philosopher, educator*
Spear, Thomas Turner *history educator*
Tedeschi, John Alfred *historian, librarian*
Vansina, Jan Maria Jozef *historian, educator*
Vowles, Richard Beckman *language educator, foreign language*
Weinbrot, Howard David *English educator*

Milwaukee
Bicha, Karel Denis *historian, educator*
Carozza, Davy Angelo *Italian language educator*
Dunleavy, Janet Frank Egleson *English language educator*
Dziewanowski, Marian Kamil *history educator*
Friedman, Melvin Jack *language professional, literature educator*
Gallop, Jane (Anne) *women's studies educator, writer*
Hachey, Thomas Eugene *British and Irish history educator, consultant*
Halloran, William Frank *English educator*
Hassan, Ihab Habib *English and comparative literature educator, author*
Horsman, Reginald *history educator*
Jaksic, Ivan A. *history educator*
McCanles, Michael Frederick *English language educator*
Olson, Frederick Irving *retired history educator*
Roeming, Robert Frederick *foreign language educator*
Schwartz, Joseph *English language educator*
Stromberg, Roland Nelson *historian*
Swanson, Roy Arthur *classicist, educator*

Oshkosh
Burr, John Roy *philosophy educator*

Ripon
Ashley, Robert Paul, Jr. *English literature educator*
Miller, George H. *historian, educator*
Northrop, Douglas Anthony *English educator, college official and dean*

River Falls
Smith, Clyde Curry *historian, educator*

Stevens Point
Paul, Justus Fredrick *historian, educator*

Superior
Feldman, Egal *historian, educator*

WYOMING

Laramie
Chisum, Emmett Dewain *historian, archeologist, researcher*
Gressley, Gene Maurice *history educator*
Hardy, Deborah Welles *history educator*
Nye, Eric William *English language educator*
Williams, Roger Lawrence *historian, educator*

TERRITORIES OF THE UNITED STATES

PUERTO RICO

San Juan
Ocasio-Melendez, Marcial Enrique *history educator*

CANADA

ALBERTA

Edmonton
Clements, Patricia Dawn *English educator, university dean*
McMaster, Juliet Sylvia *English language educator*
Prideaux, Gary Dean *linguistics educator*
Smith, Richard Carlisle *history educator*

BRITISH COLUMBIA

Burnaby
Buitenhuis, Peter Martinus *language professional, educator*
Kitchen, John Martin *historian, educator*

Gibsons
Millard, Peter Tudor *English language educator*

Vancouver
Aguzzi-Barbagli, Danilo Lorenzo *literature educator*
Batts, Michael Stanley *German language educator*
Bentley, Thomas Roy *literary educator, writer, consultant*
Conway, John S. *history educator*
Durrant, Geoffrey Hugh *retired English language educator*
Jordan, Robert Maynard *language and literature professional, educator*
Kubicek, Robert Vincent *history educator*
Overmyer, Daniel Lee *Asian studies educator*
Pacheco-Ransanz, Arsenio *Hispanic and Italian studies educator*
Pulleyblank, Edwin George *history educator emeritus, linguist*
Saint-Jacques, Bernard *linguistics educator*
Sikora, Richard Innes *philosophy educator*
Unger, Richard Watson *history educator*
White, Ruth Lillian *French language educator, researcher*

MANITOBA

Winnipeg
Kroetsch, Robert Paul *English language educator, author*
Wolfart, H. C. *linguistics scholar, author, editor*

NEW BRUNSWICK

Douglas
Cogswell, Frederick William *English language educator, poet, editor, publisher*

Fredericton
Elkhadem, Saad Eldin Amin *foreign language and literature educator, author, editor, publisher*
Kennedy, Richard Frederick *English language educator*

Saint John
Condon, Thomas Joseph *university historian*

NOVA SCOTIA

Halifax
Carrigan, David Owen *history educator*
Flint, John E. *historian, educator*
Gray, James *English literature educator*

Liscomb
Hemlow, Joyce *language and literature educator, author*

Wolfville
Zeman, Jarold Knox *history educator*

ONTARIO

Downsview
Thomas, Clara McCandless *retired English language educator, biographer*

Hamilton
Blewett, David Lambert *English literature educator*
Lee, Alvin A. *literary educator, scholar, author*
Mc Kay, Alexander Gordon *classics educator*

Kingston
Akenson, Donald Harman *historian, educator*
Dick, Susan Marie *English language educator*
Hamilton, Albert Charles *English language educator*
Mac Kenzie, Norman Hugh *retired English educator, writer*
Riley, Anthony William *German language and literature educator*

London
Collins, Thomas Joseph *English language educator*
Creighton, Douglas George *French language educator*
Gerber, Douglas Earl *classics educator*

Mississauga
Astington, John Harold *English educator*

Nepean
Kallmann, Helmut Max *music historian, retired music librarian*

North York
Adelman, Howard *philosophy educator*
†Coles, Don Langdon *English literature educator*
Granatstein, Jack Lawrence *history educator*

Ottawa
Dray, William Herbert *philosophy educator*
Hamelin, Marcel *historian, educator*
Staines, David McKenzie *English educator*

Peterborough
Symons, Thomas H. B. *historian, educator*

Rockwood
Eichner, Hans *German language and literature educator*

Thornbury
Keyes, Gordon Lincoln *history educator*

Toronto
Birnbaum, Eleazar *language professional*
Blissett, William Frank *English literature educator*
Bouissac, Paul Antoine *language professional*
Conacher, Desmond John *classics educator*
Dryer, Douglas Poole *retired philosophy educator*
Goffart, Walter André *history educator*
Graham, Victor Ernest *French language educator*
Grendler, Paul Frederick *history educator*
Johnson, Robert Eugene *historian, academic administrator*
McAuliffe, Jane Dammen *Middle Eastern and Islamic studies educator*
Millgate, Jane *language professional*
Millgate, Michael (Henry) *retired English educator*
Morey, Carl Reginald *musicologist, academic administrator*
Morgan, Peter F. *English educator, philosophy educator*
Redford, Donald Bruce *historian, archaeologist*
Saddlemyer, Ann (Eleanor Saddlemyer) *educator, critic, theater historian*
Schogt, Henry Gilius *foreign language educator*
Skvorecky, Josef Vaclav *English educator, novelist*
Webster, Jill Rosemary *historian, educator*
Wetzel, Heinz *foreign language educator*
Wevers, John William *retired Semitic languages educator*
Zemans, Joyce Pearl *art historian, arts administrator*

Waterloo
Cornell, Paul Grant *history educator*
Haworth, Lawrence Lindley *philosophy educator*
Suits, Bernard Herbert *philosophy educator*

PRINCE EDWARD ISLAND

Charlottetown
Baker, Ronald James *English language educator, university administrator*

QUEBEC

Montreal
Beugnot, Bernard Andre Henri *French literature educator*
Duquette, Jean-Pierre *French language and literature educator*
Hamel, Reginald *history educator*
Hoffmann, Peter Conrad Werner *history educator*
Kinsley, William Benton *literature educator*
Leblanc, Hugues *philosophy educator*
McLelland, Joseph Cumming *philosophy educator, former university dean*
Morin, Yves-Charles *linguistics educator, researcher*
Paikowsky, Sandra Roslyn *art historian*
Shea, William Rene *historian, philosopher of science, educator*
Silverthorne, Michael James *classics educator*
†Yates, Robin David Sebastian *Chinese history educator*

North Hatley
Jones, Douglas Gordon *retired literature educator*

Outremont
Domaradzki, Theodore Felix *Slavic studies educator, editor*

Quebec
†Letourneau, Jocelyn *history educator*
Porter, John Robert *art history educator, curator, writer*

Rock Forest
Lamirande, Emilien *historian, educator*

SASKATCHEWAN

Saskatoon
Brewster, Elizabeth Winifred *English language educator, poet, novelist*
Kent, Christopher Andrew *history educator*

MEXICO

Morelia
Warren, J. Benedict *retired history educator*

AUSTRALIA

Bundoora
Isaac, Rhys Llywelyn *historian, educator*

Sydney
Salsbury, Stephen Matthew *historian, educator*

AUSTRIA

Gaz
Weisstein, Ulrich Werner *English literature educator*

Salzburg
†Mueller, Ulrich *literature educator*

Vienna
Steinbruckner, Bruno Friedrich *foreign language educator*

ENGLAND

Coventry
Trigg, Roger Hugh *philosophy educator*

Eastbourne
Baylen, Joseph O. *retired history educator*

Hove
Kitchin, Laurence Tyson *liberal arts and drama educator, author*

Liverpool
Reilly, Thomas *humanities educator*

London
Blackbourn, David Gordon *history educator*
Martines, Lauro *historian, writer*
†Secord, James Andrew *researcher, educator*

Milford on Sea
Styan, John Louis *English literature and theater educator*

Oxford
Carey, John *English language educator, literary critic*
Howe, Daniel Walker *historian, educator*

FRANCE

Paris
Konvitz, Josef Wolf *history educator, international civil servant*
Ritcheson, Charles Ray *university administrator, history educator*

GERMANY

Munster
Spevack, Marvin *English educator*

Nuremberg
Doerries, Reinhard René *modern history educator*

Weimar
Little, William A. *foreign language educator, researcher*

ISRAEL

Jerusalem
Davis, Moshe *historian*

THE PHILIPPINES

Musuan
Lao, Mardonio Magadan *history educator, researcher, farmer*

SCOTLAND

Aberdeen
Jones, Robert Victor *physicist, natural philosophy educator*
Rousseau, George Sebastian *eighteenth century studies educator, chamber musician*

Cellardyke
Roff, William Robert *history educator, writer*

Saint Andrews
Lenman, Bruce Philip *historian, educator*

SPAIN

Barcelona
Jackson, Gabriel *historian*

TURKEY

Ankara
Inalcik, Halil *historian, educator*

ADDRESS UNPUBLISHED

Angell, Richard Bradshaw *philosophy educator*
Aptheker, Herbert *historian, lecturer*
Baxter, Stephen Bartow *retired history educator*
Bok, Sissela *philosopher, writer*
Bolsterli, Margaret Jones *English educator, farmer*
Bosse, Malcolm Joseph, Jr. *professional language educator, author*
Boyle, Richard John *art historian, author*
Brodnax, Margaret O'Bryan *retired English language educator*
Cachia, Pierre Jacques *Middle East languages and culture educator, researcher*
Chandler, Alfred Dupont, Jr. *historian, educator*
Chandra, Pramod *art history educator*
Chellas, Brian Farrell *philosophy educator*
Chinoy, Helen Krich *theater historian*
Clark, Thomas Lloyd *English linguistics educator*
Cobb, John Cecil, Jr. (Jack Cobb) *Latin America area specialist, communications specialist and executive*
Coffman, Stanley Knight, Jr. *English educator, former college president*
Condit, Doris Elizabeth *historian*
Culverwell, Albert Henry *historian*
Curry, Richard Orr *history educator and freelance writer*
Curti, Merle Eugene *historian, educator*
Edel, Abraham *philosophy educator*
Edmunds, (Arthur) Lowell *philology educator*
Fong, Wen Chih *art historian, educator, author*
Franklin, Joe Hope *historian, educator, author*
Furley, David John *classics educator*
Galbraith, John Semple *history educator*
Geiselhart, Lorene Annetta *English educator*
Gentry, Francis G. *German language educator*
Gilb, Corinne Lathrop *history educator*
Gillespie, Gerald Ernest Paul *comparative literature educator, writer*
Gordon, Cyrus Herzl *Orientalist, educator*
Greene, Elinore Aschah *speech and drama professional, writer*
Gromen, Richard John *historian, educator*
Hart, Arthur Alvin *historian, author*
Haskins, James *English language educator, writer*
Hawkes, John *humanities educator, author*
Heilbrun, Carolyn Gold *English literature educator*
Herbst, Jurgen *history and education educator*
Herington, Cecil John *classics educator*
Hetzron, Robert *linguist, educator*
Howard, Michael Eliot *historian, educator*
Huerta, Mary Zapata *English and foreign language educator*
Hughes, Thomas Parke *history educator*
Hutcheon, Linda Ann *English language educator*
Ivry, Alfred Lyon *foreign language and literature educator*
†Jacobs, William Jay *historian, writer*
†Jex, William Winkelman *humanities educator and administrator*
Johnson, Clifton Herman *historian, archivist, former research center director*
Jordan, William Bryan, Jr. *art historian*
Jourdain, Alice Marie *philosopher, retired educator*
Kalish, Donald *philosophy educator*
Kastor, Frank Sullivan *English language educator*
Kolko, Gabriel *historian, educator*
Korsgaard, Christine Marion *philosophy educator*
Kramer, Dale Vernon *English language educator*
Kwiat, Joseph J. *English educator, playwright*
Lawson Donadio, Carolina Anna *foreign language educator, translator*
Lederman, Marie Jean *English language educator*
Levack, Arthur Paul *history educator emeritus*
Lewis, Norman *English language educator, writer*
Link, Arthur Stanley *history educator, editor*
Link, Mae Mills (Mrs. S. Gordden Link) *space medicine historian and consultant*
Longsworth, Robert Morrow *English educator*
Loughran, James Newman *philosophy educator, former university president*
MacDonald, Robert Alan *language educator*
Maehl, William Harvey *historian, educator*
Maehl, William Henry *historian, university administrator, educational consultant*
Marshall, Richard *art historian, curator*
Masten, Jeffrey A. *English educator*
McCormick, John Owen *retired comparative literature educator*
McDermott, Agnes Charlene Senape *philosophy educator*
†Molloy, Sylvia *Latin American literature educator, writer*
Morgan, Edmund Sears *history educator*
Morrissey, Charles Thomas *historian, educator*
Mucklow, Neale Harmon *philosophy educator*
Murdock, Mary-Elizabeth *history educator*
Murphy, Francis *English language educator*
Nagel, Thomas *philosopher, law educator*
Nebel, Henry Martin, Jr. *literature historian, educator*
Nelson-Humphries, Tessa (Tessa Unthank) *English language educator*
Niedzielski, Henri Zygmunt *French and English language educator*
Olson, James Clifton *historian, university president*
Olson, Paul Richard *Spanish literature educator, editor*
Ortega, Rafael Clemente *English and Romance language educator*
Pace, R(alph) Wayne *organizational behavior educator*
Palter, Robert Monroe *philosophy and history educator*
Peyser, Joseph Leonard *historical researcher, translator, author*
Pflanze, Otto Paul *history educator*
Reuman, Robert Everett *philosophy educator*
Riasanovsky, Nicholas Valentine *historian, educator*
Richardson, Robert Dale, Jr. *English language educator*
Rickard, Ruth David *retired history and political science educator*
Robb, David Metheny, Jr. *art historian*
Rollins, Alfred Brooks, Jr. *historian, educator*
Romeo, Luigi *linguist, educator*
Rothman, Julius Lawrence *retired English language educator*
Sabat-Rivers, Georgina *Latin American literature educator*
Schnucker, Robert Victor *history and religion educator*
Seidensticker, Edward George *Japanese language and literature educator*
Seymour, Richard Kellogg *linguist, educator*
Shillingsburg, Miriam Jones *English educator, academic administrator*
Sices, David *language educator, translator*
Smith, Charlotte Reed *retired music educator*
Smither, Howard Elbert *musicologist*
Smock, Raymond William *historian, government official*
Snyder, Susan Brooke *retired English literature educator*
Solomon, Robert Charles *philosopher, educator*
Stein, Arnold *English educator*
Stewart, Zeph *classicist, educator*
Stolarik, M. Mark *history educator*
Street, John Charles *linguistics educator*
Sutton, Julia Sumberg *musicologist, dance historian*
Thackray, Arnold Wilfrid *historian, foundation executive*
Topik, Steven Curtis *history educator*
Trelease, Allen William *historian, educator*
Wallace, William Augustine *philosophy and history educator*
Waller, Gary Fredric *English language educator, poet*
Warlick, Roger Kinney *history educator, assistant dean*
Weber, Eugen *historian, educator, author*
Wolters, Oliver William *history educator*
Wruck, Erich-Oskar *German language educator, administrator*
Yolton, John William *philosopher, educator*
Zwerver, Peter John *linguistics educator*

HUMANITIES: LIBRARIES

UNITED STATES

ALABAMA

Birmingham
†Bulow, Jack Faye *library director*
Spence, Paul Herbert *librarian*
Stephens, Jerry Wayne *librarian, library director*
Stewart, George Ray *librarian*

Mobile
Bahr, Alice Harrison *librarian*
†Baillio, O. Dallas, Jr. *library official*
Damico, James Anthony *library director*

Montgomery
Bell, Katie Roberson *library educator*

Thomaston
Counselman, Anne *librarian*

Troy
Thompson, Jean Tanner *retired librarian*

Tuscaloosa
Osburn, Charles Benjamin *librarian, university dean*

ALASKA

Anchorage
†Rollins, Alden Milton *documents librarian*

Fairbanks
McCarthy, Paul H. *library science educator*

Juneau
Schorr, Alan Edward *librarian, publisher*

ARIZONA

Green Valley
White, Herbert Spencer *research library educator, university dean*

Mesa
Anderson, Herschel Vincent *librarian*

Phoenix
Edwards, Ralph M. *librarian*
Fox, Frances Juanice *retired librarian, educator, retired*
Hanley, Fred William *librarian, educator*
†Landers, Teresa Price *librarian*

Scottsdale
Meyer, Madeline Anna *librarian*

Sun City West
Williams, William Harrison *retired librarian*

Tempe
Borovansky, Vladimir Theodore *librarian*
Metros, Mary Teresa *librarian*

Tucson
Altman, Ellen *librarian, educator*
Anderson, Rachael Keller *library administrator*
Dickinson, Donald Charles *library science educator*
Hurt, Charles D. *college librarian*
Hurt, Charlie Deuel, III *library school director, educator*
Laird, Wilbur David, Jr. *librarian*
Miller, Liz Rodriguez *public library system director, librarian*
†Pintozzi, Chestalene *librarian*
Wolfe, William Jerome *librarian, English language educator*

ARKANSAS

Arkadelphia
Martin, Marilyn Joan *library director*

Fayetteville
Harrison, John Arthur *library administrator*

Fort Smith
Larson, Larry *librarian*

Jonesboro
Peters, Mary Helen *library media specialist*

Little Rock
Compton, Susan LaNell *retired librarian*
Jones, Philip Lindsey *librarian*
Martin, Rosemary Scarbrough *public library administrator*
Mulkey, Jack Clarendon *library director*

Lonoke
Ross, Philip Rowland *library director*

Pine Bluff
Burdick, David *library director*

CALIFORNIA

Aptos
Heron, David Winston *librarian*

Bakersfield
Duquette, Diane Rhea *library director*

Belvedere Tiburon
Crockett, Ethel Stacy *librarian*

Berkeley
Buckland, Michael Keeble *librarian, educator*
Danton, Joseph Periam *librarian, educator*
Hanff, Peter Edward *librarian, bibliographer*
Harlan, Robert Dale *library and information studies educator, academic administrator*
†Hoehn, Raymond Philip, Jr. *map librarian*
Minudri, Regina Ursula *library director, consultant*
Van House, Nancy Anita *library educator*

Carlsbad
Lange, Clifford E. *librarian*

Commerce
Conover, Robert Warren *librarian*

Corona
Leo, Karen Ann *library administrator*

Cupertino
Fletcher, Homer Lee *librarian*

Davis
Grossman, George Stefan *library director, law eductor*
Sharrow, Marilyn Jane *library administrator*

El Centro
Gotti, Margaret Lynn *library administrator*

Encino
Wood, Raymund Francis *retired librarian*

Fremont
†Wood, Linda May *librarian*

Fresno
Gorman, Michael Joseph *library director, educator*
Kallenberg, John Kenneth *librarian*

Fullerton
Ayala, John *librarian, dean*

Inglewood
Alaniz, Miguel José Castañeda *library director*

Irvine
Euster, Joanne Reed *librarian*

La Jolla
†Mirsky, Phyllis Simon *librarian*

Long Beach
Lathrop, Ann *librarian, educator*
Scepanski, Jordan Michael *librarian, administrator*

Los Angeles
Borko, Harold *information scientist, psychologist, educator*
†Brecht, Albert Odell *library and information technology administrator*
Bulmer, Connie J. *film librarian*
Chang, Henry Chung-Lien *library administrator*
Ciccone, Amy Navratil *art librarian*
Coolbaugh, Carrie Weaver *librarian*
Cuadra, Carlos Albert *information scientist, management executive*
Gilman, Nelson Jay *library director*
Goldberg Kent, Susan *library director*
†Kent, Susan Goldberg *library director, consultant*
†Patron, Susan Hall *librarian, writer*
Polan, Morris *librarian*
Richardson, John Vinson, Jr. *library science educator*
Shank, Russell *librarian, educator*
†Steele, Victoria Lee *librarian*
†Sutherland, Michael Cruise *librarian*
Werner, Gloria S. *librarian*

Mill Valley
Dillon, Richard Hugh *librarian, author*

Modesto
Ferreira, Judith Anne *librarian*
Kreissman, Starrett *librarian*

Monterey
Reneker, Maxine Hohman *librarian*

Monterey Park
Wilson, Linda *librarian*

Mountain View
Di Muccio, Mary Jo *retired librarian*

Napa
†Trice, Thomas Granville *library director, history educator*

Newport Beach
†Kienitz, LaDonna Trapp *librarian, city official*

North Hollywood
Schlosser, Anne Griffin *librarian*

Northridge
Curzon, Susan Carol *library administrator*

Oakland
Gomez, Martin *library director*
Shinomiya, Yaeko *librarian*

Ontario
Luce, Susan Marie *library director*

Palmdale
Storsteen, Linda Lee *librarian*

Palo Alto
Dassoff, Christine Ellen *library administrator*

Pasadena
Buck, Anne Marie *library director, consultant*
Dowell, David Ray *library administrator*
Harmsen, Tyrus George *librarian*

Redlands
†Burgess, Larry Eugene *library director, history educator*

Sacramento
Killian, Richard M. *library director*
Snow, Marina Sexton *reference librarian, playwright*

Salinas
Spinks, Paul *retired library director*

San Bernardino
Anderson, Barbara Louise *retired library director*
Burgess, Michael *library science educator, publisher*
†Ewing, Robert Stirling *library administrator*

San Diego
Sannwald, William Walter *librarian*

San Francisco
Dowlin, Kenneth Everett *librarian*
Frantz, John Corydon *librarian*
Geiger, Richard George *librarian*

San Jose
Fish, James Henry *library director*
Schmidt, Cyril James *librarian*

San Luis Obispo
Perkins, Dale Warren *library director*

San Marcos
Ciurczak, Alexis *librarian*

San Marino
Robertson, Mary Louise *archivist, historian*
Woodward, Daniel Holt *librarian, researcher*

Santa Ana
†Adams, John M. *library director*
Richard, Robert John *library director*

Santa Barbara
Boisse, Joseph Adonias *library administrator*
Brun, Christian Magnus From *university librarian*
Dougan, Robert Ormes *librarian*
Keator, Carol Lynne *library director*
†Korenic, Lynette Marie *librarian*
Lockett, Barbara Ann *librarian*

Santa Clara
Hopkinson, Shirley Lois *library and information science educator*

Santa Cruz
Dyson, Allan Judge *librarian*
†Welborn, Victoria Lee *science librarian, educator*

Santa Monica
Ackerman, Helen Page *librarian, educator*

Sebastopol
Sabsay, David *library consultant*

Sherman Oaks
Miller, Margaret Haigh *librarian*

Sierra Madre
Brudvig, Glenn Lowell *library director*

Stanford
Derksen, Charlotte Ruth Meynink *librarian*
Keller, Michael Alan *librarian, educator, musicologist*
Ross, Alexander Duncan *art librarian*
Weber, David C(arter) *librarian*

Stockton
Meyer, Ursula *library director*

Torrance
Buckley, James W. *librarian*

Ventura
Adeniran, Dixie Darlene *library administrator*

Yorba Linda
†Naulty, Susan Louise *archivist*

COLORADO

Aurora
†Nicholas, Thomas Peter *library administrator, community television consultant, producer*

Boulder
†Carter, Laura Lee *academic librarian, psychologist*
Gralapp, Marcelee Gayl *librarian*

Colorado Springs
Budington, William Stone *retired librarian*
Margolis, Bernard Allen *library administrator, antique book merchant and appraiser*

Denver
Ashton, Rick James *librarian*
Miller, Sarah Pearl *librarian*
Schertz, Morris *library director*

Englewood
Wynar, Bohdan Stephen *librarian, author, editor*

Fort Collins
Chambers, Joan Louise *dean of libraries*
Saferite, Linda Lee *library director*

Golden
Lerud, Joanne Van Ornum *library administrator*
Mathews, Anne Jones *international consultant, library director*

Greeley
Seager, Daniel Albert *university librarian*

Lakewood
Knott, William Alan *library director, library management and building consultant*

Littleton
Smart, Marriott Wieckhoff *research librarian consultant, information manager,*

Pueblo
Bates, Charles Emerson *library administrator*
Penny, Laura Jean *librarian*

CONNECTICUT

Bloomfield
Martin, Vernon Emil *librarian*

Bridgeport
Johmann, Nancy *librarian*
†Sheridan, Eileen *librarian*

Fairfield
Bryan, Barbara Day *librarian*
Kijanka, Dorothy M. *library administrator*

Hartford
Kaimowitz, Jeffrey Hugh *librarian*
Wilkie, Everett Cleveland, Jr. *librarian*

Middletown
Adams, John Robert *librarian*

New Britain
Donahugh, Robert Hayden *library administrator*
Sohn, Jeanne *librarian*

New Haven
Abell, Millicent Demmin *university library administrator*
Bartholomew, Alan Alfred *librarian, educator*
Bennett, Scott Boyce *librarian*
†Crossey, (John) Moore Davison *librarian*
Franklin, Ralph William *library director, literary scholar*
†Lorkovic, Tatjana *librarian*
Oliver-Warren, Mary Elizabeth *library science educator*
†Rodriguez, Cesar *librarian*
Stuehrenberg, Paul Frederick *librarian*

New London
†Daragan, Patricia A. *librarian*
Rogers, Brian Deane *librarian*

Southbury
Usher, Elizabeth Reuter (Mrs. William A. Scar) *retired librarian*

Storrs
†McGlamery, Thornton Patrick *map librarian*

Storrs Mansfield
Stevens, Norman Dennison *retired library director*

Westport
Poundstone, Sally *library director*

DELAWARE

Georgetown
Painter, John Cecil *library director*

Wilmington
†Tise, Mary Shackelford *public librarian*
Titus, H. Mark *librarian*
Williams, Richmond Dean *library appraiser, consultant*

DISTRICT OF COLUMBIA

Washington
Atiyeh, George Nicholas *library administrator, educator*
Baum, Ingeborg Ruth *librarian*
Bledsoe, Ralph Champion *archivist*
Bold, Frances Ann *librarian*
Broering, Naomi Cordero *librarian*
Bush, Robert Donald *historical preservation organization executive*
Carlin, John William *archivist, former governor*
†Carr, Timothy Bernard *librarian*
Chin, Cecilia Hui-Hsin *librarian*
Chwalek, Adele Ruth *library administrator*
Clemmer, Dan Orr *librarian*
Cylke, Frank Kurt *librarian*
Daffron, MaryEllen *librarian*
†Davis, Hiram Logan *librarian*
Deel, Frances Quinn *retired librarian*
Emperado, Mercedes Lopez *librarian*
Fawcett, John Thomas *archivist*
Fifer Canby, Susan Melinda *library administrator*
Filstrup, E. Christian *librarian, writer*
Franklin, Hardy R. *library director*
Gernand, Bradley Elton *archivist, manuscripts librarian*
Gifford, Prosser *library administrator*
Gundersheimer, Werner Leonard *library director*
Haley, Roger Kendall *librarian*
Harlem, Susan Lynn *librarian*
Heanue, Anne Allen *librarian*
Hedges, Kamla King *library director*
Heiss, Harry Glen *archivist*
Jones, Catherine Ann *library administrator*
Karklins, Vija L. *librarian*
Kenyon, Carleton Weller *librarian*
Kohlhorst, Gail Lewis *librarian*
Lorenz, John George *librarian, consultant*
Marcum, Deanna Bowling *library administrator*
Martin, Susan Katherine *librarian*
Mikel, Sarah Ann *librarian*
Moulton, David Aubin *library director*
Newton, Virginia *archivist, historian, librarian*
Perella, Susanne Brennan *librarian*
Peterson, Trudy Huskamp *national archivist*
Ratner, Rhoda Sue *librarian*
Renninger, Mary Karen *librarian*
Reynolds, Gary Kemp *librarian*
Rovelstad, Mathilde Verner *library science educator*
Sahanek, Tatana *librarian, editor*
Sampson, Daphne Rae *library director*
Scott, Catherine Dorothy *librarian, information consultant*
Siggins, Jack Arthur *librarian*
†Smith, Barbara Jeanne *librarian*
†Stackpole, Laurie Eveleth *library director*
Turtell, Neal Timothy *librarian*
Walton, Kathleen Endres *librarian*
Wand, Patricia Ann *librarian*
Wattenmaker, Richard Joel *archive director, art scholar*
Weiher, Claudine Jackson *government archives official*
Young, Peter Robert *librarian*

FLORIDA

Atlantis
Gough, Carolyn Harley *library director*

Bal Harbour
Gray, Phyllis Anne *librarian*

Boca Raton
Bettmann, Otto Ludwig *picture archivist, graphic historian*

Boynton Beach
Farace, Virginia Kapes *librarian*

Clearwater
†Hallam, Arlita Warrick *library system administrator*
Werner, Elizabeth Helen *librarian, Spanish language educator*

Coral Gables
Rodgers, Frank *librarian*

Gainesville
†Brown, Myra Suzanne *librarian*
Canelas, Dale Brunelle *library director*
Goggin, Margaret Knox *librarian, educator*
Harrer, Gustave Adolphus *librarian, educator*
Willocks, Robert Max *retired librarian*

Jacksonville
Farkas, Andrew *library director, educator, writer*
Williams, Judith L. *library administrator*

Lakeland
Reich, David Lee *library director*

Miami
Comras, Rema *library director*
Kozlowski, Ronald Stephan *librarian*
†Sommerville, Mary Robinson *library director*
Treyz, Joseph Henry *librarian*

Naples
Chartrand, Robert Lee *information scientist*

Orlando
Allison, Anne Marie *librarian*
Hyslop, Gary Lee *librarian*

Palm Bay
Regis, Nina *librarian, educator*

Saint Petersburg
Hargrave, Victoria Elizabeth *librarian*
Runge, De Lyle Paul *retired library director, consultant*

Tallahassee
Beach, Cecil Prentice *librarian*
Robbins, Jane Borsch *library science educator, information science educator*
Rockwood, Ruth H. *former library science educator*
Summers, Frank William *librarian*
Summers, Lorraine Dey Schaeffer *librarian*
Trezza, Alphonse Fiore *librarian, educator*
Wilkins, (George) Barratt *librarian*
Zachert, Martha Jane *retired librarian*

Tampa
Harkness, Mary Lou *librarian*
Tabor, Curtis Harold, Jr. *library director*

Winter Park
Rogers, Rutherford David *librarian*

GEORGIA

Athens
Potter, William Gray, Jr. *library director*
Surrency, Erwin Campbell *librarian, educator*

Atlanta
Brown, Lorene B(yron) *library educator, educational administrator*
Cann, Sharon Lee *librarian*
Churchwell, Charles Darrett *librarian*
Drake, Miriam Anna *librarian, educator*
Dubberly, Ronald Alvah *library director*
Jeschke, Channing Renwick *librarian*
Lawson, A(bram) Venable *retired librarian*
Roberts, Edward Graham *librarian*
Russell, Ralph Ernest *librarian, educator*
Schewe, Donald Bruce *archivist, library director*
Yates, Ella Gaines *library consultant*

Augusta
Rowland, Arthur Ray *librarian*

Bainbridge
Frieling, Thomas Jerome *library director*

Cochran
Ambardekar, Raj *library administrator*

Gainesville
Brasel, Michael Louis *library director*

Lilburn
Forsee, Joe Brown *library director*

Macon
Schmidt, Charles J. *library administrator*

Marietta
Lazenby, Gail R. *library director*

Rome
Mosley, Mary Mac *retired librarian*
Overbeck, James A. *library director, educator*

Savannah
Ball, Ardella Patricia *library science educator*

Woodbine
Christian, John H. *librarian*

Young Harris
Richardson, Robert Janecek *library director*

HAWAII

Honolulu
Kane, Bartholomew Aloysius *state librarian*
Stevens, Robert David *librarian, educator*
†Wageman, Lynette Mena *librarian*

IDAHO

Boise
Bolles, Charles Avery *librarian*

Moscow
Force, Ronald Wayne *librarian*

Sandpoint
Murray, James Michael *librarian, law librarian, legal educator, lawyer*

ILLINOIS

Carbondale
Bauner, Ruth Elizabeth *library administrator, reference librarian*
†Koch, David Victor *librarian, administrator*
†Koch, Loretta Peterson *librarian, educator*

Champaign
Krummel, Donald William *librarian, educator*
†Scheetz, George Henry *library director*
Wajenberg, Arnold Sherman *retired librarian, educator*
Wert, Lucille Mathena *librarian, educator*

Chicago
Berry, John Willard *librarian, consultant*
Brown, Richard Holbrook *library administrator, historian*
Elbaz, Sohair Wastawy *library director, consultant*
Gerdes, Neil Wayne *library director*
Gross, Dorothy-Ellen *library director, dean*
Hayden, Carla Diane *librarian, educator*
King, David Edgar *librarian, editor*
Knoblauch, Mark George *librarian*
†Ma, Tai-Loi *library curator, Chinese studies specialist*
Miletich, Ivo *library and information scientist, bibliographer, educator, linguist, literature research specialist*
Park, Chung Il *librarian*
Runkle, Martin Davey *library director*
Scott, Alice H. *librarian*
†Shedlock, James *library director, consultant*
Sullivan, Peggy (Anne) *librarian*
Veit, Fritz *librarian*
Waite, Ellen Jane *vice president*
Whiteley, Sandra Marie *librarian, editor*
Winger, Howard Woodrow *library educator*

De Kalb
Kies, Cosette Nell *library science educator, consultant*
Young, Arthur Price *librarian, educator*

Decatur
Moorman, John A. *librarian*

Edwardsville
†Fortado, Robert Joseph *librarian, educator*

Elgin
Zack, Daniel Gerard *library director*

Evanston
Bishop, David Fulton *library administrator*
Cates, Jo Ann *librarian, management consultant*
Crawford, Susan *library director, educator*
Wright, Donald Eugene *retired librarian*

Galesburg
Kirk, Sherwood *librarian*

Jacksonville
Gallas, Martin Hans *librarian*

Joliet
Johnston, James Robert *library director*

Kankakee
†Van Fossan, Kathryn Ruth *library director*

Lake Forest
Miller, Arthur Hawks, Jr. *librarian, consultant*

Maywood
Ellington, Mildred L. *librarian*

Naperville
†Pearson, Roger Lee *library administrator*

Normal
Peterson, Fred McCrae *librarian*

Peoria
Herring, Susan Kay *library director*
Lindgren, William Dale *librarian*

Quincy
Tyer, Travis Earl *librarian*

River Forest
Marco, Guy Anthony *library educator*
McCusker, Mary Lauretta *library science educator*

Rockford
Chitwood, Julius Richard *librarian*
†Rosenfeld, Joel Charles *librarian*

Schaumburg
Chitwood, Lera Catherine *information professional, manufacturing company manager*

Springfield
Petterchak, Janice A. *library director*

Urbana
Brichford, Maynard Jay *archivist*
†Burger, Robert Harold *librarian*
Choldin, Marianna Tax *librarian, educator*
†Davis, Elisabeth Bachman *librarian, library administration educator*
Mc Clellan, William Monson *library administrator*
†O'Brien, Nancy Patricia *librarian, educator*
Shtohryn, Dmytro Michael *librarian, educator*
Watson, Paula D. *library administrator*

Wheaton
Thompson, Bert Allen *retired librarian*

Wheeling
Hammer, Donald Price *librarian*
Long, Sarah Ann *librarian*
Mc Clarren, Robert Royce *librarian*

Wilmington
Anderson, Mary Jane *public library director*

INDIANA

Auburn
Mountz, Louise Carson Smith *retired librarian*

Bloomington
Cagle, William Rea *librarian*
Rudolph, Lavere Christian *library director*
†Yeager, Janice Skinner *library director*

Evansville
Howard, Edward Allen *library administrator, consultant*

Fort Wayne
Jackson, Paul Howard *librarian, educator*
Krull, Jeffrey Robert *library director*

Gary
Moran, Robert Francis, Jr. *library director*

Hammond
†Meyers, Arthur Solomon *library director*

Huntington
Kaehr, Robert Eugene *librarian, educator*

Indianapolis
Bundy, David Dale *librarian, educator*
Ewick, Charles Ray *librarian*
Fischler, Barbara Brand *librarian*
Gnat, Raymond Earl *librarian*
Young, Philip Howard *library director*

La Porte
Grott, Geraldine *librarian*

Lafayette
Posey, Edwin Dalfield *librarian*
VanHandel, Ralph Anthony *librarian*

Notre Dame
Hayes, Stephen Matthew *librarian*
Miller, Robert Carl *library director*

Richmond
Farber, Evan Ira *librarian*
Kirk, Thomas Garrett, Jr. *librarian*

Saint Meinrad
Daly, Simeon Philip John *librarian*

South Bend
Mullins, James Lee *library director*

Terre Haute
Little, Robert David *library science educator*
Martin, Betty Carolyn *library director*

West Lafayette
Markee, Katherine Madigan *librarian, educator*
Mobley, Emily Ruth *library dean, educator*
†Nixon, Judith May *librarian*
†Tucker, John Mark *librarian, educator*

IOWA

Ames
Eaton, Nancy Ruth Linton *librarian, dean*

Camanche
Rittmer, Elaine Heneke *library media specialist*

Cedar Rapids
Armitage, Thomas Edward *library director*

Davenport
Potter, Corinne Jean *librarian*
Runge, Kay Kretschmar *library director*

Des Moines
†Cochran, Susan Mills *librarian*
Estes, Elaine Rose Graham *librarian*
†Smith, Sharman Bridges *state librarian*

Grinnell
McKee, Christopher Fulton *librarian, naval historian, educator*

Iowa City
Bentz, Dale Monroe *librarian*

West Branch
Mather, Mildred Eunice *retired archivist*
†Walch, Timothy George *library administrator*

KANSAS

Emporia
†Hale, Martha Larsen *librarian*

Enterprise
Wickman, John Edward *librarian, historian*

Lawrence
Koepp, Donna Pauline Petersen *librarian*

Topeka
Marvin, James Conway *librarian, consultant*

University Of Kansas
†Craig, Susan Virginia *librarian*
†Neeley, Kathleen Louise *librarian*

Wichita
Rademacher, Richard Joseph *librarian*

KENTUCKY

Danville
Campbell, Stanley Richard *library services director*

Frankfort
Nelson, James Albert *librarian, state official*

Lexington
Birchfield, Martha *librarian*
Mason, Ellsworth Goodwin *librarian*
Sineath, Timothy Wayne *library educator, university dean*
†Steensland, Ronald Paul *librarian*
Willis, Paul Allen *librarian*

Louisville
Deering, Ronald Franklin *librarian, minister*
Dorr, Ralze Wheeler *librarian*
VanMeter, Vandelia L. *library director*

Morehead
Besant, Larry Xon *librarian, administrator, consultant*

Owensboro
Eaton, Clara Barbour *librarian*

LOUISIANA

Baton Rouge
Hoover, Jimmie Hartman *librarian, educator*
Jaques, Thomas Francis *librarian*
Patterson, Charles Darold *librarian, educator*

Chalmette
Wheeler, Genevieve Stutes *library administrator, educator*

Lacombe
Hendricks, Donald Duane *librarian*

Lafayette
†Branch, Sonya Meyer *library director*
Carstens, Jane Ellen *retired library science educator*

Metairie
Walsh, Maurice David, Jr. *former librarian, business executive*

New Orleans
Leinbach, Philip Eaton *librarian*
Taylor, Kenneth Byron, Jr. *librarian, minister, religion educator*
Wilson, C. Daniel, Jr. *library director*

Pineville
Martin, W. Terry *librarian*

Ruston
Wicker, William Walter *librarian*

Shreveport
Pelton, James Rodger *librarian*

MAINE

Bangor
Rea, Ann W. *librarian*

Bar Harbor
Dworak, Marcia Lynn *library director, library building consultant*

Damariscotta
Haas, Warren James *librarian, consultant*

Gardiner
Nowell, Glenna Greely *librarian, consultant*

Orient
Chenevert, Edward Valmore, Jr. *retired librarian, real estate broker*

Portland
Parks, George Richard *librarian*

Waterville
Muehlner, Suanne Wilson *library director*

MARYLAND

Annapolis
Papenfuse, Edward Carl, Jr. *archivist, state official*
Werking, Richard Hume *librarian, historian, academic administrator*

Baltimore
Brown, Florence S. *librarian, administrator*
Magnuson, Nancy *librarian*

Beltsville
Andre, Pamela Q. J. *library director*

Bethesda
Knachel, Philip Atherton *librarian*
Lindberg, Donald Allan Bror *library administrator, pathologist, educator*
Smith, Ruth Lillian Schluchter *librarian*
Tilley, Carolyn Bittner *technical information specialist*
Tsuneishi, Warren Michio *librarian*

Catonsville
†Wilt, Lawrence J.M. *librarian*

College Park
Burke, Frank Gerard *archivist*
†Fawcett, Sharon Kay Atchison *archivist*
Wasserman, Paul *library and information science educator*

Columbia
Wolter, John Amadeus *librarian, government official*

Gaithersburg
Klein, Sami Weiner *librarian*

Kensington
Rather, Lucia Porcher Johnson *library administrator*

Potomac
Broderick, John Caruthers *retired librarian, educator*

Rockville
Brandhorst, Wesley Theodore *information manager*
Griffen, Agnes Marthe *library administrator*
Missar, Charles Donald *librarian*

Savage
Filby, Percy William *library consultant*

Silver Spring
Avram, Henriette Davidson *librarian, government official*
†Brown, Carolyn Thompson *librarian*
Hackett, John Francis *archivist*
Sweetland, Loraine Fern *librarian, educator*
von Hake, Margaret Joan *librarian*

MASSACHUSETTS

Amesbury
Dowd, Frances Connelly *librarian*

Amherst
Bozone, Billie Rae *librarian, consultant*
Bridegam, Willis Edward, Jr. *librarian*
Talbot, Richard Joseph *library administrator*
Tenenbaum, Jeffrey Mark *academic librarian*

Boston
Allen, Nancy Schuster *librarian*
Armstrong, Rodney *librarian*
Chen, Ching-chih *information science educator, consultant*
Curley, Arthur *library director*
†Desnoyers, Megan Floyd *archivist, educator*
Kowal, Ruth Elizabeth *library administrator*
Patterson, Robert Logan *librarian, country and western dance promoter*

Bridgewater
Neubauer, Richard A. *library science educator, consultant*

Brookline
Tuchman, Maurice Simon *library director*

Cambridge
Bond, William Henry *librarian, educator*
Carpenter, Kenneth E. *librarian, bibliographer*
Cole, Heather Ellen *librarian*
†Collins, John William, III *librarian*
De Gennaro, Richard *library director*
†Flannery, Susan Marie *library administrator*
Hamilton, Malcolm Cowan *librarian, editor, indexer, personnel educator*
Horrell, Jeffrey Lanier *library administrator*
Lucker, Jay K. *library administrator, consultant*

Stoddard, Roger Eliot *librarian*
Wendorf, Richard Harold *library director, educator*
Willard, Louis Charles *librarian*

Fall River
Sullivan, Ruth Anne *librarian*

Framingham
Kuklinski, Joan Lindsey *librarian*

Lawrence
†Dionne, Joseph Robert *public library director, fundraising consultant*

Lexington
Freitag, Wolfgang Martin *librarian, educator*

Newton
†Glick-Weil, Kathy *library director*

Northampton
Piccinino, Rocco Michael *librarian*

Quincy
Watson, Warren Edward *retired library administrator*

Salem
La Moy, William Thomas *library director, editor*

Shrewsbury
Piggford, Roland Rayburn *library and information services consultant*

Springfield
Brennen, Patrick Wayne *library director*
Keough, Francis Paul *librarian*
Stack, May Elizabeth *library director*
Utley, F. Knowlton *library director, educator*

Swampscott
Fountain, Eugenia Ferris *library director*

Wakefield
Kelley, John Dennis *librarian*

Waltham
Hahn, Bessie King *library administrator, lecturer*
Hayes, Sherman Lee *library director*

Williamstown
Erickson, Peter Brown *librarian, scholar, writer*
Gibson, Sarah Ann Scott *art librarian*
Wikander, Lawrence Einar *librarian*

Worcester
Baughman, Susan S. *library director*
Dunlap, Ellen S. *library administrator*
Johnson, Penelope B. *librarian*
McCorison, Marcus Allen *librarian, cultural organization administrator*

MICHIGAN

Adrian
Dombrowski, Mark Anthony *librarian*

Allendale
Murray, Diane Elizabeth *librarian*

Ann Arbor
Beaubien, Anne Kathleen *librarian*
Bidlack, Russell Eugene *librarian, educator, former dean*
Carlen, Sister Claudia *librarian*
†Daub, Peggy Ellen *library administrator*
Dougherty, Richard Martin *library and information science educator*
Dunlap, Connie *librarian*
Hessler, David William *information management educator, information systems consultant*
Riggs, Donald Eugene *librarian, university dean*
Slavens, Thomas Paul *information and library studies educator*
Wagman, Frederick Herbert *librarian, educator, deceased*
Wall, Carroll Edward *librarian, publisher*
†Wan, Weiying *library curator*
Warner, Robert Mark *archivist, historian, university dean*
Williams, John Troy *librarian, educator*

Dearborn
Coady, Reginald Patrick *library director*
Marquis, Rollin Park *retired librarian*

Detroit
Audia, Christina *librarian*
Curtis, Jean Trawick *library director*
Klont, Barbara Anne *librarian*
Mika, Joseph John *library director, consultant*
Spyers-Duran, Peter *librarian, educator*
†Sutton, Lynn Sorensen *librarian*

East Lansing
Chapin, Richard Earl *librarian*
De Benko, Eugene *librarian, consultant*

Farmington Hills
†Papai, Beverly Daffern *library director*

Flint
Heymoss, Jennifer Marie *librarian*

Grand Rapids
Garcia, Joseph Everett *public library director*
Jacobsen, Arnold *archivist*
Monsma, Marvin Eugene *library director*
†Raz, Robert Eugene *librarian*

Houghton
Krenitsky, Michael V. *librarian*

Kalamazoo
†Amdursky, Saul Jack *library director*
Grotzinger, Laurel Ann *university librarian*
Lowrie, Jean Elizabeth *librarian, educator*

Midland
Byers, Rosemarie *library director*

Port Huron
Wu, Harry Pao-Tung *librarian*

Rochester
†Hage, Christine Lind *library administrator*

Saint Clair Shores
†Woodford, Arthur MacKinnon *library director, historian*

Thompsonville
Perry, Margaret *librarian, writer*

Ypsilanti
Beck, Mary Clare *librarian*

MINNESOTA

Bloomington
Huttner, Marian Alice *library administrator*

Collegeville
Haile, Getatchew *archivist, educator*

Duluth
Pearce, Donald Joslin *retired librarian*

Minneapolis
Asp, William George *librarian*
†Johnson, Donald Clay *librarian, curator*
Shaughnessy, Thomas William *librarian, consultant*
Smith, Eldred Reid *library educator*

Northfield
Hong, Howard Vincent *library administrator, philosophy educator, editor, translator*
Metz, T(heodore) John *librarian, consultant*

Rochester
Key, Jack Dayton *librarian*
Leachman, Roger Mack *librarian*

Saint Paul
Holbert, Sue Elisabeth *archivist, writer, consultant*
†Jacob, Rosamond Tryon *librarian*
Johnson, Margaret Ann *library administrator*
Kane, Lucile Marie *archivist, historian*
MacDonald, Roderick *library director*
Magnuson, Norris Alden *librarian, history educator*
Wagner, Mary Margaret *library and information science educator*

Saint Peter
Haeuser, Michael John *library administrator*

MISSISSIPPI

Cleveland
Macon, Myra Faye *library director*

Columbus
Atkinson, Gloria L. *archivist*

Indianola
Powell, Anice Carpenter *librarian*

Itta Bena
Henderson, Robbye Robinson *library director*

Jackson
Capers, Charlotte *retired state archives and history administrator*
Parks, James Franklin, Jr. *librarian*

Ridgeland
Morgan, Madel Jacobs *retired archives and library administrator*

Tupelo
Radojcsics, Anne Parsons *librarian*

MISSOURI

Blue Springs
Nelson, Freda Nell Hein *librarian*

Columbia
Alexander, Martha Sue *librarian*
Almony, Robert Allen, Jr. *librarian, businessman*
Carroll, Carmal Edward *librarian, educator, clergyman*
†Howden, Norman, III *library science educator, consultant*

Hannibal
Dothager, Julie Ann *librarian*

Independence
Ferguson, John Wayne, Sr. *librarian*
Strang, Marian Boundy *librarian*

Jefferson City
Winn, Kenneth Hugh *archivist, historian*

Kansas City
Bradbury, Daniel Joseph *library administrator*
La Budde, Kenneth James *librarian*
Pedram, Marilyn Beth *reference librarian*
Sheldon, Ted Preston *library director*
Zeller, Marilynn Kay *librarian*

Lake Lotawana
Zobrist, Benedict Karl *library director, historian*

Nevada
Hizer, Marlene Brown *library director*

Saint Louis
Baker, Shirley Kistler *university library administrator*
Cole, William Porter *librarian*
†Gaertner, Donell J. *library director*
Guenther, Charles John *librarian, writer*
Holt, Glen Edward *library administrator*
†Holt, Leslie Edmonds *librarian*

Springfield
Linnemeyer-Busch, Annie *library director*

MONTANA

Billings
Cochran, William Michael *librarian*

Helena
Fitzpatrick, Lois Ann *library administrator*

NEBRASKA

Lincoln
Robson, John Merritt *library and media administrator*
Wagner, Rod *library director*

Omaha
Dickerson, Lon Richard *library administrator*
Tollman, Thomas Andrew *librarian*

NEVADA

Carson City
Rocha, Guy Louis *archivist, historian*

Las Vegas
†Batson, Darrell Lynn *librarian, consultant*
Hunsberger, Charles Wesley *library consultant*

NEW HAMPSHIRE

Berlin
Doherty, Katherine Mann *librarian, writer*

Concord
Wiggin, Kendall French *state librarian*

Exeter
Thomas, Jacquelyn May *librarian*

Hampton
Morton, Donald John *librarian*

Hanover
Lathem, Edward Connery *librarian, editor, educator*
Otto, Margaret Amelia *librarian*
†Richards, Daniel Thomas *library director*

Manchester
Constance, Joseph William, Jr. *library director*

Newmarket
Getchell, Sylvia Fitts *librarian*

NEW JERSEY

Demarest
Ahr, Ernest Stephan *business archive executive*

East Brunswick
Karmazin, Sharon Elyse *library director*

Elizabeth
Keenan, Joseph James, Jr. *library director*

Highland Park
Coughlin, Caroline Mary *library consultant, educator*

Hightstown
Brodman, Estelle *librarian, retired educator*

Hoboken
Widdicombe, Richard Palmer *librarian*

Irvington
McConnell, Lorelei Catherine *library director*

Jersey City
LiBrizzi, Rose Marie Meola *library administrator, counselor*
Patterson, Grace Limerick *library director*

Laurel Springs
Cleveland, Susan Elizabeth *library administrator, researcher*

Lawrenceville
Iversen, David Stewart *librarian*

Lodi
Karetzky, Stephen *library director, educator, researcher*

Lyndhurst
Sieger, Charles *librarian*

New Brunswick
Anderson, James Doig *library and information science educator*
Becker, Ronald Leonard *archivist*
Edelman, Hendrik *library and information science educator*
†House, Renee S. *theological librarian, minister*
Turock, Betty Jane *library and information science educator, educational association administrator*

Princeton
Ferguson, Stephen *librarian*
Fox, Mary Ann Williams *librarian*
Henneman, John Bell, Jr. *library bibliographer*
Joyce, William Leonard *librarian*

Trenton
Butorac, Frank George *administrative librarian*
Russell, Joyce Anne Rogers *librarian*

NEW MEXICO

Albuquerque
†Dodson-Barnhart, Jan Mary *library development specialist, writer*
Snell, Patricia Poldervaart *librarian, consultant*
Thorson, Connie Capers *library educator*
Wolf, Cynthia Tribelhorn *librarian, library educator*

Las Cruces
†Myers, R. David *library director, dean*

NEW YORK

Albany
Aceto, Vincent John *librarian, educator*
Galvin, Thomas John *information science policy educator, librarian, information scientist*
Katz, William Armstrong *library science educator*
Paulson, Peter John *librarian, publishing company executive*
Shubert, Joseph Francis *librarian*

Bohemia
Manley, Gertrude Ella *librarian, media specialist*

Bronx
Caffin, Louise Anne *library media educator*
Humphry, James, III *librarian*
McCabe, James Patrick *library director*
Rosenstock, Morton *librarian*

Brooklyn
Clune, John Richard *library administrator*
Corry, Emmett Brother *librarian, educator, researcher, archivist*
Sharify, Nasser *librarian, educator, author*
Stevenson, Gale *librarian*

Buffalo
Bobinski, George Sylvan *librarian, educator*
Chrisman, Diane J. *librarian*
Cloudsley, Donald Hugh *library administrator*
Rooney, Paul Monroe *former library administrator*
†Zimmerman, Nancy Picciano *library science educator*

Canaan
Walker, William Bond *retired librarian*

Chappaqua
Whittingham, Charles Arthur *library administrator, publisher*

Clifton Park
Farley, John Joseph *library science educator emeritus*

Clinton
Anthony, Donald Charles *librarian, educator*

Cornwall On Hudson
Weiss, Egon Arthur *retired library administrator*

Corona
Jackson, Andrew Preston *library director*

Cortland
†Gration, Selby Upton *library director*

Delmar
Nitecki, Joseph Zbigniew *librarian*

East Setauket
Thom, Joseph M. *librarian*

Flushing
Cooke, Constance Blandy *librarian*
†Cooper, Marianne (Abonyi Cooper) *librarian, educator*

Great Neck
Pohl, Gunther Erich *retired library administrator*

Hamilton
Bergen, Daniel Patrick *librarian, retired educator*
Noyes, Judith Gibson *library director*

Hempstead
Andrews, Charles Rolland *library administrator*
Freese, Melanie Louise *librarian, professor*

Hyde Park
Newton, Verne Wester *library director*

Ithaca
Finch, C. Herbert *archivist, library administrator, historian*
†Law, Gordon Theodore, Jr. *library director*
Miller, J(ames) Gormly *retired librarian, educator*
Skipper, James Everett *librarian*

Jamaica
Barry, J. Kevin *librarian*
†Benson, James Allen *library science educator, academic administrator*
Hammer, Deborah Marie *librarian*
†Lin, Shu-Fang Hsia *librarian*
Strong, Gary Eugene *librarian*

Kings Point
Billy, George John *library director*

Lagrangeville
LaMont, Barbara Gibson *librarian*

New York
Ashton, Jean Willoughby *library director*
Belliveau, Gerard Joseph, Jr. *librarian*
Berger, Pearl *library director*
Berliner, Barbara *librarian, consultant*
†Berner, Andrew Jay *library director, writer*
Birnbaum, Henry *librarian*
†Bourke, Thomas Anthony *librarian, writer*
Bowen, Jean *music librarian, consultant*
Brewer, Karen *librarian*
Bristah, Pamela Jean *librarian*
Browar, Lisa M. *librarian*
Cassell, Kay Ann *librarian*
Cohen, Selma *reference librarian, researcher*
Colby, Robert Alan *retired library science educator*
Deuss, Jean *librarian*
†Downing, Arthur *librarian*
El-Erian, Tahani *library administrator*
Ellenbogen, Rudolph Solomon *library curator*
Gatch, Milton McCormick, Jr. *library administrator, clergyman, educator*
Gold, Leonard Singer *librarian, translator*
Gossage, Wayne *library director, management consultant, executive recruiter*
Gottlieb, Jane Ellen *librarian*
Graves, Fred Hill *librarian*
Green, David Edward *librarian, priest, translator*
†Heinrich, Amy Vladeck *library director*
Hewitt, Vivian Ann Davidson (Mrs. John Hamilton Hewitt, Jr.) *librarian*
Isaacson, Melvin Stuart *library director*
Jones, Anne *librarian*
Kasinec, Edward Joseph *library administrator*
LeClerc, Paul *library director*
Logsdon, Richard Henry *retired librarian and educator*
Lohf, Kenneth A. *librarian, writer*
LoSchiavo, Linda Bosco *library director*
Lubetski, Edith Esther *librarian*
Lundquist, John Milton *librarian, author, lecturer, travel writer*
†Mackey, Patricia Elaine *librarian*
Mattson, Francis Oscar *retired librarian and rare books curator*
McCormick, Donald E. *librarian, archivist*
Meyerhoff, Erich *librarian, administrator*
Miller, Philip Efrem *librarian*
Mirsky, Sonya Wohl *librarian, curator*
Moore, Jane Ross *librarian*
Palmer, Robert Baylis *librarian*
Pierce, Charles Eliot, Jr. *library director, educator*
Placzek, Adolf Kurt *librarian*
Rabinowitz, Mayer Elya *librarian, educator*
Rachow, Louis A(ugust) *librarian*
Richmond, Eero *music librarian, composer*
Rochell, Carlton Charles *librarian*
Root, Nina J. *librarian*
Sheehy, Eugene Paul *retired librarian, author*
†Van Dyk, Stephen Henry *librarian*
Wertsman, Vladimir Filip *librarian, information specialist, author*

Ogdensburg
Rusaw, Sally Ellen *librarian*

Oneonta
Johnson, Richard David *retired librarian*

Patchogue
Gibbard, Judith R. *library director*

Pleasantville
Murdock, William John *librarian*

Port Washington
†Ciccariello, Priscilla Chloe *librarian*

Poughkeepsie
Emerson, William R. *retired library executive, historian*
Henry, Charles Jay *library director*
Van Zanten, Frank Veldhuyzen *library system director*

Rhinebeck
McLaughlin, Dona Hougen *library director*

Rochester
†Chu, Ellin Resnick *librarian, consultant*
Matzek, Richard Allan *library director*
†Panz, Richard *library director*
Pitkin, Patricia Albanese *library administrator*
Swanton, Susan Irene *library director*
Wyatt, James Franklin *librarian*

Roslyn
Gelfand, Morris Arthur *librarian, publisher*

Sherrill
Rosendale, Suzanne Moore *library media specialist*

Somers
Lane, David Oliver *retired librarian*

Staten Island
Auh, Yang John *librarian, academic administrator*

Syracuse
Abbott, George Lindell *librarian*
†Daniels, Bruce Eric *library director*
Eisenberg, Michael Bruce *information studies educator*
Stam, David Harry *librarian*

Tarrytown
†Bowen, Christopher Edward *library director*

Tuckahoe
Silk, Eleana S. *librarian*

Vails Gate
Fife, Betty H. *librarian*

West Point
Watson, Georgianna *librarian*

White Plains
Manville, Stewart Roebling *archivist*

Yonkers
Miller, Jacqueline Winslow *library director*

NORTH CAROLINA

Chapel Hill
Campbell, Jerry Dean *librarian*
Carpenter, Raymond Leonard *information science educator*
Holley, Edward Gailon *library science educator, former university dean*
Kilgour, Frederick Gridley *librarian, educator*
Moran, Barbara Burns *librarian, educator*
Pruett, James Worrell *librarian, musicologist*

Charlotte
Cannon, Robert Eugene *librarian, public administrator, fund raiser*
Sintz, Edward Francis *librarian*

Davidson
Jones, Arthur Edwin, Jr. *library administrator, English and American literature educator*
Park, Leland Madison *librarian*

Durham
Canada, Mary Whitfield *librarian*
†Feinglos, Susan Jean *library director*
†Speller, Benjamin Franklin, Jr. *librarian, educator*
Thorn, Rosemary Kost *librarian*

Fayetteville
Thrasher, Jerry Arthur *library director*

Greensboro
Kovacs, Beatrice *library studies educator*
Miller, Marilyn Lea *library science educator*
Viele, George Brookins *library executive*
Wright, Kieth Carter *librarian, educator*

Greenville
Lennon, Donald Ray *archivist, historian*

Hendersonville
Peckham, Howard Henry *librarian, educator*

High Point
†Ellis, Kem Byron *public library administrator*

Raleigh
Littleton, Isaac Thomas, III *retired university library administrator, consultant*
Moore, Thomas Lloyd *librarian*

Saluda
Mowery, Bob Lee *librarian*

Washington
Timour, John Arnold *retired librarian, medical bibliography and library science educator*

Wilmington
Haselden, Clyde LeRoy *librarian*

Winston Salem
Berthrong, Merrill Gray *retired library director*
Channing, Rhoda Kramer *library director*
Roberts, William Hugh, III *library director, consultant*

NORTH DAKOTA

Mayville
Karaim, Betty June *librarian*

OHIO

Akron
Friedman, Richard Everett *librarian*
Rebenack, John Henry *retired librarian*

Athens
Lee, Hwa-Wei *librarian, educator*

Bedford
Parch, Grace Dolores *librarian*

Bluffton
Smucker, Barbara Claassen *former librarian, writer*

Chagrin Falls
Richmond, Phyllis Allen *library and information science educator*

Cincinnati
Bestehorn, Ute Wiltrud *retired librarian*
†Brestel, Mary Beth *librarian*
Hunt, James Robert *librarian*
†Monnig, Donna Sue *librarian*
Proffitt, H. Kevin *archivist*
Stonestreet, Robert *library director*
Warnken, Paula Neuman *university library director, educator*
†Wellington, Jean Susorney *librarian*
Wilson, Lucy Jean *librarian*
Zafren, Herbert Cecil *librarian, educator*

Cleveland
Abid, Ann B. *art librarian*
Gapen, Delores Kaye *librarian, educator*
Mason, Marilyn Gell *library administrator, writer, consultant*
Pike, Kermit Jerome *library director*
Rader, Hannelore *library director, consultant*

Columbus
Black, Larry David *library director*
Branscomb, Lewis Capers, Jr. *librarian, educator*
Sawyers, Elizabeth Joan *librarian, administrator*
Studer, William Joseph *library director*
Tiefel, Virginia May *librarian*

Dayton
Chait, William *librarian, consultant*
Helling, James T. *library director*
Klinck, Cynthia Anne *library director*
O'Brien, Elmer John *librarian, educator*
Wallach, John S(idney) *library administrator*

Grove City
Black, Frances Patterson *library administrator*

Lima
Dicke, Candice Edwards *library educator*

Medina
Matthews, Gertrude Ann Urch *retired librarian, writer*

Middleburg Heights
Maciuszko, Kathleen Lynn *librarian, educator*

Oberlin
English, Ray *library administrator*

Oxford
Sessions, Judith Ann *librarian, university library dean*

Perrysburg
Danford, Ardath Anne *retired librarian*

Rootstown
Sayre, Jean Williams *librarian, educator*

Springfield
Montag, John Joseph, II *librarian*
Pearson, Norman Ralston *librarian*

Van Wert
Duprey, Wilson Gilliland *retired librarian*

Wooster
Hickey, Damon D. *library director*

Youngstown
Trucksis, Theresa A. *library director*

OKLAHOMA

Norman
Hodges, Thompson Gene *librarian*
Kemp, Betty Ruth *librarian*
Lee, Sul Hi *library administrator*
Leonhardt, Thomas Wilburn *librarian, technical services director*
Sherman, Mary Angus *public library administrator*

Oklahoma City
Brawner, Lee Basil *librarian*

Stillwater
Johnson, Edward Roy *library director*

Tulsa
†Huttner, Sidney Frederick *librarian*
Woodrum, Patricia Ann *librarian*

OREGON

Astoria
Foster, Michael William *librarian*

Beaverton
Pond, Patricia Brown *library science educator, university administrator*

Corvallis
Hunt, Donald R. *retired librarian*

Eugene
Hildebrand, Carol Ilene *librarian*
Morrison, Perry David *librarian, educator*
Stirling, Isabel Ann *science librarian*

Portland
Browne, Joseph Peter *retired librarian*
Cooper, Ginnie *library director*
Eshelman, William Robert *librarian, editor*
Morgan, James Earl *librarian, administrator*

Salem
Oberg, Larry Reynold *librarian*
Turnbaugh, Roy Carroll *archivist*
†Weide, Janice Lee *librarian*

PENNSYLVANIA

Allentown
Allen, Anna Foster *librarian*
Stephanoff, Kathryn Ann *library director*

Allison Park
Hadidian, Dikran Yenovk *librarian, clergyman*

Beaver Falls
Moran, Gerald Dwight *academic librarian*

Bethel Park
Marrs, Sharon Carter *librarian*

Bethlehem
Sacks, Patricia Ann *librarian, consultant*

Bryn Mawr
Fanus, Pauline Rife *librarian*
Tanis, James Robert *library director, history educator, clergyman*

Butler
†Day, Margaret Ann *research librarian, information specialist*

Carlisle
Stachacz, John Charles *librarian*

Clarion
Mc Cabe, Gerard Benedict *library administrator*

Erie
Ridge, Michele Moore *librarian*

Greensburg
Duck, Patricia Mary *librarian*

Harrisburg
Parker, Sara Ann *librarian*

Kennett Square
Vainstein, Rose *librarian, educator*

Lancaster
Filler, Mary Ann *librarian*

New Kensington
Miller, Albert Jay *retired librarian, educator*

Philadelphia
Arnold, Lee *library director*
Axam, John Arthur *library consultant*
Carter, Edward Carlos, II *librarian, historian*
Gendron, Michèle Marguerite Madeleine *librarian*
Hamlin, Arthur Tenney *librarian*
Mosher, Paul H. *research library administrator, author, consultant*
Myers, James Nelson *librarian*
Shelkrot, Elliot Louis *librarian*

Pittsburgh
Bearman, Toni Carbo *information scientist*
Croneberger, Robert Bruce, Jr. *library director*
Josey, E(lonnie) J(unius) *librarian, educator, former state administrator*
Kent, Allen *library and information sciences educator*
†Minnigh, Joel Douglas *library director*
Woolls, Esther Blanche *library science educator*

Punxsutawney
Dinsmore, Roberta Joan Maier *library director*

Riegelsville
Banko, Ruth Caroline *library director*

Schuylkill Haven
Loder, Michael Wescott *librarian*

Scranton
Campion, Carol-Mae Sack *librarian*

Selinsgrove
Deekle, Peter Van *library director*

State College
Doms, Keith *retired library director*
Forth, Stuart *librarian*

Swarthmore
Durkan, Michael Joseph *librarian*

Titusville
Crowe, Virginia Mary *retired librarian*

University Park
Cline, Nancy M. *librarian*

Wayne
Garrison, Guy Grady *librarian, educator*
Townsend, Philip W., Jr. *library director*

Wilkes Barre
Mech, Terrence Francis *library director*

RHODE ISLAND

Jamestown
Logan, Nancy Allen *library media specialist*

Newport
†Schnare, Robert Edey, Jr. *library director*

Providence
Adams, Thomas Randolph *bibliographer, librarian, historian*
Bundy, Annalee Marshall *library director*
Caldwell-Wood, Naomi Rachel *library media specialist*
Edelstein, Jerome Melvin *bibliographer*
†Lynden, Frederick Charles *librarian*
Taylor, Merrily Ellen *university librarian*
Weaver, Barbara Frances *librarian*

Warwick
Charette, Sharon Juliette *library administrator*

SOUTH CAROLINA

Charleston
Basler, Thomas G. *librarian, administrator, educator*
Buvinger, Jan *library director*

Clemson
Boykin, Joseph Floyd, Jr. *librarian*

Columbia
Callaham, Betty Elgin *librarian*
Johnson, James Bek, Jr. *library director*
Rawlinson, Helen Ann *librarian*
Toombs, Kenneth Eldridge *librarian*
Warren, Charles David *library administrator*

Hartsville
Martin, Neal Anderson *library director*

Orangeburg
Thompson, Marguerite Myrtle Graming (Mrs. Ralph B. Thompson) *librarian*

Rock Hill
Du Bois, Paul Zinkhan *library director*

SOUTH DAKOTA

Brookings
†Raney, Leon A. *librarian*

Sioux Falls
Dertien, James LeRoy *librarian*
Thompson, Ronelle Kay Hildebrandt *library director*

TENNESSEE

Chattanooga
McFarland, Jane Elizabeth *librarian*

Collegedale
Bennett, Peggy Elizabeth *librarian, library director, educator*

Greeneville
Smith, Myron John, Jr. *librarian, author*

Jackson
Hazlewood, Judith Evans *librarian*

Jefferson City
Benson, Stanley Hugh *librarian*

Johnson City
Stokes, Thomas Edward *librarian*

Knoxville
Griffiths, José-Marie *information science educator*
Watson, Patricia L. *library director*

Maryville
Worley, Joan Hiett *library director*

Memphis
Drescher, Judith Altman *library director*
Pourciau, Lester John *librarian*
Wallis, Carlton Lamar *librarian*

Murfreesboro
Youree, Beverly B. *library science educator*

Nashville
Binkley, Yildiz Barlas *library director*
Getz, Malcolm *library administrator, economist, educator*
Gleaves, Edwin Sheffield *librarian*
†Hook, William John *library administrator*
†Stark, Caroline *library director*
Stewart, David Marshall *librarian*

Sewanee
Dunkly, James Warren *theological librarian*

TEXAS

Abilene
Specht, Alice Wilson *library director*

Alamo
McKelvy, Nicole Andrée *librarian*

Arlington
Burson, Betsy Lee *librarian*
Younkin, C. George *archivist*

Austin
Ardis, Susan Barber *librarian, educator*
Billings, Harold Wayne *librarian, editor*
Branch, Brenda Sue *library director*
Carpenter, Elizabeth Sutherland *library consultant, author, equal rights leader, lecturer*
Davis, Donald Gordon, Jr. *librarian, educator*
Gooch, William DeWitt *librarian*
Gracy, David Bergen, II *archivist, information science educator, writer*
Holt, David Earl *librarian*
Jackson, Eugene Bernard *librarian*
Jackson, William Vernon *library science and Latin American studies educator*
Middleton, Harry Joseph *library administrator*
Oram, Robert W. *library administrator*
†Rascoe, Paul Stephen *librarian, researcher*

Beaumont
†Gray, Maurine *library director*

Cedar Hill
Hickman, Traphene Parramore *library director, storyteller, library and library building consultant*

Clarendon
Roper, Beryl Cain *library director*

College Station
Hoadley, Irene Braden (Mrs. Edward Hoadley) *librarian*
Wilson, Don Whitman *archivist, historian*

Corpus Christi
Canales, Herbert Glenn *librarian*

Dallas
Bockstruck, Lloyd DeWitt *librarian*
Bradshaw, Lillian Moore *retired library director*
Ibach, Robert Daniel, Jr. *library director*
Pastine, Maureen Diane *librarian*
Salazar, Ramiro S. *library administrator*
Witmer, John Albert *librarian*

Denton
Grose, B. Donald *library administrator*
†Poole, Eva Duraine *librarian*
Snapp, Elizabeth *librarian, educator*

El Paso
Strait, Viola Edwina Washington *librarian*

Fort Worth
Allmand, Linda F(aith) *library director*
Ard, Harold Jacob *library administrator*
de Tonnancour, Paul Roger Godefroy *library administrator*

Garland
†Lindsey, Lowell L. *library director*

Grand Prairie
Ritterhouse, Kathy Lee *librarian*

Houston
Chang, Robert Huei *library director*
Downes, Robin *library director*
Henington, David Mead *library director*
Hornak, Anna Frances *library administrator*
Liddell, Leon Morris *librarian, educator*
Newbold, Benjamin Millard, Jr. *library manager, education consultant*
Radoff, Leonard Irving *librarian, consultant*
Shapiro, Beth Janet *librarian*
Suter, Jon Michael *academic library director, educator*
Wilson, Patricia Potter *library science and reading educator, educational and library consultant*

Lubbock
Murrah, David J. *archivist, historian*
Rippel, Jeffrey Alan *library director*
Wood, Richard Courtney *library director, educator*

Marshall
Magrill, Rose Mary *library director*

Mcallen
†McGee, William Howard John *library system coordinator*
Mittelstaedt, Gerard E. *library director*

Mesquite
Williams, John Elbert, Jr. *library services director*

Midland
†Wegner, Sandra Sue *library director*

Palestine
Williams, Franklin Cadmus, Jr. *bibliographer*

Pasadena
†Clifford, Ann Tharp *library director*

Port Isabel
Smith, Mary Lou *librarian*

Richardson
†Lovelace, Julianne *library director*

San Angelo
Chatfield, Mary Van Abshoven *librarian*

San Antonio
Garcia, June Marie *library director*
Jones, Daniel Hare *librarian*
Kozuch, Julianna Bernadette *librarian, educator*
Kronick, David A. *librarian*
Nance, Betty Love *librarian*
Young, Olivia Knowles *retired librarian*

Seguin
Moline, Sandra Lois *librarian*

Seminole
Molinar, Lupe Rodriquez *librarian, library director*

Terrell
Johnson, Doris Theressa *library director*

Tyler
Albertson, Christopher Adam *librarian*
Cleveland, Mary Louise *librarian, media specialist*

Waco
Bonnell, Pamela Gay *library administrator*
Hair, William Bates, III *librarian*
Lindsey, Jonathan Asmel *development executive, educator*
Progar, Dorothy *retired library director*

UTAH

Provo
†Gillum, Gary Paul *librarian*
Hall, Blaine Hill *librarian*
†Jensen, Richard Dennis *librarian*
Marchant, Maurice Peterson *librarian, educator*
Smith, Nathan McKay *library and information sciences educator*

Salt Lake City
Anderson, Grant Allen *librarian*
Buttars, Gerald Anderson *librarian*
Day, Joseph Dennis *librarian*
Hanson, Roger Kvamme *librarian*
Longsworth, Eileen Catherine *library director*
†Morrison, David Lee *librarian, educator*
Owen, Amy *library director*

VERMONT

Burlington
Martin, Rebecca Reist *librarian*

South Burlington
Kebabian, Paul Blakeslee *librarian*

VIRGINIA

Alexandria
Berger, Patricia Wilson *retired librarian*
Budde, Mitzi Marie Jarrett *librarian*
Mulvihill, John Gary *information services administrator*
O'Brien, Patrick Michael *library administrator*
Strickland, Nellie B. *library program director*

Arlington
Fling, Jacqueline Ann *library administrator*
Nida, Jane Bolster (Mrs. Dow Hughes Nida) *retired librarian*

Castleton
Hahn, James Maglorie *former librarian, farmer*

Charlottesville
Berkeley, Edmund, Jr. *archivist, educator*
Berkeley, Francis Lewis, Jr. *retired archivist*
Frantz, Ray William, Jr. *retired librarian*
Frieden, Charles Leroy *university library administrator*
Healey, James Stewart *library science educator*
Self, James Reed *librarian*
Stubbs, Kendon Lee *librarian*
†Watson, Linda Anne *library director*

Chesapeake
Forehand Stillman, Margaret P. *library director*

Farmville
Boyer, Calvin James *librarian*

Fredericksburg
Dennis, Donald Daly *retired librarian*

Harrisonburg
Lehman, James Orten *library director*
Palmer, Forrest Charles *librarian, educator*

Leesburg
Fall, Dorothy Eleanor *librarian*

Lexington
Brown, Barbara Jeanne *librarian*
Gaines, James Edwin, Jr. *retired librarian*
Leach, Maurice Derby, Jr. *librarian*

Mc Lean
Hashim, Elinor Marie *librarian*

Norfolk
Williams, Sue Darden *library director*

Portsmouth
Burgess, Dean *library director*

Rapidan
Grimm, Ben Emmet *former library director and consultant*

Richmond
Costa, Robert Nicholas *library director*
Ford, Barbara Jean *library studies educator*
Trotti, John Boone *librarian, educator*

Roanoke
Kirkwood, Richard Edwin *librarian*

Springfield
Gawalt, Gerard W(ilfred) *historian, writer*

Virginia Beach
Sims, Martha J. *library director*

Williamsburg
Marshall, Nancy Haig *library administrator*

WASHINGTON

Bellevue
Mutschler, Herbert Frederick *retired librarian*

Bellingham
Rhoads, James Berton *archivist, former government official, consultant, educator*

College Place
Jonish, Arley Duane *retired bibliographer*

Everett
†Nesse, Mark A. *library director*

Kirkland
Rosett, Ann Doyle *librarian*

Olympia
Zussy, Nancy Louise *librarian*

Pullman
Roberts, Elizabeth Porcher *library director*

Seattle
Bengtson, Betty Grimes *library administrator*
†Blase, Nancy Gross *librarian*
Boylan, Merle Nelson *librarian*
Chisholm, Margaret Elizabeth *retired library education administrator*
Gallagher, Marian Gould *librarian, educator*
Hiatt, Peter *library educator*
Privat, Jeannette Mary *bank librarian*
Ptacek, William H. *library director*
†Stroup, Elizabeth Faye *librarian*
Van Orden, Phyllis Jeanne *librarian, educator*

Spokane
Bender, Betty Wion *librarian*
Burr, Robert Lyndon *library director*
Wirt, Michael James *library director*

Tacoma
Crisman, Mary Frances Borden *librarian*

Walla Walla
Yaple, Henry Mack *library director*

WEST VIRGINIA

Bradley
Chesley, Eddie A. *librarian, educator*

Charleston
Basham, Debra Ann *archivist*
Glazer, Frederic Jay *librarian*

Glenville
Tubesing, Richard Lee *library director*

Institute
Scott, John Edward *librarian*

Morgantown
Pyles, Rodney Allen *archivist, county official*

Shepherdstown
Elliott, Jean Ann *library administrator*

WISCONSIN

Eau Claire
Marquardt, Steve Robert *library director*
Thompson, Glenn Judean *library science educator*

Kenosha
Baker, Douglas Finley *library director*

Madison
Bunge, Charles Albert *library science educator*
Dewey, Gene Lawrence *librarian*
†Weingand, Darlene Erna *librarian educator, consultant*

Milwaukee
Huston, Kathleen Marie *library administrator*
McKinney, Venora Ware *librarian*

Oshkosh
Jones, Norma Louise *librarian, educator*

Sheboygan
Winkle, Sharon Louise *library administrator*

Thiensville
Roselle, William Charles *librarian*

WYOMING

Cheyenne
Johnson, Wayne Harold *librarian, county official*
LeBarron, Suzanne Jane *librarian*

Laramie
Cottam, Keith M. *librarian, educator, administrator*

TERRITORIES OF THE UNITED STATES

GUAM

Barrigada
Uyehara, Harry Yoshimi *library educator*

Mangilao
Hamerly, Michael T. *librarian*

PUERTO RICO

Rio Piedras
†Maura, Mariano A. *library and information science educator*

San Juan
González Echevarria, Amelia L. *librarian, counselor*
Muñoz-Solá, Haydeé Socorro *library administrator*

CANADA

ALBERTA

Calgary
MacDonald, Alan Hugh *librarian, university administrator*
Meek, Gerry *library director*

Edmonton
McDougall, Donald Blake *retired government official, librarian*
McKee, Penelope Melna *library director*

Lethbridge
Rand, Duncan D. *librarian*

BRITISH COLUMBIA

Abbotsford
Sifton, Patricia Anne *library educator*

Nanaimo
Meadows, Donald Frederick *librarian*

Vancouver
Aalto, Madeleine *library director*
Coley, Betty *librarian*
Piternick, Anne Brearley *librarian, educator*
Rothstein, Samuel *librarian, educator*

Victoria
Hamilton, Donald Emery *librarian*

MANITOBA

Winnipeg
Converse, William Rawson Mackenzie *librarian*

†Weismiller, David R. *library administrator*

NEWFOUNDLAND

Saint John's
Penney, Pearce John *retired librarian*

NOVA SCOTIA

Halifax
Amey, Lorne James *library science educator*
Birdsall, William Forest *librarian*
Dykstra, Mary Elizabeth *library and information science educator*

ONTARIO

Guelph
McLeod, Norman Carl *librarian*

Hamilton
Hill, Graham Roderick *librarian*
McAnanama, Judith *library executive*

London
Edgar, Shirley Anne *librarian, educator*
†Osborne, Reed E. *library executive*

Mississauga
Mills, Donald McKenzie *librarian*
Ryan, Noel *librarian, consultant*

North York
Bryant, Josephine Harriet *library executive*
Davidson-Arnott, Frances E. *library science educator*
Land, Reginald Brian *library administrator*

Oakville
Wilburn, Marion Turner *library and information scientist educator, consultant*

Ottawa
Brown, Jack Ernest *information scientist*
Frappier, Gilles *librarian*
Scott, Marianne Florence *librarian, educator*
Spicer, Erik John *retired Canadian parliamentary librarian*
Sylvestre, Jean Guy *former national librarian*
Wallot, Jean-Pierre *archivist, historian*

Peterborough
†Brown, Wendy Evelynn *library director*

Scarborough
Bassnett, Peter James *librarian*

Thunder Bay
Harrison, Karen Ann *library director*

Toronto
Burgis, Grover Cornelius *librarian*
Fasick, Adele Mongan *library science educator*
Moore, Carole Irene *librarian*
Packer, Katherine Helen *retired library educator*
Schwenger, Frances *library director*

Windsor
Dirksen, Jean *library administrator*
Israel, Fred Carl *library director*

QUEBEC

Hull
†Boyer, Denis *library director*

Montreal
Gardner, Richard Kent *retired librarian, educator, consultant*
Large, John Andrew *library and information service educator*
Ormsby, Eric Linn *library administrator, researcher*
Panneton, Jacques *librarian*
Sauvageau, Philippe *library director*
Sykes, Stephanie Lynn *library director, archivist, museum director*

Quebec
Paradis, Andre *librarian*

Rosemere
Adrian, Donna Jean *librarian*

SASKATCHEWAN

Regina
Powell, Trevor John David *archivist*

Saskatoon
Kennedy, Marjorie Ellen *librarian*

MEXICO

Mexico City
Rodriguez, Adolfo *library director, historian*

AUSTRALIA

Belair
Briggs, Geoffrey Hugh *retired librarian*

Kensington
Rayward, Warden Boyd *librarian, educator*

CZECH REPUBLIC

Prague
Kalkus, Stanley *librarian, administrator, consultant*

ITALY

Rome
Casolino, Vincenzo *library director*

THAILAND

Bangkok
Stueart, Robert D. *university information services director, educator*

ADDRESS UNPUBLISHED

Adamovich, Shirley Gray *retired librarian, state official*
†Baker, Zachary Moshe *librarian*
Boyd, Alex *library director*
Callard, Carole Crawford *librarian, educator*
Campbell, Henry Cummings *librarian*
Cartier, Celine Paule *librarian, administrator, consultant*
Clement, Hope Elizabeth Anna *librarian*
Cluff, E. Dale *librarian, educator, administrator*
Cooke, Eileen Delores *retired librarian*
Curley, Elmer Frank *librarian*
Driver, Lottie Elizabeth *librarian*
Edmonds, Anne Carey *librarian*
†Else, Carolyn Joan *library system administrator*
Erickson, Alan Eric *librarian*
Flinner, Beatrice Eileen *library and media sciences educator*
Fowlie, Eldon Leslie *retired library administrator*
Gardner, William Michael *library administrator*
Gilbert, Nancy Louise *librarian*
Gould, Martha Bernice *retired librarian*
Gregor, Dorothy Deborah *librarian*
†Hill, Malcolm Kendall *library administrator*
Hoke, Sheila Wilder *retired librarian*
Howard, Joseph Harvey *retired librarian*
Jenkins, Darrell Lee *librarian*
Kaser, David *retired librarian, educator, consultant*
Kaufman, Paula T. *librarian*
Klatt, Melvin John *library consultant*
Komidar, Joseph Stanley *librarian*
Leather, Victoria Potts *college librarian*
Loder, Victoria Kosiorek *information broker*
Martin, Louis Edward *retired library director*
Martin, Murray Simpson *librarian, writer, consultant*
McBurney, Margot B. *librarian*
Miele, Anthony William *retired librarian*
Miller, Charles Edmond *library administrator*
†Miller, Glenn *library director, retired*
Moody, Roland Herbert *retired librarian*
Morgan, Jane Hale *retired library director*
†Nelson, Helen Martha *retired library director*
Patterson, Robert Hudson *library director*
Rafael, Ruth Kelson *archivist, librarian, consultant*
Richards, Vincent Philip Haslewood *librarian*
Rohlf, Robert Henry *retired library director, library consultant*
Rouse, Roscoe, Jr. *librarian, educator*
Sadler, Graham Hydrick *library administrator*
Scoles, Clyde Sheldon *library director*
Segal, JoAn Smyth *library consultant, organization administrator*
Sheldon, Brooke Earle *librarian, educator*
Smith, Howard McQueen *librarian*
Smith, Sallye Wrye *librarian*
Spaulding, Frank Henry *librarian*
†Spencer, David Mills *library administrator*
Stallworth-Barron, Doris A. Carter *librarian, educator*
Stavely, Keith Williams Fitzgerald *librarian*
Suput, Ray Radoslav *librarian*
Tashjean, Catherine Richardson *librarian*
Teeple, Fiona Diane *librarian, lawyer*
Trenery, Mary Ellen *librarian*
Williams, Gordon Roland *librarian*
Williams, Richard Clarence *retired librarian*
Yeo, Ronald Frederick *librarian*

HUMANITIES: MUSEUMS

UNITED STATES

ALABAMA

Birmingham
†Burnham, James A. *museum director and consultant*

Florence
Wright, Mildred Anne (Milly Wright) *conservator, researcher*

Huntsville
Buckbee, Edward O'Dell *museum administrator*

Jacksonville
Quick, Edward Raymond *museum director*

Mc Calla
Gentry, Vicki Paulette *museum director*

Mobile
Richelson, Paul William *curator*
†Schenk, Joseph B. *museum director*

Tuscaloosa
Jones, Douglas Epps *natural history museum director*

ALASKA

Fairbanks
†Jonaitis, Aldona Claire *museum administrator, art historian*

Juneau
Lonner, Thomas Dunstan *museum director*

ARIZONA

Flagstaff
Thompson, Philip Mason *museum director*

Mesa
Mead, Tray C. *museum administrator*

Phoenix
Grinell, Sheila *museum director*
Sullivan, Martin Edward *museum director*

Portal
Zweifel, Richard George *curator*

Tempe
Zeitlin, Marilyn Audrey *museum director*

Tucson
Bermingham, Peter *museum director*
Davis, Daniel Edward *museum director*
Hancocks, David Morgan *museum director, architect*
Yassin, Robert Alan *museum administrator, curator*

ARKANSAS

Little Rock
DuBois, Alan Beekman *art museum administrator, curator*
Wolfe, Townsend Durant, III *art museum director, curator*

State University
Jones, Charlott Ann *museum director, art educator*

CALIFORNIA

Bakersfield
Enriquez, Carola Rupert *museum director*

Berkeley
Benedict, Burton *retired museum director, anthropology educator*

Costa Mesa
Labbe, Armand Joseph *museum curator, anthropologist*

Fresno
Sobey, Edwin J. C. *museum director, oceanographer, consultant*

Garden Grove
Bledsoe, Jane Kathryn *art museum director, art historian*

Hollywood
Byrnes, James Bernard *museum director emeritus*

La Jolla
Beebe, Mary Livingstone *curator*
Davies, Hugh Marlais *museum director*

Lodi
Bennett, Michael William *museum and historical society director*

Long Beach
Glenn, Constance White *art museum director, educator, consultant*
†Nelson, Harold Bernhard *museum director*

Los Angeles
Cohen, Daniel Morris *museum administrator, marine biology researcher*
Ela, Patrick Hobson *museum director*
Holo, Selma Reuben *museum director, educator*
Hopkins, Henry Tyler *art educator, university gallery director*
†Kaye, Carole *museum director and curator*
Koshalek, Richard *museum director, consultant*
Kuwayama, George *curator*
Pal, Pratapaditya *museum curator*
Powell, James Lawrence *museum president*
Rudolph, Jeffrey N. *museum director*

Los Osos
Dorland, Frank Norton *art conservator*

Newport Beach
Botwinick, Michael *museum director*

North Hollywood
Bull, David *fine art conservator*

Oakland
Burns, Catherine Elizabeth *art dealer*
Power, Dennis Michael *museum director*

Pacific Grove
Adams, Margaret Bernice *retired museum official*

Palm Springs
†Frauchiger, Fritz Arnold *museum director*
†Golden, Morton Jay *museum director*

Palo Alto
Gubins, Samuel *museum administrator*

Pasadena
Gilman, Richard Carleton *museum executive, retired college president*

Redding
Becker, Stephen Arnold *museum director*

Riverside
Green, Jonathan William *museum administrator and educator, artist, author*

Sacramento
Mette, Joe *museum director*

San Diego
Brezzo, Steven Louis *museum director*
DiMattio, Terry *historic site administrator*
Petersen, Martin Eugene *museum curator*

San Francisco
†Berggruen, John Henry *art gallery executive*
Lane, John Rodger *art museum director*
Leviton, Alan Edward *museum curator*
Lindsay, George Edmund *museum director*
Parker, Harry S., III *art museum administrator*
Shangraw, Clarence Frank *museum official*
Thomas, William Geraint *museum administrator*

San Jose
Callan, Josi Irene *museum director*

San Marino
Skotheim, Robert Allen *museum administrator*
Wark, Robert Rodger *art curator*

Santa Barbara
†Breunig, Robert G. *natural history museum director*
Gebhard, David *museum director, educator*
Karpeles, David *museum director*

Santa Clara
†Schapp, Rebecca Maria *museum director*

Santa Cruz
Prentiss, Charles Gary *museum director*

Santa Monica
Walsh, John, Jr. *museum director*

Sausalito
Elliott, James Heyer *retired university art museum curator, fine arts consultant*

Stanford
Seligman, Thomas Knowles *museum administrator*

Watsonville
Hernandez, Jo Farb *museum and curatorial consultant*

Yucaipa
Griesemer, Allan David *museum director*

COLORADO

Boulder
Danilov, Victor Joseph *museum management program director, consultant, writer, educator*
Hay, William Winn *former museum director, natural history and geology educator*
Lanham, Urless Norton *curator*

Colorado Springs
Hoge, Robert Wilson *museum curator*
LeMieux, Linda Dailey *museum director*
Warner, Michael D. *museum director*

Denver
Foxley, Matthew C. *art gallery administrator*
Graham, Linda Marie *museum director, photographer*

CONNECTICUT

Hartford
Faude, Wilson Hinsdale *museum director*
White, David Oliver *museum executive*

Mystic
†Carr, J. Revell *museum executive, curator*
Johnston, Waldo Cory Melrose *museum director*

New Haven
Casteras, Susan Paulette *museum curator, educator*
Hickey, Leo J(oseph) *museum curator, educator*
Kane, Patricia Ellen *museum curator*
Noon, Patrick *museum curator*
Robinson, (David) Duncan *museum administrator, art historian*
†Vogel, Susan Mullin *museum director*

New London
Knowles, Elizabeth Pringle *art museum director*

Norwich
Gualtieri, Joseph Peter *museum director*

Stamford
Kinsman, Robert Donald *art museum administrator, cartoonist*
Mayhall, Dorothy Ann *museum director, curator of art, sculptor*
†Rasmussen, Gerald Elmer *museum director*
Scribner, Barbara Colvin *museum administrator*

Weston
Daniel, James *curator, business executive, writer, former editor,*

DELAWARE

Wilmington
Bruni, Stephen Thomas *art museum director*
Elzea, Rowland Procter *art museum curator*
Otey, Orlando *music executive, educator, pianist, theorist*

Porter, Glenn *museum and library administrator*
Woodward, Anne Spivey *museum director*

Winterthur
Hummel, Charles Frederick *museum official*
Lanmon, Dwight Pierson *museum director*

DISTRICT OF COLUMBIA

Washington
Abbott, Rebecca Phillips *museum director*
Beach, Milo C. *art museum director*
Benezra, Neal *curator*
Berenbaum, Michael G. *museum director, theology educator*
Bier, Carol Manson *museum curator*
Bowron, Edgar Peters *art museum curator, administrator*
Boyd, Susan Anne *curator*
Brannan, Beverly Wood *curator of photography*
Bretzfelder, Deborah May *museum exhibit designer, photographer*
Cikovsky, Nicolai, Jr. *curator, art history educator*
Cowart, Jack *museum executive*
Crew, Spencer *museum administrator*
Demetrion, James Thomas *art museum director*
Evelyn, Douglas Everett *museum executive*
†Frankel, Diane *museum institute administrator*
Freedberg, Sydney Joseph *retired museum curator, retired fine arts educator*
Freudenheim, Tom Lippmann *museum administrator*
Fu, Shen C. Y. *curator, art historian*
Furgol, Edward Mackie *museum curator, historian*
Grasselli, Margaret Morgan *curator*
Hand, John Oliver *museum curator*
Heyman, Ira Michael *museum executive, law educator, former government official*
Hoffmann, Robert Shaw *museum administrator, educator*
Ketchum, James Roe *curator*
Kilbourne, John Dwight *museum and library director*
Lawton, Thomas *art gallery director*
Levy, David Corcos *museum director*
Lowe, Harry *museum director*
Marsh, Caryl Amsterdam *curator, psychologist*
Mellon, Paul *retired art gallery executive*
Micozzi, Marc Stephen *museum director, physician, educator*
Moffett, Charles Simonton *museum director, curator, writer*
†Neufeld, Michael John *curator, historian*
Panzer, Mary Caroline *museum curator*
Phillips, Laughlin *museum president, former magazine editor*
Rahill, Margaret Fish *retired museum curator*
Ravenhill, Philip Leonard *curator, art historian*
Reaves, Wendy Wick *museum curator*
Robison, Andrew Cliffe, Jr. *museum curator*
Russell, H. Diane *museum curator, educator*
†Scouten, Rex W. *curator*
Sheehan, Michael Terrence *arts administrator, historian, consultant*
Shestack, Alan *museum administrator*
Sopher, Vicki Elaine *museum director*
Stanton, Robert *historic site director*
Sultan, Terrie Frances *curator*
Viola, Herman Joseph *museum director*
Weil, Stephen Edward *museum official*
West, W. Richard, Jr. *museum director*
Williams, Sylvia Hill *museum director*
Wolanin, Barbara Ann Boese *art curator, art historian*

FLORIDA

Boca Raton
Selby, Roger Lowell *museum director*

Daytona Beach
Libby, Gary Russell *museum director*

Fort Myers
Halgrim, Robert P. *museum director*

Gainesville
Bennett, Thomas Peter *museum director, educator, biologist*
Bishop, Budd Harris *museum administrator*
Dickinson, Joshua Clifton, Jr. *museum director, educator*
Valdés, Karen W. *art gallery director, educator*
Wing, Elizabeth Schwarz *museum curator, educator*

Jacksonville
Adams, Henry *museum director*
Dundon, Margo Elaine *museum director*
Schlageter, Robert William *museum administrator*

Miami
Etling, Russell Hull *museum director, production company executive*
Parris, Nina Gumpert *curator, writer, researcher*

Naples
†Gardner, Frank *museum director*

Orlando
Morrisey, Marena Grant *art museum administrator*

Pensacola
Rasmussen, Robert *museum director*

Saint Petersburg
Duval, Cynthia *museum curator, administrator*

Sarasota
Warner, Lee Howland *cultural program director*

Tallahassee
Palladino-Craig, Allys *museum director*

Tampa
Maass, R. Andrew *museum director*

West Palm Beach
Donovan, Ellen L. *museum director*
Orr-Cahall, Christina *art gallery director, art historian*

Winter Park
Ruggiero, Laurence Joseph *museum director*

GEORGIA

Atlanta
Davis, Eleanor Kay *museum administrator*
Hiers, Mary A. *museum director*
Vigtel, Gudmund *museum director emeritus*

Columbus
Butler, Charles Thomas *museum director, curator*

Fort Benning
Grube, Dick DeWayne *museum director*

Kennesaw
†Cissell, John *national park superintendent*

Macon
Anderson, Nancy *museum director*
Bundy, John Franklin, Jr. *national monument superintendent*
Oliver, Katherine C. *museum director*

Roswell
Forbes, John Ripley *museum executive, educator*

Saint Simons Island
King, Linda Orr *museum director*
†Tennent, Michael D. *park ranger administrator*

Savannah
Cave, Kent R. *national park ranger*

HAWAII

Honaunau
†Shimoda, Jerry Yasutaka *national historic park administrator*

Honolulu
Duckworth, Walter Donald *museum executive, entomologist*
Ellis, George Richard *museum administrator*
Klobe, Tom *art gallery director*
†Magee, Donald Edward *national park service administrator*
†Matelic, Candace Tangorra *museum studies educator, consultant, museum director*

Kaneohe
Lagoria, Georgianna Marie *curator, writer, editor, visual art consultant*

IDAHO

Pocatello
Jackson, Allen Keith *museum administrator*

ILLINOIS

Carbondale
Whitlock, John Joseph *museum director*

Chicago
Balzekas, Stanley, Jr. *museum director*
Boyd, Willard Lee *museum administrator, educator, lawyer*
Consey, Kevin Edward *museum administrator*
Druick, Douglas Wesley *museum administrator*
Edelstein, Teri J. *museum administrator, educator*
†Flynn, John J. *museum curator*
†Gray, Paul L. *art dealer*
Haas, Jonathan *museum research organization executive*
Heltne, Paul Gregory *museum executive*
Jakstas, Alfred John *museum conservator, consultant*
Kahn, James Steven *museum director*
Kamyszew, Christopher D. *museum curator, executive educator, art consultant*
†Knappenberger, Paul Henry, Jr. *science museum director*
Kubida, Judith Ann *museum administrator*
Lewis, Phillip Harold *museum curator*
Mueller, Gregory M. *museum curator, botanist, researcher*
Nordland, Gerald *art museum administrator, historian, consultant*
†Sautter, Dianne Lee *children's museum director*
†Travis, David B. *curator*
Wardropper, Ian Bruce *museum curator, educator*
Wilson, Karen Lee *museum curator*
Wood, James Nowell *museum director and executive*
Zukowsky, John Robert *curator*

Homewood
MacMaster, Daniel Miller *retired museum official*

Lerna
†Vance, Thomas Carter *historic site director*

Springfield
Hallmark, Donald Parker *museum director*
Mc Millan, R(obert) Bruce *museum executive, anthropologist*

INDIANA

Bloomington
Calinescu, Adriana Gabriela *museum curator, art historian*
Gealt, Adelheid Maria *museum director*

Elkhart
Kovach, John Michael *museum director, historian*

Evansville
Streetman, John William, III *museum official*

Goshen
Morris, Robert Julian, Jr. *art gallery owner*

Indianapolis
Gantz, Richard Alan *museum administrator*
Waller, Aaron Bret, III *museum director*

Muncie
†Clark, Nicholas L. *museum director, ethnic consultant*
Joyaux, Alain Georges *art museum director*

Notre Dame
†Porter, Dean Allen *art museum director, art historian, educator*

IOWA

Davenport
†Bradley, William Steven *art museum director*

Iowa City
Prokopoff, Stephen Stephen *art museum director, educator*

KANSAS

Dodge City
Clifton-Smith, Rhonda Darleen *art center director*

Fort Leavenworth
†Allie, Stephen J. *museum curator*

Lawrence
Norris, Andrea Spaulding *art museum director*

University Of Kansas
Humphrey, Philip Strong *university museum director*

KENTUCKY

Lexington
Fowler, Harriet Whittemore *art museum director*

Louisville
Becker, Gail Roselyn *museum director*
Morrin, Peter Patrick *museum director*

Murray
Hunt, Mark Alan *museum director*

Owensboro
Hood, Mary Bryan *museum director, painter*

LOUISIANA

Baton Rouge
†Gikas, Carol Sommerfeldt *museum director*

New Orleans
Bullard, Edgar John, III *museum director*
Casellas, Joachim *art gallery executive*
Fagaly, William Arthur *curator*
Freeman, Montine McDaniel *museum trustee*
Glasgow, Vaughn Leslie *museum curator and administrator*

Shreveport
Shannon, George Ward, Jr. *museum director, anthropologist, archaeologist*

MAINE

Augusta
Phillips, Joseph Robert *museum director*

Brunswick
Watson, Katharine Johnson *art museum director, art historian*

Kennebunk
Escalet, Frank Diaz *art gallery owner, artist, educator*

Orono
Hartgen, Vincent Andrew *museum director, educator, artist*
Weber, Jean MacPhail *museum director*

Portland
Nosanow, Barbara Shissler *museum director*

Rockland
Crosman, Christopher Byron *art museum administrator*

MARYLAND

Annapolis
Cheevers, James William *museum curator*

Baltimore
Bastedo, Ralph W(alter) *museum administrator, educator*
Fisher, Jay McKean *museum curator*
Fishman, Bernard Philip *museum director*
Hanle, Paul Arthur *museum administrator*
Johnston, William Ralph *museum curator*
Lamp, Frederick John *museum curator*
Lehman, Arnold Lester *museum official, art historian*
Ott, John Harlow *museum administrator*
Randall, Lilian Maria Charlotte *museum curator*
Reeder, Ellen Dryden *museum curator*
Richardson, Brenda *musuem administrator*
Somerville, Romaine Stec *arts administrator*
Spicer, Joaneath A. *museum curator*
Tyler, John W. *historic site administrator*

Vikan, Gary Kent *art museum administrator*
Weidman, Gregory Rowlett *curator, historic interiors consultant*

Colton Point
Humphries, Michael Elwood *museum director*

Elkton
Smith, James Morton *museum administrator, historian*

MASSACHUSETTS

Amherst
Parkhurst, Charles *retired museum director, art historian*
Sandweiss, Martha A. *museum director, author, American studies educator*

Boston
Brovarski, Edward Joseph *curator, Egyptologist*
Cederholm, Theresa Miriam Dickason *museum director*
Curran, Emily Katherine *museum director*
Ellis, David Wertz *museum director*
Fairbanks, Jonathan Leo *museum curator*
Freed, Rita Evelyn *curator, Egyptologist, educator*
Hawley, Anne *museum director*
Hills, Patricia Gorton Schulze *curator*
Howlett, D(onald) Roger *art gallery executive, art historian*
Krakow, Barbara Levy *art gallery executive*
Meister, Mark Jay *museum director, professional society administrator*
Nylander, Jane Louise *museum director*
†Rogers, Malcolm Austin *museum curator, art historian*
Vermeule, Cornelius Clarkson, III *museum curator*
Washburn, H. Bradford, Jr. *museum administrator, cartographer, photographer*
Wentworth, Michael Justin *curator*
Wu, Tung *curator, art historian, art educator, artist*
Zahn, Carl Frederick *museum publications director, designer, photographer*
Zannieri, Nina *museum director*

Brewster
Lindquist, Susan Pratzner *museum executive*

Cambridge
Cohn, Marjorie Benedict *curator, art historian, educator*
Cuno, James *art museum director*
Gaskell, Ivan George Alexander De Wend *art museum curator*
Mongan, Agnes *museum curator, art historian, educator*
Mowry, Robert Dean *art museum curator, educator*
Rathbone, Perry Townsend *art museum director*
Seamans, Warren Arthur *museum director*
Slive, Seymour *museum director, fine arts educator*

Deerfield
Friary, Donald Richard *museum administrator*

Duxbury
Vose, Robert Churchill, Jr. *former art gallery executive*

Fitchburg
Timms, Peter Rowland *art museum administrator*

Lincoln
Master-Karnik, Paul Joseph *art museum director*

New Bedford
Young, Janie Chester *museum consultant*

North Andover
Rivard, Paul Edmund *museum director*

Plymouth
†Ehrlich, Richard L. *museum executive*

Salem
Fetchko, Peter J. *museum administrator*
Finamore, Daniel Robert *museum curator*

Springfield
Muhlberger, Richard Charles *former museum administrator, writer*
Sturges, Hollister, III *museum director*

Waltham
Arena, Albert A. *museum director*
Belz, Carl Irvin *museum director*

Wellesley
Freeman, Judi H. *museum curator, art historian*

Williamstown
Conforti, Michael Peter *museum director, art historian*
Hamilton, George Heard *curator*

Worcester
Barnhill, Georgia Brady *print curator*
Harkavy, Donna *curator*
Jareckie, Stephen Barlow *museum curator*
King, Anthony Gabriel *museum administrator*
Welu, James A. *art museum director*

MICHIGAN

Ann Arbor
Bailey, Reeve Maclaren *museum curator*
Hennessey, William John *museum director*

Dearborn
Skramstad, Harold Kenneth *museum administrator, consultant*

Detroit
Darr, Alan Phipps *curator, historian*
Peck, William Henry *museum curator, art historian, archaeologist, author, lecturer*

Sachs, Samuel, II *museum director*
Shaw, Nancy Rivard *museum curator, art historian, educator*

East Lansing
Bandes, Susan Jane *museum director, educator*
Dewhurst, Charles Kurt *museum director, curator, folklorist, English educator*

Flint
Germann, Steven James *museum director*
Mahey, John Andrew *museum director*

Grand Rapids
†Chester, Timothy J. *museum director*
Frankforter, Weldon DeLoss *retired museum administrator*
Sobol, Judith Ellen *museum director, art historian*

Kalamazoo
Bridenstine, James Aloysius *museum director*
Norris, Richard Patrick *museum director, history educator*

MINNESOTA

Minneapolis
Halbreich, Kathy *museum director*
King, Lyndel Irene Saunders *art museum director*
Maurer, Evan Maclyn *art museum director*

Saint Paul
Appelhof, Ruth Stevens *museum director, curator, art historian*
Czarniecki, Myron James, III *art museum director, cultural planner*
Osman, Stephen Eugene *historic site administrator*
Peterson, James Lincoln *museum executive*

MISSISSIPPI

Hattiesburg
Graves, Sid Foster, Jr. *library and museum director*

Jackson
Hiatt, Jane Crater *arts agency administrator*
Knapp, Richard S. *planetarium director*

MISSOURI

Hannibal
Sweets, Henry Hayes, III *museum director*

Hermann
†Renn, Erin McCawley *museum administrator*

Kansas City
McKenna, George LaVerne *art museum curator*
Scott, Deborah Emont *curator*
Svadlenak, Jean Hayden *museum administrator, consultant*
Ucko, David Alan *museum director*
Wilson, Marc Fraser *art museum administrator and curator*

Saint Joseph
Chilcote, Gary M. *museum director, reporter*

Saint Louis
Burke, James Donald *museum administrator*
Crandell, Dwight Samuel *museum director*
Ketner, Joseph Dale *museum director, art historian*
Owyoung, Steven David *curator*

Springfield
Berger, Jerry Allen *museum director*

MONTANA

Billings
Moss, Lynda Bourque *museum director*

Crow Agency
Ditmanson, Dennis L. *national monument administrator*

Missoula
Brown, Robert Munro *museum director*

West Glacier
Lusk, Harlan Gilbert *national park superintendent*
Mihalic, David Anthony *national park administrator*

NEBRASKA

Boys Town
†Lynch, Thomas Joseph *museum manager*

Chadron
Hanson, Charles Easton, Jr. *museum director, consultant*

Lincoln
Diamond, Judy *museum administrator*
Neubert, George W. *museum director, sculptor*

Omaha
Beal, Graham William John *museum director*

NEVADA

Reno
Bandurraga, Peter Louis *museum director, historian*

NEW HAMPSHIRE

Concord
Zusy, Catherine *curator*

Hanover
Hart, Katherine Wainwright *curator*

Portsmouth
O'Toole, Dennis Allen *museum director*

NEW JERSEY

Cape May
Cadge, William Fleming *gallery owner, photographer*

Farmingdale
Smith, Sibley Judson, Jr. *historic site administrator*

Lincroft
Morehouse, Dorothy Van Winkle *museum director*

Morristown
Klindt, Steven *art museum director*

New Brunswick
Cate, Phillip Dennis *art museum director*

Newark
Auth, Susan Handler *curator, educator*
Bischoff, William Ludwig *curator*
Blount, Alice McDaniel *museum curator*
Bossert, Carol Jo *museum administrator*
†Hull, Joan Carol *historical society executive, consultant*
Reynolds, Valrae *museum curator*

Oakland
Peterson, John Douglas *museum administrator*

Princeton
Horn, Elizabeth Gates *museum curator*
Rosenbaum, Allen *art museum administrator*

Trenton
†Sloshberg, Leah Phyfer *museum director*

NEW MEXICO

Albuquerque
Black, Craig Call *retired museum administrator*
†Matthew, Kathryn Kahrs *museum director*
†Moore, James Collins *museum director*
Walch, Peter Sanborn *museum director, publisher*

Las Cruces
Way, Jacob Edson, III *museum director*

Placitas
Smith, Richard Bowen *retired national park superintendent*

Roswell
Ebie, William D. *museum director*

Santa Fe
Cerny, Charlene Ann *museum director*
Livesay, Thomas Andrew *museum administrator, lecturer*

Silver City
Bettison, Cynthia Ann *museum director, archaeologist*

Taos
Witt, David L. *curator, writer*

NEW YORK

Albany
Levine, Louis David *museum director, archaeologist*
Miles, Christine Marie *museum director*

Binghamton
Balla, Wesley G. *museum curator, historian*

Bronxville
Prakapas, Eugene Joseph *art gallery director*

Brooklyn
Buck, Robert Treat, Jr. *museum director, educator*
Faunce, Sarah Cushing *museum curator*
Ferber, Linda S. *museum curator*
Kotik, Charlotta *curator, museum administrator*
†Madigan, Richard Allen *museum director*
†Shubert, Gabrielle S. *museum executive director*

Buffalo
†Bannon, Anthony L. *museum director*
Bayles, Jennifer Lucene *museum education curator*
Brutvan, Cheryl Ann *curator, art history educator*
Schultz, Douglas George *art museum director*
Siener, William Harold *museum director, historian, consultant*

Cooperstown
MacLeish, Archibald Bruce *museum director*

Corning
Ahrens, Kent *museum director, art historian*
Spillman, Jane Shadel *curator, researcher, writer*
†Whitehouse, David Bryn *museum director*

Flushing
Friedman, Alan Jacob *museum director*

Geneva
Roenke, Henry Merrill, Jr. *curator*

Huntington
Coraor, John Edward *museum director*
Noll, Anna Cecilia *curator*

Ithaca
Green, Nancy Elizabeth *curator, writer*
Robinson, Franklin Westcott *museum director, art historian*
Trautmann, Charles Home *museum director, civil engineer*

Katonah
Simpson, William Kelly *curator, Egyptologist, educator*

New York
Baer, Norbert Sebastian *art conservation educator, chemist*
Bandy, Mary Lea *museum official*
Baragwanath, Albert Kingsmill *curator*
Barnett, Vivian Endicott *curator*
Bates, Michael Lawrence *curator*
Batscha, Robert Michael *museum executive*
Belkov, Meredith Ann *landmark administrator*
Biddle, Flora Miller *art museum administrator*
Bothmer, Dietrich Felix von *museum curator, archaeologist*
†Brown, Eric Lucasen *art gallery director, art dealer*
Brundage, Susan *art dealer, gallery director*
Castelli, Leo *art dealer*
Castleman, (Esther) Riva *museum curator*
Cohen, Mildred Thaler *art gallery director*
†Danese, Renato *art gallery director*
De Ferrari, Gabriella *curator, writer*
de Montebello, Philippe Lannes *museum administrator*
Desai, Vishakha N. *gallery director, society administrator*
Dinaburg, Mary Ellen *art education and curatorial consultant*
Draper, James David *art museum curator*
Emmerich, Andre *art gallery executive, author*
Esman, Rosa Mencher *art gallery executive*
Feldman, Ronald *art gallery director*
Fletcher, Harry George, III *curator*
Freed, Stanley Arthur *museum curator*
Futter, Ellen Victoria *museum administrator*
Galassi, Peter *museum curator*
Ginsburg, Sigmund G. *museum administrator*
†Glimcher, Arnold B. *art gallery executive*
Haskell, Barbara *curator*
Hawkins, Ashton *museum executive, lawyer*
Heckscher, Morrison Harris *museum curator, architectural historian*
Hollander, Stacy Candice Foster *museum curator*
Hoving, Thomas *museum and cultural affairs consultant, author*
Howat, John Keith *museum executive*
Ives, Colta Feller *museum curator, educator*
Kallir, Jane Katherine *art gallery director, author*
Kingsley, April *art critic, curator, historian, art educator*
Kleeberg, John Martin *museum curator*
Kramer, Linda Konheim *curator, art historian*
Krens, Thomas *museum director*
Lerner, Martin *museum curator*
Lowry, Glenn David *art gallery director*
Luers, William Henry *art museum administrator*
Lupton, Ellen *curator, graphic designer*
Macdonald, Robert Rigg, Jr. *museum director*
Martin, Mary-Anne *art gallery owner*
Martin, Richard Harrison *curator, art historian*
McFadden, David Revere *museum director and curator*
Mertens, Joan R. *museum curator, art historian*
Messer, Thomas Maria *museum director*
Metcalf, William Edwards *museum curator*
Miller, Laurence Glenn *art gallery owner and director*
Morris, Robert Lee *gallery administrator, jewelry designer*
Muller, Priscilla Elkow *curator*
Munhall, Edgar *curator, art history educator*
Murdock, Robert Mead *art consultant, curator*
Newman, Bruce Murray *antiques dealer*
Novacek, Michael John *curator, museum administrator*
Oldenburg, Richard Erik *auction house executive*
Olian, JoAnne Constance *curator, art historian*
Parker, James *retired curator*
Pekarik, Andrew Joseph *museum administrator*
Pesner, Carole Manishin *art gallery owner*
Pilgrim, Dianne Hauserman *art museum director*
Pisano, Ronald George *art consultant*
Platnick, Norman I. *curator, arachnologist*
Rosenbaum, Joan Hannah *museum director*
Rosenthal, Nan *curator, author*
Ross, David A. *art museum director*
Ryskamp, Charles Andrew *museum executive, educator*
Schuster, Karen Sutton *administrator*
Shadwell, Wendy Joan *curator, writer*
Shanley, Ellen *costume curator*
Sidamon-Eristoff, Anne Phipps *museum official*
Simon, Ronald Charles *curator*
Smith, Paul J. *museum adminstrator*
Stahl, Alan Michael *curator*
Stone, Allan Barry *art gallery director*
Storr, Robert *curator painting and sculpture, artist, writer*
Tobach, Ethel *retired curator*
Tucker, Marcia *museum director, curator*
Varnedoe, John Kirk Train *museum curator*
Vuilleumier, Francois *curator*
Waldman, Diane *museum deputy director*
Wertkin, Gerard Charles *museum director, lawyer*
Wright, Gwendolyn *art center director, writer, educator*

Poughkeepsie
Gaudieri, Alexander V. J. *museum administrator*

Purchase
Gedeon, Lucinda Heyel *museum director*

Rochester
Adams, G. Rollie *museum executive*
†Bolger, Stuart B. *museum director, architectural historian*
Enyeart, James L. *museum director*
Fulton, Marianne *curator*
Hall, Donald S. *planetarium administrator*
Hayes, Charles Franklin, III *museum research director*
Holcomb, Grant, III *museum director*
Stapp, William Francis *museum curator, photographic historian*

Setauket
MacKay, Robert Battin *museum director*

Southampton
Lerner, Abram *retired museum director, artist*

Staten Island
†Hartman, Hedy Ann *museum executive*
Lipton, Barbara *museum director, curator*

Stillwater
Lindsay, W. Douglas, Jr. *historic site administrator*

Syracuse
Kuchta, Ronald Andrew *art museum director, educator*

Ticonderoga
Westbrook, Nicholas Kilmer *museum administrator, historian*

Tupper Lake
Welsh, Peter Corbett *museum consultant, historian*

Utica
Bloch, Milton Joseph *museum administrator*
Schweizer, Paul Douglas *museum director*

Wantagh
Smits, Edward John *museum consultant*

Waterford
Gold, James Paul *museum director*

West Point
Meschutt, David Randolph *curator, historian*
†Moss, Michael Eric *museum director*

Woodstock
Cox, James David *art gallery executive*

Youngstown
Dunnigan, Brian Leigh *historic site administrator*

NORTH CAROLINA

Asheville
Cecil, William A. V., Sr. *landmark director*

Chapel Hill
Bolas, Gerald Douglas *art museum administrator, art history educator*
Riggs, Timothy Allan *museum curator*

Charlotte
Evans, Bruce Haselton *art museum director*

Durham
Krakauer, Thomas Henry *museum director*

Gastonia
Stout, Richard Alan *museum director*

Manteo
Hartman, Thomas *historical site adminstrator*

Raleigh
†Creel, Wesley Stuart *museum executive*
Kuhler, Renaldo Gillet *museum official, scientific illustrator*
Schneiderman, Richard Steven *museum official*

Salisbury
Shalkop, Robert Leroy *retired museum consultant*

Wilmington
Janson, Anthony Frederick *art educator, former museum curator*
Scheu, David Robert, Sr. *historic site director*
Seapker, Janet Kay *museum director*

Winston Salem
Cawood, Hobart Guy *historic site administrator*
Gray, James Alexander *historic preservation official*
Rauschenberg, Bradford Lee *museum research director*

OHIO

Akron
Kahan, Mitchell Douglas *art museum director*

Canton
Albacete, Manuel Joseph *museum director*
†Werstler, Richard Emerson *museum director*

Cincinnati
Burt, DeVere *museum administrator*
Desmarais, Charles Joseph *museum director, writer, editor*
King, Elaine A. *curator, art historian, critic*
Long, Phillip Clifford *museum director*
Rogers, Millard Foster, Jr. *art museum director*
Timpano, Anne *museum director, art historian*

Cleveland
Bergman, Robert Paul *museum administrator, art historian, educator, lecturer*
Taylor, J(ocelyn) Mary *museum administrator, zoologist, educator*
Turner, Evan Hopkins *retired art museum director*

Columbus
Rogers, Sarah Jeanne *curator*

Dayton
Hilliard, Jack Briggs *museum curator*
Nyerges, Alexander Lee *museum director*
Ruffer, David Gray *museum director, former college president*

Fremont
Bridges, Roger Dean *historical agency administrator*

Mentor
Miller, Frances Suzanne *historic site curator*

Oberlin
Moore, Anne Frances *museum director*

Oxford
Kelm, Bonnie G. *art museum director, educator*

Reynoldsburg
Lynch, Rose Peabody *art gallery executive*

Toledo
Steadman, David Wilton *museum official*
Wittmann, Otto *art museum executive*

Vandalia
Smith, Marjorie Aileen Matthews *museum director*

OKLAHOMA

Anadarko
Ellison, Rosemary *curator*

Norman
Toperzer, Thomas Raymond *art museum director*

Oklahoma City
Kent, Sherman Tecumseh *museum administrator, educator*
Pitts, Bill *museum director*
Price, B. Byron *museum director*
Shorney, Margo Kay *art gallery owner*

Shawnee
McCaffree, Brother Benedict Bradford *historian*

Tulsa
†Manhart, Marcia Y(ockey) *art museum director*
Troccoli, Joan Carpenter *museum director*

OREGON

Portland
Eichinger, Marilynne H. *museum administrator*
Gilkey, Gordon Waverly *curator, artist*
Jenkins, Donald John *art museum administrator*
McKinley, Loren Dhue *museum director*
†Nevue, Sarah Paulson *museum administrator*
Tramposch, William Joseph *museum director, consultant*

PENNSYLVANIA

Allentown
Blume, Peter Frederick *museum director*

Chadds Ford
Duff, James Henry *museum director, environmental administrator*

Doylestown
Purpura, Peter Joseph *museum curator, exhibition designer*

Erie
Vanco, John L. *art museum director*

Fort Washington
Hague, Stephen George *museum director*

Gettysburg
Cisneros, Jose A. *historical site administrator*

Harrisburg
Fortier, John Bertram *museum director, historian*

Kennett Square
Naeve, Milo Merle *museum curator*

Morrisville
†Hemenway, Aice Pearson *museum director*

Philadelphia
Bantel, Linda Mae *art museum director*
d'Harnoncourt, Anne *museum director*
Dyson, Robert Harris *museum director, archaeologist*
Hiesinger, Kathryn Bloom *museum curator*
Laverty, Bruce *curator*
Lindsey, Jack Lee *curator*
Percy, Ann Buchanan *museum curator*
Scott, Robert Montgomery *museum executive, lawyer*
Sewell, Darrel Leslie *art museum curator*
Shoemaker, Innis Howe *art museum curator*

Pittsburgh
†Brown, Ellsworth Howard *museum administrator*
Dawson, Mary Ruth *curator*
Johnston, Phillip Michael *museum director, curator*
King, James Edward *museum director*
McIntosh, DeCourcy Eyre *museum director*
Weis, Konrad Max *museum administrator, retired chemical company executive*
Whetzel, Joshua Clyde, Jr. *museum executive, conservationist*

Reading
Dietrich, Bruce Leinbach *planetarium and museum administrator, astronomer, educator*

Springfield
Wilkinson, William Durfee *museum director*

Strasburg
Lindsay, George Carroll *former museum director*

University Park
Willumson, Glenn Gardner *curator, art educator*

Valley Forge
McDermott, Dona M. *historical park administrator*

Wayne
Andes, Charles Lovett *museum executive, technology association executive*

Wyndmoor
Wint, Dennis Michael *museum director*

RHODE ISLAND

Providence
Hay, Susan Stahr Heller *museum curator*
Stark, David Ethan *museum curator*

Saunderstown
Leavitt, Thomas Whittlesey *museum director, educator*

SOUTH CAROLINA

Camden
†Craig, Joanna Burbank *historic site director*

Charleston
Brumgardt, John Raymond *museum administrator*

Columbia
Cilella, Salvatore George, Jr. *museum director*

Florence
Burns, William A. *museum administrator, author*

Murrells Inlet
Noble, Joseph Veach *fine arts administrator*

Pawleys Island
Tarbox, Gurdon Lucius, Jr. *retired museum executive*

Sumter
Teer, Kay Stoltz *museum director*

SOUTH DAKOTA

Keystone
Wenk, Daniel N. *landmark site administrator*

Vermillion
Banks, Margaret Downie *curator, educator*

TENNESSEE

Chattanooga
Scarbrough, Cleve Knox, Jr. *museum director*

Gatlinburg
Pope, Randall Ray *retired national park superintendent*

Memphis
†Carmean, E. A., Jr. *art museum director, art historian*
Lewin, Ann White *museum director, educator*
Noble, Douglas Ross *museum administrator*

Nashville
†Riggins-Ezzell, Lois *museum administrator*

TEXAS

Austin
Crain, William Henry *retired curator*
Stetson, Daniel Everett *museum director*

Beaumont
Smith, David Ryan *museum director*

Dallas
Vogel, Donald Stanley *gallery executive, artist*

El Paso
Sipiora, Leonard Paul *retired museum director*

Fort Worth
Auping, Michael G. *curator*
Pillsbury, Edmund Pennington *museum director*

Gun Barrel City
Smith, Thelma Tina Harriette *gallery owner, artist*

Houston
†Delehanty, Suzanne *museum director*
Latimer, Roy Truett *museum executive*
Lee, Janie C. *art gallery owner*
Marzio, Peter Cort *museum director*
Tucker, Anne Wilkes *curator, photographic historian and critic, lecturer*
†Warren, David Boardman *museum director, art curator*

Lubbock
†Edson, Gary Francis *museum director*

Midland
Ott, Wendell Lorenz *art museum director, artist*

Orange
Eldredge, Bruce Beard *museum director*

San Antonio
Barnes, Gail *historic site administrator*
†Chiego, William J. *museum director*
Hyland, Douglas K. S. *museum administrator, educator*
Parsons, Merribell Maddux *museum consultant*

UTAH

Provo
Mason, James Albert *museum director, university dean*

Salt Lake City
Hague, Donald Victor *museum director*
Leonard, Glen M. *museum administrator*
Oman, Richard George *museum curator*

VERMONT

Bennington
†Miller, Steven H. *museum diector*

Manchester
Kouwenhoven, Gerrit Wolphertsen *museum director*

Shaftsbury
Williams, Robert Joseph *museum director, educator*

Shelburne
Mason, Benjamin Lincoln *museum director*
Sheldon, David Frederick *museum director, headmaster*

VIRGINIA

Alexandria
Evans, Grose *former curator, retired educator*
Fitzgerald, Oscar P., IV *museum administrator*
Lundeberg, Philip Karl *curator*
†Majors, Steven William *director art museum, artist, art consultant*

Appomattox
Montgomery, Jon B. *museum administrator*

Arlington
Ewers, John Canfield *museum administrator*
Friedheim, Jerry Warden *museum executive*

Hampton
Johnston, Ralph Thomas *museum director*

Louisa
Lanyon, Wesley Edwin *retired museum curator, ornithologist*

Mount Vernon
†Rees, James Conway, IV *historic site administrator*

Norfolk
Martin, Roy Butler, Jr. *museum director, retired broker*

Richmond
Blatt, Elizabeth Kempske *museum administrator*
Jewell, Byron Frank *museum administrator*
†Lee, Katharine Caecilia *art museum administrator*
Miller, Nan Louise *museum director*
Witschey, Walter Robert Thurmond *science museum administrator, archaeologist, computer systems consultant*

Staunton
†Klaffky, Susan Elizabeth *museum director, consultant, researcher*

Sweet Briar
Lane, Rebecca Massie *museum director*

Waynesboro
Rippe, Peter Marquart *museum administrator*

Williamsburg
Garrison, George Hartranft Haley *curator of scripophily*

Yorktown
Gould, Alec *historic park administrator*
Riggs, David Foster *museum curator, historian*

WASHINGTON

Bellevue
Douglas, Diane Miriam *museum director*
Warren, James Ronald *retired museum director, author, columnist*

Olympia
Lind, Carl Bradley *retired museum director*

Port Townsend
Harrington, LaMar *curator, museum director*
Warren, Patricia J. *museum director*

Pullman
Watkinson, Patricia Grieve *museum director*

Seattle
Andrews, Richard Otis *museum director*
O'Donnell, Wilson Edward *museum director*
West, Richard Vincent *art museum official*

Wenatchee
†Williams, Keith Roy *museum director*

WISCONSIN

Green Bay
Koski, Ann Louise *museum director*

Madison
Fleischman, Stephen *art center director*
Garver, Thomas Haskell *curator, art consultant, writer*
†Panczenko, Russell *museum director*
Pillaert, E(dna) Elizabeth *museum curator*
Westphal, Klaus Wilhelm *university museum director*

Manitowoc
Logan, Lox Albert, Jr. *museum director*

Milwaukee
†Carter, Curtis Lloyd *art musuem director*
Green, Edward Anthony *museum director*
Moynihan, William J. *museum executive*
†Rosen, Barry Howard *museum director, history educator*

Oshkosh
Landwehr, William Charles *museum director*
Poberezny, Thomas *museum adminstrator*

Sheboygan
Kohler, Ruth DeYoung *arts center executive*

WYOMING

Casper
Mobley, Karen Ruth *art gallery director*

Cody
Hassrick, Peter Heyl *museum director*

Laramie
Guerin, Charles Allan *museum director, artist*

Rock Springs
Chadey, Henry F. *museum director*

TERRITORIES OF THE UNITED STATES

VIRGIN ISLANDS

Saint Thomas
Silvestro, Clement Mario *museum director, historian*

CANADA

ALBERTA

Calgary
Janes, Robert Roy *museum director, archaeologist,*

Drumheller
Naylor, Bruce Gordon *museum director*

Edmonton
Stepney, Philip Harold Robert *museum director*

Sherwood Park
Finlay, James Campbell *retired museum director*

BRITISH COLUMBIA

North Vancouver
Joyner, John Brooks *museum director*

Vancouver
Holmes, Willard *art gallery director*

Victoria
Barkley, William Donald *museum executive director*
Segger, Martin Joseph *museum director, art history educator*

MANITOBA

Oak Hammock Marsh
Wrigley, Robert Ernest *museum director, ecologist*

Winnipeg
Di Cosimo, Joanne Violet *museum director*

NEW BRUNSWICK

Fredericton
Lumsden, Ian Gordon *art gallery director*

NEWFOUNDLAND

Saint John's
Grattan, Patricia Elizabeth *art gallery director*
Mills, David B. *museum director*

NOVA SCOTIA

Halifax
Riordon, John Bernard *museum director*

ONTARIO

London
Poole, Nancy Geddes *art gallery director, writer*

North York
Cumming, Glen Edward *art gallery director*
Yarlow, Loretta *art museum director*

Ottawa
Bell, Phillip Michael *curator*
Emery, Alan Roy *museum executive*
McAvity, John Gillis *museum director, association executive, museologist*

Suthren, Victor J. H. *museum director*
Thomson, Shirley Lavinia *museum director*

Richmond Hill
Tushingham, (Arlotte) Douglas *museum administrator*

Toronto
McNeill, John *museum administrator*
Rombout, Luke *museum designer, administrator*

PRINCE EDWARD ISLAND

Charlottetown
Severance, Christopher Churchill *museum director*

QUEBEC

Montreal
Brisebois, Marcel *museum director*

Quebec
Laliberté-Bourque, Andrée *museum director*

SASKATCHEWAN

Regina
Oko, Andrew Jan *art gallery director, curator*

MEXICO

Mexico City
del Conde, Teresa *museum director, art historian, researcher*
Lacouture, Felipe Ernesto *museum consultant*

AUSTRIA

Vienna
Oberhuber, Konrad Johannes *art museum curator, educator*

ENGLAND

London
Serota, Nicholas Andrew *art gallery director*

FRANCE

Paris
Rosenberg, Pierre Max *museum director*

JAPAN

Miyazaki
Meyer, Ruth Krueger *museum administrator, art historian*

ADDRESS UNPUBLISHED

Armstrong, Thomas Newton, III *retired museum director*
Boulet, Roger Henri *art gallery director, curator*
Brown, James Monroe, III *museum administrator*
Brumberg, G. David *historical center administrator, history bibliographer*
Carter, John Swain *museum administrator, consultant*
Castile, Jesse Randolph (Rand) *retired museum director*
Chenhall, Robert Gene *former museum director, consultant, author*
†Cissel, John Ferrill *national part superintendent*
Coke, Frank Van Deren *museum director, photographer*
Cook, Alexander Burns *museum curator, artist, educator*
Danoff, I. Michael *art center director, writer, educator*
Dressel, Barry *museum administrator*
English, Bruce Vaughan *museum director and executive, environmental consultant*
Friedman, Martin *retired art center director*
Fry, Doris Hendricks *museum curator*
Greaves, James Louis *art conservator*
Grogan, Kevin *museum director*
Hellmers, Norman Donald *historic site director*
Houlihan, Patrick Thomas *museum director*
Jacobowitz, Ellen Sue *former museum administrator*
Kochta, Ruth Martha *art gallery owner*
Kuehne, Richard Edward *museum administrator*
Leff, Sandra H. *gallery director, consultant*
Lutts, Ralph Herbert *museum administrator, scholar, educator*
McKinney, Donald *art gallery director, art dealer*
Mezzatesta, Michael Philip *art museum director*
Millard, Charles Warren, III *museum director, writer*
Moore, William Jason *museum director*
Nasgaard, Roald *museum curator*
Nelson-Mayson, Linda Ruth *art museum curator*
Nihart, Franklin Brooke *museum consultant, writer and editor*
Nold, Carl Richard *state historic parks and museums administrator*
Pennington, Mary Anne *art museum director, museum management consultant, art educator*
Perrot, Paul Norman *museum director*
Pisney, Raymond Frank *international consulting services executive*
Pitts, Terence Randolph *curator and museum director*
Platou, Joanne (Dode) *museum director*
Porter, Daniel Reed, III *museum director*
Powell, Earl Alexander, III *art museum director*
Radice, Anne-Imelda *museum director*
Randall, Richard Harding, Jr. *art gallery director*
Rifkin, Ned *museum director*
†Rosenthal, Martha Newman *museum executive*
Schneider, Janet M. *arts administrator, curator, painter*
Sennema, David Carl *museum consultant*
Shapiro, Michael Edward *museum administrator, curator, art historian*
Smith, Jean Chandler *former museum official*
Stearns, Robert Leland *curator*
Stewart, Robert Gordon *former museum curator*
†Stryker, Richard Ripley, Jr. *museum director*
Stuart, Joseph Martin *art museum administrator*
Summerfield, John Robert *textile curator*
Talbot, Howard Chase, Jr. *retired museum administrator*
Welles, John Galt *retired museum director*
Wieser, Siegfried *planetarium executive director*
Yates, Charles Richardson *former arts center executive*
Yochelson, Bonnie Ellen *museum curator, art historian*

INDUSTRY: MANUFACTURING. *See also* FINANCE: FINANCIAL SERVICES.

UNITED STATES

ALABAMA

Alexander City
Adams, John C. *apparel company executive*
Gade, Marvin Francis *retired paper company executive*
Howell, H. Scott *apparel manufacturing company executive*

Birmingham
Bruno, Joseph S. *meat products company executive*
Cabaniss, William Jelks, Jr. *machining company executive, former state legislator*
Chrencik, Frank *chemical company executive*
Daniel, Kenneth Rule *former iron and steel manufacturing company executive*
de Windt, Edward Mandell *manufacturing executive*
Fowler, C. Thomas *power equipment manufacturing executive*
Gaffney, Michael Scully *diversified manufacturing company executive*
Grayson, William Jackson, Jr. *manufacturing executive*
Harbert, Bill Lebold *construction corporation executive*
Holton, J(erry) Thomas *concrete company executive*
Johnsey, Walter F. *manufacturing executive*
Kerr, Robert William *pipe fitting company executive*
Neal, Phil Hudson, Jr. *manufacturing company executive*
Rozendale, David S. *engineering and construction firm executive*
Sklenar, Herbert Anthony *industrial products manufacturing company executive*
Styslinger, Lee Joseph, Jr. *manufacturing company executive*
Temple, William Norman *foundry executive*
Todd, James Averill, Jr. *steel company executive*
Tyrrell, Thomas Neil *metal processing executive*
Wright, J. Raymond *manufacturing company executive*

Gadsden
†Weaver, John B. *electronics executive, metal products executive*

Gulf Shores
Wingard, Raymond Randolph *transportation products executive*

Huntsville
Holloway, Richard Allen *electronics company executive*
King, Olin B. *electronics systems company executive*
Ramsey, V. Bruce *electronics executive*
Sapp, A. Eugene, Jr. *electronics executive*

Lanett
Fowler, Conrad Murphree *retired manufacturing company executive*

Leeds
Ritchey, James Salem *office furniture manufacturing company executive*

Mobile
†Busby, James Louie *electronics company executive*

Montgomery
†Adair, Charles E. *medical products distribution company executive*
Blount, Winton Malcolm, Jr. *manufacturing company executive*
Caddell, John Allen *construction and engineering company executive*
Findlay, R. B. *paper company executive*
Shorter, Walter Wyatt *forest products executive*
Taylor, James Marion, II *automotive wholesale executive*
†Williamson, William A., Jr. *medical products executive*

Muscle Shoals
Roy, Amit H. *agricultural executive*

Opelika
Jenkins, Richard Lee *manufacturing company executive*

Perdue Hill
Schwartz, Arthur Leonard *pulp company executive, lawyer*

Sylacauga
Felker, G(eorge) Stephen *textile company executive*
Monk, Richard Hunley, Jr. *textile company executive*

Theodore
Williams, Robert Augustus *manufacturing company executive*

Tuscaloosa
Williams, Ernest Going *paper company executive*

ALASKA

Anchorage
Linford, Mary Suzanne (Sue Linford) *food distibution executive*
Williams, Mark *food products executive*

Juneau
Johnson, Marlene A. *business executive*
Loescher, Robert Wayne *holding company executive*

ARIZONA

Carefree
Byrom, Fletcher Lauman *chemical manufacturing company executive*
Menk, Louis Wilson *retired manufacturing company executive*
Trimble, George Simpson *industrial executive*

Green Valley
Blickwede, Donald Johnson *retired steel company executive*
Ehrenfeld, John Henry *grocery company executive*

Mesa
DeRosa, Francis Dominic *chemical company executive*
Woods, Joe Eldon *general contractor*

Phoenix
Carter, Ronald Martin, Sr. *pharmaceutical company executive*
Chalmers, James A. *consulting company executive*
†Day, Timothy Townley *food company executive*
†Dion, Philip Joseph *consumer products and services executive, real estate and construction company executive*
†Flatt, Michael Oliver *manufacturing company executive*
Franke, William Augustus *corporate executive*
Giedt, Bruce Alan *paper company executive*
Goldman, Murray Abraham *semiconductor executive*
†Kitchell, Samuel Farrand *construction company executive*
Kyl, John Henry *former business executive*
Lies, Richard Lorenz, Jr. *cosmetics executive*
Mardian, Daniel *construction company director*
McClelland, Norman P. *food products executive*
Mc Clelland, W. Kent *food products executive*
Norling, James A. *electronics company executive*
Patti, Andrew S. *consumer products company executive*
Paul, Elias *food company consultant*
Pruitt, J. Doug *construction executive*
Reins, Ralph Erich *automated service company executive*
Rethore, Bernard Gabriel *diversified company executive*
†Rogers, A. Kay *construction company executive*
Thompson, Charles Edward *electronics company executive*
Weinstein, Allan M. *medical device company executive*
†White, Edward Allen *electronics company executive*

Prescott
Parkhurst, Charles Lloyd *electronics company executive*

Scottsdale
Grenell, James Henry *retired manufacturing company executive*
Howard, William Gates, Jr. *electronics company executive*
Linthicum, Gary Rex *construction company executive*
Malsack, James Thomas *retired manufacturing company executive*
Rawles, Lewis Gene *manufacturing executive*
Ruhlman, Terrell Louis *business executive*
Stuart, Derald Archie *aerospace company consultant*
Walsh, Edward Joseph *toiletries and food company executive*

Sierra Vista
Meyer, William Trenholm *defense company official, real estate executive*

Sun City
Van Horssen, Arden Darrell *retired manufacturing executive*

Sun City West
Anderson, Ernest Washington *manufacturing company executive*

Tempe
Begay, Jefferson Lee *general contracting company executive*

Tucson
Bates-Silva, Mary Louise *land and cattle company executive*
Eckdahl, Donald Edward *manufacturing company executive*
Maxon, Don Carlton *construction company executive, mining company executive*
Meeker, Robert Eldon *retired manufacturing company executive*
Mullikin, Vernon Eugene *aerospace executive*
Sundt, Harry Wilson *construction company executive*
Sundt, Robert Stout *construction company executive*
Troup, Thomas James *electronics company executive*

ARKANSAS

Bentonville
Hobbs, Lewis Ray *merchandise executive*

Conway
Morgan, Charles Donald, Jr. *manufacturing executive*

Fort Smith
Flanders, Donald Hargis *manufacturing company executive*
Goins, Randall *grain company executive*
Hendrickson, Boyde W. *health products executive*
Marquard, William Albert *diversified manufacturing company executive*
Qualls, Robert L. *manufacturing executive, banker, former state official, educator*
Udouj, Herman J. *diversified industries company executive*
†Wenderoth, Collier, Jr. *food products executive*

Hiwasse
Sutherland, Gail Russell *retired industrial equipment manufacturing company executive*

Hot Springs Village
Schroeder, Donald Perry *retired food products company executive*

Little Rock
Dyke, James Trester *building materials distributing company executive*
Givens, John Kenneth *manufacturing executive*
McMullin, Carleton Eugene *automotive business executive*

North Little Rock
Harrison, Stephen Earle *manufacturing executive*
Mc Elroy, Bobbie *furniture manufacturing executive*

Pine Bluff
Lea, George A., Jr. *retail food executive*

Rogers
Hudson, James T. *food company executive*
Hudson, Michael T. *food company executive*

Siloam Springs
†Butler, Lynch *food products executive*

Springdale
Johnston, Gerald McArthur *food company executive*
Tollett, Leland Edward *food company executive*
Tyson, Donald John *food company executive*

Stuttgart
Bell, Richard Eugene *grain and food company executive*
Hillman, Tommy *food products company executive*
Jessup, Stewart E. *agricultural products executive*

CALIFORNIA

Alamo
Pritchett, Thomas Ronald *retired metal and chemical company executive*

Anaheim
Wrigley, William *corporation executive*

Aptos
Mechlin, George Francis *electrical manufacturing company executive*

Arcadia
Eck, Dennis K. *supermarket chain executive*
Nelson, Garrett R. *retail food company executive*

Artesia
Korsmeier, Gary *dairy products executive*

Atherton
Goodman, Sam Richard *electronics company executive*
Hogan, Clarence Lester *retired electronics executive*
Mc Intyre, Henry Langenberg *former business executive, lawyer*

Bakersfield
Akers, Tom, Jr. *cotton broker, consultant*
Groefsema, Bruce *agricultural products executive*
Hart, Donald Milton *automotive and ranching executive, former mayor*
Lundquist, Gene Alan *cotton company executive*
†Pratt, Brian *heavy manufacturing executive*

Belmont
Glenn, Thomas Michael *science and technology executive*

Berkeley
Berlekamp, Elwyn Ralph *former electronics company executive, mathematics educator*
Carman, James Martin *business administration educator, consultant*
Cutter, David Lee *pharmaceutical company executive*

Beverly Hills
Casey, Joseph T. *corporate executive*
dePaolis, Potito Umberto *food company executive*
Farwell, Lloyd S. *hotel executive*
Hoch, Orion Lindel *corporate executive*
Leonis, John Michael *aerospace executive*
Loeffler, Richard Harlan *retail and technology company executive*
Singleton, Henry Earl *industrialist*
Willson, James Douglas *aerospace executive*

Big Bear Lake
Dankanyin, Robert John *manufacturing executive*

Brea
Hulsey, Neven C. *metal products executive*

Buena Park
Arimoto, Masahiko *electronics company executive*
Raup, Ronald B. *electronics executive*

Burbank
Gold, Stanley P. *chemical company executive, manufacturing company executive*

Raulinaitis, Pranas Algis *electronics executive*

Calabasas
Ghose, Rabindra Nath *technology research company executive*
Kitchen, Lawrence Oscar *aircraft and aerospace corporation executive*
Marafino, Vincent Norman *aerospace company executive*

Camarillo
†Cleary, Thomas Charles *technology company executive*
Denmark, Bernhardt *manufacturing executive*

Campbell
Sack, Edgar Albert *electronics company executive*
†Walker, William R. *manufacturing executive, light*

Carlsbad
Anderson, Paul Irving *management executive*
Callaway, Ely Reeves, Jr. *golf club manufacturer*
Crooke, Stanley Thomas *pharmaceutical company executive*
Graham, Robert Klark *lens manufacturer*
Schumacher, John Christian *semiconductor materials and air pollution control equipment manufacturing company executive*

Carpinteria
Ehrlich, Grant C(onklin) *business consultant*

Central Valley
Emmerson, A. A. *sawmill executive*

Chatsworth
Adams, Charles Richard *manufacturing executive*
Alagem, Beny *electronics executive*

Chula Vista
Kerley, James J. *manufacturing executive*
†Palumbo, Donald R. *metal products executive*

Colusa
Carter, Jane Foster *agriculture industry executive*

Compton
Collins, Patrick W. *grocery stores company executive*
McNamara, E. Michael *cosmetics executive*
†Palmer, Curtis Howard *diversified company executive, lawyer*

Coronado
Brunton, Paul Edward *retired diversified industry executive*

Costa Mesa
†Foell, Ronald R. *builder*
†Panic, Milan *pharmaceutical and health products company executive*
Sognefest, Peter William *manufacturing company executive*

Covina
Fillius, Milton Franklin, Jr. *food products company executive*

Crockett
Somerset, Harold Richard *sugar company executive*

Culver City
Leve, Alan Donald *electronic materials manufacturing company owner, executive*

Cupertino
Bossen, David August *electronics company executive*
Burg, John Parker *signal processing executive*
Gingerich, John Charles *manufacturing company executive*
Mathias, Leslie Michael *electronic manufacturing company executive*
McAdams, Robert, Jr. *electronics executive*
Togasaki, Shinobu *corporate executive*

Cypress
Baugh, Coy Franklin *corporate executive*
†Kiuchi, Takashi Tachi *electronics company executive*
Naganuma, Kazue *automotive executive*

Danville
Arrol, John *corporate executive*
Liggett, Lawrence Melvin *vacuum equipment manufacturing company executive*

Dublin
Neff, James Dennis *manufacturing company executive, consultant*
†Webb, James William *food products executive*
†Whetten, John D. *food products executive*
Witt, Robert Louis *materials manufacturing and sales company executive, lawyer*

El Monte
†Christ, Clifford Charles *electronics executive*

El Segundo
Caslow, Richard Walker, Jr. *manufacturing company executive*
Clough, Charles Marvin *electronics company executive*
Croft, Leonard Mathias *toy company executive*
Eskridge, James Arthur *toy company executive*
†Lidow, Eric *electrical parts manufacturing company executive*
Tennant, Samuel McKibben *aerospace systems company executive*

Emeryville
†Penhoet, Edward *biochemicals company executive*
Winger, Dennis Lawrence *medical products company executive*

Encino
†Kerr, William Alexander *glass company executive*
Krueger, Kenneth John *corporate executive, nutritionist, educator*
Roderick, Robert Lee *aerospace executive*

Escalon
Barton, Gerald Lee *food company executive*

Escondido
Packer, Russell Howard *automotive company executive*

Fair Oaks
Chernev, Melvin *retired beverage company executive*

Folsom
Close, Gary E. *pharmaceuticals executive*

Fountain Valley
Price, Westcott Wilkin, III *health care company executive*

Fresno
O'Donnell, Thomas Howard *wheelchair manufacturing executive*

Fullerton
Crosson, Albert J. *food products executive*
Miller, Arnold *electronics executive*
Rosso, Louis T. *scientific instrument manufacturing company executive*
Stollsteimer, John F. *food company executive*

Gardena
†Kanner, Edwin Benjamin *electrical manufacturing company executive*
†Mignanelli, Thomas D. *automobile company executive*
Winston, Morton Manuel *equipment executive*

Geyserville
Mc Clelland, John Peter *winery executive*

Gilroy
Blattman, H. Eugene *foods corporation executive*

Glendale
Crull, Timm F. *food company executive*
†Ravenhall, Colin *chemicals executive*
Schult, Robert W. *food products executive*
Seegman, Irvin P. *manufacturing company executive*

Glendora
Cahn, David Stephen *cement company executive*

Goleta
†Frank, Harold Roy *metal products executive*
Thom, Richard David *aerospace executive*

Gridley
Tanimoto, George *agricultural executive, farmer*

Hawthorne
Weiss, Max Tibor *aerospace company executive*

Hayward
Hwang, Kou Mau *pharmaceutical executive*

Healdsburg
Reed, Thomas Care *business executive*

Hesperia
Butcher, Jack Robert *manufacturing executive*

Hillsborough
Keller, John Francis *retired wine company executive, mayor*

Hollywood
Parks, Robert Myers *appliance manufacturing company executive*

Indian Wells
Harris, Milton M. *distributing company executive*
Reed, A(lfred) Byron *retired apparel and textile manufacturing company*

Irvine
Alspach, Philip Halliday *manufacturing company executive*
Beckman, Arnold Orville *analytical instrument manufacturing company executive*
Combs, John Francis *manufacturing company executive*
Haggerty, Charles A. *electronics executive*
Herbert, Gavin Shearer *health care products company executive*
Moyer, Albert J. *company executive, financial analyst*
†Noda, Hiroshi *automotive company executive*
Qureshey, Safi U. *electronics manufacturing company executive*
Santoro, Carmelo James *electronics executive*
Sonoguchi, Kazuo *automotive company executive*
Williams, James E. *food products manufacturing company executive*

Irwindale
Groom, John Miller *food company executive*

Jackson
Halvorson, William *automotive executive*

La Jolla
Drell, William *chemical company executive*
Geckler, Richard Delph *metal products company executive*
Monday, John Christian *manufacturing company executive*
Penhune, John Paul *science company executive, electrical engineer*
Richey, Phil Horace *former manufacturing executive, consultant*
Stevens, Paul Irving *manufacturing company executive*
Todd, Harry Williams *aircraft propulsion system company executive*
Wallace, Robert George *retired construction company executive, civil engineer*

La Mesa
Burns, Kenneth Dean *company executive, retired air force officer*

La Puente
Reilly, John E. *automotive executive*
†Rieske, Gordon *food products executive*

Lafayette
Lewis, Sheldon Noah *technology consultant*

Laguna Beach
Bezar, Gilbert Edward *retired aerospace company executive, volunteer*
Wolf, Karl Everett *aerospace and communications corporation executive*
Youngquist, Andrew Lance *construction executive*

Laguna Hills
Rossiter, Bryant William *chemistry consultant*

Laguna Niguel
Nelson, Alfred John *retired pharmaceutical company executive*

Livermore
Bennett, Alan Jerome *electronics executive, physicist*

Livingston
Fox, Robert August *food company executive*

Long Beach
Alibrandi, Joseph Francis *diversified industrial company executive*
Hood, Robert H., Jr. *aircraft manufacturing company executive*
McGuire, James Charles *aircraft company executive*
McMillan, James Thomas *aerospace company executive*
Seita, Yukifusa *electronics executive*
Sun, Chieh *electronics company executive*

Los Altos
Beer, Clara Louise Johnson *retired electronics executive*
Mullaley, Robert Charles *manufacturing company executive*
Oder, Frederic Carl Emil *retired aerospace company executive, consultant*
†Robinson, Jacques Alan *electric manufacturing company executive*

Los Angeles
Anderson, Robert *retired manufacturing company executive*
Ash, Roy Lawrence *business executive*
Broadhurst, Norman Neil *manufacturing executive*
Bromberg, Robert *aerospace company executive*
Burns, Dan W. *manufacturing company executive*
†Butler, Donald Earnest *company executive*
Campion, Robert Thomas *manufacturing company executive*
†Colburn, Philip William *automotive company executive*
Currie, Malcolm Roderick *aerospace and automotive executive, scientist*
Dingwell, Everett W. *food products company executive*
Drake, Hudson Billings *aerospace and electronics company executive*
Dundon, Brian R. *motor company executive*
Forester, Bernard I. *recreational equipment company executive*
Giacoletto, Joseph Richard *electronics company executive*
Gillcrist, Paul Thomas *manufacturing executive, retired naval officer*
Godbold, Wilford Darrington, Jr. *enclosure manufacturing company executive, lawyer*
Goff, Stanley Norman *furniture retailing and manufacturing company executive*
Golden, Milton M. *paint company executive*
Grant, David Browne *manufacturing executive*
Handschumacher, Albert Gustave *retired corporate executive*
Hutchins, Joan Morthland *manufacturing executive, farmer*
Irani, Ray R. *oil, gas and chemical company executive*
Jenkins, William *building materials and property development company executive*
Kelleher, Robert *apparel executive*
Kendall, William Denis *medical electronic equipment company executive*
Korn, Lester Bernard *business executive, diplomat*
Kurtzman, Alan *cosmetics company executive*
Mager, Artur *retired aerospace company executive, consultant*
Mall, William John, Jr. *aerospace executive, retired air force officer*
Murphy, Gerald D. *agricultural products, grain company executive*
Norian, Roger W. *plastic manufacturing company executive*
Palevsky, Max *industrialist*
Perkins, William Clinton *company executive*
Perna, Frank, Jr. *manufacturing company executive*
Perry, William Joseph *food processing company executive*
†Proies, Michael Constantine *apparel company executive*
†Rabinowitz, Leonard *apparel executive*
Ramer, Lawrence Jerome *corporation executive*
Ruth, Craig *business executive*
Rutledge, William P. *manufacturing company executive*
Seaver, Richard Carlton *oil field equipment company executive, lawyer*
Segil, Larraine Diane *materials company executive*
Settles, F. Stan, Jr. *manufacturing executive, educator*
Tamkin, S. Jerome *business executive, consultant*
Thomas, Christopher Robert *food products company executive*
Wyatt, James Luther *drapery hardware company executive*
Ziering, Sigi *medical company executive*

Lynwood
Jorgensen, Earle M. *metal products executive*

Malibu
Smith, George Foster *retired aerospace company executive*

Menlo Park
Bremser, George, Jr. *electronics company executive*
Cook, Paul M. *technology company executive*
Evans, Bob Overton *electronics executive*
Fergason, James L. *optical company executive*
Frisco, Louis Joseph *retired materials science company executive, electrical engineer*
Graham, Howard Holmes *manufacturing executive*
Hiller, Stanley, Jr. *manufacturing company executive*
Postlewait, Harry Owen *chemical company executive*
†Saldich, Robert Joseph *electronics company executive*
Taft, David Dakin *chemical executive*

Mill Valley
Winskill, Robert Wallace *manufacturing executive*

Milpitas
Brown, David A. *computer hardware company executive*
†Davis, Jeffrey L. *electronics company executive*
†Granchelli, Ralph S. *company executive*

Modesto
Ferrucci, Raymond Vincent *retired food company executive*
Shastid, Jon Barton *wine company executive*
†Webb, Erman A. *food products executive*
†Webb, Michael A. *food products executive*

Montecito
Meghreblian, Robert Vartan *manufacturing executive, physicist*

Moorpark
†Kavli, Fred *manufacturing executive*

Mountain View
Clark, James H. *electronics executive*
Cusumano, James Anthony *chemical company executive, former recording artist*
Elkus, Richard J., Jr. *electronics company executive*
Koo, George Ping Shan *electronics executive*
Saifer, Mark Gary Pierce *pharmaceutical executive*
Slade, Bernard Newton *electronics company executive*

Newport Beach
†Kaye, Michael S. *corporate executive*
†Lyon, William *builder*

Novato
Womack, Thomas Houston *manufacturing company executive*

Oakland
†Ausfahl, William Friend *household products company executive*
Saunders, Ward Bishop, Jr. *retired aluminum company executive*
Serenbetz, Robert *manufacturing executive*
Sullivan, G. Craig *chemical executive*

Oakville
Mondavi, Robert Gerald *winery executive*

Ojai
Weill, Samuel, Jr. *automobile company executive*

Ontario
Keel, Michael Clarence *aerospace company executive*

Orange
Skilling, David van Diest *manufacturing executive*
Stacho, Zoltan Aladar *construction and engineering company executive*
Steffensen, Dwight A. *medical products and data processing services executive*

Pacific Palisades
Crane, Richard Clement *paper manufacturing company executive*

Palm Desert
Brown, James Briggs *retired business forms company executive*

Palm Springs
Greenbaum, James Richard *liquor distributing company executive, real estate developer*

Palo Alto
Burke, Edmund Charles *retired aerospace company executive*
DeLustro, Frank Anthony *biomedical company executive, research immunologist*
Early, James Michael *electronics research consultant*
Freiman, Paul E. *pharmaceutical company executive*
Gerstel, Martin Stephen *pharmaceutical company executive*
Gilbert, Keith Duncan *electronics executive*
Goff, Harry Russell *retired manufacturing company executive*
†Gribaldo, Albert C. *holding company executive*
Halperin, Robert Milton *retired electrical machinery company executive*
Hewlett, William (Redington) *manufacturing company executive, electrical engineer*
Hornak, Thomas *electronics company executive*
Kennedy, W(ilbert) Keith, Jr. *electronics company executive*
†Mario, Ernest *pharmaceutical company executive*
O'Rourke, J. Tracy *manufacturing company executive*
Packard, David *manufacturing company executive, electrical engineer*
Platt, Lewis Emmett *electronics company executive*
†Powers, Richard P. *pharmaceutical executive*
†Proctor, Peter *pharmaceutical executive*
Reagan, Joseph Bernard *aerospace executive*
Rivette, Gerard Bertram *manufacturing company executive*
Staprans, Armand *electronics executive*
Watkins, Dean Allen *electronics executive, educator*
Wayman, Robert Paul *electronics company executive*
†Wilson, James F. *pharmaceutical executive*

Palos Verdes Peninsula
Dalton, James Edward *aerospace executive, retired air force officer*
Grant, Robert Ulysses *retired manufacturing company executive*
Leone, William Charles *retired manufacturing executive*

Wilson, Theodore Henry *retired electronics company executive, aerospace engineer*

Paramount
†McCune, William Minton *construction company executive*
†Strong, Warren Robert *construction company executive*

Pasadena
Adler, Fred Peter *electronics company executive*
Bennett, Joel Herbert *construction company executive*
Chamberlain, Willard Thomas *retired metals company executive*
Jenkins, Royal Gregory *manufacturing executive*
Marlen, James S. *chemical-plastics-building materials manufacturing company executive*
Miller, Charles Daly *lumber company executive*
Neal, Philip Mark *diversified manufacturing executive*
Pieroni, Leonard J. *engineering and construction company executive*
Smith, Howard Russell *manufacturing company executive*
Sudarsky, Jerry M. *industrialist*
Tollenaere, Lawrence Robert *retired industrial products company executive*

Pebble Beach
Crossley, Randolph Allin *retired corporate executive*

Piedmont
Smith, Charles Conard *refractory company executive*

Pittsburg
Chuderewicz, Leonard H. *heavy industry executive*

Pleasanton
Busboom, Larry D. *food products company executive*
Giacolini, Earl L. *agricultural products company executive*
Hutchcraft, Arthur Stephens, Jr. *aluminum and chemical company executive*
†Marcy, Charles Frederick *food products company executive*
Perry, James R. *construction company executive*
Stager, Donald K. *construction company executive*
Tauscher, William Young *pharmaceutical and cosmetic products executive*
Weiss, Robert Stephen *medical manufacturing and services company financial executive*

Portola Valley
Graham, William James *packaging company executive*
Millard, Stephens Fillmore *electronics company executive*
Purl, O. Thomas *retired electronics company executive*

Ramona
Vaughn, Robert Lockard *aerospace and astronautics company executive*

Rancho Cucamonga
Nelson, William O. *pharmaceutical company executive*

Rancho Mirage
Strickman, Arthur Edwin *retired retail executive*

Rancho Santa Fe
Jordan, Charles Morrell *retired automotive designer*

Rancho Santa Margarita
Wong, Wallace *medical supplies company executive, real estate investor*

Redlands
Skomal, Edward Nelson *aerospace company executive, consultant*

Redondo Beach
Kagiwada, Reynold Shigeru *advanced technology manager*

Redwood City
Ellison, Lawrence J. *computer software company executive*
Kalinske, Thomas J. *video game and toy company executive*
Swinerton, William Arthur *retired construction company executive*

Riverside
Crean, John C. *housing and recreational vehicles manufacturing company executive*
†Forney, Guy Sherman *electronics components manufacturing executive*
Kummer, Glenn F. *construction and automotive executive*
Weide, William Wolfe *housing and recreational vehicles manufacturer*
Yeager, Jacques Stalder, Sr. *construction company executive*

Sacramento
Aldrich, Thomas Albert *consultant, former brewing executive*
Baccigaluppi, Roger John *agricultural company executive*
Mack, Edward Gibson *retired business executive*

Salinas
†Taylor, Steven Bruce *agriculture company executive*

San Bruno
†Agresti, Jack Joseph *construction company executive*

San Carlos
Gutow, Bernard Sidney *packaging manufacturing company executive*

San Clemente
Fertik, Ira J. *medical laser company executive*

San Diego
Anjard, Ronald Paul, Sr. *business and industry executive, consultant, educator, technologist, importer*
Arledge, Charles Stone *former aerospace executive, entrepreneur*
Boarman, Patrick Madigan *economics and business administration educator, public official*
Bradley, Francis Xavier *aluminum company executive*
Conner, Dennis *manufacturing executive, yachtsman*
Darmstandler, Harry Max *business executive, retired air force officer*
Dendo, Albert Ulysses *electronics executive*
Devine, Brian Kiernan *pet food and supplies company executive*
Duddles, Charles Weller *food company executive*
Garry, Frederick Wilton *electrical manufacturing company executive*
Goode, John Martin *manufacturing company executive*
Hawran, Paul William *pharmaceutical executive*
Holman, J(ohn) Leonard *retired manufacturing corporation executive*
Howell, Thomas Edwin *manufacturing company executive*
Ivans, William Stanley *electronics company executive*
Koehler, John Edget *electronics company executive*
†Kull, Lorenz A. *scientific research company executive*
Lewis, Alan James *pharmaceutical executive, pharmacologist*
Maier, Paul Victor *pharmaceutical executive*
Mullane, John Francis *pharmaceutical company executive*
Nassif, Thomas Anthony *business executive, former ambassador*
Nichols, Charles Lee *professional services executive*
Price, Robert E. *manufacturing company executive*
Ray, Gene Wells *industrial executive*
†Reyes, Greg *electronics executive*
Rice, Clare I. *electronics company executive*
†Smull, Scott *electronics executive*

San Francisco
Brindley, Robert E. *food products executive*
Chiaverini, John Edward *construction company executive*
Colbert, Lester Lum, Jr. *technology products executive*
Dewey, Edward Allen *construction company executive*
D'Ornellas, Robert W. *food products executive*
Fannon, John *paper company executive*
Gates, Milo Sedgwick *construction company executive*
Grubb, David H. *construction company president*
Gumucio, Fernando Raul *foods and beverage company executive*
Haas, Peter E., Sr. *retired manufacturing company executive*
Haas, Robert Douglas *apparel manufacturing company executive*
Haas, Walter A., Jr. *retired apparel company executive, professional baseball executive*
Hull, Cordell William *business executive*
James, George Barker, II *apparel industry executive*
Jewett, George Frederick, Jr. *forest products company executive*
Kreitzberg, Fred Charles *construction management company executive*
Macdonald, A. Ewan *food products executive*
Malson, Rex Richard *drug and health care corporation executive*
Marcus, Robert *aluminum company executive*
McDowell, David E. *pharmaceutical executive*
Merrill, Harvie Martin *manufacturing executive*
Miller, Paul James *coffee company executive*
Monson, Arch, Jr. *fire alarm manufacturing company executive*
Mullenix, Travis H. *food products company executive*
Peppercorn, John Edward *chemical company executive*
Powell, Sandra Theresa *timber company executive*
Richards, John M. *wood and paper products company executive*
Saras, James J. *agricultural products, grain company executive*
Siegel, Louis Pendleton *forest products executive*
Smith, Lee Clark *apparel company executive*
†Smith, Theodore W. *construction executive*
Thacher, Carter Pomeroy *diversified manufacturing company executive*
Tusher, Thomas William *apparel company executive*
Wertheimer, Robert E. *paper company executive*
Wilson, Ian Robert *food company executive*
Woodard, Clarence James *manufacturing company executive*
Zellerbach, William Joseph *retired paper company executive*

San Jose
†Campbell, Gordon A. *electronics executive*
Conner, Finis F. *electronics company executive*
Faggin, Federico *electronics executive*
Fiebiger, James Russell *manufacturing company executive*
Frauenfelder, Lewis *electronics executive*
Heiman, Frederic Paul *electronics company executive*
Hootnick, Laurence R. *electronics company executive*
Jarrat, Henri Aaron *semiconductor company executive*
Kasson, James Matthews *electronics executive*
Leavy, Paul Matthew *management consultant*
Lee, Sung W. *electronics executive*
Mitchell, David T. *electronic computing equipment company executive*
Pausa, Clements Edward *electronics company executive*
†Praisner, Jan A. *electronics executive*
†Rasdal, William D. *electronics executive*
Rha, Y. B. *electronics executive*
†Risinger, Paul N. *electronics executive*
†Rodgers, Thomas J. *electronics executive*
Rosendin, Raymond Joseph *electrical contracting company executive*
Scalise, George Martin *electronics company executive*
Schroeder, William John *electronics executive*
Scifres, Donald R. *semiconductor laser, fiber optics and electronics company executive*
†Smith, Rodney *electronics executive*
†Sola, Jure *electronics executive*
†Stafford, James F. *electronics executive*
†Steel, Gordon *electronics executive*
†Stein, Alfred J. *electronics executive, computer software company executive*
†Wang, Franny *electronics executive*
†Wang, Stanley *electronics executive*
Young, Katherine Curtin *manufacturing executive*

San Marcos
Page, Leslie Andrew *disinfectant manufacturing company executive*

San Mateo
Aadahl, Jorg *corporate executive*
Boyd, Robert Jamison *construction equipment company executive*
Everett, Lois Almen *executive director*
Felker, James M. *environmental engineering company executive*
Riskas, Harry James *construction company executive*

Santa Ana
Baik, Hyo Whi *automotive import company executive*
Buster, Edmond Bate *metal products company executive*
Place, Geoffrey *consumer goods manufacturing company executive*
Ware, James Edwin *retired international company executive*
Washburn, Lawrence Robert *manufacturing executive*

Santa Barbara
Blasingame, Benjamin Paul *electronics company executive*
Bongiorno, James William *electronics company executive*
Laverty, Roger Montgomery, III *food products executive, lawyer*
Potter, David Samuel *former automotive company executive*
Prindle, William Roscoe *consultant, retired glass company executive*

Santa Clara
Amelio, Gilbert Frank *electronics company executive*
Baird, Mellon Campbell, Jr. *electronics industry executive*
†Carey, D. John *electronics executive*
Grove, Andrew S. *electronics company executive*
House, David L. *electronics components company executive*
Krause, L. William *manufacturing company executive*
Moore, Gordon E. *electronics company executive*
Morgan, James C. *electronics executive*
Stockton, Anderson Berrian *electronics company executive, consultant, genealogist*

Santa Clarita
DeMieri, Joseph L. *manufacturing company executive*

Santa Cruz
Broadway, Nancy Ruth *landscape design and construction company executive, consultant, model and actress*

Santa Monica
†Nettleship, Patricia Sharyn *investment group executive*

Santa Ynez
Ellion, M. Edmund *aerospace executive*

Santee
Vanier, Kieran Francis *business forms printing company executive*

Seal Beach
Bacon, Paul Caldwell *training system company executive, aviation consultant, engineering test pilot*
Beall, Donald Ray *multi-industry high-technology company executive*
Black, Kent March *electronics company executive*
Iacobellis, Sam Frank *aerospace company executive*
Merrick, George Boesch *aerospace company executive*
Yarymovych, Michael Ihor *manufacturing company executive*

Sherman Oaks
Hanlin, Russell L. *citrus products company executive*
Laney, Michael L. *manufacturing executive*

Simi Valley
Mow, William *apparel executive*
Nesi, Vincent *apparel executive*

Solana Beach
Brody, Arthur *industrial executive*
Hamilton, James Marvie *automotive company scientist*
Kempf, Paul Stuart *optics company executive*

South Pasadena
White-Thomson, Ian Leonard *mining company executive*

South San Francisco
Crowley, Jerome Joseph, Jr. *manufacturing company executive*
Halligan, Thomas Walsh *construction company executive*
Henderson, Thomas James *construction company executive*
Raab, G. Kirk *biotechnology company executive*

Stockton
†Cuff, William, IV *food company executive*
Hosie, William Carlton *food products company executive*

Sun Valley
Kamins, Philip E. *diversified manufacturing company executive*

Sunnyvale
Evans, Barton, Jr. *analytical instrument company executive*
Fialer, Philip Anthony *research scientist, electronics company executive*
Hind, Harry William *pharmaceutical company executive*
†Holbrook, Anthony *manufacturing company executive*
Leeson, David Brent *electronics company executive*
Lewis, John Clark, Jr. *manufacturing company executive*
†Rankin, M. Douglas *electronics executive*
Rugge, Henry Ferdinand *medical products executive*
Sanders, Walter Jeremiah, III *electronics company executive*
†Simon, Ralph E. *electronics executive*
†Spilker, James J., Jr. *electronics executive*
†Thompson, Edward Francis *corporate executive*
Tramiel, Sam *microcomputer and video game company executive*
Trimble, Charles R. *electronics executive*
Zelencik, Stephen J. *electronics company executive*

Sylmar
Sholder, Jason Allen *medical products company executive*

Thousand Oaks
Binder, Gordon M. *health and medical products executive*
Colburn, Keith W. *electronics executive*
DeLorenzo, David A. *food products executive*
Fitzgerald, Janet Marie *cosmetic company executive, training consultant*

Toluca Lake
Belcher, Donald David *manufacturing company executive*

Torrance
Amemiya, Koichi *motor vehicle company executive*
Bruinsma, Theodore August *retired business executive*
Burnham, Daniel Patrick *manufacturing company executive*
Chandler, Richard Hill *medical products company executive*
Fledderjohn, Karl Ross *manufacturing executive*
Mann, Michael Martin *electronics company executive*
†Perrish, Albert *steel company executive*
†Pitts, Robert Lynn *automotive company executive*
Rohrberg, Roderick George *welding consultant*
†Togo, Yukiyasu *automotive executive*
Woodhull, John Richard *electronics company executive*

Tustin
Hester, Norman Eric *chemical company technical executive, chemist*

Valley Ford
Clowes, Garth Anthony *electronics executive, consultant*

Van Nuys
Bodine, Ralph E. *food products company executive*
Halamandaris, Harry *aerospace executive*

Walnut Creek
†Cadieux, Robert D. *chemical company executive*
Graham, Dee McDonald *food company executive*
Hamlin, Kenneth Eldred, Jr. *retired pharmaceutical company executive*
Roach, John D. C. *manufacturing company executive*

Watsonville
Costanzo, Patrick M. *constuction executive*
Roberts, Richard Heilbron *construction company executive*
Solari, R. C. *heavy construction company executive*

Whittier
Brown, Thomas Andrew *aircraft and weaponry manufacturing executive*

Woodland Hills
Conley, Robert Francis *aircraft and space industry executive*
Firestone, Morton H. *business management executive*
Goldberg, David Charles *electrical contracting executive*
†Morishita, Akihiko *trading company executive*
Weiser, Paul David *manufacturing company executive*

Yorba Linda
Eriksen, Otto Louis *retired manufacturing company executive*
Forth, Kevin Bernard *beverage distributing industry consultant*

COLORADO

Arvada
Holden, George Fredric *brewing company executive, policy specialist, consultant*

Aspen
Levin, Barton John *aviation products and services company executive*

Boulder
Andrews, James Rowland *electronics executive, consultant*
Clark, Melvin Eugene *chemical company executive*
Daughenbaugh, Randall Jay *chemical company executive*
Hoerig, Gerald Lee *chemical company executive*
Lodewyk, Eric *chemist, pharmaceutical executive*
Miller, Norman Richard *diversified manufacturing company executive*
†Soll, Larry *pharmaceutical executive*
Stull, Dean P. *chemical company executive*
†Van Vorous, Ted *manufacturing company executive*

Broomfield
Davis, Delmont Alvin, Jr. *manufacturing company executive*
Haas, John Allen *manufacturing company executive*

Clark
Bartoe, Otto Edwin, Jr. *aircraft company executive*

Colorado Springs
Ehrhorn, Richard William *electronics company executive*
Hill, Roger Wendell *sugar company executive*
Robinson, Robert James *retired manufacturing executive*
†Schauer, Ralph Floyd *microelectronics company executive*
Shepard, Mikki Maureen Allison *personal care company executive*

Denver
Bard, Richard H. *financial service company executive*
Barry, Henry Ford *chemical company executive*
†Bury, Thomas L. *construction executive*
†Chandler, Thomas Franklin *food products executive*
Crawford, Richard A., Jr. *corporate executive*
Gates, Charles Cassius *rubber company executive*
Gibson, Thomas Joseph *diversified holding company executive*
Holmes, Fred Gillespie *sugar company executive*
Lee, Richard Kenneth *building products company executive*
Leprino, James G. *food products executive*
Livingston, Johnston R. *manufacturing executive*
May, Francis Hart, Jr. *retired building materials manufacturing executive*
Miller, Donald E. *rubber company executive*
†Mizel, Larry A. *housing construction company executive*
†Nields, Morgan Wesson *medical supply company executive*
Stephens, William Thomas *forest products manufacturing company executive*
Swenka, Arthur John *food products executive*
Weil, Jack Baum *clothing manufacturing company executive*

Englewood
Mahoney, Gerald Francis *manufacturing company executive*
†Timbers, Michael James *information technology executive*

Fort Collins
Fields, Robert Charles *retired printing company executive*
Hafford, Patricia Ann *electronic company executive*

Golden
Babb, Alvin Charles *beverage company executive*
Coors, Jeffrey H. *technology manufacturing executive*
Coors, William K. *brewery executive*
Harreld, James Bruce *food company executive*
Johnson, Marvin Donald *brewery executive*

Greeley
Mapelli, Roland Lawrence *food company executive*
Monfort, Kenneth *cattle production and meat processing executive*
Morgensen, Jerry Lynn *construction company executive*
Mueller, Donald Dean *food company executive*

Lakewood
Owen, Robert Roy *manufacturing company executive*

Littleton
Plusk, Ronald Frank *manufacturing company executive*
Thompson, Curtis Brooks *manufacturing company executive*

Longmont
Hahn, Yubong *electro-optics company executive*

Louisville
Poppa, Ryal Robert *manufacturing company executive*

CONNECTICUT

Ansonia
Nichols, Russell James *manufacturing company executive*

Bethel
Perrin, Charles R. *light manufacturing executive*

Bloomfield
Kaman, Charles Huron *diversified technologies corporation executive*

Branford
Krupp, James Arthur Gustave *manufacturing materials executive, consultant*
Mancheski, Frederick John *automotive company executive*
Penner, Harry Harold Hamilton, Jr. *pharmaceutical company executive, lawyer*

Bridgeport
Buckley, Eugene *aircraft company executive*
Semple, Cecil Snowdon *retired manufacturing company executive*

Bristol
Barnes, Carlyle Fuller *manufacturing executive*
Barnes, Wallace *manufacturing executive*
Fenoglio, William Ronald *manufacturing company executive*
Wells, Arthur Stanton *manufacturing company executive*

Danbury
Baker, Leonard Morton *manufacturing company executive*
Barth, Elmer Ernest *wire and cable company executive*
Kennedy, Robert Delmont *chemical company executive*
Lichtenberger, Horst William *chemical company executive*
Soviero, Joseph C. *chemical company executive*

Darien
Gammie, Anthony Petrie *pulp and paper manufacturing company executive*
O'Brien, Joseph Patrick, Jr. *apparel and textile company executive*
Saari, Leonard Mathew *paper company executive, lawyer*
Sprole, Frank Arnott *retired pharmaceutical company executive, lawyer*

Fairfield
Bunt, James Richard *electric company executive*
Currier, Jeffrey L. *manufacturing executive*
Johnson, Alvin Roscoe *manufacturing executive*
Sutphen, Harold Amerman, Jr. *retired paper company executive*
Welch, John Francis, Jr. (Jack Welch) *electrical manufacturing company executive*
Wheeler, Henry Clark *manufacturing company executive*

Farmington
Frago, William S. *manufacturing executive*
Powers, John Austin *alcoholic beverage company executive*
Scott, David J. *beverage executive*
Sheeran, William James *engineering executive*
van Rooy, Jean-Pierre *international executive*

Greenwich
Allain, Emery Edgar *retired paper company executive*
Bantle, Louis Francis *tobacco company executive*
Barber, Charles Finch *retired metals company executive, financial services company executive*
Combe, Ivan DeBlois *drug company executive*
Damon, Edmund Holcombe *plastics company executive*
Dorme, Patrick John *electronic company executive*
Holten, John V. *food products executive*
Ix, Robert Edward *food company executive*
Jeffrey, Kim *food products executive*
Lozyniak, Andrew *manufacturing company executive*
Mallardi, Joseph L. *manufacturing company executive*
Mann, Marvin L. *electronics executive*
Messud, Françis-Michel *manufacturing company executive*
†Nixon, James Alexander *cosmetic company executive*
†Rooney, Francis Charles, Jr. *corporate executive*
Rossi, Ralph L. *tobacco company executive*
Scheifele, Richard Paul *cosmetic and chemicals manufacturing company executive*
Simonnard, Michel André *manufacturing executive*
Squier, David Louis *manufacturing executive*
Vance, Don Kelvin *baking industry consultant*
Wada, Sadami (Chris) *manufacturing executive*
Wearly, William Levi *business executive*

Groton
Auerbach, Michael Howard *chemical company research executive*
Hinman, Richard Leslie *pharmaceutical company executive*

Hartford
Butterworth, Kenneth W. *manufacturing company executive*
Coburn, Richard Joseph *company executive, electrical engineer*
Daniell, Robert F. *diversified manufacturing company executive*
Evans, William John *aerospace company executive*
Freeman, David *chemical company executive*
Hermann, Robert Jay *manufacturing company engineering executive, consultant*
Krieble, Robert H. *corporation executive*
Paul, William F. *manufacturing company executive*
Rolls, John Allison *electronics company executive*
†Walters, Kirk W. *financial services holding company executive*

Madison
Golembeski, Jerome John *wire and cable company executive*

Meriden
†Friedheim, Michael *footwear and apparel company executive*
†Stapleton, Richard D. *construction company executive*
†Wetmore, Byron F. *construction company executive*

Middlebury
Binns, James W. *watch manufacturing company executive*
Fickenscher, Gerald H. *chemicals company executive*
Galie, Louis Michael *electronics company executive*
Mazaika, Robert J. *chemicals executive*

Middletown
Gerber, Murray A. *molding manufacturing company executive*

Naugatuck
Flannery, Joseph Patrick *manufacturing company executive*

New Britain
Ayers, Richard H. *manufacturing company executive*
Hadlow, David Moore *manufacturing executive*
Weddle, Stephen Shields *manufacturing company executive*

New Canaan
Bartlett, Dede Thompson *company executive*
Burns, Ivan Alfred *grocery products and industrial company executive*
Day, Castle Nason *food company executive*
Foley, Patrick Martin *computer manufacturing company executive*
Hodgson, Richard *electronics company executive*
Johnston, Douglas Frederick *industrial holding company executive*
Phypers, Dean Pinney *retired computer company executive*
Powell, Harold Fryburg *food products executive*
Rutledge, John William *former watch company executive*
Sachs, John Peter *carbon company executive*
Thompson, George Lee *manufacturing company executive*

Toumey, Hubert John (Hugh Toumey) *textile company executive*

New Haven
†Calvi, Paul *chemicals executive*
Grossi, Richard J. *electric utility company executive*
James, Paul Charles *tire company executive*
Mazzarella, Andrew James *automotive products executive, accountant*
Wentz, Howard Beck, Jr. *manufacturing company executive*

North Branford
Mead, Lawrence Myers, Jr. *retired aerospace executive*

North Haven
Seton, Fenmore Roger *manufacturing company executive, civic worker*

Norwalk
Crump, James G., Jr. *printing company executive*
†Digiovanna, Charles Vincent *chemical manufacturer*
Grace, Julianne Alice *manufacturing company executive*
Hart, James W., Jr. *manufacturing executive*
Hirsch, Leon Charles *medical company executive*
Johnstone, Chauncey Olcott *pharmaceutical company executive*
Josefsen, Turi *medical supply company executive*
Kelley, Gaynor Nathaniel *instrumentation manufacturing company executive*
Korthoff, Herbert William *medical devices company executive*
Leonard, Stewart J. *dairy company executive*
Maarbjerg, Mary Penzold *office equipment company executive*
McDonell, Horace George, Jr. *instrument company executive*
Peltz, Alan Howard *manufacturing company executive*
Smith, Wendell Murray *graphic arts control and equipment manufacturing executive*
Sturm, Donald L. *construction executive*
Vanderbilt, Hugh Bedford, Sr. *mineral and chemical company executive*
†Vinciguerra, Salvatore Joseph *scientific instrument company executive*
York, Theodore *electronics executive*

Old Greenwich
Mc Donough, Richard Doyle *retired paper company executive*
Mc Quinn, William P. *corporation executive*
Plancher, Robert Lawrence *manufacturing company executive*
Rukeyser, Robert James *manufacturing executive*

Orange
Ratcliffe, George Jackson, Jr. *business executive, lawyer*
Sinclair, Robert J. *automotive executive*

Plainville
Glassman, Gerald Seymour *metal finishing company executive*

Ridgefield
Doran, Charles Edward *textile manufacturing executive*
Knortz, Herbert Charles *retired conglomerate company executive*
Levine, Paul Michael *paper industry executive, consultant*
Malhotra, Surin M. *aerospace manufacturing executive*
McGovern, R(ichard) Gordon *food company executive*
Sadow, Harvey S. *health care company executive*

Riverside
McCullough, Robert Willis *former textile executive*

Rocky Hill
Geckle, Robert Alan *manufacturing company executive*

Salisbury
Blum, Robert Edward *business executive*

Sandy Hook
Karkut, Emil Joseph *manufacturing company executive*

Shelton
Smith, Craig Richards *manufacturing executive*

Somers
Blake, Stewart Prestley *retired ice cream company executive*

South Windsor
Gentile, George Michael *manufacturing company finance executive*
†Gerber, H. Joseph *manufacturing executive*

Southport
Haas, Ward John *research and development executive*
Kingsley, John McCall, Jr. *manufacturing company executive*
Perry, Vincent Aloysius *corporate executive*
Roache, Edward Francis *retired manufacturing company executive*
Ruger, William Batterman *firearms manufacturing company executive*
Wheeler, Wilmot Fitch, Jr. *diversified manufacturing company executive*

Stamford
Allaire, Paul Arthur *office equipment company executive*
Anderson, Susan Stuebing *business equipment company executive*
Ashton, Harris John *business executive*
Ball, John A. *forest products company executive*
Beiser, Gerald J. *paper products company executive*
Bell, W. James *manufacturing company executive*
Bitter, Frank Gordon *manufacturing executive*
†Breslawsky, Marc C. *manufacturing executive*
Britton, Robert Austin *manufacturing company executive*

Burchfield, William H. *forest products company executive*
Cahill, John C. *general industry company executive*
Calarco, Vincent Anthony *specialty chemicals company executive*
Carlin, Gabriel S. *corporate executive*
Carpenter, Edmund Mogford *manufacturing executive*
Cassetta, Sebastian Ernest *industry executive*
Coleman, Ernest Albert *plastics and materials consultant*
Davis, Ronald Vernon *beverage products executive*
Evans, Robert Sheldon *manufacturing executive*
Fernandez, Nino Joseph *manufacturing company executive*
Filter, Eunice M. *business equipment manufacturing executive*
Fortune, Philip Robert *metal manufacturing company executive*
†Friedman, Joel Stephen *manufacturing company executive*
Fuller, Mark Adin, Jr. *forest products company executive*
Gladstone, Herbert Jack *manufacturing company executive*
Griffin, Donald Wayne *diversified chemical company executive*
Gross, Ronald Martin *forest products executive*
Harvey, George Burton *office equipment company executive*
Hedge, Arthur Joseph, Jr. *environmental executive*
Heist, Lewis Clark *forest products company executive*
Hicks, Wayland R. *electronic business equipment executive*
Hollander, Milton Bernard *electronics corporate executive*
Hood, Edward Exum, Jr. *retired electrical manufacturing company executive*
Horrigan, D. Gregory *metal products executive*
Hudson, Franklin Donald *diversified company executive*
Hull, James Charles *industrial company executive*
Jaffe, Elliot S. *women's clothing retail chain executive*
Johnstone, John William, Jr. *chemical company executive*
Kubisen, Steven Joseph, Jr. *chemical and plastics management consultant*
Lennard, Gerald *metal products executive*
Lockhart, Michael D. *electric company executive*
Magidson, Michael D. *metals products executive*
Martin, Patrick *business equipment company executive*
Morley, John C. *electronic equipment company executive*
Nutter, Wallace Lee *paper manufacturing executive*
Oatway, Francis Carlyle *lumber products, paper company executive*
O'Malley, Thomas D. *diversified company executive*
Owen, Nathan Richard *manufacturing company executive*
Peterson, Carl Eric *banker, metals company executive*
†Purcell, John R. *holding company executive*
Rizzuto, Leandro Peter *corporate executive*
Ryan, Raymond D. *retired steel company executive, insurance and marketing firm executive*
Salisbury, John Francis *distillery and chemical company executive, corporate lawyer*
Sigler, Andrew Clark *forest products company executive*
Silver, R. Philip *metal products executive*
Weyher, Harry Frederick, III *metals company executive*
Ziegler, William, III *diversified industry executive*

Stratford
Salzberg, Emmett Russell *new product developer*

Trumbull
Schmitt, William Howard *cosmetics company executive*
Shaw, Ronald Gordon *manufacturing company executive*

Wallingford
De George, Lawrence Joseph *diversified company executive*
†Reiner, Bert Leo *consumer product engineering/ manufacturing consultant*

Waterbury
Leever, Harold *chemical company executive*
Olsen, T. Fred *timing instruments manufacturing company executive*
Zampiello, Richard Sidney *metals and trading company executive*
Zeitlin, Bruce Allen *superconducting material technology executive*

West Hartford
Clear, Albert F., Jr. *retired hardware manufacturing company executive*
Doran, James Martin *retired food products company executive*
Raffay, Stephen Joseph *manufacturing company executive*

West Simsbury
Brinkerhoff, Peter John *manufacturing company executive*

Weston
Liberatore, Nicholas Alfred *business consultant*

Westport
Breitbarth, S. Robert *manufacturing company executive*
McKane, David Bennett *business executive*
Stashower, Michael David *retired manufacturing company executive*

Windsor
Mangold, John Frederic *manufacturing company executive, former naval officer*

Windsor Locks
Walker, K. Grahame *manufacturing company executive*

Woodbridge
Alvine, Robert *industrialist, entrepreneur, international business leader*

Woodbury
Farrell, Edgar Henry *building components manufacturing executive, lawyer*

DELAWARE

Milford
†Burris, John E. *food products executive*

Millsboro
Townsend, P(reston) Coleman *agricultural business executive*

New Castle
Roddy, Edward Joseph *plastic pipe company executive*

Newark
Webb, Richard Stephen *manufacturing executive*

Rockland
Rubin, Alan A. *pharmaceutical and biotechnology consultant*

Wilmington
Aiken, Robert McCutchen *retired chemical company executive, management consultant*
Arrington, Charles Hammond, Jr. *retired chemical company executive*
Beardwood, Bruce Allan *chemical company executive*
†Black, Robert C. *chemical company executive*
Danzeisen, John R. *chemical company executive*
DeBlieu, Ivan Knowlton *plastic pipe company executive, consultant*
Gadsby, Robin Edward *chemical company executive*
Galli, Paolo *chemical company executive*
Gibson, Joseph Whitton, Jr. *retired chemical company executive*
Gossage, Thomas Layton *chemical company executive*
Hendricks, Rayman Michael *chemical company executive*
Jaffe, Edward E(phraim) *retired research and development executive*
Kane, Edward Rynex *retired chemical company executive, corporate director*
Karrh, Bruce Wakefield *industrial company executive*
Kearns, James Francis *textile technology company executive*
Lange, James Braxton *chemical company executive*
†Manzer, Leo E. *chemicals executive*
Miller, Hugh Edward *business executive*
Mollica, Joseph A. *pharmaceutical executive*
Molz, Robert Joseph *manufacturing company executive*
Morrione, Paolo *polypropylene company executive*
Ockun, Robert J. *manufacturing executive*
Rose, Selwyn H. *chemical company executive*
Schmutz, John F. *chemical company executive, corporate lawyer*
Sganga, John B. *furniture holding company executive*
†Wattman, Kenneth E. *chemical company executive*
Wilhite, Colbert Roland *chemical and oil company executive*
†Willard, A. Keith *chemicals executive*
Woods, Robert A. *chemical company executive*
Woolard, Edgar S., Jr. *chemical company executive*

DISTRICT OF COLUMBIA

Washington
Alexander, Benjamin Harold *professional services firm executive, past government official*
†Beckner, Everet Hess *diversified research and development laboratory executive*
Benitez, Juan Antonio *electronics company executive*
†Blanchette, Robert Wilfred *business executive, lawyer*
Boren, James Harlan *business executive, association executive*
Briggs, Harold Melvin *corporate executive*
Caldwell, John L. *corporate executive*
Carr, David Kenneth *corporate executive*
Chen, Yuki Y. Kuo *industrial supplies company executive*
Choquette, William H. *construction company executive*
†Clark, William Patrick *construction, engring & transportation co exec, lawyer, rancher*
Cook, Richard Kelsey *aerospace industry executive*
Davis, Lance Alan *research and development executive, metallurgical engineer*
Davis, True *corporate executive*
Esters, Donald J. *audio and video company executive*
Farley, John Michael *steel industry executive*
Ferebee, John Spencer, Jr. *corporate executive*
Gracey, James Steele *corporate director, retired coast guard officer, consultant*
Green, Edward Crocker *health consulting firm executive*
Griffin, Robert Thomas *automotive company executive*
Grossi, Ralph Edward *agricultural conservation organization executive, farmer, rancher*
Juliana, James Nicholas *ordnance company executive*
Kinard, Helen Marie Pawnee Madison *corporate executive*
Lamb, Vincent P. *industrial executive*
Lebow, Irwin Leon *electronics engineering consultant*
Lewis, W. Walker *cosmetics executive*
Luth, William Clair *research manager*
Lutley, John H. *precious metals company executive*
Marshall, C. Travis *manufacturing executive, government relations specialist*
McKinney, James Clayton *electronics executive, electrical engineer*
Moore, Robert Madison *food industry executive, lawyer*
Peapples, George Alan *automotive executive*
Persavich, Warren Dale *diversified manufacturing company executive*
Price, Mark Michael *building development consultant*
Rales, Steven M. *automotive parts company executive*
Rowlands, T. Dewi *aerospace executive*
Sherman, George M. *manufacturing company executive*
Slater, Doris Ernestine Wilke *business executive*
Thomas, W. Dennis *paper company executive, former government official*
Thompson, Richard Leon *pharmaceutical company executive, lawyer*
Trowbridge, Alexander Buel, Jr. *corporate director, consultant*

FLORIDA

Anna Maria
Kaiser, Albert Farr *diversified corporation executive*

Atlantis
Minshall, Drexel David *retired manufacturing company executive*

Boca Grande
Nimitz, Chester William, Jr. *manufacturing company executive*

Boca Raton
Alvarado, Ricardo Raphael *retired corporate executive, lawyer*
Boer, F. Peter *chemical company executive*
Bolduc, J. P. *specialty chemicals and specialized health care company executive*
Butler, J. Murfree *chemical company executive*
Fetter, Richard Elwood *retired industrial company executive*
Houraney, William George *company executive*
Ingwersen, Martin Lewis *shipyard executive*
Klein, Robert *manufacturing company executive*
Rasmussen, Lynn C. *fashion accessories company executive*
Walsh, Robert Charles *chemical company executive*

Bonita Springs
Cairns, Raymond Eldon, Jr. *consultant, retired chemical company executive*
Sargent, Charles Lee *recreation vehicle and pollution control systems manufacturing company executive*

Boynton Beach
Jensen, Reuben Rolland *former automotive company executive*
Johnson, Edward A. *manufacturing executive*
Smith, Charles Henry, Jr. *industrial executive*

Bradenton
Atkinson, Arlis D. *wall and ceiling contractor*
Feeley, John Paul *retired paper company executive*
Price, Edgar Hilleary, Jr. *business consultant*
Riha, William Edwin *beverage company executive*
Roeder, Myron A. *agricultural products company executive*

Cape Coral
Peters, Donald Cameron *construction company executive*

Casselberry
Vincent, Thomas James *retired manufacturing company executive*

Clearwater
Chamberlin, Terry McBride *sailing equipment company executive*
St. Clair, Jane Elizabeth *management executive*
Smith, Marion Pafford *avionics company executive*
Yoho, Robert Wayne *company executive*

Clermont
Dyson, Raymond Clegg *building contractor, construction consultant*

Clewiston
Boy, John Buckner *sugar company executive*

Coral Gables
Burini, Sonia Montes de Oca *apparel manufacturing and public relations executive*
Cegnar, Ronald William *food company executive*
Higginbottom, Samuel Logan *retired aerospace company executive*

Deerfield Beach
Assaf, Ronald G. *electronics executive*

Delray Beach
Fuente, D. I. *office supply manufacturing executive*
Goldenberg, George *retired pharmaceutical company executive*
Himmelright, Robert John, Jr. *rubber company executive*
Saffer, Alfred *retired chemical company executive*
Smith, John Joseph, III *textile company executive, educator*

Fort Lauderdale
Caporella, Nick A. *diversified company executive*
Carney, Dennis Joseph *former steel company executive, consulting company executive*
Keats, Harold Alan *corporate executive*
Morse, Edward J. *automotive executive*
Peterson, Colin Hampton *electronics company executive*
Reigrod, Robert Hull *manufacturing executive*
Sklar, Alexander *electrical company executive*

Fort Myers
Censits, Richard John *electronic controls company executive*
Hudson, Leonard Harlow *contractor*
O'Dell, William Francis *retired business executive, author*
Wendeborn, Richard Donald *retired manufacturing company executive*

Gainesville
Chang, Weilin Parrish *construction educator, administrator, researcher*

Green Cove Springs
Watson, Thomas Campbell *economic development consulting company executive*

Gulf Stream
Stone, Franz Theodore *retired fabricated metal products manufacturing executive*

Hallandale
Cornblatt, Max *automotive batteries manufacturing company executive*

Hialeah
†Strauss, Robert C. *manufacturing executive*

Hillsboro Bch
Gibbons, Joseph John *builders supply company financial executive*

Hobe Sound
Casey, Edward Paul *manufacturing company executive*
Craig, David Jeoffrey *retired manufacturing company executive*
Henley, Henry Howard, Jr. *retired manufacturing company executive*
McChristian, Joseph Alexander *international business executive*

Indialantic
Bush, Norman *research and development executive*

Jacksonville
†Baker, John Daniel, II *crushed stone company executive*
Belin, Jacob Chapman *paper company executive*
DuBow, Lawrence Jay *drug company executive*
Foster, Ronald H. *construction company executive*
Haskell, Preston Hampton, III *construction company executive*
Jackson, Julian Ellis *food company executive*
Lyon, Sherman Orwig *rubber and chemical company executive*
†McGehee, Frank Sutton *paper company executive*
McGehee, Thomas Rives *paper company executive*
Robbins, George William, III *chemical company executive*
Welch, Philip Burland *electronics and office products company executive*

Key Largo
Brown, David *retired petrochemical corporation executive*
Daly, William Gerald *business executive*
Davidson, Thomas Noel *business executive*

Lakeland
Harritt, Norman L. *manufacturing company executive*
Hatten, William Seward *manufacturing company executive*

Largo
Keller, Gary William *printing manufacturing executive, accountant*

Leesburg
Talley, William Giles, Jr. *container manufacturing company executive*

Longboat Key
Prizer, Charles John *chemical company executive*

Longwood
Blumberg, Herbert Kurt *corporate executive*
Reade, Richard Sill *manufacturing executive*
Yon, Eugene T. *process control company executive*

Maitland
Crosby, Philip Bayard *company executive, author*
St. John, John *food company executive*

Marathon
Janicki, Robert Stephen *retired pharmaceutical company executive*

Marco Island
Butler, Frederick George *retired drug company executive*
Guerrant, David Edward *retired food company executive*

Melbourne
Hartley, John T., Jr. *electronic systems, semiconductor, communications and office equipment executive*

Miami
Anscher, Bernard *manufacturing executive, investor, management consultant*
Autrey, Frank Eugene *engineering company executive*
Bauer, Peter Alexander *clothing executive*
Blackburn, James Ross, Jr. *business executive, retired airline pilot*
Braman, Norman *automotive executive, football club executive*
Conese, Eugene Paul, Sr. *manufacturing company executive*
Frigo, James Peter Paul *industrial hardware company executive*
Golub, Alan *clothing company executive*
†May, Peter William *business executive*
†Peltz, Nelson *manufacturing company executive*
Weldon, Norman Ross *manufacturing company executive*

Mulberry
†Badcock, Wogan Stanhope, Jr. *manufacturing company executive*

Naples
Baldwin, Ralph Belknap *retired manufacturing company executive, astronomer*
Barth-Wehrenalp, Gerhard *chemical company executive*
Biondo, Michael Thomas *retired paper company executive*
Frazer, John Howard *tennis association executive, retired manufacturing company executive*
Freedman, Stanley Marvin *manufacturing company executive*
Gushman, John Louis *former corporation executive, lawyer*
Kapnick, Harvey Edward, Jr. *retired corporate executive*
Maloon, James Harold *business executive, economist*
Price, Thomas Benjamin *former textile company executive*
Reed, John Franklin *instrument manufacturing company executive*
Sharpe, Robert Francis *equipment manufacturing company executive*
Smith, Willis Allen *retired consultant, former food company executive*
Van der Eb, Henry Gerard *retired packaging company executive*
von Arx, Dolph William *food products executive*

New Smyrna Beach
Skove, Thomas Malcolm *retired manufacturing company financial executive*

Niceville
Burns, John Joseph *consultant, retired aerospace executive, retired air force officer*
Litke, Donald Paul *business executive, retired military officer*

North Palm Beach
Hushing, William Collins *retired corporate executive*
Kenna, Edgar Douglas *manufacturing company executive*
Rimmer, Jack *retired chemical company executive*
Staub, W. Arthur *health care products executive*

Orange Park
Webb, Robert Lee *chemical company executive*

Orlando
Brownlee, Thomas Marshall *lighting manufacturing company executive*
†Hughes, David Henry *manufacturing company executive*
Jones, Joseph Wayne *food and beverage company executive, entrepreneur*

Oviedo
Whitworth, Hall Baker *forest products company executive*

Palm Beach
Habicht, Frank Henry *industrial executive*
Isenberg, Abraham Charles *shoe manufacturing company executive*
Jackson, John Tillson *corporate executive*
Rumbough, Stanley Maddox, Jr. *industrialist*
Winkler, Joseph Conrad *former recreational products manufacturing executive*

Palm Beach Gardens
Howse, Robert Davis *business executive*

Palm City
Wishart, Ronald Sinclair *retired chemical company executive*

Panama City
†Snapp, Manco *chemicals executive*

Pinellas Park
Hall, Charles Allen *aerospace and energy company executive*

Pompano Beach
Schwartz, Joseph *retired container company executive*
Zimmer, Paul Howard *housing and transportation manufacturing company executive*

Ponte Vedra Beach
Elston, William Steger *food products company executive*
Klacsmann, John Anthony *retired chemical company executive*
Phelan, Martin DuPont *retired film company executive*
Spence, Richard Dee *paper products company executive, former railroad executive*

Port Saint Lucie
Mottram-Doss, Renée *corporate executive*

Riviera Beach
Horowitz, Dennis *electronic components company executive*

Royal Palm Beach
Graham, Carl Francis *consultant, former chemical products company executive, chemist*

Saint Augustine
Tadlock, R. Jerry *manufacturing and logistics consultant*

Saint Petersburg
Mc Lean, Thomas Edwin *retired manufacturing company executive*
Mills, William Harold, Jr. *construction company executive*
Roeder, Ross Eugene *consulting company executive*
Sheen, Robert Tilton *manufacturing company executive*
Stewart, Joseph Lester *rubber company executive*

Sarasota
Berkoff, Charles Edward *pharmaceutical executive*
Dlesk, George *retired pulp and paper industry executive*
Glasser, Otto John *former business executive, former air force officer*
Hoffman, Oscar Allen *retired forest products company executive*
Roth, James Frank *manufacturing company executive, chemist*
Soran, Robert L. *manufacturing executive*
Swenson, Harold Francis *crisis management consultant*
Wigton, Paul Norton *steel company consultant, former executive*

South Bay
Fairbanks, J. Nelson *sugar company executive*

Stuart
Conklin, George Melville *retired food company executive*
DeRita, Thomas, Jr. *automobile company executive*
Derrickson, William Borden *manufacturing executive*
Leibson, Irving *industrial executive*
Mc Kenna, Sidney F. *technical company executive*
McQuillan, William Hugh *building company executive*
Snider, Harlan Tanner *former manufacturing company executive*
Wasiele, Harry W., Jr. *diversified electrical manufacturing company executive*
Wood, Harleston Read *retired manufacturing executive*

Tampa
Brown, Troy Anderson, Jr. *electrical distributing company executive*
†Byrnes, Donald J. *consumer products company executive*
Flom, Edward Leonard *retired steel company executive*
Hyatt, Kenneth E(rnest) *building materials company executive*
Johnson, Ewell Calvin *research and engineering executive*
Martens, Ernesto *glass products company executive*
Matlock, Kenneth Jerome *building materials company executive*
McNeel, Van Louis *chemical company executive*
Naimoli, Vincent Joseph *diversified operating and holding company executive*
†Robinson, Charles E. *building materials executive*
Sada, Federico G. *glass manufacturing executive*
†Whiting, Paul L. *holding company executive*

Tarpon Springs
Vajk, Hugo *manufacturing executive*

Tequesta
Milton, Robert Mitchell *chemical company executive*
Peterson, James Robert *retired writing instrument manufacturing executive*

Titusville
Haise, Fred Wallace, Jr. *aerospace company executive, former astronaut*

Vero Beach
Allik, Michael *diversified industry executive*
Cartwright, Alton Stuart *electrical manufacturing company executive*
Conway, Earl Cranston *manufacturing company executive, educator*
Furrer, John Rudolf *retired manufacturing business executive*
MacTaggart, Barry *retired corporate executive*
Reed, Sherman Kennedy *chemical consultant*
Ritterhoff, C(harles) William *retired steel company executive*
Wiegner, Edward Alex *multi-industry executive*

West Palm Beach
Broadhead, James Lowell *business executive*
Davis, Robert Edwin *manufacturing executive*
Giacco, Alexander Fortunatus *chemical industry executive*
Hudson, Alice Peterson *chemistry consulting laboratory executive*
Lasnick, Julius *fabric company executive*
Luckett, Paul Herbert, III *manufacturing executive*
Nelson, Richard Henry *manufacturing company executive*
Rinker, Marshall Edison, Sr. *cement company executive*
Scheckner, Sy *former greeting card company executive*
Schuler, John Hamilton *holding company executive*
Vecellio, Leo Arthur, Jr. *construction company executive*

Windermere
Alexander, Judd Harris *retired paper company executive*
Hylton, Hannelore Menke *retired manufacturing executive*

Winter Haven
O'Connor, R. D. *health care executive*

Winter Park
Kost, Wayne L. *business executive*
Link, Raymond Arthur *construction company executive*
Weir, William C., III *lighting manufacturing company executive*

GEORGIA

Atlanta
Abrams, Bernard William *construction manufacturing and property development executive*
Abrams, Edward Marvin *construction company executive*
Anderson, Ray C. *carpet company executive*
Baran, William Lee *food company executive*
Benatar, Leo *packaging company executive*
Bevington, E(dmund) Milton *electrical machinery manufacturing company executive*
Biggers, William Joseph *retired manufacturing company executive*
Blount, Ben B., Jr. *apparel executive*
Boeke, Eugene H., Jr. *construction executive*
Brands, James Edwin *medical products executive*
†Burkart, Alan Ray *chemical company executive*
Cantrell, Wesley Eugene, Sr. *office equipment company executive*
Casey, Charles Francis *diversified company executive*
Chitwood, Harold Otis *food company executive*
Coan, Gaylord O. *agribusiness executive*
Corr, James Vanis *furniture manufacturing executive, investor, lawyer, accountant*
Correll, Alston Dayton, Jr. *forest products company executive*
Dennison, Stanley Scott *retired lumber company executive, consultant*
Dezell, James Elton, Jr. *educational systems and computer company executive*
Dolive, Earl *retired business executive*
Edwards, Howard Dawson *business executive, physicist, academic administrator*
Edwards, Louis Ward, Jr. *diversified manufacturing company executive*
Ford, Basil H. *packaging company executive*
Furr, Anthony Lloyd *corporate executive*
Gallagher, Thomas C. *diversified manufacturing executive*
Gianturco, Maurizio Antonio *beverage company executive*
Goizueta, Roberto Crispulo *food and beverage company executive*
†Green, William S. *corporate executive, engineer*
Hahn, Thomas Marshall, Jr. *forest products corporation executive*
Herlong, D. C. *agribusiness executive*
Honan, James Terry *construction company executive*
Hubble, Don Wayne *manufacturing company executive*
Ivester, Melvin Douglas *beverage company executive*
Jones, Christine Massey *furniture company executive*
Jones, Edward Marshall *automotive parts distributing company executive*
Kuse, James Russell *chemical company executive*
Lanier, John Hicks *apparel company executive*
Lee, R(aymond) William, Jr. *apparel company executive*
Lennon, A. Max *food products company executive*
Liebmann, Seymour W. *construction consultant*
Malaspina, Alex *soft drink company executive*
Mc Kenzie, Harold Cantrell, Jr. *retired manufacturing executive*
†Nickels, Robert Edward *plastic manufacturing company executive*
†Pinto, William A. *construction executive*
Prince, Larry L. *automotive parts and supplies company executive*
Reeder, Michael S. *consulting firm executive*
Reith, Carl Joseph *apparel industry executive*
†Richardson, Maurice M. *manufacturing executive*
Rollins, R. Randall *diversified services company executive*
†Russell, Herman Jerome *business executive*
Sands, Don William *agricultural products company executive retired*
Satrum, Jerry R. *chemicals company executive*
Scalley, John J. *automotive parts company executive*
Schimberg, Henry Aaron *soft drink company executive*
Schumacher, Robert Alan *forest products company executive*
Schwartz, Herbert Marshall *business executive*
Schweitzer, Conrad *timber company executive*
Scott, Charles R. *diversified company executive*
Shepherd, Stephen Beers *construction executive*
Smith, W. P., Jr. *food products executive*
Stevens, James M. *food processing executive*
Sutton, Berrien Daniel *beverage company executive*
Tolar, Carroll T. *paper company executive, mechanical engineer*
Tucker, Robert Dennard *health care products executive*
Ware, Carl *bottling company executive*
†Weiss, David *construction executive*
West, Richard Charles *construction company executive*
Zaban, Erwin *diversified manufacturing company executive*

Baxley
Reddy, Yenamala Ramachandra *metal processing executive*

Brunswick
Brubaker, Robert Paul *food products executive*
Iannicelli, Joseph *chemical company executive, consultant*

Carrollton
Richards, Roy, Jr. *wire and cable manufacturing company executive*

Chatsworth
†Ralston, Merrell Edward *textiles executive*
†Williams, Edward *textile executive*

Columbus
Andrews, Gerald Bruce *textile executive*
†Butler, Stephen T. *manufacturing executive, light, wholesale distribution executive*
Lampton, Mason Houghland *construction company executive*
Leebern, Donald M. *distilled beverage executive*

Conyers
†Florent, Gerald Philex *electronics executive, screen playwriter*
Mc Clung, Jim Hill *light manufacturing company executive*

Dalton
Maffett, Joe Baxter *carpet manufacturing company executive*
Shaw, Julius C. *carpet manufacturing company executive*
Shaw, Robert E. *carpeting company executive*

Duluth
Torian, Merville Russell, Sr. *construction company executive*

Eton
†Weaver, Linda *textiles executive*

Gainesville
Kartzinel, Ronald *pharmaceutical company executive, neuroscientist*

Griffin
†Newton, John T. *towel and baby products manufacturing company executive*

Kennesaw
Gay, Albert Loyal, Jr. *mining company executive*

Lilburn
Graham, Richard *container company executive*

Macon
Drinkard, Lawrence W. *health services executive*

Madison
†Meixner, Richard *manufacturing executive, light*

Marietta
Breese, John Allen *chemical industry executive*
Diercks, Chester William, Jr. *capital goods manufacturing company executive*
†Warren, James Walter, Jr. *pharmaceutical company executive*
†Welander, Bo *chemicals executive*

Moultrie
Vereen, William Jerome *uniform manufacturing company executive*

Norcross
Adams, Kenneth Francis *automobile executive*
Brown, Adrian Worley *manufacturing company executive*
†Campbell, Robert L. *holding company executive, computer software company executive*
Currey, Bradley, Jr. *paper company executive*
Drack, Paul E. *aluminum company executive*
Kelly, William S. *automotive service executive*
Pippin, John Eldon *electronics engineer, electronics company executive*
Sage, Gordon *metal products executive*

Peachtree City
†Weingarten, Stephen C. *electronics executive*

Roswell
Grosklaus, James G. *pulp and paper company executive*

Savannah
Cartledge, Raymond Eugene *retired paper company executive*
Gillespie, Daniel Curtis, Sr. *retired non-profit company executive, consultant*
Granger, Harvey, Jr. *manufacturing company executive*
Scott, Walter Coke *retired sugar company executive, lawyer*
Skipper, Henry T., Jr. *manufacturing company executive*
Spitz, Seymour James, Jr. *retired fragrance company executive*
Sprague, William Wallace, Jr. *food company executive*
Taylor, James Marshall *food products executive*

Sea Island
Mattis, Louis Price *pharmaceutical and consumer products company executive*

Smyrna
†Chanoki, Fred *electronics component manufacturing company executive*
†Murata, Akira *manufacturing executive*

Thomaston
Hightower, Neil Hamilton *textile manufacturing company executive*

Thomasville
Crozer, Robert P. *food products company executive*
Flowers, Langdon Strong *foods company executive*
Flowers, William Howard, Jr. *food company executive*
Mc Mullian, Amos Ryals *food company executive*
Varnedoe, Heeth, III *food products company executive*
Wood, Charles Martin, III *food company executive*

West Point
Glover, Clifford Clarke *retired construction company executive*
Holland, John B. *textiles executive*
Jennings, Joseph Leslie, Jr. *textile executive*
Terry, Richmond Bohler *textiles executive*

HAWAII

Honolulu
Andrasick, James Stephen *agribusiness company executive*
Barbieri, David Arthur *company executive*
Buyers, John William Amerman *agribusiness and specialty foods company executive*
Ching, Larry Fong Chow *construction company executive*
Clark, Henry Benjamin, Jr. *retired food company executive, community service volunteer*
Couch, John Charles *diversified company executive*
Gary, James Frederick *business and energy advising company executive*
†Heenan, David A. *diversified products company executive*
Hughes, Robert Harrison *former agricultural products executive*
Kugle, J. Alan *food company executive, lawyer*
Robertson, Gregg Westland *diversified company executive*
Schnack, Gayle Hemingway Jepson (Mrs. Harold Clifford Schnack) *corporate executive*

IDAHO

Boise
†Beebe, Stephen A. *agricultural products company executive*
Cleary, Edward William *retired diversified forest products company executive*
Dorman, Rex Lee *forest products executive*
Ferguson, E. Robert *construction and engineering company executive*
Fery, John Bruce *forest products company executive*
Harad, George Jay *manufacturing company executive*
Kemp, J. Robert *beef industry consultant, food company executive*
Littman, Irving *forest products company executive*
McClary, James Daly *retired contractor*
Minnick, Walter Clifford *building materials company executive*
Norrie, K. Peter *manufacturing executive*
†Parkinson, Joseph L. *electronics company executive, lawyer*
Parrish, Richard B. *manufacturing executive*
Sullivan, James Kirk *forest products company executive*
†Tinstman, Robert A. *construction, real estate executive*

Hayden
Wogsland, James Willard *retired heavy machinery manufacturing executive*

Ketchum
Kreitler, Richard Rogers *company executive*

ILLINOIS

Abbott Park
Burnham, Duane Lee *pharmaceutical company executive*
Coughlan, Gary Patrick *pharmaceutical company executive*
†Hightower, Belinda Ann *pharmaceutical company official, researcher*
Hodgson, Thomas Richard *health care company executive*
Lussen, John Frederick *pharmaceutical laboratory executive*
Thompson, David Allen *health care company executive*

Addison
Brunken, Gerald Walter, Sr. *manufacturing company executive*
Turner, Eugene Andrew *manufacturing executive*

Antioch
Strang, Charles Daniel *marine engine manufacturing company executive*

Arlington Heights
Church, Herbert Stephen, Jr. *retired construction company executive*
†Ray, C. Eugene *chemicals executive*
Staiano, Edward F. *electronics company executive*

Aurora
†Candlish, Malcolm *manufacturing executive*

Barrington
Kartalia, Mitchell P. *electrical equipment manufacturing executive*
Kroha, Bradford King *electronics manufacturing corporation executive*
Marshall, Gordon Bruce *construction company executive*
Moses, Bruce Hadley *manufacturing company executive*
Spak, Lorin Mitchell *office products industry executive*

Batavia
Tweedy, Robert Hugh *retired equipment company executive*

Bedford Park
Wenstrup, H. Daniel *chemical executive*

Bloomingdale
Pedicini, Louis James *manufacturing company executive*
†Wolande, Charles Sanford *corporate executive*

Bloomington
Poulson, Howard D. *agricultural products company executive*

Blue Island
Mueller, John D. *electric company executive*

Broadview
Andrla, Valerie Etta *manufacturing company executive*
Hohage, Frederick William *automotive parts company executive*

Burr Ridge
Danly, Donald Robert *retired manufacturing company executive*

Calumet City
Self, Madison Allen *chemical company executive*

Carlinville
Schweizer, Melvin *food products executive*
Southwell, Leonard J. *dairy corporation executive*

Carol Stream
Catone, Lucio *manufacturing executive*
Pond, Byron O. *manufacturing company executive*

Cary
Bowen, John Richard *former chemical company executive*

Champaign
Lyon, James Cyril *chemical society executive*
Richards, Daniel Wells *company executive*

Chester
Welge, Donald Edward *food manufacturing executive*

Chicago
Anderson, Richard C. *clothing company executive*
Appleton, Arthur Ivar *retired electric products manufacturing company executive, horse breeder*
Archambault, Bennett *corporate executive*
Athens, Andrew A. *steel company executive*
Badger, Charles H. *manufacturing company executive*
Banta, Merle Henry *graphics equipment and service company executive*
Bergere, Carleton Mallory *contractor*
Bonser, Sidney Henry *diversified manufacturing company executive*
Boonstra, Cornelis *food products company executive*
Brake, Cecil Clifford *diversified manufacturing executive*
Brookstone, Arnold F. *paper packaging company executive*
Bryan, John Henry *food and consumer products company executive*

Burhoe, Brian W. *automotive service executive*
Burt, Robert Norcross *diversified manufacturing company executive*
Callahan, Michael J. *chemicals and manufacturing company executive*
Campbell, Calvin Arthur, Jr. *mining and plastics molding equipment manufacturing company executive*
†Cappadoccia, Ronald *food products executive*
†Carl, John L. *petroleum industry executive*
Cavalier, Frank N. *construction company executive, civil engineer*
†Christopher, Robert Allan *manufacturing company executive*
Clarke, Richard Stewart *security company executive*
Claypool, William, III *hardware, garden equipment manufacturing company executive*
Conant, Howard Rosset *steel company executive*
Connolly, Eugene B., Jr. *building materials company executive*
Considine, Frank William *container corporation executive*
Cooper, Charles Gilbert *toiletries and cosmetics company executive*
Cotter, Daniel A. *diversified company executive*
Cotting, James Charles *manufacturing company executive*
Covalt, Robert Byron *chemicals executive*
Crawford, William F. *corporate executive, consultant*
Crown, Lester *manufacturing company executive*
Darnall, Robert J. *steel company executive*
Donnelley, James Russell *printing company executive*
Dorf, Jerome *clothing corporation executive*
Drexler, Lloyd *business executive*
Drexler, Richard Allan *manufacturing company executive*
Dykema, Henry L. *manufacturing company financial executive*
Egloff, Fred Robert *manufacturers representative, writer, historian*
Eisenberg, James *food company executive*
Ergas, Jean-Pierre Maurice *packaging company executive*
Ewers, R. Darrell *food products company executive*
Farley, William F. *corporation executive*
Francois, William Armand *packaging company executive, lawyer*
Friedland, Richard Stewart *electronics company executive*
†Fulton, Paul *food product executive*
Gallagher, John Pirie *corporation executive*
Gardner, Edward G. *manufacturing company executive*
Gidwitz, Gerald *cosmetics company executive*
Gidwitz, Ronald J. *personal care products company executive*
Giesen, Richard Allyn *business executive*
Goldberg, Arthur M. *gaming and fitness company executive*
Goldstein, Norman Ray *alcoholic beverage company executive*
Gordon, Ellen Rubin *candy company executive*
†Gordon, Melvin Jay *food company executive, diversified executive*
Goss, Howard S(imon) *manufacturing executive*
Guenzel, Paul Walter *corporate executive*
Haas, Howard Green *bedding manufacturing company executive*
Hall, William King *manufacturing company executive*
Hamister, Donald Bruce *electronics company executive*
Hand, Elbert O. *clothing manufacturing and retailing company executive*
Harris, Irving Brooks *cosmetics executive*
†Harris, King William *manufacturing company executive*
Holland, Eugene, Jr. *lumber company executive*
Horne, John R. *farm equipment company executive*
Johnson, Joan B. *cosmetics company executive*
Johnson, Paul Joseph *manufacturing company executive*
†Jones, Dennis Paul *food and consumer goods company executive*
†Kabelin, Jerrald T. *diversified manufacturing company executive*
†Keller, Eileen R. *chemical company executive accountant*
Kent, Conrad S. *chemicals executive*
Kirby, William Joseph *corporation executive*
Klein, Michael Sherman *manufacturing executive*
Lannert, Robert Cornelius *manufacturing company executive*
Lappin, Richard C. *corporate executive*
Lewis, Harriet Gerbert *plumbing fixtures manufacturing company executive*
Liddy, Edward M. *manufacturing company executive*
Light, Kenneth Benjamin *manufacturing company executive*
Linde, Ronald Keith *corporate executive, private investor*
Lockwood, Frank James *manufacturing company executive*
Lohman, Gordon R. *manufacturing executive*
†Lowenstine, James R. *metal products manufacturing company executive*
Malott, Robert Harvey *manufacturing company executive*
Marcuse, Manfred Joachim *paper products executive*
Marineau, Philip Albert *food company executive*
†Mason, Earl Leonard *steel company executive*
Mc Carter, John Wilbur, Jr. *corporation executive*
McCarville, Mark John *food company executive*
McKee, Keith Earl *manufacturing technology executive*
McMillan, C. Steven *manufacturing company executive*
Molloy, James B. *corrugated packaging executive*
Moore, John Ronald *manufacturing executive*
Murphy, Michael Emmett *food company executive*
†Murphy, Newton Jerome *steel company executive, holding company executive*
Nichol, Norman J. *manufacturing executive*
Nicholas, Arthur Soterios *manufacturing company executive*
O'Hara, Paul M. *clothing manufacturing company executive*
Onasch, Donald Carl *business executive*
Parrish, Overton Burgin, Jr. *pharmaceutical corporation executive*
Patel, Homi Burjor *apparel company executive*
Pigott, Richard J. *food company executive*
†Pitser, Tom G. *manufacturing executive, heavy*
Pritzker, Robert Alan *manufacturing company executive*
Proops, Jay D. *agricultural products executive*
Richman, William Sheldon *furniture company executive*
Rollhaus, Philip Edward, Jr. *diversified manufacturing company executive*
Rosenberg, Gary Aron *construction executive, lawyer*
Ross, Edward W. *diversified corporation executive*
†Rotunno, Joseph Rocco *construction company executive*
Schechter, Allen E(dward) *retired publishing company executive*
Schwartz, Charles Phineas, Jr. *replacement auto parts company executive, lawyer*
Siegel, Arthur *corporate executive*
Smithburg, William Dean *food manufacturing company executive*
Solomonson, Charles D. *corporate executive*
Sopranos, Orpheus Javaras *manufacturing company executive*
Stack, Stephen S. *manufacturing company executive*
Steinfeld, Manfred *furniture manufacturing executive*
†Stewart, S. Jay *chemical company executive*
Stone, Alan *container company executive*
Stone, Roger Warren *container company executive*
Strubel, Richard Perry *manufacturing company executive*
Stuart, Robert *container manufacturing executive*
Tannenberg, Dieter E. A. *manufacturing company executive*
Toll, Daniel Roger *corporate executive, civic leader*
Turner, Jack Henry *can manufacturing company executive*
Umsted, Louis Franklin *manufacturing executive*
Weil, John David *envelope company executive*
Weinberg, Harvey A. *apparel company executive*
†Weiss, Stanley C. *electrical and electronics products wholesale distribution executive*
Wellington, Robert Hall *manufacturing company executive*
†Wilks, Charles E. *chemicals executive*
Williams, Richard Lucas, III *electronics company executive, lawyer*
Zeffren, Eugene *toiletries company executive*
Zmuda, Sharon Louise *construction executive*
Zoon, William K. *packaging company executive*

Crystal Lake
Althoff, J(ames) L. *construction company executive*
Anderson, Lyle Arthur *manufacturing company executive*
Smyth, Joseph Vincent *manufacturing company executive*

Danville
Pittelkow, Richard T. *grain company executive*

De Kalb
Bickner, Bruce Pierce *agriculture executive*
Troyer, Alvah Forrest *seed corn company executive, plant breeder*

Decatur
Andreas, Michael Dwayne *agricultural business executive*
Kraft, Burnell D. *agricultural products company executive*
Randall, James R. *manufacturing company executive*
Staley, Henry Mueller *manufacturing company executive*

Deerfield
Batts, Warren Leighton *diversified industry executive*
Chapman, Douglas Kenneth *office equipment executive*
†Clement, Philip A. *electronics executive*
†Flynn, Robert Emmett *food products company executive*
†Goings, Everett Vernon *cosmetics executive*
Graham, William B. *pharmaceutical company executive*
Kushner, Jeffrey L. *manufacturing company executive*
Larrimore, Randall Walter *manufacturing company executive*
Loucks, Vernon R., Jr. *healthcare products and services company executive*
†Ringler, James M. *cookware company executive*
Rucci, Anthony Joseph *health care products and services executive*
Simon, David Sidney *consumer goods manufacturing executive*
White, Tony L. *health and medical products executive*
Zywicki, Robert Albert *electrical distribution company executive*

Des Plaines
Carroll, Barry Joseph *manufacturing and real estate executive*
Farley, James Newton *manufacturing executive, engineer*
Frank, James S. *automotive executive*
Lamey, William Lawrence, Jr. *manufacturing company executive*
Li, Norman N. *chemicals executive*
Malchow, Dennis *food products executive*
Meinert, John Raymond *clothing manufacturing and retailing executive, investment banker*
Soble, David S. *steel company executive*
†Spungin, Joel D. *wholesale office supplies and equipment executive*

Downers Grove
†Cantu, Carlos *holding company executive*

Elgin
Brinckman, Donald Wesley *industrial company executive*
Ericson, Burton E. *diversified corporation executive*
Furst, Warren Arthur *retired holding company executive*
Gwillim, Russell Adams *manufacturing company executive*
Saliba, Jacob *manufacturing executive*

Elk Grove Village
†Braznell, Gerald K. *printing company executive*
Nadig, Gerald George *manufacturing executive*

Elmhurst
†Duchossois, Richard Louis *manufacturing executive, racetrack executive*
Garvin, Thomas Michael *food products company executive*
Gerber, C. Allen *food products executive*
Townsend, Merton LeRoy *metal products executive*
Wyman, Thomas H. *food products executive*

Evanston
Harlow, Robert Dean *packaging company executive*

Fairview Heights
†Smith, John R. *agricultural products executive*
Sullivan, Joseph Patrick *agricultural product company executive*

Flossmoor
Vogt, John Henry *corporate executive*

Franklin Park
Dean, Howard M., Jr. *food company executive*
†Roche, Burke Bernard *manufacturing company executive*
Simpson, Michael *metals service center executive*
Watts, Ernest Francis *manufacturing company executive*
†Wilson, Steve *metal products executive*

Freeport
Ferguson, Daniel C. *diversified company executive*

Geneseo
Cherry, Robert Earl Patrick *retired food company executive*

Glencoe
Bendix, William Emanuel *business director, consultant*
Rubin, David Robert *corporate executive*
Silver, Ralph David *distilling company director*

Glenview
Bible, Geoffrey Cyril *tobacco company executive*
Blattner, Simon James, III *manufacturing executive*
†Durrett, Joseph Park *food company executive*
Hudnut, Stewart Skinner *manufacturing company executive, lawyer*
McCarthy, Gerald Michael *electronics executive*
Nichols, John Doane *diversified manufacturing corporation executive*
Pearlman, Jerry Kent *electronics company executive*
Powers, John Glenn, Jr. *manufacturing company executive*
Ptak, Frank S. *manufacturing executive*
Sherman, Elaine C. *gourmet foods company executive, educator*
Smith, Harold B. *manufacturing executive*
White, John Francis *retired corporate executive*
Winett, Samuel Joseph *manufacturing company executive*

Harvey
Krengel, Theodore H. *diversified metal manufacturing company executive*
Shotts, David Allison *manufacturing executive*

Highland Park
†Hulseman, Robert L. *manufacturing company executive*
Maas, Duane Harris *distilling company executive*
Rudo, Milton *retired manufacturing company executive, consultant*
Singer, Norman Sol *food products executive, inventor*
Smith, Malcolm Norman *manufacturing company executive*

Hinsdale
†Bauer, C. William *contractor*
Flynn, Donald Francis *waste management executive*
Gustafson, F. Edward *food company executive*
†Johnson, Lowell W. *management consultant*
Lowenstine, Maurice Richard, Jr. *retired steel executive*
Ochiltree, Ned A., Jr. *retired metals manufacturing executive*

Hoffman Estates
Dennis, Steven Pellowe *retail executive*

Homewood
Gray, Melvin *construction services company executive*
Manson, Bruce Malcolm *construction company executive*

Huntley
Glickman, Louis *industrial sewing equipment executive*
Suzuki, Mikio *machine manufacturing executive*

Indianhead Park
Frisque, Alvin Joseph *retired chemical company executive*

Ingleside
Propst, Catherine Lamb *biotechnology company executive*

Island Lake
Benson, John Earl *construction executive*

Itasca
Fowler, Jack W. *printing company executive*
†Garratt, Reginald George *electronics executive*

Kenilworth
Hodson, Thomas William *health care company executive*
Weiner, Joel David *retired food products executive*

Kildeer
Harrod, Scott *consulting manufacturing executive*

Lake Bluff
Albrecht, Edward Daniel *metals manufacturing company executive*
Wacker, Frederick Glade, Jr. *manufacturing company executive*

Lake Forest
Anderluh, John Russell *business forms and information management company executive*
Bernthal, Harold George *health care company executive*
Deters, James Raymond *retired manufacturing and services company executive*
Hammar, Lester Everett *health care manufacturing company executive*
Hanlon, James Allison *confectionery company executive*
†McClure, Michael Clyde *corporate executive*
O'Mara, Thomas Patrick *manufacturing company executive*
Reichert, Jack Frank *manufacturing company executive*
Yaconetti, Dianne Mary *business executive*

Libertyville
Burrows, Brian William *research and development manufacturing executive*
Thompson, David Jerome *chemical company executive, biochemist, nutritionist*

Lincolnshire
Freund, Charles Gibson *retired holding company executive*
Reilly, John Paul *manufacturing company executive*
Tucker, Arlie G. *manufacturing executive*

Lisle
Birck, Michael John *manufacturing company executive, electrical engineer*
Krehbiel, Frederick August, II *electronics company executive*
Krehbiel, John H., Jr. *electronics company executive*
Psaltis, John Costas *manufacturing company executive*
Reum, W. Robert *manufacturing executive*

Lombard
†Robinson, Richard Clark *engineering company executive*

Long Grove
Liuzzi, Robert C. *chemical company executive*
Obert, Paul Richard *manufacturing company executive, lawyer*

Maywood
†Canavan, William J. *food products executive*

Melrose Park
Bernick, Howard Barry *manufacturing company executive*
Cernugel, William John *hair care products company financial executive*
Lavin, Bernice E. *cosmetics executive*
Umans, Alvin Robert *manufacturing company executive*

Mendota
Hume, Horace Delbert *manufacturing company executive*

Moline
Becherer, Hans Walter *agricultural equipment manufacturing executive*
England, Joseph Walker *heavy equipment manufacturing company executive*
Hallene, Alan Montgomery *retired elevator and escalator company executive*
Hanson, Robert Arthur *retired agricultural equipment executive*
Leroy, Pierre Elie *manufacturing executive*
Stowe, David Henry, Jr. *agricultural and industrial equipment company executive*

Mount Prospect
Alexy, R. James *manufacturing company executive*
†Randhava, Serge *electronics executive*
Rogers, Richard F. *construction company executive, architect, engineer*
Wilks, Alan Delbert *chemical research and technology executive, researcher*

Mundelein
Kennedy, George Danner *chemical company executive*
†MacLean, Barry L. *plastic and metal products company executive*
Mills, James Stephen *medical supply company executive*

Naperville
Clark, Worley H., Jr. *specialty chemical company executive*
Frank, Dieter *technical consultant, retired chemical company executive*
Katai, Andrew Andras *chemical company executive*
Mooney, Edward Joseph, Jr. *chemical company executive*
Sadowski, Anthony James *chemical company executive, physical chemist*
Schaack, Philip Anthony *retired beverage company executive*
†Wellek, Richard Lee *business executive*

Niles
Herb, Marvin J. *food products executive*
Powell, David *manufacturing company executive*

Normal
Ohinouye, Tsuneo *automobile manufacturing executive*

North Chicago
Clark, Paul Newton *pharmaceutical company executive*

Northbrook
Boyce, Donald Nelson *diversified industry executive*
†Burgman, J. A. *manufacturing executive, light*
Fortune, Patrick John *packaging company executive*
Hedberg, Richard J. *chemicals company executive*
Hoffman, Charles Steven *fertilizer company executive*
Ingle, M(orton) Blakeman *corporate executive*
Kasperson, Richard Willet *retired pharmaceutical company executive*
Lenon, Richard Allen *chemical corporation executive*
Nordman, Richard Dennis *chemical company executive*
Piccolo, C. A. Lance *healthcare company executive*
Riskind, Kenneth Jay *metals company executive*

Sayatovic, Wayne Peter *manufacturing company executive*
Terra, Daniel James *chemical company executive*
Tucker, Frederick Thomas *electronics company executive*
Turner, Billie B. *chemical company executive*

Northfield
Carlin, Donald Walter *retired food products executive, consultant*
Hough, Richard T. *chemical company executive*
Leslie, John Hampton *manufacturing executive*
Morrison, Robert Scheck *food processing company executive*
O'Brien, Maurice James *business executive*
Smeds, Edward William *food company executive*
Stepan, Frank Quinn *chemical company executive*

Northlake
Di Matteo, James S. *food products executive*

Oak Brook
†Burzynski, William *chemicals executive, manufacturing executive, heavy*
Flynn, Patrick J. *food products company executive*
Greenberg, Jack M. *food products executive*
Holsinger, Wayne Townsend *apparel manufacturing executive*
Iorgulescu, Jorge *international chemicals executive, chemical engineer*
Jones, John Earl *construction company executive*

Oak Park
Douglas, Kenneth Jay *food products executive*
Thompson, Charles Edwin *import consultant and manufacturer*

Olympia Fields
Purdy, Charles Robert *corporate executive*

Oregon
Abbott, David Henry *manufacturing company executive*

Orland Park
Gittelman, Marc Jeffrey *manufacturing and financial executive*

Palatine
Kern, Byron Mehl *retired chemical company executive*
Lee, Tien Shuey *chemical firm executive*
Makowski, M. Paul *electronics research executive*

Palos Park
Nelson, Lawrence Evan *business consultant*

Park Ridge
Adkins, Howard Eugene *aluminum company executive*
Weber, Philip Joseph *retired manufacturing company executive*

Peoria
Fites, Donald Vester *tractor company executive*
Gould, David Scott *equipment manufacturing company executive*
Guerindon, Pierre Claude *construction equipment company executive*

Peru
Carus, Milton Blouke *chemical company executive, publisher*

Plainfield
Aldinger, Thomas Lee *construction executive*

Quincy
Liebig, Richard Arthur *retired manufacturing company executive*
Shade, Thomas L. *agricultural products executive*

Rochelle
†Ray, Gary J. *food products executive*

Rock Falls
Bippus, David Paul *manufacturing company executive*

Rockford
†Gaylord, Edson I. *manufacturing company executive*
Horst, Bruce Everett *manufacturing company executive*
Muck, George Arthur *food products executive*
O'Donnell, William David *construction firm executive*
O'Hare, Don R. *corporate executive*
†Wilson, Fred C. *manufacturing company executive*

Rolling Meadows
Brennan, Charles Martin, III *construction company executive*
Cushing, Robert Charles *beverage company executive*
†Ferguson, C. David *electronics company executive*

Rosemont
Isenberg, Howard Lee *manufacturing company executive*

Round Lake
Johnston, William David *health care company executive*

Saint Charles
Stone, John McWilliams, Jr. *electronics executive*

Savoy
Bosworth, Douglas LeRoy *farm implement company executive*

Schaumburg
Brenner, Arnold S. *electronics company executive*
Galvin, Christopher B. *electronics company executive*
Galvin, Robert W. *electronics executive*
Hickey, John Thomas *electronics company executive*
Katzir, Levy *electronics company executive*
†Mitchell, John Francis *electronics company executive*
Poth, Edward Cornelius *construction company executive*
Schulmeyer, Gerhard *manufacturing executive*
Schwab, Susan Carol *electronics company executive*
Tooker, Gary Lamarr *electronics company executive*
Weisz, William Julius *electronics company executive*

Shelbyville
Hullinger, Golden E. *manufacturing company executive*

Skokie
Alexander, John Charles *pharmaceutical company executive, physician*
†Buonanno, Vincent J. *metal products executive*
†Caldwell, Wiley North *retired distribution company executive*
†DeSchutter, Richard U. *pharmaceutical company executive*
Fluno, Jere David *business executive*
Goldberg, Arthur Lewis *manufacturing company executive*
Herting, Robert Leslie *pharmaceutical executive*
Johansson, Nils A. *manufacturing executive*
Krucks, William *electronics manufacturing executive*
Mayes, Frank Gorr *food company executive*
Rubow, W. Steven *food company executive*
Van Wagner, Bruce *telecommunications equipment distribution company executive*
†Weinberg, David *chemicals executive*
†Zakin, Jonathan Newell *computer industry executive*

South Elgin
Burdett, George Craig *plastics industry executive*

Sterling
Gurnitz, Robert Ned *steel industry company executive*
Knight, Herbert Borwell *manufacturing company executive*

Sycamore
Grace, John Eugene *business forms company executive*

Vernon Hills
Wilson, J. Steven *lumber company executive*

Villa Park
Brown, C(harles) Foster, III *construction services and building products executive*
Rogers, Peter Norman *food company executive*

Waukegan
Chapman, James Claude *marine equipment manufacturing executive*
Cherry, Peter Ballard *electrical products corporation executive*
Cherry, Walter Lorain *electronics executive, engineer*
†Martin, Darnell *medical care products corporation executive*

Wheaton
Burnham, Robert Danner *electronics executive, scientist*
Spedale, Vincent John *manufacturing executive*

Wheeling
Carmichael, Leonard Lawrence *manufacturing executive, accountant*
†Wesley, Norman H. *metal products executive*

Wilmette
Barth, David Keck *industrial distribution industry consultant*
Bro, Kenneth Arthur *plastic manufacturing company executive*

Winnetka
Bartlett, William McGillivray *hospital and scientific products company executive*
Gavin, James John, Jr. *diversified company executive*
Hartman, Robert S. *retired paper company executive*
Keller, John Paul *industrial company executive*
Menke, Allen Carl *industrial corporation executive*
Puth, John Wells *consulting company executive*

INDIANA

Batesville
Hillenbrand, Daniel A. *manufacturing company executive*
Hillenbrand, W. August *manufacturing company executive*
Rosebrough, Walter M., Jr. *manufacturing executive*
Smith, Lonnie Max *diversified industries executive*

Bluffton
Lawson, William Hogan, III *electrical motor manufacturing executive*

Burns Harbor
Brown, Gene W. *steel company executive*

Carmel
Herr, Earl Binkley, Jr. *pharmaceutical company executive*
Shoup, Charles Samuel, Jr. *chemicals and materials executive*
†Stauder, Alfred Max *wire products company executive*

Columbus
Baker, James Kendrick *auto parts manufacturing company executive*
Boll, Charles Raymond *engine company executive*
†Claypool, Edward Lavern *engine company executive*
Draeger, Wayne Harold *manufacturing company executive*
Evans, Loren Kenneth *manufacturing company executive*
Henderson, James Alan *engine company executive*
Jolly, Bruce Dwight *manufacturing company executive*
Miller, Joseph Irwin *automotive manufacturing company executive*
Orben, Robert Allen *engine company executive*
Schacht, Henry Brewer *diesel engine manufacturing company executive*
Stoner, R(ichard) B(urkett) *manufacturing company executive, member of Democratic national committee*

Crown Point
Haines, Robert Earl *retired industrial construction executive*

Elkhart
Bryant, Donald Loudon *pharmaceutical company executive*
Corson, Keith Daniel *business executive*
Corson, Thomas Harold *manufacturing company executive*
Decio, Arthur Julius *manufacturing company executive*
Groom, Gary Lee *recreational vehicle manufacturing executive*
Hill, Thomas Stewart *electronics executive, consultant, engineer*
Holtz, Glenn Edward *bank instrument manufacturing executive*
Kerich, James Patrick *manufacturing company executive*
Kloska, Ronald Frank *manufacturing company executive*
Mischke, Frederick Charles *manufacturing company executive*
O'Hagan, William D. *metal products executive*
†Renbarger, Larry D. *prefabricated housing manufacturing executive*
†Van Es, Richard John, Jr. *electronics executive*

Evansville
Egan, Raymond C. *pharmaceutical comapny executive*
†Graham, Dellas *business executive*
Koch, Robert Louis, II *manufacturing company executive, mechanical engineer*
Muehlbauer, James Herman *manufacturing executive*

Fort Wayne
Burns, Thagrus Asher *manufacturing company executive, former life insurance company executive*
Connavino, Nicholas Anthony *food company executive*
Latz, G. Irving, II *manufacturing company executive*
Loutsenhizer, Marvin Jerry *manufacturing executive*
Marine, Clyde Lockwood *agricultural business consultant*
†McAllister, Gene Robert *electronics company executive, electrical engineer*
Morehart, Donald Hadley *food products executive*
Overmyer, John Eugene *manufacturing company executive*
Quinby, Charles Edward, Jr. *manufacturing company executive*
Rifkin, Leonard *metals company executive*

Fowler
Brouillette, Donald G. *grain company executive*

Goshen
†Liegl, Peter J. *company executive*
Schrock, Harold Arthur *manufacturing company executive*

Granger
Brissey, Ruben Marion *retired container company executive*

Hammond
Ash, Frederick Melvin *manufacturing company executive*
Bahls, Gene Charles *agricultural products company executive*

Indianapolis
Bennett, Bruce W. *construction company executive, civil engineer*
Bindley, William Edward *pharmaceutical executive*
Ciotti, Eugene Barney *paper packaging company executive*
†DeMars, Dan Richard *construction executive*
Green, James Murney *software products executive*
Hunt, Robert Chester *construction company executive*
Janis, F. Timothy *technology company executive*
Justice, Brady Richmond, Jr. *medical services executive*
Kerr, M. D. *highway and street contracting company executive*
King, J. B. *pharmaceutical company executive, lawyer*
†Klusas, Roman J. *chemical company executive*
Lanford, Luke Dean *electronics company executive*
Lantz, George Benjamin, Jr. *business executive, college executive, consultant*
Lent, James A. *analytical equipment company executive*
Long, William Allan *retired forest products company executive*
Lugar, Thomas R. *manufacturing executive*
Mc Farland, H. Richard *food company executive*
Mutz, Oscar Ulysses *manufacturing and distribution executive*
Nugent, Thomas D. *food products executive*
Perelman, Melvin *pharmaceutical company executive*
Pettinga, Cornelius Wesley *pharmaceutical company executive*
†Race, John Stephen *electronics manufacturing and technology executive*
Reeve, Ronald Cropper, Jr. *manufacturing executive*
Richmond, James Ellis *restaurant company executive*
Salentine, Thomas James *pharmaceutical company executive*
Schmidt, William C. *chemical company executive*
Schwindt, Robert F. *diagnostic medical products executive*
Step, Eugene Lee *retired pharmaceutical company executive*
Swaim, David Dee *diversified company financial executive*
†Taurel, Sidney *pharmaceutical executive*
Tobias, Randall L. *pharmaceutical company executive*
Tomlinson, Joseph Ernest *manufacturing company executive*
Walsh, John Charles *metallurgical company executive*
Wood, Richard Donald *pharmaceutical company executive*
Zapapas, James Richard *pharmaceutical company executive*

Jasper
Birk, Jim *business and home furnishings company executive*
Habig, Douglas Arnold *manufacturing company executive*
Habig, Thomas Louis *manufacturing executive*
Kohler, Jeffrey Martin *office furniture manufacturing executive*
Oser, Roman Bernard *manufacturing company executive*
Thyen, Herbert Edward *furniture company executive*
Thyen, John T. *furniture company executive*
Thyen, Ronald Joseph *furniture company executive*

Lafayette
Meyer, Brud Richard *pharmaceutical company executive*
Naumann, Hans Richard Ernst *manufacturing executive*
Price, David Robert *construction company executive*

Michigan City
Ruby, Burton Bennett *men's apparel manufacturer*

Middlebury
Guequierre, John Phillip *manufacturing company executive*
†Wells, Walter E. *prefabricated housing manufacturing executive*

Mishawaka
Hagiwara, Kokichi *steel company executive*
Kapson, Jordan *automotive executive*

Muncie
Fisher, John Wesley *manufacturing company executive*
Owsley, Alvin *manufacturing executive, lawyer*
Schlesinger, Albert Reuben *diversified products company executive, controller*

Munster
Corsiglia, Robert Joseph *electrical construction company executive*
Luerssen, Frank Wonson *retired steel company executive*

New Palestine
Saunders, Toni Lynne *construction company executive*

Noblesville
Almquist, Donald John *retired electronics company executive*

Seymour
Terkhorn, Henry K. *food company executive*

South Bend
Altman, Arnold David *business executive*
Armour, James Author *military vehicle manufacturing company executive*
McKernan, Leo Joseph *manufacturing company executive*

Warsaw
Dalton, William Matthews *retired foundry executive*

West Lafayette
Feinberg, Richard Alan *consumer science educator, consultant*
Hoover, William Leichliter *forestry and natural resources educator, financial consultant*
Kampen, Emerson *chemical company executive*
McDonald, Robert Bond *chemical company executive*
Nelson, John Howard *food company research executive*
Shoup, Ronald Edward *chemicals executive*

IOWA

Ames
Gaertner, Richard Francis *manufacturing research center executive*

Bettendorf
Evans, David Lynn *management consultant, executive*

Cedar Rapids
Dunmire, Ronald Warren *manufacturing company executive*
Schrimper, Vernon L. *manufacturing, marketing executive*

Davenport
Juckem, Wilfred Philip *manufacturing company executive*

Des Moines
Frohock, Joan (Joan Walton) *industrial supply company executive*
†Roberts, Ted *manufacturing executive*
Urban, Thomas Nelson *agricultural products company executive*

Dubuque
Bertsch, Frank Henry *furniture manufacturing company executive*
Crahan, Jack Bertsch *manufacturing company executive*
McDonald, Robert Delos *manufacturing company executive*
Tully, Thomas Alois *building materials executive, consultant, educator*
Wahlert, Robert Henry *food company executive*

Fairfield
Schaefer, Jimmie Wayne, Jr. *agricultural company executive*

Forest City
Hanson, John Kendrick *recreational vehicle manufacturing company executive*

Le Mars
†Wells, Fay R. food products executive
†Wells, Fred D. food products executive

Marion
Starr, David Evan corporate executive

Mason City
†Alexandres, Richard Bernard manufacturing company executive
MacNider, Jack retired cement company executive

Muscatine
Carver, Martin Gregory tire manufacturing company executive
Dahl, Arthur Ernest former manufacturing executive, consultant
Howe, Stanley Merrill manufacturing company executive
Johnson, Donald Lee agricultural materials processing company executive
†Kent, James H. food products company executive
Koll, Richard Leroy retired chemical company executive

Newton
Hadley, Leonard Anson appliance manufacturing corporation executive
†Haines, Richard Joseph appliance manufacturing executive
Schiller, Jerry A. retired manufacturing company executive

Pella
†Andringa, Mary Vermeer manufacturing executive
Bevis, James Wayne manufacturing company executive
Farver, Mary Joan building products company executive

Sioux City
Rocklin, Isadore J. manufacturing executive, consultant, engineer

Spencer
Pearson, Gerald Leon food company executive

Springville
Nyquist, John Davis retired radio manufacturing company executive

Waterloo
Mast, Frederick William construction company executive

West Branch
Sulg, Madis corporation executive

West Des Moines
Pomerantz, Marvin Alvin container corporation executive
Richard, Harold Irvin agricultural business executive
Trebilcock, William Everett food products executive

KANSAS

Dodge City
Chaffin, Gary Roger business executive

Hesston
Yost, Lyle Edgar farm equipment manufacturing company executive

Hutchinson
Dick, Harold L. manufacturing executive

Industrial Airport
Mendelson, Lewis Aaron manufacturing company executive

Kansas City
DeFabis, Mike food products company executive

Lenexa
Ascher, James John pharmaceutical executive

Salina
Cosco, John Anthony health care executive, educator

Shawnee Mission
Arneson, George Stephen manufacturing company executive, management consultant
†Campbell, Mark S. food products executive
Dineen, Robert Joseph diversified manufacturing company executive
Dougherty, Robert Anthony manufacturing company executive
Gamet, Donald Max appliance company executive
Mischler, Paul grain company executive
Myhre, Roger L. agricultural products executive
Pierson, John Theodore, Jr. manufacturer
†Smith, Howard E. manufacturing executive, light
Smith, Robert Hugh engineering construction company executive
Strubbe, Thomas R. diagnostic testing industry executive
Sunderland, Robert cement company executive

Silver Lake
Rueck, Jon Michael manufacturing executive

Topeka
Fink, H. Bernerd corporate professional
Fink, Ruth Garvey diversified company executive

Wichita
Eby, Martin Keller, Jr. construction company executive
Hanna, William W. chemical company executive
Karp, Harvey Lawrence metal products manufacturing company executive
Meyer, Russel William, Jr. aircraft company executive
Peterman, Bruce Edgar aircraft company executive
†Watson, Dean agricultural products

KENTUCKY

Bowling Green
Holland, John Ben clothing manufacturing company executive

Covington
Mc Ginness, William George, III manufacturing company executive

Georgetown
Warren, Alex McLean, Jr. automotive executive

Gilbertsville
Mathues, Thomas Oliver retired automobile company executive

Lexington
Deitchle, Gerald Wayne restaurant company executive
Heitzman, Robert Edward retired materials handling equipment manufacturing company executive

Louisville
Ayotte, Robert C. metal products executive
Bujake, John Edward, Jr. beverage company executive
Frazier, Owsley B. beverage company executive
Fuller, Thomas Ralph retired manufacturing company executive
Heiden, Charles Kenneth former army officer, metals company executive
Kinsey, William Charles building materials company executive
Kohnhorst, Earl Eugene tobacco company executive
Mateus, Lois manufacturing executive
McDowell, James W., Jr. milk products company executive
Mountz, Wade retired health service management executive
Mueller, James E. agricultural products executive
†Niblock, William Robert manufacturing executive
P'Pool, Gerald W. manufacturing executive
Quinn, Joseph Michael coatings industry executive
†Robinson, Mark Alexander, III heavy construction, mining equipment executive
Rollo, F. David hospital management company executive, radiology educator
Rompf, Clifford G., Jr. distillery executive
Shaver, Jesse Milton, Jr. manufacturing company executive
Smith, Wayne Thomas healthcare company executive
Street, William May beverage company executive
Tucker, Ray Moss agricultural products cooperative executive

Owensboro
Hulse, George Althouse steel company executive
Wright, Patrick E. grain company executive

Prospect
Dunbar, Wallace Huntington manufacturing company executive

LOUISIANA

Baton Rouge
†Powell, Larry R. chemicals executive
†Prinzo, Felix J. chemicals executive
Schulz, Michael Anthony, Jr. construction company executive, real estate developer
Turner, Bert S. construction executive

Calhoun
Robbins, Marion Le Ron agricultural research executive

Covington
Krauss, Steven James clothing executive
†Wilcox, Richard grain company executive

Geismar
Coombs, Douglas A. L. chemical company executive

Lake Charles
Heiserman, Russell Lee electronics educator

New Orleans
Allen, F(rank) C(linton), Jr. manufacturing executive, lawyer
†Cospolich, James Donald electrical engineering executive, consultant
Deasy, William John construction, marine dredging, engineering and mining company executive
Howson, Robert E. construction company executive

West Monroe
Johnson, Thomas H. manufacturing company executive

MAINE

Brunswick
Dixon, Thomas Francis aviation company executive
Porter, Richard Sterling retired metal processing company executive, lawyer

Ellsworth
Goodyear, Austin electronics and retail company executive

Madawaska
†St. Jean, Andre paper executive
Vollmann, John Jacob, Jr. cosmetic packaging executive

Portland
Nixon, Philip Andrews diversified company executive

Sanford
Zandman, Felix electronics executive

MARYLAND

Annapolis
Hyde, Lawrence Henry, Jr. industrial company executive
Muller, Richard W. (Wilhelm Gustav Muller) retired textile importer

Baldwin
Bressler, Philip Jack food products executive, consultant

Baltimore
Byrnes, Robert Michael diversified manufacturing company executive
Deoul, Neal electronics company executive
Foreman, Ellen S. manufacturing executive
Glassgold, Israel Leon construction company executive, engineer, consultant
Green, Bernard food products executive
Hall, Richard Leland food processing company consultant
Haysbert, Raymond Victor food company executive
Legum, Jeffrey Alfred automobile company executive
Lucas, Barbara B. electrical equipment manufacturing executive
McCarty, Harry Downman tool manufacturing company executive
Morris, Edwin Thaddeus construction consultant
Reeder, Oliver Howard paint products manufacturing executive
Scheeler, Charles construction company executive
Slatkin, Murray paint sundry distribution executive
Strull, Gene technology consultant, retired electrical manufacturing company executive
Wilgis, Herbert E., Jr. corporate executive

Beltsville
Kasprick, Lyle Clinton medical products company executive
†Swales, Thomas G. electronics executive

Bethesda
Augustine, Norman Ralph industrial executive
Baird, Charles Fitz minings and metals company executive
Bregman, Jacob Israel environmental consulting company executive
Egan, John Frederick electronics executive
Richards, Merlon Foss retired diversified technical services company executive
Weinberger, Alan David corporate executive
Wilbourn, Edgar Sherman, III construction company executive, consultant
Young, A. Thomas defense, aerospace, energy and information systems company executive

Bozman
Peterson, H. William chemical executive, consultant

Chevy Chase
Bissinger, Frederick Lewis retired manufacturing executive, consultant

Clinton
Garner, William Darrell health services executive, management consultant

Columbia
Byington, S. John medical products executive, lawyer
Lapides, Jeffrey Rolf corporate executive
Peck, Charles Edward retired construction and mortgage executive
van Remoortere, Francois Petrus chemical company research and development executive

Cumberland
Fiedler, Lee N. automotive products executive

Easton
Peterson, James Kenneth manufacturing company executive

Elkridge
Calton, Gary Jim chemical company executive, medical educator

Ellicott City
Weingarten, Murray manufacturing executive

Forestville
Povey, Thomas George office systems company executive

Gaithersburg
Cook, Vincent N. information processing and business machinery company executive
Ewing, Frank Marion lumber company executive, industrial land developer
Oettinger, Frank Frederic electronics executive, researcher
Schrenk, W(illi) Juergen chemicals executive

Hanover
Miller, James L. food products executive

Hunt Valley
Mulligan, Martin Frederick clothing executive, professional tennis player

Huntingtown
Mitchell, Robert Greene industrial manufacturing executive, consultant

Landover
Bachand, Stephen E. manufacturing company executive
Hechinger, John W., Jr. home improvement company executive

Lanham Seabrook
Bowen, Robert Stevenson diversified company executive

Laurel
Abbagnaro, Louis Anthony corporate executive

Monkton
Ryker, Norman J., Jr. retired manufacturing company executive

Potomac
Karson, Emile international business executive

Rockville
Drzewiecki, Tadeusz Maria corporate executive, defense consultant
†Forest, Harvey electronics executive
†Goldenberg, Melvyn Joel company executive
Halperin, Jerome Arthur pharmacopeial convention executive
Miller, Kenneth Michael electronics executive
Shepherd, Alan J. construction executive, management consultant

Saint Michaels
Jones, Raymond Edward, Jr. brewing executive

Salisbury
Perdue, Franklin P. poultry products company executive
Perdue, James food products executive

Sandy Spring
Gibian, Thomas George chemical company executive

Silver Spring
Coates, Robert Jay retired electronic scientist
Porter, Dwight Johnson former electric company executive, foreign affairs consultant
Schneider, William Charles aerospace consultant

Sparks
Felton, John Walter spice company executive
Harrison, James Joshua, Jr. food products executive
McCormick, Charles Perry, Jr. food products company executive

Towson
DiCamillo, Gary Thomas manufacturing executive

Upper Marlboro
Bowles, Liza K. construction executive
MacFadyen, David Jerry building research executive

White Hall
Radigan, Frank Xavier pharmaceutical company executive

MASSACHUSETTS

Acton
Golden, John Joseph, Jr. manufacturing company executive
†Russo, Peter Robert, Jr. data instrument company executive

Amherst
Mc Garrah, Robert Eynon business administration educator
Torras, Joseph Hill pulp and paper company executive

Andover
Butler, Fred Jay, Jr. manufacturing company executive

Attleboro
Hammerle, Fredric Joseph metal processing executive

Bedford
Gilmartin, John A. medical products company executive

Billerica
Gray, Charles Agustus chemical company research executive
McCaffrey, Robert Henry, Jr. retired manufacturing company executive
†Rennie, John Coyne aerospace company executive

Boston
Bodman, Samuel Wright, III specialty chemicals and materials company executive
Burnes, Kennett Farrar chemical company executive
Cabot, Louis Wellington chemical manufacturing company executive
Cabot, Thomas Dudley chemical company executive
Connell, William Francis diversified company executive
†Cyker, Marvin Myer dental equipment company executive
Dumaine, F. C. diversified corporation executive
Fruitt, Paul N. manufacturing executive
Furman, John Rockwell wholesale lumber company executive
Glass, Milton Louis retired manufacturing company executive
Gordon, Philip H. jewelry industry executive
†Hall, Donald holding company executive
Hall, Lyle Gillis manufacturing company executive
Holey, Ronald Loren retired construction company executive
Kames, Kenneth F. manufacturing company executive
Macera, Salvatore industrial executive
Macomber, John D. construction executive
McClean, Graham J. commercial printing company executive
Metcalf, Arthur George Bradford electronics company executive
Mitchell, W. Randle, Jr. textile company executive
Parks, Paul corporate executive
Phillips, Derwyn Fraser manufacturing company executive
†Schorr, Marvin G. technology company executive
Skelly, Thomas Francis manufacturing company executive
Spilhaus, Karl Henry textiles executive, lawyer
†Swift, Humphrey Hathaway manufacturing executive
†Vanderweil, Raimund Gerhard, Jr. consulting firm executive, mechanical engineer
Wainberg, Alan footwear company executive

Boxboro
Murphy, Paul James high technology company executive

Braintree
Fish, Edward Anthony, Jr. construction company executive
Latham, Allen, Jr. manufacturing company consultant

Brockton
Droukas, Ann Hantis management executive

Brookline
Perry, Frederick Sayward, Jr. corporate executive

Burlington
Bright, Willard Mead manufacturing company executive
Crow, Howard Morrison, Jr. electronics company executive
Hall, John Reginald, II retired army officer, electronics company executive
Lynch, John Joseph electronics company executive
Prosperi, Robert manufacturing company executive
Reno, John Findley corporate executive

Cambridge
Annis, Martin technology company executive
Berger, Harvey James pharmaceutical company executive, physician, educator
Booth, I(srael) MacAllister photography products company executive
Bullock, Francis Jeremiah pharmaceutical research executive
Chubb, Stephen Darrow medical corporation executive
Duecker, Heyman Clarke chemical executive, researcher
Epstein, Henry David electronics company executive
Frosch, Robert Alan retired automobile manufacturing executive, physicist
Gerrish, Hollis G. confectionery company executive
Kalelkar, Ashok Satish consulting company executive
Kliem, Peter Otto imaging company executive
Modigliani, Lazzaro G. chemicals executive
Snider, Eliot I. lumber company executive
Termeer, Henricus Adrianus biotechnology company executive
Tobin, James Robert biotechnology company executive
Vincent, James Louis biotechnology company executive
Wardell, William Michael drug development executive

Canton
Ferrera, Kenneth Grant food distribution company executive
Hirsh, Jane pharmaceutical executive
Lewis, Henry Rafalsky manufacturing company executive

Charlestown
Talmage, John H. food company executive
Waldfogel, Morton Sumner prefabricated housing/plywood company executive

Chelsea
Dunn, Norman Samuel plastics and textiles company executive

Chestnut Hill
Bresky, H. Harry diversified manufacturing company executive
Rodrigues, Joseph E. grain company executive

Concord
Link, David M. medical products consultant

Danvers
†Gaut, Norman Eugene electronics firm executive
Langford, Dean Ted electronics executive
Waite, Charles Morrison food company executive

Dover
Bonis, Laszlo Joseph business executive, scientist
Roberts, Francis Donald manufacturing company executive

East Orleans
McDermott, Thomas Curtis health care and consumer products company executive

East Wareham
Dormitzer, Henry, II retired manufacturing company executive

Easthampton
Perkins, Homer Guy manufacturing company executive

Falmouth
Litschgi, Richard John computer manufacturing company executive

Foxboro
Morris, Gerald Francis manufacturing company executive
Pitt, Earle William manufacturing company executive

Framingham
Gray, John Bullard manufacturing company executive
Merser, Francis Gerard manufacturing company executive, consultant
Perini, David B. construction company executive
Perini, Joseph R. corporate executive
Waters, James Logan analytical instrument manufacturing executive
Wilson, John Benedict office supplies company executive

Gloucester
Warhover, Stephen Hunt food company executive

Haverhill
Mignanelli, James Robert manufacturing executive

Hingham
Zetcher, Arnold B. apparel executive

Hopkinton
Ruettgers, Michael Cadet electronics executive

Lawrence
Ochiltree, Stuart A. cosmetics company executive

Lexington
Berstein, Irving Aaron biotechnology and medical technology executive
Bishop, Robert Calvin pharmaceutical company executive
Bleck, Max Emil aircraft company executive
Hoopes, Walter Ronald chemical company executive
Picard, Dennis J. electronics company executive
Seaman, Robert LeRoy technology company executive
Smith, Robert Louis construction company executive

Lincoln
Fernald, George Herbert, Jr. retired photographic company executive
Green, David Henry manufacturing company executive

Lowell
Hoffman, Paul Roger aerospace executive
Rayfield, Allan Laverne electronics company executive
Tucci, Joseph M. computer software and services executive
Vanderslice, Thomas Aquinas electronics executive

Manchester
Cabot, John G. L. chemical manufacturing company executive

Mansfield
Forney, G(eorge) David, Jr. electronics company executive
Meelia, Richard J. healthcare products executive
Roskothen, Michael S. health care supply company executive

Marion
†Walsh, William Egan, Jr. electronics executive

Marlborough
Axline, Robert Paul electronics executive
†Koutros, Stephen Anthony business executive, computer consultant

Methuen
†Pollack, Herbert William electronics executive

Middleboro
Collison, Curtis Lee, Jr. processed food and beverage company executive
Llewellyn, John Schofield, Jr. food company executive

Milford
Graziano, Chancey Lee business executive

Natick
Deutsch, Marshall E(manuel) medical products company executive, inventor

Needham
Cohen, Lewis Cobrain security products firm executive
Kung, Patrick Chung-Shu biotechnology executive
Pucel, Robert Albin electronics research engineer

Newburyport
†Strem, Michael Edward chemicals executive

Newton
Gerrity, J(ames) Frank, II building materials company executive
Stein, Seymour electronic scientist

North Dartmouth
Tuttle, Clifford Horace, Jr. electronics manufacturing company executive

North Grafton
Nelson, John Martin corporate executive

North Reading
†Ford, Gilbert (Gib Ford) sporting goods company executive
O'Neil, John P(atrick) athletic footwear company executive

Norwell
†Samra, Hisham pharmaceutical executive

Somerville
Verderber, Joseph Anthony capital equipment company executive

South Hadley
Kraske, Karl Vincent paper company executive

Springfield
Gallup, John Gardiner retired paper company executive

Stoughton
Duerden, John H. sports apparel company executive
Duncan, Paul R. athletic footwear company executive
Fireman, Paul B. footwear and apparel company executive

Stow
Olsen, Kenneth Harry manufacturing company executive

Sturbridge
Flynn, Richard Jerome manufacturing company executive

Sudbury
Henderson, Ernest, III health care executive

Taunton
Weeks, Sinclair, Jr. silverware manufacturing company executive

Tewksbury
DeMoulas, Telemachus A. retail grocery company executive

Wakefield
†Carr, Greg C. electronics executive

Waltham
Bernstein, Stanley Joseph manufacturing executive
Farrington, Thomas Alex business executive
Floyd, John Taylor electronics executive
Hatsopoulos, John Nicholas high-technology company executive
Hennessey, Robert John pharmaceutical company executive
Jewett, John Persinger electronics executive, lawyer
Sakhuja, Ravinder Kumar electronics executive
Weaver, William Charles manufacturing executive
Weinert, Henry M. biomedical company executive

Watertown
†Montagu, Jean Ivan electro-optic company executive

Wayland
Blair, John consulting scientist

Wellesley
Gailius, Gilbert Keistutis manufacturing company executive
Gerson, Samuel J. apparel executive
Kucharski, John Michael scientific instruments manufacturing company executive
Marcus, William Michael rubber and vinyl products manufacturing company executive
Ritt, Paul Edward communications and electronics company executive
Rubinovitz, Samuel diversified manufacturing company executive

West Bridgewater
Wyner, Justin L. laminating company executive

West Falmouth
Scranton, William Maxwell manufacturing company executive, consultant

Westborough
†Dickson, John H. utilities executive
Skates, Ronald Louis computer manufacturing executive
†Solvell, Stefan pharmaceutical executive

Westfield
†Reed, John E. manufacturing executive
†Reed, Stewart B. manufacturing executive

Weston
Chu, Jeffrey Chuan business executive, consultant
Rogers, Howard Gardner consultant, photographic company research director emeritus
Saad, Theodore Shafick retired microwave company executive

Williamsburg
Healy, Robert Danforth manufacturing executive

Williamstown
Lee, Arthur Virgil, III biotechnology company executive
McGill, Robert Ernest, III retired manufacturing company executive
Welch, Neal William retired electric company executive

Wilmington
†Altschuler, Samuel electronics company executive
†McCard, Harold Kenneth aerospace company executive

Winthrop
Moses, Ronald Elliot retired toiletries products executive

Woburn
Flummerfelt, J. Kent electronics executive
†Reid, Martin J. electronics executive
St. Onge, Vincent A. electronics executive
Tomaszewski, James M. electronics executive

Worcester
Fuller, Gilbert Amos manufacturing company executive

Wrentham
Teplow, Theodore Herzl valve company executive

MICHIGAN

Ada
Beutner, Roger Earl manufacturing executive

Addison
Knight, V. C. manufacturing executive

Ann Arbor
Buchanan, Robert Alexander pharmaceutical company executive, physician
Carnahan, Robert Dean business development executive
†Cresswell, Ronald Morton pharmaceutical and biotechnology company executive
Decker, Raymond Frank scientist, technology transfer executive
Eberbach, Steven John consumer electronics company executive
Grisham, Rita Miller automotive executive
Moss, Cruse Watson automobile company executive
Packard, P. Kim diversified products company executive
Saussele, Charles William marking systems company executive

Auburn Hills
Farrar, Stephen Prescott company executive
Gerson, Ralph Joseph corporate executive
Grava, Alfred H. automotive and business equipment manufacturing company executive
Kerr, John E. automotive executive
Schuler, V. Edmund light manufacturing executive

Battle Creek
Costley, Gary Edward food company executive
Elliott, Charles W. food products company executive
Knowlton, Thomas A. food products executive
Langbo, Arnold Gordon food company executive
McKay, Eugene Henry, Jr. food company executive
Nichols, Robert Lee food company executive
Stewart, Joseph Melvin food products executive

Benton Harbor
Hopp, Daniel Frederick manufacturing company executive, lawyer
Putnam, Charles Duane manufacturing company executive
Samartini, James Rogers appliance company executive
Whitwam, David Ray appliance manufacturing company executive

Beulah
Edwards, Wallace Winfield retired automotive company executive

Bingham Farms
Williams, Edson Poe retired automotive company executive

Birmingham
†Robinette, Gary E. lumber executive, wholesale distribution executive, retail executive
VanDeusen, Bruce Dudley company executive

Bloomfield Hills
Bates, Baron Kent automobile company executive
Burgess, Robert K. construction company executive
Caldwell, Will M. former automobile company executive
Caplan, John David retired automotive company executive, research director
Frey, Stuart Macklin automobile manufacturing company executive
Harlan, John Marshall construction company executive
Knudsen, Semon Emil manufacturing company executive
Leonard, Michael A. automotive executive
Marko, Harold Meyron diversified industry executive
Maxwell, Jack Erwin manufacturing company executive
Smith, Richard Allen retired manufacturing company executive
Vlasic, Robert Joseph food company executive

Cadillac
†Gravelle, Peter W. durable goods manufacturing company executive
†Kempton, George Roger manufacturing company executive

Cass City
Althaver, Lambert Ewing manufacturing company executive
†Walpole, Robert heavy manufacturing executive

Dearborn
Benton, Philip Eglin, Jr. retired automobile company executive
Bixby, Harold Glenn manufacturing company executive
†Devine, John M. automotive company executive
Ford, William Clay automotive company executive
Gilmour, Allan Dana automotive company executive
Hagenlocker, Edward E. automobile company executive
Kasle, Roger H. steel company executive
Lundy, J(oseph) Edward retired automobile company executive
Manning, Mervyn H. automobile manufacturing company executive
Mc Cammon, David Noel automobile company executive
McTague, John Paul automobile manufacturing company executive, chemist
Poling, Harold Arthur retired automobile company executive
Powers, William Francis automobile manufacturing company executive
Ross, Louis Robert automotive company executive
Sagan, John former automobile company executive
Trotman, Alexander J. automobile manufacturing company executive
Whipple, Kenneth automotive company executive

Detroit
Bahr, Mark A. construction company executive
Chapin, Roy Dikeman, Jr. automobile company executive
Cunningham, Alexander Alan retired automotive company executive
Dauch, Richard E. automobile manufacturing company executive
Eaton, Robert James automotive company executive
Ferguson, James Peter distilling company executive
Fisher, Max Martin diversified company executive
Gerwert, Philip Edward automotive executive
Giocondi, Gino J. automotive company executive
Gormley, Dennis James manufacturing and distribution company executive
Hanson, David Bigelow construction company executive, engineer
Hay, Frederick Dale automotive supply company executive
Jarrell, John W. automobile company executive
Kalman, Andrew manufacturing company executive
Levy, Edward Charles, Jr. manufacturing company executive
Lutz, Robert Anthony automotive company executive
Maibach, Ben C., III construction company executive
Mc Millan, James manufacturing executive
Meilgaard, Morten Christian food products executive, international consultant
†Moore, James Terrence, II industrial distribution company executive

Murphy, Thomas Aquinas *former automobile manufacturing company executive*
Musone, Fred James *manufacturing and logistic executive*
Nordmann, Gary Arnold *corporate executive*
Penske, Roger S. *manufacturing and transportation executive*
Raden, Louis *tape and label corporation executive*
Rakolta, John *construction company executive*
Reuss, Lloyd Edwin Armin *automobile manufacturing company executive*
Rines, John Randolph *automotive company executive*
St. John, Anthony Paul *automotive executive*
Sax, Stanley Paul *manufacturing company executive*
Smith, F. Alan *automobile manufacturing company executive*
Smith, John Francis, Jr. *automobile company executive*
Stella, Frank Dante *food service and dining equipment executive*
Stone, Robert B. *automotive company executive*
Stroh, Peter Wetherill *brewery executive*
Szary, Richard M. *manufacturing company executive*
Vaughan, Clifford James *automotive manufacturing company executive*
Young, Donald E. *computer manufacturing company executive*
Young, Shirley *automotive industry executive, strategic marketing consultant*

Dundee
Byland, Peter *construction materials company executive*
Yhouse, Paul Alan *manufacturing executive*

Farmington
Britt, Gerald F. *food products company executive*
Lomason, Harry Austin, II *automotive company executive*

Farmington Hills
Landry, Thomas Henry *construction executive*

Ferndale
Braude, Edwin Simon *manufacturing company executive*
Lenz, Randolph W. *manufacturing company executive*

Flint
Hackworth, Donald E. *automotive manufacturing company executive*
Lovejoy, William Joseph *automotive company executive*

Franklin
†Navarre, Robert Ward *manufacturing company executive*

Fremont
Clark, Stephen R. *children's food and clothing company executive*
Johnston, Robert Lloyd, Jr. *food products executive*

Grand Rapids
Baker, Hollis MacLure *furniture manufacturing company executive*
Buick, James Gordon *corporate executive*
Fulton, James A. *financial executive*
Gantos, LeRoy Douglas *retail clothing executive*
†Koop, Donald J. *food products distribution executive*
Maxfield, Michael Gerald *forest products and restaurant company executive*
Meijer, Hendrik *retail company executive*
Myers, Jerry K. *medal products executive*
Perez, Peter Manuel *woodworking products company executive*
Pew, Robert Cunningham, II *office equipment manufacturing company executive*
Rougier-Chapman, Alwyn Spencer Douglas *furniture manufacturing company executive*
Wege, Peter M. *office furniture manufacturing company executive*

Grosse Ile
Frisch, Kurt Charles *educator, administrator*

Grosse Pointe
Gofrank, Frank Louis *retired machine tool company executive*
Mc Bride, Robert Dana *steel company executive*
Valk, Robert Earl *corporate executive*
Wilkinson, Warren Scripps *manufacturing company executive*

Grosse Pointe Farms
Obolensky, Marilyn Wall (Mrs. Serge Obolensky) *metals company executive*

Harbor Springs
Judge, John Emmet *manufacturing company marketing executive*

Hickory Corners
Hubbard, William Neill, Jr. *pharmaceutical company executive*

Holland
Haworth, Gerrard Wendell *office systems manufacturing company executive*
Haworth, Richard G. *office furniture manufacturer*
Johanneson, Gerald Benedict *office products company executive*

Jackson
†Hockenbrocht, David William *manufacturing and oil company executive*
Kelly, Robert Vincent, Jr. *metal company executive*
†Smith, John J. *manufacturing company executive*
Vischer, Harold Harry *manufacturing company executive*

Kalamazoo
Connable, Alfred Barnes *retired business executive*
Cyrus, Kenneth M. *pharmaceutical company executive, lawyer*
Dykstra, David Allen *corporate executive*
Edmondson, Keith Henry *chemical company executive*
Hite, Judson Cary *retired pharmaceutical company executive*
Markin, David Robert *motor company executive*
Parfet, Donald Reid *pharmaceutical executive*
†Smith, Ley S. *pharmaceutical company executive*
Vescovi, Selvi *pharmaceutical company executive*
†Zabriskie, John L. *healthcare and agricultural products manufacturing company executive*

Lansing
Anderton, James Franklin, IV *holdings company executive*

Livonia
Utley, John Eddy *automotive supplies executive*

Madison Heights
Kafarski, Mitchell I. *chemical processing company executive*

Marine City
Cronenworth, Charles Douglas *manufacturing company executive*

Midland
Cuthbert, Robert Lowell *product specialist*
Downey, Joseph L. *chemical company executive*
Falla, Enrique Crabb *chemical company executive*
Hampton, Leroy *retired chemical company executive*
Hazleton, Richard A. *chemicals executive*
†Heinlein, Gregory John *chemical company executive*
Ludington, John Samuel *manufacturing company executive*
Oreffice, Paul Fausto *retired chemical company executive*
Popoff, Frank Peter *chemical company executive*
†Stavropoulos, William S. *chemical executive*
Tabor, Theodore Emmett *chemical company research manager*

Monroe
Foster, Ronald G. *automotive parts company executive*
Knabusch, Charles Thair *manufacturing company executive*

Muskegon
Johnson, Dale A. *manufacturing company executive*
Mason, Robert Joseph *automotive parts company executive*
Werner, R(ichard) Budd *business executive*

Novi
Kirkpatrick, Elwood *milk products company and association executive*

Plymouth
Bates, J(ohn) Bertram *retired chemical company executive*
Merrill, Kenneth Coleman *retired automobile company executive*
Mondry, Ira *electronic appliance company executive*
Vlcek, Donald Joseph, Jr. *food distribution company executive*

Pontiac
Mahone, Barbara Jean *automotive company executive*
Smith, Roger Bonham *automotive manufacturing executive*

Port Huron
Hoover, Herbert Arnold *chemical manufacturing company executive*

Redford
Koci, Ludvik Frank *automotive manufacturing company executive*

Rochester Hills
Cook, Leonard Clarence *manufacturing company executive*
Stryker, James William *automotive executive, former military officer*

Rockford
Gleason, Thomas Daues *shoe company executive*

Romulus
Gulda, Edward James *automotive executive*

Saint Clair Shores
Gordon, Steven Stanley *automotive parts company executive*

Saint Joseph
Michelotti, Carl Anthony *electronics company executive*

South Haven
Nequist, John Leonard *retired food company executive*

Southfield
Borden, John Anthony *manufacturing company executive*
Dorfman, Henry S. *meat products company executive*
Dorfman, Joel Marvin *meat products company executive*
Jeffrey, Walter Leslie *corporation executive*
Mikelberg, Arnold *meat packing company executive*
Ohtake, Yoshito *metal products executive*
Rossiter, Robert E. *diversified corporation executive*
Rowe, Arthur Edgar *manufacturing company executive*
Tauber, Joel David *manufacturing company executive*
Welch, Martin E., III *manufacturing company executive*
†Wiggins, Timothy J. *metal products executive*
†Wisne, Anthony E. *metal products executive*
†Wisne, Lawrence A. *metal products executive*

Taylor
Billig, Erwin H. *manufacturing company executive*
Lyon, Wayne Barton *manufacturing company executive*
Manoogian, Alex *manufacturing company executive*
Manoogian, Richard Alexander *manufacturing company executive*
Rosowski, Robert Bernard *manufacturing company executive*
Ullrich, John Frederick *diversified manufacturing company executive*

Tecumseh
Herrick, Kenneth Gilbert *manufacturing company executive*
Herrick, Todd W. *manufacturing company executive*

Troy
Anderson, Iain Mair *automobile manufacturing company executive*
Behnke, Bruce Ivan *manufacturing company executive*
Buschmann, Siegfried *manufacturing executive*
Corace, Joseph Russell *automotive parts company executive*
Gardon, John Leslie *paint company research executive*
Handleman, David *audio products company executive*
†Klingmann, Horst *automotive company executive*
McDonald, Alonzo Lowry, Jr. *manufacturing executive*
Montross, Albert Edward *electronics company executive*
Powers, James *record and tape company executive*
Reickert, Erick Arthur *automotive executive*
Sharf, Stephan *automotive company executive*
Sloan, Hugh Walter, Jr. *automotive industry executive*
Williams, David Perry *manufacturing company executive*

Utica
Williams, Robert Joseph, Sr. *automotive executive*

Warren
Agley, Randolph J. *pharmaceutical company executive*
Bell, Bradley J. *household appliance manufacturing company executive*
Campbell, David Douglas *automotive company executive*
†Dedeurwaerder, Jose Joseph *automotive executive*
Foxworth, John Edwin, Jr. *automotive executive, philatelist*
Gothard, Donald Lee *auto company executive*
Haas, Ronald Henry *automotive company executive, mechanical engineer*
Lett, Philip Wood, Jr. *defense consultant*
†Plummer, Raymond J. *furniture manufacturing executive*
Viano, David Charles *automotive safety research scientist*

Zeeland
Campbell, J. Kermit *office products company executive*
De Pree, Max O. *furniture manufacturing company executive*
Ruch, Richard Hurley *manufacturing company executive*

MINNESOTA

Alexandria
Templin, Kenneth Elwood *paper company executive*

Austin
Hodapp, Don Joseph *food company executive*
Knowlton, Richard L. *food and meat processing company executive*

Avon
†Blattner, William Henry *construction company executive*

Bayport
Hulings, A. D. *manufacturing company execuitve*
Johnson, Alan *retired window/patio door manufacturer*
Meissner, Harold C. *window manufacturing company executive*

Bloomington
Jodsaas, Larry Elvin *computer components company executive*

Burnsville
†Weksel, William *electronics executive*

Dresbach
Saline, Lindon Edgar *industrial company executive*

Eagan
Scott, Andrew *corporate executive*

Eden Prairie
Berra, John Michael *measurement and control instrumentation company executive*
Heath, Vernon H. *manufacturing company executive*
Rusch, Thomas William *manufacturing executive*
†Steel, John M. *electronics executive*
†Thorstad, Dale J. *manufacturing company executive*

Edina
Brown, Charles Eugene *retired electronics company executive*
Prince, Robb Lincoln *manufacturing company executive*

Grand Rapids
Radecki, Anthony Eugene *paper company executive*

Hopkins
†Haley, Thomas William *corporate executive*
Rappaport, Gary Burton *defense equipment and computer company executive*
Tempero, Kenneth Floyd *pharmaceutical company executive, physician, clinical pharmacologist*

Inver Grove
Webster, Elroy *diversified supplies and machinery executive*

Marshall
Schwan, Alfred *food products executive*

Mendota Heights
Frechette, Peter Loren *dental products executive*

Minneapolis
Asplin, Edward William *retired packaging company executive*
Atwater, Horace Brewster, Jr. *food company executive*
Benson, Donald Erick *holding company executive*
Berg, Stanton Oneal *firearms and ballistics consultant*
Blood, Edward Linford *consumer products company executive*
Bonsignore, Michael Robert *electronics company executive*
Brummer, Donald E. *food company executive*
Carlson, Curtis LeRoy *corporate executive*
†Carlson, Gerald K. *metal products executive*
Eames, Earl Ward, Jr. *management educator, development specialist*
Findorff, Robert Lewis *retired air filtration equipment company executive*
†Flaten, Alfred N. *food and consumer products executive*
Galloway, Robert Lee *manufacturing executive*
George, William Wallace *manufacturing company executive*
Gherty, John E. *food products and agricultural products company executive*
Goldfus, Donald Wayne *glass company executive*
Groves, Franklin Nelson *construction company executive*
Gumucio, Marcelo Andres *electronics executive*
Hale, Roger Loucks *manufacturing company executive*
Hodder, William Alan *fabricated metal products company executive*
Holgaard, Conrad J. *company executive*
†Jacobs, Irwin Lawrence *diversified corporate executive*
Johnson, Clark Eugene, Jr. *electronics and computer company executive, magnetics physicist*
Johnson, Sankey Anton *manufacturing company executive*
Johnson, Vernon A. *retired labor saving equipment company executive*
Kramp, Richard William *biotechnology executive*
Lee, Joe R. *food products company executive*
†Lettmann, John William *cereal manufacturing company executive*
Luiso, Anthony *international food company executive*
Luthringshauser, Daniel Rene *manufacturing company executive*
MacMillan, Whitney *food products and import/export company executive*
McBurney, Thomas Ross *food company executive*
McGlynn, Michael James *bakery company executive*
Melrose, Kendrick Bascom *manufacturing company executive*
Morris, David Hugh *manufacturing and marketing executive*
†Morrison, John Lewis *former food company executive, investor*
Mortenson, M. A., Jr. *construction executive*
Nelson, Glen David *medical products executive, physician*
Nestor, Susan E. *health services executive*
Neumann, L. N. *grain company executive*
Olson, Ronald Dale *grain company executive*
†Pajor, Robert E. *paint and plastics company executive*
Rauenhorst, Gerald *design and construction company executive*
Renier, James J. *diversified electronic equipment manufacturing company executive*
Roe, John H. *manufacturing company executive*
Rogers, David *apparel executive*
Sampson, John Eugene *food company executive*
Schulze, Arthur Robert, Jr. *food company executive*
†Severinson, Kenneth J. *athletic and electronic equipment manufacturing executive*
†Smith, Norman E. *metal products executive*
Snyder, Richard Allen *manufacturing executive, accountant, treasurer*
Spoor, William Howard *food company executive*
Sullivan, Austin P(adraic), Jr. *diversified food company executive*
Toupin, Harold Ovid *chemical company executive*
Van Dyke, William Grant *manufacturing company executive*
Wallin, Winston Roger *manufacturing company executive*
Walsh, Paul S. *food products executive*
†Watkins, James David *food products executive*
†Wegmiller, Donald Charles *health care corporation executive*
Weyler, Walter Eugen *manufacturing company executive*
†Wilbur, David E., Jr. *chemicals executive*
Willes, Mark Hinckley *food industry executive*
Wurtele, Christopher Angus *paint and coatings company executive*

Minnetonka
Henningsen, Peter, Jr. *diversified industry executive*
Mc Guire, William W. *health maintenance organization executive*
Randall, Dean Bowman *retired electronics manufacturing company executive*

Moorhead
Nyquist, Robert *sugar company executive*

Osseo
†Spencer, Dale A. *medical products executive*

Plymouth
Fowler, James D., Jr. *manufacturing company financial executive*
Friswold, Fred Ravndahl *manufacturing executive*
Kahler, Herbert Frederick *diversified business executive*

Rochester
Carlson, Roger Allan *manufacturing company executive, accountant*

Saint Paul
Andersen, Anthony L. *chemical company executive*
Andersen, Elmer Lee *manufacturing and publishing executive, former governor of Minnesota*

Baker, Thomas F. *agricultural grain company executive*
Baukol, Ronald Oliver *manufacturing company executive*
Betz, Charles W. *manufacturing company executive*
Cummings, Roger David *powder coatings consultant, sales executive*
Desimone, Livio Diego *diversified manufacturing company executive*
Ehramjian, Vartkes Hagop *manufacturing company financial executive*
Fogg, Richard Lloyd *food products company executive*
Garretson, Donald Everett *retired manufacturing company executive*
Grieve, Pierson MacDonald *specialty chemicals and services company executive*
Hanson, Allen Dennis *grain marketing and processing cooperative executive*
Huber, Allan J. *diversified manufacturing company executive*
Jones, Thomas Neal *manufacturing executive, mechanical engineer*
Kuhrmeyer, Carl Albert *manufacturing company executive*
Lehr, Lewis Wylie *diversified manufacturing company executive*
Ling, Joseph Tso-Ti *manufacturing company executive, environmental engineer*
Mitsch, Ronald Allen *chemical company executive*
Nugent, Daniel Eugene *business executive*
Ostby, Ronald *dairy and food products company executive*
Peterson, Robert Austin *manufacturing company executive retired*
†Pustovar, Thomas M. *manufacturing executive, heavy*
Rastogi, Anil Kumar *medical device manufacturer executive*
Schuman, Allan L. *chemical company executive*
Shannon, Michael Edward *specialty chemical company executive*
Thwaits, James Arthur *manufacturing executive*
†Wanek, Stephen J. *electronics executive*
Wollner, Thomas Edward *manufacturing company executive*

Stillwater
Carter, Orwin L. *chemical executive*

Wayzata
Blodgett, Frank Caleb *retired food company executive*
Hoffman, Gene D. *food company executive, consultant*
Swanson, Donald Frederick *retired food company executive*

West Saint Paul
Markwardt, Kenneth Marvin *former chemical company executive*

MISSISSIPPI

Brookhaven
†Perkins, Thomas Hayes, III *furniture company executive*

Diamondhead
Jaumot, Frank Edward, Jr. *automobile parts manufacturing company executive*

Greenwood
†Eastland, Woods Eugene *agricultural products executive*

Houlka
Washington, Gerald *manufacturing executive*

Jackson
Campbell, James Boyd *office supply company executive*
Irby, Stuart Charles, Jr. *construction company executive*
Williams, James Kelley *diversified resources company executive*

Madison
Harpole, Jerry Lee *agri-business executive*

Mc Comb
Bancroft, Joseph C. *metal products company executive*

Meridian
Balliet, James Lee *manufacturing company executive*
†Peavey, Hartley Davis *electronics company executive*
†Peavey, Melia McRae *electronics company executive*

Morton
†Rogers, John M. *food Products executive*

Nettleton
Sides, Kermit Franklin *furniture company executive*

Pascagoula
St. Pe, Gerald J. *manufacturing company executive*

Scott
†Malkin, Roger D. *agricultural products executive*
†Robinson, Frederic M. *agricultural products company executive*

Tupelo
†Bland, Alvin E. *manufacturing executive*

Yazoo City
Arnold, David Walker *chemical company executive, engineer*
Hawkins, William F. *chemical company executive*

MISSOURI

Blue Springs
Olsson, Björn Eskil *railroad supply company executive*

Bridgeton
Brauer, Stephen Franklin *manufacturing company executive*
McSweeney, Michael Terrence *manufacturing executive*

Carthage
Cornell, Harry M., Jr. *furnishings company executive*
Glauber, Michael A. *manufacturing company executive*
Jefferies, Robert Aaron, Jr. *furniture company executive, lawyer*
Wright, Felix E. *manufacturing company executive*

Centralia
Lomo, Leif *electrical manufacturing company executive*

Chesterfield
Carpenter, Will Dockery *chemical company executive*
†Gervais, Russell F. *plastics company executive*
Jacobsen, James Conrad *apparel manufacturing executive*
King, William Terry *manufacturing company executive*
Malvern, Donald *retired aircraft manufacturing company executive*
McCarthy, Paul Fenton *aerospace executive, former naval officer*
Palazzi, Joseph L(azarro) *manufacturing executive*
†Ritzie, Robert F. *metal products executive*
Toombs, Eugene Martin, III *manufacturing executive*

Clayton
Buechler, Bradley Bruce *plastic processing company executive, accountant*

Columbia
Frew, Bud L. *agricultural products company executive*
Rothwell, Robert Clark *agricultural products executive*

Grandview
Brown, Bob Oliver *retired manufacturing company executive*

Kansas City
Bartlett, Paul Dana, Jr. *agribusiness executive*
Berardi, John Francis *food products and chemical manufacturing executive*
Berkley, Eugene Bertram (Bert Berkley) *envelope company executive*
Carr, Jack Richard *candy company executive*
Clarkson, William Edwin *construction company executive*
Cleberg, Harry C. *food products company executive*
Dees, Stephen Phillip *petroleum, farm and food products company executive, lawyer*
Evans, Gary *food products executive*
Hebenstreit, James Bryant *agricultural products executive, bank and venture capital executive*
Hicks, Lawrence Wayne *manufacturing company executive*
Kittoe, Larry *grain company executive*
Knadle, Richard D. *grain product company executive*
Kronschnabel, Robert James *manufacturing company executive*
Lyons, Frederick William, Jr. *pharmaceutical company executive*
Moseley, Furman C. *timber company executive*
Pratt, Donald Henry *manufacturing company executive*
Rice, H. Wayne *food products executive*
Sullivan, Charles A. *food products executive*
Temple, Joseph George, Jr. *pharmaceutical company executive*
Ward, Louis Larrick *candy company executive*

Lamar
†Riegel, T. E. *manfacturing executive, light*

Mexico
Hummer, Paul F., II *manufacturing company executive*
Stover, Harry M. *corporate executive*

Saint Louis
Abelov, Stephen Lawrence *uniform clothing company executive*
Abrahamson, Barry *chemical company executive*
Adams, Albert Willie, Jr. *lubrication company executive*
Beare, Gene Kerwin *electric company executive*
Beracha, Barry Harris *brewery executive*
Bock, Edward John *retired chemical manufacturing company executive*
Bracken, Robert W. *food products executive*
Brock, Louis Clark *business executive, former professional baseball player*
Brodsky, Philip Hyman *chemical executive, research director*
Broers, J. Terry *medical products manufacturing company executive*
Browde, Anatole *electronics company executive, consultant*
Brown, Jay Wright *food manufacturing company executive*
Burnet, Roger Hasted *construction company executive*
Burnett, Roger H. *construction executive*
Busch, August Adolphus, III *brewery executive*
Cleary, Thomas John *aluminum products company executive*
Coco, Charles Edward *food products company executive*
Conerly, Richard Pugh *retired corporation executive*
Cori, Carl Tom *chemicals executive*
Cox, Robert M., Jr. *electrical products manufacturing company executive*
Cunningham, Charles Baker, III *manufacturing company executive*
Davis, W. L., III *electrical products company executive*
Dill, Charles Anthony *manufacturing and computer company executive*
Elsesser, James R. *food products company executive*
Faught, Harold Franklin *electrical equipment manufacturing company executive*
†Fox, Sam *business executive*
Gelman, Warren Jay *metals trading company executive*
Gilbert, Allan Arthur *manufacturing executive*
Gomes, Edward Clayton, Jr. *construction company executive*
Graff, George Stephen *aerospace company executive*
Griffin, W(illiam) L(ester) Hadley *shoe company executive*
Groennert, Charles Willis *electric company executive*
Gupta, Surendra Kumar *chemical firm executive*
Harmon, Robert Lee *corporate executive*
Heininger, S(amuel) Allen *retired chemical company executive*
Hermann, Robert Ringen *conglomerate company executive*
Hirsch, Raymond Robert *chemical company executive, lawyer*
Holten, James Joseph *meat processing company executive*
Horstmeyer, John A. *manufacturing company executive*
Johnsen, Richard Alan *manufacturing executive*
Jones, Robert E. *company executive*
Kerwin, Richard G. *grain company executive*
Kessler, Nathan *technology consultant*
Knight, Charles Field *electrical equipment manufacturing company executive*
Kuhlmann, Fred L. *brewery consultant, lawyer, baseball executive*
Kummer, Fred S. *construction company executive*
Lambright, Stephen Kirk *brewing company executive*
Lanese, Herbert J. *air and aerospace transportation manufacturing executive*
Lorenzini, Paul G. *manufacturing executive*
Mc Carthy, Francis F. *construction executive*
McCorkle, Michael *construction company executive*
McDonnell, John Finney *aerospace and aircraft manufacturing company executive*
McDonnell, Sanford Noyes *aircraft company executive*
McGinnis, W. Patrick *diversified company executive*
McGrath, Edward A. *electrical equipment company executive*
McKenna, William John *textile products executive*
McKinney, John Benjamin *steel company executive*
Monroe, Thomas Edward *industrial corporation executive*
†Mulcahy, J. Patrick *food company executive*
Neville, James Morton *food company executive, lawyer*
O'Brien, Thomas Francis *manufacturing company executive*
Pellett, Thomas Rowand *retired food company executive*
†Privott, W. J. *agricultural products company executive*
Pylipow, Stanley Ross *retired manufacturing company executive*
†Ramey, Peter M. *holding company executive*
Randolph, Joe Wayne *machine manufacturing executive*
†Reding, Nicholas Lee *chemical company executive*
Rich, Harry E. *footwear and specialty retailing financial executive*
†Robert, Bruce G. *manufacturing executive, light*
Sanders, Fred Joseph *aerospace company executive*
Sathe, Sharad Somnath *chemical company executive*
Scott, Hugh, III *diesel engine distributor*
Shanahan, Michael Francis *manufacturing executive, hockey team executive*
†Shapiro, Robert B. *manufacturing executive*
†Smith, Wayman Flynn, III *brewery executive, lawyer*
Smurfit, Michael William Joseph *manufacturing company executive*
Sonnino, Carlo Benvenuto *electrical manufacturing company executive*
Stearley, Robert Jay *retired packaging company executive*
Stefoff, James Edward *retired clothing company executive*
Stiritz, William P. *food company executive*
Stokes, Patrick T. *brewery company executive*
Stonecipher, Harry Curtis *manufacturing company executive*
Suter, Albert Edward *manufacturing company executive*
Thayer, Gerald Campbell *beer company executive*
Throdahl, Monte Corden *former chemical company executive*
Tober, Lester Victor *shoe company executive*
Tulloch, George Sherlock, Jr. *electrical equipment distribution company executive, lawyer*
Waggle, Doyle Hans *food company executive, scientist/researcher*
Walker, Earl E. *manufacturing executive*
Wells, Ben Harris *retired beverage company executive*
Wenzel, Fred William *apparel manufacturing executive*
Wood, Frederick S. *manufacturing company executive*

Springfield
Hanman, Gary Edwin *dairy company executive*

MONTANA

Deer Lodge
Baehr, Robert E. *electrical contractor*

Great Falls
Sletten, John Robert *construction company executive*
Weissman, Jerrold *metal products executive*

Helena
†Morrison, John Haddow, Jr. *engineering company executive*

Whitefish
Daggett, Charles Edward *construction company executive*

NEBRASKA

Dakota City
Broyhill, Roy Franklin *manufacturing executive*
Grigsby, Lonnie Oscar *food company executive*
Leman, Eugene D. *meat industry executive*
Peterson, Robert L. *meat processing executive*

Lincoln
Fisher, Calvin David *food manufacturing company executive*

Norfolk
Froehlich, Virgil *food products company executive*
Wilson, Robert *food products executive*

Omaha
Albert, Michael L. *food broker*
Ferer, Harvey Dean *metals company executive*
Fletcher, Philip B. *food products company executive*
†Geary, Richard *construction company executive*
Jugel, Richard Dennis *corporate executive, management consultant*
Kaiman, Jerome J. *supermarket executive*
Key, Stephen Lewis *food company executive*
Knobbe, Urban *food products executive*
Lindsay, James Wiley *agricultural company executive*
†Lozier, Allan G. *manufacturing company executive*
†Regan, Timothy James *grain company executive*
Scott, Walter, Jr. *construction company executive*

NEVADA

Carson City
Noland, Robert LeRoy *retired manufacturing company executive*

Incline Village
Strack, Harold Arthur *retired electronics company executive, retired air force officer, planner, analyst, author, musician*
Wahl, Howard Wayne *retired construction company executive, engineer*

Las Vegas
†Bausher, Leslie J. *home building company executive*
Kaiser, Glen David *construction company executive*
Root, Alan Charles *diversified manufacturing company executive*

Reno
Mathewson, Charles Norman *manufacturing company executive*
†Weideking, W. *automotive holding company*

NEW HAMPSHIRE

Concord
Hosmer, Bradley Edwin *corporate executive*

Exeter
Beck, Albert *manufacturing company executive*
Kozlowski, L. Dennis *manufacturing company executive*
†Power, Richard D. *manufacturing executive*

Franklin
Wiehl, John Jack *foundry executive*

Hampton
D'Amato, Anthony Salvatore *food products company executive*
Montrone, Paul Michael *scientific instruments company executive*
Vogel, Phillip T. *manufacturing executive*

Hanover
Lawrence, Louis James, Jr. *automotive company executive*

Hill
Thierry, John Adams *heavy machinery manufacturing company executive, lawyer*

Keene
Burkart, Walter Mark *manufacturing company executive*
†Koontz, James L. *manufacturing executive*

Londonderry
Dean, Richard T. *pharmaceutical company executive*

Lyndeborough
Morison, John Hopkins *casting manufacturing company executive*

Nashua
Gregg, Hugh *former cabinet manufacturing company executive, former governor New Hampshire*
Hemming, Walter William *business financial consultant*
Hippauf, Georgette Laurin *company executive*
Moskowitz, Ronald *electronics executive*

New London
Nye, Thomas Russell *retired drafting, reproduction and surveying company executive*

North Hampton
White, Ralph Paul *automotive executive, consultant*

Peterborough
Calvin, Jerry Gene *industrial executive*

Portsmouth
Hynes, Carolyn Elizabeth *consumer products company executive*

Salem
Cooper, Warren Stanley *manufacturing executive*
King, Thomas L. *diversified manufacturing company executive*

Sunapee
Cary, Charles Oswald *aviation executive*
Rauh, John David *manufacturing company executive*

Walpole
Szmit, Frederick Andrew *paper manufacturing company executive*

Winchester
MacKay, Neil Duncan *plastic company executive*

NEW JERSEY

Allendale
Hollands, John Henry *electronics consultant*

Alpine
Yuelys, Alexander *former cosmetics company executive*

Annandale
Drakeman, Donald Lee *corporate executive, lawyer*
†Drakeman, Lisa N. *biotechnology company executive*

Atlantic City
Maland, Tim *hospitality company executive*

Basking Ridge
Miller, Richard Wesley *telecommunications company executive*
Munch, Douglas Francis *pharmaceutical and health industry consultant*

Bernardsville
Abeles, James David *manufacturing company executive*

Bound Brook
Gould, Donald Everett *retired chemical company executive*

Bridgewater
Albert, Robert Bertrand *chemical executive*
Allen, Randy Lee *corporate executive*
Iovine, Carmine P. *chemicals executive*
Kennedy, James Andrew *chemical company executive*
Weingast, Marvin *laboratory director*

Butler
Klaas, Nicholas Paul *management and technical consultant*

Camden
Denton, Arnold Eugene *retired food company executive*
Ford, Joseph Raymond *manufacturing company executive*
Johnson, David Willis *food products executive*
Weise, Frank Earl, III *food products company executive*

Cedar Knolls
Lingnau, Lutz *pharmaceutical executive*

Chatham
Glatt, Mitchell Steven *corporate executive*

Cherry Hill
†Gibson, Thomas Richard *automobile import company executive*
Higurashi, Takeshi *automotive executive*
Muller, George T. *automotive executive*
Riesenbach, Marvin S. *automotive corporation executive*

Clark
Levy, Jean *cosmetics company executive*

Clinton
Acerra, Michele (Mike Acerra) *engineering and construction company executive*
DeGhetto, Kenneth Anselm *engineering and construction company executive*
Deones, Jack E. *corporate executive*
†Hansen, Arthur Magne *engineering and manufacturing executive*
Wolsky, Murray *corporation executive*

Colonia
Wiesenfeld, Bess Gazevitz *business executive, real estate developer*

Cranbury
Daoust, Donald Roger *pharmaceutical and toiletries company executive, microbiologist*
Raymond, Maurice A. *corporate director research*

Cranford
Cleaver, William Pennington *retired sugar refining company executive, consultant*
Eisenberg, R. Neal *restoration company executive*
Thomson, Robert Hennessey *manufacturing executive*

Dayton
†Hess, Alan Marshall *toy company executive*

Denville
Minter, Jerry Burnett *electronic component company executive, engineer*

Dover
Mc Donald, John Joseph *electronics executive*

East Hanover
Hassan, Frederich *pharmaceutical executive*
Leveille, Gilbert Antonio *food products executive*
Rejeange, Jacques F. *pharmaceutical executive*
†Rothwell, Timothy Gordon *pharmaceutical company executive*
Towey, Robert *pharmaceutical company executive*

East Orange
†Weck, Thomas Lincoln *consulting company executive*

East Rutherford
Gerstein, David Brown *hardware manufacturing company executive, professional basketball team executive*

Edison
Carretta, Richard Louis *beverage company executive*
Cavanaugh, James Henry *corporate executive, former government official*
Huber, Peter C. *diversified chemicals manufacturing company executive*
Romano, Dominick V. *food products executive*

Elmwood Park
Hazama, Hajime *electronics executive*
Wygod, Martin J. *pharmaceuticals executive*

Englewood
Hess, Blaine R. *manufacturing company executive*
Neis, Arnold Hayward *pharmaceutical company executive*

Englewood Cliffs
Abdela, Angelo Solomon *manufacturing company executive*
†Baumgarten, Herbert Joseph *chemical company executive, lawyer*
Byrne, John N. *food company executive*
Feliciotti, Enio *food company executive*
Meendsen, Fred Charles *food company executive*
Scott, John William *food processing executive*
†Shimoyama, Hideo *construction company executive*
Shoemate, Charles Richard *food company executive*
Shrem, Charles Joseph *metals corporation executive*

Englishtown
Rudins, Leonids (Lee Rudins) *retired chemical company executive, financial executive*

Fair Lawn
†Brandt, Ronald Elliot *chemical company executive*
†Matsumoto, Atsushi *electronics executive*
†Ozawa, Ted *electronics executive*

Fairfield
Boccone, Andrew Albert *chemical company executive*
Giambalvo, Vincent *manufacturing company executive*
Meilan, Celia *food products executive*
Stein, Robert Alan *electronics company executive*

Fairview
Anton, Harvey *textile company executive*

Farmingdale
Schluter, Peter Mueller *electronics company executive*

Flemington
†Gilbert, Jack Alan *company executive*
McGregor, Walter *medical products company designer, inventor, consultant, educator*

Florham Park
Jameson, J(ames) Larry *cable company executive*
Kluge, J. Hans *company executive*
†Smith, Randy P. *metal products executive*
†Sperber, Martin *pharmaceutical company executive, pharmacist*
Whitley, Arthur Francis *retired international consulting company executive, engineer, lawyer*

Fords
Chryss, George *chemical company executive, consultant*
Kaufman, Alex *chemicals executive*
Lynch, Charles Andrew *chemical company executive*

Fort Lee
Barr, Edward Evan *chemical company executive*
Gauci, Charles Leon *health care company executive*
†Smith, Jeffrey E. *pharmaceutical executive*
Vignolo, Biagio Nickolas, Jr. *chemical company executive*

Fort Monmouth
Schwering, Felix Karl *electronics engineer, researcher*
Thornton, Clarence Gould *electronics engineering executive*

Franklin Lakes
Andrews, Willard Douglas *retired medical products manufacturer, consultant*
Berger, Murry P. *food company executive*
†Castellini, Clateo *medical products manufacturing executive*
Friedman, Martin Burton *chemical company executive*
Howe, Wesley Jackson *medical supplies company executive*

Freehold
Laden, Karl *toiletries company executive*
Shapiro, Michael *supermarket corporate officer*

Garfield
Kodaka, Kunio *plastics company executive*

Hackensack
Araki, K. *electronics company executive*

Haddonfield
Shaub, Harold Arthur *food products executive*

Hainesport
Sylk, Leonard Allen *housing company executive, real estate developer*

Harrison
Winnerman, Robert Henry *home building company executive*

Hazlet
Miller, Duane King *health and beauty care company executive*
Morrison, James Frederick *flavor and fragrance company administrator*

Hightstown
DeSesa, Michael Anthony *chemical company executive*

Hoboken
Bonsal, Richard Irving *textile marketing executive*

Holmdel
Kogelnik, Herwig Werner *electronics company executive*

Hopatcong
Reese, Harry Edwin, Jr. *electronics executive*

Iselin
Clarke, David H. *industrial products executive*
Garfinkel, Harmon Mark *specialty chemicals company executive*
Guyett, Robert Losee *specialty chemicals and metals executive*
LaTorre, L. Donald *chemical company executive*
Mackinnon, Robert *medical products executive*
Raos, John G. *manufacturing executive*
Smith, Orin Robert *chemical company executive*
Vitt, David Aaron *medical manufacturing company executive*
White, Sir (Vincent) Gordon Lindsay *textile company executive*

Jamesburg
Denton, John Joseph *retired pharmaceutical company executive*

Jersey City
Alfano, Michael Charles *pharmaceutical company executive*
Block, Leonard Nathan *drug company executive*
Luthi, Wilfried T. *manufacturing executive*
Manischewitz, Bernard *food products company executive*
Zuckerberg, David Alan *pharmaceutical company executive*

Kearny
†Goodman, Leonard *personal products company executive*

Kendall Park
Hershenov, Bernard Zion *electronics research and development company executive*

Kenilworth
Conklin, Donald Ransford *pharmaceutical company executive*
Darrow, William Richard *pharmaceutical company executive*

Keyport
Warren, Craig Bishop *flavor and fragrance company executive, researcher*

Lakehurst
Millar, John Francis *industrial products company executive*

Linden
Covino, Charles Peter *metal products company executive*
Hansen, Christian Andreas, Jr. *chemical company executive*
Tamarelli, Alan Wayne *chemical company executive*

Livingston
†Ho, Robert P. *plastics company executive*
†Wang, Walter *chemicals executive*
†Wang, Y. C. *chemicals executive*

Long Branch
†Sacco, Robert Anthony *financial executive*

Lyndhurst
Albosta, Richard Francis *engineering and construction company executive*
Mosher, Howard Ira *automotive executive*

Madison
†Collins, David Edmond *pharmaceutical company executive, lawyer*
Comey, J. Martin *pharmaceutical company executive*
D'Andrade, Hugh A(lfred) *pharmaceutical company executive, lawyer*
Kogan, Richard Jay *pharmaceutical company executive*
Luciano, Robert Peter *pharmaceutical company executive*
McCulloch, James Callahan *manufacturing company executive*
Stafford, John Rogers *pharmaceutical and household products company executive*

Mahwah
Hirooka, Sueyuki *electronics company executive*

Medford
Kesty, Robert Edward *chemical manufacturing company executive*
Vereb, Michael Joseph *pharmaceutical and cosmetic executive*

Middletown
Roesner, Peter Lowell *manufacturing company executive*

Millington
Thompson, Larry Flack *semiconducrtor equipment company executive*

Monmouth Junction
Neff, Peter John *chemicals, mining and metal processing executive*

Montclair
Conant, Herbert D. *construction executive*
Dubrow, Marsha Ann *high technology company executive, composer*
Mc Carthy, Daniel Christopher, Jr. *manufacturing company executive*

Montvale
Bassermann, Michael N. *automotive executive*
Borman, Earle Kirkpatrick, Jr. *chemical company executive*
Corrado, Fred *food company executive*
Kennedy, John Raymond *pulp and paper company executive*
Larkin, Michael Joseph *retail food executive*
†Quinot, Jean Michel *chemicals executive*
Steinberg, Charles Allan *electronics manufacturing company executive*

Moorestown
Andrews, Ronald Allen *laboratory director, physicist, researcher*
Springer, Douglas Hyde *retired food company executive, lawyer*

Morris Plains
de Vink, Lodewijk J. R. *consumer pharmaceutical products company executive*
Goodes, Melvin Russell *manufacturing company executive*
Kumar, Surinder *food company executive*
Williams, Joseph Dalton *pharmaceutical company executive*

Morristown
Azzato, Louis Enrico *manufacturing company executive*
Baldwin, Robert Hayes Burns *business executive*
Barpal, Isaac Ruben *technology and operations executive*
Bauhs, David J. *manufacturing executive*
Belzer, Alan *diversified manufacturing company executive*
Bickerton, John Thorburn *retired pharmaceutical executive*
Bossidy, Lawrence Arthur *industrial manufacturing executive*
Callahan, Edward William *chemical engineer, manufacturing company executive*
Cameron, Nicholas Allen *diversified corporation executive*
Colby, Lewis James, Jr. *manufacturing company executive*
Fredericks, Robert Joseph *language company executive*
Herman, Robert Lewis *cork company executive*
Hittinger, William Charles *electronics company executive*
Kirby, Fred Morgan, II *corporation executive*
Tokar, Edward Thomas *manufacturing company executive*

Mount Laurel
Calzolano, John Joseph *engineering and construction company executive*
Instone, John Clifford *manufacturing company executive*

Mount Olive
Stein, J. Dieter *chemical company executive*

Mountain Lakes
Case, Manning Eugene, Jr. *corporate executive*

New Brunswick
Bern, Ronald Lawrence *consulting company executive*
Campbell, Robert E. *retired health care products company executive*
Gussin, Robert Zalmon *health care company executive*
Larsen, Ralph S(tanley) *health care company executive*
Markey, Andrew Joseph *health care products company executive*
Roth, Herbert, Jr. *corporate executive*
Stewart, Joseph Turner, Jr. *retired pharmaceutical company executive*
Szarka, Laslo Joseph *pharmaceutical company executive*

New Providence
Chatterji, Debajyoti *manufacturing company executive*
Maloney, George Thomas *health industry executive*

New Vernon
Huck, John Lloyd *pharmaceutical company executive*
Margetts, W. Thomas *automobile parts company executive, lawyer*

Newark
Christodoulou, Aris Peter *pharmaceutical executive, investment banker*
Fink, Aaron Herman *box manufacturing company executive*
Hermann, Steven Istvan *textile executive*
Howe, Carroll Victor *construction equipment company executive*

North Bergen
Andriani, Marino N. *electronics company executive*
Chazen, Jerome A. *apparel company executive*
Lanier, Thomas *chemical and export company executive*
Miller, Samuel Martin *apparel company finance executive*
Nobile, John Frank *food flavor company executive*
Scarne, John *game company executive*

North Brunswick
Barcus, Gilbert Martin *medical products executive, business educator*

North Haledon
Brown, James Joseph *manufacturing company executive*

Northvale
Peer, George Joseph *metals company executive*

Nutley
Conrad, Herbert J. *pharmaceutical executive*
English, Robert Joseph *electronic corporation executive*
Lerner, Irwin *pharmaceutical company executive*
Seyffarth, Linda Jean Wilcox *corporate executive, controller*

Oakland
†Cooke, A. Curts *business executive*

Old Bridge
†Meisel, Philip L. *chemical company executive*
Mount, Karl A. *manufacturing executive*

Old Tappan
Dubnick, Bernard *retired pharmaceutical company administrator*

Oradell
Regazzi, John Henry *retired corporate executive*

Paramus
Maclin, Ernest *biomedical diagnostics company executive*
Wilcha, John Samuel *food products company executive*

Park Ridge
Koch, Craig R. *automobile rental and leasing company executive*

Parsippany
Askins, Wallace Boyd *manufacturing company executive*
Bernthal, Frederick W. *chemical company executive*
Brualdi, Ulysses J., Jr. *electrical company executive*
Dvorkin, Donald *electronic design and marketing company executive*
Fleisher, Seymour *manufacturing company executive*
Graham, Stuart Edward *construction company executive*
Greeniaus, H. John *food products company executive*
Hopp, Manfred Ernst *chemical company executive*
Kirkman, James A. *food products executive*
Kleinberg, Lawrence H. *food industry executive*
Lane, Stephen L. *electronic equipment company executive*
Manfredi, John Frederick *food products executive*

Paterson
Danziger, Glenn Norman *chemical sales company executive*

Peapack
Tyler, Richard Dale, Jr. *air conditioning manufacturing company executive*

Pennsauken
O'Brien, James Jerome *construction management consultant*

Piscataway
†Burzin, Klaus *chemicals executive*
Cagan, Robert H. *manufacturing company research executive, biochemist*
Classon, Rolf Allan *pharmaceutical company executive*
Goodwin, Douglas Ira *steel distribution company executive*
Kampouris, Emmanuel Andrew *corporate executive*
Moliteus, Magnus *pharmaceutical and biotechnology company executive*

Princeton
Autera, Michael Edward *health care products company executive*
Barker, Richard Gordon *corporate research and development executive*
Begel, Thomas M. *manufacturing company executive*
Carnes, James Edward *electronics executive*
Chandler, George Alfred *manufacturing executive*
Cryer, Dennis Robert *pharmaceutical company executive, researcher*
Dovey, Brian Hugh *health care products company executive, venture capitalist*
†Ebright, George Watson *health care company executive*
Fill, Dennis C. *pharmaceutical company executive*
Gips, Walter Fuld, Jr. *manufacturing company executive*
Gramlich, James Vandle *chemical products company executive*
Hayes, Edwin Junius, Jr. *business executive*
Hendrickson, Robert Frederick *pharmaceutical company executive*
Jacobson, Herbert Leonard *electronics company executive*
Minton, Dwight Church *manufacturing company executive*
Perhach, James Lawrence *pharmaceutical company executive*
Sullivan, John Mark *manufacturing company executive*
Zissman, Lorin *marketing research, consulting company executive*

Rahway
†Ashkenazi, Ely Ezra *electronics company executive*
Cohen, Abraham Ezekiel *retired health care company executive*
Horan, John J. *pharmaceutical company executive*

Ramsey
Founds, Henry William *pharmaceutical executive, microbiologist*
Kusumoto, Sadahei *light manufacturing company executive*
Markowitz, Arthur Walter *food brokerage executive*

Red Bank
Hertz, Daniel Leroy, Jr. *entrepreneur*
Sorsby, James Larry *home building company executive*

Ridgefield Park
Kim, Ok-Nyun *manufacturing executive*

Ridgewood
Healey, Frank Henry *retired research executive*

Rochelle Park
Laskey, Richard Anthony *medical device company executive*
Schapiro, Jerome Bentley *chemical company executive*

Rumson
Brennan, William Joseph *manufacturing company executive*

Saddle Brook
Anderson, David J. *metals company executive*
†Barbieri, Rocco A. *manufacturing company executive*
†Byrne, John J. *chemicals executive*

Saddle River
McClelland, William Craig *paper company executive*

Salem
Seabrook, John Martin *retired food products executive, chemical engineer*

Scotch Plains
Abramson, Clarence Allen *pharmaceutical company executive, lawyer*
Cleminshaw, Frank Foster *electronic company executive*

Secaucus
Bidermann, Maurice *textiles executive*
Bolt, J. Andrew *textiles executive*
Gerstein, Hilda Kirschbaum *clothing company executive*
Heller, Fred *illumination manufacturing company executive*
†Imura, Akiya *industrial and consumer electronics company executive*
Kraft, Richard A. *electronics executive*
Unanue, Joseph *food products executive*

Short Hills
Jackson, William Ward *chemical company executive*

Shrewsbury
Duff, Thomas M. *textiles executive*

Skillman
Wang, Jonas Chia-Tsung *pharmaceutical executive*

Somerset
Aronson, Louis Vincent, II *manufacturing executive*
Goldberg, Arthur M. *food products executive, lawyer*
†Gunji, Hiromi *manufacturing executive*
Kroll, William John, Jr. *manufacturing company executive*

Somerville
Benz, Harry R. *business executive*
Dormann, Juergen *chemical company executive*
Drew, Ernest Harold *chemical company executive*

South Plainfield
Becker, Erich Peter *metals company executive*

Sparta
Granieri, Michael Nicholas *electronics executive, educator*

Springfield
Adams, James Mills *chemicals executive*

Teaneck
Feinberg, Robert S. *plastics manufacturing company executive, marketing consultant*
Gordon, Maxwell *pharmaceutical company executive*
Margolis, Sidney O. *textile and apparel company executive*

Toms River
Gottesman, Roy Tully *chemical company executive*
Gross, Leroy *sugar company executive*

Trenton
Agocs, Stephen F. *instrument and electronic equipment manufacturing company executive*
Brandinger, Jay Jerome *electronics executive, state official*
Peacock, Douglas W. *manufacturing executive*

Union
Lapidus, Norman Israel *food broker*
Schiffman, Robert S. *environmental test equipment manufacturing executive*

Vineland
†Pranckun, John *manufacturing executive*
†Redwine, Richard H. *manufacturing executive, light*

Warren
Jackson, John Wyant *medical products executive*
Wright, Richard G. *optical and health care company executive*

Watchung
Knudson, Harry Edward, Jr. *retired electrical manufacturing company executive*
Nadeau, Earl Raymond *electronics executive*

Wayne
†Atlee, Frank V. *chemical company executive*
Boekenheide, Russell William *forest products company executive*
Coslow, Richard David *electronics company executive*
Eckardt, Carl R. *chemical and building materials executive*
Heyman, Samuel J. *chemicals and building materials manufacturing company executive*
Howes, William Browning *forest products company executive*
Jeffrey, Robert George, Jr. *industrial company executive*
Kagan, Irving *specialty chemicals and building materials executive*
Nicastro, Francis Efisio *defense electronics and retailing executive*
Sergey, John Michael, Jr. *manufacturing company executive*
Trice, William Henry *paper company executive*
Wolynic, Edward Thomas *specialty chemicals technology executive*

West Caldwell
Jacobs, Howard *distribution executive*
†Terranova, Paul *former corporate executive*

West New York
Gruenberg, Elliot Lewis *electronics company executive*

West Orange
†Housman, Harry J. *pharmaceutical company executive*
Sosnow, Lawrence Ira *health care company executive*

West Paterson
†Fry, Darryl Diamond *chemical company executive*
Ruibal, Charles Adrian *chemical company executive*

West Trenton
Roshon, George Kenneth *manufacturing company executive*

Westfield
Alayeto, George I. *food products company executive*
Connell, Grover *food company executive*
Connell, Ted *food products company executive*
Connell, Terry *agricultural products company executive*
Lloyd, Eugene Walter *construction company executive*
McLean, Vincent Ronald *former manufacturing company financial executive*
†Torcivia, Benedict J., Sr. *construction company executive*
†Torcivia, Benedict Joseph, Jr. *construction company executive*

Westwood
Bennett, Thomas E. *machinery company executive*
Black, Theodore Halsey *retired manufacturing company executive*
Folley, Clyde H. *diversified manufacturing executive*
Gerlinger, Karl *automotive executive*
McBride, Thomas Francis *machinery company executive*
Mulligan, William G(oeckel) *machinery manufacturing company executive*
Nachtigal, Patricia *equipment manufacturing company executive, general counsel*
†Perrella, James Elbert *manufacturing company executive*

Whippany
Golden, John F. *packaging company executive*

Whitehouse Station
Darien, Steven Martin *pharmaceutical executive*
Lewent, Judy C. *pharmaceutical executive*
†Spiegel, Francis Herman, Jr. *pharmaceutical company executive*

Woodbridge
Amato, Vincent Vito *business executive*
Murray, Arthur G. *food products executive*

Woodbury
Wallace, Jesse Wyatt *pharmaceutical company executive*

Woodcliff Lake
†Robson, Brian *electronics executive*

NEW MEXICO

Albuquerque
†De Santis, Nunzio Pasquale *nuclear pharmacy executive*
Friberg, George Joseph *electronics company executive*
King, James Nedwed *construction company executive, lawyer*
Korman, Nathaniel Irving *research and development company executive*
Minahan, Daniel Francis *manufacturing company executive, lawyer*
Rust, John Laurence *manufacturing company executive*
Stamm, Robert Jenne *building contractor, construction company executive*

Carlsbad
Watts, Marvin Lee *minerals company executive, chemist, educator*

Roswell
†Nasi, John Roderick *manufacturing executive*

Santa Fe
Dennison, Charles Stuart *institutional executive*

NEW YORK

Albany
Standish, John Spencer *textile manufacturing company executive*

Amherst
Alfiero, Salvatore Harry *manufacturing company executive*
Arrison, Clement R. *manufacturing company executive*
Fujita, Peter Kozo *tire manufacturing executive*
Graf, Paul Edward *electronics company executive*
Roby, Edgar Maclin *electronic equipment manufacturing company executive*

Ardsley
Barth, Richard *pharmaceutical executive*
Habermeier, Jeurgen *chemical company executive*
O'Brien, Charles O. *chemical company executive*
Sullivan, Joseph Thomas *chemical executive, chemical engineer*

Armonk
Eastman, Dean Eric *science research executive*
Forese, James John *business machine company executive*
Lynett, Lawrence Wilson *electronics company executive*
Turner, Mary Lee *data processing executive*

Athens
Lew, Roger Alan *manufacturing company executive*

Bethpage
Anderson, John Robert *manufacturing executive*

Binghamton
Pomeroy, John Eric *electronics company executive*

Briarcliff Manor
Bingham, J. Peter *electronics research executive*

Bronx
Barton, Lewis *food manufacturing company executive*
Potkin, Harvey *food company executive*
Revelle, Donald Gene *manufacturing and health care company executive, consultant*

Brooklyn
Hood, Ernest Alva, Sr. *pharmaceutical company executive*
Oussani, James John *stapling company executive*

Buffalo
Chapman, Frederick John *manufacturing executive*
Clark, Randall Livingston *manufacturing company executive*
Crandall, Robert Mason *pharmaceutical executive*
Fay, Albert Hill *building materials executive*
Foley, Timothy Francis *food company executive*
Goodell, Joseph Edward *manufacturing executive*
†Hall, Miles W. *electronics company executive*
†Hein, August Henry *transportation company executive*
Larson, Wilfred Joseph *chemical company executive*
Laurenzo, Vincent Dennis *industrial management company executive*
Leland, Harold Robert *research and development corporation executive, electronics engineer*
Minter, Edgar Frederick *industrial executive*
Pierce, Frederick Smythe *envelope company executive*
Rich, Robert E., Sr. *frozen foods company executive*
Rich, Robert E., Jr. *food products company executive*
Starks, Fred William *chemical company executive*
†Stevens, Raymond Donald, Jr. *chemical company executive*

Carmel
Laporte, Cloyd, Jr. *retired manufacturing executive, lawyer*

Cedarhurst
Cohen, David B. *optical company executive*

Chestnut Ridge
Bickel, Henry Joseph *electronics company executive*

Clarence
Mehaffy, Thomas N. *retired tire company executive*

Clifton Park
Favreau, Donald Francis *corporate executive*
Scher, Robert Sander *instrument design company executive*

Cooperstown
Reynolds, Jack Mason *manufacturing company executive*

Corning
Behm, Forrest Edwin *glass manufacturing company executive*
Booth, C(hesley) Peter Washburn *manufacturing company executive*
Campbell, Van C. *manufacturing company executive*
Duke, David Allen *glass company executive*
Dulude, Richard *glass manufacturing company executive*
Ecklin, Robert Luther *glass company executive*
Flynn, James Leonard *manufacturing executive*
Houghton, James Richardson *glass manufacturing company executive*
Luther, David Byron *glass company executive*
Riesbeck, James Edward *glass company executive*
Stuart, Ben R. *manufacturing company executive*

Cortland
Miller, John David *manufacturing company executive*

Dobbs Ferry
Clarke, Richard M. *chemicals executive*
Wilcauskas, Eugene *chemicals executive*

East Aurora
Bingham, William *toy manufacturing executive*
Hawk, George Wayne *retired electronics company executive*

East Rochester
Rauscher, Tomlinson Gene *electronics company executive, management consultant*

Ellenville
Baer, Albert Max *metal products executive*

Farmingdale
Blum, Melvin *chemical company executive, researcher*
Dordelman, William Forsyth *food company executive*
Engelhardt, Dean Lee *biotechnology company executive*
†Hinkaty, Charles John *drug company executive*
Horowitz, Sidney *manufacturing executive*
Smith, Joseph Seton *electronics company executive, consultant*

Fayetteville
Pachter, Irwin Jacob *pharmaceutical consultant*

Florida
Bronstein, David G. *food products executive*

Flushing
Farkas, Edward Barrister *airport program/project manager, engineer*
Grace, Richard Anthony *construction company executive*
Henshel, Harry Bulova *watch manufacturer*

Garden City
Fristedt, Hans *manufacturing company executive*
Guttenplan, Harold Esau *food company executive*
Krieger, Benjamin William *paper company executive*
Larsson, Hans Lennart *match company executive*
†Lipka, David H. *food company executive*

Glen Cove
Burnham, Harold Arthur *pharmaceutical company executive, physician*
Krasnoff, Abraham *business executive*
Maxwell, J. Douglas, Jr. *chemical service company executive*

Glen Head
Feinberg, Irwin L. *retired manufacturing company executive*

Glens Falls
†Carota, Richard J. *paper company executive*
Malkki, Olli *paper company executive*

Grand Island
Rader, Charles George *chemical company executive*

Great Neck
Machiz, Leon *electronic equipment manufacturing executive*

Greene
Raymond, George Gamble, Jr. *material handling equipment company executive*

Greenlawn
Engle, Merle L. *manufacturing executive*

Greenvale
Pall, David B. *manufacturing company executive, chemist*

Harrison
Mc Coy, William Daniel *manufacturing executive*

Hartsdale
Carroll, Albert *corporate executive*

Hauppauge
Arams, Frank Robert *electronics company executive*
Hausman, Howard *electronics executive*
Katz, Burton *electronics distribution company executive*
Miller, Ronald M. *manufacturing executive*
Shalam, John Joseph *car stereo and cellular telephone company executive*

Hoosick Falls
Dodge, Cleveland Earl, Jr. *manufacturing executive*

Ithaca
Moore, Charles Hewes, Jr. *industrial and engineered products executive*
Porter, Michael R. *manufacturing executive*

Jamaica
Dragone, Allan R. *manufacturing company executive*

Jamestown
Anderson, R. Quintus *diversified company executive*
†Nauleau, Heidi A. *holding company executive, metal products executive*
Okwumabua, Benjamin Nkem *corporate executive*

Jericho
Berger, Charles Martin *food company executive*

Lake Success
Fujii, Kenji *medical equipment executive*

Larchmont
Sonneborn, Henry, III *former chemical company executive, business consultant*

Laurel Hollow
Tantleff, Irwin *food products executive*

Lindenhurst
Boltz, Mary Ann *aerospace materials company executive, travel agency executive*

Liverpool
†Greenway, William Charles *electronics executive, design engineer*
Morabito, Bruno Paul *machinery manufacturing executive*
Winahradsky, Michael Francis *drug company executive*

Lockport
Hoyme, Chad Earl *packaging company executive*
Shah, Ramesh Keshavlal *automotive company executive*

Locust Valley
Schor, Joseph Martin *pharmaceutical executive, biochemist*

Long Island City
Carson, Kent (Lovett Carson) *paper company executive*
Fife, Bernard *automobile products manufacturing company executive*

Madison
Blount, Robert Grier *pharmaceutical company executive*

Mamaroneck
Holz, Harold A. *chemical and plastics manufacturing company executive*
Mizrahi, Abraham Mordechay *cosmetics and health care company executive, retired physician*

Manhasset
Keen, Constantine *retired manufacturing company executive*

Melville
Kaufman, Stephen P. *electronics company executive*
†Kissinger, Walter Bernhard *automotive test and service equipment manufacturing executive*
Lengel, David Lee *electronics manufacturing executive*
Nassberg, Edward *chemicals executive*

Mineola
Wurzel, Leonard *retired candy manufacturing company executive*

Mount Kisco
Eckhoff, Carl D. *manufacturing executive*
Laster, Richard *biotechnology executive*

New City
Feld, Joseph *construction executive*

New Hartford
Muzyka, Donald Richard *specialty metals executive, metallurgist*

New Hyde Park
Frankel, Arnold J. *chemical company executive*
†Smoot, E. Philip *chemicals executive*
Wingate, David Aaron *manufacturing company executive*

New Rochelle
Tassone, Gelsomina (Gessie Tassone) *metal processing executive*

New York
Ablon, Ralph E. *manufacturing company executive*
Agate, Robert M. *diversified manufacturing company executive*
Alexander, Norman E. *diversified manufacturing company executive*
Alvarez-Recio, Emilio De La Torre *personal care products company executive*
Anderson, George W. *metal industry executive, retired*
Andrews, E. Lee *paper company executive*
Anneken, William B. *apparel company executive*
Asch, Arthur Louis *apparel company executive*
Ashrafi, Dariush *apparel company executive*
Bagnoli, Vincent James, Jr. *construction company executive, engineer*
Bailey, Glenn Waldemar *manufacturing company executive*
Banks, Russell *chemical company executive*
Banner, Stephen Edward *company executive, lawyer*
Barnes, B. Jack *manufacturing executive*
Bass, Max S. *natural resources and chemical production company executive*
Baumann, Karl H. *health and medical products executive*
Bergen, D. Thomas *business executive*
Bertuccioli, Bruno *petrochemical company executive*
†Bigham, James John *agribusiness company executive*
†Black, Daniel James *chemical company executive*
Blinken, Robert James *manufacturing and communications company executive*
Block, Paul J. *cosmetic company executive*
Blumenthal, W(erner) Michael *manufacturing company executive, former secretary of treasury, investment banker*
Bordiga, Benno *automotive parts manufacturing company executive*
Bottner, Irving Joseph *cosmetic company executive*
Bowling, James Chandler *food products company consultant*
Brennan, Donald P. *aircraft parts manufacturing executive*
Bresani, Federico Fernando *business executive*
Briess, Roger Charles *brewing and food industry executive*
Bronfman, Edgar M., Jr. *food products executive*
Bronfman, Edgar Miles *beverage company executive*
Brophy, Francis L. *chemical company executive*
Burns, John Joseph, Jr. *manufacturing executive*
Burns, Robin *cosmetics company executive*
Burns, Ward *textile company executive*
Burrows, Selig Saul *industrialist*
†Busch, Andrew *textile executive*
Cafiero, Eugene Anthony *manufacturing company executive*
Call, Neil Judson *corporate executive*
Canavan, Bernard *retired pharmaceuticals executive, physician*
Carret, Philip Lord *corporate executive*
†Chaney, William R. *former cosmetics executive*
Charron, Paul Richard *apparel company executive*
Chernow, David A. *former distillery executive, consultant*
Christesen, Russell J. *construction company executive*
†Chu, David *apparel executive*
Clark, Robert Henry, Jr. *holding company executive*
Clarke, Kenneth Kingsley *electrical equipment company executive*
Claro, Jaime *metal trading company executive*
†Coffin, Dwight Clay *grain company executive*
Cohen, Arnold *apparel executive*
Coleman, Martin Stone *office furniture company executive*
Collamore, Thomas Jones *corporate executive*
Cullman, Edgar M., Jr. *tobacco products company executive*
Cutler, Richard J. *metal products executive*
Dabah, Haim *apparel executive*
Dabah, Isaac *apparel company executive*
Daniel, Richard Nicholas *fabricated metals manufacturing company executive*
Day, John W. *international corporation executive*
De Blasio, Michael Peter *electronics company executive*
De Jaegher, Jean F. *textile and apparel company executive*
Diamondstone, Lawrence *paper company executive*
Di Paolo, Nicholas P. *corporate executive, real estate investor*
Dixon, Paul Edward *chemical company executive, lawyer*
D'Lower, Del *manufacturing executive*
Dooskin, Herbert P. *manufacturing company executive*
Doza, Lawrence O. *food company executive, accountant*
Dreier, Douglas H. *construction executive*
Dueves, Henry C. *computer company executive*
Elia, Claudio *manufacturing executive*
Eliopoulos, Nicholas *construction company executive*
Everaert, P. J. *electronics executive*
Falk, Harvey L. *apparel company executive*
Farber, John J. *chemical company executive*
Fass, Sim *medical products executive*
Flaherty, William E. *chemicals and metals company executive*
Ford, Silas M. *personal care, household products company executive*
French, Harold Stanley *food company executive*
Fribourg, Michel *international agribusiness executive*
†Fromme, Irwin *industrial raw materials marketing company executive*
Fujitani, Yoshitaka *heavy manufacturing executive*
Furlaud, Richard Mortimer *pharmaceutical company executive*
Gaertner, Christopher Wolfgang *electronics company executive*
Gannon, Jerome Aylward *construction and contracting management executive*
Gardner, James Richard *pharmaceutical company executive*
Gelb, Richard Lee *pharmaceutical corporation executive*
†Geller, Jeffrey Lawrence *financier*
Gessner, Charles Herman *apparel company executive*
Gleason, Edward L. *manufacturing executive*
†Gleason, John Francis *paint and chemical coatings company executive*
Glisenti, Paolo *chemical, oil company executive*
Goelet, Robert G. *corporate executive*
Goodale, Toni Krissel *development consultant*
Gould, Harry Edward, Jr. *industrialist*
Greaney, Patrick Joseph *electronics executive*
Green, Jay M. *diversified manufacturing and development company executive*
Greenfield, Gordon Kraus *software company executive*
†Greenhouse, Barry David *historic and archeological consulting firm executive*
Grisanti, Eugene Philip *flavors and fragrances company executive*
Gross, Lawrence Robert *manufacturing executive*
Grunfeld, Ernst *metals company executive*
Gutterman, Gerald S. *diversified manufacturing company executive*
Gwilt, John Ruff *pharmaceutical company executive*
Haas, Frederick Carl *paper and chemical company executive*
Harder, Lewis Bradley *ore bodies development company executive*
†Hardy, Thomas George *chemical agricultural products and fertilizer company executive*
Harkrader, Milton Keene, Jr. *corporate executive*
Harper, Charles Michel *food company executive*
Harris, Richard Max *corporate executive*
Hatfield, Robert Sherman *former packaging company executive*
Heimbold, Charles Andreas, Jr. *pharmaceutical company executive*
Helpern, David Moses *shoe corporation executive*
Herbits, Stephen Edward *alcoholic beverage company executive*
Hinerfeld, Norman Martin *manufacturing company executive*
Hinrichs, Horst *manufactoring executive*
Hirata, H. *grain company executive*
Hirota, Yutaro *metal products executive*
Horn, Charles G. *textile executive*
Hoser, Albert *electronics executive*
Hoyt, Henry Hamilton, Jr. *pharmaceutical and toiletry company executive*
Hsu, Charles Jui-cheng *manufacturing company executive, advertising agent*
Inoue, Minoru *manufacturing executive*
Isogai, Masaharu *women's apparel executive*
Kahn, Walter *steel company executive*
Kamiel, Jerald *apparel executive*
Kamihara, Takashi *electronics firm executive*
Kanade, I. *manufacturing executive*
†Kasaks, Sally Frame *apparel executive*
Katz, Howard Carl *coffee company executive*
Katz, Norman *manufacturing company executive*
Kaufman, Martin N. *metal processing company executive*
Kelly, David Austin *food and chemical products executive*
Kempa, Gerald *manufacturing company executive*
Klatsky, Bruce J. *apparel company executive*
Klein, John E. *agricultural products company executive*
Koenig, Marvin *heavy manufacturing executive*
Kohut, John Walter *corporate executive*
Koplik, Michael R. *durable goods company executive*
Koplik, Perry H. *durable goods company executive*
Kressel, Henry *venture capitalist*
Krominga, Lynn *cosmetic and health care company executive, lawyer*
Lala, Dominick J. *manufacturing company executive*
†Landegger, Carl Clement *machinery and pulp manufacturing executive*
Lane, Leonard Charles *manufacturing company executive*
Lane, William W. *electronics executive*
Lang, Eugene M. *technology development company executive*
Lanza, Frank C. *electronics executive*
La Penta, Robert Vincent *electronics company executive*
Lauder, Estée *cosmetics company executive*
†Lauder, Evelyn *cosmetics executive*
Lauder, Leonard Alan *cosmetic and fragrance company executive*
Laws, Robert E. *diversified company executive*
Lebensfeld, Harry *manufacturing company executive*
Lepri, Daniel B. *light manufacturing executive*
Levin, Jerry Wayne *cosmetics executive*
Levinson, Robert Alan *textile company executive*
Lewinton, Christopher *business executive*
†Lewis, Loida Nicolas *food products holding company executive*
Lichtenstein, Seymour *clothing manufacturing company executive*
Lifton, Robert Kenneth *diversified companies executive*
†Longchampt, Michel *steel executive*
Lord, Marvin *apparel company executive*
Lorentzen, Carl Warren *chemical company executive*
Louis-Cotton d'Englesqueville, Francois Pierre *automobile company executive*
Luftglass, Murray Arnold *manufacturing company executive*
Luke, John A., Jr. *paper, packaging and chemical company executive*
Luke, John Anderson *paper company executive*
MacGrath, C. Richard *retired business executive*
Makin, Edward *food products executive*
Mango, Wilfred Gilbert, Jr. *construction company executive*
Marcus, Hyman *business executive*
Margolin, Arthur Stanley *distillery company executive*
Margolis, David I(srael) *corporate executive*
†Martinez, Julio J. *chemical company executive*
Matthews, Peter F. *electrical contracting company executive*
Maxwell, Hamish *diversified consumer products company executive*
May, William Frederick *manufacturing executive*
Mc Cullough, Donald Frederick *textile manufacturing executive*
Mc Donnell, Edward Francis *distillery executive*
McFadden, Mary Josephine *fashion industry executive*
McKinnon, Floyd Wingfield *textile executive*
McNeary, Joseph Allen *apparel executive*
McNeill, Alfred Thomas, Jr. *construction executive*
Mercer, Robert B. *automobile corporation executive*
Meyaart, Paul Jan *distilling company executive*
Miller, Morgan Lincoln *textile manufacturing company executive*
Miller, Paul *health care products company executive*
Milliken, Roger *textile company executive*
Miyaoka, K. *grain company executive*
Mobius, Michael *chemicals executive*
Model, Iris *cosmetics executive*
Mouchly-Weiss, Harriet *business executive*
Muller, Robert Joseph, Jr. *manufacturing company executive*
Munera, Gerard Emmanuel *manufacturing company executive*
Munroe, George Barber *former metals company executive*
Murphy, John Arthur *tobacco, food and brewing company executive*
†Murray, Robert William *diversified company executive*
Murray, William *food products executive*
Natori, Josie Cruz *apparel executive*
Nelson, Merlin Edward *international business consultant, company director*
Newman, Edwin David *textile company executive*
†Nussbaumer, Gerhard Karl *metals company executive*
O'Connell, Frank Joseph *apparel company executive*
O'Grady, William M. *manufacturing executive*
Ohtsu, Masakazu *electronics executive*
Opel, John R. *business machines company executive*
Opotowsky, Stuart Berger *holding company executive*
Oram, John L. *chemical company executive*
Ostberg, Henry Dean *corporate executive*
Paalz, Anthony L. *beverage company executive*
Parmelee, Harold J. *construction company executive*
Penicnak, A. John *manufacturing company executive*
Phillips, Lawrence S. *apparel company executive*
Pietersen, William Gerard *pharmaceutical company executive*
Pietrini, Andrew Gabriel *automotive aftermarket executive*
Pomerantz, John J. *manufacturing executive*
Pomerantz, Laura *apparel company executive*
Poppel, Seth Raphael *corporate executive*
Preston, James E. *cosmetics company executive*
†Puschel, Philip P. *textiles executive*
†Raasch, Ernest Martin *company executive*
Ramat, Charles S. *apparel executive*
Reis, Arthur Robert, Jr. *men's furnishings manufacturer*
Ricciardi, Lawrence R. *food products company executive, lawyer*
Riklis, Meshulam *manufacturing and retail executive*
Riley, William *corporate executive, writer*
Roath, Robert S. *food products executive*
Rochlis, James Joseph *manufacturing company executive*
Rosenberg, Burton M. *apparel company executive*
Rosenberg, Robert Charles *housing corporation executive*
Rosenthal, Milton Frederick *minerals and chemical company executive*
Rothstein, Fred H. *clothing executive*
Roubos, Gary Lynn *diversified manufacturing company executive*
Rubin, Joel Edward *consulting company executive*
Ruthchild, Geraldine Quietlake *training and development consultant, writer, poet*
Ruvane, John Austin *pharmaceutical industry consultant*
Sacks, David G. *retired distilling company executive, lawyer*
Safiol, George E. *electronics company executive*
Sarnelle, Joseph R. *electronic publishing specialist, magazine and newspaper editor*
Schick, Elliot *business executive*
Schmitter, Charles Harry *electronics manufacturing company executive, lawyer*
Schneider, Bernard *industrial machinery executive*
Schneider, Norman M. *food manufacturing company executive*
Schuchert, Joseph *light manufacturing executive*
Schulhof, Michael Peter *entertainment, electronics company executive*
†Schumacher, Hans Heinrich *steel company executive*
Schwartz, Bernard L. *electronics company executive*
†Secrist, Richard A. *industrial company executive*
Shanley, William C., III *sugar company executive*
†Sherman, Saul S. *manufacturing company executive*
Shineman, Edward William, Jr. *retired pharmaceutical executive*
Silverman, Jeffrey Stuart *manufacturing executive*
Slone, Adolph *liquor manufacturing executive*
Smith, Brian J. *diversified chemical executive*
Smith, R. Jeffery *grain company executive*
Smithson, Luther Harris *diversified electronics research company executive*
Smolinski, Edward Albert *holding company executive, lawyer, accountant, deacon*
Solomon, Howard *pharmaceutical company executive*
Solomon, Zachary Leon *apparel manufacturing company executive*
Somnolet, Michel Pierre *cosmetics company financial executive*
†Soren, Howard *textiles executive*
Sprague, Peter Julian *semiconductor company executive, lecturer*
Staheli, Donald L. *grain company executive*
Standen, Michael *metal products company executive*
Steele, Harry Gerard *diversified company executive*
Steere, William Campbell, Jr. *pharmaceutical company executive*
Steiner, Jeffrey Josef *industrial manufacturing company executive*
Stern, Leonard Norman *pet supply manufacturing company executive*
Stookey, John Hoyt *chemical company executive*
Sullivan, Eugene John Joseph *manufacturing company executive*
Swanson, David Heath *agricultural company executive*
Taguchi, Tadao *electronics company executive*
Tapella, Gary Louis *manufacturing company executive*

†Targoff, Michael Bart *defense corporation executive, lawyer*
Thurman, Ralph Holloway *health care company executive*
†Tisch, Andrew Herbert *corporate executive*
†Tison, Joseph Southwood *food products company executive*
Townsend, M. Wilbur *manufacturing company executive*
Tumminello, Stephen Charles *consumer electronics manufacturing executive*
Turner, Roderick L. *retired consumer packaged products manufacturing company executive*
Turner, Stuart *paper company executive*
Ventres, Romeo John *manufacturing company executive*
von der Heyden, Karl Ingolf Mueller *manufacturing company executive*
Wachner, Linda Joy *apparel marketing and manufacturing executive*
Waddell, John Comer *electronics distribution company executive*
Walker, Sally Barbara *retired glass company executive*
Way, Kenneth L. *seat company executive*
Weinstein, Martin *aerospace manufacturing executive, materials scientist*
Weisenburger, Randall *company executive*
†Williams, Robert L. *pharmaceutical executive*
Wolfson, Harold *corporate executive*
Wolinsky, David *metal processing company executive*

Niagara Falls
Collins, Christopher Carl *manufacturing executive*
King, George Gerard *chemical company executive*
Kirchner, Bruce McHarg *manufacturing company executive*

Niskayuna
Mangan, John Leo *retired electrical manufacturing company executive, international trade and trade policy specialist*

Northport
Brown, John Edward *textile company executive*
Reinertsen, Norman *retired aircraft systems company executive*

Norwich
Tecklenburg, Harry *pharmaceutical products executive*

Oneonta
Smith, Geoffrey Adams *special purpose mobile unit manufacturing executive*

Orangeburg
Brill-Edwards, Harry Walter *manufacturing executive*

Orchard Park
Franklin, Murray Joseph *retired steel foundry executive*
†McGroarty, Bruce James *building products manufacturing executive*

Pittsford
Ouellette, Bernard Charles *pharmaceutical company executive*
Palermo, Peter M., Jr. *photography equipment company executive*

Plainview
Stanton, Walter Oliver *electronics company exective*

Pleasantville
Schadt, James Phillip *consumer products executive*

Port Chester
†Cameron, Dort *electronics executive*

Port Jefferson Station
Niles, Walter H. *aviation manufacturing company executive, retired*

Purchase
Barnes, Randall Curtis *beverage company executive*
Butler, Robert Clifton *forest products industry executive*
Calloway, D. Wayne *food and beverage products company executive*
Casebolt, Victor Alan *paper company executive*
Deering, Allan Brooks *beverage company executive*
Dettmer, Robert Gerhart *beverage company executive*
Dillon, John T. *paper company executive*
†Fulleylove, Brian *textiles executive*
Georges, John A. *paper company executive*
Grendi, Ernest W. *electrical equipment and water supply company executive*
Hunziker, Robert McKee *paper company executive*
MacInnis, Frank T. *construction company executive, holding company executive*
Suwyn, Mark A. *paper company executive*
Turk, Milan Joseph *chemical company executive*
Wright, David L. *food and beverage company executive*

Rego Park
LeFrak, Samuel J. *housing and building corporation executive*

Rochester
Brennan, John Edward *manufacturing company executive*
Clark, W. Richard *eyewear manufacturing company executive*
DeLeo, Dennis Michael *photographic company executive*
Fisher, George Myles Cordell *electronics equipment company executive, mathematician, engineer*
Gaudion, Donald Alfred *former diversified manufacturing executive*
Giles, Peter *photographic equipment manufacturing executive*
Gill, Daniel E. *optical manufacturing company executive*
Harris, Richard M., Jr. *paper company executive*
Harvey, Douglass Coate *retired photographic company executive*
†Hubbard, Samuel T., Jr. *paper manufacturing company*
Kanaley, James Edward *optical company executive*
Kohrt, Carl Fredrick *manufacturing executive, scientist*
Latella, Robert Natale *brewing company executive, lawyer*
LeChase, Raymond Wayne *construction company executive*
McCarthy, John Russell *photographic company executive*
McDonald, David J. *food products company executive*
Mc Isaac, George Scott *business policy educator, past business executive*
Merrell, Stanley Wilson *manufacturing company executive*
Oberlies, John William *construction company executive*
Prezzano, Wilbur John *photographic products company executive*
Resnick, Alan Howard *health care and optics executive*
†Reulecke, Heimo *pharmaceutical executive*
Reveal, Ernest Ira *food company executive*
Sieg, Albert Louis *photographic company executive*
Smith, Paul Lester *photography company executive*
Thomas, Leo J. *imaging company executive*
Wehle, John L., Jr. *brewing company executive*
Whitmore, Kay Rex *retired photographic company executive*

Rye
Gurfein, Stuart James *jewelry manufacturing company executive*
Netter, Kurt Fred *building products company executive*
Ross, Charles Worthington, IV *metals company executive*
Savin, Robert Shevryn *health care products company executive*

Rye Brook
Masson, Robert Henry *paper company executive*

Scarsdale
Blitman, Howard Norton *construction company executive*
Hayman, Seymour *former food company executive*
Johnson, Boine Theodore *instruments company executive, mayor*

Schenectady
Adler, Michael S. *control systems and electronic technologies*
Grant, Ian Stanley *engineering company executive*
Petersen, Kenneth Clarence *chemical company executive*
Wilson, Delano Dee *consulting company executive*

Scotia
Jonsson, Kjartan A. *manufacturing executive, consulting company executive, engineer*

Seaford
Setzler, William Edward *chemical company executive*

Seneca Falls
Bradshaw, Eugene Barry *pump company executive, lawyer*
Morphy, John *manufacturing company executive*
Tarnow, Robert L. *manufacturing corporation executive*

Smithtown
Artzt, Russell M. *computer software company executive*
Sporn, Stanley Robert *retired electronic company executive*

Somers
Abu Zayyad, Ray S. *electronics executive*
Case, Richard Paul *electronics executive*
Finnerty, Louise Hoppe *beverage and food company executive*
Low, Paul Revere *business machine company executive*

Suffern
Sutherland, George Leslie *retired chemical company executive*

Syosset
Bainton, Donald J. *diversified manufacturing company executive*
Guthart, Leo A. *electronics executive*
Kata, Edward John *industrial products manufacturing company executive*

Syracuse
Heffner, Ralph H. *agricultural products company executive*
Incaudo, Claude J. *food products company executive*
Josephson, John Eric *food retail executive*
Kenna, E. Douglas *retired plastics company executive*
Lanzafame, Samuel James *manufacturing company executive*

Tarrytown
Jarrett, Eugene Lawrence *chemical company executive*
Kane, Stanley Bruce *food products executive*
Sasayama, Takao *electronics company executive*
†Schleifer, Leonard S. *pharmaceuticals company executive*
Toda, Keishi *electronics executive*
Vagelos, Pindaros Roy *pharmaceutical company executive*
†Weil, David S. *plastics manufacturing executive*

Thornwood
Chin, Carolyn Sue *business executive*

Troy
Duchessi, Nancy A. *manufacturing technology company administrator*

Uniondale
Frashier, Gary Even *corporation executive*

Utica
Slattery, James Arthur *electronics company executive*

Valley Stream
Golden, Hyman *beverage products company executive*

Vestal
Koffman, Milton Aaron *corporate executive*

Walden
Hanau, Kenneth John, Jr. *packaging company executive*

Webster
Duke, Charles Bryan *research and development manufacturing executive, physics educator*

West Babylon
Ziegler, Mandell Stanley *composite sheet manufacturing executive*

West Nyack
Painter, Carl Eric *manufacturing company executive*

Westbury
Cullen, John B. *food products company executive*
Kennedy, Bernard D. *food products executive*
Martin, Daniel Richard *pharmaceutical company executive*

White Plains
†Aurichio, Joseph Louis *electrical and electronic manufacturing executive*
†Benjamin, Colin Henry *metals company executive*
†Chilewich, Simon *commodity trading company, cattle, meat packing company executive*
Greene, Leonard Michael *aerospace manufacturing executive, institute executive*
Henningsen, Victor William, Jr. *food company executive*
Konney, Paul Edward *consumer products company executive, lawyer*
Sora, Sebastian Antony *business machines manufacturing executive, educator*

Yonkers
†Petrillo, Carl Edward *construction company executive*

Yorktown Heights
LaRussa, Joseph Anthony *optical company executive*

Youngstown
Alpert, Norman *chemical company executive*

NORTH CAROLINA

Advance
Huber, Thomas Martin *container company executive*

Asheville
Armstrong, Robert Baker *textile company executive*
Coli, Guido John *chemical company executive*
Conroy, David James *retired chemical and diversified manufacturing executive*
Dillon, Gary Gene *manufacturing company executive*
Vander Voort, Dale Gilbert *textile company executive*

Beaufort
Cullman, Hugh *retired tobacco company executive*

Belmont
Stowe, Daniel Harding, Sr. *textile executive*
Stowe, Robert Lee, III *textile company executive*

Burlington
Flagg, Raymond Osbourn *biology executive*

Chapel Hill
Blasius, Donald Charles *appliance company executive*
Hitchings, George Herbert *retired pharmaceutical company executive, educator*
Thakor, Haren Bhaskerrao *manufacturing company executive*

Charlotte
Belk, Thomas Milburn *apparel executive*
Bowden, James Alvin *construction company financial executive*
Copeland, John Wesley *textile company executive*
Daniels, William Carlton, Jr. *construction executive*
Davidson, Charles Tompkins *construction company executive*
Dickson, Rush Stuart *holding company executive*
Goryn, Sara *textiles executive, real estate developer, psychologist*
Hannah, Thomas E. *textiles executive*
Harrison, J. Frank, Jr. *soft drink company executive*
Hodges, Charles Thomas *construction company executive*
Holland, William Ray *diversified company executive*
Iverson, Francis Kenneth *metals company executive*
Lea, Scott Carter *retired packaging company executive*
McKeon, Robert B. *textiles executive*
McVerry, Thomas Leo *manufacturing company executive*
Moore, James L., Jr. *beverage company executive*
Murata, Junichi *electronics company executive*
Patterson, Joseph H. *chemical company executive*
Priestley, G. T. Eric *manufacturing company executive*
Regelbrugge, Roger Rafael *steel company executive*
Rosamond, Patricia Ann *construction company executive*
Schmidt, Peter *construction company executive*
Siegel, Samuel *metals company executive*
Singer, David Vincent *bottling company executive*
Ver Hagen, Jan Karol *manufacturing company executive*

Drexel
Richetta, Fred J. *manufacturing and operations executive*

Dunn
Muller, Donald Bruce *chemical executive*

Durham
Burger, Robert Mercer *semiconductor device research executive*
Chilton, Mary-Dell Matchett *chemical company executive*
Easterlin, Donald Jacob, III *construction executive*
Fair, Richard Barton *electronics executive, educator*
†Fisher, Richard Wayne *chemical company executive*
Hutchins, John Richard, III *fiber optics electronic company executive*
Ricci, Robert Ronald *manufacturing company executive*
Sanders, Charles Addison *pharmaceutical company executive, physician*
†Sumner, Gord *electronics research executive*

Eden
Bishopric, Welsford Farrell *textile executive*
Fraser, Kenneth William, Jr. *textile company executive*
Staab, Thomas Robert *textile company financial executive*

Farmville
Monk, Albert C., III *manufacturing executive*

Fayetteville
Hendrick, J. R., III *automotive executive*

Flat Rock
Demartini, Robert John *textile company executive*

Gastonia
Kimbrell, Willard Duke *textile company executive*
Lawson, William David, III *cotton company executive*

Greensboro
†Berggren, Thage *automotive executive*
Danahy, James Patrick *textile executive*
Englar, John David *textile company executive, lawyer*
Greenberg, Frank S. *textile company executive*
Greenberg, George *mill company executive*
†Halstead, William B. *metal products executive*
Hayes, Charles A. *mill company executive*
Henderson, George, III *textiles executive*
Howard, Paul Noble, Jr. *retired construction company executive*
Howard, Richard Turner *construction company executive*
Hughes, Donald R. *textile executive*
Korb, William Brown, Jr. *manufacturing company executive*
Kretzer, William T. *textile company executive*
Mann, Lowell Kimsey *retired manufacturing executive*
Mebane, George Allen *corporate executive, rancher*
Morris, Edwin Alexander *retired apparel manufacturing company executive*
Pilcher, Walter Harold *apparel company executive*
Polley, David E. *textile manufacturing executive*
Poole, Earle Gower *clothing manufacturing company executive*
†Roland, Frank H. *metal products executive, chemicals executive*
Trogdon, Dewey Leonard, Jr. *textile executive*
Vetack, Richard S. *textiles executive*

Hickory
Shuford, Harley Ferguson, Jr. *furniture manufacturing executive*

High Point
Fenn, Ormon William, Jr. *furniture company executive*
Jones, Ronald Lee *furniture manufacturing executive*
Marsden, Lawrence Albert *retired textile company executive*
Millner, Thomas *manufacturing and holding company executive*

Kannapolis
Ridenhour, Joseph Conrad *textile company executive*

Kinston
Fuchs, David *clothing manufacturing company executive*
Schechter, Sol *clothes company executive*

Maiden
†Pruitt, Thomas P., Jr. *textiles executive*
†Schrum, Ed P. *manufacturing company executive*

Morganton
Jokinen, John Victor *furniture company executive*

Mount Airy
Woltz, Howard Osler, Jr. *steel and wire products company executive*

Mount Holly
†Dickson, Alan T. *mill and holding company executive*

North Wilkesboro
Lovette, Blake Duane *food company executive*
Matthews, John Carroll *manufacturing executive*

Pine Knoll Shores
Benson, Kenneth Victor *manufacturing company executive, lawyer*

Pinehurst
O'Neill, John Joseph, Jr. *business consultant, former chemical company executive*

Raleigh
Cresimore, James Leonard *food broker*
Klein, Verle Wesley *corporate executive, retired naval officer*
Leddicotte, George Comer *business executive, consultant*
†Risher, James A. *electronics executive*
Wright, Thomas James *chemical company executive*

Research Triangle Park
Cipau, Gabriel *pharmaceutical executive*
Gaither, John Stokes *chemical company executive*
Niedel, James E. *pharmaceuticals executive*

†Smyth, George *electronics company executive, researcher*

Rocky Mount
Simpson, Dennis Arden *lighting contracting company executive*

Sanford
Beckwith, Hugh Foster, Jr. *textile company executive*

Southern Pines
Lipton, Clifford Carwood *retired glass company executive*

Thomasville
O'Brien, Charles G. *furniture manufacturing company executive*
Starr, Frederick Brown *furniture manufacturing executive*

Weaverville
†McGauran, Michael *manufacturing executive, light*

Weldon
Barringer, Paul Brandon, II *lumber company executive*
Conger, Stephen Halsey *lumber company executive*

Wilmington
Crigler, T. P. *foreign products and investments executive*
Silloway, Benton, Jr. *food products executive*
Thompson, Donald Charles *electronics company executive, former coast guard officer*

Wilson
†Coghill, Marvin W. *tobacco company executive*
Kehaya, Ery W. *tobacco holding company executive*
Murray, J. Alec G. *manufacturing executive*
Ross, Guy Matthews, Jr. *international leaf tobacco executive*

Winston Salem
Christopher, Floyd Hudnall, Jr. *corporate executive*
Emken, Robert Allan *diversified company executive*
Ford, Yancey William, Jr. *tobacco company executive*
Hanes, Ralph Philip, Jr. *textile company executive*
Maselli, John Anthony *food products company executive*
Piazza, John *hosiery company executive*
Smith, Zachary Taylor, II *retired tobacco company executive*
Sticht, J. Paul *retired food products and tobacco company executive*

NORTH DAKOTA

Fargo
Ommodt, Donald Henry *dairy company executive*

Grand Forks
Gjovig, Bruce Quentin *manufacturing consultant*

OHIO

Akron
Albrecht, Frederick Ivan *food products executive*
Altenau, Alan Giles *tire and rubber company executive*
Barnett, James Wallace *manufacturing executive*
Brennan, David Leo *manufacturing company executive, lawyer, developer*
Brock, James Robert *manufacturing company executive*
Culler, Eugene R. *automotive products company executive*
Ennis, Charles Roe *manufacturing company executive, lawyer*
Gault, Stanley Carleton *manufacturing company executive*
Glass, James Richard *retired tire and rubber manufacturing company executive*
Hackbirth, David William *aluminum company executive*
Kaufman, Donald Leroy *aluminum products company executive*
†McMillan, Robert Allan *chemical company executive*
Ockene, Alan L. *tire manufacturing executive*
Prus, Francis Vincent *tire company executive*
Reynolds, A. William *manufacturing company executive*
Shaffer, Oren George *manufacturing company executive*
†Smith, Terry *metal products executive*
Tobler, D. Lee *chemical and aerospace company executive*
Wells, Hoyt Mellor *manufacturing executive*
†Wells, Norman, Jr. *metal products executive*

Ashtabula
Bonner, David Calhoun *chemical company executive*

Barberton
Stewart, Joe J. *manufacturing executive*

Bowling Green
Guthrie, Mearl Raymond, Jr. *business administration educator*

Bratenahl
Jones, Trevor Owen *automobile supply company executive, management consultant*

Brecksville
Galloway, Ethan Charles *technology development executive, former chemicals executive*

Brookville
Juhl, Daniel Leo *manufacturing and marketing firm executive*

Canton
Ashton, P. J. *metal products executive*
Barone, Robert Paul *manufacturing company executive*
Birkholz, Raymond James *metal products manufacturing company executive*
Elsaesser, Robert James *retired manufacturing executive*
Koontz, Raymond *retired security equipment company executive*
Timken, W. Robert, Jr. *manufacturing company executive*
Toot, Joseph F., Jr. *bearing manufacturing company executive*

Cedarville
Gordin, Dean Lackey *retired agricultural products executive*

Chagrin Falls
Daniel, Clarence Huber *former manufacturing company executive, consultant*
Frohring, Paul Robert *former business executive*
Groeger, Joseph Herman *retired metal company executive*

Cincinnati
Atteberry, William Duane *diversified manufacturing company executive*
Barach, Philip G. *shoe company executive*
Baxter, Raoul *meat packing company executive*
Breth, James Raymond *scrap metals company executive*
†Byer, P. Roger *holding company executive*
Chase, William Rowell *manufacturing executive*
Christensen, Paul Walter, Jr. *gear manufacturing company executive*
Church, John Franklin, Jr. *paper company executive*
Coombe, V. Anderson *valve manufacturing company executive*
Crowe, James Joseph *shoe company executive, lawyer*
Derstadt, Ronald Theodore *health care administrator*
Geier, James Aylward Develin *manufacturing company executive*
Gibson, George M. *manufacturing company executive*
Glover, Richard M. *manufacturing company executive*
Griffin, William Ralph *manufacturing executive*
Harrell, Samuel Macy *grain company executive*
Hudson, Bannus B. *footwear manufacturing and apparel retail executive*
Keener, C(harles) Richard *food company information systems executive*
Kellar, Lorrence Theodore *retail food and manufacturing executive*
Lindner, Keith E. *food company executive*
Maisel, Michael *clothing executive*
Meyer, Daniel Joseph *machinery company executive*
Moore, Alfred Anson *corporate executive*
Munn, Stephen P. *manufacturing company executive*
Pennacchio, Joseph *apparel executive*
Petry, Thomas Edwin *manufacturing company executive*
Pichler, Joseph Anton *food products executive*
Pruett, Samuel H. *manufacturing executive*
†Ralston, Robert O. *manufacturing executive*
Slater, John Greenleaf *manufacturing company executive*
Smale, John Gray *diversified industry executive*
Smittle, Nelson Dean *electronics executive*
Sottile, Benjamin Joseph *greeting card company executive*
Stern, Joseph Smith, Jr. *former footwear manufacturing company executive*
Thompson, Morley Punshon *textile company executive*
Voet, Paul C. *specialty chemical company executive*
Walker, Ronald F. *corporate executive*
Wilson, Frederic Sandford *pharmaceutical company executive*
Yocum, Ronald Harris *chemical company executive*

Cleveland
Anderson, Harold Albert *engineering and building executive*
Ball, Robert L. *metal products company executive*
Beggs, Lyman M. *manufacturing executive*
Bersticker, Albert Charles *chemical company executive*
Bonda, Alva Ted *electronics company executive*
Breen, John Gerald *manufacturing company executive*
Brophy, Jere Hall *manufacturing company executive*
Butler, William E. *manufacturing company executive*
Carlson, Harry *electric company executive*
Carragher, Frank Anthony *chemical company executive*
Cligrow, Edward Thomas, Jr. *manufacturing executive*
Cochran, Earl Vernon *manufacturing executive*
Cutler, Alexander MacDonald *manufacturing company executive*
†Dunford, Edsel D. *electronics executive*
Epstein, Marvin Morris *retired construction executive*
Every, Russel B. *business executive*
†Forsythe, Frank S. *iron ore company executive*
Goodger, John Verne *electronics and computer systems executive*
Gorman, Joseph Tolle *corporate executive*
Grabner, George John *manufacturing executive*
Hamilton, William Milton *retired industrial company executive*
Hardis, Stephen Roger *manufacturing company executive*
Hart, Alvin Leroy *electric manufacturing company executive*
Hauserman, William Foley *manufacturing company executive*
Hayes, Scott Birchard *raw materials company executive*
Hoag, David H. *steel company executive*
Holsworth, William C. *food company executive*
†Huge, Arthur William *steel company financial executive, civil engineer*
Hushen, John W. *manufacturing company executive*
Ivy, Conway Gayle *paint company executive*
Kamm, Jacob Oswald *manufacturing executive, economist*
Kelly, J. Peter *steel company executive*
Kerr, Thomas Adolphus *retired construction company executive*
Krasney, Samuel Joseph *multi-industry company executive*
Lamore, George L. *manufacturing company executive*
Lefebvre, Gabriel Felicien *retired chemical company executive*
Luke, Randall Dan *retired tire and rubber company executive, lawyer*
Luntz, Theodore Michael *recycling company executive*
Mac Laren, David Sergeant *manufacturing corporation executive, inventor*
Mandel, Jack N. *manufacturing company executive*
Mandel, Morton Leon *industrial corporation executive*
Mc Fadden, John Volney *retired manufacturing company executive*
Mendelson, Ralph Richard *water heater manufacturing executive*
Miller, Carl George *manufacturing executive*
†Miller, Sydell Lois *cosmetics executive, marketing professional*
Moore, Louis Lee *medical instrumentation company executive*
Myers, David N. *construction executive*
Nolan, Cary J. *medical products manufacturer*
†Ortino, Hector Ruben *chemical company executive*
Parker, Patrick Streeter *manufacturing executive*
†Paul, Robert Gregory *electronic company executive*
Ramig, Alexander, Jr. *paint company executive, chemist*
Ratner, Albert B. *building products company executive, land developer*
Ratner, Max *building products company executive, land developer*
†Rego, Anthony C. *food products executive*
Reid, James Sims, Jr. *automobile parts manufacturer*
Reitman, Robert Stanley *manufacturing and marketing executive*
Renner, Simon Edward *steel company executive*
Roberts, Clyde Francis *business executive*
†Robinson, John C. *manufacturing executive, light*
Rodewig, John Stuart *manufacturing company executive*
Rosenthal, Leighton A. *aviation company executive*
Sabo, Richard Steven *electrical company executive*
Schey, Ralph Edward *manufacturing executive*
Schloemer, Paul George *diversified manufacturing company executive*
Stone, Harry H. *business executive*
Sullivan, Dennis W. *power systems company executive*
Swift, David L. *manufacturing company executive*
Tinker, H(arold) Burnham *chemical company executive*
Trzcinski, Ronald E. *mattress and bedding company executive*
Unger, Paul A. *packaging executive*
Walker, Martin Dean *specialty chemical company executive*
Weiss, Morry *greeting card company executive*
Williams, Gordon Bretnell *construction company executive*
Willis, George Edmund *chemical processing and electrical manufacturing executive*
Wright, Marshall *retired manufacturing executive, former diplomat*

Columbus
Crane, Jameson *plastics manufacturing company executive*
Dennis, Richard Irwin *company executive*
Eickelberg, John Edwin *process control company executive*
Evans, Daniel E. *sausage manufacturing and restaurant chain company executive*
Gerlach, John B. *business executive*
Gunnels, Lee O. *pallet manufacturing company executive*
Heffner, Grover Chester *retired corporate executive, retired naval officer*
Kidder, C. Robert *battery manufacturing company executive*
Knilans, Michael Jerome *supermarkets executive*
Lazar, Theodore Aaron *retired manufacturing company executive, lawyer*
McConnell, John Henderson *metal and plastic products manufacturing executive, professional sports team executive*
Mussey, Joseph Arthur *health and medical product executive*
Pfening, Frederic Denver, III *manufacturing company executive*
Trevor, Alexander Bruen *computer company executive*
†Wehr, Lynn *food products executive*
Wigington, Ronald Lee *retired chemical information services executive*
Yenkin, Bernard Kalman *paint company executive*

Concord
Whedon, Ralph Gibbs *manufacturing executive*

Cuyahoga Falls
Hooper, Blake Howard *manufacturing executive*

Dayton
Diggs, Matthew O'Brien, Jr. *air conditioning and refrigeration manufacturing executive*
Duval, Daniel Webster *manufacturing company executive*
Enouen, William Albert *paper corporation executive*
Haynes, Gerald Wayne *aerospace manufacturing administrator*
Holmes, David Richard *computer and business forms company executive*
James, Robert Charles *business equipment manufacturing company executive*
Ladehoff, Leo William *metal products manufacturing executive*
†MacLeod, Thomas D. *feed company executive*
Mason, Steven Charles *forest products company executive*
†Mathile, Clayton Lee *corporate executive*
Mc Swiney, James Wilmer *retired pulp and paper manufacturing company executive*
Medford, Dale Leon *industrial company executive*
Morse, Kenneth Pratt *manufacturing executive*
Price, Harry Steele, Jr. *construction materials company executive*
Redding, Peter Stoddard *manufacturing company executive*
Rinzler, Allan *consulting company executive*
Shuey, John Henry *diversified products company executive*
Torley, John Frederic *iron and steel company executive*

Defiance
Elberson, Elwood L. *food company executive*

Delaware
Berg, John Paul *container manufacturing company executive*
Dempsey, John Cornelius *manufacturing company executive*
Eells, William Hastings *retired automobile company executive*
Reitz, Elmer A. *manufacturing company executive*

Dublin
Clement, Henry Joseph, Jr. *diversified building products executive*
Greaves, J. Randall *metals, electronics manufacturing company executive*
†Heffron, Robert F. *manufacturing company executive*
Lamp, Benson J. *tractor company executive*
Toller, William Robert *chemical and oil company executive*

Elyria
†Carbonari, Bruce A. *metal products executive*
Uveges, George *company executive*

Fairlawn
Bonsky, Jack Alan *chemical company executive, lawyer*
Gibson, Charles Colmery *former rubber manufacturing executive*
Isles, Marvin Lee *manufacturing executive*

Findlay
Gorr, Ivan William *retired rubber company executive*
Kremer, Fred, Jr. *manufacturing company executive*
Reinhardt, James Alec *rubber industry executive*

Franklin
Smith, Lynn Howard *manufacturing company executive*

Gates Mills
Veale, Tinkham, II *former chemical company executive, engineer*

Grove City
Funk, John William *emergency vehicle manufacturing executive, packaging company executive, lawyer*

Hamilton
Belew, David Lee *retired paper manufacturing company executive*

Holland
Stewart, Daniel Robert *retired glass company executive*

Holmesville
Bolender, James Henry *tire and rubber manufacturing executive*

Hudson
Rosskamm, Martin *fabric manufacturing company executive*

Huron
Clark, Thomas Garis *rubber products manufacturer*

Independence
Callsen, Christian Edward *medical device company executive*

Jackson Center
Thompson, Wade Francis Bruce *manufacturing company executive*

Lakewood
Bradley, J.F., Jr. *retired manufacturing company executive*

Lancaster
Fox, Robert Kriegbaum *manufacturing company executive*

Lima
Pranses, Anthony Louis *retired electric company executive, organization executive*

Macedonia
Roth, Edwin Morton *manufacturing executive*

Mansfield
Gorman, James Carvill *pump manufacturing company executive*
†Roesler, Karl *electronics executive*

Marietta
Broughton, Carl L(ouis) *food company executive*

Marysville
Hines, Anthony Loring *automotive executive*

Mason
†Soos, James E. *electronics executive*

Massillon
†Genshaft, Neil *meat packing company executive*

Maumee
Allen, Darryl Frank *industrial company executive*
Anderson, Richard Paul *agricultural company executive*
Frank, Thomas Edward *food products executive*
Selland, Howard M. *manufacturing executive*

Mayfield Heights
O'Brien, Frank B. *manufacturing executive*
Rankin, Alfred Marshall, Jr. *business executive*
Smith, Ward *manufacturing company executive, lawyer*

Medina
Gossett, Robert M. *rubber industry executive*
†Karman, James Anthony *manufacturing executive*
Morris, John Hite *chemical industry executive*
Smith, Richey *chemical company executive*
Sullivan, Thomas Christopher *coatings company executive*

Miamisburg
†Byrne, John J. *manufacturing executive, light*
Mariotti, John Louis *plastics & rubber manufacturing company executive*
Northrop, Stuart Johnston *manufacturing company executive*

Middletown
Graham, Thomas Carlisle *steel company executive*

Milford
Kenton, James Alan *healthcare products executive*
Klosterman, Albert Leonard *technical development business executive, mechanical engineer*

New Bremen
Dicke, James Frederick, II *manufacturing company executive*

North Olmsted
Tanis, John Jacob *manufacturing company executive*

North Ridgeville
Haddox, Arden Ruth Stewart *automotive aftermarket manufacturing executive*

Painesville
Humphrey, George Magoffin, II *plastic molding company executive*

Perrysburg
Eastman, John Richard *retired manufacturing company executive*

Pickerington
Zacks, Gordon Benjamin *manufacturing company executive*

Randolph
Pecano, Donald Carl *truck, trailer and railcar manufacturing executive*

Reynoldsburg
Woodward, Greta Charmaine *construction company executive*

Solon
Richard, Edward H. *manufacturing company executive, former municipal government official*

Streetsboro
Kearns, Warren Kenneth *business executive*

Sugar Grove
Bonner, Herbert Dwight *construction management educator*

Sylvania
Lock, Richard William *packaging company executive*

Toledo
Boeschenstein, William Wade *glass products manufacturing executive*
Boller, Ronald Cecil *glass company executive*
Dana, Charles H. *manufacturing company executive*
Hiner, Glen Harold, Jr. *materials company executive*
Hirsch, Carl Herbert *manufacturing company executive*
Laimbeer, William *manufacturing company executive*
Lanigan, Robert J. *packaging company executive*
Lemieux, Joseph Henry *manufacturing company executive*
Mac Guidwin, Mark J. *manufacturing executive*
Morcott, Southwood J. *automotive parts manufacturing company executive*
Reimer, Borge R. *motor vehicle parts manufacturer*
Robb, A. M. *glass manufacturing executive*
Romanoff, Milford Martin *building contractor*
Saxby, Lewis Weyburn, Jr. *glass fiber manufacturing company executive*
Solari, Larry Thomas *manufacturing company executive*
Strobel, Martin Jack *motor vehicle and industrial component manufacturing and distribution company executive*
Weber, Max O. *retired glass fiber products manufacturing company executive*

Troy
Deering, Joseph William *manufacturing executive*

Vandalia
Farley, Paul Emerson *manufacturing company executive*

Walbridge
†Rudolph, Frederick William *contractor*

Warren
Alli, Richard James, Sr. *electronics executive, service executive*
†Caiazza, Donald J. *manufacturing executive heavy*
Rennert, Ira Leon *heavy manufacturing executive*

Washington Court House
Rivers, Ronald D. *manufacturing executive*

West Chester
Rishel, James Burton *manufacturing executive*

Westerville
Smith, C. Kenneth *corporate executive*

Wickliffe
Bares, William G. *chemical company executive*
Coleman, Lester Earl *chemical company executive*
Rosica, Gabriel Adam *corporate executive, engineer*

Willoughby
Chiarucci, Vincent A. *diversified manufacturing company executive*
Figgie, Harry E., Jr. *corporate executive*
Manning, William Dudley, Jr. *retired specialty chemical company executive*

Wooster
Gates, Richard Daniel *manufacturing company executive*

Morgan, James A. *rubber products company executive*
Williams, Walter W. *consumer products manufacturing executive*

Worthington
Davis, Samuel Bernhard *manufacturing executive*

Youngstown
Courtney, William Francis *food and vending service company executive*
Cushwa, William Wallace *machinery parts company executive*
Major, Richard Demarest *manufacturing company executive*
Marks, Esther L. *metals company executive*
Powers, Paul J. *manufacturing company executive*

OKLAHOMA

Bartlesville
Dunlap, James Robert *contractor, state legislator*

Bethany
Mercer, Ronald L. *retired manufacturing executive*

Bixby
Makhani, Madan Pal Singh *foundry executive*

Broken Arrow
Elad, Emanuel *industrial instrumentation executive*

Edmond
Griggy, Kenneth Joseph *food company executive*

Miami
Dines, James Melvin *manufacturing company executive*

Oklahoma City
Bishop, William T. *food company executive*
Comchoc, Rudolph A. *food distribution company executive*
†Devening, Robert Randolph *pharmaceutical company executive*
Grounds, Frances Ann *cosmetics sales professional, photographer, journalist*
Kilbourne, Lewis Buckner *food service company executive*
Locke, William Sweet *manufacturing executive*
Mc Pherson, Frank Alfred *manufacturing corporate executive*
Meyers, Theodore A. *food products executive*
Smith, Robert Walter *food company executive*
Smoak, David S. *food company executive*
Winn, Harry L., Jr. *food products financial executive*

Poteau
Harper, S. Birnie *bakery executive*

Sand Springs
Ackerman, Robert Wallace *steel company executive*

Tulsa
Bump, Larry J. *international engineering and construction company executive*
Bynum, George T., III (Ted Bynum) *biomedical company executive*
Calvert, Delbert William *chemical company executive*
†Cappy, Joseph E. *automobile company executive*
Collins, John Roger *aerospace manufacturing company executive*
†Flint, Charles W., III *corporate executive*
Jatras, Stephen James *electronics company executive*
Kaefer, Gene John *manufacturing executive*
Narwold, Lewis Lammers *paper products manufacturer*
Thomas, Robert Eggleston *former corporate executive*
Williams, Joseph Hill *retired diversified industry executive*

OREGON

Ashland
Farrimond, George Francis, Jr. *management educator*

Beaverton
Bosch, Samuel Henry *electronics company executive*
†Friedley, David P. *electronics manufacturing company executive*
Hayes, Delbert J. *athletic company executive*
Knight, Philip H(ampson) *shoe manufacturing company executive*
Long, Tom *manufacturing company executive*

Eugene
Heidenheim, Roger Stewart *automotive and electronic consultant*
Wiley, Carl Ross *timber company executive*

Forest Grove
†Coleman, Deborah Ann *electronics company executive*

Hillsboro
Gerlach, Robert Louis *research and development executive, physicist*

Medford
†Williams, William H. *food products executive, retail executive*

Milwaukie
Jones, Alan C. *grocery company executive*

Portland
Bishop, C. M., Jr. *textile company executive*
Bull, Bergen Ira *equipment manufacturing company executive*
Cooley, Edward H. *castings manufacturing company executive*
Drake, Brian William *photography company executive*

Flowerree, Robert Edmund *retired forest products company executive*
Foehl, Edward Albert *chemical company executive*
Frazier, J(ohn) Phillip *manufacturing company executive*
Fronk, William Joseph *retired machinery company executive*
Gray, John Delton *retired manufacturing company executive*
Kinnune, William P. *forest products executive*
Marvin, Roy Mack *metal products executive*
McKennon, Keith Robert *chemical company executive*
Merlo, Harry Angelo *forest products executive*
Nagel, Stanley Blair *construction and investment executive*
Pamplin, Robert Boisseau, Sr. *textile manufacturing executive*
Pope, Peter T. *forest products company executive*
Russell, Marjorie Rose *manufacturing company executive*
Steinfeld, Ray, Jr. *food products executive*
Stoyanov, Milan *lumber products company executive*
Strain, Douglas Campbell *precision instrument company executive*
Swindells, William, Jr. *lumber and paper company executive*
Thurston, George R. *lumber company executive*
Warren, Robert Carlton *manufacturing company executive*
Whitsell, Helen Jo *lumber executive*
†Winecki, William *food products executive*

Sisters
Baxter, John Lincoln, Jr. *manufacturing company executive*

Springfield
Detlefsen, William David, Jr. *research and development executive*

Sunriver
Fosmire, Fred Randall *retired forest products company executive*

Tigard
Berglund, Carl Neil *electronics company executive*

Wilsonville
Kimberley, A. G., Jr. *industrial products, factory representative, management executive*
Meyer, Jerome J. *diversified technology company executive*

Woodburn
Bradley, Lester Eugene *retired steel and rubber products manufacturing executive*

PENNSYLVANIA

Allentown
Anderson, Paul Edward *cement company executive*
Armor, John N. *chemical company research manager*
Baker, Dexter Farrington *manufacturing company executive*
Baraket, Edmund S., Jr. *general contractor, contracting consultant*
†Dimechkie, Riad N. *food company executive*
Donaldson, John Anthony *manufacturing executive*
Donley, Edward *manufacturing company executive*
Foster, Edward Paul (Ted Foster) *process industries executive*
Lovett, John Robert *chemical company executive*
Samuels, Abram *stage equipment manufacturing company executive*
Shire, Donald Thomas *retired air products and chemicals executive, lawyer*
†Snyder, Frank R. *building materials manufacturing executive*

Allison Park
Backus, John King *former chemical company research administrator*

Avondale
Friel, Daniel Denwood, Sr. *manufacturing executive*

Bala Cynwyd
Driscoll, Edward Carroll *construction management firm executive*
Furlong, Edward V., Jr. *paper company executive*
Halloran, Harry Richard *contracting company executive*
Lotman, Herbert *food processing executive*

Belle Vernon
Wapiennik, Carl Francis *manufacturing firm executive, planetarium and science institute executive*

Bensalem
Faijean, Francois *metal products executive*
Wachs, David V. *apparel executive*

Berwyn
Burch, John Walter *mining equipment company executive*
†Silverman, Stanley Wayne *chemical company executive*
Van Sant, Robert William *manufacturing company executive*

Bethlehem
Arnot, David Sheldon *steel company executive*
Barnette, Curtis Handley *steel company executive, lawyer*
Boylston, Benjamin Calvin *steel company executive*
Church, Thomas Trowbridge *former steel company executive*
Gates, Elmer D. *business executive*
Hartmann, Robert Elliott *manufacturing company executive*
Jordan, John Allen, Jr. *steel company executive*
Kerchner, Charles Frederick, Jr. *electronics executive, engineer*
Roberts, Malcolm John *steel company executive*
Rushton, Brian Mandel *chemical company executive*
Weller, Andrew Michael *steel company executive*
Williams, Walter Fred *steel company executive*

Blue Bell
Carey, Joseph A., Jr. *electronics executive*
Henkels, Paul MacAllister *engineering and construction company executive*
Keppler, William Edmund *multinational company executive*
Unruh, James Arlen *business machines company executive*

Boiling Springs
Hoefling, John Alan *former army officer, corporation executive*

Brackenridge
Bozzone, Robert P. *steel company executive*

Bradford
Rice, Lester *electronics company executive*

Butler
†Green, Charles Thomas *hardware distribution company executive*
†Rath, Frank E., Sr. *electronics executive*
†Rath, Frank E., Jr. *electronics executive*

Camp Hill
Grass, Martin Lehrman *business executive*
†Peters, Ralph Edgar *business executive*

Canonsburg
Harker, Joseph Edward *construction, industrial and steel company executive*

Central City
Brown, Robert Alan *retired construction materials company executive*

Chambersburg
Rumler, Robert Hoke *agricultural consultant, retired association executive*

Clairton
†Dick, David E. *construction company executive*
†Dick, Douglas Patrick *construction company executive*

Clarks Summit
Alperin, Irwin Ephraim *clothing company executive*
Ross, Adrian E. *retired drilling manufacturing company executive*

Coatesville
Meyers, Frederick M. *diversified industrial products and service company executive*
Myers, Frederick M. *metal products executive*

Collegeville
Dupuis, Claude Paul *pharmaceutical company executive*
Kun, Kenneth A. *business executive*
Smalley, Christopher Joseph *pharmaceutical company professional*
Tretter, James Ray *pharmaceutical company executive*

Conshohocken
†Benoliel, Peter Andre *chemical company executive*
Spaeth, Karl Henry *chemical company executive, lawyer*

Coopersburg
Spira, Joel Solon *electronics company executive*

Devon
Brody, Aaron Leo *food and packaging consultant*

Easton
Bartolacci, Guido Jamess *retail company executive*
Gurin, Richard Stephen *manufacturing company executive*

Eighty Four
Capone, Alphonse William *retired industrial executive*

Elizabethville
†DeSoto, Pete *company executive*

Emmaus
Bowers, Klaus D(ieter) *retired electronics research development company executive*

Erie
De Witt, William Gerald *retired paper company executive*
Fessler, Donald Francis *business executive*
Freeman, William A. *manufacturing company executive*
Hedrick, Charles Lynnwood *holding company executive*
Hey, John Charles *electronics company executive*
Stolley, James S. *manufacturing executive*

Exton
Lewis, Thomas B. *specialty chemical company executive*

Fairless Hills
Szuhy, Lawrence Gregory *automotive company executive*

Fairview
Duval, Albert Frank *paper company executive*

Feasterville
†Liberati, Maria Theresa *fashion production company executive*

Forty Fort
Falkowitz, Daniel *clothing manufacturing company executive*

Gladwyne
Mc Donald, Robert Emmett *company executive*

Greentown
Forcheskie, Carl S. *former apparel company executive*

Greenville
Stuver, Francis Edward *former railway car company executive*

Gwynedd
Bryant, Robert Parker *retired food service and lodging executive*

Hanover
Kline, Donald *food company executive*
†Warehime, John A. *food products executive*

Harleysville
†Rhodes, Gary Lynn *food company executive*

Harrisburg
Goell, James Emanuel *electronics company executive*
Hudson, William Jeffrey, Jr. *manufacturing company executive*
Marley, James Earl *manufacturing company executive*
McInnes, Harold A. *manufacturing company executive*
Narigan, Harold W. *manufacturing company executive*
Raab, Walter Ferdinand *manufacturing company executive*

Hatboro
Hull, Lewis Woodruff *manufacturing company executive*

Haverford
Bogash, Richard *retired pharmaceutical company executive*
Talucci, Samuel James *retired chemical company executive*

Hazleton
Denise, Robert Phillips *craft company executive*

Hershey
Duncan, Charles Lee *food products company executive*
Wolfe, Kenneth L. *food products manufacturing company executive*
Zimmerman, Richard Anson *food company executive*
Zoumas, Barry Lee *food products company executive, nutritionist*

Hollidaysburg
Bloom, Lawrence Stephen *retired clothing company executive*

Horsham
Boswell, Gary Taggart *electronics company executive*
Brenner, Ronald John *pharmaceutical industry executive*
Hakimoglu, Ayhan *electronics company executive*
Hook, Jerry B. *pharmaceutical company executive*
McNulty, Carrell Stewart, Jr. *manufacturing company executive, architect*

Huntingdon Valley
Jaffe, Marvin Eugene *pharmaceutical company executive, neurologist*

Indiana
Jones, Shelley Pryce *chemical company executive, writer*

Irvine
Koedel, John Gilbert, Jr. *forge company executive*

Jeannette
†Smiy, Paul R. *manufacturing executive, heavy*

Jenkintown
Beavers, Ellington McHenry *chemical company executive*
Coccagna, Fred Joseph, Jr. *flooring manufacturing executive*
Reese, Francis Edward *retired chemical company executive, consultant*

Johnstown
Pasquerilla, Frank James *real estate developer and manager*

Kennett Square
May, Harold Edward *chemical company executive*

Kimberton
Douglas, Bryce *former pharmaceutical company executive*

King Of Prussia
Langton, Raymond Benedict, III *manufacturing company executive*
Poste, George Henry *pharmaceutical company executive*
†Traynor, Sean Gabrial *manufacturing executive*
Wilson, Hugh Shannon *retired manufacturing company executive, consultant*
†Winkhaus, Hans-Dietrich *chemicals executive*
Wulff, Harald P. *chemicals executive*

Lancaster
†Burlefinger, Erich *electronics executive*
Deaver, Everette Allen *diversified manufacturing company executive*
Hennessey, Joseph E. *chemicals executive*
High, S. Dale *diversified company executive*
†Liddell, W. Kirk *specialty contracting and distribution company executive, lawyer*
Lorch, George A. *manufacturing company executive*

Langhorne
Davies, John Edward *biotechnology company executive*

Lansdale
Riebman, Leon *electronics company executive*

Latrobe
Underwood, James Martin *business executive*

Lebanon
McMindes, Roy James *aggregate company executive*

Ligonier
Pilz, Alfred Norman *manufacturing company executive*

Lititz
Smith, Thomas Clair *manufacturing company executive*

Lyon Station
Bowers, Richard Philip *manufacturing executive*
Breidegam, DeLight Edgar, Jr. *battery company executive*

Malvern
Holveck, David P. *pharmaceutical company executive*
Zurawski, Vincent Richard, Jr. *biotechnology company executive, research scientist*

Marcus Hook
†Rallis, John *manufacturing holding company executive*

Meadville
Foster, Catherine Rierson *manufacturing company executive*

Media
Peabody, William Tyler, Jr. *retired paper manufacturing company executive*
Resnick, Stewart Allen *diversified company executive*
Rothchild, Loren *toy manufacturing executive*

Mendenhall
Elliott, R. Keith *specialty chemical company executive*

Middleburg
Kline, David Lamar *concrete block manufacturing company executive*

Milford
Anchel, Edward *manufacturing executive*

Millersburg
Kirkwood, James Mace *pharmaceutical company executive*

Monroeville
Maclay, William Nevin *retired manufacturing and construction company executive*
Ryan, Christopher Richard *construction company executive*

Morgantown
McGraw, James Michael *manufacturing company executive*

Morrisville
Muth, Robert James *metal company executive, lawyer*

New Brighton
O'Leary, John Patrick, Jr. *packaging company executive*

New Hope
Braymer, Marguerite Annetta *optical company executive*
Williamson, Frederick Beasley, III *rubber company executive*

New Kensington
Bridenbaugh, Peter Reese *industrial research executive*

Newtown
Henshaw, Jonathan Cook *manufacturing company executive*
Wilkinson, Harry J. *technical company executive*

Newtown Square
Magee, William H. *chemical company executive*
Wood, Donald W. *chemical company executive*

North Wales
Taylor, Robert Morgan *electronics executive*

Paoli
Blankley, Walter Elwood *manufacturing company executive*

Peach Glen
Carey, Dean Lavere *fruit canning company executive*

Philadelphia
Agersborg, Helmer Pareli K. *pharmaceutical company executive, researcher*
Avery, William Joseph *packaging manufacturing company executive*
Azoulay, Bernard *chemicals company executive*
Bakhru, Ashok Naraindas *paper company executive*
Bauman, Robert Patten *diversified company executive*
Callé, Craig R.L. *packaging executive*
Clark, Paul James *chemical company executive*
Driscoll, Lee Francis, Jr. *corporate director, lawyer*
Featherman, Bernard *steel company executive*
Ferber, Arthur Henry *engineering executive*
†Fritsch, Robert Bruce *manufacturing company executive*
Garrison, Walter R. *corporate executive*
Harper, Edwin Leland *manufacturing executive*
Jones, Loren Farquhar *electronics executive*
Katherine, Robert Andrew *chemical company executive*
Kramer, Henry *metal processing executive*
Leaman, J. Richard, Jr. *paper company executive*
Lewis, George Withrow *business executive*
Llewellyn, J. Bruce *food products executive*
†McKenna, Michael Joseph *manufacturing company executive*
Mulroney, John Patrick *chemical company executive*
†Naples, Ronald James *manufacturing company executive*
Naylor, Robert Ernest, Jr. *chemical company executive*
Sorgenti, Harold Andrew *petroleum and chemical company executive*
White, Albert J. *health products executive*
Wilson, James Lawrence *chemical company executive*
†Wilson, Ronald D. *soft drink bottling company executive*
†Yoh, Harold L., III *company executive*

Pittsburgh
Agnew, Franklin Ernest, III *former food company executive*
Aronson, Arthur H. *steel company executive*
Barone, Eugene J. *medical products executive*
Bogdanovich, Joseph James *food company executive*
Burley, Jack Lynn *food products executive*
Burnham, Donald Clemens *manufacturing company executive*
Chenery, Robin *metals manufacturing executive*
Clark, Gary M. *electronics executive*
Corry, Charles Albert *steel and energy company executive*
Courtsal, Donald Preston *manufacturing company executive, financial consultant*
Danforth, Douglas Dewitt *manufacturing company executive*
Dauler, L. Van V., Jr. *chemicals executive*
Doerr, Ronald H. *steel company executive*
Edelman, Harry Rollings, III *engineering and construction company executive*
Fairbanks, Frank Bates *manufacturing company executive*
Figgins, David Forrester *construction company executive*
Fischer, Richard Lawrence *metal products executive*
Foxen, Richard William *manufacturing company executive*
Frank, Alan I W *manufacturing company executive*
Freeman, Edmund J. *heavy manufacturing executive*
Grefenstette, Carl G. *medical products and real estate executive*
Hoffman, Ronald Robert *aluminum company executive*
Horn, Jerry Dean *health products executive*
Horowitz, Don Roy *instrument company executive*
Huntington, James Cantine, Jr. *equipment manufacturing company executive*
Isherwood, John S. *beverage company executive*
Johannes, George Robert *construction executive*
Jordan, Michael Hugh *electrical and electronics company executive*
Kronk, Claude F. *heavy manufacturing executive*
Kushner, Robert Arnold *steel company executive, lawyer*
Lauterbach, Hans *pharmaceutical company executive*
Lauterbach, Robert Emil *steel company executive*
LeBoeuf, Raymond Walter *manufacturing company executive*
Lego, Paul Edward *retired corporation executive*
Limbach, Walter F. *construction company executive*
Marshall, Thomas *chemical company executive*
Mastro, A. F. *chemical company executive*
McConomy, Thomas Arthur *chemical company executive*
Moore, Frederick C. *manufacturing executive*
Mueller, Gerd Dieter *financial and administrative executive*
Mulloney, Peter Black *steel, oil and gas executive*
Oehmler, George Courtland *corporate executive*
O'Neill, Paul Henry *aluminum company executive*
O'Reilly, Anthony John Francis *food company executive*
Patton, Richard Bolling *food company executive*
Paul, Robert Arthur *steel company executive*
Phillips, James Macilduff *material handling company executive, engineering and manufacturing executive*
Porter, Irwin W. *food store chain executive*
Prine, Charles W., Jr. *construction executive*
Purdum, Robert L. *steel manufacturing company executive*
†Puskar, Milan *pharmaceuticals executive*
Roth, William George *manufacturing company executive*
Rust, William James *retired steel company executive*
Ruttenberg, Harold Joseph *manufacturing executive*
Ryan, John Thomas, Jr. *business executive*
Ryan, John Thomas, III *safety equipment company executive*
Sante, William Arthur, II *aerospace and manufacturing company executive*
Sardi, Maurice Charles *contract furniture company executive*
Scorsone, Vincent Robert *aluminum company executive*
Sculley, David W. *food company executive*
Sieckmann, Walter *industrial manufacturing and engineering company executive*
Simmons, Richard P. *steel company executive*
Smith, Phillip Hartley *steel company executive*
Stahl, Laddie L. *electrical engineer, manufacturing company executive*
Thomas, W(illiam) Bruce *retired steel, oil, gas company executive*
Turnbull, Gordon Keith *metal company executive, metallurgical engineer*
Wehmeier, Helge H. *chemical, health care and imaging technologies company executive*
White, Richard L. *chemicals company executive*
Wilcock, James William *corporation executive, retired capital equipment manufacturing company executive*
Will, James Fredrick *steel company executive*
Williams, Louis Stanton *glass and chemical manufacturing executive*

Plymouth Meeting
Boyer, David Scott *manufacturing company executive*

Pocopson
Mulligan, James Francis *retired business executive, lawyer*

Radnor
†Stetson, John Batterson, IV *construction executive*
Yoh, Harold Lionel, Jr. *engineering, construction and management company executive*

Reading
Beaver, Howard Oscar, Jr. *wrought specialty alloys manufacturing company executive*
Cardy, Robert Willard *speciality steel company executive*
Cottrell, G. Walton *manufacturing executive*
Crain, C. William *apparel company executive*
Ehlerman, Paul Michael *industrial battery manufacturing company executive*
Fiore, Nicholas Francis *special alloys and materials company executive*
Harner, Paul B. *gray iron foundry executive*
Hawkins, Arthur *battery manufacturing executive*
Hawkins, Arthur Michael *automotive executive*
Johnson, Gerard G. *apparel company executive*
Pearson, Douglas N. *battery manufacturing company executive*
Pugh, Lawrence R. *apparel executive*
†Redner, Richard *food products executive*
Roedel, Paul Robert *steel company executive*

Saint Marys
Johnson, J. M. Hamlin *manufacturing company executive*

Scranton
Guerrise, Patrick P. *manufacturing company executive*

Sewickley
McKibbin, John Meek, III *aluminum company executive*
Snyder, William Penn, III *manufacturing company executive*

Shippensburg
Luhrs, H. Ric *toy manufacturing company executive*

Sinking Spring
Wilson, Terrence Raymond *manufacturing executive*

Southampton
DaCosta, Edward Hoban *plastics and electronics manufacturing company executive*
McSparran, Robert B. *food products executive*
Zocholl, Stanley Ernest *electronics executive*

Spring City
Blanchard, Norman Harris *retired pharmaceutical company executive*

Spring Grove
Norris, Thomas Clayton *paper company executive*
Wand, Richard Walton *paper company executive*

Spring House
Payn, Clyde Francis *technology company executive, consultant*

Swarthmore
Heaps, Marvin Dale *food services company executive*
Kaufman, Antoinette D. *business services company executive*

Swiftwater
Woods, Walter Earl *biomedical manufacturing executive*

Tamaqua
Urenovitch, Joseph Victor *chemical company executive*

Telford
Luscinski, Steven Michael *corporate executive*

Trevose
McCaughan, John F. *chemical company executive*

Unionville
Forney, Robert Clyde *retired chemical industry executive*
Irwin, Robert Hugh Crawford *manufacturing company executive*

University Park
Jordan, Bryce *corporate director, retired university president*

Valley Forge
Besson, Michel Louis *manufacturing company executive*
Dachowski, Peter Richard *manufacturing executive*
Hilyard, James Emerson *manufacturing company executive*
†Smith, George E. *chemical company executive*

Verona
†Kirchner, Louis John *industrial manufacturing company executive*
Potts, Gerald Neal *manufacturing company executive*

Washington
Kastelic, Robert Frank *aerospace company executive*
Piatt, Jack Boyd *manufacturing executive*

Waverly
Matthews, Richard J. *pharmaceutical research company executive*

Wayne
†Bartholdson, John Robert *industrial company executive*
Curry, Thomas James *manufacturers representative*
DeCarlo, A. J. *lumber company executive*
†Essner, Robert Alan *pharmaceutical executive*
Mundt, Ray B. *diversified industry executive*
Peterson, Raymond A. *paper company executive*
Wolcott, Robert Wilson, Jr. *consulting company executive*

Waynesboro
Benchoff, James Martin *manufacturing company executive*
Holzman, Howard Eugene *health services executive*

West Chester
Bogle, Hugh Andrew *chemical company executive*
Kim, James Joo-Jin *electronics company executive*
Mecca, Joseph Nicholas *logistics and manufacturing company executive*
Rubin, Henri *electronics executive*

West Point
Abrams, William Bernard *pharmaceutical company executive, physician*

Wilkes Barre
Hobbs, William Barton Rogers *company executive*
Polishan, Paul Frank *clothing company executive*

Williamsport
Wygant, James Peter *food company executive*

Willow Grove
Kulicke, C(harles) Scott *business executive*
†VanLuvanee, Donald Robert *electronics executive*

Worcester
McAdam, Will *electronics consultant*
Myers, Allan Ross *construction executive*

Wynnewood
Bozzelli, Andrew Joseph, Jr. *valve company executive*
Connor, James Edward, Jr. *retired chemical company executive*
Kelly, Paul E., Jr. *metal products executive*
Kelly, Paul Edward, Sr. *metals company executive*

Wyomissing
Garr, Carl Robert *manufacturing company executive*

York
†Borgelt, Burton C. *dental and optical supply manufacturing company executive*
Dresher, James T. *manufacturing executive*
Forchheimer, Otto Louis *retired chemical company executive*
Garner, Edward Markley, II *manufacturing executive*
Jamison, Steven R. *construction company executive*
Pokelwaldt, Robert N. *manufacturing company executive*

Zionsville
Fleming, Richard *chemical company executive*

RHODE ISLAND

Bristol
Wilcox, Harry Wilbur, Jr. *retired corporate executive*

East Providence
Hay, Robert J. *plastics manufacturing executive*

Greenwich
Valenti, Leo Frank *electronics company executive*

North Kingstown
Paolino, Richard Francis *manufacturing company executive*
Sharpe, Henry Dexter, Jr. *manufacturing company executive*

Pawtucket
Neff, Edward August *manufacturing company executive*
Schwartz, Stephen Allan *toy company executive*
Tracy, Allen Wayne *manufacturing company executive*

Providence
Ames, Robert San *retired manufacturing company executive*
Bready, Richard Lawrence *manufacturing company executive*
Choquette, Paul Joseph, Jr. *construction company executive*
Cooper, Gordon Mayo *retired manufacturing company executive*
Dimeo, Thomas P. *construction company executive, real estate developer*
Gilbane, Jean Ann (Mrs. Thomas F. Gilbane) *construction company executive*
Gilbane, Thomas F., Jr. *building company executive*
Gilbane, William James *building company executive*
Hardymon, James Franklin *diversified products company executive*
Hartmann, George Herman *retired manufacturing company executive*
Little, Dennis Gage *diversified business executive*
Roy, Norman E. *construction company executive*
Wayland, William Francis *diversified manufacturing company executive*

Rumford
†Marshall, John L., III *construction company executive*

West Kingston
†Landsman, Emanuel Elbert *manufacturing company executive*

West Warwick
Galkin, Robert Theodore *company executive*

SOUTH CAROLINA

Anderson
Elks, William Chester, Jr. *manufacturing executive*
Hendrix, James Easton *textiles executive*

Arcadia
Dent, Frederick Baily *mill executive, former ambassador, former secretary of commerce*

Camden
Daniels, John Hancock *agricultural products company executive*

Catawba
Malenick, Donald H. *metals manufacturing company executive*

Charleston
Addlestone, Nathan Sidney *metals company executive*
Kent, Harry Ross *construction executive, lay worker*
Martin, Roblee Boettcher *retired cement manufacturing executive*
Thompson, W(ilmer) Leigh *pharmaceutical company executive, physician, pharmacologist*

Clinton
Cornelson, George Henry, IV *retired textile company executive*
Vance, Robert Mercer *textile manufacturing company executive, banker*

Columbia
Kahn, Herman Bernard *construction company executive*
Spector, Joseph Robert *retired diversified manufacturing executive*
Tomlin, Patrick Leslie *condominium development executive*

Florence
Dixon, Gale Harllee *drug company executive*

Fort Mill
Elisha, Walter Y. *textile manufacturing company executive*
Horten, Carl Frank *textile manufacturing company executive*
Montgomery, Terry Gray *textiles researcher*
White, James Spratt, IV *textiles executive, lawyer*

Greenville
†Albers, Gerald E. *aircraft parts manufacturing*
Chastain, Roger W. *textile company executive*
Dean, Warren Michael *construction company executive*
Friedman, Steven M. *textile company executive*
Hodges, Harland E. *apparel executive*
Hunter, Jerry E. *textile company executive*
Maddrey, E. E., II *textile company executive*
Nemirow, Arnold Myles *manufacturing executive*
Pamplin, Robert Boisseau, Jr. *agricultural company executive, minister, writer*
Parente, Emil J. *chemical engineering executive*
†Price, Arthur D. *food products executive*
Rainsford, Bettis C. *textile company executive*
Roe, Thomas Anderson *building supply company executive*
Stone, Charles Rivers *apparel manufacturing company executive*
Varin, Roger Robert *textile executive*

Greer
Gallman, Clarence Hunter *textile executive*
Lane, James Garland, Jr. *diversified industry executive*
Scruggs, Jack Gilbert *retired chemical executive*

Hartsville
Browning, Peter Crane *packaging company executive*
Coker, Charles Westfield *diversified manufacturing company executive*
Coxe, Thomas C., III *paper and plastic products manufacturing company executive*
McGee, James Gladney, Jr. *diversified products company executive*

Hilton Head Island
Cunningham, William Henry *retired food products executive*
Harty, James D. *former manufacturing company executive*
Mersereau, Hiram Stipe *wood products company consultant*
Pritchard, Dalton Harold *retired electronics research engineer*
Ranney, Maurice William *chemical company executive*
Rulis, Raymond Joseph *manufacturing company executive, consultant*
Russell, Allen Stevenson *retired aluminum company executive*
Stoll, Richard Edmund *retired manufacturing executive*

Johns Island
Mackaness, George Bellamy *retired pharmaceutical company executive*

Ladson
Hyatt, David Hudson *manufacturing executive*

Lake Wylie
Peacock, A(lvin) Ward *textile company executive*

Salem
Van Buren, William Benjamin, III *retired pharmaceutical company executive*

Seneca
Hudgin, Donald Edward *retired research company executive, editor, consultant*

Spartanburg
Sovey, L. Terrell, Jr. *textile executive, insurance agent*

Townville
Wright, George Cullen *electronics company executive*

Wellford
Stone, George Eliot *textile executive*

Williamston
Davis, Michael Todd *textile company administrator*

SOUTH DAKOTA

Aberdeen
Glover, James Todd *manufacturing company executive*

Sioux Falls
Austad, Oscar *recreational supplies company executive*
Christensen, David Allen *manufacturing company executive*
Pederson, Arnold S. *chemical company executive*

TENNESSEE

Ashland City
Lindahl, Herbert Winfred *appliance manufacturing executive*

Brentwood
†Duncan, John Lapsley *manufacturing company executive*
†Spies, Robert J. *manufacturing executive, light*

Bristol
Riggs, Benjamin Clapp, Jr. *building products manufacturing company executive*

Chattanooga
Frierson, Daniel K. *textile company executive*
Fry, James C. *textile company executive*
St. Goar, Herbert *food corporation executive*
Schuessler, Morgan McQueen *textile company executive*

Cordova
Bellantoni, Maureen Blanchfield *manufacturing executive*
Colbert, Robert B., Jr. *apparel company executive*
Cooke, Edward William *corporate executive, former naval officer*
Dean, Jimmy *meat processing company executive, entertainer*

Dandridge
Comer, Evan Philip *manufacturing company executive*

Ducktown
Hopkins, David Lee *medical manufacturing executive*

Dyersburg
De Keyzer, Patrick Maurice *manufacturing company executive*
Wiggins, Jerome Meyer *apparel textile industry financial executive*

Hixson
Sheehy, Thomas Daniel *apparel and textile manufacturing company executive*

Jackson
Lipshie, Joseph *apparel manufacturing company executive*

Johnson City
†Conerly, Steve Garland *dairy foods company executive, economist*

Kingsport
Coover, Harry Wesley *manufacturing company executive*
Deavenport, Earnest W., Jr. *chemical executive*
Findley, Don Aaron *manufacturing company executive*
Giggey, James Walker *chemical company executive*
Head, William Iverson, Sr. *retired chemical company executive*
Hubbard, Randall Dee *manufacturing company executive*
Scarff, Edward L. *diversified company executive*

Knoxville
†Baldonado, Orlino Castro *engineering and technical services company executive*
Faires, Ross N. *manufacturing company executive*
Martin, James Robert *plastics company executive*
Olmstead, Francis Henry, Jr. *plastics industry executive*
Stegmayer, Joseph Henry *housing industry executive*
Stringfield, Hezz, Jr. *contractor, financial consultant*

La Vergne
Findley, Charles H. *manufacturing company executive*
Forrest, Henry J. *manufacturing company executive*

Lookout Mountain
Rymer, S. Bradford, Jr. *retired appliance manufacturing company executive*

Memphis
Andrews, William Eugene *construction and services company executive*
Apple, John Boyd *elevator company executive*
Ballou, Howard Burgess *commercial plumbing designer*
Berry, Robert Vaughan *electrical, electronic manufacturing company executive*
Bruce, Marvin Ernest *automotive products executive*
Buckman, Robert Henry *chemical company executive*
Cannon, Robert Emmet *consumer products manufacturing company executive*
Dunnigan, T. Kevin *electrical and electronics manufacturing company executive*
Fondren, William Merle, Jr. *hardware distribution company executive*
Formanek, Peter Raemin *automobile parts company executive*
Jenkins, Ruben Lee *chemical company executive*
Kelley, Robert C. *construction industry executive*
Langford, Walter Martin *retired greeting card and gift wrap manufacturing executive*
McMinn, William A. *chemicals company executive*
Reeves, Sam T. *argicultural products company executive*
†Rohrbach, N. J. *paper company executive*

Morristown
Cordover, Ronald Harvey *business executive, venture capitalist*

Nashville
Arnett, James William *restaurant executive*
Bausman, Dennis Charles *construction company executive*
DiLorenzo, Joseph L. *health care company executive*
†Don, James K. *health care company executive*
Fitzgerald, Edmund Bacon *electronics industry executive*
Gulmi, James Singleton *apparel manufacturing company executive*
Harris, J(acob) George *health care company executive*
†Head, Michael B. *electronics company executive*
Hohlfeld, Pauline *pharmaceutical executive*
Hummell, Burton Howard *food distribution company executive*
Kaizaki, Yoichiro *automotive executive*
Langstaff, George Quigley, Jr. *retired footwear company executive*
Mahanes, David James, Jr. *retired distillery executive*
†Nunnelly, Walter Sandels, III *corporate executive*
Ono, Masatoshi *tire manufacturing executive*
Richards, James E. *pharmaceutical executive*
Shelton, Larry Brandon *apparel company executive*
†Warren, Frank M., Jr. *construction company executive*
Wire, William Shidaker, II *retired apparel and footwear manufacturing company executive*

Oak Ridge
Macfarlane, Alastair Iain Robert *business executive*

Pleasant View
Davis, Alfred Lewis *manufacturing company executive*

Smyrna
Moffatt, Leslie Mack *aluminum company executive*

TEXAS

Austin
Adams, Warren Sanford, II *retired food company executive, lawyer*
Alich, John Arthur, Jr. *manufacturing company executive*
Brager, Walter S. *retired food products corporation executive*
Cook, Chauncey William Wallace *retired food products company executive*
Culp, Joe C(arl) *electronics executive*
Dell, Michael S. *manufacturing executive*
Edwards, Wayne Forrest *paper company executive*
Hurd, Richard Nelson *pharmaceutical company executive*
Jenkins, Marie Hooper *manufacturing company executive*
†McBee, Frank Wilkins, Jr. *industrial manufacturing executive*
Rollins, Henry Moak *former oil drilling equipment company executive, consultant*
Stratton, Robert *electronics company executive*
Vykukal, Eugene Lawrence *wholesale drug company executive*

Bellaire
Lancaster, Carroll Townes, Jr. *corporate executive*

Carrollton
Miller, Marvin Edward *building materials company executive*
Pasman, James S., Jr. *aluminum company executive*

College Station
Lusas, Edmund William *food processing research executive*

Conroe
Cabaret, Joseph Ronald *defense company executive*

Corpus Christi
Grubbs, Donald Ray *welder, educator*
Heinz, Walter Ernst Edward *retired chemical executive*
†Kane, Sam *meat company executive*
Turner, Elizabeth Adams Noble (Betty Turner) *healthcare executive, former mayor*

Dallas
Albers, John Richard *beverage company executive*
Anderson, Jack Roy *health care company executive*
Ash, Mary Kay Wagner *cosmetics company executive*
Ausere, Joe Morris *food manufacturing company executive*
Aylesworth, William Andrew *electronics company executive*
Barnes, Robert Vertreese, Jr. *masonry contractor executive*
Bartlett, Richard Chalkley *cosmetics executive, writer*
Bell, John Lewis McCulloch *manufacturing executive*
Bradford, William Edward *oil field equipment manufacturing company executive*
Bucy, J. Fred *retired electronics company executive*
Campbell, Roy E. *diversified company executive*
Casey, John T. *medical products executive*
Cherryholmes, James Gilbert *construction consultant, real estate agent*
Cruikshank, Thomas Henry *energy services and engineering executive*
Dorris, Carlos E. *chemicals executive*
†Engels, Lawrence Arthur *metals company executive*
†Ergott, Harold L., Jr. *electronics company executive*
Fisher, Gene Jordan *retired chemical company executive*
Gifford, Porter William *retired construction materials manufacturing company executive*
Gillilan, William J, III *construction company executive*
Guerin, Dean Patrick *food products executive*
Haggar, Edmond Ralph *apparel manufacturing company executive*
Hegi, Frederick B., Jr. *mobile home manufacturing executive*
Hill, John Rutledge, Jr. *retired construction materials company executive*
Hirl, J. Roger *petrochemical company executive*
Hirsch, Laurence Eliot *construction executive, mortgage banker*
Hirsh, Bernard *supply company executive, consultant*
Hodge, George Lowrance *cosmetics company executive*
Hughes, Joe Kenneth *retired beverage company executive*
Humann, Walter Johann *corporation executive*
Hurst, John L., III (Jack Hurst) *chemical company executive*
Junkins, Jerry R. *electronics company executive*
Keiffer, Edwin Gene *electronics industry company executive*

Knowles, True H. *food products executive*
Lane, Marvin Maskall, Jr. *electronics company executive*
Lawson, Andrew Lowell, Jr. *defense industry company executive*
†Lehman, Donald Ray *chemical company executive*
Lord, Esther A. *corporate executive*
Maguire, Cary McIlwaine *oil company executive*
Margerison, Richard Wayne *diversified industrial company executive*
Marino, Peter Andrew *electronics company executive*
†McKinney, Joseph F. *diversified manufacturing holding company executive*
Millican, Bill T. *construction company executive*
†Mitchell, William B. *electronics company executive*
Murphy, John Joseph *manufacturing company executive*
Pearce, Ronald *retired cosmetic company executive*
Quinn, David W. *building company executive*
Rabin, Stanley Arthur *metal products manufacturer*
Rivera, Richard E. *food products executive*
Robbins, Ray Charles *manufacturing company executive*
Robertson, Beverly Carruth *steel company executive*
Rochon, John Philip *cosmetics company executive*
Rogers, Ralph B. *industrial business executive*
Rogers, Robert D. *steel company executive*
Rosenstein, Ira M. *beverage products executive*
Rosson, Glenn Richard *building products and furniture company executive*
St. John, Bill Dean *diversified equipment and services company executive*
Sammons, Elaine D. *corporate executive*
Serpan, Roger L. *cement and concrete company executive*
Simmons, Harold C. *sugar company executive*
Simmons, James F. *textiles executive*
†Smith, Andrew J. *chemicals executive*
Snetzer, Michael Alan *multi-industry executive*
Snyder, Richard Wesley *manufacturing executive*
†Termini, Deanne Lanoix *research company executive*
Thompson, Charles Kerry *company executive*
Thrash, Purvis James, Sr. *retired oil field equipment and service company executive*
Turpin, Jack A. *electronics executive*
†Walker, Fergus Joseph, Jr. *manufacturing company executive*
Wallace, William Ray *fabricated steel manufacturing company executive*
Weber, William P. *electronics company executive*
Williams, Gordon L. *aircraft manufacturing executive*
†Williams, Sterling Lee *electronics executive*
Wilson, Lawrence Alexander *construction company executive*
†Winspear, William W. *home improvement company executive*
Yanagisawa, Samuel Tsuguo *electronics executive*
Ytterberg, Ralph Warren *company executive*
Zimmerman, S(amuel) Morton (Mort Zimmerman) *electrical and electronics engineering executive*
Zumwalt, Richard Dowling *flour mill executive*

Deer Park
†Stabell, Walter W. *chemicals executive*

Denton
Brown, John Fred *steel company executive*
Jernigan, Marian Sue *fashion merchandising educator*

Diboll
Grum, Clifford J. *manufacturing company executive*

Edinburg
Livas, Eduardo, Jr. *milling company executive*

Fort Worth
Appel, Bernard Sidney *electrical company executive*
Arena, M. Scott *pharmaceutical company executive*
Brandt, Roger Del *pharmaceutical company executive*
Chapman, Ira B., II *food products executive*
Crane, Neal Dahlberg *manufacturing company executive*
Cunningham, Raymond Clement *glass company executive*
Joiner, Webb Francis *helicopter manufacturing company executive*
Leone, George Frank *pharmaceutical executive*
Ravel, Dilip N. *pharmaceutical executive*
Roberts, Leonard H. *retail executive*
Schollmaier, Edgar H. *pharmaceutical products company executive*
Thornton, Charles Victor *metals executive*
Wheaton, David Joe *aerospace manufacturing company executive*

Garland
Adams, Christopher Steve, Jr. *defense electronics corporation executive, former air force officer*
†Ray, Richard T. *manufacturing executive, heavy*

Georgetown
Gerding, Thomas Graham *medical products company executive*

Granbury
Wisler, Charles Clifton, Jr. *retired cotton oil company executive*

Houston
†Abramson, Morrie Kaplan *electronics executive*
Ahart, Jan Fredrick *electrical manufacturing company executive*
Austin, Harry Guiden *engineering and construction company executive*
Boren, William Meredith *manufacturing executive*
Boudreaux, Thomas Lee *energy company executive*
Buchanan, Dennis Michael *manufacturing and holding company executive*
Cain, Gordon A. *chemicals company executive*
Cameron, William Duncan *plastics company executive*
Cizik, Robert *manufacturing company executive*
Clemons, Ralph Hardy, Jr. *diversified manufacturing company executive*
Code, James Manley Wayne *manufacturing executive*
Crawford, David Coleman *retired diversified manufacturing company executive*
Daerr, Richard Leo, Jr. *multi-services company executive, lawyer*
Dodson, D. Keith *engineering and construction company executive*
Fabricant, Jill Diane *technology company executive*
†Fant, Eugene Robert *steel company executive*
Fort, John Franklin, III *manufacturing company executive*
French, Arthur Leeman, Jr. *process control and instrumentation company executive*
Friedkin, Thomas H. *automotive executive*
Fuchs, Bernard *apparel executive*
Galt, Barry J. *diversified company executive*
Goff, Robert Burnside *retired food company executive*
Gore, Thomas Jackson *construction executive*
Hafner, Joseph A., Jr. *food company executive*
†Haynes, William Eli *chemical company executive*
Heimbinder, Isaac *construction company executive, lawyer*
Helland, George Archibald, Jr. *equipment manufacturing company executive, former government official, management consultant*
Henning, George Thomas, Jr. *chemical company executive*
Hurwitz, Charles Edwin *manufacturing company executive*
Johnson, Frederick Dean *former food company executive*
Ketelsen, James Lee *diversified industry executive*
King, Carl B. *tool company executive*
Klausmeyer, David Michael *scientific instruments manufacturing company executive*
Levy, Gerard G. *industrial gases executive*
Loewenbaum, G. Walter, II *cement, oil and gas company executive*
Martin, J. Landis *manufacturing company executive, lawyer*
Mason, Franklin Rogers *automotive executive*
McCurdy, Larry Wayne *automotive parts company executive*
Mead, Dana George *diversified industrial manufacturing company executive*
Mendenhall, Oniel Charles *retail executive*
Menscher, Barnet Gary *steel company executive*
Nuss, Eldon Paul *casket manufacturer*
Parker, Jonathan Edward *beverage products company executive*
Peterkin, George Alexander, Jr. *marine transportation company executive*
Pfeiffer, Carl E. *manufacturing company executive*
Pieper, Wylie Bernard *diversified company executive*
†Prince, Edward R., Jr. *holding company*
Riedel, Alan Ellis *manufacturing company executive, lawyer*
Riley, Harold John, Jr. *manufacturing executive*
†Rock, Douglas Lawrence *manufacturing executive*
Roorda, John Francis, Jr. *business consultant*
†Rose, George Max *chemical company executive*
Schlindwein, James A. *food products company executive*
Sebastian, Michael James *manufacturing company executive*
Sheley, Donald Ray, Jr. *manufacturing company executive*
Snyder, Robert C. *metals company executive*
Templeton, Robert Earl *engineering and construction company executive*
Tronchon, Claude *chemical executive*
Vaughn, Donald Charles *international engineering and construction company executive*
Waggoner, James Virgil *chemicals company executive*
†Waycaster, Bill *chemicals executive*
Wilson, Carl Weldon, Jr. *construction company executive, civil engineer*
Woods, James Dudley *manufacturing company executive*
Zabcik, Daniel D. *manufacturing executive*
Zdobylak, Andrew Martin *corporate executive, homebuilder*
Zech, William Albert *manufacturing company executive*
Zerr, Emil Martin *construction company executive*

Humble
Kieta, Douglas Lloyd *construction company executive*

Hurst
Mc Keen, Chester M., Jr. *business executive*

Irving
Groussman, Dean G. *retail executive*
†Levy, Irvin L. *diversified company executive*

Longview
Folzenlogen, P. D. *petrochemical executive*

Lufkin
Denman, Joe Carter, Jr. *retired forest products company executive*
†Smith, Douglas V. *manufacturing executive, heavy*

Marshall
Poindexter, Kenneth Wayne *automobile executive*

Mesquite
Bullock, Norma Kathryn Rice *chemical research professional*

Midland
Reed, Joel Leston *diversified manufacturing company executive*
Wagner, Cyril, Jr. *metals manufacturing company executive*

Midlothian
Forward, Gordon E. *cement company executive*

Montgomery
Holman, Charles Richardson *chemical company executive*

Pasadena
Brown, Robert Griffith *chemicals executive, chemist, chemical engineer*

Pittsburg
Pilgrim, Lonnie (Bo Pilgrim) *poultry production company executive*
Voss, William R. *poultry feed company executive*

Plano
Andrews, Judy Coker *electronics company executive*
Bain, Travis Whitsett, II *manufacturing and retail executive*
Heard, David Dennis *food products company executive*
White, Michael Dennis *food manufacturing company executive*

Richardson
Edge, Harold Lee *manufacturing executive*
Hiegel, James Edward *apparel executive*
†Norris, John Windsor, Jr. *manufacturing company executive*
Orr, David E. *electronics executive*
Paluck, Robert John *electronics executive*
†Rogers, Gerald D. *electronics executive*

Richmond
Barratt, Cynthia Louise *pharmaceutical company executive*

San Antonio
Anderson, Noble *dairy products executive*
Berg, Thomas *manufacturing executive*
†Bolner, Clifton Joseph *food company executive*
Brown, Robert *manufacturing executive*
Cloud, Bruce Benjamin, Sr. *construction company executive*
DeVries, Jack *engine manufacturing executive*
Elkin, Irvin J. *milk marketing cooperative executive*
Fink, Lyman Roger *retired manufacturing executive*
Issleib, Lutz E. *beverage company executive*
Larson, Doyle Eugene *electronics company executive, retired air force officer*
Leeper, Michael Edward *retired army officer, retired corporation executive*
†Lenschow, William *food products executive*
†Lyles, Mark Bradley *high technology company executive, dentist*
Martinez, Pete R. *beverage company executive*
Prill, Arnold *diversified metal repair company executive*
Terracina, Roy David *food executive*
†Willome, John *construction executive*
Zachry, Henry Bartell, Jr. *construction company executive*

Silsbee
Ashcraft, David Lee *forest products company executive*

Stafford
Selecman, Charles Edward *business executive*

Sugar Land
Bartolo, Adolph Marion *food company executive*
Hanna, Robert C. *food products executive*
Kempner, Isaac Herbert, III *sugar company executive*

Temple
†McLane, Robert Drayton, Jr. *food products company executive*

The Woodlands
Ashley, Lawrence Atwell, Jr. *former construction executive, management consultant*
Neumann, W. Michael *chemicals executive*

Tyler
Blair, James Walter, Jr. *machinery company executive*
Warner, John Andrew *foundry executive*

Valley Mills
Evans, Clifford Jessie *manufacturing executive, land developer*

Wichita Falls
Sarni, Vincent Anthony *manufacturing company executive*

UTAH

Ogden
†Beardall, James C. *lumber company executive*
Corry, Lawrence Lee *sugar company executive*
Garrison, U. Edwin *military, space and defense products manufacturing company executive*
†Nickerson, Guy Robert *lumber company executive*
Wilson, James Rigg *aircraft manufacturing company executive*

Orem
Ashton, Alan C. *computer software company executive*

Provo
Wilson, Richard Dale *executive training, consulting company*

Salt Lake City
Anderson, Joseph Andrew, Jr. *retired apparel company executive, retail consultant*
Baker, Charles DeWitt *research and development company executive*
Cook, M(elvin) Garfield *chemical company executive*
Frary, Richard Spencer *international consulting company executive*
Gregory, Herold La Mar *chemical company administrator*
Hembree, James D. *retired chemical company executive*
Huntsman, Jon M. *chemical company executive*
Norton, Delmar Lynn *candy company executive, video executive*
Oyler, James Russell, Jr. *manufacturing executive*
Steiner, Richard Russell *conglomerate executive*

South Jordan
Bangerter, Norman Howard *building contractor, developer, former governor*

West Jordan
Sudweeks, Walter Bentley *chemicals company scientist*

VERMONT

Arlington
Nowicki, George Lucian *retired chemical company executive*

Bennington
Killen, Carroll Gorden *electronics company executive*

Brattleboro
†Cohen, Lester *food products executive*
Cohen, Richard *grocery company executive*

Danby
Mitchell, John McKearney *manufacturing company executive*

Saint Johnsbury
Trelfa, Richard Thomas *paper company executive*

South Burlington
†Pizzagalli, Angelo *construction company executive*
Pizzagalli, James *construction executive*

Vergennes
Grant, Edwin Randolph *retail and manufacturing executive*

Waterbury
Cohen, Bennett R. ("Ben" Cohen) *food products executive*
Greenfield, Jerry *food products executive*
†Holland, Robert, Jr. *food products executive*

Windsor
Furnas, Howard Earl *business executive, educator, retired government official*

VIRGINIA

Alexandria
Arensmeyer, Robert M. *pharmaceutical company executive*
Cooper, Kenneth Banks *business executive, former army officer*
Dies, Douglas Hilton *international trade consultant*
Forman, David C. *pharmaceutical company executive*
Huffman, Delton Cleon, Jr. *pharmaceuticals executive*
Keith, Donald Raymond *retired army officer, business executive*
Lantz, Phillip Edward *corporate executive, consultant*
Marsh, Robert Thomas *corporate executive, retired air force general*
Mc Lucas, John Luther *aerospace company executive*
Shuster, Robert G. *electronics company executive, consultant*
Stempler, Jack Leon *aerospace company executive*
Vander Myde, Paul Arthur *engineering services executive*

Altavista
Moore, Robert Stuart *furniture company executive*

Arlington
Bannan, Kathryn E. *pharmaceutical affairs executive*
Bennett, John Joseph *professional services company executive*
Brunson, Burlie Allen *defense contractor executive*
Cox, Henry *research company executive, research engineer*
†General, John Arthur *defense intelligence systems company executive*
Knowlton, William Allen *business executive, consultant*
Malley, Robert Joseph *manufacturing company executive*
Milburn, Richard Allan *management executive*

Bassett
Spilman, Robert Henkel *furniture company executive*

Broad Run
Hinkle, Barton Leslie *retired electronics company executive*

Broadway
Keeler, James Leonard *food products company executive*

Catlett
Scheer, Julian Weisel *business executive, author*

Chantilly
Miller, Donald Eugene *aerospace electronics executive*
†Winn, Paul T. *electronics executive*

Charlottesville
Haigh, Robert William *business administration educator*
Landel, Robert Davis *business administration educator, consultant*
MacAvoy, Thomas Coleman *glass manufacturing executive, educator*
Norgren, C. Neil *retired manufacturing company executive*
Rader, Louis T. *corporation executive, educator*
Rotch, William *business administration educator*
Tewksbury, Charles G. *textiles technology executive*
†Wilver, Wayne R. *electronics executive*

Danville
Barker, Willie G., Jr. *agriculture executive*
Dibrell, Louis Nelson, III *tobacco company executive*

Dayton
†Willertsen, Steven *food products executive*

Dumfries
Heiser, Joseph Miller, Jr. *retired army officer, business executive, author*

Fairfax
Benton, Robert *automotive executive*

Edwards, James Owen *engineering and construction company executive*
Hatch, Robert Winslow *food and furniture corporation executive*
Moore, Robert Edward *electronics executive*
Sheehan, Edward James *technical consultant, former government official*
Uffelman, Malcolm Rucj *electronics company executive, electrical engineer*
West, Bob *pharmaceutical company executive*
Willauer, Whiting Russell *systems integration company executive*

Fairfax Station
Starry, Donn Albert *former aerospace company executive, former army officer*

Falls Church
Mellor, James Robb *electronics executive*
Oesterling, Wendy Lee *sales and marketing executive*
Post, Howard Allen *forest industry specialist*
†Walters, Victor *holding company executive*

Glen Allen
Fife, William Franklin *retired drug company executive*
†Minor, George Gilmer, Jr. *drug and hospital supply company executive*
†Minor, George Gilmer, III *drug and hospital supply company executive*
Murphey, Robert Stafford *pharmaceutical company executive*

Great Falls
MacGowan, Charles Frederic *retired chemical company executive*

Hampton
Holloway, Paul Fayette *aerospace executive*

Harrisonburg
Darazsdi, James Joseph *food processing executive*
Muth, George Edward *former art and drafting supply company executive*

Heathsville
Winkel, Raymond Norman *avionics manufacturing executive, retired naval officer*

Herndon
Epstein, Samuel D. *electronics executive*
†Gorog, William Francis *corporate executive*
†Guerreri, Carl Natale *electronic company executive*

Hopewell
Leake, Preston Hildebrand *tobacco research executive*

Manassas
Geerdes, James (Divine Geerdes) *chemical company executive*
Parrish, Frank Jennings *food company executive*

Marion
Hadley, Stanton Thomas *international manufacturing and marketing company executive, lawyer*

Mc Lean
Anderson, David Lloyd *defense industry executive*
Dempsey, James Raymon *industrial executive*
Franklin, Jude Eric *electronics executive*
Mars, Forrest E., Jr. *candy company executive*
Mars, John F. *candy company executive*
Mehuron, William Otto *electronics company executive*
Ryan, John Franklin *multinational company executive*
†Schar, Dwight C. *construction company executive*
†Warga, John *construction company executive*

Newport News
Banks, Charles A. *manufacturing executive*
Becker, Ivan Endre *retired plastics company executive*
Fricks, William Peavy *shipbuilding company executive*
Luke, James Phillip *manufacturing executive*
Peebles, David L. *light manufacturing executive*
Smith, Walter Tilford *shipbuilding company executive*

Norfolk
†Grant, Walter Leroy *food products executive*
Julian, Michael *grocery company executive*
Liles, Jack S. *construction company executive*

Reston
Bannister, Dan R. *professional and technical services company executive*
Christ, Thomas Warren *electronics research and development company executive, sociologist*
Lewis, Arthur Dee *corporation executive*
Lewis, Gene Evans *retired medical equipment company executive*
Murdoch, Robert Waugh *cement and construction materials company executive*
Piecuch, John M. *manufacturing company executive*
Rose, Michel *construction materials company executive*
†Spierkel, Greg *electronics executive*
Zigel, James M. *aircraft manufacturing executive*

Richmond
Barry, Timothy Francis *construction company executive*
Bourke, William Oliver *retired metal company executive*
Brandt, Yale M. *metal products executive*
Bruckart, Walter E. *electronics company executive*
Bunzl, Rudolph Hans *retired diversified manufacturing company executive*
Dresser, Paul Alton, Jr. *paper and forest products executive*
Easterling, William K. *plastics and chemicals executive*
Estridge, Ronald B. *paper company executive*
Fox, Joseph Carter *pulp and paper manufacturing company executive*
Gottwald, Bruce Cobb *chemical company executive*
Gottwald, Floyd Dewey, Jr. *chemical company executive*
Gottwald, John D. *manufacturing executive*
Hagan, Randall Lee *manufacturing executive*
Helwig, Arthur Woods *chemical company executive*
Holder, Richard Gibson *metal products executive*
Jezuit, Leslie James *manufacturing company executive*
Jones, David Eugene *pharmaceutical company executive*
Lindholm, John Victor *business executive*
Nielsen, Steven B. *medical products executive*
†Noonan, John Michael *aluminum company executive*
Olsson, Sture Gordon *manufacturing executive*
Pauley, Stanley Frank *manufacturing company executive*
Peery, Troy Alfred, Jr. *home furnishing company executive*
Pendleton, Eugene Barbour, Jr. *business executive*
Reynolds, David Parham *metals company executive*
Reynolds, Randolph Nicklas *aluminum company executive*
Robins, Edwin Claiborne, Sr. *retired pharmaceutical company executive*
Rogers, James Edward *paper company executive*
†Sauer, Conrad Frederick, IV *food products executive*
Sweeney, Arthur Hamilton, Jr. *metal manufacturing executive, retired army officer*
Taylor, Julian Howard *metals company executive*
Thorp, Benjamin A., III *paper manufacturing company executive*
Walker, Charles B. *chemicals company executive*
Watts, Robert Glenn *retired pharmaceutical company executive*
Whelan, Karen Mae Leppo *manufacturing executive*
Williams, Robert C. *paper company executive*

Roanoke
Edwards, J. Randolph *medical products executive*

Ruckersville
†Minkle, L. Steven *manufacturing executive, light*

Smithfield
Luter, Joseph Williamson, III *meat packing and processing company executive*

Spring Grove
Daniel, Robert Williams, Jr. *business executive, former congressman*

Suffolk
Birdsong, George Yancy *manufacturing company executive*

Vienna
Savoca, Antonio Litterio *technology company executive*

Virginia Beach
Alexander, William Powell *food products executive*

Williamsburg
Godwin, R. Wayne *chemicals company executive*
†Pinotti, Joseph R. *light manufacturing executive*

Winchester
†Bryant, Arthur Herbert, II *rubber and plastics company executive*
Holland, James Tulley *plastic products company executive*
Murtagh, John Edward *chemist, alcohol production consultant*

WASHINGTON

Anacortes
Randolph, Carl Lowell *chemical company executive*

Auburn
Bingham, Charles W. *wood products company executive*
Creighton, John W., Jr. *forest products company executive*
Weyerhaeuser, George Hunt *forest products company executive*

Bellevue
Fluke, John Maurice, Jr. *electrical equipment manufacturing company executive*
Hamachek, Tod Russell *manufacturing executive*
Hovind, David J. *manufacturing company executive*
Pigott, Charles McGee *transportation equipment manufacturing executive*
Puckett, Allen Weare *health care information systems executive*

Bellingham
Bestwick, Warren William *retired construction company executive*
Helsell, Robert M. *construction executive*

Camas
Hanby, John Estes, Jr. *technology management executive*

East Sound
Anders, William Alison *aerospace and defense manufacturing executive*

Everett
†Smith, John R. *electronics executive*
†Wambolt, Ronald Ralph *electronics company executive*
†Winn, George Michael *electrical equipment company executive*

Federal Way
Curtis, Arnold Bennett *lumber company executive*

Friday Harbor
Daum, David Ernest *machinery manufacturing company executive*

Issaquah
Tenenbaum, Michael *steel company executive*
Wainwright, Paul Edward Blech *construction company executive*

Kennewick
Wistisen, Martin J. *agricultural business executive*

Kent
Goo, Abraham Meu Sen *retired aircraft company executive*
Hebeler, Henry Koester *retired aerospace and electronics executive*
Sourapas, Steve James *manufacturing executive*

Kirkland
Bernard, James William *chemical distribution company executive*
Parrish, John Brett *manufacturing executive*

Longview
Wollenberg, Richard Peter *paper manufacturing company executive*

Medina
Schlotterbeck, Walter Albert *manufacturing company executive, lawyer*

Mercer Island
Gould, Alvin R. *international business executive*

Nondland
Pollack, Joseph *diversified company executive*

Pasco
Yoshino, George *food products executive*

Port Ludlow
Gullander, Werner Paul *retired consultant, retired corporate executive*

Redmond
Darnell, Larry *plant manager*
Martin, Richard Otto *medical device company executive*
Sennstrom, John Harold *manufacturing company executive*
†Walsh, Patrick J. *medical products executive*

Richland
Nolan, John Edward *retired electrical corporation executive*

Seattle
Albrecht, Richard Raymond *airplane manufacturing company executive, lawyer*
Behnke, Carl Gilbert *beverage franchise executive*
Hoerni, Jean Amédée *electronics consultant*
Holtby, Kenneth Fraser *aircraft manufacturing company consultant*
†Johnson, Raymond A. *apparel executive*
Jones, Frank Ray *biotechnology company executive, researcher*
Leland, David D. *timber company executive*
†Nordstrom, James F. *department store executive*
Reed, William G., Jr. *paper company executive*
Schoenfeld, Walter Edwin *manufacturing company executive*
Shrontz, Frank Anderson *airplane manufacturing executive*
Stear, Edwin Byron *corporate executive*
Strand, Ray Walter *general contractor*
Wheaton, Harry James *corporate executive*
†Whitacre, John *apparel executive*
Wiborg, James Hooker *chemicals distribution company executive*

Tacoma
†Belluschi, Peter Guido *retired wood products executive*
Carlson, Frederick Paul *electronics executive*
Ferris, James Leonard *paper company executive*
Hill, Steven Richard *business executive*
Hutchings, George Henry *food company executive*
Meyer, Richard Schlomer *food company executive*
Stockdale, Ronald Allen *grocery company executive*
Sutherland, Douglass B. *tent and awning company executive, mayor*

Washougal
Vogel, Ronald Bruce *food products executive*

WEST VIRGINIA

Charleston
Gunnoe, Nancy Lavenia *food executive, artist*
Wehrle, Henry Bernard, Jr. *diversified manufacturing company executive*

Nitro
Magaw, Roger Wayne *construction company executive*

Parkersburg
Cochran, Douglas Eugene *building products company executive*
Wakley, James Turner *manufacturing company executive*

Ravenswood
Meyers, Gerald A. *metal products executive*

Weirton
Elish, Herbert *manufacturing company executive*

Wheeling
Chbosky, Fred G. *steel company executive*
Exley, Ben, III *pharmaceutical company executive*
Good, Laurance Frederic *company executive*
Wareham, James Lyman *steel company executive*

WISCONSIN

Appleton
Barlow, F(rank) John *mechanical contracting company executive*
Boldt, Oscar Charles *construction company executive*
Buchanan, Robert Campbell *corporate professional*
Rankin, Arthur David *paper company executive*
Schumaker, Dale H. *paper manufacturing company executive*
†Spanbauer, James *chemicals executive*
†Wirth, Lawrence *chemicals executive*

Arcadia
†Wanek, Ronald G. *manufacturing executive*

Baraboo
Brooks, Edward *dairy products company executive*
Storhoff, Donald C. *agricultural products company executive*

Beloit
Sovey, William Pierre *manufacturing company executive*

Brookfield
Corby, Francis Michael, Jr. *manufacturing company executive*
DeLuca, Donald Paul *manufacturing company executive*
Grade, Jeffery T. *manufacturing company executive*
†Grove, Richard Charles *power tool company executive*
McKay, John A. *mining equipment manufacturing executive*

Cedarburg
Schaefer, Gordon Emory *food company executive*

Dodgeville
Comer, Gary C. *apparel company executive*

Eau Claire
Berney, Joseph Henry *appliance manufacturing company executive*
†Menard, John R. *lumber company executive*

Fond Du Lac
Chamberlain, Robert Glenn *retired tool manufacturing executive*

Fort Atkinson
Nesbitt, Arthur Wallace *mail order and manufacturing executive*

Green Bay
Backer, David F. *packing company executive*
De Meuse, Donald Howard *paper products manufacturing executive*
Hempel, Kathleen Jane *paper company executive*
Kemerling, James Lee *paper company executive*
Kress, George F. *packaging company executive*
†Resch, Richard J. *furniture manufacturing executive*
Rowley, John F. *manufacturing executive*
†Walsh, Eric *food products executive*

Hartford
Lopina, Lawrence Thomas *manufacturing executive*

Kenosha
Cornog, Robert A. *manufacturing executive*
Huml, Donald Scott *manufacturing company executive*
Jacobson, Dennis Leonard *business executive*
†Morrone, Frank *electronic manufacturing executive*
Steigerwaldt, Donna Wolf *clothing manufacturing company executive*
†Vignieri, Charles Joseph *meat packing company executive*

Kewaskum
†Peterson, Lowell N. *light manufacuring executive*
†Reigle, James D. *manufacturing executive*

Kohler
Kohler, Herbert Vollrath, Jr. *diversified manufacturing company executive*

La Crosse
Cleary, Russell George *retired brewery executive*
Eber, David Henry *manufacturing company executive*
Gelatt, Charles Daniel *manufacturing company executive*

Madison
Felten, Edward Joseph *business executive accountant*
Frautschi, Walter Albert *contract and publications printing company executive*
Lonnebotn, Trygve *battery company executive*
Shain, Irving *retired chemical company executive and university chancellor*
Thompson, Bjorn J. *food products company executive, mechanical engineer*

Manitowish Waters
Laidig, William Rupert *retired paper company executive*

Manitowoc
†Butler, Fred M. *manufacturing executive, heavy, water transportation executive*

Marion
Simpson, Vinson Raleigh *manufacturing company executive*

Medford
Sebold, Duane David *food manufacturing executive*

Menasha
Baird, Roger Allen *retired corporation executive*
†Cianciola, Charles Sal *paper manufacturing company executive*

Mequon
Dohmen, Frederick Hoeger *retired wholesale drug company executive*

Milwaukee
Beals, Vaughn Le Roy, Jr. *motorcycle and recreational vehicle manufacturing executive*
Bishop, Charles Joseph *manufacturing company executive*
Bomberger, Glen R. *manufacturing company executive*
Burgess, Richard Ball *food products executive*
Burns, Ronald James *manufacturing equipment company executive*
Chapman, William Paul *retired automatic control manufacturing company executive*
Davis, Thomas William *steel industry manufacturing executive*

Feitler, Robert *shoe company executive*
Hopkins, Edward Donald *manufacturing executive*
†Hudson, Katherine Mary *manufacturing company executive*
Jacobs, Burleigh Edmund *foundry executive*
†Johnston, Michael Francis *battery manufacturing company executive*
Keuler, Roland Leo *retired shoe company executive*
Keyes, James Henry *manufacturing company executive*
Killian, William Paul *industrial corporate executive*
MacDonough, John N. *beverage company executive*
Manning, Kenneth Paul *food company executive*
Marringa, Jacques Louis *manufacturing company executive*
Martin, Vincent Lionel *manufacturing company executive*
Morris, G. Ronald *automotive executive*
Mosher, George Allan *manufacturing company executive*
†Nagarkatti, Jai Prakash *chemical company executive*
Novak, Victor Anthony *semi-retired manufacturing company executive*
Osborn, Guy A. *food products company executive*
O'Toole, Robert Joseph *manufacturing company executive*
Parker, Charles Walter, Jr. *consultant, retired equipment company executive*
†Rich, Robert C. *manufacturing executive*
Sanderson, Gary Warner *food company executive*
†Smith, Everett G. *chemicals executive*
Sterner, Frank Maurice *industrial executive*
Stratton, Frederick Prescott, Jr. *manufacturing executive*
Taylor, Donald *retired manufacturing company executive*
Yontz, Kenneth Fredric *medical and chemical company executive*

Neenah
Bergstrom, Dedric Waldemar *retired paper company executive*
Brophy, George Thomas *building products company executive*
Parker, Richard E. *building products manufacturing company executive*
Shepard, D. C. *wood products manufacturing company executive*

Oshkosh
Drebus, Richard William *pharmaceutical company executive*
Goodson, Raymond Eugene *automotive executive*
Hulsebosch, Charles Joseph *truck manufacturing company executive*

Pewaukee
Dickson, John R. *food products company executive, dairy products company executive*

Port Edwards
Veneman, Gerard Earl *paper company executive*

Port Washington
Frazier, Warner Carlisle *manufacturing company executive*

Racine
Batten, Michael Ellsworth *manufacturing company executive*
Campbell, Edward Joseph *retired machinery company executive*
Carpenter, Richard M. *chemical company executive*
Gunnerson, Robert Mark *manufacturing company executive, accountant, lawyer*
Johnson, Samuel Curtis *wax company executive*
Konz, Gerald Keith *manufacturing company executive*
Richter, Earl Edward *manufacturing company executive*
Savage, Richard T. *manufacturing company executive*

Spring Green
Sisson, Everett Arnold *industrial developer, business executive*

Waukesha
Huggins, Marion Dixon, Jr. *manufacturing company executive*
Norris, Robert F. *food products company executive*
†Platner, John Leland *process equipment company executive*

Waupun
†Sperger, Courtland *food products executive*

Wausau
Slayton, John Arthur *electric motor manufacturing executive*

Wisconsin Rapids
Engelhardt, LeRoy A. *retired paper company executive*
Mead, George Wilson, II *paper company executive*

WYOMING

Afton
Call, Reuel *corporate executive*

Casper
Jozwik, Francis Xavier *agricultural business executive*
Stroock, Thomas Frank *manufacturing company executive*

Jackson
Gordon, Stephen Maurice *manufacturing company executive, rancher*

Sheridan
Jones, Nancy C. *construction executive*

TERRITORIES OF THE UNITED STATES

PUERTO RICO

San Juan
del Valle, Manuel Luis *distillery executive*

CANADA

ALBERTA

Calgary
Child, Arthur James Edward *food company executive*
Gordon, Lorne Bertram *corporate executive*
Southern, Ronald D. *diversified corporation executive*

Edmonton
Bateman, William Maxwell *retired construction company executive*
O'Briain, Niall P. *wood products company executive*
Stollery, Robert *construction company executive*

Fort Saskatchewan
Weir, D. Robert *company executive*

BRITISH COLUMBIA

North Vancouver
Gibbs, David George *retired food processing company executive*

Vancouver
Bender, Graham I. *forest products executive*
Bentley, Peter John Gerald *forest industry company executive*
Buell, Thomas Allan *lumber company executive*
Donald, Ian *wood products company executive*
Grunder, Arthur Neil *forest products industry executive*
Knudsen, Conrad Calvert *corporate executive*
Smith, Raymond Victor *paper products manufacturing executive*
Solloway, C. Robert *forest products company executive*

MANITOBA

Winnipeg
Bulman, W. John A. *printing company executive*
MacKenzie, George Allan *diversified company executive*
Searle, Stewart A. *transportation equipment holding company executive*

NEW BRUNSWICK

Fredericton
Grotterod, Knut *retired paper company executive*

Moncton
Walker, Tennyson A. *corporation executive*

NOVA SCOTIA

Halifax
†Pincock, Douglas George *electronics company executive*

Lunenburg
Morrow, James Benjamin *retired sea products company executive*

North Sydney
Nickerson, Jerry Edgar Alan *manufacturing executive*

Stellarton
Gogan, James Wilson *corporate executive*
Rowe, Allan Duncan *food products executive*
Sobey, David Frank *food company executive*

ONTARIO

Brampton
Greenhough, John Hardman *business forms company executive*
Prevost, Edward James *paint manufacturing executive*
Toole, David George *pulp and paper products executive*

Cambridge
Turnbull, Robert Scott *manufacturing company executive*
White, Joseph Charles *manufacturing and retailing company executive*

Concord
Gingl, Manfred *manufacturing company executive*

Fort Erie
Watson, Stewart Charles *construction company executive*

Galt
Dobbie, George Herbert *textile manufacturing executive*

Hamilton
McMulkin, Francis John *steel company executive*
Priestner, Edward Bernard *manufacturing company executive*
Telmer, Frederick Harold *steel products manufacturing executive*

Kitchener
Pollock, John Albon *broadcasting and manufacturing company executive*

Markham
Burns, H. Michael *health care company executive*
Stronach, Frank *automobile parts manufacturing executive*

Mississauga
Barkin, Martin *pharmaceutical company executive, physician*
Johnson, Charles E., Jr. *paper company executive*
Lewis, William Leonard *food products executive*
MacNaughton, John David Francis *aerospace company executive*
Strachan, Graham *pharmaceutical company executive*

North York
Lanthier, Ronald Ross *retired manufacturing company executive*
Wleugel, John Peter *manufacturing company executive*

Owen Sound
Adams, John David Vessot *manufacturing company executive*

Rexdale
Lutgens, Harry Gerardus *food company executive*

Toronto
Arnold, Neil David *farm and industrial equipment company executive*
Blundell, William Richard Charles *electric company executive*
Cameron, Peter Alfred Gordon *corporate executive*
Cohen, Marshall *diversified international corporation executive*
Connell, Philip Francis *food industry executive*
Dale, Robert Gordon *business executive*
Eagles, Stuart Ernest *business executive*
Eisen, Leonard *food and retail company executive*
Freeman, Graham P. M. *food company executive*
Goodrich, Maurice Keith *business forms, systems and services company executive*
Griffin, Scott *manufacturing executive*
Horsey, William Grant *corporation executive*
Koken, Bernd Krafft *forest products company executive*
Lowe, Donald Cameron *corporate executive*
Mercier, Eileen Ann *management consultant*
Oberlander, Ronald Y. *paper manufacturing company executive*
Oland, Sidney M. *brewing and entertainment company executive*
Porter, Ivan *company executive*
Rusnell, Joanne D. *brewery, entertainment business executive*
Seagram, Norman Meredith *corporate executive*
Soler, Arthur R. *food products executive*
Thomas, Alan Richard *natural resources products executive*
Turner, Peter Merrick *retired manufacturing company executive*
Vance, James *retired manufacturing company executive, lawyer*
Van Houten, Stephen H. *manufacturing company executive*

Unionville
Suddick, Patrick Joseph *defense systems company executive*

Willowdale
McDonald, William Henry *financial executive*

Windsor
Kippen, Richard Marlin *wine and spirits company executive*
Landry, G. Yves *automotive company executive*

QUEBEC

Athelstan
Ness, Owen McGregor *retired aluminum company executive*

Longueuil
Caplan, L(azarus) David *manufacturing company executive*
Smith, Elvie Lawrence *corporate director*

Montreal
Ashby, Roger Arthur *pulp and paper products company executive*
Beauchamp, Jacques *wood products executive*
Bougie, Jacques *metal processing executive*
Bronfman, Charles Rosner *distillery executive*
Gagné, Paul E. *paper company executive*
Hantho, Charles Harold *textile executive*
Herling, Michael *steel company executive*
Ivanier, Paul *steel products manufacturing company executive*
Molson, Eric H. *beverage company executive*
Nadeau, Bertin F. *diversified company executive*
Pal, Prabir Kumar *aluminium company executive*
Pinard, Raymond R. *pulp and paper consultant*
Plourde, Gerard *company executive*
Poissant, Charles-Albert *paper manufacturing company executive*
Redfern, John D. *manufacturing company executive*
Royer, Raymond *transportation equipment manufacturing company executive*
Rugeroni, Ian *aluminum company executive*
Schuele, Alban Wilhelm *chemical company executive*
Simons, John H. *electronics manufacturing company executive*
Smith, James Hamilton *paper, packaging, construction material and chemicals company executive*
Williams, Paul H. *textile executive*

Outremont
Gouin, Serge *corporate executive*
Larose, Roger *former pharmaceutical company executive, former university administrator*

Pointe Claire
Wrist, Peter Ellis *pulp and paper company executive*

Saint Jerome
Rolland, Lucien G. *paper company executive*

Saint Lambert
Brossard, Maurice *biotechnology company executive*

Saint Laurent
Kivenko, Kenneth *aerospace industry executive*

Verdun
Ferguson, Michael John *electronics and communications educator*

SASKATCHEWAN

Regina
Dalla-Vicenza, Mario Joseph *steel company financial executive*
Phillips, Roger *steel company executive*

Saskatoon
Carr, Roy Arthur *agricultural products applied research, development & communication processing organization executive*

MEXICO

Mexico City
Brown, Kenneth Charles *manufacturing company executive*

AUSTRALIA

Melbourne
Lawson, Francis Colin *chemical company executive*

BAHAMAS

Nassau
Dingman, Michael David *industrial company executive*

BELGIUM

Antwerp
De Craene, Jacques Maria *plastics company executive, retired judge, arbitrator*

Brussels
Loutrel, Claude Yves *corporate official*

Chaumont Gistoux
Holleweg dit Wegman, Willy *management expert, educator, entrepreneurship development specialist*

ENGLAND

Ascot
Grubman, Wallace Karl *chemical company executive*

Berkshire
Hall, Arnold Alexander *aeronautical, mechanical and electrical executive*

Brentford
Wendt, Henry, III *pharmaceutical company executive*

East Sussex
Wilson, Leroy *retired glass manufacturing company executive*

London
Bates, Malcolm Rowland *corporate director*
Dalby, Alan James *pharmaceutical company executive*
†Gleason, Howard Wesley *consulting company executive*
Greener, Anthony *beverage company executive*
†Huismans, Sipko *diversified company executive*
Shaw, Sir Neil McGowan *sugar, cereal and starch refining company executive*
Sheehy, Sir Patrick *manufacturing and service company executive*
Taylor, Jonathan Francis *agribusiness executive*

Malmesbury
Shober, Edward Wharton *bioscience company executive*

Middlesex
Finlay, Robert Derek *food company executive*

Poole
Stokes, Donald Gresham *vehicle company executive*

Richmond
Fraser, Campbell *business consultant*

Suffolk
Clement, John *food products company executive*

Weybridge Surrey
Olney, Robert C. *diversified products manufacturing executive*

FINLAND

Helsinki
Salonen, Heikki Olavi *corporate executive*

FRANCE

Courbevoie
Desmarescaux, Philippe *chemical company executive, engineer*

Genlis
van Raalte, John A. *research and engineering management executive*

Paris
Collomb, Bertrand Pierre *cement company executive*
Lecerf, Olivier Maurice Marie *construction company executive*

Saint Quentin
†Poupart-LaFarge, Olivier Marie *financial executive*

Sevres
†Asscher, Jean Claude *electronic executive*

GERMANY

Munich
†von Pierer, Heinrich *manufacturing executive*

HONG KONG

Hong Kong
Sherrill, Joseph Harlan, Jr. *tobacco company executive*
Wong, Wing Keung *trading, electronics company executive, physician*

Wanchai
van Hoften, James Dougal Adrianus *business executive, former astronaut*

IRELAND

Arklow
Barber, Jerry Randel *medical device company executive*

ISRAEL

Haifa
Galil, Uzia *electronics company executive*

ITALY

Rome
Lynch, Edward Stephen *corporate executive*

Turin
Agnelli, Giovanni *automotive executive*

JAPAN

Tokyo
Franklin, William Emery *lumber company executive*
Ishikawa, Rokuro *construction company executive*
Johnson, Keith Gilbert *heavy equipment company executive*
Kaku, Ryuzaburo *precision instruments manufacturing company executive*
Makino, Shojiro (Mike Makino) *chemicals executive*
Ohga, Norio *electronics executive*
Smith, Robert Lee *photographic company executive*

Toyota Aichi
Toyoda, Eiji *automobile manufacturing company executive*

Yamashina
†Inamori, Kazuo *chemicals executive*

LUXEMBOURG

Luxembourg
Kasperczyk, Jürgen *business executive, government official, educator*

NEW CALEDONIA

Noumea
Curlook, Walter *mining company executive*

SCOTLAND

Edinburgh
Miller, James *construction company executive*

SINGAPORE

Singapore
Wilhelm, Ralph Vincent, Jr. *electronics company executive, ceramics engineer*

SPAIN

Madrid
Feltenstein, Harry David, Jr. *chemical executive*

SWEDEN

Linkoping
Schröder, Harald Bertel *aerospace industry executive*

Stockholm
Scharp, Anders *manufacturing company executive*

SWITZERLAND

Basel
†Moret, Marc *chemicals executive*

Fribourg
Hatschek, Rudolf Alexander *electronics company executive*

Zurich
Barnevik, Percy Nils *electrical company executive*

TAIWAN

Taipei
Ch'in, Michael Kuo-hsing *international conference and travel management executive*

ADDRESS UNPUBLISHED

Adams, William White *retired manufacturing company executive*
Adelman, Robert Paul *retired construction company executive, lawyer*
Albino, George Robert *business executive*
Alig, Frank Douglas Stalnaker *construction company executive*
Alm, John Richard *beverage company executive*
Amini, Bijan Khajehnouri *technology company executive*
Anderer, Joseph Henry *textile company executive*
Anderson, Fletcher Neal *chemical executive*
Anderson, Joseph Norman *executive consultant, former food company executive, former college president*
Andersson, Craig Remington *retired chemical company executive*
Andreuzzi, Denis *chemical company executive*
Andrews, William Frederick *manufacturing executive*
Angiuoli, Ralph *tobacco company executive*
Anspach, Herbert Kephart *retired appliance company executive, patent attorney*
Archibald, Nolan D. *household and industrial products company executive*
Armstrong, John Allan *business machine company research executive*
Arthur, Lloyd *agricultural products company executive*
Aschauer, Charles Joseph, Jr. *corporate director, former company executive*
Atkisson, Curtis Trumbull, Jr. *auto parts company executive*
Auriemma, Louis Francis *printing company executive*
Azarnoff, Daniel Lester *pharmaceutical company consultant*
Ballhaus, William Francis *retired scientific instruments company executive*
Bane, Keith James *electronics industry executive*
†Banus, Peter Mario *healthcare executive*
Barca, George Gino *winery executive, finanial investor*
Barnebey, Kenneth Alan *food company executive*
Barron, Charles Elliott *retired electronics executive*
Bass, Robert Olin *manufacturing executive*
Beadle, John Grant *manufacturing company executive*
Beighey, Lawrence Jerome *packaging company executive*
Belle Isle, Albert Pierre *electronics company executive*
Benmark, Leslie Ann *chemical company executive*
Bennett, Richard Thomas *retired manufacturing executive*
Beringer, William Ernst *retired electrical equipment executive, lawyer*
Berra, Robert Louis *chemicals consultant*
Bierwirth, John Cocks *retired aerospace manufacturing executive*
Biggs, Arthur Edward *retired chemical manufacturing company executive*
Birkenstock, James Warren *business machine manufacturing company executive*
Blair, Charles Melvin *manufacturing company executive, scientist*
Blanchard, Richard Frederick *construction executive*
Bloom, Frank *corporation executive, consultant*
†Boe, Ralph Jacob *carpet manufacturing executive*
Borten, William H. *research company executive*
Bossier, Albert Louis, Jr. *shipbuilding company executive*
†Boyce, Michael Ross *inorganic chemical and mineral executive*
Brancato, Leo John *manufacturing company executive*
Brengel, Fred Lenhardt *manufacturing company executive*
Brinckerhoff, Richard Charles *retired manufacturing company executive*
Brodie, Theodore Hamilton *construction company executive*
Brooker, Robert Elton, Jr. *manufacturing company executive*
Brooks, William Sidney *construction executive*
Brown, Barton *retired automotive company executive*
Burch, Hamlin Doughty, III *retired sheet metal professional*
Burlant, William Jack *retired chemical company executive*
Butler, Jack Fairchild *semiconductors company executive*
Buxton, Winslow Hurlbert *diversified manufacturing company executive*
†Calcaterra, Edward Lee *construction company executive*
Calvert, James Francis *manufacturing company executive, retired admiral*
Camisa, George Lincoln *beverage company executive*
†Campbell, John A. *lumber company executive*
Campbell, Richard Alden *electronics company executive*
Carmody, Thomas Roswell *business products company executive*
Carpenter, Myron Arthur *manufacturing company executive*
Carter, Joseph Edwin *former nickel company executive, writer*
Chamberlain, George Arthur, III *manufacturing company executive, venture capitalist*
Chaykin, Robert Leroy *manufacturing and marketing executive*
Chen, Di *electro-optic company executive, consultant*
Chmielinski, Edward Alexander *electronics company executive*
Chryssis, George Christopher *business executive*
Closset, Gerard Paul *forest products company executive*
Clouston, Ross Neal *retired food and related products company executive*
Cohn, Leonard Allan *retired chemical company executive*
Colton, Nelson Burton *industrial company executive*
Cooley, James William *retired executive researcher*
Copper, James Robert *manufacturing company executive*
Corddry, Paul I(mlay) *retired food products company executive*
Correnti, John David *steel company executive*
Costello, James Joseph *retired electrical manufacturing company executive*
Cox, John Francis *retired cosmetic company executive*
Cox, Wilford Donald *retired food company executive*
Craft, Edmund Coleman *automotive parts manufacturing company executive*
Cramer, William F. *capitol goods executive*
Crean, John Gale *hat manufacturer*
Cross, Alexander Dennis *business consultant, former chemical and pharmaceutical executive*
Cull, Robert Robinette *electric products manufacturing company executive*
Culwell, Charles Louis *retired manufacturing company executive*
Cunnane, James Joseph *manufacturing executive*
Czapor, Edward P. *automobile company executive*
Czarnecki, Gerald Milton *manufacturing executive*
D'Agostino, Stephen I. *bottling company executive*
Daly, William James *retired health industry distributing company executive*
Danis, Peter G., Jr. *office products company executive*
Daugherty, Alfred Clark *manufacturing company executive*
Davis, Darrell L. *automotive executive*
Decker, Gilbert Felton *manufacturing company executive*
de Kruif, Jack H. *manufacturing executive*
Denisco, Ralph Andrew *ice cream industry executive*
Derbes, Daniel William *manufacturing executive*
Diener, Royce *corporate director, retired health care services company executive*
DiLiddo, Bart A. *chemical engineer, business executive, consultant*
Di Marco, Gabriel Robert *tobacco company executive*
Dobelis, George *manufacturing company executive*
Dohrmann, Russell William *manufacturing company executive*
Dole, Robert Paul *retired appliance manufacturing company executive*
Doskocil, Larry *food company executive*
Dowden, Albert Ricker *corporate executive, lawyer*
Doyle, John Laurence *manufacturing company executive*
Dozier, Glenn Joseph *medical, surgical products distribution executive*
Dragon, William, Jr. *footwear and apparel company executive*
Dressler, David Charles *retired aerospace company executive*
Drew, Walter Harlow *retired paper manufacturing company executive*
Driscoll, William Michael *corporation executive*
Durden, Charles Dennis *former manufacturing company executive, consultant*
Durham, G. Robert *diversified manufacturing company executive*
Durr, Robert Joseph *construction firm executive, mechanical engineer*
Earle, Arthur Percival *textile executive*
Eberle, Charles Edward *paper and consumer products executive*
Ellsworth, Robert F. *manufacturing executive*
Elverum, Gerard William, Jr. *retired electronic and diversified company executive*
Ely, Paul C., Jr. *electronics company executive*
Erdeljac, Daniel Joseph *manufacturing company executive*
Ericson, Rolf Eric George *manufacturing company executive*
Evanoff, George C. *biotechnology company executive*
Fein, Seymour Howard *pharmaceutical executive*
Feinberg, Herbert *apparel and beverage executive*
Fenger, Manfred *retired manufacturing executive*
Ferris, Michael J(ames) *chemical company executive*
Fife, William J., Jr. *metal products executive*
Finkel, David *medical products executive*
Finney, Robert G. *electronics company executive*
Fitch, Robert McLellan *business and technology consultant*
Fitch, Steven Joseph *retired chemicals executive*
Flaschen, Steward Samuel *high technology company executive*
Flitcraft, Richard Kirby, II *former chemical company executive*
Florescue, Barry William *business executive*
Ford, Jerry Lee *products company executive*
Fossier, Mike Walter *consultant, retired electronics company executive*
Foster, Edson L. *retired mining and manufacturing company executive, consultant*
Foster, Paul David, Jr. *agribusiness executive*
Frame, Russell William *retired electronics executive*
Frawley, Patrick Joseph, Jr. *health care executive*
French, Clarence Levi, Jr. *retired shipbuilding company executive*
Frieling, Gerald Harvey, Jr. *specialty steel company executive*
Fritz, Rene Eugene, Jr. *manufacturing executive*
Fuller, James Chester Eedy *retired chemical company executive*
Geoppinger, William Anthony *meat processing company executive*
Georgas, John William *beverage manufacturing company executive*
George, William Ickes *manufacturing company executive*
†Gilgore, Sheldon Gerald *pharmaceutical products company executive*
Gillespie, Robert James *manufacturing company executive*
Gillette, Stanley C. *apparel manufacturing company executive*
Gilreath, Warren Dean *retired packaging company executive*
Giordano, Richard Vincent *chemicals executive*
Godino, Rino Lodovico *retired petroleum and chemical company executive*
Goldsmith, Robert Holloway *manufacturing company executive*
Good, Daniel James *manufacturing executive*
†Gostin, Judson Jacob *electronics company executive*
Grandy, James Frederick *retired electronics business executive, consultant*
Grauman, Robert A. *healthcare executive*
Gray, Donna Mae *former agricultural products executive, bookkeeper*
Gray, Richard Alexander, Jr. *retired chemical company executive*
Green, David Thomas *retired surgical company research and development executive, inventor*
Greenberg, Milton *corporation executive*
Greenblatt, Sherwin *manufacturing company executive*
Gregg, Michael W. *manufacturing executive*
Griffith, Daniel Boyd *automotive products executive*
Grubiak, James Frank *chewing gum executive*
Gulcher, Robert Harry *aircraft company executive*
Gurney, Daniel Sexton *race car manufacturing company executive, racing team executive*
Hager, Robert Worth *retired aerospace company executive*
Hall, Anthony Robert *pharmaceuticals and consumer products company executive*
Hammond, Robert Lee *retired feed company executive*
Hanes, John T. *food products executive*
Harbison, Earle Harrison, Jr. *chemical company executive*
Harrell, Henry Howze *tobacco company executive*
†Harris, Jerrold B. *scientific company executive*
Harris, Neison *manufacturing company executive*
Haskew, George M., Jr. *utility executive*
Hatchett, Edward Earl *retired aerospace manufacturing company executive*
Hausman, Arthur Herbert *electronics company executive*
Hayes, John Patrick *retired manufacturing company executive*
Heckel, John Louis (Jack Heckel) *aerospace company executive*
Heggie, Robert James *steel company executive*
Heidke, Ronald Lawrence *photographic products company executive*
Heilmann, Christian Flemming *corporate executive*
Heller, Ronald Gary *manufacturing company executive, lawyer*
Hemann, Raymond Glenn *aerospace research company executive*
Herbert, Ira C. *food processing company executive*
Herbert, John Warren *forest products executive*
Hiatt, Arnold *shoe manufacturer, importer, retailer*
Hiller, William Arlington *agriculture executive*
Hirsch, Horst Eberhard *business consultant*
Hoglund, William Elis *retired automotive company executive*
Holcombe, William Jones *manufacturing company executive*
Holster, Robert Marc *health care information company executive*
Horovitz, Zola Philip *pharmaceutical company executive*
Hughes, Thomas H. *retired health care executive*
Iacocca, Lido Anthony (Lee Iacocca) *former automotive manufacturing executive, venture capitalist*
Irani, Raymond Reza *electro-mechanical company executive*
Jacoby, Stanley Arthur *retired manufacturing executive*
Jaicks, Frederick Gillies *retired steel company executive*
Jedenoff, George Alexander *steel consultant*
Jeelof, Gerrit *electronics executive*
Jenkins, Lawrence Eugene *retired aeronautics company executive*
Johnson, Irving Stanley *pharmaceutical company executive, scientist*
Johnson, Marc *corporate executive*
Johnson, Rogers Bruce *retired chemical company executive*
Johnson, Warren Donald *retired pharmaceutical executive, former air force officer*
Jones, David John *aerospace executive*
Judelson, David N. *company executive*
Kahl, John J., Jr. *manufacturing executive, small business owner*
Kapcsandy, Louis Endre *building construction and manufacturing executive, chemical engineering consultant*
Katz, Leon *packaging company executive*
Kelly, Alonzo Hyatt, Jr. *retired automotive company engineering executive*
Kelly, Anthony Odrian *flooring manufacturing company executive*
Kerber, Ronald Lee *industrial corporation executive*
Kern, Irving John *retired food company executive*
Kerstetter, Michael James *retired manufacturing company executive*
King, Susan Bennett *retired glass company executive, dean*
Kiselik, Paul Howard *manufacturing company executive*
Kleiman, Ansel *retired electronics company executive*
Knecht, Roland Edward *retired household goods manufacturing company executive*
Kondo, Masatoshi S. *pharmaceutical executive, educator*
Kongabel, H. Fred *industrial construction company executive*
Krause, Werner William *plastics company executive*
Kudrnac, Kristian Ivoj *chemical executive*
Kulik, Rosalyn Franta *food company executive, consultant*
Kuske, Edward Alan *chemical company executive*
Labrecque, Richard Joseph *manufacturing company executive*
Landon, Robert Gray *retired manufacturing company executive*
Lane, Bernard Bell *furniture company executive*
Langdale, John Wesley *timber executive*
Langenberg, Frederick Charles *business executive*
Lathlaen, Robert Frank *retired construction company executive*
Lavington, Michael Richard *venture capital company executive*
Lazay, Paul Duane *telecommunications manufacturing company executive*
Leff, Joseph Norman *yarn manufacturing company executive*
Lehman, John F., Jr. *industrialist*
Lennox, Donald D(uane) *automotive and housing components company executive*
Leslie, James Hill *paper company executive*
Levenson, Harvey Stuart *manufacturing company executive*
Lewis, Martin R. *paper company executive*

Lewis, Rita Hoffman *plastic products manufacturing company executive*
Liffers, William Albert *retired chemical company executive*
Lindars, Laurence Edward *retired health care products executive*
Lindsay, Franklin Anthony *business executive, author*
Linfante, Charles Vincent *dental, medical, optical products company executive*
Lippincott, Philip Edward *retired paper products company executive*
Locke, Charles Stanley *manufacturing company executive, director*
Logan, John Francis *electronics company executive, management consultant*
Long, Robert Livingston *consultant, photographic equipment executive*
Lotz, Arthur William *retired engineering and construction company executve*
Lowden, John L. *retired corporate executive*
Lucas, William Ray *aerospace consultant*
†Luke, David Lincoln, III *paper company executive*
Lux, John H. *corporate executive*
Mabry, Guy O. *manufacturing company executive*
MacLachlan, Alexander *chemical company executive, retired*
Madden, Richard Blaine *forest products executive*
Manchester, Kenneth Edward *electronics executive, consultant*
Marrington, Bernard Harvey *retired automotive company executive*
Martin, Albert Charles *manufacturing executive, lawyer*
Martin, Robert A. *electronics company executive*
Mason, Frank Henry, III *automobile company executive, leasing company executive*
Mathis, Allen Washington, Jr. *manufacturing executive*
May, Kenneth Nathaniel *food industry consultant*
McCabe, Charles Law *retired manufacturing company executive, management consultant*
McGillivray, Donald Dean *agricultural products executive*
Mc Intyre, Robert Allen, Jr. *business turnaround executive*
McKenna, Quentin Carnegie *tool company executive*
McKenzie, Herbert A(lonza) *pharmaceutical company executive*
McNeeley, Donald Robert *steel company executive*
McNeil, Steven Arthur *food company executive*
McSweeny, John Edward *defense industry executive*
Mehlfeldt, Horst K. *tire manufacturing company*
Melvin, T. Stephen *manufacturing company executive*
Messmore, David William *construction executive, former psychologist*
Michalik, Edward Francis *construction company executive*
Miles, John Frederick *retired manufacturing company executive*
Miller, Harold Edward *retired manufacturing conglomerate executive, consultant*
Miller, Leland Bishop, Jr. *food processing and financial consultant*
Miller, Lowell Donald *pharmaceutical company research executive*
Miller, Merle Leroy *retired manufacturing company executive*
Miller, Michael Everett *chemical company executive*
Miskowski, Lee R. *retired automobile executive*
Mitchel, F(rederick) Kent *retired food company executive*
Monaco, Joseph R. *metals company executive*
Moore, Vernon Lee *agricultural consultant, retired food products company executive*
Morgenstein, William *shoe company executive*
Morris, Albert Jerome *pest control company executive*
Moses, Robert Davis *retired diversified industry executive*
Mott, Stewart Rawlings *business executive, political activist*
Mudd, Sidney Peter *former beverage company executive*
Mueller, Robert Louis *business executive*
Munisteri, Joseph George *construction executive*
Murphy, Bernard Thomas *electronics executive, researcher, consultant*
Musa, Samuel Albert *electronics company executive*
Myers, Albert G., Jr. *textile manufacturer*
Nash, Robert Fred *grocery company executive*
Neese, Elbert Haven *retired paper machinery manufacturing executive*
Neff, Jack Kenneth *apparel manufacturing company executive*
Nelson, Robert Gary *textile executive*
Nesheim, Robert Olaf *food products executive*
Nevin, John Joseph *tire and rubber manufacturing executive*
Newman, Phillip Barbour, III *distilling company executive*
Nielsen, Emiel Theodore, Jr. *retired manufacturing company executive*
Noe, Elnora (Ellie Noe) *retired chemical company executive*
Nord, Eric Thomas *manufacturing executive*
Nordlund, Donald Elmer *manufacturing company executive*
Norman, David A. *business equipment company executive*
Nugent, G. Eugene *manufacturing company executive*
Oaks, Maurice David *retired pharmaceutical company executive*
O'Donnell, Kevin *retired metal working company executive*
Oelman, Robert Schantz *retired manufacturing executive*
Ordal, Caspar Reuben *business executive*
Oster, Lewis Henry *manufacturing executive, engineering consultant*
†Pardue, Michael Edward *electronics company executive*
Parfet, William Upjohn *medical supplies manufacturing company executive*
Pariser, Rudolph *chemical company executive, consultant*
Parker, George *retired pen manufacturing company executive*
Parker, Thomas Lee *business executive*
Pearce, Paul Francis *retired aerospace electronics company executive*
Peck, Daniel Farnum *chemical company executive*
Perelman, Leon Joseph *paper manufacturing executive, university president*
Peterson, Roland Oscar *retired electronics company executive*
Petok, Samuel *retired manufacturing company executive*
Phillips, William George *retired food products executive*
Phoenix, Paul Joseph *steel manufacturing company executive*
Piergallini, Alfred A. *food products executive*
Pitstick, Leslie James *food products company executive*
Pollak, Edward Barry *chemical manufacturing company executive*
†Powell, Earl W. *chemicals executive*
Powell, Thomas Edward, III *biological supply company executive*
Pratt, Edmund Taylor, Jr. *pharmaceutical company executive*
Precopio, Frank Mario *chemical company executive*
Preston, Seymour Stotler, III *manufacturing company executive*
Price, Robert *electronics consultant*
Pruis, John J. *business executive*
Rajki, Walter Albert *manufacturing company executive*
Ramseier, Roger I. *aerospace and defense products company executive*
Ramsey, Claude Swanson, Jr. *former industrial executive*
Reeves, John Edwin, Jr. *manufacturing company executive*
Rhodes, Peter Edward *label company executive*
Richman, Paul *semiconductor industry executive, educator*
Richman, Peter *electronics executive*
Robinson, David Earl *pharmaceutical executive*
Robinson, Edward Joseph *cosmetics company executive*
Rogers, Herbert F. *manufacturing company executive*
Roller, Thomas Benjamin *manufacturing company executive*
Romans, Donald Bishop *corporate executive*
Rooke, David Lee *retired chemical company executive*
Roper, John Lonsdale, III *shipyard executive*
Roy, P. Norman *manufacturing company executive*
Rudy, Raymond Bruce, Jr. *retired food company executive*
Rutledge, Kenneth Dean *food company executive*
Ryan, George William *manufacturing executive*
Rydz, John S. *manufacturing executive*
Sakaino, Kozo *automobile company executive*
Salathe, John, Jr. *manufacturing company executive*
Salbaing, Pierre Alcee *retired chemical company executive*
Saltarelli, Eugene A. *retired engineering and construction company executive, consultant*
Samek, Michael Johann *corporation executive*
Samper, Joseph Phillip *retired photographic products company executive*
Sande, Thomas Paul *toy manufacturing company executive*
Sanders, Wayne R. *manufacturing executive*
Sauvey, Donald (Robert) *retired musical instrument company executive*
Scheele, Paul Drake *former hospital supply corporate executive*
Schlensker, Gary Chris *landscaping company executive*
Schmergel, Gabriel *pharmaceutical company executive*
Schmidt, Richard Edward *manufacturing company executive*
Schomer, Fred K. *financial executive*
Schroeter, Louis C. *retired pharmaceutical company executive*
Schulze, Erwin Emil *manufacturing company executive, lawyer*
Schwartz, Robert *automotive manufacturing company executive, marketing executive*
Schwartz, Samuel *business consultant, retired chemical company executive*
Schwartzberg, Martin M. *chemical company executive*
Schwier, Frederick Warren *manufacturing company executive*
Sella, George John, Jr. *chemical company executive*
Shea, Bernard Charles *retired pharmaceutical company executive*
Shepherd, Mark, Jr. *retired electronics company executive*
Shipley, Lucia Helene *retired chemical company executive*
Shriber, Maurice Norden *research and manufacturing company executive*
Siegel, Jack Morton *retired biotechnology company executive*
Silkett, Robert Tillson *food business consultant*
Silverman, Michael *manufacturing company executive*
Simeral, William Goodrich *retired chemical company executive*
Simon, Michael Paul *general contractor, realtor*
Slagle, Jacob Winebrenner, Jr. *food products executive*
Smith, Frederick Coe *manufacturing executive*
Smith, Goff *industrial equipment manufacturing executive*
Smith, James T. *electronics company executive*
Smith, James Thomas *food products executive*
Smith, Paul James *manufacturing company executive*
Snetsinger, David Clarence *retired animal feed company executive*
Somers, Louis Robert *retired food company executive*
Sommer, Howard Ellsworth *textile executive*
Sorensen, Robert Holm *diversified technology company executive, retired*
Southerland, S. Duane *manufacturing company executive*
Spector, Michael Joseph *agribusiness executive*
Spliethoff, William Ludwig *chemical company executive*
Stamper, Malcolm Theodore *aerospace company executive*
Stark, Donald Gerald *pharmaceutical executive*
Starr, Leon *retired chemical research company executive*
Stern, Arthur Paul *electronics company executive, electrical engineer*
Stern, Milton *chemical company executive*
Stewart, Peter Beaufort *retired beverage company executive*
Stickler, Fred Charles *manufacturing company executive*
Stivers, William Charles *forest products company executive*
Strauss, Simon David *manufacturing executive*
Sturgis, William Beaufort *packaging company executive*
Sundry, Arthur P. *business executive*
Swanger, Sterling Orville *appliance manufacturing company executive*
Swihart, John Marion *retired aircraft manufacturing company executive*
Switzer, Ralph Joseph, Jr. *diversified industry executive*
Tagliattini, Maurizio *construction executive, historian, writer*
Tallett, Elizabeth Edith *biopharmaceutical company executive*
Talley, Robert Morrell *aerospace company executive*
Thom, Douglas Andrew *paper company executive*
Thomas, Tom *retired plastics company executive*
Thompson, Ralph Newell *former chemical corporation executive*
Thornburg, Frederick Fletcher *diversified business executive, lawyer*
Tippett, Willis Paul, Jr. *automotive and textile company executive, retired*
Tombros, Peter George *pharmaceutical company executive*
Travers, Oliver S., Jr. *manufacturing company executive*
Turnbull, John Neil *retired chemical company executive*
†Valade, Robert Charles *apparel company executive*
Van Tassel, James Henry *retired electronics executive*
van't Hoff, Winfried C. J. *retired diversified manufacturing executive*
Volkhardt, John Malcolm *food company executive*
Vosburg, Noble E. *fur company executive*
Waldschutz, Gerhard *corporate executive*
†Walker, Kenneth Dale *automotive parts company executive*
Walter, James W. *diversified manufacturing executive*
Warren, Alfred S., Jr. *automobile manufacturing company executive*
Warson, Toby Gene *retired corporate executive*
Weinberger, Siegbert Jacob *food company executive*
Welch, Oliver Wendell *retired pharmaceutical executive*
Wesson, William Simpson *retired paper company executive*
Wheaton, Warde Franklin *manufacturing company executive*
White, Gerald Andrew *chemical company executive*
Wiesen, Donald Guy *retired diversified manufacturing company executive*
Wigdor, Lawrence Allen *chemical company executive*
Will, Joanne Marie *food and consumer services executive, communications consultant, writer*
Williams, Carolyn Elizabeth *manufacturing executive*
Winters, Nola Frances *food company executive*
Witcher, Daniel Dougherty *retired pharmaceutical company executive*
Witt, Hugh Ernest *technology consultant*
Wolf, Hans Abraham *retired pharmaceutical company executive*
Wollert, Gerald Dale *retired food company executive, investor*
Womack, Richard Marvin *manufacturing company executive*
Wommack, W(illiam) W(alton) *retired manufacturing company executive*
Wood, Elwood Steven, III *chemical company executive*
Woodall, Jack David *manufacturing company executive*
Wootton, Mack Edward *food products company executive*
Wright, Thomas William *automotive parts company executive*
Young, John Alan *electronics company executive*
Young, Peter Holden, Jr. *wholesale food company executive*
Zanetti, Joseph Maurice, Jr. *corporate executive*

INDUSTRY: SERVICE

UNITED STATES

ALABAMA

Birmingham
Bruno, Anthony J. *consumer products executive*
Bruno, Ronald G. *food service executive*
Floyd, John Alex, Jr. *editor, marketing executive, horticulturist*
Gunter, John Richmond *communications executive*
Harris, Aaron *management consultant*
Henderson, Louis Clifton, Jr. *management consultant*
Jones, Arthur McDonald, Sr. *consumer products company executive*
Parker, John Malcolm *management and financial consultant*
Sturgeon, Charles Edwin *management consultant*
Whitehead, Lewis E, Jr. *automotive consultant, management consultant*

Florence
Peck, Richard Hyde *hospital administrator*

Homewood
Miller, John W. *management and financial consultant*

Huntsville
McRary, John Walter, III *defense contract research and development company executive*
Meadlock, James W. *computer graphics company executive*
Taylor, James F., Jr. *computer graphics company executive*

Mobile
Beall, Samuel E., III *food service executive*
Boone, Louis Eugene *business and management educator, author*
Grady, Charles E. *marketing executive*
Hunt, Pflip Gardnyr *food service company executive*
†Parker, Donald Lester *technology company executive*

Montgomery
Mendel, Perry *day care company executive*
Robinson, Peter Clark *general management executive*
Salay, Carolyn Jeanne *advertising agency executive*
Schloss, Samuel Leopold, Jr. *retired food service executive, consultant*

Ohatchee
Ellis, Bernice Allred *personnel executive*

Tuscaloosa
Barban, Arnold Melvin *advertising educator*
Plumley, Joseph Pinkney, Jr. *public relations educator*

ALASKA

Anchorage
Brady, Carl Franklin *retired aircraft charter company executive*
Clement, Ronald E. *communications executive*

Juneau
†Knowles, Tony *restaurant operator, former mayor*

Kasaan
†Thompson, Louis A. *company executive*

Ketchikan
Kraft, Richard Joe *sales executive*
Laurance, Leonard Clark *marketing researcher, educator and consultant*

ARIZONA

Benson
Bennett, William Paul, Jr. *automotive marketing company executive*

Cave Creek
O'Reilly, Thomas Eugene *human resources consultant*

Chandler
Goyer, Robert Stanton *communication educator*
Williams, James Eugene, Jr. *management consultant*

Green Valley
Crystall, Joseph N. *communications company executive*

Mesa
Garfield, Ernest *bank consultant*
Murphy, Edward Francis *sales executive*
†Whiteman, John O. *rental company executive*

Paradise Valley
De Shazor, Ashley Dunn *business consultant*
Grimm, James R. (Ronald Grimm) *multi-industry executive*
Hann, J(ames) David *information systems company executive*
Swanson, Robert Killen *management consultant*

Peoria
Schindler, William Stanley *retired public relations executive*

Phoenix
Armstrong, Nelson William, Jr. *gaming company executive*
Arriola, David Bruce *resort and hotel marketing executive*
Babinec, Gehl P. *convenience store company executive*
Cox, Robert Gene *management consultant*
†Crim, Jack C. *diversified industry executive*
Derasmo, Vito Joseph (Bill Derasmo) *marketing professional*
Drain, Albert Sterling *business management consultant*
Evans, Ronald Allen *lodging chain executive*
†Fassler, Joseph K. *food service executive*
Gochnauer, Richard Wallis *consumer products company executive*
Grier, James Edward *hotel company executive, lawyer*
Hallier, Gerard Edouard *hotel chain executive*
Heller, Mitchell Thomas *hotel company executive*
Hill, Edward G. *food marketing executive*
Lemon, Leslie Gene *consumer products and services company executive, lawyer*
Manion, Jerry Robert *hotel chain executive*
Reining, Beth LaVerne (Betty Reining) *public relations consultant, journalist*
†Rubeli, Paul E. *gaming company executive*
Snell, Richard *holding company executive*
Teets, John William *diversifed company executive*
Turner, William Cochrane *international management consultant*
Ward, Yvette Hennig *advertising executive*
Wilfried, Grau *hotel executive officer*

Prescott
Harris, Earl Edward *business educator*

Scottsdale
Adams, Robert Granville *marketing professional*
Christensen, Howard Alan *consulting firm executive*
Doglione, Arthur George *data processing executive*
Donnelly, Charles Francis *management consultant*
Gall, Donald Alan *data processing executive*
Maturi, Raymond Rockne *healthcare information services company executive*
Pavlik, Nancy *convention services executive*
Peterson, Louis Robert *retired consumer products company executive*
Sullivan, George Edmund *editorial and marketing company executive*
Willoughby, Carroll Vernon *retired motel chain executive*
Wright, James Corwin *international management consultant*

Sedona
Converti, Vincenzo *computer systems company executive*
Wolfe, Al *marketing and advertising consultant*

Show Low
Collins, Copp *federal, corporate, institutional consultant*

Sun City West
Curtin, Richard Daniel *management consultant, retired air force officer, space pioneer*
Stevens, George Richard *business consultant, public policy commentator*

Tempe
Arters, Linda Bromley *public relations consultant, writer*
Bennett, ElDean *mass communication educator, broadcaster*
Gwinner, Robert Fred, Jr. *marketing educator*
Hald, Alan P. *computer company executive*
McKeever, Jeffrey D. *computer company executive*
Wales, Hugh Gregory *marketing educator, business executive*

Tucson
Auslander, Steven Lawrence *advertising executive, newspaper editor*
Barton, Stanley Faulkner *management consultant*
Hampel, Alvin *advertising executive*
Jones, Frank Wyman *management consultant, mechanical engineer*
King, Marcia *management consultant*
Lewis, Wilbur H. *educational management consultant*
Luningham, Robert Donald *radio marketing consultant*
Myers, Douglas Scott *advertising executive*
Paley, Alfred Irving *value engineering and consulting company executive, lecturer*
Rose, Hugh *management consultant*
†Willert, Sister St. Joan *health care corporation executive*

ARKANSAS

Bentonville
Schmidt, Mark Alan *information systems executive*

Conway
Kline, Rodger S. *marketing professional*

Harrison
Selby, Clark Linwood, Jr. *sales executive*

Hot Springs Village
Dellow, Reginald Leonard *advertising executive*

Little Rock
Andrews, Collins Adams, III *data processing company executive*
†Hendren, James Knox *software development executive*

Lowell
Hunt, Johnnie B. *trucking company executive*

Pine Bluff
Long, Edward Arlo *business consultant, retired manufacturing company executive*

CALIFORNIA

Agoura Hills
Guarino, Salvatore Frank *hotel executive*
Maquipour, Iraj *consulting company executive*
Naylor-Jackson, Jerry *entertainer, public relations consultant, producer*
Schmidt, Frank Broaker *executive recruiter*

Alameda
Billings, Thomas Neal *computer and publishing executive, management consultant*

Alamo
Whalen, John Sydney *management consultant*

Alhambra
Szymanski, Joyce Ann *publicist*

Anaheim
Barnett, Holly Billings *public relations executive*
Conlin, William Patrick *computer company executive*
Kallay, Michael Frank, II *medical devices company official*
Noorda, Raymond J. *computer software company executive*

Arrowhead
Bauer, Ralph Leroy *business executive*

Atherton
Lowry, Larry Lorn *management consulting company executive*

Atwater
DeVoe, Kenneth Nickolas *food service executive, mayor*

Belvedere Tiburon
Denton, Charles Mandaville *corporate consultant*

Berkeley
Aaker, David Allen *marketing educator*
Holton, Richard Henry *business educator*
Hurley, Morris Elmer, Jr. *management consultant*
Poulos-Woolley, Paige M. *public relations executive*
Pritchard, Arthur Osborn *retired business administrator*
Tyndall, David Gordon *business educator*

Beverly Hills
Barbakow, Jeffery C. *motion picture and television company executive*
Berg, Jeffrey Spencer *talent agency executive*
David, Clive *events planning executive*
Dillon, Gregory Russell *hotel executive*
Galbraith, James Ronald *hotel executive*
Hilton, Barron *hotel executive*
Hilton, Eric Michael *hotel industry executive*
†Moore, J. Jamison *consulting firm executive, economist*
Ribero, Michael Antonio *marketing executive*
†Riess, Gordon Sanderson *management consultant*
Schine, Gerard David *entertainment company executive*
Toffel, Alvin Eugene *corporate executive, business and governmental consultant*
Zarem, Abe Mordecai *management consulting executive*

Burbank
Katz, Marty *motion picture executive*
McQueen, Sherman John, Jr. *entertainment company executive*

Burlingame
Heath, Richard Raymond *investment executive*
Mc Dowell, Jack Sherman *political consultant*

Calabasas
Bartizal, Robert George *computer systems company executive, business consultant*
Gressak, Anthony Raymond, Jr. *sales executive*

Camarillo
Sime, Donald Rae *business administration educator*

Cambria
DuFresne, Armand Frederick *management and engineering consultant*
Morse, Richard Jay *human resources and organizational development consultant, manufacturers' representative company executive*

Carlsbad
Rudolph, Charles Herman *computer software development executive*
Wilson, Donald Grey *management consultant*

Carmel
Creighton, John Wallis, Jr. *consultant, author, former management educator*
Eppler, Jerry Mack *management consultant*
Krugman, Stanley Lee *international management consultant*
Skidmore, Howard Franklyn *public relations counsel*
Smith, Gordon Paul *management consulting company executive*

Carpinteria
Lessler, Richard Sigmund *advertising executive*

Castro Valley
Denning, Eileen Bonar *management consultant*

Century City
Blatt, Neil A. *cinema corporation executive*

Chatsworth
Bartling, Judd Quenton *research corporation executive*

Clayton
Wooten, Robert James *executive*

Cloverdale
Collins, John Wendler *consumer products company executive*

Concord
Allen, Toby *resort executive*

Corona Del Mar
Wickman, Paul Everett *public relations executive*

Costa Mesa
Damsky, Robert Philip *communications executive*
Patterson, Dennis Joseph *management consultant*

Crestline
Merrill, Steven William *research and development executive*

Culver City
Williams, Kenneth Scott *entertainment company executive*

Cupertino
Flynn, Ralph Melvin, Jr. *sales executive, marketing consultant*
Graziano, Joseph A. *computer company executive*
Krambeck, Robert Harold *communications and computer executive/researcher*
Marshall, Robert Charles *computer company executive*
Schmidt, Stephen C. *computer company executive*
Spindler, Michael H. *computer company executive*
Tesler, Lawrence Gordon *computer company executive*
Treybig, James G. *computer company executive*

Cypress
Recchia, Richard D. *automotive sales executive*

Daly City
Hargrave, Sarah Quesenberry *marketing, public relations company executive*

Dana Point
Jelinek, Robert *advertising executive, writer*
Krogius, Tristan Ernst Gunnar *international marketing consultant, lawyer*

Danville
Mattoon, Henry Amasa, Jr. *advertising and marketing consultant, writer*

Del Mar
Comrie, Sandra Melton *human resource executive*
La Bonté, C(larence) Joseph *weight management and lifestyle company executive*

Diablo
Pelandini, Thomas Francis *mmarketing executive*

El Cajon
Laffoon, Carthrae Merrette *management consultant*
McInerney, Joseph Aloysius *hotel executive*

El Segundo
Amerman, John W. *toy company executive*
Autolitano, Astrid *consumer products executive*
Barad, Jill Elikann *toy company executive*
Brill, James Lathrop *finance executive*
†Collazo, Jose Antonio *computer company executive*
†Honeycutt, Van B. *computer services company executive*
†Leff, Robert S. *computer company executive*
Level, Leon Jules *information services executive*
Wagman, David S. *computer company executive*

Encino
Dor, Yoram *health care executive*

Escondido
†Pershing, Richard Wilson *communications company executive, consultant*

Foster City
†Roberts, Lawrence Gilman *telecommunications company executive*
†Sewall, William Dana *data processing manager*

Fremont
Evenhuis, Henk J. *research company exexcutive*

Fresno
Levy, Joseph William *department stores executive*
Pinkerton, Richard LaDoyt *management educator*

Fullerton
Hollander, Gerhard Ludwig *computer company executive*
Malakoff, James Leonard *management information executive*
Nowel, David John *marketing professional*
Patton, David Wayne *health care executive*
Taylor, James Walter *marketing educator*

Garden Grove
Banks, Ernest (Ernie Banks) *moving company executive, retired professional baseball player*

Glendale
Herzer, Richard Kimball *franchising company executive*
Lathe, Robert Edward *management and financial consultant*
Marr, Luther Reese *communications executive, lawyer*
Misa, Kenneth Franklin *management consultant*
†Rosenberg, Robert M. *food chain executive*

Glendora
Milhous, Robert E. *advertising executive*
Roland, Donald Edward *advertising executive*
Scheller, Sanford Gregory *printing company executive*
Yochem, Barbara June *sales executive, lecturer*

Granada Hills
Shoemaker, Harold Lloyd *infosystem specialist*

Greenbrae
†Finkelstein, James Arthur *management consultant*

Half Moon Bay
Fennell, Diane Marie *marketing executive, process engineer*
†Gross, Kenneth Paul *management consultant*

Hayward
Connors, Dennis Michael *infosystems executive*
Tribus, Myron *management consultant, engineer, educator*

Healdsburg
Canfield, Grant Wellington, Jr. *management consultant*

Hollister
Parker, Patrick Johnston *entrepreneur, philantropist*

Inglewood
Turner, Norris *marketing professional*

Irvine
Allen, Joseph *public relations executive*
†Bonfield, Peter Leahy *information technology executive*
Bradley, Charles James, Jr. *corporate human resources executive*
Colino, Richard Ralph *communications consultant*
Demetrescu, Mihai Constantin *computer company executive, scientist*
Earhart, Donald Marion *management consultant, health care company executive*
Habermann, Norman *restaurant group executive*
Kossoff, Leslie Lynn *quality improvement professional, educator*
†Krantz, Barry E. *restaurant executive*
Manara, James Anthony *software executive, consultant*
Nelson, Robert E. *public relations executive, political consultant*
Nishida, Atsutoshi *computer company executive*
†Quershey, Safi U. *computer company executive*
Rollans, James O. *service company executive*
Rough, David S. *marketing professional, consultant*
†Swan, Richard Alan *executive recruiter*
Yuen, Thomas Chi Kwan *business executive*

La Habra
Burkle, Ronald W. *food service executive*
Chase, Cochrane *advertising agency executive*

La Jolla
Bardwick, Judith Marcia *management consultant*
Harris, T George *management and psychology editor*
Mogul, Leslie Anne *marketing communications executive*
Sandoval, Rik (Charles Sandoval) *broadcasting executive*
Streichler, Jerry *human and technology resource development consultant*

La Puente
Sheridan, Christopher Frederick *human resources executive*

La Quinta
Houze, William Cunningham *executive recruiter, management consultant*

Lafayette
Coffey, Susanne Norton *communications company executive*
Hemphill, Norma Jo *special event planning and tour company executive*
Kahn, Robert Irving *management consultant*

Laguna Hills
Linton, Frederick M. *strategic planning consultant*
Mc Guire, Joseph William *business educator*
Miller, Eldon Earl *corporate business publications consultant, retired manufacturing company executive*

Larkspur
†Wilde, Paul K. *computer company executive*

Livermore
†Porter, James R. *computer company executive*
Wood, Donald Craig *marketing professional*

Loma Linda
Maurice, Don *personal care industry executive*

Long Beach
†Creel, Diane Claypoole *marketing professional*
Giles, Jean Hall *retired corporate executive*
Vogel, William Charles *advertising executive*

Los Alamitos
Weinberger, Frank *information systems advisor*

Los Altos
Allen, Michael Graham *management consultant*
Bell, Chester Gordon *computer engineering company executive*
Hammond, Donald Leroy *computer company executive*

Los Angeles
Altfeld, Sheldon Isaac *communications executive*
Armstrong, C. Michael *computer business executive*
Bermingham, Richard P. *restaurant and food products company executive*
Bloch, Paul *public relations executive*
Bohle, Sue *public relations executive*
Boonshaft, Hope Judith *public relations executive*
Busse, Michael Clifford *newspaper advertising executive*
Coleman, Roger William *institutional food distribution company executive*
Counts, James Curtis *management consultant*
Crosby, Peter Alan *management consultant*
Dill, Donald *consumer products company executive*
Doll, Lynne Marie *public relations agency executive*
Domantay, Norlito Valdez (Lito Domantay) *communications executive*
Dorman, Thomas Patrick *marketing professional, consultant*
Duke, William Edward *public affairs executive*
Einstein, Clifford Jay *advertising executive*
Eisaman, Josiah Reamer, III *advertising executive*
Farrell, Joseph *movie market analyst, producer, entertainment research company executive, writer, sculptor, designer*
Feidelson, Marc *advertising executive*
Fenimore, George Wiley *management consultant*
Ferry, Richard Michael *executive search firm executive*
Fisher, Lawrence W. *public relations company executive*
Gal, Kenneth Maurice *advertising executive*
†Gerber, Charles *communications company executive*
Geving, Steve William *executive chef*
Ginsburg, Seymour *computer science educator*
†Golan, Menahem *motion picture company executive, film director*
Gottfried, Ira Sidney *management consulting executive*
Greene, Alvin *service company executive, management consultant*
Gregory, Thomas Lang *restaurant chain executive*
Grody, Mark Stephen *public relations executive*
Harbaugh, George Milton *hotel executive*
Harbison, John Robert *management consultant*
†Hartsough, Gayla Anne Kraetsch *management consultant*
Heinisch, Robert Craig *sales and marketing executive, consultant*
†Hoffman, Marvin *computer company executive*
Humphreys, Robert Lee *advertising agency executive*
Iannaccone, Emil Anthony *advertising agency executive*
Irving, Jack Howard *technical consultant*
Jacobsen, Laren *programmer, analyst*
Johnson, Patricia Gayle *public relations executive, writer*
Kline, Richard Stephen *public relations executive*
Klinger, Allen *computer science and engineering educator*
Kristoff, James *production company executive*
Krouse, Diane Murray *advertising company executive*
Krueger, Robert William *management consultant*
Kupchick, Alan Charles *advertising executive*
Laba, Marvin *management consultant*
Lee, Burns Wells *public relations executive*
Lee, R. Marilyn *employee relations executive*
Leener, Jack Joseph *advertising executive*
Lewis, Craig Graham David *public relations executive*
†Livingston, Alan Wendell *communications executive*
†Lukasik, Stephen Joseph *information technology executive*
Margol, Irving *personnel consultant*
McGaughey, Emmett Connell *advertising agency executive*
McLaren, Fred B. *supermarket chain executive*
Meuli, Judith K. *communications executive, real estate developer, small business owner*
Montgomery, Richard Alan *sales executive*
Nicholaw, George *communications executive*
Olson, Dale C. *public relations executive*
Patel, Chandra Kumar Naranbhai *communications company executive, educator, researcher*
Pearlstein, Leonard *advertising agency executive*
Quinn, Tom *communications executive*
†Record, John F. *public relations executive*
Richardson, Rand Michael *public relations executive*
†Sassoon, Vidal *hair stylist*

Segal, Morton *public relations executive*
Silverman, Bruce Gary *advertising executive*
Sitrick, Michael Steven *communications executive*
Smith, Joseph Benjamin *communications company executive*
Snyder, David Markel *marketing executive*
†Spindler, Paul *public relations executive*
Spofford, Robert Houston *advertising agency executive*
Stevens, Roy W. *distilled spirits executive*
Tardio, Thomas A. *public relations executive*
Tellem, Susan Mary *public relations executive*
Tobia, Stephen Francis, Jr. *marketing professional, consultant*
Tomash, Erwin *retired computer equipment company executive*
Triplett, Arlene Ann *travel company executive*
Van Stekelenburg, Mark *food service executive*
Warren, Mark Edward *shipping company executive, lawyer*
Whitman, Kenneth Jay *advertising executive*

Los Gatos
Grubb, William Francis X. *consumer software executive, marketing executive*
Henley, Jeffrey O. *restaurant executive*

Malibu
†Tallal, Scott Victor *television research consultant*

Mammoth Lakes
Buchanan, Lee Ann *public relations executive*

Manhattan Beach
Stern, Daniel Alan *business management consultant*
Weinstock, Herbert Frank *public relations executive*

Marina Del Rey
Collins, Russell Ambrose *advertising executive, creative director*
Gold, Carol Sapin *international management consultant, speaker*
Smith, Steven Warren *public relations executive*
Tennant, John Randall *management advisory company executive*

Menlo Park
†Chait, Arthur Lyle *management consultant*
Kurtzig, Sandra L. *software company executive*
Morrell, James Wilson *consulting company executive*
Parker, Donn Blanchard *information security consultant*
Phipps, Allen Mayhew *management consultant*
Scandling, William Fredric *retired food service company executive*
Shows, Winnie M. *public relations company executive, professional speaker*
Sommers, William Paul *management consultant*
White, Phillip E. *technology company executive*

Mill Valley
Barbarich, Stanley Joseph *marketing executive*
†Hurtado, Corydon Dicks *management consultant*

Milpitas
Berkley, Stephen Mark *computer peripherals manufacturing company executive*
Corrigan, Wilfred J. *data processing and computer company executive*
†Rostoker, Michael David *computer company executive, lawyer*
Wells, George Douglas *corporate executive*

Moffett Field
Baldwin, Betty Jo *computer specialist*

Monterey
Cutino, Bert Paul *chef, restaurant owner*

Monterey Park
†Mastaler, Richard Michael *healthcare executive*

Moraga
Grassi, James Edward *recreational facility executive director*
Sonenshein, Nathan *marine consulting company executive, retired naval officer*

Mountain View
Amdahl, Gene Myron *computer company executive*
Braun, Michael Alan *data processing executive*
Breitmeyer, Jo Anne *sales and marketing executive*
†Fiester, Clark George *communications company executive*
Mc Nealy, Scott *computer company executive*
Morris, Arlene Myers *marketing professional*
†Qureishi, A. Salam *computer software and services company executive*
†Raybould, Barry John *computer software company executive*
Rulifson, Johns Frederick *computer company executive, computer scientist*
Tierney, Patrick John *information services executive*

Napa
LaRocque, Marilyn Ross Onderdonk *public relations executive*
Leavitt, Dana Gibson *management consultant*

Newark
Joyce, Stephen Francis *human resource executive*

Newport Beach
Kelly, James P. *computer company executive*
Lipson, Melvin Alan *technology and business management consultant*
†Nadel, Steven J. *marine instruments adjusting company executive*
†Roberts, Ralph S. *restaurant chain executive*
Rueb, Richard V., Sr. *information systems management consultant*
Soliman, Anwar S. *restaurant company executive*

North Hollywood
Kapnick, Richard Allan *international marketing and advertising consultant, educator, executive television producer, editor and publisher, broadcaster*

Northridge
Stark, Martin J. *management consultant*

Oakland
Barakat, Samir F. *economic and strategic business consulting executive*
Crane, Robert Meredith *health care executive*
Cutter, Edward A(hern) *consumer products company executive, lawyer*
Laverne, Michel Marie-Jacques *international relations consultant*
†Potash, Jeremy Warner *public relations executive*
Potash, Stephen Jon *international public relations practitioner*

Oildale
Gallagher, Joseph Francis *marketing executive*

Ontario
Fry, Linda Sue *hotel sales director, food products company executive*

Orinda
Brown, Thomas Raymond *marketing company executive*

Palm Springs
Arnold, Stanley Norman *manufacturing consultant*

Palo Alto
Allen, Louis Alexander *management consultant*
Hecht, Lee Martin *software company executive*
Kaufman, Michael David *management executive*
Merrin, Seymour *computer marketing company executive*
Quraishi, Marghoob A. *management consultant*
Scott, Edward William, Jr. *computer company executive*

Palos Verdes Estates
†Davidson, Keith Thomas *industry association executive*

Palos Verdes Peninsula
Savage, Terry Richard *information systems executive*

Pasadena
†Atwood, Carol Ann *healthcare executive*
Kaplan, Gary *executive recruiter*
Lynch, Gerald John *management consultant*
Ott, George William, Jr. *management consulting executive*
Watkins, John Francis *management consultant*

Paso Robles
Boxer, Jerome Harvey *computer and management consultant, vintner, accountant*

Petaluma
Crawford, George Truett *management systems company executive, consultant*

Portola Valley
Hurd, Cuthbert C. *computer company executive, mathematician*
Moses, Franklin Maxwell *retired chemical marketing executive*

Poway
Remer, Vernon Ralph *travel consultant*

Rancho Mirage
Rotman, Morris Bernard *public relations consultant*

Rancho Palos Verdes
Marlett, De Otis Loring *retired management consultant*

Rancho Santa Fe
Gruenwald, George Henry *new products development management consultant*
Matthews, Leonard Sarver *advertising executive, consultant*
Schirra, Walter Marty, Jr. *business consultant, former astronaut*

Redding
Miller, Rodger Dale *private investigator, intelligence analyst*

Redwood City
Bertram, Jack Renard *information systems specialist*
Jenkins, Robert Lee *management consultant*
Jobs, Steven Paul *computer corporation executive*
Tyabji, Hatim Ahmedi *computer systems company executive*
†Warmenhoven, Daniel John *communications equipment executive*

Reseda
Leahy, T. Liam *management consultant*

Riverside
Chute, Phillip Bruce *management consultant*

Rohnert Park
Johnston, Edward Elliott *insurance and management consultant*

Ross
Goulet, William Dawson *marketing professional*

Rutherford
Staglin, Garen Kent *finance and computer service company executive*

Sacramento
Blackwell, Frederick Wayne *computer science educator*
†Franz, Jennifer Danton *public opinion and marketing researcher*
†Hunt, Dennis *public relations executive*
Metzger, Bobbie Ann *public relations executive*

Saint Helena
Kamman, Alan Bertram *communications consulting company executive*

San Anselmo
Goodman, Carolyn *advertising executive*

San Bruno
Arthur, Greer Martin *maritime container leasing firm executive*

San Carlos
Bellack, Daniel Willard *advertising and public relations executive*
Curry, William Sims *procurement manager*

San Clemente
Fall, John Robert *management and computer consultant*
Stenzel, William A. *consulting services executive*

San Diego
Boyd, Robert Giddings, Jr. *mental health facility administrator*
Cornett, William Forrest, Jr. *local government management consultant*
Fagot, Joseph Burdell *corporate executive*
Gill, Gail Stoorza *public relations executive*
Goodall, Jackson Wallace, Jr. *restaurant company executive*
Hale, David Fredrick *health care company executive*
Hooper, Jere Mann *consultant, retired hotel executive*
†Jacobs, Irwin Mark *communications executive*
Kennedy, Peter Smithson *personnel consultant*
†Lee, Christopher Heinz *destination management consultant*
Long, Marie Katherine *public relations consultant, researcher*
†Lowenthal, Arline Mae *marketing research executive*
MacCracken, Peter James *marketing executive, communications executive*
†Martinez, Albert *computer peripherals company executive*
Miles, Gordon Hugh *restaurant company executive, lawyer*
Nelson, Craig Alan *management consultant*
Norrod, James Douglas *computer subsystems company executive*
Nugent, Robert J., Jr. *fast food company executive*
Perrill, Frederick Eugene *information systems executive*
Ringer, Jerome *public relations executive*
Shevel, Wilbert Lee *information systems executive*
Silverberg, Lewis Henry *management consultant*
Tepedino, Francis Joseph *business management company executive*
Tillinghast, Charles Carpenter, III *marketing company executive*
Wallace, Ted *wholesale goods distribution executive*
Warner, John Hilliard, Jr. *technical services, military and commercial systems and software company executive*
Ziegaus, Alan James *public relations executive*
Zisch, William E. *technical services executive*

San Francisco
Amidei, L. Neal *public relations counselor*
Bachrach, Ira Nathaniel *marketing executive*
Bara, Jean Marc *advertising executive*
†Bellows, William *public relations executive*
†Burkett, William Cleveland *management consultant*
Butenhoff, Susan *public relations executive*
Colnett, Ronald Harry *advertising executive*
Currier, Frederick Plumer *market research company executive*
†Danko, Gary J. *chef*
Edgar, James Macmillan, Jr. *management consultant*
Farley, Leon Alex *executive search consultant*
Feld, Michael Sperry *advertising executive*
†Gehb, Michael *public relations executive*
Gertler, Alfred Martin *public relations executive*
Goldberg, Fred Sellmann *advertising executive*
Gunst, Robert Allen *consumer products executive*
Gunther, Herbert Chao *advertising agency executive*
Handlery, Paul Robert *hotel executive*
Hargadon, Bernard Joseph, Jr. *consumer goods company executive*
Harlan, Neil Eugene *retired healthcare company executive*
Harrison, E(rnest) Frank(lin) *management educator, consultant, author, former university president and chancellor*
Hayes, Thomas Jay, III *management consultant, retired construction and engineering company executive, retired army officer*
†Hindery, Leo Joseph, Jr. *media company executive*
Howley, Peter Anthony *communications executive*
Humenesky, Gregory *personnel and labor relations executive*
Hurlbert, Roger William *information service industry executive*
Kalt, Howard Michael *public relations executive*
Keesling, Francis Valentine, Jr. *management consultant*
Klammer, Joseph Francis *management consultant*
LaFollette, Charles Sanborn *business consultant*
Lautz, Lindsay Allan *retained executive search consultant*
Lockhart, James Blakely *public affairs executive*
McEvoy, Nan Tucker *publishing company executive*
Miller, Burton Leibsle *sales executive*
†Moore, Richard *public relations executive*
Mundell, David Edward *leasing company executive*
Noonan, William Moss *information systems executive, consultant*
Otus, Simone *public relations executive*
Riney, Hal Patrick *advertising executive*
Rosenberg, Sydney J. *security company executive*
Rusco, Gene Earl *radio broadcasting executive*
Russell, Carol Ann *personnel service company executive*
Salzman, Richard William *artist representative*
Skeen, John Kenneth *sales executive*
Stetler, Russell Dearnley, Jr. *private investigator*
Sturdivant, Frederick David *consultant, business educator*
Thompson, Gary W. *public relations executive*
Thor, Peter K. *marketing executive*
Wernick, Sandie Margot *advertising and public relations executive*
Westerfield, Putney *management consulting executive*
Whitaker, Clem, Jr. *advertising and public relations executive*
White, Rene *public relations executive*
Wilbur, Brayton, Jr. *distribution company executive*
Willner, Jay R. *consulting company executive*
Woolsey, David Arthur *leasing company executive*
Yu, Eleanor Ngan-Ling *advertising company executive*

San Jose
Almon, William Joseph *data processing company executive*
Dean, Burton Victor *management educator*
Dougherty, John James *computer software company executive, consultant*
Franson, Paul Oscar, III *public relations executive*
Hamilton, Judith Hall *computer company executive*
Harkins, Craig *management consultant*
Jordan, Thomas Vincent *advertising educator, consultant*
Kasley, Helen Mary *corporate secretary, legal counsel*
McCoy, James M. *data processing, computer company executive*
Nogawa, Kiyoshi *computer company executive*
Ostrom, Philip Gardner *computer company executive*
Schofield, John Trevor *environmental management company executive*
†Sollman, George Henry *telecommunications company executive*
Sweeny, Mary Ellen *public relations and advertising executive*

San Leandro
Odron, Edward Andrew *supermarket executive*

San Lorenzo
Morrison, Martin Earl *computer systems analyst*

San Marcos
Lee, John Francis *retired international management consulting company executive, author*

San Mateo
Briggs, Thorley D. *environmetal consultant*
Goldman, Bernard *leasing company executive*
Hawkins, William (Trip), III *software executive*
Helfert, Erich Anton *management consultant, author, educator*
Jordan, Michelle Henrietta *public relations company executive*
Poppel, Harvey Lee *management consultant*
†Probst, Lawrence F., III *computer company executive*

San Pedro
Price, Harrison Alan *business research company executive*

San Rafael
†Bartz, Carol *software company executive*
Friesecke, Raymond Francis *management consultant*
Kennedy, James Waite *management consultant, author*
Nelson, James Carmer, Jr. *advertising executive, writer*
Thompson, John William *international management consultant*
Wilson, Ian Holroyde *management consultant, futurist*

San Ramon
Lee, Robert *telecommunications executive*

Santa Ana
Dukes, David R. *computer company executive*
Holtz, Joseph Norman *marketing executive*
Lacy, Linwood A., Jr. *computer company executive*
Maw, Sam H. *restaurant chain executive*

Santa Barbara
Ahlers, B. Orwin *marketing executive*
Amory, Thomas Carhart *management consultant*
Boehm, Eric Hartzell *information management executive*
Boxer, Rubin *software company owner, former research and development company executive*
Emmons, Robert John *corporate executive*
Grayson, Robert Allen *marketing executive, educator*
Jacobson, Saul P. *consumer products company executive*
†Morgan, Alfred V. *business executive*
Schultz, Arthur Warren *communications company executive*
Weaver, Sylvester Laflin, Jr. *communications consultant*

Santa Clara
Barrett, Craig R. *computer company executive*
Cunningham, Andrea Lee *public relations executive*
Endo, Makoto *computer company executive*
Marken, Gideon Andrew, III *advertising and public relations executive*
Menkin, Christopher (Kit Menkin) *leasing company executive*
Vincent, David Ridgely *management consulting executive*

Santa Cruz
Brough, Bruce Alvin *public relations and communications executive*
Corrick, Ann Marjorie *communications executive*

Santa Fe Springs
Butterworth, Edward Livingston *retail company executive*

Santa Monica
Anderson, Robert Helms *computer and management company executive*
Esber, Edward Michael, Jr. *software company executive*
Janulaitis, M. Victor *consulting company executive*
Karlin, Robert *automotive sales executive*
Mc Kinney, Montgomery Nelson *advertising executive*
†Price, David *recreational facilities executive*
†Roberts, Kevin *recreational facility executive*
Salveson, Melvin Erwin *business executive, educator*
Salzer, John Michael *technical and management consultant*

Santa Rosa
Cavanagh, John Charles *advertising agency executive*
Mackay, Kenneth Donald *environmental services company executive*
Schudel, Hansjoerg *international business consultant*

Santa Ynez
Stern, Marvin *management consultant*

Saratoga
Lynch, Milton Terrence *retired advertising agency executive*

Sausalito
Treat, John Elting *management consultant*

Scotts Valley
Filler, Gary B. *computer company executive*
Shugart, Alan F. *electronic computing equipment company executive*

Seal Beach
Burge, Willard, Jr. *software company executive*
Thompson, Craig Snover *corporate communications executive*

Sherman Oaks
Ghent, Peer *management consultant*
Holst, Sanford *author, strategic consulting executive*
Light, Robert M. *broadcasting association executive*
Lindgren, Timothy Joseph *supply company executive*
Strauss, John *public relations executive*
Winkler, Lee B. *business consultant*

Signal Hill
Jarman, Donald Ray *public relations professional, minister, retired*

Solana Beach
Cvar, Duane Emil *marketing professional*

South San Francisco
†Walsh, Gary L. *consumer products company executive*

Stanford
Miller, William Frederick *research company executive, educator, business consultant*

Stockton
Jacobs, Marian *advertising agency owner*
Shao, Otis Hung-I *corporate executive, educator*

Studio City
Nieto del Rio, Juan Carlos *marketing executive*

Sun City
Newman, Glen Carroll *superintendent of schools*

Sunnyvale
Armistead, Robert Ashby, Jr. *scientific research company executive*
Previte, Richard *computer company executive*
White, Eugene R. *computer manufacturing company executive*
Zemke, (E.) Joseph *computer company executive*

Taft
Smith, Lee L. *hotel executive*

Thousand Oaks
Dorsey, Kimberly Lynne *public relations executive*
Dunaway, Robert Lee *sales and marketing executive*
Smyth, Glen Miller *management consultant*

Torrance
Carey, Kathryn Ann *advertising and public relations agency executive, consultant*
Kay, Kenneth Jeffrey *health care company executive*
Kulpa, John Edward *management executive, former air force officer*
Kurita, Masahiro *computer company executive*
Niwa, Norio *computer company executive*
Signorovitch, Dennis James *communications executive*
Walti, Randal Fred *management consultant*

Tustin
Bartlett, Arthur Eugene *franchise executive*
Jay, David Jakubowicz *management consultant*
Kelley, Robert Paul, Jr. *management consultation executive*

Twentynine Palms
Fultz, Philip Nathaniel *management analyst*

Upland
Hext, Kathleen Florence *regulatory compliance consultant*

Van Nuys
Blinder, Martin S. *business consultant, art dealer*
Kagan, Stephen Bruce (Sandy Kagan) *travel agency executive*
Simon, David Harold *retired public relations executive*

Venice
Chiat, Jay *advertising agency executive*
Clow, Lee *advertising agency executive*
Giaquinta, Gerald J. *public relations executive*
Kuperman, Robert Ian *advertising agency executive*
Thomas, Bob *public relations executive*
Wolf, Robert Howard *advertising executive, marketing consultant*

Villa Park
Britton, Thomas Warren, Jr. *management consultant*

Walnut Creek
Garlough, William Glenn *marketing executive*
†Maslin, Harvey Lawrence *staffing service company executive*
McCauley, Bruce Gordon *financial consultant*

West Hollywood
Helin, James Dennis *advertising agency executive*
Holt, Dennis F. *media buying company executive*
Kingsley, Patricia *public relations executive*
Levine, Michael *public relations executive, author*
Pozo, Santiago *marketing executive*
Wald, Donna Gene *advertising executive*

Westlake Village
†Bevan, L. Darrell *telecommunication company executive, entrepreneur*
Doherty, Patrick Francis *communications executive, educator*
Murdock, David H. *diversified company executive*

Woodland Hills
Freeman, Philip Conrad, Jr. *computer systems company executive*
Maeda, J. A. *data processing executive*

Woodside
Kaisel, Stanley Francis *management consultant*

Yountville
Goeglein, Richard John *hotel/casino chain executive*
Kay, Douglas Casey *leasing company executive*

COLORADO

Aspen
McDade, James Russell *management consultant*
Murray, Robert Bruce *theatre administrator*

Boulder
Bryson, Gary Spath *cable television and telephone company executive*
Burns, Daniel Hobart *management consultant*
Fleener, Terry Noel *marketing professional*
Fukae, Kensuke *infosystems specialist*
Goeldner, Charles Raymond *business educator*
Jerritts, Stephen G. *computer company executive*

Colorado Springs
Cole, Julian Wayne (Perry Cole) *computer educator, consultant, programmer, analyst*
Guthrie, David Neal *marketing executive*
May, Melvin Arthur *computer software company executive*
Meagher, Thomas Francis Vincent *research and development company executive*
Midkiff, Donald Wayne *program manager*
Tanous, Michael Allan *consulting company executive*

Denver
Ames, A. Gary *communications company executive*
Blatter, Frank Edward *travel agency executive*
†Browne, Spencer I. *construction sales and financing executive*
Callender, Jonathan Ferris *environmental consultant*
Clinch, Nicholas Bayard, III *business executive*
Dolsen, David Horton *mortician*
Frederickson, Charles Richard *restaurant executive*
Giesen, John William *advertising executive*
Greenberg, David Ethan *communications consultant*
Johnston, Gwinavere Adams *public relations consultant*
Laff, Seymour *health care executive*
†Lazarus, Steven S. *management consultant, marketing consultant*
Leiweke, Timothy *sales executive, marketing professional*
Mc Kinney, Alexis *public relations consultant*
Neu, Carl Herbert, Jr. *management consultant*
Notari, Paul Celestin *communications executive*
Ramon, David A. *consumer products company executive*
Reisinger, George Lambert *management consultant*
Roberts, Neil Fletcher *management consulting company executive*
†Sawicki, Thomas *health care company executive*
Schotters, Bernard William *communications company executive*
†Shaw, Ward Eric *information company executive*
†Smith, Derrin Ray *information systems company executive*
Stephens, Phillip *screenwriter, producer*

Englewood
Hagan, Thomas Patrick *advertising executive*
Karsh, Philip Howard *advertising executive*
Milford, Peggy R. *communications executive*
Neiser, Brent Allen *public affairs consultant*
Rounds, Donald Michael *public relations executive*
†Vierra, Fred A. *communications executive*

Evergreen
Benson, Robert Slater *restaurant executive*

Golden
Deere, Cyril Thomas *retired computer company executive*
Guettich, Bruce Michael *sporting goods company executive*
Togerson, John Dennis *computer software company executive*

Lakewood
†Spisak, John Francis *environmental company executive*
Walton, Roger Alan *public relations executive, mediator, writer*

Littleton
Fisher, Louis McLane, Jr. *environmental engineering firm executive*
Martinen, John A. *travel company executive*
Strang, Sandra Lee *airline official*

Loveland
Churchill, Jerry M. *environment company marketing executive*

Parker
Jankura, Donald Eugene *hotel executive, educator*

Pueblo
Arveschoug, Steven Neil *communications executive, state representative*
Carter, Jack Ralph *broadcasting administrator, television personality*

Ridgway
Glenn, Gerald Marvin *marketing, engineering and construction executive*

Steamboat Springs
Langstaff, Gary Lee *food service marketing executive*

CONNECTICUT

Andover
Domagala, Richard Edward *mail marketing analyst*

Avon
Cain, Marcy *communication executive*

Bethany
Viens, Harry Henry, Jr. *communications executive*

Bloomfield
Handel, Morton Emanuel *management consultation executive*
Mackey, William Arthur Godfrey *computer software company executive*

Bridgeport
†Kiam, Victor Kermit, II *consumer products company executive*

Cheshire
Burton, Robert William *retired office products executive*

Cos Cob
Ketchum, Alton Harrington *retired advertising executive*

Danbury
Baruch, Eduard *management consultant*
Cassidy, Robert Joseph *consumer products company executive*
Dudley, Alfred Edward *home and auto products company executive*
McNabb, Frank William *consumer products company executive*
†Sweeney, Timm Raymond Paul *marketing research consultant*

Darien
Buchanan, Robert Edgar *retired advertising agency executive*
Cowherd, Edwin Russell *management consultant*
Earle, Harry Woodward *printing company executive*
Grace, John Kenneth *communications executive*
Hubner, Robert Wilmore *retired business machines company executive, consultant*
Mundt, Barry Maynard *management consultant*

Deep River
Healy, William Kent *environmental services executive*

East Haddam
Clarke, Logan, Jr. *management consultant*

East Hartford
Tanaka, Richard I. *computer products company executive*

East Windsor
Kaufmann, Sylvia Nadeau *office equipment sales company executive*

Essex
McLaughlin, David J. *management consultant*
Russell, Thomas Wright, Jr. *retired manufacturing executive*

Fairfield
Ambrosino, Ralph Thomas, Jr. *retired telecommunications executive*
Blau, Barry *advertising agency executive*
Cole, Richard John *marketing executive*
Dean, George Alden *advertising executive*
Hergenhan, Joyce *public relations executive*
Hodgkinson, William James *marketing executive*
Kantrowitz, Jonathan Daniel *educational software company executive, lawyer*
Urquhart, John Alexander *management consultant*

Greens Farms
McManus, John Francis, III *advertising executive*

Greenwich
†Amen, Robert Anthony *investor and corporate relations consultant*
Ball, John Fleming *advertising and film production executive*
†Barham, Robert Young, Jr. *communications company executive*
Carmichael, William Daniel *consultant, educator*
Chase, William Howard *public policy consultant, editor*
Chisholm, William Hardenbergh *management consultant*
Coudert, Victor Raphael, Jr. *marketing and sales executive*
Davidson, Thomas Maxwell *international management company executive*
Donley, James Walton *management consultant*
Finn, Richard Galletly Francis *personal products executive*
Gierer, Vincent A., Jr. *tobacco and wine holding company executive*
Hasner, Rolf Kaare *management consultant*
Keegan, Richard John *advertising agency executive*
Keeshan, William Francis, Jr. *advertising executive*
Kestnbaum, Albert S. *advertising executive*
Lewis, Audrey Gersh *financial marketing consultant*
MacDonald, Gordon Chalmers *management consultant*
†Oakley, Gary William *consulting company executive*
Paulson, Paul Joseph *advertising executive*
Schlafly, Hubert Joseph, Jr. *communications executive*
Scott, John Constante *marketing company executive*
Srere, Benson M. *communications company executive, consultant*
Wallach, Philip C(harles) *financial, public relations consultant*
Whitmore, George Merle, Jr. *management consulting company executive*
Willis, William Harold, Jr. *management consultant, executive search specialist*
Wyman, Ralph Mark *corporate executive*
†Ziegler, Randall Keith *food service executive*

Guilford
Ragan, James Thomas *communications executive*

Hartford
Braithwaite, Ralph Rhey *executive search consultant*
Hertel, Suzanne Marie *personnel administrator*
Morrissey, Robert John *communications executive*
Roberts, Henry Reginald *management consultant, former life insurance company executive*

Ivoryton
LeCompte, Roger Burton *management consultant*

Lakeville
Bookman, George B. *public relations consultant*
Lovitt, George Harold *advertising executive*
Manassero, Henri J. P. *hotel executive*

Madison
Keim, Robert Phillip *retired advertising executive, consultant*

Meriden
Gilbertson, Robert G. *computer company executive*

Milford
†Blau, Stanley Marvin *information systems company executive*
Eadie, Cynthia *advertising executive*
†Reichert, Bruce Robert *travel industry executive*

New Canaan
Crossman, William Whittard *retired wire cable and communications executive*
Halan, John Paul *human resources executive*
McClure, Grover Benjamin *management consultant*
Mc Mennamin, George Barry *advertising agency executive*
Means, David Hammond *retired advertising executive*
Stack, J. William, Jr. *management consultant*
Ward, Richard Vance, Jr. *management executive*

New Haven
Van Sinderen, Alfred White *former telephone company executive*
Waters, Donald Joseph *information services administrator*

Norwalk
Balmuth, Marc I. *consumer products company executive*
†Booth, George Keefer *finanical service executive*
Brandt, Richard Paul *communications and entertainment company executive*
Caravatt, Paul Joseph, Jr. *communications company executive*
Carswell, Bruce *communications executive*
Clarke, Don R. *consumer products company executive*
†Johnson, James Lawrence *telephone company executive*
Manning, James Forrest *computer executive*
Nelson, David Leonard *process management systems company executive*
Neuman, Curtis William *computer systems company executive*
Watson, H. Mitchell, Jr. *business machines company executive*

Old Greenwich
Fernous, Louis Ferdinand, Jr. *consumer products company executive*

Old Saybrook
Phillips, William Eugene *advertising agency executive*

Orange
Rowell, Harry Brown, Jr. *technology company executive*

Pomfret
Woodbridge, Henry Sewall *management consultant*

Ridgefield
Lodewick, Philip Hughes *equipment leasing company executive*
Phelps, Judson Hewett *marketing sales executive*

Riverside
Battat, Emile A. *management executive*
Geismar, Richard Lee *communications executive*
Juneja, Diljit Singh *retired management consultant*
McSpadden, Peter Ford *retired advertising agency executive*
Pearson, Robert Greenlees *writing services company executive*

Salisbury
Block, Zenas *management consultant, educator*

Shelton
Lobsenz, Herbert Munter *data base company executive*
Shapiro, Glenn Alan *marketing executive, consultant*

Sherman
Lee, Wallace Williams, Jr. *retired hotel executive*

Simsbury
Hildebrandt, Frederick Dean, Jr. *management consultant*
Nolan, Robert *management consulting company executive*

Somers
Hooper, Donald Robert *corporate chief executive officer*

South Windsor
Gerber, Heinz Joseph *computer automation company executive*

Southbury
Cassidy, James Joseph *public relations counsel*

Stamford
Ast, Steven Todd *executive search firm executive*
Axthelm, M. Bonnie *advertising executive*

Barlow, Clark W. telephone company executive
Carroll, Thomas Sylvester business executive
Condon, Joseph F. engineering and services company executive
Dell, Warren Frank, II management consultant
Dorf, Robert L. public relations executive, marketing and management consultant
Forbes, Walter Alexander consumer services company executive
Garbacz, Gerald George information services company executive
†Goldstein, Frederick Arya marketing executive
Gudger, Robert H. retired printing company executive
Hague, John William, Jr. security company executive
Kavetas, Harry L. finance leasing company executive
Kobak, James Benedict management consultant
†Leferman, Norman Bruce marketing professional
Loeffel, Bruce software company executive, consultant
MacEwen, Edward Carter communications executive
Marlowe, Edward research company executive
Miller, Wilbur Hobart business diversification consultant
Murphy, Robert Blair management consulting company executive
Nightingale, William Joslyn management consultant
Obernauer, Marne corporate executive
Ogden, Dayton executive search consultant
†Porfeli, Joseph J. computer and software development company, computer leasing company executive
Quest, James Howard advertising executive
Sarbin, Hershel Benjamin management consultant, business publisher, lawyer
†Schiff, Craig Mitchell computer company executive
Serrani, Thom management consultant, former mayor
Silver, Charles Morton communications company executive
Sullivan, James Thomas printing company executive
Sveda, Michael management and research consultant
Trivisonno, Nicholas Louis communications company executive, accountant
Villarreal, Homero Atenógenes human resources executive
Vos, Frank advertising and marketing executive
Wall, Stephen James senior executive consultant
Wallfesh, Henry Maurice business communications company executive, editor, writer
White, Richard Booth management consultant
†Wise, Robert computer services company executive
Yardis, Pamela Hintz computer consulting company executive
Yoder, Patricia Doherty public relations executive
Zuckert, Donald Mack marketing executive

Stonington
†Bennett, Gary Paul technical services company executive

Storrs Mansfield
Glasser, Joseph manufacturing and marketing executive

Suffield
Leavitt, Joel consumer products company executive

West Hartford
Glotzer, Mortimer M. quality assurance consultant

Weston
Murray, Thomas Joseph advertising executive

Westport
Aasen, Lawrence Obert public relations executive
Allen, Robert Hugh retired communications corporation executive
Bishop, William Wade advertising executive
De Lay, Robert Francis marketing executive, consultant
Dickson, Sally I. retired public relations executive
Hambleton, George Blow Elliott management consultant
Hanslip, Edward Robert management consultant, marketing professional
Lederer, Jack Lawrence personnel director, human resources specialist
Nathan, Irwin business systems company executive
Radigan, Joseph Richard human resources executive
Sadler, David Gary financial institution crisis management consultant
Savage, Robert Heath advertising executive
Singer, Henry A. behavioral scientist, institute director
†Stewart, Martha Kostyra caterer, author, lecturer

Wilton
Black, Rita Ann communications executive
Cassidy, George Thomas international business development consultant
Farley, James Parker retired advertising agency executive
Heymann, Stephen T. marketing management consultant
McCreight, John A. management consultant
Mc Dannald, Clyde Elliott, Jr. management consultation company executive
Nickel, Albert George advertising agency executive

Windsor
Clarke, Cordelia Kay Knight Mazuy marketing management executive
Cowen, Bruce David environmental service company executive
Kamerschen, Robert Jerome consumer products executive

Woodbridge
Ostfeld, Alexander Marion advertising agency executive

Woodstock
Boote, Alfred Shepard marketing researcher, educator

DELAWARE

Hockessin
Bischoff, Joyce Arlene information systems consultant, lecturer

Middletown
Jackson, Donald Richard marketing professional

Millsboro
Jones, Lowell Robert safety and industrial hygiene consultant

New Castle
Keillor, Sharon Ann computer company executive

Wilmington
Ceci, Anthony Thomas executive secretary
Emanuel, Abraham Gabriel photo processing company executive, consultant
Kjellmark, Eric William, Jr. management consultant, opera company director
Mackenzie, Malcolm Lewis advertising executive
Shipley, Samuel Lynn advertising and public relations executive
Wieland, Ferdinand hotel executive, entrepreneur
Wyer, William Clarke management consultant, development executive

DISTRICT OF COLUMBIA

Washington
Adams, A. John Bertrand public affairs consultant
Alexander, Clifford L., Jr. management consultant, lawyer, former secretary of army
Allen, Richard Vincent international business consultant, bank executive
Arsht, Leslye Alene public relations executive
Baker, Melvin C. advertising executive
Baruch, Jordan Jay management consultant
Bauer, Robert Albert public policy consultant
Bradley, Melvin LeRoy communications company executive
Brewster-Walker, Sandra JoAnn public relations executive, publishing executive, genealogist, historian, consultant
†Bryan, A. Bradford, Jr. hotel corporation executive
†Buben, Jeffrey Alan restaurant owner, chef
Burch, Michael Ira public relations executive, former government official
Carberry, Michael Glen public relations executive
Carlstrom, Robert E., Jr. government and public relations executive
Cherian, Joy consulting company executive
Clay, Don Richard environmental consulting firm executive
Cody, Thomas Gerald management consultant, writer
Cope, Jeannette Naylor human resources consultant
Dach, Leslie Alan public relations executive
Dealy, John Francis management consultant, lawyer, educator, arbitrator
†Deaver, Michael Keith public relations consultant
Denysyk, Bohdan marketing professional
Dobriansky, Paula Jon business and communications executive
Ehrlich, Clifford John hotel executive
Elliott, Thomas Michael management services executive, educator, consultant
Erwin, Frank William personnel research and publishing executive
†Evans, Michael Brock environmentalist
Fahmy, Ibrahim Mounir hotel executive
Fairchild, Samuel Wilson professional services company executive, former federal agency administrator
Farrell, June Martinick public relations executive
Fields, Stuart Howard employee relations specialist
Flanagan, Francis Dennis retired corporate executive
Fletcher, James Andrew information systems specialist
Foreman, Carol Lee Tucker corporate executive
Fuller, Edwin Daniel hotel executive
Furash, Edward E. management consultant
Goldstein, Irving communications company executive
Grant, Carl N. communications executive
Gray, Robert Keith communications company executive
Grumbacher, Jacqueline W. communications executive
Hannaford, Peter Dor public relations executive
Harrison, Emmett Bruce, Jr. public relations counselor
Harrison, Patricia de Stacy public relations consulting company executive
Havlicek, Franklin J. communications executive
Helms, Richard McGarrah international consultant, former ambassador
Higgins, James Henry, III marketing executive
Holland, James Ricks public relations executive, association executive
Holmes, Bradley Paul information technology management consultant
†Hoog, Thomas W. public relations executive
Hoving, John Hannes Forester consulting firm executive
Howe, Fisher management consultant, former government official
Huberman, Benjamin defense consultant
Hunter, Ronald V. administrator
†Ingrassia, Anthony Frank human resource specialist
Jagoda, Barry Lionel media adviser, communications consultant
Johnson, John A. communications company executive
†Kahler, Kathryn Schiller communications executive
Kalbfeld, Brad Marshall television and radio executive, editor
Karalekas, Anne publishing executive
Kelly, Francis Joseph strategic communications company executive
Kennedy, Roger George park services executive
Kotler, Milton marketing company executive
Kraus, Margery management consultant
Kusnet, David communications executive, speechwriter
Lawson, D. Dale public relations executive
Lee, Ronald Barry marketing company executive, retired military officer
†Leibach, Dale W. public relations executive
Leslie, John William public relations and advertising executive
Lewis, Jordan David management consultant, author, international speaker, educator
Lewis, William Walker management consultant
Lilley, William, III communications business consultant
†Loiello, John Peter public affairs executive, consultant
Lombard, Judith Marie human resource policy specialist
†Lowder, Rachael Della company executive, consultant
Lowe, Florence Segal retired public relations executive
Lowrie, Gerald M. communications executive
Luikart, Fordyce Whitney management consultant
Maddock, Jerome Torrence information services specialist
Mansfield, Edward Patrick, Jr. advertising executive
Mantyla, Karen sales executive
Marriott, Alice Sheets (Mrs. John Willard Marriott) restaurant chain executive
Marriott, John Willard, Jr. hotel and food service chain executive
Marriott, Richard Edwin hotel and contract services executive
Marumoto, William Hideo management consultant
McBride, Jonathan Evans executive search company executive
McLaughlin, John Joseph broadcast executive, television producer, political commentator, journalist
Millian, Kenneth Young public policy consultant
Moore, Bob Stahly communications executive
Mueller, Ronald Raymond public relations executive
Nelson, Richard Copeland hotel executive
Norman, William Stanley travel and tourism executive
Novak, Paul hotel industry executive
O'Connor, Tom corporate executive, management consultant
Olson, Walter Justus, Jr. management consultant
Palumbo, Benjamin Lewis public affairs consulting company executive
†Payne, Michael Lee association management executive
Pedersen, Wesley Niels public relations and public affairs executive
†Pettus, Mary Catherine public relations executive
Pfeiffer, Leonard, IV executive recruiter, consultant
Pines, Wayne Lloyd public relations counselor
Powell, Joseph Lester (Jody Powell) public relations executive
Pucie, Charles R., Jr. public affairs executive
Pyle, Robert Noble public relations executive
Rabin, Kenneth Hardy public relations executive
Rabin, Steve Arthur public affairs executive
Rafshoon, Gerald Monroe communications executive
Rainey, Jean Osgood public relations executive
Rausch, Howard information service executive
†Raviv, Sheila public relations executive
Reed, Travis Dean public relations consultant
Rice, Lois Dickson former computer company executive
Rimpel, Auguste Eugene, Jr. management and technical consulting executive
Rosebush, James Scott international management and public affairs consultant, former government official
Rosenthal, Aaron management consultant
†Ruffer, Michael R. hotel company executive
Schick, Michael William public relations executive
Schlossberg, Stephen I. management consultant
Schriever, Bernard Adolph management consultant
Sheinbaum, Gilbert Harold international management consultant
Sikes, Alfred C. communications executive
Sills, Hilary H. public relations executive
Silverman, Alvin Michaels public relations consultant
Simmons, Richard De Lacey mass media executive
Sisco, Joseph John management consultant, corporation director, educator, government official
Slagle, Larry B. human resources specialist
Smith, Alan W., Jr. management consultant
Tanham, George Kilpatrick retired research company executive
Tate, Sheila Burke public relations executive
†Taylor, Gerald H. communications comapny executive
Thelian, Lorraine public relations executive
Tiefel, William Reginald hotel company executive
Timmons, William Evan corporate executive
Timperlake, Edward Thomas public relations executive
Trent, Darrell M. academic and corporate executive
Van Dyk, Frederick Theodore corporate executive
Veblen, Thomas Clayton management consultant
Wade, Robert Hirsch Beard international consultant, former government and educational association official
Walker, Ronald Hugh executive search company executive
Weeks, Julie Rae marketing executive
Weiner, Jonathan management consultant
Wertheim, Mitzi Mallina technology company executive
Wesberry, James Pickett, Jr. financial management consultant, auditor, international organization executive
Wexler, Anne government relations and public affairs consultant
Wheeler, Thomas Edgar communications technology executive
Widner, Ralph Randolph civic executive
Winnefeld, James Alexander defense analyst, former naval officer, author
Worden, Joan M. public relations executive
Worthington, John Rice communications company executive, lawyer
Yulish, Charles Barry public affairs executive
Zimmerman, John H. communications company executive
Zion, Roger H. consulting firm executive, former congressman

FLORIDA

Altamonte Springs
†Kirchman, Kenneth Paul computer software services company executive

Amelia Island
Harman, John Robert, Jr. management consultant

Aventura
†Susser, Allen restaurateur, chef

Boca Grande
Dyche, David Bennett, Jr. management consultant

Boca Raton
Albrecht, Arthur John advertising agency executive
Bradley, George H. furniture company executive
Costello, Albert Joseph diversified consumer products executive
Dorfman, Allen Bernard international management consultant
Dunhill, Robert W. advertising direct mail executive
Epstein, Barry R. public relations counselor
Finegold, Ronald computer service executive
Krause, Heinz Werner computer and communications executive
†Lemasters, John N., III management and marketing consultant
Miller, Kenneth Roy management consultant
Monroe, William Lewis human resources executive
Posner, Sidney advertising executive
Rosner, M. Norton business systems and financial services company executive
Rothbaum, Ira advertising and marketing executive
Turner, Lisa Phillips human resources executive

Bonita Springs
St. Mary, Edward Sylvester direct mail marketing company executive

Boynton Beach
†Akridge, William David hotel management company executive
Bloede, Victor Gustav retired advertising executive
Koteen, Jack management consultant, writer

Bradenton
Burton, Ralph Joseph international development consultant
Jones, Horace Charles former sales company executive
Ridings, Dorothy Sattes communications executive, newspaper publisher

Brandon
Williamson, Robert Charles marketing executive

Cape Coral
Brevoort, Richard William public relations executive

Casselberry
Medin, A. Louis computer company executive

Clearwater
Alogna, John Joseph advertising agency executive
Eshenbaugh, William Arthur sales executive
Raymund, Steven A. computer company executive

Coral Gables
Cobb, Charles E., Jr. corporate executive, former ambassador
Hammes, Terry Marie advertising, public relations and marketing executive
Ramsey, John Hansberry executive search firm executive, investment banker

Deerfield Beach
Moran, James M. automotive sales executive
Van Arnem, Harold Louis capital and technology equipment leasing company executive

Deland
Fortmueller, Heinz William Erich quality assurance professional
McCormick, Lyle Bernard, Jr. management consultant

Delray Beach
Charyk, Joseph Vincent retired satellite telecommunications executive

Fort Lauderdale
Bayles, Samuel Heagan advertising agency executive
Bleckner, Edward, Jr. data communication products company executive
Cumerford, William Richard fund raising and public relations executive
Du Mont, Dolph Joseph management consultant
Fine, Howard Alan travel industry executive
Gerbino, John advertising executive
†Golnick, Howard Marshall advertising executive
†Golnick, Leon Shaffer advertising and marketing executive
Gude, Nancy Carlson systems consultant
Honahan, H(enry) Robert motion picture theatre executive
Jotcham, Thomas Denis marketing communications consultant
Kobert, Norman Noah asset management consultant
Lederman, Michael G. consumer products company executive
Russo, Thomas Joseph hospitality and consumer durables industry executive
Smith, Scott Clybourn communications company executive
Sorensen, Allan Chresten service company executive
Vasquez, William Leroy marketing professional, educator
Zirkle, David H. data processing company executive

Fort Myers
Fromm, Winfield Eric retired corporate executive, engineering consultant and investor
Ryan, William Joseph communications company executive
Zupko, Arthur George consultant to drug industry, retired college administrator

Fort Pierce
Chapman, John Davol communications brokerage executive

Fort Walton Beach
Brown, Gary Allen defense analysis company executive

Gainesville
†Johnson, Charles William consulting firm executive

Gulf Breeze
Strength, Janis Grace management executive, educator

Hallandale
Kemp, Bernard organizational development consultant

Havana
Penson, Edward Martin *management consulting company executive*

Hialeah
Edelcup, Norman Scott *management and financial consultant*

Highland Beach
Collins, John Joseph *telecommunications executive*
Gaffey, Thomas Michael, Jr. *consumer products executive*
Summers, James Irvin *retired advertising executive*
Wegman, Harold Hugh *management consultant*

Hollywood
Angstrom, Wayne Raymond *communications executive*
Cowan, Irving *real estate owner, developer*

Indian Rocks Beach
Mortensen, James E. *management consultant*
Sullivan, Paul William *communications specialist*

Jacksonville
Birk, John R. *marketing/financial services executive*
Cary, Cornelius Adams *executive search firm executive*
Davis, A. Dano *grocery store chain executive*
Goff, Charles Wesley, Jr. *management consultant*
Hatch, Donald James (Jim Hatch) *business leadership and planning executive*
Kelly, Patrick Chastain *sales executive*
Massey, William Walter, Jr. *sales executive*
Schramm, Bernard Charles, Jr. *advertising agency executive*
Sederbaum, William *marketing executive*
Sekely, George Frank *computer and communications executive*

Jensen Beach
Sculfort, Maurice Charles *advertising agency executive*

Jupiter
Marker, Robert Sydney *management consultant*
Taylor, Claude J. *sales executive, consultant*

Kennedy Space Center
Young, Richard Stuart *technical services executive*

Key Biscayne
Duffy, Earl Gavin *hotel executive*

Key Largo
Chevins, Anthony Charles *advertising agency executive*

Key West
Ellinghaus, William Maurice *communications executive*
Fizdale, Richard *advertising agency executive*
Lynch, William Thomas, Jr. *advertising agency executive*
Nolan, Robert D. *advertising company executive*
Oates, James G. *advertising executive*
Smith, John J. (Jack Smith) *advertising agency executive*

Lady Lake
Langevin, Thomas Harvey *higher education consultant*

Lake Buena Vista
Lomonosoff, James Marc *marketing executive*
†Nunis, Richard Arlen *amusement parks executive*
Parke, Robert Leon *communications executive*

Lake Worth
Stevens, William John *management consultant, former association executive*

Lakeland
Hollis, Mark C. *supermarket company executive*
Jenkins, Howard M. *supermarket executive*
Meads, Walter Frederick *executive recruitment consultant*
Miller, Robert Allen *hotel executive*
Siedle, Robert Douglas *management consultant*

Lantana
†Rawls, L(oyd) Neal *communications executive*

Largo
Ray, Roger Buchanan *retired communications executive, lawyer*

Leesburg
Entorf, Richard Carl *management consultant*

Longboat Key
Cornelius, James Alfred *advertising executive*
Schoenberg, Lawrence Joseph *computer services company executive*

Longwood
†Bernabei, Raymond *management consultant*
Brooker, Robert Elton *corporate executive*
Faller, Donald E. *marketing and operations executive*

Manalapan
Johnstone, Edmund Frank *advertising executive*

Melbourne
Boyd, Joseph Aubrey *communications company executive*
Gabriel, Roger Eugene *management consulting executive*
Hogan, Henry Leon, III *business executive, retired air force officer*
Suojanen, Waino W. *management educator*
Vilardebo, Angie Marie *management consultant, parochial school educator*

Miami
Anders, Walter Charles *human resources administrator*
Arison, Micky *cruise line company executive*
Cole, Todd G. *management consultant transportation*
Conrad, Barry L. *hotel and restaurant executive*
Cubas, Jose M(anuel) *advertising agency executive*
Evans, Peter Kenneth *advertising executive*
Gibbons, Barry J. *food service executive*
Hanlon, David Patrick *hotel and casino executive*
Henson, John Denver *international management consulting firm executive*
Hertz, David Bendel *management consultant, educator, lawyer*
†Meyer, Hank *public relations and publicity consultant*
Myers, Joyce Anne *fast food chain company executive*
Navarro, Antonio (Luis) *public relations executive*
Parker, David Raymond *services industry executive*
Porter, Charles King *advertising executive*
Rothchild, Howard Leslie *advertising executive*
†Rubin, Bruce S. *public relations executive*
Silva, Felipe *former tobacco company executive*
†Smirnoff, Bear *recreational facility executive*
Stickler, Daniel Lee *health care management consultant*
Strong, Charles Robert *waste management administrator*
Taylor, Ann Louise *marketing executive*
Wackenhut, George Russell *security services executive*
Wackenhut, Richard Russell *security company executive*
Weiser, Ralph Raphael *recovery company executive*
Weiser, Sherwood Manuel *hotel and corporation executive, lawyer*
Wragg, Joanna DiCarlo *public relation executive, newspaper editor*

Miami Beach
Shapiro, Samuel Bernard *management consultant*

Mount Dora
Hensinger, Margaret Elizabeth *horticultural and agricultural advertising and marketing executive*

Naples
Berman, Robert S. *marketing consultant*
Buccello, Henry Louis *advertising executive*
Daniels, Myra Janco (Mrs. Draper Daniels) *advertising agency executive*
Hochschwender, Herman Karl *international consultant*
Marshall, Charles *communications company executive*
Moore, Mechlin Dongan *business consultant*
Quigley, Jack Allen *service company executive*
Richmond, Robert Linn *management consultant*
Weeks, Richard Ralph *marketing educator*

New Port Richey
Oliveto, Frank Louis *recreation consultant*

Nokomis
Halladay, Laurie Ann *public relations consultant, former franchise executive*

North Palm Beach
Bubrick, George Joseph *corporate executive*
Chane, George Warren *management consultant*
Yackira, Michael William *power company executive*

Ocala
Booth, George Warren *artist, advertising executive*

Oldsmar
Brunner, George Matthew *management consultant, former business executive*

Opa Locka
Nelsen, Martin Claude *management services professional*

Orlando
Connolly, Joseph Francis, II *government consultant*
Davis, William Albert *theme park director*
Moltzon, Richard Francis *manufacturing executive*
Pantuso, Vincent Joseph *food service consultant*
Wilkerson, John Lee *telecommunications executive*
Yesawich, Peter Charles *advertising executive*

Ormond Beach
Barker, Robert Osborne (Bob Barker) *management and public relations consultant*
Coke, C(hauncey) Eugene *consulting company executive, scientist, educator, author*

Palm Beach
Alimanestianu, Calin *retired hotel consultant*
Druck, Kalman Breschel *public relations counselor*
Robb, David Buzby, Jr. *financial services company executive, lawyer*
†Tremain, Alan *hotel executive*
Walsh, Cornelius Stephen *leasing company executive*

Palm Beach Gardens
Mendelson, Richard Donald *former communications company executive*

Panama City
Dykes, James Edgar *advertising educator, consultant*

Pembroke Pines
Ladin, Eugene *communications company executive*

Placida
Grissom, Joseph Carol *retired leasing and investments business executive*

Pompano Beach
Crandell, K(enneth) James *management and strategic planning consultant, entrepreneur*
Freimark, Jeffrey Philip *retail supermarket executive*
Slovin, Bruce *diversified holding company executive*
Toppel, Harold H. *diversified company executive*

Ponte Vedra Beach
Wilson, J. Tylee *business executive*

Punta Gorda
Harrington, John Vincent *retired communications company executive, engineer, educator*

Saint Augustine
LeBeau, Hector Alton, Jr. *management consultant, former confectionary company executive*

Saint Petersburg
Layton, William George *computer company executive, management consultant, human resources executive*
†Pyle, William Carmody *human resource management educator, researcher*
Sembler, Mel *company executive, former ambassador*
Silver, Lawrence Alan *marketing executive*
Söderberg, Bo Sigfrid *marketing executive*
Stevens, Edward Ira *information systems educator*

Sanford
Corp, William Thomas, Sr. *purchasing executive*

Sarasota
Beck, Robert Alfred *hotel administration educator*
Feder, Allan Appel *management executive, consultant*
Fendrick, Alan Burton *retired advertising executive*
Gittelson, Bernard *public relations consultant, author, lecturer*
Gray, Hope Diffenderfer *industrial relations specialist*
Greene, Richard Efraim *data processing executive*
Hagen, George Leon *computer systems consultant*
Herbert, James Paul *advertising executive*
Lewis, Brian Kreglow *computer consultant*
Mattran, Donald Albert *management consultant, educator*
Neeley, Delmar George *human resources executive*
Scherstem, H. Donald *management consultant, realtor, mortgage broker*
Simon, Joseph Patrick *food services executive*
White, Will Walter, III *public relations consultant, writer*

Seminole
Silver, Paul Robert *marketing executive, consultant*

Tallahassee
†Boutwell, Wallace Kenneth, Jr. *management consultant, health care executive*
Marshall, Stanley *former educator, business executive*

Tampa
†Cameron, Susan *computer services company executive*
Christopher, Wilford Scott *public relations consultant*
DeVine, B. Mack *management consultant*
Frankowiak, James Raymond *public relations executive*
Hayes, Don A. *data processing company executive*
Heuer, Martin *temporary services executive*
†Hoyland, Fred *diversified products supply company executive*
Tompkins, William David *corporate professional*
Whipple, Thomas A. *food marketing professional*

Tarpon Springs
Dempster, Richard Vreeland *environmental company executive*

Tavernier
Mabbs, Edward Carl *management consultant*

Tequesta
Vollmer, James E. *consulting company executive*

Tierra Verde
Kubiet, Leo Lawrence *newspaper advertising and marketing executive*

Venice
Bluhm, Barbara Jean *communications agency executive*
Dodderidge, Richard William *retired marketing executive*
Ogan, Russell Griffith *business executive, retired air force officer*

Vero Beach
Bradford, Charles Lobdell *management consultant*
Fisher, Andrew *management consultant*
Mc Namara, John J(oseph) *advertising executive, writer*
Nichols, Carl Wheeler *retired advertising agency executive*

West Palm Beach
†Davis, Karen *sales executive*
Diener, Bert *former food broker, artist*
†Hawthorne, David Eugene *service hotel and resorts executive*
Patterson, Lydia Ross *industrial relations specialist, consulting company executive*
Ronan, William John *management consultant*

Winter Park
Perkins, James Patrick *advertising executive*

GEORGIA

Ailey
Windsor, James Thomas, Jr. *printing company executive, newspaper publisher*

Alpharetta
Mills, Stephen Nathaniel *computer software company executive*

Athens
Lane, Walter Ronald, Jr. *advertising executive, educator*

Atlanta
Alford, Walter Helion *telecommunications executive, lawyer*
Allio, Robert John *management consultant, educator*
Barnes, Harry G., Jr. *human rights activist, retired ambassador*
Barnett, Elizabeth Hale *organizational consultant*
Barr, James Milton *business consultant*
Blank, Arthur M. *home and lumber retail chain executive*
Bobo, Genelle Tant (Nell Bobo) *office administrator*
Brown-Olmstead, Amanda *public relations executive*
Burge, William Lee *retired business information executive*
Carroll, James Michael *retailing executive*
Chaiet, Alan Howard *advertising agency executive*
Chasen, Sylvan Herbert *computer applications consultant, investment advisor*
Cohn, Bob *public relations executive*
Cole, David Andrew *management consultant executive*
Collura, Kathryn Jean *communications executive, consultant*
Cooper, Thomas Luther *retired printing company executive*
Copeland, Alvin Charles *fast food company executive*
Dillon, John Robert, III *communications executive*
Dysart, Benjamin Clay, III *environmental management consultant, conservationist, engineer*
Eden, Margie Cohen *public relations executive*
Farley, Charles P. *public relations executive*
Fitzgerald, David Patrick *advertising agency executive*
Francisco, Edgar Wiggin, III *management information systems consultant*
Frank, William Pendleton *sales and marketing executive*
Fuqua, John Brooks *retired consumer products and services company executive*
Gable, Carl Irwin *business consultant, private investor, lawyer*
†Gelardi, Robert Charles *trade association executive, consultant*
Goldstein, Burton Benjamin, Jr. *communications executive*
Goodwin, George Evans *public relations executive*
Hansen, Jorgen Hartmann *hotel corporation executive*
House, Donald Lee, Sr. *software executive, private investor, management consultant*
Johnson, William B. *hotel executive*
Kaiser, Fred *computer leasing company executive*
MacIntyre, R. Douglas *information technology executive*
Martindale, Larry *hotel executive*
Massey, Charles Knox, Jr. *advertising agency executive*
†McCall, Charles W. *computer company executive*
McDonald, John C. *telecommunications company executive*
Miles, John Karl *marketing executive*
Montgomery, James Morton *public relations, marketing executive, association executive*
Overstreet, Jim *public relations executive*
Raper, Charles Albert *retired management consultant*
†Reed, Bill *purchasing agent*
Reiman, Joey *advertising executive*
Rollins, Gary Wayne *service company executive*
Rosenberg, George A. *public relations company executive*
Schulze, Horst H. *hotel company executive*
†Seeger, Guenter Otto *chef*
Sherry, Henry Ivan *marketing consultant*
†Shivers, Jane *corporate communications executive, director*
Shutze, Virgil Cox *advertising executive*
Simms, Arthur Benjamin *management consultant, financier*
Sloan, Stanley *management consultant*
Sonnenfeld, Jeffrey Alan *management educator*
Steinfals, Christian Werner *hotel executive*
Stormont, Richard Mansfield *hotel executive*
Strong-Tidman, Virginia Adele *marketing and advertising executive*
Summerlin, Glenn Wood *advertising executive*
Swan, James Robert Duncan *hotel executive*
Tarkenton, Francis Asbury *computer comany executive, sports commentator, management consultant, former professional football player*
Thomas, Mable *communications company executive, former state legislator*
Thomas, Patrick Herbert *information services company executive*
Turner, Michael Griswold *advertising executive*
Verrill, F. Glenn *advertising executive*
†Walz, Jack *advertising executive*
Ward, Jackie M. *computer company executive*
Wells, Everett Clayton, Jr. *economic development executive*
White, Ronald Leon *financial management consultant*
Whitehead, John Jed *computer systems company executive*
†Wilson, Jimmy *computer service company executive*
Zunde, Pranas *information science educator, researcher*

Austell
Friedrich, Stephen Miro *credit bureau company executive*

Columbus
Slay, Ken *sales executive*
Zallen, Harold *corporate executive, scientist, former university official*

Covington
Womack, Samuel Edward *computer company executive*

Dacula
Bascom, Perry Bagnall *retired marketing sales executive*

Duluth
Galfas, Timothy, II *franchising and turnaround administrator*
Taylor, Maria Centofanti *marketing professional*

Macon
†King, Damon Dee *hospital executive*

Marietta
Johnson, Herbert Frederick *sales executive, former university administrator, librarian*
Overton, Bruce *personnel executive, consultant*
Smith, Baker Armstrong *management executive, lawyer*
Spann, George William *management consultant*

Newnan
Andrews, Rowena *public relations executive*

Norcross
Esher, Brian Richard *environmental company executive*
Johnson, Gary Ray *sales and marketing executive*
Newman, James Michael *communications company executive*
†Stanley, Robert L. *computer services executive*
†Strange, J. Leland *computer company executive*

Pine Mountain
Callaway, Howard Hollis *business executive*

Roswell
Burgess, John Frank *management consultant, former utility executive, former army officer*
Hill, Dennis James *trade show exhibition manager, consultant*
Jordan, DuPree, Jr. *management consultant, educator, journalist, publisher, business executive*

Saint Simons Island
Riedeburg, Theodore *management consultant*

Savannah
Cooper, Robert H. *marketing executive*
Daubenspeck, Robert Donley *advertising agency executive*
Lowe, William C. *business products and systems company executive*
Otter, John Martin, III *television advertising consultant, retired*
Schafer, Thomas Wilson *advertising agency executive*
†Terry, Elizabeth Bennett *chef, restaurant owner*
Theis, Francis William *business executive*

Smyrna
Lenker, Max V. *consumer products company executive*
Wilding, Diane *marketing, financial and information systems executive*

Tucker
Rogers, Richard Hilton *hotel company executive*

HAWAII

Hilo
Evans, Franklin Bachelder *marketing educator emeritus*

Honolulu
Ablon, R. Richard *service company executive*
†Bossert, Philip Joseph *information systems executive*
Brechin, Garry David *leasing company executive, real estate company executive*
Cornuelle, Herbert Cumming *retired corporate executive*
Devenot, David Charles *human resource executive*
Jongeward, George Ronald *systems analyst*
Kelley, Richard Roy *hotel executive*
Kelly, James Andrew *policy reseach executive, former government official*
†Kim, Donald Chang Won *consulting engineering company executive*
Murabayashi, Harris Nozomu *retired management analyst*
O'Neill, Charles Kelly *marketing executive, former advertising agency executive*
Simpson, Andrea Lynn *energy communications executive*
Stebbins, Dennis Robert *environmental management consultant*
†Tanabe, Barbara Jean *communications company executive*
Tatibouet, André Stephan *condominium and resort management firm executive*
Yamato, Kei C. *international business consultant*

Kaneohe
Smales, Fred Benson *corporate executive*

IDAHO

Boise
Beaumont, Pamela Jo *marketing professional*
Garber, Jerold Allan *broadcasting executive*
Gloth, Alec Robert *retail grocery executive*
Joyce, Claude Clinton *data processing executive*
Maulin, Jack Doolin *construction company executive*
Wilson, Barbara Louise *communications executive*

Ketchum
†Ring, Terry William *company executive, environmentalist*

ILLINOIS

Alton
Minsker, Robert Stanley *consultant, former industrial relations executive*

Arlington Heights
Smedley, Bernard Ronald (Bernie Smedley) *communications executive*

Barrington
Andler, Donald Andrew *marketing executive*
Edwards, Wilbur Shields *communications company executive*
Ligare, Kathleen Meredith *strategy and marketing executive*
Massé, Laurence Raymond *personnel search firm executive*
Mathis, Jack David *advertising executive*
Smith, William Lewis *hotel executive*
Woltz, Kenneth Allen *consulting executive*

Carbondale
Wills, Walter Joe *agricultural marketing educator*

Carmi
Edwards, Judith Elizabeth *advertising executive*

Champaign
Knox, Charles Milton *purchasing agent, consultant*

Chicago
Adams, Hall, Jr. (Cap Adams) *advertising agency executive*
Allen, Belle *management consulting firm executive, communications company executive*
Amberg, Thomas Law *public relations executive*
Ashwill, Terry M. *advertising executive*
Avedisian, Armen George *industrialist, financier*
Bailey, Robert, Jr. *advertising executive*
Balousek, John B. *advertising executive*
Banik, Douglas Heil *advertising executive*
Bard, John Franklin *consumer products executive*
Barnette, Dennis Arthur *management consultant*
Barrett, Paulette Singer *public relations executive*
†Barry, Richard A. *public relations executive*
†Bartolotta, Paul Wenzel *chef*
Bayer, Gary Richard *advertising executive*
Beattie, Janet Holtzman *accounting firm executive*
Beattie, Mary Jarvis *public relations executive*
Bechina, Melvin Jeremiah *leasing company executive*
Bensinger, Peter Benjamin *consulting firm executive*
Berger, Kay *public relations executive*
Bergstrom, Betty Howard *consulting executive*
Bernatowicz, Frank Allen *management consultant, expert witness*
Beugen, Joan Beth *communications company executive*
Biggles, Richard Robert *marketing executive*
Bjorneberg, Paul Grant *public relations executive*
Bliwas, Ronald Lee *advertising agency executive*
Bowen, William Joseph *management consultant*
Breslin, Michael Edward *advertising agency executive, lawyer*
Bruno, Kay Anderson *public relations executive, speaker*
†Brunson, Kathleen M. *public relations executive*
Buckley, Joseph Paul, III *polygraph specialist*
Bueschel, David Alan *management consultant*
Burack, Elmer Howard *management educator*
Burrell, Thomas J. *marketing communication executive*
Campbell, Janie Lee *patient services executive, researcher, abstractor*
Campbell, Patricia K. *public relations executive, writer, journalist*
Chaitin, Anthony *management services executive*
Chorengel, Bernd *international hotel corporation executive*
Choyke, Phyllis May Ford (Mrs. Arthur Davis Choyke, Jr.) *management executive, editor, poet*
†Claypoole, Robert Edwin *distribution service company executive*
Cohan, George Sheldon *advertising and public relations executive*
Conidi, Daniel Joseph *private investigation agency executive*
†Connolly, Peter Dominic *hotel executive, lawyer*
Coulson, John Selden *retired marketing executive*
Cox, Allan James *management consultant*
Cushman, Aaron D. *public relations executive*
Daley, Rosie *cook, writer*
Dammeyer, Rodney Foster *distribution company executive*
Davis, J. Steve *advertising agency executive*
De Francesco, John Blaze, Jr. *public relations company executive*
Delony, Patty Litton *management consultant*
†Donovan, John Vincent *consulting company executive*
Doty, Carl K. *retired printing company executive*
Dunford, Michael S. *marketing professional*
Echols, M(ary) Evelyn *travel consultant*
Edelman, Daniel Joseph *public relations executive*
Feldman, Burton Gordon *printing company executive*
Feldstein, Joel Robert *public relations executive*
Fickinger, Wayne Joseph *advertising executive*
Fisher, Wendy Astley-Bell *marketing executive*
Flagg, Michael James *communications and graphics company executive*
Flanagan, Joseph Patrick *advertising executive*
Foley, Joseph Lawrence *sales executive*
Foote, William Chapin *strategic planning and corporate development executive*
Ford, Larry John *computer company executive*
Freidheim, Cyrus F., Jr. *management consultant*
Frommelt, Jeffrey James *management consulting firm executive*
Fulgoni, Gian Marc *market research company executive*
Fullmer, Paul *public relations counselor*
Furcon, John Edward *management and organizational consultant*
Gardner, Bettiann *hair care products executive*
Gardner, Howard Alan *travel marketing executive, travel writer and editor*
Gillette, Susan Downs *advertising executive*
Glasner, LeRoy A. *public relations executive*
Glasser, James J. *leasing company executive*
Goldring, Norman Max *advertising executive*
Golin, Alvin *public relations company executive*
Golomski, William Arthur *consulting company executive*
Grant, Paul Bernard *industrial relations educator*
Haffner, Charles Christian, III *retired printing company executive*
Haley, Clifton Edward *car rental company executive*
Hallagan, Robert E. *management consultant*
Hansen, Carl R. *management consultant*
Hassan, M. Zia *management educator*
Haupt, Roger A. *advertising executive*
Heidrick, Gardner Wilson *management consultant*
Heidrick, Robert Lindsay *management consultant*
Hermann, Edward Robert *occupational and environmental health consultant*
Hoey, Rita Marie *public relations executive*
Holmes, Colgate Frederick *hotel executive*
Holzer, Edwin *advertising executive*
Hunt, Steven J(ames) *media and advertising executive*
Husting, Peter Marden *advertising agency executive*
Iltis, John Frederic *advertising and public relations company executive*
Isaacs, Roger David *public relations executive*
Jarc, Frank Robert *printing company executive*
†Jasculca, Richard J. *public relations executive*
†Johnson, Cathleen *public relations executive*
Johnson, Robert Bruce *public relations executive*
†Joho, Jean Charles *chef, restaurateur*
Katz, Marilyn Faye *communications consultant, political strategist*
Kelly, Robert Donald *management consultant*
Kestnbaum, Robert Dana *management consultant*
Kobs, James Fred *advertising agency executive*
Kopec, Joseph Arthur *public relations executive*
Koten, John A. *retired communications executive*
Kozitka, Richard Eugene *consumer products company executive*
Kraus, Herbert Myron *public relations executive*
Lane, Kenneth Edwin *retired advertising agency executive*
LaSage, John David *public relations firm executive*
Lauer, Robert Lee *consumer products executive*
Leahigh, Alan Kent *public relations executive*
Lebedow, Aaron Louis *consulting company executive*
Lehman, George Morgan *food sales executive*
Leigh, Sherren *communications executive, editor, publisher*
Lesly, Philip *public relations counsel*
†Lester, June *library, information management educator*
Lewy, Ralph I. *hotel executive*
Lowry, James Hamilton *management consultant*
Malkin, Judd D. *diversified corporation executive*
Mason, Bruce *advertising agency executive*
McConnell, E. Hoy, II *advertising executive*
McCullough, Richard Lawrence *advertising agency executive*
Mc Kenna, Thomas Joseph *advertising executive*
McNeely, Stephen Allen *outdoor advertising company executive*
Menchin, Robert Stanley *marketing executive*
Meyer, Edward Paul *advertising executive*
Miller, Bernard Joseph, Jr. *advertising executive*
Miller, William H. *public relations executive*
Mitchell, Lee Mark *communications executive, investment fund manager, lawyer*
†Nachman, Frederick *public relations executive*
Nadherny, Ferdinand *executive recruiting company executive*
Nelson, H(arry) Donald *communications executive*
Nicastro, Neil David *business executive, lawyer*
Nisenholtz, Martin Abram *telecommunications executive, educator*
O'Hare, Linda Parsons *management consultant*
Olins, Robert Abbot *communications research executive*
O'Shea, Lynne Edeen *advertising executive, educator*
Page, Janice Ellen *retail executive*
Paul, Ronald Neale *management consultant*
Philipps, Louis Edward *data systems manufacturing company executive*
Pilkington, Alan Ralph *advertising executive*
Pincus, Theodore Henry *public relations executive*
Plank, Betsy Ann (Mrs. Sherman V. Rosenfield) *public relations counsel*
Plotkin, Manuel D. *management consultant, educator, former corporate executive and government official*
Preschlack, John Edward *management consultant*
Pritzker, Thomas Jay *lawyer, business executive*
Proctor, Barbara Gardner *advertising agency executive*
Prosperi, David Philip *public relations executive*
Provus, Barbara Lee *executive search consultant*
†Queeney, Jack *public relations executive*
Radell, Nicholas John *management consultant*
Raphaelson, Joel *retired advertising agency executive*
Reggio, Vito Anthony *management consultant*
†Reid, Daniel James *public relations executive*
Reilly, Robert Frederick *valuation consultant*
Reitman, Jerry Irving *advertising agency executive*
Rible, Morton *manufacturing executive, lawyer*
Rich, S. Judith *public relations executive*
Richardson, Jerome Johnson *food service company executive*
Robbins, Henry Zane *public relations and marketing executive*
†Roger, John W. *parks and recreation director*
Rose, Merrill *public relations counselor*
Rosenthal, Albert Jay *advertising agency executive*
Rydholm, Ralph Williams *advertising agency executive*
Scott, Louis Edward *advertising agency executive*
Seaman, Irving, Jr. *public relations consultant*
Seidner, Frederic Jay *public relations executive*
Shepherd, Daniel Marston *executive recruiter*
Shirley, Virginia Lee *advertising executive*
Sibbald, John Ristow *management consultant*
Singer, Emel *staffing industry executive*
Sive, Rebecca Anne *public affairs company executive*
Soto, Ramona *training specialist*
Spencer, Rozelle Jeffery *moving and storage company executive*
Staley, Augustus Eugene, III *advertising executive*
Steingraber, Frederick George *management consultant*
Stern, Carl William, Jr. *management consultant*
Stone, James Howard *management consultant*
Stotter, David W. *marketing executive*
Strenski, James B. *communications executive*
Struggles, John Edward *management consultant*
Sweet, Charles Wheeler *executive recruiter*
Swift, Dolores Monica Marcinkevich *public relations executive*
Talbot, Pamela *public relations executive*
Tassani, Sally Marie *communications executive, marketing consultant*
Taylor, George Allen *advertising agency executive*
Teichner, Lester *management consulting executive*
Thomas, John Thieme *management consultant*
Trauscht, Donald C. *security services executive*
†Trczinski, Robert A. *public relations executive*
Tritter, Richard Paul *strategic consulting executive*
Tyler, W(illiam) Ed *printing company executive*
Uvena, Frank John *retired printing company executive, lawyer*
Vilim, Nancy Catherine *advertising agency executive*
Wackerle, Frederick William *management consultant*
Wang, Gung H. *management consultant*
Weaver, Donna Rae *company executive*
Weber, Daniel E. *marketing professional*
Weber, Donald B. *advertising and marketing executive*
†Weingart, Jeanne *public relations executive*
Westbrooks, Alphonso *public relations executive*
Williams, Mark H. *advertising agency executive*
Winninghoff, Albert C. M. *advertising company executive*
Wright, Patricia Donovan *communications executive*

Crete
Langer, Steven *human resources management consultant and industrial psychologist*

De Kalb
Wit, Daniel *international consultant*

Decatur
Blake, William Henry *credit and public relations consultant*

Deerfield
Brunner, Vernon Anthony *marketing executive*
Charlson, David Harvey *executive search company professional*
Eramo, John Jeffrey *marketing executive*
Gaples, Harry Seraphim *computer service company executive*
Hersher, Richard Donald *management consultant*
Kinzelberg, Harvey *leasing company executive*
†Polich, James W. *environmental services consultant*
†Slavin, Craig Steven *management and franchising consultant*
†Wieseneck, Robert L. *credit manager*

Des Plaines
†Bardagy, Robert A. *computer leasing company executive*
†Frank, James Alan *marketing professional*
Geisler, Rosemary P. *computer dealer, marketing executive*
Le Menager, Lois M. *incentive merchandise and travel company executive*
†Pontikes, William N. *computer rental and leasing company executive*
Yarnell, Jeffrey Alan *regional credit executive*

Downers Grove
Armstrong, Richard A. *diversified service company executive*
Erickson, Robert Daniel *management services company executive*
Pollard, Charles William *diversified services company executive*
Pollock, John Glennon *facilities management services company executive*

Dwight
Oughton, James Henry, Jr. *corporate executive, farmer*

East Saint Louis
Lindsley, James Bruce *sales and marketing executive*

Elburn
Hansen, H. Jack *management consultant*

Elgin
Burian, Robert J *human resources executive*

Elk Grove Village
Edwardson, John Albert *airline executive*
Flaherty, John Joseph *quality assurance company executive*

Elmhurst
†Baker, Robert I. *business executive*

Evanston
Fryburger, Vernon Ray, Jr. *advertising and marketing educator*
†Jelinek, Richard Carl *hospital management consultant company executive, educator*
Kaatz, Ronald B. *advertising educator, consultant*
Kotler, Philip *marketing educator, consultant, educator*
Lavengood, Lawrence Gene *management educator, historian*
Magee, Robert Paul *accounting and information systems educator*
Manheim, Marvin Lee *business management educator, consultant*
Neuschel, Robert Percy *educator, former management consultant*
Rolfe, Michael N. *management consulting firm executive*
Tornabene, Russell C. *communications executive*
Worthy, James Carson *educator*

Evergreen Park
Lucas, Shirley Agnes Hoyt *management executive*

Frankfort
Dennis, Peter Ray *environmental corporate executive*

Glen Ellyn
Conti, Paul Louis *management consulting company executive*
Sigalos, George Peter *corporate executive*

Glencoe
Gordon, Bernard *management and communications consultant*
Niefeld, Jaye Sutter *advertising executive*

Glenview
Franklin, Lynne *business communications consultant, writer*
Lacy, Herman Edgar *management consultant*
Mc Cormick, James Charles *leasing and financial services company executive*
Stern, Gerald Joseph *advertising executive*

Hawthorn Woods
Schmitz, Shirley Gertrude *marketing and sales executive*

Highland Park
Asher, Frederick *former mail order company executive*
Harris, Thomas L. *public relations executive*
Herbert, Edward Franklin *public relations executive*
Markman, Raymond Jerome *marketing executive*

Hinsdale
Berry, Virgil Jennings, Jr. *management consultant*
Bloom, Stephen Joel *distribution company executive*
Cannon, Patrick Francis *public relations executive*
Cohen, Burton David *franchising executive, lawyer*
†Passaneau, Robert J. *computer company executive*
Whitney, William Elliot, Jr. *advertising agency executive*

Hodgkins
Winn, Elwood F. *consumer product company executive*

Hoffman Estates
Costello, John H., III *business and marketing executive*
Martinez, Arthur C. *retail company executive*
Rooney, John Edward, Jr. *communications company executive*

Inverness
Hetzel, William Gelal *executive search consultant*

Itasca
Rowsey, Michael *printing company executive*

Kankakee
Berkenkamp, Fred Julius *management consultant*

Kenilworth
Guelich, Robert Vernon *retired management consultant*

La Grange
Carroll, Thomas John *advertising executive*

Lake Bluff
Fromm, Henry Gordon *retired manufacturing and marketing executive*
Gage, Calvin William *retired marketing executive*
Grant, John Robert *management consultant*
Stetson, John Charles *corporate executive*

Lake Forest
Carter, Donald Patton *advertising executive*
Ditka, Michael Keller *restaurateur, former professional football coach*
Kenly, Granger Farwell *marketing consultant, college official*
Mohr, Roger John *advertising agency executive*
Rand, Kathy Sue *public relations executive*

Lansing
†Kutzko, Nicholas, Jr. *marketing professional*

Libertyville
Ransom, Margaret Palmquist *public relations executive*

Lincolnshire
Iosue, Carmine A. *marketing executive*

Lisle
†Guglielmi, Peter Anthony *data and voice communications executive*
Long, Charles Franklin *corporate communications executive*
Schwemm, John Butler *printing company executive, lawyer*
Tyson, Kirk W. M. *management consultant*

Lombard
Johnson, Dennis Lester *marketing consultant*
Yeager, David P. *management consultant*

Long Grove
Tarjan, Robert Wegg *information services executive*

Melrose Park
Lavin, Leonard H. *personal care products company executive*

Mount Prospect
†Ottenfeld, Marshall *marketing research company executive*

Naperville
Cline, Richard Gordon *business executive*
Fritz, Roger Jay *management consultant*

Niles
Schreiber, Jeffrey Lee *computer sales executive*

Northbrook
Clarey, John Robert *executive search consultant*
†Courtheoux, Richard James *management consultant*
Freedman, Walter G. *corporate services executive*
Jacobs, Richard Alan *management consultant*
Kubek, Ralph A. *management consultant, accountant*
Marshall, Irl Houston, Jr. *residential and commercial cleaning company executive*
Pinsof, Nathan *retired advertising executive*
†Simon, Steve *public relations executive*
Tolan, James Francis *corporate and financial communications executive, marketing consultant, financial analyst*
Turner, Lee *travel company executive*
Wajer, Ronald Edward *management consultant*
Weinstein, Ira Phillip *advertising executive*
Ziemann, Edward Frances *food service company executive, sales and marketing professional*

Northfield
Mayer, Richard Philip *food executive*
Smart, Jackson Wyman, Jr. *business executive*

Oak Brook
Buntrock, Dean Lewis *waste management company executive*
Cantalupo, James Richard *restaurant company executive*
†Challenger, James Edgar, Jr. *computer software executive*
DeLorey, John Alfred *printing company executive*
Kramer, Janice Kay *real estate marketing executive*
Maher, David L. *drug store company executive*
Quinlan, Michael Robert *fast food franchise company executive*
Rensi, Edward Henry *restaurant chain executive*
Root, Lynal A. *fast food company executive*
Schrage, Paul Daniel *fast food executive*

Oak Brook Mall
†Laskowski, Richard E. *retail hardware company executive*

Oak Park
Devereux, Timothy Edward *advertising agency executive*
Notaro, Michael R. *data processing and computer service executive*
Tomek, Laura Lindemann *marketing executive*

Orland Park
Leonard, Robert Dougherty *communications company executive*

Palatine
Claassen, W(alter) Marshall *employment company executive*
Medin, Lowell Ansgard *security company executive*
†Roggeveen, Richard *operation services executive, executive recruiter*

Park Ridge
Margolies, Raymond *management consulting company executive*
Rosenheim, Howard Harris *management consultant*

Plainfield
Chase, Maria Elaine Garoufalis *publishing company executive*

River Forest
Hamper, Robert Joseph *marketing executive*
Wanamaker, Robert Joseph *advertising company executive*

Rolling Meadows
†Cain, R. Wayne *rental leasing company executive*
Sturmon, Patricia Montgomery *public relations executive*

Rosemont
Stanton, James Adkins *technology equipment leasing company executive, consultant*
Trznadel, Frank Dwight, Jr. *leasing company executive*
Walsh, Martin R. *computer company executive*

Schaumburg
Heaton, Syd N. *computer company executive*
Hill, Raymond Joseph *packaging company executive*
Morgan, David Ernest *computer and communications research executive*
Oldberg, Carl Malcolm *public relations executive*
Stephens, Norval Blair, Jr. *marketing consultant*

Shelbyville
Gloede, Richard *management consulting executive*

Skokie
Bakalar, John Stephen *printing and publishing company executive*
†Buckardt, Everett L. *marketing executive*
Kranz, Norman *advertising executive*
Sayers, Gale *computer company executive, retired professional football player*
White, William James *information management and services company executive;*

Springfield
Stroh, Raymond Eugene *personnel executive*

Urbana
Mayer, Robert Wallace *emeritus finance educator*
Rotzoll, Kim Brewer *advertising and communications educator*
Sandage, Charles Harold *advertising educator*

Vernon Hills
Powers, Anthony Richard, Jr. *educational sales professional*

Villa Park
Williams, David Arthur *marketing professional*

Westchester
†Ingalls, Harold W. *vice president, CFO, environmental services company*
†Schulte, Margaret Florence *personnel firm executive*

Western Springs
Carroll, Jeanne *public relations executive*

Wheaton
Corum, William Thomas, III *computer information systems executive*
Holman, James Lewis *financial and management consultant*
Jack, Nancy Rayford *supplemental resource company executive, consultant*
Jett, Charles Cranston *management consultant*
Mellott, Robert Vernon *advertising executive*

Wheeling
Koch, Peter F. *management consultant*

Wilmette
Kurtzman, Allan Roger *advertising executive*

Winnetka
Bogart, Homer Gordon *marketing executive*
Folds, Charles Weston *merchandising consultant*
Greeley, Joseph May *retired advertising executive*
Kahn, Paul Frederick *executive search company executive*

Wood Dale
Kearns, Janet Catherine *corporate secretary*

Woodridge
Allen, Charles Joseph, II *advertising agency executive*

INDIANA

Auburn
Kempf, Jane Elmira *marketing executive*

Bloomington
Burton, Philip Ward *advertising executive, educator*
Gordon, Paul John *business management educator*
Patterson, James Milton *marketing specialist, educator*
Sullivan, Michael Francis, III *executive*

Boggstown
Gray, Carlos Gibson *restaurateur, seedsman, entertainer*

Carmel
Ferrero, Louis Peter *computer services company executive*

Columbus
Durham, James Michael, Sr. *marketing executive*
Higgins, Harold Bailey *executive search company executive*

Danville
†Dawes, Dennis William *hospital executive*

East Chicago
Crum, James Francis *waste recycling company executive*

Elkhart
Speas, Charles Stuart *personnel director*
Tatum, Rita *communications executive*

Evansville
Kitch, Frederick David *advertising executive*

Fort Wayne
Dorman, Barry *waste management executive*
†Wolf, Don Allen *hardware wholesale executive*

Hammond
Yovich, Daniel John *educator*

Highland
Purcell, James Francis *consultant, former utility executive*

Indianapolis
Bower, Sandra Irwin *communications executive*
Carr, William H(enry) A. *public relations executive, author*
†DeHaan, Christel *vacation exchange and travel company executive*
Durbin, Robert Cain *hotel executive*
Gilman, Alan B. *restaurant company executive*
Glazner, Raymond Charles *technical services manager*
Haynes, Thomas Joseph *marketing executive*
Hillman, Charlene Hamilton *public relations executive*
Kacek, Don J. *management consultant, business owner*
Krueger, Alan Douglas *communications company executive*
MacVittie, Paula Rae *advertising executive*
Marsh, Don Ermal *supermarket executive*
Nyhart, Eldon Howard *employee benefits consultant, lawyer*
Pattyn, Remi Ceasar *management consultant*
Ruben, Gary A. *marketing and communications consultant*
Slaymaker, Gene Arthur *public relations executive*
†Spanogle, Robert William *marketing and advertising company executive, association administrator*
Walker, Frank Dilling *market research executive*
Walker, Thomas Cole *telephone company executive*

Muncie
Barber, Earl Eugene *consulting firm executive*
Emerson, Duane E. *corporate executive*

Notre Dame
Bella, Salvatore Joseph *management educator*

Peru
Bronson, Kenneth Caldean *newspaper company executive*

Seymour
Bollinger, Don Mills *grocery company executive*

South Bend
Burkhart, Charles Barclay *outdoor advertising executive*
Meyer, John Bernard *public relations executive*
Vandenberg, Sister Patricia Clasina *health system executive*

Speedway
†Knoy, Ernest Crone *management consultant*

Valparaiso
Schlender, William Elmer *management sciences educator*
Taylor, Kenard Lyle, Jr. *senior manager training*

Wabash
Flott, Leslie William *quality control professional*
Scales, Richard Lewis *manufacturer's representative*

West Lafayette
Johnson, Robert Willard *management educator*
Schendel, Dan Eldon *management consultant, business educator*

IOWA

Cedar Rapids
Damrow, Richard G. *advertising executive*
Stadlen, Diane Elizabeth *marketing professional*

Chariton
Pickens, Earl *consumer products company executive*

Des Moines
†Hoak, James McClain, Jr. *communications corporation executive, lawyer*
Martin, Christina Marie *public relations executive*
Meredith, Edwin Thomas, III *media executive*
Stoffer, Terry James *advertising executive*
Winick, Alfred Zell *data services corporation executive*

Fairfield
Hawthorne, Timothy Robert *direct response advertising and communications company executive*

Plainfield
Lynes, James William, Sr. *communications company executive*

West Des Moines
Marshall, Russell Frank *research company executive*

Starr, V. Hale *communications executive*

KANSAS

Emporia
O'Reilly, Hugh Joseph *restaurant executive*

Hutchinson
Dillon, David Brian *retail grocery executive*

Junction City
Werts, Merrill Harmon *management consultant*

Lawrence
Mackenzie, Kenneth Donald *management consultant, educator*

Leavenworth
Haag, Donald Richard *director facilities and services*

Lenexa
Rayburn, George Marvin *business executive, investment executive*

Olathe
†Summe, Gregory Louis *management consultant*

Overland Park
Mealman, Glenn *corporate marketing executive*

Salina
Ryan, Stephen Collister *funeral director*

Shawnee Mission
Boyd, John Kent *advertising executive*
Findlay, Theodore Bernard *management consultant*
Herring, Raymond Mark *marketing and planning executive*
Mindlin, Richard Barnett *market research executive*
Putman, Dale Cornelius *management consultant, lawyer*

Topeka
Franklin, Benjamin Barnum *dinner club executive*
Hilpert, Dale W. *retail shoe company executive*
Randall, Elizabeth Ellen *personnel manager*
Vidricksen, Ben Eugene *food service executive, state legislator*

Wichita
Barents, Brian Edward *marketing executive*
Gates, Walter Edward *rental company executive, business owner*
Lahti, Richard *quality improvement administrator*
Lair, Robert Louis *catering company executive*
Reinemund, Steven S. *restaurant chain executive*
†Roberts, Alice *reservations service executive*
Thomsen, Marcia Rozen *marketing executive*

KENTUCKY

Ashland
Carter, David Edward *communications executive*

Franklin
Herndon, Wallace Eugene, Jr. *human resources manager*

Lexington
Chesser, Roger Moreton *broadcasting executive*
Host, W. James *public relations and advertising executive*

Louisville
Brown, Owsley, II *diversified consumer products company executive*
Brown, William Lee Lyons, Jr. *consumer products company executive*
Cranor, John *food service executive*
Davis, Finis E. *printing company executive*
McLellan, Harold Linden *health care company executive*
Minchin, Michael M., Jr. *food industry consultant*
Neely, J. Randall *public relations executive*
Peden, Katherine Graham *industrial consultant*
Sandefur, Thomas Edwin, Jr. *tobacco company executive*
Smith, Hal W. *restaurant management company executive*
Swann, Rande Nortof *public relations executive*
Wenz, Rodney E. *public relations executive*

LOUISIANA

Belle Chasse
Yandle, Sylvester Elwood, II *sales executive, inventor*

Lafayette
†Sides, Larry Eugene *advertising executive*

Marrero
Hebert, Clifford Joseph *data processing executive*

Metairie
Benson, Jerome *automotive sales executive*
†Gereighty, Andrea Saunders *polling company executive, poet*
Goss, Donald Davis *consultant, author, lecturer*
†Grimm, John Lloyd *business executive, marketing professional*

Monroe
†Reppond, Jim D. *communications executive*
Rose, Charles David *consulting company executive*

New Orleans
Cook, Victor Joseph, Jr. *marketing educator, consultant*
Lambert, Olaf Cecil *hotel executive*
Levy, Sam *consumer products company executive*
Schwegmann, John F. *consumer products company executive*
Womack, Edgar Allen, Jr. *technology executive*

Shreveport
Tullis, John Ledbetter *retired wholesale distributing company executive*

Thibodaux
Delozier, Maynard Wayne *marketing educator*

MAINE

Augusta
Roberts, Donald Albert *advertising, public relations, marketing and media consultant*

Brooklin
Schmidt, Klaus Dieter *management consultant, university administrator, marketing and management educator*

Camden
Lavenson, James H. *hotel industry executive*
Lavenson, Susan Barker *hotel corporate executive, consultant*

Center Lovell
Adams, Herbert Ryan *management consultant, retired clergyman, educator, publishing executive*

Ellsworth
Eustice, Russell Clifford *consulting company executive*

Hartland
Larochelle, Richard Clement *tanning company executive*

Kennebunk
Alling, Charles Booth, Jr. *management consultant*

Portland
Cecil, Alex Thomson *travel executive*
Kendrick, Peter Murray *communications executive, investor*
Potter, Lillian Florence *business executive secretary*
Shaffer, James Burgess *communications executive*

Sedgwick
Mc Millan, Brockway *former communications executive*

Waterville
Zukowski, Walter Henry *administrative science educator*

York
†Peterson, Karen Ida *marketing research company executive*

MARYLAND

Annapolis
Cabral, Judith Ann *telecommunications executive*
Coogle, Joseph Moore, Jr. *management consultant*
Montague, Brian John *consulting company executive*

Arnold
Barrett, John Anthony *printing company financial executive*

Baltimore
Brotman, Phyllis Block *advertising and public relations executive*
Creagh, David Michael *public radio executive*
Dale, James Michael *advertising executive, writer*
Dall'Acqua, Charles Robert *marketing executive*
Dickman, James Gary *marketing professional*
Dodge, Calvert Renaul *education and training executive, author, educator*
Eisner, Henry Wolfgang *advertising executive*
Elias, Amy Pumpian *public relations executive*
Fried, Herbert Daniel *advertising executive*
Gibbons, Thomas Michael *communications executive*
Greenspan, Arnold Michael *computer company executive*
†Harris, Milton Michael *management consultant*
Hooper, William Edwin *advertising agency executive*
Hug, Richard Ernest *environmental company executive*
Kleiner, Arnold Joel *television executive*
Leonard, John Wirth *English educator, retailer*
Nuckolls, Robert Theodore *cemetery executive*
O'Keefe, Kevin *public relations executive*
Park, Mary Woodfill *information consultant*
Pollard, Shirley *employment training director, consultant*
Talbot, Donald Roy *consulting services executive*

Beltsville
Appell, Louise Sophia *consulting company executive*
Quirk, Frank Joseph *management consulting company executive*

Bethesda
Altobello, Daniel Joseph *service executive*
Barber, Arthur Whiting *communications company executive*
Barquín, Ramón Carlos *consulting company executive*
Brown, Earle Palmer *advertising agency executive*
Brown, Jeremy Earle *advertising executive*
Cooper, Roger Merlin *information technology executive, federal government official, educator*
†Crockett, Bruce Larmour *communications company executive*
Dresing, Robert K. *health care executive*
Ernst, Roger *consultant, university educator*
Estrin, Melvyn J. *computer products company executive*
Fowler, Emil Eugene *nuclear technology consultant*
Hanley, (Charles) Robert, Jr. *computer systems executive, real estate developer*
Helm, Lewis Marshall *public affairs executive*
Kampf-Singman, Cindy Alise *public relations executive*
King, Charles McDonald, Jr. *association foundation executive*
Kriegsman, William Edwin *consulting firm executive*
Lauret, Curtis Bernard, Jr. *international marketing professional*
Levin, Carl *public and government relations consultant*
McClure, Brooks *management consultant*
Mc Gurn, Barrett *communications executive, writer*
†Millard, Kenneth E. *communications company executive*
Pompa, James Robert *computer industry executive*
Pras, Robert Thomas *hotel executive*
Shellow, Robert *management service company executive, consultant*
†Southard, Bill *public relations executive*
Southwick, Paul *retired public relations executive*
Spector, Melbourne Louis *management consultant*
Spivak, Alvin A. *retired public relations executive*
†Van Dyke, Joseph Gary Owen *computer consulting executive*
Wertheimer, Franc *retired corporate executive*

Bowie
Purcell, Steven Richard *international management consultant, engineer, economist*

Brooklandville
Darcy, George Robert *public relations executive*
Miller, Paul George *computer company executive*

Chestertown
Gordon, James Braund *management consultant*

Chevy Chase
Corrigan, Robert Foster *business consultant, retired diplomat*
Michaelis, Michael *management and technical consultant*
Schlegel, John Frederick *management consultant, speaker, trainer*
†Weber, Shirley Bowers *retired management analyst, networking communicator*
Zurkowski, Paul George *information company executive*

Cockeysville Hunt Valley
Kunisch, Robert Dietrich *business services company executive*
Whitehurst, William Wilfred, Jr. *management consultant*

College Park
Greer, Thomas Vernon *business consultant and educator*
Holder, Sallie Lou *training and meeting management consultant*

Columbia
Bitonti, James Anthony *business machinery company executive*
Bretz, Thurman Wilbur *corporate professional*
Letaw, Harry, Jr. *technology corporation executive*
†McIndoe, Darrell Bruce, Sr. *communications executive*
Morgan, Walter Edward *management consultant*
Steele, Richard J. *management consultant*
†Willoughby, Anthony R. *satellite support services executive*

Crofton
Kelley, Albert Benjamin *consulting company executive*

Easton
Burns, Michael Joseph *operations and sales-marketing executive*
Read, William Lawrence *business executive, former naval officer*

Ellicott City
Gleaves, Leon Rogers *marketing and sales executive*
Neil, Fred Applestein *public relations executive*

Fort Washington
Fielding, Elizabeth M(ay) *public relations executive, editor, writer*
McKenzie, Ruth Bates Harris *diversity human relations consultant, writer*

Frederick
Floerchinger, Thomas Allen *computer company executive*
†Nathanson, Kim *computer support executive*
†Nathanson, Rick *computer company sales and support services executive*

Gaithersburg
†Eyman, L. Dean *environmental company executive*
Flickinger, Harry Harner *organization and business executive, management consultant*
Isbister, James David *pharmaceutical business executive*
Wohl, Ronald H. *management consultant, readability expert*

Germantown
Shaw, Jack Allen *communications company executive*

Greenbelt
†Reid, Hubert M. *computer software company executive, electronics executive*

Hagerstown
Wolford, Patricia Weber *management company executive*

Hanover
Hay, Lewis *food marketing executive*

Landover
Huggins, David *custom software development executive*

Lanham Seabrook
Herman, Kenneth *food marketing executive*
Lucido, Chester Charles, Jr. *marketing company executive*
Youman, Lillian Hobson Lincoln *building services contractor*

Lusby
Simpich, William Morris *public affairs consultant*

Lutherville Timonium
Chapman, Robert Breckenridge, III *management consulting company executive*

Monrovia
†Cooney, William Joseph, Jr. *communications company executive*

Phoenix
†Byrd, Harvey Clifford, III *information management company executive*

Potomac
Fink, Daniel Julien *management consultant*
Terragno, Paul James *information industry executive*

Queenstown
Beall, Robert Milton *restaurant executive*

Riverdale
Hedgepeth, Leroy J. *park director*

Rockville
†Burns, Kevin J. *computer software services executive*
Carey, John Edward *information services executive*
Cramer, Mercade Adonis, Jr. *computer company executive*
Jochum, George T. *management company executive*
Leslie, John Walter *development consultant*
Naft, Barry Niel *waste management administrator, chemical engineer*
Nash, Jonathon Michael *program manager, mechanical engineer*
Nguyen, Truyen Thanh *computer and communications company executive*
†Rosenthal, Richard Scott *information management company executive*
Shaw, Robert William, Jr. *management consultant, venture capitalist*
Shelton, Wayne Vernon *professional services and systems integration company executive*
Sontag, Peter Michael *travel management company executive*

Saint Leonard
Andrews, John Stewart *management consultant*

Silver Spring
Bainum, Stewart *health care and lodging company executive*
Cain, David Lee *corporate executive*
†Hazard, Robert Culver, Jr. *hotel executive*
Hersey, David Floyd *information resources management consultant, government official;*
Kendrick, James Earl *business consultant*
Kotler, Martin *management consultant*
Lynch, Sonia *data processing consultant*
Orkand, Donald Saul *management consultant*
Perlmutter, Jerome Herbert *communications specialist*
Shih-Carducci, Joan Chia-mo *cooking educator, biochemist, medical technologist*

Stevensville
Kepley, Thomas Alvin *management consultant*

MASSACHUSETTS

Acton
Barrett, James *computer software company executive*
Leighton, Charles Milton *specialty consumer products company executive*
Tod, G. Robert *consumer marketing executive*

Amherst
Buell, Victor Paul *marketing educator, author, editor*
Singleton, Philip Arthur *corporate executive*

Attleboro
Glenn, James *sales executive*

Bedford
†Carpenter, Chadwick H., Jr. *computer software company executive*
Horowitz, Barry Martin *systems research and engineering company executive*
Landry, John Bernard, III *data processing executive*
†Wilson, Raymond P. *communications systems marketing professional*

Belmont
Allison, Elisabeth Kovacs *information company executive*
Klein, Martin Samuel *management consulting executive*
Rowe, Richard R. *on-line information and management services company executive*

Beverly
Barger, Richard Wilson *hotel executive*
Bemberis, Ivars *marketing professional*

Billerica
Leblois, Axel *computer company executive*
Mackenzie, Ward D. *computer company executive*

Boston
Andrews, Kenneth Richmond *business administration educator*
Arnold, John David *management counselor, consultant*
Berenson, Paul Stewart *advertising executive*
Britton, Richard Lindsay *advertising executive*
Brown, David A.B. *strategy consultant*
Buchin, Stanley Ira *management consultant, educator*
Burns, James John *information systems executive*
Carter, Lewis Aaron, Jr. *public relations executive*
Clarke, Terence Michael *public relations and advertising executive*
Coleman, John Joseph *telephone company executive*
Cone, Carol Lynn *public relations executive*
Connors, John Michael, Jr. *advertising agency executive*
Cornwall, Deborah Joyce *consulting firm executive, management consultant*
†Coughlin, Margaret Ann *marketing communications executive*
Crandall, Rhona *personnel manager*
†Daley, James A. *hotel executive*
Dawson, James Ambrose *printing industry executive*
Donahue, Douglas Aidan, Jr. *business executive*
Doorley, Thomas Lawrence, III *management consulting firm executive*
End, William Thomas *business executive*
Eskandarian, Edward *advertising agency executive*
Fausch, David Arthur *public relations executive*
Fitzgibbons, James M. *diversified company executive*
Fonvielle, William Harold *management consultant*
†Friedmann, Robert Frederick *advertising executive*
Goldman, David *consumer products company executive*
Gould, John Joseph *communications executive*
Hayes, Andrew Wallace, II *consumer products company executive*
Hill, George Jackson, III *advertising agency executive*
Hillman, Carol Barbara *communications executive*
Houston, Douglas White *advertising company executive, creative director*
†Humphrey, John William *management and sales training executive, human resources consultant*
Hurd, J. Nicholas *executive recruiting consultant, former banker*
Isham, Carolynn Clough *advertising executive*
Jackson, Cleotha *human resource director*
Judson, Arnold Sidney *management consultant*
Kapioltas, John *hotel company executive*
Luongo, C. Paul *public relations executive*
McLennan, Bernice Claire *human resources professional*
†Metzger, Mark Kavanaugh *public relations company executive*
Miller, John A., Jr. *public relations executive*
†Morrissey, Peter A. *public relations executive*
Murray, Robert J. *consumer products company executive*
O'Block, Robert Paul *management consultant*
†Pile, Walter Mitchell, Jr. *advertising agency executive*
Powers, Charles William *environmental ethicist*
Rhinesmith, Stephen Headley *international management consultant*
†Rose, John M., Jr. *advertising executive*
Rosenberg, James William *marketing executive*
Saunders, Donald Leslie *hotel executive, commercial real estate company executive*
Saunders, Roger Alfred *hotel group executive*
Shapiro, Eli *business consultant, educator, economist*
Singer, Thomas Eric *industrial company executive*
Slosberg, Mike *advertising executive*
Sonnabend, Roger Philip *hotel company executive*
Stone, John Ware *management consultant*
Sullivan, John Louis, Jr. *retired search company executive*
Teixeira, Joseph *advertising executive*
Turillo, Michael Joseph, Jr. *management consultant*
Wilkes, Brent Ames *management consultant*
Willens, Alan Rush *management consultant*
Williams, Robert D. *cable television advertiser*
Wilson, Robert Gould *management consultant*
Wortzel, Lawrence Herbert *marketing educator*
Zeien, Alfred M. *consumer products company executive*

Boxboro
Nitta, Kenjiro *Computer company executive*

Braintree
Harris, Jeffrey Sherman *direct marketing company executive*
†O'Donnell, Michael Paul *restaurant executive*

Brookline
Walter, Helen Joy *executive director, teacher*

Burlington
†Labovitz, George Harold *business executive, educator*

Buzzards Bay
Roper, Burns Worthington *retired opinion research company executive*

Cambridge
Allen, Thomas John *management educator*
Dennis, Jack Bonnell *computer consultant*
FitzGerald, Maura *public relations executive*
Fleischer, Dorothy Ann *administrative assistant*
Forrester, Jay Wright *management specialist, educator*
Greeno, J(ohn) Ladd *consulting company executive*
Kerpelman, Larry Cyril *consulting firm executive*
LaMantia, Charles Robert *management consulting company executive*
Levy, Stephen Raymond *diversified high technology company executive*
Littlefield, Paul Damon *management consultant*
Manzi, Jim *computer software company executive*
Marolda, Anthony Joseph *management consulting company executive*
Mueller, Robert Kirk *management consulting company executive*
†Neale, Timothy Arthur *hospital administrator*
Norkus, Michael *management consultant*
†Robinson, David G. *management consultant*
Tema-Lyn, Laurie *management consultant*
†Urban, Glen L. *management educator*
Weber, Larry *public relations executive*

Canton
Ferrera, Arthur Rocco *food distribution company executive*
Galligan, Thomas Joseph, III *retail footwear company executive*
Miller, Carl Eugene *marketing executive*
Pitts, Virginia M. *human resources executive*

Chatham
Anderson, Barbara Graham *philanthropic resources development consultant*

Cohasset
Rabstejnek, George John *management consultant*

Concord
Bloom, Edwin John, Jr. *human resources consultant*
Daltas, Arthur John *management consultant*
Hogan, Daniel Bolten *management consultant*

Dedham
Culver, Edward Holland *marketing executive*

Redstone, Sumner Murray *entertainment company executive*

Dennis
Weilbacher, William Manning *advertising and marketing consultant*

Dover
Borel, Richard Wilson *communications executive, consultant*
Fulchino, Paul Edward *management consultant*
Ryburn, Samuel McChesney *marketing executive*

Duxbury
Albritton, William Hoyle *training and consulting executive, lecturer, writer*

East Bridgewater
Jenkins, David B. *supermarket chain executive*

Edgartown
Piper, George Earle *retailing design and financial consulting company executive*

Framingham
†Campbell, Kirk *information systems executives*
†McGovern, Patrick J. *communications executive*

Franklin
Hoffman, S. Joseph *advertising agency executive*

Gardner
McCarthy, Albert Henry *human resources executive*

Gloucester
Hausman, William Ray *fund raising and management consultant*
Lauenstein, Milton Charles *management consultant*

Groton
†Rhoads, Richard H. *printing company executive*

Harvard
†Becker, Ray Everett *data processing executive*

Hopkinton
Nickerson, Richard Gorham *research company executive*
Preston, William Hubbard *consultant to specialty businesses*

Housatonic
Levy, Sy *advertising and direct marketing executive*

Hull
Anderson, Timothy Christopher *consulting company executive*

Kingston
Walters, Alan Stanley *distribution company executive*

Lexington
Alloway, Robert Malcombe *computer consulting executive*
Brick, Donald Bernard *consulting company executive*
Ciampa, Dan *management consultant*
Duboff, Robert Samuel *marketing professional*
Eberle, William Denman *international management consultant*
Fray, Lionel Louis *management consultant*
Gilbert, David *computer company executive*
Phalon, Philip Anthony *marketing executive*
Risch, Martin Donald *marketing-management consulting company executive*
Ross, Douglas Taylor *retired software company executive*

Lincoln
Kalba, Kas *international communications consultant*
Sprague, John Louis *management consultant*

Longmeadow
Locklin, Wilbert Edwin *management consultant*

Lowell
Hosking, Douglas Gordon *printing company executive*

Marblehead
Rogow, Bruce Joel *information technology consultant*

Marshfield Hills
Stacey, Kathleen Mary *advertising and public relations executive*

Marstons Mills
Martin, Vincent George *management consultant*

Maynard
Palmer, Robert B. *computer company executive*
Smith, John F. *computer company executive*

Medford
†Smith, Hale *data processing services executive*

Middleton
Stover, Matthew Joseph *communications company executive*

Nantucket
Mercer, Richard Joseph *retired advertising executive, freelance writer*

Natick
Donovan, R. Michael *management consultant*
Neumeyer, John Leopold *research company administrator, chemistry educator*
Planitzer, Russell E. *computer company executive*
Strayton, Robert Gerard *public communications executive*

Newton
Bewick, John Arters *consulting firm executive*
Chlamtac, Imrich *computer company executive, educator*
Coleman, Gerald Christopher *management consultant*
†Heck, William Henry *hotel executive*
Kaplan, Steven F. *business management executive*
Kosowsky, David I. *retired biotechnical company executive*

North Andover
Buchanan, Ellery Rives *sales executive*
Olney, Peter Butler, Jr. *retired management consulting firm executive*

North Billerica
Sodini, Peter J. *food service executive*

Norwood
†Stata, Raymond *data processing and computer company executive*

Palmer
Dupuis, Robert Simeon *sales executive*

Provincetown
Brock, Alice May *restaurateur, author*

Quincy
Bierman, George William *technical consulting executive, food technologist*
Levin, Robert Joseph *retail grocery chain store executive*
Shuster, Herbert Victor *corporate executive, consultant*
Young, Richard William *corporate director*

Randolph
Rosenberg, Robert Michael *restaurant franchise company executive*

Rockport
Wiberg, Lars-Erik *human resources consultant*

Salem
Ettinger, Mort *marketing educator*

Sheffield
Velmans, Loet Abraham *retired public relations executive*

Springfield
Canavan, John James, Jr. *employment services executive*

Sudbury
Bradstreet, Bernard Francis *computer company executive*
Kaplan, Aline Michele *advertising executive*
Read, Philip Lloyd *computer design and manufacturing executive*

Taunton
Wall, Erving Henry, Jr. *sales agency executive, state senator*

Tewksbury
Miamis, James D. *retail grocery chain executive*

Wakefield
Bartl, Frederick J. *marketing professional*

Waltham
Curnan, Susan Patricia Anne *human development and social policy educator, executive director, consultant*
Kasputys, Joseph Edward *data processing executive, economist*
†Lowe, Justus Frederick, Jr. *software company executive*
Monia, Joan *management consultant*
Poduska, John William, Sr. *computer company executive*
Stambaugh, Armstrong A., Jr. *restaurant and hotel executive*
Storer, Donald Edgar *corporate executive*
†Walske, Steven C. *computer software company executive*

Wellesley
Allen, Michael W *management consultant*
Nagler, Leon Gregory *management consultant*
Papageorgiou, John Constantine *management science educator*

Wellesley Hills
Coco, Samuel Barbin *venture consultant*

West Boylston
McKenna, William Stuart *sales and marketing executive*

West Chatham
McHale, Thomas Anthony *sales and marketing consultant*

Westborough
Young, Douglas Ryan *technology company executive*

Westfield
Tower, Horace Linwood, III *consumer products company executive*

Weston
Paresky, David S. *travel company executive*
Sack, Burton Marshall *restaurant company executive*
Sullivan, Barbara Boyle *management consultant*

Westwood
†Polimeno, Lawrence A. *computer softwear company executive*
Thomas, Abdelnour Simon *software company executive*

Wilbraham
Anderson, Eric William *retired food service company executive*
O'Shaughnessy, Joseph A. *restaurant company executive*

Williamsburg
Snow, Elizabeth Jean *poet, inventor, farmer, small business owner*

Wilmington
DiFillippo, Anthony Francis *service company executive*
†Rand, Albert *computer systems company executive*
Rice, Frederick Colton *environmental management consultant*

Winchester
Cecich, Donald Edward *business executive*
Taggart, Ganson Powers *management consultant*

Woburn
Mehra, Raman Kumar *data processing executive, automation and control engineering researcher*

Worcester
Candib, Murray A. *business executive, retail management consultant*
Densmore, William Phillips *management consultant*
Ullrich, Robert Albert *business management educator*

Yarmouth Port
Brundage, Gloria Swegman *public relations executive*

MICHIGAN

Ada
DeVos, Richard Marvin *network marketing company executive*
DeVos, Richard Marvin, Jr. (Dick DeVos) *direct sales company executive*
Grochoski, Gregory Thomas *marketing company research executive*
Van Andel, Jay *home and personal products company executive*

Ann Arbor
Agno, John G. *management consultant*
Belcher, Louis David *marketing and operations executive, former mayor*
Foley, Daniel Ronald *business and personnel executive*
Martin, Claude Raymond, Jr. *marketing consultant, educator*
Monaghan, Thomas Stephen *restaurant chain executive*
Ryan, William Frank *management consultant*
Terpstra, Vern *marketing educator*
Warshaw, Martin Richard *marketing educator*

Auburn Hills
Wagner, Bruce Stanley *marketing communications executive*

Battle Creek
Thar, Ferdinand August (Bud Thar) *trade company executive*

Benton Harbor
Goldin, Sol *marketing consultant*

Bingham Farms
Berline, James H. *advertising executive, public relations agency executive*

Bloomfield Hills
Adams, Charles Francis *advertising and real estate executive*
Adams, Thomas Brooks *advertising consultant*
Benton, William Pettigrew *advertising agency executive*
Bissell, John Howard *marketing executive*
Carr, Robin *advertising executive*
Casey, John Patrick (Jack Casey) *public relations executive, political analyst*
Johnson, John K. *advertising executive*
McNeil, Joseph Malcolm *advertising executive*
Mills, Peter Richard *advertising executive*
Pingel, John Spencer *advertising executive*
Tunstall, Sharon Sue *advertising executive*
Ward, Richard C. *advertising executive*
Weil, John William *technology management consultant*

Dearborn
Caldwell, John Thomas, Jr. *communications executive*
Jelinek, John Joseph *public relations executive*

Detroit
Barden, Don H. *communications executive*
Bassett, Tina *communications executive*
Beltaire, Beverly Ann *public relations executive*
Czarnecki, Walter P. *truck rental company executive*
Flint, Robert H. *printing ink company executive*
Franco, Anthony M. *public relations executive*
Go, Robert A. *management consultant*
Henry, William Lockwood *sales and marketing executive*
McCracken, Caron Francis *data processing consultant*
†Ragains, Charles C. *public relations executive*
Roberts, Seymour M. (Skip Roberts) *advertising agency executive*
Schweitzer, Peter *advertising agency executive*
Werba, Gabriel *public relations consultant*

East Lansing
Hollander, Stanley Charles *marketing educator*
Jones, Kensinger *advertising executive*
Miracle, Gordon Eldon *advertising educator*
Wilson, R. Dale *marketing educator, consultant*

Farmington Hills
Prady, Norman *advertising executive, writer, marketing consultant*

Franklin
Sessamen, Donald William *communications company executive*

Grand Rapids
Miglore, Joseph James *furniture manufacturing executive*

Grosse Pointe
Blevins, William Edward *management consultant*
Droll, Marian Clarke *energy company public affairs executive*
Mecke, Theodore Hart McCalla, Jr. *management consultant*
Thurber, Donald MacDonald Dickinson *public relations counsel*
Wilson, Henry Arthur, Jr. *management consultant*

Harbor Springs
Graham, Robert C. *management consultant*

Kalamazoo
Freed, Karl Francis *professional planner*
Lawrence, William Joseph, Jr. *retired corporate executive*

Livonia
Brandon, David A. *marketing and publishing executive*

Midland
Hanes, James Henry *consulting business executive, lawyer*
Maneri, Remo R. *management consultant*

Novi
Andrus, Leonard Carl *marketing executive*
Kinsey, Charles John *industrial auctioneer, consultant, cattle breeder, farmer*

Plymouth
Moore, Joan Elizabeth *human resources executive, lawyer*

Redford
Flint, H. Howard, II *printing company executive*

Rochester Hills
Ferguson, Harley Robert *service company executive*
†Pfister, Karl Anton *industrial company executive*

Royal Oak
Stephens, Martha Foster *advertising executive*

Southfield
Barnett, Marilyn *advertising agency executive*
Caponigro, Jeffrey Ralph *public relations counselor*
Considine, John Joseph *advertising executive*
Darin, Frank Victor John *management consultant*
Johnson, Richard Alan *advertising executive*
Kalter, Alan *advertising agency executive*
Koch, Albert Acheson *management consultant*
Maibach, Ben C., Jr. *service executive*
Matthes, Gerald Stephen *advertising agency executive*
Neman, Thomas Edward *advertising and marketing executive*
Smith, Nancy Hohendorf *sales and marketing executive*

Stevensville
†Vegter, William Charles *wholesale supply executive*

Troy
Adderley, Terence E. *corporate executive*
Baker, Ernest Waldo, Jr. *advertising executive*
†Jablonski, Dale Z. *public relations and publishing executive*
Kelly, William R. *employment agency executive*
Sandy, William Haskell *training and communications systems executive*
Simons, Leonard Norman Rashall *advertising executive*
Smith, Glen B. *consumer products company executive*
†Stanaljczo, Gregg *computer services executive*
Thompson, Robert Eugene *employment agency executive*

Warren
Dow, Peter Anthony *advertising agency executive*
Gilbert, Suzanne Harris *advertising executive*
Hopp, Anthony James *advertising agency executive*
Schirmer, Robert Hamilton *advertising executive*
Schultz, Louis Michael *advertising agency executive*
Tausch, William Joseph *advertising agency executive*

West Bloomfield
Meyers, Gerald Carl *management consultant, author, educator, lecturer, former automobile company executive*

MINNESOTA

Bloomington
McGrath, Dennis Britton *public relations executive*
Meyer, Scott D. *public relations firm executive*
Mona, David L. *public relations executive*
Thorndyke, Lloyd Milton *computer company executive*

Burnsville
Gardner, Dennis (Den Gardner) *public relations executive*

Eden Prairie
Knotek, Robert Frank *management consultant, educator*
Lau, Michele Denise *advertising consultant, sales trainer, television personality*
†Levy, David Franklin *sales and marketing executive*
†Roth, Thomas *marketing executive*
†Schulze, Richard M. *consumer products executive*

Edina
Burdick, Lou Brum *public relations executive*

Excelsior
Deikel, Theodore *marketing company executive*

Hopkins
†Peterson, D. Bruce *data processing computer services company executive*

Hutchinson
Graf, Laurance James *communications executive*

Minneapolis
Alcott, James Arthur communications executive
Bartels, Juergen E. hotel company executive
Bartkowski, William Patrick public relations executive
Beardsley, John Ray public relations firm executive
Bileydi, Sumer advertising agency executive
†Blau, Robert Alan marketing executive
Boubelik, Henry Fredrick, Jr. car rental company executive
Burns, Neal Murray advertising agency executive
Cardozo, Richard Nunez marketing, entrepreneurship and business educator
Cox, David Carson media company executive
DeNero, Henry T. department store chain executive
Dunlap, William DeWayne, Jr. advertising agency executive
Ferner, David Charles non-profit management and development consultant
Firestone, Jon advertising executive
Fischer, Robert William financial executive
Gage, Edwin C., III (Skip Gage) travel, marketing services executive
†Gavin, Sara public relations executive
Goldstein, Mark David advertising agency executive
Gottier, Richard Chalmers computer company executive
Grieman, John Joseph communications executive
Gustafson, Richard Charles rental and leasing company executive
Haugen, Rolf Eugene leasing company executive
†Herrick, Gregory Evans technology corporation executive
†Jeffries, Mary L. public relations executive
Koutsky, Dean Roger advertising executive
Liszt, Howard Paul advertising executive
McKenna, Robert J. car rental company executive
Morgan, Arthur Edward technology company executive
Morgan, Carol Miró marketing executive
Olson, Clifford Larry management consultant, entrepreneur
Perlman, Lawrence technology company executive
Pfleider, James Kenneth motivation company executive
Pile, Robert Bennett advertising executive, writer, consultant
Poehling, Robert Edward plumbing supply company executive
Read, John Conyers management consultant
Retzler, Kurt Egon diversified management company executive, hospitality, travel and marketing company executive
Sanger, Stephen W. consumer products company executive
Schultz, Louis Edwin management consultant
Somrock, John Douglas electronic marketing and manufacturing executive
Speer, David James public relations executive
Spring, John Benham car rental company executive
Stubbs, Jan Didra travel industry executive
Sullivan, Michael Patrick food service executive
Sveinson, Pamela J. human resources executive
†Tanner, Travis travel company executive
Tree, David L. advertising agency executive
Wainwright, Charles Anthony advertising company executive
Waldera, Wayne Eugene crisis management specialist
Waller, Joel N. consumer products executive
Welch, David C. advertising agency executive
Wickesberg, Albert Klumb retired management educator
Willis, Raymond Edson strategic management and organization educator
Yourzak, Robert Joseph management consultant, engineer, educator

Minnetonka
Gillies, Donald Richard advertising agency and marketing consultant
List, Charles Edward management and organization development consultant

Rochester
Husband, Richard Lorin, Sr. consulting company executive
Milner, Harold William hotel executive
Spencer, Edson White computer systems company executive

Saint Paul
†Anderson, John Freeman marketing executive
Boehnen, David Leo grocery company executive, lawyer
Feinberg, David Erwin publishing company executive
Haverty, Harold V. forms and check printing company executive
Hill, James Stanley computer consulting company executive
Podolak, Douglas John marketing consultant
Sullivan, William E. public relations executive
Trubeck, William Lewis air transportation company executive

Victoria
Courtney, Eugene Whitmal computer company executive

Wayzata
Detlefsen, Guy-Robert management consultant
Mithun, Raymond O. advertising agency executive, banker, real estate and insurance executive

MISSISSIPPI

Columbus
Hudnall, Jarrett, Jr. management and marketing educator

Jackson
Gunn, Frank Michael direct marketing professional

Mississippi State
McGilberry, Joe Herman food service executive

Starkville
Yancey, Jimmie Isaac marketing professional

MISSOURI

Ballwin
Tyler, William Howard, Jr. advertising executive, educator

Chesterfield
Huffer, Dan L. public relations executive
Welshans, Merle Talmadge management consultant

Clayton
†Vecchiotti, Robert Anthony management and organizational consultant

Columbia
Denney, Arthur Hugh consultant

Fenton
Maritz, William E. communications company executive

Florissant
†Cochran, Robert Emmett sales executive
Kelly, James Joseph printing company executive
Pomeroy, Robert Lee food distribution executive

Hazelwood
†Dalton, Dick Newton communications executive

Kansas City
Barnes, Donald Gayle management consultant
Benner, Richard Edward, Jr. management and marketing consultant, investor
Bywaters, David R. management consultant
Callo, Joseph Francis corporate communications consultant, writer
Courson, Marna B. P. public relations executive
Dillingham, John Allen marketing professional
Durwood, Edward D. motion picture corporation executive
†Durwood, Stanley H. entertainment industry executive
Egan, Charles Joseph, Jr. greeting card company executive, lawyer
Frederick, Joseph Francis, Jr. hotel executive
Freund, Ronald S. management consultant, marketing company executive
†Gilbert, John R. advertising and public relations agency executive
Grossman, Jerome Barnett retired service firm executive
Hagans, Robert Frank industrial clothing cleaning company executive
Hall, Donald Joyce greeting card company executive
Henson, Paul Harry telecommunications corporate executive
Hockaday, Irvine O., Jr. greeting card company executive
Julian, Lanny printing company executive
Kunz, Larry P. lumber and building materials company executive
Pistilli, Philip hotel executive
Robertson, Leon H. management consultant, educator
Solberg, Elizabeth Transou public relations executive
Strandjord, Mary Jeannine telecommunications executive

Lees Summit
Hurley, Marjorie Bryan marketing consultant

Rolla
Datz, Israel Mortimer information systems specialist

Saint Ann
†Drury, Charles Louis, Jr. hotel executive

Saint Charles
Gross, Charles Robert personnel executive, legislator, appraiser

Saint Louis
Akerson, Alan W. public relations company executive
†Anderson, William K. public relations executive
Barnes, Zane Edison communications company executive
Barney, Steven Matthew human resources executive
Bartlett, Walter E. communications company executive
Bateman, Sharon Louise public relations executive
Brown, Melvin F. executive
Cejka, Susan Ann executive search company executive
†Davis, Irvin broadcasting company executive
Devantier, Paul W. communications executive, broadcaster
Dommermuth, William P. marketing consultant, educator
†Elliott, Susan Spoehrer data processing executive
Epner, Steven Arthur computer consultant
Essman, Alyn V. photographic studios company executive
Ferguson, Gary Warren public relations executive
Fillenwarth, Albert F. advertising agency financial executive
Finnigan, Joseph Townsend public relations executive
Forrestal, Patrick George sales promotion agency executive
Graham, John Dalby public relations executive
Hilgert, Raymond Lewis management and industrial relations educator, consultant, arbitrator
Hillard, Robert Ellsworth public relations consultant
Johnson, Kennett Conrad advertising agency executive
Jones, Ronald Woodbridge human resources specialist, small business owner
Kerrick, Gray corporate communications executive
Khoury, George Gilbert printing company executive, baseball association executive
Kornblet, Donald Ross communications company executive
Loynd, Richard Birkett consumer products company executive
Lucking, Peter Stephen marketing consultant, industrial engineering consultant
McGinty, John marketing consultant
Miller, Theresa Ann management consultant
Mills, Linda S. public relations executive
Morice, James L. public relations executive
O'Brien, Albert James management consultant
Ractliffe, Robert Edward George management executive
Rocklage, Sister Mary Roch health system executive
Saligman, Harvey consumer products and services company executive
Siemer, Paul Jennings public relations executive
Snyder, Peter Larsen public relations executive
Stork, Donald Arthur advertising executive
Taylor, Jack C. automobile company executive
Weaver, William Clair, Jr. (Mike Weaver) human resources development executive
Willman, John Norman management consultant
Wilson, Harry Burgoyne retired public relations company executive
Zavaglia, Greg J. management consultant

Springfield
Cox, Lester Lee broadcasting executive
Denton, D. Keith management educator

Warrenton
Dapron, Elmer Joseph, Jr. communications executive

MONTANA

Billings
Williamson, Jerry Dean radio station executive

Helena
Barnhart, Beverly Homyak management consultant

NEBRASKA

Dakota City
Andriessen, Roel management consulting company executive

Lincoln
Preister, Donald George greeting card manufacturer, state senator
†Schultz, Kathleen Anne executive director

Omaha
Eggers, James Wesley executive search consultant
Frazier, Chet June advertising agency executive
Frederickson, Keith Alvin advertising agency executive
†Gupta, Vinod business lists company executive
Phares, Lynn Levisay public relations communications executive
Scott, Robert Michael data processing executive

Scottsbluff
Fisher, J. R. marketing executive

NEVADA

Boulder City
Ferraro, Arthur Kevin broadcasting executive

Jean
Schaeffer, Glenn William casino corporate financial executive

Las Vegas
Aranow, Peter Jones service company executive
Arce, Phillip William hotel and casino executive
Barnes, Wesley Edward energy and environmental executive
Basile, Richard Emanuel retired management consultant, educator
Bennett, William Gordon casino executive
Caro, Mike gaming authority
Goodwin, Nancy Lee corporate executive
Hardie, George Graham casino executive
Kenny, Erin Leigh advertising executive, state legislator
Landau, Ellis gaming company executive
Levy, Franklin I. mail order food service company executive
Martin, Thomas E. motel chain executive
Mc Kenzie, Jeremy Alec food service and baking company executive
Popeil, Ron consumer products company executive
Reichartz, W. Dan hotel executive
†Ritchie, James E. hotel executive
Rogich, Sig advertising executive
Sandvick, Frederick gaming company executive, lawyer, accountant
Shepard, Kathryn Irene public relations executive
Smith, Fred Wesley communications company executive
Thomas-Orr, Betty Jo retired public relations specialist
Turner, Clyde T. service executive
Vanatta, Chester B. business executive, educator
Wada, Harry Nobuyoshi training company executive
Wiener, Valerie communications company owner
Wynn, Kenneth Richard design and furnishings company executive
Wynn, Stephen A. hotel, entertainment facility executive

Reno
Carr, Thomas Jefferson, Jr. gaming executive
Gibbons, Dawn managwment consultant
Hendricksen, Holmes G. hotel executive
Wells, Richard H. gaming research executive

NEW HAMPSHIRE

Bedford
Cronin, Timothy Cornelius, III computer manufacturing executive
Hall, Pamela S. environmental consulting firm executive

Concord
Roberts, George Bernard, Jr. business and government affairs consultant, former state legislator
†White, Jeffrey George healthcare consultant, educator

Dublin
Biklen, Paul retired advertising executive

Durham
Beckett, John Angus management educator, consultant
Flynn, Paul Bartholomew marketing executive

Exeter
Brownell, David Paul business executive
Jackson, Patrick John public relations counsel

Grantham
Hansen, Herbert W. management consultant

Hampton
†Best, Jacob Hilmer (Jerry), Jr. hotel chain executive
Canas, Jon hotel executive
†Weber, Kenneth J. hotel executive

Hampton Falls
Buckingham, Richard L(eroy) computer company executive

Hanover
Huppe, Alex public relations executive
Webster, Frederick Elmer, Jr. marketing educator, consultant

Hillsboro
Marsh, Richard J. strategic management consultant

Jackson
Synnott, William Raymond retired management consultant

Jaffrey
Schott, John (Robert) international consultant, educator

Keene
Lyon, Ronald Edward management consultant, computer consultant

Nashua
Clough, Charles Elmer consumer products company executive
Hargreaves, David William communications company executive
Stein, Robert consumer products company executive
Webber, Howard Rodney computer company executive
Weinstein, Jeffrey Allen consumer products company executive, lawyer

New London
Wheaton, Perry Lee management consultant

Salem
†Chasse, François consulting company executive

Sunapee
Chait, Lawrence G. marketing consultant

Waterville Valley
Grimes, Howard Ray management consultant

Wolfeboro
Steadman, David Rosslyn Ayton business executive, corporate director

NEW JERSEY

Absecon
Steinruck, Charles Francis, Jr. management consultant, lawyer

Allenhurst
Hinson, Robert William advertising executive, consultant

Allenwood
Shortess, Edwin Steevin marketing consultant

Atlantic City
Blaziek, William Louis casino and hotel executive
†Gluck, Henry resort complex executive
Harris, Paul Smith human resources professional
†Wagner, Roger Philip hotel executive

Avalon
Yochum, Philip Theodore retired motel and cafeteria chain executive

Basking Ridge
Ferguson, Forest D. marketing executive
Heckendorf, Glenn sales and marketing executive
†Laurie, Marilyn communications and computer company executive
Willcoxon, Sam Randolph communications executive

Berkeley Heights
†Collard, Ross Theo management consultant
Thomsen, Thomas Richard communications company executive

Bernardsville
DiDomenico, Mauro, Jr. communication executive
Dixon, Richard Wayne retired communications company executive

Bridgewater
McFarland, Richard M. executive recruiting consultant
Pickett, Doyle Clay employment and training counselor, consultant
Skidmore, James Albert, Jr. management, computer technology and engineering services company executive

Butler
Ward, Robert Allen, Jr. advertising executive

Caldwell
Chatlos, William Edward management consultant

Camden
Holman, Joseph S. automotive sales executive

Carlstadt
Daniels, Robert Alan *marketing executive*

Carteret
Corliss, Robert *sporting goods company executive*

Chatham
Kaulakis, Arnold Francis *management consultant*
Lenz, Henry Paul *management consultant*
Rockwood, Thomas Julian *management services executive, information technolgy consultant*
Woods, Reginald Foster *management consulting executive*

Cherry Hill
Sax, Robert Edward *food service equipment company executive*
Schelm, Roger Leonard *information systems specialist*

Chester
Maddalena, Lucille Ann *management executive*

Clark
Augeri, Joseph *personal care industry executive*
†Stepanski, Anthony Francis, Jr. *computer company executive*

Convent Station
Weber, Joseph H. *communications company executive*

Cranbury
Cuthbert, Robert Allen *pet products company executive*
Fiore, Anthony N. *marketing company executive, strategic planning consultant*
Koras, William *concessions, restaurants and publishing company executive*

Cresskill
Bogner, Stephen D. *marketing professional*

Edison
†Hare, Richard Bergin *market research company executive*
Marash, Stanley Albert *consulting company executive*
Shulman, Hyman *food service executive*

Elizabeth
Clare, Thomas J. *consumer products company executive*
Infusino, Thomas P. *food distribution company executive*

Englewood
Miles, Virginia (Mrs. Fred C. Miles) *marketing consultant*

Englewood Cliffs
Cantwell, John Walsh *advertising executive*
Schlatter, Konrad *corporate executive*

Fair Lawn
Hayden, Neil Steven *communications company executive*
Motin, Revell Judith *data processing executive*

Fairfield
Dean, John L. *sales and marketing executive, educator*
Mehta, Narinder Kumar *marketing executive*

Far Hills
Barnum, William Douglas *communications company executive*
Holt, Jonathan Turner *public relations executive*
Ross, Stephen Bruce *public affairs consultant*

Florham Park
Fischer, Pamela Shadel *public relations executive*
Naimark, George Modell *marketing and management consultant*

Fort Lee
†Berdy, Jack M. *software and consultation company executive*
Lynaugh, Joseph T. *health care executive*
Seitel, Fraser Paul *public relations executive*
†Sigona, Ralph John *international business consultant*

Freehold
Handlin, Amy Harwood *marketing educator*

Glen Ridge
Agnew, Peter Tomlin *employee benefit consultant*

Hackensack
Borg, Malcolm Austin *communications company executive*
Judge, Jean Frances *management consultant*

Haddonfield
Bauer, Raymond Gale *sales professional*

Hamburg
Buist, Richardson *corporate executive, retired banker*

Hightstown
Kilborne, William Skinner *retired business consultant*

Holmdel
Haskell, Barry Geoffry *communications company research administrator*
Jukes, Terence Douglas *marketing professional*
Netravali, Arun N. *communications executive*

Lawrenceville
Coleman, Wade Hampton, III *management consultant, mechanical engineer, former banker*

Lebanon
Kone, Russell Joseph *advertising agency executive, film producer*

Linden
Foege, Rose Ann Scudiero *human resources professional*

Little Silver
Finch, Rogers Burton *association management consultant*
Labbett, John Edgar *pet food products executive*

Livingston
Mandelbaum, Howard Arnold *marketing/management consultant*

Long Branch
Evangelista, Paula Lee *public policy and communications director*

Madison
Byrd, Stephen Fred *human resource consultant*
†Goodman, Michael B(arry) *communications educator*
O'Brien, Mary Devon *communications executive, consultant*
Siegel, George Henry *international business development consultant*

Maplewood
†Safian, Gail Robyn *public relations executive*

Matawan
Kesselman, Bruce Alan *marketing executive, consultant, composer, writer*

Mendham
Fenner, Peter David *communications executive, management consultant*

Middletown
Levi, Ilan Mosche *computer and communications company executive*

Millington
Donaldson, John Cecil, Jr. *consumer products company executive*

Montvale
†Burnett, Ed *direct marketing executive*
Gallagher, Michael Robert *consumer products company executive*

Moonachie
Colburn, Janet *data processing administrator*
Robinson, Hugh R. *retired marketing executive*

Moorestown
Bennington, William Jay *public relations executive*
Schwerin, Horace S. *marketing research executive*

Morristown
Bergstein, Stanley Francis *horse racing executive*
†Cortellessa, Dominick Ralph *information systems executive*
Miller, Hasbrouck Bailey *financial and travel services company executive*
Powell, David Greatorex *public affairs executive*
†Shanahan, William Stephen *consumer products company executive*
Shumate, Paul William, Jr. *communications executive*
Teiger, David *management consultant*
Wajnert, Thomas C. *leasing company executive*

Mount Laurel
Grey, Richard E. *toy company executive*
Hart, Larry Edward *communications company executive*
Klein, Anne Sceia *public relations executive*
Taylor, Henry Roth *marketing executive*

Mountain Lakes
Williams, Edward David *consulting executive*

Mountainside
Abrams, Joseph *computer company executive*
DiPietro, Ralph Anthony *marketing and management consultant, educator*
Lipton, Bronna Jane *marketing communications executive*

Murray Hill
Field, Michael Stanley *information services company executive*
Musa, John Davis *computer and infosystems executive, software reliability engineering researcher and expert*
†Taylor, Volney *marketing company executive*

New Brunswick
Budd, Richard Wade *communications scientist, educator, lecturer, consultant, university dean*
Burke, James Edward *consumer products company executive*
Ruben, Brent David *communication educator*

New Providence
Longfield, William Herman *health care company executive*
Sundberg, Carl-Erik Wilhelm *telecommunications executive, researcher*

Newark
Kaltenbacher, Philip D(avid) *industrialist, former public official*
Koeppe, Alfred C. *telecommunications company executive*
Lederman, Peter (Bernd) *environmental services executive, consultant, educator*
Lieberman, Leonard *retired supermarket executive*

Northvale
Goodman, Stanley Leonard *advertising executive*

Oakland
†Berrie, Russell *sales executive, business owner*

Ocean
Schell, James Edward, II *computer company executive, consultant*
Winograd, Audrey Lesser *advertising executive*

Old Bridge
Engel, John Jacob *communications executive*
†Fields, Edward *management consultant*

Old Tappan
Ferriter, Warren Joseph *information systems executive*

Oradell
Dinsmore, Gordon Griffith *management consultant*

Orange
Chlopak, Donna Gayle *marketing and management consultant*

Palmyra
Overholt, Miles Harvard, III *management consultant, family therapist*

Paramus
Baczko, Joseph R. *consumer products executive*

Park Ridge
Kaplan, Daniel I. *leasing company executive*
Kennedy, Brian James *marketing executive*
Olson, Frank Albert *car rental company executive*

Parsippany
†Belmonte, Steven Joseph *hotel chain executive*
Cochran, Larry B. *amusement park executive*
Dudrow, Peter Warren *human resources executive, consultant*
Harber, Joseph F. *food marketing executive*
Haselmann, John Philip *marketing executive*
Hoyt, Monty *communications executive*
Jenkins, Katherine Erskine *advertising executive*
Muratore, Robert Peter *advertising executive*
Nalewako, Mary Anne *corporate secretary*
Parrish, Barry Jay *marketing executive*
Rowland, Jan Brownstein *marketing statistician*
Visocki, Nancy Gayle *infosystems design consultant*
†Wiedenmayer, Christopher M. *writing instrument manufacturer, distributor*

Perrineville
Hoffman, Maryhelen H. Paulick *communications company executive*

Pleasantville
Freeman, Lillie Brooks *communications company administrator*

Point Pleasant
Perdunn, Richard Francis *management consultant*

Princeton
†Cooper, Michael R. *opinion research corporation executive*
Crespi, Irving *public opinion and market research consultant*
Davies, Robert Abel, III *consumer products company executive*
Davis, Richard K. *management consultant executive*
†Devine, Hugh James, Jr. *marketing executive, consultant*
Fouss, James H. *marketing executive*
Gillespie, Richard Joseph *advertising agency executive*
Greenberg, Joel S. *management consultant, engineer*
Hillier, James *communications executive, researcher*
Lawrence, Barbara *information manager*
Morris, Mac Glenn *advertising bureau executive*
O'Connor, Neal William *former advertising agency executive*
Popper, Robert David *computer and management consultant*
Rich, Jude T. *management consulting firm executive*
Roth, William Matson *former corporate executive*
Sethi, Shyam Sunder *management consultant*
†Sussman, Steven David *management consulting executive*
†Tregoe, Benjamin Bainbridge *management consultant, researcher*
Weinstein, Stephen Brant *communications executive, researcher, writer*
Williams, Brown F *television media services company executive*

Ramsey
DeLio, Richard Michael *management consultant*
Oliver, Joseph J. *consumer products company executive*

Randolph
Raber, Marvin *consultant, retired utility company executive*

Red Bank
Liao, Paul Foo-Hung *communications research company executive, physicist*
Reinhart, Peter Sargent *corporate executive, lawyer*

River Edge
Hochhauser, Richard Michael *marketing professional*
†Lennon, Michael T. *public relations executive*
Sommer, Robert George *public relations executive*

Roseland
Casale, Robert J. *communications executive*
†Kranson, Gerald Irwin *employee benefits consultant, lawyer*
Lafer, Fred Seymour *data processing company executive*
Taub, Henry *retired computer services company executive*
Turner, William J. *data processing company executive*
Weinbach, Arthur Frederic *computing services company executive*
Weston, Josh S. *data processing company executive*

Rumson
Christianson, Lloyd Fenton *management consultant*

Saddle River
Leavitt, Horace Madison, Jr. *communications company executive, former naval officer*
Warrington, Clayton Linwood, Jr. *advertising executive*

Scotch Plains
Barnard, Kurt *retail marketing forecaster, publisher*

Secaucus
Brown, Ira Bernard *data processing executive*
Marcus, Alan C. *public relations consultant*
Rakov, Barbara Streem *marketing executive*
Schenck, Frederick A. *business executive*

Short Hills
Harwood, Jerry *market research executive*
Meredith, George Davis *advertising executive, publisher*
Schaefer, Charles James, III *advertising agency executive, consultant*
Schaffer, Edmund John *management consultant, retired engineering executive*
Stefanile, Lawrence Vincent *management counsulting company executive*

Somerset
Aronson, Dana Lynne *program/public relations executive*
†King, David T. *communications company financial executive*
†Marinari, Donald J. *advertising executive*
Neff, Richard B. *consumer products company executive*
Noonan, William Francis *public relations company executive*

Somerville
Deieso, Donald Allan *environmental goods and services executive*
Hildebrandt, Bradford Walter *consulting company executive*

Spring Lake
Ernst, John Louis *management consultant*
McEntee, Robert Edward *management consultant*

Summit
†Beyer, Charlotte Bishop *investment management marketing executive, consultant*
Bostwick, Randell A. *retired retail food company executive*
Fuess, Billings Sibley, Jr. *advertising executive*
Nessen, Ward Henry *former typography company executive, lawyer*
Pace, Leonard *retired management consultant*
Sheldon, William Charles *marketing professional*

Teaneck
†Brophy, John Martin *information management services executive*
Gund, Sharon Smallwood *information services company executive*
Jugenheimer, Donald Wayne *advertising and communications educator, university administrator*

Tenafly
Gibbons, Robert Philip *management consultant*

Three Bridges
Lawrence, Gerald Graham *management consultant*

Titusville
Marden, Kenneth Allen *advertising executive*
†May, J. Joel *health care management consultant*

Toms River
Kanarkowski, Edward Joseph *data processing company executive*

Trenton
Robinson, Susan Mittleman *data processing executive*

Ventnor City
Bolton, Kenneth Albert *management consultant*

Vernon
Gillman, Richard *hotel, casino company executive*

Verona
Greenwald, Robert *public relations executive*

Warren
Blass, Walter Paul *consultant, management educator*

Wayne
Blauvelt, John Clifford *diversified consumer products company executive*
Bridges, Beryl Clarke *marketing executive*
Donald, Robert Graham *retail food chain personnel executive*
Hirsch, Gary D. *supermarket executive*
Louttit, William A. *supermarket chain executive*

West Bridgewater
Hulse, Robert Douglas *high technology executive*

West Caldwell
Page, Frederick West *business consultant*
Sostilio, Robert Francis *office equipment marketing executive*

Westfield
Cushman, Helen Merle Baker *retired management consultant*

Wharton
Rodzianko, Paul *energy company executive*

Whippany
Golden, Michael Frank *packaging sales company executive*
Mimnaugh, John M. *advertising executive*

Woodbridge
Cuti, Anthony J. *consumer products company executive*

Wyckoff
Anstatt, Peter Jan *marketing services executive*
Lavery, Daniel P. *marketing management consultant*

NEW MEXICO

Albuquerque
Bleiweis, Paul Benjamin *environmental services executive*
Geary, David Leslie *communications executive, educator, consultant*
Hale, Bruce Donald *marketing professional*
Hancock, Don Ray *researcher*
Smith, Elvin T. *communications executive*
Tope, Dwight Harold *retired management consultant*
Young, Joan Crawford *advertising executive*

Los Alamos
Sharp, Jane Ellyn *operations executive*

Sandia Park
Greenwell, Ronald Everett *communications executive*

Tesuque
Poedtke, Carl Henry George, Jr. *management consultant*

NEW YORK

Albany
Ferguson, Henry *international management consultant*
Murphy, Thomas Joseph *strategic communications consultant*
Quellmalz, Henry *printing company executive*
Sacklow, Stewart Irwin *advertising executive*

Amherst
Cohen, Herman Nathan *private investigator*

Amityville
Brennan, Patrick Thomas *meteorology company executive*

Ardsley
Barton, Joan Chi-Hung Lo *sales executive*
†Pires, Mary Ann *public relations consultant*

Armonk
Berlin, Caren Ann *marketing professional*
Bolduc, Ernest Joseph *management consultant*
Bolton, John Roger *public relations executive*
Gerstner, Louis Vincent, Jr. *diversified company executive*
Levy, Kenneth James *advertising executive*
†Mc Groddy, James Cleary *computer company executive*
†Rizzo, Paul J. *information processing company executive*
Sayers, Ken W(illiam) *writer and public relations executive*
York, Jerome B. *computer company executive*

Babylon
Meirowitz, Claire Cecile *public relations executive*

Batavia
Maher, John Francis *personnel executive*

Bedford Hills
Diebold, John *management consultant*

Briarcliff Manor
Dolmatch, Theodore Bieley *management consultant*
Haddad, Jerrier Abdo *engineering management consultant*
†Reynolds, Michael Joseph *consulting company executive*

Bronx
Kitzie, John, Jr. *retail electronic products executive*
Kucic, Joseph *management consultant, industrial engineer*

Bronxville
Blank, Richard Mark *advertising licensing and product development executive*

Brooklyn
Ahrens, Thomas H. *production company executive*
Frisch, Ivan Thomas *computer and communications company executive*
Geller, Sheldon *comsumer products company executive*
Shaw, Doris *creative marketing consultant*

Buffalo
†Campbell, David N. *data processing executive*
Miner, John Burnham *industrial relations educator, writer*
†Orlowski, Ronald Joseph *wood preserving company executive*
†Paul, Philip Franklin, Jr. *management consultant*
Pegels, C. Carl *management science and systems educator*
Phillips, Stanley F *restaurant company executive*
Rice, Victor Albert *global industrial company executive*
Schutte, Alden Frederick *advertising executive*
Thompson, Michael F. *food service executive*
Williams, Reginald Victor, III *marketing communications company executive*

Carle Place
Kahn, Leonard Richard *communications and electronics company executive*

Chappaqua
Maloney, John Frederick *retired marketing and opinion research specialist*

Cold Spring Harbor
Nightingale, Geoffrey J. *communications company executive, consultant*

Copake Falls
Chalk, Howard Wolfe *marketing company executive*

Corning
Peck, Arthur John, Jr. *diversified manufacturing executive*

Croton On Hudson
Plotch, Walter *management consultant, fund raising counselor*

Delmar
Button, Rena Pritsker *public relations company executive*

Dix Hills
Fisher, Fenimore *business development consultant*

Dundee
Pfendt, Henry George *retired information systems executive, management consultant*

East Amherst
Bauer, Paul David *retired food service executive*

East Hampton
Munson, Lawrence Shipley *management consultant*

East Meadow
†Fuchs, Jerome Herbert *management consultant*

East Northport
Hayo, George Edward *management consultant*

Ellenville
Straus, R. Peter *communications company executive, broadcasting executive*

Elmsford
Caswell, Hollis Leland *computer company executive, electrical engineer*
Shaviv, Eddie *marketing and sales executive*

Fairport
Van Bortel, Howard Martin *automarketing consultant*

Farmingdale
Goodstein, Edward Marc *communications executive*

Fayetteville
Cantwell, John Dalzell, Jr. *management consultant*
Pulos, Arthur Jon *industrial design executive*
Wallace, Spencer Miller, Jr. *hotel executive*

Floral Park
Corbett, William John *government and public relations consultant, lawyer*
Heyderman, Mark Baron *sales and marketing company executive*

Florida
Koppele, Gary S. *food service executive*

Forest Hills
Miller, Donald Ross *management consultant*

Fresh Meadows
Ganz, Samuel *human resource and management professional*

Garden City
Bovino, Charles Anthony *rental car company executive, lawyer*
Conlon, Thomas James *marketing executive*
Crom, James Oliver *professional training company executive*
Doucette, Mary-Alyce *computer company executive*
Roche, John Edward *human resources management consultant, educator*
Vittoria, Joseph V. *car rental company executive*

Garrison
Chasins, Edward A. *communications company executive*

Glen Cove
Greenberg, Allan *advertising and marketing research consultant*

Glendale
†Peetz-Larsen, Hans *trading company executive*

Great Neck
Donenfeld, Kenneth Jay *management consultant*
Friedland, Louis N. *retired communications executive*
Gillett, Charles *travel executive*
Goldberg, Melvin Arthur *communications executive*
Lampel, Ronald B. *human resources executive*

Greenfield Center
Templin, John Leon, Jr. *healthcare consulting executive*

Greenwich
Leone, Louis J. *marketing and communications executive*

Hancock
DeLuca, Ronald *consultant, former advertising agency executive*

Harrison
Fuchs, Hanno *communications consultant*
Krantz, Melissa Marianne *public relations company executive*

Hauppauge
Hershberg, David E. *communications corporation executive*
Reich, William Michael *advertising executive*
Stemple, Joel Gilbert *computer company executive*
Vignola, William J. *communications executive*

Hempstead
Pell, Arthur Robert *human resources development consultant, author*

Hewlett
Kislik, Louis A. *marketing company executive*

Howard Beach
Krein, Catherine Cecilia *public relations professional*

Huntington Station
Liguori, Frank Nickolas *temporary personnel company executive*

Irvington
Steinberg, James Ian *marketing executive*
Turk, Stanley Martin *advertising agency executive*

Islandia
Wang, Charles B. *computer software company executive*

Islip Terrace
Hartley-Leonard, Darryl *hotel company executive*

Ithaca
Farley, Jennie Tiffany Towle *industrial and labor relations educator*
Park, Roy Hampton, Jr. *advertising media executive*
Whyte, William Foote *industrial relations educator, author*
Windmuller, John Philip *industrial relations educator, consultant*

Jamaica
Crivelli, Joseph Louis *security specialist*

Jericho
Rosen, Robert Arnold *management company executive, real estate investor*

Katonah
White, Harold Tredway, III *management consultant*

Kingston
Agerwala, Tilak Krishna Mahesh *computer company executive*
Lanitis, Tony Andrew *market researcher*

Lancaster
Neumaier, Gerhard John *environment consulting company executive*

Larchmont
Greenwald, Carol Schiro *professional services marketing research executive*
Josevie, Arnold Jean Phillipe *physicist, scientific consultant*
Plumez, Jean Paul *advertising agency executive, consultant*
Schwatka, Mark Andrew *advertising agency executive*
Silverstone, David *advertising executive*
Wielgus, Charles Joseph *information services company executive*

Long Beach
Siegel, Herbert Bernard *certified professional management consultant*

Malverne
Freund, Richard L. *communications company executive, consultant, lawyer*

Mamaroneck
Mines, Herbert Thomas *executive recruiter*

Manhasset
†Hinds, Glester Samuel *financier, advertising executive, tax consultant*

Melville
Jagoda, Donald Robert *sales promotion agency executive*
†Jurick, Robert Herbert *marketing executive*
Krusos, Denis Angelo *communications company executive*
Large, G. Gordon M. *data processing company executive*
Maller, Robert Russell *certified management consultant, banker*
Ray, Gordon Thompson *communications executive*

Middle Island
†Andrews, Gaylen *advertising executive*
†Linick, Andrew S. *marketing executive*

Mineola
McGonigle, James Gregory *training consultant*
Rushmore, Stephen *hotel consulting and appraisal specialist*

Mount Vernon
Leonard, John Harry *advertising executive*

New City
Wasserman, Walter Leonard *magnetics company executive*

New Hyde Park
Anderson, Ronald Howard *consumer packaged goods company marketing executive*
Baldwin, Thomas James *restaurant chain financial executive, accountant, educator*

New Paltz
Nyquist, Thomas Eugene *consulting business executive, mayor*

New Rochelle
Jacobs, Doran *travel marketing executive*
Vernon, Lillian *mail order company executive*

New York
Abernathy, James Logan *public relations executive*
Achenbaum, Alvin Allen *marketing and management consultant*
Agisim, Philip *advertising and marketing company executive*
Aiello, Stephen *public relations executive*
Albright, Warren Edward *advertising executive*
Alexander, Roy *public relations executive, editor, author*
Allen, Alice Catherine Towsley *public relations professional, writer, consultant*
Alloggiamento, Nancy Thomas *advertising agency executive, consultant, business owner*
Ammirati, Ralph *advertising agency executive*
Anchlia, Than Mal *wholesale distribution executive*
Ancona, Barry *publishing and marketing consultant*
Anderson, Arthur Allan *management consultant*
Anderson, Gavin *public relations consultant*
Anderson, Ron *advertising executive*
Andolsen, Alan Anthony *management consultant*
Anfield, Frank A. *advertising executive*
Ankerson, Robert William *management consultant*
Antonacci, Lori (Loretta Marie Antonacci) *marketing executive, consultant*
Antonuccio, Joseph Albert *hospitality industry executive*
Applebaum, Stuart S. *public relations executive*
Arlow, Arnold Jack *advertising agency executive*
Arnold, Thomas Elijah, Jr. (Tim Arnold) *advertising executive, blues guitar player*
Aronson, Donald Eric *professional services firms consultant*
Aronstam, Neil Lee *media marketing firm executive*
†Ashley, Diane S. *advertising executive*
Austad, Vigdis *computer software company executive*
Avrett, John Glenn *advertising executive*
Axelrod, Norman N(athan) *technology application and technical planning consultant*
Ayers, Emory Daniel *management consultant*
Bacher, Judith St. George *executive search consultant*
Backer, William Montague *retired advertising agency executive*
Baker, Stephen *advertising executive, author*
Baker, Wilder DuPuy *advertising executive*
†Balick, Kenneth D. *securities and investment bank executive*
Balkind, Aubrey *advertising executive*
Bamberger, Gabrielle *public relations executive*
Baron, Theodore *public relations executive*
Barrett, Herbert *artists management executive*
†Bartlett, Thomas Foster *international management consultant*
Bates, Don *public relations and marketing executive*
Baum, Willow Ann *public relations executive*
Bauman, Martin Harold *executive search firm executive*
Beard, Eugene P. *advertising agency executive*
Beaumont, Richard Austin *management consultant*
Becker, Ivan *advertising executive*
Becker, Michael Lewis *advertising executive*
Becker, Robert A. *advertising executive*
Becker, Stanley R. *advertising executive*
Beckwith, Rodney Fisk *management consulting firm executive*
Beers, Charlotte Lenore *advertising agency executive*
Beinecke, William Sperry *corporate executive*
Bell, David Arthur *advertising agency executive*
Bellows, Howard Arthur, Jr. *marketing research executive*
Ben-Eli, Michael Uri *management consultant*
Benner, Mary Wright *marketing professional*
Bennett, Georgette *communications and planning consultant*
Bennett, Saul *public relations agency executive*
Benway, Joseph Calise *advertising agency financial executive*
Berenson, Robert Leonard *advertising agency executive*
Bergen, John Donald *communications, public affairs executive*
Berger, Arnold Robert *advertising executive*
Bergin, John Francis *advertising agency executive*
Berlin, Andrew Mark *advertising agency executive*
Berman, Mira *advertising agency executive*
Bernard, David George *management consultant*
Bernbach, John Lincoln *advertising executive*
Biebelberg, David Mark *marketing professional*
Biederman, Barron Zachary (Barry Biederman) *advertising agency executive*
Bijur, Arthur William *advertising executive*
Bishop, Susan Katharine *executive search company executive*
Blades, Carol Brady *public relations executive*
Blaney, John *advertising executive*
Bloomgarden, Kathy Finn *public relations executive*
Bock, Joseph Reto *industrial relations executive*
Bohan, Thomas E. *advertising company executive*
Boice, Craig Kendall *management consultant*
Bollman, Mark Brooks, Jr. *communications executive*
Bona, Frederick Emil *public relations executive*
Bond, Jonathan Halbert *advertising executive*
Booth, Margaret A(nn) *communications company executive*
Bornet, Stephen Folwell *public relations and marketing communications executive*
Bostock, Roy Jackson *advertising agency executive*
Boucher, Henry Joseph (Bud Boucher) *management consultant*
Bowen, John Sheets *advertising agency executive*
Bowman, Robert A. *hotel company executive*
Bradstock, John *advertising executive*
Brady, Adelaide Burks *public relations agency executive, giftware catalog executive*
Brilliant, Robert Lee *advertising agency executive*
Brody, Alexander *advertising executive*
†Brody, Martin *food service company executive*
Bronkesh, Annette Cylia *public relations executive*
Brooks, Timothy H. *media executive*
Brown, Edward Glenn *chef, restaurateur*
Brown, Hobson, Jr. *executive search firm consultant and executive*
Brumback-Henry, Sarah Elizabeth *industrial psychologist, management and corporate consultant*
Bruzs, Boris Olgerd *management consultant*
Buchwald, Elias *public relations executive*
Bullen, Richard Hatch *former corporate executive*
Bullock, H. Ridgely *management and investment executive, lawyer*
Bungey, Michael *advertising executive*
Burg, Mitchell Marc *advertising executive*
†Burge, Christopher *auction house executive*
Burger, Chester *retired management consultant*
Burke, Daniel Barnett *retired communications corporation executive*
Burkhardt, Ronald Robert *advertising executive*
Burns, Ronald S. *advertising company executive*
Burson, Harold *public relations executive*
Burton, Robert Gene *printing and publishing executive*
†Butrom, Carl *broadcasting executive*
†Cabot, Jane Fenderson *public relations executive*
Cadwell, Franchellie Margaret *advertising agency executive, writer*
Caggiano, Joseph *advertising executive*
Calabrese, Rosalie Sue *arts management consultant, writer*
Callen, John Holmes, Jr. *executive search consultant*
Calvillo, Ricardo C. *communications executive*
Campbell, William I. *cigarette company executive*

Cannon, James Anthony advertising executive
Canter, Stanley D. retired marketing consulting company executive
Cappello, Juan C. business executive
Cappon, Andre Alfred management consultant
Carey, Thomas Hilton advertising agency executive
Carnella, Frank Thomas information executive
Carra, Andrew Joseph advertising executive
Carter, Carolyn Houchin advertising agency executive
Case, Eugene Lawrence advertising agency executive
Casper, Jack H. advertising executive
Cavior, Warren Joseph communications executive
Chajet, Clive communications consultant
Chandler, Robert Leslie public relations executive
†Chapin, Theodore Steinway entertainment company executive
Cheney, Richard Eugene public relations executive
Chernin, Fredric David advertising agency executive
Child, Julia McWilliams (Mrs. Paul Child) cooking expert, television personality, author
Cholak, Paul Michael financial services personnel executive
Chorazy, Sandra Marie advertising agency executive
Chu, Roderick Gong-Wah management consultant
Churchill, Mary Carey public relations executive
†Ciociola, Melvin J. advertising agency executive
Citron, Richard Ira management consultant
Clark, J. Thomas advertising agency executive
Clarke, Frank William advertising agency executive
Cohen, Alan Norman business executive
Cohn, Theodore management consultant
Colonel, Sheri Lynn advertising agency executive
Conforti, Joanne advertising executive
Conroy, Dennis Joseph management consultant
Conway, David Antony communications executive, marketing professional
†Cooney, Lenore public relations executive
Cooper, Andrew public relations executive
Cooper, R. John, III advertising agency executive, lawyer
Corbin, Herbert Leonard public relations executive
Costello, Richard Neumann advertising agency executive
Cox, James Oliver, III public relations company executive
†Coyne, Nancy Carol advertising executive
Crawford, Bruce Edgar advertising executive
Crisci, Mathew G. marketing executive
Crosland, Philip Crawford advertising company executive
Culligan, John William retired corporate executive
Cullman, Edgar Meyer diversified consumer products company executive
Cunningham, Patrick Joseph advertising agency executive
Cutler, Laurel advertising agency executive
Daily, John Charles software company executive
Dane, Maxwell former advertising executive
Dangler, Richard Reiss corporate service companies executive, entrepreneur
Daniel, David Ronald management consultant
Danzig, Jerome Alan (Jerry) management consultant
Danzig, Sarah Palfrey retired advertising agency executive, writer
Davidson, Donald William advertising executive
†Davidson, Wayne A. pharmaceutical and consumer products company executive
Davis, Susan Lynn public relations executive
Dean, Sidney Walter, Jr. business and marketing executive
Deare, Jennifer Laurie marketing professional
DeBow, Jay Howard Camden public relations company executive
DeBow, Thomas Joseph, Jr. advertising executive
De Deo, Joseph E. advertising executive
Delano, Lester Almy, Jr. advertising executive
Della Femina, Jerry advertising agency executive
DeMichele, Robert Michael management corporation executive
Dent, V. Edward former advertising and communications company executive
Dessi, Adrian Frank marketing, communications executive
DeVito, Francis Joseph advertising agency executive
Diamond, Harris corporate communications executive, lawyer
Dilenschneider, Robert Louis public relations company executive
Dimling, John Arthur marketing executive
Doner, Frederick Nathan advertising and communications executive
Dooner, John Joseph, Jr. advertising executive
Doppelt, Earl H. communications corporation executive
Drobis, David R. public relations company executive
Druckenmiller, Robert T. public relations executive
Dubin, Morton Donald management consultant, film producer
Duffy, David L. public relations executive
Duke, Robin Chandler Tippett retired public relations executive
Dunst, Laurence David advertising executive
Dusenberry, Philip Bernard advertising executive
Dworin, Steve advertising executive
Dzodin, Harvey Cary communications executive
Eckstut, Michael Kauder management consultant
Edelman, Richard Winston public relations executive
Edson, Andrew Stephen public relations executive
Eggers, Ernest Russell management consultant
Einhorn, Eric John advertising executive
Elkes, Terrence Allen communications executive
Ellig, Bruce Robert personnel executive
Elliott, John, Jr. advertising agency executive
Elliott, Tim C. advertising agency executive
Epstein, Harriet Pike public relations executive
Erhardt, Edward Richard advertising company executive
Eswein, Bruce James, II human resources executive
Evans, Alfred Lee, Jr. advertising executive
Evans, Thomas Chives Newton communications executive
Evans, Van Michael advertising agency executive, consultant
Faber, Neil advertising executive
Fabian, George Stephen advertising agency executive
Fader, Ellen Strahs communications company executive
Falk, Edgar Alan public relations consulting executive, author
†Farella, Steven advertising executive
Farinelli, Jean L. public relations firm executive
Feigin, Barbara Sommer advertising executive
Feinberg, Robert Edward advertising agency executive, writer
†Feldman, Robert C. public relations executive
Feldtmose, John Nielsen management consulting executive
Ferrell, John Frederick advertising executive
Ferries, John Charles advertising executive
†Ferris, Robert public relations executive
Ferris, Robert Dominick public relations executive
Fink, Stuart Simon business management educator
Finn, David public relations company executive, artist
Finn, Joan Lockwood public relations executive, writer, educator
Finn, Peter public relations executive
Finnerud, Kenneth Percival marketing executive
Fishel, Stanley Irvyng advertising executive
Fisher, Robert Allen advertising executive
Fitzpatrick, Nancy S. advertising executive
Flaherty, Tina Santi corporate communications executive
Flaum, Sander Allen advertising and marketing executive
Fluhr, Howard consulting firm executive
Fogge, Len advertising executive
Ford, John Charles communications executive
Forman, Leonard P. media company executive
Foster, James Henry advertising and public relations executive
Foxworth, Jo advertising agency executive
Frank, Robert Allen advertising executive
Frank, William Fielding computer systems design executive, consultant
†Franken, Martin public relations company executive
Frantz, Jack Thomas advertising executive
Freedman, Allen Royal business executive, lawyer
Freeman, Clifford Lee advertising agency executive
Freeman, Michael J. consumer products company executive
Friedman, Frances public relations executive
Fuersich, Janet Theresa compensation consultant, corporate executive
Fujiwara, Nobuo trading company executive
Furman, Anthony Michael public relations executive
Fursland, Richard Curtis public relations executive
Gaines, Jay S. executive recruiter
Gardiner, E. Nicholas P. executive search executive
Gardner, Ralph David advertising executive
Gargano, Amil advertising agency executive
Garvin, Andrew Paul information company executive, author, consultant
Geduldig, Alfred corporate communications consultant
Geier, Philip Henry, Jr. advertising executive
Geller, Robert James advertising agency executive
Geltzer, Sheila Simon public relations executive
Georgescu, Peter Andrew advertising executive
Gerson, Irwin Conrad advertising executive
Gibbs, Richard Leslie public relations executive
Gibson, William B. advertising, marketing executive
Gilliatt, Neal advertising executive, consultant
Ginsberg, Frank Charles advertising executive
Ginsburg, Ellin Louis public relations executive
Glasberg, Paula Drillman advertising executive
Glos, Margaret Beach management company executive, real estate developer
Gold, Jay D. broadcasting company executive
Gold, Mari S. public relations executive
Goldberg, Leslie Daniel advertising executive
Goldin, Alan Gary advertising executive
Goldsmith, Clifford Henry former tobacco company executive
Goldsmith, Gary L. advertising executive
Goldstein, Gary S. executive recruiter
Goldstein, Richard A. consumer products company executive
Goodman, Thomas Andrew public relations executive
Gossett, Oscar Milton advertising executive
Gottlieb, Jerrold Howard advertising executive
Grace, Jason Roy advertising agency executive
Grant, Dale B. consulting company executive
Greenawalt, Peggy Freed Tomarkin advertising executive
Greenberg, Jerome advertising executive
Greene, David Elsworth advertising agency executive, accountant
Greene, Howard Paul communications executive
Greenland, Leo advertising executive
Greenwald, James L. broadcasting and communications executive
Griffin, Judith Ann strategic planning and operating executive
Griffith, Katherine Scott communications executive
Groberg, James Jay information sciences company executive
Grossman, Jack advertising agency executive
Grossman, Ronald financial executive, lawyer
Gugel, Craig Thomas advertising and new media executive
Guimaraes, George Gomes advertising agency executive
Gumbinner, Paul S. advertising and executive recruitment agency executive
†Gunn, John Reginald medical institution executive, consultant
Haddock, Robert Lynn information services entrepreneur, writer
Halper, Harlan Richard executive search consultant
Halpern, Nathan Loren communications company executive
Hamilton, Bill advertising executive
Hammond, Lou Rena Charlotte public relations executive
Harkna, Eric advertising executive
Hatheway, John Harris advertising agency executive
Hawkey, Penelope J. advertising agency executive
†Hayes, John advertising agency executive
Hearle, Douglas Geoffrey public relations consultant
Heekin, James Robson, III advertising executive
Heinzerling, Larry Edward communications executive
Heller, Arthur advertising agency executive
Hennes, Robert Taft former management consultant, investment executive
Henning, Alyson Balfour advertising executive
Hillman, Patrick advertising agency executive
Hilton, Andrew Carson management consultant, former manufacturing company executive
†Hodes, Bernard S. advertising agency executive
Hoffenberg, Harvey advertising executive
Hooper, Ian (John Derek Glass) marketing communications executive
Hope, Michael S. entertainment and communications company executive
Hopple, Richard Van Tromp, Jr. advertising agency executive
Horowitz, David H. communications industry executive, lawyer, consultant
Hosokawa, David advertising executive
Howard, Elizabeth corporate communications and marketing executive
Howes, Alfred S. business and insurance consultant
†Hubbell, Robert C. public relations executive
Hubler, Bruce Albert management executive
Hudson, Dawn Emily advertising executive
Humphreys, Richard advertising executive
Hundt, Paul Robert diversified industry executive, lawyer
Ittleson, H(enry) Anthony bicycle vacation company executive
Jackson, Richard George advertising agency executive
Jacoby, Robert Harold management consulting executive
Jaffe, Caroline Ruth association communications executive
James, Robert Leo advertising agency executive
Johnson, Harold Earl personnel executive
Johnson, John William, Jr. executive recruiter
Jonas, Gilbert public relations and fund raising executive
Jones, Caroline Robinson advertising executive
Jordan, Thomas Richard public relations executive
Josephs, Ray public relations and advertising executive, writer, international relations consultant
Josephson, Marvin talent and literary agency executive
Kalmus, Allan Henry public relations executive
Kanuk, Leslie Lazar management consultant, educator
Kaplan, Larry public relations executive
Kaplan, Lloyd Arthur public relations executive
Karalekas, George Steven advertising agency executive, political consultant
Karp, Martin Everett management consultant
Karp, Richard M. advertising agency executive
Katz, Marcia public relations company executive
Kavner, Robert M. communications company executive
Kay, Allen Steven advertising executive
Keating, Robert Edward public relations executive
Keenan, Michael Edgar advertising executive
Keeshan, Michael advertising agency executive
†Kekst, Gershon public relations consultant
Kelley, Sheila Seymour public relations executive, crisis consultant
Kelmenson, Leo-Arthur advertising executive
Kelne, Nathan editorial and public relations consultant
Kenney, Matthew chef
Kenny, Roger Michael executive search consultant
Kern, Martin H(arold) supermarket chain executive
Kieren, Thomas Henry management consultant
Killeffer, Louis MacMillan advertising executive
Kinser, Richard Edward management consultant
Kinsolving, Charles McIlvaine, Jr. marketing executive
Kirk, Donald James consultant, accounting educator
Kish, Joseph Laurence, Jr. management consultant
Knisley, Patrick Allen advertising company executive
Knox, George L(evi), III consumer products company executive
Kogstad, Rolf Egil sales company executive
Kohlenberg, Stanley marketing executive
Koplovitz, Kay communication network executive
Korman, Jess J. advertising executive
Kornhauser, Henry advertising executive
Kotcher, Raymond Lowell public relations executive
Kovacs, Elizabeth Ann professional society administrator
Kovak, Ellen B. public relations firm executive
Kraus, Norma Jean industrial relations executive
Kraushar, Jonathan Pollack communications and media consultant
Kreisberg, Neil Ivan advertising executive
Kreston, Martin Howard advertising, marketing, public relations, and publishing executive
Krinsky, Robert Daniel consulting firm executive
Krisher, Patterson Howard management consultant
Kroeger, Lin J. management consultant
Kroll, Alexander S. advertising agency executive
Krone, Helmut consultant, former advertising executive
Kubin, Michael Ernest advertising and marketing executive
Kullberg, Gary Walter advertising agency executive
Kummel, Eugene H. advertising agency executive
Kurnit, Paul David advertising executive
Kurnit, Shepard advertising agency executive
†Kuropat, Rosemary Louise marketing executive
Kurz, Mitchell Howard marketing communications executive
Lafferty, Charles Douglas Joseph advertising agency executive
Lambert, Eleanor (Mrs. Seymour Berkson) public relations executive, fashion authority, journalist
Lamont, Lee art management executive
Lang, George restaurateur
Langer, Andrew J. advertising agency executive
Langton, Cleve Swanson advertising executive
Lannamann, Richard Stuart executive recruiting consultant
Lareau, Marybeth Bass marketing professional
Laughren, Terry marketing executive
Lavey, Kenneth Henry advertising agency executive, designer
Lawrence, James Bland advertising executive
Lawrence, Ruddick Carpenter public relations executive
Lazarus, Rochelle Braff advertising executive
Leber, Lester advertising agency executive
LeBow, Bennett S. communications executive
Leeds, Douglas Brecker advertising agency executive, theatre producer
Leet, Mildred Robbins corporate executive, consultant
Le Mener, Georges Philippe hotel executive
†Lerer, Kenneth public relations executive
Leslie, John Webster, Jr. communications company executive
Leslie, Seymour Marvin communications executive
Lesser, Lawrence J. advertising agency executive
Leubert, Alfred Otto Paul international business consultant
Levenstein, Alan Peter advertising executive
†Levesque, Roger Raymond trading company executive
Levine, Carl Morton motion picture exhibition, real estate executive
Levine, Martin Robert executive search and recruiting company executive
†Levins, Ilyssa public relations executive
Levitt, Mitchell Alan management consultant
†Levy, Reynold communication company executive
Levy, Walter Kahn management consultant executive
Lewis, Edwin A. communications company executive
Lewis, George Ralph consumer goods company executive
†Lindheim, James Bruce public relations executive
Lipton, Charles public relations executive
Lipton, Joan Elaine advertising executive
†Livingston, Sharon Hollander advertising executive
Lockwood, Molly Ann communications company executive
Logan, Vicki advertising executive
†Lois, George advertising agency executive
Lotas, Judith Patton advertising executive
Love, Kenneth Del design company director, consultant
Lowe, Frank Budge business executive
Lucht, John Charles management consultant, executive recruiter, writer
Lundy, Daniel Francis communications company executive
Lynch, John T. management consultant
Mack, Joseph P. advertising agency executive
MacKay, Malcolm executive search consultant
Mackerodt, Fred public relations specialist
†Madden, Thomas J., III management consultant
Maggin, Bruce communications executive
Makrianes, James Konstantin, Jr. management consultant
Malgieri, Nick chef, author, educator
Mallozzi, Cos M. public relations executive
Manning, Burt advertising executive
Manoff, Richard Kalman advertising executive, nutrition policy consultant
Mansi, Joseph Anneillo public relations company executive
Marcosson, Thomas I. service company executive
Margaritis, John Paul public relations executive
Margolis, Milton Joseph marketing executive
Margulis, Les advertising executive
Mark, Reuben consumer products company executive
Marshall, Daniel Stuart advertising executive
Marston, Robert Andrew public relations executive
Maxey, Thomas F. advertising agency executive
McBride, David Alan business information services executive
McCabe, Edward Arthur communications company executive
McCall, David Bruce advertising executive
McCandless, Carolyn Keller entertainment, media company executive
McConnell, Charles Warren marketing management executive
McCormick, James Michael management consultant
McCoy, Millington F. management recruitment company executive
McCracken, A. Michael accounting firm executive
McGarry, John Patrick, Jr. advertising agency executive
McGinnis, Arthur Joseph, Jr. public relations executive
McKelvey, Andrew J. advertising executive
McLean, Edward Peter executive search consultant
McNamara, John Jeffrey advertising executive
McNamee, Daniel Vincent, III management consultant
McNamee, Louise advertising agency executive
†McQuade, Charles Brian data processing executive
Meek, Phillip Joseph communications executive
Meigher, S. Christopher, III communications and media investor
Menk, Carl William executive search company executive
Menninger, Edward Joseph public relations executive
Meranus, Arthur Richard advertising agency executive
Messing, Mark P. advertising executive
Messinger, Scott James advertising executive
Messner, Thomas G. advertising executive, copywriter
Meyer, Edward Henry advertising agency executive
Meyer, Fred Josef advertising executive
Meyer, Pearl executive compensation consultant
Meyerson, Morton communications executive
Miano, Louis Stephen advertising executive
Michenfelder, Joseph Francis public relations executive
Miles, Michael Arnold consumer products executive
Miller, Ernest Charles management consultant
Miller, Robert advertising executive
Minicucci, Robert A. management consultant
Minor, Raleigh Colston management consultant
Mitchell, Richard Boyle advertising executive
Mittelstadt, Charles Anthony advertising executive
†Molino, Patricia Mary communications executive
Montgomery, Walter George communications executive, consultant
†Moore, Mary advertising agency executive
Moran, Juliette M. management consultant
Moreira, Marcio Martins advertising executive
Morgen, Lynn public relations executive
†Morin, William J. management consultant
†Morley, Michael public relations executive
Morley, Michael B. public relations executive
Morris, Mark Ronald advertising agency executive
Morris, Michael Howard public relations executive
Morris, Stephen Burritt marketing information executive
Mosbacher, Martin Bruce public relations executive
Moss, Charles advertising agency executive
Muller, Frank B. advertising executive
Muro, Roy Alfred independent media service corporation executive
Murphy, James E. public relations and marketing executive
Murphy, Jill public relations executive
Nash, Edward L. advertising agency executive
Neff, Thomas Joseph executive search firm executive
Neft, David Samuel marketing professional
Nelson, Bruce Sherman advertising agency executive
Nesbit, Robert Grover management consultant
Neuhaus, Sydney Ann public relations executive
Newman, Geraldine Anne advertising executive
Newman, Jane advertising agency executive
Nicholson, William Thomas advertising executive
Nieman, John Francis advertising executive
Noonan, Susan Abert public relations counselor
Norcia, Stephen William advertising executive
Nord, Peter Robert advertising executive
Novak, Eugene Francis advertising executive
O'Brien, Richard Francis advertising agency executive
O'Connell, Carmela Digristina appraisal executive, consultant
†Okada, Takuya food service and retail executive
Oliver, Alexander R. management consultant
Olshan, Kenneth S. advertising agency executive

Olsinski, Peter Kevin *international outplacement executive*
Olson, Thomas Francis, II *communications company executive*
O'Neill, Francis Xavier, III *marketing executive*
O'Neill, Harry William *survey research company executive*
Osnos, Gilbert Charles *management consultant*
Ostrow, Joseph W. *advertising executive*
Ostrow, Samuel David *public relations executive*
O'Sullivan, Eugene Henry *retired advertising executive*
O'Toole, John E. *advertising executive*
Owett, Adam Thomas *advertising creative director, writer*
Paddock, Anthony Conaway *financial consultant*
Palmer, Robert J(oseph) *advertising executive, winery owner*
Paluszek, John L. *public relations firm executive*
Pappas, Alceste Thetis *consulting company executive, educator*
Parfit, Gavin J. *international management executive*
†Parker, Joan *public relations executive*
Parrish, Thomas Kirkpatrick, III *marketing consultant*
Parsons, Andrew John *management consultant*
†Paster, Howard G. *public relations/public affairs company executive*
Patterson, James Brendan, Jr. *advertising agency executive*
Patton, Joanna *advertising executive*
Paul, Robert David *management consultant*
Payson, Martin David *entertainment company executive, lawyer*
Pearson, Clarence Edward *management consultant*
Peasback, David R. *recruiting company executive*
Peebler, Charles David, Jr. *advertising executive*
Perelman, Ronald Owen *diversified holding company executive*
Perless, Ellen *advertising executive*
Perlmutter, Diane F. *communications executive*
Peterson, Nadeen *advertising agency executive*
†Petrocelli, Anthony Joseph *management executive, consultant*
†Phelan, Kathleen McGrath *public relations executive*
Phillips, Elizabeth Joan *marketing executive*
Phillips, Graham Holmes *advertising executive*
Phillips, John David *management consultant*
Phillips, Joyce Martha *human resources executive*
Pickholz, Jerome Walter *advertising agency executive*
Piliguian, Tro *advertising executive*
Plavoukos, Spencer *advertising executive*
Pluzynski, Edward Dale *advertising executive*
Pollak, Tim *advertising agency executive*
Pollock-O'Brien, Louise Mary *public relations executive*
Pompadur, I. Martin *communications executive*
Poppe, Fred Christoph *advertising agency executive*
Pounder, Richard A. *advertising executive*
Puris, Martin Ford *advertising agency executive*
Quintero, Ronald Gary *management consultant*
Rauch, Arthur Irving *management consultant*
Ravitz, Robert Allan *advertising agency executive*
Raynolds, John F., III *executive search consultant*
Reges, Marianna Alice *marketing executive*
Reichel, Walter Emil *advertising executive*
†Reilly, Edward J. *public relations executive*
Reinhard, Keith Leon *advertising executive*
Resnik, Frank Edward *tobacco company executive*
Reuben, Alvin Bernard *entertainment executive*
†Reynolds, James *management consultant*
Rhodes, Dennis Earl *public relations executive*
Rhodes, John Bower *management consultant*
Rich, Kenneth Malcolm *executive search and management consultant*
Rindlaub, John Wade *advertising agency executive*
Rinehart, Jonathan *public relations executive*
Riordan, James Quentin *retired company executive*
Robbins, John Clapp *management consultant*
Robbins, Kenneth L. *advertising agency executive*
Roberts, Francis Stone *advertising executive*
Robertson, Michael Brian *advertising executive*
Robinson, L. Donald *advertising executive*
Rogers, Kenneth R. *advertising executive*
Roman, Kenneth, Jr. *corporate communications executive*
Rooney, Terence *public relations executive*
Rose, Zeldon E. *public relations consultant*
Rosen, Marcella *advertising executive*
Rosenbaum, Steven Ira *public relations and publishing executive, photographer*
Rosenfeld, Ronald Marvin *advertising executive*
Rosenshine, Allen Gilbert *advertising agency executive*
Rosenthal, Peter *public relations executive*
Rossi, Dominick F., Jr. *advertising agency executive*
Rothenberg, Robert Philip *public relations counselor*
Rothholz, Peter Lutz *public relations executive*
Rothschild, Diane *advertising agency executive*
Rothstein, Richard *public relations executive*
Rotter, Steve *advertising executive*
Roughsedge, Carolyn Dunn *advertising agency executive*
Rowland, Herbert Leslie *public relations executive*
Ruben, William Samuel *marketing consultant*
Rubenstein, Howard Joseph *public relations executive*
Rubenstein, Stanley Ellis *public relations consultant*
Rubin, Edwin Manning *advertising executive*
Rubin, Mel *advertising executive*
Rudd, Nicholas *marketing communications company executive*
Ruder, William *public relations executive*
Ruello, Samuel Angus *management consultant*
Russo, Anthony Joseph *public relations professional*
Ruth, Carol A. *public relations executive*
Rutman, Mark Charles *public relations executive*
Ryle, Joseph Donald *public relations executive*
Sacks, Temi J. *public relations executive*
†Sadove, Stephen Irving *consumer products company executive*
Sard, George *public relations company executive*
Sarnoff, Albert *communications executive*
Sauerhaft, Stan *public relations executive, consultant*
Savas, Emanuel S. *public management educator*
Scardino, Michael Christopher *advertising executive*
†Schaffer, Kenneth B. *communications executive, satellite engineer, inventor, consultant*
Schaub, Sherwood Anhder, Jr. *management consultant*
†Schiffman, Stephan *management consultant, writer*
Schlaifer, Charles *advertising executive*
Schmertz, Herbert *public relations and advertising executive*
Schmetterer, Robert Allen *advertising executive*
Schoonover, Jean Way *public relations consultant*
Schriever, Fred Martin *energy, environmental and information technology executive*
†Schulman, Mark Allen *market research company executive*
Schulman, Paul Martin *advertising executive*
Schupak, Leslie Allen *public relations company executive*
Schur, Jeffrey *advertising executive*
Schwab, Frank, Jr. *management consultant*
†Schwartz, Alan Victor *advertising executive*
Schwartz, R. Malcolm *management consultant*
Scott, William Clement, III *entertainment industry executive*
Seadler, Stephen Edward *business and computer consultant, social scientist*
Seaman, Alfred Jarvis *retired advertising agency executive*
Secunda, Eugene *marketing communications executive, educator*
Segal, Joel Michael *advertising executive*
Segal, Stephen Martin *advertising executive*
Seiden, Henry (Hank Seiden) *advertising executive*
Seidman, Herta Lande *international trade and information company executive*
Selkowitz, Arthur *advertising agency executive*
†Senter, Alan Zachary *communications company executive*
Shaffer, Russell K. *advertising agency executive*
Shaine, Theodore Harris *advertising agency executive*
Shair, David Ira *human resources executive*
Shapiro, Marvin Lincoln *communications company executive*
Sheets, Michael Jay *consumer products company executive*
Sherman, Eugene Jay *marketing executive, economist*
Sherman, Norman Mark *advertising agency executive*
Shevack, Brett David *advertising agency executive*
Shpilberg, David *management consultant, artificial intelligence researcher*
Silberman, H. Lee *public relations executive*
Silverman, Marylin A. *advertising agency executive*
Simmons, J. Gerald *management consultant*
Simmons, Samuel Lee *corporate executive*
Sinclair, Daisy *advertising executive, casting director*
Sirowitz, Leonard *advertising agency executive*
Smith, George S., Jr. *communications financial executive*
Smith, Guy Lincoln, IV *strategic communications company executive*
Smith, Jim *advertising executive*
Smith, Murray Livingstone *advertising executive*
Softness, John *public relations executive*
Soika, Helmut Emil *retirement plan administrator*
Soter, George Nicholas *advertising executive*
Souham, Gérard *communications executive*
Spiegel, Arthur Henry, III *managing director, president*
Spielvogel, Carl *international marketing executive*
†Spivak, Joan Carol *medical public relations specialist*
Springer, John Shipman *public relations executive*
Stack, Edward William *business management and foundation executive*
Stanton, Alexander *public relations executive*
Stanton, Edward M. *public relations company executive*
Stanton, Frank *communications executive*
Stauffer, Michael Kirk *communications executive, consultant*
Stawasz, Cherie *public relations executive*
Steedman, Doria Lynne Silberberg *advertising agency executive*
Steinberg, Stephen Arthur *information systems executive*
Stern, Leslie Warren *management consultant*
Sternglass, Lila M. *advertising agency executive*
Stevens, Art *public relations executive*
Stewart, Jeff *advertising agency executive*
Stewart, Kirk T. *public relations executive*
Stoddard, Laurence Ralph, Jr. *advertising executive*
Strand, Curt Robert *hotel executive*
Straus, Irving Lehman *public relations executive*
Strear, Joseph D. *public relations executive*
Stroock, Mark Edwin, II *public relations company executive*
Stuart, John McHugh, Jr. *public relations consultant, retired foreign service officer*
Sturges, John Siebrand *management consultant*
Sulcer, Frederick Durham *advertising executive*
Swanzey, Robert Joseph *data processing executive*
Swid, Stephen Claar *business executive*
Swift, John Francis *health care advertising company executive*
Tagliarino, Scott Alan *public relations executive*
Taney, J. Charles *advertising agency executive*
Tarter, Fred Barry *advertising executive*
Taschetti, Vincent S. *advertising executive*
Tavon, Mary E. *public relations, marketing and communications executive*
Tellefsen, Gerald *management consultant*
Telles, Martin Jack *marketing executive*
Teran, Timothy Eric Alba *marketing professional*
Thompson, William Cannon, Jr. *advertising agency executive*
Thorne, John Watson, III *advertising and marketing executive*
Tilson, Dorothy Ruth *word processing executive*
†Tisch, James S. *diversified holding company executive*
†Tisch, Jonathan Mark *hotel company executive*
Torrenzano, Richard *public affairs executive*
Tortorella, Albert James *public relations executive, consultant*
Tripodi, Louis Anthony *advertising agency executive*
Troeger, Curtis Ralph *advertising executive*
Trueman, Walter *retired advertising agency executive*
Truesdell, Wesley Edwin *public relations and investor relations consultant*
Truitt, Richard Hunt *public relations agency executive*
Trygg, Steve Lennart *advertising executive*
Tucker, Paul Thomas *information systems executive*
Turkel, Stanley *hotel consultant, management executive*
Turner, Hester Hill *management consultant*
Ullmark, Hans *advertising agency executive*
Ulrich, Max Marsh *executive search consultant*
Upson, Stuart Barnard *advertising agency executive*
Vale, Norman *advertising executive*
Van Brunt, Albert Daniel *advertising agency executive*
Van Campen, Stephen Bernard *executive recruiter, consultant*
Vargas, Eduardo *advertising executive*
Vermeer, Maureen Dorothy *sales executive*
†Veru, Theodore *advertising agency executive*
Vignone, Ronald John *advertising agency executive*
Volpe, Thomas J. *advertising executive*
Wachsman, Phyllis Geri *advertising executive*
Wadsworth, Robert David *advertising agency executive*
Wagner, Christina Breuer *media company executive*
Walke, David Michael *public relations executive*
Walker, Joan H. *public relations executive*
Walkley, Barbara Ann *public relations executive*
Wallace, Thomas Robert *public relations executive*
Wang, Julie Caroline *public relations executive*
Warner, John Edward *advertising executive*
Warwick, John Petersen *advertising executive*
Wasserman, Bert W. *communications and publishing company executive*
†Wathne, Stefan, Jr. *consulting company executive*
Wax, Edward L. *advertising executive*
Waylett, Thomas Robert *management consultant executive*
Wechsler, Raymond Henry *management company executive*
Weida, Lewis Dixon *marketing analyst, consultant*
Weiner, Richard *public relations executive*
Weisberg, Jonathan Mark *public relations executive*
Weiss, Mark *public relations executive*
†Weissman, Morris *printing compnany company executive*
Weissman, Norman *public relations executive*
Weithas, William Vincent *advertising agency executive*
Wells, Victor Hugh, Jr. *advertising agency executive*
Wessinger, W. David *management consultant*
Whisnand, Roy Van Arsdel *investment management executive*
White, Richard David *managing director*
Wilhite, Clayton Edward *advertising executive*
Williams, David Benton *advertising agency executive*
Winkel, Fred Michael *marketing professional*
Woit, Erik Peter *corporate executive, lawyer*
Wooden, Ruth A. *public service advertising executive*
Woodrum, Robert Lee *executive search consultant*
Woodside, William Stewart *service company executive, museum official*
Wright, Jeanne Elizabeth Jason *advertising executive*
Wunderman, Lester *advertising agency executive*
Wyatt, Mary Jean (M.J. Wyatt) *public relations executive*
Wyse, Lois *advertising executive, author*
Yunich, David Lawrence *consumer goods consultant*
Zehring, Karen *information executive*
Zelnick, Strauss *entertainment company executive*

Newburgh
Cloudman, Francis Harold, III *computer company executive*

Newtonville
Weber, Barbara M. *sales executive, consultant*

Nyack
Karp, Peter Simon *marketing executive*
Keil, John Mullan *advertising agency executive*

Orchard Park
Morgan, James Durward *computer company executive*
Noll, John F. *sales and marketing executive, investment banker*

Ossining
Reynolds, Calvin *management consultant, business educator*

Palmyra
Blazey, Mark Lee *management consultant*

Pelham
Moore, Ellis Oglesby *retired public affairs consultant*

Plainview
Austin, Larry *travel company executive*

Pleasantville
Willis, William Henry *marketing executive*

Port Chester
Ailloni-Charas, Dan *marketing executive*
Blumenfeld, Seth David *communications company executive*

Port Washington
Hackett, John Byron *advertising agency executive, lawyer*
Johnson, Tod Stuart *market research company executive*

Poughkeepsie
Ashford, Rosalind Mary *advertising and marketing executive*

Pound Ridge
Cooper, Daniel *management consultant*
Throckmorton, Joan Helen *advertising agency executive*

Purchase
Akers, John Fellows *information processing company executive*
Lautenbach, Terry Robert *information systems and communications executive*
Oskin, David William *human resources specialist*
Sonnenberg, Hardy *data processing company research and development executive, engineer*

Rhinebeck
Smith, Lewis Motter, Jr. *advertising and direct marketing executive*

Rochester
†Axelrod, Joel Nathan *marketing executive*
Chin-Kee-Fatt, Hollis Romauld *marketing professional*
DeToro, Irving John *management consultant*
Fisher, Robert Joseph *marketing and corporate executive*
Gartner, Joseph Charles *business systems administrator*
Hoot, William John *retired brewery executive*
Hutchins, Frank McAllister *advertising executive*
Klinsky, Arnold *communications executive*
Mc Kelvey, Jean Trepp *industrial relations educator*
McKie, W. Gilmore *human resources executive*
Morey, James Newman *advertising executive*
Sapos, Mary Ann *advertising agency executive*
Wegman, Robert B. *food service executive*

Rockville Centre
Mc Grath, John Joseph *retired management consultant*

Roosevelt
Wisner, Roscoe William, Jr. *human resources executive*

Roslyn
Vizza, Robert Francis *hospital executive, former university administrator, marketing educator*

Rye
Metzger, Frank *management consultant*

Rye Brook
Dangoor, David Ezra Ramsi *consumer goods company executive*

Saint Bonaventure
Khairullah, Zahid Yahya *management sciences and marketing educator, consultant*

Scarsdale
Blinder, Abe Lionel *management consultant*
Clark, Merrell Mays *management consultant*
Kaufman, Robert Jules *communications consultant, lawyer*
Oswald, George Charles *advertising executive, management and marketing consultant*
Rubin, A. Louis *advertising executive*

Schenectady
Golub, Lewis *supermarket company executive*
Golub, Neil *supermarket chain executive*

Seneca Falls
Lambertsen, Mary Ann *human resources executive*

Shrub Oak
Roston, Arnold *information specialist, educator, advertising executive, artist, editor*

Somers
Paxton, Dan Richards *human resources executive*
Thoman, G. Richard *computer company executive*

Southampton
Lieberman, Carol Cooper *healthcare marketing communications consultant, city planning administrator*

Staatsburg
Gury, Jeremy *writer, advertising executive, artist*

Stanfordville
Owens, Mary Jo *electronic guidance services company executive*

Staten Island
Fafian, Joseph, Jr. *management consultant*
Mencher, Stuart Alan *sales and marketing executive*

Syracuse
Goetzmann, Harry Edward, Jr. *leasing company executive*
Mower, Eric Andrew *communications and marketing executive*
Suhowatsky, Stephen Joseph *distribution company executive*

Tappan
Fox, Muriel *public relations executive*

Tarrytown
Gsand, William L. *computer company executive*
Hurley, William Joseph *information systems executive*
Hyman, Leonard Stephen *finanical consultant, economist, author*
Schmidt, Klaus Franz *advertising executive*

Thornwood
Bassett, Lawrence C *management consultant*

Troy
Bonney, William Lawless *data processing and telecommunications educator*
Schwartz, Robert William *management consultant*

Trumansburg
Mc Connell, John Wilkinson *labor relations educator, labor arbitrator, former socio-economics educator*

Unadilla
Compton, John Robinson *printing company executive*

Uniondale
Fortunoff, Alan Meyer *retail company executive*

Valhalla
Emerson, Rose *career consultant*

West Islip
Softness, Donald Gabriel *marketing and manufacturing executive*

Westbury
Olsten, Stuart *personnel services company executive*

Westhampton Beach
Maas, Jane Brown *advertising executive*

White Plains
Colwell, Howard Otis *advertising executive*
Dowd, Peter Jerome *public relations executive*
Fudge, Ann Marie *marketing executive*
Lorelli, Michael Kevin *personal care products executive*
Machover, Carl *computer graphics consultant*
Roll, Irwin Clifford (Win Roll) *advertising, marketing and publishing executive*

Welsh, Dennie M. *business machines company executive*

Woodbury
†Wertheim, Harvey J. *human resource specialist*

Yaphank
Ahern, John James *software company executive*

Yorktown Heights
Green, Paul Eliot, Jr. *communications scientist*
Rosenblatt, Stephen Paul *marketing and sales promotion company executive*

NORTH CAROLINA

Asheville
Etter, Robert Miller *retired consumer products executive, chemist*

Burlington
Eddins, James William, Jr. *marketing executive*
Weavil, David Carlton *clinical laboratory services executive*

Carthage
Thomas, Carol Taylor *general services coordinator*

Cary
Sussenguth, Edward Henry *computer company executive, computer network designer*

Chapel Hill
Jerdee, Thomas Harlan *business administration educator, organization psychology researcher and consultant*
Lauterborn, Robert F. *advertising educator*
Pavão, Leonel Maia (Lee Pavão) *advertising executive*

Charlotte
Abernathy, Joseph Duncan *data processing executive*
Box, Alan *communications executive*
Bradshaw, Howard Holt *management consulting company executive*
†Glosson, Buster C. *consulting and business development company executive, retired military officer*
Harris, Ernest Clay, Sr. *marketing consultant, engineer*
Hudgins, Catherine Harding *business executive*
Mazze, Edward Mark *marketing consultant, business educator*
Neal, William Weaver, III *systems integration and software executive*
O'Connor, R. Dennis *consumer products company executive*
†Peterson, Jim Lee *food service executive*
Sanford, James Kenneth *public relations executive*
Thomas, Joe Carroll *human resources director*

Durham
Otterbourg, Robert Kenneth *public relations consultant, writer*
Ryan, Gerard Spencer *inn executive*
Squire, Alexander *management consultant*

Fremont
Ackerman, Lennis Campbell *management consultant retired*

Greensboro
Allen, Jesse Owen, III *management development and organizational behavior*
Sanders, William Eugene *marketing executive*
Spears, Alexander White, III *tobacco company executive*

Greenville
†Behr, Lawrence Van Der Poel *telecommunications executive*

Hickory
George, Boyd Lee *consumer products company executive*

Lake Lure
Newbrough, Edgar Truett *retired management consultant*

Lincolnton
Gaither, Ann Heafner *sales executive*

Matthews
Rivenbark, Jan Meredith *food service products corporate executive*

New Bern
Mack, Clifford Glenn *investment banker, management consultant*

North Wilkesboro
Herring, Leonard Gray *marketing company executive*

Pine Knoll Shores
Griffin, Thomas Lee, Jr. *industrial and federal government specialist*

Pinehurst
Gilmore, Voit *travel executive*
Nuzzo, Salvatore Joseph *defense, electronics company executive*
Owings, Malcolm William *retired management consultant*
Stingel, Donald Eugene *management consultant*

Pinetops
†Robertson, Richard Blake *management consultant*

Raleigh
Breytspraak, John, Jr. *management consultant*
Doherty, Robert Cunningham *advertising executive*
Eberly, Harry Landis *retired communications company executive*
Grubb, Donald Hartman *paper industry company executive*
Leak, Robert E. *management consultant*
Lewis, Richard Jay *marketing educator, university dean*
Ofner, J(ames) Alan *management consultant*
Shaw, Robert Gilbert *restaurant executive, senator*
Tompkins, James Arthur *consulting firm executive, industrial engineer*

Research Triangle Park
Bursiek, Ralph David *information systems company executive*
Tracy, Philip R. *computer company executive*

Rocky Mount
Autry, Robert F. *restaurant chain executive*
Harrington, Jesse Moye, III *restaurant chain executive*
Laughery, Jack Arnold *restaurant chain executive*

Sanford
†Ward, Robert Allen *textile company executive*

Shelby
†Carver, Earl (Randy Carver) *marketing and sales consultant, video director and producer*

Southern Pines
Mataxis, Theodore Christopher *consultant, lecturer, writer, retired army officer, educator*
Vanderwoude, J. Stephen *communications company executive*

Vass
Glassman, Edward *management creativity consultant, columnist*

Weaverville
Parsons, Vinson Adair *retired computer software company executive*

Wilson
†Peters, A. Winniett *leaf tobacco merchant, exporter*

Winston Salem
Atkinson, G. Douglas, Sr. *marketing executive, consultant*
Ehmann, Carl William *consumer products executive, researcher*
Griswold, George *marketing, advertising and public relations executive*
Gunzenhauser, Gerard Ralph, Jr. *management consultant, investor*
Johnston, James Wesley *tobacco company executive*
MacKinnon, Sally Anne *retired fast food company executive*

NORTH DAKOTA

Fargo
Wallwork, William Wilson, III *leasing company executive*

Turtle Lake
Grosz, Albert Mick *sales executive*

OHIO

Akron
Aggarwal, Sundar Lal *technology management consultant*
Crawford, Robert John *credit company executive*
Kelley, John Paul *communications consultant*
McCormick, William Edward *environmental consultant*
Sonnecken, Edwin Herbert *management consultant*
†Taylor, Gary Lee *marketing executive*

Alliance
Rockhill, Jack Kerrigan *collections company executive*

Beachwood
Seelbach, William Robert *management consultant*
Zelikow, Howard Monroe *management and financial consultant*

Berea
Irwin, Richard Loren *systems management association executive*

Bowling Green
Lunde, Harold Irving *management educator*

Canfield
Bachmeyer, Robert Wesley *retired hospital administration consultant*

Centerville
Perrich, Jerry Robert *environmental consulting company executive*

Chagrin Falls
Church, Irene Zaboly *personnel services company executive*
Eastburn, Richard A. *retired consulting firm executive*
Fisher, Will Stratton *illumination consultant*
Gelb, Victor *management consultant*

Cincinnati
Artzt, Edwin Lewis *consumer products company executive*
Bogart, Judith Saunders *public relations executive*
Brown, Dale Patrick *advertising executive*
Brunner, Gordon F(rancis) *household products company executive*
Dubuc, Kenneth E *management consultant*
Eager, William Earl *information systems corporation executive*
†Eaton, Edwin Harvey, Jr. *household cleaning products company executive, comptroller*
Ferriss, David Platt *advertising consultant*
Flanagan, Martha Lang *corporate secretary*
Fokker, J. P. *waste management executive*
Freshwater, Paul Ross *consumer goods company executive*
Harville, Thomas T. *consumer goods company executive*
Henry, J(ohn) Porter, Jr. *sales consultant*
Hicks, Irle Raymond *retail food chain executive*
Hutton, Edward Luke *diversified public corporation executive*
Johnson, C. Scott *management consultant*
Levy, Sam Malcolm *advertising executive*
Lockhart, John Mallery *management consultant*
Maier, Craig Frisch *restaurant executive*
McNulty, John William *retired public relations executive, automobile company executive*
Milligan, Lawrence Drake, Jr. *consumer products executive*
†Moler, James Clark *marketing research executive*
Moore, Thomas A. *consumer products company executive*
Pepper, John Ennis, Jr. *consumer products company executive*
†Ryan, J. Patrick *fund raising consulting company executive*
†Shipley, Tony L(ee) *software company executive*
Snead, Richard Thomas *retail company executive*
†Sperzel, George E., Jr. *personal care industry executive*
Stolley, Alexander *advertising executive*
Sullivan, Dennis James, Jr. *public relations executive*
Terhar, Louis F. *waste management administrator*
†Thomas, Jeffrey Noel *aviation consulting company executive, management consultant*
Wehling, Robert Louis *household products company executive*
Westheimer, Ruth Welling *retired management consultant*

Cleveland
Alspaugh, Robert Odo *industrial management consultant*
Bailey, John Turner *public relations executive*
Bogomolny, Richard Joseph *retail food chain executive*
Cardwell, James William *business strategy consultant*
†Chaikin, A. Scott *public relations executive*
Clutter, Bertley Allen, III *management company executive*
Danco, Léon Antoine *management consultant, educator*
Drotning, John Evan *industrial relations specialist*
Dupuy, William L. *public relations executive*
Eaton, Henry Felix *public relations executive*
Foltz, Clinton Henry *advertising executive*
Fruchtenbaum, Edward *greeting card company executive*
Henry, Edward Frank *computer accounting service executive*
Johnson, John Frank *professional recruitment executive*
Klipfell, John Martin, III *greeting card company executive*
Kuendig, William Norman, II *management consultant, actuarial consultant*
Lang, H. Jack *advertising executive, author*
Lowenthal, Henry *greeting card company executive*
Marcus, Donald Howard *advertising agency executive*
Mason, Robert McSpadden *technology management educator, consultant*
McGinty, Thomas Edward *management consultant*
Mecredy, James R. *management consultant*
Miller, John Robert *environmental recycling company executive*
Morin, Patrick Joyce *advertising executive*
Newman, Joseph Herzl *advertising executive*
Perkovic, Robert Branko *international management consultant*
Perry, Chris Nicholas *advertising executive*
†Pollack, Florence Zaks *management consultant*
Pucko, Diane Bowles *public relations executive*
Remington, Charles Bradford *professional services firm executive*
Roop, James John *public relations executive*
†Schonberg, Alan Robert *management recruiting executive*
Semelsberger, Kenneth J. *household products company executive*
Skinner, Charles Scofield *technology management service executive, consultant, mechanical engineer*
†Smith, James C. *telecommunications industry executive*
Stevens, Edward *public relations executive*
Stone, Irving I. *greeting card company executive*
Taw, Dudley Joseph *sales executive*
Ulchaker, Stanley Louis *public relations consultant*
Watt, Ronald William *public relations executive*
Young, Davis *public relations executive*
†Zimmerman, Michael Glenn *marketing/communications executive*

Columbus
Ackerman, Kenneth Benjamin *management consultant, writer*
Becher, Paul Ronald *health benefits executive*
Brown, Rowland Chauncey Widrig *information systems, strategic planning and ethics consultant*
Burke, Kenneth Andrew *advertising executive*
LaLonde, Bernard Joseph *educator*
McClain, Thomas E. *communications executive*
McMorrow, Richard Mark *research company executive*
Muller, Mervin Edgar *information systems educator, consultant*
Ryan, Robert Seibert *consulting company executive*
Taylor, Celianna I. *information systems specialist*
Tipton, Clyde Raymond, Jr. *communications and resources development consultant*
Wedge, Thomas Willim *occult consultant, criminologist*
Williams, David Fulton *industrial distribution company executive*

Dayton
Boren, Arthur Rodney *sales management executive*
†Breitenbach, Thomas George *health systems executive*
Darragh, John K. *printing company executive*
Deardorff, Darryl K. *business consultant, accountant*
Kegerreis, Robert James *management consultant, marketing educator*
Nevin, Robert Charles *information systems executive*
Office, Gerald Simms, Jr. *restaurant chain executive*

Dublin
Brownley, John Forrest *fast food company executive*
Casey, John K. *restaurant chain executive*
Freytag, Donald Ashe *management consultant*
Near, James W. *restaurant and franchise executive*
Ourant, Edwin L. *fast food restaurant chain executive*
Rome, John L. *restaurant chain executive*
Schauf, Lawrence E. *restaurant corporation executive*
Schinagl, Erich Friedrich *health care company executive, physician*
Smith, K(ermit) Wayne *computer company executive*
Teter, Gordon F. *fast food chain company executive*
Thomas, R. David *food services company executive*
Welter, William Michael *marketing and advertising executive*

Gahanna
Myers, Phillip Fenton *financial services company executive*

Hilliard
†Van Fossen, Larry Jack *service company executive*

Lancaster
Katlic, John Edward *management consultant*
Phillips, Edward John *consulting firm executive*

Lima
Borra, P. C. *health care company executive*

Mansfield
Ellison, Lorin Bruce *management consultant*

Maple Heights
Sargent, Liz Elaine (Elizabeth Sargent) *safety consulting executive*

Marysville
Rogula, James Leroy *consumer products company executive*

Miamisburg
Burshtan, Alvin *wholesale company executive*
Simpson, Jack Ward *computer company executive*

Milford
Fischer, Robert Andrew *computer executive*

Niles
Travaglini, Raymond Dominic *corporate executive*

Oberlin
Gladieux, Bernard Louis *management consultant*

Peninsula
Ludwig, Richard Joseph *ski resort executive*

Port Clinton
Subler, Edward Pierre *advertising executive*

Saint Clairsville
Dankworth, Margaret Anne *management consultant*

Salem
Fehr, Kenneth Manbeck *computer systems company executive*

Solon
Stauffer, Thomas George *hotel executive*

Streetsboro
Weiss, Joseph Joel *consulting company executive*

Strongsville
†Koppenhafer, Merle Edward *marketing company executive*

Tipp City
Taylor, Robert Homer *quality assurance professional, pilot*

Toledo
Bick, David Greer *health care marketing executive*
Block, Allan James *communications executive*
Christiansen, Eric George *marketing specialist*
†Lipner, William E. *information systems executive*
Northup, John David *management consultant, inventor*
Paquette, Jack Kenneth *management consultant, antiques and toy soldier*

Vandalia
Subotnick, Stuart *food service executive*

Warren
Florence, Jerry DeWayne *sales and marketing executive*

West Chester
Ofte, Donald *environmental executive, former management consultant*

Westerville
Kollat, David Truman *management consultant*
Paulson, Kenneth Michael *quality control executive*

Wooster
Schmitt, Wolfgang Rudolph *consumer products executive*

Xenia
Nutter, Zoe Dell Lantis *public relations executive, retired*

Zanesville
Truby, John Louis *corporate executive*

OKLAHOMA

Broken Arrow
Striegel, Peggy Simsarian *advertising executive*

Norman
Carver, Charles Ray *retired information systems company executive*

Oklahoma City
Ackerman, Raymond Basil *advertising agency executive*
Blackwell, John Adrian, Jr. *computer company executive*
†Funk, Robert Allen *personnel executive*

Hail, John Wesley *marketing professional*
Lynn, C(harles) Stephen *franchising company executive*
Raydon, Max E. *consumer products company executive*
Ruhrup, Clifton Brown *sales executive*
†Stauth, Robert E. *food service executive*

Oktaha
Taylor, Clayton Charles *management and political legislative consultant*

Stillwater
Matoy, Elizabeth Anne *personnel executive*

Tulsa
Gentry, Bern Leon, Sr. *minority consulting company executive*
Herbster, James Richard *information services executive, oil company executive*
King, Roy Lee *computer company executive*
Morrow, Laura Annette *marketing professional*
Mourton, J. Gary *communications executive*
Rubottom, Donald Julian *management consultant*

OREGON

Albany
Norman, E. Gladys *business computer educator, consultant*

Baker City
Graham, Beardsley *management consultant*

Beaverton
Chang, David Ping-Chung *business consultant, architect*
Jones, Tom D. *software company executive*
Masi, Edward A. *computer company executive*

Eugene
Bennett, Robert Royce *engineering and management consultant*
Chackel, Charles Victor *communications executive*
Piele, Philip Kern *education infosystems educator*
Torrey, James D. *communications executive, consultant*
Tull, Donald Stanley *marketing educator*

Grants Pass
Naylor, John Thomas *telephone company executive*

Lake Oswego
Piccard-Krone, Karen Aliotte *public relations executive, political consultant*

Medford
Hennion, Reeve Lawrence *communications executive*
Keener, John Wesley *management consultant*

Milwaukie
White, John *food marketing executive*

Portland
†Anderegg, Karen Klok *consumer products executive*
Boyman, John Edward George *individual/ organizational transition consultant*
†Burns, Bruce *food service executive*
Butler, Leslie Ann *advertising executive, portrait artist*
†Cartwright, Philip Crawford *marketing executive*
Congdon, Marsha B. *telecommunications executive*
Conkling, Roger Linton *consultant, business administration educator, retired utility executive*
Findlay, Susan Halton *company executive*
Kupel, Frederick John *counselor*
Maclean, Charles (Bernard) *transition, performance recognition and workplace violence prevention consultant*
Martin, Lucy Z. *public relations executive*
Morton, Clifford A. *holding company executive*
Smith, Milton Ray *computer company executive, lawyer*
Stott, Peter Walter *forest products company executive*
Sugg, John Logan (Jack Sugg) *advertising executive*
†Wieden, Dan G. *advertising executive*

Salem
Johnson, Robert Raymond *management consultant, educator*

Wilsonville
†Rhines, Walden C. *information system specialist*
†Richards, Waldo J. *computer software and systems company executive*

PENNSYLVANIA

Alexandria
Horn, John Chisolm *management consultant*

Allentown
Armstrong, W(illiam) Warren *advertising agency executive*
Jackson, William MacLeod *management consultant*
Musselman, Jamie P. *advertising executive*

Altoona
†Duncan, David James *health services adminstrator, educator*

Ardmore
Scott, Bill *advertising agency executive*

Aston
Barnett, Samuel Treutlen *international company executive*

Bala Cynwyd
Elkman, Stanley *advertising executive*
McAdams, Brian *advertising executive*

Bensalem
Bishop, Howard Stuart *management consultant*

Berwyn
Brundage, Russell Archibald *retired data processing executive*
†Westphal, Rainer John *software company executive*

Bethlehem
Fairbairn, Ursula Farrell *human resources executive*
Penny, Roger Pratt *management executive*
von Bernuth, Carl W. *diversified corporation executive, lawyer*

Blue Bell
Blechschmidt, Edward Allan *information services and systems executive*
Braun, Reto *computer systems company executive*
Nardello, Robert A. *medical software company executive*

Buckingham
Altier, William John *management consultant*

Butler
Thomas, Russell Alvin *hardware company executive*
Zehfuss, Lawrence Thomas *hardware supply company executive*

Chambersburg
Furr, Quint Eugene *marketing executive*

Collegeville
†De Rosen, Michel *business executive*

Dallas
Sutton, Royal Keith *marketing professional*

Drexel Hill
Perkins, Ralph Linwood *business executive, public health administration specialist*

Erwinna
Geldmacher, Robert Carl *software corporation executive*

Evans City
Salisbury, Judith Muriel *marketing consultant*

Exton
†Patterson, Kent E. *environmental services consultant, hydrogeologist*
Sanford, Richard D. *computer company executive*

Ferndale
Folk, James *sales executive*

Fleetwood
Lewis, Dana Kenneth *marketing company executive, consultant*

Fort Washington
Blumberg, Donald Freed *management consultant*
Deric, Arthur Joseph *management consultant, lawyer*

Gettysburg
Hallberg, Budd Jaye *management consulting firm executive*

Gladwyne
Stick, Alyce Cushing *information systems consultant*

Greensburg
Boyd, Robert Wright, III *lamp company executive*

Harrisburg
Kimmel, Robert Irving *corporate communication design consultant, former state government official*
Moritz, Milton Edward *security consultant*
Neilson, Winthrop Cunningham, III *communications executive, financial communications consultant*
Souder, Robert R. *personnel director*
Stabler, Donald Billman *business executive*

Huntingdon Valley
Appell, Kathleen Marie *management consultant, legal administrator*

Johnstown
Menna, Christine Ann *public relations executive*

King Of Prussia
Olson, Bob Moody *marketing executive*

Lancaster
Kelly, Robert Lynn *advertising agency executive*

Langhorne
Brennan, John James *marketing executive*

Lower Burrell
Kinosz, Donald Lee *quality consultant*

Malvern
Hall, James E. *computer software executive*
McIntosh, L(orne) William *marketing executive*

Middletown
Kaynak, Erdener *marketing educator, consultant editor*

Milford
Gowan, Joseph Patrick, Jr. *entertainment and food services company executive*
Snyder, Richard Lee *consumer products company executive*

Montgomeryville
†Emory, Thomas Mercer, Jr. *data communications equipment manufacturing executive*

Mount Joy
Dillow, G. Benjamin *human resources director, consultant*
Eichler, Franklin Roosevelt *petroleum products distributor and services company executive*

Mountainhome
Buttz, Charles William *outdoor advertising executive*

Narberth
Newhall, John Harrison *management consultant*

Nazareth
Herrick, Robert Ford *personnel consultant*

New Holland
Ruggeri, Riccardo *automotive sales executive*

Newtown
Goodell, Christina Marie *human resources and employee benefit consultant*
Keyes, Fenton *educational consultant, writer*

Newtown Square
Bower, Ward Alan *management consultant, lawyer*

Oakmont
†Pruitt, Charles William, Jr. *long term health care executive, educator*

Paoli
Ferrell, David Lee *public relations consultant*
Welch, Linda Ogden *sales executive*

Philadelphia
Barrett, James Edward, Jr. *management consultant*
Belinger, Harry Robert *business executive, retired*
Black, Albert Pershing, Jr. *health care executive*
Blades, Herbert William *diversified consumer products company executive*
DuBois, Ruth Harberg *human service agency executive*
Dunn, Wendell Earl, III *management consultant, educator*
Feninger, Claude *industry management services company executive*
Finney, Graham Stanley *management consultant*
Fuller, John Garsed Campbell *food and drug company executive*
Garfinkel, Judith *marketing professional*
Gilbert, Harry Ephraim, Jr. *hotel executive*
Goodchild, John Charles, Jr. *advertising and public relations executive*
Greenberg, Marshall Gary *marketing research consultant*
Guenther, George Carpenter *travel company executive*
Jordan, Clifford Henry *management consultant*
Korsyn, Irene Hahne *marketing executive*
Landis, Edgar David *services business company executive*
†Lee, Joseph William *sales executive*
Lefton, Al Paul, Jr. *advertising executive*
Louchheim, Frank Pfeifer *management consultant*
Melnick, William *advertising executive*
Mitchell, Howard Estill *human resources educator, consultant*
Munch, David Edward *newspaper executive*
Neubauer, Joseph *food services company executive*
Oliva, Terence Anthony *marketing educator*
Reich, Morton Melvyn *marketing communications company executive*
Roberts, Brian Leon *communications executive*
Rouse, Andrew Miles *management consultant*
Schluth, Michael Vernon *advertising executive*
Seiders, Joseph Robert *service company corporate executive, lawyer*
Small, Henry Gilbert *information scientist, researcher*
Spiro, Walter Anselm *advertising and public relations agency executive*
Tierney, Brian Patrick *advertising and public relations executive*
van Zyl, Jacobus Lodewyk *advertising executive*
Waas, Les *advertising executive*
Wiksten, Barry Frank *communications executive*
Wilder, Robert George *advertising and public relations executive*

Pittsburgh
Alvarez, Paul Hubert *communications and public relations consultant*
Aronson, Mark Berne *corporate executive*
Bender, Charles Christian *retail home center executive*
Boyd, William, Jr. *business advisor, banker*
Burger, Herbert Francis *advertising agency executive*
†Byham, William Clarence *instructional technology company executive*
Cowden, Jere Lee *management consultant*
Dempsey, Jerry Edward *service company executive*
Drake, Kingsley Dimitri *professional service company executive*
Fine, Milton *hotel company executive, lawyer*
Fischer, Ben *labor relations educator*
Fisher, James Aiken *industrial marketing executive*
Genge, William Harrison *advertising executive, writer*
Gerhard, Harry E., Jr. *counter trader, management and trade consultant*
Grant, Daniel Gordon *information services company executive*
Hedquist, Jan B. *advertising company executive*
Hershey, Colin Harry *management consultant*
Humphrey, Watts Sherman *technical executive, author*
Marasco, Francis Anthony *human resources executive*
Neel, John Dodd *memorial park executive*
Patten, Charles Anthony *management consultant, arbitrator, retired manufacturing company executive, author*
Rago, Ann D'Amico *public relations professional*
†Rangos, Alexander W. *waste management enironmental services administrator*
†Rangos, John G., Sr. *waste management company executive*
Shapira, David S. *food chain executive*
Sieber, Suzanne Mahoney *sales executive*
Simmermon, James Everett *credit bureau executive*
Walsh, Michael Francis *advertising executive*
Weaver, Charles Henry *business consulting executive*
Zandin, Kjell Bertil *management consulting executive*

Plymouth Meeting
Katz, Gerald *management consultant*
Siegal, Jacob J. *management and financial consultant*

Port Royal
Wert, Jonathan Maxwell, II *management consultant*

Radnor
†Draeger, Kenneth W. *high technology company executive*
Harrison, Robert Drew *management consultant*
Marland, Alkis Joseph *leasing company executive, computer science educator, financial planner*
Paier, Adolf Arthur *computer software and services company executive*
†Peters, Douglas Scott *health care executive*

Reading
Dersh, Rhoda E. *management consultant, business executive*
Knerr, Reinhard H. *communications executive*

Saint Marys
Shobert, Erle Irwin, II *management consultant*

Sewickley
†Wedeen, Marvin Meyer *hospital executive*

Shippensburg
Stone, Susan Ridgaway *marketing educator*

Skytop
Popham, Lewis Charles, III *hotel corporation director, former university dean*

Southampton
Omlor, John Joseph *management consultant*

Southeastern
Minter, Philip Clayton *retired communications company executive*

Tannersville
Moore, James Alfred *ski company executive, lawyer*

Unionville
De Marino, Donald Nicholson *international business executive, former federal agency administrator*

University Park
Gouran, Dennis Stephen *communications educator*
Rigby, Paul Herbert *management educator, college dean*

Valley Forge
Rassbach, Herbert David *marketing executive*
Schaefer, Adolph Oscar, Jr. *advertising agency executive*

Villanova
Kraftson, Raymond H. *business executive*
Nydick, Robert Lincoln, Jr. *university educator*

Warren
McComas, Murray Knabb *direct mail company executive*

Warrendale
Krysinski, Linda Ann *marketing systems analyst*

Warrington
Shaw, Milton Herbert *conglomerate executive*

Wayne
Carroll, Robert W. *retired business executive*
Coane, James Edwin, III *information technology executive*
Martino, Rocco Leonard *computer systems executive*

West Chester
Gould, Irving *computer company executive*
McKeldin, William Evans *management consultant*
Tomlinson, Charles Wesley, Jr. *advertising executive*

Wexford
Hindash, Abbas Asad *quality assurance and strategic analysis professional*

Willow Grove
Asplundh, Christopher B. *tree service company executive*
Asplundh, Robert H. *tree service company executive*

Yardley
Newsom, Carolyn Cardall *management consultant*

York
Hetzel, Dennis Richard *communications executive*
Horn, Russell Eugene, Jr. *printing executive*

RHODE ISLAND

Barrington
Horton, John Alden *advertising agency executive*

Block Island
Coxe, Weld *management consultant*

Bristol
†Esty, David Cameron *marketing and communications executive*

East Greenwich
Weiss, Alan *management consultant, author*
†Wiley, Barry Holland *marketing executive*

Lincoln
Burgdoerfer, Jerry J. *marketing and distribution executive*

Newport
Hayward, John Tucker *management consultant*

Pawtucket
Hassenfeld, Alan Geoffrey *toy company executive*
O'Neill, John T. *toy company executive*
Verrecchia, Alfred J. *toy company executive*

Providence
Kreykes, William *health care management executive*
White, Erskine Norman, Jr. *management company executive*

Wakefield
Eddy, Edward Danforth *academic administrator, educator*

West Greenwich
Breakstone, Robert Albert *consumer products, financial computer products and services, and government executive*

West Warwick
Clary, Alexia Barbara *management company executive*

SOUTH CAROLINA

Beaufort
Day, John Sidney *management sciences educator*

Charleston
†De Wolff, Louis *management consultant*

Clemson
Burch, Elmer Earl *management educator*

Columbia
Case, George Tilden, Jr. *marketing professional*
Floyd, Frank Albert, Jr. *management executive*
Martin, Charles Wallace *travel executive, retired university administrator*
Wilson, George Larry *computer software company executive*

Easley
Dark, Alvin Ralph *public relations executive*
Goldman, Joseph Elias *advertising executive*
Sundstrom, Harold Walter *public relations executive*

Florence
Costa, Manuel Antone *recreational facility manager*

Fort Mill
Kelbley, Stephen Paul *consumer products executive*

Greenville
Collins, Marshall J., Jr. *consumer products company executive*
Fitzgerald, Eugene Francis *management consultant*
Henderson, James Marvin *advertising agency executive*
Morton, James Carnes, Jr. *public relations executive*

Hartsville
Fogle, G. Lee *credit union executive, consultant*

Hilton Head Island
Little, Thomas Mayer *public relations executive*
McDowell, Theodore Noyes *public relations consultant*
Patton, Joseph Donald, Jr. *management consultant*

North Augusta
Pritchard, Constance Jenkins *human resources specialist, trainer, consultant*

Ridgeland
Smart, Jacob Edward *management consultant*

Rock Hill
Click, John William *communication educator*

Saint Helena Island
Herzbrun, David Joseph *retired advertising executive, consultant*

Spartanburg
†Jennings, Thomas Adolphus *hospital administrator*

SOUTH DAKOTA

Brookings
Swiden, Ladell Ray *travel company executive*

Edgemont
Bennett, Charles Leo *management consultant, rancher*

North Sioux City
Waitt, Ted W. *computer company executive*

Sioux Falls
†Johnson, Warren R. *marketing executive, consultant*
Taplett, Lloyd Melvin *human resources management consultant*

Vermillion
Clifford, Sylvester *retired communication educator*

Yankton
†Rezac, Pamela Jean *hospital executive*

TENNESSEE

Chattanooga
Falcon, Charles *consumer products company executive*
Johnston, Hampton L. *photography corporation executive*
Knight, Ralph H. *consumer products company executive*

Collierville
Shepard, Raymond Guy *purchasing executive*

Gallatin
Ellis, Joseph Newlin *retired distribution company executive*

Germantown
†Fischer, Paul A. *media marketing executive*

Greeneville
Austin, Tom Noell *retired tobacco company executive*

Jacksboro
Goforth, E. Jack *security firm executive*

Jackson
Ewing, Frank Crockett *marketing entrepreneur, photographer*

Johnson City
Yavas, Ugur *marketing educator*

Kingsport
McKinley, John Henry *sales executive*

Knoxville
Eisenberg, Lee B. *communications executive*
Haslam, James A., II *petroleum sales executive*
Haslam, James A., III *petroleum sales executive*
Herndon, Anne Harkness *sales executive*
Jordan, (William) Hamilton (McWhorter) *corporate and international communications consultant*
Mayfield, T. Brient, IV *media and computer executive*
Vance, Stanley Charles *management educator*

La Follette
McDonald, Miller Baird *management consultant, columnist, historian*

La Vergne
†Taylor, John L. *communications executive*

Lenoir City
Gerwels, Laurenn Barker *public relations executive*

Memphis
Abston, Dunbar, Jr. *management executive*
Driscoll, James Joseph, Jr. *advertising executive*
Granger, David Mason *broadcasting and communications executive*
Hyde, Joseph R., III *retail auto parts executive*
Langton, Bryan D. *hotel executive*
Ledsinger, Charles Albert, Jr. *hotel, gaming executive*
McCommon, Hubert *benefits, training and development administrator*
Moore, Jackson Watts *corporate executive*
Peternell, Ben Clayton *hospitality company executive*
†Rose, Michael David *hotel corporation executive*
Satre, Philip Glen *corporate executive, lawyer*
†Smith, Donald N. *Restaurant chain executive*
Sullivan, Eugene Joseph *food service company executive*
Summer, Harry Harmon *marketing educator and consultant*
†Walker, Deloss *advertising agency executive*

Nashville
Bolinger, John C., Jr. *management consultant*
†Brown, Tony Ersic *record company executive*
†Bryson, James Edward *marketing professional*
Cawthon, William Connell *operations management consultant*
Clark, James Hamel *public relations executive, author*
Clouse, Robert Wilburn *communication executive, educator*
Cristina, Francis McDermott (Frank Cristina) *corporate security company executive*
Dye, Hank *public relations executive*
Ellis, Weldon Thompson, Jr. *management specialist, consultant, author*
Faust, A. Donovan *communications executive*
Henry, Taylor Hill, Jr. *restaurant executive*
Hobbs, Betty Goad *credit union executive*
Kaludis, George *management consultant, book company executive, educator*
Lawrence, Thomas Patterson *public relations executive*
Martin, Charles Neil, Jr. *health care management company executive*
Moore, William Grover, Jr. *management consultant, former air freight executive, former air force officer*
Stout, Lonnie James, II *restaurant operations company executive*
Van Mol, Louis John, Jr. *public relations executive*

Oak Ridge
†Fee, Gordon *management consulting executive*
Whittle, Charles Edward, Jr. *consultant, lecturer*

Tullahoma
Franke, John Charles *human resources executive*
Gossick, Lee Van *corporate executive, retired air force officer*

TEXAS

Arlington
†Sawyer, Raymond Lee, Jr. *motel chain executive*

Austin
Braasch, Steven Mark *advertising executive*
Chavarria, Ernest Montes, Jr. *international trade, business and finance consultant, lecturer*
Culp, George Hart *computer executive, consultant*
†Decaro, Angelo Anthony, Jr. *data processing executive*
Delaney, Richard Michael *broadcast executive*
Dozier, Dirk A. *restaurant professional*
Hart, Roderick P. *communications educator, researcher, author*
Hefner, Robert Eugene *technology management consultant*
Payne, John Ross *rare books and archives appraisal-consulting company executive, library science educator*
Shaw, James *computer systems analyst*
†Skidmore, Gary J. *marketing executive*
Topfer, Morton Louis *computer company executive*
Vande Hey, James Michael *corporate executive, former air force officer*
Walls, Carl Edward, Jr. *communications company official*
Winegar, Albert Lee *computer systems company executive*
Young, Harrison, II *software development and marketing executive*

Beaumont
†Soleman, William T. *industrial services executive*

Burleson
Prior, Boyd Thelman *management consultant*

Carrollton
†Byrne, James J. *computer service company executive*

College Station
Conole, Richard Clement *management consultant*
Gunn, Clare Alward *consultant, writer, retired educator*

Comfort
DeFoore, John Norris *management consultant*

Corpus Christi
McKinnon, Michael Dee *broadcast executive*

Dallas
Arnold, George Lawrence *advertising company executive*
Bahr, Conrad Charles, III *financial management executive, consultant*
Ballard, Marshall *drilling company executive*
Barnett, Patricia Ann *public relations professional*
Chappelear, Claude Keplar *data systems corporation executive*
†Corbett, Roger Lee *marketing executive*
Cummings, Brian Thomas *public relations company executive*
Curtiss, Jeffrey Eugene *media company executive*
Dedman, Robert Henry *sales executive*
Dillon, Donald Ward *management consultant*
Dozier, David Charles, Jr. *marketing public relations and advertising executi*
Erwin, O. Scott *golf recreational facility executive, consultant*
†Fisherkeller, Paul Francis *food service executive*
Flores, Marion Thomas *advertising executive*
†Frank, Richard M. *restaurant corporation executive*
†Friedheim, Stephen Bailey *public relations executive*
Grimes, David Lynn *communications company executive*
Grogan, Timothy James *information technology executive*
Harber, M(ichael) Eric *manager, management consultant*
Hoffman, Harold Wayne *advertising agency executive*
Kline, Harry Byrd *lecture bureau executive*
Kluge, John Werner *broadcasting and advertising executive*
Korba, Robert W. *communications executive*
Lane, Alvin Huey, Jr. *management consultant*
Leigh-Manuell, Robert Allen *training executive, educator*
Levenson, Stanley Richard *public relations and advertising executive*
Lifson, Kalman Alan *management consultant, retail executive*
Lucier, James Alfred *advertising executive*
MacMahon, Paul *advertising executive*
McCarthy, Michael Joseph *communications company executive*
McDonald, Gail Margaret *human resources, government relations and communications executive*
Miller, Madelyn Sue *advertising executive, food and travel writer*
†Murphy, Randall Kent *training consultant*
Pace, Carolina Jolliff *communications executive, commercial real estate investor*
†Pratt, Jack E., Sr. *hotel executive*
†Richards, Stanford Harvey *advertising agency executive, design studio executive*
Robinson, Hugh Granville *consulting management company executive*
Roger, Richard R. *personal care industry executive*
†Rosebery, Richard Jay *electronics company executive*
Sculley, John *computer company executive*
Sheinberg, Israel *computer company executive*
Simmons, Glenn Reuben *management executive*
Slater, Donald J. *restaurant executive*
Spiegel, Lawrence Howard *advertising executive*
Steorts, Nancy Harvey *international management consultant*
Stuart, Norton Arlington, Jr. *data processing manufacturing executive*
Taylor, Ramona Garrett *executive assistant*
Utley, John M. *corporate professional*
Vanderveld, John, Jr. *waste disposal company executive*
†Walthall, David N. *advertising executive*
Werner, Seth Mitchell *advertising executive*
Wilber, Robert Edwin *corporate executive*
Williams, Gary Alan *management consultant*
Wyly, Charles Joseph, Jr. *corporate executive*

Dripping Springs
Ballard, Mary Melinda *financial communications and investment banking firm executive*

El Paso
Cassidy, Richard Thomas *hotel executive, defense industry consultant, retired army officer*
Roberts, Ernst Edward *marketing consultant*
Suissa, Mireille Renee *company executive, computer consultant*

Ennis
Mitchell, Robert Lynn *business supply company executive*

Fort Worth
Boyce, Allan R. *human resources executive*
Dagnon, James Bernard *human resources executive*
†Metzler, Thomas M. *service company executive*
Peters, Lawrence H. *management educator, consultant*
Ray, Paul Richard, Jr. *executive search consultant*
Turner, Loyd Leonard *advertising executive, public relations executive*
†Williamson, Doug *data processing executive*

Georgetown
Weyrauch, Paul Turney *retired army officer*

Grapevine
Friedman, Barry *financial marketing consultant*
Holley, Cyrus Helmer *management consulting service executive*
Smith, Lee Herman *business executive*

Horseshoe Bay
Lesikar, Raymond Vincent *business administration educator*

Houston
Bonham, Donald L. *food service executive*
Brackley, William Lowell *aviation management consultant*
Brown, Jean William *advertising and public relations executive*
Caltrider, Thomas Lewis *environmental company executive*
Cameron, Bruce Francis *data processing executive*
Castillo, Leonel Jabier *communications and promotions executive, consultant*
Cernan, Eugene A. *management company executive, former astronaut*
Clark, Ron D(ean) *cosmetologist*
Cofran, George Lee *management consultant*
Cole, Aubrey Louis *management consultant, forest products company executive*
Del Franco, Ray *consumer products company executive*
Dosher, John Rodney *consulting management consultant*
Dubois, Jules Edward *security firm executive, consultant*
Gilbert, Harold Stanley *warehousing company executive*
Hart, James Whitfield, Jr. *corporate public affairs executive, lawyer*
†Heiker, Vincent Edward *information systems executive*
Holmes, Darrell *tourism consultant*
†Jackson, Robert Sherwood *waste management executive*
Jeanneret, Paul Richard *management consultant*
Johns, H. Douglas *computer company executive*
Kopec, Frank John *advertising agency executive*
Kors, R. Paul *search company executive*
Larkin, William Vincent, Jr. *oil field service company executive*
Levit, Max *food service executive*
Lowrey, E. James *food service company executive*
Mampre, Virginia Elizabeth *communications executive*
Mauck, William M., Jr. *executive recruiter, small business owner*
McKim, Paul Arthur *management consultant, retired petroleum executive*
Myers, Norman Allan *marketing professional*
Onstead, Randall *consumer goods company executive*
Onstead, Robert R. *consumer goods company executive*
Orme, Denis Arthur *management consultant*
Palmer, James Edward *public relations executive*
Patterson, William Wayne *electronics company executive*
Penny, Charles Richard *retired advertising executive*
Pfeiffer, Eckhard *computer company executive*
Ruckelshaus, William Doyle *waste disposal services company executive*
Seaman, Roual Duane *data processing company executive*
Snider, Robert Larry *management consultant*
Vaeth, Nancy Ann *sales executive*
†Watson, Max P., Jr. *computer software company executive*
Welch, Byron Eugene *communications educator*

Humble
Hawk, Phillip Michael *service corporation executive*

Huntsville
†Smyth, Joseph Philip *travel industry executive*

Hurst
Jackson, Donald *waste management executive*

Irving
Daniel, Donald *advertising executive*
Dinicola, Robert *consumer products company executive*
Faulkner, David J. *computer company executive*
Judge, Stephen *advertising executive*
Levy, Lester A. *sanitation company executive*
Lindner, James D. *computer company executive*
Martin, Kenneth Douglas *consumer products company executive*
Munger, Sharon *market research firm executive*
Temerlin, Liener *advertising agency executive*
Wicks, William Withington *retired public relations executive*

Kerrville
Cremer, Richard Eldon *marketing professional*

Lufkin
Brookshire, Wiley Eugene *consumer products company executive*

Plano
Alberthal, Lester M., Jr. *information processing services executive*
Collumb, Peter John *communications company executive*
Donald, James L. *communications company executive*
Hinton, Norman Wayne *information services executive*
Linderman, Dean *data processing services company executive*
Resnik, Linda Ilene *marketing and information executive, consultant*
†Scott, Terry Lee *communications company executive*

Richardson
Fahrlander, Henry William, Jr. *management consultant*
Hagan, Joseph Lawrence *communications executive*

San Angelo
Coe, Robert Stanford *retired management educator*

San Antonio
Butt, Charles C. *food service executive*
Carpenter, John Wilson, III *management consultant, retired air force officer, educational administrator*
Cory, William Eugene *retired consulting company executive*
Davis, Walter Barry *quality assurance professional*
Ellis, James D. *communications executive, corporate lawyer*
Franklin, Larry Daniel *communications company executive*
Henderson, Arvis Burl *data processing executive, biochemist*
Keck, James Moulton *retired advertising and marketing executive, retired air force officer*
Lahourcade, John Brosius *service company executive*
Leavitt, Audrey Faye Cox *television programming executive*
McClinton, Dorothy Hardaway *former business educator*
†Michigami, Michael Masao *data processing executive*
Ritchie, Richard Lee *communications company executive, former railroad and forest products company executive*
†Walker, Tim *printing company executive*
Whitt, Robert Ampudia, III *advertising executive, marketing professional*
Wimpress, Gordon Duncan, Jr. *corporate consultant, foundation executive*
Witherspoon, John Marshall *advertising executive*

San Marcos
Martin, Jerri Whan *public relations executive*

Spring
Cooley, Andrew Lyman *corporation executive, former army officer*

Sugar Land
Kempner, James Carroll *sugar company executive*
Preng, David Edward *management consultant*

Temple
Dickson, Joseph M. *management consultant, former health care administrator*

Waco
Meyer, Paul James *communications company executive*

UTAH

Logan
Wilkinson, Richard Francis, Jr. *marketing executive*

Orem
Bastian, Bruce Wayne *software company executive*

Park City
Ebbs, George Heberling, Jr. *management consulting company executive*

Provo
Bartlett, Leonard Lee *communications educator, retired advertising agency executive, advertising historian*
Buck, William Fraser, II *marketing executive*
Harlow, LeRoy Francis *organization and management educator emeritus, author*

Salt Lake City
Adamson, Jack *communications executive*
Bolinder, Robert Donald *former supermarket executive*
Carlson, Ralph Jennings *communications executive*
Elkins, Glen Ray *service company executive*
Jones, Clark David *restaurant executive, accountant*
Kinard, J. Spencer *television news executive*
Lund, Victor L. *retail food company executive*
Norton, Howard Cherrington *leasing company executive*
Parkinson, Richard A. *consumer products company executive*
Phillips, Ted Ray *advertising agency executive*
Scott, Howard Winfield, Jr. *temporary help services company executive*

Sandy
York, Theodore Robert *consulting company executive*

VERMONT

Charlotte
McCoubrey, R. James *advertising executive*

Chester
Coleman, John Royston *innkeeper, author*

Essex Junction
Crouse, Roger Leslie *information analyst, quality consultant, facilitator*
Sweetser, Gene Gillman *quality assurance professional, state legislator*

Gaysville
Dawson, Wilfred Thomas *marketing executive, consultant*

Londonderry
Bigelow, David Skinner, III *management consultant*

Manchester
Yager, Hunter *advertising executive*

Norwich
Fitzhugh, William Wyvill, Jr. *printing company executive*
Smith, Markwick Kern, Jr. *management consultant*

Rutland
Ferraro, Betty Ann *corporate administrator, state senator*

Stowe
Fiddler, Barbara Dillow *sales and marketing professional*

Thetford Center
Brown, Robert Goodell *management consultant*

Waterbury
Pelton, Joan Elisabeth Mason *music company executive*

White River Junction
Fayerweather, John *management and international business specialist, educator*

Woodstock
Browning, Robert Masters *management consultant*

VIRGINIA

Alexandria
Broide, Mace Irwin *public affairs consultant*
Bussler, Robert Bruce *management consultant*
Collins, Frank Charles, Jr. *industrial and service quality specialist*
Cooper, B. Jay *public relations executive*
Covone, James Michael *automotive parts manufacturer and distribution company executive*
Dawson, Samuel Cooper, Jr. *retired motel company executive*
Day, Melvin Sherman *information company executive*
Devine, Donald J. *management and political consultant*
Hagan, Robert Leslie *retired consulting company executive*
Hansan, Mary Anne *marketing professional*
Hartsock, Linda Sue *educational and management development executive*
†Joseph, Lennox Edmond *training and consulting company executive*
Laurent, Lawrence Bell *communications executive, former journalist*
Locigno, Paul Robert *public affairs executive*
Loevi, Francis Joseph, Jr. *consulting company executive*
Loving, William Rush, Jr. *public relations company executive, consultant*
McMillan, Charles William *consulting company executive*
Newburger, Beth Weinstein *medical telecommunications company executive*
Osborn, William C. *personnel organization executive*
Richardson, Robert Charlwood, III *management consultant, retired air force officer*
Smith, J. Brian *advertising executive, public affairs consultant, campaign management firm executive*
Smith, William Young *consultant, former air force officer*
Wilding, James Anthony *airports manager*

Annandale
Speakes, Larry Melvin *public relations executive*

Arlington
†Anderson, Maynard Carlyle *national and international security executive*
†Brehm, William Keith *systems company executive*
Cetron, Marvin Jerome *management executive*
Faris, Frank Edgar *marketing executive*
Freeman, Neal Blackwell *communications corporation executive*
Gianturco, Delio E. *management consultant*
Gormley, Dennis Michael *consulting company executive*
Greinke, Everett Donald *corporate executive, international programs consultant*
†Hengels, Charles Francis *marketing professional, educator*
Hess, Milton Siegmund *computer company executive*
Jarvis, Elbert, II (Jay Jarvis) *human resources executive*
Kilduff, Bonnie Elizabeth *director of expositions*
Kingsley, Daniel Thain *public affairs executive*
London, J. Phillip *information technology company executive*
Martin, Edgar Thomas *telecommunications consultant, lawyer*
Meyer, Richard Townsend *service company executive*
Oleson, Ray Jerome *computer service company executive*
Riegel, Kurt Wetherhold *environmental protection, occupational safety and health*
Rosenthal, Robert M. *automotive sales executive*
Rossotti, Charles Ossola *computer consulting company executive*
Smith, Janet Erlene *advertising executive*
Thompson, Gerald Jordan *management consultant*
Zorthian, Barry *communications executive*

Blacksburg
Weaver, Pamela Ann *hospitality research professional*

Burke
Ansley, Darlene H. *communications executive*
Pollard, Joseph Augustine *advertising and public relations consultant*

Chantilly
O'Brien, Robert John, Jr. *public relations executive, former government official, air force officer*
†Ramsey, Forrest G. *computer company executive*

Charlottesville
Colley, John Leonard, Jr. *educator, author, management consultant*
Dunn, Mary Jarratt *public relations executive*
Freeman, R. Edward *business educator*
Taylor, William B. *history educator*
Wolcott, John Winthrop, III *corporate executive*

Chesapeake
Orr, Joel Nathaniel *computer graphics consultant*

Danville
Owen, Claude Bernard, Jr. *tobacco company executive*

Fairfax
Bennett, Verna Green *employee relations executive*
†Giuntini, Philip Merritt *management consultant, software developer*
Gross, Patrick Walter *business executive, management consultant*
Jones, Carleton Shaw *information systems company executive, lawyer*
Kieffer, Jarold Alan *policy and management consultant, writer, editor*
Klauberg, William Joseph *technical services company executive*
Palmer, James Daniel *information technology educator*
Pan, Elizabeth Lim *information systems company executive*
Pitchell, Robert J. *business executive*
Walker, Betsy Ellen *computer products and services company executive*

Falls Church
Beach, Robert Oliver, II *computer company executive*
Brown, Gerald Curtis *retired army officer, engineering executive*
Cohn, Samuel Maurice *economic and management consultant*
Harley, William Gardner *retired communications consultant*
†McNichols, Gerald Robert *consulting company executive*
Nelson, Thomas William *management consultant, former government official*
Webb, William John *public relations counsel*

Free Union
Hart, Jean Hardy *information systems specialist, consultant, editor*

Grundy
Smith, Jack *food service executive*

Hampton
Drummond, James Everman *technology transfer company executive, former army officer*

Harrisonburg
Ramsey, Jackson Eugene *management educator*

Herndon
Larese, Edward John *management company executive*

Hume
Barr, Joseph Walker *retired corporate director*

Kilmarnock
Maxwell, W(ilbur) Richard *management consultant*

Leesburg
Ecker, G. T. Dunlop *hospital administration executive*

Lightfoot
Morris, Robert Louis *management consultant*

Mc Lean
Adler, Larry *marketing executive*
Capone, Lucien, Jr. *management consultant, former naval officer*
Ceremsak, Karen Marie *communications executive, public relations and marketing communications executive*
Deal, George Edgar *management and industrial executive*
De Carbonnel, François Eric *management consultant*
Estren, Mark James *management and media consultant, TV producer*
Gardenier, Turkan Kumbaraci *statistical company executive, researcher*
Graybeal, Sidney Norman *national security executive, former government official*
James, Daniel J. *management consultant*
Jennings, Jerry D. *communications company executive*
Johnson, Frank Stanley, Jr. *communications executive, retired government official*
Kim, Hack Hyun *telecommunications executive*
Kiviat, Philip Jay *computer services company executive*
Kolombatovic, Vadja Vadim *management consulting company executive*
Leto, James J. *artificial intelligence executive*
Ling, Suilin *management consultant*
Parker, Scott Lane *management consultant*
Paschall, Lee McQuerter *retired communications consultant*
†Shenoy, Sudhakar Venkatraya *computer software company executive*
Sitkoff, Theodore *public management executive*
Sowle, Donald Edgar *management consultant*
Tuttle, William G(ilbert) T(ownsend), Jr. *research executive*
Watson, Jerry Carroll *advertising executive*

Merrifield
Pascoe, Charles Thomas, Jr. *computer systems company executive*

Middleburg
Cooke, Jack Kent *diversified company executive*

Moneta
Ulmer, Walter Francis, Jr. *consultant, former army officer*

Norfolk
Blount, Robert Haddock *corporate executive, retired naval officer*
†Valentine, Herman Edward *computer company executive*

Onancock
Puckorius, Theodore D. *consulting company executive*

Reston
Ackerson, Jeffrey Townsend *computer systems executive*
†Berry Cabán, Cristóbal Santiago *business executive*
Blanchard, Townsend Eugene *service companies executive*
Brosseau, Irma Finn *business executive, management consultant*
Calio, Anthony John *scientist, business executive*
Cerf, Vinton Gray *telecommunications company executive*
Duggan, James H. *technical services company executive*
Schleede, Glenn Roy *energy market and policy consultant*

Richmond
Adams, John Buchanan, Jr. *advertising agency executive*
Altschul, B J *public relations counselor*
Cothran, Phyllis L. *personal care industry executive*
Evans, James Stanley *communications company executive*
Gross, Paul Allan *health service executive*
Jacobs, Harry Milburn, Jr. *advertising executive*
Lanahan, John Stevenson *management consultant*
Laverge, Jan *tobacco company executive*
Ligon, William Austin *consumer products company executive*
McDonald, Frank Albert, Jr. *personnel director*
Mc Grath, Lee Parr *author, public relations executive*
Miller, James Christopher *paper industry information systems specialist*
Neathawk, Roger Delmore *marketing company executive*
Newbrand, Charles Michael *advertising firm executive*
Raper, Mark Irvin *public relations executive*
Roop, Ralph Goodwin *retired oil marketing company executive*
Stephens, E. Barrie *business executive*
Stettinius, Wallace *communications executive*
Trott, Sabert Scott, II *marketing professional*

Roanoke
Shaftman, Fredrick Krisch *telephone communications executive*

Seaford
Jenkins, Margaret Bunting *human resources executive*

Springfield
Bruen, John Dermot *computer systems company executive*
Fedewa, Lawrence John *information technology company executive*

Sterling
LaFroscia, Ernest John *business executive*
Witek, James Eugene *public relations executive*

Verona
de Vaux, Peter Fordney *advertising consultant*

Vienna
Bartlett, John Wesley *consulting firm executive*
Brandel, Ralph Edward *management consultant*
†Butler, Donald *rental leasing company executive*
†Campagna, Joseph *rental, leasing company executive*
†Clark, Katherine Karen *software company executive*
Hale, Thomas Morgan *professional services executive*
Jandreau, James Lawrence *program manager*
Van Stavoren, William David *management consultant, retired government official*
Walker, Edward Keith, Jr. *business executive, retired naval officer*

Virginia Beach
Brickell, Edward Ernest, Jr. *management executive*
Lisota, Gary Martin *business executive, retired naval officer*
Tarbutton, Lloyd Tilghman *motel executive, franchise consultant*
Weller, Robert N(orman) *hotel executive*
Wick, Robert Thomas *retired supermarket executive*

Warrenton
Molloy, Michael John *public relations professional*

White Stone
Wroth, James Melvin *former army officer, computer company executive*

Williamsburg
Baker, Donald Scott *communications executive*
Dittman, Duane Arthur *management consultant*
Finn, A. Michael *public relations executive*
†Verkuil, Paul Robert *corporate executive*

WASHINGTON

Anacortes
Spaulding, John Pierson *public relations executive, marine consultant*

Bainbridge Island
Bowden, William Darsie *interior designer, retired*

Bellevue
Otterholt, Barry L. *technology management consultant*
Reudink, Douglas Otto John *communications company executive, researcher*

Edmonds
Sankovich, Joseph Bernard *cemetery management consultant*

Federal Way
McNeese, Jack Marvin *communications executive*

Gig Harbor
Huyler, Jean Wiley *media and interpersonal communications consultant, hypnotherapist*
Robinson, James William *retired management consultant*

Kirkland
Alberg, Tom Austin *communications executive, lawyer*
†Craves, Robert Edward *marketing professional*
McCaw, Craig O. *communications executive*

Langley
Bitts, Todd Michael *sales and marketing consultant*

Liberty Lake
DeMerritt, Ted C. *microprocessor company executive*

Olympia
Ogden, Valeria Juan *management consultant, state representative*

Redmond
Bingham, Robert Frederick *communication company executive*
Gates, William Henry, III *software company executive*
Herres, Phillip Benjamin *computer software executive*

Seattle
Aoki, John H. *hotel chain executive*
Beetham, Stanley Williams *international management consultant*
Bounds, Christopher E. *food service executive*
DeBon, George A. *security services company executive*
Dederer, Michael Eugene *public relations company executive*
Duryee, David Anthony *management consultant*
Evans, Trevor Heiser *advertising executive*
Ladd, James Roger *international business consultant*
MacDonald, Andrew Stephen *management consulting firm executive*
Marriott, David M. *public relations executive*
Marshall, Scott *advertising agency executive*
McAleer, William Harrison *software company financial executive*
McNeely, Mark Hall *advertising executive*
McReynolds, Neil Lawrence *consultant*
Murray, Connel Lyle *advertising and public relations executive, consultant*
O'Leary, Thomas Howard *resources executive*
Rockey, Jay *public relations company executive*
Ross, Austin *health care executive*
Smith, Jeffrey L. (The Frugal Gourmet) *cook, writer*
Steele, Frank Channel *sales executive*
†Treadway, James *hotel chain executive*
†Walker, Douglas *computer developement company executive*
Whitty, Raymond John *hotel company executive*
Widener, Peri Ann *business development executive*

Sequim
Hansey, Renee Jeanne *retired communications executive*

Spokane
Agnew, Thomas Edward *communications executive*
Nicolai, Eugene Ralph *public relations consultant, editor, writer*
Storey, Francis Harold *business consultant, retired bank executive*
Woodard, Alva Abe *business consultant*

Tacoma
Brevik, J. Albert *communications consultant*

Vashon
Munson, Dee Taylor Allison *food marketing executive*

WEST VIRGINIA

Charleston
Burns, Thomas C. *communication company executive*
Mc Gee, John Frampton *communications company executive*
†Peck, Harry *public relations executive*
†Ryan, Charles Edward *public relations executive, advertising executive*

Elkins
Payne, Gloria Marquette *business eductor*

Huntington
Barenklau, Keith Edward *safety services company executive*
Underwood, Cecil H. *company executive, past governor of West Virginia*

Parkersburg
Fahlgren, H(erbert) Smoot *advertising agency executive*

Philippi
Shearer, Richard Eugene *industrial consultant*

Wheeling
Kirkpatrick, Forrest Hunter *management consultant*

WISCONSIN

Appleton
McManus, John Francis *association executive, writer*

Brookfield
Diesem, John Lawrence *information systems executive*
†Haase, Bronson J. *communications company executive*
Hanson, Leila Fraser *sales and marketing executive*
Nelson, William George, IV *software company executive*
Welnetz, David Charles *human resources executive*

Chippewa Falls
Ewald, Robert Hansen *computer company executive*

Cudahy
Naimoli, Raymond Anthony *infosystems specialist, financial consultant*

Green Bay
Bush, Robert G. *food service executive*
Meng, John C. *food service executive*

Greendale
DeLorenzo, David Joseph *public relations executive*
Tucker, William Thomas, III *computer software company executive*

Hales Corners
Hodgson, Craig Robert *radio station executive*

Hartland
Mc Neil, Donald Lewis *retired multiple association management company executive*

Jefferson
†Morgan, Gaylin F. *public realtions executive*

Kenosha
Grover, Robert Lawrence *tool company executive*

Lancaster
Johnson, Hal Harold Gustav *marketing educator emeritus*

Madison
†Conway, Robert Edward *corporate executive*
Formisano, Roger Anthony *professor of business*
Johnson, Alton Cornelius *management educator*
Miller, Richard Ulric *business and industrial relations educator*
Pampel, Roland D. *computer company executive*
Thompson, Howard Elliott *business educator*

Menasha
Aurand, Calvin W., Jr. *specialized printing company executive*

Mequon
Felde, Martin Lee *advertising agency executive, accountant*

Milwaukee
Arbit, Bruce *direct marketing executive, consultant*
Balbach, George Charles *technology company executive*
Chait, Jon Frederick *corporate executive, lawyer*
†Colbert, Virgis William *brewery company executive*
Elias, Paul S. *marketing executive*
Fromstein, Mitchell S. *temporary office services company executive*
Garnier, Robert Charles *management consultant*
†Hunter, Victor Lee *marketing executive, consultant*
Joseph, Jules K. *retired public relations executive*
Kahlor, Robert Arnold *communications company executive*
Kerr, Dorothy Marie Burmeister *consultant, marketing executive*
Marcus, Stephen Howard *hospitality and entertainment company executive*
McCollow, Thomas James *communications company executive*
Palay, Gilbert *temporary help services company executive*
Randall, William Seymour *leasing company executive*
†Roll, Teresa J. *restaurant chain executive*
Scheinfeld, James David *travel agency executive*
Shiely, John Stephen *company executive, lawyer*
Weber, Charles Edward *management educator*
Zigman, Robert S. *public relations executive*

Neenah
Underhill, Robert Alan *consumer products company executive*

Onalaska
Wilson, Anthony Vincent *business executive, mechanical engineer*

Pewaukee
Quadracci, Harry R. *printing company executive*
Quadracci, Harry V. *printing company executive, lawyer*
Ranus, Robert D. *food marketing executive*

Plymouth
Gentine, Lee Michael *marketing professional*

Racine
Bernberg, Bruce Arthur *consumer products publishing, printing executive*
George, William Douglas, Jr. *consumer products company executive*
Klein, Gabriella Sonja *communications executive*

South Milwaukee
Kitzke, Eugene David *research management executive*

Waukesha
Scott, Rodger Gene *personnel executive*

Waunakee
Berthelsen, John Robert *printing company executive*

Wisconsin Rapids
Brennan, Patrick Francis *printing paper manufacturing executive*

WYOMING

Casper
Kennerknecht, Richard Eugene *sales executive*
Perkins, Dorothy A. *marketing professional*

Cheyenne
Wagner, Samuel Albin Mar *records management executive, educator*

Sheridan
Taylor, Judith Ann *sales executive*

Wilson
Fritz, Jack Wayne *communications and marketing company executive*

TERRITORIES OF THE UNITED STATES

PUERTO RICO

Caparra
Pont, Marisara *public relations executive*

VIRGIN ISLANDS

Cruz Bay
Blitz, Peggy Sanderfur *corporate travel management company official*

Saint Thomas
Miner, Robert Gordon *creative promotional consultant, auctioneer, writer, publisher, actor*

CANADA

ALBERTA

Calgary
†Hume, James Borden *corporate professional, foundation executive*

De Winton
Shutiak, James *management consultant*

Edmonton
Cowie, Bruce Edgar *communications executive*

BRITISH COLUMBIA

Burnaby
†Canfield, Brian A. *communications company executive*

Vancouver
Campbell, Bruce Alan *market research consultant*
Lambert, Michael Malet *hotel company executive*
Rae, Barbara Joyce *employee placement company executive*

MANITOBA

Winnipeg
Fraser, John Foster *management company executive*
Liba, Peter Michael *communications executive*
Matthews, Patrick John *consumer products company executive*

NOVA SCOTIA

Dartmouth
Callaghan, J. Clair *corporate executive*

Halifax
Gratwick, John *management consulting executive, writer, consultant*
Thompson, William Grant *management executive*

ONTARIO

Etobicoke
Beckley, Michael John *hotel executive*
Snedden, James Douglas *health service management consultant*

Hamilton
Chadwick, Bruce Allen *advertising agency executive*

Kingston
Stanley, James Paul *printing company executive*

London
Henderson, Robert Jules *food service executive*
Hennessey, Frank Martin *strategic planning executive*

Mississauga
MacKinnon, David Cameron *research and development company executive*

North York
Denham, Frederick Ronald *management consultant*

Oakville
Barlow, Kenneth James *management consultant*

Ottawa
Clermont, Georges Charles *corporate executive*
Kitchen, Paul Howard *government and association management consultant*
Sharp, Mitchell William *adviser to prime minister*
Thibault, J(oseph) Laurent *service company executive*

Richmond Hill
Marshall, Donald Stewart *computer systems company executive*

Toronto
Bandeen, Robert Angus *management corporation executive*
Bonnycastle, Lawrence Christopher *retired corporate director*
Brown, W. Michael *publishing company executive*
Bunting, Christopher Henry *public relations executive*
Campbell, Donald Graham *communications company executive*
Christopher, Raymond Joseph *computer services executive*
Clarkson, Max Boydell Elliott *printing company executive, business educator*
Deacon, David Emmerson *advertising executive*
Decle, Denis Christopher *advertising executive*
DeMone, Robert Stephen *hotel company executive*
Elting, Everett E. *advertising agency executive*
Friendly, Lynda Estelle *theatre marketing and communications executive*
Graham, James Edmund *service management executive*
Gregor, Tibor Philip *management consultant*
Harvey, George Edwin *communications company executive*
Houston, Stanley Dunsmore *public relations executive*
Irwin, Samuel Macdonald *toy company executive*
Jacob, Ellis *entertainment company executive*
Livergant, Harold Leonard *health services executive*
Matathia, Ira Leslie *advertising agency executive*
†Meenan, James Joseph *communications executive*
Miller, Anthony G. *advertising executive*
Miller, Kenneth Merrill *computing services company executive*
Osborne, Ronald Walter *communications executive*
Pankratz, Henry J. *management consultant*
Rathke, Sheila Wells *advertising and public relations executive*
Reid, Terence C. W. *corporation executive*
Rogers, Edward Samuel *communications company executive*
Ross, Henry Raymond *advertising executive and legal counsel;*
Silk, Frederick C.Z. *consumer products company executive*

Unionville
Nichols, Harold Neil *corporate executive, former pipeline company executive*

Windsor
Giffen, John A. *distillery executive*

QUEBEC

Leclercville
Morin, Pierre Jean *retired management consultant*

Montreal
Audet, Henri *communications executive*
Beauregard, Luc *public relations executive*
Berube, Jacques B. *communications company executive*
Boucher, Raymond Gabriel *advertising executive*
Bouthillier, André *public relations executive, consultant*
Bussieres, Yvan *supermarket chain executive*
Crawford, Purdy *consumer products and services company executive*
Desjardins, Pierre *consumer goods company executive*
Des Marais, Pierre, II *communications holding company executive*
Ducros, Pierre Y. *information technology consulting and systems management executive*
Kearney, Robert *retired communications company executive*
Lamarre, Daniel *public relations company executive*
Levitt, Brian Michael *consumer products and services company executive, lawyer*
MacKinnon, Rodrick Keith *corporate administration executive, lawyer*
Neveu, Jean *printing company executive*
Richardson, Gisele *management company executive*
Saint-Jacques Vallée, Madeleine *advertising agency executive*
Savard, Claude A. *food service executive*
†Sirois, Charles *communications executive*
Thind, Tej Pal *international management consultant*
Tousignant, Jacques *human resources executive, lawyer*
Zakaib, Lorne *industrial technology executive*

Mount Royal
Chauvette, Claude R. *building materials company administrator*
Glezos, Matthews *consumer products and services company executive*

Quebec
Courtois, B. A. *communications executive*
Lafleur, Guy *public relations executive, professional hockey player*

Saint Sauveur des Monts
Dunsky, Menahem *retired advertising agency executive, communications consultant, painter*

Verdun
Delisle, Gilles Yvan *telecommunications executive*

Westmount
Gordonsmith, John Arthur Harold *collection agency executive*

SASKATCHEWAN

Regina
Sifton, Michael Clifford *broadcaster, publisher*

MEXICO

Mexico City
Azcarraga Milmo, Emilio *communication company executive*
Dudley, Craig James *executive recruiter*
Velasco, Eugenio *advertising executive*

BELGIUM

Strombeek Bever
Mancel, Claude Paul *household product company executive*

BRAZIL

Maceio
Fox, James Frederick *public relations counsel*

CHILE

Santiago
Beshears, Charles Daniel consultant, former insurance executive
Whelan, James Robert communications executive, international trade and investment consultant, author, educator

DENMARK

Charlottenlund
Andreassen, Poul business executive

ENGLAND

London
Ambler, Timothy Felix John management science researcher
Barocci, Robert Louis advertising agency executive
Bell, Theodore Augustus advertising executive
Bokaemper, Stefan hotel executive
Coelho, Joseph Richard research analyst
Gummer, Peter Selwyn public relations executive
Habgood, Anthony John corporate executive
Harris, Howard Elliott consulting company executive
†Kissmann, Edna communications executive
Lanigan, Denis George retired advertising agency executive
Leaf, Robert Stephen public relations executive
McNulty, Dermot public relations executive
Montero, Fernan Gonzalo advertising executive
Owers, Brian Charles holding company executive
Saatchi, Maurice communications and marketing company executive
Sorrell, Martin Stuart advertising and marketing executive
Steen, Norman Frank marketing executive
Thompson, John More managment consultant
Treasure, John Albert Penberthy advertising executive

Stroud
Robinson, John Beckwith development management consultant

Suffolk
Stauderman, Bruce Ford advertising executive, writer

Windlesham
Tarallo, Angelo Nicholas industrial gas and health care company executive, lawyer

FRANCE

Bonnes
Ogilvy, David Mackenzie advertising executive

Boulogne-Billancourt
Dellis, Frédy Michel car rental company executive

Levallois
de Pouzilhac, Alain Duplessis advertising executive

Paris
Marcus, Claude advertising executive

GERMANY

Godesberg
Hutton, Winfield Travis management consultant, educator

Guersloh
Wössner, Mark Matthias business executive

Hemsbach
Froessl, Horst Waldemar business executive, data processing developer

HONG KONG

Hong Kong
Pisanko, Henry Jonathan command and control communications company executive

Kowloon
Burns, Robert Henry hotel executive

ISRAEL

Haifa
Peled, Abraham computer company executive

Herzliya
Bitan, Giora Yoav computer systems executive

JAPAN

Tokyo
Inagaki, Masao advertising agency executive
Kajima, Shoichi general contractor executive
Kogure, Gohei advertising executive
Miyazawa, Akira advertising executive
Narita, Yutaka advertising executive
Oshita, Koji advertising executive

Tsukuba
Kobayashi, Susumu data processing executive, super computer consultant

PANAMA

Panama City
Thoman, Henry Nixon food industry executive

SINGAPORE

Singapore
Burandt, Gary Edward advertising agency executive
McMahon, Paul Francis international management consultant

SOUTH AFRICA

Johannesburg
Crockett, Phyllis Darlene communications executive

SPAIN

Santiago De Compostela
Balseiro Gonzalez, Manuel management executive, consultant

SWEDEN

Stockholm
Johnson, Antonia Axson corporate executive
Robinson, Hobart Krum management consulting company executive

SWITZERLAND

Biel
Scheftner, Gerold marketing executive

Geneva
Ballin, William Christopher international shipping, investments, and energy advisor

Valais
Chase, Morris international management consultant

Vaud
Joseph, Michael Anthony marketing executive

ADDRESS UNPUBLISHED

Adams, Jonathan L. advertising agency executive
Aden, Arthur Laverne office systems company executive
Allen, Theodore Earl computer company executive
†Altman, Lyle D. communications company executive
Ambrose, James Richard consultant, retired government official
Anderson, Vernon Russell technology company executive, entrepreneur
Andriole, Stephen John information systems executive
Angotti, Anthony John advertising executive
Anselmini, Jean-Pierre communication corporation executive
Baldauf, Jill Christine advertising executive
Ballard, Marion Scattergood software development professional
Bamberger, Gerald Francis plastics marketing consultant
Barger, William James management consultant
Barnes, Steven J. retired food franchising company executive
Barrett, Joseph Michael advertising and marketing consultant, actor
Barton, Peter Richard, III communications executive
Beasley, Barbara Starin sales executive, marketing professional
Bell, P. Jackson computer executive
Benke, Norman R. trucking company executive
Bennett, John Roscoe computer company executive
Benney, Douglas Mabley marketing executive, consultant
Berger, Frank Stanley consultant
Bernstein, Alan Barry security services company executive
Binder, Amy Finn public relations company executive
Blacker, Harriet public relations executive
Blaine, Davis Robert valuation consultant executive
Blake, John Edward car rental company executive
Blaney, Connie Gayle importer and broker
Blasco, Alfred Joseph business and financial consultant
Bliss, William Stanley, Jr. corporate marketing consultant
†Blum, Bruce Alan hotel executive
Bolingbroke, Robert A. consumer products company executive
Bonner, Jack public relations company executive
Boone, Alicia Kay Lanier marketing communications consultant, writer
Borda, Richard Joseph management consultant
Bowen, J(ohn) William management consultant
Braden, George Walter, II (Lord of Carrigaline) company executive
Bradford, Robert Edward supermarket executive
Branscomb, Anne Wells communications consultant
Brennan, Donna Lesley public relations company executive
Brennen, Stephen Alfred international business consultant
Brewer, David Meredith retired computer company executive
Brickman, Ravelle public relations writer and consultant
Broedling, Laurie Adele human resources executive, psychologist, educator
Brooks, Gary management consultant
Brown, Bart A., Jr. consumer products company executive
Burge, James Darrell personnel, government relations executive
Burge, John Wesley, Jr. management consultant
Burton, Anne M. public relations professional
Butler, Robert Leonard sales executive
Butler, Robert Thomas retired advertising executive
Butts, Virginia corporate public relations executive
Buzard, James Albert management consultant
Caine, Raymond William, Jr. retired public relations executive
Callahan, Richard J. communications company executive
Canning, John J. leasing and finance company executive
Carder, Paul Charles advertising executive
Cardy, Andrew Gordon hotel executive
Carey, Dennis Clarke executive search consultant
Carter, Jaine M(arie) human resources development company executive
Casey, Martin M. food service executive
Cashman, William James, Jr. information processing marketing executive
Castle, James Cameron information systems executive
Castle, Robert Woods advertising agency executive
Chain, Beverly Jean communications executive
Chamberlain, William Edwin, Jr. management consultant
Chapman, Kristin Heilig public relations consultant
Chereskin, Alvin advertising executive
Clarizio, Josephine Delores corporate services executive, former manufacturing and engineering company executive, foundation executive
Cohen, Mark Steven public affairs specialist
Collins, William Michael public relations executive
Cooper, Francis Loren advertising executive
Cork, Edwin Kendall business and financial consultant
Cormier, Jean G. communications company executive
Cortese, Richard Anthony computer company executive
Cotter, Richard Vern management consultant, author, educator
Covalt, Genevieve corporate executive secretary
Crawford, William Walsh retired consumer products company executive
Crosson, John Albert advertising executive
Croxton, Fred(erick) E(mory), Jr. retired information specialist, consultant
Cunningham, Isabella Clara Mantovani advertising educator
Curchoe, Carl A. printing company executive
Dalziel, Robert David retired telecommunications executive
Davis, Joanne Mary advertising executive
Davis, Joseph Edward retired supermarket chain executive
Denneny, James Clinton, Jr. business consultant
Denny, James McCahill retail executive
Dirks, Leslie Chant communications and electronics company executive
Dirvin, Gerald Vincent retired consumer products company executive
Dixon, Louis Frederick information sciences and telecommunications consulting executive
Dodson, Donald Mills restaurant executive
Dolan, Peter Robert marketing executive
Doland, Judy Ann administrative assistant, retired financial rating company associate
Dolman, John Phillips (Tim), Jr. (Tim Dolman) communications company executive
Donovan, James Robert business equipment company executive
Dorsey, Frank James grocery company executive
Doud, Wallace C. retired information systems executive
Dowie, Ian James management consultant
Drexler, Michael David advertising agency executive
Duffy, Martin Edward management consultant, economist
Dyckman, Suzanne Barbara secretary, administrative assistant
Easton, Glenn Hanson, Jr. management and insurance consultant, federal official, naval officer
†Ecton, Donna R. business consultant
Elkind, Mort William creative and business consultant
Elliot, Jared financial management consultant
Ellis, Steven George public relations and international political consultant
Emerling, Carol G(reenbaum) consumer products company executive
Emerson, Daniel Everett retired communications company executive, executive advisor
Erb, Richard Louis Lundin resort and hotel executive
Evans, Victor Miles retired funeral home/cemetery company executive
Factor, Mallory public relations firm executive
Fajardo, Katharine Lynn public relations and marketing executive
Fay, Conner Martindale management consultant
Feld, Carole Leslie marketing executive
Feller, Robert William Andrew baseball team public relations executive, retired baseball player
Fenichel, Norman Stewart public relations and advertising agency executive
Finkelstein, Seymour business consultant
Fischmar, Richard Mayer company financial executive, consultant
Fitzpatrick, Sean Kevin advertising agency executive
Fleisher, David L. business communications and market research services executive
Fleming, Charles Clifford, Jr. retired airline and jet aircraft sales company executive
Ford, Cynthia Ann advertising executive
Forester, Jean Martha Brouillette innkeeper, retired librarian and educator
Forster, Ann Dorothy publicist
Fort, Randall Martin corporate executive, former federal official
Fortier, D'Iberville communications consultant
Fortinberry, Glen W. advertising executive
Frankfurt, Stephen O. advertising agency executive
Freeman, Ralph Carter management consultant
Freter, Mark Allen marketing and public relations executive, consultant
Furman, Harry Sutton lumber distribution company executive
Gendell, Gerald Stanleigh retired public affairs executive
Gershel, Seth David sales executive
Gilford, Leon business executive and consultant
Gillett, George Nield, Jr. communications executive
Glass, Kenneth Edward management consultant
†Glassman, Stanley Alan health care management consultant
Gluys, Charles Byron retired marketing management consultant
Goldberg, Victor Joel retired data processing company executive
Goldman, Alfred Emanuel marketing research consultant
Gordon, Janine M. advertising agency executive
Gottlieb, Alan Merril advertising, fundraising and broadcasting executive, writer
Grace, Marcia Bell advertising executive
Gray, John Lathrop, III retired advertising agency executive
Greenfield, Helen Meyers inspection and testing service executive, publishing company executive, real estate executive
Greenway, John Selmes hotel owner
Groome, Reginald Kehnroth hotel executive
Gruber, Thomas A. marketing executive
Gschwind, Donald management and engineering consultant
Gumpert, Gustav public relations executive
Gunderson, Ted Lee security consultant
Gunn, George R., Jr. advertising executive
Gurwitch, Arnold Andrew communications executive
†Hadden, Earl French consultant, information technology
Haegele, John Ernest business executive
Haeger, Phyllis Marianna retired association management company executive
Hairston, John Thomas, Jr. food retail executive
Half, Robert personnel recruiting executive, author
Hall, Adrienne Ann international marketing executive
Hamilton, Thomas Michael marketing executive
Hamlin, Sonya B. communications specialist
Hardy, Clarence Earl, Jr. human resources executive
Harris, Gregory Scott management services executive
Harris, Nell H. retired public relations executive, real estate broker, writer
Harris, Robert Norman advertising and communications educator
Harris, William John retired management holding company executive, consultant
Hawkins, Lawrence Charles management consultant, educator
Hayes, Gladys Lucille Allen community care official, poet, writer
Hayes, Janet Gray retired business manager, former mayor
Hewitt, James J. retired credit corporation executive
Hiatt, Robert Nelson consumer products executive
Hirsh, Norman Barry management consultant
Hite, Elinor Kirkland oil company human resources manager
Hock, Morton entertainment advertising executive
Hollis, William S. management consultant
Hooper, Gerry Don information systems professional, consultant
Hoover, William R(ay) computer service company executive
Hudnut, David Beecher retired leasing company executive, lawyer
Illson, James Elias management consultant
Isaac, Steven Richard advertising executive
Jacobsen, Arthur business and financial consultant
Jankus, Alfred Peter retired international management and marketing consultant
Jernstedt, Richard Don public relations executive
Joanou, Phillip advertising executive
Johnson, Mary Elizabeth Susan health care planner
Johnston, Thomas John management consultant
Jones, Regina Nickerson public relations executive
Kampmeier, Curtis Neil management consultant
Kaprielian, Walter advertising executive
Karalis, John Peter computer company executive, lawyer
Karp, David communications executive, writer
Keller, Paul advertising agency executive
King, William Douglas retired executive
Kirschenmann, Henry George, Jr. management consultant, former government official, accountant
Klein, Charlotte Conrad public relations executive
Knipp, Helmut hospitality industry executive
Koelling, Herbert Lee printing company executive
Korda, Reva advertising executive, writer
Korgaonkar, Pradeep Kashinath marketing educator
Korwek, Alexander Donald management consultant
Krakow, Amy Ginzig advertising and marketing executive, writer
†Kramer, Peter Robin computer company executive
Kuhn, James Paul management consultant
Kushner, Harvey David management consultant
Lacey, John William Charles management consultant
Lamalie, Robert Eugene retired executive search company executive
Lamattina, Lawrence E. advertising agency executive
Lantz, Kenneth Eugene consulting firm executive
Larson, Mel retired hotel facility executive, corporate executive, helicopter pilot
Lavidge, Robert James marketing research executive
Lawrence, Zan computer consultant
Lee, William Chien-Yeh communications executive, educator
Leff, Ilene J(oan) management consultant, corporate and goverment executive
Lehman, Christopher M. international business consultant
Leizear, Charles William retired information services executive
Levy, Arthur James public relations executive, writer
Linda, Gerald advertising and marketing executive
Lipman, Ira Ackerman security service company executive
Littman, Earl advertising and public relations executive
Livingston, Thomas Mathias advertising agency executive, writer
Locke, Norton hotel management and construction company executive
Lockwood, Robert W. management consultant
Love, Rodney J. food distribution executive
Lowrie, Walter Olin management consultant
Lubinsky, Menachem Yechiel communications executive
Makepeace, Darryl Lee consulting company executive
Mallenbaum, Allan Eliyahu marketing executive
Mangan, Frank Thomas advertising executive
Manley, John Hugo computing technology executive, educator
†Marinaccio, Paul John, Jr. marketing executive, writer
Marks, Russell Edward, Jr. management consultant
Marple, Gary Andre management consultant
Martin, Edwin William, Jr. pharmaceutical marketing consultant, copywriter
Mason, William Randy sales executive
McArdle, John Edward management consultant
†McCarthy, Joseph W. motel chain executive
McCullough, R. Michael management consultant
Mc Kay, Dean Raymond computer company executive
Mc Kinney, David E(wing) information processing products company executive
McWilliams, Bruce Wayne marketing professional
Meads, Donald Edward management services company executive
Melsheimer, Mel P(owell) consumer products business executive
Melvin, Daniel Sean radio station executive

Metz, Frank Andrew, Jr. *data processing executive*
Mickelson, Elliot Spencer *quality assurance professional*
Miller, Joseph Edward, Jr. *media company executive*
Moeller, Robert John *management consultant*
Mogelever, Bernard *public relations executive*
Moore, Richard Earl *communications creative director*
Moritz, Charles Worthington *business information and services company executive*
Mortimer, Doyle Moss *business consultant, state legislator, business owner*
Mulcahy, Robert Edward *management consultant*
Musial, Stan(ley) (Frank Musial) *hotel and restaurant executive, former baseball team executive, former baseball player*
Myhren, Trygve Edward *communications company executive*
Newman, Sheldon Oscar *computer company executive*
Nicklaus, Charles Edward *sales training executive*
Niemann, Lewis Keith *lamp manufacturing company executive*
Nolan, Kathleen D. *public relations executive*
Norlander, John Allen *hotel executive*
Norton, Nathaniel Goodwin *marketing executive*
Novas, Joseph, Jr. *advertising agency executive*
O'Connor, Mary Scranton *public relations executive*
O'Connor, Richard Donald *advertising company executive*
Olson, Kenneth Harvey *computer company executive*
Oppenheimer, Joseph *infosystems consultant, television producer*
Opperman, Danny Gene *packaging professional, consultant*
Osmer-McQuade, Margaret *business executive, broadcast journalist*
Ostfeld, Leonard S. *computer company executive*
O'Sullivan, Paul Kevin *business executive, management and instructional systems consultant*
Owen, John Laverty *human resources executive, consultant*
Owens, Charles Vincent, Jr. *diagnostic company executive and consultant*
Parsons, Irene *management consultant*
Paul, Frank *retired consulting company executive*
Paul, Gordon Wilbur *marketing educator*
Perlov, Dadie *management consultant, association executive*
Petrie, John Richard *advertising agency executive, writer*
Pew, Thomas W., Jr. *advertising executive*
Philippi, Ervin William *mortician*
Phillips, Gabriel *travel marketing executive*
Phillips, George Michael *communications executive*
Phillips, John David *communications executive*
Plumb, Pamela Pelton *consulting company executive, former mayor and councilwoman*
Posner, Kenneth Robert *hotel corporation executive*
Post, Richard Bennett *retired human resources executive*
Potter, James Earl *retired international hotel management company executive*
Prather, Gerald Luther *management consultant, retired air force officer, judge*
Pressman, Thane Andrew *consumer products executive*
Preston, Richard McCann *creative company executive, writer*
Prokopis, Emmanuel Charles *communications company executive*
Puryear, Alvin Nelson *management educator*
Quinnan, Edward Michael *management consultant*
Ralston, Joanne Smoot *public relations counseling firm executive*
Rampen, Leonardus Eduard *broadcasting company executive*
Rasor, Dina Lynn *investigator, journalist*
Reade, Robert Mellor *advertising consultant, retired convenience store executive*
Reid, Michael J. *international management consultant and educator*
Reynolds, John Charles *communications company executive, management consultant*
Rhein, Murray Harold *management consultant*
Robins, Norman Alan *strategic planning consultant, former steel company executive*
Robinson, Linda Gosden *communications executive*
Robison, James Everett *management consulting company executive*
Rosen, Arthur Marvin *advertising executive*
Rosenfield, James Harold *communications executive*
Rosenthal, William Forshaw *advertising executive*
Roth, Richard J. *marketing and advertising consulant*
Rountree, Neva Dixon *public relations executive*
Ryan, John William, Jr. *construction-related consulting company executive*
Saffir, Leonard *public relations executive*
Salzman, Marilyn B. Wolfson *service company executive*
Samuels, Cynthia Kalish *communications executive*
Sanders, William George *public relations executive*
Sands, I. Jay *corporate executive, business, marketing and real estate consultant, lecturer, realtor, analyst*
Savage, Neve Richard *marketing executive*
Sayer, John Samuel *retired information systems consultant*
Schein, Harvey L. *communications executive*
Schmutz, Charles Reid *university foundation executive*
Schoen, Linda Allen *public affairs administrator*
Schrager, James E. *financial company executive, educator*
Schreckinger, Sy Edward *advertising executive, consultant*
Schulberg, Jay William *advertising agency executive*
†Schulstad, Eugene P. *computer company executive*
†Schulte, Richard Frank *marketing company executive*
Schuster, Gary Francis *corporate relations specialist, former news correspondent*
Schwartz, Stephen Blair *retired information industry executive*
Schweickart, Jim *advertising executive, broadcast consultant*
†Schweig, Margaret Berris *meeting and special events consultant*
Sease, Gene Elwood *public relations company executive*
Seelig, Gerard Leo *management consultant*
Semerad, Roger Dale *management consultant*
Shafran, Hank *public relations agency executive*
Shanas, Bert Z. *public relations executive, journalist*
Shapiro, Richard Charles *sales and marketing executive*
Sharlach, Jeffrey Roy *marketing company executive*
Shaw, Jerome *computer executive*
Sheeline, Paul Cushing *hotel executive*
Shelton, Karl Mason *management consultant*
Shields, John Joseph *computer manufacturing executive*
Shoup, Harold Arthur *advertising executive*
Simecka, Betty Jean *convention and visitors bureau executive*
Sincoff, Michael Z. *human resources and marketing professional*
†Singer, David Michael *marketing and public relations company executive*
Sinicropi, Anthony Vincent *industrial relations and human resources educator*
Slott, Phil *advertising agency executive*
Smith, Barbara Anne *healthcare management company consultant*
Smith, Darwin Eatna *lawyer, retired manufacturing executive*
Smith, Donald Nickerson *food service executive*
Smith, Thomas Winston *cotton marketing executive*
Snoddon, Larry Erle *public relations executive*
Sollender, Joel David *management consultant, financial executive*
Souveroff, Vernon William, Jr. *corporate executive, investor, author*
Spirn, Michele Sobel *communications professional, writer*
Spittler, Jayne Zenaty *advertising executive*
Sroge, Maxwell Harold *marketing consultant, publishing executive*
Stans, Maurice Hubert *retired business consultant, former government official*
Stefano, Ross William *business executive*
Steinback, Kenneth B. *computer sales company executive*
†Steiner, William *direct marketing advertising agency executive, consultant*
Stengel, Ronald Francis *management consultant*
†Stevens, Berton Louis, Jr. *data processing manager*
Stewart, Marsha Beach *sales executive, entertainment executive*
Stewart, Richard Alfred *business executive*
Stromberg, Arthur Harold *retired professional services company executive*
Stults, Walter Black *management consultant, former trade organization executive*
Sullivan, William Courtney *retired communications executive*
Tachmindji, Alexander John *systems engineering consultant*
Tarr, Curtis W. *business executive*
Teichroew, Daniel *information science educator*
Thomas, Martha Wetterhall *advertising agency executive*
Thompson, Chester Franklin *advertising executive*
Thompson, Richard Stephen *management consultant*
Tisdale, Stuart Williams *holding company executive*
Todea, Rockling *organizational development consultant*
Toevs, Alden Louis *management consultant*
Tomas, Jerold F. V. *business executive, management consultant*
Transou, Lynda Lew *advertising executive*
Travisano, Frank Peter *professional management consultant/business broker*
Triolo, Peter *advertising agency executive, marketing educator, consultant*
Troy, B. Theodore *direct mail advertising executive*
Tutwiler, Margaret DeBardeleben *communications executive*
Tytler, Linda Jean *communications and public affairs executive, retired state legislator*
Uehlinger, John Clark *marketing executive*
Unger, Sonja Franz *package company executive, travel consultant, ceramist*
Ussery, Luanne *communications consultant*
Vajeeprasee Thongsak, Thomas *business planning executive*
Vander Wiel, Kenneth Carlton *computer services company executive*
Van Horn, Lecia Joseph *legal secretary*
Verret, John Cyril *advertising executive*
Virgo, Julie Anne Carroll *management consultant*
Wadley, M. Richard *consumer products executive*
Wagner, Richard *business executive, former baseball team executive*
Walker, Henry Gilbert *health care executive, consultant*
Walsh, William Albert *management consultant, former naval officer*
Walter, John Robert *printing company executive*
Weise, Theodore Lewis *delivery service executive*
Weismantel, Gregory Nelson *management consultant and software executive*
Weiss, William Lee *retired communications executive*
Wheeler, George Charles *quality assurance professional*
Whitmer, Joseph Morton *benefits consulting firm executive, retired*
Wiley, David Owen *public relations executive*
Will, Mari Maseng *communications consultant*
Williams, Earle Carter *retired professional services company executive*
Williams, Louis Clair, Jr. *public relations executive*
Willig, Karl Victor *computer firm executive*
Willis, Gary K. *computer company executive*
Wolf, William Martin *computer company executive, consultant*
Worth, Gary James *communications executive*
Wright, Linda Jean *government relations executive*
Yocam, Delbert Wayne *communication company executive*
Zeller, Joseph Paul *advertising executive*
Zinnen, Robert Oliver *general management executive*
Zizza, Salvatore J. *diversified company executive*
Zoellick, Robert Bruce *corporate executive, lawyer*
Zuckerman, Martin Harvey *personnel director*
Zweifel, Donald Edwin *automobile dealer, civic affairs volunteer*

INDUSTRY: TRADE

UNITED STATES

ALABAMA

Birmingham
Garrison, Paul F. *retail executive*
George, Frank Wade *small business owner, antiquarian book dealer*
Hess, Emil Carl *retail apparel company executive*
Hubbard, Kenneth Earl *retail executive*
Pizitz, Richard Alan *retail and real estate group executive*
Wabler, Robert Charles, II *retail and distribution executive*

Mobile
Delchamps, Randolph *grocery store executive*

Montgomery
†Klein, Richard Lee *wholesale pharmaceutical executive*

Pelham
†Walker, William W, III *wholesale distribution executive*

Tuscaloosa
Blackburn, John Leslie *small business owner*

ALASKA

Anchorage
Cairns, John J(oseph) *retail executive*
Vandergriff, Jerry Dodson *computer store executive*

Wrangell
†Sturtevant, Margaret D. *retail executive*

ARIZONA

Phoenix
Zine, Larry Joseph *retail executive*

Scottsdale
McGaw, Kenneth Roy *wholesale distribution executive*

Tucson
Wood, Evelyn Nielsen *reading dynamics business executive*

ARKANSAS

Bentonville
Bruce, Robert Thomas *retail executive*
Carter, Paul R. *retail executive*
Coughlin, Thomas Martin *wholesale goods company executive*
Dietzman, Leslie *retail executive*
Fields, Bill *discount department stores executive*
Gildehaus, Roger Lee *retail company executive*
Glass, David D. *department store company executive, professional baseball team executive*
Gorman, David H. *retail company executive*
Martin, Bobby L. *retail corporation executive*
Shewmaker, Jack Clifford *retired retail executive, rancher, consultant*
Walton, S. Robson *discount department store chain executive*
White, Nicholas J. *retail company executive*

Hot Springs National Park
Tanenbaum, Bernard Jerome, Jr. *corporate executive*

Little Rock
Dillard, William, II *department store chain executive*
Dillard, William T. *department store chain executive*
Long, Walter Edward *international trade company executive, consultant*

CALIFORNIA

Anaheim
†Abramson, Norman *retail executive*
Brownhill, H. Bud *small business owner, canine behavior therapist*

Arcadia
Stangeland, Roger Earl *retail chain store executive*

Berkeley
Alpert, Norman Joseph *merchandising executive*

Beverly Hills
Orenstein, (Ian) Michael *philatelic dealer, columnist*

Big Bear Lake
Essman, Robert Norvel *small business owner, graphics designer*

Brisbane
Orban, Kurt *foreign trade company executive*

Burbank
Brankovich, Mark J. *restaurateur*
Droz, Henry *distribution company executive*

Cathedral City
Jackman, Robert Alan *retail executive*

Cerritos
†Webb, Lewis M. *retail executive*

Colton
Brown, Jack H. *supermarket company executive*

Compton
Allumbaugh, Byron *grocery company executive*
Willmott, Peter Sherman *retail executive*

Dublin
Cope, Kenneth Wayne *chain store executive*
Del Santo, Lawrence A. *retail merchandising company executive*
Prince, Jimmie Dan *retail food chain executive*

El Segundo
Pickett, Michael D. *computer hardware and software distributor*

Emeryville
Weaver, Velather Edwards (Val Weaver) *small business owner*

Folsom
Whitmire, Melburn G. *pharmaceutical distribution company executive*

Fountain Valley
Smith, Marie Edmonds *real estate agent, property manager*

Fresno
Blum, Gerald Henry *department store executive*

Fullerton
Svinos, John Georgios *software consulting firm executive*

Garden Grove
Virgo, Muriel Agnes *swimming school owner*

Irvine
Hoshi, Katsuo Kai *international business executive*

Irwindale
Hughes, Roger K. *dairy and grocery store company executive*

Los Alamitos
†Egas, Sandy Steers *import/export and travel consultant*

Los Angeles
Haas, Edward Lee *business executive, consultant*
Hawley, Philip Metschan *retired retail executive, consultant*
Hecht, Harold Michael *retail executive*
Roeder, Richard Kenneth *business owner, lawyer*
Rosenthal, Stuart A. *retail executive*
Seigel, Daniel A. *retail executive*
Sinay, Joseph *retail executive*
†Stanton, Eric *wholesale distribution executive*
Tuthill, Walter Warren *retail executive*
Underwood, Vernon O., Jr. *grocery stores executive*
Wilkerson, Kenneth L. *retail department stores executive*
Williams, Theodore Earle *industrial distribution company executive*

Mc Kinleyville
Morris, Marjorie Hale *retail executive, appraiser, artist, writer*

Menlo Park
Katz, Robert Lee *business executive*

Milpitas
Latimer, Linda Gay *small business owner*

Modesto
Piccinini, Robert M. *grocery store chain executive*
Sprinkle, Charles Ray *wholesale grocery company executive*

Monrovia
Jemelian, John Nazar *merchant, financial executive*

Newark
Ferber, Norman Alan *retail executive*
Moldaw, Stuart G. *venture capitalist, retail clothing stores executive*

Oakland
Albers, William Marion *retail food distribution executive*
Davis, Roderick William *retail executive*
Dunn, David Cameron *entrepreneur, business executive*
Gantt, M. Dean *retail food company executive*
Hoopes, Lorenzo Neville *former retailing executive*
Jacobus, Russell Lee *retail store executive*
Ludwig, LeRoy Frank *retail store executive*
Marshall, George Dwire *supermarket chain executive*
Totman, Patrick Steven *lawyer, retail executive*

Pacific Palisades
Diehl, Richard Kurth *retail business consultant*

Palos Verdes Peninsula
Slayden, James Bragdon *retired department store executive*

Port Hueneme
Pathak, Sunit Rawly *business owner, consultant, journalist*

Sacramento
Collings, Charles LeRoy *supermarket executive*
McFarlane, William F. *wholesale nut company executive*

San Bernardino
Sagmeister, Edward Frank *small business owner, career officer, consultant*

San Diego
Lynn, Mitchell Gordon *retail company executive*
Monson, Forrest Truman *shop owner, clergyman*

San Francisco
Daniels, Alfred Harvey *merchandising executive*
Dean, Norman Emerson (Ned Dean) *coffee company executive*
†Drexler, Millard S. *retail executive*
Fisher, Donald G. *casual apparel chain stores executive*
Fromm, Alfred *distributing company executive*
Goldstein, Joyce Esersky *restaurant owner*
Handler, Mark S. *retail executive*
Seelenfreund, Alan *distribution company executive*
Simone, Thomas B. *distribution company executive*
Ullman, Myron Edward, III *retail executive*

San Jose
Finnigan, Robert Emmet *business owner*
Mc Connell, John Douglas *retail corporation executive, owner*

San Juan Capistrano
Purdy, Alan MacGregor *financial executive*

San Marcos
Radder, Bruce Milton *business owner*

San Marino
Meyer, William Danielson *retired department store executive*

Santa Ana
Fitzgerald, Robert Lynn *small business owner*
Shahin, Thomas John *dry cleaning wholesale supply company executive*

Santa Barbara
Lynch, Martin Andrew *retail company executive*

Stockton
Simon, Karen Jordan *retail executive*

Torrance
Kwiker, Louis A. *business executive*

Van Nuys
†Sofro, Barney *retail executive*

Walnut Creek
Combs, William G. *drug retailing company executive*
Jones, Ebon Richard *retail executive*
Long, Robert Merrill *retail drug company executive*
Plomgren, Ronald Arthur *retail executive*
Wolcott, Oliver Dwight *international trading company executive*

West Sacramento
†Teel, James E. *supermarket and drug store retail executive*
†Teel, Joyce *supermarket and drugstore retail executive*

Woodland Hills
†Wasserman, Gerald B. *wholesale distribution executive*
†Weider, Joseph *wholesale distribution executive*

COLORADO

Aurora
Magalnick, Elliott Ben *retail medical supply company executive*

Boulder
Johnson, Maryanna Morse *business owner*
McKenzie, James Milton *excavating company executive*

Colorado Springs
Macon, Jerry Lyn *software company owner, software publisher*
Noyes, Richard Hall *bookseller*

Denver
Davis, Joseph Samuel *retired department store executive, consultant*
Green, Steven J. *retail executive*

Englewood
Blair, Stewart D. *small business owner*

Evergreen
Baxter, Millie McLean *business owner, educator*

CONNECTICUT

Cheshire
Bozzuto, Michael Adam *wholesale grocery company executive*

Greenwich
Goodman, Lawrence Baron *retail executive*
Pivirotto, Richard Roy *former retail executive*
Tournillon, Nicholas Brady *trade finance, international investments company executive*

Hartford
Goodwin, Rodney Keith Grove *international bank and trade company executive*

New Britain
†Davidson, Phillip Thomas *retail company executive*

New London
Lumadue, Donald Dean *hobby and crafts company executive*

Norwalk
Bennett, Carl *retired discount department store executive*
†Cheifetz, David S. *small business owner*

Rocky Hill
Hollis, Peter B. *retail executive*
Reese, Paul Wesley, Jr. *retail executive*

Stamford
Quinnell, Bruce Andrew *retail book chain executive*
Rickard, Norman Edward *office equipment company executive*
Steinberg, Burt *retail executive*

Suffield
Leavitt, Julian J. *wholesale food company executive*

Weston
Thorner, Peter *retail executive*

Westport
McCaig, Joseph J. *retail food chain executive*
Wexler, Herbert Ira *retail company executive*

DELAWARE

Wilmington
Nichols, David L. *retail executive*

DISTRICT OF COLUMBIA

Washington
Aires, Randolf H. *retail company executive*
Cohen, Israel *chain store executive*
Gordon, Shana *trade company executive*
Liebes, Raquel *import/export company executive, educator*
Malcolm, Ellen Reighley *small business owner*
McAllister, Patricia Anne *retail company executive*
Merchant, Carl William, II *retail executive*
Mulligan, Robert J. *retail store executive, accountant*
Pelavin, Diane Christine *small business owner, research analyst*
Rosensweig, Stanley Harold *retail executive*
Sievers, Robert H. *wholesale distributing company executive*
Singer, Thomas Kenyon *international business consultant, farmer*
Smith, Jack Carl *foreign trade consultant*
Wurtzel, Alan Leon *retail company executive*

FLORIDA

Boca Raton
Africk, Jack *duty free company executive*
Elliott, Robert M., Jr. *retail executive*

Bradenton
Beall, Robert Matthews, II *retail chain executive*

Clearwater
Hoornstra, Edward H. *retail company executive*
Turley, Stewart *retail company executive*

Deerfield Beach
Moran, Patricia Genevieve *corporate executive*

Fort Lauderdale
Hayes, Peter John *retail executive*

Gainesville
Steadham, Charles Victor, Jr. *entertainment agent, producer*

Hialeah
Wolter, Duane Roland *retail executive*

Highland Beach
Frager, Albert S. *retired retail food company executive*

Homestead
†Risi, Louis J., Jr. *business executive*

Interlachen
Hoffman, Edward Richard, III (Dick Hoffman) *retail and manufacturing executive*

Jacksonville
Kufeldt, James *retail grocery store executive*
Mann, Timothy *corporate executive*
McCook, Richard Paul *grocery chain financial executive*
McKellar, C. H. *grocery chain executive*

Lakeland
Jenkins, Charles H., Jr. *grocery company executive*

Largo
Boyle, John William *retail executive*

Longboat Key
Goldsmith, Jack Landman *former retail company executive*

Marco Island
Lesser, Joseph M. *retired business executive, retail store executive*

Miami
†Chaplin, Harvey *wine and liquor wholesale executive*

Mount Dora
Edgerton, Richard *restaurant and hotel owner*

Naples
Scarlett, Harold O. *retired retail executive, consultant*

Orlando
†Kindlund, Newton C. *retail executive*

Palm Bay
Jurgevich, Nancy J. *retail executive, educator*

Palm Beach
Black, Leonard Julius *retail store consultant*

Palm Beach Gardens
Brackett, Sally Lee Martin *small business owner*

Sanibel
Perkinson, Diana Agnes Zouzelka *import company executive*

Sarasota
Meyer, B. Fred *small business executive, home designer and builder, product designer*

Tampa
Floto, Ronald John *supermarket executive*

Winter Haven
Lansdale, Daryl L. *retail executive*

GEORGIA

Atlanta
Allen, Ivan, Jr. *office products company owner*
Brill, Ronald Mitchel *retail executive*
Haverty, Rawson *retail furniture company executive*
Kalafut, George Wendell *distribution company executive, retired naval officer*
†LeClercq, Jacques Jean *retail grocery executive*
Marcus, Bernard *retail executive*
Moderow, Joseph Robert *package distribution company executive*
Roney, Shirley Fletcher *retail company executive*
Ross, E. Dennis *retail executive*
†Watts, Robert *wholesale distribution executive*

Covington
Penland, John Thomas *import/export and development companies executive*

Smyrna
Head, John Francis, Jr. *distributing company executive*

HAWAII

Hanalei
Ching, Lawrence Lin Tai *retail executive*

Honolulu
Niles, Geddes Leroy *private investigator*

Kahului
Piros, Cecille Patao *business owner*

IDAHO

Boise
Carley, John Blythe *retail grocery executive*
Connolly, David I. *retail executive*
Michael, Gary G. *retail supermarket and drug chain executive*
Rudd, Gerald Ray *retail food and drug company executive*
Shaver, Carl Hutchens *retail executive*
Walk, Ronald Douglas *retail grocery chain executive*

Post Falls
Chamberlain, Barbara Kaye *small business owner*

ILLINOIS

Arlington Heights
Johnson, Clifford R. *retired retail executive, consultant*

Barrington
Rechtsteiner, Steven Allen *import/export company executive*

Bensenville
Lewis, Darrell L. *retail executive*

Chicago
†Andrews, Bernard W. *retail company executive*
Baloun, John Charles *wholesale grocery company executive*
Bergel, Richard *department store chain executive*
Bookshester, Dennis Steven *retail company executive*
Brennan, Bernard Francis *retail chain store executive*
Brennan, Edward A. *merchandising, insurance and real estate executive*
†Christianson, Stanley David *corporate executive*
Condon, Edward John, Jr. *retail and financial services executive*
Dehmlow, Louis Henry Theodore *wholesale and distribution company executive*
Doolittle, Sidney Newing *retail executive*
Flick, Warren Edmond *retail executive*
Gingiss, Benjamin Jack *retired formal clothing stores executive*
Goldstein, Alfred George *retail executive*
Haselton, Forrest Ronald *retail company executive*
Kahn, Harold *retail executive*
Kasenter, Robert Albert *retail executive*
Kroch, Carl Adolph *retail executive*
†Menzer, John Bruce *financial executive*
Meyer, Charles Appleton *former retailing executive*
Norum, David P. *retail company executive*
Parsons, John Russell *retail company executive*
Pavik, Malvin A. *department stores executive*
Piccirilli, Robert James, Jr. *small business owner*
Reice, Charles Thomas *department store, food service and lodging executive*
Shute, David *retail executive, lawyer*
Telling, Edward Riggs *former retail, insurance, real estate and financial services executive*
Vrablik, Edward Robert *import/export company executive*
Williams, Thurmon *retail company executive*
Wood, Arthur MacDougall *retired retail executive*

Decatur
Cain, Richard Duane *small business owner*

Deerfield
Hunter, Charles David *retail company executive*
Jorndt, Louis Daniel *retail drug store chain executive*
Walgreen, Charles Rudolph, III *retail store executive*

Des Plaines
Schmidt, Robert L. *export company executive*

Elgin
Butera, Paul *retail grocery company executive*
Seigle, Harry Jay *building supply company executive*

Glencoe
Nebenzahl, Kenneth *rare book and map dealer, author*

Hinsdale
Hodnik, David F. *retail company executive*
Rinder, George Greer *retired retail company executive*
Shea, John J. *catalog and retail company executive*
†Wisniewski, Henry George *wholesale distribution executive*
Withers, Alton Merrill *retail store executive*

Hoffman Estates
Baffico, Paul Anthony *retail executive*
Saunders, Eric Don *retail company executive*

Lake Forest
Stirling, Ellen Adair *retail executive*

Melrose Park
Di Matteo, Dominick, Jr. *supermarket chain executive*

Morton Grove
McKenna, Andrew James *paper distribution and printing company executive, baseball club executive*

Naperville
Schultz, Theodore Edward *retail executive*
†Wake, William S. *wholesale distribution executive*

Northbrook
Segal, Gordon I. *retail executive*

Northlake
Jasper, Paul Tucker *food company executive*

Oak Brook
Peterson, Roger Eric *hardware wholesale company executive*

Quincy
†Niemann, Richard Henry *grocery executive*

Rolling Meadows
Mynatt, John Rupert, Jr. *soft drink bottling executive*

Schaumburg
Kadish, Steven A. *retail executive*
Rashkow, Ronald *home improvement company executive*

Skokie
Grainger, David William *distribution company executive*

Sumner
Trent, Wendell Campbell *business owner*

Vernon Hills
Ferkenhoff, Robert J. *retail executive*

Wheeling
†Burrows, George J. *wholesale distribution executive*

Wilmette
Mc Nitt, Willard Charles *business executive*
Williams, Emory *former retail company executive, banker*

Winnetka
Weldon, Theodore Tefft, Jr. *retail company executive*

INDIANA

Elkhart
†Snyder, James R. *wholesale distribution executive, textiles executive*

Fort Wayne
Curtis, Douglas Homer *small business owner*
McClelland, Michael *wholesale distribution executive*
†Reitz, William *supermarket company executive*

Indianapolis
Dougherty, Douglas Wayne *retail executive*
Hall, Newell J. *chain drug store company executive*
Nugent, Johnny *tractor company executive, state senator*
Peters, Garry Lowell *wholesale grocery executive*
Seitz, Melvin Christian, Jr. *distributing company executive*
Seneff, Smiley Howard *business owner*
†Smith, Eric *wholesale distribution executive*
Stout, William Jewell *department store executive*

Noblesville
Wechter, Larry Scot *retail food executive*

IOWA

Chariton
Pearson, Ronald Dale *retail food stores corporation executive*
Vredenburg, Dwight Charles *retired supermarket chain executive*

Des Moines
†McKitrick, James Thomas *retail executive*
†Roberts, Howard L. *wholesale distribution executive*

KANSAS

Hutchinson
†Smith, Steve *retail executive*

Kansas City
Baska, James Louis *wholesale grocery company executive*
Carolan, Douglas *wholesale company executive*
Phillips, Gary Lynn *wholesale grocery distribution company executive*

Shawnee Mission
Watanabe, Hirosuko *grain merchandising company executive*

Wichita
Jones, Lawrence Marion *food distribution company executive*

KENTUCKY

Louisville
Brennan, William Bernard, Jr. *small business owner*

Scottsville
Turner, Cal, Sr. (H. Calister Turner) *discount stores executive*

LOUISIANA

Bossier City
Johnson, Ruby LaVerne *retail executive*

Metairie
Ammon, James E. *retail executive*

New Orleans
Besthoff, Sydney J., III *drug store company executive*

MAINE

Falmouth
Mansfield, Kenneth Eugene *retail executive*

Freeport
Gorman, Leon A. *mail order company executive*
Poole, Norman A. *retail executive*

Scarborough
Brackett, Norman E. *retail company executive*
Farrington, Hugh G. *wholesale food and retail drug company executive*
Moody, James L., Jr. *retail food distribution company executive*

MARYLAND

Baltimore
Cullen, James Patrick *international trading company executive*
Green, Benjamin Louis *wholesale food distribution executive*
Stein, Bernard Alvin *business consultant*

Bethesda
Bucherre, Veronique *environmental company executive*

Ellicott City
Hoffberger, Jerold Charles *corporation executive*

Frederick
Anderson, William Bert *import company executive*

Gaithersburg
Nemecek, Albert Duncan, Jr. *retail company executive, investment banker, management consultant*

Hyattsville
Manos, Pete Lazaros *supermarket executive*

Jessup
†Smelkinson, Robert N. *wholesale distribution executive*

Landover
Hechinger, John Walter *hardware chain executive*

Potomac
Shapiro, Richard Gerald *retired department store executive, consultant*

MASSACHUSETTS

Amherst
Rodovich, Arlene Guyotte *administrator, small business owner*

Auburn
Baker, David Arthur *small business owner, manufacturer*

Boston
Goldberg, Avram Jacob *consulting and investing company executive, arbitrator*
Kane, Louis Isaac *merchant*
Kwasnick, Paul Jack *retail executive*
Rosenberg, Manuel *retail company executive*
Rutstein, Stanley Harold *apparel retailing company executive*

Braintree
Berman, Stanley *retail executive*
Flowers, Robert L. *retail executive*
Grossman, Everett Philip *retail executive*
†Tobin, Robert G. *supermarket chain executive*

Cambridge
Krueger, Winslow Bruce, Jr. *retail executive*

Canton
Brouillard, John Charles *retail company executive*
†Ferrera, Alfred William *food distribution company executive*
Holt, Donald Edward, Jr. *retail executive*
O'Donnell, Eugene J. *department stores executive*
†Socol, Jerry M. *retail executive*

Chestnut Hill
†Reichman, Joel H. *retail executive*

Cohasset
Lyne, Austin Francis *sporting goods business executive*

Framingham
Feldberg, Sumner Lee *retail company executive*
Wishner, Steven R. *retail executive*

Hingham
Hinkley, Clark J. *retail executive*

Holyoke
Radner, Sidney Hollis *retired rug company executive*

Marlborough
Palihnich, Nicholas Joseph, Jr. *retail chain executive*

New Bedford
Hodgson, James Stanley *antiquarian bookseller*

North Chatham
McCarthy, Joseph Harold *consultant, former retail food company executive*

Quincy
McGlinchey, Joseph Dennis *retail corporation executive*

Salem
†Rich, Howard *retail executive*

Stoughton
Cammarata, Bernard *retail company executive*

Wellesley
Anathan, James Mone, III *retail executive*
†Roche, Daniel F. *retail executive*

West Bridgewater
†Roberts, David *wholesale distribution executive*

Westminster
Moran, M. Marcus, Jr. *retail executive*

MICHIGAN

Canton
†Spitler, Kenneth F. *wholesale distribution executive*

Detroit
Borman, Paul *retail chain company executive*

Farmington
Stark, Werner E. *food broker*

Flint
Hamady, Jack Ameen *retail food company executive*

Grand Rapids
Holton, Earl D. *retail company executive*
Meijer, Douglas *retail company executive*
Meijer, Frederik *retail company executive*
Meijer, Mark *retail executive*
Morin, William Raymond *bookstore chain executive*
Quinn, Patrick Michael *wholesale food executive*

Grosse Pointe
Allen, Lee Harrison *wholesale company executive, industrial consultant*

Jackson
Fowler, John Russell *retail executive*
Rosenfeld, Mark Kenneth *retail store executive*

Lake Orion
†Brendel, Albert E. *small business owner, mechanical engineer*

Muskegon
†Bliss, David C. *retail executive*

Paw Paw
Warner, James John *small business owner*

Plymouth
Maresca, Daniel G. *retail executive*

Pontiac
Robinson, Jack Albert *retail drug stores executive*
Seeley, Fred Cooley *retail executive*

Richmond
Huvaere, Richard Floyd *auto dealer*

Saint Clair Shores
Seppala, Katherine Seaman (Mrs. Leslie W. Seppala) *retail company executive*

Troy
Antonini, Joseph E. *discount department store executive*
Carlson, David Martin *retail executive*
†Chinni, Charles Ross *retail executive*
†Perkins, Donald S. *department store chain executive*
Strome, Stephen *distribution company executive*
Thomas, Joseph R. *retail chain stores executive*

MINNESOTA

Eden Prairie
Morrissey, John Edward *wholesale grocery company executive*

Edina
Emmerich, Karol Denise *former retail company executive, consultant*

Hopkins
Beeler, Donald Daryl *retail executive*

Long Lake
Lurton, H. William *retired retail executive*

Minneapolis
Dabill, Phillip Alvin *wholesale foods executive*
Gilpin, Larry Vincent *retail executive*
Heider, David Arthur *hardware wholesale company executive*
Macke, Kenneth A. *retail executive*
Mammel, Russell Norman *retired food distribution company executive*
Markopoulos, Andrew John *retail executive*
†St Germain, George *retail executive*
Stodder, John Wesley *jewelry company executive*
Trestman, Frank D. *distribution company executive*
†Ulrich, Robert J. *retail discount chain stores executive*
Wright, Michael William *wholesale food company executive*

Minnetonka
Eugster, Jack Wilson *retail executive*

Plymouth
Froemming, Herbert Dean *retail executive*

Saint Paul
Nash, Nicholas David *retailing executive*

MISSISSIPPI

Indianola
Crouse, Ted *grocery company executive*

Jackson
Holman, William Henry, Jr. *retail executive*
McCarty, William Bonner, Jr. *retail grocery executive*

MISSOURI

Chesterfield
Upbin, Hal Jay *consumer products executive*

Columbia
Pugh, Robert Kenneth *textbook distributing company executive*

Cuba
Work, Bruce Van Syoc *business consultant*

Hazelwood
Mohrmann, Robert E. *wholesale distribution executive*
Seitz, Harold A. *supermarket executive*
†Wetterau, Theodore C. *diversified food wholesaler*

Kansas City
Frigon, Henry Frederick *diversified company executive*
Stanley, David *retail company executive*

Saint Charles
Dauphinais, George Arthur *import company executive*

Saint Louis
Battram, Richard L. *retail executive*
Bridgewater, Bernard Adolphus, Jr. *footwear company executive*
Crutsinger, Robert Keane *diversified food wholesale company executive*
Edison, Bernard Alan *retired retail apparel company executive*
Farrell, David Coakley *department store executive*
Loeb, Jerome Thomas *retail executive*
Newman, Andrew Edison *retail executive*
Newman, Eric Pfeiffer *retail chain store executive*
†Richey, Donald L. *retail executive*
Schnuck, Craig *grocery stores company executive*
Sneider, Martin Karl *retail company executive*
Williams, Frank James, Jr. *department store chain executive, lawyer*

Saint Peters
Krey, Mary Ann Reynolds *beer wholesaler executive*

Sibley
Morrow, Elizabeth *business owner, sculptress, museum association administrator, educator*

MONTANA

Billings
Marcovitz, Leonard Edward *retail executive*

Helena
Brown, Jan Whitney *small business owner*

NEBRASKA

Herman
Korshoj, Franklin Delano *retail lumberyard owner*

Lincoln
Rawley, Ann Keyser *small business owner, picture framer*

Omaha
Ramm, Richard W. *retail executive*

Wymore
Meyer, Melvin A. *lumber and hardware executive, freelance designer*

NEVADA

Las Vegas
Ackerman, H. Don *automotive dealership executive*
Fehr, Gregory Paris *marketing and distribution company executive*

NEW HAMPSHIRE

Hampton
Coviello, Robert Frank *retail executive*

New Castle
Friese, George Ralph *retail executive*

North Hampton
Goldberger, Stephen A. *retail stores executive*

North Salem
†Stone, Robert Eldred *small business owner, museum director*

NEW JERSEY

Basking Ridge
Echikson, Richard *retail consultant*

Camden
Edgerton, Brenda Evans *soup company executive, treasurer*

Carteret
Didieo, James *sporting goods stores executive*
Timinski, Robert *sporting goods store executive*

Chatham
Manning, Frederick William *retired retail executive*

Cherry Hill
Lamm, Harvey H. *foreign car and parts importer*

Edison
Burke, James *wholesale executive*
Lubetkin, Charles Schiller *retail executive*

Elizabeth
Gellert, George Geza *food importing company executive*

Englewood Cliffs
Brandreth, John Breckenridge, II *chemical importer*

Freehold
Foster, Eric H., Jr. *retail executive*

Hackensack
Walsh, Joseph Michael *magazine distribution executive*

Lyndhurst
†Rim, B. C. *wholesale distribution executive, retail executive*

Montvale
O'Gorman, Peter Joseph *retail company executive*
Rowe, James W. *food chain executive*
Ulrich, Robert Gardner *retail food chain executive, lawyer*
Wood, James *supermarket executive*

New Monmouth
Donnelly, Gerard Kevin *retail executive*

Newark
†Stavitsky, Jeffrey *wholesale distribution executive*

Oakhurst
Seltzer, Ronald *retail company executive*

Paramus
Goldstein, Michael *retail executive*
Lazarus, Charles *retail toy company executive*
Nakasone, Robert C. *retail toy and game company executive*
Stone, Lawrence *retail executive*

Secaucus
Fisher, Herbert *retail executive*
Lazarus, Arlie Gary *retail corporate executive*
Rockland, Barry Clifford *retail financial executive*
Zorn, Eric Stuart *retail department store chain executive*

Short Hills
Brous, Philip *retail consultant*

Totowa
Badke, Ronald E. *retail shoe company executive*
Solomon, Edward David *chain store executive*

Verona
Brightman, Robert Lloyd *importer, textile company executive, consultant*

Whippany
Curwin, Ronald *home equipment stores executive*

Woodbridge
Futterman, Jack *retail executive*

NEW MEXICO

Albuquerque
Friederich, Jan *retail grocery executive*

NEW YORK

Bronx
Hankin, Leonard J. *merchant*

Brooklyn
Shulman, Max L. *corporate executive*
Zelin, Jerome *retail executive*

Buffalo
Barcelona, Charles B. *wholesale food company executive*

Nanula, Savino P. *supermarket and convenience store company executive*
Petrocco, William Patrick *retail executive*

Canandaigua
†Sands, Richard E. *food products executive*

Endicott
Murray, Charles Coursen *footwear manufacturing and retail company executive*

Florida
Madera, Cornelius J. J., Jr. *supermarket chain executive, lawyer, mayor*
Mench, John William *retail store executive, electrical engineer*
Rosenberg, A. Richard *supermarket company executive*
Rosenberg, William *supermarket company executive*

Hauppauge
Carpenter, Angie M. *small business owner, editor*

Hunter
Jaeckel, Christopher Carol *memorablia company executive, antiquarian*

Katonah
Levine, Pamela Gail *business owner*

Lewiston
Newlin, Lyman Wilbur *bookseller, consultant*

Liverpool
Kogut, John Anthony *retail executive, pharmacist*
O'Leary, Daniel J. *retail trade executive*

Long Island City
Lang, William Charles *retail executive*
†Weitz, Bruce *retail executive*

Melville
Kett, Herbert Joseph *retail executive*
Patrick, Allan *drug store and variety store executive*

Middletown
Waddill, Graham Walker *retail executive*

New Rochelle
Schaffer, Monroe S. *grocery company executive*

New York
Ainslie, Michael Lewis *art-related holding company executive*
Alprin, William Samuel *women's accessory company executive*
Andruskevich, Thomas A(nthony) *corporate executive*
Aronson, Arnold H. *retail company executive*
Babcock, Michael Joseph *retail company executive*
Becker, Isidore A. *business executive*
Bravo, Rose Marie *retail executive*
Brecker, Manfred *retail company executive*
Brenner, Gita Kedar Voivodas *small business owner, research and editing consultant*
Brumm, James Earl *trading company executive*
Cannon, John Haile *retail executive*
Capone, Robert *retail store executive*
Catsimatidis, John Andreas *retail chain executive, airline executive*
Chung, Chia Mou (Charles) *oriental art business owner*
Coffin, John Devereux *import-export company executive*
Cooke, Gordon Richard *retail executive*
Destino, Ralph, Jr. *retail executive*
Devine, W. John *retail executive*
Dworkin, David Lee *retail executive*
Farah, Roger *retail company executive*
Farkas, Robin Lewis *retail company executive*
Fields, Douglas Philip *building supply and home furnishings wholesale company executive*
Fields, Harry *industry executive*
Finkelstein, Edward Sydney *department store executive*
Friedman, Robert N. *retail executive*
Gilinsky, Stanley Ellis *department store executive*
Gray, C(harles) Jackson *retail executive*
Hassler, Howard E. *retail stores executive*
Hennig, Frederick E. *retail company executive*
Jarvis, Gale Rall *retail executive*
Krensky, Harold *retired retail store executive, investor*
Lachman, Lawrence *business consultant, former department store executive*
Margolis, Karl L. *retail company executive*
Matthews, Norman Stuart *department store executive*
Michelson, Gertrude Geraldine *retired retail company executive*
Miller, Philip Boyd *retail executive*
Mizuno, Masaru *retail executive*
Mondlin, Marvin *retail executive, antiquarian book dealer*
Orlowsky, Martin L. *retail company executive*
Peters, Arthur King *international trade executive, author, consultant*
Quint, Ira *retail executive*
Rawl, Arthur Julian *retail executive, accountant, consultant, author*
†Regan, Muriel *small business owner*
Riggio, Stephen *book store chain executive*
†Rizk, Mohammed M. *import/export executive*
†Roberti, William Vincent *retail executive*
Sasaki, Mikio *import/export company exeutive*
Seegal, Herbert Leonard *department store executive*
Sells, Harold E. *retail company executive*
Sherman, Jeffrey Barry *retail executive*
Stanton, Ronald P. *export company executive*
Steinberg, Michael *department store executive*
Stern, Madeleine Bettina *rare books dealer, author*
Straus, Kenneth Hollister *former retail store executive*
Strauss, Edward Robert *carpet company executive*
Sugimoto, Yoshihisa *import/export company executive*
Tanler, Ronald F. *retail executive*
Tendler, David *international trade company executive*
Thomson, William Barry *retail company executive*
Tutun, Edward H. *retired retail executive*

Pelham
Bornand, Ruth Chaloux *small business owner*

Purchase
Carleton, Robert L. *consumer products company executive*

Rochester
McCurdy, Gilbert Geier *retired retailer*

Rye
Goldstein, Stanley P. *retail company executive*
Huth, Robert D. *retail company executive*
Kingsford, William Charles *retail executive*

Schenectady
Lennon, Frank M. *retail executive*

Tonawanda
†Buzzard, Clay E. *wholesale distribution executive*

NORTH CAROLINA

Asheville
Laney, Landy B. *supermarket chain executive*

Black Mountain
Ingle, Robert P. *retail groceries company executive*

Burlington
†Byrd, C. R. *retail executive*
†Byrd, Jimmy L. *retail executive*

Charlotte
Belk, Irwin *retail executive*
Gambrell, Sarah Belk *retail executive*
Henson, Reid M. *wholesale company executive*
Levine, Leon *retail executive*
McKeon, Robert B. *retail chain stores executive*
Reiser, Charles Edward, Jr. *hospital software company executive*
†Rogers, Curtis L., Jr. *wholesale distribution executive*

Greensboro
Hutson, Alan Robert *apparel company executive*
Kennedy, Charles G. *wholesale distribution executive*

Henderson
Church, John Trammell *retail stores company executive*
Harvin, Lucius H., III *department store company executive, lawyer*
Rose, David Cameron *discount store executive*

Hendersonville
Heltman, Robert Fairchild *distribution executive*

Hickory
Lynn, Tony Lee *import company executive*

Matthews
Dunn, Edward S., Jr. *supermarket chain stores executive*

North Wilkesboro
Emerine, Wendell R. *retail executive*

Raleigh
†Pope, John W. *retail executive*

Salisbury
Ketner, Ralph Wright *retail food company executive*
Smith, Tom Eugene *retail food company executive*

NORTH DAKOTA

Bismarck
Meisner, Dee Dolores Annette *small business owner*

OHIO

Akron
Albrecht, Frederick Steven *grocery company executive, lawyer*
†Wiskind, Milton I. *wholesale distribution executive, chemicals executive*

Cincinnati
Beekman, Philip E. *retail company executive*
Burt, David A. *grocery and drugstore company executive*
Edelstein, Chaim Y. *retail executive*
Hodge, Robert Joseph *retail executive*
Marcus, Leonard *retail company executive*
Mooney, Timothy M. *retail executive*
Moore, Michael C. *retail executive*
†Pancoast, Scott R. *distribution company executive*
Price, Thomas Emile *export and investment company executive*
Sherman, Jeffrey *retail executive*
Socol, Howard *department store executive*
Strubbe, John Lewis *retired food chain store executive*
Zimmerman, James M. *retail company executive*

Cleveland
Andrus, Donald R. *department store company executive*
Charnas, Michael (Mannie Charnas) *packaging company executive*
Cole, Jeffrey A. *retail stores executive*
Crosby, Fred McClellan *retail home and office furnishings executive*
Fufuka, Natika Njeri Yaa *retail executive*
Kordalski, Anthony Tadausz *retail department store executive*
Milgrim, Franklin Marshall *merchant*

Columbus
Callander, Kay Eileen Paisley *business owner, retired gifted talented education educator, writer*
Flyg, William Theodore *retail executive*
Gilman, Kenneth B. *retail executive*
Hopkins, Thomas Gene *retail company executive*
Nutt, Fred L., Jr. *retail store executive*
Schottenstein, Saul *retail company executive*
†Turpin, Cheryl Nido *retail executive*
Wexner, Leslie Herbert *retail executive*

Dayton
Glaser, Herbert Otto *retail executive*
Gray, Edman Lowell *metal distribution company executive*
Hartley, Milton E. *retail executive*

Dublin
Walter, Robert D. *wholesale pharmaceutical distribution executive*

Fairfield
Carr, William Anthony *retail company executive*
Murphy, Dennis F. *retail executive*

Groveport
†Ricart, Paul F., Sr. *automotive retail executive*
†Ricart, Rhett C. *retail automotive executive*

Hilliard
Keyes, James Lyman, Jr. *diesel engines distributor company owner*

Hudson
Monro, James Alexander, Jr. *retail executive*
Rosskamm, Alan *retail company executive*

Maumee
Walrod, David James *retail grocery chain executive*

Miamisburg
Batista, John Veloso *wholesale food company executive*
Robinson, Samuel L. *wholesale grocery company executive*
Twyman, Jack *wholesale grocery company executive, management services company executive*

Oxford
Paulin, Henry Sylvester *antiques dealer, emeritus educator*

Powell
Kriegel, David L. *retail executive*

Toledo
Fuhrman, Charles Andrew *country club proprietor, real estate management executive, lawyer*

Twinsburg
Hoven, D. Dwayne *retail executive*
Raven, Gregory Kurt *retail executive*

Youngstown
Catoline, Pauline Dessie *small business owner*
Schwartz, David *retail executive*

OKLAHOMA

Oklahoma City
Austin, Gerald Grant *wholesale food distribution company executive*
Davis, Emery Stephen *wholesale food company executive*
Moll, John Edgar *wholesale grocery company executive*
Richards, David John *food distribution company executive*
†Roach, Wayne E. *retail automotive executive*
Werries, E. Dean *food distribution company executive*
Williams, Richard Donald *retired wholesale food company executive*

Tulsa
Howerton, Alvin *retail executive*
†Rippley, Robert *wholesale distribution executive*

OREGON

Hillsboro
Grant, James Rusk *business owner*

Medford
McKinstry, Gregory John Duncan *retail executive*

Portland
Bauer, Louis Edward *retail bookstore executive, educator*
Blanford, J(ohn) William *department store company executive*
Danielson, Craig *wholesale grocery corporation executive*
Greenstein, Merle Edward *import/export company executive*
Hill, Ray Thomas, Jr. *export and import company executive*
Miller, Robert G. *retail company executive*
Ramsby, Mark Delivan *lighting designer and consultant*

Prineville
†Wick, G. Phil *retail executive*

Riddle
Markham, William E. *timber and logging company owner*

Saint Helens
Federici, Tony *small business owner, state legislator*

PENNSYLVANIA

Ardmore
†Callahan, Thomas P. *wholesale distribution executive*

Bensalem
Sidewater, Arthur *retired retail executive, consultant*

Berwyn
Fry, Clarence Herbert *retail executive*

Bristol
McEwen, Joseph, Jr. *distributing company executive*

Butler
Kane, Marilyn Elizabeth *small business owner*

Camp Hill
Bergonzi, Frank Michael *retail drug store chain executive*
Grass, Alexander *retail company executive*
Miller, Ronald Anthony *distribution company executive*
Slane, Charles Joseph *chain drug store executive*

Carlisle
Lewis, Claude, Jr. *retired shoe company executive*
Ruble, Duane Russell *retail drug store executive*

East Butler
Mielcuszny, Albert John *wholesale distribution executive*
Pentz, Paul *hardware company executive*

Harrisburg
†Spector, Morton *wholesale distribution executive*
Vanderveen, Peter *wholesale grocery company executive*

Hummelstown
Murphy, S(usan) (Jane Murphy) *small business owner*

Media
Price, Donald *retail executive*

New Holland
Kennedy, William T. *retail executive*

Parker
Meixsell, Berrae Nevin (Mike Meixsell) *retail executive*

Philadelphia
Leibovitz, Mitchell G. *retail executive*
Marshall, Donald Tompkins *industrial distribution executive*
Sirkis, Robert Lane *retail industry executive*
Stampone, Frederick Albert *retail executive*
Strawbridge, Francis Reeves, III *department store executive*
Strawbridge, G. Stockton *retail executive*
Strawbridge, Peter S. *department store executive*
Strawbridge, Steven Lowry *retail executive*
White, Warren Wurtele *retailing executive*

Pittsburgh
Civello, Anthony Ned *retail drug company executive, pharmacist*
Day, Maurice Jerome *automobile parts distributing company executive*
Hamburg, Lester Albert *wholesale appliance company executive*
Hannan, Robert William *retail pharmaceutical company executive*
Heller, Lawrence Aaron *business owner, association executive*
Tobin, William Thomas *retail executive*

Reading
Lakin, Edwin A. *retail executive*
†Redner, Earl W. *retail executive*

Sharon
Epstein, Louis Ralph *retired wholesale grocery executive*
Rosenblum, Harold Arthur *grocery distribution executive*

Shippensburg
Thompson, Elizabeth Jane *small business owner*

Shiremanstown
Nesbit, William Terry *small business owner, consultant*

Sunbury
Weis, Sigfried *supermarket chain executive*

Washington
Erdner, Jon W. *small business owner, securities trader*

Wayne
Gozon, Richard C. *paper distribution executive*

West Conshohocken
Schumacher, Elizabeth Swisher *garden ornaments shop owner*

Williamsport
Largen, Joseph *retailer, furniture manufacturer, book wholesaler*

Yardley
Desai, Cawas Jal *distribution company executive*

RHODE ISLAND

Rumford
Pike, Allen W. *supermarket company executive*

SOUTH CAROLINA

Charleston
Belk, John M. *retail company executive*

Columbia
Clark, David Randolph *wholesale grocer*

Greenville
Bauknight, Clarence Brock *wholesale and retail company executive*

Mauldin
Yingling, William E., III *retail company executive*

Spartanburg
Littlejohn, Broadus Richard, Jr. *retail supermarket chain executive*

SOUTH DAKOTA

Mitchell
Randall, Ronald Fisher *grocery store chain executive*

TENNESSEE

Alcoa
†Piper, A. Coleman *retail executive*

Brentwood
Zimmerman, Raymond *retail chain executive*

Bristol
Cauthen, Charles Edward, Jr. *business consultant, former retail executive*

Knoxville
Harris, Charles Edgar *retired wholesale distribution company executive*
Jenkins, Roger Lane *retail executive*

La Vergne
Mason, Steven Jude *wholesale company executive*
Pfeffer, Philip Maurice *distribution company executive*

Memphis
Clarkson, Andrew MacBeth *retail executive*
Dunavant, William Buchanan, Jr. *small business owner*
Hendren, Gary E. *retail executive*
†Wein, Bernard J. *retail executive*

Morristown
Johnson, Evelyn Bryan *flying service executive*

Nashville
Zibart, Michael Alan *wholesale book company executive*

TEXAS

Amarillo
Marmaduke, John H. *retail executive*

Arlington
†Snyder, Don *retail automotive executive*
Thompson, Carson R. *retail, manufacturing company executive*

Austin
Girling, Robert George William, III *business owner*
Houston, Samuel Lee *computer software company executive*

Carrollton
Butler, Abbey J. *pharmaceutical distribution company executive*
Senecal, Eugene Gerald *retail executive*

Dallas
Beck, Abe Jack *retired business executive, retired air force officer*
Cullum, Robert B., Jr. *retail executive, property developer*
Dole, S. R., Jr. *retail executive*
Kirkpatrick, Patricia Kay *retail buyer*
Longyear, Russell Hammond *retail executive*
Matthews, Clark J(io), II *retail executive, lawyer*
McDougall, Ronald Alexander *restaurant executive*
Parker, Barry James Charles *retail executive*
St. James, Lyn *business owner, professional race car driver*
Shapiro, Robert Alan *retail executive*
Stone, Donald James *retired retail executive*
†Thompson, Jere William *retail food company executive*

Fort Worth
Bolen, Bob *retail merchant, university administrator*
Herlihy, James Edward *retail executive*
Michero, William Henderson *retired retail trade executive*
Pavony, William H. *retail executive*
Roach, John Vinson, II *retail company executive*

Houston
Barrett, Lyle Eugene *retail buyer, designer, artist*
Baugh, John Frank *wholesale company executive*
Bjornson, Carroll Norman *business owner*
Gallerano, Andrew John *retail company executive*
Irving, Herbert *food distribution company executive*
Levit, Milton *grocery supply company executive*
Orton, Stewart *retail company executive, merchant*
†Reeder, Jeffrey K. *retail executive*
Sheffield, Don B. *wholesale distribution company executive*
Steadman, Richard Cooke *retail corporate executive*
Tooker, Carl E. *department store executive*
Trinh, Victor *small business owner*
Utsey, John Blaine *retail store executive*
Van Horn, Verne Hile, III *retail executive*
Woodhouse, John Frederick *food distribution company executive*

Irving
Gerstein, Irving R. *jewelry company executive*

League City
†Langstaff, David Hamilton *commercial industry executive*

Plano
Neppl, Walter Joseph *retired retail store executive*
Oesterreicher, James E. *department stores executive*
Wells, John Andrew *retail executive*

Richardson
Wagers, Robert Shelby *entrepreneur*

San Antonio
Gresham, Gary Stuart *wholesale grocery executive, accountant*
Sheerin, Maggie *small business owner, artist*
†Wise, Doug *retail executive*

Seabrook
Spears, James Grady *small business owner*

Sulphur Springs
McKenzie, Kenneth *retail grocery executive*
†McKenzie, Michael K. *wholesale executive*

Wimberley
Ellis, John *small business owner*

UTAH

Brigham City
Call, Osborne Jay *retail executive*

Logan
†Watterson, Scott *wholesale fitness equipment distribution executive*

Salt Lake City
Bergeson, Scott *retail executive*
Brewer, Stanley R. *wholesale grocery executive*
Day, Gerald W. *wholesale grocery company executive*
Jensen, Willard Scott *warehouse executive*
†Smith, Jeffrey P. *supermarket chain executive*
Smith, Richard D. *supermarkets and drug stores executive*
†Warner, Bart C. *retail executive*

VERMONT

Brookfield
Gerard, James Wilson *book distributor*

VIRGINIA

Alexandria
Eisenberg, David Henry *drug store executive*

Arlington
Seely, James Michael *consultant, retired naval officer, small business owner*
Walker, Walter Gray, Jr. *small business owner, program statistician*
Zazulia, Irwin *retail store executive*

Danville
Oakes, Timothy Wayne *tobacco import-export company executive*

Fairfax
Pugh, Arthur James *retired department store executive, consultant*
Schrock, Simon *retail executive*

Lynchburg
Frazier, Robert James *small business owner*

Mc Lean
Vandemark, Robert Goodyear *retired retail company executive*

Mechanicsville
†Bennett, Donald Dalton *grocery stores executive*

Newport News
†Noland, Lloyd U., III *wholesale utility supplies company executive*

Norfolk
Alessi, Keith Ernest *retail executive*

Purcellville
Sharples, Winston Singleton *automobile importer and distributor*

Quantico
Joy, James R. *retail executive*

Richmond
Cramer, Morgan Joseph, Jr. *international management executive*
Kasen, Stewart Michael *retail executive*
Lewis, Frances Aaronson *retail company executive*
Lewis, Sydney *retail company executive*
Rexinger, Daniel Michael *retail company executive*
Sharp, Richard L. *retail company executive*
Sniffin, John Harrison *retail executive*

Salem
Brand, Edward Cabell *retail executive*

Staunton
Hammaker, Paul M. *retail executive, business educator, author*

Suffolk
†Spain, William J., Jr. *wholesale distribution executive*

WASHINGTON

Bellingham
Orem, Joseph Clifton *sales professional*

Kirkland
†Brotman, Jeffrey H. *variety stores executive*
†Pugmire, Robert *wholesale distribution executive*
Sinegal, James D. *variety store wholesale business executive*

Mercer Island
Greenwood, Wilbur Rowe, III *small business owner*

Redmond
Nagel, Daryl David *retail executive*

Seattle
Denniston, Martha Kent *business owner, author*
Fix, Wilbur James *department store executive*
McMillan, John A. *retail executive*
Nordstrom, Bruce A. *department store executive*
Nordstrom, John N. *department store executive*
Read, Charles Raymond, Sr. *business executive*

Spokane
Herbison, John (Steve) *wholesale and retail company executive*

WEST VIRGINIA

Charleston
Lipton, Allen David *retail executive*

WISCONSIN

Kenosha
Tielke, James Clemens *retail and manufacturing executive*

La Crosse
Metcalf, Jerry D. *wholesale food distribution company executive*

Madison
Griepp, Milton Charles *distribution executive*
†Reuhl, George *retail executive*

Menomonee Falls
Herma, John *retail executive*
Kellogg, William S. *retail executive*

Milwaukee
Anderson, Alan R. *department store executive*
Bluestone, Stanton J. *department store chain executive*
MacDonald, Michael R. *retail executive*

Platteville
Brodbeck, William Jan *retail executive*

Sheboygan
†Dickelman, James Howard *retail chain executive*

Waukesha
DeWees, James H. *retail company executive*
Lusic, Ronald R. *retail company executive*

WYOMING

Jackson
Law, Clarene Alta *innkeeper, state legislator*

TERRITORIES OF THE UNITED STATES

GUAM

Agana
Perez, Gerald S. A. *retail executive educator*

VIRGIN ISLANDS

Saint Thomas
Cockayne, Robert Barton *retail company executive*

CANADA

BRITISH COLUMBIA

North Vancouver
Jarrett, Anthony *retired business executive*

MANITOBA

Winnipeg
Cohen, Albert Diamond *retail executive*

ONTARIO

Brampton
Beaumont, Donald A. *department store chain executive*

Cornwall
Hornby, Thomas Richard *wholesale distribution executive*

Etobicoke
Graham, Allister P. *diversified company executive*

London
Crncich, Tony Joseph *retired pharmacy chain executive*

Markham
Lewis, Michael *small business owner*

Mississauga
Williams, James B. *retail electronics company executive*

Ottawa
Labbé, Paul *export corporation executive*

Toronto
Kay, James Fredrick *retailer*
Keenan, Anthony Harold Brian *catalog company executive*
Kosich, George John *retail executive*
Macaulay, Hugh L. *retail company executive*
McGiverin, Donald Scott *retail company executive*
Minto, Clive *retail company executive*
Posluns, Wilfred M. *manufacturing and retailing company executive*
Shaffer, Donald S. *retail executive*
Sharpe, Charles Richard *retail company executive*
Smith, Stephen Alexander *retail and wholesale food distribution company executive*
Wolfe, Jonathan A. *food wholesaler, retailer*

Willowdale
Binder, Herbert R. *drug store chain executive*
Bloom, David Ronald *retail drug company executive*
Swartz, Malcolm Gilbert *retail executive, restaurateur*

QUEBEC

Pointe Claire
Cohen, Charles F. *retail executive*

MEXICO

Garza Garcia
Paez, Rafael Roberto *holding company executive*

JAPAN

Tokyo
Ito, Masatoshi *retail executive*

ADDRESS UNPUBLISHED

Aved, Barry *retail executive*
Baker, Edward Kevin *retail executive*
Biagi, Richard Charles *retail executive, real estate consultant*
Bittke, Brian Edmund *food distribution company executive*
Blum, Gerald Harris *department store executive*
Brinkmann, Klaus Peter *wholesale distribution executive*
Burden, John W., III *retail company executive*
Campbell, Edward Clinton *small business owner, violin maker*
Cantarella, Francesco Paquin *retail executive*
Chevalier, Paul Edward *retired retail executive, lawyer, art gallery executive*
Clark, Maxine *retail executive*
Coons, Marion McDowell *retail food stores executive*
Couri, John A. *distribution executive*
Crandall, Albert Earl *retail executive, accountant, entrepreneur*
Depkovich, Francis John *retired retail chain executive*
†Dozier, O(llin) Kemp *tobacco wholesale company executive*
Dyer, Arlene Thelma *retail company owner*
Edwards, Patrick Ross *former retail company executive, lawyer, management consultant*
Fields, Leo *former jewelry company executive, investor*
Folkman, David H. *apparel wholesale executive*
Geoffroy, Charles Henry *retired travel company executive*
Goldman, Gerald Hillis *beverage distribution company executive*
Goldner, Sheldon Herbert *export-import company executive*
Guillemette, Gloria Vivian *small business owner, dressmaker, designer*
Hair, Danny G. *retail company executive*
Howard, Matthew Aloysius *retail company executive*
Howell, William Robert *retail company executive*
Johnson, Harold Edward *retail executive*
Johnson, Victor L. *retail executive*
Jones, Robert Henry *automotive distribution executive*
King, S(anford) MacCallum *business owner, consultant*
Kraiss, Glenn S. *retail executive*
Lacy, Alan Jasper *retail executive*
Lebor, John F(rancis) *retired department store executive*
Lipsey, Joseph, Jr. *water bottling company executive, retail and wholesale corporation executive*
Lively, H(oward) Randolph, Jr. *retail company executive*
Martini, Robert Edward *wholesale pharmaceutical and medical supplies company executive*
Meyer, Lasker Marcel *retail executive*
Miller, Michael Paul *toy company executive*
Milstein, Monroe Gary *retail executive*
Mrkonic, George Ralph, Jr. *retail executive*
Nishimura, Joseph Yo *retired retail executive, accountant*
Paterson, Robert E. *trading stamp company executive*
Peskin, Kenneth *retail executive*
Policano, Joseph Daniel *import company executive*
Questrom, Allen I. *retail executive*
Quist, Beth Dobson *small business owner*
Raab, Herbert Norman *retail executive*
Raskin, Michael A. *retail company executive*
Rau, Robert Nicholas *pipe distribution executive*
Riklis, Marcia *retail executive*
Rodbell, Clyde Armand *distribution executive*
Rosenbaum, Irving M. *retail store executive*
Ruland, Midlred Ardelia *retail executive, retail buyer*
Runge, Donald Edward *food wholesale company executive*
Rupp, Glenn N. *sporting goods executive*
Samson, Alvin *former distributing company executive, consultant*
Sewell, Phyllis Shapiro *retail chain executive*
Sherwood, (Peter) Louis *retail executive*
Smyth, John McDonnell, III *merchant, lawyer*
Stern, Charles *foreign trade company executive*
Teitelbaum, Irving *retail executive*

Trutter, John Thomas *consulting company executive*
Vernon, Carl Atlee, Jr. *retired wholesale food distributor executive*
Vila, Adis Maria *corporate executive, former government official, lawyer*
Waddle, John Frederick *former retail chain executive*
Waters, David Rogers *retail executive*
Wien, Stuart Lewis *retired supermarket chain executive*
Wiesner, John Joseph *retail executive*
Williams, Robert Lyle *corporate executive, consultant*
Worley, Gordon Roger *retail chain financial executive*

INDUSTRY: TRANSPORTATION

UNITED STATES

ALABAMA

Andalusia
†Smith, J. E. Gene *electric power industry executive*

Birmingham
Brough, James A. *airport terminal executive*
Harbert, Raymond J. *transportation executive*

Gulf Shores
Wallace, John Loys *aviation services executive*

Huntsville
Richter, William, Jr. *aerospace company executive*

Point Clear
Elmer, William Morris *retired pipe line executive*

ALASKA

Anchorage
Harris, Orville D. *transportation executive*
Lorch, William Charles *transportation executive*
Sullivan, George Murray *transportation consultant, former mayor*

ARIZONA

Mesa
Haggerty, Allen Charles *transportation company executive*

Phoenix
Beauvais, Edward R. *airline executive*
†Bertholf, Neilson Allan, Jr. *aviation executive*
Conway, Michael J. *airline company executive*
Elien, Mona Marie *air transportation professional*
Emerson, Frederick George *transportation company executive*
Shoen, Edward Joseph *transportation and insurance companies executive*
Whalen, Martin J. *transportation executive, lawyer*
Woods, Bobby Joe *transportation executive*

Scottsdale
Garelick, Martin *transportation executive*

Tempe
Miller, Marc Douglas *airline pilot*

Tucson
Burg, Walter A. *airport terminal executive*
Gissing, Bruce *retired aerospace company executive*
Peete, Russell Fitch, Jr. *aircraft appraiser*

ARKANSAS

Fort Smith
Yarbrough, Jerry A. *transportation company executive*
Young, Robert A., III *freight systems executive*

Harrison
Garrison, F. Sheridan *transportation executive*

Huntsville
Carr, Gerald Paul *former astronaut, business executive, former marine officer*

Lowell
Bergant, Paul R. *trucking company executive, lawyer*
Palmer, Stephen *trucking company executive*
Thompson, James Kirk *transportation executive*

Pine Bluff
Seawell, William Thomas *former airline executive*

Rogers
Scott, Harold Lee, Jr. *distribution executive*

Springdale
Pogue, William Reid *former astronaut, foundation executive, business and aerospace consultant*

CALIFORNIA

Bayside
Pierce, Lester Laurin *retired pilot, aviation consultant*

Berkeley
Kanafani, Adib *transportation think-tank administrator, civil engineering educator*

Borrego Springs
Scannell, William Edward *aerospace company executive, consultant, psychologist*

Burbank
Aaronson, Robert Jay *aviation executive*
O'Donnell, Scott Richard *aviation administrator*
Volk, Robert Harkins *aviations company executive*

Burlingame
Loughead, Thomas A. *transportation executive*

Calabasas
Caren, Robert Poston *aerospace company executive*

Cambria
Crowther, H. David *aerospace company corporate communications executive*

Corona Del Mar
Tether, Anthony John *aerospace executive*

Costa Mesa
Mittermeier, Janice *commercial airport executive*

Culver City
Real, Jack Garret *helicopter company executive*

Edwards
Brand, Vance Devoe *astronaut, government official*

El Segundo
Aldridge, Edward C., Jr. *aerospace transportation executive*

Encino
Bucks, Charles Alan *airline industry consultant, former executive*
Gasich, Welko Elton *retired aerospace executive, management consultant*

Foster City
Dove, Millard *retired transportation executive*

Fremont
Smith, Bernald Stephen *retired airline pilot, aviation consultant*

Gilroy
Borton, George Robert *airline captain*

Hermosa Beach
Kokalj, James Edward *retired aerospace administrator*

Irvine
Otth, Edward John, Jr. *retired marine systems executive, retired naval officer*

La Jolla
Wertheim, Robert Halley *national security consultant*

La Mesa
Hansen, Grant Lewis *retired aerospace and information systems executive*

Lancaster
Crew, Aubrey Torquil *aerospace inspector*

Long Beach
Anderson, Gerald Verne *retired aerospace company executive*
Dorrenbacher, Carl James *aerospace transportation executive*
Myers, John Wescott *aviation executive*
Schaufele, Roger Donald *aircraft company executive*

Los Angeles
Cotter, George Edward *former airline company executive*
Gregg, Lucius Perry, Jr. *aerospace executive*
Harris, T. C. *water transportation executive*
Kent, William *pilot, cameraman, special effects expert*
Kresa, Kent *aerospace executive*
Morris, Larry Garner *transportation company executive*
Yee, Stephen *airport executive*

Malibu
Ensign, Richard Papworth *transportation executive*

Menlo Park
Leach, John Frank *transportation executive*
O'Brien, Raymond Francis *transportation executive*

Mission Viejo
Foulds, Donald Duane *aerospace executive*

Moffett Field
Dean, William Evans *aerospace agency executive*

Oakland
Haskell, Arthur Jacob *retired steamship company executive*
Lillie, John Mitchell *transportation company executive*

Palmdale
†Weiss, Richard R. *rocket propulsion technology executive*

Palo Alto
†Berry, Robert Emanuel *aerospace company executive*
Moffitt, Donald Eugene *transportation company executive*
Morrison, David Fred *freight company executive*

Palos Verdes Peninsula
Ryker, Charles Edwin *former aerospace company executive*
Waaland, Irving Theodore *retired aerospace design executive*

Ramona
Hoffman, Wayne Melvin *retired airline official*

Redwood City
Guinasso, Victor *delivery service executive*

Waller, Stephen *air transportation executive*

Redwood Shores
Abrahamson, James Alan *transportation executive, retired military officer*

Sacramento
Engel, Thomas P. *airport executive*

San Diego
†Guerin, John P. *air transportation company executive*
Mattingly, Thomas K. *astronaut*
Reading, James Edward *transportation executive*

San Francisco
Anschutz, Philip F. *transportation executive*
Collar, Leo Linford *marine transportation company executive*
Hickerson, Glenn Lindsey *leasing company executive*
Mohan, D. Mike *transportation company executive*
Ryan, Randel Edward, Jr. *airline pilot*
Turpen, Louis A. *airport terminal executive*
Wood, Donald Frank *transportation educator, consultant*

San Mateo
Trabitz, Eugene Leonard *aerospace company executive*

Shingle Springs
Crotti, Joseph Robert *aviation executive*

Sunnyvale
Guastaferro, Angelo *aerospace company executive*

Torrance
Savitz, Maxine Lazarus *aerospace company executive*

Van Nuys
Cooper, Leroy Gordon, Jr. *former astronaut, business consultant*

Visalia
Miller, Carl Duane *transportation company executive*

Woodland Hills
Hawkins, Willis Moore *aerospace and astronautical consultant*

Yorba Linda
Bailey, Don Matthew *aerospace and electronics company executive*

COLORADO

Denver
Boulware, Richard Stark *airport administrator*
Burgess, Larry Lee *aerospace executive*
DeLong, James Clifford *air transportation executive*
LaRoche, Gloria Rosemarie *pilot*
Teets, Peter B. *aerospace executive*

Englewood
Claussen, Bonnie Addison, II *aerospace company executive*

Littleton
Kleinknecht, Kenneth Samuel *retired aerospace company executive, former federal space agency official*

Trinidad
Potter, William Bartlett *business executive*

CONNECTICUT

Fairfield
Peirce, George Leighton *airport administrator*
Taylor, James Blackstone *aviation company executive*

Greenwich
Crowe, John Carl *aviation consultant, retired airline executive*

Shelton
Bowron, John B. *transportation executive*
Crowe, Jeffrey C. *transportation executive*

Stamford
Barker, James Rex *water transportation executive*
Tregurtha, Paul Richard *marine transportation and construction materials company executive*

DELAWARE

Dagsboro
Lally, Richard Francis *aviation security consultant, former association executive, former government official*

Wilmington
†Rollins, John W., Jr. *transportation executive, environmental services administrator*

DISTRICT OF COLUMBIA

Washington
†Allen, Joseph P. *aerospace company executive*
Chennault, Anna Chen *aviation executive, author, lecturer*
Cocke, Erle, Jr. *international business consultant*
Donovan, George Joseph *industry executive, consultant*
Downey, Mortimer Leo, III *transportation executive*
†Downs, Thomas Michael *transportation facility administrator*
Farrell, Joseph Michael *steamship company executive*
Fuhrman, Robert Alexander *aerospace company executive*
Hinson, David Russell *airline company executive, federal agency administrator*
Josephson, Diana Hayward *aerospace executive*
Lion, Paul Michel, III *transportation engineer, executive*
Luffsey, Walter Stith *transportation executive*
Mederos, Carolina Luisa *transportation policy consultant*
Melton, Augustus Allen, Jr. *airport executive*
Meurlin, Keith W. *airport terminal executive*
Newman, William Bernard, Jr. *railroad executive*
Olcott, John Whiting *aviation executive*
Overbeck, Gene Edward *retired airline executive, lawyer*
Parker, Robert Allan Ridley *astronaut*
Sullivan, Dennis F. *transportation company executive, engineer*
Thayer, Russell, III *airlines executive*

FLORIDA

Boca Raton
Goldstein, Bernard *transportation company executive*

Boynton Beach
Crane, L(eo) Stanley *retired railroad executive*

Cape Coral
Mc Grath, William Restore *transportation planner, traffic engineer*

Clearwater
Howes, James Guerdon *airport director*
Krosser, Howard S. *aerospace company executive*

Fisher Island
Trippe, Kenneth Alvin Battershill *shipping industry executive*

Fort Lauderdale
Durfey, Robert Walker *sea transportation consultant*

Jacksonville
Aftoora, Patricia Joan *transportation executive*
Carpenter, Alvin Rauso *transportation executive*
Currie, Earl James *transportation company executive*
Davis, Jerry Ray *railroad company executive*
Hamilton, William Berry, Jr. *shipping company executive*
Hardrick, Charles M. *airport executive*
Kirk, Robert Leonard *transportation company executive*
†Nicosia, Joseph A. *transportation company executive*
Thornton, Winfred Lamotte *railroad executive*

Jupiter
Skully, Richard Patrick *airline consultant*

Miami
Bastian, James Harold *air transport company executive, lawyer*
Brock, James Daniel *retired airline executive, consultant*
Burns, Mitchel Anthony *transportation services company executive*
Conese, Eugene P., Jr. *aircraft maintenance executive*
Dellapa, Gary J. *airport terminal executive*
Dickinson, Robert H. *water transportation executive*
Downey, Ellen *transportation company executive*
Fain, Richard David *cruise line executive*
Huston, Edwin Allen *transportation company executive*
Kunstler, David B. *airline company executive*
Lazaga, Jose Ignacio *airline executive*
Sapp, Neil Carleton *international airline pilot, industrial consultant*
Stephens, Franklin Wilson *transportation executive*

Naples
Gresham, Robert Coleman *transportation consultant*
Johnson, Walter L. *transportation company executive*

Oldsmar
Burrows, William Claude *aerospace executive, retired air force officer*

Orlando
Gustafson, Robert A. *air transportation and holding company executive*
Hanus, Thomas J. *air transportation services executive*
Harris, Martin Harvey *aerospace company executive*
McGee, William G. *air transportation company executive*
Pearlman, Louis Jay *aviation and promotion company executive*
†Shaw, Brewster Hopkinson, Jr. *astronaut*

Pompano Beach
Wright, Joseph Robert, Jr. *corporate executive*

Ponte Vedra Beach
Fiorentino, Thomas Martin *transportation executive, lawyer*

Saint Augustine
Zellers, Carl Fredrick, Jr. *railway executive*

Sarasota
Lindsay, David Breed, Jr. *aircraft company executive, former editor and publisher*

Tampa
†Bean, George J. *airport executive*
†Johnson, James E. *airport executive*
†Snyder, Richard G. *transportation services executive*

GEORGIA

Athens
Dively, Frank Eugene *airport executive*

Atlanta
Allen, Ronald W. *airline company executive*
Callison, James W. *former airline executive, lawyer*
Connor, Charles William *airline pilot*
†Gittens, Angela *airport executive*
Heil, Russell Howard *air transportation company executive*
Kelley, James P. *delivery service executive*
Miller, Thomas Marshall *air transportation executive*
Nelson, Kent C. *delivery service executive*
Oppenlander, Robert *retired airline executive*
Raines, Mary Elizabeth *airline executive*
†Stogner, James *airport executive*
Thakker, Ashok *aerospace engineering company executive*

Columbus
Oropeza, Mark *airport director*

Macon
Hails, Robert Emmet *aerospace consultant, business executive, former air force officer*

Savannah
Breidenbach, Fred A. *aerospace company executive*
Glenn, Albert H. *aerospace company executive*
Graham, Patrick Samuel *air transportation executive*
Johnson, Victor L. *trucking executive*

HAWAII

Honolulu
†Derieg, Thomas F. *airline executive*
Pfeiffer, Robert John *transportation executive*
Speicher, William Clayton *transportation executive*
Ueberroth, John A. *air transportation executive*

IDAHO

Boise
Agee, William J. *transportation, engineering and construction company executive*
Ilett, Frank, Jr. *trucking company executive*

ILLINOIS

AMF Ohare
†Aron, Adam M. *air transportation executive*
Guyette, James M. *airline executive*
Hartigan, James J. *retired airline executive*
Pope, John Charles *airline company executive*

Bedford Park
Batory, Ronald Louis *transportation executive*

Chicago
Burton, Raymond Charles, Jr. *transportation company executive*
Chartier, Janellen Olsen *airline service coordinator*
Foster, Hugh Warren *transportation company executive*
Fuller, D. Ward *transportation equipment company executive*
†Harrison, E. Hunter *rail transportation executive*
Heineman, Ben Walter *corporation executive*
Nord, Henry J. *transportation executive*
Reed, John Shedd *former railway executive*
Royer, Kathleen Rose *pilot*
Schmiege, Robert *railroad executive*
Smith, Robert Drake *railroad executive*
Swartz, William John *transportation resources company executive/retired*
White, John Abiathar *pilot, consultant*
Wolf, Stephen M. *airline executive*
Zell, Samuel *transportation leasing company executive*

Des Plaines
Koffman, Morley *trucking executive*

Geneva
Barney, Charles Richard *transportation company executive*

Glen Ellyn
Logan, Henry Vincent *transportation executive*

Lake Forest
Hillman, Stanley Eric Gordon *former corporate executive*

Lombard
Yeager, Phillip Charles *transportation company executive*

Maywood
Welty, William John *transportation executive, accountant*

Naperville
Fleisher, Robert E. R. *trucking executive*
Olliver, Denis G. *transportation company executive*
Olson, Donald W. *transportation executive*

Oak Brook
Duerinck, Louis T. *retired railroad executive, attorney*

Park Ridge
Carr, Gilbert Randle *retired railroad executive*

Prophetstown
Thompson, George Howard *livestock transportation company executive*

Rockford
†Delavan, John *freight transportation company executive*
Donovan, Paul *aerospace executive*

Rosemont
Baldwin, Gerald Erwin *airline pilot*
Burkhardt, Edward Arnold *transportation company executive*

Saint Charles
Zito, James Anthony *retired railroad company executive*

Schaumburg
Bauchiero, James *transportation executive*
Krebs, Robert Duncan *transportation company executive*

Skokie
Altschul, Alfred Samuel *airline executive*

INDIANA

Carmel
Russell, Richard L. *van line executive*
Smith, John Burnside *transportation company executive*
Smith, Michael L. *transportation company executive*

Columbus
Hartley, James Michaelis *aerospace systems, printing and hardwood products manufacturing executive*

Evansville
Fagan, Thomas Perry *transportation executive*
Shaffer, Michael L. *transportation company executive*

Indianapolis
Orcutt, Daniel C. *airport terminal executive*
Wallace, F. Blake *aerospace executive, mechanical engineer*

Jeffersonville
Bobzien, H.J., Jr. *transportation company executive*

Terre Haute
Frantz, Welby Marion *transportation executive*

West Lafayette
Drake, John Warren *aviation consultant*

IOWA

Cedar Rapids
†Smith, Herald Alvin, Jr. *transportation executive*
†Smith, John M. *trucking executive*

Des Moines
†Ruan, John *transportation executive*

KANSAS

Overland Park
Powell, George Everett, Jr. *motor freight company executive*
Powell, George Everett, III *trucking company executive*

Shawnee Mission
Burdick, Robert William *transportation company executive*
Burm, Forrest Henry *transportation executive*
†Smith, Michael L. *transportation executive*

Wichita
Bell, Baillis F. *airport terminal executive*
Cheesman, John Michael *aeronautics company executive, civic leader*

KENTUCKY

Franklin
Clark, James Benton *railroad industry consultant, former executive*

LOUISIANA

Baton Rouge
Graves, Robert Glen *transportation company executivw*

Houma
Saia, Louis P., III *transportation executive*

New Orleans
Amoss, W. James, Jr. *shipping company executive*
†Cazayoux, Charles *airport executive*
Johnsen, Erik Frithjof *transportation executive*
Lykes, Joseph T., III *shipping company executive*
McCormick, Eugene F., Jr. *transportation company executive*

MAINE

Bath
O'Keefe, Patrick *transportation executive*

MARYLAND

Annapolis
Colussy, Dan Alfred *aviation executive*
Groves, George L., Jr. *air freight service company executive*
Moellering, John Henry *aviation maintenance company executive*
Waugh, Robert James *aerospace company executive*

Baltimore
Clark, Raymond Skinner *retired transportation and distribution company executive*
Cunningham, M(urray) Hunt, Jr. *aerospace company executive, mechanical engineer, author*
Harp, Solomon, III *airport executive*
†Henderson, Duncan *airport administrator*
Kirk, Robert L. *rail transportation executive*
Swani, Parvesh *transportation company executive*

Bethesda
Lewis, David Eldridge *airport development executive*
Tellep, Daniel Michael *aerospace executive, mechanical engineer*

Chevy Chase
Coleman, Joseph Michael *truck lease consultant*

College Park
Keller, Samuel William *aerospace administrator*

Preston
Suggs, Leo H. *transportation executive*

Rockville
Fthenakis, Emanuel John *diversified aerospace company executive*
Porter, John Robert, Jr. *space technology company executive, geochemist*

Stevensville
Deen, Thomas Blackburn *transportation research executive*

MASSACHUSETTS

Boston
Davis, David William *transportation consultant*
†Giesser, Richard A. *transportation executive, financial and management consultant*
Klotz, Charles Rodger *shipping company executive*
†Tocco, Stephen *airport administrator*

Brookline
Frankel, Ernst Gabriel *shipping and aviation business executive, educator*

Cambridge
John, Richard Rodda *transportation executive*

Framingham
Ballou, Kenneth Walter *retired transportation executive, university dean*

Marlborough
Birstein, Seymour Joseph *aerospace company executive*

North Billerica
Fink, David A. *rail transportation executive*

Wakefield
Roberts, Louis Wright *transportation executive*

Wilmington
Buckley, Robert Paul *aerospace company executive*

MICHIGAN

Ann Arbor
Waller, Patricia Fossum *transportation executive, researcher, psychologist*

Birmingham
Kosak, Anthony James *transportation company executive*

Detroit
Braun, Robert C. *airport executive*

Grand Rapids
Auwers, Stanley John *motor carrier executive*

Kalamazoo
Tessler, Allan R. *trucking company executive*

Monroe
White, Gary L. *trucking executive*

Warren
Morelli, William Annibale, Sr. *aerospace manufacturing company executive*

MINNESOTA

Minneapolis
Harper, Donald Victor *transportation and logistics educator*
Nyrop, Donald William *airline executive*

Saint Paul
Anderson, Tim *airport terminal executive*
Checchi, Alfred A. *airline company executive*
Engle, Donald Edward *retired railway executive, lawyer*
Gehrz, Robert Gustave *retired railroad executive*
Mitchell, Pamela Ann *airline pilot*
Washburn, Donald Arthur *business executive*

MISSISSIPPI

Jackson
†Vanderleest, Dirk *airport executive*

Pass Christian
Clark, John Walter, Jr. *shipping company executive*

MISSOURI

Blue Springs
Reed, Tony Norman *aviation company executive*

Fenton
Greenblatt, Maurice Theodore *transportation executive*
Stadler, Gerald P. *transportation executive*

Kansas City
Edwards, George W., Jr. *railway company executive*
Gile, Herbert R., Jr. *airport terminal executive*
Solomon, John Davis *aviation executive*

Lake Saint Louis
German, John George *transportation consultant*

Saint Joseph
Head, J. Michael *transportation executive*

Saint Louis
†Cahill, John Conway *air transportation company executive*
Capellupo, John P. *air transportation executive*
Delaney, Robert Vernon *logistics and transportation executive*
Jenks, Downing Bland *railroad executive*
Nelson, Michael Underhill *aerospace company executive, association executive*
O'Neill, John Robert *airline executive*

NEBRASKA

Lincoln
Acklie, Duane William *transportation company executive*

Omaha
Davidson, Richard K. *railroad company executive*
Werner, Clarence L. *transportation executive*

NEVADA

Reno
Horton, Gary Bruce *transportation company executive*
Jordan, Joseph Rembert *airline pilot*

NEW JERSEY

Bound Brook
Furst, E(rrol) Kenneth *transportation executive, accountant*

Elizabeth
Power, Frank Raymond *transportation company executive*

Flemington
Kettler, Carl Frederick *airline executive*

Jersey City
†Field, James Samuel *stevedore company executive*

Lebanon
Lager, Henry S. *transporation executive*
Pollazzi, Roger G. *transportation executive*

Montclair
Morris, John Lunden *international transportation executive*

Newark
Bonaventura, Vincent E. *transportation executive*
†Capra, Ralph *transportation executive*
Stults, Laurence Allen *airline pilot*

Peapack
Weiss, Allan Joseph *transport company executive, lawyer*

Plainsboro
Lindsay, Nathan James *aerospace company executive, retired career officer*

Raritan
Alatzas, George *delivery service company executive*

Rockleigh
†Plaskett, Thomas G. *transportation company executive*

Teterboro
†Engle, Phillip *airport executive*

Wayne
Drossman, Jay Lewis *aerospace executive*

NEW MEXICO

Farmington
Risley, Larry L. *air transportation executive*

Las Cruces
Borman, Frank *former astronaut, laser patent company executive*

NEW YORK

Albany
Vachon, Russell Bertrand *transportation executive*

Babylon
Collis, Charles *aircraft company executive*

Buffalo
†Stone, Robert A. *airport administrator*

Carmel
Shen, Chia Theng *former steamship company executive, religious institute official*

Dexter
Hayes, Eugene P. *airport administrator*

Elmsford
Bouw, Pieter *airline company executive*

Garden City
McNicholas, David Paul *automobile rental company executive*

Great Neck
Pollack, Paul Robert *airline service company executive*
Satinskas, Henry Anthony *airline services company executive*

Huntington
Jackson, Richard Montgomery *former airline executive*
Myers, Robert Jay *retired aerospace company executive*

Jackson Heights
Grebey, Clarence Raymond, Jr. *airline executive*

Jamaica
†Kelly, Robert *airport executive*
Mc Kinnon, Clinton Dan *aerospace transportation executive*
†Prendergast, Thomas F. *railroad executive*
Rowe, Richard Lloyd *aviation executive, management consultant*

Manhasset
Frankum, James Edward *airlines company executive*

Mount Kisco
Wilson, Robert R. H. *airline company executive*

New York
Apostolakis, James John *shipping company executive*
Ascher, Michael *transportation executive*
Branson, Richard *airline executive, entrepreneur, adventurer*
Danaher, Frank Erwin *transportation technologist*
Evans, James Hurlburt *retired transportation and natural resources executive*
Evans, Mary Johnston *transportation company director*
Francis, Richard Herman *transportation executive*
Gitner, Gerald L. *aviation and investment banking executive*
Goldstein, Jack *transportation executive*
Gregorio, Luis Justino Lopes *transportation executive*
Hyman, Morton Peter *shipping company executive*
Johnsen, Niels Winchester *ocean shipping company executive*
Kondas, Nicholas Frank *shipping company executive*
Lloyd-Jones, Donald J. *transportation executive*
Love, Richard Emerson *equipment manufacturing company executive*
Machida, Naoshi *airline company executive*
Recanati, Raphael *shipping and banking executive*
Whitman, Bruce Nairn *flight safety executive*
Winokur, Herbert Simon, Jr. *transportation company executive*

Rouses Point
Casey, William Rossiter *international transport executive*

NORTH CAROLINA

Chapel Hill
Bauer, Frederick Christian *motor carrier executive*

Charlotte
†Macomber, Tricia *airport executive*
Orr, T(homas) J(erome) (Jerry Orr) *airport terminal executive*
Tolan, David Joseph *transportation executive*

Cherryville
Carlton, James D. *trucking company executive*
Huffstetler, Palmer Eugene *lawyer, transportation executive*
Mayhew, Kenneth Edwin, Jr. *transportation company executive*
Younger, Kenneth G. *freight carrier corporation executive*

High Point
Ebeling, John Altman *trucking company executive*

Kannapolis
Thigpen, Alton Hill *motor transportation company executive*

Raleigh
Jacob, Jerry Rowland *airline executive*

Winston Salem
Davis, Thomas Henry *airline executive*
MacKinnon, William Howard *airline executive*

OHIO

Akron
Clapp, Joseph Mark *motor carrier company executive*
†Sullivan, Daniel Joseph, III *transportation executive*
Wickham, Michael W. *transportation executive*

Brecksville
Worden, Alfred Merrill *former astronaut, research company executive*

Cincinnati
†Hubbard, Peter E. *transportation company executive*
Murphy, Eugene F. *aerospace, communications and electronics executive*
Siebenburgen, David A. *airline company executive*

Cleveland
Collinson, John Theodore *former railroad company executive*
Damsel, Richard A. *transportation company executive*
Dannemiller, John C. *transportation company executive*

Columbus
Hedrick, Larry Willis *airport executive*
Newland, Ron *airport executive*

North Olmsted
Zilli, Harry Angelo, Jr. *rail transportation executive*

Oberlin
Startup, Charles Harry *airline executive*
Williams, Eleanor Joyce *air traffic control specialist*

Toledo
†Margolies, Jay Owen *transportation company executive*

Xenia
Bigelow, Daniel James *aerospace executive*

OKLAHOMA

Tulsa
Kitchen, Brent A. *airport executive*
†Klein, Joseph Matthew *transportation company executive*
Kruse, David Louis, II *transportation company executive*

OREGON

Oakland
Smelt, Ronald *retired aircraft company executive*

Portland
Hebe, James L. *trucking executive*

PENNSYLVANIA

Allentown
Doughty, George Franklin *airport administrator*
Rossetti, Joseph Paul *trucking industry executive*

Bethlehem
Billingsley, Charles Edward *transportation company executive*
Lewis, Andrew Lindsay, Jr. (Drew Lewis) *transportation and natural resources executive*
Stuart, Gary Miller *railroad executive*

Conshohocken
Cunningham, James Gerald, Jr. *transportation company executive*

Gettysburg
Mainwaring, Thomas Lloyd *motor freight company executive*

Gladwyne
Hasselman, Richard B. *consultant, retired railroad executive*

Highspire
†Sokol, John L. *transportation executive*

Lebanon
Arnold, Edward Henry *transportation executive*

New Oxford
Frock, J. Daniel *transportation executive, retired manufacturing company executive*

Philadelphia
Hagen, James Alfred *rail transportation executive*
†Loney, Mary Rose *airport administrator*
Walls, William Walton, Jr. *helicopter company executive*
Wilson, Bruce Brighton *transportation executive*

Pittsburgh
Hoffman, Donald Howard *transportation executive*
†Stuenkel, William C. *airport administrator*
Uher, Richard A. *rail transportation executive*

Villanova
Sullivan, Richard Cyril *retired transportation executive*

Yardley
Terry, John Joseph *transportation investor*

SOUTH CAROLINA

Charleston
†Chapin, Fred *airport executive*

Columbia
Conrad, Paul Ernest *transportation consultant*

SOUTH DAKOTA

Sioux Falls
Smith, Murray Thomas *transportation company executive*

TENNESSEE

Chattanooga
†Quinn, Patrick *tranportation executive*

Memphis
Cox, Larry D. *airport terminal executive*
Smith, Frederick Wallace *transportation company executive*
†Starnes, Michael S. *trucking executive*

Nashville
†Loveall, Clellon Lewis *transportation administrator, civil engineer*
Osborne, Charles William *transportation executive*

TEXAS

Austin
McCullough, Benjamin Franklin *transportation researcher, educator*
Nasworthy, Carol Cantwell *education and public policy researcher*

Bridge City
Smith, Phillip Carl *marine and ship pilot, rancher*

Corpus Christi
Hext, George D. *airport terminal executive*

Dallas
Baker, Robert Woodward *airline executive*
Barrett, Colleen Crotty *airline executive*
†Cambron, Robert L. *airport terminal executive*
Crandall, Robert Lloyd *airline executive*
†Fegan, Jeffrey P. *airport executive*
Fenter, Felix West *aerospace company executive*
Kelleher, Herbert David *airline executive, lawyer*
Richardi, Ralph Leonard *airline executive*
Sturns, Vernell *airport terminal executive*
Wallace, William C. *airline executive*
†Weller, Edgar O. *transportation executive*
Whitman, Reginald Norman *railroad official*
Ziebarth, Karl Rex *international transportation consultant*

Dickinson
Bush, Robert Thomas *shipping company executive*

Fort Worth
Anderson, John Quentin *rail transportation executive*
Greenwood, William E. *rail transportation executive*
Grinstein, Gerald *transportation executive*
Miller, Brian Keith *airline executive*

Harlingen
Farris, Robert Gene *transportation company executive*

Houston
Barry, Allan Ronald *ship pilot, corporate executive*
Bean, Alan LaVern *retired astronaut, artist*
†Bethune, Gordon *airline executive*
†Bonderman, David *airline company executive*
Brandenstein, Daniel Charles *astronaut, retired naval officer*
†Culbertson, Frank L. *astronaut*
Elmer, Augustus *shipping company executive*
Ferguson, John C. *airport terminal executive*
Ferguson, Robert R., III *airline company executive*
†Gaines, Paul B. *airport executive*
Hartsfield, Henry Warren, Jr. *astronaut*
Musgrave, Story *astronaut, surgeon, pilot, physiologist, educator*
Pickering, Robert Earl, Jr. *airline executive, consultant*
Thagard, Norman E. *astronaut, physician, engineer*
Young, John Watts *astronaut*

Irving
†Andersen, Carsten Steen *freight forwarding company executive*
†Wilson, Sam N. *transportation services executive*

Lindale
Carter, Thomas Smith, Jr. *retired railroad executive*

Roanoke
Steward, Jerry Wayne *air transportation executive consultant*

San Antonio
†Gonzalez, Efren *airport executive*
Kutchins, Michael Joseph *airport executive*
Lowry, A. Robert *federal government railroad arbitrator*

Temple
Rostovich, Sharon Renea *airport executive*

Thorndale
Fish, Howard Math *aerospace industry executive*

Waco
†Hall, Joe E. *trucking company executive*

UTAH

Ogden
Dilley, William Gregory *aviation company executive*

Salt Lake City
Bozich, Anthony Thomas *transportation industry consultant, retired motor freight company executive*

VIRGINIA

Alexandria
Donohue, Thomas Joseph *transportation association executive*
†McMahan, Jesse Thomas *aerospace consulting firm executive*
Pulling, Ronald Wilson, Sr. *aviation systems planner, civil engineer, consultant*

Arlington
†Beyer, Barbara Lynn *aviation consultant*
†Hochstein, Anatoly Boris *maritime ports and waterways educator, researcher, consultant*
Lloyd, James T. *air carrier corporation executive, corporate lawyer*
Mason, Phillip Howard *aircraft company executive, retired army officer*
Matthews, Sir Stuart *aviation industry executive*
Schofield, Seth Eugene *air transport company executive*
Schwab, Michael R. *air transportation company executive*
Stokes, B. R. *transportation consultant*
†Sutton, George W. *aerospace company executive*

Chesterfield
Congdon, John Rhodes *transportation executive*

Dulles
†Thompson, David Walker *astronautics company executive*

Falls Church
Morris, Robert Alan *aerospace industry executive*

Great Falls
Hughes, Alan Richard *aerospace company executive*

Herndon
Bridges, James R. *air transportation executive*
†Pollard, Charles W. *transportation services executive*

Marshall
Hayward, Charles Winthrop *retired railroad company executive*

Midlothian
Parsons, Robert Eugene *transportation consultant*

Newport News
Cox, Alvin Earl *shipbuilding executive*
Phillips, William Ray, Jr. *shipbuilding executive*

Norfolk
Goode, David Ronald *transportation company executive*
McKinnon, Arnold Borden *transportation company executive*
Middleton, Donald Earl *transportation company executive*
†Rudder, Paul R. *transportation executive*
Scott, Kenneth R. *transportation executive*
Shannon, John Sanford *railway executive, lawyer*
Turbyfill, John Ray *railway executive*
Watts, Dave Henry *corporate executive*

Richmond
Aron, Mark G. *transportation executive, lawyer*
Boswell, Thomas Wayne *transportation executive*
Hintz, Robert Louis *transportation company executive*
Hoppin, Thomas Edward *transportation executive*
Watkins, Hays Thomas *retired railroad executive*

Springfield
Finkel, Karen Evans *school transportation association executive, lawyer*

Sterling
Harris, Paul Lynwood *aerospace transportation executive*

Vienna
†Sides, James Ralph *aerospace executive*

Virginia Beach
Kreyling, Edward George, Jr. *railroad executive*

Winchester
Jamison, Richard Bryan *airport consultant*

WASHINGTON

Bellevue
Baker, Jackson Arnold *container shipping company executive*

Seattle
Beighle, Douglas Paul *business executive*
Cella, John J. *freight company executive*
Clarkson, Lawrence William *airplane company executive*
Cline, Robert Stanley *air freight company executive*
Condit, Philip Murray *aerospace executive, engineer*
Elliott, Jeanne Marie Koreltz *transportation executive*
Givan, Boyd Eugene *aircraft company executive*
Jaeger, David Arnold *aerospace company executive*
Raisbeck, James David *aircraft design executive*
Schmidt, Peter Gustav *shipbuilding industry executive*
Smith, Donald William *airport manager*
Thornton, Dean Dickson *retired airplane company executive*
Vecci, Raymond Joseph *airline executive*

Yakima
Robbins, Gary Samuel *airport manager*

WEST VIRGINIA

Harpers Ferry
Nash, Bradley DeLamater *transportation executive*

WISCONSIN

Green Bay
Lewis, Gary *trucking executive*
Olson, James Richard *transportation company executive*

Milwaukee
Bateman, C. Barry *airport terminal Executive*
Mayer, Henry Michael *mass transit consultant*
Teerlink, Richard Francis *motor company executive*
Ziperski, James Richard *lawyer, trucking company executive*

Neenah
Fetzer, Edward Frank *transportation company executive*

WYOMING

Worland
Woods, Lawrence Milton *airline company executive*

CANADA

ALBERTA

Calgary
Caron, Ernie Matthew *airport executive*
Jenkins, Kevin J. *airline company executive*
McCaig, Jeffrey James *transportation company executive*
McCaig, John Robert *transportation executive*
Paquette, Richard *airport executive*

Edmonton
Eng, Howard *airport administrator*
†Hutchison, Geoffrey Richard *airport general manager*

NOVA SCOTIA

Enfield
Randell, Joseph David *airline executive*

Halifax
Renouf, Harold Augustus *business consultant*

ONTARIO

Almonte
Morrison, Angus Curran *aviation executive*

Burlington
Jackson, Donald Kenneth *transportation company executive*

Mississauga
Dallison, Frank Keith *transportation company executive*
Kuhn, Hansjoerg Karl (George Kuhn) *transportation executive*
Tobias, Kal *transportation executive*

Ottawa
Ansary, Hassan Jaber *transportation executive*
Coleman, John Morley *transportation research director*
Sheflin, Michael John Edward *transportation commissioner*

Sault Sainte Marie
Savoie, Leonard Norman *transportation company executive*

Toronto
McCoomb, Lloyd Alexander *transportation executive*

QUEBEC

Dorval
Brown, Robert Ellis *transportation company executive, former Canadian government official*

Mirabel
Ginzburg, Rubin *airport executive, electrical engineer*

Montreal
Beaudoin, Laurent *industrial, recreational and transportation company executive*
Black, William Gordon *transportation executive*
Bourgeault, Jean-Jacques *air transportation executive*
Deegan, Derek James *transportation executive*
Labelle, Eugene Jean-Marc *airport director general*
Lanyi, Alexander Sandor *rail transportation executive*
†Lawless, Ronald Edward *transportation executive*
Smith, Brian Ray Douglas *rail transportation executive, lawyer*
Stinson, William W. *transportation executive*
Taylor, Claude I. *airlines executive*
Tellier, Paul M. *Canadian railway transportation executive*

Quebec
Rochette, Louis *shipowner*

Saint Laurent
Harris, Hollis Loyd *airline executive*

Saint Sauveur
Hanigan, Lawrence *retired railway executive*

DENMARK

Vedbaek
Nordqvist, Erik Askbo *shipping company executive*

GERMANY

Munich
Born, Gunthard Karl *aerospace executive*

SWEDEN

Stockholm
†Carlzon, Jan (Gosta) *airline company executive*
Lindberg, Helge *aviation consultant*

ADDRESS UNPUBLISHED

Aldrin, Buzz *former astronaut, science consultant*
Ames, Donald Paul *retired aerospace company executive, researcher*
Armstrong, Neil A. *former astronaut*
Baer, Robert J. *transportation company executive*
Barringer, J(ohn) Paul *transportation executive, retired diplomat and career service executive*
Brazier, Don Roland *retired railroad executive*
Brennan, Robert J. *shipping company executive*
Brown, Donald Douglas *transportation company executive, retired air force officer, consultant*
Burkett, Ben Vern, Sr. *aircraft support company executive*
Butterfield, Alexander Porter *business executive, former government official, retired air force officer*
Caporali, Renso L. *aerospace executive*
Carpenter, Malcolm Scott *astronaut, oceanographer*
Culbertson, Philip Edgar *aerospace company executive*
Dasburg, John Harold *airline executive*
Davis, George Lynn *retired aerospace company executive*
Del Balzo, Joseph Michael *aviation consulting company executive*
Dely, Steven *aerospace company executive*
Eischen, Michael Hugh *retired railroad executive*
Fenello, Michael John *aviation consultant, retired government agency executive*
Freitag, Peter Roy *transportation specialist*
Glennon, Harrison Randolph, Jr. *retired shipping company executive*
Graebner, James Herbert *transportation executive*
Greenwald, Gerald *air transportation executive*
Gunn, Michael William *airline executive*
Heitz, Edward Fred *freight traffic consultant*
Horton, Robert Baynes *railroad company executive*
Hurst, John Emory, Jr. *retired airline executive*
Johnston, Gerald Andrew *aerospace company executive, retired*
King, Edward William *retired transportation executive*
Ledford, Jack Clarence *retired aircraft company executive, former air force officer*
Lesko, Harry Joseph *transportation company executive*
Lillibridge, John Lee *retired airline executive*
Loeffler, David E. *transportation executive*
Marshall, Charles Noble *railroad executive*
Marshall, David Lawrence *freight forwarding and mining company executive*
Masiello, Rocco Joseph *airlines and aerospace manufacturing executive*
Masson, Gayl Angela *airline pilot*
Mast, Stewart Dale *retired airport manager*
Matthews, L. White, III *railroad executive*
Maxfield, Kenneth Wayne *transportation company executive*
McKinnon, Richard Anthony *airline executive*
Morse, Leon William *traffic, physical distribution and transportation management executive, consultant*
Murray, Leonard Hugh *railroad executive*
Newby, Jill Jeanine *airline pilot*
Quesnel, Gregory L. *transportation company executive*
Ransome, Ernest Leslie, III *transportation and retail company executive*
Regalado, Raul L. *airport parking executive*
Renda, Dominic Phillip *airline executive*
Rose, James Turner *aerospace consultant*
Ruegg, Donald George *retired railway company executive*
Schaefer, C. Barry *railroad executive, lawyer, investment banker*
Shepard, Alan Bartlett, Jr. *astronaut, real estate developer*
Shockley, Edward Julian *aerospace company executive*
Smith, Billie M. *retired aircraft company executive*
Snow, John William *railroad executive*
Snowden, Lawrence Fontaine *retired aircraft company executive, retired marine corps general officer*
Sze, Andy Hok-Fan *transportation executive*
Voss, Omer Gerald *truck company executive*
†Wilson, Gary Lee *airline company executive*
†Winston, Charles David *transportation company executive*
Zander, Glenn R. *airline company executive*

INDUSTRY: UTILITIES, ENERGY, RESOURCES

UNITED STATES

ALABAMA

Birmingham
Barker, Thomas Watson, Jr. *energy company executive*
Bowden, Travis J. *utilities executive*
Bowron, Richard Anderson *retired utilities executive*
Dahl, Hilbert Douglas *mining company executive*
Franklin, H. Allen *electric company executive*
Gardner, Ronald Bruce *gas company executive*
†Guthrie, Bill Myers *utility executive*
Hairston, W(illiam) George, III *nuclear power company executive*
Harris, Elmer Beseler *electric utility executive*
Hutchins, William Bruce, III *utility company executive*
Kuehn, Ronald L., Jr. *natural resources company executive*
†Lysinger, Rex Jackson *energy company executive*
Matthews, William Elliott, IV *gas company executive*
Robin, Theodore Tydings, Jr. *electric company executive, engineer*
Smith, Peter Garthwaite *energy consultant*
†Warren, William Michael, Jr. *utilities company executive*
Williams, N. Thomas *gas company executive*

Clanton
Imgrund, William *oil company executive*

Shoal Creek
Ahearn, John Francis, Jr. *retired oil and gas company executive*

ALASKA

Anchorage
Hopkins, Stephen Davis *mining company executive*
†Pritchard, David J. *oil company executive*
Wade, William Edward, Jr. *oil company executive*

Fairbanks
Beistline, Earl Hoover *mining consultant*

Juneau
Albanese, Thomas *minerals company executive*

ARIZONA

Benson
Kimball, Donald W. *electric utility corporate executive*

Carefree
Birkelbach, Albert Ottmar *retired oil company executive*

Morenci
†Snider, Tim *mining executive*

Phoenix
De Michele, O. Mark *utility company executive*
Ekstrom, Walter F. *utility company executive*
Gillis, William Freeman *telecommunications executive*
Huffman, Edgar Joseph *oil company executive*
Norberg, Jaron B. *public service company executive*
Ryan, Patrick John *mining company executive*
St. Clair, Thomas McBryar *mining and manufacturing company executive*
Yearley, Douglas Cain *mining and manufacturing company executive*

Scottsdale
†Holliger, Fred Lee *oil company executive*

Sun City West
Black, Robert Frederick *former oil company executive*
O'Brien, Gerald James *utilities executive*
Vrable, John Bernard *retired oil corrosion engineer, consultant*

Tempe
Clevenger, Jeffrey Griswold *mining company executive*
Hickson, Robin Julian *mining company executive*

Tucson
Banzhaf, Steven Michael *utility company executive, lawyer*
Bayless, Charles Edward *lawyer, utility executive*
Champagne, John F., Jr. *mining company executive*
Davidson, Dalwyn Robert *electric utility executive*
Davis, James Luther *retired utilities executive, lawyer*
Heller, Frederick *retired mining company executive*
Osborne, Thomas Cramer *mineral industry consultant*
Peeler, Stuart Thorne *petroleum industry executive and independent oil operator*
Peters, Charles William *research and development company manager*
Saul, Kenneth Louis *retired utility company executive*

ARKANSAS

El Dorado
McNutt, Jack Wray *oil company executive*
Murphy, Charles Haywood, Jr. *petroleum company executive*
Vaughan, Odie Frank *oil company executive*
Watkins, Jerry West *retired oil company executive, lawyer*

Fayetteville
Scharlau, Charles Edward, III *natural gas company executive*

Flippin
Sanders, Steven Gill *telecommunications executive*

Little Rock
Bobbitt, Max E. *telecommunications executive*
Ford, Joe Thomas *telephone company executive, former state senator*
Gardner, Kathleen D. *gas company executive, lawyer*
King, Jack L. *electric power industry executive*
†Maulden, Jerry L. *utility company executive*
†Whillock, Carl Simpson *electric cooperative executive, former academic administrator*

Russellville
Jones, James Rees *retired oil company executive*

CALIFORNIA

Alhambra
Anderson, Gordon MacKenzie *petroleum service contractors executive*
Garber, C(harles) Stedman, Jr. *oil and mining industry executive*
Shannon, Edfred L., Jr. *gas and oil drilling company executive*

Beverly Hills
Brann, Alton Joseph *oilfield services executive*

Corona Del Mar
Hill, Melvin James *oil company executive*

Costa Mesa
Wall, James Edward *petroleum, pharmaceutical executive*

Dana Point
Frederickson, Arman Frederick *minerals company executive*

Downey
Orden, Ted *gasoline service stations executive*

Hanford
Drosdick, John Girard *oil company executive*

Hillsborough
Willoughby, Rodney Erwin *retired oil company executive*

Irvine
Keating, James J. *oil industry executive*

La Canada Flintridge
Read, William McClain *retired oil company executive*
Simmons, John Wesley *oil company executive*

La Jolla
Morse, Jack Hatton *utilities consultant*

Long Beach
Rea, William *oil industry executive*
Winget, Clifford *oil industry executive*

Los Angeles
Arnault, Ronald J. *petroleum company executive*
†Asquith, Ronald H. *petroleum corporate executive*
Babikian, George H. *petroleum products company executive*
Beach, Roger C. *oil company executive*
Bowlin, Michael Ray *oil company executive*
Cook, Lodwrick Monroe *petroleum company executive*
Edwards, Howard Lee *petroleum company executive*
Farman, Richard Donald *gas company executive*
Laurance, Dale R. *oil company executive*
†Martin, David R. *oil company executive*
McIntyre, Robert Malcolm *utility company executive*
McSweeny, William Francis *petroleum company executive, author*
Middleton, James Arthur *oil and gas company executive*
Mitchell, Warren I. *utility company executive*
Rensch, Joseph Romaine *public utility holding company executive*
Snyder, Sam A. *oil company executive, lawyer*
Stegemeier, Richard Joseph *oil company executive*
Van Horne, R. Richard *oil company executive*
Wood, Willis Bowne, Jr. *utility holding company executive*
Wycoff, Robert E. *petroleum company executive*

Los Olivos
Cruft, Edgar Frank *mining company executive*

Martinez
Meyer, Jarold Alan *oil company research executive*

Newport Beach
Armstrong, Robert Arnold *petroleum company executive*
Clark, Earnest Hubert, Jr. *tool company executive*

Oxnard
Parriott, James Deforis *retired oil company executive, consultant*

Pacific Palisades
Klein, Joseph Mark *retired mining company executive*
Mulryan, Henry Trist *mineral company executive, consultant*

Palo Alto
Willrich, Mason *utility company executive, consultant*

Palos Verdes Estates
Christie, Hans Frederick *retired utility company subsidiaries executive, consultant*

Pasadena
Finnell, Michael Hartman *corporate executive*
Mc Duffie, Malcolm *oil company executive*
†Stassi, Ronald V. *electric power industry executive*
Van Amringe, John Howard *retired oil industry executive, geologist*
†Waters, Daniel W. *electrical power industry executive*

Playa Del Rey
Weir, Alexander, Jr. *utility consultant, inventor*

Rosemead
Allen, Howard Pfeiffer *electric utility executive, lawyer*
Barry, David N., III *utility executive*
Bennett, Brian O'Leary *utilities executive*
Bryson, John E. *utilities company executive*
Bushey, Richard Kenneth *utility executive*
Noel, Michael Lee *utility executive*
Ray, Harold Byrd *utilities executive*

Sacramento
Crabbe, John Crozier *telecommunications consultant*

San Diego
Cota, John Francis *utility executive*
Haney, Raymond Lee *gas and electric company executive*
Igasaki, Masao, Jr. *retired utilities company executive, controller*
†Page, Thomas Alexander *utility executive*
Saunders, Russell Joseph *utility company executive*
Thomas, Jack E. *utility company executive*

San Francisco
Bonney, John Dennis *oil company executive*
Brandin, Alf Elvin *retired mining and shipping company executive*
Bray, Arthur Philip *management science corporation executive*
Carter, George Kent *oil company executive*
Clarke, Richard Alan *electric and gas utility company executive, lawyer*
Conger, Harry Milton *mining company executive*
Crain, William Edwin *oil company executive*
Derr, Kenneth T. *oil company executive*
Flittie, Clifford Gilliland *retired petroleum company executive*
Ginn, Sam L. *telephone company executive*
Grier, William E. *petroleum company executive*
Guinn, Sam *telecommunications industry executive*
High, Thomas W. *utilities company executive*
Keller, George Matthew *retired oil company executive*

Kleeman, Michael Jeffrey telecommunications and computer consultant
Littlefield, Edmund Wattis mining company executive
Lowry, Edwin R. petroleum company executive
Maneatis, George A. retired utility company executive
McCrea, Peter oil company executive
Mielke, Frederick William, Jr. retired utility company executive
Neerhout, John, Jr. petroleum company executive
Peterson, Richard Hamlin utility executive, lawyer
Price, Willis Joseph retired oil company executive
Quigley, Philip J. telecommunications industry executive
Reinsch, Harry Orville power company executive
Renfrew, Charles Byron oil company executive, lawyer
Ross, John J. petroleum products company executive
Shackelford, Barton Warren retired utility executive
Shiffer, James David utility executive
Skinner, Stanley Thayer utility company executive, lawyer
Smith, Gordon Ray utilities executive
Sproul, John Allan retired public utility executive
Sullivan, James N. fuel company executive
†Walsh, Robert Francis oil company executive
Zaccaria, Adrian utilities executive

San Juan Capistrano
Der Garabedian, Paul energy and environmental company executive

San Mateo
Sanders, Charles Franklin corporate executive

San Rafael
Latno, Arthur Clement, Jr. telephone company executive
Premo, Paul Mark oil company executive

Santa Ana
Mickelson, H(erald) Fred electric utility executive

Santa Barbara
Bilhorn, William W. international mining company consultant

Santa Clara
†Pribilla, Peter telecommunications industry executive

Santa Ynez
Byrne, Joseph retired oil company executive

Stockton
†Kreikemeier, Kenneth G. pipe manufacturing company executive

Sunnyvale
†Money, Arthur L. electronics executive

Thousand Oaks
Sparrow, Larry J. telecommunications executive

Torrance
†Suzuki, Takuya telecommunications executive

Turlock
Williams, Delwyn Charles telephone company executive

Ventura
Field, A. J. former oil drilling company executive, engineering consultant

Walnut Creek
Humphrey, William Albert mining company executive

Woodland Hills
Talbot, Matthew J. oil company executive, rancher

COLORADO

Boulder
Fox, Joseph Leland utilities executive
†Raudenbush, Michael H. nuclear energy industry executive
Thomas, Daniel Foley telecommunications company executive

Colorado Springs
Hampton, Rex Herbert gold mining company executive, consultant
King, Peter Joseph, Jr. retired gas company executive
O'Shields, Richard Lee retired natural gas company executive
Robinson, Ronald Alan oil company executive
Whitney, Jonathan Robert gas company executive

Denver
†Anderson, Donald H. gas industry executive
Bowman, Joseph Searles petroleum consultant
†Breitenbach, Eugene Allen oil company executive
Cann, William Hopson former mining company executive
Cole, David Rodney mining executive
Dana, Richard E. oil industry executive
Danos, Robert McClure retired oil company executive
Davis, Marvin petroleum company executive, entrepreneur
Fagin, David Kyle natural resource company executive
Fancher, George H., Jr. oil company executive, petroleum engineer
†Hock, Delwin D. utilities company executive
Leather, Richard Brenk mineral company executive
Lewis, Jerome A. petroleum company executive, investment banker
Macey, William Blackmore oil company executive
Magness, Bob John telecommunications executive
McCoy, James Henry oil company executive
Miller, Arlyn James oil company executive
Murdy, Wayne William mining company executive, financial officer
Owens, Marvin Franklin, Jr. oil company executive
Philip, Thomas Peter mining executive
Rendu, Jean-Michel Marie mining executive
†Riess, J. M. gas and oil industry executive
Thompson, Lohren Matthew oil company executive
Timothy, Robert Keller telephone company executive
Trueblood, Harry Albert, Jr. oil company executive
Valot, Daniel L. oil industry executive
Wynkoop, Donal Brooke electric power company executive

Englewood
Anderson, James Thomas telecommunications executive
Arrington, Steve oil company executive
Barr, Kenneth John retired mining company executive
Fisher, Donne Francis telecommunications executive
Malone, John C. telecommunications executive
McCormick, Richard David telecommunications company executive
†Osterhoff, James Marvin telecommunications company executive
Parker, Gordon Rae natural resource company executive
Ward, Milton Hawkins mining company executive

Lakewood
Battey, Charles W. gas industry executive
Hall, Larry D. energy company executive, lawyer
Hurst, Leland Lyle natural gas company executive
Shafer, J. M. utility administrator

Larkspur
Bierbaum, J. Armin petroleum company executive, consultant

Littleton
Clift, William Orrin oil company executive, consultant

Westminster
Kober, Carl Leopold exploration company executive

CONNECTICUT

Berlin
Ellis, William Ben utility executive

Bridgeport
McGregor, Jack Edwin natural resource company executive

Darien
Kutz, Kenneth John retired mining executive
Smith, Elwin Earl mining and oil company executive

Greenwich
Bennett, Jack Franklin oil company executive
Donahue, Donald Jordan mining company executive
Hicks, Paul B., Jr. retired petroleum company executive
Lawi, David Steven energy, agriservice and thermoplastic resins industries executive
Neafsey, John Patrick oil company executive
Nelson, Don Harris gas and oil industry executive
Schmidt, Herman J. former oil company executive

Guilford
Morgan, Leon Alford retired utility executive

Hamden
Gordon, Angus Neal, Jr. retired electric company executive

Hartford
Fox, Bernard Michael utilities company executive, electrical engineer
Opeka, John Frank utility executive, electrical engineer

Milford
†Kessman, Alan Stuart telecommunications executive

Mystic
Townsend, Thomas Perkins former mining company executive

New Canaan
†Crawford, Kevin Francis mining company executive
McIvor, Donald Kenneth retired petroleum company executive, university administrator
Wolfley, Alan corporate executive

New Haven
Donofrio, Richard Michael telecommunications company executive
Fassett, John D. retired utility executive, consultant
Fiscus, Robert L. electric power industry executive
†Miglio, Daniel Joseph telecommunications company executive
Monteith, Walter Henry, Jr. utility company executive

Old Greenwich
Hittle, Richard Howard corporate executive, international affairs consultant

Orange
Bowerman, Richard Henry utility company executive, lawyer

Ridgefield
Mattausch, Thomas Edward public relations consultant, business owner

Southport
Damson, Barrie Morton oil and gas exploration company executive

Stamford
Block, Edward Martel consultant, former telephone company executive
Duke, Robert Dominick mining executive, lawyer
Farrell, Joseph Christopher mining executive, services executive
Gardiner, Hobart Clive petroleum company executive
Gault, John Franklin telecommunications industry executive
Jacobson, Ishier retired utility executive
Kinnear, James Wesley, III retired petroleum company executive
Lee, Charles Robert telecommunications company executive
Lee, John J. petroleum, fertilizer company executive
Mc Kinley, John Key retired oil company executive
Pansini, Michael Samuel energy company executive, consultant

Waterford
Sillin, Lelan Flor, Jr. retired utility executive

Westport
Krist, Peter Christopher former petroleum company executive
Nedom, H. Arthur petroleum consultant
Weil, Ernst oil industry executive

Wilton
Hoefling, Rudolf Joachim power generating company executive

DELAWARE

Wilmington
Campbell, Roger D. utility company executive
Connelly, Donald Preston electric and gas utility company executive
Corn, Jack W. oil company executive
Cosgrove, Howard Edward, Jr. utility executive
Croom, John Henry, III utility company executive
Daly, John Dennis utility company executive
Dunham, Archie W. petroleum and chemical products company executive
†Krol, John A. diversified chemicals executive
Landon, Harry Raymond utility company executive
Timmons, Earl L. oil company executive

DISTRICT OF COLUMBIA

Washington
†Bloch, Peter B. nuclear power commission administrator
Davis, Herbert Lowell utility company executive
Dawson, Rhett electric power company executive, lawyer
Deland, Michael Reeves energy executive
Dennis, Patricia Diaz communications Attorney
Derrick, John Martin, Jr. electric company executive
Endahl, Lowell Jerome retired electrical cooperative executive
Hirsch, Robert Louis energy and management consultant
†Johnson, John C. petroleum company executive
Kuhn, Thomas R. trade association executive
Maher, Patrick Joseph utility company executive
McCollam, William, Jr. utility company executive
McGee, Robert Merrill oil company executive
†Mitchell, Edward Franklin utility company executive
†Modiano, Albert Louis gas, oil industry executive
Paige, Hilliard Wegner corporate director, consultant
Roberts, Bert C., Jr. telecommunications company executive
Shawhan, Samuel Frazier, Jr. telecommunications executive
Smiley, D. E. petroleum company executive
Thompson, William Reid public utility executive, lawyer
Weiss, Stanley Alan mining, chemicals and refractory company executive
Winzenried, Jesse David retired petroleum executive
Wraase, Dennis Richard utilities company executive, accountant

FLORIDA

Atlantic Beach
Zechella, Alexander Philip oil company executive, former naval officer

Boca Raton
Gralla, Eugene natural gas company executive

Bonifay
Quattlebaum, Walter Emmett, Jr. telephone company executive

Boynton Beach
Babler, Wayne E. retired telephone company executive, lawyer

Captiva
Ronald, Peter utility executive

Delray Beach
Epley, Marion Jay oil company executive
Reef, Arthur industry business consultant

Destin
Cunningham, James Everett retired energy services company executive

Jacksonville
Francis, James Delbert oil company executive

Juno Beach
Petillo, James Thomas diversified utility company executive

Largo
Dolan, John E. consultant, retired utility executive
Loader, Jay Gordon retired utility company executive

Miami
Driscoll, Garrett Bates telecommunications executive
Hern, Kenneth Truman oil and gas industry executive

Naples
Bush, John William business executive, federal official
Ivancevic, Walter Charles former gas distribution company executive
Johnson, Zane Quentin retired petroleum company executive
Kay, Herbert retired natural resources company executive
Rowe, Jack Field retired electric utility executive

Orlando
Ispass, Alan Benjamin utilities executive
Pope, Theodore Campbell, Jr. utilities executive, consultant
Todd, Troy W. telecommunications company executive

Palm Beach
Donnell, John Randolph petroleum executive
Smith, Lloyd Hilton independent oil and gas producer

Palm Beach Gardens
Harnett, Joseph Durham oil company executive

Palm City
White, Eugene James retired technology company executive

Pensacola
McCrary, Douglas L. utility company executive
Platz, Terrance Oscar utilities company executive

Pinellas Park
Perry, Paul Alverson utility executive

Ponte Vedra Beach
Green, Norman Kenneth retired oil industry executive, former naval officer
Milbrath, Robert Henry retired petroleum executive

Saint Petersburg
Critchfield, Jack Barron utilities company executive
Greene, George E., III utility company executive
Hancock, John Allan utility company executive
Hines, Andrew Hampton, Jr. utilities executive
†Keesler, Allen John, Jr. utilites executive
Neiser, Richard William utility executive
Soechtig, Jacqueline Elizabeth telecommunications executive

Sarasota
Jaeger, Leonard Henry former public utility executive

Sun City Center
McGrath, John Francis utility executive

Tampa
†Anderson, Girard F. utility company executive
Campbell, David Ned retired electric utility executive, business consultant
†Guzzle, Timothy L. energy corporation executive
Leavengood, Victor Price telephone company executive
†Rankin, Thompson L. utilities executive, agricultural executive
Starkey, William Edward telephone company executive
Taggart, James Knox electric utility executive

Tequesta
Hart, Frederick Donald retired utility association and manufacturing executive

Venice
Torrey, Richard Frank utility executive

Vero Beach
Corr, Thomas L. oil industry executive
Mc Afee, Jerry retired oil company executive, chemical engineer

West Palm Beach
Pledger, Thomas Rolon holding company executive

Winter Park
Spake, Ned Bernarr energy company executive

GEORGIA

Americus
Jernigan, Bob utility company executive

Athens
Wood, Betty A. utilities executive

Atlanta
Ackerman, F. Duane utility company executive
Addison, Edward L. retired utility holding company executive
Baker, Henry Grady, Jr. utilities company executive
Benson, Thomas Hayden utility company executive
Bolch, Carl Edward, Jr. corporation executive, lawyer
Boren, Thomas Garner utility executive
Brinkley, Donald R. oil industry executive
Chilton, Horace Thomas pipeline company executive
Clendenin, John L. telecommunications company executive
Dahlberg, Alfred William electric company executive
Frost, Norman Cooper retired telephone company executive
Hemby, John Carlyle, Jr. utility company executive
Holmes, Malcolm Herbert telecommunications company executive
†Jobe, Warren Yancey electric utility company executive
†Jones, David R. gas company executive
Knobloch, Carl William, Jr. oil and gas services executive
†McCoy, William O. telecommunications executive
McGuire, Raymond L. telecommunications company executive
Miller, James Hugh, Jr. retired public utility executive
Norris, T. H. retired oil industry executive
Olson, Frank L. electrical power industry executive
†Pate, Zack Taylor, Jr. nuclear power company executive
Ramsey, Ira Clayton pipeline company executive
Sessoms, Walter Woodrow telecommunications executive

Skinner, B. Franklin *retired telecommunications executive*
Voss, William Charles *retired oil company executive*
Weber, Donald W. *telephone company executive*
Woodward, Richard Hollis, Jr. *utility company executive, lawyer*

Gainesville
Leet, Richard Hale *oil company executive*

Norcross
Born, Allen *mining executive*

Sandersville
Thiele, Paul Frederick *mining company executive*

Tucker
Kilgore, Tom D. *electric power company executive*

HAWAII

Honolulu
†Bates, George E. *oil industry executive*
†Clarke, Robert F. *utilities company executive*
Reed, Robert George, III *petroleum company executive*
Toole, Lee K. *telecommunications company executive*
Williams, Carl Harwell *utilities executive*
Williamson, Harwood Danford *utility company executive*

Kailua
Engelbardt, Robert Miles *telecommunications executive*

IDAHO

Boise
Bowers, Daniel Kent *electric power industry executive*
Glynn, William C. *natural gas company executive*

Coeur D Alene
Brown, Arthur *mining executive*
Griffith, William Alexander *former mining company executive*
†Sabala, James Anthony *mining company executive*
Wheeler, Dennis Earl *mining company executive, lawyer*

Idaho Falls
Newman, Stanley Ray *oil refining company executive*

ILLINOIS

Argonne
Heine, James Arthur *utilities plant manager*

Arlington Heights
†Wilson, Debra *oil, gas industry executive*

Aurora
†Fisher, Thomas Lee *gas company executive*

Barrington
Perry, I. Chet *petroleum company executive*

Chicago
Akerson, Daniel Francis *telecommunications industry executive*
Anderson, Paul Milton *steel company executive*
Ban, Stephen Dennis *natural gas industry research institute executive*
Barnett, Robert L. *utilities executive*
Brooker, Thomas Kimball *oil company executive*
Brown, Richard Harris *telecommunications industry executive*
Callahan, Ronald E. *petroleum company executive*
Carr, Robert Clifford *petroleum company executive*
†Conrad, John R. *utilities corporate executive*
Early, Patrick Joseph *oil and gas company executive*
Eisner, Michael C. *electric power industry executive*
Engel, Joel Stanley *telecommunications executive*
†Fligg, James Edward *oil company executive*
Fuller, Harry Laurance *oil company executive*
Hubbard, Antoinette Ziegler *telecommunications executive*
Lowrie, William G. *oil company executive*
Morrow, Richard Martin *retired oil company executive*
Murtaugh, Rodger W. *oil company executive*
Notebaert, Richard C. *telecommunications industry executive*
O'Connor, James John *utility company executive*
Peirson, Walter Russell *oil company executive*
Reed, Cordell *utility company executive*
Reeves, Michael Stanley *public utility executive*
Rutigliano, Louis J. *telecommunications industry executive*
Skinner, Samuel Knox *utilities executive, lawyer*
†Sobel, Arnold I. *mining executive*
Terry, Richard Edward *public utility holding company executive*
Thomas, Lawrason Dale *oil company executive*
†Whitley, Douglas L. *telecommunications industry executive*
Williams, Carl Chanson *oil company executive*

Decatur
Haab, Larry David *utility company executive*
Kelley, Wendell J. *retired utilities executive*
Wells, Charles William *utility executive*
Womeldorff, Porter John *utilities executive*

Deerfield
Chieger, Kathryn Jean *oil company executive*

East Saint Louis
Reilly, Michael K. *mining executive*

Fairview Heights
Hughes, John W. *mining executive*
Vyas, Chand Bhaourbhai *coal company executive*

Geneva
Pershing, Robert George *retired telecommunications company executive*

Glen Ellyn
Lischer, Ludwig Frederick *consultant, former utility company executive*

Glenview
Cozad, James William *retired oil company executive*

Hinsdale
Gauthier, Clarence Joseph *retired utility executive*

Lawrenceville
†Sudhaus, William S. *petroleum company executive*
Wright, John D. R. *oil industry executive*

Lincolnshire
Guist, Fredric Michael *minerals, chemicals and waste services corporation executive*

Lombard
†Riordan, John Francis *oil and gas corporate executive*

Marion
Lincoln, Lucian Abraham *coal company executive*

Naperville
†Lannon, John Joseph *energy holding company executive*
Reuss, Robert Pershing *telecommunications executive, consultant*
Triggiani, Leonard Vincent *corporate executive*

Northbrook
Demaree, David Harry *utilities executive*

Orland Park
English, Floyd Leroy *telecommunications company executive*

Peoria
Slone, R. Wayne *utility company executive*
Viets, Robert O. *utilities executive*

Rock Island
Whitmore, Charles Horace *utility executive, lawyer, management consultant*

Springfield
Greenwalt, Clifford Lloyd *utility executive*
Jackson, Robert William *utility company executive*

INDIANA

Bloomington
†Smith, J. Steven *electric power industry executive*

Evansville
Able, Warren Walter *natural resource company executive, physician*
Kiechlin, Robert Jerome *retired coal company executive, financial consultant*
Reherman, Ronald Gilbert *gas and electric company executive*

Fort Wayne
Menge, Richard Cramer *electric utility executive*

Hammond
Adik, Stephen Peter *energy company executive*
Neale, Gary Lee *utilities executive*
Schroer, Edmund Armin *utility company executive*

Indianapolis
Ellerbrook, Niel Cochran *gas company executive*
Griffiths, David Neil *utility executive*
Husted, Ralph Waldo *former utility executive*
Krueger, Betty Jane *telecommunications company executive*
Lindemann, Donald Lee *utility executive*
Morris, James Thomas *utilities executive*
Todd, Zane Grey *utility executive*
Woods, Marcus Eugene *electric utility company executive, lawyer*

Lawrenceburg
Dautel, Charles Shreve *retired mining company executive*

Michigan City
Higgins, William Henry Clay, III *retired telecommunications consultant*

New Castle
Dudley, Harry Bruce *oil company executive*

Plainfield
Menscer, Darrell V. *utility company executive*
†Noland, Jon David *utilities executive, lawyer*

South Bend
Pfeil, Richard John *electric company executive*

Westfield
Nolan, Paul T. *telephone company executive*

IOWA

Akron
Johnson, Marlys Dianne *utility company executive*

Cedar Rapids
†Carlson, LeRoy Theodore, Jr. *telecommunications industry executive*
Kucharski, Robert Joseph *power industry financial executive*
Root, Larry Donald *utilities executive*

Davenport
Bright, Stanley J. *utilities executive*

Des Moines
Christiansen, Russell *utility company executive*
Lyon, James Robert *utilities executive*

Sioux City
Delk, Ira Edwin *utilities and diversified company executive*
Engle, Richard Carlyle *utilities executive*
Harward, Gary John *utility company executive*
Wharton, Beverly Ann *utility company executive*

KANSAS

Independence
Swearingen, Harold Lyndon *oil company executive*

Mc Pherson
Williams, Larry Emmett *oil company executive*

Pittsburg
Nettels, George Edward, Jr. *mining executive*

Shawnee Mission
Deaver, Darwin Holloway *former utility executive*

Stilwell
Keith, Dale Martin *utilities management consultant*

Topeka
†Brown, William Ernest *utility executive*
Hayes, John Edward, Jr. *electric power industry executive*
Kuether, Ronald Clarence *utility company executive*

Westwood
Esrey, William Todd *telecommunications company executive*

Wichita
Cadman, Wilson Kennedy *retired utility company executive*
Johnson, Kenneth O. *petroleum company executive*
Koch, Charles de Ganahl *oil industry executive*
Lusk, William Edward *real estate, oil company executive*
Varner, Sterling Verl *retired oil company executive*

KENTUCKY

Ashland
Boyd, James Robert *oil company executive*
Brothers, John Alfred *oil company executive*
Chellgren, Paul Wilbur *petroleum company executive*
Dansby, John Walter *oil company executive*
Hall, John Richard *oil company executive*
Hartl, William Parker *oil company executive*
Justice, Franklin Pierce, Jr. *oil company executive*
Lacy, James Daniel *oil company executive*
Luellen, Charles J. *retired oil company executive*
Mc Cowan, Robert Taylor *oil company executive*
Spears, Richard W. *oil company executive*
Weaver, Carlton Davis *retired oil company executive*
Yancey, Robert Earl, Jr. *oil company executive*
Zachem, Harry M. *oil company executive*

Lexington
Knapp, Vaughn Robert *coal company executive*
Newton, John Thomas *utility company executive*
Whitley, Michael R. *utilities executive*

London
†Spencer, Thomas W. *mining executive, energy executive*

Louisville
Davidson, Michael Walker *energy company executive*
Hale, Roger W. *utilities company executive*
Higgins, Walter M., III *electric power industry executive*
Royer, Robert Lewis *retired utility company executive*

Owensboro
Best, Robert Wayne *gas transmission company executive, lawyer*
Vickery, Robert Bruce *oil industry executive, consultant*

Russell
Crimmins, Sean T(homas) *oil company executive*
Gates, Deborah Wolin *petroleum company executive, lawyer*

LOUISIANA

New Orleans
Andrus, Gerald Louis *utilities holding company consultant*
Bachmann, Richard Arthur *oil company executive*
Jackson, Jerry Donald *utility company executive, lawyer*
Kilanowski, Michael Charles, Jr. *oil, natural gas, minerals exploration company executive, lawyer*
Laborde, Alden James *oil company executive*
Laborde, John Peter *retired international energy company executive*
Latiolais, René Louis *natural resources company executive, chemical engineer*
Lewis, Floyd Wallace *former electric utility executive*
Lind, Thomas Otto *barge transportation company executive*
Mealey, George Allan *mining executive*
Moffett, James Robert *oil and gas company executive*
Murrish, Charles Howard *oil and gas exploration company executive, geologist*
Sibley, David Emile *oil company executive*
Stephens, Richard Bernard *natural resource company executive*
†Wilkinson, Joel *oil company executive*
Williamson, Ernest Lavone *petroleum company executive*
Wright, Thomas Joe *electric utility executive*

Shreveport
Bremer, Richard H. *electric power company executive*
Grigsby, Chester Poole, Jr. *oil and investments company executive*
†Smith, Clair S., Jr. *oil industry executive*
†Smith, Clair Scott, III *petroleum company executive*
†Wion, J. Mike *oil industry executive*

MAINE

Bangor
Roderick, Richard Michael *petroleum distribution and real estate company financial executive*

Portland
Haynes, Peter Lancaster *utility holding company executive*

Surry
Kilgore, John Edward, Jr. *former petroleum company executive*

York Harbor
Curtis, Edward Joseph, Jr. *gas industry executive, management consultant*

MARYLAND

Annapolis
Ellis, George Fitzallen, Jr. *energy services company executive*

Baltimore
Crooke, Edward A. *utility company executive*
Files, Jon M. *utilities executive*
Ihrie, Robert *oil, gas and real estate company executive*
McGowan, George Vincent *public utility executive*
Poindexter, Christian Herndon *utility company executive*
Rosenberg, Henry A., Jr. *petroleum executive*
Smith, James F. *oil industry executive*
Snyder, William Russell *oil company executive*
Wheeler, John Ernest, Jr. *oil company executive*

Bethesda
Asbell, Fred Thomas *telecommunications company executive*
Olmsted, Jerauld Lockwood *telephone company executive*
Pritchard, Wilbur Louis *telecommunications engineering executive*
†Timbers, William Homer, Jr. *nuclear fuel company executive*

Cabin John
Dragoumis, Paul *electric utility company executive*

Clarksburg
Hyde, Geoffrey *satellite communications research executive*

Germantown
Golding, Leonard Sheldon *telecommunications executive, scientist*

Glen Arm
Jackson, Theodore Marshall *retired oil company executive*

Kensington
Marienthal, George *telecommunications company executive*

Rockville
Griffith, Jerry Dice *energy consultant*
Pollack, Louis *telecommunications company executive*

Silver Spring
Jacobs, George *telecommunications engineering consulting company executive*

MASSACHUSETTS

Andover
Maguire, Robert Edward *retired public utility executive*

Boston
Burns, Richard Michael *public utility company executive*
Davis, George Wilmot *electric utility executive*
Eichorn, John Frederick Gerard, Jr. *utility executive*
Harrington, William David *utility executive*
†O'Brien, Paul Charles *telephone company executive*
Pardus, Donald Gene *utility executive*
†Reznicek, Bernard William *power company executive*
Tyrrell, Joseph Patrick *public utility executive*
†Weadock, Daniel Peter *corporate executive*

Burlington
†Reno, John F. *communications equipment company executive*

Cambridge
Buckler, Sheldon A. *energy company executive*

Centerville
Anderson, Gerald Edwin *utilities executive*
Scherer, Harold Nicholas, Jr. *electric utility company executive, engineer*

Chelsea
†Kaneb, Gary *oil industry executive*

Edgartown
Walsh, Philip Cornelius *mining consultant*

Harwich Port
Staszesky, Francis Myron *electric company consultant*

Lexington
Phillips, Thomas L. *corporate executive*

Marblehead
Dolan, John Ralph *retired corporation executive*
Pruyn, William J. *energy industry executive*

Needham
Cogswell, John Heyland *retired telecommunications executive, financial consultant*

Revere
Taubert, Frederick Wayne *oil company executive*

Waltham
Howard, Robert Clark *energy company executive*
McManmon, Thomas Arthur, Jr. *oil industry executive*
Slifka, Alfred A. *oil corporation executive*

Watertown
Semonian, Robert Alexander *energy and lighting consultant*

Westborough
Bok, Joan Toland *utility executive*
Greenman, Frederic Edward *utility executive*
Houston, Alfred Dearborn *energy company executive*
Rowe, John William *utility executive*
Young, Roger Austin *natural gas distribution company executive*

MICHIGAN

Dearborn
Smith, Stanton Kinnie, Jr. *utility executive*

Detroit
†Cordes, James F. *gas transmission company executive*
Dortch, Heyward *utility company executive*
Earley, Anthony Francis, Jr. *utilities company executive, lawyer*
Easlick, David Kenneth *telephone company executive*
†Ewing, Stephen E. *natural gas company executive*
Garberding, Larry Gilbert *utilities companies executive*
Glancy, Alfred Robinson, III *public utility company executive*
Lobbia, John E. *utility company executive*
McCrackin, William K. *gas company executive*
McIntyre, Ronald Llewellyn *electric utility executive*
Schiffer, Daniel L. *gas company executive*
Simpkin, Lawrence James *utilities executive*
Vititoe, William Paul *natural gas company executive*
†Wilkes, James E. *telecommunications industry executive*

Grosse Pointe
Trebilcott, James Joseph *former utility executive*

Jackson
Howell, Stephen Haviland *utility executive*
Lincoln, Raynard C., Jr. *utility company executive*
McCormick, William Thomas, Jr. *electric and gas company executive*
Patrick, Ueal Eugene *oil company executive*

Lake Leelanau
Shannahan, John Henry Kelly *energy consultant*

Midland
Boulanger, Rodney Edmund *energy company executive*

Owosso
Hoddy, George Warren *electric company executive, electrical engineer*

Port Huron
Kirby, Ward Nelson *gas company executive*
Thomson, Robert James *natural gas distribution company executive*

MINNESOTA

Duluth
Sandbulte, Arend John *utility executive*

Eden Prairie
Emison, James W. *petroleum company executive*

Farmington
†Johnson, Eldon Wayne *electric utility manager*

Fergus Falls
Emmen, Dennis R. *electric utility executive*
†MacFarlane, John Charles *utility company executive*

Minneapolis
Blair, Craig John *utilities executive*
Cadogan, William J. *telecommunications company executive*
Etchelecu, Albert Dominic *energy company executive*
Gudorf, Kenneth Francis *business executive*
Jensen, Roland Jens *utility company executive*
†Theisen, Edwin Mathew *utility company executive*
Wyman, James Thomas *petroleum company executive*

Saint Paul
Estenson, Noel K. *gas, oil industry executive*
Frame, Clarence George *retired oil and gas refining company executive*
Robertson, Jerry Earl *retired mining and manuracturing company executive*

MISSISSIPPI

Jackson
†Cavanaugh, William, III *electric utility company executive*
Dallas, Thomas Abraham *retired utility company executive*
Lampton, Leslie B., Sr. *oil industry executive*
Lutken, Donald C. *utility company executive*
Stampley, Norris Lochlen *former electric utility executive*

MISSOURI

Chesterfield
Armstrong, Theodore Morelock *corporate utilities executive*

Joplin
Fancher, Robert Burney *electric utility executive, entrepreneur*
Lamb, Robert Lewis *electric utility executive*

Kansas City
Baker, John Russell *utilities executive*
Cowley, Samuel Parkinson *utility company executive, lawyer*
Fields, Curtis Grey *public utility executive*
Jennings, A. Drue *utility company executive*
Molz, Otis *oil industry executive*

Liberty
Ferrell, James Edwin *energy company executive*

Maryland Heights
Baker, Newell Alden *oil company executive*

Saint Louis
Adorjan, J(ulius) Joe *electric company executive*
Bentele, Raymond F. *retired minerals corporate executive*
†Brandt, Donald Edward *utilities company executive*
Cornelius, William Edward *utilities company executive*
Dougherty, Charles Joseph *retired utility executive*
Elliott, Howard, Jr. *gas distribution company executive*
Goldstein, Samuel R. *oil company executive*
†Hunter, Michael Thomas *natural gas pipeline company executive*
Leer, Steven F. *mining executive*
Liberman, Lee Marvin *utility executive*
Mueller, Charles William *electric utility executive*
Munk, Peter *oil industry executive*
Novelly, Paul A. *petrochemical and refining company executive*
Quenon, Robert Hagerty *mining consultant, retired holding company executive*
Samples, Ronald Eugene *coal company executive*
Sigurdson, Erik D. *oil industry executive*
Thompson, James Clark *utilities executive*

Springfield
Boehm, Robert Kenneth *telecommunications consultant*
Jura, James J. *electric utility executive*

MONTANA

Bigfork
Shennum, Robert Herman *retired telephone company executive*

Billings
Reed, Kenneth G. *petroleum company executive*

Butte
Burke, John James *utility executive*
Gannon, Robert P. *utility company executive*
Mc Elwain, Joseph Arthur *retired power company executive*
Sherick, John Matthew (Jack Sherick) *technical services company executive*

NEBRASKA

Lincoln
Tavlin, Michael John *telecommunications company executive*

Omaha
Cohen, Paul G(erson) *management consultant*
Grewcock, William L. *mining company executive*
Lochiano, Rocco *natural gas company executive*
†Parks, J. Michael *telecommunications executive*
Power, Kenneth D. *utilities company executive*
Severa, Gordon L. *utility executive*

NEVADA

Las Vegas
Laub, William Murray *retired utility executive*
Lenzie, Charles Albert *utility company executive*
Trimble, Thomas James *utility company executive, lawyer*

Reno
Keepers, William L. *utility company executive*

Zephyr Cove
Proctor, Robert Swope *retired petroleum company executive*

NEW HAMPSHIRE

Manchester
Cameron, David Pierre Guyot, Jr. *utility company executive, lawyer*

Portsmouth
Bulmer, Edward E. *oil industry executive*
Powers, Henry Martin, Jr. *oil company executive*

Tillinghast, John Avery *utilities executive*

Rochester
Dupont, Edward Charles, Jr. *petroleum distribution company executive, state senator*

NEW JERSEY

Basking Ridge
Allen, Robert Eugene *communications and computer company executive*
Bodman, Richard Stockwell *telecommunications executive*
Collis, Sidney Robert *retired telephone company executive*
Condon, Verner Holmes, Jr. *retired utility executive*

Berkeley Heights
Marx, William B., Jr. *telecommunications industry executive*

Bloomingdale
Baeder, Donald Lee *petroleum and chemical company executive, financial consultant*

Chatham
Bast, Ray Roger *retired utility company executive*

Chester
Gurian, Mal *telecommunications executive*

Collingswood
Mohrfeld, Richard Gentel *heating oil distributing company executive*

Edison
Francis, Peter T. *gas and oil industry executive*
Huber, Michael W. *petroleum company executive*
Schenk, George *oil industry executive*

Fair Haven
Gagnebin, Albert Paul *retired mining executive*

Far Hills
Ellsworth, Duncan Steuart, Jr. *retired utility company executive*

Fort Lee
Schiessler, Robert Walter *retired chemical and oil company executive*
Weitzer, Bernard *telecommunications executive*

Hammonton
Levitt, Gerald Steven *natural gas company executive*

Holmdel
Heirman, Donald Nestor *telecommunications engineering company manager*

Lake Hopatcong
Dowling, Robert Murray *oil company executive*

Linwood
Voigt, John Jacob *telecommunication executives, international investment banker*

Montvale
†Chambers, Patrick Joseph, Jr. *utility company executive*

Moorestown
Fischer, Frank Ernest *utility executive*

Morristown
†Baldassari, Dennis *utilities executive*
Berndt, John Edward *telecommunications company executive*
Reed, Rex Raymond *retired telephone company executive*

Murray Hill
Cohen, Melvin Irwin *telephone company executive*
Dyer, Alexander Patrick *industrial gas manufacturing company executive*
Mayo, John Sullivan *telecommunications company executive*

Newark
Codey, Lawrence R. *electric power company executive*
Crimmins, Thomas Michael, Jr. *utilities company executive*
Ferland, E. James *electric utility executive*
Marano, Rocco John *telephone company executive*
Riepl, Francis Joseph *utilities executive*

Nutley
Mallard, Stephen Anthony *retired utility company executive*

Parsippany
Clark, Philip Raymond *nuclear utility executive, engineer*
Graham, John Gourlay *utility company executive*
Leva, James Robert *electric utility company executive*
Morrell, Michael Preston *utility executive*

Piscataway
Burke, Jacqueline Yvonne *telecommunications executive*

Pittstown
Jacob, Harry Myles *mining executive*

Pleasantville
Huggard, Ernest Douglas *utility company executive*

Princeton
Farley, Edward Raymond, Jr. *mining and manufacturing company executive*
Holst, Willem *oil company executive*
Mc Cullough, John Price *retired oil company executive*
Penick, Joe Edward *petroleum consultant*
Wise, John James *oil company executive*

Red Bank
Chynoweth, Alan Gerald *retired telecommunications executive, consultant*
Koch, Udo *oil industry executive*

Saddle River
Amman, Robert J. *telecommunications financial services company executive*

Scotch Plains
Avery, James Stephen *oil company executive*

Summit
Mathis, James Forrest *retired petroleum company executive*
Pollak, Henry Otto *retired utility research executive, educator*

Surf City
Aurner, Robert Ray, II *oil company, auto diagnostic, restaurant franchise and company development executive*

Voorhees
Johnstone, George W. *utility company executive*
LaFrankie, James V. *water utility holding company executive*
Lewis, Marilyn Ware *water company executive*

Wall
Colford, Francis Xavier *gas industry executive*

Wayne
Crane, Thomas R., Jr. *oil industry executive*

Whippany
Spina, Dennis J. *gas industry executive*

Woodbridge
D'Amico, Andrew John *oil company executive*

NEW MEXICO

Albuquerque
Ackerman, John Tryon *gas company executive*
Eglinton, William Matthew *utility company executive*
Gorham, Frank DeVore, Jr. *petroleum company executive*

Farmington
Little, Sylvia Ford *oil industry executive*
Swetnam, Monte Newton *petroleum exploration executive*

Hobbs
Garey, Donald Lee *pipeline and oil company executive*

Roswell
Anderson, Donald Bernard *oil company executive*
Anderson, Robert Orville *oil and gas company executive*

Santa Fe
Pickrell, Thomas Richard *retired oil company executive*

NEW YORK

Albany
†Murray, Francis J., Jr. *energy executive*
†Valentino, F. William *energy executive*

Aurora
Slocum, George Sigman *energy company executive*

Babylon
Lopez, Joseph Jack *oil company executive, consultant*

Beacon
Pollart, Dale F(lavian) *petroleum company research executive*

Bedford
Jalkut, Richard Alan *telecommunications executive*

Binghamton
Carrigg, James A. *utility company executive*
Farley, Daniel W. *lawyer, utility company executive*
Komar, Paul *utility company executive*

Brooklyn
Catell, Robert Barry *gas utility executive*
Matthews, Craig Gerard *gas company executive*
Murphy, Edward Patrick, Jr. *gas utility company executive*
Peter, Helmut W. *gas company executive*

Buffalo
Ackerman, Philip Charles *utility executive, lawyer*
Brown, John M. *gas company executive*
†Kennedy, Bernard Joseph *utility executive*

Garden City
Glass, Arthur L. *mining company executive*

Huntington Station
Pierce, Charles R. *electric company consultant*

Jericho
Fitteron, John Joseph *petroleum products company executive*
†Liebowitz, Leo *oil company executive*

Johnstown
Zinnecker, Robert Wallace *telecommunications company executive*

Manhasset
Anderson, Arthur N. *retired utility company executive*

Melville
Miller, Robert C. *telecommunications industry executive*

New Hyde Park
Chardavoyne, David Edwin *utility executive*

New York
Allen, Ralph Dean *telecommunications corporate executive*
Alonzo, Martin Vincent *mining and aluminum company executive, investor, financial consultant*
Alpert, Warren *oil company executive, philanthropist*
Araskog, Rand Vincent *diversified telecommunications multinational company executive*
Baird, Dugald Euan *telecommunications industry executive*
Belknap, Norton *petroleum company consultant*
Bernstein, Alan Arthur *oil company executive*
Carey, Edward John *utility executive*
Case, Hadley *oil company executive*
Cecil, Robert Salisbury *telecommunications company executive*
Ciccone, Peter M. *telephone company executive*
†Collins, J. Barclay, II *oil company executive, lawyer*
Delaney, Robert Vincent *former gas company executive, economic development consultant*
Delz, William Ronald *petroleum company executive*
Douglas, Paul Wolff *retired mining executive*
†Engen, D(onald) Travis *diversified telecommunications company executive*
Ferguson, William Charles *telecommunications executive*
Flynn, Richard Michael *utilities executive*
Fontaine, Edward Paul *mining company executive*
Gelfand, Neal *oil company executive*
Genin, Roland *energy executive*
Giusti, Gino Paul *natural resources company executive*
Gouilloud, Michel *oil industry servicing and equipment company executive*
Greene, Carl William *utility company executive*
Grimm, Donald E. *petroleum company executive*
Hess, Leon *oil company executive*
Hodapp, Siegfried *petroleum industry executive*
Hornby, Geoffrey *oil industry executive*
Host, Stig *oil company executive*
Jamin, Gerald Alan *petroleum company executive*
Kramer, Philip *retired petroleum refining executive*
Levy, Walter James *oil consultant*
Luce, Charles Franklin *former utilities executive, lawyer*
Malozemoff, Plato *mining executive*
†Mandl, Alex J(ohann) *telecommunications company executive*
McCann, Raymond J. *utility company executive*
McGovern, Thomas Aquinas *utility executive*
McGrath, Eugene R. *utility company executive*
Noia, Alan James *utility company executive*
Norz, Charles Henry *oil company executive*
Osborne, Richard de Jongh *mining and metals company executive*
Passage, Stephen Scott *energy company executive*
†Portas, Jose *oil industry executive*
Richards, Reuben Francis *natural resource company executive*
Schroder, Raymond A. *petroleum company executive*
†Seidenberg, Ivan G. *telecommunications company executive*
Shaw, William *diversified telecommunications company executive*
Soutar, Charles Frederick *utilities executive*
Staley, Delbert C. *telecommunications executive*
Steinmetz, Richard Bird, Jr. *holding company executive, lawyer*
Underweiser, Irwin Philip *mining company executive, lawyer*
Warner, Rawleigh, Jr. *oil company executive*
Wohlstetter, Charles *telephone company executive*
Wright, Robert F. *petroleum products company executive*

Niskayuna
Fitzroy, Nancy deLoye *technology executive, engineer*

Pearl River
Caliendo, G. D. (Jerry Caliendo) *public utility executive*
Griffin, Thomas Aquinas, Jr. *utility executive*
McBennett, Robert Joseph *utility executive*
Smith, James Francis *utilities executive*

Penfield
Amish, Keith Warren *retired utility executive*

Poughkeepsie
Mack, John Edward, III *utility company executive*

Purchase
Dwyer, Andrew T. *utility and utility service company executive*

Rochester
Henderson, Robert Cameron *utility executive*
Laniak, David Konstantyn *utility company executive*

Schenectady
Robb, Walter Lee *retired electric company executive, management company executive*

Setauket
Vetog, Edwin Joseph *retired gas utility executive*

Staten Island
Barton, Jerry O'Donnell *telecommunications executive*

Syosset
Vermylen, Paul Anthony, Jr. *oil company executive*

Syracuse
Davis, William E. *utility executive*
Endries, John Michael *utility executive*
Fleming, William Sloan *energy, environmental and technology company executive*
Hennessey, John Philip *electric power industry executive*
Lavine, Gary J. *utility executive*
Mangan, Charles Vincent *utility company executive*

Wappingers Falls
Nolan, John Thomas, Jr. *retired oil industry administrator*

West Nyack
Gillespie, John Fagan *mining executive*

White Plains
Bijur, Peter I. *petroleum company executive*
Brazell, James Ervin *oil company executive, lawyer*
Cahill, William Joseph, Jr. *utility company executive*
Davidson, Carl B. *oil company executive*
DeCrane, Alfred Charles, Jr. *petroleum company executive*
Dickinson, Richard Raymond *retired oil company executive*
Doyle, William Patrick *oil company executive*
Krowe, Allen Julian *oil company executive*
Lynch, Patrick *petroleum company executive*
Smith, Elizabeth Patience *oil industry executive, lawyer*
Tell, William Kirn, Jr. *oil company executive, lawyer*

NORTH CAROLINA

Brevard
Wall, Robert Wilson, Jr. *former utility executive*

Cary
Jones, James Arthur *retired utilities executive*

Charlotte
Davenport, Dona Lee *telecommunications consultant*
Grigg, William Humphrey *utility executive*
Lee, William States *retired utility executive*
†Maxheim, John Howard *utility executive*
Osborne, Richard Jay *electric utility company executive*
†Priory, Richard Baldwin *electric utility executive*
Thies, Austin Cole *retired utility company executive*

Gastonia
†Dickey, Crawford Marshall *gas distribution executive*
†Zeigler, Charles E., Jr. *utility company executive*

Greensboro
Griffin, Haynes Glenn *telecommunications industry executive*

Hendersonville
Haynes, John Mabin *retired utilities executive*

Pinehurst
Amspoker, James Mack *retired gas company executive*

Raleigh
Barham, Charles Dewey, Jr. *electric utility executive, lawyer*
Cox, Herbert Bartle *natural gas company executive*
Davis, James Minor, Jr. *utility company executive, mechanical engineer*
Smith, Sherwood Hubbard, Jr. *utilities executive*

Winston Salem
†Williams, Arthur T., Jr. *gas, oil industry executive*
†Williams, Arthur T., III *oil, gas industry executive*

NORTH DAKOTA

Bismarck
Schuchart, John Albert, Jr. *utility executive*

OHIO

Akron
†Alexander, Anthony J. *electric power industry executive*
Holland, Willard Raymond, Jr. *electric utility executive*
Spetrino, Russell John *retired utility company executive, lawyer*

Canton
Heller, Charles Andrew, Jr. *electric utilities company executive*

Cincinnati
†Clark, Raymond Robert *utilities company executive*
Dewey, Richard Lee *telephone company executive*
Ehrnschwender, Arthur Robert *former utility company executive*
†Hibbard, Dwight H. *telecommunications company executive*
†Randolph, Jackson Harold *utility company executive*
Raskin, Fred Charles *transportation and utility holding company executive*
Rogers, James Eugene *electric utility executive*
Victor, William Weir *retired telephone company executive, consultant*

Cleveland
Bell, Edward Francis *telecommunications company executive*
Blodgett, Omer William *electric company design consultant*
†Bowman, Charles H. *petroleum company executive*
Chase, R. F. *oil industry executive*
Connelly, John James *oil company technical specialist*
Donaldson, Richard Miesse *retired oil company executive, lawyer*
Edelman, Murray R. *utility company executive*
Farling, Robert J. *utility company executive*
Ginn, Robert Martin *retired utility company executive*
Hastings, Donald F. *electric company executive*
Long, Kenneth Robert *natural gas company executive, lawyer*
Maugans, Edgar Hurley *utility company executive*
†Moore, Michael Thomas *mining executive*
Percy, S. W. *oil industry executive*
Phillips, Lyman C. *utility company executive*
Romano, Louis, Jr. *industrial gas company executive*
Scovil, Samuel Kingston *mining company executive*
Thompson, Renold Durant *mining and shipping executive*
Vargo, Ronald Paul *oil company executive*
Webster, James Colin Eden *oil company executive*
White, Fred Rollin, Jr. *mining and shipping company executive*

Columbus
DeMaria, Peter James *utility company executive*
Disbrow, Richard Edwin *retired utility executive*
Draper, E(rnest) Linn, Jr. *electric utility executive*
Feck, Luke Matthew *utility executive*
†Lhota, William J. *electric company executive*
Maloney, Gerald P. *utility executive*
†Massey, Robert John *telecommunications executive*
Mc Caffrey, Thomas R. *utilities company executive*
Schafer, William Harry *electric power industry executive*
Tilley, C. Ronald *gas company executive*
Vassell, Gregory S. *electric utility consultant*

Dayton
†Forster, Peter Hans *utility company executive*
†Hill, Allen M. *public utility executive*
†Soin, Rajesh K. *business executive*

Findlay
Yammine, Riad Nassif *oil company executive*

Hudson
Griech, Frederick G. *telephone company executive*

Independence
Hawkinson, Gary Michael *utility holding company executive*
Meyer, Gerald Justin *energy company executive*

Massillon
Dawson, Robert Earle *utilities executive*

Pepper Pike
Bray, Pierce *business consultant*
†Murray, Robert Eugene *coal company executive*

Perrysburg
Williamson, John Pritchard *utility executive*

Toledo
Saunders, Donald Herbert *utility company executive*
Smart, Paul M. *utility company executive, lawyer*

Worthington
Curtis, Nevius Minot *utility executive, retired*

OKLAHOMA

Ardmore
Hentschel, David A. *oil company executive*

Bartlesville
Allen, W. Wayne *oil industry executive*
Armstrong, Oliver Wendell *retired oil company executive*
Bowerman, Charles Leo *oil company executive*
Cox, Glenn Andrew, Jr. *petroleum company executive*
†McGinnis, James Wesley *Petroleum company executive*
†Mulva, James Joseph *oil company executive*
Silas, Cecil Jesse *retired petroleum company executive*
Smalley, Kenneth Lee *oil company executive*

Enid
Tozzi, Richard Raymond *oil and gas company executive*
Ward, Llewellyn O(rcutt), III *oil company executive*

Oklahoma City
Campbell, David Gwynne *petroleum executive, geologist*
Hambrick, Marvin K. *energy company executive*
Harlan, Ross Edgar *retired utility company executive, writer, lecturer, consultant*
Harlow, James Gindling, Jr. *utility executive*
Horner, Russell Grant, Jr. *diversified company executive*
Kirkpatrick, John Elson *oil company executive, retired naval reserve officer*
McKenny, Jere Wesley *energy firm executive*
Mee, Herb, Jr. *natural resource/environmental services executive*
Nichols, J. Larry *energy company executive, lawyer*
O'Keeffe, Hugh Williams *oil industry executive*
Peace, H. W., II *oil company executive*
Ryan, Patrick J. *electric utility company executive*
†Stacy, Alan *gas industry executive*

Ponca City
Leonard, Samuel Wallace *oil company executive*

Tulsa
Anderson, Peer LaFollette *petroleum corporation executive*
†Bailey, Keith E. *petroleum pipeline company executive*
Barnes, James E. *energy company executive*
Berlin, Steven Ritt *oil company financial official*
Braumiller, Allen Spooner *oil and gas exploration company executive, geologist*
Brolick, Henry John *energy company executive*
Dickerson, Frank Secor, III *energy company executive*
Dotson, George Stephen *drilling company executive*
Fate, Martin Eugene, Jr. *utility company executive*
Hall, Ronald E. *oil company executive*
Helmerich, Hans Christian *oil company executive*
Horkey, William Richard *retired diversified oil company executive*
Howe, Robert Melvin *oil company executive*
Hulings, Norman McDermott, Jr. *energy consultant, former company executive*
Ingram, Charles Clark, Jr. *energy company executive*
Jones, Vernon Thomas *petrochemical company executive*
King, Peter Cotterill *former utilities executive*
Kirchner, King Pouder *oil company executive*
Lowd, Judson Dean *oil and gas processing equipment manufacturing executive*
†Mattei, Charles A. *oil company executive*
Neas, John Theodore *petroleum company executive*
Newman, Richard Oakley *utilities executive, consultant*
O'Toole, Allan Thomas *electric utility executive*
Parker, Robert Lee, Jr. *drilling company executive*
Williford, Richard Allen *oil executive, flight simulator company executive*

Vinita
Beavers, Roy L. *retired utility executive, essayist*

OREGON

Corvallis
Godfrey, Samuel Addison *retired telephone company executive*

Portland
Frisbee, Don Calvin *retired utilities executive*
Gleason, Alfred M. *telecommunications executive*
Hardy, Randall Webster *utility executive*
Hobbs, C. D. *utilities executive*
Jungers, Francis *oil consultant*
McCall, Robert H. *oil and chemical company executive*
McCall, William Calder *oil and chemical company executive*
Nofziger, Sally Alene *diversified utility company executive*
Reiten, Richard G. *electric power industry executive*
†Ridgley, Robert Louis *gas company executive, lawyer*
Short, Robert Henry *retired utility executive*

Sunriver
Jamison, Harrison Clyde *former oil company executive, petroleum exploration consultant*

PENNSYLVANIA

Allentown
Gabel, Ronald Glen *telecommunications executive*
Gadomski, Robert Eugene *chemical and industrial gas company executive*
Hecht, William F. *electric power industry executive*
Kauffman, John Thomas *utility executive*
Wagner, Harold A. *industrial gas and chemical company executive*

Bryn Mawr
Ballam, Samuel Humes, Jr. *retired corporate director*
Braha, Thomas I. *oil industry executive*
Dunlop, Robert Galbraith *retired petroleum company executive*

Coraopolis
Koepfinger, Joseph Leo *utilities executive*

Farmington
Witt, Charles E. *coal company executive*

Gladwyne
†Castle, Joseph Lanktree, II *energy company executive, consultant*
Patten, Lanny Ray *industrial gas industry executive*

Indiana
Kegel, William George *mining company executive*

Johnstown
Simmons, Elroy, Jr. *retired utility executive*
Wise, Robert Lester *utilities executive*

Monroeville
Penman, Paul Duane *nuclear power laboratory executive*

Newtown
Denoon, Clarence England, Jr. *business executive*

Oil City
Baum, Herbert Merrill *motor oil company executive*
†Conrad, Conrad A. *oil company executive*
Olson, Robert Edward *coal mining executive*
Wood, Quentin Eugene *oil company executive*

Philadelphia
Binder, Lucy Simpson *retired utility company executive*
Calman, Robert Frederick *mining executive*
Campbell, Robert H. *oil company executive*
Cullen, James G. *telecommunications industry executive*
Gilmore, Richard G. *electric power company executive*
Heilig, William Wright *coal and manufacturing company executive*
Hutchinson, Pemberton *coal company executive*
Kelleher, John M. *telephone company executive*
King, Gwendolyn S. *utility company executive, former federal official*
Knoll, David E. *petroleum refining company executive*
McNeill, Corbin Asahel, Jr. *utility executive*
Paquette, Joseph F., Jr. *utility company executive*
Smith, Raymond W. *telecommunications company executive*
Thompson, Sheldon Lee *refining company executive*
Valentini, Robert M. *telecommunications industry executive*
Wetzel, Gilbert A. *telephone company executive*

Pittsburgh
Abrew, Frederick Henry *utility company executive*
Bartley, Burnett Graham, Jr. *oil company and manufacturing executive*
Brown, Bobby R. *coal company executive*
Carey, John J. *utilities executive*
Chun, Sun W. *energy technology administrator*
Davidson, George A., Jr. *utility company executive*
Froehlich, Fritz Edgar *telecommunications educator and scientist*
†Gilbey, John Walter Guy *mining company executive, geologist*
Hammer, Harold Harlan *oil company financial executive*
†Johnson, Lester Deane *oil and gas company executive*
Karis, William George *coal company executive*

La Rue, Henry Aldred consultant, former oil company executive
McDonald, C. W. mining executive
Mc Featters, Dale Stitt retired electric company executive
Moeller, Audrey Carolyn energy company executive, corporate secretary
Moritz, Donald I. energy company executive
Murdy, James L. petroleum company executive
Murphy, John Nolan mining executive, researcher, electrical engineer
†Ramdin, R. H. mining executive
†Riazzi, Richard gas industry executive
Schwass, Gary L. utilities executive
Stern, Theodore electric company executive
von Schack, Wesley W. energy holding company executive
Welfer, Thomas, Jr. utility company executive
Williams, Charles David oil and steel company executive

Radnor
Burtis, Theodore Alfred oil company executive

Reading
Hafer, Frederick Douglass utility executive

Uniontown
Eberly, Robert Edward oil and gas production company executive

Valley Forge
†Mauch, Robert Carl gas industry executive
Sutton, James Andrew diversified utility company executive

Wayne
Lefevre, Thomas Vernon retired utility company executive, lawyer

Wynnewood
Boyer, Vincent Saull energy consultant

RHODE ISLAND

Barrington
O'Toole, John Dudley retired utility executive, consultant

Cumberland
Hogan, Kenneth William gas utility executive

Lincoln
Gulvin, David Horner electric company executive

Providence
Watkins, William, Jr. electric power industry executive

SOUTH CAROLINA

Columbia
Crews, Esca Holmes, Jr. utility company executive
Gressette, Lawrence M., Jr. utilities executive
Hallman, Harry Morgan, Jr. retired oil company executive
†Kenyon, Bruce Davis utilities executive
†Novinger, Cathy Blackburn utility company executive

Hilton Head Island
Owen, Warren Herbert utility executive
Simpson, John Wistar energy consultant, former manufacturing company executive

Johns Island
Behnke, Wallace Blanchard, Jr. consultant, engineer, retired utility executive

Moncks Corner
Rainear, Robert E. utilities executive

North Charleston
Zucker, Jerry energy systems manufacturing executive

North Myrtle Beach
Atkinson, Harold Witherspoon utilities consultant, real estate broker

SOUTH DAKOTA

Huron
Wilkens, Robert Allen utilities executive, electrical engineer

Pierre
Dunn, James Bernard mining company executive, state legislator

Rapid City
Lien, Bruce Hawkins minerals and oil company executive

TENNESSEE

Collierville
Cox, Terry Allen telecommunications executive

Knoxville
Ince, Richard W. energy company executive
Malec, William Frank utilities company executive
Yates, Robert Lynn utilities executive

Nashville
Cordaro, Matthew Charles utility executive, energy developer, engineer
Ingram, E. Bronson oil production equipment industries executive
Merrills, Roy telecommunications industry executive

Oak Ridge
Jasny, George Roman retired energy company executive

Smithville
Enoch, Leslie Blythe, II gas industry executive, lawyer

TEXAS

Austin
Deisler, Paul Frederick, Jr. retired oil company executive
Haas, Joseph Marshall petroleum consultant
Preeg, William Edward oil company executive

Beaumont
Long, Alfred B. retired oil company executive, consultant
Smith, Floyd Rodenback utilities executive

Blanco
Finley, James Edward independent oil operator

Chandler
Sanders, Sharon Raye (Sharri) telecommunications executive, educator

College Station
Neff, Ray Quinn electric power educator, consultant

Corpus Christi
†Carey, Robert R. electirc power industry executive
Haas, Paul Raymond petroleum company executive
Paulson, Bernard Arthur oil company executive, consultant

Dallas
Biegler, David W. gas company executive
Blackburn, Charles Lee oil company executive
Blessing, Edward Warfield petroleum company executive
Bonnivier, B. William utility company executive
Boyce, Charles A. oil company executive, lawyer, arbitrator
Brooks, E. R. (Dick Brooks) utility company executive
Brown, Benjamin A. gas, oil industry executive
Carson, Virginia Hill oil and gas executive
Copp, Emmanuel Anthony oil company executive
Cunyus, George Marvin oil company executive
Farrington, Jerry S. utility holding company executive
Faulkner, Mike energy company executive
Fielder, Charles Robert oil industry executive
Fowler, Robert Glen exploration company executive
Fraker, Walter Vere oil company executive
Goss, James Walter oil company executive
Haddock, Ronald Wayne oil company executive
Harbin, John Pickens oil well company executive
Hauptfuhrer, Robert Paul oil company executive
Hunt, Ray Lee petroleum company executive
†Hurford, Gary Thomas oil company executive
Jeffett, Frank Asbury former oil company and insurance company executive, business consultant
Jennings, James Burnett oil company executive
Jones, Dale P. oil service company executive
Jones, Everett Riley, Jr. oil company executive
Keiser, Robert Lee gas and oil industry executive
Mattison, Harry D. utility company executive
Maycock, Ian David oil executive
McCord, William Charles retired diversified energy company executive
McCormick, James Edward oil company executive
McCullough, George Bierce oil company executive
McGlothlin, Ray, Jr. petroleum company executive
Meek, Paul Derald oil and chemical company executive
†Miercort, Clifford Roy coal mining company executive
Moneypenny, Edward William oil and gas mining executive
Moore, Robert Clay petroleum industry executive, lawyer
Nicholson, G. Randy petroleum company executive
†Norsworthy, Lamar petroleum company executive
Notestine, Wilbur Edmund energy company executive, lawyer
Nurenberg, David oil company executive
Nye, Erle Allen utilities executive, lawyer
Parsons, Ervin Ivy, Jr. petroleum company executive
Perry, George Wilson oil and gas company executive
Perry, Kenneth Walter integrated oil company executive
Pickens, Thomas Boone, Jr. oil company executive
Pryor, Richard Walter telecommunications executive, retired air force officer
Quasha, Alan G. oil and gas company executive
†Reid, Jack Powell oil company executive
Shoup, Andrew James, Jr. oil company executive
Singer, Sanford Robert diversified energy company executive
Sizer, Phillip Spelman consultant, retired oil field services executive
Watson, Edward L. electric utility executive
Westerman, Howard G. oil and gas company executive
†Wilson, Richard A. oil/gas industry support services executive
Winters, J. Otis oil industry consultant

El Paso
Dell'Osso, Luino, Jr. natural gas pipeline executive
Henderson, Walter G. utility company executive
Hoskins, Curtis Lynn utility executive
Wiggs, David Harold, Jr. utilities company executive
Wise, William Allan oil company executive, lawyer

Fort Worth
Bass, Perry Richardson oil company executive
Hyde, Clarence Brodie, II oil company executive
†Messman, Jack L. oil executive
†Snyder, John C. oil and gas industry executive
Tarpley, James Merrell utility company executive
Woofter, R. D. utilities company executive
Zimmerman, Bill J. oil company executive, lawyer

Galveston
Ewing, George H. pipeline company executive

Houston
Adair, Red (Paul Neal Adair) oil well problem control specialist
†Alderson, David P., III oil company executive
Allison, William V. oil industry executive
Anderson, William (Albion), Jr. oil and gas producer, investment banker
Andrews, Glenn T. oil company executive
Bankston, Gene Clifton oil and gas consultant
Barney, Charles Lester petroleum company executive
Barracano, Henry Ralph retired oil company executive, consultant
Barrow, Thomas Davies oil and mining company executive
Beghini, Victor Gene oil company executive
Bell, Howard Earl natural gas distribution executive
Bennett, Richard Gerald gas company executive
†Blanton, Jack Sawtelle oil company executive
Bonneville, Richard Briggs petroleum exploration and production executive
Bookout, John Frank, Jr. oil company executive
Bowen, W. J. retired gas company executive
Bowersox, Thomas H. executive
Bracy, Michael Blakeslee energy company executive
Bryan, James Lee oil field service company executive
Bryan, J(ames) P(erry), Jr. energy company executive
Burguieres, Philip energy service and manufacturing company executive
†Burrow, Harold gas company executive
†Butters, David J. oil industry executive
Capps, Ethan LeRoy oil company executive
Carameros, George Demitrius, Jr. natural gas company executive
†Carmichael, David M. petroleum industry executive
†Carroll, Loren Kenneth oil company executive
Carroll, Philip Joseph oil company executive
Carter, John Boyd, Jr. oil operator, bank executive
Chalmers, David B. petroleum executive
Clayton, William Lewis retired utility executive
Cline, C. Bob natural gas company executive
Comer, Clarence C. oil, gas and cement company executive
Conger, Franklin Barker oil company executive
Dagley, Larry Jack energy company executive
Danburg, Jerome Samuel oil company executive
Davis, Leon oil company executive
DesBarres, John P. energy company executive
Di Corcia, Edward Thomas oil industry executive
Drury, Leonard Leroy retired oil company executive
Dunlap, James Lapham petroleum company executive
Dur, Philip Alphonse gas, oil industry executive, retired naval officer
Edens, Donald Keith oil company executive
Elers, Karl Emerson mining company executive
Ellerbeck, Ronald L. oil industry executive
Ferrand, Jean C. oil company executive
Foster, Joe B. oil company executive
Frank, George Willard (Will Frank) oil company executive, consultant
Frank, J. Louis oil company executive
Fulwiler, Robert Neal oil company executive
†Funkhouser, Paul William oil company executive, lawyer
Gallas, Daniel O. oil pipeline company executive
Garner, Thomas Ward petroleum company executive
Garrison, Martha oil industry executive
Gattis, James Ralph oil company executive
Gerard, Roy Dupuy oil company executive
Gibson, Jerry Leigh oil company executive
Goodman, Herbert Irwin petroleum company executive
Gower, Bob G. gas and oil industry executive
Haas, Merrill Wilber geologist, oil company executive
Halbouty, Michel Thomas geologist, petroleum engineer, petroleum operator
Hardin, George Cecil, Jr. petroleum consultant
Harrison, Otto R. oil industry executive
†Hayslett, Roderick James gas company executive
Hedrick, Kirby L. petroleum company executive
Hemeyer, Terry oil company executive
Hendrix, Dennis Ralph energy company executive
Hesse, Martha O. natural gas company executive
Hoglund, Forrest Eugene petroleum company executive
Homeyer, Howard C. energy consultant
†Honea, T. Milton, Jr. gas industry executive
Howard, R. L. oil industry executive
†Howell, Paul Neilson oil company executive
Huff, John Rossman oil service company executive
Jackson, Terrence J. coal company executive
Jamieson, John Kenneth oil field services company executive
Johnson, Ashmore Clark, Jr. oil company executive
Johnson, Kenneth Oscar oil company executive
Johnson, Wayne D. gas industry executive
Jordan, Don D. electric company executive
Jorden, James Roy oil company engineering executive
Kelley, David Lee oil company executive, petroleum engineer
†Kellstrom, William A. gas company executive
Kerr, Baine Perkins oil company executive
Kinder, Richard Dan natural gas pipeline, oil and gas company executive
Kirkland, John David oil and gas company executive, lawyer
Kuntz, Hal Goggan petroleum exploration company executive
Lackey, S. Allen petroleum company executive, corporate lawyer
Lasseter, Charles Erwin energy company executive
Lassiter, Ronald Corbett oil company executive
Lay, Kenneth Lee diversified energy company executive
Leonard, Gilbert Stanley oil company executive
LeSuer, Kenneth Ray oil company executive
Liedtke, John Hugh petroleum company executive
Little, Jack Edward oil company executive
Long, William Everett retired utility executive
Loveland, Eugene Franklin petroleum executive
Ludwig, Vernell Patrick gas pipeline company executive
Luigs, Charles Russell gas and oil drilling industry executive
Mackie, David F. gas company executive
Mai, Klaus L. oil research company executive
Manson, Lewis Auman energy research executive
Martin, Jerry C. oil company executive
Matthews, Thomas Michael energy company executive
†Mazanec, George L. natural gas company executive
Mc Call, Robert R. retired oil company executive
Mc Fedries, Robert, Jr. power industry executive, chemical engineer
Meyer, Randall retired oil company executive
Monroe, L. A. J. oil well drilling company executive
Mosbacher, Robert Adam oil and gas industry executive, political organization executive
Mottale, Mois oil industry executive
†Murray, Patrick M. oilfield service company executive
Muse, Ewell Henderson, III gas company executive
Nanz, Robert Hamilton petroleum consultant
Nestvold, Elwood Olaf oil service company executive
Nicandros, Constantine Stavros oil company executive
Nyberg, Donald Arvid oil company executive
O'Connor, Lawrence Joseph, Jr. energy consultant
O'Neal, Bob H. utilities company executive
Panatier, M. J. gas industry executive
Parish, Louis Leon oil company executive
Pate, James Leonard oil company executive
Paul, James Robert oil and gas mining company executive
Pester, Jack Cloyd oil company executive
Pitcher, Max Grow exploration company executive, geologist
Prentice, James Stuart energy company executive, chemical engineer
Rabb, Carlos C., Jr. petroleum company executive
Reynolds, John Terrence oil industry executive
Richardson, Frank H. retired oil industry executive
Roff, J(ohn) Hugh, Jr. energy company executive
Rossler, Willis Kenneth, Jr. petroleum company executive
Sadler, M. Whitson petroleum company executive
Schell, William H. oil company executive
Segner, Edmund Peter, III natural gas company executive
†Smith, Dan F. oil company executive
Snedeker, Robert D. air transportation executive
Spencer, W. E. oil company executive
†Spillard, Ernest John oil company executive
Spincic, Wesley James oil company executive, consultant
†Stanley, John R. petroleum company executive
Stewart, Cornelius James, II utilities company executive
Sykora, Donald D. utility company executive
Tauber, Orner J., Sr. petrochemical company executive
Thorn, Terence Hastings gas industry executive
†Tilton, Glenn F. oil company executive
Tramuto, James Arnold utilities public affairs executive, lawyer
Trusty, Roy Lee former oil company executive
Warner, Darrell G. petroleum company executive
Watson, C. L. (Chuck Watson) gas industry executive
White, Robert Winslow oilfield service company executive
†Wilkes, L. A. oil industry executive
†Wilkinson, G. Thomas gas and oil industry executive
†Will, Edward Edmund oil company executive
Wilson, Edward Converse, Jr. oil and natural gas production company executive
Winslow, Robert Albert gas, oil industry executive
Wolf, Erving oil company executive
Wray, Marc Frederick minerals company executive
Wyatt, Oscar Sherman, Jr. energy company executive

Humble
†Megill, Robert Edgar retired oil company executive, consultant

Ingram
Hughes, David Michael oil service company executive, rancher

Irving
Bayne, James Elwood oil company executive
Cattarulla, Elliot Reynold oil company executive
Hess, Edwin John oil company executive
Kirkley, T. A. oil company executive
Le Vine, Duane Gilbert petroleum company executive
Lutz, Matthew Charles geologist, oil company executive
O'Brien, William Daniel oil industry executive
Robinson, Edgar Allen oil company executive
Ward, Patrick J. oil industry executive

Lewisville
Bickel, Herbert Jacob, Jr. corporation executive

Midland
Grover, Rosalind Redfern oil and gas company executive
Vinson, Morty Conrad (Morty Vinson) oil company executive, rancher

Montgomery
Farmer, Joe Sam petroleum company executive

Plano
Schuh, Frank Joseph drilling engineering company executive, consultant
Thompson, J. Ken gas, oil industry executive

Port Arthur
Gipson, Robert Malone oil industry executive

Pottsboro
Hanning, Gary William utility executive, water company executive, consultant

Richardson
McDaniel, Dolan Kenneth oil exploration service company executive

Salado
Parks, Lloyd Lee oil company executive

San Antonio
Adams, James R. telecommunications executive
Benninger, Edward C., Jr. petroleum and natural gas company executive
Burke, Michael Donald oil and gas company executive
†Button, Damon oil industry executive
Greehey, William Eugene energy company executive
Hemminghaus, Roger Roy energy company executive, chemical engineer
Horner, Richard Elmer retired telecommunications company executive
Juren, Dennis Franklin petroleum company executive
Klaerner, Curtis Maurice former oil company executive
Miller, Larry Joseph oil and gas company executive

Moe, Palmer L. *gas company executive*
West, Robert Van Osdell, Jr. *retired petroleum executive*
Whitacre, Edward E., Jr. *telecommunications executive*

Sealy
Young, Milton Earl *retired petroleum production company executive*

Sugar Land
†Brumit, Lawrence Edward, III *oil field service company executive*
McMahon, Edward Francis *oil industry executive, consultant*
Oller, William Maxwell *retired energy company executive, retired naval officer*
Welch, William Henry *oil service company executive, consultant*

The Woodlands
Clark, Bernard F. *natural gas company executive*
Covey, F. Don *energy company executive*
Mitchell, George P. *gas and petroleum company executive*
Sharman, Richard Lee *telecommunications executive, consultant*
Smith, Philip S. *oil and gas company executive*

Tyler
Frankel, Donald Leon *oil service company executive*

Winnsboro
Fairchild, Raymond Eugene *oil company executive*

UTAH

Brigham City
†Anderson, Robert Wayne *oil company financial officer*
†Germer, Richard Eliason *oil company executive*

Orem
Jacobson, Alfred Thurl *petroleum executive*

Salt Lake City
†Cash, R. D. *natural gas and oil executive*
Cash, R(oy) Don *gas and petroleum company executive*
Groussman, Raymond G. *diversified utility and energy company executive, lawyer*
Heiner, Clyde Mont *energy company executive*
Holding, R. Earl *oil company executive*
Joklik, Günther Franz *mining company executive*
Keener, Robert W. *retired gas company executive*
Losse, John William, Jr. *mining company executive*
Scowcroft, John Major *petroleum refinery process development executive*

VERMONT

Barnard
Larson, John Hyde *retired utilities executive*

Brattleboro
Weigand, James Gary *utility company executive, former military officer*

Manchester
Freed, Walter Everett *petroleum company executive, state representative*

Rutland
Griffin, James Edwin *utilities executive*

VIRGINIA

Alexandria
Smith, Jeffrey Greenwood *industry executive, retired army officer*

Arlington
Campanella, Anton J. *telephone company executive*
Scott, Sally Elaine *telecommunications manager*
Wakefield, Richard Alan *energy consulting firm executive*

Chantilly
Johnson, Stuart *telecommunications industry executive*

Fairfax
†Acord, Herbert (Kent) *oil company executive*
Bork, Walter Albert *oil company executive*
Boutte, David Gray *oil industry executive, lawyer*
Hoenmans, Paul John *oil company executive*
Murray, Allen Edward *oil company executive*
Noto, Lucio A. *gas and oil industry executive*

Hot Springs
Richey, Herbert Southall, II *coal company executive*

Lebanon
†Spindler, G. R. *mining company executive*

Lexington
Tyree, Lewis, Jr. *retired compressed gas company executive, inventor, technical consultant*

Lynchburg
†Pryor, Charles Wingfield, Jr. *nuclear technology company executive*

Manakin Sabot
Robertson, Linwood Righter *electric utility executive*

Mc Lean
Waylan, Cecil Jerome *telecommunications executive*

Middleburg
McGhee, George Crews *petroleum producer, former government official*

Richmond
Bartell, James Elliot *oil company executive*
Berry, William Willis *retired utility executive*
Capps, Thomas Edward *utilities company executive, lawyer*
Clement, Alvis Macon *former utilities executive*
Davis, John Kennerly, Jr. *utility holding company executive*
Munsey, Virdell Everard, Jr. *utility executive*
Rhodes, James T. *electric power industry executive*
†Stallard, Hubert R. *telecommunications industry executive*
Stallard, Hugh R. *telephone company executive*

Suffolk
Hines, Angus Irving, Jr. *petroleum marketing executive*

Upperville
di Zerega, Thomas William *former energy company executive, lawyer*

Virginia Beach
Happy, Jack Nelson *oil company executive*

Williamsburg
Baranowski, Frank Paul *energy consultant, former government official*

WASHINGTON

Bellevue
Groten, Barnet *energy company executive*
†Sonstelie, Richard Robert *utilities executive*
Stephenson, Robert Baird *energy company executive*
Thorpe, James Alfred *retired utilities executive*
†Weaver, William Schildecker *electric power industry executive*

Redmond
†Butynski, Donald *electric power industry executive*

Richland
Counsil, William Glenn *electric utility executive*

Seattle
Smith, Andrew Vaughn *telephone company executive*

Sequim
Beaton, Roy Howard *retired nuclear industry executive*

Spokane
Eliassen, Jon Eric *utility company executive*
Harvey, J. R. *utilities company executive*
Redmond, Paul Anthony *utility executive*

WEST VIRGINIA

Bridgeport
Timms, Leonard Joseph, Jr. *gas company executive*

Charleston
Bennett, Robert Menzies *retired gas pipeline company executive*
Grant, Richard Lee *utility company executive*
Kettering, Glen Lee *utilities executive, lawyer*
†Lilly, Peter Byron *coal company executive*
†Robinson, R. Larry *gas industry executive*

Sistersville
Wright, John Charles Young *oil and gas company executive*

WISCONSIN

Delavan
Donnelly, James Charles *manufacturing company executive*

Madison
†Barr, Jim, III *telecommunications company executive*
Davis, Erroll Brown, Jr. *utility executive*
Gehl, Eugene Othmar *power company executive, lawyer*
Mackie, Frederick David *retired utility executive*

Milwaukee
†Abdoo, Richard A. *utilities company executive*
Britt, Russell William *utility executive*
Burstein, Sol *consultant, retired utility company executive, engineer*
Goetsch, John Hubert *utility company executive*
Hoffer, Robert Morrison *retired holding company executive*
Schrader, Thomas F. *utilities executive*

Racine
†Remmel, Jerry G. *utilities executive*

Thiensville
Kostecke, B. William *utilities executive*

WYOMING

Afton
Call, William A. *petroleum products company executive*

Laramie
Laman, Jerry Thomas *mining company executive*

Riverton
Bebout, Eli Daniel *oil executive*

CANADA

ALBERTA

Calgary
Blair, Sidney Robert *petroleum company executive*
Furnival, George Mitchell *petroleum and mining consultant*
Grimes, Edward Clifford *oil industry executive, consultant*
Hagerman, Allen Reid *oil and gas company executive*
Haskayne, Richard Francis *petroleum company executive*
Hopper, Wilbert Hill *retired oil industry executive*
Hriskevich, Michael Edward *oil and gas consultant*
Hugh, George M. *pipeline company executive*
Little, Brian F. *oil company executive*
Maclagan, John Lyall *retired petroleum company executive*
Maier, Gerald James *natural gas transmission and marketing company executive*
McCready, Kenneth Frank *electric utility executive*
McIntyre, Norman F. *petroleum industry executive*
Mc Kinnon, F(rancis) A(rthur) Richard *utility executive*
†Mungan, Necmettin *petroleum consultant*
Pick, Michael Claude *international exploration consultant*
Pierce, Robert Lorne *petrochemical, oil and gas company executive*
Price, Arthur Richard *petroleum company executive*
Reid, David Evans *pipeline company executive*
Seaman, Daryl Kenneth *oil company executive*
Stanford, James M. *oil company executive*
Travis, Vance Kenneth *petroleum business executive*
Wagner, Norman Ernest *former energy company executive, former university president*
Zaruby, Walter Stephen *holding company executive*

Edmonton
Horton, William Russell *retired utility company executive*
Twa, Craighton Oliver *power company executive*
Wood, John Denison *utility company executive*

Red Deer
Donald, Jack C. *oil company executive*

BRITISH COLUMBIA

Vancouver
Birch, Murray Patrick *oil industry executive*
Keevil, Norman Bell *mining executive*
Phillips, Edwin Charles *gas transmission company executive*
Willson, John Michael *mining company executive*
Wilson, Graham McGregor *energy company executive*

West Vancouver
Petrina, Anthony J. *mining executive, retired*

White Rock
Huntington, A. Ronald *retired coal terminal executive*

MANITOBA

Pinawa
Allan, Colin James *nuclear research and development company executive*

Winnipeg
Lang, Otto E. *industry executive, former Canadian cabinet minister*

NOVA SCOTIA

Halifax
Comeau, Louis Roland *electric power industry executive*
Smith, Ronald Emory *telecommunications executive*

ONTARIO

Don Mills
Di Tomaso, Nick *oil industry executive*
Mascitelli, Joel *oil industry executive*

Etobicoke
Hyland, Geoffrey Fyfe *energy company executive*

Kanata
Griffiths, Anthony F. *telecommunications industry executive*

Mississauga
Leech, James William *manufacturing and technology company executive*

North York
Woodruff, Laurie *oil industry executive*

Toronto
Balderrama, Fernando Hiriart *electrical utility company executive*
Bone, Bruce Charles *mining and manufacturing executive*
Bush, John Arthur Henry *mining company executive, lawyer*
Cooper, Marsh Alexander *mining company executive*
Ediger, Nicholas Martin *energy resources company executive, consultant*
James, William *mining company executive*
Light, Walter Frederick *telecommunications executive*
Marshall, Paul Macklin *oil company executive*
Martin, Robert William *former utilities company executive*
Munk, Peter *mining executive*
Nuttall, Grant *retired oil company executive*
Osler, Gordon Peter *retired utility company executive*
Pelley, Marvin Hugh *mining executive*
Peterson, Robert Byron *petroleum company executive*
Pickard, Franklin George Thomas *mining company executive*
Powis, Alfred *natural resources company executive*
Roman-Barber, Helen *corporate executive*
Ryan, James Franklin *oil company executive*
Shaw, Ian Alexander *accountant, mining company executive*
Sopko, Michael D. *mining company executive*
Thomas, Kenneth Glyndwr *mining executive*
Walker, Ronald C. *oil company executive*
Zimmerman, Adam Hartley *retired mining and forest industries executive*

QUEBEC

Montreal
Andrew, Frederick James *telecommunications company executive*
Burns, James William *business executive*
Caillé, André *gas distribution company executive*
Cyr, J. V. Raymond *telecommunications company executive*
Dufresne, Guy Georges *mining company executive*
Fridman, Josef Josel *telecommunications company executive*
Gaulin, Jean *gas distribution company executive*
Monty, Jean Claude *telecommunications company executive*
O'Brien, David Peter *oil company executive*
Wilson, Lynton Ronald *telecommunications company executive*

Varennes
St. Jean, Guy *electric power industry executive*

Westmount
Spalding, James Stuart *retired telecommunications company executive*

SASKATCHEWAN

Saskatoon
Childers, Charles Eugene *potash mining company executive*

MEXICO

Aristoteles
Akel, Ollie James *oil company executive*

AUSTRALIA

Melbourne
Mc Gimpsey, Ronald Alan *oil company executive*

BELGIUM

Brussels
†Cornelis, François *oil industry executive*
Portal, Gilbert Marcel Adrien *oil company executive*

CHINA

Beijing
Gish, Norman Richard *oil industry executive*

ENGLAND

London
Gillam, Patrick John *oil company executive*
Kirkby, Maurice Anthony *oil company executive*
Lesser, Frederick Alan *mining and chemical company executive*
Smernoff, Richard Louis *oil company executive*

FRANCE

Paris
Roux, Ambroise Marie Casimir *business executive*
Suard, Pierre Henri Andre *power company executive*

JAPAN

Osaka
Osumi, Masato *utility company executive*

THE NETHERLANDS

The Hague
Herkstroter, Cornelius *oil industry executive*
Van Wachem, Lodewijk Christiaan *petroleum company executive*

SWEDEN

Lidingo
†Wickberg, Jens Erik *industrial executive*

TAJIKISTAN

Penjikent
Arne, Kenneth George *mining executive, mineral consultant*

ADDRESS UNPUBLISHED

Addy, Frederick Seale *retired oil company executive*
Arlidge, John Walter *utility company executive*
Arnold, William Howard *nuclear fuel executive*

Arthur, John Morrison retired utility executive
Barrack, William Sample, Jr. petroleum company executive
Barrow, Frank Pearson, Jr. retired energy company executive
Bartling, Theodore Charles oil company executive
Baumgartner, John H. refining and petroleum products company executive
Bell, Thomas Rowe retired natural gas transmission company executive
Bergman, Klaus utility executive, lawyer
†Braswell, Arnold Webb executive consultant
Brinegar, Claude Stout retired oil company executive
Brophy, Theodore Frederick telephone company executive
Browne, Cecil Thayer utility company executive
Browne, Edmund John Phillip oil company executive
Bruce, James Edmund retired utility company executive
Bumbery, Joseph Lawrence diversified telecommunications company executive
Bush, Charles Vernon telecommunications executive
Butler, Eugene L. oil field equipment company executive
Carver, Calvin Reeve public utility company director
Catacosinos, William James utility company executive
Chittick, David Rupert environmental management consultant
Cliff, Ronald Laird energy company executive
Cookson, Albert Ernest telephone and telegraph company executive
Cooper, E. Camron retired oil company executive
Creigh, Thomas, Jr. utility executive
Cummer, William Jackson former oil company executive, investor
Davis, John Sidney oil and gas company executive
Davis, Laurence Laird coal company executive
Di Giovanni, Anthony retired coal mining company executive
Dille, Earl Kaye utility company executive
Donnelly, Joseph Lennon utility company executive
Dorros, Irwin retired telecommunications executive
Ellwanger, Mike (Cyril Albert Ellwanger) retired utility executive
Estes, Jack Charles oil service company executive, scientist
Ewing, Wayne Turner coal company executive
Fippinger, Grace J. retired telecommunications company executive
Fitzgeorge, Harold James former oil and gas company executive
Ford, Judith Ann retired natural gas distribution company executive
Gogarty, William Barney oil company executive, consultant
Gordon, Richard Joseph gas distribution company executive
Green, Richard Calvin, Jr. utility company executive
Greenberg, Arnold Elihu water quality specialist
Greer, Carl Crawford petroleum company executive
Gundersen, Wayne Campbell management consultant, oil and gas consultant
Hall, Milton Reese retired oil company executive
Hamilton, Allan Corning retired oil company executive
Hamilton, Lyman Critchfield, Jr. telecommunications industry executive
Hancock, John Coulter telecommunications company executive
Hansen, Shirley Jean energy consulting executive, professional association administrator
Hardesty, Christopher Scott oil and mining company executive
Harris, Howard Hunter oil company executive
Harton, John James utility executive
Hayes, Charles Raymond utility company executive
Hebner, Paul Chester retired oil company executive, consultant
Heiney, John Weitzel former utility executive
Hesse, Christian August mining and tunneling industries consultant
Hinson, Howard Houston petroleum company executive
Hitchborn, James Brian telecommunications executive
Hobbs, J. Edwin retired utility executive
Holland, James Paul utility company executive
Holmer, Edwin Carl retired petrochemical company executive
Houser, William Douglas telecommunications company executive, former naval officer
Howard, James Joseph, III utility company executive
Howard, Joel L. electric power company executive
Huffman, James Thomas William oil exploration company executive
Hughitt, Jeremiah Keefe utility executive
Humke, Ramon L. utility executive
Hunt, Joe Harold retired utility company executive
Hunter, Donald utility company executive
Hyde, Robert Burke, Jr. retired oil industry executive
Inglis, James telecommunications company executive
Johnson, Craig R. utilities executive
Jones, Jack Dellis oil company executive
Joyce, Burton Montgomery natural resources company executive
Judge, Rosemary Ann oil company executive
†Kaufman, Raymond L. energy company executive
Kebblish, John Basil retired coal company executive, consultant
Kerr, James Winslow pipe line company executive
Kertz, Hubert Leonard telephone company executive
King, William Collins oil company executive
Kinzer, James Raymond retired pipeline company executive
Kirkorian, Roy telecommunications executive
Kruizenga, Richard John retired energy company executive
Le Van, Daniel Hayden gas industry executive
Lewis, Alexander, Jr. oil company executive
Lilly, Edward Guerrant, Jr. retired utility company executive
Lively, Edwin Lester retired oil company executive
Loftin, Raymond Victor, Jr. oil and gas company executive
Lupberger, Edwin Adolph utility executive
Maffie, Michael Otis utility executive
Malpas, Robert company executive
Markle, Roger A(llan) retired oil company executive
Mc Carthy, Walter John, Jr. retired utility executive
McConnell, Elliott Bonnell, Jr. oil company executive
McGough, John Paul conveyor and power transmission company executive
Melvin, Ben Watson, Jr. petroleum and chemical manufacturing executive
†Menchaca, Peggy Sue Beard energy company executive
Mitchell, Claybourne, Jr. retired utilities executive
Montgomery, Roy Delbert retired gas utility company executive
Monty, Charles Embert utility company executive
Morrell, Gene Paul liquid terminal company executive
Morrow, George Lester retired oil and gas executive
Murrill, Paul Whitfield former utility executive, former university administrator
Nicholson, Leland Ross retired utilities company executive, energy consultant
Ogden, Sylvester O. coal company executive
O'Hare, James Raymond energy company executive
Pack, Allen S. retired coal company executive
Peckham, Donald Eugene retired utilities company executive
Perkins, Frederick Myers retired oil company executive
Perkins, Thomas Keeble oil company researcher
Pope, Robert Glynn telecommunications executive
Raymer, Donald George utility company executive
Raymond, Lee R. oil company executive
Regan, William Joseph, Jr. energy company executive
Reynolds, Jack W. retired utility company executive
Rickards, Leonard Myron oil company executive
Roe, Thomas Coombe former utility company executive
Rogers, Justin Towner, Jr. retired utility company executive
Sasdi, George P. utilities company executive
Saunby, John Brian petrochemical company executive
Schenck, Jack Lee retired electric utility executive
Schenker, Leo retired utility company executive
Schumacher, Robert Joseph petroleum company executive
Scott, Isadore Meyer former energy company executive
Sello, Allen Ralph oil company executive
Severinghaus, Nelson, Jr. mining company executive
Smith, Paul Vergon, Jr. corporate executive, retired oil company executive
Smith, Richard Grant retired telecommunications executive, electrical engineer
Steward, H. Leighton oil company executive
Stratman, Joseph Lee petroleum refining company executive, consultant, chemical engineer
Struebing, Robert Virgil retired oil company executive
Sugarman, Samuel Louis retired oil transportation and trading company executive, horse breeder
Swango, William Franklin coal company executive
Templeton, John Alexander, II coal company executive
Thompson, Jack Edward mining company executive
Threet, Jack Curtis oil company executive
Tonkyn, Richard George retired oil and gas company executive, researcher, consultant
Tucker, H. Richard oil company executive
Tucker, Hal Beall retired electric utility executive
Tucker, Paul William retired petroleum company executive
Werth, Andrew M. telecommunications executive
White, Willis Sheridan, Jr. retired utilities company executive
Whitehouse, Alton Winslow, Jr. retired oil company executive
Williams, Joseph Theodore oil and gas company executive
Wise, Jim Price energy company executive
Witte, Merlin Michael oil company executive
Wright, Randolph Earle retired petroleum company executive
Yates, Elton G. retired petroleum industry executive
Yearwood, Donald Robert oil and shipping executive

LAW: JUDICIAL ADMINISTRATION

UNITED STATES

ALABAMA

Albertville
Johnson, Clark Everette, Jr. judge

Anniston
Harwell, Edwin Whitley judge

Birmingham
Acker, William Marsh, Jr. federal judge
Blackburn, Sharon Lovelace federal judge
Campbell, Elizabeth Todd judge
Clemon, U. W. federal judge
Guin, Junius Foy, Jr. federal judge
Hancock, James Hughes federal judge
Mitchell, Tamara O. judge
Nelson, Edwin L. federal judge
Pointer, Sam Clyde, Jr. federal judge
Propst, Robert Bruce federal judge
Putnam, Terry Michael federal judge
Smith, Edward Samuel federal judge

Dothan
Little, Charles Lawson judge, lawyer

Florence
Haltom, Elbert Bertram, Jr. federal judge
Tease, James Edward judge

Gadsden
Sledge, James Scott federal judge

Mobile
Butler, Charles Randolph, Jr. federal judge
Cox, Emmett Ripley federal judge
Hand, William Brevard federal judge
Howard, Alex T., Jr. federal judge
Kahn, Gordon Barry federal bankruptcy judge
McCall, Daniel Thompson, Jr. retired justice
Milling, Bert William, Jr. federal judge
Pittman, Virgil federal judge
Thomas, Daniel Holcombe federal judge

Montgomery
Albritton, William Harold, III federal judge
Almon, Reneau Pearson state supreme court justice
Black, Robert Coleman lawyer
†Butts, Terry L. state supreme court justice
†Carnes, Edward E. federal judge
De Ment, Ira federal judge
Dubina, Joel Fredrick federal judge
Godbold, John Cooper federal judge
Hobbs, Truman McGill federal judge, lawyer
Hornsby, (E.C.) Sonny judge
Houston, James Gorman, Jr. state supreme court justice
Ingram, Kenneth Frank state supreme court justice
Johnson, Frank Minis, Jr. federal judge
Maddox, (Alva) Hugh state supreme court justice, author
McPherson, Vanzetta Penn federal judge
Patterson, John Malcolm judge
Steele, Rodney Redfearn federal judge
Thompson, Myron H. federal judge
Torbert, Clement Clay, Jr. state supreme court justice
Varner, Robert Edward federal judge

Tuscaloosa
Wright, George Searcy federal judge, educator

ALASKA

Anchorage
Branson, Albert Harold (Harry Branson) magistrate judge, educator
Fitzgerald, James Martin federal judge
Holland, H. Russel federal judge
Rabinowitz, Jay Andrew state supreme court justice
Sedwick, John Weeter judge
Singleton, James Keith federal judge
von der Heydt, James Arnold federal judge, lawyer

Barrow
Jeffery, Michael Ives judge

Fairbanks
Kleinfeld, Andrew Jay federal judge

ARIZONA

Bisbee
Holland, Robert Dale retired magistrate, consultant

Phoenix
Broomfield, Robert Cameron federal judge
Canby, William Cameron, Jr. federal judge
Carroll, Earl Hamblin federal judge
Carter, James Edward judge
Copple, William Perry federal judge
Curley, Sarah Sharer federal bankruptcy judge
Feldman, Stanley George state supreme court chief justice
Hardy, Charles Leach federal judge
Kaufman, Roger Wayne state judge
McNamee, Stephen M. federal judge
Moeller, James state supreme court justice
Muecke, Charles Andrew (Carl Muecke) federal judge
Myers, Robert David judge
Rose, C. Kimball judge
Rosenblatt, Paul Gerhardt federal judge
Schroeder, Mary Murphy federal judge
Strand, Roger Gordon federal judge
Tang, Thomas federal judge
Zastrow, John Thurman judge

Tucson
Bilby, Richard Mansfield federal judge
Browning, William Docker federal judge
Lacagnina, Michael Anthony judge
Livermore, Joseph McMaster judge
Marquez, Alfredo C. federal judge
Roll, John McCarthy federal judge

ARKANSAS

Batesville
Harkey, John Norman state judge

El Dorado
Anthony, Carol A. judge
Barnes, Harry F. federal judge

Fayetteville
Waters, H. Franklin federal judge

Fort Smith
Hendren, Jimm Larry federal judge
Kimbrough, Warren Oakley judge
Stites, Beverly R. judge

Harrison
Henley, J. Smith federal judge

Hot Springs National Park
Britt, Henry Middleton retired judge
Vaccaro, Charles G. federal judge

Little Rock
Arnold, Morris Sheppard federal judge
Arnold, Richard Sheppard federal judge
Corbin, Donald L. judge
Eisele, Garnett Thomas federal judge
Forster, John Fredrick, Jr. judge
Fussell, Robert Foreman federal judge
Glaze, Thomas A. state supreme court justice
Harris, Oren retired federal judge
Holt, Jack Wilson, Jr. state supreme court chief justice
Howard, George, Jr. federal judge
Newbern, William David state supreme court justice
Reasoner, Stephen M. federal judge
Roy, Elsijane Trimble federal judge
Scott, Mary Davies federal judge
Wilson, William R., Jr. judge
Woods, Henry federal judge
Wright, Susan Webber federal judge

Texarkana
Stroud, John Fred, Jr. state supreme court justice

CALIFORNIA

Abingdon
Williams, Glen Morgan federal judge

Alameda
Bartalini, C. Richard judge

Fresno
Beck, Dennis L. federal judge
Coyle, Robert Everett federal judge
Crocker, Myron Donovan federal judge
Price, Edward Dean federal judge
Wanger, Oliver Winston federal judge, educator

La Mirada
Brennan, Joan Stevenson federal judge
Henderson, Thelton Eugene federal judge
Legge, Charles Alexander federal judge
Walker, Vaughn R. federal judge
Zirpoli, Alfonso Joseph federal judge

Long Beach
Pokras, Sheila Frances judge

Los Angeles
Alarcon, Arthur Lawrence federal judge
Armstrong, Orville judge
Ashland, Calvin Kolle federal judge
Baird, Lourdes G. federal judge
Bufford, Samuel Lawrence federal judge
Byrne, William Matthew, Jr. federal judge
Chavez, Victor Edwin judge
Crispo, Lawrence Walter judge
Davies, John G. federal judge
Fenning, Lisa Hill federal judge
Gadbois, Richard A., Jr. federal judge
Gold, Arnold Henry judge
Groh, Rupert James, Jr. judge
Hatter, Terry Julius, Jr. federal judge
Hauk, A. Andrew federal judge
Hill, Irving judge
Hupp, Harry L. federal judge
Ideman, James M. federal judge
†Ito, Lance Allan judge
Jaffe, F. Filmore judge
Johnson, Earl, Jr. judge, author
Kelleher, Robert Joseph federal judge
Keller, William D. federal judge
Kenyon, David V. federal judge
Klein, Joan Dempsey judge
Kronenberg, John Robert retired magistrate judge
Lasarow, William Julius federal judge retired
Lax, Kathleen Thompson federal judge
Letts, J. Spencer federal judge
Lew, Ronald S. W. federal judge
March, Kathleen Patricia federal judge
Marshall, Consuelo Bland federal judge
Mund, Geraldine bankruptcy judge
Norris, William Albert federal judge
Pfaelzer, Mariana R. federal judge
Rafeedie, Edward federal judge
Rea, William J. federal judge
Real, Manuel Lawrence federal judge
Stephens, Albert Lee, Jr. federal judge
Takasugi, Robert Mitsuhiro federal judge
Tashima, Atsushi Wallace federal judge
Tevrizian, Dickran M., Jr. federal judge
Turchin, Carolyn judge
Waters, Laughlin Edward federal judge
Williams, David Welford federal judge
Wilson, Stephen Victor federal judge

Modesto
Hedrick, Joseph Watson, Jr. retired judge
Mayhew, William A. judge

Monterey Park
Tucker, Marcus Othello judge

Newport Beach
Curtis, Jesse William, Jr. retired federal judge
Kaufman, Marcus Maurice retired judge, lawyer

Oakland
Champlin, Malcolm McGregor retired municipal judge
Jensen, D. Lowell federal judge, lawyer, government official
Newsome, Randall Jackson federal judge
Tchaikovsky, Leslie J. judge
Wolfe, Cameron Withgot, Sr. federal judge

Palm Desert
Whelan, Francis C. federal judge

Palo Alto
Bird, Rose Elizabeth former state chief justice, law educator

Pasadena
Boochever, Robert federal judge
Fernandez, Ferdinand Francis federal judge
Goodwin, Alfred Theodore federal judge
Hall, Cynthia Holcomb federal judge
Kozinski, Alex federal judge
Nelson, Dorothy Wright (Mrs. James F. Nelson) federal judge
Rymer, Pamela Ann federal judge

Pomona
McCoy, Charles Wirth, Jr. superior court judge

Ramona
Jordan, David Francis, Jr. retired judge

Sacramento
Dahl, Loren Silvester federal judge
Karlton, Lawrence K. federal judge
Levi, David F. federal judge
MacBride, Thomas Jamison federal judge
Moulds, John F. federal judge
Nicholson, George judge
Russell, David E. federal judge
Schwabe, Peter Alexander, Jr. judge
Schwartz, Milton Lewis federal judge
Shubb, William Barnet federal judge
Wilkins, Philip Charles judge

San Diego
Adler, Louise DeCarl bankruptcy judge
Brewster, Rudi Milton federal judge

Enright, William Benner *judge*
Gilliam, Earl Ben *federal judge*
Gonzalez, Irma Elsa *federal judge*
Hargrove, John James *federal judge*
Huff, Marilyn L. *federal judge*
Keep, Judith N. *federal judge*
McKee, Roger Curtis *federal magistrate judge*
Meyers, James William *federal judge*
Nielsen, Leland C. *federal judge*
Rhoades, John Skylstead, Sr. *federal judge*
Schwartz, Edward J. *federal judge*
Thompson, David Renwick *federal judge*
Thompson, Gordon, Jr. *federal judge*
Wallace, J. Clifford *federal judge*

San Francisco
Anderson, Carl West *judge*
Arabian, Armand *state supreme court justice*
Armstrong, Saundra Brown *federal judge*
Baxter, Marvin Ray *state supreme court judge*
Browning, James Robert *federal judge*
Dail, Joseph Garner, Jr. *judge*
Grant, Isabella Horton *judge*
Haerle, Paul Raymond *judge*
Hamilton, Phyllis Jean *judge*
Jarvis, Donald Bertram *judge*
Kennard, Joyce L. *judge*
Kline, John Anthony *state court justice*
Lucas, Malcolm Millar *state supreme court chief justice*
Lynch, Eugene F. *federal judge*
Merrill, Charles Merton *federal judge*
Montali, Dennis *federal judge*
Mosk, Stanley *state supreme court justice*
Noonan, John T., Jr. *federal judge, legal educator*
Orrick, William Horsley, Jr. *federal judge*
Patel, Marilyn Hall *federal judge*
Poole, Cecil F. *federal judge*
Ramsey, Robert Lee *judge, lawyer*
Schwarzer, William W *federal judge*
Sneed, Joseph Tyree, III *federal judge*
Weigel, Stanley Alexander *judge*
Wilken, Claudia Ann *judge*

San Jose
Ingram, William Austin *federal judge*
Morgan, Marilyn *federal judge*
Stacy, Richard A. *adminstrative law judge*
Ware, James W. *federal judge*
Whyte, Ronald M. *federal judge*
Williams, Spencer M. *federal judge*

Santa Ana
Barr, James Norman *federal judge*
Ferguson, Warren John *federal judge*
Lydick, Lawrence Tupper *federal judge*
Riddle, Lynne *judge*
Ryan, John Edward *federal judge*
Stotler, Alicemarie Huber *federal judge*
Wilson, John James *federal judge*

Santa Barbara
Aldisert, Ruggero John *federal judge*
Riblet, Robin L. *judge*

South Pasadena
Saeta, Philip Max *judge*

Woodland
Petre, Donna Marie *county judge*

Woodland Hills
Pregerson, Harry *federal judge*

COLORADO

Denver
Abram, Donald Eugene *federal magistrate judge*
Babcock, Lewis Thornton *federal judge*
Brumbaugh, Roland John *federal judge*
Carrigan, Jim Richard *federal judge*
Clark, Patricia Ann *federal judge*
Ebel, David M. *federal judge*
Erickson, William Hurt *state supreme court justice*
Finesilver, Sherman Glenn *federal judge*
Kirshbaum, Howard M. *judge*
Lohr, George E. *state supreme court justice*
Matsch, Richard P. *federal judge*
McWilliams, Robert Hugh *federal judge*
Moore, John Porfilio *federal judge*
Mullarkey, Mary J. *state supreme court justice*
Nottingham, Edward Willis, Jr. *federal judge*
Pringle, Bruce D. *federal magistrate*
Rovira, Luis Dario *state supreme court justice*
Sparr, Daniel Beattie *federal judge*
Weinshienk, Zita Leeson *federal judge*

Golden
Rodgers, Frederic Barker *judge*

CONNECTICUT

Bridgeport
Eginton, Warren William *federal judge*
Goettel, Gerard Louis *federal judge*
Nevas, Alan Harris *federal judge*
Shiff, Alan Howard William *federal judge*

Fairfield
Lumbard, Joseph Edward, Jr. *federal judge*

Hartford
Berdon, Robert Irwin *state supreme court justice*
Bieluch, William Charles *judge*
Callahan, Robert J. *state supreme court justice*
Clarie, T. Emmet *federal judge*
Covello, Alfred Vincent *federal judge*
Eagan, F(rancis) Owen *magistrate judge*
Heiman, Maxwell *state appellate court judge, lawyer*
Newman, Jon O. *federal judge*
Palmer, Richard N. *judge*
Peters, Ellen Ash *state supreme court chief justice*
Shea, David Michael *state supreme court justice*
Wright, Douglass Brownell *judge, lawyer*

New Britain
Meskill, Thomas J. *federal judge*

New Haven
Burns, Ellen Bree *federal judge*
Cabranes, José Alberto *federal judge*
†Calabresi, Guido *federal judge*
Dorsey, Peter Collins *federal judge*
Winter, Ralph Karl, Jr. *federal judge*
Zampano, Robert Carmine *federal judge*

New London
Santaniello, Angelo Gary *state supreme court justice*

Sharon
Murphy, Thomas Francis *federal judge*

Shelton
Mahoney, J. Daniel *federal judge*

Waterbury
Daly, T(homas) F(rancis) Gilroy *federal judge*

DELAWARE

Wilmington
Balick, Helen Shaffer *federal judge*
Del Pesco, Susan Marie Carr *state judge*
Farnan, Joseph James, Jr. *federal judge*
Gebelein, Richard Stephen *judge, former state attorney general*
Latchum, James Levin *federal judge*
Longobardi, Joseph J. *federal judge*
McKelvie, Roderick R. *federal judge*
Robinson, Sue Lewis *federal judge*
Roth, Jane Richards *federal judge*
Schwartz, Murray Merle *federal judge*
Seitz, Collins Jacques *federal judge*
Stapleton, Walter King *federal judge*
Veasey, Eugene Norman *state supreme court justice, lawyer*
Walsh, Joseph Thomas *state supreme court justice*

DISTRICT OF COLUMBIA

Washington
Andewelt, Roger B. *federal judge*
Archer, Glenn LeRoy, Jr. *federal circuit judge*
Bacon, Sylvia *judge*
Barnett, John H. *judge*
Bartnoff, Judith *judge*
Bayly, John Henry, Jr. *judge*
Beghe, Renato *federal judge*
Bennett, Marion Tinsley *federal judge*
Bernstein, Edwin S. *federal judge*
Blackmun, Harry Andrew *U.S. supreme court justice*
Brennan, William Joseph, Jr. *former U.S. supreme court justice*
Breyer, Stephen Gerald *U.S. supreme court justice*
Bruggink, Eric G. *federal judge*
Bryant, William B. *federal judge*
†Bryson, William Curtis *federal judge*
Buckley, James Lane *federal judge*
Burnett, Arthur Louis, Sr. *judge*
Chabot, Herbert L. *federal judge*
Clapp, Charles E., II *federal judge*
Clevenger, Raymond C., III *federal judge*
Cohen, Mary Ann *federal judge*
Colvin, John O. *federal judge*
Cooper, Jean Saralee *judge*
Cotter, B. Paul, Jr. *judge*
Couvillion, David Irvin *federal judge*
Cowen, Wilson *federal judge*
Cox, Walter Thompson, III *federal judge*
Crawford, Susan Jean *federal judge, lawyer*
Dawson, Howard Athalone, Jr. *federal judge*
Edwards, Harry T. *chief federal judge*
Everett, Robinson Oscar *federal judge, law educator*
Farley, John Joseph, III *federal judge*
Fay, William Michael *federal judge*
Ferren, John Maxwell *federal judge*
Friedman, Daniel Mortimer *federal judge*
Futey, Bohdan A. *federal judge*
Gerber, Joel *federal judge*
Gibson, Reginald Walker *federal judge*
Ginsburg, Douglas Howard *federal judge, educator*
Ginsburg, Ruth Bader *U.S. supreme court justice*
Goldberg, Stanley Joshua *federal judge*
Goodrich, George Herbert *judge*
Green, Joyce Hens *federal judge*
Green, June Lazenby *federal judge*
Greene, Harold H. *federal judge*
Halpern, James S. *federal judge*
Hamblen, Lapsley Walker, Jr. *federal judge*
Harkins, Kenneth R. *federal judge*
Harris, Stanley S. *federal judge*
Heifetz, Alan William *federal judge*
Henderson, Karen LeCraft *federal judge*
Hodges, Robert H., Jr. *federal judge*
Holdaway, Ronald M. *federal judge*
Horn, Marian Blank *federal judge*
Ivers, Donald Louis *federal judge*
Jackson, Thomas Penfield *federal judge*
Jacobs, Julian I. *federal judge*
Johnson, Norma Holloway *federal judge*
Kennedy, Anthony McLeod *U.S. supreme court justice*
Kline, Norman Douglas *federal judge*
Korner, Jules Gilmer, III *federal judge*
Kramer, Kenneth Bentley *federal judge, former congressman*
Lamberth, Royce C. *federal judge*
Lawrence, Glenn Robert *federal administrative law judge*
Litt, Nahum *federal judge*
Lourie, Alan David *federal judge*
Lydon, Thomas J. *federal judge*
Mack, Julia Cooper *judge*
MacKinnon, George E. *federal judge*
Mankin, Hart Tiller *federal judge*
Margolis, Lawrence Stanley *federal judge*
Mathias, John Joseph *federal administrative law judge*
Mayer, Haldane Robert *federal judge*
McArdle, Paul Francis *judge*
Megan, Thomas Ignatius *judge*
Mencher, Bruce Stephan *judge*
Merow, James F. *federal judge*
Michel, Paul Redmond *federal judge*
Miller, Christine Odell Cook *federal judge*
Miller, Jack Richard *federal judge*
Mitchell-Rankin, Zinora Mona *judge*
Nebeker, Frank Quill *federal judge*
Newman, Pauline *federal judge*
Nies, Helen Wilson *federal judge*
Nims, Arthur Lee, III *federal judge*
Oberdorfer, Louis F. *federal judge*
O'Connor, Sandra Day *U.S. supreme court justice*
Parker, Edna G. *federal judge*
Parr, Carolyn Miller *federal court judge*
Penn, John Garrett *federal judge*
Plager, S. Jay *federal judge*
Powell, Lewis Franklin, Jr. *retired U.S. supreme court justice*
Pratt, John Helm *federal judge*
Queen, Evelyn E. Crawford *judge, law educator*
Rader, Randall Ray *federal judge*
Randolph, Arthur Raymond *federal judge, lawyer*
Raum, Arnold *federal judge*
Rehnquist, William Hubbs *U.S. supreme court chief justice*
Reilly, Gerard Denis *judge*
Rich, Giles Sutherland *federal judge*
Richey, Charles Robert *federal judge*
Robinson, Deborah A. *judge*
Robinson, Wilkes Coleman *federal judge*
†Rogers, Judith W. *federal judge*
Ruwe, Robert P. *federal judge*
Scalia, Antonin *U.S. supreme court justice*
Schall, Alvin Anthony *judge*
Scott, Irene Feagin *federal judge*
Sentelle, David Bryan *federal judge*
Shields, Perry *federal judge*
Smith, Loren Allan *federal judge*
Smith, Roy Philip *federal judge*
Sporkin, Stanley *federal judge*
Steadman, John Montague *judge*
Steinberg, Jonathan Robert *federal judge*
Stevens, John Paul *U.S. supreme court justice*
Sullivan, Eugene Raymond *federal judge*
Swift, Stephen Jensen *federal judge*
Tannenwald, Theodore, Jr. *federal judge*
Tansill, Frederick Riker *retired judge*
Tatel, David Stephen *federal judge*
Terry, John Alfred *judge*
Thomas, Clarence *U.S. supreme court justice*
Tidwell, Moody Rudolph *federal judge*
Turner, James Thomas *federal judge*
Vittone, John Michael *federal judge*
Wagner, Curtis Lee, Jr. *federal judge*
Wald, Patricia McGowan *federal judge*
Weinstein, Diane Gilbert *federal judge, lawyer*
Wells, Thomas B. *federal judge*
Whalen, Laurence J. *federal judge*
Whitaker, Meade *federal judge*
White, Byron R. *former U.S. supreme court justice*
Wiese, John Paul *federal judge*
Williams, Stephen Fain *federal judge*
Winfield, Susan Rebecca *judge*
Yock, Robert John *federal judge*
Yoder, Ronnie A. *federal administrative law judge*

FLORIDA

Coral Gables
Davis, Mattie Belle Edwards *retired county judge*

Fort Lauderdale
Gonzalez, Jose Alejandro, Jr. *federal judge*
Roettger, Norman Charles, Jr. *federal judge*
Rosenstein, Samuel M. *federal judge*
Snow, Lurana S. *judge*
Thomas, Everette Earl *federal judge*
Zloch, William J. *federal judge*

Fort Myers
Shafer, Robert Tinsley, Jr. *judge*

Jacksonville
Black, Susan Harrell *federal judge*
Hill, James Clinkscales *federal judge*
Hodges, William Terrell *federal judge*
Melton, Howell Webster, Sr. *federal judge*
Moore, John Henry, II *federal judge*
Schlesinger, Harvey Erwin *federal judge*
Tjoflat, Gerald Bard *federal judge*

Key Biscayne
Kraft, C. William, Jr. *federal judge*

Miami
Aronovitz, Sidney M. *federal judge*
Atkins, C(arl) Clyde *federal judge*
Barkett, Rosemary *federal judge*
Brown, Stephen Thomas *magistrate judge*
Cristol, A. Jay *federal judge*
Davis, Edward Bertrand *federal judge*
Dyer, David William *federal judge*
Fay, Peter Thorp *federal judge*
Ferguson, Wilkie D., Jr. *federal judge*
Garber, Barry L. *judge*
Graham, Donald Lynn *federal judge*
Highsmith, Shelby *federal judge*
Hoeveler, William M. *federal judge*
Johnson, Linnea R. *judge*
Kehoe, James W. *federal judge*
King, James Lawrence *federal judge*
Marcus, Stanley *federal judge*
Moore, Kevin Michael *federal judge*
Moreno, Federico Antonio *federal judge*
Nesbitt, Lenore Carrero *federal judge*
Ungaro-Benages, Ursula Mancusi *federal judge*

Orlando
Conway, Anne Callaghan *federal judge*
Fawsett, Patricia Combs *federal judge*
Sharp, George Kendall *federal judge*
Young, George Cressler *federal judge*

Panama City
Smith, Larry Glenn *retired state judge*

Pensacola
Collier, Lacey Alexander *federal judge*
Frye, John William, III *retired senior circuit judge*
Novotny, Susan M. *judge*
Vinson, C. Roger *federal judge*

Plant City
Bruton, James DeWitt, Jr. *retired judge*

Saint Petersburg
Grube, Karl Bertram *judge*
Roney, Paul H(itch) *federal judge*

Tallahassee
Grimes, Stephen Henry *state supreme court chief justice*
Harding, Major Best *state supreme court justice*
Hatchett, Joseph Woodrow *federal judge*
Kogan, Gerald *state supreme court justice*
McDonald, Parker Lee *state supreme court justice*
Overton, Benjamin Frederick *state supreme court justice*
Paul, Maurice M. *federal judge*
Shaw, Leander Jerry, Jr. *state supreme court justice*
Stafford, William Henry, Jr. *federal judge*
Sundberg, Alan Carl *former state supreme court justice, lawyer*

Tampa
Adams, Henry Lee, Jr. *federal judge*
Baynes, Thomas Edward, Jr. *judge, lawyer, educator*
Bucklew, Susan Cawthon *federal judge*
Castagna, William John *federal judge*
Corcoran, C. Timothy, III *judge*
Kovachevich, Elizabeth Anne *federal judge*
Krentzman, Ben *federal judge*
Menendez, Manuel, Jr. *judge*
Merryday, Steven D. *federal judge*
Nimmons, Ralph Wilson, Jr. *federal judge*
Paskay, Alexander L. *federal judge, law educator*

West Palm Beach
Eschbach, Jesse Ernest *federal judge*
Knott, James Robert *state judge, retired lawyer*
Paine, James Carriger *federal judge*
Ryskamp, Kenneth Lee *federal judge*
Vitunac, Ann E. *judge*

GEORGIA

Atlanta
Alexander, William Henry *judge*
Andrews, Gary Blaylock *state judge, lawyer*
Benham, Robert *state supreme court justice*
Bihary, Joyce *federal judge*
Birch, Stanley Francis, Jr. *federal judge*
Camp, Jack Tarpley, Jr. *federal judge*
Carnes, Julie E. *federal judge*
Clark, Thomas Alonzo *federal judge*
Dougherty, John Ernest *federal judge*
Edmondson, James Larry *federal judge*
Evans, Orinda D. *federal judge*
Feldman, Joel Martin *magistrate judge*
Fletcher, Norman S. *state supreme court justice*
Forrester, J. Owen *federal judge*
Freeman, Richard Cameron *federal judge*
Hall, Robert Howell *federal judge*
Henderson, Albert John *federal judge*
Kravitch, Phyllis A. *federal judge*
Moye, Charles Allen, Jr. *federal judge*
Murphy, Margaret Hackett *federal bankruptcy judge*
Nichols, Horace Elmo *state justice*
O'Kelley, William Clark *federal judge*
Shoob, Marvin H. *federal judge*
Tidwell, George Ernest *federal judge*
Tuttle, Elbert Parr *federal judge*
Ward, Horace Taliaferro *federal judge*

Augusta
Bowen, Dudley Hollingsworth, Jr. *federal judge*

Brunswick
Alaimo, Anthony A. *federal judge*

Columbus
Elliott, James Robert *federal judge*
Laney, John Thomas, III *federal judge*

Decatur
Shulman, Arnold *judge, lawyer*

Forsyth
Clarke, Harold Gravely *retired state supreme court chief justice*

Macon
Anderson, Robert Lanier, III *federal judge*
Fitzpatrick, Duross *federal judge*
Gerson, Robert Walthall *judge, retired lawyer*
Hershner, Robert Franklin, Jr. *federal judge*
Owens, Wilbur Dawson, Jr. *federal judge*

Marietta
Smith, George Thornewell *retired state supreme court justice*

Newnan
Morgan, Lewis Render *federal judge*

Rome
Murphy, Harold Loyd *federal judge*
Vining, Robert Luke, Jr. *federal judge*

Savannah
Edenfield, Berry Avant *federal judge*

HAWAII

Honolulu
Ashford, Clinton Rutledge *judge*
Choy, Herbert Young Cho *federal judge*
Ezra, David A. *federal judge*
Fong, Harold Michael *federal judge*
Kay, Alan Cooke *federal judge*
King, Samuel Pailthorpe *federal judge*
Klein, Robert Gordon *judge*

Kailua
Pence, Martin *federal judge*

IDAHO

Boise
Bakes, Robert Eldon *retired state supreme court justice*
Boyle, Larry Monroe *federal judge*
Callister, Marion Jones *federal judge*
Hagan, Alfred Chris *federal judge*
Johnson, Byron Jerald *state supreme court judge*
Lodge, Edward James *federal judge*

McDevitt, Charles Francis *state supreme court justice*
Mc Quade, Henry Ford *state justice*
Nelson, Thomas G. *federal judge*
Silak, Cathy R. *judge*
Trott, Stephen Spangler *federal judge, musician*

ILLINOIS

Belleville
Ferguson, John Marshall *retired federal magistrate judge*
Stevens, C. Glenn *judge*

Benton
Foreman, James Louis *retired judge*
Gilbert, J. Phil *federal judge*

Chicago
Alesia, James H(enry) *federal judge*
Andersen, Wayne R. *federal judge*
Aspen, Marvin Edward *federal judge*
Barliant, Ronald *federal judge*
Bauer, William Joseph *federal judge*
Bilandic, Michael A. *state supreme court chief justice, former mayor*
Bowman, George Arthur, Jr. *federal judge*
Bua, Nicholas John *retired federal judge*
Bucklo, Elaine Edwards *federal judge*
Coar, David H. *federal judge*
Conlon, Suzanne B. *federal judge*
Cousins, William, Jr. *judge*
Cummings, Walter J. *federal judge*
Duff, Brian Barnett *federal judge*
Easterbrook, Frank Hoover *federal judge*
Fairchild, Thomas E. *federal judge*
Flanagan, Kathy Marie *circuit court judge*
Flaum, Joel Martin *federal judge*
Garnett, Marion Winston *judge*
Gottschall, Joan B. *judge*
Grady, John F. *federal judge*
Hall, Sophia Harriet *judge*
Hart, William Thomas *federal judge*
Holderman, James F., Jr. *federal judge*
Johnson, Glenn Thompson *judge*
Kanne, Michael Stephen *federal judge, educator*
Katz, Edwin I. *federal judge*
Kelly, Richard Smith *judge*
Kocoras, Charles Petros *federal judge*
Lassers, Willard J. *judge*
Lefkow, Joan Humphrey *judge*
Leighton, George Neves *retired federal judge*
Leinenweber, Harry D. *federal judge*
Lindberg, George W. *federal judge*
Marovich, George M. *federal judge*
Marovitz, Abraham Lincoln *judge*
Marshall, Prentice Henry *federal judge*
McGarr, Frank James *retired federal judge, dispute resolution consultant*
Moran, James Byron *federal judge*
Nordberg, John Albert *federal judge*
Norgle, Charles Ronald, Sr. *federal judge*
Pallmeyer, Rebecca Ruth *federal judge*
Pascale, Daniel Richard *judge*
Pell, Wilbur Frank, Jr. *federal judge*
Plunkett, Paul Edward *federal judge*
Posner, Richard Allen *federal judge*
Rothschild, George William *judge, lawyer*
Rovner, Ilana Kara Diamond *federal judge*
Shadur, Milton I. *judge*
Sonderby, Susan Pierson *federal bankruptcy judge*
Squires, John Henry *federal bankruptcy judge*
Toles, Edward Bernard *retired judge*
Will, Hubert Louis *federal judge*
Williams, Ann Claire *federal judge*
Wynn, Thomas Joseph *county judge, educator*
Zagel, James Block *federal judge*

Danville
Baker, Harold Albert *federal judge*

East Saint Louis
Beatty, William Louis *federal judge*
Cohn, Gerald Bernard *federal judge*
Stiehl, William D. *federal judge*

Elgin
Kirkland, Alfred Younges, Sr. *federal judge*

Fairview Heights
Cunningham, Joseph Francis, Jr. *retired state supreme court justice*

Hennepin
Bumgarner, James McNabb *judge*

Homewood
Dietch, Henry Xerxes *judge*

Pekin
Heiple, James Dee *state supreme court justice*

Peoria
McDade, Joe Billy *federal judge*
Mihm, Michael Martin *federal judge*
Morgan, Robert Dale *federal judge*

Rock Island
Telleen, John Martin *retired judge*

Rockford
Reinhard, Philip G. *federal judge*
Roszkowski, Stanley Julian *federal judge*

Springfield
Lessen, Larry Lee *federal judge*
Miller, Benjamin K. *state supreme court justice*
Mills, Richard Henry *federal judge*
Wood, Harlington, Jr. *federal judge*

Tonica
Ryan, Howard Chris *retired state supreme court justice*

Wheaton
Provenzale, Maryellen Kirby *judge, educator*

Wilmette
Nelson, James F. *judge, religious organization administrator*

INDIANA

Evansville
Brooks, Gene Edward *federal judge*
Capshaw, Tommie Dean *federal judge*

Fort Wayne
Lee, William Charles *federal judge*

Hammond
Lozano, Rudolpho *federal judge*
Rodovich, Andrew Paul *lawyer, federal magistrate*

Indianapolis
Barker, Sarah Evans *federal judge*
Bayt, Robert Louis *federal bankruptcy judge*
DeBruler, Roger O. *state supreme court justice*
Dillin, S. Hugh *federal judge*
Endsley, J(ohn) Patrick *federal magistrate judge*
Givan, Richard Martin *state supreme court justice, retired*
Godich, John Paul *federal magistrate judge*
McKinney, Larry J. *federal judge*
Shepard, Randall Terry *judge*
Sullivan, Frank, Jr. *judge*
Tinder, John Daniel *federal judge*
Vandivier, Richard White *federal judge*

South Bend
Grant, Robert Allen *federal judge*
Manion, Daniel Anthony *federal judge*
Miller, Robert L., Jr. *federal judge*
Ripple, Kenneth Francis *federal judge*
Rodibaugh, Robert Kurtz *federal judge*
Sharp, Allen *chief federal judge*

IOWA

Cedar Rapids
Hansen, David Rasmussen *federal judge*
Mc Manus, Edward Joseph *federal judge*
Melloy, Michael J. *federal judge*

Council Bluffs
Peterson, Richard William *lawyer, magistrate judge*

Des Moines
Bremer, Celeste F. *judge*
Fagg, George Gardner *federal judge*
Harris, K. David *state supreme court justice*
Larson, Jerry L. *state supreme court justice*
Longstaff, Ronald E. *federal judge*
McGiverin, Arthur A. *state supreme court justice*
Snell, Bruce M., Jr. *state supreme court justice*
Stuart, William Corwin *federal judge*
Vietor, Harold Duane *federal judge*
Wolle, Charles Robert *federal judge*

Iowa City
Schultz, Louis William *judge*

Osceola
Reynoldson, Walter Ward *state supreme court chief justice*

Sioux City
Deck, Paul Wayne, Jr. *federal judge*
O'Brien, Donald Eugene *federal judge*

KANSAS

Kansas City
Lungstrum, John W. *federal judge*
O'Connor, Earl Eugene *federal judge*
Van Bebber, George Thomas *federal judge*
Vratil, Kathryn Hoefer *federal judge*

Lawrence
Tacha, Deanell Reece *federal judge*

Leavenworth
Stanley, Arthur Jehu, Jr. *federal judge*

Olathe
Chipman, Marion Walter *judge*

Topeka
Abbott, Bob *state supreme court justice*
Allegrucci, Donald Lee *state supreme court justice*
Carpenter, William Randolph, Jr. *judge*
Crow, Sam Alfred *federal judge*
Davis, Robert Edward *judge*
Holmes, Richard Winn *state supreme court justice*
Lockett, Tyler Charles *state supreme court justice*
McFarland, Kay Eleanor *state supreme court justice*
Miller, Robert Haskins *retired state chief justice*
Pusateri, James Anthony *federal bankruptcy judge*
Rogers, Richard Dean *federal judge*
Saffels, Dale Emerson *federal judge*
Six, Fred N. *state supreme court justice*

Wichita
Bell, Charles Robert, Jr. *judge*
Brown, Wesley Ernest *federal judge*
Kelly, Patrick F. *federal judge*
Theis, Frank Gordon *federal judge*

KENTUCKY

Ashland
Wilhoit, Henry Rupert, Jr. *federal judge*

Danville
Lively, Pierce *federal judge*

Fort Thomas
Pendery, Edward Stuart *deputy county judge*

Frankfort
Leibson, Charles M. *state supreme court justice*
Stephens, Robert F. *state supreme court chief justice*
Wintersheimer, Donald Carl *state supreme court justice*

Lexington
Forester, Karl S. *federal judge*
Lee, Joe *federal judge*
Varellas, Sandra Motte *judge*

London
Coffman, Jennifer B. *federal judge*
Siler, Eugene Edward, Jr. *federal judge*

Louisville
Allen, Charles Mengel *federal judge*
Boggs, Danny Julian *federal judge*
Heyburn, John Gilpin, II *federal judge*
Martin, Boyce Ficklen, Jr. *federal judge*
Mather, Roland Donald *judge*
Roberts, J. Wendell *federal judge*
Simpson, Charles R., III *federal judge*

Paducah
Johnstone, Edward Huggins *federal judge*

Pikeville
Hood, Joseph M. *federal judge*

LOUISIANA

Alexandria
Little, F. A., Jr. *federal judge*

Baton Rouge
Cole, Luther Francis *former state supreme court associate justice*
Noland, Christina A. *magistrate judge*
Parker, John Victor *federal judge*
Polozola, Frank Joseph *federal judge*

Lafayette
Davis, William Eugene *federal judge*
Doherty, Rebecca Feeney *federal judge*
Duhe, John Malcolm, Jr. *federal judge*
Haik, Richard T., Sr. *federal judge*
Methvin, Mildred E. *judge*
Putnam, Richard Johnson *federal judge*
Shaw, John Malach *federal judge*
Tynes, Pamela Anne *federal judge*

Lake Charles
Hunter, Edwin Ford, Jr. *federal judge*
McLeod, William Lasater, Jr. *judge, former state legislator*
Trimble, James T., Jr. *federal judge*

New Orleans
Beer, Peter Hill *federal judge*
Boyle, Edward J., Sr. *federal judge*
Calogero, Pascal Frank, Jr. *state supreme court chief justice*
Carr, Patrick E. *judge*
Clement, Edith Brown *federal judge*
Dennis, James Leon *state supreme court justice*
Duplantier, Adrian Guy *federal judge*
Feldman, Martin L. C. *federal judge*
Heebe, Frederick Jacob Regan *federal judge*
Livaudais, Marcel, Jr. *federal judge*
Marcus, Walter F., Jr. *state supreme court justice*
McNamara, A. J. *federal judge*
Mentz, Henry Alvan, Jr. *federal judge*
Mitchell, Lansing Leroy *federal judge*
Schwartz, Charles, Jr. *federal judge*
Sear, Morey Leonard *federal judge, educator*
Watson, Jack Crozier *state supreme court justice*
Wisdom, John Minor *federal judge*

Shreveport
Payne, Roy Steven *judge*
Politz, Henry Anthony *federal judge*
Stagg, Tom *federal judge*
†Stewart, Carl E. *judge*
Walter, Donald Ellsworth *federal judge*
Wiener, Jacques Loeb, Jr. *federal judge*

Tallulah
Ragland, Alwine Mulhearn *judge*

MAINE

Auburn
Clifford, Robert William *judge*

Bangor
Brody, Morton Aaron *federal judge*

Portland
Bradford, Carl O. *judge*
Carter, Gene *federal judge*
Coffin, Frank Morey *federal judge*
Glassman, Caroline Duby *state supreme court justice*
Goodman, James A. *federal judge*
Hornby, David Brock *federal judge*
McKusick, Vincent Lee *former state supreme judicial court chief justice, lawyer*
Roberts, David Glendenning *state supreme court justice*
Wathen, Daniel Everett *state supreme court chief justice*

Rockland
Collins, Samuel W., Jr. *judge*

Wells
Grimes, William Alvan *retired state supreme court chief justice*

Windham
Henry, Harriet Putnam *judge*

MARYLAND

Annapolis
Eldridge, John Cole *judge*
Murphy, Robert C(harles) *judge*

Baltimore
Black, Walter Evan, Jr. *federal judge*
Blake, Catherine C. *judge*
Cardin, Meyer M. *retired judge*
Derby, Ernest Stephen *federal judge*
Garbis, Marvin Joseph *federal judge*
Hargrove, John R. *federal judge*
Harvey, Alexander, II *federal judge*
Kaufman, Frank Albert *federal judge*
Legg, Benson Everett *federal judge*
Maletz, Herbert Naaman *federal judge*
†Motz, Diana Gribbon *judge*
Motz, John Frederick *federal judge*
Murnaghan, Francis Dominic, Jr. *federal judge*
Nickerson, William Milnor *federal judge*
Niemeyer, Paul Victor *federal judge*
Northrop, Edward Skottowe *federal judge*
Rodowsky, Lawrence Francis *judge*
Smalkin, Frederic N. *federal judge*
Young, Joseph H. *federal judge*

Greenbelt
Chasanow, Deborah K. *federal judge*
Kenkel, James Edward *judge*
Mannes, Paul *federal judge*
Messitte, Peter Jo *judge*

Leonardtown
Briscoe, John Hanson *judge, lawyer, former state legislator*

Upper Marlboro
Chasanow, Howard Stuart *judge, lecturer*

MASSACHUSETTS

Boston
Abrams, Ruth Ida *state supreme court justice*
Aldrich, Bailey *federal judge*
Alexander, Joyce London *judge*
Allard, David Henry *judge*
Boudin, Michael *federal judge*
Bowler, Marianne Bianca *judge*
Bownes, Hugh Henry *federal judge*
Campbell, Levin Hicks *federal judge*
Collings, Robert Biddlecombe *federal judge*
Connolly, Thomas Edward *state court judge*
Dacey, Kathleen Ryan *judge*
Dreben, Raya Spiegel *judge*
Harrington, Edward F. *federal judge*
Hillman, William Chernick *federal bankruptcy judge*
Keeton, Robert Ernest *federal judge*
Lasker, Morris E. *federal judge*
Liacos, Paul Julian *state supreme judicial court chief justice*
Mazzone, A. David *federal judge*
Nelson, David S. *federal judge*
Saris, Patti B. *federal judge*
Skinner, Walter Jay *federal judge*
Stearns, Richard Gaylore *judge*
Tauro, Joseph Louis *federal judge*
Todd, J. Owen *judge*
Wilkins, Herbert Putnam *judge*
Wolf, Mark Lawrence *federal judge*
Woodlock, Douglas Preston *federal judge*
Young, William Glover *federal judge*
Zobel, Hiller Bellin *judge*
Zobel, Rya Weickert *federal judge*

Cambridge
Kaplan, Benjamin *judge*

Hingham
Ford, Joseph *retired superior court judge*

Longmeadow
Keady, George Cregan, Jr. *judge*

Melrose
Fremont-Smith, Thayer *judge*

Springfield
Freedman, Frank Harlan *federal judge*
Ponsor, Michael A. *federal judge*

Worcester
Gorton, Nathaniel M. *federal judge, lawyer*
Queenan, James F., Jr. *judge*

MICHIGAN

Ann Arbor
Guy, Ralph B., Jr. *federal judge*
Joiner, Charles Wycliffe *judge*
Kirkendall, John Neal *judge*
La Plata, George *federal judge*
Pepe, Steven Douglas *federal judge*

Bay City
Churchill, James Paul *federal judge*
Cleland, Robert Hardy *federal judge*

Detroit
Duggan, Patrick James *federal judge*
Edmunds, Nancy Garlock *federal judge*
Feikens, John *federal judge*
Friedman, Bernard Alvin *federal judge*
Gadola, Paul V. *federal judge*
Gilmore, Horace Weldon *federal judge*
Graves, Ray Reynolds *federal judge*
Hackett, Barbara (Kloka) *federal judge*
Kaufman, Richard C. *judge*
Keith, Damon Jerome *federal judge*
Kennedy, Cornelia Groefsema *federal judge*
Levin, Charles Leonard *state supreme court justice*
Mallett, Conrad LeRoy, Jr. *state supreme court justice*
Morgan, Virginia *magistrate judge*
O'Meara, John Corbett *federal judge*
Riley, Dorothy Comstock *state supreme court justice*
Rosen, Gerald Ellis *federal judge*
Ryan, James Leo *federal judge*
Sullivan, Joseph B. *retired judge*
Taylor, Anna Diggs *federal judge*
Woods, George Edward *federal judge*
Zatkoff, Lawrence P. *federal judge*

Flint
Newblatt, Stewart Albert *federal judge*

Grand Rapids
Bell, Robert Holmes *federal judge*

Brenneman, Hugh Warren, Jr. *federal magistrate judge*
Engel, Albert Joseph *federal judge*
Gibson, Benjamin F. *chief federal judge*
Gregg, James D. *federal judge*
Hillman, Douglas Woodruff *federal judge*
Howard, Laurence Edward *federal judge*
Miles, Wendell A. *federal judge*
Quist, Gordon Jay *federal judge*
Stevenson, Jo Ann C. *federal bankruptcy judge*

Kalamazoo
Enslen, Richard Alan *federal judge*
Rowland, Doyle Alfred *federal judge*

Lansing
Boyle, Patricia Jean *judge*
Brickley, James H. *judge*
Cavanagh, Michael Francis *state supreme court chief justice*
Harrison, Michael Gregory *judge*
McKeague, David William *district judge*
Suhrheinrich, Richard Fred *federal judge*

Pontiac
Grant, Barry M(arvin) *judge*

Port Huron
DeMascio, Robert Edward *federal judge*

Southfield
Doctoroff, Martin Myles *judge*

MINNESOTA

Duluth
Heaney, Gerald William *federal judge*

Minneapolis
Alton, Ann Leslie *judge, lawyer, educator*
Amdahl, Douglas Kenneth *retired state supreme court justice*
Arthur, Lindsay Grier *retired judge, editor, author*
Doty, David Singleton *federal judge*
Dreher, Nancy C. *federal judge*
Larson, Earl Richard *federal judge*
Lebedoff, Jonathan Galanter *federal judge*
MacLaughlin, Harry Hunter *federal judge*
Murphy, Diana E. *federal judge*
Rosenbaum, James Michael *federal judge*

Minnetonka
Rogers, James Devitt *judge*

Saint Paul
Alsop, Donald Douglas *federal judge*
Coyne, M(ary) Jeanne *state supreme court justice*
Gardebring, Sandra S. *judge*
Keith, Alexander MacDonald *state supreme court chief justice*
Kishel, Gregory Francis *federal judge*
Kyle, Richard House *federal judge*
Lay, Donald Pomeroy *federal judge*
Loken, James Burton *federal judge*
Magnuson, Paul Arthur *federal judge*
Mason, John Milton (Jack Mason) *judge*
Noel, Franklin Linwood *federal magistrate judge*
Page, Alan Cedric *judge*
Renner, Robert George *federal judge*
Rogosheske, Walter Frederick *lawyer, former state justice*
Simonett, John E. *state supreme court justice*
Tomljanovich, Esther M. *judge*

MISSISSIPPI

Aberdeen
Davidson, Glen Harris *federal judge*
Davis, Jerry Arnold *judge*
Senter, Lyonel Thomas, Jr. *federal judge*

Biloxi
Bramlette, David C., III *federal judge*
Gex, Walter Joseph, III *federal judge*
Roper, John Marlin *federal magistrate judge*

Gulfport
Russell, Dan M., Jr. *federal judge*
Walker, Harry Grey *retired state supreme court justice*

Hattiesburg
Pickering, Charles W. *federal judge*

Jackson
Anderson, Reuben V. *state supreme court justice*
Barbour, William H., Jr. *federal judge*
Barksdale, Rhesa Hawkins *federal judge*
Hawkins, Armis Eugene *state supreme court chief justice*
Jolly, E. Grady *federal judge*
Lee, Tom Stewart *federal judge*
Pittman, Edwin Lloyd *state supreme court justice*
Prather, Lenore Loving *state supreme court presiding justice*
Sugg, Robert Perkins *former state supreme court justice*
Sullivan, Michael David *state supreme court justice*
Wingate, Henry Travillion *federal judge*

Oxford
Biggers, Neal Brooks, Jr. *federal judge*

MISSOURI

Jefferson City
Benton, W. Duane *judge*
Covington, Ann K. *judge, lawyer*
Donnelly, Robert True *retired state supreme court justice*
Holstein, John Charles *state supreme court justice*
Limbaugh, Stephen Nathaniel, Jr. *judge*
Price, William Ray, Jr. *state supreme court judge*
Robertson, Edward D., Jr. *state supreme court chief justice*
Thomas, Elwood Lauren *state supreme court justice*

Kansas City
Bartlett, D. Brook *federal judge*
Berrey, Robert Wilson, III *lawyer, judge*
Bowman, Pasco Middleton, II *federal judge*
Gaitan, Fernando J., Jr. *federal judge*
Gibson, Floyd Robert *federal judge*
Gibson, John Robert *federal judge*
Hunter, Elmo Bolton *federal judge*
Koger, Frank Williams *federal judge*
Maughmer, John Townsend *federal judge*
Sachs, Howard F(rederic) *federal judge*
See, Karen Mason *federal judge*
Stevens, Joseph Edward, Jr. *federal judge*
Ulrich, Robert Gene *judge*
Whipple, Dean *federal judge*
Wright, Scott Olin *federal judge*

Moberly
Blackmar, Charles Blakey *state supreme court justice*

Saint Louis
Barta, James Joseph *federal judge*
Cahill, Clyde S. *federal judge*
Filippine, Edward Louis *federal judge*
Gunn, George F., Jr. *federal judge*
Hamilton, Jean Constance *federal judge*
Hungate, William Leonard *retired federal judge, former congressman*
Jackson, Carol E. *federal judge*
Limbaugh, Stephen Nathaniel *federal judge*
McMillian, Theodore *federal judge*
Perry, Catherine D. *judge*
Reinhard, James Richard *judge*
Shaw, Charles Alexander *judge*
Stohr, Donald J. *federal judge*

Springfield
Clark, Russell Gentry *federal judge*
Collinson, William R. *federal judge*

MONTANA

Billings
Battin, James Franklin *judge, former congressman*
Fagg, Russell *judge, lawyer*
Shanstrom, Jack D. *federal judge*

Great Falls
Hatfield, Paul Gerhart *federal judge, lawyer*

Helena
Gray, Karla Marie *state supreme court justice*
Harrison, John Conway *state supreme court justice*
Hunt, William E., Sr. *state supreme court justice*
Lovell, Charles C. *federal judge*
McDonough, Russell Charles *retired state supreme court justice*
Trieweiler, Terry Nicholas *state supreme court justice*
Turnage, Jean A. *state supreme court chief justice*
Weber, Fred J. *state supreme court justice*

Missoula
Erickson, Leif B. *federal judge*

NEBRASKA

Columbus
Whitehead, John C. *state judge*

Lincoln
Beam, Clarence Arlen *federal judge*
Boslaugh, Leslie *judge*
Caporale, D. Nick *state supreme court justice*
Fahrnbruch, Dale E. *state supreme court justice*
Hastings, William Charles *retired state supreme court chief justice*
Kopf, Richard G. *federal judge*
Lanphier, David J. *judge*
Minahan, John C., Jr. *federal judge*
Piester, David L(ee) *magistrate judge*
Urbom, Warren Keith *federal judge*
White, C. Thomas *state supreme court justice*

Omaha
Cambridge, William G. *federal judge*
Grant, John Thomas *retired state supreme court justice*
Jaudzemis, Kathleen A. *judge*
Peck, Richard Cleon *judge*
Shanahan, Thomas M. *judge*
Strom, Lyle Elmer *federal judge*

NEVADA

Carson City
Gunderson, Elmer Millard *state supreme court justice, law educator*
Rose, Robert E(dgar) *state supreme court justice*
Springer, Charles Edward *state supreme court justice*
Young, C. Clifton *judge*

Las Vegas
Foley, Roger D. *federal judge*
George, Lloyd D. *federal judge*
Johnston, Robert Jake *federal magistrate judge*
Jones, Robert Clive *judge*
Pro, Philip Martin *federal judge*
Riegle, Linda B. *federal judge*

Reno
Brunetti, Melvin T. *federal judge*
Hagen, David W. *judge*
Hug, Procter Ralph, Jr. *federal judge*
McKibben, Howard D. *federal judge*
Reed, Edward Cornelius, Jr. *federal judge*
Thompson, James Harold *judge*
Wiggins, Charles Edward *federal judge*

NEW HAMPSHIRE

Concord
Barbadoro, Paul J. *federal judge*
Barry, William H., Jr. *federal judge*
Batchelder, William F. *state supreme court justice*
Brock, David Allen *state supreme court chief justice*
Cann, William Francis *judge*
Devine, Shane *federal judge*
Horton, Sherman D., Jr. *state supreme court justice*
Johnson, William R. *state supreme court justice*
Loughlin, Martin Francis *federal judge*
McAuliffe, Steven James *federal judge*
Stahl, Norman H. *federal judge*
Thayer, W(alter) Stephen, III *state supreme court justice*

NEW JERSEY

Atlantic City
Knight, Edward R. *judge, law educator, psychologist*

Camden
Brotman, Stanley Seymour *federal judge*
Gerry, John Francis *federal judge*
Irenas, Joseph Eron *federal judge*
Rodriguez, Joseph H. *federal judge*
Simandle, Jerome B. *federal judge*
Wizmur, Judith H. *federal judge*

Cherry Hill
Laskin, Lee B. *judge, laywer, former state senator*

Elizabeth
Beglin, Edward W., Jr. *judge*

Freehold
Fisher, Clarkson Sherman, Jr. *judge*

Hackensack
Kestin, Howard H. *judge*

Morristown
Clifford, Robert L. *state supreme court justice*
Pollock, Stewart Glasson *state supreme court justice*

Newark
Ackerman, Harold A. *federal judge*
Alito, Samuel Anthony, Jr. *federal judge*
Barry, Maryanne Trump *federal judge*
Bassler, William G. *federal judge*
Bissell, John W. *federal judge*
Chesler, Stanley Richard *federal judge*
Debevoise, Dickinson Richards *federal judge*
Gambardella, Rosemary *federal judge*
Garth, Leonard I. *federal judge*
Lechner, Alfred James, Jr. *federal judge*
Lifland, John C. *federal judge*
Politan, Nicholas H. *federal judge*
Sarokin, H. Lee *federal judge*
Tuohey, William F. *federal judge*
Winfield, Novalyn L. *federal bankruptcy judge*
Wolin, Alfred M. *federal judge*

Oakhurst
Wilentz, Robert Nathan *state supreme court justice*

Paterson
Reiss, Sidney H. *judge, lawyer*

Springfield
†Coleman, James H., Jr. *state supreme court justice*

Stockton
Griffin, Bryant Wade *retired judge*

Trenton
Brown, Garrett Edward, Jr. *federal judge*
Cowen, Robert E. *federal judge*
Fisher, Clarkson Sherman *federal judge*
Gindin, William Howard *federal judge*
Greenberg, Morton Ira *federal judge*
Handler, Alan B. *state supreme court justice*
O'Hern, Daniel Joseph *state supreme court justice*
Parell, Mary Little *federal judge, former banking commissioner*
Thompson, Anne Elise *federal judge*
Wolfson, Freda L. *judge*

NEW MEXICO

Albuquerque
Conway, John E. *federal judge*
Deaton, William Weldon, Jr. *federal judge*
Easley, Mack *retired state supreme court chief justice*
Hansen, Curtis LeRoy *federal judge*
McFeeley, Mark B. *federal judge*
Mechem, Edwin Leard *judge*
Parker, James Aubrey *federal judge*

Las Cruces
Bratton, Howard Calvin *federal judge*

Las Vegas
Flores, Benny E. *judge*

Roswell
Baldock, Bobby Ray *federal judge*

Santa Fe
Baca, Joseph Francis *state supreme court chief justice*
Campos, Santiago E. *federal judge*
Franchini, Gene Edward *state supreme court justice*
Kelly, Paul Joseph, Jr. *federal judge*
Ransom, Richard Edward *state supreme court justice*
Seth, Oliver *federal judge*
Vazquez, Martha Alicia *judge*
Yalman, Ann *judge*

NEW YORK

Albany
Bellacosa, Joseph W. *judge*
Cholakis, Constantine George *federal judge*
Kaye, Judith Smith *judge*
Miner, Roger Jeffrey *federal judge*
Simons, Richard Duncan *judge*
Smith, Ralph Wesley, Jr. *federal judge*
Titone, Vito Joseph *judge*

Bedford
Bonsal, Dudley Baldwin *federal judge*

Binghamton
McAvoy, Thomas James *federal judge*

Bronx
Bamberger, Phylis Skloot *judge*
Roberts, Burton Bennett *administrative judge*

Brooklyn
Amon, Carol Bagley *federal judge*
Azrack, Joan M. *judge*
Bartels, John Ries *federal judge*
Bramwell, Henry *federal judge*
Dearie, Raymond Joseph *federal judge*
Duberstein, Conrad B. *federal judge*
Glasser, Israel Leo *federal judge*
Johnson, Sterling, Jr. *federal judge*
Korman, Edward R. *federal judge*
Nickerson, Eugene H. *federal judge*
Raggi, Reena *federal judge*
Ross, Allyne R. *federal judge*
Ryan, Leonard Eames *administrative law judge*
Sifton, Charles Proctor *federal judge*
Trager, David G. *judge, lawyer, educator*
Weinstein, Jack Bertrand *federal judge*

Buffalo
Arcara, Richard Joseph *federal judge*
Curtin, John T. *federal judge*
Elfvin, John Thomas *federal judge*
Jasen, Matthew Joseph *state justice*
Joslin, Norman Earl *judge*
McGuire, Beryl Edward *retired federal judge*
Skretny, William Marion *federal judge*

Garden City
Harwood, Stanley *retired judge, lawyer*

Hauppauge
Hurley, Denis R. *federal judge*
Wexler, Leonard D. *federal judge*

Hempstead
Altimari, Frank X. *federal judge*

Mineola
Mogil, Bernard Marc *judge*
Murphy, George Austin *judge*

New York
Abram, Prudence Beatty *federal judge*
Aquilino, Thomas Joseph, Jr. *federal judge, law educator*
Baer, Harold, Jr. *judge*
Brozman, Tina L. *federal judge*
Buchwald, Naomi Reice *federal magistrate judge*
Cannella, John Matthew *federal judge*
Carman, Gregory Wright *federal judge*
Cedarbaum, Miriam Goldman *federal judge*
Cooper, Irving Ben *federal judge*
DiCarlo, Dominick L. *federal judge*
Duffy, Kevin Thomas *federal judge*
Edelstein, David Northon *federal judge*
Feinberg, Wilfred *federal judge*
Freedman, Helen Edelstein *justice*
Gershon, Nina *federal judge*
Goldberg, Richard W. *federal judge*
Griesa, Thomas Poole *federal judge*
Grubin, Sharon E. *federal judge*
Jacobs, Dennis G. *federal judge*
Kearse, Amalya Lyle *federal judge*
Keenan, John Fontaine *federal judge*
Knapp, Whitman *federal judge*
Koeltl, John George *judge*
Kram, Shirley Wohl *federal judge*
Kupferman, Theodore R. *state justice*
Lee, Barbara A. *federal magistrate judge*
Leisure, Peter Keeton *federal judge*
Leval, Pierre Nelson *federal judge*
Lowe, Mary Johnson *federal judge*
Martin, John S., Jr. *federal judge*
McKenna, Lawrence M. *federal judge*
McLaughlin, Joseph Michael *federal judge, law educator*
Motley, Constance Baker (Mrs. Joel Wilson Motley) *federal judge, former city official*
Mukasey, Michael B. *federal judge*
Musgrave, R. Kenton *federal judge*
Owen, Richard *federal judge*
Patterson, Robert Porter, Jr. *federal judge*
Pierce, Lawrence Warren *federal judge*
Pollack, Milton *federal judge*
Preska, Loretta A. *federal judge*
Restani, Jane A. *federal judge*
Roberts, Kathleen Anne *judge*
Rosenberger, Ernst Hey *judge*
Sand, Leonard B. *federal judge*
Schwartz, Allen G. *federal judge*
Sotomayor, Sonia *federal judge*
Sprizzo, John Emilio *federal judge*
Sweet, Robert Workman *federal judge*
Torres, Edwin *state judge, writer*
Tsoucalas, Nicholas *federal judge*
Walker, John Mercer, Jr. *federal judge*
Ward, Robert Joseph *federal judge*
Watson, James Lopez *federal judge*
Williams, Milton Lawrence *judge, educator*
Wood, Kimba M. *federal judge*

Poughkeepsie
Berk, Jeremiah E. *federal judge*
Rosenblatt, Albert Martin *state supreme court justice*

Riverhead
Stark, Thomas Michael *state supreme court justice*

Rochester
Kehoe, L. Paul *judge*
Larimer, David George *federal judge*
Telesca, Michael Anthony *federal judge*
Van Graafeiland, Ellsworth Alfred *federal judge*

Syracuse
McCurn, Neal Peters *federal judge*
Munson, Howard G. *federal judge*
Scullin, Frederick James, Jr. *federal judge*

Uniondale
Mishler, Jacob *federal judge*
Platt, Thomas Collier, Jr. *federal judge*
Seybert, Joanna *judge*
Spatt, Arthur Donald *federal judge*

Utica
Cardamone, Richard J. *federal judge*

Webster
Witmer, G. Robert *retired state supreme court justice*

Westbury
Eisenberg, Dorothy *federal judge*

White Plains
Brieant, Charles La Monte *federal judge*
Broderick, Vincent Lyons *federal judge*
Hardin, Adlai Stevenson, Jr. *judge*
Schwartzberg, Howard *federal judge*

NORTH CAROLINA

Asheville
Voorhees, Richard Lesley *federal judge*

Chapel Hill
Martin, Harry Corpening *state supreme court justice, retired*

Charlotte
McMillan, James Bryan *federal judge, retired*
Mullen, Graham C. *federal judge*
Potter, Robert Daniel *federal judge*
Taylor, Paul Bradford *judge*

Elizabeth City
Boyle, Terrence W. *federal judge*

Greensboro
Bullock, Frank William, Jr. *federal judge*
Gordon, Eugene Andrew *judge*
Osteen, William L., Sr. *federal judge*
Tart, Jerry Gordon *federal judge*
Tilley, Norwood Carlton, Jr. *federal judge*

Greenville
Howard, Malcolm Jones *federal judge*

Morganton
Ervin, Samuel James, III *federal judge*

New Bern
McCotter, Charles Kennedy, Jr. *magistrate judge*

Pilot Mountain
Long, James M. *judge*

Raleigh
Britt, W. Earl *federal judge*
Denson, Alexander Bunn *federal magistrate judge*
Dupree, Franklin Taylor, Jr. *federal judge*
Eagles, Sidney Smith, Jr. *judge*
Exum, James Gooden, Jr. *state supreme court chief justice*
Frye, Henry E. *state supreme court justice*
Mitchell, Burley Bayard, Jr. *state supreme court chief justice*
Small, Alden Thomas *federal judge*
Webb, John *state supreme court justice*
Whichard, Willis Padgett *state supreme court justice*

Wilmington
Fox, James Carroll *federal judge*

Winston Salem
Eliason, Russell Allen *federal judge*
Erwin, Richard Cannon *federal judge*
Ward, Hiram Hamilton *federal judge*

NORTH DAKOTA

Bismarck
Conmy, Patrick A. *federal judge*
Erickstad, Ralph John *judge, retired state supreme court chief justice*
Levine, Beryl Joyce *state supreme court justice*
Meschke, Herbert Leonard *state supreme court justice*
Neumann, William Allen *judge*
Paulson, William Lee *state justice*
Pederson, Vernon R. *judge*
Sandstrom, Dale Vernon *state supreme court judge*
VandeWalle, Gerald Wayne *state supreme court chief justice*
Van Sickle, Bruce Marion *federal judge*

Fargo
Benson, Paul *federal judge*
Bright, Myron H. *federal judge, educator*
Hill, William A(lexander) *bankruptcy judge*
Magill, Frank John *federal judge*
Webb, Rodney Scott *federal judge, lawyer*

Grand Forks
Senechal, Alice R. *judge, lawyer*

Minot
Kerian, Jon Robert *judge*

Williston
Burdick, Eugene Allan *retired judge, lawyer, surrogate judge*

OHIO

Ada
Hanson, Eugene Nelson *judge*

Akron
Bell, Samuel H. *federal judge*
Contie, Leroy John, Jr. *federal judge*
Dowd, David D., Jr. *federal judge*
Shea-Stonum, Marilyn *judge*
White, Harold F. *bankruptcy judge, retired federal judge*

Bowling Green
Baird, James Abington *judge*

Cincinnati
Edwards, George Clifton, Jr. *retired judge*
Jones, Nathaniel Raphael *federal judge*
Nelson, David Aldrich *federal judge*
Perlman, Burton *federal judge*
Rubin, Carl Bernard *federal judge*
Spiegel, S. Arthur *federal judge*
Weber, Herman Jacob *federal judge*

Cleveland
Aldrich, Ann *federal judge*
Baxter, Randolph *federal judge*
Burke, Lillian Walker *retired judge*
†Celebrezze, Anthony *federal judge*
Krenzler, Alvin Irving *federal judge*
Krupansky, Robert Bazil *federal judge*
Lambros, Thomas Demetrios *federal judge*
Manos, John M. *federal judge*
Matia, Paul Ramon *federal judge*
Porter, James Morris *state judge*
Snow, David Forrest *judge*
White, George W. *federal judge*

Columbus
Beckwith, Sandra Shank *federal judge*
Calhoun, Donald Eugene, Jr. *federal judge*
Douglas, Andrew *state supreme court justice*
Graham, James Lowell *federal judge*
Holschuh, John David *federal judge*
King, Norah McCann *federal judge*
Kinneary, Joseph Peter *federal judge*
Leach, Russell *judge*
Mc Cormac, John Waverly *judge*
Moyer, Thomas J. *state supreme court chief justice*
Norris, Alan Eugene *federal judge*
Pfeifer, Paul E. *state supreme court justice*
Resnick, Alice Robie *state supreme court justice*
Sellers, Barbara Jackson *federal judge*
Smith, George Curtis *federal judge*
Sweeney, Asher William *state supreme court justice*
Sweeney, Francis E. *state supreme court justice*
Wright, J. Craig *state supreme court associate justice*

Dayton
Knapp, James Ian Keith *judge*
Love, Rodney Marvin *retired judge, former congressman*
Merz, Michael *federal judge*
Porter, Walter Arthur *judge*

Medina
Batchelder, Alice M. *federal judge*

Middletown
Jones, Fred E. *state judge*

Toledo
Krasniewski, Walter Jacob *federal judge*
Potter, John William *federal judge*
Speer, Richard Lyle *federal judge*
Walinski, Nicholas Joseph *federal judge*
Young, Don J. *federal judge*

Warren
Nader, Robert Alexander *judge, lawyer*

OKLAHOMA

Lawton
Moore, Roy Dean *judge*

Muskogee
Seay, Frank Howell *federal judge*

Norman
Trimble, Preston Albert *retired judge*

Oklahoma City
Alley, Wayne Edward *federal judge, retired army officer*
Bohanon, Luther L. *federal judge*
Bohanon, Richard Lee *federal judge*
Brett, Thomas Marshall *judge*
Cauthron, Robin J. *federal judge*
Daugherty, Frederick Alvin *federal judge*
Hargrave, Rudolph *state supreme court justice*
†Henry, Robert H. *federal judge, former attorney general*
Hodges, Ralph B. *state supreme court justice*
Holloway, William Judson, Jr. *federal judge*
Irwin, Pat *federal magistrate judge*
Lavender, Robert Eugene *state supreme court justice*
Leonard, Timothy Dwight *federal judge*
Opala, Marian P(eter) *state supreme court justice*
Parks, Ed H. *judge*
Russell, David L. *federal judge*
Summers, Hardy *state supreme court justice*
Thompson, Ralph Gordon *federal judge*
West, Lee Roy *federal judge*
Wilson, Alma *state supreme court justice*

Tulsa
Beasley, William Rex *judge*
Brett, Thomas Rutherford *federal judge*
Cook, Harold Dale *federal judge*
†Goodman, Jerry L(ynn) *judge*
Martin, Robert Finlay, Jr. *retired judge*
Seymour, Stephanie Kulp *federal judge*
Taylor, Joe Clinton *judge*
Wagner, John Leo *federal judge, lawyer*

OREGON

Eugene
Coffin, Thomas M. *federal magistrate judge*
Higdon, Polly Susanne *federal judge*
Hogan, Michael R(obert) *federal judge*

Portland
Beatty, John Cabeen, Jr. *judge*
Belloni, Robert Clinton *federal judge*
Frye, Helen Jackson *federal judge*
Hess, Henry Leroy, Jr. *bankruptcy judge*
Hill, Wilmer Bailey *administrative law judge*
Johnson, Nely Lupovici *judge*
Jones, Robert Edward *federal judge*
Juba, George E. *federal judge*
Kilkenny, John F. *federal judge, lawyer*
Leavy, Edward *federal judge*
Marsh, Malcolm F. *federal judge*
O'Scannlain, Diarmuid Fionntain *federal judge*
Panner, Owen M. *federal judge*
Perris, Elizabeth L. *federal judge*
Redden, James Anthony *federal judge*
Roth, Phillip Joseph *judge*
Skopil, Otto Richard, Jr. *federal judge*

Salem
Carson, Wallace Preston, Jr. *state supreme court chief justice*
Fadeley, Edward Norman *state supreme court justice*
Graber, Susan P. *judge*
O'Connell, Kenneth John *state justice*
Peterson, Edwin J. *retired supreme court justice, law educator*
Unis, Richard L. *state supreme court justice*
Van Hoomissen, George Albert *state supreme court justice*

PENNSYLVANIA

Allison Park
Craig, David W. *judge, author*

Easton
Van Antwerpen, Franklin Stuart *federal judge*

Erie
Bentz, Warren Worthington *federal bankruptcy judge*
Mencer, Glenn Everell *federal judge*
Nygaard, Richard Lowell *federal judge*

Harrisburg
Caldwell, William Wilson *federal judge*
Rambo, Sylvia H. *federal judge*

Philadelphia
Angell, M(ary) Faith *federal magistrate judge*
Bartle, Harvey, III *federal judge*
Bechtle, Louis Charles *federal judge*
Becker, Edward Roy *federal judge*
Broderick, Raymond Joseph *federal judge*
Brody, Anita Blumstein *federal judge*
Buckwalter, Ronald Lawrence *federal judge*
Cahn, Edward N. *federal judge*
Dalzell, Stewart *federal judge*
Ditter, John William, Jr. *federal judge*
DuBois, Jan Ely *federal judge*
Fullam, John P. *federal judge*
Gawthrop, Robert Smith, III *federal judge*
Giles, James T. *federal judge*
Green, Clifford Scott *federal judge*
Hutchinson, William David *federal judge*
Hutton, Herbert J. *federal judge*
Joyner, J(ames) Curtis *federal judge*
Katz, Marvin *federal judge*
Kelly, James McGirr *federal judge*
Kelly, Robert F. *federal judge*
Ludwig, Edmund Vincent *federal judge*
McGlynn, Joseph Leo, Jr. *federal judge*
†McKee, Theodore A. *federal judge*
Melinson, James Robert *judge*
Newcomer, Clarence Charles *federal judge*
Nix, Robert N(elson) C(ornelius), Jr. *state supreme court chief justice*
O'Neill, Thomas Newman, Jr. *federal judge*
Padova, John R. *federal judge*
Pollak, Louis Heilprin *federal judge, educator*
Powers, Richard Augustine, III *federal judge*
Reed, Lowell A., Jr. *federal judge*
Richette, Lisa Aversa *judge*
Scholl, David Allen *federal judge*
Scirica, Anthony Joseph *federal judge*
Shapiro, Norma Sondra Levy *federal judge*
Sloviter, Dolores Korman *federal judge*
Stout, Juanita Kidd *judge*
Van Artsdalen, Donald West *federal judge*
Waldman, Jay Carl *federal judge*
Weiner, Charles R. *federal judge*
Yohn, William Hendricks, Jr. *federal judge*

Pittsburgh
Ambrose, Donetta W. *federal judge*
Bloch, Alan Neil *federal judge*
Brosky, John G. *judge*
Cohill, Maurice Blanchard, Jr. *district court judge*
Cosetti, Joseph Louis *federal judge*
Diamond, Gustave *federal judge*
Dumbauld, Edward *federal judge*
Fitzgerald, Judith Klaswick *federal judge*
Flaherty, John P., Jr. *state supreme court justice*
Lee, Donald John *federal judge*
Lewis, Timothy K. *federal judge*
Mansmann, Carol Los *federal judge, law educator*
Mc Cune, Barron Patterson *federal judge*
Mitchell, Robert C. *federal judge*
Ross, Eunice Latshaw *judge*
Sensenich, Ila Jeanne *magistrate judge*
Smith, David Brookman *federal judge*
Standish, William Lloyd *federal judge*
Weber, Gerald Joseph *federal judge*
Weis, Joseph Francis, Jr. *federal judge*
Zappala, Stephen A. *state supreme court justice*
Ziegler, Donald Emil *federal judge*

Reading
Huyett, Daniel Henry, III *federal judge*
Troutman, E. Mac *federal judge*

Scranton
Conaboy, Richard Paul *federal judge*
Kosik, Edwin Michael *federal judge*
Nealon, William Joseph, Jr. *federal judge*
O'Malley, Carlon Martin *judge*

Wilkes Barre
Rosenn, Max *federal judge*

Williamsport
McClure, James Focht, Jr. *federal judge*
Muir, Malcolm *federal judge*

RHODE ISLAND

Providence
Boyle, Francis Joseph *federal judge*
Hagopian, Jacob *federal judge*
Lagueux, Ronald Rene *federal judge*
Murray, Florence Kerins *state supreme court justice*
Selya, Bruce Marshall *federal judge*
Torres, Ernest C. *federal judge*
Votolato, Arthur Nicholas, Jr. *federal judge*
Weisberger, Joseph Robert *chief state supreme court justice*

SOUTH CAROLINA

Aiken
Simons, Charles Earl, Jr. *federal judge*

Anderson
Anderson, George Ross, Jr. *federal judge*

Charleston
Blatt, Solomon, Jr. *federal judge*
Carr, Robert Stuart *federal magistrate judge*
Hawkins, Falcon Black, Jr. *federal judge*
Norton, David C. *federal judge*
Sanders, Alexander Mullings, Jr. *judge*

Columbia
Anderson, Joseph Fletcher, Jr. *federal judge*
Bristow, Walter James, Jr. *retired state judge*
Chapman, Robert Foster *federal judge*
Hamilton, Clyde Henry *federal judge*
Perry, Matthew J., Jr. *federal judge*
Shedd, Dennis W. *federal judge*
Toal, Jean Hoefer *lawyer, state supreme court justice*

Darlington
Chandler, Archie Lee *state supreme court justice*

Florence
Houck, Charles Weston *federal judge*

Greenville
Herlong, Henry Michael, Jr. *federal judge*
Traxler, William Byrd, Jr. *federal judge*
Wilkins, William Walter, Jr. *federal judge*

Myrtle Beach
Harwell, David Walker *retired state supreme court chief justice*

Orangeburg
†Williams, Karen Johnson *federal judge*

Spartanburg
Russell, Donald Stuart *federal judge*

Sumter
Finney, Ernest Adolphus, Jr. *state supreme court chief justice*

SOUTH DAKOTA

Fort Pierre
Hoyt, Irvin N. *judge*

Pierre
Amundson, Robert A. *state supreme court justice*
Henderson, Frank Ellis *state supreme court justice*
Miller, Robert Arthur *state supreme court chief justice*
Porter, Donald James *federal judge*
Sabers, Richard Wayne *state supreme court justice*
Wuest, George W. *retired state supreme court justice*

Rapid City
Battey, Richard Howard *federal judge*
Bogue, Andrew Wendell *federal judge*

Sioux Falls
Ecker, Peder Kaloides *former judge*
Gibbs, Frank P. *federal judge*
Jones, John Bailey *federal judge*
Nichol, Fred Joseph *federal judge*
Piersol, Lawrence L. *federal judge*
Wollman, Roger Leland *federal judge*

TENNESSEE

Chattanooga
Edgar, R(obert) Allan *federal judge*
Kelley, Ralph Houston *judge*
Milburn, Herbert Theodore *federal judge*
Powers, John Y. *federal judge*
Summitt, Robert Murray *circuit judge*

Cookeville
Morton, Leland Clure *federal judge*

Crossville
O'Brien, Charles H. *state supreme court chief justice*

Greeneville
Hull, Thomas Gray *federal judge*

Jackson
Todd, James Dale *federal judge*

Knoxville
Anderson, Edward Riley *state supreme court justice*
Jarvis, James Howard, II *federal judge*
Jordan, Robert Leon *federal judge*
Murrian, Robert Phillip *federal judge, educator*
Swann, Bill *judge*

Memphis
Allen, James Henry *magistrate judge*
Brown, Aaron Clifton, Jr. *magistrate judge*
Brown, Bailey *federal judge*
Donald, Bernice B. *judge*
Gibbons, Julia Smith *federal judge*
Horton, Odell *federal judge*
McCalla, Jon P. *federal judge*

McRae, Robert Malcolm, Jr. *federal judge*
Turner, Jerome *federal judge*
Wellford, Harry Walker *federal judge*

Nashville
Daughtrey, Martha Craig *federal judge*
Echols, Robert L. *federal judge*
Higgins, Thomas A. *federal judge*
Merritt, Gilbert Stroud *federal judge*
Nixon, John Trice *federal judge*
Reid, Lyle *judge*
Sandidge, Kent, III *magistrate judge*
Wiseman, Thomas Anderton, Jr. *federal judge*

Signal Mountain
Cooper, Robert Elbert *state supreme court justice*

TEXAS

Amarillo
Robinson, Mary Lou *federal judge*

Arlington
Wright, James Edward *judge*

Austin
†Baird, Charles F. *judge*
†Benavides, Fortunato Pedro (Pete Benavides) *judge*
Clinton, Sam Houston *judge*
Derounian, Steven Boghos *lawyer, retired judge*
Gammage, Robert Alton (Bob Gammage) *state supreme court justice*
Garwood, William Lockhart *federal judge*
Gonzalez, Raul A. *state supreme court justice*
Greenhill, Joe Robert *former chief justice state supreme, lawyer*
Hecht, Nathan Lincoln *state supreme court justice*
Hightower, Jack English *state supreme court justice, former congressman*
Johnson, Sam D. *federal judge*
Maloney, Frank *judge, lawyer*
†Mansfield, Stephen W. *judge*
McCormick, Michael Jerry *judge*
Miller, Charles E. *judge*
Nowlin, James Robertson *federal judge*
Phillips, Thomas Royal *judge*
Pope, Andrew Jackson, Jr. (Jack Pope) *retired state supreme court chief justice*
Ray, Cread L., Jr. *retired state supreme court justice*
Reavley, Thomas Morrow *federal judge*
Sparks, Sam *federal judge*
Thornberry, William Homer *federal judge*
Williams, Mary Pearl *judge, lawyer*

Beaumont
Cobb, Howell *federal judge*
Fisher, Joseph Jefferson *federal judge*
Schell, Richard A. *federal judge*

Brownsville
Garza, Reynaldo G. *federal judge*
Vela, Filemon B. *federal judge*

Corpus Christi
Head, Hayden Wilson, Jr. *district judge*
Schmidt, Richard S. *federal judge*

Dallas
Buchmeyer, Jerry *federal judge*
Fish, A. Joe *federal judge*
Fitzwater, Sidney Allen *federal judge*
Higginbotham, Patrick Errol *federal judge*
Jackson, Lee Franklin *judge*
Kendall, Joe *federal judge*
Maloney, Robert B. *federal judge*
Price, Robert Eben *judge*
Robertson, Ted Zanderson *judge*
Sanders, Harold Barefoot, Jr. *federal judge*
Sanderson, William Fletcher, Jr. *federal judge*
Solis, Jorge Antonio *federal judge*
Youngblood, Michelle Karen Wolstein *judge*

Del Rio
Thurmond, George Murat *judge*

El Paso
Hudspeth, Harry Lee *federal judge*
Ruesch, Janet Carol *federal magistrate judge*

Fort Worth
Belew, David Owen, Jr. *judge*
Hicks, Maryellen Whitlock *lawyer, judge*
Mahon, Eldon Brooks *federal judge*
McBryde, John Henry *federal judge*
McGlinchey, Alexander Herbert *federal judge*
Means, Terry Robert *federal judge*

Galveston
Gibson, Hugh *federal judge*
Kent, Samuel B. *federal judge*

Houston
Black, Norman William *federal judge*
Brown, Karen Kennedy *federal judge*
Bue, Carl Olaf, Jr. *retired federal judge*
Clark, Letitia Z. *federal judge*
Cowan, Finis Ewing *federal judge*
DeMoss, Harold R., Jr. *federal judge*
Harmon, Melinda Furche *federal judge*
Hittner, David *federal judge*
Hoyt, Kenneth M. *federal judge*
Hughes, Lynn Nettleton *federal judge*
Johnson, Nancy K. *judge*
Jones, Edith Hollan *federal judge*
King, Carolyn Dineen *federal judge*
Lake, Simeon Timothy, III *federal judge*
Love, Miron Anderson *judge*
Powell, William Rossell, Jr. *retired judge*
Rainey, John David *federal judge*
Rosenthal, Lee H. *federal judge*
Singleton, John Virgil, Jr. *retired federal judge, lawyer*
Smith, Jerry Edwin *federal judge*
Stacy, Frances H. *judge*
Steen, Wesley Wilson *former judge, lawyer*
Tennant, Geraldine B. *judge*
Werlein, Ewing, Jr. *federal judge, lawyer*

Laredo
Kazen, George Philip *federal judge*

Levelland
Walker, James Kenneth *judge*

Lubbock
Cummings, Sam R. *federal judge*
Woodward, Halbert Owen *federal judge*

Lufkin
Hannah, John Henry, Jr. *judge*

Mcallen
Hinojosa, Ricardo H. *federal judge*

Midland
Smith, Robin Doyle *judge*

Pampa
Cain, Donald Ezell *judge*

San Antonio
Clark, Leif Michael *federal judge*
Garcia, Hipolito Frank (Hippo Garcia) *federal judge*
Garza, Emilio M(iller) *federal judge*
King, Ronald Baker *federal judge*
Krier, Cynthia Taylor *lawyer, former state legislator*
Nowak, Nancy Stein *judge*
Prado, Edward Charles *federal judge*
Suttle, Dorwin Wallace *federal judge*

Sherman
Brown, Paul Neeley *federal judge*

Temple
Skelton, Byron George *federal judge*

Tyler
Guthrie, Judith K. *federal judge*
Justice, William Wayne *federal judge*
Parker, Robert M. *federal judge*
Steger, William Merritt *federal judge*

Waco
Smith, Walter S., Jr. *federal judge*

Wharton
Abell, Thomas Henry *judge*

UTAH

Cedar City
Fenton, Patrick H. *lawyer, judge*

Ogden
Stewart, Isaac Daniel, Jr. *state supreme court justice*

Salt Lake City
Anderson, Aldon J. *judge*
Anderson, Stephen Hale *federal judge*
Clark, Glen Edward *federal judge*
Durham, Christine Meaders *state supreme court justice*
Greene, John Thomas, Jr. *federal judge*
Hall, Gordon R. *retired state supreme court chief justice*
Howe, Richard Cuddy *state supreme court justice*
Jenkins, Bruce Sterling *federal judge*
McKay, Monroe Gunn *federal judge*
Sam, David *federal judge*
Winder, David Kent *federal judge*
Zimmerman, Michael David *state supreme court chief justice*

VERMONT

Bennington
Gagliardi, Lee Parsons *federal judge*

Brattleboro
Oakes, James L. *federal judge*

Burlington
Parker, Fred I. *federal judge*

Montpelier
Allen, Frederic W. *state supreme court justice*
Morse, James L. *state supreme court justice*

North Bennington
Holden, James Stuart *federal judge*

Rutland
Billings, Franklin Swift, Jr. *federal judge*

VIRGINIA

Abingdon
Kinser, Cynthia D. *judge*
Widener, Hiram Emory, Jr. *federal judge*
Wilson, Samuel Grayson *federal judge*

Alexandria
Brinkema, Leonie Milhomme *federal judge*
Bryan, Albert V., Jr. *federal judge*
Cacheris, James C. *federal judge*
Ellis, Thomas Selby, III *federal judge*
Hilton, Claude Meredith *federal judge*

Arlington
Nejelski, Paul Arthur *judge*
Van Doren, Emerson Barclay *administrative judge*

Charlottesville
Crigler, B. Waugh *federal judge*
Michael, James Harry, Jr. *federal judge*
Wilkinson, James Harvie, III *federal judge*

Danville
Kiser, Jackson L. *federal judge*

Falls Church
Burg, Ruth Cooper (Thelma Breslauer) *administrative judge*
Morse, Marvin Henry *judge*

Reiter, Joseph Henry *judge*
Spector, Louis *retired federal judge, lawyer, arbitrator, consultant*

Fredericksburg
Jamison, John Ambler *retired circuit court judge*

Lynchburg
Harris, Dale Hutter *judge, lecturer*

Mc Lean
Luttig, J. Michael *federal judge*

Newport News
Bateman, Fred Willom *retired judge*

Norfolk
Adams, David Huntington *judge*
Bonney, Hal James, Jr. *federal judge*
Clarke, J. Calvitt, Jr. *federal judge*
Doumar, Robert George *federal judge*
Hoffman, Walter Edward *federal judge*
Jackson, Raymond A. *federal judge*
Kellam, Richard B. *judge*
MacKenzie, John A. *federal judge*
Morgan, Henry Coke, Jr. *federal judge, lawyer*
Prince, William Taliaferro *federal judge*
Smith, Rebecca Beach *federal judge*

Richmond
Butzner, John Decker, Jr. *federal judge*
Carrico, Harry Lee *state supreme court chief justice*
Compton, Asbury Christian *state supreme court justice*
Downs, George Warthen *federal judge*
Gordon, Thomas Christian, Jr. *former justice*
Merhige, Robert Reynold, Jr. *federal judge*
Payne, Robert E. *federal judge*
Poff, Richard Harding *state supreme court justice*
Spencer, James R. *federal judge*
Stephenson, Roscoe Bolar, Jr. *state supreme court justice*
Tice, Douglas Oscar, Jr. *federal judge*
Williams, Richard Leroy *federal judge*

Roanoke
Pearson, Henry Clyde *federal judge*
Turk, James Clinton *federal judge*

Staunton
Cochran, George Moffett *retired judge*

Winchester
Whiting, Henry H. *state supreme court justice*

WASHINGTON

Bainbridge Island
Warns, Raymond H. *judge*

Bellevue
Andersen, James A. *state supreme court chief justice*

Federal Way
Hayek, Carolyn Jean *retired judge*

Olympia
Brachtenbach, Robert F. *state supreme court justice*
Dolliver, James Morgan *state supreme court justice*
Durham, Barbara *state supreme court justice*
Guy, Richard P. *state supreme court justice*
Johnson, Charles William *state supreme court justice*
Smith, Charles Z. *state supreme court justice*
Utter, Robert French *state supreme court justice*

Republic
Sauer, Norman Gardiner *judge, attorney*

Seattle
Beezer, Robert Renaut *federal judge*
Coughenour, John Clare *federal judge*
Dimmick, Carolyn Reaber *federal judge*
Dwyer, William L. *federal judge*
Farris, Jerome *federal judge*
Fletcher, Betty B. *federal judge*
Koelsch, M. Oliver *federal judge*
Mc Govern, Walter T. *federal judge*
Noe, James Alva *judge*
Rothstein, Barbara Jacobs *federal judge*
Weinberg, John Lee *federal judge*
Wilson, David Eugene *magistrate judge*
Wright, Eugene Allen *federal judge*
Zilly, Thomas Samuel *federal judge*

Spokane
Green, Dale Monte *retired judge*
Imbrogno, Cynthia *judge*
Klobucher, John Marcellus *federal judge*
Nielsen, William Fremming *federal judge*
Quackenbush, Justin Lowe *chief federal judge*
Van Sickle, Frederick L. *federal judge*

Tacoma
Bryan, Robert J. *federal judge*

Yakima
Hovis, James Brunton *federal judge*
McDonald, Alan Angus *federal judge*

WEST VIRGINIA

Beckley
Hallanan, Elizabeth V. *federal judge*

Bluefield
Faber, David Alan *federal judge*

Charleston
Brotherton, William T., Jr. *state supreme court justice*
Copenhaver, John Thomas, Jr. *federal judge*
Haden, Charles H., II *federal judge*
Hall, Kenneth Keller *federal judge*
Knapp, Dennis Raymond *federal judge*
McHugh, Thomas Edward *state supreme court justice*
Michael, M. Blane *federal judge*

Workman, Margaret Lee *state supreme court justice*

Clarksburg
Keeley, Irene Patricia Murphy *federal judge*
Kidd, William Matthew *federal judge*

Elkins
Maxwell, Robert Earl *federal judge*

Lewisburg
Sprouse, James Marshall *federal judge*

WISCONSIN

Appleton
Froehlich, Harold Vernon *judge, former congressman*

Chippewa Falls
Sazama, Thomas John *circuit judge*

Madison
Abrahamson, Shirley Schlanger *state supreme court justice*
Bablitch, William A. *state supreme court justice*
Crabb, Barbara Brandriff *federal judge*
Day, Roland Bernard *state supreme court justice*
Heffernan, Nathan Stewart *state supreme court chief justice*
Martin, Robert David *federal judge, law educator*
Shabaz, John C. *federal judge*
Wilcox, Jon P. *judge*

Milwaukee
Curran, Thomas J. *federal judge*
Evans, Terence Thomas *federal judge*
Goodstein, Aaron E. *federal magistrate judge*
Gordon, Myron L. *federal judge*
Ihlenfeldt, Dale Elwood *judge*
Randa, Rudolph Thomas *federal judge*
Reynolds, John W. *federal judge*
Shapiro, James Edward *federal judge*
Stadtmueller, Joseph Peter *federal judge*
Warren, Robert Willis *federal judge*

Monroe
Deininger, David George *state circuit court judge*

Nashotah
Hansen, Robert Wayne *judge, editor*

Sheboygan
Buchen, John Gustave *retired judge*

WYOMING

Cheyenne
Barrett, James E. *federal judge*
Beaman, William Charles *magistrate judge, legal clerk*
Brimmer, Clarence Addison *federal judge*
Brorby, Wade *federal judge*
Brown, Charles Stuart *retired state supreme court justice*
Cardine, Godfrey Joseph *state supreme court justice*
Golden, Michael *state supreme court justice*
Johnson, Alan Bond *federal judge*
Macy, Richard J. *state judge*
Thomas, Richard Van *state supreme court justice*

Cody
Patrick, H. Hunter *lawyer, judge*

Green River
Marty, Lawrence A. *lawyer, magistrate judge*

Story
Mc Ewan, Leonard *former judge*

TERRITORIES OF THE UNITED STATES

AMERICAN SAMOA

Pago Pago
Kruse, F. Michael *judge*
†Togafau, Malaetasi Mauga *judge*

GUAM

Agana
Cruz, Benjamin Joseph Franquez *territory judge*
Unpingco, John Walter Sablan *federal judge*

Barrigada
Diaz, Ramon Valero *retired judge*

NORTHERN MARIANA ISLANDS

Saipan
Dela Cruz, Jose Santos *state supreme court chief justice*
Laureta, Alfred *federal judge*
Munson, Alex Robert *judge*

PUERTO RICO

San Juan
Acosta, Raymond Luis *federal judge*
Cerezo, Carmen Consuelo *federal judge*
Fusté, José Antonio *federal judge*
Gierbolini-Ortiz, Gilberto *federal judge*
Hernandez-Denton, Federico *commonwealth supreme court justice*
Laffitte, Hector Manuel *federal judge*
Perez-Gimenez, Juan Manuel *federal judge*
Pieras, Jaime, Jr. *federal judge*
Schmidt-Monge, Roberto *federal judge*

Torruella, Juan R. *federal judge*

VIRGIN ISLANDS

Charlotte Amalie
Moore, Thomas Kail *chief judge*

Christiansted
Finch, Raymond Lawrence *judge*
Resnick, Jeffrey Lance *federal judge*

Saint Thomas
Hodge, Verne Antonio *judge*

CANADA

ALBERTA

Edmonton
Fraser, Catherine Anne *Canadian chief justice*
Miller, Tevie *supernumary justice, academic administrator*
Stevenson, William Alexander *retired justice of Supreme Court of Canada*

BRITISH COLUMBIA

Vancouver
Lysyk, Kenneth Martin *judge*
†McEachern, Allan *Canadian justice*

MANITOBA

Winnipeg
Lyon, Sterling Rufus *justice*
†Scott, R. J. *justice*
Scott, Richard Jamieson *chief justice*

NEW BRUNSWICK

Fredericton
†Hoyt, William Lloyd *Canadian chief justice*

NEWFOUNDLAND

Saint John's
Goodridge, Noel Herbert Alan *state supreme court chief justice*
Logan, Rodman Emmason *jurist*

NORTHWEST TERRITORIES

Yellowknife
de Weerdt, Mark Murray *judge*

NOVA SCOTIA

Halifax
†Clarke, Lorne O. *provincial judge*
Glube, Constance Rachelle *Canadian chief justice*

ONTARIO

Dunrobin
Dickson, Brian *retired chief justice of Canada, ambassador*

Hamilton
Marshall, Thomas David *judge*

Ottawa
Cory, Peter de Carteret *Canadian Supreme Court justice*
†Couture, J. C. *Canadian federal judge*
Cullen, Jack Sydney George Bud *federal judge*
Décary, Robert *judge*
Desjardins, Alice *federal judge*
Gonthier, Charles Doherty *Canadian supreme court justice*
Heald, Darrel Verner *retired Canadian federal judge*
†Isaac, Julius A. *Canadian federal judge*
Jerome, James Alexander *Canadian federal justice*
La Forest, Gérard Vincent *justice*
Lamer, Antonio *Canadian supreme court chief justice*
L'Heureux-Dube, Claire *judge*
MacGuigan, Mark R. *Canadian federal judge*
MacKay, William Andrew *judge*
Mahoney, Patrick Morgan *retired judge*
Major, John Charles *judge*
McLachlin, Beverley *supreme court judge*
Muldoon, Francis Creighton *Canadian federal judge*
Pratte, Louis *Canadian federal judge*
Sopinka, John *Canadian supreme court justice*
Stone, Arthur Joseph *judge*
Wilson, Bertha *Canadian justice*

Toronto
Boland, Janet Lang *judge*
Dubin, Charles Leonard *federal judge*
Gotlib, Lorraine *justice, former lawyer*
McMurtry, R. Roy *chief justice*

Willowdale
Harris, Sydney Malcolm *retired judge*

PRINCE EDWARD ISLAND

Charlottetown
Carruthers, Norman Harry *Canadian province supreme court justice*

QUEBEC

Montreal
Bisson, Claude *retired chief justice of Quebec*
Gold, Alan B. *former Canadian chief justice*
Mailhot, Louise *judge*
Rothman, Melvin L. *judge*

Quebec
Tourigny, Christine *judge*

SASKATCHEWAN

Regina
Bayda, Edward Dmytro *judge*

THE NETHERLANDS

The Hague
Allison, Richard Clark *judge*

ADDRESS UNPUBLISHED

Adams, Arlin Marvin *retired judge, counsel to law firm*
Adams, Oscar William, Jr. *retired state supreme court justice*
Bartunek, Joseph Wenceslaus *magistrate judge*
Bertelsman, William Odis *federal judge*
Bistline, Stephen *retired state supreme court justice*
Bootle, William Augustus *retired federal judge*
Boulden, Judith Ann *federal judge*
Box, Dwain D. *former judge*
Brightmire, Paul William *retired judge*
Brown, Robert Laidlaw *state supreme court justice*
Bunton, Lucius Desha, III *federal judge*
Burger, Warren Earl *former chief justice of U.S. supreme court, academic administrator*
Burke, Edmond Wayne *retired judge*
Callow, Keith McLean *judge*
Callow, William Grant *retired state supreme court justice*
Ceci, Louis J. *former state supreme court justice*
Christensen, Albert Sherman *federal judge*
Coffey, John Louis *federal judge*
Cograve, John Edwin *retired judge*
Cohn, Avern Levin *federal judge*
Colaianni, Joseph Vincent *judge*
Collins, Robert Frederick *federal judge*
Cook, Julian Abele, Jr. *federal judge*
Cudahy, Richard D. *federal judge*
Cyr, Conrad Keefe *federal judge*
Davies, Ronald Norwood *federal judge*
Dore, Fred Hudson *retired state supreme court chief justice*
Drennen, William Miller *federal judge*
Eaton, Joe Oscar *federal judge*
Flannery, Thomas Aquinas *federal judge*
Foster, Robert Lawson *retired judge, deacon*
Garcia, Edward J. *federal judge*
Garrity, Wendell Arthur, Jr. *federal judge*
Goffe, William Arthur *federal judge*
Griffin, Robert Paul *former state supreme court justice*
Grody, Donald *judge, lawyer, arbitrator, actor*
Hanson, William Cook *judge*
Hawkins, Michael Daly *federal judge*
Hoffman, Leonard Elbert, Jr. *judge*
Hogan, Thomas Francis *federal judge*
Holland, Randy James *state supreme court justice*
House, Charles Staver *judge*
Jones, Phyllis Gene *judge*
Kauger, Yvonne *state supreme court justice*
Kelly, Aurel Maxey *retired judge*
Kenner, Carol J. *federal judge*
Krupansky, Blanche *retired judge*
Laycraft, James Herbert *judge*
Le Dain, Gerald Eric *retired Canadian Supreme Court justice*
Lee, Dan M. *state supreme court justice*
Linde, Hans Arthur *state supreme court justice*
Lindsay, Reginald Carl *federal judge*
Logan, James Kenneth *federal judge*
Low, Harry William *judge*
Mai, Harold Leverne *retired federal judge*
McCown, Hale *retired judge*
Metzner, Charles Miller *federal judge*
Meyer, Louis B. *superior court judge, retired state supreme court justice*
Montgomery, Seth David *retired state supreme court chief justice*
Morgan, Robert Edward *state supreme court justice*
Murray, Herbert Frazier *retired federal judge*
Mydland, Gordon James *judge*
Nangle, John Francis *federal judge*
Newman, Theodore Roosevelt, Jr. *judge*
Papadakos, Nicholas Peter *retired state supreme court justice*
Peccarelli, Anthony Marando *judge*
Phillips, James Dickson, Jr. *federal judge*
Prager, David *retired state supreme court chief justice*
Quillen, William Tatem *state judge, lawyer, educator*
Quirico, Francis Joseph *retired state supreme court justice*
Reinhardt, Stephen Roy *federal judge*
Rice, Walter Herbert *federal judge*
Robreno, Eduardo C. *federal judge*
Rodriguez, Elias C. *federal judge*
Ross, Donald Roe *federal judge*
Schwebel, Stephen Myron *judge, arbitrator*
Shea, Donald Francis *state supreme court justice*
Sheedy, Patrick Thomas *judge*
Silberman, Laurence Hirsch *federal judge*
Simmons, Paul Allen *retired federal judge*
Smith, Fern M. *federal judge*
Souter, David Hackett *U.S. supreme court justice*
Spears, Franklin Scott *retired supreme court justice*
Staker, Robert Jackson *federal judge*
Stamos, John James *judge*
Stamp, Frederick Pfarr, Jr. *federal judge*
Stanton, Louis Lee *federal judge*
Taylor, Gary L. *federal judge*
Thornburg, Lacy Herman *judge*
Tillman, Massie Monroe *federal judge*
Turnoff, William Charles *judge*
Vollmer, Richard Wade *federal judge*
Wahl, Rosalie E. *state supreme court justice*
Wyman, Louis Crosby *state justice, former senator, former congressman*

LAW: LAW PRACTICE AND ADMINISTRATION

UNITED STATES

ALABAMA

Andalusia
Fuller, William Sidney *lawyer*

Anniston
Klinefelter, James Louis *lawyer*

Auburn
Little, Ted David *lawyer*
Samford, Thomas Drake, III *lawyer*

Birmingham
Alexander, James Patrick *lawyer*
Balch, Samuel Eason *lawyer*
Blan, Ollie Lionel, Jr. *lawyer*
Brown, Ephraim Taylor, Jr. *lawyer*
Carruthers, Thomas Neely, Jr. *lawyer*
Coleman, Brittin Turner *lawyer*
Cooper, Jerome A. *lawyer*
Cornelius, Walter Felix *lawyer*
Davis, Julian Mason, Jr. *lawyer*
Denson, William Frank, III *lawyer*
Farley, Joseph McConnell *lawyer*
†Friedman, Linda A. *lawyer*
Friend, Edward Malcolm, Jr. *lawyer*
Friend, Edward Malcolm, III *lawyer*
Gaede, Anton Henry, Jr. *lawyer*
Gewin, James W. *lawyer*
Hardin, Edward Lester, Jr. *lawyer*
Heldman, Alan Wohl *lawyer*
Johnson, Joseph H., Jr. *lawyer*
Lacy, Alexander Shelton *lawyer*
Long, Thad Gladden *lawyer*
Mays, Joseph Barber, Jr. *lawyer*
Mc Millan, George Duncan Hastie, Jr. *lawyer, former state official*
McWhorter, Hobart Amory, Jr. *lawyer*
Mills, William Hayes *lawyer*
Molen, John Klauminzer *lawyer*
Monroe, Walter Harris, III *lawyer*
Morgan, Carolyn F. *lawyer*
Newfield, Mayer Ullman *lawyer*
Oliver, Samuel William, Jr. *lawyer*
Peyser, Roxane D. *lawyer*
Redden, Lawrence Drew *lawyer*
Riegert, Robert Adolf *law educator, consultant*
Rogers, Ernest Mabry *lawyer*
Rountree, Asa *lawyer*
Rubright, James Alfred *natural resources company executive*
Savage, Kay Webb *lawyer, health center administrator, accountant*
Selfe, Edward Milton *lawyer*
Smith, John Joseph *lawyer*
Spotswood, Robert Keeling *lawyer*
Stabler, Lewis Vastine, Jr. *lawyer*
Stelzenmuller, Cyril Vaughn *lawyer*
Upchurch, Samuel E., Jr. *lawyer*
Vinson, Laurence Duncan, Jr. *lawyer*
Weeks, Arthur Andrew *lawyer, educator*
Whitaker, Charles Larimore *lawyer*
Williams, Parham Henry, Jr. *lawyer*
Wrinkle, John Newton *lawyer*
Zeigler, Alan Karl *lawyer*

Dadeville
Adair, Charles Robert, Jr. *lawyer*

Decatur
Caddell, John A. *lawyer*

Demopolis
Lloyd, Hugh Adams *lawyer*

Huntsville
Cleary, James Roy *lawyer*
Huckaby, Gary Carlton *lawyer*
Potter, Ernest Luther *lawyer*
Smith, Robert Sellers *lawyer*
Sullivan, Michael Maurice *lawyer*

Mobile
Armbrecht, William Henry, III *lawyer*
Braswell, Louis Erskine *lawyer*
Brock, Paul Warrington *lawyer*
Bryant, Thomas Earle, Jr. *lawyer*
Harris, Benjamin Harte, Jr. *lawyer*
Helmsing, Frederick George *lawyer*
Holberg, Ralph Gans, Jr. *lawyer*
Holland, Lyman Faith, Jr. *lawyer*
Holmes, Broox Garrett *lawyer*
Kimbrough, William Adams, Jr. *lawyer*
Lyons, Champ, Jr. *lawyer*
Lyons, George Sage *lawyer, oil industry executive, former state legislator*
McKnight, Charles Noel *lawyer*
Puhala, James Joseph *lawyer*
Sessions, Jefferson Beauregard, III *lawyer*
Thornton, J. Edward *lawyer*
Windom, Stephen Ralph *lawyer*

Montgomery
Byars, Walter Ryland, Jr. *lawyer*
Dees, Morris Seligman, Jr. *lawyer*
Franco, Ralph Abraham *lawyer*
Graddick, Charles Allen *lawyer*
Hamner, Reginald Turner *lawyer*
Hawthorne, Frank Howard *lawyer*
Hester, Douglas Benjamin *lawyer, federal official*
Hill, Thomas Bowen, III *lawyer*
Leslie, Henry Arthur *lawyer, retired banker*
McFadden, Frank Hampton *lawyer, business executive, former judge*
Morris, L. Daniel, Jr. *lawyer*
Nachman, Merton Roland, Jr. *lawyer*
Norris, Robert Wheeler *lawyer, military officer*
Salmon, Joseph Thaddeus *lawyer*
Teague, Barry Elvin *lawyer*
Volz, Charles Harvie, Jr. *lawyer*
Wampold, Charles Henry, Jr. *lawyer*

Opelika
Samford, Yetta Glenn, Jr. *lawyer*

Orange Beach
Adams, Daniel Fenton *legal educator*

Selma
Stewart, Edgar Allen *lawyer*

Troy
Brantley, Oliver Wiley *retired lawyer*

Tuscaloosa
Christopher, Thomas Weldon *legal educator, administrator*
Cook, Camille Wright *law educator*
Hoff, Timothy *lawyer, educator, priest*
Watkins, John Cumming, Jr. *law educator*
Williams, Vergil Lewis *criminal justice educator*

ALASKA

Anchorage
Baily, Douglas Boyd *lawyer*
Brown, Harold MacVane *lawyer*
De Lisio, Stephen Scott *lawyer*
Edwards, George Kent *lawyer*
Greenstein, Marla Nan *lawyer*
Groh, Clifford J., Sr. *lawyer*
Lowe, Robert Charles *lawyer, banker*
Melcher, Jerry Eugene *lawyer*
Roberts, John Derham *lawyer*
†Smith, John Anthony *lawyer*
Wilson, Joseph Morris, III *lawyer*

Fairbanks
Rice, Julian Casavant *lawyer*

Juneau
Collins, Patricia A. *lawyer, judge*

Kodiak
Jamin, Matthew Daniel *lawyer, magistrate judge*

ARIZONA

Carefree
Hutchison, Stanley Philip *lawyer*

Globe
Malott, James Raymond, Jr. *lawyer*

Mesa
Allen, Merle Maeser, Jr. *lawyer*
Shelley, James LaMar *lawyer*

Nogales
†Castro, Raul Hector *lawyer, former ambassador, former governor*

Peoria
Degnan, Thomas Leonard *lawyer*

Phoenix
Allen, Robert Eugene Barton *lawyer*
†Alsentzer, William James, Jr. *lawyer*
Bacon, Roxana Collins *lawyer*
Bain, C. Randall *lawyer*
Baird, J. Ernest *lawyer, state representative*
Baker, William Dunlap *lawyer*
Bakker, Thomas Gordon *lawyer*
Begam, Robert George *lawyer*
Bergin, Daniel Timothy *lawyer, banker*
Blanchard, Charles Alan *lawyer, former state senator*
Burke, Timothy John *lawyer*
Cabot, Howard Ross *lawyer*
Cameron, James Duke *lawyer, former state supreme court justice*
Cohen, Jon Stephan *lawyer*
Cohen, Ronald Jay *lawyer*
Colburn, Donald D. *lawyer*
Cooledge, Richard Calvin *lawyer*
Coppersmith, Sam *lawyer*
Corson, Kimball Jay *lawyer*
Crockett, Clyll Webb *lawyer*
Daughton, Donald *lawyer*
Davies, David George *lawyer*
Dawson, John Joseph *lawyer*
Deeny, Robert Joseph *lawyer*
Derdenger, Patrick *lawyer*
Dunipace, Ian Douglas *lawyer*
Durrant, Dan Martin *lawyer*
Eaton, Berrien Clark *retired lawyer, author*
Everroad, John D. *lawyer*
Feinstein, Allen Lewis *lawyer*
Fenzl, Terry Earle *lawyer*
Fine, Charles Leon *lawyer*
Frank, John Paul *lawyer, author*
Freeman, Susan Maud *lawyer*
Gaines, Francis Pendleton, III *lawyer*
Gerard, Philip C. *lawyer*
Gilbert, Donald R. *lawyer*
Goddard, Terry *lawyer*
Goldstein, Stuart Wolf *lawyer*
Greenfield, Arthur Paul *lawyer*
Griller, Gordon Moore *court administrator*
Halpern, Barry David *lawyer*
Harris, Jean E. *lawyer*
Harrison, Mark I. *lawyer*
Hayden, William Robert *lawyer*
Hicks, William Albert, III *lawyer*
Hoecker, Thomas Ralph *lawyer*
Hoffman, Robert B. *lawyer*
Howard, William Matthew *lawyer, business executive, arbitrator, author*
Hoxie, Joel P. *lawyer*
Huntwork, James R. *lawyer*
Inman, William Peter *lawyer*
Irwin, R. Neil *lawyer*
Jacobson, (Julian) Edward *lawyer*
James, Charles E., Jr. *lawyer*
Jirauch, Charles W. *lawyer*
Johnson, James Wayne *lawyer*
Kennedy, Thomas J. *lawyer*
Klausner, Jack Daniel *lawyer*
Kreutzberg, David W. *lawyer*
Kurn, Neal *lawyer*
Lee, Stephen E. *lawyer, educator*
Lowry, Edward Francis, Jr. *lawyer*
Madden, Paul Robert *lawyer, director*
Mallender, William Harry *lawyer*
Mallery, Richard K. *lawyer*

Mangum, John K. *lawyer*
Manning, Michael C. *lawyer*
Marks, Merton Eleazer *lawyer*
Martin, Don P. *lawyer*
Martori, Joseph Peter *lawyer*
Mason, Anthony Halstead *lawyer, corporate executive*
May, Bruce Barnett *lawyer*
Mc Clennen, Louis *lawyer, educator*
McDaniel, Joseph Chandler *lawyer*
McRae, Hamilton Eugene, III *lawyer*
Melczer, Joseph T., III *lawyer*
Merritt, Nancy-Jo *lawyer*
Meyer, Paul Joseph *lawyer*
Miller, Louis Rice *lawyer*
Miller, Norman L. *lawyer*
Mitchell, George Hall *lawyer*
Moya, Patrick Robert *lawyer*
Muchmore, Charles J. *lawyer*
Novak, Edward Frank *lawyer*
Novak, Peter John *lawyer*
Olsen, Alfred Jon *lawyer*
Olsen, Gordon *retired lawyer*
Olson, Robert Howard *lawyer*
Parrett, Sherman O. *lawyer*
Peck, Deana S. *lawyer*
Porter, Amy R. *lawyer*
Pulaski, Charles Alexander, Jr. *lawyer*
Rathwell, Peter John *lawyer*
Romley, Richard M. *lawyer*
Rudolph, Gilbert Lawrence *lawyer*
Ruffner, Jay Sturgis *lawyer*
Ryan, Thomas Grady *lawyer*
Savage, Stephen Michael *lawyer*
Sherk, Kenneth John *lawyer*
Spitzer, Marc Lee *lawyer*
Storey, Norman C. *lawyer*
Susman, Alan Howard *lawyer*
Sutton, Samuel J. *lawyer, educator*
Terry, Peter Anthony *lawyer*
Traeger, Charles Henry, III *lawyer*
Trost, Eileen Bannon *lawyer*
Tubman, William Charles *lawyer*
Udall, Calvin Hunt *lawyer*
Ulrich, Paul Graham *lawyer, author, publisher, editor*
Wales, Harold Webster *lawyer*
Walker, Richard K. *lawyer*
Wall, Donald Arthur *lawyer*
Whisler, James Steven *lawyer, mining and manufacturing executive*
Wiley, Jay D. *lawyer*
Williams, Quinn Patrick *lawyer*
Winthrop, Lawrence Fredrick *lawyer*
Wolf, G. Van Velsor, Jr. *lawyer*
Woolf, Michael E. *lawyer*
Yarnell, Michael Allan *lawyer*

Prescott
Burke, Richard Kitchens *lawyer, educator*
Kleindienst, Richard Gordon *lawyer*

Scottsdale
Barbee, Joe Ed *lawyer*
Cole, George Thomas *lawyer*
Handy, Robert Maxwell *patent lawyer*
Haynie, Howard Edward *lawyer*
Jackson, Don Merrill *lawyer*
Kitchel, Denison *retired lawyer, writer*
Krupp, Clarence William *lawyer, personnel and hospital administrator*
Lisa, Isabelle O'Neill *mergers and acquisitions executive, law firm administrator*
Starr, Isidore *law educator*

Tempe
Duecy, Charles Michael *retired lawyer*
Evans, Lawrence Jack, Jr. *lawyer*
Matheson, Alan Adams *law educator*

Tucson
Brodkey, Andrew Alan *lawyer, copper company executive*
Dobbs, Dan Byron *lawyer*
Dolph, Wilbert Emery *lawyer*
Eckhardt, August Gottlieb *law educator*
Franklin, John Orland *lawyer*
Froman, Sandra Sue *lawyer*
Gantz, David Alfred *lawyer, university official*
Gieseler, Eugene C. *lawyer*
Grand, Richard D. *lawyer*
Henderson, Roger C. *law educator, former dean*
Heurlin, Bruce R. *lawyer*
Jimmerson, J. Michael *lawyer*
Kimble, William Earl *lawyer*
Lesher, Robert Overton *lawyer*
Mc Donald, John Richard *lawyer*
McNulty, Michael Francis *lawyer*
Morrow, James Franklin *lawyer*
O'Leary, Thomas Michael *lawyer*
Pace, Thomas M. *lawyer*
Pickrell, Timothy E. *lawyer*
Schorr, S. L. *lawyer*
Schottland, Charles Irwin *retired legal educator*
Seligman, Joel *law educator*
Shultz, Silas Harold *lawyer*
Strong, John William *lawyer, educator*

Window Rock
Zion, James William *lawyer*

ARKANSAS

Blytheville
Fendler, Oscar *lawyer*

Conway
Brazil, William Clay *lawyer*

Cotter
Naylor, George LeRoy *lawyer, rail transportation executive*

Eureka Springs
Epley, Lewis Everett, Jr. *lawyer*

Fayetteville
Ahlers, Glen-Peter, Sr. *library director, educator, consultant*
Bassett, Woodson William, Jr. *lawyer*
Davis, Wylie Herman *lawyer, educator*
Kincaid, Hugh Reid *lawyer*
Pearson, Charles Thomas, Jr. *lawyer*

Fort Smith
Dotson, Donald L. *lawyer*
Jesson, Bradley Dean *lawyer*
Pommerville, Robert W. *corporate lawyer*

Helena
Roscopf, Charles Buford *lawyer*

Little Rock
Anderson, Philip Sidney *lawyer*
Campbell, George Emerson *lawyer*
Cross, J. Bruce *lawyer*
Darr, James Earl, Jr. *lawyer*
Drummond, Winslow *lawyer*
Duffey, William Simon, Jr. *lawyer*
Dumeny, Marcel Jacque *lawyer*
Fogleman, John Albert *lawyer, retired judge*
Foster, Lynn *law librarian, lawyer*
Gunter, Russell Allen *lawyer*
Haught, William Dixon *lawyer*
Jennings, Alston *lawyer*
Martin, William Aubert *law association executive, lawyer, retired air force officer*
May, Ronald Alan *lawyer*
Murphey, Arthur Gage, Jr. *law educator*
Nelson, Edward Sheffield *lawyer, former utility company executive*
Pagan, John Ruston *law educator*
Patten, Gerland Paul *lawyer*
Purtle, John Ingram *lawyer, former state supreme court justice*
Shults, Robert Luther, Jr. *lawyer*
Smith, Sandra Lynn *lawyer*
Warner, Cecil Randolph, Jr. *lawyer*
Witherspoon, Carolyn Brack *lawyer*
†Wright, Robert Ross, III *lawyer, educator*

Monticello
Ball, William Kenneth *lawyer*

Newport
Boyce, Edward Wayne, Jr. *lawyer*
Thaxton, Marvin Dell *lawyer, farmer*

North Little Rock
Hays, Patrick Henry *lawyer, mayor*
Marshall, Terrell *lawyer*
Patty, Claibourne Watkins, Jr. *lawyer*

Osceola
Wilson, Ralph Edwin *lawyer, justice*

Pine Bluff
Jones, John Harris *lawyer, banker*
Ramsay, Louis Lafayette, Jr. *lawyer, banker*

Springdale
Cypert, Jimmy Dean *lawyer*

West Memphis
Fogleman, Julian Barton *lawyer*
Nance, Cecil Boone, Jr. *lawyer*

CALIFORNIA

Alameda
Stonehouse, James Adam *lawyer*

Alpine
Samuelson, Derrick William *lawyer*

Anaheim
Rohrer, George John *lawyer*

Arcadia
Mc Cormack, Francis Xavier *lawyer, former oil company executive*

Bakersfield
Martin, George Francis *lawyer*
Owen, Fred Wynne *lawyer*

Baldwin Park
Gregory, George G. *lawyer*

Berkeley
Barnes, Thomas G. *law educator*
Barnett, Stephen R. *law educator*
Barton, Babette B. *lawyer, educator*
Berring, Robert Charles, Jr. *law educator, law librarian, former dean*
Buxbaum, Richard M. *law educator, lawyer*
Cole, Robert H. *law educator*
Concepciõn, David Alden *arbitrator, educator*
Coons, John E. *legal educator, lawyer*
Cooter, Robert *law educator*
Crawford, James E. *law educator, lawyer*
De Goff, Victoria Joan *lawyer*
Dwyer, John P. *law educator*
Eisenberg, Melvin A. *law educator*
Feeley, Malcolm M. *law educator, political scientist*
Feller, David E. *arbitrator*
Fletcher, William A. *law educator*
Gordley, James Russell *law educator*
Halbach, Edward Christian, Jr. *legal educator*
Haley, George Patrick *lawyer*
Hetland, John Robert *lawyer, educator*
Holst, James E. *lawyer*
Johnson, Phillip E. *law educator*
Jorde, Thomas *law educator*
Kadish, Sanford Harold *law educator*
Kagan, Robert Michael *law educator*
Kay, Herma Hill *law educator*
Kuttner, Stephan George *law history educator*
Lieberman, David *law educator*
Mayali, Laurent *legal history educator*
McNulty, John Kent *lawyer, educator*
Mishkin, Paul J. *lawyer, educator*
Moran, Rachel *lawyer, educator*
Newman, Frank Cecil *legal educator, retired state supreme court justice*
Nonet, Philippe *law educator*
Post, Robert Charles *law educator*
Riesenfeld, Stefan Albrecht *law educator, consultant*
Rubinfeld, Daniel Lee *law educator, consultant*
Scheiber, Harry N. *law educator*
Shapiro, Martin *law educator*
Skolnick, Jerome H. *law educator*
Smith, Michael E. *legal educator, lawyer*
Sweet, Justin *law educator, lawyer*

Vetter, Jan *legal educator*
Waldron, Jeremy James *law educator*
Zimring, Franklin E. *law educator*

Beverly Hills
Bloom, Jacob A. *lawyer*
Brown, Hermione Kopp *lawyer*
Bugliosi, Vincent T. *lawyer*
Dekom, Peter James *lawyer*
Factor, Max, III *lawyer, investment adviser*
Foonberg, Jay G. *lawyer, accountant*
Jessup, W. Edgar, Jr. *lawyer*
Lebo, William C., Jr. *hotel corporation executive, lawyer*
Ramer, Bruce M. *lawyer*
Roberts, Norman Leslie *lawyer*
Rosky, Burton Seymour *lawyer*
Schiff, Gunther Hans *lawyer*
Tyre, Norman Ronald *lawyer*

Brea
Lowe, Randall Brian *lawyer*

Burbank
Cunningham, Robert D. *lawyer*
Keister, Jean Clare *lawyer*
Litvack, Sanford Martin *lawyer*
Nolan, Peter Francis *lawyer, entertainment company executive*
Shapiro, Joe *lawyer, entertainment company executive*

Burlingame
Cotchett, Joseph Winters *lawyer, author*
Ocheltree, Richard Lawrence *lawyer, retired forest products company executive*
Ziegler, R.W., Jr. *lawyer, consultant*
Zimmerman, Bryant Kable *lawyer*

Carlsbad
McCracken, Steven Carl *lawyer*

Carmel
Robinson, John Minor *lawyer, retired business executive*

Cerritos
Sarno, Maria Erlinda *lawyer, scientist*

Chatsworth
Arnold, Stanley Richard *lawyer*
Klein, Jeffrey S. *lawyer, newspaper executive*

Chico
Ruge, Neil Marshall *retired law educator*

Chino
Determan, John David *lawyer*
Van Wagner, Ellen *lawyer, educator*

Chula Vista
Allen, David Russell *lawyer*
Madsen, Richard Wellington *lawyer*

Claremont
Ansell, Edward Orin *lawyer*

Concord
Williscroft, Beverly Ruth *lawyer*

Coronado
Merkin, William Leslie *lawyer*

Costa Mesa
Anderson, Jon David *lawyer*
Currie, Robert Emil *lawyer*
Daniels, James Walter *lawyer*
Davidson, Janet Toll *lawyer*
Frieden, Clifford E. *lawyer*
Gritchen, Lyle Steven *lawyer*
Hamilton, James William *lawyer*
Hay, Howard Clinton *lawyer*
Jones, H(arold) Gilbert, Jr. *lawyer*
McIntyre, Joel Franklyn *lawyer*
Reveal, Ernest Ira, III *lawyer*
Speers, Roland Root, II *lawyer*
Thurston, Morris Ashcroft *lawyer*

Culver City
Kay, Kelly W. *lawyer*
von Kalinowski, Julian Onesime *lawyer*
Weiss, Eric Robert *lawyer*

Cupertino
†Eisenstat, Albert A. *lawyer, corporate executive*
Sarnoff, Jill Robin *lawyer*

Cypress
Olschwang, Alan Paul *lawyer*

Davis
Ayer, John Demeritt *law educator*
Bartosic, Florian *lawyer, artibrator, educator*
Bruch, Carol Sophie *lawyer, educator*
Dykstra, Daniel James *lawyer, educator*
Feeney, Floyd Fulton *legal educator*
Imwinkelried, Edward John *law educator*
Jordan, Ellen Rausen *law educator, consultant*
Juenger, Friedrich Klaus *lawyer, educator*
Perschbacher, Rex Robert *law educator*
Wolk, Bruce Alan *law educator*
Wydick, Richard Crews *lawyer, educator*

El Cerrito
Garbarino, Joseph William *labor arbitrator, economics and business educator*

El Segundo
Kuelbs, John Thomas *lawyer*
Reames, Timothy Paul *lawyer, toy company executive*

Emeryville
Dezurick, Paul Anthony *lawyer*
Edginton, John Arthur *lawyer*
Hoover, Jessica Mary *lawyer*

Encino
Kaufman, Albert I. *lawyer*

Singer, Gerald Michael *lawyer, educator, author, arbitrator and mediator*
Smith, Selma Moidel *lawyer, composer*

Fair Oaks
Luther, Florence Joan (Mrs. Charles W. Luther) *lawyer*

Fairfield
Moore, Marianna Gay *law librarian, consultant*

Foster City
Lonnquist, George Eric *lawyer*
Malone, Michael Glen *lawyer*

Fresno
Jamison, Oliver Morton *retired lawyer*
Mather, Allen Frederick *lawyer*
Ott, Michael Duane *lawyer*
Palmer, Samuel Copeland, III *lawyer*

Fullerton
Goldstein, Edward David *lawyer, former glass company executive*
May, William Hathaway *instrument corporation executive, lawyer*

Glendale
Baker, Sheldon S. *lawyer*
Ball, James Herington *lawyer*
Davidson, Suzanne Mouron *lawyer*
†Evans, Godfrey B. *lawyer*
Hoffman, Donald M. *lawyer*
Lieber, Edward Joseph *lawyer*
Martin, John Hugh *lawyer, retired*

Grass Valley
Lawrence, Dean Grayson *retired lawyer*

Hayward
Stern, Ralph David *lawyer, county and municipal*

Healdsburg
Kamm, Thomas Allen *lawyer, retired naval officer*

Hollywood
Burkow, Judith Beth *lawyer*

Huntington Beach
Shaffer, Richard James *lawyer, former manufacturing company executive*

Irvine
Bastiaanse, Gerard C. *lawyer*
Clark, Karen Heath *lawyer*
Hilker, Walter Robert, Jr. *lawyer*
Holman, Diane Rosalie *lawyer*
Jeffers, Michael Bogue *lawyer*
Marshall, Ellen Ruth *lawyer*
McCann, Dean Merton *lawyer, former pharmaceutical company executive*
Muller, Edward Robert *lawyer*
Ristau, Kenneth Eugene, Jr. *lawyer*
Sovie, Donald E. *lawyer*
Tennyson, Peter Joseph *lawyer*
Thomas, Joseph Allan *lawyer*
Tunney, Francis Richard, Jr. *lawyer, corporate executive*
Waggener, Susan Lee *lawyer*
Williams, S. Linn *lawyer*
Wintrode, Ralph Charles *lawyer*

La Canada Flintridge
Costello, Francis William *lawyer*
Wallace, James Wendell *lawyer*

La Jolla
Kirchheimer, Arthur E(dward) *lawyer, business executive*
Shannahan, William Paul *lawyer*
Siegan, Bernard Herbert *lawyer, educator*
Wilkins, Floyd, Jr. *retired lawyer, consultant*
ZoBell, Karl *lawyer*

Laguna Hills
Leydorf, Frederick Leroy *lawyer*
Mc Closkey, Paul N., Jr. *lawyer, former congressman*

Larkspur
Chilvers, Robert Merritt *lawyer*
Marker, Marc Linthacum *lawyer, investment company executive*

Long Beach
Chapman, Mayer *lawyer*
Owen, Christina L. *lawyer*
Taylor, Reese Hale, Jr. *lawyer, former government administrator*
Williams, Donald Clyde *lawyer*
Wise, George Edward *lawyer*

Los Angeles
Aaron, Benjamin *law educator, arbitrator*
Abel, Richard L. *legal educator, lawyer*
Abrams, Norman *law educator, university administrator*
Adamek, Charles Andrew *lawyer*
Adell, Hirsch *lawyer*
Adler, Douglas B. *lawyer*
Adler, Erwin Ellery *lawyer*
Alleyne, Reginald H., Jr. *legal educator*
Anderson, Alison Grey *law educator*
Apfel, Gary *lawyer*
April, Rand Scott *lawyer*
Arant, Eugene Wesley *lawyer*
Argue, John Clifford *lawyer*
Arnold, Dennis B. *lawyer*
Asimow, Michael R. *lawyer, educator*
Avery, Robert Dean *lawyer*
Barash, Anthony Harlan *lawyer*
Bardach, Sheldon Gilbert *lawyer*
Barrall, James D. C. *lawyer*
Barton, Alan Joel *lawyer*
Barza, Harold A. *lawyer*
Battaglia, Philip Maher *lawyer*
Bauman, John Andrew *law educator*
Baumann, Richard Gordon *lawyer*
Beard, Ronald Stratton *lawyer*
Bell, Wayne Steven *lawyer*
Belleville, Philip Frederick *lawyer*
Bender, Charles William *lawyer*

Bendix, Helen Irene *lawyer*
Bergman, Paul Bruce *law educator*
Bernacchi, Richard Lloyd *lawyer*
Bernhard, Herbert Ashley *lawyer*
Bice, Scott Haas *lawyer, educator*
Biederman, Donald Ellis *lawyer*
Bierstedt, Peter Richard *lawyer, entertainment industry consultant*
Binder, David A. *lawyer, educator*
Bishop, Leah Margaret *lawyer*
Bishop, Sidney Willard *lawyer*
Black, Donna Ruth *lawyer*
Blackman, Lee L. *lawyer*
Blitz, Stephen M. *lawyer*
Bloom, Alan *lawyer*
Blumberg, Grace Ganz *law educator, lawyer*
Bobbitt, Leroy *lawyer*
Bodkin, Henry Grattan, Jr. *lawyer*
Bogaard, William Joseph *lawyer*
Bogen, Andrew E. *lawyer*
Bomes, Stephen D. *lawyer*
Bonner, Robert Cleve *lawyer*
Bortman, David *lawyer*
Bosl, Phillip L. *lawyer*
Bost, Thomas Glen *lawyer*
Bottger, William Carl, Jr. *lawyer*
Bower, Allan Maxwell *lawyer*
Bower, Paul George *lawyer*
Boyd, Harry Dalton *lawyer, former insurance company executive*
Bradshaw, Carl John *investor, lawyer, consultant*
Branca, John Gregory *lawyer, consultant*
Brassell, Roselyn Strauss *lawyer*
Braun, David A(dlai) *lawyer*
Breidenbach, Francis Anthony *lawyer*
Bressan, Paul Louis *lawyer*
Bricker, Seymour (Murray) *lawyer*
Bridges, B. Ried *lawyer*
Brinsley, John Harrington *lawyer*
Broiles, Steven Anthony *lawyer*
Broussard, Thomas Rollins *lawyer*
Brown, Edmund Gerald (Pat Brown) *lawyer, former governor of California*
Brown, Louis Morris *lawyer, educator*
Burch, Robert Dale *lawyer*
Burke, William M. *lawyer*
Burke, Yvonne Watson Brathwaite (Mrs. William A. Burke) *lawyer*
Burns, Marvin Gerald *lawyer*
Byrd, Christine Waterman Swent *lawyer*
Byrne, Jerome Camillus *lawyer*
Calhoun, Gordon James *lawyer*
Capron, Alexander Morgan *lawyer, educator*
Carlson, Robert E. *lawyer*
Carlson, Terrance L. *lawyer*
Carr, Willard Zeller, Jr. *lawyer*
Castro, Leonard Edward *lawyer*
Cathcart, David Arthur *lawyer*
Catron, William G. *lawyer*
Cavanagh, John Edward *lawyer*
Chernick, Richard *lawyer*
Chiate, Kenneth Reed *lawyer*
Ching, Anthony *lawyer*
Christol, Carl Quimby *lawyer, political science educator*
Chu, Morgan *lawyer*
Churchill, James Allen *lawyer*
†Clark, Marcia Rachel *prosecutor*
Clark, R. Bradbury *lawyer*
Clark, Richard *lawyer*
Cochran, Johnnie L., Jr. *lawyer*
Cohan, John Robert *lawyer*
Cohen, Cynthia Marylyn *lawyer*
Cohen, Gary J. *lawyer*
Cole, Curtis Allen *lawyer*
Coleman, Rexford Lee *lawyer, educator*
Collier, Charles Arthur, Jr. *lawyer*
Colton, Robert Craig *lawyer*
Cooper, Leon Melvin *lawyer*
Coppola, Robert E. *lawyer*
Cross, James Edwin *lawyer*
Curtis, John E., Jr. *lawyer*
Curtiss, Thomas, Jr. *lawyer, educator*
Daniels, John Peter *lawyer*
Darby, G. Harrison *lawyer*
Davis, Edmond Ray *lawyer*
De Brier, Donald Paul *lawyer*
de Castro, Hugo Daniel *lawyer*
DeLuce, Richard David *lawyer*
De Meules, James Head *lawyer*
Deukmejian, George *lawyer, former governor*
Diamond, Stanley Jay *lawyer*
Dickerson, Jaffe Dean *lawyer*
Dodds, Douglas Allen *lawyer*
Dolan, Peter Brown *lawyer*
Dolinko, David Howard *law educator*
Donovan, John Arthur *lawyer*
Doty, George Richard *lawyer*
Drapkin, Steven G. *lawyer*
Dukeminier, Jesse *law educator*
Dunlavey, Dean Carl *lawyer*
Eichler, Peter M. *lawyer*
Ellsworth, David G. *lawyer*
Emanuel, William Joseph *lawyer*
English, Stephen Raymond *lawyer*
Erickson, Ralph Ernest *lawyer*
Estrich, Susan Rachel *law educator*
Etra, Donald *lawyer*
Eule, Julian Nathan *law educator*
Fairbank, Robert Harold *lawyer*
Farmer, Robert Lindsay *lawyer*
Fein, Ronald Lawrence *lawyer*
Fennelly, Jane Corey *lawyer*
Fenster, Fred A. *lawyer*
Field, Richard Clark *lawyer*
Fields, Bertram Harris *lawyer*
Fields, Henry Michael *lawyer*
Fine, Richard Isaac *lawyer*
Fisher, Raymond Corley *lawyer*
Fitzpatrick, William Joseph *lawyer*
Fohrman, Burton H. *lawyer*
Forbath, William E. *law educator*
Ford, Donald Hainline *lawyer*
Forgnone, Robert *lawyer*
Frackman, Russell Jay *lawyer*
Fragner, Matthew Charles *lawyer*
Francis, Merrill Richard *lawyer*
Fredman, Howard S *lawyer*
French, Susan F. *law educator*
Frimmer, Paul Norman *lawyer*
Fromholz, Haley James *lawyer*
Fudge, Jack D. *lawyer*
Fybel, Richard D. *lawyer*
Gale, Mary Ellen *law educator*
†Garcia, Terry Donato *lawyer*
Gebb, Sheldon Alexander *lawyer*
Gentile, Joseph F. *lawyer, educator*
Gest, Howard David *lawyer*
Getto, Ernest John *lawyer*
Gilbert, Judith Arlene *lawyer*
Girard, Robert David *lawyer*
Glad, Edward Newman *lawyer*
Glick, Earl A. *lawyer*
Goette, Richard A. *lawyer*
Gold, Bernard *lawyer*
Goldman, Allan Bailey *lawyer*
Goldman, Benjamin Edward *lawyer*
Goldman, Donald A. *lawyer*
Goldstein, Robert David *law educator*
Goodman, Max A. *lawyer, educator*
Gordon, David Eliot *lawyer*
Gorman, Joseph Gregory, Jr. *lawyer*
Gould, Charles Perry *lawyer*
Gould, David *lawyer*
Gralnek, Donald D. *lawyer*
Grausam, Jeffrey Leonard *lawyer*
Gray, Jan Charles *lawyer*
Green, William Porter *lawyer*
Griffey, Linda Boyd *lawyer*
Groman, Arthur *lawyer*
Gross, Allen Jeffrey *lawyer*
Grosz, Philip J. *lawyer*
Gurfein, Peter J. *lawyer*
Gutterridge, Larry G. *lawyer*
Hahn, Elliott Julius *lawyer*
Haight, James Theron *lawyer, corporate executive*
Haile, Lawrence Barclay *lawyer*
Halgren, Jack *lawyer*
Halkett, Alan Neilson *lawyer*
Hall, Carlyle Washington, Jr. *lawyer*
Halstead, Harry Moore *lawyer*
Hampton, Gordon Francis *lawyer*
Handler, Carole Enid *lawyer, city planner*
Handler, Joel F. *law educator*
Handzlik, Jan Lawrence *lawyer*
Hanrahan, Thomas P. *lawyer*
Hansell, Dean *lawyer*
Hanson, John J. *lawyer*
†Harter, Robert Jackson, Jr. *lawyer, transportation holding company executive*
Hartigan, John Francis *lawyer*
Hastings, Robert Pusey *lawyer*
Hathaway, Harry L. *lawyer*
Havel, Richard W. *lawyer*
Hayes, Byron Jackson, Jr. *lawyer*
Haythorn, J. Denny *law librarian*
Hayutin, David Lionel *lawyer*
Hayutin, Marc I. *lawyer*
Hazen, Steven Kelsey *lawyer*
Heather, Fred Doenges *lawyer, educator*
Heinke, Rex S. *lawyer*
Hemminger, Pamela Lynn *lawyer*
Hennigan, James Michael *lawyer*
Hernandez, Antonia *lawyer*
Heyert, Martin David *lawyer*
Heyler, Grover Ross *retired lawyer*
Hibner, Don Telfer, Jr. *lawyer*
Hieronymus, Edward Whittlesey *lawyer*
Higgins, John Joseph *corporate lawyer*
Highberger, William Foster *lawyer*
Hight, B. Boyd *lawyer*
Hinerfeld, Robert Elliot *lawyer*
Hirsch, Barry L. *lawyer*
Hogan, Steven L. *lawyer*
Holliday, Thomas Edgar *lawyer*
Holtzman, Robert Arthur *lawyer*
Houck, John Burton *retired lawyer*
Howell, Kenneth Kennedy *lawyer*
Hudson, Jeffrey Reid *lawyer*
Huebner, Harlan Pierce *lawyer*
Hufstedler, Seth Martin *lawyer*
Hufstedler, Shirley Mount (Mrs. Seth M. Hufstedler) *lawyer, former federal judge*
Hunter, Larry Dean *lawyer*
Hyman, Milton Bernard *lawyer*
Iamele, Richard Thomas *law librarian*
Irell, Lawrence E(lliott) *lawyer*
Irwin, Philip Donnan *lawyer*
James, Peter W. *lawyer*
Janofsky, Leonard S. *lawyer, association executive*
Johnson, Jonathan Edwin, II *lawyer*
Johnson, Martin Marion *lawyer*
Jordan, Judd L. *lawyer*
Jordan, Robert Leon *lawyer, educator*
Kadison, Stuart L. *lawyer*
Karlin, Michael Jonathan Abraham *lawyer*
Karst, Kenneth Leslie *legal educator*
Katz, Jason Lawrence *lawyer, insurance executive*
Kaus, Otto Michael *lawyer*
Kelly, Daniel Grady, Jr. *lawyer*
Kendig, Ellsworth Harold, Jr. *lawyer*
Kindel, James Horace, Jr. *lawyer*
King, Robert Lucien *lawyer*
Kinney, James Howard *lawyer*
Kirwan, Betty-Jane *lawyer*
Kirwan, Ralph DeWitt *lawyer*
Klee, Kenneth Nathan *lawyer*
Klein, William A. *lawyer, educator*
Kleinberg, Marvin H. *lawyer*
Klopf, Jeffrey A. *lawyer*
Klowden, Michael Louis *lawyer*
Koch, Albin Cooper *lawyer*
Koelzer, George Joseph *lawyer*
Kruse, Scott August *lawyer*
Kuechle, John Merrill *lawyer*
Kulzick, Kenneth Edmund *lawyer, writer*
Kupietzky, Moshe J. *lawyer*
Lane, Robert Gerhart *lawyer*
Lappen, Chester I. *lawyer*
Latham, Joseph Al, Jr. *lawyer*
Lauchengco, Jose Yujuico, Jr. *lawyer*
Lawrence, Barry Howard *lawyer*
Laybourne, Everett Broadstone *lawyer*
Lederman, Bruce Randolph *lawyer*
Leibow, Ronald Louis *lawyer*
Lesser, Joan L. *lawyer*
Letwin, Leon *legal educator*
Leung, Frankie Fook-Lun *lawyer*
Levine, Thomas Jeffrey Pello *lawyer*
Liebeler, Wesley J. *law educator, lawyer*
Light, John Robert *lawyer*
Lindholm, Dwight Henry *lawyer*
Link, George Hamilton *lawyer*
Lipsig, Ethan *lawyer*
Lishner, Laurence H. *lawyer*
Littleton, Christine A. *law educator*
Loeb, Ronald Marvin *lawyer*
Long, Gregory Alan *lawyer*
Lowenstein, Daniel Hays *lawyer, educator*
Lublinski, Michael *lawyer*
Lucero, Gene A. *lawyer*
Ludlam, James Edward *lawyer*
Lurvey, Ira Harold *lawyer*
Lynch, Patrick *lawyer*
Lyons, James Elliott *lawyer*
MacLaughlin, Francis Joseph *lawyer*
Mancino, Douglas Michael *lawyer*
Marciniak, Thaddeus J. *lawyer*
Marshall, Arthur K. *lawyer, judge, arbitrator, educator, writer*
Mason, Cheryl White *lawyer*
McBurney, George William *lawyer*
McDermott, Thomas John, Jr. *lawyer*
Mc Donough, John Richard *lawyer*
McDonough, Patrick Joseph *lawyer*
McGee, Henry W., Jr. *legal educator, lawyer*
Mc Govern, William Montgomery, Jr. *law educator*
McKnight, Frederick L. *lawyer*
McLane, Frederick Berg *lawyer*
Mc Laughlin, Joseph Mailey *lawyer*
Melkonian, Harry G. *lawyer, rancher*
Mellinkoff, David *lawyer, educator*
Menkel-Meadow, Carrie Joan *law educator*
Merritt, Bruce Gordon *lawyer*
Metzger, Robert Streicher *lawyer*
Meyer, Michael Edwin *lawyer*
Miley, Samuel A. *lawyer, electrical equipment company executive*
Millard, Neal Steven *lawyer*
Miller, Gavin *lawyer*
Miller, Milton Allen *lawyer*
Mintz, Marshall Gary *lawyer*
Mitchell, Briane Nelson *lawyer*
Morava, Carol *lawyer*
Mori, Jun *lawyer*
Morris, Herbert *lawyer, educator*
Morris, Stephen James Michael *lawyer*
Morrison, Robert Lewin *lawyer*
Mosk, Richard Mitchell *lawyer*
Moskowitz, Joel Steven *lawyer*
Moss, Gary Curtis *lawyer*
Mossawir, Harve H., Jr. *lawyer*
Mosten, Forrest Steven *lawyer, educator*
Mueller, John C. *lawyer*
Muller, Peter *lawyer, entertainment company executive, retail company executive, consultant*
Munzer, Stephen R. *law educator*
Nahai, Hamid *lawyer*
Neely, Sally Schultz *lawyer*
Neiter, Gerald Irving *lawyer*
Nelson, Grant Steel *lawyer, educator*
Nelson, J. Robert *lawyer*
Newhouse, Brian E. *lawyer*
Newman, David Wheeler *lawyer*
Nibley, Robert Ricks *retired lawyer*
Nicholas, William Richard *lawyer*
Niemeth, Charles Frederick *lawyer*
†Niemiec, Peter Jude *lawyer*
Niese, William A. *lawyer, newspaper publishing executive*
Niles, John Gilbert *lawyer*
Noble, Richard Lloyd *lawyer*
Nocas, Andrew James *lawyer*
Nochimson, David *lawyer*
Norris, Edwin L. *lawyer*
Norris, Floyd Hamilton *lawyer*
Obrzut, Ted *lawyer*
O'Connell, Kevin *lawyer*
Oder, Kenneth William *lawyer*
O'Donnell, Pierce Henry *lawyer*
Olpin, Owen *lawyer*
Olsen, Frances Elisabeth *law educator, theorist*
Olsen, Roger Milton *lawyer*
Olson, Gary *lawyer*
Olson, Ronald Leroy *lawyer*
O'Malley, Joseph James *lawyer*
Ordin, Andrea Sheridan *lawyer*
Orr, Ronald Stewart *lawyer*
Ostroff, Peter I. *lawyer*
Owen, Michael Lee *lawyer*
Owens, Stephen Thomas *lawyer*
Pace, Richard Randall *lawyer, educator*
Packard, Robert Charles *lawyer*
Paparelli, Angelo A. *lawyer*
Papiano, Neil Leo *lawyer*
Parsky, Gerald Lawrence *lawyer*
Patterson, Charles Ernest *lawyer*
Paul, Lee Gilmour *lawyer*
Peck, Austin H., Jr. *lawyer*
Pepe, Stephen Phillip *lawyer*
Pereyra-Suarez, Charles Albert *lawyer*
Perry, Ralph Barton, III *lawyer*
Peters, Richard T. *lawyer*
Peterson, Linda S. *lawyer*
Petroni, Donald Victor *lawyer*
Pieper, Darold D. *lawyer*
Pircher, Leo Joseph *lawyer*
Poindexter, William Mersereau *lawyer*
Pollock, John Phleger *lawyer*
Pope, Alexander H. *lawyer, former county official*
Porter, Verna Louise *lawyer*
Power, John Bruce *lawyer*
Praw, Albert Z. *lawyer*
Preonas, George Elias *lawyer*
Presant, Sanford Calvin *lawyer*
Privett, Howard J. *lawyer*
Rabinovitz, Joel *lawyer, educator*
Rae, Matthew Sanderson, Jr. *lawyer*
Raeder, Myrna Sharon *lawyer, educator*
Ramseyer, J. Mark *law educator*
Ramseyer, Loretta Lynne *lawyer*
Rapaport, Mark Samuel *lawyer*
Rappeport, Ira J. *lawyer*
Rath, Howard Grant, Jr. *lawyer*
Ray, Gilbert T. *lawyer*
Reeves, Barbara Ann *lawyer*
Reiner, Ira *lawyer*
Rich, J(ay) Peter *lawyer*
Richardson, Douglas Fielding *lawyer*
Richman, Frederick Alexander *lawyer*
Ring, Michael Wilson *lawyer*
Roberts, Thomas G. *lawyer*
Roberts, Virgil Patrick *lawyer, business executive*
Robertson, Hugh Duff *lawyer*
Robinson, Martha Stewart *retired legal educator*
Rogan, Patrick Goode *lawyer*
Roney, John Harvey *lawyer*
Rosen, Robert Charles *lawyer*
Rosenthal, Sol *lawyer*
Rosett, Arthur Irwin *lawyer, educator*
Rothman, Frank *lawyer, motion picture company executive*
Rubinroit, Howard J. *lawyer*
Ryan, Reade Haines, Jr. *lawyer*
Salvaty, Benjamin Benedict *lawyer*
Samet, Jack I. *lawyer*
Samuels, Donald L. *lawyer*
Sanders, Joseph Stanley *lawyer*
Savikas, Victor George *lawyer*
Saxe, Deborah Crandall *lawyer*
Scheifly, John Edward *retired lawyer*
Schmutz, Arthur Walter *lawyer*
Schroeder, Bill E. *lawyer*
Schurr, Carolyn *lawyer*
Schwartz, Gary T. *law educator*
Scott, A. Timothy *lawyer*
Selwood, Pierce Taylor *lawyer*
Shames, Henry Joseph *lawyer*
Shapiro, Marvin Seymour *lawyer*
Shapiro, Robert Leslie *lawyer*
Sheehan, Lawrence James *lawyer*
Sheppard, Thomas Richard *lawyer*
Sherrell, John Bradford *lawyer*
Sherwood, Allen Joseph *lawyer*
Sherwood, Arthur Lawrence *lawyer*
Sherwood, Linda Kathleen *lawyer*
Shortz, Richard Alan *lawyer*
Shultz, John David *lawyer*
Silbergeld, Arthur F. *lawyer*
Simpson, Allyson Bilich *lawyer*
Smith, Byron Owen *lawyer*
Smith, Chester Leo *lawyer*
Sobelle, Richard E. *lawyer*
Soltman, Neil M. *lawyer*
Southern, Robert Allen *lawyer*
Span, Robert Steven *lawyer*
Spooner, Mark Jordan *lawyer*
Spuehler, Donald Roy *retired lawyer, writer, mythologist*
Stamm, Alan *lawyer*
Stephens, George Edward, Jr. *lawyer*
Stern, Stephen Jeffrey *lawyer*
Stinehart, William, Jr. *lawyer*
Stone, Lawrence Maurice *lawyer, educator*
Stone, Richard James *lawyer*
Stoterau, H. Peter *lawyer*
Stromberg, Ross Ernest *lawyer*
Sullivan, Peter M. *lawyer*
Tan, William Lew *lawyer*
Tarr, Ralph William *lawyer, former federal government official*
Thompson, Shawna Margaret *lawyer*
Tinsley, Walton Eugene *lawyer*
Tobisman, Stuart Paul *lawyer*
Treister, George Marvin *lawyer*
Trimble, Phillip Richard *law educator*
Troy, Joseph Freed *lawyer*
Trygstad, Lawrence Benson *lawyer*
Ukropina, James R. *lawyer*
Unterman, Thomas E. *lawyer*
Van de Kamp, John Kalar *lawyer*
Vandeman, George Allen *lawyer*
Vanderet, Robert Charles *lawyer*
Van Emburgh, Joanne *lawyer*
Varat, Jonathan D. *law educator*
Vaughan, Joseph Robert *lawyer*
Vaughn, William Weaver *lawyer*
Vena, David Henry *lawyer*
Verrone, Patric Miller *lawyer, writer*
Vogel, Charles Stimmel *lawyer*
Volpert, Richard Sidney *lawyer*
Vradenburg, George, III *lawyer, corporate executive*
Wagner, D. William *lawyer*
Walcher, Alan Ernest *lawyer*
Wasserman, William Phillip *lawyer*
Wayte, (Paul) Alan *lawyer*
Weaver, Don L. *lawyer*
Weinstock, Harold *lawyer*
Weiss, Walter Stanley *lawyer*
Weitzman, Howard L. *lawyer*
Wessling, Robert Bruce *lawyer*
Wheat, Francis Millspaugh *retired lawyer*
Whisman, Linda Anne *law librarian*
White, Robert Joel *lawyer*
Wigmore, John Grant *lawyer*
Williams, Richard Thomas *lawyer*
Wolas, Herbert *lawyer*
Wolf, Lesley Sara *lawyer*
Wolfen, Werner F. *lawyer*
Woods, Daniel James *lawyer*
Wright, Kenneth Brooks *lawyer*
Wyatt, Joseph Lucian, Jr. *lawyer, educator*
York, Gary Alan *lawyer*
Young, Bless Stritar *lawyer*
Zarefsky, Ralph *lawyer*
Zelon, Laurie Dee *lawyer*
Ziffren, Kenneth *lawyer*
Ziffren, Lester *lawyer*
Zohn, Martin Steven *lawyer*

Los Gatos
Allan, Lionel Manning *lawyer, consultant*

Malibu
Coben, William Allen *lawyer*
Phillips, Ronald Frank *legal educator, law school dean*

Manhattan Beach
Scott, Michael Dennis *lawyer*

Marina Del Rey
Adams, Thomas Merritt *lawyer*
Grobe, Charles Stephen *lawyer, accountant*

Martinez
Bray, Absalom Francis, Jr. *lawyer*

Menlo Park
Bader, William Reece *lawyer*
Everett, Michael Thomas *lawyer*
Ferris, Robert Albert *lawyer, venture capitalist*
Gilburne, Miles R. *lawyer*
Pooley, James Henry Anderson *lawyer, author*
Surbeck, Leighton Homer *retired lawyer*

Mission Viejo
Ruben, Robert Joseph *lawyer*

Modesto
Owens, Jack Byron *lawyer*

Montara
Gyemant, Robert Ernest *lawyer*

Monte Rio
Pemberton, John de Jarnette, Jr. *lawyer, educator*

Monterey
Bomberger, Russell Branson *lawyer, educator*
Fenton, Lewis Lowry *lawyer*
Haddad, Louis Nicholas *paralegal*
Malone, James L. *lawyer, diplomat*
Stern, Gerald Daniel *lawyer*

Moraga
Countryman, Vern *law educator*

Napa
Fawcett, F(rank) Conger *lawyer*
Kuntz, Charles Powers *lawyer*

Newport Beach
Adams, William Gillette *lawyer*
Baskin, Scott David *lawyer*
Guilford, Andrew John *lawyer*
Johnson, Thomas Webber, Jr. *lawyer*
Katayama, Arthur Shoji *lawyer*
Klein, Maurice J. *lawyer*
Lowe, Kathlene Winn *lawyer*
Mallory, Frank Linus *lawyer*
Martens, Don Walter *lawyer*
Millar, Richard William, Jr. *lawyer*
Mortensen, Arvid LeGrande *lawyer, insurance company executive*
Phillips, Layn R. *lawyer*
Rooklidge, William Charles *lawyer*
Simon, John Roger *lawyer*
Singer, Gary James *lawyer*
Tanner, R. Marshall *lawyer*
Wentworth, Theodore Sumner *lawyer*
Willard, Robert Edgar *lawyer*

North Hollywood
Kreger, Melvin Joseph *lawyer*
Runquist, Lisa A. *lawyer*

Novato
Obninsky, Victor Peter *lawyer*

Oakland
Allen, Jeffrey Michael *lawyer*
Buckley, Mike Clifford *lawyer, electronics company executive*
Burnison, Boyd Edward *lawyer*
Cline, Wilson Ettason *retired administrative law judge*
Davis, Frances M. *lawyer, corporate executive*
Deming, Willis Riley *lawyer*
Fogel, Paul David *lawyer*
Heafey, Edwin Austin, Jr. *lawyer*
Kaplan, Alvin Irving *lawyer, adjudicator, investigator*
Kennedy, Raoul Dion *lawyer*
Miller, Kirk *lawyer*
Miller, Thomas Robbins *lawyer, publisher*
Patton, Roger William *lawyer, educator*
Quinby, William Albert *lawyer*
Saperstein, Guy T. *lawyer*
Skaff, Andrew Joseph *lawyer, public utilities, energy and transportation executive*
Sun, Cossette Tsung-hung Wu *law library director*
Tracy, James Jared, Jr. *law firm administrator*
Wick, William David *lawyer*
Winokur, Robert M. *lawyer*
Wood, James Michael *lawyer*

Oceanside
Robinson, William Franklin *retired legal consultant*
Schuck, Carl Joseph *lawyer*

Orange
Sawdei, Milan A. *lawyer*

Orinda
Brookes, Valentine *retired lawyer*
McCormick, Loyd Weldon *lawyer*

Pacific Palisades
Cale, Charles Griffin *lawyer*
Flattery, Thomas Long *lawyer, legal administrator*
Jones, Edgar Allan, Jr. *law educator, arbitrator, lawyer*
Rothenberg, Leslie Steven *lawyer, ethicist*
Schwartz, Murray Louis *lawyer, educator, academic administrator*
Sevilla, Stanley *lawyer*

Palm Desert
Humphrey, Charles Edward, Jr. *lawyer*

Palm Springs
DeVore, Daun Aline *lawyer*

Palo Alto
Adams, Marcia Howe *lawyer*
Borovoy, Roger Stuart *lawyer*
Bradley, Donald Edward *lawyer*
Climan, Richard Elliot *lawyer*
Furbush, David Malcolm *lawyer*
Gunderson, Robert Vernon, Jr. *lawyer*
Haslam, Robert Thomas, III *lawyer*
Hinckley, Robert Craig *lawyer*
Johnston, Alan Cope *lawyer*
Mendelson, Alan Charles *lawyer*
Monroy, Gladys H. *lawyer*
Moretti, August Joseph *lawyer*
Nordlund, Donald Craig *corporate lawyer*
Patterson, Robert Edward *lawyer*
Phair, Joseph Baschon *lawyer*
Saltoun, Andre Meir *lawyer*
Sonsini, Larry W. *lawyer*
Van Atta, David Murray *lawyer*
Wheeler, Raymond Louis *lawyer*

Palos Verdes Peninsula
Yeomans, Russell Allen *lawyer, translator*

Paramount
Hall, Howard Harry *lawyer*

Pasadena
Bakaly, Charles George, Jr. *lawyer, mediator*
D'Angelo, Robert William *lawyer*
Hale, Charles Russell *lawyer*
Hunt, Gordon *lawyer*
Myers, R(alph) Chandler *lawyer*
O'Neill, J. Norman, Jr. *lawyer*
Pianko, Theodore A. *lawyer*
Rapaport, David Alan *corporate legal executive*
Stone, Willard John *retired lawyer*
Tanner, Dee Boshard *lawyer*
Yohalem, Harry Morton *lawyer*

Paso Robles
Knecht, James Herbert *lawyer*

Pebble Beach
Dennison, David Short, Jr. *lawyer*
Maxeiner, Clarence William *lawyer, construction company executive*

Pleasanton
†Gustafson, Lawrence Raymond *lawyer*
Miller, William Charles *lawyer*
Petty, George Oliver *lawyer*

Plymouth
Andreason, John Christian *lawyer*

Pomona
Coombs, Walter Paul *retired lawyer, social science educator*

Portola Valley
Cooper, John Joseph *lawyer*
Hanson, Raymond Lester *retired lawyer*
Nycum, Susan Hubbell *lawyer*

Rancho Mirage
Kuhlmey, Walter Trowbridge *lawyer*

Rancho Santa Fe
Arms, Brewster Lee *retired corporate lawyer, investor*

Redlands
Ely, Northcutt *lawyer*

Redondo Beach
McCann, Joseph John, Jr. *lawyer*

Redwood City
Bentley, John Martin *lawyer*
Bonino, Mark G. *lawyer*
Coddington, Clinton Hays *lawyer*
Silvestri, Philip Salvatore *lawyer*
Tight, Dexter Corwin *lawyer*
Wilhelm, Robert Oscar *lawyer, civil engineer, developer*

Riverside
Aderton, Jane Reynolds *lawyer*
Trask, Grover C. *lawyer*

Rolling Hills Estates
Rumbaugh, Charles Earl *lawyer, corporate executive*

Roseville
Robbins, Stephen J. M. *lawyer*

Sacramento
Andrew, John Henry *lawyer, retail corporation executive*
Bell, Robert William *lawyer*
Blackman, David Michael *lawyer*
Brookman, Anthony Raymond *lawyer*
Friedman, Morton Lee *lawyer*
Goodart, Nan L. *lawyer, educator*
Kolkey, Daniel Miles *lawyer*
LeBaron, Edward Wayne, Jr. *lawyer*
O'Haire, Karen A. *lawyer*
Plant, Forrest Albert *lawyer*
Ramirez, Raul Anthony *lawyer, former federal judge*
Richardson, Frank Kellogg *lawyer, former state justice*
Salamy, Farris Najeeb *lawyer*
Schaber, Gordon Duane *law educator, former judge*
Van Camp, Brian Ralph *lawyer*
Zeff, Ophelia Hope *lawyer*
Zumbrun, Ronald Arthur *lawyer*

San Andreas
Arkin, Michael Barry *lawyer, arbitrator*

San Anselmo
Murphy, Barry Ames *lawyer*

San Clemente
Khachigian, Kenneth Larry *lawyer*

San Diego
Alpert, Michael Edward *lawyer*
Ames, Robert Forbes *lawyer*
Bohrer, Robert Arnold *law educator*
Bowie, Peter Wentworth *lawyer, educator*
Bradley, Lawrence D., Jr. *lawyer*
Branson, Harley Kenneth *lawyer, finance executive*
Brooks, John White *lawyer*
Celentino, Anne Elizabeth *lawyer*
Copeland, Robert Glenn *lawyer*
Damoose, George Lynn *lawyer*
Hofflund, Paul *lawyer*
Huston, Kenneth Dale *lawyer*
Hutcheson, J(ames) Sterling *lawyer*
Kammer, William Nolan *lawyer*
Kripke, Kenneth Norman *lawyer*
Lathrop, Mitchell Lee *lawyer*
LeBeau, Charles Paul *lawyer*
Lerach, William S. *lawyer*
Lucchino, Lawrence *lawyer, sports executive*
Mayer, James Hock *mediator, lawyer*
McGinnis, Robert E. *lawyer*
McManus, Richard Philip *lawyer*
Mittermiller, James Joseph *lawyer*
Monahan, David Emory *lawyer*
Morris, Grant Harold *legal educator*
Morris, Sandra Joan *lawyer*
Mulvaney, James Francis *lawyer*
O'Malley, James Terence *lawyer*
Peterson, Nad A. *lawyer, corporate executive*
Pettis, Ronald Eugene *lawyer*
Pray, Ralph Marble, III *lawyer*
Pugh, Richard Crawford *lawyer*
Reavey, William Anthony, III *lawyer*
St. George, William Ross *lawyer, retired naval officer, consultant*
Shaw, Richard Allan *lawyer*
Shearer, William Kennedy *lawyer, publisher*
Shelton, Dorothy Diehl Rees *lawyer*
Shippey, Sandra Lee *lawyer*
Snyder, David Richard *lawyer*
Sterrett, James Kelley, II *lawyer*
Stiska, John C. *lawyer*
Sullivan, William Francis *lawyer*
Weaver, Michael James *lawyer*
Whitmore, Sharp *lawyer*

San Francisco
Abbott, Barry A. *lawyer*
Adams, Lee Stephen *lawyer, banker*
Alexander, Robert C. *lawyer*
Allan, Walter Robert *lawyer*
Allen, Jose R. *lawyer*
Andrews, David Ralph *lawyer*
Archer, Richard Joseph *lawyer*
Arnold, Kenneth James *lawyer, publishing company executive*
Ashby, Teri Helena *lawyer*
Bagdonas, Kathy Joann *lawyer*
Baker, Cameron *lawyer*
Bancroft, James Ramsey *lawyer, business executive*
Barbagelata, Robert Dominic *lawyer*
Bare, Joseph Edward, Jr. *retired lawyer*
Bates, John Burnham *lawyer*
Bates, William, III *lawyer*
Baxter, Ralph H., Jr. *lawyer*
Beck, Edward William *lawyer*
Bedford, Daniel Ross *lawyer*
Bedford, Lyman D. *lawyer*
Belli, Melvin Mouron *lawyer, lecturer, writer*
Bennett, James Patrick *lawyer*
Benvenutti, Peter J. *lawyer*
Berns, Philip Allan *lawyer*
Bertain, G(eorge) Joseph, Jr. *lawyer*
Blackstone, George Arthur *retired lawyer*
Bonapart, Alan David *lawyer*
Bookin, Daniel H. *lawyer*
Borowsky, Philip *lawyer*
Boucher, Harold Irving *lawyer*
Boyd, William Sprott *lawyer*
Brandel, Roland Eric *lawyer*
Brick, Steven A. *lawyer*
Bridges, Robert Lysle *retired lawyer*
Briggs, Susan Shadinger *lawyer*
Bromley, Dennis Karl *lawyer*
Brosnahan, James Jerome *lawyer*
Broussard, Allen E. *lawyer, former state supreme court justice*
Brown, Albert Jacob *lawyer*
Brown, Anthony P. *lawyer*
Brown, David Julian *lawyer*
Brown, Donald Wesley *lawyer*
Brown, Margaret deBeers *lawyer*
Brown, Robert L. *lawyer*
Bryan, Robert Russell *lawyer*
Budge, Hamilton Whithed *lawyer*
Burns, Brian Patrick *lawyer, business executive*
Callan, Terrence A. *lawyer*
Campbell, Scott Robert *lawyer, former food company executive*
Canty, James M. *lawyer*
Carlson, John Earl *lawyer*
Carmichael, Lynne A. *lawyer*
Carter, John Douglas *lawyer*
Cartmell, Nathaniel Madison, III *lawyer*
Casillas, Mark *lawyer*
Caulfield, Barbara Ann *lawyer*
Chao, Cedric C. *lawyer*
Cheatham, Robert William *lawyer*
Coblentz, William Kraemer *lawyer*
Coffin, Judy Sue *lawyer*
Cole, Richard Charles *lawyer*
Coleman, Thomas Young *lawyer*
Collas, Juan Garduño, Jr. *lawyer*
Connell, William D. *lawyer*
Corcoran, Maureen Elizabeth *lawyer*
Cowan, Stephen A. *lawyer*
Cranston, Mary B. *lawyer*
Crawford, Roy Edgington, III *lawyer*
Cumming, George Anderson, Jr. *lawyer*
Daggett, Robert Sherman *lawyer*
Danoff, Eric Michael *lawyer*
Daugherty, Richard Bernard *lawyer*
Davies, Paul Lewis, Jr. *retired lawyer*
Davis, Roger Lewis *lawyer*
Davis, Roland Chenoweth *lawyer*
Dawes, Paul Harvey *lawyer*
De Benedictis, Dario *arbitrator, mediator*
Dell, Robert Michael *lawyer*
Diamond, Philip Ernest *lawyer*
Diekmann, Gilmore Frederick, Jr. *lawyer*
Doxsee, Lawrence Edward *corporate lawyer*
Dran, Robert Joseph *lawyer*
Dryden, Robert Eugene *lawyer*
Dunne, Kevin Joseph *lawyer*
Dupree, Stanley M. *lawyer*
Dyer, Noel John *lawyer*
Edwards, Robin Morse *lawyer*
Ehrlich, Thomas *law educator*
Eigner, Richard Martin *lawyer*
Elderkin, E(dwin) Judge *retired lawyer*
Enersen, Burnham *lawyer*
Engel, G(eorge) Larry *lawyer*
Ericson, Bruce Alan *lawyer*
Filippi, Frank Joseph *lawyer*
Finigan, Vincent P., Jr. *lawyer*
Fink, Scott Alan *lawyer*
Folberg, Harold Jay *lawyer, mediator, educator, university dean*
Foster, David Scott *lawyer*
Fredericks, Dale Edward *lawyer*
Freeman, Tom M. *lawyer*
Friedman, K. Bruce *lawyer*
Friese, Robert Charles *lawyer*
Fuller, Maurice DeLano, Jr. *lawyer*
Furth, Frederick Paul *lawyer*
Gaither, James C. *lawyer*
Garvey, Joanne Marie *lawyer*
Gee, Juliet Leslie *lawyer*
Gill, Margaret Gaskins *lawyer*
Gillmar, Stanley Frank *lawyer*
Golub, Howard Victor *lawyer*
Gordon, Robert Allen, Jr. *lawyer*
Gowdy, Franklin Brockway *lawyer*
Gresham, Zane Oliver *lawyer*
Guggenhime, Richard Johnson *lawyer*
Gutterman, Alan Spencer *lawyer*
Hannawalt, Willis Dale *lawyer*
Hanschen, Peter Walter *lawyer*
Hardy, David *lawyer, corporate executive*
Harris, Richard Eugene Vassau *lawyer*
Hartman, John E. *lawyer*
Hassard, Howard *lawyer*
Hasson, Kirke Michael *lawyer*
Haven, Thomas Edward *lawyer*
Heilbron, David M(ichael) *lawyer*
Heilbron, Louis Henry *lawyer*
Heng, Donald James, Jr. *lawyer*
Henson, Ray David *legal educator, consultant*
Hinman, Harvey DeForest *lawyer*
Hofmann, John Richard, Jr. *lawyer*
Holden, Frederick Douglass, Jr. *lawyer*
†Holman, Thomas C. *lawyer*
Homer, Barry Wayne *lawyer*
Howard, Carl (Michael) *lawyer*
Hudner, Philip *lawyer, rancher*
Hunter, William Dennis *lawyer*
Irwin, William Rankin *lawyer*
James, David Lee *lawyer, international advisor, author*
Johnson, Martin Wayne *lawyer*
Johnson, Reverdy *lawyer*
Joseph, Allan Jay *lawyer*
Judson, Philip Livingston *lawyer*
Jung, David Joseph *law educator*
Kaapcke, Wallace Letcher *lawyer*
Kadushin, Karen D. *lawyer*
Kallgren, Edward Eugene *lawyer*
Kane, Mary Kay *law educator*
Kasanin, Mark Owen *lawyer*
Katz, Ronald Stanley *lawyer*
Kaufman, Christopher Lee *lawyer*
Kemp, Alson Remington, Jr. *lawyer, legal educator*
Kenny, David Culber *lawyer*
Kern, John McDougall *lawyer*
Kimport, David Lloyd *lawyer*
Kirkham, Francis Robison *lawyer*
Kirkham, James Francis *lawyer*
Klafter, Cary Ira *lawyer*
Klinger, Marilyn Sydney *lawyer*
Klott, David Lee *lawyer*
Knebel, Jack Gillen *lawyer*
Koeppel, John A. *lawyer*
Kolb, Theodore Alexander *lawyer*
Kozloff, Theodore J. *lawyer*
Krevans, Rachel *lawyer*
Kuhl, Paul Beach *lawyer*
Ladar, Jerrold Morton *lawyer*
Lambert, Frederick William *lawyer, educator*
Lane, Fielding H. *lawyer*
Larson, John William *lawyer*
Lasky, Moses *lawyer*
Lathrope, Daniel John *legal educator, administrator*
Laurie, Ronald Sheldon *lawyer*
Lee, Brant Thomas *lawyer, federal official*
Lee, John Jin *lawyer*
Lee, Richard Diebold *law educator*
Levi, Julian Hirsch *lawyer, educator*
Levit, Victor Bert *lawyer, foreign representative, civic worker*
Libbin, Anne Edna *lawyer*
Lipkin, Jeffrey Alan *lawyer*
Lipton, Alvin E(lliot) *lawyer*
Little, Jan Nielsen *lawyer*
Livsey, Robert Callister *lawyer*
London, Barry Joseph *lawyer*
Lotito, Michael Joseph *lawyer*
Lundquist, Weyman Ivan *lawyer*
Mac Gowan, Mary Eugenia *lawyer*
MacGuinness, Rosemary Anne *lawyer, real estate broker*
Maddux, Parker Ahrens *lawyer*
Madison, James Raymond *lawyer*
Mann, Bruce Alan *lawyer*
Marchant, David J. *lawyer*
Marcus, Richard Leon *lawyer*
Markun, Rachel *lawyer, educator*
Martin, Joseph, Jr. *lawyer, former ambassador*
Martin, Stephen James *lawyer*
Mathiason, Garry George *lawyer*
Mattes, Martin Anthony *lawyer*
McAniff, Edward John *lawyer*
McCandless, Sandra Ravich *lawyer*
McElhinny, Harold John *lawyer*
McKee, William David *lawyer*
McKelvey, Judith Grant *lawyer, educator, university dean*
Mc Laughlin, Jerome Michael *lawyer, shipping company executive*
McLeod, Robert Macfarlan *lawyer, arbitrator*
McNally, Thomas Charles, III *lawyer*
McNamara, Thomas Neal *lawyer*
McQuaid, J. Dennis *lawyer*
Mellor, Michael Lawton *lawyer*
Mellor, Robert E. *lawyer*
Merritt, James Edward *lawyer*
Metzler, Roger James, Jr. *lawyer*
Mihan, Ralph George *lawyer*
Miller, James Lynn *lawyer*
Miller, William Napier Cripps *lawyer*
Minnick, Malcolm David *lawyer*
Mitchell, Bruce Tyson *lawyer*
Moll, Charles J., III *lawyer*
Molligan, Peter Nicholas *lawyer*
Morrissey, John Carroll *lawyer*
Murray, G(lenn) Richard, Jr. *lawyer*
Musfelt, Duane Clark *lawyer*
Musser, Sandra G. *lawyer*
Nelson, David Edward *lawyer*
Nemir, Donald Philip *lawyer*
Niehans, Daniel Jurg *lawyer*
Odgers, Richard William *lawyer*
Offer, Stuart Jay *lawyer*
Olson, Walter Gilbert *lawyer*
Park, Roger Cook *law educator*
Pasahow, Lynn H(arold) *lawyer*
Penskar, Mark Howard *lawyer*
†Pfister, Peter J. *lawyer*
Pickett, Donn Philip *lawyer*
Placier, Philip R. *lawyer*
Platt, Peter Godfrey *lawyer*
Plishner, Michael Jon *lawyer*
Popofsky, Melvin Laurence *lawyer*
Preovolos, Penelope Athene *lawyer*
Pringle, Robert Bernard *lawyer*
Prunty, Bert Sherman, Jr. *lawyer*
Ragan, Charles Ransom *lawyer*
Ratner, David Louis *legal educator*
Raven, Robert Dunbar *lawyer*
Read, Gregory Charles *lawyer*
Reese, John Robert *lawyer*
Rembe, Toni *lawyer*
Renne, Louise Hornbeck *lawyer*
Rice, Denis Timlin *lawyer*
Richards, Norman Blanchard *lawyer*
Robertson, Armand James, II *lawyer*
Robertson, David Govan *lawyer*
Robinson, Jerry H. *lawyer*
Rockwell, Alvin John *lawyer*
Roemer, Elizabeth K. *lawyer*
Roethe, James Norton *lawyer*
Rosch, John Thomas *lawyer*
Rosen, Sanford Jay *lawyer*
Rosston, Edward William *lawyer*
Rowland, John Arthur *lawyer*
Rubin, Michael *lawyer*
Ryland, David Ronald *lawyer*
Salomon, Darrell Joseph *lawyer*
Sanger, John Morton *lawyer, urban planner*
Schlesinger, Rudolf Berthold *lawyer, educator*
Schwartz, Louis Brown *legal educator*
Sears, George Ames *lawyer*
Seegal, John Franklin *lawyer*
Selman, Roland Wooten, III *lawyer*
Sevier, Ernest Youle *lawyer*
Shenk, George H. *lawyer*

Simmons, Raymond Hedelius, Jr. *lawyer*
Singer, Allen Morris *lawyer*
Small, Marshall Lee *lawyer*
Smegal, Thomas Frank, Jr. *lawyer*
Smith, Gregory Allan *lawyer*
Smith, Kerry Clark *lawyer*
Snow, Tower Charles, Jr. *lawyer*
Sparks, John Edward *lawyer*
Sparks, Thomas E., Jr. *lawyer*
Spiegel, Hart Hunter *retired lawyer*
Stanzler, Jordan *lawyer*
Staring, Graydon Shaw *lawyer*
Steer, Reginald David *lawyer*
Stephens, Shand Scott *lawyer*
Stotter, Lawrence Henry *lawyer*
Stratton, Richard James *lawyer*
Sugarman, Myron George *lawyer*
Sugarman, Paul William *lawyer*
Sullivan, Robert Edward *lawyer*
Sutcliffe, Eric *lawyer*
Sutton, John Paul *lawyer*
Sze, Helen Wang Yee *lawyer*
Taylor, Robert P. *lawyer*
Taylor, William James (Zak Taylor) *lawyer*
Thomas, William Scott *lawyer*
Thompson, Robert Charles *lawyer*
Thornton, D. Whitney, II *lawyer*
Tierney, Kevin Hugh *law educator*
Tiffany, Joseph Raymond, II *lawyer*
Tingle, James O'Malley *lawyer*
Tobin, James Michael *lawyer*
Trautman, William Ellsworth *lawyer*
Traynor, J. Michael *lawyer*
Veaco, Kristina *lawyer*
Venning, Robert Stanley *lawyer*
Walker, Ralph Clifford *lawyer*
Walsh, Francis Richard *law educator*
Walsh, James Joseph *lawyer*
Wang, William Kai-Sheng *legal educator*
Warmer, Richard Craig *lawyer*
Weisberg, D. Kelly *law educator*
Welborn, Caryl Bartelman *lawyer*
Welch, Thomas Andrew *lawyer*
Werson, James Byrd *lawyer*
Westberg, Robert Myers *lawyer*
Whelan, John William *lawyer, educator, consultant*
White, Mark N. *lawyer*
Widman, Gary Lee *lawyer, former government official*
Wild, Nelson Hopkins *lawyer*
Willson, Prentiss, Jr. *lawyer*
Wingate, C. Keith *legal educator*
Wolfe, Cameron Withgot, Jr. *lawyer*
Wollen, W. Foster *lawyer*
Woods, James Robert *lawyer*
Wyle, Frederick S. *lawyer*
Yamakawa, David Kiyoshi, Jr. *lawyer*
Yost, Nicholas Churchill *lawyer*
Young, Bryant Llewellyn *lawyer, business executive*
Ziering, William Mark *lawyer*
Zimmerman, Bernard *lawyer*

San Jose
Anderson, Edward V. *lawyer*
Fowler, John Wellington *lawyer*
Granneman, Vernon Henry *lawyer*
Greenstein, Martin Richard *lawyer*
Kennedy, George Wendell *lawyer*
Laskin, Barbara Virginia *legal association administrator*
Mitchell, David Walker *lawyer*
Morgan, William Robert *lawyer*
Rappaport, Stuart R. *lawyer*
Smirni, Allan Desmond *lawyer*
Williams, John Lyle *lawyer*

San Juan Capistrano
Curtis, John Joseph *lawyer*

San Luis Obispo
Daly, John Paul *lawyer*

San Marcos
Dixon, William Cornelius *lawyer*

San Marino
Baldwin, James William *lawyer*
Galbraith, James Marshall *lawyer, business executive*
Mortimer, Wendell Reed, Jr. *lawyer*

San Mateo
Bell, Frank Ouray, Jr. *lawyer*
Kane, Robert Francis *lawyer, former ambassador, consultant*

San Rafael
Roth, Hadden Wing *lawyer*
Stout, Gregory Stansbury *lawyer*

San Ramon
Kahane, Dennis Spencer *lawyer*
O'Connor, Paul Daniel *lawyer*

Santa Ana
Blaine, Dorothea Constance Ragetté *lawyer*
Capizzi, Michael Robert *lawyer*
Fay-Schmidt, Patricia Ann *paralegal*
Fouste, Donna H. *legal administrator*
Heckler, Gerard Vincent *lawyer*
Jaffer, Rashida Amin *lawyer*
Storer, Maryruth *law librarian*
Zaenglein, William George, Jr. *lawyer*

Santa Barbara
Anderson, Darla Rae *lawyer*
†Carlson, Arthur W. *lawyer*
Gaines, Howard Clarke *lawyer*
Harris, James Dexter *lawyer*
Jensen, Allen Reed *lawyer*
McEwan, Willard Winfield, Jr. *lawyer, judge*

Santa Clara
Alexander, George Jonathon *legal educator, former dean*
DeLong, James J. *lawyer*
Glancy, Dorothy Jean *lawyer, educator*

Santa Monica
Boltz, Gerald Edmund *lawyer*
Bonesteel, Michael John *lawyer*
Brown, Scott McLean *lawyer*
Dickson, Robert Lee *lawyer*
Garner, Donald K. *lawyer*
Jones, William Allen *lawyer, entertainment company executive*
Loo, Thomas S. *lawyer*
McMillan, M. Sean *lawyer*
Merideth, Frank E., Jr. *lawyer*
Powers, Marcus Eugene *lawyer*
Prewoznik, Jerome Frank *lawyer*
Risman, Michael *lawyer, business executive, securities company executive*
Schlei, Norbert Anthony *lawyer*
Sheller, John Willard *lawyer*
Sperling, George Elmer, Jr. *lawyer*
Tunney, John Varick *lawyer, former senator*
Walker, Charles Montgomery *lawyer*
Weatherup, Roy Garfield *lawyer*

Santa Rosa
Steinberger, Richard Lynn *lawyer, corporate executive*

Sausalito
Berkman, William Roger *lawyer, army reserve officer*
Overton, John Blair *lawyer*
Trimmer, Harold Sharp, Jr. *lawyer, international telecommunications consultant*

Seal Beach
Calise, William Joseph, Jr. *lawyer*
Hirsch, David L. *lawyer, corporate executive*
Kee, Sharon Phillips *lawyer*
Mueth, Joseph Edward *lawyer*

Sierra Madre
Calleton, Theodore Edward *lawyer*

Solana Beach
Hecker, Bruce Albert *lawyer*

Solvang
Morrow, Richard Towson *lawyer*

Stanford
Ayres, Ian *law educator*
Babcock, Barbara Allen *lawyer, educator*
Barton, John Hays *law educator*
Baxter, William Francis *lawyer, educator*
Brest, Paul A. *law educator*
Campbell, Thomas J. *law educator*
Cohen, William *law educator*
Dickson, Lance E. *law librarian, educator*
Ely, John Hart *lawyer, university dean*
Franklin, Marc Adam *law educator*
Friedman, Lawrence M. *law educator*
Gilson, Ronald Jay *law educator*
Goldstein, Paul *lawyer, educator*
Grey, Thomas C. *lawyer, law educator*
Gunther, Gerald *lawyer, educator*
Heller, Thomas C. *law educator*
Kelman, Mark Gregory *law educator*
Lawrence, Charles R. *law educator*
Lopez, Gerald P. *law educator*
†Mann, J. Keith *arbitrator, law educator*
Mc Bride, Thomas Frederick *lawyer, former university dean, government official*
Mendez-Longoria, Miguel Angel *law educator*
Polinsky, A. Mitchell *law and economics educator*
Rabin, Robert L. *lawyer, educator*
Rhode, Deborah Lynn *law educator*
Roster, Michael *lawyer*
Scholes, Myron S. *law and finance educator*
Scott, Kenneth Eugene *lawyer, educator*
Simon, William H. *legal educator*
Sofaer, Abraham David *lawyer, legal advisor, federal judge, legal educator*
Wald, Michael S. *law educator*
Williams, Howard Russell *lawyer, educator*

Stockton
Blewett, Robert Noall *lawyer*
Curtis, Orlie Lindsey, Jr. *lawyer*

Studio City
Yorty, Samuel *lawyer, former mayor*

Sunnyvale
Handschuh, G. Gregory *lawyer*
Ludgus, Nancy Lucke *lawyer*

Tarzana
Grill, Lawrence J. *lawyer, accountant, management company executive*

Torrance
Finer, William A. *lawyer*
Kaufman, Sanford Paul *lawyer*
Petillon, Lee Ritchey *lawyer*
Riess, Susan Elizabeth *lawyer*

Van Nuys
Mikesell, Richard Lyon *lawyer, financial counselor*

Walnut Creek
Blackburn, Michael Philip *lawyer*
Curtin, Daniel Joseph, Jr. *lawyer*
Garrett, James Joseph *lawyer, partner*
Ginsburg, Gerald J. *lawyer, business executive*
Jackson, Dale Edward *lawyer*
Jones, Orlo Dow *lawyer, drug store executive*
Madden, Palmer Brown *lawyer*
Merritt, Robert Edward *lawyer, educator*
Newmark, Milton Maxwell *lawyer*
Pagter, Carl Richard *lawyer*
Skaggs, Sanford Merle *lawyer*

West Covina
Hamilton, Robert William *lawyer*
McHale, Edward Robertson *retired lawyer*

West Hollywood
Walton, Brian *lawyer, union negotiator*

Westlake Village
Jessup, Warren T. *retired lawyer*
Pang, Peter Chiusing *lawyer, business consultant*

Woodland Hills
Strote, Joel Richard *lawyer*

Woodside
Poole, Gordon Leicester *lawyer*

Yuba City
Falls, Edward Joseph *lawyer, insurance executive, educator*

COLORADO

Aspen
Jalili, Mahir *lawyer*

Aurora
McPherson, Gary Lee *lawyer, state representative*
Schilling, Edwin Carlyle, III *lawyer*

Boulder
Bintliff, Barbara Ann *law librarian, educator*
Corbridge, James Noel, Jr. *law educator*
Echohawk, John Ernest *lawyer*
Fiflis, Ted J. *lawyer, educator*
Moses, Raphael Jacob *lawyer*
Oesterle, Dale Arthur *law educator*
Peterson, Courtland Harry *law educator*
Porzak, Glenn E. *lawyer*
Rich, Ben Arthur *lawyer, university official*
Steuben, Norton Leslie *lawyer, educator*
Tippit, John Harlow *lawyer*

Cherry Hills Village
Meyer, Milton Edward, Jr. *lawyer, artist*

Colorado Springs
Buell, Bruce Temple *lawyer*
†Eisner, William *lawyer*
Faber, Michael Warren *lawyer*
Flynn, James T. *lawyer*
Kendall, Phillip Alan *lawyer*
O'Rourke, Dennis *lawyer*
Payne, Billy (William A. Payne) *real estate lawyer, sports association executive*
Rouss, Ruth *lawyer*
Thomas, Darrell Denman *lawyer*

Denver
Alfers, Stephen Douglas *lawyer*
Austin, H(arry) Gregory *lawyer*
Bain, Donald Knight *lawyer*
Belitz, Paul Edward *lawyer*
Benson, Robert Eugene *lawyer*
Benson, Thomas Quentin *lawyer*
Benton, Auburn Edgar *lawyer*
Bermant, George Wilson *lawyer*
Blair, Andrew Lane, Jr. *lawyer, educator*
Blunk, Forrest Stewart *lawyer*
Brega, Charles Franklin *lawyer*
Burford, Anne McGill *lawyer*
Burke, Kenneth John *lawyer*
Butler, David *lawyer*
Bye, James Edward *lawyer*
Cain, Douglas Mylchreest *lawyer*
Campbell, Leonard Martin *lawyer*
Cantwell, William Patterson *lawyer*
Carr, James Francis *lawyer*
Carver, Craig R. *lawyer*
Cassidy, Samuel H. *lawyer, lieutenant governor, state legislator*
Chapman, Karen Louise *lawyer*
Cheroutes, Michael Louis *lawyer*
Chidester, Alfred C. *lawyer*
Collins, Martha Traudt *lawyer*
Conover, Frederic King *lawyer*
Cooper, Paul Douglas *lawyer*
Cope, Thomas Field *lawyer*
Cordova, Donald E. *lawyer*
Cox, William Vaughan *lawyer*
Curtis, George Bartlett *lawyer*
Dauer, Edward Arnold *law educator*
Dean, James Benwell *lawyer*
De Gette, Diana Louise *lawyer, state legislator*
Dempsey, Howard Stanley *lawyer, mining executive, investment banker*
Devine, Sharon Jean *lawyer*
Downey, Arthur Harold, Jr. *lawyer*
Dunham, Stephen Sampson *lawyer*
Eiberger, Carl Frederick *trial lawyer*
Eklund, Carl Andrew *lawyer*
Erisman, Frank *lawyer*
Espenoza, Cecelia M. *law educator*
Farley, John Michael *lawyer*
Faxon, Thomas Baker *lawyer*
Featherstone, Bruce Alan *lawyer*
Feder, Harold Abram *lawyer*
Fiske, Terry Noble *lawyer*
Flowers, William Harold, Jr. *lawyer*
Fognani, John Dennis *lawyer*
Gilman, Carol Elizabeth *lawyer*
Grant, Patrick Alexander *lawyer, former state legislator*
Green, Jersey Michael-Lee *lawyer*
Greene, Leslie Speed *lawyer*
Grissom, Garth Clyde *lawyer*
Gutterman, Sheila Maydet *lawyer*
Harhai, Stephen John *lawyer*
Harris, Dale Ray *lawyer*
Harry, Robert Hayden *lawyer*
Hartley, James Edward *lawyer*
Hawley, Robert Cross *lawyer*
Hendrix, Lynn Parker *lawyer*
Hoagland, Donald Wright *lawyer*
Hobson, Harry Lee, Jr. *lawyer*
Hodges, Joseph Gilluly, Jr. *lawyer*
Hoffman, Daniel Steven *lawyer, legal educator*
Holleman, Paul Douglas *lawyer*
Holme, Richard Phillips *lawyer*
Hopfenbeck, George Martin, Jr. *lawyer*
Hopkins, Donald J. *lawyer*
Hubbard, Kenneth Dean *lawyer*
Husband, John Michael *lawyer*
Irvin, Robert D. *lawyer*
Jackson, Richard Brooke *lawyer*
Jacobs, Paul Alan *lawyer*
Jones, Richard Michael *lawyer*
Keely, George Clayton *lawyer*
Keller, Glen Elven, Jr. *lawyer*
Keppler, Peter *lawyer*
Kintzele, John Alfred *lawyer*
Kirgis, Frederic L. *retired lawyer*
Law, John Manning *retired lawyer*
Lesher, Donald Miles *lawyer*
Levy, Mark Ray *lawyer*
Low, John Wayland *lawyer*
Lutz, John Shafroth *lawyer*
Mandelson, Richard S. *lawyer*
Martin, James Russell *lawyer*
Martz, Clyde Ollen *lawyer, educator*
Mauro, Richard Frank *lawyer, investment manager*
Maxfield, Thomas H. *lawyer*
Merker, Steven Joseph *lawyer*
Miller, Gale Timothy *lawyer*
Miller, Robert Nolen *lawyer*
Moorhead, John B. *lawyer*
Moye, John Edward *lawyer*
Muldoon, Brian *lawyer*
Muller, Nicholas Guthrie *lawyer, business executive*
Murane, William Edward *lawyer*
Murret, Eugene John, Sr. *judicial administrator*
Musgraves, Robert E. *lawyer*
Musyl, Marc J. *lawyer*
Nanda, Ved Prakash *law educator, university official*
Newton, James Quigg, Jr. *lawyer*
North, Phillip J. *lawyer*
O'Keefe, Edward Franklin *lawyer*
Otten, Arthur Edward, Jr. *lawyer, corporate executive*
Owen, James Churchill, Jr. *lawyer*
Palmer, David Gilbert *lawyer*
Peck, Neil *lawyer*
Petros, Raymond Louis, Jr. *lawyer*
Phillips, Paul David, Jr. *lawyer*
Poulson, Robert Dean *lawyer*
Pringle, Edward E. *legal educator, former state supreme court chief justice*
Prochnow, James R. *lawyer*
Purdy, Sherry Marie *lawyer*
Quail, Beverly J. *lawyer*
Quiat, Gerald M. *lawyer*
Ramsey, John Arthur *lawyer*
Ray, Bruce David *lawyer*
Rich, Robert Stephen *lawyer*
Ris, William Krakow *lawyer*
Roslund, Carol L. *lawyer*
Rubright, Royal Cushing *lawyer*
Ruppert, John Lawrence *lawyer*
Sasso, Cassandra Gay *lawyer*
Savitz, David Barry *lawyer*
Sayre, John Marshall *lawyer, former government official*
Seawell, Donald Ray *lawyer, publisher, arts center executive, producer*
Shea, Kevin Michael *lawyer*
Shearer, Cynthia Hodge *lawyer*
Shepherd, John Frederic *lawyer*
Skaer, Laura Elizabeth *lawyer*
Snyder, Stephen Edward *lawyer*
Spencer, Margaret Gilliam *lawyer*
Stockmar, Ted P. *lawyer*
Sutton, Raymond L., Jr. *lawyer*
Terry, Ward Edgar, Jr. *lawyer*
Thomasch, Roger Paul *lawyer*
Tipton, John J. *lawyer*
Tomlinson, Warren Leon *lawyer*
Tracey, Jay Walter, Jr. *retired lawyer*
Troy, Richard Hershey *lawyer*
Ulrich, Theodore Albert *lawyer*
†Vela, David *lawyer*
Vigil, Charles S. *lawyer*
Walker, Timothy Blake *lawyer, educator*
Wallace, Victor L., II *lawyer*
Watson, William D. *lawyer*
Welch, Carol Mae *lawyer*
Wheeler, Malcolm Edward *lawyer, law educator*
Williams, Michael Anthony *lawyer*
Williams, Wayne De Armond *lawyer*
Wohlgenant, Richard Glen *lawyer*
Woodward, Lester Ray *lawyer*
Wunnicke, Brooke *lawyer*
Yegge, Robert Bernard *lawyer, college dean emeritus, educator*

Durango
Burnham, Bryson Paine *retired lawyer*

Eagle
Sullivan, Selby William *lawyer, business executive*

Englewood
DeMuth, Laurence Wheeler, Jr. *lawyer, utility company executive*
Loughrey, Kevin *lawyer*
Reilly, Laura J. *lawyer*
Russ, Charles Paul, III *lawyer, corporate executive*

Fort Collins
Rogers, Garth Winfield *lawyer*

Golden
Lopez, Judith Carroll *lawyer*
Outerbridge, Cheryl *lawyer*
Wilson, James Robert *lawyer*

Greeley
Houtchens, Barnard *lawyer*

Lakewood
Guyton, Samuel Percy *retired lawyer*

Littleton
Spelts, Richard John *lawyer*

Montrose
Krumins, Girts *lawyer, management consultant*

Pueblo
Altman, Leo Sidney *lawyer*
O'Callaghan, Robert Patrick *lawyer*

Rifle
George, Russell Lloyd *lawyer, legislator*

CONNECTICUT

Ansonia
Carvalko, Joseph R., Jr. *lawyer*

Avon
Wiechmann, Eric Watt *lawyer*

Bloomfield
Anderson, Buist Murfee *lawyer*
Messemer, Glenn Matthew *lawyer*
Reid, Hoch *lawyer*

Branford
Leckerling, Jon Peter *lawyer*

Bridgeport
Margulies, Martin B. *lawyer, educator*
Tobin, Richard J. *lawyer*

Bristol
Besser, John Edward *lawyer*

Danbury
Geoghan, Joseph Edward *lawyer, chemical company executive*
Hull, Treat Clark *superior court trial referee*
Rowland, Thomas William *lawyer, sugar company executive*
Skolan-Logue, Amanda Nicole *lawyer, consultant*

Darien
Brown, James Shelly *lawyer*
Kaynor, Sanford Bull *lawyer*

East Hartford
Whiston, Richard Michael *lawyer*

Enfield
Berger, Robert Bertram *lawyer*

Fairfield
Caruso, Daniel F. *lawyer, judge, former state legislator*
Heineman, Benjamin Walter, Jr. *lawyer*
Kenney, James Francis *lawyer*
Sealy, Albert Henry *lawyer*

Glastonbury
Schroth, Peter W(illiam) *lawyer, management and law educator*

Greenwich
Bam, Foster *lawyer*
Bentley, Peter *lawyer*
Cantor, Samuel C. *lawyer*
Cantwell, Robert *lawyer*
Drake, Philip Meurer *lawyer*
duPont, Augustus Irénée *lawyer*
Fisher, Everett *lawyer*
Forrow, Brian Derek *lawyer, corporation executive*
Gillespie, Alexander Joseph, Jr. *lawyer*
Gorin, Robert Seymour *lawyer*
Graham, Diana *lawyer*
Jones, Edwin Michael *lawyer, former insurance company executive*
Kurtz, Melvin H. *lawyer, cosmetics company executive*
Laudone, Anita Helene *lawyer*
Lawler, Richard Francis *lawyer*
Lowenstein, Peter David *lawyer*
Lynch, William Redington *lawyer*
McKee, Thomas J. *lawyer*
Mendenhall, John Ryan *retired lawyer, transportation executive*
More, Douglas McLochlan *lawyer*
Paul, Roland Arthur *lawyer*
Rodenbach, Edward Francis *lawyer*
Rose, Richard Loomis *lawyer*
Stern, Dennis M. *lawyer*

Hamden
Peterson, George Emanuel, Jr. *lawyer, business executive*

Hartford
Alfano, Charles Thomas, Sr. *lawyer*
Anthony, J(ulian) Danford, Jr. *lawyer*
Asmar, Mark Abdon *lawyer*
Berall, Frank Stewart *lawyer*
Blumberg, Phillip Irvin *law educator*
Buck, Gurdon Hall *lawyer, urban planner, real estate broker*
Buckingham, Harold Canute, Jr. *lawyer*
Cain, George Harvey *lawyer, business executive*
Cantor, Donald Jerome *lawyer*
Cole, William Kaufman *lawyer*
Cullina, William Michael *lawyer*
Donahue, John McFall *lawyer*
Elliot, Ralph Gregory *lawyer*
Ewing, Robert *lawyer*
Fain, Joel Maurice *lawyer*
Garfield, Gerald *lawyer*
Godfrey, Robert Douglas *lawyer*
Green, Raymond Bert *lawyer*
Guenter, Raymond Albert *lawyer, banker*
Harrison, Thomas Flatley *lawyer*
Irish, Leon Eugene *lawyer, educator, insurance company executive*
†Johnson, Dwight Alan *lawyer*
Kelly, Peter Galbraith *lawyer*
Keyles, Sidney Alan *lawyer*
Knickerbocker, Robert Platt, Jr. *lawyer*
Korzenik, Armand Alexander *lawyer*
Lane-Reticker, Edward *lawyer, educator*
Lotstein, James I. *lawyer*
Lyon, James Burroughs *lawyer*
McKeon, George A. *lawyer*
Merriam, Dwight Haines *lawyer, land use planner*
Merrill, George Vanderneth *lawyer, investment executive*
Middlebrook, Stephen Beach *lawyer*
Miller, Jeffrey Clark *lawyer*
Morrison, Francis Henry *lawyer*
Murtha, John Stephen *lawyer*
Nolan, John Blanchard *lawyer*
O'Connor, Richard Dennis *lawyer*
Owen, H. Martyn *lawyer*
Pinney, Sidney Dillingham, Jr. *lawyer*
Quinn, Andrew Peter, Jr. *lawyer, insurance executive*
Richter, Donald Paul *lawyer*
Rome, Donald Lee *lawyer*
Ryan, David Thomas *lawyer*
Schatz, S. Michael *lawyer*
Schatzki, George *law educator*
See, Edmund M. *lawyer*
Seidl, Jane Patricia *lawyer*
Siegel, Robert Gordon *lawyer*
Space, Theodore Maxwell *lawyer*
Spear, H(enry) Dyke N(ewcome), Jr. *lawyer*
Speziale, John Albert *lawyer*
Stone, Dennis J. *law librarian, educator*
Taylor, Allan Bert *lawyer*
Thomas, Calvert *lawyer*
Trachsel, William Henry *corporate lawyer*
Voigt, Richard *lawyer*
Wolman, Martin *lawyer*
Yoskowitz, Irving Benjamin *lawyer, manufacturing company executive*
Zakarian, Albert *lawyer*

Madison
Haas, Frederick Peter *lawyer*

Meriden
Luby, Thomas Stewart *lawyer*

Middlebury
Davis, Joanne Fatse *lawyer*

Milford
Berchem, Robert Lee, Sr. *lawyer*

New Britain
Pearl, Helen Zalkan *lawyer*

New Canaan
Wallace, Kenneth Donald *lawyer*

New Haven
Ackerman, Bruce Arnold *lawyer, educator*
Amar, Akhil Reed *law educator*
Balkin, Jack M. *law educator*
Brilmayer, R. Lea *legal educator, lawyer*
Brown, Ralph Sharp *law educator*
Burt, Robert Amsterdam *lawyer, educator*
Carter, Stephen Lisle *law educator*
Clark, Elias *law educator*
Cohen, Morris Leo *law librarian, educator*
Coleman, Jules L. *law educator*
Damaska, Mirjan Radovan *law educator*
Dearington, Michael *lawyer*
Deutsch, Jan Ginter *law educator*
Duke, Steven Barry *law educator*
Ellickson, Robert Chester *law educator*
Elliott, Edwin Donald, Jr. *law educator, federal administrator, environmental lawyer*
Fiss, Owen M. *law educator*
Gastwirth, Donald Edward *lawyer, literary agent*
Gewirtz, Paul D. *lawyer*
Goldstein, Abraham S. *lawyer, educator*
Goldstein, Joseph *law educator*
Gordon, Robert W. *law educator*
Graetz, Michael J. *law educator*
Greenfield, James Robert *lawyer*
Hansmann, Henry Baethke *law educator*
Holder, Angela Roddey *lawyer, educator*
Johnstone, Quintin *legal educator*
Klevorick, Alvin K. *law and economics educator*
Koh, Harold Hongju *law educator*
Kronman, Anthony Townsend *lawyer, educator*
Langbein, John Harriss *lawyer, educator*
Lipson, Leon *law educator*
Logue, Frank *arbitrator, mediator, urban consultant, former mayor New Haven*
Marshall, Burke *law educator*
Mashaw, Jerry L. *lawyer, educator*
Priest, George L. *law educator*
Reisman, William M. *lawyer, educator*
Romano, Roberta *law educator*
Rose-Ackerman, Susan *law and political economy educator*
Simon, John Gerald *law educator*
Stith, Kate *legal educator*
Tilson, John Quillin *lawyer*
Wizner, Stephen *law educator*

New Milford
Edmondson, John Richard *lawyer, pharmaceutical manufacturing company executive*

Newington
Sabatini, Vincent Fernando *lawyer*

Norfolk
Lambros, Lambros John *lawyer, petroleum company executive*

Norwalk
Bergere, C(lifford) Wendell, Jr. *lawyer*
Bermas, Stephen *lawyer*
Cammaker, Sheldon Ira *lawyer*

Orange
Clark, John Phelps *lawyer, automotive executive*

Redding
Russell, Allan David *lawyer*

Riverside
Lovejoy, Allen Fraser *retired lawyer*

Shelton
Harvey, Michael Lee *lawyer, transportation executive*

Sherman
Piel, William, Jr. *retired lawyer*

Simsbury
Long, Michael Thomas *lawyer, manufacturing company executive*

Southport
Greene, Herbert Bruce *lawyer, merchant banker*

Stamford
Adams, Taggart D. *lawyer*
Barton, James Miller *lawyer*
Bowen, Patrick Harvey *lawyer, consultant*
Conti, Lee Ann *lawyer*
†Critelli, Michael J. *lawyer, manufacturing executive*
Davison, Endicott Peabody *lawyer*
Dederick, Ronald Osburn *lawyer*
Dolian, Robert Paul *lawyer*
Ginsky, Marvin H. *lawyer, corporate executive*
Kloster, Burton John, Jr. *lawyer*
Knag, Paul Everett *lawyer*
Lee, Charles Tomerlin *lawyer*
Lowman, George Frederick *lawyer*
Margolis, Emanuel *lawyer, educator*
McGeeney, John Stephen *lawyer*
McGrath, Richard Paul *lawyer*
Merritt, William Alfred, Jr. *lawyer, telecommunications company executive*
Nichols, Ralph Arthur *lawyer*
Perle, Eugene Gabriel *lawyer*
Riggs, Douglas A. *lawyer*
Schectman, Herbert A. *lawyer, corporate executive*
Schoonmaker, Samuel Vail, III *lawyer*
Sisley, G. William *lawyer*
Skidd, Thomas Patrick, Jr. *lawyer*
Spindler, John Frederick *lawyer*
Stapleton, James Francis *lawyer*
Strone, Michael Jonathan *lawyer*
Twardy, Stanley Albert, Jr. *lawyer*
Weitzel, William Conrad, Jr. *lawyer*
Wiggins, Rosalind Zeldina *lawyer*
Wilhelm, Gayle Brian *lawyer*

Stonington
Dupont, Ralph Paul *lawyer, educator*
Van Rees, Cornelius S. *lawyer*

Torrington
Wall, Robert Anthony, Jr. *lawyer*

Waterbury
Glass, Robert Davis *state legal administrator*

West Hartford
Conard, Frederick Underwood, Jr. *lawyer*
Libassi, Frank Peter *lawyer, dean*
Whitman, Robert *lawyer, educator*

Westport
Albani, Suzanne Beardsley *lawyer*
Cederbaum, Eugene E. *lawyer*
Coleman, Joel Clifford *lawyer*
Daw, Harold John *lawyer*

Wilton
Buchanan, William Hobart, Jr. *lawyer, publishing company executive*
Fricke, Richard John *lawyer*
Green, John Orne *lawyer*
Lamb, Frederic Davis *lawyer*
Raikes, Charles FitzGerald *lawyer*

Windsor
Stigler, David Mack *lawyer*

Woodbury
Marsching, Ronald Lionel *lawyer, former precision instrument company executive*

DELAWARE

Dover
Ennis, Bruce Clifford *lawyer*

Newark
Mullen, Regina Marie *lawyer*

Wilmington
Bader, John Merwin *lawyer*
†Baumann, Julian Henry, Jr. *lawyer*
Bell, Daniel Long, Jr. *lawyer, utilities executive*
Bowler, Mary E. *lawyer*
Carpenter, Edmund Nelson, II *lawyer, retired*
Clark, Esther Frances *legal educator*
Connolly, Arthur Guild *lawyer, partner emeritus*
DiLiberto, Richard Anthony, Jr. *lawyer*
Du Pont, Pierre Samuel, IV *lawyer, former governor of Delaware*
Elliott, Richard Gibbons, Jr. *lawyer*
†Engelmann, Glenn Matthew *lawyer*
Fenton, Wendell *lawyer*
Frank, George Andrew *lawyer*
Gilliam, James H., Jr. *lawyer*
Green, James Samuel *lawyer*
Gross, Lawrence Alan *lawyer*
Herdeg, John Andrew *lawyer*
Kimmel, Morton Richard *lawyer*
Kirkpatrick, Andrew Booth, Jr. *lawyer*
Malloy, John Richard *lawyer, chemical company executive*
Meitner, Pamela *lawyer, educator*
Mekler, Arlen B. *lawyer, chemist*
Morris, Kenneth Donald *lawyer*
Partnoy, Ronald Allen *lawyer*
Rich, Michael Joseph *lawyer*
†Riegel, John Kent *corporate lawyer*
Rothschild, Steven James *lawyer*
Shapiro, Irving Saul *lawyer*
Skolas, John Argyle *lawyer*
Stone, F. L. Peter *lawyer*
†Sullivan, Lawrence Matthew *lawyer*
Sutton, Richard Lauder *lawyer*
Turk, S. Maynard *lawyer*
Ward, Rodman, Jr. *lawyer*
Welch, Edward P. *lawyer*
Wier, Richard Royal, Jr. *lawyer, inventor*
Willis, Franklin Knight *lawyer, environmental services company executive*

DISTRICT OF COLUMBIA

Washington
Aaronson, David Ernest *lawyer, educator*
†Abbott, Alden Francis *lawyer, government official, educator*
Abeles, Charles Calvert *retired lawyer*
Ablard, Charles David *lawyer*
Abrecht, Mary Ellen Benson *lawyer*
Acheson, David Campion *lawyer, author, policy analyst*
Acker, Lawrence G. *lawyer*
Ackerson, Nels J(ohn) *lawyer*
Adams, John Jillson *lawyer*
Adams, Thomas Lynch, Jr. *lawyer*
Adamson, Terrence Burdett *lawyer*
Adler, Howard, Jr. *lawyer*
Adler, Howard Bruce *lawyer*
Adler, Robert Martin *lawyer*
Aisenberg, Irwin Morton *lawyer*
Alberger, William Relph *lawyer, government official*
Albertson, Fred W(oodward) *retired lawyer, radio engineer*
Albertson, Terry L. *lawyer*
Alexander, Bettina M. *lawyer*
Alexander, Clifford Joseph *lawyer*
Alexander, Donald Crichton *lawyer*
Allen, Toni K. *lawyer*
Allen, William Hayes *lawyer*
Allera, Edward John *lawyer*
Altman, Jeffrey Paul *lawyer*
Aluise, Timothy John *lawyer*
Ambrose, Myles Joseph *lawyer*
Anderson, David Lawrence *lawyer*
Anderson, Frederick Randolph, Jr. *lawyer, law educator*
Anderson, John Bayard *lawyer, educator, former congressman*
Andrews, Mark Joseph *lawyer*
Andrews, William S. *lawyer*
Angarola, Robert Thomas *lawyer*
Anthony, David Vincent *lawyer*
Applebaum, Harvey Milton *lawyer*
Areen, Judith Carol *law educator*
Arent, Albert Ezra *lawyer*
Armitage, Robert Allen *lawyer*
†Ashton, Richard M. *federal lawyer*
Atkin, James Blakesley *lawyer*
Atkinson, Francis Bolling (Frank Atkinson) *lawyer*
Atwood, James R. *lawyer*
Aucutt, Ronald David *lawyer*
Avery, George Allen *lawyer*
Avil, Richard D., Jr. *lawyer*
Axelrod, Jonathan Gans *lawyer*
Ayer, Donald Belton *lawyer*
Ayres, Richard Edward *lawyer*
Bachman, Kenneth Leroy, Jr. *lawyer*
Baer, William J. *lawyer*
Bailey, Patricia Price *lawyer, government official*
Baird, Bruce Allen *lawyer*
Baker, David Harris *lawyer*
Baker, Keith Leon *lawyer*
Ball, (Robert) Markham *lawyer*
Baran, Jan Witold *lawyer, educator*
Bardin, David J. *lawyer*
Barnes, Dennis Norman *lawyer*
Barnes, Donald Michael *lawyer*
Barnes, Mark James *lawyer*
Barnes, Michael Darr *lawyer*
Barnes, Peter *lawyer*
Barnett, Robert Bruce *lawyer*
Barr, Michael Blanton *lawyer*
Barr, William Pelham *lawyer, former attorney general of United States*
Barrett, William H. *lawyer*
Barron, Jerome Aure *law educator*
Bartlett, John Laurence *lawyer*
Bartlett, Michael John *lawyer*
Barusch, Ronald Charles *lawyer*
Baskir, Lawrence M. *lawyer*
Basseches, Robert Treinis *lawyer*
Bassman, Robert Stuart *lawyer*
Bates, John Cecil, Jr. *lawyer*
Baumgarten, Jon A. *lawyer*
Bayh, Birch Evans, Jr. *lawyer, former senator*
Baynard, Ernest Cornish, III *lawyer*
Bear, Dinah *lawyer*
Beatty, Richard Scrivener *lawyer*
Becker, Brandon *lawyer*
Becker, William Watters *lawyer*
Beckett, William Wade *lawyer*
Beckler, Richard William *lawyer*
Beckwith, Edward Jay *lawyer*
Bednar, Richard John *lawyer, law educator*
Beerbower, Cynthia Gibson *lawyer*
Beisner, John Herbert *lawyer*
Beizer, Robert A. *lawyer*
Belford, Jane Golden *lawyer*
Bell, James Frederick *lawyer*
Bell, Olin Nile *lawyer*
Beller, Herbert N. *lawyer*
Bello, Judith Hippler *lawyer*
Belman, Murray Joel *lawyer*
Belmar, Warren *lawyer*
Belter, Leonard W. *lawyer*
Bendernagel, James F., Jr. *lawyer*
Benjamin, Ben E. *lawyer*
Bennett, Alexander Elliot *lawyer*
†Bennett, Marian Clae *lawyer*
Bennett, Robert Stephen *lawyer*
Ben-Veniste, Richard *lawyer*
Berl, Joseph M. *lawyer*
Berlack, Evan Raden *lawyer*
Berlin, Kenneth *lawyer*
Berman, Marshall Fox *lawyer*
Berman, Paul J. *lawyer*
Berner, Frederic George, Jr. *lawyer*
Bernhard, Berl *lawyer*
Bernstein, Caryl Salomon *lawyer*
Bernstein, Mitchell Harris *lawyer*
Berry, Max Nathan *lawyer*
Berryman, Richard Byron *lawyer*
Berz, David R. *lawyer*
Best, Judah *lawyer*
Bevan, Robert Lewis *lawyer*
Bickart, David O. *lawyer*
Bickel, David Robert *lawyer*
Biddle, Timothy Maurice *lawyer*
Bieber, Sander M. *lawyer*
Bierman, James Norman *lawyer*
Bingaman, Anne K. *lawyer*
Bishop, Wayne Staton *lawyer*
Bittman, William Omar *lawyer*
Black, Stephen F. *lawyer*
Blaine, Barbara S. *lawyer*
Blair, William McCormick, Jr. *lawyer*
Blake, Jonathan Dewey *lawyer*
Blazek-White, Doris *lawyer*
Bleakley, Peter Kimberley *lawyer*
Bleicher, Samuel Abram *lawyer*
Bliss, Donald Tiffany, Jr. *lawyer*
Bloch, Richard Isaac *labor arbitrator*
Bloch, Susan Low *law educator*
Bloom, David I. *lawyer*
Blume, Jack Paul *retired lawyer*
Blumenfeld, Sue Deborah *lawyer*
Blumenthal, Ronnie *lawyer*
Blumenthal, William *lawyer*
Bodner, John, Jr. *lawyer*
Boehm, Steven Bruce *lawyer*
Boese, John T. *lawyer*
Bogard, Lawrence Joseph *lawyer*
Boggs, George Trenholm *lawyer*
Boland, Christopher Thomas, II *lawyer*
Bolton, John Robert *lawyer, former government official*
Bonner, Walter Joseph *lawyer*
Bono, Gaspare Joseph *lawyer*
Bonvillian, William Boone *lawyer*
Born, Brooksley Elizabeth *lawyer*
Borsari, George Robert, Jr. *lawyer, broadcaster*
Boskey, Bennett *lawyer*
Bowe, Richard Welbourn *lawyer*
Boyd, Stephen Mather *arbitrator, mediator, lawyer*
Boyle, Terrence John *lawyer*
Braden, Efrem Mark *lawyer*
Bradford, William Allen, Jr. *lawyer*
Bradford, William Hollis, Jr. *lawyer*
Brady, Phillip Donley *lawyer*
Brady, Richard Allen *lawyer*
Branson, David John *lawyer*
Brenner, Janet Maybin Walker *lawyer*
Briggs, Alan Leonard *lawyer*
Broches, Aron *international lawyer, arbitrator*

Brockway, David Hunt lawyer
Bronstein, Alvin J. lawyer
Brooke, Edward William lawyer, former senator
Brooks, Daniel Townley lawyer
Broom, Richard Stuart lawyer
Brown, Barbara Berish lawyer
Brown, Charles Freeman lawyer
Brown, David Nelson lawyer
Brown, Donald Arthur lawyer
Brown, George Leslie legislative affairs and business development consultant, former manufacturing company executive, former lieutenant governor
Brown, Michael Arthur lawyer
Brown, Omer Forrest, II lawyer
Brown, Preston lawyer
Brown, Thomas Philip, III lawyer
Browne, Richard Cullen lawyer
Brownstein, Philip Nathan lawyer
Bruce, E(stel) Edward lawyer
Bruce, John Foster lawyer
Bruce, Robert Rockwell lawyer
Bruder, George Frederick lawyer
Brunner, Thomas William lawyer
Brunsvold, Brian Garrett lawyer, educator
Bryant, Arthur H. lawyer
Buc, Nancy Lillian lawyer
Bucholtz, Harold Ronald lawyer
Buckley, Christopher Henry, Jr. lawyer
Buckley, Jeremiah Stephen lawyer
Bucklin, Donald Thomas lawyer
Buechner, Jack W(illiam) lawyer, government affairs consultant
Buente, David T. environmental lawyer
Buergenthal, Thomas lawyer, educator, international judge
Buffon, Charles Edward lawyer
†Buki, Dennis Gabor lawyer
Burack, Michael Leonard lawyer
Burch, John Thomas, Jr. lawyer
Buresh, C. John lawyer
Burk, Francis Lewis, Jr. lawyer, federal
Burka, Robert Alan lawyer
Burns, Stephen Gilbert lawyer
Burt, Jeffrey Amsterdam lawyer
Busby, David lawyer
Buscemi, Peter lawyer
Busey, George Brian lawyer
Butler, Michael Francis lawyer
Calamaro, Raymond Stuart lawyer
Calhoun, Michael Jeffery lawyer
Calvani, Terry lawyer, former government official
Campbell, Edmund Douglas lawyer
Campbell, James Sargent lawyer
Candon, Mary Eva lawyer
Canfield, Edward Francis lawyer, business executive
Caplin, Mortimer Maxwell lawyer, educator
Cardozo, Michael Hart lawyer
Carey, Hugh L. lawyer, former governor
†Carey, John Patrick, III lawyer
Carey, Sarah Collins lawyer
Carlisle, Linda Elizabeth lawyer
Carneal, George Upshur lawyer
Carney, Robert Thomas lawyer
Carome, Patrick Joseph lawyer
Carpenter, Sheila Jane lawyer
Carr, Lawrence Edward, Jr. lawyer
Carr, Ronald Gene lawyer
Carroll, Raoul Lord lawyer, investment banker
Carrow, Milton Michael lawyer, educator
Carter, Barry Edward lawyer, educator, administrator
Case, Stephen H. lawyer
Casellas, Gilbert F. lawyer, federal agency administrator
Casey, Bernard J. lawyer
Cashen, Henry Christopher, II lawyer, former government official
Casserly, James Lund lawyer
Cassidy, Robert Charles, Jr. lawyer
Cassler, Robert Leslie lawyer
Casson, Joseph Edward lawyer
Cavanaugh, Gordon lawyer
Chabot, Philip Louis, Jr. lawyer
Chameides, Steven B. lawyer
Chanin, Leah Farb law library administrator, lawyer, consultant, law educator
Chanin, Michael Henry lawyer
Chanin, Robert Howard lawyer
Cheston, Sheila Carol lawyer
Chierichella, John W. lawyer
Chopko, Mark E. lawyer
Christensen, Karen Kay lawyer
Christian, Betty Jo lawyer
Christian, Ernest Silsbee, Jr. lawyer
Christina, Thomas Michael lawyer
Church, Dale Walker lawyer
Chused, Richard Harris law educator
Cicconi, James William lawyer
Clagett, Brice McAdoo lawyer, writer
Clark, Robert William, III lawyer
Clark, Roger Arthur lawyer
Clegg, Roger Burton lawyer
Clifford, Clark McAdams lawyer
Close, David Palmer lawyer
Clubb, Bruce Edwin lawyer
Cobb, Calvin Hayes, Jr. lawyer
Coerper, Milo George lawyer
Coffield, Shirley A. lawyer
Cohen, Charles I. lawyer
Cohen, Edward Barth lawyer
Cohen, Lewis Isaac lawyer
Cohen, Stephen Bruce law educator
Cohn, Herbert B. lawyer
Cohn, Ronald Dennis lawyer
Cohn, Sherman Louis lawyer, educator
Colbert, Edward Tuck lawyer
Colby, William Egan lawyer, international consultant
Cole, Charles Glaston lawyer
Cole, John Pope, Jr. lawyer
Coleman, William Thaddeus, Jr. lawyer
Collins, Daniel Francis lawyer
Collins, Jeremiah C. lawyer
Colman, Richard Thomas lawyer
Colson, Earl M. lawyer
Colton, Sterling Don lawyer, business executive
Conklin, Kenneth Edward lawyer, industry executive
Conlon, Michael William lawyer
Connell, Gerald A. lawyer
Constandy, John Peter lawyer
Conti, William J. lawyer
Converse, Robert E., Jr. lawyer
Cook, Harry Clayton, Jr. lawyer
Cooney, John Fontana lawyer
Cooper, Alan Samuel lawyer
Cooper, Richard Melvin lawyer
Cope, John R(obert) lawyer
†Coppelman, Peter David lawyer, government official
Cortese, Alfred William, Jr. lawyer, consultant
Coursen, Christopher Dennison lawyer
Cox, Chapman Beecher lawyer, corporate executive
Cox, Kenneth Allen lawyer, communications consultant
Craft, Robert Homan, Jr. lawyer
Cragin, Charles Langmaid lawyer
Craig, Gregory Bestor lawyer
Crampton, Scott Paul lawyer
Crowell, Eldon Hubbard lawyer
†Cruden, John Charles lawyer
Crump, John lawyer
Cullen, Thomas Francis, Jr. lawyer
Cummings, Frank lawyer
Curtin, Kevin Gerard lawyer
Curtin, William Joseph lawyer
Custer, Benjamin Scott, Jr. lawyer
Cutler, Lloyd Norton lawyer, company director
Cymrot, Mark Alan lawyer
Czarra, Edgar F., Jr. lawyer
Daddario, Emilio Quincy lawyer
Dalley, George Albert lawyer
Damus, Robert George lawyer
Daniel, Aubrey Marshall, III lawyer
Daniels, Diana M. lawyer
Daniels, Michael Paul lawyer
Dankner, Donald K. lawyer
Danziger, Martin Breitel lawyer
Dash, Samuel lawyer, educator
Dauster, William Gary lawyer, economist
Davidow, Joel lawyer
†Davidson, Daniel I. lawyer
Davidson, Daniel Morton lawyer
Davidson, Michael lawyer
Davidson, Tom William lawyer
†Davis, Franklin Gary lawyer
Davis, Ross Dane lawyer
Davison, Calvin lawyer
Day, J(ames) Edward lawyer, former postmaster general
Days, Drew S., III lawyer, law educator
Dean, Paul Regis law educator
Deckelbaum, Nelson lawyer
Dees, C. Stanley lawyer
DeGrandi, Joseph Anthony lawyer
deKieffer, Donald Eulette lawyer
Deleon, Patrick Henry lawyer
de Leon, Sylvia A. lawyer
Dembling, Paul Gerald lawyer, former government official
Dempsey, David B. lawyer
DeMuth, Christopher Clay lawyer, foundation executive
Denger, Michael L. lawyer
Dennin, Joseph Francis lawyer, former government official
Denniston, John Baker lawyer
Denvir, James Peter, III lawyer
Determan, Sara-Ann lawyer
Devaney, Dennis Martin lawyer, legal educator
DiCello, Francis P. lawyer
Dickstein, Sidney lawyer
Diercks, Walter Elmer lawyer
Dietrich, Paul George lawyer
diGenova, Joseph E. lawyer
Dobkin, James Allen lawyer, engineer, artist
Docter, Charles Alfred lawyer, former state legislator
Dolan, Edward Charles lawyer
Dolan, Michael William lawyer
Donegan, Charles Edward lawyer, educator
Donohoe, Charles Richard general patent counsel
Doolittle, Jesse William, Jr. lawyer
Dorsen, David M(ilton) lawyer
Dowd, John Maguire lawyer
Dowd, Thomas F. lawyer
Dowley, Joseph Kyran lawyer, member congressional staff
Downey, Arthur Thomas, III lawyer
Downs, Clark Evans lawyer
Doyle, Gerard Francis lawyer
Doyle, Joyce Ann lawyer
Drabkin, Murray lawyer
Drinan, Robert Frederick lawyer, former congressman, educator, clergyman
DuBoff, Scott M. lawyer
Duke, Paul Robert lawyer
Duncan, Charles Tignor lawyer
Duncan, John Dean, Jr. lawyer
Dunn, H. Stewart, Jr. lawyer
Dunn, Loretta Lynn lawyer
Dunne, John Richard lawyer
Dunner, Donald Robert lawyer
Durney, Michael Cavalier lawyer
Duvall, Donald Knox lawyer
Dwyer, Jeffry R. lawyer
Dye, Alan Louis lawyer
Dye, Stuart S. lawyer
Dyk, Timothy Belcher lawyer, educator
Earle, Ralph, II lawyer
Earle, Richard Alan lawyer
Eastman, Ronald D. lawyer
Eastment, Thomas James lawyer
Easton, John Jay, Jr. lawyer
Eckart, Dennis Edward lawyer, former congressman
Eddy, David Corbett lawyer
Edelman, Marian Wright (Mrs. Peter B. Edelman) lawyer
Edelman, Peter Benjamin lawyer
Edes, Nik Bruce lawyer
Edles, Gary J. lawyer
Edson, Charles Louis lawyer, educator
Edwards, Tony M. lawyer
Efron, Marc Fred lawyer
Efron, Samuel lawyer
Efros, Ellen Ann lawyer
Ehrenhaft, Peter David lawyer
Eisenberg, Jonathan Neil lawyer
Eisenberg, Meyer lawyer
Eisenberg, Milton lawyer
Eisenstat, David H. lawyer
Eisner, Neil Robert lawyer
†Elcano, Mary S. lawyer, federal agency administrator
Ellicott, John LeMoyne lawyer
Elliott, Robert John lawyer
Elliott, Warren G. lawyer
Ellis, Courtenay lawyer
Ellis, Lee T., Jr. lawyer
Elmer, Brian Christian lawyer
Elrod, Eugene Richard lawyer
Elwood, William Edward lawyer
Emerson, John Bonnell lawyer, partner
Emery, Nancy Beth lawyer
Emmett, Robert Addis, III lawyer
Englert, Roy Theodore lawyer
Engman, Lewis August lawyer, trade association executive, former government official
Ennis, Bruce J. lawyer
Epstein, David lawyer, arbitrator
Epstein, Gary Marvin lawyer
Epstein, Lionel Charles lawyer
Epstien, Jay Alan lawyer
†Erichsen, Peter Christian lawyer, government official
Ernst, Daniel Robinson law educator, legal historian
Eskridge, William Nichol, Jr. law educator
Esslinger, John Thomas lawyer
Etters, Ronald Milton lawyer
Evans, David C. lawyer
Everett, Ralph Bernard lawyer
Ewing, Ky Pepper, Jr. lawyer
Fahrenkopf, Frank Joseph, Jr. lawyer
Fairbanks, Richard Monroe, III lawyer, former ambassador at large
Falk, David B. lawyer, professional athletic representative
Falk, James Harvey, Sr. lawyer
Fant, Lester G., III lawyer
Farabow, Ford Franklin, Jr. lawyer
Farer, Tom Joel legal educator, writer, consultant
Farmer, Donald A(rthur), Jr. lawyer
Farmer, Thomas Laurence lawyer
Farrell, J. Michael lawyer
Fasman, Zachary Dean lawyer
Faust, Marcus G. lawyer
Favretto, Richard J. lawyer
Fedders, John Michael lawyer
Feffer, Gerald Alan lawyer
Feighan, Edward Farrell lawyer, former congressman
Feinberg, Kenneth Roy lawyer, law educator
Feld, Jonathan S. lawyer
Feldhaus, Stephen Martin lawyer
Feldman, Adrienne Arsht lawyer, broadcasting company executive, banking executive
Feldman, Clarice Rochelle lawyer
Feldman, Mark B. lawyer
Feldman, Myer lawyer
Feldman, Roger David lawyer
Feller, Lloyd Harris lawyer
Fellner, Baruch Abraham lawyer
Fels, Nicholas Wolff lawyer
Fendrich, Roger Paul lawyer
Fenton, Kathryn Marie lawyer
Ferguson, Thomas Crooks lawyer
Ferman, Irving lawyer, educator
Ferrara, Ralph C. lawyer
Ferris, Charles Daniel lawyer, former government official
Feuerstein, Donald Martin lawyer
Field, Andrea Bear lawyer
Fielding, Fred Fisher lawyer
Fields, Wendy Lynn lawyer
Finkel, Eugene Jay lawyer
Finn, Timothy John lawyer
Fiorini, John E., III lawyer
Firestone, Charles Morton lawyer, educator
Fishburne, Benjamin P., III lawyer
Fisher, Bart Steven lawyer, educator
Fisher, Benjamin Chatburn lawyer
Fisher, Joel Hilton lawyer
Fitzhugh, David Michael lawyer
Fitzpatrick, James Franklin lawyer
Flagg, Ronald Simon lawyer
Flannery, Ellen Joanne lawyer
Fleischaker, Marc L. lawyer
Fleit, Martin lawyer
Fleming, Mack Gerald lawyer
Flowe, Carol Connor lawyer
Fogt, Howard W., Jr. lawyer
†Fois, Andrew lawyer, educator
Ford, Robert Nelson government lawyer
Foreman, Anne N. lawyer
Foreman, Dennis I. federal official, lawyer
Forester, John Gordon, Jr. lawyer
Forrest, Herbert Emerson lawyer
Forster, Cecil R., Jr. lawyer
Fortune, Terence John lawyer
Fortuno, Victor M. lawyer
Frame, Nancy Davis lawyer
Frank, Richard Asher lawyer, health products executive
Frank, Theodore David lawyer
Frankle, Edward Alan lawyer
Freedman, Anthony Stephen lawyer
Freedman, Walter lawyer
Freer, Robert Elliott, Jr. lawyer
Freije, Philip Charles lawyer
Frey, Andrew Lewis lawyer
Friedlander, Charles lawyer
Friedlander, James Stuart lawyer
Friedlander, Michael E. lawyer
Friedman, Alvin lawyer
Friedman, Paul Lawrence lawyer
†Friedman, Paul Richard government lawyer
Froehlich, Laurence Alan lawyer
Frost, Edmund Bowen lawyer
Fugate, Wilbur Lindsay lawyer
Fullerton, Lawrence Rae lawyer
Fulton, Richard Alsina lawyer
Futrell, John William institute executive, lawyer
Gaguine, Benito lawyer
Gale, Joseph H. lawyer
Gardner, William Leonard lawyer
Garland, Merrick Brian lawyer
Garrett, Theodore Louis lawyer
Garrish, Theodore John lawyer
Garvey, John Leo lawyer, educator
Gary, Marc lawyer
Gaynor, Kevin Allen lawyer
†Gelacak, Michael S. legal administrator
Geller, Kenneth Steven lawyer
Gellhorn, Ernest Albert Eugene lawyer
Geltman, Edward A. lawyer
Geniesse, Robert John lawyer
George, W. Peyton lawyer
Gerson, Stuart Michael lawyer
Gertig, June Munford lawyer
Gibbs, Lawrence B. lawyer
Gideon, Kenneth Wayne lawyer
Gilfoyle, Nathalie Floyd Preston lawyer
Gilliland, James Sevier lawyer
Ginsburg, Charles David lawyer
Ginsburg, Gilbert J. lawyer, law educator
Ginsburg, Martin David lawyer, educator
Gitner, Geoffrey P. lawyer
Glancz, Ronald Robert lawyer
Glanzer, Seymour lawyer
Gleason, Jean Wilbur lawyer
Glick, Leslie Alan lawyer
Glick, Warren W. lawyer, banker
Glosser, Jeffrey Mark lawyer
Goelzer, Daniel Lee lawyer
Goldberg, Avrum M. lawyer
Goldberg, Larry Joel lawyer
Goldberg, Seth A. lawyer
Goldblatt, Steven Harris law educator
Golden, Cornelius Joseph, Jr. lawyer
Goldfarb, Ronald Lawrence lawyer
Goldman, Eugene I. lawyer
Goldsmith, Willis Jay lawyer
Goldstein, Frank Robert lawyer
Goldstein, Michael B. lawyer
Goldstein, N. Linda lawyer
Goodrich, Nathaniel Herman lawyer, former government official
Gorelick, Jamie Shona lawyer
Gorinson, Stanley M. lawyer
Gorman, Joyce J(ohanna) lawyer
Gostin, Lawrence lawyer
Gottschalk, Thomas A. lawyer
Grabow, John Charles lawyer
Graefe, Frederick H. lawyer
Graham, Thomas Richard lawyer
Grant, David Alistair lawyer
Gray, Clayland Boyden lawyer
Green, Donald Hugh lawyer
Green, Richard Alan lawyer
Green, Robert Lamar, Jr. lawyer
Green, Thomas Charles lawyer
Greenberg, Robert E. lawyer
Greenberger, I. Michael lawyer
Greene, Ronald J. lawyer
Greene, Timothy Geddes lawyer
Greenebaum, Leonard Charles lawyer
Greenspan, Michael Alan lawyer
Greenwald, Gerald Bernard lawyer
Greif, Joseph lawyer
Grenier, Edward Joseph, Jr. lawyer
Gribbon, Daniel McNamara lawyer
Grier, Phillip Michael lawyer, association executive
Griffin, Joseph Parker lawyer, educator
Grimes, Larry Bruce lawyer
Groner, Samuel Brian lawyer
Gross, Richard Alan lawyer
Grossman, Joanne Barbara lawyer
Guandolo, John lawyer
Gulland, Eugene D. lawyer
Gustini, Raymond J. lawyer
Gutman, Harry Largman lawyer
Gutter, Samuel I. lawyer
Guttman, Egon law educator
Haft, Robert J. law educator
Hahn, Gilbert, Jr. lawyer
Hahn, John Stephen lawyer
†Halamandaris, Val J(ohn) lawyer, association executive
Haley, George Williford Boyce lawyer
Hall, Edwin King lawyer
Hall, Elliott Sawyer lawyer
Halpern, James Bladen lawyer
Halvorson, Newman Thorbus, Jr. lawyer
Hammond, Robert Alexander, III lawyer
Hansen, Orval lawyer, former congressman
Hanson, Jean Elizabeth lawyer
Hardesty, Charles Howard, Jr. lawyer
Harding, Bertrand M., Jr. lawyer
Hardy, Robert Gerald lawyer
Harkrader, Carleton Allen lawyer
Harman, William Boys, Jr. lawyer
Harper, Conrad Kenneth lawyer and government official
Harrington, Anthony Stephen lawyer
Harris, Don Victor, Jr. lawyer
Harris, Jeffrey lawyer
Harris, Judith Linda lawyer
†Harris, Scott Blake lawyer
Harris, Steven B. lawyer
Harrison, Donald lawyer
Harrison, Earl David lawyer, real estate executive
Harrison, Ellen Kroll lawyer
Harrison, Marion Edwyn lawyer
†Hart, Christopher Alvin lawyer
Harvey, David Michael lawyer
Hass, Lawrence Joel lawyer
Hassett, Joseph Mark lawyer
Hathaway, Fred William lawyer
Hauser, Richard Alan lawyer
Havens, Charles W., III lawyer
Hawke, John Daniel, Jr. lawyer
Hawkins, Edward Jackson lawyer
Hayes, David J. lawyer
Hayes, Webb Cook, III lawyer
Haynes, R. Michael lawyer
Haynes, William J(ames), II lawyer
Hays, Michael DeWayne lawyer
Haythe, Winston McDonald law educator, consultant, real estate investor
Head, Anita Kessler law educator
Heckman, Jerome Harold lawyer
Heffernan, James Vincent lawyer
Heffron, Howard A. lawyer
Hefter, Laurence Roy lawyer
Heintz, John Edward lawyer
Heller, Jack Isaac lawyer
Heller, John Roderick, III lawyer, business executive
Hemley, M. Rogue lawyer
Henderson, Douglas Boyd lawyer
Henderson, Thomas Henry, Jr. lawyer, legal association executive
Henke, Michael John lawyer, educator
Hennessy, Ellen Anne lawyer, educator
Henry, Harold lawyer
Herlach, Mark Dayton lawyer
Herzog, Richard Barnard lawyer
Herzstein, Robert Erwin lawyer
Hewitt, Paul Buck lawyer
Hibbert, Robert George lawyer, food company executive
Hickey, Edward Joseph, Jr. lawyer, diplomatic consultant
Higgins, John Edward, Jr. lawyer
Hill, Jerry C. lawyer
Hill, Stephen S. lawyer
Hills, Carla Anderson lawyer, former federal official
Hills, Roderick M. lawyer, business executive, former government official
Hinds, Richard De Courcy lawyer
Hirsch, Robert Bruce lawyer
Hirschhorn, Eric Leonard lawyer
Hobbs, Caswell O., III lawyer
Hobbs, J. Timothy, Sr. lawyer
Hobbs, Vivian Lee lawyer
Hobelman, Carl Donald lawyer
Hobson, James Richmond lawyer
Hochberg, Jerome A. lawyer
Hodgson, Morgan Day lawyer
Hodson, Kenneth Joe lawyer, criminal justice consultant, retired army officer
Hoffman, E. Leslie lawyer
Hoffman, Joel Elihu lawyer
†Ho-Gonzalez, William lawyer
Holden, James Phillip lawyer
Holder, Eric H. prosecutor
Holmer, Alan Freeman lawyer

Holmstead, Jeffrey R. lawyer
Hope, Judith Richards lawyer
Horahan, Edward Bernard, III lawyer
Hordell, Michael A. lawyer
Horlick, Gary Norman lawyer, legal educator
Horn, Charles M. lawyer
Horn, Donald Herbert lawyer
Horne, Michael Stewart lawyer
Horsky, Charles Antone lawyer
Hosenball, S. Neil lawyer
Houlihan, David Paul lawyer
House, W(illiam) Michael lawyer
Howard, Glen Scott lawyer
Howard, Jeffrey Hjalmar lawyer
Howard, Kenneth Calvin, Jr. lawyer
Howrey, Edward F. lawyer
Hughes, James Charles lawyer
Hughes, Marija Matich law librarian
Humphreys, Robert Russell lawyer
Hunnicutt, Charles Alvin lawyer
Hutt, Peter Barton lawyer
Hylden, Thomas lawyer
Hyman, Lester Samuel lawyer
Ingoldsby, Thomas M. lawyer
Irving, John Stiles, Jr. lawyer
Isbell, David Bradford lawyer, legal educator
Isenbergh, Max lawyer, musician, educator
Israel, Barry John lawyer
Iwry, J. Mark lawyer
Jackson, Neal A. lawyer
Jacobsen, Magdalena Gretchen mediator, federal agency executive
Jacobson, David Edward lawyer
Janetatos, Jack Peter lawyer
Jankowsky, Joel lawyer
Jaskiewicz, Leonard Albert retired lawyer
Javits, Joshua Moses lawyer
Jessup, Philip Caryl, Jr. lawyer, museum executive
Jetton, C. Loring, Jr. lawyer
†Jin, Leslie R. lawyer
Joelson, Mark Rene lawyer
†Johnson, Broderick D. lawyer
Johnson, David Raymond lawyer
Johnson, John Griffith, Jr. lawyer
Johnson, Oliver Thomas, Jr. lawyer
Johnson, Philip McBride lawyer
Johnson, Richard Clark lawyer
Johnson, Richard Tenney lawyer
Jones, Aidan Drexel lawyer
Jones, Boisfeuillet, Jr. lawyer, newspaper executive
Jones, Erika Ziebarth lawyer
Jones, Gerald Winfield lawyer
Jones, Richard Herbert lawyer, former government official
Jones, Theodore Lawrence lawyer
Jordan, Emma Coleman law educator
Jordan, Robert Elijah, III lawyer
Jordan, Vernon Eulion, Jr. lawyer, former association official
Joseph, Daniel Mordecai lawyer
Jost, Peter Hafner lawyer
Journey, Drexel Dahlke lawyer
Kabel, Robert James lawyer
Kafka, Gerald Andrew lawyer
Kahan, Jonathan Seth lawyer
Kahn, Edwin Leonard lawyer
Kamm, Linda Heller lawyer
Kammerer, Kelly Christian lawyer
Kaplan, Gilbert B. lawyer
Kaplin, William Albert lawyer, educator, consultant
Kapp, Robert Harris lawyer
Kaseman, A. Carl, III lawyer
Kass, Benny Lee lawyer
Kaswell, Maryann McCarthy lawyer
Katz, Sherman E. lawyer
Katzen, Sally lawyer
Kaufman, Thomas Frederick lawyer, legal educator
Kautter, David John lawyer
Kay, Kenneth Robert lawyer
Keane, William K. lawyer
Keener, Mary Lou lawyer
Keeney, E. Andrew lawyer
Keeney, John Christopher lawyer
Keeney, John Christopher, Jr. lawyer
†Keeney, Regina Markey lawyer
Kehoe, Patrick Emmett law librarian, educator
Keiner, R(obert) Bruce, Jr. lawyer
Kellison, James Bruce lawyer
Kellogg, Frederic Rogers lawyer
Kelly, Nancy Frieda Wolicki lawyer
Kelly, William Charles, Jr. lawyer
Kenney, Robert James, Jr. lawyer
Kent, Alan Heywood lawyer
Kent, M. Elizabeth lawyer
Kerxton, Alan Smith lawyer
Kessler, Judd Lewis lawyer
Keys, John R., Jr. lawyer
Kies, Kenneth J. lawyer
Kieve, Loren lawyer
Kiko, Philip George lawyer
Killory, Diane Silberstein lawyer
Kimball, Raymond Joel lawyer
Kimmitt, Robert Michael lawyer, banker, diplomat
†King, Marilou Meehan lawyer, association executive
King, Michelle Davis lawyer
King, Rufus lawyer
Kirby, Thomas Wesley lawyer
Kirtland, John C. lawyer
Kittrell, Steven Dan lawyer
Kittrie, Nicholas N(orbert Nehemiah) law educator, international consultant, author
Klain, Ronald Alan lawyer
Klawiter, Donald Casimir lawyer
†Klein, Joel Irwin lawyer
Klein, Michael Roger lawyer, business executive
Klepper, Martin lawyer
Knapp, George M. lawyer
Knapp, Rosalind Ann lawyer
Knebel, John Albert lawyer, former government official
Knotts, Joseph B. lawyer
Koch, George William lawyer
Koch, Kathleen Day lawyer
Kolasky, William Joseph, Jr. lawyer
Kolman, Mark Herbert lawyer
Konschnik, David Michael lawyer
Korth, Fred lawyer
Korth, Fritz-Alan lawyer
Kovacs, William Lawrence lawyer
Kraemer, Jay Roy lawyer
†Kramer, Aaron J. lawyer
Kramer, Albert H. lawyer
Kramer, Kenneth Stephen lawyer
Kramer, William David lawyer
Krasner, Wendy L. lawyer
Krasnostein, David M. lawyer
Krasnow, Erwin Gilbert lawyer
Kreczko, Alan James lawyer
Kriesberg, Simeon M. lawyer
Kroener, William Frederick, III lawyer
Kronstein, Werner J lawyer
Krump, Gary Joseph lawyer
Kupperman, Helen Slotnick lawyer
Kurrelmeyer, Louis Hayner lawyer
Lahr, Jack Leroy lawyer
Lambert, Jeremiah Daniel lawyer
Lambert, Steven Charles lawyer
Lamm, Carolyn Beth lawyer
Landfair, Stanley W. lawyer
Lane, Bruce Stuart lawyer
Lane, John Dennis lawyer
Lane, Mark lawyer, educator, author
Laporte, Gerald Joseph Sylvestre lawyer
Larroca, Raymond G. lawyer
Larry, David Heath lawyer
Lassman, Malcolm lawyer
Latham, Weldon Hurd lawyer
Latimer, Allie B. lawyer, government official
Laughlin, Felix B. lawyer
Lavine, Henry Wolfe lawyer
Lazarus, Arthur, Jr. lawyer
Lazarus, Kenneth Anthony lawyer
Leary, Thomas Barrett lawyer
Lehner, George Alexander, Jr. lawyer
Lehr, Dennis James lawyer
Leibold, Arthur William, Jr. lawyer
Leiden, Warren Robert law association executive
Leigh, Monroe lawyer
Leiter, Richard Allen law educator, law librarian
Lenhart, James Thomas lawyer
Leon, Richard J. lawyer, former government official
Leonard, Will Ernest, Jr. lawyer
Leshy, John D. lawyer, legal educator
Lessenco, Gilbert Barry lawyer
Lessy, Roy Paul, Jr. lawyer
Lettow, Charles Frederick lawyer
Leva, Marx lawyer
Levine, Henry David lawyer
Levine, Joseph Manney lawyer
Levine, Theodore A. lawyer
Levinson, Daniel Ronald lawyer
Levitas, Elliott Harris lawyer
Levy, David Matthew lawyer
Levy, Mark Irving lawyer
Lew, Ginger lawyer
Lewin, Martin J. lawyer
Lewis, David John lawyer
Lewis, E. Grey lawyer
Lewis, Gregory Scott lawyer
Lewis, William Henry, Jr. lawyer
Libin, Jerome B. lawyer
Lichtenstein, Elissa Charlene legal association executive
Liebman, Ronald Stanley lawyer
Lighthizer, Robert E. lawyer
Lillard, John Franklin, III lawyer
†Lindsey, Seth Mark lawyer, federal agency administrator
Linowitz, Sol Myron lawyer
Lipstein, Robert A. lawyer
†Lister, Sara Elisabeth lawyer
Litan, Robert Eli lawyer, economist
Litman, Harry Peter lawyer, educator
Livingston, Donald Ray lawyer
Loeffler, Robert Hugh lawyer
Loevinger, Lee lawyer
Long, Charles Thomas lawyer
Lopatin, Alan G. lawyer
†Lorne, Simon Michael lawyer
Love, Margaret Colgate lawyer
Love, Michael Kenneth lawyer
Luce, Gregory M. lawyer
Lund, Wendell Luther lawyer
Luskin, Robert David lawyer
Lybecker, Martin Earl lawyer
Lynam, Terence Joseph lawyer
Lyons, Dennis Gerald lawyer
Lyons, Ellis lawyer
MacBeth, Angus lawyer
Macdonald, David Robert lawyer
†MacHare, Peter Allen law librarian
Mackall, Laidler Bowie lawyer
Mackiewicz, Edward Robert lawyer
MacLeod, William Cyrus lawyer, economist
Macrory, Patrick Francis John lawyer
Madden, Murdaugh Stuart lawyer
Madden, William J., Jr. lawyer
Madigan, Kimberly A. mediator, lawyer
Madigan, Michael J. lawyer
Maechling, Charles, Jr. lawyer, educator, writer
Magielnicki, Robert L. lawyer
Maiwurm, James John lawyer
Majev, Howard Rudolph lawyer
Mallory, Charles King, III lawyer
Manatt, Charles T. lawyer
Manbeck, Harry Frederick, Jr. lawyer
Manly, Marc Edward lawyer
Mann, Donegan lawyer
Manning, George Taylor lawyer
Manson, Joseph Lloyd, III lawyer
Manthei, Richard Dale lawyer, health care company executive
Marans, J. Eugene lawyer
Marcuss, Stanley Joseph lawyer
Margeton, Stephen George law librarian
Margolis, Daniel Herbert lawyer
Margolis, Eugene lawyer, government official
Marinaccio, Charles Lindbergh lawyer
Mark, Alan Samuel lawyer
Markoski, Joseph Peter lawyer
Marks, Andrew H. lawyer
Marks, Herbert Edward lawyer
Marks, Leonard Harold lawyer
Marks, Richard Daniel lawyer
†Markus, Kent Richard lawyer
Marquez, Joaquin Alfredo lawyer
Martin, David Briton Hadden, Jr. lawyer
Martin, Guy lawyer
Martin, Keith lawyer
Martin, Thomas Stephen lawyer
Martyak, Joseph J. lawyer
Marvin, Douglas Raymond lawyer
Marzulla, Roger Joseph lawyer
Mathias, Charles McCurdy lawyer, former senator
†Mattingly, J. Virgil, Jr. federal lawyer
May, Gregory Evers lawyer
May, Richard Edward lawyer
May, Timothy James lawyer
Mayers, Daniel Kriegsman lawyer
Mayfield, Richard Heverin lawyer
Mayo, George Washington, Jr. lawyer
Mays, Janice Ann lawyer
Mazo, Mark Elliott lawyer
McAvoy, John Joseph lawyer
McBride, Michael Flynn lawyer
McCabe, Edward Aeneas lawyer, financial services corporation executive
Mc Carthy, Charles Joseph lawyer, former government official
McCarthy, Charles Richard lawyer
McCarthy, David Jerome, Jr. legal educator
Mc Carty, Robert Lee lawyer
McClain, William Thomas lawyer
McCobb, John Bradford, Jr. lawyer
McCoy, Jerry Jack lawyer
McCoy, Neal S. lawyer
McCoy, Patricia Ann law educator, lawyer
McDavid, J. Gary lawyer
McDavid, Janet Louise lawyer
Mc Dermott, Albert Leo lawyer
McDermott, Edward Aloysious lawyer
McDermott, Robert Francis, Jr. lawyer
McElveen, Junius Carlisle, Jr. lawyer
McGarry, J. Michael, III lawyer
Mc Giffert, David Eliot lawyer, former government official
Mc Glothlin, James Harrison lawyer
McGovern, Michael Barbot lawyer
McGrath, Kathryn Bradley lawyer
McGuire, Patricia A. lawyer, academic administrator
McGuirl, Marlene Dana Callis law librarian, educator
McHugh, James Lenahan, Jr. lawyer
McMahon, Joseph Einar lawyer, consultant
Mc Phee, Henry Roemer lawyer
Mc Pherson, Harry Cummings, Jr. lawyer
McQuinn, Michael Rand lawyer
Means, Thomas Cornell lawyer
Medalie, Richard James lawyer
Medero, Joanne Trimble lawyer
Melamed, Arthur Douglas lawyer
Meloy, Sybil Piskur lawyer
Meltzer, Steven Lee lawyer
Mercer, Lee William lawyer, corporate executive, former government agency administrator
Meserve, Richard Andrew lawyer
Meyer, Dennis Irwin lawyer
Meyer, Lawrence George lawyer
Meyers, Tedson Jay lawyer
Michaelson, Martin lawyer
Mickey, Paul F(ogle), Jr. lawyer
Mikva, Abner Joseph lawyer, retired federal judge
Millenson, Debra Ann lawyer
Miller, Andrew Pickens lawyer
Miller, Charles A. lawyer
Miller, H. Todd lawyer
Miller, Herbert John, Jr. lawyer
Miller, John T., Jr. lawyer, educator
Miller, Lawrence A. lawyer
Miller, Marshall Lee lawyer
Miller, Warren Lloyd lawyer
†Milliken, Christine Topping legal association administrator, lawyer
Milstein, Elliott Steven legal educator, academic administrator
Mintz, Seymour Stanley lawyer
Mirabelli, Mario V. lawyer
Mitchell, Roy Shaw lawyer
Mizroch, John F. lawyer
Moates, G. Paul lawyer
Mobbs, Michael Hall lawyer
Mode, Paul J., Jr. lawyer
Moe, Richard Palmer lawyer
Mogel, William Allen lawyer
Montgomery, George Cranwell lawyer, former ambassador
Mooney, Marilyn lawyer
Moring, John Frederick lawyer
Morris, William lawyer
Mostoff, Allan Samuel lawyer, consultant
Muckenfuss, Cantwell Faulkner, III lawyer
Mueller, Robert Swan, III lawyer, former federal official
Muir, J. Dapray lawyer
Muller, Scott William lawyer
Munsell, Elsie Louise lawyer
Muntzing, L(ewis) Manning lawyer
Murphy, Betty Jane Southard (Mrs. Cornelius F. Murphy) lawyer
Murphy, James Paul lawyer
Murphy, John Condron, Jr. lawyer
Murphy, Stephen P. lawyer
Murphy, Terence Roche lawyer
Murray, John Einar lawyer, retired army officer, federal official
Murry, Harold David, Jr. lawyer
Myers, John Holt lawyer
Nace, Barry John lawyer
Napier, John Light lawyer
Natalie, Ronald Bruce lawyer
Nauheim, Stephen Alan lawyer
Navarro, Bruce Charles lawyer
Neimark, Sheridan lawyer
Nelson, Robert Louis lawyer
Nemeroff, Michael Alan lawyer
Ness, Andrew David lawyer
Neuman, Robert Henry lawyer
Nevins, Louis H. lawyer
Nicholas, Robert B. lawyer
Nichols, Henry Eliot lawyer, savings and loan executive
Nolan, John Edward, Jr. lawyer
Norberg, Charles Robert lawyer
Norcross, David Frank Armstrong lawyer
Nordhaus, Robert Riggs lawyer
Nordquist, Myron Harry lawyer
Northrop, Carl Wooden lawyer
Norton, Floyd Ligon, IV lawyer
Norton, Gerald Patrick lawyer
Nutter, Franklin Winston lawyer
Oakley, Robert Louis law librarian, educator
O'Brien, Francis Anthony lawyer
O'Brien, William James, II lawyer
O'Connor, Charles Aloysius, III lawyer
O'Connor, Charles P. lawyer
O'Connor, John Jay, III lawyer
O'Connor, Nancy Morrison lawyer
Odle, Robert Charles, Jr. lawyer
O'Donnell, Terrence lawyer
Offutt, Gerald M. lawyer
†Ogden, David William lawyer
O'Hara, James Thomas lawyer
O'Hare, Patrick K. lawyer
Olender, Jack Harvey lawyer
Olmer, Lionel Herbert lawyer
Olmstead, Cecil Jay lawyer
Olson, John Frederick lawyer
Olson, Theodore Bevry lawyer, government official
O'Neill, Brian Dennis lawyer
O'Neill, John H., Jr. lawyer
O'Neill, William Patrick lawyer
Onek, Joseph Nathan lawyer
Ongman, John Will lawyer
Oppenheimer, Franz Martin lawyer
Oppenheimer, Jerry L. lawyer
O'Rourke, C. Larry lawyer
Osnos, David Marvin lawyer
O'Sullivan, Lynda Troutman lawyer
O'Toole, Francis J. lawyer
Overman, Dean Lee lawyer, investor, author
Owen, Roberts Bishop lawyer
Oyler, Gregory Kenneth lawyer
†Padgett, Nancy Weeks law librarian, consultant, lawyer
Page, Joseph Anthony law educator
Painter, William Hall law educator
Palmer, Alan Kenneth lawyer
Palmer, David Brent lawyer
Palmeter, N. David lawyer
Paoletta, Mark R. A. federal lawyer
Paper, Lewis J. lawyer
Papkin, Robert David lawyer
Patchan, Joseph lawyer
Pate, Michael Lynn lawyer
Patten, Thomas Louis lawyer
Patton, Thomas Earl lawyer
Paul, Robert Dennis lawyer
Paul, William McCann lawyer
Paup, Michael Lee lawyer
Payne, Kenneth Eugene lawyer
Pearlman, Ronald Alan lawyer
Peavy, Robert A. lawyer
Peck, Robert Stephen lawyer, educator
Pedersen, Norman A. lawyer
Pedersen, William Francis, Jr. lawyer
Pehrson, Gordon Oscar, Jr. lawyer
Pendergast, William Ross lawyer
Perkins, Jack Edwin lawyer
Perkins, Samuel Thomas lawyer
Perlik, William R. lawyer
Perlman, Matthew Saul lawyer
Perry, B(illy) Dwight lawyer
Perry, Spence William lawyer
Petrash, Jeffrey Michael lawyer
Pettit, John Whitney lawyer
Pfeiffer, Margaret Kolodny lawyer
Pfeiffer, Steven Bernard lawyer
Phemister, Thomas Alexander lawyer
Philion, Norman Joseph, III lawyer
Philips, Malcolm H. lawyer
Phillips, Carter Glasgow lawyer
Phillips, Cyrus Eastman, IV lawyer
Pickering, John Harold lawyer
Pietrowski, Robert Frank, Jr. lawyer
Pilecki, Paul Steven lawyer
Pinco, Robert G. lawyer
†Pinzler, Isabelle Katz lawyer
Pipkin, James Harold, Jr. lawyer
Pitt, Harvey Lloyd lawyer
Pittman, Steuart Lansing lawyer
Plaine, Daniel J. lawyer
Plotkin, Harry Morris lawyer
Podberesky, Samuel lawyer
Poe, Luke Harvey, Jr. lawyer
Pogue, Lloyd Welch lawyer
Polebaum, Elliot Edward lawyer
Pomeroy, Harlan lawyer
Poppler, Doris Swords lawyer
Porter, Richard Howard lawyer
Portnoy, Ian Karl lawyer
Postol, Lawrence Philip lawyer
Potter, Trevor Alexander McClurg lawyer
Potts, Ramsay Douglas lawyer, aviator
Potts, Stephen Deaderick lawyer
Poulson, Richard Jasper Metcalfe lawyer
Povich, David lawyer
Pozen, Walter lawyer
Preston, Colleen Ann lawyer
Preston, Richard McKim lawyer
Prettyman, Elijah Barrett, Jr. lawyer
Price, Griffith Baley, Jr. lawyer
Price, Joseph Hubbard lawyer
Principi, Anthony Joseph lawyer
Proctor, John P. lawyer
Proto, Neil Thomas lawyer, educator
Pugh, Keith E., Jr. lawyer
Pusey, William Anderson lawyer
Quale, John Carter lawyer
Quarles, James Linwood, III lawyer
Quigley, Thomas J. lawyer
Quint, Arnold Harris lawyer
Quintiere, Gary G. lawyer
Rabb, Harriet Schaffer lawyer, educator
Rademaker, Stephen Geoffrey lawyer
Rader, Robert Michael lawyer
Raimo, Bernard, Jr. (Bernie) lawyer
Ramey, Carl Robert lawyer
Rauh, Carl Stephen lawyer
Raul, Alan Charles lawyer
Reade, Claire Elizabeth lawyer
Reaves, John Daniel lawyer, playwright, actor
Reback, Joyce Ellen lawyer
Rehm, John Bartram lawyer
Reichardt, Glenn Richard lawyer
Reid, George Bernard, Jr. lawyer
Reid, Inez Smith lawyer, educator
Reid, Robert Newton lawyer, mortgage and financial consultant
Rein, Bert Walter lawyer
Reynolds, Joseph Hurley lawyer
Reynolds, Nicholas S. lawyer
Rezneck, Daniel Albert lawyer
Rhodes, John Jacob lawyer, former congressman
Rice, Paul Jackson lawyer, educator
†Rich, Bruce Miller lawyer, environmental foundation executive
Richards, Suzanne V. lawyer
Richardson, Elliot Lee lawyer
Richmond, David Walker lawyer
Richmond, Marilyn Susan lawyer
Rickard, Lisa Ann lawyer
Rieser, Joseph A., Jr. lawyer
Rill, James Franklin lawyer
Rinzel, Daniel Francis lawyer
Rishe, Melvin lawyer
Risher, John Robert, Jr. lawyer
Rissetto, Harry A. lawyer
Rivers, Richard Robinson lawyer
Roach, Arvid Edward, II lawyer
Robbins, Robert B. lawyer
Roberts, James Harold, III lawyer
Robinson, Davis Rowland lawyer
Robinson, Douglas George lawyer
Robinson, Laurie Overby lawyer
Rockefeller, Edwin Shaffer lawyer
Rockler, Walter James lawyer
Rocque, Vincent Joseph lawyer
Rodemeyer, Michael Leonard, Jr. lawyer
Rodgers, Paul lawyer, government official
Rogers, James Albert lawyer
Rogers, Paul Grant lawyer, former congressman

Rogers, William Dill *lawyer*
Rogovin, Mitchell *lawyer*
Rohner, Ralph John *lawyer, educator, university dean*
Roiter, Eric D. *lawyer*
Roll, David Lee *lawyer*
Romansky, Michael A. *lawyer*
Romeo, Peter John *lawyer*
Rose, Henry *lawyer*
Rose, James McKinley, Jr. *lawyer, government official*
Rose, Jonathan Chapman *lawyer*
†Roseborough, Teresa Wynn *lawyer*
†Rosenberg, Mark Louis *lawyer*
Rosenberg, Ruth Helen Borsuk *lawyer*
Rosenblatt, Peter Ronald *lawyer, former ambassador*
Rosenbloom, H. David *lawyer*
Rosenthal, Douglas Eurico *lawyer, author*
Rosenthal, Steven Siegmund *lawyer*
Ross, Douglas *lawyer*
Ross, Stanford Gordon *lawyer, former government official*
Rossides, Eugene Telemachus *lawyer, writer*
Rossotti, Barbara Jill Margulies *lawyer*
Rostow, Eugene Victor *lawyer, educator, economist*
Roth, Alan J. *lawyer, congressional aide*
Rothstein, Paul Frederick *lawyer, educator*
Rousselot, Peter Frese *lawyer*
Rouvelas, Emanuel Larry *lawyer*
Rowden, Marcus Aubrey *lawyer, former government official*
Rowe, Richard Holmes *lawyer*
Roycroft, Howard Francis *lawyer*
Rubin, Kenneth Allen *lawyer*
Rubin, Seymour Jeffrey *lawyer, educator*
Ruckert, Edward M. *lawyer*
Ruddy, Frank S. *lawyer, former ambassador*
Rudnick, Robert Alan *lawyer*
†Ruiz, Vanessa *lawyer*
Rule, Charles Frederick (Rick Rule) *lawyer*
Russell, Michael James *lawyer*
Russin, Jonathan *lawyer, consultant*
Ruttenberg, Charles Byron *lawyer*
Ruttinger, George David *lawyer*
Ruyak, Robert Francis *lawyer*
Ryan, Frederick Joseph, Jr. *lawyer, public official*
Ryan, Jerry William *lawyer*
Ryan, Joseph *lawyer*
Ryerson, Paul Sommer *lawyer*
Sacher, Steven Jay *lawyer*
Sachs, Stephen Howard *lawyer*
Sackler, Arthur Brian *lawyer*
Sacks, David Arnold *lawyer*
Sagalkin, Sanford *lawyer*
Sagawa, Shirley Sachi *lawyer*
Sagle, Robert Franklin *lawyer*
Salem, George Richard *lawyer*
Saltzburg, Stephen Allan *law educator, consultant*
Sanford, Bruce William *lawyer*
Santos, Leonard Ernest *lawyer*
Sapienza, John Thomas *lawyer*
Sauntry, Susan Schaefer *lawyer*
Savarese, Ralph J. *lawyer*
Scharff, Joseph Laurent *lawyer*
Schenker, Carl Richard, Jr. *lawyer*
Schifter, Richard *lawyer, government official*
Schildhause, Sol *lawyer*
Schmeltzer, Edward *lawyer*
Schmidt, John R. *lawyer*
Schmidt, Paul Wickham *lawyer*
Schmidt, Richard Marten, Jr. *lawyer*
Schneider, Matthew Roger *lawyer*
Schotland, Roy Arnold *lawyer, educator*
Schotland, Sara Deutch *lawyer*
Schrag, Philip Gordon *law educator*
Schropp, James Howard *lawyer*
Schwaab, Richard Lewis *lawyer, educator*
Schwartz, Daniel C. *lawyer*
Schwartz, Harry Kane *lawyer*
Schwartz, Robert S. *lawyer*
Schwartz, Victor Elliot *lawyer*
Schwarz, Carl W. *lawyer*
Schweitzer, William H. *lawyer*
Sclafani, Frances Ann *lawyer, federal agency executive*
Scott, Edward Philip *lawyer*
Scott, Michael *lawyer*
Scott, Thomas Jefferson, Jr. *lawyer, electrical engineer*
Scrimenti, Belinda Jayne *lawyer*
Sczudlo, Raymond Stanley *lawyer*
Sears, John Patrick *lawyer*
Sears, Mary Helen *lawyer*
Segal, Donald E. *lawyer*
Seidman, Ellen Shapiro *lawyer, government official*
Seltzer, Bradley Marshall *lawyer*
Sender, Stanton P. *lawyer*
Sernoff, Louis R. *lawyer*
Shafer, Raymond Philip *lawyer, business executive*
Shaffer, Jay Christopher *lawyer*
Shaheen, Michael Edmund, Jr. *lawyer, government official*
Shanks, Robert Bruce *lawyer*
Shapiro, David Israel *lawyer*
Shapiro, George Howard *lawyer*
Shelley, Herbert Carl *lawyer*
Shenefield, John Hale *lawyer*
Sher, Linda Rosenberg *lawyer*
Sherer, Samuel Ayers *lawyer, urban planning consultant*
Sherry, Robert Joseph *lawyer*
Sherzer, Harvey Gerald *lawyer*
†Shimberg, Steven Jay *lawyer*
Shniderman, Harry Louis *lawyer*
Shook, Langley R. *lawyer*
Shrinsky, Jason Lee *lawyer*
Shriver, Robert Sargent, Jr. *lawyer*
Shulman, Stephen Neal *lawyer*
Shuman, Michael Harrison *lawyer, policy analyst*
Siegel, Allen George *lawyer*
Siemer, Deanne Clemence *lawyer*
Sierck, Alexander Wentworth *lawyer*
Silberg, Jay Eliot *lawyer*
Silver, Daniel B. *lawyer*
Silver, Harry R. *lawyer*
Simchak, Matthew Stephen *lawyer*
Simon, Justin Daniel *lawyer*
Simon, Karla Weber *law educator*
Simon, Kenneth Mark *lawyer*
Simon, Rita James *legal educator*
Simons, Barbara M. *lawyer*
Simons, Lawrence Brook *lawyer*
Simowitz, Lee H. *lawyer*
Simpson, John W. *lawyer*
Sims, Joe *lawyer*
Singer, Daniel Morris *lawyer*
Singer, Norman H. *lawyer*
Singleton, Harry Michael *lawyer*
Skall, Gregg P. *lawyer*
Skinner, William Polk *lawyer*
Slattery, James Charles *lawyer, real estate executive*
Smith, Brian William *lawyer, former government official*
Smith, Daniel Clifford *lawyer*
Smith, Geoffrey R.W. *lawyer*
Smith, George Patrick, II *lawyer, educator*
Smith, John Lewis, III *lawyer*
Smoot, Oliver Reed, Jr. *lawyer, trade association executive*
Smyth, Paul Burton *lawyer*
Sneed, James H. *lawyer*
Snider, Jerome Guy *lawyer*
Snyder, Allen Roger *lawyer*
Sohn, Louis Bruno *lawyer, educator*
Sokler, Bruce Douglas *lawyer*
Solomons, Mark Elliott *lawyer*
Sommer, Alphonse Adam, Jr. *lawyer*
Sonde, Theodore Irwin *lawyer*
Spaeder, Roger Campbell *lawyer*
Spencer, Samuel *lawyer*
Spingler, Frank Joseph *lawyer*
Springer, James van Roden *lawyer*
Stafford, Barbara Rose *lawyer*
Stahr, Elvis J(acob), Jr. *lawyer, conservationist, educator*
Stansbury, Philip Roger *lawyer*
Stauffer, Ronald Eugene *lawyer*
Stayin, Randolph John *lawyer*
Steadman, Charles Walters *lawyer, corporate executive, writer*
Steel, Adrian L., Jr. *lawyer*
Stein, Michael Henry *lawyer*
Steinbach, Sheldon Elliot *lawyer*
Steinberg, Mark Robert *lawyer*
Steinhardt, Ralph Gustav, III *law educator*
Stephens, Jay B. *lawyer*
Steptoe, Mary Lou *lawyer*
Stern, Gerald Mann *lawyer*
Stern, Samuel Alan *lawyer*
†Sterrett, Samuel Black *lawyer, former judge*
Stevens, Herbert Francis *lawyer, law educator*
Stevenson, John Reese *lawyer*
Stevenson, Russell B., Jr. *lawyer*
Stewart, George Cope, III (Scoop Stewart) *lawyer*
Stewart, John Irwin, Jr. *lawyer*
Stillman, Elinor Hadley *lawyer*
Stock, Stuart Chase *lawyer*
Stoer, Eric F. *lawyer*
Stoll, Richard G(iles) *lawyer*
Stone, Donald Raymond *lawyer*
Stranahan, Robert Paul, Jr. *lawyer*
Strauss, Stanley Robert *lawyer*
Strickler, Frank Hunter *lawyer*
Stromberg, Clifford Douglas *lawyer*
Stropp, Robert H., Jr. *lawyer*
Stuart, Raymond Wallace *lawyer*
†Studley, Jamienne Shayne *lawyer*
Stumpf, Mark Howard *lawyer*
†Sugrue, Thomas Joseph *lawyer*
Sullivan, Brendan V., Jr. *lawyer*
Sullivan, Timothy *lawyer*
Susman, Thomas Michael *lawyer, lobbyist*
Sussman, Monica Hilton *lawyer*
Sutherlund, David Arvid *lawyer*
Swankin, David Arnold *lawyer, consumer advocate*
Swart, Robert H. *lawyer*
†Swerdzewski, Joseph *lawyer*
Swift, Evangeline Wilson *lawyer*
Swygert, H. Patrick *lawyer, educational administrator*
Tabor, John Kaye *retired lawyer*
Tague, Peter Winston *law educator*
Tallent, Stephen Edison *lawyer, educator*
Tannenwald, Peter *lawyer*
Tauber, Mark J. *lawyer*
Taylor, Carl Larsen *lawyer*
Taylor, James, Jr. *lawyer*
Taylor, Ralph Arthur, Jr. *lawyer*
Taylor, Richard Powell *lawyer*
Teague, Randal Cornell, Sr. *lawyer*
Tegtmeyer, Rene Desloge *lawyer*
Temko, Stanley Leonard *lawyer*
Temple, Riley Keene *lawyer*
Tendler, Paul Marc *lawyer*
Terry, Gary A. *lawyer, former trade association executive*
Terwilliger, George James, III *lawyer*
Theroux, Eugene *lawyer*
Thomas, Ritchie Tucker *lawyer*
Thompson, Mozelle Willmont *lawyer, federal agency administrator*
Thornburgh, Dick (Richard L. Thornburgh) *lawyer, former United Nations official, former U.S. attorney general, former governor*
Timberg, Sigmund *lawyer*
Timmer, Barbara *lawyer*
Tirana, Bardyl Rifat *lawyer*
Tisch, Ronald Irwin *lawyer*
Tompkins, Joseph Buford, Jr. *lawyer*
Toohey, Daniel Weaver *lawyer*
Topelius, Kathleen E. *lawyer*
Townsend, John Michael *lawyer*
Toy, Charles David *lawyer*
Treacy, Vincent Edward *lawyer*
Trooboff, Peter Dennis *lawyer*
Trosten, Leonard Morse *lawyer*
Troyer, Thomas Alfred *lawyer*
Truitt, Thomas Hulen *lawyer*
Tucker, Stefan Franklin *lawyer*
Tufaro, Richard Chase *lawyer*
Tuohey, Mark Henry, III *lawyer*
Turkus, Albert H. *lawyer*
Turnage, Fred Douglas *lawyer*
Tushnet, Mark Victor *law educator, associate dean*
Tuttle, Jon F. *lawyer*
Tuyakbaev, Zharmakhan Aitbajevich *prosecutor*
Tydings, Joseph Davies *lawyer, former senator*
Uehlein, E(dward) Carl, Jr. *lawyer*
Urgenson, Lawrence A. *lawyer*
Vacketta, Carl Lee *lawyer, educator*
Valdez, Abelardo Lopez *lawyer*
Valentine, Steven Richards *lawyer*
Vander Clute, Norman Roland *lawyer*
Vanderstar, John *lawyer*
Vanderver, Timothy Arthur, Jr. *lawyer*
van Horne, Jon W. *lawyer*
Van Vlack, Charles W. *lawyer, trade association executive*
Verner, James Melton *lawyer*
Verrill, Charles Owen, Jr. *lawyer*
Vickery, Ann Morgan *lawyer*
Vieth, G. Duane *lawyer*
Vince, Clinton Andrew *lawyer*
Vincze, L. Stephan *lawyer*
Vlcek, Jan Benes *lawyer*
Wade, Robert Paul *lawyer*
Wadlow, R. Clark *lawyer*
Waits, John A. *lawyer*
Walker, Mary Ann *lawyer*
Wallace, Don, Jr. *law educator*
Wallace, James Harold, Jr. *lawyer*
Wallace, Robert Bruce *lawyer, educator*
Wallison, Frieda K. *lawyer*
Wallman, Steven Mark Harte *lawyer*
Walsh, James Patrick *lawyer*
Walsh, Michael J. *lawyer*
Walton, Morgan Lauck, III *lawyer*
Ward, Alan S. *lawyer*
Ward, Erica Anne *lawyer, educator*
Waris, Michael, Jr. *lawyer*
Warnke, Paul Culliton *lawyer*
Warren, Edward W. *lawyer*
Wasilewski, Vincent Thomas *retired lawyer*
Waters, Jennifer Nash *lawyer*
Waters, Timothy J. *lawyer*
Watkin, Virginia Guild *lawyer*
Watson, Jack H., Jr. *lawyer*
Waxman, Margery Hope *lawyer*
†Waxman, Seth Paul *lawyer*
Webber, Richard John *lawyer*
Webster, George Drury *lawyer*
Webster, Robert Kenly *lawyer*
Webster, William Hedgcock *lawyer*
Wegener, Mark Douglas *lawyer*
Weich, Ronald H. *lawyer*
Weidenfeld, Edward Lee *lawyer*
Weinberg, Edward *lawyer*
Weinberg, Robert Lester *lawyer, educator*
Weinman, Howard Mark *lawyer*
Weinmann, John Giffen *lawyer, diplomat*
Weinstein, Harris *lawyer*
Weiss, Edith Brown *law educator*
Weiss, Ellyn Renee *lawyer*
Weiss, James Robert *lawyer*
Weiss, Jerome Paul *lawyer*
Weiss, Mark Anschel *lawyer*
Weiss, Stephen Joel *lawyer*
Weissbard, Samuel Held *lawyer*
Weissman, William R. *lawyer*
Wellen, Robert Howard *lawyer*
Weller, Janet Louise *lawyer*
Wenner, Charles Roderick *lawyer*
West, Gail Berry *lawyer*
Wheeler, Edward Kendall *lawyer*
Whelan, Roger Michael *lawyer, educator*
Whitaker, A(lbert) Duncan *lawyer*
White, Christian S. *lawyer*
White, Lee Calvin *lawyer*
Whiting, Richard Albert *lawyer*
Wiegley, Roger Douglas *lawyer*
Wilburn, Mary Nelson *lawyer, writer, educator*
Wilcher, LaJuana Sue *lawyer*
Wilcher, Shirley J. *lawyer*
Wiley, Richard Emerson *lawyer*
Willard, Richard Kennon *lawyer*
Willett, Edward Farrand, Jr. *lawyer*
Williams, B. John, Jr. *lawyer, former federal judge*
Williams, John Edward *lawyer*
Williams, Karen Hastie *lawyer*
Williams, T. Raymond *lawyer*
Williamson, Edwin Dargan *lawyer, former federal official*
Williamson, Thomas Samuel, Jr. *lawyer*
Willmore, Robert Louis *lawyer*
Wilson, Gary Dean *lawyer*
Wilson, R. Merinda D. *lawyer*
Wine, L. Mark *lawyer*
Winston, Judith Ann *lawyer*
Winter, Douglas E. *lawyer, writer*
Wintrol, John Patrick *lawyer*
Wirtz, William Willard *lawyer*
Wiseman, Alan M(itchell) *lawyer*
Wiss, Marcia A. *lawyer*
Witherspoon, Sharon *lawyer*
Wolff, Alan William *lawyer*
Wolff, Elroy Harris *lawyer*
Wollenberg, J. Roger *lawyer*
Wood, John Martin *lawyer*
Work, Charles Robert *lawyer*
Worsley, James Randolph, Jr. *lawyer*
Worthy, K(enneth) Martin *lawyer*
Wright, Lawrence A. *federal judge*
Wruble, Bernhardt Karp *lawyer*
Wyss, John Benedict *lawyer*
Yablon, Jeffery Lee *lawyer*
Yannucci, Thomas David *lawyer*
Yarowsky, Jonathan R. *lawyer*
Young, William Fielding *lawyer*
Yurow, John Jesse *lawyer*
Yuspeh, Alan Ralph *lawyer*
Zausner, L. Andrew *lawyer*
Zax, Leonard A. *lawyer*
Zeifang, Donald P. *lawyer*
Zevnik, Paul A. *lawyer*
Zielinski, Charles Anthony *lawyer*
Zimmerman, Edwin Morton *lawyer*
Zipp, Joel Frederick *lawyer*
Zuckman, Harvey Lyle *legal educator*
Zweben, Murray *lawyer, consultant*
Zwick, Kenneth Lowell *lawyer*

FLORIDA

Alachua
Gaines, Weaver Henderson *lawyer*

Aventura
Peshkin, Samuel David *lawyer*

Bal Harbour
Field, Cyrus Adams *lawyer*
Hastings, Lawrence Vaeth *lawyer, physician, educator*

Boca Grande
Baldwin, William Howard *lawyer, retired foundation executive*
Brock, Mitchell *lawyer*

Boca Raton
Barton, William Blackburn *retired lawyer*
Beber, Robert H. *lawyer, financial services executive*
Beck, Jan Scott *lawyer*
Camilleri, Michael *lawyer, educator*
Erdman, Joseph *lawyer*
Hedrick, Frederic Cleveland, Jr. *lawyer*
MacIntyre, A(lfonso) Everette *lawyer*
Reinstein, Joel *lawyer*

Bonita Springs
Olander, Ray Gunnar *retired lawyer*

Boynton Beach
Brome, Robert Harrison *lawyer*
Miller, Emanuel *retired lawyer, banker*
Saxbe, William Bart *lawyer, former government official*
Snell, Thaddeus Stevens, III *lawyer, retired building materials manufacturing company executive*

Bushnell
Hagin, T. Richard *lawyer*

Cape Coral
Seemann, Ernest Albright *lawyer*

Clearwater
Berman, Elihu H. *lawyer*
Birmingham, Richard Gregory *lawyer*
Churuti, Susan Hamilton *lawyer*
Free, E. LeBron *lawyer*
Jagger, Robert Edwin *lawyer*

Coconut Creek
Godofsky, Stanley *lawyer*

Coconut Grove
Denaro, Gregory *lawyer*
McAmis, Edwin Earl *lawyer*

Coral Gables
Getman, Dennis Jon *lawyer*
Kniskern, Joseph Warren *lawyer*
Rosenn, Keith Samuel *lawyer, educator*

Deerfield Beach
Brown, Colin W(egand) *lawyer, diversified company executive*
Rung, Richard Allen *lawyer, retired air force officer, retired educator*

Delray Beach
Barlow, Joel *retired lawyer*
Groening, William Andrew, Jr. *lawyer, former chemical company executive*
Larry, R. Heath *lawyer*
Shister, Joseph *labor arbitrator, law educator*

Fort Lauderdale
Adams, Daniel Lee *lawyer*
Copelan, John Jefferson, Jr. *lawyer*
Dressler, Robert A. *lawyer*
Ferris, Robert Edmund *lawyer*
Gardner, Russell Menese *lawyer*
Hargrove, John Russell *lawyer*
Hiaasen, Carl Andreas *lawyer*
Hirsch, Jeffrey Allan *lawyer*
Joseph, Paul R *law educator*
Lataif, Lawrence P. *lawyer*
Marcus, Richard Alan *lawyer, distribution company executive*
Moss, Stephen B. *lawyer*
O'Bryan, William Monteith *lawyer*
†Richmond, Gail Levin *law educator*
†Roehrenbeck, Carol *law librarian, educator*
Turner, Hugh Joseph, Jr. *lawyer*
Walton, Rodney Earl *lawyer*
Weinstein, Peter M. *lawyer, state senator*

Fort Myers
Allen, Richard Chester *retired lawyer, educator*
Erickson, Roy Lydeen *lawyer*
Medvecky, Robert Stephen *lawyer*
Morse, John Harleigh *lawyer*

Gainesville
Boyes, Patrice Flinchbaugh *lawyer, environmental executive*
Eder, George Jackson *lawyer, economist*
Mautz, Robert Barbeau *lawyer, educator*
Moberly, Robert Blakely *lawyer, educator*
Probert, Walter *lawyer, educator*
Quarles, James Cliv *law educator*
Smith, David Thornton *lawyer, educator*
†Taylor, Grace Elizabeth Woodall (Betty Taylor) *lawyer, educator, law library administrator*
Van Alstyne, W. Scott, Jr. *lawyer, educator*
Weyrauch, Walter Otto *legal educator*
White, Jill Carolyn *lawyer*

Hobe Sound
Beddow, Thomas John *retired lawyer*
Etherington, Edwin Deacon *lawyer, business executive, educator*
Havens, Oliver Hershman *lawyer, consultant*
Markoe, Frank, Jr. *lawyer, business and hospital executive*
Matheson, William Lyon *lawyer, farmer*
Simpson, Russell Gordon *lawyer, mayor, counselor to not-for-profit organiz*

Hollywood
Blazzard, Norse Novar *lawyer*
Thomas, Thomas A. *lawyer*

Homosassa
Clement, Howard Wheeler *lawyer*

Jacksonville
Ade, James L. *lawyer*
Ansbacher, Lewis *lawyer*
Bullock, Bruce Stanley *lawyer*
Christian, Gary Irvin *lawyer*
Commander, Charles Edward *lawyer, real estate consultant*
Criser, Marshall M. *lawyer*
Dawes, Michael Francis *lawyer*
Drew, Horace Rainsford, Jr. *lawyer*
Ehrlich, Raymond *lawyer*
Farmer, Guy Otto, II *lawyer*
Fawbush, Andrew Jackson *lawyer*
Freeman, Judson, Jr. *lawyer*
Fruit, Melvyn Herschel *lawyer, management consultant*
Gabel, George DeSaussure, Jr. *lawyer*
Getman, Willard Etheridge *lawyer*
Glocker, Theodore Wesley, Jr. *lawyer*
Kent, Frederick Heber *lawyer*
Legler, Mitchell Wooten *lawyer*
McWilliams, John Lawrence, III *lawyer*
Moseley, James Francis *lawyer*

Nelson, Julie D. *lawyer*
O'Neal, Michael Scott, Sr. *lawyer*
Pillans, Charles Palmer, III *lawyer*
Prom, Stephen George *lawyer*
Rinaman, James Curtis, Jr. *lawyer*
Sadler, Luther Fuller, Jr. *lawyer*
Slade, Thomas Bog, III *lawyer, investment banker*
Vail, Patricia *lawyer*
Wallis, Donald Wills *lawyer*
Webster, David A. *lawyer*

Key Largo
Mattson, James Stewart *lawyer, environmental scientist, educator*

Key West
Coudert, Ferdinand Wilmerding *lawyer*

Lakeland
Dufoe, William Stewart *lawyer*
Kibler, David Burke, III *lawyer*
Kittleson, Henry Marshall *lawyer*
Koren, Edward Franz *lawyer*

Largo
†Slattery, James Lee *lawyer*

Longboat Key
Freeman, Richard Merrell *corporate director, lawyer*
Heitler, George *lawyer*

Longwood
Miller, William Jones *lawyer*
Tomasulo, Virginia Merrills *retired lawyer*

Marco Island
Fisher, Chester Lewis, Jr. *retired lawyer*
Poletti, Charles *lawyer*

Melbourne
Cacciatore, S. Sammy, Jr. *lawyer*

Miami
Alonso, Antonio Enrique *lawyer*
Altro, David A. *lawyer*
Armstrong, James Louden, III *lawyer*
Astigarraga, Jose I(gnacio) *lawyer*
Baena, Scott Louis *lawyer*
Basile, Michael *lawyer*
Bemis, Lawrence Perry *lawyer*
Berley, David Richard *lawyer*
Berman, Bruce Judson *lawyer*
Brown, Morton Paul *lawyer*
Burnett, Henry *lawyer*
Carman, Gary Michael *lawyer*
Cesarano, Gregory Morgen *lawyer*
Cesarano, Michael Chapman *lawyer*
Clarke, Mercer Kaye *lawyer*
Cole, Robert Bates *lawyer*
Connor, Terence Gregory *lawyer*
Dady, Robert Edward *lawyer*
Deaktor, Darryl Barnett *lawyer*
Dimond, Alan Theodore *lawyer*
Dyer, John Martin *lawyer, marketing educator*
England, Arthur Jay, Jr. *lawyer, former state justice*
Ferrer, Esteban A. *lawyer*
Fletcher, John Sheidley *lawyer*
Freitag, Dean Marco *lawyer*
Furia, Arthur Joseph *lawyer*
Garcia-Pedrosa, Jose Ramon *lawyer*
Gassen, Joseph Albert *lawyer, former judge*
Godofsky, Lawrence *lawyer*
Gold, Alan Stephen *lawyer, educator, judge*
Gong, Edmond Joseph *lawyer*
Gonzalez-Pita, J. Alberto *lawyer*
Gragg, Karl Lawrence *lawyer*
Greer, Alan Graham *lawyer*
Hall, Andrew Clifford *lawyer*
Harris, Steven Michael *lawyer*
Hector, Louis Julius *lawyer*
Herron, James Michael *lawyer*
Hoffman, Larry J. *lawyer*
Houlihan, Gerald John *lawyer*
Hudson, Robert Franklin, Jr. *lawyer*
Hurtgen, Peter Joseph *lawyer*
Kenin, David S. *lawyer*
King, Shepard *lawyer*
Kline, Charles C. *lawyer*
Klock, Joseph Peter, Jr. *lawyer*
Korchin, Judith Miriam *lawyer*
Kutner, Maurice Jay *lawyer*
Lampen, Richard Jay *lawyer, investment banker*
Landy, Burton Aaron *lawyer*
Leite, Eduardo Cerqueira *lawyer*
Light, Alfred Robert *lawyer, political scientist*
Long, Maxine Master *lawyer*
Louis, Paul Adolph *lawyer*
Mathews, Byron Burnett, Jr. *lawyer*
Moore, Michael T. *lawyer*
Mudd, John Philip *lawyer*
Munn, Janet Teresa *lawyer*
Myers, Kenneth M. *lawyer*
Nuernberg, William Richard *lawyer*
Osman, Edith Gabriella *lawyer*
Pasano, Michael S. *lawyer*
Paul, Robert *lawyer*
Pearson, Daniel S. *lawyer*
Pearson, John Edward *lawyer*
Quentel, Albert Drew *lawyer*
Reid, R(alph) Benjamine *lawyer*
Ross, David Lee *lawyer*
Ryce, Donald Theodore *lawyer*
Sacher, Barton Stuart *lawyer*
Samole, Myron Michael *lawyer*
Schulman, Clifford A. *lawyer*
Seitz, Patricia Ann *lawyer*
Sharett, Alan Richard *lawyer, environmental litigator, mediator and arbitrator, educator*
Shepherd, Frank Andrew *lawyer*
Shevin, Robert Lewis *lawyer*
Silber, Norman Jules *lawyer*
Smith, Chesterfield Harvey *lawyer*
Smith, Samuel Stuart *lawyer*
Sonnett, Neal Russell *lawyer*
Stanley, Sherry A. *lawyer*
Stokes, Paul Mason *lawyer*
Strait, Loraine Hall *lawyer*
Stratos, Kimarie Rose *lawyer, sports agent*
Suarez, Xavier Louis *lawyer, former mayor*
Tarkoff, Michael Harris *lawyer*
Tew, Jeffrey Allen *lawyer*
Tifford, Arthur W. *lawyer*
Valle, Laurence Francis *lawyer*
Walters, David McLean *lawyer*
Weigel, Rainer R. *lawyer*
Weinstein, Alan Edward *lawyer*
Weinstein, Andrew H. *lawyer*
Werth, Susan *lawyer*
Whisenand, James Dudley *lawyer*

Miami Lakes
Dominik, Jack Edward *lawyer*

Naples
Beam, Robert Thompson *retired lawyer*
Budd, David Glenn *lawyer*
Crehan, Joseph Edward *lawyer*
Dodds, Robert James, Jr. *retired lawyer*
Dutton, Clarence Benjamin *lawyer*
Emerson, John Williams, II *lawyer*
Farese, Lawrence Anthony *lawyer*
McCaffrey, Judith Elizabeth *lawyer*
O'Neill, William Robert *lawyer*
Passidomo, John Michael *lawyer*
Peck, Bernard Sidney *lawyer*
Putzell, Edwin Joseph, Jr. *lawyer, mayor*
Roberts, William B. *lawyer, business executive*
Schauer, Wilbert Edward, Jr. *lawyer, manufacturing company executive*
Snyder, Marion Gene *lawyer, former congressman*
Stevens, William Kenneth *lawyer*
Westman, Carl Edward *lawyer*

New Port Richey
Focht, Theodore Harold *lawyer, educator*

Oldsmar
Hirschman, Sherman Joseph *lawyer, educator*
Sloane, Thomas Charles *lawyer*

Orlando
Ball, G. Thomas *lawyer*
Bassett, Robert Cochem *lawyer, publisher*
Baumgardner, Theodore Rogers *lawyer*
Blackford, Robert Newton *lawyer*
Canan, Michael J. *lawyer, author*
Cardwell, David Earl *lawyer*
Conti, Louis Thomas Moore *lawyer*
Duane, William Francis *lawyer*
DuRose, Richard Arthur *lawyer*
Eagan, William Leon *lawyer*
Fulton, Richard T. *lawyer*
Handley, Leon Hunter *lawyer*
Henry, William Oscar Eugene *lawyer*
Herrington, John Stewart *lawyer*
Horan, John Patrick *lawyer*
Ioppolo, Frank Sebastian *lawyer*
Jontz, Jeffry Robert *lawyer*
Leonhardt, Frederick Wayne *lawyer*
Linscott, Jerry R. *lawyer*
Mock, Frank Mackenzie *lawyer*
Morris, Max F. *lawyer*
Reed, John Alton *lawyer*
Rolle, Christopher Davies *lawyer*
Rosenthal, Paul Edmond *lawyer*
Rush, Fletcher Grey, Jr. *lawyer*
Sharp, Joel H., Jr. *lawyer*
Simon, James Lowell *lawyer*
Skambis, Christopher Charles, Jr. *lawyer*
Urban, James Arthur *lawyer*

Osprey
Maddocks, Robert Allen *lawyer, manufacturing company executive*

Palm Beach
Adler, Frederick Richard *lawyer, financier*
Bane, Charles Arthur *lawyer*
Beasley, James W., Jr. *lawyer*
Chopin, L. Frank *lawyer*
Cole, Jonathan Edward *lawyer*
Crawford, Sandra Kay *lawyer*
Fogelson, David *retired lawyer*
Ford, Thomas Patrick *lawyer*
Graubard, Seymour *lawyer*

Palm City
Burton, John Routh *lawyer*
Huntington, Earl Lloyd *lawyer, retired natural resources company executive*

Pensacola
Adams, Joseph Peter *retired lawyer, consultant*
Bozeman, Frank Carmack *lawyer*
Geeker, Nicholas Peter *lawyer, judge*
Moulton, Wilbur Wright, Jr. *lawyer*

Pompano Beach
Szilassy, Sandor *retired lawyer, library director, educator*

Ponte Vedra Beach
Kuhn, Bowie K. *lawyer, former professional baseball commissioner, consultant*

River Ranch
Swett, Albert Hersey *retired lawyer, business executive, consultant*

Saint Augustine
Davis, Bertram George *lawyer, association executive*

Saint Petersburg
Battaglia, Anthony Sylvester *lawyer*
Brandimore, Stanley Albert *lawyer, holding company executive*
DiFilippo, Fernando, Jr. *lawyer*
Escarraz, Enrique, III *lawyer*
Mann, Sam Henry, Jr. *lawyer*
Oleck, Howard Leoner *legal educator, writer*
Schultz, G. Robert *lawyer*
Woodard, Joseph Lamar *law librarian, law educator*

Sanibel
Kiernan, Edwin A., Jr. *lawyer, corporation executive*

Sarasota
Browdy, Alvin *lawyer*
Christopher, William Garth *lawyer*
Greenfield, Robert Kauffman *lawyer*
Hull, J(ames) Richard *retired lawyer, business executive*
Ives, George Skinner *arbitrator, former government official*
Kimbrough, Robert Averyt *lawyer*
Mackey, Leonard Bruce *lawyer, former diversified manufacturing corporation executive*
Raimi, Burton Louis *lawyer*
Schwartz, Norman L. *lawyer*

South Miami
Fletcher, John Greenwood II *lawyer, consultant*

Tallahassee
Aurell, John Karl *lawyer*
Barnett, Martha Walters *lawyer*
Boyd, Joseph Arthur, Jr. *lawyer*
Carson, Leonard Allen *lawyer*
Clarkson, Julian Derieux *lawyer*
Coleman, Hume Field *lawyer*
Collette, Charles T. (Chip Collette) *lawyer*
D'Alemberte, Talbot (Sandy D'Alemberte) *lawyer, educator*
Ervin, Robert Marvin *lawyer*
Griffith, Elwin Jabez *lawyer, university administrator*
Holifield, Bishop Clarke *lawyer*
Morse, Joshua Marion, III *lawyer, educator*
Owen, William Cone *lawyer*
Pelham, Thomas Gerald *lawyer*
Peterson, Rodney Delos *mediator, forensic economist*
Reid, Sue Titus *law educator*
Roberts, B. K. *lawyer, former judge*
Saunders, Ron *lawyer, former state legislator*
Schroeder, Edwin Maher *law educator*
Zaiser, Kent Ames *lawyer*

Tampa
Acton, Emeline *lawyer*
Adkins, Edward Cleland *lawyer*
Aitken, Thomas Dean *lawyer*
Barkin, Marvin E. *lawyer*
Barton, Bernard Alan, Jr. *lawyer*
Beytin, Kenneth Alan *lawyer*
Bierley, John Charles *lawyer*
Burnette, Guy Ellington, Jr. *lawyer*
Butler, Paul Bascomb, Jr. *lawyer*
Campbell, Richard Bruce *lawyer*
†Carideo, James Vincent *lawyer, telephone company executive*
Culverhouse, Hugh Franklin *lawyer, professional sports team executive*
Cutler, Edward I. *lawyer*
Davis, Richard Earl *lawyer*
Dawson, Richard Thomas *lawyer*
Doliner, Nathaniel Lee *lawyer*
Ellwanger, Thomas John *lawyer*
Gassler, Frank Henry *lawyer*
Germany, John Fredrick *lawyer*
Gilbert, Leonard Harold *lawyer*
Gillen, William Albert *lawyer*
Gonzalez, Joe Manuel *lawyer*
Griffin, Christopher L. *lawyer*
Hemke, Donald Edward *lawyer*
Hoyt, Brooks Pettingill *lawyer*
Jones, John Arthur *lawyer*
Karl, Frederick Brennan *lawyer, former state justice*
Kelly, Thomas Paine, Jr. *lawyer*
Kiernan, William Joseph, Jr. *lawyer, real estate investor*
LeFevre, David E. *lawyer, professional sports team executive*
Levine, Jack Anton *lawyer*
Litschgi, A. Byrne *lawyer*
MacDonald, Thomas Cook, Jr. *lawyer*
Martin, Gary Wayne *lawyer*
McAdams, John P. *lawyer*
McDevitt, Sheila Marie *lawyer, energy company executive*
O'Neill, Albert Clarence, Jr. *lawyer*
O'Sullivan, Brendan Patrick *lawyer*
Roberson, Bruce H. *lawyer*
Rosenkranz, Stanley William *lawyer*
Sams, Robert Alan *lawyer*
Schwenke, Roger Dean *lawyer*
Soble, James Barry *lawyer*
Sparkman, Steven Leonard *lawyer*
Stafford, Josephine Howard *lawyer*
Stallings, (Charles) Norman *lawyer*
Taub, Theodore Calvin *lawyer*
Thomas, Wayne Lee *lawyer*
Villareal, Dewey R. *lawyer*
Wagner, Frederick William (Bill Wagner) *lawyer*

Venice
Miller, Allan John *lawyer*

Vero Beach
Anderson, Rudolph J., Jr. *lawyer*
Phillips, Ellis Laurimore, Jr. *legal educator, foundation executive*

West Palm Beach
Baker, Bernard Robert, II *lawyer*
Beall, Kenneth Sutter, Jr. *lawyer*
Burck, Arthur Albert *lawyer, corporate merger expert*
†Coyle, Dennis Patrick *lawyer*
Flanagan, L. Martin *lawyer*
Freeland, James M. Jackson *lawyer, educator*
Hill, Thomas William, Jr. *lawyer, educator*
Jorandby, Richard Leroy *lawyer*
Miller, Richard Jackson *lawyer*
Montgomery, Robert Morel, Jr. *lawyer*
Moore, George Crawford Jackson *lawyer*
Mora, Abraham Martin *lawyer*
O'Brien, Thomas George, III *lawyer*
O'Flarity, James P. *lawyer*
Petersen, David L. *lawyer*
Royce, Raymond Watson *lawyer, rancher, citrus grower*
Sammond, John Stowell *lawyer*
Smith, David Shiverick *lawyer, former ambassador*
Wagner, Arthur Ward, Jr. *lawyer*
Worsham, Ernest Lee *lawyer*

Winter Haven
Chase, Lucius Peter *lawyer, retired corporate executive*

Winter Park
Brooten, Kenneth Edward, Jr. *lawyer*
Fowler, Mark Stapleton *lawyer, corporation counsel*
Kiely, Dan Ray *lawyer, banking and real estate development executive*
Patterson, Robert Youngman, Jr. *retired lawyer, utility executive*

GEORGIA

Alpharetta
Feuss, Linda Anne Upsall *lawyer*

Athens
Beaird, James Ralph *legal educator*
Carlson, Ronald Lee *lawyer, educator*
Ellington, Charles Ronald *lawyer, educator*
Phillips, Walter Ray *lawyer, educator*
Puckett, Elizabeth Ann *law librarian, law educator*
Spurgeon, Edward Dutcher *law educator*
Watson, William A. J. *law educator*
Wellman, Richard Vance *legal educator*

Atlanta
Abrams, Harold Eugene *lawyer*
Alexander, Miles Jordan *lawyer*
Anderson, Peter Joseph *lawyer*
Ashe, Robert Lawrence, Jr. *lawyer*
Attridge, Richard Byron *lawyer*
Baker, David S. *lawyer*
Barkoff, Rupert Mitchell *lawyer*
Bassett, Peter Q. *lawyer*
Batson, Richard Neal *lawyer*
Baxter, Harry Stevens *lawyer*
Beckham, Walter Hull, III *lawyer*
Beckman, Gail McKnight *law educator*
Bennett, Jay D. *lawyer*
Bird, Wendell Raleigh *lawyer*
Blackburn, William Stanley *lawyer*
Blackstock, Jerry Byron *lawyer*
Blank, A(ndrew) Russell *lawyer*
Bloodworth, A(lbert) W(illiam) Franklin *lawyer*
Boisseau, Richard Robert *lawyer*
Boman, John Harris, Jr. *retired lawyer*
Bonds, John Wilfred, Jr. *lawyer*
Bondurant, Emmet Jopling, II *lawyer*
Boone, J. William *lawyer*
Booth, Gordon Dean, Jr. *lawyer*
Bowden, Henry Lumpkin, Jr. *lawyer*
Bradley, William H. *lawyer*
Branch, Thomas Broughton, III *lawyer*
Brannon, Lester Travis, Jr. *lawyer*
Bratton, James Henry, Jr. *lawyer*
Brooks, Wilbur Clinton *lawyer*
Brown, John Robert *lawyer, priest, philanthropist*
Cadenhead, Alfred Paul *lawyer*
Candler, John Slaughter, II *retired lawyer*
Cheatham, Richard Reed *lawyer*
Chilivis, Nickolas Peter *lawyer*
Chisholm, Tommy *lawyer, utility company executive*
Clark, William Franklin *lawyer*
Clarke, Thomas Hal *lawyer*
Cohen, Ezra Harry *lawyer*
Cohen, George Leon *lawyer*
Cohen, N. Jerold *lawyer*
Collins, Steven M. *lawyer*
Cooper, Frederick Eansor *lawyer*
Copeland, Floyd Dean *lawyer*
Coxe, Tench Charles *lawyer*
Crews, William Edwin *lawyer*
Cutshaw, Kenneth Andrew *lawyer*
Dalton, John J. *lawyer*
Davis, Frank Tradewell, Jr. *lawyer*
Denny, Richard Alden, Jr. *lawyer*
Downs, Harry *lawyer and retired corporate legal executive*
Doyle, Michael Anthony *lawyer*
DuBose, Charles Wilson *lawyer*
Durrett, James Frazer, Jr. *lawyer*
Eason, William Everette, Jr. *lawyer*
Egan, Michael Joseph *lawyer*
Ehrlichman, John Daniel *lawyer, company executive, author, former assistant to President of United States*
Eisner, Rebecca Suzanne *lawyer*
Elliott, A(rthur) James *lawyer*
Epstein, David Gustav *lawyer*
Erck, Theodore Augustus, Jr. *lawyer*
Etheridge, Jack Paul *arbitrator, mediator, former judge*
Felton, Jule Wimberly, Jr. *lawyer*
Fleming, Julian Denver, Jr. *lawyer*
Forbes, Theodore McCoy, Jr. *lawyer, arbitrator, mediator*
Foreman, Edward Rawson *lawyer*
Franklin, Charles Scothern *lawyer*
Gambrell, David Henry *lawyer*
Garner, Robert Edward Lee *lawyer*
Gifford, Anita Sheree *lawyer*
Girth, Marjorie Louisa *lawyer, educator*
Goldman, Joel Stanley *lawyer*
Goldstein, Elliott *lawyer*
Grant, Walter Matthews *lawyer, diversified consumer products executive*
Graves, Judson *lawyer*
Greer, Bernard Lewis, Jr. *lawyer*
Grove, Russell Sinclair, Jr. *lawyer*
Haas, George Aaron *lawyer*
Hackett, Stanley Hailey *lawyer*
Harkey, Robert Shelton *lawyer*
Harlin, Robert Ray *lawyer*
Harmon, Nolan B. *lawyer*
Harney, Thomas C. *lawyer*
Hasson, James Keith, Jr. *lawyer*
Hawks, Barrett Kingsbury *lawyer*
Hill, Harold Nelson, Jr. *lawyer*
Hill, Paul Drennen *lawyer, banker*
Hoenig, Gerald Jay *lawyer, insurance company executive*
Hoff, Gerhardt Michael *lawyer, insurance company executive*
Hopkins, George Mathews Marks *lawyer, business executive*
Houpt, Corinne Anderson *lawyer*
Howard, Harry Clay *lawyer*
Huie, William Stell *lawyer*
Hunter, Forrest Walker *lawyer*
Ide, Roy William, III *lawyer*
Izard, John *lawyer*
Janney, Donald Wayne *lawyer*
Jeffries, McChesney Hill *retired lawyer*
Jenkins, Albert Felton, Jr. *lawyer*
Jones, Frank Cater *lawyer*
Jones, Glower Whitehead *lawyer*
Kelley, James Francis *lawyer*
Kelly, James Patrick *lawyer*
Killorin, Edward Wylly *lawyer, tree farmer*
Kinzer, William Luther *lawyer*
Klamon, Lawrence Paine *lawyer*
Kneisel, Edmund M. *lawyer*
Knowles, Marjorie Fine *lawyer, educator, dean*
Lackland, Theodore Howard *lawyer*
Lamon, Harry Vincent, Jr. *lawyer*
Landon, James Henry *lawyer*
Lawing, Jack L. *lawyer, corporate executive*

Lee, Kathryn Ellen *corporate lawyer*
Leonard, David Morse *lawyer*
Lester, Charles Turner, Jr. *lawyer*
Levy, David *lawyer*
Linkous, William Joseph, Jr. *lawyer*
Lipshutz, Robert Jerome *lawyer, former government official*
Lokey, Hamilton *retired lawyer*
Lowe, Jonathan Wayne *lawyer*
Lower, Robert Cassel *lawyer, educator*
Lunsford, Julius R(odgers), Jr. *lawyer*
Lurey, Alfred Saul *lawyer*
Macey, Morris William *lawyer*
Marshall, John Donald, Jr. *lawyer*
Marshall, John Treutlen *lawyer*
Marshall, Thomas Oliver, Jr. *lawyer*
McEvoy, James F. *lawyer*
McNeill, Thomas Ray *lawyer*
Mobley, John Homer, II *lawyer*
Moeling, Walter Goos, IV *lawyer*
Molm, John Ralph *lawyer*
Moore, John W. *lawyer*
Mull, Gale W. *lawyer*
Murphy, Michael Conlon *lawyer*
Neely, Edgar Adams, Jr. *lawyer*
Newton, Richard Aaron *lawyer*
Ordover, Abraham Philip *lawyer*
Owen, Robert Hubert *lawyer, real estate broker*
Parker, John Garrett *lawyer*
Parks, John Robert *lawyer*
Partain, Eugene Gartly *lawyer*
Patrick, Robert Winton, Jr. *lawyer*
Patterson, William Robert *lawyer*
Patton, Matthew Henry *lawyer*
Persons, J. Robert *lawyer*
Persons, Oscar N. *lawyer*
Phillips, Barry *lawyer*
Piassick, Joel Bernard *lawyer*
Pike, Larry Samuel *lawyer*
Poe, H. Sadler *lawyer*
Polstra, Larry John *lawyer*
Poole, John Jordan *lawyer*
Porter, James Alexander *lawyer*
Pratt, John Sherman *lawyer*
Ramsay, Ernest Canaday *lawyer*
Reed, Glen Alfred *lawyer*
Reinhardt, Daniel Sargent *lawyer*
Ridley, Clarence Haverty *lawyer*
Rogers, C. B. *lawyer*
Russell, Harold Louis *lawyer*
Saidman, Gary K. *lawyer*
Savell, Edward Lupo *lawyer*
Sawyer, Christopher Glenn *lawyer*
Scharuda, Victoria *lawyer*
Schroder, Jack Spalding, Jr. *lawyer*
Schulte, Jeffrey Lewis *lawyer*
Schwartz, Dale Marvin *lawyer*
Sibley, Horace Holden *lawyer*
Sibley, James Malcolm *retired lawyer*
Smith, Alexander Wyly, Jr. *lawyer*
Smith, James Louis, III *lawyer*
Smith, Jeffrey Michael *lawyer*
Smith, Sidney Oslin, Jr. *lawyer*
Smith, Walton Napier *lawyer*
Speer, G. William *lawyer*
Stanhope, William Henry *lawyer*
Steed, Robert Lee *lawyer, humor columnist*
Stokes, James Sewell *lawyer*
Strauss, Robert David *lawyer*
Swann, Jerre Bailey *lawyer*
Swift, Frank Meador *lawyer*
Tanner, W(alter) Rhett *lawyer*
Taylor, George Kimbrough, Jr. *lawyer*
Taylor, Virginia S. *lawyer*
Tennant, Thomas Michael *lawyer*
Thompson, Larry Dean *lawyer*
Varner, Chilton Davis *lawyer*
Vickery, Trammell Eugene *lawyer*
Walsh, W. Terence *lawyer*
Webb, Brainard Troutman, Jr. *lawyer, distribution company executive*
West, Ruth Tinsley *lawyer*
White, Benjamin Taylor *lawyer*
Whitley, Joe Dally *lawyer*
Williams, David Howard *lawyer*
Williams, Neil, Jr. *lawyer*
Wilson, Alexander Erwin, Jr. *lawyer, management consultant*
Wilson, James Hargrove, Jr. *lawyer*
Wolensky, Michael K. *lawyer*
Womack, Mary Pauline *lawyer*
Wright, Peter Meldrim *lawyer*
Zink, Charles Talbott *lawyer*

Augusta
Lee, Lansing Burrows, Jr. *lawyer, corporate executive*

Canton
Hasty, William Grady, Jr. *lawyer*

Columbus
Brinkley, Jack Thomas *lawyer, former congressman*
Lasseter, Earle Forrest *lawyer*
McGlamry, Max Reginald *lawyer*
Page, William Marion *lawyer*
Rothschild, Alan Friend *lawyer*

Dalton
Kinnamon, Gregory Harold *lawyer*

Decatur
Middleton, James Boland *lawyer*
Oakley, Mary Ann Bryant *lawyer*

Dillard
Wilkinson, Albert Mims, Jr. *lawyer*

Dublin
Greene, Jule Blounte *lawyer*

Duluth
Cardin, Charles Edward *lawyer*

Fort Valley
Marchman, Robert L., III *lawyer, pecan farmer*

Gainesville
Schuder, Raymond Francis *lawyer*

Lawrenceville
Henson, Gene Ethridge *retired legal administrator*

Lookout Mountain
Hitching, Harry James *retired lawyer*

Macon
Ennis, Edgar William, Jr. *lawyer*
Rutledge, Ivan Cate *retired legal educator, arbitrator*
Sell, Edward Scott, Jr. *lawyer*
Snow, Cubbedge, Jr. *lawyer*

Marietta
Belcher, Julianna *lawyer*
Burkey, J(acob) Brent *lawyer, company executive*
Hammond, John William *lawyer*
Ingram, George Conley *lawyer*

Metter
Doremus, Ogden *lawyer*

Norcross
Helander, Robert Charles *lawyer*

Savannah
Dickey, David Herschel *lawyer, accountant*
Forbes, Morton Gerald *lawyer*
Kenrich, John Lewis *lawyer*
McAlpin, Kirk Martin *lawyer*
Painter, Paul Wain, Jr. *lawyer*
Rawson, William Robert *lawyer, retired manufacturing company executive*
Stillwell, Walter Brooks, III *lawyer*

Smyrna
Welch, Jennifer Diane *lawyer*

Watkinsville
Wright, Robert Joseph *lawyer*

HAWAII

Honolulu
Akinaka, Asa Masayoshi *lawyer*
Bloede, Victor Carl *lawyer, academic executive*
Broder, Sherry Phyllis *lawyer*
Cades, Julius Russell *lawyer*
Callies, David Lee *lawyer, educator*
Case, James Hebard *lawyer*
Char, Vernon Fook Leong *lawyer*
Chuck, Walter G(oonsun) *lawyer*
Devens, Paul *lawyer*
D'Olier, H(enry) Mitchell *lawyer*
Fernandes Salling, Lehua *lawyer, state senator*
Fong, Peter C. K. *lawyer, judge*
Gay, E(mil) Laurence *lawyer*
Gelber, Don Jeffrey *lawyer*
Heller, Ronald Ian *lawyer*
Katayama, Robert Nobuichi *lawyer*
Lilly, Michael Alexander *lawyer*
Marks, Michael J. *lawyer, corporate executive*
Mattoch, Ian L. *lawyer*
Miller, Richard Sherwin *legal educator*
Moore, Willson Carr, Jr. *lawyer*
Okinaga, Lawrence Shoji *lawyer*
Omori, Morio *lawyer*
†Pollack, Richard W. *lawyer*
Porter, Michael Pell *lawyer*
Quinn, William Francis *lawyer*
Roberti, Mario Andrew *lawyer, former energy company executive*
Turbin, Richard *lawyer*

Kula
Rohlfing, Frederick William *lawyer, judge*

Lahaina
Nelson, Robert Bruce *lawyer*

Wailuku
Kinaka, William Tatsuo *lawyer*

IDAHO

Boise
Board, Dwight Vernon *lawyer*
Klein, Edith Miller *lawyer, former state senator*
Lance, Alan George *lawyer, legislator, attorney general*
Leroy, David Henry *lawyer, state and federal official*
Marcus, Craig Brian *lawyer*
O'Riordan, William Hugh *lawyer*
Risch, James E. *lawyer*
Shurtliff, Marvin Karl *lawyer*
VanHole, William Remi *lawyer*

Ketchum
Hogue, Terry Glynn *lawyer*

Lewiston
Peterson, Philip Everett *legal educator*
Ware, Marcus John *lawyer*

Moscow
Seeger, Leinaala Robinson *law librarian, educator*

Pocatello
Nye, W. Marcus W. *lawyer*

Rupert
Bellwood, Sherman Jean *arbitrator, consultant, retired judge*

ILLINOIS

Abbott Park
Sazdanoff, Catherine Ann *lawyer*

Alton
Hoagland, Karl King, Jr. *lawyer*
Struif, L. James *lawyer*

AMF Ohare
Bateman, Sylvia Lilaine *lawyer*

Aurora
Alschuler, Sam *lawyer*
Lowe, Ralph Edward *lawyer*
Tyler, Lloyd John *lawyer*

Barrington
Victor, Michael Gary *lawyer, physician*
Wyatt, James Frank, Jr. *lawyer*

Belleville
Bauman, John Duane *lawyer*
Boyle, Richard Edward *lawyer*
Coghill, William Thomas, Jr. *lawyer*
Heiligenstein, Christian E. *lawyer*
Hess, Frederick J. *lawyer*
Parham, James Robert *lawyer*

Bloomington
Bragg, Michael Ellis *lawyer*
Goebel, William Mathers *lawyer*
Jordan, Leo John *lawyer*
Montgomery, William Adam *lawyer*
Sullivan, Laura Patricia *lawyer, insurance company executive*

Carbondale
Clemons, John Robert *lawyer*
Kionka, Edward James *lawyer*
Lesar, Hiram Henry *lawyer, educator*
Matthews, Elizabeth Woodfin *law librarian, law educator*

Carrollton
Strickland, Hugh Alfred *lawyer*

Carthage
Glidden, John Redmond *lawyer*

Champaign
Bender, Paul Edward *lawyer*
Cribbet, John Edward *legal educator, former university chancellor*
Frampton, George Thomas *legal educator*
Kindt, John Warren, Sr. *lawyer, educator, consultant*
Krause, Harry Dieter *lawyer, educator*
Maggs, Peter Blount *lawyer, educator*
Mamer, Stuart Mies *lawyer*
Miller, Harold Arthur *lawyer*
Nowak, John E. *law educator*
Phipps, John Tom *lawyer*
Rotunda, Ronald Daniel *law educator, consultant*
Surles, Richard Hurlbut, Jr. *law librarian*

Chicago
Abbott, Kenneth Wayne *law educator*
Abrahamson, Vicki Lafer *lawyer*
Abrams, Lee Norman *lawyer*
Acker, Frederick George *lawyer*
Adair, Wendell Hinton, Jr. *lawyer*
Adams, Roy M. *lawyer, writer*
Adelman, Stanley Joseph *lawyer*
Adelman, Steven Herbert *lawyer*
Agnew, David M. *lawyer*
Aland, Robert H. *lawyer*
Aldrich, Thomas Lawrence *lawyer*
Alexander, William Henry *lawyer*
Alexis, Geraldine M. *lawyer*
Allard, Jean *lawyer, urban planner*
Allen, Ronald Jay *law educator*
Allen, Thomas Draper *lawyer*
Alschuler, Albert W. *law educator*
Altheimer, Alan J. *lawyer*
Altman, Louis *lawyer, author, educator*
Ambrose, Gerald A. *lawyer*
Anagnost, Themis John *lawyer*
Anderson, David A. *lawyer*
Anderson, Donald W. *lawyer*
Anderson, J. Trent *lawyer*
Anderson, John Thomas *lawyer*
Anderson, Kimball Richard *lawyer*
Anderson, William Cornelius, III *lawyer*
Angelo, Percy L. *lawyer*
Angst, Gerald L. *lawyer*
Anthony, Michael Francis *lawyer*
Anvaripour, M. A. *lawyer*
Apcel, Melissa Anne *lawyer*
Appel, Nina Schick *law educator, dean*
Arlow, Allan Joseph *lawyer*
Armstrong, Edwin Richard *lawyer, publisher, editor*
Aronson, Simon H. *lawyer*
Aronson, Virginia L. *lawyer*
Arroyo, Robert Edward *lawyer*
Artwick, Frederic J. *lawyer*
Athas, Gus James *lawyer*
Auerbach, Marshall Jay *lawyer*
Austin, Richard William *lawyer*
Austin, Robert B. *lawyer*
Auwarter, Franklin Paul *lawyer*
Axley, Frederick William *lawyer*
Badel, Julie *lawyer*
Baer, John Richard Frederick *lawyer*
Baetz, W. Timothy *lawyer*
Bailey, Robert Short *lawyer*
Baird, Douglas Gordon *law educator*
Baird, Russell Miller *lawyer*
Baker, James Edward Sproul *retired lawyer*
Baker, Pamela *lawyer*
Banoff, Sheldon Irwin *lawyer*
Barker, William Thomas *lawyer*
Barnard, Morton John *lawyer*
Barnard, Robert N. *lawyer*
Barnes, James Garland, Jr. *lawyer*
Barr, John Robert *lawyer*
Barrett, Roger Watson *lawyer*
Barron, Howard Robert *lawyer*
Barry, Norman J., Jr. *lawyer*
Bartlit, Fred Holcomb, Jr. *lawyer, educator*
Baruch, Hurd *lawyer*
Bashwiner, Steven Lacelle *lawyer*
Baugher, Peter V. *lawyer*
Baumgartner, William Hans, Jr. *lawyer*
Beall, Ingrid Lillehei *lawyer*
Beck, Philip S. *lawyer*
Becker, Mary E. *law educator*
Becker, Theodore Michaelson *lawyer*
Beckstrom, John H. *lawyer, educator*
Beem, Jack Darrel *lawyer*
Beggan, John Francis *lawyer*
Belmore, F. Martin *lawyer*
Bennett, M(ary) Elizabeth *lawyer*
Bennett, Russell Odbert *lawyer*
Bentley, Peter John Hilton *lawyer*
Berens, Mark Harry *lawyer*
Berger, Robert Michael *lawyer*
Berghoff, John C., Jr. *lawyer*
Bergstrom, Robert William *lawyer*
Berkeley, Jill Brenda *lawyer*
Berland, Abel Edward *lawyer, realtor*
Berman, Bennett I. *lawyer*
Bernard, Frank Charles *lawyer*
Berner, Robert Lee, Jr. *lawyer*
Bernick, David M. *lawyer*
Berning, Larry D. *lawyer*
Bernstein, H. Bruce *lawyer*
Bernstein, Howard L. *lawyer*
Bernstein, Stuart *lawyer*
Berolzheimer, Karl *lawyer*
Berry, Alan M. *lawyer*
Betke, James E. *lawyer*
Bezman, Victor H. *lawyer*
Biebel, Paul Philip, Jr. *lawyer*
Bielawski, Alan P. *lawyer*
Bierig, Jack R. *lawyer*
Bitner, John Howard *lawyer*
Bixby, Frank Lyman *lawyer*
Blackman, Jana Cohen *lawyer*
Blakemore, Thomas F. *lawyer*
Blanco, Jim L. *lawyer*
Blatt, Richard Lee *lawyer*
Block, Neal Jay *lawyer*
Bloom, Christopher Arthur *lawyer*
Blount, Michael Eugene *lawyer*
Boberg, Wayne D. *lawyer*
Bockelman, John Richard *lawyer*
Bodine, Laurence *lawyer, editor, marketer*
Bogert, George Taylor *lawyer*
Boies, Wilber H. *lawyer*
Boley, John N. *lawyer*
Bomchill, Fern Cheryl *lawyer*
Boodell, Thomas Joseph, Jr. *lawyer*
Borders, Thomas C. *lawyer*
Bosselman, Fred Paul *law educator*
Botica, Matthew J. *lawyer*
Bouma, Robert Edwin *lawyer, diversified company executive*
Bowe, William John *lawyer*
Bowen, Stephen Stewart *lawyer*
Bower, Bruce Lester *lawyer*
Bower, Glen Landis *lawyer*
Bowytz, Robert B. *lawyer*
Boyd, David J. *lawyer*
Bramnik, Robert Paul *lawyer*
Breakstone, Donald S. *lawyer*
Brennan, James Joseph *lawyer*
Brennan, Richard J. *lawyer*
Brice, Roger Thomas *lawyer*
Bridewell, David Alexander *lawyer*
Bridgman, Thomas Francis *lawyer*
Brizzolara, Charles Anthony *lawyer*
Brooks, Robert Liss *lawyer*
Brophy, Joan Edmonds *lawyer*
Brown, Alan Crawford *lawyer*
Brown, Donald James, Jr. *lawyer*
Brown, Gregory K. *lawyer*
Bruner, Stephen C. *lawyer*
Bryson, Cheryl Blackwell *lawyer*
Buchholz, Edward J. *lawyer*
Bulger, Brian Wegg *lawyer*
Bunge, Jonathan Gunn *lawyer*
Burdelik, Thomas L. *lawyer*
Burditt, George Miller, Jr. *lawyer*
Burgett, George L. *lawyer*
Burke, Thomas Joseph, Jr. *lawyer*
Burkey, Lee Melville *lawyer*
Busey, Roxane C. *lawyer*
†Butts, Edward A. *lawyer*
Byman, Robert Leslie *lawyer*
Cahan, James N. *lawyer*
Campbell, Christian Larsen *lawyer*
Caplis, Kevin J. *lawyer*
Carlin, Dennis J. *lawyer*
Carlson, Stephen Curtis *lawyer*
Carlson, Walter Carl *lawyer*
Carpenter, David William *lawyer*
Carren, Jeffrey P. *lawyer*
Carroll, James J. *lawyer*
Carroll, John M. *lawyer*
Carroll, William Kenneth *law educator, psychologist, theologian*
Carton, Laurence Alfred *lawyer*
Cassling, Donald Roger *lawyer*
Chabraja, Nicholas D. *lawyer*
Chaffetz, Hammond Edward *lawyer*
Chandler, Kent, Jr. *lawyer*
Chanen, Franklin Allen *lawyer*
Chapman, Howard Stuart *lawyer*
Cheely, Daniel Joseph *lawyer*
Chefitz, Joel Gerald *lawyer*
†Cherner, Paul Jordan *lawyer*
Cherney, James Alan *lawyer*
†Childers, J. Richard *lawyer*
Chiles, Stephen Michael *lawyer*
Christensen, George B. *lawyer, retired*
Cicero, Frank, Jr. *lawyer*
Citron, Diane *lawyer*
Clark, James Allen *lawyer, educator*
Clark, James E. *lawyer*
Clay, John Ernest *lawyer*
Clemens, Richard Glenn *lawyer*
Closen, Michael Lee *law educator*
Cohen, Christopher B. *lawyer*
Cohen, Melanie Rovner *lawyer*
Cole, Thomas Amor *lawyer*
Collen, Sheldon Orrin *lawyer*
Colman, Jeffrey D. *lawyer*
Comiskey, Michael Peter *lawyer*
Congalton, Susan Tichenor *lawyer*
Conklin, Thomas William *lawyer*
Conlon, William F. *lawyer*
Connelly, Vincent J. *lawyer*
Conviser, Richard James *law educator, lawyer, publications company executive*
Conway, Michael Maurice *lawyer*
Cooney, Robert John *lawyer*
Copeland, Edward Jerome *lawyer*
Corboy, Philip Harnett *lawyer*
Corcoran, James Martin, Jr. *lawyer, writer, lecturer*
Corwin, Sherman Phillip *lawyer*
Costello, John William *lawyer*
Cotton, Eugene *lawyer*
Coughlan, Kenneth Lewis *lawyer*
Coughlin, Joseph E. *lawyer*
Covey, Frank Michael, Jr. *lawyer, educator*
Covington, George Morse *lawyer*
Crane, Charlotte *law educator*
Crane, Mark *lawyer*
Craven, George W. *lawyer*
Crawford, Dewey Byers *lawyer*
Creamer, Robert Allan *lawyer*
Cremin, Susan Elizabeth *lawyer*
Crihfield, Philip J. *lawyer*
Crisham, Thomas Michael *lawyer*
Cronin, Robert E. *lawyer*
Crossan, John Robert *lawyer*
†Crown, James Schine *lawyer*
Crumbaugh, David Gordon *lawyer*

Crusto, Mitchell Ferdinand *lawyer, environmental management consultant*
Cunningham, Robert James *lawyer*
Curley, Robert E. *lawyer*
Currie, David Park *lawyer, educator*
Cusack, John Thomas *lawyer*
Custer, Charles Francis *lawyer*
Daley, James P. *lawyer*
Daley, Susan Jean *lawyer*
Dam, Kenneth W. *lawyer, law educator*
D'Amato, Anthony *law educator*
Davidson, Stanley J. *lawyer*
Davis, Michael W. *lawyer*
Davis, Muller *lawyer*
Davis, Ralph E. *lawyer*
Davis, Scott Jonathan *lawyer*
DeCarlo, William S. *lawyer*
Dechene, James Charles *lawyer*
Decker, Richard Knore *lawyer*
de Hoyos, Debora M. *lawyer*
Deignan, Robert E. *lawyer*
Deitrick, William Edgar *lawyer*
Delp, Wilbur Charles, Jr. *lawyer*
Denvir, Robert F. *lawyer*
DePaul, Carol Stone *lawyer*
D'Esposito, Julian C., Jr. *lawyer*
Despres, Leon Mathis *lawyer, former city official*
Detuno, Joseph Edward *lawyer*
DeWolfe, John Chauncey, Jr. *lawyer*
De Yoe, David P. *lawyer*
Dilling, Kirkpatrick Wallwick *lawyer*
Dilworth, Robert Holden *lawyer*
Dixon, Stewart Strawn *lawyer*
Dockterman, Michael *lawyer*
Dondanville, John Wallace *lawyer*
Donenfeld, J. Douglas *lawyer*
Donlevy, John Dearden *lawyer*
Donohoe, Jerome Francis *lawyer*
Donohue, John Joseph *law educator*
Donovan, Thomas B. *lawyer*
Dorman, Jeffrey Lawrence *lawyer*
Dorr, Williams Peter *lawyer*
Douglas, Charles W. *lawyer*
Douglass, Andrew Ian *lawyer, financial executive*
Downing, Robert Allan *lawyer*
Doyle, John Robert *lawyer*
Dropkin, Allen Hodes *lawyer*
Drymalski, Raymond Hibner *lawyer, banker*
Duez, David Joseph *lawyer*
Duhl, Michael Foster *lawyer*
Duncan, John Patrick Cavanaugh *lawyer*
Durchslag, Stephen P. *lawyer*
Durso, John J. *lawyer*
Dykstra, Paul Hopkins *lawyer*
Early, Bert Hylton *lawyer, legal search consultant*
Eaton, Larry Ralph *lawyer*
Eckel, John M. *lawyer*
Edelman, Alvin *lawyer*
Edwards, Charles Lloyd *lawyer*
Egan, Kevin James *lawyer*
Eggert, Russell Raymond *lawyer*
Ehrman, Joseph S. *lawyer*
Eimer, Nathan Philip *lawyer*
Ekdahl, Jon Nels *lawyer, corporate secretary*
Elden, Gary Michael *lawyer*
Ellwood, Scott *lawyer*
Elson, Alex *lawyer, legal educator*
Elson, John S. *legal educator*
Emerson, Carter Whitney *lawyer*
Ephraim, Donald Morley *lawyer*
Epstein, Richard A. *law educator*
Erens, Jay Allan *lawyer*
Ericson, Robert W. *lawyer*
Erlebacher, Arlene Cernik *lawyer*
Esrick, Jerald Paul *lawyer*
Ettinger, Joseph Alan *lawyer*
Even, Francis Alphonse *lawyer*
Everett, Jonathan Jubal *lawyer*
Everson, Leonard Charles *lawyer*
Fahner, Tyrone C. *lawyer, former state attorney general*
Fayhee, Michael R. *lawyer*
Fazio, Peter Victor, Jr. *lawyer*
Feagley, Michael Rowe *lawyer*
Fein, Roger Gary *lawyer*
Feinstein, Fred Ira *lawyer*
Feldman, Scott M. *lawyer*
Fellows, Jerry Kenneth *lawyer*
Ferencz, Robert Arnold *lawyer*
Ferguson, Bradford Lee *lawyer*
Ferrini, James Thomas *lawyer*
Fiduccia, Paul C. *lawyer*
Field, Henry Frederick *lawyer*
Field, Robert Edward *lawyer*
Fifield, William O. *lawyer*
Finke, Robert Forge *lawyer*
Fischel, Daniel R. *law educator*
Fischer, Fredric H. *lawyer*
Fisher, Herbert Hirsh *lawyer*
Fishman, Irving S. *lawyer*
Fishman, Ross Howard *lawyer*
Fitch, Morgan Lewis, Jr. *patent lawyer*
Flanagin, Neil *lawyer*
Fletcher, James L. *lawyer*
Flynn, Peter Anthony *lawyer*
Foote, Edward L. *lawyer*
Ford, Michael W. *lawyer*
Forrester, J(ohn) Paul *lawyer*
Fort, Jeffrey C. *lawyer*
Foudree, Bruce William *lawyer*
Fox, Jacob Logan *lawyer*
Fox, Paul T. *lawyer*
Franch, Richard Thomas *lawyer*
Francis, Clinton William *legal educator*
Franklin, Richard Mark *lawyer*
Fraumann, Willard George *lawyer*
Freed, Mayer Goodman *law educator*
Freehling, Paul Edward *lawyer*
Freeman, Lee Allen, Jr. *lawyer*
Freeman, Louis S. *lawyer*
Friedland, Joanne Benazzi *lawyer*
Friedman, Lawrence Milton *lawyer*
Friedman, Roselyn L. *lawyer*
Fross, Roger Raymond *lawyer*
Fullagar, William Watts *lawyer*
Fuller, Perry Lucian *lawyer*
Furda, Gregory H. *lawyer*
Furlane, Mark Elliott *lawyer*
Fuson, Douglas Finley *lawyer*
Gaggini, John Edmund *lawyer*
Gaines, Kenneth R. *lawyer*
Gancer, Donald Charles *lawyer*
Gangemi, Columbus Rudolph, Jr. *lawyer, educator*
Garber, Samuel Baugh *lawyer, retail company executive*
Garbutt, Eugene James *lawyer*
Gareis, Robert J. *lawyer*
Garth, Bryant Geoffrey *law educator, foundation executive*
Garvey, Michael J. *lawyer*
Garvey, Richard J. *lawyer*
Gates, Stephen Frye *lawyer*
Gaynor, James M., Jr. *lawyer*
Gearen, John J. *lawyer*
Geiman, J. Robert *lawyer*
Geis, Norman Winer *lawyer*
George, John Martin, Jr. *lawyer*
Geraghty, Thomas F. *law educator*
Geraldson, Raymond I. *lawyer*
Geraldson, Raymond I., Jr. *lawyer*
Gerber, Lawrence *lawyer*
Gerek, William Michael *lawyer*
Gerlits, Francis Joseph *lawyer*
Gerson, Jerome Howard *lawyer*
Gerstman, George Henry *lawyer*
Gertz, Elmer *lawyer, author, educator*
Getz, Bettina *lawyer*
Getzendanner, Susan *lawyer, former federal judge*
Giampietro, Wayne Bruce *lawyer*
Gibbons, William John *lawyer*
Gilbert, Howard N(orman) *lawyer*
Gilford, Steven Ross *lawyer*
Gill, Michael J. *lawyer*
Gilson, Jerome *lawyer, writer*
Ginsberg, Lewis Robbins *lawyer*
Given, Ronald B. *lawyer*
Gladden, James Walter, Jr. *lawyer*
Gleeson, Paul Francis *lawyer*
Glieberman, Herbert Allen *lawyer*
Glovka, Richard Paul *lawyer*
Goeke, Joseph R. *lawyer*
Golan, Stephen Leonard *lawyer*
Gold, Norman Myron *lawyer*
Goldberg, Stephen B. *law educator*
Goldblatt, Stanford Jay *lawyer*
Golden, Bruce Paul *lawyer*
Golden, William C. *lawyer*
Goldman, Louis Budwig *lawyer*
Goldschmidt, Lynn Harvey *lawyer*
Goodman, Elliott I(rvin) *lawyer*
Goodman, Gary Alan *lawyer*
Goodman, Stuart Lauren *lawyer*
Gordon, Phillip *lawyer*
Gordon, William A. *lawyer*
Goschi, Nicholas Peter *lawyer*
Goss, Richard Henry *lawyer*
Gottlieb, Gidon Alain Guy *law educator*
Gould, Arthur Irwin *lawyer*
Grady, Mark F. *law educator*
Graham, David F. *lawyer*
Graham, Robert L. *lawyer*
Gralen, Donald John *lawyer*
Grant, Robert Nathan *lawyer*
Gray, James S. *lawyer*
Gray, Milton Hefter *lawyer*
Grayck, Marcus Daniel *lawyer*
Greenbaum, Kenneth *lawyer*
Greenberger, Ernest *lawyer*
Greenblatt, Ray Harris *lawyer*
Greenblatt, Russell Edward *lawyer, consultant*
Gregg, Jon Mann *lawyer*
Gregory, Byron L. *lawyer*
Griffin, Hugh C. *lawyer*
Griffith, Donald Kendall *lawyer*
Grimm, Terry M. *lawyer*
Grimm, Victor E. *lawyer*
Grossi, Francis Xavier, Jr. *lawyer, educator*
Grossman, Robert Mayer *lawyer*
Gunn, Robert Murray *lawyer, farmer*
Guthman, Jack *lawyer*
Haarlow, John B. *lawyer*
Hablutzel, Margo Lynn *lawyer*
Haddad, James Brian *lawyer, law educator*
Haderlein, Thomas M. *lawyer*
Hagan, Robert K. *lawyer*
Hahn, Frederic Louis *lawyer*
Haines, Martha Mahan *lawyer*
Hales, Daniel B. *lawyer*
Hall, Joan M. *lawyer*
Hamilton, Thomas Mackin, Jr. *lawyer*
Hammesfahr, Robert Winter *lawyer*
Hanbury, Marshall E. *lawyer*
Handler, Steven P. *lawyer*
Hannah, Wayne Robertson, Jr. *lawyer*
Hannay, William Mouat, III *lawyer*
Hanson, Richard A. *lawyer*
Hanson, Ronald William *lawyer*
Hanzlik, Paul F. *lawyer*
Hardgrove, James Alan *lawyer*
Hardy, David Jerry *lawyer*
Harmon, Robert Lon *lawyer*
Harrington, Carol A. *lawyer*
Harrington, James Timothy *lawyer*
Harris, Donald Ray *lawyer*
Harrold, Bernard *lawyer*
Hartigan, Neil F. *lawyer, former state official*
Hasten, Michael V. *lawyer*
Hayes, David John Arthur, Jr. *legal association executive*
Hayward, Thomas Zander, Jr. *lawyer*
Head, Patrick James *lawyer*
Heatwole, Mark M. *lawyer*
Heindl, Warren Anton *law educator, retired*
Heine, Spencer H. *corporate lawyer, real estate executive*
Heinz, John Peter *lawyer, educator*
Heinz, William Denby *lawyer*
Heisler, Quentin George, Jr. *lawyer*
Heiss, Robin *lawyer*
Heitland, Ann Rae *lawyer*
Heller, Stanley J. *lawyer, physician*
Helman, Robert Alan *lawyer*
Helmholz, R(ichard) H(enry) *law educator*
Henning, Joel Frank *lawyer, author, publisher, consultant*
Henning, Mark G. *lawyer*
Henry, Frederick Edward *lawyer*
Henry, Robert John *lawyer*
Hensel, Paul H. *lawyer*
Herman, Sidney N. *lawyer*
Herpe, David A. *lawyer*
Herzel, Leo *lawyer*
Herzog, Fred F. *legal educator*
Hess, Peter A. *lawyer*
Hess, Sidney J., Jr. *lawyer*
Hesse, Carolyn Sue *lawyer*
Hester, Thomas Patrick *lawyer*
Hickey, John Thomas, Jr. *lawyer*
Hickman, Frederic W. *lawyer*
Hilborn, Michael G. *lawyer, real estate development executive*
Hiller, David Dean *lawyer*
Hilliard, David Craig *lawyer*
Hinchliff, James Thomas *lawyer*
Hirshman, Harold Carl *lawyer*
Hirshman, Linda Redlick *law educator*
Hitch, James T., III *lawyer*
Hoban, George Savre *lawyer*
Hodes, Scott *lawyer*
Hoeft, Steven H. *lawyer*
Hofer, Roy Ellis *lawyer*
Hoff, William Bruce, Jr. *lawyer*
Hoffman, Douglas W. *lawyer*
Hoffman, Richard Bruce *lawyer*
Hoffman, Valerie Jane *lawyer*
Hoffmann, Howard M. *lawyer*
Hollins, Mitchell Leslie *lawyer*
Holmen, Neil E. *lawyer*
Holmes, Stephen T. *political science and law educator*
Horwath, Leslie Kathleen *lawyer*
Horwich, Allan *lawyer*
Hoskins, Richard Jerold *lawyer*
Howe, Jonathan Thomas *lawyer*
Howell, R(obert) Thomas, Jr. *lawyer, food company executive*
Hron, Michael G. *lawyer*
Hucker, Brian S. *lawyer*
Huebsch, Robert P. *lawyer*
Huggins, Rollin Charles, Jr. *lawyer*
Hughes, Joyce Anne *law educator*
Hummel, Gregory William *lawyer*
Hunt, Lawrence Halley, Jr. *lawyer*
Hurlbert, Robert P. *lawyer*
Hussey, Charles E., II *lawyer*
Huston, DeVerille Anne *lawyer*
Huston, Steven Craig *lawyer*
Hutchins, Harley *lawyer*
Hutchinson, Leland E. *lawyer*
Inbau, Fred Edward *lawyer, educator, author*
Isenbergh, Joseph *law educator*
Jacobson, David Cary *lawyer*
Jacobson, Harold LeLand *lawyer*
Jacobson, Marian Slutz *lawyer*
Jacobson, Richard Joseph *lawyer*
Jacoby, John Primm *lawyer*
Jacover, Jerold Alan *lawyer*
Jager, Melvin Francis *lawyer*
Jahns, Jeffrey *lawyer*
Jakubik, Jerome W. *lawyer*
Jambor, Robert Vernon *lawyer*
†Jast, Raymond Joseph *lawyer*
†Jenkins, Neil Edmund *lawyer*
Jerrick, Ronald M. *lawyer*
Jock, Paul F., II *lawyer*
Johnson, C. Richard *lawyer*
Johnson, Daniel Leroy *lawyer*
Johnson, Elmer William *lawyer*
Johnson, Gary Thomas *lawyer*
Johnson, H. Arvid *lawyer*
Johnson, Lael Frederic *lawyer*
Johnson, Richard Fred *lawyer*
Johnston, Alan Rogers *lawyer*
Johnston, Thomas Watts *lawyer*
Jones, Richard Cyrus *lawyer*
Jones, Thomas M. *lawyer*
Jordan, Michelle Denise *lawyer*
Joseph, Robert Thomas *lawyer*
Joslin, Rodney Dean *lawyer*
Juhl, Loren Earl *lawyer*
Junewicz, James J. *lawyer*
Jurek, Kenneth J. *lawyer*
Kamin, Chester Thomas *lawyer*
Kanwit, Glen Harris *lawyer*
Kaplan, Harold L. *lawyer*
Kaplan, Jared *lawyer*
Kaplan, Sidney Mountbatten *lawyer*
Kaplan, Wayne S. *lawyer*
Karaba, Frank Andrew *lawyer*
Karge, Stewart W. *lawyer*
Kastel, Howard L. *lawyer*
Katten, Melvin L. *lawyer*
Katz, Harold Ambrose *lawyer, former state legislator*
Katz, Stuart Charles *lawyer, concert jazz musician*
Kaufman, Andrew Michael *lawyer*
Keck, Robert Clifton *lawyer*
Kelley, Duane Matthew *lawyer*
Kelly, Charles Arthur *lawyer*
Kelman, Robert Andrew *lawyer*
Kempf, Donald G., Jr. *lawyer*
Kenney, Frank Deming *lawyer*
Kenny, Edmund Joyce *lawyer*
Kessler, Stanton A. *lawyer*
Kiley, Roger J. *lawyer*
King, Clark Chapman, Jr. *lawyer*
King, Michael Howard *lawyer*
King, Sharon L. *lawyer*
Kins, Juris *lawyer*
Kipnis, Mark S. *lawyer*
Kipperman, Lawrence I. *lawyer*
Kirkland, John Leonard *lawyer*
Kissel, Richard John *lawyer*
Kite, Steven B. *lawyer*
Klegerman, Neal Alan *lawyer*
Klenk, James Andrew *lawyer*
Knight, Christopher Nichols *lawyer*
Knox, James Edwin *lawyer*
Knuti, Robert A. *lawyer*
Kohn, Shalom L. *lawyer*
Kohn, William Irwin *lawyer*
Kolek, Robert Edward *lawyer*
Komie, Stephen Mark *lawyer*
Koran, Janet M. *lawyer*
Kortright, Richard T. *lawyer*
Koven, Howard Richard *lawyer*
Kowitt, Arthur Jay *lawyer*
Kravitt, Jason Harris Paperno *lawyer*
Kriss, Robert J. *lawyer*
Kroll, Barry Lewis *lawyer*
Krueger, Herbert William *lawyer*
Krupka, Robert George *lawyer*
Kucera, Daniel Jerome *lawyer*
Kunkle, William Joseph, Jr. *lawyer*
Kurland, Philip B. *lawyer, educator*
Kuta, Jeffrey Theodore *lawyer*
Ladd, Jeffrey Raymond *lawyer*
Laidlaw, Andrew R. *lawyer*
Landan, Henry Sinclair *lawyer*
Landes, William M. *law educator*
Landow-Esser, Janine Marise *lawyer*
Landsman, Stephen A. *lawyer*
Lane, Robert G. *lawyer*
Lane, Ronald Alan *lawyer*
Laner, Richard Warren *lawyer*
Lang, Richard A. *lawyer*
Langhenry, John Godfred, Jr. *lawyer*
Lapidus, Allan E. *lawyer*
LaRue, Paul Hubert *lawyer*
LaRue, Paul Hubert, Jr. *lawyer*
Lasky, Laurence D. *lawyer*
Lassar, Scott R. *lawyer*
Latimer, Kenneth Alan *lawyer*
LeDuc, John Andre *lawyer*
Lee, William Marshall *lawyer*
Leiseca, Sergio A. Jr. *lawyer*
Leisten, Arthur Gaynor *lawyer*
Lemein, Gregg D. *lawyer*
Lev, Allen P. *lawyer*
Levenfeld, Milton Arthur *lawyer*
Levi, John G. *lawyer*
Levin, Charles Edward *lawyer*
Levin, Jack S. *lawyer*
Levin, Michael David *lawyer*
Levine, Laurence Harvey *lawyer*
Levit, Louis William *lawyer*
Levy, Richard Herbert *lawyer*
Lewis, Julius *lawyer*
Lieberman, Myron *lawyer*
Lind, Jon Robert *lawyer*
Linklater, William Joseph *lawyer*
Lippe, Melvin Karl *lawyer*
Lipton, Lois Jean *lawyer*
Lipton, Richard M. *lawyer*
List, David Patton *lawyer*
Listrom, Linda L. *lawyer*
Litwin, Burton Howard *lawyer*
Livingston, Theodore A., Jr. *lawyer*
Lloyd, William F. *lawyer*
Lockwood, Gary Lee *lawyer*
Looman, James R. *lawyer*
Lorch, Kenneth F. *lawyer*
Lorenz, Richard Theodore, Jr. *lawyer*
Lott, David Stuart *lawyer*
Lubet, Steven *law educator*
Lubin, Donald G. *lawyer*
Lucas, Jo Desha *law educator, editor*
Lucas, John Kenneth *lawyer*
Lundergan, Barbara Keough *lawyer*
Lundy, Joseph R. *lawyer*
Lurie, Paul Michael *lawyer*
Luscombe, George A. II *lawyer*
Lutter, Paul Allen *lawyer*
Lutz, Karl Evan *lawyer*
Lynch, John Peter *lawyer*
MacCarthy, Terence Francis *lawyer*
Macey, Jonathan R. *law educator*
Macneil, Ian Roderick *lawyer, educator*
Maher, David Willard *lawyer*
Maher, Francesca Marciniak *lawyer*
Malato, Stephen H. *lawyer*
Malkin, Cary Jay *lawyer*
Malone, James Laurence, III *lawyer*
Malovance, Gregory J. *lawyer*
Malstrom, Robert A. *lawyer*
Mancoff, Neal Alan *lawyer*
Mandell, Floyd A. *lawyer*
Mangler, Robert James *lawyer*
Mann, H. George *lawyer*
Maram, Barry S. *lawyer*
Marcus, Stephen A. *lawyer*
Margolis, Jeremy *lawyer*
Marks, Dennis A. *lawyer*
Marks, Jerome *lawyer*
Marovitz, James Lee *lawyer*
Marshall, Eric C. *lawyer*
Marshall, John David *lawyer*
Marshall, Prentice H., Jr. *lawyer*
Martin, Arthur Mead *lawyer*
Martin, R. Eden *lawyer*
Marwedel, Warren John *lawyer*
Marx, David, Jr. *lawyer*
Mason, Henry Lowell, III *lawyer*
Matis, Nina B. *lawyer*
Mattos Neto, Sebastiao De Souza *lawyer*
Mattson, Stephen Joseph *lawyer*
Maxson, M. Finley *lawyer*
Mayer, Frank D., Jr. *lawyer*
Mayers, Barbara W. *lawyer*
McBreen, Maura Ann *lawyer*
McCaleb, Malcolm, Jr. *lawyer*
McCarthy, Paul *lawyer*
Mc Clure, James J., Jr. *lawyer, former municipal executive*
McCombs, Hugh R., Jr. *lawyer*
Mc Connell, Michael W. *law educator*
McCormick, Steven D. *lawyer*
McCracken, Thomas James, Jr. *lawyer*
McCue, Howard McDowell, III *lawyer, educator*
McCue, Judith W. *lawyer*
McDermott, John H(enry) *lawyer*
McDermott, Robert B. *lawyer*
McDonald, Thomas Alexander *lawyer*
McDonough, John Michael *lawyer*
Mc Dougall, Dugald Stewart *retired lawyer*
McDowell, William S. *lawyer*
McGivern, Arthur J. *corporate lawyer, food products company executive*
McGrath, William Joseph *lawyer*
McGuigan, John V. *lawyer*
McKenzie, Robert E. *lawyer*
McLaughlin, T. Mark *lawyer*
McLean, Robert David *lawyer*
McMahon, Thomas Michael *lawyer*
McMenamin, John Robert *lawyer*
McNeill, Thomas B. *lawyer*
McQueen, Thomas K. *lawyer*
McVisk, William Kilburn *lawyer*
McWhirter, Bruce J. *lawyer*
McWilliams, Dennis Michael *lawyer*
Mehlman, Mark Franklin *lawyer*
Melbinger, Michael S. *lawyer*
Meleney, John Alexander *lawyer*
Melton, David Reuben *lawyer*
Meltzer, Bernard David *legal educator*
Menson, Richard L. *lawyer*
Merrill, Thomas Wendell *lawyer, law educator*
Meyer, J. Theodore *lawyer*
Meyer, Michael Louis *lawyer*
Michalak, Edward Francis *lawyer*
Migdal, Sheldon Paul *lawyer*
Millard, Richard Steven *lawyer*
Miller, Geoffrey Parsons *law educator*
Miller, Maurice James *lawyer*
Miller, Michael I. *lawyer*
Miller, Paul J. *lawyer*
Miller, Stephen Ralph *lawyer*
Miller, Theodore Norman *lawyer*
Millner, Robert B. *lawyer*
Mills, Martha Alice *lawyer*
Milnikel, Robert Saxon *lawyer*
Milstein, Albert *lawyer*
Minichello, Dennis *lawyer*
Minow, Newton Norman *lawyer*
Mitchell, Daniel Ray *lawyer*
Mlsna, Timothy Martin *lawyer*
Moelmann, Lawrence R. *lawyer*
Moltz, Marshall Jerome *lawyer*
Mone, Peter John *lawyer*
Montgomery, Charles Barry *lawyer*
Moran, John Thomas, Jr. *lawyer*

Morency, Paula J. *lawyer*
Morrison, John Horton *lawyer*
Morrison, Michael P. *lawyer*
Morrison, Portia Owen *lawyer*
Morrissey, Francis Daniel *lawyer*
Morrow, John Ellsworth *lawyer*
Morsch, Thomas Harvey *lawyer*
Mrozek, Donald L. *lawyer*
Muchin, Allan B. *lawyer*
Muench, John E. *lawyer*
Mullen, J. Thomas *lawyer*
Mumford, Manly Whitman *lawyer*
Munitz, Gerald F. *lawyer*
Munson, James Calfee *lawyer*
Murdock, Charles William *lawyer, educator*
Murray, Daniel Richard *lawyer*
Murray, Gregory S. *lawyer*
Murray, James Cunningham, Jr. *lawyer*
Murtaugh, Christopher David *lawyer*
Murtaugh, Michael K. *lawyer*
Myers, Lonn William *lawyer*
Nachman, James L. *lawyer*
Nachman, Norman Harry *lawyer*
Nash, Robert Coutts *lawyer*
Neal, Stephen C. *lawyer*
Nebel, Kai Allen *lawyer*
Nechin, Herbert Benjamin *lawyer*
Neis, James M. *lawyer*
Nelsen, Timothy Alan *lawyer*
Nelson, Richard David *lawyer*
Nelson, Thomas R. *lawyer*
Nemerovski, Steven H. *lawyer*
Nesburg, Alan D. *lawyer*
Newey, Paul Davis *lawyer*
Newlin, Charles Fremont *lawyer*
Newman, Terry E. *lawyer*
Nicklin, Emily *lawyer*
Nicolaides, Mary *lawyer*
Nissen, William John *lawyer*
Nitikman, Franklin W. *lawyer*
Nixon, Harvey *lawyer*
Nord, Robert Eamor *lawyer*
Notz, John Kranz, Jr. *lawyer*
Nowacki, James Nelson *lawyer*
Nussbaum, Bernard J. *lawyer*
Nye, Sandra Gayle *lawyer, psychiatric social worker, consultant*
O'Brien, James Phillip *lawyer*
O'Brien, Patrick William *lawyer*
O'Connor, Daniel J. *lawyer*
O'Connor, John Killeen *lawyer*
Odorizzi, Michele L. *lawyer*
Oesterle, Eric Adam *lawyer*
O'Flaherty, Paul Benedict *lawyer*
O'Hagan, James Joseph *lawyer*
O'Hare, John Mitchell *lawyer*
O'Leary, Daniel Vincent, Jr. *lawyer*
O'Leary, Frank J. *lawyer*
Olian, Robert Martin *lawyer*
O'Malley, John Daniel *legal educator, banker*
Orbon, Margaret J. *lawyer*
Organ, Joseph B. *lawyer*
Oswald, William H. *lawyer*
Overgaard, Mitchell Jersild *lawyer*
Overton, George Washington *lawyer*
Ozog, Edward J. *lawyer*
Pallasch, B. Michael *lawyer*
Palm, Gary Howard *lawyer, educator*
Palmer, John Bernard, III *lawyer*
Palmer, Robert Towne *lawyer*
Palmore, Roderick Alan *lawyer*
Panich, Danuta Bembenista *lawyer*
Pape, Arthur Edward *lawyer*
Parsons, Keith I. *lawyer*
Partridge, Mark Van Buren *lawyer*
Parzen, Stanley Julius *lawyer*
Pascal, Roger *lawyer*
Pattishall, Beverly Wyckliffe *lawyer*
Patton, Stephen Ray *lawyer*
Pavalon, Eugene Irving *lawyer*
Pearl, Melvin E. *lawyer, film producer*
Pelton, Russell Meredith, Jr. *lawyer*
Perkins, James L. *lawyer*
Perlberg, Jules Martin *lawyer*
Perlman, Judy Platt *lawyer*
Perlstadt, Sidney Morris *lawyer*
Perry, Michael John *law educator*
Petersen, Donald Sondergaard *lawyer*
Petersen, William Otto *lawyer*
Peterson, Gerald C. *lawyer*
Petrakis, Peter *lawyer*
Phelps, Paul Michael *lawyer*
†Piecewicz, Walter Michael *lawyer*
Piekarski, Victor J. *lawyer*
Pierce, Daniel Marshall *lawyer, mayor*
Pitt, George *lawyer*
Platz, George Arthur, III *lawyer*
Poe, Douglas Allan *lawyer*
Polaski, Anne Spencer *lawyer*
Pollock, Earl Edward *lawyer*
Polsby, Daniel D. *law educator*
Pope, Daniel James *lawyer*
Pope, Jerome W. *lawyer*
Postlewaite, Philip Frederick *law educator*
Powles, Peter B. *lawyer*
Pratt, Robert Windsor *lawyer*
Presser, Stephen Bruce *lawyer, educator*
Prior, Gary L. *lawyer*
Pritikin, David T. *lawyer*
Pritikin, James B. *lawyer, employee benefits consultant*
Prochnow, Douglas Lee *lawyer*
Prochnow, Herbert Victor, Jr. *lawyer*
Proctor, Edward George *lawyer*
Pugliese, Robert J. *lawyer*
Quinlan, William Joseph, Jr. *lawyer*
Ralph, William J. *lawyer*
Rank, John Thomas *lawyer*
Rankin, James Winton *lawyer*
Ranney, George A., Jr. *lawyer*
Rapoport, David E. *lawyer*
Rasor, Robert D. *lawyer*
Ratner, Gerald *lawyer*
Rattner, William Edward *lawyer*
Rauch, George Washington *lawyer*
Raymond, Spencer Henry *lawyer*
Rearick, J. Arden *lawyer*
Redish, Martin Harris *legal educator*
Reed, Janet Lynn *lawyer*
Reed, Keith Allen *lawyer*
Refo, Patricia Lee *lawyer*
Reich, Allan J. *lawyer*
Reicin, Ronald Ian *lawyer*
Reiter, Michael A. *lawyer*
Relias, John Alexis *lawyer*
Resnick, Donald Ira *lawyer*
Reuben, Don Harold *lawyer*
Reum, James Michael *lawyer*
Reynolds, Thomas A., Jr. *lawyer*
Reynolds, Thomas A., III *lawyer*
Rhind, James Thomas *lawyer*
Rhoads, Paul Kelly *lawyer*
Rhodes, Charles Harker, Jr. *lawyer*
Richardson, William F. *lawyer*
Richman, John Marshall *lawyer, business executive*
Richmond, William Patrick *lawyer*
Rieger, Mitchell Sheridan *lawyer*
Rissman, Burton Richard *lawyer*
Ritchie, Albert *lawyer*
Ritchie, William Paul *lawyer*
Rizzo, Ronald Stephen *lawyer*
Robinson, Martin F. *lawyer*
Robinson, Theodore Curtis, Jr. *lawyer*
Roche, James McMillan *lawyer*
Roebuck, John Clifford *lawyer*
Rogers, Eddy J. *lawyer*
Roin, Howard James *lawyer*
Rooney, Matthew A. *lawyer*
Ropski, Gary Melchior *lawyer*
Rosemarin, Carey Stephen *lawyer*
Rosenberg, Richard M. *lawyer*
Rosenbloom, Lewis Stanley *lawyer*
Rosenblum, Michael F. *lawyer*
Ross, Jeffrey Kenneth *lawyer*
Roston, David C. *lawyer*
Rowder, William Louis *lawyer*
Rubin, E(rwin) Leonard *lawyer*
Rubin, Robert J. *lawyer*
Rubinowitz, Leonard S. *lawyer, educator*
Ruder, David Sturtevant *lawyer, educator, government official*
Rudnick, Paul David *lawyer*
Rudstein, David Stewart *law educator*
Rundio, Louis Michael, Jr. *lawyer*
Rupert, Donald William *lawyer*
Russell, James H. *lawyer*
Russell, Paul Frederick *lawyer*
Rutkoff, Alan Stuart *lawyer*
Ryan, Robert Collins *lawyer*
Ryan, Thomas F. *lawyer*
Ryder, David R. *lawyer*
Sabl, John J. *lawyer*
Salpeter, Alan N. *lawyer*
Sanders, David P. *lawyer*
Sanders, Richard Henry *lawyer*
Sandquist, Elroy Charles, Jr. *lawyer*
Sangerman, Harry M. *lawyer*
Saunders, George Lawton, Jr. *lawyer*
Saunders, Terry Rose *lawyer*
Savner, David A. *lawyer*
Sawdey, Richard Marshall *lawyer*
Sawyier, Calvin P. *lawyer*
Sawyier, David R. *lawyer*
Schauer, Louis Frank *lawyer*
Schiffman, David M. *lawyer*
Schiller, Donald Charles *lawyer*
Schiller, Eric M. *lawyer*
Schimberg, A(rmand) Bruce *retired lawyer*
Schindel, Donald Marvin *lawyer*
Schink, James Harvey *lawyer*
Schippers, David Philip *lawyer*
Schlickman, J. Andrew *lawyer*
Schlitter, Stanley Allen *lawyer*
Schneider, Dan W. *lawyer, consultant*
Schneider, Robert Jerome *lawyer*
Schoonhoven, Ray James *retired lawyer*
Schorer, Joseph U. *lawyer*
Schoumacher, Bruce Herbert *lawyer*
Schreck, Robert A., Jr. *lawyer*
Schriver, John T., III *lawyer*
Schuette, Michael *lawyer*
Schulhofer, Stephen Joseph *law educator*
Schulte, Stephen Charles *lawyer*
Schultz, Kurt Lee *lawyer*
Schulz, Keith Donald *corporate lawyer*
Schuyler, Daniel Merrick *lawyer, educator*
Schwartz, Donald Lee *lawyer*
Scogland, William Lee *lawyer*
Scott, Theodore R. *lawyer*
Scullion, Annette Murphy *lawyer, educator*
Seamons, Quinton Frank *lawyer*
Seely, Robert Fleming *lawyer*
Seewald, Elsbeth M. *law firm executive, fraternal organization administrator*
Seidenfeld, Glenn Kenneth *lawyer*
Seki, Hoken S. *lawyer*
Selander, Larry *lawyer*
Seligman, Richard Michael *lawyer*
Serritella, James Anthony *lawyer*
Serritella, William David *lawyer*
Serwer, Alan Michael *lawyer*
Sfikas, Peter Michael *lawyer, educator*
Shadur, Robert H. *lawyer*
Shank, William O. *lawyer*
Shannon, Peter Michael, Jr. *lawyer*
Shapiro, Harold David *lawyer, educator*
Shapiro, Stephen Michael *lawyer*
Shapo, Helene S. *law educator*
Shapo, Marshall Schambelan *lawyer, educator*
Sheldon, Harvey M. *lawyer*
Shepherd, Stewart Robert *lawyer*
Shepro, Richard W. *lawyer*
Sherck, Timothy C. *lawyer*
Shields, Thomas Charles *lawyer*
Shindler, Donald A. *lawyer*
Sido, Kevin Richard *lawyer*
Siegel, Howard Jerome *lawyer*
Sigal, Michael Stephen *lawyer*
Silberman, Alan Harvey *lawyer*
Silets, Harvey Marvin *lawyer*
Simon, John Bern *lawyer*
Simon, John P. *lawyer*
Simon, Seymour *lawyer, former state supreme court justice*
Siske, Roger Charles *lawyer*
Skilling, Raymond Inwood *lawyer*
Sklarsky, Charles B. *lawyer*
Slavitt, Earl Benton *lawyer*
Slocomb, Paul D. *lawyer*
Smart, Allen Rich, II *lawyer*
Smedinghoff, Thomas J. *lawyer*
Smith, Arthur B(everly), Jr. *lawyer*
Smith, Gordon Howell *lawyer*
Smith, John Gelston *lawyer*
Smith, Lawrence R. *lawyer*
Smith, Mary Anne *lawyer*
Smith, Michele *lawyer*
Smith, Tefft W. *lawyer*
Snider, Lawrence K. *lawyer*
Snyder, Jean Maclean *lawyer*
†Snyder, William E. *lawyer*
Solomon, Jack Avrum *lawyer, automotive distributor, art dealer*
Solotorovsky, Julian *lawyer*
Solovy, Jerold Sherwin *lawyer*
Sonderby, Peter R. *lawyer*
Spector, David M. *lawyer*
Spellmire, George W. *lawyer*
Spencer, Lewis Douglas *lawyer*
Sperling, Robert Y. *lawyer*
Spindler, George S. *lawyer, oil industry executive*
Spiotto, James Ernest *lawyer*
Springer, David Edward *lawyer*
Sproger, Charles Edmund *lawyer*
Sprowl, Charles Riggs *lawyer*
Stack, John Wallace *lawyer*
Stahl, Charles Eugene *lawyer*
Stahl, David M. *lawyer*
Stanley, James Richard *lawyer*
Stanley, Justin Armstrong *lawyer*
Staples, James G. *lawyer*
Starkman, Gary Lee *lawyer*
Stassen, John Henry *lawyer*
Stein, Carey M. *lawyer*
Steinberg, Morton M. *lawyer*
Steiner, Barbara S. *lawyer*
Stephan, Edmund Anton *lawyer*
Steptoe, Philip P., III *lawyer*
Stern, Robert Louis *lawyer*
Sternstein, Allan J. *lawyer*
Stickler, K. Bruce *lawyer*
Stillman, Nina Gidden *lawyer*
Stinson, James R. *lawyer*
Stoll, John Robert *lawyer, educator*
Stone, Geoffrey Richard *law educator, lawyer*
Stone, Howard Lawrence *lawyer*
Stone, Randolph Noel *law educator*
Storer, John W. *lawyer, consultant*
Strasburger, Joseph Julius *retired lawyer*
Streff, William Albert, Jr. *lawyer*
Strobel, Pamela B. *lawyer*
Strobel, Russ M. *lawyer*
Studwell, Thomas W. *lawyer*
Sullivan, Cornelius J. *lawyer*
Sullivan, Marcia Waite *lawyer*
Sullivan, Thomas Patrick *lawyer*
Sunstein, Cass R. *law educator*
Sussman, Arthur M. *law educator*
Sutherland, Joe Allen *lawyer*
Sutter, William Paul *lawyer*
Swaney, Thomas Edward *lawyer*
Sweeney, James Raymond *lawyer*
Sweeney, Michael J. *lawyer*
Swett, Daniel Robert *lawyer*
Swibel, Steven Warren *lawyer*
Swiger, Elinor Porter *lawyer*
Szala, Scott J. *lawyer*
Szczepanski, Slawomir Zbigniew Steven *lawyer*
Tabin, Julius *patent lawyer, physicist*
Talbot, Earl Armour *lawyer*
Tallant, David, Jr. *lawyer*
Tarun, Robert Walter *lawyer*
Taylor, Roger Lee *lawyer*
Theobald, Edward Robert *lawyer*
Thies, Richard Brian *lawyer*
Thomas, Dale E. *lawyer*
Thomas, Frederick Bradley *lawyer*
Thomas, Stephen Paul *lawyer*
Thompson, James Robert, Jr. *lawyer, former governor*
Thomson, George Ronald *lawyer, educator*
Thorne-Thomsen, Thomas *lawyer*
Tibble, Douglas Clair *lawyer*
Tillett, Samuel Raymond *lawyer*
Tippins, Bedell A. *lawyer*
Tobin, Thomas F. *lawyer*
Tompsett, William C. *lawyer*
Tone, Jeffrey R. *lawyer*
†Tone, Michael P. *lawyer*
Tone, Philip Willis *lawyer, former federal judge*
Toohey, James Kevin *lawyer*
Topol, Clive M. *lawyer*
Torbert, Preston M. *lawyer*
Torshen, Jerome Harold *lawyer*
Towne, L. Stanton *lawyer*
Tozer, Forrest Leigh *lawyer*
Trapp, James McCreery *lawyer*
Treece, John W. *lawyer*
Trienens, Howard Joseph *lawyer*
Truskowski, John Budd *lawyer*
Tsoris, Stephen A. *lawyer*
Tucker, Watson Billopp *lawyer*
Turow, Scott F. *lawyer, author*
Tyler, Thomas Shephard *lawyer*
Tymm, William E. *lawyer*
Valdes, Miguel A. *lawyer*
Vieregg, Robert Todd *lawyer*
Vittum, Daniel Weeks, Jr. *lawyer*
Vogler, James R. *lawyer*
Voortman, John J. *lawyer*
Vree, Roger Allen *lawyer*
Wahlen, Edwin Alfred *lawyer*
Waintroob, Andrea Ruth *lawyer*
Waite, Norman, Jr. *lawyer*
Wall, Robert F. *lawyer*
Walsh, Joseph A., Jr. *lawyer*
Walter, Douglas Hanson *lawyer*
Walter, Priscilla Anne *lawyer*
Walton, Stanley Anthony, III *lawyer*
Waltz, Jon Richard *lawyer, educator, author*
Wander, Herbert Stanton *lawyer*
Wanke, Ronald Lee *lawyer*
Ward, Daniel Patrick *lawyer*
Warnecke, Michael O. *lawyer*
Watson, Lee Ann *lawyer*
Watson, Robert R. *lawyer*
Weaver, William Townsend *laywer*
Webb, Dan K. *lawyer*
Weber, Frederic *lawyer*
Weber, Merrill Evan *lawyer, business executive*
Weinberg, David B. *lawyer*
Weinberger, Seth Jay *lawyer*
Weinkopf, Friedrich J. *lawyer*
Weinsheimer, William Cyrus *lawyer*
Weissman, Michael Lewis *lawyer*
Wexler, Raymond P. *lawyer*
Wexler, Richard Lewis *lawyer*
Whalen, Wayne W. *lawyer*
White, Barry A. *lawyer*
White, Craig Mitchell *lawyer*
White, H. Blair *lawyer*
White, Linda Diane *lawyer*
White, R. Quincy *lawyer*
White, William J. *lawyer*
Whitehead, James S. *lawyer*
Wiggins, Charles Henry, Jr. *lawyer*
Wilcox, Mark Dean *lawyer*
Wilczek, Robert Joseph *lawyer*
Wildman, Max Edward *lawyer*
Williams, Douglas H. *lawyer*
Williams, George Howard *lawyer, association executive*
Williams, H. Randolph *lawyer*
Williams, John Cobb *lawyer*
Williamson, Joel V. *lawyer*
Williamson, Richard Salisbury *lawyer*
Wilson, Bruce G. *lawyer*
Wilson, Harry L. *lawyer*
Wilson, Roger Goodwin *lawyer*
Wise, William Jerrard *lawyer*
Witcoff, Sheldon William *lawyer*
Witwer, Samuel Weiler, Sr. *lawyer*
Wojcik, Lawrence A. *lawyer*
Wolf, Charles Benno *lawyer*
Wolf, Neal Lloyd *lawyer*
Wolfe, David Louis *lawyer*
Wolfson, Larry M. *lawyer*
Wood, James Clarence *lawyer*
Wootton, Robert Ray *lawyer*
Wright, Judith Margaret *law librarian, educator*
Zabel, Sheldon Alter *lawyer, educator*
Zaremski, Miles Jay *lawyer*
Zavis, Michael William *lawyer*
Zemans, Frances Kahn *legal association executive*
Zemm, Sandra Phyllis *lawyer*
Zenner, Sheldon Toby *lawyer*
Zolno, Mark S. *lawyer*
Zulkey, Edward John *lawyer, author*

Chicago Heights
Cifelli, John Louis *lawyer*

Crystal Lake
Knox, Susan Marie *paralegal*

De Kalb
Witmer, John Harper, Jr. *lawyer*

Decatur
Dunn, John Francis *lawyer, state representative*
Mohan, J. Patrick *lawyer*
Stetzner, Leah Manning *lawyer, utilities executive*

Deerfield
Abbey, G(eorge) Marshall *lawyer, former health care company executive, general counsel*
Ames, Craig L. *lawyer*
Gash, Lauren Beth *lawyer, state legislator*
Hannafan, Kay H. Pierce *lawyer*
Oettinger, Julian Alan *lawyer, pharmacy company executive*
Smith, Marschall Imboden *lawyer*
Staubitz, Arthur Frederick *lawyer, healthcare products company executive*
Vollen, Robert Jay *lawyer*
Williams, Robert Jene *lawyer, rail car company executive*

Des Plaines
Brodl, Raymond Frank *lawyer, former lumber company executive*
Demouth, Robin Madison *lawyer, corporate executive*
Jacobs, William Russell, II *lawyer*
Munden, Robin Ghezzi *lawyer*

Downers Grove
Divis, Deborah B. *lawyer*

East Moline
Silliman, Richard George *retired lawyer, retired farm machinery company executive*

Edwardsville
Carlson, Jon Gordon *lawyer*

Elk Grove Village
Sutton, Norma J. *lawyer, educator*

Elmwood Park
Spina, Anthony Ferdinand *lawyer*

Evanston
Alexander, Ellen Jo *lawyer, arbitrator, mediator*
Gormley, R(obert) James *retired lawyer*
Polzin, John Theodore *lawyer*
Taronji, Jaime, Jr. *lawyer*
Van Demark, Ruth Elaine *lawyer*
Vanneman, Edgar, Jr. *lawyer*
Weston, Michael C. *lawyer*

Fairview Heights
Barkofske, Francis Lee *lawyer, coal company executive*

Flossmoor
Garrison, Ray Harlan *lawyer*

Freeport
Matschullat, Dale Lewis *lawyer*

Galva
Massie, Michael Earl *lawyer*

Garden Prairie
Channick, Herbert S. *lawyer, arbitrator, retired real estate and broadcasting corporation executive*

Genoa
Cromley, Jon Lowell *lawyer*

Glen Ellyn
Larson, Ward Jerome *lawyer, retired banker*

Glencoe
Baer, Joseph Winslow *retired lawyer, mediator, arbitrator*
Stewart, Charles Leslie *lawyer*

Glenview
Berkman, Michael G. *lawyer, chemical consultant*
Dawson, Suzanne Stockus *lawyer*
Miller, Edward Boone *lawyer*

Highland
Rikli, Donald Carl *lawyer*

Highland Park
Dolin, Albert Harry *lawyer*
Haight, Edward Allen *lawyer*
Karol, Nathaniel H. *lawyer, consultant*

Hinsdale
Lee, Patricia Hureston *lawyer*
Mulhern, Joseph Patrick *lawyer*
Sheehan, Dennis William *lawyer, business executive*

Joliet
Dunn, Thomas Aquinas *lawyer, state legislator*

Kenilworth
McKittrick, William Wood *lawyer*

La Grange
Kerr, Alexander Duncan, Jr. *lawyer*

Lafox
Seils, William George *lawyer*

Lake Forest
Emerson, William Harry *lawyer, oil company executive*
Sikorovsky, Eugene Frank *retired lawyer*

Libertyville
Ranney, George Alfred *lawyer, former steel company executive*

Lisle
Aprati, Robert L. *lawyer, car rental company executive*
Hecht, Louis Alan *lawyer*
Sandrok, Richard William *lawyer*

Long Grove
Gallichio, Kathleen Anne *lawyer, insurance and financial services company executive*

Marengo
Franks, Herbert Hoover *lawyer*

Mattoon
Horsley, Jack Everett *lawyer, author*

Melrose Park
Gass, Raymond William *lawyer, consumer products company executive*

Moline
Cottrell, Frank Stewart *lawyer, manufacturing executive*
Morrison, Deborah Jean *lawyer*

Mundelein
Burns, Kenneth Jones, Jr. *lawyer, consultant*

Naperville
Rovner, Jack Alan *lawyer*
Shaw, Michael Allan *lawyer, mail order company executive*
Ulrich, Werner *patent lawyer*

Niles
†Walker, A. Harris *lawyer, manufacturing executive*

Northbrook
Cohen, Seymour *lawyer*
Lapin, Harvey I. *lawyer*
Salomon, Richard Adley *business executive, lawyer*

Northfield
Lawrie, Henry DeVos, Jr. *lawyer*
Porter, Helen Viney (Mrs. Lewis M. Porter, Jr.) *lawyer*
Sernett, Richard Patrick *lawyer*

Oak Brook
Barnes, Karen Kay *lawyer*
Bergerson, J. Steven *lawyer*
Caldarazzo, Richard Joseph *lawyer*
Getz, Herbert A. *lawyer*
Gibson, James Thomas, Jr. *lawyer, consultant, antique dealer*
Johnson, Grant Lester *lawyer, retired manufacturing company executive*
Riley, Georgianne Marie *lawyer*

Park Forest
Goodrich, John Bernard *lawyer, consultant*

Park Ridge
Curtis, Philip James *lawyer*

Pekin
Clevenger, Robert Vincent *lawyer*

Peoria
Allen, Lyle Wallace *lawyer*
Christison, William Henry, III *lawyer*
Dabney, Seth Mason, III *lawyer*
Eissfeldt, Theodore L. *lawyer*
Ryan, Michael Beecher *lawyer, former government official*
Strodel, Robert Carl *lawyer*
Sullivan, Paul J. *legal administrator*
Thompson, William Scott *lawyer*

Princeton
Johnson, Watts Carey *lawyer*

River Forest
Li, Tze-chung *lawyer, educator*

Riverwoods
Bartlett, Robert William *lawyer, publishing executive*

Rock Island
Wallace, Franklin Sherwood *lawyer*

Rockford
Anderson, LaVerne Eric *lawyer*
Barrick, William Henry *lawyer*
Reno, Roger *lawyer*
Schilling, Richard M. *lawyer, corporate executive*
Van Vleet, William Benjamin *lawyer, life insurance company executive*

Saint Charles
Mc Kay, Thomas, Jr. *lawyer*

Schaumburg
Collins, James Francis *lawyer*
Keene, Floyd Stanley *lawyer*
Meltzer, Brian *lawyer*
Weise, Richard Henry *lawyer, corporate executive*
Wine-Banks, Jill Susan *lawyer*

Skokie
Bogomolny, Robert Lee *lawyer*

Springfield
Cadigan, Patrick Joseph *lawyer*
†Gottfried, Theodore Alexander *lawyer*
Oxtoby, Robert Boynton *lawyer*
Rowe, Max L. *lawyer, corporate executive, management consultant, judge*
Van Meter, Abram DeBois *lawyer, retired banker*

Streator
Harrison, Frank Joseph *lawyer*

Urbana
Balbach, Stanley Byron *lawyer*
Fitz-Gerald, Roger Miller *lawyer*

Villa Park
Fenech, Joseph C. *lawyer*
Kohlstedt, James August *lawyer*
Leston, Patrick John *lawyer*

Waukegan
Beeler, Thomas Joseph *lawyer, manufacturing company executive*
Hall, Albert Leander *lawyer*

Western Springs
Hanson, Heidi Elizabeth *lawyer*

Wheaton
Botti, Aldo E. *lawyer*
Butt, Edward Thomas, Jr. *lawyer*
Roberts, Keith Edward, Sr. *lawyer*

Winnetka
Abell, David Robert *lawyer*
Crowe, Robert William *lawyer, mediator*
Davis, Britton Anthony *lawyer*
Kapnick, Richard Bradshaw *lawyer*
Mc Millen, Thomas Roberts *lawyer, arbitrator, mediator, retired judge*

Woodstock
Gitlin, H. Joseph *lawyer*
Hale, Hamilton Orin *retired lawyer*

INDIANA

Bloomington
Aman, Alfred Charles, Jr. *law educator*
Heidt, Robert Harold *law educator, consultant*

Brownsburg
Gregory, Susan B. *lawyer*

Carmel
Read, Frank Thompson *law educator*

Columbus
Hamilton, Peter Bannerman *lawyer, manufacturing company executive*

Connersville
Kuntz, William Henry *lawyer, mediator*

Elkhart
Bowers, Richard Stewart, Jr. *lawyer*
Gassere, Eugene Arthur *lawyer, business executive*
Harman, John Royden *lawyer*
Treckelo, Richard M. *lawyer*

Evansville
Clouse, John Daniel *lawyer*

Fort Wayne
Abbott, Jacquelyn Meng *lawyer*
Baker, Carl Leroy *lawyer*
Gerberding, Miles Carston *lawyer*
Hunter, Jack Duval *lawyer*
Keefer, J(ames) Michael *lawyer*
Niewyk, Anthony *lawyer*
Peebles, Carter David *lawyer*
Pope, Mark Andrew *lawyer*
Shoaff, Thomas Mitchell *lawyer*
Steinbronn, Richard Eugene *lawyer*

Hammond
Eichhorn, Frederick Foltz, Jr. *lawyer*
Goodman, Samuel J. *lawyer*

Indianapolis
Albright, Terrill D. *lawyer*
Allen, David James *lawyer*
Aschleman, James Allan *lawyer*
Badger, David Harry *lawyer*
Beckwith, Lewis Daniel *lawyer*
Beeler, Virgil L. *lawyer*
Betley, Leonard John *lawyer*
Blackwell, Henry Barlow, II *lawyer*
Boldt, Michael Herbert *lawyer*
Born, Samuel Roydon, II *lawyer*
Bruess, Charles Edward *lawyer*
Buttrey, Donald Wayne *lawyer*
Capehart, Homer Earl, Jr. *lawyer*
Carney, Joseph Buckingham *lawyer*
Carpenter, Susan Karen *lawyer*
Choplin, John M., II *lawyer*
Cofield, Howard John *lawyer*
Cross, Leland Briggs, Jr. *lawyer*
Deer, Richard Elliott *lawyer*
DeLaney, Edward O'Donnell *lawyer*
Dutton, Stephen James *lawyer*
Emerson, Andrew Craig *lawyer, insurance executive*
Evans, Daniel Fraley, Jr. *lawyer*
Fisher, James R. *lawyer*
FitzGibbon, Daniel Harvey *lawyer*
Fruehwald, Kristin G. *lawyer*
Fuller, Samuel Ashby *lawyer, mining company executive*
Funk, David Albert *law educator*
Grayson, John Allan *lawyer*
Henderson, Eugene Leroy *lawyer*
Highfield, Robert Edward *lawyer*
Hodowal, John Raymond *lawyer, holding company executive, utility company executive*
Huston, Michael Joe *lawyer*
Irwin, H. William *lawyer*
Jegen, Lawrence A., III *law educator*
Johnstone, Robert Philip *lawyer*
Kahlenbeck, Howard, Jr. *lawyer*
Kappes, Philip Spangler *lawyer*
Kashani, Hamid Reza *lawyer, computer consultant*
Kemper, James Dee *lawyer*
Kerr, William Andrew *lawyer, educator*
Kitchen, John Milton *lawyer*
Klaper, Martin Jay *lawyer*
Kleiman, David Harold *lawyer*
Knebel, Donald Earl *lawyer*
Kreuscher, Wayne Charles *lawyer*
Lee, Stephen W. *lawyer*
Lefstein, Norman *lawyer, educator*
Lewis, Dale Kenton *retired lawyer*
Lobley, Alan Haigh *lawyer*
†Lofton, Thomas Milton *lawyer*
Maine, Michael Roland *lawyer*
Mallon, David Joseph, Jr. *lawyer*
McDermott, James Alexander *lawyer*
Merrill, William H., Jr. *lawyer, corporate professional*
Miller, David W. *lawyer*
Nolan, Alan Tucker *retired lawyer*
Paul, Stephen Howard *lawyer*
Petersen, James L. *lawyer*
Ponder, Lester McConnico *lawyer, educator*
Powlen, David Michael *lawyer*
Quayle, Marilyn Tucker *lawyer, wife of former vice president of U.S.*
Ralph, Roger Paul *arbitrator*
Reynolds, Robert Hugh *lawyer*
Roberts, William Everett *lawyer*
Rusthoven, Peter James *lawyer*
Ryder, Henry C(lay) *lawyer*
Scaletta, Phillip Ralph, III *lawyer*
Scanlon, Thomas Michael *lawyer*
Schlegel, Fred Eugene *lawyer*
Scism, Daniel Reed *lawyer*
Segar, Geoffrey *retired lawyer*
Shideler, Shirley Ann Williams *lawyer*
Shula, Robert Joseph *lawyer*
Smith, Stephen Kendall *lawyer*
Snyder, Jack Ralph *lawyer*
Stayton, Thomas George *lawyer*
Steger, Evan Evans, III *lawyer*
Stein, Richard Paul *lawyer*
Strauss, Jerome Manfred *lawyer, banker*
Sutherland, Donald Gray *lawyer*
Swhier, Claudia Versfelt *lawyer*
Tabler, Bryan G. *lawyer*
Tabler, Norman Gardner, Jr. *lawyer*
Townsend, Earl Cunningham, Jr. *lawyer, writer*
Trigg, Donald Clark *lawyer, insurance company executive*
Wampler, Lloyd Charles *retired lawyer*
Webster, Daniel Robert *lawyer*
Whale, Arthur Richard *lawyer*
White, James Patrick *law educator*
Wilson, Charles Edward *lawyer*
Wishard, Gordon Davis *lawyer*
Wood, William Jerome *lawyer*
Woodard, Harold Raymond *lawyer*
Worrell, David Charles *lawyer*
Zoeller, David Louis *lawyer*

Jeffersonville
Hoehn, Elmer Louis *lawyer, state and federal agency administrator, educator, consultant*
Pettyjohn, Shirley Ellis *lawyer, real estate executive*

Mount Vernon
Bach, Steve Crawford *lawyer*

Muncie
Radcliff, William Franklin *lawyer*
Sissel, George Allen *lawyer, manufacturing executive*

Nashville
McDermott, Renée R(assler) *lawyer*

Notre Dame
Grazin, Igor Nikolai *law educator, former state official*
Gunn, Alan *law educator*
Gurulé, Jimmy *legal educator*
Robinson, John Hayes *law educator*
Shaffer, Thomas Lindsay *law educator*

Princeton
Fair, Robert James *lawyer*

South Bend
Bancroft, Bruce Richard *lawyer*
Carey, John Leo *lawyer*
Clarke, Thomas Crawford *lawyer*
Ford, George Burt *lawyer*
Kalamaros, Edward Nicholas *lawyer*
Lake, Brian James *lawyer*
McGill, Warren Everett *lawyer, consultant*
Reinke, William John *lawyer*
Seall, Stephen Albert *lawyer*
Szarwark, Ernest John *lawyer*
Vogel, Nelson J., Jr. *lawyer*

Terre Haute
Bopp, James, Jr. *lawyer*
Pease, Edward Allan *lawyer, former state legislator, university official*

Unionville
Franklin, Frederick Russell *retired legal association executive*

Valparaiso
Ehren, Charles Alexander, Jr. *lawyer, educator*
Persyn, Mary Geraldine *law librarian, law educator*

IOWA

Burlington
Hirsch, David Alan *lawyer*
Hoth, Steven Sergey *lawyer*

Cedar Rapids
Albright, Justin W. *lawyer*
†Brown, Larry G. *corporate lawyer*
Faches, William George *lawyer*
Nazette, Richard Follett *lawyer*
Riley, Tom Joseph *lawyer*
Wilson, Robert Foster *lawyer*

Charles City
Mc Cartney, Ralph Farnham *lawyer*

Dallas Center
McDonald, John Cecil *lawyer*

Davenport
Le Grand, Clay *former state justice*
Shaw, Donald Hardy *lawyer*

Decorah
Belay, Stephen Joseph *lawyer*

Des Moines
Begleiter, Martin David *law educator, consultant*
Belin, David William *lawyer*
Clark, Beverly Ann *lawyer*
Claypool, David L. *lawyer*
Conlin, Roxanne Barton *lawyer*
Dahl, Harry Waldemar *lawyer*
Duncan, Hearst Randolph *lawyer*
Edwards, John Duncan *law educator, librarian*
Fisher, Thomas George *lawyer*
Grefe, Rolland Eugene *lawyer*
Hansell, Edgar Frank *lawyer*
Harris, Charles Elmer *lawyer*
Hill, Luther Lyons, Jr. *lawyer*
Hockenberg, Harlan David *lawyer*
Jensen, Dick Leroy *lawyer*
Josten, Robert E. *lawyer*
Langdon, Herschel Garrett *lawyer*
Leighton, Paul Joe *lawyer*
Merriman, John Allen *lawyer, insurance executive*
Nyemaster, Ray *lawyer*
Peddicord, Roland Dale *lawyer*
Power, Joseph Edward *lawyer*
Proctor, William Zinsmaster *lawyer*
Shoff, Patricia Ann *lawyer*
Slade, Llewellyn Eugene *lawyer, engineer*
Vorbrich, Lynn Karl *lawyer, utility executive*
Wine, Donald Arthur *lawyer*

Dubuque
Ernst, Daniel Pearson *lawyer*
†Hammer, David Lindley *lawyer, author*

Forest City
Beebe, Raymond Mark *lawyer*

Iowa City
Bonfield, Arthur Earl *lawyer, educator*
Cain, Patricia A. *law educator*
Downer, Robert Nelson *lawyer*
Dudziak, Mary Louise *law educator, lecturer*
Gittler, Josephine *law educator*
Green, Michael David *law educator*
Hines, N. William *law educator, administrator*
Kurtz, Sheldon Francis *lawyer, educator*
Saks, Michael Jay *law educator*
Stensvaag, John-Mark *legal educator, lawyer*
Tomkovicz, James Joseph *law educator*
Vernon, David Harvey *lawyer, educator*
Weston, Burns Humphrey *law educator*
Widiss, Alan I. *lawyer, educator*

Marshalltown
Brennecke, Allen Eugene *lawyer*

Muscatine
Coulter, Charles Roy *lawyer*
Schoeffel, Jon Michael *lawyer*

Nevada
Countryman, Dayton Wendell *lawyer*

Newton
Bennett, Edward James *lawyer*

Shenandoah
Rose, Jennifer Joan *lawyer*

Sioux City
Madsen, George Frank *lawyer*
Marks, Bernard Bailin *lawyer*
Nymann, P. L. *lawyer*

West Des Moines
Bump, Wilbur Neil *retired lawyer*
Davis, James Casey *lawyer*
Neiman, John Hammond *lawyer*

KANSAS

Beloit
Conroy, Thomas Hyde *lawyer*

Concordia
Buechel, William Benjamin *lawyer*

Fairway
Marquardt, Christel Elisabeth *lawyer*

Hugoton
Nordling, Bernard Erick *lawyer*

Hutchinson
Hayes, John Francis *lawyer*

Kansas City
Simpson, Laura Kay *lawyer*

Lawrence
Casad, Robert Clair *legal educator*
Smith, Glee Sidney, Jr. *lawyer*
Wilson, Paul Edwin *lawyer, educator*

Leawood
Snyder, Willard Breidenthal *lawyer*

Lyons
Hodgson, Arthur Clay *lawyer*

Mc Pherson
Shriver, Garner Edward *lawyer, former congressman*

Olathe
Snowbarger, Vincent Keith *lawyer, state representative*

Overland Park
Balloun, Joseph Eugene *lawyer*
Gaar, Norman Edward *lawyer, former state senator*
Krauss, Carl F. *lawyer*
Murphy, Stephen P. *corporate lawyer*
Ruse, Steven Douglas *lawyer*
Sampson, William Roth *lawyer*
Short, Joel Bradley *lawyer, consultant, software publisher*
Stanton, Roger D. *lawyer*
Van Dyke, Thomas Wesley *lawyer*
Waxse, David John *lawyer*
Webb, William Duncan *lawyer, investment executive*

Prairie Village
Lytle, Robert Frank *lawyer*

Shawnee Mission
Bennett, Robert Frederick *lawyer, former governor*
Biggs, J. O. *lawyer, general industry company executive*
Bond, Richard Lee *lawyer, state senator*
Cahal, Mac Fullerton *lawyer, publisher*
Clay, George Harry *lawyer*
Connelly, John Matthew *lawyer, insurance company executive*
Nulton, William Clements *lawyer*
Rubin, Charles Elliott *lawyer, sports agent*
Steinkamp, Robert Theodore *lawyer*

Topeka
Ayres, Ted Dean *lawyer, academic counsel*
Elrod, Linda Diane Henry *lawyer, educator*
Kuether, John Frederick *law educator*
Marshall, Herbert A. *lawyer*
†Platis, Tom Gust *lawyer, oil company executive*
Rosenberg, John K. *lawyer*
Skoog, Ralph Edward *lawyer*
Spring, Raymond Lewis *legal educator*

Wellington
Ferguson, William McDonald *retired lawyer, rancher, author, banker, former state official*

Westwood
Devlin, James Richard *lawyer*

Wichita
Curfman, Lawrence Everett *lawyer*
Davis, Robert Louis *lawyer*
Docking, Thomas Robert *lawyer, former state lieutenant governor*
Rainey, William Joel *lawyer*
Sowers, Wesley Hoyt *lawyer, management consultant*
Thompson, M(orris) Lee *lawyer*
Williams, Ronald Paul *lawyer*

KENTUCKY

Ashland
Compton, Robert H. *lawyer*
Feazell, Thomas Lee *lawyer, oil company executive*

Benton
Lewis, Richard Hayes *lawyer, former state legislator*

Bowling Green
Campbell, Joe Bill *lawyer*
Russell, Joyce M. *lawyer, apparel executive*

Covington
Head, Joseph Henry, Jr. *lawyer*
Kerr, Thomas Robert *lawyer*

Florence
Walker, H. Lawson *lawyer*

Frankfort
Carroll, Julian Morton *lawyer, former governor*
Palmore, John Stanley, Jr. *lawyer*

Glasgow
†Baker, Walter A. *lawyer, state senator*

Highland Heights
Bell, Sheila Trice *lawyer*
Carr, George Francis, Jr. *lawyer*
Jones, William Rex *lawyer, educator*
Seaver, Robert Leslie *law educator*

Hopkinsville
Dixon, John Morris, Jr. *lawyer*

Lexington
Beshear, Steven L. *lawyer*
Breathitt, Edward Thompson, Jr. *lawyer, railroad executive*
Eberle, Todd Bailey *lawyer, educator*
Goldman, Alvin Lee *lawyer, educator*
Lewis, Thomas Proctor *legal educator*
McCann, William H., Sr. *lawyer*
Miller, Harry B(enjamin) *lawyer*
Oberst, Paul *law educator*
Philpott, James Alvin, Jr. *lawyer*
Rogers, Lon B(rown) *lawyer*
Schaeffer, Edwin Frank, Jr. *lawyer*
Ward, Richard C. *lawyer*

Louisville
Aberson, Leslie Donald *lawyer*
†Allen, Charles Ethelbert, III *lawyer*
Ardery, Joseph Lord *lawyer*
Ardery, Philip Pendleton *lawyer*
Benfield, Ann Kolb *lawyer*
Burse, Raymond Malcolm *lawyer*
Conner, Stewart Edmund *lawyer*
Cowan, Frederic Joseph *lawyer*
Crutcher, Michael Bayard *lawyer*
Davidson, Gordon Byron *lawyer*
Dudley, George Ellsworth *lawyer*
Ethridge, Larry Clayton *lawyer*
Ferguson, Jo McCown *lawyer*
Fitch, Howard Mercer *lawyer, labor arbitrator, travelogue exhibitor and producer*
Helm, Joseph Burge *lawyer*
Hunter, William Jay, Jr. *lawyer*
Klotter, John Charles *retired legal educator*
Lay, Norvie Lee *legal educator*
Luber, Thomas J(ulian) *lawyer*
Maddox, Robert Lytton *lawyer*
McCall, John Richard *lawyer*
Meuter, Maria Coolman *lawyer*
Osborn, John Simcoe, Jr. *lawyer*
Ratterman, David Burger *lawyer*
Runyon, Keith Leslie *lawyer, newspaper editor*
Schmidt, Stephen Robert *lawyer*
Silverthorn, Robert Sterner, Jr. *lawyer*
Skees, William Leonard, Jr. *lawyer*
Straus, R(obert) James *lawyer*
Talbott, Ben Johnson, Jr. *lawyer*
Volz, Marlin Milton *legal educator*
Wyatt, Wilson Watkins *lawyer*
Zingman, Edgar Alan *lawyer*

Madisonville
Monhollon, Leland *lawyer*

Newport
Siverd, Robert Joseph *lawyer*

Owensboro
Cocklin, Kim Roland *lawyer*

Paducah
Westberry, Billy Murry *lawyer*

Scottsville
Wilcher, Larry Keith *lawyer*

LOUISIANA

Alexandria
Brady, James Joseph *lawyer*
Gist, Howard Battle, Jr. *lawyer*
Ward-Steinman, Irving *lawyer*

Baton Rouge
Bayard, Alton Ernest, III *lawyer*
Beckner, Donald Lee *lawyer*
Blackman, John Calhoun, IV *lawyer*
Bybee, Jay Scott *lawyer, educator*
Byrd, Warren Edgar, II *lawyer*
Gibbs, Arnold James *lawyer*
Hawkland, William Dennis *law educator*
Lamonica, P(aul) Raymond *lawyer, academic administrator, educator*
Leonard, Paul Haralson *retired lawyer*
Mayfield, William Stephen *law educator*
Mc Clendon, William Hutchinson, III *lawyer*
Middleton, Frank Walters, Jr. *lawyer*
Pugh, George Willard *legal educator*
Yiannopoulos, Athanassios Nicholas *law educator*

Hammond
Matheny, Tom Harrell *lawyer*

Lafayette
Cook, David Sherman *lawyer*
Davidson, James Joseph, III *lawyer*
Mickel, Joseph Thomas *lawyer*

Lake Charles
Cox, James Joseph *lawyer*
Everett, John Prentis, Jr. *lawyer*
McHale, Robert Michael *lawyer*
Shaddock, William Edward, Jr. *lawyer*

Mandeville
Christian, John Catlett, Jr. *lawyer*
Deano, Edward Joseph, Jr. *lawyer, state legislator*

Metairie
Denegre, George *lawyer*
Gauthier, Wendell Haynes *lawyer*
†Perlis, Sharon A. *lawyer*

Monroe
Curry, Robert Lee, III *lawyer*
Sartor, Daniel Ryan, Jr. *lawyer*

New Orleans
Acomb, Robert Bailey, Jr. *lawyer, educator*
Alsobrook, Henry Bernis, Jr. *lawyer*
Ates, J. Robert *lawyer*
Barham, Mack Elwin *lawyer, educator*
Barnett, Walter Michael *lawyer*
Barry, Francis Julian, Jr. *lawyer*
Benjamin, Edward Bernard, Jr. *lawyer*
Bernstein, Joseph *lawyer*
Bieck, Robert Barton, Jr. *lawyer*
Brown, Wood, III *lawyer*
Buckley, Samuel Olliphant, III *lawyer*
Cassibry, Fred James *lawyer, retired federal court judge*
Cheatwood, Roy Clifton *lawyer*
Claverie, Philip deVilliers *lawyer*
Coleman, James Julian, Jr. *lawyer, industrialist, real estate executive*
Combe, David Alfred *law librarian, educator*
Combe, John Clifford, Jr. *lawyer*
Correro, Anthony James, III *lawyer*
Couch, Harvey Crowley, III *law educator*
Couhig, Robert Emmet *lawyer*
Dennery, Moise Waldhorn *lawyer, educator*
Dittmann, Albert Stephen, Jr. *lawyer*
Fantaci, James Michael *lawyer*
Fishman, Louis Yarrut *lawyer*
Force, Robert *law educator*
Franco, Philip Anthony *lawyer*
Friedman, Joel William *law educator*
Garcia, Patricia A. *lawyer*
Gelfand, M. David *lawyer, educator*
Gelpi, C. James (Jim Gelpi) *lawyer*
Goins, Richard Anthony *lawyer, educator*
Hall, Luther Egbert, Jr. *retired lawyer*
Healy, George William, III *lawyer*
Hilbert, Peter Louis, Jr. *lawyer*
Hinton, James Forrest, Jr. *lawyer*
Howard, Ernest E., III *lawyer, natural resource company executive*
Keller, Thomas Clements *lawyer*
Kemp, James Bradley, Jr. *lawyer*
Lavelle, Paul Michael *lawyer*
Leger, Walter John, Jr. *lawyer*
Lemann, Thomas Berthelot *lawyer*
Lovett, William Anthony *law and economics educator*
Lowe, Robert Charles *lawyer*
Marcus, Bernard *lawyer*
Martinez, Andrew Tredway *lawyer*
McDougal, Luther Love, III *law educator*
McMillan, Lee Richards, II *lawyer*
Mintz, Albert *lawyer*
Molony, Michael Janssens, Jr. *lawyer*
Morrell, Arthur Anthony *lawyer, state legislator*
Nehrbass, Seth Martin *lawyer*
Nuzum, Robert Weston *lawyer*
Plaeger, Frederick Joseph, II *lawyer*
Poitevent, Edward Butts, II *lawyer*
Purtell, Lawrence Robert *lawyer*
Redmon, Harry Smith, Jr. *lawyer*
Riess, George Febiger *lawyer, educator*
Rosen, Charles, II *lawyer*
Rosen, William Warren *lawyer*
Sarpy, Leon *lawyer*
Shinn, Clinton Wesley *lawyer*
Simon, H(uey) Paul *lawyer*
Sims, John William *lawyer*
Sinor, Howard Earl, Jr. *lawyer*
Snyder, Charles Aubrey *lawyer*
Stapp, Dan Ernest *retired lawyer, utility executive*
Surprenant, Mark Christopher *lawyer*
Sweeney, Joseph Modeste *lawyer, educator*
Tarver, Michael Keith *lawyer*
Trostorff, Alexander Peter *lawyer*
Vance, Robert Patrick *lawyer*
Waechter, Arthur Joseph, Jr. *lawyer*
Weigel, John J. *lawyer*
Weiss, Kenneth Andrew *lawyer, law educator*
†Willems, Constance Charles *lawyer*
Woodward, Madison Truman, Jr. *lawyer*

Shreveport
Achee, Roland Joseph *lawyer*
Carmody, Arthur Roderick, Jr. *lawyer*
Gentry, Hubert, Jr. *lawyer*
Pugh, Robert Gahagan *lawyer*
Ramey, Cecil Edward, Jr. *lawyer*
Woodman, Walter James *lawyer*

MAINE

Alfred
Jordan, Anne Harrison *lawyer*

Augusta
Cohen, Richard Stockman *lawyer*

Bath
Weiss, David Raymond *lawyer*

Camden
Shuman, Samuel Irving *lawyer, law educator*

Castine
Wiswall, Frank Lawrence, Jr. *lawyer, educator*

Freeport
Lea, Lola Stendig *lawyer*

Lewiston
Gauvreau, Norman Paul *lawyer*

Lincolnville
Nichols, David Arthur *mediator, retired state justice*

Portland
Allen, Charles William *lawyer*
Coughlan, Patrick Campbell *lawyer*
Graffam, Ward Irving *lawyer*
Hirshon, Robert Edward *lawyer*
Lancaster, Ralph Ivan, Jr. *lawyer*
Loper, Merle William *law educator*
Mooers, Daniel William *lawyer*
Murray, Peter Loos *lawyer, educator*
Philbrick, Donald Lockey *lawyer*
Santomenna, Robert Charles *lawyer*
Skolnik, Barnet David *lawyer*
Smith, William Charles *lawyer*
Stier, Robert H., Jr. *lawyer*
Wroth, L(awrence) Kinvin *lawyer, educator*
Zarr, Melvyn *lawyer, educator*

South Portland
Connell, Lawrence *lawyer*

Wells
Carleton, Joseph George, Jr. *lawyer, state legislator*

MARYLAND

Annapolis
Dembrow, Dana Lee *lawyer*
Evans, William Davidson, Jr. *lawyer*
Levitan, Laurence *lawyer, former state senator*
Lustbader, Philip Lawrence *lawyer*

Arnold
Green, John Cawley *lawyer*

Baltimore
Adkins, Edward James *lawyer*
Angelos, Peter G. *lawyer*
Archibald, James Kenway *lawyer*
Astrachan, James Barry *lawyer*
Ayres, Jeffrey Peabody *lawyer*
Bair, Robert Rippel *lawyer*
Baldwin, John Chandler *lawyer*
Barnhouse, Robert Bolon *lawyer*
Bartlett, James Wilson, III *lawyer*
Beall, George *lawyer*
Berman, Barry David *lawyer*
Bernhardt, Herbert Nelson *lawyer, educator*
Blanton, Edward Lee, Jr. *lawyer*
Boone, Harold Thomas *retired lawyer*
Bowen, Lowell Reed *lawyer*
Brewster, Gerry Leiper *lawyer*
Brumbaugh, John Maynard *lawyer, educator*
Burch, Francis Boucher, Jr. *lawyer*
Cahill, William Walsh, Jr. *lawyer*
Carbine, James Edmond *lawyer*
Carey, Anthony Morris *lawyer*
Carey, Jana Howard *lawyer*
Carlin, Paul Victor *legal association executive*
Carney, Bradford George Yost *lawyer, educator*
Chaplin, Peggy Fannon *lawyer*
Chiarello, Donald Frederick *lawyer*
Chiu, Hungdah *lawyer, legal educator*
Civiletti, Benjamin R. *lawyer, former U.S. attorney general*
Clapp, Roger Alvin *lawyer*
Coe, Ward Baldwin, Jr. *retired lawyer*
Cook, Bryson Leitch *lawyer*
Crowe, Thomas Leonard *lawyer*
Curran, Robert Bruce *lawyer*
Daly, Warren B., Jr. *lawyer*
Davison, Warren Malcolm *lawyer*
Dilloff, Neil Joel *lawyer*
Doory, Robert Leonard, Jr. *lawyer*
Dunne, Richard Edwin, III *lawyer*
Ellin, Marvin *lawyer*
Engel, Paul Bernard *lawyer*
†Eyler, James R. *lawyer*
Fenton, Charles E. *lawyer*
Fergenson, Arthur Friend *lawyer*
Finch, Walter Goss Gilchrist *lawyer, engineer, accountant, retired army officer*
Finnerty, Joseph Gregory, Jr. *lawyer*
Fisher, Morton Poe, Jr. *lawyer*
Friedman, Louis Frank *lawyer*
Gately, Mark Donohue *lawyer*
Gauvey, Susan K. *lawyer*
Gillece, James Patrick, Jr. *lawyer*
Goldman, Brian Arthur *lawyer, accountant*
Goldscheider, Sidney *lawyer*
Goldstein, Franklin *lawyer*
Graham, John Stuart, III *lawyer*
Gray, Frank Truan *lawyer*
Grieb, Elizabeth *lawyer*
Hafets, Richard Jay *lawyer*
Haines, Thomas W. W. *lawyer*
Hanks, James Judge, Jr. *lawyer*
†Hayes, Dennis C. *lawyer*
Hillman, Robert Sandor *lawyer*
Hirsh, Theodore William *lawyer*
Hochberg, Bayard Zabdial *lawyer*
Honemann, Daniel Henry *lawyer*
Hubbard, Herbert Hendrix *lawyer*
Hughes, Harry Roe *lawyer*
Immelt, Stephen J. *lawyer*
Johnston, George W. *lawyer*
Jones, John Martin, Jr. *lawyer*
Junghans, Paula Marie *lawyer*
Lebowitz, Harvey M. *lawyer*
Levin, Betsy *lawyer, educator, university dean*
Levin, Edward Jesse *lawyer*
Levine, Richard E. *lawyer*
Lewis, Alexander Ingersoll, III *lawyer*
Liebmann, George William *lawyer*
Loewy, Steven A. *lawyer*
Lohr, Walter George, Jr. *lawyer*
Machen, Arthur Webster, Jr. *lawyer*
McClung, A(lexander) Keith, Jr. *lawyer*
Mc Kenney, Walter Gibbs, Jr. *lawyer, publishing company executive*
McPherson, Donald Paxton, III *lawyer*
McWilliams, John Michael *lawyer*
Melvin, Norman Cecil *lawyer*
Miller, Decatur Howard *lawyer*
Mogol, Alan Jay *lawyer*
Moser, M(artin) Peter *lawyer*
Nilson, George Albert *lawyer*
O'Connell, Kevin Michael *lawyer*
Ohly, D. Christopher *lawyer*
Orman, Leonard Arnold *lawyer*
Owen, Stephen Lee *lawyer*
Pappas, George Frank *lawyer*
Patz, Edward Frank *lawyer*
Plant, Albin MacDonough *lawyer*
Plummer, Risque Wilson *lawyer*
Pokempner, Joseph Kres *lawyer*
Pollak, Mark *lawyer*
Prince, Charles O., III *lawyer*
Proctor, Kenneth Donald *lawyer*
Provorny, Frederick Alan *lawyer*
Putzel, Constance Kellner *lawyer*
Rafferty, William Bernard *lawyer*
Redden, Roger Duffey *lawyer*
Reno, Russell Ronald, Jr. *lawyer*
Reynolds, William Leroy *lawyer, educator*
Rosenthal, William J. *lawyer*
Sack, Sylvan Hanan *lawyer*
Sagett, Jan Jeffrey *lawyer, former government official*
Sandler, Paul Mark *lawyer*
Scriggins, Larry Palmer *lawyer*
Sfekas, Stephen James *lawyer*
Shapiro, Harry Dean *lawyer*
Sharpe, Donald Edward *lawyer*
Short, Alexander Campbell *lawyer*
Smouse, H(ervey) Russell *lawyer*
Stalfort, John Arthur *lawyer*
Stewart, C(ornelius) Van Leuven *lawyer*
Sykes, Melvin Julius *lawyer*
Teret, Stephen Paul *health law educator*
Trimble, William Cattell, Jr. *lawyer*
Tyler, George Thomas *lawyer*
Walker, Irving Edward *lawyer*
Wasserman, Richard Leo *lawyer*
White, Pamela Janice *lawyer*
Winn, James Julius, Jr. *lawyer*
Wintriss, Lynn *lawyer*
Wolf, Fred, III *lawyer*
Yarmolinsky, Adam *lawyer, educator, university administrator*

Bel Air
Crocker, Michael Pue *lawyer*
Miller, Max Dunham, Jr. *lawyer*

Bethesda
Abrams, Samuel K. *lawyer*
Alper, Jerome Milton *lawyer*
Anestos, Harry Peter *lawyer*
Bauersfeld, Carl Frederick *lawyer*
Brickfield, Cyril Francis *lawyer, association executive*
Burton, Charles Henning *lawyer*
Calvert, Gordon Lee *retired legal association executive*
Cass, Millard *lawyer, arbitrator*
Elman, Philip *lawyer*
Eule, Norman L. *lawyer*
Hall, William Darlington *lawyer*
Herman, Stephen Allen *lawyer*
Jayson, Lester Samuel *lawyer, educator*
Meier, Louis Leonard, Jr. *lawyer*
O'Brien, Lawrence Francis, III *lawyer*

O'Connell, Quinn *lawyer*
Pankopf, Arthur, Jr. *lawyer*
Pitofsky, Robert *lawyer, educator, university administrator*
Pritchard Schoch, Teresa Noreen *lawyer, law librarian, executive*
Ross, William Warfield *lawyer*
Schmeltzer, David *lawyer*
Schurman, Joseph Rathborne *lawyer*
Toomey, Thomas Murray *lawyer*

Brookeville
Johns, Warren LeRoi *lawyer*

Catonsville
Stowe, David Henry *arbitrator*

Chevy Chase
Casey, Thomas J. *lawyer*
Chase, Nicholas Joseph *lawyer, educator*
Gellermann, Marian DeBelle *lawyer*
Harr, Karl Gottlieb, Jr. *lawyer*
Ikenberry, Henry Cephas, Jr. *lawyer*
Ketcham, Orman Weston *lawyer, former judge*
Stetler, C. Joseph *lawyer*
Vance, Sheldon Baird *lawyer, former diplomat*

Cockeysville Hunt Valley
Edgett, William Maloy *lawyer, labor arbitrator*

Columbia
Baker, Russell Tremaine, Jr. *lawyer*
Ulman, Louis Jay *lawyer*

Dundalk
Arnick, John Stephen *lawyer, legislator*

Easton
Jacobs, Michael Joseph *lawyer*
Maffitt, James Strawbridge *lawyer*
Woods, William Ellis *lawyer, pharmacist, association executive*

Ellicott City
†Wehland, Granville Warren Pearson *lawyer, consultant*

Fort Washington
Alexander, Gary R. *lawyer, state legislator*

Frederick
Hogan, Ilona Modly *lawyer*

Gaithersburg
Schaefer, William G. *lawyer*

Garrett Park
Friedman, Edward David *lawyer, arbitrator*

Greenbelt
Ekstrand, Richard Edward *lawyer, educator*
Jascourt, Hugh D. *lawyer, arbitrator, mediator*

Hagerstown
Poole, D. Bruce *lawyer*

Hyattsville
Houle, Philip P. *lawyer*

Kensington
Daisley, William Prescott *lawyer*
Revoile, Charles Patrick *lawyer*

Lanham Seabrook
McCarthy, Kevin John *lawyer*

Lutherville Timonium
Bond, Calhoun *lawyer, retired*

Potomac
Affeldt, David Allan *lawyer, legal consultant*
Conner, Troy Blaine, Jr. *lawyer, writer*
Elisburg, Donald Earl *lawyer*
Peter, Phillips Smith *lawyer*
Reichart, Stuart Richard *lawyer*

Riverdale
Love, Richard Harvey *lawyer*

Rockville
Barkley, Brian Evan *lawyer, political consultant*
Chapin, James Chris *lawyer*
Doub, William Offutt *lawyer*
Gordon, Joan Irma *lawyer*
Gordon, Michael Robert *lawyer*
Kadish, Richard L. *lawyer*
Molitor, Graham Thomas Tate *lawyer*
Nelson, Joseph Conrad *lawyer, business executive, educator*
Nystrom, Harold Charles *lawyer, labor consultant*
Parler, William Carlos *lawyer*
Shadoan, George Woodson *lawyer*
Stern, Joyce Reuben *lawyer*
Titus, Roger Warren *lawyer*

Seabrook
Brugger, George Albert *lawyer*

Silver Spring
Craig, Paul Max, Jr. *lawyer*
Hannan, Myles *lawyer, banker*
Mitchell, Milton *lawyer*
Pellerzi, Leo Maurice *lawyer*

Sparks
Single, Richard Wayne, Sr. *lawyer*

Takoma Park
†Tucker, Kathleen M. *lawyer*

Towson
Howell, Harley Thomas *lawyer*
Johnston, Edward Allan *lawyer*
Lerch, Richard Heaphy *lawyer*
Levasseur, William Ryan *lawyer*
Peacock, James Daniel *lawyer*

Westminster
Bryson, Brady Oliver *lawyer*
Dulany, William Bevard *lawyer*

MASSACHUSETTS

Ashfield
Pepyne, Edward Walter *lawyer, former educator*

Ashland
Borgeson, Earl Charles *law librarian, educator*

Bedford
Dulchinos, Peter *lawyer*
Nunes, Geoffrey *lawyer, corporate executive*

Belmont
Luick, Robert Burns *lawyer*

Boston
Abraham, Nicholas Albert *lawyer, real estate developer*
Achatz, John *lawyer*
Ames, James Barr *lawyer*
Anderson, Arthur Irvin *lawyer*
Annas, George J. *health law educator*
Aresty, Jeffrey M. *lawyer*
Astrue, Michael James *lawyer*
Auerbach, Joseph *lawyer, educator*
Bae, Frank S. H. *law educator, law librarian*
Bangs, Will Johnston *lawyer*
Batchelder, Samuel Lawrence, Jr. *corporate lawyer*
Bates, Jeffrey C. *lawyer*
Beard, Charles Julian *lawyer*
Beard, John Edwards *lawyer*
Becker, Fred Ronald *lawyer*
Belin, Gaspard d'Andelot *lawyer*
Bellefontaine, Edgar John *law librarian, lawyer*
Benjamin, William Chase *lawyer*
Bergen, Kenneth William *lawyer*
Berlew, Frank Kingston *lawyer*
Berman, Kenneth R. *lawyer*
Bernhard, Alexander Alfred *lawyer*
Berry, Janis Marie *lawyer*
Bines, Harvey Ernest *lawyer, educator, writer*
Bohnen, Michael J. *lawyer*
Bok, John Fairfield *lawyer*
Borenstein, Milton Conrad *lawyer, manufacturing company executive*
Bornheimer, Allen Millard *lawyer*
Borod, Ronald Sam *lawyer*
Boyden, W(alter) Lincoln *lawyer*
Brody, Richard Eric *lawyer*
Brountas, Paul Peter *lawyer*
Brown, Judith Olans *lawyer, educator*
Brown, Matthew *lawyer*
Brown, Michael Robert *lawyer*
Browne, Kingsbury *lawyer*
Buccella, William Victor *lawyer*
Buchanan, Robert McLeod *lawyer*
Burgess, John Allen *lawyer*
Burleigh, Lewis Albert *lawyer*
Burns, Thomas David *lawyer*
Burr, Francis Hardon *lawyer*
Cabot, Charles Codman, Jr. *lawyer*
Campbell, Richard P. *lawyer*
Caner, George Colket, Jr. *lawyer*
Cashel, Thomas William *lawyer, educator*
Casner, Truman Snell *lawyer*
Caso, Gasper *librarian, lawyer*
Chapin, Melville *lawyer*
Cogan, John Francis, Jr. *lawyer*
Cohn, Andrew Howard *lawyer*
Comegys, Walker Brockton *lawyer*
Connolly, Paul K., Jr. *lawyer*
Connors, Donald Louis *lawyer, land use planner*
Coolidge, Francis Lowell *lawyer*
Craver, James Bernard *lawyer*
Cronin, Philip Mark *lawyer*
Curtin, John Joseph, Jr. *lawyer*
Cutler, Arnold Robert *lawyer*
Daley, Paul Patrick *lawyer*
Davis, Harold Truscott *retired lawyer*
Delaney, John White *lawyer*
Delinsky, Stephen R. *lawyer*
Denniston, Brackett Badger, III *lawyer*
de Rham, Casimir, Jr. *lawyer*
Deutsch, Stephen B. *lawyer*
Dignan, Thomas Gregory, Jr. *lawyer*
Dillon, James Joseph *lawyer*
Dineen, John K. *lawyer*
Dusseault, C. Dean *lawyer*
Ehrlich, M. Gordon *lawyer*
Elliott, Byron Kauffman *lawyer, business executive*
Erickson, Kenneth W. *lawyer*
Evans, Donald John *lawyer*
Farrah, Elias George *lawyer*
Fay, Michael Leo *lawyer*
Fazzone, David A. *lawyer*
Feldman, Roger David *lawyer*
Felter, John Kenneth *lawyer*
Fischer, Eric Robert *lawyer, educator*
Fischer, Thomas Covell *law educator, consultant, writer, lawyer*
Fisher, Champe Andrews *lawyer*
Floor, Richard Earl *lawyer*
Fox, Francis Haney *lawyer*
Frankenheim, Samuel *lawyer*
Fraser, Robert Burchmore *lawyer*
Freehling, Daniel Joseph *law educator, law library director*
Freishtat, Harvey W. *lawyer*
Fremont-Smith, Marion R. *lawyer*
Galvani, Paul B. *lawyer*
Garcia, Adolfo Ramon *lawyer*
Gaudreau, Russell A., Jr. *lawyer*
Gault, Robert Mellor *lawyer*
Gens, Peter David *lawyer*
Gerstmayr, John Wolfgang *lawyer*
Gesmer, Henry *lawyer*
Gilmore, Daniel J., III *lawyer*
Giso, Frank, III *lawyer*
Glazer, Michael H. *lawyer*
Glosband, Daniel Martin *lawyer*
Goodman, Bruce Gerald *lawyer*
Goodman, Louis Allan *lawyer*
Goodman, Sherri Wasserman *lawyer*
Gorham, William Hartshorne *lawyer*
Greco, Michael S. *lawyer*
Greer, Gordon Bruce *lawyer*
Guthary, Barry Curtis *lawyer*
Haddad, Ernest Mudarri *lawyer*
Haley, Joseph William *lawyer*
Hall, Henry Lyon, Jr. *lawyer*
Hamilton, John Dayton, Jr. *lawyer*
Hand, John *lawyer*
Harrington, John Michael, Jr. *lawyer*
Harvey, William Burnett *retired law educator*
Hassan, William Ephriam, Jr. *lawyer*
Haussermann, Oscar William, Jr. *lawyer*
Hawkey, G. Michael *lawyer*
Haydock, Robert, Jr. *lawyer*
Hayes, Robert Francis *lawyer*
Heigham, James Crichton *lawyer*
Hoffman, Christian Matthew *lawyer*
Hoffman, David Alan *lawyer*
Holland, Hubert Brian *lawyer*
Hoort, Steven Thomas *lawyer*
Hotchkiss, Andra Ruth *lawyer*
Howe, Jas. Murray *lawyer*
Jaroch, Timothy D. *lawyer*
Johannsen, Peter George *lawyer*
Johnston, Richard Alan *lawyer*
Jones, Jeffrey Foster *lawyer*
Jones, Sheldon Atwell *lawyer*
Jordan, Alexander Joseph, Jr. *lawyer*
Kanin, Dennis Roy *lawyer*
Kaplan, Lawrence Edward *lawyer*
Karelitz, Robert N(elson) *lawyer*
Katz, Peter *lawyer*
†Katzmann, Gary Stephen *lawyer*
Kearns, Ellen Cecelia *lawyer*
Keating, Michael Burns *lawyer*
Kehoe, William Francis *lawyer*
Keller, Stanley *lawyer*
Kelly, Thomas J. *lawyer*
Kenney, Raymond Joseph, Jr. *lawyer*
Kerry, Cameron F. *lawyer*
King, William Bruce *lawyer*
Kirchick, William Dean *lawyer*
Kirk, Paul Grattan, Jr. *lawyer, former political organization official*
Klem, Christopher A. *lawyer*
Koffel, William Barry *lawyer*
Kopelman, Leonard *lawyer*
Korb, Kenneth Allan *lawyer*
Lamere, Robert Kent *lawyer*
Lampert, James B. *lawyer*
Lane, Newton Alexander *lawyer*
Lapatin, Philip Stuart *lawyer*
Largey, Kathleen Kiernan *lawyer, marketing director*
Last, Michael P. *lawyer*
Latham, James David *lawyer*
Leibensperger, Edward Paul *lawyer*
Leone, Peter R. *lawyer*
Lettieri, Richard Joseph *lawyer*
Ley, Andrew James *lawyer*
†Licata, Arthur Frank *lawyer*
Lockwood, Rhodes Greene *retired lawyer*
Loeser, Hans Ferdinand *lawyer*
Looney, William Francis, Jr. *lawyer*
Loring, Arthur *lawyer, financial services company executive*
Lynch, Francis Charles *lawyer*
Lynch, Sandra Lea *lawyer*
Lyons, Paul Vincent *lawyer*
MacDougall, Peter *lawyer*
Mandell, Samuel W. W. *corporate lawyer*
Marcellino, James J. *lawyer*
Martin, Stanley A. *lawyer*
Matthews, Roger Hardin *lawyer*
McChesney, S. Elaine *lawyer*
Mc Donough, William *corporate lawyer*
McGovern, A. Lane *lawyer*
McHugh, Edward Francis, Jr. *lawyer*
Menoyo, Eric Felix *lawyer*
Mercer, Douglas *lawyer*
Meserve, Robert William *lawyer*
Meserve, William George *lawyer*
Messing, Arnold Philip *lawyer*
Metzer, Patricia Ann *lawyer*
Michael, Michael L. *lawyer, brokerage house executive*
Mikels, Richard Eliot *lawyer*
Miller, Alan Gershon *lawyer*
Miller, Alan Robert *lawyer*
Miller, John B. *lawyer*
Moncreiff, Robert P. *lawyer*
Mooney, Michael Edward *lawyer*
Moran, James J., Jr. *lawyer*
Moriarty, George Marshall *lawyer*
Moss, Guy B. *lawyer*
Motley, Thomas, Jr. *lawyer*
Muldoon, Robert Joseph, Jr. *lawyer*
Mullaney, Joseph E. *lawyer*
Munro, Meredith Vance *lawyer*
Mygatt, Susan Hall *lawyer*
Myrick, Ronald Ernest *lawyer, educator*
Neely, Thomas Emerson *lawyer*
Newberg, Joseph H. *lawyer*
Nichols, William Deming *lawyer*
Norris, Melvin *lawyer*
Notopoulos, Alexander Anastasios, Jr. *lawyer*
Nutt, Robert L. *lawyer*
O'Dell, Edward Thomas, Jr. *lawyer*
O'Donnell, Thomas Lawrence Patrick *lawyer*
O'Leary, Joseph Evans *lawyer*
O'Neill, Philip Daniel, Jr. *lawyer, educator*
O'Neill, Timothy P. *lawyer*
Orenstein, Theodore Paul *lawyer*
Osteen, Carolyn McCue *lawyer*
Packer, Rekha Desai *lawyer*
Park, William Wynnewood *law educator*
Parker, Christopher William *lawyer*
Partan, Daniel Gordon *lawyer, educator*
Patterson, John de la Roche, Jr. *lawyer*
Pechilis, William John *lawyer*
Perera, Lawrence Thacher *lawyer*
Perkins, James Wood *lawyer*
Perkins, John Allen *lawyer*
Perkins, Malcolm Donald *lawyer*
Perkins, Samuel *lawyer*
Perocchi, Paul Patrick *lawyer*
Pierce, Joel Farwell *lawyer*
Ploszaj, Stephen Charles *lawyer*
Pomeroy, Robert Corttis *lawyer*
Popeo, R. Robert *lawyer*
Rabadjija, Neven *lawyer*
Raish, David Langdon *lawyer*
Reck, Joel M(arvin) *lawyer*
Resnik, Peter L. *lawyer*
Ritt, Roger Merrill *lawyer*
Rizzo, William Ober *lawyer*
Rose, Alan Douglas *lawyer*
Rossman, Stuart T. *lawyer*
Rostow, Charles Nicholas *lawyer, educator*
St. Clair, James Draper *lawyer*
Samp, Edward Joseph, Jr. *lawyer*
Saparoff, Peter M. *lawyer*
†Sapers, Carl Martin *lawyer*
Sargeant, Ernest James *lawyer*
Savrann, Richard Allen *lawyer*
Saxe, Edward A. *lawyer*
Schmelzer, Henry Louis Phillip *lawyer, financial company executive*
Schram, Ronald Byard *lawyer*
Scott, A. Hugh *lawyer*
Scott, Arnold Duane *lawyer*
Sears, John Winthrop *lawyer*
Segal, Robert Mandal *lawyer*
Shapiro, Sandra *lawyer*
Shepard, Henry Bradbury, Jr. *lawyer*
Sherman, Elliot Mark *lawyer*
Silberman, Robert A. S. *lawyer*
Simons, Steven J(ay) *lawyer*
Sirkin, Joel H. *lawyer*
Slinger, Michael Jeffery *law library director*
Smith, Edwin Eric *lawyer*
Smith, Philip Jones *lawyer*
Snyder, Richard Joseph *lawyer*
Soden, Richard Allan *lawyer*
Solet, Maxwell David *lawyer*
Sommerfeld, Nicholas Ulrich *lawyer*
Sonnenschein, Adam *lawyer*
Southard, William G. *lawyer*
Spackman, David Glendinning *lawyer*
Stein, Marshall David *lawyer*
Steinhauer, Gillian *lawyer*
Stevenson, Philip Davis *lawyer*
Stokes, James Christopher *lawyer*
†Storer, Thomas Perry *lawyer*
Storey, James Moorfield *lawyer*
Streeter, Henry Schofield *lawyer*
Sugarman, Paul Ronald *lawyer, educator, academic administrator*
Swaim, Charles Hall *lawyer*
Swope, Jeffrey Peyton *lawyer*
Taylor, Hal Winslow *lawyer*
Taylor, Thomas William *lawyer*
Teller, Richard E. *lawyer*
Trimmier, Roscoe, Jr. *lawyer*
Tsongas, Paul Efthemios *lawyer, former senator*
Tuchmann, Robert *lawyer*
Vaccarelli, Marie C. *lawyer*
Van, Peter *lawyer*
Vance, Verne Widney, Jr. *lawyer*
van Gestel, Allan *lawyer*
Vaughan, Herbert Wiley *lawyer*
Waddick, Sheryl F. Baiky *lawyer*
Walker, Gordon T. *lawyer*
Weaver, Paul David *lawyer*
Weiner, Stephen Mark *lawyer*
Weinstein, David Carl *lawyer*
Weitzel, John Patterson *lawyer*
Weltman, David Lee *lawyer*
Westcott, John McMahon, Jr. *lawyer*
White, Barry Bennett *lawyer*
Whitlock, John L. *lawyer*
Whitters, James Payton, III *lawyer, university administrator*
Wieckowski, Zdislaw Wladyslaw *lawyer*
Williams, John Taylor *lawyer*
Williams, Robert Dana *lawyer*
Winter, Donald Francis *lawyer*
Wirth, Peter *lawyer*
Wodlinger, Eric W. *lawyer*
Wolf, David *lawyer*
Woodburn, Ralph Robert, Jr. *lawyer*
Woolsey, John Munro, Jr. *lawyer*
Young, Raymond Henry *lawyer*
Zack, Arnold Marshall *lawyer, mediator, arbitrator*
Zupcofska, Peter F. *lawyer*

Braintree
Kent, Richard Edmund *lawyer*
†O'Toole, Lawrence William *lawyer, educational finance professional*
Paven, Nathan Samuel *lawyer*

Brookline
Burnstein, Daniel *lawyer*
Feinberg, Robert I(ra) *lawyer*

Cambridge
Alevizos, Susan Bamberger *lawyer, santouri player, author*
Alevizos, Theodore G. *lawyer, singer, author*
Alford, William P. *lawyer, educator*
Andrews, William Dorey *lawyer, educator*
Areeda, Phillip *lawyer, educator*
Bartholet, Elizabeth *law educator*
Baum, Michael Scott *lawyer, consultant*
Bebchuk, Lucian Arye *law educator*
Bellow, Gary *lawyer, educator*
Bok, Derek *law educator, former university president*
Chapin, Richard *arbitrator, consultant*
Chayes, Abram *law educator, lawyer*
Clark, Robert Charles *lawyer, educator, dean*
Cox, Archibald *lawyer, educator*
Dershowitz, Alan Morton *lawyer, educator*
Donahue, Charles, Jr. *law educator, author*
Downey, Richard Ralph *lawyer, consultant*
Edley, Christopher F., Jr. *law educator*
Fallon, Richard H., Jr. *law educator*
Field, Martha Amanda *law educator, lawyer*
Fisher, Roger Dummer *lawyer, educator, negotiation expert*
Fried, Charles *lawyer, educator*
Frug, Gerald E. *law educator*
Glauner, Alfred William *lawyer, engineering company executive*
Glendon, Mary Ann *law educator*
Gonson, S. Donald *lawyer*
Herwitz, David Richard *law educator*
Horwitz, Morton J. *law educator*
Kaplow, Louis *law educator*
Kassman, Herbert Seymour *lawyer, management consultant*
Katz, Milton *legal educator, public official*
Kaufman, Andrew Lee *law educator*
Kennedy, David W. *law educator*
Kennedy, Randall L. *law educator*
Kraakman, Reinier H. *law educator*
Leibowitz, Ann Galperin *lawyer*
Loss, Louis *lawyer, retired educator*
Mack, Robert Whiting *lawyer*
Mansfield, John H. *lawyer, educator*
Marshall, Margaret Hilary *lawyer*
Martin, Harry Stratton, III *law librarian*
Meltzer, Daniel J. *law educator*
Michelman, Frank I. *lawyer, educator*
Miller, Arthur Raphael *legal educator*
Minow, Martha L. *law educator*
Mnookin, Robert Harris *lawyer, educator*
Nesson, Charles R. *lawyer, educator*
Oldman, Oliver *law educator*
Parker, Richard Davies *lawyer, educator*
Rakoff, Todd D. *law educator*
Riesman, David *lawyer, social scientist*

Roche, John Jefferson *lawyer*
Rosenberg, David *law educator*
Ryan, Allan Andrew, Jr. *lawyer, author, lecturer*
Sander, Frank Ernest Arnold *law educator*
Sargentich, Lewis D. *legal educator*
Schauer, Frederick Franklin *legal educator*
Scott, Hal S. *law educator*
Shapiro, David Louis *lawyer, educator*
Shavell, Steven *law educator*
Steiner, Henry Jacob *law and human rights educator*
Stone, Alan A. *law educator, psychiatry educator*
Stone, Andrew Grover *lawyer*
Ta, Tai Van *lawyer, researcher*
Tribe, Laurence Henry *lawyer, educator*
Vagts, Detlev Frederick *lawyer, educator*
von Mehren, Arthur Taylor *lawyer, educator*
Vorenberg, James *lawyer, educator, university dean*
Warren, Alvin Clifford, Jr. *lawyer*
Weiler, Paul Cronin *law educator*
Weinreb, Lloyd Lobell *law educator*
Westfall, David *lawyer, educator*
Wolfman, Bernard *lawyer, educator*

Canton
Friend, William Kagay *lawyer*

Chatham
Pacun, Norman *lawyer*

Chelmsford
Grossman, Debra A. *lawyer, real estate manager, radio talk show host*

Chestnut Hill
Bursley, Kathleen A. *lawyer*
†Geller, Eric P. *lawyer, cinema company executive*

Concord
Berger, Raoul *lawyer, educator, violinist*
White, James Barr *lawyer, real estate investor, consultant*

Dedham
Lake, Ann Winslow *lawyer*

Framingham
Gaffin, Gerald Eliot *lawyer*
Meltzer, Jay H. *lawyer, retail company executive*

Greenfield
Lee, Marilyn (Irma) Modarelli *law librarian*

Hingham
Dassori, Frederic Davis, Jr. *lawyer*
Lane, Frederick Stanley *lawyer*

Holliston
Scibelli, Arthur Peter, Jr. *lawyer*

Ipswich
Getchell, Charles Willard, Jr. *lawyer, publisher*

Lexington
Eaton, Allen Ober *lawyer*
Hoffmann, Christoph Ludwig *lawyer*

Lincoln
Schwartz, Edward Arthur *lawyer, foundation executive*

Maynard
Siekman, Thomas Clement *lawyer*

Medford
Berman, David *lawyer, poet*
Salacuse, Jeswald William *lawyer, educator*

Middleboro
Beeby, Kenneth Jack *lawyer, food products executive*

Milton
Place, David Elliott *lawyer*

Nantucket
Lobl, Herbert Max *lawyer*

Natick
Savage, James Cathey, III *lawyer, military officer, educator*

Newton
Baron, Charles Hillel *lawyer, educator*
Coquillette, Daniel Robert *lawyer, educator*
Hauser, Harry Raymond *lawyer*
Horbaczewski, Henry Zygmunt *lawyer, publishing executive*
Katz, Sanford Noah *lawyer, educator*
†Landers, Renée Marie *law educator, government lawyer*

Newton Center
Ault, Hugh Joseph *legal educator*

North Reading
Green, Jack Allen *lawyer*

Norwell
Mullare, T(homas) Kenwood, Jr. *lawyer*

Norwood
Rasmussen, David George *lawyer*

Pittsfield
Poland, Susan Lee *lawyer*

Plymouth
Barreira, Brian Ernest *lawyer*

Salem
Griffin, Thomas McLean *retired lawyer*
Moran, Philip David *lawyer*

Sharon
Segersten, Robert Hagy *lawyer, investment banker*

Springfield
Dunn, Donald Jack *law librarian, law educator, lawyer*
Miller, J(ohn) Wesley, III *lawyer, writer*
Milstein, Richard Sherman *lawyer*
Oldershaw, Louis Frederick *lawyer*

Stoughton
Douglas, John Breed, III *lawyer*

Wakefield
Hunt, Samuel Pancoast, III *lawyer, corporate executive*

Waltham
Touster, Saul *legal educator*

Wayland
Bullard, Robert Oliver, Jr. *lawyer*

Wellesley
Aldrich, Richard Orth *lawyer*
Carlson, Christopher Tapley *lawyer*
Shea, Robert McConnell *lawyer*

Westborough
Frank, Jacob *lawyer*

Weston
Haas, Jacqueline Crawford *lawyer*
Thomas, Roger Meriwether *lawyer*

Wilbraham
Wise, Warren Roberts *lawyer*

Winchester
Bigelow, Robert P. *arbitrator, writer*

Worcester
Cowan, Fairman Chaffee *lawyer*
Dewey, Henry Bowen *retired lawyer*
Fries, Donald Eugene *lawyer, insurance executive*
Kelly, John Francis *lawyer*

Worthington
Hastings, Wilmot Reed *lawyer*

MICHIGAN

Ada
Mitchell, Kim Sarahjane *lawyer*

Ann Arbor
Aleinikoff, T. Alexander *law educator*
Allen, Layman Edward *law educator, research scientist*
Britton, Clarold Lawrence *lawyer, consultant*
Chambers, David Laurance, III *legal educator*
Cooper, Edward Hayes *lawyer, educator*
DeVine, Edmond Francis *lawyer*
Duquette, Donald Norman *law educator*
Eisenberg, Rebecca S. *law educator*
Ellmann, William Marshall *lawyer, mediator, arbitrator, researcher*
Fox, Merritt B. *law educator*
Friedman, Richard D. *law educator*
Frier, Bruce W. *law educator*
Gilbert, Robert Edward *lawyer*
Gray, Whitmore *law educator, lawyer*
Green, Thomas Andrew *lawyer, law and history educator*
Huetteman, Raymond Theodore, Jr. *lawyer*
Israel, Jerold Harvey *law educator*
Jackson, John Howard *lawyer, educator*
Joscelyn, Kent Buckley *lawyer, research scientist*
Kahn, Douglas Allen *legal educator*
Kamisar, Yale *lawyer, educator*
Kauper, Thomas Eugene *lawyer, educator*
Kennedy, Frank Robert *lawyer*
Krier, James Edward *law educator, author*
Lempert, Richard Owen *lawyer, educator*
MacKinnon, Catharine A. *lawyer, law educator, legal scholar, writer*
Miller, William Ian *legal educator*
Payton, Sallyanne *law educator*
Pierce, William James *law educator*
Reed, John Wesley *lawyer, educator*
Roach, Thomas Adair *lawyer*
St. Antoine, Theodore Joseph *legal educator*
Sandalow, Terrance *law educator*
Schneider, Carl Edward *law educator*
Simpson, A. W. B. *law educator*
Southwick, Arthur Frederick *legal educator*
Stein, Eric *retired law educator*
Vining, (George) Joseph *law educator*
Waggoner, Lawrence William *law educator*
Westen, Peter *law educator*
White, James Boyd *law educator*
White, James Justesen *legal educator*
Whitman, Christina Brooks *law educator*

Battle Creek
Clark, Richard McCourt *lawyer, food company executive*

Benton Harbor
Frey, Robert Imbrie *lawyer*

Bingham Farms
Martin, J(oseph) Patrick *lawyer, arbitrator, educator*

Birmingham
Bromberg, Stephen Aaron *lawyer*
Buesser, Anthony Carpenter *lawyer*
Elsman, James Leonard, Jr. *lawyer*
Gold, Edward David *lawyer*
Hirschhorn, Austin *lawyer*
Schaefer, John Frederick *lawyer*
Wittlinger, Timothy David *lawyer*

Bloomfield Hills
Andrews, Frank Lewis *lawyer*
Avant, Grady, Jr. *lawyer, financial executive*
Baker, Robert Edward *lawyer, retired financial corporation executive*
Bruegel, David Robert *lawyer*
Cannon, John Kemper *lawyer*
Clippert, Charles Frederick *lawyer*
Cumbey, Constance Elizabeth *lawyer, author, lecturer*
Dawson, Stephen Everette *lawyer*
Googasian, George Ara *lawyer*
Kasischke, Louis Walter *lawyer*
LoPrete, James Hugh *lawyer*
Mc Donald, Patrick Allen *lawyer, arbitrator, educator*
Meyer, George Herbert *lawyer*
Nolte, Henry R., Jr. *lawyer, former automobile company executive*
Norris, John Hart *lawyer*
Pappas, Edward Harvey *lawyer*
Preston, David Michael *lawyer*
Rader, Ralph Terrance *lawyer*
Snyder, George Edward *lawyer*
Thurber, John Alexander *lawyer*
Williams, Walter Joseph *lawyer*

Dearborn
Christy, Perry Thomas *lawyer, air transport company executive*
Currier, Gene Mark *lawyer*
Kienbaum, Karen Smith *lawyer*
Martin, John William, Jr. *lawyer, automotive industry executive*
Pestillo, Peter John *lawyer, automotive executive*
Simon, Evelyn *lawyer*
Taub, Robert Allan *lawyer*

Detroit
Amerman, John Ellis *lawyer*
Amsden, Ted Thomas *lawyer*
Babcock, Charles Witten, Jr. *lawyer*
Banas, Christine Leslie *lawyer*
Barringer, Leland David *lawyer*
Battista, Robert James *lawyer*
Brady, Edmund Matthew, Jr. *lawyer*
Brand, George Edward, Jr. *lawyer*
Braun, Richard Lane, II *lawyer*
Brodhead, William McNulty *lawyer, former congressman*
Brown, Stratton Shartel *lawyer*
Brustad, Orin Daniel *lawyer*
Burstein, Richard Joel *lawyer*
Bushnell, George Edward, Jr. *lawyer*
Candler, James Nall, Jr. *lawyer*
Charfoos, Lawrence Selig *lawyer*
Charla, Leonard Francis *lawyer*
Choate, Robert Alden *lawyer*
Cohan, Leon Sumner *lawyer, retired electric company executive*
Collier, James Warren *lawyer*
Connor, Laurence Davis *lawyer*
Cothorn, John Arthur *lawyer*
Darlow, Julia Donovan *lawyer*
Dart, Judith C(andelor) Lalka *lawyer*
Dobranski, Bernard *law educator*
Draper, James Wilson *lawyer*
Driker, Eugene *lawyer*
Dudley, Arthur, II *lawyer*
Dudley, John Henry, Jr. *lawyer*
Dunn, William Bradley *lawyer*
Dykema, John Russel *retired lawyer*
Eggertsen, John Hale *lawyer*
Garzia, Samuel Angelo *lawyer*
Gelder, John William *lawyer*
Getz, Ernest John *lawyer*
Grow, Richard Dennis *lawyer*
Gushee, Richard Bordley *lawyer*
Hampton, Verne Churchill, II *lawyer*
Hatie, George Daniel *lawyer*
Heaphy, John Merrill *lawyer*
Herstein, Carl William *lawyer*
Holmes, Peter Douglas *lawyer*
Howbert, Edgar Charles *lawyer*
Kessler, Philip Joel *lawyer*
Keydel, Frederick Reid *lawyer*
Kienbaum, Thomas Gerd *lawyer*
King, John Lane *lawyer*
Kinnaird, Charles Roemler *lawyer*
Kuehn, George E. *lawyer, beverage company executive*
Lamborn, LeRoy Leslie *legal educator*
Lawrence, John Kidder *lawyer*
Ledwidge, Patrick Joseph *lawyer*
Lenga, J. Thomas *lawyer*
Lockman, Stuart M. *lawyer*
Lombard, Arthur J. *law educator*
Longhofer, Ronald Stephen *lawyer*
Lucow, Milton *lawyer*
Majzoub, Mona Kathryne *lawyer*
Mamat, Frank Trustick *lawyer*
Massie, Noel David *lawyer*
Maurer, David L. *lawyer*
Maycock, Joseph Farwell, Jr. *lawyer*
McKim, Samuel John, III *lawyer*
McNair, Russell Arthur, Jr. *lawyer*
Miller, George DeWitt, Jr. *lawyer*
Mitseff, Carl *lawyer*
O'Hair, John D. *lawyer, prosecutor*
Parker, George Edward, III *lawyer*
Paul, Richard Wright *lawyer*
Pearce, Harry Jonathan *lawyer*
Phillips, Elliott Hunter *lawyer*
Ponitz, John Allan *lawyer*
Richie, Leroy C. *lawyer, automotive executive*
Robinson, James Kenneth *lawyer*
Roche, Douglas David *lawyer, bar examiner*
Rossen, Jordan *lawyer*
Rossman, Richard Alan *lawyer*
Rozof, Phyllis Claire *lawyer*
Russell, Robert Gilmore *lawyer*
Ruwart, David Peter *lawyer*
Santo, Ronald Joseph *lawyer*
Saurbier, Scott Alan *lawyer*
Saxton, William Marvin *lawyer*
Saylor, Larry James *lawyer*
Schultz, Dennis Bernard *lawyer*
Schwartz, Alan E. *lawyer*
Schwartz, Jerome Merrill *lawyer*
Scott, John Edward Smith *lawyer*
Semple, Lloyd Ashby *lawyer*
Shaevsky, Mark *lawyer*
Shannon, Margaret Anne *lawyer*
Sott, Herbert *lawyer*
Sparrow, Herbert George, III *lawyer*
Thelen, Bruce Cyril *lawyer*
Thorpe, Norman Ralph *lawyer, automobile company executive, retired air force officer*
Thurber, Peter Palms *lawyer*
Toll, Sheldon Samuel *lawyer*
Volz, William Harry *legal educator, administrator*
Waldmeir, Peter William *lawyer*
Warren, William Gerald *lawyer*
Weiss, Robert Benjamin *lawyer*
Williams, J. Bryan *lawyer*
Winsten, I. W. *lawyer, law educator*
Wise, John Augustus *lawyer*
Wynne, James Earl *lawyer*
Ziegler, John Augustus, Jr. *lawyer*
Zuckerman, Richard Engle *lawyer, educator*

Dundee
Moir, Robert Jesse *manufacturing company executive, lawyer*

East Lansing
Bonham, Vence Lee, Jr. *lawyer, educator*
Hackett, Wesley Phelps, Jr. *lawyer*
Kurz, Mary Elizabeth *lawyer*
Lashbrooke, Elvin Carroll, Jr. *legal educator, consultant*

Farmington
Shoop, Deborah *lawyer*

Farmington Hills
Birnkrant, Sherwin Maurice *lawyer*
Haliw, Andrew Jerome, III *lawyer, engineer*

Flint
Lehman, Richard Leroy *lawyer*
†Pelavin, Michael Allen *lawyer*

Franklin
Rassel, Richard Edward *lawyer*

Grand Rapids
Barnes, Thomas John *lawyer*
Boyden, Joel Michael *lawyer*
Bradshaw, Conrad Allan *lawyer*
Brady, James S. *lawyer*
Bransdorfer, Stephen Christie *lawyer*
Curtin, Timothy John *lawyer*
Deems, Nyal David *lawyer, mayor*
DeWitt, Jon Francis *lawyer*
Fry, David Stow *lawyer*
Heiden, Thomas John *lawyer*
Kara, Paul Mark *lawyer*
Mc Callum, Charles Edward *lawyer*
McGarry, John Everett *lawyer*
Mears, Patrick Edward *lawyer*
Pestle, John William *lawyer*
Sytsma, Fredric Alan *lawyer*
Titley, Larry J. *lawyer*
VanderLaan, Robert D. *lawyer*
Van't Hof, William Keith *lawyer*

Grosse Pointe
Brucker, Wilber Marion *lawyer*
Darke, Richard Francis *lawyer*
Gilbride, William Donald *lawyer*
Mogk, John Edward *legal educator, association executive*
Pytell, Robert Henry *lawyer, former judge*

Grosse Pointe Farms
Axe, John Randolph *lawyer, financial executive*

Hickory Corners
Bristol, Norman *lawyer, arbitrator, former food company executive*

Ishpeming
Andriacchi, Dominic Francis *lawyer*

Jackson
Marcoux, William Joseph *lawyer*

Kalamazoo
Brown, Eric Vandyke, Jr. *lawyer*
Hooker, Richard Alfred *lawyer*
Hustoles, Thomas Paul *lawyer*
Ritter, Charles Edward *lawyer*

Lansing
Baker, Frederick Milton, Jr. *lawyer*
Demlow, Daniel J. *lawyer*
Fink, Joseph Allen *lawyer*
Fitzgerald, John Warner *legal educator*
Foster, Joe C., Jr. *lawyer*
Lindemer, Lawrence Boyd *lawyer, former utility executive, former state justice*
McLellan, Richard Douglas *lawyer*
Rooney, John Philip *law educator*
Stockmeyer, Norman Otto, Jr. *law educator, consultant*
Valade, Alan Michael *lawyer*
Wilkinson, William Sherwood *lawyer*

Livonia
Hanket, Mark John *lawyer*
McCuen, John Francis, Jr. *lawyer*

Midland
Jenkins, James Robert *lawyer, corporate executive*

Monroe
Lipford, Rocque Edward *lawyer, corporate executive*

Muskegon
Van Leuven, Robert Joseph *lawyer*

New Buffalo
Laird, Evalyn Walsh *lawyer*

Oak Park
McManus, Martin Joseph *lawyer, priest*

Plymouth
Morgan, Donald Crane *lawyer*

Pontiac
Berlow, Robert Alan *lawyer*

Saint Clair Shores
Shehan, Wayne Charles *lawyer*

Southfield
Cohen, Norton Jacob *lawyer*
Dawson, Dennis Ray *lawyer, manufacturing company executive*
Hotelling, Harold *law and economics educator*
Jacobs, John Patrick *lawyer*
Link, Robert Allen *lawyer, financial company executive*
Morganroth, Fred *lawyer*
Morganroth, Mayer *lawyer*
Satovsky, Abraham *lawyer*

Taylor
Bright, Gerald *lawyer, manufacturing company executive*
Leekley, John Robert *lawyer*

Traverse City
Wolfe, Richard Ratcliffe *lawyer*

Troy
Alterman, Irwin Michael *lawyer*
Cantor, Bernard Jack *patent lawyer*
Crane, Louis Arthur *retired labor arbitrator*
Hartwig, Eugene Lawrence *lawyer*
Kruse, John Alphonse *lawyer*
LaDuke, Nancie *lawyer, corporate executive*

MINNESOTA

Bemidji
Kief, Paul Allan *lawyer*

Burnsville
Knutson, David Lee *lawyer, state senator*

Duluth
Balmer, James Walter *lawyer*

Hopkins
Hunter, Donald Forrest *lawyer*

Mankato
Gage, Fred Kelton *lawyer*

Minneapolis
Abrams, Richard Brill *lawyer*
Ackman, Lauress V. *lawyer*
Adams, Thomas Lewis *lawyer*
Adamson, Oscar Charles, II *lawyer*
Anderson, Eric Scott *lawyer*
Anderson, Laurence Alexis *lawyer*
Anderson, Thomas Willman *lawyer*
Baillie, James Leonard *lawyer*
Barnard, Allen Donald *lawyer*
Bartle, Emery W(arness) *lawyer*
Bearmon, Lee *lawyer*
Berens, William Joseph *lawyer*
Berg, Thomas Kenneth *lawyer*
Bergerson, Stephen Richard *lawyer*
Beukema, John Frederick *lawyer*
Blanton, W. C. *lawyer*
Bleck, Michael John *lawyer*
Bloom, Roger Fredric *lawyer*
Boelter, Philip Floyd *lawyer*
Borger, John Philip *lawyer*
Brand, Steve Aaron *lawyer*
Breimayer, Joseph Frederick *patent lawyer*
Bress, Michael E. *lawyer*
Brink, David Ryrie *lawyer*
Brosnahan, Roger Paul *lawyer*
Bruner, Philip Lane *lawyer*
Buratti, Dennis P. *lawyer*
Burk, Robert S. *lawyer*
Burke, Martin Nicholas *lawyer*
Burns, Robert A. *lawyer*
Busdicker, Gordon G. *lawyer*
Carlson, Don D. *lawyer*
Carlson, Thomas David *lawyer*
Carpenter, Norman Roblee *lawyer*
Champlin, Steven Kirk *lawyer*
Christiansen, Jay David *lawyer*
Ciresi, Michael Vincent *lawyer*
Comstock, Rebecca Ann *lawyer*
Conn, Gordon Brainard, Jr. *lawyer*
Cook, Jay F. *lawyer*
Crosby, Thomas Manville, Jr. *lawyer*
Cutler, Kenneth Lance *lawyer*
Davies, R. Scott *lawyer*
Dorsey, Peter *lawyer*
Drawz, John Englund *lawyer*
Eastwood, J. Marquis *lawyer*
Eck, George Gregory *lawyer*
Endorf, Verlane L. *lawyer*
Feld, Barry Charles *law educator*
Finzen, Bruce Arthur *lawyer*
Fisher, Michael Bruce *lawyer*
Fisher, Orville Earl, Jr. *lawyer, venture capital consultant*
†FitzGerald, Richard Joseph, Jr. *lawyer, educator*
Flannery, George Perry *lawyer*
Flom, Gerald Trossen *lawyer*
Frase, Richard Stockwell *law educator*
Frecon, Alain *lawyer*
French, John Dwyer *lawyer*
Fronek, David N. *lawyer*
Gagnon, Craig William *lawyer*
Garon, Philip Stephen *lawyer*
Garton, Thomas William *lawyer*
Gearty, Edward Joseph *lawyer*
Gifford, Daniel Joseph *lawyer, educator, antitrust consultant*
Gill, Richard Lawrence *lawyer*
Goodman, Elizabeth Ann *lawyer*
Gordon, John Bennett *lawyer*
Gottschalk, Stephen Elmer *lawyer*
Grayson, Edward Davis *lawyer, manufacturing company executive*
Greener, Ralph Bertram *lawyer*
Griffith, G. Larry *lawyer*
Hagglund, Clarance Edward *lawyer, publishing company owner*
Hardman, James Charles *lawyer, motor carrier executive*
Harris, John Edward *lawyer*
Hasselquist, Maynard Burton *retired lawyer*
Hayward, Edward Joseph *lawyer*
Heiberg, Robert Alan *lawyer*
Hempel, William J. *lawyer*
Hemphill, Stuart R. *lawyer*
Hendrixson, Peter S. *lawyer*
Henson, Robert Frank *lawyer*
Hibbs, John Stanley *lawyer*
Hibbs, William R. *lawyer*
Hinderaker, John Hadley *lawyer*
Hippee, William H., Jr. *lawyer*
Hitch, Horace *lawyer*
Hobbins, Robert Leo *lawyer*
Howland, Joan Sidney *law librarian, law educator*
Hudec, Robert Emil *lawyer, educator*
Jackson, J. David *lawyer*
Jarboe, Mark Alan *lawyer*
Johnson, Eugene Laurence *lawyer*
Johnson, Gary M. *lawyer*
Johnson, Larry Walter *lawyer*
Johnson, Paul Owen *lawyer*
Johnson, Scott William *lawyer, manufacturing company executive*
Jones, Bradley Mitchell *lawyer*
Kampf, William Ira *lawyer*
Kaplan, Sheldon *lawyer*
Karan, Bradlee *lawyer, educator*
Karigan, James Andrew *lawyer*
Kelly, A. David *lawyer*
Keppel, William James *lawyer*
Keyes, Jeffrey J. *lawyer*
Kilbourn, William Douglas, Jr. *law educator*
Kirby, John D. *lawyer*
Kirshbaum, Jane Kaplan *lawyer*
Kitchak, Peter Ramon *lawyer*
Klaas, Paul Barry *lawyer*
Koeppen, Bart *law educator, consultant*
Koneck, John M. *lawyer*
Krohnke, Duane W. *lawyer*
Landry, Paul Leonard *lawyer*
Lareau, Richard George *lawyer*
Larson, Dale Irving *lawyer*
Lazar, Raymond Michael *lawyer, educator*
Lebedoff, David M. *lawyer, author*
Lebedoff, Randy Miller *lawyer*
Levine, John David *lawyer*
Levy, Robert Joseph *lawyer, educator*
Lindgren, D(erbin) Kenneth, Jr. *lawyer*
Lubben, David J. *lawyer*
Magnuson, Roger James *lawyer*
Mahoney, Jerry C. D. *lawyer*
Malfeld, Diane D. *lawyer*
Manning, William Henry *lawyer*
Manthey, Thomas Richard *lawyer*
Martin, Kathleen Minder *lawyer*
Martin, Phillip Hammond *lawyer*
Matthews, James Shadley *lawyer*
McClintock, George Dunlap *lawyer*
Mellum, Gale Robert *lawyer*
Meshbesher, Ronald I. *lawyer*
Minish, Robert Arthur *lawyer*
Mitau, Lee R. *lawyer*
Moe, Thomas O. *lawyer*
Mooty, John William *lawyer*
Morris, C. Robert *law educator*
Morrison, Fred LaMont *law educator*
Nelson, Richard Arthur *lawyer*
Nelson, Steven Craig *lawyer*
Nilles, John Michael *lawyer*
Norton, Elizabeth Wychgel *lawyer*
O'Keefe, Daniel P. *lawyer*
O'Neill, Brian Boru *lawyer*
Palmer, Brian Eugene *lawyer*
Palmer, Deborah Jean *lawyer*
Payne, William Bruce *lawyer*
Pluimer, Edward J. *lawyer*
Potuznik, Charles Laddy *lawyer*
Pratte, Robert John *lawyer*
Price, Joseph Michael *lawyer*
Rachie, Cyrus *lawyer*
Radmer, Michael John *lawyer, educator*
Ranheim, David A. *lawyer*
Rebane, John T. *lawyer*
Reilly, George *lawyer*
Rein, Stanley Michael *lawyer*
Reinhart, Robert Rountree, Jr. *lawyer*
Reister, Raymond Alex *lawyer*
Reuter, James William *lawyer*
Rockenstein, Walter Harrison, II *lawyer*
Rockwell, Winthrop Adams *lawyer*
Saeks, Allen Irving *lawyer*
Safley, James Robert *lawyer*
Sanner, Royce Norman *lawyer*
Satorius, John Arthur *lawyer*
Savelkoul, Donald Charles *lawyer*
Scallen, Stephen Burns *law educator*
Scheerer, Paul J. *lawyer*
Schnell, Robert Lee, Jr. *lawyer*
Schnobrich, Roger William *lawyer*
Schoettle, Ferdinand P. *lawyer, educator*
Schwartzbauer, Robert Alan *lawyer*
Sheehy, Lee Edward *lawyer*
Sherry, Suzanna *law educator*
Shiels, Barbara L. *lawyer*
Shnider, Bruce Jay *lawyer*
Silverman, Robert Joseph *lawyer*
Spencer, David James *lawyer*
Steilen, James R. *lawyer*
Stern, Leo G. *lawyer*
Stroup, Stanley Stephenson *lawyer, educator*
Struyk, Robert John *lawyer*
†Stuart, John Malcolm *public defender*
Symchych, Janice M. *lawyer*
Tinkham, Thomas W. *lawyer*
Todd, John Joseph *lawyer*
Torres, Gerald *law educator*
Trucano, Michael *lawyer*
Tygesson, Gary Lincoln *lawyer*
Ueland, Sigurd, Jr. *lawyer*
Vander Molen, Thomas Dale *lawyer*
Wahoske, Michael James *lawyer*
Weissbrodt, David Samuel *law educator*
Whitehill, Clifford Lane *lawyer*
Whitlock, William Abel *lawyer*
Wille, Karin L. *lawyer*
Windhorst, John William, Jr. *lawyer*
Wine, Mark Philip *lawyer*
Woods, Robert Edward *lawyer*
Younger, Judith Tess *lawyer, educator*
Zalk, Robert H. *lawyer*

Minnetonka
Palmer, John Marshall *lawyer*

Minnetonka Mills
Hoard, Heidi Marie *lawyer*

Pipestone
Scott, William Paul *lawyer*

Rochester
Lantz, William Charles *lawyer*
Seeger, Ronald L. *lawyer*
Wicks, John R. *lawyer*

Saint Cloud
Lindula, Pamela O'Hara *lawyer*
Pribble, Edward David Lalor *labor and employment arbitrator, lawyer*

Saint Louis Park
Rothenberg, Elliot Calvin *lawyer, writer*

Saint Paul
Carruthers, Philip Charles *lawyer*
Clary, Bradley Grayson *lawyer, educator*
Collins, Theodore Joseph *lawyer, educator*
Crippin, Byron Miles, Jr. *lawyer, religious organization professional, consultant*
Culp, Bethany Kelly *lawyer*
Daly, Joseph Leo *law educator*
Dietz, Charlton Henry *lawyer*
Ebert, Robert Alvin *retired lawyer, retired airline executive*
Friel, Bernard Preston *lawyer*
Galvin, Michael John, Jr. *lawyer*
Geis, Jerome Arthur *lawyer, legal educator*
Goodrich, Leon Raymond *lawyer*
Hammond, Frank Joseph *lawyer*
Hansen, Robyn L. *lawyer*
Haynsworth, Harry Jay, IV *lawyer, educator*
Heidenreich, Douglas Robert *lawyer*
Johnson, Paul Oren *lawyer*
Jones, C. Paul *lawyer, educator*
Kane, Thomas Patrick *lawyer*
Kaner, Harvey Sheldon *lawyer, executive*
Kirwin, Kenneth F. *law educator*
Levi, Arlo Dane *lawyer*
Maclin, Alan Hall *lawyer*
McNeely, John J. *lawyer*
Oppenheimer, James Richard *lawyer*
Popovich, Peter Stephen *lawyer, former state supreme court chief justice*
Rosengren, William R. *lawyer, corporation executive*
Ryan, Lehan Jerome *lawyer*
Seymour, McNeil Vernam *lawyer*
Sippel, William Leroy *lawyer*
Ursu, John Joseph *lawyer*
Whelpley, Dennis Porter *lawyer*

Slayton
Anderson, Merlyn Dean *lawyer*

South Saint Paul
Pugh, Thomas Wilfred *lawyer*

Stillwater
O'Brien, Daniel William *lawyer, corporation executive*

Wayzata
Alton, Howard Robert, Jr. *lawyer, real estate and food company executive*
Bergerson, David Raymond *lawyer*
Reutiman, Robert William, Jr. *lawyer*

MISSISSIPPI

Brandon
Samsel, Maebell Scroggins (Midge Samsel) *paralegal*

Clarksdale
Curtis, Chester Harris *lawyer, retired bank executive*

Cleveland
Alexander, William Brooks *lawyer, former state senator*
Howorth, Lucy Somerville *lawyer*

Gulfport
Allen, Harry Roger *lawyer*
Harral, John Menteith *lawyer*

Hattiesburg
Riley, Thomas Jackson *lawyer*

Jackson
Barnett, Robert Glenn *lawyer*
Butler, George Harrison *lawyer*
†Chustz, J. Steve *lawyer*
Clark, Charles *lawyer*
Clark, David Wright *lawyer*
Fuselier, Louis Alfred *lawyer*
Hosemann, C. Delbert, Jr. *lawyer*
Langford, James Jerry *lawyer*
Lilly, Thomas Gerald *lawyer*
Miller, Hainon Alfred *lawyer, investor*
Moize, Jerry Dee *lawyer*
Phillips, George L. *prosecutor*
Price, Alfred Lee *lawyer, mining company executive*
Wise, Sherwood Willing *lawyer*

Learned
Barrett, Richard *lawyer*

Oxford
Dunbar, Wylene Wisby *lawyer, writer*

Pascagoula
Carlson, John Henry *lawyer*

Ruleville
Crook, Robert Lacey *lawyer*

Tupelo
Bush, Fred Marshall, Jr. *lawyer*

MISSOURI

Chesterfield
Klarich, David John *lawyer, state senator*
Pollihan, Thomas Henry *lawyer*

Clayton
Belz, Mark *lawyer*

Columbia
Fisch, William Bales *lawyer*
Parrigin, Elizabeth Ellington *lawyer*
Welliver, Warren Dee *lawyer, retired state supreme court justice*
Westbrook, James Edwin *lawyer, educator*

Fenton
Stolar, Henry Samuel *corporate lawyer*

Grandview
Dietrich, William Gale *lawyer, real estate developer, consultant*

Hazelwood
Purvines, Verne Ewald, Jr. *lawyer*

Independence
Walsh, Rodger John *lawyer*

Jefferson City
Bartlett, Alex *lawyer*
Deutsch, James Bernard *lawyer*
Gaw, Robert Steven *lawyer, state representative*
Tettlebaum, Harvey M. *lawyer*

Kansas City
Anderson, Christopher James *lawyer*
Bates, William Hubert *lawyer*
Becker, Thomas Bain *lawyer*
Beckett, Theodore Charles *lawyer*
Beihl, Frederick *lawyer*
Berkowitz, Lawrence M. *lawyer*
Black, John Sheldon *lawyer*
Blackwell, Menefee Davis *lawyer*
Bradshaw, Jean Paul, II *lawyer*
Brenner, Daniel Leon *lawyer*
Brouillette, Gary Joseph *lawyer*
Brown, Peter W. *lawyer*
Bruening, Richard P(atrick) *lawyer*
Canfield, Robert Cleo *lawyer*
Chisholm, Donald Herbert *lawyer*
Clarke, Milton Charles *lawyer*
Conway, Thomas James *lawyer*
Cooper, Corinne *law educator*
Crawford, Howard Allen *lawyer*
Cross, William Dennis *lawyer*
Davis, John Charles *lawyer*
Deacy, Thomas Edward, Jr. *lawyer*
Driscoll, Robert Louis *lawyer*
Edgar, John M. *lawyer*
Eldridge, Truman Kermit, Jr. *lawyer*
Field, Lyman *lawyer*
Foster, Mark Stephen *lawyer*
Freilich, Robert H. *lawyer, educator*
French, Linda Jean *lawyer*
Frost, Earle Wesley *lawyer, retired judge*
Gardner, Brian E. *lawyer*
Giffin, Reggie Craig *lawyer*
Gorman, Gerald Warner *lawyer*
Hoffman, John Raymond *lawyer*
Hoskins, William Keller *lawyer, pharmaceutical company executive*
Hubbell, Ernest *lawyer*
Johnson, Mark Eugene *lawyer*
Kilroy, John Muir *lawyer*
Kilroy, William Terrence *lawyer*
King, Richard Allen *lawyer*
Kroenert, Robert Morgan *lawyer*
Langworthy, Robert Burton *lawyer*
Lindsey, David Hosford *lawyer*
Lombardi, Cornelius Ennis, Jr. *lawyer*
Loudon, Donald Hoover *lawyer*
Lysaught, Patrick *lawyer*
Manka, Ronald Eugene *lawyer*
Martucci, William Christopher *lawyer*
Matheny, Edward Taylor, Jr. *lawyer*
McLarney, Charles Patrick *lawyer*
McManus, James William *lawyer*
Mick, Howard Harold *lawyer*
Milton, Chad Earl *lawyer*
Mordy, James Calvin *lawyer*
Newsom, James T. *lawyer*
Northrip, Robert Earl *lawyer*
Palmer, Dennis Dale *lawyer*
Pelofsky, Joel *lawyer*
Popham, Arthur Cobb, Jr. *lawyer*
Popper, Robert *law educator, former dean*
Robb, Gary Charles *lawyer*
Semegen, Patrick William *lawyer*
Session, William Terrell *lawyer*
Setzler, Edward Allan *lawyer*
Shaw, John W. *lawyer*
Smithson, Lowell Lee *lawyer*
Spalty, Edward Robert *lawyer*
Spencer, Richard Henry *lawyer*
Toll, Perry Mark *lawyer*
Tripp, David Richard *lawyer*
Vandever, William Dirk *lawyer*
Varner, Barton Douglas *lawyer*
Vering, John Albert *lawyer*
Viani, James L. *lawyer*
Wiggins, Kip Acker *lawyer*
Woods, Richard Dale *lawyer*
Wrobley, Ralph Gene *lawyer*
Wyrsch, James Robert *lawyer, educator, author*

Kirkwood
Gibbons, Michael Randolph *lawyer*

Lebanon
Hutson, Don *lawyer*

Lees Summit
Hall, Glenn Allen *lawyer, state representative*

Maryland Heights
Sobol, Lawrence Raymond *lawyer*

Nevada
Ewing, Lynn Moore, Jr. *lawyer*

Saint Joseph
Kranitz, Theodore Mitchell *lawyer*

Saint Louis
Appleton, R. O., Jr. *lawyer*
Arnold, John Fox *lawyer*
Attanasio, John Baptist *law educator*
Atwood, Hollye Stolz *lawyer*
Aylward, Ronald Lee *lawyer*
Babington, Charles Martin, III *lawyer*
Baldwin, Edwin Steedman *lawyer*
Barken, Bernard Allen *lawyer*
Barrie, John Paul *lawyer, educator*
Bascom, C. Perry *lawyer*
Bean, Bourne *lawyer*
Becker, David Mandel *legal educator, author, consultant*
Berger, John Torrey, Jr. *lawyer*
Bernstein, Merton Clay *lawyer, educator, arbitrator*
Bottini, Thomas H. *lawyer*
Breece, Robert William, Jr. *lawyer*
Brickey, Kathleen Fitzgerald *law educator*
Brickson, Richard Alan *lawyer*
Brody, Lawrence *lawyer, educator*
Brownlee, Robert Hammel *lawyer*
Bryan, Henry C(lark), Jr. *lawyer*
Carmody, Gerard Timothy *lawyer*
Carp, Richard Lawrence (Larry Carp) *lawyer*
Carr, Gary Thomas *lawyer*
Clear, John Michael *lawyer*

Conran, Joseph Palmer *lawyer*
Cornfeld, Dave Louis *lawyer*
Crampton, William DeVer *tax lawyer*
Crebs, P(aul) Terence *lawyer*
Davis, Steven L. *lawyer*
Denneen, John Paul *lawyer*
Donohue, Carroll John *lawyer*
Dorsey, Gray Lankford *law educator emeritus*
Dorwart, Donald Bruce *lawyer*
Dowd, Edward L., Jr. *prosecutor*
Duesenberg, Richard William *lawyer*
Erwin, James Walter *lawyer*
Falk, William James *lawyer*
Fournie, Raymond Richard *lawyer*
Fryer, Edwin Samuel *lawyer*
Garr, Louis Joseph, Jr. *lawyer, retail company executive*
Gerard, Jules Bernard *law educator*
Gershenson, Harry *lawyer*
Gladding, Nicholas C. *lawyer*
Godiner, Donald Leonard *lawyer*
Goebel, John J. *lawyer*
Goldstein, Michael Gerald *lawyer*
Goldstein, Steven *lawyer*
Goodman, Harold S. *lawyer*
Gray, Charles Elmer *lawyer, rancher, investor*
Green, Dennis Joseph *lawyer*
Guerri, William Grant *lawyer*
Hansen, Charles *lawyer*
Harris, Whitney Robson *lawyer*
Hays, Ruth *lawyer*
Hecker, George Sprake *lawyer*
Hellmuth, Theodore Henning *lawyer*
Hempstead, Gerard Francis *lawyer*
Hillis, Mark B. *lawyer*
Immel, Vincent Clare *retired law educator*
Inkley, John James, Jr. *lawyer*
Jackson, Rebecca R. *lawyer*
Jaudes, William E. *lawyer*
Johnson, E. Perry *lawyer*
Jones, William Catron *legal educator*
Kauffman, William Ray *lawyer*
Keller, Juan Dane *lawyer*
Klobasa, John Anthony *lawyer*
Lander, David Allan *lawyer*
Lause, Michael Francis *lawyer*
Lebowitz, Albert *lawyer, author*
Lents, Don Glaude *lawyer*
Levin, Ronald Mark *law educator*
Lieberman, Edward Jay *lawyer*
Lipeles, Maxine Ina *lawyer*
Logan, Joseph Prescott *lawyer*
Lucy, Robert Meredith *lawyer*
Luedde, Charles Edwin Howell *lawyer, corporation executive*
Luepke, Henry Francis, Jr. *lawyer*
Mandelker, Daniel Robert *law educator*
Mandelstamm, Jerome Robert *lawyer*
Massey, Raymond Lee *lawyer*
Mattern, Keith Edward *lawyer*
McCarter, Charles Chase *lawyer*
McCracken, Ellis W., Jr. *lawyer, corporation executive*
Mc Daniel, James Edwin *lawyer*
McKinnis, Michael B. *lawyer*
Meisel, George Vincent *lawyer*
Merrill, Charles Eugene *lawyer*
Metcalfe, Walter Lee, Jr. *lawyer*
Miller, Frank William *legal educator*
Mohan, John J. *lawyer*
Moore, McPherson Dorsett *lawyer*
Mulligan, Michael Dennis *lawyer*
Newman, Charles A. *lawyer*
Newman, Joan Meskiel *lawyer*
Noel, Edwin Lawrence *lawyer*
O'Connell, Dennis E. *lawyer*
Oetter, Bruce Christian *lawyer*
O'Keefe, Michael Daniel *lawyer*
Olson, Robert Grant *lawyer*
O'Malley, Kevin Francis *lawyer, writer, educator*
O'Toole, Terrence J. *lawyer*
Palans, Lloyd Alex *lawyer*
Peper, Christian Baird *lawyer*
Pickle, Robert Douglas *lawyer, diversified industry executive*
Poscover, Maury B. *lawyer*
Rataj, Edward William *lawyer*
Reynolds, James E. *lawyer*
Riddle, Veryl Lee *lawyer*
Ritter, Robert Forcier *lawyer*
Ritterskamp, Douglas Dolvin *lawyer*
Rubenstein, Jerome Max *lawyer*
Sachs, Alan Arthur *lawyer, corporate executive*
Sale, Llewellyn, III *lawyer*
Sanders, Steven Paul *lawyer*
Sant, John Talbot *lawyer*
Searls, Eileen Haughey *lawyer, librarian, educator*
Sestric, Anthony James *lawyer*
Shands, Courtney, Jr. *lawyer*
Shaw, John Arthur *lawyer*
Suhre, Walter Anthony, Jr. *retired lawyer and brewery executive*
Teasdale, Kenneth Fulbright *lawyer*
Thomas, Rhonda Churchill *lawyer*
Tremayne, Bertram William, Jr. *lawyer*
Turley, Michael Roy *lawyer*
Van Cleve, William Moore *lawyer*
Vandover, Samuel Taylor *lawyer*
Wack, Thomas E. *lawyer*
Walsh, Thomas Charles *lawyer*
Weil, Paul P. *lawyer*
Weiss, Charles Andrew *lawyer*
Wilson, Margaret Bush *lawyer, civil rights leader*
Withers, W. Wayne *lawyer*
Wolff, Frank Pierce, Jr. *lawyer*
Woodruff, Bruce Emery *lawyer*
Young, Marvin Oscar *lawyer*

Springfield
Carlson, Thomas Joseph *lawyer, mayor, real estate developer*
Hulston, John Kenton *lawyer*
Lowther, Gerald Halbert *lawyer*
†McDonald, William Henry *lawyer*
Starnes, James Wright *lawyer*

MONTANA

Billings
Haughey, James McCrea *lawyer, artist*
Jones, James Leonard *lawyer*
Murphy, Gregory Gerard *lawyer*
Sites, James Philip *lawyer, consul*
Thompson, James William *lawyer*
Towe, Thomas Edward *lawyer*

Bozeman
Harris, Christopher Kirk *lawyer*

Butte
Peterson, John Leonard *lawyer, judge*
Poore, James Albert, III *lawyer*

Great Falls
Doherty, Steve *lawyer, state legislator*
Manning, John Willard *lawyer*
Overfelt, Clarence Lahugh *lawyer*

Helena
†Meadows, Judith Adams *law librarian, educator*

Missoula
Haddon, Sam Ellis *lawyer*
Sogard, Jeffrey W. *lawyer*

NEBRASKA

Lincoln
Hewitt, James Watt *lawyer*
Luedtke, Roland Alfred *lawyer*
Oldfather, Charles Eugene *lawyer*
Swihart, Fred Jacob *lawyer*

Omaha
Barmettler, Joseph John *lawyer*
Christensen, Curtis Lee *lawyer*
Council, Brenda Joyce *lawyer*
Dolan, James Vincent *lawyer*
Forbes, Franklin Sim *lawyer, educator*
Hamann, Deryl Frederick *lawyer, bank executive*
Harr, Lawrence Francis *lawyer*
Hruska, Roman Lee *lawyer, retired senator*
Jensen, Sam *lawyer*
Monaghan, Thomas Justin *prosecutor*
Nethers, Elena Soto *lawyer*
†Richard, Oliver Gonzard, III (Rick Richard) *lawyer, business executive*
Rock, Harold L. *lawyer*
Wright, Norman Harold *lawyer*

NEVADA

Carson City
†Jackson, James Jeffrey *lawyer*
Van Wagoner, Robert Louis *lawyer*

Gardnerville
Manoukian, Noel Edwin *lawyer, former state supreme court chief justice*

Incline Village
Eastin, Keith E. *lawyer*

Las Vegas
Brebbia, John Henry *lawyer*
Galane, Morton Robert *lawyer*
Hilbrecht, Norman Ty *lawyer*
Hosier, Gerald Douglas *lawyer*
Levin, Bruce Alan *lawyer, real estate developer*
Lovell, Carl Erwin, Jr. *lawyer*
Mahan, James Cameron *lawyer*
Riddell, Richard Harry *retired lawyer*
Sawyer, Grant *lawyer*
Smith, Stephanie Marie *lawyer*

Reno
Broili, Robert Howard *lawyer*
Guild, Clark Joseph, Jr. *lawyer*
Hibbs, Loyal Robert *lawyer*
Hill, Earl McColl *lawyer*
Martz, John Roger *lawyer*
Mildon, Marie Roberta *association executive*
Richards, Paul A. *lawyer*

NEW HAMPSHIRE

Concord
Rath, Thomas David *lawyer, former state attorney general*

Dover
Catalfo, Alfred, Jr. (Alfio Catalfo) *lawyer*

Dublin
Wolfe, Albert Blakeslee *lawyer*

Franconia
Merwin, John David *lawyer, former governor*

Hanover
Bollinger, Lee Carroll *law educator*

Hollis
Merritt, Thomas Butler *lawyer*

Keene
Bell, Ernest Lorne, III *lawyer*
Plaut, Nathan Michael *retired lawyer*

Laconia
Carbon, Susan Berkson *lawyer, consultant*

Manchester
Coolidge, Daniel Scott *lawyer*
Mc Lane, John Roy, Jr. *lawyer*
Middleton, Jack Baer *lawyer*
Millimet, Joseph Allen *retired lawyer*
Monson, John Rudolph *lawyer*
Nixon, David Lee *lawyer*
Zachos, Kimon Stephen *lawyer*

Nashua
Hanson, Arnold Philip *retired lawyer*

New London
Cleveland, James Colgate *lawyer, former congressman*

Oxford
Richardson, John Carroll *lawyer, tax legislative consultant*

Portsmouth
Doleac, Charles Bartholomew *lawyer*
Tober, Stephen Lloyd *lawyer*
Volk, Kenneth Hohne *lawyer*

NEW JERSEY

Barnegat
Schmoll, Harry F., Jr. *lawyer, educator*

Barnegat Light
Gibbs, Frederick Winfield *lawyer, communications company executive*

Bridgewater
Conroy, Robert John *lawyer*

Camden
Coleman, John Michael *lawyer, food products executive*
Cottrol, Robert James *lawyer, history educator*
Fairbanks, Russell Norman *law educator, university dean*
Pomorski, Stanislaw *lawyer, educator*

Chatham
Barnes, William Oliver, Jr. *lawyer*

Cherry Hill
Boyer, Peter Jay *lawyer*
Dunfee, Thomas Wylie *law educator*
Gillespie, Colleen Patricia *lawyer*
Luchak, Frank Alexander *lawyer*
Myers, Daniel William, II *lawyer*
Rabil, Mitchell Joseph *lawyer*
Rose, Joel Alan *legal consultant*
Weinstein, Steven David *lawyer*

Clifton
Feinstein, Miles Roger *lawyer*

Clinton
Kennedy, Harold Edward *lawyer*
Moser, Elizabeth Marie *lawyer*

East Brunswick
McDonough, Patrick Joseph, Jr. *lawyer*

East Orange
Brown, Paulette *lawyer*

East Rutherford
Wadler, Arnold L. *lawyer*

Edison
Applebaum, Charles *lawyer*
Behr, Omri M. *lawyer*
Corman, Randy *lawyer*
Kott, Joseph Hilton *lawyer, bank executive*

Elizabeth
Klein, Peter Martin *lawyer, transportation company executive*

Englewood Cliffs
Green, Alvin *lawyer, corporate executive*
Storms, Clifford Beekman *lawyer*

Fair Haven
Labrecque, Theodore Joseph *lawyer*

Flemington
Roth, Lee Britton *lawyer*

Florham Park
Hardin, William Downer *lawyer*
Laulicht, Murray Jack *lawyer*
Stanton, Patrick Michael *lawyer*

Fort Lee
Abut, Charles C. *lawyer*
Goldberg, Harry Finck *lawyer, business consultant*
Jacobs, Marisa Frances *lawyer*

Franklin Lakes
Galiardo, John William *lawyer*

Hackensack
Fahy, John J. *lawyer*
Massler, Howard Arnold *lawyer, corporate executive*
Pollinger, William Joshua *lawyer*
Schuber, William Patrick *lawyer*

Hackettstown
Mulligan, Elinor Patterson *lawyer*

Haddonfield
Adler, John Herbert *lawyer, state legislator*
Iavicoli, Mario Anthony *lawyer*

Harrington Park
McGlynn, Richard Bruce *lawyer*

Hightstown
†Bronner, William Roche *lawyer*

Ho Ho Kus
Tobin, John Everard *retired lawyer*

Iselin
Dornbusch, Arthur A., II *lawyer*

Jersey City
Basso, Kathleen Alyssa *lawyer*
Meyer, Howard Robert *lawyer*

Kenilworth
Hoffman, John Fletcher *lawyer*

Liberty Corner
Apruzzese, Vincent John *lawyer*

Livingston
Pantages, Louis James *lawyer*

Lyndhurst
Lasky, David *lawyer, corporate executive*

Madison
Fogarty, John Thomas *lawyer*
Gnichtel, William Van Orden *lawyer*

Mahwah
Bryan, Thomas Lynn *lawyer, educator*

Manahawkin
†Docheff, Ivan *lawyer*

Manalapan
Stone, Fred Michael *lawyer*

Mantoloking
Morris, Robert *lawyer, writer*

Maplewood
MacWhorter, Robert Bruce *retired lawyer*

Metuchen
Vercammen, Kenneth Albert *lawyer*

Montclair
Brown, Geraldine Reed *lawyer, consulting executive*
Draper, Daniel Clay *lawyer*
Mochary, Mary Veronica *lawyer*
Tobia, Ronald Lawrence *lawyer*
Ward, Roger Coursen *lawyer*

Montvale
Beattie, James Raymond *lawyer*
Kanter, Carl Irwin *lawyer*
Kennedy, Quentin J., Sr. *lawyer, paper company executive*

Morristown
Aspero, Benedict Vincent *lawyer*
Berkley, Peter Lee *lawyer*
Bromberg, Myron James *lawyer*
Campion, Thomas Francis *lawyer*
Clemen, John Douglas *lawyer*
Graham, Paul E(ugene) *lawyer*
Herzberg, Peter Jay *lawyer*
Hyland, William Francis *lawyer*
Kandravy, John *lawyer*
Katzenbach, Nicholas deBelleville *lawyer*
Kreindler, Peter Michael *lawyer*
Krumholz, Dennis Jonathan *lawyer*
Lavey, Stewart Evan *lawyer*
Lunin, Joseph *lawyer*
Martin, Alvin Charles *lawyer*
Maskaleris, Stephen Nicholas *lawyer*
McCarthy, G. Daniel *lawyer*
Mc Elroy, William Theodore *lawyer*
Nittoly, Paul Gerard *lawyer*
O'Grady, Dennis Joseph *lawyer*
Pantel, Glenn Steven *lawyer*
Reid, Charles Adams, III *lawyer*
Rose, Robert Gordon *lawyer*
Rosenthal, Meyer L(ouis) *lawyer*
Samet, Andrew Benjamin *lawyer*
Scott, Susan *lawyer*
Sharkey, Vincent Joseph *lawyer*
Szuch, Clyde Andrew *lawyer*
Tierney, Raymond Moran, Jr. *lawyer*
Whitmer, Frederick Lee *lawyer*

Mount Olive
Cornish, Jeannette Carter *lawyer*

Mountainside
Cardoni, Horace Robert *retired lawyer*

Murray Hill
Bonnes, Charles Andrew *lawyer*

Neptune
†Falvo, Peter S., Jr. *lawyer*

New Brunswick
Lee, Barbara Anne *lawyer, educator*
†Woodward, John Taylor, III *lawyer*

New Providence
Flink, Richard Allen *lawyer, manufacturing company executive*

Newark
Askin, Frank *law educator*
Cahn, Jeffrey Barton *lawyer*
Caldwell, Wesley Stuart, III *lawyer, lobbyist*
Colli, Bart Joseph *lawyer*
Day, Edward Francis, Jr. *lawyer*
Del Tufo, Robert J. *lawyer, former state prosecutor*
Eittreim, Richard MacNutt *lawyer*
English, Nicholas Conover *lawyer*
English, Woodruff Jones *lawyer*
Flaherty, John Edmund *lawyer*
Futter, Victor *lawyer*
Genzer, Stephen Bruce *lawyer, educator*
Gilbert, Stephen Alan *lawyer*
Greenbaum, Jeffrey J. *lawyer*
Griffinger, Michael R. *lawyer*
Haring, Eugene Miller *lawyer*
Harrison, Roslyn Siman *lawyer*
Karp, Donald Mathew *lawyer, banker*
Knee, Stephen H. *lawyer*
Kott, David Russell *lawyer*
Lawatsch, Frank Emil, Jr. *lawyer*
Levin, Simon *lawyer*
McGuire, William B(enedict) *lawyer*
McKinney, John Adams, Jr. *lawyer*
Mitchell, James Lowry *lawyer, former government official*
Muscato, Andrew *lawyer*
Paul, James Caverly Newlin *law educator, former university dean*
Reilly, William Thomas *lawyer*
Robertson, William Withers *lawyer*
Roth, Allan Robert *lawyer, educator*
Tischman, Michael Bernard *lawyer*
Von Glahn, Keith G. *lawyer*
Wachenfeld, William Thomas *lawyer, foundation executive*
Wyer, James Ingersoll *lawyer*

Yamner, Morris *lawyer*

North Brunswick
Phillips, Daniel Miller *lawyer*

Oakhurst
Konvitz, Milton Ridbaz *legal educator*

Oakland
Bloom, Arnold Sanford *lawyer*

Ocean
Abrams, Robert Allen *lawyer*

Oldwick
Hitchcock, Ethan Allen *lawyer*
Purcell, Richard Fick *lawyer, food companies advisor and counsel*

Paramus
†Ascher, David Mark *lawyer*
Yegen, Christian Conrad, Jr. *lawyer, business executive*

Park Ridge
†Tschirhart, Paul M. *corporate lawyer*

Parsippany
Bridwell, Robert Kennedy *lawyer*
Florio, Jim *lawyer, former governor*
Jolles, Ira Hervey *lawyer*
Kallmann, Stanley Walter *lawyer*
Karpf, Ilene Phyllis *lawyer*

Piscataway
Smith, Robert G. *lawyer, assemblyman, educator*

Pottersville
Lynch, James Henry, Jr. *lawyer*

Princeton
Ackourey, Peter Paul *lawyer*
Anderson, Ellis Bernard *retired lawyer, pharmaceutical company executive*
Banse, Robert Lee *lawyer*
Beidler, Marsha Wolf *lawyer*
Brennan, William Joseph, III *lawyer*
Burgess, Robert Kyle *lawyer*
Connor, Geoffrey Michael *lawyer*
Cuoco, Daniel Anthony *lawyer*
Harris, Robert *lawyer, investment company executive*
Hill, James Scott *lawyer*
Johnston, Robert Chapman *lawyer*
Judge, Marty M. *lawyer*
Nucciarone, A. Patrick *lawyer*
Orleans, Jeffrey Howard *lawyer*
Rosen, Norman Edward *lawyer*
Wood, Joshua Warren, III *lawyer, foundation executive*
Wright, Thomas H., Jr. *lawyer*

Rahway
Byles, Daniel William *lawyer*
McDonald, Mary M. *lawyer*

Red Bank
Auerbach, Philip Gary *lawyer*
Rogers, Lee Jasper *lawyer*

Ridgewood
Harris, Micalyn Shafer *lawyer*

Roseland
Berkowitz, Bernard Solomon *lawyer*
D'Avella, Bernard Johnson, Jr. *lawyer*
Drasco, Dennis J. *lawyer*
Eakeley, Douglas Scott *lawyer*
Fleischman, Joseph Jacob *lawyer*
Greenberg, Stephen Michael *lawyer, businesss executive*
Kemph, Carleton Richard *lawyer*
Kohl, Benedict M. *lawyer*
Korf, Gene Robert *lawyer*
Lowenstein, Alan Victor *lawyer*
MacKay, John Robert, II *lawyer*
Shoulson, Bruce Dove *lawyer*
Slutsky, Kenneth Joel *lawyer*
Steinhart, Ashley *lawyer*
Stern, Herbert Jay *lawyer*
Sturtz, Ronald M. *lawyer*
Wells, Theodore V., Jr. *lawyer*
Wovsaniker, Alan *lawyer*

Salem
Petrin, Helen Fite *lawyer, consultant*

Scotch Plains
Klock, John Henry *lawyer*

Secaucus
Endyke, Mary Beth *lawyer*
Kilburn, Edwin Allen *lawyer*

Short Hills
Greenberg, Carl *lawyer*
Hazlehurst, Robert Purviance, Jr. *lawyer*
Siegfried, David Charles *lawyer*

Shrewsbury
Hopkins, Charles Peter, II *lawyer*

Somerset
Kozlowski, Thomas Joseph, Jr. *lawyer, trust company executive*

Somerville
Hutcheon, Peter David *lawyer*

South Hackensack
Ragals, William Charles, Jr. *lawyer, business executive*

South Plainfield
Saltz, Ralph *corporate lawyer*

Summit
Kenyon, Edward Tipton *lawyer*
Mulreany, Robert Henry *retired lawyer*

Parsons, Judson Aspinwall, Jr. *lawyer*

Tenafly
Badr, Gamal Moursi *Arab laws consultant*

Toms River
Whitman, Russell Wilson *lawyer*

Trenton
Bigham, William J. *lawyer*
Domm, Alice *lawyer*
†Poritz, Deborah T. *state attorney general*
Sterns, Joel Henry *lawyer*
Stockman, Gerald Richard *lawyer*

Union City
Stier, Edwin H. *lawyer*

Warren
Knox, William T., IV *lawyer*

Wayne
Buckstein, Mark Aaron *lawyer, educator*
Droste, Donald Casper *corporate lawyer, diversified manufacturing company executive*
Garcia C., Elisa Dolores *lawyer*

Weehawken
Hayden, Joseph A., Jr. *lawyer*

West Orange
Kushen, Allan Stanford *lawyer, retired*
Mandelbaum, Barry Richard *lawyer*
Richmond, Harold Nicholas *lawyer*

West Paterson
Vandervoort, Peter *lawyer*

Woodbridge
Becker, Frederic Kenneth *lawyer*
Brauth, Marvin Jeffrey *lawyer*
Brown, Morris *lawyer*
Buchsbaum, Peter A. *lawyer*
Cirafesi, Robert J. *lawyer*
Greenbaum, Robert S. *lawyer*
Hoberman, Stuart A. *lawyer*
Jaffe, Sheldon Eugene *lawyer*
Molloy, Brian Joseph *lawyer*

Woodbury
White, John Lindsey *lawyer*

NEW MEXICO

Albuquerque
Anspach, Judith Ford *law librarian, law educator*
Bardacke, Paul Gregory *lawyer, former attorney general*
Bennett, Marianne *lawyer, health care company executive*
Cargo, David Francis *lawyer*
Caruso, Mark John *lawyer*
Haltom, B(illy) Reid *lawyer*
Hanna, Robert Cecil *lawyer, lecturer, hotelier*
Hart, Frederick Michael *law educator*
Jones, Donald L. *lawyer*
Loubet, Jeffrey W. *lawyer*
Meiering, Mark C. *lawyer*
Ramo, Roberta Cooper *lawyer*
Riordan, William F. *lawyer*
Roehl, Jerrald J(oseph) *lawyer*
Roehl, Joseph E. *lawyer*
Schoen, Stevan Jay *lawyer*
Serna, David C. *lawyer*
Sisk, Daniel Arthur *lawyer*
Slade, Lynn H. *lawyer*
Stephenson, Barbera Wertz *lawyer*
Thompson, Rufus E. *lawyer*
Wellborn, Charles Ivey *lawyer*
Youngdahl, James Edward *lawyer*

Las Cruces
Lutz, William Lan *lawyer*
Sandenaw, Thomas Arthur, Jr. *lawyer*

Roswell
Olson, Richard Earl *lawyer, state legislator*

Santa Fe
Bejnar, Thaddeus Putnam *lawyer, law librarian*
Burton, John Paul (Jack Burton) *lawyer*
Citrin, Phillip Marshall *retired lawyer*
Cuming, George Scott *retired lawyer, retired gas company official*
Dodds, Robert James, III *lawyer*
Jaramillo, Arthur Lewis *lawyer*
Pollock, Marvin Erwin *lawyer*
†Quintana, Sammy J. *lawyer*
Samora, Joseph E., Jr. *lawyer*
Schwarz, Michael *lawyer*
Stephenson, Donnan *lawyer, former state supreme court justice*
Stevens, Ron A. *lawyer, public interest organization administrator*

Seneca
Monroe, Kendyl Kurth *lawyer*

Silver City
Foy, Thomas Paul *lawyer, state legislator, banker*

Univ Of New Mexico
Ellis, Willis Hill *lawyer, educator*

NEW YORK

Albany
Ashe, Bernard Flemming *lawyer*
Beach, John Arthur *lawyer*
Begg, Robert Thomas *law library adminstrator, law librarian, lawyer*
Brown, Judith Anne *law librarian*
Carpenter, Howard Grant, Jr. *lawyer, savings and loan association executive*
Case, Forrest N., Jr. *lawyer*
Catalano, Jane Donna *lawyer*
Engel, David Anthony *lawyer*
Hagoort, Thomas Henry *lawyer*

Holt-Harris, John Evan, Jr. *lawyer*
Salkin, Patricia E. *law educator*
Siegel, David Donald *law educator*
Sprow, Howard Thomas *lawyer, educator*
Wallender, Michael Todd *lawyer*

Ardsley
Benjamin, Jeff *lawyer*

Armonk
Evangelista, Donato A. *lawyer, computer and infosystems manufacturing company executive*
Quinn, James W. *lawyer*
Weill, Richard L. *lawyer*

Babylon
Hennelly, Edmund Paul *lawyer, oil company executive*

Bayside
D'Amato, Domenico Donald *lawyer*

Bedford
Atkins, Ronald Raymond *lawyer*

Binghamton
Anderson, Warren Mattice *lawyer*
Gerhart, Eugene Clifton *lawyer*
Hinman, George Lyon *lawyer*

Briarcliff Manor
Bornmann, Carl M(alcolm) *lawyer*

Bronx
Balka, Sigmund Ronell *lawyer*
Cornfield, Melvin *lawyer, university institute director*
Garance, Dominick (D. G. Garan) *lawyer, author*
Sussman, David William *lawyer*
Wolf, Robert Thomas *lawyer*

Bronxville
Armstrong, John Kremer *lawyer, artist*
Cook, Charles David *international lawyer, arbitrator, consultant*
Root, Stuart Dowling *lawyer, former banker and government official*

Brooklyn
Graham, Arnold Harold *lawyer, educator*
Herman, Susan N. *legal educator*
Kehl, Shelley Sanders *lawyer, academic administrator*
Lewis, Felice Flanery *lawyer, educator*
Onken, George Marcellus *lawyer*
Poser, Norman Stanley *law educator*
Provine, John C. *lawyer*
Raskind, Leo Joseph *law educator*
Schussler, Theodore *lawyer, physician, educator*

Buffalo
Barney, Thomas McNamee *lawyer*
Bean, Edwin Temple, Jr. *lawyer*
Blaine, Charles Gillespie *lawyer*
Carmichael, Donald Scott *lawyer, business executive*
Cordes, Alexander Charles *lawyer*
Day, Donald Sheldon *lawyer*
Duke, Emanuel *lawyer*
Floyd, David Kenneth *lawyer, judge*
Foschio, Leslie George *lawyer*
Fuzak, Victor Thaddeus *lawyer*
Gardner, Arnold Burton *lawyer*
Garvey, James Anthony *lawyer*
Gerstman, Sharon Stern *lawyer*
Glanville, Robert Edward *lawyer*
Goldberg, Neil A. *lawyer*
Grasser, George Robert *lawyer*
Gray, F(rederick) William, III *lawyer*
Hall, David Edward *lawyer*
Halpern, Ralph Lawrence *lawyer*
†Head, Christopher Alan *lawyer*
Headrick, Thomas Edward *lawyer, educator*
Heilman, Pamela Davis *lawyer*
Kaeser, Clifford Richard *lawyer, food service industry executive*
Kieffer, James Marshall *lawyer*
Lammert, Richard Alan *corporate lawyer*
Lippes, Gerald Sanford *lawyer, business executive*
MacLeod, Gordon Albert *lawyer*
Moriarty, Robert Brian *lawyer*
Newman, Stephen Michael *lawyer*
Pearson, Paul David *lawyer, mediator*
Rachlin, Lauren David *lawyer*
Reif, Louis Raymond *lawyer, utilities executive*
Sahlem, James Robert *law librarian*
Salisbury, Eugene W. *lawyer, justice*
Saperston, Howard Truman, Sr. *lawyer*
Schroeder, Harold Kenneth, Jr. *lawyer*
Shanahan, Thomas J. *lawyer*
Sharpe, Daniel Roger *lawyer*
Sherwood, Arthur Morley *lawyer*
Spaulding, Robert Mark *lawyer*
†Vacco, Dennis C. *lawyer*
Wickser, John Philip *lawyer*
Wisbaum, Wayne David *lawyer*

Campbell Hall
Stone, Peter George *lawyer, publishing company executive*

Canaan
Pennell, William Brooke *lawyer*

Catskill
Kingsley, John Piersall *lawyer*

Chappaqua
Fischer, David C. *lawyer*

Corning
Hauselt, Denise Ann *lawyer*
Ughetta, William Casper *lawyer, manufacturing company executive*

Croton On Hudson
Hoffman, Paul Shafer *lawyer*

Cutchogue
O'Connell, Francis Joseph *lawyer, arbitrator*

Dobbs Ferry
Juettner, Diana D'Amico *lawyer, educator*

Maiocchi, Christine *lawyer*
Newman, Edwin Stanley *lawyer, publishing company executive*

East Aurora
Brott, Irving Deerin, Jr. *lawyer, judge*

East Meadow
Adler, Ira Jay *lawyer*

Fayetteville
Evans, Nolly Seymour *lawyer*

Garden City
Cook, George Valentine *lawyer*
Corsi, Philip Donald *lawyer*
Fishberg, Gerard *lawyer*
Gordon, Jay F(isher) *lawyer*
Larocca, James Lawrence *lawyer*
Lioz, Lawrence Stephen *lawyer, accountant*
Minicucci, Richard Francis *lawyer, former hospital administrator*
Tucker, William Philip *lawyer, writer*
Westermann, David *lawyer, educator, electronics industry executive*

Glen Cove
Deming, Donald Livingston *lawyer*
Mills, Charles Gardner *lawyer*

Glens Falls
Bartlett, Richard James *lawyer, former university dean*
McMillen, Robert Stewart *lawyer*

Great Neck
Busner, Philip H. *lawyer, arbitrator, judge*
Gellman, Yale H. *lawyer*
Glushien, Morris P. *lawyer, arbitrator*
Samanowitz, Ronald Arthur *lawyer*
Unger, Robert Martin *lawyer, author, professional speaker, singer*
Wachsman, Harvey Frederick *lawyer, neurosurgeon*

Greene
Sternberg, Paul J. *lawyer*

Greenvale
Halper, Emanuel B(arry) *real estate lawyer, developer, consultant, author*

Hamburg
Killeen, Henry Walter *lawyer*

Hempstead
Agata, Burton C. *lawyer, educator*
Freedman, Monroe Henry *lawyer, educator*
Mahon, Malachy Thomas *lawyer, educator*
Regan, John J. *law educator*

Henrietta
Snyder, Donald Edward *corporate executive*

Huntington
Augello, William Joseph *lawyer*
Glickstein, Howard Alan *law educator*
Jordan, Daniel Patrick, Jr. *law librarian*
Munson, Nancy Kay *lawyer*
Pratt, George Cheney *law educator, retired federal judge*

Huntington Station
Schoenfeld, Michael P. *lawyer*

Ithaca
Alexander, Gregory Stewart *law educator*
Barcelo, John James, III *law educator*
Barney, John Charles *lawyer*
Clermont, Kevin Michael *law educator*
Cramton, Roger Conant *lawyer, legal educator*
Eisenberg, Theodore *law educator*
†Germain, Claire Madeleine *law librarian, educator*
Hammond, Jane Laura *retired law librarian, lawyer*
Hay, George Alan *law and economics educator*
Henderson, James A., Jr. *law educator*
Hillman, Robert Andrew *law educator, university dean*
Kent, Robert Brydon *law educator*
Martin, Peter William *lawyer, educator*
Osgood, Russell King *law educator*
Palmer, Larry Isaac *lawyer, educator*
Relihan, Walter J., Jr. *lawyer*
Roberts, E. F. *lawyer, educator*
Rossi, Faust F. *lawyer, educator*
Schwab, Stewart Jon *law educator*
Shiffrin, Steven H. *law educator*
Simson, Gary Joseph *law educator*
Stamp, Neal Roger *lawyer*
Summers, Robert Samuel *lawyer, author, educator*

Jamaica
Angione, Howard Francis *lawyer, editor*
Beard, Joseph James *law educator*
Berman, Richard Miles *lawyer*
Re, Edward Domenic *law educator, retired federal judge*
Reams, Bernard Dinsmore, Jr. *lawyer, educator*
Tschinkel, Andrew Joseph, Jr. *law librarian*

Jamestown
Idzik, Martin Francis *lawyer*

Jamesville
DeCrow, Karen *lawyer, author, lecturer*

Jericho
Blau, Harvey Ronald *lawyer*

Kew Gardens
Silver, Jonathan *lawyer*

Kinderhook
Benamati, Dennis Charles *law librarian, editor, consultant*

Lake Success
Lee, Brian Edward *lawyer*

Larchmont
Berridge, George Bradford *retired lawyer*

Bloom, Lee Hurley *lawyer, public affairs consultant, retired household products manufacturing executive*
Emery, Jonathan Willard *lawyer*
Engel, Ralph Manuel *lawyer*
Pelton, Russell Gilbert *lawyer*
Seton, Charles B. *lawyer*

Lido Beach
Billauer, Barbara Pfeffer *lawyer, educator*

Liverpool
Wolfson, Warren David *lawyer, specialty retail store executive*

Lockport
Penney, Charles Rand *lawyer, civic worker*

Long Island City
Cushing, Robert Hunter *lawyer, real estate investment executive*
Modell, Michael Steven *lawyer, business executive*

Manhasset
Barrett, James P. *lawyer*
Carucci, Samuel Anthony *lawyer*
Hayes, Arthur Michael *lawyer*

Melville
Green, Carol H. *lawyer, educator, journalist*
Klatell, Robert Edward *lawyer, electronics company executive*
McMillan, Robert Ralph *lawyer*

Mineola
Bartlett, Clifford Adams, Jr. *lawyer*
English, John F. *lawyer*
Hendler, Samuel I. *lawyer*
Klein, Arnold Spencer *lawyer*
Meyer, Bernard Stern *lawyer, former judge*
Paterson, Basil Alexander *lawyer*
Rains, Harry Hano *lawyer, arbitrator, mediator*
Schaffer, David Irving *lawyer*
Smolev, Terence Elliot *lawyer, educator*

Montauk
Garvey, Richard Anthony *lawyer*

Monticello
Cooke, Lawrence Henry *lawyer, former state chief judge*

Mount Kisco
Goodhue, Mary Brier *lawyer, former state senator*
Icahn, Carl C. *arbitrator, options specialist, corporation executive*

New City
Rosenbaum, Joseph Irving *lawyer, educator*

New Hartford
Jones, Hugh Richard *lawyer*

New Hyde Park
Offner, Eric Delmonte *lawyer*

New Rochelle
Behren, Robert Alan *lawyer, accountant*
Blotner, Norman David *lawyer, real estate broker, corporate executive*
Burns, Joseph William *lawyer*
Frenkel, Michael *lawyer*
Gunning, Francis Patrick *lawyer, insurance association executive*
Malach, Herbert John *lawyer*

New York
Abberley, John J. *lawyer*
Abrams, Alan M. *lawyer*
Abrams, Bertram Alan *lawyer*
Abrams, Floyd *lawyer*
Abrams, Marc R. *lawyer*
Ackman, Milton Roy *lawyer*
Adams, John Hamilton *lawyer*
Adler, Joel A. *lawyer*
Aibel, Howard J. *lawyer*
Aidinoff, M(erton) Bernard *lawyer*
Aksen, Gerald *lawyer, educator*
Albenda, David *lawyer*
Albert, Neale Malcolm *lawyer*
Albert, Rory Judd *lawyer*
Alcott, Mark Howard *lawyer*
Alden, Steven Michael *lawyer*
Alessandroni, Venan Joseph *lawyer*
Allen, Leon Arthur, Jr. *lawyer*
Alpern, Andrew *lawyer, architect*
Alpert, Gordon Myles *lawyer*
Alter, David *lawyer*
Alter, Eleanor Breitel *lawyer*
Amberg, Stanley Louis *lawyer*
Amdur, Martin Bennett *lawyer*
Amhowitz, Harris J. *lawyer, educator*
Amsterdam, Anthony Guy *law educator*
Anderson, Eugene Robert *lawyer*
Andrews, Gordon Clark *lawyer*
Andrus, Roger Douglas *lawyer*
Angland, Joseph *lawyer*
Anthoine, Robert *lawyer, educator*
Appel, Alfred *lawyer*
Appelbaum, Alan *lawyer*
Archer, James G. *lawyer*
Archer, Kenneth Davidson *lawyer, insurance executive*
Arenson, Gregory K. *lawyer*
Arenstein, Robert David *lawyer*
Armstrong, James Sinclair *retired lawyer, foundation director*
Armstrong, Michael Francis *lawyer*
Arning, John Fredrick *lawyer*
Arouh, Jeffrey Alan *lawyer*
Arquit, Kevin James *lawyer*
Arther, Richard Oberlin *polygraphist, educator*
Ashinoff, Reid L. *lawyer*
Ashton, Robert W. *lawyer, foundation administrator*
Atkins, Peter Allan *lawyer*
Atkins, Robert Emmett, Jr. *lawyer*
Auerbach, William *lawyer*
Axelrod, Charles Paul *lawyer*
Axinn, Stephen Mark *lawyer*
Bachelder, Joseph Elmer, III *lawyer*
Backman, Gerald Stephen *lawyer*
Badertscher, David Glen *law librarian, consultant*
Baer, Thomas James *lawyer*
Baeza, Mario Leon *lawyer*
Bagger, Richard Hartvig *lawyer*
Bainton, J(ohn) Joseph *lawyer*
Baity, John Cooley *lawyer*
Baker, David Remember *lawyer*
Baker, Edwin Herbert *lawyer*
Baker, Stuart David *lawyer*
Ball, John H(anstein) *lawyer*
Bamberger, Michael Albert *lawyer*
Bancroft, Alexander Clerihew *lawyer*
Bancroft, Margaret Armstrong *lawyer*
Banker, Stephen M. *lawyer*
Bankston, Archie Moore, Jr. *lawyer*
Barandes, Robert *lawyer*
Barasch, Clarence Sylvan *lawyer*
Barasch, Mal Livingston *lawyer*
Barbash, Joseph *lawyer, arbitrator*
Barist, Jeffrey A. *lawyer*
Barnett, Richard Blair *lawyer*
Baron, Mitchell Neal *lawyer*
Barr, Thomas D. *lawyer*
Barrett, William L. D. *lawyer*
Barron, Francis Patrick *lawyer*
Barry, David Earl *lawyer*
Barry, Desmond Thomas, Jr. *lawyer*
Barth, Mark Harold *lawyer*
Bartlett, Joseph Warren *lawyer*
Baskin, Stuart Jay *lawyer*
Bason, George R., Jr. *lawyer*
Bassen, Ned Henry *lawyer*
Bauer, Douglas F. *lawyer*
Bauer, Ralph Glenn *lawyer, maritime arbitrator*
Baumgardner, John Ellwood, Jr. *lawyer*
Baumgarten, Paul Anthony *lawyer*
Baumgarten, Sidney *lawyer*
Baumrin, Bernard Stefan Herbert *lawyer, educator*
Bazerman, Steven Howard *lawyer*
Bear, Donald *law firm executive director*
Bear, Larry Alan *lawyer, educator*
†Beattie, Richard Irwin *lawyer*
Beeney, Garrard Russ *lawyer*
Beerbower, John Edwin *lawyer*
Begley, Louis *lawyer, writer*
Behrendt, John Thomas *lawyer*
Beinecke, Candace Krugman *lawyer*
Belford, Richard David *lawyer*
Bell, Derrick Albert *legal educator, author, lecturer*
Bell, James Halsey *lawyer*
Bell, Jonathan Robert *lawyer*
Bellwin, Janna H. J. *lawyer*
Belnick, Mark Alan *lawyer*
Benedict, James Nelson *lawyer*
Benenson, Mark Keith *lawyer*
Benjamin, Harvey E. *lawyer, sports executive*
Benkard, James W. B. *lawyer*
Bennett, Reynold *lawyer*
Benshoof, Janet L. *lawyer, association executive*
Berend, Robert William *lawyer*
Bergan, Philip James *lawyer*
Bergen, G. S. Peter *lawyer*
Berger, Curtis Jay *law educator*
Berger, George *lawyer*
Berger, Vivian Olivia *lawyer, educator*
Bergstein, Daniel Gerard *lawyer*
Berk, Alan S. *law firm executive*
Berle, Peter Adolf Augustus *lawyer, association executive*
Berlin, Emily *lawyer*
Berman, Joshua Mordecai *lawyer, manufacturing company executive*
Berman, Julius *lawyer*
Bermann, George Alan *law educator, lawyer*
Bernard, Richard Phillip *lawyer*
Bernstein, Bernard *lawyer, corporate executive*
Bernstein, Daniel Lewis *lawyer*
Berry, Charles Gordon *lawyer*
Berry, Edna Janet *lawyer, chemist*
Beshar, Christine *lawyer*
Best, Geoffry D. C. *lawyer*
Bettman, Gary Bruce *lawyer*
Beuchert, Edward William *lawyer*
Bezahler, Donald Jay *lawyer*
Bezanson, Thomas Edward *lawyer*
Bezikos, Lynne A. *lawyer*
Bialkin, Kenneth Jules *lawyer*
Bialo, Kenneth Marc *lawyer*
Bicks, David Peter *lawyer*
Bidwell, James Truman, Jr. *lawyer*
Bienenstock, Martin J. *lawyer*
Bierman, Steven M. *lawyer*
Birenbaum, Jonathan *lawyer*
Birnbaum, Edward Lester *lawyer*
Birnbaum, Irwin Morton *lawyer*
Birnbaum, Robert Jack *lawyer*
Birnbaum, Sheila L. *lawyer, educator*
Bizar, Irving *lawyer*
Black, Barbara Aronstein *legal history educator*
Black, James Isaac, III *lawyer*
Black, Jerry Bernard *lawyer*
Blackiston, Henry Curtis, III *lawyer*
Blackman, Kenneth Robert *lawyer*
Blackwell, Richard Manning *lawyer*
Blake, Richard Charles *lawyer*
Blakeslee, Edward Eaton *lawyer, insurance executive*
Blanc, Roger David *lawyer*
Blasi, Vincent A. *lawyer, educator*
Blattmachr, Jonathan George *lawyer*
Blind, William Charles *lawyer*
Bliwise, Lester Martin *lawyer*
Block, Dennis Jeffery *lawyer*
Bloom, Robert Avrum *lawyer*
Bloomer, Harold Franklin, Jr. *lawyer*
Blumberg, Gerald *lawyer*
Blume, Lawrence Dayton *lawyer*
Blumkin, Linda Ruth *lawyer*
Blumstein, Allan *lawyer*
Boast, Molly Shryer *lawyer*
Bockstein, Herbert *lawyer*
Boes, Lawrence William *lawyer*
Bonomi, John Gurnee *lawyer*
Booth, Edgar Hirsch *lawyer*
Booth, Mitchell B. *lawyer*
Borchard, William Marshall *lawyer*
Borisoff, Richard Stuart *lawyer*
Borsody, Robert Peter *lawyer*
Boshkov, Stefan Robert *lawyer*
Bowden, William P., Jr. *lawyer, banker*
Bowie, Jonathan Munford *lawyer*
Boxer, Leonard *lawyer*
Bozorth, Squire Newland *lawyer*
Bradley, E. Michael *lawyer*
Bradner, William Murray, Jr. *lawyer*
Braun, Jeffrey Louis *lawyer*
Breglio, John F. *lawyer*
Brenner, Frank *lawyer, venture capitalist*
Brenner, Paul R. *lawyer*
Bresler, Martin I. *lawyer*
Bressler, Bernard *lawyer*
Briggs, Taylor Rastrick *lawyer*
Bring, Murray H. *lawyer*
Britell, Peter Stuart *lawyer*
Broadwater, Douglas Dwight *lawyer*
Broder, Douglas Fisher *lawyer*
Brodsky, Edward *lawyer*
Brodsky, Samuel *lawyer*
Brome, Thomas Reed *lawyer*
Bronstein, Richard J. *lawyer*
Brooks, Lorimer Page *patent lawyer*
Brooks, Russell Edwin *lawyer*
Bross, Steward Richard, Jr. *lawyer*
Broude, Richard Frederick *lawyer, educator*
Broughton, Phillip Charles *lawyer*
Browdy, Joseph Eugene *lawyer*
Brown, Charles Dodgson *lawyer*
Brown, Daniel Herbert *lawyer, manufacturing company executive*
Brown, Francis Cabell, Jr. *lawyer*
Brown, Meredith M. *lawyer*
Brown, Paul M. *lawyer*
Brown, Peter Megargee *lawyer, writer, lecturer*
Brown, Ralph Sawyer, Jr. *lawyer, business executive*
Browne, Jeffrey Francis *lawyer*
Brownwood, David Owen *lawyer*
Bruckmann, Mark F. *lawyer*
Brundige, Robert W., Jr. *lawyer*
Bryan, Barry Richard *lawyer*
Bschorr, Paul Joseph *lawyer*
Burak, H(oward) Paul *lawyer*
Burgweger, Francis Joseph Dewes, Jr. *lawyer*
Burke, Thomas Edmund *lawyer*
Burns, Arnold Irwin *lawyer*
Burrows, Michael Donald *lawyer*
Bursky, Herman Aaron *lawyer*
Butler, Samuel Coles *lawyer*
Butler, William Joseph *lawyer*
Butowsky, David Martin *lawyer*
Buttenwieser, Lawrence Benjamin *lawyer*
Cahn, Joshua Binion *lawyer*
Caldwell, Paulette M. *law educator*
Callahan, Joseph Patrick *lawyer*
Calvey, Brian J. *lawyer*
Campbell, Scott G. *lawyer*
Campbell, Woodrow Wilson, Jr. *lawyer*
Campo, Benjamin Paul *lawyer*
Cane, Myles Adrian *lawyer, not-for-profit organization executive*
Cannell, John Redferne *lawyer*
Canoni, John David *lawyer*
Cantor, Melvyn Leon *lawyer*
Carb, Stephen Ames *lawyer*
Carberry, Charles Michael *lawyer*
Cardinali, Albert John *lawyer*
Cardozo, Benjamin Mordecai *lawyer*
Cardozo, Michael A. *lawyer*
Carey, J. Edwin *lawyer*
Carling, Francis *lawyer*
Carlson, David Bret *lawyer, consultant*
Carlson, Theodore Joshua *lawyer, retired utility company executive*
Carroll, J. Speed *lawyer*
Carroll, Joseph J(ohn) *lawyer*
Carter, James Hal, Jr. *lawyer*
Caso, Ronald George *lawyer, accountant*
Castel, P. Kevin *lawyer*
Catuzzi, J. P., Jr. *lawyer*
Ceresney, Ian *lawyer*
Chalif, Seymour H. *lawyer*
Chapin, Hugh A. *lawyer*
Chapnick, David B. *lawyer*
Chappell, John Charles *lawyer*
Chazen, Hartley James *lawyer*
Chell, Beverly C. *lawyer*
Cherovsky, Erwin Louis *lawyer, writer*
Chester, John Geoffrey *lawyer*
Chevigny, Paul Graves *lawyer, educator*
Chiarchiaro, Frank John *lawyer*
Chilstrom, Robert Meade *lawyer*
Chin, Sylvia Fung *lawyer*
Chirelstein, Marvin A. *law educator*
Christaldi, Brian *lawyer*
Christensen, Henry, III *lawyer*
Christensen, Thomas Gordon Steffen *law educator*
Christy, Arthur Hill *lawyer*
Chromow, Sheri P. *lawyer*
Clark, Cameron *lawyer*
Clark, Carolyn Cochran *lawyer*
Clark, Jonathan Montgomery *lawyer*
Clark, Merrell Edward, Jr. *lawyer*
Clark, Ramsey *lawyer*
Clary, Richard Wayland *lawyer*
Clayton, Joe Don *lawyer*
Clemente, Constantine Louis *lawyer, health care company executive*
Cliff, Walter Conway *lawyer*
Close, Michael John *lawyer*
Coffee, John Collins, Jr. *legal educator*
Cogan, James Richard *lawyer*
Cohen, Edmund Stephen *lawyer*
Cohen, Edward Herschel *lawyer*
Cohen, Henry Rodgin *lawyer*
Cohen, Jerome Alan *lawyer, educator*
Cohen, Joel J. *lawyer, investment banker*
Cohen, Richard Gerard *lawyer*
Cole, Lewis George *lawyer*
Coll, John Peter, Jr. *lawyer*
Collins, Daniel G. *law educator*
Collins, Wayne Dale *lawyer*
Collins, William T. *lawyer*
Collinson, Dale Stanley *lawyer*
Collyer, Michael *lawyer*
Comfrey, Kathleen Marie *lawyer*
Conboy, Kenneth *lawyer, former federal judge*
Concannon, Richard James *lawyer*
Connelly, Albert R. *lawyer*
Connor, John Thomas, Jr. *lawyer*
Conrad, Winthrop Brown, Jr. *lawyer*
Constance, Thomas Ernest *lawyer*
Constantine, Jan Friedman *lawyer*
Conston, Henry Siegismund *lawyer*
Cook, Michael Lewis *lawyer*
Cook, Robert Stansfield, Jr. *lawyer*
Cooney, John Patrick, Jr. *lawyer*
Cooper, Deborah Ellen *lawyer*
Cooper, Michael Anthony *lawyer*
Cooper, Stephen Herbert *lawyer*
Coplan, Norman Allan *lawyer*
Corbin, Sol Neil *lawyer*
Corcoran, James P. *lawyer*
Corry, John Adams *lawyer*
Costikyan, Edward N(azar) *lawyer*
Cotter, James Michael *lawyer*
Cowan, Martin B. *lawyer*
Cowan, Wallace Edgar *lawyer*
Cowen, Edward S. *lawyer*
Cowen, Robert Nathan *lawyer*
Cowles, Frederick Oliver *lawyer*
Cox, Marshall *lawyer*
Craft, Randal Robert, Jr. *lawyer*
Cramer, Edward Morton *lawyer, music company executive*
Crames, Michael J. *lawyer*
Crane, Benjamin Field *lawyer*
Crary, Miner Dunham, Jr. *lawyer*
Creel, Thomas Leonard *lawyer*
Crisona, James Joseph *lawyer*
Critchlow, Charles Howard *lawyer*
Cross, Peter A. *lawyer*
Cubitto, Robert J. *lawyer*
Cuneo, Donald Lane *lawyer, educator*
Cunha, Mark Geoffrey *lawyer*
Cunningham, Noel B. *lawyer, educator*
Cuomo, Mario Matthew *lawyer, former governor*
Curran, William James, III *lawyer*
Curtis, Frank R. *lawyer*
Curtis, Sheldon *lawyer*
Curtis, Susan Grace *lawyer*
Cutler, Kenneth Burnett *lawyer, investment company executive*
Dacey, Eileen M. *lawyer*
Daitz, Ronald Frederick *lawyer*
Dale, Harvey Philip *law educator*
Dallas, William Moffit, Jr. *lawyer*
Damrosch, Lori Fisler *law educator*
Danilek, Donald J. *lawyer*
Dannhauser, Stephen J. *lawyer*
Danzig, Aaron Leon *lawyer*
Darrell, Norris, Jr. *lawyer*
Darrow, Jill E(llen) *lawyer*
Darrow, Katherine Prager *lawyer, publishing executive*
D'Auria, Anthony J. *lawyer*
Davidson, George Allan *lawyer*
Davidson, Mark Edward *lawyer*
Davidson, Robert Bruce *lawyer*
Davis, Edward Shippen *lawyer*
Davis, Evan Anderson *lawyer*
Davis, Frederick Townsend *lawyer*
Davis, Peggy Cooper *law educator*
Davis, Richard Joel *lawyer, former government official*
Davis, Richard Ralph *lawyer*
Davis, Steven Howard *lawyer*
Davis, Wendell, Jr. *lawyer*
Dayan, Rodney S. *lawyer*
Deane, James Richard *lawyer*
Debo, Vincent Joseph *lawyer*
DeCarlo, Donald Thomas *lawyer, insurance company executive*
Delikat, Michael *lawyer*
Delman, Stephen Bennett *lawyer*
Delson, Robert *lawyer*
Demarest, Daniel Anthony *retired lawyer*
De Natale, Andrew Peter *lawyer*
Denham, Robert Edwin *lawyer, investment company executive*
de Saint Phalle, Pierre Claude *lawyer*
De Sear, Edward Marshall *lawyer*
Devers, Peter Dix *lawyer*
de Zagon, Baroness Monique S. *lawyer*
Diamant, Aviva F. *lawyer*
Diamond, David Howard *lawyer*
DiBenedetto, Joseph A. *lawyer*
diBuono, Anthony Joseph *lawyer, business executive*
Dicker, Marvin *lawyer*
DiDonna, Richard A. *lawyer, diversified company executive*
Diskant, Gregory L. *lawyer*
Dolan, James Francis *lawyer*
Doman, Nicholas R. *lawyer*
Dominianni, Emilio Anthony (Mike Dominianni) *lawyer, accountant*
Donald, Norman Henderson, III *lawyer*
Dormire, Corwin Brooke *lawyer*
Dorsen, Harriette K. *lawyer*
Dorsen, Norman *lawyer, educator*
Douglas, Philip Le Breton *lawyer*
Doyle, Joseph Anthony *lawyer*
Doyle, Paul Francis *lawyer*
Drebsky, Dennis Jay *lawyer*
Dreizen, Alison M. *lawyer*
Dreyfuss, Rochelle Cooper *law educator*
Druker, Isaac E. *lawyer*
Dubin, James Michael *lawyer*
Dubin, Seth Harris *lawyer*
DuBois, Jonathan Delafield *lawyer*
Dubroff, Charles Mark *lawyer*
Duffy, Edmund Charles *lawyer*
Duffy, W. Leslie *lawyer*
Dundas, Philip Blair, Jr. *lawyer*
Dune, Steve Charles *lawyer*
Dunham, Corydon Busnell *lawyer, broadcasting executive*
Dunham, Wolcott Balestier, Jr. *lawyer*
Dunn, M(orris) Douglas *lawyer*
Dworkin, Ronald Myles *legal educator*
Dykhouse, David Wayne *lawyer*
Earle, Victor Montagne, III *lawyer*
Ebin, Robert Felix *lawyer*
Eckhaus, Jay Elliot *business executive, lawyer*
Edelbaum, Philip R. *lawyer*
Edelman, Herbert Stephen *lawyer*
Edelman, Paul Sterling *lawyer*
Edelson, Gilbert Seymour *lawyer*
Edgar, Harold Simmons Hull *legal educator*
Edmonds, Robert Scott *lawyer*
Edwards, Christine Annette *lawyer*
Edwards, James Malone *lawyer*
Edwards, Robert Randle *law educator*
Effel, Laura *lawyer*
Ehrenbard, Robert *lawyer*
Ehrenkranz, Joel S. *lawyer*
Einarson, Baldvin Oliver *lawyer*
Einhorn, Harold *lawyer*
Eisert, Edward Gaver *lawyer*
Ekern, George Patrick *lawyer*
Elicker, Gordon Leonard *lawyer*
Elkin, Jeffrey H. *lawyer*
Ellis, Carolyn Terry *lawyer*
Elsen, Sheldon Howard *lawyer*
Emil, Arthur D. *lawyer*
Epling, Richard Louis *lawyer*
Eppner, Gerald Allen *lawyer*
Epstein, Jeremy G. *lawyer*
Epstein, Melvin *lawyer*
Epstein, Michael Alan *lawyer*
Ercklentz, Enno Wilhelm, Jr. *lawyer*
†Estreicher, Samuel *lawyer, educator*
Etra, Aaron *lawyer*
Eustice, James Samuel *lawyer, educator*
Evans, Martin Frederic *lawyer*
Evans, Thomas William *lawyer*
Everett, James William, Jr. *lawyer*
Faber, Peter Lewis *lawyer*
Fabricant, Neil *lawyer, educator*

Fagen, Leslie Gordon *lawyer*
Fales, Haliburton, II *lawyer*
Falvey, Patrick Joseph *lawyer*
Farley, Robert Donald *lawyer, business executive*
Farnham, George Railton *lawyer*
Farnsworth, E(dward) Allan *lawyer, educator*
Farnsworth, Philip Richeson *lawyer, broadcasting and publishing executive*
Fass, Peter Michael *lawyer, educator*
Faulkner, Walter Thomas *lawyer*
Feder, Arthur A. *lawyer*
Feder, Saul E. *lawyer*
Feit, Glenn M. *lawyer*
Felcher, Peter L. *lawyer*
Feldberg, Michael Svetkey *lawyer*
Feldman, Franklin *lawyer, printmaker*
Feldman, Jerome Ira *lawyer, patent development executive*
Feldman, Justin Newton *lawyer*
Felfe, Peter Franz *lawyer*
Felsher, Celia Ann *lawyer*
†Fenster, Albert M. *lawyer*
Fensterstock, Blair Courtney *lawyer*
Ferguson, Milton Carr, Jr. *lawyer*
Ferguson, Robert A. *law educator*
Ferguson, Robert Harry Munro *lawyer*
Fernandez, Jose Walfredo *lawyer*
Fier, Elihu *lawyer*
Filler, Ronald Howard *lawyer*
Finch, Edward Ridley *lawyer, former diplomat, author, lecturer*
Fineman, Martha Albertson *law educator*
Fink, Robert Steven *lawyer, writer, educator*
Finkelstein, Bernard *lawyer*
First, Harry *legal educator*
Fischman, Bernard D. *lawyer*
Fishbein, Peter Melvin *lawyer*
Fisher, Ann Bailen *lawyer*
Fisher, Harold Leonard *lawyer, banker*
Fisher, Herbert Franklin *lawyer*
Fisher, Robert I. *lawyer*
Fishman, Fred Norman *lawyer*
Fishman, Mitchell Steven *lawyer*
Fiske, Robert Bishop, Jr. *lawyer*
Flannery, Anne Catherine *lawyer*
Fleder, Robert Charles *lawyer*
Fleischer, Arthur, Jr. *lawyer*
Fleischman, Edward Hirsh *lawyer*
Fleishman, Wendy Ruth *lawyer*
Fleming, Peter Emmet, Jr. *lawyer*
Fletcher, Anthony L. *lawyer*
Fletcher, George P. *law educator*
Fletcher, Raymond Russwald, Jr. *lawyer*
Flint, George Squire *lawyer*
Flom, Joseph Harold *lawyer*
Flowers, William Ellwood *lawyer*
Flumenbaum, Martin *lawyer*
Fodor, Susanna Serena *lawyer*
Fogg, Blaine Viles *lawyer*
Fontana, Vincent Robert *lawyer*
Forstadt, Joseph Lawrence *lawyer*
Forster, Arnold *lawyer, author*
Fortenbaugh, Samuel Byrod, III *lawyer*
Foster, David Lee *lawyer*
Fox, Donald Thomas *lawyer*
Fraidin, Stephen *lawyer*
Fraiman, Genevieve Lam *lawyer*
Franck, Thomas Martin *law educator*
Frank, Lloyd *lawyer, chemical company executive*
Frankel, Benjamin Harrison *lawyer*
Frankel, Marvin E. *lawyer*
Frankl, Kenneth Richard *lawyer*
Franklin, Blake Timothy *lawyer*
Fredericks, Wesley Charles, Jr. *lawyer*
Freedman, Gerald M. *lawyer*
Freedman, Theodore Levy *lawyer*
Freilicher, Morton *lawyer*
French, John, III *lawyer*
Freund, Fred A. *lawyer*
Freund, James Coleman *lawyer*
Fried, Burton Theodore *lawyer*
Fried, Donald David *lawyer*
Fried, Walter Jay *lawyer*
Friedman, Alan Roy *lawyer*
Friedman, Bart *lawyer*
Friedman, John Maxwell, Jr. *lawyer*
Friedman, Leon *law educator, lawyer*
Friedman, Robert Laurence *lawyer*
Friedman, Samuel Selig *lawyer*
Friedman, Stephen James *lawyer*
Friedman, Victor Stanley *lawyer*
Friedman, Wilbur Harvey *lawyer*
Frisch, Harry David *lawyer, consultant*
Frischling, Carl *lawyer*
Frost, Diana *lawyer*
Frost, William Lee *lawyer*
Fryer, Judith Dorothy *lawyer*
Fuhrer, Arthur K. *lawyer*
Fuld, James Jeffrey *lawyer*
Fuld, Stanley H. *lawyer*
Fullem, Lawrence Robert *lawyer*
Fuzesi, Stephen, Jr. *lawyer, communications executive*
Gabay, Donald David *lawyer*
Galant, Herbert Lewis *lawyer*
Gallagher, Terence Joseph *lawyer*
Gallantz, George Gerald *lawyer*
Galston, Clarence Elkus *lawyer*
Gambro, Michael S. *lawyer*
Gans, Walter Gideon *lawyer*
Ganz, Howard L. *lawyer*
Ganzi, Victor Frederick *lawyer*
Garber, Robert Edward *lawyer, insurance company executive*
Garfinkel, Barry Herbert *lawyer*
Garland, Sylvia Dillof *lawyer*
Garnett, Stanley Iredale, II *lawyer, utility company executive*
Gartner, Murray *lawyer*
Gassel, Philip Michael *lawyer*
Gelb, Joseph W. *lawyer*
Gelb, Judith Anne *lawyer*
Geldzahler, Janet Thiele *lawyer*
Gelfman, Robert William *lawyer*
Genova, Joseph Steven *lawyer*
Geoghegan, Patricia *lawyer*
George, Beauford James, Jr. *lawyer, educator*
Gerard, Fred N. *lawyer*
Gerard, Whitney Ian *lawyer*
Gerber, Robert Evan *lawyer*
Gerber, Roger Alan *lawyer, business executive*
Gerra, Ralph A., Jr. *lawyer*
Gershuny, Donald Nevin *lawyer*
Gewirtz, Elliot *lawyer*
Giannetti, Thomas Leonard *lawyer*
†Gibbs, L(ippman) Martin *lawyer*
Gifford, William C. *lawyer*
Gilbert, Phil Edward, Jr. *lawyer*
Gill, E. Ann *lawyer*
Gillers, Stephen *law educator*
Gillespie, George Joseph, III *lawyer*
Gilman, Charles Alan *lawyer*
Gilpatric, Roswell Leavitt *lawyer*
Ginsberg, Ernest *lawyer, banker*
Girden, Eugene Lawrence *lawyer*
Gitter, Max *lawyer*
Glassman, Steven J. *lawyer*
Glekel, Jeffrey Ives *lawyer*
Glickstein, Steven *lawyer*
Goetz, Cecelia Helen *lawyer, retired judge*
Goetz, Maurice Harold *lawyer*
Gold, Martin Elliot *lawyer, educator*
Gold, Simeon *lawyer*
Gold, Stuart Walter *lawyer*
Goldberg, David *lawyer, law educator*
Goldberg, Victor Paul *law educator*
Goldblatt, David Ira *lawyer*
Golden, Arthur F. *lawyer*
Golden, William Robert, Jr. *lawyer*
Goldfield, Alfred Sherman *lawyer*
Goldman, Charles Norton *lawyer, corporation executive*
Goldman, Donald Howard *lawyer*
Goldman, Lawrence Saul *lawyer*
Goldman, Marvin Gerald *lawyer*
Goldschmid, Harvey Jerome *law educator*
Goldsmith, Donald Alan *lawyer*
Goldsmith, Lee Selig *lawyer, physician*
Goldstein, Alvin *lawyer*
Goldstein, Bernard Herbert *lawyer*
Goldstein, Charles Arthur *lawyer*
Goldstein, Howard Warren *lawyer*
Goldstein, Jonathan *lawyer*
Goldstein, Marcia Landweber *lawyer*
Goldstone, Steven F. *lawyer*
Gooch, Anthony Cushing *lawyer*
Goodale, James Campbell *lawyer*
Goodfriend, Herbert Jay *lawyer*
Goodhartz, Gerald *law librarian*
Goodkind, Louis William *lawyer*
Goodman, Gary A. *lawyer*
Goodridge, Allan D. *lawyer*
Goodwillie, Eugene William, Jr. *lawyer*
Goodwin, Bernard *lawyer, executive, educator*
Gordon, Jeffrey Neil *law educator*
Gordon, Michael Mackin *lawyer*
Gordon, Nicole Ann *lawyer*
Gormley, Nancy H. *lawyer, electric power industry executive*
Gottesman, Callman *lawyer*
Gould, Milton Samuel *lawyer, business executive*
Grad, Frank Paul *lawyer*
Graff, George Leonard *lawyer*
Graham, Jesse Japhet, II *lawyer*
Grant, Stephen Allen *lawyer*
Grashof, August Edward *lawyer*
Green, Robert S. *lawyer*
Greenawalt, Robert Kent *lawyer*
Greenawalt, William Sloan *lawyer*
Greenbaum, Maurice Coleman *lawyer*
Greenberg, Daniel Herbert *lawyer*
Greenberg, Ira George *lawyer*
Greenberg, Jack *lawyer*
Greenberg, Joshua F. *lawyer, educator*
Greenberg, Ronald David *law educator*
Greenberger, Howard Leroy *lawyer, educator*
Greene, Bernard Harold *lawyer*
Greenfield, Jay *lawyer*
Greenman, Jane Friedlieb *lawyer*
Greer, Allen Curtis, II *lawyer*
Greer, James Alexander, II *lawyer*
Greig, Robert Thomson *lawyer*
Greilsheimer, James Gans *lawyer*
Groban, Robert Sidney, Jr. *lawyer*
Gropper, Allan Louis *lawyer*
Gross, Ernest Arnold *lawyer*
Gross, Steven Ross *lawyer*
Grossman, Dan Steven *lawyer*
Grossman, Sanford *lawyer*
Grubman, Allen J. *lawyer*
Gruenberger, Peter *lawyer*
Grumbach, George Jacques, Jr. *lawyer*
Grunewald, Raymond Bernhard *lawyer*
Gruson, Michael *lawyer*
†Gunther, Jack Disbrow, Jr. *lawyer*
Guth, Paul C. *lawyer*
Gutman, Jeremiah Sheldon *lawyer*
Hackett, Kevin R. *lawyer*
Haffner, Alfred Loveland, Jr. *intellectual property lawyer*
Haft, Marilyn Geisler *lawyer*
Hagendorn, William *lawyer*
Hager, Charles Read *lawyer*
Haggerty, Robert Henry *lawyer*
Haidt, Harold *lawyer*
Haig, Robert Leighton *lawyer*
Haims, Bruce David *lawyer*
Haje, Peter Robert *lawyer*
Halberstam, Malvina *legal educator, lawyer*
Hall, John Herbert *lawyer*
Halliday, Joseph William *lawyer*
Halperin, Richard E. *lawyer, holding company executive*
Hamblen, L. Jane *lawyer*
Hamburg, Charles Bruce *lawyer*
Hamel, Rodolphe *lawyer, pharmaceutical company executive*
Hamm, David Bernard *lawyer*
Hammerling, Robert Charles *lawyer*
Hammerman, Stephen Lawrence *lawyer, financial services company executive*
Hammond, Steven Alan *lawyer*
Handelsman, Lawrence Marc *lawyer*
Handler, Arthur M. *lawyer*
Handler, Milton *lawyer*
Harbison, James Wesley, Jr. *lawyer*
Harley, Colin Emile *lawyer*
Harnett, Thomas Aquinas *lawyer*
Harper, Emery Walter *lawyer*
Harper, Gerard Edward *lawyer*
Harris, Allen *lawyer, educator*
Harris, Arlene *lawyer*
Harris, Ellen W. *lawyer*
Harris, Joel B(ruce) *lawyer*
Harrison, S. David *lawyer*
Hart, Kenneth Nelson *lawyer*
Hart, Robert M. *lawyer*
Hartzell, Andrew Cornelius, Jr. *lawyer*
Hauser, Rita Eleanore Abrams *lawyer*
Hawes, Douglas Wesson *lawyer*
Hawke, Roger Jewett *lawyer*
Hayden, Raymond Paul *lawyer*
Hayes, Gerald Joseph *lawyer*
Haynes, Jean Reed *lawyer*
Healy, Harold Harris, Jr. *lawyer*
Healy, Nicholas Joseph *lawyer, educator*
Hearn, George Henry *lawyer, steamship corporate executive*
Heckart, Robert Lee *lawyer*
Heine, Edward Joseph, Jr. *lawyer*
Heineman, Andrew David *lawyer*
Heisler, Stanley Dean *lawyer*
Heitner, Kenneth Howard *lawyer*
Helfgott, Samson *lawyer*
Hellawell, Robert *law educator*
Hellenbrand, Samuel Henry *lawyer, diversified industry executive*
Heller, Edwin *lawyer*
Heller, Robert Martin *lawyer*
Hellerstein, Alvin Kenneth *lawyer*
Hellerstein, Jerome Robert *lawyer*
Heming, Charles E. *lawyer*
Henderson, Donald Bernard, Jr. *lawyer*
Hendrickson, Robert Augustus *lawyer*
Hendry, Andrew Delaney *lawyer, consumer products company executive*
Henkin, Louis *lawyer, law educator*
Henry, Elizabeth Powers *lawyer*
Henry, Sally McDonald *lawyer*
Herman, Kenneth Beaumont *lawyer*
Herold, Karl Guenter *lawyer*
Hersch, Dennis Steven *lawyer*
Herz, Andrew Lee *lawyer*
Hetherington, John Warner *lawyer*
Hewitt, Carl Herbert *lawyer*
Hiden, Robert Battaile, Jr. *lawyer*
Higginbotham, A. Leon, Jr. *lawyer, educator*
Higginson, James Jackson *lawyer*
Higgs, John H. *lawyer*
Highleyman, Samuel Locke, III *lawyer*
Hill, Alfred *lawyer, educator*
Hirsch, Barry *lawyer*
Hirsch, Jerome Seth *lawyer*
Hirschfeld, Michael *lawyer*
Hirshfield, Stuart *lawyer*
Hirshon, Sheldon Ira *lawyer*
Hirshowitz, Melvin Stephen *lawyer*
Hochman, Charles Bruce *lawyer*
Hodes, Robert Bernard *lawyer*
Hoff, Jonathan M(orind) *lawyer*
Hoffman, John Ernest, Jr. *retired lawyer*
Hoffman, Mathew *lawyer*
Hoffmann, Malcolm Arthur *lawyer*
Hogan, William E. *law educator, lawyer*
Holderness, Algernon Sidney, Jr. *lawyer*
Holderness, G(eorge) Malcolm *lawyer*
Hollander, David *lawyer*
Holman, Bud George *lawyer*
Holtzman, Alexander *lawyer, consultant*
Holtzmann, Howard Marshall *lawyer, judge*
Holtzschue, Karl Bressem *lawyer, author, educator*
Hoover, James Lloyd *law librarian, educator*
Hopkins, Thomas Arscott *lawyer*
Hopper, Walter Everett *lawyer*
Hornick, Robert Newton *lawyer*
Horowitz, Raymond J. *lawyer*
Hovdesven, Arne *lawyer*
Howe, Richard Rives *lawyer*
Howell, Wesley Grant, Jr. *lawyer*
Hoynes, Louis LeNoir, Jr. *lawyer*
Hruska, Alan J. *lawyer*
Hudspeth, Stephen Mason *lawyer*
Huettner, Richard Alfred *lawyer*
Hughes, Kevin Peter *lawyer*
Huhs, John I. *lawyer*
Hulbert, Richard Woodward *lawyer*
Hull, Philip Glasgow *lawyer*
Hunt, Franklin Griggs *lawyer*
Hupper, John Roscoe *lawyer*
Hurley, Geoffrey Kevin *lawyer*
Hurlock, James Bickford *lawyer*
Hyde, David Rowley *lawyer*
Hyman, Alan Barry *lawyer*
Hyman, Jerome Elliot *lawyer*
Iannuzzi, John Nicholas *lawyer, author, educator*
Idzik, Daniel Ronald *lawyer*
Indursky, Arthur *lawyer*
Ingram, Samuel William, Jr. *lawyer*
Insel, Michael S. *lawyer*
Iovenko, Michael *lawyer*
Irvin, Patricia Louise *lawyer*
Isaacson, Allen Ira *lawyer*
Isquith, Fred Taylor *lawyer*
Issler, Harry *lawyer*
Ivanick, Carol W. Trencher *lawyer*
Jablons, Jane Ellen *lawyer*
Jackson, Thomas Gene *lawyer*
Jackson, William Eldred *lawyer*
Jacob, Edwin J. *lawyer*
Jacob, Marvin Eugene *lawyer*
Jacobs, Arnold Stephen *lawyer*
Jacobs, James B. *law educator*
Jacobs, Jane Brand *lawyer*
Jacobs, Robert Alan *lawyer*
Jacobson, Gary Steven *lawyer*
Jacobson, Jerold Dennis *lawyer*
Jaffe, Alan Steven *lawyer*
Jaffin, Charles Leonard *lawyer*
Jander, Klaus Heinrich *lawyer*
Jánszky, Andrew Béla *lawyer*
Jassy, Everett Lewis *lawyer*
Javits, Eric Moses *lawyer*
Jefferies, Jack P. *lawyer*
Jessup, John Baker *lawyer*
Jeydel, Richard K. *lawyer*
Jinnett, Robert Jefferson *lawyer*
Joffe, Robert David *lawyer*
Johnson, James Gann, Jr. *lawyer*
Johnston, Harry Melville, III *lawyer*
Jones, Lucian Cox *lawyer*
Jones, Ronald David *lawyer*
Jones, William Kenneth *law educator*
Jordon, Deborah Elizabeth *lawyer*
Joseph, Gregory Paul *lawyer*
Joseph, L. Anthony, Jr. *lawyer*
Joseph, Leonard *lawyer*
Josephson, William Howard *lawyer*
Juceam, Robert E. *lawyer*
Kaden, Ellen Oran *lawyer, broadcasting corporation executive*
Kaden, Lewis B. *law educator*
Kadet, Samuel *lawyer*
Kafin, Robert Joseph *lawyer*
Kahen, Harold I. *lawyer*
Kahn, Anthony F. *lawyer*
Kahn, Richard Dreyfus *lawyer*
Kailas, Leo George *lawyer*
Kalish, Arthur *lawyer*
Kalish, Myron *lawyer*
Kals, Stephen A. *lawyer*
Kamin, Sherwin *lawyer*
Kaminer, Peter H. *lawyer*
Kaminsky, Arthur Charles *lawyer*
Kandel, William Lloyd *lawyer, educator, author*
Kane, Daniel Hipwell *lawyer*
Kaplan, Carl Eliot *lawyer*
†Kaplan, Helene Lois *lawyer*
Kaplan, Joseph Solte *lawyer*
Kaplan, Lewis A. *lawyer*
Kaplan, Madeline *legal administrator*
Kaplan, Mark Norman *lawyer*
Kaplan, Peter James *lawyer*
Kaplan, Philip Thomas *lawyer*
Karasz, Peter *lawyer*
Karatz, William Warren *lawyer*
Karmel, Roberta Segal *lawyer, educator*
Karotkin, Stephen K. *lawyer*
Kartiganer, Joseph *lawyer*
Kasowitz, Marc Elliot *lawyer*
Kassebaum, John Philip *lawyer*
Katsh, Salem Michael *lawyer*
Katz, Gregory *lawyer*
Katz, Jerome Charles *lawyer*
Katz, Ronald S. *lawyer*
Katz, Stanley Nider *law history educator, association executive*
Kaufman, Arthur Stephen *lawyer*
Kaufman, Frank Joseph *lawyer*
Kaufman, Robert Max *lawyer*
Kaufmann, Jack *lawyer*
Kavaler, Thomas J. *lawyer*
Kavoukjian, Michael Edward *lawyer*
Kaye, Stephen Rackow *lawyer*
Kaynor, William Akin *lawyer*
Kazanjian, John Harold *lawyer*
Kean, Hamilton Fish *lawyer*
Keany, Sutton *lawyer*
Kennedy, John Joseph *lawyer, educator*
Kennedy, Michael John *lawyer*
Kennedy, Thomas H. *lawyer*
Kenney, John Joseph *lawyer*
Keogh, Kevin *lawyer*
Kern, George Calvin, Jr. *lawyer*
Kern, Jerome H. *lawyer*
Kernochan, John Marshall *lawyer, educator*
Kessel, Mark *lawyer*
Kessler, Jeffrey L. *lawyer*
Kessler, Ralph Kenneth *lawyer, manufacturing company executive*
Kevlin, Mary Louise *lawyer*
Kezsbom, Allen *lawyer*
Kheel, Theodore Woodrow *lawyer, labor arbitrator and mediator*
Kidd, John Edward *lawyer, corporate executive*
Kill, Lawrence *lawyer*
Kimball, Richard Arthur, Jr. *lawyer*
King, Henry Lawrence *lawyer*
King, Lawrence Philip *lawyer, educator*
Kinney, Stephen Hoyt, Jr. *lawyer*
Kinsolving, Augustus Blagden *lawyer*
Kinzler, Thomas Benjamin *lawyer*
Kirby, John Joseph, Jr. *lawyer*
Kirschbaum, Myron *lawyer*
Kirschner, Marc Steven *lawyer*
Klaperman, Joel Simcha *lawyer*
Klein, William, II *lawyer*
Kleinbard, Edward D. *lawyer*
Kleinberg, Norman Charles *lawyer*
Kleinberg, Robert Irwin *lawyer*
Kline, Eugene Monroe *lawyer*
Klingsberg, David *lawyer*
Klink, Fredric J. *lawyer*
Kmiotek, Jacqueline J. *lawyer*
Knapp, Charles Lincoln *law educator*
Knickerbocker, Daniel Candee, Jr. *legal educator*
Knight, Robert Huntington *lawyer, bank executive*
Knight, Townsend Jones *lawyer*
Knutson, David Harry *lawyer, banker*
Kobak, James Benedict, Jr. *lawyer, educator*
Kober, Jane *lawyer*
Kobrin, Lawrence Alan *lawyer*
Koegel, William Fisher *lawyer*
Koenigsberg, I. Fred *lawyer*
†Kohlberg, Jerome, Jr. *lawyer, business executive*
Kolb, Daniel Francis *lawyer*
Kolbe, Karl William, Jr. *lawyer*
Kolbert, Kathryn *lawyer, educator*
Komaroff, Stanley *lawyer*
Koob, Charles Edward *lawyer*
Koral, Alan M. *lawyer*
Korn, Harold Leon *law educator*
Kornberg, Alan William *lawyer*
Kornblit, Sandra Cohen *lawyer*
Kornhauser, Lewis *law educator*
Kornreich, Edward Scott *lawyer*
Korotkin, Michael Paul *lawyer*
Kostelanetz, Boris *lawyer*
Kourides, Peter Theologos *lawyer*
Kraemer, Lillian Elizabeth *lawyer*
Kraft, Marcijane *lawyer*
Kramer, Alan Sharfsin *lawyer*
Kramer, George P. *lawyer*
†Kramer, Kenneth Merin *lawyer*
Kramer, Morris Joseph *lawyer*
Kranwinkle, Conrad Douglas *lawyer*
Krasner, Daniel Walter *lawyer*
Kraus, Douglas M. *lawyer*
Kreitzman, Ralph J. *lawyer*
Kreutzer, Franklin David *lawyer*
Krieger, Sanford *lawyer*
Krinsly, Stuart Zalmy *lawyer, manufacturing company executive*
Kroll, Arthur Herbert *lawyer, law educator*
Krouse, George Raymond, Jr. *lawyer*
Krupman, William Allan *lawyer*
Krupp, Frederic D. *lawyer, environmental agency executive*
Kufeld, William Manuel *lawyer*
Kuh, Richard Henry *lawyer*
Kuklin, Anthony Bennett *lawyer*
Kumble, Steven Jay *lawyer*
Kunstler, William Moses *lawyer, educator, lecturer, author*
Kuntz, Lee Allan *lawyer*
Kurtyka, Ruthanne *lawyer*
Kurtz, Jerome *lawyer, educator*
Kury, Bernard Edward *lawyer*
Kurzweil, Harvey *lawyer*
LaBarre, Dennis W. *lawyer*
Lacey, Frederick Bernard *lawyer, former federal judge*
Lacovara, Philip Allen *lawyer*
Lacy, Robinson Burrell *lawyer*
Lambert, Paul Christopher *lawyer, former ambassador*
Lamia, Thomas Roger *lawyer*
Lanchner, Bertrand Martin *lawyer, advertising executive*
Land, David Potts *lawyer*
Landa, Howard Martin *lawyer, business executive*
Landau, Walter Loeber *lawyer*
Landes, Robert Nathan *lawyer*

Lane, Alvin S. *lawyer*
Lane, Arthur Alan *lawyer*
Lang, John Francis *lawyer*
Lang, Robert Todd *lawyer*
Lang, Stephen R. *lawyer*
Lange, Marvin Robert *lawyer*
Lans, Asher Bob *lawyer*
LaPier, Theodore *lawyer*
Larkin, Leo Paul, Jr. *lawyer*
La Rossa, James M(ichael) *lawyer*
Larsen, Robert Dhu *lawyer*
Lascher, Alan Alfred *lawyer*
Lauer, Eliot *lawyer*
Laufer, Donald L. *lawyer*
Lavinsky, Larry Monroe *lawyer, consultant*
Law, Sylvia A. *law educator*
Layton, Robert *lawyer*
Lebow, Mark Denis *lawyer*
Lederer, Peter David *lawyer*
Lederman, Lawrence *lawyer, writer, educator*
Lee, David James *lawyer*
Lee, Jerome G. *lawyer*
Lee, Paul L. *lawyer*
Leebron, David Wayne *law educator*
Lefkowitz, Howard N. *lawyer*
Lefkowitz, Lawrence *lawyer*
Lehman, Mark E. *lawyer*
Lehrer, Sander *lawyer*
Leichtling, Michael Alfred *lawyer*
Leisure, George Stanley, Jr. *lawyer*
Leland, Richard G. *lawyer*
Leness, George Crawford *lawyer*
Leonard, Edwin Deane *lawyer*
Lerner, Ralph E. *lawyer*
Lesch, Michael Oscar *lawyer*
Levie, Joseph Henry *lawyer*
Levin, Ezra Gurion *lawyer*
Levine, Edward Leslie *lawyer*
Levine, Laurence William *lawyer*
Levine, Lawrence Steven *lawyer*
Levine, Mark Leonard *lawyer*
Levine, Robert Jay *lawyer*
Levine, Ronald Jay *lawyer*
Levison, Harold George *lawyer*
Levitan, David M(aurice) *lawyer, educator*
Levitan, James A. *lawyer*
Levy, Joseph *lawyer*
Levy, Mark Allan *lawyer*
Levy, Stanley Herbert *lawyer*
Lewis, Grant Stephen *lawyer*
Lewis, James Berton *law educator*
Lewis, Robert Charles *lawyer*
Lewyn, Thomas Mark *lawyer*
Lifland, William Thomas *lawyer*
Liftin, John Matthew *lawyer*
Liggio, Carl Donald *lawyer*
Lilley, Albert Frederick *lawyer*
Lillie, James Woodruff, Jr. *lawyer*
Liman, Arthur Lawrence *lawyer*
Lindblom, Marjorie Press *lawyer*
Lindenbaum, Sandford Richard *lawyer*
Lindley, David Morrison *lawyer*
Lindsay, George Nelson *lawyer*
Lindsay, George Peter *lawyer*
Lindskog, David Richard *lawyer*
Linsenmeyer, John Michael *lawyer*
†Lipton, Charles Jules *lawyer*
Lipton, Martin *lawyer*
Lipton, Robert Steven *lawyer*
Litman, Helena D. *lawyer*
Lochner, Philip Raymond, Jr. *lawyer*
Loeb, Steven Michael *lawyer*
Loengard, Richard Otto, Jr. *lawyer*
LoFrisco, Anthony F. *lawyer*
Logan, Francis Dummer *lawyer*
Logan, Kenneth Richard *lawyer*
Lokken, Lawrence *law educator*
London, Martin *lawyer*
Longstreth, Bevis *lawyer*
Lorch, Ernest Henry *lawyer*
Lore, Martin Maxwell *lawyer*
Losh, Clifford William *lawyer*
Loss, Margaret Ruth *lawyer*
Lotwin, Stanford Gerald *lawyer*
Lowenfeld, Andreas Frank *legal educator, arbitrator*
Lowenfels, Fred M. *lawyer*
Lowenfels, Lewis David *lawyer*
Lowenstein, Louis *legal educator*
Lowy, George Theodore *lawyer*
Lunding, Christopher Hanna *lawyer*
Lundquist, James Harold *lawyer*
Lupert, Leslie Allan *lawyer*
Lupkin, Stanley Neil *lawyer*
Luria, Mary Mercer *lawyer*
Lurie, Alvin David *lawyer*
Lusky, Louis *legal educator*
Lustenberger, Louis Charles, Jr. *lawyer*
Lustgarten, Ira Howard *lawyer*
Lutringer, Richard Emil *lawyer*
Lynch, Gerard E. *law educator*
Lynn, Theodore Stanley *lawyer*
Lynton, Harold Stephen *lawyer*
Lyon, Carl Francis, Jr. *lawyer*
Macan, William Alexander, IV *lawyer*
MacCallum, Robert Kenneth *lawyer*
MacCrate, Robert *lawyer*
Macioce, Frank Michael, Jr. *lawyer, financial services company executive*
Mack, Dennis Wayne *lawyer*
MacKinnon, John Alexander *lawyer*
MacRae, Cameron Farquhar, III *lawyer*
Madden, Donald Paul *lawyer*
Madsen, Stephen Stewart *lawyer*
Mahon, Arthur J. *lawyer*
Maidman, Richard Harvey Mortimer *lawyer*
Malina, Michael *lawyer*
Malkin, Peter Laurence *lawyer*
Malman, Laurie L. *law educator*
Maloney, Michael Patrick *lawyer, corporate executive*
Mamorsky, Jeffrey Dean *lawyer*
Mandelstam, Charles Lawrence *lawyer*
Maneker, Morton M. *lawyer*
Maney, Michael Mason *lawyer*
Mann, James Brooks *lawyer*
Manning, Jerome Alan *lawyer*
Manning, William Joseph *lawyer*
Mantle, Raymond Allan *lawyer*
Marcus, Barry Philip *lawyer*
Marcus, Eric Peter *lawyer*
Marcus, Norman *lawyer*
Marcusa, Fred Haye *lawyer*
Marden, John Newcomb *lawyer*
Mark, Jonathan I. *lawyer*
Marke, Julius Jay *law librarian, educator*
Marks, Theodore Lee *lawyer*
Marlin, Richard *lawyer*
Marshall, John Patrick *lawyer*
Marshall, Sheila Hermes *lawyer*
Martin, George J., Jr. *lawyer*
Martin, Malcolm Elliot *lawyer*
Martone, Patricia Ann *lawyer*
Marx, Owen Cox *lawyer*
Marzulli, John Anthony, Jr. *lawyer*
Mashberg, Gregg M. *lawyer*
Masin, Michael Terry *lawyer*
Masinter, Edgar Martin *lawyer*
Maskin, Arvin *lawyer*
Maslow, Will *lawyer, association executive*
Masters, Jon Joseph *lawyer*
Mathers, William Harris *lawyer*
Matteson, William Bleecker *lawyer*
Matthews, Edwin Spencer, Jr. *lawyer*
Maulsby, Allen Farish *lawyer*
Max, Herbert B. *lawyer*
Maxfield, Guy Budd *lawyer, educator*
Mayden, Barbara Mendel *lawyer*
Mayer, Carl Joseph *lawyer, town official*
Mayer, Theodore V.H. *lawyer*
Mayerson, Sandra Elaine *lawyer*
Mazza, Thomas Carmen *lawyer*
McBaine, John Neylan *lawyer*
McBryde, Thomas Henry *lawyer*
McCaffrey, Carlyn Sundberg *lawyer*
Mc Cann, John Joseph *lawyer*
McCarthy, Bernard William *lawyer*
McClimon, Timothy John *lawyer*
McClung, Richard Goehring *lawyer*
McCormick, Hugh Thomas *lawyer*
McDavid, William Henry *lawyer*
McDermott, Richard T. *lawyer, educator*
McDonald, Willis, IV *lawyer*
McDowell, Jay Hortenstine *lawyer*
McEnroe, John Patrick *lawyer*
McGanney, Thomas *lawyer*
McGinnis, John Oldham *lawyer, educator*
Mc Goldrick, John Gardiner *lawyer*
McGonigal, Richard M. *lawyer*
McGrath, Thomas J. *lawyer, writer, film producer*
McGunigle, Brian Edward *lawyer*
McHenry, Barnabas *lawyer*
Mc Inerney, Denis *lawyer*
McLaughlin, Joseph *lawyer*
McLaughlin, Joseph Thomas *lawyer*
McLearn, Michael Baylis *lawyer*
McMahon, Colleen *lawyer*
McMeen, Elmer Ellsworth, III *lawyer, guitarist*
McNally, John Joseph *lawyer*
Mc Namara, J(ohn) Donald *lawyer, business executive*
Mc Nicol, Donald Edward *lawyer*
†Mead, Wayland McCon *lawyer*
Meaders, Paul Le Sourd *lawyer*
Medford-Rosow, Traci *lawyer*
Medina, Standish Forde, Jr. *lawyer*
Medwick, Craig Steven *lawyer*
Mendelsohn, Walter *lawyer*
Mercorella, Anthony J. *lawyer, former state supreme court justice*
Meron, Theodor *law educator, researcher*
Merow, John Edward *lawyer*
Mescon, Richard Alan *lawyer*
Mestres, Ricardo Angelo, Jr. *lawyer*
Meyer, Edward N. *lawyer*
Michaelson, Arthur M. *lawyer*
Michel, Clifford Lloyd *lawyer, investment executive*
Milgrim, Roger Michael *lawyer*
Millard, John Alden *lawyer*
Miller, Charles Hampton *lawyer*
Miller, David *lawyer, advertising executive*
Miller, Harvey R. *lawyer, bankruptcy reorganization specialist*
Miller, Lawrence Edward *lawyer*
Miller, Richard Steven *lawyer*
Miller, Sam Scott *lawyer*
Millstein, Ira M. *lawyer, lecturer*
Minkel, Herbert Philip, Jr. *lawyer*
Minkowitz, Martin *lawyer, former state government official*
Mishkin, Edwin B. *lawyer*
Mishkin, Jeffrey Alan *lawyer*
Missan, Richard Sherman *lawyer*
Modlin, Howard S. *lawyer*
Moerdler, Charles Gerard *lawyer*
Moloney, Thomas Joseph *lawyer*
Monaghan, Henry P. *lawyer, educator*
Monge, Jay Parry *lawyer*
Montgomery, Robert Humphrey, Jr. *lawyer*
Moore, Donald Francis *lawyer*
Moore, John Joseph *lawyer*
Moore, Thomas Ronald *lawyer*
Moorhead, Thomas Burch *lawyer, pharmaceutical company executive*
Morgan, Frank Edward, II *lawyer*
Morgenthau, Robert Morris *lawyer*
Morris, Eugene Jerome *lawyer*
Morris, John E. *lawyer*
Mortimer, Peter Michael *lawyer*
Moskin, Morton *lawyer*
Moss, William John *lawyer*
Most, Jack Lawrence *lawyer, consultant*
Mottola, Gary F. *lawyer*
Mullen, Peter P. *lawyer*
Mulvihill, Roger Denis *lawyer*
Mundheim, Robert Harry *law educator*
Murase, Jiro *lawyer*
Murphy, Arthur William *lawyer, educator*
Murphy, Daniel Hayes, II *lawyer*
Murray, Paul Brady *lawyer, banker*
Myerson, Toby Salter *lawyer*
Naftalis, Gary Philip *lawyer, educator*
Nance, Allan Taylor *lawyer*
Narasimhan, Subha *law educator*
Nash, Paul LeNoir *lawyer*
Nassau, Michael Jay *lawyer*
Nathan, Frederic Solis *lawyer*
Nazareth, Annette LaPorte *lawyer*
Neidell, Martin H. *lawyer*
Nelson, Richard R. *law educator*
Nelson, William Edward *lawyer, educator*
Nemser, Earl Harold *lawyer*
Neuborne, Burt *law educator*
Neuwirth, Alan James *lawyer*
Neveloff, Jay A. *lawyer*
Nevling, J. Kelley, Jr. *lawyer*
Newcomb, Danforth *lawyer*
Newcombe, George Michael *lawyer*
Newman, Fredric Samuel *lawyer, business executive*
Newman, Howard Neal *law educator, lawyer*
Newman, Lawrence *lawyer*
Newman, Lawrence Walker *lawyer*
Newman, Norman *lawyer*
Newman, Scott David *lawyer*
Newton, Blake Tyler, III *lawyer*
Nicholls, Richard H. *lawyer*
Nimetz, Matthew *lawyer*
Nimkin, Bernard William *retired lawyer*
Nolan, Terrance Joseph, Jr. *lawyer*
Nonna, John Michael *lawyer*
Norfolk, William Ray *lawyer*
Nusbacher, Gloria W. *lawyer*
Oberman, Michael Stewart *lawyer*
O'Brien, Donal Clare, Jr. *lawyer*
O'Brien, Kevin J. *lawyer*
O'Brien, Thomas Ignatius *lawyer*
O'Brien, Timothy James *lawyer*
O'Dea, Dennis Michael *lawyer*
Odell, Stuart Irwin *lawyer*
O'Donnell, John Logan *lawyer*
Ogden, Alfred *lawyer*
O'Grady, John Joseph, III *lawyer*
O'Hara, Alfred Peck *lawyer*
†O'Hara, Robert Sydney, Jr. *lawyer*
O'Hare, Jean Ann *lawyer*
Olick, Arthur Seymour *lawyer*
Olick, Philip Stewart *lawyer*
Oliensis, Sheldon *lawyer*
Olmstead, Clarence Walter, Jr. *lawyer*
Olson, Wanda Jean *lawyer*
O'Neil, John Joseph *lawyer*
O'Neill, Daniel Joseph *lawyer*
Oppenheimer, Martin J. *lawyer*
Orce, Kenneth W. *lawyer*
Orkin, Leonard *lawyer*
Ornitz, Richard Martin *lawyer, business executive*
O'Rorke, James Francis, Jr. *lawyer*
Osborn, Donald Robert *lawyer*
Osgood, Robert Mansfield *lawyer*
Ostling, Paul James *lawyer*
Ostrager, Barry Robert *lawyer*
O'Sullivan, Thomas J. *lawyer*
Ott, Gilbert Russell, Jr. *lawyer*
Oxman, David Craig *lawyer*
Pack, Leonard Brecher *lawyer*
Padilla, James Earl *lawyer*
Paisner, Bruce Lawrence *lawyer, television and film executive*
Paladino, Daniel R. *lawyer, beverage corporation executive*
Palladino, Vincent Neil *lawyer*
Palmieri, Victor Henry *lawyer, business executive*
Panken, Peter Michael *lawyer*
Papernik, Joel Ira *lawyer*
Parent, Louise Marie *lawyer*
Parish, J. Michael *lawyer, writer*
Parker, Douglas Martin *lawyer*
Parker, Kellis E., Sr. *legal educator, lawyer, musician*
Parkinson, Thomas Ignatius, Jr. *lawyer*
Parr, Ferdinand Van Siclen, Jr. *lawyer*
Parver, Jane W. *lawyer*
Patrikis, Ernest T. *lawyer*
Paul, Eve W. *lawyer*
Paul, James William *lawyer*
Paul, Robert Carey *lawyer*
Pearsall, Otis Pratt *lawyer*
Peaslee, James M. *lawyer*
Peerce, Stuart Bernard *lawyer*
Peet, Charles D., Jr. *lawyer*
Pegram, John Braxton *lawyer*
Peloso, John Francis Xavier *lawyer*
Pelster, William C. *lawyer*
Pelz, Robert Leon *lawyer*
Pennoyer, Paul Geddes, Jr. *lawyer*
Pennoyer, Robert M. *lawyer*
Pepper, Allan Michael *lawyer*
Peppers, Jerry P. *lawyer*
Perell, Edward Andrew *lawyer*
Perkiel, Mitchel H. *lawyer*
Perkins, Roswell Burchard *lawyer*
Perlmuth, William Alan *lawyer*
Perrotta, Fioravante Gerald *lawyer*
Perschetz, Martin L. *lawyer*
Pershan, Richard Henry *lawyer*
Peters, Alton Emil *lawyer*
Peterson, Charles Gordon *retired lawyer*
Pettibone, Peter John *lawyer*
Pfeffer, David H. *lawyer*
Phillips, Anthony Francis *lawyer*
Phillips, Barnet, IV *lawyer*
Phillips, Charles Gorham *lawyer*
Phillips, Pamela Kim *lawyer*
Pickholz, Marvin G. *lawyer*
Pidot, Whitney Dean *lawyer*
Pierce, Morton Allen *lawyer*
Pierpoint, Powell *lawyer*
Pietrzak, Alfred Robert *lawyer*
Pike, Laurence Bruce *retired lawyer*
Pitts, Thomas E. *lawyer*
Plant, David William *lawyer*
Podos-Untermeyer, Salle *lawyer*
Polak, Vivian Louise *lawyer*
Polak, Werner L. *lawyer*
Pollack, Stanley P. *lawyer*
Pollak, Martin Marshall *lawyer, patent development company executive*
Portnoy, Sara S. *lawyer*
Posen, Susan Orzack *lawyer*
Potter, Hamilton Fish, Jr. *lawyer, consultant, author*
Povell, Roy Albert *lawyer*
Powell, James Henry *lawyer*
Powell, Richard Gordon *retired lawyer*
Preble, Laurence George *lawyer*
Preiskel, Barbara Scott *lawyer, association executive*
Prem, F. Herbert, Jr. *lawyer*
Prentice, Eugene Miles, III *lawyer*
Price, Robert *lawyer, media executive, investment banker*
Primps, William Guthrie *lawyer*
Prince, Kenneth Stephen *lawyer*
Profusek, Robert Alan *lawyer*
Puleo, Frank Charles *lawyer*
Purcell, James Lawrence *lawyer*
Quaintance, Robert Forsyth, Jr. *lawyer*
Quale, Andrew Christopher, Jr. *lawyer*
Quinlan, Guy Christian *lawyer*
Quinn, Yvonne Susan *lawyer*
Raab, Sheldon *lawyer*
Rabb, Bruce *lawyer*
Rabb, Maxwell M. *lawyer, former ambassador*
Rabin, Jack *lawyer*
Rahm, David Alan *lawyer*
Rahm, Susan Berkman *lawyer*
Raisler, Kenneth Mark *lawyer*
Rakoff, Jed Saul *lawyer, author*
Ralli, Constantine Pandia *lawyer*
Rand, Harry Israel *lawyer*
Rand, William *lawyer, former state justice*
Rankin, Clyde Evan, III *lawyer*
Rapaczynski, Andrzej *law educator*
Rapoport, Bernard Robert *lawyer*
Rappaport, Charles Owen *lawyer*
Ravitch, Beverly *lawyer*
Raylesberg, Alan Ira *lawyer*
Redlich, Norman *lawyer, educator*
Reibstein, Richard Jay *lawyer*
Reich, Larry Sam *lawyer*
Reich, Seymour David *lawyer, former fraternal organization executive*
Reich, Yaron Z. *lawyer*
Reid, John Phillip *law educator*
Reid, Sarah Layfield *lawyer*
Reilly, Edward Arthur *lawyer*
Reinhold, Richard Lawrence *lawyer*
Reinstein, Paul Michael *lawyer*
Reinthaler, Richard Walter *lawyer*
Reis, Muriel Henle *lawyer, broadcast executive, commentator*
Reiss, Steven Alan *lawyer, law educator*
Relson, Morris *patent lawyer*
Rembar, Charles (Isaiah) *lawyer, writer*
Resor, Stanley Rogers *lawyer*
Reverdin, Bernard J. *lawyer*
Revesz, Richard Luis *law educator*
Reynolds, Clayton S. *lawyer*
Ribicoff, Abraham A. *lawyer, former senator*
Rice, Donald Sands *lawyer*
Rice, Joseph Lee, III *lawyer*
Rich, R(obert) Bruce *lawyer*
Richards, David A. J. *lawyer, educator*
Richards, David Alan *lawyer*
Richman, Martin Franklin *lawyer*
Rifkind, Robert S(inger) *lawyer*
Rifkind, Simon Hirsch *lawyer*
Ring, Renee E. *lawyer*
Ringel, Dean *lawyer*
Ringer, James Milton *lawyer*
Ritter, Robert Joseph *lawyer*
Roberts, Sidney I. *lawyer*
Robertson, Edwin David *lawyer*
Robinowitz, Stuart *lawyer*
Robinson, Barbara Paul *lawyer*
Robinson, Irwin Jay *lawyer*
Robinson, Lee Harris *lawyer*
Rocklen, Kathy Hellenbrand *lawyer, banker*
Rodman, Leroy Eli *lawyer*
Rodriguez, Vincent Angel *lawyer*
Roe, Mark J. *law educator*
Roessler, Ronald James *lawyer*
Rogers, Edmund Pendleton, III *lawyer*
Rolfe, Ronald Stuart *lawyer*
Romans, John Niebrugge *lawyer*
Romney, Richard Bruce *lawyer*
Rooney, Paul C., Jr. *lawyer*
Rosdeitcher, Sidney Samuel *lawyer*
Rose, Jerome Gerald *lawyer*
Rose, Milton Curtiss *lawyer*
Rosen, J(oshua) Philip *lawyer*
Rosen, Richard Lewis *lawyer, real estate developer*
Rosenberg, Alan Stewart *lawyer*
Rosenberg, Jerome I. *lawyer*
Rosenberg, Marianne *lawyer*
Rosenberg, Maurice *lawyer, educator*
Rosenberg, Stephen *lawyer*
Rosenfeld, Arthur H. *lawyer, publisher*
Rosenfeld, Steven B. *lawyer*
Rosensaft, Menachem Zwi *lawyer, author, community activist*
Rosow, Stuart L. *lawyer*
Ross, Michael Aaron *lawyer*
Roth, Judith Shulman *lawyer*
Roth, Michael I. *lawyer, financial executive*
Roth, Paul Norman *lawyer*
Rothenberg, Peter Jay *lawyer*
Rothman, Bernard *lawyer*
Rothman, Henry Isaac *lawyer*
Rothman, Howard Joel *lawyer*
Rover, Edward Frank *lawyer*
Rovine, Arthur William *lawyer*
Rozel, Samuel Joseph *lawyer*
Rubenfeld, Stanley Irwin *lawyer*
Rubenstein, Joshua Seth *lawyer*
Rubin, Herbert *lawyer*
Rubin, Jane Lockhart Gregory *lawyer*
Rubin, Richard Allan *lawyer*
Rubin, Stephen Wayne *lawyer*
Rubino, Victor Joseph *law institute executive*
Rubinstein, Aaron *lawyer*
Rubinstein, Frederic Armand *lawyer*
Rudoff, Sheldon *lawyer, former religious organization executive*
Ruebhausen, Oscar Melick *lawyer*
Ruegger, Philip Theophil, III *lawyer*
Ruggiero, Thomas William *lawyer*
Rusmisel, Stephen R. *lawyer*
Russell, John St. Clair, Jr. *lawyer*
Russo, Gregory Thomas *lawyer*
Russo, Thomas Anthony *lawyer*
Ryan, J. Richard *lawyer*
Ryan, Michael Clifford *lawyer*
Ryan, Michael Lee *lawyer*
Sabel, Bradley Kent *lawyer*
Sachs, David *lawyer*
Sack, Robert David *lawyer*
Sacks, Ira Stephen *lawyer*
Safer, Jay Gerald *lawyer*
Sager, Lawrence Gene *law educator*
Sahid, Joseph Robert *lawyer*
Saiman, Martin S. *lawyer*
Salberg, Melvin *lawyer*
†Salter, Kevin Thornton *lawyer*
Sanders, Fredric M. *lawyer*
Sandler, Richard Jay *lawyer*
Sandler, Ross *law educator*
Sanger, Gail *lawyer*
Sargent, James Cunningham *lawyer*
Satine, Barry Roy *lawyer*
Saunders, Paul Christopher *lawyer*
Savrin, Louis *lawyer*
Scala, Gale G. *lawyer*
Schacht, Ronald Stuart *lawyer*
Schachter, Oscar *lawyer, educator, arbitrator*
Schade, Malcolm Robert *lawyer*
Schaffer, Seth Andrew *lawyer*
Schallert, Edwin Glenn *lawyer*
Schapiro, Donald *lawyer*
Schechter, Daniel Philip *lawyer*
Scheler, Brad Eric *lawyer*
Schenk, Deborah Huffman *law educator*
Scher, Irving *lawyer*
Scher, Stanley Jules *lawyer*
Schirmeister, Charles F. *lawyer*
Schizer, Zevie Baruch *lawyer*
Schlein, Carol Leslie *lawyer*
Schlesinger, Sanford Joel *lawyer*
Schmertz, Eric Joseph *lawyer, educator*
Schmolka, Leo Louis *law educator*
Schnall, Flora *lawyer*
Schneider, Howard *lawyer*
Schneider, Willys Hope *lawyer*
Schneiderman, Irwin *lawyer*
Schreiber, Paul Solomon *lawyer*

Schreyer, Leslie John *lawyer*
Schroeder, Edmund R. *lawyer*
Schueller, Thomas George *lawyer*
Schulte, Stephen John *lawyer, educator*
Schuur, Robert George *lawyer*
Schwab, Terrance Walter *lawyer*
Schwarcz, Steven Lance *lawyer*
Schwartz, Herbert Frederick *lawyer*
Schwartz, Marvin *lawyer*
Schwartz, Renee Gerstler *lawyer*
Schwartz, William *lawyer, educator*
Schwarz, Melvin A. *lawyer*
Schwind, Michael Angelo *law educator*
Scott, Helen S. *law educator*
Seaman, Robert Lee *lawyer*
Secunda, Don Elliott *lawyer, realtor*
Sederbaum, Arthur David *lawyer*
Segall, Harold Abraham *lawyer*
Seidler, Norman Howard *lawyer*
Seifert, Thomas Lloyd *lawyer*
Seigel, Stuart Evan *lawyer*
Seltzer, Richard C. *lawyer*
Selver, Paul Darryl *lawyer*
Semaya, Francine L. *lawyer*
Senzel, Martin Lee *lawyer*
Serbaroli, Francis J. *lawyer, educator, writer*
Serota, James Ian *lawyer*
Serota, Susan Perlstadt *lawyer*
Setrakian, Berge *lawyer*
Severs, Charles A., III *lawyer*
Seward, George Chester *lawyer*
Sexton, John Edward *lawyer, educator*
Sexton, Richard *lawyer, diversified manufacturing company executive*
Shachar, Avishai *lawyer*
Shanman, James Alan *lawyer*
Shapiro, George M. *lawyer*
Shapiro, Howard Alan *lawyer*
Shapiro, Ivan *lawyer*
Shapiro, Jerome Gerson *lawyer*
Sharpe, Jean Elizabeth *lawyer*
Shaw, L. Edward, Jr. *lawyer*
Shays, Rona Joyce *lawyer*
Shea, Edward Emmett *lawyer, educator, author*
Shea, James William *lawyer*
Sheehan, Robert W. *lawyer*
Shelby, Jerome *lawyer*
Shepard, Robert M. *lawyer, investment banker, engineer*
Sherman, Randolph S. *lawyer*
Sherman, Saul Lawrence *lawyer, government official*
Shientag, Florence Perlow *lawyer*
Shimer, Zachary *lawyer*
Shorter, James Russell, Jr. *lawyer*
Shoss, Cynthia Renée *lawyer*
Shupack, Paul Martin *law educator*
Shwartz, Robert N. *lawyer*
Shyer, John D. *lawyer*
Sidamon-Eristoff, Constantine *lawyer*
Siegel, Jeffrey Norton *lawyer*
Siegel, Martin Jay *lawyer, investment advisor*
Siegel, Stanley *lawyer, educator*
Silberberg, Richard Howard *lawyer*
Silberman, John Alan *lawyer*
Silberman, Linda Joy *lawyer, educator*
Silkenat, James Robert *lawyer*
Silleck, Harry Garrison *lawyer*
Silverberg, Michael Joel *lawyer*
Silverman, Arthur Charles *lawyer*
Silverman, Moses *lawyer*
Silverman, Samuel Joshua *lawyer*
Silvers, Eileen S. *lawyer*
Simon, Caroline K(lein) *lawyer*
Simone, Joseph R. *lawyer*
Simons, Albert, III *lawyer*
Simpson, Linda Ann *lawyer*
Sinsheimer, Warren Jack *lawyer*
Siphron, Joseph Rider *lawyer*
Sisk, Robert Joseph *lawyer*
Siskind, Arthur *lawyer, director*
Siskind, Donald Henry *lawyer*
Sitrick, James Baker *lawyer*
Sive, David *lawyer*
Skigen, Patricia Sue *lawyer*
Skirnick, Robert Andrew *lawyer*
Sklarew, Cary Stewart *lawyer*
Slain, John Joseph *legal educator*
Slate, William Kenneth, II *international dispute resolution association executive*
Slater, Jill Sherry *lawyer*
Slonaker, Norman Dale *lawyer*
Small, Jeffrey *lawyer, law educator*
Small, Jonathan Andrew *lawyer*
Smalley, David Vincent *lawyer*
Smart, L(ouis) Edwin, Jr. *lawyer, business executive*
Smit, Hans *law educator, academic administrator, lawyer*
Smith, Bradley Youle *lawyer*
Smith, Edward Paul, Jr. *lawyer*
Smith, R. Evan *lawyer*
Smith, Robert Everett *lawyer*
Smith, Stuart A. *lawyer*
Smith, Vincent Milton *lawyer*
Snitow, Charles *lawyer*
Solinger, David Morris *lawyer*
Solomon, Joseph *lawyer*
Somerville, Theodore Elkin *lawyer*
Songster, John Hugh *legal administrator*
Sorensen, Theodore Chaikin *lawyer, former special counsel to President of U.S.*
Sorkin, Laurence Truman *lawyer*
Sovern, Michael Ira *law educator*
Soyster, Margaret Blair *lawyer*
Spatt, Robert Edward *lawyer*
Spear, Harvey M. *lawyer*
Sperling, Allan George *lawyer*
Spivack, Gordon Bernard *lawyer, lecturer*
Spizzirri, Richard Dominic *lawyer*
Squire, Walter Charles *lawyer*
Stanger, Abraham M. *lawyer*
Stein, Stephen William *lawyer*
Steinberg, Arthur Jay *lawyer*
Steinberg, Howard Eli *lawyer, holding company executive*
Steiner, Lee Nathan *lawyer*
Stephenson, Alan Clements *lawyer*
Stergios, Peter Doe *lawyer*
Stern, Joseph A. *lawyer*
Stern, Lewis Arthur *lawyer*
Sternman, Joel W. *lawyer*
Steuer, Richard Marc *lawyer*
Stevenson, Justin Jason, III *lawyer*
Stever, Donald Winfred *lawyer*
Stewart, Charles Evan *lawyer*
Stewart, Duncan James *lawyer*
Stewart, Richard Burleson *lawyer, educator*
Steyer, Roy Henry *retired lawyer*
†Stiles, Ned Berry *lawyer*
Stocker, Jule E(lias) *lawyer*
Stoll, Neal Richard *lawyer*
Stone, David Philip *lawyer*
Stone, Lewis Bart *lawyer*
Stone, Merrill Brent *lawyer*
Stone, Richard B. *law educator*
Storette, Ronald Frank *lawyer*
Stratton, Walter Love *lawyer*
Straub, Chester John *lawyer*
Strauber, Donald I. *lawyer*
Straus, Alan Gordon *lawyer*
Strauss, Audrey *lawyer*
Strauss, Peter L(ester) *law educator*
Strickon, Harvey Alan *lawyer*
Strom, Milton Gary *lawyer*
Strossen, Nadine *law educator, human rights activist*
Strum, Jay Gerson *lawyer*
Strupp, David John *lawyer*
Struve, Guy Miller *lawyer*
Sugarman, Irwin J. *lawyer*
Sugarman, Robert Gary *lawyer*
Suhr, J. Nicholas *lawyer*
Sulger, Francis Xavier *lawyer*
Sussman, Alexander Ralph *lawyer*
Sutter, Laurence Brener *lawyer*
Sweeney, Thomas Joseph, Jr. *lawyer*
Symmers, William Garth *international maritime lawyer*
Tabak, Ronald Jerome *lawyer*
Tallackson, Jeffrey Stephen *lawyer*
Tanenbaum, Gerald Stephen *lawyer*
Taubin, Robin Livingston *lawyer*
Taylor, John Chestnut, III *lawyer*
Taylor, Richard Trelore *retired lawyer*
Taylor, Telford *lawyer, educator*
Teclaff, Ludwik Andrzej *law educator, consultant, author, lawyer*
Tehan, John Bashir *lawyer*
Teiman, Richard B. *lawyer*
Tengi, Frank R. *lawyer, insurance company executive*
Tenney, Dudley Bradstreet *lawyer*
Terrell, J. Anthony *lawyer*
Terry, Frederick Arthur, Jr. *lawyer*
Terry, James Joseph, Jr. *lawyer*
Testa, Michael Harold *lawyer*
Thackeray, Jonathan E. *lawyer*
Thalacker, Arbie Robert *lawyer*
Thoman, Mark *lawyer*
Thomas, Robert Morton, Jr. *lawyer*
Thomas, Roger Warren *lawyer*
Thompson, Robert L., Jr. *lawyer*
Thornton, John Vincent *lawyer, educator*
Thoyer, Judith Reinhardt *lawyer*
Tillinghast, David Rollhaus *lawyer*
Todd, Ronald Gary *lawyer*
Toepke, Utz Peter *lawyer*
Tondel, Lawrence Chapman *lawyer*
Tortoriello, Robert Laurence *lawyer*
Tracy, Janet Ruth *legal educator, librarian*
Tramontine, John O. *lawyer*
Traub, Richard Kenneth *lawyer*
Traum, Jerome S. *lawyer*
Trost, J. Ronald *lawyer*
Trubin, John *lawyer*
Tuck, Edward Hallam *lawyer*
Tulchin, David Bruce *lawyer*
Tung, Ko-Yung *lawyer*
Turner, E. Deane *lawyer*
Tyler, Harold Russell, Jr. *lawyer, former government official*
Udell, Richard *lawyer*
Ufford, Charles Wilbur, Jr. *lawyer*
Underberg, Mark Alan *lawyer*
Unger, Ronald Lawrence *lawyer*
Urowsky, Richard J. *lawyer*
Urquia, Rafael, II *lawyer*
Uviller, H. Richard *law educator*
Vance, Andrew Peter *lawyer*
Vance, Cyrus Roberts *lawyer, former government official*
Van Gundy, Gregory Frank *lawyer*
Varet, Michael A. *lawyer*
Vega, Matias Alfonso *lawyer*
Versfelt, David Scott *lawyer*
Victor, A. Paul *lawyer*
Viener, John D. *lawyer*
Vig, Vernon Edward *lawyer*
Vitkowsky, Vincent Joseph *lawyer*
Vogel, Eugene L. *lawyer*
Volckhausen, William Alexander *lawyer, banker*
Volk, Stephen Richard *lawyer*
von Mehren, Robert Brandt *lawyer*
Wachtel, Harry H. *lawyer, chain store executive*
Wachtel, Norman Jay *lawyer*
Wade, George Joseph *lawyer*
Wadsworth, Dyer Seymour *lawyer*
Wailand, George *lawyer*
Wainwright, Carroll Livingston, Jr. *lawyer*
Waks, Jay Warren *lawyer*
Waksman, Ted Stewart *lawyer*
Wald, Bernard Joseph *lawyer*
Waldbaum, Maxim Howard *lawyer*
Wales, Gwynne Huntington *lawyer*
Walker, Charles R., III *lawyer*
Walker, John Lockwood *lawyer*
Walker, Mark A. *lawyer*
Wallace, Walter C. *lawyer, government official*
Wallach, Eric Jean *lawyer*
Wallance, Gregory J. *lawyer*
Walpin, Gerald *lawyer*
Walsh, Kevin A. *lawyer*
Walton, Eileen Rowan *lawyer*
Warden, John L. *lawyer*
Warhaftig, Solomon L. *lawyer*
Warner, Edward Waide, Jr. *lawyer*
Warren, Irwin Howard *lawyer*
Warren, William Bradford *lawyer*
Warren, William Clements *lawyer, educator*
Warshauer, Irene Conrad *lawyer*
Warsoff, Stanley L. *lawyer*
Washburn, David Thacher *lawyer*
Watson, John King, Jr. *lawyer*
Watson, Solomon Brown, IV *lawyer, business executive*
Wattman, Malcolm Peter *lawyer*
Watts, David Eide *lawyer*
Wechsler, Herbert *retired legal educator*
Weil, Gilbert Harry *lawyer*
Weil, Peter Henry *lawyer*
Weinberg, Herschel Mayer *lawyer*
Weinberg, Jeffrey J. *lawyer*
Weinberger, Harold Paul *lawyer*
Weiner, Earl David *lawyer*
Weiner, Stephen Arthur *lawyer*
Weinschel, Alan Jay *lawyer*
Weinstein, Mark Michael *lawyer*
Weinstein, Ruth Joseph *lawyer*
Weinstock, Leonard *lawyer*
Weir, Peter Frank *lawyer*
†Weisbrod, Carl Barry *lawyer, public official*
Weiss, Brian *lawyer*
Weiss, George C. *lawyer*
Weiss, Melvyn I. *lawyer*
Weiswasser, Stephen Anthony *lawyer, broadcast executive*
Weld, Jonathan Minot *lawyer*
Welikson, Jeffrey Alan *lawyer*
Welles, James Bell, Jr. *lawyer*
Wellington, Harry Hillel *lawyer, educator*
Weltchek, Paul Richard *lawyer*
Wemple, William *lawyer*
Wender, Ira Tensard *lawyer*
Werner, Robert L. *lawyer*
Wesely, Edwin Joseph *lawyer*
West, Stephen Kingsbury *lawyer*
Westin, David Lawrence *lawyer*
Wetzler, Monte Edwin *lawyer*
Weyher, Harry Frederick *lawyer*
Whelan, Stephen Thomas *lawyer*
White, Harry Edward, Jr. *lawyer*
White, Thomas Edward *lawyer*
Whitworth, John Harvey, Jr. *lawyer*
Whoriskey, Robert Donald *lawyer*
Wickes, R(ichard) Paul *lawyer*
Wilcox, John Caven *lawyer, corporate consultant*
Wildes, Leon *lawyer, educator*
Wilkinson, Donald Michael, Jr. *lawyer*
Wilkinson, John Hart *lawyer*
Williams, Anthony *lawyer*
Williams, Lowell Craig *lawyer, employee relations executive*
Williams, Omer S. J. *lawyer*
Williams, Thomas Allison *lawyer*
Williams, Vaughn Charles *lawyer*
Williamson, Douglas Franklin, Jr. *lawyer*
Willis, Everett Irving *lawyer*
Willis, William Ervin *lawyer*
Willkie, Wendell Lewis, II *lawyer*
Wilson, Paul Holliday, Jr. *lawyer*
Windels, Paul, Jr. *lawyer*
Wing, John Russell *lawyer*
Winger, Ralph O. *lawyer*
Winterer, Philip Steele *lawyer*
Wise, Robert F., Jr. *lawyer*
Wisehart, Arthur McKee *lawyer*
Woglom, Eric Cooke *lawyer*
Wohl, Ronald Gene *lawyer*
Wolf, Gary Wickert *lawyer*
Wolfe, James Ronald *lawyer*
Wolff, Jesse David *lawyer*
Wolff, Kurt Jakob *lawyer*
Wolff, Sanford Irving *lawyer*
Wolfson, Michael George *lawyer*
Wolkoff, Eugene Arnold *lawyer*
Wolowitz, Steven *lawyer*
Wolson, Craig Alan *lawyer*
Woo, Frances Mei Soo *lawyer*
Woodbury, Thomas Bowring, II *lawyer, public utility executive*
Woods, Laurie *lawyer*
Worenklein, Jacob Joshua *lawyer*
Worley, Robert William, Jr. *lawyer*
Wray, Cecil, Jr. *lawyer*
Wright, Franklin Leatherbury, Jr. *lawyer, banker*
Wright, P(aul) Bruce *lawyer*
Wulf, Melvin Lawrence *lawyer*
Wyckoff, Edward Lisk, Jr. *lawyer*
Wyser-Pratte, John Michael *lawyer*
Yanowitch, Michael H. *lawyer*
Yassky, Lester *lawyer, banker*
Yerman, Fredric Warren *lawyer*
Yonkman, Fredrick Albers *lawyer, management consultant*
Young, Alice *lawyer*
Young, John Edward *lawyer*
Young, Nancy *lawyer*
Young, William F. *legal educator*
Youngwood, Alfred Donald *lawyer*
Zabel, William David *lawyer*
Zaitzeff, Roger Michael *lawyer*
Zedrosser, Joseph John *lawyer*
Zerin, Steven David *lawyer*
Ziegler, Michael Lewis *lawyer*
Ziegler, Richard Ferdinand *lawyer*
Ziegler, William Alexander *lawyer*
Zifchak, William C. *lawyer*
Zimand, Harvey Folks *lawyer*
Zimmerman, Diane Leenheer *law educator, lawyer*
Zimmerman, George Abraham *lawyer*
Zimmett, Mark Paul *lawyer*
Zirin, James David *lawyer*
Zoeller, Donald J. *lawyer*
Zoogman, Nicholas Jay *lawyer*
Zornow, David M. *lawyer*
Zukerman, Michael *lawyer*
Zweibel, Joel Burton *lawyer*
Zylberberg, Abraham Lieb *lawyer*

Niagara Falls
Anton, Ronald David *lawyer*

Oneida
Matthews, William D(oty) *lawyer, consumer products manufacturing company executive*
Rudnick, Marvin Jack *lawyer*

Orchard Park
Sullivan, Mortimer Allen, Jr. *lawyer*

Ossining
Daly, William Joseph *lawyer*

Oyster Bay
Robinson, Edward T., III *lawyer*

Pearl River
Meyer, Irwin Stephan *lawyer, accountant*
Riley, James Kevin *lawyer*

Peconic
Mitchell, Robert Everitt *lawyer*

Pelham
Simon, Robert G. *lawyer*

Pittsford
Kieffer, James Milton *lawyer*

Pleasantville
Ahrensfeld, Thomas Frederick *lawyer*
Needleman, Harry *lawyer*

Soden, Paul Anthony *lawyer*

Port Washington
Feldman, Jay Newman *lawyer, telecommunications executive*
Read, Frederick Wilson, Jr. *lawyer, educator*

Poughkeepsie
Dolan, Thomas Joseph *lawyer*
McEnroe, Caroline Ann *legal assistant*
Millman, Jode Susan *lawyer*
Ostertag, Robert Louis *lawyer*
St. John, Howard Chambers *lawyer, bank executive*

Pound Ridge
Bright, Craig Bartley *lawyer*

Purchase
Guedry, James Walter *lawyer, paper corporation executive*
Joyce, Joseph James *lawyer, food products executive*
Kelly, Edmund Joseph *lawyer, investment banker*
McKenna, Matthew Morgan *lawyer*
Melican, James Patrick, Jr. *lawyer*
Wallach, Ira David *lawyer, business executive*
Wilderotter, James Arthur *lawyer*

Richmond Hill
Scheich, John F. *lawyer*

Riverdale
Edelman, Samuel Irving *lawyer, financial executive*
Phocas, George John *international lawyer, business executive*

Riverhead
Maggipinto, V. Anthony *lawyer*

Rochester
Braunsdorf, Paul Raymond *lawyer*
Buckley, Michael Francis *lawyer*
Clement, Thomas Earl *lawyer*
Donovan, Kreag *lawyer*
Doyle, Justin P *lawyer*
Fink, Thomas A. *lawyer*
Fischer, Richard Samuel *lawyer*
Fox, Edward Hanton *lawyer*
George, Richard Neill *lawyer*
Goldman, Joel J. *lawyer*
Gootnick, Margery Fischbein *lawyer*
Gumaer, Elliott Wilder, Jr. *lawyer*
Hampson, Thomas Meredith *lawyer*
Harris, Wayne Manley *lawyer*
Hellrung, Stephen Andrew *lawyer*
Hoffberg, David Lawrence *lawyer*
Holmes, Jay Thorpe *lawyer*
Hood, John B. *lawyer*
Kraus, Sherry Stokes *lawyer*
Kunkel, David Nelson *lawyer*
Kurland, Harold Arthur *lawyer*
Law, Michael R. *lawyer*
Lundback, Staffan Bengt Gunnar *lawyer*
McCrory, John Brooks *retired lawyer*
Morrison, Patrice B. *lawyer*
Palermo, Anthony Robert *lawyer*
Paley, Gerald Larry *lawyer*
Parsons, George Raymond, Jr. *lawyer*
Reed, James Alexander, Jr. *lawyer*
Robfogel, Susan Salitan *lawyer*
Rosenbaum, Richard Merrill *lawyer*
Schumacher, Jon Lee *lawyer*
Scutt, Robert Carl *lawyer*
Smith, John Stuart *lawyer*
Stewart, Sue Stern *lawyer*
Stonehill, Eric *lawyer*
Tomaino, Michael Thomas *lawyer*
Trueheart, Harry Parker, III *lawyer*
Turri, Joseph A. *lawyer*
Tyler, John Randolph *lawyer*
Underberg, Alan J. *lawyer*
Van Graafeiland, Gary P. *lawyer*
Waite, Stephen Holden *lawyer*
Wild, Robert Warren *lawyer*
Willett, Thomas Edward *lawyer*
Witmer, George Robert, Jr. *lawyer*

Rockville Centre
Halliday, Walter John *lawyer*

Rome
Griffith, Emlyn Irving *lawyer*

Rye
Flanagan, Eugene John Thomas *retired lawyer*
Varona, Daniel Robert *lawyer, insurance company executive*

Saratoga Springs
Aldrich, Alexander *lawyer*

Scarsdale
Hoffman, Richard M. *lawyer*
Howard, John Brigham *lawyer, foundation executive*
O'Brien, Edward Ignatius *lawyer, private investor*
Wertheimer, Sydney Bernard *lawyer*

Schoharie
Duncombe, Raynor Bailey *lawyer*

Silver Bay
Parlin, Charles C., Jr. *retired lawyer*

Smithtown
Holland, Marvin Arthur *lawyer*
Pruzansky, Joshua Murdock *lawyer*

Staten Island
Henry, Paul James *lawyer, health care administrator*
Pennington, Catherine Ann *legal technology consultant*

Syracuse
Baldwin, Robert Frederick, Jr. *lawyer*
Barclay, H(ugh) Douglas *lawyer, former state senator*
Beeching, Charles Train, Jr. *lawyer*
Cirando, John Anthony *lawyer*
DiLorenzo, Louis Patrick *lawyer*
Ferguson, Tracy Heiman *lawyer, educational administrator*
Fitzpatrick, James David *lawyer*
Fraser, Henry S. *lawyer*

Gaal, John lawyer
Hayes, David Michael lawyer
Herzog, Peter Emilius legal educator
Hole, Richard Douglas lawyer
King, Bernard T. lawyer
King, Chester Harding, Jr. lawyer
Kopp, Robert Walter lawyer
Lawton, Joseph J., Jr. lawyer
Moses, Robert Edward lawyer
Murray, Raymond William, Jr. lawyer
Pellow, David Matthew lawyer
Shattuck, George Clement lawyer
Taylor, Richard Fred, Jr. lawyer
Wiecek, William Michael law educator

Tarrytown
Oelbaum, Harold lawyer, corporate executive

Troy
Jones, E. Stewart, Jr. lawyer

Tuxedo Park
Brown, Walston Shepard lawyer

Uniondale
Brown, Kenneth Lloyd lawyer
Pierce, Stanley lawyer
Shapiro, Barry Robert lawyer
Waldhof, Sharka Eva lawyer

Valley Stream
Blakeman, Royal Edwin lawyer

Wainscott
Wainwright, Stuyvesant, II lawyer

White Plains
Alin, Robert David lawyer
Berlin, Alan Daniel lawyer, international energy and legal consultant
Burke, Raymond F. lawyer
Carey, John lawyer, judge
Gjertsen, O. Gerard lawyer
Goldberg, Steven H. law educator
Jensen, Eric Finn lawyer
Johnson, Daniel Robert lawyer
Johnson, Janet A. law educator, academic dean
McQuaid, John G. lawyer
Munneke, Gary Arthur law educator, consultant
Payson, Martin Fred lawyer
Rosenberg, Michael lawyer
Teitell, Conrad Laurence lawyer, author
Triffin, Nicholas law librarian, law educator
Vergari, Carl Anthony lawyer
Wefer, Donald Peters lawyer
Westerman, Gayl Shaw law educator

Wolcott
Bartlett, Cody Blake lawyer, educator

Woodbury
Lemle, Robert Spencer lawyer

Woodmere
Bobroff, Harold lawyer
Raab, Ira Jerry lawyer

Yorktown Heights
Samalin, Edwin lawyer, educator

NORTH CAROLINA

Asheville
Baldwin, Garza, Jr. lawyer, manufacturing company executive
Bissette, Winston Louis, Jr. lawyer, mayor
Davis, Roy Walton, Jr. lawyer
Hyde, Herbert Lee lawyer
Johnston, John Devereaux, Jr. law educator
Sharpe, Keith Yount lawyer

Black Mountain
Pinkerton, Linda F. lawyer

Buies Creek
Davis, Ferd Leary, Jr. law educator, lawyer, consultant

Chapel Hill
Broun, Kenneth Stanley lawyer, educator
Clifford, Donald Francis, Jr. law educator
Crohn, Max Henry, Jr. lawyer
Gasaway, Laura Nell law librarian, educator
Gressman, Eugene lawyer
Haskell, Paul Gershon law educator
Lawrence, David Michael lawyer, educator
Loeb, Ben Fohl, Jr. lawyer, educator
Oliver, Mary Wilhelmina law librarian, educator
Powell, Burnele Venable law educator
Sharpless, Richard Kennedy lawyer
Wegner, Judith Welch lawyer, educator, university dean

Charlotte
Ayscue, Edwin Osborne, Jr. lawyer
Belthoff, Richard Charles, Jr. lawyer
Buchan, Jonathan Edward, Jr. lawyer
Clodfelter, Daniel Gray lawyer
Cogdell, Joe Bennett, Jr. lawyer
Dagenhart, Larry Jones lawyer
Davis, Jeffrey J. lawyer
Davis, William Maxie, Jr. lawyer
Ferguson, James Elliot, II lawyer
Gage, Gaston Hemphill lawyer
Grier, Joseph Williamson, Jr. lawyer
Griffith, Steve Campbell, Jr. lawyer
Hanna, George Verner, III lawyer
Helms, Fred Bryan lawyer
McBryde, Neill Gregory lawyer
McConnell, David Moffatt lawyer
Norwood, Philip Weltner lawyer
Orsbon, Richard Anthony lawyer
Raper, William Cranford lawyer
Taylor, David Brooke lawyer, banker
Thigpen, Richard Elton, Jr. lawyer
Ubell, Donald Paul lawyer
Van Allen, William Kent lawyer
Vinroot, Richard Allen lawyer, mayor
Walker, Clarence Wesley lawyer
Wood, William McBrayer lawyer

Woolard, William Leon lawyer, electrical distributing company executive

Durham
Bartlett, Katharine Tiffany law educator
Baxter, Lawrence Gerald law educator, consultant
Beale, Sara Sun law educator
Bernstein, Herbert L. law educator
Carrington, Paul DeWitt lawyer, educator
Chambers, Julius LeVonne lawyer
Christie, George Custis lawyer, educator, author
†Costa, Santo Joseph lawyer
Cox, James D. law educator
Danner, Richard Allen law educator, dean
Dellinger, Walter Estes, III lawyer
Demott, Deborah Ann lawyer, educator
Fish, Peter Graham law educator
Haagen, Paul Hess law educator
Hauerwas, Stanley Martin law educator, theologian
Havighurst, Clark Canfield law educator
Holton, Charles R. lawyer
Horowitz, Donald Leonard lawyer, educator, researcher, political scientist, arbitrator
Kirk-Duggan, Michael Allan retired law and computer sciences educator
Lange, David L. law educator
Lorelli, Charles A. lawyer, chemical company executive
Markham, Charles Buchanan lawyer
Maxwell, Richard Callender lawyer, educator
McMahon, John Alexander lawyer, educator
Mosteller, Robert P. law educator
†Powell, H. Jefferson law educator
Reppy, William Arneill, Jr. law educator
Robertson, Horace Bascomb, Jr. law educator
Rowe, Thomas Dudley, Jr. law educator
Schroeder, Christopher H. law educator
Shimm, Melvin Gerald law educator
Sparks, Bertel Milas lawyer, educator
Van Alstyne, William Warner law educator
Warren, David Grant lawyer, educator
Weistart, John C. law educator
Welborn, Reich Lee lawyer

Gastonia
Alala, Joseph Basil, Jr. lawyer, accountant
Stott, Grady Bernell lawyer

Gibsonville
Foster, C(harles) Allen lawyer

Greensboro
Davis, Herbert Owen lawyer
Erwin, Martin Nesbitt lawyer
Floyd, Jack William lawyer
Gumbiner, Kenneth Jay lawyer
Harllee, JoAnn Towery lawyer, educator
Hopkins, John David lawyer
Hunter, Bynum Merritt lawyer
Koonce, Neil Wright lawyer
Melvin, Charles Edward, Jr. lawyer
Moore, Beverly Cooper lawyer
Rowlenson, Richard Charles lawyer
St. George, Nicholas James lawyer, manufactured housing company executive
Schell, Braxton lawyer
Smith, John McNeill, Jr. lawyer
Smith, Lanty L(loyd) lawyer, business executive
Swan, George Steven lawyer, educator

High Point
Sheahan, Robert Emmett lawyer, management employment and environment law consultant

Horse Shoe
Howell, George Washington lawyer, consultant

Morganton
Simpson, Daniel Reid lawyer

New Bern
Kellum, Norman Bryant, Jr. lawyer
Skipper, Nathan Richard, Jr. lawyer

Raleigh
Andrews, William Parker, Jr. lawyer
Carlton, Alfred Pershing, Jr. lawyer
Case, Charles Dixon lawyer
Dannelly, William D. lawyer
Davis, Egbert Lawrence, III lawyer
Dixon, Wright Tracy, Jr. lawyer
Eason, Joseph W. lawyer
Edwards, Charles Archibald lawyer
Ellis, Lester Neal, Jr. lawyer
Foley, Peter Michael lawyer
Graham, William Edgar, Jr. lawyer, retired utility company executive
Head, Allan Bruce bar association executive
Joyner, Gary Kelton lawyer
Joyner, Walton Kitchin lawyer
Maupin, Armistead Jones lawyer
Miller, Ralph Bradley lawyer, former state legislator
Miller, Robert James lawyer
Patterson, William S. lawyer
Powell, Durwood Royce lawyer
Poyner, James Marion retired lawyer
Ragsdale, George Robinson lawyer
Roach, Wesley Linville lawyer, insurance executive
Robson, Charles Baskervill, Jr. lawyer
Rosen, Lee Spencer lawyer
Sanford, Terry lawyer, educator, former U.S. senator, former governor, former university president
Shyllon, Prince E.N. lawyer, law educator
Suhr, Paul Augustine lawyer

Rocky Mount
Condon, Breen O'Malley lawyer
Cooper, Roy Asberry, III lawyer, state senator
Parsons-Salem, Diane Lora lawyer

Salisbury
Trexler, Wynn Ridenhour paralegal

Sanford
Raisig, Paul Jones, Jr. lawyer

Tabor City
Jorgensen, Ralph Gubler lawyer

Tarboro
Hopkins, Grover Prevatte lawyer

Tryon
Stinson, George Arthur lawyer, former steel company executive

Williamston
Cowen, Robert Henry lawyer

Wilmington
Block, Franklin Lee lawyer

Wilson
Herring, Jerone Carson lawyer, bank executive

Winston Salem
Barnhardt, Zeb Elonzo, Jr. lawyer
Benfield, Marion Wilson, Jr. lawyer, educator
Blynn, Guy Marc lawyer
Copenhaver, W. Andrew lawyer
Corbett, Leon H., Jr. lawyer, educator, university official
Davis, Linwood Layfield lawyer
Davis, William Allison, II lawyer
Donahue, Daniel William lawyer
Farr, Henry Bartow, Jr. lawyer
Foy, Herbert Miles, III lawyer, educator
Gitter, Allan Reinhold lawyer
Greason, Murray Crossley, Jr. lawyer
Healy, Joseph Francis, Jr. lawyer, arbitrator, retired airline executive
Leonard, R. Michael lawyer
Newton, George Durfee, Jr. lawyer
†Petree, William Horton lawyer
Ray, Michael Edwin lawyer
Sandridge, William Pendleton, Jr. lawyer
Schollander, Wendell Leslie, Jr. lawyer
Steele, Thomas McKnight law librarian, law educator
Strayhorn, Ralph Nichols, Jr. lawyer
Sullivan, William Beaumont lawyer
Vance, Charles Fogle, Jr. lawyer
Walker, George Kontz law educator
Wells, Dewey Wallace lawyer
Womble, William Fletcher lawyer
Zagoria, Sam D(avid) arbitrator, author, educator

NORTH DAKOTA

Bismarck
Maichel, Joseph Raymond lawyer, business executive
Murry, Charles Emerson lawyer, official
Nelson, Keithe Eugene lawyer, state court administrator
Olson, John Michael lawyer
Strutz, William A. lawyer
Torgerson, Les bar association administrator

Grand Forks
Vogel, Robert lawyer, educator
Widdel, John Earl, Jr. lawyer

Jamestown
Hjellum, John retired lawyer

OHIO

Akron
Bartlo, Sam D. lawyer
Calise, Nicholas James lawyer
Childs, James William lawyer, legal educator
Fisher, James Lee lawyer
Haller, Sonja Maria lawyer
Heider, Jon Vinton lawyer, corporate executive
Holloway, Donald Phillip lawyer
†Lloyd, Philip Armour lawyer
Lombardi, Frederick McKean lawyer
Ong, John Doyle lawyer
Richert, Paul law educator
Schulz, Mary Elizabeth lawyer
Trotter, Thomas Robert lawyer

Barberton
Moss, Robert Drexler lawyer

Batavia
Rosenhoffer, Chris lawyer

Bowling Green
Hanna, Martin Shad lawyer
Holmes, Robert Allen lawyer, educator, consultant, lecturer

Canton
Bennington, Ronald Kent lawyer
Dettinger, Warren Walter lawyer
Lindamood, John Beyer lawyer
Mokodean, Michael John lawyer, accountant

Chagrin Falls
Streicher, James Franklin lawyer

Chesterland
Driggs, Charles Mulford lawyer
Durn, Raymond Joseph lawyer
Kancelbaum, Joshua Jacob lawyer

Cincinnati
Adams, Edmund John lawyer
Anderson, James Milton lawyer
Anderson, William Hopple lawyer
Anthony, Thomas Dale lawyer
Bahlman, William Thorne, Jr. retired lawyer
Blum, William Lee lawyer
Bridgeland, James Ralph, Jr. lawyer, mayor
Bromberg, Barbara Schwartz lawyer
Bromberg, Robert Sheldon lawyer
Carlson, Jennie Peaslack lawyer
Carro, Jorge Luis law librarian, educator
Carson, Nolan Wendell lawyer
Chesley, Stanley Morris lawyer
Christenson, Gordon A. law educator
Cissell, James Charles lawyer
Cody, Thomas Gerald lawyer
Cowan, Jerry Louis lawyer
Craig, L. Clifford lawyer
Dehner, Joseph Julnes lawyer
DeLong, Deborah lawyer
Diller, Edward Dietrich lawyer
Dornette, W(illiam) Stuart lawyer, educator
Elleman, Lawrence Robert lawyer

Erickson, Richard J. lawyer
Fagin, Richard litigation consultant
Faller, Susan Grogan lawyer
Fink, Jerold Albert lawyer
Finkelmeier, Philip Renner law librarian, lawyer
Freedman, William Mark lawyer
Garfinkel, Jane E. lawyer
Gettler, Benjamin lawyer, manufacturing company executive
Goodman, Stanley lawyer
Greenberg, Gerald Stephen lawyer
Guggenheim, Richard E. lawyer, shoe company executive
Hardy, William Robinson lawyer
Harris, Irving lawyer
Heinlen, Ronald Eugene lawyer
Hermanies, John Hans lawyer
Hess, Donald C. lawyer
Hill, Thomas Clark lawyer
Hoffheimer, Daniel Joseph lawyer
Hubschman, Henry Allan lawyer
Johnson, James J. lawyer
Kelley, John Joseph, Jr. lawyer
Kiel, Frederick Orin lawyer
Kite, William McDougall lawyer
Koepcke, F. Kristen corporate lawyer
Kordons, Uldis lawyer
Lawrence, James Kaufman Lebensburger lawyer
Lindberg, Charles David lawyer
Lloyd, David Livingstone, Jr. lawyer
Longenecker, Mark Hershey, Jr. lawyer
Lutz, James Gurney lawyer
Manley, Robert Edward lawyer, economist
Mann, David Scott lawyer
Mattingly, Paul R. lawyer
Maxwell, Robert Wallace, II lawyer
McClain, William Andrew lawyer
McCoy, John Joseph lawyer
McDowell, John Eugene lawyer
McGavran, Frederick Jaeger lawyer
Mc Henry, Powell lawyer
Meranus, Leonard Stanley lawyer
Monroe, Murray Shipley lawyer
Mooney, Donald James, Jr. lawyer
Naylor, Paul Donald lawyer
Nechemias, Stephen Murray lawyer
Neumark, Michael Harry lawyer
Olson, Robert Wyrick lawyer
O'Reilly, James Thomas lawyer, educator, author
Parker, R. Joseph lawyer
Phalen, Thomas Francis, Jr. lawyer
Phillips, T. Stephen lawyer
Puchta, Charles George lawyer
Ralston, James Allen lawyer
Reichert, David lawyer
Rich, Robert Edward lawyer
Roberts, Richard Stewart lawyer
Roe, Clifford Ashley, Jr. lawyer
Rose, Donald McGregor lawyer
Schmidt, Thomas Joseph, Jr. lawyer
Schuck, Thomas Robert lawyer
Scoggins, Samuel McWhirter lawyer
Shore, Thomas Spencer, Jr. lawyer
Silbersack, Mark Louis lawyer
†Streckfuss, James Arthur lawyer, historian
Swigert, James Mack lawyer
Tatgenhorst, (Charles) Robert lawyer
Taylor, Wayne Fletcher lawyer
Terp, Thomas Thomsen lawyer
Tobias, Charles Harrison, Jr. lawyer
Tobias, Paul Henry lawyer
Townsend, Robert J. lawyer
Vander Laan, Mark Alan lawyer
Wales, Ross Elliot lawyer
Warrington, John Wesley lawyer
Weeks, Steven Wiley lawyer
Yurchuck, Roger Alexander lawyer

Cleveland
Abram, Marian Christine lawyer
Adamo, Kenneth R. lawyer
Adams, Albert T. lawyer
Alfred, Stephen Jay lawyer
Andorka, Frank Henry lawyer
Andrews, Oakley V. lawyer
Arison, Barbara J. lawyer
Ashmus, Keith Allen lawyer
Atkinson, William Edward lawyer
Ault, Charles Rollin lawyer
Austin, Arthur Donald, II lawyer, educator
Azoff, Elliot Stephen lawyer
Babin, Mara L. lawyer
Bacon, Brett Kermit lawyer
Bamberger, Richard H. lawyer
Barnard, Thomas Harvie lawyer
Barnes, Geoffrey K. lawyer
Barnes de Resendiz, Susan lawyer
Barr, Douglas N. lawyer
Bates, Walter Alan former lawyer
Baughman, R(obert) Patrick lawyer
Baumgartner, Bruce O. lawyer
Baxter, Howard H. lawyer
Bennett, Paul Edward lawyer
Berger, Sanford Jason lawyer, securities dealer, real estate broker
Berick, James Herschel lawyer
Berry, Dean Lester lawyer
Besse, Ralph Moore lawyer
Bilchik, Gary B. lawyer
Binford, Gregory Glenn lawyer
Bixenstine, Kim Fenton lawyer
Blattner, Robert A. lawyer
Bodurtha, James H. lawyer
Borowitz, Albert Ira lawyer, author
Branagan, James Joseph lawyer
Braverman, Herbert Leslie lawyer
Bravo, Kenneth Allan lawyer
Brennan, Maureen A. lawyer
Brooks, Arthur V. N. lawyer
Brown, Seymour R. lawyer
Brown, Troy R. lawyer
Brucken, Robert Matthew lawyer
Bryenton, Gary Lynn lawyer
Buchmann, Alan Paul lawyer
Buescher, Stephen L. lawyer
Bumpass, T. Merritt, Jr. lawyer
Burke, Kathleen B. lawyer
Burlingame, John Hunter lawyer
Burns, Donald Andrew lawyer
Cairns, James Donald lawyer
Calfee, John Beverly retired lawyer
Calfee, William Lewis lawyer
Campbell, Paul Barton lawyer
Canary, Nancy Halliday lawyer
Carlson, James R. lawyer
Carrick, Kathleen Michele law librarian
Case, Betsey Brewster lawyer
Chapman, Diane P. lawyer

Clarke, Charles Fenton lawyer
Collin, Thomas James lawyer
Colombo, Louis A. lawyer
Cooper, Hal Dean lawyer
Coquillette, William Hollis lawyer
Cornell, John Robert lawyer
Coughlin, Barring lawyer
Coyle, Martin Adolphus, Jr. lawyer
Crist, Paul Grant lawyer
Cudak, Gail Linda lawyer
Currivan, John Daniel lawyer
Dakin, Carol F. lawyer
Dampeer, John Lyell lawyer
Daniels, Anthea Rena lawyer
Dempsey, James Howard, Jr. lawyer
Doris, Alan S(anford) lawyer
Downie, John Francis lawyer
Downing, George lawyer
Drinko, John Deaver lawyer
Duffy, John C., Jr. lawyer
Duncan, Ed Eugene lawyer
Dunn, John P. lawyer
Dunn, Leslie D. lawyer
Durham, Mary Lynn lawyer
Duvin, Robert Phillip lawyer
Dye, Sherman retired lawyer
Edwards, John Wesley, II lawyer
Ekelman, Daniel Louis lawyer
Eyre, Paul P. lawyer
Fabens, Andrew Lawrie, III lawyer
Fairweather, John C. lawyer
Falsgraf, William Wendell lawyer
Fay, Regan Joseph lawyer
Fay, Robert Jesse lawyer
Feinberg, Paul H. lawyer
Feliciano, José Celso lawyer
Fletcher, Robert lawyer, horologist
Friedman, Harold Edward lawyer
Friedman, Hyman lawyer
Friedman, James Moss lawyer
Fullmer, David R. lawyer
Garner, James Parent lawyer
Garver, Theodore Meyer lawyer
Gerhart, Peter Milton law educator
Gibson, Wendy Joan lawyer
Giles, Homer Wayne lawyer
Ginsberg, Edward lawyer
Ginsburg, Edward S. lawyer
Glaser, Robert Edward lawyer
Goins, Frances Floriano lawyer
Gold, Gerald Seymour lawyer
Goldfarb, Bernard Sanford lawyer
Goler, Michael David lawyer
Griswold, James B. lawyer
Groetzinger, Jon, Jr. lawyer, consumer products executive
Grossman, Theodore Martin lawyer
Gruettner, Donald W. lawyer
Grundstein, Nathan David lawyer, management science educator, management consultant
Gutfeld, Norman E. lawyer
Haiman, Irwin Sanford lawyer
Hamilton, J. Richard lawyer
Hammer, Daniel William lawyer
Hanna, Harry Adolphus lawyer
Hardy, Michael Lynn lawyer
Heddesheimer, Walter Jacob lawyer
Hermann, Philip J. lawyer
Hochman, Kenneth George lawyer
Hoerner, Robert Jack lawyer
Hollington, Richard Rings, Jr. lawyer
Hopkins, John S., III lawyer
Hopps, Sidney Bryce lawyer
Horvitz, Michael John lawyer
Inglis, Patricia Marcus lawyer
Jacobs, Leslie William lawyer
Janke, Ronald Robert lawyer
Jeavons, Norman Stone lawyer
Jorgenson, Mary Ann lawyer
Kacir, Barbara Brattin lawyer
Kahrl, Robert Conley lawyer
Kaiser, Gordon S., Jr. lawyer
Kapp, C. Terrence lawyer
Karch, George Frederick, Jr. lawyer
Karch, Sargent lawyer
Katcher, Richard lawyer
Katz, Lewis Robert legal educator
Kelly, Dennis Michael lawyer
Kilbane, Thomas Stanton lawyer
Kirchick, Calvin B. lawyer
Knopp, Albert J. lawyer
Kola, Arthur Anthony lawyer
Kramer, Andrew Michael lawyer
Kramer, Eugene Leo lawyer
Kuhn, David Alan lawyer
Kundtz, John Andrew lawyer
Kurit, Neil lawyer
Lawniczak, James Michael lawyer
Lease, Robert K. lawyer
Leavitt, Jeffrey Stuart lawyer
Leech, John Dale lawyer
Leidner, Harold Edward lawyer
Leiken, Earl Murray lawyer
Lemke, Judith A. lawyer
Lenn, Stephen Andrew lawyer
Leonard, Irvin Alan lawyer
Leukart, Richard Henry, II lawyer
Lewis, John Bruce lawyer
Lewis, John Francis lawyer
Lewis, Robert Lawrence lawyer, educator
Liegl, Joseph Leslie lawyer
Lindberg, Lawrence V. lawyer
Lynch, John Edward, Jr. lawyer
Madsen, H(enry) Stephen retired lawyer
Margulies, Jeffrey J. lawyer
Markey, Robert Guy lawyer
Markus, Richard M. lawyer
Marting, Michael G. lawyer
Mason, Thomas Albert lawyer
McAndrews, James Patrick retired lawyer
Mc Cartan, Patrick Francis lawyer
McCarthy, Mark Francis lawyer
Mc Clelland, James Craig lawyer
Mc Elhaney, James Wilson lawyer, educator
McKee, Thomas Frederick lawyer
McLaughlin, Patrick Michael lawyer
McNamee, Bernard Joseph lawyer
Meaney, Michael Joseph lawyer
Mehlman, Maxwell Jonathan law educator
Meisel, George Ira lawyer
Melsher, Gary W. lawyer
Meyer, G. Christopher lawyer
Miller, Ivan Lawrence lawyer
Miller, Richard Hamilton lawyer, broadcasting company executive
Millstone, David J. lawyer
Milner, Irvin Myron lawyer
Moody, Lizabeth Ann law educator
Moore, Anthony R. lawyer
Moore, Kenneth Cameron lawyer
Morrison, Donald William lawyer
Moscarino, George J. lawyer
Newborn, Karen B. lawyer
Newman, John M., Jr. lawyer
Nims, Michael A. lawyer
Novatney, John F., Jr. lawyer
Oberdank, Lawrence Mark lawyer, arbitrator
Ollinger, W. James lawyer
Orr, Parker Murray former lawyer
Paris, Zachary T. lawyer
Perris, Terrence George lawyer
Perry, George Williamson lawyer
Pinkney, Betty Kathryn lawyer
Plesec, William Thomas lawyer
Podboy, Alvin Michael, Jr. lawyer, law library director
Pogue, Richard Welch lawyer
Portwood, John Harding lawyer, electric products manufacturing executive
Preston, Robert Bruce retired lawyer
Price, Charles T. lawyer
Ptaszek, Edward Gerald, Jr. lawyer
Putka, Andrew Charles lawyer
Pyke, John Secrest, Jr. lawyer, polymers company executive
Rains, Merritt Neal lawyer
Ransom, William Harrison lawyer
Rapp, Robert Neil lawyer
Rasmussen, Frank Morris lawyer
Rawson, Robert H., Jr. lawyer
Reale, William A. lawyer
Rekstis, Walter J., III lawyer
Reppert, Richard Levi lawyer
Robiner, Donald Maxwell lawyer
Roj, William Henry lawyer
Rorimer, Louis lawyer
Rosenbaum, Jacob I. lawyer
Ruben, Alan Miles lawyer, educator
Ruxin, Paul Theodore lawyer
Rydzel, James A. lawyer
Sager, John William lawyer
Sawyer, Raymond Terry lawyer
Sayler, Richard H. lawyer
Schaefer, David Arnold lawyer
Schiller, James Joseph lawyer
Schneider, David Miller lawyer
Schnell, Carlton Bryce lawyer
Seger, Thomas M. lawyer
Seikel, Oliver Edward lawyer
Shanker, Morris Gerald lawyer, educator
Shapiro, Fred David lawyer
Sharp, Robert Weimer lawyer
Shaw, Russell Clyde lawyer
Shelley, John Fletcher lawyer
Sicherman, Marvin Allen lawyer
Sigalow, Steven E. lawyer
Skulina, Thomas Raymond lawyer
Sloan, David W. lawyer
Smith, Barbara Jean lawyer
Smith, James A. lawyer
Smith, Steven Ray law educator
Snyder, Kenneth F. lawyer
Sogg, Wilton Sherman lawyer
Solomon, Randall L. lawyer
Springel, Barry L. lawyer
Stanley, Hugh Monroe, Jr. lawyer
Steinbrink, William H. lawyer
Steindler, Howard Allen lawyer
Stevens, Thomas Charles lawyer
Stinchcomb, Robert G. lawyer
Stinson, Robert Charles lawyer
†Storey, Robert Davis lawyer
Strauch, John L. lawyer
Strauss, David J. lawyer
Streeter, Richard Edward lawyer
Striefsky, Linda A(nn) lawyer
Strimbu, Victor, Jr. lawyer
Stuhan, Richard George lawyer
Swartzbaugh, Marc L. lawyer
Szaller, James Francis lawyer
Taft, Seth Chase retired lawyer
Thomson, Maynard F. lawyer
Toohey, Brian Frederick lawyer
Toomajian, William Martin lawyer
Traci, Donald Philip retired lawyer
Trevor, Leigh Barry lawyer
Updegraft, Kenneth E., Jr. lawyer
von Mehren, George M. lawyer
Waldeck, John Walter, Jr. lawyer
Wallace, R. Byron lawyer
Wallach, Mark Irwin lawyer
Wamsley, James Lawrence, III lawyer
Watson, Richard Thomas lawyer
Weaver, Robin Geoffrey lawyer, educator
Weber, Robert Carl lawyer
Weible, Robert A. lawyer
Weiler, Jeffry Louis lawyer
White, Paul Dunbar lawyer
Whiteman, Joseph David lawyer, manufacturing company executive
Whiting, Hugh Richard lawyer
Whitney, Richard Buckner lawyer
Wilharm, John H., Jr. lawyer
Williams, Clyde E., Jr. lawyer
Woodring, James H. lawyer
Yosowitz, Sanford lawyer, metal sales and fabricating executive
Young, James Edward lawyer
Zambie, Allan John lawyer
Zangerle, John A. lawyer

Columbus
Adams, John Marshall lawyer
Anderson, Jon Mac lawyer
Anderson, Sandra Jo lawyer
Arthur, William Edgar lawyer
Ayers, James Cordon lawyer
Bahls, Steven Carl lawyer, legal educator
Bailey, Daniel Allen lawyer
Barnes, Wallace Ray lawyer
Belville, Barbara Ann lawyer
Bibart, Richard L. lawyer
Boardman, William Penniman lawyer, banker
Bridgman, G(eorge) Ross lawyer
Briggs, Marjorie Crowder lawyer
Brinkman, Dale Thomas lawyer
Brooks, Richard Dickinson lawyer
Brown, Herbert Russell lawyer, writer
Brown, Philip Albert lawyer
Brubaker, Robert Loring lawyer
Buchenroth, Stephen Richard lawyer
Burtch, John Hamrick lawyer
Carnahan, John Anderson lawyer
Carpenter, Michael H. lawyer
Case, William R. lawyer
Celebrezze, Anthony J., Jr. lawyer
Chester, John Jonas lawyer
Christensen, John William lawyer
Clovis, Albert Lee lawyer, educator
Cogan, J. Kevin lawyer
Cole, Ransey Guy, Jr. lawyer
Cook, Samuel Ronald, Jr. lawyer
Cushman, James Butler lawyer
Cvetanovich, Danny L. lawyer
Day, Roger F. lawyer
DeRousie, Charles Stuart lawyer
Di Lorenzo, John Florio, Jr. lawyer
Dreher, Darrell L. lawyer
Druen, William Sidney lawyer
Dugan, Charles Francis, II lawyer
Edwards, John White lawyer
Eggenschwiler, James E. lawyer
Elam, John Carlton lawyer
†Eyerly, Gloria A. lawyer
Fahey, Richard Paul lawyer
Fisher, Lloyd Edison, Jr. lawyer
Fried, Samuel lawyer
†Fu, Paul Shan law librarian, consultant
Gall, Maryann Baker lawyer
Gibson, Rankin MacDougal lawyer
Grant, Dennis Duane lawyer
Greek, Darold I. lawyer
Gross, James Howard lawyer
Gunsett, Daniel J. lawyer
Habash, Stephen J. lawyer
Hairston, George W. lawyer
Hale, Daniel Gordon lawyer
Hardymon, David Wayne lawyer
Hire, Charles H. lawyer
Hoberg, John William lawyer
Howarth, Robert F., Jr. lawyer
Hughes, Donald Allen, Jr. law librarian and educator
Jenkins, George L. lawyer
Jenkins, John Anthony lawyer
Johnson, Mark Alan lawyer
Johnston, Philip Crater lawyer
Keller, John Kistler lawyer
Kennedy, James Patrick lawyer
Kincaid, Robert M., Jr. lawyer
King, G. Roger lawyer
King, James R. lawyer
Knepper, William Edward lawyer
Kocher, Walter William lawyer, food company executive
Kozyris, Phaedon John law educator, consultant
Kuehnle, Kenton Lee lawyer
Kurtz, Charles Jewett, III lawyer
Lahey, John H. lawyer
Lehman, Harry Jac lawyer
Long, Thomas Leslie lawyer
Maloon, Jerry L. lawyer, physician, medicolegal consultant
Martin, William Giese lawyer
Maynard, Robert Howell lawyer
Mayo, Elizabeth Broom lawyer
McAlister, Robert Beaton lawyer
McConnaughey, George Carlton, Jr. lawyer
McCutchan, Gordon Eugene lawyer, insurance company executive
McKenna, Alvin James lawyer
McMahon, John Patrick lawyer
McNealey, J. Jeffrey lawyer, corporate executive
Miller, Malcolm Lee retired lawyer
Miller, Terry Morrow lawyer
Minister, Michael E. lawyer
Minor, Charles Daniel lawyer
Minor, Robert Allen lawyer
Minor, Robert Walter lawyer
Mirman, Joel Harvey lawyer
Moloney, Thomas E. lawyer
Mone, Robert Paul lawyer
Moritz, Michael Everett lawyer
Moul, William Charles lawyer
Nelson, Helaine Queen lawyer
Oman, Richard Heer lawyer
Petricoff, M. Howard lawyer, educator
Petro, James Michael lawyer, politician
Phillips, James Edgar lawyer
Pliskin, Marvin Robert lawyer
Pohlman, James Erwin lawyer
Powell, Ernestine Breisch retired lawyer
Pressley, Fred G., Jr. lawyer
Quigley, John Bernard law educator
Radnor, Alan T. lawyer
Rakestraw, Warren Vincent lawyer
Ramey, Denny L. bar association executive director
Reasoner, Willis Irl, III lawyer
Ridgley, Thomas Brennan lawyer
Robinson, Barry R. lawyer
Robol, Richard Thomas lawyer
Rose, Michael Dean lawyer, educator
Rowland, Ronald Lee lawyer
Royalty, Kenneth Marvin lawyer
Ryan, Joseph W., Jr. lawyer
Schrag, Edward A., Jr. lawyer
Scott, Thomas Clevenger lawyer
Selcer, David Mark lawyer
Senff, Mark D. lawyer
Shamansky, Robert Norton lawyer
Shayne, Stanley H. lawyer
Sheward, Richard S. lawyer
Sidman, Robert John lawyer
Siehl, Richard W. lawyer
Smith, Norman T. lawyer
Stedman, Richard Ralph lawyer
Stein, Jay Wobith legal research and education consultant
Stern, Geoffrey lawyer, disciplinary counsel
Stinehart, Roger Ray lawyer
Taft, Sheldon Ashley lawyer
Taggart, Thomas Michael lawyer
Tait, Robert Ed lawyer
Tarpy, Thomas Michael lawyer
Taylor, Joel Sanford lawyer
Tell, A. Charles lawyer
Thomas, Duke Winston lawyer
Todd, William Michael lawyer
Turano, David A. lawyer
Van Heyde, J. Stephen lawyer
Vorys, Arthur Isaiah lawyer
Warner, Charles Collins lawyer
Wentworth, Andrew Stowell lawyer
Whipps, Edward Franklin lawyer
Wightman, Alec lawyer
Williams, Gregory Howard lawyer, educator
Wright, Harry, III lawyer

Dayton
Bartlett, Robert Perry, Jr. lawyer
Berrey, Robert Forrest lawyer
Burick, Lawrence T. lawyer
Chernesky, Richard John lawyer
Finn, Chester Evans lawyer
Gottschlich, Gary William lawyer
Hadley, Robert James lawyer
Hayman, Jeffrey Lloyd corporate lawyer
Heyman, Ralph Edmond lawyer
Hitter, Joseph Ira lawyer
Jenks, Thomas Edward lawyer
Kinlin, Donald James lawyer
†Koziar, Stephen Francis, Jr. lawyer, power company executive
Lewis, Welbourne Walker, Jr. lawyer
Lowry, Bruce Roy lawyer
Macklin, Crofford Johnson, Jr. lawyer
McDonnell, Sue Kartin lawyer
McSwiney, Charles Ronald lawyer
Rapp, Gerald Duane lawyer, manufacturing company executive
Rogers, Richard Hunter lawyer, business executive

Delphos
Clark, Edward Ferdnand lawyer

Dresden
Reidy, Thomas Anthony lawyer

East Liverpool
Lang, Francis Harover lawyer

Findlay
Jetton, Girard Reuel, Jr. lawyer, retired oil company executive
Teeple, Richard Duane lawyer

Independence
Linnert, Terrence Gregory lawyer

Kent
Giffen, Daniel Harris lawyer, educator

Lancaster
Libert, Donald Joseph lawyer

Lima
Robenalt, John Alton lawyer

Logan
Dillon, Neal Winfield lawyer

Marietta
Fields, William Albert lawyer
Hausser, Robert Louis lawyer

Maumee
Kline, James Edward lawyer
Marsh, Benjamin Franklin lawyer

Medina
Ballard, John Stuart law educator, former mayor

Middletown
Rathman, William Ernest lawyer, minister

Milford
Vorholt, Jeffrey Joseph lawyer, telecommunications company executive

Mount Vernon
Turner, Harry Edward lawyer

Newark
Mantonya, John Butcher lawyer

Norwalk
Carpenter, Paul Leonard lawyer

Oregon
St. Clair, Donald David lawyer

Oxford
Brown, Edward Maurice retired lawyer, business executive

Pepper Pike
Mc Innes, Robert Malcolm lawyer, business consultant

Perrysburg
Spitzer, John Brumback lawyer

Portsmouth
Horr, William Henry lawyer

Reynoldsburg
Goostree, Robert Edward political science and law educator

Sandusky
Tone, Kenneth Edward lawyer

Springfield
Browne, William Bitner lawyer
Rush, Kenneth G. lawyer

Toledo
Anderson, Dale Kenneth retired lawyer
Baker, Richard Southworth lawyer
Boesel, Milton Charles, Jr. lawyer, business executive
Boggs, Ralph Stuart lawyer
Brown, Charles Earl lawyer
Colasurd, Richard Michael lawyer
Craig, Harald Franklin lawyer
Dalrymple, Thomas Lawrence lawyer
Fisher, Donald Wiener lawyer
Hawkins, Donald Merton lawyer
Hiett, Edward Emerson retired lawyer, glass company executive
James, Harold Arthur lawyer
La Rue, Carl Forman lawyer
Leech, Charles Russell, Jr. lawyer
McCormick, Edward James, Jr. lawyer
O'Connell, Maurice Daniel lawyer
Stewart, Mark Carroll lawyer
Tuschman, James Marshall lawyer

Twinsburg
†Staph, Jack A. corporate lawyer

Warren
Rossi, Anthony Gerald lawyer

Wickliffe
Hsu, Roger Y. K. *lawyer*
Kidder, Fred Dockstater *lawyer*

Willoughby
Harthun, Luther Arthur *lawyer*

Wooster
Colclaser, H. Alberta *lawyer, retired government official*

Youngstown
Mumaw, James Webster *lawyer*
Nadler, Myron Jay *lawyer*
Nunziato, Carl Anthony *lawyer, banker*
Roth, Daniel Benjamin *lawyer, business executive*
Sokolov, Richard Saul *lawyer*
Spector, Earl M. *lawyer, retail executive*
Stevens, Paul Edward *lawyer*
Tucker, Don Eugene *retired lawyer*
Wolfcale, Arthur Dale *lawyer*

Zanesville
Micheli, Frank James *lawyer*

OKLAHOMA

Anadarko
Pain, Charles Leslie *lawyer*

Antlers
Stamper, Joe Allen *lawyer*

Bartlesville
Paul, William George *lawyer*

Chandler
Mather, Stephanie J. *lawyer*

Edmond
Payne, William Howard *lawyer*
Shadid, Randel Coy *lawyer*

Enid
Jones, Stephen *lawyer*
Musser, William Wesley, Jr. *lawyer*

Guymon
Wood, Donald Euriah *lawyer*

Kingfisher
Baker, Thomas Edward *lawyer, accountant*

Mcalester
Cornish, Richard Pool *lawyer*

Muskogee
Ruby, Russell (Glenn) *lawyer*

Norman
Brown, Elvin J. *lawyer*
Elkouri, Frank *legal educator*
Fairbanks, Robert Alvin *lawyer*
Hemingway, Richard William *lawyer, educator*
Pain, Betsy M. *lawyer*
Petersen, Catherine Holland *lawyer*
†Singleton, Alma Nickell *law librarian*

Oklahoma City
Allen, Robert Dee *lawyer*
Angel, Arthur Ronald *lawyer, consultant*
Ball, Leonard F. *lawyer, architectural firm executive*
Boston, William Clayton *lawyer*
Cantrell, Charles Leonard *lawyer, educator*
Champlin, Richard H. *lawyer, insurance company executive*
Coats, Andrew Montgomery *lawyer, former mayor*
Court, Leonard *lawyer*
Cunningham, Stanley Lloyd *lawyer*
Durland, Jack Raymond *lawyer*
Emerson, Marvin Chester *legal association administrator*
Epperson, Kraettli Quynton *lawyer, educator*
Fellers, James Davison *lawyer*
Ford, Michael Raye *lawyer*
Hemry, Jerome Eldon *lawyer*
Hendrick, Howard H. *lawyer, state senator*
Lambird, Mona Salyer *lawyer*
Legg, William Jefferson *lawyer*
Lester, Andrew William *lawyer*
Loving, Susan B. *lawyer, former state official*
Milsten, Robert B. *lawyer*
Mock, Randall Don *lawyer*
Moler, Edward Harold *lawyer*
Necco, Alexander David *lawyer, educator*
Nesbitt, Charles Rudolph *lawyer, energy consultant*
Reynolds, Norman Eben *lawyer*
Ross, William Jarboe *lawyer*
Scott, Willard Philip *lawyer, corporate executive*
Snider, John Joseph *lawyer*
Steinhorn, Irwin Harry *lawyer, educator, corporate executive*
†Stringer, L. E. Dean *lawyer*
Turpen, Michael Craig *lawyer*
Verity, George Luther *lawyer*
Walsh, Lawrence Edward *lawyer*
Woodruff, Judson Sage *lawyer*

Pauls Valley
Hope, Garland Howard *lawyer, retired judge*

Ponca City
Northcutt, Clarence Dewey *lawyer*

Tulsa
Arrington, John Leslie, Jr. *lawyer*
Banker, Barbara L. *lawyer*
Belsky, Martin Henry *law educator, lawyer*
Biolchini, Robert Fredrick *lawyer*
Blackstock, LeRoy *lawyer*
Bryant, Hubert Hale *lawyer*
Cooper, Richard Casey *lawyer*
Crawford, B(urnett) Hayden *lawyer*
Daniel, Samuel Phillips *lawyer*
Doverspike, Terry Richard *lawyer*
Farrell, John L., Jr. *lawyer, business executive*
Frey, Martin Alan *lawyer, educator*
Gaberino, John Anthony, Jr. *lawyer*
Gable, G. Ellis *lawyer*
Graham, Tony M. *lawyer*
Howard, Gene Claude *lawyer, former state senator*
Imel, John Michael *lawyer*
Kihle, Donald Arthur *lawyer*
Killin, Charles Clark *lawyer*
Kothe, Charles Aloysius *lawyer*
Langholz, Robert Wayne *lawyer, investor*
Lewis, John Furman *lawyer, oil company executive*
Luthey, Graydon Dean, Jr. *lawyer*
Milsten, David Randolph *lawyer*
Parr, Royse Milton *lawyer*
Pritchard, William Winther *lawyer, drilling company executive*
Quinn, Francis Xavier *arbitrator and mediator, author, lecturer*
Schwartz, Bernard *lawyer, educator*
Stuart, Harold Cutliff *lawyer, business executive*
Walker, Floyd Lee *lawyer*

Vinita
Curnutte, Mark William *lawyer*

OREGON

Astoria
Haskell, Donald McMillan *lawyer*

Brookings
Maxwell, William Stirling *retired lawyer*

Eugene
Clark, Chapin DeWitt *law educator*
Mumford, William Porter, II *lawyer*
Owens, A(rnold) Dean *lawyer*
Sahlstrom, E(lmer) B(ernard) *lawyer*
Scoles, Eugene Francis *legal educator, lawyer*

Lebanon
Kuntz, Joel Dubois *lawyer*

Medford
O'Connor, Karl William *lawyer*

Pendleton
Bloom, Stephen Michael *lawyer, judge*
Kottkamp, John Harlan *lawyer*

Portland
Abravanel, Allan Ray *lawyer*
Anderson, Herbert H. *lawyer, farmer*
Arthur, Michael Elbert *lawyer*
Babcock, Robert Evans *lawyer*
Bakkensen, John Reser *lawyer*
Booth, Brian Geddes *lawyer*
Brenneman, Delbert Jay *lawyer*
Byerly, Bruce Lloyd *lawyer*
Cable, John Franklin *lawyer*
Cantlin, Richard Anthony *lawyer*
Carlsen, Clifford Norman, Jr. *lawyer*
Carmack, Mildred Jean *lawyer*
Chernoff, Daniel Paregol *patent lawyer*
Crow, William Beryl *lawyer*
Crowell, John B., Jr. *lawyer, former government official*
Dahl, Joyle Cochran *lawyer*
Davidson, Crow Girard *lawyer*
Dean, E. Joseph *lawyer*
DeChaine, Dean Dennis *lawyer*
Deering, Thomas Phillips *lawyer*
Dotten, Michael Chester *lawyer*
Drummond, Gerard Kasper *lawyer, retired minerals company executive*
Eakin, Margaretta Morgan *lawyer*
Edwards, Richard Alan *lawyer*
Epstein, Edward Louis *lawyer*
Ericsson Dailey, Dianne K. *lawyer*
Faust, John Roosevelt, Jr. *lawyer*
Fell, James F. *lawyer*
Feuerstein, Howard M. *lawyer*
Fogg, George Kephart *lawyer*
Foley, Ridgway Knight, Jr. *lawyer, writer*
Franzke, Richard Albert *lawyer*
Froebe, Gerald Allen *lawyer, partner*
Georges, Maurice Ostrow *lawyer*
Gill, Rockne *lawyer*
Girard, Leonard Arthur *lawyer*
Glasgow, William Jacob *lawyer*
Glick, Richard Myron *lawyer*
Griffith, Stephen Loyal *lawyer*
Hager, Orval O. *retired lawyer, consultant*
Halle, John Joseph *lawyer*
Hanna, Harry Mitchell *lawyer*
Helmer, M. Christie *lawyer*
Hergenhan, Kenneth William *lawyer*
Hinkle, Charles Frederick *lawyer, clergyman, educator*
Hoffman, Jack Leroy *lawyer*
Holman, Donald Reid *lawyer*
Holmes, Michael Gene *lawyer*
Howorth, David Bishop *lawyer*
Johansen, Judith A. Bearzi *lawyer*
Johnson, Alexander Charles *lawyer, electrical engineer*
Josephson, Richard Carl *lawyer*
Kanter, Stephen *law educator, college dean*
Kennedy, Jack Leland *lawyer*
Kester, Randall Blair *lawyer*
Larpenteur, James Albert, Jr. *lawyer*
Leedy, Robert Allan, Sr. *retired lawyer*
Lindley, Thomas Ernest *environmental lawyer, law educator*
Livingston, Louis Bayer *lawyer*
Love, William Edward *lawyer*
Maloney, Robert E., Jr. *lawyer*
Martin, Chrys Anne *lawyer*
McCarty, Chester Earl *lawyer, retired air force officer*
Miller, William Richey, Jr. *lawyer*
Mowe, Gregory Robert *lawyer*
Nash, Frank Erwin *lawyer*
Nunn, Robert Warne *lawyer*
O'Hanlon, James Barry *retired lawyer*
Pruitt, Charles Joseph *lawyer*
Richardson, Campbell *lawyer*
Richter, Peter Christian *lawyer*
Roberts, Gary *lawyer*
Rosenbaum, Lois Omenn *lawyer*
Roy, Richard E. *lawyer*
Rubin, Bruce Alan *lawyer*
Rutzick, Mark Charles *lawyer*
Ryan, John Duncan *lawyer*
Sand, Thomas Charles *lawyer*
Schuster, Philip Frederick, II *lawyer*
Simpson, Robert Glenn *lawyer*
Spiekerman, James Frederick *lawyer*
Stevason, John C. *lawyer*
Stewart, Milton Roy *lawyer*
Sullivan, Edward Joseph *lawyer, educator*
Tilbury, Roger Graydon *lawyer, rancher*
Van Valkenburg, Edgar Walter *lawyer*
Waggoner, James Clyde *lawyer*
Walters, Stephen Scott *lawyer*
Weaver, Delbert Allen *lawyer*
Webb, Jere Michael *lawyer*
Westwood, James Nicholson *lawyer*
Whinston, Arthur Lewis *lawyer*
White, Douglas James, Jr. *lawyer*
Wiener, Norman Joseph *lawyer*
Wilson, Owen Meredith, Jr. *lawyer*
Wood, Marcus Andrew *lawyer*
Wren, Harold Gwyn *arbitrator, lawyer, legal educator*
Wright, Charles Edward *lawyer*
Wyse, William Walker *lawyer*
Zalutsky, Morton Herman *lawyer*

Salem
†Breen, Richard F., Jr. *law librarian, lawyer, educator*
Mannix, Kevin Leese *lawyer*

Tigard
Replogle, William H(enry), II *lawyer*

PENNSYLVANIA

Allentown
Agger, James H. *lawyer*
Brown, Robert Wayne *lawyer*
Frank, Bernard *lawyer*
Holt, Leon Conrad, Jr. *lawyer, business executive*
Nagel, Edward McCaul *lawyer, former utilities executive*
Parks, Jeffrey A. *lawyer*
Platt, William Henry *lawyer*

Allison Park
Herrington, John David, III *lawyer*
Miller, William Evans, Jr. *retired lawyer*

Ardmore
Chadwick, H. Beatty *lawyer*

Bala Cynwyd
Cades, Stewart Russell *lawyer, communications company executive*
Garrity, Vincent Francis, Jr. *lawyer*
Manko, Joseph Martin, Sr. *lawyer*
Quay, Thomas Emery *lawyer*
Shepard, Geoffrey Carroll *insurance company executive*

Beaver
Ledebur, Linas Vockroth, Jr. *lawyer*

Berwyn
Huffaker, John Boston *lawyer*
Markle, John, Jr. *lawyer*
Odell, Herbert *lawyer*
Watters, Edward McLain, III *lawyer*
Wood, Thomas E. *lawyer*

Blue Bell
Barron, Harold Sheldon *lawyer*
Crawford, Christine Ann *lawyer*
Elliott, John Michael *lawyer*
Swansen, Samuel Theodore *lawyer*
Young, Jere Arnold *lawyer, management consultant*

Broomall
Stewart, Allen Warren *lawyer*

Carlisle
†Dineen, Daniel Thomas *lawyer*
Glenn, Peter G. *lawyer, educator*

Coatesville
Sprague, William Douglas *lawyer, company executive*

Conshohocken
Gutkin, Arthur Lee *lawyer*
Rounick, Jack A. *lawyer*

Feasterville
McEvilly, James Patrick, Jr. *lawyer*

Gibsonia
Heilman, Carl Edwin *lawyer*

Gladwyne
Acton, David *lawyer*

Greensburg
McDowell, Michael David *lawyer, utility executive*

Harrisburg
Allen, Heath Ledward *lawyer*
Ball, William Bentley *lawyer*
Cawley, James Hughes *lawyer*
Cline, Andrew Haley *lawyer*
Cramer, John McNaight *lawyer*
Diehm, James Warren *lawyer, educator*
Hanson, Robert DeLolle *lawyer*
Kelly, Robert Edward, Jr. *lawyer*
Klein, Michael D. *lawyer*
Kury, Franklin Leo *lawyer*
Termini, Roseann Bridget *lawyer*
Warshaw, Allen Charles *lawyer*
Zimmerman, LeRoy S. *lawyer, former state attorney general*

Haverford
Frick, Sidney Wanning *lawyer*
McGlinn, Frank Cresson Potts *lawyer*
Stroud, James Stanley *retired lawyer*
Szabad, George Michael *lawyer, former mayor*

Herminie
McAbee, Cheryl Rosilyn *lawyer*

Huntingdon Valley
Forman, Howard Irving *lawyer, former government official*
Toll, Robert Irwin *lawyer, real estate developer*

Indiana
Engler, W. Joseph, Jr. *lawyer*

Jenkintown
Nerenberg, Aaron *lawyer*

Jersey Shore
†Nassberg, Richard T. *lawyer*

Johnstown
Antonazzo, Nicholas Orlando *lawyer, corporate real estate executive*
Glock, Earl Ferdinand *lawyer*
Glosser, William Louis *lawyer*

Jones Mills
Fish, Paul Waring *lawyer*

King Of Prussia
Bramson, Robert Sherman *lawyer*
Dubbs, Robert Morton *lawyer, health services company executive*

Lake Harmony
Polansky, Larry Paul *court administrator, consultant*

Lancaster
Brown, Joseph Allen *lawyer, business executive*
Duroni, Charles Eugene *retired lawyer, food products executive*
Nast, Dianne Martha *lawyer*
Whare, Wanda Snyder *lawyer*
Zimmerman, D(onald) Patrick *lawyer, educator*

Langhorne
Brafford, William Charles *lawyer*

Lansdale
Esterhai, John Louis *lawyer*

Lock Haven
Snowiss, Alvin L. *lawyer*

Macungie
Gavin, Austin *retired lawyer*

Malvern
Cameron, John Clifford *lawyer, health science facility administrator*
Churchill, Winston John *lawyer, investment firm executive*
DeHaven, Michael Allen *lawyer*
Ewing, Joseph Neff, Jr. *lawyer*
†Klapinsky, Raymond Joseph *lawyer*

Mechanicsburg
Brawner, Gerald Theodore *lawyer*

Media
Elman, Gerry Jay *lawyer*
Lambert, George Robert *lawyer*

Mendenhall
Reinert, Norbert Frederick *patent lawyer, retired chemical company executive*

Millersburg
Woodside, Robert Elmer *lawyer, former judge*

Morrisville
Heefner, William Frederick *lawyer*

Norristown
Aman, George Matthias, III *lawyer*
Flint, Daniel Waldo Boone *lawyer*
Folmar, Larry John *lawyer*
Wetherill, Eikins *lawyer, stock exchange executive*

Philadelphia
Aaron, Kenneth Ellyot *lawyer*
Abbott, Frank Harry *lawyer*
Abrahams, Robert David *lawyer, author*
Abramowitz, Robert Leslie *lawyer*
Ackerman, Alvin S. *lawyer*
Adams, Barbara *lawyer*
Ake, John Notley *lawyer, former investment services executive*
Albert, Jeffrey B. *lawyer*
Anders, Jerrold Paul *lawyer*
Anderson, Edward Clive *lawyer*
Apfel, Jerome B. *lawyer*
Armstrong, Stephen Wales *lawyer*
Aronstein, Martin Joseph *lawyer, educator*
Auten, David Charles *lawyer*
Baccini, Laurance Ellis *lawyer*
Bachman, Arthur *lawyer*
Baker, C. Edwin *law educator*
Bales, John Foster, III *lawyer*
Ballengee, James McMorrow *lawyer*
Barrett, John J(ames), Jr. *lawyer*
Bartolini, Anthony Louis *lawyer*
Baughman, Jon A. *lawyer*
Berger, David *lawyer*
Berger, Harold *lawyer, engineer*
Bergholtz, Norbert F. *lawyer*
Berkley, Emily Carolan *lawyer*
Berkman, Richard Lyle *lawyer*
Berlin, Norman B. *lawyer*
Bernard, John Marley *lawyer, educator*
Bernstein, George L. *lawyer, accountant*
Bershad, Jack R. *lawyer*
Bildersee, Robert Alan *lawyer*
Binder, David Franklin *lawyer, author*
Black, Allen Decatur *lawyer*
Bloom, Michael Anthony *lawyer*
Bogutz, Jerome Edwin *lawyer*
Boss, Amelia Helen *law educator, lawyer*
Bradley, Raymond Joseph *lawyer*
Braverman, Elliott Kenneth *lawyer*
Brenan, Denis V. *lawyer*
Brier, Bonnie Susan *lawyer*
Bright, Joseph Coleman *lawyer*
Brinkworth, Donald A. *lawyer, general counsel*
Briscoe, Jack Clayton *lawyer*
Britt, Earl Thomas *lawyer*
Brown, Richard P., Jr. *lawyer*

Brown, Stephen D. *lawyer*
Brown, William Hill, III *lawyer*
Browne, Michael Leon *lawyer*
Browne, Stanhope Stryker *lawyer*
†Buller, Carter R. *lawyer*
Burbank, Stephen Bradner *law educator*
Calvert, Jay H., Jr. *lawyer*
Carnecchia, Baldo M., Jr. *lawyer*
Carroll, Mark Thomas *lawyer*
Carroll, Thomas Colas *lawyer, educator*
Casper, Charles B. *lawyer*
Cherken, Harry Sarkis, Jr. *lawyer*
Cheston, George Morris *lawyer*
Child, John Sowden, Jr. *lawyer*
Chimples, George *lawyer*
Clark, Frederic William *lawyer*
Clark, John Arthur *lawyer*
Clothier, Isaac H., IV *lawyer*
Cloues, Edward Blanchard, II *lawyer*
Cohen, Deborah Fuchs *lawyer*
Cohen, Felix Asher *lawyer*
Cohen, Frederick *lawyer*
Cohen, Sylvan M. *lawyer*
Collings, Robert L. *lawyer*
Comfort, Robert Dennis *lawyer*
Comisky, Hope A. *lawyer*
Comisky, Marvin *retired lawyer*
Cooney, J(ohn) Gordon *lawyer*
Cox, Roger Frazier *lawyer*
Cramer, Harold *lawyer*
Crawford, James Douglas *lawyer*
Crough, Daniel Francis *lawyer, insurance company executive*
Damsgaard, Kell Marsh *lawyer*
D'Angelo, Christopher Scott *lawyer*
Dean, Michael M. *lawyer*
DeBunda, Salvatore Michael *lawyer*
De Lone, H. Francis *lawyer*
Deming, Frank Stout *lawyer*
Dennis, Edward S(pencer) G(ale), Jr. *lawyer*
Denworth, Raymond K. *lawyer*
Dichter, Mark S. *lawyer*
Dilks, Park Bankert, Jr. *lawyer*
Donner, Henry Jay *lawyer*
Donoghue, Norman E., II *lawyer*
Donohue, James J. *lawyer*
Doran, Thomas E. *lawyer*
Doran, William Michael *lawyer*
Dorfman, John Charles *lawyer*
Drake, William Frank, Jr. *lawyer*
Dryer, Jonathan *lawyer*
Dubin, Leonard *lawyer*
†Dubin, Stephen Victor *lawyer*
Durham, James W. *lawyer*
Dworetzky, Joseph Anthony *lawyer, city official*
Edwards, Stephen Allen *lawyer*
Elliott, William Homer, Jr. *lawyer*
Emerson, S. Jonathan *lawyer*
Emory, Hugh Mercer *lawyer*
Esser, Carl Eric *lawyer*
Fader, Henry Conrad *lawyer*
Fala, Herman C. *lawyer*
Falk, I. Lee *lawyer*
Fallon, Christopher Chaffee, Jr. *lawyer*
Feirson, Steven B. *lawyer*
Feldman, Albert Joseph *lawyer*
Fiebach, H. Robert *lawyer*
Fine, Lawrence B. *lawyer*
Finet, Scott *law librarian*
Fisher, Linda A. *lawyer*
Fitts, Michael Andrew *law educator*
Flaherty, John Edward, Jr. *lawyer*
Flanagan, Joseph Patrick, Jr. *lawyer*
Flaxman, Howard Richard *lawyer*
Fox, Lawrence J. *lawyer*
Fox, Reeder Rodman *lawyer*
Frank, Harvey *lawyer, writer*
Freedman, Robert Louis *lawyer*
Frenkel, Douglas N. *law educator*
Friedell, Ellen Silberstein *lawyer*
Friedman, Frank Bennett *lawyer*
Friedman, Steven Lewis *lawyer*
Frimmer, Rick Leslie *lawyer*
Fryman, Louis William *lawyer*
Gadsden, Christopher Henry *lawyer*
Gadsden, Thomas P. *lawyer*
Garcia, Rudolph *lawyer*
Genkin, Barry Howard *lawyer*
Gerhart, Frederick John *lawyer*
Glanton, Richard H. *lawyer*
Glassman, Howard Theodore *lawyer*
Glassmoyer, Thomas Parvin *lawyer*
Glazer, Ronald Barry *lawyer*
Gold, William Buchanan, Jr. *lawyer*
Goldberg, Jay Lenard *lawyer*
Goldberg, Marvin Allen *lawyer, business consultant*
Goldberg, Richard Robert *lawyer*
Goldsmith, Howard Michael *lawyer*
Goldstein, William Marks *lawyer*
Goodman, Frank I. *law educator, lawyer*
Goodrich, Herbert Funk, Jr. *lawyer*
Gorman, Robert A. *law educator*
Gornish, Gerald *lawyer*
Gough, John Francis *lawyer*
Granoff, Gail Patricia *lawyer*
Grant, M. Duncan *lawyer*
Grant, Richard W. *lawyer*
Greenberg, Peter Steven *lawyer*
Greenfield, Bruce Harold *lawyer, banker*
Grossi-Tyson, Laura *lawyer*
Grove, David Lavan *lawyer*
Haley, Vincent Peter *lawyer*
Hamilton, Stephen David Derwent *lawyer*
Hangley, William Thomas *lawyer*
Harkins, John Graham, Jr. *lawyer*
Hatoff, Howard Ira *labor lawyer*
Hauptfuhrer, George Jost, Jr. *lawyer*
Haviland, Bancroft Dawley *lawyer*
Haydanek, Ronald Edward *lawyer and consultant*
Hazard, Geoffrey Cornell, Jr. *law educator*
Heim, Robert Charles *lawyer*
Henderson, J(oseph) Welles *lawyer*
Hennessy, Joseph H. *lawyer*
Henrich, William Joseph, Jr. *lawyer*
Henry, Ragan A. *lawyer, broadcaster*
Herman, Charles Jacob *lawyer*
Hess, Hans Ober *lawyer*
Hodavance, Robert S. *lawyer*
Hoelscher, Robert James *lawyer*
Hoffman, Alan Jay *lawyer*
Hoffman, Jerome A. *lawyer*
Holloway, Hiliary Hamilton *lawyer, banker*
Holmes, Norman Leonard *lawyer*
Honnold, John Otis, Jr. *law educator*
Horvath, Joseph John *lawyer, insurance company executive*
Humenuk, William Anzelm *lawyer*
Humes, James Calhoun *lawyer, communications consultant, author*
Hunter, James Austen, Jr. *lawyer*
Iskrant, John Dermot *lawyer*
Jaffe, Paul Lawrence *lawyer*
Jamieson, David Donald *lawyer*
Jellinek, Miles Andrew *lawyer*
Jennings, James Walsh *lawyer*
Jones, Robert Jeffries *lawyer*
Jones, Robert Mead, Jr. *lawyer*
Justice, Jack Burton *lawyer*
Kahn, James Robert *lawyer*
Kane, Jonathan *lawyer*
Kane-Vanni, Patricia Ruth *lawyer, consultant*
Kauffman, Bruce William *lawyer, former state supreme court justice*
Kaufman, David Joseph *lawyer*
Keene, John Clark *lawyer, educator*
Kellett, Morris C. *lawyer*
†Kelly, Elizabeth Slusser *law librarian, educator*
Kempin, Frederick Gustav, Jr. *lawyer, educator*
Kendall, Robert Louis, Jr. *lawyer*
Kenty, David Earl *lawyer*
Kenworthy, Thomas Bausman *lawyer*
Kessler, Alan Craig *lawyer*
Kessler, Mark Keil *lawyer*
Kittredge, Thomas M. *lawyer*
Klasko, Herbert Ronald *lawyer, law educator, writer*
Klauder, N. Jeffrey *lawyer*
Klaus, William Robert *lawyer*
Klayman, Barry Martin *lawyer*
Klein, Howard Bruce *lawyer, law educator*
Klein, Samuel Edwin *lawyer*
Kline, Thomas Richard *lawyer*
Koenig, C(arl) Frederick, III *lawyer*
Kohn, Harold Elias *lawyer*
Kraemer, Michael Frederick *lawyer*
Kramer, Meyer *lawyer, editor, clergyman*
Krampf, John Edward *lawyer*
Krzyzanowski, Richard Lucien *lawyer, corporate executive*
Kübler, Friedrich Karl *law educator*
Kupperman, Louis Brandeis *lawyer*
Kurland, Seymour *lawyer*
Laddon, Warren Milton *lawyer*
Landis, Robert M. *lawyer*
LaValley, Frederick J. M. *lawyer*
Ledwith, James Robb *lawyer*
Ledwith, John Francis *lawyer*
Leech, Noyes Elwood *lawyer, educator*
Leonard, Thomas Aloysius *lawyer*
Lesnick, Howard *legal educator*
Levin, A. Leo *law educator, retired government official*
Levin, Murray Simon *lawyer*
Levin, Susan Bass *lawyer*
Levy, Dale Penneys *lawyer*
Lewis, Christopher Alan *lawyer*
Lewis, John Hardy, Jr. *lawyer*
Libonati, Michael Ernest *lawyer, educator, writer*
Lichtenstein, Lawrence Jay *lawyer*
Lichtenstein, Robert Jay *lawyer*
Lillie, Charisse Ranielle *lawyer, educator*
Lipman, Frederick D. *lawyer*
Lisker, Deborah J(ane) *lawyer*
Loewenstein, Benjamin Steinberg *lawyer*
Lombard, John James, Jr. *lawyer*
Loveless, George Group *lawyer*
Lowery, William Herbert *lawyer*
Lucey, John David, Jr. *lawyer*
Lundy, Joseph E. *lawyer*
MacGregor, David Bruce *lawyer*
Maclay, Donald Merle *lawyer*
Madeira, Edward W(alter), Jr. *lawyer*
Madva, Stephen Alan *lawyer*
Magargee, W(illiam) Scott, III *lawyer*
Magaziner, Fred Thomas *lawyer*
Mai, Elizabeth Hardy *lawyer*
Mann, Bruce H. *law educator*
Mann, Theodore R. *lawyer*
Mannino, Edward Francis *lawyer*
Mason, Theodore W. *lawyer*
Masterson, Thomas A. *lawyer*
Mather, Barbara W. *lawyer*
Mathes, Stephen Jon *lawyer*
Mattoon, Peter Mills *lawyer*
Maxey, David Walker *lawyer*
McKeever, John Eugene *lawyer*
McMenamin, Richard F. *lawyer*
McQuiston, Robert Earl *lawyer*
Meigs, John Forsyth *lawyer*
Mesirov, Leon Isaac *lawyer*
Meyers, Howard L. *lawyer*
Milbourne, Walter Robertson *lawyer*
Miller, Henry Franklin *lawyer*
Miller, Leslie Anne *lawyer*
Miller, Margery K. *lawyer*
Milone, Francis Michael *lawyer*
Minisi, Anthony S. *lawyer*
Mirabello, Francis Joseph *lawyer*
Mooney, Charles William, Jr. *law educator*
Morikawa, Dennis J. *lawyer*
Morris, Thomas Bateman, Jr. *lawyer*
Morse, Stephen J. *law educator*
Moss, Arthur Henshey *lawyer*
Murrell, Thomas W., III *lawyer*
Myers, Kenneth Raymond *lawyer*
Narin, Stephen B. *lawyer*
Newbold, Arthur *lawyer*
Nofer, George Hancock *lawyer*
O'Brien, William Jerome, II *lawyer*
O'Connor, Joseph A., Jr. *lawyer*
O'Donnell, G. Daniel *lawyer*
O'Leary, Dennis Joseph *lawyer*
Ominsky, Harris *lawyer*
O'Reilly, Timothy Patrick *lawyer*
Oswald, Stanton S. *lawyer*
Pagliaro, James Domenic *lawyer*
Palmer, Richard Ware *lawyer*
Panzer, Mitchell Emanuel *lawyer*
Patrick, George W. *lawyer*
Phillips, Dorothy Kay *lawyer*
Pillai, K. G. Jan *law educator, lawyer*
Pokotilow, Manny David *lawyer*
Pollack, Michael *lawyer*
Posner, Edward Martin *lawyer*
Poul, Franklin *lawyer*
Powell, Walter Hecht *labor arbitrator*
Pratter, Gene E. K. *lawyer*
Price, Robert Stanley *lawyer*
Promislo, Daniel *lawyer*
Putney, Paul William *lawyer*
Rabinowitz, Samuel Nathan *lawyer*
Rachofsky, David J. *lawyer*
Rackow, Julian Paul *lawyer*
Rainey, Arthur H. *lawyer*
Ralph, Thomas A. *lawyer*
Reagan, Harry Edwin, III *lawyer*
Redeker, James Russell *lawyer*
Reed, Alan L. *lawyer*
Reed, Michael Haywood *lawyer*
Reich, Abraham Charles *lawyer*
Reiss, John Barlow *lawyer*
Reitz, Curtis Randall *lawyer, educator*
Rizzo, Richard C. *lawyer*
Roberts, Carl Geoffrey *lawyer*
Roomberg, Lila Goldstein *lawyer*
Root, Stanley William, Jr. *lawyer*
Rosenbleeth, Richard Marvin *lawyer*
Rosenbloom, Sanford M. *lawyer*
Rosenfield, Bruce Alan *lawyer*
Rosenstein, James Alfred *lawyer*
Rosoff, William A. *lawyer*
Ross, Daniel R. *lawyer*
Ross, Murray Louis *lawyer, business executive*
Rulon, Richard R. *lawyer*
Sabat, Richard J. *lawyer*
Samson, Peter *lawyer*
Sartorius, Peter S. *lawyer*
Satinsky, Barnett *lawyer*
Sax, Helen Spigel *lawyer*
Schaub, Harry Carl *lawyer*
Scher, Howard Dennis *lawyer*
Schneider, Carl W. *lawyer*
Schneider, Richard Graham *lawyer*
Schwartz, Robert M. *lawyer*
Scott, Donald Allison *lawyer*
Scott, Michael Timothy *lawyer*
Scott, William Proctor, III *lawyer*
Segal, Bernard Gerard *lawyer*
Segal, Irving Randall *lawyer*
Segal, Robert Martin *lawyer*
Segrè, Nina *lawyer*
Shakow, David Joseph *law educator*
Shapiro, Cheryl Beth *lawyer*
Shapiro, Raymond L. *lawyer*
Sharbaugh, Thomas J. *lawyer*
Shaw, Mari Gursky *lawyer*
Shecter, Howard L. *lawyer*
Shestack, Jerome Joseph *lawyer*
Shiekman, Laurence Zeid *lawyer*
Shipman, Lynn Karen *lawyer*
Shusterman, Murray H. *lawyer*
Shuter, Bruce Donald *lawyer*
Siskind, Ralph Walter *lawyer*
Smith, John Francis, III *lawyer*
Snyder, Lee H. *lawyer*
Snyder, Ralph Sheldon *lawyer*
Solano, Carl Anthony *lawyer*
Somers, Hans Peter *lawyer*
Spaeth, Edmund Benjamin, Jr. *lawyer, law educator, former judge*
Spector, Martin Wolf *lawyer, business executive*
Spencer, Steven D. *lawyer*
Stack, Stephen A., Jr. *lawyer*
Stakias, G. Michael *lawyer*
Starr, Allan H. *lawyer*
Steinberg, Robert Philip *lawyer*
Stern, Joan Naomi *lawyer*
Sternberg, Donna Udin *lawyer*
Stewart, Robert Forrest, Jr. *lawyer*
Stiller, Jennifer Anne *lawyer*
Strasbaugh, Wayne Ralph *lawyer*
Strickler, Matthew M. *lawyer*
Stuntebeck, Clinton A. *lawyer*
Subak, John Thomas *lawyer*
Sugarman, Robert Jay *lawyer*
Summers, Clyde Wilson *law educator*
Suplee, Dennis Raymond *lawyer*
Swichar, Edward *lawyer*
Tashman, Myles Richard *lawyer*
Temin, Michael Lehman *lawyer*
Thomas, Frank M., Jr. *lawyer*
Thurston, David E. *lawyer, general counsel*
Tiger, Ira Paul *lawyer*
Torregrossa, Joseph Anthony *lawyer*
Undercofler, J(onas) Clayton *lawyer*
Vaira, Peter Francis *lawyer*
Volpicelli, Stephen L. *lawyer*
Wagner, Thomas Joseph *lawyer, insurance company executive*
Wald, Martin *lawyer*
Walker, Kent *lawyer*
Walsh, Donald Peter *lawyer, retired oil company executive*
Walters, Christopher Kent *lawyer*
Wambold, Judson J. *lawyer*
Warner, Theodore Kugler, Jr. *lawyer*
Weil, Jeffrey George *lawyer*
Weisberg, Morris L. *retired lawyer*
West, James Joseph *lawyer*
Wetzel, Carroll Robbins *lawyer*
Whiteside, William Anthony, Jr. *lawyer*
Whitman, Bradford F. *lawyer*
Wiener, Ronald Martin *lawyer*
Wiener, Thomas Eli *lawyer*
Wild, Richard P. *lawyer*
Williams, Robert Deland *lawyer*
Witt, Thomas Powell *lawyer*
Wolf, Robert B. *lawyer*
†Wolff, Deborah H(orowitz) *lawyer*
Wolkin, Paul Alexander *lawyer, former institute executive*
Wood, William Philler *lawyer*
Wright, Minturn Tatum, III *lawyer*
Wrobleski, Jeanne Pauline *lawyer*
Wysocki, F(elix) Michael *lawyer*
Young, Andrew Brodbeck *lawyer*
Zemaitis, Thomas Edward *lawyer*
Ziff, Lloyd Richard *lawyer*
Ziga, Kathleen *lawyer*
Ziomek, Thomas John *lawyer*

Pittsburgh

Aaron, Marcus, II *lawyer*
Aaronson, Joel P. *lawyer*
Alstadt, Lynn Jeffery *lawyer*
Aranson, Michael J. *lawyer*
Armstrong, Jack Gilliland *lawyer*
Baier, George Patrick *lawyer, electrical engineer*
Baldauf, Kent Edward *lawyer*
Basinski, Anthony Joseph *lawyer*
Beck, Paul Augustine *lawyer*
Bevan, William, III *lawyer*
Black, Alexander *lawyer*
Bleil, Walter G. *lawyer*
Blenko, Walter John, Jr. *lawyer*
Bonessa, Dennis R. *lawyer*
Borkovic, David Allen *lawyer*
Brennan, Carey M. *lawyer*
Briskman, Louis J. *lawyer*
Brown, David Ronald *lawyer*
Buerger, David Bernard *lawyer*
†Burke, Linda Beerbower *lawyer, aluminum manufacturing company executive, mining executive*
Candris, Laura A. *lawyer*
Chamberlain, Denise Kay *lawyer, banking counsel*
Cheever, George Martin *lawyer*
Christof, Joseph S. D., II *lawyer*
Clark, Richard A. *lawyer*
Colen, Frederick Haas *lawyer*
Colville, Robert E. *lawyer*
Coney, Aims C., Jr. *lawyer, labor-management negotiator*
Connors, Eugene Kenneth *lawyer*
Conti, Joy Flowers *lawyer*
Cooper, Thomas Louis *lawyer*
Cowan, Barton Zalman *lawyer*
Craig, Edward Armstrong, III *lawyer*
Daniel, Robert Michael *lawyer*
Davis, John Phillips, Jr. *lawyer*
Davis, Lewis U., Jr. *lawyer*
DeForest, Walter Pattison, III *lawyer*
Dell, Ernest Robert *lawyer*
Demmler, John Henry *lawyer*
Demmler, Ralph Henry *lawyer*
DiPietro, Melanie *lawyer*
Donnelly, Thomas Joseph *lawyer*
Doty, Robert Walter *lawyer*
Dugan, John F. *lawyer*
Ehrenwerth, David Harry *lawyer*
Evans, Bruce Dwight *lawyer*
Ewalt, Henry Ward *lawyer*
Farley, Andrew Newell *lawyer*
Ferguson, Sanford Barnett *lawyer*
Fernsler, John Paul *lawyer*
Fishman, Libby G. *lawyer*
Flatley, Lawrence Edward *lawyer*
Flinn, Michael J. *lawyer*
Fort, James Tomlinson *lawyer*
Fox, Cyril A., Jr. *law educator*
Frank, Ronald W. *lawyer, financier*
Frolik, Lawrence Anton *law educator, lawyer, consultant*
Gallagher, Daniel P., Jr. *lawyer*
Garrett, Sylvester *arbitrator*
Gerlach, G. Donald *lawyer*
Gold, Harold Arthur *lawyer*
Goldberg, Mark Joel *lawyer*
Graf, Edward Louis, Jr. *lawyer, finance executive*
Hackney, William Pendleton *lawyer*
Hardie, James Hiller *lawyer*
Harff, Charles Henry *lawyer, diversified industrial company executive*
Harmon, Megan Elizabeth *lawyer*
Hartman, Ronald G. *lawyer*
Harty, James Quinn *lawyer*
Harvey, Calvin Rea *lawyer*
Hellman, Arthur David *law educator, consultant*
Helwig, Gilbert John *lawyer*
Hershey, Dale *lawyer*
Hershey, Nathan *lawyer, educator*
Hickman, Leon Edward *lawyer, business executive*
Hill, John Howard *lawyer*
Hitt, Leo N. *lawyer, educator*
Hoffstot, Henry Phipps, Jr. *lawyer*
Hollinshead, Earl Darnell, Jr. *lawyer*
Holz, Richard Lee *lawyer*
Hough, Thomas Henry Michael *lawyer*
Johnson, Robert Alan *lawyer*
Jones, Craig Ward *lawyer*
Katarincic, Joseph Anthony *lawyer*
Kearney, Kerry A. *lawyer*
Kearns, John J., III *lawyer*
Kenrick, Charles William *lawyer*
Kent, Robert Warren *lawyer*
Kerr, William Gregg *lawyer*
Ketter, David Lee *lawyer*
Klett, Edwin Lee *lawyer*
Knapp, George Robert *lawyer*
Knox, Charles Graham *lawyer*
Krasik, Carl *lawyer*
London, Alan E. *lawyer*
Lovett, Robert G. *lawyer*
Mansmann, J. Jerome *lawyer*
May, Charles Kent *lawyer*
Mc Cartney, Robert Charles *lawyer*
McConomy, James Herbert *lawyer*
McCullough, M. Bruce *lawyer*
McGough, Walter Thomas *lawyer*
McGough, Walter Thomas, Jr. *lawyer*
McKenna, J. Frank, III *lawyer*
McLaughlin, John Sherman *lawyer*
Medonis, Robert Xavier *lawyer*
Meisel, Alan *law educator*
Mellott, Cloyd Rowe *lawyer*
Messner, Robert Thomas *lawyer, banking executive*
Miller, Harbaugh *lawyer*
Miller, James Robert *lawyer*
Miller, Patricia G. *lawyer*
Morton, James Davis *lawyer*
Mulroy, Thomas Michael *lawyer*
Munsch, Martha Hartle *lawyer*
Murdoch, David Armor *lawyer*
Murray, John Edward, Jr. *lawyer, educator, university president*
Murrin, Regis Doubet *lawyer*
Myers, Marlee S. *lawyer*
Nordenberg, Mark Alan *legal educator, university administrator*
Norris, James Harold *lawyer*
Ober, Russell John, Jr. *lawyer*
O'Connor, Donald Thomas *lawyer*
O'Connor, Edward Gearing *lawyer*
Olson, Stephen M(ichael) *lawyer*
Patton, Robert Frederick *lawyer, banker*
Perfido, Ruth S. *lawyer*
Phillips, Larry Edward *lawyer*
Plowman, Jack Wesley *lawyer*
Pohl, Paul Michael *lawyer*
Pois, Joseph *lawyer, educator*
Pomeroy, Thomas Wilson, Jr. *lawyer, former state supreme court justice*
Post, Peter David *lawyer*
Powderly, William H., III *lawyer*
Propst, John Leake *lawyer*
Prorok, Robert Francis *lawyer*
Prosperi, Louis Anthony *lawyer*
Pugliese, Robert Francis *lawyer, business executive*
Quinn, John E. *lawyer*
Randolph, Robert DeWitt *lawyer*
Reed, W. Franklin *lawyer*
Reif, Eric Peter *lawyer*
Restivo, James John, Jr. *lawyer*
Ritchey, Patrick William *lawyer*
Robinson, William M. *lawyer*
Rose, Evans, Jr. *lawyer*
Rosenberger, Bryan David *lawyer*
Sandman, Dan D. *lawyer*
Scanlon, Eugene Francis *lawyer*
Scheinholtz, Leonard Louis *lawyer*
Schliebs, Charles Allan *lawyer*
Schmidt, Edward Craig *lawyer*

Schmidt, Thomas Mellon *lawyer*
Schwab, Arthur James *lawyer*
Schwendeman, Paul William *lawyer*
Sell, William Edward *legal educator*
Shane, Peter Milo *law educator, lawyer*
Silverman, Arnold Barry *lawyer*
Singer, Paul Meyer *lawyer*
Smith, Charles Raymond, Jr. *lawyer*
Smith, William J. *lawyer*
Stein, Arland Thomas *lawyer*
Strader, James David *lawyer*
Stroyd, Arthur Heister *lawyer*
Swaim, Joseph Carter, Jr. *lawyer*
Sweeney, Clayton Anthony *lawyer, business executive*
Symons, Edward Leonard, Jr. *lawyer, educator, investment advisor*
Thompson, Thomas Martin *lawyer*
Tungate, David E. *lawyer, educator*
Turner, Harry Woodruff *lawyer*
Ubinger, John W., Jr. *lawyer*
Van Kirk, Thomas L. *lawyer*
Walton, Jon David *lawyer*
Ward, Thomas Jerome *lawyer*
Webb, William Hess *lawyer*
Wentley, Richard Taylor *lawyer*
Wiegand, Bruce *lawyer*
Woodward, Thomas Aiken *lawyer*
Wright, Thomas David *lawyer, entrepreneur*
Yorsz, Stanley *lawyer*
Zimmerman, Scott Franklin *lawyer*

Punxsutawney
Lorenzo, Nicholas Francis, Jr. *lawyer*

Reading
Linton, Jack Arthur *lawyer*
Rothermel, Daniel Krott *lawyer, holding company executive*
Welty, John Rider *lawyer*

Ridley Park
Clark, John H., Jr. *lawyer*

Saint Davids
Bovaird, Brendan Peter *lawyer*

Scranton
Cimini, Joseph Fedele *law educator, lawyer, former magistrate*
Haggerty, James Joseph *lawyer*
Howley, James McAndrew *lawyer*
Myers, Morey Mayer *lawyer*
Preate, Ernest D., Sr. *lawyer*

Solebury
Valentine, H. Jeffrey *legal association executive*

Southeastern
Husick, Lawrence Alan *lawyer*

Spring City
Mayerson, Hy *lawyer*

Tunkhannock
Jones, Edward White, II *lawyer*

Valley Forge
Croney, J. Kenneth *lawyer*
Moulton, Hugh Geoffrey *lawyer, business executive*
Posner, Ernest Gary *lawyer*

Villanova
Bersoff, Donald Neil *lawyer, psychologist*
Carrasco, Gilbert Paul *law educator*
Mulroney, Michael *lawyer, law educator, graduate program director*
Perritt, Henry Hardy, Jr. *law educator*

Washington
Allison, Jonathan *lawyer*
Richman, Stephen I. *lawyer*

Wayne
Baldwin, Frank Bruce, III *lawyer*
Griffith, Edward, II *lawyer*
Hedges, Donald Walton *lawyer*
Woodbury, Alan Tenney *lawyer*

West Chester
Judson, Franklyn Sylvanus *lawyer, consultant*

Whitehall
Cunconan-Lahr, Robin Lynn *lawyer*

Wilkes Barre
Musto, Joseph John *lawyer*

Williamsport
Ertel, Allen Edward *lawyer, former congressman*

RHODE ISLAND

Cranston
Ferguson, Christine C. *lawyer, state agency administrator*
Simonian, John S. *lawyer*

East Greenwich
Dence, Edward William, Jr. *lawyer, banker*
Flynn, Richard James *lawyer*

Kingston
Kennard, Mary Elizabeth *lawyer*

Newport
Cohen, Arthur Abram *lawyer*
Levie, Howard S(idney) *lawyer, educator, author*

Pawtucket
Robbins, Donald Michael *lawyer*
Shank, Stephen George *lawyer, toy manufacturing executive*

Providence
Arcaro, Harold Conrad, Jr. *lawyer, educator*
Borod, Richard Melvin *lawyer*
Caprio, Frank T. *lawyer, state legislator*
Carlotti, Stephen Jon *lawyer*
Cianci, Vincent Albert, Jr. *lawyer, mayor*
Cohen, Linda Marks *lawyer, securities negotiator*
Courage, Thomas Roberts *lawyer*
Curran, Joseph Patrick *lawyer*
Donnelly, Kevin William *lawyer*
Dowling, Sarah T. *lawyer, state official*
Farmer, Malcolm, III *lawyer*
Farrell, Margaret Dawson *lawyer*
Field, Noel Macdonald, Jr. *lawyer*
Gasbarro, Pasco, Jr. *lawyer*
Gorham, Bradford *lawyer*
Grimm, William Richard *lawyer*
Hopkins, Jacques Vaughn *lawyer*
Johnson, Vahe Duncan *lawyer*
†Juchatz, Wayne Warren *lawyer*
Kean, John Vaughan *lawyer*
Kersh, DeWitte Talmadge, Jr. *lawyer*
Licht, Richard A. *lawyer*
Lipsey, Howard Irwin *lawyer*
Long, Beverly Glenn *lawyer*
Mandell, Mark Steven *lawyer*
McCann, Gail Elizabeth *lawyer*
Newcomb, Martha Freeman *lawyer*
Olsen, Hans Peter *lawyer*
Pendergast, John Joseph, III *lawyer*
Pierce, Richard Hilton *lawyer*
Reed, Walter Gurnee Dyer *lawyer*
Robinson, William Philip, III *lawyer*
Salter, Lester Herbert *lawyer*
Sherman, Deming Eliot *lawyer*
Silver, Paul Allen *lawyer*
Soutter, Thomas D. *retired lawyer*
Staples, Richard Farnsworth *lawyer*
Svengalis, Kendall Frayne *law librarian*
Tobin, Bentley *lawyer*
Walker, Howard Ernest *lawyer*
Weissfeld, Joachim Alexander *lawyer*
White, Benjamin Vroom, III *lawyer*

Tiverton
Davis, Stephen Edward *lawyer*

Warwick
Knowles, Charles Timothy *lawyer, state legislator*
Sholes, David Henry *lawyer, former state senator*

Westerly
Hennessy, Dean McDonald *lawyer, multinational corporation executive*

SOUTH CAROLINA

Aiken
Buchanan, Robert Lee, Jr. *lawyer*

Anderson
Glenn, Michael Douglas *lawyer*
Watkins, William Law *retired lawyer*

Beaufort
Harvey, William Brantley, Jr. *lawyer, former lieutenant governor*

Camden
Furman, Hezekiah Wyndol Carroll *lawyer*

Charleston
Cannon, Hugh *lawyer*
Farr, Charles Sims *lawyer*
Good, Joseph Cole, Jr. *lawyer*
Grimball, William Heyward *lawyer*
Robinson, Neil Cibley, Jr. *lawyer*
Young, Joseph Rutledge, Jr. *lawyer*

Clemson
Cox, Headley Morris, Jr. *lawyer, educator*

Columbia
Adams, Gregory Burke *lawyer, educator*
Bailey, George Screven *lawyer*
Baker, Donald *lawyer*
†Baum, Marsha Lynn *law educator*
Blanton, Hoover Clarence *lawyer*
Clifford, Amie Lois *prosecutor*
Elliott, John Dewey *lawyer*
Finkel, Gerald Michael *lawyer*
Foster, Robert Watson, Sr. *legal educator*
Haimbaugh, George Dow, Jr. *lawyer, educator*
Knight, Henry Scarborough, Jr. *lawyer*
Matthews, Steve Allen *lawyer*
Mc Cullough, Ralph Clayton, II *lawyer, educator*
Nelson, William Shannon, II *lawyer*
Nexsen, Julian Jacobs *lawyer*
Rogers, Timothy Folk *lawyer*
Scarborough, Claude Mood, Jr. *lawyer*
Sloan, Frank Keenan *lawyer, writer*
Tate, Harold Simmons, Jr. *lawyer*
Wedlock, Eldon Dyment, Jr. *law educator*
Wells, Robert Steven *law association executive*
Wolfe, George B. *lawyer*

Easley
Grantham, George Leighton *lawyer, banker, utility company executive*

Fort Jackson
Conrad, Paul Edward *lawyer*

Georgetown
Moore, Albert Cunningham *lawyer, insurance company executive*

Greenville
Foulke, Edwin Gerhart, Jr. *lawyer*
Freeman, David Lynn *lawyer*
Hagood, William Milliken, III *lawyer*
Haskins, Terry Edward *lawyer, politician*
Horton, James Wright *retired lawyer*
Thompson, Robert Thomas *lawyer*
Todd, John Dickerson, Jr. *lawyer*
Traxler, William Byrd *lawyer*
Walker, Wesley M. *lawyer*
Walters, Johnnie McKeiver *lawyer*

Greenwood
Sigety, Charles Edward *lawyer, medical products executive*

Hartsville
DeLoach, Harris E(ugene), Jr. *lawyer, manufacturing company executive*
Shelley, James Herbert *lawyer, paper company executive*

Hilton Head Island
Becker, Karl Martin *lawyer, investment company executive*
Rose, William Shepard, Jr. *lawyer, former federal official*
Scarminach, Charles Anthony *lawyer*

Landrum
Hilton, Ordway *document examiner*

Lexington
Wilkins, Robert Pearce *lawyer*

Mount Pleasant
McConnell, John William, Jr. *lawyer*

Newberry
Pope, Thomas Harrington, Jr. *lawyer*

Spartanburg
Williams, John Cornelius *lawyer*

SOUTH DAKOTA

Britton
Farrar, Frank Leroy *lawyer, former governor*

Dakota Dunes
Putney, Mark William *lawyer, utility executive*

Parker
Zimmer, John Herman *lawyer*

Pierre
Johnson, Julie Marie *lawyer, lobbyist, governor's cabinet*
Thompson, Charles Murray *lawyer*

Rapid City
Foye, Thomas Harold *lawyer*
Viken, Linda Lea Margaret *lawyer*

Sioux Falls
Kirby, Dan Laird *lawyer*
LaFave, LeAnn Larson *lawyer*

Yankton
Hirsch, Robert William *lawyer*

TENNESSEE

Brentwood
Bodzy, Glen Alan *lawyer*

Chattanooga
Bahner, Thomas Maxfield *lawyer*
Proctor, John Franklin *lawyer*
Witt, Raymond Buckner, Jr. *lawyer*

Clarksville
Smith, Gregory Dale *lawyer*

Cleveland
Fisher, Richard Ashley *lawyer*

Fayetteville
Dickey, John Harwell *public defender*

Germantown
Ewing, William Hickman, Jr. *lawyer*

Hermitage
Lockmiller, David Alexander *lawyer, educator*

Knoxville
Arnett, Foster Deaver *lawyer*
Christenbury, Edward Samuel *lawyer*
Dillard, W. Thomas *lawyer*
Hagood, Lewis Russell *lawyer*
Howard, Lewis Spilman *lawyer*
Lucas, John Allen *lawyer*
Phillips, Jerry Juan *law educator*
Phillips, Thomas Wade *lawyer*
Rayson, Edwin Hope *lawyer*
Reynolds, Glenn Harlan *law educator*
Roth, Stephen Evans *lawyer*
Schmidt, Benno Charles, Jr. *lawyer, educator*
Vogel, Howard H. *lawyer*
Waters, John B. *lawyer*
Wheeler, John Watson *lawyer*

Lookout Mountain
Leitner, Paul R. *lawyer*

Memphis
Allen, Newton Perkins *lawyer*
Armstrong, Walter Preston, Jr. *lawyer*
Broadhurst, Jerome Anthony *lawyer*
Brode, Marvin Jay *lawyer, former state legislator*
Buchignani, Leo Joseph *lawyer*
Burch, Lucius Edward, Jr. *lawyer*
Clark, Ross Bert, II *lawyer*
Cody, Walter James Michael *lawyer, former state official*
Friedman, Robert Michael *lawyer*
Gilman, Ronald Lee *lawyer*
Greenberg, Susan Lynn *lawyer*
Harpster, James Erving *lawyer*
Harvey, Albert C. *lawyer*
Johnson, Harry A., III *lawyer*
Manire, James McDonnell *lawyer*
Noel, Randall Deane *lawyer*
Norville, Craig Hubert *lawyer*
Pierotti, John William *prosecutor*
Russell, James Franklin *lawyer*
Springfield, James Francis *retired lawyer, banker*
Streibich, Harold Cecil *lawyer*
Tate, Stonewall Shepherd *lawyer*

Nashville
Alexander, Andrew Lamar (Lamar Alexander) *lawyer, former secretary of education, former governor*
Allred, Michael Sylvester *lawyer*
Bass, James Orin *lawyer*
Belton, Robert *law educator*
Berry, William Wells *lawyer*
Bloch, Frank Samuel *law educator*
Blumstein, James Franklin *legal educator, lawyer, consultant*
Bostick, Charles Dent *lawyer, educator*
Brown, Joe Blackburn *lawyer*
Campbell, Gilbert R., Jr. *lawyer*
Cantrell, Luther E., Jr. *lawyer*
Charney, Jonathan Isa *legal educator, lawyer*
Cheek, James Howe, III *lawyer*
Covington, Robert Newman *lawyer, educator*
Culbertson, Katheryn Campbell *lawyer*
Ely, James Wallace, Jr. *legal educator*
Fish, Donald Winston *lawyer, health care company executive*
Frazier, Keith David *lawyer*
Gillmor, John Edward *lawyer*
Hall, Donald J. *law educator*
Hardin, Hal D. *lawyer, former U.S. attorney, former judge*
Hart, Richard Banner *lawyer*
Harwell, Aubrey Biggs *lawyer*
†Hood, Howard Allison *law librarian*
Langevoort, Donald Carl *law educator*
Ledyard, Robins Heard *lawyer*
Levinson, L(eslie) Harold *lawyer, educator*
Lyon, Philip K(irkland) *lawyer*
Maier, Harold Geistweit *legal educator, lawyer*
Martin, Henry Alan *lawyer*
May, Joseph Leserman (Jack) *lawyer*
McCoy, Thomas Raymond *lawyer, educator*
Reichman, Jerome H. *law educator*
Sanders, Paul Hampton *lawyer, retired educator, arbitrator/mediator*
Schoenblum, Jeffrey A. *law educator*
Sims, Wilson *lawyer*
Soderquist, Larry Dean *lawyer, educator*
Thompson, Almose Alphonse *lawyer, educator*
Trautman, Herman Louis *lawyer, educator*

TEXAS

Abilene
Boone, Billy Warren *lawyer, judge*
Wilson, Stanley P. *retired lawyer*

Amarillo
Madden, Wales Hendrix, Jr. *lawyer*
Neal, A. Curtis *retired lawyer*
Smithee, John True *lawyer, state legislator*

Austin
Ahrens, Carolyn *lawyer*
Allday, Martin Lewis *lawyer*
Allison, John Robert *lawyer, educator, author*
Anderson, David Arnold *law educator*
Baade, Hans Wolfgang *legal educator, law expert*
Barndt, Richard V. *law educator*
Binder, Bob *lawyer*
Bissex, Walter Earl *lawyer*
Bobbitt, Philip Chase *lawyer, educator, writer*
Bruff, Harold Hastings *law educator*
Byrd, Linward Tonnett *lawyer, rancher*
Cantilo, Patrick Herrera *lawyer*
Carson, Loftus C., II *law educator*
Churgin, Michael Jay *law educator*
Cook, J. Rowland *lawyer*
Davis, Robert Larry *lawyer*
Dawson, Robert Oscar *lawyer, educator*
Dodge, Joseph M. *law educator*
Dougherty, John Chrysostom, III *lawyer*
Dzienkowski, John Stephen *law educator*
Finn, Patricia Gloria *lawyer*
Fishkin, James S. *law educator*
Gambrell, James Bruton, III *lawyer, educator*
Gangstad, John Erik *lawyer*
Gergen, Mark P. *law educator*
Getman, Julius Gerson *law educator, lawyer*
Gibson, William Willard, Jr. *law educator*
Goldstein, E. Ernest *lawyer*
Golemon, Ronald Kinnan *lawyer*
Gonzales, Alexander J. *lawyer*
Goode, Steven *law educator*
Graglia, Lino Anthony *lawyer, educator*
Greene, John Joseph *lawyer*
Greig, Brian Strother *lawyer*
Hamilton, Dagmar Strandberg *lawyer, educator*
Hamilton, Robert Woodruff *law educator*
Hardin, Dale Wayne *retired law educator*
Harrison, Richard Wayne *lawyer*
Hazel, J. Patrick *law educator*
Hedrick, John Richard *lawyer*
Helburn, Isadore B. *arbitrator, mediator, educator*
Henderson, George Ervin *lawyer*
Huie, William Orr *legal educator*
Hunter, William Morgan *lawyer*
Ikard, Frank Neville, Jr. *lawyer*
Ingram, Denny Ouzts, Jr. *lawyer, educator*
Jentz, Gaylord Adair *law educator*
Johnson, Calvin Harsha *law educator*
Johnson, Corwin Waggoner *lawyer, educator*
Jordan, Barbara C. *lawyer, educator, former congresswoman*
Knight, Gary *lawyer, educator, publisher*
Laycock, Harold Douglas *law educator, writer*
Levinson, Sanford Victor *legal educator*
Markovits, Inga *law educator*
Markovits, Richard Spencer *lawyer, educator*
Mauzy, Oscar Holcombe *lawyer, retired state supreme court justice*
McDaniel, Myra Atwell *lawyer, former state official*
McGinnis, Robert Campbell *lawyer*
Mersky, Roy Martin *law educator, librarian*
Mullenix, Linda Susan *lawyer, educator*
Oates, Carl Everette *lawyer*
Orr, David L. *lawyer*
Painton, Russell Elliott *lawyer, mechanical engineer*
Pickens, Franklin Ace *lawyer*
Powe, L. A. Scot, Jr. *law educator*
Powers, Pike, Jr. *lawyer*
Powers, William Charles, Jr. *law educator*
Rabban, David M. *law educator*
Ratliff, Jack *law educator*
Rau, Alan Scott *law educator*
Rider, Brian Clayton *lawyer*
Robertson, David Wyatt *lawyer, educator*
Robertson, John A. *law educator*

Ruud, Millard Harrington *former legal association administrator, retired educator*
Sampson, John J. *law educator*
Shapiro, Sander Wolf *lawyer*
Sherman, Edward Francis *lawyer, educator*
Sherman, Max Ray *lawyer, academic executive, former state senator*
Sims, Robert Barry *lawyer*
Smith, Ernest E. *lawyer, educator*
Stephen, John Erle *lawyer, consultant*
Strauser, Robert Wayne *lawyer*
Sturley, Michael F. *law educator*
Sullivan, Teresa Ann *law and sociology educator, academic administrator*
Sutton, John F., Jr. *law educator, university dean, lawyer*
Temple, Larry Eugene *lawyer*
Thomajan, Robert *lawyer, management and financial consultant*
Tigar, Michael Edward *lawyer, educator*
Tottenham, Terry Oliver *lawyer*
Wagner, William Bradley *lawyer*
Webb, Wayne Earl, Jr. *lawyer, engineer*
Weddington, Sarah Ragle *lawyer, educator*
Weinberg, Louise *lawyer, educator, author*
Weintraub, Russell Jay *lawyer, educator*
Wellborn, Olin Guy, III *law educator*
Westbrook, Jay Lawrence *law educator*
Wright, Charles Alan *lawyer, educator, author*
Yudof, Mark G. *lawyer, educator, academic administrator*
Zimmerman, Louis Seymour *lawyer*

Bangs
McDonald, Charles Eugene *lawyer*

Beaumont
Johnson, Cecil L. *lawyer*

Bellville
Dittert, J. Lee, Jr. *lawyer*

Big Spring
Morrison, Walton Stephen *lawyer*

Cleburne
MacLean, John Ronald *lawyer*
Urban, Carlyle Woodrow *retired lawyer*

Corpus Christi
Bonilla, Tony *lawyer*
Branscomb, Harvie, Jr. *lawyer*
Bucklin, Leonard Herbert *lawyer*
Cockrell, William F(oster), Jr. *lawyer*
McMillen, James Thomas *lawyer*
Miller, Carroll Gerard, Jr. (Gerry Miller) *lawyer*
Vanaman, Charles Arthur *lawyer*
Wood, James Allen *lawyer*

Corsicana
Dawson, Leighton Brooks *lawyer*

Dallas
Abney, Frederick Sherwood *lawyer*
Acker, Rodney *lawyer*
Adkins, M. Douglas *lawyer*
Admire, Ben H. *lawyer*
Agnich, Richard John *lawyer, electronics company executive*
Akin, Henry David *lawyer*
Alford, Margaret Suzanne *lawyer*
Anderson, Barbara McComas *lawyer*
Anderson, E. Karl *lawyer*
Anglin, Michael Williams *lawyer*
Armour, James Lott *lawyer*
Babcock, Charles Lynde, IV *lawyer*
Baer, Henry *lawyer*
Baggett, W. Mike *lawyer*
Bangs, Nelson A. *lawyer, soft drink company executive*
Barbee, Linton E. *lawyer*
Barnes, Hershell Louis, Jr. *lawyer*
Bass, John Fred *lawyer*
Beane, Jerry Lynn *lawyer*
Berry, Buford Preston *lawyer*
Besing, Ray Gilbert *lawyer*
Birkeland, Bryan Collier *lawyer*
Bishop, Bryan Edwards *lawyer*
Bishop, R. Doak *lawyer*
Blachly, Jack Lee *lawyer*
Blau, Charles William *lawyer, former government official*
Bliss, Robert Harms *lawyer*
Block, Steven Robert *lawyer*
Bonesio, Woodrow Michael *lawyer*
Bonney, Samuel Robert *lawyer*
Boone, Michael Mauldin *lawyer*
Boone, Oliver Kiel *lawyer*
Boren, Benjamin N. *lawyer*
Boyd, Dan Stewart *lawyer*
Brin, Royal Henry, Jr. *lawyer*
Bromberg, Henri Louie, Jr. *lawyer*
Bromberg, John E. *lawyer*
Bumpas, Stuart Maryman *lawyer*
Burke, William Temple, Jr. *lawyer*
Busbee, Kline Daniel, Jr. *lawyer, law educator*
Bux, William John *lawyer*
Campfield, Regis William *law educator*
Carlton, Dean *lawyer*
Castle, John Raymond, Jr. *lawyer*
Clark, John W., Jr. *lawyer*
Coleman, Robert Winston *lawyer*
Collins, Michael Homer *lawyer*
Conant, Allah B., Jr. *lawyer*
Copley, Edward Alvin *lawyer*
Costello, John Francis, Jr. (Jack Costello) *lawyer*
Cowart, T(homas) David *lawyer*
Cowling, David Edward *lawyer*
Crain, Gayla Campbell *lawyer*
Creel, Luther Edward, III *lawyer*
Crowley, James Worthington *retired lawyer, business consultant, investor*
Crowson, James Lawrence *lawyer, financial company executive*
Curran, Geoffrey Michael *lawyer*
Dale, Erwin Randolph *lawyer, author*
Davis, Clarice McDonald *lawyer*
Davis, Walter Richard *lawyer*
DeBusk, Manuel Conrad *lawyer*
Dillard, Robert Lionel, Jr. *lawyer, former life insurance executive*
Doke, Marshall J., Jr. *lawyer*
Dunlap, George Carter *lawyer*
Dutton, Diana Cheryl *lawyer*
Dyess, Bobby Dale *lawyer*
Eddleman, William Roseman *lawyer*
Emery, Herschell Gene *lawyer*
Engleman, Donald James *lawyer*
Evans, Roger *lawyer*
Everbach, Otto George *lawyer*
Everett, C. Curtis *lawyer*
Fanning, Barry Hedges *lawyer*
Fanning, Robert Allen *lawyer*
Feld, Alan David *lawyer*
Feldman, H. Larry *lawyer*
Fennell, Thomas E. *lawyer*
Fenner, Suzan Ellen *lawyer*
Finn, Frank *lawyer*
Fishman, Edward Marc *lawyer*
Flanagan, Christie Stephen *lawyer*
Flegle, Jim L. *lawyer*
Fordyce, Edward Winfield, Jr. *lawyer*
Forsythe, Earl Andrew *lawyer, steel company executive*
Fortado, Michael George *lawyer*
Freling, Richard Alan *lawyer*
French, Joseph Jordan, Jr. *lawyer*
Frisbie, Curtis Lynn, Jr. *lawyer*
Galvin, Charles O'Neill *law educator*
Gandy, Dean Murray *lawyer*
Gaswirth, Ronald M. *lawyer*
Gilchrist, Henry *lawyer*
Gilliam, John A. *lawyer*
Gilmore, Jerry Carl *lawyer*
Ginsburg, Lawrence David *lawyer*
Glancy, Walter John *lawyer*
Godfrey, Cullen Michael *lawyer*
Goodell, Sol *retired lawyer*
Goodstein, Barnett Maurice *lawyer*
Gores, Christopher Merrel *lawyer*
Goyne, Roderick A. *lawyer*
Grissom, Gerald Homer *lawyer*
Grundman, Valentine Rock, Jr. *lawyer*
Gump, Richard Anthony *lawyer*
Gutman, Richard Edward *lawyer*
Hamon, Richard Grady *lawyer*
Harper, Harlan, Jr. *lawyer*
Harrell, Gwendolyn Baumann *lawyer*
Harrell, Morris *lawyer*
Hart, John Clifton *lawyer*
Hartnett, Will Ford *lawyer*
Hauer, John Longan *lawyer*
Hawkins, Jack Wade *lawyer*
Haworth, Charles Ray *lawyer*
Henkel, Kathryn G. *lawyer*
Hennessy, Daniel Kraft *lawyer*
Hicks, Marion Lawrence, Jr. (Larry Hicks) *lawyer*
Hinshaw, Chester John *lawyer*
Hollingsworth, John Mark *lawyer*
Horton, Paul Bradfield *lawyer*
Howie, John Robert *lawyer*
Huffman, Gregory Scott Combest *lawyer*
Hughes, Vester Thomas, Jr. *lawyer*
Humble, Monty Garfield *lawyer*
Hunt, David Ford *lawyer*
Hunter, Marsha L. *lawyer*
Jayson, Melinda Gayle *lawyer*
†Jennings, Susan Jane *lawyer*
Jobe, Larry Alton *legal association executive*
Johnson, James Harold *lawyer*
Johnson, Judith Kay *lawyer*
Johnson, Richard Craig *lawyer*
Jones, John Gornal *lawyer*
Joplin, Julian Mike *lawyer*
Jordan, Robert W. *lawyer*
Jordan, William Davis *lawyer*
Keithley, Bradford Gene *lawyer*
Keller, William L. *lawyer*
Kennedy, Marc J. *lawyer*
Kent, David Charles *lawyer*
Kimbrough, Allen Wayne *lawyer*
Kinnebrew, Jackson Metcalfe *lawyer*
Kneipper, Richard Keith *lawyer*
Kuhn, Willis Evan, II *lawyer, mediator*
LaBrec, David John *lawyer*
Lacy, John Ford *lawyer*
Lafving, Brian Douglas *lawyer*
La Jone, Jay Allen *lawyer*
Lan, Donald Paul, Jr. *lawyer*
Lancaster, John Lynch, III *lawyer*
Lang, Douglas Steward *lawyer*
Lang-Miers, Elizabeth Ann *lawyer*
Lee, George Terry, Jr. *lawyer*
Levin, Richard C. *lawyer*
Levine, Harold *lawyer*
Little, Jack Merville *lawyer*
Livingstone, William Edwin, III *lawyer*
Lombard, Richard Spencer *lawyer*
Lowden, Scott Richard *lawyer*
Lowenberg, Michael *lawyer*
Luther, David Gaston, Jr. *lawyer*
Lynch, Thomas Wimp *lawyer*
Madrid, Jay Joseph *lawyer*
Mahoney, Margaret Ann *lawyer*
Mankoff, Ronald Morton *lawyer*
Maris, Stephen S. *lawyer, educator*
Martin, Boe Willis *lawyer*
Martin, Richard Kelley *lawyer*
Massman, Richard Allan *lawyer*
McCLure, William B., Jr. *lawyer*
McCormack, William Arthur *lawyer*
Mc Elhaney, John Hess *lawyer*
McGowan, Patrick Francis *lawyer*
McGregor, Martin Luther, Jr. *lawyer*
McKnight, Joseph Webb *law educator, historian*
McLain, Maurice Clayton *lawyer, real estate executive*
McLane, David Glenn *lawyer*
†McNamara, Anne H. *lawyer, corporate executive*
McNamara, Lawrence John *lawyer*
McNamara, Martin Burr *lawyer, oil and gas company executive*
McWilliams, Mike C. *lawyer*
Mears, Rona Robbins *lawyer*
Mebus, Robert Gwynne *lawyer*
Menges, John Kenneth, Jr. *lawyer*
Micciche, Daniel John *lawyer*
Middleton, Linda Jean Greathouse *lawyer*
Mighell, Kenneth John *lawyer*
Mills, Jerry Woodrow *lawyer*
Montoya, Regina T. *lawyer, television and radio commentator*
Moore, Stanley Ray *lawyer*
Morgan, Steven Michael *lawyer*
Morris, Rebecca Robinson *lawyer*
Mow, Robert Henry, Jr. *lawyer*
Mueller, Mark Christopher *lawyer*
Mullinax, Otto B. *lawyer*
Nelson, Steven Douglas *lawyer*
Nicewander, Dan Leon *lawyer, rancher*
Nichols, Henry Louis *lawyer*
Nihill, Julian Dumontiel *lawyer*
Nordlund, William Chalmers *lawyer*
Oliver, Thomas William *lawyer*
Palmer, Ronald Leigh *lawyer*
Parker, Angelo Pan *lawyer*
Patterson, Joseph Redwine *lawyer*
Peart, Sherry Hartman *lawyer*
Penegar, Kenneth Lawing *law educator*
Perkins, Alan J. *lawyer*
Peterson, Edward Adrian *lawyer*
Pettey, Walter Graves, III *lawyer*
Pew, John Glenn, Jr. *lawyer*
Phelan, Robin Eric *lawyer*
Pingree, Bruce Douglas *lawyer*
Pleasant, James Scott *lawyer*
Portman, Glenn Arthur *lawyer*
Price, John Aley *lawyer*
Pritzker, Jay Arthur *lawyer*
Purnell, Maurice Eugene, Jr. *lawyer*
Radford, Norman DePue, Jr. *lawyer*
Raggio, Kenneth Gaylord *lawyer*
Raggio, Louise Ballerstedt *lawyer*
Ray, George Einar *lawyer*
Reid, Rust Endicott *lawyer*
Rendell, Robert Sloat *lawyer*
Rice, Darrel Alan *lawyer*
Riggs, Arthur Jordy *retired lawyer*
Ringle, Brett Adelbert *lawyer*
Ritchie, Robert Field *lawyer*
Roberts, Harry Morris, Jr. *lawyer*
Robinson, Lawrence Dewitt *lawyer*
Roche, William Joseph *lawyer*
Rodgers, John Hunter *lawyer*
Rosenberg, David Howard *lawyer, mediator, marketing executive*
Rudberg, Joe Arthur *lawyer*
Rundell, Thomas Gardner *lawyer*
St. Claire, Frank Arthur *lawyer*
†Satterwhite, William T. *lawyer, energy company executive*
Savage, Wallace Hamilton *lawyer*
Schoenbrun, Larry Lynn *lawyer*
Schreiber, Sally Ann *lawyer*
Schulman, Michael Robert *lawyer*
Schwartz, Charles Morris *lawyer*
Sechrest, William B. *lawyer*
See, Robert Fleming, Jr. *lawyer*
Sheeder, Robert Elwood *lawyer*
Siegel, Thomas Louis *lawyer*
Smith, Larry Van *lawyer*
Springer, Stanley G. *lawyer*
Stalcup, Joe Alan *lawyer, clergyman*
Staley, Joseph Hardin, Jr. *lawyer*
Steinberg, Lawrence Edward *lawyer*
Stilwell, John Quincy *lawyer*
Stockard, James Alfred *lawyer*
Storey, Charles Porter *lawyer*
Strauss, Robert Schwarz *lawyer, former ambassador*
Swanson, Wallace Martin *lawyer*
Thau, William Albert, Jr. *lawyer*
True, Roy Joe *lawyer*
Tubb, James Clarence *lawyer*
Tucker, Laurey Dan *lawyer*
Tygrett, Howard Volney, Jr. *lawyer*
Veach, Robert Raymond, Jr. *lawyer*
Vestal, Tommy Ray *lawyer*
Vetter, James George, Jr. *lawyer*
Walden, Linda L. *lawyer*
Walkowiak, Vincent Steven *lawyer*
Wallenstein, James Harry *lawyer*
Weekley, Frederick Clay, Jr. *lawyer*
Weiland, Stephen Cass *lawyer*
Wells, Leonard Nathaniel David, Jr. *lawyer*
Werner, Joseph Granberry *lawyer*
West, William Beverley, III *lawyer*
White, James Richard *lawyer*
Williams, James Alexander *lawyer*
Willingham, Clark Suttles *lawyer*
Wilson, Claude Raymond, Jr. *lawyer*
Winborn, Terry Lee *lawyer*
Winkel, Judy Kay *lawyer*
Winn, Edward Burton *lawyer*
Wise, Marvin Jay *lawyer*
Wright, Wallace Mathias *lawyer*
Young, Barney Thornton *lawyer*
Zisman, Barry Stuart *lawyer*

Denton
Lawhon, John E., III *lawyer, former county official*
Waage, Mervin Bernard *lawyer*

Diboll
Ericson, Roger Delwin *lawyer, forest resource company executive*

El Paso
Ainsa, Francis Swinburne *lawyer*
Feuille, Richard Harlan *lawyer*
Marshall, Richard Treeger *lawyer*
McCotter, James Rawson *lawyer*
Smith, Tad Randolph *lawyer*

Euless
Paran, Mark Lloyd *lawyer*

Fort Worth
Becker, James William *lawyer, natural resource and transportation holding company executive*
Brown, C. Harold *lawyer*
Brown, Richard Lee *lawyer*
Chalk, John Allen *lawyer*
Collins, Whitfield James *lawyer*
Crumley, John Walter *lawyer*
Dean, Beale *lawyer*
Franks, Jon Michael *lawyer, mediator*
Greenhill, William Duke *lawyer*
Kelly, Dee J. *lawyer*
Keltner, David E. *lawyer, judge*
Mack, Theodore *lawyer*
McConnell, Michael Arthur *lawyer*
McMackin, John William *lawyer*
Minton, Jerry Davis *lawyer, former banker*
Munn, Cecil Edwin *lawyer*
Ratliff, William D., III *lawyer*
Ratliff, William Durrah, Jr. *lawyer*
Sharpe, James Shelby *lawyer*
Tilley, Rice M(atthews), Jr. *lawyer*

Galveston
Bircher, Edgar Allen *lawyer*
Caldwell, Garnett Ernest *lawyer*
Schwartz, Aaron Robert *lawyer, former state legislator*

Granbury
Fletcher, Riley Eugene *lawyer*

Grand Prairie
Martin-Nagle, Carol Renee *lawyer*

Grapevine
Hatch, John D. *lawyer, consultant*

Hallettsville
Baber, Wilbur H., Jr. *lawyer*

Harlingen
Ephraim, Charles *lawyer*
Johnson, Orrin Wendell *lawyer*

Heath
Kolodey, Fred James *lawyer*

Horseshoe Bay
Moore, Lawrence Jack *lawyer*

Houston
Abercia, Ralph *lawyer, financial advisor*
Addison, Linda Leuchter *lawyer*
Adelman, Graham Lewis *lawyer*
Alexander, Neil Kenton *lawyer*
Allender, John Roland *lawyer*
Anders, Milton Howard *lawyer*
Anderson, Eric Severin *lawyer*
Anderson, Robert Dennis *lawyer*
Anderson, Thomas Dunaway *retired lawyer*
Arnold, Gordon Thomas *lawyer*
Atlas, Nancy Friedman *lawyer, mediator, arbitrator*
Atlas, Scott Jerome *lawyer*
Austin, Page Insley *lawyer*
Backus, Marcia Ellen *lawyer*
Bagwell, Louis Lee *lawyer*
Baker, James Addison, III *lawyer, former government official*
Bambace, Robert Shelly *lawyer*
Barnett, Edward William *lawyer*
Barrett, John Adams *lawyer*
Bech, Douglas York *lawyer*
Bellatti, Lawrence Lee *lawyer*
Berg, David Howard *lawyer*
Berry, Thomas Eugene *lawyer*
Bistline, F. Walter, Jr. *lawyer*
Blackshear, A. T., Jr. *lawyer*
Bliss, Ronald Glenn *lawyer*
Bluestein, Edwin A., Jr. *lawyer*
Bonica, John R. *lawyer*
Boston, Charles D. *lawyer*
Botley, Calvin *lawyer, magistrate judge*
Bousquet, Thomas Gourrier *lawyer*
Boyd, John E. *lawyer*
Brann, Richard Roland *lawyer*
Brantley, John Randolph *lawyer*
Bridges, David Manning *lawyer*
Brinsmade, Lyon Louis *lawyer*
Brinson, Gay Creswell, Jr. *lawyer*
Buckingham, Edwin John, III *lawyer*
Burch, Voris Reagan *lawyer*
Caddy, Michael Douglas *lawyer*
Caldwell, James Wiley *lawyer*
Calhoun, Frank Wayne *lawyer, former state legislator*
Campbell, Bert Louis *lawyer*
Carmody, James Albert *lawyer*
Carroll, James Vincent, III *lawyer*
Carsey, Lamberth S. *lawyer*
Caudill, William Howard *lawyer*
Chafin, James Scott *lawyer*
Cheavens, Joseph D. *lawyer*
Clark, Pat English *lawyer*
Clarke, Robert Logan *lawyer*
Clemenceau, Paul B. *lawyer*
Clore, Lawrence H. *lawyer*
Cochran, Les *lawyer*
Coghlan, Kelly Jack *lawyer*
Cook, B. Thomas *lawyer*
Cook, Eugene Augustus *lawyer*
Couch, J. O. Terrell *lawyer, former oil company executive*
Cox, James Talley *lawyer*
Crites, Omar Don, Jr. *lawyer*
Crooker, John H., Jr. *lawyer*
Cunningham, Tom Alan *lawyer*
Curfiss, Robert Clinton *lawyer*
Curry, Alton Frank *lawyer*
Dack, Christopher Edward Hughes *lawyer*
Davis, Martha Algenita Scott *lawyer*
DeMent, James Alderson, Jr. *lawyer*
Denny, Otway B., Jr. *lawyer*
Derrick, James V., Jr. *lawyer*
Dillon, Clifford Brien *retired lawyer*
Dimitry, Theodore George *lawyer*
Dinkins, Carol Eggert *lawyer*
Douglas, James Matthew *law educator*
Douglass, John Jay *lawyer, educator*
Driscoll, Michael Hardee *lawyer*
Dunlop, Fred Hurston *lawyer*
Dutton, Uriel Elvis *lawyer*
Dykes, Osborne Jefferson, III *lawyer*
Eastland, S. Stacy *lawyer*
Ebert, Alfred H., Jr. *lawyer*
Epstein, Jon David *lawyer, educator*
Estes, Carl Lewis, II *lawyer*
Eubank, J. Thomas *lawyer*
Ewell, Vincent Fletcher *lawyer*
Fant, Douglas Vernon *lawyer*
Farenthold, Frances Tarlton *lawyer*
Farnsworth, T. Brooke *lawyer*
Feldcamp, Larry Bernard *lawyer*
Feldt, J(ohn) Harrell *lawyer*
Finch, Michael Paul *lawyer*
Fortenbach, Ray Thomas *retired lawyer*
Foster, Charles Crawford *lawyer, educator*
French, Layne Bryan *lawyer, investor, community volunteer*
Fullenweider, Donn Charles *lawyer*
Gagnon, Stewart Walter *lawyer*
Gano, John *lawyer*
Garrett, Jasper Patrick *lawyer*
Garten, David B. *lawyer*
Gayle, Gibson, Jr. *lawyer*
Gillmore, Kathleen Cory *lawyer*
Gissel, L. Henry, Jr. *lawyer*
Goldstein, Jack Charles *lawyer*
†Gormley, W. Clarke *lawyer*
Gover, Alan Shore *lawyer*
Graham, Michael Paul *lawyer*
Gray, Archibald Duncan, Jr. *lawyer*
Gruben, Karl Taylor *law librarian*
Gunter, Joseph Clifford, III *lawyer*
Halloran, Bernard Thorpe *lawyer*
Hanen, Andrew Scott *lawyer*
Harper, Alfred John, II *lawyer*
Harrington, Bruce Michael *lawyer, investor*

Hartrick, Janice Kay lawyer
Harvin, David Tarleton lawyer
Harvin, William Charles lawyer
Hermann, Robert John lawyer, corporate executive
Hicks, Taylor M., Jr. lawyer
Hinton, Paula Weems lawyer
Hollyfield, John Scoggins lawyer
Holstead, John Burnham lawyer
Hoover, Howard S., Jr. lawyer
Hoyt, Mont Powell lawyer
Hudson, Frank N. lawyer, real estate developer
Hudspeth, Chalmers Mac lawyer, educator
Huelbig, Larry Leggett lawyer
Hurd, Charles W. lawyer
Hutcheson, Joseph Chappell, III lawyer
Illig, Carl lawyer
Jacobus, Charles Joseph lawyer, title company executive, author
Jamail, Joseph Dahr, Jr. lawyer
Jansen, Donald Orville lawyer
Jewell, George Hiram lawyer
Jones, Frank Griffith lawyer
Jordan, Charles Milton lawyer
Jordan, W. Carl lawyer
Kaplan, Lee Landa lawyer
Katz, M. Marvin lawyer
Kay, Joel Phillip lawyer
Kelly, Hugh Rice lawyer
Kelly, William Franklin, Jr. lawyer
Knull, William H., III lawyer
Knull, Yolanda Chavez lawyer
Koenig, Rodney Curtis lawyer, rancher
Kosut, Kenneth Paul lawyer
Kratochvil, L(ouis) Glen lawyer
Krebs, Arno William, Jr. lawyer
Krieger, Paul Edward lawyer
LaBoon, Robert Bruce lawyer
Lake, Kathleen C. lawyer
†Lannie, Paul Anthony lawyer
Larkin, Lee Roy lawyer
Lavenant, Rene Paul, Jr. lawyer
Lawhon, William Griffith lawyer
Lawrie, Robert George lawyer
Lawson, Ben F. lawyer, international legal consultant
Lee, William Gentry lawyer
Lilienstern, O. Clayton lawyer
Lionberger, Richard Lee lawyer
Loeffler, James Joseph lawyer
Love, Jeffrey Benton lawyer
Lovelace, Byron Keith lawyer, management consultant
Maloney, James Edward lawyer
Marley, Everett Armistead, Jr. lawyer
Marshall, J. Howard, II lawyer
Marston, Edgar Jean, III lawyer
Martin, Neil lawyer
Massad, Stephen Albert lawyer
Mayer, John lawyer
Mayor, Richard Blair lawyer
McClure, Daniel M. lawyer
McDaniel, Jarrel Dave lawyer
McDonald, Gail Jacolev lawyer
McEvily, Daniel Vincent Sean lawyer, author
McMahon, Catherine Driscoll lawyer
McQuarrie, Claude Monroe, III lawyer
Melo, Thomas M. lawyer
Miller, Barry Rixmann lawyer
Miller, Robert Daniel lawyer
Moehlman, Michael Scott lawyer
Moncure, John Lewis lawyer
Morris, (William) Carloss lawyer, insurance company executive
†Morris, Malcolm Stewart lawyer
Morrison, Jennifer Ann lawyer, oil company executive
Mueller, Carl Gustav, Jr. lawyer
Murphy, Ewell Edward, Jr. lawyer
Myers, Franklin lawyer, oil service company executive
Nations, Howard Lynn lawyer
Nickens, Jacks Clarence lawyer
Niebruegge, Michael E. lawyer
Nimmer, Raymond T. lawyer, law educator
Nolen, Roy Lemuel lawyer
Northrop, Monroe lawyer
O'Kehie, Collins Emeka lawyer, consultant
Oldham, Darius Dudley lawyer
Oliver, Rufus W., III lawyer
Oncken, Henry Kuck lawyer
Ongert, Steven Walter lawyer, mediator
O'Quinn, John M. lawyer
Orloff, Gary W(illiam) lawyer, former energy company executive
O'Toole, Austin Martin lawyer
Paine, Louis Burr, Jr. lawyer
Pallenik, Christine M. lawyer
Parsley, Robert Horace lawyer
Pravel, Bernarr Roe lawyer
Pugsley, Frank Burruss lawyer
Radnofsky, Barbara A. lawyer
Randolph, Robert Raymond lawyer
Ray, Hugh Massey, Jr. lawyer
Reasoner, Harry Max lawyer
Roberts, Cecil Kenneth lawyer
Robertson, George Leonard lawyer
Robertson, James Woolsey lawyer
Rogers, Arthur Hamilton, III lawyer
Rozzell, Scott Ellis lawyer
Ryan, Cornelius O'Brien lawyer
Salch, Steven Charles lawyer
Sales, James Bohus lawyer
Sanders, John Moncrief lawyer
Sapp, Walter William lawyer, energy company executive
Saunders, Charles Albert lawyer
†Schechter, Arthur Louis lawyer
Schwartz, Charles Walter lawyer
Schwartzel, Charles Boone lawyer
Secrest, Ronald Dean lawyer
Selke, Charles Richard lawyer, mediator, real estate professional
Sewell, Ben Gardner lawyer
Shaddock, Carroll Sidney lawyer
Sheinfeld, Myron M. lawyer, educator
Silva, Eugene Joseph lawyer
Simon, Barry Philip lawyer
Sing, William Bender lawyer
Smith, Frank Forsythe, Jr. lawyer
Smith, William Randolph lawyer
Smullen, James Dennis lawyer
Soliz, Joseph Guy lawyer
Sonfield, Robert Leon, Jr. lawyer
Spalding, Andrew Freeman lawyer
Staine, Ross lawyer
Stapp, William Edward lawyer
Stephens, Delia Marie Lucky lawyer
Still, Charles Henry lawyer
Stradley, William Jackson lawyer
Streng, William Paul lawyer, educator
Stryker, Steven Charles lawyer
Stuart, Walter Bynum, IV lawyer
Susman, Morton Lee lawyer
Susman, Stephen Daily lawyer
Swanson, Roy Joel lawyer
Szalkowski, Charles Conrad lawyer
Terrell, G. Irvin lawyer
Tetzlaff, Theodore R. lawyer
Toedt, D(ell) C(harles), III lawyer
Travis, Andrew David lawyer
Truesdell, Carolyn Gilmour lawyer
Vaden, Frank Samuel, III lawyer, engineer
Vance, Carol Stoner lawyer
Van Fleet, George Allan lawyer
Van Slyke, Paul Christopher lawyer
Varner, David Eugene lawyer, energy company executive
Wakefield, Stephen Alan lawyer
Walker, Jerry Vanzant lawyer
Wallingford, John Rufus lawyer
Watson, John Allen lawyer
Webb, Jack M. lawyer
Webb, Robert Allen lawyer, educator
Weber, Fredric Alan lawyer
Welch, Harry Scoville lawyer, retired gas pipeline company executive
Welch, Robert Morrow, Jr. lawyer
Wells, Benjamin Gladney lawyer
Westmoreland, Kent Ewing lawyer
Wharton, Thomas H(eard), Jr. lawyer
Wheelan, R(ichelieu) E(dward) lawyer
White, John David lawyer
White, Sue Jean lawyer
Wickliffe, Jerry L. lawyer
†Wiese, Larry Clevenger lawyer
Wilde, Carlton D. lawyer
Wilde, William Key lawyer
Williams, Percy Don lawyer
Williamson, Peter David lawyer
Williamson, Sam lawyer
Wilson, James William lawyer
Winton, James C. lawyer
Wood, Ivan, Jr. lawyer
Worden, Larry Lee lawyer
Wray, Thomas Jefferson lawyer
Wright, Robert Payton lawyer
Yokubaitis, Roger T. lawyer
York, James Martin lawyer
Youngblood, J. Craig lawyer
Zivley, Walter Perry lawyer

Hurst
Marling, Lynwood Bradley lawyer

Irving
Baird, David Leach, Jr. lawyer, petroleum and chemical company executive
Elliott, Frank Wallace lawyer, educator
Hansen, Nick Dane lawyer
Simon, Dolph B(ertram) H(irst) lawyer, jewelry company executive
Zahn, Donald Jack lawyer

Katy
Fudge, Edward William lawyer

Kilgore
Rorschach, Richard Gordon lawyer

Kingwood
Sale, James Prowant, Jr. lawyer

Lancaster
Fewel, Harriett lawyer

Longview
Beckworth, Lindley Gary, Jr. lawyer

Lubbock
Cochran, Joseph Wesley law librarian, educator
Duncan, Robert Lloyd lawyer
Glass, Carson McElyea lawyer
Nagy, Joe Howard lawyer
Purdom, Thomas James lawyer

Mc Kinney
White, Nathan Emmett, Jr. lawyer

Midland
Bullock, Maurice Randolph lawyer
Chappell, Clovis Gillham, Jr. lawyer
Morrow, William Clarence lawyer
Sykes, Robert Reed lawyer, former judge

Odessa
Gilliland, William Elton retired lawyer

Pampa
Warner, John William lawyer

Pasadena
Zimmerer, Ann(a) Morgan lawyer, consulting psychologist, genealogist

Plano
Bonet, Frank Joseph lawyer
Friedlander, D. Gilbert lawyer
Kranzow, Ronald Roy lawyer

Pottsboro
Thomas, Ann Van Wynen lawyer, educator

Richardson
Edwards, Carl Elmo, Jr. lawyer

Round Rock
LaShelle, Charles Stanton lawyer, insurance company executive

San Antonio
Aldave, Barbara Bader law educator, lawyer
Allison, Stephen Philip lawyer
Auerbach, Ernest Sigmund lawyer, company executive, writer
Barton, James Cary lawyer
Bates, David Quentin, Jr. lawyer, pharmaceutical executive
Biery, Evelyn Hudson lawyer
Dazey, William Boyd retired lawyer
Durbin, Richard Louis, Jr. lawyer
Fagan, Wayne Irwin lawyer
Fox, Michael W. lawyer
Freeman, Philip Dayne lawyer
Fretthold, Timothy Jon lawyer
Guenther, Jack Egon lawyer
Hardberger, Phillip Duane judge, lawyer, journalist
Johnston, Murray Lloyd, Jr. lawyer
Labay, Eugene Benedict lawyer
Lynch, Robert Martin lawyer, educator
Macon, Jane Haun lawyer
Macon, Richard Laurence lawyer
Matthews, Dan Gus lawyer
Matthews, Wilbur Lee lawyer
Padgett, Shelton Edward lawyer
Ross, James Ulric lawyer, accountant, educator
Schlueter, David Arnold law educator
Spears, Sally lawyer
Steen, John Thomas, Jr. lawyer
Vazquez, Gilbert Falcon lawyer
Westbrook, Joel Whitsitt, III lawyer

Stratford
Woods, John William lawyer

Temple
Pickle, Jerry Richard lawyer

Waco
Mc Call, Abner Vernon law educator, retired university administrator
Smith, Cullen lawyer
Thomson, Basil Henry, Jr. lawyer, corporate
Wendorf, Hulen Dee law educator, author, lecturer
Wilson, John Ross retired law educator

Yoakum
Williams, Walter Waylon lawyer, pecan grower

UTAH

Logan
Hillyard, Lyle William lawyer

Ogden
Harris, R. Robert lawyer
†Mecham, Glenn Jefferson lawyer, mayor

Park City
Kennicott, James W. lawyer

Provo
Abbott, Charles Favour, Jr. lawyer
Bramhall, Eugene Hulbert lawyer
Kimball, Edward Lawrence legal educator, lawyer
Lundberg, Constance K. law educator
Smith, Maurice Edward lawyer, business consultant
Thomas, David Albert law educator
Whitman, Dale Alan lawyer, educator

Salt Lake City
Baucom, Sidney George lawyer
Berman, Daniel Lewis lawyer
Buchi, Mark Keith lawyer
Christensen, Ray Richards lawyer
Frei, Michael Clark lawyer
Holbrook, Donald Benson lawyer
Holtkamp, James Arnold lawyer, legal educator
Lunt, Jack lawyer
Mabey, Ralph R. lawyer
Manning, Brent V. lawyer
McIntosh, Terrie Tuckett lawyer
Melich, Mitchell lawyer
Metz, Lawrence Anthony lawyer
Mock, Henry Byron lawyer, writer, consultant
Nebeker, Stephen Bennion lawyer
Nielsen, Greg Ross lawyer
Oaks, Dallin Harris lawyer, church official
Ockey, Ronald J. lawyer
Roberts, Jack Earle lawyer, ski resort operator, wood products company executive, real estate developer
Thurman, Samuel David legal educator
Wadsworth, Harold Wayne lawyer
Welch, Thomas Kenyon lawyer

VERMONT

Brattleboro
Cummings, Charles Rogers lawyer

Burlington
Dinse, John Merrell lawyer
Liggett, Lee Brown lawyer
Martin, Allen lawyer
Prentice, Frederick Sheldon lawyer
Wick, Hilton Addison lawyer

Hinesburg
Ross, Charles Robert lawyer, consultant

Middlebury
Langrock, Peter Forbes lawyer
Palmer, Michael Paul lawyer, mediator, educator

Montpelier
Brock, James Sidney lawyer
Diamond, M. Jerome lawyer, former state official
Guild, Alden lawyer

Morrisville
Simonds, Marshall lawyer

Norwich
Platto, Charles lawyer

Randolph
Angell, Philip Alvin, Jr. lawyer

Rutland
Keyser, Frank Ray, Jr. lawyer, former governor
Stafford, Robert Theodore lawyer, former senator

South Royalton
Williams, Norman law educator, city planner

Waitsfield
Raphael, Albert Ash, Jr. lawyer

Waterbury
Adams, Charles Jairus lawyer

VIRGINIA

Alexandria
Abell, Richard Bender lawyer, federal official
Alexander, Fred Calvin, Jr. lawyer
Armstrong, C(harles) Torrence lawyer
Blumenthal, David A. lawyer
Brittigan, Robert Lee lawyer
Brown, Frank Eugene, Jr. lawyer
Cohen, Bernard S. lawyer
Dicks, John G., III lawyer
Duncan, Stephen Mack lawyer
Evans, H(arold) Bradley, Jr. lawyer
Georges, Peter John lawyer
Hussey, Ward MacLean lawyer, government official
Kopp, Eugene Paul lawyer
Mathis, William Lowrey lawyer
McClure, Roger John lawyer
Middleton, J. Howard, Jr. lawyer
Miller, Martin John lawyer
Overholt, Hugh Robert lawyer, retired army officer
Rollins, Thomas Michieli lawyer
Schultz, Franklin M. lawyer
Straub, Peter Thornton lawyer
Sturtevant, Brereton retired lawyer, former government official
Swinburn, Charles lawyer
Thomas, William Griffith lawyer
Tierney, Philip lawyer
Vance, Bernard Wayne lawyer, government official
Van Cleve, Ruth Gill retired lawyer, government official
Watson, George William lawyer, legal consultant
Wegner, Helmuth Adalbert lawyer, retired chemical company executive
Wilner, Morton Harrison retired lawyer
Zarro, Janice Anne lawyer

Annandale
Richstein, Abraham Richard lawyer

Arlington
Anthony, Robert Armstrong lawyer, law educator
Ashcraft, Elizabeth Eva lawyer, educator
Bader, Michael Haley lawyer, broadcasting executive
Belen, Frederick Christopher lawyer
Boykin, Lykes M. lawyer, real estate company executive
Brenner, Edgar H. lawyer
Burgess, David lawyer
Carretta, Albert Aloysius lawyer, educator
Chapple, Thomas Leslie lawyer
Cohen, Sheldon Irwin lawyer
Collins, Philip Reilly lawyer, educator
Damich, Edward John law educator
Drayton, William lawyer, management consultant
Elliott, R Lance lawyer
Freeman, Orville Lothrop lawyer, former governor of Minnesota
Gillick, John Edward lawyer
Goodman, Steven Mark lawyer, journalism educator
Hugler, Edward C. lawyer, federal and state government
Huston, Harris Hyde legal consultant
Jackson, William Paul, Jr. lawyer
Korman, James William lawyer
Kosarin, Jonathan Henry lawyer
Kovacic, William Evan law educator
Krauss, Michael Ian law educator
Levinson, Lawrence Edward lawyer, corporation executive
Malone, William Grady lawyer
Mathis, Mark Jay lawyer
McDermott, Francis Owen lawyer
Muris, Timothy Joseph law educator
Quigg, Donald James lawyer
Smith, Numa Lamar, Jr. lawyer
Stover, David Frank lawyer
Van Landingham, Leander Shelton, Jr. lawyer
Wall, Barbara Wartelle lawyer

Ashland
d'Evegnee, Charles Paul lawyer

Blacksburg
Jensen, Walter Edward lawyer, educator

Bristol
Jones, James Parker lawyer

Charlottesville
Abraham, Kenneth Samuel law educator
Alford, Neill Herbert, Jr. law educator
Bergin, Thomas Francis lawyer
Bevier, Lillian Riemer law educator
Bonnie, Richard Jeffrey legal educator, lawyer
Cohen, Edwin Samuel lawyer, educator
Dooley, Michael P. law educator
Eustis, Albert Anthony lawyer, diversified industry corporate executive
Fitzgerald, Joseph Michael, Jr. lawyer
Goetz, Charles John law educator, economic consultant
Henderson, Stanley Dale lawyer, educator
Hetherington, John Alan Crawford legal educator
Hodous, Robert Power lawyer
Howard, Arthur Ellsworth Dick law educator
Ibbeken, David H. law educator
Jeffries, John Calvin, Jr. law educator
Johnson, Alex Moore lawyer, educator
Kitch, Edmund Wells lawyer, educator, private investor
Landess, Fred S. lawyer
Leslie, Douglas L. law educator
Levmore, Saul law educator
Lillich, Richard B. law educator
Lilly, Graham C. law educator
Low, Peter W. legal educator
Martin, David Alan law educator
Mc Culloch, Frank W. lawyer, government official, educator, arbitrator
McGee, Gary Calvin lawyer
Meador, Daniel John lawyer, educator
Merrill, Richard Austin lawyer
Middleditch, Leigh Benjamin, Jr. lawyer, educator
Monahan, John T. law educator, psychologist
Moore, John Norton lawyer, diplomat, educator
Mott, William Chamberlain lawyer, retired naval officer
Ortiz, Daniel Roy law educator

Perkins, William Allan, Jr. *retired lawyer*
Robinson, Glen O. *law educator*
Rutherglen, George A. *law educator*
Sinclair, Kent *law educator*
Slaughter, Edward Ratliff, Jr. *lawyer*
Stroud, Robert Edward *lawyer*
Turner, Robert Foster *lawyer, educator, former government official, writer*
Wadlington, Walter James *law educator*
†Wenger, Larry Bruce *law librarian, law educator*
White, George Edward *law educator, lawyer*
White, Thomas Raeburn, III *law educator, consultant*
Whitehead, John Wayne *law educator, organization administrator, author*

Chesapeake
Jones, John Lou *arbitrator, retired railroad executive*

Culpeper
Davies, John Jenkyn, III *lawyer*

Danville
Conway, French Hoge *lawyer*
Talbott, Frank, III *lawyer*

Dumfries
Mc Dowell, Charles Eager *lawyer, retired military officer*

Fairfax
Arntson, Peter Andrew *lawyer*
Bloomquist, Dennis Howard *lawyer*
Brown, Gary Wayne *lawyer*
Church, Randolph Warner, Jr. *lawyer*
Durenberger, David Ferdinand *lawyer*
Folk, Thomas Robert *lawyer*
Groves, Hurst Kohler *lawyer, oil company executive*
Hopson, Everett George *retired lawyer*
Perdue, Christine H. *lawyer*
Sanderson, Douglas Jay *lawyer*
Spitzberg, Irving Joseph, Jr. *lawyer, corporate executive*

Falls Church
Calkins, Gary Nathan *lawyer, retired*
†Christman, Bruce Lee *lawyer*
Diamond, Robert Michael *lawyer*
Duesenberg, Robert H. *lawyer*
Ehrlich, Bernard Herbert *lawyer, association executive*
Elderkin, Helaine Grace *lawyer*
†Feagles, Gail Winter *lawyer*
Hazel, John Tilghman, Jr. *lawyer, real estate developer*
†Holman, John P. *lawyer*
†Honigberg, Carol Crossman *lawyer*
Jennings, Thomas Parks *lawyer*
Keesling, Karen Ruth *lawyer*
†Lawrence, Robert Allen *lawyer*
Rooney, Kevin Davitt *lawyer*
Von Drehle, Ramon Arnold *lawyer*
Wright, Wiley Reed, Jr. *lawyer*
Young, John Hardin *lawyer*

Franklin
Cobb, G. Elliott, Jr. *lawyer*

Fredericksburg
Snapp, Roy Baker *lawyer*

Gloucester
Powell, Bolling Raines, Jr. *lawyer, educator*

Great Falls
Jacobson, Richard Lee *lawyer, educator*
†Neidich, George Arthur *lawyer*
Railton, William Scott *lawyer*
Sims, John Rogers, Jr. *lawyer*

Halifax
Greenbacker, John Everett *lawyer*

Harrisonburg
Dansby, Harry Bishop *lawyer*
Hodges, Ronald Dexter *lawyer*

Heathsville
McKerns, Charles Joseph *lawyer*

Herndon
Pollard, Charles William *lawyer*

Ivy
Wilcox, Harvey John *lawyer*

Lanexa
Kirk, Maurice Blake *lawyer, educator*

Leesburg
Finnegan, Edward James *lawyer*

Lexington
Beveridge, Albert Jeremiah, III *lawyer*
Kirgis, Frederic Lee, Jr. *legal educator*
Sullivan, Barry *lawyer, educator*
Sundby, Scott Edwin *law educator*
Wiant, Sarah Kirsten *law library director, educator*

Lynchburg
Burnette, Ralph Edwin, Jr. *lawyer*

Manassas
†Foote, John Holland *lawyer*

Marshall
Seder, Arthur Raymond, Jr. *lawyer*

Maurertown
Macleod, John Amend *lawyer*

Mc Lean
Appler, Thomas L. *lawyer*
Brown, Thomas C., Jr. *lawyer*
Cabaniss, Thomas Edward *lawyer*
Corson, J. Jay, IV *lawyer*
Gammon, James Alan *lawyer*
Herge, J. Curtis *lawyer*
†Kargula, Michael R. *corporate lawyer*
Kennedy, Cornelius Bryant *lawyer*
Klinedinst, Duncan Stewart *lawyer*
Marino, Michael Frank *lawyer*
Moorstein, Mark Alan *lawyer*
Murphy, Thomas Patrick *lawyer*
Nassikas, John Nicholas *lawyer*
Neel, Samuel Ellison *lawyer*
Ney, Robert Terrence *lawyer*
Perry, Charles S. *lawyer*
Prichard, Edgar Allen *lawyer*
Rau, Lee Arthur *lawyer*
Rhyne, Charles Sylvanus *lawyer*
Stitt, David Tillman *lawyer*
Stump, John Sutton *lawyer*
Tansill, Frederick Joseph *lawyer*
Traver, Courtland Lee *lawyer*
Trotter, Haynie Seay *lawyer*

McLean
Hoffmann, Martin Richard *lawyer*

Middleburg
Beddall, Thomas Henry *lawyer*

Newport News
Cuthrell, Carl Edward *lawyer, educator, clergyman*
Fisher, Timothy Scott *lawyer*

Norfolk
Baird, Edward Rouzie, Jr. *lawyer*
Crenshaw, Francis Nelson *lawyer*
Lefcoe, Vann H. *lawyer*
Rephan, Jack *lawyer*
Ryan, Louis Farthing *lawyer*
Smith, Richard Muldrow *lawyer*
Spainhour, Tremaine Howard *lawyer*
Timms, A. Jackson *lawyer*
Tolmie, Donald McEachern *lawyer*

Norton
Earls, Donald Edward *lawyer*

Orange
Dunnington, Walter Grey, Jr. *lawyer, retired food and tobacco executive*

Palmyra
White, Luther Wesley *lawyer*

Portsmouth
Spong, William Belser, Jr. *lawyer, educator*

Reston
Humphreys, David John *lawyer, trade association executive*
Schelling, John Paul *lawyer, consultant*
Wood, Stephannie Anne *lawyer*

Richmond
Ackerly, Benjamin Clarkson *lawyer*
Anderson, Leonard Gustave *retired lawyer, retired business executive*
Baliles, Gerald L. *lawyer, former governor*
Batzli, Terrence Raymond *lawyer*
Belcher, Dennis Irl *lawyer*
Benedetti, Joseph B. *lawyer, state senator*
Blanchard, Lawrence Eley, Jr. *lawyer, corporation executive*
Booker, Lewis Thomas *lawyer*
Brame, Joseph Robert, III *lawyer*
Brasfield, Evans Booker *lawyer*
Brent, Andrew Jackson *lawyer*
Brissette, Martha Blevins *lawyer*
†Broaddus, William Gray *lawyer*
Brockenbrough, Henry Watkins *lawyer*
Brooks, Robert Franklin, Sr. *lawyer*
Buford, Robert Pegram *lawyer*
Burke, John K(irkland), Jr. *lawyer*
Burrus, Robert Lewis, Jr. *lawyer*
Bush, Thomas Norman *lawyer*
Carrell, Daniel Allan *lawyer*
Carter, Joseph Carlyle, Jr. *lawyer*
Catlett, Richard H., Jr. *retired lawyer*
Clinard, Robert Noel *lawyer*
Cohn, David Stephen *lawyer*
Cutchins, Clifford Armstrong, IV *lawyer*
Davenport, Bradfute Warwick, Jr. *lawyer*
Davis, Douglas Whitfield *lawyer*
Denny, Collins, III *lawyer*
Douglass, William Birch, III *lawyer*
Dray, Mark S. *lawyer*
Ellis, Andrew Jackson, Jr. *lawyer*
Epps, Augustus Charles *lawyer*
Farnham, James Edward *lawyer*
Framme, Lawrence Henry, III *lawyer*
Freeman, George Clemon, Jr. *lawyer*
Gary, Richard David *lawyer*
Gasch, Manning *lawyer*
Geisler, Ernest Keith, Jr. *lawyer*
Grandis, Leslie Allan *lawyer*
Graves, H. Brice *lawyer*
Griffith, Garth Ellis *lawyer*
Guthrie, Rebecca Claire *lawyer*
Hackney, Virginia Howitz *lawyer*
Hall, Phoebe Poulterer *lawyer, judge*
Hall, Stephen Charles *lawyer*
Hancock, William Glenn *lawyer*
Harbaugh, Joseph Delbert *legal educator, consultant*
Harper, James Allie, Jr. *lawyer, arbitrator, administrative hearing officer*
Hettrick, George H. *lawyer*
Holton, A. Linwood, Jr. *lawyer*
Horsley, Waller Holladay *lawyer*
Howell, George Cook, III *lawyer*
Huntley, Robert Edward Royall *lawyer, business executive, former university president*
Kay, John Franklin, Jr. *lawyer*
Kearfott, Joseph Conrad *lawyer*
King, Donald Edward *lawyer*
Lanam, Linda Lee *lawyer*
Landin, David Craig *lawyer*
Ledbetter, David Oscar *lawyer*
Levit, Jay J(oseph) *lawyer*
Martenstein, Thomas Ewing *lawyer*
Mathews, Roderick Bell *lawyer*
McClard, Jack Edward *lawyer*
McElligott, James Patrick, Jr. *lawyer*
McVey, Henry Hanna, III *lawyer*
Mezzullo, Louis Albert *lawyer*
Milmoe, Patrick Joseph *lawyer*
Moore, Thurston Roach *lawyer*
Morris, Dewey Blanton *lawyer*
Oakey, John Martin, Jr. *lawyer*
Pasco, Hansell Merrill *retired lawyer*
Patterson, Robert Hobson, Jr. *lawyer*
Peters, David Frankman *lawyer*
Pinckney, C. Cotesworth *lawyer*
Pope, Robert Dean *lawyer*
Powell, Kenneth Edward *investment banker*
Powell, Lewis Franklin, III *lawyer*
Powell, Virginia W. *lawyer*
Rainey, Gordon Fryer, Jr. *lawyer*
Reveley, Walter Taylor, III *lawyer*
Roach, Edgar Mayo, Jr. *lawyer*
Rolfe, Robert Martin *lawyer*
Rosbe, William Louis *lawyer*
Rubinstein, Phyllis M. *lawyer*
Rudlin, David Alan *lawyer, educator*
Schwarzschild, Patricia Michaelson *lawyer*
Shands, William Ridley, Jr. *lawyer*
Sharer, John Daniel *lawyer*
Slater, Thomas Glascock, Jr. *lawyer*
Slaughter, Alexander Hoke *lawyer*
Smith, R. Gordon *lawyer*
Spahn, Gary Joseph *lawyer*
Spain, Jack Holland, Jr. *lawyer*
Spivey, Joseph M., III *lawyer*
Strickland, William Jesse *lawyer*
Thomas, John Charles *lawyer, former state supreme court justice*
Thompson, Paul Michael *lawyer*
Totten, Randolph Fowler *lawyer*
Troy, Anthony Francis *lawyer*
Twomey, Wililam Eldred, Jr. *lawyer*
Walsh, James Hamilton *lawyer*
Walsh, William Arthur, Jr. *lawyer*
Warthen, Harry Justice, III *lawyer*
Watts, Stephen Hurt, II *lawyer*
Wellford, Hill B., Jr. *lawyer*
Wheeler, R(ichard) Kenneth *lawyer*
White, Hugh Vernon, Jr. *lawyer*
Whittemore, Anne Marie *lawyer*
Wilson, Sara Redding *lawyer*
Witt, Walter Francis, Jr. *lawyer*
Word, Thomas S., Jr. *lawyer*

Roanoke
Bowers, David Allen *lawyer, mayor*
Butler, Manley Caldwell *lawyer*
Fishwick, John Palmer *lawyer, retired railroad executive*
Woodrum, Clifton A., III *lawyer, state legislator*

Vienna
Alberta, Mark Edward *lawyer*
Fasser, Paul James, Jr. *labor arbitrator*
Howard, Daggett Horton *lawyer*
Pesner, Susan M. *lawyer*
Razzano, Frank Charles *lawyer*

Virginia Beach
Sekulow, Jay Alan *lawyer*

Warm Springs
Deeds, Robert Creigh *lawyer, state legislator*

West Point
†Causey, J(ohn) P(aul), Jr. *lawyer*

Williamsburg
Braun, Richard Lane *lawyer, university administrator*
Geddy, Vernon Meredith, Jr. *lawyer*
Heller, James Stephen *law librarian*
Marcus, Paul *lawyer, educator*
Sipes, Larry L. *lawyer*
Smolla, Rodney Alan *lawyer, educator*
Sullivan, Timothy Jackson *law educator, academic administrator*
Whyte, James Primrose, Jr. *former law educator*

WASHINGTON

Bainbridge Island
Nagle, James Francis *lawyer*

Bellevue
Elliott, Richard Wayne *lawyer*
Hannah, Lawrence Burlison *lawyer*
Scaringi, Michael Joseph *lawyer, consultant*
Smith, George Lester *lawyer*
Sullivan, James Jerome *lawyer, consultant*

Bellingham
Packer, Mark Barry *lawyer, financial consultant, foundation official*

Colfax
Webster, Ronald B. *lawyer*

Friday Harbor
McCreary, Dustin Campbell *lawyer, arbitrator*

Kirkland
Dorkin, Frederic Eugene *lawyer*

Olympia
Norwood, Deborah Anne *law librarian*

Pullman
Savage, Sally P. *lawyer*

Redmond
Erxleben, William Charles *lawyer, data processing executive*

Richland
Barr, Carlos Harvey *lawyer*

Seattle
Alkire, John D. *lawyer*
Allen, Joanna Cowan *lawyer*
Allison, John Robert *lawyer*
Anderson, Peter MacArthur *lawyer*
Andrews, J. David *lawyer*
Barry, Christopher John *lawyer*
Birmingham, Richard Joseph *lawyer*
Black, W. L. Rivers, III *lawyer*
Blom, Daniel Charles *lawyer, investor*
Blumenfeld, Charles Raban *lawyer*
Boeder, Thomas L. *lawyer*
Boman, Marc Allen *lawyer*
Boruchowitz, Bob *lawyer*
Brady, Viola Catt *lawyer, psychologist*
Brothers, Lynda Lee *lawyer*
Burkhart, William Henry *lawyer*
Butler, Timothy Harold *lawyer*
Carlson, Stanley Andrew *lawyer*
Cavanaugh, Michael Everett *lawyer*
Char, Patricia Helen *lawyer*
Claflin, Arthur Cary *lawyer*
Clinton, Gordon Stanley *lawyer*
Clinton, Richard M. *lawyer*
Collins, Theodore John *lawyer*
Corker, Charles Edward *retired lawyer, educator*
Corr, Kelly *lawyer*
Cosway, Richard *legal educator*
Cross, Harry Maybury *retired law educator, consultant*
Dahl, Lance Christopher *lawyer*
Dalton, Thomas George *paralegal, social worker, legal consultant*
Danelo, Peter Anthony *lawyer*
Davis, John MacDougall *lawyer*
Derham, Richard Andrew *lawyer*
DeVore, Paul Cameron *lawyer*
Dickinson, Calhoun *lawyer*
Ellis, James Reed *lawyer*
Fitzpatrick, Thomas Mark *lawyer*
Freeman, Antoinette Rosefeldt *lawyer*
Gates, William H. *lawyer*
Giles, Robert Edward, Jr. *lawyer*
Gittinger, D. Wayne *lawyer*
Glover, Karen E. *lawyer*
Goeltz, Thomas A. *lawyer*
Graham, Stephen Michael *lawyer*
Gray, Marvin Lee, Jr. *lawyer*
Greenan, Thomas J. *lawyer*
Greene, John Burkland *lawyer*
Haggard, Joel Edward *lawyer*
Haman, Raymond William *lawyer*
Hansen, Wayne W. *lawyer*
Hazelton, Penny Ann *law librarian, educator*
Henderson, Dan Fenno *lawyer, retired law educator*
Higgins, Nancy McCready *lawyer, director*
Hilpert, Edward Theodore, Jr. *lawyer*
Hofmann, Douglas Allan *lawyer*
Horton, Elliott Argue, Jr. *lawyer, business consultant*
Huston, John Charles *law educator*
Hutcheson, Mark Andrew *lawyer*
Isaki, Lucy Power Slyngstad *lawyer*
Israel, Allen D. *lawyer*
Jameson, Henry C. *lawyer*
Johnson, Bruce Edward Humble *lawyer*
Judson, C(harles) James (Jim Judson) *lawyer*
Kane, Alan Henry *lawyer*
Kane, Christopher *lawyer*
Kaplan, Barry Martin *lawyer*
Kareken, Francis A. *lawyer*
Kellogg, Kenyon P. *lawyer*
Killeen, Michael John *lawyer*
Koehler, Reginald Stafford, III *lawyer*
Kuhrau, Edward W. *lawyer*
Kummert, Richard Osborne *lawyer, educator*
Leitzell, Terry Lee *lawyer*
Lemly, Thomas Adger *lawyer*
Lombard, David Norman *lawyer*
Maulding, Barry Clifford *lawyer*
McAteer, James Francis *lawyer*
McCann, Richard Eugene *lawyer*
McKay, John *lawyer*
McKay, Michael Dennis *lawyer*
McKeown, Mary Margaret *lawyer*
McKey, Thomas J. *lawyer*
Mickelwait, Lowell Pitzer *lawyer*
Moch, Robert Gaston *lawyer*
Moore, James R. *lawyer*
Moore, Malcolm Arthur *lawyer*
Mullin, J(ack) Shan *lawyer*
Mussehl, Robert Clarence *lawyer*
Nellermoe, Leslie C. *lawyer*
Nelson, Marshall J. *lawyer*
Niemi, Janice *lawyer, former state legislator*
Noll, Jonathan Boyd *lawyer*
Oehler, Richard William *lawyer*
Olsen, Harold Fremont *lawyer*
Palm, Gerald Albert *lawyer*
Parker, Omar Sigmund, Jr. *lawyer*
Parks, Patricia Jean *lawyer*
Parsons, A. Peter *lawyer*
Paul, Thomas Frank *lawyer*
Perey, Ron *lawyer*
Petrie, Gregory Steven *lawyer*
Powell, George Van Tuyl *lawyer*
Prentke, Richard Ottesen *lawyer*
Prosterman, Roy L. *law educator, development specialist*
Pusch, William Gerard *lawyer*
Pym, Bruce Michael *lawyer*
Redman, Eric *lawyer*
Rieke, Paul Victor *lawyer*
Ritter, Daniel Benjamin *lawyer*
Ruddy, James W. *lawyer*
Runstad, Judith Manville *lawyer*
Rupp, John Norris *lawyer*
Sandler, Michael David *lawyer*
Shulkin, Jerome *lawyer*
Smith, Payton *lawyer*
Soltys, John Joseph, Jr. *lawyer*
Spitzer, Hugh D. *lawyer*
Squires, William Randolph, III *lawyer*
Steinberg, Jack *lawyer*
Stewart, Robert Andrew *lawyer*
Sweeney, David Brian *lawyer*
Tallman, Richard C. *lawyer*
Thorson, Lee A. *lawyer*
†Tomlinson, Robert John *lawyer, energy executive*
Treiger, Irwin Louis *lawyer*
Voorhees, Lee R., Jr. *lawyer*
Wagner, Patricia H. *lawyer*
Wagoner, David Everett *lawyer*
Wall, William E. *lawyer, former utility executive*
Wallis, Richard James *lawyer*
Wells, Christopher Brian *lawyer*
Wells, Judee Ann *lawyer*
Whalen, Jerome Demaris *lawyer*
Whitford, Joseph P. *lawyer*
Williams, J. Vernon *lawyer*
Wright, Willard Jurey *lawyer*

Spokane
Foley, Thomas Stephen *lawyer, former speaker House of Representatives*
Koegen, Roy Jerome *lawyer*
Lamp, John Ernest *lawyer*

Tacoma
Gordon, Joseph Harold *lawyer*
Graves, Ray *lawyer*
Lane, Robert Casey *lawyer*

Miller, Judson Frederick *lawyer, former military officer*
Purnell, Carolyn Jean *lawyer*
Rodin, Michael F. *lawyer, corporate*
Rudolph, Wallace Morton *legal educator*
Steele, Anita Martin (Margaret Anne Martin) *law librarian, legal educator*
Thompson, Ronald Edward *lawyer*

Vancouver
Kleweno, Gilbert H. *lawyer*

Vashon
Biggs, Barry Hugh *lawyer*

Walla Walla
Hayner, Herman Henry *lawyer*

Yakima
Suko, Lonny Ray *lawyer*
Wright, J(ames) Lawrence *lawyer*

WEST VIRGINIA

Charles Town
Layva, David *lawyer*

Charleston
Brown, James Knight *lawyer*
Davis, James Hornor, III *lawyer*
Freeman, Thomas G., II *lawyer*
Gage, Charles Quincey *lawyer*
Goodwin, Claude Elbert *lawyer, former gas utility executive*
Kizer, John Oscar *lawyer*
Lawson, Robert William, Jr. *retired lawyer*
McClaugherty, John Lewis *lawyer*
Murchison, David Roderick *lawyer*
Neely, Richard *lawyer*
†Rogers, John Alfrod *lawyer*
Slack, John Mark, III *lawyer*
Snyder, Giles D. H. *lawyer*
Southworth, Louis Sweetland, II *lawyer*
Stacy, Charles Brecknock *lawyer*

Huntington
Jenkins, John E., Jr. *lawyer, educator*
St. Clair, James William *lawyer*

Lewisburg
Ford, Richard Edmond *lawyer*

Martinsburg
Rice, Lacy I., Jr. *lawyer*

Morgantown
Fisher, John Welton, II *law educator, magistrate judge, university official*
Fusco, Andrew G. *lawyer*
Morris, William Otis, Jr. *lawyer, educator, author*

Summersville
Yeager, Charles William *lawyer, newspaper publisher*

Wheeling
Phillips, John Davisson *retired lawyer*

WISCONSIN

Columbus
Callahan, Carroll Bernard *lawyer*

Elm Grove
Gorske, Robert Herman *retired lawyer*

Glendale
Gefke, Henry Jerome *lawyer*

Janesville
Steil, George Kenneth, Sr. *lawyer*

La Crosse
Klos, Jerome John *lawyer*
Nix, Edmund Alfred *lawyer*

Lake Geneva
Braden, Berwyn Bartow *lawyer*

Madison
Auen, Michael H. *lawyer*
Baldwin, Gordon Brewster *lawyer, educator*
Barnhill, Charles Joseph, Jr. *lawyer*
Bartell, Jeffrey Bruce *lawyer*
†Bochert, Linda H. *lawyer*
Bugge, Lawrence John *lawyer*
Chatterton, William Alonzo *lawyer*
†Chiarkas, Nicholas L. *lawyer, state agency administrator*
Curry, Robert Lee *lawyer*
Erhard, Michael Paul *lawyer*
Field, Henry Augustus, Jr. *lawyer*
Finman, Ted *lawyer, educator*
Foster, George William, Jr. *lawyer, educator*
†Glesner, Richard Charles *lawyer, law examiner*
Helstad, Orrin L. *lawyer, legal educator*
Heymann, S. Richard *lawyer*
Hildebrand, Daniel Walter *lawyer*
Holbrook, John Scott, Jr. *lawyer*
Hurst, James Willard *legal educator*
†Ishikawa, Jesse Steven *lawyer*
Jones, James Edward, Jr. *retired law educator*
Langer, Richard J. *lawyer*
Lautenschlager, Peggy Ann *prosecutor*
†Linstroth, Tod B. *lawyer*
Melli, Marygold Shire *law educator*
Murphy, Robert Brady Lawrence *lawyer*
Pellino, Charles Edward, Jr. *lawyer*
Prange, Roy Leonard, Jr. *lawyer*
Ragatz, Thomas George *lawyer*
Raushenbush, Walter Brandeis *law educator*
†Rogers, Joel *law, political science and sociology educator*
Ryan, Thomas Joseph *lawyer*
Skilton, John Singleton *lawyer*
Temkin, Harvey L. *lawyer*
Thompson, Cliff F. *lawyer, educator*
Wagner, Burton Allan *lawyer*
Walsh, David Graves *lawyer*
White, William Fredrick *lawyer*
Whitney, Robert Michael *lawyer*
Wilcox, Michael Wing *lawyer*

Manitowoc
Muchin, Arden Archie *lawyer, director*

Mequon
Burroughs, Charles Edward *lawyer*

Middleton
Hofeldt, John W. *lawyer*

Milwaukee
†Abraham, Jeffrey L. *lawyer*
Abraham, William John, Jr. *lawyer*
†Ahrens, Gary Andrew *lawyer*
Alverson, William H. *lawyer*
Babler, Wayne E., Jr. *lawyer*
Bannen, John T. *lawyer*
Barbee, Lloyd Augustus *lawyer*
Barnes, Paul McClung *lawyer*
Barron, Russell J. *lawyer*
Bauer, Bruce Richard *lawyer*
Beckwith, David E. *lawyer*
Bell, Darryl Stephen *lawyer*
Berkoff, Marshall Richard *lawyer*
Biehl, Michael Melvin *lawyer*
Biller, Joel Wilson *lawyer, former foreign service officer*
Binder, Robert Lawrence *lawyer*
Bowen, Michael Anthony *lawyer, writer*
Braza, Mary Kathryn *lawyer*
Brody, James Patrick *lawyer*
Bruce, Jackson Martin, Jr. *lawyer*
Busch, John Arthur *lawyer*
Cannon, David Joseph *lawyer*
†Canter, Richard J. *lawyer*
Case, Karen Ann *lawyer*
Casey, John Alexander *lawyer*
Casper, Richard Henry *lawyer*
Christiansen, Jon Peter *lawyer*
Christiansen, Keith Allan *lawyer*
Clark, James Richard *lawyer*
Cleary, John Washington *lawyer*
Connolly, Gerald Edward *lawyer*
Connolly, L. William *lawyer*
Croak, Francis R. *lawyer*
Cutler, Richard Woolsey *lawyer*
Daily, Frank J(erome) *lawyer*
Davis, Walter Stewart *lawyer*
Drummond, Robert Kendig *lawyer*
Duback, Steven Rahr *lawyer*
Ehrmann, Thomas William *lawyer*
Eisenberg, Howard Bruce *law educator*
Ericson, James Donald *lawyer, insurance executive*
Fischer, Michael Davin *lawyer*
Florsheim, Richard Steven *lawyer*
Frautschi, Timothy Clark *lawyer*
Friedman, James Dennis *lawyer*
Gallagher, Richard S. *lawyer*
Gemignani, Joseph Adolph *lawyer*
Ghiardi, James Domenic *lawyer, educator*
Goodkind, Conrad George *lawyer*
Groethe, Reed *lawyer*
Groiss, Fred George *lawyer*
Haas, George Edward *lawyer*
†Haberman, F. William *lawyer*
Habush, Robert Lee *lawyer*
†Haggerty, Nancy Leary *lawyer*
†Hanson, David James *lawyer*
Harrington, John Timothy *lawyer*
Hase, David John *lawyer*
Hatch, Michael Ward *lawyer*
Hazelwood, John A. *lawyer*
Hoelter, Timothy K. *lawyer, manufacturing company executive*
Hoffman, Nathaniel A. *lawyer*
Holz, Harry George *lawyer*
†Husmann, Michael E. *lawyer*
†Jackson, W. Charles *lawyer*
†Johannes, Robert J. *lawyer*
Jost, Lawrence John *lawyer*
Kamps, Charles Q. *lawyer*
Kelly, Francis Daniel *lawyer*
Kennedy, John Patrick *lawyer, corporate executive*
Kessler, Joan F. *lawyer*
Kinnamon, David Lucas *lawyer*
Kringel, Jerome Howard *lawyer*
†Krueger, Raymond Robert *lawyer*
Kubale, Bernard Stephen *lawyer*
Kurtz, Harvey A. *lawyer*
LaBudde, Roy Christian *lawyer*
Lavers, Richard Marshall *lawyer*
Le Duc, Don Raymond *lawyer, educator*
Levit, William Harold, Jr. *lawyer*
Loeb, Leonard L. *lawyer*
Lueders, Wayne Richard *lawyer*
MacGregor, David Lee *lawyer*
MacIver, John Kenneth *lawyer*
Maio, F. Anthony *lawyer*
Martin, Quinn William *lawyer*
Maynard, John Ralph *lawyer*
McCauley, Michael Stephen *lawyer*
McGaffey, Jere D. *lawyer*
McGinnity, Maureen Annell *lawyer*
McSweeney, Maurice J. (Marc) *lawyer*
†Medved, Paul Stanley *lawyer*
Meldman, Clifford Kay *lawyer*
Meldman, Robert Edward *lawyer*
†Miller, Gordon K. *lawyer*
†Morgan, Geoffrey Richard *lawyer*
Mulcahy, Robert William *lawyer*
Noelke, Paul *lawyer*
Noyes, Anne Louise *lawyer*
†Obenberger, Thomas E. *lawyer*
†Olson, David R. *lawyer*
Olson, John Marshall *lawyer*
O'Shaughnessy, James Patrick *lawyer*
Paige, Norma *lawyer, corporate executive*
Pelisek, Frank John *lawyer*
Phillips, Thomas John *lawyer*
Pindyck, Bruce Eben *lawyer, corporate executive*
Podell, Richard Jay *lawyer*
Powell, Edmund William *lawyer*
Precourt, Lyman Arthur *lawyer*
†Prentiss, Paul E. *lawyer*
Richman, Stephen Erik *lawyer*
Ryan, Patrick Michael *lawyer*
Sapp, John Raymond *lawyer*
Schnur, Robert Arnold *lawyer*
Scrivner, Thomas William *lawyer*
†Shapiro, Robyn Sue *lawyer, educator*
Shriner, Thomas L., Jr. *lawyer*
†Smith, David B. *lawyer*
Teschner, Richard Rewa *retired lawyer*
Van Vugt, Eric J. *lawyer*
Wallace, Harry Leland *lawyer*
Walmer, Edwin Fitch *lawyer*
Wawrzyn, Ronald M. *lawyer*
Weber, Robert George *lawyer*
Whyte, George Kenneth, Jr. *lawyer*
Wiedenman, Jere Wayne *lawyer*
Wiley, Edwin Packard *lawyer*
Will, Trevor Jonathan *lawyer*
Willis, William J. *lawyer*
†Winsten, Saul Nathan *lawyer*

Monroe
Kittelsen, Rodney Olin *lawyer*

Neenah
Stanton, Thomas Mitchell *lawyer, educator*

Oshkosh
Dempsey, Timothy Michael *lawyer*

Phelps
Coccia, Michel Andre *retired lawyer*

Racine
Coates, Glenn Richard *lawyer*
Hart, Robert Camillus *lawyer, company executive*
Pavlick, Walter Eugene *lawyer, manufacturing company executive*
Swanson, Robert Lee *lawyer*

Rhinelander
Saari, John William, Jr. *lawyer*

River Hills
Silverman, Albert A. *retired lawyer, manufacturing company executive*

Shorewood
Surridge, Stephen Zehring *lawyer, writer*

Stevens Point
Makholm, Mark Henry *lawyer, former insurance company executive*

Sun Prairie
Eustice, Francis Joseph *lawyer*

Waukesha
Macy, John Patrick *lawyer*

Wausau
Drengler, William Allan John *lawyer*
Orr, San Watterson, Jr. *lawyer*

WYOMING

Casper
Bostwick, Richard Raymond *retired lawyer*
Lowe, Robert Stanley *lawyer*

Cheyenne
Freudenthal, Steven Franklin *lawyer*
Hanes, John Grier *lawyer, state legislator*
Mc Clintock, Archie Glenn *lawyer*
Rooney, John Joseph *lawyer, former state supreme court justice*
Rose, Robert R., Jr. *lawyer*

Cody
Housel, Jerry Winters *lawyer*

Jackson
Schuster, Robert Parks *lawyer*
Watt, James Gaius *lawyer, former government official, legal consultant*

Laramie
Kinney, Lisa Frances *lawyer*
Smith, Thomas Shore *lawyer*

Riverton
Girard, Nettabell *lawyer*

TERRITORIES OF THE UNITED STATES

GUAM

Agana
Tock, Joseph *lawyer*

PUERTO RICO

Carolina
Figueroa, Iván *lawyer*

San Juan
Colorado, Antonio José *lawyer*
Diaz-Cruz, Jorge Hatuey *lawyer, former state supreme court justice*
Rua, Milton Francisco *lawyer*
Trías-Monge, Jose *lawyer, former territory supreme court chief justice*

VIRGIN ISLANDS

Charlotte Amalie
Bolt, Thomas Alvin Waldrep *lawyer*

Saint Thomas
Feuerzeig, Henry Louis *lawyer*

MILITARY ADDRESSES OF THE UNITED STATES

ATLANTIC

APO
Guinot, Luis, Jr. *lawyer, ambassador*

EUROPE

APO
Doyle, Justin Emmett *lawyer, government official*

CANADA

ALBERTA

Calgary
Ballem, John Bishop *lawyer, novelist*
Hughes, Margaret Eileen *law educator, former dean*
Lougheed, Peter *lawyer, former Canadian official*
Matthews, Francis Richard *lawyer*
Perrin, Robert Maitland *solicitor, oil company executive*

Edmonton
Patrick, Lynn Allen *lawyer, construction company executive*
Shoctor, Joseph Harvey *barrister, producer, civic worker*

Smith
Rodnunsky, Sidney *lawyer, educator, Prince of Kiev, Prince of Trabzon, Prince and Duke of Rodari, Duke of Chernigov, Count of Riga, Count of Saint John of Alexandria*

BRITISH COLUMBIA

Brentwood Bay
Carrothers, Alfred William Rooke *retired law educator*

Vancouver
Bonner, Robert William *lawyer*
Head, Ivan Leigh *law educator*
Howard, John Lindsay *lawyer, forest industry company executive*
Ladner, Thomas E. *lawyer*
Nemetz, Nathaniel Theodore *lawyer, former chief justice of British Columbia*
Peterson, Leslie Raymond *barrister*
Smethurst, Robert Guy *lawyer*

Victoria
Partridge, Bruce James *lawyer, educator*

MANITOBA

Winnipeg
Anderson, David Trevor *law educator*
Cherniack, Saul Mark *retired barrister, solicitor*
Wiebe, Bernie *conflict resolution studies educator*

NEW BRUNSWICK

Rothesay
Fairweather, Robert Gordon Lee *lawyer*

NOVA SCOTIA

Halifax
†Dexter, Robert Paul *lawyer*
Dickey, John Horace *lawyer*
Macdonald, Joseph Albert Friel *lawyer*

Waverly
†Swan, Judith *marine lawyer*

ONTARIO

Etobicoke
Gulden, Simon *lawyer, foods and beverages company executive*

Hamilton
Stanbury, Robert Douglas George *lawyer, executive*

Kingston
Manning, Charles Terrill *retired lawyer*

Mississauga
Allen, Clive Victor *lawyer, communications company executive*
Davies, Michael Norman Arden *lawyer, electric company executive*

North York
Arthurs, Harry William *legal educator, former university president*
Castel, Jean Gabriel *lawyer*

Oakville
O'Reilly, Denis *aluminum company executive, lawyer*

Ottawa
Beaudoin, Gérald-A(rmand) *lawyer, educator, senator*
d'Aquino, Thomas *lawyer, business council chief executive*
Goulard, Guy Yvon *lawyer*
Iacobucci, Frank *lawyer, educator, jurist*
Tassé, Roger *lawyer, former Canadian government official*
Urie, John James *lawyer, retired Canadian federal judge*
Weatherill, John Frederick William *arbitrator*

Scarborough
Krajicek, Mark Andrew *lawyer*

Toronto
Aird, John Black *lawyer, university official, former lieutenant governor*
Apple, B. Nixon *lawyer*
Bristow, David Ian *lawyer*
Chester, Robert Simon George *lawyer*
Cowan, Charles Gibbs *lawyer, corporate executive*
Davis, William Grenville *lawyer, former Canadian government official*
Dickens, Bernard Morris *law educator*
Donais, Gary Warren *lawyer*
Elliott, R(oy) Fraser *lawyer, holding and management company executive*
Eyton, John Trevor *lawyer, business executive*
Farquharson, Gordon MacKay *lawyer*
Gee, Gregory Williams *lawyer*
Godfrey, John Morrow *lawyer, retired Canadian government official*
Graham, John Webb *lawyer*
Innanen, Larry John *lawyer, food products executive*
Liston, Alan A. *lawyer*
Lyons, Joseph Chisholm *lawyer*
Macdonald, Donald Stovel *lawyer*
Peterson, David Robert *lawyer, former Canadian government official*
Scheininger, Lester *lawyer, administrator religious organization*
Wolfe, Harold Joel *lawyer, business executive*

QUEBEC

Montreal
Benson, Kenneth Samuel *corporate executive*
Brierley, John E. C. *legal educator, former university dean*
Courtois, Edmond Jacques *lawyer*
Gillespie, Thomas Stuart *lawyer*
Guenette, Francoise *legal affairs executive*
Kirkpatrick, John Gildersleeve *lawyer*
Lacoste, Paul *lawyer, educator, university official*
Lalonde, Marc *lawyer, former Canadian government official*
Mercier, Francois *lawyer*
Messier, Pierre *lawyer, manufacturing company executive*
Montcalm, Norman Joseph *lawyer*
Popovici, Adrian *law educator*
Pound, Richard William Duncan *lawyer, accountant*
Pratte, Lise *lawyer, corporate secretary*
Régnier, Marc Charles *lawyer, corporate executive*
Robb, James Alexander *lawyer*
Sheppard, Claude-Armand *lawyer*
Somerville, Margaret Anne Ganley *law educator*
Tremblay, Andre Gabriel *lawyer, educator*
Trudeau, Pierre Elliott *lawyer, former Canadian prime minister*
Vennat, Michel *lawyer*

Quebec
Aubut, Marcel *lawyer, sports association official*
†Dinan, Robert Michael *lawyer*
Gauthier, Paule *lawyer*
LeMay, Jacques *lawyer*
Normand, Robert *lawyer*
Verge, Pierre *legal educator*

Westmount
Fortier, L. Yves *barrister*

SASKATCHEWAN

Regina
Balfour, Reginald James *lawyer*
Laschuk, Roy Bogdan *lawyer*
MacKay, Harold Hugh *lawyer*

Saskatoon
Ish, Daniel Russell *law educator, academic adminstrator*

AUSTRALIA

Sydney
Bleveans, John *lawyer*

BELGIUM

Brussels
Barnum, John Wallace *lawyer*
Bustin, George Leo *lawyer*
Glazer, Barry David *lawyer*
Liebman, Howard Mark *lawyer*
Oberreit, Walter William *lawyer*
Orly, Elvira Jolan *lawyer*
Smith, Turner Taliaferro, Jr. *lawyer*

ENGLAND

London
Adams, George Bell *lawyer*
Albert, Robert Alan *lawyer*
Batla, Raymond John, Jr. *lawyer*
Beharrell, Steven Roderic *lawyer*
Bigbie, John Taylor *lawyer, banker*
Chubb, Joseph *lawyer*
Cole, Richard A. *lawyer*
Fabricant, Arthur E. *lawyer, corporate executive*
Fox, Hazel Mary *law educator, editor*
Gaines, Peter Mathew *lawyer*
Gordon, Jeffrey I. *lawyer*
Haubold, Samuel Allen *lawyer*
Hudson, Manley O., Jr. *lawyer*
Johnson, Thomas Edward *lawyer*
Kies, David M. *lawyer*
Kingham, Richard Frank *lawyer*
McLeod, Wilson Churchill *lawyer*
Metzger, Barry *lawyer*
Morrison, William David *lawyer*
Nelson, Bernard Edward *lawyer*
Newburg, Andre W. G. *lawyer*
Randour, Paul A(lfred) *lawyer*
Smart, Claude Harlan, Jr. *lawyer*
Stevens, Robert Bocking *lawyer, educator*
Thomas, Allen Lloyd *lawyer, private investor*
Van Meter, John David *lawyer*

FRANCE

Neuilly-sur-Seine
O'Neill, Lawrence Daniel *lawyer, consultant*

Paris
Abboud, Ann Creelman *lawyer*
Baum, Axel Helmuth *lawyer*
Cochran, John M., III *lawyer*
Cone, Sydney M., III *lawyer*
Craig, William Laurence *lawyer*
Davidson, Alfred Edward *lawyer*
Iseman, Joseph Seeman *lawyer*
Landers, Steven E. *lawyer*
Lubick, Donald Cyril *lawyer*
MacCrindle, Robert Alexander *lawyer*
McGurn, William Barrett, III *lawyer*
Rawlings, Boynton Mott *lawyer*
Riggs, John Hutton, Jr. *lawyer*
Salans, Carl Fredric *lawyer*
Shapiro, Isaac *lawyer*
Wolrich, Peter M. *lawyer*

GERMANY

Finning
English, Charles Brand *retired lawyer*

Kaiserslautern
Immesberger, Helmut *lawyer*

GRENADA

Saint George's
Helgerson, John Walter *lawyer*

HONG KONG

Hong Kong
Allen, Richard Marlow *lawyer*
Choo, Yeow Ming *lawyer*
Chu, Franklin Dean *lawyer*
Collins, Charles Roland *lawyer*
Halperin, David Richard *lawyer*
Nee, Owen D., Jr. *lawyer*
Tanner, Douglas Alan *lawyer*

ISRAEL

Jerusalem
Rosenne, Meir *lawyer, government agency administrator*

ITALY

Rome
Alegi, Peter Claude *lawyer*

JAPAN

Nagoya
Kato, Masanobu *lawyer, educator*

Osaka
Solberg, Norman Robert *lawyer*

Tokyo
Drabkin, David *lawyer*
Kawachi, Michael Tateo *lawyer*
Reid, Edward Snover, III *lawyer*

NORWAY

Stavanger
Fitzpatrick, Whitfield Westfeldt *lawyer*

PANAMA

Panama City
†Fabrega P., Jorge *lawyer, writer, legal books publisher*

THE PHILIPPINES

Manila
Quasha, William Howard *lawyer*

POLAND

Warsaw
Soltysinski, Stanislaw J. *law educator*

PORTUGAL

Funchal
Mayda, Jaro *lawyer, educator, author, consultant*

ROMANIA

Bucharest
Moses, Alfred Henry *lawyer*

SAUDI ARABIA

Riyadh
Taylor, Frederick William, Jr. *lawyer*

SINGAPORE

Singapore
Reed, John G. *lawyer*

SWITZERLAND

Fribourg
Gurley, Franklin Louis *lawyer, military historian*

Geneva
Abram, Morris Berthold *lawyer, educator, diplomat*
De Pfyffer, Andre *lawyer*

Lucerne
Sherwin, James Terry *lawyer, window covering company executive*

Zurich
Panitz, Lawrence Herbert *lawyer*

THAILAND

Bangkok
Lyman, David *lawyer*

ADDRESS UNPUBLISHED

Aaron, Roy Henry *lawyer, business consultant*
Abzug, Bella Savitzky *lawyer, former congresswoman*
Adams, Paul Winfrey *lawyer, business executive*
Anderson, Geoffrey Allen *lawyer*
Anderson, Keith *retired lawyer, retired banker*
Arenella, Peter Lee *law educator*
Ariyoshi, George Ryoichi *lawyer, business consultant, former governor Hawaii*
Armstrong, William Henry *lawyer*
Arnold, Jerome Gilbert *lawyer*
Askey, William Hartman *lawyer, federal magistrate judge*
Axelrad, Irving Irmas *lawyer, motion picture producer*
Babb, Frank Edward *lawyer, executive*
Baddour, Phillip A. *lawyer, state legislator*
Bagley, William Thompson *lawyer*
Bailey, Francis Lee *lawyer*
Bailey, Henry John, III *retired lawyer, educator*
Bain, William Donald, Jr. *lawyer, chemical company executive*
Bangs, John Kendrick *lawyer, foundation executive, former chemical company executive*
Banks, Robert Sherwood *lawyer*
Barnhill, Henry Grady, Jr. *lawyer*
Barrett, Jane Hayes *lawyer*
Bates, Charles Turner *lawyer, educator*
Battle, Frank Vincent, Jr. *lawyer*
Beatty, Michael L. *lawyer*
Beckey, Sylvia Louise *lawyer*
Beldock, Myron *lawyer*
Bell, Haney Hardy, III *lawyer*
Benjamin, Edward A. *lawyer*
Bergan, William Luke *lawyer*
Berger, Lawrence Douglas *lawyer*
Berry, Robert Worth *lawyer, educator, retired army officer*
Bierbower, James J. *lawyer*
Birchfield, John Kermit, Jr. *lawyer*
Blatt, Harold Geller *lawyer*
Blow, George *lawyer*
Bluemle, Robert Louis *lawyer*
Boho, Dan L. *lawyer*
Borden, Mark G. *lawyer*
Bork, Robert Heron *lawyer, author, former federal judge*
Borow, Richard Henry *lawyer*
Borton, Robert Ernest *lawyer*
Bower, Jean Ramsay *court administrator, lawyer*
Brantz, George Murray *retired lawyer*
Braun, Jerome Irwin *lawyer*
Brink, Richard Edward *lawyer*
Brodhead, David Crawmer *lawyer*
Brodsky, David M. *lawyer*
Brower, Charles Nelson *lawyer, judge*
Brown, William Houston *lawyer*
Bryant, Cecil Farris *lawyer, retired insurance company executive*
Bujold, Tyrone Patrick *lawyer*
Bunn, George *legal educator, writer*
Burlingame, James Montgomery, III *lawyer*
Burroughs, John Townsend *lawyer*
Califano, Joseph Anthony, Jr. *lawyer, public health policy educator, writer*
†Campbell, Todd J. *lawyer, federal official*
Casey, Robert Reisch *lawyer*
Casselman, William E., II *lawyer*
Cassidy, John Harold *lawyer*
Casterline, Cecil W. *lawyer*
Cattani, Maryellen B. *lawyer*
Chamberlin, Michael Meade *lawyer*
Chase, Seymour M. *lawyer*
Chepiga, Pamela Rogers *lawyer*
Chervin, Joseph *lawyer*
Christensen, Robert A. *lawyer*
Clark, Donald Otis *lawyer*
Clarke, Edward Owen, Jr. *lawyer*
Cobb, Miles Alan *lawyer*
Cockrill, Ann Teresa *lawyer*
Coleman, John James *lawyer*
Coleman, Robert Lee *retired lawyer*
Colodny, Edwin Irving *lawyer, retired airline executive*
Connelly, Sharon Rudolph *lawyer, federal official*
Cooper, Charles Justin *lawyer, former government official*
Coplin, Mark David *lawyer*
Corbin, Robert Keith *lawyer, former state attorney general*
Corwin, Laura J. *lawyer*
Cotton, Aylett Borel *retired lawyer*
Crawford, Muriel Laura *lawyer, author, educator*
Cronson, Robert Granville *lawyer*
Cross, Elmo Garnett, Jr. *lawyer, state senator*
Csia, Susan Rebecca *lawyer, oil company executive*
Culvahouse, Arthur Boggess, Jr. *lawyer*
Davenport, Chester *lawyer*
Davis, Roger Edwin *lawyer, retired discount chain executive*
Diamond, Stuart *lawyer, journalist*
Diehl, Deborah Hilda *lawyer*
Doty, James Robert *lawyer*
Dowd, Clark Wayne *lawyer, state legislator*
Dubuc, Carroll Edward *lawyer*
Duncan, Donald William *retired lawyer*
Dungan, Malcolm Thon *lawyer*
Dunn, Warren Howard *retired lawyer, brewery executive*
Dunne, Katherine Anne *lawyer*
Dutile, Fernand Neville *law educator*
Dymond, Lewis Wandell *lawyer, mediator, educator*
Dziubla, Robert W. *lawyer*
Edwards, Jerome *lawyer*
Ellenberger, Jack Stuart *law librarian*
Ellis, Emory Nelson, Jr. *retired lawyer*
English, Richard D. *lawyer, diplomat, government official*
Erb, James J. *lawyer*
Erlenborn, John Neal *lawyer, educator, former congressman*
Everdell, William *lawyer*
Fabrick, Howard David *lawyer*
Fanwick, Ernest *corporate lawyer*
Farmakides, John Basil *lawyer*
Ferraro, Geraldine Anne *lawyer, former congresswoman*
Field, Arthur Norman *lawyer*
Finder, Theodore Roosevelt *retired lawyer*
Fiorito, Edward Gerald *lawyer*
Flick, John Edmond *lawyer*
Ford, Ashley Lloyd *lawyer, retired consumer products company executive*
Fowler, Donald Raymond *retired lawyer, educator*
Franklin, Michael Harold *arbitrator, lawyer, consultant*
Frasca, Joanne M. *lawyer*
Frega, Patrick R. *lawyer*
Frisch, Robert Emile *lawyer*
Fuller, Robert Ferrey *lawyer, investor*
Gamble, E. James *lawyer, accountant*
Gardner, Warner Winslow *lawyer*
George, Joyce Jackson *lawyer, former judge*
Gillam, Max Lee *lawyer*
Giusti, William Roger *lawyer*
Gobel, John Henry *lawyer*
Goforth, William Clements *lawyer*
Goldstein, Mark *lawyer*
Grabemann, Karl W. *lawyer*
Green, Mark Joseph *lawyer, author*
Green, Oliver Francis, Jr. *lawyer*
Griffin, Campbell Arthur, Jr. *lawyer*
Griffith, Clark Calvin, II *lawyer*
Grove, Kalvin M(yron) *lawyer*
Gudenberg, Harry Richard *arbitrator, mediator*
Gunnels, Lawrence *lawyer*
Guttentag, Joseph Harris *lawyer, educator*
Hackel-Sims, Stella Bloomberg *lawyer, former government official*
Hackett, Robert John *lawyer*
Hafner, Thomas Mark *lawyer*
Haley, George Brock, Jr. *lawyer*
Hall, Jack Gilbert *lawyer, business executive*
Hall, John Hopkins *retired lawyer*
Halleck, Charles White *lawyer, former judge*
Handler, Harold Robert *lawyer*
Hanzlik, Rayburn DeMara *lawyer*
Harnack, Don Steger *lawyer*
Harriman, John Howland *lawyer*
Harrison, Charles Maurice *lawyer, former communications company executive*
Hausman, Bruce *lawyer*
Hauver, Constance Longshore *lawyer*
Healy, Richard Joseph *lawyer*
Heath, Richard Eddy *lawyer*
Heiman, David Gilbert *lawyer*
Helms, W. Richard *lawyer*
Hemmer, James Paul *lawyer*
Herwitz, Carla Barron *lawyer*
Hewes, Laurence Ilsley, III *lawyer, management and legal consultant*
Hicks, Vicki Jean *lawyer*
Higginbotham, John Taylor *lawyer*
Hoch, Roland Franklin *lawyer, retired utilities corporation executive*
Hoffman, Alan Craig *lawyer*
Hoffman, S. David *lawyer, engineer, educator*
Holt, Marjorie Sewell *lawyer, retired congresswoman*
Honeystein, Karl *lawyer, entertainment company executive*
Horsburgh, Beverly *law educator*
Horwitz, Donald Paul *lawyer*
Howell, Donald Lee *lawyer*
Hughey, Richard Kohlman *lawyer, author, legal publisher*
Hunt, Ronald Forrest *lawyer*
Hyman, Seymour Charles *arbitrator*
Iklé, Richard Adolph *lawyer*
Irvine, John Alexander *lawyer*
Jackson, Elmer Joseph *lawyer, oil and gas company executive*
Jacobs, Alan *lawyer*
Jaicomo, Ronald James *lawyer*
Jamieson, Michael Lawrence *lawyer*
Jensen, Robert Neal *lawyer*
Jensen, Robert Trygve *lawyer*
Jones, Jerrauld C. *lawyer*
Jones, Keith Alden *lawyer*
Kafes, William Owen *lawyer*
Kaster, Laura A. *lawyer*
Katz, Martin Howard *lawyer*
Keating, Louis Jeremiah *lawyer*
Kennedy, William Francis *lawyer*
Keys, Jerry Malcom *lawyer*
King, David Roy *lawyer*
King, John Francis *lawyer*
Kirven, Gerald *lawyer*
Klaus, Charles *retired lawyer*
Kleban, Kenneth A. *lawyer*
Kleiman, Bernard *lawyer*
Koplow, David Alexander *law educator*
Kratt, Peter George *lawyer*
Kurtz, Lloyd Sherer, Jr. *lawyer*
Kyle, Henry Carper *lawyer*
Lackland, John *lawyer*
Lagos, George Peter *lawyer*
Lambert, Samuel Waldron, III *lawyer*
Lancaster, Robert Samuel *lawyer, educator*
Landau, Kenneth Jeffrey *lawyer*
Lande, James Avra *lawyer, engineering and construction company executive*
Lea, Lorenzo Bates *lawyer*
Leb, Arthur Stern *lawyer*

Lemon, Eric V. *lawyer*
Lerner, Harry *lawyer, consultant*
Levetown, Robert Alexander *lawyer*
Levine, Meldon Edises *lawyer, former congressman*
Levy, David *lawyer, insurance company executive*
Liebeler, Susan Wittenberg *lawyer*
Lightstone, Ronald *lawyer*
Linde, Maxine Helen *lawyer, business executive, private investor*
Lisk, Pamela Konieczka *lawyer*
Ludwikowski, Rett Ryszard *law educator, researcher*
Lurie, William L. *lawyer, association executive*
Magurno, Richard Peter *lawyer*
Malin, Ronald H. *lawyer, real estate associate, consultant*
Mallory, William Barton, III *lawyer*
Manne, Henry Girard *lawyer, educator*
Marinis, Thomas Paul, Jr. *lawyer*
Marlatt, Jerry Ronald *lawyer*
Marr, Carmel Carrington *lawyer, retired state official*
†Marshall, Kathryn Sue *lawyer*
Matthews, Cari Pineiro *lawyer, author*
Mattingly, William Earl *lawyer*
Mayer, James Joseph *retired corporate lawyer*
McCabe, David Allen *lawyer*
McCarthy, J. Thomas *lawyer, educator*
McCarthy, Vincent Paul *lawyer*
Mc Connell, Edward Bosworth *legal organization administrator, lawyer*
McConnell, James Guy *lawyer*
McCormick, Michael D. *lawyer*
Mc Curley, Robert Lee, Jr. *lawyer*
McKean, Robert Jackson, Jr. *retired lawyer*
McKinlay, Donald Carl *lawyer*
McNeil, Heidi Loretta *lawyer*
McNutt, Suzzanne Marie *lawyer*
Mc Pherson, Robert Donald *retired lawyer*
Mc Quade, Lawrence Carroll *lawyer, corporate executive*
McSorley, Cisco *lawyer*
Medlock, Donald Larson *lawyer*
Mercer, Edwin Wayne *lawyer*
Meyer, Max Earl *lawyer*
Miller, Edward Albert *lawyer*
Miller, Jeffrey Grant *law educator*
Miller, Jesse D. *lawyer*
Miller, Reed *lawyer*
Miller, Richard Alan *lawyer, former merger and acquisition and forest products company executive*
Miller, Thormund Aubrey *lawyer*
Miller, William Talbot *lawyer*
Millimet, Erwin *lawyer*
Mingle, James John *lawyer*
Mintz, M. J. *lawyer*
Mlyniec, Wallace John *law educator, lawyer, consultant*
Moody, Graham Blair *lawyer*
Morgan, Melanie Karyn *lawyer*
Mulligan, William Hughes *lawyer, former federal judge*
Mullin, Roger William, Jr. *lawyer, former truck manufacturing company executive*
Munford, Luther Townsend *lawyer*
Murphy, Lewis Curtis *lawyer, former mayor*
Murphy, Sandra Robison *lawyer*
Murray, Fred F. *lawyer*
Muskie, Edmund Sixtus *lawyer, former secretary of state, former senator*
†Myers, Daniel N. *lawyer, association executive*
Myers, Jesse Jerome *lawyer, construction company executive*
Nagle, David R. *lawyer, former congressman*
Natcher, Stephen Darlington *lawyer, business executive*
Nelson, Carl Roger *retired lawyer*
†Nelson, Ralph Stanley *lawyer*
Nelson, Shelley Marie *lawyer*
Newman, Carol L. *lawyer*
Nichols, Wade Hampton, III *lawyer*
Nolen, William Giles *lawyer, accountant*
Norman, Albert George, Jr. *lawyer*
Norris, Martin Joseph *lawyer*
Ober, Richard Francis, Jr. *lawyer, banker*
O'Brien, J. Willard *lawyer, educator*
O'Connell, Philip Raymond *retired lawyer, paper company executive*
O'Flinn, Peter Russell *lawyer*
O'Mahoney, Robert M. *lawyer*
Orloff, Neil *lawyer*
Osimitz, Dennis Victor *lawyer*
Otis, Lee Liberman *lawyer, educator*
Padgett, George Arthur *retired lawyer*
†Palizzi, Anthony N. *lawyer, retail corporation executive*
Patrick, Deval Laurdine *lawyer*
Patton, James Richard, Jr. *lawyer*
Paul, Herbert Morton *lawyer, accountant, taxation educator*
Paulus, Norma Jean Petersen *lawyer, state school system administrator*
Penzer, Mark *lawyer, editor, corporate trainer, former publisher*
Pierluisi, Pedro Rafael *lawyer*
Piga, Stephen Mulry *lawyer*
Pitcher, Griffith Fontaine *lawyer*
Polikoff, Benet, Jr. *lawyer*
Pollard, Henry *lawyer*
Pooley, Beverley John *law educator, librarian*
Prince, Andrew Steven *lawyer, former government official*
Prugh, George Shipley *lawyer*
Pusateri, Lawrence Xavier *lawyer*
Pustilnik, David Daniel *lawyer*
Quigley, Leonard Vincent *lawyer*
Quillen, Cecil Dyer, Jr. *lawyer, consultant*
Quinlan, J(oseph) Michael *lawyer*
Rabinowitz, Mark Allan *lawyer*
Ramsey, Stephen Douglas *lawyer*
Reath, George, Jr. *lawyer*
Reeder, James Arthur *lawyer*
Reeder, Robert Harry *retired lawyer*
Reese, Harry Browne *lawyer, educator*
Rehmus, Charles Martin *law educator, arbitrator*
Reiche, Frank Perley *lawyer, former federal commissioner*
Reiss, Jerome *lawyer*
Reister, Ruth Alkema *lawyer, business executive*
Reiter, Glenn Mitchell *lawyer*
Reminger, Richard Thomas *lawyer*
Reycraft, George Dewey *lawyer*
Reynolds, William Bradford *lawyer*
Rivers, Kenneth Jay *judicial administrator, consultant*
Roberts, Alfred Wheeler, III *law firm executive*
Roberts, John Glover, Jr. *lawyer*
Rock, Richard Rand *lawyer, former state senator*
Rohrback, Robert Lee, Jr. *lawyer*
Rose, Carol Marguerite *law educator*
Rosenberg, Sheli Zysman *lawyer, financial management executive*
Rosenn, Harold *lawyer*
Roth, Michael *lawyer*
Rothwell, Albert Falcon *retired lawyer, retired natural resource company executive*
Royer, Donald E. *lawyer*
Saliterman, Richard Arlen *lawyer, educator*
Sallus, Marc Leonard *lawyer*
Sampson, Ronald Gary *lawyer*
Santman, Leon Duane *lawyer, former federal government executive*
Savage, Charles Francis *lawyer*
Sax, Joseph Lawrence *lawyer, educator*
Saxon, John David *lawyer, educator*
Schmults, Edward Charles *lawyer*
Schoor, Michael Mercier *lawyer, lobbyist*
Schroeder, Paul J., Jr. *lawyer*
Schuck, Peter Horner *lawyer, educator*
Schwab, Eileen Caulfield *lawyer, educator*
Sellars, Victor Carol Gene *lawyer*
Shattuck, Cathie Ann *lawyer, former government official*
Shaver, Daniel P. *law educator, civilian military employee*
Sheldon, Terry Edwin *lawyer, business consultant, advisor*
Shirley, George Pfeiffer *lawyer, educational consultant*
Shook, Ann Jones *lawyer*
Shughart, Donald Louis *lawyer*
Shutler, Kenneth Eugene *lawyer*
Simonton, Robert Bennet *lawyer*
Sinclair, Virgil Lee, Jr. *lawyer, writer*
Skratek, Sylvia Paulette *mediator, arbitrator, dispute systems designer*
Slavitt, David Walton *retired lawyer*
Smith, Edward Reaugh *retired lawyer, cemetery and funeral home consultant*
Smith, Lauren Ashley *lawyer, journalist, clergyman, physicist*
Smith, Robert Michael *lawyer*
Spanninger, Beth Anne *lawyer*
Spicer, S(amuel) Gary *lawyer, writer*
Spollen, John William *lawyer*
Springer, Paul David *lawyer, motion picture company executive*
Starr, Kenneth Winston *lawyer*
Stegall, Daniel Richard *lawyer*
Stein, Milton Michael *lawyer*
Stein, Stanley Richard *lawyer, fast food company executive*
†Stern, Todd David *lawyer*
Stetler, David J. *lawyer*
†Stevenson, Bryan Allen *lawyer, administrator*
Stream, Arnold Crager *lawyer, writer*
Streeter, Richard Henry *lawyer*
Strock, William C. *lawyer*
Strong, William Sutherland *lawyer*
Tamen, Harriet *lawyer*
Tancredi, Laurence Richard *law and psychiatry educator, administrator*
Tapley, James Leroy *retired lawyer, railway corporation executive*
Taylor, James E. *lawyer*
Terry, John Hart *lawyer, former utility company executive, former congressman*
Tessler, Allan Roger *lawyer*
Thiele, Howard Nellis, Jr. *lawyer*
Thomas, Melissa Ann *lawyer*
Thomas, Patricia Anne *retired law librarian*
Tillmon, Bobbi *lawyer*
Toensing, Victoria *lawyer*
Tolentino, Casimiro Urbano *lawyer*
Tomasko, Mark Daniel *lawyer*
Towery, Matthew Allen, Sr. *lawyer*
Trigg, Paul Reginald, Jr. *lawyer*
Trilling, Helen Regina *lawyer*
Trimble, Paul Joseph *lawyer*
Turner, James P. *lawyer*
Valcic, Susan Joan *lawyer*
Voight, Elizabeth Anne *lawyer*
Voorhees, James Dayton, Jr. *lawyer*
Voorhees, John Schenck *lawyer*
Walch, W. Stanley *lawyer*
Waldo, Burton Corlett *lawyer*
Walker, Craig Michael *lawyer*
Walker, James William, Jr. *lawyer*
Walker, John Sumpter, Jr. *lawyer*
Walker, Mary L. *lawyer*
Wallack-Roselli, Rina Evelyn *lawyer*
Walner, Robert Joel *lawyer*
Weber, Julian L. *lawyer, former publishing and entertainment company executive*
Webster, Robert David *lawyer*
Weclew, Robert George *lawyer, educator*
Weiland, Charles Hankes *lawyer*
Weinberg, Robert Leonard *retired lawyer*
Wesely, Marissa Celeste *lawyer*
West, Stephen Allan *lawyer*
Westreich, Benzion Joseph *lawyer*
White, Richard Clarence *lawyer*
Widlus, Hannah Beverly *lawyer*
Wildhack, William August, Jr. *lawyer*
Wiley, Richard Arthur *lawyer*
†Willey, Frank Patrick *lawyer, insurance company executive*
Williams, William John, Jr. *lawyer*
Wilner, Thomas Bernard *lawyer*
Wilson, Hugh Steven *lawyer*
Wiltbank, Joseph Kelley *lawyer, university counsel, sports association executive*
Wittner, Loren Antonow *lawyer, former public relations executive*
Wood, David Charles *lawyer, finance company executive*
Wood, Diane Pamela *lawyer*
Yarbro, Alan David *lawyer*
Yarbrough, Marilyn Virginia *lawyer, educator*
Yeager, Mark L. *lawyer*
York, Alexandra *lawyer*
Yost, William Arthur, III *lawyer*
Young, Michael Kent *lawyer, educator*

MEDICINE. *See* HEALTHCARE: MEDICINE.

MILITARY

UNITED STATES

ALABAMA

Alexander City
Shuler, Ellie Givan, Jr. *heritage center administrator*

Fort Rucker
Adams, Ronald Emerson *army officer*
†Petrosky, Daniel J. *army officer*

Huntsville
†Stevens, Edward Parker *military officer*

Madison
Frakes, Lawrence Wright *retired career officer, businessman*
Jellett, James Morgan *retired army officer, aerospace defense consultant*

Maxwell AFB
Pendley, William Tyler *naval officer, international relations educator*

Montgomery
Pickett, George Bibb, Jr. *retired military officer*

ALASKA

Fort Richardson
Schnell, Roger Thomas *retired military officer, state official*

ARIZONA

Phoenix
Beltrán, Anthony Natalicio *military non-commissioned officer, deacon*
Voorhees, John Henry *military officer*

Tucson
Guice, John Thompson *retired air force officer*
Wickham, John Adams, Jr. *retired army officer*

Yuma
Hudson, John Irvin *retired marine officer*

ARKANSAS

Mountain Home
Baker, Robert Leon *naval medical officer*

CALIFORNIA

Beale AFB
Carpenter, Adelbert Wall *air force officer*

Bonita
Curtis, Richard Earl *former naval officer, former company executive, business consultant*

Borrego Springs
Shinn, Allen Mayhew *retired naval officer, business executive*

Camp Pendleton
†Higginbotham, Geoffrey B. *military officer*

Cedar Ridge
Yeager, Charles Elwood (Chuck Yeager) *retired air force officer*

Coronado
Butcher, Bobby Gene *retired military officer*
Worthington, George Rhodes *naval officer*

Escondido
Briggs, Edward Samuel *naval officer*

Folsom
Aldridge, Donald O'Neal *military officer*

Fort Ord
†Simpson, Kenneth Warren *army officer*

Healdsburg
Eade, George James *retired air force officer, research executive, defense consultant*

Laguna Hills
Faw, Duane Leslie *retired military officer, law educator, lay worker, author*

Long Beach
Mears, Gary H. *career military officer*

Los Angeles
Chernesky, John Joseph, Jr. *naval officer*

Monterey
Hoivik, Thomas Harry *military educator, international consultant*
Schrady, David Alan *operations research educator*

Napa
Smith, Robert Bruce *former security consultant, retired army officer*

Pebble Beach
Carns, Michael Patrick Chamberlain *air force officer*
Fergusson, Robert George *retired army officer*
Mauz, Henry Herrward, Jr. *retired naval officer*

Point Mugu
Newman, William E. *naval officer*

Riverside
Wright, John MacNair, Jr. *retired army officer*

San Diego
Cockell, William Arthur, Jr. *naval officer*
Fontana, J. D. *naval research administration*
Robinson, David Brooks *naval officer*

San Francisco
†Tedeschi, Ernest Francis, Jr. *naval officer*

Santa Barbara
Conley, Philip James, Jr. *retired air force officer*

Saratoga
Henderson, William Darryl *army officer, writer*

Sonora
†Smith, Carlton Myles *military officer*

Sunnyvale
Schumacher, Henry Jerold *former career officer, business executive*

COLORADO

Cheyenne Mountain AFB
†Dekok, Roger G. *air force officer*
Horner, Charles Albert *air force officer*

Colorado Springs
Allery, Kenneth Edward *air force officer*
Barry, William Patrick *military officer*
Bowen, Clotilde Dent *retired army officer, psychiatrist*
Breckner, William John, Jr. *retired air force officer, corporate executive, consultant*
Forgan, David Waller *retired air force officer*
Metzler, Philip Lowry, Jr. *air force officer*
Mitchell, John Henderson *retired army officer, management consultant*
Munro, Michael Donald *entertainment and hospital consultant, professional voice talent*
Sawyer, Thomas William *air force officer*
Schaeffer, Reiner Horst *air force officer, retired librarian, foreign language professional*
Stewart, Robert Lee *retired army officer, astronaut*
Todd, Harold Wade *retired air force officer, consultant*

Denver
Avrit, Richard Calvin *defense consultant*

Englewood
France, John Lyons *air force officer*

Fort Collins
†Roberts, Archibald Edward *retired army officer, author*

U S A F Academy
†Hopkins, James William *career officer, educator*
Hosmer, Bradley Clark *retired military officer, educational consultant*
Porter, David Bruce *air force officer, behavioral scientist, educator*

CONNECTICUT

Groton
Simpson, W. M. *career officer administrator*

Niantic
Hunt, Francis Howard *retired navy laboratory official*

West Haven
Callison, Charles Stuart *retired foreign service officer, development economist*

DISTRICT OF COLUMBIA

Bolling AFB
Jones, William Edward *air force officer*

Washington
Adams, Andrew Joseph *army officer*
Anderson, Marcus A. *career officer*
Anselmo, Philip Shepard *naval officer*
Bennett, David Michael *naval officer*
Bennitt, Brent Martin *naval officer*
Boorda, Jeremy Michael (Mike Boorda) *naval officer*
Briggs, Steven Russell *naval officer*
†Burg, Robert Jules *naval officer*
Caruana, Patrick Peter *career officer*
†Ceroni, Andrew Joseph, Jr. *air force officer*
†Cisneros, Marc Anthony *military officer*
Coady, Philip James, Jr. *naval officer*
†Conaway, John Bolyn *national guard officer*
Corcoran, Thomas Joseph *retired foreign service officer, former ambassador*
Dantone, Joseph John, Jr. *naval officer*
Davis, James Richard *military officer*
Davis, Walter J., Jr. *vice admiral*
†Deegan, Gene Austin *marine corps officer*
†DeLuca, Anthony J. *director small and minority business program in United State Air Force*
DiBattiste, Carol A. *assistant U.S. attorney, lawyer*
†Dula, Brett M. *military officer*
Dyke, Charles William *retired army officer*
Earner, William Anthony, Jr. *naval officer*
Falter, Vincent Eugene *retired army officer, consultant*
†Farmen, William Newton *career officer*
Fedorochko, William, Jr. *retired army officer, policy analyst*

Finerty, Martin Joseph, Jr. *military officer, researcher*
†Fisher, Stephen Todd *naval officer*
Fogleman, Ronald Robert *military officer*
Franklin, Charles E. *career officer*
Frost, S. David *retired naval officer*
Fuller, Lawrence Joseph *military officer, lawyer*
†Gardner, Donald Ray *career officer*
†Garner, Jay Montgomery *career officer*
†Genega, Stanley G. *career officer, federal agency administrator*
Goodpaster, Andrew Jackson *retired army officer*
Graves, Ernest, Jr. *retired army officer, engineer*
†Gray, Kenneth Darnell *career officer, judge*
†Gregory, Frederick D. *career officer, space agency administrator*
Griffith, Ronald H. *military career officer*
†Haines, Milton L. (Lee Haines) *air force officer*
Hancock, William John *career officer*
Harrison, Jerry Calvin *army officer*
†Heflebower, Charles R. *career officer*
†Hicks, Robert Ruiz, Jr. *army officer*
Hoar, Joseph P. *military officer*
Huston, John Wilson *air force officer, historian*
Jeremiah, David Elmer *naval officer*
†Jones, Thomas Curtis *army officer*
†Joulwan, George A. *career military officer*
Kalleres, Michael Peter *career officer*
†Kern, Paul John *army officer*
†Kilmartin, Thomas John, III *army officer*
Klugh, James Richard *military officer*
†Koenig, Harold Martin *U.S. Navy deputy surgeon general*
†Konetzni, Albert H., Jr. *naval officer*
†Kostelnik, Michael Charles *military officer*
†Kramek, Adm. Robert E. *U.S. coast guard officer*
LaPlante, John Baptiste *naval officer*
Laughton, Katharine L. *career officer*
Leaf, Howard Westley *retired air force officer, military official*
†Little, John Hadley *army officer*
†Loeffke, Bernard *career officer*
Loftus, Stephen Francis *naval officer*
Lynch, Thomas C. *career military officer*
Maddox, David M. *career military officer*
Marfiak, Thomas Fletcher *career officer*
Mathis, William Walter *career officer*
†McCaffrey, Barry Richard *army officer*
McClain, Charles William, Jr. (Bill McClain) *army officer*
McGinty, Michael Dennis *air force officer*
McMiller, Anita Williams *army officer, transportation professional, educator*
McPeak, Merrill Anthony *business executive, consultant, retired officer*
Menoher, Paul Edwin, Jr. *army officer*
Merino Castro, José Toribio *retired Chilean naval officer*
Miller, Kenneth Gregory *air force officer*
Montelongo, Michael *career officer*
†Moore, Walter Bruce *career officer*
Moorer, Thomas Hinman *retired naval officer*
Morehouse, David C. *military lawyer*
Mundy, Carl Epting, Jr. *commandant of the marine corps*
Murashige, Allen *defense analysis executive*
†Musselman, James Arthur *army officer*
†Navas, William Antonio, Jr. *military officer, civil engineer*
†Nowak, John Michael *air force officer*
O'Berry, Carl Gerald *air force officer, electrical engineer*
Odom, William Eldridge *army officer, educator*
†Ord, Robert L., III *military officer*
†Orsini, Eric Andrew *army official*
†Oster, Jeffrey Wayne *marine corps officer*
Oswald, Robert Bernard *science administrator, nuclear engineer*
†Page, William Candler, Jr. *career officer*
Paulsen, Thomas Dean *naval officer*
Pearson, Jeremiah W., III *military career officer, federal agency official*
Phillips, Richard L(overidge) *marine corps officer*
Pirie, Robert Burns, Jr. *defense analyst*
†Profitt, Glenn Arliss, II *air force officer*
Reason, Joseph Paul *naval officer*
†Rees, Raymond F. *military officer*
Riddell, Richard Anderson *naval officer*
†RisCassi, Robert W. *career military officer*
Rokke, Ervin Jerome *air force officer, university president*
St. John, Adrian, II *retired army officer*
Sanford, Frederic Goodman *career officer*
Sareeram, Ray Rupchand *naval officer*
Scowcroft, Brent *retired air force officer, government official*
Shea, Donald William *career officer*
Simmons, Edwin Howard *marine corps officer, historian*
Slatkin, Nora *government official*
Smith, Leighton Warren, Jr. *naval officer*
Smith, William Dee *naval officer*
Snyder, Daniel James *military career officer*
†Stiner, Carl Wade *army officer*
Studeman, William Oliver *naval officer*
Sullivan, Gordon R. *career officer*
†Taylor, Wesley Bayard, Jr. *army officer*
Thomas, Richard *civilian military employee*
†Tohlen, David Ray *air force officer*
†Weiler, Todd Alan *army official*
Wheeler, Albin Gray *U.S. Army career officer, educator, retail executive, law firm executive*
†Willis, Mary Catherine *brigadier general*
†Yakeley, Jay B., III *naval officer*
Yatsevitch, Gratian Michael *retired army officer, diplomat, engineer*
Zlatoper, Ronald Joseph *career officer*

FLORIDA

Daytona Beach
Gauch, Eugene William, Jr. *former air force officer*

Destin
Carlton, Paul Kendall *former air force officer, consultant*

Eglin AFB
Stewart, J. Daniel *air force development and test center administrator*

Fernandina Beach
Rogers, Robert Burnett *naval officer*

Haines City
Clement, Robert William *air force officer*

Jacksonville
Howe, Jonathan Trumbull *naval officer*
Lestage, Daniel Barfield *retired naval officer, physician*

Lake Wales
Mumma, Albert G. *retired naval officer, retired manufacturing company executive, management consultant*

Longwood
Smyth, Joseph Patrick *retired naval officer, physician*

Lutz
Bedke, Ernest Alford *retired air force officer*

Mac Dill AFB
†Downing, Wayne Allan *career officer*
LeMoyne, Irve Charles *career officer*
†Weinstein, Mark Steven *air force officer*

Niceville
†Hagwood, Henry Melvin, Jr. *career officer*
Phillips, Richard Wendell, Jr. *air force officer*

Ocala
Parker, Harry Lee *retired military officer, counselor*

Orange Park
Enney, James Crowe *former air force officer, business executive*

Orlando
Laning, Richard Boyer *naval officer, writer, retired*
Smetheram, Herbert Edwin *business executive*
Tillotson, Frank Lee *naval officer*

Ormond Beach
Riley, Daniel Edward *air force officer*

Palm City
Senter, William Oscar *retired air force officer*

Pensacola
†Tobin, Paul Edward, Jr. *naval officer*
Weisner, Maurice Franklin *former naval officer*

Punta Gorda
Hepfer, John William, Jr. *consultant, retired air force officer*
Wilson, Dwight Liston *former military officer, investment advisor*

Sarasota
Loving, George Gilmer, Jr. *retired air force officer*

Tampa
Matheny, Charles Woodburn, Jr. *retired army officer, retired civil engineer, former city official*

Tyndall AFB
†Horn, Clinton Van *air force officer*

Valrico
Nelson, Norman Daniel *career officer*

GEORGIA

Atlanta
Carey, Gerald John, Jr. *former air force officer, research institute director*
McGuinn, Michael Edward, III *retired army officer*
†Miller, Frank L., Jr. *army officer*

Columbus
Cavezza, Carmen James *career officer*

Duluth
Holutiak-Hallick, Stephen Peter, Jr. *military officer*

Fort Benning
Ramsey, Russell Wilcox *national security affairs educator*
†White, Jerry Allen *career officer*

Fort Gordon
†Spaulding, Vernon Charles, Jr. *military officer, gastroenterologist*

Fort McPherson
Champion, Charles Howell, Jr. *army officer*
Reimer, Dennis J. *career military officer*

Georgetown
Connelly, Donald Webb *former military officer, business executive*

Kings Bay
Ellis, Winford Gerald *military career officer, federal agency administrator*

Peachtree City
Eichelberger, Charles Bell *retired career officer*
Yeosock, John John *army officer*

Roswell
Graham, Charles Passmore *retired army officer*

Stockbridge
Davis, Raymond Gilbert *retired career officer, real estate developer*

Valdosta
†Kinnan, Timothy Alan *air force officer*

Warner Robins
DePriest, C(harles) David *engineer, retired air force officer*
Nugteren, Cornelius *air force officer*

HAWAII

Camp H M Smith
†Christmas, George Ronald *career officer*
Macke, Richard Chester *naval officer*
Toney, Robert L. *naval officer*

Fort Shafter
Ivey, Claude Tarlton *military officer*

Honolulu
Barr, Jon Michael *naval officer, federal official*
Berg, Dennis Ray *air force officer*
Driskill, Thomas Malcolm, Jr. *military officer*
†Fields, Harold Thomas, Jr. *career officer*
Greer, Howard Earl *former naval officer*
Hays, Ronald Jackson *naval officer*
Rutherford, Robert L. *career military officer*
Weyand, Frederick Carlton *retired military officer*

Kaneohe
McGlaughlin, Thomas Howard *publisher, retired naval officer*

Pearl Harbor
Fitzgerald, James Richard *naval officer*

IDAHO

Boise
Manning, Darrell V. *national guard officer*

ILLINOIS

Fort Sheridan
†Lenhardt, Alfonso Emanual *army officer*

Great Lakes
Gaston, Mack Charles *naval officer*

Hoffman Estates
Pagonis, William Gus *retired army officer*

Lemont
Herriford, Robert Levi, Sr. *army officer*

Mattoon
Phipps, John Randolph *retired army officer*

Savanna
Foulk, David Wingerd *military civilian executive*

Scott A F B
†Hemingway, Thomas L. *career officer*

IOWA

Des Moines
Durrenberger, William John *retired army general, educator, investor*

KANSAS

Fort Leavenworth
Miller, John Edward *army officer*

Fort Riley
†House, Randolph Watkins *military officer*

KENTUCKY

Fort Knox
†Funk, Paul Edward *army officer*

Fort Thomas
†Goetz, Robert Clifford *army officer*

LOUISIANA

New Orleans
†Harness, Francis William *naval officer*
†Livingston, James Evertte *marine corps officer*
Smith, John Webster *retired naval officer, company executive*

MARYLAND

Aberdeen Proving Ground
Coburn, John G. *career officer*

Annapolis
Baldwin, John Ashby, Jr. *retired naval officer*
Barber, James Alden *military officer*
†Gallis, John Nicholas *naval officer, healthcare executive*
Larson, Charles Robert *naval officer*
Long, Robert Lyman John *naval officer*
McDonough, Joseph Corbett *former army officer, aviation consultant*

Baltimore
Wilmot, Louise C. *charitable organization executive*

Bethesda
Cooper, William Ewing, Jr. *retired army officer*
Daniel, Charles Dwelle, Jr. *consultant, retired army officer*
Hauck, Frederick Hamilton *retired naval officer, astronaut, business executive*
O'Shaughnessy, Gary William *military officer*
Owen, Thomas Barron *retired naval officer, space company executive*
Schinski, Vernon David *navy officer*
Taylor, Jimmie Wilkes *naval officer*
Wishart, Leonard Plumer, III *army officer*
Zimble, James Allen *naval officer, physician*

Chevy Chase
Delano, Victor *retired naval officer*

Columbia
Kime, J. William *career officer, engineer*

Crownsville
Lawrence, William Porter *former naval officer, academic administrator*

Easton
Quinn, William Wilson *army officer, manufacturing executive*

Edgewater
Holm, Jeanne Marjorie *author, consultant, government official, former air force officer*
†Malley, Kenneth Cornelius *military officer*

Lutherville
Sagerholm, James Alvin *retired naval officer*

Oxford
Mc Kee, Kinnaird Rowe *retired naval officer*

Rockville
Cowart, Elgin Courtland, Jr. *naval medical officer*
Harvey, Donald Phillips *retired naval officer*
Ramsey, William Edward *retired naval officer, space systems executive*
Trost, Carlisle Albert Herman *retired naval officer*

Silver Spring
Brog, David *consultant, former air force officer*

Trappe
Anderson, Andrew Herbert *retired army officer*

MASSACHUSETTS

Boston
Amirault, Richard B. *career officer*
Doebler, James Carl *naval officer, engineering executive*
Holloway, Bruce Keener *former air force officer*

Medford
Galvin, John Rogers *educator, retired army officer*

North Dartmouth
Cressy, Peter Hollon *naval officer, academic administrator*

Quincy
Miller, George David *retired air force officer, marketing consultant*

South Hamilton
Patton, George Smith *military officer*

Westford
Stansberry, James Wesley *air force officer*

MICHIGAN

Ann Arbor
Ploger, Robert Riis *retired military officer, engineer*

Warren
Horton, William David, Jr. *army officer*

MINNESOTA

Minneapolis
Chen, William Shao-Chang *retired army officer*

MISSISSIPPI

Madison
Robinson, John David *retired army officer*

Pass Christian
McCardell, James Elton *retired naval officer*

Stennis Space Center
Gaffney, Paul Golden, II *military officer*

Vicksburg
†Howard, Bruce Kenneth *army officer, environmental engineer*

MISSOURI

Chesterfield
Willis, Frank Edward *retired air force officer*

Florissant
Reese, Alferd George *retired army civilian logistics specialist*

Fort Leonard Wood
†Broyles, Thomas Edwin *career officer, healthcare facility executive*

Saint Louis
†Prather, Thomas Levi, Jr. *army officer*
Williamson, Donald Ray *retired career Army officer*

MONTANA

Helena
Blair, Gary Charles *military officer*

Mc Lean
Cowhill, William Joseph *retired naval officer, consultant*
Davis, Bennie Luke *air force officer*
Haddock, Raymond Earl *career officer*
Hopkins, Thomas Matthews *former naval officer*
Hyde, John Paul *retired air force officer*
Rogers, Alan Victor *former career officer*

Middleburg
Collins, James Lawton, Jr. *retired army officer*

Mount Jackson
Sylvester, George Howard *retired air force officer*

Newington
Miggins, Michael Denis *retired career officer, arms control analyst*

Norfolk
Clemins, Archie Ray *naval officer*
Davey, John Michael *military career officer*
Garlette, William Henry Lee *army officer*
Haskins, Michael Donald *naval officer*
Katz, Douglas Jeffrey *naval officer*
Moses, Paul Davis *career officer*
Olson, Phillip Roger *naval officer*
Robb, Nathaniel Heyward, Jr. *national guard officer, real estate executive*
†Terry, William E. *rear admiral*
Train, Harry Depue, II *retired naval officer*

Portsmouth
McDaniel, William J. *career military officer*

Reston
Brown, James Robert *retired air force officer*
Wilkinson, Edward Anderson, Jr. *retired naval officer, business executive*

Richmond
Dilworth, Robert Lexow *career officer, adult education educator*

Springfield
Becton, Julius Wesley, Jr. *army officer*

Vienna
Chandler, Hubert Thomas *former army officer*
Davis, Cabell Seal, Jr. *naval officer*
Dunn, Bernard Daniel *former naval officer, consultant*
Hatch, Harold Arthur *retired military officer*
Hughes, Thomas Joseph *retired naval officer*
Jackson, Dempster McKee *retired naval officer*
Leonard, Edward Paul *naval officer, dentist, educator*
Webb, William Loyd, Jr. *army officer*

Virginia Beach
Oldfield, Edward Charles, Jr. *retired naval officer, communications company executive*
Sanderson, James Richard *naval officer, planning and investment company consultant*

Williamsburg
Boatright, James Francis *air force official*
Cantlay, George Gordon *retired army officer*

WASHINGTON

Anacortes
Higgins, Robert (Walter) *military officer, physician*

Bothell
McDonald, Michael Lee *career naval officer*

Fort Lewis
Davis, Harley Cleo *career officer*
†Marsh, Caryl Glenn *career officer*

Lynnwood
Jenes, Theodore George, Jr. *retired military officer*

Richland
Traister, Robert Edwin *naval officer, engineer*

Tacoma
Russell, James Sargent *retired naval officer*

Yakima
Baker, Herbert Geoffrey *career officer*

WEST VIRGINIA

Harpers Ferry
Carter, Powell Frederick *retired naval officer*

Powellton
†Lopez, Thomas Joseph *naval officer*

WISCONSIN

Madison
Slack, Jerald David *adjutant general of Wisconsin, civil engineer*

Stone Lake
Kissinger, Harold Arthur *retired army officer*

MILITARY ADDRESSES OF THE UNITED STATES

ATLANTIC

APO
Hobbs, Roy Jerry *military career officer, health services administrator*
†Magruder, Lawson William, III *military officer*

FPO
†Bill, David Spencer, III *naval officer*
†Krekich, Alexander Joseph *naval officer*

EUROPE

APO
Borling, John Lorin *military officer*
Boyd, Charles Graham *military officer*
†Brady, Robert Edward *career officer, dentist*
†Daniel, Eugene Lee *career officer*
†Dickey, James Stuart *military officer*
†Downer, Lee Alan *air force officer*
†Hennessee, James Franklin *military officer*
†Link, Charles Dale *air force officer*
†Lotzbire, Bruce John *air force officer*
†Meigs, Montgomery Cunningham, Jr. *military officer*
Oaks, Robert C. *air force officer*
Ray, Norman Wilson *career officer*
†Witt, Buford Randolph *air force officer*
Yates, Walter Harvey, Jr. *career officer*

FPO
Allen, Lloyd Edward, Jr. *naval officer*
Picotte, Leonard Francis *naval officer*
Pletcher, John Harold, Jr. *air force officer*
Ryan, Thomas D. *naval officer*

PACIFIC

APO
†Brown, Daniel G. *military officer*
Chung, Tchang-Bok *management analyst, consultant*
†Jenkins, Robert Gordon *air force officer*
Running, Nels *career officer*

FPO
†Franks, Tommy Ray *army officer*
Hickey, Robert Philip, Jr. *naval officer*

CANADA

ONTARIO

Etobicoke
MacKenzie, Lewis Wharton *military officer*

Ottawa
de Chastelain, A(lfred) John G(ardyne) D(rummond) *Canadian army officer, diplomat*

Stittsville
Tellier, Henri *retired Canadian military officer*

QUEBEC

Montreal
Manson, Paul David *retired military officer, electronics executive*

ADDRESS UNPUBLISHED

Austin, Robert Clarke *naval officer*
†Bates, Jared Lewis *army officer*
Bauman, Richard Arnold *coast guard officer*
Block, Emil Nathaniel, Jr. *military officer*
†Blume, Jay Donald, Jr. *air force officer*
Boyd, Stuart Robert *military officer*
Brooks, James Sprague *retired national guard officer*
Brooks, Thomas Aloysius, III *retired naval officer*
Buker, Robert Hutchinson, Sr. *army officer, thoracic surgeon*
Campbell, Arlington Fichtner *military officer*
Carlson, Elvin Palmer *military officer*
Carter, William George, III *army officer*
Chelberg, Robert Douglas *army officer*
Cole, Brady Marshall *retired naval officer*
Cook, Douglas W. *career officer*
Crippen, Robert Laurel *former naval officer and astronaut*
Davis, Henry Jefferson, Jr. *former naval officer*
Dozier, James Lee *former army officer*
†Elam, Fred Eldon *career army officer*
Evans, Marsha Johnson *naval officer*
Fischer, Eugene H. *air force officer*
Foote, Evelyn Patricia *retired army officer, consultant*
Gavin, Herbert James *consultant, retired air force officer*
Granuzzo, Andrew Aloysius *career officer*
Gray, David Lawrence *retired air force officer*
Gurke, Sharon McCue *naval officer*
Guthrie, Wallace Nessler, Jr. *naval officer*
Hall, Thomas Forrest *naval officer*
Harper, Henry H. *military officer, retired*
Harris, Marcelite Jordan *air force officer*
Hoover, John Elwood *former military officer, consultant, writer*
Hostettler, Stephen John *naval officer*
†Hurd, Joseph Elbert *air force officer*
Johnston, James Monroe, III *air force officer*
Jones, David Charles *retired air force officer, former chairman Joint Chiefs of Staff*
Kelley, Larry Dale *retired military officer*
Kempf, Cecil Joseph *naval officer*
Krulak, Charles Chandler *marine officer*
Kutyna, Donald Joseph *air force officer*
Lautenbacher, Conrad Charles, Jr. *naval officer*
†Luck, Gary Edward *career officer*
Maness, Anthony Ray *retired naval officer*
Manganaro, Francis Ferdinand *naval officer*
Matthews, John Louis *retired military officer, educator*
Mc Fadden, George Linus *retired army officer*
McKinnon, Daniel Wayne, Jr. *naval officer*
Moore, William Leroy, Jr. *career officer, physician*
Morgan, Thomas Rowland *retired marine corps officer*
Mow, Douglas Farris *former naval officer, consultant*
Mullen, William Joseph, III *military analyst, retired army officer*
Nelson, Ben, Jr. *air force officer*
Ninos, Nicholas Peter *retired military officer, medical consultant*
Oliver, David Rogers, Jr. *naval officer*
Otstott, Charles Paddock *army officer*
Owens, William Arthur *military officer*
Palmer, Dave Richard *educator, military officer*
Parent, Rodolphe Jean *Canadian air force official, pilot*
Partington, James Wood *naval officer*
Pearson, John Davis *naval officer*
Powell, Harvard Wendell *former air force officer, business executive*
Price, Robert Ira *coast guard officer*
Retz, William Andrew *naval officer*
Rhame, Thomas Gene *army officer*
Richards, Thomas Carl *air force officer, governmental official*
Rogers, Bernard William *military officer*
Santarelli, Eugene David *air force officer*
Sausser, Robert Gary *retired army officer*
†Scholes, Edison Earl *army officer*
Schrader, Harry Christian, Jr. *retired naval officer*
Schumacher, William Jacob *retired army officer*
Shapiro, Sumner *retired naval officer, business executive*
Shaw, John Frederick *retired naval officer*
Slewitzke, Connie Lee *retired army officer*
Springer, Robert Dale *retired air force officer, consultant, lecturer*
Strohsahl, George Henry, Jr. *retired rear admiral, consultant*
Sullivan, Michael Patrick *marine officer*
Sunell, Robert John *retired army officer*
†Swanson, Dane C. *navy pilot*
Swanson, Dane Craig *naval officer, pilot*
Taylor, Allen John *U.S. Coast Guard officer*
Tourino, Ralph Gene *career officer*
Vincent, Hal Wellman *marine corps officer, investor*
Watts, Ronald Lester *retired military officer*
Weir, Kenneth Wynn *marine corps officer, experimental test pilot*
†Wheeler, Jack Cox *army officer*
Williamson, Myrna Hennrich *retired army officer, lecturer, consultant*
Wilson, Richard Alexander *career officer*

RELIGION

UNITED STATES

ALABAMA

Birmingham
†Bass, Richard O., Sr. *bishop*
Nelson, Dotson McGinnis, Jr. *clergyman*
†Roby, Jasper *bishop*

Helena
Smith, John Lee, Jr. *minister, former association administrator*

Huntsville
Loshuertos, Robert Herman *clergyman*

Mobile
Duvall, Charles Farmer *bishop*
Lipscomb, Oscar Hugh *archbishop*

Montgomery
Bullard, Mary Ellen *retired religious study center administrator*

ALASKA

Anchorage
Hurley, Francis T. *archbishop*
Parsons, Donald D. *bishop*
Williams, Charles D. *bishop*

Bethel
†Andrew, John P. *church official*

Fairbanks
Charleston, Steve *bishop*
Kaniecki, Michael Joseph *bishop*

Juneau
Kenny, Michael H. *bishop*

ARIZONA

Paradise Valley
Sapp, Donald Gene *minister*

Phoenix
Galvan, Elias Gabriel *bishop*
Galvin, Elias *bishop*
Hamilton, Ronald Ray *minister*
Harte, John Joseph Meakins *bishop*
O'Brien, Thomas Joseph *bishop*

Sun City
Lapsley, James Norvell, Jr. *minister, pastoral theology educator*

Sun City West
Randall, Claire *church executive*
Schmitz, Charles Edison *evangelist*

Tucson
Elrod, Jerry David *clergyman*
Moreno, Manuel D. *bishop*
Tirrell, John Albert *religious organization executive, consultant*

ARKANSAS

Conway
Reddin, George *religious organization administrator*

El Dorado
Lee, Vernon Roy *minister*

Garfield
Webb, Lance *bishop*

Little Rock
Donovan, Herbert Alcorn, Jr. *bishop*
Mc Donald, Andrew J. *bishop*
Walker, L. T. *bishop*

North Little Rock
Holmes, James Frederick *minister*

Pine Bluff
Adair, Toby Warren, Jr. *minister*

Russellville
Chesnut, Franklin Gilmore *clergyman*
Inch, Morris Alton *theology educator*

Searcy
Miller, Ken Leroy *religious studies educator, consultant, writer*

Texarkana
Henry, James Alvin *minister, benefits executive*

CALIFORNIA

Acton
†Butman, Harry Raymond *clergyman, author*

Anaheim
Nguyen, Tai Anh *minister*

Barstow
Jones, Nathaniel *bishop*

Berkeley
Faulk, I. Carlton *religious organization executive*
Faulk, Sylvia *religious organization executive*
Gall, Donald Arthur *minister*
Schmalenberger, Jerry Lew *pastor, seminary administrator*
Schommer, Trudy Marie *pastoral minister, religion education*
Stuhr, Walter M. *seminary educator, clergyman*
Welch, Claude (Raymond) *theology educator*

Buena Park
Elliott, Darrell Kenneth *minister, legal researcher*

Calabasas
Bleiweiss, Robert Morton *religious magazine editor, labor newspaper publisher*

Carmichael
Probasco, Calvin Henry Charles *clergyman, college administrator*

Century City
Thomas, Issac David Ellis *clergy member*

Chatsworth
Dart, John Seward *religion news writer*

Claremont
Beardslee, William Armitage *religious organization administrator, educator*
Hick, John Harwood *theologian, philosopher, educator*
Kucheman, Clark Arthur *religion educator*
†Parker, Pierson *minister, religion educator*
Sanders, James Alvin *minister, biblical studies educator*

Costa Mesa
Williams, William Corey *Old Testament educator, consultant*

Culver City
†Wilson, Nancy Linda *church officer*

Cupertino
Winslow, David Allen *chaplain, naval officer*

El Cerrito
Dillenberger, John *theology educator emeritus, minister*
Schomer, Howard *retired clergyman, educator, social policy consultant*

Escondido
Ortiz, Angel Vicente *church administrator*

Etna
Auxentios, (Bishop) *clergyman*
Chrysostomos, (González-Alexopoulos) *bishop, clergyman, psychologist, educator*

Fresno
Schofield, John-David Mercer *bishop*
Steinbock, John T. *bishop*
Wilson, Warren Samuel *clergyman, bishop*

Garden Grove
Ballesteros, Juventino Ray, Jr. *minister*
Schuller, Robert Harold *clergyman, author*

Gilroy
†Henry-John, Emmanuel Sylvester *preacher, counselor*

Glendale
Courtney, Howard Perry *clergyman*

Glendora
Richey, Everett Eldon *religion educator*

Hollywood
Hovsepian, Vatche *clergyman*

La Jolla
Freedman, David Noel *religion educator*

La Mirada
Nash, Sylvia Dotseth *religious organization executive, consultant*

Laguna Hills
Lindquist, Raymond Irving *clergyman*
Wheatley, Melvin Ernest, Jr. *retired bishop*

Lake Forest
Lindsell, Harold *clergyman*

Los Alamitos
Booth, John Nicholls *minister, magician, writer, photographer*

Los Angeles
Berg, Philip *religious denomination administrator*
Borsch, Frederick Houk *bishop*
†Bowers, John William *church official*
†Brown, E. Lynn *minister*
†Cravens, Virginia Lee *church official*
†Eastman, Donald *church officer*
Eger, Denise Leese *rabbi*
Fitzgerald, Tikhon (Lee R. H. Fitzgerald) *bishop*
Helms, Harold Edwin *minister*
Holland, John Ray *minister*
Mahony, Roger M. Cardinal *archbishop*
Mc Pherson, Rolf Kennedy *clergyman, church official*
Milligan, Sister Mary *theology educator, religious consultant*
Neal, Joseph C., Jr. *church administrator*
Perry, Troy D. *clergyman, church administrator*
Phillips, Keith Wendall *minister*
†Rogers, James Wilson *church official*
Talton, Chester Lovelle *bishop*
Wolf, Alfred *rabbi*
Wooten, Cecil Aaron *religious organization administrator*

Malibu
Wilson, John Francis *religion educator*

Menlo Park
Davis, William Emrys *religious organization official*

Mill Valley
Crews, William Odell, Jr. *seminary administrator*

Monterey
Ryan, Sylvester D. *bishop*

Northridge
Kuzma, George Martin *bishop*

Oakland
Benham, Priscilla Carla *religion educator, college president*
Crompton, Arnold *minister, educator*
Cummins, John Stephen *bishop*
Miller, Lyle G. *bishop*
Patten, Bebe Harrison *minister*
Talbert, Melvin George *bishop*

Orange
Goble, Thomas Lee *clergyman*
Mc Farland, Norman Francis *bishop*

Palm Desert
Hunt, Barnabas John *priest, religious order administrator*

Palo Alto
Brown, Robert McAfee *minister, religion educator*

Pasadena
Sano, Roy I. *bishop*
†Torres, Ralph Chon *minister*

Rancho Mirage
Stenhouse, Everett Ray *clergy administrator*

Redwood City
Logie, Dennis Wayne *minister*

Reedley
Dick, Henry Henry *minister*

Richmond
Ayers, G. W. *church adminstrator*

Sacramento
Cole, Glen David *minister*
†Lamb, Jerry A. *bishop*
Meier, George Karl, III *pastor, lawyer*
Quinn, Francis A. *bishop*
Smith, Freda M. *minister*

San Anselmo
Mudge, Lewis Seymour *theologian, educator, university dean*
Waetjen, Herman Charles *theologian, educator*

San Bernardino
†Barnes, Gerald R. *bishop*

San Diego
Boller, John Hall, Jr. *minister*
Brom, Robert H. *bishop*
Downing, David Charles *minister*
Hughes, Gethin B. *bishop*
Owen-Towle, Carolyn Sheets *clergywoman*
Phillips, Randall Clinger *minister, university administrator*

San Fernando
Gosselin, Kenneth Stuart *minister*

San Francisco
Anthony, of Sourozh (Anthony Emmanuel Gergiannakis) *bishop*
Quinn, John R. *archbishop*
Rosen, Moishe *religious organization administrator*
Sparer, Malcolm Martin *rabbi*
Swing, William Edwin *bishop*
Yamaoka, Seigen Haruo *bishop*

San Rafael
Scanlan, John Joseph *retired bishop*

Santa Barbara
Campbell, Robert Charles *clergyman, religious organization administrator*
Hubbard, David Allan *minister, educator, religious association administrator*
Long, Charles Houston *history of religion educator*
Moholy, Noel Francis *clergyman*

Santa Clara
DuMaine, R. Pierre *bishop*

Santa Cruz
Lease, Gary Lloyd *religion educator, dean*

Santa Monica
Boyd, Malcolm *minister, religious author*
Williams, George Masayasu *religious organization administrator, editor*

Santa Rosa
†Ziemann, G. Patrick *bishop*

Sebastopol
†DeMartini, Rodney J. *executive director religious organization, priest*

Sherman Oaks
Bower, Richard James *minister*

Solana Beach
Friedman, Maurice Stanley *religious educator*

Solvang
Chandler, E(dwin) Russell *religious journalist, author*

South Lake Tahoe
Null, Paul Bryan *minister*

Stanford
Harvey, Van Austin *religious studies educator*

Stockton
Montrose, Donald W. *bishop*

Studio City
Garver, Oliver Bailey, Jr. *bishop*

Tustin
†Crouch, Paul Franklin *minister, church official*
Krumm, John McGill *bishop*

Vista
Rader, Paul Alexander *minister, administrator*

Walnut Creek
†Stover, W. Robert *lay worker, temporary services executive*

Whittier
Connick, Charles Milo *retired religion educator, clergyman*

Yorba Linda
Miller, Robert Lindsey *bishop*

COLORADO

Boulder
Lester, Robert Carlton *religious studies educator*

Brighton
Vang, Timothy Teng *church executive*

Colorado Springs
Bishop, Leo Kenneth *clergyman, educator*
Bubna, Paul F. *church administrator*
Davey, J. A. *church administrator*
Fox, Douglas Allan *religion educator*
Hanifen, Richard Charles *bishop*
Mangham, R. H. *church administrator*
Nanfelt, P. N. *church administrator*
Perkins, Floyd Jerry *theology educator*
†Rambo, David L. *religious organization administrator*
Sinclair, William Donald *church official, fundraising consultant, political activist*
Wheeland, D. A. *church administrator*
Wood, Stephen *minister*

Denver
†Barger, Louise Baldwin *religious organization administrator*
Brownlee, Judith Marilyn *Wiccan minister, psychotherapist*
Burrell, Calvin Archie *minister*
Fischer, James Adrian *clergyman*
Hayes, Edward Lee *religious organization administrator*
Horn, Gilbert *minister*
Sheeran, Michael John Leo *priest, educational administrator*
Stafford, J. Francis *archbishop*
Swenson, Mary Ann *bishop*
Weissenbuehler, Wayne *bishop*
Winterrond, William J. *bishop*

Fort Collins
Rolston, Holmes, III *theologian, educator, philosopher*

Lafayette
Short, Ray Everett *minister, sociology educator emeritus, author, lecturer*

Pueblo
Tafoya, Arthur N. *bishop*

CONNECTICUT

Bethany
Forman, Charles William *religious studies educator*

Bridgeport
Egan, Edward M. *bishop*
Norris, Louise *religious organization executive*

Danbury
Malino, Jerome R. *rabbi*

East Hartford
Scholsky, Martin Joseph *priest*

Fairfield
Allaby, Stanley Reynolds *clergyman*

Hartford
Cronin, Daniel Anthony *bishop*
Reed, David Benson *bishop*
†Winter, Miriam Therese (Gloria Frances Winter) *nun, religious education educator*
Zikmund, Barbara Brown *minister, seminary president, church history educator*

Middletown
Crites, Stephen Decatur *religion educator*

New Haven
Brewer, Charles H., Jr. *bishop*
Childs, Brevard Springs *religious educator*
Dittes, James Edward *psychology of religion educator*
Johnson, Robert Clyde *theology educator*
Kavanagh, Aidan Joseph *priest, university educator*
Keck, Leander Earl *theology educator*
Malherbe, Abraham Johannes, VI *religion educator, writer*
Meeks, Wayne A. *religious studies educator*
Robbins, William Randolph *minister*
Sanneh, Lamin *religion educator*
Weinstein, Stanley *Buddhist studies educator*

Ridgefield
Kelley, Edward Allen *publisher*

Salisbury
Bevan, Charles Albert, Jr. *minister*

Stamford
†McCabe, Sister Daniel Marie *nun, religious organization executive*

Storrs
Mc Innes, William Charles *priest, campus ministry director*

Wethersfield
Payne, Edward Carlton *archbishop*

DELAWARE

New Castle
Blackshear, L. T., Sr. *bishop*

Wilmington
Grenz, Linda L. *Episcopal priest*
Harris, Robert Laird *minister, theology educator emeritus*
Linderman, Jeanne Herron *priest*
Tennis, Calvin Cabell *bishop*
†Weeks, Thomas Wesley *bishop*

DISTRICT OF COLUMBIA

Washington
Allen, William Jere *minister*
Alpern, Robert Zellman *religious organization lobbyist/administrator*
†Anderson, Carl Albert *theology school dean, lawyer*
Bittker, David *religious organization administrator*
†Bleichner, Howard P. *theological studies administrator*
†Broomfield, Oree, Sr. *bishop*
Burke, John *priest*
Cacciavillan, Agostino *archbishop*
Cenkner, William *religion educator, academic administrator*
Colson, Charles Wendell *lay minister, writer*
Di Lella, Alexander Anthony *biblical studies educator*
Doyle, Francis Xavier *religious organization administrator*
Dugan, Robert Perry, Jr. *minister, religious organization administrator*
Easley, William Webster, Jr. *minister*
Fitzmyer, Joseph Augustine *theology educator, priest*
Godsey, John Drew *minister, theology educator emeritus*
Gros, Jeffrey *ecumenical theologian*
Haines, Ronald H. *bishop*
Halverson, Richard Christian *minister, chaplain*
Harty, Sheila Therese *theologian, writer, editor*
Haught, John Francis *theology educator*
Hellwig, Monika Konrad *theology educator*
Hickey, James Aloysius Cardinal *archbishop*
Hotchkin, John Francis *church official, priest*
Hug, James Edward *religious organization administrator*
James, Frederick Calhoun *bishop*
Jansen, E. Harold *bishop*
Jensen, Joseph (Norman) *priest, educator*
Kane, Annette P. *religious organization executive*
King, Thomas M. *theology educator, priest*
Le Mone, Archie *religious organization administrator*
†Lynch, Robert N. *clergy member*
Marrett, Michael McFarlene *chaplain*
Mc Lean, George Francis *philosophy of religion educator, clergyman*
Miller, Mary Hotchkiss *lay worker*
Moore, Jerry *religious organization administrator*
Novak, Michael (John) *religion educator, author, editor*
Pfnausch, Edward *religious association administrator*
Rabinowitz, Stanley Samuel *rabbi*
Stookey, Laurence Hull *clergyman, theology educator*
Tribett, Brenda Diane Bell *religious organization administrator*
Trisco, Robert Frederick *church historian, educator*
Vandegrift, John Raymond *priest, librarian*

FLORIDA

Boca Raton
Sarna, Nahum Mattathias *biblical studies educator*

Brooksville
Slaatte, Howard Alexander *minister, philosophy educator*

Clearwater
Beckwith, William Hunter *clergyman*

Daytona Beach
Bronson, Oswald Perry *religious organization administrator, clergyman*

Deland
Fant, Clyde Edward, Jr. *religion educator*

Delray Beach
Silver, Samuel Manuel *rabbi, author*

Fernandina Beach
Hildebrand, Richard Allen *bishop*

Fort Lauderdale
Grestner, Jonathan Neil *religious studies educator*
Skiddell, Elliot Lewis *rabbi*

Fort Myers
Koehler, Robert Brien *priest*

Fort Pierce
Garment, Robert James *clergyman*

Gainesville
Creel, Austin Bowman *religion educator*

Jacksonville
Afflick, Clive Henry *minister, counselor*
Bartholomew, John Niles *church administrator*
Blackburn, Robert McGrady *retired bishop*
Cerveny, Frank Stanley *bishop*
Kensey, Calvin D. *bishop*
Snyder, John Joseph *bishop*
Vines, Charles Jerry *minister*
Voss, Carl Hermann *clergyman, humanities educator, author*

Jupiter
McCall, Duke Kimbrough *clergyman*

Lakeland
Hughes, Harold Hasbrouck, Jr. *bishop*

Largo
Williams, Harry George *minister*

Miami
Cohen, Jacob *bishop*
Hoy, William Ivan *minister, religion educator*
Lehrman, Irving *rabbi*
Schofield, Calvin Onderdonk, Jr. *bishop*
Weeks, Marta Joan *priest*

Naples
Hennessy, Brother Paul Kevin *religion educator*

New Port Richey
Sorensen, John Frederick *retired minister*

New Smyrna Beach
Hollis, Reginald *archbishop*

Orlando
Dorsey, Norbert M. *bishop*
Grady, Thomas J. *bishop*
Howe, John Wadsworth *bishop*
Santiago, Carlos *minister*
Sconiers, M. L. *bishop*

Palm Beach Gardens
Symons, J. Keith *bishop*

Pensacola
Mountcastle, William Wallace, Jr. *philosophy and religion educator*
†Smith, John M. *bishop*

Plant City
Patronelli, Raymond *church administrator*

Plymouth
Voelker, Charles Robert *archbishop, academic dean*

Ruskin
Nissen, Carl Andrew, Jr. *minister, retired procurement analyst*

Saint Petersburg
Favalora, John Clement *bishop*
Harris, Rogers S. *bishop*

Sarasota
Augsburger, Aaron Donald *clergyman*
Jones, Tracey Kirk, Jr. *minister, educator*

Tallahassee
Rubenstein, Richard Lowell *theologian, educator*

Tampa
Davis, W. E. *clergyman, bishop*
Franzen, Lavern Gerhard *bishop*
Neusner, Jacob *humanities and religious studies educator*

Venice
Nevins, John J. *bishop*

West Palm Beach
Knudsen, Raymond Barnett *clergyman, association executive, author*

Winter Park
Armstrong, (Arthur) James *minister, religion educator, religious organization executive, consultant*
Britton, Erwin Adelbert *clergyman, college administrator*
Edge, Findley Bartow *clergyman, religious education educator*

Zellwood
Wallcraft, Mary Jane Louise *religious organization executive, songwriter, author*

GEORGIA

Atlanta
Allan, Frank Kellog *bishop*
Cannon, William Ragsdale *bishop*
Donoghue, John Frances *archbishop*
Dunahoo, Charles *religious publisher, religious organization administrator*
Gilchrist, Paul R. *religious organization administrator*
Husband, J. D. *bishop*
Knox, James Lloyd *bishop*
Lowery, Joseph E. *clergyman*
McMaster, Belle Miller *religious organization administrator*
Parks, R(obert) Keith *missionary, religious organization administrator*
Skillrud, Harold Clayton *minister*
Stokes, Mack (Marion) Boyd *bishop*
Sutherland, Raymond Carter *clergyman, English educator emeritus*
Westerhoff, John Henry, III *clergyman, theologian, educator*
White, Gayle Colquitt *religion writer, journalist*
Williams, Ervin Eugene *religious organization administrator*
†Williams, W. Clyde *religious organization administrator*

Augusta
Oliver, John William Posegate *minister*

Decatur
Gericke, Paul William *minister, educator*
Winn, Albert Curry *clergyman*

Macon
Alexander, David Lee *clergyman*
†Bell, L. M. *bishop*
Hicks, C. J. *bishop*
Looney, Richard Carl *bishop*

Marietta
Derrick-White, Elizabeth *chaplain, international affairs consultant*

Monroe
Johnson, Robert Hoyt *minister*

Norcross
Kyle, John Emery *mission executive*

Riverdale
Waters, John W *minister, educator*

Savannah
†Boland, John K. *bishop*
Lessard, Raymond W. *bishop*

Townsend
Collins, David Browning *religious institution administrator*

HAWAII

Honolulu
†DiLorenzo, Francis X. *bishop*
Russi, John Joseph *priest, educational administrator*

Kailua
Bezanson, Ronald Scott, Jr. *clergyman, army chaplain*

Oceanview
Gilliam, Jackson Earle *bishop*

IDAHO

Boise
Brown, Tod David *bishop*
Thornton, John S., IV *bishop*

Post Falls
Capener, Regner Alvin *minister, electronics engineer*

ILLINOIS

Arlington Heights
Dickau, John C. *religious organization executive*

Belleville
†Gregory, Wilton D. *bishop*

Bensenville
Matera, Richard Ernest *minister*

Cairo
Cobb, J. *bishop*

Carol Stream
Fricke, H. Walter *minister*

Chicago
Almen, Lowell Gordon *church official*
†Bacher, Robert Newell *church official*
Banks, Deirdre Margaret *church organization administrator*
Barbour, Claude Marie *minister*
Barnard, Susan C. *church administrator*
Baumhart, Raymond Charles *church administrator*
Berg, Mildred M. *church administrator*
Berman, Howard Allen *rabbi*
Bernardin, Joseph Louis Cardinal *archbishop, university chancellor*
Betz, Hans Dieter *theology educator*
Browning, Don Spencer *religion educator*
Burhoe, Ralph Wendell *religion and science educator*
Campbell, Edward Fay, Jr. *religion educator*
Carr, Anne Elizabeth *theology educator*
Chadwick, Joanne *church administrator*
Chilstrom, Herbert Walfred *bishop*
Doniger, Wendy *history of religions educator*
Duecker, Robert Sheldon *bishop*
Farrakhan, Louis *religious leader*
Fiechter, Charlotte E. *church administrator*
Ford, L. H. *bishop*
Fortune, Michael Joseph *religion educator*
Gerrish, Brian Albert *theologian, educator*
Griswold, Frank Tracy, III *bishop*
Haertel, Charles Wayne *minister*
Hefner, Philip James *theologian*
Hicks, Sherman Gregory *bishop*
Hollies, Linda Hall *minister, educator, author, publisher*
Homans, Peter *psychology and religious studies educator*
Iakovos, (Iakovos Garmatis) *bishop*
Inskeep, Kenneth W. *church administrator*
James, A. Lincoln, Sr. *minister, religious organization executive*
Klutz, C. H. *church administrator*
Larsen, Paul Emanuel *religious organization administrator*
LeFevre, Perry Deyo *minister, theology educator*
Lotocky, Innocent Hilarius *bishop*
Marshall, Cody *bishop*
Marty, Martin Emil *religion educator, editor*
Mayo, J. Haskell, Jr. *bishop*
†McAuliffe, Richard L. *church official*
McCullough, Michael William, Jr. *minister, educator, researcher, writer, missionary, gospel singer, consultant*
McGinn, Bernard John *religious educator*
Miller, Charles S. *clergy member, church administrator*
Minnick, Malcolm L., Jr. *clergy member, church administrator*
Moller-Gunderson, Mark Robert *minister, administrator*
Moller-Gunderson, Mary Ann *clergy member, church administrator*
Mortensen, Audrey R. *church administrator*
Myers, Jim *church administrator*
Peterson, Marybeth A. *church administrator*
Powell, Allen Royal *bishop*
Rajan, Fred E. N. *clergy member, church administrator*
Reynolds, Frank Everett *religious studies educator*
Rusch, William Graham *religious organization administrator*
Sauer, Kenneth H. *bishop*
Schroeder, W(illiam) Widick *religion educator*
Schupp, Ronald Irving *clergyman, civil rights leader*
Seitz, Tim *church administrator*
Shafer, Eric Christopher *minister*
Sherwin, Byron Lee *religion educator, college official*
Simon, Mordecai *religious association administrator, clergyman*
Simon, Ralph *rabbi*
Sorensen, W. Robert *clergy member, church administrator*
Stegemoeller, Harvey A. *clergy member, church administrator*
Stein, A. C. *clergy member, church administrator*
Thomsen, Mark William *religious organization administrator*
Tracy, David *theology educator*
Trexler, Edgar Ray *minister, editor*
Varsbergs, Vilis *minister, former religious organization administrator*
Wagner, Joseph M. *church administrator*
Wall, James McKendree *minister, editor*
†Wiwchar, Michael *bishop*
Yee, Edmond *church administrator*
Yu, Anthony C. *religion and literature educator*

Darien
Sieracki, Aloysius Alfred *religious organization administrator*

Decatur
Morgan, E. A. *church administrator*

Dolton
†Bennett, Joe *bishop*

Elgin
Deeter, Joan G. *church administrator*
†Miller, Donald Eugene *minister, educator*
Minnich, Dale E. *religious administrator*
Myers, Anne M. *church administrator*
Nolen, Wilfred E. *church administrator*
Ratthahao, Sisouphanh *minister*
Steiner, Duane *religious administrator*
Timmons, Glenn F. *church administrator*
Ziegler, Earl Keller *minister*

Evanston
Fisher, Neal Floyd *minister*
Parker, James Floyd *minister, pension fund executive*
Thompson, Tyler *minister, philosophy educator*
Walker, Harold Blake *minister*

Evergreen Park
Smith, Lawrence J. *bishop*

Flossmoor
Walker, George W. *bishop*

Highland
Baumer, Martha Ann *minister*

Homewood
McClellan, Larry Allen *minister, writer*

Joliet
Imesch, Joseph Leopold *bishop*
Kaffer, Roger Louis *bishop*

Kankakee
Sayes, James Ottis *religion educator, minister*

Lincoln
Wilson, Robert Allen *religion educator*

Mendota
Du Bois, Clarence Hazel, Jr. *clergy member*

Naperville
Landwehr, Arthur John *minister*

Oak Park
Cary, William Sterling *retired church executive*

Palos Heights
Nederhood, Joel H. *church organization executive, minister*

Peoria
MacBurney, Edward Harding *bishop*
Myers, John Joseph *bishop*
Parsons, Donald James *retired bishop*

Rock Island
Bergendoff, Conrad John Immanuel *clergyman*

Rockford
†Doran, Thomas George *bishop*
Hasley, Ronald K. *bishop*
Weissbard, David Raymond *minister*

Schaumburg
Miller, Vernon Dallace *minister*
Nettleton, David *religious administrator*

South Holland
Mulder, Dennis Marlin *religious organization executive*

Springfield
Byers, Gary William *religious organization administrator*
Kaitschuk, John Paul *bishop*
Ryan, Daniel Leo *bishop*
Shotwell, Malcolm Green *minister*
Worthing, Carol Marie *minister*

Summit Argo
Abramowicz, Alfred L. *bishop*

Villa Park
Binder, John *minister, religious organization executive*
Effa, Herman *clergy member, religious organization administrator*
†Loewer, Jackie *church official*
†Norman, Ronald *church officer*
Russell, Richard *religious organization admnstrator*

Wheaton
Estep, John Hayes *religious denomination executive, clergyman*
Pint, Sister Rose Mary *nun, religious order administrator, health care executive*

Winnetka
Hudnut, Robert Kilborne *clergyman, author*

INDIANA

Anderson
Conrad, Harold August *retired religious pension board executive*
Dale, Doris *religious organization executive*
Dye, Dwight Latimer *minister*
Foggs, Edward L. *church administrator*
Grubbs, J. Perry *church administrator*
Hayes, Sherill D. *religious organization administrator*
Patton, Norman S. *church administrator*
Rist, Robert G. *religious publishing executive*

Elkhart
Bender, Ross Thomas *minister*
Lapp, James Merrill *clergyman, marriage and family therapist*
Oltz, Richard John *publishing executive, minister*

Evansville
Gettelfinger, Gerald Andrew *bishop*

Fort Wayne
Beals, Duane *church administrator*
Bunkowske, Eugene Walter *religious studies educator*
Carpenter, Charles *religious organization administrator*
D'Arcy, John Michael *bishop*
Henschen, Bob *religious foundation executive*
Liechty, Eric *church administrator*
†Maier, Walter Arthur *church official*
Mann, David William *minister*
McFarlane, Neil *church administrator*
Moran, John *religious organization administrator*
Schmiel, David Gerhard *clergyman, religious education administrator*
Speicher, Opal *church administrator*
Stucky, Ken *clergy member, religious publication editor, church organization administrator*
von Gunten, David *church administrator*

Gary
Gaughan, Norbert F. *bishop*

Huntington
Kopp, Clarence Adam, Jr. *clergyman*
†Seilhamer, Ray A. *bishop*

Indianapolis
Austin, Spencer Peter *minister*
Bates, Gerald Earl *bishop*
Behar, Lucien E. *church administrator*
Bonney, M. Doane *religious organization director*
Brannon, Ronald Roy *minister*
Bray, Donald Lawrence *religious organization executive, minister*
Buechlein, Daniel Mark *bishop*
Cassel, Herbert William *religion educator*
Castle, Howard Blaine *religious organization administrator*
Crow, Paul Abernathy, Jr. *clergyman, religious council executive, educator*
Dickinson, Richard Donald Nye *clergyman, educator, theological seminary administrator*
Ellis, Carollyn *religious organization administrator*
Ellis, Raymond W. *religious organization executive, consultant*
Foster, David Mark *bishop*
Foulkes, John R. *minister*
†Golder, Morris Ellis *minister*
Grant, Claudia Ewing *minister*
Haines, Lee Mark, Jr. *religious denomination administrator*
Haslam, Robert B. *religious publication editor*
Ilangyi, Bya'ene Akulu *bishop*
Johnson, James P. *religious organization executive*
Kempski, Ralph Aloisius *bishop*
Kilgore, Gary M. *church administrator*
Manworren, Donald B. *church administrator*
†Nzeyimana, Noah *bishop*
Palmer, Lester Davis *minister*
Polston, Mark Franklin *minister*
Riemenschneider, Dan LaVerne *religious organization administrator*
Sayre, Larry D. *religious organization executive*
Sindlinger, Verne E. *bishop*
Ton, L. Eugene *church official*
Updegraff Spleth, Ann L. *church executive, pastor*
Watkins, Harold Robert *minister*
Welsh, Robert K. *religious organization executive*
Wilson, Earle Lawrence *church administrator*
Wilson, Harry Cochrane *clergyman*
Woodring, DeWayne Stanley *religion association executive*
Young, Richard *religious organization executive*

Kokomo
Hall, Milton L. *bishop*

Lafayette
Higi, William L. *bishop*

Marion
McIntyre, Robert Walter *church official*

Noblesville
Wilson, Norman Glenn *church administrator, writer*

Notre Dame
†Blenkinsopp, Joseph *biblical studies educator*
Cunningham, Lawrence Springer *theology educator*
Hesburgh, Theodore Martin *clergyman, former university president*
Malloy, Edward Aloysius *priest, university administrator, educator*
McBrien, Richard Peter *theology educator*
McCormick, Richard Arthur *priest, religion educator, writer*
O'Meara, Thomas Franklin *priest, educator*
White, James Floyd *theology educator*
Yoder, John Howard *theology educator*

Plainfield
Hay, John Franklin *church administrator*

Richmond
Maurer, Johan Fredrik *religious denomination administrator*
†Smuck, Harold Vernon *retired minister, religious organization administrator*

South Bend
Gray, Francis Campbell *bishop*
Gray, Frank C. *bishop*
Sumrall, Lester Frank *missionary, evangelist*

Veedersburg
Marshall, Carolyn Ann M. *church official, consultant*

Winona Lake
Ashman, Charles H. *retired minister*
Davis, John James *religion educator*
Julien, Thomas Theodore *religious denomination administrator*
Lewis, Edward Alan *religious organization administrator*

IOWA

Amana
Setzer, Kirk *religious leader*

Ankeny
Hartog, John, II *theology educator, librarian*

Cedar Rapids
Barta, James Omer *priest, psychology educator, church administrator*
Roth, Sister M. Augustine *nun, educator*

Davenport
O'Keefe, Gerald Francis *bishop, retired*

Decorah
Farwell, Elwin D. *minister, educational consultant*

Des Moines
†Bowlin, Patrick L. *church officer*
†Charron, Joseph L. *bishop*
†Epp, Telfer L. *church official*
Epting, C. Christopher *bishop*
Jordan, Charles Wesley *bishop*
Mitchell, Orlan E. *clergyman, former college president*
†Smith, Ray E. *church officer*

Dubuque
Drummond, Richard Henry *religion educator*
Hanus, Jerome *archbishop*
Pike, George Harold, Jr. *religious organization executive, clergyman*

Iowa City
Baird, Robert Dahlen *religious educator*
Bayne, David Cowan *priest, lawyer, law educator*
Forell, George Wolfgang *religion educator*
Holstein, Jay Allen *Judaic studies educator*
Werger, Paul Myron *bishop*

Orange City
Scorza, Sylvio Joseph *religion educator*

Sioux City
Soens, Lawrence D. *bishop*

Storm Lake
Miller, Curtis Herman *bishop*

Waterloo
†Lindberg, Duane R. *minister*

West Union
Vettrus, Richard James *minister*

KANSAS

Dodge City
Schlarman, Stanley Gerard *bishop*

Kansas City
Cade, Walter *church administrator*
Forst, Marion Francis *bishop*
Keleher, James P. *bishop*
†Loosen, Sister Sister Ann Marita *nun, health care executive*
Strecker, Ignatius J. *archbishop*

Leavenworth
McGilley, Sister Mary Janet *nun, educator, writer, academic administrator*

Newton
Preheim, Vern Quincy *religious organization administrator, minister*

North Newton
Fast, Darrell W. *minister*

Salina
Ashby, John Forsythe *bishop*
Fitzsimons, George K. *bishop*

Shawnee Mission
Haggard, Forrest Deloss *minister*
Holter, Don Wendell *retired bishop*
Olsen, Stanley Severn *minister*

Topeka
Mutti, Albert Frederick *minister*
Smalley, William Edward *bishop*

Wichita
Eastburn, Jeannette Rose *religious publishing executive*
Gerber, Eugene J. *bishop*
Zehr, Clyde James *church administrator*

KENTUCKY

Erlanger
Hughes, William Anthony *bishop*

Lexington
Landon, John William *minister, social worker, educator*
Williams, James Kendrick *bishop*

Louisville
Andrews, James Edgar *church official, minister*
Carpenter, Marj Collier *religious organization news director*
Clements, Kerry *religious organization administrator*
Coffin, John *religious organization administrator*
Dale, Judy Ries *religious organization administrator*
†Goff, Jim *religious organization administrator*
Granady, Juanita H. *religious organization administrator*
Hendricks, William Lawrence *theology educator*
Jenkins, C(arle) Frederick *religious organization executive, minister, lawyer*
Kelly, Thomas Cajetan *archbishop*
Kirkpatrick, Clifton *minister, church administrator*
Lundy, Mary Ann Weese *religious organization administrator*
Miller, John Ulman *minister, author*
Schaefer, J. Scott *religious organization administrator*
Turner, Gene *religious organization administrator*
Wingenbach, Gregory Charles *minister, religious-ecumenical agency director*
Zimmerman, Gideon K. *minister*

Owensboro
McRaith, John Jeremiah *bishop*

Pineville
Whittaker, Bill Douglas *minister*

Wilmore
Faupel, David William *minister, theological librarian*
Kinlaw, Dennis Franklin *clergyman, society executive*

LOUISIANA

Alexandria
Hargrove, Robert Jefferson, Jr. *bishop*
†Jacobs, Sam G. *bishop*
Keller, Christoph, Jr. *bishop*

Baton Rouge
Hughes, Alfred Clifton *bishop*
Oden, William Bryant *bishop, educator*
Swaggart, Jimmy Lee *evangelist, gospel singer*
Witcher, Robert Campbell *bishop*

Harvey
Romagosa, Elmo Lawrence *clergyman, retired editor*

Houma
Boudreaux, Warren Louis *retired bishop*
†Jarrell, Charles Michael *bishop*

Lafayette
O'Donnell, Edward Joseph *bishop, former editor*

Lake Charles
Speyrer, Jude *bishop*

Metairie
†Cheveallier, J. Clint *religious organization executive*

New Iberia
Henton, Willis Ryan *bishop*

New Orleans
Brown, James Barrow *bishop*
Jenkins, Howard J. *church education administrator*
Schulte, Francis B. *archbishop*

Pineville
Boswell, Bill Reeser *religious organization executive*

Saint Bernard
Lee, Melvin Joseph *minister*

Shreveport
Friend, William Benedict *bishop*
†Gilmore, Marshall *bishop*
Jones, Ernest Edward *minister, religious organization administrator*
Webb, Donald Arthur *minister*

Springhill
Schoenrock, James V. *religious organization administrator*

MAINE

Bangor
Turner, Marta Dawn *youth program specialist*

Brunswick
Geoghegan, William Davidson *religion educator, minister*

Leeds
Lynn, Robert Wood *theologian, educator, dean*

Lewiston
Baxter, William MacNeil *priest*

Old Orchard Beach
Holmes, Reed M. *clergyman, former religious organization administrator*

Portland
Chalfant, Edward Cole *bishop*
Gerry, Joseph John *bishop*
O'Leary, Edward Cornelius *bishop*

Presque Isle
Gallagher, John *church administrator*

Readfield
Metzler, Glenn Elam *minister*

Winthrop
Skeete, F. Herbert *bishop*

MARYLAND

Arnold
Smith, Clifford Lee *clergyman*

Baltimore
Houck, John Roland *clergyman*
Macleod, Donald *clergyman, educator*
Mocko, George Paul *minister*
Murphy, Philip Francis *bishop*
Newman, William C. *bishop*
Ricard, John H. *bishop, educator*
Strickland, Marshall Hayward *bishop*
Zaiman, Joel Hirsh *rabbi*

Brentwood
†Fiedler, Maureen Ellen *nun*

Catonsville
Wynn, John Charles *clergyman, retired religion educator*

Gaithersburg
Hall, Arthur Raymond, Jr. *minister*
Rupert, (Lynn) Hoover *minister*

Hagerstown
Coles, Robert Nelson, Sr. *religious organization administrator*

Rockville
†Meade, Kenneth Albert *minister*
Sanks, Charles Randolph, Jr. *minister, psychotherapist*

Silver Spring
†Baptiste, Harold W. *religious organization administrator*
Beach, Bert Beverly *clergyman*
Dimino, Joseph T. *archbishop*
Doerr, Edd *religious liberty organization administrator*
Folkenberg, Robert S. *religious organization administrator*
Gilbert, Donald Floyd *church administrator*
Thompson, George Ralph *church denomination administrator*
Yeakel, Joseph Hughes *clergyman*

MASSACHUSETTS

Amherst
Wills, David Wood *minister, educator*

Boston
Bettenhausen, Elizabeth Ann *theology educator*
Braver, Barbara Leix *religious organization communications administrator*
Harris, Barbara C(lementine) *bishop*
Korff, Yitzchok Aharon *rabbi*
Mason, Herbert Warren, Jr. *religion and history educator, author*
Nesmith, Richard Duey *clergyman, theology educator*
Wheelwright, Steven C. *religious organization administrator, business educator*
Williams, Rhys *minister*
Worthley, Harold Field *minister, educator*

Brewster
Coburn, John Bowen *retired bishop*

Brighton
Law, Bernard Francis Cardinal *archbishop*

Brockton
Hart, Daniel Anthony *bishop*

Brookfield
Kring, Walter Donald *minister*

Brookline
Gyger, Terrell Lee *minister*
Papademetriou, George Constantine *priest, director, educator*
Tournas, Methodios (Methodios of Boston) *bishop, academic administrator*

Cambridge
Fiorenza, Francis P. *religion educator*
Gomes, Peter John *clergyman, educator*
Graham, William Albert *religion educator*
Hanson, Paul David *religion educator*
Hart, Donald Purple *bishop*
Kaufman, Gordon Dester *theology educator*
Koester, Helmut Heinrich *theologian, educator*
Potter, Ralph Benajah, Jr. *theology and social ethics educator*
Schuessler Fiorenza, Elisabeth *theology educator*
Septimus, Bernard Mark *religion educator*
Thomas, Owen Clark *clergyman, educator*
Williams, George Huntston *church historian, educator*
Williams, Preston Noah *theology educator*

Chestnut Hill
Daly, Robert Joseph *theology educator*

Dedham
Spoolstra, Linda Carol *minister, educator, religious organization administrator*

East Orleans
Rath, George Edward *bishop*

Fall River
O'Malley, Sean *bishop*

Harvard
Sutherland, Malcolm Read, Jr. *clergyman, educator*

Hyde Park
Riley, Lawrence Joseph *bishop*

Lexington
Schultz, Samuel Jacob *clergyman, educator*

Longmeadow
Stewart, Alexander Doig *bishop*

Marlborough
Lohr, Harold Russell *bishop*

Newton
†Capon, Edwin Gould *church organization administrator, clergyman*
Deats, Paul Kindred, Jr. *religion educator, clergyman*

North Easton
†Holland, David Vernon *minister*

Northampton
Derr, Thomas Sieger *religion educator*
Donfried, Karl Paul *minister, theology educator*
Flesher, Hubert Louis *religion educator*

Norwood
Freni, Anthony *church administrator*

Sheffield
Unsworth, Richard Preston *minister, school administrator*

Somerville
Bailey, James Martin *minister, ecumenical executive, public relations consultant*

South Easton
Clarke, Cornelius Wilder *superintendent, minister*

South Hamilton
Kalland, Lloyd Austin *minister*

Springfield
Marshall, John Aloysius *bishop*

Swampscott
Mulcahy, John J. *bishop*

Waltham
Johnson, William Alexander *clergyman, philosophy educator*
Reisman, Bernard *theology educator*

West Newton
Elya, John Adel *bishop*

Weymouth
Parsons, Edwin Spencer *clergyman, educator*

Williamstown
Eusden, John Dykstra *theology educator, minister*
Petersen, Norman Richard, Jr. *religious studies educator*

Worcester
Dufault, Wilfrid Joseph *religious organization administrator*
Isaksen, Robert L. *bishop*
Reilly, Daniel Patrick *bishop*
Torraco, Stephen Francis *priest, theologian, educator*

MICHIGAN

Ann Arbor
Guthrie, Harvey Henry, Jr. *clergyman*
Hess, Bartlett Leonard *clergyman*

Berrien Springs
Andreasen, Niels-Erik Albinus *religious educator*

Bloomfield Hills
Hertz, Richard Cornell *rabbi*
Plaut, Jonathan Victor *rabbi*

Detroit
†Anderson, Moses B. *bishop*
†Crutcher, Gabriel *bishop*
Gumbleton, Thomas J. *bishop*
Hardon, John Anthony *priest, research educator*
Maida, Adam Joseph *archbishop*
Mc Gehee, H(arry) Coleman, Jr. *bishop*
Negrepontis, Michael (Timothy) *bishop*
Ross, Mary O. *religious organization administrator*
Ursache, Victorin (His Eminence The Most Reverend Archbishop Victorin) *archbishop*
Wood, R. Stewart *bishop*

East Lansing
Shaw, Robert Eugene *minister, administrator*

Farmington
Wine, Sherwin Theodore *rabbi*

Ferndale
Dunn, Elwood *minister*

Gaylord
Cooney, Patrick Ronald *bishop*

Grand Rapids
Anderson, Roger Gordon *minister*
Babcock, Wendell Keith *religion educator*
Beeke, Joel Robert *minister, theology educator, writer*
Borgdorff, Peter *church adminstrator*
Brink, William P. *clergyman*
DeHaan, John *religious organization administrator*
DeVries, Robert K. *religious book publisher*
Hofman, Leonard John *minister*
Mulder, Gary *religious publisher*
Rozeboom, John A. *religious organization administrator*
†Schwanda, Tom *religious studies educator*
Vander Meer, Harry *church administrator*
Vander Weele, Ray *religious organization administrator*
Van Tol, William *religious organization administrator*
Vinton, Samuel R., Jr. *religious organizatoin administrator*

Grass Lake
Popp, Nathaniel *bishop*

Grosse Pointe
Canfield, Francis Xavier *priest, English language educator*

Holland
Cook, James Ivan *clergyman, religion educator*

Kalamazoo
Lee, Edward L. *bishop*

Lansing
Holle, Reginald Henry *bishop*
Povish, Kenneth Joseph *bishop*

Livonia
†Davis, Lawrence Edward *church official*

Marquette
Burt, John Harris *bishop*
†Garland, James H. *bishop*
Ray, Thomas Kreider *bishop*
Skogman, Dale R. *bishop*

Pinckney
Hernandez, Ramon Robert *clergyman*

Saginaw
Untener, Kenneth E. *bishop*
Williams, Herbert J. *bishop*
Wilson, J. Parrish *religious organization administrator*

Southfield
†Ibrahim, Ibrahim N. *bishop*

Spring Arbor
Dillman, Charles Norman *religion educator*
Thompson, Stanley B. *church administrator*

MINNESOTA

Alexandria
Hultstrand, Donald Maynard *bishop*

Bloomington
Cuthill, Robert T. *church administrator*
McDill, Thomas Allison *minister*
Thomas, Margaret Jean *clergywoman, religious research consultant*

Chisago City
Bergstrand, Wilton Everet *minister*

Collegeville
Henry, Patrick G. *religious research administrator*

Crookston
Balke, Victor H. *bishop*

Duluth
Aadland, Thomas Vernon *minister*
Schwietz, Roger L. *bishop*

Edina
Putnam, Frederick Warren, Jr. *bishop*

Fergus Falls
Egge, Joel *clergy member, academic administrator*
Olson, Jarle *clergy member, Church administrator*
Overgaard, Robert Milton *religious organization administrator*
Westby, Armin *clergy member, church administrator*

Golden Valley
†Cepure, Uldis *church official*

Little Falls
Zirbes, Mary Kenneth *social justice ministry coordinator*

Mankato
Orvick, George Myron *church denomination executive, minister*

Minneapolis
Anderson, Robert Marshall *bishop*
Brown, Laurence David *retired bishop*
Cedar, Paul Arnold *church executive, minister*
Fleischer, Daniel *minister, religious organization administrator*
Graham, William Franklin (Billy Graham) *evangelist*
†Hamel, William John *church administrator, minister*
Hull, Bill *clergy member, church administrator*
Kapanke, John *church edministrator*
†Lee, Robert Lloyd *pastor, religious association executive*
Miller, William Alvin *clergyman, author*
Palms, Roger Curtis *religious magazine editor, clergyman*
Sowada, Alphonse Augustus *bishop*
Swatsky, Ben *church administrator*
Wang, L. Edwin *church official*

Moorhead
Rimmereid, Arthur V. *bishop*

New Ulm
Lucker, Raymond Alphonse *bishop*

Northfield
Crouter, Richard Earl *religion educator*
Foss, Harlan Funston *religious education educator, academic administrator*

Rochester
Hudson, Winthrop Still *minister, history educator*
Larson, April U. *bishop*
Nycklemoe, Glenn Winston *bishop*

Roseville
†Be Vier, William A. *religious studies educator*

Saint Paul
Carlson, Marjorie J. *retired church administrator*
Flynn, Harry Joseph *bishop*
Hopper, David Henry *religion educator*
McMillan, Mary Bigelow *retired minister, volunteer*
Merrill, Arthur Lewis *retired theology educator*
Preus, David Walter *bishop, minister*
Roach, John Robert *archbishop*

Winona
Vlazny, John George *bishop*

MISSISSIPPI

Biloxi
Howze, Joseph Lawson Edward *bishop*

Clinton
Hensley, John Clark *religious organization administrator, minister*

Gulfport
Freret, René Joseph *minister*

Hattiesburg
Gordon, Granville Hollis *church official*

Indianola
Matthews, David *clergyman*

Jackson
Allin, John Maury *bishop*
†Graham, Charlotte Ann *religion writer, consultant*
Gray, Duncan Montgomery, Jr. *retired bishop*
Houck, William Russell *bishop*
McKnight, William Edwin *minister*

Kosciusko
Kearley, F. Furman *minister, religious educator, magazine editor*

Long Beach
Horton, Jerry Smith *minister*

Meridian
Lindstrom, Donald Fredrick, Jr. *priest*

MISSOURI

Branson
†Todd, Cecil William *ministry director*

Hazelwood
McClintock, Eugene Jerome *minister*
Rose, Joseph Hugh *clergyman*
Urshan, Nathaniel Andrew *minister, church administrator*

Highlandville
Pruter, Karl Hugo *bishop*

Independence
Booth, Paul Wayne *minister*
Hansen, Francis Eugene *minister*
†Lindgren, A. Bruce *church administrator*
Mitchell, Earl Wesley *clergyman*
Sheehy, Howard Sherman, Jr. *minister*
†Spencer, Geoffrey F. *church administrator*
†Swails, Norman E. *church officer*
Tyree, Alan Dean *clergyman*

Jefferson City
Kelley, Pat *minister, state legislator*
Mc Auliffe, Michael F. *bishop*

Joplin
Burke, Charles Don *church administrator, minister*
Gee, James David *minister*
†Minor, Ronald Ray *minister*
Wilson, Aaron Martin *religious studies educator, college executive*

Kansas City
Anderson, David *church administrator*
Berard, Dennis *church administrator*
Boland, Raymond James *bishop*
Bowers, Curtis Ray, Jr. *chaplain*
Brannon, Wilbur *church administrator*
Buchanan, John Clark *bishop*
Butler, Martin *church administrator*
Cloud, Randall R. *church administrator*
Estep, Michael R. *church administrator*
Frank, Eugene Maxwell *bishop*
Fullerton, Fred *church administrator*
Gray, Helen Theresa Gott *religion editor*
Grider, Joseph Kenneth *theology educator, writer*
Gunter, Moody *church administrator*
Hall, Miriam *church administrator*
Hendrix, Ray *church administrator*
Jenkins, Orville Wesley *retired religious administrator*
Johnson, Jerald D. *religious organization administrator*
†Knight, John Allan *clergyman, philosophy and religion educator*
†Owens, Donald D. *church officer*
†Prince, William J. *church officer*
Skiles, Paul *church administrator*
Smee, John *church administrator*
Stone, Jack *religious organization administrator*
Sullivan, Bill *church administrator*
Vogel, Arthur Anton *clergyman*

Laddonia
Scheffler, Lewis Francis *pastor, educator, research scientist*

Neosho
Hargis, Billy James *minister*

Poplar Bluff
Black, Ronnie Delane *religious organization administrator, mayor*
Carr, Charles Louis *religious organization administrator*
Duncan, Leland Ray *mission administrator*

Saint Louis
†Barry, A. L. *church official*
Boldt, H. James *church administrator*
†Carberry, John J. Cardinal *former archbishop*
†Curley, John E., Jr. *religious health association director*
Haake, Arthur C. *church administrator*
King, Robert Henry *minister, church denomination executive, former educator*
Krenzke, Richard L. *church administrator, clergy member, social worker*
Mahsman, David Lawrence *religious publications editor*
Mall, Ida *church administrator*
†Mennicke, August Theodore *church officer*
Merrell, James Lee *religious editor, clergyman*
Meyer, John *church administrator*
Meyer, William F. *church administrator*
Muller, Lyle Dean *religious organization administrator*
Ong, Walter Jackson *priest, English educator, author*
O'Shoney, Glenn *church administrator*
Pfautch, Roy *minister, public affairs consultant*
†Rigali, Justin F. *archbishop*
Rockwell, Hays Hamilton *bishop*
†Rosin, Walter L. *religious organization administrator*
†Ryan, Barbara Ann *church official*
Saperstein, Marc Eli *religious history educator, rabbi*
Sauer, Robert C. *religious organization administrator*
Shaw, James *church administrator*
Suggs, James C. *publishing executive*
Ward, R. J. *bishop*
Weber, Gloria Richie *minister, retired state representative*
Wilke, LeRoy *church administrator*

Springfield
Cunningham, Robert Cyril *clergyman, editor*
Dailey, Parker Stokes *minister*
Flower, Joseph Reynolds *administrative executive*
Leibrecht, John Joseph *bishop*
Trask, Thomas Edward *religious organization administrator*
Triplett, Loren O. *religious organization administrator*

MONTANA

Great Falls
Milone, Anthony M. *bishop*

Helena
†Brunett, Alexander J. *bishop*
Jones, Charles Irving *bishop*

NEBRASKA

Grand Island
MacDonald, Joseph Faber *bishop*
Mc Namara, Lawrence J. *bishop*

Lincoln
†Bruskewitz, Fabian W. *bishop*
Wiersbe, Warren Wendell *clergyman, author, lecturer*

Norfolk
Stites, Ray Dean *minister, college president*

Omaha
Curtiss, Elden F. *bishop*
Krotz, James Edward *bishop*
McDaniels, B. T. *bishop*

Scottsbluff
Scovil, Larry Emery *minister*

West Point
Paschang, John Linus *retired bishop*

NEVADA

Las Vegas
Walsh, Daniel Francis *bishop*

Reno
Savoy, Douglas Eugene *bishop, religion educator, explorer, writer*
Straling, Phillip Francis *bishop*

NEW HAMPSHIRE

Center Sandwich
Booty, John Everitt *historiographer*

Concord
Theuner, Douglas Edwin *bishop*

Hanover
Green, Ronald Michael *ethics and religious studies educator*

Hillsboro
Gibson, Raymond Eugene *clergyman*
Walmsley, Arthur Edward *bishop*

Loudon
Moore, Bea *religious organization executive*

Manchester
O'Neil, Leo E. *bishop*

New London
Pearson, Roy Messer, Jr. *clergyman*

NEW JERSEY

Bloomfield
Becker, Robert Clarence *clergyman*

Camden
McHugh, James T. *bishop*

Cherry Hill
Belin, Henry A., Jr. *bishop*
Schad, James L. *bishop*

Clifton
Rodimer, Frank Joseph *bishop*

East Orange
Medley, Alex Roy *executive minister*

Englewood
Essey, Basil *bishop*
Hertzberg, Arthur *rabbi, educator*
Khouri, Antoun *church administrator*
Saliba, Philip E. *archbishop*

Fort Lee
Kim, Gil *minister*

Hopatcong
Harsanyi, Andrew *bishop*

Lakewood
Levovitz, Pesach Zechariah *rabbi*

Lodi
Meno, John Peter *chorepiscopus*
Samuel, Athanasius Yeshue *archbishop*

Madison
Irons, Neil L. *bishop*
Yrigoyen, Charles, Jr. *church denomination executive*

Mahwah
Padovano, Anthony Thomas *theologian, educator*

Metuchen
Hughes, Edward T. *bishop*

Mullica Hill
Demola, James, Sr. *church administrator*

New Brunswick
†Bowden, Henry Warner *religion educator*

Newark
Mc Carrick, Theodore Edgar *archbishop*
McKelvey, Jack M. *bishop*
Spong, John Shelby *bishop*

Plainsboro
Yun, Samuel *minister, educator*

Princeton
Allen, Diogenes *clergyman, philosophy educator*
Armstrong, James Franklin *religion educator*
Armstrong, Richard Stoll *minister, ministry and evangelism educator*
Davies, Horton Marlais *clergyman, religion educator*
Diamond, Malcolm Luria *retired religion educator, therapist*
Douglass, Jane Dempsey *theology educator*
Gordon, Ernest *clergyman*
Hardy, Daniel Wayne *theological center director, theologian, educator*
Metzger, Bruce Manning *clergyman, educator*
Miller, Patrick Dwight, Jr. *religion educator, minister*
Paris, Peter Junior *religion educator, minister*
West, Charles Converse *theologian, educator*

Rutherford
Gerety, Peter Leo *archbishop*

Short Hills
Pilchik, Ely Emanuel *rabbi, writer*

South Orange
Fleming, Edward J. *priest, educator*
Goldman, Harvey S. *therapist, rabbi*

Summit
May, Ernest Max *charitable organization official*

Tenafly
Stowe, David Metz *clergyman*

Tinton Falls
Priesand, Sally Jane *rabbi*

Trenton
Courtney, Esau *bishop*
Farina, David *church administrator*
Pettit, Vincent King *bishop*
Reiss, John C. *bishop*

Union City
†Arias, David *bishop*

West Milford
Stelpstra, William John *minister*

Westville
Doughty, A. Glenn *minister*

Wharton
Loughlin, William Joseph *priest, religious organization administrator*

NEW MEXICO

Albuquerque
Ford, Wallace Roy *clergyman, religious organization executive*
George, Roy Kenneth *minister*
Griffin, W. C. *bishop*
Kellshaw, Terence *bishop*
Kelshaw, Terence *bishop*
Sanchez, Robert Fortune *archbishop*
Sheehan, Michael Jarboe *archbishop*

Farmington
Plummer, Steven Tsosie *bishop*

Las Cruces
Ramirez, Ricardo *bishop*

Roswell
Pretti, Bradford Joseph *lay worker, insurance company executive*

NEW YORK

Albany
Bowen, Mary Lu *ecumenical developer*
Gay, Charles *church administrator*
Grove, William Boyd *bishop*
Hubbard, Howard James *bishop*

Bronx
Bryant, Roy, Sr. *bishop*
Dulles, Avery *priest, theologian*
Hennessy, Thomas Christopher *clergyman, educator, retired university dean*
†McShane, Joseph M. *priest, dean, theology educator*
Parker, Everett Carlton *clergyman*

Bronxville
L'Huillier, Peter (Peter) *archbishop*

Brooklyn
Abrahamsen, Samuel *retired Judaic studies educator*
Al-Hafeez, Humza *minister, editor*
†Baltakis, Paul Antanas *bishop*
Daily, Thomas V. *bishop*
Grayson, D. W. *bishop*
Leiman, Sid Zalman *Judaic studies educator*
Sullivan, Joseph M. *bishop*
†Williams, Carl E., Sr. *bishop*

Buffalo
Head, Edward Dennis *bishop*
Jerge, Marie Charlotte *minister*
Lamb, Charles F. *minister*
Loew, Ralph William *clergyman, columnist*

Canton
O'Connor, Daniel William *retired religious studies and classical languages educator*

East Aurora
Hayes, Bonaventure Francis *priest*

Far Rockaway
Kelly, George Anthony *clergyman, author, educator*

Flushing
Valero, René Arnold *clergyman*
Vasilachi, Gheorghe Vasile *priest, vicar*

Garrison
Egan, Daniel Francis *priest*

Hamilton
Carter, John Ross *philosophy and religion educator*

Ithaca
Gold, Daniel *religious studies educator*
Katz, Steven Theodore *religion studies educator*
Little, George Daniel *clergyman*

Jamaica
Clemmons, Ithiel *bishop*

Kingston
Tsirpanlis, Constantine N. *theology, classics and history educator*

Lawrence
Wurzburger, Walter Samuel *rabbi, philosophy educator*

Lily Dale
Merrill, Joseph Hartwell *religious association executive*
Wittich, Brenda June *religious organization executive, minister*

Lima
Reynolds, Lewis Dayton *administrator*
Spencer, Ivan Carlton *clergyman*

Lindenhurst
Hamilton, Daniel Stephen *clergyman*

Manhasset
†Fendt, John W. *minister, religious organization administrator*
Spitz, Charles Thomas, Jr. *clergyman*

Marcy
Fay, Rowan Hamilton *minister*

Mount Vernon
Richardson, W. Franklyn *religious organization administrator*

New Hyde Park
Daley, John Terence *priest*

New York
Alicea-Baez, Johnny *religious organization administrator*
Ashjian, Mesrob *archbishop*
Barsamian, Khajag Sarkis *primate*
Bronkema, Frederick Hollander *minister, church official*
Brown, Raymond Edward *educator, priest*
Browning, Edmond Lee *bishop*
Cato, John David *religious organization administrator*
Chinnis, Pamela P. *religion organization administrator*
Church, Frank Forrester *minister, author, columnist*
Cohen, Samuel Israel *clergyman, organization executive*
Cone, James Hal *theologian, educator, author*
Dennis, Walter Decoster *suffragan bishop*
Donohue, William Anthony *religious organization administrator*
Dreyfus, Alfred Stanley *rabbi*
Driver, Tom Faw *theology educator, writer, justice/peace advocate*
Geer, John Farr *religious organization administrator*
Ginsberg, Hersh Meier *rabbi, religious organization executive*
Graham, Alma Eleanor *magazine editor, writer, educational consultant*
Grein, Richard Frank *bishop, pastoral theology educator*
Gross, Abraham *rabbi, educator*
Habecker, Eugene Brubaker *religious association executive*
Hawley, John Stratton *religious studies educator*
Holmgren, Laton Earle *clergyman*
Hopkins, Harold Anthony, Jr. *bishop*
Howard, M(oses) William, Jr. *minister, seminary president*
Iakovos, (Demetrios A. Coucouzis) *archbishop*
Kazanjian, Shant *religious organization administrator*
Kloos, Edward John Michael, Jr. *minister*
Kreitman, Benjamin Zvi *rabbi, Judaic studies educator*
Laurus, (Laurus Skurla) *archbishop*
†Lookstein, Haskel *rabbi*
Mallory, Kenneth W. *religious organization administrator*
Marcus, Beth E. *religious organization administrator*
McGeady, Sister Mary Rose *religious organization administrator, psychologist*
†McWilliam, Joanne Elizabeth *religion educator*
Menuez, D. Barry *religious organization administrator*
Miller, Israel *rabbi, university administrator*
Moore, Paul, Jr. *bishop*
Morris, Clayton Leslie *priest*
Mulder, Edwin George *minister, church official*
Nadich, Judah *rabbi*
Najarian, Haigazoun *church administrator*
Norgren, William Andrew *religious denomination administrator*
O'Connor, John Joseph Cardinal *archbishop, former naval officer*
O'Keefe, Vincent Thomas *clergyman, educational administrator*
Paulsen, Diana *religious organization administrator*
Perry, David *priest*
Poppen, Alvin J. *religious organization administrator*
Powers, Edward Alton *minister, educator*
Proudfoot, Wayne Lee *religion educator*
Read, David Haxton Carswell *clergyman*
Reed, John W. *religious organization administrator*
Riddle, Sturgis Lee *minister*
Roth, Sol *rabbi*
Salisbury, Nancy *convent director*
Schindler, Alexander Moshe *rabbi, organization executive*
Schorsch, Ismar *clergyman, Jewish history educator*
Shriver, Donald Woods, Jr. *theology educator*
Siegel, Morton Kallos *religious organization administrator, educational administrator*
Simpson, Mary Michael *priest, psychotherapist*
Solheim, James Edward *church executive, journalist*
Stolper, Pinchas Aryeh *religious organization executive, rabbi*
Strelzer, Martin *religious organization administrator*
Tannenbaum, Bernice Salpeter *religious organization executive*
†Tertzakian, Hovhannes *bishop*
Twiname, John Dean *minister, health care executive*
Verbridge, Gerald *religious organization administrator*
Weiss, David *religion educator*
Wiener, Marvin S. *rabbi, editor, executive*

Nyack
Lehman, Paul V. *minister*
Mann, Kenneth Walker *retired minister, psychologist*

Ogdensburg
†Loverde, Paul S. *bishop*

Orchard Park
Reid, Thomas Fenton *minister*

Ozone Park
Taylor, Joyce *religious organization executive*

Pawling
Peale, Ruth Stafford (Mrs. Norman Vincent Peale) *religious leader*

Poughkeepsie
Glasse, John Howell *retired philosophy and theology educator*

Rochester
Burrill, William George *bishop*
Clark, Matthew Harvey *bishop*
Mandt, John F. *religious organization executive*
May, Melanie Ann *theologian*

Rockville Centre
McGann, John Raymond *bishop*

Syosset
Lazor, Theodosius (His Beatitude Metropolitan Theodosius) *archbishop*

Syracuse
Cole, Ned *bishop*
Costello, Thomas Joseph *bishop*
O'Keefe, Joseph Thomas *bishop*
Schiess, Betty Bone *priest*
Wiggins, James Bryan *religion educator*

Troy
Phelan, Thomas *clergyman, academic administrator, educator*

Trumansburg
Billings, Peggy Marie *religious organization administrator, educator*

West Nyack
†Irwin, Ronald Gilbert *minister*

Westbury
De Pauw, Gommar Albert *priest, educator*

White Plains
Gurahian, Vincent *church official, former judge*
Stith, Forrest Christopher *bishop*

Yonkers
Gunner, Murray *Jewish organization administrator*

NORTH CAROLINA

Asheville
Davenport, L. B. *bishop*

Black Mountain
Kennedy, William Bean *theology educator*
Weinhauer, William Gillette *retired bishop*

Boiling Springs
Lamb, Robert Lee *religious studies educator*

Chapel Hill
Dixon, John Wesley, Jr. *retired religion and art educator*
Van Seters, John *biblical literature educator*

Charlotte
Battle, George Edward, Jr. *minister*
Begley, Michael Joseph *bishop*
Blaschke, Robert Carvel *education coordinator*
†Curlin, William G. *bishop*
Freeman, Sidney Lee *minister, educator*
Jones, Lewis Bevel, III *bishop*
Ross, David Edmond *church official*
Sherman, Joseph Howard *clergyman*

Davidson
McKelway, Alexander Jeffrey *religion studies educator*

Dunn
Blackman, Danny *religious organization administrator*
Davis, Dolly *religious organization administrator*
Ellis, W. L. *religious arganization administrator*
Hammond, James Thurman *educator, clergyman*
Heath, Preston *clergy member, religious organization administrator*
Sauls, Don *religious organization administrator, clergyman*
Taylor, David *clergy member, religious administrator*

Durham
Campbell, Dennis Marion *theology dean, educator, university administrator*
Meyers, Eric Mark *religion educator*
Smith, Harmon Lee, Jr. *clergyman, moral theology educator*
Steinmetz, David Curtis *religion educator, publisher, minister*
Westbrook, Don Arlen *minister*
Willimon, William Henry *minister, educator*

Elizabethtown
Taylor, David Wyatt Aiken *retired clergyman*

Gastonia
Williams, Raymond F. *regigious organization executive*

Greensboro
Hull, James Ernest *religion and philosophy educator*
Lolley, William Randall *minister*
Rights, Graham Henry *minister*
†Williams, Milton A. *bishop*

Greenville
Jackson, Bobby Rand *minister*

Hendersonville
Sims, Bennett Jones *minister, educator*

Hickory
McDaniel, Michael Conway Dixon *bishop, theology educator*

High Point
Wood, Stephen Wray *minister*

Kinston
Sanders, Brice Sidney *bishop*

Lake Junaluska
Bryan, Monk *retired bishop*
Hale, Joseph Rice *church organization executive*
Stokes, John Lemacks, II *clergyman, university administrator*
Tullis, Edward Lewis *retired bishop*

Liberty
Garner, Mildred Maxine *retired religious studies educator*

Manteo
Miller, William Lee, Jr. *minister*

Morganton
MacLeod, John Daniel, Jr. *religious organization administrator*

Mount Olive
Boyd, Julia Margaret (Mrs. Shelton B. Boyd) *lay church worker*

Pinehurst
Black, Bobby C. *chaplain*

Raleigh
Collins, Thomas Asa *minister*
Estill, Robert Whitridge *retired bishop*
Gossman, Francis Joseph *bishop*
Miller, John Henry *clergyman*
Minnick, Carlton Printess, Jr. *bishop*

Reidsville
Hart, Richard Wesley *religious organization administrator, pastor*

Salisbury
Speaks, Ruben Lee *bishop*

Southern Pines
Lowry, Charles Wesley *clergyman, lecturer*

Wake Forest
Binkley, Olin Trivette *clergyman, seminary president emeritus*

Weaverville
Edwards, Otis Carl, Jr. *theology educator*

Wilmington
Wright, Thomas Henry *bishop*

Wilson
†Gibbons, Larry Eugene *minister*

Winston Salem
Fitzgerald, Ernest Abner *retired bishop*
Harrelson, Walter Joseph *minister, religion educator emeritus*
Martin, James Alfred, Jr. *religious studies educator*
†McElveen, William Henry *minister*
Spach, Jule Christian *church executive*

NORTH DAKOTA

Bismarck
Kinney, John Francis *bishop*
Lardy, Sister Susan Marie *prioress*
Montz, Florence Stolte *church official*

Fargo
Fairfield, Andrew H. *bishop*
Foss, Richard John *bishop*
Sullivan, James Stephen *bishop*

OHIO

Akron
Kelley, Robert W. *bishop*
†Sheldon, Gilbert Ignatius *clergyman*

Ashland
†Waters, Ronald W. *church executive, pastor*

Canton
Boulton, Edwin Charles *bishop*

Cincinnati
Crumes, William Edward *bishop*
Harrington, Jeremy Thomas *clergyman, publisher*
Hendricks, Harry *church administrator*
Herring, Milton S. *church administrator*
Huron, Roderick Eugene *religious organization administrator*
†Lakey, Othal H. *bishop*
Linsey, Nathaniel L. *bishop*
Molitor, Sister Margaret Anne *nun, former college president*
Perry, Norman Robert *priest, magazine editor*
Pilarczyk, Daniel Edward *archbishop*
Sweeten, Gary Ray *religious counseling educator*
Thompson, Herbert, Jr. *bishop*

Circleville
Norman, Jack Lee *church administrator, consultant*
Tipton, Daniel L. *religious organization executive*

Cleveland
Buhrow, William Carl *religious organization administrator*
Dipko, Thomas E. *minister, national church executive*
Epp, Eldon Jay *religion educator*
Holck, Frederick H. George *priest, educator*
Lelyveld, Arthur Joseph *rabbi*
Miller, Warren *bishop*
Norris, Dennis E. *religious organization executive*
Pataki, Andrew *bishop*
Pilla, Anthony Michael *bishop*
Sherry, Paul Henry *minister, religious organization administrator*
Williams, Arthur Benjamin, Jr. *bishop*

Columbus
Craig, Judith *bishop*
Plagenz, George Richard *minister, journalist, columnist*
†Simms, Lowelle *synod executive*

Dayton
†Mathews, John *bishop*
†McCrabb, Donald R. *religious ministry director*

Englewood
Shearer, Velma Miller *clergywoman*

Findlay
Martin, Jim G. *church renewal consultant*
Rave, James A. *bishop*
Wilkin, Richard Edwin *clergyman, religious organization executive*

Granville
Fisher, Robert Allison *minister, church administrator*

Grover Hill
Harr, Joseph *religious organization administrator*

Lakewood
Berman, Phillip Lee *author, institute administrator*

London
Hughes, Clyde Matthew *religious denomination executive*

Lorain
Szucs, Zoltan Daniel *religious organization executive, minister, psychologist, educator*

Mayfield Heights
Marino, Michael *church administrator*

Napoleon
Walker, Frank Houston, Jr. *minister*

Oberlin
Zinn, Grover Alfonso, Jr. *religion educator*

Parma
Moskal, Robert M. *bishop*

Steubenville
Scanlan, Michael *priest, academic administrator*

Toledo
Hoffman, James R. *bishop*
James, William *bishop*

University Heights
Kelly, Joseph Francis *theology educator*

West Milton
†Peters, Stephen Paul *pastor*

Wickliffe
Pevec, Anthony Edward *bishop*

OKLAHOMA

Bartlesville
Owen, Raymond Harold *minister*
Woodruff, William Jennings *theology educator*

Bethany
Leggett, James Daniel *church administrator*
Moore, Ronald Quentin *minister*
Shelton, Muriel Moore *religious education administrator*

Broken Arrow
Janning, Sister Mary Bernadette *nun, retired association executive*

Lawton
Young, J. A. *bishop*

Norman
Fuerbringer, Alfred Ottomar *clergyman*

Oklahoma City
Andrews, Robert Frederick *religious organization administrator, retired bishop*
Beltran, Eusebius Joseph *archbishop*
Jones, Robert Lee *religion educator*
Lewis, C. A. *church administrator*
Moody, Robert M. *bishop*
Ponder, Alonza *church administrator*
Simmons, Jesse Doyle *minister, educator*
Solomon, Dan Eugene *bishop*
Underwood, Bernard Edward *religious organization administrator*

Purcell
Lucas, Roy Edward, Jr. *minister*

Stillwater
Lawson, F. D. *bishop*

Tulsa
Cooke, Marvin Lee *religious organization administrator, consultant, minister*
Cox, William Jackson *bishop*
Gottschalk, Sister Mary Therese *nun, hospital administrator*
Henderson, Robert Waugh *retired religion educator, minister*
Rex, Lonnie Royce *religious organization administrator*
Roberts, (Granville) Oral *clergyman*
Slattery, Edward J. *bishop*

OREGON

Bend
Connolly, Thomas Joseph *bishop*
Hanes, Clifford Ronald *religious denomination administrator*

Eugene
Osborn, Ronald Edwin *minister, church history educator*
Sanders, Jack Thomas *religious studies educator*

Grants Pass
Oestmann, Irma Emma *minister, artist, educator*

Gresham
Nicholson, R. Stephen *organization administrator*

Lake Oswego
Ladehoff, Robert Louis *bishop*

Newport
Langrock, Karl Frederick *former academic administrator*

Portland
Carver, Loyce Cleo *clergyman*
Dew, William Waldo, Jr. *bishop*
Huenemann, Ruben Henry *clergyman*
Levada, William Joseph *archbishop*
Richards, Herbert East *minister emeritus, commentator*
Sevetson, Donald James *minister, church administrator*
Steiner, Kenneth Donald *bishop*

Wilsonville
Gross, Hal Raymond *bishop*

PENNSYLVANIA

Akron
Lapp, John Allen *religious organization administrator*

Allentown
Jodock, Darrell Harland *minister, religion educator*
Welsh, Thomas J. *bishop*

Altoona
Miller, Gerald E. *bishop*

Ambridge
Frey, William Carl *bishop, academic administrator*

Bethlehem
†Sommers, Gordon L. *religious organization administrator*
†Wickmann, David L. *clergyman*

Camp Hill
Johnston, Thomas McElree, Jr. *church administrator*

Clearfield
Pride, Douglas Spencer *minister*

Coopersburg
Eckardt, Arthur Roy *religion studies educator emeritus*

Cornwall
Ehrhart, Carl Yarkers *retired minister, retired college administrator*

Cranberry Township
Bashore, George Willis *bishop*

Doylestown
Maser, Frederick Ernest *clergyman*

Drexel Hill
Thompson, William David *minister, homiletics educator*

Elizabethtown
Brown, Dale Weaver *clergyman, theologian, educator*
Mann, Lowell D. *religious organization executive*

Erie
Rowley, Robert Deane, Jr. *bishop*
Trautman, Donald W. *bishop*

Fogelsville
Ault, James Mase *bishop*

Grantham
Byers, John A. *bishop*
Chubb, Harold D. *church official*
†Shafer, R. Donald *church official*
Sider, Harvey Ray *minister, church administrator*

Greensburg
Winters, Sister Mary Ann *religious organization administrator*

Greenville
Farina, Andrew *church administrator*

Harrisburg
Dattilo, Nicholas C. *bishop*
Edmiston, Guy S., Jr. *bishop*
May, Felton Edwin *bishop*
McNutt, Charlie Fuller, Jr. *bishop*

Hatfield
Garis, Mark *church administrator*

Hollidaysburg
Adamec, Joseph Victor Otto *bishop*

Huntingdon
Durnbaugh, Donald Floyd *church history educator, researcher*

Johnstown
Miloro, Frank P. *church official, religious studies educator*
Nicholas, (Richard G. Smisko) *bishop*
†Smisko, Nicholas Richard *bishop, educator*
Yurcisin, John *church official*

Kutztown
Ring, Rodney Everett *religion educator*

Lake Ariel
Massa, Conrad Harry *religious studies educator*

Lancaster
Dubble, Curtis William *pastor*
Glick, Garland Wayne *retired theological seminary president*

Latrobe
Murtha, John Francis *priest, academic administrator, history educator*

Lewisburg
Jump, Chester Jackson, Jr. *clergyman, church official*
Main, A. Donald *bishop*

Lititz
Acker, Raymond Abijah *minister*

Merion Station
Littell, Franklin Hamlin *theologian, educator*

Myerstown
Schock, Franklin H. *clergy member, church administrator*

Philadelphia
Bartlett, Allen Lyman, Jr. *bishop*
Bevilacqua, Anthony Joseph Cardinal *cardinal*
Butz, Geneva Mae *pastor*
Goldin, Judah *Hebrew literature educator*
Gossett, Joyce *religious organization administrator*
Hammond, Charles Ainley *clergyman*
Harvey, William J. *religious service organization, religious publication editor*
Jones, O. T. *bishop*
Kee, Howard Clark *religion educator*
Kraft, Robert Alan *history of religion educator*
Krol, John Cardinal *retired archbishop*
Marple, Dorothy Jane *retired church executive*
Matter, Edith Ann *religion educator*
Sandler, Abraham *minister*
Sulyk, Stephen *archbishop*
Turner, Franklin Delton *bishop*
Waskow, Arthur Ocean *theologian, educator*

Pittsburgh
Green, Isaac *church administrator*
Harvey, Thomas J. *priest, social service organization executive*
Hathaway, Alden Moinet *bishop*
Koedel, Robert Craig *minister, historian, educator*
Leiter, Donald Eugene *religious organization executive*
Maximos, (Maximos Demetrios Aghiorgoussis) *bishop*
McCoid, Donald James *bishop*
Mc Dowell, John B. *bishop*
Muto, Susan Annette *religion educator, academic administrator*
†Procyk, Judson M. *bishop*
Schaub, Marilyn McNamara *religion educator*
Vaughn, Gordon E. *bishop*
Wuerl, Donald W. *bishop*

Reading
Cate, Patrick O'Hair *mission executive*

Rydal
Black, Thomas Donald *retired religious organization administrator*
Kirkland, Bryant Mays *clergyman*

Sagamore
Cornell, William Harvey *clergyman*

Saint Davids
Maahs, Kenneth Henry, Sr. *religion educator*

Scranton
De Celles, Charles Edouard *theologian, educator*
Timlin, James Clifford *bishop*

Sellersville
Raub, Donald Wilmer *minister, author*

Seneca
Spring, Paull E. *bishop*

Sewickley
Newell, Byron Bruce, Jr. *clergyman, former naval officer*

South Canaan
Herman *archbishop*

Swarthmore
Cornelsen, Rufus *clergyman*
Frost, Jerry William *religion and history educator, library administrator*

Shaull, Richard *theologian, educator*
Swearer, Donald Keeney *Asian religions educator, writer*

Valley Forge
Buckles, Michael A. *religious organization executive*
Collemer, Craig A. *religious organization administrator*
Gonzales, Hector M. *church administrator*
González, Héctor *church official*
Kim, Jean B. *religious organization executive*
McPhee, Richard S. *church administrator*
Penfield, Carole H. (Kate Penfield) *minister, church official*
Renquest, Richard A. *religious organization executive*
Smith, G. Elaine *religious organization executive*
Smith, Gordon E. *religious arganization executive*
Sundquist, John A. *religious organization executive*
Wade, Cheryl H. *church official*
Weiss, Daniel Edwin *clergyman, educator*
Wright-Riggins, Aidsand F. *religious organization executive*

Villanova
†Palmer, Donald Curtis *interdenominational missionary society executive*

Warren
Waterston, William King *minister, educator, academic administrator*

Wayne
Green, Norman Marston, Jr. *minister*

Wernersville
Mackey, Sheldon Elias *minister*

Wilkes Barre
Thomas, Reginald Harry, Sr. *minister*

Willow Grove
Duff, Donald James *religious organization administrator*

Wyncote
Burton, DeWitt A. *bishop*
Sasso, Sandy *rabbi*

Wynnewood
†Sider, Ronald J. *theology educator, author*

RHODE ISLAND

Providence
Frerichs, Ernest Sunley *religious studies educator*
Gelineau, Louis Edward *bishop*
Goldscheider, Calvin *Jewish studies educator, sociologist*
Hunt, George Nelson *bishop*
Milhaven, John Giles *religious studies educator*
Mulvee, Robert Edward *bishop*
Pearce, George Hamilton *archbishop*
Reeder, John P., Jr. *religious studies educator*
Thomson, Paul van Kuykendall *priest, educator*

Westerly
†Looper, George Kirk *religious society executive*

SOUTH CAROLINA

Anderson
Hearne, Stephen Zachary *minister, educator*

Charleston
Salmon, Edward Lloyd, Jr. *bishop*
Thompson, David B. *bishop*

Columbia
Adams, John Hurst *bishop*
Aull, James Stroud *bishop*
Beckham, William Arthur *bishop*
Bethea, Joseph Benjamin *bishop*
Blount, Evelyn *religious organization administrator*
Brubaker, Lauren Edgar *minister, educator*

Due West
Ruble, Randall Tucker *theologian, educator, academic administrator*

Gastonia
Carson, John Little *historical theology educator, clergyman*

Georgetown
Allison, Christopher FitzSimons *bishop*

Goose Creek
Johnson, Johnnie *bishop*

Greenville
Kowalski, Paul Randolph *minister*
McKnight, Edgar Vernon *religion educator*
Smith, Morton Howison *religious organization administrator, educator*

Hilton Head Island
Radest, Howard Bernard *clergyman, educator*

Leesville
Crumley, James Robert, Jr. *retired clergyman*

Mauldin
Phillips, James Oscar *minister*

SOUTH DAKOTA

Rapid City
Chaput, Charles J. *bishop*

Sioux Falls
Carlson, Robert James *bishop*
Cowles, Ronald Eugene *church administrator*
Dudley, Paul V. *bishop*

Eitrheim, Norman Duane *bishop*
Nelson, Suzanne Mosey *association executive, non-profit management consultant*

TENNESSEE

Antioch
Reeds, Roger *church administrator*
Thomas, Roy Lee *minister*
Vallance, James *church administrator, religious publication editor*
Waddell, R. Eugene *minister*
Worthington, Melvin Leroy *minister, writer*

Brentwood
†Atchison, David Warren *church officer*
Bennett, Harold Clark *clergyman, religious organization administrator*

Chattanooga
Hall, Thor *religion educator*
Mohney, Ralph Wilson *minister*
Ragon, Robert Ronald *clergyman*
†Wheeler, Evelyn A. *communications specialist*

Cleveland
Albert, Leonard *religious organization executive*
Alford, Delton L. *religious organization executive*
Betancourt, Esdras *religious organization executive*
Chambers, O. Wayne *religious organization executive*
Crisp, Sam *church administrator*
Fisher, Robert Elwood *minister, church official*
Hughes, Ray Harrison *minister, church official*
Jackson, Joseph Essard *religious organization administrator*
Jones, E. L. *church administrator*
Moffett, B. J. *church administrator*
Murray, Billy Dwayne, Sr. *church administrator*
Nichols, John D. *church administrator*
O'Neal, Timothy D. *church administrator*
Pemberton, Donald T. *church administrator*
Rayburn, Billy J. *Church administrator*
Reyes, Jose Antonio, Sr. *minister*
Riley, Jerlena *church administrator*
Robinson, Julian B. *church administrator*
Sheeks, Bill F. *minister*
Sustar, T. David *religious organization executive*
Taylor, William Al *church administrator*
Tomlinson, Milton Ambrose *clergyman*
Varlack, Adrian *church administrator*
Vaughan, Roland *church administrator*
Vest, R. Lamar *church administrator*
White, Robert *church administrator*

Hermitage
Chambers, Curtis Allen *clergyman, church communications executive*

Jackson
Maynard, Terrell Dennis *minister*

Johnson City
Shaw, Angus Robertson, III *minister*

Knoxville
Bell, H. Jenkins *clergyman, bishop*
Kitts, Elbert Walker *minister*
O'Connell, Anthony J. *bishop*
Sanders, William Evan *bishop*

La Follette
Eads, Ora Wilbert *clergyman, church official*

Loudon
Jones, Robert Gean *religion educator*

Memphis
Adamson, John *church administrator*
Brooks, P. A., II *bishop*
Cunningham, Ronald M. *religious education director*
Dickson, Alex Dockery *bishop*
Hamilton, W. W. *church administrator*
Howell, Stephen Wayne *church organization administrator, clergyman*
Macklin, F. Douglas *bishop*
†Magrill, Joe Richard, Jr. *religious organization administrator, minister*
Perry, Floyde E., Jr. *bishop*
Porter, W. L. *bishop*
†Steib, James Terry *bishop*
Thomas, Nathaniel Charles *clergyman*
Todd, Virgil Holcomb *clergyman, religion educator*
†Wade, Edgar L. *church administrator*

Nashville
Abstein, William Robert, II *minister*
Adkins, Cecelia N. *church administrator*
Burgess, Roger *retired church official*
Buttrick, David Gardner *religion educator*
†Chapman, Morris Hines *denominational executive*
Draper, James Thomas (Jimmy Draper) *clergyman*
Forlines, Franklin Leroy *minister, educator*
Forstman, Henry Jackson *theology educator, university dean*
Fry, Malcolm Craig *clergyman*
Hamm, Richard L. *church administrator*
Hampton, Ralph Clayton, Jr. *pastoral studies educator, clergyman*
Harrod, Howard Lee *religion educator*
†Henry, James B. *church officer*
Ireson, Roger William *religious organization administrator, minister, educator*
Jemison, Theodore Judson *religious organization administrator*
Jones, Kathryn Cherie *pastor*
†Kmiec, Edward Urban *bishop*
Land, Richard Dale *minister, religious organization administrator*
Mills, Liston Oury *theology educator*
Picirilli, Robert Eugene *clergyman, college dean, writer*
Seale, James Millard *religious organization administrator, clergyman*
Spencer, Harry Chadwick *minister*
Walker, Arthur Lonzo *religious organization administrator*
Whaley, Vernon *church administrator*

Sewanee
Hughes, Robert Davis, III *theological educator*

Springfield
Fagan, A. Rudolph *minister*

Sweetwater
Johnson, Charlie James *minister*

TEXAS

Alice
Tetlie, Harold *priest*

Amarillo
Matthiesen, Leroy Theodore *bishop*

Austin
Ahlschwede, Arthur Martin *church educational official*
Mc Carthy, John Edward *bishop*
Wahlberg, Philip Lawrence *former bishop, legislative liaison*

Beaumont
†Galante, Joseph A. *bishop*
Ganter, Bernard J. *bishop*
McGary, Betty Winstead *minister, counselor, individual, marriage, and family therapist*

Brownsville
Fitzpatrick, John J. *bishop*

Corpus Christi
Doty, James Edward *pastor, psychologist*
Gracida, Rene Henry *bishop*
Pivonka, Leonard Daniel *priest*

Dallas
Allen, John Carlton *minister*
Clark, C. A. W. *church administrator*
Grahmann, Charles V. *bishop*
Harris, David, Jr. *minister*
Haynes, J. Neauell *clergyman, bishop*
Herbener, Mark Basil *bishop*
Jenkins, Chester P. *religious organization, church administration*
†Jones, E. Edward, Sr. *church officer*
Morgan, Larry Ronald *minister*
Scott, Manuel *church administrator*
Slater, Oliver Eugene *bishop*
Thurston, Stephen John *pastor*
Valentine, Foy Dan *clergyman*
Wiles, Charles Preston *minister*

De Soto
Jackson, Johnny W. *minister*
Lee, J. E. *bishop*

Denton
Leslie, Marvin Earl *minister*

Early
Chapman, Dan G. *minister*

El Paso
Pena, Raymundo Joseph *bishop*

Fort Worth
Calkins, Loren Gene *church executive, clergyman*
Delaney, Joseph P. *bishop*
†Edwards, Samuel Lee *religious organization executive*
Elliott, John Franklin *clergyman*
Gilbert, James Cayce *minister*
Gross, John Birney *retired minister*
Newport, John Paul *philosophy of religion educator, former academic administrator*
Rogers, Charles Ray *minister, religious organization administrator*
Suggs, Marion Jack *minister, college dean*
Teegarden, Kenneth Leroy *clergyman*

Gary
Speer, James *religious organization administrator*

Houston
Benitez, Maurice Manuel *bishop*
Fiorenza, Joseph A. *bishop*
Henderson, Nathan H. *bishop*
Joyce, James Daniel *clergyman*
Karff, Samuel Egal *rabbi*
Meeks, Herbert Lessig, III *pastor, former school system administrator*
Nelson, John Robert *theology educator, clergyman*
Nielsen, Niels Christian, Jr. *theology educator*
Sampson, Franklin Delano *minister*
Sellers, James Earl *theological educator*
Sudbury, John Dean *religious foundation executive, petroleum chemist*
Woodard, Robert E. *bishop*

Jacksonville
Blaylock, James Carl *clergyman, librarian*
†Higgs, Grady L. *religious organization administrator*
Pruitt, William Charles, Jr. *minister, educator*

League City
Ellis, Walter Leon *minister*

Longview
Brannon, Clifton Woodrow, Sr. *evangelist, lawyer*

Lubbock
Hulsey, Sam Byron *bishop*
†Rodriguez, Placido *bishop*
Watson, W. H. *bishop*

Orange
Delarue, Louis C(harles) *priest*

Plano
Lee, Allan Wren *clergyman*

Red Oak
Henderson, Edwin Harold *minister*

Richardson
Conrad, Flavius Leslie, Jr. *minister*

San Angelo
Pfeifer, Michael David *bishop*

San Antonio
Caudill, Howard Edwin *bishop, educator*
Flores, Patrick F. *archbishop*
Iglehart, T. D. *bishop*
Jacobson, David *rabbi*
Mc Allister, Gerald Nicholas *retired bishop, clergyman*
Nix, Robert Lynn *minister*
Ranson, Guy Harvey *clergyman, religion educator*
Walker, William Oliver, Jr. *religion educator*

Spring
Hunt, T(homas) W(ebb) *retired religion educator*

Texarkana
Cross, Irvie Keil *religious organization executive*
Silvey, James L. *religious publisher*
Tucker, Bobby Glenn *minister*

Tyler
†Carmody, Edmond *bishop*

Van
Cottrell, Ralph *religious organization executive*

Van Alstyne
Daves, Don Michael *minister*

Victoria
Fellhauer, David E. *bishop*

Waco
Chewning, Richard Carter *religious business ethics educator*
Flanders, Henry Jackson, Jr. *religious studies educator*
Wood, James E., Jr. *religion educator, author*

Waxahachie
Tschoepe, Thomas *bishop*

UTAH

Bountiful
Carter, Richard Bert *retired church official, retired government official*

Salt Lake City
Bates, George Edmonds *bishop*
Eyring, Henry Bennion *bishop*
Faust, James E. *church official*
Haight, David B. *church official*
Hinckley, Gordon B. *church official*
Maxwell, Neal A. *church official*
Monson, Thomas Spencer *church official, publishing company executive*
†Niederauer, George H. *bishop*
Packer, Boyd K. *church official*
Paramore, James Martin *church executive*
Perry, L. Tom *church official, merchant*
Scott, Richard G. *church official*
Smith, Eldred Gee *church leader*
Weigand, William Keith *bishop*
Wirthlin, Joseph B. *church official*

VERMONT

Burlington
†Angell, Kenneth Anthony *bishop*
Swenson, Daniel Lee *bishop*

Middlebury
Ferm, Robert Livingston *religion educator*

Newport
Guerrette, Richard Hector *priest, management consultant*

Northfield
Wick, William Shinn *clergyman, chaplain*

Norwich
Post, Avery Denison *church official*

Pawlet
Buechner, Carl Frederick *minister, author*

Springfield
Garinger, Louis Daniel *religion educator*

VIRGINIA

Arlington
Keating, John Richard *bishop*

Blacksburg
Grover, Norman LaMotte *theologian, philosopher*

Charlottesville
Childress, James Franklin *theology and medical educator*
Fletcher, John Caldwell *religious studies educator, bioethicist*
Fogarty, Gerald Philip *church history educator, priest*
Hartt, Julian Norris *religion educator*
Novak, David *Judaic studies educator, rabbi*
Sachedina, Abdulaziz *religious studies educator*
Scharlemann, Robert Paul *religious studies educator, clergyman*
Scott, Nathan Alexander, Jr. *minister, educator, literary critic*

Covington
Grove, Jeffery Lynn *minister*

Emory
Dawsey, James Marshall *religious studies educator, minister*

Hampton
Henderson, Salathiel James *minister*

Lexington
Hodges, Louis Wendell *religion educator*

Lincoln
LeSourd, Leonard Earle *publisher, editor*

Lynchburg
Gilbert, Larry Alan *religious institute administrator*

Madison Heights
Falwell, Jerry L. *clergyman*

Mc Lean
Eastman, Albert Theodore *bishop*
Lotz, Denton *minister, church official*
Wümpelmann, Knud Aage Abildgaard *clergyman, religious organization administrator*

Mechanicsville
Balser, Glennon *church administrator*

Norfolk
Vest, Frank Harris, Jr. *bishop*

Penn Laird
Wise, Charles Conrad, Jr. *educator, past government official, author*

Portsmouth
Thomas, Ted, Sr. *minister*

Reston
Lowry, Frederick Sherwood *minister, association director*
Walzer, William Charles *church official, interdenominational religious publishing agency executive*

Richmond
Aigner, Emily Burke *lay worker*
Anderson, James Frederick *clergyman*
Bagby, Daniel Gordon *minister*
Briggs, Edward Burton, Jr. *religion writer*
Brown, Aubrey Neblett, Jr. *minister, editor*
Fuller, Reginald Horace *clergyman, biblical studies educator*
Hart, Philip Ray *religion educator, minister*
Lee, Peter James *bishop*
Leith, John Haddon *clergyman, theology educator*
McDonough, Reginald Milton *religious organization executive*
Moore, John Sterling, Jr. *minister*
Rogers, Isabel Wood *religious studies educator*
Stockton, Thomas B. *bishop*
Sullivan, Walter Francis *bishop*
Swezey, Charles Mason *Christian ethics educator, administrator*

Roanoke
Light, Arthur Heath *bishop*
Marmion, William Henry *retired bishop*

Rockbridge Baths
Patteson, Roy Kinneer, Jr. *clergyman, administrator*

Salem
Bansemer, Richard Frederick *bishop*

Sweet Briar
Armstrong, Gregory Timon *religious studies educator, minister*

Virginia Beach
Williams, John Rodman *theologian, educator*

Warsaw
Hirsch, Charles Bronislaw *retired religion educator and administrator*

Williamsburg
Finn, Thomas Macy *religion educator*

Woodbridge
Townsend, Kenneth Ross *priest*

WASHINGTON

Belfair
Walker, E. Jerry *retired clergyman*

College Place
Thompson, Alden Lloyd *biblical studies educator, author*

Greenbank
Tuell, Jack Marvin *retired bishop*

Richland
Johnson, Arnold Gordon *clergyman*

Seattle
Averill, Lloyd James, Jr. *religion educator*
Burrows, Elizabeth MacDonald *religious organization executive, educator*
Mackey, Sally Schear *retired religious organization administrator*
McConnell, Calvin Dale *clergyman*
Murphy, Thomas Joseph *archbishop*
Raible, Peter Spilman *minister*
Robb, John Wesley *religion educator*
Warner, Vincent W. *bishop*

Spanaway
Westbrook, T. L. *bishop*

Spokane
Keller, Robert M. *bishop*
Polley, Harvey Lee *retired missionary and educator*
Skylstad, William S. *bishop*
Terry, Frank Jeffrey *bishop*

Tacoma
Alger, David Townley *religious organization director*
Wiegman, Eugene William *minister, former college administrator*
Wold, David C. *bishop*

Yakima
George, Francis *bishop*

WEST VIRGINIA

Charleston
Atkinson, Robert Poland *bishop*
Scott, Olof Henderson, Jr. *priest*

Fairmont
Black, L. Alexander *bishop*

Grafton
Poling, Kermit William *minister*

Morgantown
Meitzen, Manfred Otto *religious studies educator*

Wheeling
Schmitt, Bernard W. *bishop*

WISCONSIN

Amery
Mickelson, Arnold Rust *consultant, religious denominational official*

Appleton
Herder, Robert H. *bishop*

Cedarburg
Clark, Harry Wilber *administrator*

Eau Claire
Wantland, William Charles *bishop, lawyer*

Fond Du Lac
Stevens, William Louis *bishop*

Green Bay
Banks, Robert J. *bishop*

La Crosse
†Bubar, Joseph Bedell, Jr. *church official*
†Burke, Raymond L. *bishop*
Paul, John Joseph *bishop*

Madison
Bullock, William Henry *bishop*
Enslin, Jon S. *bishop*
Fox, Michael Vass *Hebrew educator, rabbi*
Wirz, George O. *bishop*

Milwaukee
†Mueller, Wayne Dennis *pastor, administrator, educator*
Weakland, Rembert G. *archbishop*

Oak Creek
Robertson, Michael Swing *religious association administrator*

Oshkosh
Barwig, Regis Norbert James *priest*
Burke, Redmond A. *priest, librarian, educator*

Racine
Jacobson-Wolf, Joan Elizabeth *minister*

Rice Lake
Knutson, Gerhard I. *bishop*

Sun Prairie
Mischke, Carl Herbert *religious association executive, retired*

Superior
Fliss, Raphael M. *bishop*

Watertown
Henry, Carl Ferdinand Howard *theologian*

WYOMING

Cheyenne
Hart, Joseph H. *bishop*

Cody
Murphy, Warren Charles *rector*

Laramie
Jones, Bob Gordon *bishop*

TERRITORIES OF THE UNITED STATES

AMERICAN SAMOA

Pago Pago
Weitzel, John Quinn *bishop*

FEDERATED STATES OF MICRONESIA

Chuuk
Neylon, Martin Joseph *bishop*

GUAM

Agana
Apuron, Anthony Sablan *archbishop*

NORTHERN MARIANA ISLANDS

Saipan
Camacho, Tomas Aguon *bishop*

PUERTO RICO

Caguas
†Hernandez Rivera, Enrique *bishop*

Mayaguez
†Casiano Vargas, Ulises *bishop*

Ponce
Torres Oliver, Juan Fremiot *bishop*

Santurce
Aponte Martinez, Luis Cardinal *archbishop*

VIRGIN ISLANDS

Charlotte Amalie
†Thomas, Elliott G. *bishop*

Saint Croix
Talbot, Frederick Hilborn *bishop, former Guyanese diplomat*

CANADA

ALBERTA

Calgary
Curtis, John Barry *bishop*
O'Byrne, Paul J. *bishop*

Camrose
Campbell, John Douglas *minister*

Cochrane
†Schmidt, Allen Edward *religious foundation administrator*

Edmonton
Daciuk, Myron Michael *bishop*
Doyle, Wilfred Emmett *retired bishop*
Genge, Kenneth Lyle *bishop*
Mac Neil, Joseph Neil *archbishop*

McLennan
Légaré, Henri Francis *archbishop*

Saint Paul
Roy, Raymond *bishop*

BRITISH COLUMBIA

Kamloops
Cruickshank, James David *bishop*
Sabatini, Lawrence *bishop*

Nelson
Mallon, Peter *bishop*

Prince Rupert
Hannen, John Edward *bishop*

Richmond
Plomp, Teunis (Tony Plomp) *minister*

Salt Spring Island
Shepherd, R. F. *retired bishop*

Surrey
Farley, Lawrence *clergyman*

Vancouver
Exner, Adam *archbishop*
Wakefield, Wesley Halpenny *church official*

Victoria
De Roo, Remi Joseph *bishop*
Frame, John Timothy *bishop*

West Vancouver
Bentall, Shirley Franklyn *lay church leader, author*

MANITOBA

Churchill
Rouleau, Reynald *bishop*

Saint Boniface
Hacault, Antoine Joseph Leon *archbishop*

The Pas
Sutton, Peter Alfred *archbishop*

Winnipeg
Harder, Helmut George *religious organization administrator*
Hermaniuk, Maxim *retired archbishop*
Jarmus, Stephan Onysym *priest*
Sjoberg, Donald *bishop*
Wall, Leonard J. *bishop*

NEW BRUNSWICK

Fredericton
Lemmon, George Colborne *bishop*

Moncton
Chiasson, Donat *archbishop*

NEWFOUNDLAND

Corner Brook
Payne, Sidney Stewart *archbishop*

Saint John's
Harvey, Donald F. *bishop*
†Hiscock, Boyd L. *minister, religious organization administrator*
†King, Roy D. *religious organization administrator*
Mate, Martin *bishop*
Troy, J. Edward *bishop*

NORTHWEST TERRITORIES

Iqaluit
Williams, John Christopher Richard *bishop*

Yellowknife
Croteau, Denis *bishop*

NOVA SCOTIA

Antigonish
Campbell, Colin *bishop*

Halifax
†Burke, Austin E. *archbishop*

Parrsboro
Hatfield, Leonard Fraser *retired bishop*

ONTARIO

Almonte
Penney, Alphonsus Liguori *archbishop*

Barrie
Clune, Robert Bell *bishop*

Brampton
Bastian, Donald Noel *bishop, retired*

Burlington
Elgersma, Ray *relief and development organization executive*
Hamilton, Donald Gordon *religious association administrator*
Karsten, Albert *religious organization administrator*

Cambridge
Hooper, Wayne Nelson *clergy member*

Cornwall
La Rocque, Eugene Philippe *bishop*

Etobicoke
†Coleman, K. Virginia *diaconal minister*

Guelph
Steffer, Robert Wesley *clergyman*

Hamilton
†Asbil, Walter *bishop*
Tonnos, Anthony *bishop*

Kanata
Hunter, Edward Stewart *clergy member*

Kingston
Read, Allan Alexander *minister*
Spence, Francis John *archbishop*

Kitchener
Huras, William David *bishop*
Winger, Roger Elson *church administrator*

London
MacBain, William Halley *minister, theology educator, seminary chancellor*
†O'Driscoll, Perry R. *archbishop*
Peterson, Leslie Ernest *bishop*
Scott, W. Peter *bishop*
Sherlock, John Michael *bishop*

Milton
Georgije, Djokic *bishop*

Mississauga
†Griffin, William Arthur *clergyman, religious organization executive*

Niagara Falls
Mullan, Donald William *bishop*

North Bay
†Bell, J. Stewart *clergy member*
†Plouffe, Jean-Louis *bishop*

Oshawa
†Devnich, D. D. *religious organization administrator*

Ottawa
Landriault, Jacques Emile *retired bishop*
Ryan, William Francis *priest*
Squire, Anne Marguerite *religious leader*

Pembroke
Windle, Joseph Raymond *bishop*

Peterborough
Doyle, James Leonard *bishop*

Rexdale
Joseph, Emanuel *church administrator*

Saint Catharines
Fulton, Thomas Benjamin *retired bishop*
O'Mara, John Aloysius *bishop*

Sault Sainte Marie
Ferris, Ronald Curry *bishop*

Scarborough
†Mikloshazy, Attila *bishop*

Schumacher
Lawrence, Caleb James *bishop*

Timmins
Cazabon, Gilles *bishop*

Toronto
Athanassoulas, Sotirios (Sotirios of Toronto) *bishop*
Carter, Gerald Emmett *retired archbishop*
Ching, Julia *philosophy and religion educator*
Chodos, Robert Irwin *editor, writer*
Finlay, Terence Edward *bishop*
Jay, Charles Douglas *religion educator, college administrator, clergyman*
Owens, Joseph *clergyman*
Plaut, Wolf Gunther *minister, author*
Synan, Edward Aloysius, Jr. *clergyman, former institute president*
Wilson, Lois M. *minister*

Unionville
Rusnak, Michael *bishop*

Waterloo
Kraus, Michael *minister*
Mills (Kutz-Harder), Helga *religious organization executive*

Windsor
Whitney, Barry Lyn *religious studies educator*

QUEBEC

Amos
†Drainville, Gerard *bishop*

Chicoutimi
Couture, Jean Guy *bishop*

Hull
Ebacher, Roger *archbishop*

Joliette
Audet, Rene *bishop*
†Lussier, Gilles *monsignor*

LaSalle
†Kristensen, John *church organization administrator*

Longueuil
Hubert, Bernard *bishop*

Mont Laurier
Gratton, Jean *clergyman*

Montreal
†Abi-Saber, Georges *archbishop*
Charron, André Joseph Charles Pierre *theologian, educator, former dean*
†Hakim, Michel *religious leader*
Hall, Douglas John *minister, educator*
†Hutchison, Andrew S. *bishop*
Kannengiesser, Charles A. *theology educator*
Turcotte, Jean-Claude Cardinal *archbishop*

Outremont
†Derderian, Hovnan *church official*

Quebec
Stavert, Alexander Bruce *bishop*

Rimouski
Blanchet, Bertrand *archbishop*
Levesque, Louis *bishop*

Rouyn-Noranda
Hamelin, Jean-Guy *bishop*

Saint Hyacinthe
Langevin, Louis-de-Gonzaque *bishop*

Saint Jerome
Valois, Charles *bishop*

Sherbrooke
Fortier, Jean-Marie *archbishop*

Sillery
Couture, Maurice *archbishop*

Trois Rivieres
Noël, Laurent *bishop, educator*

Valleyfield
Lebel, Robert *bishop*

SASKATCHEWAN

Gravelbourg
Delaquis, Noel *bishop*

Prince Albert
Morand, Blaise E. *bishop*

Regina
Bays, Eric *bishop*
Holm, Roy K. *church administrator*

Saltcoats
Farquharson, Walter Henry *minister, church official*

Saskatoon
Filevich, Basil *bishop*
Jacobson, Sverre Theodore *retired minister*
Mahoney, James P. *bishop*
Morgan, Thomas Oliver *bishop*

YUKON TERRITORY

Whitehorse
Lobsinger, Thomas *bishop*

MEXICO

Chihuahua
Almeida Merino, Adalberto *archbishop*

Col Tepeyac Insurgentes
Godinez Flores, Ramon *auxiliary bishop*

Matamoros
Chavolla Ramos, Francisco Javier *bishop*

Mexico City
Guizar, Ricardo Diaz *clergyman*

Saltillo
Villalobos Padilla, Francisco *bishop*

Veracruz
Ranzahuer, Guillermo Gonzalez *bishop*

ARGENTINA

Buenos Aires
Gennadios, (Gennadios Chrysoulakis) *bishop*

BELGIUM

Brussels
Jadot, Jean Lambert Octave *clergyman*

BRAZIL

Rio de Janeiro
Sales, Eugenio de Araujo Cardinal *archbishop*

ENGLAND

London
Gilbert, Patrick Nigel Geoffrey *organization executive*
Hornyak, Eugene Augustine *bishop*
Van Culin, Samuel *religious organization administrator*

Oxford
Gulbrandsen, Natalie Webber *religious association administrator*
Ryscavage, Richard Joseph *Jesuit priest, social services administrator*

Saint Leonards on Sea
Holloway, Julia Bolton *retired educator*

FEDERATED STATES MICRONESIA

Truk
Samo, Amando *bishop*

FRANCE

Bordeaux
Gouyon, Paul Cardinal *archbishop*

GHANA

Kumasi
Sarpong, Peter Kwasi *bishop*

HONG KONG

Hong Kong
Kwong, Peter Kong Kit *bishop*

Kowloon
Chiang, Samuel Edward *theological educator, humanities educator*

INDIA

New Delhi
Gregorios, Paulos Mar *archbishop, metropolitan of Delhi*

Yavatmal
Ward, Daniel Thomas *bishop*

IRAN

Tehran
Dinkha, Mar, IV *church administrator*

ISRAEL

Jerusalem
Schindler, Pesach *rabbi, educator, author*

ITALY

Rome
Audet, Leonard *theologian*
Bafile, Corrado *cardinal*

Baum, William Wakefield Cardinal *former church official*

JAPAN

Aichi-ken
Yukei, Hasebe Yoshikazu *religious studies educator*

Nishinomiya
Ogida, Mikio *history of religion educator*

Tenri
Miyata, Gen *history of religion educator*

NORWAY

Lillestr0m
Borgen, Ole Edvard *bishop, educator*

THE PHILIPPINES

Pasay
Lim, Sonia Yii *minister*

SAINT LUCIA

Castries
Felix, Kelvin Edward *archbishop*

VATICAN CITY

Vatican City
John Paul, His Holiness Pope, II (Karol Jozef Wojtyla) *bishop of Rome*
Szoka, Edmund Casimir Cardinal *cardinal*

ADDRESS UNPUBLISHED

Allan, Hugh James Pearson *retired bishop*
Ambrozic, Aloysius Matthew *archbishop*
Anderson, Charles D. *bishop*
Anderson, John Firth *church administrator, librarian*
Arnold, Duane Wade-Hampton *minister, educator*
Baker, Josephine L. Redenius (Mrs. Milton G. Baker) *minister, civic leader, retired career officer, former public relations company executive*
Belshaw, George Phelps Mellick *bishop*
Bishop, Cecil *bishop*
Blank, Richard Glenn *religious organization administrator, counselor*
Bollback, Anthony George *minister*
Borecky, Isidore *bishop*
Bosco, Anthony Gerard *bishop*
Bothwell, John Charles *archbishop*
Chapman, Robert L. *bishop*
Charlton, Gordon Taliaferro, Jr. *retired bishop*
Christopher, Sharon A. Brown *bishop*
Cliff, Judith Anita *author, biblical studies lecturer*
Clymer, Wayne Kenton *bishop*
Cobb, John Boswell, Jr. *clergyman, educator*
Cole, Clifford Adair *clergyman*
Crabtree, Davida Foy *minister*
Crudup, W. *bishop*
Daly, James Joseph *bishop*
D'Angelo, Ronald Holmes *priest, psychotherapist*
Davis, Theodore Roosevelt *bishop, contractor*
Dirksen, Richard Wayne *canon precentor, organist, choirmaster*
Dixon, Ernest Thomas, Jr. *retired bishop*
Docker, John Thornley *religious organization administrator, minister*
Dudick, Michael Joseph *bishop*
Ellis, Howard Woodrow *evangelist, creative agent, clergyman, artist, author*
Emerson, R. Clark *priest, business administrator*
†Flory, Shirlene *church officer*
†Garner, Darlene C. *church officer*
Gemignani, Michael Caesar *clergyman, retired educator*
Gervais, Marcel Andre *bishop*
Grant, Jacquelyn *minister, religion educator*
Gregory, Myra May *religious organization administrator, educator*
Griffin, James Anthony *bishop*
Hambidge, Douglas Walter *archbishop*
Handy, William Talbot, Jr. *bishop*
Hazuda, Ronald A. *church administrator*
Hearn, J(ames) Woodrow *bishop*
Heistand, Joseph Thomas *retired bishop*
Hilton, Clifford Thomas *clergyman*
Hummel, Gene Maywood *retired bishop*
Hurn, Raymond Walter *religious order administrator*
Isom, Dotcy Ivertus, Jr. *bishop*
Iverson, David M. *church executive*
Ives, Samuel Clifton *minister*
Jackson, David Gordon *religious organization administrator*
John, K. K. (John Kuruvilla Kaiyalethe) *minister*
Joslin, David Bruce *bishop*
Joye, Afrie Songco *minister*
Kalkwarf, Leonard V. *minister*
Keeler, William Henry *cardinal*
Keyser, Charles Lovett, Jr. *bishop*
King, Felton *bishop*
Kucera, Daniel William *bishop*
†Kung (Gong) Pin-Mei, Ignatius Cardinal (Ignatius Kung (Gong) Cardinal Pin-Mei) *cardinal*
Landes, George Miller *biblical studies educator*
Lawson, David Jerald *bishop*
Lee, Mordecai *religious agency administrator*
Lehman, Edwin *minister, head of religious organization*
Lohmuller, Martin Nicholas *bishop*
Loppnow, Milo Alvin *clergyman, former church official*
†Losten, Basil Harry *bishop*
Luetkehoelter, Gottlieb Werner (Lee) *retired bishop, clergyman*
Madera, Joseph J. *bishop*
Malone, James William *bishop*
McCandless, J(ane) Bardarah *retired religion educator*
Mc Kay, Samuel Leroy *clergyman*
McQuilkin, John Robertson *religion educator, academic administrator, writer*
Melczek, Dale J. *bishop*
Melvin, Billy Alfred *clergyman*
Meyer, Paul William *biblical literature educator emeritus*
Milhouse, Paul William *bishop*
†Mills, Robert Harry *church administrator*
Moore, E. Harris *bishop*
Muckerman, Norman James *priest, writer*
Mumford, Patricia Rae *religious organization administrator*
Nottingham, William Jesse *church mission executive, minister*
Osborne, James Alfred *religious organization administrator*
Parsons, Elmer Earl *retired clergyman*
Patterson, Donis Dean *bishop*
Peers, Michael Geoffrey *archbishop*
Pelotte, Donald Edmond *bishop*
Procter, John Ernest *former publishing company executive*
Quick, Norman *bishop*
Righter, Walter Cameron *bishop*
Rooks, Charles Shelby *minister*
Rose, Robert John *bishop*
Rose, T. T. *bishop*
Salatka, Charles Alexander *archbishop*
Sams, John Roland *retired mission executive, missionary*
Sayre, Francis Bowes, Jr. *clergyman*
Schuelke, John Paul *religious organization administrator*
Scott, Robert Hal *minister*
Scott, Waldron *mission executive*
Shimpfky, Richard Lester *bishop*
Sloyan, Gerard Stephen *religious studies educator, priest*
Soro, Mar Bawai *bishop*
Spence, Glen Oscar *clergyman*
Stendahl, Krister *retired bishop*
Strasser, Gabor *priest, management consultant*
Sullivan, James Lenox *clergyman*
Sullivan, Leon Howard *clergyman*
Swanson, Paul Rubert *minister*
†Vachon, Louis-Albert Cardinal *archbishop*
van Dyck, Nicholas Booraem *minister, foundation official*
Van Valin, Clyde Emory *bishop*
Weinkauf, Mary Louise Stanley *clergywoman*
Wilhelm, Joseph Lawrence *archbishop*
Wills, Charles Francis *former church executive, retired career officer*
Wright, Earl Jerome *pastor, bishop*
Zayek, Francis Mansour *bishop*

SCIENCE: LIFE SCIENCE

UNITED STATES

ALABAMA

Auburn
Bailey, Wilford Sherrill *parisitology educator, science administrator, university president*
Ball, Donald Maury *agronomist, consultant*
Klesius, Phillip Harry *microbiologist, researcher*
Lemke, Paul Arenz *botany educator*

Birmingham
Bradley, John M(iller), Jr. *forestry executive*
Brown, Jerry William *cell biology and anatomy educator*
Finley, Sara Crews *medical geneticist, educator*
Gerlach, Gary G. *botanical garden director, columnist*
Navia, Juan Marcelo *biologist, educator*
Oglesby, Sabert, Jr. *retired research institute administrator*
Rouse, John Wilson, Jr. *research institute administrator*
Schneyer, Charlotte Alper *physiologist, researcher, educator*

Mobile
Gottlieb, Sheldon Fred *biologist, educator*

Tuscaloosa
Darden, William Howard, Jr. *biology educator*
Wetzel, Robert George *botany educator*

Tuskegee Institute
Khan, Abu T. *environmental toxicologist, educator*

ALASKA

Anchorage
Bender, Thomas Richard *science administrator, epidemiologist*

Auke Bay
Snyder, George Richard *laboratory director*

Fairbanks
Kessel, Brina *ornithologist, educator*
†White, Robert Gordon *educator, researcher, research director*

Juneau
Willson, Mary F. *ecology researcher, educator*

ARIZONA

Phoenix
Anderson, Edward Frederick *biology educator*
†Iliff, Warren Jolidon *zoo administrator*
Kimball, Bruce Arnold *soil scientist*
Radin, John William *agriculturalist, physiologist*
Witherspoon, James Donald *biology educator*

Rio Rico
Le, Ton Da *horticulturist, researcher*

Sun City
Morse, True Delbert *business and agricultural consultant, former undersecretary of agriculture*
Steffan, Wallace Allan *entomologist, educator*

Tempe
Aronson, Jerome Melville *plant physiology educator*
Gerking, Shelby Delos, Jr. *zoologist, educator*
Herald, Cherry Lou *research educator, research director*
Patten, Duncan Theunissen *ecologist educator*

Tucson
Acker, Robert Flint *microbiologist*
Alcorn, Stanley Marcus *plant pathology educator*
Bohn, Hinrich Lorenz *soil science educator*
Bowers, William Sigmord *entomology educator*
Cortner, Hanna Joan *science administrator, research scientist, educator*
Foster, Kennith Earl *life sciences educator*
Fritts, Harold Clark *dendrochronology educator, researcher*
Fuller, Wallace Hamilton *research scientist, educator*
Gerba, Charles Peter *microbiologist, educator*
Green, Robert Scott *biotechnology company executive*
Hull, Herbert Mitchell *plant physiologist, researcher*
McCormick, Floyd Guy, Jr. *agricultural educator, college administrator*
†McCusker, J. Stephen *zoo director*
Metcalfe, Darrel Seymour *agronomist, educator*
Neuman, Shlomo P. *hydrology educator*
Osterberg, Charles Lamar *marine radioecologist, oceanographer*
Pepper, Ian L. *environmental microbiologist, research scientist, educator*
Shannon, Robert Rennie *optical sciences center administrator, educator*
Shubinski, Raymond *planetarium director*
†Strausfeld, Nicholas *neurobiology and entomology educator*
Sypherd, Paul Starr *microbiologist*
Winfree, Arthur Taylor *biologist, educator*
Yocum, Harrison Gerald *horticulturist, botanist, educator, researcher*

ARKANSAS

Bella Vista
Musacchia, X(avier) J(oseph) *physiology and biophysics educator*

Fayetteville
Brown, Connell Jean *retired animal science educator*
Clayton, Frances Elizabeth *cytologist, scientist, educator*
Evans, William Lee *biologist*
Morris, Justin Roy *food scientist, enologist, consultant*
Musick, Gerald Joe *entomology educator*
Rutledge, Elliott Moye *soil scientist, educator*
West, Charles Patrick *agronomist, educator*
Wolf, Duane Carl *microbiologist*

Jefferson
Casciano, Daniel Anthony *biologist*
†Schwetz, Bernard Anthony *toxicologist*

Little Rock
Barron, Almen Leo *microbiologist*
Hinson, Jack Allsbrook *research toxicologist, educator*

CALIFORNIA

Alameda
Blatt, Beverly Faye *biologist, consultant*

Albany
†Weber, Barbara C. *research entomologist*

Arcadia
Morse, Judy *science foundation administrator*

Arcata
Barratt, Raymond William *biologist, educator*

Atherton
Starr, Chauncey *research institute executive*

Azusa
Kimnach, Myron William *botanist, horticulturist, consultant*

Berkeley
Anderson, John Richard *entomologist, educator*
†Baldwin, Bruce Gregg *botany educator, researcher*
Barrett, Reginald Haughton *wildlife management educator, biology educator*
Berkner, Klaus Hans *laboratory administrator, physicist*
Bern, Howard Alan *science educator, research biologist*
Burnside, Mary Beth *biology educator, researcher*
Casida, John Edward *entomology educator*
Chemsak, John Andrew *entomologist*
Cozzarelli, Nicholas Robert *molecular biologist, educator*
Dahlsten, Donald Lee *enviromental biology and forest entomology educator*
Dempster, Lauramay Tinsley *botanist*
DePaolo, Donald James *earth science educator*
Duesberg, Peter Heinz Hermann *molecular biology educator*
Frankie, Gordon William *entomology educator*
Furman, Deane Philip *parasitologist, emeritus educator*
Getz, Wayne Marcus *biomathematician, researcher, educator*
Kaplan, Donald Robert *biologist, educator*
King, Mary-Claire *epidemiologist, educator, geneticist*
Lennette, Edwin Herman *virologist*
Licht, Paul *zoologist, educator*
Lidicker, William Zander, Jr. *zoologist, educator*
Loher, Werner J. *entomology educator*
McColl, John Graham *plant and soil biology educator*
McKillop, William Lawie *forest economics educator*
Nandi, Satyabrata *zoology educator*
Ornduff, Robert *botany educator*
Pitelka, Frank Alois *zoologist, educator*
Purcell, Alexander Holmes *entomologist, educator*
Reginato, Robert Joseph *soil scientist*
Schachman, Howard Kapnek *molecular biologist, educator*
†Schekman, Randy W. *molecular biology administrator, biochemist*
Scott, Eugenie Carol *science foundation director, anthropologist*
Shank, Charles Vernon *science administrator, educator*
Spear, Robert Clinton *environmental health educator, consultant*
Still, Gerald G. *plant physiologist, research director*
Teeguarden, Dennis Earl *forest economist*
Thornton, John Irvin *forensic scientist, educator*
Twiss, Robert Hamilton, Jr. *environmental planning educator*
Vaux, Henry James *forest economist, educator*
Vedros, Neylan Anthony *microbiologist*
Wake, David Burton *biology educator, researcher*
Wake, Marvalee Hendricks *biology educator*
†White, Timothy Douglas *biology educator*
Wohletz, Leonard Ralph *soil scientist, consultant*
Wood, David L. *entomologist, educator*

Beverly Hills
Spence, Mary Anne *geneticist, medical association executive*

Bishop
MacMillen, Richard Edward *biological sciences educator, researcher*

Bodega Bay
Hand, Cadet Hammond, Jr. *marine biologist, educator*
Jeffery, William Richard *developmental biology educator*

Cambria
Villeneuve, Donald Avila *biology educator*

Chico
Ediger, Robert Ike *botanist, educator*
Kistner, David Harold *biology educator*

Claremont
†Benjamin, Richard Keith *mycologist, botany educator*
Purves, William Kirkwood *biologist, educator*
Taylor, Roy Lewis *botanist, educator*

Clovis
Ensminger, Marion Eugene *animal science educator, author*

Coalinga
Harris, John Charles *agriculturalist*

Colton
Halstead, Bruce Walter *biotoxicologist*

Corona Del Mar
Brokaw, Charles Jacob *educator, cellular biologist*

Cupertino
Anderson, Charles Arthur *former research institute administrator*
Cheeseman, Douglas Taylor, Jr. *wildlife tour executive, photographer, educator*

Davis
Addicott, Fredrick Taylor *retired botany educator*
Allard, Robert Wayne *geneticist, educator*
Barbour, Michael G(eorge) *botany educator, ecological consultant*
Baskin, Ronald Joseph *zoologist, physiologist, biophysicist educator, dean*
Carman, Hoy Fred *agricultural sciences educator*
Chang, Robert Shihman *virology educator*
Colvin, Harry Walter, Jr. *physiology educator*
Crane, Julian Coburn *agriculturist,retired educator*
Eldridge, Bruce Frederick *entomology educator, researcher*
Epstein, Emanuel *plant physiologist*
Freedland, Richard Allan *retired biologist, educator*
Gifford, Ernest Milton *biologist, educator*
Grey, Robert Dean *biology educator*
†Hammock, Bruce Dupree *research entomologist and toxicology educator*
Hartmann, Hudson Thomas *agriculturist, educator*
Hess, Charles Edward *environmental horticulture educator*
Horwitz, Barbara Ann *physiologist, educator, consultant*
Hsieh, Dennis P. H. *environmental toxicology educator*
Hughes, John P. *equine research adminstrator*
Kado, Clarence Isao *molecular biologist*
Kimsey, Lynn Siri *entomologist, educator*
Kofranek, Anton Miles *floriculturist, educator*
Kunkee, Ralph Edward *viticulture and enology educator*
Laidlaw, Harry Hyde, Jr. *entomology educator*
Learn, Elmer Warner *agricultural economics educator, retired*
Martin, George Conner *pomology educator*
Meyer, Margaret Eleanor *microbiologist, educator*
Moyle, Peter Briggs *fisheries and biology educator*
Murphy, Terence Martin *biology educator*
Pappagianis, Demosthenes *microbiology educator, physician*
Pearcy, Robert Woodwell *botany educator*
Qualset, Calvin O. *agronomy educator*
Rappaport, Lawrence *plant physiology and horticulture educator*
Rick, Charles Madeira, Jr. *geneticist, educator*
Rost, Thomas Lowell *plant biology educator*
Schoener, Thomas William *zoology educator, researcher*
Shapiro, Arthur Maurice *biology educator*
Sillman, Arnold Joel *physiologist, educator*
Stewart, James Ian *agricultural water scientist, cropping system developer, consultant*
†Van Bruggen, Ariena Hendrika Cornelia *plant pathologist*
Watt, Kenneth Edmund Ferguson *zoology educator*
Williams, William Arnold *agronomy educator*
Wilson, Barry William *biology educator*

Del Mar
Farquhar, Marilyn Gist *cell biology and pathology educator*

Duarte
Lundblad, Roger Lauren *research director*
Ohno, Susumu *research scientist*
Smith, Steven Sidney *molecular biologist*

El Centro
Flock, Robert Ashby *retired entomologist*

El Segundo
Wallace, Arthur *agricultural educator*

Foster City
Baselt, Randall Clint *toxicologist*

Fullerton
Brattstrom, Bayard Holmes *biology educator*
Jones, Claris Eugene, Jr. *botanist, educator*

Gilroy
Barham, Warren Sandusky *horticulturist*

Hayward
Flora, Edward Benjamin *research and development company executive, mechanical engineer*

Hopland
Jones, Milton Bennion *agronomist, educator*

Irvine
Ayala, Francisco José *geneticist, educator*
Bennett, Albert Farrell *biology educator*
†Bryant, Peter James *biologist, educator*
Cheney, Darwin Leroy *research foundation executive, medical educator*
Cunningham, Dennis Dean *microbiology, molecular genetics educator*
Ericson, Jonathon Edward *environmental science educator, researcher*
Fan, Hung Y. *virology educator, consultant*
Fitch, Walter M(onroe) *molecular biologist, educator*
Gutman, George Andre *molecular biologist, educator*
Lambert, Robert Lowell *scientific investigator*
Lenhoff, Howard Maer *biological sciences educator, academic administrator, activist*
Menzel, Daniel Bruce *toxicology educator*
Silverman, Paul Hyman *parasitologist, former university official*

Kensington
Stent, Gunther Siegmund *molecular biologist, educator*

La Canada Flintridge
Clauser, Francis H. *applied science educator*

La Jolla
Alvariño De Leira, Angeles (Angeles Alvariño) *biologist, oceanographer*
Bloom, Floyd Elliott *physician, research scientist*
Dulbecco, Renato *biologist, educator*
Fishman, William Harold *cancer research foundation executive, biochemist*
Guillemin, Roger C. L. *physiologist*
Haxo, Francis Theodore *marine biologist*
Hunter, Tony (Anthony Rex Hunter) *molecular biologist, educator*
Jones, Galen Everts *microbiologist, educator*
Lewin, Ralph Arnold *biologist*
†Myer, James Albert *research science company executive*
Saier, Milton H, Jr. *biology educator*
West, John Burnard *physiologist, educator*
Wilkie, Donald Walter *biologist, aquarium museum director*
†Woodruff, David Scott *biologist, educator*
†Yang, Zhen *research scientist*

Lafayette
Sandberg, Robert Alexis *former research organization administrator*

Lemon Grove
Whitehead, Marvin Delbert *plant pathologist*

Loma Linda
Longo, Lawrence Daniel *physiologist, gynecologist*

Long Beach
Anand, Rajen S. *physiologist*
Swatek, Frank Edward *microbiology educator*

Los Altos
Fraser-Smith, Elizabeth Birdsey *biologist*
Frey, Christian Miller *research center executive*

Los Angeles
Anderson, W. French *genticist, biochemist, physician*
Baker, Robert Frank *molecular biologist, educator*
Birren, James Emmett *university research center executive*
Bok, Dean *cell biologist, educator*
Collias, Elsie Cole *zoologist*
Eisenberg, David Samuel *molecular biologist, educator*
Eiserling, Frederick Allen *microbiologist, educator*
Finch, Caleb Ellicott *neurobiologist, educator*
Gibson, Arthur Charles *biologist, educator*
Goldstein, Mark A. *zoo director*
Gordon, Malcolm Stephen *biology educator*
Langer, Glenn Arthur *cellular physiologist, educator*
Lindstedt-Siva, (Karen) June *marine biologist, oil company executive*
Lunt, Owen Raynal *biologist, educator*
Martin, Walter Edwin *biology educator*
Mockary, Peter Ernest *clinical laboratory scientist, researcher*
Mohr, John Luther *biologist, environmental consultant*
Mommaerts, Wilfried Francis Henry Maria *physiologist, educator*
Rice, Susan F. *zoological park executive*
Schopf, James William *paleobiologist*
Seto, Joseph Tobey *virologist, educator*
Smulders, Anthony Peter *biology educator*
Sonnenschein, Ralph Robert *physiologist*
Szego, Clara Marian *cell biologist, educator*
Teutsch, Champion Kurt *psycho-geneticist*
Wei, Jen Yu *physiologist, researcher, educator*
Wright, Ernest Marshall *physiologist, consultant*

Martinez
Thomas, Walter Dill, Jr. *forest pathologist, consultant*

Menlo Park
Alexander, Theron *behavioral scientist, psychologist, writer*
†Cardon, Lon Ray *geneticist researcher*
Crane, Hewitt David *science advisor*
Fuhrman, Frederick Alexander *physiology educator*
Jorgensen, Paul J. *research company executive*
MacGregor, James Thomas *toxicologist*
Oronsky, Arnold Lewis *scientific research company executive, medical educator*
Sutherland, Robert Melvin *life sciences professional, educator*
Tietjen, James *research institute administrator*

Merced
Olsen, David Magnor *science educator*

Moffett Field
†Morrison, David *science administrator*
†Munechika, Ken Kenji *research center administrator*

Monterey
Packard, Julie *aquarium administrator*

Mountain View
Lu, Wuan-Tsun *microbiologist, immunologist*

Northridge
Oppenheimer, Steven Bernard *biology educator*
Sparling, Mary Lee *biology educator*

Oakland
Whitsel, Richard Harry *biologist, entomologist*

Orinda
Bowyer, Jane Baker *science educator*

Pacific Grove
Epel, David *biologist, educator*
Powers, Dennis Alpha *biology educator*

Pacific Palisades
Lewis, Frank Harlan *botanist, educator*

Palm Desert
Sausman, Karen *zoological park administrator*

Palo Alto
Balzhiser, Richard Earl *research and development company executive*
Briggs, Winslow Russell *plant biologist, educator*
Eggers, Alfred John, Jr. *research corporation executive*
Elliott, David Duncan, III *science research company executive*
Johnson, Noble Marshall *research scientist*
Krupp, Marcus Abraham *medical research director*
Pake, George Edward *research executive, physicist*
Wiedmann, Tien-Wen Tao *medical scientist, educator*
Zuckerkandl, Emile *molecular evolutionary biologist, scientific institute executive*

Parlier
Schaefer, Charles Herbert *physiologist, educator*

Pasadena
Abelson, John Norman *biology educator*
Allman, John Morgan *neurobiology educator*
Attardi, Giuseppe M. *biology educator*
Beer, Reinhard *atmospheric scientist*
Campbell, Judith Lynn *molecular biologist educator*
Davidson, Eric Harris *molecular and developmental biologist, educator*
†Friedman, Louis Dill *association executive, aerospace engineer*
Lewis, Edward B. *biology educator*
Meyerowitz, Elliot Martin *biologist, educator*
North, Wheeler James *marine ecologist, educator*
Owen, Ray David *biology educator*
Patterson, Paul H. *biology educator, neuroscientist*
Revel, Jean-Paul *biology educator*
Rounds, Donald Edwin *cell biologist*
Stehsel, Melvin Louis *biology educator*
Wayland, J(ames) Harold *biomedical scientist, educator*

Pomona
Burrill, Melinda Jane *animal science educator*
Keating, Eugene Kneeland *animal scientist, educator*

Redwood City
Neville, Roy Gerald *scientist, chemical management and environmental consultant*

Richmond
Balakrishnan, Krishna (Balki Balakrishnan) *biotechnologist, corporate executive*
Beall, Frank Carroll *science director and educator*
Hedgpeth, Joe *molecular biologist, business executive*
Wilcox, W(ebster) Wayne *forest products pathologist, educator*
Zavarin, Eugene *forestry science educator*

Riverside
Barnes, Martin McRae *entomologist*
Bartnicki-Garcia, Salomon *microbiologist, educator*
Bergh, Berthold Orphie (Bob Bergh) *plant research scientist, human genetics educator*
Bovell, Carlton Rowland *biology educator, microbiologist*
Clegg, Michael Tran *genetics educator, researcher*
†Coggins, Charles William *plant physiology educator*
Embleton, Tom William *horticultural science educator*
Erwin, Donald Carroll *plant pathology educator*
Hall, Anthony Elmitt *plant physiologist*
Letey, John Joseph, Jr. *soil scientist, educator*
†Moore, John Alexander *biologist*
Page, Albert Lee *soil science educator, researcher*
Quinton, Paul Marquis *physiology educator*
Reuther, Walter *horticulture educator*
Sherman, Irwin William *biological sciences educator, university official*
Spencer, William Franklin, Sr. *soil scientist, researcher*
Talbot, Prue *biology educator*

Van Gundy, Seymour Dean *nematologist, plant pathologist, educator*
Zentmyer, George Aubrey *plant pathology educator*

Saint Helena
Amerine, Maynard Andrew *enologist, educator*

San Clemente
Walker, Joseph *retired research executive*

San Diego
Bieler, Charles Linford *development director, zoo executive director emeritus*
†Chory, Joanne *plant biologist*
Crick, Francis Harry Compton *research scientist, educator*
Cross, C. Michael *marine museum administrator*
Eckhart, Walter *molecular biologist, educator*
Fisher, Kathleen Mary *biology educator*
Helinski, Donald Raymond *biologist, educator*
Hemmingsen, Barbara Bruff *microbiology educator*
McGraw, Donald Jesse *biologist, historian of science, writer*
Myers, Douglas George *zoological society administrator*
Risser, Arthur Crane, Jr. *zoo administrator*
Schaechter, Moselio *microbiology educator*
Thomas, Charles Allen, Jr. *molecular biologist, educator*
Vause, Edwin Hamilton *research foundation administrator*
Zedler, Joy Buswell *ecological sciences educator*

San Francisco
Anderson, David E. *zoological park administrator*
Bibel, Debra Jan *microbiologist, immunologist*
Blackburn, Elizabeth Helen *molecular biologist*
Cape, Ronald Elliot *biotechnology company executive*
Chickering, Allen Lawrence *research institute executive*
Clements, John Allen *physiologist*
†de Hostos, Eugenio Luis *cell biologist*
Dewitt, John Belton *conservation executive*
Eschmeyer, William Neil *marine scientist*
Furst, Arthur *toxicologist, educator*
Ganong, William F(rancis) *physiologist, physician*
Garoutte, Bill Charles *neurophysiologist*
Glass, Laurel Ellen *gerontologist, developmental biologist, physician, retired educator*
Goodman, Joel Warren *microbiologist, research scientist*
Heyneman, Donald *parasitology educator*
Iacono, James Michael *research center administrator*
†Karentz, Deneb *biology educator*
†LaBudde, Samuel Freeman *biologist, environmental activist*
Lyon, David William *research executive*
McKnight, Steven Lanier *molecular biologist*
Mostov, Keith Elliot *cell biologist, educator*
†Thiers, Harry Delbert *biology educator, research mycologist*
Vyas, Girish Narmadashankar *virologist, immunohematologist*
Wetzel, Cherie Lalaine Rivers *biologist*

San Jacinto
†Jones, Marshall Edward *retired environmental educator*

San Jose
†Crommie, Michael R. *research scientist*
†Zaro, Brad A. *research company executive, biologist*

San Leandro
Earle, Sylvia Alice *research biologist, oceanographer*

San Luis Obispo
Brown, Howard C. *horticulture educator, consultant*
Jen, Joseph Jwu-Shan *food scientist, educator*

San Mateo
Potts, David Malcolm *population specialist, administrator*

San Rafael
March, Ralph Burton *retired entomology educator*

Santa Ana
Miller, Eric *zoologist*

Santa Barbara
Alldredge, Alice Louise *biological oceanography educator*
Badash, Lawrence *science history educator*
Childress, James J. *marine biologist, biological oceanographer*
Doutt, Richard Leroy *entomologist, lawyer, educator*
Kryter, Karl David *research scientist*
Philbrick, Ralph *botanist*
Schneider, Edward Lee *botanic garden administrator*
Tucker, Shirley Lois Cotter *botany educator, researcher*

Santa Cruz
Beevers, Harry *biologist*
Dasmann, Raymond Fredric *ecologist*
Langenheim, Jean Harmon *biology educator*

Santa Monica
Augenstein, Bruno W. *research scientist*
Demond, Joan *marine biologist*
Shubert, Gustave Harry *research executive, consultant, social scientist*

Santa Rosa
Sibley, Charles Gald *biologist, educator*

South San Francisco
Levinson, Arthur David *molecular biologist*
Masover, Gerald Kenneth *microbiologist*

Stanford
Atkin, J. Myron *science educator*
†Bailey, Frank Ronald *technology educator, science administrator*
Baker, Bruce S. *molecular biologist*
Banks, Peter M. *aerospace science director*
Bjorkman, Olle Erik *plant biologist, educator*
†Botstein, David *geneticist, educator*
Campbell, Allan McCulloch *bacteriology educator*

Cavalli-Sforza, Luigi Luca *genetics educator*
Cohen, Stanley Norman *geneticist, educator*
Davis, Mark M. *microbiologist, educator*
Davis, Ronald Wayne *genetics researcher, biochemistry educator*
†Ehrlich, Anne Howland *research associate*
Ehrlich, Paul Ralph *biology educator*
Falkow, Stanley *microbiologist, educator*
Fernald, Russell Dawson *biologist, researcher*
Francke, Uta *medical geneticist, genetics researcher, educator*
Ganesan, Ann Katharine *molecular biologist*
Green, Paul Barnett *biology educator*
Hanawalt, Philip Courtland *biology educator, researcher*
Heller, Horace Craig *biologist, educator*
Jones, Patricia Pearce *biologist, educator*
Long, Sharon Rugel *molecular biologist, plant biology educator*
Mooney, Harold Alfred *plant ecologist*
†Mullins, James I. *virologist, educator*
Shapiro, Lucille *molecular biology educator*
Shooter, Eric Manvers *neurobiology educator, consultant*
Spudich, James A. *biology educator*
†Tsien, Richard Winyu *biology educator*
Yanofsky, Charles *biology educator*

Stockton
McNeal, Dale William, Jr. *biological sciences educator*

The Sea Ranch
Hayflick, Leonard *microbiologist, cell biologist, gerontologist, educator, writer*

Thousand Oaks
Malmuth, Norman David *program manager*

Tiburon
Robinson, Gordon Pringle *forester*

Ventura
Arita, George Shiro *biology educator*

Watsonville
Carpenter, Philip David *laboratory administrator, environmental and organic chemist*

Westlake Village
Small, Richard David *research scientist*

Westminster
Allen, Merrill James *marine biologist*

Westwood
Brydon, Harold Wesley *entomologist, writer*

Woodland
Phan, Chuong Van *biotechnologist*
Stevens, M. Allen *geneticist, administrator*

COLORADO

Boulder
Armstrong, David Michael *biology educator*
Byerly, Radford, Jr. *science policy official*
Clifford, Steven Francis *science research director*
Danna, Kathleen Janet *virologist, plant molecular biologist, educator*
De Fries, John Clarence *behavioral genetics educator, institute administrator*
Derr, Vernon Ellsworth *government research administrator*
Glover, Fred William *artificial intelligence and optimization research director, educator*
Hanley, Howard James Mason *research scientist*
Horowitz, Isaac M. *control research consultant, writer*
†Jakosky, Bruce M. *planetary scientist*
Mc Intosh, J(ohn) Richard *biologist, educator*
Meier, Mark F. *research scientist, glaciologist, educator*
Prescott, David Marshall *biology educator*
Serafin, Robert Joseph *science center administrator, electrical engineer*
Shanahan, Eugene Miles *flow measurement instrumentation company executive*
Staehelin, Lucas Andrew *cell biology educator*

Carbondale
Cowgill, Ursula Moser *biologist, educator, environmental consultant*

Colorado Springs
Engfer, Susan Marvel *zoological park executive*
Markert, Clement Lawrence *biology educator*

Denver
†Curnow, Richard D. *biologist, research ecologist*
Freiheit, Clayton Fredric *zoo director*
Hartman, Emily Lou *botanist, educator, researcher*
Horwitz, Kathryn Bloch *molecular biologist*
Neville, Margaret Cobb *physiologist, educator*
Pfenninger, Karl H. *cell biology and neuroscience educator*
Puck, Theodore Thomas *geneticist, biophysicist, educator*
Schanfield, Moses Samuel *geneticist, educator*
Talmage, David Wilson *microbiology and medical educator, physician, former university administrator*

Durango
Steinhoff, Harold William *retired research institute executive*

Fort Collins
Altman, Jack *plant pathologist, educator*
Burns, Denver P. *forestry research administrator*
Follett, Ronald Francis *soil scientist*
Hanan, Joe John *horticulture educator*
Hecker, Richard Jacob *research geneticist*
Keim, Wayne Franklin *retired agronomy educator, plant geneticist*
†Laughlin, Charles William *agriculture educator, research administrator*
Maga, Joseph Andrew *food science educator*
Mortvedt, John Jacob *soil scientist*

Niehaus, Merle H. *agricultural educator, international agriculture consultant*
Niswender, Gordon Dean *physiologist, educator*
Ogg, James Elvis *microbiologist, educator*
Peterson, Gary Andrew *agronomics researcher*
Roos, Eric Eugene *plant physiologist*
Seidel, George Elias, Jr. *animal scientist, educator*
Smith, Dwight Raymond *ecology and wildlife educator, writer*
Smith, Ralph Earl *virologist*
Stendell, Rey *ecological research director*
Wilber, Charles Grady *forensic science educator, consultant*

Frisco
Bybee, Rodger Wayne *science education administrator*

Golden
Kazmerski, Lawrence Lee *scientist, research facility executive*
Stokes, Robert Allan *science research facility executive, physicist*

Grand Junction
Young, Ralph Alden *soil scientist, educator*

Greeley
Caffarella, Edward Philip *educational technology educator*

Livermore
Evans, Howard Ensign *entomologist, educator*

Sterling
Jackson, L. Duane *agriculturist*

Westminster
Dotson, Gerald Richard *biology educator*

CONNECTICUT

East Glastonbury
Smith, David Clark *research scientist*

East Hartford
Lundeberg, Roger Victor *inventor, scientist, writer*

Farmington
Bronner, Felix *physiologist, biophysicist, educator, painter*
Rothfield, Lawrence I. *microbiology educator*

Groton
Routien, John Broderick *mycologist*
Tassinari, Melissa Sherman *toxicologist*

Guilford
Baillie, Priscilla Woods *aquatic ecologist*

Hartford
Crawford, Richard Bradway *biologist, biochemist, educator*
†Schneider, Craig William *biology educator, research botanist*

Madison
Kilbourne, Edwin Dennis *virologist, educator*

Milford
Calabrese, Anthony *marine biologist*

Monroe
Turko, Alexander Anthony *biology educator*

Mystic
Connell, Hugh P. *aquarium executive*

New Haven
Adelberg, Edward Allen *genetics educator*
Altman, Sidney *biology educator*
†Anderson, John Frederick *science administrator, entomologist, researcher*
†Aronson, Peter Samuel *medical scientist, physiology educator*
†Bormann, Frederick Herbert *forest ecology educator*
Boulpaep, Emile Louis J. B. *physiology educator, foundation administrator*
Buss, Leo William *biologist, educator*
Chandler, William Knox *physiologist*
Cohen, Lawrence Baruch *neurobiologist, educator*
DuBois, Arthur Brooks *physiologist, educator*
Galston, Arthur William *biology educator*
Goldsmith, Mary Helen M. *biology educator*
Gordon, John Charles *forestry educator*
Hartman, Willard Daniel *marine biologist, educator*
Hoffman, Joseph Frederick *physiology educator*
Novick, Alvin *biology educator*
Rawson, Robert Orrin *physiologist*
Ruddle, Francis Hugh *genetics educator*
†Ruddle, Nancy Hartman *microbiology educator*
Sigler, Paul Benjamin *molecular biology educator, protein crystallographer*
Slayman, Carolyn Walch *geneticist, educator*
Smith, David Martyn *forestry educator*
Smith, William Hulse *forestry and environmental studies educator*
Stolwijk, Jan Adrianus Jozef *physiologist, biophysicist*
Stowe, Bruce Bernot *biology educator*
Summers, William Cofield *science educator*
Tanaka, Kay *genetics educator*
Trinkaus, John Philip *cell and developmental biologist*
Waggoner, Paul Edward *agricultural scientist*
Wagner, Günter Paul *biologist educator*
Wyman, Robert J. *biology educator, neurophysiologist, neurogeneticist*

New London
Goodwin, Richard Hale *botany educator*

Norwalk
Marnane, Joseph Peter *maritime center executive*

Southport
Hill, David Lawrence *research corporation executive*

Storrs
Hinckley, Lynn Schellig *microbiologist*
Marcus, Philip Irving *virology educator, researcher*
†Pilar, Guillermo Roman *physiology and neurobiology educator*

Storrs Mansfield
Anderson, Gregory Joseph *botanical sciences educator*
Guttay, Andrew John Robert *agronomy educator, researcher*
Koths, Jay Sanford *floriculture educator*
Laufer, Hans *developmental biologist, educator*
†Schwenk, Kurt *evolutionary biology educator*

Wallingford
†Molinoff, Perry Brown *biology educator*

West Haven
Gerritsen, Mary Ellen *vascular and cell biologist*

DELAWARE

Newark
Borgaonkar, Digamber Shankarrao *cytogeneticist, educator*
Campbell, Linzy Leon *microbiologist, educator*
Mills, George Alexander *science administrator*
Somers, George Fredrick *biology educator*

Wilmington
Hartzell, Charles R. *research administrator, biochemist, cell biologist*
†Howard, Richard James *biologist*
Kassal, Robert James *polymer research scientist*
Steinberg, Marshall *toxicologist*

Winterthur
Buchter, Thomas *horticulturist, garden director*

DISTRICT OF COLUMBIA

Washington
Abdalla, Abdalla Ahmed *agricultural educator*
Affronti, Lewis Francis, Sr. *microbiologist, educator*
Aiuto, Russell *science educators association executive*
Anderson, Donald Morgan *entomologist*
Apple, Martin Allen *scientific society executive*
Beehler, Bruce McPherson *research zoologist, ornithologist*
Bellanti, Joseph A. *microbiologist, educator*
Bergmann, Fred Heinz *genetic scientist, government official*
Bernstein, Harvey Michael *research foundation executive, engineer*
†Best, William Jennings *research scientist*
Bishop, William Peter *research scientist*
Borgiotti, Giorgio Vittorio *research scientist, engineering consultant*
Brown, Lester Russell *research institute executive*
Buffington, John Douglas *ecologist, researcher*
†Carhart, Homer W. *science administrator, safety engineer*
Case, Larry D. *agricultural education specialist*
Challinor, David *scientific institute administrator*
Coleman, Bernell *physiologist, educator*
†Colglazier, E. William *science academy administrator, physicist*
†Conway, Stuart Nelson *forestry project administrator*
Cooper-Smith, Jeffrey Paul *botanic garden administrator*
Davis, Donald Ray *entomologist*
DeGiovanni-Donnelly, Rosalie Frances *biology researcher, educator*
DeJong, Gerben *hospital research executive*
Drouilhet, Paul Raymond, Jr. *science laboratory director, electrical engineer*
Elias, Thomas Sam *botanist, author*
Eno, Amos Stewart *natural resource foundation administrator*
Falci, Kenneth Joseph *food and nutrition scientist*
Feulner, Edwin John, Jr. *research foundation executive*
Finney, Essex Eugene, Jr. *agricultural research administrator*
Fox, Laurel R. *community and population ecologist, researcher*
Frederick, Lafayette *botanist*
†Goforth, Wayne Reid *research administrator, biologist*
Goldstein, Murray *health organization official*
Grafton, Robert Bruce *science foundation official*
Gross, David Joseph *aquarium director*
†Hammonds, Timothy Merrill *scientific association executive, economist*
Harriman, Philip Darling *geneticist, science foundation executive*
Hazen, Robert Miller *research scientist, musician*
Henkin, Robert Irwin *neurobiologist, internal medicine, nutrition and neurology educator, scientific products company executive, taste and smell disease physician*
Hess, Wilmot Norton *science administrator*
Hope, William Duane *zoologist, curator*
Kennedy, Eugene Richard *microbiologist, university dean*
Koven, Joan Follin Hughes *marine biologist*
Krombein, Karl vonVorse *entomologist*
Krugman, Stanley Liebert *science administrator, geneticist*
Lilienfield, Lawrence Spencer *physiology and biophysics educator*
Little, Elbert Luther, Jr. *botanist, dendrologist*
Lorber, Mortimer *physiology educator, researcher*
Lovejoy, Thomas Eugene *tropical and conservation biologist, association executive*
Madden, Joseph Michael *microbiologist*
McGinley, Ronald James *entomologist, researcher*
Melnick, Vijaya Lakshmi *biology educator, research center director*
Meyers, Wayne Marvin *microbiologist*
Murphy, Robert Earl *scientist, government agency administrator*
Nightingale, Elena Ottolenghi *geneticist, physician, administrator*
O'Hern, Elizabeth Moot *microbiologist, writer*
O'Neil, Joseph Francis *association executive*
Podgorny, Richard Joseph *biologist, science administrator*
Post, Boyd Wallace *forester*
Pyke, Thomas Nicholas, Jr. *government science and engineering administrator*
Ralls, Katherine *zoologist*
Ritter, Donald Lawrence *environmental policy institute administrator*
Robbins, Robert John *biologist, computer scientist, educator*
Roberts, Howard Richard *food scientist, association administrator*
Robinson, Michael Hill *zoological park director, biologist*
Schad, Theodore MacNeeve *science research administrator, consultant*
Schiff, Stefan Otto *zoologist, educator*
Simpson, Michael Marcial *science specialist, consultant*
Skog, Laurence Edgar *botanist*
Sparrowe, Rollin D. *wildlife biologist*
Steinberg, Marcia Irene *science foundation program director*
Stoner, Allan L. *science foundation director*
Thomas, Jack Ward *wildlife biologist*
Tidball, M. Elizabeth Peters *educator, author*
Torrey, Barbara Boyle *research council administrator*
Train, Russell Errol *environmentalist*
Trull, Francine Sue *research foundation administrator, lobbyist*
Wasshausen, Dieter Carl *systematic botanist*
West, Robert MacLellan *science education consultant*
Wilkinson, Christopher Foster *toxicologist, educator*
Wilkinson, Ronald Sterne *science administrator, environmentalist, historian*
†Wood, Robert Winfield *science administrator, biophysicist*
Woods, Walter Ralph *animal scientist, research administrator*

FLORIDA

Boca Raton
Lucà-Moretti, Maurizio *scientist, nutrition researcher*
Reid, George Kell *biology educator, researcher, author*
Samuels, William Mason *physiology association executive*

Bonita Springs
Dacey, George Clement *retired laboratory administrator, consultant*

Bowling Green
†Klein, Philip Howard *park ranger*

Boynton Beach
Mirman, Irving R. *scientific adviser*

Bradenton
Hare, John, IV *planetarium director*
Maynard, Donald Nelson *horticulturist, educator*
Waters, Will Estel *horticulturist, researcher, educator*

Chuluota
Hatton, Thurman Timbrook, Jr. *retired horticulturist, consultant*

Clearwater
Bramante, Pietro Ottavio *physiology educator, retired pathology specialist*
Byrd, Mary Laager *life science researcher*
Whedon, George Donald *medical administrator, researcher*

Fort Pierce
Calvert, David Victor *soil science educator*

Gainesville
Agrios, George Nicholas *plant pathology educator*
Besch, Emerson Louis *physiology educator, past academic administrator*
Cantliffe, Daniel James *horticulture educator*
Childers, Norman Franklin *horticulture educator*
Dilcher, David Leonard *paleobotany educator*
Drury, Kenneth Clayton *biological scientist*
†Edwardson, John Richard *agronomist*
Gerberg, Eugene Jordan *entomologist*
Gutekunst, Richard Ralph *microbiology educator*
Hoy, Marjorie Ann *entomology educator, researcher*
Jones, Richard Lamar *entomology educator*
†Kucharek, Thomas A. *plant pathologist, educator*
Locascio, Salvadore Joseph *horticulturist*
Meredith, Julia Alice *nematologist, biologist, researcher*
Oberlander, Herbert *insect physiologist, educator*
Otis, Arthur Brooks *physiologist, educator*
†Popenoe, Hugh Llywelyn *soils educator*
Purcifull, Dan Elwood *plant virologist, educator*
Quesenberry, Kenneth Hays *agronomy educator*
Schmidt-Nielsen, Bodil Mimi (Mrs. Roger G. Chagnon) *physiologist*
Stern, William Louis *botanist, educator*
Teixeira, Arthur Alves *food engineer, consultant*
Vasil, Indra Kumar *botanist*
Wilcox, Charles Julian *geneticist, educator*
Williams, Norris Hagan, Jr. *biologist, educator, curator*

Gulf Breeze
Mayer, Foster Lee, Jr. *toxicologist*
Menzer, Robert Everett *toxicologist, educator*

Homestead
Revuelta, René Sergio *marine scientist, educator*
Roberts, Larry Spurgeon *zoologist*

Jacksonville
Bodkin, Lawrence Edward *research development company executive, gemologist, inventor*

Lake Alfred
Kender, Walter John *horticulturist, educator*
Rouseff, Russell Lee *food chemistry educator, researcher*

Lake Placid
Layne, James Nathaniel *vertebrate biologist*

Lehigh Acres
Moore, John Newton *retired natural science educator*

Longboat Key
Maha, George Edward *research facility administrator, consultant*

Melbourne
Abbott, Robert Tucker *zoologist, author*
Helmstetter, Charles Edward *microbiologist*
Storrs, Eleanor Emerett *research institute consultant*

Miami
Bezdek, Hugo Frank *scientific laboratory administrator*
Bunge, Richard Paul *cell biologist, educator*
Chavin, Walter *biological science educator and researcher*
Clark, John Russell *ecologist*
Colwin, Arthur Lentz *biologist, educator*
Correll, Helen Butts *botanist, researcher*
Hayashi, Teru *zoologist, educator*
Myrberg, Arthur August, Jr. *marine biological sciences educator*
Powers, Joseph Edward *marine biologist*
Zeiller, Warren *former aquarium executive, consultant*

Miami Beach
Abraham, William Michael *physiologist*

North Miami
Polley, Richard Donald *microbiologist, polymer chemist*

Ona
Rechcigl, Jack Edward *soil and environmental sciences educator*

Orlando
Andrews, Brad Francis *zoological park administrator*
Smith, Paul Frederick *plant physiologist, consultant*

Osprey
Cort, Winifred Mitchell *microbiologist, biochemist*

Pensacola
Loesch, Harold C. *retired marine fisheries biologist, consultant*
Ray, Donald Hensley *biologist*

Port Charlotte
Parvin, Philip E. *retired agricultural researcher and educator*

Port Manatee
Falls, William Wayne *aquaculturist*

Port Richey
Baiardi, John Charles *retired scientific laboratory director*

Quincy
Teare, Iwan Dale *agronomy educator, research scientist*

Saint Augustine
Greenberg, Michael John *biologist, research director*

Saint Petersburg
Byrd, Isaac Burlin *fishery biologist, fisheries administrator*

Sarasota
Gilbert, Perry Webster *emeritus educator*
Mahadevan, Kumar *marine laboratory director, researcher*
Seibert, Russell Jacob *botanist, research associate*

Tallahassee
Adams, James Alfred *natural science educator*
Friedmann, E(merich) Imre *biologist, educator*
Friedmann, Roseli Ocampo *microbiologist, educator*
Harris, Natholyn Dalton *food science educator, researcher*
†Koontz, Christine Miller *research faculty*
Lipner, Harry *physiologist, educator*
Makowski, Lee *science administrator, biology and chemistry educator*
Meredith, Michael *science educator, researcher*
Taylor, J(ames) Herbert *cell biology educator*

Tampa
Baker, Carleton Harold *physiology educator*
Hinsch, Gertrude Wilma *biology educator*
Lim, Daniel Van *microbiology educator*
†Salisbury, Charles A. (Lex) *zoo director, educator*

Venice
Hardenburg, Robert Earle *horticulturist*

Vero Beach
Grobman, Arnold Brams *retired biology educator and academic administrator*
Grobman, Hulda Gross (Mrs. Arnold B. Grobman) *horticulturist, retired public health educator*
Ward, William Binnington *agricultural communicator*

West Palm Beach
Freudenthal, Ralph Ira *toxicology consultant*
Sturrock, Thomas Tracy *botany educator, horticulturist*

Winter Haven
Grierson, William *retired agricultural educator*

Winter Park
Dawson, Ray Fields *research scientist, educator, consultant, tropical agriculturist*

GEORGIA

Alpharetta
Balows, Albert *microbiologist, educator*

Athens
Agosin, Moises Kankolsky *zoology educator*
Albersheim, Peter *biology educator*
Avise, John Charles *geneticist, educator*

Boyd, Louis Jefferson *agricultural scientist, educator*
Fuller, Melvin Stuart *botany educator*
Giles, Norman Henry *educator, geneticist*
Green, Frank C. *agricultural administrator*
†Lewis, A. Jefferson, III *botanical garden administrator*
Payne, William Jackson *microbiologist, educator*
Plummer, Gayther L(ynn) *climatologist, ecologist, researcher*
Van Eseltine, William Parker *microbiologist, educator*

Atlanta
Barnard, Susan Muller *zookeeper*
Circeo, Louis Joseph, Jr. *research center director, civil engineer*
Clifton, David Samuel, Jr. *research executive, economist*
Flemming, David Paul *biologist*
Humphrey, Charles Durham *microbiologist, biomedical researcher*
Jeffery, Geoffrey Marron *medical parasitologist*
Johnson, Barry Lee *public health research administrator*
La Farge, Timothy *plant geneticist*
Langdale, Noah Noel, Jr. *research educator, former university president*
Long, Leland Timothy *geophysics educator, seismologist*
Lucchesi, John Charles *genetics educator*
McGowan, John Edward, Jr. *microbiology educator*
Navalkar, Ramchandra Govindrao *microbiologist, immunologist*
Spitznagel, John Keith *microbiologist, immunologist*
Tornabene, Thomas Guy *microbiologist, researcher, administrator*

Columbus
Riggsby, Ernest Duward *science educator*

Evans
Little, Robert Colby *physiologist, educator*

Griffin
Arkin, Gerald Franklin *agricultural research administrator, educator*
Doyle, Michael Patrick *food microbiologist, educator, researcher, administrator*
Duncan, Ronny Rush *agriculturist, researcher*
Shuman, Larry Myers *soil chemist*
Wilkinson, Robert Eugene *plant physiologist*

Macon
Volpe, Erminio Peter *biologist, educator*

Norcross
Darst, Bobby Charles *soil chemist, administrator*
Dibb, David Walter *research association administrator*
Wagner, Robert Earl *agronomist*

Sapelo Island
Alberts, James Joseph *scientist, researcher*

Savannah
Eaves, George Newton *lecturer, consultant, research administrator*

Thomasville
Buckner, James Lee *forester, biologist*

Tifton
Austin, Max Eugene *horticulture educator*
Douglas, Charles Francis *agronomist*
Miller, John David *retired agronomist*
Rogers, Charlie Ellic *entomologist*

Tucker
O'Neil, Daniel Joseph *science research executive, university consultant*

Watkinsville
Langdale, George Wilfred *research soil scientist*
Wedig, John Harrison *toxicologist, consultant*

HAWAII

Haleiwa
Woolliams, Keith Richard *arboretum and botanical garden director*

Hilo
Nagao, Mike Akira *horticulturist, county administrator*

Honolulu
Abbott, Isabella Aiona *biology educator*
Ashton, Geoffrey Cyril *geneticist, educator*
Fok, Agnes Kwan *cell biologist, educator*
†Fujioka, Roger Sadao *research microbiology educator*
Hubbard, Harold Mead *research executive*
Kamemoto, Fred Isamu *zoologist*
Kamemoto, Haruyuki *horticulture educator*
Kay, Elizabeth Alison *zoology educator*
Lamoureux, Charles Harrington *botanist, arboretum administrator*
†Mandel, Morton *molecular biologist*
Sagawa, Yoneo *horticulturist, educator*
Sherman, Martin Nmi *entomologist*
Siegel, Barbara Z(enz) *biology research scientist, educator*
Smith, Albert Charles *biologist, educator*

Kailua
Blue, Steven Joshua *nutritional physiologist*

IDAHO

Aberdeen
Sparks, Walter Chappel *horticulturist, educator*

Hayden Lake
Olson, Phillip David LeRoy *agriculturist, chemist*

Island Park
Heinz, Don J. *agronomist*

Kimberly
Carter, David LaVere *soil scientist, researcher, consultant*

Moscow
Crawford, Don Lee *microbiologist*
MacFarland, Craig George *natural resource management professional*
Roberts, Lorin Watson *botanist, educator*
Scott, J(ames) Michael *research biologist*

Pocatello
McCune, Mary Joan Huxley *microbiology educator*
Seeley, Rod Ralph *physiology educator*

ILLINOIS

Argonne
Schriesheim, Alan *research administrator*

Brookfield
Pawley, Ray Lynn *zoological park herpetology curator*
Rabb, George Bernard *zoologist*

Carbondale
Bozzola, John Joseph *botany educator, researcher*
Burr, Brooks Milo *zoology educator*
Verduin, Jacob *botany educator*

Champaign
Batzli, George Oliver *ecology educator*
Espeseth, Robert D. *park and recreation planning educator*
Getz, Lowell Lee *zoology educator*
Levin, Geoffrey Arthur *botanist*
Ridlen, Samuel Franklin *agriculture educator*
Smith, Robert Lee *agriculturalist*
Sprugel, George, Jr. *ecologist*

Chicago
Altmann, Jeanne *zoologist, educator*
Altmann, Stuart Allen *biologist, educator*
Arzbaecher, Robert C(harles) *research institute executive, electrical engineer, researcher*
†Beattie, Ted Arthur *zoological gardens administrator*
Beecher, William John *zoologist, museum director*
†Bell, Kevin J. *zoological park administrator*
Buss, Daniel Frank *environmental scientist*
Chakrabarty, Ananda Mohan *microbiologist*
Charlesworth, Brian *biologist, genetics and evolution educator*
Cohen, Edward Philip *microbiology and immunology educator, physician*
Dumbacher, John Philip *evolutionary biologist*
†Ernest, J. Terry *ocular physiologist, educator*
†Esposito, Rochelle Easton *geneticist, educator*
†Fine, Beth Anne *genetic counselor, educator*
Fisher, Lester Emil *zoo administrator*
†Fozzard, Harry Allen *physiologist, cardiologist*
Fuchs, Elaine V. *molecular biologist, educator*
Fukui, Yoshio *biology educator*
Greenberg, Bernard *entomologist, educator*
Haselkorn, Robert *virology educator*
Kass, Leon Richard *life sciences educator*
†Leiden, Jeffrey Marc *molecular biologist, cardiologist*
Mahowald, Anthony Peter *geneticist, cell biologist, educator*
Mateles, Richard Isaac *biotechnologist*
McCrone, Walter Cox *research institute executive*
McKinley, Vicky Lynn *biology educator*
†Meritt, Dennis Andrew *zoo administrator*
Miller, Patrick William *research administrator, educator*
Nakajima, Yasuko *medical educator*
Overton, Jane Vincent Harper *biology educator*
Pick, Ruth *research scientist, physician, educator*
Pumper, Robert William *microbiologist*
Roizman, Bernard *virologist, educator*
Rosenberg, Robert Brinkmann *research organization executive*
Rothman-Denes, Lucia Beatriz *biology educator*
Rymer, William Zev *research scientist, administrator*
Scott, John Brooks *research institute executive*
Straus, Helen Lorna Puttkammer *biologist, educator*
Van Valen, Leigh Maiorana *biologist, educator*
Wadden, Richard Albert *environmental science educator, consultant, researcher*
†Wade, Michael John *ecology and evolution educator, researcher*
Woodruff, Teresa K. *cell biologist*

De Kalb
Zar, Jerrold H(oward) *biology educator, statistician*

Decatur
Harris, Donald Wayne *research scientist*

Des Plaines
Lee, Bernard Shing-Shu *research company executive*

Dundee
Burger, George Vanderkarr *wildlife ecologist, researcher*

Evanston
Dallos, Peter John *neurobiologist, educator*
King, Robert Charles *biologist, educator*
Novales, Ronald Richards *zoologist, educator*
†Pinto, Lawrence Henry *neurobiologist, educator*
Wu, Tai Te *biological sciences and engineering educator*

Forest Park
Orland, Frank *oral microbiologist, educator*

Glenview
†Wilcoxson, Roy Dell *plant pathology educator and researcher*

Harvey
Liem, Khian Kioe *medical entomologist*

Hines
Trimble, John Leonard *sensor psychophysicist, biomedical engineer*

Lisle
†Bingham, Carleton Dille *science administrator, chemist*
†Donnelly, Gerard Thomas *arboretum director*

Lombard
Velardo, Joseph Thomas *molecular biology and endocrinology educator*

Macomb
Anderson, Richard Vernon *ecology educator, researcher*

Maywood
Blumenthal, Harold Jay *microbiologist, educator*

Murphysboro
Miller, Donald Morton *physiology educator*

Naperville
Hauptmann, Randal Mark *molecular biologist*

Peoria
Grundbacher, Frederick John *geneticist, educator*

Springfield
Munyer, Edward A. *zoologist, museum adminstrator*

Urbana
Banwart, Wayne Lee *agronomy, environmental science educator*
Beavers, Alvin Herman *soil science educator*
Becker, Donald Eugene *animal science educator*
Bryant, Marvin Pierce *bacteriologist, microbiologist, educator*
Buck, William Boyd *toxicology educator*
Buetow, Dennis Edward *physiology educator*
Burger, Ambrose William *agronomy educator*
Chow, Poo *wood technologist, scientist*
Cole, Michael Allen *microbiologist, educator*
Crang, Richard Francis Earl *plant and cell biologist, research center administrator*
Dickinson, David Budd, Jr. *horticulture educator*
Dziuk, Philip John *animal scientist educator*
†Endress, Anton G. *horticulturist, educator*
†Everly, Jack Crittenden *agriculturist, educator*
Ford, Richard Earl *plant virologist, educator, academic administrator*
Frazzetta, Thomas H. *evolutionary biologist, functional morphologist, educator*
Friedman, Stanley *insect physiologist, educator*
Garrigus, Upson Stanley *animal science and international agriculture educator*
†Glaser, Janet H. *science administrator, biochemistry educator*
†Glawe, Dean A. *mycology educator*
Greenough, William Tallant *psychobiologist, educator*
Harlan, Jack Rodney *geneticist, emeritus educator*
Harper, James Eugene *plant physiologist*
Heichel, Gary Harold *agronomy educator*
Hixon, James Edward *physiology educator*
Hoeft, Robert Gene *agriculture educator*
Hoffmeister, Donald Frederick *zoology educator*
Horwitz, Alan Fredrick *cell and molecular biology educator*
Hymowitz, Theodore *plant geneticist, educator*
Isaacson, Richard Evan *microbiologist*
Knake, Ellery Louis *weed science educator*
Konisky, Jordan *microbiology educator*
Lodge, James Robert *dairy science educator*
Mc Glamery, Marshal Dean *agronomy, weed science educator*
Meyer, Richard Charles *microbiologist*
Nanney, David Ledbetter *genetics educator*
Ogren, William Lewis *physiologist, educator*
Prosser, C. Ladd *physiology educator, researcher*
Rebeiz, Constantin Anis *plant physiology educator*
Ricketts, Gary Eugene *animal scientist*
Seigler, David Stanley *botanist, chemist, educator*
Shurtleff, Malcolm C. *plant pathologist, consultant, educator, extension specialist*
†Sinclair, James Burton *plant pathology educator, consultant*
Sonka, Steven T. *agricultural economics educator, consultant*
Splittstoesser, Walter Emil *plant physiologist*
Stout, Glenn Emanuel *water resources center administrator*
Waldbauer, Gilbert Peter *entomologist, educator*
Whitt, Gregory Sidney *molecular phylogenetics, evolution educator*
Wolfe, Ralph Stoner *microbiology educator*

Woodstock
Kuhajek, Eugene James *chemical research executive*

INDIANA

Bloomington
Clevenger, Sarah *botanist, computer consultant*
DeVoe, Robert Donald *visual physiologist*
Gest, Howard *microbiologist, educator*
Hagen, Charles William, Jr. *botany educator*
Hammel, Harold Theodore *physiology and biophysics educator, researcher*
Hegeman, George Downing *microbiology educator*
Heiser, Charles Bixler, Jr. *botany educator*
Hites, Ronald Atlee *environmental science educator, chemist*
Mc Clung, Leland Swint *microbiologist, educator*
Nolan, Val, Jr. *biologist, lawyer*
Preer, John Randolph, Jr. *biology educator*
Ruesink, Albert William *biologist, plant sciences educator*
Weinberg, Eugene David *microbiologist, educator*
Young, Frank Nelson, Jr. *biology educator, entomologist*

Butler
Ford, Lee Ellen (Leola Ford) *scientist, educator, retired lawyer*

Crawfordsville
†Simmons, Emory G. *mycologist*

Evansville
Denner, Melvin Walter *life sciences educator*
Guthrie, Catherine S. Nicholson (Catherine S. Nicholson-Guthrie) *research scientist*

Shaw, Margery Wayne Schlamp *geneticist, physician, lawyer*

Fort Wayne
Szuhaj, Bernard Francis *food research director*

Greensburg
Ricke, David Louis *agricultural and environmental consultant*

Indianapolis
Avery, Dennis Teel *agricultural analyst*
Barman, Charles Roy *science educator*
Christian, Joe Clark *medical genetics researcher, educator*
Gehring, Perry James *toxicologist, chemical company executive*
Gibson, James Edwin *toxicologist*
Hodes, Marion Edward *genetics educator, physician*
Ochs, Sidney *neurophysiology educator*

Lafayette
†Nicholson, Ralph Lester *botanist, educator*
Stob, Martin *physiology educator*

Muncie
Hendrix, Jon Richard *biology educator*
Henzlik, Raymond Eugene *zoophysiologist, educator*
Mertens, Thomas Robert *biology educator*

New Albany
Baker, Claude Douglas *biology educator, researcher*

Notre Dame
Craig, George Brownlee, Jr. *entomologist*
Fuchs, Morton S. *biology educator*
Jensen, Richard Jorg *biology educator*
Pollard, Morris *microbiologist, educator*

West Lafayette
Allen, Durward Leon *biologist, educator*
Altman, Joseph *biological sciences educator*
Axtell, John David *genetics educator, researcher*
Barber, Stanley Arthur *agronomy educator*
†Bracker, Charles E. *plant pathology educator and researcher*
Ferris, Virginia Rogers *nematologist, educator*
Franzmeier, Donald Paul *agronomy educator, soil scientist*
Harmon, Bud Gene *animal sciences educator, consultant*
Ho, Cho-Yen *scientific research director*
Hunt, Michael O'Leary *wood science and engineering educator*
Janick, Jules *horticultural scientist, educator*
Johannsen, Chris Jakob *agronomist, educator, administrator*
Knudson, Douglas Marvin *forestry educator*
Le Master, Dennis Clyde *forest economics and policy educator*
Low, Philip Funk *soil chemistry educator, consultant, researcher*
Mannering, Jerry Vincent *agronomist, educator*
McFee, William Warren *soil scientist*
Mengel, David Bruce *agronomy and soil science educator*
Michaud, Howard Henry *conservation educator*
Nelson, Philip Edwin *food scientist, educator*
Ohm, Herbert Willis *agronomy educator*
Ortman, Eldon E. *entomologist, educator*
Schreiber, Marvin Mandel *agronomist, educator*
Sherman, Louis Allen *biologist, researcher*
White, Joe Lloyd *soil scientist, educator*

IOWA

Ames
Anderson, Lloyd Lee *animal science educator*
Berger, P(hilip) Jeffrey *animal science educator, quantitative geneticist*
Black, Charles Allen *soil scientist, educator*
Bremner, John McColl *agronomy and biochemistry educator*
Burris, Joseph Stephen *agronomy educator*
Cantrell, Ronald Paul *agronomy educator, plant breeder*
Freeman, Albert E. *agricultural science educator*
Hallauer, Arnel Roy *geneticist*
Hatfield, Jerry Lee *plant physiologist, biometeorologist*
Isely, Duane *biology and botany educator*
Johnson, Lawrence Alan *cereal technologist, educator, researcher, administrator*
Kalton, Robert Rankin *crop scientist*
Karlen, Douglas Lawrence *soil scientist*
Keeney, Dennis Raymond *soil science educator*
Kirkham, Don *soil physicist, educator*
†Moore, Kenneth James *agronomy educator*
Redmond, James Ronald *zoology educator, researcher*
Thompson, Louis Milton *agronomy educator, scientist*
Voss, Regis Dale *agronomist, educator*
Wallin, Jack Robb *research plant pathology educator*
Willham, Richard Lewis *animal science educator*
Young, Jerry Wesley *animal nutrition educator*

Cambridge
Frederick, Lloyd Randall *soil microbiologist*

Des Moines
Rogers, Rodney Albert *biologist, educator*
Rosen, Matthew Stephen *botanist, consultant*

Grinnell
Christiansen, Kenneth Allen *biologist, educator*

Iowa City
Cruden, Robert William *botany educator*
Daniels, Lacy *microbiology educator*
Hausler, William John, Jr. *microbiologist, educator, public health laboratory administrator*
Kessel, Richard Glen *zoology educator*
Milkman, Roger Dawson *genetics educator, molecular evolution researcher*
Osborne, James William *radiation biologist*
Stay, Barbara *zoologist, educator*
Wunder, Charles C(ooper) *physiology and biophysics educator, gravitational biologist*

Johnston
Duvick, Donald Nelson *plant breeder*

Muscatine
Kautz, John T. *agricultural business executive*

Waterloo
Kimm, Robert George *animal science educator*

KANSAS

Hays
Coyne, Patrick Ivan *physiological ecologist*

Kansas City
Behbehani, Abbas M. *clinical virologist, educator*
†Doull, John *toxicologist, pharmacologist*
Goldberg, Ivan D. *microbiologist, educator*
Greenwald, Gilbert Saul *physiologist*

Lawrence
Armitage, Kenneth Barclay *biology educator, ecologist*
Bovee, Eugene Cleveland *protozoologist, emeritus educator*
Byers, George William *retired entomology educator*
Haufler, Christopher Hardin *botany educator*
Johnston, Richard Fourness *biologist*
Lane, Meredith Anne *botany educator, museum director*
†Lichtwardt, Robert William *mycologist*
Michener, Charles Duncan *entomologist, biologist, educator*
Paretsky, David *microbiology educator*
Schiefelbusch, Richard L. *research administrator*

Manhattan
Barkley, Theodore Mitchell *biology educator*
Ealy, Robert Phillip *horticulture and landscape architecture educator*
Janke, Rhonda Rae *agronomist, educator*
Johnson, Terry Charles *biologist, researcher*
Kaufman, Donald Wayne *research ecologist*
Kirkham, M. B. *plant physiologist, educator*
†Posler, Gerry Lynn *agronomist, educator*
Sears, Rollin George *wheat geneticist, small grains researcher*
Vetter, James Louis *food research association administrator*

Mission
Novak, Alfred *retired biology educator*

Neosho Falls
Bader, Robert Smith *biology, zoology educator and researcher*

Parsons
Lomas, Lyle Wayne *agricultural research administrator, educator*

Salina
Piper, Jon Kingsbury *ecologist, researcher*

Shawnee Mission
Clifford, James Michael *clinical research administrator*
Goetz, Kenneth Lee *cardiovascular physiologist*

Topeka
Clarke, Gary Kendrick *zoologist*
Karr, Gerald Lee *agricultural economist, state senator*

University Of Kansas
Ashe, James S. *entomologist, educator*

KENTUCKY

Lexington
Barnhart, Charles Elmer *animal sciences educator*
Bhattacharya-Chatterjee, Malaya *cancer research scientist*
Diana, John Nicholas *physiologist*
Frye, Wilbur Wayne *soil science educator, researcher, administrator*
Grabau, Larry J. *crop physiologist, educator*
Kasperbauer, Michael John *plant physiology educator, researcher*
†Little, Charles Oran *agriculture director, animal scientist*
Mitchell, George Ernest, Jr. *animal scientist, educator*
†Nathan, Richard Arnold *research and development company executive*
Pass, Bobby Clifton *entomology educator*
Pirone, Thomas Pascal *plant pathology educator*
Reed, Michael Robert *agricultural economist*
Rodriguez, Juan Guadalupe *entomologist*
Schneider, George William *horticulturist, educator, researcher*
Shepherd, Robert James *plant pathology researcher, educator*

Louisville
Early, Glen Alan *biology educator*
Thorp, James Harrison, III *aquatic ecologist*

Richmond
Branson, Branley Allan *biology educator*

LOUISIANA

Baton Rouge
†Beckman, Joseph Alfred *research and development administrator*
Hansel, William *biology educator*
Larkin, John Montague *microbiology educator, researcher*
Liuzzo, Joseph Anthony *food science educator*
Martin, Freddie Anthony *agronomist, educator*
Patrick, William Hardy, Jr. *wetland biogeochemist, educator, laboratory director*
Remsen, James Vanderbeek, Jr. *biologist, museum curator*
Shaw, Richard Francis *fisheries administrator, oceanography educator*
Willis, Guye Henry, Jr. *soil chemist*

Boyce
Chilton, St. John Poindexter *retired plant pathology educator, farm owner*

Chauvin
Sammarco, Paul William *ecologist*

New Orleans
Beard, Elizabeth Letitia *physiologist, educator*
Bennett, Joan Wennstrom *biology educator*
Christman, John Francis *science administrator, former university administrator*
Defenbaugh, Richard Eugene *marine ecologist*
Dickinson, Catherine Schatz *microbiologist*
Fingerman, Milton *biologist, educator*
Forman, L. Ronald *park and zoological garden administrator*
Huot, Rachel Irene *cell biologist*
Ivens, Mary Sue *microbiologist, mycologist*
Navar, Luis Gabriel *physiology educator, researcher*
Orihel, Thomas Charles *parasitology educator, research scientist*
Rossowska, Magdalena Joanna *physiology educator, research scientist*
Welden, Arthur Luna *biology educator*

Shreveport
Jamison, Richard Melvin *virologist, educator*

MAINE

Alna
Herz, Michael Joseph *marine environmental scientist*

Bar Harbor
Davisson, Muriel Trask *geneticist*
Hoppe, Peter Christian *biologist, geneticist*
Paigen, Kenneth *geneticist, educator*

Brunswick
Huntington, Charles Ellsworth *biologist, educator*

Damariscotta
Hauschka, Theodore Spaeth *biologist, researcher, educator*

Lewiston
Chute, Robert Maurice *retired biologist, educator, poet*

New Vineyard
West, Arthur James, II *biologist*

Orono
Campana, Richard John *retired plant pathology educator, writer, consultant*
Clapham, William Montgomery *plant physiologist*
Knight, Fred Barrows *forester, entomologist, educator*
†Kornfield, Irv *zoology educator*

Waterville
Bennett, Miriam Frances *biologist, educator*

Wells
Neilson, Elizabeth Anastasia *health sciences educator, association executive, author, editor*

MARYLAND

Aberdeen Proving Ground
Frasier, John T. *research administrator*

Annapolis
Anderson, William Carl *association executive, environmental engineer, consultant*

Baltimore
Beemon, Karen Louise *biology educator*
Brady, Joseph Vincent *behavioral biologist, educator*
Brand, Ludwig *biology educator, biophysicist*
Brock, Mary Anne *research biologist, consultant*
Brown, Donald David *biology educator*
Edidin, Michael Aaron *biologist*
Fambrough, Douglas McIntosh, Jr. *biology educator, researcher*
Fowler, Bruce Andrew *toxicologist, marine biologist*
Gall, Joseph Grafton *biologist, researcher, educator*
Goldberg, Alan Marvin *toxicologist, educator*
Habermann, Helen Margaret *plant physiologist, educator*
Hansen, Barbara Caleen *physiology educator, scientist*
Hartman, Philip Emil *biology educator*
Huang, Ru Chih Chow *molecular biology educator*
Kelly, Thomas Jesse, Jr. *molecular biologist*
Kingsbury, David T. *microbiologist, science administrator*
Littlefield, John Walley *physiology educator, geneticist, cell biologist, pediatrician*
Nathans, Daniel *biologist*
Permutt, Solbert *physiologist, physician*
Pollard, Thomas Dean *biologist, educator*
Privalov, Peter L. *biology and biophysics educator*
†Rutledge, Brian Aaron *zoo director*
Schleif, Robert F. *biology educator*
Smith, Hamilton Othanel *molecular biologist, educator*
Stewart, Doris Mae *biology educator*
Suskind, Sigmund Richard *microbiology educator*
Trpis, Milan *vector biologist, scientist, educator*

Beltsville
Adams, Jean Ruth *entomologist*
†Chapela, Ignacio H. *biologist, researcher*
Diener, Theodor Otto *plant pathologist*
Duke, James Alan *botanist, author, consultant*
Faust, Robert McNeer *science research administrator*
Guttman, Helene Nathan *research science executive*
Hoberg, Eric Paul *parasitologist*
Marten, Gordon Cornelius *research agronomist, educator, federal agency administrator*
Murphy, Charles Franklin *agriculturist*
†Sexton, Thomas John *science administrator, research physiologist*
Shands, Henry Lee *plant geneticist, administrator*
Terrill, Clair Elman *animal scientist, geneticist, consultant*

Bethesda
†Ahmed, S. Basheer *research company executive, educator*
Bick, Katherine Livingstone *scientist, international liaison consultant*
Brady, Roscoe Owen *neurogeneticist, educator*
Brinley, F(loyd) J(ohn), Jr. *health science institution executive, physician*
Bryan, Billie Marie (Mrs. James A. Mackey) *biologist*
Butler, Sydney J. *zoological and aquarium association administrator*
Catravas, George Nicholas *biologist*
Cohen, Allan Yale *social science research administrator*
Collins, Francis S. *medical research scientist*
Dawid, Igor Bert *biologist*
Delappe, Irving Pierce *scientist, government official*
Di Paolo, Joseph Amedeo *geneticist*
Dubner, Ronald *neurobiologist*
Duma, Richard Joseph *microbiologist, physician, pathologist, researcher, educator*
Frank, Martin *physiology educator, health scientist, association executive*
Fraser, James Cavender *research center executive*
Fraumeni, Joseph F., Jr. *scientific researcher, medical educator, physician, military officer*
Gallo, Robert Charles *research scientist*
Garges, Susan *microbiologist*
Gartland, William Joseph, Jr. *research institute administrator*
Gilbert, Daniel Lee *physiologist*
Gruber, Jack *medical virologist, biomedical research administrator*
Halstead, Scott Barker *foundation administrator*
Hancock, Charles Cavanaugh, Jr. *scientific association administrator*
Harding, Fann *health scientist, administrator*
Hausman, Steven Jack *health science administrator*
Hodgdon, Harry Edward *association executive, wildlife biologist*
Holmes, Randall Kent *microbiology educator, physician, university administrator*
Horakova, Zdenka Zahutova *retired toxicologist, pharmacologist*
Jackson, Michael John *physiologist, association executive*
Jones, John Courts *wildlife biologist*
Jordan, Elke *molecular biologist, government medical research institute executive*
Keith, Jerry M. *molecular biologist*
Kelly, William Clark *science administrator*
Kety, Seymour S(olomon) *physiologist, neuroscientist*
Law, Lloyd William *geneticist*
Malone, Winfred Francis *health scientist*
†Martino, Robert Louis *computational scientist and engineer, researcher*
Miller, Louis Howard *biologist, researcher*
Moss, Bernard *virologist, researcher*
Packard, Barbara Baugh *science institute administrator, physician, physiologist*
Pastan, Ira Harry *biomedical science researcher*
Petralia, Ronald Sebastian *entomologist, neurobiologist, educator*
Pospisil, George Curtis *biomedical research administrator*
Potter, Michael *genetics researcher, medical researcher*
Purcell, Robert Harry *virologist*
Robbins, Keith Cranston *research scientist*
Robinson, David Mason *physiologist*
Rosen, Saul Woolf *research scientist, health facility administrator*
Salmoiraghi, Gian Carlo *physiologist, educator*
Sanford, Katherine Koontz *cancer researcher*
Shulman, Lawrence Edward *biomedical research administrator, rheumatologist*
Sokoloff, Louis *physiologist, neurochemist*
Sponsler, George Curtis, III *research administrator, lawyer*
Stolz, Walter Sargent *health scientist administrator*
White, Beverly J. *cytogeneticist*
Woolley, George Walter *biologist, geneticist, educator*
Wurtz, Robert Henry *physiologist, scientist*
Yamada, Kenneth Manao *cell biologist*

Chester
Pelczar, Michael Joseph, Jr. *microbiologist, educator*

Chevy Chase
Anderson, Owen Raymond *scientific and educational organization executive*
Choppin, Purnell Whittington *research administrator, virology researcher, educator*
Cowan, William Maxwell *neurobiologist*
Harter, Donald Harry *research administrator, medical educator*

Claiborne
Moorhead, Paul Sidney *geneticist*

Cockeysville
Marsik, Frederic John *microbiologist*

Cockeysville Hunt Valley
Brown, Adrienne Jean *microbiology diagnostic testing company official*

College Park
Clark, Eugenie *zoologist, educator*
Colwell, Rita Rossi *microbiologist, molecular biologist*
Fanning, Delvin Seymour *soil science educator*
†Gantt, Elisabeth *botany educator and researcher*
Gouin, Francis Romeo *physiologist*
Heath, James Lee *food science educator, researcher*
Miller, Alan Stanley *ecology center administrator, law educator*
Miller, Raymond Jarvis *agronomy educator*
Patterson, Glenn Wayne *botany educator*
Popper, Arthur N. *zoology educator*
Quebedeaux, Bruno *horticulture educator*
Stark, Francis C., Jr. *horticulturist, educator*
Vandersall, John Henry *dairy science educator*
Weil, Raymond Richard *soil scientist*

Columbia
Keeton, Morris Teuton *research institute director*

Frederick
Housewright, Riley Dee *microbiologist, former society executive*
Lewis, Robert Alan *biologist, physiologist, environmental scientist, researcher, educator, administrator, author*
Rice, Jerry Mercer *medical research center administrator*
Vande Woude, George Franklin *molecular biologist, cancer researcher*

Gaithersburg
Buckley, Gerard Duke *science facility administrator*
Semerjian, Hratch Gregory *research and development executive*

Galena
Haenlein, George Friedrich Wilhelm *dairy scientist, educator*

Garrett Park
Baldwin, Calvin Benham, Jr. *retired medical research administrator*

Greenbelt
†Krulisch, Lee *science facility administrator*

Hancock
Popenoe, John *horticultural consultant, retired botanical garden administrator*

Kensington
Jackson, William David *research executive*

Laurel
Ellis, David H. *biologist, research behaviorist*
Robbins, Chandler S(eymour) *research biologist*

Libertytown
Lindblad, Richard Arthur *health services administrator, drug abuse epidemiologist*

Potomac
Bollum, Frederick James *biotechnology executive*

Riverdale
Ahl, Alwynelle Self *zoology, ecology and veterinary medical executive*

Rockville
†Gordis, Enoch *science administrator, internist*
Gougé, Susan Cornelia Jones *microbiologist*
Landon, John Campbell *medical research company executive*
Mertz, Walter *retired government research executive*
Poljak, Roberto J(uan) *research director, biotechnology educator*
Rafajko, Robert Richard *medical research company executive*

Salisbury
Moultrie, Fred *geneticist*

Silver Spring
Hanson, Angus Alexander *geneticist*
Kohler, Max Adam *consulting hydrologist, weather service administrator*
Leedy, Daniel Loney *ecologist*
Phillips, Craig *aquarium administrator*

Sykesville
Buck, John Bonner *retired biologist*

Temple Hills
Whidden, Stanley John *physiologist, physician*

MASSACHUSETTS

Amherst
Belt, Edward Scudder *sedimentologist, educator*
Coppinger, Raymond Parke *biologist, educator*
Godfrey, Paul Joseph *science foundation director*
Hillel, Daniel *soil physics and hydrology educator, researcher, consultant*
Holmes, Francis William *plant pathologist*
McNeal, Ann P. Woodhull *physiology professor*
Palser, Barbara F. *botany researcher, retired educator*
Rohde, Richard A. *plant pathologist educator*
Stein, Otto Ludwig *botany educator*
Tippo, Oswald *botanist, educator, university administrator*

Bedford
Griffin, Donald R(edfield) *zoology educator*
Taylor, C(harles) Richard *biological sciences educator*

Beverly
Roberts, Richard John *molecular biologist*

Billerica
Kolb, Charles Eugene *research corporation executive*

Boston
Barger, A(braham) Clifford *physiology educator*
Broitman, Selwyn Arthur *microbiologist, educator*
†Coffin, John Miller *molecular biologist, educator*
Cohen, Jonathan Brewer *molecular neurobiologist, biochemist*
Davison, Peter Fitzgerald *retired science administrator, consultant*
Essex, Myron Elmer *microbiology educator*
Faller, Douglas V. *cancer research scientist, physician*
Gibbons, Ronald John *microbiologist, educator*
Green, Howard *cellular physiologist, educator, administrator*
Hornig, Donald Frederick *scientist*
Hubel, David Hunter *physiologist, educator*
Kahn, Carl Ronald *research laboratory administrator*
Kunkel, Louis Martens *research scientist, educator*
Lanner, Michael *research administrator, consultant*

Lees, Sidney *research facility administrator, bioengineering educator*
Malamy, Michael Howard *molecular biology and microbiology educator*
Park, James Theodore *microbiologist, educator*
Peterson, Roger Tory *ornithologist, artist*
Prescott, John Hernage *aquarium executive*
Prior, Ronald L. *animal scientist, nutritionist*
Sager, Ruth *geneticist*
Slechta, Robert Frank *biologist, educator*
Strauss, Phyllis R. *biology educator*
†Tosteson, Daniel Charles *physiologist, medical school dean*

Cambridge
Allen, Lew, Jr. *laboratory executive, former air force officer*
Ashton, Peter Shaw *tropical forest science educator*
Baltimore, David *microbiologist, educator*
Bazzaz, Fakhri A. *plant biology educator, administrator*
Beranek, Leo Leroy *scientific foundation executive, acoustical design consultant*
Berg, Howard C. *biology educator*
Bogorad, Lawrence *biologist*
Boss, Kenneth Jay *biology educator, museum curator*
Branton, Daniel *biology educator*
†Buchwald, Jed Zachary *science history educator*
Cook, Robert Edward *plant ecology researcher, educator*
Cumings, Edwin Harlan *biology educator*
Demain, Arnold Lester *microbiologist, educator*
Dowling, John Elliott *biology educator*
Einsweiler, Robert Charles *research director*
Erikson, Raymond Leo *biology educator*
Fink, Gerald Ralph *geneticist, biochemist*
Forman, Richard T. T. *ecology educator*
Fox, Maurice Sanford *molecular biologist, educator*
Gage, (Leonard) Patrick *research company executive*
Gilbert, Walter *molecular biologist, educator*
Goldberg, Ray Allan *agribusiness educator*
Goldblith, Samuel Abraham *food science educator*
Goldman, Ralph Frederick *research physiologist, educator*
Griffin, Robert G. *chemistry administrator*
Hartl, Daniel Lee *genetics educator*
Hastings, John Woodland *biologist, educator*
Horvitz, Howard Robert *biology educator, researcher*
Hubbard, Ruth *biology educator*
Hynes, Richard Olding *biology educator*
Jacobson, Ralph Henry *laboratory executive, former air force officer*
King, Jonathan Alan *molecular biology educator*
Knoll, Andrew Herbert *biology educator*
†Lander, Eric S. *biologist, educator*
Lerman, Leonard Solomon *science educator, scientist*
Levi, Herbert Walter *biologist, educator*
Levins, Richard *science educator*
Liem, Karel Frederik *biologist, educator*
Lodish, Harvey Franklin *biologist, educator*
Lynch, Harry James *biologist*
Magee, John Francis *research company executive*
Maniatis, Thomas Peter *molecular biology educator*
Mayr, Ernst *emeritus zoology educator, author*
McMahon, Thomas Arthur *biology and applied mechanics educator*
Mendelsohn, Everett Irwin *science educator*
Mitchell, Ralph *microbiologist*
Pardue, Mary Lou *biology educator*
Penman, Sheldon *biology educator*
Pfister, Donald Henry *biology educator*
Pierce, Naomi Ellen *biology educator, researcher*
Rich, Alexander *molecular biologist, educator*
Robbins, Phillips Wesley *biology educator*
Schultes, Richard Evans *ethnobotanist, museum executive, educator, conservationist*
†Shieber, Stuart Merrill *natural sciences educator*
Shultz, Leila McReynolds *botanist, educator*
Signer, Ethan Royal *biology educator*
Sinskey, Anthony John *microbiology educator*
Solbrig, Otto Thomas *population biologist, educator*
†Steller, Hermann *neurobiologist, educator*
Tanaka, Toyoichi *science educator*
Tannenbaum, Steven Robert *toxicologist, chemist*
Tonegawa, Susumu *biology educator*
Torriani-Gorini, Annamaria *microbiologist*
Tsipis, Kosta Michael *science educator*
Walker, Graham Charles *biology educator*
Wilson, Edward Osborne *biologist, educator*
Wogan, Gerald Norman *toxicology educator*
Wurtman, Judith Joy *research scientist*

Canton
Lyman, Charles Peirson *comparative physiologist*

Grafton
Haggerty, John Edward *research center administrator, former army officer*

Great Barrington
Stonier, Tom *educator, author*

Lexington
Fillios, Louis Charles *retired science educator*
Gibbs, Martin *biologist, educator*
Melngailis, Ivars *solid state research executive*
Stern, Ernest *science research executive, electrical engineer*

Lincoln
Holberton, Philip Vaughan *biotechnology company executive*

Lowell
Coleman, Robert Marshall *biology educator*

North Falmouth
Morse, Robert Warren *research administrator*

Northampton
Burk, Carl John *biological sciences educator*
Munson, Richard Howard *horticulturist*
Olivo, Margaret Ellen Anderson (Margaret Ellen Anderson) *physiologist, educator*

Norwood
Pence, Robert Dudley *biomedical research administrator, hospital administrator*

Quincy
Hagar, William Gardner, III *photobiology educator*

Shrewsbury
Pederson, Thoru Judd *biologist, research institute director*

Somerville
Wong, Po Kee *research company executive, educator*

South Hadley
Townsend, Jane Kaltenbach *zoologist, educator*

Vineyard Haven
Billingham, Rupert Everett *zoologist, educator*

Waltham
Decker, C(harles) David *research and development executive*
†Galinat, Walton C. *research scientist*
Ganong, William Francis, III *speech sciences research executive*
Gerety, Robert John *microbiologist, pharmaceutical company executive, pediatrician, vaccinologist*
Huxley, Hugh Esmor *molecular biologist, educator*
Levitan, Irwin Barry *neuroscience educator, academic administrator*
†Rufeh, Firooz *energy research firm administrator*
Schiff, Jerome Arnold *biologist, educator*

Watertown
El-Bisi, Hamed Mohamed *scientist*

West Falmouth
Vaccaro, Ralph Francis *marine biologist*

Westborough
Nichols, Guy Warren *institute executive, former utilities executive*

Williamstown
Art, Henry Warren *biology educator*
†Lovett, Charles M. *genetics educator*

Woburn
Gelb, Arthur *science association executive, electrical and systems engineer*

Woods Hole
Ballard, Robert Duane *marine scientist*
Burris, John Edward *biologist*
Copeland, Donald Eugene *research marine biologist*
Ebert, James David *research biologist, educator*
Grice, George Daniel *marine biologist, science administrator*
Inoué, Shinya *microscopy and cell biology scientist, educator*
Woodwell, George Masters *ecologist, educator, author, lecturer*

Worcester
Bagshaw, Joseph Charles *molecular biologist, educator*

Yarmouth Port
Stauffer, Robert Allen *former research company executive*

MICHIGAN

Ann Arbor
Allen, Sally Lyman *biologist*
Anderson, William R. *botanist, educator, curator, director*
Beeton, Alfred Merle *laboratory director, limnologist, educator*
Bryant, Barbara Everitt *academic researcher, market research consultant, former federal agency administrator*
Cantrall, Irving J(ames) *entomologist, educator*
Davenport, Horace Willard *physiologist*
Dawson, William Ryan *zoology educator*
Easter, Stephen Sherman, Jr. *biology educator*
Evans, Francis Cope *ecologist*
Faulkner, John Arthur *physiologist, educator*
Gans, Carl *zoologist, educator*
Gelehrter, Thomas David *medical and genetics educator, physician*
Ginsburg, David *human genetics educator, researcher*
Goad, Linda May *research scientist*
Gray, Robert Howard *toxicology educator, researcher*
Hawkins, Joseph Elmer, Jr. *retired acoustic physiologist, educator*
Horowitz, Samuel Boris *biomedical researcher, educational consultant*
Kaufman, Peter Bishop *biological sciences educator*
Kleinsmith, Lewis Joel *cell biologist, educator*
Kostyo, Jack Lawrence *physiology educator*
Losada, Marcial Francisco *research scientist, psychologist*
Lowe, John Burton *molecular biology educator, pathologist*
Moore, Thomas E. *biology educator, museum director*
Neidhardt, Frederick Carl *microbiologist*
Richardson, Rudy James *toxicology and neurosciences educator*
Savageau, Michael Antonio *microbiology and immunology educator*
Shappirio, David Gordon *biologist, educator*
Steiner, Erich Ernst *botany educator*
†Stoermer, Eugene Filmore *biologist, educator*
Vesecky, John F. *science educator, electrical engineering educator, researcher*
Wagner, Warren Herbert, Jr. *botanist, educator*
Williams, John Andrew *physiology educator, consultant*
Yocum, Charles Fredrick *biology educator*
†Zhou, Xiaoyuan *paleobiologist, researcher*

Big Rapids
Barnes, Isabel Janet *microbiology educator, college dean*

Dearborn
Schneider, Michael Joseph *biologist*

Detroit
Jeffries, Charles Dean *microbiology educator, scientist*
Krawetz, Stephen Andrew *molecular biology and genetics educator*
Lerner, Stephen Alexander *microbiologist, physician, educator*
†Macoska, Jill Anne *urology and cancer biology educator, researcher*
Miller, Dorothy Anne Smith *cytogenetics educator*
Novak, Raymond Francis *research institute director, pharmacology educator*
Phillis, John Whitfield *physiologist, educator*
Tunac, Josefino Ballesteros *biotechnology administrator*

East Lansing
Bergen, Werner Gerhard *animal science educator, nutritionist*
Bukovac, Martin John *horticulturist, educator*
Butcher, James Walter *biologist*
Dennis, Frank George, Jr. *horticulture educator*
Dilley, David Ross *plant physiologist, researcher*
Fischer, Lawrence Joseph *toxicologist, educator*
Fluck, Michele M(arguerite) *biology educator*
Fromm, Paul Oliver *physiology educator*
Gast, Robert Gale *agriculture educator, experiment station administrator*
Gerhardt, Philipp *microbiologist, educator*
Hackel, Emanuel *science educator*
Hildebrand, Verna Lee *human ecology educator*
Hull, Jerome, Jr. *horticultural extension specialist*
†Kamrin, Michael Arnold *toxicology educator*
Kende, Hans Janos *plant physiology educator*
Kevern, Niles Russell *aquatic ecologist, educator*
†Lacy, Melvyn Leroy *plant pathology educator and reseacher*
Lockwood, John LeBaron *plant pathologist*
Lucas, Robert Elmer *soil scientist*
Lund, Lois A. *food science and human nutrition educator*
McMeekin, Dorothy *botany, plant pathology educator*
Nelson, Ronald Harvey *animal science educator, researcher*
Ohlrogge, John B. *botany and plant pathology educator*
Patterson, Maria Jevitz *microbiology-pediatric infectious disease educator*
Ries, Stanley K. *plant physiologist, university educator*
Root-Bernstein, Robert Scott *biologist, educator*
Sparks, Harvey Vise, Jr. *physiologist*
Tesar, Milo Benjamin *agricultural researcher and educator*
Tiedje, James Michael *microbiology educator, ecologist*
Velicer, Leland Frank *veterinarian, microbiologist, virologist, educator*

Grand Rapids
†Lewis, John Robert *zoo administrator*

Hickory Corners
Lauff, George Howard *biologist*

Kalamazoo
Marshall, Vincent de Paul *industrial microbiologist, researcher*

Rochester
Unakar, Nalin Jayantilal *biological sciences educator*

Ypsilanti
Caswell, Herbert Hall, Jr. *retired biology educator*

MINNESOTA

Apple Valley
†Seal, Ulysses S. *animal scientist*

Duluth
Heller, Lois Jane *physiologist, educator, researcher*
Johnson, Arthur Gilbert *microbiology educator*

Mapleton
John, Hugo Herman *natural resources educator*

Marcell
Aldrich, Richard John *agronomist, educator*

Minneapolis
Dworkin, Martin *microbiologist, educator*
Gorham, Eville *science educator*
Grim, Eugene Donald *physiology educator*
Haase, Ashley Thomson *microbiology educator, scientist*
†Howe, Craig Walter Sandell *medical organization executive, internist*
Kallok, Michael John *physiologist, research administrator*
Meyer, Maurice Wesley *physiologist, dentist, neurologist*
Olson, Theodore Alexander *former environmental biology educator*
Rahman, Yueh-Erh *biologist*
Reynolds, David G(eorge) *physiologist, educator*
Tufte, Obert Norman *retired research executive*
Watson, Dennis Wallace *microbiology educator, scientist*

Moorhead
Gee, Robert LeRoy *agriculturist, dairy farmer*

Morris
Ordway, Ellen *biology educator, entomology researcher*

Northfield
Burton, Alice Jean *biology educator*

Park Rapids
Tonn, Robert James *entomologist*

Rochester
Shepherd, John Thompson *physiologist*
Szurszewski, Joseph Henry *physiologist*
Wood, Earl Howard *physiologist, educator*

Saint Cloud
†Thrune, Elaine M. *biotechnician*

Saint Paul
Baker, Donald Gardner *retired soil science educator*
Barnwell, Franklin Hershel *zoology educator*
Burnside, Orvin Charles *agronomy educator, researcher*
Bushnell, William Rodgers *agricultural research scientist*
Caldwell, Elwood Fleming *food science educator, researcher, editor*
Cheng, H(wei) H(sien) *soil scientist, agriculture and environmental scie*
Chiang, Huai Chang *entomologist, educator*
Crookston, Robert Kent *agronomy educator*
Davis, Margaret Bryan *paleoecology researcher, educator*
Ek, Alan Ryan *forestry educator*
Enfield, Franklin D. *geneticist*
Herman, William Sparkes *zoology educator*
Kommedahl, Thor *plant pathology educator*
Leonard, Kurt John *plant pathologist, university program director*
Magee, Paul Terry *geneticist and molecular biologist, college dean*
McKinnell, Robert Gilmore *zoology, genetics and cell biology educator*
McLaughlin, David Jordan *botanist*
Morrow, Patrice Ann *biology educator*
Phillips, Ronald Lewis *plant geneticist, educator*
Schafer, John Francis *plant pathologist*
Stadelmann, Eduard Joseph *plant physiologist, educator*
Tate, Jeffrey L. *biology institute administrator*
Tester, John Robert *biologist, educator*
Tordoff, Harrison Bruce *retired zoologist, educator*
Wendt, Hans W. *life scientist*
Zeyen, Richard John *plant pathology educator*

MISSISSIPPI

Jackson
Hutchison, William Forrest *parasitologist, educator*

Lorman
†Williams, Richard, Jr. *animal scientist*

Meridian
Blackwell, Cecil *science association executive*

Mississippi State
Dorough, H. Wyman *toxicologist, educator, consultant*
†Reddy, Kambham Raja *plant physiology educator*
Thompson, Warren S. *forestry educator, university dean*
†White, Charles H. *food science and technology educator*

Oxford
Foster, George Rainey *soil erosion research scientist*

Picayune
Pardue, Larry G. *botanical garden administrator, educator*

Poplarville
Edwards, Ned Carmack, Jr. *agronomist, university program director*

Stennis Space Center
Baker, Robert Andrew *environmental research scientist*

Stoneville
Hardee, D. D. *laboratory director, research program leader*
Ranney, Carleton David *plant pathology researcher, administrator*

University
Keiser, Edmund Davis, Jr. *biologist, educator*
Kushlan, James A. *biology educator*

Vicksburg
Mather, Bryant *research administrator*

West Point
Vicks, JoAnn *biology educator*

MISSOURI

Blue Springs
†Yahn-Kramer, Bettie Lynn *forester, horticulturist*

Cape Girardeau
Blackwelder, Richard E(liot) *entomologist, zoology educator, archivist*

Columbia
Blevins, Dale Glenn *agronomy educator*
Blount, Don H. *physiology educator*
Brown, Olen Ray *medical microbiology research educator*
Burdick, Allan Bernard *geneticist*
Calabrese, Diane Marie *entomologist, writer*
Coe, Edward Harold, Jr. *geneticist, agronomist, educator*
Darrah, Larry Lynn *plant breeder*
Davis, James O(thello) *physician, educator*
Duncan, Donald Pendleton *retired forestry educator*
Finkelstein, Richard Alan *microbiologist*
Ignoffo, Carlo Michael *insect pathologist-virologist*
Lambeth, Victor Neal *horticulturist, researcher*
Martin, Mark Edward *molecular biologist, biochemist*
Mc Ginnes, Edgar Allen, Jr. *forestry educator*
Mitchell, Roger Lowry *agronomy educator*
Novacky, Anton Jan *plant pathologist, educator*
Poehlmann, Carl John *agronomist, researcher*
†Schoettger, Richard A. *physiologist, marine biology researcher, science administrator*
Yanders, Armon Frederick *biological sciences educator, research administrator*

Eureka
Coles, Richard W(arren) *biology educator, research administrator*
†Lindsey, Susan Lyndaker *zoologist*

Jefferson City
Reidinger, Russell Frederick, Jr. *fish and wildlife scientist*

Kansas City
Cook, Mary Rozella *psychophysiologist*
Hagsten, Ib *animal scientist, educator*
†Leikam, Dale Francis *agronomist*
Mc Kelvey, John Clifford *research institute executive*
†Wourms, Mark Kenneth *zoological park director*

Saint Charles
Radke, Rodney Owen *agricultural research executive*

Saint Louis
Allen, Garland Edward *biology educator, science historian*
Asa, Cheryl Suzanne *biologist*
Baile, Clifton A. *biologist, researcher*
†Crawford, Walter Clyde, Jr. *ornithologist*
Curran, Michael Walter *scientist*
Curtiss, Roy, III *biology educator*
Ewan, Joseph (Andorfer) *botanist, biohistorian, research bibliographer*
Feir, Dorothy Jean *entomologist, physiologist, educator*
Green, Maurice *molecular biologist, virologist, educator*
Hamburger, Viktor *retired biology educator*
Hoessle, Charles Herman *zoo director*
Laskowski, Leonard Francis, Jr. *microbiologist*
†Nichols, Colin Graham *bioscience educator*
†Phillips, Oliver *botany educator*
Raven, Peter Hamilton *botanical garden director, botany educator*
Sexton, Owen James *vertebrate ecology educator, conservationist*
Stahl, Philip Damien *physiology and cell biology educator*
†Stevens, Warren Douglas *botanist*
Templeton, Alan Robert *biology educator*
Varner, Joseph Elmer *biology educator, researcher*

MONTANA

Bozeman
Hovin, Arne William *agronomist, educator*
†Lavin, Matthew T. *horticultural educator*
Onsager, Jerome Andrew *research entomologist*
Pittendrigh, Colin Stephenson *retired biologist, educator*
Todd, Kenneth S., Jr. *parasitologist, educator*

Butte
†De Voe, Irving Woodrow *microbiologist, educator*

Corvallis
Koch, Peter *wood scientist*

Hamilton
Garon, Claude Francis *laboratory administrator, researcher*
Munoz, John Joaquin *research microbiologist*
Rudbach, Jon Anthony *biotechnical company executive*

Helena
Opitz, John Marius *clinical geneticist, pediatrician*

Miles City
Heitschmidt, Rodney Keith *rangeland ecologist*

Missoula
Jenni, Donald Alison *zoology educator*
Nakamura, Mitsuru James *microbiologist, educator*
Wright, Barbara Evelyn *microbiologist*

Polson
Flamm, Barry Russell *ecologist*
Stanford, Jack Arthur *biological station administrator*

Red Lodge
Kauffman, Marvin Earl *geoscience consultant*

NEBRASKA

Clay Center
Laster, Danny Bruce *animal scientist*

Gering
Weihing, John Lawson *plant pathologist, state senator*

Humboldt
Rumbaugh, Melvin Dale *geneticist, agronomist*

Lincoln
Adams, Charles Henry *retired animal scientist, educator*
Francis, Charles Andrew *agronomy educator, consultant*
Gardner, Charles Olda *plant geneticist and breeder, design consultant, analyst*
Genoways, Hugh Howard *biologist*
Hanway, Donald Grant *retired agronomist, educator*
Johnson, Virgil Allen *retired agronomist*
Jones, Alice Jane *soil scientist, educator, federal agency administrator*
Massengale, Martin Andrew *agronomist, university president*
McClurg, James Edward *research laboratory executive*
Morris, M(ary) Rosalind *cytogeneticist, educator*
Sander, Donald Henry *soil scientist, researcher*
†Schepers, James Stuart *soil scientist*
Schmidt, John Wesley *agronomy educator*
Swartzendruber, Dale *soil physicist, educator*
Taylor, Stephen Lloyd *food toxicology educator*
Thorson, Thomas Bertel *zoologist, educator*

Omaha
Andrews, Richard Vincent *physiologist, educator*
Badeer, Henry Sarkis *physiology educator*
Dubes, George Richard *geneticist*
†Maher, L. James, III *molecular biologist*
Simmons, Lee Guyton, Jr. *zoological park director*

NEVADA

Las Vegas
Hess, John Warren *scientific institute administrator, educator*
Pridham, Thomas Grenville *research microbiologist*

North Las Vegas
†Whiteman, Steven *science adminstrator*

Reno
Bohmont, Dale Wendell *agricultural consultant*
Fox, Carl Alan *research institute executive*
Johnson, Arthur William, Jr. *planetarium executive*

NEW HAMPSHIRE

Durham
Aber, John David *global ecosystem research adminstrator*
Harter, Robert Duane *soil scientist, educator*
Pistole, Thomas Gordon *microbiology educator, researcher*

Hanover
Flaccus, Edward *retired biology educator*
Lubin, Martin *cell physiologist educator*
Roos, Thomas Bloom *biological scientist, educator*
Spiegel, Evelyn Sclufer *biology educator, researcher*
Spiegel, Melvin *retired biology educator*

Lebanon
Mc Cann, Frances Veronica *physiologist, educator*
Munck, Allan Ulf *physiologist, educator*

New Castle
Stevenson, Robert Edwin *microbiologist, culture collection executive*

Sanbornton
Andrews, Henry Nathaniel, Jr. *botanist, scientist, educator*

Silver Lake
Pallone, Adrian Joseph *research scientist*

NEW JERSEY

Annandale
Rosensweig, Ronald Ellis *research scientist*

Camden
Kirk, James Robert *research development and quality assurance executive*

Chatham
Gonzalez, Efren William *science information services administrator*

East Brunswick
Chang, Stephen S. *food scientist, educator, researcher, inventor*

East Hanover
Nemecek, Georgina Marie *molecular pharmacologist*

Fairfield
Prince, Daniel Lloyd *molecular biologist, virologist, validation scientist, industrial microbiologist, computer network administrator, consultant*

Florham Park
Eidt, Clarence Martin, Jr. *research and development executive*

Fort Lee
Manniello, John Baptiste Louis *research scientist*

Highland Park
Green, James Weston *educator, physiologist*

Hoboken
Abel, Robert Berger *science administrator*

Jamesburg
Chase, Aurin Moody, Jr. *biology educator*

Madison
Campbell, William Cecil *biologist*

Montvale
Bowman, Patricia Imig *microbiologist*

Mount Arlington
Cohen, Irving David *science administrator*

Neptune
Axelrod, Herbert Richard *ichthyologist, publishing executive*

New Brunswick
Ballou, Janice Marie *research director*
Day, Peter Rodney *geneticist, educator*
Ehrenfeld, David William *biology educator, author*
Funk, Cyril Reed, Jr. *agronomist, educator*
Gupta, Ayodhya Prasad *entomologist, immunologist, cell biologist*
Hayakawa, Kan-Ichi *food science educator*
Lachance, Paul Albert *food science educator, clergyman*
Maramorosch, Karl *virologist, educator*
Psuty, Norbert Phillip *marine sciences educator*
Solberg, Myron *food scientist, educator*
Tedrow, John Charles Fremont *soils educator*

New Providence
Mitchell, James Winfield *science administrator*

Newark
Beyer-Mears, Annette *physiologist*
Chinard, Francis Pierre *physiologist, physician*
Jakubowski, Hieronim *biochemistry educator*
Weis, Judith Shulman *biology educator*

Paramus
†Gunther, Timothy *zoo director*

Piscataway
Denhardt, David Tilton *molecular and cell biology educator*
Liu, Alice Yee-Chang *biology educator*
Messing, Joachim Wilhelm *molecular biology educator*
Passmore, Howard Clinton, Jr. *geneticist, biological sciences educator*
Pramer, David *microbiologist, educator, research administrator*
Schlesinger, Robert Walter *microbiologist, microbiology educator emeritus*
Witkin, Evelyn Maisel *geneticist*

Princeton
Broach, James Riley *molecular biology educator*
Cole, Nancy Stooksberry *educational research executive*
Cox, Edward Charles *biology educator*
Fernandes, Prabhavathi Bhat *molecular biologist*
Flint, Sarah Jane *molecular biologist, educator*
Gould, James L. *biology educator*
Grant, Peter Raymond *biologist, researcher, educator*
Harford, James Joseph *retired aerospace association executive*
Horn, Henry Stainken *biology educator*
†Jacobs, William Paul *botanist, educator*
Levine, Arnold Jay *molecular biology educator, researcher*
Merrill, Leland Gilbert, Jr. *retired environmental science educator*
Morrill, William Ashley *research executive*
Seizinger, Bernd Robert *molecular geneticist, physician, researcher*
Shenk, Thomas Eugene *molecular biology educator*
Silhavy, Thomas Joseph *molecular biology educator*
Steinberg, Malcolm Saul *biologist, educator*
Tilghman, Shirley Marie *biology educator*
Weinmann, Roberto *molecular biologist, educator*

Rahway
Linemeyer, David Lee *molecular biologist*
Reynolds, Glenn Franklin *medicinal research scientist*
†Scolnick, Edward Mark *science administrator*

Somerville
Grant, Robert James *animal nutritional research manager*

Stockton
Kent, George Cantine, Jr. *zoology educator*

Tenafly
Kronenwett, Frederick Rudolph *microbiologist*

Teterboro
Gambino, S(alvatore) Raymond *medical laboratory executive, educator*

Wayne
White, Doris Gnauck *science educator, biochemical and biophysics researcher*

NEW MEXICO

Albuquerque
Corliss, John Ozro *zoology educator*
Findley, James Smith *biology and zoology educator, museum director*
†Henderson, Rogene Faulkner *toxicologist, researcher*
Hsi, David Ching Heng *plant pathologist and geneticist, educator*
Moore, John Ashton *zoo director*
Narath, Albert *laboratory administrator*
Newsom, Melvin Max *retired research company executive*
Rosenberg, Arthur James *research science company executive*
Sanchez, Victoria Wagner *science educator*
Ward, Charles Richard *extension and research entomologist, educator*

Carlsbad
Cooper, Richard *zoological park administrator*

Las Cruces
Kilmer, Neal Harold *physical scientist*
Schemnitz, Sanford David *wildlife biology educator*

Los Alamos
†Gancarz, Alexander John *science administrator, research chemist*
Gregg, Charles Thornton *research company executive*
†McComas, David John *science administrator, space physicist*

NEW YORK

Albany
Hitchcock, Karen Ruth *biology educator, university dean, academic administrator*
†Schmidt, John Thomas *neurobiologist*
Stewart, Margaret McBride *biology educator, researcher*
Tieman, Suzannah Bliss *neurobiologist*

Annandale On Hudson
Kiviat, Erik *ecologist, administrator, educator*

Bedford Hills
Marshall, William Emmett *biotechnology company executive, biochemistry researcher*

Briarcliff Manor
Callahan, Daniel John *institute director*

Bronx
Bloom, Barry R. *microbiologist, immunologist, educator*
Conway, William Gaylord *zoologist, zoo director, conservationist*
Forero, Enrique *botanical garden research director*
Lattis, Richard Lynn *zoo director*
Lilly, Frank *oncogenetic biomedical researcher*
Schaller, George Beals *zoologist*
Stanley, Pamela Mary *cell biologist*
Waelsch, Salome Gluecksohn *geneticist, educator*

Bronxville
Hutchison, Dorris Jeannette *retired microbiologist, educator*

Brooklyn
Altura, Burton Myron *physiologist, educator*
Carswell, Lois Malakoff *botanical gardens executive, consultant*
Forest, Charlene Lynn *cell biologist, educator*
Gabriel, Mordecai Lionel *biologist, educator*
Gootman, Phyllis Myrna *educator*
Jacobson, Leslie Sari *biologist, educator*
Pagala, Murali Krishna *physiologist*
Schiffman, Gerald *microbiologist, educator*
Scholtz, Elizabeth *botanical garden administrator*
Sultzer, Barnet Martin *microbiology and immunology researcher, educator*

Buffalo
Bishop, Beverly Petterson *physiologist*
Duax, William Leo *biological researcher*
He, Guang Sheng *research scientist*
Kostyniak, Paul John *toxicology educator*
McHale, Magda Cordell *academic administrator, trend analyst*
Ortolani, Minot Henry *zoo director*
Tomasi, Thomas B. *cell biologist, administrator*

Cobleskill
Ingels, Jack Edward *horticulture educator*

Cold Spring Harbor
Watson, James Dewey *molecular biologist, educator*
Wigler, Michael H. *molecular biologist*

Cooperstown
Harman, Willard Nelson *malacologist, educator*

Craryville
Payson, Ronald Sears *biology educator*

East Setauket
Briggs, Philip Terry *biologist*

Elmira
Hall, Geraldine Cristofaro *biology educator*

Elmsford
Sklarew, Robert Jay *biomedical research educator, consultant*

Flushing
Boylan, Elizabeth Shippee *biology educator, academic administrator*
Commoner, Barry *biologist, educator*
Schnall, Edith Lea (Mrs. Herbert Schnall) *microbiologist, educator*

Fredonia
Benton, Allen Haydon *biology educator*

Geneseo
Forest, Herman Silva *biology educator*

Geneva
Siebert, Karl Joseph *food science educator, consultant*
Wilcox, Wayne F. *plant pathologist, educator, researcher*

Hamilton
Kessler, Dietrich *biology educator*

Highland
Rosenberger, David A. *research scientist, cooperative extension specialist*

Homer
Gustafson, John Alfred *biology educator*

Ithaca
Adler, Kraig (Kerr) *biology educator*
Alexander, Martin *microbiology educator, researcher*
Arntzen, Charles Joel *bioscience educator*
Bates, David Martin *botanist, educator*
Bergstrom, Gary Carlton *physiologist*
Blackler, Antonie William Charles *biologist*
Coffman, William Ronnie *plant breeding educator*
Crepet, William Louis *botanist, educator*
Davies, Peter John *plant physiology educator, researcher*
Earle, Elizabeth Deutsch *biology educator*
Eisner, Thomas *biologist, educator*
Fick, Gary Warren *agronomy educator, forage crops researcher*
Foote, Robert Hutchinson *animal physiology educator*
Gillett, James Warren *toxicologist*
Grunes, David Leon *research soil scientist, educator, editor*
Hairston, Nelson George, Jr. *ecologist, educator*
Halpern, Bruce Peter *physiologist, consultant*
Hardy, Ralph Wilbur Frederick *science administrator, biochemist, molecular biologist*
Jagendorf, Andre Tridon *plant physiologist*
Kennedy, Wilbert Keith, Sr. *agronomy educator, retired university official*
Kingsbury, John Merriam *botanist, educator*
†Korf, Richard Paul *mycology educator*
Kramer, John Paul *entomologist, educator*
Kubota, Joe *soil scientist*
Ledford, Richard Allison *food science educator, food microbiologist*
Lengemann, Frederick William *physiology educator, scientist*
Mortlock, Robert Paul *microbiologist, educator*
†Niklas, Karl J. *plant biology educator*
Novak, Joseph Donald *science educator, knowlege studies specialist*
Pimentel, David *entomologist, educator*
Plaisted, Robert Leroy *plant breeder, educator*
Seeley, Harry Wilbur, Jr. *microbiology educator*
Staples, Richard Cromwell *microbiologist, researcher*
Vandenberg, John Donald *entomologist*
Walcott, Charles *neurobiology and behvior educator*

Wasserman, Robert Harold *biology educator*
Welch, Ross Maynard *plant physiologist, researcher, educator*
Wootton, John Francis *physiology educator*

Lake Placid
Sato, Gordon Hisashi *retired biologist, researcher*

Middleport
Schwan, Judith Alecia *photographic researcher*

Millbrook
Likens, Gene Elden *ecologist*

New Hyde Park
Isenberg, Henry David *microbiology educator*

New Rochelle
Beardsley, Robert Eugene *microbiologist, educator*

New York
Anderson, O(rvil) Roger *biology educator, marine biology and protozoology, researcher*
Anderson, Sydney *biologist, museum curator*
Ben-Hur, Ehud *research scientist*
Binkowski, Edward Stephan *research analysis director, lawyer, educator*
Blobel, Günter *cell biologist, educator*
Bock, Walter Joseph *zoology educator*
Calame, Kathryn Lee *microbiologist, educator*
Carlson, Marian Bille *geneticist, researcher, educator*
Cheung, Ambrose Lin-Yau *microbiologist, researcher*
Choi, Ye-Chin *microbial geneticist*
Chua, Nam-Hai *plant molecular biologist, educator*
Cohen, Joel Ephraim *scientist, educator*
Cronholm, Lois S. *biology educator*
Desnick, Robert John *human geneticist*
Despommier, Dickson Donald *microbiology educator, parasitologist, researcher*
Ellison, Solon Arthur *microbiology and dentistry educator*
Ginsberg, Harold Samuel *virologist, educator*
Godson, Godfrey Nigel *molecular geneticist, educator*
Goff, Stephen Payne *molecular biologist, educator*
Grafstein, Bernice *physiology and neuroscience educator, researcher*
Hanafusa, Hidesaburo *virologist*
Hirschhorn, Rochelle *genetics educator*
Hommes, Frits Aukustinus *biology educator*
Huang, Alice Shih-hou *microbiology and molecular genetics educator*
Hutner, Seymour Herbert *microbiologist, protozoologist*
Jacobson, Willard James *science educator*
Jagiello, Georgiana M. *geneticist, educator*
King, Marvin *research executive*
Kong, Deyong *research center administrator*
Kramer, Fred Russell *molecular biologist*
Lederberg, Joshua *geneticist, educator*
Lee, Chin O. *physiologist, educator*
Luck, David Jonathan Lewis *biologist, educator*
Maas, Werner Karl *microbiology educator*
Manski, Wladyslaw Julian *microbiology educator, medical scientist*
Mayo, Joan Bradley *microbiologist, epidemiologist*
Model, Peter *molecular biologist*
Nelson, Gareth Jon *zoologist, curator, educator*
Ott, Jurg *geneticist, educator*
Pietruski, John Michael, Jr. *biotechnology company executive, pharmaceuticals executive*
Pogo, Beatriz Teresa Garcia-Tunon *cell biologist, virologist, educator*
Pollack, Robert Elliot *biological sciences educator, writer, scientist*
Robbins, Edith Schultz *microscopy educator*
Rothman, James Edward *cell biologist, educator*
Rozen, Jerome George, Jr. *research entomologist, museum curator and research administrator*
Segal, Sheldon Jerome *biologist, educator, foundation administrator*
Shelanski, Michael L. *cell biologist, educator*
Siekevitz, Philip *biology educator*
Silverstein, Samuel Charles *cellular biology and physiology educator, researcher*
Telang, Nitin T. *cancer biologist, educator*
Tietjen, John Henry *biology and oceanography educator, consultant*
Trager, William *biology educator*
Underwood, Joanna DeHaven *environmental research and education organizations president*
†Wharton, Danny Carroll *zoo biologist*
Windhager, Erich Ernst *physiologist, educator*
Winston, Judith Ellen *marine biologist, curator*
Wynder, Ernst Ludwig *science foundation director, epidemiologist*
Young, Michael Warren *geneticist, educator*
Zinder, Norton David *genetics educator, university dean*

Pearl River
Barik, Sudhakar *microbiologist, researcher*

Plattsburgh
Graziadei, William Daniel, III *biology educator, researcher*

Purchase
Ehrman, Lee *geneticist*

Ridge
Black, Lindsay MacLeod *plant virologist*

Rochester
Chang, Jack Che-man *photoscience research laboratory director*
Clarkson, Thomas William *toxicologist, educator*
Coleman, Paul David *neurobiology researcher, educator*
Iglewski, Barbara Hotham *microbiologist, educator*
Morrow, Paul Edward *toxicology educator*
Muchmore, William Breuleux *zoologist, educator*
Olmsted, Joanna Belle *cell biology educator*

Saranac Lake
North, Robert John *biologist*

Schenectady
†Bedard, Donna Lee *microbiologist*

Stanley
Jones, Gordon Edwin *horticulturist*

Staten Island
Wisniewski, Henryk Miroslaw *pathology and neuropathology educator, research facility administrator, research scientist*

Stony Brook
Carlson, Elof Axel *genetics educator*
Kim, Charles Wesley *microbiology educator*
Lennarz, William Joseph *research biologist, educator*
Levinton, Jeffrey S. *biology educator, oceanographer*
Rohlf, F. James *biometrician, educator*
Schubel, Jerry Robert *marine science educator, scientist, university dean and official*
Steigbigel, Roy Theodore *infectious disease physician and scientist, educator*
Wurster, Charles Frederick *environmental scientist, educator*

Syosset
Hershey, Alfred Day *geneticist*

Syracuse
Burgess, Robert Lewis *ecologist, educator*
Collette, Alfred Thomas *biology and science education educator*
Delmar, Mario *cardiac physiology educator*
Dunham, Philip Bigelow *biology educator, physiologist*
Kriebel, Mahlon Edward *physiology educator, inventor*
McNaughton, Samuel Joseph *ecology educator*
Phillips, Arthur William, Jr. *biology educator*
Russell-Hunter, W(illiam) D(evigne) *zoology educator, research biologist, writer*
Tanenbaum, Stuart William *biotechnologist, educator*
†Wang, Chun-Juan Kao *mycology educator*

Troy
Breed, Helen Illick *ichthyologist, educator*
†Ehrlich, Henry Lutz *biology educator*
Pfau, Charles Julius *biology educator, researcher*
Wilson, Jack Martin *university administrator, scientific association executive, physics educator*

Tuxedo Park
Heusser, Calvin John *biology educator, researcher*
Rossman, Toby Gale *genetic toxicology educator, researcher*

Upton
Petrakis, Leonidas *research scientist, educator, administrator*

Utica
Antzelevitch, Charles *research center executive*
McIntyre, Judith Watland *ornithologist, biology educator*

Valhalla
Ferrone, Soldano *microbiology and immunology educator, physician*

White Plains
Peyton, Donald Leon *retired standards association executive*

NORTH CAROLINA

Archdale
Riddick, Douglas Smith *horticultural industrialist, industrial designer*

Atlantic Beach
Barnes, James Thomas, Jr. *aquarium administrator*

Burlington
Tolley, Jerry Russell *clinical laboratory executive*

Cary
Mochrie, Richard D. *physiology educator*

Chapel Hill
Andrews, Richard Nigel Lyon *environmental policy educator, environmental studies administrator*
Frankenberg, Dirk *marine scientist*
Gilbert, Lawrence Irwin *biologist, educator*
Hairston, Nelson George *animal ecologist*
Judd, Burke Haycock *geneticist*
Kuenzler, Edward Julian *ecologist and environmental biologist*
Manire, George Philip *bacteriologist, educator*
McBay, Arthur John *toxicologist, consultant*
Mueller, Nancy Schneider *retired biology educator*
Scott, Tom Keck *biologist, botanist, educator*
Shapiro, Lee Tobey *planetarium administrator, astronomer*
Stiven, Alan Ernest *population biologist, ecologist*
Stumpf, Walter Erich *cell biology educator, researcher*
Warren, Donald William *physiology educator, dentistry educator*
Weiss, Charles Manuel *environmental biologist*
Wyrick, Priscilla Blakeney *microbiologist*

Charlotte
Cornell, James Fraser, Jr. *entomologist, educator*
†Smiley, E. Thomas *tree pathologist*

Durham
Barrett, J. Carl *cancer researcher, molecular biologist*
Billings, William Dwight *ecology educator*
Blum, Jacob Joseph *physiologist, educator*
Cook, Clarence Edgar *research facility executive*
Counce-Nicklas, Sheila Jean *cell biology educator*
Cruze, Alvin M. *research institute executive*
Culberson, William Louis *botany educator*
Gillham, Nicholas Wright *geneticist, educator*
Kramer, Paul Jackson *plant physiologist, educator, writer, editor*
Lieberman, Melvyn *biology educator*
Livingstone, Daniel Archibald *zoology educator*
McClellan, Roger Orville *toxicologist*
Naylor, Aubrey Willard *botany educator*
Nicklas, Robert Bruce *cell biologist*
†Richardson, Curtis J. *ecology educator*
Rouse, Doris Jane *physiologist, research administrator*
Sassaman, Anne Phillips *science administrator*
Schmidt-Nielsen, Knut *physiologist, educator*
Searles, Richard Brownlee *botany educator, marine biology researcher*
Somjen, George Gustav *physiologist*
Wainwright, Stephen A. *zoology educator, design consultant*
Wilbur, Karl Milton *zoologist, educator*
Wilbur, Robert Lynch *botanist, educator*

Greenville
Maier, Robert Hawthorne *biology educator*
Thurber, Robert Eugene *physiologist, researcher*

Hendersonville
Brittain, James Edward *science and technology educator, researcher*
Kehr, August Ernest *geneticist, researcher*

Kure Beach
†Lanier, James Alfred, III *aquarium administrator*

Pinehurst
Stroud, Richard Hamilton *aquatic biologist, scientist, consultant*

Raleigh
Atchley, William Reid *geneticist, evolutionary biologist, educator*
†Benson, D(avid) Michael *plant pathologist*
Bergsma, Daniel *retired medical foundation executive, consultant*
Bishop, Paul Edward *microbiologist*
Cockerham, Columbus Clark *retired geneticist, educator*
Cook, Maurice Gayle *soil science educator, consultant*
Cooper, Arthur Wells *ecologist, educator*
Cummings, Ralph Waldo *soil scientist, educator, researcher*
Davey, Charles Bingham *soil science educator*
De Hertogh, August Albert *horticulture educator, researcher*
Dunphy, Edward James *crop science extension specialist*
Goodman, Major Merlin *botanical sciences educator*
Hardin, James W. *botanist, herbarium curator, educator*
Hodgson, Ernest *toxicology educator*
Kelman, Arthur *plant pathologist, educator*
Moreland, Donald Edwin *plant physiologist*
Scandalios, John George *geneticist, educator*
Shih, Jason Chia-Hsing *biotechnology educator*
Speck, Marvin Luther *microbiologist, educator*
Stoskopf, Michael Kerry *educator*
Stuber, Charles William *genetics educator, researcher*
Timothy, David Harry *biology educator*
†Triantaphyllou, Hedwig Hirschmann *plant pathologist*
Wilson, Richard Ferrol *plant physiologist, educator*
Wollum, Arthur George, II *microbiologist, researcher, educator*

Research Triangle Park
de Serres, Frederick Joseph *genetic toxicologist*
Drake, John Walter *geneticist*
Heck, Henry D'Arcy *toxicologist*
Li, Steven Shoei-lung *geneticist, educator*
Wooten, Frank Thomas *research facility executive*

Southern Pines
Towell, William Earnest *forester, former association executive*

Wilmington
Brauer, Ralph Werner *physiologist, educator*
Merritt, James Francis *biological sciences educator*
Roer, Robert David *physiologist, educator*
Zechman, Fred William, Jr. *physiologist, educator, administrator*

Winston Salem
Flory, Walter S., Jr. *geneticist, botanist, educator*
Herndon, Claude Nash *retired geneticist, physician*

Winterville
Myers, Robert Durant *biologist, research director, medical educator*

NORTH DAKOTA

Dunseith
Gorder, Steven F. *association administrator*

Fargo
†Joppa, Leonard Robert *research geneticist, agronomist, educator*
†Lund, H. Roald *plant scientist, educator*
Schmidt, Claude Henri *retired research administrator*
Williams, Norman Dale *geneticist, researcher*
Zimmerman, Don Charles *plant physiologist, biochemist*

Jamestown
†Kirby, Ronald Eugene *fish and wildlife research administrator*

Mandan
Halvorson, Ardell David *research leader, soil scientist*
Halvorson, Gary Alfred *soil scientist*

OHIO

Athens
Cohn, Norman Stanley *botany educator, university dean*
Ungar, Irwin Allan *botany educator*

Bowling Green
Clark, Eloise Elizabeth *biologist, university official*
Heckman, Carol A. *biology educator*
Rockett, Carlton Lee *biological sciences educator*

Broadview Heights
†Hahn, Sang Ki *genetist*

Cincinnati
Maruska, Edward Joseph *zoo administrator*
Nebert, Daniel Walter *molecular geneticist, research administrator*
Safferman, Robert Samuel *microbiologist*
Scarpino, Pasquale Valentine *environmental microbiologist*
Sjoerdsma, Albert *research institute executive*
Sperelakis, Nicholas *physiology and biophysics educator, researcher*

Cleveland
†Caplan, Arnold I. *biology educator*
†Holley, Brian E. *botanical garden director*
Singer, Marcus Joseph *biologist, educator*
Steinberg, Arthur G(erald) *geneticist*
Taylor, Steve Henry *zoologist*

Columbus
†Axsmith, Brain J. *botany educator*
Bagby, Frederick Lair, Jr. *retired research institute executive*
Banwart, George Junior *food microbiology educator*
†Boerner, Ralph E. J. *forest soil ecologist, plant biology educator*
Deep, Ira Washington *plant pathology educator*
Disinger, John Franklin *natural resources educator*
Fawcett, Sherwood Luther *research laboratory executive*
†Floyd, Gary Leon *cell biologist, educator*
Fry, Donald Lewis *physiologist, educator*
Glaser, Ronald *microbiology educator, scientist*
Haury, David Leroy *science education specialist*
Kapral, Frank Albert *medical microbiology and immunology educator*
Lal, Rattan *soil scientist, researcher*
Logan, Terry James *soil chemist, educator*
Miller, Frederick Powell *agronomy educator*
Morrow, Grant, III *genetecist*
Newcomb, Lawrence Howard *agricultural educator*
Olesen, Douglas Eugene *research institute executive*
Pappas, Peter William *zoology educator*
Peterle, Tony John *zoologist, educator*
Pieper, Heinz Paul *physiology educator*
†Rayner, John Norman *science educator*
Reece, Robert William *zoological park administrator*
Reeve, John Newton *molecular biology and microbiology educator*
Roth, Robert Earl *environmental educator*
Triplehorn, Charles A. *entomology educator, insects curator*
Waldron, Acie Chandler *agronomy and entomology educator*
Warmbrod, James Robert *agriculture educator, university administrator*
Yohn, David Stewart *virologist, science administrator*
Zartman, David Lester *animal sciences educator, researcher*

Dayton
Bigley, Nancy Jane *microbiology educator*
Isaacson, Milton Stanley *research and development company executive, engineer*
Martino, Joseph Paul *research scientist*
Thomas, Donald Charles *microbiology educator, former university dean and administrator*

Delaware
Fry, Anne Evans *zoology educator*

Kent
Cooke, G. Dennis *biological science educator*
Cooperrider, Tom Smith *botanist*

Oberlin
†Stinebring, Warren Richard *microbiologist, educator*

Oxford
Eshbaugh, W(illiam) Hardy *botanist, educator*
Heimsch, Charles *retired botany educator*
Miller, Harvey Alfred *botanist, educator*
Risser, Paul Gillan *botanist, academic administrator*
Williamson, Clarence Kelly *microbiologist, educator*

Powell
Hanna, Jack Bushnell *zoo director*
Lombardi, Celeste *zoological park administrator*

Rootstown
Gilloteaux, Jacques Jean-Marie Anthime *cell biologist, researcher*

Wooster
Ferree, David Curtis *horticultural researcher*
Lafever, Howard Nelson *plant breeder, geneticist, educator*

OKLAHOMA

Durant
Smith, Samuel Joseph *soil scientist*

Edmond
Caire, William *biologist, educator, assistant dean*

El Reno
†Phillips, William A. *research animal scientist*

Norman
Boke, Norman Hill *botanist*
Carpenter, Charles Congden *zoologist, educator*
Cross, George Lynn *foundation administrator, former university president*
Estes, James Russell *botanist*
Hinshaw, Lerner Brady *physiology educator*
Hutchison, Victor Hobbs *biologist, educator*
Mares, Michael Allen *ecologist, educator*
Schnell, Gary Dean *zoology educator, administrator*

Oklahoma City
Alexander, Patrick Byron *zoological society executive*
Branch, John Curtis *biology educator, lawyer*
Murphy, Juneann Wadsworth *microbiologist, educator*
Scott, Lawrence Vernon *microbiology educator*
Scribner, Ronald Kent *microbiologist*

Ponca City
Bolene, Margaret Rosalie Steele *bacteriologist, civic worker*

Stillwater
Bantle, John Albert, II *zoology educator*
Campbell, John Roy *animal scientist educator, academic administrator*
Durham, Norman Nevill *microbiologist, scientist, educator*
Grischkowsky, Daniel Richard *research scientist, educator*
Langwig, John Edward *retired wood science educator*
Owens, Fredric Newell *animal nutritionist, educator*
Ownby, Charlotte Ledbetter *anatomy educator*
†Stone, John Floyd *soil physics researcher and educator*

Tulsa
Johnson, Gerald, III *cardiovascular physiologist, researcher*
†Zucconi, David G. *zoo and museum director*

OREGON

Ashland
Coffey, Marvin Dale *biology educator*

Aurora
Martin, Lloyd Wayne *research agriculturist*

Beaverton
†Boone, David Ridgway *environmental microbiology educator*

Charleston
Shapiro, Lynda P. *biology educator, director*

Corvallis
†Brown, George *research forester and educator*
Chambers, Kenton Lee *botany educator*
†Farkas, Daniel Frederick *food science and technology educator*
Frakes, Rod Vance *plant geneticist, educator*
Frazier, William A. *retired horticulturist*
Fuchigami, Leslie Hirao *horticulturist, researcher*
Kronstad, Warren Ervind *genetics educator, researcher*
Leong, Jo-Ann Ching *microbiologist, educator*
Liston, Aaron Irving *botanist*
Moore, Thomas Carrol *botanist, educator*
Morita, Richard Yukio *microbiology and oceanography educator*
Pearson, Albert Marchant *food science and nutrition educator*
Tarrant, Robert Frank *soil science educator, researcher*
Trappe, James Martin *mycologist*
Westwood, Melvin Neil *horticulturist, pomologist*
Young, J. Lowell *soil chemist, biologist*
Zobel, Donald Bruce *botany educator*

Eugene
DeVries, Philip James *tropical field ecologist, butterfly biologist*
Holzapfel, Christina Marie *biologist*
Matthews, Brian W. *molecular biology educator*
Sprague, George Frederick *geneticist*

Gresham
Poulton, Charles Edgar *natural resources consultant*

Newport
Weber, Lavern John *marine science administrator, educator*

Pendleton
Lund, Steve *agronomist, research administrator*
Smiley, Richard Wayne *research center administrator, researcher*

Portland
Bragdon, Paul Errol *educator*
Campbell, Charles Joy *fishery biologist*
Crosa, Jorge Homero *bacterial geneticist, educator, consultant*
Hagenstein, William David *forester, consultant*
Spencer, Peter Simner *neurotoxicologist*

Yachats
Gerdemann, James Wessel *plant pathologist, educator*

PENNSYLVANIA

Annville
Verhoek, Susan Elizabeth *botany educator*

Collegeville
Popp, James Alan *toxicologist, toxicology executive*

Danville
Morgan, Howard Edwin *physiologist*

Douglassville
Burke, Peter Arthur *microbiologist, chemist*

Doylestown
George, William Leo *plant geneticist, educator*
Mishler, John Milton (Yochanan Menashsheh ben Shaul) *natural sciences educator, academic administrator*

Edinboro
Miller, G(erson) H(arry) *research institute director, mathematician, computer scientist, chemist*

Elkins Park
Fussell, Catharine Pugh *biological researcher*

Gladwyne
Allen, Theresa Ohotnicky *neurobiologist, consultant*

Grove City
Brenner, Frederic James *biology educator, ecological consultant*

Harrisburg
Wei, I-Yuan *research and development consultant and director*

Haverford
Perloe, Sidney Irwin *primatologist, educator*
Thimann, Kenneth Vivian *biology educator*

Hershey
Hopper, Anita Klein *molecular genetics educator*
Rapp, Fred *virologist*
Stump, Troy Elwood *zoo director*

Holland
Umbreit, Wayne William *bacteriologist, educator*

Huntingdon Valley
Liberti, Paul Alfonso *biotechnology executive, inventor, entrepreneur, consultant*

Lewisburg
Sojka, Gary Allan *biologist, educator, university official*

Malvern
Breslin, Elizabeth Walker *biological scientist*

Media
Hand, Brian Edward *science association administrator*

Narberth
Nathanson, Neal *virologist, epidemiologist, educator*

New Kensington
Lederman, Frank L. *scientist, research center administrator*

Philadelphia
Bayer, Margret Helene Janssen *biologist, research scientist*
Beauchamp, Gary Keith *physiologist*
†Birnbaum, Morris Jay *cell biology educator, researcher*
Brinster, Ralph Lawrence *biologist*
Brobeck, John Raymond *physiology educator*
Brownstein, Barbara Lavin *geneticist, educator, university official*
Cheston, Morris, Jr. *zoological park administrator*
Cheston, Warren Bruce *research institute administrator*
Cox, Robert Harold *physiology educator*
Crowell, Richard Lane *microbiologist*
Davis, Robert Harry *physiology educator*
DiBerardino, Marie Antoinette *developmental biologist, educator*
Eisenstein, Toby K. *microbiology educator*
Erickson, Ralph O. *botany educator*
Fisher, Aron Baer *physiology and medicine educator*
†Fox, Jonathan Charles *biomedical scientist, educator*
Furth, John Jacob *molecular biologist, pathologist, educator*
Goldman, Yale E. *physiologist, educator*
Hand, Peter James *neurobiologist, educator*
Hung, Paul Porwen *biotechnologist, educator, consultant*
Janzen, Daniel Hunt *biology educator*
Johnson, E(lmer) Marshall *biology educator, reproductive toxicologist*
Kaji, Akira *microbiology scientist, educator*
Kleinzeller, Arnost *physiologist, physician, emeritus educator*
Knudson, Alfred George, Jr. *medical geneticist*
Koprowski, Hilary *medical scientist*
Krutsick, Robert Stanley *science center executive*
Lefer, Allan Mark *physiologist*
Levin, Michael H(oward) *environmentalist*
Live, Israel *microbiologist, educator*
Lu, Ponzy *molecular biology educator*
Meyer, Paul William *arboretum director, horticulturist*
Morahan, Page S. *microbiologist, educator*
Niewiarowski, Stefan *physiology educator, biomedical research scientist*
Oppenheimer, Jane Marion *biologist, historian, educator*
†Patrick, Ruth (Mrs. Charles Hodge) *limnologist, diatom taxonomist, educator*
Patterson, Donald Floyd *human, medical and veterinary genetics educator*
Peachey, Lee DeBorde *biology educator*
Pepe, Frank A. *cell and developmental biology educator*
Perry, Robert Palese *molecular biologist, educator*
†Poethig, Richard Scott *geneticist, biology educator*
Porter, Roger John *medical research administrator, neurologist, pharmacologist*
Schaedler, Russell William *microbiologist, physicians, educator*
Schneider, Adele Sandra *clinical geneticist*
Shockman, Gerald David *microbiologist, educator*
Siegman, Marion Joyce *physiology educator*
Silvers, Willys Kent *geneticist*
Skalka, Anna Marie *molecular biologist, virologist*
Thomson, Keith Stewart *science museum administrator, writer*
Waldron, Ingrid Lore *biology educator*
Young, Robert Crabill *medical researcher, science facility administrator, internist*
Yunis, Jorge Jose *geneticist, pathologist, educator, poet*

Pittsburgh
Aul, Donald J. *biochemist, researcher*
Borle, André Bernard *physiologist*
Edmonds, Mary Patricia *biological sciences educator*
Feingold, David Sidney *microbiology educator*
Fletcher, Ronald Darling *microbiologist educator*
Gollin, Susanne Merle *cytogeneticist, cell biologist*
Henry, Susan Armstrong *biology educator, university dean*
Ho, Chien *biological sciences educator*
Hoffee, Patricia Anne *molecular genetics educator*
Jones, Elizabeth Winifred *biology educator*
Kanade, Takeo *science educator, institute administrator*
Kaufman, William Morris *research institute administrator, engineer*
Kiger, Robert William *botanist, science historian, educator*
McGovern, John Joseph *former air pollution control association executive, consultant*
McWilliams, Betty Jane *science administrator, communication disorders educator, researcher*
Parkes, Kenneth Carroll *ornithologist*
Partanen, Carl Richard *biology educator*
Wang, Allan Zuwu *cell biologist*
†Warner, Richard David *research foundation executive*
Youngner, Julius Stuart *microbiologist, educator*

Quakertown
de Limantour, Clarice Barr *food scientist*

State College
Bergman, Ernest L. *biologist*
Hettche, L. Raymond *research director*

Swarthmore
Flemister, Launcelot Johnson *physiologist, educator*
Gilbert, Scott Frederick *biologist, educator, author*

Titusville
Peaslee, Margaret Mae Hermanek *zoology educator*

University Park
Bollag, Jean-Marc *soil biochemistry educator, consultant*
Brenchley, Jean Elnora *microbiologist, researcher*
Buskirk, Elsworth Robert *physiologist, educator*
Cosgrove, Daniel Joseph *biology educator*
Cowen, Barrett Stickney *microbiologist*
Dunson, William Albert *biology educator*
Fowler, H(oratio) Seymour *retired science educator*
Fox, Richard Henry *soil science educator*
Hagen, Daniel Russell *physiologist*
Kim, Ke Chung *entomology and biodiversity educator, researcher*
Lindstrom, Eugene Shipman *biologist, academic administrator*
Macdonald, Digby Donald *scientist, science administrator*
Manbeck, Harvey B. *agricultural engineer, wood engineer, educator*
†Maynard, Julian D. *acoustician, physicist, educator*
Nelson, Paul Edward *science educator*
Traverse, Alfred *palynology educator, clergyman*
Tukey, Loren Davenport *pomology educator, researcher*

Villanova
Steg, Leo *research and development executive*

Wayne
Hess, Eugene Lyle *biologist, retired association executive*

West Chester
†Garber, Charles Allen *research company executive, consultant*
Pollock, Roy Van Horn *pharmaceutical company animal health researcher*
Weston, Roy Francis *environmental consultant*

West Mifflin
Clayton, John Charles *scientist, researcher*

West Point
Hilleman, Maurice Ralph *virus research scientist*

Wilkes Barre
Hayes, Wilbur Frank *biology educator*
Ogren, Robert Edward *biologist, educator*

Willow Grove
Rieders, Fredric *forensic toxicologist*
Spikes, John Jefferson, Sr. *forensic toxicologist, pharmacologist*

RHODE ISLAND

Kingston
Goos, Roger Delmon *mycologist*
Harlin, Marilyn Miler *marine botany educator, researcher, consultant*
Hufnagel, Linda Ann *biology educator, researcher*
†Miller, Robert H. *soil scientist, dean*

Portsmouth
Pearson, Oscar Harris *plant breeder, geneticist*

Providence
†Coleman, Annette Wilbois *biology educator*
Gerbi, Susan Alexandra *biology educator*
Goss, Richard Johnson *biologist, educator*
Knopf, Paul Mark *immunoparasitologist, neuro-immunologist*
Marshall, Jean McElroy *physiologist*
Miller, Kenneth Raymond *biologist, educator*
Rothman, Frank George *biology educator, biochemical genetics researcher*
†Savage, Anne *zoologist, researcher*
Schmitt, Johanna Marie *plant population biologist, educator*

SOUTH CAROLINA

Aiken
Smith, Michael Howard *ecologist*

Charleston
Brusca, Richard Charles *zoologist, researcher, educator*
Cheng, Thomas Clement *parasitologist, immunologist, educator, author*

Clemson
Hays, Sidney Brooks *retired entomology educator*
Morr, Charles Vernon *food science educator*

Columbia
Abel, Francis Lee *physiology educator*
Cole, Benjamin Theodore *biologist*
Dawson, Wallace Douglas, Jr. *geneticist*
†Krantz, Palmer Eric, III *zoo director*
Vernberg, Frank John *marine and biological sciences educator*
Watabe, Norimitsu *biology and marine science educator*

Conway
Moore, Richard Harlan *biology educator, university official*

Florence
Kittrell, Benjamin Upchurch *agronomist*

Gaffney
Kowalczyk, Jeanne Stuart *biology educator*

Greenwood
Fox, Richard Shirley *zoology educator*

Hilton Head Island
Adams, William Hensley *ecologist, educator*

Spartanburg
Leonard, Walter Raymond *retired biology educator*

SOUTH DAKOTA

Brookings
Hugghins, Ernest Jay *biology educator*
Morgan, Walter *retired poultry science educator*
Sword, Christopher Patrick *microbiologist, university dean*

Porcupine
†Tall, Joann *ecologist*

Vermillion
Langworthy, Thomas Allan *microbiologist, educator*

Volga
Moldenhauer, William Calvin *soil scientist*

TENNESSEE

Cookeville
Coorts, Gerald Duane *horticulturist, educator, college dean*

Johnson City
Rasch, Ellen Myrberg *cell biology educator*
†Renzaglia, Karen Sue *botany educator*

Knoxville
Conger, Bob Vernon *plant and soil science educator*
†Harris, William Franklin, III *biologist, environmental science director and educator*
Holton, Raymond William *botanist, educator*
Hughes, Karen Woodbury *botany educator, academic administrator*
Maxson, Linda Ellen *biologist, educator*
Mc Hargue, Carl Jack *research laboratory administator*
Sharp, Aaron John *botanist, educator*
Swingle, Homer Dale *horticulturist, educator*
White, David Cleaveland *microbial ecologist, environmental toxicologist*
Williamson, Handy, Jr. *agricultural economist, educator*
Wust, Carl John *microbiology and medical biology educator*

Maryville
Hall, Marion Trufant *botany educator, arboretum director*

Memphis
Bardos, Denes Istvan *research scientist, medical company executive*
Chung, King-Thom *microbiologist, educator*
Freeman, Bob A. *microbiology educator*
Howe, Martha Morgan *microbiologist, educator*
Miller, Neil Austin *biology educator*
Ryan, Kevin William *research virologist, educator*
†Wilson, Charles Glen *zoo administrator*
Wise, George Urban *botanic garden administrator, horticulturist, entomologist*

Mount Juliet
Kerr, Charles Randall *consultant, former florist*

Nashville
Granner, Daryl Kitley *physiology and medicine educator*
Mosig, Gisela *molecular biology educator*
Orgebin-Crist, Marie-Claire *biology educator*
Page, Terry Lee *biology educator*
Pincus, Theodore *microbiologist, educator*
Spiller, Hart *microbiologist*
Tomlinson, Gus *biology educator*
Wang, Taylor Gunjin *science administrator, astronaut, educator*

Norris
Kelly, James Michael *soil scientist*

Oak Ridge
Auerbach, Stanley Irving *ecologist, environmental scientist, educator*
Boyle, William R. *science administrator*
Gooch, Patricia Carolyn *cytogeneticist*
Hosker, Rayford Peter, Jr. *air pollution research scientist*
Luxmoore, Robert John *soil and plant scientist*
†Russell, Liane Brauch *geneticist*
Slusher, Kimberly Goode *researcher*
Tyndall, Richard Lawrence *microbiologist, researcher*
Veigel, Jon Michael *corporate professional*

Sewanee
Croom, Henrietta Brown *biology educator*
Yeatman, Harry Clay *biologist, educator*

TEXAS

Abilene
Fleshman, Jim J. *zoological park administrator*

Austin
Albin, Leslie Owens *biology educator*
Biesele, John Julius *biologist, educator*
Bronson, Franklin H. *zoology educator*
Brown, Dennis Taylor *molecular biology educator*
Delevoryas, Theodore *botanist, educator*
Durden, Christopher John *entomologist, paleontologist, museum curator*
Fryxell, Greta Albrecht *botany educator, oceanographer*
Grant, Verne Edwin *biology educator*
Hubbs, Clark *zoologist, researcher*
Jacobson, Antone Gardner *zoology educator*
Kalthoff, Klaus Otto *zoology educator*
Northington, David K. *research center director, botanist, educator*
Park, Thomas Joseph *biology researcher, educator*
Simpson, Beryl Brintnall *botany educator*
Starr, Richard Cawthon *botany educator*
Sutton, Harry Eldon *geneticist, educator*
Thornton, Joseph Scott *research institute executive, materials scientist*
Turner, Billie Lee *botanist, educator*
Walker, James Roy *microbiologist*
Wheeler, Marshall Ralph *zoologist, educator*

Brooks AFB
Convertino, Victor Anthony *physiologist, educator, research scientist*
Cox, Ann Bruger *biological scientist, editor, researcher*

Brownsville
Farst, Don David *zoo director, veterinarian*

Bryan
Röller, Herbert Alfred *biology and medical scientist, educator*
Van Arsdel, Eugene Parr *tree pathologist, consultant meteorologist*

Bushland
Unger, Paul Walter *soil scientist*

College Station
Black, Samuel Harold *microbiology and immunology educator*
Borlaug, Norman Ernest *agricultural scientist*
†Brown, Robert Dale *wildlife science educator, department head*
Bryant, Vaughn Motley, Jr. *botany and anthropology educator*
Fisher, Richard Forrest *soils educator, academic administrator*
Hall, Timothy C. *biology educator, consultant*
Harris, William James, Jr. *research administrator, educator*
Kohel, Russell James *geneticist*
Milford, Murray Hudson *soil science educator*
Neill, William Harold, Jr. *biological science educator*
Rosberg, David William *plant sciences educator*
Sanchez, David Alan *science administrator*
Smith, Roberta Hawkins *plant physiologist*
Summers, Max (Duanne) *entomologist, scientist, educator*
Wilding, Lawrence Paul *pedology educator, soil science consultant*

Dallas
Bollon, Arthur Peter *scientist, educator, biotechnology company executive*
Brown, Michael Stuart *geneticist*
Harbaugh, Lois Jensen *secondary science educator*
Hudspeth, Albert James *biomedical researcher, educator*
Land, Geoffrey Allison *science administrator*
Mc Cann, Samuel McDonald *physiologist, educator*
Murad, John Louis *clinical microbiology educator*
Neaves, William Barlow *cell biologist, educator*
Reinert, James A. *entomologist, educator*
Senkayi, Abu Lwanga *environmental soil scientist*
Vanatta, John Crothers, III *physiologist, physician, educator*

Denton
Schwalm, Fritz Ekkehardt *biology educator*

El Paso
Harris, Arthur Horne *biology educator*

Galveston
Baron, Samuel *microbiologist, physician*
Budelmann, Bernd Ulrich *zoologist, educator*
Giam, Choo-Seng *marine science educator*
Prakash, Satya *biology educator*
Santschi, Peter Hans *marine sciences educator*
Thompson, Edward Ivins Brad *biological chemistry and genetics educator, molecular endocrinologist, department chairman*
Würsig, Bernd Gerhard *marine biology educator*
†Zimmerman, Roger Joseph *fisherie biologist*

Georgetown
Girvin, Eb Carl *biology educator*

Harlingen
Ryall, A(lbert) Lloyd *horticulturist, refrigeration engineer*

Houston
Ablott, Vance Randall *science foundation administrator*
Baughn, Robert Elroy *microbiology educator*
Brown, Jack Harold Upton *physiology educator, university official, biomedical engineer*
Caskey, Charles Thomas *biology and genetics educator*
DeBakey, Lois *science communications educator, writer, lecturer, editor, scholar*
DeBakey, Selma *science communication educator, writer, editor, lecturer*
Few, Arthur Allen, Jr. *science educator*
Goldstein, Margaret Ann *biologist*
Huntoon, Carolyn Leach *physiologist*
Jurtshuk, Peter, Jr. *microbiologist, educator*
†Mitchell, David L. *phycology researcher*
O'Malley, Bert William *cell biologist, educator, physician*
Sass, Ronald Lewis *biology and chemistry educator*
Schultz, Stanley George *physiologist, educator*

Irving
Potter, Robert Joseph *technical research and business executive*

Kerrville
Kunz, Sidney *entomologist*

Kingsville
Perez, John Carlos *biology educator*

Lubbock
Dregne, Harold Ernest *agronomy educator*
Hentges, David John *microbiology educator*
Maunder, Addison Bruce *agronomic research company executive*
Schake, Lowell Martin *animal science educator*
Skoog, Gerald Duane *science educator*
Wendt, Charles William *soil physicist, educator*

Nacogdoches
Worrell, Albert Cadwallader *forest economics educator*

Overton
Randel, Ronald Dean *physiologist, educator*

Port Aransas
Wohlschlag, Donald Eugene *zoologist, marine ecologist, educator emeritus*

Richardson
Gray, Donald Melvin *molecular and cell biology educator*

San Angelo
Menzies, Carl Stephen *agricultural research administrator, ruminant nutritionist*

San Antonio
Betts, Austin Wortham *retired research company executive*
Blystone, Robert Vernon *developmental cell biologist, educator, textbook consultant*
Bowman, Barbara Hyde *biologist, geneticist, educator*
Burch, James Leo *science research institute executive*
Carson, Robin D. *zoological park administrator*
Corrigan, Helen González *cytologist*
Gates, Mahlon Eugene *applied research executive, former government official, former army officer*
Goland, Martin *research institute executive*
Kalter, Seymour Sanford *virologist, educator*
Lindholm, Ulric Svante *engineering research institute executive, retired*
Masoro, Edward Joseph, Jr. *physiology educator*
Stone, William Harold *geneticist, educator*
Winters, Wendell Delos *microbiology educator, researcher, consultant*

San Marcos
Longley, Glenn *biology educator, research director*

Stephenville
†Simpson, Charles Edmond *crop science educator*

The Woodlands
Porter, W. Arthur *research center executive*

Tyler
†Caldwell, Hayes *zoological park administrator*

Warda
Kunze, George William *retired soil scientist*

Weslaco
Amador, Jose Manuel *plant pathologist, research center administrator*
Collins, Anita Marguerite *research geneticist*
King, Edgar G. *agricultural researcher*
Lingle, Sarah Elizabeth *research scientist*

UTAH

Logan
Anderson, Jay LaMar *horticulture educator, researcher, consultant*
Bennett, James Austin *retired animal science educator*
Salisbury, Frank Boyer *plant physiologist, educator*
Sidle, Roy Carl *research hydrologist*
Vest, Hyrum Grant, Jr. *horticultural sciences educator*
†Wagner, Frederic Hamilton *biology educator, dean, research ecologist*

Provo
Blake, George Rowland *soil science educator, water resources research administrator*
†McArthur, Eldon Durant *geneticist, researcher*

Salt Lake City
Brierley, James Alan *research administrator*
†Emerson, Sharon B. *biology researcher and educator*
Johnson, Stephen Charles *exercise physiology and sport science educator*
King, R. Peter *science educator, academic center director*
Leonard, Claire Offutt *pediatric geneticist educator*
Roth, John Roger *geneticist, biology educator*
Straight, Richard Coleman *photobiologist*

Vernal
Folks, F(rancis) Neil *biologist, researcher*

VERMONT

Burlington
Albertini, Richard Joseph *molecular geneticist, educator*
Bartlett, Richmond Jay *soil chemistry educator, researcher*
†Forcier, Lawrence Kenneth *research forester*
Heinrich, Bernd *biologist, zoology educator*
Hendley, Edith Di Pasquale *physiology and neuroscience educator*

Greensboro
Hill, Lewis Reuben *horticulturist, nursery owner, author*

Middlebury
Hitchcock, Harold Bradford *retired biology educator, zoologist*
Landgren, Craig Randall *biology educator*
Saul, George Brandon, II *biology educator*

South Burlington
Johnson, Robert Eugene *physiologist*

VIRGINIA

Alexandria
Woolley, Mary Elizabeth *research administrator*

Amonate
†Stout, Ernest Ray *molecular biology educator, research biochemist, botanist*

Annandale
Faraday, Bruce John *scientific research company executive, physicist*

Arlington
Aukland, Elva Dayton *retired biologist, educator*
Bridgewater, Albert Louis *science foundation administrator*
Brown, Nicholas *retired aquarium administrator*
Cameron, Maryellen *science association administrator, geologist, educator*
Corell, Robert Walden *science administration educator*
Gaines, Alan McCulloch *government official, educator*
Gottschalk, John Simison *biologist*
Haq, Bilal Ul *national science foundation program director, researcher*
Hess, LaVerne Derryl *research laboratory scientist*
†Junker, Bobby Ray *research and development executive, physicist*
Knipling, Edward Fred *retired research entomologist, agricultural administrator*
Lambert, Richard Bowles, Jr. *science foundation program director, oceanographer*
†Lynch, John Thomas *science foundation administrator, physicist*
Mense, Allan Tate *research scientist, engineer*
Moraff, Howard *science foundation program director*
O'Neill, Brian *research organization administrator*
Sullivan, Cornelius Wayne *marine biology researcher, educator*
†Talmadge, John Barnes *science foundation administrator*
Williams, Luther Steward *biologist, federal agency administrator*
Zehner, Lee Randall *biotechnologist, research director*

Blacksburg
Barden, John Allan *horticulturist*
Colmano, Germille *physiology educator, biophysics researcher*
Cowles, Joe Richard *biology educator*
Siau, John Finn *wood scientist, educator*
Smeal, Paul Lester *retired horticulture educator*
Yousten, Allan Arthur *microbiologist, educator*

Charlottesville
Berne, Robert Matthew *physiologist, educator*
†Connor, Edward Francis *biology and ecology educator*
Desjardins, Claude *physiology educator*
Friesen, Wolfgang Otto *biology educator*
Garrett, Reginald Hooker *biology educator, researcher*
Gottesman, Irving Isadore *psychiatric genetics educator, consultant*
Hamilton, Howard Laverne *zoology educator*
Hornberger, George Milton *environmental science educator*
Kadner, Robert Joseph *microbiology educator*
Kelly, Thaddeus Elliott *medical geneticist*
Murray, Joseph James, Jr. *zoologist*
Somlyo, Andrew Paul *physiology, biophysics and cardiology educator*
Stoner, Glenn Earl *science educator*
Wagner, Robert Roderick *microbiologist, oncology educator*
Wilbur, Henry Miles *zoologist*
Wright, Theodore Robert Fairbank *biologist, educator*

Chesapeake
Gibbs, William Eugene *scientific consultant*

Culpeper
Covey, Charles William *marine consultant*

Fairfax
Gray, Clarence Cornelius, III *international agronomist*
Pixley, John Sherman, Sr. *research company executive*

Falls Church
Hart, C(harles) W(illard), Jr. *zoologist, curator*

Front Royal
Douglas, J(ocelyn) Fielding *toxicologist, consultant*

Gloucester Point
Perkins, Frank Overton *marine scientist, educator*

Hampton
Stern, Joseph Aaron *services contracting executive*

Lexington
Hickman, Cleveland Pendleton, Jr. *biology educator*

Mc Lean
Layson, William McIntyre *research consulting company executive*
Mc Hugh, John Laurence *marine biologist, educator*
Talbot, Lee Merriam *ecologist, environmental specialist, consultant*

Norfolk
†Alden, Raymond William, III *marine biologist, laboratory director*

Richmond
Bradley, Sterling Gaylen *microbiology and pharmacology educator*
Wolf, Barry *genetics, pediatric educator*
Yu, Robert Kuan-jen *biochemistry educator*

Vienna
Giovacchini, Robert Peter *toxicologist, manufacturing executive, retired*
Jahn, Laurence Roy *retired biologist, institute executive*
Schneider, Peter Raymond *research scientist, juvenile justice consultant*

Virginia Beach
Merchant, Donald Joseph *microbiologist*

Williamsburg
Griffith, Melvin Eugene *entomologist, public health official*
Spitzer, Cary Redford *avionics consultant, electrical engineer*

Winchester
Horsburgh, Robert Laurie *entomologist*

WASHINGTON

Anacortes
Sulkin, Stephen David *marine biology educator*

Bellingham
Critchlow, B. Vaughn *research facility administrator, researcher*
Landis, Wayne G. *environmental toxicologist*
Naylor, Harry Brooks *microbiologist*
Ross, June Rosa Pitt *biologist*

Eatonville
Geddes, Gary Lee *wildlife park director*

Edmonds
Paul, Ronald Stanley *research institute executive*

Friday Harbor
Blinks, John Rogers *physiology and biophysics educator*
Willows, Arthur Owen Dennis *neurobiologist, zoology educator*

Olympia
Steiger, Gretchen Helene *marine mammalogist, research biologist*

Prosser
Miller, David Eugene *soil scientist, researcher*
Proebsting, Edward Louis, Jr. *retired research horticulturist*

Pullman
Bertramson, B. Rodney *agronomist*
Hosick, Howard Lawrence *cell biology educator, academic administrator*
Nakata, Herbert Minoru *retired microbiology educator, academic administrator*

Richland
Colson, Steven Douglas *research director, chemistry educator*
Wehner, Alfred Peter *inhalation toxicologist, biomedical scientist*
Wiley, William Rodney *microbiologist, administrator*

Seattle
Alexander, Edward Russell *disease research administrator*
Aron, William *marine biology administrator*
Bevan, Donald Edward *retired marine science educator, university dean*
Bliss, Lawrence Carroll *botany educator*
Boersma, P. Dee *ecology educator*
Bronsdon, Melinda Ann *microbiologist*
†Clark, Edward Alan *immunologist, microbiologist, educator*
Cleland, Robert Erksine *plant physiologist, educator*
Coyle, Marie Bridget *microbiology educator, laboratory director*
del Moral, Roger *botany educator, ecologist, wetland consultant*
Donaldson, Lauren R. *fisheries biology and radiobiology educator emeritus*
Edmondson, W(allace) Thomas *limnologist, educator*
Edwards, John Stuart *zoology educator, researcher*
Evans, Charles Albert *microbiology educator*
Gessel, Stanley Paul *emeritus soil science educator*
Groman, Neal Benjamin *microbiology educator*
Hall, Benjamin Downs *genetics and botany educator*
†Hartwell, Leland Harrison *geneticist, educator*
Hauschka, Stephen Denison *developmental biologist, educator*
Hille, Bertil *physiology educator*
†Holbrook, Karen Ann *biology educator and researcher, dean*
Hood, Leroy Edward *molecular biologist, educator*
Karr, James Richard *ecologist, researcher, educator*
Kohn, Alan J. *zoology educator*
Kruckeberg, Arthur Rice *botanist, educator*
Laird, Charles David *zoology and genetics educator, researcher*
Leopold, Estella Bergere *botany and environmental studies educator*
Mc Donald, James Michael, Jr. *research institute consultant*
Meeuse, Bastiaan Jacob Dirk *biologist, educator, researcher*
Motulsky, Arno Gunther *geneticist, physician, educator*
Nakatani, Roy Eiji *biologist, educator*
Nester, Eugene William *microbiology educator*
Ning, Xue-Han (Hsueh-Han Ning) *physiologist, researcher*
Olstad, Roger Gale *science educator*
Orians, Gordon Howell *biology educator*

Paine, Robert Treat *zoology educator*
Pigott, George Morris *food engineering educator, consulting engineer*
Pollack, Sylvia Byrne *educator, researcher, counselor*
Ratner, Buddy Dennis *bioengineer, educator*
Riddiford, Lynn Moorhead *zoologist, educator*
Schellenberg, Gerard David *geneticist, researcher*
Smith, Orville Auverne *physiology educator*
Staley, James Trotter *microbiology educator*
Thomas, David Phillip *forestry educator, college administrator*
Tukey, Harold Bradford, Jr. *horticulture educator*
Wooster, Warren S(criver) *marine science educator*
Wott, John Arthur *arboretum and botanical garden executive, horticulture educator*

Tacoma
Champ, Stanley Gordon *scientific company executive*
Otten, Thomas *zoological park director*

Vancouver
†Matlock, John Hudson *science administrator, materials engineer*

Wenatchee
†Elfving, Don C. *horticulturist, administrator*
Schrader, Lawrence Edwin *plant physiologist, educator*

WEST VIRGINIA

Beckley
Baligar, Virupax C. *research soil scientist*
Voigt, Paul Warren *research geneticist*

Elkins
Van Gundy, James Justin *biology educator*

Fairmont
Shan, Robert Kuocheng *biology educator*

Kearneysville
†Biggs, Alan Richard *plant pathologist, educator*

Morgantown
Hedge, George Albert *physiologist*
Keller, Edward Clarence, Jr. *foundation executive, ecologist, statistician, geneticist, educator*
Nath, Joginder *genetics and biology educator, researcher*
Ong, Tong-man *microbiologist, educator*
Smith, Robert Leo *ecologist, wildlife biologist*
Snyder, Irvin Stanley *microbiologist, educator*

WISCONSIN

DeForest
Miller, Paul Dean *breeding company executive, geneticist*

Hartland
Abramoff, Peter *biology educator*

Madison
Armstrong, Gregory Davenport *arboretum administrator*
Arny, Deane Cedric *former plant pathology educator, researcher*
Barnes, Robert F *agronomist*
Beck, Stanley Dwight *retired entomology educator, researcher*
Binning, Larry Keith *horticulture educator*
Bisgard, Gerald Edwin *biosciences educator, researcher*
Bjoraker, Walter Thomas *agricultural and vocational educator emeritus*
Borisy, Gary G. *molecular biology educator*
Brock, Thomas Dale *microbiology educator*
Bula, Raymond J. *agronomist*
Burkholder, Wendell Eugene *entomologist*
Cassens, Robert Gene *food scientist*
Cliver, Dean Otis *virologist, educator*
Daie, Jaleh *researcher, science educator, administrator*
Dick, Elliot Colter *virologist, epidemiologist, educator*
Erickson, John Ronald *research administrator*
Evert, Ray Franklin *botany educator*
Gilboe, David Dougherty *physiology educator*
Goodman, Robert Merwin *agriculturalist, plant biologist, university educator*
Graham, Linda Kay Edwards *biology educator*
Greaser, Marion Lewis *science educator*
Hagedorn, Donald James *phytopathologist, educator, agricultural consultant*
Hall, David Charles *zoo director, veterinarian*
Hearn, John Patrick *biologist, educator*
Helgeson, John Paul *physiologist, researcher*
Hopen, Herbert John *horticulture educator*
Iltis, Hugh Hellmut *plant taxonomist and evolutionist, educator*
Jeanne, Robert Lawrence *entomologist, educator, researcher*
Kaesberg, Paul Joseph *virology researcher*
Kirk, Thomas Kent *research scientist*
Koval, Charles Francis *entomologist, agricultural administrator, educator*
Marth, Elmer Herman *bacteriologist, educator*
McCabe, Robert Albert *wildlife ecology educator*
Nelson, Oliver Evans, Jr. *geneticist, educator*
Newcomb, Eldon Henry *retired botany educator*
Olson, Norman Fredrick *food science educator*
Pariza, Michael Willard *research institute executive, microbiology and toxicology educator*
Pella, Milton Orville *retired science educator*
Peterson, David Maurice *plant physiologist, researcher*
Ris, Hans *zoologist, educator*
Rueckert, Roland Rudyard *virologist, educator*
Rutledge, Jackie Joe *genetics educator*
Schatten, Gerald Phillip *cell biologist, educator*
Sequeira, Luis *plant pathology educator*
Sheffield, Lewis Glosson *physiologist*
Skoog, Folke Karl *botany educator*
Smalley, Eugene Byron *plant pathology educator, forest pathologist, mycologist*
Susman, Millard *geneticist, educator*
Szybalski, Waclaw *molecular geneticist, educator*
Tibbitts, Theodore William *horticulturist, researcher*
Vailas, Arthur C. *biomechanics educator*
Walker, Duard Lee *medical educator*
Welker, Wallace Irving *neurophysiologist, educator*
†White, John Graham *scientist*

Milwaukee
Boese, Gilbert Karyle *cultural organization executive*
Ficken, Millicent Sigler *zoology educator*
Remsen, Charles Cornell, III *microbiologist, research administrator, educator*
Risch, Richard William *horticultural manager*
Smith, James John *physiologist*
Taylor, Jerry Lynn *microbiologist, educator*
Weise, Charles Martin *zoology educator*
Wikenhauser, Charles Joseph *zoological park director*

Neenah
Proctor, Nick Hobert *toxicologist, pharmacologist*

Stevens Point
LeGrande, William Hunt *biology educator*

WYOMING

Bondurant
Shepard, Paul Howe *ecology educator, author, lecturer*

Cheyenne
Schuman, Gerald Eugene *soil scientist*

Laramie
Caldwell, Daniel Ralston *microbiology educator*
Christensen, Martha *mycologist, educator*
Dunn, Thomas Guy *biology educator, university administrator*
Hartman, Ronald Lee *plant systematist*
Speight, James Glassford *research company executive*

Moose
Craighead, Frank Cooper, Jr. *ecologist*

TERRITORIES OF THE UNITED STATES

PUERTO RICO

Bayamon
Santacana, Guido E. *physiology educator*

Corozal
Rodriguez Garcia, Jose A. *agronomist, investigator*

San Juan
†Crawford, William Pingree *forester*
Fernández-Coll, Fred *microbiologist, food technology laboratory director*
Lugo, Ariel E. *ecologist, botanist, federal agency administrator*
Orkand, Richard Kenneth *neurobiologist, researcher, educator*
Rodriguez-del Valle, Nuri *microbiology educator*

MILITARY ADDRESSES OF THE UNITED STATES

ATLANTIC

APO
Knowlton, Nancy *biologist*
Rubinoff, Ira *biologist, research administrator, conservationist*

CANADA

ALBERTA

Calgary
Jones, Geoffrey Melvill *physiology research educator*
†Mossop, Grant Dilworth *geological institute director*
Parkinson, Dennis *biology educator, soil biology researcher*
Yoon, Ji-Won *virology, immunology and diabetes educator, research administrator*

Edmonton
Bentley, Charles Fred *consulting agrologist*
Cormack, Robert George Hall *botany educator*
Cossins, Edwin Albert *biology educator, academic administrator*
Hiruki, Chuji *plant virologist, science educator*

Lethbridge
Sonntag, Bernard H. *agrologist, research executive*

BRITISH COLUMBIA

Bamfield
Druehl, Louis Dix *biology educator*

Burnaby
Borden, John Harvey *entomologist, educator*
Brandhorst, Bruce Peter *biology educator*

Nanaimo
Margolis, Leo *marine biologist*
Ricker, William Edwin *biologist*

New Denver
†McCrory, Colleen *ecologist*

New Westminster
Waygood, Ernest Roy *plant physiology educator*

Sidney
Bigelow, Margaret Elizabeth Barr *mycologist educator*
Davis, John Christopher *zoologist, aquatic toxicologist*
Kendrick, William Bryce *biology educator, author, publisher*
Mann, Cedric Robert *retired institute administrator, oceanographer*

Summerland
†Beveridge, Herbert James Thomas *research scientist*
Dueck, John *agricultural researcher, plant pathologist*
Looney, Norman Earl *pomologist, plant physiologist*

Vancouver
Blair, Robert *animal science administrator, educator, researcher*
Campbell, Jack James Ramsay *microbiology educator*
Chitty, Dennis Hubert *zoology educator*
Copp, Douglas Harold *physiologist, educator*
†Finlay, Barton Brett *science educator*
Hoar, William Stewart *zoologist, educator*
Jones, David Robert *zoology educator*
Larkin, Peter Anthony *zoology educator, university dean and official*
Lindsey, Casimir Charles *zoologist*
March, Beryl Elizabeth *animal scientist, educator*
McBride, Barry Clarke *microbiology and oral biology educator, research microbiologist*
Mc Lean, Donald Millis *microbiology, pathology educator, physician*
Miller, Robert Carmi, Jr. *microbiology educator, university administrator*
Newman, Murray Arthur *aquarium administrator*
Phillips, Anthony George *neurobiology educator*
Phillips, John Edward *zoologist, educator*
†Pitcher, Tony John *fishery science educator, author*
Randall, David John *physiologist, zoologist, educator*
†Rennie, Paul Steven *science administrator, biochemist, surgeon*
Shaw, Michael *biologist, educator*
Wellington, William George *plant science and ecology educator*

Victoria
Bousfield, Edward Lloyd *biologist*
Drew, T. John *life science research administrator*
†Trust, Trevor John *microbiology educator and researcher*

West Vancouver
Donaldson, Edward Mossop *research scientist, government official*

MANITOBA

Brandon
Robertson, John Alden *agrologist, researcher*

Pinawa
†Wright, Michael George *science administrator, research metallurgist*

Winnipeg
Eales, John Geoffrey *zoology educator*
Findlay, Glen Marshall *agrologist*
†Haber, Steve *plant pathologist, researcher*
Hamerton, John Laurence *geneticist, educator*
Suzuki, Isamu *microbiology educator, researcher*
†Tipples, Keith Howard *research scientist*

NEW BRUNSWICK

Saint Andrews
Scott, William Beverley *ichthyologist*

NEWFOUNDLAND

Saint John's
Coady, Larry *marine biology research administrator*
Crim, Lawrence *marine life research administrator*
Davis, Charles Carroll *aquatic biologist, educator*
Jeffrey, N. E. *marine biology administrator*
Thomas, Martin Lewis H. *marine ecologist, educator*

NOVA SCOTIA

Dartmouth
Bhartia, Prakash *defense research management executive, researcher, educator*
Mann, Kenneth Henry *marine ecologist*

Halifax
Easterbrook, Kenneth Brian *retired microbiologist*
Hall, Brian Keith *biology educator, author*
O'Dor, Ron *physiologist, marine biology educator*
Pringle, John D. *ecological research administrator*

Wallace
Bidwell, Roger Grafton Shelford *biologist, educator*

ONTARIO

Caledon
Fallis, Albert Murray *microbiology educator*

Deep River
Newcombe, Howard Borden *biologist, consultant*

Downsview
Forer, Arthur H. *biology educator, researcher, editor*
Moens, Peter B. *biology researcher and educator*

Guelph
Beveridge, Terrance James *microbiology educator, researcher*
Bewley, John Derek *botany researcher, educator*
†Buchanan-Smith, Jock Gordon *animal science educator*
Jorgensen, Erik *forest pathologist, educator, consultant*
Kasha, Kenneth John *crop science educator*
Oaks, B. Ann *plant physiologist, educator*
Sells, Bruce Howard *biomedical sciences educator*

Kingston
Bisby, Mark Ainley *physiology educator*
Leggett, William C. *biology educator, educational administrator*
Turpin, David Howard *biology educator, educational administrator*
Wyatt, Gerard Robert *biology educator, researcher*

London
Dales, Samuel *microbiologist, virologist, educator*
Locke, Michael *zoology educator*
†Poznansky, Mark J. *research institute administrator, educator*

Nepean
Bishop, Claude Titus *retired biological sciences research administrator, editor*

North York
Davey, Kenneth George *biologist, university official*

Ottawa
†Alexander, Charles *geologist*
†Batra, Tilak Raj *research scientist*
Carty, Arthur John *research council administrator*
Dence, Michael Robert *research director*
Gruchy, Charles George *conservation institute director*
Hughes, Stanley John *mycologist*
Morand, Peter *research agency executive*
Nordin, Vidar John *forestry educator, consultant*
†Perron, Pierre O. *science administrator*
Perry, Malcolm Blythe *biologist*
†Seifert, Keith Anthony *mycologist*
Sinha, Ramesh Chandra *plant pathologist*
Soper, James Herbert *botanist, curator*
Storey, Kenneth Bruce *biology educator*
Topp, George Clarke *soil physicist*

Peterborough
Hutchinson, Thomas Cuthbert *ecology and environmental educator*

Port Rowan
†Francis, Charles MacKenzie *wildlife biologist*

Sault Sainte Marie
†Winget, Carl Henry *science administrator, forest ecologist*

Toronto
Atwood, Harold Leslie *physiology and zoology educator*
†Heath, Michele Christine *botany educator*
Kerr, David Wylie *natural resource company executive*
†Kushner, Donn Jean *microbiologist, children's author*
Liversage, Richard Albert *cell biologist*
MacLennan, David Herman *research scientist, educator*
Mustard, James Fraser *research institute executive*
†Pawson, Anthony J. *molecular biologist*
Stadelman, William Ralph *chemical institution executive*
Tobe, Stephen Solomon *zoology educator*
Tsui, Lap-Chee *molecular genetics educator*
White, Calvin John *zoo executive, financial manager, zoological association executive*
Worton, Ronald Gibert *geneticist, educator*

Waterloo
Hynes, Hugh Bernard Noel *biology educator*
McCauley, Robert William *biologist, educator*

Yarker
Smallman, Beverley N. *biology educator*

QUEBEC

Ile Perrot
Tomlinson, George Herbert *retired industrial company research executive*

Lac Beauport
†Lane, Peter *ornithologist*

Laval
Frisque, Gilles *forestry engineer*
Kluepfel, Dieter *microbiologist*
Pavilanis, Vytautas *microbiology educator, physician*

Lennoxville
†Deschenes, Jean-Marc *agriculturist, researcher*

Montreal
Adamkiewicz, Vincent Witold *microbiology and immunology educator, researcher*
Carroll, Robert Lynn *biology educator, vertebrate paleontologist, museum curator*
Chang, Thomas Ming Swi *medical scientist, biotechnologist*
Dansereau, Pierre *ecologist*
Gibbs, Sarah Preble *biologist, educator*
Jolicoeur, Paul *molecular biologist*
Maclachlan, Gordon Alistair *biology educator, researcher*
Murphy, Beverley Elaine Pearson *scientist, administrator, physician, educator*
Pinsky, Leonard *geneticist*
Plaa, Gabriel Leon *toxicologist, educator*
Sattler, Rolf *plant morphologist, educator*
Sonea, Sorin I. *microbiologist*
Stanners, Clifford Paul *molecular biologist, cell biologist, biochemistry educator*

Quebec
†Bourget, Edwin Robert *marine ecologist, educator*
Joly, Jean Robert *microbiologist, medical educator*
Potvin, Pierre *physiologist, educator*
Trudel, Marc J. *botanist*
†Villeneuve, Jean-Pierre *science association director, educator*

Saint Jean-sur-Richelieu
†Demars, Denis *research institution director*

Sainte Anne de Bellevue
Grant, William Frederick *geneticist, educator*
MacLeod, Robert Angus *microbiology educator, researcher*
Steppler, Howard Alvey *agronomist*

Sainte Foy
Cardinal, André *phycologist, educator*

SASKATCHEWAN

Regina
Davis, Gordon Richard Fuerst *biologist, translator*

Saskatoon
Babiuk, Lorne Alan *virologist, immunologist, research administrator*
Baker, Robert John *agronomy educator*
Bell, John Milton *agricultural science educator*
Harvey, Bryan Laurence *crop science educator*
Huang, Pan Ming *soil science educator*
Shokeir, Mohamed Hassan Kamel *medical geneticist, educator*
†Steck, Warren Franklin *former entomology researcher, science administrator*

MEXICO

Mexico City
Rajaram, Sanjaya *agricultural scientist, plant breeder*

ARGENTINA

Buenos Aires
Balve, Beba Carmen *research center administrator*

AUSTRALIA

Parkville
Foote, Simon James *molecular biologist*

Randwick
Hall, Peter Francis *physiologist*

CUBA

Havana
Kouri, Gustavo Pedro *virologist*

ENGLAND

Cambridge
Carpenter, Adelaide Trowbridge Clark *geneticist*

Cranbrook
Hattersley-Smith, Geoffrey Francis *retired government research scientist*

Oxford
May, Robert McCredie *biology educator*

FRANCE

Orsay
Fiszer-Szafarz, Berta (Berta Safars) *research scientist*

Paris
LeGoffic, Francois *biotechnology educator*
Robert, Leslie Ladislas *research center administrator, consultant*

GERMANY

Hamburg
Müller-Eberhard, Hans Joachim *medical research scientist, administrator*

Hannover
Döhler, Klaus Dieter *pharmaceutical and development company executive*

Katlenburg
Hagfors, Tor *institute director*

Munich
Berg, Jan Mikael *science educator*

HONG KONG

Kowloon
Kung, Shain-dow *molecular biologist, educator*

ITALY

Camerino
Miyake, Akio *biologist, educator*

Naples
Tarro, Giulio *virologist*

JAPAN

Fukuoka
Aizawa, Keio *biology educator*

Iwate
Kawauchi, Hiroshi *hormone science educator*

Kanagawa
Okui, Kazumitsu *biology educator*

Osaka
Sakaguchi, Genji *food microbiologist, educator*
Watanabe, Toshiharu *ecologist, educator*

Tochigi
Ishii, Akira *medical parasitologist, malariologist, allergologist*

Tokyo
Takahashi, Keiichi *zoology educator*

KENYA

South Nyanza
Khan, Zeyaur Rahman *entomologist*

PERU

Lima
French, Edward Ronald *plant pathologist*

POLAND

Warsaw
Koscielak, Jerzy *scientist, science administrator*

SAUDI ARABIA

Riyadh
Chaudhary, Shaukat Ali *ecologist, plant taxonomist*

SCOTLAND

Gullane
Collins, Jeffrey Hamilton *research facility administrator, electrical engineering educator*

SWITZERLAND

Lausanne
Stingelin, Valentin *research center director, mechanical engineer*

TAIWAN

Taichung
Lee, Kuo-Chuan *horticulture educator*

THAILAND

Bangkok
Friedman, Ronald Marvin *cellular biologist*

ADDRESS UNPUBLISHED

Ahearne, John Francis *scientific research society administrator, researcher*
Ahlquist, Paul Gerald *molecular biology researcher, educator*
Arnott, Howard Joseph *biology educator, university dean*
Barrett, Izadore *retired fisheries research administrator*
Berlowitz Tarrant, Laurence *biotechnologist, university administrator*
Bernard, Richard Lawson *geneticist, retired*
Birchem, Regina *cell biologist, environment consultant, educator, writer*
Block, Barbara Ann *biology educator*
Boell, Edgar John *biology educator*
Bonner, John Tyler *biology educator*
Bricken, William Marion *scientist*
Brill, Winston Jonas *microbiologist, educator, research director, publisher and management consultant*
Brody, Edward Norman *molecular biologist, educator*
Bullock, Theodore Holmes *biologist, educator*
Burlew, John Swalm *research scientist*
Bush, Guy Louis *biology educator*
Carlquist, Sherwin *biology and botany educator*
Catlin, B. Wesley *microbiologist*
Cheverton, William Kearns *science corporation executive, consultant*
Coia, Robert Salvatore *biology educator, consultant*
Cole, Jerome Foster *research company executive*
Coleman, Nancy Pees *environmental toxicologist*
Creech, John Lewis *retired scientist, consultant*
Cutler, Winnifred Berg *biologist*
Davis, Emma R. *horticulturist*
De Antoni, Edward Paul *cancer control research scientist*
Detra, Ralph William *research laboratory administrator*
†Di Sabato, Louis Roman *zoo administrator*
Dugan, Patrick Raymond *microbiologist, university dean*
Eicher, George John *aquatic biologist*
Ellner, Paul Daniel *clinical microbiologist*
Erlenmeyer-Kimling, L. *psychiatric and behavior genetics researcher, educator*
Field, George Sydney *retired research director*
Florence, Paul Smith *agronomist, business owner*
Folkens, Alan Theodore *clinical and pharmaceutical microbiologist*
Foy, Charles Daley *retired soil scientist*
Franklin, Jerry Forest *ecologist*
Galas, David John *molecular biology educator, researcher*
Gennaro, Antonio L. *biology educator*
Gill, William Robert *soil scientist*
Glick, J. Leslie *biotechnology entrepreneur*
Goin, Olive Bown *biologist*
Goldstein, Walter Elliott *biotechnology executive*
Grill, Laurence Kay *molecular biologist*
Gross, Paul Randolph *biologist, academic administrator*
Hall, John Marshall *food industry consultant*
Hamilton, William Howard *laboratory executive*
Harris, Elliott Stanley *toxicologist*
Hartman, Margaret J. *biologist, educator, university official*
Heine, Ursula Ingrid *biologist, researcher, artist*
Hölldobler, Berthold Karl *zoologist, educator*
Inouye, David William *zoology educator*
Jackson, Victor Louis *retired naturalist*
Jacobs, Hyde Spencer *soil chemistry educator*
†Johnson, Marshall Wain *entomologist, educator*
Katz, Anne Harris *biologist, educator, writer, aviator*
Kemnitzer, Susan Coady *science foundation administrator*
King, John Quill Taylor *science center administrator, college administrator emeritus*
Kirsteuer, Ernst Karl Eberhart *biologist, curator*
Kolb, James A. *science association director, writer*
Kozlowski, Theodore Thomas *botany educator, research director, author, editor*
Krogh, Lester Christensen *retired research and development executive*
Kuper, George Henry *research and development institute executive*
LaMunyon, Craig Willis *biology researcher*
Leath, Kenneth Thomas *research plant pathologist, educator*
Lechevalier, Hubert Arthur *microbiology educator*
Leder, Philip *geneticist, educator*
Lindsay, Dale Richard *research administrator*
Markovitz, Alvin *molecular biologist, geneticist*
Maroni, Donna Farolino *science administrator, retired*
McFarland, Victor Alan *toxicologist*
Melnick, Joseph L. *virologist, educator*
Menn, Julius Joel *research scientist*
Micks, Don Wilfred *biologist, educator*
Moore, Donald Eugene *retired botanical garden administrator, communications executive*
Moscona, Aron Arthur *biology educator, scientist*
Myers, Jack Edgar *biologist, educator*
†Nantermet, Philippe Guy *research scientist*
Neel, James Van Gundia *geneticist, educator*
Nelson, Wallace Warren *retired superintendent experimental station, agronomy educator*
Nicoll, Charles Samuel *physiologist, educator*
†O'Brien, Stephen James *geneticist*
Palade, George Emil *biologist, educator*
Parmelee, David Freeland *biologist, educator*
Peiss, Clarence Norman *physiology educator, college dean*
Peter, Richard Ector *zoology educator*
Pielou, Evelyn C. *biologist*
Pinter, Gabriel George *physiologist*
Rabson, Robert *plant physiologist, administrator*
Ramanarayanan, Madhava Prabhu *science administrator, researcher, educator*
Read, Paul E. *horticulture educator*
Reetz, Harold Frank, Jr. *industrial agronomist*
†Rogers, Jack David *plant pathologist, educator*
Rucker, Charles Thomas *science facility administrator*
Schmidt, Jean Marie *microbiology educator*
Schwab, John Harris *microbiology and immunology educator*
Simon, Melvin I. *molecular biologist, educator*
Simpson, Frederick James *retired research administrator*
Sjostrand, Fritiof Stig *biologist, educator*
Skinner, James Stanford *physiologist, educator*
Snell, George Davis *geneticist*
Sokal, Robert Reuven *biology educator, author*
South, Frank Edwin *physiologist, educator*
Southwick, Charles Henry *zoologist, educator*
Stark, Nellie May *forest ecology educator*
Striker, Gary E. *scientist, research institution administrator*
Tandler, Bernard *cell biology educator*
Tenney, Stephen Marsh *physiologist, educator*
Tzimopoulos, Nicholas D. *science and mathematics education specialist*
Vaughan, John Charles, III *horticultural products executive*
Warren, Henry Clay, Jr. *retired naturalist*
Wilkinson, Stanley Ralph *agronomist*
Williams, Timothy James *sanctuary manager, naturalist*
Yang, Xiangzhong *research scientist, administrator, educator*

SCIENCE: MATHEMATICS AND COMPUTER SCIENCE

UNITED STATES

ALABAMA

Birmingham
Jones, Warren Thomas *computer science educator*
Peeples, William Dewey, Jr. *mathematics educator*

Florence
Johnson, Johnny Ray *mathematics educator*

Huntsville
†Meadlock, Nancy B. *computer graphics company executive*
Pruitt, Alice Fay *mathematician, engineer*
Zant, Robert Franklin *computer information educator*

Mobile
Morelock, James Crutchfield *mathematician*

Pelham
Turner, Malcolm Elijah *biomathematician, educator*

Tuscaloosa
Davis, Anthony Michael John *mathematics educator*
Drake, Albert Estern *retired statistics educator, farming administrator*

ALASKA

Anchorage
Chang, Ping-Tung *mathematics educator*
Mann, Lester Perry *mathematics educator*

ARIZONA

Mesa
Stott, Brian *software company executive*

Phoenix
Friesen, Oris Dewayne *software engineer, historian*

Prescott
Anderson, Arthur George *laboratory director, former computer company executive, consultant*

Tempe
Krus, David James *statistician*
Smith, Harvey Alvin *mathematics educator, consultant*
Wang, Alan Ping-I *mathematics educator*
Yau, Stephen Sik-sang *computer science and engineering educator, computer scientist, researcher*

Tucson
Clay, James Ray *mathematics educator*
Neuts, Marcel Fernand *statistician, educator*
Re Velle, Jack B(oyer) *statistician, consultant*
Willoughby, Stephen Schuyler *mathematics educator*

ARKANSAS

Batesville
Carius, Robert Wilhelm *mathematics and science educator, retired naval officer*

Little Rock
Townsend, James Willis *computer scientist*

Searcy
Oldham, Bill W. *mathematics educator*

CALIFORNIA

Arcadia
Seitz, Charles Lewis *computer scientist and engineer*

Arcata
Hunt, Robert Weldon *mathematics educator, consultant*

Berkeley
Arveson, William Barnes *mathematics educator*
†Basch, Reva *information services company executive*
Bergman, George Mark *mathematician, educator*
Bickel, Peter John *statistician, educator*
Blum, Manuel *computer science educator*
Bourne, Samuel G. *mathematician, consultant, educator*
Chern, Shiing-Shen *mathematics educator*
Chorin, Alexandre Joel *mathematician, educator*
Cooper, William Secord *information science educator*
Culler, David Ethan *computer science educator*
Fateman, Richard J. *computer science educator, researcher*
Feldman, Jerome Arthur *computer scientist, educator*
Ferrari, Domenico *computer science educator*
Freedman, David Amiel *statistics educator, consultant*
Graham, Susan Lois *computer science educator, consultant*
Harrison, Michael Alexander *computer scientist, educator, entrepreneur*
Henkin, Leon Albert *mathematician, educator*
Hirsch, Morris William *mathematics educator*
Jewell, Nicholas Patrick *statistics educator*
Kahan, William M. *mathematics educator, consultant*
Kaplansky, Irving *mathematician, educator, research institute director*
Karp, Richard Manning *computer sciences educator*
Le Cam, Lucien Marie *mathematics educator*
Lehmann, Erich Leo *statistics educator*
Osserman, Robert *mathematician, educator*
Patterson, David Andrew *computer scientist, educator, consultant*
Ramamoorthy, Chittor V. *computer science educator*
Ratner, Marina *mathematician, educator, researcher*
Schoenfeld, Alan Henry *mathematics and education educator*
Sequin, Carlo H. *computer science educator*
Smith, Alan Jay *computer science educator, consultant*
Speed, Terence Paul *statistician, educator*
Tarter, Michael Ernest *biostatistician, educator*
Thomas, Paul Emery *mathematics educator*
Wolf, Joseph Albert *mathematician, educator*
†Xie, Ganquan *mathematician, computational geophysical scientist, educator*

Carlsbad
Halberg, Charles John August, Jr. *mathematics educator*

Carmichael
Givant, Philip Joachim *mathematics educator, real estate investment executive*

Carson
Suchenek, Marek Andrzej *computer science educator*

Chico
Wolff, Howard Keith *computer science educator, consultant*

Claremont
Bentley, Donald Lyon *mathematics and statistics educator*
Coleman, Courtney Stafford *mathematician, educator*
Cooke, Kenneth Lloyd *mathematician, educator*
Elderkin, Richard Howard *mathematician, educator*

Grabiner, Sandy *mathematics educator*
Henriksen, Melvin *mathematician, educator*
Mullikin, Harry Copeland *mathematics educator*
White, Alvin Murray *mathematics educator, consultant*

Costa Mesa
Savage, Sandra Hope Skeen *mathematics educator, curriculum writer*

Culver City
Berland, James Fred *software developer, computer management consultant*

Danville
Lowery, Lawrence Frank *mathematic science and computer educator*

Davis
Alder, Henry Ludwig *mathematics educator*
Rocke, David Morton *statistician, educator*

Fremont
Lautzenheiser, Marvin Wendell *computer software engineer*

Fresno
Cohen, Moses Elias *mathematician, educator*

Fullerton
Kagiwada, Harriet Hatsune Natsuyama *mathematician*

Glendale
Burger, John Barclay *systems architect, computer scientist*

Hayward
Sabharwal, Ranjit Singh *mathematician*

Irvine
Bennett, Bruce Michael *mathematics educator, musician*
†Hoffman, Donald David *cognitive and computer science educator*
Li, Peter Wai-Kwong *mathematics educator*
Wan, Frederic Yui-Ming *mathematician, educator*

La Jolla
Freedman, Michael Hartley *mathematician, educator*
Haimo, Deborah Tepper *mathematics educator*
Halkin, Hubert *mathematics educator, research mathematician*
Martin, James John, Jr. *retired consulting research firm executive, systems analyst*
Reissner, Eric (Max Erich Reissner) *applied mechanics researcher*
Rodin, Burton *mathematics educator*
Rosenblatt, Murray *mathematics educator*
Terras, Audrey Anne *mathematics educator*
Wulbert, Daniel Eliot *mathematician, educator*

Lafayette
Moore, Calvin C. *mathematics educator, administrator*

Los Angeles
Afifi, Abdelmonem A. *biostatistics educator, academic dean*
Arbib, Michael Anthony *computer scientist, educator, neuroscientist, cybernetician*
Bekey, George Albert *computer scientist, educator, engineer*
Chacko, George Kuttickal *systems science educator, consultant*
Chu, Wesley Wei-Chin *computer science educator, consultant*
Estrin, Gerald *computer scientist, engineering educator, academic administrator*
Golomb, Solomon Wolf *mathematician, electrical engineer, educator, university official*
Gordon, Basil *mathematics educator*
Greenberger, Martin *computer and information scientist, educator*
Harris, Theodore Edward *mathematician, educator*
Hu, Sze-Tsen *mathematics educator*
Kalaba, Robert Edwin *applied mathematician*
Kleinrock, Leonard *computer scientist*
†Petak, William John *systems management educator*
Port, Sidney Charles *mathematician, educator*
Rector, Robert Wayman *mathematics and engineering educator, former association executive*
Redheffer, Raymond Moos *mathematician, educator*
Shapley, Lloyd Stowell *mathematics and economics educator*
Waterman, Michael Spencer *mathematics educator, biology educator*

Menlo Park
Bourne, Charles Percy *information scientist, educator*

Milpitas
Hodson, Roy Goode, Jr. *retired logistician*

Monterey
Gaskell, Robert Eugene *mathematician, educator*
Hamming, Richard Wesley *computer scientist*

Moss Landing
Lange, Lester Henry *mathematics educator*

Orange
†Stickney, Douglas Henry *biostatistician, consultant*

Pacific Palisades
Becker, Joseph *information scientist*

Palo Alto
†Feigenbaum, Edward Albert *computer science educator*
Goldberg, Jacob *computer scientist, researcher*
Itnyre, Jacqueline Harriet *programmer*
Lamport, Leslie B. *computer scientist*
Spinrad, Robert Joseph *computer scientist*
Taylor, Robert William *research director*
Weiser, Mark David *computer scientist, researcher*

Pasadena
Chandy, Kanianthra Mani *computer sciences educator, consultant*
Cohen, Donald Sussman *mathematician, educator*
Franklin, Joel Nicholas *mathematician, educator*
Luxemburg, Wilhelmus Anthonius Josephus *mathematics educator*
Mead, Carver Andress *computer science educator*
Saffman, Philip G. *mathematician*
Simon, Barry *mathematician, physicist, educator*
Todd, John *mathematician, educator*
Whitham, Gerald Beresford *mathematics educator*

Pomona
Bernau, Simon John *mathematics educator*

Portola Valley
Kuo, Franklin F. *computer scientist, electrical engineer*

Ramona
Bennett, James Chester *computer consultant, real estate developer*

Redondo Beach
Burris, Harrison Robert *computer and software developer*

Riverside
Bhanu, Bir *computer information scientist, educator, director university program*
Ratliff, Louis Jackson, Jr. *mathematics educator*
Shapiro, Victor Lenard *mathematician*

Sacramento
Sawiris, Milad Youssef *statistician, educator*

San Diego
Burgin, George Hans *computer scientist, educator*
Burke, John *science technology company executive*
Garrison, Betty Bernhardt *mathematics educator*
Hales, Alfred Washington *mathematics educator, consultant*
Karin, Sidney *research and development executive*
Willerding, Margaret Frances *mathematician*

San Francisco
Backus, John *computer scientist*
Christensen, David William *mathematician, engineer*
Farrell, Edward Joseph *retired mathematics educator*
Rautenberg, Robert Frank *consulting statistician*

Santa Barbara
Fan, Ky *mathematician, educator*
Johnsen, Eugene Carlyle *mathematician and educator*
Marcus, Marvin *mathematician, educator*
Minc, Henryk *mathematics educator*
Newman, Morris *mathematician*
Rosenberg, Alex *mathematician, educator*
Simons, Stephen *mathematics educator, researcher*
Zelmanowitz, Julius Martin *mathematics educator, university administrator*

Santa Clara
Alexanderson, Gerald Lee *mathematician, educator, writer*
Halmos, Paul Richard *mathematician, educator*

Santa Cruz
Huskey, Harry Douglas *information and computer science educator*

Santa Monica
Ware, Willis Howard *computer scientist*

Santee
Peters, Raymond Eugene *computer systems company executive*

Saratoga
Park, Joseph Chul Hui *computer scientist*

Simi Valley
Stratton, Gregory Alexander *computer specialist, administrator, mayor*

Stanford
Anderson, Theodore Wilbur *statistics educator*
Brown, Byron William, Jr. *biostatistician, educator*
Brumfiel, Gregory Wayne *mathematics educator*
Carlsson, Gunnar Erik *mathematics educator*
Cover, Thomas M. *statistician, electrical engineer, educator*
Dantzig, George Bernard *applied mathematics educator*
Efron, Bradley *mathematics educator*
Feferman, Solomon *mathematics and philosophy educator, researcher*
Johnstone, Iain Murray *statistician, educator, consultant*
Karlin, Samuel *mathematics educator, researcher*
Keller, Joseph Bishop *mathematician, educator*
Knuth, Donald Ervin *computer sciences educator*
Lieberman, Gerald J. *statistics educator*
McCarthy, John *computer scientist, educator*
Moses, Lincoln E. *statistician, educator*
Nilsson, Nils John *computer science educator, researcher*
Olshen, Richard A. *statistician, educator*
Ornstein, Donald Samuel *mathematician, educator*
Phillips, Ralph Saul *mathematics educator*
Royden, Halsey Lawrence *mathematics educator*
Switzer, Paul *statistics educator*
Ullman, Jeffrey David *computer science educator*
Winograd, Terry Allen *computer science educator*

Thousand Oaks
Sladek, Lyle Virgil *mathematician, educator*

Woodland Hills
Fitzpatrick, Dennis Michael *information systems executive*

COLORADO

Aurora
Barth, David Victor *computer systems designer, consultant*

Boulder
Crow, Edwin Louis *mathematical statistician, consultant*
Mycielski, Jan *mathematician, educator*

Colorado Springs
Couger, James Daniel *computer scientist, writer*
Cray, Seymour R. *computer designer*
Simmons, George Finlay *mathematics educator*

Denver
†Cutter, Gary Raymond *biostatistician, epidemiologist*

Durango
Spencer, Donald Clayton *mathematician*

Fort Collins
Allgower, Eugene Leo *mathematics educator*
Mielke, Paul William, Jr. *statistician*
Tweedie, Richard Lewis *statistics educator, consultant*

CONNECTICUT

East Hartford
Ahlberg, John Harold *mathematician, educator*

Fairfield
Eigel, Edwin George, Jr. *mathematics educator, retired university president*
Shaffer, Dorothy Browne *retired mathematician, educator*

Farmington
Miser, Hugh Jordan *systems analyst, operations researcher, consultant*

Middletown
Comfort, William Wistar *mathematics educator*
Hager, Anthony Wood *mathematics educator*
Linton, Fred Ernest Julius *mathematics educator*
Reid, James Dolan *mathematics educator, researcher*
Rosenbaum, Robert Abraham *mathematics educator*

New Haven
Feit, Walter *mathematics educator*
Fischer, Michael John *computer science educator*
†Holford, Theodore Richard *biostatistician, educator*
†Howe, Roger Evans *mathematician, educator*
Jacobson, Nathan *mathematics educator*
Lang, Serge *mathematics educator*
Massey, William S. *mathematician, educator*
McDermott, Drew Vincent *computer science educator*
Mostow, George Daniel *mathematics educator*
Piatetski-Shapiro, Ilya *mathematics educator*
Rickart, Charles Earl *mathematician, educator*
Seligman, George Benham *mathematics educator*
Szczarba, Robert Henry *mathematics educator, mathematician*
Tamagawa, Tsuneo *mathematics educator*
Tufte, Edward Rolf *statistics educator, publisher*

Southbury
March, Xavier *systems analyst*

Storrs
Spencer, Domina Eberle *mathematics educator*

West Hartford
Welna, Cecilia *mathematics educator*

Wilton
Brown, James Thompson, Jr. *computer information scientist*

DELAWARE

Dover
Vawter, William Snyder *computer software consultant*

Newark
Colton, David Lem *mathematician, educator*
Stakgold, Ivar *mathematics educator*
Stark, Robert Martin *mathematician, civil engineer, educator*

DISTRICT OF COLUMBIA

Washington
Bogdan, Victor Michael *mathematics educator, scientist*
Chiazze, Leonard, Jr. *biostatistician, epidemiologist, educator*
Chou, Wushow *information scientist, federal agency official*
Denning, Dorothy Elizabeth Robling *computer scientist*
Flournoy, Nancy *statistician, educator*
Gastwirth, Joseph Lewis *statistician, educator*
Goldfield, Edwin David *statistician*
Goldhaber, Jacob Kopel *retired mathematician, educator*
Gray, Mary Wheat *statistician, lawyer*
Hammer, Carl *computer scientist, former computer company executive*
Hedges, Harry George *computer scientist, educator*
Hoffman, Kenneth Myron *mathematician, educator*
†Killion, Ruth Ann *statistical researcher*
Lewis, Forbes Downer *computer science educator, researcher*
Loosbrock, Carol Marie *information management professional*
Maisel, Herbert *computer science educator*
†Matthews, Dale Samuel *information scientist, media futurist*
Okay, John Louis *information scientist*
Perry, William James *mathematical scientist, government official*
Raphael, Louise Arakelian *mathematician, educator*
Sandefur, James Tandy *mathematics educator*
Saworotnow, Parfeny Pavlovich *mathematician, educator*
Shaw, William Frederick *statistician*
Stokes, Arnold Paul *mathematics educator*
Tidball, Charles Stanley *computer scientist, educator*
Tortora, Robert D. *mathematician*
Walsh, William H., Jr. *statistical research director*
Weiss, Leonard *mathematician, engineer, senate staff director*

FLORIDA

Coral Gables
Howard, Bernard Eufinger *computer science and mathematics educator*

Delray Beach
Hegstrom, William Jean *mathematics educator*

Fort Lauderdale
Kemper Littman, Marlyn *information scientist, educator*

Gainesville
Bednarek, Alexander Robert *mathematician, educator*
Dinculeanu, Nicolae *mathematician*
Emch, Gerard Gustav *mathematics and physics educator*
Keesling, James Edgar *mathematics educator*
Pop-Stojanovic, Zoran Rista *mathematics educator*

Highland Beach
Schor, Stanley Sidney *mathematical sciences educator*

Indialantic
Carroll, Charles Lemuel, Jr. *mathematician*

Jacksonville
Robinson, Christine Marie *mathematics educator*

Lakeland
Sheppard, Albert Parker, Jr. *mathematics educator*

Melbourne
Lakshmikantham, Vangipuram *mathematics educator*

Miami
Zanakis, Steve H. *management/science/information systems educator*

Naples
Ciano, James Francis *computer systems analyst*
Hainsworth, Melody May *information professional, researcher*

Ocala
Johnson, Winston Conrad *mathematics educator*

Orlando
Deo, Narsingh *computer science educator*
Medin, Julia Adele *mathematics educator, researcher*
Sathre, Leroy *mathematics educator, consultant*

Palm Bay
Olejar, Paul Duncan *former information science administrator*

Saint Petersburg
Kazor, Walter Robert *statistical process control and quality assurance consultant*
Schell, Joan Bruning *information specialist, business science librarian*
Shi, Feng Sheng *mathematician*

Sarasota
Eachus, Joseph J(ackson) *computer scientist, consultant*

Tallahassee
Goodner, Dwight Benjamin *mathematician, emeritus educator*
†Hunter, Christopher *mathematics educator*
Navon, Ionel Michael *mathematics educator*
Nichols, Eugene Douglas *mathematics educator*
Stino, Farid K.R. *biostatistician, educator, researcher, consultant*

Tampa
Bryant, Herbert McCoy, Jr. (Herbie DeLaney) *statistician*
Saff, Edward Barry *mathematics educator*
Williams, Thomas Arthur *biomedical computing consultant, psychiatrist*

West Palm Beach
Bower, Ruth Lawther *retired mathematics educator*
Still, Mary Jane (M. J. Still) *mathematics educator*

GEORGIA

Athens
Neter, John *statistician*
Speering, Robin *computer specialist, educator*

Atlanta
Ames, William Francis *mathematician, educator*
Foley, James David *computer science educator, consultant*
Hale, Jack K. *mathematics educator, research center administrator*
Imlay, John Prescott, Jr. *computer information science executive*
Johnson, Ellis Lane *mathematician*
Oliker, Vladimir *mathematician, educator*
Vaishnavi, Vijay Kumar *computer science educator, researcher*
Wilkins, J. Ernest, Jr. *mathematician*
Williams, Charles Murray *computer information systems educator, consultant*

Savannah
Albert, Theodore Merton *computer scientist*
Wheeler, Ed Ray *mathematics educator*

HAWAII

Hilo
Gersting, Judith Lee *computer science educator, researcher*

Honolulu
Swanson, Richard William *statistician*

IDAHO

Boise
Mech, William Paul *mathematics educator, director honors program*

Calder
Rechard, Ottis William *mathematics and computer science educator*

Moscow
Bobisud, Larry Eugene *mathematics educator*

ILLINOIS

Bloomington
Friedman, Joan M. *educator*
Prescott, Richard Paul, Jr. *computer company consultant*

Champaign
Kuck, David Jerome *computer system researcher, administrator*
Philipp, Walter Viktor *mathematician, educator*

Chicago
Ash, J. Marshall *mathematician, educator*
†Bloch, Spencer J. *mathematician*
Calderon, Alberto P. *mathematician, educator*
Dupont, Todd F. *mathematics and computer science educator*
Ejiogu, Lem Onyeaduzim *software engineer*
Graves, Robert Lawrence *mathematician, educator*
Hanson, Floyd Bliss *applied mathematician, computational scientist, mathematical biologist*
Kruskal, William Henry *statistician, educator*
MacLane, Saunders *mathematician, educator*
Madansky, Albert *statistics educator*
May, J. Peter *mathematics educator*
Pless, Vera *mathematics and computer science educator*
Reingold, Haim *mathematics educator*
Roberts, Harry Vivian *statistics educator*
†Safar, Michael *information scientist*
Stigler, Stephen Mack *statistician, educator*
Swan, Richard Gordon *mathematics educator*
Wirszup, Izaak *mathematician, educator*
†Zelmanov, Efim Isaakovich *mathematician educator*
Zimmer, Robert J. *mathematician*

De Kalb
Sons, Linda Ruth *mathematics educator*

East Peoria
Grisham, George Robert *mathematics educator*

Elgin
Juister, Barbara Joyce *mathematics educator*

Evanston
Aagaard, James Stuart *computer system developer*
Bareiss, Erwin Hans *computer scientist, mathematician, nuclear engineer, educator*
Bellow, Alexandra *mathematician, educator*
Davis, Stephen Howard *applied mathematics educator*
Devinatz, Allen *mathematics educator*
Dwass, Meyer *mathematician, educator*
Fisher, Stephen David *mathematics educator, university official*
Gasper, George, Jr. *mathematics educator*
Haberman, Shelby Joel *statistician, educator*
Ionescu Tulcea, Cassius *research mathematician, educator*
Jerome, Joseph Walter *mathematics educator*
Kalai, Ehud *decision sciences educator, researcher in economics and decision sciences*
Krulee, Gilbert Koreb *computer scientist, educator*
Leslie, Joshua Allensworth *mathematics educator*
Matkowsky, Bernard Judah *applied mathematician, educator*
Olmstead, William Edward *mathematics educator*
Saari, Donald Gene *mathematician*
Schank, Roger Carl *computer science and psychology educator*
Tamhane, Ajit C. *statistician, engineer, educator*
Zelinsky, Daniel *mathematics educator*

Godfrey
McDaniels, John Louis *mathematics educator*

Hinsdale
Butler, Margaret Kampschaefer *retired computer scientist*

Normal
Brown, Francis Robert *mathematics educator*
Jones, Graham Alfred *mathematics educator*

River Forest
Koenig, Michael Edward Davison *information science educator*

Urbana
Albrecht, Felix Robert *mathematics educator*
Bateman, Paul Trevier *mathematician, educator*
Burkholder, Donald Lyman *mathematician, educator*
Carroll, Robert Wayne *mathematics educator*
Doob, Joseph Leo *mathematician, educator*
Edelsbrunner, Herbert *computer scientist, mathematician*
Fossum, Robert Merle *mathematician, educator*
Goldberg, Samuel Irving *mathematics educator*
Gray, John Walker *mathematician, educator*
Haken, Wolfgang *mathematics educator*
Henson, C. Ward *mathematician, educator*
Jerrard, Richard Patterson *mathematics educator*
Jockusch, Carl Groos, Jr. *mathematics educator*
Knight, Frank Bardsley *mathematics educator*
Lawrie, Duncan H. *computer science educator, consultant*
Liebman, Judith Rae Stenzel *operations research educator*
Merkelo, Henri *electronics and computer scientist*
Sameh, Ahmed Hamdy *computer science educator*
Suzuki, Michio *mathematics educator*
Tondeur, Philippe Maurice *mathematician, educator*
Williams, Martha Ethelyn *information science educator*

Wheaton
Reszka, Alfons *computer systems architect*

INDIANA

Bloomington
Davis, Charles Hargis *information scientist, educator*
Prosser, Franklin Pierce *computer scientist*
Purdom, Paul Walton, Jr. *computer scientist*
Puri, Madan Lal *mathematics educator*

Fort Wayne
Beineke, Lowell Wayne *mathematics educator*
Mansfield, Maynard Joseph *computer science educator, academic dean*

Greencastle
Anderson, John Robert *retired mathematics educator*
Gass, Clinton Burke *mathematics educator*

Hammond
Yackel, James William *mathematician, academic administrator*

Indianapolis
Cliff, Johnnie Marie *mathematics and chemistry educator*
Ho, Thomas Inn Min *computer scientist, educator*
Reid, William Hill *mathematics educator*
Yovits, Marshall Clinton *computer and information science educator, university dean*

Kokomo
Schraut, Kenneth Charles *mathematician, educator*

Lafayette
de Branges de Bourcia, Louis *mathematics educator*
Gautschi, Walter *mathematics educator*
Rubin, Jean Estelle *mathematics educator*

Muncie
Robold, Alice Ilene *mathematician, educator*

Notre Dame
Kogge, Peter Michael *computer scientist, educator*
Pollak, Barth *mathematics educator*
Sommese, Andrew John *mathematics educator*
Stoll, Wilhelm *mathematics educator*
Wong, Warren James *mathematics educator*

West Lafayette
Abhyankar, Shreeram S. *mathematics and industrial engineering educator*
Conte, Samuel Daniel *computer scientist, educator*
Gupta, Shanti Swarup *statistician, educator*
Haas, Felix *former mathematics educator, university administrator*
Lynch, Robert Emmett *mathematics educator*
Rice, John Rischard *computer scientist, researcher, educator*

IOWA

Ames
David, Herbert Aron *statistics educator*
Fuller, Wayne Arthur *statistics educator*
Kempthorne, Oscar *retired statistics educator*

Grinnell
Adelberg, Arnold Melvin *mathematics educator, researcher*
Ferguson, Pamela Anderson *mathematics educator, educational administrator*
Herman, Eugene Alexander *mathematics educator*

Iowa City
Hogg, Robert Vincent, Jr. *mathematical statistician, educator*
Johnson, Eugene Walter *mathematician*
Kleinfeld, Erwin *mathematician, educator*
Potra, Florian Alexander *mathematics educator*
Robertson, Timothy Joel *statistician, educator*

KANSAS

Kansas City
Hassanein, Khatab M. *biostatistics educator, consultant*

Lawrence
Bulgren, William Gerald *computer science educator, researcher*
Himmelberg, Charles John, III *mathematics educator, researcher*

Wichita
Zytkow, Jan Mikolaj *computer science educator*

KENTUCKY

Lexington
Anderson, Richard L(oree) *mathematician, educator*
Mostert, Paul Stallings *mathematician, educator*

LOUISIANA

Baton Rouge
Goldstein, Jerome Arthur *mathematics educator*

Lafayette
Heatherly, Henry Edward *mathematics educator*

New Orleans
Birtel, Frank Thomas *mathematician, philosopher, educator*
LaValle, Irving Howard *decision analysis educator*
Sharma, Bhu Dev *mathematics educator, researcher*

MAINE

Bailey Island
Carter, William Caswell *computer systems scientist*

Brunswick
Tucker, Allen Brown, Jr. *computer science educator*

MARYLAND

Annapolis
Sheppard, John Wilbur *computer research scientist*

Baltimore
Boardman, John Michael *mathematician, educator*
Igusa, Jun-Ichi *mathematician, educator*
Kosaraju, S. Rao *computer science educator, researcher*
Kramer, Morton *biostatistician, epidemiologist*
Lidtke, Doris Keefe *computer science educator*
Meyer, Jean-Pierre Gustave *mathematician, educator*
†Nevin, Joseph Francis *computer systems engineer*
Shiffman, Bernard *mathematician, educator*
Shokurov, Vyacheslav Vladimirovich *mathematics educator*
Slepian, Paul *mathematician, educator*
Wierman, John Charles *mathematician, educator*
Wilson, W. Stephen *mathematics educator*

Bel Air
Eichelberger, Robert John *retired government research and development administrator, consultant*

Bethesda
Clema, Joe Kotouc *computer scientist*
Freedman, Laurence Stuart *statistician*
Moshman, Jack *statistical consultant*
Navarro, Joseph Anthony *statistician, consultant*
Schoch, Claude Martin *computer scientist, publishing company executive*
Vasta, Bruno Morreale *information scientist, chemist*
Weiss, George Herbert *mathematician, consultant*

College Park
Aloimonos, Yiannis John *computer sciences educator*
Antman, Stuart Sheldon *mathematician, educator*
Efrat, Isaac *mathematician, financial analyst*
Ehrlich, Gertrude *retired mathematics educator*
Embody, Daniel Robert *biometrician*
†Hendler, James Alexander *computer science educator, consultant*
Kirwan, William English, II *mathematics educator, university official*
Kotz, Samuel *statistician, educator, translator*
Mikulski, Piotr Witold *mathematics educator*
Miller, Raymond Edward *computer science educator*
Minker, Jack *computer scientist, educator*
Rosenfeld, Azriel *computer science educator, consultant*
Stewart, Gilbert Wright *computer science educator*
†White, Marilyn Domas *information science educator*

Gaithersburg
Deprit, Andre Albert *mathematician, consultant*
Jefferson, David *computer scientist*
†Martin, Roger John *computer scientist*
Penniman, W. David *information scientist, management consultant*
Rosenblatt, Joan Raup *mathematical statistician*
Witzgall, Christoph Johann *mathematician*

Garrett Park
McDowell, Eugene Charles *systems analyst*

Huntingtown
Merrion, Arthur Benjamin *mathematics educator, tree farmer*

Hyattsville
Choi, Jai Won *mathematical statistician, researcher*

Laurel
Gieszl, Louis Roger *mathematician*

Riverdale
Kanal, Laveen N. *computer science educator, data processing company executive*

Rockville
Bryant, Edward Clark *statistician*
Dubey, Satya Deva *biomedical and statistical scientist, researcher, executive*
Fischer, Irene Kaminka *retired research geodesist, mathematician*
Hunt, Joseph A. *statistical survey research executive*
Kalton, Graham *survey statistician, research scientist*
Menkello, Frederick Vincent *computer scientist*

Temple Hills
Wilcox, Richard Hoag *information scientist*

MASSACHUSETTS

Arlington
Whitehead, George William *retired mathematician*

Boston
Berkey, Dennis D. *mathematics educator*
D'Agostino, Ralph Benedict *mathematician, statistician, educator, consultant*
Falb, Peter Lawrence *mathematician, educator, investment company executive*
Moseby, LeBaron Clarence, Jr. *mathematics and computer science educator*
Pratt, John Winsor *statistics educator*
Salzberg, Betty Joan *computer science educator*
Stone, Arthur Harold *mathematics educator*
Taqqu, Murad Salman *mathematics educator*
Warga, Jack *mathematician, educator*
Zelen, Marvin *statistics educator*

Cambridge
Anderson, Donald Gordon Marcus *mathematics educator*
Bartee, Thomas Creson *computer scientist, educator*
Bernstein, Joseph N. *mathematician, researcher, educator*
Berwick, Robert Cregar *computer science educator*
Bott, Raoul *mathematician, educator*
Carrier, George Francis *applied mathematics educator*
Chernoff, Herman *statistics educator*
†Conrades, George Henry *information systems company executive*
Corbato, Fernando Jose *electrical engineer and computer science educator*
Dertouzos, Michael Leonidas *computer scientist, electrical engineer, educator*
Diaconis, Persi W. *mathematical statistician, educator*
Dudley, Richard Mansfield *mathematician, educator*
Gleason, Andrew Mattei *mathematician, educator*
Greenspan, Harvey Philip *applied mathematician, educator*
Grosz, Barbara Jean *computer science educator*
Helgason, Sigurdur *mathematician, educator*
Jackson, Francis Joseph *research and development company executive*
Kac, Victor G. *mathematician, educator*
Kazhdan, David *mathematician, educator*
Kleiman, Steven Lawrence *mathematics educator*
Kostant, Bertram *mathematician, educator*
Light, Richard Jay *statistician, education educator*
Lynch, Nancy Ann *computer scientist, educator*
Mackey, George Whitelaw *mathematician, educator*
Malkus, Willem Van Rensselaer *mathematics educator*
Minsky, Marvin Lee *mathematician, educator*
Moses, Joel *computer scientist, educator*
Mosteller, Frederick *mathematical statistician, educator*
Mumford, David Bryant *mathematics educator*
Oettinger, Anthony Gervin *mathematician, educator*
Orlin, James Berger *mathematician, management scientist, educator*
Papert, Seymour Aubrey *mathematician, educator, writer*
Roberts, Edward Baer *technology management educator*
Roberts, Nancy *computer educator*
Rockart, John Fralick *information systems reseacher*
Rota, Gian-Carlo *mathematician, educator*
Rubin, Donald Bruce *statistician, educator, research company executive*
Schmid, Wilfried *mathematician*
Segal, Irving Ezra *mathematics educator*
Singer, Isadore Manuel *mathematician, educator*
Stanley, Richard P. *mathematics educator*
Strang, William Gilbert *mathematician, educator*
Stroock, Daniel Wyler *mathematician, educator*
Taubes, Clifford H. *mathematician, educator*
†Toomre, Alar *applied mathematician, theoretical astronomer*
Valiant, Leslie Gabriel *computer scientist*
Yau, Shing-Tung *mathematics educator*

Duxbury
Thrasher, Dianne Elizabeth *mathematics educator, computer consultant*

Falmouth
Bonn, Theodore Hertz *computer scientist, consultant*

Framington
Scherr, Allan Lee *computer scientist, executive*

Greenfield
Robinson, John Alan *logic and computer science educator*

Jamaica Plain
Cushing, Steven *software educator, researcher, consultant*

Lincoln
LeGates, John Crews Boulton *information scientist*

Lowell
Ruskai, Mary Beth *mathematics researcher, educator*

Medford
Nitecki, Zbigniew Henry *mathematician, educator*
Reynolds, William Francis *mathematics educator*

Medway
Yonda, Alfred William *mathematician*

Quincy
Hayes, Bernardine Frances *computer systems analyst*

Sharon
Olum, Paul *mathematician, former university president*

Waltham
Brown, Edgar Henry, Jr. *mathematician, educator*

Wellesley
Hildebrand, Francis Begnaud *mathematics educator*
Shuchat, Alan Howard *mathematician, educator*

Westfield
Buckmore, Alvah Clarence, Jr. *computer scientist, ballistician*

Westport Point
Fanning, William Henry, Jr. *computer scientist*

Williamstown
Hill, Victor Ernst, IV *mathematics educator, musician*
Morgan, Frank *mathematician*

Winchester
Shannon, Claude Elwood *mathematician, educator*

Worcester
Malone, Joseph James *mathematics educator, researcher*

McQuarrie, Bruce Cale *mathematics educator*

MICHIGAN

Ann Arbor
Bartle, Robert Gardner *mathematics educator*
Beutler, Frederick Joseph *information scientist*
Brown, Morton B. *biostatistics educator*
Conway, Lynn Ann *computer scientist, educator*
Duren, Peter Larkin *mathematician, educator*
Gehring, Frederick William *mathematician, educator*
Herzog, Bertram *computer scientist, educator*
Hill, Bruce Marvin *statistician, scientist, educator*
Hochster, Melvin *mathematician, educator*
Jones, Phillip Sanford *mathematics educator emeritus*
Kish, Leslie *research statistician, educator*
Kister, James Milton *mathematician, educator*
Lewis, Donald John *mathematics educator*
Schriber, Thomas Jude *computer and information systems educator, researcher*

Auburn Hills
Neumann, Charles Henry *mathematics educator*

Dearborn
Brown, James Ward *mathematician, educator, author*

Detroit
Rajlich, Vaclav Thomas *computer science educator, researcher, consultant*
Schreiber, Bertram Manuel *mathematics educator*

East Lansing
Frame, James Sutherland *retired mathematics educator*
Hocking, John Gilbert *mathematics educator*
Hoppensteadt, Frank Charles *mathematician, university dean*
Moran, Daniel Austin *mathematician*
Phillips, Richard Edward *mathematics educator*
Stapleton, James Hall *statistician, educator*
Wojcik, Anthony Stephen *computer science educator*

Farmington
Salabounis, Manuel *computer information scientist, mathematician*

Flint
Kugler, Lawrence Dean *mathematics educator*

Kalamazoo
Calloway, Jean Mitchener *mathematician, educator*
Clarke, Allen Bruce *mathematics educator, retired academic administrator*

Marquette
Geiger, David Scott *mathematician, researcher*

Novi
Chow, Chi-Ming *retired mathematics educator*

Saline
Cornell, Richard Garth *biostatistics educator*

Warren
Ginsberg, Myron *computer scientist*

Ypsilanti
Gledhill, Roger Clayton *statistician, engineer, mathematician, educator*
Randolph, Linda Jane *mathematics educator*
Ullman, Nelly Szabo *statistician, educator*

MINNESOTA

Arden Hills
Ousley, James E. *systems integrator*

Minneapolis
Aris, Rutherford *applied mathematician, educator*
Brasket, Curt Justin *systems analyst, chess player*
Friedman, Avner *mathematician, educator*
Infante, Ettore Ferrari *mathematician, educator, university administrator*
Loud, Warren Simms *mathematician*
Markus, Lawrence *retired mathematics educator*
Miller, Willard, Jr. *mathematician, educator*
Nitsche, Johannes Carl Christian *mathematics educator*
Pedoe, Daniel *mathematician, writer, artist*
Pour-El, Marian Boykan *mathematician, educator*
Rosen, Judah Ben *computer scientist*
Serrin, James Burton *mathematics educator*
Slagle, James Robert *computer science educator*
Warner, William Hamer *applied mathematician*

Moorhead
Heuer, Gerald Arthur *mathematician, educator*

New Brighton
Shier, Gloria Bulan *mathematics educator*

Northfield
Appleyard, David Frank *mathematics and computer science educator*
Schuster, Seymour *mathematician, educator*
†Steen, Lynn Arthur *mathematician, educator*

Saint Paul
Bingham, Christopher *statistics educator*

MISSISSIPPI

Hattiesburg
Miller, James Edward *computer scientist, educator*

Jackson
Galloway, Patricia Kay *systems analyst, ethnohistorian*

University
Paterson, Alan Leonard Tuke *mathematics educator*

MISSOURI

Columbia
Basu, Asit Prakas *statistician*
Beem, John Kelly *mathematician, educator*
Schrader, Keith William *mathematician*
Springsteel, Frederick Neil *computer science educator*
Williams, Frederick *statistics educator*
Zemmer, Joseph Lawrence, Jr. *mathematics educator*

Kansas City
Flora, Jairus Dale, Jr. *statistician*

Nevada
Hornback, Joseph Hope *mathematics educator*

Rolla
Grimm, Louis John *mathematician, educator*
Ingram, William Thomas, III *mathematics educator*
Zobrist, George Winston *computer scientist, educator*

Saint Louis
Baernstein, Albert, II *mathematician*
Ball, William Ernest *computer science educator*
Benson, Robert John *computer science educator, administrator*
Boothby, William Munger *mathematics educator*
Coerver, Elizabeth Ann *data base consultant*
Jenkins, James Allister *mathematician, educator*
Jensen, Gary Richard *mathematics educator*
Nussbaum, A(dolf) Edward *mathematician, educator*
Pollack, Seymour Victor *computer science educator*
Rodin, Ervin Yechiel László *mathematician*
Tamke, George William *electronics and electrical equipment executive*
Wilson, Edward Nathan *mathematician, educator*
Zuker, Michael *biomathematician*

MONTANA

Big Timber
Yuzeitis, James Richard *information specialist*

Missoula
Banaugh, Robert Peter *computer science educator*

NEBRASKA

Lincoln
Wiegand, Sylvia Margaret *mathematician, educator*

NEVADA

Las Vegas
Miel, George Joseph *computer scientist*

NEW HAMPSHIRE

Durham
Appel, Kenneth I. *mathematician, educator*

Hanover
Baumgartner, James Earl *mathematics educator*
Bogart, Kenneth Paul *mathematics educator, consultant*
Crowell, Richard Henry *mathematician, educator*
Kurtz, Thomas Eugene *mathematics educator*
Lahr, Charles Dwight *mathematics educator, college dean*
Lamperti, John Williams *mathematician, educator*
Slesnick, William Ellis *mathematician, educator*
Snell, James Laurie *mathematician, educator*

Kingston
Johnston, Robert Everett *information management administrator*

Londonderry
Nelson, Lloyd Steadman *statistics consultant*

NEW JERSEY

Englewood
Lapidus, Arnold *mathematician*

Glassboro
Stone, Don Charles *computer science educator*

Jersey City
Poiani, Eileen Louise *mathematics educator, college administrator, higher education planner*

Lakewood
Sloyan, Sister Stephanie *mathematics educator*

Montclair
Stevens, John Galen *mathematics and computer science educator*

Murray Hill
Graham, Ronald Lewis *mathematician*
Sloane, Neil James Alexander *mathematician, researcher*

Neshanic Station
Muckenhoupt, Benjamin *retired mathematics educator*

New Brunswick
Amarel, Saul *computer scientist, educator*
Daubechies, Ingrid *mathematics educator*
†Gelfand, Israel Moseevich *mathematician*
Kruskal, Martin David *mathematical physicist, educator*
Kulikowski, Casimir Alexander *computer science educator, research program director*
Scanlon, Jane Cronin *mathematics educator*
Strawderman, William E. *statistics educator*
Taft, Earl Jay *mathematics educator*

New Providence
Fishburn, Peter Clingerman *research mathematician, economist*
Shepp, Lawrence Alan *mathematician, educator*
Wyner, Aaron Daniel *mathematician*

Princeton
Almgren, Frederick Justin, Jr. *mathematician*
Bien, Frederic Vincent *mathematics educator*
Borel, Armand *mathematics educator*
Browder, William *mathematician, educator*
Caffarelli, Luis Angel *mathematician, educator*
Deligné, Pierre R. *mathematician*
Dobkin, David Paul *computer science educator*
Fefferman, Charles Louis *mathematics educator*
Fornaess, John Erik *mathematics educator*
Gear, Charles William *computer scientist*
Griffiths, Phillip A. *mathematician, academic administrator*
Gunning, Robert Clifford *mathematician, educator*
Hunter, John Stuart *statistician, consultant*
Kobayashi, Hisashi *computer scientist, communication theorist, educator*
Kohn, Joseph John *mathematician, educator*
Langlands, Robert Phelan *mathematician*
Levin, Simon Asher *mathematician, ecologist, educator*
Lieberman, David Ira *mathematician, administrator*
Majda, Andrew J. *mathematician, educator*
Mather, John Norman *mathematics educator*
†Nash, John C. *research mathematician*
Orszag, Steven Alan *applied mathematician, educator*
Singer, Burton Herbert *statistics educator*
Tarjan, Robert Endre *computer scientist, educator*
Umscheid, Ludwig Joseph *computer specialist*
†Weil, Andre *mathematics educator and researcher*
Wiles, Andrew J. *mathematician, educator*
Zierler, Neal *mathematician*

South Orange
Houle, Joseph E. *mathematics educator*

Summit
Slepian, David *mathematician, communications engineer*

Teaneck
Zwass, Vladimir *computer scientist, educator*

Union City
Conklin, Anna Immaculata Zotti *mathematics and language arts educator*

Watchung
Schaefer, Jacob Wernli *military systems consultant*

NEW MEXICO

Albuquerque
Bell, Stoughton *computer scientist, mathematician, educator*
†Sobolewski, John Stephen *computer information scientist, director computer services, consultant*

Belen
Gutjahr, Allan Leo *mathematics educator, researcher*

Las Cruces
Harary, Frank *mathematician, computer scientist, educator*
Reinfelds, Juris *computer science educator*
Southward, Glen Morris *statistician, educator*

Los Alamos
Wade, Rodger Grant *financial systems analyst*

Pecos
Price, Thomas Munro *computer consultant*

NEW YORK

Albany
Halsey, Richard Sweeney *information scientist, educator*
Mullin, Lenore Marie Restifo *computer scientist, researcher*
Rosenkrantz, Daniel J. *computer science educator*

Amherst
Brown, Stephen Ira *mathematics educator*
Eberlein, Patricia James *mathematician, computer scientist, educator*

Ardsley
Gayle, Joseph Central, Jr. *computer information professional*

Aurora
Shilepsky, Arnold Charles *mathematics educator, computer consultant*

Binghamton
Hilton, Peter John *mathematician, educator*
Klir, George Jiri *systems science educator*
Su, Stephen Y. H. *computer science and engineering educator, consultant*

Bronx
Koranyi, Adam *mathematics educator*
Rose, Israel Harold *mathematics educator*
Seltzer, William *statistician, social researcher, former international organization director*
Tong, Hing *mathematician, educator*

Brooklyn
Bachman, George *mathematics educator*
Hochstadt, Harry *mathematician, educator*
Pennisten, John William *computer scientist, linguist, actuary*
Weill, Georges Gustave *mathematics educator*

Buffalo
Berner, Robert Frank *statistics educator*
Bross, Irwin Dudley Jackson *biostatistician*
Coburn, Lewis Alan *mathematics educator*
Hauptman, Herbert Aaron *mathematician, educator, researcher*
Menasco, William Wyatt *mathematics educator*
Piech, Margaret Ann *mathematics educator*
Priore, Roger L. *biostatistics educator, consultant*
Shapiro, Stuart Charles *computer scientist, educator*

Farmingdale
Guggenheimer, Heinrich Walter *mathematician, educator*
Marshall, Clifford Wallace *mathematics educator*

Flushing
Mendelson, Elliott *mathematician, educator*

Garden City
Zirkel, Gene *computer science educator and mathematics*

Geneseo
Small, William Andrew *mathematics educator*

Hamilton
Lantz, David Carson *mathematics educator*
Nevison, Christopher Harry *computer science educator*
Pownall, Malcolm Wilmor *mathematics educator*
Tucker, Thomas William *mathematics professor*

Ithaca
Bramble, James Henry *mathematician, educator*
Conway, Richard Walter *computer scientist, educator*
Earle, Clifford John, Jr. *mathematician*
Fuchs, Wolfgang Heinrich *mathematics educator*
Gries, David Joseph *computer science researcher, educator*
Guckenheimer, John *mathematician*
Hartmanis, Juris *computer scientist, educator*
Heath, David Clay *mathematics educator, consultant*
Payne, Lawrence Edward *mathematics educator*
Salton, Gerard *computer science educator*
Shore, Richard Arnold *mathematics educator*
Trotter, Leslie Earl *operations research educator, consultant*

Morrisville
Rouse, Robert Moorefield *mathematician, educator*

New Paltz
Fleisher, Harold *computer scientist*
Richbart, Carolyn Mae *mathematics educator*

New York
Abbey, Scott Gerson *computer information scientist*
Bass, Hyman *mathematician, educator*
Bauer, Frances Brand *research mathematician*
Berman, Simeon Moses *mathematician, educator*
Birman, Joan S. *mathematician, educator*
Bloomfield, Peter *statistics educator*
Blumstein, Reneë J. *research and statistical consultant*
Chow, Yuan Shih *mathematician, educator*
Chu, C. K. *applied mathematician, educator*
†Chudnovsky, David Volfovich *mathematician, computer designer*
Chudnovsky, Gregory Volfovich *mathematician, educator*
Cohn, Harvey *mathematician*
Derman, Cyrus *mathematical statistician*
Di Paola, Robert Arnold *mathematics and computer science educator*
Edwards, Harold Mortimer *mathematics educator*
Frankel, Martin Richard *statistician, educator, consultant*
Gallagher, Patrick Ximenes *mathematics educator, researcher*
Goldfeld, Dorian *mathematics educator*
Gomory, Ralph Edward *mathematician, manufacturing company executive, foundation executive*
Gross, Jonathan Light *computer scientist, mathematician, educator*
Hilton, Alice Mary *cybernetics and computing systems consultant, author, mathematician, art historian*
Hunte, Beryl Eleanor *mathematics educator, consultant*
Jacquet, Hervé Michel *mathematics educator*
Kurnow, Ernest *statistician, educator*
Lax, Peter David *mathematics educator*
Lucas, Henry Cameron, Jr. *information systems educator, writer, consultant*
Mc Cracken, Daniel Delbert *computer science educator, author*
McKean, Henry P. *mathematics institute administrator*
Meier, Paul *statistician, mathematics educator*
Moise, Edwin Evariste *mathematician, educator*
Mok, Ngaiming *mathematics educator*
Morawetz, Cathleen Synge *mathematician*
Moyne, John Abel *computer scientist, linguist, educator*
Nirenberg, Louis *mathematician, educator*
Padberg, Manfred Wilhelm *mathematics educator*
Posamentier, Alfred Steven *mathematics educator, university administrator*
Sellers, Peter Hoadley *mathematician*
Sohmer, Bernard *mathematics educator, administrator*
†Tian, Gang *mathematics educator*
Traub, J(oseph) F(rederick) *computer scientist, educator*
Vogel, Stephen Eugene *systems analyst*
Weitzner, Harold *mathematics educator*
Widlund, Olof Bertil *computer science educator*

Orangeburg
Siegel, Carole Ethel *mathematician*

Rochester
Alling, Norman Larrabee *mathematics educator*
Arden, Bruce Wesley *computer science and electrical engineering educator*
Gitler, Samuel Carlos *mathematics educator, researcher*
Hollingsworth, Jack Waring *mathematics and computer science educator*
Segal, Sanford Leonard *mathematics educator*
Simon, William *biomathematician, educator*

Stony Brook
†Anderson, Michael Thomas *mathematics researcher, educator*

Douglas, Ronald George *mathematician*
Feinberg, Eugene Alexander *mathematics educator*
Glimm, James Gilbert *mathematician*
Hill, C(lyde) Denson *mathematician, educator*
Lawson, H(erbert) Blaine, Jr. *mathematician, educator*
Tucker, Alan Curtiss *mathematics educator*

Syracuse
Berra, P. Bruce *computer educator*
Cargo, Gerald Thomas *mathematics educator*
Church, Philip Throop *mathematician, educator*
Dudewicz, Edward John *statistician*
Graver, Jack Edward *mathematics educator*
Hansen, Per Brinch *computer scientist*
Pardee, Otway O'Meara *computer science educator*

Troy
Berg, Daniel *science and technology educator*
Cole, Julian D. *mathematician, educator*
Drew, Donald Allen *mathematical sciences educator*
Jacobson, Melvin Joseph *applied mathematician, acoustician, educator*
McNaughton, Robert Forbes, Jr. *computer science educator*

Washingtonville
Perrego, Virginia *mathematics educator*

West Point
Barr, Donald Roy *statistics and operations research educator, statistician*
Barrett, Lida Kittrell *mathematics educator*

White Plains
Merritt, Susan Mary *computer science educator, university dean*

Yorktown Heights
Agarwal, Ramesh Chandra *applied mathematician, researcher*
Allen, Frances Elizabeth *computer scientist*
†Cocke, John *computer scientist*
d'Heurle, François Max *research scientist, engineering educator*
Hoffman, Alan Jerome *mathematician, educator*
Jaffe, Jeffrey Martin *computer scientist*
Mandelbrot, Benoit B. *mathematician, scientist, educator*
Winograd, Shmuel *mathematician*
Wong, Chak-Kuen *computer scientist*

NORTH CAROLINA

Chapel Hill
Chi, Vernon Longstreet *computer science educator, administrator*
Coulter, Elizabeth Jackson *biostatistician, educator*
Simons, Gordon Donald, Jr. *statistician*
Stasheff, James Dillon *mathematics educator*
Wahl, Jonathan Michael *mathematics educator*
Wogen, Warren Ronald *mathematics educator*

Charlotte
Johnson, Phillip Eugene *mathematics educator*

Cullowhee
Willis, Ralph Houston *mathematics educator*

Davidson
Klein, Benjamin Garrett *mathematics educator*
Stroud, Junius Brutus, III *mathematics educator*

Durham
Allard, William Kenneth *mathematician*
Keepler, Manuel *mathematics educator, researcher*
Loveland, Donald William *computer science educator*
Rose, Donald James *computer science educator*
Vitter, Jeffrey Scott *computer science educator, consultant*
Warner, Seth L. *mathematician, educator*
Winkler, Robert Lewis *statistics educator, researcher, author, consultant*
Woodbury, Max Atkin *polymath, educator*

Greensboro
Posey, Eldon Eugene *mathematician, educator*

Hillsborough
Cooley, Philip Chester *computer modeller*

Morrisville
Smith, Malbert, III *computer technology executive, psychologist*

Raleigh
Mason, David Dickenson *statistics educator*
†Nelson, Larry A. *statistics educator, consultant*
Peterson, Elmor Lee *mathematical scientist, educator*
Rawlings, John Oren *statistician, researcher*
Wesler, Oscar *mathematician, educator*

Research Triangle Park
Karr, Alan Francis *statistics educator, academic administrator*

Salisbury
Tlalka, Jacek *mathematics educator*

Swansboro
Mullikin, Thomas Wilson *mathematics educator*

Winston Salem
Kerr, Sandria Neidus *mathematics and computer science educator*

OHIO

Ashtabula
Taylor, Norman Floyd *computer educator, administrator*

Athens
Wen, Shih-Liang *mathematics educator*

Cincinnati
Flick, Thomas Michael *mathematics educator, educational administrator*
Semon, Warren Lloyd *retired computer sciences educator*

Cleveland
Clark, Robert Arthur *mathematician, educator*
de Acosta, Alejandro Daniel *mathematician, educator*
Goffman, William *mathematician, educator*
Hajek, Otomar *mathematics educator*
Nelson, Raymond John *mathematics and philosophy educator*
Sterling, Leon Samuel *computer scientist, researcher, educator*
Szarek, Stanislaw Jerzy *mathematics educator*
Woyczynski, Wojbor Andrzej *mathematician, educator*

Columbus
Chandrasekaran, Balakrishnan *computer and information science educator*
Dowling, Thomas Allan *mathematics educator*
Kindig, Fred Eugene *statistics educator, arbitrator*
Santner, Thomas *statistician, educator*

Dayton
Bedell, Kenneth Berkley *computer specialist, educator*
Garcia, Oscar Nicolas *computer science educator*
Khalimsky, Efim *mathematics and computer science educator*
Stander, Joseph William *mathematics educator, former university official*

Defiance
Mirchandaney, Arjan Sobhraj *mathematics educator*

Delaware
Mendenhall, Robert Vernon *mathematics educator*

Kent
Cummins, Kenneth Burdette *retired science and mathematics educator*
Powell, Robert Ellis *mathematics educator, former college dean*
Stackelberg, Olaf Patrick Von *mathematician*
Varga, Richard Steven *mathematics educator*

Mansfield
Gregory, Thomas Bradford *mathematics educator*

Oberlin
Andrews, George Harold *mathematics educator*

Oxford
†Park, Chull *mathematician, educator*

Vermilion
Vance, Elbridge Putnam *mathematics educator*

OKLAHOMA

Ada
Walker, Billy Kenneth *computer science educator, academic administrator*

Edmond
Loman, Mary LaVerne *retired mathematics educator*

Stillwater
Folks, J. Leroy *statistician, educator*
Lu, Huizhu *computer scientist, educator*

OREGON

Beaverton
Rattner, Justin *supercomputer research manager*

Bend
Mayer, Richard Dean *mathematics educator*

Corvallis
Petersen, Bent Edvard *mathematician, educator*

Eugene
Andrews, Fred Charles *mathematics educator*

Florence
Gray, Augustine Heard, Jr. *computer consultant*

Monmouth
Forcier, Richard Charles *information technology educator, computer applications consultant*

Portland
Ahuja, Jagdish Chand *mathematics educator*

Tualatin
Brown, Robert Wallace *mathematics educator*

PENNSYLVANIA

Abington
Ayoub, Ayoub Barsoum *mathematician, educator*

Bala Cynwyd
Ackoff, Russell Lincoln *systems sciences educator*

Bethlehem
Ghosh, Bhaskar Kumar *statistics educator, researcher*
Rivlin, Ronald Samuel *mathematics educator emeritus*

Chester
Frank, Amalie Julianna *computer science, electrical engineering and mathematics educator, consultant*

Haverford
Greene, Curtis *mathematics educator*

Lewisburg
Ray, David Scott *mathematics educator*

Meadville
Cable, Charles Allen *mathematician*

Mercer
Brady, Wray Grayson *mathematician, educator*

Morrisville
Bush, Harold Ehrig *computer consultant*

Philadelphia
Albright, Hugh Norton *mathematics educator*
Badler, Norman Ira *computer and information science educator*
Banerji, Ranan Bihari *mathematics and computer science educator*
Calabi, Eugenio *mathematician, educator*
Collons, Rodger Duane *decision sciences educator*
de Cani, John Stapley *statistician, educator*
Donagi, Ron *mathematics educator*
Freyd, Peter John *mathematician, computer scientist, educator*
Garfield, Eugene *information scientist, author, publisher*
Goldstine, Herman Heine *mathematician, association executive*
Hildebrand, David Kent *statistics educator*
Iglewicz, Boris *statistician, educator*
Kadison, Richard Vincent *mathematician, educator*
Knopp, Marvin Isadore *mathematics educator*
Mode, Charles J. *mathematician, educator*
Morrison, Donald Franklin *statistician, educator*
Porter, Gerald Joseph *mathematician, educator*
Prywes, Noah Shmarya *computer scientist, educator*
Scandura, Joseph Michael *education researcher, software engineer*
Shatz, Stephen Sidney *mathematician, educator*
Stringer, Gail Griffin *information systems administrator*
Warner, Frank Wilson, III *mathematics educator*

Pittsburgh
Balas, Egon *applied mathematician, educator*
Berliner, Hans Jack *computer scientist*
Bryant, Randal Everitt *computer science educator, consultant*
Chao, Chong-Yun *mathematics educator*
Deskins, Wilbur Eugene *mathematician, educator*
Duffin, Richard James *mathematician, educator*
Fienberg, Stephen Elliott *statistician*
Gurtin, Morton Edward *mathematics educator*
Hall, Charles Allan *numerical analyst, educator*
Kadane, Joseph B. *statistics educator*
Kolodner, Ignace Izaak *mathematician, educator*
Lehoczky, John Paul *statistics educator*
Moore, Richard Allan *mathematics educator*
Rheinboldt, Werner Carl *mathematics educator, researcher*
Shaw, Mary M. *computer science educator*
Siewiorek, Daniel Paul *computer science educator, researcher*
Thompson, Gerald Luther *operations research and applied mathematics educator*

State College
Arnold, Douglas Norman *mathematics educator*

Swarthmore
Kelemen, Charles F. *computer science educator*

University Park
Andrews, George Eyre *mathematics educator*
Antle, Charles Edward *statistics educator*
Brownawell, Woodrow Dale *mathematics educator*
Lindsay, Bruce George *statistics educator*

Villanova
Beck, Robert Edward *computer scientist, educator*

Wayne
Clelland, Richard Cook *statistics educator, university administrator*

RHODE ISLAND

Kingston
Driver, Rodney David *mathematics educator, former state legislator*
Roxin, Emilio Oscar *mathematics educator*
Verma, Ghasi Ram *mathematics educator*

Providence
Banchoff, Thomas Francis *mathematics educator*
Charniak, Eugene *computer scientist, educator*
Dafermos, Constantine Michael *applied mathematics educator*
Davis, Philip J. *mathematician*
Fitzpatrick, William Peter *computer programmer/analyst, state legislator*
Fleming, Wendell Helms *mathematician, educator*
Freiberger, Walter Frederick *mathematics educator, actuarial science consultant, educator*
Kushner, Harold Joseph *mathematics educator*
Savage, John Edmund *computer science educator, researcher*
Shu, Chi-Wang *mathematics educator, researcher*
Silverman, Joseph Hillel *mathematics educator*
van Dam, Andries *computer scientist, educator*
Wegner, Peter *computer science educator*

SOUTH CAROLINA

Charleston
Hoel, David Gerhard *statistician, scientist, educator*

Clemson
Kenelly, John Willis, Jr. *mathematician, educator*

Columbia
Culik, Karel *computer scientist, educator*
Eastman, Caroline Merriam *computer science educator*
Ott, Jack M. *mathematics educator*

Florence
Strong, Roger Lee *mathematics educator*

Newberry
Layton, William Isaac *mathematics educator*

Spartanburg
Wilde, Edwin Frederick *mathematics educator*

TENNESSEE

Brownsville
Kalin, Robert *retired mathematics educator*

Chattanooga
Tracy, Carol Cousins *mathematics educator*

Knoxville
Sherman, Gordon Rae *computer science educator*
Soni, Kusum Kapila *mathematics educator*

Maryville
Inscho, Barbara Pickel *mathematics educator*

Memphis
Franklin, Stanley Phillip *computer scientist, mathematician, cognitive scientist, educator*
Hodges, Velma Quinn *mathematics educator*
Schelp, Richard Herbert *mathematics educator*

Murfreesboro
Aden, Robert Clark *retired computer information systems educator*

Nashville
Banks, John Houston *mathematics educator*
†Blair, Joyce Allsmiller *computer science educator*
Crooke, Philip Schuyler *mathematics educator*
Fischer, Patrick Carl *computer scientist, educator*
Gavish, Bezalel *computer science operations research, information systems educator*
Jonsson, Bjarni *mathematician, educator*
Schumaker, Larry Lee *mathematics educator*

Oak Ridge
Gardiner, Donald Andrew *statistician, consultant*
Kliewer, Kenneth Lee *computational scientist, research administrator*
Raridon, Richard Jay *computer specialist*
†Ward, Robert Cleveland *research mathematician, science administrator*

Sewanee
Puckette, Stephen Elliott *mathematics educator, mathematician*

TEXAS

Abilene
Retzer, Kenneth Albert *mathematics educator*

Arlington
Greenspan, Donald *mathematician, educator*
Han, Chien-Pai *statistics educator*

Austin
Bledsoe, Woodrow Wilson *mathematics and computer sciences educator*
Clark, Charles T(aliferro) *retired business statistics educator*
Dijkstra, Edsger Wybe *computer science educator, mathematician*
Garner, Harvey Louis *computer scientist, consultant, electrical engineering educator*
Gillman, Leonard *mathematician, educator*
Kozmetsky, George *computer science educator*
Lam, Simon Shin-Sing *computer science educator*
Misra, Jayadev *computer science educator*
Uhlenbeck, Karen Keskulla *mathematician, educator*
Wyllys, Ronald Eugene *information science educator, dean*

College Station
Blakley, George Robert, Jr. *mathematician, computer scientist*
Chui, Charles Kam-Tai *mathematics educator*
Ewing, Richard Edward *mathematics, chemical and petroleum engineering educator*
Parzen, Emanuel *statistical scientist*
Ringer, Larry Joel *statistics educator*

Dallas
Browne, Richard Harold *statistician, consultant*

Denton
Renka, Robert Joseph *computer science educator, consultant*

El Paso
Quevedo, Hector Adolf *operations research analyst, environmental scientist*

Fort Worth
Doran, Robert Stuart *mathematician, educator*
Sullenberger, Ara Broocks *mathematics educator*

Houston
Auchmuty, Giles *applied mathematics educator*
Brown, Dennison Robert *mathematician, educator*
Dennis, John Emory, Jr. *mathematics educator*
Freeman, Marjorie Schaefer *mathematics educator*
Gardner, Everette Shaw, Jr. *information sciences educator*
Hardt, Robert Miller *mathematics educator*
Harvey, F. Reese *mathematics educator*
Hempel, John P. *mathematics educator*
Kennedy, Ken *computer science educator*
Munson, John Backus *computer systems consultant, retired computer engineering company executive*
Scott, David Warren *statistics educator*
Tapia, Richard Alfred *mathematics educator*
Wang, Chao-Cheng *mathematician, engineer*
Wells, Raymond O., Jr. *mathematics educator, researcher*
Wright, Clark Phillips *computer systems specialist*

Kingsville
Cecil, David Rolf *mathematician, educator*
Morey, Philip Stockton, Jr. *mathematics educator*

Lubbock
Amir-Moez, Ali Reza *mathematician, educator*
Conover, William Jay *statistics educator*

Richardson
Pervin, William Joseph *computer science educator*

San Antonio
Ahmad, Shair *mathematics educator*
Bennett, Gerard Paul *computer scientist*
Grubb, Robert Lynn *computer system designer*
Trench, William Frederick *mathematics educator*
Tucker, Roy Nelson *mathematics educator, minister*

Temple
Rajab, Mohammad Hasan *biostatistician, educator*

Waco
Odell, Patrick Lowry *mathematics educator*

UTAH

Logan
Cheng, Heng-Da *computer scientist*

Provo
Moore, Hal G. *mathematician, educator*
Robinson, Donald Wilford *mathematics educator*

Salt Lake City
Horn, Susan Dadakis *statistics educator*
Wilcox, Calvin Hayden *mathematics educator*

VERMONT

Norwich
Snapper, Ernst *mathematics educator*

VIRGINIA

Alexandria
McDaniel, William Howard Taft, Jr. *computer information systems educator*
Olson, Warren Kinley *operations research analyst, engineer, physicist*

Arlington
Cherniavsky, John Charles *computer scientist*
Ciment, Melvyn *mathematician*
Green, Judy *mathematics educator*
Long, Madeleine J. *mathematics and science educator*
Murray, Jeanne Morris *computer scientist, educator, consultant*
Schafer, Alice Turner *mathematics educator*
Voigt, Robert Gary *numerical analyst*
Waring, John Alfred *former research writer, lecturer, consultant*
Young, Paul Ruel *computer scientist, administrator*

Blacksburg
Good, Irving John *statistics educator, philosopher of science*
Krutchkoff, Richard Gerald *statistics educator, researcher*
Olin, Robert Floyd *mathematics educator and reseacher*

Charlottesville
Brydges, David Chandos *mathematician*
Catlin, Avery *engineering and computer science educator, writer*
Horgan, Cornelius Oliver *applied mathematics and applied mechanics educator*
Lasiecka, Irena M. *mathematics educator*
Mansfield, Lois Edna *mathematics educator, researcher*
Martin, Nathaniel Frizell Grafton *mathematician, educator*
Ortega, James McDonough *mathematician, educator*
Paige, Eugene Carroll, Jr. *mathematics educator, consultant*
Pang, Maybeline Miusze (Chan) *software and system engineer and analyst*
Roberts, William Woodruff, Jr. *applied mathematics educator, researcher*
Rosenblum, Marvin *mathematics educator*
Scott, Leonard Lewy, Jr. *mathematician, educator*
Simmonds, James Gordon *mathematician, educator*
Taylor, Samuel James *mathematics educator*
Thomas, Lawrence Eldon *mathematics educator*
Triggiani, Roberto *mathematics educator*
Wulf, William Allan *computer information scientist, educator*

Fairfax
Denning, Peter James *computer scientist, engineer*
Hanuschak, George Alan *statistician*
Sage, Andrew Patrick, Jr. *systems information and software engineering educator*
Shrier, Stefan *mathematician, educator*

Gloucester
Cooke, Dorothy Helena Cosby *mathematics educator, counselor*

Hampton
Proctor, Amelia Doleman *mathematics educator*

Herndon
Arnberg, Robert Lewis *mathematician*

Mc Lean
Gardenier, John Stark, II *statistician, management scientist*
Schneck, Paul Bennett *computer scientist*

Norfolk
Maly, Kurt John *computer science educator*
Marchello, Joseph Maurice *mathematics and physical science educator*

Reston
Fredette, Richard Chester *computer specialist*

Richlands
Witten, Thomas Jefferson, Jr. *mathematics educator*

Richmond
Charlesworth, Arthur Thomas *mathematics and computer science educator*

Springfield
Bradunas, Edward Terence *data processing management and technology management consultant*

Vienna
de Planque, Emile, III *computer consultant*
Lillard, Mark Hill, III *computer consulting executive, former air force officer*

Williamsburg
Johnson, Charles Royal *research mathematician, educator*
Rodman, Leiba *mathematics educator*

WASHINGTON

Ellensburg
Comstock, Dale Robert *mathematics educator*

Orcas
Greever, John *retired mathematics educator*

Pullman
Hildebrandt, Darlene Myers *information scientist*
Kallaher, Michael Joseph *mathematics educator*

Richland
Cochran, James Alan *mathematics educator*

Seattle
Breslow, Norman Edward *biostatistics educator, researcher*
Criminale, William Oliver, Jr. *applied mathematics educator*
Hewitt, Edwin *mathematician, educator*
Jans, James Patrick *mathematics educator*
Kevorkian, Jirair *applied mathematics, aeronautics and astronautics educator*
Klee, Victor La Rue *mathematician, educator*
Lee, John Marshall *mathematics educator*
Michael, Ernest Arthur *mathematics educator*
Murray, James Dickson *mathematical biology educator*
Nijenhuis, Albert *mathematician, educator*
Noe, Jerre Donald *computer science educator*
O'Malley, Robert Edmund, Jr. *mathematics educator*
Pyke, Ronald *mathematics educator*
Segal, Jack *mathematics educator*
Wellner, Jon August *statistician, educator*

WEST VIRGINIA

Morgantown
Butcher, Donald Franklin *statistics educator, computer scientist*
De Vore, Paul Warren *technology educator*
Holtan, Boyd DeVere *mathematics educator*
Vest, Marvin Lewis *mathematical educator*

WISCONSIN

Madison
Askey, Richard Allen *mathematician*
Beck, Anatole *mathematician, educator*
de Boor, Carl *mathematician*
Draper, Norman Richard *statistician, educator*
Harvey, John Grover *mathematics educator*
Hickman, James Charles *business and statistics educator, business school dean*
Johnson, Millard Wallace, Jr. *mathematics and engineering educator*
Johnson, Richard Arnold *statistics educator, consultant*
Kurtz, Thomas Gordon *mathematics educator*
Levin, Jacob Joseph *mathematician, educator*
Moore, Edward Forrest *computer scientist, mathematician, former educator*
Robinson, Stephen Michael *applied mathematician, educator*
Wahba, Grace *statistician, educator*

Milwaukee
Lawrence, Willard Earl *mathematics, statistics and computer science educator emeritus*

Whitewater
Verma, Krishnanand *mathematics educator, researcher, administrator, consultant*

WYOMING

Cheyenne
Southworth, Rod Brand *computer science educator*

TERRITORIES OF THE UNITED STATES

PUERTO RICO

Mayaguez
Collins, Dennis Glenn *mathematics educator*

Rio Piedras
Bangdiwala, Ishver Surchand *statistician, educator*

CANADA

ALBERTA

Edmonton
Davis, Wayne Alton *computer science educator*
†Moody, Robert Vaughan *mathematician, educator*

BRITISH COLUMBIA

Burnaby
†Borwein, Peter Benjamin *mathematician*

Vancouver
Boyd, David William *mathematician, educator*
Clark, Colin Whitcomb *mathematics educator*
Feldman, Joel Shalom *mathematician*
Granirer, Edmond Ernest *mathematician, educator*
Miura, Robert Mitsuru *mathematician, researcher, educator*
Seymour, Brian Richard *mathematician*
Sion, Maurice *mathematics educator*
Swanson, Charles Andrew *mathematics educator*
Zidek, James Victor *statistician, educator*

Victoria
Manning, Eric *computer science and engineering educator, university dean, researcher*

NOVA SCOTIA

Halifax
Fillmore, Peter Arthur *mathematician, educator*

ONTARIO

Hamilton
Banaschewski, Bernhard *mathematics educator*
Parnas, David Lorge *computer scientist, engineer, educator*

Kingston
Campbell, L(ouis) Lorne *mathematics educator*
Coleman, Albert John *mathematics educator*

London
Anderson, Oliver Duncan *consulting statistician, educator*
Bauer, Michael Anthony *computer scientist, educator*
Borwein, David *mathematics educator*
Ehrman, Joachim Benedict *mathematics educator*

Ottawa
Dawson, Donald Andrew *mathematics educator, researcher*
Dlab, Vlastimil *mathematics educator, researcher*
†Fellegi, Ivan Peter *statistician*
Macphail, Moray St. John *mathematics educator emeritus*

Toronto
Arthur, James Greig *mathematics educator*
Cook, Stephen Arthur *mathematics and computer science educator*
Coxeter, Harold Scott Macdonald *mathematician*
Davis, (Horace) Chandler *mathematics educator*
Fraser, Donald Alexander Stuart *mathematics educator*
Friedlander, John Benjamin *mathematics educator*
Gotlieb, Calvin Carl *computer scientist, educator*
Greiner, Peter Charles *mathematics educator, researcher*
Halperin, John Stephen *mathematics educator*
Murasugi, Kunio *mathematician, educator*
Rooney, Paul George *mathematics educator*
†Sigal, Israel Michael *mathematics educator*
Tall, Franklin David *mathematician, neurolinguistic programming master practitioner*

Waterloo
Aczel, Janos Dezso *mathematics educator*
Gladwell, Graham Maurice Leslie *mathematician, civil engineering educator*
Paldus, Josef *mathematics educator*
Sprott, David Arthur *statistics and psychology educator*
Stewart, Cameron Leigh *mathematics educator*

QUEBEC

Montreal
De Mori, Renato *computer science educator, researcher*
Dubuc, Serge *mathematics educator*
Herz, Carl Samuel *mathematician*
Levine, Martin David *computer science and electrical engineering educator*
Maag, Urs Richard *statistics educator*
Moser, William Oscar Jules *mathematics educator*
Saint-Pierre, Jacques *statistics educator, consultant*
Suen, Ching Yee *computer scientist and educator, researcher*

Quebec
Theodorescu, Radu Amza Serban *mathematician, educator*

AUSTRALIA

Canberra
Gani, Joseph Mark *statistics educator, administrator, researcher*

AUSTRIA

Vienna
Niederreiter, Harald Guenther *mathematician, researcher*

BELGIUM

Lens
Peat, Randall Dean *defense analysis company executive, retired air force officer*

Louvain la Neuve
Sintzoff, Michel *computer scientist, educator*

BRAZIL

Sao Paulo
Berman, Marcelo Samuel *mathematics and physics educator, cosmology*

CHINA

Beijing
Chen, Peide *mathematics educator*

ENGLAND

Leicester
Harijan, Ram *technology transfer researcher*

London
Ralston, Anthony *computer scientist, mathematician, educator*

FRANCE

Paris
Yuechiming, Roger Yue Yuen Shing *mathematics educator*

GERMANY

Darmstadt
Hofmann, Karl Heinrich *mathematics educator*

Munster
Maltese, George John *mathematics educator*

Paderborn
Belli, Fevzi *computing science educator, consultant*

HONG KONG

Kowloon
Hsieh, Din-Yu *applied mathematics educator*

ISRAEL

Jerusalem
Peleg, Bezalel *mathematician*

ITALY

Padua
Rosati, Mario *mathematician, educator*

JAPAN

Chiba
Yamada, Shinichi *mathematician, computer scientist, educator*

Hachioji
Shimoji, Sadao *applied mathematics educator, engineer*

LEBANON

Beirut
Jurdak, Murad Eid *mathematics educator*

SAUDI ARABIA

Dhahran
Warne, Ronson Joseph *mathematics educator*

SWITZERLAND

Zurich
Lanford, Oscar Erasmus, III *mathematics educator*
Nievergelt, Jurg *computer science educator*

ADDRESS UNPUBLISHED

Bajcsy, Ruzena Kucerova *computer science educator*
Bednarz, Nadine *mathematics educator, director research center*
Birkhoff, Garrett *mathematician, educator*
†Borwein, Jonathan Michael *mathematics educator*
Box, George Edward Pelham *statistics educator*
Browder, Felix Earl *mathematician, educator*
Butson, Alton Thomas *mathematics educator*
Choi, Man-Duen *mathematics educator*
Colvin, Burton Houston *mathematician, government official*
Elliott, David LeRoy *mathematician, educator, engineering educator*
Faltings, Gerd *mathematician, educator*
Fell, James Michael Gardner *mathematics educator, researcher*
Fitting-Gifford, Marjorie Ann *mathematician, educator, consultant*

Freitag, Harlow *retired computer scientist and corporate executive*
Frieder, Gideon *computer science and engineering educator*
Fuller, Nancy MacMurray *mathematics educator, tutor*
Galfo, Armand James *statistics educator*
Goldberg, Samuel *retired mathematician, foundation officer*
Gray, James Peyton *computer scientist*
Greenwood, Frank *information scientist*
Halberstam, Heini *mathematician*
Hamblen, John Wesley *computer scientist, genealogist*
Hildebrandt, Theodore Ware *computer scientist*
†Hill, Shirley Ann *mathematics educator*
Horton, Wilfred Henry *mathematics educator*
Hughes, Richard Gene *computer executive, consultant*
Husain, Taqdir *mathematics educator*
Israel, Robert Allan *statistician*
Jones, Anita Katherine *computer scientist, educator*
Kadota, Takashi Theodore *mathematician, electrical engineer*
Karnaugh, Maurice *computer scientist, educator*
Keisler, H(oward) Jerome *mathematics educator*
Komkov, Vadim *mathematician, educator*
Krantz, Steven George *mathematics educator*
Laning, J. Halcombe *retired computer scientist*
Lasry, Jean-Michel *mathematics educator*
Liskov, Barbara Huberman *software engineering educator*
Low, Emmet Francis, Jr. *mathematics educator*
McGehee, Richard Paul *mathematics educator*
Padberg, Harriet Ann *mathematics educator*
Pratt, Terrence Wendall *information research scientist*
Pritzker, Leon *statistician, consultant*
Roberts, Marie Dyer *computer systems specialist*
Roitman, Judith *mathematician*
Sagan, Hans *mathematician, educator, author*
Skelton, John Edward *computer technology consultant*
Stern, Nancy Fortgang *mathematics and computer science, educator*
Suppes, Patrick *statistics, education, philosophy and psychology educator*
Temam, Roger M. *mathematician*
Thorington, John M., Jr. *computer graphics company executive*
Tompsett, Michael Francis *research director*
Walter, Martin Edward *mathematician, educator*
Weiner, Louis Max *retired mathematics educator*
Winder, Robert Owen *retired mathematician, computer engineer executive*
Wylie, Clarence Raymond, Jr. *mathematics educator*
Yntema, Mary Katherine *retired mathematics educator*

SCIENCE: PHYSICAL SCIENCE

UNITED STATES

ALABAMA

Auburn
Carr, Howard Earl *physicist, educator*
Molz, Fred John, III *hydrologist, educator*
Perez, Joseph Dominique *physics educator*

Birmingham
Bauman, Robert Poe *physicist*
Bugg, Charles Edward *biochemistry educator, scientist*
Lammertsma, Koop *chemist, consultant*
Longenecker, Herbert Eugene *biochemist, former university president*
Montgomery, John Atterbury *research chemist, consultant*
Moore, William Gower Innes *biochemist*
Robinson, Edward Lee *retired physics educator, consultant*
Shealy, David Lee *physicist, educator*
Thompson, Wynelle Doggett *chemistry educator*
Urry, Dan Wesley *research biophysicist, educator, science facility administrator*

Dauphin Island
Porter, John Finley, Jr. *physicst, conservationist, retired educator*

Harvest
Norman, Ralph Louis *physicist, consultant*

Huntsville
Allan, Barry David *research chemist, government official*
Anderson, Elmer Ebert *physicist, educator*
Decher, Rudolf *physicist*
de Loach, Anthony Cortelyou *solar physicist*
Dimmock, John Oliver *university research center director*
Garriott, Owen Kay *astronaut, scientist*
Johnson, Charles Leslie *aerospace physicist, consultant*
McKnight, William Baldwin *physics educator*
Mc Manus, Samuel Plyler *chemist, academic administrator*
Parnell, Thomas Alfred *physicist*
Perkins, James Francis *physicist*
Schwinghamer, Robert John *materials scientist*
Smith, Robert Earl *space scientist*
Stuhlinger, Ernst *physicist*
Vaughan, William Walton *atmospheric scientist*
Wright, John Collins *chemistry educator*

Jacksonville
Reid, William James *retired physicist, educator*

Madison
Rosenberger, Franz Ernst *physics educator*

Mobile
Fox, Sidney Walter *chemist, educator*

New Market
Lee, Thomas J. *aerospace scientist*

Normal
Caulfield, Henry John *physics educator*

Sheffield
†Meagher, James Francis *atmospheric research executive*

Tuscaloosa
Cava, Michael Patrick *chemist, educator*
Cole, George David *physicist*
Coulter, Philip Wylie *physicist, educator*
Izatt, Jerald Ray *physics educator*
LaMoreaux, Philip Elmer *geologist, hydrogeologist, consultant*
Mancini, Ernest Anthony *geologist, educator, researcher*
Miyagawa, Ichiro *physicist*
Van Artsdalen, Ervin Robert *physical chemist, educator*

ALASKA

Anchorage
Evans, William Frederick *research chemist*

Fairbanks
Eichelberger, John Charles *volcanologist, educator*
Guthrie, Russell Dale *vertebrate paleontologist*
Helfferich, Merritt Randolph *geophysical research administrator*
†Hopkins, David Moody *geologist*
Roederer, Juan Gualterio *physics educator*
Speck, Robert Charles *geological engineer*
Weeks, Wilford Frank *geophysics educator, glaciologist*
Weller, Gunter Ernst *geophysics educator*

ARIZONA

Amado
Weekes, Trevor C. *astrophysicist*

Coolidge
Hiller, William Clark *physics educator, engineering educator, consultant*

Flagstaff
Barnes, Charles Winfred *geology educator, administrator*
Colbert, Edwin Harris *paleontologist, museum curator*
†McEwen, Alfred Sherman *planetary geologist*
Millis, Robert Lowell *astronomer*
†Shoemaker, Carolyn Spellmann *planetary astronomer*
Shoemaker, Eugene Merle *geologist*
†Spudis, Paul D. *geologist*

Green Valley
Bates, Charles Carpenter *oceanographer*

Peoria
Bernstein, Eugene Merle *physicist, retired educator*

Phoenix
Allen, John Rybolt L. *chemist, biochemist*
Phillips, Edwin Arthur *meteorologist*
Wing, David Allan *biochemistry educator*

Scottsdale
McPherson, Donald J. *metallurgist*
Newman, William Louis *geologist*

Sun City
Dapples, Edward Charles *geologist, educator*

Sun City West
Mariella, Raymond P. *chemistry educator, consultant*

Tempe
Burgoyne, Edward Eynon *chemistry educator*
Buseck, Peter Robert *geochemistry educator*
Cowley, John Maxwell *physics educator*
Dietz, Robert Sinclair *retired geology educator*
Goronkin, Herbert *physicist*
†Greeley, Ronald *geology educator*
Juvet, Richard Spalding, Jr. *chemistry educator*
Mayer, James Walter *materials science educator*
Nigam, Bishan Perkash *physics educator*
Page, John Boyd *physics educator*
Pettit, George Robert *chemistry educator, cancer researcher*
Péwé, Troy Lewis *geologist, educator*
Quadt, Raymond Adolph *metallurgist, cement company executive*
Skibitzke, Herbert Ernst, Jr. *hydrologist*
Smith, David John *physicist, educator*
Starrfield, Sumner Grosby *astrophysics educator, researcher*
Tillery, Bill W. *physics educator*
Vandenberg, Edwin James *chemist, educator*
Whitehurst, Harry Bernard *chemistry educator*
Wyckoff, Susan *astronomy researcher*

Tucson
Angel, James Roger Prior *astronomer*
Barrett, Bruce Richard *physics educator*
Bartocha, Bodo *scientist, educator*
†Beckers, Jacques Maurice *astrophysicist*
Broadfoot, Albert Lyle *physicist*
Carruthers, Peter Ambler *physicist, educator*
†Chapman, Clark Russell *research astronomer*
†Crawford, David L. *astronomer*
Davis, Stanley Nelson *hydrologist, educator*
Dessler, Alexander Jack *space physics and astronomy educator, scientist*
De Young, David Spencer *astrophysicist*
Dickinson, Robert Earl *atmospheric scientist, educator*
Dodd, Charles Gardner *physical chemist*
Falco, Charles Maurice *physicist, educator*
†Fang, Li-Zhi *physicist, educator*
Forster, Leslie Stewart *chemistry educator*
†Freiser, Henry *chemistry educator*
Gruhl, James *energy scientist, artist*
Hartmann, William Kenneth *astronomy scientist*
Haynes, Caleb Vance, Jr. *geology and archaeology educator*
Hill, Henry Allen *physicist, educator*
Hoffmann, William Frederick *astronomer*
Howard, Robert Franklin *observatory administrator, astronomer*
Hruby, Victor Joseph *chemistry educator*
Hubbard, William Bogel *planetary sciences educator*
Hunten, Donald Mount *planetary scientist, educator*
Jackson, Kenneth Arthur *physicist, researcher*
Jefferies, John Trevor *astronomer, astrophysicist, observatory administrator*
Kessler, John Otto *physicist, educator*
Kiersch, George Alfred *geological consultant, retired educator*
Krider, E. Philip *atmospheric scientist, educator*
Lamb, Willis Eugene, Jr. *physicist, educator*
Lane, Leonard J. *hydrologist*
Law, John Harold *biochemistry educator*
Levy, Eugene Howard *planetary sciences educator, researcher*
†Marcialis, Robert Louis *planetary astronomer*
Nagy, Bartholomew Stephen *geochemist, educator*
Parmenter, Robert Haley *physics educator*
Peyghambarian, Nasser *optical science educator*
Powell, Richard C. *physicist, educator, researcher*
Roemer, Elizabeth *astronomer, educator*
Rountree, Janet Caryl *astrophysicist*
Schaefer, John Paul *chemist, corporate executive*
†Scotti, James Vernon *astronomer*
Smiley, Terah Leroy *geosciences educator*
Sonett, Charles Philip *physicist*
Strittmatter, Peter Albert *astronomer, educator*
Swalin, Richard Arthur *scientist, company executive*
Tifft, William Grant *astronomer*
Willis, Clifford Leon *geologist*
Wolfe, William Louis *optics educator*
Wolff, Sidney Carne *astronomer, observatory administrator*

ARKANSAS

Bella Vista
Johnson, A(lyn) William *chemistry educator, researcher and consultant*

Fayetteville
Steele, Kenneth Franklin, Jr. *hydrology educator, resource center director*

Little Rock
Williams, Norman F. *geologist, researcher*

Searcy
Pryor, Joseph Ehrman *chemistry educator*

CALIFORNIA

Altadena
Gurnis, Michael Christopher *geological sciences educator*

Anaheim
Loeblich, Helen Nina Tappan *paleontologist, educator*

Apple Valley
Mays, George Walter, Jr. *educational technology educator, consultant*

Arcata
Wayne, Lowell Grant *air pollution scientist, consultant*

Atascadero
Ogier, Walter Thomas *retired physics educator*

Atherton
Fisher, Leon Harold *physicist, emeritus educator*

Auburn
Hess, Patrick Henry *chemist*

Bakersfield
Dorer, Fred Harold *chemistry educator*

Bayside
Cocks, George Gosson *retired chemical microscopy educator*

Bellflower
Martin, Melissa Carol *radiological physicist*

Berkeley
Alpen, Edward Lewis *biophysicist, educator*
Alvarez, Walter *geology educator*
Ames, Bruce N(athan) *biochemist, molecular biologist*
Ames, Giovanna Ferro-Luzzi *biochemistry educator*
Arnon, Daniel I(srael) *biochemist, educator*
Arons, Jonathan *astrophysicist, educator*
Attwood, David Thomas *physicist, educator*
Baletta, William *physics research administrator*
Barker, Horace Albert *biochemist, microbiologist*
Barnett, R(alph) Michael *theoretical physicist, educational agency administrator*
Bartlett, Neil *chemist, educator*
†Bartlett, Paul A. *biochemist*
Bergman, Robert George *chemist, educator*
Berry, William Benjamin Newell *geologist, educator, former museum administrator*
Bolt, Bruce Alan *seismologist, educator*
Bowyer, Stuart C(harles) *astrophysicist, educator*
Brewer, Leo *physical chemist, educator*
Bukowinski, Mark Stefan Tadeusz *geophysics educator*
Calvin, Melvin *chemist, educator*
Carmichael, Ian Stuart Edward *geologist, educator*
Cerny, Joseph, III *chemistry educator, scientific laboratory administrator, university dean and official*
Chamberlain, Owen *nuclear physicist*
Chamberlin, Michael John *biochemistry educator*
Chandler, David *scientist, educator*
Chew, Geoffrey Foucar *physicist*
Clarke, John *physics educator*
Clemens, William Alvin *vertebrate paleontology educator*
Cohen, Marvin Lou *physics educator*
Cole, Roger David *biochemist, educator*
Curtis, Garniss Hearfield *geology educator*
Dauben, William Garfield *chemist, educator*
Davis, Marc *astrophysics educator*
de Lumen, Benito O. *science educator*
de Pater, Imke *astronomy educator*
Ely, Robert Pollock, Jr. *physics educator, researcher*
Fowler, Thomas Kenneth *physicist*
Fuhs, G(eorg) Wolfgang *environmental research manager*
Gaillard, Mary Katharine *physics educator*
Glaser, Donald Arthur *physicist*
†Godfrey, Charles Bruce *chemist, laboratory executive*
Goldhaber, Gerson *physicist, educator*
†Graham, James *astronomy educator*
Gregory, Joseph Tracy *paleontologist, educator*
Hahn, Erwin Louis *physicist, educator*
Hearst, John Eugene *chemistry educator*
Heathcock, Clayton Howell *chemistry educator, researcher*
Heiles, Carl Eugene *astronomer, educator*
Heineman, Heinz *chemist*
Heinemann, Heinz *chemist, researcher, consultant*
Helmholz, August Carl *physicist, educator emeritus*
Hoffman, Darleane Christian *chemistry educator*
Holdren, John Paul *energy and resource educator, researcher, author, consultant*
Jackson, J(ohn) David *physicist, educator*
Jeanloz, Raymond *geophysicist, educator*
Jeffries, Carson Dunning *physicist, educator*
Jolly, William Lee *chemistry educator*
Kahn, Steven Michael *astrophysicist, educator*
Kerth, Leroy T. *physics educator*
†Kim, Sung-Hou *chemistry educator, biophysical and biological chemist*
King, Ivan Robert *astronomy educator*
Kirsch, Jack Frederick *biochemistry educator*
Kittel, Charles *physicist, educator emeritus*
Klinman, Judith Pollock *biochemist, educator*
Koshland, Daniel Edward, Jr. *biochemist, educator*
Lee, Yuan T(seh) *chemistry educator*
Leemans, Wim Pieter *physicist*
Leopold, Luna Bergere *geology educator*
Lester, William Alexander, Jr. *chemist, educator*
Linn, Stuart Michael *biochemist, educator*
Lipps, Jere Henry *paleontology educator*
Malina, Roger F. *astronomer*
Mandelstam, Stanley *physicist*
Markowitz, Samuel Solomon *chemistry educator*
Mathies, Richard Alfred *chemistry educator*
†Matson, Pamela Anne *environmental science educator*
Mc Evilly, Thomas Vincent *seismologist*
McKee, Christopher Fulton *astrophysics and astronomy educator*
Mel, Howard Charles *biophysics educator*
Miller, William Hughes *theoretical chemist, educator*
Moore, C. Bradley *chemistry educator*
Muller, Richard August *physicist, author*
Nero, Anthony Vincent, Jr. *physicist, environmental scientist*
Perez-Mendez, Victor *physics educator*
Perry, Dale Lynn *chemist*
Pines, Alexander *chemistry educator, researcher*
Pitzer, Kenneth Sanborn *chemist, educator*
Rasmussen, John Oscar *chemist, scientist*
Raymond, Kenneth Norman *chemistry educator, research chemist*
Reynolds, John Hamilton *physicist, educator*
Ritchie, Robert Oliver *materials science educator*
Rosenblatt, Gerd Matthew *chemist*
Sadoulet, Bernard *astrophysicist, educator*
Sauer, Kenneth *chemistry educator*
Saykally, Richard James *chemistry educator*
†Schoenlein, Robert W. *research scientist*
Schultz, Peter G. *chemistry educator*
Seaborg, Glenn Theodore *chemistry educator*
Searcy, Alan Winn *chemist, educator*
Sessler, Andrew Marienhoff *physicist*
Shen, Yuen-Ron *physics educator*
Shu, Frank Hsia-San *astronomy educator, researcher, author*
Shugart, Howard Alan *physicist, educator*
†Silk, Joseph Ivor *astronomy educator*
Siri, William E. *physicist*
Smoot, George Fitzgerald, III *astrophysicist*
Somorjai, Gabor Arpad *chemist, educator*
Spinrad, Hyron *astronomer*
†Stacy, Angelica M. *chemistry educator*
Steiner, Herbert Max *physics educator*
Strauss, Herbert Leopold *chemistry educator*
Streitwieser, Andrew, Jr. *chemistry educator*
Symons, Timothy James McNeil *physicist*
Thomas, Gareth *metallurgy educator*
Thompson, Anthony Wayne *metallurgist, educator, consultant*
Tinoco, Ignacio, Jr. *chemist, educator*
Townes, Charles Hard *physics educator*
Trilling, George Henry *physicist, educator*
Tsina, Richard Vasil *chemistry educator*
Valentine, James William *paleobiology, educator, author*
Vollhardt, Kurt Peter Christian *chemistry educator*
†Welch, William John *astronomer, educator*
Zumino, Bruno *physics educator, researcher*

Bonita
Wood, Fergus James *geophysicist, consultant*

Burlingame
Hotz, Henry Palmer *physicist*

Cameron Park
Buckles, Robert Edwin *chemistry educator*

Carlsbad
Smith, Warren James *optical scientist, consultant, lecturer*

China Lake
Bennett, Jean Louise McPherson *physicist, research scientist*

Claremont
Beilby, Alvin Lester *chemistry educator*
Chambers, Robert Jefferson *educator, observatory administrator*
Helliwell, Thomas McCaffree *physicist, educator*
Kronenberg, Klaus J(ohannes) *physicist*
Kubota, Mitsuru *chemistry educator*
Long, Franklin Asbury *chemistry educator*
White, Kathleen Merritt *geologist*

Corona Del Mar
Britten, Roy John *biophysicist*

Coronado
Hudson, George Elbert *retired research physicist*

Costa Mesa
Lattanzio, Stephen Paul *astronomy educator*

Cupertino
Nelson, Richard Burton *physicist, engineer, patent consultant*
Wiley, Richard Haven *chemist, educator*

Davis
Andrews, Lawrence James *chemistry educator, academic administrator*
Axelrod, Daniel Isaac *geology and botany educator*
Black, Arthur Leo *biochemistry educator*
Bradbury, Edwin Morton *biochemistry educator*
Cahill, Thomas Andrew *physicist, educator*
Carlson, Don Marvin *biochemist*
Conn, Eric Edward *plant biochemist*
Day, Howard Wilman *geology educator*
Doi, Roy Hiroshi *biochemist, educator*
Goldman, Marvin *biophysicist, educator*
Hedrick, Jerry Leo *biochemistry and biophysics educator*
Higgins, Charles Graham *geology educator*
Hullar, Theodore Lee *environmental educator*
Jungerman, John Albert *physics educator*
Keizer, Joel Edward *chemistry educator, theoretical scientist*
Mukherjee, Amiya K *metallurgy and materials science educator*
Nash, Charles Presley *chemistry educator*
Shelton, Robert Neal *physics educator, researcher*
Smith, Lloyd Muir *chemist, educator*
Stumpf, Paul Karl *biochemistry educator emeritus*
Verosub, Kenneth Lee *geology educator, researcher*
Volman, David Herschel *chemistry educator*
Wooten, Frederick (Oliver) *applied science educator*
Yang, Shang Fa *biochemistry educator, plant physiologist*

Del Mar
Reid, Joseph Lee *physical oceanographer, educator*
†Stevenson, Robert Everett *oceanography consultant*

Duarte
Greenstein, Jesse Leonard *astronomer, educator*

El Cajon
Burnett, Lowell Jay *physicist, educator*

El Cerrito
Griffith, Ladd Ray *retired chemical research director*
Gwinn, William Dulaney *physical chemist, educator, consultant*

El Granada
Heere, Karen R. *astrophysicist*

El Segundo
Paulikas, George Algis *physicist*
Radys, Raymond George *laser scientist*

Emeryville
Marcus, Frank *biochemist*
Masri, Merle Sid *biochemist, consultant*

Encinitas
Goldberg, Edward Davidow *geochemist, educator*

Encino
Hawthorne, Marion Frederick *chemistry educator*

Fountain Valley
Gittleman, Morris *metallurgist,consultant*

Fremont
Berry, Michael James *scientist*
Gill, Stephen Paschall *physicist, mathematician*

Fresno
Kauffman, George Bernard *chemistry educator*

Fullerton
Hufnagel, Raymond Joseph, Jr. *aerospace and commercial executive*
McAuliffe, Clayton Doyle *chemist*
Shapiro, Mark Howard *physicist, educator, academic dean, consultant*

Glendale
Farmer, Crofton Bernard *atmospheric physicist*

Hayward
Hirschfeld, Sue Ellen *geological sciences educator*
Warnke, Detlef Andreas *geologist, educator*

Hemet
Berger, Lev Isaac *physicist, educator*

Hercules
Zhu, Mingde *chemist*

Inglewood
Lewis, Roy Roosevelt *physicist*

Irvine
Bander, Myron *physics educator, university dean*
Bradshaw, Ralph Alden *biochemistry educator*
Bron, Walter Ernest *physics educator*
Cho, Zang Hee *physics educator*
Clark, Bruce Robert *geology consultant*
Lanyi, Janos Karoly *biochemist, educator*
McLaughlin, Calvin Sturgis *biochemistry educator*
McWilliams, Roger Dean *physicist, educator*
Nalcioglu, Orhan *physicist*
Nomura, Masayasu *biological chemistry educator*
†Overman, Larry Eugene *chemistry educator*
Reines, Frederick *physicist, educator*
Rentzepis, Peter M. *chemistry educator*
Rowland, Frank Sherwood *chemistry educator*
Rynn, Nathan *physics educator, consultant*
Trolinger, James Davis *laser scientist*
†Van Vranken, David Lee *chemist*
Wallis, Richard Fisher *physicist, educator*
White, Stephen Halley *biophysicist, educator*
Wolfsberg, Max *chemist, educator*
Woodruff, Truman O(wen) *physicist, emeritus educator*

Kensington
Connick, Robert Elwell *chemistry educator*

La Canada Flintridge
Pickering, William Hayward *physics educator, scientist*

La Habra
Woyski, Margaret Skillman *retired geology educator*

La Jolla
Arnold, James Richard *chemist, educator*
Asmus, John Fredrich *physicist*
Backus, George Edward *theoretical geophysicist*
Barnett, Tim P. *meteorologist*
Benson, Andrew Alm *biochemistry educator*
Boger, Dale L. *chemistry educator*
Bray, Nancy A. *oceanographic administrator*
Brueckner, Keith Allan *theoretical physicist, educator*
Buckingham, Michael John *oceanography educator*
Burbidge, E. Margaret *astronomer, educator*
Christensen, Halvor Niels *biochemist, educator*
†Continetti, Robert E. *chemistry educator*
Cox, Charles Shipley *oceanography researcher, educator*
Craig, Harmon *geochemist, oceanographer*
Dashen, Roger Frederick *physics educator, consultant*
Doolittle, Russell Francis *biochemist, educator*
Edelman, Gerald Maurice *biochemist, educator*
†Engvall, Eva *biochemist*
Feher, George *physics and biophysics scientist, educator*
Fisher, Frederick Hendrick *oceanographer*
Geiduschek, E(rnest) Peter *biophysics and molecular biology educator*
†Ghadiri, M. Reza *chemistry educator*
Goodman, Murray *chemistry educator*
Grier, Herbert Earl *scientist, consultant*
Grine, Donald Reaville *geophysicist, research executive*
Itano, Harvey Akio *biochemistry educator*
†Joyce, Gerald F. *biochemist, educator*
Kadonaga, James Takuro *biochemist*
Keeling, Charles David *oceanography educator*
Kerr, Donald MacLean, Jr. *physicist*
Knox, Robert Arthur *oceanographer, academic administrator*
Lal, Devendra *nuclear geophysics educator*
Lauer, James Lothar *physicist, educator*
Lerner, Richard Alan *chemistry educator, scientist*
MacDonald, Gordon James Fraser *geophysicist*
MacDougall, John Douglas *earth science educator*
Marti, Kurt *chemistry educator*
McCammon, James Andrew *chemistry educator*
Mc Elroy, William David *biochemist, educator*
McIlwain, Carl Edwin *physicist*
Mullis, Kary Banks *biochemist*
Munk, Walter Heinrich *geophysics educator*
Namias, Jerome *meteorologist*
†Nicolaou, Kyriacos Costa *chemistry educator*
O'Neil, Thomas Michael *physicist, educator*
†Orcutt, John Arthur *geophysicist*
Patton, Stuart *biochemist, educator*
Ride, Sally Kristen *physics educator, scientist, former astronaut*
Rosenbluth, Marshall Nicholas *physicist, educator*
Rotenberg, Manuel *physics educator*
Sclater, John George *geophysics educator*
Sham, Lu Jeu *physics educator*
Sharpless, K. Barry *chemist*
Shor, George G., Jr. *geophysicist, oceanographic administrator, engineer*
Shuler, Kurt Egon *chemist, educator*
Somerville, Richard Chapin James *atmospheric scientist, educator*
Spiess, Fred Noel *oceanographer, educator*
Suhl, Harry *physics educator*
Van Lint, Victor Anton Jacobus *physicist*
Wall, Frederick Theodore *chemistry educator*
Watson, Kenneth Marshall *physics educator*
Wong, Chi-Huey *chemistry educator*
York, Herbert Frank *physics educator, government official*

La Puente
Reddy, Nagendranath K. *biochemist, researcher*

Laguna Beach
Wilson, James Newman *retired laboratory executive*

Laguna Hills
Batdorf, Samuel B(urbridge) *physicist*
Howard, Hildegarde (Mrs. Henry Anson Wylde) *paleontologist*
Iberall, Arthur Saul *physicist, publisher*

Livermore
Alder, Berni Julian *physicist*
†Campbell, Edward Michael *research physicist, science administrator*
†Glinsky, Michael Edwin *research physicist*
Hulet, Ervin Kenneth *retired nuclear chemist*
Kidder, Ray Edward *physicist, consultant*
Kirkwood, Robert Keith *applied physicist*
Leith, Cecil Eldon, Jr. *retired physicist*
Max, Claire Ellen *physicist*
Nuckolls, John Hopkins *physicist, researcher*
Schock, Robert Norman *geophysicist*
Shotts, Wayne J. *nuclear scientist, federal agency administrator*
Tarter, Curtis Bruce *physicist, science administrator*
Wong, Joe *physical chemist*

Loma Linda
Slattery, Charles Wilbur *biochemistry educator*
Wilcox, Ronald Bruce *biochemistry educator, researcher*

Long Beach
Bauer, Roger Duane *chemistry educator, science consultant*
Hu, Chi Yu *physicist, educator*
Jensen, James Leslie *chemistry educator, dean*

Los Altos
Barker, William Alfred *physics educator*
Fraknoi, Andrew *astronomy educator, astronomical society executive*
Hall, Charles Frederick *space scientist, government administrator*
Johnson, Richard Damerau *aerospace scientist*
Jones, Robert Thomas *aerospace scientist*
Twersky, Victor *mathematical physicist, educator*
van Tamelen, Eugene Earle *chemist, educator*

Los Angeles
Adamson, Arthur Wilson *chemistry educator*
Aki, Keiiti *seismologist, educator*
Aller, Lawrence Hugh *astronomy educator, researcher*
Benson, Sidney William *chemistry researcher*
Bhaumik, Mani Lal *physicist*
Bird, Peter *geology educator*
Braginsky, Stanislav Iosifovich *physicist, geophysicist, researcher*
Byers, Nina *physics educator*
Campbell, Kenneth Eugene, Jr. *vertebrate paleontologist*
Chapman, Orville Lamar *chemist, educator*
Chester, Marvin *physics educator*
Cline, David Bruce *physicist, educator*
Coleman, Charles Clyde *physicist, educator*
Coleman, Paul Jerome, Jr. *physicist, educator*
Cornwall, John Michael *physics educator, consultant, researcher*
Coroniti, Ferdinand Vincent *physics educator, consultant*
Cram, Donald James *chemistry educator*
Dalton, Larry Raymond *chemistry educator, researcher, consultant*
Dawson, John Myrick *plasma physics educator*
†Diederich, Francois Nico *chemistry educator*
Domaradzki, Julian Andrzej *physics educator*
Dows, David Alan *chemistry educator*
Dunn, Arnold Samuel *biochemistry educator*
Dunn, Bruce Sidney *materials science educator*
Edwards, Kenneth Neil *chemist, consultant*
†Fischer, Alfred George *geology educator*
Foote, Christopher Spencer *chemist, educator*
Fried, Burton David *physicist, educator*
Fulco, Armand John *biochemist*
Ganas, Perry Spiros *physicist*
Glitz, Dohn George *biochemistry educator*
†Haegel, Nancy M. *materials, optics sciences educator*
Hall, Clarence Albert, Jr. *geologist, educator*
†Heath, James R. *chemistry educator*
Hellwarth, Robert Willis *physicist, educator*
Houk, Kendall Newcomb *chemistry educator*
Igo, George Jerome *physics educator*
Jaffe, Sigmund *educator, chemist*
Jones, Walter Harrison *chemist*
†Jung, Michael Ernest *chemistry educator*
Kaplan, Isaac Raymond *chemistry educator, corporate executive*
†Kaula, William Mason *geophysicist, educator*
Kikuchi, Ryoichi *physics educator*
Kivelson, Margaret Galland *physicist*
Knopoff, Leon *geophysics educator*
Kolin, Alexander *retired biophysics researcher*
Krupp, Edwin Charles *astronomer*
Kunc, Joseph Anthony *physics and engineering educator, consultant*
Laaly, Heshmat Ollah *research chemist, roofing consultant, author*
Lee, Amy Shiu *biochemist, educator*
Levine, Raphael David *chemistry educator*
Logan, Joseph Granville, Jr. *physicist*
Maki, Kazumi *physicist, educator*
Markland, Francis Swaby, Jr. *biochemist, educator*
Neufeld, Elizabeth Fondal *biochemist, educator*
Nimni, Marcel Ephraim *biochemistry educator*
Olah, George Andrew *chemist, educator*
Onak, Thomas Philip *chemistry educator*
Paulson, Donald Robert *chemistry educator*
Reiss, Howard *chemistry educator*
Roberts, Sidney *biological chemist*
Saxon, David Stephen *physics educator, university official*
Scott, Robert Lane *chemist, educator*
Shapiro, Isadore *materials scientist, consultant*
Smathers, James Burton *medical physicist, educator*
Smith, Emil L. *biochemist, consultant*
Smith, William Ray *retired biophysicist, engineer*
Steinberg, Morris Albert *metallurgist*
Stellwagen, Robert Harwood *biochemistry educator*
Szwarc, Michael *polymer scientist*
Thorne, Richard Mansergh *physicist*
Trimble, Stanley Wayne *hydrology and geography educator*
Ufimtsev, Pyotr Yakovlevich *physicist, electrical engineer, educator*
Whitten, Charles Alexander, Jr. *physics educator*
Wittry, David Beryle *physicist, educator*
Wong, Alfred Yiu-fai *physics educator*
Woodruff, Fay *paleoceanographer, geological researcher*
Wu, Robert Chung Yung *space sciences educator*
Wurtele, Morton Gaither *meteorologist, educator*

Los Gatos
Knudsen, William Claire *geophysicist*

Magalia
Joffre, Stephen Paul *consulting chemist*

Malibu
Chester, Arthur Noble *physicist*
Forward, Robert L(ull) *physicist, writer, consultant*
Margerum, J(ohn) David *chemist*
Pepper, David M. *physicist, educator, author, inventor*

Menlo Park
Bukry, John David *geologist*
Funkhouser, Lawrence William *retired geologist*
Holzer, Thomas Lequear *geologist*
Lachenbruch, Arthur Herold *geophysicist*
Lindh, Allan Goddard *seismologist*
†McMillen, Donald F. *chemist*
†Savage, James Crampton *geophysicist*
Tokheim, Robert Edward *physicist*
Vickers, Roger Spencer *physicist, program director*
Vidale, John Emilio *geologist*
Wallace, Robert Earl *geologist*

Milpitas
Lee, Kenneth *physicist*

Moffett Field
Kittel, Peter *research scientist*
Ragent, Boris *physicist*
Seiff, Alvin *planetary scientist, atmosphere physics and aerodynamics consultant*
†Yelle, Roger V. *physical chemist*

Montecito
Wheelon, Albert Dewell *physicist*

Monterey
Collins, Curtis Allan *oceanographer*
Shull, Harrison *chemist, educator*
Van Der Bijl, Willem *meteorology educator*
Weaver, William Bruce *astronomer, research administrator*

Monterey Park
Waiter, Serge-Albert *retired scientist, consultant*

Moraga
Hollingsworth, Robert Edgar *nuclear consultant*

Mountain View
Blachman, Nelson M(erle) *physicist*

North Hollywood
Thomson, John Ansel Armstrong *biochemist*

Novato
Simon, Lee Will *astronomer*

Oakland
Jukes, Thomas Hughes *biological chemist, educator*
Kropschot, Richard H. *physicist, science laboratory administrator*
Massey, Walter Eugene *physicist, science foundation administrator*
Mikalow, Alfred Alexander, II *deep sea diver, marine surveyor, marine diving consultant*

Orinda
Hartsough, Walter Douglas *physicist*
Heftmann, Erich *biochemist*

Pacific Grove
Brewer, Peter George *ocean geochemist*

Pacific Palisades
Csendes, Ernest *chemist, corporate and financial executive*
Fink, Robert Morgan *biological chemistry educator*
Salter, Robert Mundhenk, Jr. *physicist, consultant*

Palm Springs
Krick, Irving Parkhurst *meteorologist*

Palo Alto
Ballam, Joseph *physicist, educator*
Bienenstock, Arthur Irwin *physicist, educator*
Colin, Lawrence *aerospace scientist*
Cutler, Leonard Samuel *physicist*
Eng, Lawrence Fook *biochemistry educator, neurochemist*
†Flory, Curt A. *research physicist*
Fried, John H. *chemist*
Heinemann, Klaus W. *physical sciences research administrator*
Holmes, John Richard *physicist, educator*
Loewenstein, Walter Bernard *nuclear power technologist*
Panofsky, Wolfgang Kurt Hermann *physicist, educator*
†Street, Robert A. *research physicist*
Stringer, John *materials scientist*
†Theeuwes, Felix *physical chemist*
Ullman, Edwin Fisher *research chemist*

Palos Verdes Peninsula
Reynolds, Harry Lincoln *physicist*

Pasadena
Albee, Arden Leroy *geologist, educator*
Allen, Clarence Roderic *geologist, educator*
Anderson, Don Lynn *geophysicist, educator*
Anson, Fred Colvig *chemistry educator*
Babcock, Horace W. *astronomer*
Baldeschwieler, John Dickson *chemist, educator*
Barnes, Charles Andrew *physicist, educator*
Beauchamp, Jesse Lee (Jack Beauchamp) *chemistry educator*
†Beaudet, Robert Arthur *chemistry educator*
Beichman, Charles Arnold *astrophysicist, academic director*
Bejczy, Antal Károly *research scientist, research facility administrator*
Bercaw, John Edward *chemistry educator, consultant*
†Bjorkman, Pamela *crystallographer*
Blandford, Roger David *astronomy educator*
Boehm, Felix Hans *physicist, educator*
Breckinridge, James Bernard *research physicist*
†Buratti, Bonnie J. *aerospace scientist*
†Carlstrom, John E. *astronomy educator*
Chahine, Moustafa Toufic *atmospheric scientist*
Chan, Sunney Ignatius *chemist*
Cohen, Judith Gamora *astronomy educator*
Cohen, Marshall Harris *astronomer, educator*
Culick, Fred Ellsworth Clow *physics and engineering educator*
Davidson, Norman Ralph *biochemistry educator*
Dervan, Peter Brendan *chemistry educator*
Dimotakis, Paul Emmanuel *aeronautics and physics educator*
Dougherty, Dennis A. *chemistry educator*
Dressler, Alan Michael *astronomer*
†Duxbury, Thomas C. *planetary scientist*
Epstein, Samuel *geologist, educator*
Fowler, William Alfred *retired physics educator*
Frautschi, Steven Clark *physicist, educator*
†Fu, Lee-Lueng *oceanographer*
Goddard, William Andrew, III *chemist, applied physicist, educator*
Goldreich, Peter Martin *astrophysics and planetary physics educator*
Goodstein, David Louis *physics educator*
Gray, Harry Barkus *chemistry educator*
Grubbs, Robert Howard *chemistry educator*
Heindl, Clifford Joseph *physicist*
†Helin, Eleanor Kay *astronomer, geologist*
Helmberger, Donald Vincent *geophysical educator, researcher*
Hitlin, David George *physicist, educator*
Hopfield, John Joseph *biophysicist, educator*
Ingersoll, Andrew Perry *planetary science educator*
Jastrow, Robert *physicist*
Johnson, Torrence Vaino *astronomer*

Johnson, William Lewis *materials science educator*
Kanamori, Hiroo *geophysics educator*
Kavanagh, Ralph William *physics educator*
Koonin, Steven Elliot *physicist, professor*
Leonard, Nelson Jordan *chemistry educator*
Lewis, Nathan Saul *chemistry educator*
Liepmann, Hans Wolfgang *physicist, educator*
Marcus, Rudolph Arthur *chemist, educator*
McGill, Thomas Conley *physics educator*
Mc Koy, Basil Vincent Charles *theoretical chemist, educator*
Murray, Bruce C. *planetary scientist, educator, administrator*
Neugebauer, Gerry *astrophysicist, educator*
Neugebauer, Marcia *physicist, administrator*
†Patterson, Clair Cameron *nuclear chemist, biogeochemist, educator*
Politzer, Hugh David *physicist, educator*
Preskill, John Phillip *physics educator*
Roberts, John D. *chemist, educator*
Sandage, Allan Rex *astronomer*
Sargent, Wallace Leslie William *astronomer, educator*
Schmidt, Maarten *astronomy educator*
Schwarz, John Henry *theoretical physicist, educator*
Searle, Leonard *astronomer, researcher*
†Sekanina, Zdenek *astronomer*
Sharp, Robert Phillip *geology educator, researcher*
Stevenson, David John *planetary scientist*
Stone, Edward Carroll *physicist, educator*
Terhune, Robert William *optics scientist*
Tombrello, Thomas Anthony, Jr. *physics educator, consultant*
Vogt, Rochus Eugen *physicist, educator*
Wasserburg, Gerald Joseph *geology and geophysics educator*
Wernicke, Brian Philip *geologist, educator*
†Westphal, James Adolph *planetary science educator*
Wyllie, Peter John *geologist, educator*
†Yeomans, Donald Keith *astronomer*
Zachariasen, Fredrik *physics educator*
Zewail, Ahmed Hassan *chemistry and physics educator, editor, consultant*

Pleasant Hill
Weiss, Lionel Edward *geology educator*

Pomona
Aurilia, Antonio *physicist, educator*
Dev, Vasu *chemistry educator*
Eagleton, Robert Don *physics educator*

Rancho Santa Fe
Creutz, Edward Chester *physicist, museum consultant*

Redwood City
Nacht, Sergio *biochemist*
Speziale, A. John *organic chemist, consultant*

Richmond
Holmquist, Walter Richard *research chemist, molecular evolutionist, mathematics educator*
Thomas, John Richard *chemist*
Ward, Carl Edward *research chemist*

Ridgecrest
Bennett, Harold Earl *physicist, optics researcher*
St. Amand, Pierre *geophysicist*

Riverside
Green, Harry Western, II *geology/geophysics educator*
Norman, Anthony Westcott *biochemistry educator*
Orbach, Raymond Lee *physicist, educator*
Rabenstein, Dallas Leroy *chemistry educator*
White, Robert Stephen *physics educator*
Wild, Robert Lee *physics educator*
Wilkins, Charles L. *chemistry educator*

Sacramento
Gibson, Edward Fergus *physicist, educator*
Nussenbaum, Siegfried Fred *chemistry educator*

San Carlos
True, Richard Brownell *scientist*

San Diego
Cobble, James Wikle *chemistry educator*
Cunningham, Bruce Arthur *biochemist*
Daub, Clarence Theodore, Jr. *astronomer, educator*
Gastil, Russell Gordon *geologist, educator*
Gu, Zu-Han *research scientist*
†Lao, Lang Li *nuclear fusion research physicist*
Lyon, Waldo Kampmeier *physicist*
Malin, Michael Charles *space scientist, former geology educator*
Martin, Donald Ray *chemist, educator, consultant*
Moe, Chesney Rudolph *physics educator*
Morris, Richard Herbert *physicist, educator*
Ohkawa, Tihiro *physicist*
Pecsok, Robert Louis *chemist, educator*
Pincus, Howard Jonah *geologist, engineer, educator*
Roeder, Stephen Bernhard Walter *chemistry and physics educator*
Shneour, Elie Alexis *biochemist*
†Stambaugh, Ronald *physicist, researcher*
†Strait, Edward J. *research physicist*
†Taylor, Tony S. *research scientist*
Wright, Jon Alan *physicist*

San Francisco
Boyer, Herbert Wayne *biochemist*
Burlingame, Alma Lyman *chemist, educator*
Cluff, Lloyd Sterling *earthquake geologist*
Dickinson, Wade *physicist, research and development company executive*
Djerassi, Carl *chemist, educator, writer*
Featherstone, John Douglas Bernard *biochemistry educator*
Grodsky, Gerold Morton *biochemistry educator*
†Kollman, Peter A. *chemistry educator*
Krebs, Ernst Theodor, Jr. *biochemist*
Landahl, Herbert Daniel *biophysicist, mathematical biologist, researcher, consultant*
Majumdar, Sharmila *research scientist, educator*
Mandra, York T. *geology educator*
Posin, Daniel Q. *physics educator, television lecturer*
†Rutter, William J. *biochemist, educator*

San Jose
Brewer, Richard George *physicist*
Coburn, John Wyllie *physicist, researcher*
†Eigler, Donald Mark *physicist*
Forster, Julian *physicist, consultant*
Gruber, John Balsbaugh *physics educator, university administrator*
Houle, Frances Anne *physical chemist*
†Ito, Hiroshi *research chemist*
†Lutz, Chris P. *research physicist*
Neptune, John Addison *chemistry educator, consultant*
†Parkin, Stuart S. P. *materials scientist*
Rabolt, John Francis *optics scientist*
Winters, Harold Franklin *physicist*
†Yannoni, Costantino Sheldon *research chemist*

San Leandro
Stallings, Charles Henry *physicist*

San Luis Obispo
Bailey, Christina Anne *chemistry educator*
Grismore, Roger *physics educator, researcher*

San Pedro
Simmons, William *physicist, aerospace research executive*

Santa Barbara
Ahlers, Guenter *physicist, educator*
Awramik, Stanley Michael *geology educator*
†Buratto, Steven K. *chemistry educator, researcher*
Byers, Horace Robert *former meteorology educator*
Caldwell, David Orville *physics educator*
†Carlson, Jean M. *physics educator*
Christman, Arthur Castner, Jr. *scientific advisor*
Crowell, John C(hambers) *geology educator, researcher*
Dudziak, Walter Francis *physicist*
Eck, Robert Edwin *physicist*
Eisberg, Robert Martin *physics educator, computer software author and executive*
Ford, Peter C. *chemistry educator*
Gossard, Arthur Charles *physicist*
Heeger, Alan Jay *physicist*
Kennett, James Peter *geology and oceanography educator*
Kohn, Walter *educator, physicist*
Langer, James Stephen *physicist, educator*
†Macdonald, Ken Craig *geophysicist*
Meinel, Aden Baker *optics scientist*
Montgomery, Michael Davis *advanced technology consultant, hotelier*
†Morse, Daniel E. *biochemistry educator, science administrator*
Norris, Robert Matheson *geologist*
Peale, Stanton Jerrold *physics educator*
Scalapino, Douglas James *physics educator*
†Sowle, David Hugh *physicist*
†Stubbs, Christopher W. *physics educator*
Tilton, George Robert *geochemistry educator*
Wilson, Leslie *biochemist, cell biologist, biology educator*
Witherell, Michael S. *physics educator*
Wudl, Fred *chemistry educator, consultant*

Santa Clara
Carruthers, John Robert *scientist*
Gozani, Tsahi *nuclear physicist*
†Hobart, James L. *laser scientist*

Santa Clarita
Buck, Douglas Earl *chemist*

Santa Cruz
Brown, George Stephen *physicist*
Bunnett, Joseph Frederick *chemist, educator*
Drake, Frank Donald *astronomy educator*
Faber, Sandra Moore *astronomer, educator*
Flatté, Stanley Martin *physicist, educator*
Griggs, Gary Bruce *earth sciences educator, oceanographer, geologist, consultant*
Heusch, Clemens August *physicist, educator*
Hill, Terrell Leslie *chemist, biophysicist*
Kraft, Robert Paul *astronomer, educator*
Laporte, Leo Frederic *earth sciences educator*
Lay, Thorne *geosciences educator*
Noller, Harry Francis, Jr. *biochemist, educator*
Osterbrock, Donald E(dward) *astronomy educator*
Sands, Matthew Linzee *physicist, educator*
Silver, Mary Wilcox *oceanography educator*
Williams, Quentin Christopher *geophysicist, educator*
Wipke, W. Todd *chemistry educator*
Woosley, Stanford Earl *astrophysicist*

Santa Maria
Musser, C. Walton *physical scientist, consultant*

Santa Monica
Intriligator, Devrie Shapiro *physicist*

Santa Rosa
de Wys, Egbert Christiaan *geochemist*
Mc Donald, David William *chemist, educator*

Solana Beach
Agnew, Harold Melvin *physicist*

Solvang
Shelesnyak, Moses Chaim *biodynamicist, physiologist*

Stanford
Allen, Matthew Arnold *physicist*
Andersen, Hans Christian *chemistry educator*
Bai, Taeil Albert *research physicist*
Baldwin, Robert Lesh *biochemist, educator*
†Bashaw, Matthew Charles *physicist*
Beasley, Malcolm Roy *physics educator*
Berg, Paul *biochemist, educator*
Bershader, Daniel *aerophysics educator*
Bonner, William Andrew *chemistry educator*
†Boxer, Steven G. *physical chemistry educator*
Brauman, John I. *chemist, educator*
Brown, Gordon E., Jr. *earth scientist, educator*
Bube, Richard Howard *materials scientist*
Chu, Steven *physics educator*
Coleman, Robert Griffin *geology educator*
Collman, James Paddock *chemistry educator*
Cutler, Cassius Chapin *physicist, educator*
Deal, Bruce Elmer *physical chemist, educator*
Ernst, Wallace Gary *geology educator*
Fetter, Alexander Lees *theoretical physicist, educator*
Flinn, Paul Anthony *materials scientist*
Geballe, Theodore Henry *physics educator, communications technology consultant*
Graham, Stephan Alan *earth sciences educator*
Hagstrom, Stig Bernt *materials science and engineering educator*
Hanna, Stanley Sweet *physicist, educator*
Harbaugh, John Warvelle *applied earth sciences educator*
Harrison, Walter Ashley *physicist, educator*
Herring, William Conyers *physicist, emeritus educator*
Johnson, William Summer *chemistry educator*
Kaiser, Armin Dale *biochemist, educator*
Kennedy, Donald *environmental science educator, former academic administrator*
Kornberg, Arthur *biochemist*
Kornberg, Roger David *biochemist, structural biologist*
Kovach, Robert Louis *geophysics educator*
Krauskopf, Konrad Bates *geology educator*
Lehman, (Israel) Robert *biochemistry educator, consultant*
Levinthal, Elliott Charles *physicist, educator*
Little, William Arthur *physicist, educator*
McConnell, Harden Marsden *biophysical chemistry researcher, chemistry educator*
Nix, William Dale *materials scientist, educator*
Osheroff, Douglas Dean *physicist, researcher*
Pecora, Robert *chemistry educator*
Petrosian, Vahé *astrophysicist, educator*
Rees, John Robert *physicist*
Remson, Irwin *retired hydrogeology educator*
Richter, Burton *physicist, educator*
Ross, John *physical chemist, educator*
Sa, Luiz Augusto Discher *physicist*
Schawlow, Arthur Leonard *physicist, educator*
Schimke, Robert Tod *biochemist, educator*
Schneider, Stephen Henry *climatologist, environmental policy analyst, researcher*
Shaw, Herbert John *physics educator emeritus*
Solomon, Edward Ira *chemistry educator and researcher*
Spicer, William Edward, III *physicist, educator*
†Stevenson, David A. *materials science educator*
Stryer, Lubert *biochemist, educator*
Sturrock, Peter Andrew *space science and astrophysics educator*
Taube, Henry *chemistry educator*
Taylor, Richard Edward *physicist, educator*
Teller, Edward *physicist*
Thompson, George Albert *geophysics educator*
Trost, Barry Martin *chemist, educator*
Wagoner, Robert Vernon *astrophysicist, educator*
Walt, Martin *physicist, consulting educator*
†Waymouth, Robert *chemistry educator*
†Wender, Paul Anthony *chemistry educator*
Wojcicki, Stanley George *physicist, educator*
Zare, Richard Neil *chemistry educator*
Zoback, Mark David *geophysicist, educator*

Stockton
Whiteker, Roy Archie *retired chemistry educator*

Sunnyvale
DeMello, Austin Eastwood *astrophysicist, concert artist, poet, writer*
Thissell, James Dennis *physicist*

Thousand Oaks
Rathmann, George Blatz *genetic engineering company executive*
Wang, I-Tung *atmospheric scientist*

Torrance
Rogers, Howard H. *chemist*

Tustin
Clarke, Joyce Anne *biochemist*

Vacaville
Coulson, Kinsell Leroy *meteorologist*

Walnut Creek
Kieffer, William Franklinn *chemistry educator*

Westlake Village
Easton, William Heyden *geology educator*

Woodland Hills
Sharma, Brahama Datta *chemistry educator*

Woodside
Ashley, Holt *aerospace scientist, educator*

COLORADO

Arvada
Knight, William V. *geologist*

Boulder
Albritton, Daniel L. *environmental scientist*
Alldredge, Leroy Romney *retired geophysicist*
Anthes, Richard Allen *meteorologist*
Archambeau, Charles Bruce *physics educator, geophysics research scientist*
Bailey, Dana Kavanagh *radiophysicist, botanist*
†Baker, Daniel Neil *physicist*
Bartlett, David Farnham *physics educator*
Begelman, Mitchell C. *astrophysicist, educator*
Brault, James William *physicist*
Calvert, Jack George *atmospheric chemist, educator*
Caruthers, Marvin Harry *biochemistry educator*
Cary, John Robert *physics educator*
Cech, Thomas Robert *chemistry and biochemistry educator*
Chappell, Charles Franklin *meteorologist, consultant*
Choquette, Philip Wheeler *geologist, educator*
Conti, Peter Selby *astronomy educator*
Cristol, Stanley Jerome *chemistry educator*
Dryer, Murray *physicist*
Fleming, Rex James *meteorologist*
Garstang, Roy Henry *astrophysicist, educator*
Gossard, Earl Everett *physicist*
Hall, John Lewis *physicist, researcher*
Hermann, Allen Max *physics educator*
Hildner, Ernest Gotthold, III *solar physicist, science administrator*
Hofmann, David John *atmospheric science researcher, educator*
Hogg, David Clarence *physicist*
Holzer, Thomas E. *astronomer*
Joselyn, Jo Ann *space scientist*
Kauffman, Erle Galen *geologist, paleontologist*
Kellogg, William Welch *meteorologist*
King, Edward Louis *retired chemistry educator*
Koch, Tad Harbison *chemistry educator, researcher*
†Lally, Vincent Edward *atmospheric scientist*
Lineberger, William Carl *chemistry educator*
Low, Boon Chye *physicist*
Mahanthappa, Kalyana Thipperudraiah *physicist, educator*
Malde, Harold Edwin *retired federal government geologist*
†McCray, Richard Alan *astrophysicist, educator*
†Middleton, Paulette Bauer *atmospheric chemist*
Norcross, David Warren *physicist, researcher*
Pankove, Jacques Isaac *physicist*
Phelps, Arthur Van Rensselaer *physicist, consultant*
Robinson, Peter *paleontology educator, consultant*
Smythe, William Rodman *physicist, educator*
Snow, Theodore Peck *astrophysics educator*
Speiser, Theodore Wesley *astrophysics, planetary and atmospheric sciences educator*
Sullivan, Donald Barrett *physicist*
Tatarskii, Valerian Il'ich *physics researcher*
Tolbert, Bert Mills *biochemist, educator*
†Tolbert, Margaret A. *geochemistry educator*
Trenberth, Kevin Edward *atmospheric scientist*
Wahl, Floyd Michael *geologist*
Washington, Warren Morton *meteorologist*
Wieman, Carl E. *physics educator*

Colorado Springs
Christensen, Thomas Michael *surface physicist*
Henrickson, Eiler Leonard *geologist, educator*
Hoffman, John Raleigh *physicist*
Schwartz, Donald *chemistry educator*

Denver
Behrendt, John Charles *research geophysicist*
Boudreau, Robert Donald *meteorology educator*
Chappell, Willard Ray *physics educator, environmental scientist*
Eaton, Gareth Richard *chemistry educator, university dean*
Hamilton, Warren Bell *research geologist, educator*
Hetzel, Fredrick William *biophysicist, educator*
Iona, Mario *retired physics educator*
Liu, Chaoqun *staff scientist*
Miller, Stanley Custer, Jr. *physicist, retired educator*
Mullineaux, Donal Ray *geologist*
Neumann, Herschel *physics educator*
Pakiser, Louis Charles, Jr. *geophysicist*
Selbin, Joel *chemistry educator*
Smith, Dwight Morrell *chemistry educator*
Todd, Donald Frederick *geologist*
Weihaupt, John George *geosciences educator, scientist, university administrator*

Englewood
Mc Adams, Ronald Earl *geologist*
Wilson, James Ernest *geological consultant, writer*

Evergreen
Haun, John Daniel *petroleum geologist, educator*
Link, Peter Karl *geologist*
Phillips, Adran Abner (Abe Phillips) *geologist, oil and gas exploration consultant*

Fort Collins
Bamburg, James Robert *biochemistry educator*
Bernstein, Elliot Roy *chemistry educator*
Collins, Royal Eugene *physicist, engineering consultant, former educator*
Curthoys, Norman P. *biochemistry educator, consultant*
Elkind, Mortimer Murray *biophysicist, educator*
Fixman, Marshall *chemist, educator*
†Gray, William Mason *meteorologist, atmospheric science educator*
Johnson, Robert Britten *geology educator*
Ladanyi, Branka Maria *chemist, educator*
†Landsea, Christopher W. *meteorologist, educator*
Meyers, Albert Irving *chemistry educator*
Mosier, Arvin Ray *chemist, researcher*
Patton, Carl Elliott *physics educator*
†Runnells, Donald DeMar *geochemist, consultant*
Schumm, Stanley Alfred *geologist, educator*

Golden
Grose, Thomas Lucius Trowbridge *geologist, educator*
Hutchinson, Richard William *geology educator, consultant*
Kennedy, George Hunt *chemistry educator*
Kotch, Alex *chemistry educator*
Krauss, George *metallurgist*
Morrison, Roger Barron *geologist, executive*
Ponder, Herman *geologist*
Sims, Paul Kibler *geologist*
Tilton, John Elvin *mineral economics educator*
Weimer, Robert Jay *geology educator, energy consultant, civic leader*
White, James Edward *geophysicist*

Grand Junction
Rutz, Richard Frederick *physicist, researcher*

Lafayette
McNeill, William *environmental scientist*

Longmont
Little, Charles Gordon *geophysicist*

Snowmass
Lovins, Amory Bloch *physicist, energy consultant*

University Of Colorado
DePuy, Charles Herbert *chemist, educator*
Leone, Stephen Robert *chemical physicist, educator*
Miller, Gifford Hubbs *geologist*

Wheat Ridge
Meier, Thomas Joseph *geologist, consultant, engineering firm executive*

CONNECTICUT

Avon
Goodson, Richard Carle, Jr. *chemist, hazardous waste management consultant*

Brookfield
Schetky, Laurence McDonald *metallurgist, researcher*

Danbury
†Joyce, William H. *chemist*

Farmington
Herbette, Leo Gerard *biophysics educator*
Osborn, Mary Jane Merten *biochemist*
Spencer, Richard Paul *biochemist, educator, physician*

Greenwich
Heath, Gloria Whitton *aerospace scientist, consultant*

Groton
Cooper, Richard Arthur *oceanographer*
Pinson, Ellis Rex, Jr. *chemist, consultant*
Swindell, Archie Calhoun, Jr. *research biochemist, statistician*

Guilford
Engelman, Donald Max *molecular biophysics and biochemistry educator*

Hartford
†Solomon, Peter R. *physicist, physical chemist, engineering executive*

Manchester
Galasso, Francis Salvatore *materials scientist*

Middletown
Beveridge, David Lewis *chemistry educator*
Fry, Albert Joseph *chemistry educator*
Haake, Paul *chemistry and biochemistry educator*
Horne, Gregory Stuart *geologist, educator*
Sease, John W(illiam) *chemistry educator*
Upgren, Arthur Reinhold, Jr. *astronomer, educator, outdoor lighting consultant*

New Britain
Baskerville, Charles Alexander *geologist, educator*
Dimmick, Charles William *geology educator*

New Canaan
Harper, Anne Hopson *environmental scientist, administrator*

New Haven
Adair, Robert Kemp *physicist, educator*
†Aylor, Donald Earl *biophysicist, research meteorologist, plant pathology educator and reseacher*
Bennett, William Ralph, Jr. *physicist, educator*
Berner, Robert Arbuckle *geochemist, educator*
Bernstein, Ira Borah *physics educator*
Berson, Jerome Abraham *chemistry educator*
Bromley, David Allan *physicist, educator*
Chang, Richard Kounai *physics educator*
Chupka, William Andrew *chemical physicist, educator*
Coleman, Joseph Emory *biophysics and biochemistry educator*
Crothers, Donald Morris *biochemist, educator*
Gordon, Robert Boyd *geophysics educator*
†Gore, John Christopher *medical physicist*
Handschumacher, Robert Edmund *biochemistry educator*
Henrich, Victor Eugene *physicist, educator*
Herzenberg, Arvid *physicist, educator*
Hinds, Edward Allen *physicist, educator*
Hoffleit, Ellen Dorrit *astronomer*
Hohenberg, Pierre Claude *research physicist*
Jorgensen, William L. *chemistry educator*
Klein, Martin Jesse *physicist, educator, science historian*
Konigsberg, William Henry *molecular biophysics and biochemistry educator, administrator*
Lasaga, Antonio C. *geochemistry educator, researcher*
Mac Dowell, Samuel Wallace *physics educator*
Moore, Peter Bartlett *biochemist, educator*
Oemler, Augustus, Jr. *astronomy educator*
Ostrom, John H. *vertebrate paleontologist, educator, museum curator*
Parker, Peter D.M. *physicist, educator, researcher*
Reifsnyder, William Edward *meteorologist*
Richards, Frederic Middlebrook *biochemist, educator*
Rodgers, John *geologist, educator*
Saltzman, Barry *meteorologist, educator*
Sandweiss, Jack *physicist, educator*
†Schepartz, Alanna *biochemist, educator*
†Schmuttenmaer, Charles A. *chemistry educator*
Shulman, Robert Gerson *biophysics educator*
Skinner, Helen Catherine Wild *biomineralogist*
Slayman, Clifford Leroy, Jr. *biophysicist, educator*
Söll, Dieter *biochemistry educator*
Steitz, Joan Argetsinger *biochemistry educator*
Turekian, Karl Karekin *geochemistry educator*
Wasserman, Harry Hershal *chemistry educator*
Wiberg, Kenneth Berle *chemist, educator*
Wolf, Werner Paul *physicist, educator*
Zeller, Michael Edward *physicist*
Zinn, Robert James *astronomer*

New London
Mellberg, Leonard Evert *physicist*

New Milford
Fabricand, Burton Paul *physicist, educator*
†Wedral, Elaine Regina *food chemist*

New Preston
Duffis, Allen Jacobus *polymer chemistry extrusion specialist*

Newtown
Bockelman, Charles Kincaid *physics educator*

Norwalk
Ettre, Leslie Stephen *chemist*

Old Lyme
Anderson, Theodore Robert *physicist*

Redding
Foster, Edward John *engineering physicist*

Ridgefield
Farina, Peter R. *biochemist*

Shelton
Zeller, Claude *physicist, researcher*

Stamford
Hagner, Arthur Feodor *geologist, educator*
Porosoff, Harold *chemist, research and development director*
Toy, Arthur Dock Fon *chemist*

Storrs
Bartram, Ralph Herbert *physicist*
Bobbitt, James McCue *chemist*
Devereux, Owen Francis *metallurgy educator*
Stwalley, William Calvin *physics and chemistry educator*

Storrs Mansfield
Azaroff, Leonid Vladimirovitch *physics educator*
Klemens, Paul Gustav *physicist, educator*
Schuster, Todd Mervyn *biophysics educator, biotechnology company executive*

Wallingford
Augustyn, Walter Henry *physicist*

Westport
Tucker, Gardiner Luttrell *physicist, former paper company executive*

Woodbury
Skinner, Brian John *geologist, educator*

DELAWARE

Dover
Wasfi, Sadiq Hassan *chemistry educator*

Greenville
†Levitt, George *retired chemist*
Schroeder, Herman Elbert *scientific consultant*

Newark
Böer, Karl Wolfgang *physicist, educator*
Burmeister, John Luther *chemistry educator*
Daniels, William Burton *physicist, educator*
Evans, Dennis Hyde *chemist, educator*
Evenson, Paul Arthur *physics educator*
Hutton, David Glenn *environmental scientist, consultant, chemical engineer*
Jordan, Robert Reed *geologist, educator*
Mather, John Russell *climatologist, educator*
Murray, Richard Bennett *physics educator*
Ness, Norman Frederick *astrophysicist, educator, administrator*
Schultz, Jerold Marvin *materials scientist, educator*
Wetlaufer, Donald Burton *biochemist, educator*
Wu, Jin *oceanographer, educator, engineer*

Newport
Kirkland, Joseph J. *research chemist*

Wilmington
†Anderson, Paul S. *research chemist*
Crippen, Raymond C. *chemist, consultant*
Crittenden, Eugene Dwight, Jr. *chemical company executive*
†Jacobson, Howard W. *research chemist*
Kissa, Erik *retired chemist, consultant*
Moore, Carl Gordon *chemist, educator*
Parshall, George William *research chemist*
†Resnick, Paul R. *research chemist*
†Scherer, George W. *research chemist*
Simmons, Howard Ensign, Jr. *chemist, research administrator*
Smook, Malcolm Andrew *chemist, chemical company executive*
Wasserman, Edel *scientist, executive*

DISTRICT OF COLUMBIA

Washington
Abelson, Philip Hauge *physicist*
Alexander, Joseph Kunkle, Jr. *physicist*
Alter, Harvey *chemist, association executive*
Bednarek, Jana Maria *biochemist*
Berendzen, Richard *astronomer, educator, author*
Boyce, Peter Bradford *astronomer, professional association executive*
Brinckman, Frederick Edward, Jr. *retired research chemist, consultant*
Byer, Robert Louis *applied physics educator, university dean*
†Carrigan, Richard Alfred *environmental scientist, chemist*
Carter, Ashton Baldwin *physicist, government agency executive*
Chubb, Talbot Albert *physicist*
Coffey, Timothy *physicist*
Córdova, France Anne-Dominic *astrophysics scientist, administrator*
Crandall, David Hugh *physicist*
Darby, Joseph Branch, Jr. *metallurgist, government official*
Davidson, Eugene Abraham *biochemist, university administrator*
Dorman, Craig Emery *oceanographer, academic administrator*
Douglas, Bruce Colman *geophysicist*
Dutro, John Thomas, Jr. *geologist, paleontologist*
El Khadem, Hassan Saad *chemistry educator, researcher*
Fiske, Richard Sewell *geologist*
Fleischer, Michael *chemist*
Fowler, Earle Cabell *physicist, administrator*
Friedman, Herbert *physicist*
Garavelli, John Stephen *biochemistry research scientist*
Garvey, Gerald Thomas *physicist, researcher*
Girard, James Emery *chemistry educator*
Goldstein, Allan Leonard *biochemist, educator*
Grant, Richard Evans *paleontologist, museum curator*
Hallgren, Richard Edwin *meteorologist*
†Hammer, Charles F. *chemistry educator*
Harwit, Martin Otto *astrophysicist, educator, museum director*
Haskins, Caryl Parker *scientist, author*
Heindel, Ned Duane *chemistry educator*
Holland, Christie Anna *biochemist, virologist*
Holloway, John Thomas *physicist*
†Hooke, William Hines *meteorologist*
Imam, M. Ashraf *materials scientist, educator*
†Jackson, Shirley Ann *physicist*
†Johnston, Kenneth John *astronomer*
Karle, Isabella L. *chemist*
Karle, Jerome *physicist, researcher*
Keyworth, George Albert, II *physicist, consulting company executive*
Kier, Porter Martin *paleontologist*
†Knopman, Debra S. *hydrologist, federal agency administrator*
Kouts, Herbert John Cecil *physicist*
Krebs, Martha *physicist, federal agency administrator*
Lash, Jonathan *environmental law executive*
Ledley, Robert Steven *biophysicist*
Lehmberg, Robert Henry *research physicist*
Lintz, Paul Rodgers *physicist, engineer, patent examiner*
Lozansky, Edward Dmitry *physicist, author, consultant*
Mandula, Jeffrey Ellis *physicist*
Mason, Brian Harold *geologist, curator*
Mayer, Walter Georg *physics educator*
Maynard, Nancy Gray *biological oceanographer*
Mead, Gilbert D(unbar) *geophysicist, lawyer*
Meijer, Paul Herman Ernst *educator, physicist*
†Michel, David J. *metallurgist, crystallographer*
Morehouse, David Frank *geologist*
Morrison, David Lee *chemist, research institute executive*
Nelson, David Brian *physicist*
†Obenschain, Stephen Philip *physicist*
O'Connor, Thomas Edward *petroleum geologist, world bank officer*
Oertel, Goetz K. H. *physicist, professional association administrator*
Oliver, William Albert, Jr. *paleontologist*
Oran, Elaine Surick *physicist*
Ordway, Frederick Ira, III *educator, consultant, researcher, author*
Perros, Theodore Peter *chemist, educator*
Pojeta, John, Jr. *geologist*
Pope, Michael Thor *chemist*
Press, Frank *geophysicist, educator*
Prewitt, Charles Thompson *geochemist*
Raab, Harry Frederick, Jr. *physicist*
Rao, Desiraju Bhavanarayana *meteorologist, oceanographer, educator*
Rittner, Edmund Sidney *physicist*
Romanowski, Thomas Andrew *physics educator*
Roscher, Nina Matheny *chemistry educator*
Rosenberg, Norman Jack *agricultural meteorologist, educator*
Scott, Raymond Peter William *chemistry research educator, writer*
Siegel, Frederic Richard *geology educator*
Singer, Maxine Frank *biochemist*
Smith, Philip Meek *science policy consultant, writer*
Soderberg, David Lawrence *chemist*
Solomon, Sean Carl *geophysicist, lab director*
Stanley, Daniel Jean *geological oceanographer, senior scientist*
Stanley, Ronald Alwin *environmental scientist, poet*
Sullivan, Kathryn D. *geologist, astronaut*
Theon, John Speridon *meteorologist*
†Tilford, Shelby G. *earth science director, physical chemist, meteorlgist*
Tousey, Richard *physicist*
Uberall, Herbert Michael Stefan *physicist, educator*
Villforth, John Carl *health physicist*
Wang, Franklin Fu Yen *materials scientist, educator*
Watters, Thomas Robert *geologist, museum administrator*
Weiler, Kurt Walter *radio astronomer*
Wetherill, George West *geophysicist, planetary scientist*
White, John Arnold *physics educator, research scientist*
White, Robert Mayer *meteorologist*
Whitmore, Frank Clifford, Jr. *geologist*
Yochelson, Ellis L(eon) *paleontologist*
Yoder, Hatten Schuyler, Jr. *petrologist*

FLORIDA

Alachua
Schneider, Richard T(heodore) *optics research executive, engineer*

Bartow
McFarlin, Richard Francis *industrial chemist, researcher*

Boca Raton
Carraher, Charles Eugene, Jr. *chemistry educator, dean*
Finkl, Charles William, II *geologist, educator*
Wiesenfeld, John Richard *chemistry educator*

Boynton Beach
Balis, Moses Earl *biochemist, educator*
Fields, Theodore *consulting medical radiation physicist*
Gilstein, Jacob Burrill *physicist*

Cape Coral
West, John Merle *retired physicist, nuclear consultant*

Cocoa Beach
Gunn, Kenneth David *explosives safety specialist, consultant*

Coral Gables
Criss, Cecil M. *chemistry educator*
Einspruch, Norman Gerald *physicist, educator*
Leblanc, Roger Maurice *chemistry educator*

Dade City
Burdick, Glenn Arthur *physicist, engineering educator*

Deland
Coolidge, Edwin Channing *chemistry educator*

Delray Beach
Zarwyn, Berthold *physical scientist*

Fort Lauderdale
Zikakis, John P. *educator, researcher, biochemist*

Fort Myers
†Missimer, Thomas Michael *geologist*

Gainesville
Andrew, Edward Raymond *physicist*
Bodor, Nicholas Stephen *medicinal chemistry researcher, educator, consultant*
Couch, Margaret Wheland *research chemist*
Cousins, Robert John *nutritional biochemist, educator*
Davis, George Kelso *nutrition biochemist, educator*
Detweiler, Steven Lawrence *physicist, educator*
Dewar, Michael James Steuart *chemistry educator*
Drago, Russell Stephen *chemist, educator*
Eichhorn, Heinrich Karl *astronomer, educator, consultant*
Gander, John Edward *biochemistry educator*
Hanrahan, Robert Joseph *chemist, educator*
Hanson, Harold Palmer *physicist, government official, editor, academic administrator*
†Harrison, Debia *chemistry educator*
Harrison, Willard W. *chemist, educator*
Holloway, Paul Howard *materials science educator*
Jacobs, Alan Martin *physicist, educator*
Katritzky, Alan Roy *chemistry educator, consultant*
Klauder, John Rider *physics educator*
Micha, David Allan *chemistry and physics educator*
Ohrn, Nils Yngve *chemistry and physics educator*
†Park, Robert McIlwraith *science and engineering educator*
Person, Willis Bagley *chemistry educator*
Putnam, Hugh Dyer *environmental scientist, educator, consultant*
Sisler, Harry Hall *chemist, educator*
Smith, Alexander Goudy *physics and astronomy educator*
Stehli, Francis Greenough *geologist, educator*
Wood, Frank Bradshaw *retired astronomy educator*
Young, David Michael *biochemistry and molecular biology educator, physician*
Zerner, Michael Charles *chemistry and physics educator, consultant, researcher*

Gonzalez
Plischke, Le Moyne Wilfred *research chemist*

Hialeah
Stewart, Burch Byron *chemist, physicist*

Indian Harbour Beach
Boan, Bobby Jack *chemist*

Jacksonville
Huebner, Jay Stanley *physicist, engineer, forensics consultant*

Key West
Trammell, Herbert Eugene *physicist, laboratory executive*

Lake Alfred
Nagy, Steven *biochemist*

Lake Worth
Kline, Gordon Mabey *chemist, editor*

Marco Island
Hurley, Patrick Mason *geology educator*

Melbourne
Babich, Michael Wayne *chemistry educator, educational administrator*
Button, Kenneth John *physicist*
Nelson, Gordon Leigh *chemist, educator*
von Ohain, Hans Joachim P. *aerospace scientist*

Miami
Blanco, Luciano-Nilo *physicist*
Cooper, William James *chemist*
Corcoran, Eugene Francis *chemist, educator*
Fine, Rana Arnold *chemical, physical oceanographer*
Man, Eugene Herbert *chemist, educator, business executive*
Mooers, Christopher Northrup Kennard *physical oceanographer, educator*
Ostlund, H. Gote *atmospheric and marine scientist, educator*
Rosenthal, Stanley Lawrence *meteorologist*
Wells, Daniel Ruth *physics educator*

Naples
Ancker-Johnson, Betsy *physicist, engineer, retired automotive company executive*
Leitner, Alfred *mathematical physicist, educator, educational film producer*
Stewart, Harris Bates, Jr. *oceanographer*

Ocala
Forgue, Stanley Vincent *physics educator*

Oldsmar
Ligett, Waldo Buford *chemist*

Orlando
Baker, Peter Mitchell *laser scientist and executive, educator*
Blue, Joseph Edward *physicist*
Llewellyn, Ralph Alvin *physics educator*
Silfvast, William T. *laser physics educator, consultant*
Ting, Robert Yen-ying *physicist*

Palm Beach Gardens
Emiliani, Cesare *geology educator, author*

Palmetto
Compton, Charles Daniel *chemistry educator*

Pensacola
Chang, Clifford W.J. *chemistry educator, researcher, consultant*

Port Saint Joe
Smith, Harry Lee *laboratory technician, chemist*

Saint Petersburg
Castle, Raymond Nielson *chemist, educator*
Hallock-Muller, Pamela *oceanography educator, biogeologist, researcher*
Hansel, Paul George *physicist, consultant*
Rester, Alfred Carl, Jr. *physicist*

Rydstrom, Carlton Lionel *chemist, paint and coating consultant*

Sanibel
Herriott, Donald Richard *optical physicist*
Horecker, Bernard Leonard *retired biochemistry educator*

Sarasota
Kerker, Milton *chemistry educator*
Myerson, Albert Leon *physical chemist*

Tallahassee
Caspar, Donald Louis Dvorak *biophysics and structural biology educator*
Choppin, Gregory Robert *chemistry educator*
Clarke, Allan J. *oceanography educator, consultant*
Crow, Jack E. *physics administrator*
Herndon, Roy Clifford *physicist*
Johnsen, Russell Harold *chemist, educator*
Kemper, Kirby Wayne *physics educator*
Lannutti, Joseph Edward *physics educator*
Mandelkern, Leo *biophysics and chemistry educator*
†Marshall, Alan George *chemistry and biochemistry educator*
Moulton, Grace Charbonnet *physics educator*
O'Brien, James Joseph *meteorology and oceanography educator*
Pfeffer, Richard Lawrence *geophysics educator*
Robson, Donald *physics educator*
Schrieffer, John Robert *physics educator, science administrator*
Smith, Eric Alan *meteorology educator*
Walborsky, Harry M. *chemistry educator, consultant*

Tampa
Binford, Jesse Stone, Jr. *chemistry educator*
DeMontier, Paulette LaPointe *chemist*
Zhou, Huanchun *chemist*

Venice
Leidheiser, Henry, Jr. *retired chemistry educator, consultant*

West Palm Beach
McGinnes, Paul R. *environmental chemist*

GEORGIA

Albany
McManus, James William *chemist, researcher*

Alpharetta
Barr, John Baldwin *chemist, reserach scientist*
Hung, William Mo-Wei *chemist*

Americus
Counts, Wayne Boyd *chemistry educator*

Athens
Allinger, Norman Louis *chemistry educator*
Black, Clanton Candler, Jr. *biochemistry educator, researcher*
Boyd, George Edward *physical chemist*
Darvill, Alan G. *biochemist, botanist, educator*
Eriksson, Karl-Erik Lennart *biochemist, educator*
Johnson, Michael Kenneth *chemistry educator*
King, Robert Bruce *chemistry educator, writer*
Landau, David Paul *physics educator*
McGuire, John Murray *chemist, researcher*
Melton, Charles Estel *physicist, educator*
Pelletier, S. William *chemistry educator*
Schaefer, Henry Frederick, III *chemistry educator*
Yamaguchi, Yukio *chemistry research scientist*
Yen, William Mao-Shung *physicist*

Atlanta
Copeland, John Alexander, III *physicist*
Cramer, Howard Ross *geologist, environmental consultant*
Dennison, Daniel Bassel *chemist*
El-Sayed, Mostafa Amr *chemistry educator*
Finkelstein, David *physicist, educator, consultant*
Fox, Ronald Forrest *physics educator*
Gokhale, Arun Mahadeo *materials science and engineering educator*
Goldstein, Jacob Herman *retired physical chemist*
Johnson, Ronald Carl *chemistry educator*
Kahn, Bernd *radiochemist, educator*
Lin, Ming-Chang *physical chemistry educator, researcher*
Long, Maurice Wayne *physicist, electrical engineer, radar consultant*
Marzilli, Luigi Gaetano *chemistry educator, consultant*
†McBay, Henry Cecil *chemist, educator*
McCormick, Donald Bruce *biochemist, educator*
Moran, Thomas Francis *chemistry educator*
Perkowitz, Sidney *physicist, educator, author*
Pierotti, Robert Amedeo *chemistry educator*
Strekowski, Lucjan *chemistry educator*
Wartell, Roger Martin *biophysics educator*

Marietta
Bridges, Alan Lynn *physicist, computer scientist, software engineer*

Peachtree City
Roobol, Norman Richard *chemistry educator, industrial painting consultant*

Savannah
Su, Helen Chien-fan *research chemist*

Statesboro
†Zellner, Benjamin Holmes *research astronomer*

Tucker
Valk, Henry Snowden *physicist, educator*

HAWAII

Hilo
Schnell, Russell Clifford *atmospheric scientist, researcher*

Honolulu
Brantley, Lee Reed *chemistry educator*
Chambers, Kenneth Carter *astronomer*
Chave, Keith Ernest *oceanographer, educator*
Cowie, Lennox Lauchlan *astrophysicist*
Hall, Donald Norman Blake *astronomer*
Hawke, Bernard Ray *planetary scientist*
Herbig, George Howard *astronomer, educator*
Ihrig, Judson La Moure *chemist*
Keil, Klaus *geology educator, consultant*
Khan, Mohammad Asad *geophysicist, educator, former energy minister and senator of Pakistan*
Mader, Charles Lavern *chemist*
†Meech, Karen Jean *astronomer*
Ogburn, Hugh Bell *chemical engineer, consultant*
Raleigh, Cecil Baring *geophysicist*
Scheuer, Paul Josef *chemistry educator*
Tuan, San Fu *theoretical physics, political science educator*
Wyrtki, Klaus *oceanography educator*
†Yamamoto, Harry Yoshimi *research institute director, educator*
Yount, David Eugene *physicist, educator*

Kamuela
Azzopardi, Marc Antoine *astrophysicist, scientist*

Princeville
Kaye, Wilbur Irving *chemist, researcher, consultant*

IDAHO

Boise
Hibbs, Robert Andrews *analytical chemistry educator*

Idaho Falls
Reich, Charles William *nuclear physicist*

Lewiston
Bjerke, Robert Keith *chemist*

Moscow
LeTourneau, Duane John *biochemist, educator*
Miller, Maynard Malcolm *geologist, educator, research foundation director, explorer, state legislator*
Renfrew, Malcolm MacKenzie *chemist, educator*
Shreeve, Jean'ne Marie *chemist, educator*

ILLINOIS

Argonne
Arzoumanidis, Gregory G. *chemist*
Berger, Edmond Louis *theoretical physicist*
Berkowitz, Joseph *physicist, physical chemist, researcher*
Blander, Milton *chemist*
Carpenter, John Marland *engineer, physicist*
Derrick, Malcolm *physicist*
†Dyrkacz, Gary R. *chemist*
Ferraro, John Ralph *chemist*
Fields, Paul Robert *research nuclear chemist, consultant*
Green, David William *chemist, educator*
Herzenberg, Caroline Stuart Littlejohn *physicist*
Jorgensen, James Douglas *research physicist*
Krauss, Alan Robert *physicist*
Martin, Ronald Lavern *physicist*
Morss, Lester Robert *chemist*
Nolen, Jerry Aften, Jr. *physicist*
Perlow, Gilbert J(erome) *physicist, editor*
Peshkin, Murray *physicist*
Schiffer, John Paul *physicist*
Steindler, Martin Joseph *chemist*
Zeidman, Benjamin *nuclear physicist*

Arlington Heights
Lewin, Seymour Zalman *chemistry educator, consultant*

Barrington
Tomomatsu, Hideo *chemist*

Batavia
Bardeen, William Allan *research physicist*
Chrisman, Bruce Lowell *physicist, administrator*
Jonckheere, Alan Mathew *physicist*
Lach, Joseph Theodore *physicist*
Nash, E(dward) Thomas *physicist*
Peoples, John, Jr. *physicist, researcher*
Tollestrup, Alvin Virgil *physicist*

Carbondale
Tao, Rongjia *physicist, educator*
Wotiz, John Henry *chemist, educator*

Champaign
Buschbach, Thomas Charles *geologist, consultant*
Cartwright, Keros *hydrogeologist, researcher*
Cohen, Jozef *psychophysicist, educator*
Gross, David Lee *geologist*
Herzog, Beverly Leah *hydrogeologist*
Mapother, Dillon Edward *physicist, university official*
Simmons, Ralph Oliver *physics educator*
Slichter, Charles Pence *physicist, educator*
Stapleton, Harvey James *physics educator*
Wolfram, Stephen *physicist, computer company executive*

Chicago
Anderson, Louise Eleanor *biochemistry educator*
Barany, Kate *biophysics educator*
Barenberg, Sumner *polymer physicist, business executive*
Blumberg, Avrom Aaron *physical chemistry educator*
Chambers, Donald Arthur *biochemistry and molecular medicine educator*
Chandrasekhar, Subrahmanyan *astrophysicist, educator*
Charlier, Roger Henri *oceanographer, geographer, educator*
Clayton, Robert Norman *chemist, educator*
Copley, Stephen Michael *materials science and engineering educator*
Cronin, James Watson *physicist, educator*
Dobbs, Frank Wilbur *chemistry educator*
Epstein, Wolfgang *biochemist, educator*
Erber, Thomas *physics educator*
Evans, Earl Alison, Jr. *biochemist*
Fano, Ugo *physicist, educator*
Fanta, Paul Edward *chemist, educator*
Fleming, Graham Richard *chemistry educator*
Freed, Karl Frederick *chemistry educator*
Fried, Josef *chemist, educator*
Frisch, Henry Jonathan *physics educator*
Fritzsche, Hellmut *physics educator*
Fujita, Tetsuya Theodore *educator, meteorologist*
Fultz, Dave *meteorology educator*
Gislason, Eric Arni *chemistry educator*
Goldsmith, Julian Royce *geochemist, educator*
Goldwasser, Eugene *biochemist, educator*
Gomer, Robert *chemistry educator*
Grossweiner, Leonard Irwin *physicist, educator*
Halpern, Jack *chemist, educator*
Harper, Doyal Alexander, Jr. *astronomer, educator*
Harvey, Ronald Gilbert *research chemist*
Hildebrand, Roger Henry *astrophysicist, physicist*
Huston, John Lewis *chemistry educator*
Hutchison, Clyde Allen, Jr. *chemistry educator*
†Iqbal, Zafar Mohd *cancer researcher, biochemist, pharmacologist, toxicologist, consultant*
Jeffay, Henry *biochemistry educator*
Kadanoff, Leo Philip *physicist*
Kouvel, James Spyros *physicist, educator*
Krawetz, Arthur Altshuler *chemist, science administrator*
Lanzl, Lawrence Herman *medical physicist*
Lederman, Leon Max *physicist, educator*
Levi-Setti, Riccardo *physicist, director*
Levy, Donald Harris *chemistry educator*
Liao, Shutsung *biochemist*
Light, John Caldwell *chemistry educator*
Lorand, Laszlo *biochemist, educator*
Lykos, Peter George *educator, scientist*
Makinen, Marvin William *biophysicist, educator*
Margoliash, Emanuel *biochemist, educator*
Mazenko, Gene Francis *physics educator*
Meyer, Peter *physicist, educator*
Moore, Paul Brian *geophysical sciences educator*
Muller, Dietrich Alfred Helmut *physicist, educator*
Nagel, Sidney Robert *physics educator*
Nambu, Yoichiro *physics educator*
Norris, James Rufus, Jr. *chemist, educator, consultant*
Oehme, Reinhard *physicist, educator*
Oka, Takeshi *physicist, chemist, astronomer, educator*
Olsen, Edward John *geologist, educator*
Oxtoby, David William *chemistry educator*
Palmer, Patrick Edward *radio astronomer, educator*
Platzman, George William *geophysicist, educator*
Rafelson, Max Emanuel, Jr. *biochemist, medical school administrator*
Raup, David Malcolm *paleontology educator*
Reiffel, Leonard *physicist, scientific consultant*
Rocek, Jan *chemist, educator*
Rosner, Jonathan Lincoln *physicist, educator*
Rosner, Robert *astrophysicist*
Sachs, Robert Green *physicist, educator, laboratory administrator*
Sager, William F. *retired chemistry educator*
Sawinski, Vincent John *chemistry educator*
Schillinger, Edwin Joseph *physics educator*
Schramm, David Norman *astrophysicist, educator*
Schug, Kenneth Robert *chemistry educator*
Sereno, Paul C. *paleontologist, educator*
Shapiro, Stanley *materials scientist*
Simpson, John Alexander *physicist*
Spector, Harold Norman *physics educator*
Steck, Theodore Lyle *biochemistry and molecular biology educator, physician*
Steiner, Donald Frederick *biochemist, physician, educator*
Stock, Leon Milo *chemist, educator*
Truran, James Wellington, Jr. *astrophysicist*
Turkevich, Anthony Leonid *chemist, educator*
Turner, Michael Stanley *physics educator*
Williams-Ashman, Howard Guy *biochemistry educator*
Winston, Roland *physicist, educator*
Wool, Ira Goodwin *biochemist, molecular biologist, educator*
York, Donald Gilbert *astronomy educator, researcher*

De Kalb
Kevill, Dennis Neil *chemistry educator*
Kimball, Clyde William *physicist, educator*
Rossing, Thomas D. *physics educator*

Downers Grove
Appelman, Evan Hugh *retired chemist*
Boese, Robert Alan *forensic chemist*
Kinsinger, Jack Burl *chemist, educator*

Evanston
Allred, Albert Louis *chemistry educator*
Basolo, Fred *chemistry educator*
†Bedzyk, Michael J. *ctystallographer, materials scientist*
†Bordwell, Frederick George *chemistry educator*
Brown, Laurie Mark *physicist, educator*
Chang, R. P. H. *materials science educator*
Cohen, Jerome Bernard *materials science educator*
Colton, Frank Benjamin *retired chemist*
Ellis, Donald Edwin *physicist, educator*
Freeman, Arthur J. *physics educator*
Halperin, William Paul *physicist, educator*
Hoffman, Brian M. *chemist, educator*
Ibers, James Arthur *chemist, educator*
Johnson, David Lynn *materials scientist, educator*
Ketterson, John Boyd *physics educator*
Klotz, Irving Myron *chemist, educator*
Lambert, Joseph Buckley *chemistry educator*
Letsinger, Robert Lewis *chemistry educator*
Lippincott, James Andrew *biochemistry and biological sciences educator*
Marks, Tobin Jay *chemistry educator*
Meshii, Masahiro *materials science educator*
Mintzer, David *physics educator*
Oakes, Robert James *physics educator*
Olson, Gregory Bruce *materials science and engineering educator, academic director*
Pines, Herman *chemistry educator, consultant*
Poeppelmeier, Kenneth Reinhard *chemistry educator*
Pople, John Anthony *chemistry educator*
Ratner, Mark Alan *chemistry educator*
Sachtler, Wolfgang Max Hugo *chemistry educator*
Seidman, David N(athaniel) *materials science and engineering educator*
Shriver, Duward Felix *chemistry educator, researcher, consultant*
Silverman, Richard Bruce *chemist, biochemist, educator*
Spears, Kenneth George *chemistry educator*
Taam, Ronald Everett *physics and astronomy educator*
Ulmer, Melville Paul *physics and astronomy educator*
Van Duyne, Richard Palmer *analytical chemistry and chemical physics educator*
Weertman, Julia Randall *materials science and engineering educator*
Wessels, Bruce W. *materials scientist, educator*

Forest Park
Johnson, Calvin Keith *research executive, chemist*

Glenview
Rorig, Kurt Joachim *chemist, research director*

Hinsdale
Kaminsky, Manfred Stephan *physicist*

Homewood
Parker, Eugene Newman *retired physicist, educator*

Lake Forest
Coutts, John Wallace *chemist, educator*
Walter, Robert Irving *chemistry educator, chemist*
Weston, Arthur Walter *chemist, scientific and business executive*

Lemont
Katz, Joseph Jacob *chemist, educator*
Tomkins, Frank Sargent *physicist*
Williams, Jack Marvin *chemist*

Lisle
Wouch, Gerald *materials scientist*

Naperville
Fields, Ellis Kirby *research chemist*
Hensley, Albert Lloyd, Jr. *research chemist, technical consultant*
Karayannis, Nicholas Marios *chemist*
Wolfram, Thomas *physicist*

Normal
Young, Robert Donald *physicist, educator*

North Chicago
Loga, Sanda *physicist, educator*

Northfield
Shabica, Charles Wright *earth science educator*

O'Fallon
Jenner, William Alexander *meteorologist, educator*

Palos Park
Crewe, Albert Victor *physicist, business executive, former research administrator*

Peoria
Chamberlain, Joseph Miles *astronomer, educator*
Cunningham, Raymond Leo *research chemist*
King, Jerry Wayne *research chemist*
Nielsen, Harald Christian *retired chemist*
Osborn, Terry Wayne *biochemist, executive*
Rothfus, John Arden *chemist*

Rock Island
†Hickerson, William Joseph, Jr. *geology researcher, educator*
Sundelius, Harold W. *geology educator*

Rockford
Walhout, Justine Simon *chemistry educator*

Schaumburg
Langsdorf, Alexander, Jr. *physicist*

Skokie
Filler, Robert *chemistry educator*

Springfield
Gallina, Charles Onofrio *nuclear scientist*

Urbana
Baker, David Hiram *biochemist, biochemistry educator*
Beak, Peter Andrew *chemistry educator*
Birnbaum, Howard Kent *materials science educator*
Brown, Theodore Lawrence *chemistry educator*
Crofts, Antony Richard *biophysics educator*
Curtin, David Yarrow *chemist, educator*
Debrunner, Peter George *physics educator*
Drickamer, Harry George *retired chemistry educator*
Dunn, Floyd *biophysicist, bioengineer, educator*
Ehrlich, Gert *science educator, researcher*
Faulkner, Larry Ray *chemistry educator, academic officer*
Forbes, Richard Mather *biochemistry educator*
Goldwasser, Edwin Leo *physicist*
Govindjee *biophysics and biology educator*
Greene, Laura Helen *physicist*
†Gruebele, Martin *chemistry educator*
Gutowsky, Herbert Sander *chemistry educator*
Hay, Richard Le Roy *geology educator*
Iben, Icko, Jr. *astrophysicist, educator*
Jackson, Edwin Atlee *physicist, educator*
Jonas, Jiri *chemistry educator*
Kirkpatrick, R(obert) James *geology educator*
Klein, Miles Vincent *physics educator*
Langenheim, Ralph Louis, Jr. *geology educator*
Lauterbur, Paul C(hristian) *chemistry educator*
Lazarus, David *physicist, educator*
Lo, Kwok-Yung *astronomer*
Makri, Nancy *chemistry educator*
Mihalas, Dimitri Manuel *astronomer, educator*
Pethick, Christopher John *physicist*
†Pirkle, William H. *chemistry educator*
Rowland, Theodore Justin *physicist, educator*
Salamon, Myron Ben *physicist, educator*
†Sargent, Malcolm Lee *research biochemist, research geneticist, botany educator and researcher*
Satterthwaite, Cameron B. *physics educator*
Schweizer, Kenneth Steven *physics educator*
Simon, Jack Aaron *geologist, former state official*
Snyder, Lewis Emil *astrophysicist*
†Suslick, Kenneth Sanders *chemistry educator*
Switzer, Robert Lee *biochemistry educator*
Wattenberg, Albert *physicist, educator*
White, W(illiam) Arthur *geologist*
Wolynes, Peter Guy *chemistry researcher, educator*

INDIANA

Anderson
Gay, David Earl, Sr. *experimental chemist*

Bloomington
Bair, Edward Jay *chemistry educator*
Bent, Robert Demo *physicist, educator*
Bonham, Russell Aubrey *chemistry educator*
Bundy, Wayne M. *retired geologist, consultant*
Campaigne, Ernest Edward *chemistry educator*
Chisholm, Malcolm Harold *chemistry educator*
Davidson, Ernest Roy *chemist, educator*
Dodd, James Robert *geologist, educator*
Edmondson, Frank Kelley *astronomer*
Goodman, Charles David *physicist, educator*
Grieco, Paul Anthony *chemistry educator*
Hamburger, Michael Wile *geology educator*
Hattin, Donald Edward *geologist, educator*
Johnson, Hollis Ralph *astronomy educator*
Macfarlane, Malcolm Harris *physics educator*
Murray, Haydn Herbert *geology educator*
Novotny, Milos Vlastislav *chemistry educator*
Parmenter, Charles Stedman *chemistry educator*
Peters, Dennis Gail *chemist*
Pollock, Robert Elwood *nuclear physicist*
Putnam, Frank William *biochemistry and immunology educator*
†Roush, William R. *chemistry educator*
Schaich, William L. *physics educator*
Vitaliano, Charles J(oseph) *geologist, educator*

Elkhart
Free, Helen M. *chemist, consultant*
Rand, Phillip Gordon *chemist*

Fort Wayne
Cox, David Jackson *biochemistry educator*
Stevenson, Kenneth Lee *chemist, educator*

Gary
Meyerson, Seymour *retired chemist*

Granger
Chmiel, Chester T. *adhesive chemist, consultant*

Hammond
Albright, John Rupp *physics educator*
Ammeraal, Robert Neal *biochemist*

Indianapolis
Aprison, Morris Herman *biochemist, neurobiologist, educator*
Bessey, William Higgins *physicist, educator*
Gibson, David Mark *biochemist, educator*
Harris, Robert Allison *biochemistry educator*
Jones, Katharine Jean *research physicist*
Koppel, Gary Allen *chemist, immunologist*
Liu, Pingyu *physicist, educator*
Long, Timothy Scott *chemist, consultant*
Mirsky, Arthur *geologist, educator*
Pearlstein, Robert M. *physics educator*
Soper, Quentin Francis *chemist*
Wong, David T. *biochemist*
Yan, Sau-Chi Betty *biochemist*

Lafayette
Brewster, James Henry *retired chemistry educator*
Christensen, Nikolas Ivan *geophysicist, educator*
Feuer, Henry *chemist, educator*
Gartenhaus, Solomon *physicist*
Judd, William Robert *engineering geologist, educator*
Loeffler, Frank Joseph *physicist, educator*
Melhorn, Wilton Newton *geosciences educator*
Porile, Norbert Thomas *chemistry educator*
Sato, Hiroshi *materials science educator*
Truce, William Everett *chemist, educator*

Muncie
Harris, Joseph McAllister *chemist*

Notre Dame
Cason, Neal Martin *physics educator*
Fehlner, Thomas Patrick *chemistry educator*
Feigl, Dorothy Marie *chemistry educator, university official*
Helquist, Paul M. *chemistry educator, researcher*
Marshalek, Eugene Richard *physics educator*
†Ross, Alberta Barkley *chemist*
Scheidt, W. Robert *chemistry educator, researcher*
Schuler, Robert Hugo *chemist, educator*
Thomas, John Kerry *chemistry educator*
Trozzolo, Anthony Marion *chemistry educator*

Terre Haute
Guthrie, Frank Albert *chemistry educator*

Valparaiso
Cook, Addison Gilbert *chemistry educator*

West Lafayette
Adelman, Steven Allen *theoretical physical chemist, chemistry educator*
Amy, Jonathan Weekes *scientist, educator*
Baird, William McKenzie *chemical carcinogenesis researcher, biochemistry educator*
Barnes, Virgil Everett, II *physics educator*
BeMiller, James Noble *biochemist, educator*
Bray, Ralph *physics educator*
Brown, Herbert Charles *chemistry educator*
Butler, Larry Gene *biochemistry educator, researcher*
Cramer, William Anthony *biochemistry and biophysics researcher, educator*
Diamond, Sidney *chemist, educator*
Dilley, Richard A. *biochemist, plant physiologist, educator*
Fischbach, Ephraim *physicist*
Grant, Edward Robert *chemistry educator*
Grimley, Robert Thomas *chemistry educator*
Hanks, Alan R. *chemistry educator*
Kim, Yeong Ell *physics educator, researcher, consultant*
Laskowski, Michael, Jr. *chemist, educator*
Leap, Darrell Ivan *hydrogeologist*
Lipschutz, Michael Elazar *chemistry educator, consultant, researcher*
Margerum, Dale William *chemistry educator*
McMillin, David Robert *chemistry educator*
Morrison, Harry *chemistry educator, university dean*
Mullen, James Gentry *physics educator*
Overhauser, Albert Warner *physicist*
†Pardue, Harry L. *chemist, educator*
Pratt, Dan Edwin *chemistry educator*
†Ramdas, Anant Krishna *physicist, optics scientist*
Rossmann, Michael George *biochemist, educator*

IOWA

Ames
Angelici, Robert J. *chemistry educator*
Barnes, Richard George *physicist, educator*
Bowen, George Hamilton, Jr. *astrophysicist, educator*
Clem, John Richard *physicist, educator*
Corbett, John Dudley *chemistry educator*
Finnemore, Douglas Kirby *physics educator*
Fritz, James Sherwood *chemist, educator*
Gschneidner, Karl Albert, Jr. *metallurgist, educator, editor, consultant*
Hansen, Robert Suttle *chemist, educator*
Horowitz, Jack *biochemistry educator*
Houk, Robert Samuel *chemistry educator*
Jacobson, Robert Andrew *chemistry educator*
Kelly, William Harold *physicist, physics educator*
Lynch, David William *physicist, educator*
Papadakis, Emmanuel Philippos *physicist, university research director, consultant*
Ruedenberg, Klaus *theoretical chemist, educator*
Russell, Glen Allan *chemist, educator*
Smith, John Francis *materials science educator*
Svec, Harry John *chemist, educator*
Wilhelm, Harley A(lmey) *chemist, educator, mechanical engineer, retired*
Yeung, Edward Szeshing *chemist*

Cedar Falls
Hanson, Roger James *physics educator*

Cedar Rapids
Boettcher, Norbe Birosel *chemist*

Grinnell
Erickson, Luther Eugene *chemist, educator*

Iowa City
Baker, Richard Graves *geology educator, palynologist*
Burton, Donald Joseph *chemistry educator*
Donelson, John Everett *biochemistry educator, molecular biologist*
Goff, Harold Milton *chemistry educator*
Goodridge, Alan Gardner *research biochemist, educator*
Gurnett, Donald Alfred *physics educator*
Koch, Donald LeRoy *geologist, state agency administrator*
†Linhardt, Robert John *medicinal chemistry educator*
Montgomery, Rex *biochemist, educator*
Pietrzyk, Donald John *chemistry educator*
Plapp, Bryce Vernon *biochemistry educator*
Titze, Ingo Roland *physics educator*
Van Allen, James Alfred *physicist, educator*
Wiley, Robert Allen *pharmaceutical educator*

Spirit Lake
Brett, George Wendell *retired geologist, philatelist*

KANSAS

Kansas City
Ebner, Kurt Ewald *biochemistry educator*

Lawrence
Ammar, Raymond George *physicist, educator*
Angino, Ernest Edward *geology educator*
Borchardt, Ronald Terrance *biochemistry and pharmaceutical chemistry educator, consultant*
Carlson, Robert Gideon *chemistry educator*
Dreschhoff, Gisela Auguste Marie *physicist, educator*
Enos, Paul *geologist, educator*
Gerhard, Lee Clarence *geologist, educator*
Harmony, Marlin Dale *chemistry educator, researcher*
Kleinberg, Jacob *chemist, educator*
Landgrebe, John Allan *chemistry educator*
Mitscher, Lester Allen *chemist, educator*
Stella, Valentino John *pharmaceutical chemistry educator*
Zeller, Edward Jacob *physics, astronomy and geology educator, consultant*

Lebanon
Colwell, John Edwin *retired aerospace scientist*

Manhattan
Fateley, William Gene *scientist, educator, inventor, administrator*
Setser, Donald Wayne *chemistry educator*
Twiss, Page Charles *geology educator*

Topeka
Cohen, Sheldon Hersh *chemistry educator*

Wichita
Andrew, Kenneth L. *research physicist, physics educator*

KENTUCKY

Bowling Green
Slocum, Donald Warren *chemist*

Highland Heights
Redding, Rogers Walker *physics educator*

Lexington
Brown, William Randall *geology educator*
Cheniae, George Maurice *plant biochemist*
Cochran, Lewis W. *physicist, university official*
DeLong, Lance Eric *physics educator, researcher*
Ehmann, William Donald *chemistry educator*
Ettensohn, Frank Robert *geologist, educator*
Hagan, Wallace Woodrow *geologist*
Kern, Bernard Donald *retired educator, physicist*
Liu, Keh-Fei Frank *physicist, educator*
Lodder, Robert Andrew *chemistry and pharmaceutics educator*
Mercer, Leonard Preston, II *biochemistry educator*
Sands, Donald Edgar *chemistry educator*
Tietz, Norbert Wolfgang *clinical chemistry educator, administrator*

Louisville
Belanger, William Joseph *chemist, polymer applications consultant*
Cohn, David V(alor) *biochemistry educator*
Johnson, Alan Arthur *physicist, educator*
Prough, Russell Allen *biochemistry educator*
Shoemaker, Gradus Lawrence *chemist, educator*
Taylor, Kenneth Grant *chemistry educator*
Teller, David Norton *neurochemist*

Paducah
Walden, Robert Thomas *physicist educator, consultant*

LOUISIANA

Baton Rouge
Coleman, James Malcolm *marine geology educator*
†Groat, Charles George *geologist, science administrator*
Hazel, Joseph Ernest *geology educator, stratigrapher*
Lambremont, Edward Nelson, Jr. *nuclear science educator*
Landolt, Arlo Udell *astronomer, educator*
Mc Glynn, Sean Patrick *physical chemist, educator*
O'Connell, Robert Francis *physics educator*
Pope, David E. *geologist, micropaleontologist*
Pryor, William Austin *chemistry educator*
Traynham, James Gibson *chemist, educator*
Van Lopik, Jack Richard *geologist, educator*
West, Philip William *chemistry educator*

Carencro
Clark, George Bryan *geophysicist*

Metairie
†Hartman, James Austin *retired geologist*

New Orleans
Allen, Gary Curtiss *geology educator*
Andrews, Bethlehem Kottes *research chemist*
Benerito, Ruth Rogan (Mrs. Frank H. Benerito) *chemist*
†Bertoniere, Noelie Rita *research chemist*
Buccino, Salvatore George *physics educator*
Harper, Robert John, Jr. *chemist, researcher*
Perdew, John Paul *physics educator, condensed matter and density functional theorist*
Rosensteel, George T. *physics educator, nuclear physicist*
Roskoski, Robert, Jr. *biochemist, educator, author*
†Schwartz, Daniel K. *chemistry educator*
Sumrell, Gene *research chemist*
†Thomas, Robert Allen *environmental policy administrator, educator*

MAINE

Belfast
Porter, Bernard Harden *consulting physicist, author, publisher*

Friendship
Owen, Wadsworth *oceanographer, consultant*

Lewiston
Stauffer, Charles Henry *retired chemistry educator*

Oakland
Koons, Donaldson *geologist, educator*

Orono
Borns, Harold William, Jr. *geologist, educator*
Csavinszky, Peter John *physicist, educator*
Norton, Stephen Allen *geological sciences educator*
Tarr, Charles Edwin *physicist, educator*

MARYLAND

Aberdeen Proving Ground
Hackley, Brennie Elias, Jr. *chemist*
Steger, Ralph James *chemist*

Adelphi
DeMonte, Vito J. *physical sciences research administrator*

Annapolis
Bontoyan, Warren Roberts *chemist, state laboratories administrator*
Brunk, William Edward *astronomer*
Clotworthy, John Harris *oceanographic consultant*
Elder, Samuel Adams *physics educator*
Howell, Barbara Fennema *research chemist*
Johnson, David Simonds *meteorologist*
†Massie, Samuel Proctor, Jr. *chemistry educator*
Rowell, Charles Frederick *chemistry educator*

Ashton
Leibowitz, Jack Richard *physicist, educator*

Baltimore
Ahearn, John Stephen *research physicist*
Albinak, Marvin Joseph *chemistry educator*
Allen, Ronald John *astrophysics educator, researcher*
Beer, Michael *biophysicist, educator*
Benton, George Stock *meteorologist, educator*
Berg, Jeremy M. *chemistry educator*
Blumenfeld, Barry Jay *physics educator*
Bowen, Kit Hansel, Jr. *chemistry educator*
†Brown, Robert Alan *physicist*
Chartrand, Mark Ray *astronomer, telecommunications consultant*
Chien, Chia-Ling *physics educator*
Chien, Chih-Yung *physics educator, researcher*
Cone, Richard Allen *biophysics educator*
Dagdigian, Paul Joseph *chemistry educator*
Dicello, John Francis, Jr. *physicist, educator*
Domokos, Gabor *research physicist*
Eichhorn, Gunther Louis *chemist*
Englund, Paul Theodore *biochemist, educator*
Feldman, Gordon *physics educator*
†Feldman, Paul Donald *physics educator, research astronomer*
Fenselau, Catherine Clarke *chemistry educator*
Fisher, George Wescott *geology educator*
†Fulton, Thomas *theoretical physicist, educator*
Green, Robert Edward, Jr. *physicist, educator*
Grossman, Lawrence *biochemist, educator*
Haig, Frank Rawle *physics educator, clergyman*
Heckman, Timothy Martin *astronomy and physics educator*
Henry, Richard Conn *astrophysicist, educator*
Huang, Pien Chien *biochemistry educator, scientist*
Inglehart, Lorretta Jeannette *physicist*
Jensen, Arthur Seigfried *consulting engineering physicist*
Judd, Brian Raymond *physicist, educator*
Kaplan, Alexander Efimovich *physics educator, engineering educator*
Kim, Chung Wook *physics educator, researcher*
Koski, Walter S. *chemistry educator, scientist*
Kowal, Charles Thomas *astronomer*
Krolik, Julian Henry *astrophysicist, educator*
Kruger, Jerome *materials science educator, consultant*
Lane, Malcolm Daniel *biological chemistry educator*
Larrabee, Martin Glover *biophysics educator*
Lee, Yung-Keun *physicist, educator*
Lin, Shin *biophysics educator*
Love, Warner Edwards *biophysics educator*
Madansky, Leon *particle physicist, educator*
Marsh, Bruce David *geologist, educator*
McCarty, Richard Earl *biochemist, biochemistry educator*
Moos, H. Warren *physicist, astronomer, educator, administrator*
Moudrianakis, Evangelos N. *cell biology and biochemistry educator, biomedical researcher*
Mulligan, Joseph Francis *physics educator*
Nickon, Alex *chemist, educator*
Norman, Colin Arthur *astrophysics educator*
Pettijohn, Francis John *geology educator*
Pevsner, Aihud *physicist, educator*
Phillips, Owen Martin *oceanographer, geophysicist, educator*
Posner, Gary Herbert *chemist, educator*
†Reich, Daniel H. *physics educator*
Robinson, Dean Wentworth *chemist, educator*
Roseman, Saul *biochemist, educator*
Roth, George Stanley *research biochemist, physiologist*
Shamoo, Adil Elias *biochemist, biophysicist, educator*
Silverstone, Harris J. *chemistry educator*
Stanley, Steven Mitchell *paleobiologist, educator*
Steiner, Robert Frank *biochemist*
†Storrs, Alexander David *astronomer*
Sweeting, Linda Marie *chemist*
†Townsend, Craig Arthur *chemistry educator*
Ts'o, Paul On-Pong *biophysical chemist, educator*
Westerhout, Gart *retired astronomer*
White, Emil Henry *chemistry educator*
†Williams, Robert Eugene *astronomer*

Beltsville
Kearney, Philip Charles *biochemist*
Tallent, William Hugh *chemist, research administrator*

Berlin
Horner, William Harry *biochemist*
Passwater, Richard Albert *biochemist, writer*

Bethesda
Atlas, David *meteorologist, research scientist*
Becker, Edwin Demuth *chemist, laboratory director*
Bennett, Lawrence Herman *physicist*
Berger, Robert Lewis *biophysicist, researcher*
Bernardini, Isa *biochemist*
Blush, Steven Michael *nuclear scientist, safety consultant*
†Brossi, Arnold R. *research chemist*
Cantoni, Giulio Leonardo *biochemist, government official*
Cassman, Marvin *biochemist*
Conrad, Edward Ezra *physicist, nuclear engineer, scientific corporation executive*
Daly, John W. *chemistry research administrator*
Ehrenstein, Gerald *biophysicist*
Fales, Henry Marshall *chemist*
Gelboin, Harry Victor *biochemistry educator, researcher*
Gerwin, Brenda Isen *research biochemist*
Ginsburg, Ann *biochemist, researcher*
Hall, John Allen *international nuclear consultant*
Holt, Helen Keil *physicist*
Kaufman, Seymour *biochemist*
Korn, Edward David *biochemist*
Lugt, Hans Josef *physicist*
Miller, Bennett *physicist, former government official*
Murayama, Makio *biochemist*
Nash, Howard Allen *biochemist, researcher*
Nirenberg, Marshall Warren *biochemist*
Podolsky, Richard James *biophysicist*
Sinclair, Warren Keith *radiation biophysicist, organization executive, consultant*
Stadtman, Earl Reece *biochemist*
Stadtman, Thressa Campbell *biochemist*
Tabor, Herbert *biochemist*
†Trus, Benes Louis *chemist*
Vaughan, Martha *biochemist*
Witkop, Bernhard *chemist*
Wright, James Roscoe *chemist*

Cabin John
Shropshire, Walter, Jr. *biophysicist emeritus, pastor*

Catonsville
Vanderlinde, Raymond Edward *clinical chemist*

Chevy Chase
Hudson, Ralph P. *physicist*
Promisel, Nathan E. *materials scientist, metallurgical engineer*

Clarksburg
Townsend, John William, Jr. *physicist, retired federal aerospace agency executive*

Cobb Island
Vanderslice, Joseph Thomas *chemist*

College Park
†Ahearn, Michael Francis *astronomer, educator*
Benesch, William Milton *molecular physicist, atmospheric researcher, educator*
Blewett, John Paul *retired physicist*
Brill, Dieter Rudolf *physicist*

Brodsky, Marc Herbert *physicist, research and publishing executive*
Castellan, Gilbert William *chemistry educator*
DeSilva, Alan W. *physics educator, researcher*
Fisher, Michael Ellis *mathematical physicist, chemist*
Gluckstern, Robert Leonard *physics educator*
Greenberg, Oscar Wallace *physicist, educator*
Griem, Hans Rudolf *physicist, educator*
Griffin, James Joseph *physics educator*
Grim, Samuel Oram *chemistry educator*
Irwin, George Rankin *physicist, mechanical engineering educator*
Jaquith, Richard Herbert *chemistry educator, retired university official*
Kerr, Frank John *astronomer, educator*
Kundu, Mukul Ranjan *physics and astronomy educator*
Lubkin, Gloria Becker *physicist*
Mc Donald, Frank Bethune *physicist*
Misner, Charles William *physics educator*
Rabin, Herbert *physics educator, university official*
Silverman, Joseph *chemistry educator, scientist*
Smith, Betty Faye *textile chemist*
Snow, George Abraham *physicist*
Webb, Richard Alan *physicist*
Weeks, John David *chemistry and physical science educator*
Zen, E-an *research geologist*

Columbia
Clark, Billy Pat *physicist*
Deutsch, Robert William *physicist*
Fisher, Dale John *chemist, instrumentation and medical diagnostic device investigator*
Khare, Mohan *chemist*
Lijinsky, William *biochemist*

Crofton
Watson, Robert Tanner *physical scientist*

Edgewater
†Gross, M(eredith) Grant *oceanographer, science administrator*

Frederick
Cragg, Gordon Mitchell *government chemist*
Garver, Robert Vernon *research physicist*
Kappe, David Syme *environmental chemist*
Smith, Sharron Williams *chemistry educator*
Wohlgemuth, John Harold *solid state physicist*

Frostburg
Tam, Francis Man Kei *physics educator*

Gaithersburg
Attix, Frank Herbert *medical physics educator, researcher*
Berger, Harold *physicist*
Cahn, John Werner *metallurgist, educator*
Casella, Russell Carl *physicist*
Caswell, Randall Smith *physicist*
†Celotta, Robert James *physicist*
Clark, Alan Fred *physicist*
Costrell, Louis *physicist*
Danos, Michael *physicist*
Dean, Stephen Odell *physicist*
Gebbie, Katharine Blodgett *astrophysicist*
Harman, George Gibson *physicist, consultant*
Hougen, Jon Torger *physical chemist, researcher*
Hsu, Stephen M. *materials scientist, chemical engineer*
Hubbell, John Howard *radiation physicist*
Kessler, Karl Gunther *physicist*
Kushner, Lawrence Maurice *physical chemist*
Kuyatt, Chris E(rnie) (Earl) *physicist, administrator*
Levelt Sengers, Johanna Maria Henrica *research physicist*
†Pierce, Daniel Thornton *physicist*
Pugh, Edison Neville *metallurgist*
Reader, Joseph *physicist*
Schwartz, Lyle H. *materials scientist, government official*
Smith, Leslie E. *physical chemist*
†Stein, Stephen Ellery *research chemist, software engineer*
Taylor, Barry Norman *physicist*
Weber, Alfons *physicist*
Wiese, Wolfgang Lothar *physicist*

Garrett Park
Melville, Robert Seaman *chemist*

Glenelg
Williams, Donald John *research physicist*

Greenbelt
Day, John H. *physicist*
Fichtel, Carl Edwin *physicist*
Gehrels, Neil *astrophysicist*
Hauser, Michael George *astrophysicist*
Holt, Stephen S. *astrophysicist*
Langel, Robert Allan, III *geophysicist*
Maran, Stephen Paul *astronomer*
Mather, John Cromwell *astrophysicist*
Mumma, Michael Jon *physicist*
†Ormes, Jonathan Fairfield *astrophysicist, science administrator, researcher*
Ramaty, Reuven Robert *physicist, researcher*
Simpson, Joanne Malkus *meteorologist*
Smith, David Edmund *geophysicist*
Stief, Louis John *chemist*
†Weinman, James A. *meteorologist*

Lanham Seabrook
Fischel, David *astrophysicist, remote sensing specialist*

Laurel
Apel, John Ralph *physicist*
Avery, William Hinckley *physicist, chemist*
Fristrom, Robert Maurice *chemist*
Kossiakoff, Alexander *chemist*
Krimigis, Stamatios Mike *physicist, researcher, space science/engineering manager, consultant*
Linevsky, Milton Joshua *physical chemist*
O'Connor, Harold J. *wildlife research administrator*

Mechanicsville
Henderson, Madeline Mary (Berry) (Berry Henderson) *chemist, researcher, consultant*

Monrovia
Atanasoff, John Vincent *physicist*

Parkton
Fitzgerald, Edwin Roger *physicist, educator*

Pasadena
Kreps, Robert Wilson *research chemist*
Young, Russell Dawson *physics consultant*

Potomac
Engelmann, Rudolf Jacob *meteorologist*
Epstein, Edward S. *meteorologist*
Whang, Yun Chow *space science educator*

Rockville
Beattie, Donald A. *energy scientist, consultant*
Bruck, Stephen Desiderius *biochemist*
Buchanan, John Donald *health physicist, radiochemist*
Day, LeRoy Edward *aerospace scientist, consultant*
Dunn, Bonnie Brill *chemist*
Finlayson, John Sylvester *biochemist*
Grady, Lee Timothy *pharmaceutical chemist*
Jamieson, Graham A. *biochemist, organization official*
Kindt, Thomas James *chemist*
Liu, Darrell Teh Yung *biochemist, researcher*
Murray, Peter *metallurgist, manufacturing company executive*
Schindler, Albert Isadore *physicist, educator*
Zoon, Kathryn Egloff *biochemist*

Saint Leonard
Sanders, James Grady *biogeochemist*

Sandy Spring
Kanarowski, Stanley Martin *chemist, chemical engineer, government official*

Silver Spring
Briscoe, Melbourne G. *oceanographer, administrator*
Douglass, Carl Dean *biochemistry consultant, former government official*
†Fiorito, Ralph Bruno *research physicist, consultant*
Gaunaurd, Guillermo C. *physicist, engineer, researcher*
Ostenso, Ned Allen *oceanographer, government official*
Rueger, Lauren John *retired physicist*
†Rule, Donald *research physicist*
Scheer, Milton David *physical chemist*
Wilson, William Stanley *oceanographer*
†Young, Jay Alfred *chemical safety and health consultant, writer, editor*

Upper Marlboro
†Anderson, Neil R. *oceanographer*

MASSACHUSETTS

Amherst
Archer, Ronald Dean *chemist, educator*
Bromery, Randolph Wilson *geologist, educator*
Byron, Frederick William, Jr. *physicist, educator, university vice chancellor*
Carpino, Louis A. *chemist, educator*
Ehrlich, Paul *chemist, educator*
Fink, Richard David *chemist, educator*
Goldstein, Joseph Irwin *materials scientist, educator*
Gordon, Joel Ethan *physics educator*
Harrison, Edward Robert *physicist, educator*
Inglis, David Rittenhouse *physicist*
Kantor, Simon William *chemistry educator*
Lenz, Robert William *polymer chemistry educator*
MacKnight, William John *chemist, educator*
Peterson, Gerald Alvin *physicist*
Porter, Roger Stephen *chemistry educator*
Quin, Louis DuBose *chemist, educator*
Ragle, John Linn *chemistry educator*
Scott, David Knight *physicist, university administrator*
Slakey, Linda Louise *biochemistry educator*
Stein, Richard Stephen *chemistry educator*
†Strom, Stephen Eric *astronomer*

Andover
†Caledonia, George E. *research company executive*
Fan, Rulin *organic chemist, researcher*

Arlington
Spengler, Kenneth C. *meteorologist, professional society administrator*

Attleboro
Griffin, Edwin H., Jr. (Hank Griffin) *chemist*

Bedford
Carr, Paul Henry *physicist*
Sizer, Irwin Whiting *biochemistry educator*

Boston
Anselme, Jean-Pierre Louis Marie *chemist*
Antoniades, Harry Nicholas *educator, research biochemist*
Aronow, Saul *physicist*
Blout, Elkan Rogers *biological chemistry educator, university dean*
Brecher, Kenneth *astrophysicist*
Brownell, Gordon Lee *physicist, educator*
Cantor, Charles Robert *biochemistry educator*
Cohen, Robert Sonné *physicist, philosopher, educator*
Gergely, John *biochemistry educator*
†Karger, Barry L. *chemistry educator*
Karnovsky, Manfred L. *biochemistry educator*
Kennedy, Eugene Patrick *biochemist, educator*
†Kirschner, Marc Wallace *biochemist, cell biologist*
Kolodner, Richard David *biochemist, educator*
Le Quesne, Philip William *chemistry educator, researcher*
Lichtin, Norman Nahum *chemistry educator*
†Loscalzo, Joseph *biochemist, cardiologist*
Malenka, Bertram Julian *physicist, educator*
Miliora, Maria Teresa *chemist, psychotherapist, psychoanalyst, educator*
Pardee, Arthur Beck *biochemist, educator*
Quelle, Frederick William, Jr. *physicist*
Raskin, Paul D. *resource management and environmental research administrator*
Scuderi, Louis Anthony *climatology educator*
Sinex, Francis Marott *biochemist, educator*
Solomon, Arthur Kaskel *biophysics educator*
Stanley, H(arry) Eugene *physicist, educator*
Villee, Claude Alvin, Jr. *biochemistry educator*
†Walsh, Christopher Thomas *biochemist, department chairman*
Webster, Edward William *medical physicist*
Weiss, Rainer *physics educator*
Zimmerman, George Ogurek *physicist, educator*

Braintree
Guertin, Robert Powell *physics educator, university dean*

Brookline
Lynton, Ernest Albert *physicist, educator, former university official*
Vallee, Bert Lester *biochemist, physician, educator*

Cambridge
Alberty, Robert Arnold *chemistry educator*
†Anderson, James Gilbert *chemistry educator*
†Ashoori, Raymond *physics educator*
Baker, James Gilbert *optics scientist*
Barger, James Edwin *physicist*
Becker, Ulrich J. *physics educator, particle physics researcher*
Bekefi, George *physics educator*
†Benedek, George Bernard *physicist, educator*
Biemann, Klaus *chemistry educator*
Billings, Marland Pratt *geologist, educator*
Birgeneau, Robert Joseph *physicist, educator*
Bloch, Konrad Emil *biochemist*
Bloembergen, Nicolaas *physicist, educator*
†Bloxham, Jeremy *geologist*
Boyle, Edward Allen *oceanography educator*
Bradt, Hale Van Dorn *physicist, x-ray astronomer, educator*
Branscomb, Lewis McAdory *physicist*
†Brooks, Harvey *physics educator*
Brown, Gene Monte *biochemist, educator*
Buchi, George Hermann *chemistry educator*
Burchfiel, Burrell Clark *geology educator*
Burke, Bernard Flood *physicist, educator*
Burnham, Charles Wilson *mineralogy educator*
Butler, James Newton *chemist, educator*
Cameron, Alastair Graham Walter *astrophysicist, educator*
Canizares, Claude Roger *astrophysicist, educator*
Chisholm, Sallie Watson *biological oceanography educator, researcher*
Ciappenelli, Donald John *chemist, electronics company executive*
Clark, George Whipple *physics educator*
Cobb, Carolus Melville *science company executive, chemical researcher*
Coleman, Sidney Richard *physicist, educator*
†Coppi, Bruno *physicist, educator*
Corey, Elias James *chemistry educator*
Covert, Eugene Edzards *aerophysics educator*
Dalgarno, Alexander *astronomy educator*
†Danheiser, Rick Lane *biochemistry educator*
Doering, William von Eggers *organic chemist, educator*
Donnelly, Thomas William *physicist*
†Doty, Paul Mead *biochemist, educator, arms control specialist*
Dresselhaus, Mildred Spiewak *physics and engineering educator*
Durant, Graham John *medicinal chemist, drug researcher*
Eagar, Thomas Waddy *metallurgist, educator*
Eagleson, Peter Sturges *hydrologist, educator*
Edsall, John Tileston *biological chemistry educator*
Ehrenreich, Henry *physicist, educator*
Elliot, James Ludlow *astronomer, educator*
Emanuel, Kerry Andrew *earth sciences educator*
Evans, David A(lbert) *chemistry educator*
Evans, Robley Dunglison *physicist*
Feld, Michael Stephen *physics educator*
Feldman, Gary Jay *physicist, educator*
Feshbach, Herman *physicist, educator*
Field, George Brooks *theoretical astrophysicist*
Field, Robert Warren *chemistry educator*
Foner, Simon *research physicist*
French, Anthony Philip *physicist, educator*
Frey, Frederick August *geochemistry researcher, educator*
Friedman, Jerome Isaac *physics educator, researcher*
Friend, Cynthia M. *chemist, educator*
Garland, Carl Wesley *chemist, educator*
†Geller, Margaret Joan *astrophysicist, educator*
Georgi, Howard *physics educator*
Gingerich, Owen Jay *astronomer, educator*
Glauber, Roy Jay *theoretical physics educator*
Goldstone, Jeffrey *physicist*
Golovchenko, Jene Andrew *physics and applied physics educator*
Gordon, Roy Gerald *chemistry educator*
Gould, Stephen Jay *paleontologist, educator*
Greene, Frederick D., II *chemistry educator*
Gregory, Bruce Nicholas *astrophysicist, educator*
Greytak, Thomas John *physics educator*
Grindlay, Jonathan Ellis *astrophysics educator*
Grove, Timothy Lynn *geology educator*
Guth, Alan Harvey *physicist, educator*
Halperin, Bertrand Israel *physics educator*
Herschbach, Dudley Robert *chemistry educator*
Hobbs, Linn Walker *materials science educator*
Hoffman, Paul Felix *geologist, educator*
Holm, Richard Hadley *chemist, educator*
Holton, Gerald *physicist, science historian*
Horowitz, Paul *physicist, educator*
Horwitz, Paul *physicist*
Houtchens, Robert Austin, Jr. *biochemist*
Huang, Kerson *physics educator*
Huchra, John Peter *astronomer, educator*
Jackiw, Roman *physicist, educator*
Jacob, Daniel James *atmospheric chemist*
†Jacobsen, Eric N. *chemistry educator*
Jaffe, Robert Loren *theoretical physicist, educator*
Javan, Ali *educator, physicist*
Jordan, Thomas Hillman *geophysicist, educator*
Joss, Paul Christopher *astrophysicist, educator*
Kamentsky, Louis Aaron *biophysicist*
Karplus, Martin *chemistry educator*
Kendall, Henry Way *physicist*
Kerman, Arthur Kent *physicist, educator*
Khorana, Har Gobind *chemist, educator*
Kim, Peter Sungbai *biochemistry educator*
King, John Gordon *physicist, educator*
King, Ronold Wyeth Percival *physics educator*
Kirby, Kate Page *physicist*
Kirshner, Robert P. *astrophysicist, educator*
Kishi, Yoshito *chemist, educator*
Kistiakowsky, Vera *physics researcher, educator*
Klemperer, William *chemistry educator*
Klibanov, Alexander Maxim *chemistry educator*
Knowles, Jeremy Randall *chemist, educator*
Layzer, David *astrophysicist, educator*
Lee, Patrick A. *physics educator*
Lewin, Walter H. G. *physics educator*
Lightman, Alan Paige *physicist, writer*
Lindzen, Richard Siegmund *meteorologist, educator*
Lippard, Stephen James *chemist, educator*
Lipscomb, William Nunn, Jr. *retired physical chemistry educator*
Litster, James David *physics educator, dean*
Livingston, James Duane *physicist, educator*
Lomon, Earle Leonard *physicist, educator, consultant*
Lorenz, Edward Norton *meteorologist, educator*
Low, Francis Eugene *physics educator*
Lyon, Richard Harold *educator, physicist*
Marsden, Brian Geoffrey *astronomer*
Martin, Paul Cecil *physicist, educator*
Marvin, Ursula Bailey *geologist*
Masamune, Satoru *chemistry educator, consultant*
Mazur, Eric *physicist, educator*
McCarthy, James Joseph *oceanography educator*
McElroy, Michael *physicist, researcher*
McNutt, Marcia Kemper *geophysicist*
Meselson, Matthew Stanley *biochemist, educator*
Molina, Mario Jose *physical chemist, educator*
Moniz, Ernest Jeffrey *physics educator*
Moran, James Michael, Jr. *astronomer*
Morgenthaler, Frederic Richard *physics educator*
Narayan, Ramesh *astronomy educator*
Negele, John William *physics educator, consultant*
Nelson, David Robert *physics educator*
Nelson, Keith Adam *chemistry educator*
Newell, Reginald Edward *physics educator*
Oppenheim, Irwin *chemical physicist, educator*
Orme-Johnson, William Henry, III *chemist, educator*
Papaliolios, Costas Demetrios *physics educator*
Paul, William *physicist, educator*
Pershan, Peter Silas *physicist, educator*
Petersen, Ulrich *geology educator*
Pettengill, Gordon H(emenway) *physicist, educator*
Poggio, Tomaso Armando *physicist, educator, computer scientist, researcher*
Press, William Henry *astrophysicist, computer scientist*
Pritchard, David Edward *physics educator*
Ptashne, Mark Steven *biochemistry educator*
Purcell, Edward Mills *physics educator*
Ramsey, Norman F. *physicist, educator*
Raymond, John Charles *physicist*
Rebek, Julius, Jr. *chemistry educator, consultant*
Rediker, Robert Harmon *physicist*
Redwine, Robert Page *physicist, educator*
Rice, James Robert *engineering scientist, geophysicist*
Robinson, Allan Richard *oceanography educator*
Roedder, Edwin Woods *geologist*
Rose, Robert Michael *materials science and engineering educator*
Rosenblith, Walter Alter *scientist, educator*
Rubin, Lawrence Gilbert *physicist, laboratory manager*
Sadoway, Donald Robert *materials science educator*
Sanders, John Lyell, Jr. *educator, researcher*
Schild, Rudolph Ernst *astronomer, educator*
Schimmel, Paul Reinhard *biochemist, biophysicist, educator*
Seyferth, Dietmar *chemist, educator*
Shapiro, Irwin Ira *physicist, educator*
Siever, Raymond *geology educator*
Silbey, Robert James *chemistry educator, researcher*
Silvera, Isaac Franklin *physics educator*
Spaepen, Frans August *applied physics researcher, educator*
Steinfeld, Jeffrey Irwin *chemistry educator, consultant, author*
Strandberg, Malcom Woodrow Pershing *physicist*
Strauch, Karl *physicist, educator*
Stubbe, JoAnne *chemistry educator*
Sullivan, Jeremiah David *physicist, educator*
Thaddeus, Patrick *physicist, educator*
Thompson, James Burleigh, Jr. *geologist, educator*
Ting, Samuel Chao Chung *physicist, educator*
Tinkham, Michael *physicist, educator*
Triantafyllou, Michael Stefanos *ocean engineering educator*
†Tromp, Jeroen *earth scientist*
Turnbull, David *physical chemist, educator*
†Verdine, Gregory Lawrence *chemist, educator*
Vessot, Robert Frederick Charles *physicist*
Villars, Felix Marc Hermann *physicist, educator*
Wald, George *biochemist, educator*
Wang, James Chuo *biochemistry and molecular biology educator*
Wang, Jian-Sheng *materials scientist*
Waugh, John Stewart *chemist, educator*
Weinberg, Robert Allan *biochemist, educator*
Westervelt, Robert Moore *physics educator*
Westheimer, Frank Henry *chemist, educator*
Whipple, Fred Lawrence *astronomer*
Whitesides, George McClelland *chemistry educator*
Whitney, Charles Allen *astronomer, writer*
Wiley, Don Craig *biochemistry and biophysics educator*
Wilson, Robert Woodrow *radio astronomer*
†Wisdom, Jack Leach *physicist, educator*
Wood, John Armstead *planetary scientist, geological sciences educator*
Wu, Tai Tsun *physicist, educator*
Wunsch, Carl Isaac *oceanographer, educator*
Yamamoto, Richard Kumeo *physics educator*
†Zur Loye, Hans-Conrad *research chemist*

Chelmsford
Shepp, Allan *chemist and physicist*

Chestnut Hill
†Fourkas, John T. *chemistry educator*

Concord
Valley, George Edward, Jr. *physicist, educator*

Cotuit
Miller, Robert Charles *retired physicist*

Dover
Chattoraj, Sati Charan *biochemistry educator, researcher*

Falmouth
Goody, Richard Mead *geophysicist*
Hollister, Charles Davis *oceanographer*

Gloucester
Socolow, Arthur Abraham *geologist*

Hanscom AFB
†Eckhardt, Donald Henry *geophysicist*
Mailloux, Robert Joseph *physicist*

Hull
Chase, David Marion *applied physicist, mathematical modeler*

Lexington
Aldrich, Ralph Edward *physicist*
Bainbridge, Kenneth Tompkins *physicist, educator*
Bartlett, Paul Doughty *chemist, educator*
Buchanan, John Machlin *biochemistry educator*
Cathou, Renata Egone *chemist, consultant*
Garing, John Seymour *retired physicist, research executive*
Jensen, Mona Dickson *chemist, researcher*
Kanter, Irving *mathematical physicist*
Kirkpatrick, Francis H(ubbard), Jr. *biophysicist, consultant*
Mollo-Christensen, Erik Leonard *oceanographer*
Nash, Leonard Kollender *chemistry educator*
Samour, Carlos Miguel *chemist*
Schloemann, Ernst Fritz (Rudolf August) *physicist, engineer*
Shull, Clifford G. *physicist, educator*
Smith, Edgar Eugene *biochemist, university administrator*
Wallace, John Edwin *retired meteorologist, consultant*
Williamson, Richard Cardinal *physicist*

Lowell
Baker, Adolph *physicist*
Carr, George Leroy *physicist, educator*
Salamone, Joseph Charles *polymer chemistry educator*
Sheldon, Eric *physics educator*
Tripathy, Sukant Kishore *chemistry educator*

Marblehead
Sanders, Frederick *meteorologist*

Medford
Cormack, Allan MacLeod *physicist, educator*
Gunther, Leon *physicist*
Klema, Ernest Donald *nuclear physicist, educator*
Mc Carthy, Kathryn A. *physicist*
Milburn, Richard Henry *physics educator*
Schneps, Jack *physics educator*
Sung, Nak-Ho *science educator*
Urry, Grant Wayne *chemistry educator*

Natick
Cukor, Peter *chemical research and development executive, educator, consultant*
Milius, Richard A. *organic chemist*
Narayan, K(rishnamurthi) Ananth *biochemist*
Wang, Chia Ping *physicist, educator*

Newton
Dunlap, William Crawford *physicist*
Guidotti, Guido *biochemist, educator*
Heyn, Arno Harry Albert *retired chemistry educator*
Weisskopf, Victor Frederick *physicist*

Newton Center
Mautner, Henry George *chemist*

Northampton
Fleck, George Morrison *chemistry educator*

Plymouth
Atkinson, Christine Gagner *chemist, environmental engineer, consultant*

Roxbury
Franzblau, Carl *biochemist, consultant, researcher*
MacNichol, Edward Ford, Jr. *biophysicist, educator*
Simons, Elizabeth R(eiman) *biochemist, educator*

Salem
Hope, Lawrence Latimer *physicist*

South Hadley
Campbell, Mary Kathryn *chemistry educator*
Harrison, Anna Jane *chemist, educator*

Sturbridge
McMahon, Maribeth Lovette *physicist*

Sudbury
Blackey, Edwin Arthur, Jr. *geologist*

Waltham
Abeles, Robert Heinz *biochemistry educator*
Cohen, Saul G. *chemist, educator*
De Rosier, David John *biophysicist, educator*
Deser, Stanley *educator, physicist*
Epstein, Irving Robert *chemistry educator*
Fasman, Gerald David *biochemistry educator*
Foxman, Bruce Mayer *chemist, educator*
Jeanloz, Roger William *biochemist, educator*
Jencks, William Platt *biochemist, educator*
Kustin, Kenneth *chemist*
Lees, Marjorie Berman *biochemist, neuroscientist*
Nisonoff, Alfred *biochemist, educator*
Petsko, Gregory Anthony *chemistry and biochemistry educator*
Rosenblum, Myron *chemist, educator*
Schweber, Silvan Samuel *physics and history educator*

Watertown
Wright, Edward S. *materials technology administrator*

Wayland
Clark, Melville, Jr. *physicist, electrical engineer, consultant*

Wellesley
Kobayashi, Yutaka *biochemist, consultant*

Westford
†Hanna, Steven Rogers *meteorologist*
Salah, Joseph Elias *research scientist, educator*

Weston
Whitehouse, David Rempfer *physicist*

Westwood
Bernfeld, Peter Harry William *biochemist*

Williamstown
Crampton, Stuart Jessup Bigelow *physicist, educator*
Fox, William Templeton *geologist, educator*
Markgraf, J(ohn) Hodge *chemist, educator*
Park, David Allen *physicist, educator*
Pasachoff, Jay Myron *astronomer, educator*
Wobus, Reinhard Arthur *geologist, educator*

Wilmington
Tuchman, Avraham *physicist, researcher*

Woods Hole
Butman, Bradford *oceanographer*
Cohen, Seymour Stanley *biochemist, educator*
Emery, Kenneth Orris *marine geologist*
Fofonoff, Nicholas Paul *oceanographer, educator*
Hart, Stanley Robert *geochemist, educator*
Steele, John Hyslop *marine scientist, oceanographic institute administrator*
Von Herzen, Richard Pierre *research scientist, consultant*

Worcester
Apelian, Diran *materials scientist, provost*
Bell, Peter Mayo *geophysicist*
Hohenemser, Christoph *physics educator, researcher*
Klein, Michael William *physics educator*
Pavlik, James William *chemistry educator*

MICHIGAN

Ann Arbor
Agranoff, Bernard William *biochemist, educator*
Akerlof, Carl William *physics educator*
Aller, Margo Friedel *astronomer*
Alpern, Mathew *physiological optics educator*
Ashe, Arthur James, III *chemistry educator*
Atreya, Sushil Kumar *astronomy educator, astrophysicist, researcher*
Bartell, Lawrence Sims *chemist, educator*
Bernstein, Isadore Abraham *biochemistry educator, researcher*
Blinder, Seymour Michael *chemistry educator*
Chupp, Timothy E. *physicist, educator, nuclear scientist, academic administrator*
Clarke, Roy *physicist, educator*
Crane, Horace Richard *educator, physicist*
Dekker, Eugene Earl *biochemistry educator*
†Dixon, Jack E. *biological chemistry educator, consultant*
Donahue, Thomas Michael *physics educator*
Farrand, William Richard *geology educator*
Filisko, Frank Edward *physicist, educator*
Gingerich, Philip Derstine *paleontologist, evolutionary biologist, educator*
Haddock, Fred T. *astronomer, educator*
Jones, Lawrence William *educator, physicist*
Kesler, Stephen Edward *economic geology educator*
Krimm, Samuel *physicist, educator*
Krisch, Alan David *physics educator*
Longone, Daniel Thomas *chemistry educator*
†Marietta, Michael *biochemistry and medicinal chemistry educator*
Massey, Vincent *biochemist, educator*
Matthews, Rowena Green *biological chemistry educator*
Neal, Homer Alfred *physics educator, researcher, university administrator*
Nordman, Christer Eric *chemistry educator*
Parkinson, William Charles *physicist, educator*
Pollack, Henry Nathan *geophysics educator*
Rea, David K. *geology and oceanography educator*
Robertson, Richard Earl *physical chemist, educator*
Roe, Byron Paul *physics educator*
Ruff, Larry *geology educator*
†Samson, Perry J. *environmental scientist, educator*
Schacht, Jochen Heinrich *biochemistry educator*
Steel, Duncan Gregory *physics educator*
Tamres, Milton *chemistry educator*
Townsend, LeRoy B. *chemistry educator, university administrator, researcher*
Van der Voo, Rob *geophysicist*
Veltman, Martinus J. *physics educator*
Weinreich, Gabriel *physicist, minister, educator*
Yeh, Gregory Soh-Yu *physicist, educator*
†Zhang, Youxue *geology educator*

Big Rapids
Mathison, Ian William *chemistry educator, academic dean*

Cross Village
Stowe, Robert Allen *catalytic and chemical technology consultant*

Dearborn
†Hoffman, David W. *research scientist*
Otto, Klaus *physicist, physical chemist*
Tai, Julia Chow *chemistry educator*

Detroit
Bohm, Henry Victor *physicist*
Brown, Ray Kent *biochemist, physician, educator*
Coleman, David Manley *chemistry educator*
Ebbing, Darrell Delmar *chemist, educator*
Frade, Peter Daniel *chemist*
Fradkin, David Milton *physicist, educator*
Gupta, Suraj Narayan *physicist, educator*
Johnson, Carl Randolph *chemist, educator*
Kirschner, Stanley *chemist*
†Liu, Gang-Yu *chemist, educator*
Oliver, John Preston *chemistry educator, academic administrator*
Orton, Colin George *medical physicist*
Ronca, Luciano Bruno *geologist, educator*
Stewart, Melbourne George, Jr. *physicist, educator*
Thomas, Robert Leighton *physicist, researcher*

East Lansing
Abolins, Maris Arvids *physics researcher and educator*
Austin, Sam M. *physics educator*
Benenson, Walter *nuclear physics educator*
Brown, Boyd Alex *physicist, educator*
Cross, Aureal Theophilus *geology and botany educator*
D'Itri, Frank Michael *environmental research chemist*
Dye, James Louis *chemistry educator*
Gelbke, Claus-Konrad *nuclear physics educator*
Harrison, Michael Jay *physicist, educator*
Kaplan, Thomas Abraham *physics educator*
Klomparens, Karen Lee *optics scientist, educator*
Luecke, Richard William *biochemist*
Macrakis, Kristie Irene *history of science educator*
McConnell, David Graham *research biochemist, educator*
Montgomery, Donald Joseph *physicist, educator*
Pollack, Gerald Leslie *physicist, educator*
Preiss, Jack *biochemistry educator*
Spence, Robert Dean *physics educator*
Summitt, (William) Robert *chemist, educator*
Tien, H. Ti *biophysics and physiology educator, scientist*
Tolbert, Nathan Edward *biochemistry educator, plant science researcher*
Wolterink, Lester Floyd *biophysicist, educator*
Yussouff, Mohammed *physicist, educator*

Flint
Wong, Victor Kenneth *physics educator, academic administrator*

Holland
Inghram, Mark Gordon *physicist, educator*

Jackson
Henderson, John William *chemistry educator*

Kalamazoo
Greenfield, John Charles *bio-organic chemist*

Leland
Small, Hamish *chemist*

Madison Heights
Chapman, Gilbert Bryant *physicist*

Metamora
Blass, Gerhard Alois *physics educator*

Midland
Chao, Marshall *chemist*
Dorman, Linneaus Cuthbert *retired chemist*
Gant, George Arlington Lee *chemist*
Mansfield, Marc Lewis *chemist, research scientist*
Speier, John Leo, Jr. *chemist*
Stull, Daniel Richard *research thermochemist, educator, consultant*
Weyenberg, Donald Richard *chemist*

Mount Pleasant
Dietrich, Richard Vincent *geologist, educator*

Rochester
Callewaert, Denis Marc *biochemistry educator*

Saint Clair Shores
Rownd, Robert Harvey *biochemistry and molecular biology educator*

Troy
Drakos, Irene Sasso *chemist*
Ovshinsky, Stanford Robert *physicist, inventor, energy and information company executive*

Warren
Herbst, Jan Francis *physicist, researcher*
Schwartz, Shirley E. *chemist*
Smith, George Wolfram *physicist, educator*
Smith, John Robert *physicist*

Ypsilanti
Barnes, James Milton *physics and astronomy educator*

MINNESOTA

Austin
Holman, Ralph Theodore *biochemistry and nutrition educator*
Schmid, Harald Heinrich Otto *biochemistry educator, academic director*

Duluth
Rapp, George Robert, Jr. (Rip) *geology and archeology educator*

Lakeville
Phinney, William Charles *retired geologist*

Minneapolis
Ackerman, Eugene *biophysics educator*
†Barany, George *chemistry educator, researcher, consultant*
Carr, Charles William *biochemist, emeritus educator*
Carr, Robert Wilson, Jr. *chemistry educator*
Crawford, Bryce Low, Jr. *chemist, educator*
Dahler, John Spillers *chemist, educator*
†Eisenreich, Steven John *chemistry educator, environmental scientist*
Gannon, Mary Carol *nutritional biochemist*
Gasiorowicz, Stephen George *physics educator*
Gehrz, Robert Douglas *astrophysicist, educator, researcher*
Goldman, Allen Marshall *physics educator*
Halley, James Woods, Jr. *physicist*
Hamermesh, Morton *physicist, educator*
Hobbie, Russell Klyver *physicist*
Hogenkamp, Henricus Petrus Cornelis *biochemistry researcher, biochemistry educator*
Hooke, Roger LeBaron *geomorphology and glaciology educator*
Humphreys, Roberta Marie *astronomer, educator*
Jones, Thomas Walter *astrophysics educator, researcher*
Kelts, Kerry R. *geology educator*
Kruse, Paul Walters, Jr. *physicist, consultant*
Kuhi, Leonard Vello *astronomer, university administrator*
Lumry, Rufus Worth, II *chemist, educator*
Marshak, Marvin Lloyd *physicist, educator*
Moscowitz, Albert Joseph *chemist, educator*
Portoghese, Philip Salvatore *medicinal chemist, educator*
Prager, Stephen *chemistry educator*
Rubens, Sidney Michel *physicist, technical advisor*
†Siepmann, Joern Ilja *chemistry educator*
Truhlar, Donald Gene *chemist, educator*
Wade, Lewis V. *mineral research director*
Wright, Herbert E(dgar), Jr. *geologist*
Yuen, David Alexander *geophysics and computational physics educator*

Northfield
Buchwald, Caryl Edward *geology educator, environmental consultant, educational consultant*
Casper, Barry Michael *physics educator*
Noer, Richard J. *physics educator, researcher*
Ramette, Richard Wales *chemistry educator*

Rochester
Kao, Pai Chih *clinical chemist*

Roseville
Berry, James Frederick *biochemistry educator*

Saint Paul
Bloomfield, Victor Alfred *biochemistry educator*
Clapp, C(harles) Edward *research chemist, soil biochemistry educator*
Farnum, Sylvia Arlyce *physical chemist*
Fuchs, James A. *biochemistry educator*
Holmen, Reynold Emanuel *chemist*
Nicholson, Morris Emmons, Jr. *metallurgist, educator*
Thompson, Mary Eileen *chemistry educator*
Walker, Charles Thomas *physicist, educator*
Walton, Matt Savage *geologist, educator*

MISSISSIPPI

Mississippi State
Howell, Everette Irl *physicist, educator*
Minyard, James Patrick, Jr. *chemist, educator*

Pascagoula
Corben, Herbert Charles *physicist, educator*

Starkville
Emerich, Donald Warren *retired chemistry educator*

Stennis Space Center
Royestess, Roy *aerospace science administrator*

MISSOURI

Cape Girardeau
Dahiya, Jai Narain *physics educator, researcher*

Columbia
Bauman, John E., Jr. *chemistry educator*
Decker, Wayne Leroy *meteorologist, educator*
Ethington, Raymond Lindsay *geology educator, researcher*
Gehrke, Charles William *biochemistry educator*
Johns, Williams Davis, Jr. *geologist, educator*
Mayer, Dennis Thomas *biochemist, educator*
Plummer, Patricia Lynne Moore *chemistry and physics educator*
Rabjohn, Norman *chemistry educator emeritus*
Unklesbay, Athel Glyde *geologist, educator*

Joplin
Malzahn, Ray Andrew *chemistry educator, university dean*

Kansas City
Ching, Wai Yim *physics educator, researcher*
Gier, Audra May Calhoon *environmental chemist*
Grosskreutz, Joseph Charles *physicist, engineering researcher, educator*
Martinez-Carrion, Marino *biochemist, educator*
Parizek, Eldon Joseph *geologist, college dean*
Rost, William Joseph *chemist*

Kirksville
Festa, Roger Reginald *chemist, educator*

Rolla
Adawi, Ibrahim Hasan *physics educator*
Alexander, Ralph William, Jr. *physics educator*
Armstrong, Daniel Wayne *chemist, educator*
Hagni, Richard Davis *geology and geophysics educator*
James, William Joseph *chemistry educator*
Mc Farland, Robert Harold *physicist, educator*
O'Keefe, Thomas Joseph *metallurgical engineer*

Saint Louis
Ackerman, Joseph J. H. *chemistry educator*
Ackers, Gary Keith *biophysical chemistry educator, researcher*
Arvidson, Raymond Ernst *planetary geology educator*
Bender, Carl Martin *physics educator, consultant*
Burgess, James Harland *physics educator, researcher*
Callis, Clayton Fowler *research chemist*
Frieden, Carl *biochemist, educator*
Friedlander, Michael Wulf *physicist, educator*
Gibbons, Patrick Chandler *physicist, educator*
Gross, Michael Lawrence *chemistry educator*
Handel, Peter H. *physics educator*
Heinrich, Ross Raymond *geophysicist, educator*
Hohenberg, Charles Morris *physics educator*
Holtzer, Alfred Melvin *chemistry educator*
Horwitt, Max Kenneth *biochemist, educator*
Israel, Martin Henry *astrophysicist, educator, academic administrator*
†Kilkenny, John E. *geologist*
Kornfeld, Rosalind Hauk *research biochemist*
Kurz, Joseph Louis *chemistry educator*
Lipkin, David *chemist*
Macias, Edward S. *chemistry educator, university official*
Marshall, Garland Ross *biochemist, biophysicist, medical educator*
Miller, James Gegan *research scientist, physics educator*
Murray, Robert Wallace *chemistry educator*
Norberg, Richard Edwin *physicist, educator*
Rosenthal, Harold Leslie *biochemistry educator*
Stauder, William Vincent *geophysics educator*
Takano, Masaharu *physical chemist*
Walker, Robert Mowbray *physicist, educator*
Weber, Morton M. *microbial biochemist, educator*
Will, Clifford Martin *physicist, educator*
Wrighton, Mark Stephen *chemistry educator*

Springfield
Criswell, Charles Harrison *analytical chemist, environmental and forensic consultant, executive*
Thompson, Clifton C. *chemistry educator, university administrator*

MONTANA

Bozeman
†Horner, John Robert *paleontologist, researcher*
Mertz, Edwin Theodore *biochemist, emeritus educator*

Butte
Beuerman, Donald Roy *chemistry educator*
Volborth, Alexis *geochemistry and geological engineering educator*

Missoula
Jakobson, Mark John *physics educator*
Murray, Raymond Carl *forensic geologist, educator*
Osterheld, R(obert) Keith *chemistry educator*
Peterson, James Algert *geologist, educator*

Troy
Sherman, Signe Lidfeldt *securities analyst, former research chemist*

Twin Bridges
Ruppel, Edward Thompson *geologist*

NEBRASKA

Crete
Brakke, Myron Kendall *retired research chemist and educator*

Lincoln
Blad, Blaine L. *agricultural meteorology educator, consultant*
Eckhardt, Craig Jon *chemistry educator*
Jolliff, Carl R. *clinical biochemist, immunologist, laboratory administrator*
Jones, Lee Bennett *chemist, educator*
O'Leary, Marion Hugh *chemistry educator*
Sellmyer, David Julian *physicist, educator*
Treves, Samuel Blain *geologist, educator, administrator*

Omaha
Gambal, David *biochemistry educator*
Watt, Dean Day *retired biochemistry educator*
Zepf, Thomas Herman *physics educator, researcher*

NEVADA

Carson City
Crawford, John Edward *geologist, scientist*

Incline Village
McCormac, Billy Murray *physicist, research institution executive, former army officer*

Las Vegas
Barth, Delbert Sylvester *environmental studies educator*
Bretthauer, Erich Walter *chemist*
Eastwood, DeLyle *chemist*
Harpster, Robert Eugene *engineering geologist*
Levich, Robert Alan *geologist*

Reno
Helm, Donald Cairney *hydrogeologist, educator*
Horton, Robert Carlton *geologist*
Leipper, Dale Frederick *physical oceanographer, educator*
Pierson, William Roy *chemist*
Pough, Frederick Harvey *mineralogist*
Price, Jonathan G. *geologist*
Ritter, Dale Franklin *geologist, research association administrator*
Sladek, Ronald John *physics educator*
Taranik, James Vladimir *geologist, educator*

Sparks
Bentley, Kenton Earl *aerospace scientist, researcher*

NEW HAMPSHIRE

Alstead
Hanson, George Fulford *geologist*

Bedford
Effenberger, John Albert *research chemist*

Durham
Tischler, Herbert *geologist, educator*

Groveton
Kegeles, Gerson *chemistry educator*

Hanover
Braun, Charles Louis *chemistry educator, researcher*
Chamberlain, Charles Page *earth science educator*
Doyle, William Thomas *physicist, educator*
Harbury, Henry Alexander *biochemist, educator*
Kantrowitz, Arthur *physicist, educator*
Montgomery, David Campbell *physicist, educator*
Perrin, Noel *environmental studies educator*
Stockmayer, Walter H(ugo) *chemistry educator*
Sturge, Michael Dudley *physicist*
Wegner, Gary Alan *astronomer*
Wetterhahn, Karen Elizabeth *chemistry educator*

Jaffrey
Walling, Cheves Thomson *chemistry educator*

Salem
Simmons, Marvin Gene *geophysics educator*

NEW JERSEY

Allendale
Castor, William Stuart, Jr. *chemist, consultant, laboratory executive, educator*

Annandale
Cohen, Morrel Herman *physicist, biologist, educator*
Gorbaty, Martin Leo *chemist, researcher*
Lohse, David John *physicist*
Sinfelt, John Henry *chemist*

Bedminster
Bovey, Frank Alden *research chemist*

Belle Mead
Hansen, Ralph Holm *chemist*

Berkeley Heights
Geusic, Joseph Edward *retired physicist*

Bound Brook
Karol, Frederick John *industrial chemist*

Bridgewater
Albrethsen, Adrian Edysel *metallurgist, consultant*

Camden
Beck, David Paul *biochemist*

Cape May
Wilson, H(arold) Fred(erick) *chemist, research scientist*

Cherry Hill
Cazes, Jack *chemist, marketing consultant, editor*
Hayasi, Nisiki *physicist, business executive, inventor*

Cinnaminson
Lippincott, Sarah Lee *astronomer, graphologist*

East Brunswick
Wagman, Gerald Howard *retired biochemist*

Edison
Lo Surdo, Antonio *physical chemist, educator*

Far Hills
McCall, David Warren *chemist, administrator, materials consultant*

Florham Park
Griffo, James Vincent, Jr. *retired biology educator*

Fort Hancock
Klein, George D. *geologist, executive*

Franklin Lakes
Hetzel, Donald Stanford *chemist*

Highland Park
Brudner, Harvey Jerome *physicist*
Feigenbaum, Abraham Samuel *nutritional biochemist*

Hoboken
Fajans, Jack *physics educator*
Kunhardt, Erich Enrique *physicist, educator*
Schmidt, George *physicist*

Holmdel
Bjorkholm, John Ernst *physicist*
Burrus, Charles Andrew, Jr. *research physicist*
Kaminow, Ivan Paul *physicist*
Mac Rae, Alfred Urquhart *physicist, electrical engineer*
Miller, David Andrew Barclay *physicist*
Mollenauer, Linn Frederick *physicist*
Shah, Jagdeep *physicist, researcher*

Kenilworth
Ganguly, Ashit Kumar *organic chemist*

Liberty Corner
Gall, Martin *project chemist, research and development manager*

Little Falls
Stiles, John Callender *physicist*

Madison
deStevens, George *chemist, educator*

Mahwah
Borowitz, Grace Burchman *chemistry educator, researcher*

Morristown
Arnow, Leslie Earle *scientist*
Van Uitert, LeGrand Gerard *chemist*

Murray Hill
Baker, William Oliver *research chemist, educator*
†Batlogg, Bertram *physicist*
Brinkman, William Frank *physicist, research executive*
Capasso, Federico *physicist, research administrator*
Coppersmith, Susan Nan *physicist*
Glass, Alastair Malcolm *physicist, research director*
Helfand, Eugene *chemist*
†Hutchinson, Albert L. *research physicist*
Morgan, Samuel P(ope) *physicist, applied mathematician*
Pinczuk, Aron *physicist*
†Sirtori, Carlo *research physicist*
†Sivco, Deborah L. *research physicist*
Stillinger, Frank Henry *chemist, educator*
†Tully, John Charles *research chemical physicist*
†van Dover, Robert Bruce *physicist*
Wernick, Jack Harry *chemist*
White, Alice Elizabeth *physicist, researcher*

Neptune
Aguiar, Adam Martin *chemist, educator*

New Brunswick
Grassle, John Frederick *oceanographer, marine sciences educator*
Ho, Chi-Tang *food chemistry educator*
Lebowitz, Joel Louis *mathematical physicist, educator*
Liao, Mei-June *biopharmaceutical company executive*
Plano, Richard James *physicist, educator*
Rosen, Robert Thomas *analytical and food chemist*
Strauss, Ulrich Paul *educator, chemist*
Temmer, Georges Maxime *physicist*

New Providence
Bishop, David John *physicist*
Gaylord, Norman Grant *chemical and polymer consultant*
Lanzerotti, Louis John *physicist*
Laudise, Robert Alfred *research chemist*
Murray, Cherry Ann *physicist, researcher*
Stormer, Horst Ludwig *physicist*
Wertheim, Gunther Klaus *physicist*

Newark
Christakos, Sylvia *biochemist, educator, researcher*
Murnick, Daniel Ely *physicist, educator*

Nutley
Udenfriend, Sidney *biochemist*
Weissbach, Herbert *biochemist*

Pennington
Halasi-Kun, George Joseph *hydrologist, educator*
Widmer, Kemble *geologist*

Piscataway
†Devlin, Thomas Joseph *physicist*
Gotsch, Audrey Rose *environmental health sciences educator, researcher*
Kear, Bernard Henry *materials scientist*
Lindenfeld, Peter *physics educator*
Lioy, Paul James *environmental health scientist*
Pond, Thomas Alexander *physics educator*
Robbins, Allen Bishop *physics educator*
Shatkin, Aaron Jeffrey *biochemistry educator*
Snitzer, Elias *physicist*
Yacowitz, Harold *biochemist, nutritionist*

Port Murray
Kunzler, John Eugene *physicist*

Princeton
Adler, Stephen Louis *physicist*
Bahcall, John Norris *astrophysicist*
Bhatt, Ravindra N. *physicist, educator*
Bonini, William Emory *geophysics educator*
†Bryan, Kirk, Jr. *research meteorologist, research oceanographer*
Chang, Clarence Dayton *chemist*
Cooke, Theodore Frederic, Jr. *chemist*
Crerar, David Alexander *geochemistry educator, consultant*
Davidson, Ronald Crosby *physicist, educator*
Dyson, Freeman John *physicist*
Fenichel, Richard Lee *biochemist*
Fisch, Nathaniel Joseph *physicist*
Fitch, Val Logsdon *physics educator*
Florey, Klaus Georg *chemist, pharmaceutical consultant*
†Forest, Carey *research physicist*
Fresco, Jacques Robert *biochemist, educator*
Gale, Paula Jane *chemist*
Gott, J. Richard, III *astrophysicist*
Grasselli, Robert Karl *physical chemist, research scientist*
Green, Joseph *chemist*
Groves, John Taylor, III *chemist, educator*
Gunn, James Edward *astrophysicist*
Haldane, Frederick Duncan Michael *physics educator*
Happer, William, Jr. *physicist, educator*
Hawryluk, Richard Janusz *physicist*
Hulse, Russell Alan *physicist*
Jenkins, Edward Beynon *research astronomer*
Jones, Maitland, Jr. *chemistry educator*
Judson, Sheldon *geology educator*
Kauzmann, Walter Joseph *chemistry educator*
†Kulsrud, Russell Marion *physicist*
Lemonick, Aaron *physicist, educator*
Libchaber, Albert Joseph *physics educator*
Lieb, Elliott Hershel *physicist, mathematician, educator*
†Los, Marinus *agrochemical researcher*
Mahlman, Jerry David *research meteorologist*
Manabe, Syukuro *climatologist*
Mc Clure, Donald Stuart *physical chemist, educator*
Mills, Robert Gail *retired physicist*
Miyakoda, Kikuro *meteorologist, lecturer*
Montgomery, Ronald Eugene *chemist, research and development director*
Navrotsky, Alexandra *geophysics educator*
Ondetti, Miguel Angel *chemist, consultant*
Oort, Abraham Hans *meteorologist, researcher, educator*
Ostriker, Jeremiah Paul *astrophysicist, educator*
Paczynski, Bohdan *astrophysicist, educator*
†Page, Lyman Alexander, Jr. *physicist*
Peebles, Phillip James E. *physicist, educator*
Phinney, Robert Alden *geophysics educator*
Rabitz, Herschel Albert *chemistry educator*
Rebenfeld, Ludwig *chemist*
Reynolds, George Thomas *physics educator, researcher, consultant*
Robertson, Nat Clifton *chemist*
Rodwell, John Dennis *biochemist*
Royce, Barrie Saunders Hart *physicist*
Rutherford, Paul Harding *physicist*
Scoles, Giacinto *chemistry educator*
Shoemaker, Frank Crawford *physicist, educator*
Simmons, Jean Elizabeth Margaret (Mrs. Glen R. Simmons) *chemistry educator*
Smagorinsky, Joseph *meteorologist*
Smith, Arthur John Stewart *physicist, educator*
†Spergel, David Nathaniel *astrophysicist*
Spiro, Thomas George *chemistry educator*
Sterzer, Fred *research physicist*
Stix, Thomas Howard *physicist, educator*
†Suppe, John *geology educator*
Taylor, Edward Curtis *chemistry educator*
Taylor, Joseph Hooton, Jr. *radio astronomer, physicist*
Torquato, Salvatore *materials science engineer, researcher*
Treiman, Sam Bard *physics educator*
Turner, Edwin Lewis *astronomy educator, researcher*
Van Houten, Franklyn Bosworth *geologist, educator*
†Verlinde, Herman L. *physics educator*
Villafranca, Joseph J. *biochemistry educator*
Weigmann, Hans-Dietrich H. *chemist*
Wheeler, John Archibald *physicist, educator*
Wightman, Arthur Strong *physicist, educator*
Wilczek, Frank Anthony *physics educator*
Wilkinson, David Todd *physics educator*
Witten, Edward *mathematical physicist*
Wong, Ching-Ping *chemist*

Rahway
Kaczorowski, Gregory John *biochemist, researcher, science administrator*
†Rasmusson, Gary Henry *medicinal chemist*
Shapiro, Bennett Michaels *biochemist, educator*

Red Bank
Harbison, James Prescott *research physicist*

Ridgefield
Goldman, Arnold Ira *biophysicist, statistical analyst*

Skillman
Kral, Frank *biophysical chemist*

Springfield
Panish, Morton B. *physicial chemist, consultant*

Summit
Gonnella, Nina Celeste *biophysical chemist*
Phillips, James Charles *physicist, educator*
Wissbrun, Kurt Falke *chemist, consultant*

Teaneck
Kramer, Bernard *physicist, educator*
Walsh, Peter Joseph *physics educator*

Trenton
Cushman, David Wayne *research biochemist*
Summerfield, Martin *physicist*
Tucker, Robert Keith *environmental scientist, research administrator*

Union
Zois, Constantine Nicholas Athanasios *meteorology educator*

Upper Montclair
Kowalski, Stephen Wesley *chemistry educator*

Wayne
Mallik, Arjun *biomedical chemist*

Westfield
Bartok, William *environmental technologies consultant*
Miller, Gabriel Lorimer *physicist, researcher*

Westwood
Schutz, Donald Frank *geochemist, corporate executive*

NEW MEXICO

Albuquerque
Beckel, Charles Leroy *physics educator*
Beeler, Gary *materials science administrator*
Binkley, J. S. *physical sciences research administrator*
Garland, James Wilson, Jr. *retired physics educator*
Graham, Robert Albert *research physicist*
Harrison, Charles Wagner, Jr. *applied physicist*
King, James Claude *physicist*
Loftfield, Robert Berner *biochemistry educator*
Osbourn, Gordon Cecil *materials scientist*
Papike, James Joseph *geology educator, science institute director*
Robinson, Charles Paul *nuclear physicist, diplomat, business executive*
Scully, Marlan Orvil *physics educator*
Sparks, Morgan *physicist*
†Van Devender, J. Pace *physical scientist*
Vook, Frederick Ludwig *physicist*

Las Cruces
Coburn, Horace Hunter *retired physics educator*
Kemp, John Daniel *biochemist, educator*

Los Alamos
Allred, John Caldwell *physicist*
†Becker, Stephen A. *physicist, designer*
Bell, George Irving *biophysics researcher*
†Bishop, Alan Reginald *research scientist*
Bradbury, Norris Edwin *physicist*
Campbell, Mary Margaret Stinecipher *research chemist, educator*
Colgate, Stirling Auchincloss *physicist*
Engelhardt, Albert George *physicist*
Flynn, Edward Robert *physicist*
Friar, James Lewis *physicist*
Gibson, Benjamin Franklin *physicist*
Ginocchio, Joseph Natale *theoretical physicist*
Goldstone, Philip David *physicist*
Grilly, Edward Rogers *physicist*
Hecker, Siegfried Stephen *metallurgist*
Jarmie, Nelson *physicist*
Johnson, Mikkel Borlaug *physicist*
Judd, O'Dean P. *physicist*
Keepin, George Robert, Jr. *physicist*
Kelly, Robert Emmett *physicist, educator*
Kubas, Gregory Joseph *research chemist*
Linford, Rulon Kesler *physicist, engineer*
Matlack, George Miller *radiochemist*
McNally, James Henry *physicist, defense consultant*
Metropolis, Nicholas Constantine *mathematical physicist*
Mitchell, Terence Edward *materials scientist*
Nix, James Rayford *nuclear physicist, consultant*
Pack, Russell T *theoretical chemist*
Penneman, Robert Allen *retired chemist*
Pynn, Roger *physicist*
Rosen, Louis *physicist*
Selden, Robert Wentworth *physicist, science advisor*
†Shaner, John Wesley *physicist*
Smith, James Lawrence *research physicist*
Strottman, Daniel David *physicist*
Terrell, (Nelson) James *physicist*
Wahl, Arthur Charles *retired chemistry educator*
Whetten, John Theodore *geologist*
†WoldeGabriel, Giday *research geologist*
Zurek, Wojciech Hubert *physicist*
Zweig, George *physicist, neurobiologist*

Mesilla Park
Tombaugh, Clyde William *astronomer, educator*

Santa Fe
Cannon, Helen Leighton *retired geologist, government official*
Cowan, George Arthur *chemist, bank executive, director*
Fisher, Robert Alan *laser physicist*
Gell-Mann, Murray *theoretical physicist, educator*
Giovanielli, Damon Vincent *physicist, consulting company executive*
Ratliff, Floyd *biophysics educator, scientist*
White, David Hywel *physics educator*

Socorro
Kottlowski, Frank Edward *geologist*
Petschek, Albert George *physics educator*

Sunspot
Altrock, Richard Charles *astrophysicist*
Leibacher, John William *astronomer*

NEW YORK

Albany
†Block, Eric *chemist*
Bosart, Lance Frank *meteorology educator*
Demerjian, Kenneth Leo *atmospheric science educator, research center director*
Frisch, Harry Lloyd *chemist, educator*
Frost, Robert Edwin *chemistry educator*
Hof, Liselotte Bertha *biochemist*
Kim, Jai Soo *physics educator*
Kuivila, Henry Gabriel *chemist, educator, consultant*
Reichert, Leo Edmund, Jr. *biochemist, endocrinologist*
Roth, Laura Maurer *physics educator, researcher*
Schneider, Allan Stanford *biochemistry and pharmacology educator, biomedical research scientist*

Alfred
Rossington, David Ralph *physical chemistry educator*

Bayport
Courant, Ernest David *physicist*

Bellport
Barton, Mark Quayle *physicist*

Binghamton
Coates, Donald Robert *geology educator, scientist*
Eisch, John Joseph *chemist, educator*

Briarcliff Manor
Bhargava, Rameshwar Nath *physicist*

Bronx
Shamos, Morris Herbert *physicist educator*
Yalow, Rosalyn Sussman *medical physicist*

Brooklyn
Castleman, Louis Samuel *metallurgist, educator*
Charton, Marvin *chemist, educator*
Eirich, Frederick Roland *chemist, educator*
Franco, Victor *theoretical physics educator*
Friedman, Gerald Manfred *geologist, educator*
Friedman, Paul *chemistry educator*
Kjeldaas, Terje, Jr. *physics educator emeritus*
Langer, Arthur Mark *mineralogist*
Mendelson, Sol *physical science educator, consultant*
Morawetz, Herbert *chemistry educator*
Sanduja, Mohan L. *chemist, researcher, executive*
Stracher, Alfred *biochemistry educator*
Tamir, Theodor *electrophysics researcher, educator*
Tesoro, Giuliana Cavaglieri *chemistry research educator, consultant*
Vogl, Otto *polymer science and engineering educator*
Wolf, Edward Lincoln *physics educator*

Buffalo
Anbar, Michael *biophysics educator*
Bardos, Thomas Joseph *chemist, educator*
Basu, Rajat Subhra *physicist, researcher*
Borst, Lyle Benjamin *physicist, educator*
Bruckenstein, Stanley *chemistry educator*
Coppens, Philip *chemist*
†Hall, Linda M. *biochemical pharmacology educator, consultant*
Jain, Piyare Lal *physics educator*
Kris, Edward Joseph *chemist*
Langway, Chester Charles, Jr. *geological sciences educator*
Reitan, Paul Hartman *geologist, educator*
Treanor, Charles Edward *physicist*
Tufariello, Joseph James *chemistry educator*
Wang, Jui Hsin *biochemistry educator*

Canton
Romey, William Dowden *geologist, educator*

Clinton
Ring, James Walter *physics educator*

Corning
Josbeno, Larry Joseph *physics educator*
Keck, Donald Bruce *physicist*
Maurer, Robert Distler *retired industrial physicist*
Meiling, Gerald Stewart *materials scientist*

Cortland
Zipp, Arden Peter *chemistry educator*

Croton On Hudson
Adelson, Alexander M. *physicist*

Dobbs Ferry
Triplett, Kelly B. *chemist*

East Hampton
Garrett, Charles Geoffrey Blythe *physicist*

East Rochester
†Gundlach, Robert William *physicist*

Farmingdale
Marcuvitz, Nathan *electrophysics educator*
Nolan, Peter John *physics educator*

Flushing
Finks, Robert Melvin *paleontologist, educator*
Gafney, Harry D. *chemistry educator*
Goldman, Norman Lewis *chemistry educator*
Hatcher, Robert Douglas *physicist, educator*
Rafanelli, Kenneth Robert *physics educator*
Speidel, David Harold *geology educator*

Fredonia
Barnard, Walther M. *geosciences educator*

Freeport
Pullman, Maynard Edward *biochemist*

Garden City
Williams, Irving Laurence *physics educator*

Geneva
Roelofs, Wendell Lee *biochemistry educator, consultant*

Glen Cove
Dehn, Joseph William, Jr. *chemist*

Greenvale
†Shields, Joan E. *chemistry educator*

Hamilton
Aveni, Anthony Francis *astronomy and anthropology educator, researcher*
Cochran, John Charles *chemistry educator*
Holbrow, Charles Howard *physicist, educator*
Linsley, Robert Martin *retired geology educator*

Hastings On Hudson
Weil, Edward David *chemist*

Hawthorne
Press, Jeffery Bruce *chemist*

Hempstead
Sparberg, Esther B. *chemist, educator*

Irvington
Devons, Samuel *educator, physicist*

Ithaca
Ashcroft, Neil William *physics educator, researcher*
Barker, Robert *biochemistry educator*
Bassett, William Akers *geologist, educator*
Batterman, Boris William *physicist, educator, academic director*
Bauer, Simon Harvey *chemistry educator*
Bauman, Dale Elton *nutritional biochemistry educator*
Berkelman, Karl *physics educator*
Bethe, Hans Albrecht *physicist, educator*
Burns, Joseph Arthur *planetary science educator*
Carpenter, Barry Keith *chemistry educator, researcher*
†Clardy, Jon Christel *chemistry educator, consultant*
Clark, David Delano *physicist, educator*
Craighead, Harold G. *physics educator*
Dodd, Jack Gordon, Jr. *physicist, educator*
Fay, Robert Clinton *chemist, educator*
Fitchen, Douglas Beach *physicist, educator*
Fleischmann, Hans Hermann Paul *physics educator*
Fréchet, Jean Marie Joseph *chemistry educator*
Freed, Jack Herschel *chemist, educator*
Gibson, Quentin Howieson *biochemist*
Gierasch, Peter Jay *astronomy educator*
Giovanelli, Riccardo *astronomer*
Gold, Thomas *astronomer, educator*
Goldsmith, Paul Felix *physics and astronomy educator*
Gottfried, Kurt *physicist, educator*
Greisen, Kenneth Ingvard *physicist, emeritus educator*
Hardy, Ralph W. F. *biochemist, biotechnology executive*
Hart, Edward Walter *physicist*
Haynes, Martha Patricia *astronomer*
Hess, George Paul *biochemist, educator*
Hoffmann, Roald *chemist, educator*
Holcomb, Donald Frank *physicist, academic administrator*
Lee, David Morris *physics educator*
Liboff, Richard Lawrence *physicist, educator*
Lumley, John Leask *physicist, educator*
McDaniel, Boyce Dawkins *physicist, educator*
McLafferty, Fred Warren *chemist, educator*
McMurry, John Edward *chemistry educator*
Meinwald, Jerrold *chemist, educator*
Mermin, N. David *physicist, educator, essayist*
Morrison, George Harold *chemist, educator*
Oglesby, Ray Thurmond *aquatic science educator*
Oliver, Jack Ertle *geophysicist*
Orear, Jay *physics educator, researcher*
Pohl, Robert Otto *physics educator*
Richardson, Robert Coleman *physics educator, researcher*
Ruoff, Arthur Louis *physicist, educator*
Sagan, Carl Edward *astronomer, educator, author*
Salpeter, Edwin Ernest *physical sciences educator*
Scheraga, Harold Abraham *physical chemistry educator*
Sievers, Albert John, III *physics educator*
Silcox, John *physicist, educator*
Slate, Floyd Owen *chemist, materials scientist, civil engineer, educator, researcher*
Terzian, Yervant *astronomy and astrophysics educator*
Thomas, J. Earl *physicist*
Tigner, Maurice *physicist, educator*
Turcotte, Donald Lawson *geophysical sciences educator*
Van Campen, Darrell Robert *chemist*
Webb, Watt Wetmore *physicist, educator*
Widom, Benjamin *chemistry educator*
Wilson, Robert Rathbun *retired physicist*
Wu, Ray Jui *biochemistry educator*
Zilversmit, Donald Berthold *nutritional biochemist, educator*

Jamaica
Greenberg, Jacob *biochemist, educator, consultant*
Lengyel, István *chemist, educator*

Kings Park
Calviello, Joseph Anthony *research electrophysicist, consultant*

Lancaster
Weinberg, Norman Louis *electrochemist*

Larchmont
Rosenberg, Paul *physicist, consultant*

Lewiston
Dexter, Theodore Henry *chemist*

Mamaroneck
Mazzola, Claude Joseph *physicist, small business owner*

Merrick
Paul, Martin Ambrose *physical chemist*

Middle Village
Farb, Edith Himel *chemist*

New York
Agosta, William Carleton *chemist, educator*
Arons, Michael Eugene *physicist, academic administrator*
Baker, Norman Hodgson, Jr. *astronomy educator*
Bederson, Benjamin *physicist, educator*
Berne, Bruce J. *chemistry educator*
Borowitz, Sidney *retired physics educator*
†Boskey, Adele Ludin *biochemistry educator, researcher*
Breslow, Ronald Charles *chemist, educator*
Campbell, George, Jr. *physicist, administrator*
Chargaff, Erwin *biochemistry educator emeritus, writer*
Cheng, Chuen Yan *biochemist, educator*
Chevray, Rene *physics educator*
Cohen, Ezechiel Godert David *physicist, educator*
Cross, George Alan Martin *biochemistry educator, researcher*
Cummins, Herman Zachary *physicist*
Dailey, Benjamin Peter *chemistry educator*
de Duve, Christian René *chemist, biologist, educator*
de Planque, E. Gail *physicist*
Diemente, Damon L. *chemistry educator*
Dunn, James Robert *geologist*
Edelman, Isidore Samuel *biochemist and medical educator*
Eisenthal, Kenneth B. *physical chemistry educator*
Erlanger, Bernard Ferdinand *biochemist, educator*
Feigelson, Philip *biochemist, educator*
Finlay, Thomas Hiram *biochemist, researcher*
Flynn, George William *chemistry educator, researcher*
Fox, Jack Jay *chemist, educator*
Fraenkel, George Kessler *chemistry educator*
Friedberg, Richard M. *physicist, educator*
Friesner, Richard A. *chemistry educator*
Gilmont, Ernest Rich *chemist*
Glassgold, Alfred Emanuel *physicist, educator*
Goldstein, Menek *neurochemistry educator*
Goulianos, Konstantin *physics educator*
Greenberger, Daniel Mordecai *physics researcher and educator*
Gross, Robert Alfred *engineering and physics educator*
Grunberger, Dezider *biochemist, researcher*
Guillen, Michael Arthur *mathematical physicist, educator, writer, television journalist*
Gyulassy, Miklos *physics educator*
Halpern, Alvin Michael *physicist, educator*
Hansen, James E. *physicist, meteorologist, federal agency administrator*
Harlow, George Eugene *mineralogist, curator*
Harris, Cyril Manton *physicist, engineering and architecture educator, consulting acoustical engineer*
Hartmann, Sven Richard *physicist, educator*
†Hendrickson, Wayne A(rthur) *biochemist, educator*
Hochstadt, Joy *biomedical research scientist, scientific and research director*
Hoffert, Martin Irving *applied science educator*
Honig, Barry Hirsh *biophysics educator*
Hutter, Rudolf Gustav Emil *physics educator*
†Kaku, Michio *theoretical nuclear physicist*
†Katz, Thomas J. *chemistry educator*
Kellogg, Herbert Humphrey *metallurgist, educator*
Khuri, Nicola Najib *physicist, educator*
Knowles, Richard James Robert *medical physicist, educator, consultant*
Komar, Arthur B. *physicist, educator*
Krasna, Alvin Isaac *biochemist, educator*
Krulwich, Terry Ann *biochemistry researcher*
Kuo, John Tsungfen *geophysicist, educator, researcher*
Laughlin, John Seth *physicist, educator*
Lax, Melvin *theoretical physicist*
Lee, Tsung-Dao *physicist, educator*
Lee, Wonyong *physicist, educator*
Lieberman, Seymour *biochemistry educator emeritus*
Low, Barbara Wharton *biochemist, biophysicist*
Luttinger, Joaquin Mazdak *retired physics educator, researcher*
Machlin, Eugene Solomon *metallurgy educator, consultant*
Marshall, Thomas Carlisle *applied physics educator*
Mauzerall, David Charles *biophysics educator, research scientist*
Mc Kenna, Malcolm Carnegie *vertebrate paleontologist, curator, educator*
Meislich, Herbert *chemistry educator emeritus*
Merrifield, Robert Bruce *biochemist, educator*
Middleton, David *physicist, applied mathematician, educator*
Nagamiya, Shoji *physicist, educator*
Nakanishi, Koji *chemistry educator, research institute administrator*
Navratil, Gerald Anton *physicist, educator*
Neumark, Gertrude Fanny *materials science educator*
Newell, Norman Dennis *paleontologist, geologist, museum curator, educator*
†Norell, Mark Allen *paleontology educator*
Novick, Robert *physicist, educator*
Nowick, Arthur Stanley *metallurgy, materials science educator*
Oppenheimer, Michael *physicist*
Oreskes, Irwin *biochemistry educator*
Osgood, Richard M., Jr. *applied physics and electrical engineering educator, research administrator*
Pais, Abraham *physicist, educator*
Parkin, Gerard Francis Ralph *chemistry educator, researcher*
Pechukas, Philip *chemistry educator*
Percus, Jerome Kenneth *physicist, educator*
Piore, Emanuel Ruben *physicist*
Pye, Lenwood David *materials science educator, researcher, consultant*
Rhodes, Yorke E(dward) *chemist*
Robinson, Enders Anthony *geophysics educator, writer*
Roeder, Robert Gayle *biochemist, educator*
Roellig, Leonard Oscar *physics educator*
Russell, Charlotte Sananes *biochemistry educator, researcher*
Sakita, Bunji *physicist, educator*
Sarachik, Myriam Paula *physics educator*
Saxena, Brij B. *biochemist, endocrinologist, educator*
Schwartz, Melvin *physics educator, laboratory administrator*
Sidran, Miriam *retired physics educator, researcher*
Simon, Eric Jacob *neurochemist, educator*
†Sleator, Tycho *physics educator*
Smith, Norman Obed *physical chemist, educator*
Sonenberg, Martin *biochemistry educator, physician*
Spector, Abraham *ophthalmic biochemist, educator, laboratory administrator*
Spiegel, Edward A. *astrophysicist, fluid dynamicist, educator*
Sprinson, David Benjamin *biochemistry educator*
Spruch, Larry *physicist, educator*
Still, William Clark, Jr. *chemistry educator*
Stork, Gilbert (Josse) *chemistry educator, investigator*
Stroke, Hinko Henry *physicist, educator*
Szer, Wlodzimierz *biochemist, educator*
Turro, Nicholas John *chemistry educator*
Verdol, Joseph Arthur *chemist*
†Werthamer, N. Richard *physicist*
†Wu, Chien Shiung *physicist*
Zakim, David *biochemist*

Niskayuna
Katz, Samuel *geophysics educator*
Lafferty, James Martin *physicist*
Mihran, Theodore Gregory *retired physicist*

Nyack
Penn, Lynn Sharon *materials scientist*

Oneonta
Hickey, Francis Roger *physicist, educator*

Orangeburg
Lajtha, Abel *biochemist*

Oswego
Silveira, Augustine, Jr. *chemistry educator*

Painted Post
Hammond, George Simms *chemist*

Palisades
Broecker, Wallace S. *geophysics educator*
Cane, Mark Alan *oceanography and climate researcher*
Fairbanks, Richard G. *geological science educator*
Hayes, Dennis Edward *geophysicist, educator*
Hays, James Douglas *geologist, educator*
Kent, Dennis Vladimir *geophysicist, researcher*
Langmuir, Charles Herbert *geology educator*
Richards, Paul Granston *geophysics educator, seismologist*
Ryan, William B. F. *geologist*
Scholz, Christopher Henry *geophysicist*
Sykes, Lynn Ray *geologist, educator*

Plattsburgh
Heintz, Roger Lewis *biochemist, educator, researcher*

Potsdam
Mackay, Raymond Arthur *chemist*
Matijevic, Egon *chemistry educator, researcher, consultant*

Poughkeepsie
Beck, Curt Werner *chemist, educator*
Deiters, Sister Joan Adele *chemistry educator, nun*
Lang, William Warner *physicist*
Maling, George Croswell, Jr. *physicist*
Pliskin, William Aaron *physicist*
Tavel, Morton Allen *physics educator, researcher*

Rochester
Abood, Leo George *biochemistry educator*
Basu, Asish Ranjan *geological sciences educator, researcher*
†Bigelow, Nicholas Pierre *physicist, educator*
Boeckman, Robert Kenneth, Jr. *chemistry educator, organic chemistry researcher*
Cline, Douglas *physicist, educator*
Coburn, Theodore James *retired physicist*
Eisenberg, Richard S. *chemistry educator*
Elder, Fred Kingsley, Jr. *physicist, educator*
Ferbel, Thomas *physics educator, physicist*
Gates, Marshall DeMotte, Jr. *chemistry educator*
George, Nicholas *optics educator, researcher*
Goldstein, David Arthur *biophysicist, educator*
Hilf, Russell *biochemist*
Kampmeier, Jack August Carlos *chemist, educator*
Kende, Andrew Steven *chemistry educator*
Khosla, Rajinder Paul *physicist*
Kingslake, Rudolf *retired optical designer*
Knauer, James Philip *physicist*
Knox, Robert Seiple *physicist, educator*
Kreilick, Robert W. *chemist, educator*
La Celle, Paul Louis *biophysics educator*
Makous, Walter Leon *visual scientist, educator*
Mandel, Leonard *physics and optics educator*
Maniloff, Jack *biophysicist, educator*
Marinetti, Guido V. *biochemistry educator*
McCrory, Robert Lee *physicist, mechanical engineering educator*
Melissinos, Adrian Constantin *physicist, educator*
Saunders, William Hundley, Jr. *chemist, educator*
Shapiro, Sidney *physicist, educator*
Simon, Albert *physicist, engineer, educator*
†Skupsky, Stanley *laser scientist*
Slattery, Paul Francis *physicist, educator*
Soures, John M. *physicist, researcher*
Thomas, John Howard *astrophysicist, engineer, educator*
Thorndike, Edward Harmon *physicist*
†Tipton, Paul Louis *physicist, educator*

Whitten, David George *chemistry educator, researcher*
Wolf, Emil *physics educator*

Rouses Point
Weierstall, Richard Paul *pharmaceutical chemist*

Saint James
Bigeleisen, Jacob *chemist, educator*

Saratoga Springs
Walter, Paul Hermann Lawrence *chemistry educator*

Scarborough
Wittcoff, Harold Aaron *chemist*

Scarsdale
Cox, Robert Hames *chemist, scientific consultant*

Schenectady
Alpher, Ralph Asher *physicist*
Anthony, Thomas Richard *research physicist*
Bulloff, Jack John *physical chemist, consultant*
†Edelheit, Lewis S. *research physicist*
Hart, Howard Roscoe, Jr. *retired physicist*
Hebb, Malcolm Hayden *physicist*
Kambour, Roger Peabody *polymer physical chemist, researcher*
Luborsky, Fred Everett *research physicist*
Peak, David *physicist, educator, researcher*
Philip, A. G. Davis *astronomer, editor, educator*
Redington, Rowland Wells *physicist, researcher*

Southold
Bachrach, Howard L. *biochemist*

Stony Brook
Alexander, John Macmillan, Jr. *chemistry educator*
Bonner, Francis Truesdale *chemist, educator, university dean*
Hanson, Gilbert Nikolai *geochemistry educator*
Herman, Herbert *materials science educator*
Kahn, Peter B. *physics educator*
†Ojima, Iwao *chemistry educator*
Pritchard, Donald William *oceanographer*
Solomon, Philip Myron *astronomer, atmospheric scientist*
Weidner, Donald J. *geophysicist educator*
Yahil, Amos *astrophysicist, educator*
Yang, Chen Ning *physicist, educator*

Syracuse
Baldwin, John Edwin *chemistry educator*
Birge, Robert Richards *chemistry educator*
Burtt, Benjamin Pickering *retired chemistry educator*
Conan, Robert James, Jr. *chemistry educator, consultant*
Fendler, Janos Hugo *chemistry educator*
Fox, Geoffrey Charles *computer science and physics educator*
Honig, Arnold *physics educator, researcher*
†Levy, H. Richard *biochemistry educator*
Martonosi, Anthony Nicholas *biochemistry educator, researcher*
Muller, Ernest H. *geology educator*
Nafie, Laurence Allen *chemistry educator*
Prucha, John James *geologist, educator*
Robinson, Joseph Edward *geology educator, consulting petroleum geologist*
Vook, Richard Werner *physics educator*
Wellner, Marcel Nahum *physics educator, researcher*

Tarrytown
Flanigen, Edith Marie *materials scientist*

Troy
Archer, Sydney *chemistry educator*
Bean, Charles Palmer *biophysicist*
Bunce, Stanley Chalmers *chemist, educator*
Corelli, John Charles *physicist, educator*
Daves, Glenn Doyle, Jr. *science educator, chemist, researcher*
Ferris, James Peter *chemist, educator*
Fleischer, Robert Louis *physics educator*
Giaever, Ivar *physicist*
Hickok, Robert Lyman, Jr. *electrophysics educator*
Koretz, Jane Faith *biophysicist*
Krause, Sonja *chemistry educator, researcher*
Levinger, Joseph Solomon *physicist, educator*
McKinley, William A. *educator, physicist*
Medicus, Heinrich Adolf *physicist, educator*
Miller, Donald Spencer *geologist, educator*
Potts, Kevin T. *emeritus chemistry educator*
Resnick, Robert *physicist, educator*
†Saxena, Arjun Nath *physicist*
Sperber, Daniel *physicist*
Wentorf, Robert Henry *physical chemist*
White, Frederick Andrew *physics educator, physicist*
Wiberley, Stephen Edward *chemistry educator, consultant*

Tuxedo Park
Hall, Frederick Keith *chemist*

Upton
Blume, Martin *physicist*
Bond, Peter Danford *physicist*
Casten, Richard Francis *physicist*
Chrien, Robert Edward *physicist*
Chung, Suh-Urk *physicist*
Dover, Carl Bellman *physicist, consultant*
Friedlander, Gerhart *nuclear chemist*
Goldhaber, Gertrude Scharff *physicist*
Goldhaber, Maurice *physicist*
Hendrie, Joseph Mallam *physicist, nuclear engineer, government official*
Kato, Walter Yoneo *physicist*
Lowenstein, Derek Irving *physicist*
Marr, Robert Bruce *physicist, educator*
Rau, Ralph Ronald *physicist*
Samios, Nicholas Peter *physicist*
Setlow, Jane Kellock *biophysicist*
Setlow, Richard Burton *biophysicist*
†Shutt, Ralph B. *research physicist*
Souw, Bernard Eng-Kie *physicist, consultant*
Studier, Frederick William *biophysicist*
Sutin, Norman *chemistry educator, scientist*
Wolf, Alfred Peter *chemist, educator*

Valhalla
Gross, Stanislaw *environmental sciences educator, activist*

Wappingers Falls
Maissel, Leon Israel *physicist, engineer*

Webster
Conwell, Esther Marly *physicist*

Wellsville
Taylor, Theodore Brewster *physicist, business executive*

West Stockholm
O'Brien, Neal Ray *geology educator*

Yorktown Heights
Chang, Chin-An *research scientist*
Fowler, Alan Bicksler *retired physicist*
†Garwin, Richard Lawrence *physicist*
Gutzwiller, Martin Charles *theoretical physicist, research scientist*
Keyes, Robert William *physicist*
Kirkpatrick, Edward Scott *physicist*
Landauer, Rolf William *physicist*
Lang, Norton David *physicist*
†Meyerson, Bernard Steele *physicist*
Ning, Tak Hung *physicist, microelectronic technologist*
Sorokin, Peter Pitirimovich *physicist*
Spiller, Eberhard Adolf *physicist*

NORTH CAROLINA

Asheville
Haggard, William Henry *meteorologist*
Smith, Norman Cutler *geologist, business executive, educator*
Squibb, Samuel Dexter *chemistry educator*

Black Mountain
Lathrop, Gertrude Adams *chemist, consultant*

Chapel Hill
†Brookhart, Maurice S. *chemist*
Buck, Richard Pierson *chemistry educator, researcher*
Bursey, Maurice M. *chemistry educator*
Butler, James Robert *geology educator*
Davis, Morris Schuyler *astronomer*
Dearman, Henry Hursell *chemistry educator*
Dennison, John Manley *geologist, educator*
Dolan, Louise Ann *physicist*
Eliel, Ernest Ludwig *chemist, educator*
Forman, Donald T. *biochemist*
Frampton, Paul Howard *physics researcher, educator*
Fullagar, Paul David *geology educator, geochemical consultant*
Goldman, Leonard Manuel *physicist, engineering educator*
Hatfield, William Emerson *chemist, educator*
Hubbard, Paul Stancyl, Jr. *physics educator*
Irene, Eugene Arthur *physical chemistry educator, researcher*
Jones, Mary Ellen *biochemist*
†Lee, Kuo-Hsiung *medicinal chemistry educator*
Macdonald, James Ross *physicist, educator*
Markham, Jordan J. *physicist, retired educator*
McKay, Kenneth Gardiner *physicist, electronics company executive*
Merzbacher, Eugen *physicist, educator*
Meyer, Thomas J. *chemistry educator*
Miller, Daniel Newton, Jr. *geologist, consultant*
Mitchell, Earl Nelson *physicist, educator*
Murray, Royce Wilton *chemistry educator*
Neumann, Andrew Conrad *geological oceanography educator*
Parr, Robert Ghormley *chemistry educator*
Roberts, Louis Douglas *physics educator, researcher*
Rogers, John James William *geology educator*
St. Jean, Joseph, Jr. *micropaleontologist, educator*
Shuman, Mark Samuel *environmental and electroanalytical chemistry educator*
Slifkin, Lawrence Myer *physics educator*
Wilson, John Eric *biochemistry educator*
Wolfenden, Richard Vance *biochemistry educator*
York, James Wesley, Jr. *theoretical physicist, educator*

Charlotte
Hall, Peter Michael *physics educator, electronics researcher*

Davidson
Burnett, John Nicholas *chemistry educator*

Durham
Bell, Robert Maurice *biochemistry educator, consultant*
Bilpuch, Edward George *nuclear physicist, educator*
Bursey, Joan Tesarek *chemist*
Chesnut, Donald Blair *chemistry educator*
Cocks, Franklin Hadley *materials scientist*
Evans, Ralph Aiken *physicist, consultant*
Fraser-Reid, Bertram Oliver *chemistry educator*
Fridovich, Irwin *biochemistry educator*
Hammes, Gordon G. *chemistry educator*
Han, Moo-Young *physicist*
Hobbs, Marcus Edwin *chemistry educator*
Jaszczak, Ronald Jack *physicist, researcher, consultant*
Joklik, Wolfgang Karl *biochemist, virologist, educator*
Mc Phail, Andrew Tennent *chemist, educator*
Meyer, Horst *physics educator*
Opara, Emmanuel Chukwuemeka *biochemistry educator*
Palmer, Richard Alan *chemistry educator*
Pearsall, George Wilbur *materials scientist, mechanical engineer, educator, consultant*
Perkins, Ronald Dee *geologist, educator*
Pilkey, Orrin H. *geology educator*
Roberson, Nathan Russell *physicist, educator*
Selkirk, James Kirkwood *biochemist*
Smith, Peter *chemist, educator, consultant*
Stroscio, Michael Anthony *physicist, educator*
Walter, Richard Lawrence *physicist, educator*
Wilder, Pelham, Jr. *chemist, pharmacologist, educator*

Greensboro
Clark, Clifton Bob *physicist*

Greenville
Clemens, Donald Faull *chemistry educator*
Frisell, Wilhelm Richard *biochemist, educator*
Sayetta, Thomas Charles *physics educator*
Snyder, Scott William *geology educator*

Hendersonville
Saby, John Sanford *physicist*

Pinehurst
Huizenga, John Robert *nuclear chemist, educator*

Pittsboro
Quinn, Jarus William *physicist, former association executive*

Raleigh
Aspnes, David Erik *physicist, educator*
Cuomo, Jerome John *materials scientist*
Davis, William Robert *physicist*
†Droessler, Earl George *geophysicist educator*
Ebisuzaki, Yukiko *chemistry educator*
Goldstein, Irving Solomon *chemistry educator, consultant*
Horton, Horace Robert *biochemistry educator*
Hugus, Z Zimmerman, Jr. *chemistry educator*
Mitchell, Gary Earl *physicist, educator*
†Murty, Korukonda Linga *nuclear science educator*
Stiles, Phillip John *physicist, educator*
Swaisgood, Harold Everett *biochemist, educator*
Whitten, Jerry Lynn *chemistry educator*

Research Triangle Park
Krenitsky, Thomas Anthony *biochemist, research director*
Rodbell, Martin *biochemist*

Salemburg
Baugh, Charles Milton *biochemistry educator, college dean*

Spring Hope
Lavatelli, Leo Silvio *retired physicist, educator*

Wilmington
Martin, Ned Harold *chemistry educator*
Worzel, John Lamar *geophysicist, educator*

Winston Salem
Mokrasch, Lewis Carl *neurochemist, educator*
Rodgman, Alan *chemist, consultant*

NORTH DAKOTA

Bismarck
Cornatzer, William Eugene *retired biochemistry educator*

Grand Forks
Duerre, John Arden *biochemist*
Jacobs, Francis Albin *biochemist, educator*
Kelley, Patricia Hagelin *geology educator*
Nordlie, Robert Conrad *biochemistry educator*
Willson, Warrack G. *physical chemist*

OHIO

Akron
†Cheng, Stephen Zheng Di *chemistry educator, polymeric material researcher*
Gent, Alan Neville *physicist, educator*
Kennedy, Joseph Paul *polymer scientist, researcher*
Piirma, Irja *chemist, educator*

Alliance
Rodman, James Purcell *astrophysicist, educator*

Athens
Eckelmann, Frank Donald *geology educator, retired*

Berea
Jensen, Adolph Robert *former chemistry educator*

Bowling Green
Brecher, Arthur Seymour *biochemistry educator*

Burbank
Koucky, Frank Louis *geology educator, archeogeology researcher*

Canton
Koniecko, Edward S(tanley) *biochemist*

Chardon
Dietrich, Joseph Jacob *retired chemist, research executive*

Cincinnati
Alexander, John J. *chemistry educator*
Carr, Albert Anthony *organic chemist*
Devitt, John William *physicist*
Ford, Emory A. *chemist, researcher*
Francis, Marion David *consulting chemist*
Goodman, Bernard *physics educator*
Gray, John Augustus *physical chemist*
Heineman, William Richard *chemistry educator*
Hubbard, Arthur Thornton *chemistry educator, electro-surface chemist*
Kang, Mohinder Singh *biochemist*
Kawahara, Fred Katsumi *research chemist*
Lienhart, David Arthur *geologist, consultant, laboratory director*
†Mark, James Edward *physical chemist*
Martin, Daniel William *acoustical physicist*
Meal, Larie *chemistry educator, consultant*
Merchant, Mylon Eugene *physicist, engineer*
Rockwell, R(onald) James, Jr. *laser and electro-optics consultant*
Rudney, Harry *biochemist, educator*
Williams, James Case *metallurgist*
Witten, Louis *physics educator*

Cleveland
Banerjee, Amiya Kumar *biochemist*
Bidelman, William Pendry *astronomer, educator*
Blackwell, John *polymer scientist, educator*
Bockhoff, Frank James *chemistry educator*
Brown, Helen Bennett *biochemist*
Carey, Paul Richard *biophysicist*
Deissler, Robert George *fluid dynamicist, researcher*
Dowell, Michael Brendan *chemist*
Hanson, Richard Winfield *biochemist, educator*
Heuer, Arthur Harold *material science and engineering educator*
Jenkins, Thomas Llewellyn *physics educator*
Klopman, Gilles *chemistry educator*
Koenig, Jack L. *chemist, educator*
Kosmahl, Henry G. *electron physicist*
Kowalski, Kenneth Lawrence *physicist, educator*
Krieger, Irvin Mitchell *chemistry educator, consultant*
Landau, Bernard Robert *biochemistry educator, physician*
Landis, Geoffrey Alan *physicist, writer*
Lando, Jerome Burton *macromolecular science educator*
Litt, Morton Herbert *macromolecular science educator, researcher*
Mawardi, Osman Kamel *plasma physicist*
Maximovich, Michael Joseph *chemist, consultant*
McGervey, John Donald *physics educator, researcher*
Olson, Walter Theodore *research scientist, consultant*
Ritchey, William Michael *chemistry educator*
Robinson, Donald Keith *physicist, educator*
Rogers, Charles Edwin *physical chemistry educator*
Savin, Samuel Marvin *geologist*
Schuele, Donald Edward *physics educator*
Taylor, Philip Liddon *physics educator*
Urbach, Frederick Lewis *chemistry educator*
Wolff, Gunther Arthur *physical chemist*
Yeager, Ernest Bill *physical chemist, electrochemist, educator*

Columbus
Behrman, Edward Joseph *biochemistry educator*
Bergstrom, Stig Magnus *geology educator*
Corbato, Charles Edward *geology educator*
Cornwell, David George *biochemist, educator*
Daehn, Glenn Steven *materials scientist*
De Lucia, Frank Charles *physicist, educator*
Elliot, David Hawksley *geologist*
Epstein, Arthur Joseph *physics and chemistry educator*
Faure, Gunter *geology educator*
Firestone, Richard Francis *chemistry educator*
Foland, Kenneth A. *geological sciences educator*
Jezek, Kenneth Charles *geophysicist, educator, researcher*
†Jossem, Edmund Leonard *physics educator*
Kolattukudy, Pappachan Ettoop *biochemist, educator*
Lipinsky, Edward Solomon *chemist*
Marzluf, George Austin *biochemistry educator*
Mayer, Victor James *earth systems science educator*
Milford, Frederick John *retired research company executive*
Miller, Terry Alan *chemistry educator*
Mills, Robert Laurence *physicist, educator*
Newsom, Gerald Higley *astronomy educator*
Noltimier, Hallan Costello *geology educator, researcher, consultant*
Osmer, Patrick Stewart *astronomer*
†Paquette, Leo Armand *chemistry educator*
Reibel, Kurt *physicist, educator*
Relle, Ferenc Matyas *chemist*
Slettebak, Arne *astronomer, educator*
Slonim, Arnold Robert *biochemist, physiologist*
Soloway, Albert Herman *medicinal chemist*
Steigman, Gary *physics and astronomy educator*
Wali, Mohan Kishen *environmental science and natural resources educator*
Webb, Thomas Evan *biochemistry educator*
Wilkins, John Warren *physics educator*
Wojcicki, Andrew Adalbert *chemist, educator*

Dayton
Battino, Rubin *chemistry educator*
Emrick, Donald Day *chemist, consultant*
Fang, Zhaoqiang *research physicist*
Gregor, Clunie Bryan *geology educator*
Janning, John Louis *research scientist, consultant*
Nam, Sang Boo *physicist*
Spicer, John Austin *physicist*
Standley, Paul Melvin *chemist*

Ironton
Mitchell, Maurice McClellan, Jr. *chemist*

Kent
†Doane, J. William *physics educator and researcher, science administrator*
Gould, Edwin Sheldon *chemist, educator*
Heimlich, Richard Allen *geologist, educator*
Tuan, Debbie Fu-Tai *chemistry educator*

Miamisburg
Avona, Vincent Leonard *chemist*

Norwalk
Germann, Richard P(aul) *chemist, chemical company executive*

Oberlin
Carlton, Terry Scott *chemist, educator*
Simonson, Bruce Miller *geologist, educator*
Wojtal, Steven Francis *geology educator, researcher*

Oxford
Baldwin, Arthur Dwight, Jr. *geology educator*
Gordon, Gilbert *chemist, educator*
Katon, John Edward *chemist, educator*
Macklin, Philip Alan *physics educator*

Painesville
†Scozzie, James Anthony *chemist*

Rootstown
Hutterer, Ferenc *biochemistry educator, researcher*

Steubenville
Kasprzak, Lucian Alexander *physics educator, researcher*

Sylvania
Kneller, William Arthur *geologist, educator*

Tiffin
Baker, David B. *environmental scientist*

Toledo
Saffran, Murray *biochemist*

†0ichards, Raymond Sears scientist, company executive

Westlake
Myers, Ira Thomas physicist

Wickliffe
Dunn, Horton, Jr. organic chemist

Wilberforce
Gupta, Vijay Kumar chemistry educator

Worthington
Idol, James Daniel, Jr. chemist, educator, inventor, consultant

Youngstown
Gillis, Bernard Thomas chemistry educator

OKLAHOMA

Ada
Stafford, Donald Gene chemistry educator

Bartlesville
Dwiggins, Claudius William, Jr. chemist
Hogan, J(ohn) Paul chemistry researcher, consultant

Broken Arrow
Chambers, Richard Lee geoscientist, researcher

Lawton
Nalley, Elizabeth Ann chemistry educator

Muskogee
Kendrick, Thomas Rudolph chemist

Norman
Atkinson, Gordon chemistry educator
Branch, David Reed astrophysicist, educator
†Christian, Sherril Duane chemistry educator
Ciereszko, Leon Stanley chemistry educator
Doviak, Richard James atmospheric scientist, engineer
Dryhurst, Glenn chemistry educator
Gal-Chen, Tzvi geophysicist, meteorologist, educator
Kessler, Edwin meteorology educator, consultant
Lamb, Peter James meteorology educator, researcher, consultant
Maddox, Robert Alan atmospheric scientist
Mankin, Charles John geology educator

Nowata
Osborn, Ann George retired chemist

Oklahoma City
Dunn, Parker Southerland retired chemical company consultant
England, Gary Alan television meteorologist
Hartsuck, Jean Ann chemist
Jackson, Gaines Bradford environmental science educator
Magarian, Robert Armen medicinal chemist, researcher, educator
Troelstra, Arne physics educator
†Walker, Bailus, Jr. environmental scientist, dean, health facility administrator
Weigel, Paul Henry biochemistry educator, researcher, consultant

Stillwater
Berlin, Kenneth Darrell chemistry educator, consultant, researcher
Gorin, George retired chemistry educator
Leach, Franklin Rollin biochemistry educator
Martin, Joel Jerome physics educator

Tulsa
Ahmadieh, Aziz metallurgy materials science educator
Breck, Howard Rolland geophysicist
Horn, Myron Kay consulting petroleum geologist, author, educator
Rummerfield, Benjamin Franklin geophysicist
Smothers, William Edgar, Jr. geophysical exploration company executive

Weatherford
Hamm, Donald Ivan retired chemistry educator, university dean

OREGON

Albany
Dooley, George Joseph, III metallurgist

Ashland
Abrahams, Sidney Cyril physicist, crystallographer
Grover, James Robb chemist, editor

Corvallis
Arp, Daniel J. biochemistry educator
Becker, Robert Richard biochemist, educator
Dalrymple, Gary Brent research geologist
Drake, Charles Whitney physicist
Evans, Harold J. plant physiologist, biochemist, educator
Huyer, Adriana oceanographer, educator
Keller, George Henrik marine geologist
Reed, Donald James biochemistry educator
Shoemaker, David Powell chemist, educator
Sleight, Arthur William chemist, educator
Thomas, Thomas Darrah chemistry educator
Van Holde, Kensal Edward biochemistry educator
†Whanger, Philip Daniel biochemistry educator and researcher, nutrition educator
Yeats, Robert Sheppard geologist, educator

Eugene
Boekelheide, Virgil Carl chemistry educator
Boggs, Sam, Jr. geology educator
Chezem, Curtis Gordon physicist, former retail executive
Crasemann, Bernd physicist, educator
Deshpande, Nilendra Ganesh physics educator
Donnelly, Russell James physicist, educator
Girardeau, Marvin Denham physics educator
Griffith, Osbie Hayes chemistry educator
Holser, William Thomas geochemistry educator, geologist
†Hutchison, James E. chemistry educator
Mazo, Robert Marc chemistry educator
Noyes, Richard Macy physical chemist, educator
Peticolas, Warner Leland physical chemistry educator
†Retallack, Gregory John geologist educator
Schellman, John A. chemistry educator
von Hippel, Peter Hans chemistry educator

Medford
Bouquet, Francis Lester physicist

Monmouth
White, Donald Harvey physicist, educator

Otter Rock
Kassner, Michael Ernest materials science educator, researcher

Portland
Claycomb, Cecil Keith biochemist, educator
Cohen, Norm chemist
Cronyn, Marshall William chemistry educator
Dunne, Thomas Gregory chemistry educator, researcher
Jones, Richard Theodore biochemistry educator
Pearson, David Petri chemist
Wetzel, Karl Joseph physics educator, university official and dean

PENNSYLVANIA

Abington
Schuster, Ingeborg Ida chemistry educator

Allentown
Goldey, James Mearns physicist
†Pez, Guido Peter research chemist

Allison Park
Xu, Zhifu chemist, researcher

Ardmore
Stanley, Edward Alexander geologist, forensic scientist, technical and academic administrator

Bethlehem
Allen, Eugene Murray chemist
Hertzberg, Richard Warren materials science and engineering educator, researcher
Kanofsky, Alvin Sheldon physicist
Sclar, Charles Bertram geology educator, researcher
Smyth, Donald Morgan chemical educator, researcher
Varnerin, Lawrence John physicist
Watkins, George Daniels physics educator
Weidner, Richard Tilghman physicist, educator

Bristol
Arkles, Barry Charles chemist

Bryn Mawr
Berliner, Ernst chemistry educator
Crawford, William Arthur geologist
Mallory, Frank Bryant chemistry educator
Platt, Lucian Brewster geology educator

Carlisle
Laws, Priscilla Watson physics educator
Long, Howard Charles physics educator emeritus

Coatesville
Bucher, John Henry metallurgical consultant, technology manager

Doylestown
Brink, Frank, Jr. biophysicst, former educator

Easton
†Sherma, Joseph chemistry educator

Elkins Park
Prince, Morton Bronenberg physicist

Erie
Karlson, Eskil Leannart biophysicist

Harrisburg
Zook, Merlin Wayne meteorologist

Haverford
Lazar, Anna chemist
Partridge, Robert Bruce astronomy educator

Hazleton
Miller, David Emanuel physics educator, researcher

King Of Prussia
Carroll, Margaret Ann chemist

Lancaster
Hess, Earl Hollinger laboratory executive, chemist

Lansdale
Schnable, George Luther chemist

Lincoln University
Williams, Willie, Jr. physicist, educator

Malvern
Fisher, Sallie Ann chemist
Frazer, Jack Winfield chemistry researcher

Meadville
Lotze, Barbara physicist

Media
Fehnel, Edward Adam chemist, educator

Monroeville
Parker, James Roger chemist

Newtown
Carlson, David Emil physicist
Leibholz, Stephen Wolfgang physicist, engineering company executive, entrepreneur
Long, Harry (On-Yuen Eng) chemist, rubber science and technology consultant

Norristown
Kopple, Kenneth D. chemistry researcher, educator

Philadelphia
Ajzenberg-Selove, Fay physicist, educator
Benfey, Otto Theodor chemist, educator, editor, historian of science
Bludman, Sidney Arnold theoretical physicist, astrophysicist
Burstein, Elias physicist, educator
Chance, Britton biophysics and physical chemistry educator emeritus
Childress, Scott Julius medicinal chemist
Cohn, Mildred biochemist, educator
Creech, Hugh John chemist
Davis, Raymond, Jr. physical chemistry researcher
Devlin, Thomas McKeown biochemist
Dymicky, Michael retired chemist
Farber, Emmanuel pathology and biochemistry educator
Fitts, Donald Dennis chemist, educator
Frankel, Sherman physicist
Glick, Jane Mills biochemistry educator
Hameka, Hendrik Frederik chemist, educator
Harker, Robert Ian geologist, educator
Havas, Peter physicist, educator
Hirschmann, Ralph Franz chemist
Intemann, Robert Louis physics educator, researcher
Kay, Jack Garvin chemist, educator
Klein, Abraham physics educator, researcher
Klein, Michael Lawrence research chemist, educator
Kritchevsky, David biochemist, educator
Langacker, Paul George physics educator
Larson, Donald Clayton physics educator, consultant
Levitt, Israel Monroe astronomer
Liebman, Paul Arno biophysicist, educator
Litwack, Gerald biochemistry researcher, educator, administrator
Magee, Wayne Edward biochemistry educator, researcher
Malamud, Daniel biochemistry educator
Maurer, Paul Herbert biochemist, educator
Nixon, Eugene Ray chemist, educator
Noordergraaf, Abraham biophysics educator
Pollack, Solomon Robert bioengineering educator
Prockop, Darwin Johnson biochemist, physician
Rosen, Gerald Harris physicist, consultant, educator
Rutman, Robert Jesse biochemist, educator
Sage, Louis E. environmental science executive
†Scherer, Norbert Franz chemistry educator
Shen, Benjamin Shih-Ping scientist, engineer, educator
Steinhardt, Paul Joseph physics educator, consultant
Vitek, Vaclav materials scientist
Wales, Walter D. physicist, educator
Weisz, Paul B(urg) physicist, chemical engineer
Zurmuhle, Robert Walter physicist

Pittsburgh
Anderson, Russell Karl, Jr. physicist, horse breeder
Berry, Guy Curtis polymer science educator, researcher
Biondi, Manfred Anthony physicist, educator
Bothner-By, Aksel Arnold chemist, horseman
Caretto, Albert Alexander chemist, educator
Carr, Walter James, Jr. research physicist, consultant
Cassidy, William Arthur geology and planetary science educator
Choyke, Wolfgang Justus physicist
Cohen, Bernard Leonard physicist, educator
Coltman, John Wesley physicist
†Dowd, Paul chemistry educator
Emmerich, Werner Sigmund physicist
Feller, Robert Livingston chemist, art conservation scientist
Finn, Frances Mary biochemistry researcher
Gerjuoy, Edward physicist, lawyer
Griffiths, Robert Budington physics educator
Janis, Allen Ira retired physicist, educator
Jasnow, David Michael physics educator
Kisslinger, Leonard Sol physicist, educator
Laughlin, David Eugene materials science educator, metallurgical consultant
Massalski, Thaddeus Bronislaw material scientist, educator
†Matyjaszewski, Krzysztof chemist, educator
Page, Lorne Albert physicist, educator
Pratt, Richard Houghton physics educator
Rosenberg, Jerome Laib chemist, educator
Rosenkranz, Herbert S. environmental toxicology educator
Sax, Martin crystallographer
Sekerka, Robert Floyd physics educator, scientist
White, Robert Marshall physicist, educator
Wolken, Jerome Jay biophysicist, educator
Wynblatt, Paul Pinhas materials science educator, researcher
Yasinsky, John Bernard nuclear scientist
Yates, John Thomas, Jr. chemistry educator, researcher
Young, Hugh David physics educator, writer, organist

Plymouth Meeting
Carriker, Roy C. physicist

Reading
Rowe, Jay E., Jr. research and development director

State College
Garrett, Steven Lurie physicist
Landy, Richard Allen former geologist, consultant
Rusinko, Frank, Jr. fuels and materials scientist

Swarthmore
Bilaniuk, Oleksa Myron physicist, educator
Hammons, James Hutchinson chemistry educator, researcher
Pasternack, Robert Francis chemistry educator

University Park
Allcock, Harry Rex chemistry educator
Amateau, Maurice Francis materials scientist, educator
†Badding, John Victor chemistry educator
Barnes, Hubert Lloyd geochemistry educator
†Benkovic, Stephen James chemist
Bernheim, Robert Allan chemistry educator
Blackadar, Alfred Kimball meteorologist, educator
Cahir, John Joseph meteorologist, educational administrator
Castleman, Albert Welford, Jr. physical chemist, educator
Coleman, Michael Murray polymer science educator
Dutton, John Altnow meteorologist, educator
Frankl, Daniel Richard educator, physicist
Garmire, Gordon Paul astronomer, educator
German, Randall Michael materials science educator, consultant
Hardy, Henry Reginald, Jr. geophysicist, educator
Herman, Roger M. physicist, educator
†Hogg, Richard physical chemistry educator
Hosler, Charles Luther, Jr. meteorologist, educator
Howell, Benjamin Franklin, Jr. geophysicist, educator
Jackman, Lloyd Miles chemistry educator
Jurs, Peter Christian chemistry educator
Lampe, Frederick Walter chemistry educator, consultant
Osborn, Elburt Franklin former geochemistry educator, research scientist
Pazur, John Howard biochemist, educator
Roy, Rustum interdisciplinary materials researcher, educator
White, William Blaine geochemist, educator
Winograd, Nicholas chemist
†Zhang, Xumu chemist, educator

Valley Forge
Erb, Doretta Louise Barker polymer applications scientist
Erb, Robert Allan physical scientist
Hergert, Herbert Lawrence chemist

Villanova
Cordes, Eugene Harold biochemist
Edwards, John Ralph chemist, educator
Phares, Alain Joseph physicist, educator

Wyncote
Baldridge, Robert Crary retired biochemistry educator

Wynnewood
Weinhouse, Sidney biochemist, educator

Wyomissing
Boyer, Robert Allen physics educator

RHODE ISLAND

Kingston
Cruickshank, Alexander Middleton chemistry educator
Nixon, Scott West oceanography science educator

Narragansett
Leinen, Margaret Sandra oceanographic researcher
Pilson, Michael Edward Quinton oceanography educator
Sherman, Kenneth oceanographer
Sigurdsson, Haraldur oceanography educator, researcher

Providence
Avery, Donald Hills metallurgist, educator, ethnographer
Beyer, Robert Thomas physicist, educator
Bray, Philip James physicist
Briant, Clyde Leonard metallurgist, researcher
Carpenter, Gene Blakely crystallography and chemistry educator
Cooper, Leon N. physicist, educator
Cutts, David physics educator
Dahlberg, Albert Edward biochemistry educator
Doll, Jimmie Dave chemistry educator
Elbaum, Charles physicist, educator, researcher
Estrup, Peder Jan physics and chemistry educator
Forsyth, Donald William geophysics educator
Gerritsen, Hendrik Jurjen physics educator, researcher
Greene, Edward Forbes chemistry educator
Houghton, Anthony physics educator, research scientist
Kang, Kyungsik physics educator
Lanou, Robert Eugene, Jr. physicist, educator
Levin, Frank S. physicist, educator
Maris, Humphrey John physicist, educator
Rieger, Philip Henri chemistry educator, researcher
Risen, William Maurice, Jr. chemistry educator
Stratt, Richard Mark chemist, educator
Tauc, Jan physics educator
Tullis, Julia Ann (Jan Tullis) geologist, educator
Ward, Harold Roy chemist, educator
Webb, Thompson geological sciences educator, researcher
Westervelt, Peter Jocelyn physics educator
Widgoff, Mildred physicist, educator

Wakefield
Moore, George Emerson, Jr. geologist, educator
Zuehlke, Richard William technical communications consultant, writer

West Kingston
Abell, Paul Irving retired chemistry educator

SOUTH CAROLINA

Aiken
Dickson, Paul Wesley, Jr. physicist
Hofstetter, Kenneth John research chemist
Miller, Phillip Edward environmental scientist

Charleston
Adelman, Saul Joseph astronomy educator, researcher
Berglund, Robin G. biochemist, former corporate executive
Delli Colli, Humbert Thomas chemist, product development specialist
Gadsden, Richard Hamilton clinical biochemistry educator
Swanson, Arnold Arthur retired biochemistry educator

Clemson
Clayton, Donald Delbert *astrophysicist, nuclear physicist, educator*
DesMarteau, Darryl Dwayne *chemistry and geology educator*
Griffin, Villard Stuart, Jr. *geology educator*

Columbia
Edge, Ronald Dovaston *physics educator*
Kanes, William Henry *geology educator, research center administrator*
Secor, Donald Terry, Jr. *geologist, educator*
Teague, Peyton Clark *chemist, educator*

Conway
Skinner, Samuel Ballou, III *physics educator, researcher*

Johns Island
Failla, Patricia McClement *biomedical and environmental research administrator*

Pendleton
Spain, James Dorris, Jr. *biochemist, educator*

Salem
Gentry, Robert Cecil *meteorological consultant, research scientist*

Spartanburg
Cavin, William Pinckney *chemist, educator*

SOUTH DAKOTA

Brookings
Duffey, George Henry *physics educator*

Rapid City
Gries, John Paul *geologist*
Lisenbee, Alvis Lee *structural geologist, educator*
Smith, Paul Letton, Jr. *geophysicist*

Spearfish
Erickson, Richard Ames *physicist, emeritus educator*

Vermillion
Neuhaus, Otto Wilhelm *biochemistry educator*

TENNESSEE

Chattanooga
Kiser, Thelma Kay *analytical chemist*

Dyersburg
Bell, Helen Cherry *chemistry educator*

Hendersonville
Hill, William Thomas *geological consultant*

Jefferson City
Bahner, Carl Tabb *retired chemistry educator, researcher*

Johnson City
Huang, Thomas Tao-shing *chemistry educator*

Kingsport
Holmes, Jerry Dell *organic chemist*
Young, Howard Seth *chemist, researcher*

Kingston
Manly, William Donald *metallurgist*

Knoxville
Alexeff, Igor *physicist, electrical engineer, educator*
Blass, William Errol *physics and astronomy educator*
Dean, John Aurie *chemist, author, chemistry educator emeritus*
Fox, John David *educator, physicist*
Lietzke, Milton Henry *chemistry educator*
Mahan, Gerald Dennis *physics educator, researcher*
Mamantov, Gleb *chemistry educator, consultant*
Painter, Linda Robinson *physics educator, dean*
Schweitzer, George Keene *chemistry educator*
Williams, Thomas Ffrancon *chemist, educator*
Wunderlich, Bernhard *physical chemistry educator*

Lenoir City
Breazeale, Mack Alfred *physics educator*

Memphis
Crane, Laura Jane *research chemist*
Desiderio, Dominic Morse, Jr. *chemistry and neurochemistry educator*
Fain, John Nicholas *biochemistry educator*
Johnston, Archibald Currie *geophysics educator, research director*
Lasslo, Andrew *medicinal chemist, educator*
Shugart, Cecil Glenn *physics educator*
Wildman, Gary Cecil *chemist*

Mount Juliet
Sweetman, Brian Jack *organic, analytical chemist, educator*

Nashville
†Bayuzick, Robert J. *material scientist, educator*
Brau, Charles Allen *physics educator*
Chytil, Frank *biochemist*
†Clarke, James Harold *environmental scientist, educator*
Cohen, Stanley *biochemistry educator*
Cunningham, Leon William *biochemist, educator*
Dettbarn, Wolf-Dietrich *neurochemist, pharmacologist, educator*
Fort, Tomlinson *chemist, chemical engineering educator*
Guengerich, Frederick Peter *biochemistry educator, toxicologist, researcher*
Hall, Douglas Scott *astronomy educator*
Hamilton, Joseph Hants, Jr. *physicist, educater*
Harris, Thomas Munson *chemistry educator, researcher*
Heiser, Arnold Melvin *astronomer*
Hercules, David Michael *chemistry educator, consultant*
Holladay, Wendell Gene *physics educator*
Inagami, Tadashi *biochemist, educator*
Kono, Tetsuro *biochemist, physiologist, educator*
Lukehart, Charles Martin *chemistry educator*
Martin, James Cullen *chemistry educator*
†Miller, Calvin Francis *geology educator*
Panvini, Robert S. *physics educator*
Stubbs, Gerald *biochemist, educator*
Tarbell, Dean Stanley *chemistry educator*
Tolk, Norman Henry *physics educator*
Weeks, Robet Andrew *materials science researcher, educator*
Wert, James Junior *materials scientist, educator*
Wilson, David James *chemistry educator*

Oak Ridge
Beasley, Cloyd Orris, Jr. *physicist, researcher*
Burtis, Carl A., Jr. *chemist*
Cawley, Charles Nash *enviromental scientist*
Eatherly, Walter Pasold *physicist, consultant*
Garrett, Jerry Dale *nuclear physicist*
Gifford, Franklin Andrew, Jr. *meteorologist*
†Huff, Dale Duane *hydrologist, educator*
Krause, Manfred Otto *physicist*
Larson, Bennett Charles *solid state physicist, researcher*
Maienschein, Fred C. *physicist*
Plasil, Franz *physicist*
Postma, Herman *physicist, consultant*
Poutsma, Marvin L. *chemical research administration*
Renshaw, Amanda Frances *physicist, nuclear engineer*
Satchler, George Raymond *physicist*
Sellin, Ivan Armand *physicist, educator, researcher*
Totter, John Randolph *biochemist*
Trivelpiece, Alvin William *physicist, corporate executive*
Weinberg, Alvin Martin *physicist*
Wilkinson, Michael Kennerly *physicist*
Zucker, Alexander *physicist, administrator*

Powell
†Gentry, Robert Vance *physicist, researcher, writer*

TEXAS

Arlington
Burkart, Burke *geology educator, researcher*
Perkins, Bob(by) F(rank) *geologist, dean*
Pomerantz, Martin *chemistry educator, researcher*
†Rajeshwar, Krishnan *chemist, educator*
Schimelpfenig, C(larence) W(illiam), Jr. *chemistry educator*
Smith, Charles Isaac *geology educator*

Austin
Bailey, Philip Sigmon *chemistry educator*
Bard, Allen Joseph *chemist, educator*
Barker, Daniel Stephen *geology educator*
Bash, Frank Ness *astronomer, educator*
Bengtson, Roger Dean *physicist*
Boggs, James Ernest *chemistry educator*
Boyer, Robert Ernst *geologist, educator*
Campion, Alan *chemistry educator*
de Vaucouleurs, Gerard Henri *astronomer, educator*
de Wette, Frederik Willem *physics educator*
De Witt, Bryce Seligman *physics educator*
De Witt-Morette, Cécile *physicist*
Douglas, James Nathaniel *astronomer, educator*
Drummond, William Eckel *physics educator*
Duncombe, Raynor Lockwood *astronomer*
Ellison, Samuel Porter, Jr. *geologist, educator*
Erskine, James Lorenzo *physics educator*
Evans, David Stanley *astronomy educator*
Fisher, William Lawrence *geologist, educator*
Folk, Robert Louis *geologist, educator*
Folkers, Karl August *chemistry educator*
Fonken, Gerhard Joseph *retired chemistry educator, academic administrator*
Fox, Marye Anne *chemistry educator*
Gardiner, William Cecil, Jr. *chemist, educator*
Gavenda, J(ohn) David *physicist*
Gentle, Kenneth William *physicist*
Gleeson, Austin Michael *physicist, educator*
Griffy, Thomas Alan *physics educator*
Hazeltine, Richard Deimel *physics educator, university institute director*
Heller, Adam *chemist, researcher*
Herman, Robert *physics educator*
Ho, Paul Siu-Chung *physics educator*
Hudspeth, Emmett LeRoy *physicist, educator*
Jefferys, William Hamilton, III *astronomer*
Lagowski, J(oseph) J(ohn) *chemist*
†Longenecker, John Bender *biochemist, nutritionist, educator*
Lundelius, Ernest Luther, Jr. *vertebrate paleontologist, educator*
Matzner, Richard Alfred *physicist, educator*
Maxwell, Arthur Eugene *oceanographer, marine geophysicist, educator*
Mohrmann, Leonard Edward, Jr. *chemist, chemical engineer*
Moore, James Robert *geological oceanographer*
Oakes, Melvin Ervin Louis *physics educator*
Pradzynski, Andrzej Henryk *chemist*
Prigogine, Vicomte Ilya *physics educator*
Reed, Lester James *biochemist, educator*
Schwitters, Roy Frederick *physicist, educator*
Sharp, John Malcolm, Jr. *geology educator*
Smoluchowski, Roman *physicist, emeritus educator*
Snell, Esmond Emerson *biochemist*
Swinney, Harry Leonard *physics educator*
Wheeler, John Craig *astrophysicist, writer*
White, John Michael *chemistry educator*
Willson, C. Grant *chemistry educator, engineering educator*
Ziegler, Daniel Martin *chemistry educator*

Baytown
Mendelson, Robert Allen *polymer scientist, rheologist*

Beaumont
Walker, John Michael *environmental hydrogeologist, consultant*

College Station
Anderson, Aubrey Lee *oceanographer, educator*
Anderson, Duwayne Marlo *earth and polar scientist, university administrator*
Arnowitt, Richard Lewis *physics educator, researcher*
Berg, Robert Raymond *geologist, educator*
Berner, Leo De Witte, Jr. *retired oceanographer*
Carter, Neville Louis *geophysicist, educator*
Conway, Dwight Colbur *chemistry educator*
Cotton, Frank Albert *chemist, educator*
†Darensbourg, Marcetta York *chemistry educator*
†Duce, Robert Arthur *atmospheric chemist, university administrator*
Fackler, John Paul, Jr. *chemistry educator*
Friedman, Melvin *geology educator, college dean*
Laane, Jaan *chemistry educator*
Martell, Arthur Earl *chemistry educator*
McIntyre, John Armin *physics educator*
McIntyre, Peter Mastin *physicist, educator*
Nachman, Ronald James *research chemist*
Natowitz, Joseph B. *chemistry educator, administrator, researcher*
O'Connor, Rod *chemist, inventor*
Orville, Richard Edmonds *atmospheric science educator*
Prescott, John Mack *biochemist, retired university administrator*
Rezak, Richard *geology and oceanography educator*
Rowe, Gilbert Thomas *oceanography educator*
Scott, Alastair Ian *chemistry educator*
Stanton, Robert James, Jr. *geologist, educator*
Stewart, Robert Henry *oceanographer, educator*
Stipanovic, Robert Douglas *chemist, researcher*
†Wild, James Robert *biochemistry and biophysics educator*

Corpus Christi
Berryhill, Henry Lee, Jr. *geologist*
Roels, Oswald Albert *oceanographer, educator, business executive*

Dallas
Blattner, Wolfram Georg Michael *meteorologist*
Brooks, James Elwood *geologist, educator*
Esquivel, Agerico Liwag *research physicist*
Estabrook, Ronald Winfield *chemistry educator*
Gibbs, James Alanson *geologist*
Green, Cecil Howard *geophysicist, consultant, educator*
Johnson, Richard Clayton *engineer, physicist*
Konrad, Dusan *chemist*
McAlester, Arcie Lee, Jr. *geologist, educator*
Montgomery, Edward Benjamin *physicist, retired educator*
Ray, Bradley Stephen *petroleum geologist*
Ries, Edward Richard *petroleum geologist, consultant*
Srere, Paul A. *biochemist, educator*
Toohig, Timothy E. *physicist*

Denton
Brostow, Witold Konrad *materials scientist, educator*
Golden, David Edward *physicist*

El Paso
Cook, Clarence Sharp *physics educator*
Hardaway, Robert Morris, III *physician, educator, retired army officer*

Fort Worth
Battista, Orlando Aloysius *scientist, author, executive, inventor*
Gutsche, Carl David *chemistry educator*
Landolt, Robert George *chemistry educator*
Quarles, Carroll Adair, Jr. *physicist, educator*
Reinecke, Manfred G. *chemistry educator*
Smith, William Burton *chemist, educator*
Webb, Theodore Stratton, Jr. *aerospace scientist, consultant*

Galveston
Bonchev, Danail Georgiev *chemist, educator*
Gorenstein, David G. *chemistry educator*
Kurosky, Alexander *biochemist, educator*
Merrell, William John, Jr. *oceanography educator*
Schoenbucher, Bruce *health physicist*

Georgetown
White, Alvin Swauger *aerospace scientist, consultant*

Granger
Horton, Claude Wendell *physicist, educator*

Horseshoe Bay
Ramey, James Melton *chemist*

Houston
Anderson, Richard Carl *geophysical exploration company executive*
Askew, William Earl *chemist, educator*
Baker, Stephen Denio *physics educator*
Bally, Albert W. *geology educator*
Bennett, George Nelson *biochemistry educator*
Berry, Julianne Elward *polymer and colloid chemist, researcher, inventor*
Bonner, Billy Edward *physics educator*
Brandt, I. Marvin *chemist, engineer*
Brooks, Philip Russell *chemistry educator, researcher*
Brotzen, Franz Richard *materials science educator*
Burke, Kevin Charles Antony *geologist*
Cantwell, Thomas *geophysicist, electrical engineer*
Chaku, Pran Nath *international consulting metallurgist*
Chamberlain, Joseph Wyan *astronomer, educator*
Chu, Paul Ching-Wu *physicist*
Chu, Wei-Kan *physicist, educator*
Curl, Robert Floyd, Jr. *chemistry educator*
De Bremaecker, Jean-Claude *geophysics educator*
Engel, Paul Sanford *educator*
Estle, Thomas Leo *physicist, educator*
Fukuyama, Tohru *organic chemistry educator*
Gibson, Everett Kay, Jr. *space scientist, geochemist*
Gibson, Robert Lee *astronaut*
Glantz, Raymon M. *biochemist, biologist, educator*
Gordon, William Edwin *physicist, engineer, educator, university official*
Hackerman, Norman *chemist, university president*
Hasling, Jill Freeman *meteorologist*
Haymes, Robert C. *physicist, educator*
Horning, Marjorie G. *biochemistry educator*
Huang, Huey Wen *physics educator*
Hungerford, Ed Vernon, III *physics educator*
Kevan, Larry *chemistry educator*
Kinsey, James Lloyd *chemist, educator*
Kit, Saul *biochemist, educator*
Kochi, Jay Kazuo *chemist, educator*
Kouri, Donald Jack *chemist, educator*
Kraus-Friedmann, Naomi *biochemistry educator*
LeBlanc, Rufus Joseph, Sr. *geology educator, consultant, researcher*
Lewis, Edward Sheldon *chemistry educator*
Liang, Edison Parktak *astrophysicist, educator, researcher*
Margrave, John Lee *chemist, educator, university administrator*
†Marsh, John *research chemist*
Mateker, Emil Joseph, Jr. *geophysicist*
Matthews, Kathleen Shive *biochemistry educator*
McCleary, Henry Glen *geophysicist*
McMillin, Jeanie Byrd *biochemist, medical educator*
Mehra, Jagdish *physicist*
Norton, Norman James *exploration geologist*
O'Dell, Charles Robert *astronomer, educator*
Page, Thornton Leigh *astrophysicist*
Reiff, Patricia Hofer *space physicist, educator*
Reso, Anthony *geologist, earth resources economist*
Rudolph, Frederick Byron *biochemistry educator*
Savit, Carl Hertz *geophysicist*
Schroepfer, George John, Jr. *biochemistry educator*
Scuseria, Gustavo Enrique *theoretical chemist*
Sisson, Virginia Baker *geology educator*
Skolnick, Malcolm Harris *biophysics researcher, educator, patent lawyer, mediator*
†Slaugh, Lynn H. *chemist*
Smalley, Richard Errett *chemistry and physics educator, researcher*
Smith, Michael Alexis *petroleum geologist*
†Speed, Stan *research chemist*
†Stehling, Ferdinand Christian *physical chemist*
Stormer, John Charles, Jr. *geology educator, mineralogist*
Talwani, Manik *geophysicist, educator*
Trammell, George Thomas *physics educator*
Vail, Peter Robbins *geologist*
Wakil, Salih Jawad *biochemistry educator*
Walters, Geoffrey King *physicist, educator*
Weinstein, Roy *physics educator, researcher*
Weisheit, Jon Carleton *physicist, educator*
Willcott, Mark Robert, III *chemist, educator, researcher*
Wold, Finn *biochemist, educator*
Zlatkis, Albert *chemistry educator*

Irving
Hendrickson, Constance Marie McRight *chemist, consultant*

Kingwood
Brinkley, Charles Alexander *geologist*
Davies, David Keith *geologist*

Lake Jackson
Tasa, Kendall Sherwood *chemistry educator*

Lubbock
Murray, Grover Elmer *geologist, educator*
Robinson, G. Wilse *molecular spectroscopist, educator*
Shine, Henry Joseph *chemistry educator*

New Braunfels
Wilson, James Lee *retired geology educator, consultant*

Odessa
Reeves, Robert Grier LeFevre *geology educator, scientist*

Orange
Adkins, John E(arl), Jr. *chemist*

Plano
Broyles, Michael Lee *geophysics and physics educator*

Richardson
Cordell, Robert James *retired geologist*
Johnson, Francis Severin *physicist*
Landisman, Mark *geophysicist, educator*
Nevill, William Albert *chemistry educator*

Richmond
Willis, David Edwin *retired geophysicist*

San Antonio
Ball, M(ary) Isabel *chemistry educator, dean*
Budalur, Thyagarajan Subbanarayan *chemistry educator*
Burton, Russell Rohan *aerospace scientist, researcher*
Doyle, Frank Lawrence *geologist, hydrologist, executive*
Hamm, William Joseph *retired physics educator*
Hanahan, Donald James *biochemist, educator*
Howard, M. Francine *chemist*
Lyle, Robert Edward *chemist*
Mills, Nancy Stewart *chemistry educator*
Siler-Khodr, Theresa Marie *biochemistry educator*

San Marcos
Cassidy, Patrick Edward *chemist, educator*

Spring
Clark, Carolyn Archer *aerosopace scientist*

The Woodlands
Levy, Robert Edward *biotechnology company executive*

Tyler
†Locklin, Allen Clement *petroleum exploration geologist*

Waco
Pedrotti, Leno Stephano *physics educator*

Wichita Falls
Sund, Eldon Harold *chemistry educator*

UTAH

Garrison
Beeston, Joseph Mack *metallurgist*

Logan
Aust, Steven Douglas *biochemistry, biotechnology and toxicology educator*
Scouten, William Henry *chemistry educator, academic administrator*

Steed, Allan J. *physical science research administrator*

Ogden
Buss, Walter Richard *geology educator*
Welch, Garth Larry *chemistry educator*

Provo
Hall, Howard Tracy *chemist*

Salt Lake City
Allison, Merle Lee *geologist*
Boyd, Richard Hays *chemistry educator*
DeCourten, Frank L. *earth science educator*
Dick, Bertram Gale, Jr. *physics educator*
Foltz, Rodger Lowell *chemistry educator, mass spectroscopist*
Giddings, J. Calvin *chemistry educator*
Grant, David Morris *chemistry educator*
Hill, George Richard *chemistry educator*
Miller, Jan Dean *metallurgy educator*
Miller, Joel Steven *solid state scientist*
Oblad, Alexander Golden *chemistry educator, research chemist*
O'Halloran, Thomas Alphonsus, Jr. *physicist, educator*
Parry, Robert Walter *chemistry educator*
Partridge, William Schaubel *retired physicist, research company executive*
†Poulter, Charles Dale *chemist, educator, consultant*
Stang, Peter John *organic chemist*
Velick, Sidney Frederick *research biochemist, educator*
Warnick, Charles Terry *research biochemist*

VERMONT

Burlington
Chiu, Jen-Fu *biochemistry educator*
Rankin, Joanna Marie *astronomy educator*
White, William North *chemistry educator*

Middlebury
Gleason, Robert Willard *chemistry educator, college dean*
†Winkler, Paul Frank, Jr. *astrophysicist, educator*

Norwich
Drake, Charles Lum *geology educator*
Naumann, Robert Bruno Alexander *chemist, physicist, educator*

Thetford
Hoagland, Mahlon Bush *biochemist, educator*

VIRGINIA

Alexandria
Berman, Alan *physicist*
Biberman, Lucien Morton *physicist*
Brenner, Alfred Ephraim *physicist*
Campbell, Francis James *retired chemist*
Masterson, Kleber Sanlin, Jr. *physicist*
Milling, Marcus Eugene, Sr. *geologist*
Mooney, John Bradford, Jr. *oceanographer, engineer, consultant*
Muir, Warren R. *chemist, toxic substances specialist*
Sayre, Edward Vale *chemist*
Shapiro, Maurice Mandel *astrophysicist*
Straus, Leon Stephan *physicist*
Toulmin, Priestley *geologist*
Wolicki, Eligius Anthony *nuclear physicist, consultant*
Yaworsky, George Myroslaw *physicist, technical and management consultant*

Annandale
Matuszko, Anthony Joseph *research chemist, administrator*

Arlington
Barnhart, Beverly Jean *physicist*
Bautz, Laura Patricia *astronomer*
Berg, John Richard *chemist, former federal government executive*
Borchers, Robert Reece *physicist and administrator*
†Cavanaugh, Margaret C. *chemist*
Dickman, Robert Laurence *physicist, researcher*
Ensminger, Luther Glenn *chemist*
Erb, Karl Albert *physicist, government official*
Gergely, Tomas *astronomer*
†Hartwig, Eric Owen *oceanographer*
Hays, James Fred *geologist, educator*
Heineken, Frederick George *biochemical engineer*
†Johnson, Charles Nelson, Jr. *physicist*
Lawrence, Ray Vance *chemist*
Romney, Carl F. *seismologist*
Sancetta, Constance Antonina *oceanographer*
Sinclair, Rolf Malcolm *physicist*
Teichert, Curt *geologist, educator*
Wayland, Russell Gibson, Jr. *geology consultant, retired government official*
Whitcomb, James Hall *geophysicist, foundation administrator*
Wodarczyk, Francis John *chemist*
Yankwich, Peter Ewald *chemistry educator*
Zirkind, Ralph *physicist*

Blacksburg
Bauer, Henry Hermann *chemistry and science educator*
Cairns, John, Jr. *environmental science educator, researcher*
†McGrath, James Edward *chemistry educator*
Mo, Luke Wei *physicist, educator*
Ogliaruso, Michael Anthony *chemist, educator*
Stewart, Kent Kallam *analytical biochemistry educator*

Charlottesville
Biltonen, Rodney Lincoln *biochemistry and pharmacology educator*
Boring, John Wayne *physicist, educator*
Bradbeer, Clive *biochemistry and microbiology educator, research scientist*
Brill, Arthur Sylvan *biophysics educator*
Carpenter, Richard Amon *chemist*
Chevalier, Roger Alan *astronomy educator, consultant*
Du Bar, Jules Ramon *geologist, retired educator*
Fredrick, Laurence William *astronomer, educator*
Gaskin, Felicia *biochemist, educator*
Goodell, Horace Grant *environmental sciences educator*
Greene, Virginia Carvel *chemist*
Grimes, Russell Newell *chemistry educator, inorganic chemist*
Grisham, Charles Milton *biochemist, educator*
Gugelot, Piet Cornelis *physics educator*
Hereford, Frank Loucks, Jr. *physicist, educator*
†Hunt, Donald Frederick *chemistry educator, researcher*
Kellermann, Kenneth Irwin *astronomer*
Kerr, Anthony Robert *scientist*
Kuhlmann-Wilsdorf, Doris *physics and materials science educator*
Martin, Robert Bruce *chemistry educator*
Meem, James Lawrence, Jr. *nuclear scientist*
Roberts, Morton Spitz *astronomer*
Sarazin, Craig Leigh *astronomer*
Shugart, Herman Henry *environmental sciences educator, researcher*
Sobottka, Stanley E. *physics educator*
Song, Xiaotong *physicist, educator*
Starke, Edgar Arlin, Jr. *metallurgist, educator*
Sundberg, Richard Jay *chemistry educator*
†Turner, Barry Earl *radio astronomer*
Vanden Bout, Paul Adrian *astronomer, physicist, educator*
Weber, Hans Jürgen *physics educator*

Dahlgren
Holt, William Henry *physicist, researcher*

Fairfax
Cary, Boyd Balford, Jr. *physicist*
Morowitz, Harold Joseph *biophysicist, educator*
Ozernoy, Leonid Moissey *astrophysicist*
Singer, S(iegfried) Fred *geophysicist, educator*
Trefil, James S. *physicist, educator*

Falls Church
Benson, William Edward (Barnes) *geologist*
Feldmann, Edward George *pharmaceutical chemist*
Spindel, William *chemistry educator, scientist, educational administrator*

Great Falls
Masters, Charles Day *geologist*

Hampden Sydney
Joyner, Weyland Thomas *physicist, educator, business consultant*
Kniffen, Donald Avery *astrophysicist, educator, researcher*
Porterfield, William Wendell *chemist, educator*

Hampton
Allario, Frank *aerospace science research administrator*
†Deepak, Adarsh *meteorologist, aerospace engineer, atmospheric scientist*
Houbolt, John Cornelius *physicist*
†McCormick, Michael Patrick *optics scientist, meteorologist*
Tenney, Darrel R. *materials science administrator*

Herndon
Crossfield, Albert Scott *aeronautical science consultant, pilot*

Kinsale
Gould, Gordon *physicist, retired optical communications executive*

Lexington
Spencer, Edgar Winston *geology educator*

Lynchburg
Morgan, Evan *chemist*

Manassas
Tidman, Derek Albert *physics researcher*

Manassas Park
Bussard, Robert William *physicist*

Mc Lean
Carter, William Walton *physicist*
Cotterill, Carl Hayden *mineral and metals company executive*
Doyle, Frederick Joseph *government research scientist*
Hoffman, Ronald Bruce *biophysicist, life scientist, human factors consultant*

Middleburg
Spilhaus, Athelstan *meteorologist, oceanographer*

Newport News
Cardman, Lawrence S. *physics educator*
Isgur, Nathan Gerald *physicist, educator*

Norfolk
Schellenberg, Karl Abraham *biochemist*

Purcellville
Conte, Joseph John, II *meteorologist, management consultant*

Reston
Barton, Paul Booth, Jr. *geologist*
Brett, Robin *geologist*
†Burton, James Samuel *physical chemist*
Clark, Sandra Helen Becker *geologist*
Cohen, Philip *hydrogeologist, retired*
Doe, Bruce Roger *geologist*
Eaton, Gordon Pryor *geologist, research director*
Hamilton, Robert Morrison *geophysicist*
Huebner, John Stephen *geologist*
McCartan, Lucy *geologist*
Naeser, Nancy Dearien *geologist, researcher*
Peck, Dallas Lynn *retired geologist*
Ross, Malcolm *mineralogist, crystallographer*
Sato, Motoaki *geologist, researcher*

Richmond
Leyden, Donald Elliott *chemist, researcher*
Wakeham, Helmut Richard Rae *chemist, consulting company executive*

Roanoke
Al-Zubaidi, Amer Aziz *physicist, educator*
Husted, John Edwin *geologist, educator*

Salem
Fisher, Charles Harold *chemistry educator, researcher*

Seaford
Hammer, Jacob Myer *physicist, consultant*

Springfield
Sebastian, Richard Lee *physicist, executive*
Steele, Lendell Eugene *research scientist*

Sweet Briar
McClenon, John Raymond *chemistry educator*

Williamsburg
Burwell, Robert Lemmon, Jr. *chemist, educator*
Goodwin, Bruce Kesseli *geology educator, researcher*
Mc Knight, John Lacy *physics educator*
Orwoll, Robert Arvid *chemistry educator*
Siegel, Robert Ted *physicist*
Starnes, William Herbert, Jr. *chemist, educator*

Winchester
Ludwig, George Harry *physicist*

Zuni
Holm, Robert Arthur *environmental scientist*

WASHINGTON

Anacortes
Businger, Joost Alois *atmospheric scientist, educator*
†Collins, Thomas L. *research physicist*

Battle Ground
Morris, William Joseph *paleontologist, educator*

Bellevue
Chen, Ching-Hong *medical biochemist, biotechnical company executive*
Fremouw, Edward Joseph *physicist*

Ellensburg
Jones, Jerry Lynn *chemistry educator*

Issaquah
Benveniste, Jacob *retired physicist*

Kalama
Liang, Jason Chia *research chemist*

Manchester
Fearon, Lee Charles *chemist*

Port Angeles
Hart, Edwin James *chemist*

Pullman
Crosby, Glenn Arthur *chemistry educator*
Dodgen, Harold Warren *chemistry and physics educator*
Fowles, George Richard *physicist, educator*
George, Thomas Frederick *chemistry educator*
Kapteyn, Henry Cornelius *physics educator*
Lutz, Julie Haynes *astronomy and mathematics educator*
McFadden, Bruce Alden *biochemistry educator*
Murnane, Margaret Mary *physics educator*
Pomeranz, Yeshajahu *research chemist, technologist*
Randall, Linda Lea *biochemist, educator*
Ryan, Clarence Augustine, Jr. *biochemistry educator*

Redmond
Sargent, Murray, III *physicist, educator, software engineer*

Richland
Beck, Joe Eugene *environmental health scientist, educator*
Bush, Spencer Harrison *metallurgist*
Campbell, Milton Hugh *chemist*
Elderkin, Charles Edwin *meteorologist*
Jacobsen, Gerald Bernhardt *biochemist*
McDowell, Robin Scott *physical chemist*
Moore, Emmett Burris, Jr. *physical chemist*
Rebagay, Teofila Velasco *chemist, chemical engineer*

Seattle
Andersen, Niels Hjorth *chemistry educator, biophysics researcher, consultant*
Anderson, Arthur G., Jr. *chemistry educator*
Arons, Arnold Boris *physicist, educator*
Baum, William Alvin *astronomer, educator*
Bernard, Eddie Nolan *oceanographer*
Bodansky, David *physicist, educator*
Bohm, Karl-Heinz Hermann *astrophysicist, educator*
Borden, Weston Thatcher *chemistry educator*
Brown, Frederick Calvin *physicist, educator*
Brown, Lowell Severt *physicist, educator*
Brown, Robert Alan *atmospheric science educator, research scientist*
Brownlee, Donald Eugene, II *astronomer, educator*
Charlson, Robert Jay *atmospheric sciences educator, scientist*
Christian, Gary Dale *chemistry educator*
Clark, Kenneth Courtright *retired physics and geophysics educator*
Cramer, John Gleason, Jr. *physics educator, experimental physicist*
Creager, Joe Scott *geology and oceanography educator*
†Crum, Lawrence A. *physicist, research educator*
Dash, J. Gregory *physicist, educator*
Dehmelt, Hans Georg *physicist*
Dunne, Thomas *geology educator*
Ellis, Stephen D. *physics educator*
Engel, Thomas *chemistry educator*
Evans, Bernard William *geologist, educator*
Favorite, Felix *oceanographer*
Fischer, Edmond Henri *biochemistry educator*
Fleagle, Robert Guthrie *meteorologist, educator*
Floss, Heinz G. *chemistry educator, scientist*
Fortson, Edward Norval *physics educator*
Geballe, Ronald *physicist, university dean*
Gerhart, James Basil *physics educator*
Gordon, Milton Paul *biochemist, educator*
Gouterman, Martin Paul *chemistry educator*
Gregory, Norman Wayne *chemistry educator, researcher*
Grenfell, Thomas Cameron *geophysicist, educator*
Hakomori, Sen-itiroh *immunochemist, biochemist, researcher, educator*
Halpern, Isaac *physicist, educator*
Halver, John Emil *nutritional biochemist*
Harrison, Don Edmunds *oceanographer, educator*
Hartmann, Dennis Lee *atmospheric science educator*
Haxton, Wick Christopher *theoretical physicist, educator*
Heath, George Ross *oceanographer, university dean*
Henley, Ernest Mark *physics educator, university dean emeritus*
Hodge, Paul William *astronomer, educator*
†Hopkins, Paul Brink *chemistry educator*
Houck, John Candee *research facility administrator, biochemist*
Ingalls, Robert Lynn *physicist, educator*
Katsaros, Kristina Barbro *atmospheric sciences educator*
Kennedy, David Michael *environmental scientist*
Krebs, Edwin Gerhard *biochemistry educator*
Kwiram, Alvin L. *physical chemistry educator, university official*
Lingafelter, Edward Clay, Jr. *chemistry educator*
Lord, Jere Johns *retired physics educator*
Lubatti, Henry Joseph *physicist, educator*
Mallory, V(irgil) Standish *geologist, educator*
Margon, Bruce Henry *astrophysicist, educator*
Merrill, Ronald Thomas *geophysicist, educator*
Miles, Edward Lancelot *marine studies educator, consultant, director*
Nelson, Wendel Lane *medicinal chemist, educator*
Pocker, Yeshayau *chemistry, biochemistry educator*
Porter, Stephen Cummings *geologist, educator*
Rabinovitch, Benton Seymour *chemist, educator emeritus*
Reed, Richard John *retired meteorology educator*
Reinhardt, William Parker *chemical physicist, educator*
Rhines, Peter Broomell *oceanographer, atmospheric scientist*
Schomaker, Verner *chemist, educator*
Spinrad, Bernard Israel *physicist, educator*
Stern, Edward Abraham *physics educator*
Stuiver, Minze *geological sciences educator*
Swanson, Donald Alan *geologist*
Szkody, Paula *astronomy educator, researcher*
Thouless, David James *physicist, educator*
Wallace, John Michael *meteorology educator*
Wallerstein, George *astronomy educator*
Weitkamp, William George *retired nuclear physicist*
Wilets, Lawrence *physics educator*
Williams, Robert Walter *physics educator*

Silverdale
Walske, M(ax) Carl, Jr. *physicist*

Spokane
Benson, Allen B. *chemist, educator, consultant*

Tacoma
Gregory, Arthur Stanley *retired chemist*

WEST VIRGINIA

Fairmont
Swiger, Elizabeth Davis *chemistry educator*

Huntington
Hubbard, John Lewis *chemist, educator, researcher*

Institute
DasSarma, Basudeb *chemistry educator*

Lewisburg
Cardis, Thomas Michael *chemist*

Morgantown
Beattie, Diana Scott *biochemistry educator*
Chen, Ping-fan *geologist*
Fodor, Gábor Béla *chemistry educator, researcher*
†Seehra, Mohindar Singh *physics educator*

WISCONSIN

Kenosha
Kolb, Vera M. *chemistry educator*

La Crosse
Rozelle, Lee Theodore *physical chemist*

Madison
Adler, Julius *biochemist, biologist, educator*
Anderson, Louis Wilmer, Jr. *physicist, educator*
Barger, Vernon Duane *physicist, educator*
Barschall, Henry Herman *physics educator*
Bentley, Charles Raymond *geophysics educator*
Blaedel, Walter John *chemist, retired educator*
Botez, Dan *physicist*
Bryson, Reid Allen *meteorology educator*
Burris, Robert Harza *biochemist, educator*
Casey, Charles Philip *organic chemist, educator*
Cassinelli, Joseph Patrick *astronomy educator*
Churchwell, Edward Bruce *astronomer, educator*
Clark, David Leigh *marine geologist, educator*
Cleland, W(illiam) Wallace *biochemistry educator*
Code, Arthur Dodd *astrophysics educator*
Connors, Kenneth Antonio *chemist*
Cornwell, Charles Daniel *physical chemist, educator*
Craddock, (John) Campbell *geologist, educator*
Crim, Forrest Fleming, Jr. *chemist, educator*
Curtiss, Charles Francis *chemist, educator*
Dahl, Lawrence Frederick *chemistry educator, researcher*
Deutsch, Harold Francis *biochemist, researcher, educator*
DeWerd, Larry Albert *medical physicist, educator*
Dott, Robert Henry, Jr. *geologist, educator*
Ebel, Marvin Emerson *physicist,educator*
Ellis, Arthur Baron *chemist, educator*
Evenson, Merle Armin *chemist, educator*
Farrar, Thomas C. *chemist, educator*
Fennema, Owen Richard *food chemistry educator*
Ferry, John Douglass *chemist*
Fry, William Frederick *physics educator*
Gallagher, John Sill, III *astronomer*

Gorski, Jack *biochemistry educator*
†Hamers, Robert J. *chemistry educator*
Hedden, Gregory Dexter *environmental science educator, consultant*
Hershkowitz, Noah *physicist, educator*
Hokin, Lowell Edward *biochemist, educator*
Houghton, David Drew *meteorologist, educator*
Inman, Ross Banks *biochemistry and biophysics educator*
Karavolas, Harry J(ohn) *biochemist, educator*
Knutson, Lynn Douglas *physics educator*
Kraushaar, William Lester *physicist, educator*
Lagally, Max Gunter *physics educator*
Lardy, Henry Arnold *biochemist, biological sciences educator*
Larsen, Edwin Merritt *retired chemist, educator*
Lawler, James Edward *physics educator*
Maher, Louis James, Jr. *geologist, educator*
Markley, John Lute *biochemistry educator*
McVoy, Kirk Warren *physicist, educator*
Moore, John Ward *chemistry educator*
Morton, Stephen Dana *chemist*
Mukerjee, Pasupati *chemistry educator*
Perlman, D(avid) *biochemist, educator*
Pondrom, Lee Girard *physicist, educator*
Pray, Lloyd Charles *geologist, educator*
Rich, Daniel Hulbert *chemist*
Richards, Hugh Taylor *physics educator*
Rowe, John Westel *retired organic chemist*
Savage, Blair deWillis *astronomer, educator*
Schatz, Paul Frederick *laboratory director*
Sih, Charles John *pharmaceutical chemistry educator*
Skinner, James Lauriston *chemist, educator*
Smith, William Leo *meteorologist, researcher, educator*
†Suomi, Verner Edward *meteorologist, administrator, inventor*
Treichel, Paul Morgan, Jr. *chemistry educator*
Vaughan, Worth Edward *chemistry educator*
Wang, Herbert Fan *geophysics educator*
West, Robert Culbertson *chemistry educator*
Yu, Hyuk *chemist, educator*
Zimmerman, Howard Elliot *chemist, educator*

Manitowoc
†Huss, Ronald John *biochemist*

Middleton
†Clay, Clarence Samuel *acoustical oceanographer*
Ferry, James Allen *physicist, electrostatics company executive*
Herb, Raymond George *physicist, manufacturing company executive*
Ostrom, Meredith Eggers *retired geologist*

Milwaukee
Aita, Carolyn Rubin *physicist*
Bader, Alfred Robert *chemist*
Greenler, Robert George *physics educator, researcher*
Haworth, Daniel Thomas *chemistry educator*
Hendee, William Richard *medical physics educator, university official*
Jache, Albert William *retired chemistry educator, scientist*
Miller, David Hewitt *environmental scientist, writer*
Nakamoto, Kazuo *chemistry educator*
Paull, Richard Allen *geologist, educator*
Walters, William LeRoy *physics educator*

Plover
Peanasky, Robert Joseph *biochemist, medical educator*

Stoughton
Huber, David Lawrence *physicist, educator*
Kuhn, Peter Mouat *atmospheric physicist*

Williams Bay
Hobbs, Lewis Mankin *astronomer*
Kron, Richard G. *astrophysicist, educator*

WYOMING

Casper
Wold, John Schiller *geologist, former congressman*

Jackson Hole
Paulson, Glenn *environmental scientist*

Laramie
Grandy, Walter Thomas, Jr. *physicist*
Lillegraven, Jason Arthur *paleontologist, educator*
Meyer, Edmond Gerald *energy and natural resources educator, resources scientist, entrepreneur, former chemistry educator, university administrator*

TERRITORIES OF THE UNITED STATES

PUERTO RICO

Arecibo
†Harmon, John Knud *astronomer*

Manati
Silva-Ruiz, Sergio Andrés *biochemist*

Mayaguez
Hernandez-Avila, Manuel Luis *physical oceanography educator, researcher, administrator, consultant*

Rincon
Morris, Victor Franklin, Jr. *meteorology educator*

CANADA

ALBERTA

Calgary
Armstrong, David Anthony *physical chemist, educator*
Campbell, Finley Alexander *geologist*
Dixon, Gordon Henry *biochemist*
Hyne, James Bissett *chemistry educator, industrial scientist, consultant*
Nigg, Benno Maurus *biomechanics educator*
Okulitch, Vladimir Joseph *geologist, university administrator*
Thorsteinsson, Raymond *geology research scientist*

Edmonton
†Charlesworth, Henry A. K. *geology educator*
Folinsbee, Robert Edward *retired geology educator*
Gough, Denis Ian *geophysics educator*
Harris, Walter Edgar *chemistry educator*
Israel, Werner *physics educator*
James, Michael N. G. *crystallographer, educator*
Jones, Richard Norman *physical chemist, researcher*
Kay, Cyril Max *biochemist*
Kebarle, Paul *chemistry educator*
Khanna, Faqir Chand *physics educator*
Kratochvil, Byron George *chemistry educator, researcher*
Lemieux, Raymond Urgel *chemistry educator*
Rostoker, Gordon *physicist, educator*
Rutter, Nathaniel Westlund *geologist, educator*
Spencer, Mary Eileen *biochemist, educator*
Stelck, Charles Richard *geology educator*
Sykes, Brian Douglas *biochemistry educator, researcher*
Umezawa, Hiroomi *physics educator, researcher*
†Usher, W. David *earth scientist*
Vance, Dennis Edward *biochemistry educator*

Fort McMurray
†Hyndman, Alexander W. *earth scientist*

BRITISH COLUMBIA

Burnaby
Arrott, Anthony Schuyler *physics educator*
†Dahn, Jeff R. *physics educator*

Maple Ridge
†Wainwright, David Stanley *intellectual property professional*

North Saanich
Weichert, Dieter Horst *seismologist, researcher*

Sidney
Best, Melvyn Edward *geophysicist*
Irving, Edward *geophysicist, educator*
Petrie, William *physicist*
van den Bergh, Sidney *astronomer*

Vancouver
†Alden, Thomas Hyde *metallogist*
Aubke, Friedhelm *chemistry educator*
Bloom, Myer *physicist, educator*
Clarke, Garry Kenneth Connal *geophysics educator*
†Comisarow, Melvin B. *chemist, educator*
Hardy, Walter Newbold *physics educator, researcher*
James, Brian Robert *chemistry educator*
Kieffer, Susan Werner *geology educator*
LeBlond, Paul Henri *oceanographer, educator*
Mathews, William Henry *geology educator*
Nafe, John Elliott *geophysicist*
Ozier, Irving *physicist, educator*
Pickard, George Lawson *physics educator*
Pincock, Richard Earl *chemistry educator*
†Richardson, John Reginald *physics educator*
Russell, Richard Doncaster *geophysicist, educator, geoscientist*
Sinclair, Alastair James *geology educator*
Smith, Michael *biochemistry educator*
Snider, Robert F. *chemistry educator, researcher*
Stewart, Ross *chemistry educator*
Underhill, Anne Barbara *astrophysicist*
Unruh, William G. *physics educator, researcher*
Vogt, Erich Wolfgang *physicist, academic administrator*
Volkoff, George Michael *educational administator, former physics educator*
Warren, Harry Verney *geological sciences educator, consulting geological engineer*
Wheeler, John Oliver *geologist*

Victoria
Barnes, Christopher Richard *geologist*
Batten, Alan Henry *astronomer*
Hutchings, John Barrie *astronomer, researcher*
Mc Carter, John Alexander *biochemistry educator*
Morton, Donald Charles *astronomer*
Oke, John Beverley *astronomy educator*
†Stetson, Peter Brailey *astronomer*
Wiles, David McKeen *chemist*
Wright, Kenneth Osborne *retired astronomer*

West Vancouver
Wynne-Edwards, Hugh Robert *entrepreneur, scientist*

White Rock
Cooke, Herbert Basil Sutton *geologist, educator*

MANITOBA

Winnipeg
Barber, Robert Charles *physics educator*
Bigelow, Charles Cross *biochemist, university administrator*
Ferguson, Robert Bury *mineralogy educator*
Hawthorne, Frank Christopher *geologist, educator*
Kanfer, Julian Norman *biochemist, educator*
Mantsch, Henry Horst *chemistry educator*
Schaefer, Theodore Peter *chemistry educator*
Smith, Ian Cormack Palmer *biophysicist*

NEW BRUNSWICK

Fredericton
Valenta, Zdenek *chemistry educator*
Vaníček, Petr *geodesist*

NEWFOUNDLAND

Saint John's
Idler, David Richard *biochemist, marine scientist, educator*
Rochester, Michael Grant *geophysics educator*
Williams, Harold *geology educator*

NOVA SCOTIA

Dartmouth
Elliott, James A. *oceanographer, researcher*
Keen, Charlotte Elizabeth *marine geophysicist, researcher*
Needler, George Treglohan *oceanographer, researcher*
Platt, Trevor Charles *oceanographer, scientist*

Halifax
Geldart, Donald James Wallace *physics educator*
Gold, Edgar *marine affairs educator, mariner, lawyer*
Leffek, Kenneth Thomas *chemist, educator*

Wallace
Boyle, Willard Sterling *physicist*

Wolfville
Bishop, Roy Lovitt *physics and astronomy educator*
Ogilvie, Kelvin Kenneth *chemistry educator*

ONTARIO

Ancaster
†Brockhouse, Bertram Neville *physicist, retired educator*

Burlington
Cragg, Laurence Harold *chemist, former university president*
Donelan, Mark Anthony *physicist*

Chalk River
Hardy, John Christopher *physicist*
Milton, John Charles Douglas *nuclear physicist*
Torgerson, David Franklyn *chemist, research facility administrator*

Deep River
Hanna, Geoffrey Chalmers *nuclear scientist*

Don Mills
Koster, Emlyn Howard *geologist, educator, Canadian agency executive*

Downsview
Pritchard, Huw Owen *chemist, educator*
Ribner, Herbert Spencer *physicist, educator*
Tennyson, Roderick C. *aerospace scientist*

Etobicoke
Bahadur, Birendra *display specialist, liquid crystal researcher*

Gloucester
Marsters, Gerald Frederick *retired aerospace science and technology executive*

Guelph
Dickinson, William Trevor *hydrologist, educator*
Karl, Gabriel *physics educator*
Simpson, John Joseph *physics educator, researcher*

Hamilton
Basinski, Zbigniew Stanislaw *metal physicist, educator*
Childs, Ronald Frank *chemistry educator, science administrator*
Datars, William Ross *physicist, educator*
Davies, John Arthur *physics and engineering educator, scientist*
Garland, William James *engineering physics educator*
Gillespie, Ronald James *retired chemistry educator, writer*
MacLean, David Bailey *chemistry educator, researcher*
Preston, Melvin Alexander *physicist, educator*
Schwarcz, Henry Philip *geologist, educator*
Spenser, Ian Daniel *chemist educator*
Sprung, Donald Whitfield Loyal *physics educator*
Walker, Roger Geoffrey *geology educator, consultant*
†Welch, Douglas Lindsay *physics educator*

Hawkestone
†Boville, Byron Walter *meteorologist*

Kingston
Ewan, George Thomson *physicist, educator*
McDonald, Arthur Bruce *physics educator*
Sayer, Michael *physics educator*
Spencer, John Hedley *biochemistry educator*
Stewart, Alec Thompson *physicist*
Szarek, Walter Anthony *chemist, educator*
Uffen, Robert James *geophysics educator, engineer*

Lions Bay
Bartholomew, Gilbert Alfred *retired physicist*

London
Bancroft, George Michael *chemical physicist, educator*
Carroll, Kenneth Kitchener *biochemist, nutritionist, educator*
Dreimanis, Aleksis *emeritus geology educator*
Fyfe, William Sefton *geochemist, educator*
Roach, Margot Ruth *biophysicist, educator*
Stewart, Harold Brown *biochemist*
Stothers, John B. *chemistry educator*
Weedon, Alan Charles *chemist, educator*

Manotick
Hobson, George Donald *retired geophysicist*

Mississauga
†Hair, Michael Lloyd *research scientist*

North York
Bohme, Diethard Kurt *chemistry educator*
Carswell, Allan Ian *physics educator*

Ottawa
Alper, Howard *chemistry educator*
Babcock, Elkanah Andrew *geologist*
Davis, B. *physical science administrator*
Fallis, Alexander Graham *chemistry educator*
Ferron, J. *mineralogy administrator*
Halliday, Ian *astronomer*
Harington, Charles Richard *vertebrate paleontologist*
Haworth, Richard Thomas *geophysicist, science director*
Herzberg, Gerhard *physicist*
Himms-Hagen, Jean Margaret *biochemist*
Holmes, John Leonard *chemistry educator*
Ingold, Keith Usherwood *chemist, educator*
Itzkovitch, Irwin J. *metallurgy administrator*
Kates, Morris *biochemist, educator*
Lossing, Frederick Pettit *retired chemist*
MacLeod, John Munroe *radio astronomer, academic administrator*
Marmet, Paul *physicist*
McKellar, Andrew Robert *physicist, researcher*
McLaren, Digby Johns *geologist, educator*
Puddington, Ira Edwin *chemist*
Ramsay, Donald Allan *physical chemist*
Redhead, Paul Aveling *physicist*
Roots, Ernest Frederick *scientific advisor emeritus*
St-Onge, Denis Alderic *geologist, research scientist*
Schneider, William George *chemist, research consultant*
Siebrand, Willem *theoretical chemist, science editor*
Templeton, Ian Malcolm *retired physicist*
Varshni, Yatendra Pal *physicist*
Veizer, Ján *geology educator*
Whitehead, J. Rennie *science consultant*
Whitham, Kenneth *science and technology consultant*

Owen Sound
Morley, Lawrence Whitaker *geophysicist, remote sensing consultant*

Richmond Hill
Bolton, Charles Thomas *astronomer*
Fernie, John Donald *astronomer, educator*
Garrison, Robert Frederick *astronomer, educator*
MacRae, Donald Alexander *astronomy educator*

Saint Catharines
Terasmae, Jaan *geology educator*

Toronto
Alcock, Charles Benjamin *materials science consultant*
†Boothroyd, Arnold Ian *astrophysicist*
Brook, Adrian Gibbs *chemistry educator*
Brumer, Paul William *chemical physicist, educator*
Dunlop, David John *geophysics educator, researcher*
Ganoza-Becker, Maria Clelia *biochemistry educator*
Goldberg, David Meyer *biochemistry educator*
Haynes, Robert Hall *biophysicist, educator*
Hofmann, Theo *biochemist, educator*
Ivey, Donald Glenn *physics educator*
Jervis, Robert E. *chemistry educator*
Kaiser, Nicholas *physicist, educator*
Kresge, Alexander Jerry *chemistry educator*
List, Roland *physicist, educator, former UN official*
Litherland, Albert Edward *physics educator*
Mak, Tak Wah *biochemist*
McNeill, K(enneth) G(ordon) *medical physicist*
Moffat, John William *physics educator*
Naldrett, Anthony James *geology educator*
Norris, Geoffrey *geology educator, consultant*
Packham, Marian Aitchison *biochemistry educator*
Polanyi, John Charles *chemist, educator*
Prugovecki, Eduard *mathematical physicist, educator, author*
Rowe, David John *physics educator*
Scott, Steven Donald *geology educator, researcher*
Seaquist, Ernest Raymond *astronomy educator*
Sheinin, Rose *biochemist, educator*
Stoicheff, Boris Peter *physicist, educator*
Taylor, Harry William *physics educator*
Tidwell, Thomas Tinsley *chemistry educator*
Tremaine, Scott Duncan *astrophysicist*
Whittington, Stuart Gordon *chemistry educator*
Yates, Keith *chemistry educator, writer*

Waterloo
Morgan, Alan Vivian *geologist, educator*
Rudin, Alfred *chemistry educator emeritus*
Thomas, Richard Lynn *geologist, researcher, educator, director university geecology center*

Windsor
†Drake, Gordon F. *physicist educator*
Drake, Gordon William Frederic *physics educator*
Jones, William Ernest *chemistry educator*
Thibert, Roger Joseph *clinical chemist, educator*

QUEBEC

Dorval
Bachynski, Morrel Paul *physicist*

Laval
David, Michel Louis *geostatistician, consultant*

Montreal
Chan, Tak Hang *chemist, educator*
Derome, Jacques Florian *meteorology educator*
de Takacsy, Nicholas Benedict *physicist, educator*
Edward, John Thomas *chemist, educator*
Eisenberg, Adi *chemist*
Fontaine, Gilles *physics educator*
Gaudry, Roger *chemist, university official*
Guindon, Yvan *research labratory director*
Hay, Allan Stuart *chemist, educator*
Johnstone, Rose Mamelak (Mrs. Douglas Johnstone) *biochemistry educator*
Langleben, Manuel Phillip *physics educator*
Leroy, Claude *physics educator, researcher*
Mark, Shew-Kuey Tommy *physics educator*
Mysak, Lawrence Alexander *oceanographer, climatologist, mathematician, educator*
Perlin, Arthur Saul *chemistry educator*
Podgorsak, Ervin B. *medical physicist, educator, administrator*
Purdy, William Crossley *chemist, educator*

Sandor, Thomas *biochemist*
Sandorfy, Camille *chemistry educator*
Solomon, Samuel *biochemistry educator, administrator*
Sourkes, Theodore Lionel *biochemistry educator*
Taras, Paul *physicist, educator*
Van Vliet, Carolyne Marina *physicist, educator*
Wallace, Philip Russell *retired physics educator*
Whitehead, Michael Anthony *chemistry educator*

Outremont
Levesque, Rene Jules Albert *retired physicist*

Pointe Claire
Bolker, Henry Irving *retired chemist, research institute director, educator*

Quebec
Engel, Charles Robert *chemist, educator*
Page, Michel *biochemist*

Rimouski
Walton, Alan *oceanographer*

Saint Jerome
Joly, Jean-Gil *medical biochemist, internist, administrator, researcher, educator*

Saint Luc
Marcoux, Jules Edouard *physicist, educator, writer*

Sainte Foy
Boudoux, Michel *environmental research executive*
Legendre, Louis *biological oceanography educator, researcher*

Sherbrooke
Deslongchamps, Pierre *chemistry educator*
Tremblay, André-Marie *physicist*

Varennes
Vijh, Ashok Kumar *chemistry educator, researcher*

Westmount
Dunbar, Maxwell John *oceanographer, educator*

SASKATCHEWAN

Saskatoon
Hirose, Akira *physics educator, researcher*
Kupsch, Walter Oscar *geologist*

MEXICO

Mexico City
Peimbert, Manuel *astronomer*

Puebla
Zehe, Alfred Fritz Karl *physics educator*

ARMENIA

Byurakan
Khachikian, Edward Yerem *astronomer*

AUSTRALIA

Bundoora
James, Bruce David *chemistry educator*

BELGIUM

Heverlee
L'abbé, Gerrit Karel *chemist*

BRAZIL

Rio de Janeiro
Costa Neto, Adelina *chemistry educator, consultant*

DENMARK

Copenhagen
Hansen, Ole *physicist*

Grasted
Wiin-Nielsen, Aksel Christopher *meteorologist educator*

Hoersholm
Jensen, Ole *energy researcher*

ENGLAND

Cambridge
Hawking, Stephen W. *astrophysicist, mathematician*
Needham, Joseph *biochemist, historian of science, Orientalist*

Oxford
Hirsch, Peter Bernhard *metallurgist*
Williams, William Stanley Cossom *physics educator and researcher*

FRANCE

Orsay
Deutsch, Claude David *physicist, educator*

Paris
Bikales, Norbert M. *chemist, science administrator*
Cousteau, Jacques-Yves *marine explorer*
Haroche, Serge *optics scientist*

GERMANY

Dusseldorf
Stuhl, Oskar Paul *scientific and regulatory consultant*

Gottingen
Sheldrick, George Michael *chemistry educator, crystallographer*
Tietze, Lutz Friedjan *chemist, educator*
Wedemeyer, Erich Hans *physicist*

Groebenzell
Chandrasekhar, B(ellur) S(ivaramiah) *physics educator*

Hamburg
Jensen, Elwood Vernon *biochemist*

Kelkheim
Haeske, Horst *physicist*

Munich
Fischer, Ernst Otto *chemist, educator*
Giacconi, Riccardo *astrophysicist, educator*

ISRAEL

Ra'ananna
Hayon, Elie M. *chemist, educator*

Rehovot
†Sharon, Nathan *biochemist*

ITALY

Milan
Sindoni, Elio *physics educator*

JAPAN

Ehime
Sakai, Yoshiro *chemistry educator*

Hamamatsu
Aoki, Ichiro *theoretical biophysics systems science educator*

Ibaraki
Ishii, Yoshinori *geophysics educator*

Koganei
Akiyama, Masayasu *chemistry educator*

Kyoto
Araki, Takeo *chemistry educator*

Okayama
Oda, Takuzo *biochemistry educator*
Ubuka, Toshihiko *biochemistry educator*

Osaka
Ikeda, Kazuyosi *physicist, poet*
Kobayashi, Mitsue *chemistry educator*
†Ueno, Hiroshi *biochemist*

Otsu
Matsuura, Teruo *chemistry educator*
Takemoto, Kiichi *chemistry educator*

Sakai-Gun
Ise, Norio *chemistry educator*

Sendai
Oikawa, Hiroshi *materials science educator*

Shimizu
Uyeda, Seiya *geophysics educator*

Tochigi
Iida, Shuichi *physicist,educator*

Tokyo
Kigoshi, Kunihiko *geochemistry educator*
Nakagaki, Masayuki *chemist*

Tondabayashi
Nozato, Ryoichi *metallurgy educator, researcher*

Toyama
Hayashi, Mitsuhiko *physics educator*

Yamaguchi
Suzuki, Nobutaka *chemistry educator*

KOREA

Pohang
Choi, Sang-il *physics educator, researcher*

THE NETHERLANDS

Amsterdam
Averill, Bruce Alan *chemistry educator*

Goor
Bonting, Sjoerd Lieuwe *biochemist, priest*

REPUBLIC OF KOREA

Taejon
Lee, Choochon *physics educator, researcher*

RUSSIA

Novosibirsk
Aleksandrov, Leonid Naumovitsh *physicist, educator, researcher*

SCOTLAND

Glasgow
Courtney, James McNiven *chemist*

Peebles
Hooper, John Edward *retired physicist, researcher*

SWEDEN

Lund
Grimmeiss, Hermann Georg *physics educator, researcher*

SWITZERLAND

Geneva
Harigel, Gert Günter *physicist*
Overseth, Oliver Enoch *physicist, educator*

Rueschlikon
Rohrer, Heinrich *physicist*

Zurich
Mueller, Stephan *geophysicist, educator*

TAIWAN

Taipei
Yang, Chin-Ping *chemist, engineering educator*

VENEZUELA

Caracas
Mendelovici, Efraim Eliahu *materials chemistry researcher*
Nakano, Tatsuhiko *chemist, researcher, educator*

ADDRESS UNPUBLISHED

Akasofu, Syun-Ichi *geophysicist*
Ames, Oakes *physicist, educator*
†Andersen, Willem Hendrik Jan *physicist*
Appelbaum, Jacob Gregory *physicist*
Atwood, Genevieve *geologist*
Autin, Ernest Anthony, II *chemist, educator*
Baldwin, George Curriden *physicist, educator*
Ball, Lawrence *retired physical scientist*
Bandeen, William Reid *retired meteorologist*
Basford, Robert Eugene *retired biochemistry educator, researcher*
Baym, Gordon Alan *physicist, educator*
Berry, Richard Stephen *chemist*
Betlach, Mary Carolyn *biochemist, molecular biologist*
Biedenharn, Lawrence C., Jr. *physicist, educator*
Bodanszky, Miklos *chemist, educator*
Braden, Charles Hosea *physicist, university administrator*
Bragagnolo, Julio Alfredo *physicist*
Brand, John Charles *chemistry educator*
Cahn, Robert Nathan *physicist*
Cairns, Theodore LeSueur *chemist*
Cane, David E. *chemistry educator*
Cavallaro, Mary Caroline *retired physics educator*
Christoffersen, Ralph Earl *chemist*
Chu, Benjamin Thomas Peng-Nien *chemistry educator*
Church, Eugene Lent *physicist, consulting scientist*
Compton, W. Dale *physicist*
Crabtree, Robert Howard *chemistry educator, consultant*
Critoph, Eugene *retired physicist, nuclear research company executive*
Csanady, Gabriel Tibor *oceanographer, meteorologist, environmental engineer*
Dale, Wesley John *chemistry educator*
Daniels, James Maurice *physicist*
Davidsen, Arthur F. *astrophysicist, educator*
DeAngelis, Thomas P. *chemist*
Deisenhofer, Johann *biochemistry educator, researcher*
De Loach, Bernard Collins, Jr. *retired physicist*
Dicke, Robert Henry *educator, physicist*
Dickinson, William Richard *retired geologist and educator*
Donath, Fred Arthur *geologist, geophysicist*
Eberly, Joseph Henry *physics educator, consultant*
Ewen, H.I. *physicist*
Fang, Joseph Pe Yong *chemistry educator*
Ford, Kenneth William *physicist*
†Foster, Norman Holland *geologist*
Franklin, Kenneth L(inn) *astronomer*
Frauenfelder, Hans *physicist, educator*
Galloway, William Joyce *physicist, consultant*
Gardner, Wilford Robert *physicist, educator*
Geller, Seymour *retired educator, researcher*
Genung, R. K. *physical sciences research administrator*
Getting, Ivan Alexander *physicist, former aerospace company executive*
Gilinsky, Victor *physicist*
Glashow, Sheldon Lee *physicist, educator*
Goldfine, Howard *microbiology and biochemistry educator, researcher*
Goldman, Charles Remington *environmental scientist, educator*
Gounaris, Anne Demetra *biochemistry educator, researcher*
Gummel, Hermann Karl *retired physicist, laboratory administrator*
Gutsch, William Anthony, Jr. *astronomer*
Haering, Rudolph Roland *retired physics educator, researcher*
Hannay, N(orman) Bruce *chemist, industrial research and business consultant*
Heeschen, David Sutphin *astronomer, educator*
Herzfeld, Charles Maria *physicist*
Hinkley, Everett David, Jr. *scientist,business executive*
Hoeg, Donald Francis *chemist, consultant, former research and development executive*
Howard, Charles L. *chemist, educator*
Howe, John Perry *materials science educator, research consultant*
Hungerford, Lugene Green *physicist*
Ingle, James Chesney, Jr. *geology educator*
Jacobs, Abigail Conway *biochemist*
Jiang, Bai-Chuan *optics researcher, educator*
Jordan, Thomas Fredrick *physics educator*
Kamen, Martin David *physical biochemist*
†Kastner, Marc Aaron *physics educator*
Kepler, Raymond Glen *physicist*
Kerwin, Larkin *physics educator*
Kolm, Henry Herbert *physicist, electric research company executive*
Kraichnan, Robert Harry *theoretical physicist, consultant*
Kravitz, Rubin *chemist*
Lamanec, Tracy *chemist, writer*
Landel, Robert Franklin *physical chemist, rheologist*
Langerak, Esley Oren *retired research chemist*
†Langmore, John Preston *biophysicist, educator*
Lemke, James Underwood *physicist*
Levenson, Marc David *optics and lasers specialist, scientist*
Levi, Barbara Goss *physicist, editor*
Lloyd, Joseph Wesley *physicist, researcher*
Lo, Shui-yin *physicist*
Loach, Paul Allen *biochemist, biophysicist, educator*
Lynds, Beverly Turner *retired astronomer*
MacQueen, Robert Moffat *solar physicist*
Maddin, Robert *metallurgist educator*
Maglich, Bogdan Cveta *physicist*
Maiman, Theodore Harold *physicist*
Marcuse, Dietrich *retired physicist*
†Martin, Charles Raymond *chemist, educator*
McLendon, George Leland *chemistry educator, researcher*
Medzihradsky, Fedor *biochemist, educator*
Mislow, Kurt Martin *chemist, educator*
Mogil, H(arvey) Michael *meteorologist, educator*
Neff, John Samuel *astronomy educator*
Neilson, Robert McKenzie, Jr. *materials scientist*
Nobles, Laurence Hewit *retired geology educator*
Norman, Joe G., Jr. *chemistry educator, college dean*
Noyes, H(enry) Pierre *physicist*
Olsen, Clifford Wayne *retired physical chemist*
Orttung, William Herbert *chemistry educator*
Oster, Ludwig Friedrich *physicist*
Palmer, James Russworth *theoretical physicist, high energy optics researcher*
Parsegian, V. Adrian *biophysicist*
Pearson, Donald Emanual *chemist, educator*
Pearson, Ralph Gottfrid *chemistry educator*
Penzias, Arno Allan *astrophysicist, research scientist, information systems specialist*
Piehl, Donald Herbert *chemist, consultant*
Pirkle, Earl Charnell *geologist, educator*
Pocock, Frederick James *scientist, consultant*
Portis, Alan Mark *physicist, educator*
Pound, Robert Vivian *physics educator*
Price, Paul Buford *physicist, educator*
Proctor, Richard J. *geologist, consultant*
Procunier, Richard Werner *environmental scientist, administrator*
Pursey, Derek Lindsay *physics educator*
Qutub, Musa Yacub *hydrogeologist, educator, consultant*
Radin, Norman Samuel *retired biochemistry educator*
Rast, Walter, Jr. *hydrologist, water quality management*
Redda, Kinfe Ken *chemist, educator*
Rice, Stuart Alan *chemist, educator*
Richards, Paul Linford *physics educator, researcher*
Richardson, Charles Clifton *biochemist, educator*
Robbins, Jessie Earl *metallurgist*
Roberts, Earl John *carbohydrate chemist*
Robertson, John Archibald Law *nuclear scientist*
Robinson, Bruce Butler *physicist*
Roychoudhuri, Chandrasekhar *physicist*
Rubin, Vera Cooper *research astronomer*
Rugge, Hugo Robert *physicist*
Russell, John Lynn, Jr. *physicist*
Sayre, David *physicist*
Schachter, Harry *biochemist, educator*
Schmitt, George Joseph *chemist*
Schonhorn, Harold *chemist, researcher*
Schurr, John Michael *chemistry educator*
†Schuster, Gary Benjamin *chemistry educator, university dean*
Schwarzschild, Martin *astronomer, educator*
Shaw, Melvin Phillip *physicist, engineering educator, psychologist*
†Sheffield, Richard Lee *physicist*
Shirley, David Arthur *chemistry educator, science administrator*
Shockley, James Thomas *physics educator*
Smith, Charles Haddon *geoscientist, consultant*
Spejewski, Eugene Henry *physicist, educator*
Spitzer, Lyman, Jr. *astronomer*
Stevenson, Paul Michael *physics educator, researcher*
Stewart, Robert William *retired physicist, government research council executive*
Sturtevant, Julian Munson *biophysical chemist*
Sullivan, Nicholas G. *science educator, speleologist*
Sullivan, Woodruff Turner, III *astronomy educator, science historian, researcher, gnomonicist*
Sundaresan, Mosur Kalyanaraman *physics educator*
Sunderman, Duane Neuman *chemist, research institute executive*
Tate, Manford Ben *guided missile scientist, investor*
Taylor, Hugh Pettingill, Jr. *geologist, educator*
Thompson, Julia Ann *physicist*
Thompson, Robert W. *theoretical physicist*
Thorne, Kip Stephen *physicist, educator*
Thuillier, Richard Howard *meteorologist*
Turco, Richard Peter *atmospheric scientist*
Vanier, Jacques *physicist*
Veronis, George *geophysicist, educator*
Walsh, Kenneth Albert *chemist*
Watson, Robert Barden *physicist*
Waymouth, John Francis *physicist, consultant*
Weertman, Johannes *materials science educator*
Weinberg, Steven *physics educator*
Weisburger, Elizabeth Kreiser *chemist, editor*
Weiss, Michael James *chemistry educator*
Weitz, Eric *chemistry educator*
Welton, Theodore Allen *theoretical physics educator, consultant*
Whistler, Roy Lester *chemist, educator, industrialist*
Wickman, Herbert Hollis *physical chemist, condensed matter physicist*

Wilson, Kenneth Geddes *physics research administrator, educator*
Wilson, M(athew) Kent *retired chemist, researcher, educator*
Wolff, Manfred Ernst *medicinal chemist, pharmaceutical company executive*
Wolff, Peter Adalbert *physicist, educator*
Wright, Ann Elizabeth *physicist, consultant*
Yates, David John C. *chemist, researcher*
Zaffaroni, Alejandro C. *biochemist, medical research company executive*
Zhou, Ming De *aeronautical scientist, educator*
Zimm, Bruno Hasbrouck *physical chemistry educator*
Ziock, Klaus Otto Heinrich *physics educator*

SOCIAL SCIENCE

UNITED STATES

ALABAMA

Birmingham
Liu, Ray Ho *forensic science program director, educator*
Nunn, Grady Harrison *political science educator emeritus*

Collinsville
Beasley, Mary Catherine *home economics educator, administrator, researcher*

Dothan
Wright, Burton *sociologist*

Huntsville
Traylor, Orba Forest *economist, lawyer, educator*

Jacksonville
Dunaway, Carolyn Bennett *sociology educator*

Maplesville
Nichols, J. Hugh *economic development consultant*

Maxwell AFB
†Wendzel, Robert Leroy *political science educator*

Mobile
Bobo, James Robert *economics educator*

Montevallo
McChesney, Robert Michael, Sr. *political science educator*

Tuscaloosa
Abdel-Ghany, Mohamed *family economics educator*
Baklanoff, Eric Nicholas *economist, educator*
Cramer, Dale Lewis *economics educator*
Fish, Mary Martha *economics educator*
Vogel, Joseph Otto *archaeologist, educator, museologist*
Wu, Hsiu Kwang *economist, educator*

ALASKA

Anchorage
Jones, Garth Nelson *public administration educator*

Fairbanks
Cutler, Howard Armstrong *economics educator, chancellor*
†Kunz, Michael Lenney *archaeologist*

ARIZONA

Flagstaff
Smith, Zachary Alden *political science and public administration educator*

Sedona
Eggert, Robert John, Sr. *economist*

Tempe
Alisky, Marvin Howard *political science educator*
Farber, Bernard *sociologist, educator*
Farris, Martin Theodore *economist, educator*
Gordon, Leonard *sociology educator*
Lounsbury, John Frederick *geographer, educator*
†Melnick, Rob *research administrator*
Metcalf, Virgil Alonzo *economics educator*
Miller, Warren Edward *political scientist*
Montero, Darrel Martin *sociologist, social worker, educator*
†O'Neil, Michael Joseph *opinion survey executive, marketing consultant*
Simon, Sheldon Weiss *political science educator*
Weigend, Guido Gustav *geographer, educator*

Tucson
Block, Michael Kent *economics and law educator, public policy association executive, former government official, consultant*
Clarke, James Weston *political science educator, writer*
†Gibson, Lay J. *geography educator*
Green, Jerrold David *political science educator, academic administrator*
Ingram, Helen Moyer *political science educator*
Marshall, Robert Herman *economics educator*
Rodeffer, Stephanie Lynn Holschlag *archaeologist, government official*
Seger, Martha Romayne *financial economist*
Smith, Vernon Lomax *economist, researcher*
Soren, David *archaeology educator, administrator*
Stini, William Arthur *anthropologist, educator*
†Thompson, Raymond Harris *anthropologist, educator*
Underwood, Jane Hainline Hammons *anthropologist, educator*
Volgy, Thomas John *political science educator, organization official*
Wahlke, John Charles *political science educator*
Whiting, Allen Suess *political science educator, writer, consultant*

Yuma
Norton, Dunbar Sutton *economic developer*

ARKANSAS

Conway
Hamblin, Daniel Morgan *economist*
Mc New, Bennie Banks *economics and finance educator*

Fayetteville
Cramer, Gail Latimer *economist*
Green, Thomas James *archaeologist*
Mc Gimsey, Charles Robert, III *anthropologist*
Purvis, Hoyt Hughes *political scientist, academic administrator, educator*

Little Rock
Ledbetter, Calvin Reville, Jr. (Cal Ledbetter) *political science educator, university dean, former legislator*

Morrilton
Thompson, Robert Lee *agricultural economist, nonprofit executive*

Pine Bluff
Engle, Carole Ruth *aquaculture economics educator*

State University
Power, Mary Susan *political science educator*

CALIFORNIA

Arcata
Emenhiser, JeDon Allen *political science educator, academic administrator*

Bakersfield
Glynn, James A. *sociology educator, author*

Berkeley
Adelman, Irma Glicman *economics educator*
Alhadeff, David Albert *economics educator*
Auerbach, Alan Jeffrey *economist*
Bellah, Robert Neelly *sociologist, educator*
Bonnell, Victoria Eileen *sociologist*
Brandes, Stanley Howard *anthropology educator, writer*
Breslauer, George William *political science educator*
Cain, Bruce Edward *political science educator, consultant*
Cheit, Earl Frank *economist, educator*
Clark, John Desmond *anthropology educator*
Colson, Elizabeth Florence *anthropologist*
Debreu, Gerard *economics and mathematics educator*
Duster, Troy *sociology educator*
Foster, George McClelland, Jr. *anthropologist*
Gilkerson, Tom Moffet *economist, company executive, education consultant*
Graburn, Nelson Hayes Henry *anthropologist, educator*
Gurgin, Vonnie Ann *social scientist*
Hakansson, Nils Hemming *financial economics and accounting educator*
Hammel, Eugene Alfred *anthropologist*
Harsanyi, John Charles *economics educator, researcher*
Henry, Charles Patrick *political science educator*
Hitch, Charles Johnston *economist, institution executive*
Howell, Francis Clark *anthropologist, educator*
Jaffee, Dwight M. *economist, educator*
Johanson, Donald Carl *physical anthropologist*
Kallgren, Joyce Kislitzin *political science educator*
Keeler, Theodore Edwin *economics educator*
Landau, Martin *political science educator*
Lane, Sylvia *economist, educator*
Lee, Ronald Demos *demographer, economist, educator*
Letiche, John Marion *economist, educator*
Lipson, Leslie Michael *political science educator*
Luker, Kristin *sociology educator*
Maisel, Sherman Joseph *economist, educator*
McFadden, Daniel Little *economics educator*
Meier, Richard Louis *futurist, planner, behavioral scientist*
Muir, William Ker, Jr. *political science educator*
Parsons, James Jerome *geographer, educator*
Quigley, John Michael *economist, educator*
Ranney, (Joseph) Austin *political science educator*
Rausser, Gordon C(lyde) *agricultural and resource economics educator*
Reich, Michael *economics educator*
Rosberg, Carl Gustaf *political science educator*
Rosen, Kenneth T. *economist*
Rowe, John Howland *anthropologist, educator*
Sarich, Vincent M. *anthropologist, educator*
Shack, William Alfred *anthropology educator, researcher, consultant*
Shapiro, Carl *economics educator and consultant*
Smolensky, Eugene *economics educator*
Sutch, Richard Charles *economics educator*
Teece, David John *economics and management educator*
Waltz, Kenneth Neal *political science educator*
Wilensky, Harold L. *political science and industrial relations educator*
Williamson, Oliver Eaton *economics and law educator*
Wolfinger, Raymond Edwin *political science educator*

Calistoga
Spindler, George Dearborn *anthropologist, educator, author, editor*

Carpinteria
Schmidhauser, John Richard *political science educator*
Wheeler, John Harvey *political scientist*

Chico
Farrer, Claire Anne Rafferty *anthropologist, folklorist, educator*
McIntyre, Valene Smith *anthropology educator*

Claremont
Arndt, Sven William *economics educator*
Benson, George Charles Sumner *political science educator*
Bjork, Gordon Carl *economist, educator*
Bond, Floyd Alden *economist, educator*
Bowman, Dean Orlando *economist, educator*
Gold, Bela *educator, economist*
Hinshaw, Randall (Weston) *economist, educator*
Lehman, James Alden *economist, educator*
Likens, James Dean *economics educator*
Neal, Fred Warner *political scientist, educator*
Palmer, Hans Christian *economics educator*
Phelps, Orme Wheelock *economics educator emeritus*
Rossum, Ralph Arthur *political science educator*
Wykoff, Frank Champion *economics educator*

Corona Del Mar
Hinderaker, Ivan *political science educator*

Davis
Cohen, Lawrence Edward *sociology educator, criminologist*
Crowley, Daniel John *anthropologist*
Elmendorf, William Welcome *anthropology educator*
Groth, Alexander Jacob *political science educator*
Hrdy, Sarah Blaffer *anthropology educator*
Ives, John David (Jack Ives) *geography and environmental sciences educator*
Jett, Stephen Clinton *geography educator, researcher*
Johnston, Warren Eugene *agricultural economics educator, consultant*
Lofland, John Franklin *sociologist, educator*
Lofland, Lyn Hebert *sociology educator*
McHenry, Henry Malcolm *anthropologist, educator*
Musolf, Lloyd Daryl *political science educator, institute administrator*
Siverson, Randolph Martin *political science educator*
Skinner, G(eorge) William *anthropologist, educator*
Smith, Michael Peter *social science educator, researcher*
Sumner, Daniel Alan *economist, educator*
Wegge, Leon Louis François *economics educator*

Encinitas
Bloomberg, Warner, Jr. *urban affairs educator emeritus*

Encino
Posnansky, Merrick *history and archaeology educator*

Escondido
Stone, Ileane Gertrude *gerontologist*

Foster City
Thomlinson, Ralph *demographer, educator*

Fresno
Dackawich, S. John *sociology educator*
O'Brien, John Conway *economist, educator, writer*

Fullerton
Foster, Julian Francis Sherwood *political science educator*

Glendale
Hadley, Paul Ervin *international relations educator*

Hayward
Smith, J(ohn) Malcolm *political science educator*

Irvine
Aigner, Dennis John *economics educator, consultant*
Burton, Michael Ladd *anthropology educator*
Cushman, Robert Fairchild *political science educator, author, editor*
Danziger, James Norris *political science educator*
Freeman, Linton Clarke *sociology educator*
Geis, Gilbert Lawrence *sociology educator emeritus*
Lave, Charles Arthur *economics educator*
Margolis, Julius *economist, educator*
Rubel, Arthur Joseph *anthropologist, educator*
Schonfeld, William Rost *political science educator, researcher*
Small, Kenneth Alan *economics educator*
Taagepera, Rein *social science educator*
Treas, Judith Kay *sociology educator*
White, Douglas R. *anthropology educator*

Kensington
Swanson, Guy Edwin *social scientist, educator*

La Jolla
Attiyeh, Richard Eugene *economics educator*
Borjas, George J(esus) *economics educator*
Cornelius, Wayne A., Jr. *political scientist, educator*
Gourevitch, Peter Alexis *political science educator, dean*
Granger, Clive William John *economist, educator*
Groves, Theodore Francis, Jr. *economics educator*
Hoston, Germaine Annette *political science educator*
Lakoff, Sanford *political scientist, educator*
Schiller, Herbert Irving *social scientist, author*
†Smith, Peter Hopkinson *political scientist, consultant, author*
Spiro, Melford Elliot *anthropology educator*
Starr, Ross Marc *economist, educator*

Laguna Beach
Bent, Alan Edward *political science educator, administrator*
Dale, Leon Andrew *economist, educator*
Fagin, Henry *public administration consultant*

Laguna Hills
Kaplan, Sidney Joseph *sociologist, educator*

Loomis
Hartmann, Frederick Howard *political science educator emeritus*

Los Angeles
Alexander, Herbert E. *political scientist*
Allen, William Richard *retired economist*
Alvarez, Rodolfo *sociology educator, consultant*
Anawalt, Patricia Rieff *anthropologist*
Anderson, Austin Gilman *economics research company consultant*
Arnold, Jeanne Eloise *anthropologist, educator*
Bennett, Charles Franklin, Jr. *biogeographer, educator*
Blakely, Edward James *economics educator*
Bloland, Paul Anson *psychology educator emeritus*
Broderick, Carlfred Bartholomew *sociology educator*
†Brubaker, William Rogers *sociology educator*
Castaneda, Carlos *anthropologist, author*
†Champagne, Duane Willard *sociology educator*
Clark, Burton Robert *sociologist, educator*
Coombs, Robert Holman *sociologist, medical educator, author*
Darby, Michael Rucker *economist, educator*
Dekmejian, Richard Hrair *political science educator*
Demsetz, Harold *economist, educator*
Earle, Timothy *anthropology educator*
Easterlin, Richard Ainley *economist, educator*
†Ellickson, Bryan Carl *economics educator*
Glaser, Daniel *sociologist*
Glassner, Barry *sociology educator, author*
Hahn, Harlan Dean *political science educator, consultant*
Harberger, Arnold Carl *economist, educator*
Heer, David Macalpine *sociology educator*
Hendrick, Hal Wilmans *human factors educator*
Hirsch, Werner Zvi *economist, educator*
Hoffenberg, Marvin *political science educator, consultant*
Intriligator, Michael David *economist, educator*
Klein, Benjamin *economics educator, consultant*
La Force, James Clayburn, Jr. *economist, educator*
Leijonhufvud, Axel Stig Bengt *economics educator*
Levine, Robert Arthur *economist, policy analyst*
Lowenthal, Abraham Frederic *international relations educator*
Malecki, Edward Stanley, Jr. *political science educator*
Maquet, Jacques Jerome Pierre *anthropologist, writer*
Morgner, Aurelius *economist, educator*
Nelson, Howard Joseph *educator, geographer*
Nixon, John Harmon *economist*
Orme, Antony Ronald *geography educator*
Riley, John Graham *economics educator*
Rosecrance, Richard Newton *political scientist, educator*
Seeman, Melvin *sociologist, educator*
Sklar, Richard Lawrence *political science educator*
Somers, Harold Milton *economist, educator*
Thompson, Earl Albert *economics educator*
Thrower, Norman Joseph William *geographer, educator*
Totten, George Oakley, III *political science educator*
Turk, Herman *sociologist, educator, researcher*
Turner, Ralph Herbert *sociologist, educator*
Williams, Robert Martin *economist, consultant*
Wilson, James Quinn *government, management educator*
Zame, William R. *economist, educator, mathematician*

Los Gatos
Webster, John Chas *human resources management consultant*

Mill Valley
Harner, Michael James *anthropologist, educator, author*

Monterey
von Pagenhardt, Robert *policy sciences educator, diplomat*

Northridge
Segalman, Ralph *sociology educator*

Oakdale
Thomas, William LeRoy *geography educator, cruise lecturer*

Oakland
†Farrell, Kenneth Royden *economist*

Oregon House
Storm, Donald John *archaeologist, historian*

Pacific Palisades
Longaker, Richard Pancoast *political science educator emeritus*

Palo Alto
Bohrnstedt, George William *educational researcher*
Cogan, John Francis *economist, researcher, educator*
Dornbusch, Sanford Maurice *sociology educator*
Eulau, Heinz *political scientist, educator*
Lewis, John Wilson *political science educator*
Scitovsky, Anne Aickelin *economist*
Smelser, Neil Joseph *sociologist*

Pasadena
Davis, Lance Edwin *economics educator*
Grether, David Maclay *economics educator*
Ledyard, John Odell *economics educator, consultant*
Munger, Edwin Stanton *political geography educator*
Oliver, Robert Warner *economics educator*
Plott, Charles R. *economics educator*
Scudder, Thayer *anthropologist, educator*

Placentia
Gobar, Alfred Julian *economic consultant, educator*

Pomona
Shieh, John Ting-chung *economics educator*

Portola Valley
Ward, Robert Edward *retired political science educator and university administrator*

Redondo Beach
McWilliams, Margaret Ann *home economics educator, author*

Riverside
Adrian, Charles Raymond *political science educator*
Griffin, Keith Broadwell *economics educator*
Kronenfeld, David Brian *anthropologist*
Turk, Austin Theodore *sociology educator*
Turner, Arthur Campbell *political science educator, author*

Sacramento
Bruce, Thomas Edward *thanatologist, psychology educator*
Flournoy, Houston Irvine *public administration educator*

Gottfredson, Don Martin *criminal justice educator*
Moore, David Sumner *forensic document examiner*
Newland, Chester Albert *public administration educator*
Post, August Alan *economist, artist*
Sherwood, Robert Petersen *retired sociology educator*

San Diego
Barckley, Robert Eugene *economics educator*
Berger, Bennett Maurice *sociology educator*
Getis, Arthur *geography educator*
Madhavan, Murugappa Chettiar *economics educator, international consultant*
Rea, Amadeo Michael *ethnobiologist, ornithologist*
Storer, Norman William *sociology educator*
Weeks, John Robert *geographer, sociology educator*

San Francisco
Burgess, Leonard Randolph *business administration and economics educator, writer*
Butz, Otto William *political science educator*
Chesnut, Carol Fitting *economist*
Cirese, Robert Charles *economist, real estate investment counselor*
Clark, M(ary) Margaret *anthropology educator*
Estes, Carroll Lynn *sociologist, educator*
Hoadley, Walter Evans *economist, financial executive, lay worker*
Luft, Harold S. *health economist*
Marston, Michael *urban economist, asset management executive*
Marvin, David Keith *international relations educator*
Pincus, Joseph *economist, educator*
Rice, Dorothy Pechman (Mrs. John Donald Rice) *medical economist*
Wilson, John Oliver *economist, educator, banker*

San Jose
Careaga, Rogelio Antonio *economics educator, consultant*
McDowell, Jennifer *sociologist, composer, playwright, publisher*

Santa Barbara
Baldwin, John David *sociologist, educator*
Clinard, Marshall Barron *sociologist, educator*
Comanor, William S. *economist, educator*
Erasmus, Charles John *anthropologist, educator*
Jochim, Michael Allan *archaeologist*
Juergensmeyer, Mark Karl *sociology educator*
Pritchett, Charles Herman *political science educator*
Shapiro, Perry *economics educator*
Tobler, Waldo Rudolph *geographer, cartographer*
Turner, Henry A. *political science educator, author*

Santa Cruz
Child, Frank Clayton *economist, educator*
Fung, K. C. *economics educator*
Musgrave, Richard Abel *economics educator*

Santa Monica
†Hensler, Deborah Rosenfield *public policy analyst, law educator*
Smith, James Patrick *economist*
Williams, Albert Paine *economist*
Wolf, Charles, Jr. *economist, educator*

Stanford
Abramovitz, Moses *economist, educator*
Almond, Gabriel Abraham *political science educator*
Amemiya, Takeshi *economist, statistician*
Anderson, Annelise Graebner *economist*
Anderson, Martin Carl *economist*
Aoki, Masahiko *economics educator*
Arrow, Kenneth Joseph *economist, educator*
Beichman, Arnold *political scientist, educator, writer*
Boskin, Michael Jay *economist, government official, university educator, consultant*
Bunzel, John Harvey *political science educator, researcher*
Campbell, Wesley Glenn *economist, educator*
Carnoy, Martin *economics educator*
David, Paul Allan *economics educator*
Davis, Kingsley *sociologist, educator, researcher*
Enthoven, Alain Charles *economist, educator*
Falcon, Walter Phillip *economist*
Flanagan, Robert Joseph *economics educator*
Friedman, Milton *economist, educator emeritus, author*
Fuchs, Victor Robert *economics educator*
George, Alexander Lawrence *political scientist, educator*
Greenberg, Joseph H. *anthropologist*
Hall, Robert Ernest *economics educator*
Harris, Donald J. *economics educator*
Hickman, Bert George, Jr. *economist, educator*
Holloway, David James *political science educator*
Howell, James Edwin *economist, educator*
Inkeles, Alex *sociology educator*
Johnston, Bruce Foster *economics educator*
Kreps, David Marc *economist, educator*
Kurz, Mordecai *economics educator*
Lau, Lawrence Juen-Yee *economics educator, consultant*
Lazear, Edward Paul *economics and industrial relations educator, researcher*
Levin, Henry Mordecai *economist, educator*
Manley, John Frederick *political scientist, educator*
March, James Gardner *social scientist, educator*
Mc Lure, Charles E., Jr. *economist*
Meier, Gerald M. *economics educator*
Milgrom, Paul Robert *economics educator*
Moore, Thomas Gale *economist, educator*
Noll, Roger Gordon *economist, educator*
North, Robert Carver *political science educator*
Paul, Benjamin David *anthropologist, educator*
Ricardo-Campbell, Rita *economist, educator*
Roberts, Donald John *economics and business educator, consultant*
Romer, Paul Michael *economics educator*
Rosaldo, Renato Ignacio, Jr. *cultural anthropology educator*
Rosenberg, Nathan *economics educator*
Rosse, James Nelson *economics educator, educational administrator*
Rowen, Henry Stanislaus *economics educator*
Sargent, Thomas John *economics educator*
Scott, W(illiam) Richard *sociology educator*
Solomon, Ezra *economist, educator*
Sowell, Thomas *economist*
Spence, A. Michael *economics educator, academic administrator*
Staar, Richard Felix *political scientist*
Taylor, John Brian *economist, educator*
Triska, Jan Francis *retired political science educator*
Van Horne, James Carter *economist, educator*

Studio City
Fisher, Joel Marshall *political scientist, legal recruiter*

Trabuco Canyon
Addy, Jo Alison Phears *economist*

Walnut Creek
Nelson, Elmer Kingsholm, Jr. *educator, writer, mediator, consultant*
Smith, Robert Houston *archeologist, religious studies educator*

COLORADO

Boulder
Boss, Russel Wayne *business administration educator*
Boulding, Elise Marie *sociologist, educator*
Codding, George Arthur, Jr. *political science educator*
Darling, Frank Clayton *former political science educator, educational institute administrator*
Greenberg, Edward Seymour *political science educator*
Greene, David Lee *physical anthropologist, educator*
Helburn, Nicholas *geography educator*
Kelso, Alec John (Jack Kelso) *anthropologist, educator*
Walker, Deward Edgar, Jr. *anthropologist, educator*
Wheat, Joe Ben *anthropologist*
White, Gilbert F(owler) *geographer, educator*

Colorado Springs
Brooks, Glenn Ellis *political science educator, educational administrator*
Feld, Werner Joachim *political scientist, educator*

Denver
Beresford, Thomas Patrick *psychiatry educator, alcoholism researcher*
Collins, Susan Margaret *archaeologist*
Mendelsohn, Harold *sociologist, educator*
Nelson, Sarah Milledge *archaeology educator*

Estes Park
Moore, Omar Khayyam *experimental sociologist*

Fort Collins
†Berry, Kenneth J. *sociology educator*
Eitzen, David Stanley *sociologist, educator*
Standing Bear, Zugguelgeres Galafach *criminologist, forensic scientist, educator*
Walsh, Richard George *agricultural economist*
Wengert, Norman Irving *political science educator*

Golden
Petrick, Alfred, Jr. *mineral economics educator, consultant*
Woolsey, Robert Eugene Donald *mineral economics, mathematics and business administration educator*

Grand Junction
Bacon, Phillip *geographer, author, consultant*

Littleton
Chapman, Richard LeRoy *public policy researcher*
Milliken, John Gordon *research economist*

Mc Coy
Wolf, Charlotte Elizabeth *sociologist*

CONNECTICUT

Bridgeport
van der Kroef, Justus Maria *political science educator*

Brooklyn
Wendel, Richard Frederick *economist, educator, consultant*

Hamden
Parker, William Nelson *economics educator*

Hartford
Curran, Ward Schenk *economist, educator*
Gunderson, Gerald Axel *economics educator, administrator*
Vohra, Ranbir *political scientist, educator*

Middletown
Lemert, Charles Clay *sociology educator*
Lovell, Michael C. *economics educator*
Miller, Richard Alan *economist, educator*
Titus, David Anson *political science educator*

New Britain
Kim, Ki Hoon *economist, educator*

New Canaan
Marcus, Edward *economist, educator*

New Haven
Apter, David Ernest *political science educator*
Bell, Wendell *sociologist, educator, futurist*
Bracken, Paul *political science educator*
Brainard, William Crittenden *economist, educator, university official*
Brewer, Garry Dwight *social scientist, educator*
Coe, Michael Douglas *anthropologist, educator*
Conklin, Harold Colyer *anthropologist, educator*
Davis, Deborah *sociology educator*
Ember, Melvin Lawrence *anthropologist, educator*
Erikson, Kai *sociologist, educator*
Hole, Frank *anthropology educator*
LaPalombara, Joseph *political science educator*
Levin, Richard Charles *economist*
MacAvoy, Paul Webster *economics educator, university dean*
Marmor, Theodore Richard *political science and public management educator*
Mayhew, David Raymond *political educator*
Myers, Jerome Keeley *sociology educator*
Peck, Merton Joseph *educator, economist*
Phillips, Peter Charles Bonest *economist, educator, researcher*
Pospisil, Leopold Jaroslav *anthropology educator*
Ranis, Gustav *economist, educator*
Reiss, Albert John, Jr. *sociology educator*
Reynolds, Lloyd George *economist, educator*
Reynolds, Mary Trackett *political scientist*
†Richard, Alison Feltes *anthropology educator*
Rouse, Irving *anthropologist, emeritus educator*
Russett, Bruce Martin *political science educator*
Scarf, Herbert Eli *economics educator*
Schultz, T. Paul *economics educator*
Shubik, Martin *economics educator*
Smith, Rogers Mood *political scientist*
Tobin, James *economics educator*
Westerfield, Holt Bradford *political scientist, educator*
Wheeler, Stanton *law and social science educator*

New London
Doro, Marion Elizabeth *political scientist, educator*

North Haven
Dahl, Robert Alan *political science educator*

Ridgefield
Tomanic, Joseph P(aul) *research scientist*

Rowayton
Sills, David Lawrence *retired sociologist*

Southbury
Atwood, Edward Charles *economist, educator*
Wescott, Roger Williams *anthropologist*

Stamford
Teeters, Nancy Hays *economist*
Williams, Ernest William, Jr. *economist, educator*

Stepney
Stokes, Charles Junius *economist, educator*

Storrs
Allen, John Logan *geographer*
Walker, David Bradstreet *political science educator*

Storrs Mansfield
Ladd, Everett Carll *political science educator, author*

Westport
Duncan, Joseph Wayman *business economist*
Nolte, Richard Henry *political science researcher, consultant*
O'Leary, James John *economist*

DELAWARE

Lewes
Chapman, Janet Carter Goodrich (Mrs. John William Chapman) *economist, educator*

Newark
Bilinsky, Yaroslav *political scientist*
Brams, Marvin Robert *economist, mental health counselor, interfaith minister*
DiRenzo, Gordon James *sociologist, psychologist, educator*
Elterich, Joachim Gustav *agricultural economics educator*
Mangone, Gerard J. *international and maritime law educator*
Raffel, Jeffrey Allen *urban affairs educator*
Scarpitti, Frank Roland *sociology educator*
Tannian, Francis Xavier *economist, educator*

Wilmington
Reeder, Charles Benton *economic consultant*

DISTRICT OF COLUMBIA

Washington
Aaron, Henry Jacob *economics educator*
Abler, Ronald Francis *geography educator*
Adams, Arvil Van *economist, educator*
Amling, Frederick *economist, educator, investment manager*
Arend, Anthony Clark *international relations educator*
Aschheim, Joseph *economist, educator*
Ballentine, J. Gregory *economist*
Banister, Judith *demographer, educator*
Barnes, Samuel Henry *political scientist, educator*
Barnett, Arthur Doak *political scientist, educator*
Becker, Mary Louise *political scientist*
Bergmann, Barbara Rose *economics educator*
Bergsten, C. Fred *economist*
Besen, Stanley Martin *economist*
†Beyer, John Carl *economist, consultant*
Birnbaum, Norman *author, humanities educator*
Blasier, Cole *political scientist*
Blaxall, Martha Ossoff *economist*
Blinder, Alan Stuart *economist*
Bloomfield, Arthur Irving *economics educator*
Bluth, B. J. (Elizabeth Jean Catherine Bluth) *sociologist, aerospace educator*
Boughton, James Murray *economist*
Bramson, Leon *social scientist, educator*
Brown, David Springer *retired public administration educator*
†Bruno, Michael Peter *economist*
Brzezinski, Zbigniew *political science educator, author*
Burcroff, Richard Tomkinson, II *economist*
Burns, Joseph M. *economist*
Butterworth, Charles E. *political science educator*
Button, Kenneth Rodman *international economist, consultant*
Cantor, Muriel Goldsman *sociologist, educator*
Carliner, Michael Simon *economist, association executive*
Carpenter, Ted Galen *political scientist*
†Carson, Carol S. *economist*
Cavanagh, John Henry *political economist*
Checchi, Vincent Victor *economist*
Chimerine, Lawrence *economist*
Chu, David S. C. *economist*
Cline, Ray Steiner *political scientist, historian*
Cline, William Richard *economist, educator*
Clodius, Robert LeRoy *economist, educator*
Coates, Joseph Francis *futurist*
Corden, Warner Max *economics educator*
Craig, John Tucker *economist, consultant*
†Davidson, James Dale *political economist, writer*
Davis, Lynn Etheridge *political scientist, government official*
Dawson, Mimi (Mimi Weyforth) *public policy consultant, former government official*
de Leeuw, Frank *economist*
†Dickens, William Theodore *economics educator*
Dillon, Wilton Sterling *anthropologist, foundation administrator*
Dine, Thomas Alan *government relations specialist*
Dizard, Wilson Paul, Jr. *international affairs consultant, educator*
Dommen, Arthur John *agricultural economist*
Downs, Anthony *urban economist, real estate consultant*
Eads, George Curtis *economics executive*
Edwards, Gilbert Franklin *sociologist, educator*
English, Richard Allyn *sociologist, social work educator*
Etzioni, Amitai Werner *sociologist, educator*
Faux, Jeff (Geoffrey Peter Faux) *economist, writer*
Fischer, Stanley *economist, educator*
Frank, Isaiah *economist, educator*
Frankel, Jeffrey Alexander *economics educator, consultant*
Fuchs, Roland John *geography educator, university administrator*
Fukushima, Kiyohiko *economist*
Galston, William Arthur *political scientist, educator*
Gelman, Norman Ira *public policy consultant*
Goode, Richard Benjamin *economist, educator*
Grandmaison, J. Joseph *political consultant*
Green, Gordon Woodrow, Jr. *economist, federal agency administrator*
Greenberg, Milton *political scientist, educator*
Greenspan, Alan *economist*
Griffin, James Bennett *anthropologist, educator*
Gubser, Peter Anton *political scientist, writer, educator*
Gutierrez-Santos, Luis Emiliano *economist*
†Hartmann, Heidi Irmgard Victoria *economist, political organization executive*
Hayes, Samuel Perkins *social scientist, educator*
Helms, Robert Brake *economist, research director*
Hess, Stephen *political scientist, author*
Hickman, R(obert) Harrison *political pollster, strategist*
Holland, Robert Carl *economist*
Horowitz, Herbert Eugene *educator, consultant, former ambassador*
Hovey, Justus Allan, Jr. *political scientist*
Hudson, Michael Craig *political science educator*
Hufbauer, Gary Clyde *economist, lawyer, educator*
Hyland, William George *international relations educator*
Jamme, Albert Joseph *archaeologist, educator*
Jasinowski, Jerry Joseph *economist, corporate executive*
Jaspersen, Frederick Zarr *economist*
Johnson, Omotunde Evan George *economist*
Johnson, Robert Henry *political science educator*
Jones, William Bowdoin *political scientist, retired diplomat, lawyer*
Kemp, Geoffrey Thomas Howard *international affairs specialist*
Kendrick, John Whitefield *economist, educator, consultant*
Kerns, Wilmer Lee *social science researcher*
Khadduri, Majid *international studies educator*
Kirkpatrick, Jeane Duane Jordan *political scientist, government official*
Kitchen, John Howard *economist*
Kling, William *economist, retired foreign service officer*
Kondratas, Skirma Anna *policy analyst*
Korologos, Tom Chris *government affairs consultant, former federal official*
Kristol, Irving *social sciences educator, editor*
Krulfeld, Ruth Marilyn *anthropologist, educator*
Laden, Ben Ellis *economist*
LaRouche, Lyndon H., Jr. *economist*
Lefever, Ernest W. *political philosopher, author, former institute president*
LeoGrande, William Mark *political science educator, writer*
Liebenson, Herbert *economist, trade association executive*
Lieber, Robert J. *political science educator, writer*
Lin, William Wen-Rong *economist*
Lindsey, Lawrence Benjamin *economist, federal official*
Liska, George *political science educator, author*
Luttwak, Edward Nicolae *policy and business consultant, writer*
Malashevich, Bruce Peter *economist*
Malmgren, Harald Bernard *economist*
Manatos, Andrew Emanuel *policy consultant, former government official*
Manley, William Tanner *economist*
Mann, Thomas Edward *political scientist*
Margolis, James David *political consulting and advertising executive*
Martinez, Herminia S. *economist, banker*
Matalin, Mary *political consultant*
Maudlin, Robert V. *economics and government affairs consultant*
McElroy, Frederick William *economics educator, consultant*
McGough, Duane Theodore *economist, government official*
Meggers, Betty J(ane) *anthropologist*
Mellor, John Williams *economist, policy consultant firm executive*
Millar, James Robert *economist, educator, university official*
Miller, James Clifford, III *economist*
Minarik, Joseph John *economist, researcher*
Miranowski, John Alfred *agricultural economist*
Moran, Ricardo Julio *economist*
Munasinghe, Mohan *development economist*
Munnell, Alicia Haydock *economist*
Nakhleh, Emile A. *governmental sciences educator*
Nehmer, Stanley *economics consultant*
Newman, Monroe *retired economist, educator*
Niskanen, William Arthur, Jr. *economist*
†Noland, Marcus *economist, educator*
Oh, John Kie-Chiang *political science educator, university official*
Olson, Charles Eric *economist*
Ooms, Van Doorn *economist*
Ornstein, Norman Jay *political scientist*
†Ortner, Donald J. *biological anthropologist, educator*
Oswald, Rudolph A. *economist*
Oweiss, Ibrahim Mohamed *economist, educator*

Perry, George Lewis *research economist, consultant*
Peterman, John L. *economist*
Peterson, William Herbert *economist*
Phillips, Karen Borlaug *economist, association executive*
Phillips, Susan Meredith *financial economist, former university administrator*
Pickenpaugh, Thomas Edward *archaeologist*
†Plewes, Thomas Jeffrey *economic statistician, government executive*
Polak, Jacques Jacobus *economist, foundation administrator*
Potvin, Raymond Herve *sociology educator, author*
Preeg, Ernest Henry *strategic and international studies center executive*
Prell, Michael Jack *economist*
Prestowitz, Clyde Vincent *economist, research administrator*
Rahn, Richard William *economist, business executive*
Randall, Robert L(ee) *ecological economist*
Ravenal, Earl Cedric *international relations educator, author*
Reich, Bernard *political science educator*
Reich, Otto Juan *political analyst, business consultant*
Reining, Priscilla Copeland *anthropologist*
Rettig, Richard Allen *social sciences educator, policy analyst, administrator*
Reynolds, Robert Joel *economist, consultant*
Rivlin, Alice Mitchell *economist*
Roberts, Markley *economist, educator*
Roberts, Paul Craig, III *economics educator, author, consultant*
Roberts, Walter Ronald *political science educator, former government official*
Roett, Riordan *political science educator, consultant*
Rosenau, James Nathan *political scientist, author*
Ruttenberg, Stanley Harvey *economist*
Ryn, Claes Gösta *political science educator, author, research institute administrator*
Salant, Walter S. *economist*
Salop, Steven Charles *economics educator*
Sanderson, Fred Hugo *economist*
Sawhill, Isabel Van Devanter *economist*
Schachter, Barry *economist*
Scheppach, Raymond Carl, Jr. *association executive, economist*
Schlesinger, James Rodney *economist*
Schotta, Charles *economist, government official*
Schuck, Victoria *political science educator*
Schultze, Charles Louis *economist, educator*
Shah-Jahan, M. M. *economist*
Shelton, Joanna Reed *economist*
†Shelton, Sally Angela *political scientist, writer, educator, editor*
Simes, Dimitri Konstantin *international affairs expert and educator*
Smith, Bruce David *archaeologist*
Smythe-Haith, Mabel Murphy *consultant on African economic development, speaker, writer*
Soldo, Beth Jean *demography educator, researcher*
Solomon, Richard Harvey *political scientist*
Solomon, Robert *economist*
Spiro, Benjamin Paul *economist, consultant*
Squier, Robert Dave *political consultant, documentary filmmaker*
Stanford, Dennis Joe *archaeologist, museum curator*
Stanley, Timothy Wadsworth *economist*
Stavrou, Nikolaos Athanasios *political science educator*
Stein, Herbert *economist*
Steiner, Gilbert Yale *political scientist*
Sterner, Michael Edmund *international affairs consultant*
Stone, Russell A. *sociology educator*
†Strauss, David *Vice Presidential Office official*
Strauss, Elliott Bowman *economic development consultant, retired naval officer*
Sturtevant, William Curtis *anthropologist*
Sundquist, James Lloyd *political scientist*
Sunley, Emil McKee *economist*
Sweeney, Richard James *economics educator*
Taylor, William Jesse, Jr. *international studies educator, research center executive*
†Teele, Thurston Ferdinand *economist*
Toder, Eric Jay *economist*
Tolchin, Susan Jane *public administration educator, writer*
Tyson, Laura D'Andrea *economist, government adviser, educator*
Van Beek, Gus Willard *archaeologist*
Walinsky, Louis Joseph *economic consultant, writer*
Walker, Charls Edward *economist, consultant*
Wallis, W(ilson) Allen *economist, educator, statistician*
Warne, William Robert *economist*
Whyte, Martin King *sociology and Chinese studies educator*
Wilensky, Gail Roggin *economist*
Williams, Abiodun *international relations educator*
Wilson, Ewen Maclellan *economist*
Woodward, Susan Ellen *economist, federal official*
Yochelson, John *political economist*

FLORIDA

Boca Raton
Feuerlein, Willy John Arthur *economist, educator*
Nystrom, John Warren *geographer, educator*

Bradenton
Balsley, Howard Lloyd *economist*

Coral Gables
Shipley, Vergil Alan *political science educator*

Fort Lauderdale
Bartelstone, Rona Sue *gerontologist*
Fosback, Norman George *stock market econometrician, researcher*

Gainesville
Barton, Allen Hoisington *sociologist*
Bernard, H. Russell *anthropology educator, scientific editor*
Carr, Glenna Dodson *economics educator*
Harris, Marvin *anthropology educator*
†Maples, William Ross *anthropology educator, consultant*
Milanich, Jerald Thomas *archaeologist, museum curator*
Schmidt, Peter R. *anthropology educator*
Thompson, Victor Alexander *political science educator*
von Mering, Otto Oswald *anthropology educator*
Zabel, Edward *economist, educator*

Hawthorne
Ross, James Elmer *economist, administrator*

Jacksonville
Godfrey, John Munro *bank economist*
Moore, David Graham *sociologist, educator*
Seroka, James Henry *social sciences educator, university administrator*

Jupiter
Biebuyck, Daniel Prosper *retired anthropologist, educator*

Mac Dill AFB
Schwendinger, Charles Joseph *public administration educator, researcher*

Maitland
Blackburn, John Oliver *economist, consultant*

Miami
Salazar-Carrillo, Jorge *economics educator*

Miami Beach
Chirovsky, Nicholas Ludomir *economics educator, historian, author*

Mount Dora
Myren, Richard Albert *criminal justice consultant*

Naples
Myers, Charles Andrew *retired economist*

North Miami Beach
Averch, Harvey Allan *economist, educator, academic administrator*

Ocala
Grissom, Robert Jesse, Sr. *criminal justice educator*

Pensacola
Killian, Lewis Martin *sociology educator*

Pompano Beach
Calatchi, Ralph Franklin *economist*

Saint Augustine
Armstrong, John Alexander *political scientist, educator*
Theil, Henri *economist, educator*

Saint Petersburg
Serrie, Hendrick *anthropology and international business educator*

Sanibel
Crown, David Allan *criminologist, educator*

Sarasota
Fabrycy, Mark Zdzislaw *retired economist*
Gordon, Sanford Daniel *economics educator*
Hamberg, Daniel *economist, educator*
Roberts, Merrill Joseph *economist, educator*

Summerland Key
Muth, John Fraser *economics educator*

Tallahassee
Ashler, Philip Frederic *international trade and development advisor*
Brueckheimer, William Rogers *social science educator*
Colberg, Marshall Rudolph *economist*
Dye, Thomas Roy *political science educator*
Earhart, Eileen Magie *retired home and family life educator*
Holcombe, Randall Gregory *economics educator*
Laird, William Everette, Jr. *economics educator, administrator*
Macesich, George *econmomics professor*
Maier-Katkin, Daniel *criminology educator, administrator*
Nam, Charles Benjamin *sociologist, demographer, educator*
Newell, Barbara Warne *economist, educator*
Paredes, James Anthony *anthropologist, educator*
†Rittberg, Eric Joseph *political consultant*
Serow, William John *economics educator*
Williams, James Howard *sociologist, research agency executive*

Tampa
MacManus, Susan Ann *political science educator, researcher*
Thomas, Carole Dolores *gerontologist*

West Palm Beach
Lively, Edwin Lowe *sociology educator*

GEORGIA

Athens
Allsbrook, Ogden Olmstead, Jr. *economics educator*
Bullock, Charles Spencer, III *political science educator, author, consultant*
Clute, Robert Eugene *political and social science educator*
Dunn, Delmer Delano *political science educator*
Garbin, Albeno Patrick *sociology educator*
Kamerschen, David Roy *economist, educator*
Knapp, Charles Boynton *economist, educator, academic administrator*
Smith, Howard Ross *economics educator, academic administrator, researcher, consultant*

Atlanta
†Bahl, Roy Winford *economist, educator, consultant*
Cameron, Rondo *economic history educator*
Cox, Albert Harrington, Jr. *economist*
Endicott, John Edgar *international relations educator*
Muth, Richard Ferris *economics educator*

Milledgeville
Bouley, Eugene Edward, Jr. *sociology and criminal justice educator*

Norcross
Conway, Hobart McKinley, Jr. *geo-economist*

HAWAII

Hilo
Wang, James Chia-Fang *political science educator*

Honolulu
Cho, Lee-Jay *social scientist, demographer*
Force, Roland Wynfield *anthropologist, museum executive*
Kuroda, Yasumasa *political science educator, researcher*
Laney, Leroy Olan *economist, banker*
Mark, Shelley Muin *economist, educator, government official*
Morse, Richard *social scientist*
Ogawa, Dennis Masaaki *American studies educator*
Paige, Glenn Durland *political scientist, educator*
Rambo, A. Terry *anthropologist, research program director*
Schubert, Glendon *political scientist, educator*
Solheim, Wilhelm Gerhard, II *anthropologist, educator*
Suh, Dae-Sook *political science educator*
Tuttle, Daniel Webster *retired political science educator*

Kaneohe
Baker, Paul Thornell *anthropology educator*

IDAHO

Boise
Overgaard, Willard Michele *retired political scientist, jurisprudent*
Scudder, David Benjamin *economist, foundation administrator*

Caldwell
Lonergan, Wallace Gunn *economics educator, management consultant*

Kamiah
Martin, Boyd Archer *political science educator emeritus*

Sandpoint
Glock, Charles Young *sociologist*

ILLINOIS

Carbondale
Best, Joel Gordon *sociology educator*
Derge, David Richard *political science educator*
Eynon, Thomas Grant *sociology educator*
Handler, Jerome Sidney *anthropology educator*
Harper, Robert Alexander *geography educator*
Snyder, Charles Royce *sociologist, educator*
Somit, Albert *political educator*
Takayama, Akira *economics educator*

Champaign
Arnould, Richard Julius *economist, educator, consultant*
Brems, Hans Julius *economist, educator*
Due, John Fitzgerald *economist, educator emeritus*
Frankel, Marvin *economist, educator*
Kanet, Roger Edward *political science educator, university administrator*
Nagel, Stuart Samuel *political science educator, lawyer*
Orr, Daniel *educator, economist*
Shupp, Franklin Richard *economist*
Sprenkle, Case Middleton *economics educator*

Charleston
Price, Dalias Adolph *geography educator*

Chicago
Aliber, Robert Z. *economist, educator*
Annable, James Edward *economist*
Arditti, Fred D. *economist, educator*
Baum, Bernard Helmut *sociologist, educator*
Becker, Gary Stanley *economist, educator*
Bidwell, Charles Edward *sociologist, educator*
Boyce, David Edward *transportation and regional science educator*
Boyer, John William *history educator, dean*
Bradburn, Norman M. *behavioral science educator*
Braidwood, Linda Schreiber *archaeologist*
Braidwood, Robert J. *archaeologist, educator*
Carlton, Dennis William *economics educator*
Chung, Joseph Sang-hoon *economics educator*
Clark, Terry Nichols *sociology educator*
Coase, Ronald Harry *economics educator*
Cohler, Bertram Joseph *social sciences educator, clinical psychologist*
Coleman, James Samuel *sociologist, educator*
†Conzen, Michael Peter *geography educator*
Cox, Charles C. *economist*
Cropsey, Joseph *political science educator*
Depoy, Phil E. *special studies think-tank executive*
Fogel, Robert William *economist, educator, historian*
Fogelson, Raymond David *anthropology educator*
Freeman, Leslie Gordon *anthropologist, educator*
Freeman, Susan Tax *anthropologist, educator*
Friedrich, Paul *anthropologist, linguist, poet*
Genetski, Robert James *economist*
Gibson, McGuire *archaeologist, educator*
Ginsburg, Norton Sydney *geography educator*
Gould, John Philip *economist, educator*
Graber, Doris Appel *political scientist, editor, author*
Hamada, Robert S(eiji) *economist, educator*
Harris, Chauncy Dennison *geographer, educator*
Hayes, William Aloysius *economics educator*
Heckman, James Joseph *economist, econometrician, educator*
Hotz, V. Joseph *economics educator*
Johnson, David Gale *economist, educator*
Johnson, Janet Helen *Egyptology educator*
Kahan, Samuel D. *economist*
Kaplan, Morton A. *political science educator*
Klarich, Nina Marie *economic development executive*
Laitin, David Dennis *political science educator*
Larson, Allan Louis *political scientist, educator, lay church worker*
Laumann, Edward Otto *sociology educator*
Lehner, Mark *archaeologist, educator*
Levine, Donald Nathan *sociologist, educator*
Liu, Ben-chieh *economist*
Lopata, Helena Znaniecka *sociologist, researcher, educator*
Malik, Raymond Howard *economist, scientist, corporate executive, multi-lingual, inventor, educator*
Marsh, Jeanne Cay *social welfare educator, researcher*
Mikesell, Marvin Wray *geography educator*
Mirza, David Brown *economist, educator*
Morris, Norval *criminologist, educator*
Neugarten, Bernice Levin *social scientist*
Nicholas, Ralph Wallace *anthropologist, educator*
Peltzman, Sam *economics educator*
†Ranney, David C. *urban economics educator*
Reed, Charles Allen *anthropologist*
Rosen, George *economist, educator*
Rosen, Sherwin *economist, educator*
Rosenblum, Victor Gregory *political science and law educator*
Rudolph, Lloyd Irving *political science educator*
Rudolph, Susanne Hoeber *political and social science educator*
Scheinkman, José Alexandre *economics educator*
Scherer, Ross Paul *retired sociology educator*
Schloss, Nathan *economist*
Schultz, Theodore William *retired educator, economist*
Shanas, Ethel *sociology educator*
Smith, Raymond Thomas *anthropology educator*
Smith, Stan Vladimir *economist, financial service company executive*
Stocking, George Ward, Jr. *anthropology educator*
Stover, Leon (Eugene) *anthropology educator, writer, critic*
Sumner, William Marvin *anthropology and archaeology educator*
Taub, Richard Paul *social sciences educator*
Tienda, Marta *demographer, educator*
Tsou, Tang *political science educator, researcher*
Warnecke, Richard Basley *sociologist, educational administrator*
Wilson, William Julius *sociologist, educator*
Wiser, James Louis *political science educator*
Zarnowitz, Victor *economist, educator*
Zonis, Marvin *political scientist, educator*

De Kalb
Skeels, Jack William *economics educator, consultant*
Wenner, Lettie McSpadden *political science educator*

Edwardsville
Virgo, John Michael *economist, researcher, educator*

Evanston
Alexis, Marcus *economics educator*
Braeutigam, Ronald Ray *economics educator*
Crotty, William *political science educator*
Domowitz, Ian *economics educator*
Eichenbaum, Martin Stewart *economist, educator, consultant*
Eisner, Robert *economics educator*
Goldman, Jerry *political science educator, researcher*
Gordon, Robert James *economics educator*
Hurter, Arthur Patrick *economist, educator*
Irons, William George *anthropology educator*
Jacob, Herbert *political science educator*
Janda, Kenneth Frank *political science educator*
Jencks, Christopher Sandys *sociology educator*
Mills, Edwin Smith *economics educator*
Moses, Leon Nathan *economist, educator*
Moskos, Charles C. *sociology educator*
Myerson, Roger Bruce *game theorist, economist, educator*
Page, Benjamin Ingrim *political science educator, researcher*
Panzar, John C. *economist, educator, consultant*
Porter, Robert Hugh *economics educator*
Reiter, Stanley *economist, educator*
Schnaiberg, Allan *sociology educator*

Glen Ellyn
Frateschi, Lawrence Jan *economist, statistician, educator*

Hinsdale
Dederick, Robert Gogan *economist*

Macomb
†Walzer, Norman Charles *economics educator*

Normal
Jelks, Edward Baker *archaeologist, educator*

Olympia Fields
Sprinkel, Beryl Wayne *economist, consultant*

Palatine
Nagatoshi, Konrad R. *anthropology educator, information systems specialist*

Park Ridge
Tongue, William Walter *economics and business consultant, educator emeritus*

Springfield
Wehrle, Leroy Snyder *economist, educator*
Whitney, John Freeman, Jr. *political science educator*

University Park
Lingamneni, Jaganmohan Rao *criminology educator*

Urbana
Baer, Werner *economist, educator*
Bruner, Edward M. *anthropology educator*
Burdge, Rabel James *sociology educator*
Carmen, Ira Harris *political scientist, educator*
Cohen, Stephen Philip *political science and history educator*
Cunningham, Clark Edward *anthropology educator*
Dovring, Folke *land economics educator, consultant*
Due, Jean Margaret *agricultural economist, educator*
Giertz, J. Fred *economics educator*
Giles, Eugene *anthropology educator*

Gorecki, Jan *sociologist, educator*
Gove, Samuel Kimball *political science educator*
Kolodziej, Edward Albert *political scientist, educator*
Leuthold, Raymond Martin *agricultural economics educator*
Linowes, David Francis *political economist, educator, corporate executive*
Mayer, Enrique José *anthropology educator*
†Nardulli, Peter F. *political science educator*
Nettl, Bruno *anthropology and musicology educator*
Schmidt, Stephen Christopher *agricultural economist, educator*
Seitz, Wesley Donald *agricultural economics educator*
Spitze, Robert George Frederick *agricultural economics educator*
Wirt, Frederick Marshall *political scientist*
Yu, George Tzuchiao *political science educator*

Western Springs
Zamora, Marjorie Dixon *retired political science educator*

Wilmette
Espenshade, Edward Bowman, Jr. *geographer, educator*

INDIANA

Bloomington
Adams, William Richard *archaeologist, lecturer, curator*
Bauman, Richard *anthropologist, educator*
Beckwith, Christopher Irving *social sciences educator, writer, composer*
†Black, William Richard *transportation geography educator*
Caldwell, Lynton Keith *social scientist, educator*
Conrad, Geoffrey Wentworth *archaeologist, educator*
Diamant, Alfred *political science educator*
Leftwich, Richard Henry *economist, educator*
O'Meara, Patrick O. *political science educator*
Ostrom, Elinor *political science educator, researcher*
Ostrom, Vincent A(lfred) *political science educator*
Patrick, John Joseph *social sciences educator*
Schmidt, Nancy J. *anthropologist, educator*
Schuessler, Karl Frederick *sociologist, educator*
Smith, Frederick Robert, Jr. *social studies educator*
Spulber, Nicolas *economics educator emeritus*
Stolnitz, George Joseph *economist, educator, demographer*
Stryker, Sheldon *sociologist, educator*
Vincent, Jeff Robert *labor studies educator*
von Furstenberg, George Michael *economics educator, researcher*

Columbus
Hackett, John Thomas *economist*

Evansville
Barber, Charles Turner *political science educator*

Greencastle
Bonifield, William C. *economist, educator*

Indianapolis
Reynolds, Alan Anthony *economist, writer, consultant*
Stone, Donald Crawford *public administrator, educator*

Monticello
Hardin, Lowell Stewart *retired economics educator*

Muncie
Carmin, Robert Leighton *retired geography educator*
Sargent, Thomas Andrew *political science educator, university program director*
Swartz, B(enjamin) K(insell), Jr. *archaeologist, educator*

New Albany
Braden, Samuel Edward *economics educator*

North Manchester
Harshbarger, Richard B. *economics educator*

Notre Dame
Aldous, Joan *sociology educator*
Arnold, Peri Ethan *political scientist*
Bartell, Ernest *economist, educator*
Craypo, Charles *labor economics educator*
Despres, Leo Arthur *sociology and anthropology educator, academic administrator*
Dowty, Alan Kent *political scientist, educator*
Goerner, Edward Alfred *political science educator*
Goulet, Denis André *political science educator, writer, development ethicist*
Hallinan, Maureen Theresa *sociologist*
Kennedy, John Joseph *political science educator*
Leege, David Calhoun *political scientist, educator*
Loescher, Gilburt Damian *international relations educator*
Mirowski, Philip Edward *economics educator*
Scully, Timothy Richard *priest, academic administrator*
Swartz, Thomas R. *economist, educator*
Valenzuela, Julio Samuel *sociologist, educator*
Walshe, Aubrey Peter *political science educator*
Weigert, Andrew Joseph *sociology educator*

South Bend
Niemeyer, Gerhart *political science educator*

Terre Haute
Johnson, Jack Thomas *political science educator*
Mausel, Paul Warner *geography educator*
Puckett, Robert Hugh *political scientist, educator*

West Lafayette
Anderson, James George *sociologist, educator*
Farris, Paul Leonard *agricultural economist*
Horwich, George *economist, educator*
Knudsen, Dean DeWayne *sociology educator*
McGee, Reece Jerome *sociology educator, researcher*
Perrucci, Robert *sociologist, educator*
Schrader, Lee Frederick *agricultural economist*
Theen, Rolf Heinz-Wilhelm *political science educator*
Tyner, Wallace Edward *economics educator*
Weinstein, Michael Alan *political science educator*
Wilson, Franklin Leondus, III *political science educator*
Wright, Gordon Pribyl *management, operations research educator*

IOWA

Ames
Flora, Cornelia Butler *sociologist, educator*
Fox, Karl August *economist, eco-behavioral scientist*
Hadwiger, Don Frank *retired political science educator, researcher*
Harl, Neil Eugene *economist, lawyer, educator*
Johnson, Stanley R. *economist, educator*
Klonglan, Gerald Edward *sociology educator*
†Meyers, William Henry *economics educator*
Starleaf, Dennis Roy *economics educator*

Cedar Falls
Austin, Calvin Murray *geography educator*

Des Moines
Miller, Kenneth Edward *sociologist, educator*

Iowa City
Albrecht, William Price *economist, educator, government official*
Barkan, Joel David *political science educator*
Forsythe, Robert Elliott *economics educator*
Fuller, John Williams *economics educator*
Green, William *archaeologist*
Helm, June *anthropologist, educator*
Kim, Chong Lim *political science educator*
Krause, Walter *retired economics educator, consultant*
Loewenberg, Gerhard *political science educator*
Ross, Russell Marion *political science educator*
Shannon, Lyle William *sociology educator*
Siebert, Calvin D. *economist, educator*

Mount Vernon
Ruppel, Howard James, Jr. *sociologist*

Oskaloosa
Porter, David Lindsey *history and political science educator, author*

KANSAS

Lawrence
Augelli, John Pat *geography educator, author, consultant, rancher*
†El-Hodiri, Mohamed A. *economics educator*
Heller, Francis H(oward) *law and political science educator emeritus*
Laird, Roy Dean *political science educator*
Lundsgaarde, Henry Peder *anthropology educator, researcher*
Seibold, Ronald Lee *sociologist, writer*
Sheridan, Richard Bert *economics educator*
Willner, Ann Ruth *political scientist, educator*

Manhattan
Babcock, Michael Ward *economics educator*
Hoyt, Kenneth Boyd *educational psychology educator*
Johnson, Marc Anton *agricultural economics educator*
Nafziger, Estel Wayne *economics educator*
Thomas, Lloyd Brewster *economics educator*

Overland Park
Burger, Henry G. *anthropologist, vocabulary scientist, publisher*

Pittsburg
Behlar, Patricia Ann *political science educator*

KENTUCKY

Bowling Green
Cravens, Raymond Lewis *political science educator*
Kalab, Kathleen Alice *sociology educator*

Lexington
Davis, Vincent *political science educator*
Hochstrasser, Donald Lee *cultural anthropologist, community health and public administration educator*
Hultman, Charles William *economics educator*
Stober, William John, II *economics educator*
Straus, Robert *behavioral sciences educator*
Ulmer, Shirley Sidney *political science educator, researcher, consultant*

Newport
Hopgood, James F. *anthropologist*

LOUISIANA

Baton Rouge
Guedry, Leo J. *agricultural economics educator*
Smyth, David John *economist*
West, Robert Cooper *geography educator*

Lafayette
Dur, Philip Francis *political scientist, educator, retired foreign service officer*

Metairie
Falco, Maria Josephine *political scientist, academic administrator*

New Orleans
Boudreaux, Kenneth Justin *finance and economics educator, consultant*
Bricker, Harvey Miller *anthropology educator*
Bricker, Victoria Reifler *anthropology educator*
Edmonson, Munro Sterling *anthropologist, educator*
Freudenberger, Herman *retired economics educator*
Jacobsen, Thomas Warren *archaeologist, educator*
†Lief, Thomas Parrish *sociologist, educator*
Mason, Henry Lloyd *political science educator*
Robins, Robert Sidwar *political science educator, administrator*
Wilford, Walton Terry *economics educator*

New Roads
Haag, William George *anthropologist, educator*

Ruston
Sale, Tom S., III *financial economist, educator*

Shreveport
Hall, John Whitling *geography educator*
Pederson, William David *political scientist, educator*

MAINE

Auburn
Phillips, Charles Franklin *economic consultant*

Augusta
Nickerson, John Mitchell *political science educator*

Brunswick
Morgan, Richard Ernest *political scientist, educator*

Camden
Weidman, Hazel Hitson *anthropologist, educator*

Canaan
Walker, Willard Brewer *anthropology educator, linguist*

Kittery Point
Howells, William White *anthropology educator*

Lewiston
Murray, Michael Peter *educator, economist*

Orono
Devino, William Stanley *economist, educator*

Phippsburg
Schuman, Howard *sociologist, educator*

Portland
Durgin, Frank Albert, Jr. *economics educator*

Waterville
Gemery, Henry Albert *economics educator*

MARYLAND

Adamstown
Ohlke, Clarence Carl *public affairs consultant*

Baltimore
Anderson, Gerard Fenton *economist, university program administrator*
Bright, Margaret *sociologist*
Cooper, Joseph *political scientist, educator*
Crenson, Matthew Allen *political science educator*
Dietze, Gottfried *political science educator*
Entwisle, Doris Roberts *sociology educator*
Flathman, Richard Earl *political science educator*
Ginsberg, Benjamin *political science educator*
Goedicke, Hans *archeology educator*
Henderson, Lenneal Joseph, Jr. *political science educator*
Howard, J. Woodford, Jr. *political science educator*
Karni, Edi *economics educator*
Katz, Richard Stephen *political science educator*
Khan, Mohammed Ali *economics educator*
Klarman, Herbert Elias *economist, educator*
Kohn, Melvin L. *sociologist*
Maccini, Louis John *economic educator*
Martin, Emily *anthropologist, educator*
Mintz, Sidney Wilfred *anthropologist*
Peabody, Robert Lee *political science educator, researcher*
Portes, Alejandro *sociologist, educator*
Rose, Hugh *retired economics educator*
Salamon, Lester Milton *political science educator*
Sorkin, Alan Lowell *economist, educator*
Stanley, Jay *sociologist, educator*
Trouillot, Michel-Rolph *anthropology educator, educational administrator*
Verdery, Katherine Maureen *anthropologist, educator*
Wolman, M. Gordon *geography educator*

Bethesda
Berns, Walter Fred *political scientist, educator*
Bowles, Walter Donald *economist, educator*
de Vries, Margaret Garritsen *economist*
Ferris, Frederick Joseph *gerontologist, social worker*
Gates, Theodore Ross *economic consultant*
Hyson, Charles David *economist, consultant*
Kingsley, Thomas Drowne *economist*
Kleine, Herman *economist*
Lystad, Mary Hanemann (Mrs. Robert Lystad) *sociologist, author, consultant*
Norwood, Bernard *economist*
Parry, Hugh Jones (James Cross) *social scientist, educator, author*
Raullerson, Calvin Henry *political scientist, consultant*
Riley, Matilda White (Mrs. John W. Riley, Jr.) *sociology educator*
Sayre, E(noch) Phillip *political scientist, state official*
Schwartz, Charles Frederick *economist, consultant*
Spangler, Miller Brant *science and technology analyst, planner, consultant*
Striner, Herbert Edward *economics educator*
Willner, Dorothy *anthropologist, educator*

Cabin John
Gallagher, Hugh Gregory *government affairs author, consultant*

Chevy Chase
Emery, Robert Firestone *economist, educator*
Geber, Anthony *economist, retired foreign service officer*
Miller, Ralph Eli *consulting economist*
Riley, John Winchell, Jr. *consulting sociologist*
Scammon, Richard Montgomery *political scientist*
Teitel, Simon *economist*
Wallerstein, Leibert Benet *economist*

Churchton
†Morrison, Joel Lynn *cartographer, geographer*

College Park
Coughlin, Peter Joseph *economics educator, researcher*
Davidson, Roger H(arry) *political scientist, educator*
Destler, I. M(ac) *political scientist, foreign policy writer*
Gurr, Ted Robert *political science educator, author*
Just, Richard Eugene *agricultural and resource economics educator consultant*
Lyon, Andrew Bennet *economics educator*
Nerlove, Marc Leon *economics educator*
Olson, Mancur Lloyd *economics educator*
Piper, Don Courtney *political science educator*
Presser, Harriet Betty *sociology educator*
†Presser, Stanley *survey researcher, educator*
Quester, George Herman *political science educator*
Schelling, Thomas Crombie *economist, educator*
Simon, Julian Lincoln *economics educator*
Ulmer, Melville Jack *economist, educator*
Williams, Aubrey Willis *anthropology educator*

Crofton
Reich, Merrill Drury *intelligence consultant, writer*

Glen Echo
Simpson, Robert Edward *economist, consultant*

Kensington
†Booz, Elisabeth Benson *geographer*

Laurel
Corrothers, Helen Gladys *criminal justice official*

Lavale
Heckert, Paul Charles *sociologist, educator*

Mitchellville
Blough, Roy *retired economist*
Manvel, Allen Dailey *fiscal economist*

Potomac
Jones, Sidney Lewis *economist, government official*
Mc Bryde, F. Webster *geographer, ecologist, consultant*

Rockville
Fischetti, Michael *public administration educator, arbitrator*
Knox, C. Neal *political and governmental affairs consultant, writer*
Niewiaroski, Trudi Osmers (Gertrude Niewiaroski) *social studies educator*
Pollard, George Marvin *economist*
Wonnacott, (Gordon) Paul *economics educator*

Royal Oak
Israel, Lesley Lowe *political consultant*

Silver Spring
Blankenheimer, Bernard *economics consultant*
Hsueh, Chun-tu *political science educator, foundation executive*
†Michelson, Stephan *economist*

Temple Hills
Day, Mary Jane Thomas *cartographer*

Woodstock
Ballweber, Hettie Lou *archaeologist*

MASSACHUSETTS

Amherst
Alfange, Dean, Jr. *political science educator*
Arkes, Hadley P. *political science and jurisprudence educator*
Beals, Ralph Everett *economist, educator*
Benson, Lucy Peters Wilson *political and diplomatic consultant*
Demerath, Nicholas Jay, III *sociology educator*
Goldman, Sheldon *political science educator*
Klare, Michael Thomas *social science educator, program director*
Mc Donagh, Edward Charles *sociologist, university administrator*
Nicholson, Walter *economist, educator*
Rossi, Alice S. *sociology educator, author*
Sarat, Austin D. *jurisprudence and political science educator*
Taubman, William Chase *political science educator*
Woodbury, Richard Benjamin *anthropologist, educator*

Andover
Mac Neish, Richard Stockton *archaeologist, educator*

Babson Park
Genovese, Francis Charles (Frank Genovese) *economist, consultant, editor*

Belmont
Bergson, Abram *economist, educator*

Boston
Amy-Moreno de Toro, Angel Alberto *social sciences educator, writer, oral historian*
Baer, Michael Alan *political scientist, educator*
Burley, Dexter Lishon *gerontologist, consultant*
Bustin, Edouard Jean *political scientist, educator*
Cheever, Daniel Sargent *international affairs educator, editor*
Dentler, Robert Arnold *sociologist, educator*
Fieleke, Norman Siegfried *economist*
Gabel, Creighton *anthropologist, educator*
Gamson, Zelda *sociologist, researcher*
Gamst, Frederick Charles *anthropology educator*
Green, Jerry Richard *economist, educator*
Hammond, Norman David Curle *archaeology educator, researcher*
Horowitz, Morris A. *economist*
Jensen, Michael Cole *economics educator*
Kurzweil, Edith *sociology educator, editor*
Levine, Sol *sociologist*
Markham, Jesse William *economist*
Merton, Robert C. *economist, educator*

Mihaly, Eugene Bramer *consultant, corporate executive, writer, educator*
†Newbrander, William Carl *health economist, management consultant*
Newhouse, Joseph Paul *economics educator*
Nixon, Ralph Edward *financial executive*
Norton, Augustus Richard *political science educator*
Palmer, David Scott *political scientist, educator*
Psathas, George *sociologist, educator*
Rossell, Christine Hamilton *political science educator*
Sanders, Irwin Taylor *sociology educator*
Sinai, Allen Leo *economist, educator*
Torto, Raymond Gerald *economist*

Brookline
Cromwell, Adelaide M. *sociology educator*

Cambridge
Abt, Clark C. *social scientist, executive, engineer, publisher, educator*
Alonso, William *population studies educator, demographer*
Alt, James Edward *political science educator*
†Athey, Susan *economist educator*
Banfield, Edward Christie *political science educator*
Barro, Robert Joseph *economics educator, consultant*
Bator, Francis Michel *economist, educator*
Bell, Daniel *sociologist*
Berger, Suzanne *political science educator*
Berliner, Joseph Scholom *economics educator*
Berndt, Ernst Rudolf *economist, educator*
Bishop, Robert Lyle *economist, educator*
Blackmer, Donald Laurence Morton *political scientist*
Bloomfield, Lincoln Palmer *political scientist*
Brown, Edgar Cary *retired economics educator*
Campbell, John Young *economics educator*
Carliner, Geoffrey Owen *economist, director*
Champion, (Charles) Hale *political science educator, former public official*
Chang, Kwang-Chih *anthropologist, educator*
Cooper, Richard Newell *economist, educator*
Coser, Lewis Alfred *sociology educator*
Diamond, Peter Arthur *economics educator*
Domar, Evsey David *economics educator*
Dominguez, Jorge Ignacio *government educator*
Dorfman, Robert *economics educator*
Dornbusch, Rudiger *economics educator*
Dunlop, John Thomas *economics educator, former secretary of labor*
Eckaus, Richard Samuel *economist, educator*
Feldstein, Martin Stuart *economist, educator*
Fisher, Franklin Marvin *economist*
Friedman, Benjamin Morton *economics educator*
Frisch, Rose Epstein *population sciences researcher*
Galbraith, John Kenneth *retired economist*
Glazer, Nathan *sociologist, educator*
Goldin, Claudia Dale *economics educator*
†Goode, William Josiah *sociology educator*
Griliches, Zvi *educator, economist*
Hall, Peter Andrew *social scientist, educator, writer*
Hart, Oliver D'Arcy *economics educator*
Hausman, Jerry Allen *economics educator, consultant*
Hoffmann, Stanley *political science, French educator*
Holbik, Karel *economics educator*
Houthakker, Hendrik S(amuel) *economics educator, consultant*
Hsiao, William C. *economist, actuary, educator*
Huntington, Samuel Phillips *political science educator*
Jacoby, Henry Donnan *economist, educator*
Jenkins, Glen Paul *economics educator*
Johnson, Willard Raymond *political science educator, consultant*
Jorgenson, Dale Weldeau *economist, educator*
Joskow, Paul Lewis *economist, educator*
Kaysen, Carl *economics educator*
Kennedy, Stephen Dandridge *economist, researcher*
Keyfitz, Nathan *educator, sociologist, demographer*
Khoury, Philip S. *social sciences educator, historian*
Kilson, Martin Luther, Jr. *government educator*
Krugman, Paul Robin *economics educator*
Lamberg-Karlovsky, Clifford Charles *anthropologist, archaeologist*
Lieberson, Stanley *sociologist, educator*
Lipsky, Michael *political science educator*
Maass, Arthur *political science and environmental studies educator*
Medoff, James Lawrence *economics educator*
Meyer, John Robert *economist, educator*
Mitten, David Gordon *classical archaeologist*
Montgomery, John Dickey *political science educator*
Moore, Mark Harrison *criminal justice, public policy educator*
Moore, Sally Falk *anthropology educator*
Neustadt, Richard Elliott *political scientist, educator*
†Nichols, Albert L. *economics consultant*
Oye, Kenneth A. *political scientist, educator*
Patterson, Orlando *sociologist*
Peattie, Lisa Redfield *urban anthropology educator*
Perkins, Dwight Heald *economics educator*
†Pfaltzgraff, Robert Louis, Jr. *political scientist, educator*
Pilbeam, David Roger *paleoanthropology educator*
Piore, Michael Joseph *educator*
Polenske, Karen Rosel *economics educator*
Poterba, James Michael *economist, educator*
Price, Don K. *political science educator*
Pye, Lucian Wilmot *political science educator*
Rathjens, George William *political scientist, educator*
Rein, Martin *educator, social worker*
Robinson, Marguerite Stern *anthropologist, educator, consultant*
Rosovsky, Henry *economist, educator*
Rotemberg, Julio Jacobo *economist, educator, consultant*
Samuelson, Paul Anthony *economics educator*
Sapolsky, Harvey Morton *political scientist, educator*
Scherer, Frederic Michael *economics educator*
Schmalensee, Richard Lee *economist, former government official, educator*
Sen, Amartya Kumar *economist*
Siegel, Abraham J. *economics educator, academic administrator*
Skolnikoff, Eugene B. *political science educator*
Solow, Robert Merton *economist, educator*
Stager, Lawrence E. *archaeologist, educator*
Stoker, Thomas M. *economics educator*
Tambiah, Stanley Jeyarajah *anthropologist*
Temin, Peter *economics educator*
Thompson, Dennis Frank *political science and ethics educator, consultant*
Thurow, Lester Carl *economics educator*
Timmer, Charles Peter *agricultural economist*
Turkle, Sherry *sociologist, psychologist, educator*
Ulam, Adam B. *history and political science educator*
van der Merwe, Nikolaas Johannes *archaeologist*
Verba, Sidney *political scientist, educator*
Vernon, Raymond *economist, educator*
Vogel, Ezra F. *sociology educator*
Vogt, Evon Zartman, Jr. *anthropologist*
Weiner, Myron *political science educator*
Willie, Charles Vert *sociology educator*
Wrangham, Richard Walter *anthropology educator*
†Zeckhauser, Richard Jay *economist, educator*
Zeidenstein, George *population educator*
Zinberg, Dorothy Shore *science policy educator*

Chestnut Hill
Belsley, David Alan *economics educator, consultant*
Kane, Edward James *economics educator*

Cohasset
Campbell, John Coert *political scientist, author*

East Orleans
Hallowell, Burton Crosby *economist, educator*

Fitchburg
Wiegersma, Nan *economics educator*

Harwich
Randolph, Robert Lee *economist, educator*

Lenox
Pierson, John Herman Groesbeck *economist, writer*

Leverett
Barkin, Solomon *economist*

Lexington
Bell, Carolyn Shaw *economist, educator*
Bernardi, John Lawrence, Jr. *economic historian, educator, consultant*
Holzman, Franklyn Dunn *economics educator*
Kindleberger, Charles P., II *economist, educator*
Papanek, Gustav Fritz *economist, educator*

Medford
Conklin, John Evan *sociology educator*

Newton
Manners, Robert Alan *anthropologist*

Northampton
Lehmann, Phyllis Williams *archaeologist, educator*
Robinson, Donald Leonard *social scientist, educator*
Rose, Peter Isaac *sociologist, writer*

South Dartmouth
Stern, T. Noel *political scientist, educator*

Waltham
Altman, Stuart Harold *economist*
Brown, Seyom *international relations educator, government consultant*
Carter, Anne Pitts *economist, educator*
Evans, Robert, Jr. *economics educator*
McCulloch, Rachel *economics researcher, educator*
Petri, Peter Alexander *economist, educator, director*
Ross, George William *social scientist, educator*
Weckstein, Richard Selig *economics consultant*

Wayland
Hagenstein, Perry Reginald *economist*

Wellesley
Eilts, Hermann Frederick *international relations educator, former diplomat*
Miller, Linda B. *political scientist*

Weston
Kraft, Gerald *economist*

Williamstown
Bolton, Roger Edwin *economist, educator*
†Burns, James MacGregor *political scientist, historian*
Sheahan, John Bernard *economist, educator*
Winston, Gordon Chester *economic educator, former academic administrator*

Worcester
Hanson, Susan Easton *geography educator*

MICHIGAN

Adrian
Weathers, Milledge Wright *retired economics educator*

Ann Arbor
Anderson, Barbara A. *sociologist, educator*
Arlinghaus, Sandra Judith Lach *mathematical geographer, educator*
Bornstein, Morris *economist, educator*
Cohen, Malcolm Stuart *economist, research institute director*
Converse, Philip Ernest *social science educator*
Courant, Paul Noah *economist, educator*
Fifield, Russell Hunt *political science educator*
Freedman, Ronald *sociology educator*
Fusfeld, Daniel Roland *economist*
Grassmuck, George Ludwig *political science educator*
Holbrook, Robert Sumner *economist, educator*
Howrey, Eugene Philip *economics educator, consultant*
Jacobson, Harold Karan *political science educator, researcher*
Johnson, Harold R. *social work and gerontology educator, academic administrator*
Johnston, Lloyd Douglas *social scientist*
Kelly, Raymond Case *anthropology educator*
Kingdon, John Wells *political science educator*
Kmenta, Jan *economics educator*
Livingstone, Frank Brown *anthropologist, educator*
Mc Cracken, Paul Winston *economist, business educator*
Mitchell, Edward John *economist, retired educator*
Morgan, James Newton *research economist, educator*
Organski, Abramo Fimo Kenneth *political scientist, educator*
Paige, Jeffery Mayland *sociologist, educator*
Parsons, Jeffrey Robinson *anthropologist, educator*
Pedley, John Griffiths *archaeologist, educator*
Pierce, Roy *political science educator*
†Shapiro, Matthew David *economist*
Singer, Eleanor *sociologist, editor*
Singer, Joel David *political science educator*
Stafford, Frank Peter, Jr. *economics educator, consultant*
Steiner, Peter Otto *economics educator, dean*
Steiss, Alan Walter *research administrator, educator*
Stolper, Wolfgang Friedrich *retired economist, educator*
Varian, Hal Ronald *economics educator*
White, Michelle Jo *economics educator*
Whitman, Marina Von Neumann *economist*
Wolpoff, Milford Howell *paleoanthropologist, educator, author*
Zimmerman, William *political science educator*

Beverly Hills
Landuyt, Bernard Francis *economist, educator*

Big Rapids
Santer, Richard Arthur *geography educator*

Buchanan
French, Robert Warren *economics educator emeritus, writer, consultant*

Detroit
Baba, Marietta Lynn *business anthropologist*
Goodman, Allen Charles *economics educator*
Gould, Wesley Larson *political science educator*
Kaplan, Bernice Antoville *anthropologist, educator*
Lasker, Gabriel Ward *anthropologist, educator*
Marx, Thomas George *economist*
Spencer, Milton Harry *economics and finance educator*
Weiss, Mark Lawrence *anthropology educator*

East Lansing
Abramson, Paul Robert *political scientist, educator*
Allen, Bruce Templeton *economics educator*
Axinn, George Harold *rural sociology educator*
Fisher, Ronald C. *economics educator*
Kreinin, Mordechai Eliahu *economics educator*
Lang, Marvel *urban affairs educator*
Larrowe, Charles Patrick *economist, educator*
Manderscheid, Lester Vincent *agricultural economics educator*
Manning, Peter Kirby *sociology educator*
Olson, Judy Mae *geography, cartography educator*
Papsidero, Joseph Anthony *social scientist, educator*
Poland, Robert Paul *business educator, consultant*
Press, Charles *retired political science educator*
Rasche, Robert Harold *economics educator*
Ricks, Donald Jay *agricultural economist*
Robbins, Lawrence Harry *anthropologist*
Schlesinger, Joseph Abraham *political scientist*
Smith, Victor Earle *economist, educator*
Sommers, Lawrence Melvin *geographer, educator*
Strassmann, W. Paul *economics educator*
Suits, Daniel Burbidge *economist*
Useem, John Hearld *sociologist, anthropologist*
Useem, Ruth Hill *sociology educator*
VerBurg, Kenneth *political scientist, educator, writer*

Hancock
Dresch, Stephen Paul *economist, state legislator*

Kalamazoo
Thomas, Philip Stanley *economics educator*

Lansing
Ballbach, Philip Thornton *political consultant*

Mount Pleasant
Grabinski, C. Joanne *gerontologist, educator*
Meltzer, Bernard N(athan) *sociologist, educator*

Okemos
Killingsworth, Charles Clinton *economist*
Solo, Robert Alexander *economist, educator*

Sault Sainte Marie
Johnson, Gary Robert *political scientist, editor*

Ypsilanti
Weinstein, Jay A. *social science educator, researcher*

MINNESOTA

Duluth
Lease, Martin Harry, Jr. *retired political science educator*

Forest Lake
Marchese, Ronald Thomas *ancient history and archaeology educator*

Marshall
Libby, Ronald Theodore *political science educator, consultant, researcher*

Minneapolis
Adams, John Stephen *geography educator*
Chipman, John Somerset *economist, educator*
Cleveland, (James) Harlan *political scientist, public affairs executive*
Erickson, W(alter) Bruce *business and economics educator, entrepreneur*
Fulton, Robert Lester *sociology educator*
Gerlach, Luther Paul *anthropologist*
Geweke, John Frederick *economics educator*
Gray, Virginia Hickman *political science educator*
Gudeman, Stephen Frederick *anthropology educator*
Holt, Robert Theodore *political scientist, dean, educator*
Hurwicz, Leonid *economist, educator*
Knoke, David Harmon *sociology educator*
Krislov, Samuel *political science educator*
Kudrle, Robert Thomas *economist, educator*
Porter, Philip Wayland *geography educator*
Reiss, Ira Leonard *sociology educator, writer*
Rogers, William Cecil *political science educator*
Schreiner, John Christian *economics consultant, software publisher*
Scoville, James Griffin *economics educator*
Shively, William Phillips *political scientist, educator*
Ward, David Allen *sociology educator*

Moorhead
Noblitt, Harding Coolidge *political scientist, educator*
Sun, Li-Teh *economics educator*
Trainor, John Felix *retired economics educator*

Morris
Kahng, Sun Myong *economics educator*

Northfield
Clark, William Hartley *political science educator*
Lamson, George Herbert *economics educator*
†Lewis, Stephen Richmond, Jr. *economist, academic administrator*
Will, Robert Erwin *economics educator*

Saint Paul
Dahl, Reynold Paul *agricultural economics educator*
Jessup, Paul Frederick *financial economist, educator*
Peterson, Willis Lester *economics educator*
Ruttan, Vernon Wesley *agricultural economist*

Saint Peter
Mc Rostie, Clair Neil *economics educator*

Scandia
Borchert, John Robert *geography educator*

MISSISSIPPI

Hattiesburg
Burrus, John N(ewell) *sociology educator*

Mississippi State
Clynch, Edward John *political science educator, researcher*

Starkville
Loftin, Marion Theo *sociologist, educator*

MISSOURI

Bolivar
Jackson, James Larry *recreation educator*

Columbia
Breimyer, Harold Frederick *agricultural economist*
Bunn, Ronald Freeze *political science educator, lawyer*
Ratti, Ronald Andrew *economics educator*
Rowlett, Ralph Morgan *archaeologist, educator*
Twaddle, Andrew Christian *sociology educator*
Yarwood, Dean Lesley *political science educator*

Saint Louis
Barnett, William Arnold *economics educator*
Beck, Lois Grant *anthropologist, educator*
Browman, David L(udvig) *archaeologist*
Etzkorn, K. Peter *sociologist, educator, author*
Greenbaum, Stuart I. *economist, educator*
Kagan, Sioma *economics educator*
Kling, Merle *political scientist, university official*
Leven, Charles Louis *economics educator*
Le Vine, Victor Theodore *political science educator*
Miller, Gary J. *political economist*
Neuefeind, Wilhelm *economics educator, university administrator*
North, Douglass Cecil *economist, educator*
Ozawa, Martha Naoko *social work educator*
Pittman, David Joshua *sociologist, educator, researcher, consultant*
†Rasmussen, David Tab *physical anthropology educator*
Salisbury, Robert Holt *political science educator*
Weidenbaum, Murray Lew *economics educator*
Witherspoon, William *investment economist*
Worseck, Raymond Adams *economist*

Springfield
Stone, Allan David *economics educator*
Van Cleave, William Robert *international relations educator*

MONTANA

Bozeman
Refsland, Gary Arlan *retired sociology educator*
Spencer, Robert C. *political science educator*
Stroup, Richard Lyndell *economics educator, writer*

Missoula
Lopach, James Joseph *political science educator*
Power, Thomas Michael *economist, educator*

NEBRASKA

Alliance
Haefele, Edwin Theodore *political theorist, consultant*

Lincoln
Babchuk, Nicholas *sociology educator, researcher*
Kivett, Marvin Franklin *anthropologist*
MacPhee, Craig Robert *economist, educator*
Ottoson, Howard Warren *agricultural economist, former university administrator*
Peterson, Wallace Carroll, Sr. *economics educator*

Omaha
Wunsch, James Stevenson *political science educator*

NEVADA

Incline Village
Jones, Robert Alonzo *economist*

Las Vegas
Goodall, Leonard Edwin *public administration educator*
Hardbeck, George William *economics educator*
Johns, Albert Cameron *political scientist*

Reno
Derby, Jill Talbot *anthropologist, educator, consultant*
Haynes, Gary Anthony *archaeologist*
Leland, Joy Hanson *anthropologist, alcohol research specialist*
Weems, Robert Cicero *economist, educator*
Weinberg, Leonard Burton *political scientist*

Sparks
Chapman, Samuel Greeley *political science educator, criminologist*

NEW HAMPSHIRE

Center Sandwich
Shoup, Carl Sumner *retired economist*

Concord
Rogers, Katherine Diane *political consultant, state legislator*

Durham
†Puffer, Winthrop Freeman, Jr. *behavioral science company executive, clergyman*
Romoser, George Kenneth *political science educator*
Rosen, Sam *economics educator emeritus*

Hanover
Bower, Richard Stuart *economist, educator*
Campbell, Colin Dearborn *economist, educator*
Clement, Meredith Owen *economist, educator*
Demko, George Joseph *geographer*
Gustman, Alan Leslie *economics educator*
Knetter, Michael Mark *economics educator*
Logue, Dennis Emhardt *financial economics educator, consultant*
Lyons, Gene Martin *political scientist, educator*
Malmstrom, Vincent Herschel *geography educator*
Masters, Roger Davis *government educator*
Rutter, Jeremy Bentham *archaeologist, educator*
Starzinger, Vincent Evans *political science educator*
Young, Oran Reed *political scientist, educator*

Henniker
Braiterman, Thea Gilda *economics educator, state legislator*

Nashua
Taeuber, Conrad *demography educator, former government statistician*

Wolfeboro
Murray, Roger Franklin *economist, educator*

NEW JERSEY

Atlantic Highlands
Kevenides, Herve Arnaud *economic and real estate consultant*

Camden
Sigler, Jay Adrian *political scientist, educator*

Cape May
Janosik, Edward Gabriel *retired political science educator*

Denville
Breed, Ria *anthropologist*

East Brunswick
Daniel, Eleanor Sauer *economist, real estate executive*

East Orange
Wolff, Derish Michael *economist, company executive*

Glen Ridge
Szamek, Pierre Ervin *research anthropologist*

Hawthorne
Cole, Leonard Aaron *political scientist, dentist*

Jersey City
D'Amico, Thomas F. *economist, educator*

Maplewood
Hammond, Caleb Dean, Jr. *cartographer, publisher*

Marlboro
Leveson, Irving Frederick *economist*

Murray Hill
Radner, Roy *economist, educator, researcher*

New Brunswick
Alexander, Robert Jackson *economist, educator*
Boocock, Sarane Spence *sociologist*
Chelius, James Robert *economics educator*
Elinson, Jack *sociology educator*
Glasser, Paul Harold *sociologist, educator, university administrator, social worker*
Jacob, Charles Elmer *political scientist, educator*
Leggett, John Carl *sociology educator*
Mandel, Ruth B. *political science educator, educational association administrator, researcher*
Mechanic, David *social sciences educator*
Midlarsky, Manus Issachar *political scientist, educator*
Roberts, Albert Roy *social work educator*
Russell, Louise Bennett *economist, educator*
Stuart, Robert Crampton *economics educator*
Tiger, Lionel *social scientist, anthropology consultant*
Toby, Jackson *sociologist, educator*

Newark
Hiltz, Starr Roxanne *sociologist, educator, computer scientist, writer, lecturer, consultant*
Holzer, Marc *public administrator educator*

Piscataway
Glickman, Norman Jay *economist, urban policy analyst*

Princeton
Ashenfelter, Orley Clark *economics educator*
Barlow, Walter Greenwood *public opinion analyst, management consultant*
Baumol, William Jack *economist, educator*
Bernanke, Ben Shalom *economist, educator*
Berry, Charles Horace *economist, educator*
Bienen, Henry Samuel *political science educator*
Bogan, Elizabeth Chapin *economist, educator*
Bradford, David Frantz *economist*
Chow, Gregory Chi-Chong *economist, educator*
Coale, Ansley Johnson *economics educator*
Coffey, Joseph Irving *international affairs educator*
Cook, Michael Allan *social sciences educator*
Deaton, Angus Stewart *economist, educator*
Doig, Jameson Wallace *political science educator*
Geertz, Clifford James *anthropology educator*
Geertz, Hildred Storey *anthropology educator*
Gilpin, Robert George, Jr. *political science educator*
Goldfeld, Stephen Michael *economics educator, university official*
Gordenker, Leon *political sciences educator*
Greenstein, Fred Irwin *political science educator*
Halpern, Manfred *political science educator*
Hirschman, Albert Otto *political economist, educator*
Issawi, Charles Philip *economist, educator*
Joyce, Carol Bertani *social studies educator*
Kateb, George Anthony *political science educator*
Kenen, Peter Bain *economist, educator*
Kuenne, Robert Eugene *economics educator*
Kuh, Charlotte Virginia *economist*
Lester, Richard Allen *economist, educator*
Malkiel, Burton Gordon *economics educator*
Montagu, Ashley *anthropologist, social biologist*
Quandt, Richard Emeric *economics educator*
Reinhardt, Uwe Ernst *economist, educator*
Rogoff, Kenneth S. *economics educator*
Rosen, Harvey Sheldon *economics educator*
Rosenthal, Howard Lewis *political science educator*
Rothschild, Michael *economics educator*
Rozman, Gilbert Friedell *sociologist, educator*
Shear, Theodore Leslie, Jr. *archaeologist, educator*
Sigmund, Paul Eugene *political science educator*
Starr, Paul Elliot *sociologist, writer, editor, educator*
Stokes, Donald Elkinton *political science educator*
Ullman, Richard Henry *political science educator*
Von Hippel, Frank Niels *public and international affairs educator*
Wallace, Walter L. *sociologist, educator*
Walzer, Michael Laban *political science educator*
Westoff, Charles Francis *demographer, educator*
White, Lynn Townsend, III *political science educator*
Willig, Robert Daniel *economics educator*
Wuthnow, Robert *sociology educator*

Red Bank
McWhinney, Madeline H. (Mrs. John Denny Dale) *economist*

Short Hills
Parks, Robert Henry *consulting economist, educator*

South Orange
Green, Donald Webb *economist*

Springfield
Shilling, A. Gary *economic consultant, investment advisor*

Teaneck
Browne, Robert Span *economist*
Brudner, Helen Gross *social sciences educator*
Cassimatis, Peter John *economics educator*
Fanshel, David *social worker*

Upper Montclair
Cordasco, Francesco *sociologist, educator, author*

NEW MEXICO

Albuquerque
Basso, Keith Hamilton *cultural anthropologist, linguist, educator*
Condie, Carol Joy *anthropologist, research facility administrator*
Harris, Fred R. *political science educator, former senator*
Heady, Ferrel *retired political science educator*
Murphy, Walter Francis *political science educator, author*
Schwerin, Karl Henry *anthropology educator, researcher*
Sickels, Robert Judd *political science educator*
Wollman, Nathaniel *economist, educator*

Las Cruces
Lease, Richard Jay *police science educator, former police officer*

Las Vegas
Riley, Carroll Lavern *anthropology educator*

Portales
Agogino, George Allen *anthropologist, educator*

Santa Fe
Arthur, William Brian *economist, educator*
Hall, Edward Twitchell *anthropologist, educator, author*
Whiteford, Andrew Hunter *anthropologist*
Williams, Stephen *anthropologist, educator*

Taos
Young, Jon Nathan *archeologist*

NEW YORK

Albany
Falk, Dean *anthropology educator*
Fitzgerald, Frank Thomas *sociology educator*
Nathan, Richard P(erle) *political scientist, educator*
Thompson, Frank Joseph *political science educator*
Thornberry, Terence Patrick *criminologist, educator*
Wright, Theodore Paul, Jr. *political science educator*
Zimmerman, Joseph Francis *political scientist, educator*

Amherst
Mills, Theodore Mason *sociologist, educator*

Armonk
Grove, David Lawrence *economist*

Averill Park
Haines, Walter Wells *retired economics educator*

Binghamton
Banks, Arthur Sparrow *political scientist, educator*
Mazrui, Ali Al'Amin *political science educator, researcher*
Salem-Murdock, Muneera *anthropologist*

Brockport
Bretton, Henry L. *political scientist, educator*

Bronx
Fishman, Joshua Aaron *sociolinguist, educator*
Heilbrun, James *economist, educator*

Bronxville
Conant, Miriam Bernheim *political scientist, educator*
Kirk, Grayson Louis *retired political science educator, retired universtiy president, trustee*

Brooklyn
Bowers, Patricia Eleanor Fritz *economist*
Harris, James Arthur, Sr. *economics educator, consultant*
Masterson, Charles Francis *retired social scientist*
Minkoff, Jack *economics educator*
Sternlight, Peter Donn *economist, retired banker*
Szenberg, Michael *economics educator, editor, consultant*

Buffalo
Abrahams, Athol Denis *geography researcher, educator*
Aurbach, Herbert Alexander *sociology educator*
Batty, J. Michael *geographer, educator*
Frake, Charles Oliver *anthropology educator*
Gort, Michael *economics educator*
Hetzner, Donald Raymund *social studies educator*
Levine, Murray *psychology educator*
Rosenthal, Donald B. *political scientist, educator*
Steegmann, Albert Theodore, Jr. *anthropology educator*
Stein, William Warner *anthropology educator*
Tedlock, Dennis *anthropology and literature educator*
Zarembka, Paul *economics educator*

Chappaqua
Brockway, George Pond *economist*

Clinton
Wertimer, Sidney *economics educator*

Conesus
Dadrian, Vahakn Norair *sociology educator*

Dobbs Ferry
Kraetzer, Mary C. *sociologist, educator, consultant*
Sutton, Francis Xavier *social scientist, consultant*

Farmingdale
Kostanoski, John Ivan *criminal justice educator*

Flushing
Hacker, Andrew *political science educator*
Nelson, Ralph Lowell *economics educator*
Patai, Raphael *former anthropology educator*
Psomiades, Harry John *political science educator*
†Smith, Charles William *social sciences educator, sociologist*

Fredonia
Dowd, Morgan Daniel *political science educator*

Garden City
Ohrenstein, Roman Abraham *economics educator, economist, rabbi*

Geneseo
Battersby, Harold Ronald *anthropologist, archaeologist, linguist*
Moore, Gary Alan *economist*

Great Neck
Hamovitch, William *economist, educator, university official*
Joskow, Jules *economic research company executive*

Hamilton
Farnsworth, Frank Albert *economics educator*
Johnston, (William) Michael *political science educator, university administrator*
Kraynak, Robert *political science educator*

Hempstead
Turgeon, Edgar Lynn *economics educator*
Wattel, Harold Louis *economics educator*

Henrietta
Carmel, Simon J(acob) *anthropologist*

Irvington
Wolf, Eric Robert *anthropologist, educator*

Ithaca
Anderson, Benedict Richard O'Gorman *political science educator*
Ascher, Robert *anthropologist, archaeologist, educator, filmmaker*
†Beneria, Lourdes *sociologist, educator*
Blau, Francine Dee *economics educator*
Briggs, Vernon Mason, Jr. *economics educator*
Call, David Lincoln *agricultural economics educator, administrator*
Easley, David *economics educator*
Fireside, Harvey Francis *political scientist, educator*
Forker, Olan Dean *agricultural economics educator*
Hockett, Charles Francis *anthropology educator*
Isard, Walter *economics educator*
Jarrow, Robert Alan *finance and economics educator, consultant*
Kahin, George McTurnan *political science and history educator*
Kahn, Alfred Edward *economist, educator, government official*
Kennedy, Kenneth Adrian Raine *biological anthropologist, forensic anthropologist*
Kirsch, A(nthony) Thomas *anthropology and Asian studies educator, researcher*
Kramnick, Isaac *government educator*
Lowi, Theodore J(ay) *political science educator*
Lyons, Thomas Patrick *economics educator*
Murra, John Victor *anthropologist, educator*
Shell, Karl *economics educator*
Smith, Robert John *anthropology educator*
Stycos, Joseph Mayone *demographer, educator*
Thaler, Richard H. *economics educator*
Thorbecke, Erik *economics educator*
Tomek, William Goodrich *agricultural economist*
Vanek, Jaroslav *economist, educator*
Williams, Robin Murphy, Jr. *sociology educator*

Mexico
Sade, Donald Stone *anthropology educator*

New Hyde Park
Reddan, Harold Jerome *sociologist, educator*

New Paltz
Schnell, George Adam *geographer, educator*

New Rochelle
Berlage, Gai Ingham *sociologist, educator*
Murphy, Austin de la Salle *economist, educator, banker*

New York
Abu-Lughod, Janet Lippman *sociologist, educator*
Adler, Freda Schaffer (Mrs. G. O. W. Mueller) *criminologist, educator*
Alford, Robert Ross *sociologist*
Alland, Alexander, Jr. *anthropology educator*
Angell, Wayne D. *economist, banker*
Anspach, Ernst *economist, lawyer*
Baldwin, David Allen *political science educator*
Bartel, Ann Pelcovits *economist*
Bernstein, Thomas Paul *political science educator*
Betts, Richard Kevin *political science educator*
Bialer, Seweryn *political science educator, author, consultant*
Blank, Blanche Davis *political science educator*
Bond, George Clement *anthropologist, educator*
Boodey, Cecil Webster, Jr. *political science educator*
Bowen, William Gordon *economist, educator, foundation administrator*
Braham, Randolph Lewis *political science educator*
Brams, Steven John *political scientist, educator, game theorist*
Brancato, Carolyn Kay *economist, consultant*
Brusca, Robert Andrew *economist*
Brush, Charles Francis *anthropologist*
Caraley, Demetrios *political scientist, educator, author*
Chichilnisky, Graciela *economics educator, mathematician, consultant*
Cochrane, James Louis *economist*
Cohen, Eli Edward *sociology educator*
Cohen, Stephen Frand *political scientist, historian, educator, author, broadcaster*
Cole, Jonathan Richard *sociologist, academic administrator*
Comitas, Lambros *anthropologist*
Dalton, Dennis Gilmore *political science educator*
Denoon, David Baugh Holden *economist, educator, consultant*
Desai, Padma *economist, educator, political scientist*
de Vries, Rimmer *economist*
Dhrymes, Phoebus James *economist, educator*
Dorris, Michael Anthony *anthropologist, writer*
Dowling, Edward Thomas *economics educator*
Duke, Anthony Drexel *sociologist, educator, philanthropist*
Edinger, Lewis Joachim *political science educator*
Edwards, Franklin R. *economist, educator, consultant*
Elliott-Smith, Paul Henry *marketing and economics consultant*
Emerson, Alice Frey *political scientist, educator emerita*
Engler, Robert *political science educator, author*
Epstein, Cynthia Fuchs *sociology educator, writer*
Fabbri, Brian John *economist, investment strategist*
Findlay, Ronald Edsel *economist*
Finger, Seymour Maxwell *political science educator, former ambassador*
Fitch, Lyle Craig *economist, administrator*
Foley, Duncan Karl *economist, educator*
Franklin, Julian Harold *political science educator*
Freedman, Audrey Willock *economist*
Freund, William Curt *economist*
Gans, Herbert J. *sociologist, educator*
Gellhorn, Walter *law and political science educator, author*
†Ginsburg, Faye D. *anthropology educator, ethnologist*
Ginzberg, Eli *economist, emeritus educator, government consultant, author*
Gordon, Diana Russell *political science educator*
Goss, Mary E. Weber *sociology educator*
Gould, Jay Martin *economist, consultant*
Gresov, Boris (Vladimir) *economist*
Grindea, Daniel *international economist*
Hahn, Fred *retired political science and history educator*
Halper, Thomas *political science educator*
Heal, Geoffrey Martin *economics educator*
Heilbroner, Robert Louis *economist, author*
Helmreich, William Benno *sociology educator, consultant*
Heydebrand, Wolf Von *sociology educator*
Hirschfield, Robert S. *political science educator*
Holloway, Ralph Leslie *anthropology educator*
Hormats, Robert David *economist, investment banker*
Hoxter, Curtis Joseph *international economic adviser, public relations and affairs counselor*
Hurewitz, J(acob) C(oleman) *retired international relations educator, author, consultant*
Hurwitz, Sol *business policy organization executive*
Ianni, Francis Anthony James *anthropologist, psychoanalyst, educator*
Jervis, Robert *political science educator*

Jones, David Milton *economist, educator*
Kamsky, Leonard *economist, retired manufacturing executive, financial advisor*
Kaplan, Leo Sylvan *social scientist, former college administrator*
Kavesh, Robert A. *economist, educator*
Kazemi, Farhad *political science educator*
Kellner, Irwin L. *economist*
Kesselman, Mark Jonathan *political science educator, writer*
Klass, Morton *anthropology educator, consultant*
Komarovsky, Mirra (Mrs. Marcus A. Heyman) *sociology educator*
Lakah, Jacqueline Rabbat *political scientist, educator*
Lancaster, Kelvin John *economics educator*
Lehman, Edward William *sociology educator, researcher*
Leontief, Wassily *economist, educator*
Lewis, Hylan Garnet *sociologist, educator*
Lichtblau, John H. *economist*
Lieberman, Charles *economist*
Lin, Wuu-Long *economist*
Lipsey, Robert Edward *economist, educator*
Macchiarola, Frank Joseph *political science, business and law educator*
Mac Namara, Donal Eoin Joseph *criminologist*
Maldonado-Bear, Rita Marinita *economist, educator*
Markowitz, Harry M. *finance and economics educator*
McCarthy, James *sociology researcher, educator*
McKesson, John Alexander, III *international relations educator*
Melamid, Alexander *economics educator, consultant*
Merton, Robert K. *sociologist, educator*
Mincer, Jacob *economics educator*
Molz, Redmond Kathleen *public administration educator*
Moore, Geoffrey Hoyt *economist*
Moskowitz, Arnold X. *strategist, economist, educator*
Mroz, John Edwin *political scientist*
Muller, Charlotte Feldman *economist, educator*
†Mundell, Robert Alexander *economics educator*
Murphy, Joseph Samson *political science educator*
Nadiri, M. Ishaq *economics educator, researcher, lecturer, consultant*
Nakamura, James I. *economics educator*
Nathan, Andrew James *political science educator*
Nelkin, Dorothy *sociology and science policy educator, researcher*
Netzer, Dick *economics educator*
Newborn, Jud *cultural anthropologist, writer*
O'Neill, June Ellenoff *economist*
Patrick, Hugh Talbot *economist, educator*
Paulus, John David *economist*
Peck, Fred Neil *economist, educator*
Persell, Caroline Hodges *sociologist, educator, author, researcher, consultant*
†Petchesky, Rosalind Pollack *political science and women's studies educator*
Phelps, Edmund Strother *economics educator*
Piven, Frances Fox *political scientist, educator*
Prewitt, Kenneth *political science educator, foundation executive*
Pye, Gordon Bruce *economist*
†Quackenbush, Margery Clouser *psychoanalyst, administrator*
Ramirez, Maria Fiorini *economist, investment advisor*
Rivlin, Benjamin *political science educator*
Robock, Stefan Hyman *economics educator emeritus*
Rosner, Lydia S. *sociology educator, author*
Ross, Jeffrey Allan *political scientist, educator*
Rothschild, Joseph *political science educator*
†Sanhueza, Hernan *demographer, physician*
Sartori, Giovanni *political scientist*
Scanlon, Rosemary *economist*
Scelsa, Joseph Vincent *sociologist*
Schilling, Warner Roller *political scientist, educator*
Schotter, Andrew Roye *economics educator, consultant*
Schwab, George David *social science educator*
Schwartz, Anna Jacobson *economic historian*
Schwartzman, David *economist, educator*
Sennett, Richard *sociologist, writer*
Shapiro, Judith R. *anthropology educator, academic administrator*
Sheldon, Eleanor Harriet Bernert *sociologist*
Sherry, George Leon *political science educator*
Silver, Morris *economist, educator*
†Silverman, Sydel Finfer *anthropologist*
Simon, Jacqueline Albert *political scientist, writer*
Small, George LeRoy *geographer, educator*
Spilerman, Seymour *sociologist, educator*
Stepan, Alfred C. *political science educator, author*
Taylor, Lance Jerome *economics educator*
Tepper, Lynn Marsha *gerontology educator*
Thomas, David Hurst *archaeologist*
Updike, Helen Hill *economist, investment manager, financial planner*
Vickrey, William Spencer *economist, emeritus educator*
Vora, Ashok *financial economist*
Walter, Ingo *economics educator*
Watts, Harold Wesley *economist, educator*
Wenglowski, Gary Martin *economist*
Westin, Alan Furman *political science educator*
Wetzler, James Warren *economist*
White, Harrison Colyar *sociology educator*
White, Lawrence J. *economics educator*
Winick, Charles *sociologist, educator*
Wojnilower, Albert Martin *economist*
Wolman, William *economist, journalist, broadcaster*
Wrong, Dennis Hume *sociologist, educator*
Yorburg, Betty (Mrs. Leon Yorburg) *sociology educator*
Zolberg, Aristide Rodolphe *political science educator, researcher*

Niagara Falls
Albanese, Jay Samuel *criminologist, educator*

Old Westbury
Ozelli, Tunch *economics educator, consultant*

Oneonta
†Anthony, David Waller *archaeologist, anthropologist, educator*

Oyster Bay
Trevor, Bronson *economist*

Potsdam
Hanson, David Justin *sociology educator, college administrator*
Whelehan, Patricia Elizabeth *anthropology educator*

Poughkeepsie
Johnson, Lucille Lewis *anthropology educator, archaeologist*
Johnson, M(aurice) Glen *political science educator*
Marshall, Natalie Junemann *economics educator*

Purchase
Ryan, Edward W. *economics educator*
Siegel, Nathaniel Harold *sociology educator*

Rochester
Bluhm, William Theodore *political scientist, educator*
D'Agostino, Anthony Carmen *anthropologist, educator*
Engerman, Stanley Lewis *economist, educator, historian*
Fenno, Richard Francis, Jr. *political science educator*
Hanushek, Eric Alan *economics educator*
Harris, Alfred *social anthropologist, educator*
Hopkins, Thomas Duvall *economics educator*
Jacobs, Bruce *political science educator*
Jones, Ronald Winthrop *economics educator*
Long, John Broaddus, Jr. *economist, educator*
Mc Kenzie, Lionel Wilfred *economist, educator*
Mueller, John Ernest *political science educator, dance critic and historian*
Niemi, Richard Gene *political science educator*
Regenstreif, S(amuel) Peter *political scientist, educator*
Rosett, Richard Nathaniel *economist, educator*
Sangree, Walter Hinchman *social anthropologist, educator*
Steamer, Robert Julius *political science educator*

Scarsdale
Cohen, Irwin *economist*

Slingerlands
Fenton, William Nelson *anthropologist, anthropology educator emeritus*

Stony Brook
Fleagle, John Gwynn *anthropology and paleontology educator*
Goodman, Norman *sociologist, researcher*
James, Estelle *economics educator*
Neuberger, Egon *economics educator*
Schneider, Mark *political science educator*
Tanur, Judith Mark *sociologist, educator*
Travis, Martin Bice *political scientist, educator*

Syracuse
Birkhead, Guthrie Sweeney, Jr. *political scientist, university dean*
Braungart, Richard Gottfried *sociology and international relations educator*
Cooke, Goodwin *international relations educator*
Frohock, Fred Manuel *political science educator*
Jensen, Robert Granville *geography educator, university dean*
Jump, Bernard, Jr. *economics educator*
Kriesberg, Louis *sociologist, educator*
Mazur, Allan Carl *sociologist, engineer, educator*
Meinig, Donald William *geography educator*
Monmonier, Mark *graphics educator, geographer*
Palmer, John L. *social sciences researcher, educator*
Samuels, Marwyn Stewart *geography educator*
Schwartz, Richard Derecktor *sociologist, educator*
Thorson, Stuart J. *political science educator*
Wadley, Susan Snow *anthropologist*

Tarrytown
Marcus, Sheldon *social sciences educator*

Troy
Brazil, Harold Edmund *political science educator*
Diwan, Romesh Kumar *economics educator*
Gorenstein, Shirley Slotkin *anthropologist, educator*
Schechter, Stephen L. *political scientist*

Wantagh
Dawson, George Glenn *economics educator emeritus*

White Plains
Rapp, Richard Tilden *economist, consultant*

Yonkers
Varma, Baidya Nath *sociologist, broadcaster, poet*

NORTH CAROLINA

Cary
†Goodwin, Barry Kent *economics educator*

Chapel Hill
Akin, John Stephen *economics educator*
Behrman, Jack Newton *economist*
Black, Stanley Warren, III *economics educator*
Blau, Peter Michael *sociologist, educator*
Brockington, Donald Leslie *anthropologist, archaeologist, educator*
Brown, Frank *social science educator*
Crane, Julia Gorham *anthropology educator*
Eisenbeis, Robert A. *business educator*
Friedman, James Winstein *economist, educator*
Gallman, Robert Emil *economics and history educator*
Gil, Federico Guillermo *political science educator*
Graham, George Adams *political scientist, emeritus educator*
Gulick, John *anthropology educator*
†Ingram, James Carlton *economist, educator*
MacRae, Duncan, Jr. *social scientist, educator*
Pfouts, Ralph William *economist, consultant*
Richardson, Richard Judson *political science educator*
Rindfuss, Ronald Richard *sociology educator*
Rondinelli, Dennis A(ugust) *business administration educator, research center director*
Schoultz, Lars *political scientist, educator*
Simpson, Richard Lee *sociologist, educator*
Smith, James Finley *economist, educator*
Steponaitis, Vincas Petras *archaeologist, anthropologist, educator*
Treml, Vladimir Guy *economist, educator*
Udry, J. Richard *sociology educator*
Waud, Roger Neil *economics educator*
Wilson, Glenn *economist, educator*
Wilson, Robert Neal *sociologist, educator*
Wright, Deil Spencer *political science educator*
Yarnell, Richard Asa *anthropologist*

Charlotte
Neel, Richard Eugene *economics educator*

Dallas
Blanton, Robert D'Alden *anthropology and history educator*

Davidson
Proctor, Jesse Harris, Jr. *political science educator*
Ratliff, Charles Edward, Jr. *economics educator*

Durham
Aldrich, John Herbert *political science educator*
Barber, James David *political scientist, educator*
Behn, Robert Dietrich *public policy educator, writer*
Braibanti, Ralph John *political scientist, educator*
Burmeister, Edwin *economics educator*
Clotfelter, Charles T. *economics educator*
Elliot, Jeffrey M. *political science educator, author*
Gittler, Joseph Bertram *sociology educator*
Handy, Rollo Leroy *economics educator, research executive*
Holsti, Ole Rudolf *political scientist, educator*
Hough, Jerry Fincher *political science educator*
Kelley, Allen Charles *economist, educator*
Keohane, Robert Owen *political scientist, educator*
Kreps, Juanita Morris *economics educator, former government official*
Kuniholm, Bruce Robellet *public policy studies institute director, history educator*
Land, Kenneth Carl *sociology educator, demographer, statistician, consultant*
Leach, Richard Heald *political scientist, educator*
Lincoln, C(harles) Eric *sociologist, educator, author*
Mickiewicz, Ellen Propper *political science educator*
Myers, George Carleton *sociology and demographics educator*
O'Barr, William McAlston *anthropologist, educator*
Tiryakian, Edward Ashod *sociology educator*

Fearrington Village
Doenges, Byron Frederick *economist, educator, former government official*

Gastonia
Kiser, Clyde Vernon *retired demographer*

Greensboro
Helms-VanStone, Mary Wallace *anthropology educator*
Hidore, John Junior *geographer, educator*
Shelton, David Howard *economics educator*
Zopf, Paul Edward, Jr. *sociologist*

Greenville
Cramer, Robert Eli *geography educator*
Williams, Melvin John *sociologist, educator*

Hillsborough
Goodwin, Craufurd David *economics educator*

Raleigh
Caldwell, John Tyler *political science educator, former university administrator*

NORTH DAKOTA

Bismarck
Sperry, James Edward *anthropologist*

Fargo
Query, Joy Marves Neale *medical sociology educator*

Grand Forks
†Hammen, John Leo, III *geographer, educator*

OHIO

Akron
Coyne, Thomas Joseph *economist, finance educator*
Marini, Frank Nicholas *public administration and political science educator*

Ashland
Ford, Lucille Garber *economist, educator, college official*

Beachwood
Wolf, Milton Albert *economist, former U.S. ambassador, investor*

Bowling Green
McCaghy, Charles Henry *sociology educator*

Chagrin Falls
Morris, Jane Elizabeth *home economics educator*

Cincinnati
Bishop, George Franklin *political social psychologist, educator*
Katz, Robert Langdon *human relations educator, rabbi*

Cleveland
Beall, Cynthia *anthropologist, educator*
Binstock, Robert Henry *public policy educator, writer, lecturer*
Burke, John Francis, Jr. *economist*
Carlsson, Bo A. V. *economics educator*
Carter, John Dale *organizational development executive*
Chatterjee, Pranab *social sciences educator*
Conaway, Orrin Bryte *political scientist, educator*
Goldstein, Melvyn C. *anthropologist, educator*
Grundy, Kenneth William *political science educator*
Jordan, Jerry Lee *economist, banker*
Kahana, Eva Frost *sociology educator*
Lavelle, Michael Joseph *economist, academic administrator*
Mayland, Kenneth Theodore *economist*
McHale, Vincent Edward *political science educator*
Murray, Thomas Henry *bioethics educator, writer*
Rosegger, Gerhard *economist, educator*
Sibley, Willis Elbridge *anthropology educator, consultant*
Stein, Herman David *social sciences educator, past university provost*

Columbus
Alger, Chadwick Fairfax *political scientist, educator*
Beck, Paul Allen *political science educator*
Bourguignon, Erika Eichhorn *anthropologist, educator*
Cunnyngham, Jon *economist, information systems educator*
Epstein, Erwin Howard *sociology educator, editor*
Gouke, Cecil Granville *economist, educator*
Hermann, Margaret Gladden *political science educator*
Huber, Joan Althaus *sociology educator*
Huff, C(larence) Ronald *public administration and criminology educator*
Ichiishi, Tatsuro *economics and mathematics educator*
Kessel, John Howard *political scientist, educator*
Ladman, Jerry R. *economist, educator*
Lundman, Richard Jack *sociology educator*
Lundstedt, Sven Bertil *behavioral and social scientist, educator*
Lynn, Arthur Dellert, Jr. *economist, educator*
Maddala, Gangadharrao Soundaryarao *economics educator*
Marble, Duane Francis *geography educator, researcher*
Namboodiri, Krishnan *sociology educator*
Patterson, Samuel Charles *political science educator*
Poirier, Frank Eugene *physical anthropology educator*
Ray, Edward John *economics educator, administrator*
Richardson, Laurel Walum *sociology educator*
Ripley, Randall Butler *political scientist, educator*
Taaffe, Edward James *geography educator*
Weisberg, Herbert Frank *political science educator*

Kent
Hall, Bernard *retired economics educator and university official*
Koller, Marvin Robert *sociology educator, writer*
Williams, Harold Roger *economist, educator*

Oxford
Rejai, Mostafa *political science educator*

Tiffin
Porter, Arthur Reno *economist, arbitrator*

Toledo
Bardis, Panos Demetrios *sociologist, social philosopher, historian, author, editor, poet, educator*

Waterford
Riley, Nancy Mae *retired vocational home economics educator*

OKLAHOMA

Norman
Affleck, Marilyn *sociology educator*
Albert, Lois Eldora Wilson *archaeologist*
Bell, Robert Eugene *anthropologist educator*
Cella, Francis Raymond *economist, research consultant*
Dauffenbach, Robert C. *economic and management administrator, educator*
Henderson, George *educational sociologist, educator*
Kondonassis, Alexander John *economist, educator*

Stillwater
Bynum, Jack Edward, Jr. *sociology educator*
Jadlow, Joseph Martin *economics educator*
Moomaw, Ronald Lee *economics educator*
Poole, Richard William *economics educator*
Shearer, John Clyde *economics consultant, labor arbitrator, international manpower consultant*

OREGON

Ashland
Houston, John Albert *political science educator*

Corvallis
Castle, Emery Neal *agricultural and resource economist, educator*
Harter, Lafayette George, Jr. *economics educator emeritus*
Towey, Richard Edward *economics educator*

Eugene
Aikens, C(lyde) Melvin *anthropology educator, archaeologist*
Davis, Richard Malone *economics educator*
Hildreth, Clifford *retired economist, educator*
Khang, Chulsoon *economics educator*
McGuire, Timothy William *economics and management educator, dean*
Mikesell, Raymond Frech *economics educator*
Stone, Joe Allan *economics educator*
Upham, Steadman *anthropology educator, university dean, academic administrator*

Monmouth
Shay, Roshani Cari *political science educator*

Portland
Davis, James Allan *gerontologist, educator*
Haviland, John Beard *anthropology and linguistics educator*
Kristof, Ladis Kris Donabed *political scientist, author*
Netusil, Noelwah Rose *economics educator*

Salem
Archer, Stephen Hunt *economist, educator*

Siletz
Jennings, Jesse David *anthropology educator*

PENNSYLVANIA

Allentown
Bednar, Charles Sokol *political scientist, educator*

Bethlehem
Frankel, Barbara Brown cultural anthropologist
Schwartz, Eli economics educator, writer

Birdsboro
Hill, Lenora Mae astrologer

Bryn Athyn
Kintner, William Roscoe political science educator emeritus

Bryn Mawr
de Laguna, Frederica anthropology educator emeritus, author, consultant
Ellis, Richard Stephens archaeology educator, field archaeologist, researcher, consultant
Porter, Judith Deborah Revitch sociologist, educator
Ridgway, Brunilde Sismondo archaeology educator
Rubinstein, Alvin Zachary political science educator, author
Walton, Clarence political science and history educator

Carlisle
Jacobs, Norman G(abriel) sociologist, educator

East Stroudsburg
Briggs, Philip James political science educator, author, lecturer

Easton
Kincaid, John political science educator, editor

Erie
Adovasio, J. M. anthropologist, archeologist, educator

Gettysburg
Plischke, Elmer political science educator

Gwynedd
Zumeta, Bertram William retired economist

Haverford
Mellink, Machteld Johanna archaeologist, educator
Northrup, Herbert Roof economist, business executive

Huntingdon
Murray, Andrew peace studies educator

Indiana
Mc Cauley, R. Paul criminologist, educator
†Walker, Donald Anthony economist, educator

Kutztown
Dougherty, Percy H. geographer, educator, politician

Lancaster
Stephenson, Donald Grier, Jr. government studies educator
Taylor, Norman William economics educator

Lewisburg
Anderson, John Whiting economics educator

Manns Choice
Jones, Oliver Hastings consulting economist

Meadville
Adams, Earl William, Jr. economics educator

Media
Smith, David Gilbert political science educator

Philadelphia
Adams, F. Gerard economist, educator
Ando, Albert K. economist, educator
Bailey, Elizabeth Ellery economics educator
Baltzell, E(dward) Digby sociology educator
Behrman, Jere Richard economics educator
Berg, Ivar Elis, Jr. social science educator
Buerkle, Jack Vincent sociologist, educator
Cass, David economist, educator
Clark, John J. economics and finance educator
Cummins, John David economics educator, consultant
Duffy, Francis Ramon sociology educator
Evan, William Martin sociologist, educator
Fox, Renée Claire sociology educator
Frankel, Francine Ruth political science educator
Frantz, Charles anthropology educator
Goodenough, Ward Hunt anthropologist, educator
Grossman, Sanford Jay economics educator
Hall, Charles P(otter), Jr. educator consultant
Johnston, Francis Edward anthropologist, educator
Katz, Solomon Hertz anthropologist, educator
Klausner, Samuel Zundel sociologist, educator
Klein, Lawrence Robert economist, educator
Kopecky, Kenneth John economics educator
Kopytoff, Igor anthropology educator
Lang, Richard Warren economist
Lee, Chong-Sik political scientist, educator
Levine, Herbert Samuel economics educator, research consultant
Mansfield, Edwin economist, educator
Menken, Jane Ava demographer, educator
Michael, Henry N. geographer, anthropologist
Miller, Ronald Eugene regional science educator
Postlewaite, Andrew William economics and public policy educator
Preston, Samuel Hulse demographer
Pritchard, James Bennett archaeologist, educator, author
Rieff, Philip sociologist
Rima, Ingrid Hahne economics educator
Rosenzweig, Mark Richard economist, educator
†Rubinstein, Robert Lawrence anthropologist, gerontologist
Sabloff, Jeremy Arac archaeologist
Sigmond, Robert M. medical economist
Smith, Donald Eugene political science educator
Summers, Anita Arrow public policy and management educator
Summers, Robert economics educator
Taubman, Paul James economics educator
Van De Walle, Etienne demographer
Wachter, Michael L. economics educator
Wallace, Anthony Francis Clarke anthropologist, educator
Weeks, Gerald psychology educator
Wolfbein, Seymour Louis economist, educator
Wolfgang, Marvin Eugene sociologist, criminologist, educator

Pittsburgh
Blumstein, Alfred urban and public affairs educator
Bobrow, Davis Bernard public policy educator
Brown, L. Keith anthropology educator
Carroll, Holbert Nicholson political science educator
Davis, Otto Anderson economics educator
Eaton, Joseph W. sociology educator
Fararo, Thomas John sociologist, educator
Ginsburg, Mark Barry sociology of education educator
Hammond, Paul Young political scientist, educator
Holzner, Burkart sociologist, educator
Howard, Lawrence Cabot international affairs educator
Katz, Arnold economics educator
Katz, Saul Milton economist, social scientist, educator
Keefe, William Joseph political science educator
Kenkel, James Lawrence economics educator
Lave, Judith Rice economics educator
LeMelle, Tilden John political science educator, editor, college official
Lidz, Charles Wilmanns sociologist
McCallum, Bennett Tarlton economics educator
Meltzer, Allan H. economist, educator
Mesa-Lago, Carmelo economist, educator
Ogul, Morris Samuel political science educator, consultant
Roth, Alvin Eliot economics educator
Simon, Herbert A(lexander) social scientist
Strauss, Robert Philip economics educator
Sussna, Edward economist, educator

Saint Davids
Heebner, Albert Gilbert economist, banker, educator

Scranton
Parente, William Joseph political science educator

State College
Ferguson, John Henry retired political science educator
Gould, Peter Robin geographer, educator
Miller, E. Willard geographer

Swarthmore
Hopkins, Raymond Frederick political science educator
Keith, Jennie anthropology educator/administrator, writer
Saffran, Bernard economist, educator

University Park
Aspaturian, Vernon Varaztat political science educator, consultant, author
Epp, Donald James economist, educator
Friedman, Robert Sidney political science educator
Klein, Philip Alexander economist
Lewis, Peirce Fee geographer, educator
Michels, Joseph William anthropology and archaeology educator
Nelsen, Hart Michael sociologist, educator
Pashek, Robert Donald economics educator emeritus
Rose, Adam Zachary economist, educator
Walden, Daniel humanities and social sciences educator
Wyand, Martin Judd economics educator, retired military officer

Villanova
Johannes, John Roland political science educator, college dean
Jones, Brian Joseph sociology educator
Langran, Robert Williams political scientist
Lesch, Ann Mosely political scientist, educator
Malik, Hafeez political scientist, educator
McFalls, Joseph A., Jr. sociology educator
Schrems, John Joseph (Jack Schrems) political science educator

West Chester
Green, Andrew Wilson economist, lawyer, educator

Wynnewood
Khouri, Fred John political science educator
Phillips, Almarin economics educator, consultant

Yardley
Somma, Beverly Kathleen medical and marriage educator

RHODE ISLAND

Kingston
Alexander, Lewis McElwain geographer, educator
Gelles, Richard James sociology and psychology educator
Zucker, Norman Livingston political scientist, educator, author

Providence
Anton, Thomas Julius political science and public policy educator, consultant
Borts, George Herbert economist, educator
Garrison, Mark Joseph political science educator, former diplomat
Goldscheider, Frances K. sociologist, educator
Goldstein, Sidney sociology educator, demographer
Goodman, Elliot Raymond political scientist, educator
Grossman, Herschel I. economics educator
Heath, Dwight Braley anthropologist, educator
Hogan, Dennis Patrick university educator
Hopmann, Philip Terrence political science educator
Lancaster, Anthony economics educator, consultant
Leis, Philip Edward anthropologist
Marsh, Robert Mortimer sociologist, educator
Moffitt, Robert Allen economics educator
Perkins, Whitney Trow political science educator emeritus
Poole, William economics educator, consultant
Putterman, Louis G. economics educator
Rueschemeyer, Dietrich sociology educator
Ryder, Harl Edgar economist, educator
Smoke, Richard political scientist, political psychologist
Speare, Alden, Jr. sociology educator
Stein, Jerome Leon economist, educator
Stultz, Newell Maynard political science educator

SOUTH CAROLINA

Anderson
Gleason, Ralph Newton economic development consultant

Charleston
Moore, William Vincent political science educator

Clemson
Trevillian, Wallace Dabney economics educator, retired dean

Columbia
Cohn, Elchanan economics educator
Feinn, Barbara Ann economist
Hatch, David Lincoln sociology educator
Heider, Karl Gustav anthropology educator
Kiker, Billy Frazier economics educator
Mishler, William, II political science educator
Morris, James Aloysius economist, educator
Norton, Hugh Stanton economist, educator
Starr, Harvey political scientist
Weatherbee, Donald Emery political scientist, educator
Wilder, Ronald Parker economics educator

Newberry
Logan, Sandra Jean economics and business educator

SOUTH DAKOTA

Brookings
Gilbert, Howard Alden economics educator
Wagner, Mary Kathryn sociology educator, former state legislator

Vermillion
Carlson, Loren Merle political science educator
Clem, Alan Leland political scientist
Dahlin, Donald C(lifford) political science educator

TENNESSEE

Knoxville
Cole, William Edward economics educator, consultant
Hammond, Edwin Hughes geography educator
Harris, Diana Koffman sociologist, educator

Memphis
Daniel, Coldwell, III economist, educator
Depperschmidt, Thomas Orlando economist, educator
Mealor, William Theodore, Jr. geography educator, university administrator, consultant

Nashville
Buckles, Stephen Gary economist, educator
Damon, William Winchell economics educator
Fels, Rendigs economist, educator
Finegan, Thomas Aldrich economist
Fowler, William Roy, Jr. anthropologist, educator
Gibbs, Jack Porter sociologist, educator
Gove, Walter R. sociology educator
Graham, George J., Jr. political scientist, educator
Hancock, M(arion) Donald political science educator
Heard, (George) Alexander retired educator and chancellor
Russell, Clifford Springer economics and public policy educator
Scheffman, David Theodore economist, management educator, consultant
Sloan, Frank Allen economics educator
Spores, Ronald Marvin anthropology educator, ethnohistorian
Westfield, Fred M. economics educator

TEXAS

Abilene
Davis, Burl Edward social sciences research consulting company executive, communications educator

Arlington
Carney, Kim economics educator
Cole, Richard Louis political scientist, educator
Farmer, James Aurther sociology educator
Furubotn, Eirik Grundtvig economics educator
Mullendore, Walter Edward economist
Nelson, Wallace Boyd economics and business administration educator
Ramsey, Charles Eugene sociologist, educator

Austin
Bean, Frank D(awson) sociology and demography educator
Blodgett, Warren Terrell public affairs educator
Buchanan, Bruce, II political science educator
Burnham, Walter Dean political science educator
Butzer, Karl W. archaeology and geography educator
Cardenas, Gilberto sociology educator, director
Christian, George Eastland political consultant
Davis, Edward Mott anthropology educator and researcher
Dusansky, Richard economist, educator
Epstein, Jeremiah Fain anthropologist, educator
Fernea, Robert Alan cultural anthropology and Middle Eastern studies educator, consultant
Glade, William Patton, Jr. economics educator
Glenn, Norval Dwight sociologist, educator
Hamermesh, Daniel Selim economics educator
Hester, Thomas Roy anthropologist
Holz, Robert Kenneth geography educator
Huff, David L. geography educator
Jannuzi, F. Tomasson economics educator
Jordan, Terry Gilbert geography educator
Kendrick, David Andrew economist, educator
Lariviere, Richard Wilfred Asian studies educator, consultant
Leiden, Carl political scientist, educator
Lopreato, Joseph sociology educator, author
Magee, Stephen Pat economics and finance educator
Marshall, F. Ray public affairs educator
Mc Donald, Stephen Lee economics educator
Roach, James Robert retired political science educator
Rostow, Elspeth Davies political science educator
Rostow, Walt Whitman economist, educator
Schmandt-Besserat, Denise archaeologist, educator
Schmitt, Karl Michael retired political scientist
Smith, Alfred Goud anthropologist, educator
Spiro, Herbert John political scientist, politician, educator, ambassador
Weintraub, Sidney economist, educator

College Station
Bass, George Fletcher archaeology educator
Copp, James Harris sociologist, educator
Greenhut, Melvin Leonard economist, educator
Jones, Bryan Davidson political science educator
Knutson, Ronald Dale economist, educator, academic adminstrator
Solecki, R. Stefan anthropologist, educator
Steffy, John Richard nautical archaeologist, educator
Van Riper, Paul Pritchard political science educator

Dallas
Cochran, Kendall Pinney economics educator
Free, Mary Moore anthropologist
Kemper, Robert Van anthropologist, educator
Murphy, John Carter economics educator
Reagan, Barbara Benton economics educator

Denton
Newell, Charldean public administration educator

El Paso
Blevins, Leon Wilford political science educator, minister
Stoddard, Ellwyn R. sociology and anthropology educator

Fort Worth
Salih, Halil Ibrahim political science educator

Georgetown
Neville, Gwen Kennedy anthropology educator

Houston
Brito, Dagobert Llanos economics educator
Bryant, John Bradbury economics educator, consultant
Condit, Linda Faulkner economist
Cuthbertson, Gilbert Morris political science educator
Davidson, Chandler sociologist, educator
Dix, Robert H. political science educator
Ebaugh, Helen Rose sociology educator, researcher
Fischer, Michael M. J. anthropology educator
Foster, Dale Warren political scientist, educator, management consultant, real estate
Gordon, Wendell Chaffee economics educator
Marcus, George E. anthropologist
McIntosh, Susan Keech anthropology educator
Pelaez, Rolando Federico economics educator, consultant,
Tarrance, Vernon Lance, Jr. behavior research executive
von der Mehden, Fred R. political science educator

Huntsville
Biles, Robert Erle political science educator
Flanagan, Timothy James criminal justice educator, university official

Irving
Cooper, Kathleen Bell economist

Lancaster
Wendorf, Denver Fred, Jr. anthropology educator

Lubbock
Cartwright, Walter Joseph sociology educator
Collins, Harker manufactuing executive, economist, publisher, marketing, financial, business and legal consultant
Gilliam, John Charles economist, educator
Havens, Murray Clark political scientist, educator
Jonish, James Edward economist, educator

Post
Earl, Lewis Harold economics and management consultant

Prairie View
Prestage, Jewel Limar political science educator

Richardson
Berry, Brian Joe Lobley geographer, political economist, urban planner

San Antonio
Bellows, Thomas John political scientist, educator
Benz, George Albert economic consultant, retired educator
Furino, Antonio economist, educator
†Hard, Robert J. archaeology educator
Hazuda, Helen Pauline sociologist
Truett, Lila Flory economics educator
Wagener, James Wilbur social science educator
Whittington, Floyd Leon economist, business consultant, retired oil company executive, foreign service officer

San Marcos
Balanoff, Howard Richard social sciences educator
Boehm, Richard Glennon geography and planning educator, writer
Schultz, Clarence Carven, Jr. sociology educator
Weinberger, George Martin political scientist, government infosystems specialist

Tyler
Ramirez, Enrique Rene social sciences educator

Waco
Miller, Robert T. political science educator
Osborne, Harold Wayne sociology educator, consultant

UTAH

Provo
Bahr, Howard Miner *sociologist, educator*
Chadwick, Bruce Albert *sociology educator*
Christiansen, John Rees *sociologist, educator*
Fry, Earl Howard *political scientist, educator*
Hollist, William Ladd *political science educator*
Kunz, Phillip Ray *sociologist, educator*
Porter, Blaine Robert Milton *psychology/sociology educator*
Snow, Karl Nelson, Jr. *public management educator, university administrator, former state senator*
Thomas, Darwin LaMar *sociology educator*
Wilson, Ramon B. *agricultural economics educator, administrator*

Salt Lake City
Lease, Ronald Charles *financial economics educator*
Lund, Dale A. *sociology educator*
†Schick, Seth Harvey *land resource economist*
Skidmore, Rex Austin *social work educator*

VERMONT

Burlington
Cutler, Stephen Joel *sociologist*
Pacy, James Steven *political science educator*
Sampson, Samuel Franklin *sociology educator*
Smallwood, Franklin *political science educator*

Middlebury
Andrews, David Henry *anthropology educator*
Colander, David Charles *economist, educator*
†Robison, Olin Clyde *political science educator, former college president*
Wilson, George Wilton *economics educator*

White River Junction
Markou, Peter John *economic developer*

VIRGINIA

Alexandria
Corson, Walter Harris *sociologist*
Kollander, Mel *social scientist, statistician*
Mann, Seymour Zalmon *political science and public administration educator emeritus, union official*
Roberts, John Benjamin, II *public policy consultant*
Spar, Edward Joel *demographer*

Arlington
Bartlett, Bruce Reeves *economist*
Brown, Robert Lyle *foreign affairs consultant*
Coe, Paul Francis *demographer, economist*
Collins, Eileen Louise *economist*
Funseth, Robert Lloyd Eric Martin *international consultant, lecturer, retired senior foreign service officer*
Henderson, John Brown *economist*
Marshall, Charles Burton *political science consultant*
Morgan, Bruce Ray *international consultant*
Norwood, Janet Lippe *economist*
Sawhill, John Crittenden *businessman, economist, university president, government official*
Sielicki-Korczak, Boris Zdzislaw *political educator, investigative consultant*
Weidemann, Celia Jean *social scientist, international business and financial development consultant*
Zakheim, Dov Solomon *economist, government official*

Bedford
Haymes, Harmon Hayden *economist, educator*

Blacksburg
Bryant, Clifton Dow *sociologist, educator*
Herndon, James Francis *retired political science educator*
Shepard, Jon Max *sociologist*

Charlottesville
Abraham, Henry Julian *political science educator*
Bierstedt, Robert *sociologist, author*
Claude, Inis Lothair, Jr. *political scientist, educator*
Derthick, Martha Ann *political science educator*
Evans, Robert Henry *political science educator*
Hadden, Jeffrey Keith *sociology and religion educator*
Henry, Laurin Luther *public affairs educator*
Holden, Matthew, Jr. *political scientist, educator, arbitrator, energy consultant*
Holt, Charles Asbury *economics educator*
Hymes, Dell Hathaway *anthropologist*
Johnson, William Richard *economist*
Kubovy, Michael *psychology educator*
Lanham, Betty Bailey *anthropologist, educator*
Leng, Shao Chuan *political science educator*
McClain, Paula Denice *political scientist*
Meiburg, Charles Owen *business administration educator*
Miller, William Lee *writer, social ethics educator*
O'Brien, David Michael *political science educator, researcher*
Perdue, Charles L., Jr. *anthropology educator*
Quandt, William Bauer *political scientist*
Ramazani, Rouhollah Karegar *government and foreign affairs educator*
Rhoads, Steven Eric *political science educator*
Sabato, Larry Joseph *political science educator*
Sherman, Roger *economics educator*
Snavely, William Pennington *economics educator*
Sykes, Gresham M'Cready *sociologist, educator, artist*
Wagner, Roy *anthropology educator, researcher*
Whitaker, John King *economics educator*

Earlysville
Caplow, Theodore *sociologist*

Fairfax
Barth, Michael Carl *economist*
Bennett, James Thomas *economics educator*
Buchanan, James McGill *economist, educator*
Dennis, Rutledge Melvin *sociology educator, researcher*
Dobson, Allen *economist*
Kash, Don Eldon *political science educator*
Lipset, Seymour Martin *sociologist, political scientist, educator*
Vaughn, Karen Iversen *economics educator*

Falls Church
Calkins, Susannah Eby *retired economist*
Green, James Wyche *sociologist, anthropologist, psychotherapist*
LeBlanc, Hugh Linus *political science educator, consultant*
Schumaker, Clarence Joseph, Jr. *sociologist, educator*
Waldo, (Clifford) Dwight *political science educator*
Weiss, Armand Berl *economist, association management executive*
Wyczalkowski, Marcin Roman *retired economist*

Harrisonburg
Cline, Paul Charles *political science educator, state legislator*
Ivory, Ming Marie *political scientist*

Herndon
Boucher, Wayne Irving *policy analyst*
Spragens, William Clark *public policy educator, consultant*

Ivy
Selden, Richard Thomas *economist, educator*

Lexington
Herrick, Bruce Hale *economics educator*
John, Lewis George *political science educator*
Phillips, Charles Franklin, Jr. *economist, educator*
White, Owen Kendall, Jr. *sociologist, educator*
Winfrey, John Crawford *economist, educator*

Locust Grove
Baratz, Morton Sachs *economic consultant, writer*

Lynchburg
Duff, Ernest Arthur *political scientist, educator*
Morland, John Kenneth *sociology and anthropology educator*

Manassas
Smith, Vme (Verna Mae Edom Smith) *sociology educator, freelance writer, photographer*

Mc Lean
Deardourff, John D. *political consultant*
Struelens, Michel Maurice Joseph Georges *political science educator, foreign affairs consultant*
Yager, Joseph Arthur, Jr. *economist*

Midlothian
Stringham, Luther Winters *economist, administrator*

Nellysford
French, Charles Ezra *economist, educational and agricultural consultant*

Norfolk
Ahrari, M. Ehsan *political science educator, researcher, consultant*
Bernsen, Harold John *political affairs consultant, retired naval officer*

Petersburg
Williams, Gertie Boothe *retired home school coordinator*

Reston
Blum, John Curtis *agricultural economist*
Goldman, Ralph Morris *political science educator*
Kelly, Robert William *economist*
Payne, Roger Lee *geographer*

Richmond
Baretski, Charles Allan *political scientist, librarian, educator, historian, municipal official*
Campbell, Thomas Corwith, Jr. *economics educator*
Geary, David Patrick *criminal justice educator, consultant, author*
Hall, James Curtis *business and economics educator*
Hellmuth, William Frederick, Jr. *economics educator*
Morris, Thomas Robbins *political science educator*

Round Hill
Pugh, Marion Stirling *archaeologist, author*

Sperryville
Armor, David J. *sociologist*

Springfield
McLaurin, Ronald De *political analyst, consultant, author, journalist*

Sweet Briar
Miller, Reuben George *economics educator*

Virginia Beach
Lichtenberg, Byron K. *futurist, manufacturing executive, space flight consultant*

Williamsburg
Blouet, Brian Walter *geography educator*
Noël Hume, Ivor *retired antiquary, consultant*
Smith, Roger Winston *political theorist, educator*
Zamora, Mario Dimarucut *anthropologist, educator*

Wise
Yun, Peter Subueng *economics educator*

WASHINGTON

Ellensburg
Jacobs, Robert Cooper *political scientist, consultant*

Friday Harbor
Palmer, Norman Dunbar *political scientist, educator, author*

Issaquah
Pearson, Belinda Kemp *economist, consultant*

La Conner
Knopf, Kenyon Alfred *economist, educator*

Port Angeles
Osborne, Richard Hazelet *anthropology and medical genetics educator*

Pullman
Blakeslee, Leroy Lawrence *agricultural economist*
Catton, William Robert, Jr. *sociology educator*
Dillman, Donald Andrew *sociologist, educator*
Sheldon, Charles Harvey *political science educator*

Seattle
Beyers, William Bjorn *geography educator*
Borgatta, Edgar F. *social psychologist, educator*
Bourque, Philip John *business economist, educator*
Chirot, Daniel *sociology and international studies educator*
Dunnell, Robert Chester *archaeologist, educator*
Gore, William Jay *political science educator*
Gross, Edward *retired sociologist, educator, lawyer*
Hamilton, Gary Glen *sociology educator*
Hellmann, Donald Charles *political science educator*
Hirschman, Charles, Jr. *sociologist, educator*
Inlow, Edgar Burke *political science educator*
†Kranda, Michael Louis *biotechnology company executive*
Lang, Kurt *sociologist, educator, writer*
Lardy, Nicholas Richard *economics educator*
Mah, Feng-hwa *economics educator*
Matthews, Donald Rowe *political scientist, educator*
Morrill, Richard Leland *geographer, educator*
Narver, John Colin *business administration educator*
Nelson, Charles Rowe *economist, educator*
Olson, David John *political science educator*
Parks, Richard William *economics educator, consultant*
Quimby, George Irving *anthropologist, former museum director*
Schall, Lawrence Delano *economics educator, consultant*
Sherman, John Clinton *geography educator*
Thornton, Judith Ann *economist*
Tucker, Gary Jay *physician, educator*
Turnovsky, Stephen John *economics educator*
van den Berghe, Pierre Louis *sociologist, anthropologist*
Wolfle, Dael Lee *public affairs educator*

Spokane
Novak, Terry Lee *public adminstration educator*

Tacoma
Bourgaize, Robert G. *economist*

Walla Walla
Stevens, David *economics educator*

WEST VIRGINIA

Bethany
Cooey, William Randolph *economics educator*

Martinsburg
Yoe, Harry Warner *retired agricultural economist*

Morgantown
Colyer, Dale Keith *agricultural economics educator*
Peterson, Sophia *international studies educator*

WISCONSIN

Beloit
Davis, Harry Rex *political science educator*

Cedarburg
Eley, Lynn W. *political science educator, former mayor*

Eau Claire
Davidson, John Kenneth, Sr. *sociologist, educator, researcher, author, consultant*

Madison
Anderson, Odin Waldemar *sociologist, educator*
Andreano, Ralph Louis *economist, educator*
Baldwin, Robert Edward *economics educator*
Barrows, Richard Lee *economics educator, academic administrator*
Bennett, Kenneth Alan *biological anthropologist*
Brock, William Allen, III *economics educator, consultant*
Bromley, Daniel Wood *economics educator, consultant*
Cohen, Bernard Cecil *political scientist, educator*
Culbertson, John Mathew *economist, educator*
Denevan, William Maxfield *geographer, educator*
Eisinger, Peter K(endall) *political science educator*
Goldberger, Arthur Stanley *economics educator*
Graf, Truman Frederick *agricultural economist, educator*
Grossman, Joel B(arry) *political science educator*
Haller, Archibald Orben *sociologist, educator*
Hansen, W. Lee *economics educator, author*
Hauser, Robert Mason *sociologist, demographer, educator*
Hester, Donald Denison *economics educator*
Levine, Solomon Bernard *business and economics educator*
Lewis, Herbert Samuel *anthropologist, educator*
Luening, Robert Adami *agricultural economics educator emeritus*
Mare, Robert Denis *sociology educator, demography researcher*
Marwell, Gerald *sociology educator, research consultant*
Mc Camy, James Lucian *former political science educator*
McCubbin, Hamilton I. *social scientist, educator, researcher*
Mueller, Willard Fritz *economics educator*
Nichols, Donald Arthur *economist, educator*
Pempel, T. J. *political science educator*
Penniman, Clara *political scientist, educator*
Robinson, Arthur Howard *geography educator*
Schmidt, John Richard *agricultural economics educator*
Sewell, William Hamilton *sociologist*
Strasma, John Drinan *economist, educator*
Strier, Karen Barbara *anthropology educator*
Thiesenhusen, William Charles *agricultural economist*
†Tuan, Yi-Fu *geography educator*
Waldron, Ellis Leigh *retired political science educator*
Wright, Erik Olin *sociology educator*
Young, Merwin Crawford *political science educator*

Milwaukee
Hawkins, Brett William *political science educator*
Lydolph, Paul Edward *geography educator*
Moberg, David Oscar *sociology educator*
Paulson, Belden Henry *political scientist*
Perlman, Richard Wilfred *economist, educator*
Quade, Quentin Lon *political science educator*
Schur, Leon Milton *educator, economist*
Shea, Donald Richard *political science educator*

Oregon
Dorner, Peter Paul *retired economist, educator*

Oshkosh
Gruberg, Martin *political science educator*

Thiensville
Lee, Tong Hun *economics educator*

West Allis
Powell, Rosalie *home economist*

Whitewater
Bhargava, Ashok *economics educator*
Refior, Everett Lee *labor economist, educator*

WYOMING

Laramie
Chai, Winberg *political science educator, foundation chair*
Gill, George Wilhelm *anthropologist*

MILITARY ADDRESSES OF THE UNITED STATES

PACIFIC

FPO
†Nance, William Bennett *economic development specialist*

CANADA

ALBERTA

Calgary
Forbis, Richard George *archaeologist*
Stebbins, Robert Alan *sociology educator*

Edmonton
Freeman, Milton Malcolm Roland *anthropology educator*
Krotki, Karol Jozef *sociology educator, demographer*
Smith, Peter John *geographer, educator*

BRITISH COLUMBIA

Burnaby
Brantingham, Patricia Louise *criminology educator*
Brantingham, Paul Jeffrey *criminology educator*
Copes, Parzival *economist, researcher*

Vancouver
Aberle, David Friend *anthropologist, educator*
Cairns, H. Alan C. *political scientist, educator*
Elkins, David J. *political science educator*
Ericson, Richard Victor *social science and law educator, university administrator*
Feaver, George A. *political science educator*
Ho, Samuel Pao-San *economics educator*
Holsti, Kalevi Jacque *political scientist, educator*
Kesselman, Jonathan Rhys *economics educator, public policy researcher*
Langdon, Frank Corriston *political science educator, researcher*
Laponce, Jean Antoine *political scientist*
Lipsey, Richard George *economist, educator*
Marchak, Maureen Patricia *anthropology and sociology educator*
Pearson, Richard Joseph *archaeologist, educator*
Robinson, John Lewis *geography educator*
Shearer, Ronald Alexander *economics educator*
Slaymaker, H. Olav *geography educator*
Stankiewicz, Wladyslaw Jozef *political scientist, educator*

Victoria
Barber, Clarence Lyle *economics educator*
Chard, Chester Stevens *archaeologist, educator*

MANITOBA

Winnipeg
Loxley, John *economics educator*

NEW BRUNSWICK

Fredericton
Kenyon, Gary Michael *gerontology educator, researcher*

NOVA SCOTIA

Halifax
Borgese, Elisabeth Mann *political science educator, author*
†Shaw, Timothy Milton *political science educator*
Stairs, Denis Winfield *political science educator*

ONTARIO

Clarksburg
Krueger, Ralph Ray *retired geography educator*

Dundas
Jones, Frank Edward *sociology educator*

Hamilton
King, Leslie John *geography educator*

Kingston
Kaliski, Stephan Felix *economics educator*
Meisel, John *political scientist*

Kitchener
Qualter, Terence Hall *retired political science educator*

London
Laidler, David Ernest William *economics educator*
Wonnacott, Ronald Johnston *economics educator*

Nepean
Cornell, Peter McCaul *economic consultant, former government official*

Niagara on the Lake
Olley, Robert Edward *economist, educator*

North York
Richmond, Anthony Henry *sociologist, emeritus educator*

Ottawa
Brooks, David Barry *resource economist*
Griller, David *economics and technology consultant*
Jubinville, Alain Maurice Joseph *retired economist, banker*
Lithwick, Norman Harvey *economics educator*
Mc Rae, Kenneth Douglas *political scientist, educator*
Paquet, Gilles *economist, university administrator*
Whyte, Anne Veronica *social science researcher, educator*

Toronto
Beigie, Carl Emerson *economist, research administrator, educator*
Clark, Samuel Delbert *sociology educator*
Dean, William George *geography educator*
Eastman, Harry Claude MacColl *economics educator*
Eayrs, James George *political scientist, educator*
George, Peter James *economist, educator*
Goldfarb, Martin *sociologist*
Grayson, Albert Kirk *Near Eastern studies educator*
Helleiner, Gerald Karl *economics educator*
Hollander, Samuel *economist, educator*
Kruger, Arthur Martin *economics educator, university official*
Munro, John Henry Alexander *economics educator, writer*
Neufeld, Edward Peter *retired economist*
Pratt, Robert Cranford *political scientist, educator*
Rapoport, Anatol *peace studies educator, mathematical biologist*
Ross, Murray George *social science educator, university president emeritus*
†Shearing, Clifford Denning *criminology and sociology educator*
Wilson, Thomas Arthur *economics educator*

Vanier
Davidson, Alexander T. *geographer, professional society administrator*

Waterloo
Fallding, Harold Joseph *sociology educator*
Nash, Peter Hugh John *geographer, educator, planner*
†Nelson, J. Gordon *geography educator*
Warner, Barry Gregory *geographer*

QUEBEC

Hull
MacDonald, George Frederick *anthropologist, Canadian museum director*

Ile des Soeurs
Dagenais, Marcel Gilles *economist, educator*

Montreal
Brecher, Irving *economics educator*
Brecher, Michael *political science educator*
Chateau, John-Peter D(avid) *economics and finance educator, mining company executive*
Dufour, Jean-Marie *economics researcher, educator*
Ikawa-Smith, Fumiko *anthropologist, educator*
Jonassohn, Kurt *sociologist, educator*
Nayar, Baldev Raj *political science educator*
Normandeau, Andre Gabriel *criminologist, educator*
Noumoff, Samuel Joseph *political scientist, researcher*
O'Brien, John Wilfrid *economist, university president emeritus, educator*
Orban, Edmond Henry *political science educator*
Raynauld, Andre *economist, educator*
Smith, Philip Edward Lake *anthropology educator*
Szabo, Denis *criminologist, educator*
Tremblay, Rodrigue *economics educator*
Trigger, Bruce Graham *anthropology educator*
Vaillancourt, Jean-Guy *sociology educator*
Waller, Harold Myron *political science educator*

Quebec
Belanger, Gerard *economics educator*
Migue, Jean Luc *economics educator*
Tremblay, Marc Adélard *anthropologist, educator*

Rimouski
†Rioux, Claude *economics educator*

Sainte Croix
Grenier, Fernand *geographer, consultant*

Sainte Foy
Denis, Paul-Yves *geography educator*

AUSTRALIA

Adelaide
Twidale, C(harles) R(owland) *geomorphologist, educator*

BRAZIL

Rio de Janeiro
DaMatta, Roberto Augusto *anthropologist*

Salvador
Davidson, Ralph Kirby *economist, retired foundation executive, consultant*

ENGLAND

Birmingham
Fry, Maxwell John *economist, educator*

Cambridge
Meade, James Edward *economist*

Claverton Down
Buchanan, Robert Angus *archaeology educator*

Cornwall
Dark, Philip John Crosskey *anthropologist, educator*

London
Douglas, Mary Tew *anthropology and humanities educator*
Junz, Helen B. *economist*
Kuper, Adam Jonathan *anthropologist, educator*
Pennant-Rea, Rupert Lascelles *banker*

FRANCE

Fontainebleu
Ayres, Robert Underwood *environmental economics and technology educator*

Paris
Gottschalk, Charles M. *international relations consultant*
Lubell, Harold *economic consultant*

GERMANY

Halle
Rode, Reinhard *political science educator*

Luneburg
Linde, Robert Hermann *economics educator*

Munich
Whetten, Lawrence Lester *international relations educator*

GREECE

Athens
Iakovidis, Spyros Eustace *archaeologist*
Kalamotousakis, George John *economist*

ISRAEL

Tel Aviv
Rubin, Barry Mitchel *foreign policy analyst, writer*

ITALY

Rome
Rossmiller, George Eddie *agricultural economist*

JAPAN

Tokyo
Ori, Kan *political science educator*

KOREA

Seoul
Steinberg, David Isaac *economic development consultant, educator*

MARTINIQUE

Anses d'Arlet
Price, Richard *anthropologist, author*

SLOVENIA

Ljubljana
Sicherl, Pavle *economics educator, consultant*

SRI LANKA

Colombo
Spain, James William *political scientist, writer, investor*

ADDRESS UNPUBLISHED

Abere, Andrew Evan *economist*
Adams, Robert McCormick *anthropologist, educator*
Adelman, Richard Charles *gerontologist, educator*
Alker, Hayward Rose *political science educator*
Alsadek, Jihad Abdalla *economist*
Anderson, Bernard E. *economist*
Arkin, William Morris *military and political analyst, writer*
Bambrick, James Joseph *labor economist, labor relations executive*
Barnett, Vincent MacDowell, Jr. *political science educator*
Bateson, Mary Catherine *anthropology educator*
Biesdorf, Heinz Bernard *retired economist, educator*
Bohannan, Paul James *anthropologist, writer, former university administrator*
Brage, Carl Willis *genealogist*
Brandl, John Edward *public affairs educator*
Cantril, Albert H(adley) *public opinion analyst*
Cash, Carol Vivian *sociologist*
Chew, Margaret Sarah *geography educator, retired*
Clark, Caleb Morgan *political scientist, educator*
Cope, Alfred Haines *political scientist, educator*
Crampton, Esther Larson *sociology and political science educator*
Daniels, Arlene Kaplan *sociology educator*
de Blij, Harm Jan *geography educator, editor*
DeFleur, Melvin Lawrence *sociologist, communication educator*
Dobriansky, Lev Eugene *economist, educator, diplomat*
Drummond, Dorothy Weitz *geography education consultant, educator, author*
Greeley, Andrew Moran *sociologist, author*
Hare, Frederick Kenneth *geography and environmental educator, university official*
Hefferan, Colien Joan *economist*
Helfgott, Roy B. *economist, educator*
Henle, Peter *economic consultant, arbitrator*
Hilliard, Sam Bowers *geography educator*
Holloway, Robert Ross *archaeologist, educator*
Holmes, Paul Luther *political scientist, educational consultant*
Johnson, Albert Wesley *political science educator*
Jones, Joan Megan *anthropologist*
Juviler, Peter Henry *political scientist, educator*
Kates, Robert William *geographer, educator, independent scholar*
Keyes, Margaret Naumann *home economics educator*
Lanzillotti, Robert Franklin *economist, educator*
Leith, James Clark *economics educator*
Levi, Maurice David *economics educator*
Ludden, John Franklin *financial economist*
Lynch, Thomas Francis *archeologist, educator*
Maranda, Pierre Jean *anthropologist, writer*
Mc Clellan, Catharine *anthropologist, educator*
Michael, Donald Nelson *social scientist, educator*
Modigliani, Franco *economics and finance educator*
Monsen, Raymond Joseph, Jr. *economist, educator, art patron*
Moore, John Runyan *agricultural and resource economics educator*
Naylor, Thomas Herbert *economist, educator, consultant*
Newman, Peter Kenneth *economist, educator*
Oksas, Joan K. *economist, educator*
Olson, William Clinton *international affairs educator, author, lecturer*
Pedersen, Knud George *economics educator, former university president*
Pillai, A(rrackal) K(asava) B. *integral development therapist, anthropology educator*
Piore, Nora Kahn *economist, health policy analyst*
Pollack, Gerald Alexander *economist, government official*
Randall, Richard Rainier *geographer*
Robinson, Marshall Alan *economics educator, foundation executive*
Rosen, Lawrence *anthropology educator*
Rossi, Peter Henry *sociology educator*
Ruchelman, Leonard Isadore *urban studies and public administration educator*
Ruderman, Armand Peter *health economics educator, consultant, volunteer*
Sebastian, Peter *international affairs consultant, former ambassador*
†Shapiro, Leo J. *social researcher*
Sharpe, William Forsyth *economics educator*
Sheppard, Harold Lloyd *gerontologist, educator*
Siddayao, Corazón Morales *economist, educator*
Sims, Kent Otway *economist*
Smith, Edward K. *economist, consultant*
Smith, V. Kerry *economics educator*
Stalon, Charles Gary *retired economics educator, institute administrator*
Steffens, Dorothy Ruth *political economist*
Steinhauser, Sheldon Eli *sociology and gerontology educator*
Striker, Cecil Leopold *archaeologist, educator*
Sutton, Willis Anderson, Jr. *sociology educator*
Swanstrom, Thomas Evan *economist*
Swindler, Daris Ray *physical anthropologist, forensic anthropologist*
Tarr, David William *political scientist, educator*
Taylor, Richard Wirth *political science educator*
terHorst, Jerald Franklin *public affairs counsel*
Textor, Robert Bayard *cultural anthropology writer, consultant, educator*
Theobald, H. Rupert *retired political scientist*
Throckmorton, William Robert, Sr. *sociologist*
Tonello-Stuart, Enrica Maria *political economist*
Volcker, Paul A. *economist*
†Weber, Mary Ellen Healy *economist*
Weil, Rolf Alfred *economist, university president emeritus*
Wilkinson, Doris Yvonne *medical sociology educator*
Willey, Gordon Randolph *retired anthropologist, archaeologist, educator*
Wolfe, Gregory Baker *international relations educator*
Wonders, William Clare *geography educator*
Wood, Robert Coldwell *political scientist*
Wright, James David *sociology educator, writer*
Zeigler, L(uther) Harmon *political science educator*

UNCLASSIFIED

UNITED STATES

DISTRICT OF COLUMBIA

Washington
Clinton, Hillary Rodham *First Lady of United States, lawyer*
Gore, Tipper (Mary Elizabeth Gore) *wife of vice president of the United States*

Retiree Index

The index below lists the names of those individuals whose biographical sketches last appeared in the forty-seventh, forty-eighth, or forty-ninth edition of *Who's Who in America*. The latest volume containing a full sketch is indicated by *47, 48,* or *49* following each name. The listees have since retired from active participation in their respective occupations.

A

Adams, Andrew Stanford, *47*
Adams, John Hanly, *48*
Adams-Ender, Clara Leach, *48*
Addicott, Warren Oliver, *49*
Addy, George Arthur, *49*
Ahern, Patrick V., *49*
Alexander, Charles Thomas, *49*
Allan, Harry Thain, *48*
Allard, James Edward, *49*
Amundson, Clyde Howard, *48*
Ancker-Johnson, Betsy, *47*
Anders, Edward, *47*
Anderson, Ansel Cochran, *47*
Anderson, Donald Paul, *48*
Anderson, John Leonard, *47*
Anderson, Thomas Paine, *47*
Annand, James Earle, *47*
Anton, Thomas, *48*
Aramony, William, *47*
Arbour, Alger, *48*
Arfa, Milton, *47*
Armour, Laurance Hearne, Jr., *49*
Ashbrook, James Barbour, *48*
Azneer, J. Leonard, *48*
Azzato, Louis Enrico, *48*

B

Babbitt, Milton Byron, *49*
Bacon, Richard Franklin, *47*
Badura-Skoda, Paul (Ludwig Badura), *49*
Bailey, R. W., *49*
Banse, Karl, *48*
Barbato, Silvio, *48*
Barrett, Robert South, IV, *48*
Barry, David N., III, *47*
Bartholomew, Byron Simpson, Jr., *49*
Batzel, Roger Elwood, *48*
Begley, R. T., *49*
Bekkum, Owen D., *47*
Benedict, Samuel S., *49*
Bennett, Edward Nevill, *48*
Benson, Kenneth Peter, *48*
Benton, Philip Eglin, Jr., *48*
Berry, Thomas Joseph, *48*
Bickmore, J. Grant, *48*
Biggy, Mary Virginia, *48*
Binkerd, Gordon Ware, *49*
Blair, William Sutherland, *47*
Blanchard, Elwood P., Jr., *48*
Boardman, Richard Stanton, *47*
Bodden, William Michael, *48*
Bohlmann, Ralph Arthur, *48*
Bonde, Olaf Carl, *48*
Bonnyman, George Gordon, *48*
Bonsignore, Joseph John, *48*
Borders, William Donald, *48*
Bowers, Emmett Wadsworth, *48*
Bowman, Robert Allott, *47*
Braden, Thomas Wardell, *48*
Bradley, Marvin R., *47*
Braker, William Paul, *49*
Brayer, Menachem Mendel, *48*
Bremner, Bruce Barton, *48*
Briggs, George Madison, *48*
Briggs, William Egbert, *48*
Brock, Thomas Walter, *47*
Bronstein, Aaron Jacob, *47*
Brooks, Maurice Edward, *49*
Brown, Glenn Robbins, Jr., *48*
Brown, Ronald, *48*
Brzana, Stanislaus Joseph, *49*
Buchanan, George Francis, *47*
Buckley, Edwin T., *47*
Budig, Gene Arthur, *49*
Buesinger, Ronald Ernest, *49*
Bugos, Joseph V., *48*
Bullard, Todd Hupp, *48*
Burba, Edwin Hess, Jr., *48*
Burleson, Willard McKenzie, Jr., *47*
Burns, James MacGregor, *47*
Burns, John Dudley, *48*
Burnsky, Paul John, *48*
Butler, George L., *48*
Butta, J. Henry, *48*
Byrd, Gill Arnette, *48*
Byrne, James Joseph, *47*

C

Cain, James Marshall, *48*
Caldwell, Carlyle G., *48*
Campbell, Eric Eldon, *48*
Carlson, Charles A., *47*
Carlson, Guy Raymond, *48*
Carlson, Richard George, *47*
Cassiday, Benjamin Buckles, Jr., *47*
Chappelear, Patsy Stallings, *48*
Chappell, Robert Earl, Jr., *48*
Charbonneau, George Allen, *48*
Chase, Goodwin, *47*
Chen, Wayne H., *47*
Chesbrough, Geoffrey Lynn, *48*
Chou, Wen-chung, *49*
Clark, James Whitley, *47*
Clark, William George, *47*
Clayton, Jonathan Alan, *47*
Clinch, Harry Anselm, *47*
Cochrane, Robert H., *48*
Coffin, David Linwood, *48*
Coffin, Gordon Lee, *47*
Cohen, Isidore Leonard, *49*
Cole, Nyla Jessamine, *47*
Coleman, Martin, *49*
Coleman, Mary Stallings, *48*
Conlin, Alfred Thomas, *49*
Connare, William Graham, *48*
Conner, John Wayne, *47*
Copeland, Ronald Max, *48*
Cox, James Melville, *47*
Cragg, Ernest Elliott, *48*
Crain, Charles Anthony, *49*
Crawford, Bryce Low, Jr., *48*
Crecine, John Patrick, *48*
Cronemiller, Philip Douglas, *48*
Crouse, Lloyd Roseville, *48*
Crow, John William, *48*
Crowell, Robert Leland, *47*
Curotto, Ricky Joseph, *48*
Cutler, Robert H., *47*

D

Daeschner, Charles William, Jr., *49*
Dailey, John Revell, *48*
Danis, Richard Ralph, Sr., *47*
Darling, George Bapst, Jr., *49*
Davie, Donald Alfred, *47*
Davis, Luther, Jr., *49*
Day, John Franklin, *48*
Dean, Frances Childers, *47*
DeAnda, James, *48*
DeBois, James Adolphus, *48*
Decker, Bernard Martin, *47*
Deecken, George Christian, *48*
Delaney, Caldwell, *47*
Dembofsky, Thomas Joseph, *47*
Demetz, Peter, *47*
de Wetter, Herman Peter, *48*
Dial, William Henry, *48*
Dickerson, Eric Demetric, *48*
Dietz, Albert George Henry, *48*
Dinitz, Simon, *47*
Di Sabato, Louis Roman, *48*
Dolan, Beverly Franklin, *48*
Dolan, Kevin Leo, *47*
Donovan, Paul V., *49*
Dornburgh, William Walter, *49*
Dunn, Robert Vincent, *47*
Dupuy, Howard Moore, Jr., *47*
Dwyer, Bernard James, *47*

E

Eakin, Tom Scott, Jr., *47*
Eaton, Conrad Paul, *47*
Eckenrode, Robert J., *48*
Eckler, John Alfred, *48*
Edwards, Helen Thom, *47*
Eichholz, Geoffrey G(unther), *48*
Eisenhardt, (Emil) Roy, *48*
Ekrom, Roy Herbert, *48*
Ellis, Grover, Jr., *47*
Else, Carolyn Joan, *48*
Englehaupt, William Myles, *48*
Erickson, Thomas Sherman, *47*
Estey, Willard Zebedee, *48*
Etling, John Charles, *48*
Evans, J(ohn) Harvey, *47*
Everitt, George Bain, *48*

F

Farley, James Duncan, *48*
Farrar, Beverly Jayne, *47*
Favreau, Joseph Lucien Gilles, *48*
Feagles, Robert West, *47*
Felt, Irving Mitchell, *48*
Ferguson, Charles Winston, *48*
Ferrario, Joseph A., *49*
Finch, Charles Baker, *48*
Finley, Murray Howard, *48*
Fisher, Harold Wallace, *47*
Fitch, Stona James, *48*
Flavin, Glennon P., *48*
Foell, Earl William, *48*
Follman, Dorothy Major, *48*
Foss, John William, *48*
Foss, William Francis, *47*
Foster, John Stuart, Jr., *48*
Franzke, (Arthur) Allan, *47*
Frey, Gerard Louis, *48*
Fulton, Paul, *48*

G

Gambill, Malcolm W., *48*
Gard, Curtis Eldon, *48*
Garwin, Richard Lawrence, *48*
Gates, Daryl Francis, *47*
Gaydos, Joseph Matthew, *47*
Gebel-Williams, Gunther, *48*
Gerard, W. Gene, *48*
Gersch, Harold Arthur, *48*
Gideon, Miriam, *49*
Gill, Raymond Joseph, *48*
Gill, Robert B., *48*
Gillon, John William, *47*
Giuggio, John Peter, *47*
Glaser, Harold, *49*
Goldberger, Marvin Leonard, *47*
Goldrick, John Richard, *48*
Goldschmied, Fabio Renzo, *47*
Goodrich, Henry Calvin, *48*
Gore, David Eugene, *47*
Grant, William A., Jr., *48*
Grant, William Downing, *48*
Gray, Ronald D., *48*
Graydon, Frank Drake, *48*
Green, Marguerite, *48*
Greenhouse, Bernard, *49*
Guffey, James Roger, *47*
Gwaltney, Eugene C., Jr., *48*

H

Haake, Earle E., *49*
Haas, Peter Edgar, Jr., *47*
Halprin, Lawrence, *48*
Hambrick, Jackson Reid, *49*
Hampton, Daniel Oliver, *47*
Hank, Bernard J., Jr., *49*
Hankinson, James Floyd, *49*
Hanna, Robert C., *48*
Hannah, Mary-Emily, *48*
Hansen, Richard W., *47*
Hare, Robert Lewis, *47*
Harrigan, John Frederick, *48*
Harrigan, Kenneth William J., *48*
Harrington, Timothy J., *49*
Harris, George Clinton, *47*
Harrison, Richard Donald, *48*
Harrower, George Alexander, *47*
Hartman, Fred George, *48*
Hartman, Richard Russell, *48*
Hastrich, Jerome Joseph, *49*
Hawkins, W. Whitley, *48*
Hayne, David Mackness, *49*
Haynes, Arden R., *48*
Heebner, David Richard, *48*
Hees, George Harris, *48*
Hefner, Robert Alan, *48*
Hegyi, Julius, *49*
Helmsing, Charles Herman, *48*
Henning, Charles Nathaniel, *47*
Herder, Stephen Rendell, *48*
Hessberg, Rufus R., *48*
Hirsch, Melvin L., *47*
Hoberman, Henry Don, *48*
Hodgson, Matthew Marshall Neil, *47*
Hogg, James R., *48*
Holding, Harvey, *48*
Howard, Helen Arlene, *48*
Hoyt, Stanley Charles, *49*
Huckel, Hubert E., *48*
Hudson, Desmond F., *47*
Hulse, John Edward, *48*
Hume, Ernest Harding, *47*
Hunt, James Robert, *47*
Hurley, Mark Joseph, *49*
Hyman, Stanley Herbert, *47*
Hytha, Robert J., *48*

I

Inkster, Norman David, *49*
Irwin, Leo Howard, *48*

J

Jelavich, Barbara, *48*
Jenkins, Carrell Ray, *47*
Jensen, Shirley Wulff, *49*
Job, Reuben Philip, *48*
Johncock, Gordon Walter, *48*
Johnston, Robert Lloyd, Jr., *48*
Jones, John Barclay, Jr., *48*
Jones, Johnie H., *49*
Jones, William Augustus, Jr., *48*
Juba, George E., *48*
Judd, Robert Carpenter, *48*

K

Kaltenbach, Hubert Leonard, *48*
Kaslow, John Francis, *48*
Katsaros, Constantine (Dean Katsaros), *47*
Kay, Ulysses Simpson, *49*
Keedy, Mervin L., *47*
Kelly, Burton Vincent, *47*
Kelso, Frank Benton, II, *48*
Kemp, Edgar Ray, Jr., *48*
Kenny, R. Timothy, *48*
Kerr, Chester Brooks, *47*
Kilpatrick, George H., *48*
Kim, Earl, *49*
King, Arthur Hood, *48*
King, Russell C., Jr., *49*
Kirchner, Leon, *49*
Kirk, Richard Augustus, *47*
Kleene, Stephen Cole, *48*
Kocisko, Stephen John, *49*
Koile, Earl, *49*
Krakauer, Albert Alexander, *49*
Krinsky, Paul Lewis, *48*
Kroeber, Clifton Brown, *48*
Kuhns, William George, *48*
Kyman, Alexander Leon, *48*

L

Laimbeer, Bill, *48*
Laird, Walter Jones, Jr., *48*
Lake, Charles William, Jr., *47*
Lallinger, E. Michael, *48*
LaMotte, William Mitchell, *47*
Largent, Steve, *48*
Laski, Frank Joseph, *47*
Lassen, John R., *49*
Lassen, Laurence E., *49*
Laswell, Troy James, *47*
Lattes, Jean-Claude J., *47*
Lawrence, Mary Georgene Wells (Mrs. Harding Lawrence), *47*
Leader, Robert Wardell, *49*
LeHane, Louis James, *49*
Lehman, William, *47*
Leidel, Frederick Otto, *48*
Leighton, Robert B(enjamin), *47*
Lemasters, John N., *48*
Lent, Berkeley, *48*
Levine, David Barry, *47*
Liao, Hsiang Peng, *48*
Liberman, Samuel, *47*
Livingston, Robert Burr, *49*
Loiselle, Gilles, *48*
Lovenberg, Walter M., *48*
Lowry, Sheldon Gaylon, *49*
Luginbuhl, William Hossfeld, *48*
Luhrs, James E., *48*
Lulu, Donald James, *47*
Lundy, Richard Alan, *48*
Lustig, Harry, *49*
Lynch, Frank William, *48*

M

MacDonald, Gerald V., *48*
MacDonald, Wesley Angus Reginald, *48*
MacLaury, Richard Joyce, *48*
MacLeod, Jack (J. M. MacLeod), *48*
MacMillan, John Lavergne, *47*
Maguire, Joseph F., *48*
Maguire, Robert Edward, *47*
Mahoney, Richard John, *49*
Mai, Harold Leverne, *48*
Mai, William Frederick, *47*
Makarova, Natalia, *48*
Mallory, Charles Shannon, *48*
Malloy, James B., *49*
Mandolini, Anthony Mario, *48*
Marcinkowski, Marion John, *48*
Marquardt, Frederic Sylvester, *47*
Marschall, Marlene Elizabeth, *48*
Marshall, Robert James, *47*
Martin, Walter Patrick, *47*
Marvin, Oscar McDowell, *48*
Masson, Pierre, *48*
Match, Robert Kreis, *48*
Maurer, Fred Dry, *47*
Maxwell, Christine, *47*
May, Robert A., *48*
Mayberry, William Eugene, *47*
McAboy, Thomas Hatfield, *48*
McAuliffe, Dennis Philip, *48*
McAuliffe, John F., *48*
McCarthy, Edward Anthony, *49*
McCaughey, Andrew Gilmour, *48*
Mc Clellan, James Edward, Jr., *48*
Mc Cutcheon, John Tinney, Jr., *48*
McDonald, Ian MacLaren, *48*
Mc Farland, Keith Nielson, *47*
Mc Gehee, Carden Coleman, *48*
McKenzie, Jack Harris, *47*
McKibben, Gordon Charles, *49*
Mc Manus, Charles Anthony, Jr., *49*
McMorris, William, *48*
Mc Tavish, John Elser, *47*
McVey, James William, *48*
Mears, Rick Ravon, *48*
Melton, Andrew Joseph, Jr., *47*
Mercier, Jean-Louis, *48*
Metzger, Sidney, *48*
Millard, David Ralph, Jr., *49*
Miller, John Henry, *47*
Miller, William Robert, *48*
Minahan, Roger Copp, *47*
Mobraaten, William Lawrence, *48*
Moir, Edward, *47*
Moore, Charles Julian, *48*
Moore, John Cordell, *48*
Moore, Thomas Charles, *48*
Moran, Thomas Joseph, *48*
Morgan, William T., *47*
Morita, Akio, *49*
Morris, Ben Rankin, *47*
Morrissette, Rosemary D., *47*
Morrow, John Howard, *48*
Morss, Charles Anthony, Jr., *47*
Morton, David, *49*
Morton, Dean O., *47*
Moss, Clement Murphy, Jr., *47*
Mossman, Stuart Alan, *48*
Moulder, James Edwin, *49*
Mowbray, John Code, *48*
Murphy, Charles Francis, Jr., *47*
Murphy, James Bryson, Jr., *47*
Murphy, James F., *48*
Murphy, Thomas Francis, *48*
Myers, Theodore Ash, *48*

N

Naughton, William Aloysius, *47*
Neary, Robert D., *48*
Nee, Frank Walter, *48*
Nelson, Wallace W., *47*
Newman, Melvin Spencer, *48*
Newman, Robert Joseph, *48*
Niedergeses, James D., *48*

O

O'Connell, Robert Thomas, *48*
Odell, Donald Austin, *48*
Ohashi, Kosuke, *47*
O'Loughlin, Earl T., *48*

Necrology

Biographees of the forty-ninth edition of *Who's Who in America* whose deaths have been reported to the editors prior to the close of compilation of this edition are listed below. For those individuals whose deaths were reported prior to January 1993, complete biographical information, including date of death and place of interment, can be found in Volume X of *Who Was Who in America.*

A

Abbott, George
Abbott, Woodrow Acton
Ackerman, James Nils
Adams, Stanley
Agusta, Benjamin J.
Alderete, Joseph Frank
Alfvén, Hannes Olof Gosta
Alicata, Joseph Everett
Allers, Franz
Andersen, Daniel Johannes
Anderson, Philip Warren
Anfinsen, Christian Boehmer
Arnold, Philip Mills
Arnow, Winston Eugene
Aspin, Les
Austin, Darrel

B

Bach, George Leland
Bach, Marcus
Bailey, Joel Furness
Bailey, Sturges Williams
Baker, John Alexander
Ball, George Wildman
Ballantine, Ian
Ballew, Nellie Hester
Barkate, John Albert
Barry, John Kevin
Battisti, Frank Joseph
Beaty, James Ralph
Becker, Ralph Elihu
Behl, Wolfgang
Bell, James Frederick
Bellamy, Robert K.
Benade, Leo Edward
Bennett, Edward Herbert, Jr.
Bergold, Harry Earl, Jr.
Berkman, Marshall L.
Bernays, Edward L.
Bernstein, Louis
Biezup, John Thomas
Birdwhistell, Ray L.
Bishop, Barry Chapman
Blackwell, Earl
Blakely, Robert John
Bloch, Robert Albert
Block, George Edward
Blum, Walter J.
Bondi, Enrico
Borst, John, Jr.
Brannon, H(ezzie) Raymond, Jr.
Briggs, Rodney Arthur
Britt, James Thomas
Broadus, James Matthew
Brown, Robert Harold
Bryant, Alan Willard
Burciaga, Juan Guerrero
Burke, William James
Burkhardt, Hans Gustav
Burns, George Washington
Byrnes, Victor Allen

C

Cahill, James David
Calamari, John Daniel
Calder, Daniel Gillmore
Cannady, Edward Wyatt, Jr.
Carey, William Joseph
Carlton, Winslow
Carmichael, Hugh
Carmichael, Mary Mulloy
Carroll, John Howard
Chamberlain, John Rensselaer
Chambers, Richard H.
Chernoff, Robert
Childress, Alice
Christopherson, Weston Robert
Clavell, James
Collado, Emilio Gabriel
Collier, Gaylan Jane
Cook, Don
Corry, Andrew Francis
Cosell, Howard (Howard William Cohen)
Cotter, William Joseph
Critchfield, Richard Patrick
Cross, Clyde Cleveland
Curtis, Mark Hubert

D

Danishefsky, Isidore
Daub, Berger Ellis
David, Paul Theodore
DeBartolo, Edward J., Sr.
Debevoise, Thomas McElrath
Dekker, Maurits
Dell, J. Howard
Denisoff, R. Serge
Dennis, Ward Brainerd
Despatie, Roger
Dilworth, James Weldon
Donovan, Allen Francis
Doolittle, Robert Frederick
Douglis, Avron
D'Souza, Anthony Frank
DuFour, R(ichard) W(illiam), Jr.
Durrell, Gerald Malcolm

E

Easley, John Allen (Jack Easley)
Egekvist, W. Soren
Ehrenkranz, Shirley Malakoff
Ellis, Eva Lillian
Ellis, Spencer Percy
Elsbree, John Francis
Elsen, Albert Edward
Enloe, Cortez Ferdinand, Jr.
Eshbach, William Wallace
Evans, Edwin Charles
Evans, John James
Evarts, Charles McCollister

F

Faiman, Robert Neil
Fain, Paul Kemp, Jr.
Falicov, Leopoldo Maximo
Faust, John William, Jr.
Fenvessy, Stanley John
Fields, Bernard Nathan
Finch, Harold Bertram, Jr.
Finger, Kenneth Franklin
Finks, James Edward
Finneburgh, Morris Lewis
Firkušny, Rudolf
Fisch, Max Harold
Fisher, Walter Dummer
Flagler, Robert Loomis
Flanders, Dwight Prescott
Fortess, Karl Eugene
Fox, Eleanor Mae Cohen
Francis, Sam
Franck, Michael
Franke, Charles H(enry)
Frazier, John Warren
Freeman, William Ernest, Jr.
French, John Henry, Jr.
Frese, Walter Wenzel
Friederici, Hartmann H.R.
Froeschle, Robert Edward
Fuchs, Fritz
Fulbright, James William
Furst, Norma Fields
Futas, Elizabeth Dorothy

G

Gallo, Dean Anderson
Garman, Willard Hershel
Garston, Gerald Drexler
Gee, Thomas Gibbs
George, Earl
Gershbein, Leon Lee
Gialanella, Philip Thomas
Gilmer, B. von Haller
Gimbutas, Marija
Glaser, Joseph Bernard
Glasser, Melvin Allan
Gleason, John Martin
Godunov, Alexander Boris
Goggins, John Francis
Goldberg, Irving Loeb
Gottmann, Jean
Grace, J. Peter
Graese, Clifford Ernest
Grant, James Pineo
Grant, Rhoda
Gray, Henry David
Greenberg, Melvin Nathaniel
Greenblatt, Milton
Grenley, Philip
Griffeth, Paul Lyman
Grist, Clarence Richard
Griswold, Erwin Nathaniel
Guarino, John Ralph
Guerry, Alexander
Günther, Marian W(aclaw) J(an)

H

Haass, Erwin Herman
Haggerty, Lawrence George
Hagstrum, Homer Dupre
Hale, James Russell
Hallbauer, Robert Edward
Hammond, Harold Francis
Hancock, Thomas
Hanson, William Bert
Harding, Victor Mathews
Harlan, Robert Warren
Harless, Byron Brittingham
Harper, Roy W.
Harrington, Fred Harvey
Harrington, Joseph, Jr.
Hartl, Albert Victor
Hawkins, Erick
Hays, Thomas R.
Hayward, Jane
Hazard, John Newbold
Heffelbower, Dwight Earl
Hem, John David
Hendon, Robert Caraway
Herbert, George Richard
Herriot, James (James Alfred Wight)
Hesse, William R.
Hidalgo, Edward
Higgins, Kenneth Raymond
Higinbotham, William Alfred
Hill, Norman Julius
Himelstein, Peggy Donn
Hoddy, Raymond Arthur
Holiga, Ludomil Andrew
Holloway, Herman M., Sr.
Horgan, Paul
Horner, Harry
Horton, Bernard Francis
Hospodor, Andrew Thomas
Houk, Vernon Neal
Hovermale, John B.
Hucker, Charles Oscar
Huddleson, Edwin Emmet, Jr.
Hugin, Adolph Charles (Eugene)
Hunt, Walter L.
Hunter, Edgar Hayes
Hunter, Howard William
Hutton, Warwick Blair

I

Ivanier, Isin
Ives, Burl (Icle Ivanhoe)

J

Jackson, Everett Gee
Jaffe, Nora
Jenks, Homer Simeon
Jesurún, Harold Méndez
John, Fritz
Johnson, David Elliot
Johnson, Lowell Ferris
Jolson, Alfred James
Jones, Charles Edward
Jorgensen, William Ernest
Julia, Raul

K

Kaplan, Oscar Joel
Karpowitz, Anthony Victor
Kelliher, Peter Maurice
Kempe, Lloyd Lute
Kennedy, Rose Fitzgerald (Mrs. Joseph P. Kennedy)
Kenney, Richard Alec
Kenny, Alexander Donovan
Kerrigan, (Thomas) Anthony
Kingsley, Sidney
Klaus, Elmer Erwin
Knoll, Erwin
Krehbiel, John H.
Kriz, Vilem Francis
Kudryk, Oleg
Kurek, Dolores Bodnar

L

Lamy, Peter Paul
Lancaster, Burt(on)
Landon, Sealand Whitney
Lanham, Elizabeth
LaRoe, Edward Terhune, III
Larson, Martin Alfred
Legget, Robert Ferguson
Leitch, Alma May
Lenneberg, Hans
Lesch, George Henry
Levandowski, Donald William
Lichstein, Herman Carlton
Lindner, Kurt Julius
Linville, Thomas Merriam
Lipson, Paul S.
Littner, Ner
Locke, John Whiteman, III
Lohr, Mary Margaret
Lott, Kench Lee, Jr.
Lotterman, Hal
Louden, James Keith
Lucey, Charles Timothy
Luther, James Howard

M

Macgregor, Wallace
Madigan, Edward R.
Mahoney, Justin J.
Malkin, Myron Samuel
Mallers, George Peter
Mallette, Alfred John
Mandel, Siegfried
Manfred, Frederick Feikema (Feike Feikema)
Manship, Charles Phelps, Jr.
Marbury, Benjamin Edward
Marquis, Robert B.
Martin, John J.
Martin, Mark
Martin, Oscar Thaddeus
Mason, Edward Allen
Masserman, Jules Homan
Mata, Eduardo
Mathias, Mildred Esther
Matteson, Robert Eliot
Maves, Paul Benjamin
May, Rollo
Mayer, Eugene Stephen
McCarty, Philip Norman
McClung, John Robinson, Jr.
McCowen, Max Creager
McCullough, David L.
Mc Donnell, John Thomas
McGrew, Thomas James
McIlhone, John Thomas
McLeod, Walton James, Jr.
McNeil, George Joseph
McRae, Carmen
Mc Whorter, Hezzie Boyd
Meister, Alton
Meredith, Ronald Edward
Merrill, James
Merrill, James Mercer
Meyer, Harold Louis
Mills, Howard McIlroy
Mims, Thomas Jerome
Moffett, William Andrew
Mollison, Richard Devol
Monroe, Burt Leavelle, Jr.
Montagna, William
Moody, G. William
Morgan, Charles Sumner
Morton, Charles Brinkley
Mosser, Thomas Joseph
Mueller, John Alfred
Mulvihill, Edward Robert
Munro, Hamish Nisbet

N

Nebergall, Roger Ellis
Neiman, Lionel Joseph
Netting, Robert M.
Nevius, Blake Reynolds
Newsom, Will Roy
Nixon, Robert Pleasants
Noonan, Ray John

O

Oakeshott, Gordon B(laisdell)
Obenhaus, Victor
O'Brien, Paul Jerry
Odeh, Aziz Salim
O'Donoghue, Michael
Olsen, Dagne B.
O'Mahony, Jeremiah Francis
Onstott, Edward Irvin
Osborn, Robert Chesley
Oser, Bernard Levussove
Overby, Lacy Rasco

P

Pallot, E. Albert
Papa, Anthony Emil
Pappas, Costas Ernest
Pappenheimer, Alwin M(ax), Jr.
Pauling, Linus Carl
Pavis, Jesse Andrew
Pekow, Eugene
Pennock, James Roland
Perkins, Edward A.
Perry, Marvin Banks, Jr.
Petrie, Milton J.
Philips, Jesse
Pickus, Albert Pierre
Pine, Granville Martin
Pipkin, Allen Compere, II
Pleasence, Donald
Pond, Martin Allen
Pope-Hennessy, John Wyndham
Post, Joseph
Pressler, Herman Paul
Prichard, Robert Williams
Primus, Pearl

R

Ragsdale, James Marcus
Rahl, James Andrew
Randall, Bob
Rask, Michael Raymond
Raymond, Victor P.
Reardon, Robert Joseph
Rector, Richard Robert
Reed, George Farrell
Regenstein, Louis
Reifman, William J.
Rhodes, Andrew James
Robbins, Daniel
Roberts, Frank
Roebling, Mary Gindhart
Rogers, David Elliott
Rogers, Ginger (Virginia Katherine McMath)
Roller, Duane Henry DuBose
Romualdi, James Philip
Root, Oren
Rosenberg, Dennis Melville Leo
Rosenthal, Samuel Robert
Rosner, Jorge
Roth, June Doris Spiewak
Rothschild, Edwin Alfred
Roussakis, Nicolas
Rowen, Hobart
Roy, Radha Raman
Rush, Kenneth
Rusk, Dean
Russell, Tomas Morgan
Ryan, Harold L.

S

Sagendorf, Bud (Forrest Cowles Sagendorf)
San Pedro, Enrique
Sawyer, John Edward
Schaaf, C(arl) Hart
Schewel, Stanford
Schilpp, Paul Arthur
Schneider, William Henry
Schramm, John Clarendon
Schulmann, Horst
Segatto, Bernard Gordon
Seltzer, Mildred M.
Setton, Kenneth M.
Seymour, Mary Powell
Shafer, Joseph Ernest
Sharbaugh, Amandus Harry
Sharf, Donald Jack

Shaw, Harry Alexander, III
Sherwood, Thorne
Shibley, Raymond Nadeem
Shore, Ferdinand John
Shoup, Wesley Dale
Shurrager, Phil Sheridan
Shutt, Edwin Holmes, Jr.
Sigel, M(ola) Michael
Sikes, Robert L. F.
Silk, Leonard Solomon
Sirna, Anthony Alfred, III
Sirois, Raymond
Sisk, Philip Laurence
Speare, Elizabeth George
Spencer, John Richard
Spurr, Charles Lewis
Stacy, Gardner W.
Stalnaker, Armand Carl
Stampfl, Rudolf Alois
Steckler, William Elwood
Stecklow, Steve
Steegmuller, Francis
Stella, Daniel Francis
Stennis, John Cornelius
Sterling, Kenneth
Stern, Henry Louis
Stewart, Charles Edward, Jr.
Stimpson, John Hallowell
Stirling, Edwin Murdoch
Stoddart, Jack Elliott
Stolp, Lauren Elbert
Stone, Ezra Chaim
Sturman, Robert Harries
Styne, Jule
Suyematsu, Toshiro
Symons, Julian Gustave

T

Taft, Robert, Jr.
Talbot, Richard Burritt
Tamm, Igor
Tandy, Jessica
Taylor, Peter Matthew Hillsman
Taylor, Thomas Hewitt, Jr.
Tenney, Charles Henry
Theisz, Erwin Jan
Theros, Elias George
Thompson, Lee Bennett
Thorpe, James, III
Timbers, William Homer
Timmerman, George Bell, Jr.
Townley, Preston
Treadgold, Donald Warren
True, Henry Alfonso, Jr.
Turner, Donald Frank

V

Van Arsdell, Paul Marion
Verdier, Philippe M(aurice)
Vest, George Graham
Vetter, Betty McGee
Vincent, Lloyd Drexell
Volpi, Walter Mark

W

Waldschmidt, Paul Edward
Ward, Donald Butler
Watts, Daniel Thomas
Weaver, John Carrier
Webb, E. N.
Wegner, Harvey Edward
Weiss, Marvin
Welliver, Albertus Delmar
Wengerd, Sherman Alexander
West, Arleigh Burton
Wheeler, Leonard
Wicker, Veronica DiCarlo
Wiesner, Jerome Bert
Wigner, Eugene Paul
Williams, Langbourne Meade
Wilson, Alice Hornbuckle
Wilson, H. Brian, Jr.
Wilson, Olin Chaddock
Wilson, Samuel, Jr.
Wittenmeyer, Charles E.
Wolfe, John F.
Wolfe, John Walton
Wolfson, Richard Frederick
Woodcock, George
Wooden, Howard Edmund
Woods, John Lucius
Woroniak, Alexander
Wragg, Laishley Palmer, Jr.
Wray, Karl

Y

Young, John Hendricks
Young, Terence

Z

Zimmer, Norman Cunningham